CHILDREN'S CATALOG

NINETEENTH EDITION

STANDARD CATALOG SERIES

JOHN GREENFIELDT, GENERAL EDITOR

CHILDREN'S CATALOG

FICTION CATALOG

MIDDLE AND JUNIOR HIGH SCHOOL
LIBRARY CATALOG

PUBLIC LIBRARY CATALOG

SENIOR HIGH SCHOOL LIBRARY CATALOG

CHILDREN'S CATALOG

NINETEENTH EDITION

EDITED BY

ANNE PRICE

NEW YORK AND DUBLIN

THE H. W. WILSON COMPANY

2006

Printed in the United States of America

Abridged Dewey Decimal Classification and Relative Index, Edition 14 is © 2004-2006 OCLC Online Computer Library Center, Incorporated. Portions reprinted with Permission. DDC, Dewey, Dewey Decimal Classification and WebDewey are registered trademarks of OCLC.

ISBN 0-8242-1073-5

Library of Congress Cataloging-in-Publication Data

Children's catalog. — 19th ed. / edited by Anne Price.
    p. cm. — (Standard catalog series)
Kept up-to-date by annual supplements.
Includes index.

ISBN 0-8242-1073-5 (alk. paper)

1. Children's literature—Bibliography.   2. Children's libraries—United States—Book lists. 3. School libraries—United States—Book lists. 4. Children—Books and reading—United States. I. Price, Anne, 1946-

Z1037.C5443 2006
011.62—dc22

        2006028647

CONTENTS

CONTENTS

PREFACE

Children's Catalog is a comprehensive list of fiction and nonfiction books, periodicals, and electronic resources for children from preschool through grade six, together with review sources and other professional aids for children's librarians and school media specialists.

In this Edition. This nineteenth edition of *Children's Catalog* includes 8,934 titles and 3,600 analytical entries. Of special note in this edition are a new abundance of books on minorities, ecology, natural sciences, and natural history. The sections for fairy tales and picture books have also been expanded. A new separate section has been added for recommended periodicals. This section is in two parts, one for children's periodicals and one for professional journals for teachers and librarians. The section listing recommended Web resources, now entitled Recommended Electronic Resources, has been expanded. Another new feature is a selection of recommended graphic novels, which are included at 741.5 in the Classified Catalog. These graphic novels have been chosen by a well-known expert in the field with special attention to their suitability for an elementary school audience.

Preparation. In producing this edition the editor has worked closely with an advisory committee of distinguished librarians, who are listed below. Over the past five years they have participated in selecting the books that have entered the Catalog. In preparation for this new edition they have re-evaluated all the material in the previous edition of the Catalog and its supplements and proposed many new titles. Reviews in the professional literature have also been an important source of information in selecting the material for this Catalog.

Scope and Purpose. The Catalog is aimed at the needs of libraries in elementary schools through the sixth grade. Materials for the librarian or school media specialist are included among both the print and the electronic resources, such as works on the history and development of children's literature, literary criticism, bibliographies, selection aids, guides to the operation of media centers, and periodicals relating to library science, reviewing, and education.

Three annual supplements, to be published in 2007, 2008, and 2009, are intended for use with this volume. Libraries and media centers serving large systems or users with special needs will undoubtedly wish to augment this list. To accommodate the precocious child the user is referred to *Middle and Junior High School Library Catalog*.

Books listed are published in the United States, or published in Canada or the United Kingdom and distributed in the United States. All titles are in print at the time this Catalog is published. Original paperback editions are included, and information is provided on paperback reprints of hardcover editions. Those concerned about the durability of paperbound editions may wish to consult a commercial rebinding service.

The convention of citing the first book in a fiction series in full with brief listings for other works in the series has been retained. In cases where more than one edition of a work illustrated by a notable artist is available, a listing of editions is provided with complete bibliographic information. Notes specify prizes or medals won and identify sequels or companion volumes.

The catalog excludes textbooks and materials in languages other than English, except for dictionaries and bilingual works. A non-English version of an English-language work is cited in the main entry for the work.

Organization. The Catalog consists of four parts. Part 1, the Classified Catalog, is arranged according to the Dewey Decimal Classification, followed by Fiction (Fic), Story Collections (S C), and Easy Books (E); Part 2, a List of Recommended Peridocials; Part 3, a List of Recommended Electronic Resources, and Part 4, an Author, Title, Subject, and Analytical Index. The section that follows this Preface, entitled How to Use Children's Catalog, contains more detailed information about the uses, content, and arrangement of the Catalog.

Acknowledgments

The H. W. Wilson Company is indebted to the publishers who supplied copies of their books and information about editions and prices. This Catalog could not have been published without the efforts of the advisory committee, who gave so generously of their time and expertise.

Members of the Advisory Committee:

Barbara Barstow
Youth Services Manager
Cuyahoga County Public Library
Parma, OH

Crystal Faris
Manager, Waldo Branch
Kansas City Public Library
Kansas City, MO

Pat Manning
Reviewer and consultant
Clearwater, FL

Linda Perkins
Library Services Manager, Children's
    Services
Berkeley Public Library
Berkeley, CA

Judith Rovenger
Youth Services Consultant
Westchester Library System
Ardsley, NY

Linda Ward-Callaghan
Lead Professional, Youth Services
Joliet Public Library
Joliet, IL

Consultant on Electronic Resources:

Frances B. Bradburn
Director, Instructional Technologies
North Carolina Department of Public Instruction
Raleigh, NC

Consultant on Graphic Novels:

Katharine L. Kan
Reviewer and consultant
Panama City, FL

HOW TO USE CHILDREN'S CATALOG

A. USES OF THE CATALOG

Children's Catalog is designed to serve these purposes:

As an aid in collection development. The annotations and grade level designation provided for each work in the Classified Catalog, along with information concerning publisher, ISBN, price, and availability, are intended to assist in the selection and ordering of titles. The arrangement of the Classified Catalog according to the Dewey Decimal Classification expedites the process of identifying elements of the collection that should be strengthened or updated. Evaluation of the suitability of any particular work will always take into account the special character of the children, the school, and the community that the library or media center serves.

As an aid in user service. Every item in this Catalog is a highly recommended work of its kind and can be given with confidence to a user who expresses a need based on topic, genre, etc. Reference work and user service are furthered by information about grade level, sequels, and companion volumes; by the descriptive and critical annotations in the Classified Catalog; and by the series and subject approach in the Index. In addition, the Index includes entries under names of illustrators and headings for Newbery and Caldecott medal winners. Analytical entries augment the local catalog by providing access to parts of composite works.

As an aid in verification of information. Full bibliographical data, recommended subject headings based upon *Sears List of Subject Headings*, a suggested classification derived from the *Abridged Dewey Decimal Classification and Relative Index,* and notes that describe editions available, awards, and publication history are provided for this purpose.

As an aid in curriculum support. The classified approach, subject indexing, annotations, and grade level designations are helpful in identifying materials appropriate for classroom use. In areas where few monographs exist, or where those that do are outdated, inaccurate, or unavailable—as in the history and geography of some countries—the user should consult current reference sources, periodical literature, and the Internet to supply the lack.

As an aid in collection maintenance. Items elected to this edition of the Catalog comprise newly published works along with works listed in the previous edition or its supplements that have retained their usefulness. Information about the range of titles available in a field facilitates decisions to rebind, replace, or discard materials in the library's collection. That a book was in a previous edition of Children's Catalog and is not in this edition should not necessarily be interpreted to mean that the book is no longer useful or that it should be weeded from the collection.

As an aid in professional development. The Catalog is useful in courses that deal with children's literature and book selection, particularly on the preschool and elementary level.

B. DESCRIPTION OF THE CATALOG

Children's Catalog is arranged in four parts: Part 1. Classified Catalog; Part 2. List of Recommended Periodicals; Part 3. List of Recommended Electronic Resources; and Part 4. Author, Title, Subject, and Analytical Index.

Part 1. Classified Catalog

The Classified Catalog is arranged with the nonfiction books first, classified by the Dewey Decimal Classification in numerical order from 000 to 999. Individual biographies are classed in 92 and follow the 920s (collective biography). Three sections follow the nonfiction: Fiction (Fic), Story Collections (S C); and Easy Books (E), consisting chiefly of picture books of interest to children from preschool to grade three.

An Outline of Classification, which serves as a table of contents to the Classified Catalog, is reproduced on page xiii. Many subjects are dealt with in more than one discipline and hence are found in more than one part of the classification. If a particular title is not found where it might be expected, the Index should be consulted to determine if the work is classified elsewhere.

Within classes, works are arranged alphabetically under the main entry, usually the author. An exception is made for works of individual biography, classed in 92, which are arranged alphabetically under the name of the person written about.

Following is a sample entry and a description of the components of a typical entry:

Toupin, Laurie
 Life in the temperate grasslands; [by] Laurie Peach Toupin. 1st ed Franklin Watts 2005 63p il map (Biomes and habitat) $25.50 (4 and up)

577.4

 1. Grassland ecology
 ISBN 0-531-12385-5   LC 2004-13282
 "Watts library"
 Contents: No trees, no problem; Tough as grass; Grazing big and small; Predators feathery, furry, and slippery; Giving mother nature a hand; In your hands
 This describes the ecology of grasslands such as the North American prairie, the South American pampas, the African veldt and the European steppes.
 This is "written in an accessible and interesting, conversational style. The [author conveys] a good deal of information about topics such as adaptation, environmental threats, seasonal changes and other essentials important to report writers and general readers." SLJ
 Includes bibliographical references

The name of the author, which is inverted and printed in bold face type, is given in conformity with *Anglo-American Cataloguing Rules*, 2nd edition, 2002 revision, with 2005 Amendments. It is followed by the title, responsibility statement, edition note, and publisher. Next are the date of publication, pagination, illustration note, map note, series note, price, and grade level. Prices given are current when the Catalog goes to press. As time passes they should be confirmed with the publisher.

The figure printed in bold face on the last line of type in the body of the entry is the classification number derived from the 14th edition of the *Abridged Dewey Decimal Classification.* The numbered term that follows is a recommended subject heading for this book. In some instances subject headings assigned to the entire book will not show that portions of the book deal with more specific topics. In such cases subject analytic entries are made in the Index. All subject headings are based on the 18th edition of *Sears List of Subject Headings.*

The ISBN (International Standard Book Number) or ISSN (International Standard Serial Number) is included to facilitate identification of the item. The Library of Congress control number is provided when available.

Notes supply additional information about the book. Most entries include both a note describing the book's content and a critical note, which is useful in evaluating books for selection and in determining which of several books on the same subject is best suited for the individual reader. Other notes list special features, such as glossaries or bibliographical references, or describe sequels and companion volumes, editions available, awards, and publication history.

Part 2. List of Recommended Periodicals

The List of Recommended Periodicals is divided into two parts: Part I, Professional journals for teachers and librarians, and Part II, Periodicals for children. Within each part the journals are listed alphabetically by title. The information given for each periodical consists of title, publisher, price, ISSN, a note indicating frequency of publication, and a brief annotation.

Part 3. List of Recommended Electronic Resources

The List of Recommended Electronic Resources is arranged alphabetically by title. Subscription-based and free resources are included in a single alphabet. For each item the following information is given: title, publisher, price (or an indication that it is free), a URL, and an annotation. Where the price is too variable to list, a note directs the user to contact the publisher for pricing information. The annotation describes the general contents and features of the resource and includes a quotation from a reviewing source where available.

Part 4. Author, Title, Subject, and Analytical Index

This is an alphabetical index to all the books entered in the Catalog. Each book is entered under author, title (if distinctive), and subject, with added entries for joint author, illustrator, editor, and publisher's series as necessary. Also included are subject, author, and title analytics for parts of composite works. Analytical entries are an important feature of the Catalog. Subject analytics afford access to parts of books not covered by the subject headings for the whole, while author and title analytics provide an approach to anthologies and collections, especially of stories and tales. In a time of restricted funding analytic entries aid in maximizing use of the library's holdings.

The classification number in bold face type is the key to the location of the main entry of the book in the Classified Catalog. Works classed in 92, individual biography, will be found under the name of the person written about.

"See" references are made from forms of names or subjects not used as headings. "See also" references are made to related or more specific headings. The suggested grade level of a book is repeated in the Index.

Examples of entries for the book cited above:

Author	**Toupin, Laurie** Life in the temperate grasslands (4 and up) **577.4**
Title	**Life** in the temperate grasslands. Toupin, L. **577.4**
Subject	**Grassland ecology** Toupin, L. Life in the temperate grasslands (4 and up) **577.4**
Publisher's series	**Biomes and habitats** [series] Toupin, L. Life in the temperate grasslands (4 and up) **577.4**

Examples of other types of entries:

Joint authors	**Hantula, Richard** (jt. auth) Asimov, I. The life and death of stars **523.8**
Illustrator	**Kellog, Steven** (il) McNulty, F. If you decide to go to the moon **629.45**
Editor	**Kimmel, Eric A.** (ed) A Hanukkah treasury. *See* A Hanukkah treasury **296.4**
Author analytic	**Singer, Marilyn** First position *In* Sport shorts **S C**
Title analytic	**First** position. Singer, M. *In* Sport shorts **S C**
Subject analytic	**Singer, Isaac Bashevis, 1904-1991** *See/See also pages in the following book(s):* Krull, K. Lives of the writers (4 and up) **920**

Outline of Classification

Reproduced below is the Second Summary of the Dewey Decimal Classification. It will serve as a table of contents for the nonfiction section of the Classified Catalog. (Fiction and Story Collections follow the nonfiction.) Note that the inclusion of this outline is not intended as a substitute for consulting the Dewey Decimal Classification itself. This outline is reproduced from Edition 14 of the Abridged Dewey Decimal Classification and Relative Index, published in 2004, by permission of OCLC Online Computer Library Center, Inc., owner of copyright.

000	**Computer science, knowledge & systems**		**500**	**Science**
010	Bibliographies		510	Mathematics
020	Library & information sciences		520	Astronomy
030	Encyclopedias & books of facts		530	Physics
040	[Unassigned]		540	Chemistry
050	Magazines, journals & serials		550	Earth sciences & geology
060	Associations, organizations & museums		560	Fossils & prehistoric life
070	News media, journalism & publishing		570	Life sciences; biology
080	Quotations		580	Plants (Botany)
090	Manuscripts & rare books		590	Animals (Zoology)
100	**Philosophy**		**600**	**Technology**
110	Metaphysics		610	Medicine & health
120	Epistemology		620	Engineering
130	Parapsychology & occultism		630	Agriculture
140	Philosophical schools of thought		640	Home & family management
150	Psychology		650	Management & public relations
160	Logic		660	Chemical engineering
170	Ethics		670	Manufacturing
180	Ancient, medieval & eastern philosophy		680	Manufacture for specific uses
190	Modern western philosophy		690	Building & construction
200	**Religion**		**700**	**Arts**
210	Philosophy & theory of religion		710	Landscaping & area planning
220	The Bible		720	Architecture
230	Christianity & Christian theology		730	Sculpture, ceramics & metalwork
240	Christian practice & observance		740	Drawing & decorative arts
250	Christian pastoral practice & religious orders		750	Painting
260	Christian organization, social work & worship		760	Graphic arts
270	History of Christianity		770	Photography & computer art
280	Christian denominations		780	Music
290	Other religions		790	Sports, games & entertainment
300	**Social sciences, sociology & anthropology**		**800**	**Literature, rhetoric & criticism**
310	Statistics		810	American literature in English
320	Political science		820	English & Old English literatures
330	Economics		830	German & related literatures
340	Law		840	French & related literatures
350	Public administration & military science		850	Italian, Romanian & related literatures
360	Social problems & social services		860	Spanish & Portuguese literatures
370	Education		870	Latin & Italic literatures
380	Commerce, communications & transportation		880	Classical & modern Greek literatures
390	Customs, etiquette & folklore		890	Other literatures
400	**Language**		**900**	**History**
410	Linguistics		910	Geography & travel
420	English & Old English languages		920	Biography & genealogy
430	German & related languages		930	History of ancient world (to ca. 499)
440	French & related languages		940	History of Europe
450	Italian, Romanian & related languages		950	History of Asia
460	Spanish & Portuguese languages		960	History of Africa
470	Latin & Italic languages		970	History of North America
480	Classical & modern Greek languages		980	History of South America
490	Other languages		990	History of other areas

CHILDREN'S CATALOG

NINETEENTH EDITION

CLASSIFIED CATALOG

000 COMPUTER SCIENCE, INFORMATION & GENERAL WORKS

001.4 Research; statistical methods

Duncan, Donna

I-search for success; a how-to-do-it manual for linking the I-search process with standards, assessment, tests, and evidence-based practice; [by] Donna Duncan and Laura Lockhart. Neal-Schuman Publishers 2005 xxi, 277p il (How-to-do-it manuals for libraries) pa $75 **001.4**

1. Research 2. Libraries

ISBN 1-55570-510-3   LC 2004-54665

"Extending the authors' previous book, *I-Search, You Search, We All Learn to Research* (Neal-Schuman, 2000), this title takes readers step-by-step through a unit for grades three and four, from planning to assessment. . . . Large boxed figures interspersed throughout the text include I-Search forms, worksheets, organizational tools, and lists of resources for further information. The accompanying CD-ROM contains the collaborative planning guide, the I-Search journal for students, and a PowerPoint presentation for professional development found in the book, with all of the figures incorporated for easy modification and printing. This is a valuable resource guide for teachers and librarians using, or planning to use, the I-Search method." Booklist

Includes bibliographical references

I-Search, you search, we all learn to research; a how-to-do-it manual for teaching elementary school students to solve information problems; [by] Donna Duncan, Laura Lockhart. Neal-Schuman 2000 159p (How-to-do-it manuals for libraries) pa $49.95 **001.4**

1. Research 2. Libraries 3. Report writing

ISBN 1-55570-381-X   LC 99-89993

"This manual introduces teachers and librarians to strategies to get students to move away from traditional research in which they merely restate information to a higher order of thinking. . . . Along the way, they will learn about choosing topics, evaluating sources, note taking, presenting findings, and working with peers to develop better skills." SLJ

The **Nobel** book of answers; the Dalai Lama, Mikhail Gorbachev, Shimon Peres, and other Nobel Prize winners answer some of life's most intriguing questions for young people; edited by Bettina Stiekel; translated by Paul De Angelis and Elisabeth Kaestner. Atheneum Bks. for Young Readers 2003 254p $14.95 (5 and up) **001.4**

1. Nobel Prizes

ISBN 0-689-86310-1   LC 2003-8721

"Will I soon have a clone? Why are leaves green? Why are some people rich and others poor? Why does 1 + 1 = 2? Why is there war? What is love? Nobel Prize winners honored for their work for peace and in science, economics, medicine, and literature speak to children about elemental issues. . . . Most of these intellectuals do an amazing job of explaining complex ideas. . . . This will be especially welcome as a discussion opener in science and social studies classrooms." Booklist

004 Data processing. Computer science

Barrett, Joanne R.

Teaching and learning about computers; a classroom guide for teachers, librarians, media specialists, and students. Scarecrow Press 2002 255p il $45 **004**

1. Computers 2. Data processing

ISBN 0-8108-4450-8   LC 2002-8350

"The 14 chapters in increasing complexity include information about word processing, spreadsheets, charts and graphics, databases, multimedia presentations, the Internet, the World Wide Web, creating Web pages, learning programming, and viruses and copyright law. . . . Every computer teacher should be in possession of this book, and it would make a terrific textbook for those who are teaching teachers." SLJ

Baxter, Roberta

Computers; by Roberta Baxter. KidHaven Press 2004 48p il (Kidhaven science library) $23.70 (3-5) **004**

1. Computers

ISBN 0-7377-3053-6   LC 2004-10946

Contents: The invention of computers; Computers at work; Computers for fun; Super fast, super powerful

This is a brief introduction to the history of computers, their uses, how they function, and possible future developments in computer technology.

Includes glossary and bibliographical references

1

Cuddy, Colleen

Using PDAs in libraries; a how-to-do-it manual. Neal-Schuman Publishers 2005 145p bibl il tab (How-to-do-it manuals for libraries) pa $65

004

1. Libraries—Automation 2. Personal digital assistants
ISBN 1-55570-543-X

"After an opening chapter that defines PDAs (personal digital assistants) and provides an overview of their history and future, this practical manual's remaining six chapters discuss PDAs in terms of networking, storage devices, peripherals, software applications, content, library reference software, security, and vulnerability issues. . . . Information throughout the book is well researched, and readers will appreciate its deft organization and clear, accessible language." Booklist

Sherman, Josepha

The history of the personal computer. Watts 2003 63p il lib bdg $24; pa $8.95 (4 and up)

004

1. Computers—History
ISBN 0-531-12166-6 (lib bdg); 0-531-16213-3 (pa)

LC 2002-8507

"Watts library"
Discusses the inventors and scientists that contributed to the development of computers and more recently, personal computers

This offers "fascinating and useful content." Libr Media Connect

Includes glossary and bibliographical references

004.6 Interfacing and communications. Networks

Brimner, Larry Dane

E-Mail. rev ed. Children's Press 2000 47p il lib bdg $25; pa $6.95 (2-4)   **004.6**
1. Electronic mail systems
ISBN 0-516-21937-5 (lib bdg); 0-516-26858-9 (pa)

LC 00-60382

"A True book"
First published 1997
A simple explanation of what e-mail is and how to use it to communicate with others through the Internet and the Information Superhighway.

Includes bibliographical references

Kazunas, Charnan

The Internet for kids; [by] Charnan & Tom Kazunas. rev ed. Children's Press 2000 47p il lib bdg $25; pa $6.95 (2-4)   **004.6**
1. Internet
ISBN 0-516-21936-7 (lib bdg); 0-516-26857-0 (pa)

LC 00-60384

"A True book"
First published 1997
A simple introduction to the Internet, the worldwide network of computers that communicate with each other, and its many uses.

Includes bibliographical references

Sherman, Josepha

The history of the Internet. Watts 2003 63p il lib bdg $24; pa $8.95 (4 and up)   **004.6**
1. Internet
ISBN 0-531-12164-X (lib bdg); 0-531-16211-7 (pa)

LC 2002-8478

"Watts library"
Explores the history of the Internet—how it was developed and refined, the people involved, and future possibilities

"Tightly written . . . [this] book gives a balanced presentation of the importance of the Internet." SLJ

Includes glossary and bibliographical references

Ward-Johnson, Chris

E-mail: a magic mouse guide; by Chris Ward-Johnson and the Magic Mouse; illustrations & layout by Laughing Gravy Design. Enslow Pubs. 2003 32p il (Magic mouse guides) $17.95 (k-3)   **004.6**
1. Electronic mail systems
ISBN 0-7660-2261-7   LC 2002-13287

Contents: What is e-mail?; On the Internet; E-mail addresses; The right address; Make it snappy!; Say it with a smile; Sending your e-mail; Looking for a message; Receiving a message; Attachments; Sending a reply; Surprise, surprise!; More about e-mail

This "title discusses sending and receiving e-mail, while telling how Ben and Hari communicate with one another. . . . The visual appeal of [this] kid-friendly [title] will make [it a] first [choice] among young readers." SLJ

Includes glossary

005.7 Data in computer systems

Lindsay, Dave

Dave's quick n' easy web pages; an introductory guide to creating web sites; written by Dave Lindsay; illustrated by Sean Lindsay; edited by Bruce Lindsay. 2nd ed. Erin Publs. 2001 116p il pa $11.95 (5 and up)   **005.7**
1. Web sites
ISBN 0-9690609-8-X
First published 1999
Basic information on creating, testing, editing, and maintaining web pages with HTML

"With this book, a word processor, and an idea, any child can create a Web site to be proud of." SLJ

Selfridge, Benjamin

A Kid's guide to creating web pages for home and school; [by] Benjamin Selfridge and Peter Selfridge. Zephyr Press 2004 110p il pa $19.95 (5 and up)   **005.7**
1. Web sites
ISBN 1-56976-180-9

"This book leads students . . . through the basic functionalities of HTML. . . . Each section focuses on a specific project and includes sample computer screens to demonstrate the basic site being developed. . . . Also in-

Selfridge, Benjamin—*Continued*
cluded are more advanced techniques for web page design, including sound, animation, and the uses of Javascript, Java, and Flash, as well as off and online resources for readers to investigate." Publisher's note

"A clear, concise how-to book. . . . The step-by-step instructions are easy to follow." SLJ

006   Special computer methods

Baker, Christopher W.
Scientific visualization; the new eyes of science. Millbrook Press 2000 48p il lib bdg $23.90 (5 and up)   **006**
1. Science—Methodology 2. Computer simulation
ISBN 0-7613-1351-6
This work "explores the ways that computers enable scientists to study the universe beyond the range of our eyes. Examples include studying the interaction of molecules or even atoms when an egg is heated in a pan, viewing the human brain through MRI images, and simulating events such as the creation of a black hole or the collision of two galaxies." Booklist

006.3   Artificial intelligence

Margulies, Phillip
Artificial intelligence; written by Phillip Margulies. Blackbirch Press 2004 48p il (Science on the edge) $23.70 (5 and up)   **006.3**
1. Artificial intelligence
ISBN 1-56711-783-X   LC 2002-13160
Contents: History of artificial intelligence; The quest for artificial intelligence; The future of artificial intelligence
Discusses the definition of artificial intelligence, the development of "thinking" machines, and what computers may be able to do in the future
Includes glossary and bibliographical references

006.8   Virtual reality

Wyborny, Sheila
Virtual reality; written by Sheila Wyborny. Blackbirch Press 2003 48p il (Science on the edge) lib bdg $23.70 (5 and up)   **006.8**
1. Virtual reality
ISBN 1-56711-789-9   LC 2002-11926
Discusses the history, present uses, and future of the technology of virtual reality
"Exemplary in [its] balanced, easy-to-grasp coverage of complex issures." Booklist
Includes bibliographical references

011.6   General bibliographies of works for specific kinds of users and libraries

Adventuring with books; a booklist for pre-K-grade 6; Amy A. McClure and Janice V. Kristo, editors, and the Committee to Revise the Elementary School Booklist; with a foreword by Rudine Sims Bishop. 13th ed. National Council of Teachers of English 2002 536p il pa $39.95
011.6
1. Children's literature—Bibliography 2. Best books
ISBN 0-8141-0073-2   LC 2003-265339
First published 1950
"In this latest edition of Adventuring with Books, teachers and librarians will find descriptions of more than 850 . . . texts suitable for student use in background research, unit study, or pleasure reading. . . . [divided] under the 24 general topics, including Science Nonfiction; Struggle and Survival; Fantasy Literature; Sports, Games, and Hobbies; and Mathematics in Our World." Publisher's note

Ammon, Bette D.
Worth a thousand words; an annotated guide to picture books for older readers; [by] Bette D. Ammon and Gale W. Sherman. Libraries Unlimited 1996 210p pa $30.95   **011.6**
1. Picture books for children—Bibliography 2. Children's literature—Bibliography 3. Books and reading
ISBN 1-56308-390-6   LC 96-31489
This is a bibliography of approximately 640 titles. "Arranged alphabetically by author, each entry briefly describes a book. The description is accompanied by a subject list that includes themes, genres, and topics to enhance the book's potential classroom use, as well as to help match books with readers. Following the annotations are specific suggestions for including each book in the curriculum. Icons representing the curriculum ideas indicate classroom applications and suitable curriculum areas. Author/illustrator, title, and subject indexes help users locate specific works." Publisher's note

Barr, Catherine
Best books for children: preschool through grade 6. 8th ed. Libraries Unlimited 2006 1783p $80
011.6
1. Children's literature—Bibliography 2. Best books
ISBN 1-59158-085-4
First published 1978
This "guide to children's books includes more than 25,000 in-print titles recommended for children in grades K-6. . . . [It offers] thematic organization, concise annotations, and complete bibliographic data plus review citations." Publisher's note

Blakemore, Catherine

Faraway places; your source for picture books that fly children to 82 countries. Adams-Pomeroy Press 2002 468p $28.95   **011.6**
1. Picture books for children—Bibliography
2. Travel—Bibliography
ISBN 0-9661009-2-1   LC 2001-132599
"The bibliography is divided by region. . . . Each region is divided alphabetically by country; each country is divided (as applicable) into Specific Locations (such as cities), General (fables, fairy tales, folktales, legends, etc.), Historical Figures, Nonfiction, Stories, Poetry and Songs, and Books. Succinct summaries of more than 900 recommended titles are offered in a narrative format under each section. . . . An impressive guide that will not only aid collection development but serve as a useful reference tool as well." Bull Cent Child Books
Includes bibliographical references

Dale, Doris Cruger

Bilingual children's books in English and Spanish; an annotated bibliography, 1942 through 2001. McFarland & Co. 2003 174p pa $39.95
        011.6
1. Children's literature—Bibliography 2. Bilingual books—English-Spanish—Bibliography
ISBN 0-7864-1316-6   LC 2002-13462
A revised edition of Bilingual books in Spanish and English for children published 1985 by Libraries Unlimited
Title page in English and Spanish
In the introduction "the author discusses the four awards that have been established for books by Latino authors or with Latino themes, the publishers that produce bilingual books for children, and journals that review the books. . . . The annotated bibliography, the main body of the work, is comprised of 433 entries, mostly picture, alphabet, and counting books. Listing is by author's name, followed by the title in English and Spanish. The remainder of the information provided, including the annotation, is written in English. The price is not provided, but other ordering information is presented. Citations for book reviews are also given. . . . The colorful picture on the cover, which depicts a Latino village scene, entices the user. . . . A welcome addition to the literature in this growing field." Am Ref Books Annu, 2003

Freeman, Judy

Books kids will sit still for 3; a read-aloud guide; [by] Judy Freeman; Catherine Barr, series editor. Libraries Unlimited 2006 915p il (Children's and young adult literature reference series) $70; pa $55   **011.6**
1. Children's literature—Bibliography 2. Best books
ISBN 1-59158-163-X; 1-59158-164-8 (pa)
First published 1984 by Alleyside with title: Books kids will sit still for
"The author features 2,000 . . . selected titles [for] children in grades K through 6. . . . All [are] published [from 1995 to 2005]. . . . Each annotated entry provides a brief plot summary, related titles, and subject designations. In addition, there are curriculum tie-ins and sug-

gested activities including drama, crafts, research, and problem solving. The book . . . [offers] tips on effective reading aloud, storytelling, and classroom and library activities. There is also a bibliography of professional books." Publisher's note

Gillespie, John Thomas

The children's and young adult literature handbook; a research and reference guide. Libraries Unlimited 2005 393p (Children's and young adult literature reference series) $55
        011.6
1. Children's literature—Bibliography 2. Children's literature—History and criticism 3. Young adult literature—Bibliography 4. Young adult literature—History and criticism
ISBN 1-56308-949-1
This is "a selection guide and collection development aid for librarians, as well as a navigation tool for researchers. Describing and evaluating more than 1,000 publications, the book covers . . . general reference, bibliographies, and biographies to review sources, literary awards, professional organizations, and special library collections. Internet and other nonprint media are included, as are major English-language resources from Britain, Canada, Australia, and South Africa." Publisher's note
"This reference should meet the needs of librarians, teachers, and scholars." Choice

Harms, Jeanne McLain

Picture books to enhance the curriculum; [by] Jeanne McLain Harms, Lucille J. Lettow. Wilson, H.W. 1996 521p $60   **011.6**
1. Picture books for children—Indexes 2. Picture books for children—Bibliography
ISBN 0-8242-0867-6   LC 94-42653
This is "a list of approximately 1,500 picture-book titles for use in literature-based programs in elementary schools implementing the whole language concept. The focus rests on language arts, graphic and performing arts, social studies, and science. Chapters cover a key to themes; a themes index listing related titles; a picture book index containing bibliographic information, a brief annotation of contents, and a list of themes; and a title index." Choice

Kaleidoscope; a multicultural booklist for grades K-8. 4th ed, Nancy Hansen-Krening, Elaine M. Aoki, and Donald T. Mizokawa, editors; and the Committee to Revise the Multicultural Booklist of the National Council of Teachers of English. National Council of Teachers of English 2003 118p il (NCTE bibliography series) pa $30.95
        011.6
1. Multiculturalism—Bibliography 2. Children's literature—Bibliography 3. Best books 4. Minorities—Bibliography
ISBN 0-8141-2539-5   LC 2003-269386
First published 1994
This highlights "fiction and nonfiction published by and about people of color. Hundreds of annotations of books published from 1999 to 2001 are divided according to type of literature, such as informational and educa-

Kaleidoscope—*Continued*
tional books, or contemporary issues, such as families, friends, and community. . . . Annotations provide bibliographic information as well as content summaries, and readers can search for books by author, illustrator, subject, and title." Publisher's note

Includes bibliographical references

Lima, Carolyn W.
A to zoo; subject access to children's picture books; [by] Carolyn W. Lima and John A. Lima. 7th ed. Libraries Unlimited 2006 xxiii, 1692p (Children's and young adult literature reference series) $80   **011.6**
1. Picture books for children—Bibliography
ISBN 1-59158-232-6   LC 2005030879
First published 1982
This "subject index to picture books for pre-school through grade 2 . . . covers nearly 28,000 in-print and out-of-print titles. . . . The volume is . . . divided into five sections: 'Subject Headings,' a list of the 1,350 subjects under which the books are classified; 'Subject Guide,' where the books are listed under the appropriate headings; 'Bibliographic Guide,' arranged by author and containing bibliographic information for each title; and title and illustrator indexes. . . . [An] essential [resource] for school and public libraries." Booklist
Includes bibliographical references

Middle and junior high school library catalog; edited by Anne Price. 9th ed. H. W. Wilson Co. 2005 1237p $275   **011.6**
1. Classified catalogs 2. School libraries—Catalogs
ISBN 0-8242-1053-0
Also available on-line version
"Standard catalog series"
First published 1965 with title: Junior high school catalog
Kept up to date by annual supplements which are included in the price of the main volume
This collection of recommended materials includes entries for more than 6,000 books, plus over 2,000 analytic entries for stories, plays, and other items from anthologies and composite works, for grades five through nine. Entries contain full bibliographic information, Dewey Decimal Classification number, subject headings, descriptive, and when possible, critical annotations. Special sections include annotated lists of recommended periodicals for professionals and for children and young adults, and an annotated list of recommended electronic resources for student research

The **New** books kids like; edited by Sharon Deeds, Catherine Chastain; prepared for Association for Library Service to Children. American Lib. Assn. 2001 179p pa $32   **011.6**
1. Children's literature—Bibliography 2. Books and reading
ISBN 0-8389-3512-5   LC 2001-18850
This is a "collection of more than 500 annotated book recommendations. Organized around 44 topics considered by the panel as 'the most frequently requested,' this . . . readers' advisory guide for children's literature . . . [includes titles] on everything from dogs and diaries to

adventure and science." Publisher's note
"This resource will be of great use to librarians, parents, and kids alike and is highly recommended for its unique approach to readers' advisory service for children." Am Ref Books Annu, 2002

Safford, Barbara Ripp
Guide to reference materials for school media centers. 5th ed. Libraries Unlimited 1998 353p $51.95   **011.6**
1. Reference books—Bibliography 2. School libraries—Catalogs 3. Instructional materials centers
ISBN 1-56308-545-3   LC 98-29867
First edition by Christine Gehrt Wynar published 1973 with title: Guide to reference books for school media centers
"Safford reviews more than 2,000 current information sources (most published between 1992 and 1997). . . . Organized by topics within broad subject categories, this work covers not only books but also CD-ROMs and other electronic reference sources in all curricular and some extracurricular areas. . . . Each entry gives complete bibliographic data; a grade level code; and a description of the work's content, organization, and special features." Publisher's note

Schon, Isabel
The best of Latino heritage 1996-2002; a guide to the best juvenile books about Latino people and cultures. Scarecrow Press 2003 269p $45.50
                                          011.6
1. Children's literature—Bibliography 2. Latin America—Bibliography
ISBN 0-8108-4669-1   LC 2002-154088
Companion volume to The best of Latino heritage, published 1997
Schon "identifies both fiction and nonfiction works useful in exposing K-12 students to Latino public figures, history, art, politics, social issues, and economics. . . . Each title receives a full bibliographic citation, suggested grade level, and a paragraph-long annotation. . . . Recommended books are in English or bilingual editions and are available from U.S. publishers. An excellent tool for collection development." Booklist
Includes bibliographical references

Recommended books in Spanish for children and young adults, 2000 through 2004. Scarecrow Press 2004 415p $45   **011.6**
1. Latin American literature—Bibliography 2. Spanish literature—Bibliography 3. Children's literature—Bibliography 4. Young adult literature—Bibliography
ISBN 0-8108-5196-2   LC 2004-11910
Also available volumes covering titles published 1991-1995 and 1996-1999
This "reference tool includes annotated entries for more than 1300 books in Spanish published between 2000 and 2004 in the U.S., Spain, Mexico, Venezuela, and Argentina. . . . Each entry includes an extensive critical annotation, title in Spanish as well as English, tentative grade level, and approximate price." Publisher's note

Silvey, Anita
100 best books for children. Houghton Mifflin 2004 184p $20   **011.6**
1. Children's literature—Bibliography 2. Best books
ISBN 0-618-27889-3   LC 2003-56899
"A former editor and reviewer for The Horn Book Magazine recommends one hundred of the best books for children, including a variety of works to suit diverse interests, reading levels, and special needs." Publisher's note

The author's "long experience as a book reviewer and editor makes her list pretty much spot-on. . . . Each title gets a short essay that not only discusses the book and what it has meant to its audience but that also supplies wonderful behind-the-scenes information. . . . A helpful list, 'Beyond the 100 Best,' points parents in the right direction for more good reads." Booklist
Includes bibliographical references

015.73 Bibliographies and catalogs of works issued or printed in the United States

Children's books in print. Bowker $179.95
                                                        015.73
1. Children's literature—Bibliography
ISSN 0069-3480
Also available CD-ROM version
Annual. First published 1969
"Gives current publisher's information for juvenile titles listed in their catalogs as 'in print.' Useful, but not complete." N Y Public Libr. Ref Books for Child Collect. 2d edition

Subject guide to Children's books in print. Bowker $270   **015.73**
1. Children's literature—Bibliography 2. Subject catalogs
ISSN 0000-0167
Also available CD-ROM version
Annual. First published 1970
This publication provides a subject approach to its companion work: Children's books in print. The headings used are based on the Sears list of subject headings supplemented by headings from LC. Entries include author, title, publisher, year of publication, binding, price, ISBN, and, in some cases, grade level. A directory of publishers and distributors is included

016.3 Bibliographies of the social sciences

Notable social studies trade books for young people. Children's Bk. Council pa $2
                                                        016.3
1. Social sciences—Bibliography 2. Best books
An annual annotated list, reprinted from an issue of the periodical Social Education, of the preceding year's best trade books in the field of social studies of interest to children in grades K-8. Prepared by the Book Review Panel of the National Council for the Social Studies—Children's Book Council Joint Committee. Titles are selected for emphasis on human relations, originality, readability and, when appropriate, illustrations. General reading levels (primary, intermediate, advanced) are indicated

016.3058 Bibliographies of racial, ethnic, national groups

The **Black** experience in children's books; selected by the New York Public Library, Black Experience in Children's Books Committee. New York Public Lib. pa $8   **016.3058**
1. African Americans—Bibliography 2. Blacks—Bibliography
First published 1946 with title: Books about Negro life for children. (1999 edition) Periodically revised
An annotated bibliography of approximately 500 titles portraying African American life in the United States and the Black experience in Africa and the Caribbean. Includes picture books, fiction, folklore, poetry, history, biography, and other nonfiction books for children from preschool through junior high school

Rand, Donna
Black Books Galore!—guide to great African American children's books about boys; [by] Donna Rand, Toni Trent Parker. Wiley 2001 209p il pa $15.95   **016.3058**
1. African Americans—Bibliography 2. Children's literature—Bibliography 3. Boys
ISBN 0-471-37527-6   LC 00-42257
An annotated bibliography of approximately 300 recommended titles, divided by age group, with illustrations of the titles covered. An index of titles by topic is included

016.5 Bibliographies of science

Outstanding science trade books for students K-12. Children's Bk. Council pa $2
                                                        016.5
1. Science—Bibliography 2. Best books
An annual annotated list, reprinted from an issue of the periodical Science and Children, of the preceding year's best trade books in the field of science of interest to children in grades K-8. Prepared by a Book Review Committee appointed by the National Science Teachers Association in cooperation with the Children's Book Council. Titles are selected for accuracy, readability and pleasing format. General reading levels (primary, intermediate, advanced) are indicated

016.8 Bibliographies of literature

Becker, Beverley C.
Hit list for children 2; frequently challenged books; [by] Beverley C. Becker and Susan M. Stan for the Office for Intellectual Freedom of the American Library Association. American Lib. Assn. 2002 65p $25   **016.8**
1. Censorship 2. Children's literature—Bibliography
ISBN 0-8389-0830-6   LC 2002-905

Becker, Beverley C.—*Continued*

Continues Hit list: frequently challenged books for children edited by Donna Reidy Pistolis, published 1996
.

This "is the second in a series that gives readers the information needed to defend challenged books with an informed response. An introduction that is identical to the first volume begins this authoritative guide. It is followed by a one- to three-page profile of the book (listed alphabetically by author), with a brief description of the story plot and characters, most recent challenges (with the reasoning behind the challenge), review sources, and sources recommending this book. In some cases articles about the book, some background sources, and awards and prizes are listed. At the conclusion there is a chapter on how ALA can help librarians faced with a censorship challenge. . . . It is an easy-to-read guide that includes an additional 28 books, with 14 books that are repeated word for word." Am Ref Books Annu, 2003

Includes bibliographical references

From biography to history; best books for children's entertainment and education; edited by Catherine Barr; foreword by James Cross Giblin; contributors, Rebecca L. Thomas, Deanna McDaniel. Bowker 1998 508p il $65.95

016.8

1. Biography—Bibliography 2. History—Bibliography

ISBN 0-8352-4012-6 LC 98-23147

"This annotated bibliography recommends biographies and related books that provide information about nearly 300 people of historical interest and the time periods in which they lived. The entries are arranged alphabetically; a brief paragraph about the individual is followed by suggested titles for 'Older Readers' (grades six to nine) and 'Younger Readers' (grades three to five). The bibliographic information is complete and most of the titles have been published in the last 10 years." SLJ

Includes bibliographical references

Hall, Susan

Using picture storybooks to teach literary devices; recommended books for children and young adults. v3. Oryx Press 2002 349p $37.95

016.8

1. Children's literature—Bibliography 2. Picture books for children—Bibliography 3. Literature—Study and teaching

ISBN 1-57356-350-1

"In this work, which updates earlier volumes published in 1990 and 1994; Hall selects picture storybooks that have received favorable reviews as resources for teaching the recognition and understanding of literary devices. Hall selects 120 picture storybooks published through the year 2000. . . . Hall's book is a useful tool for teachers in language arts programs in kindergarten through twelfth grade and for professional collections in public libraries and school library media centers." Voice Youth Advocates

Helbig, Alethea

Many peoples, one land; a guide to new multicultural literature for children and young adults; [by] Alethea K. Helbig, Agnes Regan Perkins. Greenwood Press 2001 431p $70.95

016.8

1. Children's literature—Bibliography 2. Young adult literature—Bibliography 3. Minorities—Bibliography

ISBN 0-313-30967-1 LC 00-25111

Replaces This land is our land published 1994

"This volume contains 561 entries covering works of literature published from 1994 to 1999. It offers entries for African Americans, Asian Americans, Hispanic Americans, and Native-American Indians, which are then subdivided into separate sections for books of fiction, books of poetry, and oral tradition for audiences from preschool through high school. Each numbered entry includes author, title, illustrator, publisher, publication year, ISBN, price, number of pages, age level, and grade level. A brief description of each literary work contains the major themes, plot, characters, settings, and illustration style of each work." Book Rep

"An excellent tool for readers' advisory and collection building." SLJ

Includes bibliographical references

Lynn, Ruth Nadelman

Fantasy literature for children and young adults; a comprehensive guide. 5th ed. Libraries Unlimited 2005 1128p $65

016.8

1. Fantasy fiction—Bibliography 2. Fairy tales—Bibliography

ISBN 1-59158-050-1

First published 1979 with title: Fantasy for children

This describes and categorizes "fantasy novels and story collections published between 1900 and 2004. More than 7,500 titles . . . for readers grades 3-12 are organized in chapters based on fantasy subgenres and themes, including animal, alternate worlds, time travel, witchcraft, and sorcery. Lynn provides complete bibliographic information, grade level, a brief annotation, and a list of review citations, and notes recommended titles." Publisher's note

"This is an excellent resource." Booklist

Sands, Karen

Back in the spaceship again; juvenile science fiction series since 1945; [by] Karen Sands and Marietta Frank. Greenwood Press 1999 152p (Contributions to the study of science fiction and fantasy) $97.95

016.8

1. Science fiction—Bibliography

ISBN 0-313-30192-1 LC 99-17848

"The authors delve into the elements of juvenile and young adult science-fiction series such as 'Animorphs' 'Tom Swift,' and 'Danny Dunn.' The introduction traces the history of these books and the impact that World War II and the development of rocket and atomic science had on the genre. Chapters deal with the inclusion of robots, androids, and artificial intelligence as stock conventions; animals, strange and familiar; the female presence; the role of humor; the absence or presence of scientific theory; utopias and dystopias; aliens; and coming-of-age stories." SLJ

Includes bibliographical references

Steiner, Stanley F.

Promoting a global community through multicultural children's literature; illustrations by Peggy Hokom; foreword by Alma Flor Ada. Libraries Unlimited 2001 179p pa $35

016.8

1. Children's literature—Bibliography 2. Minorities—Bibliography
ISBN 1-56308-705-7   LC 00-50702

This guide to developing a children's multicultural book collection lists over 800 titles for kindergarten through eighth grade

"A timely and informative guide for educators who are trying to promote an understanding of world cultures and our interconnectedness." SLJ

Includes bibliographical references

Thomas, Rebecca L.

Popular series fiction for K-6 readers; a reading and selection guide. Libraries Unlimited 2004 . 799p bibl (Children's and young adult literature reference series) $60   **016.8**

1. Children's literature—Bibliography
ISBN 1-59158-203-2

This "introduces users to some 1,200 of today's best and most popular fiction series appropriate for elementary readers. For each series an annotation describes the series' appeal and lists characters, location, the original publisher, the range of dates over which the series was published, genre, and grade level range." Publisher's note

"This is a useful resource, arranged in a most functional way, and any library serving children could well make use of it." SLJ

Ward, Marilyn

Voices from the margins; an annotated bibliography of fiction on disabilities and differences for young people. Greenwood Press 2002 154p $44.95   **016.8**

1. Children's literature—Bibliography 2. Young adult literature—Bibliography 3. Handicapped—Fiction—Bibliography
ISBN 0-313-31798-4   LC 2002-276832

This title "lists 200 books for children and young adults published from 1990 to 2001. . . . The juvenile fiction covered includes picture books, chapter books for middle-schoolers, and young adult novels as well as poetry. A few of the books included are nonfiction. . . . This resource is a welcome addition to the growing literature about disabilities of all kinds." Booklist

What do children and young adults read next? a reader's guide to fiction for children and young adults. Gale Res. $125   **016.8**

1. Best books 2. Children's literature—Bibliography 3. Young adult literature—Bibliography
ISSN 1540-5060

Annual. First published 2002; previously published separately as: What do children read next? and What do young adults read next?

Each volume contains over 2,000 entries arranged alphabetically by author, for fiction for children and young adults. Each annotation includes basic bibliographic in-

formation, suggested age range, subject(s) and genre, names and descriptions of major characters, time period, locale(s), plot summary, citations of selected reviews, awards received and additional titles on a similar theme

016.9   Bibliographies of geography and history

Adamson, Lynda G.

Literature connections to world history, K-6; resources to enhance and entice. Libraries Unlimited 1998 326p pa $35.50   **016.9**

1. History—Bibliography 2. Audiovisual materials—Catalogs 3. CD-ROMs—Reviews
ISBN 1-56308-504-6   LC 97-35952

This bibliography "identifies novels, biographies, history books, CD-ROMs, and videotapes to supplement history courses." Booklist

Includes bibliographical references

Barancik, Sue

Guide to collective biographies for children and young adults. Scarecrow Press 2005 447p pa $44.95   **016.9**

1. Biography—Bibliography
ISBN 0-8108-5033-8 (pa)   LC 2004-19560

"This text indexes 721 titles for children and young adults in order to provide access to 5,760 notable individuals from early to modern times. All of the referenced titles were published between 1988 and 2002." Booklist

"A current guide such as this one is essential. . . . A must-have for libraries serving grades 4 through 12." SLJ

Beck, Peggy

GlobaLinks: resources for world studies, grades K-8. Linworth Pub. 2002 148p pa $39.95

016.9

1. World history—Bibliography
ISBN 1-58683-040-6   LC 2001-50718

Also available GlobaLinks: resources for Asian studies, grades K-8

This "annotated bibliography of books, videos, CD-ROMs and Web sites includes items selected on the basis of the 10 strands of social studies. . . . For each source, whether print, non-print, Web site, or key and pen pal project, complete bibliographic information is given, as well as two to four sentences about the source and its intended audience." Book Rep

"The author's strength . . . lies not only in her selections, but also in her consistently high-quality annotations. . . . This compilation is highly recommended for the professional collection of young adult sections and school media centers." Am Ref Books Annu, 2003

016.973 Bibliographies of United States history

Adamson, Lynda G.
Literature connections to American history, K-6; resources to enhance and entice. Libraries Unlimited 1998 542p pa $39 **016.973**
1. United States—History—Bibliography
2. Audiovisual materials—Catalogs 3. CD-ROMs—Reviews
ISBN 1-56308-502-X LC 97-14283
This bibliography is divided "into two main parts. The first part lists authors and titles in the categories of historical fiction, biography, collective biography, history trade book, CD-ROM, and videotape within specific time periods according to grade levels. The second part contains annotated bibliographies of titles listed in the first part: books, CD-ROMs, and videotapes." Introduction
Includes bibliographical references

020 Library and information sciences

Misakian, Jo Ellen Priest
The essential school library glossary; [by] Jo Ellen Priest Misakian. Linworth Pub 2004 96p pa $36.95 **020**
1. School libraries—Dictionaries
ISBN 1-586-83150-X LC 2004-6746
"This useful compendium of terms from 'Abstract' to 'Online Computer Library Center' to 'W3C' is succinct and easy to read. . . . Misakian includes terms specific to library-media programs as well as those related to the whole school program. This is a valuable resource for school librarians at all stages in their career." SLJ

021.7 Promotion of libraries, information centers

Flowers, Helen F.
Public relations for school library media programs; 500 ways to influence people and win friends for your school library media center. Neal-Schuman 1998 158p pa $49.95
021.7
1. Libraries—Public relations 2. School libraries
ISBN 1-55570-320-8 LC 98-11470
The author recommends "techniques for promoting the use of the library media services by students, faculty, building administrators, and school support staff. Readers will also learn how to target administrators, the board of education, parents, community, and legislators to maintain and increase support for staff, materials, equipment, and space." Publisher's note
"Writing with a sense both of purpose and of humor, Flowers turns a book of excellent lists into a good, entertaining read." Voice Youth Advocates
Includes bibliographical references

025.04 Automated information storage and retrieval systems

Blowers, Helene
Weaving a library Web; a guide to developing children's websites; [by] Helene Blowers and Robin Bryan. American Library Association 2004 197p il pa $32 **025.04**
1. Web sites
ISBN 0-8389-0877-2 LC 2004-1806
"A detailed description of topics and issues involved in designing, implementing, and maintaining Web sites for children. . . . This book can be used as a beginner's first stop and as a webmaster's companion. It is uncomplicated and easy to read." SLJ
Includes bibliographical references

Brimner, Larry Dane
The World Wide Web. rev ed. Children's Press 2000 47p il lib bdg $25; pa $6.95 (2-4)
025.04
1. World Wide Web
ISBN 0-516-21935-9 (lib bdg); 0-516-26856-2 (pa)
LC 00-60385
"A True book"
First published 1997
A basic overview of the World Wide Web, including the history of its development and details on how to use it.
Includes bibliographical references

Gordon, Rachel Singer
Teaching the Internet in libraries. American Lib. Assn. 2001 143p pa $38 **025.04**
1. Internet searching—Study and teaching
2. Computer networks
ISBN 0-8389-0799-7 LC 00-52564
"Chapters cover the reasons and methods to initiate programs, including convincing others of the necessity of such training, the importance of choosing proper trainers and how to do so; techniques for reaching diverse audiences such as parents, senior citizens, and Hispanics; training techniques and considerations such as lists of popular searches requested by patrons; and criteria for evaluating the program. Each section of the book concludes with resources for further information." Book Rep
An "excellent and readable volume." Voice Youth Advocates
Includes bibliographical references

Haycock, Ken
Neal-Schuman authoritative guide to kids' search engines, subject directories, and portals; by Ken Haycock, Michelle Dober, and Barbara Edwards. Neal-Schuman 2003 234p il pa $55
025.04
1. Web sites 2. Internet resources 3. Internet searching
4. Computers and children
ISBN 1-55570-451-4 LC 2002-35766

Haycock, Ken—*Continued*

"Focusing on children in grades 4-9, the book begins with descriptions of search tools and the way children search the Web. The authors identify elements of search engines, present a checklist for evaluating them, and then recommend 20 of the best. . . . The book concludes with coverage of online tutors and homework help sites and a section on critical issues confronting children's use of the Internet. . . . Useful for any school or public librarian who wants to better serve his or her students using the Internet." Booklist

Includes bibliographical references

Johnson, Carolyn

Using internet primary sources to teach critical thinking skills in the sciences. Libraries Unlimited 2003 339p (Libraries Unlimited professional guides in school librarianship) $39.95

025.04

1. Science—Study and teaching 2. Internet in education

ISBN 0-313-31851-4   LC 2003-47722

Also available: Using internet primary sources to teach critical thinking skills in world literature by Roxanne M. Kent-Drury; Using internet primary sources to teach critical thinking skills in visual arts by Pamela J. Eyerdam; Using internet primary sources to teach critical thinking skills in government, economics, and contemporary world issues by James M. Shiveley and Phillip J. VanFossen

"A navigation tool for steering students to excellent scientific resources available on the Internet. The sites included are principally primary documents and other sites that provide reliable data. . . . Each lesson begins with a URL and a site summary. A series of tasks follows that would serve as a starting point for science teachers to expand upon, and are designed to trigger discussion and analytical thinking and writing. . . . The 10 appendixes offer such helpful topics as subject guides to Web sites, career data, information available in journals and other periodicals, and Web guides to standards." SLJ

Includes bibliographical references

Raatma, Lucia

Safety on the Internet; by Lucia Raatma. Child's World 2005 32p il (Living well) lib bdg $25.64 (4 and up)

025.04

1. Internet and children 2. Safety education

ISBN 1-59296-242-4   LC 2003-27212

Contents: Daniel's school report; Safe surfing; E-mail, IMS, and netiquette; Knowing to whom you are talking; Guarding your computer; When it's time to sign off; Glossary; Questions and answers about Internet safety; Helping a friend learn about Internet safety; Did you know?; How to learn more about Internet safety

This is an "overview of online safety, including choosing age-appropriate sites, e-mailing, instant messaging, netiquette, and maintaining one's privacy." SLJ

Includes glossary

Wolinsky, Art

Internet power research using the Big6 approach. rev ed. Enslow Publishers 2005 64p il (Internet library) lib bdg $22.60; pa $11.93 (5 and up)

025.04

1. Information systems 2. Research

ISBN 0-7660-1563-7; 0-7660-1564-5 (pa)

LC 2004-22185

Provides instructions for using the "Big6" research method and scenarios for applying the technique to research conducted on the Internet

The information is presented in "a friendly, informal writing style. . . . This is a helpful resource for students who want to hone their research strategies." SLJ

Includes glossary and bibliographical references

025.1   Library administration

Anderson, Cynthia

Write grants, get money. Linworth Pub. 2002 146p il pa $44.95   **025.1**

1. Grants-in-aid

ISBN 1-58683-025-2   LC 2001-38555

The author "begins with identifying the need for a grant, making a plan, and asking the right questions to help stimulate the generation of proposal ideas. Then she explains how to identify donors. . . . This title offers an excellent analysis of the grant-writing process for both novice and veteran grant writers." Book Rep

Includes glossary and bibliographical references

Curzon, Susan Carol

Managing change; a how-to-do-it manual for librarians. Rev. ed. Neal-Schuman Publishers 2005 129p (How-to-do-it manuals for librarians) pa $55

025.1

1. Libraries—Administration

ISBN 1-55570-553-7   LC 2005-22846

First published 1989

The author "outlines the step-by-step processes and . . . instructions necessary for conceptualizing the issues; planning; preparing; decision-making; controlling resistance; and implementing changes. Practical guidance for dealing with technology's impact on libraries, applying the latest research in change management, and developing new strategies for coping with change are included." Publisher's note

"The real-world approach makes the book a valuable addition to the professional collection." Booklist

Includes bibliographical references

Grantsmanship for small libraries and school library media centers; [by] Sylvia D. Hall-Ellis [et al.]; edited by Frank W. Hoffman. Libraries Unlimited 1999 173p pa $34   **025.1**

1. Grants-in-aid

ISBN 1-56308-484-8   LC 98-31247

This "guide outlines each step of the process for obtaining grants, providing examples and definitions along the way. . . . This helpful and easy-to-use handbook should be a part of every professional collection." SLJ

Includes bibliographical references

Hall-Ellis, Sylvia Dunn

Grants for school libraries; [by] Sylvia D. Hall-Ellis and Ann Jerabek. Libraries Unlimited 2003 197p il pa $35 **025.1**

1. Grants-in-aid 2. School libraries

ISBN 1-59158-079-X   LC 2003-54630

"Hall-Ellis and Jerabek provide a systematic approach to every aspect of the grant process. Each section breaks down important concepts and is clearly supported by reproducible forms, examples, and lists. Two important segments address budget and personnel considerations. The project-evaluation section includes data-collection instruments and time lines, while a final chapter discusses practical suggestions such as publicity and writing letters of appreciation. . . . This surprisingly readable guide should be on every school library media specialist's professional shelf." SLJ

Includes bibliographical references

Hallam, Arlita

Managing budgets and finances; a how-to-do-it manual for librarians and information professionals. Neal-Schuman Publishers 2005 233p il (How-to-do-it manuals for libraries) pa $65 **025.1**

1. Library finance

ISBN 1-55570-519-7

"This budgeting manual . . . offers the new or seasoned library administrators, board members, department heads, or finance professionals a way to budget carefully and clearly by offering a variety of strategies, definitions, and suggestions. The manual is divided into three parts: basics for librarians, special topics in financial management for libraries, and alternative library funding." Booklist

Includes bibliographical references

MacDonell, Colleen

Essential documents for school libraries; I've-got-it! answers to I-need-it-now! questions. Linworth Pub. 2004 132p il $44.95 **025.1**

1. Libraries—Administration

ISBN 1-58683-174-7   LC 2004-19392

Contents: Planning documents; Official reports; Publicity; Teaching documents; Programming documents; Procedure sheets and guides; Library rules and regulations; Interactive forms

"Each chapter begins with why the documents are needed, followed by practical advice for writing the documents, and examples of how the documents make an effective change in the library media program." Libr Media Connect

"An excellent addition for school librarians who always want to be prepared." SLJ

Includes bibliographical references

Thelen, Laurie Noble

Essentials of elementary library management; by Laurie Noble Thelen. Linworth Pub 2003 113p il pa $39.95 **025.1**

1. School libraries 2. Libraries—Administration

ISBN 1-58683-076-7   LC 2003-12889

Contents: Planning a new library media center; Starting over: the library media specialist in a new school district; Time management and the library media center; Budget secrets; Grant my wish; Programs to motivate a student to read; The library media specialist as collaborator and reading advocate; Encouraging staff to use new technology; Guidelines for positive student behavior; Finding and keeping volunteers and media clerks

This "guide covers the basics of school librarianship, with special emphasis on the one-person operation. Facilities planning, budgeting, technology advocacy, reading motivation, and student discipline are among the topics included. . . . A handy and functional volume that will be appreciated by both newbies and veteran media specialists 'in transition.'" SLJ

Includes bibliographical references

Where do I start? a school library handbook; Santa Clara County Office of Education, Library Services. Linworth Pub. 2001 153p il (Professional growth series) pa $39.95 **025.1**

1. School libraries 2. Instructional materials centers

ISBN 1-58683-043-0   LC 2001-32674

"This handbook is the outgrowth of library-training workshops developed for elementary school library clerks in order to introduce them to the various facets of a successful library program. Components include the institution's mission, staffing, policies, student handbooks, physical organization, environment, safety issues, bulletin boards, public relations and marketing, Internet issues, weeding, selection, booktalking, storytelling, information skills, Dewey Decimal Classification System, purchasing, filing and cataloging rules, library automation, and a glossary of library terms. . . . Although this book is basically for support staff, it includes many ideas that can be utilized by librarians." SLJ

Includes bibliographical references

025.2 Acquisitions and collection development

Building a special collection of children's literature in your library; identifying, maintaining, and sharing rare or collectible items; [edited by] Dolores Blythe Jones. American Lib. Assn. 1998 170p pa $40 **025.2**

1. Libraries—Special collections 2. Children's literature

ISBN 0-8389-0726-1   LC 97-43144

"Ten essays that offer advice on many aspects of collection development, acquisition, preservation, funding, and promotion of special collections of children's books in academic or public libraries. The informative discussions cover topics such as acquiring out-of-print materials, securing a professional appraisal of rare books, the elements of a complete catalog record, archival preparation of original materials, organizing a Friends group, preservation and security, and public relations and programming." SLJ

Includes bibliographical references

Doll, Carol Ann

Managing and analyzing your collection; a practical guide for small libraries and school media centers; [by] Carol A. Doll, Pamela Petrick Barron. American Lib. Assn. 2002 93p il pa $30

025.2

1. Libraries—Collection development
ISBN 0-8389-0821-7   LC 2001-53747

This guide to collection development is divided into chapters covering management objectives, gathering and analyzing collection data, and weeding

This is a "book that librarians will actually read from cover to cover. . . . [It] isn't overwhelming and technical. Instead, it is rather chatty with solid, useful information." Book Rep

Includes bibliographical references

Hughes-Hassell, Sandra

Collection management for youth; responding to the needs of learners; [by] Sandra Hughes-Hassell, Jacqueline C. Mancall. ALA Editions 2005 103p il pa $35

025.2

1. Libraries—Collection development 2. Instructional materials centers
ISBN 0-8389-0894-2   LC 2004-26911

"The authors present 11 . . . tools for creating a learner-centered collection with suggestions on the best methods for easy implementation of these procedures. . . . Every library media specialist wanting a more practical approach to collection management would find this book an important addition to his or her professional development library." Libr Media Connect

Includes bibliographical references

Lukenbill, W. Bernard

Community resources in the school library media center; concepts and methods; [by] W. Bernard Lukenbill. Libraries Unlimited 2004 195p bibl diag graph il tab $40

025.2

1. School libraries 2. Libraries and community
ISBN 1-59158-110-9   LC 2004-48926

"This text outlines organizational strategies for managing community resources. . . . Lukenbill includes information such as agency directories, telementoring numbers, historical documents, museum exhibits, photos, and volunteer pools. Expanding the concept of the vertical file, the author presents ideas for developing, managing, marketing, and accessing electronic photo archives, Web site links, school documents, and bulletin boards. One chapter addresses sensitive community information, censorship, privacy, and terrorism concerns. . . . A definitive tool for developing community-resource collections." SLJ

Lyga, Allyson A. W.

Graphic novels in your media center; a definitive guide; by Allyson A. W. Lyga with Barry Lyga. Libraries Unlimited 2004 180p il pa $35

025.2

1. Graphic novels—Administration 2. Book selection 3. Books and reading
ISBN 1-59158-142-7   LC 2004-46517

In the first section the authors "make cogent arguments for the inclusion of graphic novels. A second section introduces common terms and includes an extremely useful 'how to read' subsection, complete with sample pages. The remaining sections provide recommended titles for all ages, testimonials from teachers and comic book store proprietors, resource lists, and a set of 17 lesson plans." Booklist

"This indispensable, well-organized guide will provide school librarians with all of the necessary information for implementing and developing a graphic-novels collection." SLJ

Miller, Steve

Developing and promoting graphic novel collections. Neal-Schuman Publishers 2005 130p il (Teens @ the library series) pa $49.95

025.2

1. Graphic novels—Administration 2. Book selection 3. Books and reading
ISBN 1-55570-461-1   LC 2004-40159

This is an "overview of graphic novels and their use as reader development tools. Miller explores the evolution, categories, and genres of graphic novels; he then addresses the . . . details of collection development, acquisition, cataloging, and maintenance for this unique format. A special section shows how to promote graphic novels (include display ideas)." Publisher's note

"This volume is filled with practical information and savvy advice." SLJ

Includes bibliographical references

Symons, Ann K.

Protecting the right to read; a how-to-do-it manual for school and public librarians; [by] Ann K. Symons, Charles Harmon; illustrations by Pat Race. Neal-Schuman 1995 211p il (How-to-do-it manuals for libraries) pa $55

025.2

1. Libraries—Censorship 2. Intellectual freedom
ISBN 1-55570-216-3   LC 95-42444

"The authors take readers from discussion of the policies and principles of intellectual freedom to considerations specific to school and public libraries to the protection of freedom on the Internet. . . . Appendixes consist of reprints of documents put out by the ALA and the Minnesota Coalition Against Censorship." Book Rep

"Intellectual freedom issues and guiding principles get a thorough and comprehensive treatment. . . . An essential book." Voice Youth Advocates

Includes bibliographical references

Van Orden, Phyllis J.

Selecting books for the elementary school library media center; a complete guide. Neal-Schuman 2000 212p il pa $59.95

025.2

1. School libraries 2. Instructional materials centers
ISBN 1-55570-368-2   LC 99-56394

"The first four chapters give an overview of the selection process and general guidelines for establishing and applying criteria. The remaining nine chapters present measures for evaluating specific genres, including picture

Van Orden, Phyllis J.—*Continued*
books (with color plates illustrating artistic considerations), fiction (including classics and series), genre fiction, folk literature, poetry, informational literature, reference, and professional books." SLJ

025.3 Bibliographic analysis and control

ALA filing rules; [prepared by the] Filing
Committee, Resources and Technical Services
Division, American Library Association.
American Lib. Assn. 1980 50p pa $16
                                                    025.3
1. Files and filing 2. Library catalogs
ISBN 0-8389-3255-X   LC 80-22186
Successor to ALA Rules for filing catalog cards, second edition
"The rules set forth in *ALA Filing Rules*, which apply
to the arrangement of bibliographic records of library
materials in card, book, or online format, are based on
the 'file-as-is' principle." Nichols. Guide to Ref Books
for Sch Media Cent. 4th edition
According to a 1981 announcement of the American
Library Association, this may be considered as an alternative to, rather than a definite replacement for, the 1968
edition of ALA Rules for filing catalog cards. Libraries
may choose to continue using the earlier publication

Cataloging correctly for kids; an introduction to
the tools; edited by Sheila S. Intner, Joanna F.
Fountain, Jane E. Gilchrist; Association for
Library Collections and Technical Services. 4th
ed. American Library Association 2006 136p
bibl il tab pa $32   **025.3**
1. Cataloging
ISBN 0-8389-3559-1   LC 2005018838
First published 1989 by the Cataloging for Children's
Materials Committee
Among the topics discussed are: guidelines fo standardized cataloging for children; how children search; using AACR2 and MARC 21; Sears List of Subject Headings; LC Children's headings; sources for Dewey numbers; cataloging nonbook materials; authority control;
how the CIP program helps children; automating the
children's catalog; vendors of cataloging for children's
materials
Includes bibliographical references

Fritz, Deborah A. (Deborah Angela)
Cataloging with AACR2 and MARC21; for
books, electronic resources, sound recordings,
videorecordings, and serials. 2nd ed. American
Library Association 2004 various paging il loose
leaf $68   **025.3**
1. American Library Association 2. Anglo-American
cataloguing rules 3. Cataloging
ISBN 0-8389-0884-5   LC 2004-6535
First published 1998 with title: Cataloging with
AACR2R and USMARC
In this guide Fritz "provides the hands-on cross-
references between AACR2 and MARC21 required for

easy online cataloging. Designed to streamline the process and avoid errors, the book is organized in order of
MARC tags." Publisher's note
"Although it does not present every rule or MARC
tag, this fairly comprehensive and handy reference addresses all levels of cataloging expertise. Catalogers and
instructors should add this to their collection." Libr J

Gorman, Michael
The concise AACR2; prepared by Michael
Gorman. 4th ed. American Library Association
2004 179p pa $40   **025.3**
1. Anglo-American cataloguing rules 2. Cataloging
ISBN 0-8389-3548-6   LC 2004-16088
On cover: Fourth edition
"This practical guidebook . . . has been fully revised
and is now in concordance with AACR2, 2002 Revision
2004 Update. Michael Gorman . . . explains the more
generally applicable AACR2 rules for cataloging library
materials in simplified terms that make the rules more
accessible and practical for practitioners and students
who are in less complex library and bibliographic environments." Publisher's note

025.4 Subject analysis and control

Dewey, Melvil
Abridged Dewey decimal classification and
relative index; devised by Melvil Dewey. ed 14,
edited by Joan S. Mitchell, Julianne Beall, Giles
Martin, Winton E. Matthews, Jr., Gregory R. New.
OCLC 2004 1050p $99   **025.4**
1. Dewey Decimal Classification
ISBN 0-910608-73-3   LC 2003-542823
Also available online
First abridged edition published 1894
The 14th Abridged Edition is an abridgement of the
four volume 22nd Edition. Adapted to the needs of small
and growing libraries, the 14th Abridged Edition is designed primarily for school and public libraries with col-
lections of up to 20,000 titles

Sears list of subject headings. 18th ed, Joseph
Miller, editor; Joan Goodsell, associate editor.
Wilson, H.W. 2004 864p $115   **025.4**
1. Subject headings
ISBN 0-8242-1040-9
Also available Canadian companion. 6th edition published 2001
First published 1923 with title: List of subject headings for small libraries, by Minnie Earl Sears
In addition to the inclusion of five hundred new subject headings, this edition has updated the suggested classification numbers to conform to the 14th edition of the
Abridged Dewey Decimal classification. The new subject
headings reflect developments in areas such as computers, technology, personal relations, politics, and popular
culture

025.5 Services to users

Cooper, Gail
New virtual field trips; [by] Gail Cooper and
Garry Cooper. Libraries Unlimited 2001 155p pa
$27.50 **025.5**
1. Internet 2. World Wide Web 3. Field trips
ISBN 1-56308-887-8 LC 00-45091
Replaces virtual field trips, published 1997
This is an "annotated guide to 440 web sites . . . that
were selected to tie in to National Science Standards and
inquiry-based learning, and to encourage independent
studies. Organized into 13 topics covered in most K-12
school curricula, the entries include museums, libraries,
schools, scientific labs, and government and university
sites. . . . An accessible, useful resource." SLJ
Includes bibliographical references

Eisenberg, Michael
Teaching information & technology skills; the
Big6 in elementary schools; by Michael B.
Eisenberg and Robert E. Berkowitz; with Barbara
A. Jansen and Tami J. Little. Linworth Pub. 1999
Xl, 144p il pa $39.95 **025.5**
1. Computer-assisted instruction 2. Research
ISBN 0-938865-81-1 LC 99-29894
The six steps the authors "prescribe are: 'Task Defini-
tion,' 'Information Seeking Strategies,' 'Location & Ac-
cess,' 'Use of information,' 'Synthesis,' and 'Evaluation.'
. . . Sample lessons demonstrate how to integrate the
Big6 into the curriculum and to teach students how to
select appropriate resources, discriminate between needed
and superfluous information, and evaluate their progress
and success." SLJ
Includes bibliographical references

Farmer, Lesley S. Johnson
Technology-infused instruction for the
educational community; a guide for school library
specialists; [by] Lesley S.J. Farmer. Scarecrow
Press 2005 209p il pa $40 **025.5**
1. School libraries 2. Information technology
ISBN 0-8108-5118-0 LC 2004018028
"Library media teachers who provide staff development would do well to read this concise manual, which
provides a welcome shortcut for the training of teachers
and parents in the use of technology. . . . Farmer keeps
the information moving swiftly through an engaging text
that sparks ideas that readers can transfer smoothly into
practice. Useful checklists and worksheets that translate
into visuals abound." SLJ
Includes glossary and bibliographical references

Heiligman, Deborah
The New York Public Library kid's guide to
research. Scholastic Ref. 1998 134p il pa $8.95
hardcover o.p. (5 and up) **025.5**
1. Research 2. Libraries
ISBN 0-590-30716-9 (pa); 0-590-30715-0 (hc)
LC 97-28939

Provides guidance on how to do research, including
how to use libraries and their resources, the Internet, and
other sources such as interviews and surveys
"Short and complete, this book contains a wealth of
material for young researchers. . . . A book that is appealing and informative, with content appeal across the
grades." SLJ

Miller, Pat
Library skills. UpstartBooks 2003 56p il
(Stretchy library lessons) pa $15.95 **025.5**
1. Bibliographic instruction 2. Children's libraries
ISBN 1-57950-083-8 LC 2003-245
Contents: Genre relay; Caldecott challenge; Fairy tale
or folktale?; Where in the library?; Real or imagined?;
Selecting a book; Book care; Meet Melvil; What's my
line?; Life stories
This includes ten library skills lesson plans which can
be presented in 20 minutes or expanded to an hour, focusing "on basic skills such as parts of a book, fiction
and nonfiction, genres and the Dewey Decimal System."
Publisher's note
The book is "great for lesson plans for school media
specialists, and . . . [it also has] some interesting ideas
for crafts and activities for public librarians. . . . [A
must-have] for anyone working in a school library." SLJ
Includes bibliographical references

Reading activities. UpstartBooks 2003 80p il
(Stretchy library lessons) pa $15.95 **025.5**
1. Books and reading 2. Children's libraries
ISBN 1-57950-082-X LC 2003-279132
This includes ten reading activity lesson plans which
can be presented in 20 minutes or expanded to an hour,
focusing "on basic reading skills such as cause and effect, fact and opinion, main idea with supporting details,
story mapping, graphic organizers and retelling in sequence." Publisher's note
This book is "great for lesson plans for school media
specialists, and . . . [it also has] some interesting ideas
for crafts and activities for public librarians. . . . [A
must-have] for anyone working in a school library." SLJ

Research skills. UpstartBooks 2003 79p il
(Stretchy library lessons) pa $15.95 **025.5**
1. Research 2. Children's libraries
ISBN 1-57950-084-6 LC 2003-271646
This includes ten research skills lesson plans which
can be presented in 20 minutes or expanded to an hour
focusing on "using electronic and print resources, forming questions and locating answers and gathering and organizing information." Publisher's note
This book is "great for lesson plans for school media
specialists, and . . . [it also has] some interesting ideas
for crafts and activities for public librarians. . . . [A
must-have] for anyone working in a school library." SLJ
Includes bibliographical references

025.8 Maintenance and preservation of library collections

Halsted, Deborah D.

Disaster planning; a how-to-do-it manual for librarians with planning templates on CD-ROM; [by] Deborah D. Halsted, Richard P. Jasper, and Felicia M. Little. Neal-Schuman Publishers 2005 xx, 247p il (How-to-do-it manuals for librarians) pa $85 **025.8**

1. Disaster relief 2. Accidents—Prevention 3. Library resources—Conservation and restoration
ISBN 1-55570-486-7 LC 2003-65152
Includes CD-ROM

"Step-by-step instructions discuss creating a working disaster team, establishing a communications strategy, identifying relief and recovery agencies, developing response plans, and examining issues of cutting-edge library security. . . . This valuable resource is an important addition to most professional collections." Booklist
Includes bibliographical references

027 General libraries, information centers

Appelt, Kathi

Down Cut Shin Creek; the pack horse librarians of Kentucky; [by] Kathi Appelt & Jeanne Cannella Schmitzer. HarperCollins Pubs. 2001 58p il $16.99; lib bdg $17.89 (4 and up) **027**

1. Librarians 2. Great Depression, 1929-1939 3. Mountain life 4. Kentucky
ISBN 0-06-029135-4; 0-06-029244-X (lib bdg)
LC 00-59702

This describes the Pack Horse Library Project of Eastern Kentucky, which during the Great Depression delivered books to poor families in remote mountain communities.

"Appelt and Schmitzer's slim but evocative account finally gives these early outreach librarians their due. The detailed text and accompanying photographs recreate a time of extreme hardship. . . . A rich, well-documented bibliography is appended." Booklist
Includes bibliographical references

Malam, John

Library; from ancient scrolls to the World Wide Web. Bedrick Bks. 2000 32p il (Building works) lib bdg $16.95 (4 and up) **027**

1. Libraries 2. Library science
ISBN 0-87226-587-0 LC 99-57835

Reveals the inner workings of a large public library by examining the various departments and their functions, the equipment used, and the duties of the people who work there

This "book includes lending libraries and bookmobiles as well as single-themed collections such as special-needs, children's, multimedia, reference, local history, business, and rare books. . . . [An] outstanding offering." SLJ
Includes glossary

Munro, Roxie

The inside-outside book of libraries; paintings by Roxie Munro; text by Julie Cummins. Dutton Children's Bks. 1996 unp il $16.99 (2-4) **027**

1. Libraries
ISBN 0-525-45608-2 LC 96-12111

Illustrations and brief text present various types of libraries, from bookmobiles and home libraries to the New York Public Library and the Library of Congress

"Cummins's text flows smoothly and is easy to comprehend, and the vast array of facilities discussed will add greatly to children's understanding of the concept of library services. Munro's excellent watercolor illustrations are extremely detailed and reveal an incredible sense of each architectural space." SLJ

Trumble, Kelly

The Library of Alexandria; illustrated by Robina MacIntyre Marshall. Clarion Bks. 2003 72p il maps $17 (5 and up) **027**

1. Alexandrian Library (Egypt) 2. Egypt—Civilization 3. Ancient civilization
ISBN 0-395-75832-7 LC 2003-150

Contents: A city of learning; Collecting books; Pergamum; Astronomy; Geography; Mathematics; Medicine; Decline and destruction; The fate of the Library of Alexandria

An introduction to the largest and most famous library in the ancient world, discussing its construction in Alexandria, Egypt, its vast collections, rivalry with the Pergamum Library, famous scholars, and destruction by fire

This is a "well-organized and thorough resource." SLJ
Includes glossary and bibliographical references

027.4 Public libraries

Mediavilla, Cindy

Creating the full-service homework center in your library. American Lib. Assn. 2001 141p pa $35 **027.4**

1. Libraries and students 2. Public libraries 3. Latchkey children
ISBN 0-8389-0800-4 LC 00-52163

The author "describes what constitutes an effective homework center, a separate space in the library, with set hours, clearly defined services, and an assigned staff member. With real-life examples from actual homework centers, this how-to-do-it manual has . . . sample surveys, goals, objectives, publicity and recruitment flyers, homework helper application forms and contracts, staff and volunteer job descriptions, grant applications, and focus group questions." Publisher's note

"There are no other books available solely on this topic, and this resource is surely definitive." Voice Youth Advocates
Includes bibliographical references

027.62   Libraries for young people

Bauer, Caroline Feller

Leading kids to books through crafts. American
Lib. Assn. 2000 145p (Mighty easy motivators) pa
$30   **027.62**

1. Children's libraries 2. Books and reading
3. Handicraft 4. Children's literature—Bibliography

ISBN 0-8389-0769-5   LC 99-41387

"Bauer gives basic, practical information on presenting
programs that introduce preschool and primary-grade
youngsters to stories and poems and demonstrates related
crafts that are easy to prepare and execute." SLJ

Leading kids to books through magic; illustrated
by Richard Laurent. American Lib. Assn. 1996
128p il (Mighty easy motivators) pa $29

                                 027.62

1. Children's libraries 2. Books and reading 3. Magic
tricks 4. Children's literature—Bibliography

ISBN 0-8389-0684-2   LC 95-53049

"Bauer shows how she uses magic tricks to entertain
children as she leads them to good books. . . . Each section includes instructions for performing at least one trick
as well as a short, annotated list of related books and,
occasionally, a story or poem to present as part of the
magician's patter." Booklist

The author's "concise yet thorough directions accompanied by Richard Laurent's delightful line drawings
make this book a useful tool for teachers and librarians
looking for ways to promote children's enthusiasm for
reading." J Youth Serv Libr

Includes bibliographical references

Leading kids to books through puppets;
illustrated by Richard Laurent. American Lib.
Assn. 1997 156p il (Mighty easy motivators) pa
$22   **027.62**

1. Children's libraries 2. Books and reading
3. Puppets and puppet plays 4. Children's literature—
Bibliography

ISBN 0-8389-0706-7   LC 97-1357

This "book suggests ways to promote books and reading to children through simple puppetry. . . . [It offers]
a number of theme-based programs complete with stories
to act out, poems, and lists of related books." Booklist

"Even the most reluctant performer will be encouraged
by this practical, concise, easy-to-use book." SLJ

Includes bibliographical references

Read for the fun of it; active programming with
books for children; drawings by Lynn Gates
Bredeson. Wilson, H.W. 1992 xx, 372p il $75

                                 027.62

1. Books and reading 2. Children's literature
3. Children's libraries

ISBN 0-8242-0824-2   LC 91-31450

"Among the topics covered are reading aloud, reaching parents, author visits, storytelling with visual aids,
teaching children to present stories and poetry, and using
puppetry and magic tricks in storytelling." Booklist

"Diagrams, artwork, and word games are . . . scattered appropriately throughout the book. All are reproducible and available for reader use. . . . *Read for the*

Fun of it emphasizes Bauer's obvious passion for reading, making this book a delightful addition to the professional collection." J Youth Serv Libr

Includes bibliographical references

Benton, Gail

Ready-to-go storytimes; fingerplays, scripts,
patterns, music, and more; [by] Gail Benton,
Trisha Waichulaitis. Neal-Schuman 2003 239p il
$59.95   **027.62**

1. Storytelling 2. Children's libraries

ISBN 1-55570-449-2   LC 2002-5806

"The six chapters represent six themed programs that
include a welcome song, a read-aloud book, and various
enrichment activities such as fingerplays, props, songs,
coloring projects, and games. The accompanying CD includes 14 songs appropriate for the specific themes." SLJ

"This resource is excellent for beginning librarians and
teachers and for any professionals who seek new ideas
to freshen up their repertoires." Booklist

Includes bibliographical references

Bromann, Jennifer

Storytime action! 2000+ ideas for making 500
picture books interactive. Neal-Schuman 2003
295p pa $45   **027.62**

1. Children's libraries 2. Storytelling 3. Picture books
for children—Bibliography

ISBN 1-55570-459-X   LC 2002-31994

The author "provides readers with ideas and tools to
add interactivity to their programs. Tips include incorporating props, questions, movement, etc.; selecting the
right books for your style; and adding simple crafts.
Most of the book consists of an alphabetical listing (by
author) of 500 recommended titles." SLJ

This "is packed with practical and fun activities for
educators, parents, public librarians, and school media
specialists." Booklist

Includes bibliographical references

Cullum, Carolyn N.

The storytime sourcebook; a compendium of
ideas and resources for storytellers. 2nd ed.
Neal-Schuman 1999 469p pa $49.95

                                 027.62

1. Storytelling 2. Children's libraries

ISBN 1-55570-360-7   LC 99-46420

First published 1990

A guide to 146 topics and 2,200 picture books. Appropriate videos and CDs are discussed. A "Topical Calendar," arranged chronologically, suggests holidays or
notable events that can be related to a storyhour theme

Includes bibliographical references

Ernst, Linda L.

Lapsit services for the very young II; a
how-to-do-it manual. Neal-Schuman 2001 217p
(How-to-do-it manuals for libraries) $38.50

                                 027.62

1. Children's libraries 2. Storytelling

ISBN 1-55570-391-7   LC 00-45076

Replaces Lapsit services for the very young, published
1995

Ernst, Linda L.—*Continued*

The author offers "explanations of the latest in brain-development research, stages in early-child development, and an excellent Webliography. This volume is rich with book suggestions, finger rhymes, songs, extension ideas, and other program resources. Thematic indexes and camera-ready handouts make it an essential tool for busy librarians trying to serve their youngest customers." SLJ

Includes bibliographical references

Feinberg, Sandra

Running a parent/child workshop; a how-to-do-it manual for librarians; [by] Sandra Feinberg, Kathleen Deere; with special assistance from the staff of the Middle Country Public Library. Neal-Schuman 1995 166p il (How-to-do-it manuals for libraries) pa $49.95   **027.62**
1. Children's libraries
ISBN 1-55570-189-2   LC 94-46345
"The goals of the workshop, Feinberg says, are to increase parents' awareness of library services and materials, to tell them about child development and community agencies, and to provide a comfortable place for parent-child interaction. The authors provide bibliographies of materials for both children and parents. . . . Also included are sample program forms, publicity ideas, suggestions for workshop content, floor plans for workshop space, a list of references, and an index." SLJ

Fiore, Carole D.

Fiore's summer library reading program handbook. Neal-Schuman Publishers 2005 xxiii, 312p pa $65   **027.62**
1. Children's libraries 2. Books and reading
ISBN 1-55570-513-8
"This research-laden handbook . . . serves as a 'comprehensive program-planning and implementation tool' for public libraries seeking to revamp, revise, or develop a summer library reading program. . . . This is an invaluable resource, both for its concrete guidance and its abstract exploration of the meaning of summer library programs." Bull Cent Child Books

Includes bibliographical references

Holbrook, Belinda

String stories; a creative, hands-on approach for engaging children in literature. Linworth Pub. 2002 141p il pa $36.95   **027.62**
1. Storytelling 2. String figures
ISBN 1-58683-063-5   LC 2002-32443
A "collection of stories that use the ancient art of string figures to tell the tales. Holbrook opens by explaining how this art has crossed over many cultures. . . . This first chapter also covers basic string instruction for the uninitiated. . . . Instructions follow guidelines developed by the International String Figure Association and are clearly illustrated, step-by-step, with black-and-white photos. The 19 stories are arranged by level of difficulty. . . . A unique and comprehensive collection for storytellers." SLJ

Includes bibliographical references

Marino, Jane

Babies in the library! Scarecrow Press 2003 149p $23.50   **027.62**
1. Children's libraries
ISBN 0-8108-4576-8   LC 2002-12022
Contents: Babies in the library; What works for prewalkers; What works for walkers; Rhymes to take home; Puppet rhymes

The author presents "arguments for holding library programs specifically geared toward babies. Organizing and presenting her ideas in a thoughtful and philosophical manner, she addresses many relevant topics: making babies feel comfortable in the library, creating programs for prewalkers and walkers, handling registration, and offering suggestions for planning and executing programs. She also includes various activities that introduce books, rhymes, puppets, and other tools that enhance language skills." SLJ

Includes bibliographical references

Mother Goose time; library programs for babies and their caregivers; by Jane Marino and Dorothy F. Houlihan; music arrangements by Jane Marino; photographs by Susan G. Drinker. Wilson, H.W. 1992 172p il music $50   **027.62**
1. Children's libraries 2. Nursery rhymes
ISBN 0-8242-0850-1   LC 91-46986
"The book was inspired by a program designed by the authors, librarians . . . who conducted 'Mother Goose Time' sessions for more than five years at the White Plains, New York, Public Library. These interactive sessions involved sharing songs and rhymes with babies and adults. . . . There are musical arrangements for the songs; bibliographies of picture books, display books, and resource books; an evaluation of form; and various indexes categorizing the rhymes and songs by title, first line, and developmental level." J Youth Serv Libr

Includes bibliographical references

Nespeca, Sue McCleaf

Library programming for families with young children. Neal-Schuman 1994 180p il (How-to-do-it manuals for libraries) $49.95
                                       027.62
1. Children's libraries
ISBN 1-55570-181-7   LC 94-37894
The author "outlines the developmental characteristics of young children, providing book-sharing ideas for different age groups, sample family programs, current bibliographies of suggested titles, and places to write for additional information. Multicultural, intergenerational, institutional, and outreach programs are discussed separately, with suggestions for their implementation." SLJ

Includes bibliographical references

Pavon, Ana-Elba

25 Latino craft projects; [by] Ana-Elba Pavon, Diana Borrego. American Lib. Assn. 2003 80p il (Celebrating culture in your library) pa $30
                                       027.62
1. Children's libraries 2. Hispanic Americans—Social life and customs 3. Handicraft
ISBN 0-8389-0833-0   LC 2002-5750

Pavon, Ana-Elba—*Continued*

Following a "chapter on planning, the projects are organized around important Latino holidays and are inspired by *artesenias* (Latino folk art). . . . For each celebration, there is a suggested program for preschoolers, after-schooler, and families; each program incorporates the craft with songs, poems, and books. Activities include making piñatas, paper flowers, sweet tamales, and salsa." SLJ

Includes glossary and bibliographical references

Reid, Rob

Something funny happened at the library; how to create humorous programs for children and young adults. American Lib. Assn. 2003 163p $32

027.62

1. Children's libraries 2. Young adults' libraries 3. Storytelling

ISBN 0-8389-0836-5   LC 2002-8970

Contents: Tricks of the trade; Humor programs for younger children: preschool and primary school age; Humor programs for intermediate school age children; Humor programs for middle and high school students; Reader's theater; Lively library tours & visits to schools; Raps and closings; The funniest books in the library; Two last treats

This is "an excellent resource for adding wit to your library repertoire." SLJ

Includes bibliographical references

Sierra, Judy

The flannel board storytelling book. 2nd ed rev & expanded. Wilson, H.W. 1997 241p il music $60

027.62

1. Children's libraries 2. Storytelling

ISBN 0-8242-0932-X   LC 97-15107

First published 1987

"Fifty stories, poems, and songs and over three hundred patterns are included for presenting stories to children in a flannel board medium, including classic children's stories, nursery rhymes, folk tales, and songs. . . . Sierra's experience telling stories with children is reflected throughout her book." J Youth Serv Libr

Sima, Judy

Raising voices; creating youth storytelling groups and troupes; [by] Judy Sima, Kevin Cordi. Libraries Unlimited 2003 xxviii, 241p pa $32.50

027.62

1. Storytelling

ISBN 1-56308-919-X   LC 2003-47631

This offers a "blueprint for beginning and sustaining a successful group or troupe of storytellers from grades 4 to 12. . . . The book includes reproducible forms that will save a lot of work and lists of valuable resources. . . . Raising Voices is the complete, and essential, handbook for this special group of storytellers." SLJ

Includes bibliographical references

Soltan, Rita

Reading raps; a book club guide for librarians, kids, and families; [by] Rita Soltan. Libraries Unlimited 2006 354p pa $35   **027.62**

1. Children's libraries 2. Books and reading 3. Children's literature—Bibliography

ISBN 1-59158-234-2   LC 2005030842

"The author provides librarians with a guide to book discussion groups for children and adults, with plans for 100 books geared to grades 3-8. Ideas for forming groups and choosing titles, discussion questions, and ice-breakers are included. Titles range from older classics to books published in 2004 and cover all fiction genres. . . . The novice group leader will find this book helpful, and the experienced facilitator will find many new ideas." Booklist

Includes bibliographical references

Steele, Anita T.

Bare bones children's services; tips for public library generalists; [by] Anita T. Steele [and] Association for Library Service to Children. American Lib. Assn. 2001 123p pa $32

027.62

1. Children's libraries 2. Libraries and students 3. Public libraries

ISBN 0-8389-0791-1   LC 00-48492

Partial contents: Storytime and storytelling; Summer reading programs; Collection development; Displays

"Covers children's services, programming, and promotion of books and the library, along the way pointing out practical differences between children and adult library users." Publisher's note

Includes bibliographical references

Stover, Lynne Farrell

Magical library lessons; [by] Lynne Farrell Stover. UpstartBooks 2003 85p il pa $16.95

027.62

1. Children's libraries 2. Bibliographic instruction

ISBN 1-57950-094-3   LC 2004-269620

Also available More magical library lessons (2004)

"Stover presents 15 stand-alone exercises designed to teach and reinforce library skills, research techniques, and literary concepts. . . . Each entry begins with a quote and a story synopsis of a book by a popular writer. . . . An introduction, time involved, objectives, materials, procedure, a subjective evaluation, and an enrichment extension are included, as are visuals and activity sheets. Up-to-date library and literacy lessons are always welcome, and these are winners." SLJ

Includes bibliographical references

Sullivan, Michael

Fundamentals of children's services. American Library Association 2005 255p il (ALA fundamentals series) pa $45   **027.62**

1. Children's libraries

ISBN 0-8389-0907-8

This "covers the underlying principles and mission of library work for children and then discusses the collection, services, programming, and management. . . . Sec-

Sullivan, Michael—*Continued*

tions on homework, interlibrary loan, and reference services are especially well done, and lists of good story hour books for infants and toddlers as well as for older children are valuable." Booklist

Includes bibliographical references

Van Orden, Phyllis J.

Library service to children; a guide to the history, planning, policy, and research literature; [by] Phyllis Van Orden, Patricia Pawelak-Kort. Rowman & Littlefield 2005 154p pa $35

027.62

1. Children's libraries—Bibliography 2. Children—Books and reading—Bibliography

ISBN 0-8108-5169-5

"There are 428 works written or published between 1876 and 2003 in this annotated bibliography, which updates the 1992 edition of the same title. Every format is included, from journal articles to books, to brochures, to government documents, to electronic resources. . . . This is an amazingly complete resource for researchers." Booklist

Walter, Virginia A.

Children and libraries; getting it right. American Lib. Assn. 2000 155p pa $32 **027.62**

1. Children's libraries 2. Young adults' libraries

ISBN 0-8389-0795-4 LC 00-57600

Walter "examines changing routines, educational practices, and social patterns that have had a profound effect on our communities and from these trends drafts a slate of suggested goals for those of us who strive to serve children. She also examines the impact of digital technology and looks at the future of the book." SLJ

Includes bibliographical references

Weissman, Annie

Do tell! storytelling for you and your students. Linworth Pub. 2002 86p il pa $36.95

027.62

1. Storytelling 2. Children's libraries

ISBN 1-58683-074-0 LC 2002-32969

"This concise beginner's guide encourages school librarians and teachers to incorporate storytelling into the elementary curriculum. It discusses how to select a story; how to learn it; and how to present it, including voice, pace, dialects, facial expressions, sound effects, and audience participation. . . . Proverbs, myths, fables, and folktales, all in the public domain and selected with beginning storytellers in mind, make this a handy one-volume source." SLJ

Includes bibliographical references

027.8 School libraries

American Association of School Librarians

Information power; building partnerships for learning; prepared by the American Association of School Librarians [and] Association for Educational Communications and Technology. American Lib. Assn. 1998 205p il pa $37

027.8

1. School libraries 2. Instructional materials centers

ISBN 0-8389-3470-6 LC 98-23291

First published 1988

This resource "relates the library-media program to the entire educational infrastructure. The authors explicate their themes in terms of standards, indicators, levels of proficiency, goals, principles, and examples of student activities. The appendixes contain essential information on Library Power, AASL's ICON-nect project, the Library Bill of Rights, confidentiality, censorship, access equity, and ethics." SLJ

Includes bibliographical references

Bradburn, Frances Bryant

Output measures for school library media programs. Neal-Schuman 1999 95p pa $55

027.8

1. School libraries 2. Instructional materials centers

ISBN 1-55570-326-7 LC 98-45557

"Bradburn's handbook is intended to guide school library specialists in collecting data on budgets, staff, and services and in using the data to evaluate programs and argue for increased funding. Forms and work sheets as well as three case studies are included." Booklist

Includes bibliographical references

Craver, Kathleen W.

Creating cyber libraries; an instructional guide for school library media specialists. Libraries Unlimited 2002 xxvi, 222p (Greenwood professional guides in school librarianship) pa $40

027.8

1. Internet resources 2. School libraries

ISBN 0-313-32080-2 LC 2001-55619

"Nine chapters cover guidelines; policies to consider; Web-design issues; the use of portals; and strategies for maintaining, evaluating, and promoting a library Web site. Special-interest areas, such as providing a virtual reading room and online instruction, are also discussed. . . . This title is a one-stop-shopping bonanza of wonderful, useful ideas on how to create a cyber library that will meet the information needs of our patrons." Libr J

Includes bibliographical references

Exploring science in the library; resources and activities for young people; edited by Maria Sosa and Tracy Gath. American Lib. Assn. 1999 236p pa $32 **027.8**

1. Elementary school libraries 2. Science—Study and teaching

ISBN 0-8389-0768-7 LC 99-41496

Exploring science in the library—*Continued*

This "resource helps public and school librarians develop science, math, and technology resources for K-12 students, supporting the recent national efforts toward achieving science literacy." SLJ

Includes bibliographical references

Farmer, Lesley S. Johnson

Student success and library media programs; a systems approach to research and best practice; [by] Lesley S. J. Farmer. Libraries Unlimited 2003 180p bibl tab pa $45   **027.8**

1. School libraries 2. Academic achievement

ISBN 1-59158-058-7   LC 2003-53881

"Designed for school library media specialists, this book focuses on library media programs and examines the factors that influence student achievement." Publisher's note

This is a "comprehensive and thoroughly researched book. . . . An invaluable guide for media specialists." SLJ

Includes bibliographical references

Harada, Violet H.

Assessing learning; librarians and teachers as partners. Libraries Unlimited 2005 149p il pa $40   **027.8**

1. School libraries 2. Instructional materials centers

ISBN 1-59158-200-8

"After reviewing the topic of assessment, the authors look at library media centers to determine where and how students should be assessed and then examine assessment tools and explain a wide array of effective graphic organizers. . . . Close to 100 illustrations demonstrate the many forms of assessment described. Chapters are well constructed and the writing is clear." SLJ

Includes bibliographical references

The **Information-powered** school; [by] Public Education Network, American Association of School Librarians; edited by Sandra Hughes-Hassell, Anne Wheelock. American Lib. Assn. 2001 138p il pa $35   **027.8**

1. Library Power (Program) 2. School libraries 3. Instructional materials centers

ISBN 0-8389-3514-1   LC 2001-22561

"This volume presents a variety of articles highlighting various aspects and activities of Information Powered Schools and giving tips for putting the principles and practices to work. . . . Checklists, surveys, and planning forms are included to determine the status of current practices. The collaborative planning worksheets, request forms, unit evaluation and collaborative-unit evaluation forms will be of special interest to librarians already involved in this process." SLJ

Includes bibliographical references

Johnson, Mary

Primary sources in the library; a collaboration guide for library media specialists; [by] Mary J. Johnson. Linworth Pub 2003 145p il $39.95   **027.8**

1. School libraries 2. History—Study and teaching

ISBN 1-58683-075-9   LC 2003-12887

This offers ideas for school librarians for developing collaborative units with teachers in grades 4 through 12 that incorporate primary source material.

"A treasure trove of ideas, lessons, and strategies for teaching the concept of primary sources." SLJ

Includes bibliographical references

Martin, Ann M.

7 steps to an award-winning school library program; [by] Ann M. Martin; foreword by Ruth Toor. Libraries Unlimited 2005 129p diag il tab pa $35   **027.8**

1. School libraries 2. Instructional materials centers

ISBN 1-59158-173-7

Cover title: Seven steps to an award-winning school library program

"The author's purpose in this book is to describe how to use *Information Power* effectively and how to achieve the goal of winning a national award. . . . Her description of the process is organized in seven clearly explained steps. Appendixes contain helpful forms and policy statements. . . . [This is a] well-written, unique, and important book." Booklist

Ray, Virginia Lawrence

School wide book events; how to make them happen; [by] Virginia Lawrence Ray. Libraries Unlimited 2003 133p pa $25   **027.8**

1. School libraries 2. Books and reading

ISBN 1-59158-038-2   LC 2003-47724

"The author's intent is to present ideas on how to celebrate reading across grade levels and curriculum, involving teachers, administration, faculty, and students both in preparation and actual activities. She proposes that school libraries have a Book Event for the whole school. . . . All events require simple resources and are easy to follow even for school systems with extremely limited budgets." SLJ

Includes bibliographical references

School Library Journal's best; a reader for children's, young adult & school librarians; edited by Lillian N. Gerhardt; compiled by Marilyn L. Miller & Thomas W. Downen. Neal-Schuman 1997 474p il $49.95   **027.8**

1. School libraries 2. Children's libraries 3. Young adults' libraries

ISBN 1-55570-203-1   LC 96-23856

This is a collection of articles and columns culled from issues of SLJ from 1971 to the present. Contributors include Ursula Nordstrom, Margaret McElderry, Zena Sutherland, and June Jordan

"A useful overview of professional writing of the last quarter-century." Bull Cent Child Books

Includes bibliographical references

Schuckett, Sandy

Political advocacy for school librarians; you have the power! by Sandy Schuckett. Linworth Pub 2004 128p pa $39.95   **027.8**

1. School libraries 2. Libraries and community 3. Lobbying

ISBN 1-58683-158-5   LC 2004-4869

Schuckett, Sandy—*Continued*

"Schuckett motivates and explicitly details an exciting 'how-to' of political lobbying at all levels—from the school site and local board all the way to the national level. . . . School librarians need political clout, and Schuckett shows us how to get it." SLJ

Includes bibliographical references

Stein, Barbara L.

Running a school library media center; a how-to-do-it manual for librarians; [by] Barbara L. Stein, Risa W. Brown. 2nd ed. Neal-Schuman 2002 179p (How-to-do-it manuals for libraries) pa $49.95 **027.8**

1. School libraries 2. Instructional materials centers
ISBN 1-55570-439-5   LC 2002-2987
First published 1992

Contents: Getting started; Policies and procedures; Ordering and processing materials; Cataloging; Circulation; Maintaining the collection; Hiring and working with staff; Designing and using the facility; Information literacy; Programming

"This manual offers assistance to any new or seasoned library media specialist on aspects of library management. . . . Because of its comprehensive inclusion of easily accessible information, this is an important resource." SLJ

The **Whole** school library handbook; edited by Blanche Woolls and David V. Loertscher. American Library Association 2005 448p pa $45 **027.8**

1. School libraries 2. Instructional materials centers
ISBN 0-8389-0883-7   LC 2004-20198

This reference resource to the school media center includes "facts, . . . articles, checklists, organization contact information, trivia, [and] advice from the field's experts. . . . [It also features] information on fundraising, grant writing, flexible scheduling, promoting the school library, and advocating its value in the school community." Publisher's note

Includes bibliographical references

Zweizig, Douglas

Lessons from Library Power; enriching teaching and learning: final report of the evaluation of the national library power initiative: an initiative of the DeWitt Wallace-Reader's Digest Fund; [by] Douglas L. Zweizig and Dianne McAfee Hopkins; with Norman Lott Webb and Gary Wehlage. Libraries Unlimited 1999 281p pa $39.50 **027.8**

1. Library Power (Program) 2. School libraries
ISBN 1-56308-833-9   LC 99-52025

The authors "examine the specific goals and accomplishments of Library Power, the school library funding project initiated in 1988 by the DeWitt Wallace—Reader's Digest Fund. Having analyzed surveys collected from teachers, librarians, and principals, and case studies of media center practices, they conclude that collaborative planning, flexible scheduling, collection development, and professional growth can make a positive difference in libraries and the students that they support." Booklist

Includes bibliographical references

028.1 Reviews of books and other media

Baxter, Kathleen A.

Gotcha! nonfiction booktalks to get kids excited about reading; by Kathleen A. Baxter [and] Marcia Agness Kochel. Libraries Unlimited 1999 183p pa $28 **028.1**

1. Books and reading
ISBN 1-56308-683-2   LC 99-34279

This guide to booktalking discusses more than 350 titles for grades one through eight

The books are presented in a "conversational style that is extremely readable and entertaining; useful bibliographies following each section assign appropriate grade levels to the books. The authors also give general tips on organizing booktalks." SLJ

Includes bibliographical references

The **Best** in children's books; the University of Chicago guide to children's literature, 1966-1972—1985-1990; written and edited by Zena Sutherland. University of Chicago Press 1973-1991 4v **028.1**

1. Children's literature—Bibliography 2. Best books 3. Books—Reviews

Successor to Good books for children; a selection of outstanding children's books published 1950-65, compiled by Mary K. Eakin

1985-1990 volume written by Zena Sutherland, Betsy Hearne, and Roger Sutton

Volumes available are: 1966-1972 $39 (ISBN 0-226-78057-0); 1973-1978 $39 (ISBN 0-226-78059-7); 1979-1984 $50 (ISBN 0-226-78060-0); 1985-1990 $50 (ISBN 0-226-78064-3)

These volumes bring together reviews originally published in The Bulletin of the Center for Children's Books. Some 1400 recommended titles from each period are covered in each volume. The listings are arranged alphabetically by author, with title, developmental values, curricular use, reading level, subject, and type of literature indexes

The **Best** in children's nonfiction; reading, writing, and teaching Orbis Pictus Award books; edited by Myra Zarnowski, Richard M. Kerper, Julie M. Jensen. National Council of Teachers of English 2001 161p $21.95 **028.1**

1. Orbis Pictus Award 2. Children's literature—History and criticism 3. Children's literature—Bibliography
ISBN 0-8141-0489-4   LC 2001-44261

"Looking at the first ten years of NCTE's Orbis Pictus Award for excellence in children's nonfiction, the book features current and former members of the award committee discussing the issues that keep them engaged as they select each year's winner, honor books, and recommended titles. . . . Readers get to meet outstanding writers—and Orbis Pictus Award winners or honorees—as they reflect on their work during the 1990s. . . . The book concludes with an annotated list of Orbis Pictus winners and honor books from 1989 to 1999, including teaching suggestions for classroom use." Publisher's note

Includes bibliographical references

Blass, Rosanne J.
Celebrate with books; booktalks for holidays and other occasions; [by] Rosanne J. Blass. Libraries Unlimited 2005 226p pa $35

028.1

1. Children's literature—Bibliography 2. Holidays—Bibliography 3. Book talks
ISBN 1-59158-076-5

"This collection of booktalks for children in kindergarten through sixth grade emphasizes picture books, chapter books, and poetry published from 2000 to 2004. The volume begins with general holidays celebrated by cultures around the world . . . and then takes a month-by-month approach. Additional year-round celebrations . . . are appended. For each observation, at least two selections are suggested and include a complete citation, genre, age level, culture (where appropriate), summary, the booktalk itself, and a learning extension. . . . A great aid for collection development and for thematic planning." SLJ

Cianciolo, Patricia J.
Informational picture books for children. American Lib. Assn. 2000 205p pa $38

028.1

1. Picture books for children—Bibliography
ISBN 0-8389-0774-1   LC 99-39597

"Cianciolo lists the criteria for inclusion and discusses trends in informational picture books. Subsequent chapters provide lengthy critical annotations, including recommended age levels, divided into categories such as 'The Natural World,' 'Numbers and Arithmetic,' 'Peoples and Cultures,' And 'Arts and Crafts.' The approximately 250 titles are up-to-date, and though most of them would be considered nonfiction, a handful of titles are classified as fiction or include fictionalized elements." SLJ

Includes bibliographical references

Horning, Kathleen T.
From cover to cover; evaluating and reviewing children's books. HarperCollins Pubs. 1997 230p pa $14.99 hardcover o.p.   **028.1**

1. Books—Reviews 2. Children's literature—History and criticism
ISBN 0-06-446167-X (pa); 0-06-024519-0 (hc)
                               LC 96-27281

The author "begins with an overview of how children's books are published in the United States, the physical parts of the book, and categories of children's books. The next six chapters are devoted to the definition and scope of those categories." Bull Cent Child Books

"Anyone entering the field of children's book reviewing, or indeed, the wider field of children's literature, will find *From Cover to Cover* an excellent guide to analyzing books and presenting clear, useful reviews." Booklist

Includes bibliographical references

Odean, Kathleen
Great books about things kids love; more than 750 recommended books for children 3 to 14. Ballantine Bks. 2001 xxiii, 439p pa $14

028.1

1. Books and reading 2. Children's literature—Bibliography
ISBN 0-345-44131-1   LC 00-68072

This bibliography of children's books is organized under eight broad subject categories and includes such subjects as "baseball, robots, dinosaurs, knights, wizards, cars, trucks, and trains. The annotations in big clear type are more like reviews, relaxed in style, both enthusiastic and informative. . . . This is a strong parent's resource that also belongs on the professional shelf." Booklist

Includes bibliographical references

Great books for babies and toddlers; more than 500 recommended books for your child's first three years. Ballantine Bks. 2003 337p pa $14.95

028.1

1. Picture books for children—Bibliography
ISBN 0-345-45254-2   LC 2003-90307

This offers "annotations for more than five hundred books, divided into two . . . categories: Nursery Rhymes, Fingerplays, and Songs; and Picture-Story Books for the Very Young." Publisher's note

This is a "fine roundup of well-annotated, carefully selected books. . . . It is also a wonderful repository of information that will help adults make educated choices of their own and use them well—not only to help their child's language development but also just for fun." Booklist

Great books for boys; more than 600 books for boys 2 to 14. Ballantine Bks. 1998 384p pa $13.95

028.1

1. Boys—Books and reading 2. Children's literature—Bibliography 3. Young adult literature—Bibliography
ISBN 0-345-42083-7   LC 97-45926

This annotated bibliography offers recommended titles and strategies for parents, teachers, and librarians to promote reading among boys

"An excellent resource!" SLJ

Great books for girls; more than 600 recommended books for girls ages 3-14. rev ed. Ballantine Books 2002 417p pa $14.95

028.1

1. Girls—Books and reading 2. Children's literature—Bibliography 3. Young adult literature—Bibliography
ISBN 0-345-45021-3

First published 1997

This bibliography "introduces 600 titles, ranging from picture-story books for toddlers to biographies and novels for adolescents that depict girls and women who are self-sufficient, decisive, and assertive. . . . Odean's background as a children's book expert is apparent in her well-crafted, descriptive annotations. . . . The introduction and last chapter provide advice about locating good children's books, reading aloud, etc." Libr J [review of 1997 ed]

028.5 Reading and use of other information media by young people

Author talk; conversations with Judy Blume [et al.]; compiled and edited by Leonard S. Marcus. Simon & Schuster Bks. for Young Readers 2000 103p il $22 (4 and up) **028.5**
1. Authors
ISBN 0-689-81383-X   LC 99-39777
Presents interviews with fifteen well-known children's writers, including Judy Blume, Karen Cushman, Russell Freedman, James Howe, Lois Lowry, Gary Paulsen, and Laurence Yep
"In addition to the editor's well-crafted introductions to the writers, the volume contains contemporary photos and childhood snapshots, reproductions of edited manuscript pages and a selected bibliography of each author's oeuvre. An excellent choice for aspiring writers and avid readers." Publ Wkly

Bauer, Caroline Feller
This way to books; drawings by Lynn Gates. Wilson, H.W. 1983 363p il $66   **028.5**
1. Books and reading 2. Children's literature
ISBN 0-8242-0678-9   LC 82-19985
"Designed to involve children in books, this compendium is chock-full of ideas for programs, booktalks, games, crafts, and exhibits. Bauer's upbeat tone lends enthusiasm, and her numerous suggestions, which include easy-to-implement activities, short poems, directions for crafts, recipes, and unusual but effective bibliographies, will inspire readers with new ideas. . . . Teachers, librarians, and other adults working with children will find the collection worthwhile and helpful as a springboard to their own variations." Booklist

The **Cambridge** guide to children's books in English; [edited by] Victor Watson; advisory editors, Elizabeth L. Keyser, Juliet Partridge, Morag Styles. Cambridge Univ. Press 2001 814p il $75   **028.5**
1. Children's literature—Encyclopedias
ISBN 0-521-55064-5   LC 00-65163
This reference provides an "overview of historic and contemporary children's books published in English. The entries include authors, illustrators, and significant works primarily from Britain, the US, Canada, Australia, New Zealand, India, and Africa. . . . Major themes, such as fairy tales, fantasy, folktales, legends, mythology, and young adult fiction, are covered as well as less-expected entries on topics such as bias, the bush, disability, ecology, and nudity in children's books. Nonbook media are also covered by entries on animated cartoons, comics, superheroes, and television for children." Choice
Includes bibliographical references

Children's books and their creators; Anita Silvey, editor. Houghton Mifflin 1995 800p il $45
028.5
1.   Children's   literature—Bio-bibliography
2. Children's literature—History and criticism
ISBN 0-395-65380-0   LC 95-19049

This volume "compiles, in alphabetical order, 823 articles, most of them essays on contemporary creators of children's books. Writers as early as Aesop and as varied as Anna Sewell and Mark Twain are also included. . . . Each essay focuses on the subject's importance to the field of children's books and notes major contributions. . . . Silvey's editorial judgment is sound, and the entries, although varying in quality and depth, are usually well done." SLJ

Children's books: awards & prizes; includes prizes and awards for children's and young adult books; compiled and edited by The Children's Book Council. rev ed. Children's Book Council 2005 576p pa $150
028.5
1. Literary prizes—Bibliography 2. Children's literature—Bibliography 3. Young adult literature—Bibliography
ISBN 0-933633-07-6
Also available on-line version
First published 1969
This publication lists approximately 200 awards divided as follows: Part I: United States awards selected by adults; Part II: United States awards selected by young readers; Part III: Australian, Canadian, New Zealand, and United Kingdom (UK) awards; Part IV: Selected international and multinational awards; Part V: Awards classified; Part VI: Publications and lists for selecting U. S. children's and young adult books. A brief history of each award precedes the list of winners
This volume "will make a good desk reference." Booklist

Children's literature in the elementary school; [by] Charlotte S. Huck . . . [et al.] 8th ed, revised by Barbara Z. Kiefer. McGraw-Hill 2004 645p il $96.25   **028.5**
1. Children's literature—History and criticism
ISBN 0-07-256281-1   LC 2002-37955
First published 1961
Includes CD-ROM
This "text shows readers how children's literature can capture the attention of K-8 students and foster a lifelong love of reading. . . . It covers learning about children's literature, understanding children's responses to literature, the history of children's literature, beginning books, picture books, the genres of children's literature, planning the literature program, and extending and evaluating children's understanding of literature." Publisher's note
Includes bibliographical references

Codell, Esmé Raji
How to get your child to love reading. Algonquin Bks. 2003 531p il pa $18.95
028.5
1. Books and reading 2. Children's literature—Bibliography
ISBN 1-56512-308-5   LC 2003-40405
The author presents her "theory that interest (finding the right books for the child), integration (using reading as a springboard into other disciplines) and invention (when a child's unique ideas are inspired by the writing) can make the difference in how a youngster approaches

Codell, Esmé Raji—*Continued*

reading. . . . The witty, comical 'Madame Esme' (as she calls herself) offers scores of thematic book lists parents can use to inspire young readers. . . . Codell creates a contagious enthusiasm for the enormous value of children's literature." Publ Wkly

Includes bibliographical references

The **Continuum** encyclopedia of children's literature; [by] Bernice E. Cullinan and Diane G. Person, editors. Continuum 2001 861p $59.95 **028.5**

1. Children's literature—Encyclopedias 2. Children's literature—Bio-bibliography

ISBN 0-8264-1516-4 LC 00-59036

"A Giniger book"

This "encyclopedia contains 1,200 biographical-critical entries for international authors and illustrators of children's literature in English, and approximately 100 topical entries. The entries are arranged in alphabetical order and each is signed. Each author/illustrator entry briefly identifies the subject, gives birth and death date and place, awards received, further works, and bibliography. Entries vary in length." Choice

"This work would be useful for parents and teachers as well as scholars, librarians, and writers. It is well researched, well written, and easy to use." Booklist

Includes bibliographical references

The **Coretta** Scott King Awards book, 1970-1999; edited by Henrietta M. Smith. American Lib. Assn. 1999 135p pa $40 **028.5**

1. Coretta Scott King Award 2. Children's literature—History and criticism 3. American literature—African American authors 4. African Americans in literature

ISBN 0-8389-3496-X LC 99-25046

First published 1994

This work begins with discussions of the 1994-1999 award winners and honor books and then goes back year by year to 1969

"The text is broken up with quotes from the winning titles, and the book ends with photos and biographies of the authors and artists. An essential resource." Booklist

Cox Clark, Ruth E.

Tantalizing tidbits for middle schoolers; quick booktalks for the busy middle school and jr. high library media specialist; [by] Ruth E. Cox Clark. Linworth Pub. 2005 140p pa $36.95

028.5

1. Book talks 2. Books and reading 3. Children's literature—Bibliography 4. Young adult literature—Bibliography

ISBN 1-58683-195-X LC 2005013159

"In the first sections, the author provides information on annual recommended reading lists and children's book awards and describes different booktalking techniques. Section 5, the heart of the book, offers 75 booktalk examples. For each, the author provides bibliographic information, subjects and genres, references to pertinent reading lists and awards, and interest levels. This information is followed by a brief annotation, a booktalk, a page reference for an excerpt to read, a curriculum connection, and a list of similar books. A list of themes and an index

of the books and authors mentioned conclude the volume, which is highly recommended for librarians, teachers, and students." Booklist

The **Dictionary** of characters in children's literature; Beverly Ann Chin, general editor. Watts 2002 128p il $34 **028.5**

1. Children's literature—Dictionaries 2. Characters and characteristics in literature

ISBN 0-531-11984-X LC 2001-17771

"A Franklin Watts Library edition."

This reference describes over 550 characters in children's literature and includes brief book summaries, book jackets and illustrations, author anecdotes, and review excerpts

"Beverly Ann Chin does an admirable job of choosing characters from traditional and contemporary literature, as well as different cultures and time periods. The content is well organized and easy to understand." Book Rep

Includes bibliographical references

The **Essential** guide to children's books and their creators; Anita Silvey, editor. Houghton Mifflin 2002 542p $28; pa $17 **028.5**

1. Children's literature—Bio-bibliography 2. Children's literature—History and criticism

ISBN 0-618-19083-X; 0-618-19082-1 (pa)

LC 2002-32288

This "volume contains 475 alphabetically ordered entries . . . covering authors, illustrators, genres, publishing trends and more. Writers and artists sound off in entries marked 'Voices of the Creators'; incidental illustrations appear throughout." Publ Wkly

"This guide offers brief but meaty articles. . . . While the original work featured over 800 authors and topics representing classic children's literature, the updated version retains only 375 of the older work's entries. This poses a difficulty for libraries, which will want to acquire this volume for the necessary updates but also retain the prior volume for the 400-plus entries not replicated here. Recommended for most reference collections." Libr J

Includes bibliographical references

Feinberg, Barbara

Welcome to Lizard Motel; children, stories, and the mystery of making things up: a memoir. Beacon Press 2004 256p $20 **028.5**

1. Children—Books and reading 2. Imagination

ISBN 0-8070-7144-7 LC 2004-710

This "is a memoir about the place of stories in children's lives. It began when Barbara Feinberg noticed that her twelve-year-old son, Alex . . . hated reading many of the novels assigned to him in school. These stories of abandonment, kidnapping, abuse, and more—called 'problem novels'—were standard fare in his middle school classroom." Publisher's note

"Feinberg, who's spent years working with children in a creativity workshop she designed, has the independence and experience to raise important questions. Her critique . . . should stir some much-needed controversy." Publ Wkly

Includes bibliographical references

Fox, Mem

Reading magic; why reading aloud to our children will change their lives forever. Harcourt 2001 156p il $23; pa $12 **028.5**

1. Storytelling 2. Books and reading

ISBN 0-15-100624-5; 0-15-601076-3 (pa)

LC 2001-24631

"An introduction for parents about reading aloud to their children. Fox explains that babies are born learners, discusses the importance of books in the home, and stresses the value of a read-aloud ritual." SLJ

"In a cheerful, chatty style that's totally jargon-free . . . Fox makes a passionate case for reading aloud to children. . . . Her examples are personal, many from her own family and friends and from her own books, and occasional cartoons by Judy Horacek add to the fun." Booklist

Gillespie, John Thomas

The Newbery/Printz companion; booktalk and related materials for award winners and honor books; [by] John T. Gillespie and Corinne J. Naden. 3rd ed. Libraries Unlimited 2006 503p $75 **028.5**

1. Newbery Medal 2. Michael L. Printz award 3. Children's literature—History and criticism 4. Authors

ISBN 1-59158-313-6   LC 2006014955

Replaces The Newbery companion first published 1996

This guide to the "Newbery and Printz awards for children's and young adult literature provides information on each year's winners and honor books, as well as on the awards themselves and the librarians for whom they are named. For each award-winning book, there is a plot summary, list of characters and themes, background on the author, incidents for booktalking, related reads, and . . . ideas for introducing the book to young readers." Publisher's note

Includes bibliographical references

Hearne, Betsy Gould

Choosing books for children; a commonsense guide; [by] Betsy Hearne with Deborah Stevenson. 3rd ed. University of Ill. Press 1999 229p il $27.95; pa $14.95 **028.5**

1. Books and reading 2. Children's literature—Bibliography

ISBN 0-252-02516-4; 0-252-06928-5 (pa)

LC 99-6144

First published 1981 by Delacorte Press

"The focus is on books since 1950; the 14 chapter-opening illustrations mainly represent books of the last decade. Chapters divide books by age and genre; one chapter considers the value of controversial books while another affectionately revisits classics." Publ Wkly

Helbig, Alethea

Dictionary of American children's fiction, 1995-1999; books of recognized merit; [by] Alethea K. Helbig and Agnes Regan Perkins. Greenwood Press 2002 614p $115 **028.5**

1. Children's literature—Dictionaries 2. Best books

ISBN 0-313-30389-4   LC 2001-23871

Also available volumes in series covering the years 1859-1959, 1960-1984, 1985-1989 and 1990-1994

"This dictionary is arranged alphabetically by title entries, author entries, character entries, and miscellaneous entries. . . . Entries include award winning and notable books from 1995-1999, as well as a few from previous years. Descriptions of each book are concise and include an overview of the characters, plot, setting, and awards received." Book Rep

"The extensive, detailed index is an excellent resource for locating fiction about a wide range of specific topics, characters, authors, and genres. . . . Valuable as a social history of children's fiction, and recommended for academic and large public libraries." Booklist

Includes bibliographical references

Herb, Steven

Connecting fathers, children, and reading; a how-to-do it manual for librarians; [by] Steven Herb, Sara Willoughby-Herb. Neal-Schuman 2001 196p (How-to-do-it manuals for libraries) pa $45 **028.5**

1. Books and reading 2. Fathers

ISBN 1-55570-390-9   LC 2001-18315

This "book looks at both the importance and effect of father involvement in children's reading. . . . Case studies, anecdotes, and interesting sidebars abound in this well-organized, well-written source. . . . An extensive bibliography includes more than 450 children's books about fathers and fathering." SLJ

Hey! listen to this; stories to read aloud; edited by

Jim Trelease. Viking 1992 414p pa $15 hardcover o.p. **028.5**

1. Books and reading 2. Literature—Collections 3. Authors

ISBN 0-14-014653-9 (pa)   LC 91-37668

"Divided into categories such as 'Animal Tales,' 'Children of Courage,' or 'Classic Tales,' the forty-eight selections cover a wide spectrum from folktales to fantasy, classics to contemporary stories. More than half are complete stories, while the remainder are one or two chapters from longer books. Trelease skillfully weaves his choices into a cohesive whole. Beyond merely categorizing them, he refers to other authors or stories in the discussions that precede and follow each story." J Youth Serv Libr

Includes bibliographical references

Knowles, Elizabeth

Boys and literacy; practical strategies for librarians, teachers, and parents; [by] Elizabeth Knowles and Martha Smith. Libraries Unlimited 2005 xxi, 164p il pa $35 **028.5**

1. Boys—Books and reading 2. Children's literature—Bibliography 3. Young adult literature—Bibliography

ISBN 1-59158-212-1

"Boys don't seem to like to read. . . . This book briefly explores the research about this situation, outlines strategies to reverse this trend, and lists books within genres that boys enjoy reading. . . . The best part of the book is the author section. . . . For each author covered, there is a complete list of books, contact information,

Knowles, Elizabeth—*Continued*

. . . and Web sites. . . . This is a wonderful resource for teachers and parents to begin working on improving literacy with boys." Booklist

More reading connections; bringing parents, teachers, and librarians together; [by] Elizabeth Knowles and Martha Smith. Libraries Unlimited 1999 148p il pa $26.50   **028.5**

1. Books and reading
ISBN 1-56308-723-5
Also available Reading connections pa $23 (ISBN 1-56308-436-8)

The authors present "information about starting and participating in elementary and middle school book clubs. The authors introduce 13 topics such as the arts, humor, families in transition, folklore and mythology, sports fiction, the Internet, and banned books. Each chapter contains guided reading questions, a related journal article . . . and an additional annotated list of articles." SLJ

Konigsburg, E. L.

TalkTalk; a children's book author speaks to grown-ups. Atheneum Pubs. 1995 198p il $29.95   **028.5**

1. Children's literature—History and criticism
ISBN 0-689-31993-2   LC 94-32341
"A Jean Karl book"
"Nine entertaining and provocative speeches, ranging from the author's 1968 Newbery acceptance to a reassuring rationale for the continuing significance of children's books in the multimedia nineties." J Youth Serv Libr

Langemack, Chapple

The booktalker's bible; how to talk about the books you love to any audience; [by] Chapple Langemack. Libraries Unlimited 2003 199p pa $30   **028.5**

1. Book talks
ISBN 1-56308-944-0   LC 2003-47543
"This book reminds readers that booktalks . . . are an effective way to present books and can be aimed at all types of settings . . . and age groups. It explains why booktalks are needed, tells how to hold one, and offers tips for a fail-safe presentation. Each chapter provides practical examples and closes with additional reading. Appendixes include sample talks and ideas for titles as well as other helpful resources." Booklist
Includes bibliographical references

Larson, Jeanette C.

Bringing mysteries alive for children and young adults; [by] Jeanette Larson. Linworth Pub. 2004 134p il pa $39.95   **028.5**

1. Children—Books and reading 2. Teenagers—Books and reading 3. Mystery fiction
ISBN 1-58683-012-0   LC 2003-22064
Contents: Introducing mystery; Defining mystery; Appreciating mysteries; Looking at series mysteries; Suggestions for integrating mysteries into the curriculum; Programming with mysteries

"The book has excellent ideas for beginning as well as seasoned professionals." SLJ
Includes bibliographical references

Latrobe, Kathy Howard

The children's literature dictionary; definitions, resources, and teaching activities; [by] Kathy Latrobe, Carolyn S. Brodie, Maureen White. Neal-Schuman 2002 282p pa $59.95   **028.5**

1. Children's literature—Dictionaries
ISBN 1-55570-424-7   LC 2001-44434
"The first section is an alphabetical dictionary of 325 terms found in reviews, lesson plans, and other resources. Definitions of terms contain meanings and examples from popular children's literature and activities related to the term. The activities descriptions provide a starting point for teaching or demonstrating the term. This reference book supports resources and materials that librarians or teachers should have in their collection." Book Rep

Lewis, Valerie V.

Valerie & Walter's best books for children; a lively, opinionated guide; [by] Valerie V. Lewis and Walter M. Mayes. 2nd ed. Quill 2004 543p il pa $17.95   **028.5**

1. Children's literature—Bibliography 2. Books and reading
ISBN 0-06-052467-7   LC 2003-062352
First published 1998 by Avon Bks.
In this guide to over 2000 books "fiction and nonfiction are organized by age and subject for children up through about 12 years, including books for family reading. Interest/listening level is differentiated from reading level. Sidebars and inserts include additional information about books, themes or ideas, authors, and more as well as additional commentary by Mayes or Lewis." SLJ
"The tone is enthusiastic, committed, and informal. . . . A handy reference even for those who know the books." Booklist

Nespeca, Sue McCleaf

Picture books plus; 100 extension activities in art, drama, music, math, and science; [by] Sue McCleaf Nespeca, Joan B. Reeve. American Lib. Assn. 2003 133p il pa $38   **028.5**

1. Picture books for children 2. Books and reading
ISBN 0-8389-0840-3   LC 2002-11822
Contents: Why use picture books with children?; Extending picture books through art; Extending picture books through drama; Extending picture books through music; Extending picture books through math; Extending picture books through science
"This book is intended for use by teachers, librarians, and others working with children in preschool through grade three and features extension activities for use with a variety of materials. . . . Each chapter includes titles with annotations, 20 activities, and a list of resource books that will introduce readers to further activities. . . . Librarians and teachers will find many useful ideas here." Booklist
Includes bibliographical references

The **Newbery** and Caldecott awards; a guide to the medal and honor books; [by] Association for Library Service to Children. American Lib. Assn. il $18   **028.5**
1. Newbery Medal 2. Caldecott Medal
ISSN 1070-4493
Annual
"An annotated listing of winning titles since the inception of the awards (1922 and 1938 respectively). . . . Annotations serve as a reliable guide for colllection development, reader's advisory, curriculum development, and a host of other programs." Publisher's note

Newbery and Caldecott Medal books, 1966-1975; with acceptance papers, biographies and related material chiefly from The Horn Book magazine; edited by Lee Kingman. Horn Bk. 1975 xx, 321p il $22.95   **028.5**
1. Newbery Medal 2. Caldecott Medal 3. Children's literature—History and criticism 4. Authors 5. Illustrators
ISBN 0-87675-003-X
Continues Newbery Medal books, 1922-1955, Caldecott Medal books, 1938-1957 (o.p.), and Newbery and Caldecott Medal books, 1956-1965 (o.p.)
"Gives for each Newbery or Caldecott award winner his acceptance speech, a biographical note, and a book note. An excerpt from each Newbery book gives an example of the writer's style; a sample illustration from each Caldecott book is supplemented by notes on size, medium, printing process, number of illustrations and type used." Choice

Newbery and Caldecott Medal books, 1976-1985; with acceptance papers, biographies, and related material chiefly from The Horn Book magazine; edited by Lee Kingman. Horn Bk. 1986 358p il $24.95   **028.5**
1. Newbery Medal 2. Caldecott Medal 3. Children's literature—History and criticism 4. Authors 5. Illustrators
ISBN 0-87675-004-8   LC 86-15223
This volume "compiles the winning speeches, biographies and book notes for the 1976 through 1985 awards. It includes essays by Barbara Bader, Ethel Heins and Zena Sutherland." Bookbird

Newbery Medal books, 1922-1955; with their authors' acceptance papers & related material chiefly from The Horn Book magazine; edited by Bertha Mahony Miller and Elinor Whitney Field. Horn Bk. 1955 458p il $22.95
028.5
1. Newbery Medal 2. Children's literature—History and criticism 3. Authors
ISBN 0-87675-000-5
Companion volume to Caldecott Medal books, 1938-1957
"Largely biographical notes about award recipients and the acceptance papers." Ref Sources for Small & Medium-sized Libr. 5th edition

Reid, Rob
Cool story programs for the school-age crowd. American Library Association 2004 181p il pa $32
028.5
1. Books and reading 2. Children's literature
ISBN 0-8389-0887-X   LC 2004-9933
This offers plans for story programs which incorporate poetry, picture books, chapter book excerpts, and short stories.
"Eighteen well-developed plans with wacky themes that kids will love will bring literature to life with a minimum of stress for public librarians, teachers, and school media specialists. . . . A useful book with surefire suggestions for winning programs." SLJ
Includes bibliographical references

Stephens, Claire Gatrell
Coretta Scott King Award books; using great literature with children and young adults. Libraries Unlimited 2000 238p pa $27.50   **028.5**
1. Coretta Scott King Award 2. Children's literature—History and criticism 3. Young adult literature—History and criticism 4. American literature—African American authors 5. African Americans in literature
ISBN 1-56308-685-9   LC 99-51955
"Both author and illustrator award lists are followed by annotated bibliographies. Twelve of the author entries also feature biographical information. The book is chock-full of curricular units for 15 selected titles. The units include discussion questions, crossword puzzles, vocabulary exercises, performance activities, and integrated curriculum ideas. Additionally, lists of related materials and Internet sites are provided." Book Rep
Includes bibliographical references

Sutherland, Zena
Children & books; [by] Zena Sutherland; cover, frontispiece, and part opening illustrations by Trina Schart Hyman. 9th ed. Longman 1997 720p $119
028.5
1. Children's literature—History and criticism 2. Children—Books and reading
ISBN 0-673-99733-2
First edition by May Hill Arbuthnot published 1947 by Scott, Foresman
"This children's literature textbook emphasizes the best books and authors. The introductory sections about children and books in general are followed by genre overviews which emphasize the major authors in each category. A third section discusses ways to bring children and books together, while a final section covers issues such as censorship. Lavish color illustrations, viewpoint boxes, extensive bibliographies and useful appendices make this an attractive and stimulating work." Safford. Guide to Ref Materials for Sch Libr Media Cent. 5th edition

Trelease, Jim
The read-aloud handbook. 5th ed. Penguin Bks. 2001 xxvi, 402p il pa $15   **028.5**
1. Books and reading 2. Children's literature—Bibliography
ISBN 0-14-100161-5   LC 2001-21012

Trelease, Jim—*Continued*

First published 1982

This handbook explains the importance of reading aloud to children, offers guidance on how to set up a read-aloud atmosphere in the home or classroom, and "shows readers how to take full advantage of recent cultural and technological developments. A new chapter explores important lessons from Oprah, Harry Potter, and the Internet, and an updated appendix lists key Internet sites for children's literature and education." Publisher's note

Includes bibliographical references

Yolen, Jane

Touch magic; fantasy, faerie & folklore in the literature of childhood. Expanded ed. August House 2000 128p pa $11.95   **028.5**

1. Children's literature—History and criticism
2. Folklore

ISBN 0-87483-591-7   LC 00-27565

First published 1981 by Philomel Bks.

The author provides perspectives on reading, appreciating, and preserving fantasy and folklore for children. Among topics discussed are the morality of fairy tales, the definition of story, and the theme of time travel

Includes bibliographical references

York, Sherry

Children's and young adult literature by Latino writers; a guide for librarians, teachers, parents, and students. Linworth Pub. 2002 184p pa $36.95   **028.5**

1. American literature—Hispanic American authors—Bibliography 2. Young adult literature—Bibliography 3. Children's literature—Bibliography 4. Books and reading

ISBN 1-58683-062-7   LC 2002-67112

This guide includes "bibliographic information for a variety of titles in various genres including novels, chapter books, short stories, folklore, drama, poetry, and nonfiction. A list of additional resource materials, as well as publisher information and an index, is also included." Publisher's note

"This publication fills a necessary void for professionals looking for all forms of Latino literature for primary grades through high school. . . . This book should provide the framework for building a solid collection." SLJ

Picture books by Latino writers; a guide for librarians, teachers, parents, and students. Linworth Pub. 2002 116p pa $36.95   **028.5**

1. Picture books for children 2. American literature—Hispanic American authors—Bio-bibliography

ISBN 1-58683-052-X   LC 2001-58182

This "reference tool presents a selection of 65 original picture books by Latino writers. All works are set in the United States, and are either in English or have bilingual texts. . . . Lucid opening essays discuss selection criteria . . . and the need for authentic Latino literature. . . . This is an excellent resource, combining clear prose and an exemplary layout." SLJ

Includes bibliographical references

031   General encyclopedic works in American English

Compton's encyclopedia & fact-index. Success Pub. Group, P.O. Box 1167, Elmhurst, Il 60126 26v il maps set $699   **031**

1. Encyclopedias and dictionaries

First published 1922 with title: Compton's pictured encyclopedia. Frequently revised

Supplemented by: Compton's yearbook

"Recommended for home and school use by young people ages nine through eighteen. The main text, consisting of more than 5,000 articles, is supported by nearly 30,000 brief articles among the 70,000 entries in the 'fact-index.' This volume presents brief dictionary entries, biographical sketches, statistics, and capsule treatments of topics not considered in the main text." Ref Sources for Small & Medium-sized Libr. 6th edition

Grolier student encyclopedia. Grolier 2004 17v il map set $249 (3-6)   **031**

1. Encyclopedias and dictionaries

ISBN 0-7172-5865-3   LC 2003-42402

Contents: v1 Abolitionist Movement -Angola; v2 Animal - Baseball; v3 Basketball - Carroll, Lewis; v4 Carson, Rachel - Connecticut; v5 Conquistadors - Ecology; v6 Economy - Food chain; v7 Football - Harrison, William Henry; v8 Hawaii - Inuit; v9 Inventors and inventions - Longitude; v10 Louisiana - Michelangelo; v11 Michigan - Native Americans, Eastern; v12 Native American, Northwest - Olmec and Toltec; v13 Olympic games - Punctuation; v14 Pyramid - Scientific instruments; v15 Scientist - Tanzania; v16 Taste and smell - Venezuela; v17 Venus - Zoology

This is "a general encyclopedia with more than 700 entries arranged alphabetically. . . . The writing is clear and should be accessible to students in grades three and above. . . . Entries are enhanced with color photographs, illustrations, diagrams, time lines, and maps. The picture captions supplement the text nicely. . . . This set provides a solid introduction to general topics for students in the primary grades." Booklist

The **New** book of knowledge; the children's encyclopedia. Grolier 2006 21v il map set $699   **031**

1. Encyclopedias and dictionaries

ISBN 0-7172-0540-1

Also available on-line version

First published 1966 as successor to The Book of knowledge. Frequently revised

Supplemented by The New book of knowledge annual

"Intended to interest a wide range of readers from those in early childhood to students nearly ready to use an adult encyclopedia; thus, articles are written at various levels of understanding, with the main emphasis being for children in grades three to six. Longer articles are signed by contributors or consultants. Suggested activities or projects are incorporated into some articles to further the educational value." Guide to Ref Books. 11th edition

For a review of 2004 edition see: Booklist, Sept. 15, 2004

Scholastic children's encyclopedia. Scholastic Reference 2004 710p il map $19.95 (4 and up)

031

1. Encyclopedias and dictionaries
ISBN 0-439-43816-0   LC 2003-45591

"More than 600 entries are arranged alphabetically and range in length from one-half page to just over four pages. Entries are illustrated with more than 2,000 photographs, diagrams, charts, time lines, and maps. Longer entries include subheadings that divide text into easy-to-read sections. . . . Libraries serving younger students will want multiple copies of this highly usable and user-friendly tool." Booklist

The **World** Book encyclopedia. World Bk. 2006 22v il map set $1,079   **031**

1. Encyclopedias and dictionaries
ISBN 0-7166-0106-0

Also available CD-ROM version, The World Book multimedia encyclopedia, and online

First published 1917-1918 by Field Enterprises. Frequently revised

Supplemented by: World Book's year in review; another available annual supplement is World Book's science year in review

"Curriculum-oriented, this superior encyclopedia is well-edited and produced to meet the reference and informational needs of students from grade four through high school. Long standing tradition of excellence for readability, accuracy, authoritativeness, objectivity, judicious and extensive use of outstanding graphics and timeliness." N Y Public Libr. Ref Books for Child Collect

For a review of 2004 edition see: Booklist, Sept. 15, 2004

031.02 American books of miscellaneous facts

Information please almanac, atlas & yearbook. Houghton Mifflin il maps $24.95

031.02

1. Almanacs 2. Statistics 3. United States—Statistics
ISSN 0073-7860

Annual. First published 1947 by Doubleday. Publisher varies

"Statistical and factual material organized by subject area; contains special articles by experts. Illustrated, with a color map section and detailed index." N Y Public Libr Book of How & Where to Look It Up

Kane, Joseph Nathan

Famous first facts; a record of first happenings, discoveries, and inventions in American history; by Joseph Nathan Kane, Steven Anzovin, Janet Podell. 5th ed. Wilson, H.W. 1997 xxix, 1122p $160

031.02

1. Encyclopedias and dictionaries 2. United States—History—Dictionaries
ISBN 0-8242-0930-3   LC 97-31252

Also available CD-ROM version and online
First published 1933

"Aims to establish the earliest date of various occurrences, achievements, inventions, etc. Dictionary arrangement with many cross-references. Gives brief description or explanation together with the date; some references to sources." Guide to Ref Books. 11th edition

Masoff, Joy

Oh, yuck! the encyclopedia of everything nasty; illustrated by Terry Sirrell. Workman 2000 212p il pa $14.95 (4 and up)   **031.02**

1. Curiosities and wonders
ISBN 0-7611-0771-1   LC 99-43603

An alphabetical collection of articles about disgusting things, from acne, ants, and bacteria to worms, x-periments, and zits

"Amusing cartoons and well-chosen, black-and-white photographs with humorous captions support the text. . . . This delightful volume will be enjoyed by fans of grossness everywhere." SLJ

Includes bibliographical references

Pascoe, Elaine

Scholastic kid's almanac; facts, figures, and stats; written by Elaine Pascoe, Deborah Kops, and Jenifer Morse; illustrated by Bob Italiano and David C. Bell. rev ed. Scholastic Reference 2004 il map pa $12.95 (4 and up)   **031.02**

1. Encyclopedias and dictionaries
ISBN 0-439-56078-0

"A Georgian Bay book"
First published 1999

This is a compilation of facts, illustrations, graphs, and statistics alphabetically arranged under 38 topics such as aerospace, animals, arts and music, calendars and holidays, energy, environment, health, math, religion, sports, and zodiac.

The **World** almanac and book of facts. World Almanac Educ. il maps $31.95   **031.02**

1. Almanacs 2. Statistics 3. United States—Statistics
ISSN 0084-1382

Annual. First published 1868. Publisher varies

"This is the most comprehensive and well-known of almanacs. . . . Contains a chronology of the year's events, consumer information, historical anniversaries, annual climatological data, and forecasts. Color section has flags and maps. Includes detailed index." N Y Public Libr Book of How & Where to Look It Up

The **World** almanac for kids. World Almanac il maps $18.95; pa $10.95   **031.02**

1. Almanacs

Annual. First published 1995 for 1996

This volume contains information on animals, art, religion, sports, books, law, language, science and computers. Includes a section of full-color maps and flags. Illustrated throughout with pictures, diagrams, and charts

032.02 English books of miscellaneous facts

Guinness book of records. Guinness Media il
$27.95   **032.02**
1. Curiosities and wonders
ISSN 1057-4557
Also available in paperback from Bantam Bks.
Annual. First published 1955 in the United Kingdom;
in the United States 1962. Variant titles: Guinness book
of world records; Guinness world records
Editors and publisher vary
"Ready reference for current record holders in all
fields, some esoteric. Index provides access to information arranged in broad subject categories. Must be replaced annually." N Y Public Libr. Ref Books for Child
Collect

051 General serial publications in American English

Hopkins, Lee Bennett
Days to celebrate; a full year of poetry, people,
holidays, history, fascinating facts, and more;
written and edited by Lee Bennett Hopkins;
illustrated by Stephen Alcorn. Greenwillow Books
2005 112p il $17.99; lib bdg $18.89 (3-5)
051
1. Almanacs 2. Poetry—Collections 3. Holidays
ISBN 0-06-000765-6; 0-06-000766-4 (lib bdg)
LC 2003-49288
"The writers represented include Robert Frost, Langston Hughes, Richard Wilbur, and Gwendolyn Brooks.
Alcorn's large, vibrant, whimsical artwork perfectly enhances the prose and verse to make this book a delight
to the eye and the ear." SLJ

069 Museology (Museum science)

Norris, Joann
Children's museums; an American guidebook.
McFarland & Co. 1998 217p il pa $32.50
069
1. Museums
ISBN 0-7864-0443-4   LC 97-42194
"This is a listing of 242 children's museums, large
and small, valid as of 1997. . . . The entries consist of
a brief description, location, hours, admissions, and other
sites of interest nearby, concluding with contact information, including Web sites and e-mail addresses. . . . Norris' volume should prove a useful and informative guide
for school and public libraries." Booklist

070 News media, journalism, publishing

Sullivan, George
Journalists at risk; reporting America's wars;
[by] George Sullivan. Twenty-First Century Books
2006 128p il (People's history) lib bdg $26.60 (5
and up)   **070**
1. Journalism 2. War
ISBN 0-7613-2745-2   LC 2003015855
Discusses the role of reporters during war time, including the risks they take and the censorship they face,
and how their jobs have changed with each conflict since
the Civil War.
"As a case study in the fluidity of First Amendment
rights in wartime, it's thought-provoking reading."
Booklist
Includes bibliographical references

070.5 Publishing

Brookfield, Karen
Book; written by Karen Brookfield;
photographed by Laurence Pordes. Dorling
Kindersley 2000 63p il (DK eyewitness books)
$15.95; lib bdg $19.99 (4 and up)   **070.5**
1. Books
ISBN 0-7894-5892-6; 0-7894-6597-3 (lib bdg)
First published 1993 by Knopf
Text and photographs trace the evolution of the written word, how the alphabet grew out of pictures, the development of papermaking, bookbinding, children's
books, and more.

Marcus, Leonard S.
Side by side; five favorite picture-book teams
go to work. Walker & Co. 2001 64p il $22.95; lib
bdg $23.85 (4 and up)   **070.5**
1. Picture books for children 2. Authors, American
3. Illustrators
ISBN 0-8027-8778-9; 0-8027-8779-7 (lib bdg)
LC 2001-26344
This "volume introduces five sets of collaborators in
the field of picture books: Arthur Yorinks and Richard
Egielski, Alice and Martin Provensen, Julius Lester and
Jerry Pinkney, Joanna Cole and Bruce Degen, and Jon
Scieszka, Lane Smith, and Molly Leach. Each chapter
discusses how the writer and artist (and in Leach's case,
designer) got together, and highlights their collaboration
during various projects, as well as providing a wealth of
interesting details about these creative individuals and
their books. The clearly reproduced illustrations, many in
color, include photographs, sketches for book illustrations, and finished art." Booklist
Includes glossary and bibliographical references

100 PHILOSOPHY & PSYCHOLOGY

Weate, Jeremy
A young person's guide to philosophy; "I think, therefore I am". DK Pub. 1998 64p il $16.99 (5 and up) **100**
1. Philosophy 2. Philosophers
ISBN 0-7894-3074-6   LC 97-33454
Socrates, Aquinas, Descartes, Nietzsche, Simone de Beauvoir and Herbert Marcuse are among the thinkers discussed. Schools of thought and philosophical concepts are covered
"Teens who have thought about and questioned the hows, whats, and whys of human existence will find this introduction fascinating." Booklist

133.4 Demonology and witchcraft

Hill, Douglas
Witches & magic-makers; written by Douglas Hill; photographed by Alex Wilson. Dorling Kindersley 2000 61p il (DK eyewitness books) $15.99; lib bdg $19.99 (4 and up) **133.4**
1. Witchcraft 2. Magic
ISBN 0-7894-5878-0; 0-7894-6619-8 (lib bdg)
First published 1997 by Knopf
This book on "witchcraft, shamanism, and mysticism . . . introduces magical charms, talismans, and amulets from around the world. . . . This title gives a colorful overview of the topic." [review of 1997 edition]

Jackson, Shirley
The witchcraft of Salem Village. Random House 1987 c1956 146p pa $5.99 hardcover o.p. (4 and up) **133.4**
1. Witchcraft 2. Salem (Mass.)—History
ISBN 0-394-89176-7 (pa)   LC 87-4543
"Landmark books"
A reissue of the title first published 1956
"A simple, chilling account of the witchcraft trials of 1692 and '93 when, because of testimony given by a group of little girls, twenty persons were executed as witches and others died in jail. There is good introductory background and though the story's subject is by nature horrifying the book does not play on the emotions. . . . It presents a difficult theme lucidly and without condescension." Horn Book

Meltzer, Milton
Witches and witch-hunts; a history of persecution. Blue Sky Press (NY) 1999 128p $16.95 (4 and up) **133.4**
1. Witchcraft
ISBN 0-590-48517-2   LC 97-36999
Traces the origins and progression of hysteria, fear, and persecution associated with witches and witchcraft in western societies
The author "crams a lot of ideas and insights into this ambitious, unusually meaty survey." Publ Wkly
Includes bibliographical references

Roach, Marilynne K.
In the days of the Salem witchcraft trials. Houghton Mifflin 1996 92p il map $16 (4 and up) **133.4**
1. Witchcraft 2. Salem (Mass.)—History
ISBN 0-395-69704-2   LC 94-32383
"After discussing the Salem Witchcraft trials in one short chapter, this attractive volume explores the social history of the times to show the context that made such events possible. Topics include the law and punishment, magic, social status, clothing, food, household goods, occupations, recreation, common activities, government, and the political troubles leading to widespread tension and unrest. Readers will come away with a much fuller picture of who lived in Salem and how they lived. Small ink drawings decorate the pages." Booklist
Includes bibliographical references

152.1 Sensory perception

Cobb, Vicki
How to really fool yourself; illusions for all your senses; illustrated by Jessica Wolk-Stanley. Wiley 1999 120p il pa $12.95 (5 and up) **152.1**
1. Senses and sensation 2. Perception 3. Optical illusions
ISBN 0-471-31592-3   LC 98-27723
A newly illustrated edition of the title first published 1981 by Lippincott
"The book begins with an explanation of perception and explores many different sensory aspects of it through experiments, definitions of important terms (italicized), background information and how illusions affect us in everyday life." SLJ

152.14 Visual perception

Dispezio, Michael A.
Eye-popping optical illusions. Sterling 2000 80p il $17.95 (4-6) **152.14**
1. Optical illusions
ISBN 0-8069-6641-6   LC 00-58319
"Page after page of visual images demonstrate how the eye and brain can be confused by tricky perspectives, varicolored patterns, and comparative lines and shapes." Horn Book Guide
The author "includes instructions for several projects—among them, a flip book and a zootrope. Whether used independently or in the classroom this lively book will entertain and educate." Booklist

Optical illusion magic; visual tricks & amusements; [by] Michael DiSpezio. Sterling 1999 80p il $17.95 (4 and up) **152.14**
1. Optical illusions
ISBN 0-8069-6581-9   LC 99-21113
This introduction to optical illusions "explains how the eye is deceived by visual tricks. Many examples are effectively used to illustrate different patterns and types of illusions, including spirals, slants, afterimages, broken

Dispezio, Michael A.—*Continued*
lines, and 3-D." SLJ

"This entertaining, enlightening volume will be helpful for projects and fun for browsing." Booklist

Simon, Seymour

Now you see it, now you don't; the amazing world of optical illusions; drawings by Constance Ftera. rev ed. Morrow Junior Bks. 1998 64p il $17.99 (4 and up)   **152.14**

1. Optical illusions

ISBN 0-688-16152-9   LC 97-49855

First published 1976 by FourWinds Press with title: The optical illusion book

The author explains optical illusions involving lines and spaces, changeable figures, depth and distance, brightness and contrast, and color

"One of the clearest and most interesting discussions of optical illusions ever written for children." Booklist

Westray, Kathleen

Picture puzzler. Ticknor & Fields Bks. for Young Readers 1994 unp il $16 (2-4)   **152.14**

1. Optical illusions

ISBN 0-395-70130-9   LC 94-4066

This "explanation of assorted optical illusions employs . . . gouache sketches in the style of American folk art to demonstrate the visual phenomena—afterimages, blind spots, incomplete pictures, the arrangement of lines and shapes to alter perspective, color deceptions, and reversible drawings." Horn Book

"The layout and ample white space will snare reluctant readers; explanations of the illusions and how they work are adequate, although not detailed. A fresh presentation for young puzzlers." SLJ

Wick, Walter

Walter Wick's Optical tricks. Cartwheel Bks. 1998 43p il $13.95 (4 and up)   **152.14**

1. Optical illusions

ISBN 0-590-22227-9   LC 97-35672

Presents a series of optical illusions and explains what is seen

The author "has produced a stunning picture book of optical illusions. With crystal-clear photographs, he creates a series of scenes that fool the eye and the brain." Booklist

152.4   Emotions

Aliki

Feelings. Greenwillow Bks. 1984 32p il $16; pa $5.95 (k-3)   **152.4**

1. Emotions

ISBN 0-688-03831-X; 0-688-06518-X (pa)

LC 84-4098

"Small pen-and-ink cartoons with vivid coloring depict boys and girls interacting and experiencing the full range of feelings which evolve in everyday settings. This cre-

ative, unique book would be ideal for parent/child interaction or use by elementary teachers in language arts classes. Children will enjoy the comic book 'frame' format." Child Book Rev Serv

Crist, James J.

What to do when you're scared & worried; a guide for kids; [by] James Crist. Free Spirit Pub. 2004 128p il pa $9.95 (5 and up)   **152.4**

1. Fear 2. Worry

ISBN 1-57542-153-4

"Part one deals with normal anxiety, offering detailed steps for developing 10 coping mechanisms. Expert help is needed to deal with the more serious problems discussed in Part two (e.g., phobias, separation anxiety, obsessive-compulsive disorder). Throughout, the author provides information, case histories, and coping skills in a manner that is both reassuring and encouraging. . . . Illustrations lighten the tone of the subject matter." SLJ

Includes bibliographical references

153.4   Thought, thinking, reasoning

Burns, Marilyn

The book of think; or, How to solve a problem twice your size; written by Marilyn Burns; illustrated by Martha Weston. Little, Brown 1976 125p il pa $14.99 hardcover o.p. (4 and up)

     153.4

1. Thought and thinking 2. Problem solving

ISBN 0-316-11743-9 (pa)   LC 76-17848

"A Brown paper school book"

"A provocative text invites the reader to solve problems by looking for alternatives, sharpening the senses, studying people, and expressing ideas in words. Brainteasers, riddles, and suggested projects are interpolated and represented by black-and-white line drawings." Child Books, 1976

155.9   Environmental psychology

Brown, Laurene Krasny

When dinosaurs die; a guide to understanding death; [by] Laurie Krasny Brown and Marc Brown. Little, Brown 1996 32p il lib bdg $14.95; pa $5.95 (k-3)   **155.9**

1. Death 2. Bereavement

ISBN 0-316-10917-7 (lib bdg); 0-316-11955-5 (pa)

LC 95-14511

"The text explains the inevitability of death, various reasons for death (including old age, sickness, accident, and suicide), and the difference between death and sleep; it then goes on to examine feelings about death and ways, both individual and cultural, of dealing with the loss of loved ones. . . . The simple watercolor illustrations help to make some scary situations more approachable. Quiet, respectful, and unthreatening, this will probably become a primary-grades standard on the subject." Bull Cent Child Books

Includes glossary

Dennison, Amy

Our dad died; the true story of three kids whose lives changed; as told and illustrated by Amy, Allie, and David Dennison. Free Spirit Pub. 2003 107p pa $9.95 (4 and up)   **155.9**

1. Bereavement 2. Fathers 3. Loss (Psychology)

ISBN 1-57542-135-6   LC 2003-4440

Contents: Finding out that dad died; The night he died; The day before the funeral; The funeral; After the funeral; The first week; Two weeks; Six weeks; Two months; Three months; Four months; Six months; Eight months; The cemetery; One year; Fifteen months; Seventeen months; A year and a half; Twenty-two months; Messages from dad; Grandparents; The future; Suggestions; Letters to dad

"When Amy and Allie were eight and David was four, their father died unexpectedly in his sleep. For the next two years, with their mother's help and encouragement, they kept journals about their reactions to their loss. The chapters are organized chronologically from the time they learned the news through their return to school and other activities. . . . The book is a valuable resource not only for children who have lost a parent but also for the adults who interact with them." SLJ

Gellman, Marc

Lost & found; a kid's book for living through loss; [by] Marc Gellman and Thomas Hartman; illustrated by Debbie Tilley. Morrow Junior Bks. 1999 176p il $15.99 (4-6)   **155.9**

1. Loss (Psychology)

ISBN 0-688-15752-1   LC 98-27779

Describes different kinds of losses—losing possessions, competitions, health, trust, and the permanent loss because of death—and discusses how to handle these situations

The authors' "informal text is aimed straight at kids and incorporates lots of examples children can relate to. . . . A practical, heartfelt exploration." Booklist

Includes bibliographical references

Krementz, Jill

How it feels when a parent dies. Knopf 1981 110p il pa $15 hardcover o.p. (4 and up)

155.9

1. Death 2. Bereavement

ISBN 0-394-75854-4 (pa)   LC 80-8808

Also available in hardcover from P. Smith

This book is "a hopeful tribute to the healing power sustained by young survivors, who are competently interviewed and photographed in their widely varied reactions and situations. The subjects range in age from 7 to 16 and cope with a variety of deaths by suicide, accident, and illness. Adults helping children through a hard time will better understand their charges' problems through the honest opinions expressed here, and young readers might feel less alone." Booklist

158   Applied psychology

Andrews, Linda Wasmer

Meditation; [by] Linda Wasmer Andrews. F. Watts 2004 79p (Life balance) $19.50; pa $6.95 (5 and up)   **158**

1. Meditation

ISBN 0-531-12219-0; 0-531-16609-0 (pa)

LC 2003-7153

Contents: Meditation myth-busters; The relaxation response; The mind/body/spirit link; Minding your mindfulness

"Andrews emphasizes that meditation is not a flaky practice, or a particularly religious one, but one that's designed to reduce stress and help individuals manage their lives. Four chapters explain the why and how of meditating. . . . [This offers] solid, easy-to-understand information" SLJ

Includes bibliographical references

Brown, Laurene Krasny

How to be a friend; a guide to making friends and keeping them; [by] Laurie Krasny Brown and Marc Brown. Little, Brown 1998 31p il $15.99; pa $6.99 (k-3)   **158**

1. Friendship

ISBN 0-316-10913-4; 0-316-11153-8 (pa)

LC 97-10179

"Dino life guides for families"--Cover

Dinosaur characters illustrate the value of friends, how to make friends, and how to be and not to be a good friend

"Dialogue balloons personalize, enrich, and add humor to the main text. . . . How to Be a Friend will be very useful to parents, teachers, and other caregivers of young children." Horn Book

McIntyre, Thomas

The behavior survival guide for kids; how to make good choices and stay out of trouble; [by] Thomas McIntyre. Free Spirit Pub. 2003 167p pa $14.95 (5 and up)   **158**

1. Interpersonal relations 2. Conduct of life

ISBN 1-57542-132-1   LC 2003-4565

"The author provides skills and activities to learn and practice so that new behaviors can replace those that have resulted in getting students into trouble. . . . Those motivated to make better choices for how they behave in school or with friends and family will find much to help them." Voice Youth Advocates

Rogers, Fred

Making friends; photographs by Jim Judkis. Putnam 1987 unp il pa $6.99 hardcover o.p. (k-1)

158

1. Friendship

ISBN 0-698-11409-4 (pa)   LC 86-12353

"From its opening lines ('When people like each other and like to do things together, they're friends. Can you think of someone who's your friend?'), Rogers's inimitable voice reaches out to his small readers with under-

Rogers, Fred—*Continued*

standing and reassurance. He describes the pleasures of friendship as well as potential problem areas. . . . Judkis's large color photos capture the range of emotions Rogers writes about." Publ Wkly

170   Ethics (Moral philosophy)

MacGregor, Cynthia

Think for yourself; a kid's guide to solving life's dilemmas and other sticky problems; [by] Cynthia MacGregor. Lobster Press; distributed by Raincoast Books 2003 96p il pa $7.95 (3-6)

170

1. Ethics 2. Conduct of life

ISBN 1-89422-273-3

"The introduction takes readers through the various stages of problem solving. The chapters that follow include real-life scenarios organized by theme. Situations include being approached by kids selling drugs, having to thank a relative for a dreadful birthday gift, having friends who download music from the Internet, etc. . . . Attractive, cartoon illustrations introduce each section and are scattered throughout. Children fortunate enough to read this helpful title will not have to say 'uh-oh' the next time they find themselves in a tricky situation." SLJ

174   Occupational ethics

Ethics in school librarianship; a reader; edited by Carol Simpson. Linworth Pub 2003 164p pa $44.95

174

1. School libraries 2. Librarians—Ethics

ISBN 1-58683-084-8   LC 2003-7956

Contents: An ethical dilemma by Carol Simpson; Ethical issues in collection development by Kay Bishop; Ethics in access by Mary Ann Bell; Confidentiality in the school library by Harry Willems; Ethics in the use of technology by Doug Johnson; Ethics and intellectual freedom by Carrie Gardner; Ethics in intellectual property by Carol Simpson; Ethics in the administration of school library media centers by Nancy Everhart; Ethics in Internet use by Nancy Willard; Ethics in professional realtionships by Frank Hoffman

This is a compilation of "articles dealing with the ethical aspects of collection development, access, confidentiality, technology, intellectual freedom, intellectual property, administration, Internet use, and professional relationships. . . . School librarians and administrators would do well to have this thought and discussion-provoking book on hand." SLJ

Includes bibliographical references

177   Ethics of social relations

Verdick, Elizabeth

Words are not for hurting; illustrated by Marieka Heinlen. Free Spirit Pub 2004 33p il pa $11.95 (k-2)

177

1. Conversation 2. Etiquette

ISBN 1-57542-156-9   LC 2003-21273

Also available board book edition

Encourages toddlers and preschoolers to express themselves using helpful, not hurtful, words. Includes a note for parents and caregivers.

"The brightly colored drawings, which bring the minimal text to life, are especially effective at showing the range of emotions children experience when they hear unkind language. An excellent resource for sharing at home and at preschools." Booklist

179   Other ethical norms

Young, Ed

Voices of the heart. Scholastic 1997 unp il $17.95

179

1. Ethics 2. Emotions 3. Chinese language

ISBN 0-590-50199-2   LC 96-7595

"Young lists 26 emotions with their modern Chinese characters. He then devotes a page to each emotion, breaking each character into its parts and creating a collage out of the parts and the figure of a heart to express the feeling of the emotion. . . . Emotions include panic, rudeness, mercy and loyalty." Booklist

"This is a powerful combination of words and imagery that lends itself to a number of uses both in the library and the classroom, but it will need the intercession of a knowledgeable adult to make this a part of a language, art, or religion curriculum." Bull Cent Child Books

200   RELIGION

Birdseye, Debbie Holsclaw

What I believe; kids talk about faith; by Debbie Holsclaw Birdseye and Tom Birdseye; photographs by Robert Crum. Holiday House 1996 32p il $15.95 (4 and up)

200

1. Religions

ISBN 0-8234-1268-7   LC 96-11240

Six children of different religious backgrounds tell about their faith and what it means to them; includes background information on each religious tradition

"These simple personal portraits show kids who have made a strong place for religion in their everyday world. . . . An affirmation of faith that goes beyond any single faith." Booklist

Includes bibliographical references

Buller, Laura

A faith like mine; a celebration of the world's religions . . . seen through the eyes of children. DK 2005 80p il maps $19.99 (4 and up)

200

1. Religions

ISBN 0-7566-1177-6

"Buller introduces Hinduism, Islam, Judaism, Christianity, Buddhism, and Sikhism through the eyes of children. . . . The amount of information is adequate and straightforward and focuses on aspects of the religion that would appeal to children. The clear, vibrant photographs are especially inviting." SLJ

Gellman, Marc

How do you spell God? answers to the big questions from around the world; [by] Marc Gellman & Thomas Hartman; illustrated by Jos. A. Smith; with a foreword by his Holiness the Dalai Lama. Morrow Junior Bks. 1995 206p il $17.99; pa $6.95 (5 and up) **200**

1. Religions

ISBN 0-688-13041-0; 0-688-15296-1 (pa)

LC 94-28770

The authors "show how the various religions—Judaism, Christianity, Islam, Buddhism, and Hinduism—deal with the soul-searching questions central to all people. . . . There is also information on each religion's teachers, holy days and places, sanctuaries, and prayers, among other topics." Booklist

This book "is warm, friendly and, most of all, respectful of the importance and variety of belief." Book Rep

Maestro, Betsy

The story of religion; illustrated by Giulio Maestro. Clarion Bks. 1996 48p il map $17 (3-5) **200**

1. Religions

ISBN 0-395-62364-2   LC 92-38980

"Beginning with early polytheistic beliefs in multiple spirits of gods and goddesses, and their usual strong link to nature, the author moves on to introduce Taoism and teachings of Confucius, Hinduism and Buddhism, Judaism, Christianity and Islam." SLJ

"Each religion is presented in only a couple of illustrated pages of text that manage to emphasize important points. The artwork, executed in colored pencil, ink, and water color, is varied and lively, with the illustrator looking to each religion's artistic traditions for inspiration." Booklist

Osborne, Mary Pope

One world, many religions; the ways we worship. Knopf 1996 86p il map $19.95 (4 and up) **200**

1. Religions

ISBN 0-679-83930-5   LC 96-836

This is an "overview of major world religions—Judaism, Christianity, Islam, Hinduism, Buddhism, Confucianism, and Taoism. . . . Each of six essay-styled chapters addresses themes of religious tenets, deities, morality, and ritual only as they are pertinent to a particular faith." Bull Cent Child Books

"The presentation is notable for its respect to each group, succinctness, and clarity. . . . The artful, full-page, color and black-and-white photographs tell much of the story." SLJ

Includes glossary and bibliographical references

201 Religious mythology & social theology

Bulfinch, Thomas

Bulfinch's mythology   **201**

1. Mythology 2. Folklore—Europe 3. Chivalry

Hardcover and paperback editions available from various publishers

First combined edition published 1913 by Crowell. Originally published in three separate volumes 1855, 1858 and 1862 respectively

Contents: The age of fable; The age of chivalry; Legends of Charlemagne

"The classic work on mythology, Bulfinch's gives brief summations of Greek, Roman, Norse, Arthurian, and other miscellaneous myths and includes notes on the 'Iliad.' the 'Odyssey,' and the 'Aeneid.'" N Y Public Libr Book of How & Where to Look It Up

Hamilton, Virginia

In the beginning; creation stories from around the world; told by Virginia Hamilton; illustrated by Barry Moser. Harcourt Brace Jovanovich 1988 161p il lib bdg $28; pa $20 (5 and up)

201

1. Creation 2. Mythology

ISBN 0-15-238740-4 (lib bdg); 0-15-238742-0 (pa)

LC 88-6211

A Newbery Medal honor book, 1989

"Hamilton has gathered 25 creation myths from various cultures and retold them in language true to the original. Images from the tales are captured in Moser's 42 full-page illustrations, tantalizing oil paintings that are rich with somber colors and striking compositions. Included in the collection are the familiar stories (biblical creation stories, Greek and Roman myths), and some that are not so familiar (tales from the Australian aborigines, various African and native American tribes, as well as from countries like Russia, China, and Iceland). At the end of each tale, Hamilton provides a brief commentary on the story's origin and originators." Booklist

Includes bibliographical references

Philip, Neil

The illustrated book of myths; tales & legends of the world; retold by Neil Philip; illustrated by Nilesh Mistry. Dorling Kindersley 1995 192p il $19.99 (5 and up)   **201**

1. Mythology

ISBN 0-7894-0202-5   LC 95-2156

"This collection represents a wide variety of world cultures and stories. Selections are grouped by type (creation myths, fertility and cultivation, visions of the end), which helps readers understand the commonality of the tales. The standard Greek and Norse myths are here, but what makes this volume special is its inclusion of less frequently anthologized stories of the Aztecs, Haitians, Africans, and Japanese, to name a few." SLJ

Zeitlin, Steven J.

The four corners of the sky; creation stories and cosmologies from around the world; [by] Steve Zeitlin; pictures by Chris Raschka. Holt & Co. 2000 135p il lib bdg $17 (5 and up)   **201**

1. Creation 2. Cosmology 3. Mythology

ISBN 0-8050-4816-2   LC 00-22546

A collection of folk stories from around the world, each accompanied by background information, that explain the various perspectives of different peoples on how the universe and their world came to be

Zeitlin, Steven J.—*Continued*

"Raschka's stylish, culture-specific graphic designs enliven the text without literally translating the stories. A conclusion calling for tolerance across cultures and extensive source notes round out this intriguing volume that will find wide curricular support." Booklist

203   Public worship and other practices

Sturges, Philemon

Sacred places; illustrated by Giles Laroche. Putnam 2000 38p il $16.99 (4 and up)

203

1. Shrines 2. Religions
ISBN 0-399-23317-2   LC 98-31086

Describes various types of space which are sacred to different religions, including churches, mosques, synagogues, temples, and other shrines

"Sturges' approach is respectful and impartial, and the selection of sites offers some thought-provoking diversity. . . . The intricate paper construction of everything from Chartres to the River Ganges is impressive and visually absorbing." Bull Cent Child Books

204   Religious experience, life, practice

Baylor, Byrd

The way to start a day; by Byrd Baylor; illustrated by Peter Parnall. Scribner 1978 unp il lib bdg $17; pa $5.99 (1-4)   **204**

1. Worship 2. Sun worship
ISBN 0-684-15651-2 (lib bdg); 0-689-71054-2 (pa)
     LC 78-113

A Caldecott Medal honor book, 1979

Text and illustrations describe how people all over the world celebrate the sunrise

"While the format is that of a picture book, the concepts in the poetic text of this handsome volume are more appropriate for independent readers who can grasp the historic and ritual values of Baylor's thoughts." Bull Cent Child Books

In every tiny grain of sand; a child's book of prayers and praise; collected by Reeve Lindbergh; illustrated by Christine Davenier [et al.] Candlewick Press 2000 77p il $21.99 (2-5)
     204

1. Prayers 2. Worship
ISBN 0-7636-0176-4   LC 99-89379

A "collection of 77 poems and prayers, illustrated by four different artists. There are excerpts from Native American, Hindu, Jewish, Buddhist, Christian, African, and Baha'i prayers and meditations as well as offerings from individual poets." SLJ

"This is a prayerful, powerful collection." Booklist

220   Bible

Brown, Alan

The Bible and Christianity; by Alan Brown. Smart Apple Media 2003 30p il (Sacred texts) $27.10 (5 and up)   **220**

1. Bible (as subject) 2. Christianity
ISBN 1-58340-243-8   LC 2003-41645

Explains how the Old and New Testaments came to be part of the Bible used by Christians and discusses some of the important messages found in the holy scriptures.

"Colorful strips of symbolic patterns adorn the pages and accent the informative text boxes. . . . The clear captioned . . . illustrations (photos and historical art) provide additional background." Horn Book Guide

Includes glossary

220.5   Bible--Modern versions

Bible.

The Holy Bible; containing the Old and New Testaments; translated out of the original tongues; and with the former translations diligently compared and revised by King James's special command, 1611. Oxford Univ. Press

220.5

Available in various bindings and editions

The authorized or King James Version originally published 1611

The Holy Bible: new revised standard version; containing the Old and New Testaments with the Apocryphal/Deuterocanonical books. Nelson, T.

220.5

Available in various bindings and editions

This version first published 1989

"Intended for public reading, congregational worship, private study, instruction, and meditation, it attempts to be as literal as possible while following standard American English usage, avoids colloquialism, and prefers simple, direct terms and phrases." Sheehy. Guide to Ref Books. 10th edition. suppl

220.8   Nonreligious subjects treated in Bible

Bible. Selections.

Animals of the Bible; a picture book by Dorothy P. Lathrop; with text selected by Helen Dean Fish from the King James Bible. Harper & Row 1987 65p il $17.95; lib bdg $16.89 (1-4)

220.8

1. Bible—Natural history 2. Animals
ISBN 0-397-31536-8; 0-397-30047-6 (lib bdg)

Awarded the Caldecott Medal, 1938

A reissue of the title first published 1937 by Lippincott

Bible. Selections.—*Continued*

"Dorothy Lathrop's love and understanding of animals, the sensitiveness and joy with which she draws them, make her the ideal artist for such a volume. It is more than a beautiful picture book, for she has studied the fauna and flora of Bible lands until each animal and bird, each flower and tree, is true to natural history." NY Times Book Rev

220.9 Bible--Geography, history, biography, stories

Bible. Selections.

Tomie dePaola's book of Bible stories. Putnam 1989 127p il $24.99 **220.9**
1. Bible stories
ISBN 0-399-21690-1 LC 88-26468
"A collection of 17 stories from the Old Testament, 15 from the New Testament, and 4 psalms. The text is from the New International Version. . . . De Paola uses the text as written with some abridgement to make the stories an appropriate length. Done in his typical style, the illustrations feature stylized people and objects. . . . There are several illustrations for each story, many of which are full page, and most make dramatic use of color. The large format enhances the impact of the pictures." SLJ

Hoffman, Mary

Animals of the Bible; [pictures by] Jackie Morris. Phyllis Fogelman Bks. 2003 29p il $16.99 (2-4) **220.9**
1. Animals—Fiction 2. Bible stories
ISBN 0-8037-2842-5 LC 2002-18787
First published 2002 in the United Kingdom
Contents: Naming the animals; The serpent in the garden; Noah's ark; Jacob's sheep; Pharaoh's dream; Frogs and creep-crawlies; Elijah's ravens; Daniel in the lions' den; Jonah and the whale
"Nine Old Testament stories—five of them from Genesis and most very familiar—are simply told and splendidly illustrated in this lively book. . . . Lush, detailed watercolors in shades of brown, gray, and blue, and touches of red accompany the tales." SLJ

Rock, Lois

Everlasting stories; a family Bible treasury; illustrated by Christina Balit. Chronicle Bks. 2001 223p il $24.95 (3-6) **220.9**
1. Bible stories
ISBN 0-8118-3258-9 LC 00-13161
This "collection of biblical selections includes stories from the Old Testament, up to the book of Esther, and from the four Gospels and the first chapters of the Book of Acts in the New Testament. Rock recasts the biblical texts in a simple and direct, yet dignified language that simplifies without losing the essence of each story. Balit's stylized watercolor-and-gouache paintings, reminiscent of ancient Near Eastern art, appear in clever layouts on every page and add to the book's vitality." Booklist

Watts, Murray

The Bible for children from Good Books; retold by Murray Watts; illustrated by Helen Cann. Good Bks. (Pa.) 2002 352p il map $23.99 (3-6) **220.9**
1. Bible stories
ISBN 1-56148-362-1 LC 2002-20243
A collection of approximately two hundred and fifty illustrated stories from the Old and New Testaments, retold for children
"Watts' retellings from the Old and New Testaments are vivid and evocative. . . . The handsome pictures and decorated borders employ a rich palette of colors and patterns, giving the book a contemporary look." Booklist

Words of gold; a treasury of the Bible's poetry and wisdom; selected and introduced by Lois Rock; illustrated by Sarah Young. Eerdmans 1999 48p il $18 (4 and up) **220.9**
1. Bible stories
ISBN 0-8028-5199-1 LC 99-37903
First published 1997 in the United Kingdom
Presents passages from both the Old and New Testaments as lessons on life for young children
"Well organized and beautifully presented. . . . The quotations are short; printed in a clear, varied, handsome typeface; and attractively arranged among a multitude of charming illustrations, ranging from vignettes to half-page scenes. Done in a delicate folk-art technique, using gold and rich, stained-glass colors." SLJ

221.9 Bible. Old Testament-- Geography, history, biography, stories

McKissack, Patricia C.

Let my people go; Bible stories told by a freeman of color to his daughter, Charlotte, in Charleston, South Carolina, 1806-16; by Patricia and Fredrick McKissack; illustrated by James Ransome. Atheneum Bks. for Young Readers 1998 134p il $20 (4 and up) **221.9**
1. African Americans—Fiction 2. Bible stories 3. Slavery—Fiction
ISBN 0-689-80856-9 LC 97-19983
"An Anne Schwartz book"
Charlotte, the daughter of a free black man who worked as a blacksmith in Charleston, South Carolina, in the early 1800s recalls the stories from the Bible that her father shared with her, relating them to the experiences of African Americans
"The poignant juxtaposition of the Biblical characters and Charlotte's personal narrative is authentic and moving. . . . The occasional illustrations are powerful oil paintings in rich colors, emotional and evocative." SLJ
Includes bibliographical references

Sasso, Sandy Eisenberg

But God remembered; stories of women from creation to the promised land; illustrated by Bethanne Andersen. Jewish Lights Pub. 1995 31p il $16.95 (3-5)   **221.9**

1. Women in the Bible 2. Bible stories
ISBN 1-879045-43-5   LC 95-3591

The author "weaves together the stories of: Lilith, the first woman in the garden of Eden, . . . Serach the musician, who, with her song, reveals to her grandfather Jacob that his son is still alive, . . . Bityah, who draws the baby Moses from the Nile, . . . and the bold-spirited Daughters of Z, who struggle against discrimination." Publisher's note

"Although part of the pleasure of the book lies in its strong feminist voice, Sasso also tells good stories; and these will have even more value for the discussions they can generate. Andersen's evocative paintings are beautiful additions to this carefully designed book." Booklist

Ward, Elaine M.

Old Testament women; [by] Elaine Ward. Enchanted Lion 2004 32p il (Art revelations) $18.95 (5 and up)   **221.9**

1. Women in the Bible 2. Bible stories
ISBN 1-59270-011-X

These Old Testament stories about women include "explanatory paragraphs, sidebars, and captions by the author. Art masterpieces . . . illustrate each story. . . . The captions provide background on the artist and the significance of each painting or mosaic. . . . The 18 women . . . include Rachel, Leah, Ruth, and Bathsheba. . . . Bosch, Botticelli, and Poussin are among the painters whose work appears here. . . . Visually stunning." SLJ

222   Historical books of Old Testament

Bible. O.T. Genesis.

The story of the creation; words from Genesis; [pictures by] Jane Ray. Dutton Children's Bks. 1993 c1992 unp il $16 (k-3)   **222**

1. Creation 2. Bible stories
ISBN 0-525-44946-9   LC 92-20862

First published 1992 in the United Kingdom

Illustrates the story of creation, from the book of Genesis of the King James version of the Bible

"Folk-art exuberance, sapphire and emerald hues, and decorative detail mark Ray's style and reflect Creation's rich abundance." SLJ

Cato, Vivienne

The Torah and Judaism; by Vivienne Cato. Smart Apple Media 2003 30p il (Sacred texts) $27.10 (5 and up)   **222**

1. Torah 2. Judaism
ISBN 1-58340-244-6   LC 2003-41644

This explains the origins of the Torah, its structure and contents, its message and teachings, and its place in Jewish life and worship.

"Colorful strips of symbolic patterns adorn the pages and accent the informative text boxes. . . . The clear, captioned . . . illustrations (photos and historical art) provide additional background." Horn Book Guide

De Regniers, Beatrice Schenk

David and Goliath; illustrated by Scott Cameron. Orchard Bks. 1996 unp il $15.95; lib bdg $16.99   **222**

1. David, King of Israel 2. Goliath (Biblical figure) 3. Bible stories
ISBN 0-531-09496-0; 0-531-08796-4 (lib bdg)
    LC 95-22025

The biblical tale of the young shepherd who uses a slingshot to do battle with a giant and eventually becomes a king

Feiler, Bruce S.

Walking the Bible; an illustrated journey for kids through the greatest stories ever told; by Bruce Feiler; illustrated by Sasha Meret. 1st ed. HarperCollinsPublishers 2004 108p il map $16.99; lib bdg $17.89   **222**

1. Middle East 2. Bible (as subject)
ISBN 0-06-051117-6; 0-06-051118-4 (lib bdg)
    LC 2003-15861

Contents: Walking the Bible; Creating the world; Noah's ark; Abraham; Abraham in the promised land; Abraham and Isaac; Joseph in Egypt; Moses parts the Red Sea; The burning bush; Climbing Mt. Sinai

The author describes his journey through places mentioned in the Old Testament

"In this version of his adult book with the same title (Morrow, 2001), Feiler largely succeeds in slimming rather than dumbing down his account of his trip across the 10,000-mile setting of the earliest Bible stories. The author's unpretentious . . . tone and astute pacing help make the volume accessible, and his sincerity is palpable." SLJ

Fisher, Leonard Everett

David and Goliath; adapted from the Bible and illustrated by Leonard Everett Fisher. Holiday House 1993 unp il $15.95 (k-3)   **222**

1. David, King of Israel 2. Goliath (Biblical figure) 3. Bible stories
ISBN 0-8234-0997-X   LC 92-24063

Retells the Bible story in which a Hebrew shepherd boy kills the giant Philistine warrior Goliath with a slingshot

"Fisher has created majestic images that reflect the grandeur of the story in all its mythic proportions. The concise telling works in counterpoint to the thickly painted images, which Fisher has chosen carefully." Booklist

Geisert, Arthur

The ark. Houghton Mifflin 1988 48p il lib bdg $17.95; pa $7.95 (k-3)   **222**

1. Noah's ark 2. Bible stories
ISBN 0-395-43078-X (lib bdg); 0-618-00608-7 (pa)
    LC 88-15889

Geisert, Arthur—*Continued*

"Beginning with God's decision to destroy his creation—except for Noah and his family—Geisert details the story on buff-colored pages. The illustrator employs intricate cross hatching and unusual perspectives to show Noah building the ark and housing all the creatures of the earth. . . . As a result of its astonishing illustrations, as well as its compact text, this book can be used with a wide range of audiences, all of whom will no doubt want to look closely at the meticulous detail that abounds on every spread." Booklist

Goldin, Barbara Diamond

Journeys with Elijah; eight tales of the Prophet; retold by Barbara Diamond Goldin; paintings by Jerry Pinkney. Harcourt Brace & Co. 1999 77p il $20 (4 and up)   222

1. Elijah (Biblical figure) 2. Jewish legends 3. Bible stories

ISBN 0-15-200445-9   LC 96-9278

"Gulliver books"

Presents eight stories about the Old Testament prophet Elijah, set in a variety of time periods and in places all over the world where Jews have lived

"Goldin's storytelling is every bit as colorful as Pinkney's radiant, masterfully composed paintings, and both text and art testify to careful historical research." Publ Wkly

Includes bibliographical references

Koralek, Jenny

The coat of many colors; illustrated by Pauline Baynes. Eerdmans Books for Young Readers 2004 unp il $16 (k-3)   222

1. Joseph (Biblical figure) 2. Bible stories

ISBN 0-8028-5277-7   LC 2004-6575

This "retelling of the story from the Book of Genesis highlights the key events in the life of Joseph . . . and explores timeless themes of sibling rivalry and the power of forgiveness. . . . Baynes enhances the straightforward text with atmospheric illustrations rendered in muted desert shades. . . . This appealing rendition of a well-known tale is perfect for reading aloud." SLJ

Manushkin, Fran

Miriam's cup; a Passover story; illustrated by Bob Dacey. Scholastic 1998 unp il $15.95 (k-3)
222

1. Miriam (Biblical figure) 2. Passover 3. Bible stories
ISBN 0-590-67720-9   LC 96-2480

A Jewish mother preparing for Passover tells her young children, the story of Miriam, the Biblical woman who prophesied the birth of Moses

"The text and the lush double-spread watercolors, which are painted to reflect a child's perspective, are framed on a papyrus background. Each illustration bursts with movement, immersing readers and pre-readers alike in the sequence and drama of the story." Booklist

Includes bibliographical references

Marzollo, Jean

Miriam and her brother Moses; a Bible story; retold and illustrated by Jean Marzollo. Little, Brown 2003 unp il $15.95 (k-3)   222

1. Miriam (Biblical figure) 2. Moses (Biblical figure) 3. Bible stories

ISBN 0-316-74131-0

"When the wicked king Pharaoh decides that all Hebrew baby boys should be drowned, Miriam and her family come up with a plan to save [Moses]." Publisher's note

The narrative is "lively, interesting, and easy to understand. . . . Painted in watercolors and scanned and finished in Adobe Photoshop, the joyful and childlike illustrations are full of movement and color." SLJ

Ruth and Naomi; a Bible story; retold and illustrated by Jean Marzollo. Little, Brown 2005 unp il $15.99 (k-3)   222

1. Bible stories

ISBN 0-316-74139-6

"This abbreviated retelling of the experiences of two widows, Ruth and her mother-in-law, Naomi, highlights the key events from the Old Testament story. . . . This simple tale explores themes of loyalty and sacrifice, and also provides an interesting look at the farming customs of biblical times. Dialogue and a harvest song supplement the text. Painted in watercolor and Chinese ink and then finished in Adobe Photoshop, the cartoon illustrations are bright and expressive." SLJ

Paterson, Katherine

The angel and the donkey; retold by Katherine Paterson; illustrated by Alexander Koshkin. Clarion Bks. 1996 34p il $15.95 (3-5)
222

1. Balaam (Biblical figure) 2. Bible stories
ISBN 0-395-68969-4   LC 94-22430

"Paterson retells the story from the Book of Numbers in which the Moab king Balak summons soothsayer Balaam to curse the Israelites, but through the intervention of God, an angel, and a talking donkey, Balaam is inspired to bless this people instead." Bull Cent Child Books

"This faithful, graceful retelling is embellished with many equally graceful watercolor, tempera, and gouache paintings executed in a detailed and realistic manner." SLJ

Pinkney, Jerry

Noah's ark. SeaStar Bks. 2002 unp il $15.95; lib bdg $16.50 (k-3)   222

1. Noah's ark 2. Bible stories
ISBN 1-58717-201-1; 1-58717-202-X (lib bdg)
LC 2002-2010

A Caldecott Medal honor book, 2003

Retells the biblical story of the great flood and how Noah and his family faithfully responded to God's call to save life on earth

"The deep rumble of a distant voice can almost be heard in the strong, straightforward text. . . . And the muscular pencil-and-watercolor art, in Pinkney's familiar style, stands up well to the telling." Booklist

Ray, Jane

Adam and Eve and the Garden of Eden; written and illustrated by Jane Ray. 1st ed. Eerdmans Books for Young Readers 2005 unp il $17 (k-3) **222**

1. Adam (Biblical figure) 2. Eve (Biblical figure) 3. Bible stories

ISBN 0-8028-5278-5   LC 2004-6804

"Adam and Eve live harmoniously with the animals that have been named by the first man, until Eve is tempted by the serpent. In rich prose, the author describes the garden in lyrical detail. The descriptive passages are complemented by exquisite illustrations that lend a mystical aura to the narrative." SLJ

Sasso, Sandy Eisenberg

Cain & Abel; finding the fruits of peace; illustrated by Joani Keller Rothenberg. Jewish Lights Pub. 2001 32p il $16.95 (k-3) **222**

1. Cain (Biblical figure) 2. Abel (Biblical figure) 3. Bible stories

ISBN 1-58023-123-3   LC 2001-2206

Retells the story of two brothers who, after years of sharing everything, become angry enough to lose control and bring violence into the world

"In this simple yet effective book, Sasso leads children to think not only about how the brothers' personal relationship failed but also about the story's connection to today's violence. The eye-catching, folk-art-style illustrations, with thick swathes of color and inventive background designs, make as strong a statement as the text." Booklist

Spier, Peter

Noah's ark; illustrated by Peter Spier. Doubleday 1977 unp il $16.95; pa $7.99 (k-2) **222**

1. Noah's ark 2. Bible stories

ISBN 0-385-09473-6; 0-440-49693-8 (pa)
     LC 76-43630

Awarded the Caldecott Medal, 1978

"A seventeenth-century Dutch poem, 'The Flood' by Jacobus Revius, opens the otherwise almost wordless book. Skillfully translated by the artist and set in a readable, appropriately archaic type, the artlessly reverent verses add an unexpected dimension to the full-color pictures. Peter Spier's characteristic panoramas are marvels of minute detail, activity, vitality, and humor." Horn Book

Wildsmith, Brian

Exodus. Eerdmans Bks. for Young Readers 1999 c1998 unp il $20 **222**

1. Moses (Biblical figure) 2. Bible stories

ISBN 0-8028-5175-4   LC 98-18066

First published 1998 in the United Kingdom

Describes how God sent Moses to lead his people out of slavery in Egypt and into the promised land of Canaan

"The storytelling is formal but understandable to a young reader. The illustrations are dramatic, and each page is bordered in gold, with God depicted as a prismatic star." Horn Book Guide

223   Poetic books of Old Testament

Bible. O.T. Ecclesiastes.

To every thing there is a season; verses from Ecclesiastes; illustrations by Leo and Diane Dillon. Blue Sky Press (NY) 1998 unp il $16.95 **223**

ISBN 0-590-47887-7   LC 97-35124

Presents that selection from Ecclesiastes which relates that everything in life has its own time and season

"The Dillons compellingly convey the relevance of the Ecclesiastes verse throughout history, via a stunning array of artwork that embraces motifs from cultures the world over." Publ Wkly

Lindbergh, Reeve

On morning wings; adapted from Psalm 139 by Reeve Lindbergh; illustrated by Holly Meade. Candlewick Press 2002 unp il $15.99 (k-3) **223**

1. Bible. O.T. Psalms 2. God

ISBN 0-7636-1106-9   LC 2001-58169

"On morning wings" was previously published in the anthology In every tiny grain of sand: a child's book of prayers and praise, collected by Reeve Lindbergh, published by Candlewick Press, 2000

Retells, in simple words, a psalm of God's knowledge of and love for each of us

"Meade's visual story line shows four children spending an idyllic summer day together outdoors. The striking use of light, reflected in water or filtered by campfire, conveys the natural reverence of the text with seeming spontaneity." Publ Wkly

224   Prophetic books of Old Testament

Marzollo, Jean

Daniel in the lion's den; retold and illustrated by Jean Marzollo. Little, Brown 2004 unp il $14.95 (k-3) **224**

1. Daniel (Biblical figure) 2. Bible stories

ISBN 0-316-74132-9

A retelling of the Bible story in which the Prophet Daniel is saved from being eaten by lions.

The narrative is "lively, interesting, and easy to understand. . . . Painted in watercolors and scanned and finished in Adobe Photoshop, the joyful and childlike illustrations are full of movement and color." SLJ

230   Christianity. Christian theology

Self, David

Christianity; [by] David Self. World Almanac Library 2005 48p il map (Religions of the world) lib bdg $30 (5 and up) **230**

1. Christianity

ISBN 0-8368-5866-2   LC 2005041712

Self, David—*Continued*
This is a summary of the Christian religion including history, beliefs, worship, festivals, practice, and current disagreements.
"Wonderfully colorful in images, language, and fact. . . . [This is] enumerated with full-color photographs on every page, charts, maps, and tables." SLJ
Includes bibliographical references

231 God

Fitch, Florence Mary
A book about God; illustrated by Henri Sorensen. Lothrop, Lee & Shepard Bks. 1998 24p il $16; lib bdg $15.93 (k-3) **231**
1. God
ISBN 0-688-16128-6; 0-688-16129-4 (lib bdg)
LC 97-48682
A newly illustrated edition of the title first published 1953
The "text explains how people can understand God's nature by observing the world he created. Fitch describes the ways that characteristics of the sun, air, trees, mountains, and oceans reflect the character of God. Proponents of many faiths will embrace this book's message." Horn Book Guide

Paterson, John Barstow
Images of God; by John and Katherine Paterson; illustrated by Alexander Koshkin. Clarion Bks. 1998 112p il $20 (5 and up) **231**
1. God 2. Bible stories
ISBN 0-395-70734-X
LC 97-21637
Explores some of the images which biblical writers use to teach about God; images include light, rock, and wind as well as a gardener, father, and architect
"The commentary is both explanation and storytelling. It is simple yet profound. Koshkin's paintings in watercolor, tempera and gouache live up to the writing. They are full of movement, color and realistic detail." Child Book Rev Serv

232.9 Family and life of Jesus

Bible. N.T.
The Christmas story; according to the Gospels of Matthew and Luke from the King James Version; paintings by Gennady Spirin. Holt & Co. 1998 32p il $19.95 **232.9**
1. Jesus Christ—Nativity
ISBN 0-8050-5292-5
LC 97-50417
Presents the story of the birth of Christ, from Mary's meeting with the angel Gabriel to the birth of baby Jesus in a stable and the visit of the shepherds and three Wise Men
"The beautiful illustrations, with angels everywhere and Christian symbols such as lilies, are illuminated by an appropriate golden glow that gives an air of religiosity and holiness to the art." Booklist

The Easter story; according to the Gospels of Matthew, Luke & John; illustrated by Gennady Spirin. Holt & Co. 1999 31p il $19.95; lib bdg $19.95 **232.9**
1. Jesus Christ 2. Bible stories 3. Easter
ISBN 0-8050-5052-3; 0-8050-6333-1 (lib bdg)
LC 98-7087
By combining verses from the gospels of Matthew, Luke, and John, tells the Easter story from Jesus' triumphant entry into Jerusalem through his passion and resurrection to his appearance to his disciples
"From the elaborate architectural details to the stunning use of color and light, the artist's prodigious command of the page inspires awe." Publ Wkly

Crossley-Holland, Kevin
How many miles to Bethlehem? illustrated by Peter Malone. Arthur A. Levine Books 2004 unp il $16.95 (k-3) **232.9**
1. Jesus Christ—Nativity
ISBN 0-439-67642-8
LC 2003-28079
This is a telling of the Nativity story, told from the perspectives of Mary, the innkeeper, the ox, the donkey, the shepherds, the Wise Men, King Herod, the child, the lamb, and the angels.
"The language is both colloquial and lyrical. . . . Malone's illustrations are reminiscent of early Renaissance and medieval Eastern art in their wealth of detail and color. . . . The paintings evoke both sumptuous glory and a serene stillness." SLJ

De Paola, Tomie
The miracles of Jesus; retold from the Bible and illustrated by Tomie dePaola. Holiday House 1987 unp il $16.95; pa $8.95 (k-3) **232.9**
1. Jesus Christ 2. Bible stories
ISBN 0-8234-0635-0; 0-8234-1211-3 (pa)
LC 86-18297
"Thirteen miracles, with the Biblical texts only slightly shortened and simplified, are retold with the beauty and dignity of the original. The artist's typical stylized, flat, highly decorative illustrations of sturdy, pensive figures, their faces often expressing awe, in soft, warm tones, have a still, timeless quality particularly appropriate to the spirituality and eternity of the subject." SLJ

Demi
Jesus; written and illustrated by Demi. 1st ed. Margaret K. McElderry Books 2005 unp il $19.95 (3-6) **232.9**
1. Jesus Christ
ISBN 0-689-86905-3
LC 2004-12854
"Brilliantly colored artwork and text based on the King James version of the Bible tell the story of the life of Jesus, beginning with the prophesies and the annunciation and ending with his ascension into Heaven. Demi's paintings are full of bright, intricate patterns, and bold touches of gold produce a feeling of awe and splendor." SLJ

Lottridge, Celia Barker

Stories from the life of Jesus; retold from the Bible by Celia Barker Lottridge; illustrated by Linda Wolfsgruber. Doulgas & McIntyre 2004 140p il $24.95 (4 and up)   **232.9**

1. Jesus Christ 2. Bible stories

ISBN 0-88899-497-4

"A Groundwood book"

A retelling of selected events from the life of Christ based on biblical accounts

This is an "exceptional collection. . . . Each story is retold in three or four pages of clear, concise prose that is meant to be read aloud. . . . Each selection is enhanced by dramatic and atmospheric, mixed-media illustrations that are executed in warm earth tones." SLJ

Mayer, Marianna

Seeing Jesus in His own words. Phyllis Fogelman Bks. 2002 32p il $16.99   **232.9**

1. Jesus Christ

ISBN 0-8037-2742-9   LC 2001-50145

"Using a number of biblical translations . . . Mayer has assembled and interpreted in graceful language some of Jesus's most memorable sayings and keys to his basic theology. All are beautifully mounted on double-page spreads; illustrated with a variety of carefully chosen, richly colored art reproductions; and set in handsome, well-spaced typeface." SLJ

Includes bibliographical references

Thompson, Lauren

Love one another; the last days of Jesus; retold by Lauren Thompson; illustrated by Elizabeth Uyehara. Scholastic Press 2000 unp il lib bdg $15.95 (1-3)   **232.9**

1. Jesus Christ 2. Easter 3. Bible stories

ISBN 0-590-31830-6   LC 99-25157

"Drawing from all four Evangelists, Thompson retells events from the life of Jesus from his public role as preacher and teacher through the aftermath of his death and the continuing mission of his disciples." Bull Cent Child Books

"The text has a fine read-aloud rhythm. . . . The oil-on-canvas illustrations, with a sweep and agitation reminiscent of van Gogh, are almost overpowering with their bold lines, gleaming stained-glass colors, and dramatic movement." SLJ

Wildsmith, Brian

Jesus. Eerdmans Bks. for Young Readers 2000 unp il $20 (k-3)   **232.9**

1. Jesus Christ

ISBN 0-8028-5212-2   LC 00-55126

This "picture book gives an overview of Jesus' life beginning with the angel Gabriel's visit to Mary and ending with Jesus' ascension into Heaven." Horn Book Guide

"Wildsmith's pictures are framed in windowlike arches, set against backgrounds of pure colors. As with his other works, gold embellishments add majesty." Booklist

Winthrop, Elizabeth

He is risen: the Easter story; adapted from the New Testament by Elizabeth Winthrop; illustrated by Charles Mikolaycak. Holiday House 1985 unp il lib bdg $16.95 (k-3)   **232.9**

1. Jesus Christ 2. Easter 3. Bible stories

ISBN 0-8234-0547-8   LC 84-15869

"The Easter story, adapted from the King James Version of the Gospels of John and Matthew, has been slightly altered and some of the obscure passages omitted for the benefit of young readers." Child Book Rev Serv

"Mikolaycak's potent, yet emotionally controlled compositions are enclosed along with the text in narrow, rust-colored borders that echo the earthy tones of the pictures themselves. . . . The text is lengthy, and adults may want to paraphrase the story in parts to hold youngsters' attention, but older listeners will be moved by the timelessness of the language and the reverent beauty of Mikolaycak's spellbinding interpretation." Booklist

232.91   Mary, mother of Jesus

De Paola, Tomie

Mary, the mother of Jesus. Holiday House 1995 unp il $16.95 (3-5)   **232.91**

1. Mary, Blessed Virgin, Saint 2. Bible stories

ISBN 0-8234-1018-8   LC 92-54491

"Based on the New English Bible and legends about the mother of Jesus, this picture book tells the story of Mary's life in words and full-color artwork." Booklist

"The writing style is restrained, elegant, and expressive. Handsome, framed, full-page paintings; harmonizing, rectangular spot illustrations on the pages of text; and a clear, attractive typeface give a balanced, dignified appearance to the book." SLJ

Wildsmith, Brian

Mary. Eerdmans Bks. for Young Readers 2002 unp il $20 (k-3)   **232.91**

1. Mary, Blessed Virgin, Saint

ISBN 0-8028-5231-9   LC 2001-54336

This outline of the life of the mother of Jesus includes "accounts of Mary's childhood, family life with Jesus and Joseph, death, and crowning as Queen of Heaven. The simply written text reads smoothly and cohesively. . . . The artist's illustrations are sumptuous. Iridescent ink-and-watercolor pictures are highlighted with lustrous gold." SLJ

Includes bibliographical references

242   Devotional literature

Beckett, Wendy

A child's book of prayer in art. Dorling Kindersley 1995 32p il $14.95 (3-6)   **242**

1. Prayers 2. Art appreciation

ISBN 1-56458-875-0   LC 94-40362

"Linking the work of 15 different artists, from Michelangelo to Millet, to a spiritual value such as respect or forgiveness, Sister Wendy Beckett introduces children to

Beckett, Wendy—*Continued*

art as a means of discovering faith. . . . With appeal to older as well as middle readers, this is a remarkable book, not only for its innate spirituality and wisdom, but also for its harmonious partnership of great art and astute interpretation." Booklist

Brooks, Jeremy

A world of prayers; selected by Jeremy Brooks; illustrated by Elena Gomez. 1st ed. Eerdmans Books for Young Readers 2006 unp il $16 (1-4)
242

1. Prayers
ISBN 0-8028-5285-8   LC 2004017482

"A collection of 26 prayers assembled under the headings, Prayers for the Morning, Mealtime Graces, Prayers for Nighttime, and Blessings. A brief introduction and comments at the beginning of each chapter reflect on the place of prayer in our lives. Written in simple, easy-to-read language, the entreaties are recited by children in a variety of lands. . . . Dreamlike, decorative paintings that reflect the various cultures greatly enhance the selections and emphasize the books message of inclusiveness." SLJ

Field, Rachel

Prayer for a child; pictures by Elizabeth Orton Jones. Diamond anniversary ed. Simon & Schuster Books for Young Readers 2004 c1944 unp il $10.95 (k-2)   **242**

1. Prayers
ISBN 0-689-87356-5   LC 2004-5259
Awarded the Caldecott Medal, 1945
A reissue of the title first published 1944 by Macmillan

"The complete prayer, written in rhymed couplets, appears on the first page; then a few lines per page accompany serene illustrations of a girl in tender moments—stargazing out a window or smiling up at her parents. . . . This lovely book lends itself to nightly repetition (a reference to Jesus tags it for a Christian audience)." Publ Wkly

Goble, Paul

Song of creation; written and illustrated by Paul Goble. 1st ed. Eerdmans Books for Young Readers 2004 unp il $16 (k-3)   **242**

1. Creation 2. Prayers
ISBN 0-8028-5271-8   LC 2004-6576

"An author's note introduces this story as an adaptation of the song from The Liturgy of the Hours and The Book of Common Prayer. . . . Goble includes the familiar verse, in which heavens, angels, sun, moon, and the entire Earth sing songs of praise, and includes animals and plants of America as additional elements that also send out prayers to God." SLJ

"In striking graphic compositions, Goble creates magical, yet concrete, scenes of birds, beasts, fish, and more, conveying a personal and a universal reverence for and connection to nature. A beautiful, praiseworthy volume that does, indeed, sing." Booklist

Let there be light; poems and prayers for repairing the world; compiled and illustrated by Jane Breskin Zalben. Dutton Children's Bks. 2002 unp il $16.99 (3-6)   **242**

1. Prayers 2. Religious poetry
ISBN 0-525-46995-8   LC 2002-728864

This is a "collection of short, inspirational writings gathered from many cultures and religious traditions. . . . Each piece is illustrated with one or two pages of artwork—sometimes delicate, precise paintings, sometimes bold paper-cut collage, sometimes a combination of the two. . . . The positive message of this anthology of poems, quotations, and prayers, with thoughtful selections and creative illustrations, shines through like the sun that warms the world's children on the jacket illustration." Booklist

Lindbergh, Reeve

The circle of days; from Canticle of the sun by Saint Francis of Assisi; illustrated by Cathie Felstead. Candlewick Press 1998 unp il $15.99 (k-3)   **242**

1. Prayers
ISBN 0-7636-0357-0   LC 96-49848

Rhyming text gives praise and thanks for all of creation including wind and sun, plants and animals, desert, rocks, and sea

"The poem is accessible . . . and quite lyrical. Felstead uses collage and paint to create a benevolent and varied world to complement the poem." Horn Book Guide

One earth, one spirit; a child's book of prayers from many faiths and cultures; compiled by Tessa Strickland. Sierra Club Bks. for Children 1997 unp il $14.95   **242**

1. Prayers
ISBN 0-87156-978-7   LC 96-40387

Photographs of children from around the world are combined with more than fifteen prayers from different times and places to celebrate the natural world

"Poignant children's images accompany poetic expressions that reflect a reverence for the oneness of all living things. Last-page notes provide insights into each prayer's cultural source." Kobrin Letter

264   Public worship

Pinkney, Gloria Jean

Music from our Lord's holy heaven; gathered and sung by Gloria Jean Pinkney; art by Jerry Pinkney, Brian Pinkney, and Myles C. Pinkney; prelude by Troy Pinkney-Ragsdale. HarperCollins Publishers 2005 41p il $17.99; lib bdg $18.89 (2-4)   **264**

1. Hymns 2. Spirituals (Songs)
ISBN 0-06-000768-0; 0-06-000769-9 (lib bdg)
          LC 2002-18939

Contents: Music for the heart by Troy Pinkney-Ragsdale; Adoration; Spiritual wayfarers; The Good Shepherd; Melodius journey by Gloria Jean Pinkney

Pinkney, Gloria Jean—_Continued_

"Gloria Pinkney has gathered together 22 gospel songs that include familiar favorites such as 'Old Time Religion,' 'Go Down, Moses', and 'Come By Here, My Lord'. . . . Each of the spirituals is paired with a psalm that adds insight. Illustrating the joyous music are pictures by award-winning artists Jerry (husband) and Brian (son) and photographs by son Myles. Daughter Troy provides a prelude discussing the songs. . . . A CD featuring Gloria singing the songs accompanies the book. Whimsical, majestic, and moving by turns, this artful project will be enjoyed by the whole family." Booklist

271   Religious orders in church history

Kennedy, Robert Francis

Saint Francis of Assisi; a life of joy; written by Robert F. Kennedy, Jr.; illustrated by Dennis Nolan. Hyperion Books for Children 2004 31p il $18.99 (2-4)   **271**

1. Francis, of Assisi, Saint, 1182-1226 2. Christian saints

ISBN 0-7868-1875-1   LC 2003-60420

"The book paints Francis in glowing terms . . . weaving together the major threads of his life: his early kindness to beggars in his family's fabric shop; his call to and ultimate rejection of a military career; his estrangement from his wealthy father; and his ministry to lepers, the impoverished, and animals. . . . Nolan's oil paintings render realistic figures in carefully staged scenes." SLJ

Pandell, Karen

Saint Francis sings to Brother Sun; a celebration of his kinship with nature; selected and retold by Karen Pandell; illustrated by Bijou Le Tord. Candlewick Press 2005 64p il $18.99 (4 and up)   **271**

1. Francis, of Assisi, Saint, 1182-1226 2. Christian saints

ISBN 0-7636-1563-3

"The book opens with an author's note giving background about Saint Francis's poem _The Canticle of Brother Sun,_ followed by a summary of the man's life. . . . The rest of the book consists of brief vignettes from the saint's life, accompanied by an illustration. The author has used medieval biographies as sources and retold the stories in accessible language for modern readers. . . . The book is beautifully designed. Unifying elements appear throughout, such as a repeated pattern of colored tiles, the verses of The Canticle reproduced in gold superimposed on a medieval-style shield background, and Le Tords gold-embellished, primitive-style paintings." SLJ

Includes bibliographical references

Visconti, Guido

Clare and Francis; text by Guido Visconti, inspired by the biographies and written works of the two saints of Assisi collected in the Franciscan Sources. Eerdmans Books for Young Readers 2004 unp il $20 (4 and up)   **271**

1. Francis, of Assisi, Saint, 1182-1226 2. Clare, of Assisi, Saint, 1194-1253 3. Christian saints

ISBN 0-8028-5269-6   LC 2003-13441

Reviews the lives and works of two members of Assisi society, Francis and Clare, who renounced their wealth and founded religious orders dedicated to relying on God and living in peace, poverty, and humility.

"The familiar story of Francis (and to a lesser extent, Clare) is beautifully treated in this book, with luminous iconic artwork and a text that is both down-to-earth and stroking the stars." Booklist

280   Christian denominations and sects

Woog, Adam

What makes me a Protestant? by Adam Woog. KidHaven Press 2005 48p il map (What makes me a--?) $23.70 (3-5)   **280**

1. Protestantism 2. Protestant churches

ISBN 0-7377-2264-9   LC 2004-9043

Contents: How did Protestantism begin?; What forms does Protestantism take?; What do Protestants believe?; How do Protestants practice their faith?; What holidays do Protestants celebrate?

This describes Protestant origins, denominations, beliefs, practices, and holidays

"Presenting information about religion objectively for younger audiences poses a difficult challenge, but [this title does] an excellent job of it." Booklist

Includes glossary and bibliographical references

289.3   Latter-Day Saints (Mormons)

George, Charles

What makes me a Mormon? by Charles George. KidHaven Press 2004 48p il map (What makes me a--?) $23.70 (3-5)   **289.3**

1. Mormons 2. Church of Jesus Christ of Latter-day Saints

ISBN 0-7377-3083-8   LC 2004-13636

Contents: How did Mormonism begin?; What do I believe?; How do I practice my faith?; What holidays do I celebrate?

This describes Morman origins, beliefs, practices, and holidays

"Presenting information about religion objectively for younger audiences poses a difficult challenge, but [this title does] an excellent job of it." Booklist

Includes bibliographical references

289.6 Society of Friends (Quakers)

Woog, Adam
What makes me a Quaker? by Adam Woog. KidHaven Press 2004 48p il (What makes me a--?) $23.70 (3-5) **289.6**
1. Society of Friends
ISBN 0-7377-3082-X   LC 2004-13096
Contents: How did Quakerism begin?; What do Quakers believe?; How do Quakers practice their faith?; What is the future of Quakerism?
This explains Quakerism's origins, beliefs, practices, and future
"Presenting information about religion objectively for younger readers poses a difficult challenge, but [this title does] an excellent job of it." Booklist
Includes glossary and bibliographical references

289.7 Mennonite churches

Bial, Raymond
Amish home. Houghton Mifflin 1993 40p il $17; pa $5.95 (3-5) **289.7**
1. Amish
ISBN 0-395-59504-5; 0-395-72021-4 (pa)
                        LC 92-4406
Text and photographs depict the way of life of the Amish
The full-color photos depict "cozy kitchens, lovingly tended gardens, prized horses, and rolling landscapes. As well as being informative, these photographs create a mood through which readers enter another lifestyle." SLJ
Includes bibliographical references

Kenna, Kathleen
A people apart; photographs by Andrew Stawicki. Somerville House Pub. 1995 64p il $18 (4 and up) **289.7**
1. Mennonites
ISBN 0-395-67344-5   LC 94-18545
"A Nick Harris book"
This photo-essay "shows various aspects of life in Old Order Mennonite communities, including home, work, education, and worship. The well-written text does a good job of explaining the Mennonites' lifestyle and the reasons they choose to live as they do. It also explains how groups splinter off or individuals leave or are expelled because of disagreements about what is acceptable and unacceptable. . . . The full-page black-and-white photographs are marvelous and reflect the same respect for the way of life expressed in the narrative." SLJ
Includes bibliographical references

292 Classical religion (Greek and Roman religion)

Aliki
The gods and goddesses of Olympus; written and illustrated by Aliki. HarperCollins Pubs. 1994 48p il $16; pa $6.95 (2-5) **292**
1. Classical mythology
ISBN 0-06-023530-6; 0-06-446189-0 (pa)
                        LC 93-17834
"After the Uranus-Gaea, Cronus-Rhea background is sketched, the occupants of the 12 golden thrones are each described, along with Hades (underground), Hestia (hearth-bound) and Eros (hovering). The author outlines the deities' characters and attributes, sometimes including a brief incident from their lives." SLJ
"This large-format book provides a quick, brightly illustrated introduction to the ancient Greek gods and goddesses." Booklist

Burleigh, Robert
Hercules; illustrated by Raúl Colón. Silver Whistle Bks. 1999 unp il $16 (3-6) **292**
1. Hercules (Legendary character)
ISBN 0-15-201667-8   LC 98-4989
Retells the story of the final, and most difficult, labor of Hercules, known as Heracles in Greek mythology, in which he must go to Underworld and bring back the three-headed dog, Cerberus
"The narrative is spare, broken into short, poetic lines. . . . The success of this version depends heavily on Colón's watercolor and colored-pencil illustrations. His characteristically golden hues work well for the Mediterranean and mythical setting." SLJ

Colum, Padraic
The Golden Fleece and the heroes who lived before Achilles; illustrated by Willy Pogany. Macmillan 1962 c1921 316p il $18; pa $9.95 (5 and up) **292**
1. Argonauts (Greek mythology) 2. Classical mythology
ISBN 0-02-723620-X; 0-02-042260-1 (pa)
A reissue of the title first published 1921
Contents: The voyage to Colchis; The return to Greece; The heroes of the quest
"Mr. Colum preserves the spirit of the Greek tales and weaves them into a magic whole. In this he is aided by the spirited drawings." Booklist

Craft, Marie
Cupid and Psyche; as told by M. Charlotte Craft; illustrated by K. Y. Craft. Morrow Junior Bks. 1996 unp il $16 (4 and up) **292**
1. Eros (Greek deity) 2. Psyche (Greek deity) 3. Classical mythology
ISBN 0-688-13163-8   LC 95-14895
"In this Greek myth, Cupid falls in love with Psyche and treats her royally but does not reveal himself. When Psyche tries to discover his identity, Cupid leaves her,

Craft, Marie—*Continued*

but she wins him back by accomplishing three difficult tasks. Recalling an earlier artistic era, the occasionally ornate romantic paintings—some of them quite dramatic—feature detailed landscapes and beautiful figures in flowing drapery." Horn Book Guide

Hamilton, Edith

Mythology; illustrated by Steele Savage. Little, Brown 1942 497p il $27.95; pa $13.95 (5 and up) **292**

1. Classical mythology 2. Norse mythology
ISBN 0-316-34114-2; 0-316-34151-7 (pa)

Contents: The gods, kthe creation and the earliest heroes; Stories of love and adventure; Great heroes before the Trojan War; Heroes of the Trojan War; Great families of mythology; Less important myths; Mythology of the Norsemen; Genealogical tables

A retelling of Greek, Roman and Norse myths

The **Lincoln** Library of Greek & Roman mythology; editors Timothy and Susan Gall; contributing editor Rick M. Newton. The Lincoln Library Press 2006 5v il map set $224 (5 and up) **292**

1. Classical mythology—Encyclopedias
ISBN 0-912168-21-8

These "volumes cover everything that the classical mythology homework assignment is likely to require and more. . . . Nearly 500 alphabetically arranged articles range from a short paragraph to several pages in length." Booklist

Low, Alice

The Macmillan book of Greek gods and heroes; illustrated by Arvis Stewart. Macmillan 1985 184p il $18 (3-6) **292**

1. Classical mythology
ISBN 0-02-761390-9   LC 85-7170

Retellings of ancient Greek myths including the legends of Odysseus, Pandora, Pygmalion, Heracles, and Perseus

"The tales are clearly told, without embroidery. A useful index not only refers the reader to a page or pages, but briefly identifies the character or subject as well. Watercolors in glowing earth tones with touches of blue and decorative pen-and-ink drawings enhance the book's appeal." Booklist

Mayer, Marianna

Pegasus; as told by Marianna Mayer; illustrated by K.Y. Craft. Morrow Junior Bks. 1998 unp il lib bdg $15.93 (4-6) **292**

1. Pegasus (Greek mythology) 2. Classical mythology
ISBN 0-688-13383-5   LC 96-32442

Retells how Bellerophon, son of the king of Corinth, secures the help of the winged horse Pegasus in order to fight the monstrous Chimera

"Dark, painterly illustrations set in gold frames heighten the mysticism in this lyrical interpretation of the Greek myth." Horn Book Guide

McCaughrean, Geraldine

Greek gods and goddesses; retold by Geraldine McCaughrean; illustrated by Emma Chichester Clark. Margaret K. McElderry Bks. 1998 108p il $20 (4-6) **292**

1. Classical mythology
ISBN 0-689-82084-4

"McCaughrean uses the literary device of a story within a story to relate tales of Greek gods and goddesses. . . . The lively narrative offers accurate accounts of Artemis, Apollo, Demeter, Hephaestus, Aphrodite, and others. Chichester Clark has incorporated stylistic Greek art into her bright watercolor interpretations of the Olympians as they frolic on nearly every page." SLJ

Greek myths; retold by Geraldine McCaughrean; illustrated by Emma Chichester Clark. Margaret K. McElderry Bks. 1993 c1992 96p il $19.95 (4-6) **292**

1. Classical mythology
ISBN 0-689-50583-3   LC 92-61748

First published 1992 in the United Kingdom

Retells sixteen tales from Greek mythology, including Pandora's box, King Midas, The twelve labors of Heracles, and Orpheus and Eurydice

"McCaughrean's style is fresh and lively, dynamic and direct. She is faithful in essentials, but not afraid to edit. . . . The text is matched by clear, rainbow-bright illustrations. Clark's watercolors are lighthearted and engaging, and a picture or decoration enlivens every page." SLJ

Hercules; retold by Geraldine McCaughrean. Cricket Books 2005 142p il (Heroes) $15.95 (5 and up) **292**

1. Hercules (Legendary character) 2. Classical mythology
ISBN 0-8126-2737-7   LC 2005004524

First published 2003 by Oxford University Press

This is a retelling of the twelve labors of Hercules including his battles with the Cretan Bull, the many-headed Hydra, the Nemean Lion, and the three-headed guardian of hell, Cerberus.

"This volume does a creditable job of making Hercules a dimensional character whose struggles against fate and the vindictiveness of the gods arouse readers' sympathy. . . . McCaughrean enlivens the familiar story with arresting imagery." SLJ

Odysseus; retold by Geraldine McCaughrean. 1st American ed. Cricket Books 2004 148p il (Heroes) (5 and up) **292**

1. Odysseus (Greek mythology) 2. Classical mythology
ISBN 0-8126-2721-0   LC 2004-10734

This is a retelling of the "adventures of Odysseus, including his encounters with the evil Cyclops, the monsters Scylla and Charybdis, the beautiful sorceress Circe, and . . . Poseidon." Publisher's note

"With mounting suspense, wild action, and simple, rhythmic prose, this dramatic retelling of Homer's classic makes a gripping read-aloud as well as an exciting introduction to the story." Booklist

McCaughrean, Geraldine—*Continued*
Perseus; retold by Geraldine McCaughrean. Cricket Books 2005 118p (Heroes) $15.95 (5 and up)   **292**
1. Perseus (Greek mythology) 2. Classical mythology
ISBN 0-8126-2735-0
This follows the story of "Perseus as he lives the fate the oracles have declared, an impossible quest to kill the hideous, snake-haired Medusa to save his mother from marriage to an evil king." Publisher's note
This "makes a thrilling read-aloud. . . . McCaughrean blends the colloquial and contemporary into the heroic quest." Booklist

Osborne, Mary Pope
Favorite Greek myths; retold by Mary Pope Osborne; illustrated by Troy Howell. Scholastic 1989 81p il lib bdg $18.95 (3-6)   **292**
1. Classical mythology
ISBN 0-590-41338-4   LC 87-32332
Retells twelve tales from Greek mythology, including the stories of King Midas, Echo and Narcissus, the Golden Apples, and Cupid and Psyche
"Osborne's retellings are both lively and descriptive, while Howell's full-color, often iridescent illustrations set the scene and mood at the start of each tale." Publ Wkly
Includes glossary and bibliographical references

293   Germanic religion and religious mythology

Fisher, Leonard Everett
Gods and goddesses of the ancient Norse. Holiday House 2001 unp il $16.95 (3-6)
                                  293
1. Norse mythology
ISBN 0-8234-1569-4   LC 00-32040
In this guide each "double-page spread is devoted to one or two of the major gods or goddesses, accompanied by a succinct description that includes significant characteristics and responsibilities. A pronunciation guide and family tree are appended." Horn Book Guide
Includes bibliographical references

Osborne, Mary Pope
Favorite Norse myths; retold by Mary Pope Osborne; illustrated by Troy Howell. Scholastic 1996 87p il pa $7.99 hardcover o.p. (4 and up)
                                  293
1. Norse mythology
ISBN 0-590-48047-2 (pa)   LC 94-34222
A collection of rarely retold tales from the "Elder Edda" and the "Younger Edda," two six-hundred-year-old Norse manuscripts
The tales are "retold with clarity and grace. The unusual artwork combines acrylic paintings with line drawings reminiscent of Norse carvings in their simplicity and vigor. . . . The informative appendixes include glossaries of the gods, goddesses, giants, giantesses, dwarves, worlds, events, places, and things as well as discussions of symbols and runes." Booklist
Includes bibliographical references

Philip, Neil
Odin's family; myths of the Vikings; retold by Neil Philip; illustrated by Maryclare Foa. Orchard Bks. 1996 124p il $19.95 (4-6)   **293**
1. Norse mythology
ISBN 0-531-09531-2   LC 96-1965
"Philip tells the stories of the origin of the gods and frost giants, how Odin got his wisdom, the death of Baldur, the coming of Ragnarok, and eleven other Norse myths. What distinguishes Philip's anthology is its design: large print, a generous amount of white space, and full-page color art make this an eminently accessible, easily promoted collection. Foa's oil paintings (with a preponderance of red, gold and blue) have a primitive vigor." Bull Cent Child Books
Includes bibliographical references

294.3   Buddhism

Chödzin, Sherab
The wisdom of the crows and other Buddhist tales; retold by Sherab Chödzin & Alexandra Kohn; illustrated by Marie Cameron. Tricycle Press 1998 c1997 80p il pa $16.95 (4 and up)
                                  294.3
1. Buddhism
ISBN 1-883672-68-6   LC 97-30441
First published 1997 in the United Kingdom with title: The Barefoot book of Buddhist tales
A collection of thirteen retold Buddhist tales from all over Asia, illustrating various aspects of Buddhist thought
"Folktale lovers will find much to like here. Marie Cameron's clear, fresh watercolors, incorporating Asian artistic motifs and bordered with waves and origami, are handsomely rendered." Booklist
Includes bibliographical references

Demi
Buddha. Holt & Co. 1996 unp il $21.95 (4-6)
                                  294.3
1. Gautama Buddha
ISBN 0-8050-4203-2   LC 95-16906
The author "tells the story of Siddhartha's birth and the prophecies surrounding it, touches upon his childhood, and then follows his path to enlightenment." Booklist
Demi "uses clear, uncomplicated storytelling to present complex philosophical concepts. . . . The gilded illustrations (based, according to the jacket, on 'Indian, Chinese, Japanese, Burmese, and Indonesian paintings, sculptures, and sutra illustrations') are delicate, yet the colors and composition are bold, with central figures and action cascading beyond the careful borders." Bull Cent Child Books

Buddha stories. Holt & Co. 1997 unp il $21.95 (3-6)   **294.3**
1. Jataka stories
ISBN 0-8050-4886-3   LC 96-31253
This "is a picture-book collection of eleven Jataka tales retold in a formal yet straightforward style. . . . An

Demi—*Continued*

author's note gives the source of the tales as well as the historical basis for the design concept behind the elegantly sophisticated artwork. Both text and illustrations are done in gold ink on deep indigo paper, resulting in a striking visual impact." Bull Cent Child Books

Ganeri, Anita

Buddhism; [by] Anita Ganeri. World Almanac Library 2006 48p il map (Religions of the world) lib bdg $30.60 (5 and up)   **294.3**

1. Buddhism

ISBN 0-8368-5865-4   LC 2005041708

The author "presents a survey of Buddhist history, beliefs, sacred texts, festivals, and lifecycle events. . . . There is discussion of the art and folk literature associated with the religious tradition. Colorful photographs, illustrations, and art reproductions appear throughout." SLJ

Includes bibliographical references

The Tipitaka and Buddhism. Smart Apple Media 2003 30p il (Sacred texts) $27.10 (5 and up)   **294.3**

1. Buddhism

ISBN 1-58340-246-2   LC 2003-42354

A discussion of Buddhism and some of its sacred texts

"Attractive illustrations, including photographs and reproductions of religious art, make for a nice design, and students will find a wealth of information for reports." Booklist

Gedney, Mona

The life and times of Buddha. Mitchell Lane Pubs. 2005 48p il map (Biography from ancient civilizations) lib bdg $19.95 (5 and up)   **294.3**

1. Gautama Buddha

ISBN 1-58415-342-3

A biography of Siddhartha Gautama, who became known as Buddha.

This "offers a fluid and lively retelling of the basic story, including insight into the broader context of the times, an introduction to the teachings of [Buddha], and a recounting of the facts that most believers would assent to." SLJ

Includes bibliographical references

George, Charles

What makes me a Buddhist? by Charles George. KidHaven Press 2004 48p il (What makes me a--?) $23.70 (3-5)   **294.3**

1. Buddhism

ISBN 0-7377-2269-X   LC 2003-24344

Contents: A religion or a philosophy?; How did my religion begin?; What do I believe?; How do I practice my faith?; What holidays do I celebrate?; My religion today and tomorrow

This describes the beliefs, origins, practices, holidays and future of Buddhism.

"An attractive, colorful design is the background for a map and numerous color photographs and diagrams.

But best of all is the straightforward organization and the clarity of the text." Booklist

Includes bibliographical references

Lee, Jeanne M.

I once was a monkey; stories Buddha told. Farrar, Straus & Giroux 1999 unp il $16 (4 and up)   **294.3**

1. Jataka stories

ISBN 0-374-33548-6   LC 98-17651

A retelling of six Jatakas, or birth stories, which illustrate some of the central tenets of Buddha's teachings, such as compassion, honesty, and thinking clearly before acting

"The appealing character of the monkey will pull children into the tales, which convey lessons in a direct yet gentle way that is never preachy. The accompanying linocut illustrations are lovely." Booklist

Rockwell, Anne F.

The Prince who ran away; the story of Guatama Buddha; by Anne Rockwell; illustrated by Fahimeh Amiri. Knopf 2001 unp il $16.95 (3-6)   **294.3**

1. Gautama Buddha

ISBN 0-679-89188-9   LC 00-67140

"Combining aspects of folklore and biography, Rockwell creates a life of the Buddha." SLJ

The "text is clear, nicely paced, and vividly written. . . . Amiri's vibrant, tropically colored paintings . . . offer tangible, action-filled images that will help kids imagine the abstract (evil appears as candy-colored, mustachioed demons)." Booklist

Wilkinson, Philip

Buddhism; written by Philip Wilkinson; photographed by Steve Teague. DK Pub 2003 64p il (DK eyewitness guides) $15.99; lib bdg $19.99 (4 and up)   **294.3**

1. Buddhism

ISBN 0-7894-9833-2; 0-7894-9834-0 (lib bdg)

      LC 2003-51656

"This introduction to Buddhism presents a series of topics on double-page spreads, each with a paragraph of text and many excellent color photographs, accompanied by lengthy captions in small type. . . . The book provides a visually appealing introduction to Buddhism and is a good source of photos of Buddhist sites, art, and artifacts." Booklist

294.5   Hinduism

Ganeri, Anita

Hindu festivals throughout the year; [by] Anita Ganeri. Smart Apple Media 2003 30p il (Year of festivals) $24.56 (3-6)   **294.5**

1. Hindu holidays 2. Hinduism

ISBN 1-58340-372-8   LC 2003-40302

Contents: Pongal; Vasanta Panchami; Mahashivaratri; Holi; Celebrating Holi; Ramanavami; Ratha Yatra;

Ganeri, Anita—*Continued*
Raksha Bandhan; Janmashtami; Ganesha Chaturthi; Festivals of the Goddess; Divali; Celebrating Divali; Festival Calendar

Introduces the main religious festivals of Hinduism, telling the story behind each festival, describing how it is celebrated around the world, and providing instructions for related activities

"Colorful photographs and clear writing fill [this book]. . . . Each page contains a good balance of text, full-color photos, and illustrations." SLJ

Includes bibliographical references

The Ramayana and Hinduism. Smart Apple Media 2003 30p il (Sacred texts) $27.10 (5 and up)   **294.5**
 1. Hinduism
 ISBN 1-58340-242-X   LC 2003-42352
 Contents: Origins; Texts and teaching; In daily life
Explains the history and practices of the religion of Hinduism, especially as revealed through its sacred book, the Ramayana

George, Charles
What makes me a Hindu? by Charles George. KidHaven Press 2004 48p il map (What makes me a--?) $23.70 (3-5)   **294.5**
 1. Hinduism
 ISBN 0-7377-2267-3   LC 2003-24346
 This describes Hindu origins, beliefs, practices, and holidays

"Presenting information about religion objectively for younger audiences poses a difficult challenge, but [this title does] an excellent job of it." Booklist

Includes bibliographical references

Jani, Mahendra
What you will see inside a Hindu temple; [by] Mahendra Jani and Vandana Jani; with photographs by Neirah Bhargava and Vijay Dave. Skylight Paths 2005 32p il (What you will see inside–) $17.99 (3-6)   **294.5**
 1. Hinduism
 ISBN 1-59473-116-0
"This introduces the beliefs and practices of the Hindu religion. The book opens with a traditional Sanskrit word of greeting . . . setting the respectful, inviting tone of the text, which leads readers into a temple. The book explains what can be seen there and discusses Hindu beliefs, worship practices, scriptures, celebrations, blessing ceremonies, and family shrines in homes. A typical double-page spread includes one large color photograph and a few small ones illustrating several paragraphs of clear, concise text." Booklist

Novesky, Amy
The elephant prince; the story of Ganesh; illustrated by Belgin K. Wedman. Mandala 2004 il $16.95 (2-4)   **294.5**
 1. Hindu mythology
 ISBN 1-886069-16-6
 The author retells the story "of how the Hindu god Ganesh came to have the head of an elephant. . . .

Parvati tells the story to the Elephant Prince as he sits on her lap, and the constancy of her love and affection is captured beautifully in both text and illustrations. Wedman's watercolor, gouache, and gold-leaf illustrations have a shimmering loveliness and are replete with charming details." SLJ

Rasamandala Das
Hinduism. World Almanac Library 2006 48p il map (Religions of the world) $30.60 (5 and up)   **294.5**
 1. Hinduism
 ISBN 0-8368-5867-0
Hinduism is "explored in an accessible introductory manner, including information on [its] history, teachings, religious practices, culture and lifestyle, and the [faith's role] in today's global society. Vibrant full-color photographs are appropriately placed within the [text]. Ideal for . . . school reports or for general interest." SLJ

Includes bibliographical references

296 Judaism

Fisher, Leonard Everett
To bigotry, no sanction; the story of the oldest synagogue in America. Holiday House 1998 64p il $16.95 (4 and up)   **296**
 1. Touro Synagogue (Newport, R.I.) 2. Jews—United States
 ISBN 0-8234-1401-9   LC 98-12834
The author discusses "the history of the Jews in America in general and the building of the Touro Synagogue, the oldest in the U.S. in particular. Fisher does his usual excellent job of bringing history to life." Booklist

Includes bibliographical references

Keene, Michael
Judaism; [by] Michael Keene. World Almanac Library 2006 48p il map (Religions of the world) lib bdg $30 (5 and up)   **296**
 1. Judaism
 ISBN 0-836-85869-7   LC 2005041734
This "volume presents fundamental beliefs and faith foundations, current status and practices of [Judaism] around the globe, and a time line of historically significant events. . . . The [book is] enumerated with full-color photographs on every page, charts, maps, and tables. . . . [This title] will enhance the education of diverse populations." SLJ

Includes bibliographical references

296.1 Judaism--Sources

Chaikin, Miriam
Angel secrets; stories based on Jewish legend; illustrated by Leonid Gore. 1st ed. Henry Holt 2006 68p il $18.95 (4 and up)   **296.1**
 1. Angels 2. Jewish legends
 ISBN 0-8050-7150-4   LC 2004-54062

Chaikin, Miriam—*Continued*

Contents: Angels of forgetfulness; Alphabet angels; Stay stone, stay; Sign-minders; A trial in heaven; Palace of love

"This offering retells the legends of how angels work alongside God in both heaven and on Earth." SLJ

"Chaikin is both solemn and playful about holy matters, and her light touch humanizes the holy and makes God approachable. Gore's poetic illustrations in muted earth tones are similarly corporeal and etheral." Horn Book Guide

Includes bibliographical references

Angels sweep the desert floor; Bible legends about Moses in the wilderness; illustrated by Alexander Koshkin. Clarion Bks. 2002 102p il $19 (4 and up)   **296.1**

1. Moses (Biblical figure) 2. Angels—Fiction 3. Jewish legends 4. Bible stories

ISBN 0-395-97825-4   LC 2001-47501

A collection of eighteen stories based on the Bible which tell how angels respond to God's commands to ease the way for Moses and the Israelites as they cross the wilderness after being freed from slavery in Egypt

"The full-page watercolor, tempera, and gouache illustrations have a fanciful formality that complements the narrative. Capable of exciting the creative, as well as the spiritual imagination, these wonderful stories make great read-alouds." SLJ

Includes bibliographical references

Jaffe, Nina

While standing on one foot; puzzle stories and wisdom tales from the Jewish tradition; [by] Nina Jaffe and Steve Zeitlin; pictures by John Segal. Holt & Co. 1993 120p il pa $8.95 hardcover o.p. (4 and up)   **296.1**

1. Jewish legends

ISBN 0-8050-5073-6 (pa)   LC 93-13750

"Each of seventeen tales is divided into two sections: the first poses a dilemma for the main character; the second describes the clever solution. . . . The entire collection is of general interest because of the solve-it-yourself aspect . . . and the suspense or humor of the difficulties. . . . Wash drawings in black and white are whimsically stylized with figures that have a humorous, paper-doll quality." Bull Cent Child Books

Includes glossary and bibliographical references

Lester, Julius

When the beginning began; stories about God, the creatures, and us; illustrations by Emily Lisker. Silver Whistle Bks. 1999 100p il $17 (4 and up)   **296.1**

1. Creation 2. Bible stories 3. Jewish legends

ISBN 0-15-201238-9   LC 97-37352

A collection of traditional and original Jewish tales interpreting the Biblical story of the creation of the world

"Lester fuses two traditions here—the 'loving irreverence' of African-American storytelling and the imaginative inquiry of midrashim. . . . Lisker's paintings capture the stories' primal essence (and a bit of their playfulness) in bold, archetypal forms. A reverent, wise, witty, and wonderfully entertaining book." Horn Book Guide

Includes bibliographical references

296.4   Judaism--Traditions, rites, public services

Berger, Gilda

Celebrate! stories of the Jewish holidays; paintings by Peter Catalanotto. Scholastic 1998 114p il pa $8.99 hardcover o.p. (4 and up)
296.4

1. Jewish holidays

ISBN 0-439-43052-6 (pa)   LC 97-40150

"Berger examines the history of the major holidays of the Jewish faith and the Bible story that lies behind the celebration of each, as well as the customs that make these special days. The lively writing coupled with Catalanotto's dramatic watercolors ensure that this volume will become a treasured family favorite." Publ Wkly

Chaikin, Miriam

Menorahs, mezuzas, and other Jewish symbols; illustrated by Erika Weihs. Clarion Bks. 1990 102p il $17 (5 and up)   **296.4**

1. Jewish art and symbolism 2. Judaism—Customs and practices

ISBN 0-89919-856-2   LC 89-77719

Explains the history and significance of many Jewish symbols, such as the Shield of David, the menorah, and the mezuza, and discusses holiday symbols and rituals

"Embellished with bibliographical references as well as Weihs' simple yet elegant and wonderfully dramatic scratchboard illustrations, this smoothly woven patchwork of history and culture is a fine introduction that will attract browsers and be useful for children investigating the subject of symbolism in school." Booklist

Cooper, Ilene

Jewish holidays all year round; a family treasury; written by Ilene Cooper; illustrations by Elivia Savadier; captions by Josh Feinberg; in association with the Jewish Museum, New York. Abrams 2002 80p il $19.95 (4 and up)
296.4

1. Jewish holidays

ISBN 0-8109-0550-7   LC 2001-56741

As the author "explores the history and significance of the holidays and festivals of the Jewish year, she . . . links these to traditions and rituals. . . . Instructions for holiday activities (crafts, recipes, etc.) are also included. . . . Savadier's vignettes, mostly of busy, happy people, underscore the liveliness of Jewish faith." Publ Wkly

Includes bibliographical references

Fishman, Cathy

On Hanukkah; by Cathy Goldberg Fishman; illustrated by Melanie W. Hall. Atheneum Bks. for Young Readers 1998 unp il $16 (k-3)
296.4

1. Hanukkah

ISBN 0-689-80643-4   LC 96-44696

"Fishman and Hall focus on a family's celebration of a Jewish holiday. The writing is simple and direct, yet

Fishman, Cathy—*Continued*
the coverage is ample. . . . The fanciful, mixed-media paintings feature strong texturing and glowing, gilt-edged colors." Booklist

On Passover; by Cathy Goldberg Fishman; illustrated by Melanie W. Hall. Atheneum Bks. for Young Readers 1997 unp il $16; pa $5.99 (k-3)

296.4

1. Passover
ISBN 0-689-80528-4; 0-689-83264-6 (pa)

LC 97-114611

"A young girl shares the preparations and the rituals that are part of the traditional Passover seder." SLJ

"This is illustrated in beautiful Chagall-like pictures that are rooted in both the practicalities of Passover preparation and the joyful spirit of this holiday of freedom. . . . The book is a lovely introduction to the holiday." Booklist

On Rosh Hashanah and Yom Kippur; by Cathy Goldberg Fishman; illustrated by Melanie W. Hall. Atheneum Bks. for Young Readers 1997 unp il $16; pa $5.99 (k-3) **296.4**
1. Rosh ha-Shanah 2. Yom Kippur
ISBN 0-689-80526-8; 0-689-83892-1 (pa)

LC 96-23258

"Fishman explores and explains the traditions associated with the Jewish High Holidays. She focuses mainly on Rosh Hashanah . . . and in a quiet, almost reverent way uses the voice of a little girl to make readers party to a family's celebrations. . . . Hall's beautiful, rosy, expressionistic pictures are a fine complement to Fishman's text. They capture the warm glow of a family celebrating together." Booklist

Goldin, Barbara Diamond
While the candles burn; eight stories for Hanukkah; illustrated by Elaine Greenstein. Viking 1996 60p il $16.99; pa $6.99 (4 and up)

296.4

1. Hanukkah
ISBN 0-670-85875-7; 0-14-037341-1 (pa)

LC 95-50310

"In her introduction Goldin discusses the celebratory customs of Hanukkah, noting similarities and differences around the world and pointing out the themes of her selected eight tales, including faith, religious freedom, charity, and miracles. The tales are folkloric, biblical, and original. . . . Greenstein's cheerful, boldly celebratory scratchboard and watercolor illustrations are generously interspersed throughout. . . . This is a solid addition to collections looking for something a little more unusual than typical holiday fare." Bull Cent Child Books
Includes bibliographical references

Had gadya; a Passover song; paintings by Seymour Chwast; afterword by Michael Strassfeld. Roaring Brook Press 2005 unp il $16.95 (k-3) **296.4**
1. Passover 2. Songs
ISBN 1-59643-033-8   LC 2003-17831
"A Deborah Brodie book"

This is an illustrated version of "a folk song often sung at the end of the Passover Seder. [It] tells a cumulative story that begins with a man's purchase of a goat. In the tradition of chain folk stories, the cat eats the goat, the dog chases the cat, the stick beats the dog, and so on. . . . The Angel of Death appears, but then God comes and destroys the Angel of Death." Bull Cent Child Books
"The bright, acrylic folk-art paintings express the rhythm of the chant. . . . The book, complete with musical notation and Hebrew and English words, is bound to add to the pleasure of the seder." Booklist

A **Hanukkah** treasury; edited by Eric A. Kimmel; illustrated by Emily Lisker. Holt & Co. 1998 99p il $19.95 **296.4**
1. Hanukkah
ISBN 0-8050-5293-3   LC 97-24428
Presents stories, songs, recipes, and activities related to the celebration of Hanukkah
"Emily Lisker's vibrant acrylic paintings accent the text in small and full-page illustrations. Her colors and fluid lines are dramatic and joyful." Booklist

Hildebrandt, Ziporah
This is our Seder; illustrated by Robin Roraback. Holiday House 1999 unp il $15.95 (k-3)

296.4

1. Passover
ISBN 0-8234-1436-1   LC 98-4194
A simple description of the food and activities at a Seder, the ritual meal of Passover, including an explanation of their historical and symbolic significance
"The compositions are calm but busy, with plenty of background action. . . . Despite the explanatory note at the end, however, terms like 'afikomen' and rites like opening the door (for Elijah) go undefined, so that this book is best enjoyed by families who already know the special significance of Passover." Publ Wkly

Hoffman, Lawrence A.
What you will see inside a synagogue; [by] Lawrence Hoffman and Ron Wolfson; with photographs by Bill Aron. SkyLight Paths 2004 31p il (What you will see inside--) $17.99 (3-6)

296.4

1. Judaism
ISBN 1-59473-012-1   LC 2004-11178
Contents: Welcome; Gathering for Shabbat; Preparing for prayer; The holiest place in the synagogue; How Jews pray; Reading the Torah; Enjoying Shabbat; Prayer and learning go together; Fixing the world; Bar and bat mitzvah; Celebrating holidays; The High Holy Days; Showing our thanks; How we remember; L'hitra'ot. come again
"The authors focus on the synagogues and services of three branches of North American Judaism—Conservative, Reconstruction, and Reform. . . . They introduce readers to Sabbath customs, prayer, the sanctuary and its contents, the Torah, important holidays and life cycle events, and key tenets of the faith." Booklist
"This book provides a warm and thorough welcome to the center of Jewish life. . . . Numerous clear color photos and pronunciation guides for Hebrew words are included. . . . An excellent overview." SLJ

Hoyt-Goldsmith, Diane

Celebrating Hanukkah; photographs by Lawrence Migdale. Holiday House 1996 31p il $16.95; pa $6.95 (3-5)   **296.4**

1. Hanukkah

ISBN 0-8234-1252-0; 0-8234-1411-6 (pa)

LC 96-5110

"Leora, the 11-year-old daughter of a San Francisco rabbi, explains the history of Hanukkah and describes how her family observes it." Publ Wkly

The photographs "are warm and inviting, with Migdale catching celebrations at home, at school, and in the synagogue. . . . The text is equally fine, well organized and rich in detail but also friendly." Booklist

Includes glossary

Celebrating Passover; photographs by Lawrence Migdale. Holiday House 2000 32p il lib bdg $16.95 (3-5)   **296.4**

1. Passover

ISBN 0-8234-1420-5   LC 99-49006

Uses one family's celebration of Passover to describe the religious significance, traditions, customs, and symbols of this Jewish holiday

"An attractive and useful choice for the holiday shelf; recipes, songs, and a glossary are a bonus." Booklist

Kimmel, Eric A.

Wonders and miracles; a Passover companion; illustrated with art spanning three thousand years; written and compiled by Eric A. Kimmel. Scholastic Press 2004 136p il $18.95 (4 and up)   **296.4**

1. Passover

ISBN 0-439-07175-5   LC 2002-4732

Presents the steps performed in a traditional Passover Seder, plus stories, songs, poetry, and pictures that celebrate the historical significance of this holiday to Jews all over the world.

"The marvelous selection of art—paintings, photographs, artifacts, and illustrations from historical Haggadahs—illuminates each step in the service. . . . Both the presentation of information and the overall design attest to the careful and loving attention given to every detail. This inviting, handsome, and informative compendium should find a place of honor in every library." SLJ

Includes bibliographical references

Musleah, Rahel

Why on this night? a Passover haggadah for family celebration; illustrated by Louise August. Simon & Schuster Bks. for Young Readers 2000 112p $24.95; pa $13.99   **296.4**

1. Passover

ISBN 0-689-81356-2; 0-689-83313-X (pa)

LC 97-2570

Includes the basic elements of a traditional seder as well as many creative facets intended to involve children in this Jewish liturgy through song, dance, drama, explanation, and action

"A useful addition to Jewish holiday collections." SLJ

Podwal, Mark H.

The menorah story. Greenwillow Bks. 1998 unp il $15; lib bdg $14.89 (k-3)   **296.4**

1. Hanukkah

ISBN 0-688-15758-0; 0-688-15759-9 (lib bdg)

LC 97-36300

Discusses the story of the Hanukkah menorah which commemorates the miraculous victory of the Maccabees over King Antiochus and his army

"In his distinctive paintings, Podwal incorporates traditional symbols within masterfully simplified compositions." Publ Wkly

Includes bibliographical references

A sweet year; a taste of the Jewish holidays; [by] Mark Podwal. Doubleday Bks. for Young Readers 2003 unp il $12.95; lib bdg $14.99 (k-3)   **296.4**

1. Jewish holidays 2. Food

ISBN 0-385-74637-7; 0-385-90869-5 (lib bdg)

LC 2002-155442

Pictures and easy-to-read text introduce Jewish holidays, focusing on the foods associated with each

This offers "beautifully crafted poetic text and symbolic paintings in gouache and acrylics." SLJ

Includes bibliographical references

Rosen, Michael J.

Our eight nights of Hanukkah; illustrated by DyAnne DiSalvo-Ryan. Holiday House 2000 unp il lib bdg $16.95 (k-3)   **296.4**

1. Hanukkah

ISBN 0-8234-1476-0   LC 99-11001

A child describes how one family celebrates Hanukkah, including polishing the silver menorah, lighting the candles, having a special family dinner, and sharing gifts

"DiSalvo-Ryan's watercolors match the text in their warmth and wealth of familial detail. It's the inclusive message and the sharing across cultures, however, that may strike the most responsive chord with children." Booklist

Schecter, Ellen

The family Haggadah; illustrated by Neil Waldman. Viking 1999 66p il music pa $13.99   **296.4**

1. Passover

ISBN 0-670-88341-7   LC 98-28597

"This book interweaves original writing with traditional Haggadah, prayer book, and biblical texts, as well as with midrash (rabbinic stories and commentaries)." Verso of title page

"Although really intended for parents to use with their children at a family Passover seder, this attractive book may also be useful to children wanting to plan their own model celebration." Booklist

Schwartz, Lynne Sharon

The four questions; text by Lynne Sharon Schwartz; paintings by Ori Sherman. Dial Bks. 1989 unp il pa $5.99 hardcover o.p. (k-3)   **296.4**

1. Passover

ISBN 0-14-055269-3 (pa)   LC 88-18881

Schwartz, Lynne Sharon—*Continued*

This book explores the meaning of Passover by explicating the symbolism of the seder and the four questions

"Framed by the rituals of a Seder, an excellent text gives brief background on the celebration of Passover. . . . The stunningly stylized illustrations facing each page of text are a sophisticated carnival of animals that reflect a kind of Chagallian surrealism grounded by strongly outlined shapes, deep colors, and dense compositions." Bull Cent Child Books

Simon, Norma

The story of Hanukkah; illustrated by Leonid Gore. HarperCollins Pubs. 1997 unp il $15.95; pa $5.95 (2-4) **296.4**

1. Hanukkah

ISBN 0-06-027419-0; 0-06-027420-4 (pa)

LC 96-5141

A newly illustrated edition of Hanukkah, first published 1966 by Crowell

Explains the history and traditions that are a part of the Jewish holiday of Hanukkah

"A straightforward . . . text is followed by instructions for playing dreidel, a recipe for potato pancakes, and a quick overview of the Jewish calendar. . . . [This] edition features textured softly colored illustrations that seem to glow like the candles of the holiday." Horn Book

The story of Passover; illustrated by Erica Weihs. HarperCollins Pubs. 1997 unp $15.95; pa $5.95 (2-4) **296.4**

1. Passover

ISBN 0-06-027062-4; 0-06-027063-2 (pa)

LC 95-41201

A newly illustrated edition of the title first published 1965 by Crowell

Describes the origins and traditions of Passover, in particular the special meal called the Seder

"Biblically accurate and factual, Simon's book brings the Passover celebration to life for both Jewish and Gentile children." SLJ

Woog, Adam

What makes me a Jew? Kidhaven Press 2004 48p il (What makes me a-- ?) $23.70 (3-5) **296.4**

1. Judaism

ISBN 0-7377-2266-5   LC 2003-20951

Contents: How Judaism began; What I believe; The ceremonies I observe; The holidays I celebrate; The food I eat; Judaism in the modern world

This describes Jewish origins, beliefs, practices, foods, and holidays

"Presenting information about religion objectively for younger audiences poses a difficult challenge, but [this title does] and excellent job of it." Booklist

Includes bibliographical references

297 Islam, Babism, Bahai Faith

Demi

Muhammad; written and illustrated by Demi. Margaret K. McElderry Bks. 2003 unp il $19.95 (4 and up) **297**

1. Muḥammad, d. 632 2. Islam

ISBN 0-689-85264-9   LC 2002-2985

"With dramatic scenes extending past the borders of the intricately patterned frames, the art will be a continual source of interest for young people. . . . [An] excellent retelling of the Prophet's life that combines beauty and scholarship." Booklist

Includes bibliographical references

297.3 Islamic worship

Douglass, Susan L.

Ramadan; illustrations by Jeni Reeves. Carolrhoda Books 2004 48p il (On my own holidays) lib bdg $23.93; pa $4.95 (1-3) **297.3**

1. Ramadan 2. Islam

ISBN 0-87614-932-8 (lib bdg); 1-57505-584-8 (pa)

LC 2002-6781

An introduction to Islamic observances during the month of Ramadan and the subsequent festival of Eid-al-Fitr

"Reeves's abundant, framed illustrations in pastel colors provide detailed windows on the observance. . . . An easy-to-read, well-organized introduction." SLJ

Ganeri, Anita

Muslim festivals throughout the year; [by] Anita Ganeri. Smart Apple Media 2003 30p il (Year of festivals) $24.56 (3-6) **297.3**

1. Islam

ISBN 1-58340-371-X   LC 2003-40304

Contents: Friday prayers; Al-hijrah; Ashura; Milad-al-Nabi; Laylat-ul-usra; Ramadan; Laylat-ul-qadr; Id-ul-fitr; Id-ul-adha; the Hajj; Festival calendar

Introduces the main religious festivals of Islam, telling the story behind each festival, describing how it is celebrated around the world, and providing instructions for related activities.

"Colorful photographs and clear writing fill [this book]. . . . Each page contains a good balance of text, full-color photos, and illustrations." SLJ

Includes glossary and bibliographical references

Ghazi, Suhaib Hamid

Ramadan; illustrated by Omar Rayyan. Holiday House 1996 unp il $16.95; pa $6.95 (k-3) **297.3**

1. Ramadan 2. Islam

ISBN 0-8234-1254-7; 0-8234-1275-X (pa)

LC 96-5154

"The month of Ramadan, an Islamic time of fasting, feasting, sharing, and prayer, is seen through the eyes of young Hakeem. . . . Ghazi gives just the right amount

Ghazi, Suhaib Hamid—*Continued*
of background information, along with interesting details.
. . . Rayyan incorporates into his paintings Islamic symbols and architectural motifs, as well as a lively, ethnically diverse group of people." Booklist
Includes glossary

Hoyt-Goldsmith, Diane
Celebrating Ramadan; Ramadan al-mu'azzam; photographs by Lawrence Migdale. Holiday House 2001 32p il map $16.95 (3-5)   **297.3**
1. Ramadan 2. Islam
ISBN 0-8234-1581-3   LC 2001-16643
"This picture book for older readers follows devout muslim Ibraheem, a fourth-grader living in New Jersey, through the holy month of Ramadan. . . . This is a sensitive introduction to Ramadan; the quality of the photographs and the eloquent text make the book the one of the best introductions in recent memory." Booklist

Khan, Aisha Karen
What you will see inside a mosque; photographs by Aaron Pepis. Skylight Paths Pub 2003 31p il (What you will see inside--) $16.95 (3-6)
297.3
1. Islam 2. Mosques
ISBN 1-893361-60-8   LC 2002-153436
Describes what happens inside a mosque and introduces the Muslim faith.
This is an "excellent introduction. . . . Full-page photographs are supplemented by smaller photos with informative captions." SLJ

Marchant, Kerena
Id-ul-Fitr. Millbrook Press 1998 32p il (Festivals) lib bdg $21.90 (3-5)   **297.3**
1. Islam
ISBN 0-7613-0963-2   LC 97-46035
Looks at some of the ways Muslims around the world celebrate the joyous festival of Id-ul-Fitre
Includes bibliographical references

Petrini, Catherine M.
What makes me a Muslim? [by] Catherine M. Petrini. KidHaven Press 2005 48p il map (What makes me a-- ?) $23.70 (3-5)   **297.3**
1. Islam
ISBN 0-7377-2265-7   LC 2004014526
"This overview explains what Islam is, where it came from, and how it has spread over time. Petrini provides a look at the background, beliefs, practices, holidays, and challenges of the religion today. . . . The full-color photographs and religious paintings throughout the book are as informative as they are appealing." SLJ
Includes bibliographical references

299 Religions not provided for elsewhere

Fisher, Leonard Everett
The gods and goddesses of ancient China. Holiday House 2003 unp il $16.95 (3-6)
299
1. Gods and goddesses 2. China—Religion
ISBN 0-8234-1694-1   LC 2002-68802
"Beginning with an introduction that mentions Qin Shi Huangdi, China's First Supreme Emperor, Fisher offers very brief historical and cultural background to China's deities. . . . Profiles of 17 gods and goddesses follow, each one presented on a double-page spread that includes a roughly brushed portrait opposite a few paragraphs summarizing the figure's corresponding legend. . . . Fisher combines concise, accessible language, colorful art, and exciting stories about figures that aren't often covered in books for youth." Booklist
Includes bibliographical references

The gods and goddesses of ancient Egypt. Holiday House 1997 unp il $16.95; pa $6.95 (3-6)
299
1. Egyptian mythology
ISBN 0-8234-1286-5; 0-8234-1508-2 (pa)
LC 96-42068
Relates the history of the gods and goddesses worshipped by the ancient Egyptians and describes how they were depicted
"Simple profiles of Ra, Osiris, Isis, Nut, and others are accompanied by vivid paintings with bold outlines that recall hieroglyphic symbols. . . . A family tree and pronunciation guide help budding Egyptologists keep the figures straight." SLJ
Includes bibliographical references

Gods and goddesses of the ancient Maya. Holiday House 1999 unp il $16.95 (3-6)
299
1. Mayas—Religion 2. Native Americans—Religion
ISBN 0-8234-1427-2   LC 99-19900
Page numbering in Mayan numbers
Gives the history of the principal gods and goddesses of the ancient Mayans, including Hunab Ku, Itzamna, Ixtab, and Ah Puch
"Facing the pages of text are full-page paintings inspired by Mayan glyphs and stelae depicting profiled figures with sloped foreheads holding or wearing representative objects or clothing. Bold, vibrant tones highlight the features of these heavily outlined figures and form backdrops for the pages. . . . A visual treat from cover to cover." SLJ
Includes bibliographical references

Hofmeyr, Dianne
The star-bearer; a creation myth from ancient Egypt; [pictures by] Jude Daly. Farrar, Straus & Giroux 2001 unp il $16 (3-5)   **299**
1. Egyptian mythology 2. Creation
ISBN 0-374-37181-4   LC 00-37586

Hofmeyr, Dianne—*Continued*

"Lonely, the golden godchild Atum creates the god of air and goddess of dew and rain. Their less-tempestuous children, earth and sky, cling to each other and must be separated to give their creator room to further fashion a world." Horn Book Guide

"This picture book for older readers captures the magic and mystery of an early Egyptian creation myth in both its evocative language and innovative art." Booklist

Morley, Jacqueline

Egyptian myths; retold by Jacqueline Morley; illustrated by Giovanni Caselli. Bedrick Bks. 2000 64p il $22.50 (4 and up)   **299**

1. Egyptian mythology
ISBN 0-87226-589-7   LC 99-44979

First published 1999 in the United Kingdom

"Stories based on ancient temple inscriptions, hieroglyphic texts, and tomb paintings. . . . The creation tale of Ra, explanations of the moon's phases and of how mummies came to be, and the story of the first pyramid are just some of the stories included. . . . The fresh, accessible storytelling style makes this a fine choice." SLJ

299.7 Religions of North American native origin

Swamp, Jake

Giving thanks; a Native American good morning message; by Chief Jake Swamp; illustrated by Erwin Printup, Jr. Lee & Low Bks. 1995 unp il $16.95; pa $6.95 (k-3)   **299.7**

1. Mohawk Indians 2. Native Americans
ISBN 1-880000-15-6; 1-880000-54-7 (pa)
LC 94-5955

"Drawing on Six Nation (Iroquois) ceremonial tradition, the text speaks concise thanks to Mother Earth, to water, grass, fruits, animals, to the wind and rain, sun, moon and stars, to the Spirit Protectors of our past and present . . . and to the Great Spirit, giver of all. . . . The entire text is reproduced in Mohawk on the last page." SLJ

"Its simple, timeless language bears witness to the Native American reverence for the natural world and sense of unity with all living things. . . . The gifts of the earth . . . are richly depicted in paintings of wildlife and bountiful harvests." Publ Wkly

300   SOCIAL SCIENCES

301   Sociology and anthropology

Batten, Mary

Anthropologist: scientist of the people; with photographs by A. Magdalena Hurtado and Kim Hill. Houghton Mifflin 2001 64p il map (Scientists in the field) $16 (4 and up)   **301**

1. Hurtado, A. Magdalena 2. Hill, Kim 3. Anthropology 4. Guayaki Indians
ISBN 0-618-08368-5

This book "introduces readers to Magdalena [Hurtado] and Kim Hill, a husband-and-wife team who study the Aché of Paraguay. . . . Batten's graceful text covers basic science concepts (what an anthropologist really does; what evolutionary biology is) in accessible, clear language and examples just right for kids, offering fascinating hypotheses along the way." Booklist

302   Social interaction

Erlbach, Arlene

The kids' volunteering book. Lerner Publs. 1998 64p il lib bdg $22.60; pa $9.95 (4-6)   **302**

1. Volunteer work
ISBN 0-8225-2415-5 (lib bdg); 0-8225-9820-5 (pa)
LC 97-23356

Presents some opportunities for young people to perform volunteer service, and briefly profiles some children who are volunteers

"The profiles are interesting and inspiring, and substantial information is provided on the practical details of . . . a volunteer enterprise." Horn Book Guide

Includes glossary and bibliographical references

302.23   Media (Means of communication)

Ali, Dominic

Media madness; an insider's guide to media; written by Dominic Ali; illustrated by Michael Cho. Kids Can Press 2005 64p il $14.95; pa $8.95 (4 and up)   **302.23**

1. Mass media
ISBN 1-55337-174-7; 1-55337-175-5 (pa)

Host Max McLoon gives pointers on how to analyze media, and takes readers behind the scenes to reveal media workplaces in action. The book also includes activities for readers to further explore concepts or try their own media-making.

"The hip illustrations and wry sidebars prevent the book from coming off as goofy or childish, while the humorous treatment takes a bit of the edge off of otherwise 'heavy' issues like stereotypes, sexism, and violence. Light and loony, but enlightening, too." SLJ

303.6 Conflict

Gilley, Jeremy
Peace one day; illustrated by Karen Blessen.
Putnam 2005 48p il $16.99 **303.6**
1. Peace
ISBN 0-399-24330-5 LC 2004-20475
The author "tells how he persuaded world leaders to
establish World Peace Day. . . . His personal account of
filming the consequences of war in several countries . . .
draws attention to the issue, as do his accounts of meeting with world leaders. . . . Most powerful are the double-page collage illustrations . . . which blend some of
Gilley's film images of kids caught up in war and portraits of world peace leaders with colored pencil drawings, posters, and even news headlines. [This offers] passionate prose and stirring images." Booklist

Polland, Barbara K.
We can work it out; conflict resolution for
children; photographs by Craig DeRoy. Tricycle
Press 2000 64p il $13.95; pa $9.95 (k-3)
303.6
1. Interpersonal relations
ISBN 1-58246-031-0; 1-58246-029-9 (pa)
LC 00-23852
Text and photographs designed to create opportunities
for children to talk about their experiences of conflict
and the varieties of ways to resolve them
"DeRoy's candid photos of kids caught in the act,
both positive and negative, should be powerful incentives
for thought and discussion." Booklist

Stewart, Gail
Terrorism. KidHaven Press 2002 48p il map
(Understanding issues) lib bdg $23.70 (4 and up)
303.6
1. Terrorism 2. September 11 terrorist attacks, 2001
ISBN 0-7377-1287-2 LC 2001-6215
Uses the terrorist attacks of September 11, 2001 to explore the historical, political, and religious origins of political violence, its effects on individuals, and what governments can do to stop it
"Clear, colorful photographs appear on nearly every
page and illustrate the text effectively. . . . A succinct,
balanced presentation that can serve as a good starting
point for both research and discussion." Booklist

Woolf, Alex
Why are people terrorists? Raintree 2005 48p il
(Exploring tough issues) lib bdg $31.43 (4 and up)
303.6
1. Terrorism
ISBN 0-7398-6686-9 LC 2003-11571
Contents: What is terrorism?; Why do people become
terrorists?; What methods do terrorists use?; The support-
ers of terrorism; What can be done about terrorism?;
What is the war on terrorism?
Explores issues related to terrorism, such as who be-
comes a terrorist and why, and options such as the "War
Against Terrorism" for fighting against these acts of vio-

lence agains innocent people.
"Up-to-date information for young people who are
concerned about security and want to learn more about
important political issues." SLJ

304.6 Population

Smith, David J.
If the world were a village; a book about the
world's people; written by David J. Smith;
illustrated by Shelagh Armstrong. Kids Can Press
2002 32p il $15.95 (3-5) **304.6**
1. Population 2. Human geography
ISBN 1-55074-779-7
The author compresses the earth's population of over
six billion "down to a more understandable figure, 100
persons, and in 9 spreads offers data on such topics as
nationalities, languages, ages, religions, and education as
represented in a condensed global village." SLJ
"Though understated, the artwork contains accurate
details. . . . Thought-provoking and highly effective, this
world-in-miniature will open eyes to a wider view of our
planet and its human inhabitants." Horn Book
Includes bibliographical references

305.23 Young people

Freedman, Russell
Children of the Great Depression. Clarion Books
2005 118p il lib bdg $20 **305.23**
1. Children—United States 2. Great Depression, 1929-
1939 3. United States—Social conditions
ISBN 0-618-44630-3 LC 2005-06506
"Eight chapters cover the causes of the Great Depression, schooling, work life, migrant work, the lives of
children who rode the rails, entertainment, and the economic resurgence of the early '40s." SLJ
"This stirring photo-essay combines . . . unforgettable
personal details with a clear historical overview of the
period and black-and-white photos by Dorothea Lange,
Walker Evans, and many others." Booklist

Jukes, Mavis
It's a girl thing; how to stay healthy, safe, and
in charge; illustrations by Debbie Tilley. Knopf
1996 135p il lib bdg $16.99; pa $5.99 (5 and up)
305.23
1. Adolescence 2. Girls 3. Sex education
ISBN 0-679-94325-0 (lib bdg); 0-679-88771-7 (pa)
LC 93-40296
"Jukes discusses a wide variety of subjects from buying a bra to sexual harassment and abuse. In a warm,
conversational style, she covers body changes in both
boys and girls, menstruation, general health, drinking and
drugs, sexual feelings, pregnancy, contraceptives, and
sexually transmitted diseases including AIDS. The text is
sometimes humorous, but always conveys caring, respect,
and concern." SLJ
Includes bibliographical references

Kindersley, Barnabas

Children just like me; by Barnabas & Anabel Kindersley. Dorling Kindersley 1995 79p il maps $19.95 (3-6)   **305.23**
1. Children—Pictorial works
ISBN 0-7894-0201-7   LC 95-10199
"In association with United Nations Children's Fund"
This is a "compilation of facts, photographs, and interviews with thirty-seven children from thirty-two countries, including the U.S. Each child gets a full-page or double spread built around a large color photograph of the child and, often, his or her siblings; smaller photos show other family members, home and school, favorite foods and toys, homework or schoolbooks, and file photos of famous sights." Bull Cent Child Books
"A delightful, attractive look at children from around the world. . . . This book is factual, respectful, and insightful. It provides just the right balance of information and visual interest for the intended audience." SLJ

Lasky, Kathryn

Love that baby! a book about babies for new brothers, sisters, cousins, and friends; illustrated by Jennifer Plecas. Candlewick Press 2004 unp il $15.99 (k-2)   **305.23**
1. Infants
ISBN 1-56402-679-5   LC 99-57125
Describes how babies look, eat, talk, play, sleep, and more.
"Lasky dispenses thoughtful information, rock-solid advice, and suggestions for soothing a crying infant. Plecas's delightful watercolor-and-ink illustrations have touches of humor and are often set against vibrantly colored pages. . . . A loving and indispensable guide." SLJ

A **Life** like mine. DK Pub. 2002 127p il maps $24.99 (3-6)   **305.23**
1. Children
ISBN 0-7894-8859-0   LC 2002-11197
"In association with UNICEF, United Nations Children's Fund"
Looks at what life is like for children of different countries and how each child can fulfill his or her hopes and ambitions no matter how little or much their human rights are infringed
"This book gives the reader a remarkable look at the lives of children around the world. . . . The text is varied within each page and is written in language easy for a child to understand. The photographs are dispersed throughout all pages and enhance the meaning of the text." Libr Media Connect

Making it home; real-life stories from children forced to flee; with an introduction by Beverley Naidoo. Dial Books 2005 c2004 117p $17.99; pa $6.99 (4 and up)   **305.23**
1. Refugees 2. Children and war
ISBN 0-8037-3083-7; 0-14-240455-1 (pa)
                                            LC 2005045904
First published 2004 in the United Kingdom
This includes 20 "brief narratives by young people escaping their war-torn lands and lives. . . . Narrators from Kosovo, Bosnia, Afghanistan, Iraq, Congo, Liberia, Sudan, and Burundi reveal the injustices of their lives,

forced by fate to have anything but normal childhoods. A short introduction precedes each narrative or set of narratives and gives the history of the country's conflict, providing much-needed background information. . . . A centerfold features full-color photos of several of the young people." SLJ

The **Milestones** Project; celebrating childhood around the world; photography by Richard Steckel and Michele Steckel. Tricycle 2004 il $17.95   **305.23**
1. Children
ISBN 1-58246-132-5
"Milestones such as losing a first tooth, starting school, birthdays, haircuts, responsibilities, and so on are documented with stunning images of children from all corners of the globe, along with their observations. . . . The book has a clean design, with blocks of color and text and brilliantly animated photographs. This is a volume to share with younger children and to be enjoyed by many ages." SLJ

Rimm, Sylvia B.

See Jane win for girls; a smart girl's guide to success; [by] Sylvia Rimm. Free Spirit 2003 131p il pa $13.95 (5 and up)   **305.23**
1. Girls 2. Success 3. Conduct of life
ISBN 1-57542-122-4   LC 2002-155780
Adapted from the author's title for adults See Jane win, published 1999 by Crown
Presents tips, quizzes, activities, and words of wisdom from successful women for girls trying to make positive changes and choices in all areas of their lives and develop confidence, inner strength, and the desire to learn
"The message is strong and simple, the advice is practical, and readers looking for guidance and direction will respond positively to the book's format. . . . A useful self-help book and practical guide to life." SLJ
Includes bibliographical references

305.4 Women

33 things every girl should know about women's history; from suffragettes to skirt lengths to the E.R.A.; edited by Tonya Bolden. Crown 2002 240p il lib bdg $18.99; pa $12.95 (5 and up)
                                            305.4
1. Women—United States—History 2. Feminism 3. Women's rights
ISBN 0-375-91122-7 (lib bdg); 0-375-81122-2 (pa)
                                            LC 2001-47131
Uses poems, essays, letters, photographs and more to present the actions and achievements of women in the United States, from its beginnings up through the twentieth century
"This is a very strong, highly readable offering that gives context to the feminist movement." Booklist

Heinemann, Sue

The New York Public Library amazing women in American history; a book of answers for kids. Wiley 1998 192p (New York Public Library answer books for kids series) pa $12.95 (5 and up)
305.4

1. Women—United States—History

ISBN 0-471-19216-3   LC 97-18465

"A Stonesong Press book"

Consists of short answers to questions about the roles and achievements of women in America from prehistory to the end of the twentieth century

"The text is succinct, easy to read, and informative. . . . Pertinent black-and-white photos appear throughout." SLJ

Includes glossary and bibliographical references

Rossi, Ann

Created equal; women campaign for the right to vote 1840-1920. National Geographic 2005 40p il (Crossroads America) $12.95; lib bdg $21.90 (4-6)
305.4

1. Women—Suffrage 2. Women—United States—History

ISBN 0-7922-8275-2; 0-7922-8285-X (lib bdg)

A history of the movement for women's suffrage in the United States

"Period photographs, drawings, and cartoons; primary-source material; and biographical content make [this] introductory [title] interesting and accessible." SLJ

Includes glossary

305.8   Ethnic and national groups

Birdseye, Debbie Holsclaw

Under our skin; kids talk about race; by Debbie Holsclaw Birdseye and Tom Birdseye; photographs by Robert Crum. Holiday House 1997 30p il $15.95 (4 and up)
305.8

1. United States—Race relations 2. Ethnic relations

ISBN 0-8234-1325-X   LC 97-9395

Six young people discuss their feelings about their own ethnic backgrounds and about their experiences with people of different races

"This book provides an excellent starting point for discussion. It gives readers a chance to see what life is like through someone else's eyes, and in someone else's skin." SLJ

Includes bibliographical references

The **Black** Americans: a history in their own words, 1619-1983; edited by Milton Meltzer. Crowell 1984 306p il pa $12.95 hardcover o.p.
305.8

1. African Americans—History—Sources

ISBN 0-06-446055-X (pa)   LC 83-46160

This is a revised and updated edition of In their own words: a history of the American Negro, edited by Milton Meltzer and published in three volumes, 1964-1967

A history of black people in the United States, as told through letters, speeches, articles, eyewitness accounts, and other documents

Bolden, Tonya

Tell all the children our story; memories and mementos of being young and Black in America. Abrams 2001 128p il $24.95 (5 and up)
305.8

1. African American children 2. United States—Race relations

ISBN 0-8109-4496-0   LC 2001-1353

"This compilation of the African American experience, from colonial times through the twentieth century, reads and looks like a family scrapbook. . . . Photographs, excerpts from diaries and memoirs, and reproductions of artwork by black artists such as Charles Altson beautifully bring the story of each generation to life. Bolden vibrantly delivers her historical message through a contemporary perspective." Booklist

Includes bibliographical references

Cha, Dia

Dia's story cloth; written by Dia Cha; stitched by Chue and Nhia Thao Cha. Lee & Low Bks. 1996 unp il $15.95; pa $6.95 (3-5)   **305.8**

1. Hmong (Asian people)

ISBN 1-880000-34-2; 1-880000-63-6 (pa)

LC 95-41465

The story cloth made for her by her aunt and uncle chronicles the life of the author and her family in their native Laos and their eventual emigration to the United States

"An interesting and unusual title that resists neat categorization. . . . Part autobiography, part history, part description of a changing culture adapting life and art to new circumstances, the book serves as a brief introduction to the Hmong people." SLJ

Includes bibliographical references

Garza, Carmen Lomas

In my family; pictures and stories by Carmen Lomas Garza; as told to Harriet Rohmer; edited by David Schecter; Spanish translation by Francisco X. Alarcón. Children's Bk. Press 1996 unp il $15.95; pa $7.95 (k-3)   **305.8**

1. Mexican Americans 2. Bilingual books—English-Spanish

ISBN 0-89239-138-3; 0-89239-163-4 (pa)

LC 96-7471

Text in English and Spanish

"Lomas Garza uses her narrative paintings to relate her memories of growing up in Kingsville, Texas, near the Mexican border, and to reflect her pride in her Mexican American heritage. The artist portrays everyday events as well as special moments of family history in crisply colorful, vibrantly peopled paintings and provides brief, bilingual background stories for each of the 13 paintings." Booklist

Magic windows; cut-paper art and stories by Carmen Lomas Garza; as told to Harriet Rohmer; edited by David Schecter; Spanish translation by Francisco X. Alarcón. Children's Bk. Press 1999 30p il $15.95   **305.8**

1. Mexican Americans—Social life and customs 2. Bilingual books—English-Spanish 3. Mexico—Social life and customs

ISBN 0-89239-157-X   LC 98-38379

Garza, Carmen Lomas—*Continued*

"Garza creates paper windows that depict scenes from her family life, the desert, and Mexican culture. She places seventeen papercuttings, mostly made from black paper, against vibrant backgrounds of turquoise, tangerine, lime and other tropical colors. Opposite the *papel picado*, text in English and Spanish explains the artistic process, providing cultural or personal information related to the papercutting." Bull Cent Child Books

Haskins, James

Out of the darkness; the story of Blacks moving North, 1890-1940; by James Haskins and Kathleen Benson. Benchmark Bks. 2000 112p (Great journeys) lib bdg $32.79 (5 and up)

305.8

1. Bricktop, 1894-1984 2. Jones, Joe, 1896-1987 3. African Americans—History 4. United States—Race relations

ISBN 0-7614-0970-X   LC 99-19882

Uses the experiences of two individuals, Ada "Bricktop" Smith and Joe Jones, to present the story of the Great Migration of Southern Blacks to northern cities from the late 1800s to the years after World War I.

This "delivers a compelling account of the 'Great Migration' from the South to the North. . . . Black-and-white photos and quotes greatly enhance the narrative." SLJ

Includes bibliographical references

Hoobler, Dorothy

The African American family album; [by] Dorothy and Thomas Hoobler; introduction by Phylicia Rashad. Oxford Univ. Press 1995 127p il (American family albums) pa $16.95 hardcover o.p. (5 and up)   305.8

1. African Americans

ISBN 0-19-512419-7 (pa)   LC 94-34697

"Beginning with life in pre-colonial Africa, the Hooblers make superb use of personal histories, autobiographies, slave narratives, and other original documents to paint a vivid picture of life in medieval Africa, in Africa during the slave trade, and of the lives of slaves and former slaves in the U.S. Readers are introduced to a complex set of historical events, presented in a simple, yet moving manner. . . . An excellent addition to any collection." SLJ

Includes bibliographical references

The Chinese American family album; [by] Dorothy and Thomas Hoobler; introduction by Bette Bao Lord. Oxford Univ. Press 1994 128p il map (American family albums) pa $16.95 hardcover o.p.   305.8

1. Chinese Americans

ISBN 0-19-512421-9 (pa)   LC 93-11873

"This sourcebook on the Chinese immigrant experience is divided into six topics: the homeland, the voyage to America, arrival in America, first-generation life, the integration of . . . generations, and Chinese Americans today. The authors introduce each chapter with a summary essay, then let the immigrants and their descendents speak for themselves in excerpts from oral reminiscences, written histories, and fiction spanning the years from the Gold Rush to the 1980s. Period photographs and drawings, maps, and sidebars enhance the text. The result resembles a well-organized, handsomely designed scrapbook. . . . A valuable resource." SLJ

Includes bibliographical references

The Cuban American family album; [by] Dorothy and Thomas Hoobler; introduction by Oscar Hijuelos. Oxford Univ. Press 1996 127p il (American family albums) pa $16.95 hardcover o.p.   305.8

1. Cuban Americans

ISBN 0-19-512425-1 (pa)   LC 95-38103

Interviews, excerpts from diaries and letters, newspaper accounts, profiles of famous individuals, and pictures from family albums portray the Cuban American experience

Includes bibliographical references

The German American family album; [by] Dorothy and Thomas Hoobler; introductions by Werner Klemperer. Oxford Univ. Press 1996 127p il (American family albums) pa $16.95 hardcover o.p. (5 and up)   305.8

1. German Americans

ISBN 0-19-512422-7 (pa); 0-19-508133-1 (hc)

LC 95-14448

Traces the history of German immigrants to the United States through letters, diaries and newspaper accounts

Includes bibliographical references

The Irish American family album; [by] Dorothy and Thomas Hoobler; introduction by Joseph P. Kennedy II. Oxford Univ. Press 1995 128p il (American family albums) pa $16.95 hardcover o.p. (5 and up)   305.8

1. Irish Americans

ISBN 0-19-512418-7 (pa)   LC 94-19569

"Selections from diaries, letters, interviews, newspaper and magazine articles, and books provide an arresting picture of what it has meant to be of Irish heritage in America. . . . Topics such as prejudice, working conditions and labor unions; politics; and the importance of family, friends, and the Catholic Church are touched upon." SLJ

Includes bibliographical references

The Italian American family album; [by] Dorothy and Thomas Hoobler; introduction by Governor Mario M. Cuomo. Oxford Univ. Press 1994 127p il map (American family albums) pa $16.95 hardcover o.p. (5 and up)   305.8

1. Italian Americans

ISBN 0-19-512420-0 (pa)   LC 93-46918

This volume includes selections from "diaries, letters, and oral histories. . . . Each of the six chapters begins with background information and then goes on to discuss life in the old country, coming to America, first impressions, working, forming a new life, and becoming a part of America." SLJ

Includes bibliographical references

Hoobler, Dorothy—*Continued*

The Japanese American family album; [by] Dorothy and Thomas Hoobler. Oxford Univ. Press 1995 127p il map (American family albums) pa $16.95 hardcover o.p. (5 and up) **305.8**

1. Japanese Americans

ISBN 0-19-512423-5 (pa); 0-19-508131-5 (hc)

LC 94-43466

"Organized chronologically, this book captures the broad sweep of the Japanese-American experience. Each of the six chapters offers a succinct historical presentation followed by first-person accounts. Relying on oral histories and original documents, both pictorial and written, the Hooblers have truly humanized historical events." SLJ

Includes bibliographical references

The Jewish American family album; [by] Dorothy and Thomas Hoobler; introduction by Mandy Patinkin. Oxford Univ. Press 1995 127p il (American family albums) pa $16.95 (5 and up) **305.8**

1. Jews—United States

ISBN 0-19-512417-0 LC 94-43460

,This volume "begins with a five-page thumbnail sketch of Jewish history from Abraham to the rise of the State of Israel. Successive chapters detail Jewish life in 'the old country', immigration to America, and the contributions Jews have made to their new homeland." Book Rep

"What makes this title unique is the high quality of the carefully researched and varied historical information and the Hooblers' judicious selection of primary-source excerpts, many of which are by well-known writers, politicians, and celebrities." SLJ

Includes bibliographical references

The Mexican American family album; [by] Dorothy and Thomas Hoobler; introduction by Henry G. Cisneros. Oxford Univ. Press 1994 127p il (American family albums) pa $16.95 hardcover o.p. (5 and up) **305.8**

1. Mexican Americans

ISBN 0-19-512426-X (pa); 0-19-509-459-X (hc)

LC 94-7785

"Using almost exclusively first-person accounts, the Hooblers present vignettes of history, culture, and experience from the first Mexican American settlers to the Chicano Movement. . . . Gathered together, these accounts present a powerful portrait of a strong people, rich in history and culture. A must for multicultural studies." Book Rep

Includes bibliographical references

The Scandinavian American family album; [by] Dorothy and Thomas Hoobler; introduction by Hubert H. Humphrey, III. Oxford Univ. Press 1997 127p il (American family albums) pa $16.95 (5 and up) **305.8**

1. Scandinavian Americans

ISBN 0-19-512424-3 (pa); 0-19-510579-6 (hc)

LC 95-45540

"The Hooblers begin with a chapter on life in Scandinavia and the conditions that caused people to emigrate. Scandinavian-Americans who have played an influential role in our society are featured throughout the book. . . . Photographs and captions add personal narratives that explain what life was like for Scandinavian Americans." Book Rep

Includes bibliographical references

Hoyt-Goldsmith, Diane

Hoang Anh; a Vietnamese-American boy; photographs by Lawrence Migdale. Holiday House 1992 30p il map $16.95 (3-5) **305.8**

1. Vietnamese Americans

ISBN 0-8234-0948-1 LC 91-28880

A Vietnamese American boy describes the daily activities of his family in San Rafael, California, and the traditional culture and customs that shape their lives

"Color photographs of good quality are carefully placed in relation to a text that is direct, informative, and convincing." Bull Cent Child Books

Includes glossary

Kuklin, Susan

How my family lives in America. Bradbury Press 1992 unp il $16; pa $5.99 (k-3) **305.8**

1. African Americans 2. Chinese Americans 3. Puerto Ricans—United States

ISBN 0-02-751239-8; 0-689-82221-9 (pa)

LC 91-22949

"Sanu's father was born in Senegal, Eric's father came from Puerto Rico, and both of April's parents were born in Taiwan. Each section provides special words, foods, games, clothes, music and other ways in which families transmit their heritages and integrate them with the lifestyles of the United States. The photographs provide insights as to how cultures are cherished and continued." Child Book Rev Serv

"Each child's first-person narration is simple and uncomplicated, with occasional humorous touches. . . . The full-color photographs are well composed and serviceable." SLJ

Lester, Julius

Let's talk about race; illustrated by Karen Barbour. 1st ed. HarperCollinsPublishers 2005 unp il $15.99; lib bdg $16.89 (k-3) **305.8**

1. Racism 2. Prejudices

ISBN 0-06-028596-6; 0-06-028598-2 (lib bdg)

LC 2002-10979

This "picture book introduces race as just one of many chapters in a person's story. . . . Throughout the narrative, [the author] asks questions that young readers can answer, creating a dialogue about who they are and encouraging them to tell their own tales. He also discusses 'stories' that are not always true, pointing out that we create prejudice by perceiving ourselves as better than others. . . . The pairing of text and dazzling artwork is flawless." SLJ

Myers, Walter Dean

Now is your time! the African-American struggle for freedom. HarperCollins Pubs. 1991 292p il pa $12.99 hardcover o.p. (6 and up)

305.8

1. African Americans—History
ISBN 0-06-446120-3 (pa)   LC 91-314
Coretta Scott King Award for text, 1992

A history of the African-American struggle for freedom and equality, beginning with the capture of Africans in 1619, continuing through the American Revolution, the Civil War, and into contemporary times

"Myers's unique episodic approach makes this history a compelling exploration of the African-American experience. . . . This fascinating book will engender pride in heritage for young African Americans and provide insight into American history for all of us." Horn Book

Includes bibliographical references

Rappaport, Doreen

Free at last! stories and songs of Emancipation; illustrated by Shane W. Evans. Candlewick Press 2004 63p il $19.99 (3-6)   **305.8**

1. African Americans—History 2. African Americans—Civil rights 3. Southern States—Race relations
ISBN 0-7636-1440-8   LC 2003-43853

"Stories, poems, and songs about events from the Emancipation Proclamation of 1863 through the Brown v. Board of Education decision of 1954 are perfectly matched with vibrant oil paintings. The result is a glorious tribute to the lives of African-American heroes and heroines." SLJ

Sanders, Nancy I.

A kid's guide to African American history; more than 70 activities. Chicago Review Press 2000 242p il map pa $14.95 (4-6)   **305.8**

1. African Americans—History
ISBN 1-55652-417-X   LC 00-31554

This book "introduces many aspects of African American history. . . . Throughout the book, crafts and other projects offer parents and teachers practical ways to involve children in African American heritage. . . . A useful resource." Booklist

Includes bibliographical references

Wolf, Bernard

Coming to America; a Muslim family's story. Lee & Low Bks. 2003 unp il $17.95; pa $7.95 (3-5)   **305.8**

1. Arab Americans 2. Muslims—United States
ISBN 1-58430-086-8; 1-58430-177-5 (pa)
LC 2002-67115

Depicts the joys and hardships experienced by a Muslim family that immigrates to New York City from Alexandria, Egypt, in the hope of making a better life for themselves

"The tone is low-key but optimistic; the large, mostly full-page color photos seem like those of a welcomed visitor." Horn Book

306   Culture and institutions

Morris, Ann

Work. Lothrop, Lee & Shepard Bks. 1998 29p il $15; lib bdg $14.93 (k-1)   **306**
1. Work
ISBN 0-688-14866-2; 0-688-14867-0 (lib bdg)
LC 97-21607
Also available Play $15 (ISBN 0-688-14552-3)

Photographs and brief text show people all over the world at work. A section identifies the country in which each photo was taken and describes the activity portrayed

"The language is clear and straightforward, and, for the most part, the photographs support the [text] well." SLJ

306.8   Marriage and family

Cole, Joanna

The new baby at your house; photographs by Margaret Miller. rev ed. Morrow Junior Bks. 1998 unp il $16; lib bdg $15.93 (k-3)   **306.8**
1. Infants 2. Siblings
ISBN 0-688-13897-7; 0-688-13898-5 (lib bdg)
LC 97-29267

A revised and newly illustrated edition of the title first published 1985

Describes the activities and changes involved in having a new baby in the house and the feelings experienced by the older brothers and sisters

"Miller captures many intimate and touching moments with her pictures. . . . There is a good balance of families from varied ethnic backgrounds. . . . This book opens with a clear and precise note to parents that gives honest, practical advice." SLJ

Includes bibliographical references

Kuklin, Susan

Families. Hyperion Books for Children 2006 36p il $15.99 (3-5)   **306.8**
1. Family
ISBN 0-7868-0822-5

"This book consists of interviews with the children from 15 different families, including mixed-race, immigrant, gay, lesbian, and divorced, as well as single parents and families for whom religion is a focal point. The children may be adopted, have special needs, be only children or have multiple siblings. . . . The voices are natural, and the children come across as individuals. . . . Kuklin has composed sharp and vibrant photos that capture the essence of each of them. This book will be both attractive to browsers and an excellent impetus for discussing relationships and diversity in America." SLJ

MacGregor, Cynthia

Jigsaw puzzle family; the stepkids' guide to fitting it together. Impact Pub. 2005 106p (RebuildingBooks, relationships, divorce and beyond) pa $12.95 (5 and up)   **306.8**

1. Stepfamilies
ISBN 1-886230-63-3

"MacGregor offers simple guidelines, practical advice, and lots of fictional examples about living with a new blended family. . . . This title offers healthy and helpful suggestions for resolving much of the conflict that arises when family situations change." SLJ

Includes bibliographical references

Rotner, Shelley

Lots of grandparents! by Shelley Rotner and Sheila Kelly; photographs by Shelley Rotner. Millbrook Press 2001 unp il lib bdg $23.90 (k-1)   **306.8**

1. Grandparents
ISBN 0-7613-2313-9   LC 00-66827

In this photo-essay "color photographs show grandparents of different ages, ethnic groups, shapes, and sizes sharing happy times with grandchildren." SLJ

"The brief text offers sensible comments about grandparents and their bond with their grandchildren, but teachers will particularly appreciate the variety of photographs that can lead to classroom discussions." Booklist

Rubel, Nicole

Twice as nice; what it's like to be a twin. Farrar, Straus and Giroux 2004 32p il $16.50 (k-3)   **306.8**

1. Twins
ISBN 0-374-31836-0   LC 2003-54168

Presents facts, anecdotes, studies, opinions, and advice on the topic of twins

"The layout is colorful and inviting, blending light-hearted cartoon illustrations with black-and-white and full-color photos. Dialogue balloons present additional factual tidbits as well as humorous one-liners." SLJ

Snow, Judith E.

How it feels to have a gay or lesbian parent; a book by kids for kids of all ages. Harrington Park Press 2004 110p $19.95; pa $12.95 (5 and up)   **306.8**

1. Parent-child relationship 2. Homosexuality
ISBN 1-56023-419-9; 1-56023-420-2 (pa)
     LC 2003-18008

In their own words, children of different ages talk about how and when they learned of their gay or lesbian parent's sexual orientation and the effect it has had on them.

"This inspirational, eye-opening title gives readers who have gay and lesbian parents a much-deserved voice." SLJ

306.89   Separation and divorce

Bingham, Jane

Why do families break up? Raintree 2005 48p il (Exploring tough issues) lib bdg $31.43 (4 and up)   **306.89**

1. Divorce
ISBN 0-7398-6683-4   LC 2003-20285

Contents: Happily every after?; Getting along; When things go wrong; How it feels; Splitting up; Moving on

"This book looks at the reasons people divorce and discusses the stages a family goes through when a marriage breaks up. It also considers how different family members struggle with the painful effects, and the benefits of counseling. Case studies, quotes, and color photos personalize the issues, and fact boxes provide a few statistics. . . . Libraries needing self-help information for young people dealing with divorce will find Bingham's volume a useful addition." SLJ

Includes bibliographical references

Brown, Laurene Krasny

Dinosaurs divorce; a guide for changing families; [by] Laurene Krasny Brown and Marc Brown. Atlantic Monthly Press 1986 31p il $15.95; pa $7.95 (k-3)   **306.89**

1. Divorce
ISBN 0-316-11248-8; 0-316-10996-7 (pa)
     LC 86-1079

Text and illustrations of dinosaur characters introduce aspects of divorce such as its causes and effects, living with a single parent, spending holidays in two separate households, and adjusting to a stepparent

"The picture-book, almost comic-book, format, the touches of humor, and the distancing effect of the dinosaurs as surrogate humans may make the book accessible to young or extremely anxious children. A thoughtful, useful book." Horn Book

Krementz, Jill

How it feels when parents divorce. Knopf 1984 115p il pa $15 hardcover o.p. (4 and up)   **306.89**

1. Divorce
ISBN 0-394-75855-2   LC 83-48856

In a personal interview format "19 boys and girls, ranging in age from 7 to 16 years, tell of their parents' divorces and of the effects the divorce has had on them and their families." SLJ

"The full-page portraits that precede each piece are exceptionally expressive. While the accounts have many similarities, experiences and personalities are unique; Krementz' ear for language ensures that the children project their own individuality." Horn Book

Rogers, Fred

Divorce; photographs by Jim Judkis. Putnam 1996 unp il (Lets talk about it) $16.99; pa $6.99 (k-2)   **306.89**

1. Divorce
ISBN 0-399-22449-1; 0-698-11670-4 (pa)
     LC 94-2312

Rogers, Fred—*Continued*

Rogers "defines a family as anyone who gives a child food, care, love, and a place to feel safe. He explains that these main ingredients should remain constant even in the event of a divorce. Children are advised to ask about changes in living arrangements and other aspects of their lives. . . . The author prescribes activities like talking, drawing, and playing with friends to deal with normal feelings of sadness, anger, and crying. . . . Judkis's sensitive full-color photographs of three families work well with the text." SLJ

307 Communities

Ajmera, Maya

Be my neighbor; [by] Maya Ajmera & John D. Ivanko. Shakti for Children, Charlesbridge 2004 unp il $15.95; pa $6.95 (k-2)   **307**
1. Community life
ISBN 1-57091-504-0; 1-57091-685-3 (pa)
LC 2003-21230
A simple introduction to the characteristics of a neighborhood

"This beautifully crafted book explores the concept of community, using well-chosen words from the late Mr. Rogers as a starting point. . . . Illustrated with bright, beautiful full-color photos of children around the world, the gorgeous spreads are organized by themes." SLJ

Press, Judy

All around town! exploring your community through craft fun; illustrations by Karen Weiss. Williamson 2002 128p il (Williamson Little Hands book) pa $12.95 (k-2)   **307**
1. Community life 2. Handicraft
ISBN 1-885593-68-6   LC 2002-23456
"A Williamson kids Can! book"

Explores the library, police station, park, post office, and other parts of a neighborhood through craft activities such as making a butterfly book bag, paper airplane, puppy puppet, and more

"Line drawings illustrate the text with cheerful pictures of children and helpful illustrations of craft activities in various stages of completion. Preschool and primary-grade teachers will find a wealth of ideas here." Booklist

323.1   Civil and political rights of nondominant groups

Bausum, Ann

Freedom Riders; John Lewis and Jim Zwerg on the front lines of the civil rights movement; by Ann Bausum; forewords by Freedom Riders Congressman John Lewis and Jim Zwerg. National Geographic 2006 79p il por $18.95; lib bdg $28.90 (5 and up)   **323.1**
1. Lewis, John, 1940- 2. Zwerg, Jim, 1939- 3. African Americans—Civil rights 4. Southern States—Race relations
ISBN 0-7922-4173-8; 0-7922-4174-6 (lib bdg)
LC 2005012947

"Eschewing a general overview of the 1961 Freedom Rides for specific, personal histories of real participants in the dangerous bus integration protests, Bausum focuses on two college students from strikingly different backgrounds: Jim Zwerg, a white Wisconsin native who became involved during an exchange visit to Nashville, and John Lewis, a black seminarian and student leader of the nonviolence movement." Booklist

"Bausum's narrative style, fresh, engrossing, and at times heart-stopping, brings the story of the turbulent and often violent dismantling of segregated travel alive in vivid detail. The language, presentation of material, and pacing will draw readers in and keep them captivated." SLJ

Includes bibliographical references

King, Casey

Oh, freedom! kids talk about the Civil Rights Movement with the people who made it happen: illustrated with photographs; by Casey King and Linda Barrett Osborne; foreword by Rosa Parks; portraits by Joe Brooks. Knopf 1997 137p il lib bdg $19; pa $10.99 (5 and up)   **323.1**
1. African Americans—Civil rights 2. United States— Race relations
ISBN 0-679-85856-3 (lib bdg); 0-679-89005-X (pa)
LC 96-13014
Interviews between young people and people who took part in the civil rights movement accompany essays that describe the history of efforts to make equality a reality for African Americans

"King and Osborne present a carefully unbiased overview of the civil rights movement. . . . But most impressive is the way the authors use interesting interviews by students . . . [that] humanize history and add depth to the bare facts of the historical account." Book Rep

Includes bibliographical references

King, Martin Luther, Jr.

I have a dream; foreword by Coretta Scott King; paintings by fifteen Coretta Scott King Award and Honor Book artists, Ashley Bryan [et al.] Scholastic 1997 40p il $16.95   **323.1**
1. African Americans—Civil rights 2. United States— Race relations
ISBN 0-590-20516-1   LC 95-45189
"Martin Luther King, Jr.'s classic speech is creatively illustrated by 15 Coretta Scott King Award-winning artists. Signed statements from the artists explain the emotions they were trying to capture and why and how they used certain colors and tones. . . . From cover to cover this is a beautiful book." SLJ

Linda Brown, you are not alone; the Brown v. Board of Education decision: a collection; edited by Joyce Carol Thomas; illustrations by Curtis James. Jump at the Sun/Hyperion Books for Children 2003 114p il $15.99 (5 and up)

323.1

1. School integration 2. African Americans—Civil rights 3. United States—Race relations
ISBN 0-7868-0821-7

A collection of personal reflections, stories and poems of 10 well-known children's authors, such as Jerry Spinelli, Eloise Greenfield, Lois Lowry, Michael Cart, and Katherine Paterson, who were themselves young people in 1954 when the Supreme Court handed down the decision to desegregate public schools.

The authors' "personal reminiscences capture a spectrum of powerfully expressed emotions. . . . James's closely focused, lifelike pastel illustrations feature striking portraits and memorable images." Publ Wkly

McWhorter, Diane

A dream of freedom; the Civil Rights Movement from 1954 to 1968; foreword by Reverend Fred Shuttlesworth. Scholastic Nonfiction 2004 160p il $19.95 (5 and up)

323.1

1. African Americans—Civil rights 2. United States—Race relations
ISBN 0-439-57678-4

The author discusses "the national civil rights movement from Brown v. the Board of Education to the assassination of Martin Luther King Jr. . . . This account is both factual and personal. She discusses her feelings as a white child in the South, and she focuses in on the many ways in which both white and black children were involved in the movement. . . . The breadth and depth of McWhorter's book is exemplary." Booklist

323.44   Freedom of action (Liberty)

Intellectual freedom manual; compiled by the Office for Intellectual Freedom of the American Library Association. American Lib. Assn. il $52

323.44

1. Intellectual freedom 2. Libraries—Censorship
First published 1974. (7th edition 2005) Periodically revised

This guide to preserving intellectual freedom includes: ALA interpretations to the Library Bill of Rights; recommendations for special libraries and specific situations; information about legal decisions affecting school and public libraries; a section on the ALA's Intellectual Freedom Action Network

"This manual details the professional standards to which librarians aspire and offers practical information about how to achieve those goals; it's a must for any librarian's professional library." Book Rep

Includes bibliographical references

Scales, Pat R.

Teaching banned books; 12 guides for young readers. American Lib. Assn. 2001 134p pa $28

323.44

1. Books—Censorship 2. Children's literature—Study and teaching 3. School libraries
ISBN 0-8389-0807-1   LC 01-22340

The author "offers twelve strategies for teaching books that have been challenged or censored in the United States. Designed to accompany teaching about the First Amendment, 'each strategy includes a summary of the novel, a pre-reading activity, discussion questions to encourage critical thinking, and activities to broaden students' knowledge of topics in the novel.'" Bull Cent Child Books

"Scales knows her material inside out. She also knows how to inspire others to take up this cause and gives them an effective handbook to do just that." Booklist

Includes bibliographical references

323.6   Citizenship and related topics

Hamilton, John

Becoming a citizen; [by] John Hamilton. ABDO Pub. Co 2004 32p il (Government in action!) $22.78 (3-5)

323.6

1. Citizenship 2. Naturalization
ISBN 1-59197-642-1   LC 2003-69698

This describes the process of naturalization, with samples of the documents required and questions from citizenship tests.

This "has an interesting assortment of vintage and recent color photos, all well captioned, and is logically arranged." SLJ

324   The political process

Christelow, Eileen

Vote! Clarion 2003 47p il $16 (k-3)

324

1. Elections 2. Politics
ISBN 0-618-24754-8   LC 2002-152288

Using a campaign for mayor as an example, shows the steps involved in an election, from the candidate's speeches and rallies, to the voting booth where every vote counts, to the announcement of the winner

"It's hard to imagine a more accessible introduction to voting. The words are straightforward, the art whimsical and creative, and two darling dogs provide color commentary on the action." Booklist

Includes glossary

The **encyclopedia** of U.S. presidential elections; David C. Saffell, general editor. Franklin Watts 2004 128p il map (Watts reference) $39 (5 and up)

324

1. Presidents—United States—Election
ISBN 0-531-12051-1   LC 2002-38009

Chronicles the candidates, issues, platforms, campaign slogans, and influences of presidential elections in the United States from 1789 through 2000.

The encyclopedia of U.S. presidential elections—*Continued*

"Enjoyably readable, this compilation devotes a clearly written, two to three-page treatment to each election. . . . Casual readers will enjoy the way historical figures come to life, foibles and all." SLJ

Includes glossary and bibliographical references

Granfield, Linda

America votes; how our president is elected; written by Linda Granfield; illustrated by Steve Bjorkman. Kids Can Press 2003 64p il $16.95; pa $9.95 (4-6)   **324**

1. Presidents—United States—Election

ISBN 1-55337-086-4; 1-55337-087-2 (pa)

"The author explains the presidential election process, including its history, the two-party system, third parties, PACs, election fraud, also-rans, and more. This thorough overview is enlivened with examples drawn from history and children's own lives. Colorful cartoon drawings keep the pages animated and interesting." SLJ

Hamilton, John

Running for office; [by] John Hamilton. ABDO Pub. Co 2005 32p il (Government in action!) $22.78 (3-5)   **324**

1. Elections 2. Politics

ISBN 1-59197-822-X   LC 2004-46289

This describes a political campaign and discusses differences between Republicans and Democrats.

This "book has an interesting assortment of vintage and recent color photos, all well captioned, and is logically arranged." SLJ

Includes bibliographical references

Landau, Elaine

The 2000 presidential election. Children's Press 2002 48p il (Cornerstones of freedom) lib bdg $24 (2-5)   **324**

1. Presidents—United States—Election 2. United States—Politics and government—1989-

ISBN 0-516-22527-8   LC 2001-6916

Explores the people and events surrounding the 2000 presidential election

"Landau provides an insightful, informative, and orderly description of the events as they unfolded from Election Day, November 7, 2000, until December 13, 2000, when Al Gore conceded defeat. . . . A time line effectively summarizes all of the important events, and full-color photographs on nearly every page enhance the text." SLJ

Includes bibliographical references

325.73 Immigration to the United States

Anderson, Dale

Arriving at Ellis Island. World Almanac Library 2002 48p il map (Landmark events in American history) lib bdg $26.60; pa $11.95 (5 and up)   **325.73**

1. Ellis Island Immigration Station 2. United States—Immigration and emigration

ISBN 0-8368-5337-7 (lib bdg); 0-8368-5351-2 (pa)

LC 2002-24627

Discusses immigration to the United States during the nineteenth and early twentieth centuries and describes the small island in New York harbor that served as the point of entry for millions of immigrants from 1892 to 1954

The "design is attractive, with drawings, maps, paintings, and photos; primary sources, such as excerpts from diaries, letters, and newspapers, support and enhance the [text]. . . . Informative, competently written." Booklist

Includes glossary and bibliographical references

Bierman, Carol

Journey to Ellis Island; how my father came to America; by Carol Bierman with Barbara Hehner; illustrated by Laurie McGaw. Hyperion Bks. for Children 1998 48p il $17.95; pa $8.99 (3-5)   **325.73**

1. Weinstein, Julius 2. Ellis Island Immigration Station 3. United States—Immigration and emigration 4. Jews—United States

ISBN 0-7868-0377-0; 0-7868-5499-5 (pa)

LC 98-10987

An account of the ocean voyage and arrival at Ellis Island of twelve-year-old Julius Weinstein who, along with his mother and younger sister, immigrated from Russia in 1922

"Bierman accurately describes the facility's processing procedures, regulations, routines, and dormitories. . . . Well-chosen sepia photographs, including some of the family; reproductions of postcards of Ellis Island during the 1920s; and full-page watercolor-and-casein artwork illustrate the presentation giving it the look of a photo album." SLJ

Includes glossary

Freedman, Russell

Immigrant kids. Dutton 1980 72p il pa $8.99 hardcover o.p. (4 and up)   **325.73**

1. Children of immigrants 2. United States—Immigration and emigration 3. City and town life

ISBN 0-14-037594-5 (pa)   LC 79-20060

The author has "assembled an interesting collection of old photographs for a book that gives a broad view of the experiences of immigrant children in an urban environment. The text is divided into such areas as the journey to America, schools, play, work (much of it illegal), and home life. Photographs are carefully placed in relation to textual references, and the text itself is enlivened by quotations from the reminiscences of several people about their first days in the United States as child immigrants. Large, clear print and an index add to the book's usefulness." Horn Book

Hoobler, Dorothy

We are Americans; voices of the immigrant experience; by Dorothy and Thomas Hoobler. Scholastic Ref. 2003 194p il $21.95 (5 and up)

325.73

1. United States—Immigration and emigration

ISBN 0-439-16297-1   LC 2001-49612

A history of immigration to America, from speculation about the earliest immigrants to the present day

"This thoughtful, well-researched overview will be a solid addition to most collections and is most notable for the diverse array of voices that it contains." SLJ

Includes bibliographical references

I was dreaming to come to America; memories from the Ellis Island Oral History Project; selected and illustrated by Veronica Lawlor; foreword by Rudolph W. Giuliani. Viking 1995 38p il pa $6.99 hardcover o.p. (4 and up)

325.73

1. Ellis Island Immigration Station 2. United States—Immigration and emigration

ISBN 0-14-055622-2 (pa)   LC 95-1281

In their own words, coupled with hand-painted collage illustrations, immigrants recall their arrival in the United States. Includes brief biographies and facts about the Ellis Island Oral History Project

"There is a flavor of Chagall in the peasant figures dancing above the ship or hopping ashore near the turreted towers of the huge building on Ellis Island. The elegant rendering offers a timeless view of this significant journey that is at once personal and universal." Horn Book

Kroll, Steven

Ellis Island; doorway to freedom; illustrated by Karen Ritz. Holiday House 1995 32p il maps $15.95 (3-5)

325.73

1. Ellis Island Immigration Station 2. United States—Immigration and emigration

ISBN 0-8234-1192-3   LC 95-714

Describes how the immigration station on Ellis Island served as a gateway into the United States for more than sixteen million immigrants between 1892 and 1954

This is an "informative, approachable introduction. . . . Illustration done in pen and ink and in pencil and watercolor give an authentic, old-fashioned feeling to the artwork." Horn Book Guide

Includes glossary

Levine, Ellen

. . . if your name was changed at Ellis Island; illustrated by Wayne Parmenter. Scholastic 1993 80p pa $5.99 hardcover o.p. (3-5)

325.73

1. Ellis Island Immigration Station 2. United States—Immigration and emigration

ISBN 0-590-43829-8 (pa)   LC 92-27940

Describes, in question and answer format, the great migration of immigrants to New York's Ellis Island, from the 1880s to 1914. Features quotes from children and adults who passed through the station

The author "writes in a clear, direct style that's packed with information and lively case histories. . . .

There are many illustrations, sometimes full-page, sometimes small, in acrylic earth colors . . . they are an attractive part of a clear and accessible design." Booklist

Maestro, Betsy

Coming to America: the story of immigration; illustrated by Susannah Ryan. Scholastic 1996 unp il $15.95 (k-3)

325.73

1. United States—Immigration and emigration

ISBN 0-590-44151-5   LC 94-31110

"In an introductory look at immigration, all inhabitants of the United States are considered immigrants or descendants of immigrants, whether they crossed the land bridge from Asia, came across the oceans voluntarily, or were brought as slaves. The clear, simple text and bright, animated illustrations convey excitement and adventure as well as hardship and loss." Horn Book Guide

Meltzer, Milton

Bound for America; the story of the European immigrants. Benchmark Bks. 2002 112p il (Great journeys) $32.79 (5 and up)

325.73

1. United States—Immigration and emigration

ISBN 0-7614-1227-1   LC 00-51875

This history of immigration to the United States focuses on Europeans who arrived in the late 19th and early 20th century

Includes bibliographical references

Sandler, Martin W.

Island of hope; the story of Ellis Island and the journey to America. Scholastic Nonfiction 2004 144p il $18.95 (5 and up)

325.73

1. Ellis Island Immigration Station 2. United States—Immigration and emigration

ISBN 0-439-53082-2   LC 2003-54448

Relates the story of immigration to America through the voices and stories of those who passed through Ellis Island, from its opening in 1892 to the release of the last detainee in 1954.

"This engagingly written, inspirational account will give children, particularly immigrants or descendants of immigrants, some sharp insight into the trials and triumphs of their predecessors." Booklist

Includes bibliographical references

326   Slavery and emancipation

Bial, Raymond

The strength of these arms; life in the slave quarters. Houghton Mifflin 1997 40p il $16 (4 and up)

326

1. Slavery—United States 2. Plantation life 3. African Americans—Social life and customs

ISBN 0-395-77394-6   LC 96-39860

Describes how slaves were able to preserve some elements of their African heritage despite the often brutal treatment they experienced on Southern plantations

"This volume features clear, color photographs of plantation sites and artifacts, as well as a few early pho-

Bial, Raymond—*Continued*

tos of people living under slavery. . . . This makes slavery in America more concrete than many other books on the subject." Booklist

Includes bibliographical references

The Underground Railroad. Houghton Mifflin 1995 48p il map $17; pa $6.95 (4 and up)

326

1. Underground railroad 2. Slavery—United States

ISBN 0-395-69937-1; 0-395-97915-3 (pa)

LC 94-19614

Using first-person accounts, historical documents, and his own photographs, the author "focuses on the history of the Underground Railroad, building on the experiences of both riders and conductors as he outlines the political climate and the moral beliefs that allowed slavery to thrive and those that helped bring about its downfall." Publ Wkly

"Although the text covers ground often trodden by other works on this popular subject, Bial's shots of places and things which now appear tidy and innocent conjure spirits of desperate freedom-seekers as handily as do more detailed narratives." Bull Cent Child Books

Includes bibliographical references

Currie, Stephen

Escapes from slavery; [by] Stephen Currie. Lucent Books 2003 112p il map (Great escapes) $28.70 (5 and up) **326**

1. Slavery—United States

ISBN 1-59018-276-6   LC 2002-154078

Contents: Introduction: fugitive slaves; Ellen and William Craft; Josiah Henson; Harriet Tubman; William Wells Brown; Henry Brown

Narratives of five escapes from slavery, each of which was typical in many ways but featured unusual personal characteristics or circumstances that made these trips to freedom extraordinary

"These exciting tales are written in lively language and are accompanied by black-and-white illustrations and informative sidebars." SLJ

Includes bibliographical references

Ford, Carin T.

Slavery and the underground railroad; bound for freedom. Enslow 2004 48p il map lib bdg $23.93 (3-5) **326**

1. Slavery—United States 2. Underground railroad 3. Abolitionists

ISBN 0-7660-2251-X   LC 2003-6824

Contents: The growth of slavery; The life of a slave; Running from slavery; Riding the underground railroad; Working on the railroad

This "explores the roots of the Civil War, and offers a profusion of true stories about 'passengers' and 'conductors' on the underground railroad. Well-chosen, primary-source quotations, culled from a variety of sources, bring the drama up close. . . . Compelling archival images illustrate . . . [this] thoughtfully executed [volume]." Booklist

Includes glossary and bibliographical references

Fradin, Judith Bloom

5,000 miles to freedom; Ellen and William Craft's flight from slavery; [by] Judith Bloom Fradin and Dennis Brindell Fradin. National Geographic 2006 96p il $19.95; lib bdg $29.90

326

1. Craft, Ellen, 1826-1891 2. Craft, William, 19th cent. 3. Slavery—United States

ISBN 0-7922-7885-2; 0-7922-7886-0 (lib bdg)

"In 1848, light-skinned Ellen Craft, dressed in the clothing of a rich, white man, assumed the identity of Mr. William Johnson and, escorted by his black slave, William, traveled by railroad and boat to reach the North. With the passage of a more stringent Fugitive Slave Law in 1850, the couple . . . decided to travel to England. . . . In 1869, they returned to the United States, opening a school and operating a farm in Georgia. . . . This lively, well-written volume presents the events in their lives in an exciting, page-turner style that's sure to hold readers attention. Black-and-white photographs, illustrations, and reproductions enhance the text." SLJ

Greene, Jacqueline Dembar

Slavery in ancient Greece and Rome. Watts 2000 63p il map lib bdg $24 (5 and up)

326

1. Slavery 2. Classical civilization

ISBN 0-531-11693-X   LC 00-38197

"Watts library"

This book discusses the dependence of Ancient Greece and Rome "on slavery as an institution through its decline. In tandem with an attractive, open layout, judicious use of maps, photographs, and reproductions serves to break up the . . . text." SLJ

Includes glossary and bibliographical references

Hamilton, Virginia

Many thousand gone; African Americans from slavery to freedom; illustrated by Leo and Diane Dillon. Knopf 1993 151p il lib bdg $18.99; pa $12.95 (5 and up) **326**

1. Underground railroad 2. Slavery—United States

ISBN 0-394-92873-3 (lib bdg); 0-679-87936-6 (pa)

LC 89-19988

In this book the author tells "the story of slavery through a series of dramatic biographical vignettes. . . . Her book includes such famous historical figures as Frederick Douglass, Sojourner Truth and Harriet Tubman. She also presents some more obscure individuals. . . . All of these profiles drive home the sickening realities of slavery in a personal way. . . . These are powerful stories eloquently told." N Y Times Book Rev

Includes bibliographical references

Haskins, James

Bound for America; the forced migration of Africans to the New World; [by] James Haskins & Kathleen Benson; illustrated by Floyd Cooper. Lothrop, Lee & Shepard Bks. 1999 48p il $17; lib bdg $17.89 (5 and up) **326**

1. Slave trade 2. Slavery—History

ISBN 0-688-10258-1; 0-688-10259-X (lib bdg)

LC 98-24101

Haskins, James—*Continued*

Discusses the European enslavement of Africans, including their capture, branding, conditions on slave ships, shipboard mutinies, and arrival in the Americas

"This combination of clear text and judicious use of primary-source material makes crystalline the inhumanity and commercialism that kept the trade in slaves alive for 350 years." SLJ

Includes bibliographical references

Get on board: the story of the Underground Railroad. Scholastic 1993 152p il map pa $4.50 hardcover o.p. (5 and up) **326**
1. Tubman, Harriet, 1815?-1913 2. Brown, John, b. ca. 1810 3. Underground railroad 4. Slavery—United States
ISBN 0-590-45419-6 (pa) LC 92-13247

The author "relates the history of the Underground Railroad in the U.S., and introduces those who made it a success." SLJ

"Weaving together poignant personal stories and carefully researched historical data, Haskins has produced a stirring account of the founding and the workings of the Underground Railroad." Publ Wkly

Includes bibliographical references

Heinrichs, Ann

The Underground Railroad. Compass Point Bks. 2001 48p il map (We the people) lib bdg $21.26 (2-4) **326**
1. Underground railroad 2. Slavery—United States
ISBN 0-7565-0102-4 LC 00-11020

This book briefly describes the Underground Railroad, slavery, and important abolitionists in the U.S.

"Short chapters, succinct text, large print, and well-chosen illustrations make this book a good starting point for young readers embarking on a study of the topic." SLJ

Includes glossary and bibliographical references

Lester, Julius

From slave ship to freedom road; paintings by Rod Brown. Dial Bks. 1998 40p il $17.99; pa $6.99 (4 and up) **326**
1. Slavery—United States
ISBN 0-8037-1893-4; 0-14-056669-4 (pa)
LC 96-44422

"Lester uses empathy-provoking exercises, open-ended questions, and the paintings of Rod Brown to help readers understand the experience of African-American slaves." Bull Cent Child Books

"Lester's impassioned questions grow from his visceral response to Brown's narrative paintings. . . . The combination of history, art, and commentary demands interaction." Booklist

To be a slave; paintings by Tom Feelings. 30th anniversary ed. Dial Bks. 1998 160p il $20 (6 and up) **326**
1. Slavery—United States
ISBN 0-8037-2347-4 LC 98-5213

A reissue of the title first published 1968

"Through the words of the slave, interwoven with strongly sympathetic commentary, the reader learns what it is to be another man's property; how the slave feels about himself; and how he feels about others. Every aspect of slavery, regardless of how grim, has been painfully and unrelentingly described." Read Ladders for Hum Relat. 6th edition

Includes bibliographical references

McKissack, Patricia C.

Rebels against slavery; by Patricia C. McKissack and Fredrick McKissack. Scholastic 1996 181p il $15.95 (5 and up) **326**
1. Slavery—United States
ISBN 0-590-45735-7 LC 94-41089

A Coretta Scott King honor book for text, 1997

The authors "explore slave revolts and the men and women who led them, weaving a tale of courage and defiance in the face of tremendous odds. Readers learn not only about Nat Turner and Denmark Vesey, but also about Cato, Gabriel Prosser, the maroons, and the relationship between escaped slaves and Seminole Indians. The activities of abolitionists are described as well. The authors' careful research, sensitivity, and evenhanded style reveal a sad, yet inspiring story of the will to be free." SLJ

Myers, Walter Dean

Amistad: a long road to freedom. Dutton Children's Bks. 1998 99p il maps $16.99; pa $9.99 (5 and up) **326**
1. Amistad (Schooner) 2. Slavery—United States
ISBN 0-525-45970-7; 0-14-130004-3 (pa)

This is an "account of the capture in West Africa, the hellish journey aboard the slave ship on the Middle Passage, the sale in Cuba, the mutiny led by Sengbe on the *Amistad* as it sailed from Cuba, the forced landing in Connecticut, the subsequent court trials in the U.S., and the final struggle to return home. The design is clear and readable. . . . Myers includes considerable detail drawn from primary reports. . . . The narrative is exciting, not only the account of the uprising but also the tension of the court arguments." Booklist

Includes bibliographical references

Newman, Shirlee Petkin

Child slavery in modern times; [by] Shirlee P. Newman. Watts 2000 63p il lib bdg $24 (5 and up) **326**
1. Child abuse 2. Child labor 3. Slavery
ISBN 0-531-11696-4 LC 00-38199

"Watts library"

Discusses cases where children are forced to work against their wills in difficult and dangerous conditions in various countries around the world

This "includes numerous black-and-white and color photographs of exploited young people, guaranteed to raise readers' level of consciousness." SLJ

Includes bibliographical references

Rappaport, Doreen

No more! stories and songs of slave resistance; illustrated by Shane Evans. Candlewick Press 2002 60p il $17.99 (3-6)   **326**

1. Slavery

ISBN 0-7636-0984-6   LC 00-29756

"Rappaport has collected slave narratives, biographies, and songs that tell the history of resistance from the Middle Passage to the plantation and then the Underground Railroad and the Civil War." Booklist

"Evans's large, bold, dramatic oil paintings capture the despair, fear, and hope of the slaves. Taken together, the text and illustrations make a powerful statement." SLJ

327.12   Espionage and subversion

Gifford, Clive

Spies; foreword by Dame Stella Rimington. Kingfisher 2004 63p il (Kingfisher knowledge) $11.95 (5 and up)   **327.12**

1. Spies

ISBN 0-7534-5777-6

This "book provides a history of the trade, includes memorable spy stories, and discusses the future of espionage. The facts come fast and furiously, interspersed with attractive color photographs. . . . An eye-catching introduction, best for browsers." SLJ

Includes glossary

328   The legislative process

Donovan, Sandra

Making laws; a look at how a bill becomes a law; by Sandy Donovan. Lerner Publications Co 2004 56p il (How government works) lib bdg $25.26 (4-6)   **328**

1. Legislation 2. Law

ISBN 0-8225-1346-3   LC 2002-152931

Contents: It all starts with an idea: people and interest groups; Introducing . . . ; Getting a fair hearing: the committee stage; Traffic cop: the rules committee and calendars; On the floor: debating and voting; Sorting things out: conference committees; To the president: getting signed into law

"Making Laws poses the question: What if kids want to ban school on Fridays? Donovan takes readers through the entire process of how that idea might turn into a legislative bill that could become a law. . . . Students will find [this title] worthwhile." SLJ

Includes bibliographical references

Hamilton, John

How a bill becomes a law; [by] John Hamilton. Abdo Pub 2004 32p il (Government in action!) lib bdg $15.95 (3-5)   **328**

1. Legislation 2. Law

ISBN 1-59197-646-4   LC 2003-69305

This describes the steps in passing a federal law in the United States.

This "book has an interesting assortment of vintage and recent color photos, all well captioned, and is logically arranged." SLJ

Horn, Geoffrey

The Congress; by Geoffrey M. Horn. World Almanac Library 2003 48p il (World Almanac Library of American government) lib bdg $30; pa $11.95 (5 and up)   **328**

1. United States. Congress

ISBN 0-8368-5457-8 (lib bdg); 0-8368-5462-4 (pa)   LC 2002-514111

Contents: Congress and the Capitol; What the Constitution says; Getting elected and reelected; House and Senate; How a bill becomes a law; Landmark legislation; Congress in the spotlight

This describes "how the Constitution gives different jobs to each chamber of Congress, the extent and limits of their powers, and the roles each performs in the making of federal laws. . . . [It also discusses] the important officials in Congress, the legislative process, and some important laws Congress has passed. Special sections explain concepts such as pork-barrel spending, lameduck sessions, and filibusters." Publisher's note

Includes bibliographical references

330.973   United States--Economic conditions

Collins, Mary

The Industrial Revolution. Children's Press 2000 30p il (Cornerstones of freedom) lib bdg $20.50; pa $5.95 (4 and up)   **330.973**

1. Industrial revolution

ISBN 0-516-21596-5 (lib bdg); 0-516-27036-2 (pa)   LC 99-14954

A history of the Industrial Revolution focusing primarily on the United States during the nineteenth century and on the change from an agrarian society to one based on machines and factories

331.3   Workers by age group

Bartoletti, Susan Campbell

Growing up in coal country. Houghton Mifflin 1996 127p il $17; pa $7.95 (5 and up)

    331.3

1. Child labor 2. Coal mines and mining

ISBN 0-395-77847-6; 0-395-97914-5 (pa)

    LC 96-3142

This is an "account of working and living conditions in Pennsylvania coal towns. The first half of the volume details various duties in the mines, from jobs performed by the youngest boys to the tasks of adult miners, while the second half describes the company village, common customs and recreational activities, and the accidents and diseases that frequently beset the workers." Horn Book

"With compelling black-and-white photographs of children at work in the coal mines of northeastern Pennsylvania about 100 years ago, this handsome, spacious photo-essay will draw browsers as well as students doing research on labor and immigrant history." Booklist

Includes bibliographical references

Brown, Don

Kid Blink beats the world. Roaring Brook Press 2004 unp il $16.95 (2-4)   **331.3**

1. Newspaper carriers 2. Strikes 3. Child labor 4. New York (N.Y.)—History

ISBN 1-59643-003-6   LC 2003-21896

This "details the events in the summer of 1899, during which hundreds of young news vendors stood up to two of the most powerful men in the U.S.—William Randolph Hearst and Joseph Pulitzer." Booklist

"The accessible text presents a cogent, kid-empowering tale of underprivileged youngsters whose actions really made a difference. . . The loosely drawn pencil-and-watercolor illustrations convey great energy." Horn Book

Freedman, Russell

Kids at work; Lewis Hine and the crusade against child labor; with photographs by Lewis Hine. Clarion Bks. 1994 104p il $20; pa $9.95 (5 and up)   **331.3**

1. Hine, Lewis Wickes, 1874-1940 2. Child labor

ISBN 0-395-58703-4; 0-395-79726-8 (pa)

LC 93-5989

"Using the photographer's work throughout, Freedman provides a documentary account of child labor in America during the early 1900s and the role Lewis Hine played in the crusade against it. He offers a look at the man behind the camera, his involvement with the National Child Labor Committee, and the dangers he faced trying to document unjust labor conditions." SLJ

Freedman "does an outstanding job of integrating historical photographs with meticulously researched and highly readable prose." Publ Wkly

Includes bibliographical references

331.4   Women workers

Colman, Penny

Rosie the riveter; women working on the home front in World War II. Crown 1995 120p il pa $10.99 hardcover o.p. (5 and up)   **331.4**

1. Women—Employment 2. World War, 1939-1945—United States

ISBN 0-517-88567-0 (pa)   LC 94-3614

This is an account of women's employment in wartime during the Second World War. "Colman looks at the jobs women took, the impact women had on the workplace, and what happened to working women at war's end. . . . [She also discusses] the public relations campaign that not only 'wooed' women into the workplace, but also sought to change firmly entrenched attitudes about women's role in society." Booklist

"A thoughtfully prepared look at women's history and wartime society, this dynamic book is characterized by extensive research." Horn Book

Includes bibliographical references

331.5   Special categories of workers other than by age or sex

Ancona, George

Harvest. Marshall Cavendish 2001 48p il lib bdg $15.95 (4 and up)   **331.5**

1. Agricultural laborers 2. Migrant labor 3. Mexicans—United States

ISBN 0-7614-5086-6   LC 2001-17497

"This photo-documentary focuses on the lives and work of Mexican migrant workers as they pick various crops on the West coast." SLJ

"Ancona puts a face on Mexican migrant workers and uses their own words to explain their lives, also including a great deal of information about the crops they pick. . . . Ancona's photos are insightful, with scenes and subjects deftly chosen and shot." Booklist

331.7   Labor by industry and occupation

Hopkinson, Deborah

Up before daybreak; cotton and people in America; [by] Deborah Hopkinson. Scholastic Nonfiction 2005 120p il $18.99   **331.7**

1. Cotton 2. Textile industry 3. Working class

ISBN 0-439-63901-8   LC 2005008128

"From the industrial revolution to the 1950s demise of the Lowell cotton mills, Hopkinson discusses the history and sociology of king cotton, frequently emphasizing the children who labored under slave masters, endured dead-end mill jobs, or helped sharecropping parents claw out a living. . . . Stories of real people . . . sharply focus the dramatic history, as do arresting archival photos of stern youngsters manipulating hoes, cotton sags, or bobbins." Booklist

331.8   Labor unions and labor-management relations

Bartoletti, Susan Campbell

Kids on strike! Houghton Mifflin 1999 208p il $20; pa $8.95 (5 and up)   **331.8**

1. Jones, Mother, 1830-1930 2. Strikes 3. Child labor

ISBN 0-395-88892-1; 0-618-36923-6 (pa)

LC 98-50575

Describes the conditions and treatment that drove workers, including many children, to various strikes, from the mill workers strikes in 1828 and 1836 and the coal strikes at the turn of the century to the work of Mother Jones on behalf of child workers

"This well-researched and well-illustrated account creates a vivid portrait of the working conditions of many American children in the 19th and early 20th centuries." SLJ

Includes bibliographical references

332.024 Personal finance

Godfrey, Neale S.

Neale S. Godfrey's ultimate kids' money book; illustrated by Randy Verougstraete. Simon & Schuster Bks. for Young Readers 1998 122p il $19 (5 and up)   **332.024**

1. Personal finance 2. Money

ISBN 0-689-81717-7   LC 97-35433

Provides an overview of economics and money, including earning, spending, saving, checks and credit cards, banks, and the history of money

"Facts, fables, advice, strategies, games, history, vocabulary, and more are energetically packaged with cartoon art, photos, and archival documents in this exciting treatment of money and economics for kids. The eye-catching pages playfully combine bold colors and varied sizes of print with lighthearted illustrations and commendably cogent text." Booklist

Includes glossary

Hall, Margaret

Your allowance. Heinemann Lib. 2000 32p il lib bdg $14.95 (3-5)   **332.024**

1. Personal finance

ISBN 1-57572-234-8   LC 99-46698

Offers young people information on how to manage the money they have, providing advice on spending, saving, and donating money to help others

Includes glossary and bibliographical references

Thomas, Keltie

The kids guide to money cent$; written by Keltie Thomas; illustrated by Stephen MacEachern. Kids Can Press 2004 56p il $14.95; pa $7.95 (4-6)   **332.024**

1. Personal finance

ISBN 1-55337-389-8; 1-55337-391-X (pa)

"As a social-studies assignment, Alicia, Dan, and Jeff form the Money Cent$ Gang and embark on a journey into the world of consumerism, banks, credit cards, philanthropy, employment, and the stock market. Complex subjects are presented in short, easy-to-understand chapters. . . . Explanations are clear, concise, and age appropriate. . . . The accessible layout and colorful cartoon artwork will grab readers' attention." SLJ

332.4 Money

Cribb, Joe

Money; written by Joe Cribb. rev ed. DK Pub. 2005 72p il (DK eyewitness books) $15.99; lib bdg $19.99 (4 and up)   **332.4**

1. Money

ISBN 0-7566-1389-2; 0-7566-1398-1 (lib bdg)

First published 1990 by Knopf

Examines, in text and photographs, the symbolic and material meaning of money, from shekels, shells, and beads to gold, silver, checks, and credit cards. Also discusses how coins and banknotes are made, the value of money during wartime, and how to collect coins

Hall, Margaret

Money. Heinemann Lib. 2000 32p il lib bdg $14.95 (3-5)   **332.4**

1. Money

ISBN 1-57572-233-X   LC 99-46700

An introduction to money, describing how it evolved to replace the barter system, how it is used, different forms it takes, and currency in countries around the world

Includes glossary and bibliographical references

Kummer, Patricia K.

Currency; [by] Patricia K. Kummer. Franklin Watts 2004 80p il (Inventions that shaped the world) lib bdg $30.50; pa $9.95 (4 and up)   **332.4**

1. Money

ISBN 0-531-12341-3 (lib bdg); 0-531-16734-8 (pa)

     LC 2003-16309

Contents: What is currency?; Barter and early currency; Important developers of modern currency; Development of modern currency: coins and paper money; Role of currency in daily life and in the life of countries

"Kummer covers the history of currency around the world, how money is made, and its prospective use in the future. Information about early barter systems and the role that currency plays in modern society are also included. . . . [The book has] appropriate color and black-and-white photographs, reproductions, and/or diagrams on virtually every spread. [This offering is an] excellent [resource] for reports and should also appeal to readers." SLJ

Leedy, Loreen

Follow the money! written and illustrated by Loreen Leedy. Holiday House 2002 unp il $16.95 (k-3)   **332.4**

1. Money 2. Coins

ISBN 0-8234-1587-2   LC 2001-39418

A quarter describes all the ways it is used from the time it is minted until it is taken back to a bank

"Leedy includes a good deal of information, while keeping the book light, energetic, and entertaining." Booklist

Includes glossary

Maestro, Betsy

The story of money; illustrated by Giulio Maestro. Clarion Bks. 1993 43p il maps $17 (3-5)   **332.4**

1. Money

ISBN 0-395-56242-2   LC 91-24997

Also available in paperback from Mulberry Bks.

A history of money, beginning with the barter system in ancient times, to the first use of coins and paper money, to the development of modern monetary systems

"A successful, readable presentation of a complicated subject. . . . Guilio Maestro's meticulously drawn watercolor illustrations brighten each page." SLJ

332.7 Credit

Hall, Margaret

Credit cards and checks. Heinemann Lib. 2000 32p il lib bdg $14.95 (3-5)   **332.7**

1. Credit cards 2. Debit cards 3. Personal finance

ISBN 1-57572-232-1   LC 99-46697

Provides an introduction to checks, credit cards, and debit cards, explaining how they work and why people use them

Includes glossary and bibliographical references

333.73 Land

Dalgleish, Sharon

Managing the land. Chelsea House 2003 32p il (Our world: our future) $18.95 (3-6)

333.73

1. Land use 2. Land tenure 3. Urbanization 4. Environmental protection

ISBN 0-7910-7020-4   LC 2002-2534

Contents: Our world; Our future; To the center of the earth; Living off the land; Wanted! more soil for food; Creeping concrete jungles; Digging it up; Mountains made of garbage; Poisoning the land; Global warming and the land; Getting away from it all; Sacred land; Project land; Think globally; Sustaining our world

Describes the geological makeup of Earth and the ecosystems it supports; discusses issues that affect the land, including population growth, mining, landfills, pollution, erosion; and explains how people can help manage and preserve land

This book is "well-written, thought-provoking, motivating. . . . The illustrations clarify some difficult concepts as well as keep the reader's attention." Libr Media Connect

Includes glossary

333.75 Forest lands

Dalgleish, Sharon

Protecting forests. Chelsea House 2003 32p il (Our world: our future) $18.95 (3-6)

333.75

1. Forest conservation

ISBN 0-7910-7017-4   LC 2002-2533

Contents: Our world; Our future; Forest facts; Green clean-air machines; Green forest or greenhouse?; Making space; Digging under; Water on tap; Mountains of wood; Acid and aliens; Rich world or poor world?; Forest spirits; Project forests; Think globally; Sustaining our world

Describes different types of forests and where they grow, explains the role trees play in keeping the air clean, and discusses deforestation, acid rain, and forest conservation

This title is "well-written, thought-provoking, motivating. . . . The illustrations clarify some difficult concepts as well as keep the reader's attention." Libr Media Connect

Includes glossary

333.79 Energy

Bailey, Jacqui

Charged up; the story of electricity; written by Jacqui Bailey; illustrated by Matthew Lilly. Picture Window Books 2004 31p il (Science works) lib bdg $23.93 (2-4)   **333.79**

1. Electricity

ISBN 1-4048-0568-0   LC 2003-20116

Describes how electrical energy is generated in power stations and how it travels through pylons, power cables, and wires into people's homes.

This "is an excellent source of information for younger science students. . . . The authors . . . creatively use bright colors, interesting graphics, and 'everyday' household experiences to bring this difficult topic to life." Sci Books Films

Includes bibliographical references

Bowden, Rob

Energy; by Rob Bowden. KidHaven Press 2004 48p (Sustainable world) $23.70 (5 and up)

333.79

1. Renewable energy resources 2. Energy development

ISBN 0-7377-1897-8   LC 2003-52953

This "briefly introduces various forms of sustainable energy—water, wind, sun, geothermal sources—and takes a look at where sustainable technology is headed. . . . Bowden writes with admirable simplicity about complicated subjects, and he's careful to separate facts from opinions when he quotes others. [This book includes] excellent color photos . . . and gripping statistics." Booklist

Includes glossary and bibliographical references

Dalgleish, Sharon

Renewing energy. Chelsea House 2003 32p il (Our world: our future) $18.95 (3-6)

333.79

1. Energy resources

ISBN 0-7910-7018-2   LC 2002-2532

Explores what energy is, sources of energy including fossil fuels as well as alternatives, the environmental impact of using different forms of energy, and how people can conserve energy

This book is "well-written, thought-provoking, motivating. . . . The illustrations clarify some difficult concepts as well as keep the reader's attention." Libr Media Connect

Includes glossary

Hirschmann, Kris

Solar energy. KidHaven Press 2006 48p il (Our environment) lib bdg $23.70 (5 and up)

333.79

1. Solar energy

ISBN 0-7377-3049-8

"This book examines all aspects of the solar energy question-how solar energy works, its problems and potential, where it is being used today and more." Publisher's note

Juettner, Bonnie
Energy; by Bonnie Juettner. KidHaven Press 2004 48p il map (Our environment) $23.70 (5 and up)   **333.79**
1. Energy resources
ISBN 0-7377-1821-8   LC 2003-876
Contents: What does the world use for energy?; How is energy managed?; Are we running out of energy?; What will happen in the future?
"The liberal use of vibrant colors, the inclusion of a photograph or diagram on most pages, and the generous print size will appeal to reluctant readers. [This title] will help students examine cause and effect (and possible solutions), and challenge them to live green." SLJ
Includes glossary and bibliographical references

333.91 Water and lands adjoining bodies of water

Vogel, Carole Garbuny
Human impact; [by] Carole G. Vogel. F. Watts 2003 95p il (Restless sea) $29.59; pa $12.95 (5 and up)   **333.91**
1. Marine pollution 2. Human influence on nature
ISBN 0-531-12323-5; 0-531-16680-5 (pa)
                                      LC 2003-5301
Contents: Troubled waters; Sea sick; Too many fishermen; The impact of global warming; The human footprint
This "provides a detailed description of the results of population growth, global warming, and the development of coastal areas. The devastation to marine life resulting from occurrences such as oil spills and the dead zones caused by oxygen-depleted water are described through both heart-wrenching photographs and informative text." SLJ
Includes bibliographical references

333.95 Biological resources

Bortolotti, Dan
Tiger rescue; changing the future for endangered wildlife. Firefly 2003 64p il map lib bdg $19.95; pa $9.95 (4 and up)   **333.95**
1. Tigers 2. Wildlife conservation
ISBN 1-55297-599-1 (lib bdg); 1-55297-558-4 (pa)
This describes the tiger's "natural habitat, habits, physiology, and behavior in captivity. [It also includes] a time line of conservation efforts, profiles of conservationists in the field, and forecasts of the animals' future. Throughout, the author makes clear the factors that can threaten animal populations, and discusses human attitudes toward the animals throughout history. . . . Written in accessible, lively language and nicely illustrated with exciting color photos, [this] will be useful for reports and browsing." Booklist

Burnie, David
Endangered planet; [by] David Burnie. 1st ed. Kingfisher 2004 63p il maps (Kingfisher knowledge) $11.95 (5 and up)   **333.95**
1. Human influence on nature 2. Environmental degradation
ISBN 0-7534-5776-8   LC 2004-478
This "explores the delicate web of natural cycles that supports millions of species . . . and reveals how our ever-growing demand for food, fuel, and living space threatens to damage Earth's habitats beyond repair." Publisher's note
"Children will be immediately drawn to the high-quality graphics artfully laid out on brightly colored spreads. . . . The [narrative is] logically arranged into three chapters, each containing a broad overview as well as more detailed subtopics." SLJ
Includes glossary

Dalgleish, Sharon
Protecting wildlife. Chelsea House 2003 32p il (Our world: our future) $18.95 (3-6)
                                              333.95
1. Wildlife conservation
ISBN 0-7910-7021-2   LC 2002-2537
Contents: Our world; Our future; Different worlds; The variety of life; A change in the weather; Paving over habitats; Polluting habitats; Fishing or overfishing?; Souvenirs and trophies; Alien invasion; The richest place on Earth; Changing our food; Project wildlife; Think globally; Sustaining our world
This "discusses habitats, changing weather, greed, and vanishing species. . . . The busy pages with full-color photos, diagrams, and varied typeface will appeal to both browsers and report writers." SLJ
Includes glossary

Gallant, Roy A.
The wonders of biodiversity. Benchmark Bks. 2003 80p il maps (Story of science) lib bdg $19.95 (5 and up)   **333.95**
1. Biological diversity
ISBN 0-7614-1427-4   LC 2002-916
Partial contents: Beetles, bacteria, and biodiversity; Critters galore, what they are; Critters galore, where they live; Major ecosystems; Tragedy of the rain forests; Gaia
Discusses the many different life forms that have existed on Earth, their importance, and how they have changed over time
"Readers will find accurate, readable explanations for the scientific principles here addressed. . . . Up-to-date controversies and predictions conclude the [book] . . . illustrated with well-captioned photos." Horn Book Guide
Includes glossary and bibliographical references

Patent, Dorothy Hinshaw
Biodiversity; photographs by William Muñoz. Clarion Bks. 1996 109p il $18; pa $7.95 (5 and up)   **333.95**
1. Biological diversity 2. Nature conservation
ISBN 0-395-68704-7; 0-618-31514-4 (pa)
                                      LC 95-49982

Patent, Dorothy Hinshaw—*Continued*

Provides a global perspective on environmental issues while demonstrating the concept which encompasses the many forms of life on earth and their interdependence on one another for survival

"Patent imbues her lucid scientific discussion with many examples of her personal experience both in childhood and as an adult, and she employs a wide array of examples from many parts of the world to demonstrate current problems and scientific and conservation activity. Illustrated with plentiful and helpful photos." Horn Book

Includes glossary

Salmansohn, Pete

Saving birds; heroes around the world; [by] Pete Salmansohn and Stephen W. Kress. Tilbury House 2003 39p il $16.95 (5 and up)　　　**333.95**

1. Birds—Protection 2. Wildlife conservation 3. Endangered species

ISBN 0-88448-237-5　　　　　　LC 2002-6710

Profiles adults and children working in six habitats around the world to save wild birds, some of which are on the brink of extinction.

"As a teaching aid, this volume is an exceptional supplement. The six articles relating the heroic rescue of the endangered birds are accurate and enhanced by appropriate color photographs." Sci Books Films

Swinburne, Stephen R.

Once a wolf; how wildlife biologists fought to bring back the gray wolf; with photographs by Jim Brandenburg. Houghton Mifflin 1999 48p il $16 (4 and up)　　　**333.95**

1. Wolves 2. Wildlife conservation

ISBN 0-395-89827-7　　　　　　LC 98-16865

Surveys the history of the troubled relationship between wolves and humans, examines the view that these predators are a valuable part of the ecosystem, and describes the conservation movement to restore them to the wild

The "crisp color photographs showing wolves in their natural environment are exceptional. Swinburne's text adds suspense and excitement to the story. . . . This is an involving study . . . which makes fascinating reading." Bull Cent Child Books

Includes bibliographical references

Turner, Pamela S.

Gorilla doctors; saving endangered great apes. Houghton Mifflin 2005 64p il map (Scientists in the field) $17 (5 and up)　　　**333.95**

1. Gorillas 2. Wildlife conservation

ISBN 0-618-44555-2　　　　　　LC 2004-9213

This describes The Mountain Gorilla Veterinary Project which works to save the mountain gorilla population in Rwanda and Uganda.

This offers "readable text . . . accompanied by striking, full-color photographs." SLJ

Includes bibliographical references

342　Constitutional and administrative law

Finkelman, Paul

The Constitution. National Geographic 2006 32p il (American documents) $15.95; lib bdg $23.90 (4 and up)　　　**342**

1. United States. Constitution 2. Constitutional history

ISBN 0-7922-7937-9; 0-7922-7975-1 (lib bdg)

An introduction to the American Constitution, including why and how it was written and how it is amended.

This title is "clear and concise. . . . The superior layout and illustrations enhance and reinforce the [text] through a combination of high-quality reproductions, photographs, artwork, and biographical sidebars." SLJ

Includes glossary

Fritz, Jean

Shhh! we're writing the Constitution; illustrated by Tomie dePaola. Putnam 1987 64p il $15.99; pa $5.99 (2-4)　　　**342**

1. Constitutional history—United States

ISBN 0-399-21403-8; 0-698-11624-0 (pa)

LC 86-22528

"This book discusses how the Constitution came to be written and ratified. It includes the full text of the document produced by the Constitutional Convention of 1787." Bull Cent Child Books

"Jean Fritz gives a vivid, vibrant picture of the 1787 Constitutional Convention. The wonderful, full-color illustrations are a perfect match for the captivating text." Child Book Rev Serv

Krull, Kathleen

A kid's guide to America's Bill of Rights; curfews, censorship, and the 100-pound giant; illustrated by Anna DiVito. Avon Bks. 1999 226p il $15.99 (4 and up)　　　**342**

1. United States. Constitution. 1st-10th amendments 2. Civil rights

ISBN 0-380-97497-5　　　　　　LC 99-17324

"After describing how the first 10 amendments came to be added to the Constitution, the book considers each one from a historical point of view, examining Supreme Court cases and famous challenges, and explaining in what ways each amendment applies to children and teenagers. Anna Divito's cartoonlike drawings add a visually appealing touch." Booklist

Includes bibliographical references

Maestro, Betsy

A more perfect union; the story of our Constitution; illustrated by Giulio Maestro. Lothrop, Lee & Shepard Bks. 1987 48p il pa $7.99 hardcover o.p. (2-4)　　　**342**

1. Constitutional history—United States

ISBN 0-688-10192-5 (pa)　　　　　LC 87-4083

Also available Spanish language edition

The Maestros "cover the birth of the Constitution from the initial decision to hold the convention, through the

Maestro, Betsy—*Continued*
summer meetings in Philadelphia, the ratification struggle, the first election, and the adoption of the Bill of Rights." SLJ

"A simple, straightforward account using an oversize format with full-color illustration throughout. There is an excellent, fact-filled addenda that also includes the Preamble, chronologies and summaries of the Articles of the Constitution, the Bill of Rights, the Amendments and the Connecticut Compromise. This fine book places important events in historical context." Publ Wkly

344   Labor, social service, education, cultural law

Good, Diane L.
Brown v. Board of Education; a civil rights milestone. Children's Press 2004 48p il (Cornerstones of freedom, Second series) $25 (4-6)
344
1. Brown, Oliver, 1919-1961 2. Topeka (Kan.). Board of Education 3. Segregation in education
ISBN 0-516-24225-3   LC 2003-9097
Explains the history of segregation in the United States and cases that tested the law allowing "separate but equal" treatment, including the five cases that came together as Brown v. Board of Education
"Text divided into short sections, numerous photographs, and generous use of white space combine to make [this title] inviting." SLJ
Includes bibliographical references

Somervill, Barbara A.
Brown v. Board of Education; the battle for equal education; . Child's World 2005 40p il (Journey to freedom) lib bdg $28.50 (5 and up)
344
1. Brown, Oliver, 1919-1961 2. Topeka (Kan.). Board of Education 3. Segregation in education
ISBN 1-59296-229-7   LC 2003-27079
Contents: A long walk to school; Separate . . . not equal; Brown v. Board of Education; Desegregation; Linda Brown's legacy; Timeline
This book provides an account of the famous Supreme Court case which led to the outlawing of racial segregation in public schools
A "quality [title] both in content and design. . . . Excellent historical and current photos enhance the easy-to-read [text] on every spread." SLJ
Includes bibliographical references

Torrans, Lee Ann
Law for K-12 libraries and librarians. Libraries Unlimited 2003 250p pa $25   **344**
1. Libraries—Law and legislation 2. School libraries
ISBN 1-59158-036-6   LC 2003-2592
Contents: Copyright; The scope of copyright; The fair use of material protected by copyright in education; Library archiving and section 108 of the DMCA; Tracing copyright; Library bibliographies criteria for selection and the legal implications and limitations of linking; Faculty created web sites: who owns them?; Patron privacy and filtering in the school library: guarding outgoing data, monitoring incoming data; Library bibliographies: student web pages, metatags in websites and the law; Licensing in the library; Americans with disabilities and the school library; Employment in the library; Policies and procedures: a difference with significance

"Advice and regulations addressing what can be copied, taped, and used on school Web sites will be helpful for both media specialists and teachers. Comprehensive yet readable, this guide is logically organized and solidly supported by examples and references. An indispensable resource." SLJ
Includes bibliographical references

345   Criminal law

Crewe, Sabrina
The Scottsboro case; [by] Sabrina Crewe and Michael V. Uschan. Gareth Stevens Pub 2005 32p il map (Events that shaped America) lib bdg $24.67 (4 and up)   **345**
1. Trials 2. African Americans—Civil rights
ISBN 0-8368-3407-0   LC 2004-44240
An account of the 1931 court case in which nine African American youths were charged with rape
"The authors do a good job of a taking a subject that is rife with conflict, duplicity, and ugly words and actions . . . and shaping it into a useful, informative book for middle-graders. . . . [It] is attractively designed with plenty of crisply reproduced, black-and-white photos, and historical art, such as posters, in color. The writing is clear and the text doesn't pull punches." Booklist
Includes bibliographical references

Olson, Steven P.
The trial of John T. Scopes; a primary source account; by Steven P. Olson. Rosen Pub. Group 2004 64p il (Great trials of the 20th century) lib bdg $29.25 (5 and up)   **345**
1. Scopes, John Thomas 2. Evolution—Study and teaching
ISBN 0-8239-3974-X   LC 2002-153354
Contents: The meeting at the drugstore; Evolution vs. creation; The nation takes sides; The trial begins; The prosecution; The defense; Darrow vs. Bryan; The meaning of the Scopes trial
An account of the trial of John T. Scopes, prosecuted in 1925 for teaching evolution.
This title utilizes "photographs, copies of original transcripts, political cartoons, and quotations from those involved. [This] is written with respectful attention to the issues of evolution and creationism, the separation of church and state, and the power of the government. Readers interested in the law will be captivated by the complexities of the arguments." SLJ
Includes bibliographical references

346.04   Property law

Butler, Rebecca P.
Copyright for teachers and librarians.
Neal-Schuman Publishers 2004 248p il pa $59.95
346.04

1. Copyright 2. Fair use (Copyright)
ISBN 1-55570-500-6   LC 2004-46013
"The five chapters in Part I are . . . reviews of copyright law, the concept of fair use, determining what is in public domain, how to obtain permissions, and other general guidelines on such topics as licensing, loaning, penalties, plagiarism, and exemptions. The bulk of the book is in Part II, which deals with specific applications, such as Internet and public access, videos and DVDs, television, software, music, multimedia, distance learning and—oh, yes!—print! . . . An indispensable addition." SLJ
Includes bibliographical references

Complete copyright; an everyday guide for librarians; Carrie Russell, editor. American Library Association 2004 262p il spiral bdg $50
346.04

1. Copyright
ISBN 0-8389-3543-5   LC 2004-7681
Russell provides "guidance for both common copyright issues and latest trends, including the intricacies of copyright in the digital world. Through real-life examples, she also illustrates how librarians can be advocates for a fair and balanced copyright law." Publisher's note

Crews, Kenneth D.
Copyright law for librarians and educators; creative strategies and practical solutions; with contributions from Dwayne K. Buttler . . . [et al.] 2nd ed. American Library Association 2006 141p il pa $45
346.04

1. Copyright
ISBN 0-8389-0906-X   LC 2005-13804
First published 2000 with title: Copyright essentials for librarians and educators
The author "addresses 18 areas of copyright in 5 parts. He begins with the scope of protectable works as well as works without copyright protection. Next, he discusses the rights of ownership, including duration and exceptions. He then explains fair use and its related guidelines. Part 4 focuses on the TEACH Act, Section 108, and responsibilities and liabilities. Lastly, Crews examines special issues such as the Digital Millennium Copyright Act." Booklist
Includes bibliographical references

347   Civil procedure and courts

Horn, Geoffrey
The Supreme Court; by Geoffrey M. Horn. World Almanac Library 2003 48p il (World Almanac Library of American government) lib bdg $30; pa $11.95 (5 and up)
347
ISBN 0-8368-5459-4 (lib bdg); 0-8368-5464-0 (pa)
LC 2002-38091

Contents: First Monday in October; What the Constitution says; Getting Confirmed; Arguing a case; The Chief Justices; Great dissenters; Finding a balance
This describes "the organization of the Court, the extent and limits of its powers, and how it checks and balances the president and Congress. . . . the history of the Court, how a person becomes a Supreme Court justice, how cases come before the Court, the role of the chief justice, and the importance of dissenting opinions." Publisher's note
"An amazing array of historical photos, statistics, primary-source documents, tables, graphs, and case studies supports the [text]." SLJ
Includes bibliographical references

352.23   Chief executives

Horn, Geoffrey
The presidency; by Geoffrey M. Horn. World Almanac Library 2003 48p il (World Almanac Library of American government) lib bdg $30; pa $11.95 (5 and up)
352.23

1. Presidents—United States 2. United States—Politics and government
ISBN 0-8368-5458-6 (lib bdg); 0-8368-5463-2 (pa)
LC 2002-33129

Contents: A presidential inauguration; What the Constitution says; Getting elected; Using presidential power; Life in the White House; The first family; Leaving office
This discusses the jobs of the president, the history of the presidency, presidential elections and the electoral college, the transfer of power from one president to the next, the vice presidency, life in the White House, impeachment, and the role of the first lady.
"An amazing array of historical photos, statistics, primary-source documents, tables, graphs, and case studies supports the [text]. Highly readable for casual information seekers, yet perfect for research." SLJ
Includes bibliographical references

355   Military science

Chrisp, Peter
Warfare; by Peter Chrisp. Lucent Books 2004 48p il map (Medieval realms) $28.70 (5 and up)
355

1. Military history 2. Medieval civilization 3. Knights and knighthood
ISBN 1-59018-537-4   LC 2003-18308
Contents: 1. Warrior nobles; War and the Church; The Normans; 1066: the year of three battles; Castles; 2. Holy war; Siege warfare; Warrior Monks of Outremer; Muslim holy war; Chivalry; The dead of Visby; 3. The Hundred Years War; English victory; The Campaign of Crecy; 4. The Black Prince's War, Chivalry in Decline; 5. Joan of Arc; Gunpowder; Swiss footsoldiers; 6. The Wars of the Roses; New armies
This briefly describes wars and warfare in the Middle Ages, including the Norman invasions, the Crusades, knighthood and chivalry, the Hundred Years War, the campaign of Crécy, the Black Prince's War, and the Wars of the Roses
Inlcudes glossary and bibliographical references

Clinton, Catherine
The Black soldier; 1492 to the present.
Houghton Mifflin 2000 117p il $17 (5 and up)
355
1. African American soldiers
ISBN 0-395-67722-X   LC 99-48935
Chronicles the military accomplishments of African
Americans who fought for the independence and preser-
vation of the United States while struggling to be treated
as equals and recognized for their valor and achievement
"Numerous black-and-white archival photographs and
reproductions appear throughout this well-organized,
readable resource." SLJ
Includes bibliographical references

Meltzer, Milton
Weapons & warfare; from the stone age to the
space age; illustrated by Sergio Martinez.
HarperCollins Pubs. 1996 85p il $16.95; lib bdg
$16.89 (5 and up)   **355**
1. Weapons 2. Military art and science
ISBN 0-06-024875-0; 0-06-024876-9 (lib bdg)
LC 95-48464
Highlights some weapons of war explaining how and
why they were developed, various responses people have
had to them, and the impact they have had upon society
"A concise, tautly written, introductory survey of an
ever-popular subject. In straightforward, seemingly effortless prose, Meltzer presents readers with essential facts
and figures." SLJ
Includes bibliographical references

355.7   Military installations

Adams, Simon
Castles & forts; foreword by Clifford J. Rogers.
Kingfisher (NY) 2003 63p il (Kingfisher
knowledge) $11.95 (5 and up)   **355.7**
1. Fortification 2. Castles
ISBN 0-7534-5620-6   LC 2003-44631
An illustrated exploration of a wide array of castles
and fortifications throughout the world, from Norman
mottes to Maori forts, including how and why they were
built and their importance in history
This title includes "stunning, captioned photos and illustrations that emphasize the many intriguing factual details in the text." SLJ
Includes glossary

355.8   Military equipment and supplies

Byam, Michéle
Arms & armor; written by Michéle Byam. rev
ed. DK Pub 2004 72p il (DK eyewitness books)
$15.99; lib bdg $19.99 (4 and up)   **355.8**
1. Weapons 2. Armor
ISBN 0-7566-0654-3; 0-7566-0653-5 (lib bdg)
LC 2004-558979
First published 1988 by Knopf

A photo essay examining the design, construction, and
uses of hand weapons and armor from a Stone Age axe
to the revolvers and rifles of the Wild West.

361.2   Social action

Lewis, Barbara A.
The kid's guide to social action; how to solve
the social problems you choose—and turn creative
thinking into positive action; edited by Pamela
Espeland and Caryn Pernu. rev, expanded, updated
ed. Free Spirit 1998 211p il pa $18.95 (4 and up)
361.2
1. Social problems
ISBN 1-57542-038-4   LC 98-11036
"A Do something! book"
First published 1991
Resource guide for children for learning political action skills that can help them make a difference in solving social problems at the community, state, and national
levels
"Clearly but informally written, the book is packed
with well-organized, practical information and includes
plenty of inspiring quotes and anecdotes. . . . This is an
exemplary reference and curricular resource that works
as enlightening browsing material as well." Bull Cent
Child Books
Includes bibliographical references

362.1   Physical illness

Gray, Susan Heinrichs
Living with cerebral palsy. Child's World 2003
32p il (Living well) lib bdg $25.64 (4 and up)
362.1
1. Cerebral palsy
ISBN 1-56766-101-7   LC 2002-2865
This title "leads off with an introduction to a young
person who has [cerebral palsy]. Subsequent chapters explain the physiology of the illness, what causes it, and
what it's like to live with it. [The concluding section
looks] at possible treatments and potential cures. The
[text is] clear and simple, double spaced, and punctuated
by colorful exemplary photos of kids dealing with the
disease. Gray provides a surprising amount of information and develops considerable empathy in readers." SLJ
Includes glossary and bibliographical references

Peacock, Carol Antoinette
Sugar was my best food; diabetes and me; [by]
Carol Antoinette Peacock, Adair Gregory, and
Kyle Carney Gregory; illustrated by Mary Jones.
Whitman, A. 1998 55p il $13.95; pa $4.95 (3-6)
362.1
1. Diabetes
ISBN 0-8075-7646-8; 0-8075-7648-4 (pa)
LC 97-27869
Adair Gregory, an eleven-year-old boy describes how
he learned that he had diabetes, the effect of this disease
on his life, and how he learned to cope with the changes

Peacock, Carol Antoinette—*Continued*
in his life

"What is truly exceptional here is the boy's emotional candor. . . . This appealing book is packaged with a colorful cover and has charming black-and-white illustrations. . . . A useful title for children with this disease and those who want to know more about it." SLJ

Rogers, Fred
Going to the hospital; photographs by Jim Judkis. Putnam 1988 unp il pa $5.99 hardcover o.p. (k-2)   **362.1**
1. Hospitals 2. Medical care
ISBN 0-698-11574-0 (pa)   LC 87-19170
Describes what happens during a stay in the hospital, including some of the common forms of medical treatment

"The author's style is just right for this level of information book: reassuring yet candid, matter-of-fact about those aspects of hospitalization that may be frightening or painful, yet not in itself alarming." Bull Cent Child Books

Rosenberg, Maxine B.
Mommy's in the hospital having a baby; photographs by Robert Maass. Clarion Bks. 1997 28p il $14.95 (k-1)   **362.1**
1. Childbirth 2. Hospitals 3. Infants
ISBN 0-395-71813-9   LC 96-12442
Describes the care that mothers and babies receive in the hospital and tells children what to expect if they go to visit their new brother or sister

"Full-color photographs of several families and babies appear throughout, and the tone is generally upbeat and positive." SLJ

Westcott, Patsy
Living with leukemia. Raintree Steck-Vaughn Pubs. 2000 32p il lib bdg $25.69 (3-5)
                                        362.1
1. Leukemia
ISBN 0-8172-5743-8   LC 99-27219
Describes the condition of leukemia, how it affects the lives of those who have it, and how to cope with or recover from it

"The author does a commendable job of explaining the nature of the disease and its symptoms in the types affecting the young subjects." Sci Books Films
Includes glossary and bibliographical references

362.292 Alcoholism

Pringle, Laurence P.
Drinking; a risky business; [by] Laurence Pringle. Morrow Junior Bks. 1997 112p il $16 (5 and up)   **362.292**
1. Alcoholism
ISBN 0-688-15044-6   LC 97-7807
Describes the history of alcohol, its effects on the body and personality, how to deal with peer pressure to drink, and how to get help for alcoholism

"Pringle's chapters on the history of the U.S. temperance movement and the economic side of the alcohol industry set his book apart. . . . Readable and well organized." SLJ
Includes glossary and bibliographical references

362.4 Problems of and services to people with physical disabilities

Alexander, Sally Hobart
Do you remember the color blue? and other questions kids ask about blindness. Viking 2000 78p il $16.99 (4 and up)   **362.4**
1. Blind
ISBN 0-670-88043-4   LC 99-34130
Children ask questions of an author who lost her vision at the age of twenty-seven, including "How did you become blind?" "How can you read?" and "Was it hard to be a parent when you couldn't see your kids?"

"The author's clearheaded and pragmatic approach . . . refreshingly resists mythologizing, and her balanced account will give kids a feeling for a life that on the one hand seems very different and on the other could be anybody's." Bull Cent Child Books

Haughton, Emma
Living with deafness. Raintree Steck-Vaughn Pubs. 2000 32p il lib bdg $25.69 (3-5)
                                        362.4
1. Deafness 2. Deaf
ISBN 0-8172-5742-X   LC 98-32231
The author offers an "explanation of the anatomy of the ear to help children understand various types of hearing loss and their causes, from infection to fluid in the ear. Hearing aids, cochlear implants, and TTYs are described, as are various methods of communication, such as sign language, finger spelling, and lip reading." SLJ
Includes glossary

Patent, Dorothy Hinshaw
The right dog for the job; Ira's path from service dog to guide dog; photographs by William Muñoz. Walker & Co. 2004 unp il $16.95 (2-4)
                                        362.4
1. Guide dogs 2. Animals—Training 3. Animals and the handicapped
ISBN 0-8027-8914-5   LC 2003-65785
This "photo-essay follows a puppy from his training to becoming a service dog to becoming a guide dog. . . . The author . . . manages to slip in an extraordinary amount of information about the raising and training of guide dogs. . . . Myriad full-color photographs that will capture kids' interest accompany the text." SLJ

Pimm, Paul
Living with cerebral palsy. Raintree Steck-Vaughn Pubs. 2000 32p il lib bdg $25.69 (3-5)   **362.4**
1. Cerebral palsy
ISBN 0-8172-5744-6   LC 99-27202

Pimm, Paul—*Continued*

Describes the varying effects of cerebral palsy, how different people manage to live with this condition, and where to get more information

The "book conveys a strong sense of individuals finding it difficult at first to cope with the limitations of the condition and accept the recommended therapies. . . . Young readers will become aware that those affected by cerebral palsy have many of the same desires to be liked, to learn, and to have fun as they themselves have." Sci Books Films

Includes glossary and bibliographical references

Westcott, Patsy

Living with blindness. Raintree Steck-Vaughn Pubs. 2000 32p il lib bdg $25.69 (3-5)

362.4

1. Blind

ISBN 0-8172-5741-1 LC 98-32230

Explains the condition of blindness, its possible causes, and how it affects the everyday lives of those who are dealing with it

"The explanations are clear and straightforward, without creating anxiety. . . . Future prospects for treating blindness and how those affected learn to cope are treated very sensitively." Sci Books Films

Includes glossary and bibliographical references

362.5 Problems of and services to poor people

Mason, Paul

Poverty; [by] Paul Mason. Heinemann Library 2006 48p il map (Planet under pressure) lib bdg $31.43 (4 and up) **362.5**

1. Poverty

ISBN 1-4034-7743-4 LC 2005017166

"Mason presents common factors for poverty worldwide, such as lack of money and education, as well as natural disasters. He also addresses the effects of outsourcing jobs from wealthier countries to poorer ones and how poverty affects environment. The book should make the global situation clearer. [This has] numerous quality color visuals, and sidebars. Up-to-date and informative." SLJ

Includes bibliographical references

362.7 Problems of and services to young people

Krementz, Jill

How it feels to be adopted. Knopf 1982 107p il pa $15 hardcover o.p. (4 and up) **362.7**

1. Adoption

ISBN 0-394-75853-6 (pa) LC 82-48011

"Nineteen youngsters ranging in age from 8 to 16 voice their feelings about being adopted. . . . Several of the accounts are by youngsters who 'have' found their birth mothers and are in the process of getting to know them. Single-parent adoptees are included, too." Booklist

This "is an important contribution to literature on adoption and the question of searching for biological parents." SLJ

Includes bibliographical references

Warren, Andrea

Orphan train rider; one boy's true story. Houghton Mifflin 1996 80p il $16; pa $7.95 (4 and up) **362.7**

1. Nailling, Lee, 1917- 2. Orphans 3. Abandoned children

ISBN 0-395-69822-7; 0-395-91362-4 (pa)

LC 94-43688

"From 1854 to 1930, the orphan trains took homeless children from cities in the East to new homes in the West, the Midwest, and the South. In Warren's book, one man's memories of his childhood abandonment and adoption give a personal slant on the subject. Chapters telling the story of Lee Nailing, who took an orphan train west in 1926, alternate with chapters filling in background information about the trains and the experiences of other children who rode them to their destinies." Booklist

"An excellent introduction to researching or discussing children-at-risk in an earlier generation. The book is clearly written and illustrated with numerous black-and-white photographs and reproductions." SLJ

Includes bibliographical references

We rode the orphan trains. Houghton Mifflin 2001 132p il $18; pa $8.95 (4 and up)

362.7

1. Orphans

ISBN 0-618-11712-1; 0-618-11712-1 (pa)

LC 00-47279

The author "interviews eight orphan train riders concerning their childhood experiences during 'the largest children's migration in history' between 1854 and 1929 as part of a 'placing out' program run by the Children's Aid Society of New York City." Publ Wkly

"This is powerful nonfiction for classroom and personal reading and for discussion." Booklist

Includes bibliographical references

363.1 Public safety programs

Mayell, Mark

Tragedies of space exploration. Lucent Books 2004 112p il (Manmade disasters) $27.45 (5 and up) **363.1**

1. Space vehicle accidents 2. Astronautics

ISBN 1-59018-508-0 LC 2003-15618

Contents: Into the dead zone; A pair of shuttle disasters; Rescue efforts; Challenging investigations; Preventing future accidents

Analyzes the inherent risks and dangers of human space exploration, from those that affect the health of astronauts to those that result in shuttle explosions, and examines ways of reducing safety-related incidents.

"Behind-the-headlines details are fresh and thought-provoking. . . . Halftone photographs and clear drawings speak to the reality of these events. . . . [This is] rich in content and detail." SLJ

363.2   Police services

Ingram, Scott
The FBI director. Blackbirch Press 2004 32p il
(America's leaders) lib bdg $22.45 (2-4)
                                           363.2
1. United States. Federal Bureau of Investigation
ISBN 1-4103-0090-0
Describes the duties and importance of the Director of
the FBI.

Jackson, Donna M.
The wildlife detectives; how forensic scientists
fight crimes against nature; by Donna M. Jackson;
photographs by Wendy Shattil and Bob Rozinski.
Houghton Mifflin 2000 47p il $16 (4 and up)
                                           363.2
1. National Fish and Wildlife Forensics Laboratory
2. Forensic sciences 3. Game protection
ISBN 0-395-86976-5   LC 99-34857
Describes how the wildlife detectives at the National
Fish and Wildlife Forensics Laboratory in Ashland, Oregon, analyze clues to catch and convict people responsible for crimes against animals
This book features "a smoothly written text that unfolds almost like a mystery novel. . . . Engaging full-
color photographs help clarify the text and will appeal to
browsers. A list of follow-up suggestions and a glossary
of terms are appended. A book that will be welcomed by
mystery fans and anyone who cares about animals."
Booklist

Mattern, Joanne
Forensics; written by Joanne Mattern.
Blackbirch Press 2004 48p il (Science on the
edge) $23.70 (5 and up)   **363.2**
1. Forensic sciences
ISBN 1-56711-785-6   LC 2003-12995
Contents: Forensics through history; Forensics today;
The future of forensics
Discusses the investigation by scientists and detectives
of deaths that occur under mysterious circumstances, in-
cluding how forensic science developed and how tech-
nology is transforming the field
Includes glossary and bibliographical references

Meltzer, Milton
Case closed; the real scoop on detective work.
Orchard Bks. 2001 88p il $18.95 (5 and up)
                                           363.2
1. Detectives 2. Police 3. Criminal investigation
ISBN 0-439-29315-4   LC 2001-16293
"Meltzer's book covers the day-to-day work of detectives, the crime lab, and investigators outside the police
force. Separate chapters provide information . . . on
handwriting and DNA analysis, organized crime, the Pin-
kertons, and the efforts of investigative journalists. . . .
A good choice for career reports or for anyone interested
in the fascinating world of criminal investigation." SLJ
Includes bibliographical references

Pentland, Peter
Forensic science; [by] Peter Pentland and Pennie
Stoyles. Chelsea House 2003 c2002 32p il
(Science and scientists) lib bdg $18.95 (4 and up)
                                           363.2
1. Forensic sciences 2. Criminal investigation
ISBN 0-7910-7010-7   LC 2002-1279
First published 2002 in Australia
Contents: Have you ever wondered . . .?; Questions
and clues; Tools of the trade; Would you make a good
witness?; Making faces; Leaving your fingerprints; Why
are other prints useful?; Is all blood the same?; What is
DNA profiling?; Clues in your cleaning up; Teeth tell
stories too; Paper and ink; Autopsies; Meet a forensic
technician; Forensic science timeline
Surveys some of the scientific principles used in investigating crime scenes and suspects
This title has "colorful illustrations and [uses] sidebars
to present interesting tidbits of relevant information." SLJ
Includes glossary

Platt, Richard
Forensics. Kingfisher 2005 63p il (Kingfisher
knowledge) $12.95 (5 and up)   **363.2**
1. Forensic sciences 2. Criminal investigation
ISBN 0-7534-5862-4
"This book looks at the . . . topic of collecting and
analyzing evidence. Each spread focuses on a subtopic
under the categories Signs of the Crime, Who Is It? and
Crime Lab. Abundant, closeup color photographs illustrate everything from ballistics to counterfeit money. . . .
This visually appealing book gives a basic overview of
everything that goes into investigating a crime and is
good for browsing." SLJ
Includes glossary

363.34   Disasters

Bryan, Nichol
Los Alamos wildfires. World Almanac Library
2004 48p il map (Environmental disasters) lib bdg
$29.27; pa $11.95 (5 and up)   **363.34**
1. Los Alamos wildfires 2. Wildfires
ISBN 0-8368-5507-8 (lib bdg); 0-8368-5514-0 (pa)
                             LC 2003-53536
Describes the events surrounding the wildfire that
raged in New Mexico in 2000 and the resulting debate
over the policy of prescribed burning, or purposely setting fires as a means of forest management.
Includes glossary and bibliographical references

Gibbons, Gail
Emergency! Holiday House 1994 unp il $16.95;
pa $6.95 (k-3)   **363.34**
1. Vehicles
ISBN 0-8234-1128-1; 0-8234-1201-6 (pa)
                             LC 94-2109
The author "covers emergency vehicles, from ambu-
lances and fire engines to helicopters, boats and planes,
distinguishing . . . between the different types of fire
trucks and including utility trucks sent out after storms."

Gibbons, Gail—Continued
Bull Cent Child Books
"Gibbons's stylistic, flat, colorful illustrations accurately depict the events described in the text and add more for observant readers to interpret." SLJ

Langley, Andrew
Hurricanes, tsunamis, and other natural disasters; [by] Andrew Langley. 1st ed. Kingfisher 2006 63p il map (Kingfisher knowledge) $12.95 (5 and up)
363.34
1. Natural disasters
ISBN 978-0-7534-5975-1; 0-7534-5975-2
LC 2005027200
This briefly describes such natural disasters as hurricanes, tsunamis, avalanches, brush fires, earthquakes, floods, tornadoes, drought and famine, pandemics, with many color illustrations and maps.
Includes glossary and bibliographical references

Levey, Richard H.
Dust bowl! the 1930s black blizzards; by Richard H. Levey; consultant, Daniel H. Franck. Bearport Pub 2005 32p il (X-treme disasters that changed America) lib bdg $23.96 (1-3)
363.34
1. Great Plains—History 2. Dust storms
ISBN 1-59716-007-5
LC 2004-20742
Contents: A hurricane filled with dirt; Deadly drifts; The dust bowl; A dangerous practice; Dry as dust; Sizzling; Not just people; The dust bowl sweeps a nation; A better way; Heading west; Keep out!; End and a beginning; Disaster data
"Starting with Black Sunday, the day a black storm cloud of dirt raced across the Great Plains, Levey does an excellent job of explaining the physical properties of the dust storms that destroyed the country's midsection as well as the psychological hardships that the blizzards left in their wake. He manages to do all this in short, relatively simple sentences that are bolstered by an attractive, accessible design." Booklist
Includes bibliographical references

Markle, Sandra
Rescues! Millbrook Press 2006 88p il map lib bdg 25.26 (4 and up)
363.34
1. Rescue work 2. Survival after airplane accidents, shipwrecks, etc.
ISBN 978-0-8225-3413-6 (lib bdg)
LC 2005-09707
"From the collapse of a Pennsylvania coal mine in 2002 to the tsunami that struck 11 countries in 2004 to Hurricane Katrina in 2005, the 11 disasters Markle describes are straight from news headlines. In this full-color photo-essay, she uses individual experiences of rescue and survival to bring each drama close." Booklist
Includes bibliographical references

Miller, Mara
Hurricane Katrina strikes the Gulf Coast; disaster & survival; [by] Mara Miller. Enslow Publishers 2006 48p il map (Deadly disasters) $23.93 (4 and up)
363.34
1. Hurricane Katrina, 2005 2. Hurricanes 3. Rescue work
ISBN 0-7660-2803-8
LC 2005030989
Contents: Katrina gains strength; What is a hurricane?; Katrina strikes; New Orleans floods; After Katrina; The next hurricane
Includes glossary and bibliographical references

363.6 Public utilities and related services

Dalgleish, Sharon
Saving water. Chelsea House 2003 32p il (Our world: our future) $18.95 (3-6)
363.6
1. Water supply
ISBN 0-7910-7016-6
LC 2002-2522
Contents: Our world; Our future; Weird water; Living in a watery world; Water and weather; Storing water; Using water at home; Wastewater down the drain; Water for factories; Thirsty cows and crops; From drains to waterways; Dissolving—good and bad; Project water; Think globally; Sustaining our world
This "concentrates on the need to preserve the fresh water available to sustain life and to minimize both use and pollution. . . . The busy pages with full-color photos, diagrams, and varied typeface will appeal to both browsers and report writers." SLJ
Includes glossary

Kerley, Barbara
A cool drink of water. National Geographic Soc. 2002 unp il map $16.95; pa $7.95 (k-3)
363.6
1. Water supply 2. Water
ISBN 0-7922-6723-0; 0-7922-5489-9 (pa)
LC 2001-2479
Depicts people around the world collecting, chilling, and drinking water
"Children will be entranced by the beautiful images of a basic substance that connects us all. Excellent for cross-cultural discussions." Booklist

363.7 Environmental problems

Bang, Molly
Nobody particular; one woman's fight to save the bays. Holt & Co. 2000 46p il $18 (4 and up)
363.7
1. Wilson, Diane 2. Pollution 3. Environmental protection
ISBN 0-8050-5396-4
LC 99-33348
"Bang tells the story of activist Diane Wilson, a commercial shrimper who almost single-handedly forced Formosa Plastics to agree to stop polluting the Texas bays." Horn Book Guide

Bang, Molly—*Continued*

"The story, in hand-lettered text and speech balloons, is in bordered squares containing panels of black-and-white cartoon art, which are printed over double-page spreads of beautifully executed full-color depictions of the bays' ecosystem, chemical pollution, and shrimp farming. . . . A riveting, emotional story." Booklist

Bowden, Rob

Waste; by Rob Bowden. KidHaven Press 2004 48p il (Sustainable world) lib bdg $23.70 (5 and up)   **363.7**

1. Refuse and refuse disposal
ISBN 0-7377-1902-8   LC 2003-52951

This "discusses innovations in reuse and recycling, ingenious ways to use what would be discarded, and changes in taxation policy. The many full-color photographs clarify the [text]. [This] will be highly useful for both reports and in classroom discussions." SLJ

Includes bibliographical references

Brown, Laurene Krasny

Dinosaurs to the rescue! a guide to protecting our planet; [by] Laurie Krasny Brown and Marc Brown. Little, Brown 1992 unp il pa $7.99 hardcover o.p. (k-3)   **363.7**

1. Environmental protection
ISBN 0-316-11397-2 (pa)   LC 91-27177

"Joy Street books"

Text and illustrations of dinosaur characters introduce the earth's major environmental problems and suggest ways children can help

"Information is presented in a straightforward way, enlivened by energetic, brightly colored, cartoon-style illustrations. Irreverent and often humorous comments . . . appear in conversational balloons and help to lighten the decidedly earnest tone of the narrative. With plenty of practical suggestions and projects . . . this book is an ideal and upbeat way to introduce the problems in our environment and to inspire children to make a difference in the health of our planet." Horn Book

Bryan, Nichol

Bhopal; chemical plant accident. World Almanac Library 2004 48p il map (Environmental disasters) lib bdg $29.27; pa $11.95 (5 and up)   **363.7**

1. Chemical industry—Accidents 2. Bhopal Union Carbide Plant Disaster, Bhopal, India, 1984
ISBN 0-8368-5503-5 (lib bdg); 0-8368-5510-8 (pa)   LC 2003-49718

Presents an account of the 1984 chemical accident at the Union Carbide plant in Bhopal, India, and its aftermath

Includes glossary and bibliographical references

Chernobyl; nuclear disaster. World Almanac Library 2004 48p il map (Environmental disasters) lib bdg $29.27; pa $11.95 (5 and up)   **363.7**

1. Chernobyl Nuclear Accident, Chernobyl, Ukraine, 1986 2. Nuclear power plants—Environmental aspects
ISBN 0-8368-5504-3 (lib bdg); 0-8368-5511-6 (pa)   LC 2003-42291

Discusses the disastrous 1986 accident at the Chernobyl nuclear power plant in the Ukraine.

Includes glossary and bibliographical references

Danube; cyanide spill; by Nichol Bryan. World Almanac Library 2004 48p il map (Environmental disasters) lib bdg $29.27; pa $11.95 (5 and up)   **363.7**

1. Chemical spills 2. Water pollution
ISBN 0-8368-5505-1 (lib bdg); 0-8368-5512-4 (pa)   LC 2003-57694

Discusses the disastrous year 2000 overflow of a Romanian reservoir that held heavy metals and cyanide, pouring the deadly mix into rivers that feed the Danube and killing all living creatures in its path.

Includes glossary and bibliographical references

Exxon Valdez oil spill. World Almanac Library 2004 48p il map (Environmental disasters) lib bdg $29.27; pa $11.95 (5 and up)   **363.7**

1. Exxon Valdez (Ship) 2. Oil spills
ISBN 0-8368-5506-X (lib bdg); 0-8368-5513-2 (pa)   LC 2003-47991

Describes the oil tanker Exxon Valdez, the events that led up to its disastrous oil spill in 1989, and the effects of the spill on the Alaskan environment.

This is "well-illustrated. . . . [It does] a fine job of placing [the] disaster within a larger context by including detailed background about America's industrial and environmental history; quotes from eyewitnesses, politicians, and journalists; and clear explanations of the changes in policy that [the] disaster instigated." Booklist

Includes glossary and bibliographical references

Love Canal; pollution crisis. World Almanac Library 2004 48p il map (Environmental disasters) lib bdg $29.27; pa $11.95 (5 and up)   **363.7**

1. Love Canal Chemical Waste Landfill (Niagara Falls, N.Y.) 2. Pollution
ISBN 0-8368-5508-6 (lib bdg); 0-8368-5515-9 (pa)   LC 2003-57162

Traces the history and eventual cleanup of the ecological disaster known as Love Canal, which resulted from building a neighborhood over a chemical dumpsite that poisoned the environment and endangered the health of residents.

This is "well-illustrated. . . . [It does] a fine job of placing [the] disaster within a larger context by including detailed background about America's industrial and environmental history; quotes from eyewitnesses, politicians, and journalists; and clear explanations of the changes in policy that [the] disaster instigated." Booklist

Includes glossary and bibliographical references

Dalgleish, Sharon

Cleaning the air. Chelsea House 2003 32p il (Our world: our future) $18.95 (3-6)   **363.7**

1. Air pollution
ISBN 0-7910-7019-0   LC 2002-2536

Contents: Our world; Our future; Air—it's a gas!; Living in the troposphere; Holes in the ozone layer; The power of photosynthesis; Cycling carbon; Firing up the

Dalgleish, Sharon—*Continued*
factories; Electricity at home; Burning up the highway;
Pardon my methane; Acid from the sky; Project air;
Think globally; Sustaining our world

This book is "well-written, thought-provoking, motivating. . . . The illustrations clarify some difficult concepts as well as keep the reader's attention." Libr Media
Connect

Includes glossary

Gifford, Clive
Pollution; [by] Clive Gifford. Heinemann
Library 2006 48p il map (Planet under pressure)
lib bdg $31.43 (4 and up)   **363.7**
1. Pollution
ISBN 1-4034-7742-6   LC 2005017064
"Gifford discusses the many types of pollution, global
warming and the greenhouse effect, the worldwide impact on human lives and well-being, and possible solutions. . . . [This has] numerous quality color visuals, and
sidebars. Up-to-date and informative." SLJ

Includes bibliographical references

Glaser, Linda
Compost! growing gardens from your garbage;
pictures by Anca Hariton. Millbrook Press 1996
unp il lib bdg $22.90; pa $8.95 (k-2)
                                              363.7
1. Compost
ISBN 1-56294-659-5 (lib bdg); 0-76130-030-9 (pa)
                                     LC 95-10421
"A child tells how her family uses leftovers to create
compost, explaining how garbage, added to dirt in a bin,
makes rich soil for growing healthy plants. The book begins and ends with a picture of the family garden in full
glory. Soft watercolor washes and borders grace the
book's pages. 'Questions and Answers about Compost-
ing' fact sheet included." Horn Book Guide

Hall, Eleanor J.
Recycling; . KidHaven Press 2004 c2005 48p il
(Our environment) $23.70 (5 and up)
                                              363.7
1. Recycling
ISBN 0-7377-1517-0   LC 2003-21682
Contents: What is recycling?; The challenges of
recycling; The benefits of recycling; What does the future hold?
"The liberal use of vibrant colors, the inclusion of a
photograph or diagram on most pages, and the generous
print size will appeal to reluctant readers. [This title] will
help students examine cause and effect (and possible solutions), and challenge them to live green." SLJ
Includes glossary and bibliographical references

Hirschmann, Kris
Pollution. Kidhaven Press 2004 c2005 48p il
(Our environment) $23.70 (5 and up)
                                              363.7
1. Pollution
ISBN 0-7377-1563-4
Contents: What is pollution?; Air pollution; Water pol-
lution; Garbage

This briefly describes the sources and effects of air
and water pollution and refuse disposal and suggests possible solutions.

Includes glossary and bibliographical references

Martin, Laura C.
Recycled crafts box; [by] Laura C. Martin.
Storey Publishing 2004 88p il $19.95; pa $10.95
(3-6)   **363.7**
1. Recycling 2. Handicraft
ISBN 1-58017-523-6; 1-58017-522-8 (pa)
                                     LC 2003-16703
Contents: All about garbage; Getting started; Paper;
Plastics; Meta; Fabric and clothing; Glass

Discusses recycling and provides information and instructions for making art projects from a variety of
recycled materials

"Illustrated with cheerful cartoon drawings and color
photos of the finished projects, and bolstered by many
resource lists, this is a surprisingly attractive, substantive
offering." Booklist

Oxlade, Chris
Global warming. Bridgestone Bks. 2003 32p il
(Our planet in peril) lib bdg $22.60 (5 and up)
                                              363.7
1. Greenhouse effect
ISBN 0-7368-1361-6   LC 2002-9823
Contents: About global warming; The atmosphere and
the weather; The greenhouse effect; Greenhouse gases;
Upsetting the balance; Gathering evidence; Changing climates; More causes of climate change; Modeling the future; Effects of global warming; Problems for us; Stopping global warming; Waking up to global warming

"Double-page chapters introduce topics such as 'The
atmosphere and the weather' . . . through brief paragraphs of information. Numerous colorful photographs,
graphs, and diagrams with informative captions add details on each spread." SLJ

Includes bibliographical references

Parks, Peggy J.
Global warming. KidHaven Press 2004 48p il
(Our environment) $23.70 (5 and up)
                                              363.7
1. Greenhouse effect
ISBN 0-7377-1822-6   LC 2002-156050
Contents: What is global warming?; Caused by humans or caused by nature?; Signs and effects of global
warming; What can be done?
"The liberal use of vibrant colors, the inclusion of a
photograph or diagram on most pages, and the generous
print size will appeal to reluctant readers. [This title] will
help students examine cause and effect (and possible solutions), and challenge them to live green." SLJ
Includes glossary and bibliographical references

Pringle, Laurence P.

The environmental movement; from its roots to the challenges of a new century; [by] Laurence Pringle. Morrow Junior Bks. 2000 144p $16.95 (5 and up)   **363.7**

1. Environmental movement 2. Environmental protection

ISBN 0-688-15626-6   LC 99-32110

"Topics covered include the rise of the conservation movement, the roles of legislation, big business, and eco-warriors. There's also a brief look at the struggles ahead. . . . Well-chosen photographs and a comprehensive resource section round out this engaging, useful title." Booklist

Includes bibliographical references

Global warming; the threat of Earth's changing climate; [by] Laurence Pringle. SeaStar Bks. 2001 48p il $16.95; pa $6.95 (4 and up)   **363.7**

1. Greenhouse effect

ISBN 1-58717-009-4; 1-58717-28-3 (pa)

       LC 00-63740

Replaces the edition published 1990 by Arcade Pub.

"Pringle covers the science of global warming . . . from detailed discussion of atmospheric phenomena to concerns about human production of emissions." Horn Book Guide

"Well-illustrated . . . this offers students a solid, factual overview of the subject." Booklist

Includes glossary and bibliographical references

Scarborough, Kate

Nuclear waste. Bridgestone Bks. 2003 32p il (Our planet in peril) lib bdg $22.60 (5 and up)   **363.7**

1. Radioactive waste disposal 2. Nuclear energy

ISBN 0-7368-1362-4   LC 2002-10139

Contents: What is nuclear waste?; The world's energy needs; Fossil fuels; Nuclear energy; Background radiation; Nuclear power stations; Nuclear waste; Low level and intermediate waste; High level waste; Further research; Nuclear fusion; Public concerns; The future of nuclear power

"Chapters introduce topics such as . . . 'What is nuclear power?' through brief paragraphs of information. Numerous colorful photographs, graphs, and diagrams with informative captions add details on each spread." SLJ

Includes glossary and bibliographical references

363.8   Food supply

Bowden, Rob

Food and farming; by Rob Bowden. KidHaven Press 2004 il map (Sustainable world) lib bdg $23.70 (5 and up)   **363.8**

1. Food 2. Agriculture

ISBN 0-7377-1899-4   LC 2003-52952

This "first presents conventional techniques of food production, but focuses primarily on sustainable agriculture methods. . . . Bowden writes with admirable simplicity about complicated subjects, and he's careful to separate facts from opinions when he quotes others. . . . [The book includes] excellent color photos, and gripping statistics." Booklist

Includes glossary and bibliographical references

364   Criminology

Lane, Brian

Crime and detection; written by Brian Lane. Dorling Kindersley 2005 61p il (DK eyewitness books) $15.99   **364**

1. Crime 2. Forensic sciences 3. Criminal investigation

ISBN 0-7566-1386-8

First published 1998 by Knopf

Explores the many different methods used to solve crimes, covering such topics as criminal, detectives, and forensics.

364.1   Criminal offenses

St. George, Judith

In the line of fire; presidents' lives at stake. Holiday House 1999 144p il lib bdg $22.95 (4 and up)   **364.1**

1. Presidents—United States—Assassination

ISBN 0-8234-1428-0   LC 98-39030

"The first of the two main sections concerns the four slain U.S. presidents as well as their respective assassins, and also discusses the effects of these fatal events on the country. Each chapter preface relays the day's events preceding the murder in a dramatic fashion. The second half concerns the assassination attempts on six presidents and their would-be assassins. St. George includes intriguing anecdotes. . . . Nicely placed illustrations and photos add power to the text." SLJ

Includes bibliographical references

370   Education

Coles, Robert

The story of Ruby Bridges; illustrated by George Ford. Scholastic 1995 unp il lib bdg $15.95 (1-3)   **370**

1. Bridges, Ruby 2. School integration 3. New Orleans (La.)—Race relations

ISBN 0-590-57281-4   LC 92-33674

"Ruby Bridges was the first African American child to attend an all-white elementary school in New Orleans in 1960. Coles tells the brief story of her daily walk past . . . white adults, her time alone with her teacher in an otherwise empty classroom because white parents kept their children home, and the . . . moment when she prays in front of the . . . crowd for God to forgive them." SLJ

Coles "tells one girl's heroic story, part of the history of ordinary people who have changed the world. . . . Ford's moving watercolor paintings mixed with acrylic ink are predominantly in sepia shades of brown and red. They capture the physical warmth of Ruby's family and community, the immense powers against her, and her shining inner strength." Booklist

O'Neill, Laurie

Little Rock; the desegregation of Central High. Millbrook Press 1994 64p il (Spotlight on American history) lib bdg $24.90 (5 and up)

370

1. Central High School (Little Rock, Ark.) 2. School integration 3. African Americans—Civil rights 4. Arkansas—Race relations

ISBN 1-56294-354-5   LC 93-29057

This is an "account of a year in the life of the group of nine brave African-American teenagers who integrated Central High School in Little Rock, Arkansas, in 1957. O'Neill's well-written narrative documents human nature at its best and worst." SLJ

Includes bibliographical references

370.9   Education--Historical and geographic treatment

Bial, Raymond

One-room school. Houghton Mifflin 1999 48p il $15 (3-5)   **370.9**

1. Schools—United States—History 2. Education—United States—History

ISBN 0-395-90514-1   LC 98-43241

Presents a brief history of the one-room schools that existed in the United States from the 1700s to the 1950s

"Clear, beautifully composed photos on every page transport readers back to bygone days." Booklist

Includes bibliographical references

Fisher, Leonard Everett

The schoolmasters; written & illustrated by Leonard Everett Fisher. Benchmark Bks. 1997 47p il $21.36 (4 and up)   **370.9**

1. Teaching 2. Education—United States—History 3. United States—Social life and customs—1600-1775, Colonial period

ISBN 0-7614-0480-5   LC 96-16609

A reissue of the title first published 1967 by Watts

An account of the historical background of education in the United States, telling what the colonial schoolmasters were like, where they taught, how they taught, and what they taught

Loeper, John J.

Going to school in 1776. Atheneum Pubs. 1973 79p il $16 (4 and up)   **370.9**

1. Education—United States—History 2. United States—Social life and customs—1600-1775, Colonial period 3. Schools—United States—History

ISBN 0-689-30089-1   LC 72-86940

The author tells what it was like to be a child and to go to school in America in 1776. He describes children's dress, schools, teachers, school books, lessons, discipline and after-school recreation

Includes bibliographical references

371.1   Teachers, teaching, and related activities

Harada, Violet H.

Inquiry learning through librarian-teacher partnerships; [by] Violet H. Harada and Joan M. Yoshina. Linworth Pub 2004 172p il pa $39.95

371.1

1. Teaching teams 2. School libraries

ISBN 1-58683-134-8   LC 2004-662

"The authors describe what happens in an inquiry-based classroom and library media center and show teachers/librarians how to develop a curriculum that incorporates essential questions and important habits of mind, all aligned with content standards. . . . The volume contains everything a teacher-librarian team would need to create, teach, research, and assess major interdisciplinary units." SLJ

Includes bibliographical references

371.2   School administration

Aillaud, Cindy Lou

Recess at 20 below. Alaska Northwest Books 2005 unp il $15.95; pa $8.95 (k-3)   **371.2**

1. Schools—Alaska 2. Alaska

ISBN 0-88240-604-3; 0-88240-609-4 (pa)

"Aillaud, who wrote the text and took the photos here, teaches elementary physical education in Delta Junction, Alaska, a town at the end of the Alaska Highway, above the Arctic Circle. By focusing on one school activity—outdoor recess . . . she demonstrates how cold things get and how kids deal with it and still have plenty of fun. . . . Twenty-five color photographs capture marvelous details." Booklist

371.3   Methods of instruction and study

Barron, Ann E.

Technologies for education; a practical guide; [by] Ann E. Barron [et al.] 4th ed. Libraries Unlimited 2002 234p il pa $48   **371.3**

1. Teaching—Aids and devices

ISBN 1-56308-779-0   LC 2001-50746

First published 1993 with title: New technologies for education

This discusses such educational technologies as graphics and digital audio

"This useful, practical guide will be a boon for teachers and librarians. . . . The book is clearly written and easy to understand." Libr Media Connect

Includes bibliographical references

371.3025   Audiovisual materials-- Directories

AV market place. Information Today il pa $195
371.3025
1. Audiovisual materials—Directories
ISSN 1044-0445
Annual. First published 1969 with title: Audiovisual market place. Subtitle varies
"The complete business directory of: audio, audio visual, computer systems, film, video, programming—with industry yellow pages." Title page

371.5   School discipline

Bott, C. J.
The bully in the book and in the classroom; [by] C. J. Bott. Scarecrow Press 2004 185p il pa $30
371.5
1. Bullies 2. Children's literature—Bibliography 3. Young adult literature—Bibliography
ISBN 0-8108-5048-6   LC 2004-8536
This "was written to address the . . . problem of bullying in the halls, offices, and classrooms of our schools and to help educators know what to look for and how to react when they witness harassment. . . . Bott also reviews books recommended for each reading level. . . . Each review contains . . . [a] summary, activities, and quotes from the book." Publisher's note
"The volume may be useful as a beginning effort in dealing with this very real and pervasive problem." SLJ
Includes bibliographical references

Winkler, Kathleen
Bullying; how to deal with taunting, teasing, and tormenting. Enslow Pubs. 2005 104p il (Issues in focus today) lib bdg $31.93 (5 and up)
371.5
1. Bullies
ISBN 0-7660-2355-9
"Winkler examines the impact of bullying on both the victim and the victimizer. In straightforward and clear language, she uses conversations with teens, quotes from magazine and newspaper articles, interviews with professional therapists and school officials, plus excerpts from titles such as Rachel Simmons's *Odd Girl Out: The Hidden Culture of Aggression in Girls* (Harcourt, 2002) to provide a readable discussion of what bullying is, why bullies do what they do, and why victims take it." SLJ
Includes glossary and bibliographical references

371.9   Special education

Brinkerhoff, Shirley
Why can't I learn like everyone else? youth with learning disabilities; by Shirley Brinkerhoff. Mason Crest Publishers 2004 127p il (Youth with special needs) $24.95 (5 and up)   **371.9**
1. Learning disabilities
ISBN 1-59084-730-X   LC 2003-18438

Contents: Changes; Learning to get by; Anger; Another world; Conflicts; Tensions; The power of persistence; Hope
"Charlie Begay, an eighth-grade Navajo student in New Mexico who cannot read due to dyslexia, describes his personal journey of embarrassment, frustration, and low self-esteem. Following the fictional narrative is factual material about learning disabilities, covering terminology, possible signs, diagnosis, the law, coping strategies, and success stories." SLJ
"The writing is straightforward but not simplistic and liberally illustrated with photographs and occasional diagrams." Voice Youth Advocates
Includes bibliographical references

Kent, Deborah
Athletes with disabilities. Watts 2003 63p il lib bdg $24; pa $8.95 (4 and up)   **371.9**
1. Sports for the handicapped
ISBN 0-531-12019-8 (lib bdg); 0-531-16664-3 (pa)
     LC 2002-8883
"Watts library"
Contents: The love of the game; Beating the odds; Brave in the attempt; Going for the Gold; A level playing field
Explores the people and events involved in sports competitions for people with disabilities and discusses people with disabilities who play professional sports
"Information is effectively conveyed through clear, straightforward prose and accounts of individual athletes. . . . [This is] informative, often inspirational and thought-provoking." Booklist
Includes bibliographical references

Stanley, Jerry
Children of the Dust Bowl; the true story of the school at Weedpatch Camp. Crown 1992 85p il maps pa $9.95 hardcover o.p. (5 and up)
371.9
1. Migrant labor 2. Great Depression, 1929-1939 3. Education—Social aspects
ISBN 0-517-88094-6 (pa)   LC 92-393
Describes the plight of the migrant workers who traveled from the Dust Bowl to California during the Depression and were forced to live in a federal labor camp and discusses the school that was built for their children
"Stanley's text is a compelling document. . . . The story is inspiring and disturbing, and Stanley has recorded the details with passion and dignity." Booklist
Includes bibliographical references

372   Elementary education

Whitin, David Jackman
New visions for linking literature and mathematics; [by] David J. Whitin, Phyllis Whitin; [with a foreword by Judith Lindfors] National Council of Teachers of Mathematics 2004 170p il pa $32.95   **372**
1. Mathematics—Study and teaching 2. Literature—Study and teaching
ISBN 0-8141-3348-7   LC 2003023544

Whitin, David Jackman—*Continued*

"The authors of this book offer teachers of grades K-6 . . . ideas for integrating literature and mathematics, including specific criteria for evaluating mathematics-related books; practical discussions about books and strategies for introducing them to children." Publisher's note

Includes bibliographical references

372.2 Specific levels of elementary education

Howe, James

When you go to kindergarten; text by James Howe; photographs by Betsy Imershein. rev & updated ed. Morrow Junior Bks. 1994 unp il $15; pa $5.95 (k-1)   **372.2**

1. Kindergarten

ISBN 0-688-12912-9; 0-688-14387-3 (pa)

LC 93-48152

First published 1986 by Knopf

"The author tells youngsters what school might look like and how they might get there, and describes some of the possible activities. . . . Multicultural children are welcomed and taught by both male and female teachers. Smiling, busy kids engaged in many activities portray school as an exciting, interesting, and happy place." SLJ

372.4 Reading

Bouchard, Dave

The gift of reading; [by] David Bouchard, with Wendy Sutton. Orca Bk. Pubs. 2001 158p il pa $16.95   **372.4**

1. Reading 2. Books and reading

ISBN 1-55143-214-5   LC 2001-92682

This "overview of what young people need to become independent readers . . . targets families, teachers, and school administrators, claiming that nothing extravagant is required to promote reading. . . . All groups will find the grade-level reading lists and abundant literacy strategies helpful." Voice Youth Advocates

Bradbury, Judy

Children's book corner; a read-aloud resource with tips, techniques, and plans for teachers, librarians, and parents: level grades 1 and 2; photographs by Gene Bradbury. Libraries Unlimited 2004 245p il pa $32   **372.4**

1. Reading 2. Books and reading

ISBN 1-59158-047-1

Also available volumes for Grades 3 and 4 and PreK to K

This book promotes "the reading aloud of quality picture books and early chapter books by teachers, librarians, and parents. 'Read-Aloud Plans' for 53 different titles include suggestions for introducing each book, for questions to pose while reading, and for follow-up discussion. . . . This fresh and original book should be a winner for schools, libraries, and homes." Booklist

Includes bibliographical references

Hauser, Jill Frankel

Wow! I'm reading! fun activities to make reading happen; illustrations by Stan Jaskiel. Williamson 2000 141p il (Williamson Little Hands book) pa $12.95 (k-2)   **372.4**

1. Reading

ISBN 1-88559-341-4   LC 99-89816

"An introductory message for adults provides insight into the importance of letter recognition, phonetics, and writing in the reading process. The reading-readiness activities are simple enough for youngsters to follow on their own, but also present opportunities that will encourage interaction between adult and child. . . . An inviting and useful tool for parents and teachers working with little readers-to-be." SLJ

Herb, Steven

Using children's books in preschool settings; a how-to-do-it manual; [by] Steven Herb and Sara Willoughby-Herb. Neal-Schuman 1994 181p (How-to-do-it manuals for school and public librarians) pa $45.25   **372.4**

1. Reading 2. Books and reading

ISBN 1-55570-156-6   LC 94-8238

Includes sections on child and language development, literary genres and setting up a storybook corner. Problems posed by restless listeners, disliked books, and language barriers are addressed

"The treatment is a nice mixture of the theoretical and the pragmatic." Bull Cent Child Books

Includes bibliographical references

Knowles, Elizabeth

Talk about books! a guide for book clubs, literature circles, and discussion groups, grades 4-8. Libraries Unlimited 2003 147p il pa $30   **372.4**

1. Books and reading

ISBN 1-59158-023-4   LC 2003-51582

"Each of the fifteen chapters focuses on a different book that serves as a prototype for a particular subject or genre. . . . Each focal book is briefly summarized, followed by a bit of biographical information about its author. Then a list of discussion questions is offered. . . . The questions nicely probe both concrete and abstract understanding of the book. . . . In addition, each chapter includes activities for all areas of the curriculum, an annotated list of related books, an annotated list of the author's other works, dozens of Web site suggestions, and the publisher's information." Voice Youth Advocates

Includes bibliographical references

Raines, Shirley C.

Story stretchers for infants, toddlers, and twos; experiences, activities, and games for popular children's books; [by] Shirley Raines, Karen Miller, and Leah Curry-Rood; illustrations by Kathy Dobbs. Gryphon House 2002 240p il pa $19.95   **372.4**

1. Preschool education

ISBN 0-87659-274-4   LC 2002-4803

Raines, Shirley C.—*Continued*

"A book that offers numerous activities as well as a wealth of information for anyone instituting early childhood programs. The first chapter discusses emergent literacy and the role books play in this critical time. Sections on 'making the right selections' and 'techniques for reading books' will be especially valuable to new librarians, early childhood teachers, and other adults interested in promoting age-appropriate material. . . . The activities . . . include object play, music, movement, and more." SLJ

Includes bibliographical references

372.6   Language arts (Communication skills)

Bauer, Caroline Feller

Caroline Feller Bauer's new handbook for storytellers; with stories, poems, magic, and more; illustrations by Lynn Gates Bredeson. American Lib. Assn. 1993 550p il music pa $45 hardcover o.p.   **372.6**

1. Storytelling
ISBN 0-8389-0664-8 (pa)   LC 93-14959
First published 1977 with title: Handbook for storytellers

Bauer's introduction "incorporates a broad variety of media and props into the storytelling process. . . . Beginners and veterans alike can benefit from this practical approach to program planning and promotion, story selection and preparation, and activities extending various themes or occasions." Bull Cent Child Books

Includes bibliographical references

The poetry break; an annotated anthology with ideas for introducing children to poetry; illustrations by Edith Bingham. Wilson, H.W. 1995 xxv, 347p il $55   **372.6**

1. Poetry—Study and teaching
ISBN 0-8242-0852-8   LC 93-42069
This book serves as a "do-it-yourself poetry-break packet, including ideas for presentation, settings, and general poetry activities; she includes a good 250 pages of poems, suggesting a poem-specific project or topic-extending book after most of the verses." Bull Cent Child Books

Includes bibliographical references

Bruchac, Joseph

Tell me a tale; a book about storytelling. Harcourt Brace & Co. 1997 117p $16 (5 and up)   **372.6**

1. Storytelling 2. Folklore
ISBN 0-15-201221-4   LC 96-21697
Storyteller Joseph Bruchac incorporates many of his favorite tales in this discussion of the four basic components of storytelling: listening, observing, remembering, and sharing

"Youngsters will find this to be a clear guide to the age-old art form. A 'Note to Parents' about the power of stories, as well as the book's readable style, make this a useful resource for teachers and librarians as well." SLJ

Includes bibliographical references

Buzzeo, Toni

Terrific connections with authors, illustrators, and storytellers; real space and virtual links; by Toni Buzzeo, Jane Kurtz. Libraries Unlimited 1999 185p pa $26.50   **372.6**

1. Children's literature—Study and teaching 2. Book talks 3. Internet
ISBN 1-56308-744-8   LC 99-28468
This book explains "how to choose the right guest, successfully contact bookpeople to make arrangements for your event, and make the most of the visit with curriculum connections and learning extensions." Publisher's note

Includes bibliographical references

Champlin, Connie

Storytelling with puppets. 2nd ed. American Lib. Assn. 1998 249p il pa $35   **372.6**

1. Storytelling 2. Puppets and puppet plays
ISBN 0-8389-0709-1   LC 97-24810
First published 1985 under the authorship of Connie Champlin and Nancy Renfro

This book covers "such topics as puppet types and styles, developing a puppet collection, participatory storytelling, and presentation formats. . . . A very useful choice for professional shelves in both school and public libraries." Booklist

Includes bibliographical references

Ellis, Sarah

From reader to writer; teaching writing through classic children's books. Douglas & McIntyre 2000 176p $24.95   **372.6**

1. Rhetoric—Study and teaching 2. Children's literature—Study and teaching
ISBN 0-88899-372-2
"A Groundwood book"

The author discusses the work of seventeen British, Canadian and American authors of children's literature. "With each classic book, there's a 'sneak preview' (i.e., booktalk), a suggested read-aloud, exercises to help students and adult writers find their own stories, and a short annotated bibliography of related children's books." Booklist

Greene, Ellin

Storytelling; art and technique; foreword by Augusta Baker. 3rd ed. Bowker 1996 xxi, 333p il $39   **372.6**

1. Storytelling
ISBN 0-8352-3458-4   LC 96-11602
First published 1977 under the authorship of Augusta Baker and Ellin Greene

"The first part of the work gives a history of storytelling in U.S. libraries . . . followed by a chapter on the purpose and values of storytelling. Several chapters are devoted to the practice of storytelling, with attention given to selection of the stories, preparation for story hour and the actual presentation." Am Libr [review of 1987 edition]

Includes bibliographical references

Hopkins, Lee Bennett

Pass the poetry, please! 3rd ed. HarperCollins
Pubs. 1998 277p $25; pa $5.99   **372.6**
1. Poetry—Study and teaching
ISBN 0-06-027746-7; 0-06-446199-8 (pa)
LC 98-19617
First published 1972
"Written for teachers and librarians seeking ways of
getting poetry into the lives of children. . . . Through-
out, many poets are cited, from Langston Hughes to
Nikki Giovanni and from Jack Prelutsky to Robert
Frost." Booklist
"This a must-purchase." SLJ
Includes bibliographical references

Livingston, Myra Cohn

Poem-making; ways to begin writing poetry.
HarperCollins Pubs. 1991 162p $16.95 (4 and up)
372.6
1. Poetry—Study and teaching 2. Creative writing
ISBN 0-06-024019-9   LC 90-5012
"A Charlotte Zolotow book"
Introduces the different kinds of poetry and the me-
chanics of writing poetry, providing an opportunity for
the reader to experience the joy of making a poem
"As a writing guide, this book will be most useful in
creative writing groups with a teacher or leader. . . .
What Livingston does communicate on every page is the
excitement of poetry and its strange power to 'arrest our
senses' and help us see the world in a new way."
Booklist
Includes bibliographical references

MacDonald, Margaret Read

Look back and see; twenty lively tales for
gentle tellers; illustrations by Roxane Murphy.
Wilson, H.W. 1991 178p il $45   **372.6**
1. Storytelling 2. Folklore
ISBN 0-8242-0810-2   LC 91-2539
The author presents twenty non-violent folktales from
around the world, with background notes and suggestions
for storytelling uses
"Delightfully varied in mood, the tales range from silly and rowdy to contemplative and touching. . . . Mac-
Donald's useful, informative, and entertaining notes follow each story. . . . The notes alone are worth the price
of the book." J Youth Serv Libr
Includes bibliographical references

Shake-it-up tales! stories to sing, dance, drum,
and act out. August House 2000 174p il music
$24.95; pa $14.95   **372.6**
1. Storytelling 2. Folklore
ISBN 0-87483-590-9; 0-87483-570-4 (pa)
LC 00-36228
"With help from Jen and Nat Whitman, Wajuppa
Tossa, and the Mahasarakham Storytellers"
This is a collection of "participation tales from differ-
ent cultures. Each of the 20 stories is easy to learn and
MacDonald provides wonderful ideas on how to inspire
elementary-aged children to join in and become part of
the storytelling tradition." SLJ
Includes bibliographical references

The storyteller's start-up book; finding, learning,
performing, and using folktales including twelve
tellable tales. August House 1993 215p $26.95; pa
$14.95   **372.6**
1. Storytelling 2. Folklore
ISBN 0-87483-304-3; 0-87483-305-1 (pa)
LC 93-1580
The author's advice on storytelling "covers the practical ground, from selection, learning (in one hour!), performance, and setting to classroom applications. . . . A
dozen texts of proven success follow, with performance
tips and source notes. Equally valuable are the selected
and annotated bibliographies appended to every chapter."
Libr J
Includes bibliographical references

When the lights go out; twenty scary tales to
tell; illustrations by Roxane Murphy. Wilson, H.W.
1988 176p il $45; pa $30   **372.6**
1. Storytelling 2. Horror fiction 3. Folklore
ISBN 0-8242-0770-X; 0-8242-0823-4 (pa)
LC 88-14197
"Divided into six sections—Not Too Scary, Scary in
the Dark, Gross Stuff, Jump Tales, Tales to Act Out, and
Tales to Draw or Stir Up—the selections will be especially useful around Halloween, although, as the author
points out, the book can be used year round. Following
each inclusion are helpful notes on telling the stories and
a section that gives sources on origins and variants. Murphy's decorative drawings introduce chapters and are
scattered throughout the text. Several concluding chapters
list bibliographies and provide other helpful information."
Booklist
Includes bibliographical references

Pellowski, Anne

The world of storytelling. expanded and rev ed.
Wilson, H.W. 1990 xxi, 311p il $50
372.6
1. Storytelling
ISBN 0-8242-0788-2   LC 90-31151
First published 1977
A practical guide to the origins, development, and applications of storytelling
This guide "reviews the oral traditions from which literature for children grew, addresses the controversy between storytellers and folklorists, and offers a modern-
day definition for storytelling. *The world of storytelling*
also includes chapters on: types of storytelling—bardic,
folk, religious, theatrical, library and institutional, camp-
ground and playground, hygienic and therapeutic storytelling; format and style of storytelling—opening and
closing of a story session; language, voice, and audience
response; musical accompaniment; pictures and objects
used; training of storytellers—history and survey of training methods; visuality, orality, and literacy; storytelling
festivals." Publisher's note
"This is an important work for collections serving
adult students of storytelling and the oral tradition." J
Youth Serv Libr
Includes bibliographical references

Sawyer, Ruth

The way of the storyteller. Viking 1962 360p il pa $15 hardcover o.p.   **372.6**

1. Storytelling 2. Literature—Collections

ISBN 0-14-004436-1 (pa)

First published 1942

"This is not primarily a book on how to tell stories; it is rather the whole philosophy of story telling as a creative art. From her own rich experience the author writes inspiringly of the background, experience, creative imagination, technique and selection essential to this art. A part of the book is devoted to a few well-loved stories with suggestions and comments." Booklist

Includes bibliographical references

Shedlock, Marie L.

The art of the story-teller; foreword by Anne Carroll Moore. 3d ed rev, with a new bibliography by Eulalie Steinmetz. Dover Publs. 1951 xxi, 290p pa $8.95   **372.6**

1. Storytelling 2. Literature—Collections

ISBN 0-486-20635-1

First published 1915

"This has long been considered one of the . . . standard books on storytelling. . . . Suggestions for selecting and for telling stories are included as well as eighteen of Miss Shedlock's own favorites." Horn Book

Includes bibliographical references

Simpson, Martha Seif

Storycraft; 50 theme-based programs combining storytelling activities and crafts for children in grades 1-3; by Martha Seif Simpson and Lynne Perrigo; illustrated by Lynne Perrigo. McFarland & Co. 2001 283p il pa $38.50   **372.6**

1. Storytelling 2. Handicraft 3. Children's libraries 4. Children—Books and reading

ISBN 0-7864-0891-X   LC 00-67653

"A collection of popular, child-tested programs. Themes include dragons, cowboys and cowgirls, kites, and magic, and are arranged alphabetically by title of program. . . . Each unit includes suggestions for a bulletin board, background music, an opener, stories, a group-participation activity, a craft, and numerous titles to booktalk. . . . A must for public librarians looking for programs to keep kids coming to the library." SLJ

Includes bibliographical refernces

Totten, Kathryn

Seasonal storytime crafts. UpstartBooks 2002 109p il (Reading activities series) pa $16.95   **372.6**

1. Storytelling 2. Nature craft 3. Books and reading

ISBN 1-57950-075-7   LC 2002-8247

"This book focuses on craft projects that can be combined with story time activities for children in grades K-2. Divided into monthly themes, each project includes activities to complete before sharing books, rest activities . . . and related books to share. The crafts that are included in the book have clear, concise directions as well as the time it usually takes to complete the craft. . . . This book is a must for teachers and media specialists looking for simple craft activities for their students." Libr Media Connect

Includes bibliographical references

373.1   Organization and activities in secondary education

Pipkin, Gloria

At the schoolhouse gate; lessons in intellectual freedom; [by] Gloria Pipkin and ReLeah Cossett Lent; foreword by Susan Ohanian. Heinemann (Portsmouth) 2002 xx, 235p pa $21   **373.1**

1. Academic freedom 2. Censorship 3. Public schools

ISBN 0-325-00395-5   LC 2001-39909

"Two English teachers share their . . . personal battle to support students intellectual rights in the Bay County School District in Florida in the 1980s when censorship cases were looming in schools throughout the nation. . . . This book is one of inspiration, and teachers, librarians, and school administrators may find it encouraging as they face similar battles." SLJ

Includes bibliographical references

373.2   Secondary schools and programs of specific kinds

Middle school: how to deal; by Sara Borden . . . [et al.]; illustrated by Yuki Hatori; with a foreword by Karen Bokram. Chronicle Books 2005 lib bdg $15.50; pa $9.95 (4 and up)   **373.2**

1. Middle schools

ISBN 0-8118-4845-0 (lib bdg); 0-8118-4497-8 (pa)

Five middle school girls write about how to navigate middle school and deal with the changes in your life.

"The writing style is reassuring and casual. . . . The majority of rising middle-school readers will find much good advice here." Booklist

379   Public policy issues in education

Haskins, James

Separate, but not equal; the dream and the struggle. Scholastic 1998 184p il pa $4.99 hardcover o.p. (5 and up)   **379**

1. African Americans—Education 2. School integration 3. Segregation in education

ISBN 0-590-45910-4 (pa); 0-590-45911-2 (hc)

    LC 96-51507

The author traces "the history of the African American struggle for equal rights to education, from the enforced illiteracy of slavery times to the present debate about affirmative action." Booklist

"With his knack for blending historical facts and thoughtful interpretation, Haskins offers an informative, closeup look at the course of black education in America." SLJ

Includes bibliographical references

Morrison, Toni

Remember; the journey to school integration. Houghton Mifflin Co 2004 78p il $18 (3-5)
379

1. School integration 2. Discrimination in education 3. African Americans—Education 4. United States—Race relations
ISBN 0-618-45967-7   LC 2003-22884

Historical real photo/portraits combined with simple factual statement from the point of view of African American children tells the history of the school integration in this country.

"The provocative, candid images and conversational text should spark questions and discussion, a respect for past sacrifices, and inspiration for facing future challenges." SLJ

Rappaport, Doreen

The school is not white! a true story of the civil rights movement; illustrated by Curtis James. Jump at the Sun/Hyperion Books for Children 2005 unp il $16.99 (1-3)
379

1. Carter family 2. African Americans—Education 3. School integration 4. Segregation in education
ISBN 0-7868-1838-7   LC 2003-62003

"Sharecroppers on a cotton plantation, Mae Bertha and Matthew Carter believed that 'a good education would get their children out of the cotton fields.' In 1965, under a new federal law, the Carters enrolled their children in a superior all-white school, a move that cost them their jobs and their home. . . . At once spare and hard-hitting, the narrative exposes the prejudice the young Carters endured. . . . James's . . . chalk pastels effectively capture the tale's intense emotion." Publ Wkly

381   Commerce (Trade)

Fisher, Leonard Everett

The peddlers; written & illustrated by Leonard Everett Fisher. Benchmark Bks. 1998 47p il (Colonial craftsmen) lib bdg $14.95 (4 and up)
381

1. Peddlers and peddling 2. United States—Social life and customs—1600-1775, Colonial period
ISBN 0-7614-0511-9   LC 96-38412

A reissue of the title first published 1968 by Watts

Describes the enterprise and commercial development that peddlers brought to the colonies before the establishment of general stores

Krull, Kathleen

Supermarket; illustrated by Melanie Hope Greenberg. Holiday House 2001 unp il $16.95 (k-3)
381

1. Supermarkets
ISBN 0-8234-1546-5   LC 99-88042

Explains modern supermarkets and how they work, discussing how they organize, display, and keep track of the items they sell

"Written in a clear and lively style. . . . Best of all, however, are the vibrant double-page gouache cartoon-style pictures using flat, decorative forms." SLJ

Lewin, Ted

How much? visiting markets around the world. 1st ed. HarperCollins Pubs. 2006 31p il $15.99; lib bdg $16.89 (k-3)
381

1. Markets
ISBN 0-688-17552-; 0-688-17553-8 (lib bdg)
LC 2004-30198

"From pet markets in Cairo to a flea market in New Jersey, stalls and vendors in five countries are described with brief, evocative text that captures small details. . . . The elaborate watercolors have a photorealistic authenticity that softened by impressionistic dabs of color." Bull Cent Child Books

Market! Lothrop, Lee & Shepard Bks. 1996 unp il $16.95; pa $5.95 (k-3)
381

1. Markets
ISBN 0-688-12161-6; 0-688-17520-1 (pa)
LC 95-7439

"An Irish horse market, New York City's Fulton Fish Market, a countryside market in Uganda, and a city market square in Nepal are among the six venues visited in this thoughtful exploration of long-standing social practices. Lewin's richly detailed watercolors convey the color and bustle of the marketplace as a human arena common worldwide, yet having distinctive characteristics according to country." Horn Book Guide

383   Postal communication

Harness, Cheryl

They're off! the story of the Pony Express. Simon & Schuster Bks. for Young Readers 1996 unp il $17 (3-5)
383

1. Pony express
ISBN 0-689-80523-3   LC 95-43534

Relates the history of the Pony Express from when it began to carry messages across the American West in April 1860 until the telegraph replaced it in October 1861

"Harness's text is involving and filled with lively detail. Her busy and elaborate illustrations also create a panorama of the age." SLJ

Includes bibliographical references

385   Railroad transportation

Zimmermann, Karl R.

All aboard! passenger trains around the world; [by] Karl Zimmermann; photography by the author. Boyds Mills Press 2006 48p il $19.95 (5 and up)
385

1. Railroads
ISBN 1-59078-325-5   LC 2005-24990

"Zimmerman has traveled by train across six continents, and his beautiful, big color photos appear on every double-page spread of this enthusiastic account, which blends history, geography, business, and engineering with his personal focus." Booklist

Zimmermann, Karl R.—*Continued*

Steam locomotives; whistling, chugging, smoking iron horses of the past. Boyds Mills Press 2004 48p il $19.95 (4 and up) **385**
1. Locomotives 2. Steam engines
ISBN 1-59078-165-1

"In this photo-essay, Zimmermann shares his excitement for steam locomotives with young readers, tracing the development of the early engines and their impact on the history of the U.S. He includes a clear explanation . . . of how a steam engine works. The photographs, some archival and some from the present day, are excellent. . . . The engaging text clearly imparts the author's enthusiasm and love for the subject." SLJ

Includes glossary

385.09 Railroad transportation--Historical and geographic treatment

Halpern, Monica

Railroad fever; building the Transcontinental Railroad, 1830-1870; [by] Monica Halpern. National Geographic 2004 40p il map (Crossroads America) $21.90; pa $12.95 (4-6) **385.09**
1. Union Pacific Railroad Company 2. Central Pacific Railroad 3. Railroads—History 4. Frontier and pioneer life
ISBN 0-7922-6767-2; 0-7922-6767-2 (pa)
LC 2003-17858

Presents a history of the building of the transcontinental railroad and its effects on American life

"This is a first-choice purchase for its visually appealing presentation and its succinct yet thorough treatment of the topic." SLJ

Includes glossary

Houghton, Gillian

The Transcontinental Railroad; a primary source history of America's first coast-to-coast railroad. Rosen Central 2002 64p il map (Primary sources in American history) lib bdg $29.25 (5 and up) **385.09**
1. Union Pacific Railroad Company 2. Central Pacific Railroad 3. Railroads—History 4. Frontier and pioneer life
ISBN 0-8239-3684-8 LC 2001-8530

Describes the people, circumstances, and events surrounding the building of the railway system across the continent in the mid-nineteenth century.

"Clearly written [text is] accompanied by numerous reproductions of handbills, maps, period photographs, portraits, political cartoons, the National Republican platform of 1860, blueprints, and letters. . . . [This] will be useful to students and their teachers." SLJ

Includes glossary and bibliographical references

Landau, Elaine

The transcontinental railroad; [by] Elaine Landau. Franklin Watts 2005 63p il $25.50 (5 and up) **385.09**
1. Union Pacific Railroad Company 2. Central Pacific Railroad 3. Railroads—History 4. Frontier and pioneer life
ISBN 0-531-12326-X LC 2005000914

"Watts library"

"Landau describes how people traveled prior to the building of the railroads and how the concept of Manifest Destiny influenced the development of the railroads. . . . Black-and-white and color illustrations, maps, sidebars, and time lines enhance the well-organized [text]." SLJ

Includes bibliographical references

Meltzer, Milton

Hear that train whistle blow! how the railroad changed the world. Random House 2004 157p il $18.95; lib bdg $20.95 (5 and up) **385.09**
1. Railroads—History
ISBN 0-375-81563-5; 0-375-91563-X (lib bdg)
LC 2003-13255

"Landmark books"

Takes a look at the history of rail transportation, focussing on how it transformed societies from isolated communities which rarely communicated or traded into unified nations

"Illustrated with numerous archival photographs, this excellent, comprehensive history will be a welcome addition." SLJ

Thompson, Linda

The transcontinental railroad; by Linda Thompson. Rourke Pub. 2005 48p il (Expansion of America) $23.93 (4-6) **385.09**
1. Union Pacific Railroad Company 2. Central Pacific Railroad 3. Railroads—History 4. Frontier and pioneer life
ISBN 1-59515-227-X LC 2004-10035

"The story of the Transcontinental Railroad is a complicated one, with extraordinary vision, corruption, innovation, and plain backbreaking work playing roles. In this volume . . . Thompson does an excellent job of meshing the overriding ideal inherent in linking the Atlantic and Pacific coasts with the politics and greed that were also part of the project. . . . The black-and-white historical photos are well chosen." Booklist

Includes bibliographical references

387.1 Ports. Lighthouses

Gibbons, Gail

Beacons of light: lighthouses. Morrow Junior Bks. 1990 unp il $16 (k-3) **387.1**
1. Lighthouses
ISBN 0-688-07379-4 LC 89-33884

The author traces the development of lighthouses "from hilltop bonfires to the electronically controlled beacons that flash warnings to today's passing ships.

Gibbons, Gail—*Continued*

Drawings of specific lighthouses grace every page. . . . Readers are told of lighthouse keepers' duties, the changing technology of lighthouses, and their status today as high-tech markers." Booklist

"The history of lighthouses is told in a picture book format for independent readers. Although the narrative is simple, the vocabulary and some of the concepts are more difficult than is typical in picture books. . . . However, each difficult concept is clarified with supplementary illustrations or text." Bull Cent Child Books

Plisson, Philip

Lighthouses; photographs by Philip Plisson; text by Francis Dreyer; drawings by Daniel Dufour. Harry N. Abrams 2005 78p il $18.95 (4 and up) **387.1**

1. Lighthouses

ISBN 0-8109-5958-5 LC 2005011781

"Plisson's magnificent color photos will draw young people to this introduction to lighthouses and the work of tending them. Each spread in the oversize volume introduces a different aspect of the history and technology of the structures or the work of maintaining them, from the lighthouses of ancient Egypt to the automated towers of today. Dreyer's engaging text . . . will pull readers to the facts through anecdotes about lighthouse keepers' lives." Booklist

387.2 Ships

Barton, Byron

Boats. Crowell 1986 unp il lib bdg $14.89 (k-1) **387.2**

1. Boats and boating 2. Ships

ISBN 0-690-04536-0 LC 85-47900

Depicts a variety of boats and a cruise ship docking and unloading passengers

"Thick black outlines contain vivid colors . . . clean lines, bright hues, and undemanding text." Booklist

Collicutt, Paul

This boat. Farrar, Straus & Giroux 2001 unp il $15 (k-2) **387.2**

1. Boats and boating 2. Ships

ISBN 0-374-37495-3 LC 00-37174

"From a paddle-powered riverboat to a submarine to an aircraft carrier to a ship stranded in a storm, a number of different boats are presented. . . . The book is excellent for reading aloud, and the dramatic illustrations will carry across a crowd and make for excellent discussion of the boats and their functions." Booklist

Gibbons, Gail

Boat book. Holiday House 1983 unp il lib bdg $16.95; pa $5.95 (k-3) **387.2**

1. Boats and boating 2. Ships

ISBN 0-8234-0478-1 (lib bdg); 0-8234-0709-8 (pa) LC 82-15851

An introduction to "all sorts of seafaring craft . . . [including] speedboats, sailboats, canoes, cruise ships, police and fire boats, and commercial and military vessels. Various means of propulsion (wind, oars and paddles, engine power) are explained, as are the uses of each type of boat." Publ Wkly

The text "is logically presented in a noncondescending manner. Bright color illustrations throughout show an array of boats moving through the water." SLJ

Macaulay, David

Ship. Houghton Mifflin 1993 96p il $19.95; pa $12.95 (4 and up) **387.2**

1. Shipwrecks 2. Underwater exploration 3. Caribbean region—Antiquities

ISBN 0-395-52439-3; 0-395-74518-7 (pa) LC 92-1346

This book "opens with an underwater find in the Caribbean and, in story and illustration, follows the work of marine archeologists in studying the wreck. As part of the background research in Spain, one of the team finds a diary recording the building of a caravel in 1504. The rest of the book contains a 'translation' of the diary with accompanying illustrations. Though a fictional account, the narrative gives a good feel for the maritime technology of the early 16th century." Sci Books Films

O'Brien, Patrick

The great ships. Walker & Co. 2001 39p il $16.95; lib bdg $17.85 (4 and up) **387.2**

1. Ships

ISBN 0-8027-8774-6; 0-8027-8775-4 (lib bdg) LC 2001-17873

"O'Brien tells the stories of 17 of the world's most illustrious vessels (or groups of vessels). . . . The author includes accounts of Sir Francis Drake's *Golden Hind*, Blackbeard's *Queen Anne's Revenge*, Columbus's trio of Spanish caravels, and the disaster-destined *Titanic*. A double-page spread is devoted to each story, with a dramatic watercolor-and-gouache illustration on the left and history on the right. . . . A captivating and beautiful volume." SLJ

Sandler, Martin W.

On the waters of the USA; ships and boats in American life. Oxford Univ. Press 2004 63p il (Transportation in America) $19.95 (5 and up) **387.2**

1. Shipping—United States 2. Ships 3. Boats and boating

ISBN 0-19-513227-0

Explores the evolving role of boats and ships in American history, from the dugout and birchbark canoes of Native Americans to twenty-first century container ships and supertankers.

This is a "fascinating account. . . . Drawings, maps, and photographs are well placed and fully captioned. . . . The large type is reader friendly, and the writing is clear and engaging." SLJ

Includes bibliographical references

387.7 Air transportation

Barton, Byron
Airplanes. Crowell 1986 unp il lib bdg $15.89
(k-1)   **387.7**
1. Airplanes
ISBN 0-690-04532-8   LC 85-47899
Brief text and illustrations present a variety of airplanes and what they do, "as well as some of the usual
scenes surrounding each (e.g., workers checking a passenger plane). Brightly colored illustrations outlined in
heavy black convey a bold and simple first impression,
yet they portray a good number of accurate details that
preschoolers find so fascinating." SLJ

Airport. Crowell 1982 unp il lib bdg $14.89; pa
$5.95 (k-1)   **387.7**
1. Airports 2. Airplanes
ISBN 0-690-04169-1 (lib bdg); 0-06-443145-2 (pa)
LC 79-7816
"In a brightly illustrated book, the author/artist captures the hustle and bustle of passenger traffic from arrival at the terminal to take off." Kobrin Letter

388 Transportation. Ground transportation

Herbst, Judith
The history of transportation; [by] Judith Herbst.
Twenty-First Century Books 2006 56p il (Major
inventions through history) lib bdg $26.60 (5 and
up)   **388**
1. Transportation—History
ISBN 0-8225-2496-1   LC 2004-23020
Contents: The wheel; Boats; The steam engine; The
internal combustion engine; Air travel; Timeline
This history of transportation "covers the wheel, sail,
steam engine, internal combustion engine, and airplane.
. . . The text . . . is breezy but informative; unfamiliar
terms are defined. Illustrations are a mixture of period
black-and-white and color photos." SLJ
Includes bibliographical references

388.3 Vehicular transportation

Ammon, Richard
Conestoga wagons; illustrated by Bill
Farnsworth. Holiday House 2000 unp il lib bdg
$16.95 (2-5)   **388.3**
1. Carriages and carts 2. Transportation
ISBN 0-8234-1475-2   LC 99-19726
Explains how Conestoga wagons were built and driven
as well as their historical significance and importance to
the early American economy
Includes bibliographical references

388.4 Local transportation

DuTemple, Lesley A.
The New York subways. Lerner Publs. 2003
80p il (Great building feats) lib bdg $27.93 (5 and
up)   **388.4**
1. Subways 2. New York (N.Y.)—History
ISBN 0-8225-0378-6   LC 2001-6143
Traces the history of the underground transportation
system in New York City, discussing the politics involved, how it was financed, the men who built it, and
the construction techniques
"DuTemple does a fine job. . . . [Photos] sidebars,
maps, and archival material work beautifully together to
supplement the information." Booklist
Includes bibliographical references

Sandler, Martin W.
Straphanging in the USA; trolleys and subways
in American life. Oxford Univ. Press 2003 61p il
(Transportation in America) lib bdg $19.95 (5 and
up)   **388.4**
1. Subways 2. Street railroads 3. City and town life
ISBN 0-19-513229-7
An illustrated look at how the problem of moving
large numbers of people within cities has been addressed
through a series of vehicles and systems, from horse-
drawn cars to the modern subway.
"The fascinating narrative is embellished with reproductions of historical photos and illustrations and period
quotes from newspapers, magazines, and books. This offering will capture the interest of casual readers and provide researchers with plenty of information." SLJ
Includes bibliographical references

389 Metrology and standardization

Murphy, Stuart J.
Mighty Maddie; comparing weights; illustrated
by Bernice Lum. 1st ed. HarperCollins Publishers
2004 31p il (MathStart) $15.99; pa $4.99 (k-2)
389
1. Weights and measures 2. Cleanliness
ISBN 0-06-053159-2; 0-06-053161-4 (pa)
LC 2003-17610
"Level 1. Comparing weights."
As Maddie cleans up her room, she learns how to
compare the weights of various objects.
"Childlike line drawings with bright colors give readers a sense of action. This appealing book has uses beyond the math concept, and offers messages about family
life, self-image, and responsibility." SLJ

391 Costume and personal appearance

Finley, Carol
The art of African masks; exploring cultural traditions. Lerner Publs. 1999 64p il map (Art around the world) $23.93 (5 and up)   **391**
1. Masks (Facial) 2. African art
ISBN 0-8225-2078-8   LC 98-10570
Describes how different types of masks are made and used in Africa and how they reflect the culture of their ethnic groups
"Clear, sharp full-color photographs of museum artifacts are well placed on the pages. . . . Pictures of modern members of still-existing cultures add to the attractiveness of this volume." SLJ
Includes bibliographical references

Fisher, Leonard Everett
The wigmakers; written & illustrated by Leonard Everett Fisher. Benchmark Bks. 2000 c1965 44p il (Colonial craftsmen) $21.36 (4 and up)   **391**
1. Wigs 2. United States—Social life and customs—1600-1775, Colonial period
ISBN 0-7614-0933-5   LC 99-16261
A reissue of the title first published 1965 by Watts
Describes the advent of the wig as a fashion necessity in France and England, illustrates popular styles of eighteenth-century wigs, and explains the colonial wigmaker's technique in construction and care of the wig
Includes bibliographical references

Lauber, Patricia
What you never knew about tubs, toilets & showers; illustrated by John Manders. Simon & Schuster Bks. for Young Readers 2001 unp il (Around-the-house history) $16 (2-4)   **391**
1. Bathrooms—History 2. Baths—History
ISBN 0-689-82420-3   LC 99-14517
Describes people's feelings about bathing and methods of keeping clean throughout history, from the Stone Age to modern times
"The cartoonish illustrations, which include some kid-pleasing gross-out moments, reflect the breezy style of the informative text." Horn Book Guide
Includes bibliographical references

Morris, Ann
Hats, hats, hats; photographs by Ken Heyman. Lothrop, Lee & Shepard Bks. 1989 unp il $16; pa $4.95 (k-1)   **391**
1. Hats
ISBN 0-688-06338-1; 0-688-12274-4 (pa)
                                      LC 88-26676
This book introduces a variety of hats worn around the world
"The vivid color photographs, one or two per page, show people engaged in lively activities while . . . wearing their hats. Each picture offers a strong ethnic identity or a thought-provoking human interaction, with captions of only a few words in large print. An unusual index . . . gives background information about the pictures, citing the countries of origin and a few facts about each . . . kind of hat." SLJ

Shoes, shoes, shoes. Lothrop, Lee & Shepard Bks. 1995 32p il $16; pa $4.95 (k-1)   **391**
1. Shoes
ISBN 0-688-13666-4; 0-688-16166-9 (pa)
                                      LC 94-46649
"Morris gives a world-tour of shoes . . . in [a] picture book illustrated by various photographers. In rhyming text, she talks about shoes for all kinds of activities. . . . [The] book includes a map and a photograph key of the places visited." Bull Cent Child Books

Rowland-Warne, L.
Costume; written by L. Rowland-Warne; [special photography, Liz McAulay] Dorling Kindersley 2000 63p il (DK eyewitness books) $15.99; lib bdg $19.99 (4 and up)   **391**
1. Costume 2. Clothing and dress
ISBN 0-7894-5586-2; 0-7894-6584-1 (lib bdg)
First published 1992 by Knopf
Photographs and text document the history and meaning of clothing, from loincloths to modern children's clothes.

Sills, Leslie
From rags to riches; a history of girls' clothing in America; [by] Leslie Sills. 1st ed. Holiday House 2005 48p il $16.95 (5 and up)
                                      391
1. Children's clothing 2. Girls
ISBN 0-8234-1708-5   LC 2003-67600
A history of the clothing of American girls from colonial times to the present.
"The sparkling design of Sills' overview makes this a pleasure to page through. . . . A marvelous collection of paintings and photographs show off the apparel." Booklist
Includes glossary and bibliographical references

Swain, Ruth Freeman
Hairdo! what we do and did to our hair; illustrated by Cat Bowman Smith. Holiday House 2002 unp il $16.95 (1-4)   **391**
1. Hair
ISBN 0-8234-1522-8   LC 99-13350
Depicts how people have viewed, worn, and changed their hairstyles throughout history and in various cultures
"Smith's cartoons are well suited to the lighthearted tone of the narrative." SLJ
Includes bibliographical references

Yue, Charlotte
Shoes; their history in words and pictures; [by] Charlotte and David Yue. Houghton Mifflin 1997 92p il $14.95 (4 and up)   **391**
1. Shoes
ISBN 0-395-72667-0   LC 96-17220

Yue, Charlotte—*Continued*

Relates the history and lore of many of the kinds of shoes worn by men, women, and children throughout the world

"Filled with vignettes . . . and interesting, little-known facts. . . . The short chapters are chronologically arranged, providing a good historical overview of classical to modern times with just the right scope for the intended audience. Ample black-and-white drawings illustrate almost every style of footwear mentioned in the text." SLJ

Includes bibliographical references

392   Customs of life cycle and domestic life

Hoyt-Goldsmith, Diane

Celebrating a Quinceañera; a Latina's 15th birthday celebration; photographs by Lawrence Migdale. Holiday House 2002 30p il $16.95 (3-5)
           392

1. Quinceañera (Social custom) 2. Mexican Americans—Social life and customs

ISBN 0-8234-1693-3   LC 2001-59424

Describes the customs and traditions connected with the celebration of a Mexican-American girl's fifteenth birthday, marking her coming of age

This offers "eye-catching, full-color photos. . . . The clearly written, engaging text conveys both the social and religious significance of the event." SLJ

King, Elizabeth

Quinceañera; celebrating fifteen. Dutton Children's Bks. 1998 40p il $16.99 (5 and up)
           392

1. Quinceañera (Social custom) 2. Mexican Americans—Social life and customs

ISBN 0-525-45638-4   LC 97-44539

Also available Spanish language edition

Focuses on describing the celebration of this rite of passage in the life of a specific Mexican American girl, while also presenting historical background for the occasion

"The photographs are so full of spectacle and genuine warmth that we feel as though we have been invited, too." Booklist

Morris, Ann

Weddings. Lothrop, Lee & Shepard Bks. 1995 25p il map $15; lib bdg $14.93 (k-1)   **392**

1. Marriage customs and rites

ISBN 0-688-13272-3; 0-688-13273-1 (lib bdg)
            LC 94-48040

This photographic look at weddings includes a Shinto rite in Japan, an Orthodox Jewish service in Russia, a Catholic mass in Slovakia and a ceremony at City Hall in Los Angeles

Onyefulu, Ifeoma

Welcome Dede! an African naming ceremony; [by] Ifeoma Onyefulu. Frances Lincoln; distributed by Publisher's Group West 2003 unp il map pa $7.95 (k-3)   **392**

1. Birth customs 2. Ghana—Social life and customs 3. Personal names

ISBN 0-84507-311-8

"Onyefulu opens this photo-essay with an enlightening one-page introduction that succinctly addresses the significance of names in African culture. Amarlai, who lives in Ghana, has a new cousin. . . . Through Amarlai's engaging voice, the process of naming a child is described—how and why one is chosen, and by whom. Each step is documented in a series of insightful, well-positioned photographs that capture the richness of this tradition and the importance of the extended family and community." SLJ

393   Death customs

Kallen, Stuart A.

Mummies. KidHaven Press 2003 48p il map (Wonders of the world) $23.70 (4 and up)
           393

1. Mummies

ISBN 0-7377-1031-4   LC 2002-5388

Contents: The golden age of mummies; King Tut and his amazing tomb; Bog bodies; Otzi the iceman

"Kallen discusses accidental mummification as well as the art and science practiced in different civilizations around the world. . . . The mummification process is described in great detail." SLJ

"There's plenty of information to support reports, all of which is presented in . . . Kallen's straightforward, sometimes lively language." Booklist

Includes glossary and bibliographical references

Markle, Sandra

Outside and inside mummies. Walker & Co. 2005 40p il $17.95; lib bdg $18.85 (4 and up)
           393

1. Mummies

ISBN 0-8027-8966-8; 0-8027-8967-6 (lib bdg)
            LC 2004-66128

"Markle explores a global smorgasbord of mummy varieties, both those created by human procedures and those caused by nature. Crisp (if gruesome) color photos accompany the readable, informative text, which discusses not only the mummification process, but also the cutting-edge technologies used by forensic anthropologists and others to study the mummies themselves." SLJ

Includes glossary

Pemberton, Delia

Egyptian mummies; people from the past. Harcourt 2001 48p il lib bdg $18 (4 and up)
           393

1. Mummies 2. Egypt—Civilization

ISBN 0-15-202600-2   LC 00-44882

First published 2000 in the United Kingdom

Pemberton, Delia—*Continued*

"Seven mummies from the British Museum are used as an organizing device to look at the historical and medical significance of mummification. . . . Following a general overview, there are discussions of grave goods, tombs, coffins and sarcophagi, medical uses of mummies (past and present), archaeology and excavation, hieroglyphics, etc. The text is brisk and readable, and is enhanced by an abundance of well-placed color photographs." SLJ

Includes glossary and bibliographical references

Sloan, Christopher

Bury the dead; tombs, corpses, mummies, skeletons, & rituals; foreword by Bruno Frohlich. National Geographic Soc. 2002 64p il $18.95 (5 and up) **393**

1. Funeral rites and ceremonies 2. Burial
ISBN 0-7922-7192-0   LC 2001-7507
Examines the customs and practices related to burial that have existed from ancient times to the present

The author "does a terrific job of providing an intriguing, reader-friendly text that is not overshadowed by the fabulous color photographs." Booklist

Includes bibliographical references

Tanaka, Shelley

Mummies; the newest, coolest, and creepiest from around the world; [by] Shelley Tanaka; archaeological consultation by Paul Bahn. Harry N. Abrams 2005 48p il map $16.95 (4 and up) **393**

1. Mummies
ISBN 0-8109-5797-3   LC 2005-00984
"After a brief discussion of mummification and the sorts of places in which mummified bodies have been found, Tanaka organizes her text by continent. Simple outlined and colored maps display the countries featured, supplementing the author's descriptions of the local conditions. . . . The main text for each mummy or cache of mummies is generally a few paragraphs, often supported by a shorter text, both of which are illustrated by photographs or reproductions." SLJ

"Not for the squeamish, the descriptions are graphic, and, like the riveting photos, they will draw kids right into the science." Booklist

Includes bibliographical references

Secrets of the mummies; uncovering the bodies of ancient Egyptians; illustrations by Greg Ruhl; historical consultation by Peter Brand. Hyperion Bks. for Children 1999 48p il pa $7.99 hardcover o.p. (4 and up) **393**

1. Mummies 2. Egypt—Civilization
ISBN 0-7868-1539-6 (pa)   LC 99-11012
"An I was there book"

Describes the ancient Egyptian practice of preserving the dead through the process of mummification and explains what scientists have learned from unwrapping and examining mummies

Wilcox, Charlotte

Mummies, bones & body parts. Carolrhoda Bks. 2000 64p il $25.26; pa $7.95 (5 and up) **393**

1. Mummies 2. Funeral rites and ceremonies
ISBN 1-57505-428-0; 1-57505-486-8 (pa)
LC 99-50516

"Wilcox touches on many aspects of how death is treated in various cultures, including the indigenous peoples of the Americas. Embalming techniques and cryonics are discussed, as well as the fascinating jobs of experimental archaeologists and artists trained in anthropology. Scattered liberally throughout the text are uncompromising photos of important finds and scientists at work piecing together mysteries." Booklist

Includes bibliographical references

394.1   Eating, drinking; using drugs

Lauber, Patricia

What you never knew about fingers, forks, & chopsticks; illustrated by John Manders. Simon & Schuster Bks. for Young Readers 1999 unp il (Around-the-house history) $16 (2-4) **394.1**

1. Tableware 2. Table etiquette 3. Eating customs
ISBN 0-689-80479-2   LC 97-17041
Describes changes in eating customs throughout the centuries and the origins of table manners

"A delicious blend of humor and fascinating facts. . . . The lively, linear drawings incorporate amusing asides in dialogue balloons that will entertain readers as the text enlightens them about the subject." SLJ

Includes bibliographical references

Whitman, Sylvia

What's cooking? the history of American food. Lerner Publs. 2001 88p il (People's history) lib bdg $22.60 (5 and up) **394.1**

1. Food—History 2. United States—Social life and customs
ISBN 0-8225-1732-9   LC 00-9168
A look at food in the United States from colonial times to the present, describing what we have eaten, where it came from, and how it reflected events in American history

"The text is very accessible, and there are many interesting black-and-white photographs. . . . Intriguing as well as informative." Booklist

Includes bibliographical references

394.2   Customs--Special occasions

Lankford, Mary D.

Birthdays around the world; illustrated by Karen Dugan. HarperCollins Pubs. 2002 32p il $15.99; lib bdg $17.89 (3-5) **394.2**

1. Birthdays
ISBN 0-688-15431-X; 0-688-15432-8 (lib bdg)
"Brief chapters cover customs in Finland, Malaysia, Mexico, the Netherlands, New Zealand, the Philippines,

Lankford, Mary D.—*Continued*

and Sweden. Each one begins with a short description of the country's location or geography, or a historical note. Birthday foods, decorations, games, history, and present-giving habits are all described in simple language. The accompanying illustrations, done in soft pastels, depict family-centered festivities." SLJ

394.25 Carnivals

Ancona, George

Carnaval. Harcourt Brace & Co. 1999 unp il $18; pa $9 (3-6)   **394.25**

1. Carnival 2. Brazil—Social life and customs

ISBN 0-15-201793-3; 0-15-201792-5 (pa)

LC 98-47297

Text and photographs present the traditions and rituals of the annual celebration of Carnaval as experienced in the small Brazilian city of Olinda

"The prose is superb—scenes and traditions are clearly presented in a language rich with description and imagery. Stunning photographs capture the spirit of the festival." SLJ

Hoyt-Goldsmith, Diane

Mardi Gras: a Cajun country celebration; photographs by Lawrence Migdale. Holiday House 1995 32p il music $15.95 (3-5)   **394.25**

1. Carnival 2. Cajuns—Social life and customs

ISBN 0-8234-1184-2   LC 94-42707

This is a "photo essay and introduction to a Cajun Mardi Gras celebration in Eunice, Louisiana. The text follows Joel, a young fiddle player, as he prepares for and participates in the festivities. This lively and informative look at an ethnic and regional holiday is presented with clear text and bright, attractive photographs." Horn Book Guide

Includes glossary

394.26 Holidays

Ancona, George

Fiesta U.S.A. Lodestar Bks. 1995 unp il $17.99 (k-3)   **394.26**

1. Hispanic Americans—Social life and customs
2. Festivals—United States

ISBN 0-525-67498-5   LC 94-34828

"An introduction to four Hispanic holidays celebrated in the U.S.—*El Dia de los Muertos* (Day of the Dead); the processions of *Las Posadas*, which reenact Mary and Joseph's search for a place to stay in Bethlehem; the New Year's Day dance of *Los Matachines*; and *La Fiesta de los Reyes Magos*, which revolves around the story of the Three Wise Kings. . . . Ancona gives children the opportunity to view the distinctive flavors of different Hispanic communities, from San Francisco to a small town in New Mexico to New York City. The text shares the excitement and meaning of the celebrations, and focuses on how young people participate in them. Colorful, eye-catching photographs capture the mood and reinforce the narrative." SLJ

Includes glossary

The fiestas. Benchmark Bks. 2002 48p il (Viva Mexico!) $16.95 (2-4)   **394.26**

1. Festivals 2. Mexico—Social life and customs

ISBN 0-7614-1327-8   LC 00-65080

This photo-essay describes the festivals of Mexico, including carnaval, folk plays, saints days, and national holidays such as Dia de la Bandera, Cinco de Mayo, and El Dia del Charro

Includes glossary and bibliographical references

Pablo remembers; the fiesta of the Day of the Dead. Lothrop, Lee & Shepard Bks. 1993 42p il $16.95; lib bdg $16.89 (k-3)   **394.26**

1. All Souls' Day 2. Mexico—Social life and customs

ISBN 0-688-11249-8; 0-688-11250-1 (lib bdg)

LC 92-22819

During the three-day celebration of the Day of the Dead, a young Mexican boy and his family make elaborate preparations to honor the spirits of the dead

"The photography has the intimacy of high-quality family snapshots, and the tone of the text is clear and natural." Bull Cent Child Books

Includes glossary

Barth, Edna

Hearts, cupids, and red roses; the story of the valentine symbols; illustrated by Ursula Arndt. Clarion Bks. 2001 64p il $16; pa $7.95 (3-6)

394.26

1. Valentine's Day 2. Signs and symbols

ISBN 0-618-06789-2; 0-618-06791-4 (pa)

LC 2001-265787

A reissue of the title first published 1974 by Seabury Press

The history of Valentine's Day and the little-known stories behind its symbols

This offers "interesting and concise text along with lists of stories, poems, and sources." SLJ

Includes bibliographical references

Holly, reindeer, and colored lights; the story of the Christmas symbols; illustrated by Ursula Arndt. Clarion Bks. 2000 96p il $16; pa $7.95 (3-6)   **394.26**

1. Christmas 2. Signs and symbols

ISBN 0-618-06786-8; 0-618-06788-4 (pa)

LC 00-702874

A reissue of the title first published 1971 by Seabury Press

Examines the origins of Christmas symbols—trees, ornaments, Yule logs, Santa Claus, cards, Christmas colors, and many other holiday observances

"The well-written text is concise and interesting and the two-colored marginal drawings are festive. A selected list of books containing Christmas stories and poems is appended." Booklist

Includes bibliographical references

Barth, Edna—*Continued*

Lilies, rabbits, and painted eggs; the story of the Easter symbols; illustrated by Ursula Arndt. Clarion Bks. c1998 63p il $16; pa $7.95 (3-6)
394.26
1. Easter 2. Signs and symbols
ISBN 0-618-09646-9; 0-618-09648-5 (pa)
A reissue of the title first published 1970 by Seabury Press

Traces the history of Easter symbols from their Christian and pagan origins to such present-day additions as rabbits and new clothes

"The small pen drawings which illustrate the symbols and the celebrations will please the children, and an index and a bibliography of other Easter books will please the librarian." Horn Book

Shamrocks, harps, and shillelaghs; the story of the St. Patrick's Day symbols; illustrated by Ursula Arndt. Clarion Bks. 2001 95p il $16; pa $7.95 (3-6)
394.26
1. Saint Patrick's Day 2. Signs and symbols
ISBN 0-618-09649-3; 0-618-09651-5 (pa)
A reissue of the title first published 1977 by Seabury Press

"Irish history, lore, and legend are part of a wealth of information provided about Patrick the real missionary, St. Patrick's Day, and its celebration. Includes lists of stories for St. Patrick's Day and sources." LC. Child Books, 1977

Turkeys, Pilgrims, and Indian corn; the story of the Thanksgiving symbols; illustrated by Ursula Arndt. Clarion Bks. 2000 96p il $16; pa $7.95 (3-6)
394.26
1. Thanksgiving Day 2. Pilgrims (New England colonists) 3. Signs and symbols
ISBN 0-618-06783-3; 0-618-06785-X (pa)
LC 00-702873
A reissue of the title first published 1975 by Seabury Press

This book provides "information about the Pilgrims' voyage to and life in America and their dealings with the Indians. (The point is made, but not belabored, that the settled land was taken from the Indians.) Interesting sidelights are included about prominent men and women, myths such as Plymouth Rock, and harvest feasts in cultures around the world." SLJ

Includes bibliographical references

Witches, pumpkins, and grinning ghosts; the story of the Halloween symbols; illustrated by Ursula Arndt. Clarion Bks. 2000 95p il $16; pa $7.95 (3-6)
394.26
1. Halloween 2. Signs and symbols
ISBN 0-618-06780-9; 0-618-06782-5 (pa)
LC 00-712796
A reissue of the title first published 1972 by Seabury Press

Explains the origins of and relates stories associated with familiar Halloween symbols

"A diverting as well as useful account appropriately illustrated with drawings in black and orange." Booklist

Includes bibliographical references

Bulla, Clyde Robert

The story of Valentine's Day; illustrated by Susan Estelle Kwas. newly il ed. HarperCollins Pubs. 1999 unp il $14.95; lib bdg $14.89; pa $5.95 (k-3)
394.26
1. Valentine's Day
ISBN 0-06-027883-8; 0-06-027884-6 (lib bdg); 0-06-443626-8 (pa)
LC 97-37195
A newly illustrated edition of St. Valentine's Day, published 1965

Relates the history and describes the customs of this holiday from its beginning in Roman times to the present. Includes directions for making a paper valentine and sugar cookies

"Bulla's informative and entertaining guide to the holiday of romance . . . here receives fresh treatment—jazzy color-saturated illustrations with a touch of the abstract and a handsome book design." Horn Book Guide

Chase's calendar of events. Contemporary Bks. pa $64.95
394.26
1. Calendars 2. Holidays 3. Almanacs
Annual. First published 1958 with title: Chase's calendar of annual events, under the editorship of William D. and Helen M. Chase. Variant title: Chase's annual events
Accompanied by CD-ROM

"Day-by-day listing of national and state holidays, religious observances, special events, festivals and fairs, and historical anniversaries and birthdays. Covers U.S. events primarily, but some international occasions and anniversaries are included." N Y Public Libr Book of How & Where to Look It Up

Chocolate, Debbi

Kwanzaa; illustrations by Melodye Rosales. Children's Press 1990 31p il lib bdg $18; pa $4.95 (3-5)
394.26
1. Kwanzaa 2. African Americans—Social life and customs
ISBN 0-516-03991-1 (lib bdg); 0-516-43991-X (pa)
LC 89-25418
Discusses the holiday in which Afro-Americans celebrate their roots and cultural heritage from Africa

"Using clear and direct language, Chocolate provides a wealth of detail as she shares her family's Kwanzaa festival. . . . Rosales's brightly colored paintings in a realistic style draw readers into the warmth and joy of this celebration." SLJ

My first Kwanzaa book; illustrated by Cal Massey. Scholastic 1992 unp il $10.95; pa $5.99 (k-2)
394.26
1. Kwanzaa 2. African Americans—Social life and customs
ISBN 0-590-45762-4; 0-439-12926-5 (pa)
LC 92-1200
"Cartwheel books"
Introduces Kwanzaa, the holiday in which Afro-Americans celebrate their cultural heritage

"The book effectively conveys the spirit of the holiday through the text and the acrylic paint and colored-pencil illustrations, all outlined in a thin line of earthy brown." SLJ

Includes glossary

Demi

Happy, happy Chinese New Year! Crown Pubs. 2003 c1997 unp il $8.95 (k-3)   **394.26**
1. Chinese New Year 2. China—Social life and customs
ISBN 0-375-82642-4   LC 2003-43469
First published in different form 1997 with title: Happy New Year! Kung-Hsi Fa-ts'ai!
Examines the customs, traditions, food, and lore associated with the celebration of Chinese New Year

Ditchfield, Christin

Memorial Day; by Christin Ditchfield. Children's Press 2003 47p il lib bdg $25; pa $6.95 (2-4)   **394.26**
1. Memorial Day
ISBN 0-516-22783-1 (lib bdg); 0-516-27821-5 (pa)
          LC 2003-4532
"A true book"
Contents: A very special holiday; How it all got started; America at war; To protect and serve; A day of remembrance
This looks at the history of Memorial Day and how Americans celebrate it.
"The discussions . . . of how people came to wear red poppies to honor the war dead and of the Tomb of the Unknowns add interest to the presentation. . . . Appropriate black-and-white and color photographs reflect the diversity of the U.S. and enhance the [text]. [This] up-to-date [title] will add depth to holiday collections." SLJ
Includes bibliographical references

Erlbach, Arlene

Merry Christmas, everywhere! by Arlene Erlbach with Herb Erlbach; illustrated by Sharon Lane Holm. Millbrook Press 2002 48p il map lib bdg $23.90 (k-3)   **394.26**
1. Christmas
ISBN 0-7613-1956-5   LC 2001-44758
Presents Christmas greetings and traditions, with related activities, from around the world
"The artwork is bright and festive, and the instructions are easy enough for even the most craft-challenged adults to follow." SLJ
Includes bibliographical references

Fisher, Aileen Lucia

The story of Easter; by Aileen Fisher; illustrated by Stefano Vitale. HarperCollins Pubs. 1997 unp il $15.95; pa $5.95 (3-5)   **394.26**
1. Jesus Christ—Resurrection 2. Easter
ISBN 0-06-027296-1; 0-06-443490-7 (pa)
          LC 96-17395
A newly illustrated edition of Easter published 1968 by Crowell
"This book begins with the story of Jesus' crucifixion and resurrection, but focuses on the origins of various Easter and vernal equinox traditions, with an emphasis on the history of egg decorating. . . . The folk-art illustrations are defined by strong black outlines, simple shapes, and natural colors." Horn Book Guide

The **Folklore** of world holidays; Robert Griffin and Ann H. Shurgin, editors. 2nd ed. Gale Res. 1998 c1999 841p $150   **394.26**
1. Holidays 2. Festivals 3. Folklore
ISBN 0-8103-8901-0   LC 98-37030
First published 1992 under the editorship of Margaret Read MacDonald
"Provides descriptive information on nearly 2,000 beliefs, stories, superstitions, proverbs, recipes, games, pageants, fairs, processions and other lore related to more than 350 special dates from 150 countries." Publisher's note
Includes bibliographical references

Gibbons, Gail

Easter. Holiday House 1989 unp il lib bdg $16.95; pa $6.95 (k-3)   **394.26**
1. Easter
ISBN 0-8234-0737-3 (lib bdg); 0-8234-0866-3 (pa)
          LC 88-23292
Examines the background, significance, symbols, and traditions of Easter
Gibbons "simplifies complex beliefs and traditions in a straightforward way, though transitions are occasionally abrupt. Pleasing watercolors outlined in black ink illustrate the text." Booklist

Halloween is—. Holiday House 2002 unp il $16.95 (k-3)   **394.26**
1. Halloween
ISBN 0-8234-1758-1   LC 2001-59429
Describes the origins and history of Halloween traditions and festivities from ancient times to the present day
"The new version of Gibbons' *Halloween* (1984) features a larger format, new illustrations, and a revised and slightly longer text as well as the new title. . . . Libraries with multiple copies of the earlier book will still find this version useful when the holiday rush is on, and given a choice, children will reach for this bigger, brighter, new edition." Booklist

St. Patrick's Day. Holiday House 1994 unp il lib bdg $16.95; pa $6.95 (k-3)   **394.26**
1. Saint Patrick's Day
ISBN 0-8234-1119-2 (lib bdg); 0-8234-1173-7 (pa)
          LC 93-29570
"A basic introduction to the holiday—how it began, the life and works of St. Patrick, and the various ways in which the day is celebrated. The text is clear and concise, and the pages are full of information. Gibbons's simple, clean, full-page watercolor-and-ink illustrations flow logically from one to the next." SLJ

Thanksgiving Day. Holiday House 1983 unp il lib bdg $16.95; pa $6.95 (k-3)   **394.26**
1. Thanksgiving Day
ISBN 0-8234-0489-7 (lib bdg); 0-8234-0576-1 (pa)
          LC 83-175
This book presents information about the first Thanksgiving and the way that holiday is celebrated today
"Cheery shades of gold and orange and other hues animate the scenes illustrating Gibbon's incisive history of the American holiday." Publ Wkly

Gibbons, Gail—*Continued*

Valentine's Day. Holiday House 1986 unp il
$16.95; pa $6.95 (k-3)   **394.26**
  1. Valentine's Day
  ISBN 0-8234-0572-9; 0-8234-0764-0 (pa)
                                          LC 85-916
The author "briefly describes the history, meaning,
and customs of Valentine's Day in picture-book format.
Simple line drawings are brightened with the bright,
crisp colors that are the artist's hallmark. . . . On the
last two pages she shows how to make valentines and a
valentine box. A useful addition to a holiday collection
for young children and a serviceable read-aloud choice
for classrooms where Valentine's Day is celebrated."
Booklist

Giblin, James

Fireworks, picnics, and flags; [by] James Cross
Giblin; illustrated by Ursula Arndt. Clarion Bks.
1983 90p il $16; pa $8.95 (3-6)   **394.26**
  1. Fourth of July
  ISBN 0-89919-146-0; 0-89919-174-6 (pa)
                                          LC 82-9612
Traces the social history behind America's celebration
of Independence Day and explains the background of
such national symbols as the flag, the bald eagle, the
Liberty Bell, and Uncle Sam
"Giblin was the editor of Edna Barth's books on holiday symbols; according to his author's note, he knew
that Barth intended to write about the Fourth of July and
took on the project himself after her death. The result is
consistent in both format and spirit with the wellknown
Barth series, complete with Arndt's unpretentious two-
color drawings." Booklist

Gnojewski, Carol

Day of the Dead; a Latino celebration of family
and life; [by] Carol Gnojewski. Enslow
Elementary 2005 48p il (Finding out about
holidays) lib bdg $23.93 (2-4)   **394.26**
  1. All Souls' Day
  ISBN 0-7660-1780-X   LC 2004-8714
  Also available Spanish language edition
  Contents: Day of the Dead; Ancient Aztec beliefs;
Spanish conquest; My house is your house; Fiesta, flowers and food; Skull symbols
This "presents the Mexican history and traditions that
have led to modern celebrations of the Day of the Dead.
. . . Throughout the book, the value of family and tradition emerges as the center of the celebration. Clear, colorful photos, ranging from mundane to quite beautiful,
appear on every page of this attractive book. [The book]
includes a good, simple craft project." Booklist
  Includes glossary and bibliographical references

Grace, Catherine O'Neill

1621; a new look at Thanksgiving; [by]
Catherine O'Neill Grace and Margaret M. Bruchac
with Plimoth Plantation; photographs by Sisse
Brimberg and Cotton Coulson. National
Geographic Soc. 2001 47p il map $17.95 (3-5)
                                          394.26
  1. Plimoth Plantation, Inc. (Plymouth, Mass.)
  2. Thanksgiving Day 3. Pilgrims (New England colonists) 4. Wampanoag Indians
  ISBN 0-7922-7027-4   LC 2001-124
This is a "pictorial presentation of the reenactment of
the first Thanksgiving, held at Plimoth Plantation museum in October, 2000. Countering the prevailing, traditional story of the first Thanksgiving . . . this lushly illustrated photo-essay presents a more measured, balanced, and historically accurate version of the three-day
harvest celebration in 1621." SLJ
  Includes bibliographical references

Gulevich, Tanya

Encyclopedia of Easter, Carnival, and Lent;
illustrated by Mary Ann Stavros-Lanning.
Omnigraphics 2002 729p il $58 (5 and up)
                                          394.26
  1. Easter 2. Lent 3. Carnival
  ISBN 0-7808-0432-5   LC 2001-54877
"A guide to this season's joyous celebration and solemn worship, including folk customs, religious observances, history, legends, folklore, symbols, and related
days from Europe, the Americas, and around the world.
Supplemented by a bibliography, list of web sites, and
index." Title page
"This is an entertaining and solid introduction that will
be useful for both report writing and ready reference."
Booklist
  Includes bibliographical references

Hess, Debra

The Fourth of July; [by] Debra Hess.
Benchmark Books 2004 40p il map (Symbols of
America) lib bdg $25.64 (4-6)   **394.26**
  1. Fourth of July
  ISBN 0-7614-1711-7   LC 2003-4934
  Contents: Taxation without representation; A nation is
born; The American dream
  The author explains why we celebrate the Fourth of
July, offers a brief history of American independence
from Britain, and describes how the holiday is celebrated
around the country.

Hoyt-Goldsmith, Diane

Celebrating Chinese New Year; photographs by
Lawrence Migdale. Holiday House 1998 32p il
$16.95; pa $6.95 (3-5)   **394.26**
  1. Chinese New Year 2. Chinese Americans—Social
life and customs
  ISBN 0-8234-1393-4; 0-8234-1520-1 (pa)
                                          LC 98-17028
Depicts a San Francisco boy and his family preparing
for and enjoying their celebration of the Chinese New
Year, their most important holiday

Hoyt-Goldsmith, Diane—*Continued*

This book offers "big, bright photographs and a clear, easy-to-follow text. . . . Hoyt-Goldsmith's excellent book makes the Chinese New Year celebration accessible and understandable." SLJ

Includes glossary

Day of the Dead; a Mexican-American celebration; photographs by Lawrence Migdale. Holiday House 1994 30p il $16.95 (3-5)

394.26

1. All Souls' Day 2. Mexican Americans—Social life and customs

ISBN 0-8234-1094-3　　　　　　LC 93-42106

"Ten-year-old twins from Sacramento, California, tell the story of their family's Day of the Dead celebration. . . . Aztec beliefs and their intermingling with Catholic rituals are explained, and descriptions of dancing, art, and prayer repeatedly illustrate the unity of past and present during festival days." Booklist

"The excellent-quality, full-color photographs, drawings, and cut-paper illustrations are well placed and appealing. . . . Hoyt-Goldsmith provides a good deal of background, making *Day of the Dead* a solid report source." SLJ

Includes glossary

Las Posadas; an Hispanic Christmas celebration; photographs by Lawrence Migdale. Holiday House 1999 32p il music $16.95; pa $6.95 (3-5)

394.26

1. Christmas 2. Hispanic Americans—Social life and customs

ISBN 0-8234-1449-3; 0-8234-1635-6 (pa)

LC 99-17337

Follows a Hispanic American family in a small New Mexican community as they prepare for and celebrate the nine-day religious festival which occurs just before Christmas

"Numerous clear, colorful photos bring the text to life. . . . A recipe for Las Posadas cookies, biscochitos, is provided, along with *The Song of Las Posadas* in both Spanish and English." Booklist

Includes glossary

Three Kings Day; a celebration at Christmastime; photographs by Lawrence Migdale. Holiday House 2004 30p il map $16.95 (3-5)

394.26

1. Epiphany 2. Puerto Ricans—United States

ISBN 0-8234-1839-1　　　　　　LC 2003-67625

This "photo-essay introduces Three Kings Day, or Dia de los Tres Reyes, and shows the celebration as experienced by a 10-year-old girl in New York's Puerto Rican community. . . . The clearly written text conveys a good deal of information in a lively, accessible manner. The many photographs capture the joyful spirit of the holiday." Booklist

Includes glossary

Jango-Cohen, Judith

Chinese New Year; illustrations by Jason Chin. Carolrhoda Books 2005 48p il (On my own holidays) lib bdg $23.93; pa $5.95 (1-3)

394.26

1. Chinese New Year

ISBN 1-57505-653-4 (lib bdg); 1-57505-763-8 (pa)

LC 2004-4472

This "book describes the celebration of Chinese New Year. . . . Among the topics discussed are the Chinese zodiac, traditional symbols of the new year, family feasts and traditions for the holiday, and community activities, such as parades. . . . Clearly written, informative, and child-centered without talking down to children, this provides a good introduction to the holiday." Booklist

Jones, Lynda

Kids around the world celebrate! the best feasts and festivals from many lands. Wiley 1999 c2000 124p il pa $12.95 (4-6)　　　　　　**394.26**

1. Festivals 2. Holidays

ISBN 0-471-34527-X　　　　　　LC 99-14639

Introduces a variety of festivals celebrated around the world. Includes recipes and hands-on activities to give a taste of what it is like to be part of a feast or ceremony in another country

Jordan, Denise

Juneteenth; [by] Denise M. Jordan. Heinemann Library 2003 32p il (Holiday histories) $25.36; pa $7.60 (1-3)　　　　　　**394.26**

1. Juneteenth 2. African Americans—Social life and customs

ISBN 1-4034-3505-7; 1-4034-4253-3 (pa)

LC 2003-7827

"Juneteenth, which began in Texas, commemorates the end of African-American slavery. The meaning of [the] celebration is explained in basic, understandable language. . . . A lively combination of short chapters, bold text, vivid color photographs, and historical drawings and photos makes for [an] attractive [package] that will certainly hold the attention of young readers." SLJ

Junior worldmark encyclopedia of world holidays; [edited by Robert Griffin and Ann H. Shurgin] U.X.L 2000 4v il set $185 (5 and up)

394.26

1. Holidays 2. Festivals

ISBN 0-7876-3927-3　　　　　　LC 00-23425

Alphabetically arranged entries provide descriptions of celebrations around the world of some thirty holidays and festivals, including national and cultural holidays, such as Independence Day and New Year's Day, which are commemorated on different days for different reasons in a number of countries

Includes bibliographical references

Kindersley, Anabel

Celebrations; written by Anabel Kindersley; photographed by Barnabas Kindersley. DK Pub. 1997 63p il (Children just like me) $17.95 (3-5)

394.26

1. Festivals 2. Holidays

ISBN 0-7894-2027-9　　　　　　LC 97-20108

Kindersley, Anabel—*Continued*
Published in association with UNICEF
"The celebrations are arranged by season and include: Christmas in Germany, Halloween in Canada, Hanukkah in the U.S., Diwali in India, Hina Matsuri in Japan, and Egemenlik Bayrami in Turkey. Each holiday is shown on a two-page spread with a large photograph of a featured child or children and many smaller captioned photographs of the festivities and the culture. . . . A superb addition to country/cultural teaching units." SLJ

Landau, Elaine
Easter; parades, chocolates, and celebration; [by] Elaine Landau. Enslow Publishers 2004 48p il (Finding out about holidays) lib bdg $23.93 (2-4)
394.26
1. Easter
ISBN 0-7660-2172-6   LC 2003-27483
Contents: Was that the Easter Bunny?; It started this way; A holiday that is more than a day; Easter symbols; Celebrating Easter; Still more celebrations!
This introduction to Easter covers "historical origins and [includes] descriptions of the symbols from eggs and bunnies to lambs and lilies, as well as both religious and secular celebrations, such as sunrise services, parades, and egg hunts. . . . The informative text is enhanced with colorful photographs." SLJ
Includes glossary and bibliographical references

St. Patrick's Day; parades, shamrocks, and leprechauns. Enslow Pubs. 2002 48p il (Finding out about holidays) lib bdg $18.95 (2-4)
394.26
1. Saint Patrick's Day
ISBN 0-7660-1777-X   LC 2001-5560
"The story of St. Patrick is told, with legend and fact delineated. The significance of the color green is explained, as is that of shamrocks, four-leaf clovers, and pots of gold. Parades, festivals, athletic events, and special foods are all discussed. The text is clear and engaging, and the attractive color photos, reproductions, and drawings add interest and detail." SLJ
Includes glossary and bibliographical references

Valentine's day; candy, love, and hearts. Enslow Pubs. 2002 48p il (Finding out about holidays) lib bdg $18.95 (2-4)
394.26
1. Valentine's Day
ISBN 0-7660-1779-6   LC 2001-989
"Three origins of the holiday are presented, followed by ways in which the day is celebrated around the world. . . . The large print and the well-placed, attractive color photos and illustrations make this book accessible to its intended audience." SLJ
Includes glossary and bibliographical references

Lankford, Mary D.
Christmas around the world; illustrated by Karen Dugan. Morrow Junior Bks. 1995 47p il map $16; lib bdg $16.89; pa $5.95 (3-5)   **394.26**
1. Christmas
ISBN 0-688-12166-7; 0-688-12167-5 (lib bdg); 0-688-16323-8 (pa)   LC 93-38566

This book "looks at the rich diversity of Christmas traditions found in 12 distinctly different cultures. A small amount of pertinent background information serves as an introduction to each entry, but the majority of the text discusses the special ways each culture celebrates the holiday. The book's attractive layout effectively uses repetition of color and theme, with each double-page spread of text and art surrounded by a decorative border. . . . The book features a small selection of craft activities. . . . A helpful pronunciation guide, and an interesting selection of Christmas superstitions." Booklist
Includes bibliographical references

Lasky, Kathryn
Days of the Dead; photographs by Christopher G. Knight. Hyperion Bks. for Children 1994 48p il lib bdg $16.49; pa $5.95 (4-6)   **394.26**
1. All Souls' Day 2. Mexico—Social life and customs
ISBN 0-7868-2018-7 (lib bdg); 0-7868-1055-6 (pa)
LC 93-47957
The author "details the history and customs associated with this traditional Mexican celebration, briefly tells how it is linked to practices in ancient cultures, and describes a contemporary rural family's preparations and observances. . . . Large, bold, and often dramatic full-color photographs fill the pages, amplifying and extending the text." SLJ

Leeper, Angela
Juneteenth; a day to celebrate freedom from slavery; [by] Angela Leeper. Enslow 2003 48p il lib bdg $23.95 (3-5)   **394.26**
1. Juneteenth 2. African Americans—Social life and customs
ISBN 0-7660-2206-4   LC 2003-8815
Contents: What is Juneteenth?; Early African-American history; Early Juneteenth celebrations; Juneteenth becomes a holiday; Juneteenth today
"Leeper opens with a vivid description of the festivities that take place during a typical Juneteenth celebration. She explains why the day is commemorated and its origins, and includes a chapter on early African Americans. Short sentences and colorful photographs give just enough information for young readers." SLJ
Includes bibligraphical references

Matthew, Kathryn I.
Neal-Schuman guide to celebrations & holidays around the world; [by] Kathryn I. Matthew, Joy L. Lowe. Neal-Schuman Publishers 2004 xx, 452p il pa $65   **394.26**
1. Holidays—Bibliography 2. Festivals—Bibliography 3. Children's literature—Bibliography
ISBN 1-55570-479-4   LC 2003-59940
"The first section provides bibliographic information and suggested grade levels for titles on specific days. Sections that follow offer longer, more detailed explanations of the meaning and significance of a holiday and a . . . description of the content of each recommended book or media choice. 'Explorations,' or activities for sharing specific titles with students, are included." SLJ
"Selecting books that represent favorite authors who will appeal to children, the authors have designed a work

Matthew, Kathryn I.—*Continued*
that will be useful to elementary librarians and teachers looking for culturally sensitive resources and activities to teach K-8 students about more than 80 holidays." Booklist

McKissack, Patricia C.
Christmas in the big house, Christmas in the quarters; by Patricia C. McKissack and Fredrick L. McKissack; illustrated by John Thompson. Scholastic 1994 68p il pa $6.99 hardcover o.p. (4 and up) **394.26**
1. Plantation life 2. Christmas 3. Slavery—United States
ISBN 0-590-43028-9 (pa)   LC 92-33831
Coretta Scott King award for text, 1995
"The authors view the holiday from the perspectives of both slaveholder and his household in the 'Big House' and the slaves in the 'Quarters.' Rich descriptions of preparations fill the text—recipes and menus from both groups are provided—and colorful paintings reflect the antebellum period. Sprinkled throughout the book are lyrics of traditional spirituals, carols, and poetry. . . . Use of authentic language of the time helps the narrative flow, and carefully documented notes illuminate the interesting text." Horn Book
Includes bibliographical references

Moehn, Heather
World holidays; a Watts guide for children. Watts 2000 123p il lib bdg $26.80; pa $19.95 (3-6) **394.26**
1. Holidays 2. Festivals
ISBN 0-531-11714-6 (lib bdg); 0-531-16490-X (pa)
LC 99-14673
An illustrated alphabetical guide to celebrations and holidays around the world, including religious, civic, and cultural practices
"This will be just the ticket for short reports—and for young researchers studying connections between human cultures." Booklist
Includes bibliographical references

Nelson, Vaunda Micheaux
Juneteenth; by Vaunda Micheaux Nelson and Drew Nelson; illustrations by Mark Schroder. Millbrook Press 2006 48p il (On my own holidays) lib bdg $23.93 (2-4) **394.26**
1. Juneteenth 2. African Americans—Social life and customs
ISBN 978-1-57505-876-4 (lib bdg); 1-57505-976-6 (pa)   LC 2005-15334
This is an introduction to the holiday "which celebrates the belated arrival of emancipation news to Texas slaves on June 19, 1865. . . . [This] offers a solid introduction to the holiday for independent readers or for presenting to small groups." Booklist

Perl, Lila
Piñatas and paper flowers; holidays of the Americas in English and Spanish; illustrated by Victoria de Larrea. Clarion Bks. 1983 91p il pa $7.95 hardcover o.p. (4 and up) **394.26**
1. Holidays 2. Folklore—Latin America 3. Bilingual books—English-Spanish
ISBN 0-89919-155-X (pa)   LC 82-1211
Text and title page in English and Spanish; Spanish version by Alma Flor Ada
A brief overview of eight holidays and their customs as celebrated in the Americas. Holidays covered include: The New Year, Three Kings' Day; Carnival and Easter; St. John the Baptist Day; Columbus Day; Halloween; The Festival of the Sun; and Christmas

Pinkney, Andrea Davis
Seven candles for Kwanzaa; pictures by Brian Pinkney. Dial Bks. for Young Readers 1993 unp il $15.99; lib bdg $14.89; pa $5.99 (k-3) **394.26**
1. Kwanzaa 2. African Americans—Social life and customs
ISBN 0-8037-1292-8; 0-8037-1293-6 (lib bdg); 0-14-056428-4 (pa)   LC 92-3698
Describes the origins and practices of Kwanzaa, the seven-day festival during which people of African descent rejoice in their ancestral values
The "joyful text is accompanied by equally joyful scratchboard illustrations, set within colorful textilelike borders, depicting a family preparing for and celebrating the holiday." Booklist
Includes bibliographical references

Shea, Pegi Deitz
Ten mice for Tet! by Pegi Deitz Shea and Cynthia Weill; illustrations by Tô Ngoc Trang; embroidery by Pham Viêt Dinh. Chronicle Books 2003 unp il $15.95 (k-3) **394.26**
1. Vietnamese New Year 2. Counting 3. Mice—Fiction
ISBN 0-8118-3496-4   LC 2002-7456
A village of mice prepares for Tet, or Vietnamese New Year, as different numbers of mice give gifts, cook food, and celebrate in other traditional ways. Includes an afterword with facts about the holiday
"This accessible counting book is a lovely introduction to the Vietnamese New Year. . . . Remarkable, vividly colored, embroidered artwork enhances the text." SLJ

Simonds, Nina
Moonbeams, dumplings & dragon boats; a treasury of Chinese holiday tales, activities & recipes; [by] Nina Simonds, Leslie Swartz, & the Children's Museum of Boston; illustrated by Meilo So. Harcourt 2002 74p il $20 (4 and up) **394.26**
1. Festivals—China
ISBN 0-15-201983-9   LC 2001-4280
"Gulliver books"
Presents background information, related tales, and activities for celebrating five Chinese festivals—Chinese

Simonds, Nina—*Continued*
New Year, the Lantern Festival, Qing Ming, the Dragon
Boat Festival, and the Moon Festival
"The ample white space surrounding the text is filled
with small, whimsical watercolor illustrations. . . . [This]
is a useful, visually appealing addition to any holiday
collection." SLJ
Includes bibliographical references

Trawicky, Bernard
Anniversaries and holidays. 5th ed. American
Lib. Assn. 2000 311p $68   **394.26**
1. Holidays 2. Calendars 3. Birthdays
ISBN 0-8389-0695-8   LC 99-56166
First edition by Mary Emogene Hazeltine published
1928
"Covers, in calendar form, the names of important
people, holidays, religious festivals and special events for
nearly 200 countries. Annotated bibliographies about holidays, etc." N Y Public Libr. Ref Books for Child Collect. 2d edition [entry for 4th edition]

Walter, Mildred Pitts
Kwanzaa: a family affair. Lothrop, Lee &
Shepard Bks. 1995 95p il hardcover o.p. pa $3.99
(4 and up)   **394.26**
1. Kwanzaa 2. African Americans—Social life and
customs
ISBN 0-380-72735-8; 0-688-11553-5 (pa)
This is a "guide to preparing for and celebrating
Kwanzaa that encourages early planning and the sharing
of family histories. The principles and symbols are clearly explained, and the directions for making simple gifts
are accompanied by adequate line drawings. Walter's enthusiasm for her subject brightens this modest effort."
Booklist
Includes glossary and bibliographical references

Waters, Kate
Lion dancer: Ernie Wan's Chinese New Year;
by Kate Waters and Madeline Slovenz-Low;
photographs by Martha Cooper. Scholastic 1990
unp il pa $4.99 hardcover o.p. (k-3)
                    394.26
1. Chinese New Year 2. Chinese Americans—Social
life and customs
ISBN 0-590-43047-5 (pa)   LC 89-6423
Describes six-year-old Ernie Wan's preparations, at
home and in school, for the Chinese New Year celebrations and his first public performance of the lion dance
"While some of the pictures look posed, the marvelously colorful photographs successfully capture Ernie's
pride and anticipation as he is dressed in his gorgeous
costume and the excitement and swirling movement of
the subsequent parade. Illustrations of a Chinese lunar
calendar and a Chinese horoscope are extra dividends in
a useful and appealing book." Horn Book

395 Etiquette (Manners)

Aliki
Hello! good-bye! Greenwillow Bks. 1996 unp il
$15; lib bdg $14.93 (k-3)   **395**
1. Etiquette 2. Communication
ISBN 0-688-14333-4; 0-688-14334-2 (lib bdg)
                    LC 95-25090
Describes some of the many ways, both verbal and
nonverbal, that people say hello and good-bye
"Vivid cartoons rendered in watercolors and colored
pencils show plenty of action and accurately reflect the
concise text. . . . While entertaining readers, the author
offers vocabulary by providing synonyms, and then explains that sometimes words are not necessary if gestures
are used. Illustrations of people from far-away lands in
traditional dress are found throughout." SLJ

Manners. Greenwillow Bks. 1990 unp il $16; lib
bdg $15.93; pa $5.95 (k-3)   **395**
1. Etiquette
ISBN 0-688-09198-9; 0-688-09199-7 (lib bdg);
0-688-04579-0 (pa)   LC 89-34622
The author discusses etiquette and good manners
"Aliki makes manners accessible to children through
colorful cartoon-style illustrations. . . . Her lively primer
sparkles with examples of the proper and the poor."
Booklist

Holyoke, Nancy
A smart girl's guide to manners; the secrets to
grace, confidence, and being your best; illustrated
by Cathi Mingus. American Girl 2005 120p il pa
$9.95 (3-6)   **395**
1. Etiquette
ISBN 1-58485-983-0
A revised edition of Oops! The manners guide for
girls, published 1997 by Pleasant Co
This "covers the basic etiquette areas, including cell
phone and table manners, host and guest duties, and such
occasions as weddings and family gatherings. The text is
sprinkled with lots of colorful illustrations and quizzes
geared to letting readers assess their own behavior.
Though the rules echo the traditional thoughts on the
subjects, the lively writing and straight talk make them
seem fresh and relevant today." SLJ

Joslin, Sesyle
What do you do, dear? pictures by Maurice
Sendak. Harper & Row 1985 c1961 unp il pa
$6.95 hardcover o.p. (k-2)   **395**
1. Etiquette
ISBN 0-06-443113-4 (pa)   LC 84-43139
First published 1961 by Addison-Wesley
A "handbook of etiquette for young ladies and gentle-
men to be used as a guide for everyday social behavior."
The Author
"The propriety of what the well-mannered child will
do is related to extraordinary situations, as for example:
The Sheriff of Nottingham interrupts you while you are
reading, to take you to jail; you will, naturally, 'Find a
bookmark to save your place.'" Horn Book

Joslin, Sesyle—*Continued*

A "wonderful spoof on manners in a hilarious picture-book made for laughing aloud." Child Study Assoc of Am

What do you say, dear? pictures by Maurice Sendak. Harper & Row 1986 c1958 unp il lib bdg $15.89; pa $5.95 (k-2)   **395**

1. Etiquette

ISBN 0-06-023074-6 (lib bdg); 0-06-443112-6 (pa)

LC 84-43140

A Caldecott Medal honor book, 1959

First published 1958 by Addison-Wesley

A "handbook of etiquette for young ladies and gentlemen to be used as a guide for everyday social behavior." The Author

"A rollicking introduction to manners for the very young. A series of delightfully absurd situations—being introduced to a baby elephant, bumping into a crocodile, being rescued from a dragon—are posed and appropriately answered. The illustrations are among Sendak's best—and funniest." Bull Cent Child Books

Post, Peggy

Emily Post's The guide to good manners for kids; by Peggy Post & Cindy Post Senning. HarperCollins 2004 144p il $15.99; lib bdg $16.89 (5 and up)   **395**

1. Etiquette

ISBN 0-06-057196-9; 0-06-057197-7 (lib bdg)

LC 2003-26426

This offers advice on etiquette at home, at school, and other places, including letter writing and on-line communication, table manners, phone answering, and behavior at social gatherings, and public places.

"The writing is clear, friendly, and sometimes clever. . . . The advice is consistently practical and simple." SLJ

398 Folklore

Allen, Judy

Fantasy encyclopedia. 1st ed. Kingfisher 2005 144p il $19.95 (4 and up)   **398**

1. Fairies 2. Mythical animals

ISBN 0-7534-5847-0   LC 2004-29475

"This highly visual presentation introduces readers to fantasy characters within their habitats and genres. . . . More than 50 types of characters are arranged in nine chapters covering topics such as 'The Little People,' 'Mysterious Animals,' and 'Ghosts and Spirits.' . . . Student fans of the fantasy genre will find this tool exceedingly browsable, and school and public libraries will want to purchase reference and circulating copies." Booklist

Includes glossary

Beeler, Selby B.

Throw your tooth on the roof; tooth traditions from around the world; illustrated by G. Brian Karas. Houghton Mifflin 1998 unp il $16 (k-3)   **398**

1. Teeth—Folklore

ISBN 0-395-89108-6   LC 97-46042

Consists of brief statements relating what children from around the world do with a tooth that has fallen out. Includes facts about teeth

"This book will be an eye-opener for young Americans who may have assumed that the Tooth Fairy holds a worldwide visa." Publ Wkly

Buller, Laura

Myths and monsters; from dragons to werewolves; consultant, Philip Wilkinson. DK Pub. 2003 96p il (DK secret worlds) $14.99; pa $5.99 (5 and up)   **398**

1. Mythical animals 2. Monsters

ISBN 0-7894-9703-4; 0-7894-9226-1 (pa)

LC 2003-268994

This guide to myths and monsters includes "photographs of artifacts such as Egyptian mummies . . . [as well as] movie stills from *Shrek*, *Lord of the Rings*, and *Harry Potter and the Sorcerer's Stone*. . . . The text provides origins of characters such as Dracula and Medusa and describes a wide variety of creatures." SLJ

"Action photographs, authentic artwork and maps, inset Weird World facts, action captions, and highlighted Web sites work together with snappy vocabulary and intriguing facts to capture a reader's interest from the first sentence on." Libr Media Connect

Includes glossary and bibliographical references

The **Dictionary** of folklore; David Adams Leeming, general editor. Watts 2002 128p il $35 (4 and up)   **398**

1. Folklore—Dictionaries

ISBN 0-531-11985-8   LC 2001-22034

This work answers such questions as "Why was Abraham Lincoln known as 'Honest Abe?' Did George Washington really cut down his father's cherry tree? How much truth is there to the tall tale of John Henry, the 'natural-born steel-driving man,' or Paul Bunyon and Babe the Blue Ox?" Publisher's note

"The layout of the book is pleasing. It is organized in alphabetical order and the content is understandable with many cross-references. The illustrations complement the text. . . . Leeming does an excellent job of enticing the reader to be curious." Book Rep

Includes bibliographical references

Gibbons, Gail

Behold . . . the dragons! Morrow Junior Bks. 1999 unp il $16; lib bdg $15.89 (k-3)   **398**

1. Dragons 2. Folklore

ISBN 0-688-15526-X; 0-688-15527-8 (lib bdg)

LC 98-20205

Explains how myths about dragons developed, different types of dragons, what draconologists do, and how different cultures portray dragons

Gibbons, Gail—_Continued_

"Numerous bright illustrations accompany the well-researched text. This is a solid, informative presentation." Horn Book Guide

MacDonald, Margaret Read

The storyteller's sourcebook; a subject, title, and motif index to folklore collections for children, 1983-1999; by Margaret Read MacDonald and Brian W. Sturm. Gale Group 2001 712p $125

398

1. Folklore—Indexes

ISBN 0-8103-5485-3   LC 00-48395

Also available original volume covering the years 1961-1982 $125 (ISBN 0-8103-0471-6)

This sourcebook "provides descriptions of folktales and references to more than 700 published sources of folktales. . . . [Includes] indexing by subject, motif, title, ethnic group and country of origin and a comprehensive bibliography." Publisher's note

Mitton, Jacqueline

Zodiac; celestial circle of the sun; [by] Jacqueline Mitton; illustrated by Christina Balit. Frances Lincoln 2005 32p il $16.95 (2-4)

398

1. Zodiac 2. Constellations

ISBN 1-84507-074-7

"Mitton covers the 12 well-known constellations belonging to the Zodiac, beginning with a brief introduction that is followed by a spread devoted to each of the signs. . . . Striking jewel-toned, classically inspired illustrations highlighted by metallic stars complement the text. This attractive survey of the symbols of the Zodiac should serve as an appealing starting point for budding astronomers and astrologers." SLJ

Opie, Iona Archibald

The lore and language of schoolchildren; by Iona and Peter Opie. Oxford Univ. Press 1960 c1959 417p il maps   **398**

1. Folklore—Great Britain

Available in paperback from New York Review of Bks.

A collection of the "rhymes, riddles, incantations, jeers, torments, parodies, nicknames, holiday customs, and other types of lore that is . . . transmitted orally, some of it over a period of hundreds of years. The basic study was made in Great Britain and detailed analysis of geographic usage is made for Great Britain but some usage in other countries is also noted. Chiefly of interest to folklorists, teachers, librarians, and others who work with children but nostalgic appeal for the general reader." Booklist

Sierra, Judy

The gruesome guide to world monsters; illustrated by Henrik Drescher. Candlewick Press 2005 63p il $18.99 (5 and up)   **398**

1. Monsters 2. Folklore

ISBN 0-7636-1727-X   LC 2004-57470

This presents "brief introductions to dozens of ugly customers from world folklore. . . . [The author] offers wonderfully provocative warnings against creatures as diverse as the giant skunk Aniwye, the bloodsucking bat Mansusopsop, and Bloody Mary, an evil specter who lives on the other side of mirrors." SLJ

Van Laan, Nancy

With a whoop and a holler; a bushel of lore from way down south; illustrated by Scott Cook. Atheneum Bks. for Young Readers 1998 102p il map hardcover o.p. pa $10 (4 and up)

398

1. Folklore—Southern States

ISBN 0-689-84473-3; 0-689-81061-X (pa)

LC 96-24336

"An Anne Schwartz book"

A collection of tales, rhymes, riddles, superstitions, and sayings organized around the three distinct regions of the South: the Bayou, the Deep South, and Appalachia

"Cook's caricature-like illustrations draw out the fun-loving humor with an affectionate wink-and-a-nod style." Horn Book Guide

398.2 Folk literature

Sagas, romances, legends, ballads, and fables in prose form, and fairy tales, folk tales, and tall tales are included here, instead of with the literature of the country of origin, to keep the traditional material together and to make it more readily accessible. Modern fairy tales are classified with Fiction, Story collections (SC), or Easy books (E)

Aardema, Verna

Anansi does the impossible! an Ashanti tale; retold by Verna Aardema; illustrated by Lisa Desimini. Atheneum Bks. for Young Readers 1997 unp il $16; pa $5.99 (k-3)   **398.2**

1. Anansi (Legendary character) 2. Folklore—West Africa

ISBN 0-689-81092-X; 0-689-83933-2 (pa)

LC 96-20033

"An Anne Schwartz book"

"Anansi the Spider is determined to buy back the stories taken from the people and kept by the Sky God. With the assistance of his clever wife, Aso, he takes the Sky God the live python, the real fairy, and the 47 stinging hornets required to regain the stories." SLJ

"Vivid, stylized collage illustrations convey the frightening force and power of the Sky God yet also reveal Anansi's own pluck and boldness. Perfect for reading or telling aloud." Booklist

Includes glossary and bibliographical references

Borreguita and the coyote; a tale from Ayutla, Mexico; retold by Verna Aardema; illustrated by Petra Mathers. Knopf 1991 unp il pa $6.99 hardcover o.p. (k-3)   **398.2**

1. Folklore—Mexico 2. Coyote (Legendary character) 3. Sheep—Folklore

ISBN 0-679-88936-1 (pa)   LC 90-33302

A little lamb uses her clever wiles to keep a coyote from eating her up

Aardema, Verna—*Continued*

This folk tale "is energetically told and comfortably packed with many recognizable motifs. Mathers enlarges upon the humorous elements of the story in her boldly colored paintings. . . . Aardema and Mathers are felicitously paired in a tale of trickery rewarded that begs to be read aloud." Horn Book

Includes glossary

Bringing the rain to Kapiti Plain; a Nandi tale; retold by Verna Aardema; pictures by Beatriz Vidal. Dial Bks. for Young Readers 1981 unp il $16.99; pa $5.99 (k-3)   398.2
1. Folklore—Africa 2. Stories in rhyme 3. Droughts—Folklore
ISBN 0-8037-0809-2; 0-8037-0904-8 (pa)
LC 80-25886

"Retold from an African folk tale, this is a cumulative rhyming tale with the rhythm and repetition of 'The House that Jack Built.' It tells of how Ki-pat, the herdsman, works out a clever method to save the plain from a long drought." SLJ

"Effective both in the rhythm of its metered storytelling and in the brilliance of its stylized paintings, the panoramic picture book quickly engages both eye and ear." Horn Book

Koi and the kola nuts; a tale from Liberia; illustrated by Joe Cepeda. Atheneum Bks. for Young Readers 1999 unp il $16.95 (k-3)
398.2
1. Folklore—Liberia
ISBN 0-689-81760-6   LC 97-46713
"An Anne Schwartz book"

Originally published 1960 in Aardema's Tales from the story hat

A Liberian folktale in which the son of the chief must make his way in the world with only a sackful of kola nuts and the help of some creatures that he has treated with kindness

"Aardema's crisp retelling . . . is given additional humor by Cepeda's jauntily irreverent illustrations. Oil paintings with backdrops of lime, apricot, and grape give a feeling of spacious plains and skies." Bull Cent Child Books

Rabbit makes a monkey of lion; a Swahili tale; retold by Verna Aardema; pictures by Jerry Pinkney. Dial Bks. for Young Readers 1989 unp il pa $5.99 hardcover o.p. (k-3)   398.2
1. Folklore—Zanzibar 2. Animals—Folklore
ISBN 0-14-054593-X (pa)   LC 86-11523
Text adapted from The hare and the lion, published 1901 in Zanzibar tales

With the help of his friends Bush-rat and Turtle, smart and nimble Rabbit makes a fool of the mighty but slow-witted king of the forest

"Aardema's version of the tale reinforces the amusing trickster qualities of rascally Rabbit, making it a sure-fire choice for sharing with groups of children, who will instantly root for her success. Pinkney's lovely watercolor and pencil paintings in hues of green, brown, and gold fill the pages with lush scenes which evoke the East African setting." Horn Book

Who's in Rabbit's house? a Masai tale; retold by Verna Aardema; pictures by Leo and Diane Dillon. Dial Bks. for Young Readers 1977 unp il pa $6.99 hardcover o.p. (k-3)   398.2
1. Masai (African people)—Folklore 2. Animals—Folklore 3. Folklore—East Africa
ISBN 0-14-054724-X (pa)   LC 77-71514

This "tale relates the attempts of Rabbit to regain possession of her house after it is taken over by an intruder. Rabbit's friends offer suggestions on how to solve the problem, but the solution comes from 'an unexpected source.' The story, adapted from the Masai tale 'The Long One,' uses repetition of key phrases to produce a rhythmic read-aloud text. The Dillons skillfully present their artistry in a vivid, colorful and impressive manner which contributes to the story and sets the tone." Child Book Rev Serv

Why mosquitoes buzz in people's ears; a West African tale retold; pictures by Leo and Diane Dillon. Dial Bks. for Young Readers 1975 unp il $16.99; pa $6.99 (k-3)   398.2
1. Folklore—West Africa 2. Mosquitoes—Folklore 3. Animals—Folklore
ISBN 0-8037-6089-2; 0-14-054905-6 (pa)

Awarded the Caldecott Medal, 1976

This tale relates "how a mosquito's silly lie to an iguana sets in motion a cumulative series of events that finally causes Mother Owl not to call up the sun. The resulting hardship ends only after King Lion traces the problem back to its source." Booklist

"Stunning full-color illustrations—watercolor sprayed with air gun, overlayed with pastel, cut out and repasted—give an eye-catching abstract effect and tell the story with humor and power." SLJ

Adler, David A.

Chanukah in Chelm; [illustrated by] Kevin O'Malley. Lothrop, Lee & Shepard Bks. 1997 unp il lib bdg $15.89 (k-3)   398.2
1. Jews—Folklore 2. Hanukkah—Folklore
ISBN 0-688-09953-X   LC 96-53127

When the rabbi tells Mendel to get a table for the Chanukah menorah, Mendel makes the task more difficult than it should be

"Adler's witty text finds able companionship in O'Malley's old-worldly crosshatched pen and watercolor illustrations, which capture the folly of the residents of Chelm with both humor and respectful affection." Horn Book Guide

Afanas'ev, A. N. (Aleksandr Nikolaevich)

Russian fairy tales; translated by Norbert Guterman from the collections of Aleksandr Afanas'ev; illustrated by Alexander Alexeieff; folkloristic commentary by Roman Jakobson. Pantheon Bks. 1975 c1945 661p il pa $18 hardcover o.p. (4 and up)   398.2
1. Folklore—Russia 2. Fairy tales
ISBN 0-394-73090-9 (pa)

A reprint of the title first published 1945

Afanas'ev's "tales carry the reader to faraway Russian villages, long winter nights, deep snow, thatched huts,

Afanás'ev, A. N. (Aleksandr Nikolaevich)—*Continued*
forests teeming with wild animals and muzhiks (peasants), who have never progressed beyond the very beginnings of human civilization. . . . [This is a] beautiful book. I recommend it to all readers, young and old who are interested in the folktale and its unique qualities." N Y Times Book Rev
Includes bibliographical references

The **Arabian** nights entertainments; selected and edited by Andrew Lang; with numerous illustrations by H. J. Ford. Dover Publs. 1969 424p il pa $9.95 (5 and up) **398.2**
1. Arabs—Folklore 2. Fairy tales
ISBN 0-486-22289-6
First published 1898 in the United Kingdom
"A collection of popular tales assembled over many centuries, and well known in Europe from the 18th cent. It contains the stories of 'Aladdin, Alibaba, and Sindbad the sailor.' . . . The framing story in which the tales are set concerns Scheherazade, who is determined to delay her royal husband's plan of killing her—he has taken to murdering his wives because the first was unfaithful to him—by telling him a story every evening. She leaves each evening's tale incomplete until the next day, so that he has to spare her life in order to hear its conclusion. He is so entertained that he finally abandons his murderous plan." Oxford Companion to Child Lit

Aylesworth, Jim
The Gingerbread man; retold by Jim Aylesworth; illustrated by Barbara McClintock. Scholastic 1998 unp il $15.95 (k-3) **398.2**
1. Folklore
ISBN 0-590-97219-7 LC 96-52781
A freshly baked gingerbread man escapes when he is taken out of the oven and eludes a number of pursuers until he meets a clever fox
"This hearty retelling of the well-known tale is distinguished by cheery, lively illustrations. . . . The scenery resembles that of the eighteenth-century English artist Thomas Bewick. With even a recipe included, this is altogether an old-fashioned and enjoyable version of a favorite tale." Horn Book Guide

Goldilocks and the three bears; retold by Jim Aylesworth; illustrated by Barbara McClintock. Scholastic Press 2003 unp il $15.95 (k-3) **398.2**
1. Folklore 2. Bears—Folklore
ISBN 0-439-28133-4 LC 2002-15964
A little girl walking in the woods finds the house of the three bears and helps herself to their belongings
"Aylesworth's text is faithful to the traditional elements of the original, juicing up the plot with folksy, conversational asides. . . . The artist's watercolor, sepia ink, and gouache illustrations are pastel and dainty yet full of life and action." SLJ

The tale of Tricky Fox; a New England trickster tale; retold by Jim Aylesworth; illustrated by Barbara McClintock. Scholastic Press 2001 unp il $15.95 (k-3) **398.2**
1. Foxes—Folklore 2. Folklore—New England
ISBN 0-439-09543-3 LC 00-35773

Tricky Fox uses his sack to trick everyone he meets into giving him ever more valuable items
"The romping good humor of the story is carried by the old-fashioned illustrations in sepia tones." SLJ

Babbitt, Natalie
Ouch! a tale from Grimm; retold by Natalie Babbitt; illustrated by Fred Marcellino. HarperCollins Pubs. 1998 unp il $14.95; lib bdg $15.89 (k-3) **398.2**
1. Fairy tales 2. Folklore—Germany
ISBN 0-06-205066-4; 0-06-205067-2 (lib bdg)
"Michael di Capua books"
"A fortuneteller predicts that Marco will marry a princess and this comes to pass in short order. . . . The youth still must placate his evil father-in-law, the king, who demands three golden hairs from the head of the Devil." Publ Wkly
"Babbitt's language is perfect: neither too archaic nor too modern. Throughout the story, words and pictures work together to underscore the humor in the tale. . . . With comic perspectives and sly expression Marcellino introduces a farcical cast." SLJ

Badoe, Adwoa
The pot of wisdom: Ananse stories; pictures by Baba Wagué Diakité. Douglas & McIntyre 2001 63p il $18.95 **398.2**
1. Anansi (Legendary character) 2. Folklore—West Africa
ISBN 0-88899-429-X
"A Groundwood book"
The author "retells ten tales of Ananse, the West African trickster figure. Stories include a version of the tar-baby story, a tale involving secrets between husband and wife, and several entries wherein an embarrassed Ananse suffers when his tricks backfire on him." Bull Cent Child Books
"Badoe remembers hearing these trickster stories in her youth in Ghana, and she retells them with the freshness and verve of the spoken word. . . . Each tale is illustrated with a brilliantly colored polychrome tile by Diakite, the Mali-born illustrator. The tiles employ strong black linear motifs and sun-and-earth colors: gold, orange, brown, blue, lemon." Booklist

Balit, Christina
Atlantis; the legend of a lost city; adapted and retold by Christina Balit; with a note by Geoffrey Ashe. Holt & Co. 2000 c1999 unp il $16.95 (2-4) **398.2**
1. Atlantis
ISBN 0-8050-6334-X LC 99-27943
First published 1999 in the United Kingdom
Adapted and retold from Plato's Timaeus and Critias
In this retelling of Plato's legend, "the city founded by Poseidon flourishes, then falters and is finally destroyed when its inhabitants start acting more like greedy mortals than like gods. Exquisitely detailed illustrations, rich in geometric patterns, capture the tragic core of the story. A historical note is included." Horn Book Guide

Barton, Byron

The little red hen. HarperCollins Pubs. 1993 unp il $15.95; lib bdg $15.89 (k-2) **398.2**
1. Folklore 2. Chickens—Folklore
ISBN 0-06-021675-1; 0-06-021676-X (lib bdg)
LC 91-4051
Also available Board book edition and Big book edition

The little red hen finds none of her lazy friends willing to help her plant, harvest, or grind wheat into flour, but all are eager to eat the bread she makes from it

"Barton here skillfully pares down a well-known tale for the youngest readers and listeners. Vibrant hues abound in his full-page, collage-like illustrations." Publ Wkly

The three bears. HarperCollins Pubs. 1991 unp il $15.95; lib bdg $15.89 (k-1) **398.2**
1. Folklore 2. Bears—Folklore
ISBN 0-06-020423-0; 0-06-020424-9 (lib bdg)
LC 90-43151
Also available Board book edition

"Here's the familiar tale of the three bears and their blond gal pal drawn for the very youngest. Byron uses large simple shapes, bright colors, and a spare text to tell his story. . . . The size of the art makes this a good choice for mother-toddler story hours." Booklist

Bedard, Michael

The wolf of Gubbio; story by Michael Bedard; paintings by Murray Kimber. Stoddart Kids 2000 unp il $15.95 (3-6) **398.2**
1. Francis, of Assisi, Saint, 1182-1226—Legends 2. Wolves—Folklore 3. Italy—Fiction
ISBN 0-7737-3250-0

When a wolf terrorizes the town of Gubbio, a humble stranger confronts the beast and makes peace between it and the villagers. Based on one of the St. Francis of Assisi legends.

"Murray Kimber's paintings have the hieratic geometry of stained glass, all angles and forms enriched with sun-drenched russets and golds. . . . The quiet of Bedard's narrative is deeply powerful" Booklist

Ben-'Ezer, Ehud

Hosni the dreamer; an Arabian tale; pictures by Uri Shulevitz. Farrar, Straus & Giroux 1997 unp il $16 (2-4) **398.2**
1. Arabs—Folklore 2. Shepherds—Folklore 3. Deserts—Folklore
ISBN 0-374-33340-8
LC 96-18608

"Hosni is regarded as a fool by his fellow shepherds when during his trip to the city he spends all his money on a verse. But his purchase saves his life and secures his happiness and fortune." Horn Book

"Ben-Ezer uses crisp, vivid language throughout; he includes descriptions and phrases that suggest the tale's setting. Shulevitz's illustrations add a light, comic touch." SLJ

Beneduce, Ann

Jack and the beanstalk; retold by Ann Keay Beneduce; illustrated by Gennady Spirin. Philomel Bks. 1999 32p il $16.99 (2-4) **398.2**
1. Fairy tales 2. Folklore—Great Britain
ISBN 0-399-23118-8
LC 98-5722

A boy climbs to the top of a giant beanstalk, where he uses his quick wits to outsmart an ogre and make his and his mother's fortune

"Beneduce bases her version of Jack and the Beanstalk on a Victorian version, complete with a fairy guardian. . . . Spirin contributes some glorious borders for the text as well as many impressively detailed paintings, notable for their dark muted colors and mysterious, foggy look." Booklist

Berger, Barbara

All the way to Lhasa; a tale from Tibet; retelling & art by Barbara Helen Berger. Philomel Bks. 2002 unp il $15.99 (k-3) **398.2**
1. Folklore—Tibet (China)
ISBN 0-399-23387-3
LC 2001-54560
Based on a story told to the author by Lama Tharchin Rinpoche

A boy and his yak persevere along the difficult way to the holy city of Lhasa and succeed where others fail

"Berger distills the pilgrim's quest into a simply told, evocative tale. . . . Berger's paint-and-pencil illustrations are gloriously colored and filled with subtle details borrowed from Tibetan Buddhism." Booklist

Bernier-Grand, Carmen T.

Juan Bobo; four folktales from Puerto Rico; retold by Carmen T. Bernier-Grand; pictures by Ernesto Ramos Nieves. HarperCollins Pubs. 1994 58p il pa $3.95 hardcover o.p. (k-2)
398.2
1. Folklore—Puerto Rico
ISBN 0-06-444185-7 (pa)
LC 93-12936
"An I can read book"

Four folktales from rural Puerto Rico about the comical Juan Bobo's nonsensical shenanigans

The tales "are told with immediacy and spirit. The exuberant folk-style illustrations in bright tropical colors reflect the island setting and the scenes of comic confrontation. . . . A Spanish translation is provided in small print at the back." Booklist

Bierhorst, John

Is my friend at home? Pueblo fireside tales; retold by John Bierhorst; pictures by Wendy Watson. Farrar, Straus & Giroux 2001 unp il $16 (1-4) **398.2**
1. Hopi Indians—Folklore 2. Coyote (Legendary character)
ISBN 0-374-33550-8
LC 99-29214

A collection of traditional tales originally told in the Hopi pueblos of Arizona, featuring Coyote and other animal characters

"Watson's slate-and-earth-toned cartoon illustrations, featuring an endearingly frazzled, frantic cast, capture the spirit of these disarmingly absurd, unexpectedly touching tales." Horn Book

Bierhorst, John—*Continued*

The people with five fingers; a native Californian creation tale; retold by John Bierhorst; illustrated by Robert Andrew Parker. Marshall Cavendish 2000 unp il $15.95 (k-3) **398.2**
1. Native Americans—Folklore
ISBN 0-7614-5058-0   LC 99-28795
A tale shared by the different native peoples of California tells how Coyote and other animals created the world and the people who came to live in it
"The spare watercolor illustrations complement this quietly appealing story." Horn Book Guide

Blackstone, Stella
Storytime; first tales for sharing; told by Stella Blackstone; illustrated by Anne Wilson. Barefoot Books 2005 94p il $19.99 (k-1) **398.2**
1. Folklore 2. Animals—Folklore
ISBN 1-84148-345-1   LC 2004029542
"Seven familiar nursery tales are accompanied by bright, stylized, folk-art illustrations, done in paper collage and acrylic. Selections include The Cock, the Mouse and the Little Red Hen, The Gingerbread Man, The Ugly Duckling, Goldilocks, The Timid Hare (a Henny Penny story from India), The Three Little Pigs, and Stone Soup. The retellings are straightforward; most are faithful to the most commonly known versions and retain the familiar refrains. . . . The collection as a whole is delightful; the art is fresh, vibrant, and full of child appeal." SLJ
Includes bibliographical references

Blackwood, Gary L.
Legends or lies? Marshall Cavendish Benchmark 2006 72p il (Unsolved history) lib bdg $29.93 (4 and up) **398.2**
1. Legends
ISBN 0-7614-1891-1
Describes several legends that have intrigued people for centuries: the lost civilization of Atlantis, the Amazons, King Arthur, St Brendon, Pope Joan, and El Dorado
This collection of "of tidbits about lingering mysteries of the past . . . [offers] more substance than most. . . . [It offers] a full-page illustration opening each chapter; reproductions, many in color; and a generously spaced format." SLJ
Includes glossary and bibliographical references

Blia Xiong
Nine-in-one, Grr! Grr! a folktale from the Hmong people of Laos; told by Blia Xiong; adapted by Cathy Spagnoli; illustrated by Nancy Hom. Children's Bk. Press 1989 30p il $14.95; pa $7.95 (k-2) **398.2**
1. Folklore—Laos 2. Tigers—Folklore 3. Hmong (Asian people)—Folklore
ISBN 0-89239-048-4; 0-89239-110-3 (pa)
LC 89-9891
When the great god Shao promises Tiger nine cubs each year, Bird comes up with a clever trick to prevent the land from being overrun by tigers

"Simply and eloquently told, this *pourquoi* tale from a minority Laotian culture is boldly illustrated in a style adapted from the multi-imaged embroidered story cloths of the Hmong people. Its rhythmic text and appealing, brightly colored pictures make it a good choice for preschool story hours." Booklist

The **Blue** fairy book; edited by Andrew Lang; with numerous illustrations by H. J. Ford and G. P. Jacomb Hood. Dover Publs. 1965 390p il pa $10.95 (4-6) **398.2**
1. Folklore 2. Fairy tales
ISBN 0-486-21437-0
Also available in paperback $10.95 each: The Green fairy book; The Grey fairy book; The Lilac fairy book; The Olive fairy book; The Orange fairy book; The Pink fairy book; The Red fairy book; The Yellow fairy book
A reprint of the title first published 1889 by Longmans
A collection of thirty-seven fairy tales from various countries, consisting largely of old favorites from such sources as Perrault, the Brothers Grimm, Madame D'Aulnoy, Asbjörnsen and Möe, the Arabian Nights and Swift's Gulliver's travels

Bodger, Joan
Tales of court and castle; illustrated by Mark Lang. Tundra Books 2003 88p il pa $9.95 (5 and up) **398.2**
1. Folklore—Great Britain
ISBN 0-88776-614-5
This presents "retellings of seven English, Irish, and Welsh tales. Tristan, Iron John, Burd Janet, Tamlane, and others come to life with language that speaks to the stories' origins, but will engage modern readers. . . . Lang's illustrations are detailed and wonderfully moody, adding to the otherworldly appeal of the book." SLJ

Bodkin, Odds
The crane wife; retold by Odds Bodkin; illustrated by Gennady Spirin. Gulliver Bks. 1998 unp il $16 (3-5) **398.2**
1. Folklore—Japan
ISBN 0-15-201407-1   LC 96-35488
A retelling of the traditional Japanese tale about a poor sail maker who gains a beautiful but mysterious wife skilled at weaving magical sails
"Capturing the tale's mystery and tragedy, Spirin's watercolor-and-gouache paintings take their inspiration from Japanese art. Delicate shades of tawny gray and burnished gold predominate in the illustrations." Booklist

Brett, Jan
Beauty and the beast; retold and illustrated by Jan Brett. Clarion Bks. 1989 unp il lib bdg $16; pa $6.95 (1-3) **398.2**
1. Folklore—France 2. Fairy tales
ISBN 0-89919-497-4 (lib bdg); 0-395-55702-X (pa)
LC 88-16965
Through her great capacity to love, a kind and beautiful maid releases a handsome prince from the spell which has made him an ugly beast

Brett, Jan—*Continued*

"A Beauty of distinguished appearance, a delightful set of animal servants, and a suitably hideous Beast are presented in Jan Brett's distinctive, decorative style. Small details, such as tapestries mirroring the action of the tale, add to the effect of the simply written story." Horn Book Guide

Gingerbread baby. Putnam 1999 unp il $16.99 (k-3)   **398.2**
1. Folklore
ISBN 0-399-23444-6   LC 98-52310
A young boy and his mother bake a gingerbread baby that escapes from their oven and leads a crowd on a chase
"Although the story remains true to the original tale, Brett has added her own touches and a surprise ending. . . . The illustrations are pure Brett and feature warm colors against a snow-white landscape." SLJ

The mitten; a Ukrainian folktale; adapted and illustrated by Jan Brett. Putnam 1989 unp il $16.99 (k-2)   **398.2**
1. Folklore—Ukraine 2. Animals—Folklore
ISBN 0-399-21920-X   LC 88-32198
Also available Board book edition
"Grandmother knits snow-white mittens that Nikki takes on an adventure. Readers will enjoy the charm and humor in the portrayal of the animals as they make room for each newcomer in the mitten and sprawl in the snow after the big sneeze." Horn Book Guide

Town mouse, country mouse. Putnam 1994 unp il $16.99 (k-3)   **398.2**
1. Aesop—Adaptations 2. Fables 3. Mice—Folklore
ISBN 0-399-22622-2   LC 93-41227
A retelling of the Aesop fable. After trading houses, the country mice and the town mice discover there's no place like home
"In Brett's version, the town mice are as charming and naive as their country cousins. . . . Brett's narrative alternates the parallel mishaps of the two sets of mice with lively, smooth writing and a deft touch of humor. . . . The illustrations are rich with meticulous detail." SLJ

Who's that knocking on Christmas Eve. Putnam 2002 unp il $16.99 (k-2)   **398.2**
1. Christmas—Fiction 2. Folklore—Norway
ISBN 0-399-23873-5   LC 2001-48253
A boy from Finnmark and his ice bear help scare away some hungry trolls so that Kyri and her father can enjoy their Christmas Eve meal
This is a "vivid, well-paced retelling of an old Norwegian folktale. . . . Gorgeous endpapers depicting night-sky constellations studded with trolls, bears, and other mythical symbols complement the exquisitely detailed winter-wonderland artistry within." Booklist

Brown, Marcia

Once a mouse; a fable cut in wood. Atheneum Pubs. 1961 unp il $16; pa $5.99 (k-3)
          398.2
1. Folklore—India 2. Fables
ISBN 0-684-12662-1; 0-689-71343-6 (pa)
Awarded the Caldecott Medal, 1962

A "fable from the Indian 'Hitopadesa.' There is lively action in spreads showing how a hermit 'thinking about big and little' suddenly saves a mouse from a crow and then from larger enemies by turning the little creature into the forms of bigger and bigger animals—until as a royal tiger it has to be humbled." Horn Book
"The illustrations are remarkably beautiful. The emotional elements of the story . . . are conveyed with just as much intensity as the purely visual ones." New Yorker

Stone soup; an old tale; told and pictured by Marcia Brown. Scribner 1947 unp il $16.95; pa $6.99 (k-3)   **398.2**
1. Folklore—France
ISBN 0-684-92296-7; 0-689-71103-4 (pa)
A Caldecott Medal honor book, 1948
"When the people in a French village heard that three soldiers were coming, they hid all their food for they knew what soldiers are. However, when the soldiers began to make soup with water and stones the pot gradually filled with all the vegetables which had been hidden away. The simple language and quiet humour of this folktale are amplified and enriched by gay and witty drawings of clever light-hearted soldiers, and the gullible 'light-witted' peasants." Cont Libr Rev

Bruchac, Joseph

Between earth & sky; legends of Native American sacred places; written by Joseph Bruchac; illustrated by Thomas Locker. Harcourt Brace & Co. 1996 unp il map $16; pa $7 (3-5)
          398.2
1. Native Americans—Folklore
ISBN 0-15-200042-9; 0-15-202062-4 (pa)
          LC 95-10862
"In response to Little Turtle's questions about places sacred to the Delaware Indians, Old Bear explains that all people have sacred places and shares 10 legends from different tribes." Booklist
"Each tale is a model of economy, gracefully distilling its message, while Locker's landscapes capture the mysticism inherent in each setting." Horn Book Guide

The first strawberries; a Cherokee story; retold by Joseph Bruchac; pictures by Anna Vojtech. Dial Bks. for Young Readers 1993 unp il $15.99; pa $6.99 (k-3)   **398.2**
1. Cherokee Indians—Folklore 2. Strawberries—Folklore
ISBN 0-8037-1331-2; 0-14-05409-8 (pa)
          LC 91-31058
A quarrel between the first man and the first woman is reconciled when the Sun causes strawberries to grow out of the earth
"This retelling . . . is simply and clearly written, and as sweet as the berries the woman stops to taste. The attractive watercolors and colored-pencil illustrations show an idealized pastoral world." SLJ

The great ball game; a Muskogee story; retold by Joseph Bruchac; illustrated by Susan L. Roth. Dial Bks. for Young Readers 1994 unp il $15 (k-3)   **398.2**
1. Creek Indians—Folklore 2. Animals—Folklore
ISBN 0-8037-1539-0   LC 93-6269

Bruchac, Joseph—*Continued*

Bat, who has both wings and teeth, plays an important part in a game between the Birds and the Animals to decide which group is better

"Roth's dynamic collages combine cut papers of varied textures and hues to create a series of effective illustrations. Short and well told, this appealing *pourquoi* tale lends itself to reading aloud." Booklist

How Chipmunk got his stripes; a tale of bragging and teasing; as told by Joseph Bruchac & James Bruchac; pictures by Jose Aruego & Ariane Dewey. Dial Bks. for Young Readers 2001 unp il $15.99 (k-3) **398.2**
1. Native Americans—Folklore 2. Bears—Folklore 3. Squirrels—Folklore 4. Chipmunks—Folklore
ISBN 0-8037-2404-7   LC 99-16793

"Bears brags that he can do anything, so Brown Squirrel dares him to keep the sun from rising. When Bear fails, Brown Squirrel teases him and gets scratched down his back." Horn Book Guide

"This *pourquoi* story is succinctly written in simple, concrete language, and repeated chants give listeners an opportunity to participate actively in the narrative's unfolding. . . . The pictures are large enough to be seen and enjoyed by a group." Bull Cent Child Books

Raccoon's last race; a traditional Abenaki story; as told by Joseph Bruchac & James Bruchac; pictures by Jose Aruego & Ariane Dewey. Dial Books for Young Readers 2004 unp il $15.99 (k-3) **398.2**
1. Abnaki Indians—Folklore 2. Raccoons—Folklore
ISBN 0-8037-2977-4   LC 2003-9104

Tells the story of how Raccoon, the fastest animal on earth, loses his speed because he is boastful and breaks his promises.

"A solid retelling of an Abenaki legend. . . . The text reads aloud smoothly and keeps the action moving quickly. Done in pen-and-ink, gouache, and pastel, the illustrations accentuate the humor of the tale." SLJ

Turtle's race with Beaver; a traditional Seneca story; as told by Joseph Bruchac & James Bruchac; pictures by Jose Aruego & Ariane Dewey. Dial Bks. for Young Readers 2003 unp il $15.99; pa $5.99 (k-3) **398.2**
1. Seneca Indians—Folklore 2. Beavers—Folklore 3. Turtles—Folklore
ISBN 0-8037-2852-2; 0-14-240466-7 (pa)
                LC 2002-4001

When Beaver challenges Turtle to a swimming race for ownership of the pond, Turtle outsmarts Beaver, and Beaver learns to share

"Done in pen and ink, gouache, and pastel, the cheerful artwork is a wonderful match for this well-told tale." SLJ

When the Chenoo howls; native American tales of terror; [by] Joseph and James Bruchac; illustrations by William Sauts Netamuxwe Bock. Walker & Co. 1998 136p $16.95; lib bdg $17.85; pa $10.95 (4-6) **398.2**
1. Native Americans—Folklore
ISBN 0-8027-8638-3; 0-8027-8639-1 (lib bdg); 0-8027-7576-4 (pa)   LC 97-48715

"Twelve monster tales from a variety of American Indian tribes. . . . These pithily retold tales are short enough for reading aloud and easy enough to learn to tell quickly. Brief notes at the end of each tale give cultural context as well as specific written and oral sources. Full-page black-and-white pen and ink drawings and spot art effectively evoke the spooky but concrete creepiness of the tales. . . . A successful, accessible collection." Bull Cent Child Books

Includes bibliographical references

Bryan, Ashley

Ashley Bryan's African tales, uh-huh; retold and illustrated by Ashley Bryan. Atheneum Bks. for Young Readers 1998 198p il $22 (4-6)
                398.2
1. Folklore—Africa
ISBN 0-689-82076-3   LC 97-77743

This volume combines three previously published titles: The ox of the wonderful horns and other African folktales (1971), Beat the story-drum, pum-pum (1980), Lion and the ostrich chicks and other African folktales (1986)

This collection of African folktales is "told with Bryan's distinctive rhythmic word patterns and filled with humor, life lessons, and the antics of trickster Ananse. . . . Quality reproductions of the original woodcuts enrich this handsome volume." Horn Book Guide

Beautiful blackbird. Atheneum Bks. for Young Readers 2003 unp il $16.95 (k-3) **398.2**
1. Folklore—Zambia 2. Birds—Folklore
ISBN 0-689-84731-9   LC 2002-5290

In a story of the Ila people, the colorful birds of Africa ask Blackbird, whom they think is the most beautiful of birds, to decorate them with some of his "blackening brew"

"Bryan employs boldly colored, cut-paper artwork to dramatize the action. The overlapping collage images fill the pages with energy. . . . Ready-made for participative storytelling." Booklist

Burleigh, Robert

Pandora; illustrated by Raul Colón. Silver Whistle/Harcourt 2002 unp il $16 (3-6)
                398.2
1. Pandora (Legendary character)
ISBN 0-15-202178-7   LC 2001-1282

"Burleigh relates Pandora's battle to obey the stricture of Zeus that the jar remain unopened. Inevitably, she opens the vessel and releases greed, pestilence, war, and all manner of ills on an unsuspecting mankind, with only Hope remaining in the jar." Bull Cent Child Books

"The text, arranged in lines like free verse, is rhythmic and clear, with short, simple sentences. . . . The romantic watercolor/colored-pencil illustrations have narrow borders and textured grounds. Blues and greens dominate the muted palette." SLJ

Bushyhead, Robert H.

Yonder mountain; a Cherokee legend; as told by Robert H. Bushyhead; written by Kay Thorpe Bannon; foreword by Joseph Bruchac; illustrated by Kristina Rodanas. Marshall Cavendish 2002 unp il $16.95 (k-3)   **398.2**

   1. Cherokee Indians—Folklore 2. Folklore—Southern States

ISBN 0-7614-5113-7   LC 2001-32319

A Cherokee chief chooses his successor by asking three candidates to climb a mountain, thus testing their character and strength

"Beautifully illustrated with rich watercolors that fill most of the pages, this story folds its altruistic message into a vivid, entertaining tale." Booklist

Byrd, Robert

Finn MacCoul and his fearless wife; a giant of a tale from Ireland; retold and illustrated by Robert Byrd. Dutton Children's Bks. 1999 unp il $16.99 (k-3)   **398.2**

   1. Finn MacCumhaill, 3rd cent.—Fiction 2. Folklore—Ireland 3. Giants—Folklore

ISBN 0-525-45971-5   LC 98-26132

With the help of his brave and clever wife, Finn MacCoul bests the fearsome giant, Cucullin

"Cartoonish figures almost burst out of the illustrations, playing up the humor in this tall tale." Horn Book Guide

The hero and the minotaur; the fantastic adventures of Theseus; retold and illustrated by Robert Byrd. 1st ed. Dutton Children's Books 2005 unp il $16.99 (3-6)   **398.2**

   1. Theseus (Greek mythology) 2. Minotaur (Greek mythology)

ISBN 0-525-47391-2   LC 2004-21585

The author "interweaves the legends of Aegeus, Heracles, the Minotaur, Ariadne, and Icarus with the story of Theseus. Myths that are normally quite complicated become easy to decipher in this outstanding version, for Byrd tells the tales simply and clearly. . . . The pen-and-watercolor illustrations are painstakingly drawn and include numerous small period details that heighten the sense of history." SLJ

Caduto, Michael J.

Keepers of the night; Native American stories and nocturnal activities for children; [by] Michael J. Caduto and Joseph Bruchac; story illustrations by David Kanietakeron Fadden; chapter illustrations by Jo Levasseur and Carol Wood; foreword by Merlin D. Tuttle. Fulcrum 1994 146p il pa $15.95   **398.2**

   1. Native Americans—Folklore 2. Nature study 3. Night—Folklore

ISBN 1-55591-177-3   LC 94-2602

Also available Keepers of the Earth (1988); Keepers of the animals (1991) and Keepers of life (1994)

"Caduto and Bruchac use stories from various American Indian tribes as the basis for activities and lessons about the nighttime world. Written as a guide for teachers, outdoor education leaders, and other adults working with children in a nature setting, the guide gives detailed instructions for preparing, conducting, and evaluating a variety of activities that focus on the nocturnal habits of animals, on astronomy and nighttime weather, and on campfire activities, such as storytelling, dances, and games." Booklist

"The well-written chapters include discussions with illuminating scientific information." Sci Books Films

Includes glossary and bibliographical references

Casanova, Mary

The hunter; a Chinese folktale; retold by Mary Casanova; illustrations by Ed Young. Atheneum Bks. for Young Readers 2000 unp il $16.95 (k-3)   **398.2**

   1. Folklore—China

ISBN 0-689-82906-X   LC 99-32166

After learning to understand the language of animals, Hai Li Bu the hunter sacrifices himself to save his village

Casanova "tells the tale in a dignified yet moving way that is complemented by the stark artwork. Arid-looking, dun-colored paper is the background for Young's masterful brush strokes." Booklist

Cinderella; [illustrated by K.Y. Craft] SeaStar Bks. 2000 unp il $15.95; lib bdg $15.88 (2-4)   **398.2**

   1. Fairy tales 2. Folklore

ISBN 1-58717-004-3; 1-58717-005-1 (lib bdg)

LC 00-24540

Although mistreated by her stepmother and stepsisters, Cinderella meets her prince with the help of her fairy godmother

"The oil-over-watercolor paintings, based on a vision of eighteenth-century France, glow with an abundance of detail. . . . This book truly enraptures with both text and ravishing illustrations." Booklist

Clayton, Sally Pomme

Tales told in tents; stories from central Asia; written by Sally Pomme Clayton; illustrated by Sophie Herxheimer. Frances Lincoln; distributed by Publishers Group West 2005 64p il map $16.95 (2-4)   **398.2**

   1. Folklore—Asia

ISBN 1-84507-066-6

"In 12 traditional stories from the nomadic cultures of Central Asia, folklorist Clayton retells myth and folklore she heard in Kazakhstan, Afghanistan, and elsewhere. The lively tales include epic creation myths, rhyming riddles, trickster tales, songs, and stories of magic carpets and music. The large picture book is illustrated with richly colored line-and-watercolor paintings that evoke Central Asian traditional culture. . . . A rich resource, even for older readers, this anthology has stories that travel across the world." Booklist

Includes glossary

Climo, Shirley

The Egyptian Cinderella; illustrated by Ruth Heller. Crowell 1989 unp il $15.95; pa $5.95 (k-3)
398.2

1. Folklore—Egypt 2. Fairy tales
ISBN 0-690-04822-X; 0-06-443279-3 (pa)
LC 88-37547

In this version of Cinderella set in Egypt in the sixth century B.C., Rhodopes, a slave girl, eventually comes to be chosen by the Pharaoh to be his queen

"The beauty of the language is set off to perfection by Heller's arresting full-color illustrations." SLJ

The Korean Cinderella; illustrated by Ruth Heller. HarperCollins Pubs. 1993 unp il $15.95; pa $6.95 (k-3)
398.2

1. Folklore—Korea 2. Fairy tales
ISBN 0-06-020432-X; 0-06-443397-8 (pa)
LC 91-23268

In this version of Cinderella set in ancient Korea, Pear Blossom, a stepchild, eventually comes to be chosen by the magistrate to be his wife

"Heller's paintings are exotically lush and colorful as well as engaging. Climo includes an explanatory note about Cinderella variants (the Korean version in particular), and Heller explains the decorations, costumes, and settings she used in the illustrations. An agreeable retelling of the Cinderella story." Booklist

Magic & mischief; tales from Cornwall; retold by Shirley Climo; illustrated by Anthony Bacon Venti. Clarion Bks. 1999 127p il $17 (4 and up)
398.2

1. Folklore—Great Britain
ISBN 0-395-86968-4   LC 97-34091

Drawn from Robert Hunt's Popular romances of the west of England and from William Bottrell's Traditions and hearthside stories of West Cornwall

"Ten tales of Cornwall featuring supernatural beings . . . are accompanied by explanatory bits of traditional lore . . . in this handsomely presented volume. . . . Climo's style is polished and literary, and her selection of tales to retell from detailed sources leans toward the humorous happy ending with just the occasional creepy shiver." Bull Cent Child Books

Monkey business; stories from around the world; illustrated by Erik Brooks. 1st ed. H. Holt 2005 118p il $18.95 (3-6)
398.2

1. Folklore 2. Monkeys—Folklore
ISBN 0-8050-6392-7   LC 2003-63956

A collection of monkey lore, fables, and stories from around the world.

"This well-told and entertaining book . . . draws on pourquoi and folktales, mythology, facts, and trivia. . . . Numerous colored-pencil-and-watercolor illustrations capture the myriad cultures and creatures represented. This collection is unique, well written, and fun." SLJ

Coburn, Jewell Reinhart

Domitila; a Cinderella tale from the Mexican tradition; adapted by Jewell Reinhart Coburn; illustrated by Connie McLennan. Shen's Bks. 2000 unp il $16.95 (2-4)
398.2

1. Folklore—Mexico
ISBN 1-88500-813-9   LC 99-56173

By following her mother's admonition to perform every task with care and love, a poor young Mexican girl wins the devotion of the governor's son

"The full-page oil-on-cavas illustrations are bright, sumptuous, and visually enticing. The text is bordered by proverbs rendered in both Spanish and English. Well-written and strongly illustrated." SLJ

Cohen, Caron Lee

The mud pony; a traditional Skidi Pawnee tale; retold by Caron Lee Cohen; illustrated by Shonto Begay. Scholastic 1988 unp il pa $4.99 hardcover o.p. (k-3)
398.2

1. Pawnee Indians—Folklore 2. Horses—Folklore
ISBN 0-590-41526-3 (pa)   LC 87-23451

A poor boy becomes a powerful leader when Mother Earth turns his mud pony into a real one, but after the pony turns back to mud, he must find his own strength

"The text is powerful because it is spare and unadorned. It is extended well by the softly toned, full-color, impressionistic pictures." Helbig. This land is our land

Cole, Joanna

Bony-Legs; pictures by Dirk Zimmer. Four Winds Press 1983 unp il (k-3)
398.2

1. Folklore—Russia 2. Fairy tales
LC 82-7424

Available in paperback from Scholastic

"Based on the tale 'Baba-Yaga' in Russian fairy tales by Aleksandr Afanas'ev." Verso of title page

When a terrible witch vows to eat her for supper, a little girl escapes with the help of a mirror and comb given to her by the witch's cat and dog

"The rich text leaves out some of the grisly details of the original without castrating the story, and it is matched by clear yet densely lined drawings that borrow some from Ivan Bilibin's earlier illustrations, yet add amusing detail and fine design and layout of their own." SLJ

Cooper, Susan

The silver cow; a Welsh tale; retold by Susan Cooper; illustrated by Warwick Hutton. Atheneum Pubs. 1983 unp il pa $6.99 hardcover o.p. (1-4)
398.2

1. Folklore—Wales 2. Cattle—Folklore
ISBN 0-689-71512-9 (pa)   LC 82-13928

"A Margaret K. McElderry book"

A young Welsh boy is rewarded for his beautiful harp playing with a silver cow, the gift of the magic people living in the lake. The cow makes his family rich but when his father becomes greedy the magic people take their revenge

"A lilting text, complemented by luminous watercolor

Cooper, Susan—*Continued*
illustrations, captures the enchantment inherent in a traditional tale explaining the genesis of the water lilies fringing Llyn Barfog, 'the bearded lake,' set high in the Welsh hills." Horn Book

Courlander, Harold
Cow-tail switch, and other West African stories; [by] Harold Courlander and George Herzog; drawings by Madye Lee Chastain. Holt & Co. 1947 143p il pa $12.95 hardcover o.p. (4-6)
                                       398.2
   1. Folklore—West Africa 2. Ashanti (African people)—Folklore
   ISBN 0-8050-00298-7 (pa)
   A Newbery Medal honor book, 1948
   "The seventeen stories mostly gathered in the Ashanti country, are fresh to collections and are told with humor and originality. Their themes, chosen with discrimination, are frequently primitive explanations of the origin of folk sayings and customs, or show examples of animal trickery and ingenuity." Horn Book

Craft, Charlotte
King Midas and the golden touch; as told by Charlotte Craft; illustrated by K.Y. Craft. Morrow 1999 32p il $16 (2-4)
                                       398.2
   1. Midas (Legendary character)
   ISBN 0-688-13165-4   LC 98-24035
   A king finds himself bitterly regretting the consequences of his wish that everything he touches would turn to gold
   "This sophisticated retelling, set in the Middle Ages, places King Midas in a sumptuous palace. . . . The elaborate oil-over-watercolor illustrations show the wondrous, tragic effects of the golden touch." Horn Book Guide

Craft, Mahlon F.
Sleeping Beauty; illustrated by Kinuko Y. Craft; as retold by Mahlon F. Craft. SeaStar Bks. 2002 unp il $15.95; lib bdg $16.50 (2-4)
                                       398.2
   1. Fairy tales 2. Folklore—Germany
   ISBN 1-58717-120-1; 1-58717-121-X (lib bdg)
                                  LC 2002-2009
   A beautiful and beloved princess, cursed by the one fairy who was not invited to her christening, pricks her finger on her sixteenth birthday and falls asleep for one hundred years
   "Mahlon Craft relates events in formal language, using specifics that correspond to most traditional Brothers Grimm version[s]. The lush, richly detailed, oil-on-watercolor paintings perfectly complement the text." Booklist

Creswick, Paul
  Robin Hood; illustrated by N.C. Wyeth. Scribner 1984 362p il $28 (5 and up)
                                       398.2
   1. Robin Hood (Legendary character)
   ISBN 0-684-18162-2   LC 84-10662
   A reissue of a title first published 1917 by McKay

Recounts the life and adventures of Robin Hood, who, with his band of followers, lived as an outlaw in Sherwood Forest dedicated to fight against tyranny

Cruz, Alejandro
  The woman who outshone the sun; the legend of Lucia Zenteno; from a poem by Alejandro Cruz Martinez; pictures by Fernando Olivera; story by Rosalma Zubizarreta, Harriet Rohmer, David Schecter. Children's Bk. Press 1991 30p $14.95; pa $7.95 (k-3)
                                       398.2
   1. Zapotec Indians—Folklore 2. Bilingual books—English-Spanish
   ISBN 0-89239-101-4; 0-89239-126-X (pa)
                                    LC 91-16646
   Title page and text in English and Spanish
   Retells the Zapotec legend of Lucia Zenteno, a beautiful woman with magical powers who is exiled from a mountain village and takes its water away in punishment
   This "Hispanic folktale is skillfully told, and is solid and colorfully steeped with imagery of the earth and sky. Both the Spanish and English read gracefully, and the poetic use of language suits the story well for telling. The illustrations have a sense of volume that is reminiscent of Orozco." SLJ

Cummings, Pat
  Ananse and the lizard; a West African tale; retold and illustrated by Pat Cummings. Holt & Co. 2002 unp il $16.95 (k-3)
                                       398.2
   1. Anansi (Legendary character) 2. Folklore—Ghana
   ISBN 0-8050-6476-1   LC 2001-1679
   Ananse the spider thinks he will marry the daughter of the village chief, but instead he is outsmarted by Lizard
   "Cummings' lively prose and humor are a perfect match for the story. The boxed text is accompanied by gorgeous watercolor, gouache, and pencil illustrations, rich in color and lively pattern." Booklist

Curry, Jane Louise
  Hold up the sky: and other Native American tales from Texas and the Southern Plains; illustrated by James Watts. Margaret K. McElderry Bks. 2003 159p il $17.95 (4 and up)
                                       398.2
   1. Native Americans—Folklore 2. Folklore—Southern States
   ISBN 0-689-85287-8   LC 2002-16519
   Retells twenty-six tales from Native Americans whose traditional lands were in Texas and the Southern Plains, and provides a brief introduction to the history of each tribe
   "Curry has carefully researched and sensitively retold tales from fourteen Native American nations. Attractive pencil drawings enhance the stories." Horn Book Guide
   Includes bibliographical references

Curry, Jane Louise—*Continued*

The wonderful sky boat and other Native American tales of the Southeast; illustrated by James Watts. Margaret K. McElderry Bks. 2001 142p il $17 (4 and up)   **398.2**

1. Native Americans—Folklore 2. Folklore—Southern States

ISBN 0-689-83595-7   LC 00-40207

"Curry retells 28 stories from a variety of American Indian tribes from the southeastern U.S. . . . Although the stories are relatively short and the language simple, middle-grade readers unfamiliar with the characters and the conventions of American Indian tales will benefit most from having these stories read or told to them. . . . A good resource for accessible stories to use in folktale units or American Indian studies." Booklist

Includes bibliographical references

Dabcovich, Lydia

The polar bear son; an Inuit tale; retold and illustrated by Lydia Dabcovich. Clarion Bks. 1997 37p il $16; pa $5.95 (k-3)   **398.2**

1. Inuit—Folklore 2. Polar bear—Folklore

ISBN 0-395-72766-9; 0-395-97567-0 (pa)

LC 96-4780

An old woman adopts and raises a polar bear cub which grows up and provides for her even after she has had to send it away to save it from the jealous men of the village

"Illustrated in muted pastel colors, the pictures capture this stark, yet beautiful, winter world." SLJ

Daly, Jude

Fair, Brown & Trembling; an Irish Cinderella story. Farrar, Straus & Giroux 2000 unp il $16 (k-3)   **398.2**

1. Fairy tales 2. Folklore—Ireland

ISBN 0-374-32247-3   LC 99-34315

This version of the Cinderella story, in which a young girl overcomes the wickedness of her older sisters to become the bride of a prince, is based on a Irish folktale

This offers "bright illustrations in folk-art style. . . . The fairy godmother is an old henwife, who provides Trembling with splendid clothes and a milk-white horse to carry her to church—not the palace ball. . . . In a nice variation, there are many princes; they fight over Trembling, and the best one wins." Booklist

Dayrell, Elphinstone

Why the Sun and the Moon live in the sky; an African folktale; illustrated by Blair Lent. Houghton Mifflin 1968 26p il $16; pa $6.95 (k-3)   **398.2**

1. Folklore—Nigeria 2. Sun—Folklore 3. Moon—Folklore

ISBN 0-395-29609-9; 0-395-53963-3 (pa)

A Caldecott Medal honor book, 1969

First told by the author in his book: Folk stories from Southern Nigeria, West Africa, published 1910 in England

"When the Sun and the Moon extended an invitation to Water and his people to visit their earthly home, they underestimated the number of Water's followers and thus were forced to seek a habitation in the sky." SLJ

"The beautifully detailed and stylized art work is based on African sources; the artist uses cool colors for the water, a pale blue-grey for the moon, and shades of gold and white for the sun." Sutherland. The Best in Child Books

De Paola, Tomie

Adelita; a Mexican Cinderella story; written and illustrated by Tomie de Paola. Putnam 2002 unp il $16.99 (k-3)   **398.2**

1. Fairy tales 2. Folklore—Mexico

ISBN 0-399-23866-2   LC 2001-57873

After the death of her mother and father, Adelita is badly mistreated by her stepmother and stepsisters until she finds her own true love at a grand fiesta

"The prose is straightforward and crisp. . . . Making perfect use of clear, warm hues, the full-color acrylic illustrations are a feast for the eye." SLJ

Christopher, the holy giant. Holiday House 1994 unp il $16.95; pa $6.95 (k-3)   **398.2**

1. Christopher, Saint, 3rd cent.?. Legends

ISBN 0-8234-0862-0; 0-8234-1169-9 (pa)

LC 90-49926

As Reprobus carries a child across a river one stormy night, the boy gets heavier and heavier until Reprobus feels he is carrying the world on his shoulders—thus goes the legend of the name Christ-bearer, or Christopher

"DePaola's prose is simple and eloquent, and his expressive folk art style, here rendered in the intense but muted shades of the desert, is perfectly attuned to the legend's reverent tone." Publ Wkly

The clown of God; an old story; told and illustrated by Tomie de Paola. Harcourt Brace Jovanovich 1978 unp il $16; pa $7 (k-3)   **398.2**

1. Legends 2. Miracles—Folklore 3. Christmas—Folklore

ISBN 0-15-219175-5; 0-15-618192-4 (pa)

LC 78-3845

An orphan whose juggling skill led him to a career as a traveling entertainer has grown old and clumsy and returns as a hungry beggar to his birthplace. On Christmas Eve in the monastery church a miracle occurs as he summons his last strength to make his only possible offering

"Mr. de Paola has written the tale with love, tenderness, and joy. He has executed authentic Renaissance illustrations that are magnificent in design and beauty." Child Book Rev Serv

Jamie O'Rourke and the big potato; an Irish folktale; retold and illustrated by Tomie dePaola. Putnam 1992 unp il $16.99; pa $5.99 (k-3)   **398.2**

1. Folklore—Ireland

ISBN 0-399-22257-X; 0-698-11603-8 (pa)

LC 91-10626

The laziest man in all of Ireland catches a leprechaun, who offers a potato seed instead of a pot of gold for his freedom

"Illustrated in dePaola's signature style, this has an in-

De Paola, Tomie—*Continued*

viting look. Buoyant watercolors are framed by thin orange borders, but the potato simply can't be contained and bulges beyond the boundaries, graphic proof of its enormous size, an engaging read-aloud choice for Saint Patrick's Day." Booklist

The legend of the Indian paintbrush; retold and illustrated by Tomie dePaola. Putnam 1988 unp il lib bdg $16.99; pa $6.99 (k-3)   **398.2**

1. Native Americans—Folklore

ISBN 0-399-21534-4 (lib bdg); 0-399-21777-0 (pa)
                        LC 87-20160

A "folktale of the Plains Indians that reveals how the Indian Paintbrush, the state flower of Wyoming, first bloomed. An Indian boy's dream to recreate the colors of the sunset comes true when he discovers paintbrushes filled with the colors he needs. A voice in the night had promised him this because he had shared his artistic talent with his people." Child Book Rev Serv

"The native American motifs are rendered simply and authentically; the night sky and glorious sunset spreads are truly beautiful with line, color, and form perfectly balanced to capture the text." Horn Book

The legend of the poinsettia; retold and illustrated by Tomie de Paola. Putnam 1994 unp il $16.99 (k-3)   **398.2**

1. Folklore—Mexico   2. Flowers—Folklore
3. Christmas—Folklore

ISBN 0-399-21692-8   LC 92-20459

When Lucida is unable to finish her gift for the Baby Jesus in time for the Christmas procession, a miracle enables her to offer the beautiful flower we now call the poinsettia

"dePaola establishes a sense of place in his use of glowing colors and architectural details as he retells another legend of miraculous transcendence." Horn Book

Tony's bread: an Italian folktale. Putnam 1989 unp il pa $5.99 hardcover o.p. (k-3)
                           398.2

1. Folklore—Italy

ISBN 0-689-11371-3 (pa)   LC 88-7687

"A Whitebird book"

"This tale captures the flavor of an Italian folk tale with both textual and visual humor. The story of Angelo—a rich, young nobleman from Milan who attempts to win the hand of his true love, the beautiful daughter of Tony the baker—explains the origin of panettone, the delicious *Milanese* Christmas bread made with eggs, raisins, and candied fruit. . . . The pictures and story combine to make a delectable Christmas treat." Horn Book

Delacre, Lulu

Golden tales; myths, legends, and folktales from Latin America; [retold by] Lulu Delacre. Scholastic 1996 73p pa $5.99 hardcover o.p. (5 and up)   **398.2**

1. Folklore—Latin America 2. Native Americans—Folklore

ISBN 0-439-24398-X (pa)   LC 94-36724

This includes 12 "stories from four native cultures (Taino, Zapotec, Muisca, and Quechua), including

pourquoi tales, legends of the conquistadores, and folktales from before and after the age of Columbus. . . . [The author's] . . . retellings are done in a clear and confident voice and are accompanied by her robust, colorful oil paintings. . . .This impressively presented and referenced collection will inspire readers and tellers alike." Booklist

Includes bibliographical references

Demi

The donkey and the rock. Holt & Co. 1999 unp il $16.95 (k-3)   **398.2**

1. Folklore—Tibet (China)

ISBN 0-8050-5959-8   LC 98-14743

In this version of a tale with many Asian variations, a wise king, who rules a town full of foolish people in the mountains of Tibet, puts a donkey and a rock on trial to settle the dispute between two honest men

"The story is told with Demi's usual deft humor, and the illustrations, reminiscent of Chinese paper cut-outs, are aptly supplemented by Tibetan details." Horn Book Guide

The empty pot. Holt & Co. 1990 unp il $16.95; pa $6.95 (k-3)   **398.2**

1. Folklore—China

ISBN 0-8050-1217-6; 0-8050-4900-2 (pa)
                        LC 89-39062

"Ping is a Chinese boy with an emerald green thumb; he can make anything grow 'as if by magic.' One day the Emperor announces that he needs a successor. . . . He gives each child one seed, and the one who grows the best flower will take over after him. . . . On the day of the competition, [Ping] is the only child with an empty pot; all the others bring lush plants. But the Emperor has tricked everyone by distributing cooked seeds, unable to grow; and Ping, with his empty pot, is the only honest gardener—and the winner." Publ Wkly

"This simple story with its clear moral is illustrated with beautiful paintings. . . . A beautifully crafted book that will be enjoyed as much for the richness of its illustrations as for the simplicity of its story." SLJ

The hungry coat; a tale from Turkey. Margaret K. McElderry Books 2004 unp il $19.95 (k-3)
                           398.2

1. Folklore—Turkey

ISBN 0-689-84680-0   LC 2002-155129

After being forced to change to a fancy new coat to attend a party, Nasrettin Hoca tries to feed his dinner to the coat, reasoning that it was the coat that was the invited guest.

"Demi's retelling of this tale is compelling and includes many details that help bring both time and place into focus. Her paint-and-ink illustrations are resplendent with her trademark gold leaf and intricate borders." SLJ

King Midas; the golden touch. Margaret K. McElderry Bks. 2002 unp il $19.95 (2-4)
                           398.2

1. Midas (Legendary character)

ISBN 0-689-83297-4   LC 99-89389

A king finds himself bitterly regretting the consequences of his wish that everything he touches would turn to gold

Demi—*Continued*

Demi's "unsourced but briskly amusing retelling begins with the contest when Midas's preference for Pan's shrill discord so angers the great musician Apollo that he gives the king donkey's ears. . . . The gilded special effects take center stage; still, Demi's glowing colors, decorative figures, and delicate drafting are also worthy of note. . . . This handsome book breathes new life into one of the oldest of cautionary tales." Horn Book

Diane Goode's book of scary stories & songs. Dutton Children's Bks. 1994 64p il music $15.99; pa $6.99 (2-5)   **398.2**
1. Ghost stories 2. Folklore 3. Folk songs
ISBN 0-525-45175-7; 0-14-056432-2 (pa)
                                    LC 93-32610
Selections collected by Lucia Monfried
This "anthology of mildly scary stories, songs, and verse includes folktales from English and American (including Native American and African American) sources. Varied in tone and subject, the selections are consistently entertaining. Appealing, full-color illustrations, from the weird to the wonderful, appear throughout the book, lending more of a sense of humor than a sense of menace." Booklist
Includes bibliographical references

Doherty, Berlie
Fairy tales; told by Berlie Doherty; illustrated by Jane Ray. Candlewick Press 2000 223p il $19.99 (4-6)   **398.2**
1. Fairy tales 2. Folklore
ISBN 0-7636-0997-8   LC 99-89380
A collection of well-known fairy tales, such as Cinderella, Rapunzel, Aladdin and the enchanted lamp, and The fire-bird
These are "superb retellings on the earliest available sources in fresh versions sure to captivate readers anew. Ray's gold paint and folk art motifs prevail, but she also peppers the spreads with striking silhouette-collage compositions in a sumptuously designed volume." Publ Wkly

The famous adventures of Jack; decorations by Sonja Lamut. Greenwillow Bks. 2001 c2000 148p $14.95; lib bdg $14.89 (3-5)   **398.2**
1. Fairy tales 2. Folklore—Great Britain
ISBN 0-06-623618-5; 0-06-623619-3 (lib bdg)
                                    LC 00-67698
First published 2000 in the United Kingdom
In a magical land of giants and castles and beautiful princesses, Jill hears several tales about characters named Jack, then embarks on a fairy tale adventure of her own
"Children who recognize these tales will delight in their interweaving; children who don't can simply let the sparkling, silvery language transport them." Booklist

Doucet, Sharon Arms
Lapin plays possum: trickster tales from the Louisiana Bayou; adapted by Sharon Arms Doucet; pictures by Scott Cook. Farrar, Straus & Giroux 2002 62p il $18 (4-6)   **398.2**
1. Folklore—Southern States
ISBN 0-374-34328-4   LC 2001029387
Companion volume to Why Lapin's ears are long and other stories of the Louisiana Bayou (1997)

"Melanie Kroupa books"
"The three stories in this title follow Lapin as he hoodwinks rich, dim-witted Bouki, a hyena in African folklore, who has, according to Doucet's note, morphed into 'a vague dog-wolf character' in the U.S. . . . . Filled with sly, hilarious regionalisms and spiced with bayou phrases . . . This is a wonderful choice for enlivening folktale units. Cook's thickly brushed, impressionistic paintings in the earthy colors of a rich Cajun sauce show the stories' bluster and exaggerated action and will work well for read-alouds." Booklist

Doyle, Malachy
Tales from old Ireland; retold by Malachy Doyle; illustrated by Niamh Sharkey. Barefoot Bks. (NY) 2000 95p il $19.99 (3-6)
                                    398.2
1. Folklore—Ireland
ISBN 1-902283-97-X
A collection of seven Irish folk tales
Doyle's "retellings are simple and economical, yet contain all the lilting rhythm and musical quality for which Irish tales are famous. Sharkey's illustrations, prepared in oil and gesso on canvas, are a perfect match." SLJ
Includes bibliographical references

Egielski, Richard
The gingerbread boy. HarperCollins Pubs. 1997 unp il $15.95; pa $5.95 (k-3)   **398.2**
1. Folklore 2. New York (N.Y.)—Fiction
ISBN 0-06-026030-0; 0-06-443708-6 (pa)
                                    LC 95-50026
"A Laura Geringer book"
The "Gingerbread Boy pops out of an oven in an apartment somewhere in lower Manhattan. As he runs down the New York City streets, the arrogant little cookie is chased by his family, a rat, construction workers, subway musicians, and a mounted policeman." Horn Book
"Egielski's retelling is straightforward and retains the traditional refrain: 'Run run run as fast as you can'—it sounds just right, making a satisfying modern variation. The illustrations . . . adroitly evoke the city setting while giving a solid three-dimensionality and unique individuality to the Gingerbread Boy and his pursuers." SLJ

Saint Francis and the wolf; [by] Richard Egielski. 1st ed. Laura Geringer Books 2005 unp il $15.99; $16.89 (1-3)   **398.2**
1. Francis, of Assisi, Saint, 1182-1226—Legends 2. Wolves—Folklore 3. Italy—Fiction
ISBN 0-06-623870-6; 0-06-623871-4 (lib bdg)
                                    LC 2003-09615
"A wolf is terrorizing the Italian town of Gubbio. Knights, armies, and a threatening-looking war machine have all failed to put a stop to his terrible behavior. Only St. Francis, who can speak the wolf's language, is able to find a workable compromise for the creature and the town. The expressive cartoon art is done in Egielski's characteristic style and is full of child appeal." SLJ

Ehlert, Lois

Cuckoo. Cucú; a Mexican folktale; translated into Spanish by Gloria de Aragón Andújar. Harcourt Brace & Co. 1997 unp il $16; pa $7 (k-3)   **398.2**

1. Mayas—Folklore 2. Folklore—Mexico 3. Bilingual books—English-Spanish

ISBN 0-15-200274-X; 0-15-202428-X (pa)

LC 95-39560

A traditional Mayan tale which reveals how the cuckoo lost her beautiful feathers

"This tale, charmingly told in both English and Spanish, is boldly illustrated with large, brightly colored, cut-paper pictures. Inspired by folk art and crafts, the images evoke the tin work and cutout fiesta banners of Mexico." SLJ

Moon rope. Un lazo a la luna; a Peruvian folktale; translated into Spanish by Amy Prince. Harcourt Brace Jovanovich 1992 unp il $17 (k-3)   **398.2**

1. Folklore—Peru 2. Moon—Folklore 3. Bilingual books—English-Spanish

ISBN 0-15-255343-6   LC 91-36438

An adaptation of the Peruvian folktale in which Fox and Mole try to climb to the moon on a rope woven of grass

"Designed as a bilingual book from title page to the concluding double-page spread, this handsome addition to material for multicultural education impels young audiences to try reading the story in both languages. . . . The text moves smoothly, just right for reading aloud; the pictures are dramatic abstractions that glow like jewels against richly toned, calendared pages." Horn Book

Endredy, James

The journey of Tunuri and the Blue Deer; a Huichol Indian story; illustrated by Maria Hernández de la Cruz and Casimiro de la Cruz López. Bear Cub Books 2003 32p il $15.95 (1-3)   **398.2**

1. Native Americans—Folklore—Mexico

ISBN 1-59143-016-X   LC 2003-52298

Retells a traditional Huichol folktale in which the young Tunuri learns his place in the natural world when he meets the magical Blue Deer, and follows him on an enlightening journey.

"The colorful artwork is made from yarn that is applied to a piece of wood, an elaborate process that is a long-practiced art of the Huichol. The illustrations enhance the feel and authenticity of the story. Elaborate notes explain the sacred symbols, who the Huichol are, and how the art was created. A strong addition to folktale collections." SLJ

Ernst, Lisa Campbell

Little Red Riding Hood: a newfangled prairie tale. Simon & Schuster Bks. for Young Readers 1995 unp il $16; pa $5.99 (k-3)   **398.2**

1. Folklore 2. Wolves—Folklore

ISBN 0-689-80145-9; 0-689-82191-3 (pa)

LC 94-45723

In this "contemporary rendering of the old tale, Little Red Riding Hood wears a hooded sweatshirt and rides her bicycle, while Grandma is a robust farmer who turns the tables on the wolf. Ernst's inventive plot, enjoyable characters, and characteristic cartoon-style drawings demonstrate her mastery of the picture-book form." Horn Book Guide

Fang, Linda

The Ch'i-lin purse; a collection of ancient Chinese stories; retold by Linda Fang; pictures by Jeanne M. Lee. Farrar, Straus & Giroux 1994 127p il $16; pa $5.95 (5 and up)   **398.2**

1. Folklore—China

ISBN 0-374-31241-9; 0-374-41189-1 (pa)

LC 94-9909

A collection of "Chinese stories derived from the history of the Warring States Period (770-221 B.C.E.) and from operatic versions of popular tales. Retellings are vivid, lively, and read aloud well. Many have a moral, and all are entertaining. . . . The black-and-white illustrations—one per selection—are graceful, depicting widely different epochs with amazing accuracy." SLJ

Includes glossary and bibliographical references

Forest, Heather

The baker's dozen; a colonial American tale; retold by Heather Forest; illustrated by Susan Gaber. Harcourt Brace Jovanovich 1988 unp il pa $6 hardcover o.p. (k-3)   **398.2**

1. Folklore—United States

ISBN 0-15-205687-4 (pa)   LC 87-17103

"Gulliver books"

"A seventeenth-century legend describes the rise and fall of a prosperous baker whose famous St. Nicholas cookies bring him a booming business until he begins to cheat his customers. . . . A mysterious old woman curses him for his greed, and thereafter everything goes wrong. Only on her return visit, when he adds an extra cookie to her dozen, does good fortune return." Bull Cent Child Books

"Gaber's elegant watercolors are vivid and stylized, showing a dusted palette of burgundies with charcoal and burnished oranges. This is a fine explanation of a longstanding custom, and Forest backs it up with an author's note on the facts." Publ Wkly

Fowles, Shelley

The bachelor and the bean. Farrar, Straus & Giroux 2003 unp il $16 (k-3)   **398.2**

1. Jews—Folklore 2. Folklore—Morocco

ISBN 0-374-30478-5   LC 2002-23160

In this Jewish folktale from Morocco, a bachelor receives a magic pot from an imp, but it is stolen by an old woman

"Fowles' retelling . . . is lively, funny, and perfectly paced for read-alouds. But it's her watercolor-and-ink illustrations that are most distinctive. Young children will enjoy the shimmering colors and swirling patterns . . . that show the town bustle and the humor." Booklist

Fritz, Jean

Brendan the Navigator; a history mystery about the discovery of America; illustrated by Enrico Arno. Coward, McCann & Geoghegan 1979 31p il $15.99; pa $5.99 (3-5) **398.2**

1. Brendan, Saint, the Voyager, ca. 483-577
2. America—Exploration

ISBN 0-698-20473-5; 0-698-11759-X (pa)

LC 78-13247

Recounts St. Brendan's life and voyage to North America long before the Vikings arrived

"Jean Fritz's narrative is beautifully cadenced, lively and wry. Her historical postscript is all right, too, and the two-color illustrations are appropriately convoluted and Celtic." N Y Times Book Rev

Galdone, Joanna

The tailypo; a ghost story; told by Joanna Galdone; illustrated by Paul Galdone. Clarion Bks. 1984 unp il pa $7.95 hardcover o.p. (k-3) **398.2**

1. Folklore—United States

ISBN 0-395-30084-3 (pa)

LC 77-23289

First published by Seabury Press

"An old man lives in the Tennessee backwoods with his three hunting dogs, Uno, Ino and Cumptico-Calico. . . . The old man sees an odd animal squeezing through a crack in his cabin and grabs it. All he gets is its tail but he makes a snack of that and gets into bed with a satisfied appetite. But the dismembered [creature] wants its tail back. When he haunts the old man with his keening, 'Tailypo, tailypo, all I want is my tailypo' in vain, he settles for vengeance instead." Publ Wkly

"The energetic postures of the old man and his dogs form a strong accompaniment to the clean, vigorous storytelling, and the subtly underplayed color in the paintings not only suggests the ghostliness of the story but is pleasing in itself." Horn Book

Galdone, Paul

The elves and the shoemaker; retold and illustrated by Paul Galdone. Clarion Bks. 1984 unp il pa $6.95 hardcover o.p. (k-2) **398.2**

1. Folklore—Germany 2. Fairy tales

ISBN 0-89919-422-2 (pa)

LC 83-14979

"Based on Lucy Crane's translation from the German of the Brothers Grimm." Title page

A pair of elves help a poor shoemaker become successful, and the shoemaker and his wife reward them with elegant outfits

"The pictures in flashing hues emphasize the secret helpers' impishness; they seem to be performing the service more for a lark than in the name of sweet charity." Publ Wkly

The gingerbread boy. Clarion Bks. 1975 unp il $16; pa $6.95 (k-2) **398.2**

1. Folklore 2. Fairy tales

ISBN 0-395-28799-5; 0-89919-163-0 (pa)

First published by Seabury Press

"A lively version of the tale of the gingerbread boy who sprang into action as soon as he was baked and gleefully eluded all would-be captors until he was finally outwitted by a fox. The artist's gingerbread boy is a strong-legged, cocky individual, who sets out on a merry race through the countryside. The action of the tale is well-paced; large, humorous illustrations with stone fences, a covered bridge, and hearty rural folk suggest a New England background, while the triumphant fox is the epitome of all slyness." Horn Book

Henny Penny; retold and illustrated by Paul Galdone. Clarion Bks. 1968 unp il $16; pa $6.95 (k-2) **398.2**

1. Folklore 2. Animals—Folklore

ISBN 0-395-28800-2; 0-89919-225-4 (pa)

First published by Seabury Press

A folktale also popularly known as Chicken Little. "The simple retelling has a different ending which makes the fox seem somewhat less villainous—when Henny Penny and her credulous friends follow Foxy Loxy into the cave they are never seen again and the king is never told that the sky is falling, but Foxy Loxy, his wife, and seven little foxes (appealingly portrayed in a picture as a family group) still remember the fine feast they had that day." Booklist

The little red hen. Clarion Bks. 1973 unp il $15; pa $5.95 (k-2) **398.2**

1. Folklore 2. Chickens—Fiction

ISBN 0-395-28803-7; 0-89919-349-8 (pa)

First published by Seabury Press

"In a light-hearted interpretation of the old tale, a domesticated little hen, complete with mobcap and apron, busies herself in a picturesquely shabby cottage while her three house mates—a cat, a dog, and a mouse—doze blissfully. The industry of the little hen produces a cake; and only when 'a delicious smell filled the cozy little house,' do her lazy companions come to life." Horn Book

"The large, clear, colorful pictures perfectly suit the book for pre-school story hours; the simple text, with one or two lines per page, will make it a success with beginning readers." SLJ

The monkey and the crocodile; a Jataka tale from India. Clarion Bks. 1969 unp il pa $6.95 hardcover o.p. (k-2) **398.2**

1. Folklore—India 2. Fables 3. Monkeys—Folklore 4. Crocodiles—Folklore 5. Jataka stories

ISBN 0-89919-524-5 (pa)

First published by Seabury Press

Illustrated by Galdone, this is a retelling of one of the Jataka fables about Buddha in his animal incarnations. "The crocodile wants a meal of monkey, but the intended prey is far wilier than his antagonist." SLJ

The story "has the humor, plot, and movement to make it a good book for any young child, even one unused to stories: the brilliant colors, clear pictures, and brief text should make it very successful for sharing with groups of children." Horn Book

Puss in boots. Clarion Bks. 1976 unp il pa $7.95 hardcover o.p. (k-2) **398.2**

1. Folklore—France 2. Fairy tales 3. Cats—Folklore

ISBN 0-89919-192-4 (pa)

First published by Seabury Press

Galdone, Paul—*Continued*

"Galdone follows Perrault's story line faithfully, as Puss works mischief to obtain a fortune for his master. The writing, fluid and readable, makes even this familiar tale sound fresh—no mean feat. Galdone's large, humorous caricatures—easily seen for story hour—have great gusto, and Puss is the embodiment of cleverness and knavery." SLJ

The teeny-tiny woman; a ghost story. Clarion Bks. 1984 unp il $16; pa $5.95 (k-2)

398.2

1. Folklore—Great Britain 2. Ghost stories
ISBN 0-89919-270-X; 0-89919-463-X (pa)

LC 84-4311

Retold and illustrated by Galdone, this is an English folk tale about a "teeny-tiny woman who lives in a teeny-tiny house in a teeny-tiny village goes for a teeny-tiny walk, etc. Opening the gates to a churchyard, she finds a bone that will add flavor to the soup she plans for supper. Back home, she goes to bed but is alarmed by a voice . . . demanding, 'Give me back my bone!'" Publ Wkly

"Quarter-inch type will attract reticent readers, and the comfortable, cozy country and cottage scenes defuse whatever scariness young readers might conjure up. Fences, trees, balustrades and cupboards in murky, inky tones are designed to suggest watchful faces and add to the atmospheric tension of the narrative." SLJ

The three bears. Clarion Bks. 1972 unp il $15; pa $6.95 (k-2) **398.2**

1. Folklore 2. Bears—Folklore
ISBN 0-395-28811-8; 0-89919-401-X (pa)
Also available Spanish language edition
First published by Seabury Press

In Galdone's illustrations for his retelling of the tale of Goldilocks, "his three bears are beautifully groomed, civilized creatures, living a life of rustic contentment in an astonishingly verdant forest, while his Goldilocks is a horrid, be-ringletted, overdressed child who rampages wantonly through the bears' tidy home." Times Lit Suppl

The three Billy Goats Gruff. Clarion Bks. 1973 unp il $16; pa $6.95 (k-2) **398.2**

1. Folklore—Norway 2. Goats—Folklore
ISBN 0-395-28812-6; 0-89919-035-9 (pa)
First published by Seabury Press

In this retelling of the old Norwegian folk tale, "the goats flummox the wicked troll and send him over the rickety bridge to a watery grave." Publ Wkly

"Galdone's illustrations are in his usual bold, clear style. The three Billy Goats Gruff are expressively drawn, and the troll looks appropriately ferocious and ugly. The large, lively, double-page spreads are sure to win a responsive audience at story hour." SLJ

Garland, Sherry

Children of the dragon; selected tales from Vietnam; with illustrations by Trina Schart Hyman. Harcourt 2001 58p il $18 (3-6)

398.2

1. Folklore—Vietnam
ISBN 0-15-224200-7 LC 00-8300

An illustrated collection of Vietnamese folktales with explanatory notes following each story

"This handsome volume gathers six well-told traditional tales not readily available elsewhere. . . . [The book is] greatly enhanced by Hyman's strong color work, romantic sensibility, and dramatic characterizations." SLJ

Geras, Adèle

My grandmother's stories; a collection of Jewish folk tales; pictures by Anita Lobel. Knopf 2003 87p il $19.95; lib bdg $21.99 (3-5) **398.2**

1. Jews—Folklore
ISBN 0-375-82285-2; 0-375-92285-7 (lib bdg)

LC 2002-152476

A newly illustrated edition of the title first published 1990

As a young girl spends time at her grandmother's apartment, she is treated to traditional Jewish tales, including "Bavsi's Feast," "The Golden Shoes," "The Garden of Talking Flowers," and "A Phantom at the Wedding"

"Lobel's energetic and robust paintings provide the perfect accompaniment. These are stories to be shared and treasured." SLJ

Gershator, Phillis

Zzzng! Zzzng! Zzzng! a Yoruba tale; retold by Phillis Gershator; illustrated by Theresa Smith. Orchard Bks. 1998 unp il $15.95 (k-3)

398.2

1. Mosquitoes—Folklore 2. Folklore—Africa
3. Yoruba (African people)—Folklore
ISBN 0-531-09523-1 LC 95-51565
"A Richard Jackson book"

When Ear, Leg, and Arm refuse to marry Mosquito, she shows them that she is not to be ignored

"Gershator's economical but engaging text has repetitive refrains and opportunities for group participation galore; Smith's pastel and crayon illustrations, with their saturated colors and uncluttered compositions, suit the readaloud, showabout nature of the tale." Bull Cent Child Books

Gerson, Mary-Joan

Fiesta femenina; celebrating women in Mexican folktale; retold by Mary-Joan Gerson; illustrated by Maya Christina Gonzalez. Barefoot Bks. (NY) 2001 64p il map $19.99 (4 and up) **398.2**

1. Folklore—Mexico 2. Women—Folklore
ISBN 1-84148-365-6 LC 00-12965

A collection of folktales from various cultures in Mexico, all focusing on the important roles of women, such as Rosha, a young girl who rescues the sun; the goddess Tangu Yuh; Kesne, a Zapotec princess; and the Virgin Mary

"Gerson's prose is lively and engaging, drawing readers in and conveying pictures of believable people in fantastic situations. Gonzalez's primitive acrylic paintings are strong and vigorous, and their riotous use of color enhances the stories tremendously." SLJ

Includes glossary and bibliographical references

Gerson, Mary-Joan—*Continued*

Why the sky is far away; a Nigerian folktale; retold by Mary-Joan Gerson; pictures by Carla Golembe. Little, Brown 1992 unp il pa $5.95 hardcover o.p. (k-3)   **398.2**

1. Folklore—Nigeria
ISBN 0-316-30874-9 (pa)   LC 91-24949

"Joy Street books"

A revised and newly illustrated edition of the title first published 1974 by Harcourt

The sky was once so close to the Earth that people cut parts of it to eat, but their waste and greed caused the sky to move far away

"Golembe's simple, theatrical illustrations combine monotype prints and collages in brilliant colors. . . . With its playfulness and drama, this is a fine book for story hour, especially in an ecology program." Booklist

Giblin, James

The dwarf, the giant, and the unicorn; a tale of King Arthur; retold by James Cross Giblin; illustrated by Claire Ewart. Clarion Bks. 1996 47p il $15.95 (3-5)   **398.2**

1. Arthur, King 2. Arthurian romances
ISBN 0-395-60520-2   LC 92-34031

When his ship runs aground on a strange island during a storm, Arthur sets off on his charger to look for help and meets a dwarf who tells a curious story about his son and the unicorn who has befriended them both

"Ewart's impressionistic watercolor-and-colored-pencil artwork sensitively expresses the characters' emotions and creates richly colored and convincing settings. This good read-aloud is one of the few stories that show King Arthur's realm as a peaceful kingdom." Booklist

Ginsburg, Mirra

The Chinese mirror; adapted from a Korean folktale by Mirra Ginsburg; illustrated by Margot Zemach. Harcourt Brace Jovanovich 1988 unp il pa $6 hardcover o.p. (k-3)   **398.2**

1. Folklore—Korea
ISBN 0-15-21708-3 (pa)   LC 86-22940

"Gulliver books"

"A man brings a mirror—an object unknown to his fellow villagers—home from a trip to China. He secretes it in a chest, but when his curious family each indulge in a peek and see a different image (his or her own face, of course), each has a different reaction." Booklist

"This elegantly simple little story is a seamless blend of folk-tale adaptation with illustrations that were inspired by Korean genre paintings of the eighteenth century." Horn Book

Clay boy; adapted from a Russian folk tale by Mirra Ginsburg; pictures by Jos. A. Smith. Greenwillow Bks. 1997 unp il $16; lib bdg $15.89 (k-3)   **398.2**

1. Folklore—Russia
ISBN 0-688-14409-8; 0-688-14410-1 (lib bdg)
                                            LC 96-33820

Wanting a son, an old man and woman make a clay boy who comes to life and begins eating everything in sight until he meets a clever goat

"The tale is adapted from a Russian folktale, and the storytelling voice is very simple and immediate. . . . In their play with scale, the illustrations express a wonderful combination of the monstrous and the cozy." Booklist

Goble, Paul

Buffalo woman; story and illustrations by Paul Goble. Bradbury Press 1984 unp il $16; pa $5.99 (2-4)   **398.2**

1. Native Americans—Folklore 2. Bison—Folklore
ISBN 0-02-737720-2; 0-689-71109-3 (pa)
                                            LC 83-15704

A young hunter marries a female buffalo in the form of a beautiful maiden, but when his people reject her he must pass several tests before being allowed to join the buffalo nation

"Each page sparkles with the lupins and yuccas of the Southwest and teems with native birds, butterflies, and small animals, the richness of detail never detracting from the overall design of the handsome illustrations. The author-artist successfully combines a compellng version of an old legend with his own imaginative and striking visual interpretation." Horn Book

Includes bibliographical references

Crow chief; a Plains Indian story; told and illustrated by Paul Goble. Orchard Bks. 1992 unp il $16.95; pa $5.95 (2-4)   **398.2**

1. Native Americans—Folklore
ISBN 0-531-05947-2; 0-531-07064-6 (pa)
                                            LC 90-28457

"A Richard Jackson book"

Crow Chief always warns the buffalo that hunters are coming, until Falling Star, a savior, comes to camp, tricks Crow Chief, and teaches him that all must share and live like relatives together

"Stylized, stylish, and strongly decorative, Goble's distinctive paintings use symbol, design, and repetition to illustrate a retelling of a Plains Indians myth that is both a pourquoi story and a hero tale. . . . Goble discusses the legend of Falling Star, 'the Savior,' in a prefatory note that should be of special interest to storytellers." Bull Cent Child Books

The girl who loved wild horses; story and illustrations by Paul Goble. Bradbury Press 1978 unp il $14.95; pa $5.99 (k-3)   **398.2**

1. Native Americans—Folklore 2. Horses—Folklore
ISBN 0-02-736570-0; 0-689-71696-6 (pa)
                                            LC 77-20500

Awarded the Caldecott Medal, 1979

"After becoming lost in a storm, a young Indian girl joins and lives with a herd of wild horses until finally, she becomes one herself." SLJ

"Elaborate double-page spreads burst with life, revealing details of flowers and insects, animals and birds. . . . The story is told in simple language, and the author has included verses of a Navaho and Sioux song about horses. Both storytelling and art express the harmony with and the love of nature which characterize Native American culture." Horn Book

Goble, Paul—*Continued*

The legend of the White Buffalo Woman. National Geographic Soc. 1998 unp il $16.95 (3-5)
398.2

1. Native Americans—Folklore
ISBN 0-7922-7074-6   LC 97-24086

A Lakota Indian legend in which the White Buffalo Woman presents her people with the Sacred Calf Pipe which gives them the means to pray to the Great Spirit

"In his fluid retelling of the legend of the first peace pipe, Goble . . . handles sweeping Lakota history succinctly and assuredly, largely due to his compelling artwork." Publ Wkly

Includes bibliographical references

Mystic horse. HarperCollins Pubs. 2003 unp il $16.99; lib bdg $17.89 (2-4)   **398.2**

1. Pawnee Indians—Folklore 2. Horses—Folklore
ISBN 0-06-029813-8; 0-06-029814-6 (lib bdg)
LC 2002-22831

After caring for an old abandoned horse, a poor young Pawnee boy is rewarded by the horse's mystic powers

"The ink, watercolor, and gouache paintings make full use of color, texture, and form, both in the minutely detailed naturalistic flora and fauna and in the exquisite abstract patterning. A lovely rhythm makes the story good for reading aloud." Booklist

Includes bibiographical references

Remaking the earth; a creation story from the Great Plains of North America; written and illustrated by Paul Goble. Orchard Bks. 1996 unp il lib bdg $16.99 (2-4)   **398.2**

1. Native Americans—Folklore 2. Creation—Folklore
ISBN 0-531-08874-X   LC 96-4243

In this creation myth, the water birds and animals left behind when the old world was flooded dive for mud so that the Creator can make dry land again

The narrative "is based on elements taken from several Native American tribal groups. Goble has included an extensive reference list and a detailed introductory note, and he supplies additional notes by using asterisks. His double-page spreads are saturated with the richness of nature and the splendor of everyday animals." Booklist

Includes bibliographical references

Storm Maker's tipi; story and illustrations by Paul Goble. Atheneum Bks. for Young Readers 2001 unp il $18 (2-5)   **398.2**

1. Siksika Indians—Folklore 2. Native Americans—Dwellings
ISBN 0-689-84137-X   LC 00-40154

"A Richard Jackson book"

"Storm Maker saves the lives of Sacred Otter and his son and teaches them his special designs for painting the Storm Lodge tipis. Photos of actual tipis accompany Goble's distinctive illustrations . . . and there's information on the mythic origin of the tipis, a description of how an authentic buffalo skin tipi is assembled, and a reproducible template for crafting a model." Booklist

"Goble's instructive storytelling prepares readers for this stunning visual adventure." Publ Wkly

González, Lucía M.

Señor Cat's romance and other favorite stories from Latin America; retold by Lucía M. González; illustrated by Lulu Delacre. Scholastic 1997 46p il $17.95 (2-4)   **398.2**

1. Folklore—Latin America
ISBN 0-590-48537-7   LC 95-34144

"González and Delacre introduce six . . . folktales popular throughout Latin America." Booklist

González tells these tales "with style and humor. The retellings are peppered with Spanish words, all of which are easily understood through context. Each story is followed by a short glossary and an author's note with information on the tale's origins and its variants. The vivid, sprightly paintings contain many regional details." Horn Book Guide

Graham, Lorenz B.

How God fix Jonah; by Lorenz Graham; illustrated by Ashley Bryan; foreword by W.E.B. Du Bois; new foreword by Effie Lee Morris. Boyds Mills Press 2000 156p il $17.95 (4 and up)
398.2

1. Folklore—West Africa 2. Bible stories
ISBN 1-56397-698-6

A newly illustrated edition of the title first published 1946 by Reynal & Hitchcock

"These stories from the Bible are offered in the idiom of the West African native." Introduction

"Ashley Bryan's magnificent black-and-white woodblock illustrations lend an added power and dignity to the text of this most unusual and captivating book." Horn Book Guide

Grandfather tales; American-English folk tales; selected and edited by Richard Chase; illustrated by Berkeley Williams, Jr. Houghton Mifflin 1948 239p il $18; pa $7.95 (4 and up)
398.2

1. Folklore—Southern States
ISBN 0-395-06692-1; 0-395-56150-7 (pa)

Folklore gathered in Alabama, "North Carolina, Virginia and Kentucky. Written down only after many tellings, these [twenty-four] humorous tales are told in the vernacular of the region with added touches of local color provided by the storytellers as they meet together to keep Old-Christmas Eve. . . . Of special interest to storytellers." Booklist

Green, Roger Lancelyn

King Arthur and his Knights of the Round Table; retold out of the old romances; with illustrations by Aubrey Beardsley. Knopf 1993 355p il $14.95 (5 and up)   **398.2**

1. Arthur, King 2. Arthurian romances
ISBN 0-679-42311-7   LC 92-55073

Also available in paperback from Puffin Bks.

"Everyman's library children's classics"

A newly illustrated edition of the title first published 1953 in the United Kingdom

Relates the exploits of King Arthur and his knights from the birth of Arthur to the destruction of Camelot

Greene, Ellin

The little golden lamb; retold by Ellin Greene; illustrated by Roseanne Litzinger. Clarion Bks. 2000 32p il $15 (k-3)   398.2

1. Folklore 2. Sheep—Folklore

ISBN 0-395-71526-1   LC 99-36025

A retelling of the traditional tale in which a poor, but good-hearted lad finds his fortune with the aid of a little golden lamb to which everyone that touches it sticks

"Greene's storytelling style is at once classic and re-laxed, and the illustrations, in a soft, springtime palette, are fittingly buoyant." Horn Book Guide

Gregorowski, Christopher

Fly, eagle, fly! an African tale; retold by Christopher Gregorowski; pictures by Niki Daly. Margaret K. McElderry Bks. 2000 unp il $16 (k-3)   398.2

1. Folklore—Africa 2. Eagles—Folklore

ISBN 0-689-82398-3   LC 98-45302

Original two-color illustrated edition published 1982 in South Africa

A farmer finds an eagle and raises it to behave like a chicken, until a friend helps the eagle learn to find its rightful place in the sky

This "is a powerful celebration of the human spirit and its need for independence. It is beautifully comple-mented by watercolors, rich in the vibrant tones of earth and sky." Booklist

Grifalconi, Ann

The village of round and square houses. Little, Brown 1986 unp il lib bdg $16.95 (k-3)
                398.2

1. Folklore—Africa

ISBN 0-316-32862-6   LC 85-24150

A Caldecott Medal honor book, 1987

A grandmother explains to her listeners why in their village on the side of a volcano the men live in square houses and the women in round ones

The author "illustrates her own tale, told to her by a young girl who grew up in Tos. The resting purple vol-cano, suddenly erupting into orange; the eerie orange sun; the villagers covered with ash; the fiery colored skies; the dense, lush jungles—all are captured beautiful-ly by Grifalconi's art." Publ Wkly

Grimm, Jacob

The Bremen town musicians; a tale; by Jacob and Wilhelm Grimm; illustrated by Hans Fischer; translated by Anthea Bell. North-South Bks. 1998 unp il $15.95; lib bdg $15.88 (k-3)   398.2

1. Folklore—Germany 2. Animals—Folklore

ISBN 1-55858-893-0; 1-55858-894-9 (lib bdg)
                LC 97-34512

Original Swiss edition 1944; this is a reissue of the 1955 edition published by Harcourt with title: The travel-ing musicians

While on their way to Bremen, four aging animals who are no longer of any use to their masters find a new home after outwitting a gang of robbers

This offers "sprightly, imaginative drawings that match the humor of this favorite fairy tale." Booklist

Hansel and Gretel; a fairy tale; by Jacob and Wilhelm Grimm; illustrated by Dorothée Duntze; translated by Anthea Bell. North-South Bks. 2001 unp il $15.95; lib bdg $15.88 (3-6)   398.2

1. Fairy tales 2. Folklore—Germany

ISBN 0-7358-1422-8; 0-7358-1423-6 (lib bdg)
                LC 2001-34537

Translated from the German

When they are left in the woods by their parents, two children find their way home despite an encounter with a wicked witch

"Hansel and Gretel is perhaps the most terrifying fairy tale of all, and this book doesn't cover up the universal nightmare. . . . Duntze's large, beautiful, stylized pic-tures show the children huddled in their home, hearing their wild monster parent shout, 'We must get rid of the children.' . . . This is not a book for the very young, but it will lead to some great discussions among older kids studying heroes and monsters." Booklist

Haley, Gail E.

A story, a story; an African tale retold and illustrated by Gail E. Haley. Atheneum Pubs. 1970 unp il lib bdg $17; pa $5.99 (k-3)   398.2

1. Folklore—Africa 2. Anansi (Legendary character)

ISBN 0-689-20511-2 (lib bdg); 0-689-71201-4 (pa)

Awarded the Caldecott Medal, 1971

"The story explains the origin of that favorite African folk material, the spider tale. Here Ananse, the old spider man, wanting to buy the Sky God's stories, completes by his cleverness three seemingly impossible tasks set as the price for the golden box of stories which he takes back to earth." Sutherland. The Best in Child Books

Hamilton, Virginia

Bruh Rabbit and the tar baby girl; paintings by James E. Ransome. Blue Sky Press (NY) 2003 unp il $16.95 (k-3)   398.2

1. Rabbits—Folklore 2. Wolves—Folklore 3. African Americans—Folklore

ISBN 0-590-47376-X   LC 2002-15529

In this retelling of the African American story, the wily Brer Rabbit outwits Brer Wolf who has set out to trap him

"Retold in Gullah, Hamilton's narrative is meticulous-ly paced, lyrical, hilarious, and a joy to read aloud. Ransome's lush watercolors suit the story perfectly." SLJ

The girl who spun gold; illustrated by Leo & Diane Dillon. Blue Sky Press (NY) 2000 unp il $16.95 (k-3)   398.2

1. Fairy tales 2. Folklore—West Indies

ISBN 0-590-47378-6   LC 99-86365

In this West Indian retelling of "Rumpelstiltskin," Lit'mahn spins thread into gold cloth for the Quashiba, the King's new bride

"The source of this folktale is apparent in the distinc-tive and lilting West Indian dialect that pervades this hu-morous and, at times, scary telling. The lavish use of gold within the acrylic illustrations and their frames is sumptuous." SLJ

Hamilton, Virginia—*Continued*

Her stories; African American folktales, fairy tales, and true tales; told by Virginia Hamilton; illustrated by Leo & Diane Dillon. Blue Sky Press (NY) 1995 112p il $22.95 (4 and up)

398.2

1. African American women—Folklore
ISBN 0-590-47370-0   LC 94-33055
Coretta Scott King award for text, 1996
"Nineteen African-American fairy tales, animal stories, supernatural tales, legends and true narratives of a female kind are presented in this single volume." Child Book Rev Serv
"Retold from a variety of sources, the stories flow smoothly in Hamilton's expertly measured prose. The full-color illustrations, one per story, are lush and detailed. . . . These are tales to be read over and over again." Publ Wkly
Includes bibliographical references

The people could fly; American black folktales; illustrated by Leo and Diane Dillon. Knopf 1985 178p il lib bdg $18.99; pa $13 (5 and up)

398.2

1. African Americans—Folklore
ISBN 0-394-96925-1 (lib bdg); 0-679-84336-1 (pa)
LC 84-25020
Also available with audio CD $24.95 (ISBN 0-375-80471-4)
"Hamilton retells 24 representative black folktales. . . . The stories are organized into four sections: tales of animals; the supernatural; the real, extravagent, and fanciful; and freedom tales." Booklist
The author "has been successful in her efforts to write these tales in the Black English of the slave storytellers. Her scholarship is unobtrusive and intelligible. She has provided a glossary and notes concerning the origins of the tales and the different versions in other cultures. Handsomely illustrated." N Y Times Book Rev
Includes bibliographical references

The people could fly; the picture book; illustrated by Leo and Diane Dillon. Knopf 2004 unp il $16.95; lib bdg $18.99 (3-6)   **398.2**
1. Slavery—Folklore 2. African Americans—Folklore
ISBN 0-375-82405-7; 0-375-92405-1 (lib bdg)
LC 2003-25579
This is a retelling of the story first published in the author's collection, The people could fly: American black folktales, published 1985
In this retelling of a folktale, a group of slaves, unable to bear their sadness and starvation any longer, calls upon the African magic that allows them to fly away
"Familiar as it is, we have never seen the story like this. Not with all these evocative images, vivid, bright and moving, leading us on a journey through territory we thought we knew." NY Times Book Rev

A ring of tricksters; animal tales from America, the West Indies, and Africa; illustrated by Barry Moser. Blue Sky Press (NY) 1997 111p il $19.95 (3-6)   **398.2**
1. Folklore 2. Animals—Folklore
ISBN 0-590-47374-3   LC 96-37543

"Divided into sections on American, West Indian, and African tricksters, these eleven tales each feature an animal tricksters either getting his comeuppance or giving as good as he gets." Bull Cent Child Books
"Hamilton's prose infuses the dialogue with depth and dimension, while Moser's spectacular, lively watercolors nearly render the impish creatures human." Publ Wkly

When birds could talk & bats could sing; the adventures of Bruh Sparrow, Sis Wren, and their friends; told by Virginia Hamilton; illustrated by Barry Moser. Blue Sky Press (NY) 1996 63p il $17.95 (3-5)   **398.2**
1. African Americans—Folklore 2. Birds—Folklore
ISBN 0-590-47372-7   LC 95-15307
A collection of stories, featuring sparrows, jays, buzzards, and bats, based on those African American tales originally written down by Martha Young on her father's plantation in Alabama after the Civil War
"Moser's finely detailed watercolors have an inherent humor that makes the characters especially vivid, and the jacket illustration is a wonderful, slyly funny collection of bird personalities. The text, the layout, and the illustrations work together seamlessly in this beautifully designed, well-crafted collection." Booklist

Han, Suzanne Crowder

The rabbit's tail; a story from Korea; illustrated by Richard Wehrman. Holt & Co. 1999 unp il $16.95 (k-3)   **398.2**
1. Folklore—Korea 2. Rabbits—Folklore 3. Tigers—Folklore
ISBN 0-8050-4580-5   LC 98-16627
Tiger is afraid of being eaten by a fearsome dried persimmon, but when Rabbit tries to convince him he is wrong, Rabbit loses his long tail
"The tale is vividly retold. . . . An amusing entertainment about misperceptions." SLJ

Harris, John

Strong stuff; Herakles and his labors; fierce words by John Harris; powerful art by Gary Baseman. J. Paul Getty Museum 2005 unp il map $16.95 (4 and up)   **398.2**
1. Hercules (Legendary character)
ISBN 0-89236-784-9   LC 2004-7904
This is a "simplified version of the 12 labors of Hercules (Herakles as the Greeks called him). . . . Each labor is allotted a spread with bright and bold illustrations featuring Herakles locked in mortal combat with the monster of the moment, accompanied by a chatty, humorous commentary." SLJ

Hausman, Gerald

Horses of myth; [by] Gerald and Loretta Hausman; pictures by Robert Florczak. 1st ed. Dutton Children's Books 2004 100p il $19.99 (4 and up)   **398.2**
1. Horses—Folklore 2. Folklore
ISBN 0-525-46964-8   LC 2002-40809
Contents: The Arabian: Abjer, the horse of the Saharan sands; The Mustang: Snail, the horse of the Ameri-

Hausman, Gerald—*Continued*

can plains; The Mongolian pony: Humpy, the horse of the Russian steppes; The Timor: Ghost Chaser, the horse of the Tahitian shadows; The Karabair: Kourkig Jelaly, the horse of the Armenian Highlands

"These five tales each feature a different type of horse, remarkable for both its individuality and the qualities representative of its breed. . . . Florczak's illustrations adapt characteristics appropriate to the locations and time periods of each selection's origins. . . . This is an attractive volume, useful to teachers and librarians for read-alouds and of interest to horse-loving youngsters." SLJ

Hayes, Joe

Little Gold Star; a Cinderella cuento/Estrellita de oro; retold in Spanish & English by Joe Hayes; illustrated by Gloria Osuna Perez & Lucia Angela Perez. Cinco Puntos Press 2000 30p il $15.95 (k-3)   **398.2**

1. Fairy tales 2. Hispanic Americans—Folklore 3. Bilingual books—English-Spanish

ISBN 0-938317-49-0   LC 99-57104

In this variation of the Cinderella story, coming from the Hispanic tradition in New Mexico, Arciá and her wicked stepsisters have different encounters with a magical hawk and are left physically changed in ways that will affect their meeting with the prince

"The English text, which is made full-bodied by its many details, appears with a Spanish translation. The impressive acrylic illustrations, done in a sturdy folk-art style, are thick with color and bright with humor." Booklist

Henderson, Kathy

Lugalbanda:; the boy who got caught up in a war; illustrated by Jane Ray. Candlewick Press 2006 72p il $16.99   **398.2**

1. Folklore—Iraq

ISBN 0-7636-2782-8   LC 2004-65950

An ancient Sumerian tale about the youngest and weakest of eight brothers who, caught up in an ill-advised war, uses his wits and courage and eventually becomes king.

"The adventure story and the luminous, beautifully detailed watercolors of young men and gods will easily capture today's children. The background facts about the Sumerians . . . also makes this title a valuable nonfiction resource." Booklist

Hennessy, B. G. (Barbara G.)

The boy who cried wolf; retold by B.G. Hennessy; illustrated by Boris Kulikov. 1st ed. Simon & Schuster Books for Young Readers 2006 unp il $15.95 (k-2)   **398.2**

1. Folklore 2. Wolves—Folklore 3. Sheep—Folklore

ISBN 0-689-87433-2   LC 2004-21672

A boy tending sheep on a lonely mountainside thinks it a fine joke to cry "wolf" and watch the people come running—and then one day a wolf is really there, but no one answers his call.

"The story begs to be read aloud, and the large, color-ful, and amusing watercolor-and-gouache paintings are perfect for group viewing. . . . A clever take on an old favorite." SLJ

Heo, Yumi

The green frogs; a Korean folktale; retold by Yumi Heo. Houghton Mifflin 1996 unp il $16 (k-3)   **398.2**

1. Folklore—Korea 2. Frogs—Folklore

ISBN 0-395-68378-5   LC 95-19129

"Two young frogs delight in being contrary whenever their mother asks them to do something. . . . When she is dying, she asks to be buried by the creek, thinking they will contrarily bury her on a sunny hill. But the saddened frogs decide to carry out her wish." Child Book Rev Serv

"Using delicate tones, flat perspectives, and somewhat abstract figures set against busy backgrounds, [Heo] creates a quaint, comic effect. . . . This is a quirkier pourquoi tale than most, but it's too mischievous to be morbid." Horn Book

Hickox, Rebecca

The golden sandal; a Middle Eastern Cinderella story; illustrated by Will Hillenbrand. Holiday House 1998 unp il $16.95; pa $6.95 (k-3)   **398.2**

1. Fairy tales 2. Folklore—Iraq

ISBN 0-8234-1331-4; 0-8234-1513-9 (pa)
                    LC 97-5071

Based on a Cinderella story from Iraq called "The little red fish and the clog of gold" in Inea Bushnaq's Arab folktales

An Iraqi version of the Cinderella story in which a kind and beautiful girl who is mistreated by her stepmother and stepsister finds a husband with the help of a magic fish

"The story is charmingly told and illustrated with paintings on vellum, giving the pictures a soft, luxurious quality." N Y Times Book Rev

Hodges, Margaret

The boy who drew cats; adapted by Margaret Hodges; illustrated by Aki Sogabe. Holiday House 2002 unp il $16.95 (k-3)   **398.2**

1. Folklore—Japan 2. Cats—Folklore 3. Artists—Folklore

ISBN 0-8234-1594-5   LC 2001-16642

"Adapted from Lafcadio Hearn's *Japanese Fairy Tales*, Boni and Liveright: New York 1918." Verso of title page

"Drawing on a Japanese legend concerning a fifteenth-century artist, Hodges tells a . . . tale of a boy artist so skilled that his creations spring to life to confound a supernatural antagonist. Hodges's text is so expertly honed that it could easily stand on its own. Sogabe's cut-paper, watercolor, and airbrush illustrations set the stage handsomely, their bold outlines and areas of dramatic black mellowed with a cool palette." Horn Book Guide

Hodges, Margaret—*Continued*

Dick Whittington and his cat; retold by Margaret Hodges; illustrated by Melisande Potter. Holiday House 2006 unp il $16.95 (k-3)

398.2

1. Whittington, Richard, d. 1423—Legends 2. Folklore—Great Britain 3. Cats—Folklore

ISBN 0-8234-1987-8

Retells the legend of the poor boy in medieval England who trades his beloved cat for a fortune in gold and jewels and eventually becomes Lord Mayor of London.

"In this spare retelling of the British legend, the narrative keeps buoyant with droll dialogue. The humorous illustrations, created with colorful inks and gouache, enhance the story with expressive faces and movement that delight the eye." SLJ

The hero of Bremen; retold by Margaret Hodges; with illustrations by Charles Mikolaycak. Holiday House 1993 unp il $16.95; pa $6.95 (3-5)

398.2

1. Folklore—Germany

ISBN 0-8234-0934-1; 0-8234-1236-9 (pa)

LC 91-22357

Retells the German legend in which a shoemaker who cannot walk helps the town of Bremen, aided by the spirit of the great hero Roland

"Mikolaycak's realistic watercolor and colored pencil drawings have powerful lines, sculptural forms, and a strong narrative quality. . . . This eloquent retelling of a gentle, little-known tale honoring the chivalric virtues of service and sacrifice is all the more beautiful for its understated quality; the documentation is detailed and scholarly." Booklist

The kitchen knight; a tale of King Arthur; retold by Margaret Hodges and illustrated by Trina Schart Hyman. Holiday House 1990 unp il $16.95 (3-6)

398.2

1. Gareth (Legendary character) 2. Arthurian romances

ISBN 0-8234-0787-X

LC 89-11215

A retelling of the Arthurian legend of how Sir Gareth becomes a knight and rescues the lady imprisoned by the fearsome Red Knight of the Red Plain

"Hyman's richly romantic illustrations are lush watercolors, framed and broken with framed insets for closeups and framed text inside the panoramic picture. The format is horizontal, capturing the sweep of the story. While not a tale of King Arthur, it's a wonderful taste of Arthurian legend, hopefully whetting young appetites for more." SLJ

Merlin and the making of the king; illustrated by Trina Schart Hyman. Holiday House 2004 unp il $16.95 (3-6)

398.2

1. Arthur, King 2. Arthurian romances 3. Merlin (Legendary character)

ISBN 0-8234-1647-X

LC 2003-47861

"Retold from Sir Thomas Malory's Morte d'Arthur"

"With its fairly simple vocabulary and succinct style, the lyrical narrative can be enjoyed if read independently or in a group setting. The truly distinguishing feature of this book is Hyman's detailed, colorful acrylic artwork. . . . In keeping with the feel of a medieval illuminated

manuscript, each page has an attractive, elaborate border partially painted with gold ink that glows with all the richness of gold leaf." SLJ

Saint George and the dragon; a golden legend; adapted by Margaret Hodges from Edmund Spenser's Faerie Queene; illustrated by Trina Schart Hyman. Little, Brown 1984 32p il $16.95; pa $6.95 (2-5)

398.2

1. George, Saint, d. 303 2. Knights and knighthood—Folklore 3. Dragons—Folklore

ISBN 0-316-36789-3; 0-316-36795-8 (pa)

LC 83-19980

Awarded the Caldecott Medal, 1985

Retells the segment from Spenser's The Faerie Queene, in which George, the Red Cross Knight, slays the dreadful dragon that has been terrorizing the countryside for years and brings peace and joy to the land

"Hyman's illustrations are uniquely suited to this outrageously romantic and appealing legend. . . . The paintings are richly colored, lush, detailed and dramatic. . . . This is a beautifully crafted book, a fine combination of author and illustrator." SLJ

Hogrogian, Nonny

The contest; adapted and illustrated by Nonny Hogrogian. Greenwillow Bks. 1976 unp il lib bdg $15.89 (k-3)

398.2

1. Folklore—Armenia

ISBN 0-688-84042-6

A Caldecott Medal honor book, 1977

A "gently humorous retelling of an Armenian folk tale about two robbers who not only share the same occupation but are engaged to the same girl." SLJ

"The symmetrical elements of the tale, which create arabesques of humor, are well-served by the full-color, full-page illustrations and by the pencil drawings scattered through the text. Some of the colored illustrations are bordered by oriental rug patterns, and all of the paintings and drawings are strong in their depiction of Armenian physiognomy." Horn Book

One fine day. Macmillan 1971 unp il $16; pa $5.99 (k-3)

398.2

1. Folklore—Armenia 2. Foxes—Folklore

ISBN 0-02-744000-1; 0-02-043620-3 (pa)

Awarded the Caldecott Medal, 1972

When a fox drinks the milk in an old woman's jug, she chops off his tail and refuses to sew it back on unless he gives her milk back. The author-illustrator's cumulative tale, based on an Armenian folktale, tells of the many transactions the fox must go through before his tail is restored

"A charming picture book that is just right for reading aloud to small children, the scale of the pictures also appropriate for group use." Sutherland. The Best in Child Books

Hong, Lily Toy

Two of everything; a Chinese folktale; retold and illustrated by Lily Toy Hong. Whitman, A. 1993 unp il $15.95 (k-3)

398.2

1. Folklore—China

ISBN 0-8075-8157-7

LC 92-29880

Hong, Lily Toy—*Continued*

A poor old Chinese farmer finds a magic brass pot that doubles or duplicates whatever is placed inside it, but his efforts to make himself wealthy lead to unexpected complications

The author "here paints with muted colors, defining rounded forms with broad outlines. Retold with verve and gentle humor, this Chinese folktale could become a read-aloud favorite." Booklist

Hooks, William H.

Moss gown; illustrations by Donald Carrick. Clarion Bks. 1987 48p il pa $6.95 hardcover o.p. (k-3)   **398.2**

1. Fairy tales

ISBN 0-395-54793-8 (pa)   LC 86-17199

After failing to flatter her father as much as her two evil sisters, Candace is banished from his plantation and only after much time and meeting her Prince Charming, is her father able to appreciate her love

"Many children and most adults will recognize in 'Moss Gown' the Cinderella story, while the most astute may note its resemblance to 'King Lear.' But everyone will enjoy this beautifully told North Carolina tale from the oral tradition. Carrick, a master of the dark and mysterious, has created haunting illustrations that are a wonderful complement to the story." Child Book Rev Serv

Huck, Charlotte S.

The Black Bull of Norroway; a Scottish tale; retold by Charlotte Huck; pictures by Anita Lobel. Greenwillow Bks. 2001 unp il $15.95; lib bdg $15.89 (2-4)   **398.2**

1. Fairy tales 2. Folklore—Scotland

ISBN 0-688-16900-7; 0-688-16901-5 (lib bdg)
                                  LC 00-34107

A traditional Scottish tale set in Norway in which a courageous girl sets out to seek her fortune and ultimately finds true love

"The text, fluid and precise, has just enough repetition to suggest the authentic voice of a storyteller; with an emphasis on movement and texture, the full-color illustrations match its style." Horn Book Guide

Princess Furball; retold by Charlotte Huck; illustrated by Anita Lobel. Greenwillow Bks. 1989 unp il pa $6.99 hardcover o.p. (1-3)
                                        398.2

1. Fairy tales

ISBN 0-688-13107-7 (pa)   LC 88-18780

This book is about a "princess who rebels against her tyrannical father and makes the most of her gifts to survive in another kingdom and win the hand of the king. This narrative focuses on the ingenuity of a girl who plots her own destiny." N Y Times Book Rev

"The paintings glimmer with intense colors—Lobel's flair for both historical and humorous detail has never been more apparent, nor more luxuriously bold." SLJ

Hyman, Trina Schart

Little Red Riding Hood; by the Brothers Grimm retold and illustrated by Trina Schart Hyman. Holiday House 1983 unp il lib bdg $16.95; pa $6.95 (k-2)   **398.2**

1. Folklore—Germany 2. Wolves—Folklore

ISBN 0-8234-0470-6 (lib bdg); 0-8234-0653-9 (pa)
                                  LC 82-7700

This retelling "basically follows the Grimm story, although the text has been fleshed out with some extraneous details (for instance, the little girl is called Elisabeth). . . . The illustrations seem to be a labor of love; richly colored paintings of the forest teem with exquisitely detailed plant and animal life, and the interior scenes, awash with atmospheric light, are beautifully composed and executed." Horn Book

Index to fairy tales; including folklore, legends, and myths in collections. Scarecrow Press 1985-1994 4v   **398.2**

1. Folklore—Indexes 2. Fairy tales 3. Legends—Indexes 4. Mythology—Indexes

Volumes covering 1949-1972 and 1973-1977 first published by Faxon 1973 and 1979 respectively

A continuation of Index to fairy tales, myths and legends and its two supplements, compiled by Mary Huse Eastman, published 1926-1952 by Faxon (o.p.)

Volume covering 1949-1972 compiled by Norma Olin Ireland $78 (ISBN 0-8108-2011-0); volume covering 1973-1977 compiled by Norma Olin Ireland $45 (ISBN 0-8108-1855-8); volume covering 1978-1986 compiled by Norma Olin Ireland and Joseph W. Sprug $88 (ISBN 0-8108-2194-X); volume covering 1987-1992 compiled by Joseph W. Sprug $88 (ISBN 0-8108-2750-6)

"Although this is an essential reference book for the children's department, it is also a valuable source for the location of much folklore and fairy-tale material and should be available in adult book collections as well." Ref Sources for Small & Medium-sized Libr. 6th edition

The **Jack** tales; with an appendix compiled by Herbert Halpert; and illustrations by Berkeley Williams, Jr. Houghton Mifflin 1943 201p il $16; pa $5.95 (4-6)   **398.2**

1. Folklore—Southern States

ISBN 0-395-06694-8; 0-395-66951-0 (pa)

"Told by R. M. Ward and his kindred in the Beech Mountain section of Western North Carolina and by other descendants of Council Harmon (1803-1896) elsewhere in the Southern mountains; with three tales from Wise County, Virginia. Set down from these sources and edited by Richard Chase." Title page

"Humor, freshness, colorful American background, and the use of one character as a central figure in the cycle mark these 18 folk tales, told here in the dialect of the mountain country of North Carolina. A scholarly appendix by Herbert Halpert, giving sources and parallels, increases the book's value as a contribution to American folklore. Black-and-white illustrations in the spirit of the text." Booklist

Jacobs, Joseph

English fairy tales; with illustrations by John Batten. Knopf 1993 428p il $13.95 (4-6)

398.2

1. Fairy tales 2. Folklore—Great Britain
ISBN 0-679-42809-7   LC 93-13878
Also available in paperback from Dover Pubs.
"Everyman's library children's classics"
A reissue in one volume of the author's English fairy tales (1891) and More English fairy tales (1894)
A collection of more than eighty traditional stories that recount the adventures of giants, witches, princes, princesses, and animals

Jaffe, Nina

The cow of no color: riddle stories and justice tales from around the world; [by] Nina Jaffe and Steve Zeitlin; pictures by Whitney Sherman. Holt & Co. 1998 159p il $17 (4 and up)

398.2

1. Folklore
ISBN 0-8050-3736-5   LC 98-14167
In each of these stories, collected from around the world, a character faces a problem situation which requires that he make a decision about what is fair or just
"Sherman's black-and-white line drawings have a stark gracefulness that complements the tales' form and structure; the tales themselves are simply told with little embellishment." Bull Cent Child Books
Includes bibliographical references

The way meat loves salt; a Cinderella tale from the Jewish tradition; illustrated by Louise August. Holt & Co. 1998 unp il music $15.95 (k-3)

398.2

1. Jews—Folklore
ISBN 0-8050-4384-5   LC 97-41286
The youngest daughter of a rabbi is sent away from home in disgrace, but thanks to the help of the prophet Elijah, marries the son of a renowned scholar and is reunited with her family. Includes words and music to a traditional Yiddish wedding song
"Vibrant oils of reds, yellows, and blues set off the inky black, which defines the trees and rocks, and the sashes on the women's provincial gowns. Both the writing and the art contribute to the abundant good spirit." Horn Book

Jiang, Ji-li

The magical Monkey King; mischief in heaven; classic Chinese tales retold by Ji Li Jiang; illustrated by Hui Hui Su-Kennedy. HarperCollins Pubs. 2002 122p il lib bdg $14.89; pa $4.95 (3-5)

398.2

1. Folklore—China 2. Monkeys—Folklore
ISBN 0-06-029544-9 (lib bdg); 0-06-442149-X (pa)
       LC 2001-39672
The mischievous Monkey King attempts to achieve immortality the easy way, gains god-like powers, and wreaks havoc in heaven
The author "provides a lively telling, and the stories move briskly. Accompanying black-and-white pictures have the look of woodcuts." Booklist

Johnson, Paul Brett

Fearless Jack; adapted and illustrated by Paul Brett Johnson. Margaret K. McElderry Bks. 2001 unp il $16 (k-3)

398.2

1. Folklore—Appalachian Mountains
ISBN 0-689-83296-6   LC 99-89184
In this Appalachian folktale, Jack wins fame and fortune after killing ten yellow jackets with one whack
"In an Appalachian twang, complete with distinct vocabulary and speech patterns, Johnson's colorful, comical, sturdy pictures are just as energetic as the story which is told." Booklist

Jack outwits the giants; adapted and illustrated by Paul Brett Johnson. Margaret K. McElderry Bks. 2002 unp il $16 (k-3)

398.2

1. Folklore—Appalachian Mountains 2. Giants—Folklore
ISBN 0-689-83902-2   LC 2001-30811
Companion volume to Fearless Jack
In this Appalachian folktale, Jack outwits two giants who want fresh meat for breakfast
"Johnson interweaves several familiar motifs from many traditions while bringing an authentic mountain twang to his telling. Johnson's lively acrylics leave no doubt that these events are as comical as they are suspenseful; the equally lively dialogue makes this an especially good read-aloud." Horn Book Guide

Johnson-Davies, Denys

Goha the wise fool; retold by Denys Johnson-Davies; sewing by Hany El Saed Ahmed from drawings by Hag Hamdy Mohamed Fattouh. Books 2005 40p il $16.99 (2-4)

398.2

1. Folklore—Turkey
ISBN 0-399-24222-8   LC 2004-15739
A collection of fourteen tales about the folk hero Nasreddin Hoca, also known as Goha, a man with a reputation for being able to answer difficult questions in a clever way.
The book is "illustrated by a team of Cairo tent makers in the form of traditional khiyamiya tapestries, with bits of bright, solid-colored fabric stitched to roughly woven, oatmeal-toned backgrounds. Many of the tales expose familiar human foibles. . . . Others amusingly illustrate wise principles." Booklist

Johnston, Tony

The tale of Rabbit and Coyote; illustrated by Tomie de Paola. Putnam 1994 unp il $15.99; pa $5.99 (k-3)

398.2

1. Zapotec Indians—Folklore 2. Rabbit (Legendary character) 3. Coyote (Legendary character)
ISBN 0-399-22258-8; 0-698-11630-5 (pa)
       LC 92-43652
Rabbit outwits Coyote in this Zapotec tale which explains why coyotes howl at the moon
"DePaola's vivid, spicy palette of gold, red, and turquoise tones and his use of folk-art borders evoke the desert setting and complement the broad humor of Johnston's text. A glossary of the Spanish phrases that pepper the illustrations is appended." Booklist

Kajikawa, Kimiko

Yoshi's feast; illustrated by Yumi Heo. DK Ink 2000 unp il $15.95 (k-3)   **398.2**

1. Folklore—Japan

ISBN 0-7894-2607-2   LC 99-14754

"A Melanie Kroupa book"

"Yoshi's Feast was adapted from a story, 'Smells and Jingles,' in William Elliot Griffis's Japanese Fairy World: Stories from the Wonder-lore of Japan (J.H. Barhyte, 1880)."--T.p. verso; "A Melanie Kroupa Book"--T.p. verso

When Yoshi's neighbor, Sabu, the eel broiler, attempts to charge him for the delicious smelling aromas he has been enjoying, Yoshi hatches a plan to enrich them both

"Heo's dazzling collages of painting, pencil, and handmade papers bring out the outrageous action and humor in Yoshi and Sabu's conflict, extending the lively dialogue and rich text." Booklist

Karlin, Barbara

James Marshall's Cinderella; illustrated by James Marshall; retold by Barbara Karlin. Dial Bks. for Young Readers 2001 unp il $15.99; pa $6.99 (k-2)   **398.2**

1. Fairy tales 2. Folklore

ISBN 0-8037-2730-5; 0-14-230048-9 (pa)
                    LC 2001-23097

This is a reissue of Barbara Karlin's Cinderella, published 1989 by Little, Brown

"Those seeking a condensed version of the classic fairy tale will find just what they want in Karlin's brief retelling; . . . James Marshall's witty, warts-and-all illustrations add the sparkle that brings out the best in Karlin's straightforward retelling." Horn Book

Keats, Ezra Jack

John Henry; an American legend; story and pictures by Ezra Jack Keats. Pantheon Bks. 1965 unp il pa $5.99 hardcover o.p. (k-3)
                    398.2

1. John Henry (Legendary character) 2. African Americans—Folklore 3. Folklore—United States

ISBN 0-394-89052-3 (pa)   LC 86-27453

This is a picture book retelling of the legend of the Black American folk hero who drove spikes for the railroads

"The dynamic power with which John Henry wields his hammer is matched by the strong illustrations: brilliant oranges and reds contrast with grays and blacks that are often silhouettes; unusual backgrounds produce startling effects. A good picture-story to show to a group." Horn Book

Kellogg, Steven

Chicken Little; retold & illustrated by Steven Kellogg. Morrow 1985 unp il pa $5.95 hardcover o.p. (k-3)   **398.2**

1. Folklore 2. Animals—Folklore

ISBN 0-688-07045-0 (pa)   LC 84-25519

Also available Spanish language edition

Chicken Little and his feathered friends, alarmed that the sky seems to be falling, are easy prey to hungry Foxy Loxy when he poses as a police officer in hopes of tricking them into his truck

"Kellogg has enlivened the text [by] giving it some modern touches (Turkey Lurkey carries golf clubs, Foxy Loxy is caught when a 'hippoliceman' tumbles out of a patrol helicopter to land him). Children have always enjoyed the repetition and cumulation of the story, as well as the silliness of the fowls who believe the sky is falling; here there's added fun." Bull Cent Child Books

Jack and the beanstalk; retold and illustrated by Steven Kellogg. Morrow Junior Bks. 1991 unp il $16; lib bdg $16.89; pa $6.95 (k-3)   **398.2**

1. Fairy tales 2. Folklore—Great Britain 3. Giants—Folklore

ISBN 0-688-10250-6; 0-688-10251-4 (lib bdg); 0-688-15281-3 (pa)   LC 90-45990

A boy climbs to the top of a giant beanstalk, where he uses his quick wits to outsmart a giant and make his and his mother's fortune

"Seldom has the ogre at the top of the beanstalk been depicted with such gusto! The warty, fanged, pug-nosed lout dressed in animal skins and a necklace of teeth is a wonder to behold. Steven Kellogg's humorous detail provides witty embellishment for savoring. His story line is quite faithful to the Joseph Jacobs version of the story, the sturdy text offering a strong framework for the energetic illustrations." Horn Book

Mike Fink; a tall tale; retold and illustrated by Steven Kellogg. Morrow Junior Bks. 1992 unp il $16; pa $6.95 (k-3)   **398.2**

1. Fink, Mike, 1770-1823?—Fiction 2. Tall tales

ISBN 0-688-07003-5; 0-688-13577-3 (pa)
                    LC 91-46014

Relates the extraordinary deeds of the frontiersman who became King of the Keelboatmen on the Mississippi River

"Steven Kellogg's ebullient retelling of Mike's tall-tale feats—illustrated with large, glowing scenes suffused with blue and yellow and with smaller vignettes emphasizing comic detail—follows Mike's prodigious childhood exploits, his teenage wrestling practice with Rocky Mountain grizzlies, and his years as King of the Keelboatmen, and closes with a final showdown with enormous steamboats taking over the river trade." Horn Book

Paul Bunyan; a tall tale; retold and illustrated by Steven Kellogg. Morrow 1984 unp il lib bdg $16.89; pa $5.95 (k-3)   **398.2**

1. Bunyan, Paul (Legendary character) 2. Tall tales

ISBN 0-688-03850-6 (lib bdg); 0-688-05800-0 (pa)
                    LC 83-26684

"Numerous events from the legendary north woodsman's life have been linked together as Bunyan and Babe, his big blue ox, traverse the U.S." Booklist

"Kellogg uses oversize pages for busy, detail-crowded illustrations that have vitality and humor, echoing the exaggeration and ebullience of the story." Bull Cent Child Books

Kellogg, Steven—*Continued*

Pecos Bill; a tall tale; retold and illustrated by Steven Kellogg. Morrow 1986 unp il $17; pa $5.95 (k-3)　　　　**398.2**

1. Pecos Bill (Legendary character) 2. Tall tales
ISBN 0-688-05871-X; 0-688-09924-6 (pa)

LC 86-784

Incidents from the life of Pecos Bill, from his childhood among the coyotes to his unusual wedding day

"Although there's a lot going on in these pictures, they're not cluttered; both the gradations of color and the page design smooth the lines of continuous action and tumult of humorous detail. Kellogg's portrayal of Pecos Bill as a perpetual boy will appeal to children. The retelling is a smooth adaptation for introducing young listeners to longer versions or to accompany storytelling sessions centered around tall-tale heroes." Bull Cent Child Books

Sally Ann Thunder Ann Whirlwind Crockett; a tall tale; retold and illustrated by Steven Kellogg. Morrow Junior Bks. 1995 unp il $17; lib bdg $16.93; pa $5.95 (k-3)　　　　**398.2**

1. Crockett, Sally Ann Thunder Ann Whirlwind—Fiction 2. Tall tales
ISBN 0-688-14042-4; 0-688-14043-2 (lib bdg); 0-688-17113-3 (pa)　　　　LC 94-43782

Sally Ann is "Davy's wife and a match for any bear, alligator, or macho man in the West. As retold (and scrupulously sourced) by Kellogg, Sally Ann's early life outracing and outswimming her nine big brothers and beating all comers at the state fair . . . is but a prelude to her flight to the frontier and subsequent rescue of and marriage to Davy Crockett. . . . Kellogg's characteristically energetic paintings meet their match in this story's kinetic hyperbole; the fact that his Sally Ann and Davy look like rambunctious big kids will only add to their story-hour appeal." Bull Cent Child Books

The three little pigs; retold and illustrated by Steven Kellogg. Morrow Junior Bks. 1997 unp il $16; lib bdg $15.93 (k-3)　　　　**398.2**

1. Folklore 2. Pigs—Folklore 3. Wolves—Folklore
ISBN 0-688-08731-0; 0-688-08732-9 (lib bdg)

LC 96-34434

In this retelling of a well-known tale, Serafina Sow starts her own waffle-selling business in order to enable her three offspring to prepare for the future, which includes an encounter with a surly wolf

"Much of the broad humor is carried in the lively, colorful illustrations, though there's wordplay aplenty in the text and pictures too." Booklist

The three sillies. Candlewick Press 1999 unp il $16.99 (k-3)　　　　**398.2**

1. Folklore—Great Britain
ISBN 0-7636-0811-4　　　　LC 98-30646

A retelling of Joseph Jacobs' folk tale

A young man believes his sweetheart and her family are the three silliest people in the world until he meets three others who are even sillier

"Kellogg's ink-and-watercolor illustrations are wonderfully suited to the goofy goings-on. . . . While the telling itself is simple and straightforward, the dialogue balloons and plentiful asides add greatly to the humor." SLJ

Kim, So-Un

Korean children's favorite stories; retold by Kim So-un; illustrated by Jeong Kyoung-Sim. Tuttle 2004 95p il $16.95 (3-6)　　　　**398.2**

1. Folklore—Korea
ISBN 0-8048-3591-8

A newly illustrated edition of The story bag, published 1955

This collection of 13 Korean folktales "includes elements shared by many cultures, such as a flood story, and others with a unique sensibility. A variety of animals appear, including tigers, both good and bad, and snakes, depicted as dragons. The delicate watercolor illustrations make the stories accessible to children." SLJ

Kimmel, Eric A.

The adventures of Hershel of Ostropol; retold by Eric A. Kimmel; with drawings by Trina Schart Hyman. Holiday House 1995 64p il $15.95; pa $7.95 (3-5)　　　　**398.2**

1. Ostropoler, Hershele, 18th cent.—Legends 2. Jewish legends
ISBN 0-8234-1210-5; 0-8234-1404-3 (pa)

LC 95-8907

"Kimmel retells ten stories about Hershel of Ostropol, a Jewish folk hero who lived during the first part of the nineteenth century. A man quick with a humorous saying or jest, Hershel lived by his wits, traveling from town to town in Eastern Europe." Horn Book Guide

"Hyman's wild, beautifully detailed drawings . . . capture Hershel's farcical interchange with the village creatures and characters, including the miser, the bandit, and the rabbi. With their wry idiom, these are stories for telling across generations." Booklist

Anansi and the magic stick; illustrated by Janet Stevens. Holiday House 2001 unp il $16.95 (k-3)　　　　**398.2**

1. Folklore—Africa 2. Anansi (Legendary character)
ISBN 0-8234-1443-4　　　　LC 00-39608

Anansi the Spider steals Hyena's magic stick so he won't have to do the chores, but when the stick's magic won't stop, he gets more than he bargained for

"Kimmel tells it with cheerful energy, and Stevens' chaotic mixed-media illustrations, with lots of bright pink and green, show Anansi's friends and neighbors . . . caught up in the mess." Booklist

Anansi and the talking melon; retold by Eric A. Kimmel; illustrated by Janet Stevens. Holiday House 1994 unp il $16.95; pa $6.95 (k-3)　　　　**398.2**

1. Folklore—Africa 2. Anansi (Legendary character)
ISBN 0-8234-1104-4; 0-8234-1167-2 (pa)

LC 93-4239

Anansi the Spider tricks Elephant and some other animals into thinking the melon in which he is hiding can talk

"The snappy narration is well suited for individual reading or group sharing. The colorful line-and-wash illustrations are filled with movement and playful energy." SLJ

Kimmel, Eric A.—*Continued*

Anansi goes fishing; retold by Eric A. Kimmel; illustrated by Janet Stevens. Holiday House 1992 unp il $16.95; pa $6.95 (k-3)   **398.2**
1. Folklore—Africa 2. Anansi (Legendary character)
ISBN 0-8234-0918-X; 0-8234-1022-6 (pa)
LC 91-17813
Anansi the spider plans to trick Turtle into catching a fish for his dinner, but Turtle proves to be smarter and ends up with a free meal. Explains the origin of spider webs
"Children able to comprehend the wordplay will be delighted when the lazy but lovable trickster figure is outwitted by the clever turtle, and Stevens' colorful, comical illustrations are perfect for this contemporary rendition of the tale." Booklist

The birds' gift; a Ukrainian Easter story; retold by Eric A. Kimmel; illustrated by Katya Krenina. Holiday House 1999 unp il $16.95 (k-3)
398.2
1. Easter—Folklore 2. Birds—Folklore 3. Eggs—Folklore 4. Folklore—Ukraine
ISBN 0-8234-1384-5   LC 97-50209
Villagers take in a flock of golden birds nearly frozen by an early snow and are rewarded with beautifully decorated eggs the next spring
"Exquisitely detailed illustrations complete this engaging tale: pale yellow backgrounds reflect the birds' golden feathers, borders echo the designs on the eggs, and the Ukrainian costumes are lovingly rendered." Horn Book Guide

The frog princess; a Tlingit legend from Alaska; retold by Eric A. Kimmel; illustrated by Rosanne Litzinger. 1st ed. Holiday House 2006 unp il $16.95 (2-4)   **398.2**
1. Tlingit Indians—Folklore 2. Frogs—Folklore
ISBN 0-8234-1618-6   LC 2004049347
After rejecting all of her human suitors, the beautiful daughter of a Tlingit tribal leader declares that she would rather marry a frog from the lake.
The story "is gracefully told, and [readers] will enjoy the shape-shifting magic and cultural details, which are extended in the uncluttered paintings of villagers in Tlingit costume." Booklist

Gershon's monster; a story for the Jewish New Year; retold by Eric A. Kimmel; illustrated by Jon J Muth. Scholastic Press 2000 il $16.95
398.2
1. Jews—Folklore
ISBN 0-439-10839-X   LC 99-46986
"Retelling of a Hasidic legend featuring Rabbi Israel ben Eliezer"--Author's note
When his sins threaten the lives of his beloved twin children, a Jewish man finally repents of his wicked ways
"This presentation of a Hasidic legend has everything a reader could want: a suspenseful story, an insightful lesson and brilliantly conceived, airy pictures that accelerate the delivery of both." Publ Wkly

The gingerbread man; retold by Eric A. Kimmel; illustrated by Megan Lloyd. Holiday House 1993 unp il $16.95 (k-2)   **398.2**
1. Folklore
ISBN 0-8234-0824-8   LC 90-33202
A freshly baked gingerbread man escapes when he is taken out of the oven and eludes a number of animals until he meets a clever fox
"This version softens the ending with a final page of fresh, recently baked gingerbread men. This is a story that calls for energetic art, and Lloyd provides just that in warm-toned watercolors that feature the gingerbread man zipping across the pages. A compact text and suitably large pictures make this just right for groups." Booklist

The hero Beowulf; retold and adapted by Eric Kimmel from the epic poem Beowulf; pictures by Leonard Everett Fisher. Farrar, Straus and Giroux 2005 unp il $16 (3-6)   **398.2**
1. Beowulf 2. Folklore—Great Britain
ISBN 0-374-30671-0   LC 2003-54888
A simple, brief retelling of the Anglo-Saxon epic about the heroic efforts of Beowulf, son of Ecgtheow, to save the people of Heorot Hall from the terrible monster, Grendel.
"Paired to its dramatic essence, the story has enough action to satisfy even today's media-saturated youngsters. Fisher's large, solid figures in a brooding pallete are worthy of Kimmel's text." Horn Book Guide

Iron John; adapted from the Brothers Grimm by Eric A. Kimmel; illustrated by Trina Schart Hyman. Holiday House 1994 unp il $16.95; pa $6.95 (2-5)   **398.2**
1. Fairy tales 2. Folklore—Germany
ISBN 0-8234-1073-0; 0-8234-1248-2 (pa)
LC 93-7534
With help of Iron John, the wild man of the forest who is under a curse, a young prince makes his way in the world and finds his true love
"Abridged and, as the afterword explains, somewhat changed from the Grimms' tale, Kimmel's dramatic narrative flows from scene to scene with a clear sense of adventure and romance and an underlying sense of mystery. Hyman's beautifully composed illustrations . . . are notable for their rich colors and subtle interplay of light and darkness." Booklist

The rooster's antlers; a story of the Chinese zodiac; retold by Eric A. Kimmel; illustrated by YongSheng Xuan. Holiday House 1999 unp il $16.95 (k-3)   **398.2**
1. Folklore—China 2. Zodiac
ISBN 0-8234-1385-3   LC 97-46854
Relates how the Jade Emperor chose twelve animals to represent the years in his calendar. Also discusses the Chinese calendar, zodiac, the qualities associated with each animal, and what animal rules the year in which the reader was born
"Xuan's illustrations, with their thick black outlines and bold colors, capture the simplicity and strength of Kimmel's telling." Booklist

Kimmel, Eric A.—*Continued*

The runaway tortilla; illustrated by Randy Cecil. Winslow Press (Delray Beach) 2000 unp il $16.95 (k-3)   **398.2**

1. Fairy tales 2. Folklore 3. Hispanic Americans—Folklore

ISBN 1-89081-718-X   LC 00-20487

In this Southwestern version of the Gingerbread Man, a tortilla runs away from Tia Lupe and Tio Jose in Texas

"The primitive oil paintings feature a palette of sunset colors, a rotund Tia and Tio, and a lipsticked, scowling tortilla. . . . Kimmel's saucy story joins a swarm of similar, albeit popular, retellings of traditional tales with a Southwestern setting." SLJ

Seven at one blow; a tale from the Brothers Grimm; retold by Eric A. Kimmel; illustrated by Megan Lloyd. Holiday House 1998 unp il $16.95 (k-3)   **398.2**

1. Fairy tales 2. Folklore—Germany

ISBN 0-8234-1383-7   LC 97-44200

Relates how a tailor who kills seven flies at one blow manages to become king

"Lloyd's watercolor illustrations are a treat for the eye and perfectly complement the rollicking humor of the tale." SLJ

The spotted pony: a collection of Hanukkah stories; retold by Eric A. Kimmel; illustrated by Leonard Everett Fisher. Holiday House 1992 70p il $15.95 (3-6)   **398.2**

1. Jews—Folklore 2. Hanukkah—Folklore

ISBN 0-8234-0936-8   LC 91-24214

This is a collection of "stories for Hanukkah. There are eight tales, one for each night, and each has a *shammes* or 'servant' story preceding it. All of the selections are rich in plot, character, and tradition. . . . Perfect for any occasion, this collection will truly shine when its selections are told or read aloud." SLJ

Ten suns; a Chinese legend; retold by Eric A. Kimmel; illustrated by YongSheng Xuan. Holiday House 1998 unp il $15.95 (2-4)   **398.2**

1. Folklore—China

ISBN 0-8234-1317-9   LC 96-30044

When the ten sons of Di Jun walk across the sky together causing the earth to burn from the blazing heat, their father looks for a way to stop the destruction

"The dramatic retelling is enhanced by the vibrant colors and sweeping lines of the illustrations." Horn Book Guide

The three princes; a tale from the Middle East; retold by Eric A. Kimmel; illustrated by Leonard Everett Fisher. Holiday House 1994 unp il $16.95; pa $6.95 (k-3)   **398.2**

1. Folklore—Middle East

ISBN 0-8234-1115-X; 0-8234-1553-8 (pa)

LC 93-25862

A princess promises to marry the prince who finds the most precious treasure

"Sly humor and high spirits buoy Kimmel's text. . . . Fisher . . . suggests the exotic Arabian setting with a rich palette of striking tones—pink desert skies, violet vistas—and by incorporating unexpected closeups and

unusual angles in his compositions. The play of light and shadow is spectacular." Publ Wkly

Three sacks of truth; a story from France; adapted by Eric A. Kimmel; illustrated by Robert Rayevsky. Holiday House 1993 unp il $15.95 (2-4)   **398.2**

1. Fairy tales 2. Folklore—France

ISBN 0-8234-0921-X   LC 91-19265

With the aid of a perfect peach, a silver fife, and his own resources, Petit Jean outwits a dishonest king and wins the hand of a princess

"In this crisp and sprightly interpretation, storyteller Kimmel takes full advantage of the plot's sly humor, which he accentuates through many colorful, deft turns of phrase. . . . Rayevsky adds rich, predominantly earth-toned illustrations that emphasize character and expression with a slight ironic bite." Publ Wkly

The two mountains; an Aztec legend; retold by Eric A. Kimmel; illustrated by Leonard Everett Fisher. Holiday House 2000 unp il $16.95 (3-5)   **398.2**

1. Aztecs—Folklore 2. Folklore—Mexico

ISBN 0-8234-1504-X   LC 99-32881

Two married gods disobey their orders and visit Earth, are turned into mortals as punishment, and eventually become mountains so that they will always stand side by side

"Acrylic paintings of large figures in Aztec clothing posed against wide skies have a spareness that accentuates this tale's stark drama." Horn Book Guide

Knutson, Barbara

Love and roast chicken; a trickster tale from the Andes. Lerner Pub. Group 2004 unp il map lib bdg $16.95 (k-3)   **398.2**

1. Guinea pigs—Folklore 2. Foxes—Folklore 3. Folklore—Peru 4. Native Americans—South America—Folklore

ISBN 1-57505-657-7   LC 2003-18045

In this folktale from the Andes, a clever guinea pig repeatedly outsmarts the fox that wants to eat him for dinner

"Knutson's boldly outlined, vibrant woodcut-and-watercolor artwork captures the mischievous nature of the guinea pig. . . . A thoroughly enjoyable tale that deserves a place in most libraries." SLJ

Krasno, Rena

Cloud weavers; ancient Chinese legends; [by] Rena Krasno and Yeng Fong Chiang; illustrations from the collection of Yeng-Fong Chiang. Pacific View Press 2003 96p il $22.95 (5 and up)

398.2

1. Folklore—China

ISBN 1-881896-26-9   LC 2002-35911

Presents legends and tales from China, including ancient folktales, stories that reflect Chinese traditions and virtues, historical tales, and selections from literature

This collection "provides a showcase for some remarkable pieces of Chinese calendar art and advertising posters from the 1920s and 1930s. . . . Prefaces provide

Krasno, Rena—*Continued*
cultural insight for some stories, and the brisk retellings weave important background unobtrusively into the narrative." Booklist

Kurtz, Jane
Fire on the mountain; illustrated by E. B. Lewis. Simon & Schuster Bks. for Young Readers 1994 unp il pa $5.99 hardcover o.p. (1-4)
398.2
1. Folklore—Ethiopia
ISBN 0-689-81896-3 (pa)   LC 93-11477
A clever young shepherd boy uses his wits to gain a fortune for himself and his sister from a haughty rich man
"Lewis uses color to achieve intriguing contrast and articulates characters' faces with expression and power. Kurtz, who heard the story as a child in Ethiopia, retells it in a strong narrative voice: her language is simple and spare yet evocative." Booklist

Laird, Elizabeth
When the world began; stories collected in Ethiopia. Oxford Univ. Press 2000 96p il pa $13.99 hardcover o.p. (3-6)   **398.2**
1. Folklore—Ethiopia
ISBN 0-19-274189-6 (pa)   LC 00-708674
"Twenty retellings of classic Ethiopian tales, humorous to thought-provoking, introduce an array of heroes, villains, animals, and ogres. . . . The straightforward prose and the brevity of the tales make them good for reading aloud or story times. . . . Four artists provide delightful visual accompaniment." Booklist

Lee, Jeanne M.
Toad is the uncle of heaven; a Vietnamese folk tale; retold and illustrated by Jeanne M. Lee. Holt & Co. 1985 unp il pa $6.95 hardcover o.p. (k-3)
398.2
1. Folklore—Vietnam 2. Toads—Folklore
ISBN 0-8050-1147-1 (pa)   LC 85-5639
Toad leads a group of animals to ask the King of Heaven to send rain to the parched earth
"The story is simple and reminiscent of motifs common to many cultures. . . . The author's simple prose and beautiful page design, far from being static or stilted, are fluid and convey movement and earthy humor. Her tale of courage born of common sense and perseverance will satisfy a wide audience." Horn Book

Lesser, Rika
Hansel and Gretel; illustrated by Paul O. Zelinsky; retold by Rika Lesser. Dutton Children's Bks. 1999 unp il $16.99; pa $6.99 (k-3)
398.2
1. Fairy tales 2. Folklore—Germany
ISBN 0-525-46152-3; 0-698-11407-8 (pa)
LC 99-10198
A Caldecott Medal honor book, 1985
A reissue of the edition first published 1984 by Dodd, Mead

A retelling of the well-known tale in which two children are left in the woods but find their way home despite an encounter with a wicked witch
"Direct and unembellished, Lesser's retelling resembles that of the earliest German edition of Grimm, published in 1812. . . . A visual feast, the illustrations frequently recall Flemish and French genre painting of the seventeenth century, while the idyllic woodland scenes reflect a later Romantic mood." Horn Book Guide

Lester, Julius
John Henry; pictures by Jerry Pinkney. Dial Bks. for Young Readers 1994 unp il $17.99; pa $6.99 (k-3)   **398.2**
1. John Henry (Legendary character) 2. African Americans—Folklore 3. Folklore—United States
ISBN 0-8037-1606-0; 0-14-056622-8 (pa)
LC 93-34583
A Caldecott Medal honor book, 1995
"The original legend of John Henry and how he beat the steam drill with his sledgehammer has been enhanced and enriched, in Lester's retelling, with wonderful contemporary details and poetic similes that add humor, beauty, and strength. Pinkney's evocative illustrations—especially the landscapes, splotchy and impressionistic, yet very solid and vigorous—are little short of magnificent." Horn Book Guide

The last tales of Uncle Remus; as told by Julius Lester; illustrated by Jerry Pinkney. Dial Bks. 1994 156p il $18.99 (4 and up)   **398.2**
1. African Americans—Folklore 2. Animals—Folklore
ISBN 0-8037-1303-7   LC 93-7531
Also available Uncle Remus: the complete tales $30 (ISBN 0-8037-2451-9)
"Thirty-nine selections . . . drawn from the African American tradition are reclaimed and retold in this fourth and . . . final volume in Lester's Uncle Remus series. Lester's ability to communicate the oral rhythm of the stories is compelling, and his storyteller's voice offers commentary and asides in a nearly perfect combination of traditional and modern vernacular. Humor bubbles from the characterizations, plot, and language. . . . With 8 color and 26 black-and-white illustrations by Pinkney, this roundup is as refreshing and down-to-earth as was the first book in the series." Booklist
Other Uncle Remus tales in this series are:
Further tales of Uncle Remus (1989)
More tales of Uncle Remus (1988)
The tales of Uncle Remus (1987)

Lexau, Joan M.
Crocodile and hen; a Bakongo folktale; text by Joan M. Lexau; pictures by Doug Cushman. HarperCollins Pubs. 2001 45p il $14.95; lib bdg $14.89 (k-2)   **398.2**
1. Folklore—Africa 2. Crocodiles—Folklore 3. Chickens—Folklore
ISBN 0-06-028486-2; 0-06-028487-0 (lib bdg)
LC 99-45410
"An I can read book"
A revised and newly illustrated edition of the title first published 1969

Lexau, Joan M.—*Continued*

Adaptation of Why the crocodile does not eat the hen, from Notes on the folklore of the Fjort (French Congo), by R. E. Dennett

Crocodile is so confused by Hen calling him "brother" every time he gets ready to eat her that he finally goes searching for an explanation of how such a relationship can be

This story, "with simple vocabulary and repetition, is enhanced by . . . high-personality, humorous cartoons." Horn Book Guide

Light, Steven

Puss in boots; retold and illustrated by Steven Light. Abrams 2002 unp il $14.95 (k-3)

398.2

1. Fairy tales 2. Folklore—France 3. Cats—Folklore
ISBN 0-8109-4368-9   LC 2001-3746

A clever cat helps his poor master win fame, fortune, and the hand of a beautiful princess

"Inspired by the work of the French Rococo artist Jean-Honor Fragonard and by French decorative wallpapers, Light created patterned papers onto which he collaged the main illustrations for this story. The results are bright, busy, cheery spreads that suit his lighthearted retelling." SLJ

Long, Laurel

The lady & the lion; a Brothers Grimm tale; retold by Laurel Long & Jacqueline K. Ogburn; illustrated by Laurel Long. Dial Books 2003 unp il $16.99 (2-4)

398.2

1. Folklore—Germany 2. Fairy tales
ISBN 0-8037-2651-1

With help from Sun, Moon, and North Wind, a lady travels the world seeking to save her beloved from the evil enchantress who turned him first into a lion, then into a dove.

"The dramatic tale is smoothly told, but the illustrations, with even more drama and lush with romance, take center stage here. The oil paintings use flowing compositions, swirling lines, rich colors, and a profusion of subtle patterns to create a series of detailed scenes combining European and Middle Eastern elements." Booklist

Louie, Ai-Ling

Yeh-Shen; a Cinderella story from China; retold by Ai-Ling Louie; illustrated by Ed Young. Philomel Bks. 1982 unp il $16.99; pa $6.99 (2-4)

398.2

1. Folklore—China 2. Fairy tales
ISBN 0-399-20900-X; 0-698-11388-8 (pa)
          LC 80-11745

This version of the Cinderella story, in which a young girl overcomes the wickedness of her stepsister and stepmother to become the bride of a prince, is based on ancient Chinese manuscripts written 1000 years before the earliest European version

"The reteller has cast the tale in well-cadenced prose, fleshing out the spare account with elegance and grace. In a manner reminiscent of Chinese scrolls and of decorated folding screens, the text is chiefly set within verti-

cal panels, while the luminescent illustrations—less narrative than emotional—often increase their impact by overspreading the narrow framework or appearing on pages of their own." Horn Book

Lowell, Susan

The bootmaker and the elves; pictures by Tom Curry. Orchard Bks. 1997 unp il $16.95; lib bdg $17.99; pa $6.95 (k-3)

398.2

1. West (U.S.)—Folklore 2. Folklore 3. Fairy tales
ISBN 0-531-30044-7; 0-531-33044-3 (lib bdg); 0-531-07138-3 (pa)   LC 96-53303

A retelling, set in the Old West, of the traditional story about two elves who help a poor shoemaker, or in this case a bootmaker, and his wife

"Curry's acrylic rendering of these western characters is the perfect accompaniment to Lowell's laconically funny text, and it's just bigger than life enough to make this a believable tall-tale fairy tale." Bull Cent Child Books

Lunge-Larsen, Lise

The hidden folk; stories of fairies, dwarves, selkies, and other secret beings; illustrated by Beth Krommes. Houghton Mifflin 2004 72p il $18 (3-5)

398.2

1. Fairy tales 2. Folklore
ISBN 0-618-17495-8   LC 2002-5089

Brief stories featuring such creatures as flower fairies, elves, dwarves, and river spirits.

"The author draws on a rich tradition of legends and myths, retelling them in an accessible manner that will captivate readers. Handsome scratchboard illustrations decorate the pages with stylized figures and landscapes. The vivid hues and interesting textures make an eye-catching combination." SLJ

The race of the Birkebeiners; written by Lise Lunge-Larsen; illustrated by Mary Azarian. Houghton Mifflin 2001 unp il $16 (3-5)

398.2

1. Folklore—Norway
ISBN 0-618-10313-9   LC 00-53977

"Based on the account in 'Håkon Håkonssøon's Saga' penned in 1264 by Sturla Tordsson." Title page

Tells how the infant Prince Hakon is rescued by men fiercely loyal to his dead father, who ski across the rugged mountains in blizzard conditions to save him from his enemies, the Baglers

"The prose is clear and the story is engaging. . . . The woodcut pictures have been expertly rendered in rich colors and capture all of the action." SLJ

Includes bibliographical references

The troll with no heart in his body and other tales of trolls from Norway; retold by Lise Lunge-Larsen; woodcuts by Betsy Bowen. Houghton Mifflin 1999 92p il $18 (3-6)

398.2

1. Folklore—Norway
ISBN 0-395-91371-3   LC 98-43244

"Lunge-Larsen presents nine Norwegian tales about the greed and foolishness of trolls in a casual style that makes these stories ripe for reading aloud and storytell-

Lunge-Larsen, Lise—*Continued*

ing. Her liveliness of language and easy turn of phrase give these retellings a comforting tone despite the sometimes scary events. Bowen's colored-ink woodblock prints, inspired by traditional Norwegian woodcarving and design, suit the monumental nature of the subject." Bull Cent Child Books

Includes bibliographical references

Lupton, Hugh

Pirican Pic and Pirican Mor; retold by Hugh Lupton; illustrated by Yumi Heo. Barefoot Bks. (NY) 2003 unp il $16.99 (k-3)   **398.2**
1. Folklore—Scotland
ISBN 1-84148-070-3

The story of two friends who go off to pick walnuts. Their adventure begins after one friend has been busy picking the walnuts, while the other has eaten every one. Based on a Scottish folktale

This adaptation "has a robust rhythm and language that lends itself easily to reading or telling aloud. That energetic, oral immediacy is enhanced by Heo's lighthearted oil paintings. Human and animal characters sporting eccentric physiologies free-float among varying planes and perspectives in foreground-focused compositions infused with color and light." Bull Cent Child Books

Lyons, Mary E.

Roy makes a car; based on a story collected by Zora Neale Hurston; illustrated by Terry Widener. Atheneum 2005 unp il $16.95 (k-3)   **398.2**
1. Folklore—United States 2. African Americans—Folklore 3. Tall tales 4. Automobiles—Folklore
ISBN 0-689-84640-1   LC 2004-03221

Roy Tyle, the best mechanic in the state of Florida, can clean spark plugs just by looking at them, and he takes a two dollar bet that he can make an accident-proof car.

"Perfect for reading aloud, the funny rhythmic words are well matched to Widener's exaggerated acrylic illustrations." Booklist

MacDonald, Amy

Please, Malese! a trickster tale from Haiti; pictures by Emily Lisker. Farrar, Straus & Giroux 2002 unp il $16 (k-3)   **398.2**
1. Folklore—Haiti
ISBN 0-374-36000-6   LC 2001-29386
"Melanie Kroupa books"

Using his tricky ways, Malese takes advantage of his neighbors, until they catch on, after which he manages to pull an even bigger trick on them

"The stimulating, expressive language matches the fast and funny plot, and the dialogue will lend itself easily to readers' theater and storytelling. Lisker's illustrations are rendered in a tropical-punch palette of pink, yellow, and green." Bull Cent Child Books

MacDonald, Margaret Read

Celebrate the world; twenty tellable folktales for multicultural festivals; illustrations by Roxane Murphy Smith. Wilson, H.W. 1994 225p il $60
          398.2
1. Folklore 2. Festivals 3. Storytelling
ISBN 0-8242-0862-5   LC 94-6682

In this collection MacDonald "has interwoven the stories with holidays and festivals from various countries and presented tips on how to present both the story and the holiday in a storytelling program." J Youth Serv Libr

Includes bibliographical references

Conejito; a folktale from Panama; illustrated by Geraldo Valério. August House 2006 unp il $16.95 (k-3)   **398.2**
1. Folklore—Panama 2. Rabbits—Folklore
ISBN 0-87483-779-0   LC 2005-52567
"LittleFolk"

In this folktale from Panama, a little rabbit and his Tia Monica outwit a fox, a tiger, and a lion, all of whom want to eat him for lunch.

"Rhyming refrains invite the participation of young listeners. . . . Valerio's splashy tropical colors and elongated, rubbery characters . . . capture the tale's bouncing energy." Booklist

Fat cat; a Danish folktale; retold by Margaret Read MacDonald; illustrated by Julie Paschkis. August House 2001 unp il $15.95 (k-3)
          398.2
1. Folklore—Denmark 2. Cats—Folklore 3. Mice—Folklore
ISBN 0-87483-616-6   LC 00-68939

A greedy cat grows enormous as he eats everything in sight, including his friends and neighbors who call him fat

"The book's huge, bright illustrations are glorious. . . . The large, funny illustrations will carry well for a bigger crowd and, combined with refrain that invites chanting along, make this a surefire hit for reading aloud." Booklist

The girl who wore too much; a folktale from Thailand; retold by Margaret Read MacDonald with Thai text by Supaporn Vathanaprida; illustrated by Yvonne Davis. August House LittleFolk 1998 unp il $15.95 (k-3)   **398.2**
1. Folklore—Thailand 2. Bilingual books—English-Thai
ISBN 0-87483-503-8   LC 97-38807

Spoiled and vain, Aree cannot decide which of her many silken dresses and lavish jewels to wear to the dance, so she wears them all

"The story is told in rhythmic, cadenced sentences, ideal for reading aloud. The illustrations substitute modern rural Thailand for the archaic setting of the original tale and depict the characters as somewhat stylized figures dressed in brightly colored Thai silks." SLJ

A hen, a chick, and a string guitar; written by Margaret Read MacDonald; illustrated by Sophie Fatus. Barefoot Books 2005 unp il $17.99 (k-2)
          398.2
1. Animals—Folklore 2. Folklore—Chile
ISBN 1-84148-796-1   LC 2004-17830

MacDonald, Margaret Read—*Continued*

Includes audio CD

A cumulative tale from Chile that begins with a hen and ends with sixteen different animals and a guitar.

"Fatus's vibrant acrylic-and-pastel illustrations of the boy in his poncho and the assorted animals nearly dance off the page. . . . A book to share in storyhours and with toddlers learning animal sounds and counting." SLJ

Mabela the clever; retold by Margaret Read MacDonald; illustrated by Tim Coffey. Whitman, A. 2001 unp il music lib bdg $15.95 (k-3)

398.2

1. Folklore—Africa 2. Mice—Folklore 3. Cats—Folklore

ISBN 0-8075-4902-9   LC 00-8307

An African folktale about a mouse who pays close attention to her surroundings and avoids being tricked by the cat

"MacDonald's retelling of this Limba tale is engineered for storytime success. . . . Coffey's thatch-strewn paintings, rendered in acrylic on watercolor paper textured with gesso, feature lots of visibly clueless, wide-eyed mice, and his cat oozes predatory shrewdness to the very end." SLJ

Pickin' peas; retold by Margaret Read MacDonald; pictures by Pat Cummings. HarperCollins Pubs. 1998 unp il music $15.95; lib bdg $15.89 (k-3)   **398.2**

1. Rabbits—Folklore 2. Folklore—Southern States

ISBN 0-06-027235-X; 0-06-027970-2 (lib bdg)

LC 95-26133

Because a pesky rabbit picks peas from her garden, a little girl catches it and puts it in a box, but the rabbit outwits her

"Fans of Brer Rabbit stories will have a very good time with this classic tale. The retelling is fresh and is anchored by the repetition of the bouncy, catchy refrain. The illustrations are bold, bright, and action-packed." Booklist

Three-minute tales; stories from around the world to tell or read when time is short. August House 2004 160p $24.95; pa $17.95

398.2

1. Folklore 2. Storytelling

ISBN 0-87483-728-6; 0-87483-729-4 (pa)

LC 2004-46257

"Easy to tell, easy to teach to children and adults, and easy to remember, the 80 very short tales in this global collection are for sharing in the classroom, library, and home and around the campfire. . . . The informal, highly practical suggestions for beginners make storytelling sound easy." Booklist

Includes bibliographical references

Tunjur! Tunjur! Tunjur! a Palestinian folktale; retold by Margaret Read MacDonald; collected by Ibrahim Muhawi and Sharif Kanaana; illustrated by Alik Arzoumanian. Marshall Cavendish Children 2006 unp il $16.95 (k-2)   **398.2**

1. Palestinian Arabs—Folklore 2. Theft—Fiction

ISBN 9780761452256; 0-7614-5225-7

LC 2005009719

"In this lively Palestinian tale, a woman wishes for a child to love, 'even if it is nothing more than a cooking pot.' Voila! Her wish comes true, and red Little Pot appears. . . . Reluctantly, the mother lets her pot outdoors, and its adventures include meetings with a merchant and even the royal family. Little Pot manages to roll away from each encounter with valuable stolen goods tucked inside her lid, but after her petty thefts are discovered, she receives a stinky comeuppance that is sure to please read-aloud crowds. Folklorist MacDonald's briskly paced text brims with repetitive phrases that evoke the sounds and rhythm of Little Pot's tumbling, rolling movement, and Arzoumanian's richly hued, stylized acrylics, bordered with Islamic motifs, add subtle cultural detail." Booklist

The **Magic** orange tree, and other Haitian folktales; collected by Diane Wolkstein; drawings by Elsa Henriquez. Knopf 1978 212p il music (5 and up)   **398.2**

1. Folklore—Haiti

LC 77-15003

Available in paperback from Schocken Bks. $14 (0-8052-1077-6)

"A rare collection of folktales and songs is presented in this volume. Miss Wolkstein travelled throughout Haiti listening to the many storytellers in all areas. Each of the twenty-eight tales is preceded by an introduction which details the circumstances surrounding the collection of each story. The blend of cultures found in Haiti is well-depicted in her selections. The introduction in itself is as spellbinding as are the stories. . . . An added delight is the inclusion of music and words in both English and Creole." Bibliophile

Mahy, Margaret

The seven Chinese brothers; illustrated by Jean and Mou-Sien Tseng. Scholastic 1990 unp pa $5.99 hardcover o.p. (1-3)   **398.2**

1. Folklore—China 2. Fairy tales

ISBN 0-590-42057-7 (pa)   LC 88-33668

A story about "seven brothers, each of whom was blessed with an extraordinary power. Together, they use their amazing talents to avoid death at the hands of Emperor Ch'in Shih Huang, while trying to help the exhausted conscripted laborers working on the Great Wall." Child Book Rev Serv

"The handsome watercolor illustrations show a sensitivity to landscape and character portrayal . . . a hint of humor, and a flair for the dramatic. Written with Mahy's accustomed storytelling skill, this book will find an eager audience as a read-aloud for elementary school children." Booklist

Manna, Anthony L.

Mr. Semolina-Semolinus; a Greek folktale; retold by Anthony L. Manna and Christodoula Mitakidou; illustrated by Giselle Potter. Atheneum Bks. for Young Readers 1997 unp il $16 (1-3)

398.2

1. Folklore—Greece

ISBN 0-689-81093-8   LC 96-1924

"An Anne Schwartz book"

Manna, Anthony L.—*Continued*
Areti, a Greek princess, makes a man fit for her to love from almonds, sugar, and semolina, but when he is stolen away by a jealous queen, Areti searches the world for him
"This engaging tale, told in flowing prose with the charming authenticity of oral tradition, is enhanced by Potter's use of colored ink and pencil." Booklist

Marshall, James
Goldilocks and the three bears; retold and illustrated by James Marshall. Dial Bks. for Young Readers 1988 unp il $15.99; pa $5.99 (k-2)
398.2
1. Folklore 2. Bears—Folklore
ISBN 0-8037-0542-5; 0-14-056366-0 (pa)
LC 87-32983
A Caldecott Medal honor book, 1989
"Marshall's Goldilocks, the naughty little girl who disrupts a placid bear household, is no adorable blond moppet led more by curiosity than by mischievous intent. Instead, she is a sturdy, brazen, mini-hussy who stomps over the doorsill with a determined set to her mouth and a confident bounce in her step. . . . The big cartoonlike pictures depict a cozy modern setting for the respectable, suburban bears with snug rooms cluttered with books, bulbous upholstered furniture and a messy little bear's room. . . . The story contains a genuine enjoyment of Goldilock's adventures as they are reflected in Marshall's usual slapdash and rollicking illustrations." Horn Book

Hansel and Gretel; retold and illustrated by James Marshall. Dial Bks. for Young Readers 1990 unp il pa $5.99 hardcover o.p. (k-2)
398.2
1. Folklore—Germany 2. Fairy tales
ISBN 0-14-050836-8 (pa)
LC 89-26011
A poor woodcutter's children, lost in the forest, come upon a house made of cookies, cakes, and candy, occupied by a wicked witch who likes to have children for dinner
"Marshall's trademark wit and slyness mark every page of this effervescent interpretation. Never has there been a more horribly magnificent witch than his—an overstuffed, cackling harridan resplendent in scarlet costume, lipstick and rouge, her hair bedecked with incongruously delicate bows." Publ Wkly

Red Riding Hood; retold and illustrated by James Marshall. Dial Bks. for Young Readers 1987 unp il $15.99; pa $5.99 (k-2) **398.2**
1. Folklore—Germany 2. Wolves—Folklore
ISBN 0-8037-0344-9; 0-14-054693-6 (pa)
LC 86-16722
A "retelling of the familiar tale . . . maintaining the integrity of the Grimm Brothers' version, with both Grandma and Red Riding Hood eaten and later rescued by a hunter." SLJ
This version "will have both children and their parents gripped with the drama and amused by the up-to-date dialogue. . . . The humorous, slightly sinister illustrations display Marshall's wacky style to its best advantage. Funny and wonderful for reading aloud." Horn Book

The three little pigs; retold and illustrated by James Marshall. Dial Bks. for Young Readers 1989 unp il $15.99 (k-2) **398.2**
1. Folklore—Great Britain 2. Pigs—Folklore 3. Wolves—Folklore
ISBN 0-8037-0591-3
LC 88-33411
"In his spiffed-up version of the story, the three porkers follow the traditional course of straw, sticks, and bricks with the traditional results, but the players and accoutrements have a bit more zip than those in other versions. . . . The large, exuberant, cartoonlike illustrations provide much additional entertainment, jouncing readers along delightfully from one amusing scene to the next." Horn Book

Martin, Francesca
Clever Tortoise; a traditional African tale. Candlewick Press 2000 unp il $14.99 (k-3)
398.2
1. Folklore—East Africa 2. Turtles—Folklore 3. Animals—Folklore
ISBN 0-7636-0506-9
LC 99-47080
Clever Tortoise leads the other jungle animals in teaching bullying Elephant and Hippopotamus a lesson by tricking them into engaging in a tug of war with each other
"Martin tells her story in rhythmic, deceptively simple sentences, punctuated with sounds and Kiswahili words that extend the story. . . . The textured watercolor paintings are rendered in colors at once vibrant and muted, and packed with fascinating, expressive details." SLJ

Martin, Rafe
The boy who lived with the seals; illustrated by David Shannon. Putnam 1993 unp il $16.99 (1-4)
398.2
1. Chinook Indians—Folklore 2. Seals (Animals)—Folklore
ISBN 0-399-22413-0
LC 91-46023
In this Chinook legend, a lost boy who has grown up in the sea with seals returns to his tribe but is strangely changed
"Shannon's dark, romantic paintings are dramatically stylized. . . . Martin's retelling employs lyrical language while carefully retaining a clarity appropriate for the intended audience." Publ Wkly

The language of birds; illustrations by Susan Gaber. Putnam 2000 unp il $15.99 (2-4)
398.2
1. Fairy tales 2. Folklore—Russia 3. Birds—Folklore
ISBN 0-399-22925-6
LC 98-48917
A retelling of the Russian folktale in which Ivan, the younger son of a merchant, marries the czar's daughter and gains wealth by learning to understand the language of birds
"The text maintains a rolling pace and lends itself easily to reading aloud or storytelling. Acrylic paintings echo Russian folk art, with borders of birds, feathers, and bird feet running around the edges of the full-and double-page images. . . . This is an unusually robust, inviting folktale setting." Bull Cent Child Books

Martin, Rafe—*Continued*

The Shark God; story by Rafe Martin; pictures by David Shannon. Levine Bks. 2001 unp il $15.95 (k-3) **398.2**

1. Folklore—Hawaii 2. Sharks—Folklore

ISBN 0-590-39500-9   LC 00-40570

Because they freed a shark caught in a net, the fearsome Shark God rescues a brother and sister from the cruel king's imprisonment and helps them find a new, peaceful kingdom across the sea

"Shannon's vigorous illustrations provide a dramatic backdrop for this well-told tale." SLJ

The world before this one; a novel told in legend; with paper sculpture by Calvin Nicholls. Levine Bks. 2002 195p il $16.95 (4 and up) **398.2**

1. Seneca Indians—Folklore

ISBN 0-590-37976-3   LC 2001-23403

"Written in the style of a novel, this collection of 14 Seneca tales is presented through the retelling of one central story into which all of the others are artfully woven. . . . Martin offers sources for the tales along with an introductory note by Seneca Elder Peter Jemison. Each chapter includes a painstakingly detailed white paper sculpture of a character (often an animal) from one of the stories." SLJ

Matthews, Caitlin

Celtic memories; retold by Caitlin Matthews; illustrated by Olwyn Whelan. Barefoot 2003 80p il $19.99 (3-6) **398.2**

1. Celtic mythology

ISBN 1-84148-097-5

"Matthews retells six traditional stories from the Celtic people of Brittany, Ireland, Scotland, and Wales. Between the stories are single-page offerings from the same countries: blessings, songs, and a 'healing charm'. . . . The spacious book design and fresh, appealing artwork make this volume a resplendent showcase for the stories, which are well chosen and well told. Besides the watercolor illustrations of people, places, and events in the narratives, each page has an intricate, Celtic-inspired border designed for that story or verse." Booklist

Includes bibliographical references

Mayer, Marianna

The adventures of Tom Thumb; written by Marianna Mayer; illustrated by Kinuko Y. Craft. SeaStar Bks. 2001 unp il lib bdg $15.88 (1-4) **398.2**

1. Fairy tales 2. Folklore

ISBN 1-58717-065-5   LC 2001-34424

A tiny boy has adventures in a cow's mouth, a fish's belly, and the stomach of a giant

"Mayer's fine retelling is sure to capture the fancy of young readers. . . . Craft's opulent oil-over-watercolor illustrations will draw in even the most reluctant reader." SLJ

Baba Yaga and Vasilisa the brave; as told by Marianna Mayer; illustrated by K. Y. Craft. Morrow Junior Bks. 1994 unp il $16.95 (3-5) **398.2**

1. Fairy tales 2. Folklore—Russia

ISBN 0-688-08500-8   LC 90-38514

A retelling of the old Russian fairy tale in which beautiful Vasilisa uses the help of her doll to escape from the clutches of the witch Baba Yaga, who in turn sets in motion the events which lead to the once ill-treated girl's marrying the tzar

"Mayer's graceful prose conveys both the wonder and power of the tale. Complementing the text are Craft's illustrations done in a mixture of watercolor, gouache, and oils. The palette of red and gold set against a dark background resembles Russian folk-art paintings on black-lacquered wood." SLJ

Beauty and the beast; retold by Marianna Mayer; illustrated by Mercer Mayer. Four Winds Press 1978 unp il $15.95 (1-4) **398.2**

1. Folklore—France 2. Fairy tales

ISBN 0-02-765270-X   LC 78-54679

Through her great capacity to love, a kind and beautiful maid releases a handsome prince from the spell which has made him an ugly beast

"This fresh, new version of the classic French tale is a valid condensation of its lengthier ancestors. Ms. Mayer's clear, crisp style perfectly complements the book's visual qualities. Mercer Mayer's illustrations are, quite simply, superb. They are dramatic and evocative, rich in warm, earth tones and exotic detail." Child Book Rev Serv

Women warriors; myths and legends of heroic women; illustrated by Julek Heller. Morrow Junior Bks. 1999 80p il $17.95 (5 and up) **398.2**

1. Heroes and heroines 2. Women—Folklore

ISBN 0-688-15522-7   LC 98-45697

A collection of twelve traditional tales about female military leaders, war goddesses, women warriors, and heroines from around the world, including such countries as Japan, Ireland, and Zimbabwe

These stories "are told in accessible, rhythmic prose. . . . Each three-to six page selection is prefaced by comments on its origin and history and accompanied by a full-page watercolor painting showing the protagonist in action." SLJ

Includes bibliographical references

McCaughrean, Geraldine

The epic of Gilgamesh; retold by Geraldine McCaughrean; illustrated by David Parkins. Eerdmans Bks. for Young Readers 2003 c2002 95p il $18 (5 and up) **398.2**

1. Gilgamesh 2. Folklore—Iraq

ISBN 0-8028-5262-9   LC 2003-1086

Cover title: Gilgamesh the hero

A retelling, based on seventh-century B.C. Assyrian clay tablets, of the wanderings and adventures of the god king, Gilgamesh, who ruled in ancient Mesopotamia (now Iraq) in about 2700 B.C., and of his faithful companion, Enkidu

McCaughrean, Geraldine—*Continued*

This is "clearly a telling for our time, but one that honors its source. Parkins captures the epic's primitive power and universal emotions in rough, broadly rendered portraits." Horn Book

Grandma Chickenlegs; illustrated by Moira Kemp. Carolrhoda Bks. 1999 unp il $15.95 (k-3)
398.2

1. Folklore—Russia

ISBN 1-57505-415-9   LC 99-19161

In this variation of the traditional Baba Yaga story, a young girl must rely on the advice of her dead mother and her special doll when her wicked stepmother sends her to get a needle from Grandma Chickenlegs

"McCaughrean's well-paced narrative is rich in imagery and humor. . . . Kemp's colored-pencil illustrations are rendered with accessibly childlike simplicity, but she also uses sophisticated composition and perspectives to enhance the drama." Horn Book

McClintock, Barbara

Animal fables from Aesop; adapted and illustrated by Barbara McClintock. Godine 1991 unp il pa $10.95 hardcover o.p. (1-4)
398.2

1. Aesop—Adaptations 2. Fables 3. Animals—Folklore

ISBN 1-56792-144-2 (pa)   LC 91-55368

The fables "are framed at the beginning and end by scenes from a stage set, with the actors posing as animals introducing themselves to us on the opening page and bowing at our expected applause on the last. The graceful full-color illustrations are both delicate and theatrical, as the limited cast reappears in various tales . . . dressed as 18th- or 19th-century townspeople, with the dramatic gestures and facial expressions of humans. . . . The whole feel of this book is in the tradition of La Fontaine: gay, witty, full of charm and foible." N Y Times Book Rev

Cinderella; retold and illustrated by Barbara McClintock; from the Charles Perrault version. 1st ed. Scholastic Press 2005 32p il $15.99 (2-4)
398.2

1. Fairy tales 2. Folklore—France

ISBN 0-439-56145-0   LC 2003-24883

Although mistreated by her stepmother and stepsisters, Cinderella meets her prince with the help of her fairy godmother.

"McClintock's faithful adaptation combines readable text and enchanting pen-and-ink and watercolor illustrations filled with minute details of architecture and dress from the era of Louis XIV." SLJ

McDermott, Gerald

Anansi the spider; a tale from the Ashanti; adapted and illustrated by Gerald McDermott. Holt & Co. 1972 unp il $16.95; pa $6.95 (k-3)
398.2

1. Folklore—Ghana 2. Ashanti (African people)—Folklore 3. Anansi (Legendary character)

ISBN 0-8050-0310-X; 0-8050-0311-8 (pa)

A Caldecott Medal honor book, 1973

The adaptation of this traditional tale of Ghana is based on an animated film by McDermott. It tells of Anansi, a spider, who is saved from terrible fates by his six sons and is unable to decide which of them to reward. The solution to his predicament is also an explanation for how the moon was put into the sky

This offers "brief poetic text, complemented by geometric African folk-style illustrations in pure, bold colors." SLJ

Arrow to the sun; a Pueblo Indian tale; adapted and illustrated by Gerald McDermott. Viking 1974 unp il $16.99; pa $6.99 (k-3)
398.2

1. Pueblo Indians—Folklore

ISBN 0-670-13369-8; 0-14-050211-4 (pa)

Also available Spanish language edition

Awarded the Caldecott Medal, 1975

This myth tells how Boy searches for his immortal father, the Lord of the Sun, in order to substantiate his paternal heritage. Shot as an arrow to the sun, Boy passes through the four chambers of ceremony to prove himself. Accepted by his father, he returns to earth to bring the Lord of the Sun's spirit to the world of men

"The simple, brief text—which suggests similar stories in religion and folklore—is amply illustrated in full-page and doublespread pictures. . . . The strong colors and the bold angular forms powerfully accompany the text." Horn Book

Coyote: a trickster tale from the American Southwest; told and illustrated by Gerald McDermott. Harcourt Brace & Co. 1994 unp il $15; pa $6 (k-3)
398.2

1. Native Americans—Folklore 2. Coyote (Legendary character)

ISBN 0-15-220724-4; 0-15-200032-1 (pa)
LC 92-32979

"Coyote persuades the crows to help him fly, but he becomes so obnoxious and boastful that they abandon him in midair, so he falls back to earth. Told with playful illustrations against the glowing orange of a desert sky, the humorous Zuni tale explains how Coyote, who once had blue fur, got his dust-colored coat and black-tippped tail." Horn Book Guide

Jabuti the tortoise; a trickster tale from the Amazon; told and illustrated by Gerald McDermott. Harcourt 2001 unp il $16 (k-3)
398.2

1. Native Americans—Folklore 2. Amazon River valley—Folklore 3. Turtles—Folklore

ISBN 0-15-200496-3   LC 00-11977

All the birds enjoy the song-like flute music of Jabuti, the tortoise, except Vulture who, jealous because he cannot sing, tricks Jabuti into riding his back toward a festival planned by the King of Heaven

"The story succeeds by embracing what McDermott refers to as a universal trickster theme. . . . Utilizing a radiant palette to evoke the brilliance and vitality of the region, McDermott's spreads feature his familiar geometrically drawn characters that seem to vibrate against the lush-green stylized foliage set upon hot-pink backgrounds." SLJ

McDermott, Gerald—*Continued*
Musicians of the sun. Simon & Schuster Bks. for Young Readers 1997 unp il $17; pa $6.99 (k-3) **398.2**

1. Folklore—Mexico
ISBN 0-689-80706-6; 0-689-93907-3 (pa)
LC 96-19891

In this retelling of an Aztec myth, Lord of the Night sends Wind to free the four musicians that the Sun is holding prisoner so they can bring joy to the world

"This work bears the hallmarks of McDermott's style: vivid colors, illustrations informed by cultural iconography and mythology, an engaging story, and complete source notes." Bull Cent Child Books

Raven; a trickster tale from the Pacific Northwest; told and illustrated by Gerald McDermott. Harcourt Brace Jovanovich 1993 unp il $16 (k-3) **398.2**

1. Native Americans—Folklore
ISBN 0-15-265661-8
LC 91-14563

A Caldecott Medal honor book, 1994

Raven, a Pacific Coast Indian trickster, sets out to find the sun

"Raven, whether he appears as a bird or child, is always marked with a distinctive design of clear-cut red, green, and blue on black, sharply contrasting with the softer hues and forms of the backgrounds and the other characters. In this way, Raven is always recognizable, even when he shifts his shape to human form. . . . Read this picture book aloud for the full effect of its simple, rhythmic text and striking artwork." Booklist

Zomo the Rabbit; a trickster tale from West Africa; told and illustrated by Gerald McDermott. Harcourt Brace Jovanovich 1992 unp il $14.95; pa $6 (k-3) **398.2**

1. Folklore—Africa 2. Rabbits—Folklore
ISBN 0-15-299967-1; 0-15-201010-6 (pa)
LC 91-14558

"Zomo the Rabbit, an African trickster . . . goes to Sky God and requests wisdom. Sky God informs him that he must earn it and assigns him three impossible tasks." Child Book Rev Serv

"Like the spare text, the shapes here are boldly controlled—ideal for sharing with a group of very young children. Because of their rich patterns and sharp color contrasts, the images in the gouache paintings, although simple, never become simplistic." Bull Cent Child Books

McGill, Alice
Sure as sunrise; stories of Bruh Rabbit & his walkin' talkin' friends; illustrated by Don Tate. Houghton Mifflin 2004 48p il $17 (2-5) **398.2**

1. African Americans—Folklore
ISBN 0-618-21196-9
LC 2003-12289

"Drawing on the tales she heard from her African American family and community growing up in rural North Carolina more than 50 years ago, McGill tells five trickster stories with warmth, wit, and simple immediacy that's just right for reading aloud. . . . Based on clay models, the animal characters in human clothes are reminiscent of puppets in the big, clear oil-and-acrylic illustrations; their body language and exaggerated expressions are wonderful." Booklist

McGovern, Ann
Too much noise; illustrated by Simms Taback. Houghton Mifflin 1967 44p il $16; pa $6.95 (k-3) **398.2**

1. Folklore
ISBN 0-395-18110-0; 0-395-62985-3 (pa)

"The too crowded house of a familiar old tale becomes a too noisy house in this entertaining picture-book story. Bothered by the noises in his house, an old man follows the advice of the village wise man by first acquiring and then getting rid of a cow, donkey, sheep, hen, dog, and cat. Only then can he appreciate how quiet his house is. The simplicity and straightforwardness of the folktale are evident in both the telling of the cumulative story and in the amusing colored illustrations." Booklist

Menchú, Rigoberta
The honey jar; [by] Rigoberta Menchu with Dante Liano; pictures by Domi; translated by David Unger. Groundwood Books House of Anansi Press 2006 64p il $16.96 (4-6) **398.2**

1. Mayas—Folklore
ISBN 978-0-88899-670-1

This is a collection of 12 Mayan folktales that the author "heard as a child. The stories range from creation stories and pourquoi tales about animals to selections that reflect a distinctive worldview, a broad awareness of nature, and a sense of humor. Using vivid colors, the naturalistic, folk-art oil paintings . . . illustrate the stories in a manner that reflects the simple spirit and directness of the tellings. An expressive collection that lends insight into the Mayan culture in which Menchu grew up." Booklist

Includes glossary

Milligan, Bryce
Brigid's cloak; an ancient Irish story; written by Bryce Milligan; illustrated by Helen Cann. Eerdmans Bks. for Young Readers 2002 unp il $16; pa $8 (k-3) **398.2**

1. Brigid, Saint, d. ca. 525—Legends 2. Jesus Christ—Nativity 3. Folklore—Ireland
ISBN 0-8028-5224-6; 0-8028-5297-1 (pa)
LC 2001-40174

Relates a legend about the Irish slave girl who became Saint Brigid, beginning with a celestial song, a mysterious gift, and a prophecy on the night of her birth

"Borders of Celtic designs frame Cann's mixed-media pictures and add both authenticity and wonder to the tale." Booklist

Mollel, Tololwa M. (Tololwa Marti)
Ananse's feast; an Ashanti tale; retold by Tololwa M. Mollel; illustrated by Andrew Glass. Clarion Bks. 1997 31p il $14.95 (k-3) **398.2**

1. Anansi (Legendary character) 2. Ashanti (African people)—Folklore 3. Folklore—Ghana
ISBN 0-395-67402-6
LC 95-17358

Mollel, Tololwa M. (Tololwa Marti)—*Continued*

Unwilling to share his feast, Ananse the spider tricks Akye the turtle so that he can eat all the food himself, but Akye finds a way to get even

"Varied in composition and bright with layers of color, the oil-and-colored-pencil artwork captures the actions, reactions, and emotions of the two main characters with a great sense of playfulness and humor." Booklist

The orphan boy; a Maasai story; illustrated by Paul Morin. Clarion Bks. 1990 unp il $16; pa $6.95 (k-3)   398.2

1. Masai (African people)—Folklore 2. Folklore—Africa

ISBN 0-89919-985-2; 0-395-72079-6 (pa)

LC 90-2358

"A solitary old man on the wide plains welcomes into his compound an orphan boy, Kileken, who helps with the work and the cattle and brings prosperity even in times of drought. But when the old man insists on knowing the boy's secret, Kileken returns to his place in the sky. He is the steadily shining star . . . that is the planet Venus." Booklist

"Infused with an aura of mystery, Mollel's compelling story is told skillfully and dramatically. Morin's richly textured paintings, evoking in bold colors an Africa of both parched desert and lush vegetation, are worthy companions." Publ Wkly

Montes, Marisa

Juan Bobo goes to work; a Puerto Rican folktale; retold by Marisa Montes; illustrated by Joe Cepeda. HarperCollins Pubs. 2000 unp il $15.95; lib bdg $15.89 (k-3)   398.2

1. Folklore—Puerto Rico

ISBN 0-688-16233-9; 0-688-16234-7 (lib bdg)

LC 99-28799

Although he tries to do exactly as his mother tells him, foolish Juan Bobo keeps getting things all wrong

"The funny, well-paced retelling smoothly incorporates Spanish words and phrases. . . . Using bold, bright Caribbean colors, Cepeda's oil paintings amplify Juan's silliness and charm. Brush strokes add texture, and background details establish the Puerto Rican setting." Booklist

Includes glossary

Morales, Yuyi

Just a minute; a trickster tale and counting book. Chronicle Books 2003 unp il $15.95 (k-3)

398.2

1. Folklore—Mexico 2. Counting

ISBN 0-8118-3758-0   LC 2002-151386

Text in English and Spanish

In this version of a traditional tale, Senor Calavera arrives at Grandma Beetle's door, ready to take her to the next life, but after helping her count, in English and Spanish, as she makes her birthday preparations, he changes his mind.

"Like the text, the rich, lively artwork draws strongly upon Mexican culture. . . . The splendid paintings and spirited storytelling—along with useful math and multicultural elements—augur a long, full life for this original folktale." Booklist

Moroney, Lynn

Baby rattlesnake; told by Te Ata; adapted by Lynn Moroney; illustrated by Veg Reisberg. Children's Bk. Press 1989 30p il $14.95; pa $7.95 (k-2)   398.2

1. Chickasaw Indians—Folklore 2. Rattlesnakes—Folklore

ISBN 0-89239-049-2; 0-89239-111-1 (pa)

LC 89-9892

Also available Spanish language edition

In this Chickasaw Indian tale, willful Baby Rattlesnake throws tantrums to get his rattle before he's ready, but he misuses it and learns a lesson

"The short sentences, onomatopoeia, and repetition will hold the attention of the youngest listeners as will the boldly colored, stylized gouache and cut-paper illustrations that depict the endearing Rattlesnake family." Booklist

Morpurgo, Michael

The McElderry book of Aesop's fables; illustrations by Emma Chichester Clark. Margaret K. McElderry Books 2005 94p il $19.95 (k-2)

398.2

1. Aesop—Adaptations 2. Fables

ISBN 1-4169-0290-2   LC 2004-58160

First published 2004 in the United Kingdom with title: The Orchard book of Aesop's fables

Retellings of twenty-one classic Aesop fables, including "The Hare and the Tortoise" and "Belling the Cat," in updated language.

"This large, spacious hardcover is perfectly designed for reading aloud. The text appears in big, clear type on thick paper, and Clark's gorgeous watercolors show the characters. . . . Morpurgo's adaptations of 21 short tales stay true to the tradition of humanlike animal characters and lessons that eschew heavy philosophizing in favor of warnings about ordinary folk and their foolishness." Booklist

Sir Gawain and the Green Knight; as told by Michael Morpurgo; illustrated by Michael Foreman. Candlewick Press 2004 114p il $18.99 (5 and up)   398.2

1. Arthurian romances 2. Gawain (Legendary character)

ISBN 0-7636-2519-1   LC 2003-65527

The quest of Sir Gawain for the Green Knight teaches him a lesson in pride, humility, and honor

"Morpurgo's sprightly writing brings out all the humor as well as the horror of the original tale, and Foreman's profuse, evocative watercolor-and-pastel illustrations highlight the drama in each scene." SLJ

Mosel, Arlene

The funny little woman; retold by Arlene Mosel; pictures by Blair Lent. Dutton 1972 unp il pa $5.99 hardcover o.p. (k-2)   398.2

1. Folklore—Japan

ISBN 0-14-054753-3 (pa)

Awarded the Caldecott Medal, 1973

Based on Lafcadio Hearn's The old woman and her dumpling

Mosel, Arlene—*Continued*

While chasing a dumpling, a little lady is captured by wicked creatures from whom she escapes with the means of becoming the richest woman in Japan

"The tale unfolds in a simple tellable style. . . . Using elements of traditional Japanese art, the illustrator has made marvelously imaginative pictures. . . . All the inherent drama and humor of the story are manifest in the illustrations." Horn Book

Tikki Tikki Tembo; retold by Arlene Mosel; illustrated by Blair Lent. Holt & Co. 1968 unp il $16.95; pa $6.95 (k-2)   **398.2**
1. Folklore—China 2. Personal names—Folklore
ISBN 0-8050-0662-1; 0-8050-1166-8 (pa)

Also available Big book edition and Spanish language edition

A "Chinese folk tale about a first son with a very long name. When Tikki Tikki Tembo-No Sa Rembo-Chari Bari Ruchi-Pip Peri Pembo fell into the well, it took his little brother so long to say his name and get help that Tikki almost drowned." Hodges. Books for Elem Sch Libr

"In this polished version of a story hour favorite, beautifully stylized wash drawings of serene Oriental landscapes are in comic contrast to amusingly visualized folk and the active disasters accruing to the possessor of a 21-syllable, irresistibly chantable name." Best Books of the Year, 1968

Moser, Barry

The three little pigs; retold and illustrated by Barry Moser. Little, Brown 2001 unp il $14.95 (k-3)   **398.2**
1. Folklore 2. Pigs—Folklore 3. Wolves—Folklore
ISBN 0-316-58544-0   LC 00-35228

A humorous retelling of the classic story recounts the fatal episodes in the lives of two foolish pigs and how the third pig managed to avoid the same fate

"Moser has made the plot his own by embellishing the text with dynamic, full-color illustrations that set the story in contemporary times without losing its fabulist elements." Horn Book Guide

Muth, Jon J.

Stone soup; retold and illustrated by Jon J. Muth. Scholastic Press 2003 unp il $16.95 (k-3)   **398.2**
1. Folklore 2. China—Fiction
ISBN 0-439-33909-X   LC 2002-3776

"Three Zen monks arrive in a Chinese mountain village where hard times have made villagers distrustful of strangers and selfish toward one another. Undeterred by a lack of welcome, the monks set about preparing dinner soup, which . . . draws the villagers from their sheltered homes with ingredients to enrich the pot, thereby reinvigorating the community." Booklist

"Muth's muted blue-and-gray watercolors are ideally suited to portraying the inhospitable village. . . . His respect for Chinese people and their culture makes this serving of fusion cuisine delicious and satisfying." Horn Book

Myers, Christopher

Lies and other tall tales; collected by Zora Neale Hurston; adapted and illustrated by Christopher Myers. 1st ed. HarperCollins Pub. 2005 unp il $15.99; lib bdg $16.89   **398.2**
1. Hurston, Zora Neale, 1891-1960—Adaptations
2. African Americans—Folklore 3. Tall tales
ISBN 0-06-000655-2; 0-06-000656-0 (lib bdg)
     LC 2004-22252

"Myers has adapted and illustrated some of the wild, very short, wicked stories collected by . . . Zora Neale Hurston. . . . True to the spirit of the tall-tale oral tradition, Myers' quiltlike pictures in paper and fabric collage are minimalist and exaggerated, magical and mundane. . . . Perfect for sharing with many age groups." Booklist

Norman, Howard

Between heaven and earth; bird tales from around the world; illustrated by Leo & Diane Dillon. Harcourt 2004 78p il lib bdg $22 (4 and up)   **398.2**
1. Folklore 2. Birds—Folklore
ISBN 0-15-201982-0   LC 2003-7874
"Gulliver books"

A collection of folktales from around the world, all of which have a bird as a main character.

This is "a collection of stories that are rich in cultural references from the lands of their origins. . . . The Dillons' luminous watercolor-and-pencil illustrations, detailed with patterns drawn from each tale's culture of origin, will draw readers and listeners back to the stories." Booklist

The girl who dreamed only geese, and other tales of the Far North; told by Howard Norman; illustrated by Leo & Diane Dillon. Harcourt Brace & Co. 1997 147p il $22 (4 and up)
     398.2
1. Inuit—Folklore
ISBN 0-15-230979-9   LC 96-20880
"Gulliver books"

A collection of stories retold from Inuit folklore

"The narratives have a marvelous vitality and excitement. They capture the sound and cadence of the spoken word. . . . The plots reflect the diversity and humor of Inuit culture. . . . Each tale is accompanied by several large, full-color acrylic illustrations in addition to outstanding black-and-white friezes that run across the top of each page." SLJ

Oberman, Sheldon

Solomon and the ant; and other Jewish folktales; retold by Sheldon Oberman; introduction and commentary by Peninnah Schram. 1st ed. Boyds Mills Press 2006 165p $19.95 (5 and up)
     398.2
1. Jews—Folklore
ISBN 1-59078-307-7   LC 2005020115
"This collection of 43 traditional Jewish stories is authoritative as well as immensely entertaining. . . . The stories, from both Ashkenazi and Sephardic traditions, are arranged more or less chronologically—from biblical days through the talmudic period to more contemporary

Oberman, Sheldon—*Continued*

times. There are legends, medieval fables, trickster tales, and more. . . . The stories, wonderful for storytelling and sharing, are accessible even to listeners younger than the target audience, and the notes and commentary will provide older children with context and history." Booklist

Includes bibliographical references

Olson, Arielle North

Ask the bones: scary stories from around the world; selected and retold by Arielle North Olson and Howard Schwartz; illustrated by David Linn. Viking 1999 145p il $15.99; pa $5.99 (4 and up)

398.2

1. Folklore

ISBN 0-670-87581-3; 0-14-230140-X (pa)

LC 98-19108

A collection of scary folktales from countries around the world including China, Russia, Spain, and the United States

"David Linn's bone-chilling black-and-white illustrations . . . will stay with the reader long after the book is closed. Excellent for reading aloud, this collection will satisfy even jaded genre fans." Booklist

Includes bibliographical references

Orgel, Doris

The Bremen town musicians and other animal tales from Grimm; retold by Doris Orgel; illustrated by Bert Kitchen. 1st ed. Roaring Brook Press 2004 unp il $18.95; lib bdg $25.90 (k-3)

398.2

1. Folklore—Germany 2. Animals—Folklore

ISBN 0-7613-1694-9; 0-7613-2809-2 (lib bdg)

LC 2003-8989

Contents: The Bremen town musicians; The hare and the hedgehog; King of the birds; When the birds and the beasts went to war; The wolf and the seven young kids; The fox and the geese

A retelling of six Grimm's fairy tales about animals

The author provides "fresh lively retellings that will be a particular boon to storytellers. . . . Bert Kitchen's elegantly detailed animals are strongly realistic, yet imbued with character, dignity, and a beguiling whiff of humor." Horn Book

Osborne, Mary Pope

American tall tales; wood engravings by Michael McCurdy. Knopf 1991 115p il map $22 (3-6)

398.2

1. Tall tales 2. Folklore—United States

ISBN 0-679-90089-1

LC 89-37235

A collection of tall tales about such American folk heroes as Sally Ann Thunder Ann Whirlwind, Pecos Bill, John Henry, and Paul Bunyan

"As tantalizing as Osborne's storytelling are McCurdy's . . . elaborate, full-color wood engravings, which in their robust stylization dramatically render the grandeur of these engrossing yarns." Publ Wkly

Includes bibliographical references

The brave little seamstress; written by Mary Pope Osborne; illustrated by Giselle Potter. Atheneum Bks. for Young Readers 2002 unp il $16 (k-3)

398.2

1. Fairy tales 2. Folklore

ISBN 0-689-84486-7

LC 2001-33018

"An Anne Schwartz book"

A seamstress who kills seven flies with one blow outwits the king and, with the help of a kind knight, becomes a wise and kind queen

"The whimsically perky, generous text is perfectly matched to the illustrations, in Potter's signature ink-gouache-gesso-water-colors, which affix just the right amount of sauciness to the cheeky heroine." Booklist

Favorite medieval tales; retold by Mary Pope Osborne; illustrated by Troy Howell. Scholastic 1998 86p il pa $7.99 hardcover o.p. (4 and up)

398.2

1. Folklore—Europe

ISBN 0-439-14134-6 (pa)

LC 96-17285

A collection of well-known tales from medieval Europe, including "Beowulf," "The Sword in the Stone," "The Song of Roland," and "Gudren and the Island of the Lost Children"

"Inspired by medieval art and illuminated manuscripts, Howell's paintings complement the well-researched text." Horn Book Guide

Includes bibliographical references

Kate and the beanstalk; written by Mary Pope Osborne; illustrated by Giselle Potter. Atheneum Bks. for Young Readers 2000 unp il $16 (k-3)

398.2

1. Fairy tales 2. Folklore—Great Britain 3. Giants—Folklore

ISBN 0-689-82550-1

LC 99-27029

"An Anne Schwartz book"

In this version of the classic tale, a girl climbs to the top of a giant beanstalk, where she uses her quick wits to outsmart a giant and make her and her mother's fortune

"The text is straightforward but punctuated by some delicious dialogue. . . . Using a variety of mediums—pencil, ink, gouache, and watercolor—the illustrations are executed in Potter's signature folk-art style. They are immediate, innovative, and just the right size for story hours." Booklist

Osborne, Will

Sleeping Bobby; [by] Will Osborne and Mary Pope Osborne; illustrated by Giselle Potter. Atheneum Books for Young Readers 2005 unp il $16.95 (k-3)

398.2

1. Fairy tales 2. Folklore—Germany

ISBN 0-689-87668-8

LC 2004-06346

"An Anne Schwartz Book"

A retelling of the Grimm tale featuring a handsome prince who is put into a deep sleep by a curse until he is awakened by the kiss of a brave princess.

This "is written in a breezy, readable style, and most details of the original story have been included. . . . Potter's folk-style characters are dressed in Elizabethan garb with details such as puffed sleeves, high lace collars, and ruffs." SLJ

The **Oxford** companion to fairy tales; edited by Jack Zipes. Oxford Univ. Press 2000 xxxii, 601p pa $24.95 hardcover o.p.   **398.2**
1. Fairy tales—History and criticism
ISBN 0-19-860509-9 (pa)   LC 99-14271
This is a "collection of brief essays on classic tales, both modern and ancient. In alphabetical order, the companion profiles noted authors, illustrators, filmmakers, choreographers, and composers; more broadly, it covers film, art, opera, ballet, music, and commercial use. . . . Attractive, well written, and approachable, this solid guide to the fairy-tale world is without equal." Libr J
Includes bibliographical references

Park, Janie Jaehyun
The love of two stars; a Korean legend; retold and pictures by Janie Jaehyun Park. Groundwood Books 2005 unp il $16.95 (k-3)   **398.2**
1. Folklore—Korea 2. Stars—Folklore
ISBN 0-88899-672-1
"A Groundwood book"
"High in the starry sky, Kyonu works as a farmer and Jingnyo as a weaver. After they fall in love, they neglect their work, leaving the people hungry and ragged, so the king allows them to meet only on the seventh day of the seventh moon month. When that day comes, however, they can't reach one another, and their tears flood the earth. Finally, the birds . . . fly up and make a bridge across the Milky Way to enable the lovers to embrace. Park's unframed double-page illustrations, painted on gessoed paper to add attractive texture, show the romantic costume drama of the Korean lovers together and apart. At the same time, the rich, dark-blue mystery of the night sky, with stars and swirling curves, will touch kids everywhere." Booklist

Partridge, Elizabeth
Kogi's mysterious journey; adapted by Elizabeth Partridge; illustrated by Aki Sogabe. Dutton Children's Bks. 2003 unp il $17.99 (k-3)   **398.2**
1. Artists—Folklore 2. Fishes—Folklore 3. Folklore—Japan
ISBN 0-525-47078-6
Kogi paints the shore of Lake Biwa, but is unable to capture the vigor and beauty that inspire him. One day, Kogi wades into the water to release a fish, and unable to resist follows in its wake, eventually becoming a fish himself, and learning what it is to be a fish in the lake
"Partridge's spare, poetic recasting of a Japanese folktale ends with the artist and his creations coming to life again as fish. Dignified and handsome, Sogabe's carefully composed cut-paper art employs muted colors to bring Kogi's inner and outer worlds to life." SLJ

Paterson, Katherine
Parzival; the quest of the Grail Knight; retold by Katherine Paterson. Lodestar Bks. 1998 127p pa $5.99 hardcover o.p. (5 and up)   **398.2**
1. Arthurian romances
ISBN 0-14-130573-8 (pa); 0-525-67579-5 (hc)
LC 97-23891

"From the thirteenth-century epic poem by Wolfram von Eschenbach. This retelling is based on A.T. Hatto's English translation"--Publisher
A retelling of the Arthurian legend in which Parzival, unaware of his noble birth, comes of age through his quest for the Holy Grail
"Nearly 800 years old, the story has freshness, humor, grace, and depth. . . . Paterson clarifies much of the Christian doctrine that is the basis of the story, but she is never dull or pedantic." SLJ

The tale of the mandarin ducks; illustrated by Leo & Diane Dillon. Lodestar Bks. 1989 unp il $16.99; pa $6.99 (1-3)   **398.2**
1. Folklore—Japan 2. Ducks—Folklore
ISBN 0-525-67283-4; 0-14-055739-3 (pa)
LC 88-30484
"A Japanese fairy tale, in picture-book format, about a Mandarin duck caught and caged at the whim of a wealthy Japanese lord. Separated from his mate, the bird languishes in captivity until a compassionate servant girl sets him free. The lord sentences the girl and her beloved to death, but they in turn are freed and rewarded with happiness." Booklist
"Paterson's story is rich with magic, compassion and love. The Dillons' elegantly detailed watercolor and pastel drawings, in the style of 18th-century Japanese woodcuts, are exquisite." Publ Wkly

Paye, Won-Ldy
Head, body, legs; a story from Liberia; retold by Won-Ldy Paye & Margaret H. Lippert; illustrated by Julie Paschkis. Holt & Co. 2002 unp il $16.95 (k-3)   **398.2**
1. Folklore—Liberia
ISBN 0-8050-6570-9   LC 00-44856
In this tale from the Dan people of Liberia, Head, Arms, Body, and Legs learn that they do better when they work together
"This simple fable about working together is told in a straightforward text; humor is inherent in the situation. Enticing illustrations in ripe fruit colors enhance the strange, silly tale." Horn Book Guide

Mrs. Chicken and the hungry crocodile; [by] Won-Ldy Paye & Margaret H. Lippert; illustrated by Julie Paschkis. Holt & Co. 2003 unp il $16.95 (k-3)   **398.2**
1. Folklore—Liberia 2. Chickens—Folklore 3. Crocodiles—Folklore
ISBN 0-8050-7047-8   LC 2002-1755
"A version of this story was previously published in Why Leopard Has Spots: Dan Stories from Liberia by Won-Ldy Paye and Margaret H. Lippert, illustrated by Ashley Bryan, by Fulcrum Publishing, Inc., Golden, Colorado, 1998"
When a crocodile captures Mrs. Chicken and takes her to an island to fatten her up, clever Mrs. Chicken claims that she can prove they are sisters and that, therefore, the crocodile shouldn't eat her
"Told in straightforward language this trickster tale is smart and funny. . . . The stylized gouache artwork is strong and streamlined. . . . The flat paintings recall folk art, and Crocodile's checkerboard skin reflects the patterns found in her home." SLJ

Penner, Lucille Recht

Dragons; illustrated by Peter Scott. 1st ed. Random House 2004 42p il lib bdg $11.99; pa $3.99 (3-5) **398.2**

1. Dragons 2. Folklore

ISBN 0-307-26417-2 (lib bdg); 0-307-46417-3 (pa)

LC 2003-12427

"A stepping stone book"

Contents: Dragon myth; Scaly and scary

Relates myths about dragons from different countries, including where they live, what they eat, and how they look, as well as how the myths may have developed.

"Carefully differentiating between reality and myth, the author intersperses bits of dragon lore . . . through the text. . . . Color illustrations showing different types of dragons add interest." Booklist

Perrault, Charles

Cinderella; or, The little glass slipper; a free translation from the French of Charles Perrault; with pictures by Marcia Brown. Scribner 1954 unp il $16; pa $5.99 (k-3) **398.2**

1. Folklore—France 2. Fairy tales

ISBN 0-684-12676-1; 0-689-81474-7 (pa)

Awarded the Caldecott Medal, 1955

This is the classic story of the poor, good-natured girl who works for her selfish step-sisters until a fairy godmother transforms her into a beautiful 'princess' for just one night

"With soft, delicate colors and lines that subtly suggest, Miss Brown creates a thoroughly fairyland atmosphere, at the same time recreating the sophistication of the French Court with its golden coach, canopied bed, dazzling chandeliers, liveried footmen, curled and pompadoured ladies, and peruked (bewigged) courtiers." Libr J

Puss in boots; illustrated by Fred Marcellino; translated by Malcolm Arthur. Farrar, Straus & Giroux 1990 unp il $16; pa $8.95 (k-3) **398.2**

1. Folklore—France 2. Fairy tales 3. Cats—Folklore

ISBN 0-374-36160-6; 0-374-46034-5 (pa)

LC 90-82136

A Caldecott Medal honor book, 1991

"Opulently designed and handsomely illustrated, this picture book provides a fitting showcase for Perrault's artful tale of deceit and resourcefulness. Unsullied by type, the striking front of the book features a close-up portrait of the cat's face. Befitting a fairy tale, the artwork inside is suffused with a golden light that proclaims the story to be from a sunnier, more dreamlike world." Booklist

Philip, Neil

Celtic fairy tales; retold with an introduction by Neil Philip; illustrated by Isabelle Brent. Viking 1999 137p il $21.99 (4 and up) **398.2**

1. Fairy tales 2. Celts—Folklore 3. Folklore—Great Britain

ISBN 0-670-88387-5 LC 98-50081

An illustrated collection of twenty stories from many Celtic regions, including "The Battle of the Birds," "Finn MacCool and the Scotch Giant," and "The Ship that Went to America."

"There's a mix of the almost familiar and nicely exotic in this collection, which is lavishly illustrated with a glowing full-page painting for each tale and Celtic motifs on every page." Booklist

Horse hooves and chicken feet: Mexican folktales; selected by Neil Philip; illustrated by Jacqueline Mair. Clarion Bks. 2003 83p il $19 (4 and up) **398.2**

1. Folklore—Mexico

ISBN 0-618-19463-0 LC 2002-154886

This is a "selection of 14 folktales from Mexico and people of Mexican descent from the American Southwest. The stories are simply yet effectively retold. . . . Adding considerably to the overall appeal of the book are Mair's exuberant illustrations, accomplished in the style of Mexican folk art." Booklist

Includes bibliographical references

Noah and the Devil; a legend of Noah's Ark from Romania; retold by Neil Philip; illustrated by Isabelle Brent. Clarion Bks. 2001 unp il $16 (k-3) **398.2**

1. Folklore—Romania 2. Noah's ark—Folklore

ISBN 0-618-11754-7 LC 00-60325

A retelling of the story of Noah's ark, embellished with elements from Romanian folklore, including how the devil sneaked aboard, the reason Noah threw a cat overboard, and the role of a snake in saving the ark

"Philip blends the story's elements together into a believable whole in language that, while slightly elevated, is simple enough for young listeners to follow. The luminous gold-leafed watercolors . . . will delight young ones with their lovely details, ornate borders based on folk-art designs, and whimsical touches." Booklist

Includes bibliographical references

The pirate princess and other fairy tales; by Neil Philip; illustrated by Mark Weber. 1st American ed. Arthur A. Levine Books 2005 88p il $19.99 (4-6) **398.2**

1. Jewish legends 2. Fairy tales

ISBN 0-590-10855-7 LC 2004-16949

Contents: The pirate princess; The fixer; The gem prince; The treasure; The merchant and the poor man; The turkey prince; The lost princess

This "volume contains seven fairy tales adapted from the stories written by seventeenth-century Hasidic rabbi Nahman ben Simha. . . . An informative four-page introduction discusses Nahman and his storytelling. The lively collection of varied tales begins with the story of a princess who turns pirate to escape unwanted suitors and rejoin the man she loves. Several of the other stories share elements of adventure, true love, promises, quests, and fortune. . . . Weber's many gouache paintings have the stylistic feeling of Chagall. . . . They capture the wit, drama, and occasional comedy of the tales." Booklist

Includes bibliographical references

Pinkney, Jerry

Aesop's fables. SeaStar Bks. 2000 87p il $19.95 **398.2**

1. Aesop—Adaptations 2. Fables

ISBN 1-58717-000-0 LC 00-24194

Pinkney, Jerry—*Continued*

A collection of nearly sixty fables from Aesop, including such familiar ones as "The Grasshopper and the Ants," "The North Wind and the Sun," "Androcles and the Lion," "The Troublesome Dog," and "The Fox and the Stork"

Pinkney brings "vivid new life to these ancient fables by creating pencil, colored pencil, and watercolor illustrations that are subtle and delicate in color but dynamic and dramatic in composition and in size. . . . Pinkney's text proves equal to his art. His language, though formal, is subtly witty and begs to be read aloud." Booklist

The little red hen; [by] Jerry Pinkney. Dial Books for Young Readers 2006 unp il $16.99 (k-3)   **398.2**

1. Folklore 2. Chickens—Folklore
ISBN 0-8037-2935-9   LC 2005013301

A newly illustrated edition of the classic fable of the hen who is forced to do all the work of baking bread and of the animals who learn a bitter lesson from it.

This is "a lush, light-filled rendition of a folktale staple. . . . The animal's names appear in color-coded font (red for the hen, brown for the dog, etc.), making it extra-easy even for pre-readers to chime in, and the glorious, generous paintings are a real gift." SLJ

Polacco, Patricia

Luba and the wren. Philomel Bks. 1999 unp il $16.99 (k-3)   **398.2**

1. Fairy tales 2. Folklore—Russia 3. Birds—Folklore
ISBN 0-399-23168-4   LC 98-16353

In this variation on the story of "The Fisherman and His Wife," a young Ukrainian girl must repeatedly return to the wren she has rescued to relay her parents' increasingly greedy demands

"Polacco's signature illustrations are lush and vibrant. The regal colors of royal blue and crimson play against deep green, dappled brown, and ocher of the natural world." SLJ

Pollock, Penny

The Turkey Girl; a Zuni Cinderella story; retold by Penny Pollock; illustrated by Ed Young. Little, Brown 1996 unp il lib bdg $16.95 (3-5)   **398.2**

1. Zuni Indians—Folkore
ISBN 0-316-71314-7   LC 93-28947

In this Indian variant of a familiar story, some turkeys make a gown of feathers for the poor girl who tends them so that she can participate in a sacred dance, but they desert her when she fails to return as promised

"The bleakness of the tale is softened by Young's elegantly evocative pastel and oil crayon illustrations. . . . Pollock's retelling is steady and solid, and her source is clearly indicated in an author's note that gives some background on the tale." Booklist

Poole, Amy Lowry

The ant and the grasshopper; retold and illustrated by Amy Lowry Poole. Holiday House 2000 unp il $16.95 (k-3)   **398.2**

1. Aesop—Adaptations 2. Fables
ISBN 0-8234-1477-9   LC 99-18820

Retells the fable about a colony of industrious ants which busily prepares for the approaching winter while a grasshopper makes no plans for the cold weather to come

"This graceful retelling of Aesop's fable . . . is set 'in the old Summer Palace at the edge of the Emperor's courtyard.' . . . The simple, rhythmic text . . . is enriched by the strong figures, muted colors, and subtle details of each double-page spread. Ink and gouache illustrations on rice paper both literally and figuratively provide another layer; not only do they depict above-ground action, they also delineate outlines of the animals that live beneath the soil in which the ants toil." Bull Cent Child Books

How the rooster got his crown; retold and illustrated by Amy Lowry Poole. Holiday House 1999 unp il $15.95 (k-3)   **398.2**

1. Folklore—China 2. Roosters—Folklore
ISBN 0-8234-1389-6   LC 98-12311

In the early days of the world, when the sun refuses to come out for fear of a skillful archer's arrows, a small rooster saves the day by coaxing the sun out with his crowing

"The illustrations reflect the traditions of ancient scroll paintings; the pacing of the story is synchronized with the pictures so that the visual and verbal elements form a seamless unit." Horn Book Guide

Price, Kathy

The Bourbon Street musicians; illustrated by Andrew Glass. Clarion Bks. 2002 39p il $16 (3-5)   **398.2**

1. Fairy tales 2. Folklore 3. Animals—Folklore
ISBN 0-618-04076-5   LC 2001-28892

A Cajun retelling of the classic tale of four animals, past their prime, who set out together to become musicians

"Price has fashioned a bluesy African-American version of the 'Bremen Town Musicians,' and her tale is perfectly matched with Glass's wonderfully humorous, vibrant illustrations of Louisiana country. . . . The colorful use of rural dialect rolls off the tongue. . . . Glass uses oil crayons to fill the oversized pages with marvelous images of the animals and their wacky actions, creating an unforgettable bayou romp." SLJ

Includes glossary

Princess stories; a classic illustrated edition; compiled by Cooper Edens. Chronicle Books 2004 133p il $19.95 (2-4)   **398.2**

1. Fairy tales 2. Folklore
ISBN 0-8118-4032-8   LC 2003-20890

Contents: The princess and the pea; Rapunzel; The frog prince; Cinderella; Sleeping Beauty; Snow White and the seven dwarfs; The little mermaid; Beauty and the beast

"This edition of classic princess stories showcases artists from the Golden Age of Illustration, roughly the 1880s to the 1920s. . . . Arthur Rackham, Walter Crane, Jesse Wilcox Smith, Charles Robinson, Kay Nielsen, and Edmund Dulac are among the American and European artists represented. The edition is rich in language, tone, and picture and despite the disparate nature of each artist's style, it somehow comes together as a classic whole." SLJ

Pullman, Philip

Aladdin and the enchanted lamp; retold by Philip Pullman; illustrated by Sophy Williams. 1st American ed. Arthur A. Levine Books 2005 67p il $16.95 (3-5)   398.2

1. Fairy tales 2. Arabs—Folklore
ISBN 0-439-69255-5   LC 2004-8586

Recounts the tale of a poor tailor's son who becomes a wealthy prince with the help of a magic lamp he finds in an enchanted cave.

"Pullman's spin on Aladdin's serendipitous adventures is satisfyingly festooned with exotic vocabulary and details. He also enlivens the telling with knowing wit. . . . Williams' numerous paintings follow Pullman's lead, with a bazaar of burnished colors and dramatic, imagination-tickling scenes." Booklist

Puttapipat, Niroot

The musicians of Bremen; a brothers Grimm tale; retold and illustrated by Niroot Puttapipat. Candlewick Press 2005 unp il $15.99 (k-3)   398.2

1. Folklore—Germany 2. Animals—Folklore
ISBN 0-7636-2758-5   LC 2005-46907

While on their way to Bremen, four aging animals who are no longer of any use to their masters find a new home after outwitting a gang of robbers.

"Puttipipat makes music the strong focus of this lively version of the old Grimm folktale. . . . The dramatic ink-and-watercolor illustrations show the characters as real barnyard animals." Booklist

Ransome, Arthur

The Fool of the World and the flying ship; a Russian tale retold by Arthur Ransome; pictures by Uri Shulevitz. Farrar, Straus & Giroux 1968 unp il $16; pa $6.95 (k-3)   398.2

1. Folklore—Russia
ISBN 0-374-32442-5; 0-374-42438-1 (pa)
Awarded the Caldecott Medal, 1969
"An Ariel book"

Text first published 1916 in Ransome's Old Peter's Russian tales

The Fool of the World was the third and youngest son whose parents thought little of him. When the Czar announced that his daughter would marry the hero who could bring him a flying ship, Fool of the World went looking and found one. Aided in surprising ways by eight peasants with magical powers, he then had to outwit the treacherous Czar

This "is a fascinating tale, told with humor and grace and brought vividly to life by Uri Shulevitz's illustrations." N Y Times Book Rev

Rascol, Sabina I.

The impudent rooster; adapted by Sabina I. Rascol; illustrated by Holly Berry. Dutton Children's Books 2004 unp il $16.99 (k-3)   398.2

1. Roosters—Folklore 2. Folklore—Romania
ISBN 0-525-47179-0   LC 2003-53141
"From a Romanian story by Ion Creanga"

Using his amazing swallowing ability, a rooster foils the evil plans of a greedy nobleman and brings back riches to his poor master.

"The language flows smoothly and reads aloud well. The large folk-art paintings, done in watercolors and colored pencils, depict brightly clothed characters, detailed backdrops, and a hero who grows in stature along with his deeds." SLJ

Riordan, James

King Arthur; retold by James Riordan; illustrated by Victor G. Ambrus. Oxford Univ. Press 1998 95p il $25; pa $12.95 (5 and up)   398.2

1. Arthur, King 2. Arthurian romances
ISBN 0-19-274176-4; 0-19-274177-2 (pa)
                LC 98-192703

This retelling covers "the life of Arthur from his boyhood with Merlin to his death in the final battle with Mordred." Voice Youth Advocates

"Riordan draws from a number of traditional sources to create his own version of Arthurian legend. . . . Victor G. Ambrus' ink drawings with washes appear on every spread. Black-and-white pictures alternate with those brightened by brilliant watercolors, which complement the energy of Ambrus' drawing style." Booklist

Includes bibliographical references

Robbins, Ruth

Baboushka and the three kings; illustrated by Nicolas Sidjakov; adapted from a Russian folk tale. Houghton Mifflin 1960 unp il $16; pa $6.95 (1-4)   398.2

1. Folklore—Russia 2. Christmas—Folklore
ISBN 0-395-27673-X; 0-395-42647-2 (pa)
Awarded the Caldecott Medal, 1961
First published by Parnassus Press

A retelling of the Christmas legend about the old woman who declined to accompany the three kings on their search for the Christ Child and has ever since then searched for the Child on her own. Each year as she renews her search she leaves gifts at the homes she visits, acting, in this respect, as a Russian equivalent to Santa Claus

"Mystery and dignity are in the retelling. . . . At the end of the book is the story in verse set to original music." Horn Book

Rockwell, Anne F.

The boy who wouldn't obey: a Mayan legend; story and pictures by Anne Rockwell. Greenwillow Bks. 2000 unp il $15.95 (2-4)   398.2

1. Mayas—Folklore 2. Folklore—Mexico
ISBN 0-688-14881-6   LC 99-15201

When Chac, the great lord who makes rain, takes a disobedient boy as his servant, they are both in for trouble

"Inspired by the art on Mayan ceramic vases, the pen and watercolor illustrations rendered in a mellow palette of blues, pinks, and greens, with flat perspectives and decorative borders, are an attractive match for this traditional tale." Horn Book Guide

Rogasky, Barbara

Dybbuk; a version; pictures by Leonard Everett Fisher. Holiday House 2005 64p il $16.95
        398.2

1. Jewish legends 2. Ghost stories
ISBN 0-8234-1616-X   LC 2004-60624
In this retelling of a Jewish legend, a girl is possessed by the spirit of the man she was destined to, but did not, marry.

The "storytelling is rich and powerful. . . . Extending the horror are starkly composed, monumental oils in inky blacks and moonlit grays." Booklist

The golem; a version; illustrated by Trina Schart Hyman. Holiday House 1996 96p il $18.95 (4 and up)   **398.2**
1. Jewish legends
ISBN 0-8234-0964-3   LC 94-13040
This is "the legend of the golem—a monster created of clay—who, under the guidance of the chief rabbi of Prague, rescued the Jews from persecution by anti-Semitic Christians in the late 16th century. Rogasky's strong storytelling skills are evident. . . . Hyman's colorful, fairy tale-like illustrations bring the story to life." SLJ

Rohmer, Harriet

Uncle Nacho's hat; adapted by Harriet Rohmer; illustrations by Veg Reisberg; Spanish version, Rosalma Zubizarreta. Children's Bk. Press 1989 31p il pa $7.95 hardcover o.p. (k-3)
        398.2
1. Folklore—Nicaragua 2. Bilingual books—English-Spanish
ISBN 0-89239-112-X (pa)   LC 88-37090
Title page and text in English and Spanish
"Adaptation of a Nicaraguan folktale. . . . When his niece, Ambrosia, gives Uncle Nacho a new hat, he tries unsuccessfully several times to get rid of the old, holey one. Seeing him dejected because his hat keeps coming back, Ambrosia suggests he put his mind on the new one instead. Flattened primitive paintings in brilliant, clear tropical colors and motifs enhance the fun of this comedy of errors." Helbig. This land is our land

Rose, Naomi C.

Tibetan tales for little Buddhas; [by] Naomi C. Rose; translated into Tibetan by Pasang Tenzin. Clear Light Publishing 2004 63p il $16.95 (k-3)
        398.2
1. Folklore—Tibet (China) 2. Bilingual books—English-Tibetan
ISBN 1-57416-081-8   LC 2003-27230
Three traditional tales about mystical beings, yaks, an enormous sow, and yeti introduce Tibetan culture and wisdom. Includes a foreword from the Dalai Lama, map of Tibet, glossary of Tibetan terms, and description of a Tibetan chant.
"Children will enjoy the exciting fairy-tale elements. . . . Rose's vibrantly colored paintings, created with broad, blurry strokes and thick dabs of pigment, ably bring to life the characters, setting, and supernatural encounters." Booklist

Ross, Gayle

How Turtle's back was cracked; a traditional Cherokee tale; retold by Gayle Ross; illustrated by Murv Jacob. Dial Bks. for Young Readers 1995 unp il $15.99 (k-3)   **398.2**
1. Cherokee Indians—Folklore 2. Turtles—Folklore 3. Animals—Folklore
ISBN 0-8037-1728-8   LC 93-40657
"When Turtle's friend Possum kills a greedy wolf, Turtle not only takes all the credit for the deed, but boasts and flaunts his trophies. The wolves take revenge on him, but they are stupid and quarrelsome, and Turtle tricks them into throwing him into the river instead of a fire. Although he escapes death, he hits a rock and his shell is cracked into pieces." SLJ
"Ross, a storyteller of Cherokee descent, retains a sense of the oral tradition through the language and rhythm of the text. . . . Jacob . . . illustrates the tale with warm paintings full of pattern and texture, echoing the patterns on the clothing and jewelry that the animals wear." Horn Book

Rounds, Glen

Ol' Paul, the mighty logger. Holiday House 1976 93p il pa $5.95 hardcover o.p. (3-6)
        398.2
1. Bunyan, Paul (Legendary character)
ISBN 0-8234-0713-6 (pa)
First published 1936
"Being a true account of the seemingly incredible exploits and inventions of the great Paul Bunyan, profusely illustrated by drawings made at the scene by the author, Glen Rounds, and now republished in this special fortieth anniversary edition." Subtitle

Three billy goats Gruff; retold and illustrated by Glen Rounds. Holiday House 1993 il $14.95 (k-3)
        398.2
1. Folklore—Norway 2. Goats—Folklore
ISBN 0-8234-1015-3   LC 92-23951
Retells the folktale about three billy goats who trick a troll that lives under a bridge
"Spare and straightforward in text and illustrations, this interpretation of the old tale has an energy lacking in more elaborate versions. . . . Shaded, mottled crayon markings color the scenes here and there with good effect, and the broad white pages make a bright, clean background for the action." Booklist

Ryan, Pam Muñoz

Nacho and Lolita; illustrated by Claudia Rueda. 1st ed. Scholastic Press 2005 unp il $16.99 (2-4)
        398.2
1. Folklore—Mexico 2. Swallows—Folklore 3. California—Folklore
ISBN 0-439-26968-7   LC 2004-793
Also available Spanish language edition
A very rare pitacochi bird falls in love with a swallow and plucks his colorful feathers to transform dry, barren San Juan Capistrano into a haven of flowers and flowing water, which the swallows can easily find when returning from their annual migration.
"Ryan's cozy storytelling will draw listeners close,

Ryan, Pam Muñoz—*Continued*
and the Colombian-born illustrator cleverly exploits the contrast between the drought-scarred backdrops and Nacho's brilliance to achieve a vibrancy that is unusual in colored-pencil illustrations." Booklist

Sakade, Florence
Japanese children's favorite stories; compiled by Florence Sakade; illustrated by Yoshisuke Kurosaki. 3rd ed. Tuttle 2003 109p il $16.95 (2-4)
398.2
1. Folklore—Japan
ISBN 0-8048-3449-0
First published 1953
50th anniversary edition
A collection of Japanese folktales.
"This enduring collection presents 20 stories to enchant and enlighten young readers. . . . Minor text revisions have little effect on the stories. . . . The text remains simple, clear, and accessible to beginning readers and storytellers alike. The 'sparkling new color illustrations' are simply Kurosaki's original stylized scenes, repainted in bright dabs of watercolor." SLJ

Salley, Coleen
Epossumondas; written by Coleen Salley; illustrated by Janet Stevens. Harcourt 2002 unp il $16 (k-3)
398.2
1. Folklore—Southern States 2. Opossums—Folklore
ISBN 0-15-216748-X
LC 2001-4906
A retelling of a classic tale in which a well-intentioned young possum continually takes his mother's instructions much too literally
"All of the elements of a good story are here. . . . Salley's text rolls off the page (and off the tongue) easily, and is accompanied by delightful watercolor and colored-pencil art." SLJ
Other titles about Epossumondas are:
Epossumondas saves the day (2006)
Why Epossumondas has no hair on his tail (2004)

San Souci, Robert
Brave Margaret; by Robert D. San Souci; illustrated by Sally Wern Comport. Simon & Schuster Bks. for Young Readers 1999 unp il $17 (k-3)
398.2
1. Fairy tales 2. Folklore—Ireland
ISBN 0-689-81072-5
LC 98-16794
In this retelling of an Irish folktale, a brave young woman battles a sea serpent and rescues her true love from a giant
"San Souci's text is smoothly written, dramatic, and rhythmic enough to please a storyteller. Full of rich colors and textures, the large-scale illustrations, rendered in pastels, almost jump off the pages." Booklist

Cendrillon; a Caribbean Cinderella; [by] Robert D. San Souci; illustrated by Brian Pinkney. Simon & Schuster Bks. for Young Readers 1998 unp il $17 (k-3)
398.2
1. Fairy tales 2. Folklore—Martinique
ISBN 0-689-80668-X
LC 96-53142

A Creole variant of the familiar Cinderella tale set in Martinique and narrated by the godmother who helps Cendrillon find true love
"The narrative is full of French Creole words and phrases. . . . A *fruit à pain* (breadfruit) is transformed into the coach; six agoutis (a kind of rodent) become the horses. . . . Pinkney's art perfectly conveys the lush beauty and atmosphere of the island setting." SLJ

Cut from the same cloth; American women of myth, legend, and tall tale; collected and told by Robert D. San Souci; illustrated by Brian Pinkney; introduction by Jane Yolen. Philomel Bks. 1993 140p il $21.99; pa $6.99 (4 and up)
398.2
1. Folklore—United States 2. Tall tales 3. Women—Folklore
ISBN 0-399-21987-0; 0-698-11811-1 (pa)
LC 92-5233
A collection of fifteen stories about legendary American women from Anglo-American, African American, and Native American folklore
"San Souci's language is vigorous and action verbs abound; Pinkney's black-and-white block prints match the strength of the telling. The inclusion of notes on the sources and a general bibliography make this an academic resource as well as a good collection of rolicking stories." Child Book Rev Serv

Even more short & shivery; thirty spine-tingling stories; retold by Robert D. San Souci; illustrated by Jacquelin Rogers. Delacorte Press 1997 162p il $14.95; pa $10.95 (4 and up)
398.2
1. Ghost stories 2. Folklore
ISBN 0-385-32252-6; 0-385-32639-4 (pa)
LC 96-35365
A collection of scary traditional tales from all over the world
"San Souci groups together 30 tales that not only read well but also work as splendid choices for oral telling around a campfire, on a trip, in school, or at a sleepover." Booklist
Includes bibliographical references

Fa Mulan; the story of a woman warrior; [by] Robert D. San Souci; illustrated by Jean & Mou-sien Tseng. Hyperion Bks. for Children 1998 unp il $15.45; lib bdg $16.49; pa $6.99 (2-4)
398.2
1. Folklore—China
ISBN 0-7868-0346-0; 0-7868-2287-2 (lib bdg); 0-7868-1421-7 (pa)
LC 97-19291
A retelling of the original Chinese poem in which a brave young girl masquerades as a boy and fights the Tartars in the Khan's army

The faithful friend; [by] Robert D. San Souci; illustrated by Brian Pinkney. Simon & Schuster Bks. for Young Readers 1995 unp il $16; pa $5.99 (2-4)
398.2
1. Folklore—Martinique
ISBN 0-02-786131-7; 0-689-82458-0 (pa)
LC 93-40672
A Caldecott Medal honor book, 1996

San Souci, Robert—*Continued*

"A West Indian folktale from Martinique. . . . When Clement seeks the lovely Pauline as his wife, it is Hippolyte who protects the couple from the zombies and her vengeful uncle." Child Book Rev Serv

"Pinkney's scratchboard and oil artwork switches from bright daytime hues for most of the book to purples and grays for scenes with the zombies and snakes, which are very effective. . . . This excellent title contains all the elements of a well-researched folktale, and convincingly conveys the richness of the West Indian culture." SLJ

Includes bibliographical references

Little Gold Star; a Spanish American Cinderella tale; retold by Robert D. San Souci; illustrated by Sergio Martinez. HarperCollins Pubs. 2000 unp il $15.95; lib bdg $15.89 (2-4)   **398.2**
1. Fairy tales 2. Folklore—Southern States 3. Hispanic Americans—Folklore
ISBN 0-688-14780-1; 0-688-14781-X (lib bdg)
      LC 99-50290

A Spanish American retelling of the familiar story of a kind girl who is mistreated by her jealous stepmother and stepsisters. In this version, the Virgin Mary replaces the traditional fairy godmother

"Martinez' watercolors depict homes with Spanish architectural influences in an arid, southwest desert landscape; his characters have lively, expressive faces and evocative body language. . . . This is effective fairy-tale magic transported to new terrain." Bull Cent Child Books

More short & shivery; thirty terrifying tales; retold by Robert D. San Souci; illustrated by Katherine Coville and Jacqueline Rogers. Delacorte Press 1994 163p il pa $10.95 hardcover o.p. (4 and up)   **398.2**
1. Folklore 2. Ghost stories
ISBN 0-385-32250-X (pa)   LC 94-479

A collection of scary folktales from the United States, China, England, Italy, Russia, and other countries around the world

Includes bibliographical references

The secret of the stones; a folktale; retold by Robert D. San Souci; pictures by James Ransome. Phyllis Fogelman Bks. 2000 unp il $16.99 (k-3)
     398.2
1. African Americans—Folklore 2. Folklore—United States
ISBN 0-8037-1640-0   LC 93-43952

When they try to find out who is doing their chores while they are working in the field, a childless couple discovers that the two stones they have brought home are actually two bewitched orphans

"Based on a tale found in both the Bantu and African-American cultures . . . the clearly told tale (which includes dialect in the dialogue) is accompanied by expressive, deep-toned illustrations." Horn Book Guide

Short & shivery; thirty chilling tales; retold by Robert D. San Souci; illustrated by Katherine Coville. Doubleday 1987 175p il pa $5.50 hardcover o.p. (4 and up)   **398.2**
1. Folklore 2. Ghost stories
ISBN 0-440-41804-6 (pa)   LC 86-29067

"A collection of spooky stories, competently adapted and retold (sometimes quite freely) from world folklore, including Japan, Africa, and Latin America, as well as Europe and the U.S. . . . The stories drawn from collections of regional American folklore are not only the freshest, but often the scariest. Sources are fully documented. . . . There are some delicious shivers here, with plenty of fodder for an active imagination, as well as excitement." SLJ

Six foolish fishermen; [by] Robert D. San Souci; illustrated by Doug Kennedy. Hyperion Bks. for Children 2000 unp il $14.99 (k-3)
     398.2
1. Cajuns—Folklore 2. Folklore—United States
ISBN 0-7868-0385-1   LC 98-39040

Six silly friends spend a day trying to figure out how to proceed with their fishing trip when one thing after another goes wrong

"The setting and lavish Cajun dialect give the tale a strong regional flavor, while the cartoonlike illustrations of the fishermen's antics (which are observed by a frog, a turtle, and an alligator) play up the humor in this entertaining, ridiculous tale." Horn Book Guide

Sootface; an Ojibwa Cinderella story; retold by Robert D. San Souci; illustrated by Daniel San Souci. Doubleday Bks. for Young Readers 1994 unp il pa $6.99 hardcover o.p. (1-4)
     398.2
1. Ojibwa Indians—Folklore
ISBN 0-440-41363-X (pa)   LC 93-10553

"A Doubleday Book for Young Readers."

Although she is mocked and mistreated by her two older sisters, Sootface, an Ojibwa Indian maiden, wins a mighty invisible warrior for her husband with her kind and honest heart

"The San Souci version reads aloud well, and the watercolor artwork illustrates the story with quiet grace." Booklist

Sukey and the mermaid; [by] Robert D. San Souci; illustrated by Brian Pinkney. Four Winds Press 1992 unp il $16; pa $5.95 (1-4)
     398.2
1. Mermaids and mermen 2. African Americans—Folklore
ISBN 0-02-778141-0; 0-689-80718-X (pa)
     LC 90-24559

Unhappy with her life at home, Sukey receives kindness and wealth from Mama Jo the mermaid

San Souci "outdoes himself here with pungent, lyrical prose that reverberates with the cadences of the South Carolina islands. . . . The supple lines of Pinkney's fluid scratchboard technique capture the grace and spirit of this magical tale and serve as the perfect foil to its darker undertones." Publ Wkly

The talking eggs; a folktale from the American South; retold by Robert D. San Souci; pictures by Jerry Pinkney. Dial Bks. for Young Readers 1989 unp il $16 (k-3)   **398.2**
1. Folklore—Southern States
ISBN 0-8037-0619-7   LC 88-33469

A Caldecott Medal honor book, 1990

San Souci, Robert—*Continued*

A Southern folktale in which kind Blanche, following the instructions of an old witch, gains riches, while her greedy sister makes fun of the old woman and is duly rewarded

"Adapted from a Creole folk tale originally included in a collection of Louisiana stories by folklorist Alcee Fortier, this tale captures the flavor of the nineteenth-century South in its language and story line. . . . Jerry Pinkney's watercolors are chiefly responsible for the excellence of the book; his characters convey their moods with vivid facial expressions." Horn Book

A terrifying taste of short & shivery; thirty creepy tales; retold by Robert D. San Souci; illustrated by Lenny Wooden. Delacorte Press 1998 159p il $14.95; pa $10.95 (4 and up)

398.2

1. Ghost stories 2. Folklore
ISBN 0-385-32635-1; 0-385-32255-0 (pa)
LC 98-5551

"Drawing on urban legends, myths, folktales, and ghost stories from around the world and across time, the reteller serves up 30 tales of the supernatural that range from eerie to downright scary. . . . Suspenseful, accessible, and energetic, the tales are uniformly brief and gripping." SLJ

Includes bibliographical references

The twins and the Bird of Darkness; a hero tale from the Caribbean; by Robert D. San Souci; illustrated by Terry Widener. Simon & Schuster Bks. for Young Readers 2002 unp il $16.95 (3-6)

398.2

1. Folklore—Caribbean region
ISBN 0-689-83343-1
LC 99-58950

When the Bird of Darkness takes Princess Marie, twin brothers Soliday, who is brave and kind, and Salacota, who is cowardly, set off to fight the beast and rescue the princess

"San Souci's robust, exciting retelling is composed from 13 variants according to the author's note. The text is enhanced by Widener's rich acrylic illustrations, which carve from color the undulating Caribbean landscapes, stylized sculpted characters, and the horrific Bird of Darkness." Booklist

Two bear cubs; a Miwok legend from California's Yosemite Valley; retold by Robert D. San Souci; illustrated by Daniel San Souci. Yosemite Assn. 1997 unp il $14.95 (k-3)

398.2

1. Miwok Indians—Folklore 2. Bears—Folklore
3. Worms—Folklore
ISBN 0-939666-87-1
LC 97-17226

Retells the Miwok Indian legend in which a little measuring worm saves two bear cubs stranded at the top of the rock known as El Capitan

"Watercolor illustrations portray gently anthropomorphized animals in spare but traditional garb (the females wear buckskin skirts) and with amusing, humanlike poses and facial expressions. . . . Endnotes concerning Miwok customs add heft to this expertly rendered tale." Publ Wkly

A weave of words; an Armenian tale; retold by Robert D. San Souci; illustrated by Raúl Colón. Orchard Bks. 1998 unp il $16.95; lib bdg $17.99 (3-5)

398.2

1. Fairy tales 2. Folklore—Armenia
ISBN 0-531-30053-6; 0-531-33053-2 (lib bdg)
LC 97-5046

A reworking of Armenian folktales in which a lazy prince learns to read, write, and weave to win his love only to have these very talents later save him from a three-headed monster

"Rich with subtle colors and strong composition, Colón's textured paintings create a fantasy world that reflects the tale's subtlety and its dramatic force." Booklist

Sanderson, Ruth

The crystal mountain; retold and illustrated by Ruth Sanderson. Little, Brown 1999 unp il $15.95 (3-5)

398.2

1. Fairy tales 2. Folklore
ISBN 0-316-77092-2
LC 97-46991

The youngest of three sons outwits the fairy thieves who stole his mother's tapestry and marries one of the fairies he has rescued

"The story combines bits of drama, suspense, romance and magic, with some surprises, too. The oil paintings, set in 15th-century Europe, depict a rugged rolling countryside as well as the ornate tapestries of the era." Publ Wkly

The Golden Mare, the Firebird, and the magic ring; retold and illustrated by Ruth Sanderson. Little, Brown 2001 unp il $15.95 (3-5)

398.2

1. Folklore—Russia
ISBN 0-316-76906-1
LC 99-16412

"Based on elements from a number of traditional Russian fairy tales, including The Firebird, the Horse of Power and Vasilissa . . . [et al.]"--T.p. verso

A young huntsman is helped by a golden mare when he tries to perform the seemingly impossible feats commanded by the Tsar

"Sanderson's complex yet smooth text and her sumptuously elegant and atmospheric oil paintings create an entrée into a world where realism and magic co-exist." Horn Book Guide

Sanfield, Steve

The adventures of High John the Conqueror; illustrated by John Ward. Orchard Bks. 1988 113p il (4 and up)

398.2

1. African Americans—Folklore
LC 88-17946

Available in paperback from August House
"A Richard Jackson book"

"A competent retelling of 16 African-American folktales about the black trickster hero who always manages to outwit others, particularly his white master. Simply told in language comprehensible to very young readers, these tales are short, funny, and entertaining. . . . Fourteen full-page black-and-white pencil drawings illustrate some of the more dramatic moments in the stories." SLJ

Includes bibliographical references

Schmidt, Gary D.

The wonders of Donal O'Donnell; a folktale of Ireland; [by] Gary Schmidt; illustrated by Loren Long. Holt & Co. 2002 40p il $17.95 (3-6)
398.2

1. Folklore—Ireland
ISBN 0-8050-6516-4   LC 00-47301

The stories of three peddlers are told to Donal O'Donnell and his wife one stormy night and begin to heal their hearts, broken by the death of their son

"Long's green, gold, and russet paintings, many full-page portraits, sound the right deep, reverberating note for the resonance of the stories." Booklist

Schwartz, Alvin

All of our noses are here, and other noodle tales; retold by Alvin Schwartz; pictures by Karen Ann Weinhaus. Harper & Row 1985 64p il lib bdg $15.89 (k-2)
398.2

1. Folklore 2. Wit and humor
ISBN 0-06-025288-X (lib bdg)   LC 84-48330
"An I can read book"

This companion volume to There is a carrot in my ear, and other noodle tales, contains additional stories about members of the Brown family

"The illustrations show them looking very much like mice and always smiling and cheerful. Cousins, no doubt, to the Stupids, the family is bound to be as appealing to young readers. With a list of sources." Horn Book

Ghosts! ghostly tales from folklore; retold by Alvin Schwartz; illustrated by Victoria Chess. HarperCollins Pubs. 1991 63p il lib bdg $15.89; pa $3.95 (k-2)
398.2

1. Ghost stories 2. Folklore
ISBN 0-06-021797-9; 0-06-444170-9 (pa)
    LC 90-21746
"An I can read book"

Presents seven, easy-to-read ghost stories based on traditional folk tales and legends from various countries

"All of the pen-and-watercolor illustrations are tidy and cheery and creepy. . . . Retold in a style that is simple but not choppy . . . and accompanied by a page of brief notes, all the tales will lend themselves to elaboration and innovation." Bull Cent Child Books

I saw you in the bathtub, and other folk rhymes; collected by Alvin Schwartz; pictures by Syd Hoff. Harper & Row 1989 64p il pa $3.99 hardcover o.p. (k-2)
398.2

1. Folklore
ISBN 0-06-444151-2 (pa)   LC 88-16111
"An I can read book"

Presents an illustrated collection of traditional folk rhymes, some composed by children

"Kids may be surprised to see their recess yells on the printed page but will relish the confirmation of significance. Hoff's full-color cartoons interpret the rhymes literally, an approach that leads to some pretty surreal results." Bull Cent Child Books

In a dark, dark room, and other scary stories; retold by Alvin Schwartz; illustrated by Dirk Zimmer. Harper & Row 1984 63p il $15.95; pa $3.95 (k-2)
398.2

1. Folklore 2. Ghost stories 3. Horror fiction
ISBN 0-06-025271-5; 0-06-444090-7 (pa)
    LC 83-47699
"An I can read book"

This is a collection of "seven traditional tales from around the world retold in simple yet effective language. . . . The chill here springs from suspense, an eerie setting or a ghostly surprise, rather than from blood and gore. Though pared down somewhat from longer versions, the stories retain their genuine creepiness. . . . The colorfully dark illustrations are sinister without being gruesome and add a comic touch." SLJ

More scary stories to tell in the dark; collected & retold from folklore by Alvin Schwartz; drawings by Stephen Gammell. Lippincott 1984 100p il $15.99; lib bdg $16.89; pa $5.99 (4 and up)
398.2

1. Ghost stories 2. Horror fiction 3. Folklore—United States
ISBN 0-397-32081-7; 0-397-32082-5 (lib bdg);
0-06-440177-4 (pa)   LC 83-49494

This volume contains stories of ghosts, murders, graveyards and other horrors

"The stories are all short and lively, very tellable, and greatly enhanced by the gray, ghoulish, horrifying illustrations of dismembered bodies, hideous creatures, and mysterious lights. A fine compendium by a well-known collector, easily accessible to young readers." Horn Book

Includes bibliographical references

Scary stories 3; more tales to chill your bones; collected from folklore and retold by Alvin Schwartz; drawings by Stephen Gammell. HarperCollins Pubs. 1991 115p il music $15.99; lib bdg $16.89; pa $5.99 (4 and up)
398.2

1. Ghost stories 2. Horror fiction 3. Folklore—United States
ISBN 0-06-021794-4; 0-06-021795-2 (lib bdg);
0-06-440418-8 (pa)   LC 90-47474

Traditional and modern-day stories of ghosts, haunts, superstitions, monsters, and horrible scary things

"The book is well paced and continually captivates, surprises, and entices audiences into reading just one more page. Gammell's gauzy, cobwebby, black-and-white pen-and-ink drawings help to sustain the overall creepy mood." SLJ

Includes bibliographical references

Scary stories to tell in the dark; collected from American folklore by Alvin Schwartz; with drawings by Stephen Gammell. Lippincott 1981 111p il $15.99; lib bdg $16.89; pa $5.99 (4 and up)
398.2

1. Ghost stories 2. Horror fiction 3. Folklore—United States
ISBN 0-397-31926-6; 0-397-31927-4 (lib bdg);
0-06-440170-7 (pa)   LC 80-8728

Schwartz, Alvin—*Continued*

"A collection of scary, semi-scary, and humorous stories about ghosts and witches collected from American folklore. Most of the stories (poems and songs also) are very short and range from the traditional to the modern. The author includes suggestions on how to tell scary stories effectively." Bull Cent Child Books

"The scholarship in the source notes and bibliography will be useful to serious literature students." SLJ

There is a carrot in my ear, and other noodle tales; retold by Alvin Schwartz; pictures by Karen Ann Weinhaus. Harper & Row 1982 64p il lib bdg $15.89; pa $3.95 (k-2)   **398.2**
1. Folklore 2. Wit and humor
ISBN 0-06-025234-0 (lib bdg); 0-06-444103-2 (pa)
LC 80-8442

"An I can read book"

This "is a collection of six stories from sources . . . as diverse as American 'Little Moron' stories, ancient Greek tales and vaudeville pieces. Explaining in his foreword that a 'noodle is a silly person,' reteller Alvin Schwartz goes on to introduce the noodly Brown family and reveal their various foibles. . . . Most of the stories don't appear in other beginning noodle collections and will provide laughs for readers who catch the puns and absurdities the stories hinge on. The drawings by Karen Ann Weinhaus . . . show funny, pointy-proboscised folk blissfully unaware of their own goofiness." SLJ

Schwartz, Howard

Before you were born; retold by Howard Schwartz; illustrated by Kristina Swarner. 1st ed. Roaring Brook Press 2005 unp il $16.95 (k-3)
398.2
1. Jews—Folklore
ISBN 1-59643-028-1   LC 2003-17845
"A Deborah Brodie Book"

Retells a folktale in which Lailah, a guardian angel, places the indentation that everyone has on the upper lip just before a baby is born.

"In spare, serene language, Schwartz reshapes a rabbinic legend. . . . Swarner's ethereal, mixed-media illustrations illuminate the spirituality of the telling." Booklist

A coat for the moon and other Jewish tales; selected and retold by Howard Schwartz and Barbara Rush; illustrated by Michael Iofin. Jewish Publ. Soc. 1999 81p il $14.95 (4 and up)
398.2
1. Jews—Folklore
ISBN 0-8276-0596-X   LC 98-52704

A collection of Jewish folktales from around the world, including "The Lamp on the Mountain," "The Witch Barusha," "The Sabbath Walking Stick," and "The Fisherman and the Silver Fish"

"These tales incorporate everything from the magical to the bizarre, all the while imparting specific Jewish values that have transcended time and cultural dispersion. . . . Each retelling opens with a delightfully detailed pen-and-ink illustration encircled by a key sentence or phrase from the text that gives a hint of what's to come." SLJ

Invisible kingdoms; Jewish tales of angels, spirits, and demons; retold by Howard Schwartz; pictures by Stephen Fieser. HarperCollins Pubs. 2002 68p il $16.99; lib bdg $18.89 (3-5)
398.2
1. Supernatural—Fiction 2. Jews—Folklore
ISBN 0-06-027855-2; 0-06-027856-0 (lib bdg)
LC 00-38901

A collection of nine tales from countries around the world, dealing with an assortment of supernatural creatures

"The writing is lovely and fluid, with enough formality to capture the traditional style while still being accessible to young readers. . . . Fieser's occasional full-page, full-color scenes are for the most part realistic and enhance the text." SLJ

A journey to paradise and other Jewish tales; retold by Howard Schwartz; illustrated by Giora Carmi. Pitspopany Press 2000 48p il $16.95; pa $9.95 (3-5)   **398.2**
1. Jews—Folklore
ISBN 0-943706-21-1; 0-943706-16-5 (pa)

"This collection of traditional tales from the world's far-flung Jewish community is ably selected by a well-known scholar. . . . The volume is abundantly illustrated with both spot and full-spread drawings in subdued colors." Horn Book Guide

Includes bibliographical references

Seeger, Pete

Abiyoyo; based on a South African lullaby and folk story; text by Pete Seeger; illustrations by Michael Hays. Simon & Schuster Bks. for Young Readers 2001 unp il $19.95 (k-3)   **398.2**
1. Folklore—South Africa 2. Giants—Folklore
ISBN 0-689-84693-2

Also available: Abiyoyo returns (2001)

A reissue of the title first published 1986 by Macmillan

Includes audio CD

Banished from the town for making mischief, a little boy and his father are welcomed back when they make the giant Abiyoyo disappear

"Told in the familiar Seeger style, with brief musical phrases of the one-word song incorporated in the text and printed complete at the end, and with illustrations full of light and color, this rendering of a South African tale is a pleasure. The giant is imposing but not too scary for the youngest listener leaning over the book while a parent tells the story." N Y Times Book Rev

Shannon, George

More stories to solve; fifteen folktales from around the world; told by George Shannon; illustrated by Peter Sís. Greenwillow Bks. 1991 64p il pa $4.95 hardcover o.p. (3 and up)
398.2
1. Folklore 2. Riddles
ISBN 0-380-73261-0 (pa)

"Shannon combines the folktale and the riddle in a brief collection that brings together 15 international stories." Booklist

Includes bibliographical references

Shannon, George—*Continued*

More true lies; 18 tales for you to judge; told by
George Shannon; illustrated by John O'Brien.
Greenwillow Bks. 2001 64p il $14.95; lib bdg
$14.89 (3-6)   **398.2**
1. Folklore 2. Literary recreations
ISBN 0-688-17643-7; 0-06-029188-5 (lib bdg)
               LC 99-52860
Presents a collection of eighteen brief folktales in
which the reader is asked to explain how the folk charac-
ter lied and told the truth at the same time
"The combination of brevity, humor, and accessible
language should attract reluctant readers, and teachers
could use the book to inspire creative-writing exercises.
. . . O'Brien's pen-and-ink illustrations are a whimsical
complement to the tales." SLJ
Includes bibliographical references

Still more stories to solve; fourteen folktales
from around the world; told by George Shannon;
pictures by Peter Sis. Greenwillow Bks. 1994 64p
il $15 (3 and up)   **398.2**
1. Folklore 2. Riddles
ISBN 0-688-04619-3   LC 93-26529
Fourteen brief folktales in which there is a mystery or
problem that the reader is invited to solve before the resolution is presented
Includes bibliographical references

Stories to solve; folktales from around the
world; illustrated by Peter Sis. Greenwillow Bks.
1985 55p il $11.75; lib bdg $11.88 (3 and up)
           398.2
1. Folklore 2. Riddles
ISBN 0-688-04303-8; 0-688-04304-6 (lib bdg)
               LC 84-18656
"Each of these 14 delightful folktales is a short puzzle
to be solced through clevernes, common sense or careful
observations of details in the text. . . . Sis' pointillistic
pen-and-ink drawings illustrate each puzzle, and sometimes clarify the solutions." SLJ

Shepard, Aaron
King O' the Cats; told by Aaron Shepard;
illustrated by Kristin Sorra. Atheneum Books for
Young Readers 2004 unp il $16.95 (k-3)
           398.2
1. Folklore—Great Britain 2. Cats—Folklore
ISBN 0-689-82082-8   LC 2002-5292
A church sexton, known for his wild tales, has three
weird encounters with magical cats and can't convince
Father Allen that they really happened, until the priest's
cat shows an intense interest.
"Sorra's single and double-page oil scenes, dark in
tone, have the look of some animated films, with square-
faced, flat-figured humans and almost stern-looking cats.
. . . [This is] a smooth narrative that will please listeners, storytellers, and readers." SLJ

Master man; a tall tale of Nigeria; told by
Aaron Shepard; illustrated by David Wisniewski.
HarperCollins Pubs. 2001 unp il $15.95; lib bdg
$15.89 (k-3)   **398.2**
1. Folklore—Nigeria 2. Tall tales
ISBN 0-688-13783-0; 0-688-13784-9 (lib bdg)
               LC 99-48513
A boastful strong man learns a lesson harder than his
muscles when he encounters one of Nigeria's
superheroes in this Hausa tale which explains the origin
of thunder
"The lively, well-paced story finds wonderful expression in Wisniewski's cut-paper collages. Organized like
a comic book with dialogue bubbles, narrative boxes, and
multiple frames per page." Booklist

The princess mouse; a tale of Finland; told by
Aaron Shepard; illustrated by Leonid Gore.
Atheneum Bks. for Young Readers 2003 unp il
$16.95 (k-3)   **398.2**
1. Fairy tales 2. Folklore—Finland 3. Mice—Folklore
ISBN 0-689-82912-4   LC 2001-55273
A retelling of a Finnish folk tale about a young man
who plans to marry his mouse sweetheart
"Shepard's charmingly droll version of a Finnish folktale combines classic elements with unexpected, witty details. . . . The jewel-toned art has beautiful luminescence; the elongated, somewhat blocky look of the characters reinforces the fantasy; and the mice are downright
irresistible." Booklist

The sea king's daughter; a Russian legend;
retold by Aaron Shepard; illustrated by Gennady
Spirin. Atheneum Bks. for Young Readers 1997
28p il $17 (3-6)   **398.2**
1. Folklore—Russia 2. Musicians—Folklore
ISBN 0-689-80759-7   LC 96-3391
A talented musician from Novgorod plays so well that
the Sea King wants him to marry one of his daughters
"The telling is descriptive yet very accessible, with the
art, in Spirin's majestic signature style, evoking both the
mythical feel of the legend and the folk-music roots from
which the story sprang." Booklist

Sherman, Pat
The sun's daughter; a story based on an
Iroquois legend; illustrated by R. Gregory Christie.
Clarion Bks. 2005 31p il $16 (2-4)   **398.2**
1. Iroquois Indians—Folklore
ISBN 0-618-32430-5   LC 2004-17820
"Inspired by Iroquois tales of the Corn Maiden and
her sisters, this original story tells how Maize, Red Bean,
and Pumpkin walked the earth spreading a bounty of
food in their wake. . . . The story is charmingly told
with eloquent phrasing and vocabulary. The artwork,
done in a folk-art style, is energetic and exuberant, and
the brush strokes are used to dramatic effect across the
spreads." SLJ

Shulevitz, Uri

The golden goose; [by] the Brothers Grimm; retold and with pictures by Uri Shulevitz. Farrar, Straus & Giroux 1995 unp il $16; pa $5.95 (k-3)
398.2

1. Fairy tales 2. Folklore—Germany

ISBN 0-374-32695-9; 0-374-42748-8 (pa)

LC 94-44358

"The youngest of three sons is rewarded for his kindheartedness with a gleaming golden goose to which a chain of unwilling companions becomes attached. He makes a sad princess laugh with his silly procession and, after completing a task set by her disgruntled father, wins her hand." SLJ

"This is a lively rendition of an appealing tale, complemented with illustrations done in an angular, puppetlike style that recalls the story's folk origins. The skillful incorporation of an insistent refrain begs for audience participation." Horn Book Guide

The treasure. Farrar, Straus & Giroux 1978 unp il $16; pa $5.95 (k-3)
398.2

1. Folklore

ISBN 0-374-37740-5; 0-374-47955-0 (pa)

A Caldecott Medal honor book, 1980

This is the "tale of a poor man, here named Isaac, who three times dreams of a voice telling him to go to the capital and look for a treasure under the bridge by the palace. When he gets to the capital, the captain of the guard tells him of his dream: a treasure is buried under the stove of a man named Isaac back in Isaac's home city. So Isaac returns home, finds the treasure under his own stove, and lives happily ever after." SLJ

"Although the story is known in many cultures the retelling suggests the Hassidic tradition. . . . The eastern European influence is extended in the illustrations." Horn Book

Sierra, Judy

The beautiful butterfly; a folktale from Spain; retold by Judy Sierra; illustrated by Victoria Chess. Clarion Bks. 2000 32p il $15 (k-3)
398.2

1. Folklore—Spain 2. Butterflies—Folklore

ISBN 0-395-90015-8

LC 99-16616

After choosing a husband for his sweet singing voice, a beautiful butterfly mourns the fact that he is swallowed by a fish, until a king in his underwear reunites the two

"Chess adds a madcap atmosphere with gouache scenes of staring, sunken-eyed, richly dressed figures posing in a grassy, sunlit glade. Sierra. . . . tells the tale in a simple, straightforward way that will make it equally easy to read or learn." Booklist

Can you guess my name? traditional tales around the world; selected and retold by Judy Sierra; illustrated by Stefano Vitale. Clarion Bks. 2002 110p il $20 (3-6)
398.2

1. Folklore

ISBN 0-618-13328-3

LC 2002-3509

A collection of fifteen folktales from all over the world, including stories that resemble "The Three Pigs," "The Bremen Town Musicians," "Rumpelstiltskin," "The Frog Prince," and "Hansel and Gretel"

"All of the selections have dramatic dialogue and repetitive phrases and refrains, and are easy to learn. . . . Vitale's engaging folk illustrations are painted on wood. . . . This collection provides a fascinating experience with comparative literature, one that can open doors to other cultures. A must purchase for most collections." SLJ

Includes bibliographical references

The gift of the Crocodile; a Cinderella story; illustrated by Reynold Ruffins. Simon & Schuster Bks. for Young Readers 2000 unp il $17 (k-3)
398.2

1. Fairy tales 2. Folklore—Indonesia

ISBN 0-689-82188-3

LC 98-40592

In this Indonesian version of the Cinderella story, a girl named Damura escapes her cruel stepmother and stepsister and marries a handsome prince with the help of Grandmother Crocodile

"Sierra's unadorned retelling is straightforward. . . . Ruffins's brightly colored, patterned paintings, with their angular figures and wavy landscapes, express and evoke the story's island setting." Horn Book

Nursery tales around the world; selected and retold by Judy Sierra; illustrated by Stefano Vitale. Clarion Bks. 1996 114p il $20
398.2

1. Folklore

ISBN 0-395-67894-3

LC 93-2068

Presents eighteen simple stories from international folklore, grouped around six themes, such as "Runaway Cookies," "Slowpokes and Speedsters," and "Chain Tales." Includes background information and storytelling hints

"This richly illustrated compendium of folktales does double duty as a nursery story book for lap-sharing and as a sourcebook for parents and professionals. . . . Most entries feature strong rhythms and repetition that invite audience participation and develop memory. . . . Top this engaging text with Vitale's lavish oil-on-wood ethnic borders, motif vignettes, and full-page illustrations, and you have a handsome work to be valued by readers and treasured by listeners." Bull Cent Child Books

Includes bibliographical references

Tasty baby belly buttons; a Japanese folktale; illustrated by Meilo So. Knopf 1998 unp il $17; lib bdg $18.99; pa $6.99 (k-3)
398.2

1. Folklore—Japan

ISBN 0-679-89369-5; 0-679-99369-X (lib bdg); 0-440-41738-4 (pa)

LC 98-22524

Urikohime, a girl born from a melon, battles the monstrous onis, who steal babies to eat their tasty belly buttons

"Graced with occasional delicate brushwork that seems distinctly Japanese, So's fluid, sweeping watercolors add freshness to a traditional tale of swashbuckling heroics." Booklist

Silverman, Erica

Raisel's riddle; story by Erica Silverman; pictures by Susan Gaber. Farrar, Straus & Giroux 1999 unp il $16 (k-3)
398.2

1. Fairy tales 2. Jews—Folklore

ISBN 0-374-36168-1

LC 97-29421

Silverman, Erica—*Continued*

A Jewish version of the Cinderella story, in which a poor but educated young woman captivates her "Prince Charming" a rabbi's son, at a Purim ball

"Gaber's softly stippled spreads evoke a quiet seriousness appropriate to this thoughtful retelling." Bull Cent Child Books

Singer, Isaac Bashevis

Zlateh the goat, and other stories; pictures by Maurice Sendak; translated from the Yiddish by the author and Elizabeth Shub. Harper & Row 1966 90p il $15.95; pa $6.95 (4 and up)

398.2

1. Jews—Folklore

ISBN 0-06-028477-3; 0-06-440147-2 (pa)

A Newbery Award honor book, 1967

"Seven tales drawn from middle-European Jewish village life, with illustrations which extend the humor and subtlety of the situations." Hodges. Books for Elem Sch Libr

Snyder, Dianne

The boy of the three-year nap; illustrated by Allen Say. Houghton Mifflin 1988 32p il $16.95; pa $6.95 (1-3)   398.2

1. Folklore—Japan

ISBN 0-395-44090-4; 0-395-66957-X (pa)

LC 87-30674

A Caldecott Medal honor book, 1989

"Japan's contribution to the trickster folktale, in which a lazy son cons a rich man, only to be outsmarted by his own, even trickier mother. Lilting prose and shimmering illustrations combine in perfect harmony." SLJ

So, Meilo

Gobble, gobble, slip, slop; a tale of a very greedy cat; by Meilo So. 1st ed. Alfred A. Knopf 2004 unp il $15.95; lib bdg $17.99   398.2

1. Folklore—India 2. Cats—Folklore

ISBN 0-375-82504-5; 0-375-92504-X (lib bdg)

LC 2003-1772

Retold from the Indian folktale 'The cat and the parrot' appearing in 'How to tell stories to children' by Sara Cone Bryant (Boston: Houghton Mifflin, 1905)

In this story based on a folktale from India, a very greedy cat eats five hundred cakes, his friend the parrot, the nosy old woman, and much more.

"The smoothly written text reads aloud well. . . . The jewel-toned illustrations, done in ink and watercolor on rice paper, feature large, dramatic figures to capture immediate interest." SLJ

Souhami, Jessica

The little, little house. Frances Lincoln 2006 32p il $15.95 (k-2)   398.2

1. Jews—Folklore

ISBN 1-84507-108-5

"Souhami's adaptation of this eastern European Jewish folktale features a poor man named Joseph, his wife, and three children, who live together in a cramped little house. Joseph seeks advice from wise Aunty Bella, who recommends that he bring his six chickens, his rooster, his cow, and his goat inside. The results are predictably disastrous. . . . Finally, Aunty Bella gives permission to turn the animals outside again, and, suddenly, the house seems just the right size for Joseph's family." Booklist

"A delightful retelling. . . . The vibrant colors and strong contrast of the cut-paper shapes against neutral backgrounds provide great visual energy. The simple yet dramatic text makes it especially well suited to reading aloud." SLJ

Mrs. McCool and the giant Cuhullin; an Irish tale. Holt & Co. 2002 unp il $16.95 (k-3)

398.2

1. Finn MacCumhaill, 3rd cent.—Fiction 2. Folklore—Ireland 3. Giants—Folklore

ISBN 0-8050-6852-X   LC 2001-2884

The very clever Oona saves her husband, the giant Finn McCool, by outwitting Cuhullin, who seeks to prove that he is the strongest giant in the world by beating Finn

"Painted and cut-paper illustrations in bold colors and simple shapes echo the basic drama. This is a clever, amusing version of an oft-told story." Booklist

Spirin, Gennadiĭ

The tale of the Firebird; translated by Tatiana Popova. Philomel Bks. 2002 32p il $16.99 (2-4)

398.2

1. Fairy tales 2. Folklore—Russia 3. Birds—Folklore

ISBN 0-399-23584-1   LC 2001-36660

When Prince Ivan sets out to find the Firebird for his father the tsar, he must complete a series of tasks before obtaining the Firebird and winning the hand of a beautiful princess

"The storytelling is dramatic and controlled, the language rising and falling in a cadence that encourages reading aloud. . . . Detailed and dramatic, with a golden palette that echoes crown jewels, the illustrations have an adventurous fairy-tale sweep." Bull Cent Child Books

Stauffacher, Sue

The angel and other stories; retold by Sue Stauffacher; illustrated by Leonid Gore. Eerdmans Bks. for Young Readers 2002 75p il $20 (3-5)

398.2

1. Christianity—Folklore 2. Folklore—Europe

ISBN 0-8028-5203-3   LC 2002-21614

Retellings of folktales which reflect Christian oral traditions from fifteenth and sixteenth century Europe

"Gore's luminous illustrations are a fitting complement for this thought-provoking book, which offers wise counsel while respecting children enough not to preach too loudly at them." Booklist

Includes bibliographical references

Steig, Jeanne

A handful of beans; six fairy tales; retold by Jeanne Steig; with pictures by William Steig. HarperCollins Pubs. 1998 142p il $17.95 (k-3)

398.2

1. Fairy tales 2. Folklore

ISBN 0-06-205162-8   LC 97-78385

Steig, Jeanne—*Continued*

"Michael di Capua books"

"Six familiar fairy tales—'Rumpelstiltskin,' 'Beauty and the Beast,' 'Hansel and Gretel,' 'Little Red Riding Hood,' 'The Frog Prince,' and 'Jack and the Beanstalk'—are retold in a sprightly, energetic style. Jeanne Steig has a knack for slipping humor into simple language . . . and providing silly rhymes as welcome refrains and pithy conclusions." Bull Cent Child Books

Steptoe, John

Mufaro's beautiful daughters; an African tale. Lothrop, Lee & Shepard Bks. 1987 unp il $15.95; lib bdg $15.89 (k-3) **398.2**

1. Folklore—Africa

ISBN 0-688-04045-4; 0-688-04046-2 (lib bdg)

LC 84-7158

Also available Big book edition

A Caldecott Medal honor book, 1988; Coretta Scott King award for illustration, 1988

Mufaro's two beautiful daughters, one bad-tempered, one kind and sweet, go before the king, who is choosing a wife

"The pace of the text matches the rhythm of the illustrations—both move in dramatic unity to the climax. By changing perspective the artist not only captures the lush, rich background but also the personalities of the characters with revealing studies of their faces." Horn Book

The story of Jumping Mouse; a native American legend; retold and illustrated by John Steptoe. Lothrop, Lee & Shepard Bks. 1984 unp il $15.95; pa $5.95 (1-3) **398.2**

1. Native Americans—Folklore 2. Mice—Folklore

ISBN 0-688-01902-1; 0-688-08740-X (pa)

LC 82-14848

A Caldecott Medal honor book, 1985

"By keeping hope alive within himself, a mouse is successful in his quest for the far-off land. Steptoe's retelling of an unattributed tribal legend is exquisite in its use of language and in its expansive drawings which employ dazzling subtleties of light and shadow." SLJ

Stevens, Janet

Coyote steals the blanket; an Ute tale; retold and illustrated by Janet Stevens. Holiday House 1993 unp il pa $6.95 hardcover o.p. (k-3) **398.2**

1. Ute Indians—Folklore 2. Coyote (Legendary character)

ISBN 0-8234-1129-X (pa)

LC 92-54415

"When Coyote swipes a blanket, thus angering the spirit of the desert, he is pursued by a rock on a rampage. This traditional trickster tale features a scraggly, scruffy yet lovable character, a narrative that will roll right off storytellers' tongues, and hilarious pictures of boastful animals trying to halt the furious boulder." SLJ

Old bag of bones; a Coyote tale; retold and illustrated by Janet Stevens. Holiday House 1996 unp il $16.95; pa $6.95 (k-3) **398.2**

1. Shoshoni Indians—Folklore 2. Coyote (Legendary character)

ISBN 0-8234-1215-6; 0-8234-1337-3 (pa)

LC 95-31443

"Now an aging, decidedly mangy creature who yearns for youth, Coyote begs a stalwart young buffalo for 'a drop of strength.' Transformed into a strapping 'Buffote,' Coyote misjudges the extent of his new powers, as well as the virtues of age, and is stripped of his buffalo guise." Publ Wkly

"Expressive, darkly hued illustrations complement the lively retelling, loosely based on a Shoshoni tale, which blends dialogue and a clipped narration for an animated, appealing story." Horn Book Guide

Tops and bottoms; adapted and illustrated by Janet Stevens. Harcourt Brace & Co. 1995 unp il $16 (k-3) **398.2**

1. African Americans—Folklore 2. Rabbits—Folklore 3. Bears—Folklore

ISBN 0-15-292851-0

LC 93-19154

A Caldecott Medal honor book, 1996

"Bear agrees to enter into a farming partnership with Hare, but first Hare makes Bear choose which half he will receive at harvest time: tops or bottoms. Because Bear picks tops, Hare sows all root vegetables. For the second crop, Bear chooses bottoms; this time Hare grows lettuce, broccoli, and celery. Finally, the frustrated Bear demands tops and bottoms from the final season's crop. But Hare is still the winner: he grows corn [and] keeps the ears 'in the middle' for his family. . . . Steven's bold, well-composed watercolor, pencil, and gesso illustrations cover every inch of each vertically oriented double-page spread. . . . The story contains enough sly humor and reassuring predictability to captivate listeners." Horn Book

Stewig, John W.

King Midas; a golden tale; told by John Warren Stewig; pictured through the mind of Omar Rayyan. Holiday House 1999 unp il $15.95 (2-4) **398.2**

1. Midas (Legendary character)

ISBN 0-8234-1423-X

LC 98-21222

A king finds himself bitterly regretting the consequences of his wish that everything he touches would turn to gold

"Rayyan's watercolors are a phantasmagoria of irreverent details, from the statue of a fresh minotaur sticking his tongue out to a rubber duck floating in a fountain." Bull Cent Child Books

Stockings of buttermilk: American folktales; edited by Neil Philip; illustrated by Jacqueline Mair. Clarion Bks. 1999 124p il $20 (4 and up) **398.2**

1. Folklore—United States

ISBN 0-395-84980-2

LC 98-54366

These "stories and anecdotes, rooted in Europe but harvested in America, and often from African American tellers, are nearly all surprising variants on familiar folktales. . . . Philip generally lays editorial hands on the tales lightly, if at all, learnedly discusses tale types and other matters in appended notes. . . . Jacqueline Mair's small paintings add atmosphere by mimicking folk art patchwork and embroidery patterns." Booklist

Includes bibliographical references

Sturges, Philemon

The Little Red Hen (makes a pizza); retold by Philemon Sturges; illustrated by Amy Walrod. Dutton Children's Bks. 1999 unp il $15.99 (k-3)

398.2

1. Folklore 2. Chickens—Folklore

ISBN 0-525-45953-7 LC 99-20066

In this version of the traditional tale, the duck, the dog, and the cat refuse to help the Little Red Hen make a pizza but do get to participate when the time comes to eat it and then they wash the dishes

"There's a keen sense of the absurd here, and the hilarious cut-paper illustrations are right in tune with the zany plot." SLJ

Sutcliff, Rosemary

The light beyond the forest; the quest for the Holy Grail; decorations by Shirley Felts. Dutton 1980 143p pa $5.99 hardcover o.p. (4 and up)

398.2

1. Arthur, King 2. Grail—Fiction 3. Arthurian romances

ISBN 0-14-037150-8 (pa) LC 79-23396

First published 1979 in the United Kingdom

This is a retelling of the adventures of King Arthur's knights as they search for the Holy Grail. "After a vision of the Cup from the Last Supper appears, Sir Lancelot, Sir Galahad, Sir Bors, and Sir Percival quit Camelot to look for the Grail, knowing that only the world's most perfect knight will succeed. The individual adventures, which take on a loftier meaning as the journeys also become the knights' personal searches for God, will be most appreciated by special readers interested in King Arthur and his time." Booklist

Followed by The sword and the circle

The road to Camlann; decorations by Shirley Felts. Dutton 1982 142p pa $5.99 hardcover o.p. (4 and up)

398.2

1. Arthur, King 2. Arthurian romances

ISBN 0-14-037147-8 (pa) LC 82-9481

First published 1981 in the United Kingdom

"This book completes Rosemary Sutcliff's Arthurian trilogy, begun with 'The Light Beyond the Forest' and 'The Sword and the Circle.' Here Sutcliff describes the events from the coming of Mordred to the death of Lancelot. The title refers to The Last Battle, in which Arthur and his civilization perish. Sutcliff writes with her usual economy and rich prose, with a touch of archaic diction in the speeches. . . . Other than Malory, I can think of no better introduction to the whole sweep of Arthurian stories and values." SLJ

The sword and the circle; King Arthur and the Knights of the Round Table. Dutton 1981 260p pa $5.99 hardcover o.p. (4 and up)

398.2

1. Arthur, King 2. Arthurian romances

ISBN 0-14-037149-4 (pa) LC 81-9759

The second volume in the author's Arthurian trilogy, begun with: The light beyond the forest. The events in this volume precede those in the earlier volume

"The author has brought together thirteen stories associated with the Arthurian cycle, beginning with 'The Coming of Arthur' and concluding not with the passing of Arthur but with 'The Coming of Perceval.' Although she has relied on Malory's 'Morte d' Arthur' for most of her material, she has drawn upon other medieval sources for some of her best storytelling: For example 'Sir Gawain and the Green Knight' comes from a Middle English poem, and the twenty-nine-page 'Tristan and Iseult' is indebted to Godfrey of Strasburg's version." Horn Book

Followed by The road to Camlann

Taback, Simms

Kibitzers and fools; tales my zayda (grandfather) told me. Viking 2005 unp il $16.99 (k-3)

398.2

1. Jews—Folklore

ISBN 0-670-05955-2 LC 2005-03859

Thirteen brief, illustrated, traditional Jewish tales, each accompanied by an appropriate saying.

"This uproarious book celebrates the shtetl scene with energetic, mixed-media pictures in bright, folk-art style. . . . Families will want to share this." Booklist

Talbott, Hudson

Excalibur; written and illustrated by Hudson Talbott. Books of Wonder 1996 unp il $16 (3-5)

398.2

1. Arthur, King 2. Arthurian romances

ISBN 0-688-13380-0 LC 95-35388

At head of title: Tales of King Arthur

The young King Arthur asks for and receives the noble sword Excalibur from the Lady of the Lake and promises to be deserving of it through acts of valor

"The particulars of costumes, weapons, and heraldic emblems captured in the watercolors may intrigue many youngsters; others will relish Talbott's abundant detailing of bloody battles or enjoy the story for its fantasy and drama." Booklist

King Arthur and the Round Table; written and illustrated by Hudson Talbott. Books of Wonder 1995 unp il $16 (3-5)

398.2

1. Arthur, King 2. Arthurian romances

ISBN 0-688-11340-0 LC 94-43766

"Talbott recounts the battles immediately following Arthur's accession to the throne, the young king's fateful meeting with beautiful Guinevere, and the acquisition of the Round Table." Horn Book Guide

"The rich watercolor tableaux . . . paint war as bloody and painful, not all glorious. The love scenes glow golden. The Round Table, huge and decorated with the signs of the zodiac, exhibits its power more than the words do. Overall, this is a rousing addition to the current pickings of Arthurian stories." SLJ

Taylor, Harriet Peck

Brother Wolf; a Seneca tale; retold and illustrated by Harriet Peck Taylor. Farrar, Straus & Giroux 1996 unp il $15 (k-3)

398.2

1. Seneca Indians—Folklore 2. Wolves—Folklore 3. Raccoons—Folklore

ISBN 0-374-30997-3 LC 95-30775

Taylor, Harriet Peck—*Continued*

"This Seneca tale relates how Wolf and Raccoon are friends, but they enjoy teasing each other. After the teasing has turned to insults, Raccoon comes upon the sleeping Wolf and covers his eyes with tar and clay. The mixture hardens, and Wolf has to beg the birds to peck away the seal so that he can see again. . . . Wolf shows his gratitude to the birds by painting their feathers with bright dyes and offers his forgiveness to Raccoon by painting stripes on his tail. . . . The large-scale batik illustrations, with their distinctive look, will please young children with their clarity and freshness. A satisfying read-aloud." Booklist

Coyote places the stars; retold and illustrated by Harriet Peck Taylor. Bradbury Press 1993 unp il pa $5.99 hardcover o.p. (k-3)   **398.2**
1. Chinook Indians—Folklore 2. Coyote (Legendary character) 3. Stars—Folklore
ISBN 0-689-81535-2 (pa)   LC 92-46431

"Based on a Wasco Native American legend, this . . . pourquoi tale explains the designs of the constellations. It is the curious coyote who decides to discover the secrets of the heavens by creating a ladder of arrows he shoots into the sky. Once in the heavens, he moves the stars around forming the shapes of his animal friends." SLJ

"Taylor's batik-and-dye paintings are a good match for the casual, playful rhythm of her retelling." Booklist

Tchana, Katrin Hyman

Changing Woman and her sisters; retold by Katrin Hyman Tchana; illustrated by Trina Schart Hyman. Holiday House 2006 80p il $18.95 (5 and up)   **398.2**
1. Gods and goddesses 2. Folklore
ISBN 0-8234-1999-1   LC 2005052504

An illustrated collection of traditional tales which feature goddesses from different cultures, including Navajo, Mayan, and Fon. Notes explain each goddess's place in her culture, the reason for the book, and how the illustrations were developed.

"This large, handsome volume assembles well-chosen, well-told stories. . . . Hyman . . . contributed distinctive portrayals of the goddesses using a technique that melded photographs and found materials into full-page ink and acrylic paintings." Booklist

Includes bibliographical references

Sense Pass King; a story from Cameroon; retold by Katrin Tchana; illustrated by Trina Schart Hyman. Holiday House 2002 unp il $16.95 (k-3)   **398.2**
1. Folklore—Cameroon
ISBN 0-8234-1577-5   LC 00-35094

Despite a jealous king's repeated attempts to get rid of her, Ma'antah continually manages to outwit him and proves herself worthy of the name Sense Pass King

The author "gives enough details to set the scene, and her smooth pacing will keep readers on the edge of their seats. . . . Hyman's artwork suggests the African heat—layers of gold silhouettes of trees and straw-colored huts on stilts with palm-frond rooftops are artfully set off by geometrically patterned fabrics in citrus tones." Publ Wkly

Terada, Alice M.

Under the starfruit tree; folktales from Vietnam; told by Alice M. Terada; illustrations by Janet Larsen; introduction and notes by Mary C. Austin. University of Hawaii Press 1989 136p il pa $12.95 hardcover o.p. (4-6)   **398.2**
1. Folklore—Vietnam
ISBN 0-8248-1553-X (pa)   LC 89-5123
"A Kolowalu book"

"Twenty-seven tales culled from North and South Vietnam and translated by native speakers are grouped in four sections: foibles and quirks; tales from the lowlands and the highlands; the spirit world; and food, love and laughter. . . . Each narration is followed by an afterword that . . . reveals customs, beliefs and values." Publ Wkly

"Although the book's format is not particularly attractive, these 27 stories from Vietnam will certainly find a place on library shelves. . . . Occasional black-and-white drawings add some visual interest." Booklist

Includes bibliographical references

Thomas, Joyce Carol

The six fools; collected by Zora Neale Hurston; adapted by Joyce Carol Thomas; illustrated by Ann Tanksley. 1st ed. HarperCollins 2006 unp il $15.99; lib bdg $16.89 (k-3)   **398.2**
1. Hurston, Zora Neale, 1891-1960—Adaptations 2. African Americans—Folklore 3. Folklore—United States
ISBN 0-06-000646-3; 0-06-000647-1 (lib bdg)
                    LC 2004-30055

Adapted from a story collected by Zora Neale Hurston and previously published in *Every tongue got to confess*

A young man searches for three people more foolish than his fiancée and her parents.

"This adaptation of the fool story from Hurston's *Every Tongue Got to Confess* . . . is light and adept. . . . The result is wonderful in voice: rich, hilarious, and satisfying. Tanksley's oil monoprints done in a folk-art style set the story in Hurston's 1920s-'30s with humor and vibrant color in a wide-ranging palette." SLJ

The skull talks back and other haunting tales; collected by Zora Neale Hurston; adapted by Joyce Carol Thomas; illustrated by Leonard Jenkins. 1st ed. HarperCollins 2004 56p $15.99; lib bdg $16.89 (4 and up)   **398.2**
1. Hurston, Zora Neale, 1891-1960—Adaptations 2. Horror fiction 3. African Americans—Folklore
ISBN 0-06-000631-5; 0-06-000634-X (lib bdg)
                    LC 2003-22215

Contents: Big, bad Sixteen; Bill, the talking mule; High Walker; The witch who could slip off her skin; The skull talks back; The haunted house

"Thomas retells six supernatural folktales selected from Hurston's Every Tongue Got to Confess" SLJ

"Using a direct style that loses none of the colloquial immediacy of the original voices, Thomas has done a great job of retelling six of Hurston's supernatural tales, and Jenkins' monochromatic collages and silhouettes capture the delicious, shivery glow of skeletons and graveyards." Booklist

Thomas, Joyce Carol—*Continued*

What's the hurry, Fox? and other animal stories; collected by Zora Neale Hurston; illustrated by Bryan Collier; adapted by Joyce Carol Thomas. HarperCollins Publishers 2004 unp il $15.99; lib bdg $16.89 (k-3) **398.2**

1. Hurston, Zora Neale, 1891-1960—Adaptations 2. Animals—Folklore 3. Folklore—Southern States

ISBN 0-06-000643-9; 0-06-000644-7 (lib bdg)

LC 2003-7014

Presents a volume of pourquoi tales collected by Zora Neale Hurston from her field research in the Gulf states in the 1930s.

In her adaptations Thomas uses "simplicity, humor, wit, and a colloquial style true to the spirit of the originals. . . . Collier's double-page-spread pictures combine painting and collage to show the animal characters' sly human machinations. The stories are very short, leaving lots of space for storyteller and audience." SLJ

Tomie dePaola's Favorite nursery tales. Putnam 1986 127p il $24.99 (k-3) **398.2**

1. Folklore 2. Fables

ISBN 0-399-21319-8 LC 85-28302

The book begins "with a verse about reading picture books from Stevenson's *Child's Garden of Verses*, followed by Longfellow's 'Children's Hour.' The story selections—'Johnny Cake,' 'The Little Red Hen,' 'Rumpelstiltskin,' 'The Princess and the Pea,' 'The Tortoise and the Hare,' 'The House on the Hill,' and 22 more." Booklist

"DePaola's droll, witty, and very funny illustrations capture the essence of each story from a child's point of view. . . . The beautiful layout of these pages, in which the print and pictures are perfectly at ease with one another, invites confident new readers as well as adults for reading aloud." SLJ

Tresselt, Alvin R.

The mitten; an old Ukrainian folktale; retold by Alvin Tresselt; illustrated by Yaroslava; adapted from the version by E. Rachev. Lothrop, Lee & Shepard Bks. 1964 unp il pa $5.95 hardcover o.p. (k-2) **398.2**

1. Folklore—Ukraine 2. Animals—Folklore

ISBN 0-688-09238-1 (pa)

"On the coldest day of the year a little Ukrainian boy loses his fur-lined mitten, which becomes so overcrowded with animals seeking a snug shelter that it finally bursts. Brightly colored pictures show the animals dressed in typical Ukrainian costumes." Hodges. Books for Elem Sch Libr

Tseng, Grace

White tiger, blue serpent; illustrated by Jean and Mou-Sien Tseng. Lothrop, Lee & Shepard Bks. 1999 unp il $16; lib bdg $16.84 (2-4) **398.2**

1. Fairy tales 2. Folklore—China

ISBN 0-688-12515-8; 0-688-12516-6 (lib bdg)

LC 94-9757

Based on tale from Drung tribe of Yunnan Province

When his mother's beautiful brocade is snatched away by a greedy goddess, a young Chinese boy faces many perils as he attempts to get it back

"Lush paintings in the manner of fifteenth-century Chinese art animate a full-bodied folktale retelling about the search for beauty." Booklist

Van Kampen, Vlasta

It couldn't be worse! Annick Press; distributed by Firefly Bks. 2003 unp il lib bdg $18.95; pa $6.95 (k-3) **398.2**

1. Folklore

ISBN 1-55037-783-3 (lib bdg); 1-55037-782-5 (pa)

The farmer's family was so crowded in their one-room house that they knew that it couldn't get worse but couldn't see how to make it better. So the farmer's wife asked for advice

"Bright, cheery watercolors match the puckish charm of this folktale." Booklist

Van Laan, Nancy

The magic bean tree; a legend from Argentina; retold by Nancy Van Laan; paintings by Beatriz Vidal. Houghton Mifflin 1998 unp il $15 (k-3) **398.2**

1. Native Americans—Folklore 2. Folklore—Argentina

ISBN 0-395-82746-9 LC 96-38632

A young Quechuan boy sets out on his own to bring the rains back to his parched homeland and is rewarded by a gift of carob beans that come to be prized across Argentina

"Vidal's shimmering, folk art-style paintings are well matched to the elegant simplicity and drama of Van Laan's retelling." Booklist

Includes glossary and bibliographical references

Shingebiss; an Ojibwe legend; retold by Nancy Van Laan; woodcuts by Betsy Bowen. Houghton Mifflin 1997 unp il $16 (2-4) **398.2**

1. Ojibwa Indians—Folklore 2. Ducks—Folklore

ISBN 0-316-89627-6 LC 95-40274

Shingebiss the duck bravely challenges the Winter Maker and manages to find enough food to survive a long, harsh winter

Van Laan's "lyric text flows like a soft drum beat and, although lengthy, wastes no words. . . . The artist's rustic, spirited woodcuts appear within circular frames of thick, loose lines that give one the sense of peering through ice holes." Publ Wkly

Includes glossary and bibliographical references

Wada, Stephanie

Momotarō and the island of ogres; a Japanese folktale; as told to Stephanie Wada; paintings by Kano Naganobu. George Braziller 2005 47p il $19.95 (3-6) **398.2**

1. Folklore—Japan

ISBN 0-8076-1552-8

Found floating on the river inside a peach by an old couple, Momotaro grows up and fights the terrible demons who have terrorized the village for years.

"Nineteenth-century silk handscrolls, painted by mas-

Wada, Stephanie—*Continued*
ter Naganobu and housed in the New York Public Library's Spencer Collection, illustrate this handsome retelling of a much-loved Japanese folktale." Booklist

Wagué Diakité, Baba
The hatseller and the monkeys; a West African folktale; retold and illustrated by Baba Wagué Diakité. Scholastic Press 1999 unp il $15.95 (k-3)
398.2
1. Folklore—West Africa 2. Monkeys—Folklore
ISBN 0-590-96069-5   LC 98-16250
An African version of the familiar story of a man who sets off to sell his hats, only to have them stolen by a treeful of mischievous monkeys
"Ceramic-tile paintings on each spread depict the action in fluid, bold brushwork. . . . In this retelling, Diakité's use of language is as colorful and unusual as his artwork." Publ Wkly

The hunterman and the crocodile; a West African folktale; retold and illustrated by Baba Wagué Diakité. Scholastic 1997 unp il $15.95 (2-4)
398.2
1. Folklore—West Africa 2. Crocodiles—Folklore
ISBN 0-590-89828-0   LC 95-25975
"After Donso rescues a crocodile family, they turn on him and threaten to eat him. Several creatures . . . refuse his appeals for help, saying that Man has always misused them in the past. Only clever Rabbit is willing to assist him. Bold figures painted on ceramic tiles illustrate this teaching tale about 'living in harmony with nature.'" Horn Book Guide
Includes bibliographical references

The magic gourd. Scholastic Press 2003 32p il $16.95 (2-4)
398.2
1. Folklore—Mali   2.   Rabbits—Folklore
3. Chameleons—Folklore
ISBN 0-439-43960-4   LC 2002-4731
"In a time of famine, Chameleon rewards Brother Rabbit for a kind deed with a magic gourd that fills with whatever its owner desires. King Mansa Juga steals the gourd, but clever Rabbit recovers it and teaches the greedy king a lesson. Photos of exquisitely crafted ceramic plates, bowls, and tiles bordered with traditional Mali patterns illustrate this West African tale, which is retold with both economy and flair." Horn Book Guide
Includes glossary

Ward, Helen
The hare and the tortoise; a fable from Aesop; retold & illustrated by Helen Ward. Millbrook Press 1999 unp il $16.95; lib bdg $24.90 (k-3)
398.2
1. Aesop—Adaptations 2. Fables 3. Folklore
4. Rabbits—Folklore 5. Turtles—Folklore
ISBN 0-761-30988-8; 0-7613-1318-4 (lib bdg)
LC 98-26100
Retells the events of the famous race between the boastful hare and the persevering tortoise. Includes a key to the various animals pictured in the illustrations
"A straightforward, elegant, witty retelling of an old

favorite. . . . With black ink outlines meticulously delineating the creatures' fur and markings, Ward's watercolor-and-gouache paintings show each animal as both warmly cuddly and realistic." Booklist

Unwitting wisdom; an anthology of Aesop's fables; retold & illustrated by Helen Ward. Chronicle Books 2004 unp il $18.95 (3-6)
398.2
1. Aesop—Adaptations 2. Fables
ISBN 0-8118-4450-1   LC 2003-22990
Contents: Sour grapes; The trappings of power; All dressed up; Pot luck; A time to dance; A dinner invitation; Steady and slow; Upon reflection; Size isn't everything; Not flying, but falling; Fool's gold; Hard cheese
Illustrated retellings of twelve of Aesop's fables

Wardlaw, Lee
Punia and the King of Sharks; a Hawaiian folktale; adapted by Lee Wardlaw; pictures by Felipe Davalos. Dial Bks. for Young Readers 1997 unp il $16.99 (k-3)
398.2
1. Folklore—Hawaii 2. Sharks—Folklore
ISBN 0-8037-1682-6   LC 93-43955
Clever Punia, a Hawaiian fisherman's son, finds different ways to trick the King of Sharks and take his tasty lobsters away from him
"The involving story contains comforting folktale elements and an engaging protagonist. The illustrations have an appropriate folk-art flatness as well as vigor and humor." Horn Book Guide
Includes glossary

Washington, Donna L.
A pride of African tales; illustrated by James Ransome. HarperCollinsPublishers 2004 70p il $16.99; lib bdg $17.89 (3-5)
398.2
1. Folklore—Africa
ISBN 0-06-024929-3; 0-06-024932-3 (lib bdg)
LC 94-18697
A collection of African folktales originating in the storytelling tradition.
"Ransome contributes lush, naturalistic watercolors. . . . Storytellers looking for material will welcome this versatile offering, as will educators seeking to deepen children's understanding of Africa's diversity and the richness of its narrative tradition." Booklist
Includes bibliographical references

Wattenberg, Jane
Henny-Penny; retold and illustrated by Jane Wattenberg. Scholastic Press 2000 unp il lib bdg $15.95 (k-3)
398.2
1. Folklore 2. Animals—Folklore
ISBN 0-439-07817-2   LC 99-28806
While on their way to tell the king that the sky is falling, Henny Penny and her friends meet the very hungry Foxy-Loxy
"This is a hip, updated version of the old folktale. The colorful photo-collage art places Henny-Penny in locations around the world from Stonehenge to the Egyptian pyramids to the Taj Mahal." SLJ

Watts, Bernadette

Jorinda and Jorindel; by the Grimm brothers; retold by Bernadette Watts. North-South Books 2005 unp il $15.95 (k-3)   **398.2**

1. Grimm, Jacob, 1785-1863 2. Fairy tales 3. Folklore—Germany

ISBN 0-7358-1987-4

When a witch changes Jorinda into a nightingale, her sweetheart Joringel discovers through a dream how to save her.

This is an "evocative but infrequently retold tale. . . . [Some children will] pore over Watts' delicate renderings of fairy-tale scenery, while older readers will enjoy discussing the witch's motivations and fate, both left tantalizingly mysterious." Booklist

Weitzman, David L.

Rama and Sita; a tale of ancient Java; retold and illustrated by David Weitzman. Godine 2002 unp il $19.95 (3-6)   **398.2**

1. Rāma (Hindu deity) 2. Folklore—India

ISBN 1-56792-151-5   LC 2001-40964

Banished by his father to a dark forest, Prince Rama loses his wife Sita to the demon prince Ravana, but the Monkey King offers to help rescue her

"Weitzman uses the framework of a Javanese puppet show to surround the narrative. He briefly describes the puppeteer's preparations, and his elaborately detailed, gold-accented illustrations mimic the angular, long-limbed, two-dimensional look of shadow puppets. . . . Children will easily connect with . . . the exciting superhero action, which Weitzman sets down in elegant, well-paced language." Booklist

Willey, Margaret

Clever Beatrice; an Upper Peninsula conte; illustrated by Heather McWhorter. Atheneum Bks. for Young Readers 2001 unp il $16 (k-3)   **398.2**

1. Folklore—United States 2. Giants—Folklore

ISBN 0-689-83254-0   LC 00-42019

A small, but clever young girl outwits a rich giant and wins all his gold

"Set in Michigan's Upper Peninsula, this is a winning tale of brain vs. brawn. . . . Willey's telling is simple but spirited, and her dialogue, with its slight French-Canadian cadence, is pitch perfect. Heather Solomon's illustrations are remarkable: watercolors augmented with collage, they have unusual texture and depth." Horn Book

Another title about Clever Beatrice by this author is: Clever Beatrice and the best little pony (2004)

Wisniewski, David

Golem; story and pictures by David Wisniewski. Clarion Bks. 1996 unp il $15.95 (3-5)   **398.2**

1. Jewish legends

ISBN 0-395-72618-2   LC 95-21777

Awarded the Caldecott Medal, 1997

This "is the tale of a clay giant formed in the image of man to protect the Jewish people of medieval Prague from destruction by their enemies." SLJ

"The fiery, crisply layered paper illustrations, portraying with equal drama and precision the ornamental architecture of Prague and the unearthly career of the Golem, match the specificity and splendor of the storytelling." Publ Wkly

Wolkstein, Diane

The day Ocean came to visit; paintings by Steve Johnson and Lou Fancher. Gulliver Bks. 2001 unp il $16 (k-3)   **398.2**

1. Folklore—Nigeria

ISBN 0-15-201774-7   LC 00-10898

After hearing Ocean's stories, Sun invites Ocean to the house he shares with his wife, Moon, but his visitor proves to be more than his house can hold

"The richly descriptive text turns a story of domestic upheaval into a suspenseful yet happy accident. Luminous oil illustrations, set against textured clay-and-shell backgrounds . . . extend the glowing warmth of the words." Booklist

Womenfolk and fairy tales; edited by Rosemary Minard; illustrated by Suzanna Klein. Houghton Mifflin 1975 163p il $18 (3-6)   **398.2**

1. Folklore 2. Fairy tales 3. Women—Folklore

ISBN 0-395-20276-0

This collection features stories by the Brothers Grimm, Lafcadio Hearn, Andrew Lang, Joseph Jacobs, and others

"Although the tales are available in a multitude of collections, this handsomely illustrated volume brings them together in a convenient form for those searching for feminist folklore." Horn Book

Wooldridge, Connie Nordhielm

Wicked Jack; adapted by Connie Nordhielm Wooldridge; illustrated by Will Hillenbrand. Holiday House 1995 unp il $16.95; pa $6.95 (k-3)   **398.2**

1. Folklore—Southern States

ISBN 0-8234-1101-X; 0-8234-1292-X (pa)

LC 93-13248

"The mean blacksmith defeats the devil and his young sons with a chair that won't stop rocking, a sledgehammer that won't stop pounding, and a fire bush that keeps on sticking. In the delectable ending, Jack, now deceased, is turned away from the underworld by terrified demons. . . . Hillenbrand's imaginative mixed-media paintings (with smudges of coal) have thin, robust lines, angular figures, subtle colors, and a distinctive style." Booklist

Wormell, Christopher

Mice, morals, & monkey business; lively lessons from Aesop's Fables. Running Press 2005 unp il $18.95 (k-3)   **398.2**

1. Aesop—Adaptations 2. Fables

ISBN 0-7624-2404-4

"Wormell uses linocut prints to illuminate 21 of Aesop's famous life lessons. . . . The bold, black lines of the expertly rendered images and colorful accents primar-

Wormell, Christopher—*Continued*
ily in earth tones create instantly recognizable figures.
The subtle use of light and shadow adds clarity, expression, and often drama without extraneous detail." SLJ

Yeoman, John
The Seven voyages of Sinbad the Sailor;
illustrated by Quentin Blake; retold by John
Yeoman. Margaret K. McElderry Bks. 1997 c1996
119p il (5 and up)   **398.2**
1. Fairy tales 2. Arabs—Folklore
ISBN 0-689-81368-6
Available in paperback from Chrysalis Books $6.95
(ISBN 1-8436-5040-1)
First published 1996 in the United Kingdom
"Yeoman's first-person narration . . . leads readers
through Sinbad's seven shipwrecks while introducing
them to the amazing inhabitants of the islands on which
the sailor is inevitably stranded." SLJ
"Blake's ink drawings with watercolors . . . illustrate
the story with style and grace. A handsome edition in every way, this book features good storytelling, lively illustrations, and excellent design." Booklist

Yep, Laurence
The Khan's daughter; a Mongolian folktale;
illustrated by Jean and Mou-Sien Tseng. Scholastic
1996 unp il $16.95 (3-5)   **398.2**
1. Folklore—Mongolia
ISBN 0-590-48389-7   LC 95-25150
A simple shepherd must pass three tests in order to
marry the Khan's beautiful daughter
"Yep's strong folkloric narrative is amplified by splendid watercolor illustrations. . . . With engaging human
characters, frightful monsters, dramatic tension within a
warrior-based society, powerful illustrations, and plenty
of action, this is the sort of book that will appeal to diverse ages and sensibilities." Booklist

Yolen, Jane
Meow; cat stories from around the world;
illustrated by Hala Wittwer. HarperCollins 2005
40p il $16.99; lib bdg $17.89 (k-3)   **398.2**
1. Cats—Folklore 2. Folklore
ISBN 0-06-029161-3; 0-06-029162-1 (lib bdg)
                                      LC 2002-06380
"A collection of 10 cat stories, plus nursery rhymes
and lore drawn from sources around the world. Yolen
captures the heart of each story, and the resulting text
begs to be told or read aloud. . . . Wittwer's richly colored paintings fill the pages with the essence of feline
charm, power, and wit. " SLJ

Mightier than the sword; world folktales for
strong boys; collected and told by Jane Yolen;
with illustrations by Raul Colón. Silver
Whistle/Harcourt 2003 112p il $19 (4 and up)
                                        398.2
1. Folklore
ISBN 0-15-216391-3   LC 2002-9886
A collection of folktales from around the world which
demonstrate the triumph of brains over brawn

Yolen's "versions of these stories are lively, expressively written, ready for reading aloud or telling, and illustrative of her point." SLJ
Includes bibliographical references

Not one damsel in distress; world folktales for
strong girls; collected and told by Jane Yolen;
with illustrations by Susan Guevara. Silver Whistle
Bks. 2000 116p il $17 (4 and up)   **398.2**
1. Fairy tales 2. Women—Folklore
ISBN 0-15-202047-0   LC 99-18509
A collection of thirteen traditional tales from various
parts of the world, each of whose main character is a
fearless, strong, heroic, and resourceful woman
"This is a spirited collection with a lively pace. . . .
The stories sing and soar in Yolen's supple language,
and each is contained enough for a read-aloud." Booklist
Includes bibliographical references

Young, Ed
Cat and Rat; the legend of the Chinese zodiac.
Holt & Co. 1995 unp il $15.95; pa $6.95 (k-3)
                                        398.2
1. Folklore—China 2. Zodiac 3. Cats—Folklore
4. Rats—Folklore
ISBN 0-8050-2977-X; 0-8050-6049-9 (pa)
                                     LC 94-49147
"Cat and Rat were best friends, according to this Chinese legend, until the Jade Emperor of Heaven held a
race to determine which animals would be included in
the zodiac. . . . In the author's note, Young comments
on the Chinese New Year, the 12 traditional signs, and
the birth years and personality traits for each one."
Booklist
"Young tells the story in lively, spare prose. . . . His
charcoal and pastel drawings on dark blue and buff rice
paper are elegant and full of action." SLJ

Lon Po Po; a Red-Riding Hood story from
China; translated and illustrated by Ed Young.
Philomel Bks. 1989 unp il $16.99; pa $6.99 (1-3)
                                        398.2
1. Folklore—China 2. Wolves—Folklore
ISBN 0-399-21619-7; 0-698-11382-9 (pa)
                                     LC 88-15222
Awarded the Caldecott Medal, 1990
Three sisters staying home alone are endangered by a
hungry wolf who is disguised as their grandmother
"The text possesses that matter-of-fact veracity that
characterizes the best fairy tales. The watercolor and pastel pictures are remarkable: mystically beautiful in their
depiction of the Chinese countryside, menacing in the
exchanges with the wolf, and positively chilling in the
scenes inside the house." SLJ

Seven blind mice. Philomel Bks. 1992 unp il
$17.99; pa $7.99 (k-3)   **398.2**
1. Fables 2. Elephants—Folklore 3. Folklore—India
4. Mice—Folklore
ISBN 0-399-22261-8; 0-698-11895-2 (pa)
                                     LC 90-35396
A Caldecott Medal honor book, 1993
"In Young's version of the familiar Indian folktale of
the blind men and the elephant, seven blind mice ap-

Young, Ed—*Continued*

proach an elephant, ask what it is, explore various parts of the beast, and arrive at different conclusions. . . . Many preschool and primary grade teachers will find that the book reinforces their students' learning of colors, days of the week, and ordinal numbers, while heeding the story's admonition not to lose sight of the whole in their enthusiasm for identifying the parts. Graphically, this picture book is stunning, with the cut-paper figures of the eight characters dramatically silhouetted against black backgrounds. . . . At once profound and simple, intelligent and playful." Booklist

The sons of the Dragon King; a Chinese legend. Atheneum Bks. for Young Readers 2004 unp il $16.95 (3-5)   **398.2**

1. Folklore—China

ISBN 0-689-85184-7   LC 2002-154321

The nine immortal sons of the Dragon King set out to make something of themselves, and each, with help from a watchful father, finds a role that suits his individual strengths.

"The text is engrossing and includes an informative author's note. The illustrations, rendered in brush, ink, and cut paper, use softly smudged lines for the part of the story focused on the legend, and sharper, cleaner lines augmented by a minimal but dramatically effective use of color for the present-day segments. This elegant addition to folklore shelves should be a first purchase for most libraries." SLJ

What about me? Philomel Bks. 2002 unp il $16.99 (k-3)   **398.2**

1. Folklore—Middle East

ISBN 0-399-23624-4   LC 2001-45927

A young boy determinedly follows the instructions of the Grand Master in the hope of gaining knowledge, only to be surprised as how he acquires it. Based on a Sufi tale.

"Dazzling collage illustrations set the personae of the tale against muted, spatter-paint backgrounds. The figures are agile, rhythmic, graceful, and emotionally charged, interpreting the story in perfect synchronization with mood and tempo." Horn Book

Zelinsky, Paul O.

Rapunzel; retold and illustrated by Paul O. Zelinsky. Dutton Children's Bks. 1997 unp il $16.99 (3-5)   **398.2**

1. Fairy tales 2. Folklore

ISBN 0-525-45607-4   LC 96-50260

Awarded the Caldecott Medal, 1998

A retelling of the folktale in which a beautiful girl with long golden hair is kept imprisoned in a lonely tower by a sorceress

"An elegant and sophisticated retelling that draws on early French and Italian versions of the tale. Masterful oil paintings capture the Renaissance setting and flesh out the tragic figures." SLJ

Rumpelstiltskin; from the German of the Brothers Grimm; retold & illustrated by Paul O. Zelinsky. Dutton 1986 unp il lib bdg $16.99; pa $6.99 (k-4)   **398.2**

1. Folklore—Germany 2. Fairy tales

ISBN 0-525-44265-0 (lib bdg); 0-14-055864-0 (pa)

     LC 86-4482

Also available Spanish language edition

A Caldecott Medal honor book, 1987

A strange little man helps the miller's daughter spin straw into gold for the king on the condition that she will give him her first-born child.

"Zelinsky's painterly style and rich colors provide an evocative backdrop to this story. The medieval setting and costumes and the spools of gold thread which shine on the page like real gold are suggestive of an illuminated manuscript. . . . Zelinsky's smooth retelling and glowing pictures cast the story in a new and beautiful light." SLJ

Zemach, Margot

The little red hen; an old story. Farrar, Straus & Giroux 1983 unp il $14; pa $4.95 (k-2)

     398.2

1. Folklore 2. Chickens—Folklore

ISBN 0-374-34621-6; 0-374-44511-7 (pa)

     LC 83-14159

A retelling of the traditional tale about the little red hen whose lazy friends are unwilling to help her plant, harvest, or grind the wheat into flour, but all are willing to help her eat the bread that she makes from it

"The pleasingly retold, rhythmical text is appropriately extended by scrappy, cartoonish, softly glowing color illustrations. The animals are anthropomorphized just enough, and their characters perfectly caught." Child Book Rev Serv

The three little pigs; an old story. Farrar, Straus & Giroux 1989 unp il $14; pa $5.95 (k-2)

     398.2

1. Folklore—Great Britain 2. Pigs—Folklore 3. Wolves—Folklore

ISBN 0-374-37527-5; 0-374-47717-5 (pa)

     LC 87-73488

"Michael di Capua books"

Zemach "has brought a familiar, often-told tale to life with marvelous ink-and-watercolor illustrations. Her wolf, wearing a dapper green hat and radiating slyness with every inch of his furry self, cuts a spendidly sinister figure as he attempts to wile his way to three pork chop dinners. With simple, lively sentences Zemach has related the complete story, including the apple-picking and country fair episodes." Horn Book

The three wishes; an old story. Farrar, Straus & Giroux 1986 unp il $16; pa $4.95 (k-2)

     398.2

1. Folklore 2. Wishes—Folklore

ISBN 0-374-37529-1; 0-374-47728-0 (pa)

     LC 86-80956

In this "version of the familiar folk tale, a woodcutter and his wife rescue an imp in the forest. He gives them three wishes, which they foolishly manage to squander on a long chain of sausages." N Y Times Book Rev

Zemach, Margot—*Continued*

This "is a natural for the picture-book format, and Zemach has taken full advantage of the humor with her watercolor illustrations. . . . The characters are homely and affectionate, their dog an amusing echo of their own lively expressions." Bull Cent Child Books

Ziefert, Harriet

Little Red Riding Hood; retold by Harriet Ziefert; illustrated by Emily Bolam. Viking 2000 unp il $13.89; pa $3.99 (k-2)   **398.2**
1. Fairy tales 2. Folklore—Germany 3. Wolves—Folklore
ISBN 0-670-88389-1; 0-14-056529-9 (pa)
LC 99-23210

"A Viking easy-to-read"

A little girl meets a hungry wolf in the forest while on her way to visit her gandmother

This adaptation of the Grimm's fairy tale "tells the story in a brisk, straightforward style . . . [with] simple, colorful illustrations. . . . The vocabulary is appropriate for beginning readers. The lively illustrations and familiarity of the story should provide a successful reading experience." SLJ

398.8   Rhymes and rhyming games

Alter, Anna

The three little kittens; [adapted and illustrated by] Anna Alter. Holt & Co. 2001 unp il $15.95 (k-1)   **398.8**
1. Nursery rhymes 2. Cats—Poetry
ISBN 0-8050-6471-0   LC 00-57533

Three little kittens lose and find their mittens

"Humor injects vitality into Alter's entertaining take on the traditional nursery rhyme. The kittens, who are miffed at being scolded for losing their mittens, spy a scavenging mouse retreating into its hole. . . . Using colored pencil and watercolor, Alter creates such soft-looking critters that children expect the pages to feel like fur." Booklist

Anna Banana: 101 jump-rope rhymes; compiled by Joanna Cole; illustrated by Alan Tiegreen. Morrow Junior Bks. 1989 64p il pa $7.95 hardcover o.p.   **398.8**
1. Jump rope rhymes 2. Games
ISBN 0-688-08809-0 (pa)   LC 88-29108

An illustrated collection of jump rope rhymes arranged according to the type of jumping they are meant to accompany

"Heavily inked drawings provide cartoon-style humor; sources for jump-rope rhymes and an index of first lines are appended." Booklist

The **Arnold** Lobel book of Mother Goose. Knopf 1997 176p il $21; lib bdg $22.99 (k-2)   **398.8**
1. Nursery rhymes
ISBN 0-679-88736-9; 0-679-98736-3 (lib bdg)
LC 97-1762

First published 1986 with title: The Random House book of Mother Goose

This nursery rhyme collection is "a true classic, with more than three hundred verses and Lobel's vigorous, lively, narrative-filled illustrations." Horn Book Guide

Arrorró mi niño; Latino lullabies and gentle games; selected and illustrated by Lulu Delacre; musical arrangements by Cecilia Esqivel and Diana Sáez. 1st ed. Lee & Low Books 2004 unp il $16.95 (k-3)   **398.8**
1. Nursery rhymes 2. Finger play 3. Lullabies 4. Bilingual books—English-Spanish
ISBN 1-58430-159-7   LC 2003-9234

An illustrated collection of nursery rhymes, finger play games, and lullabies from the major Latino groups living in the United States today.

"The bright, beautiful oil-wash illustrations . . . reflect the diversity of the Latino experience. . . . The bilingual text appears first in Spanish, with the English translation beneath or by its side. . . . Musical notation and comments about the melodies are at the back." Booklist

The **Baby's** lap book; [compiled and illustrated by] Kay Chorao. rev ed. Dutton 1990 58p il lib bdg $17.99   **398.8**
1. Nursery rhymes
ISBN 0-525-44604-4   LC 89-23273

First published 1977

A collection of more than fifty traditional nursery rhymes accompanied by "Chorao's soft, eminently careful pencil drawings of the characters and their situations. Innocence is all pervasive, in the alternating pastel pink and yellow pages that nicely counter the light grays of the framed drawings; in the young faces, both animal and human; and in the fullness of cozy interiors and bucolic outdoor field and forest scenes. The artist's light hand is right for her interpretation, unabashedly, uncloyingly sweet, and admirably suited to its purpose." Booklist [review of 1977 edition]

Baker, Keith

Big fat hen; illustrated by Keith Baker. Harcourt Brace & Co. 1994 unp il $15   **398.8**
1. Nursery rhymes 2. Counting 3. Chickens—Folklore
ISBN 0-15-292869-3   LC 93-19160

Also available Board book edition

"The text is the old rhyme, 'One, two, buckle my shoe,' and the double-page spreads show the hen and her chicks (first appearing as eggs) enacting the words. . . . Children who want to skip the counting altogether can just enjoy the singsong text and the pictures executed in acrylic paints. The big fat hen is very large and quite beautiful, with iridescent green feathers accented with purple and red; her friends are just as lovely, all colors, some with delicate patterns in their feathers." Booklist

Cabrera, Jane

Old Mother Hubbard. Holiday House 2001 unp il $15.95 (k-2)   **398.8**
1. Nursery rhymes
ISBN 0-8234-1659-3   LC 00-59715

Based on The comic adventures of Old Mother Hubbard and her dog, by Sarah Catherine Martin, originally published in London, 1805, by John Harris

Cabrera, Jane—*Continued*

Light-hearted illustrations accompany this version of the familiar nursery rhyme about an old woman and her playful dog

"The big, close-up pictures, with thick black lines and blazing color combine slapstick and coziness. . . . The chanting rhymes and exuberant illustrations make a great read-aloud for young preschoolers." Booklist

Chapman, Jane

Sing a song of sixpence; a pocketful of nursery rhymes and tales; [by] Jane Chapman. 1st U.S. ed. Candlewick Press 2004 61p il $15.99 (k-1)
        398.8

1. Nursery rhymes
ISBN 0-7636-2545-0   LC 2003-69565

An illustrated collection of twenty-five traditional nursery rhymes and stories, including "Jack and Jill," "Wee Willie Winkie," "Little Miss Muffet," "Three Blind Mice," "Goldilocks and the Three Bears," and "The Little Red Hen"

"With clear, bright acrylic pictures, Chapman brings an action-packed collection to preschoolers. . . . The type is large and clear, and lots of boisterous pictures decorate the big, spacious pages." Booklist

Dunn, Opal

Hippety-hop, hippety-hay; growing with rhymes from birth to age three; illustrated by Sally Anne Lambert. Holt & Co. 1999 46p il music $16.95
        398.8

1. Nursery rhymes
ISBN 0-8050-6081-2   LC 98-8105

A "collection of rhymes and finger plays complete with music, movement suggestions, and information for parents and caregivers on childhood developmental stages. . . . Filled with warm colors and appealing details, Lambert's watercolor illustrations pleasantly support the verses." SLJ

Emberley, Barbara

Drummer Hoff; adapted by Barbara Emberley; illustrated by Ed Emberley. Simon & Schuster 1987 c1967 unp il $16; pa $5.95   **398.8**

1. Nursery rhymes
ISBN 0-671-66248-1; 0-671-66249-X (pa)
         LC 87-35755

Also available Board book edition

Awarded the Caldecott Medal, 1968

First published 1967 by Prentice-Hall

"A cumulative folk rhyme is adapted in spirited style and illustrated with arresting black woodcuts accented with brilliant color. The characters who participate in the building and firing of a cannon—'Sergeant Crowder brought the powder, Corporal Farrell brought the barrel,' etc.—are hilariously rugged characters, while 'Drummer Hoff who fired it off stands by, deadpan, waiting to touch off the marvelously satisfying explosion.'" Hodges. Books for Elem Sch Libr

Galdone, Paul

The cat goes fiddle-i-fee; adapted and illustrated by Paul Galdone. Clarion Bks. 1985 unp il pa $6.95 hardcover o.p. (k-1)   **398.8**

1. Nursery rhymes 2. Animals—Poetry
ISBN 0-89919-705-1 (pa)   LC 85-2686

An old English rhyme names all the animals a farm boy feeds on his daily rounds

"Galdone's line-and-watercolor illustrations have all the verve and accessible good humor associated with his work, and the varied and irresistible rhythm of the verses carries the nonsense along at a good pace, enhancing its appeal to the very young. Whether told or sung, this is a diverting selection for preschool story times." Booklist

Three little kittens. Clarion Bks. 1986 unp il $15; pa $5.95   **398.8**

1. Nursery rhymes 2. Cats—Poetry
ISBN 0-89919-426-5; 0-89919-796-5 (pa)
         LC 86-2655

Three little kittens lose, find, soil, and wash their mittens

"Galdone's characteristically exuberant pen-and-wash drawings fill these pages with feline faces, first rueful then joyful, then repentant, and finally excited about the prospects of catching 'a rat close by.' This is one of those sustained nursery rhymes that initiates youngest listeners into the concentration required for stories, and there's enough dramatic movement and color contrast in the art to hold toddlers' attention." Bull Cent Child Books

The **Helen** Oxenbury nursery collection. 1st American ed. Alfred A. Knopf 2004 91p il $19.95; lib bdg $21.99 (k-3)   **398.8**

1. Nursery rhymes 2. Poetry—Collections
ISBN 0-375-82992-X; 0-375-92992-4 (lib bdg)
         LC 2004-58446

This "anthology draws from three previous books: five poems from Tiny Tim—Verses for Children (1981), a dozen rhymes from Cakes and Custard—The Helen Oxenbury Nursery Rhyme Book (1975), and seven tales from The Helen Oxenbury Nursery Story Book (1985)." Booklist

"The stories all feature Oxenbury's trademark winsome pencil-and-watercolor pictures. They include such favorites as 'Little Red Riding Hood,' 'Henny-Penny,' and 'The Three Little Pigs,' and are retold with drama and humor." SLJ

Here comes Mother Goose; edited by Iona Opie; illustrated by Rosemary Wells. Candlewick Press 1999 107p il $21.99   **398.8**

1. Nursery rhymes
ISBN 0-7636-0683-9   LC 99-14256

Presents more than sixty traditional nursery rhymes, including "Old Mother Hubbard," "I'm a Little Teapot," and "One, Two, Buckle My Shoe"

"Wells's watercolor-and-ink pictures of somersaulting guinea pigs, mischievous rabbits, and fluffy ducklings capture the sheer joy and exuberance of the rhymes. . . . Make room on the shelves for this must-have title." SLJ

Hoberman, Mary Ann

Miss Mary Mack; a hand-clapping rhyme; adapted by Mary Ann Hoberman; illustrated by Nadine Bernard Westcott. Little, Brown 1998 unp il music $14.95 **398.8**

1. Nursery rhymes

ISBN 0-316-93118-7 LC 96-34829

Also available Board Book edition

"In this expanded version of the popular hand-clapping rhyme, the elephant (who's 'jumped so high' . . ./ He reached the sky/) . . . lands in the middle of a picnic where Mary Mack promises him her silver buttons if he doesn't go back to the zoo. Westcott's loose and humorous illustrations add to the necessarily limited text. A melody line and instructions for hand-clapping are included on the front endpapers." Horn Book Guide

I saw Esau; the schoolchild's pocket book; edited by Iona and Peter Opie; illustrated by Maurice Sendak. Candlewick Press 1992 160p il $19.99; pa $9.99 **398.8**

1. Folklore—Great Britain 2. English poetry—Collections

ISBN 1-56402-046-0; 0-7636-1199-9 (pa)

LC 91-71845

A revised and newly illustrated edition of the title first published 1947 in the United Kingdom

A collection of rhymes and riddles traditionally passed on orally from child to child

"From lamentation, pun, and insult to rebuttal, tongue-twister, and comic complaint, these schoolyard folk rhymes are vulgar, absurd, fierce, and utterly compelling. . . . [The book features] Sendak's wicked, joyful illustrations. Blending the factual and the surreal, the pictures (most in color, some in sepia or in black and white) extend the rhymes with characters and scenarios that are gross and tender. Sendak knows kids' ferocity and their fear." Booklist

James Marshall's Mother Goose. Farrar, Straus & Giroux 1979 unp il pa $6.95 hardcover o.p.

398.8

1. Nursery rhymes

ISBN 0-374-43723-8 (pa) LC 79-2574

"Clean, translucent pastel colors and jolly cartoon figures give this limited collection [of thirty-five rhymes] a cheerful countenance. . . . Several of the old favorites are here, plus a number of lesser known rhymes such as little Poll Parrot and Little Tommy Tittlemouse. The illustrations depict the action in a literal way, with a breezy, occasionally offbeat humor." Booklist

Mamá Goose; a Latino nursery treasury; [compiled by] Alma Flor Ada and F. Isabel Campoy; illustrated by Maribel Suárez; creative editing of the English by Tracy Hefferman. Hyperion Books For Children 2004 121p il $19.99 (k-2) **398.8**

1. Nursery rhymes 2. Bilingual books—English-Spanish

ISBN 0-7868-1953-7 LC 2003-57059

Presents lullabies, finger plays, nursery rhymes, games, riddles, proverbs, and more in Spanish and English.

"The format is spacious, with . . . charming watercol-

or cartoon illustrations. . . . The selections, which are just as much fun to read in English as in Spanish, are wonderful examples of paraphrasing." SLJ

My very first Mother Goose; edited by Iona Opie; illustrated by Rosemary Wells. Candlewick Press 1996 107p il $21.99 **398.8**

1. Nursery rhymes

ISBN 1-56402-620-5 LC 96-4904

"The 60 plus rhymes in this collection are mostly the old-time favorites, but include some more recent ones such as 'Shoo Fly' and 'Down by the Station.' Wells illustrates the selections with her usual winsome, quirky, anthropomorphic mice, rabbits, cats, pigs, bears, etc., and even includes some people. The lavish ink-and-watercolors are filled with action and delightful details." SLJ

The **neighborhood** Mother Goose; [illustrated by] Nina Crews. Greenwillow Books 2004 63p il $15.99; lib bdg $16.89 **398.8**

1. Nursery rhymes

ISBN 0-06-051573-2; 0-06-051574-0 (lib bdg)

LC 2003-41763

"Amistad"

A collection of nursery rhymes, both familiar and lesser known, illustrated with photographs in a city setting.

"Nina Crews' clear, beautiful color photographs and computer manipulations bring children closeup to people like them. . . . She uses computer tools to combine photos of joyful kids in her Brooklyn neighborhood with all kinds of scenarios, realistic and wild." Booklist

The **Orchard** book of nursery rhymes; rhymes chosen by Zena Sutherland; pictures by Faith Jaques. Orchard Bks. 1990 88p il $22.95

398.8

1. Nursery rhymes

ISBN 0-531-05903-0 LC 89-71002

"A collection of familiar short verses, including Mother Goose rhymes, tongue twisters, and nonsense poems, with illustrations set in 18th-century England and France." SLJ

"Sutherland's collection is a particularly fresh and satisfying entry in a crowded field. The selections are sequenced with care. . . . Sprinkled throughout the verses, Jaques's bustling illustrations brim with pleasingly old-fashioned details." Publ Wkly

Includes bibliographical references

The **Oxford** dictionary of nursery rhymes; edited by Iona and Peter Opie. 2nd ed. Oxford Univ. Press 1997 xxix, 559p il $55 **398.8**

1. Nursery rhymes—Dictionaries

ISBN 0-19-860088-7 LC 98-140995

First published 1951

An anthology of "over 500 rhymes, songs, nonsense jingles, and lullabies. . . . Complementing the rhymes are nearly a hundred illustrations, including reproductions of early art found in ballad sheets and music books, which highlight the development of children's illustrations over the last two centuries. . . . [The editors note] the earliest known publications of the rhyme, describing how it originated, illustrating changes in wording over time, and indicating variations and parallels in other lan-

The Oxford dictionary of nursery rhymes—
Continued
guages." Publisher's note

"The novice as well as the professional will find it an enjoyable read, as well as a learning experience." Am Ref Books Annu, 1999

Pat-a-cake and other play rhymes; compiled by Joanna Cole and Stephanie Calmenson; illustrated by Alan Tiegreen. Morrow Junior Bks. 1992 48p il $14; pa $6.95   **398.8**
1. Nursery rhymes 2. Finger play
ISBN 0-688-11038-X; 0-688-11533-0 (pa)
LC 91-32264

A collection of nursery rhymes and action rhymes, in such categories as finger and hand rhymes, tickling rhymes, and knee-and-foot-riding rhymes

"A charming source of bounce-and-tickle rhymes, this book features a good choice of games, an inviting format, and illustrations that make the most of the fun. . . . The simple line drawings, one to four on a page, combine an appealing informality of line with the delicacy of watercolor washes." Booklist

Includes bibliographical references

Patz, Nancy
Moses supposes his toeses are roses and 7 other silly old rhymes; retold and illustrated by Nancy Patz. Harcourt Brace Jovanovich 1983 unp il $13.95; pa $6   **398.8**
1. Nursery rhymes
ISBN 0-15-255690-7; 0-15-255691-5 (pa)
LC 82-3099

"Eight English and American nonsense rhymes have lilt, nonsense, and humor. On each page, the ebullient paintings erupt from their tidy frames with vigorous and at times grotesque people and animals painted in the style of eighteenth and nineteenth century Pennsylvania Dutch pictures." Bull Cent Child Books

¡Pio peep! traditional Spanish nursery rhymes; selected by Alma Flor Ada & F. Isabel Campoy; English adaptations by Alice Schertle; illustrated by Vivi Escrivá. HarperCollins Pubs. 2003 64p il $14.99; lib bdg $16.89 (k-3)   **398.8**
1. Nursery rhymes 2. Bilingual books—English-Spanish
ISBN 0-688-16019-0; 0-688-16020-4 (lib bdg)
LC 2001-51641

A collection of more than two dozen nursery rhymes in Spanish, from Spain and Latin America, with English translations

"Deeply rhythmic verses, compelling rhyme schemes, and words that 'play trippingly on the tongue' characterize every verse. Schertle's excellent English adaptations are not literal translations but poetic re-creations. They retain the rhythm, meter, and general meaning of the originals. . . . Escrivá's watercolor and colored-pencil illustrations use brilliant hues and detail to reconstruct a young child's world." SLJ

Polacco, Patricia
Babushka's Mother Goose. Philomel Bks. 1995 64p il $18.99; pa $6.99   **398.8**
1. Nursery rhymes
ISBN 0-399-22747-4; 0-698-11860-X (pa)
LC 94-32332

"The collection includes original rhymes written by Polacco as well as Ukrainian folktales and retellings from Mother Goose and Aesop that Polacco heard as a child from her own Babushka. The distinctive and humorous folk-art illustrations and delightful verses and stories make this book a joy to share with children." Horn Book Guide

The **Real** Mother Goose; illustrated by Blanche Fisher Wright. Checkerboard Press 1987 c1944 128p il   **398.8**
1. Nursery rhymes
LC 87-13778

Available Scholastic edition $9.95 (ISBN 0-590-22517-0)

First published 1916 by Rand McNally

A comprehensive collection of over three-hundred traditional nursery rhymes

Sierra, Judy
Schoolyard rhymes; kids' own rhymes for rope skipping, hand clapping, ball bouncing, and just plain fun; illustrated by Melissa Sweet. 1st ed. Knopf 2005 31p il $15.95; lib bdg $17.89 (k-3)   **398.8**
1. Singing games 2. Jump rope rhymes
ISBN 0-375-82516-9; 0-375-92516-3 (lib bdg)
LC 2004-4273

"Sierra has selected 50 traditional playground chants and rhymes for inclusion in this illustrated collection. . . . Sweet's comical, mixed-media art adds to the wackiness of the rhymes, with jump ropes commanding a prominent position." Booklist

Sylvia Long's Mother Goose. Chronicle Bks. 1999 109p il $22.95   **398.8**
1. Nursery rhymes
ISBN 0-8118-2088-2   LC 98-52311

"Human beings are replaced by animals, reptiles, and insects, all elegantly dressed, in this exuberant nursery-rhyme collection, which includes 82 familiar and less familiar verses." SLJ

Taback, Simms
This is the house that Jack built. Putnam 2002 unp il $15.99 (k-3)   **398.8**
1. Nursery rhymes
ISBN 0-399-23488-8   LC 00-28057

The cumulative nursery rhyme about the chain of events that started when Jack built a house

"Taback's version of the age-old cumulative rhyme is an explosion of color, energy, zaniness, and pore-over-able detail." Horn Book

This little piggy; lap songs, finger plays, clapping rhymes, and pantomime rhymes; edited by Jane Yolen; illustrated by Will Hillenbrand; musical arrangements by Adam Stemple. Candlewick Press 2006 c2005 80p il $19.99 **398.8**
1. Nursery rhymes 2. Finger play 3. Songs
ISBN 0-7636-1348-7

An "anthology of approximately 60 lap rhymes, songs, clapping rhymes, and finger and foot rhymes, all presented with explanations and simple instructions for parents to play with their babies and toddlers. . . . Hillenbrand has framed the rhymes with lovely mixed-media pictures in an array of sherbet pastel colors with happy piggy families acting out the rhymes. . . . A delightful accompanying CD includes 13 songs from the text, beautifully done with vivacious accompaniment. The result is a perfect book for one-on-one sharing." SLJ

Tomie dePaola's Mother Goose. Putnam 1985 127p il $24.99 **398.8**
1. Nursery rhymes
ISBN 0-399-21258-2 LC 84-26314

This "is a large, ample, unfussy edition of every child's first staple of literature. . . . The neat, flat illustrations are darkly outlined and colored generally in the illustrator's favorite palette of clear pinks, blues, and violets and surrounded with a lot of white space. Each verse is pictured in a simple and unmistakable interpretation. . . . A perfectly basic and lovely Mother Goose, lavish yet simple, and a splendid beginning for the youngest listener." Horn Book

Tortillitas para mamá and other nursery rhymes; Spanish and English; selected and translated by Margot C. Griego [et al.]; illustrated by Barbara Cooney. Holt & Co. 1981 unp il pa $5.95 hardcover o.p. **398.8**
1. Nursery rhymes 2. Folklore—Latin America 3. Bilingual books—English-Spanish
ISBN 0-8050-0317-7 (pa) LC 81-4823

A bilingual collection of 13 popular Latin American nursery rhymes

The purpose of this book "is to preserve a unique aspect of Hispanic culture which deserves to be passed down to all children. . . . The illustrations are strikingly beautiful, capturing the rich color and texture of some parts of South America. . . . [But their] homogenized view of Latin Americans can easily lead to the perpetuation of some familiar stereotypes." Interracial Books Child Bull

Will Moses Mother Goose. Philomel Bks. 2003 61p il $17.99 **398.8**
1. Nursery rhymes
ISBN 0-399-23744-5 LC 2003-731

Folk art paintings accompany this compilation of over sixty of the best-loved Mother Goose rhymes

"In a marvelous match of style and content Moses's . . . sprightly folk-art oil paintings make this a 'must have' Mother Goose volume. The book's tempo is set from the first page, which intersperses thumbnail vignettes with individual rhymes. . . . A turn of the page then blends the vignettes into a full-bleed panorama of busy village life." Publ Wkly

Wilner, Isabel
The baby's game book; pictures by Sam Williams. Greenwillow Bks. 2000 47p il $15.95 **398.8**
1. Games 2. Finger play 3. Nursery rhymes
ISBN 0-688-15916-8 LC 98-22120

Rhymes, illustrations, and instructions present a variety of simple games to play with babies, including foot tapping, knee rides, finger play, peek-a-boo, and tickle games

"Simple instructions for the movements accompany the rhymes; gentle pencil and watercolor illustrations depict adult and child at play as well as more whimsical scenes of animals or countryside." Horn Book

Winter, Jeanette
The house that Jack built. Dial Bks. for Young Readers 2000 unp il $13.99 **398.8**
1. Nursery rhymes
ISBN 0-8037-2524-8 LC 99-36344

Simple rebus illustrations are used to present the familiar cumulative nursery rhyme about the antics that go on in the house built by an unsuspecting Jack

"Readers can predict who will enter the story next by watching for visual clues. The small trim size of the book and the clear, vibrant colors and simple shapes of the artwork are appealing." Horn Book Guide

Zemach, Margot
Some from the moon, some from the sun; poems and songs for everyone. Farrar, Straus & Giroux 2001 unp il $17 (k-2) **398.8**
1. Nursery rhymes
ISBN 0-374-39960-3 LC 00-67695

An illustrated collection of traditional poems and songs, including "This Little Pig Went to Market," "Brave News is Come to Town," and "Bingo"

"Zemach's imaginative ink-and-watercolor illustrations are fresh, exuberant, and witty. . . . An appended album of drawings, autobiographical notes, and family photos make this book an especially lovely tribute as well as an invitation to new generations to discover Zemach's truly spectacular talent." Booklist

Includes bibliographical references

398.9 Proverbs

The **Night** has ears; African proverbs; selected and illustrated by Ashley Bryan. Atheneum Bks. for Young Readers 1999 unp il $16 (k-3) **398.9**
1. Proverbs 2. Folklore—Africa
ISBN 0-689-82427-0 LC 98-48772

"A Jean Karl book"

A collection of twenty-six proverbs, some serious and some humorous, from a variety of African tribes

"Illustrated in Bryan's distinctive multishape, multicolor style, the tempera-and-gouache art resembles stained glass. . . . A worthy supplement to cultural studies, this will also inspire students to write and illustrate their own proverbs." Booklist

400 LANGUAGE

411 Writing systems

Jeffrey, Laura S.
All about Braille; reading by touch. Enslow Publishers 2004 48p il (Transportation & communication series) lib bdg $23.93 (2-4)
411

1. Blind—Books and reading
ISBN 0-7660-2184-X   LC 2003-17617
Contents: A girl named Helen; Finger reading; Changing a secret code; Communicating and getting around; From teachers to musicians; Today and tomorrow
This offers a brief history of braille, describes the braille alphabet and how it is used for communication for the blind.
Includes glossary and bibliographical references

413 Dictionaries

Park, Linda Sue
Mung-mung! a foldout book of animal sounds; illustrated by Diane Bigda. Charlesbridge 2004 unp il $9.95 (k-2)   **413**

1. Polyglot materials 2. Vocabulary
ISBN 1-57091-486-9   LC 2003-3765
"A multilingual guessing game for the youngest children. Each spread begins with the question, 'What kind of animal says.' and features a variety of sounds in playful handwritten typefaces. Opening a flap reveals the answer. Several languages from Europe, Asia, and the Middle East are included, as well as the sound in English to tip off youngsters. Bigda's cotton-candy-colored gouache artwork displays a lightness of line and a jazzy, freeform feel that blends well with the simple fare." SLJ

Yum! Yuck! a foldout book of people sounds from around the world; [by] Linda Sue Park, Julia Durango; illustrated by Sue Rama. Charlesbridge 2005 unp il $9.95 (k-2)   **413**

1. Polyglot materials 2. Vocabulary
ISBN 1-57091-659-4   LC 2004-18955
Presenting sounds that people make to utter or cry out abruptly in various languages to express such emotion as distaste, excitement, and surprise
"This original offering is a delightful addition to the canon of multicultural picture books and a fun read-aloud guessing game." SLJ

Stojic, Manya
Hello world! greetings in 42 languages around the globe! Scholastic 2002 38p il $14.95 (k-2)
413

1. Polyglot materials 2. Vocabulary
ISBN 0-439-36202-4   LC 2001-43615
"Cartwheel books"
Children from around the world say "hello" in forty-two languages, from Amharic to Zulu
"Greetings appear with a bold nearly full-page acrylic painting of a child. . . . This deceivingly simple book encourages interest in and awareness of other languages." SLJ

419 Verbal language not spoken and written

Ault, Kelly
Let's sign! every baby's guide to communicating with grownups; written by Kelly Ault; illustrated by Leo Landry. Houghton Mifflin Co. 2005 77p il $17 (k-1)   **419**

1. Sign language
ISBN 0-618-50774-4
"After a brief and informative introduction that details the benefits of using sign language with babies, Ault presents three simple stories: Mealtime, Playtime, and Bedtime. . . . Landry's pencil-and-watercolor illustrations are child-friendly, and his depictions of the signs are both appealing and informative. . . . The signs are well chosen to reflect a child's world." SLJ

Baker, Pamela J.
My first book of sign; illustrations by Patricia Bellan Gillen. Gallaudet Univ. Press 1986 76p il $11.96 (k-3)   **419**

1. Sign language
ISBN 0-930323-20-3   LC 86-14937
"A Kendall Green publication"
Pictures of children demonstrate the forming in sign language of 150 basic alphabetically arranged words, accompanied by illustrations of the words themselves. Includes a discussion of fingerspelling and general rules for signing
"Looking like an ABC book, this is both appealing and useful. . . . Illustrations are brightly colored and have an even mixture of boys and girls of various racial backgrounds, some with hearing aids, some without." SLJ

Heller, Lora
Sign language for kids; a fun & easy guide to American sign language; [by] Lora Heller. Sterling 2004 95p il $14.95 (3-6)   **419**

1. Sign language
ISBN 1-4027-0672-3   LC 2003-19011
Color photos illustrate sign language for numbers, letters, colors, feelings, animals, and clothes
"Clear color photos and simple text combine to form an excellent introduction to American Sign Language (ASL)." SLJ

Lowenstein, Felicia
All about sign language; talking with your hands. Enslow Publishers 2004 48p il (Transportation & communication series) lib bdg $23.93 (2-4)   **419**

1. Sign language
ISBN 0-7660-2028-2   LC 2003-26608
Contents: The unspoken language; Signs of the times; The history of sign language; People who sign; Jobs with sign language; The future of sign language

Lowenstein, Felicia—*Continued*

This discusses "how sign language came about, the jobs where it is useful to know sign language, and people who are important to sign language. Also [includes] the manual alphabet." Publisher's note

Includes glossary and bibliographical references

Rankin, Laura

The handmade alphabet. Dial Bks. 1991 unp il $16.99; pa $5.99 (k-3) **419**

1. Sign language 2. Alphabet

ISBN 0-8037-0974-9; 0-14-055876-4 (pa)

LC 90-24593

Presents the handshape for each letter of the American manual alphabet accompanied by an object whose name begins with that letter

"This [is] an excellent introduction to American sign, as well as an engaging ABC book. The art work is multiethnic, visually appealing, anatomically correct, and full of life. Clever use of props, light, and reflections add to the enjoyment." SLJ

422 Etymology of standard English

Baker, Rosalie F.

In a word; 750 words and their fascinating stories and origins; by Rosalie Baker; illustrated by Tom Lopes. 1st American ed. Cobblestone Pub 2003 221p il $17.95 (5 and up) **422**

1. English language—Etymology

ISBN 0-8126-2710-5

LC 2003-25582

Contents: Cultural creations; Worldly words & power people; Math magic & science synergy; Religious rituals, fabulous folklore, & marvelous myths; Exceptional expressions; Clothing collection; Glorious gizmos & great grub; Spectacular sports; Joyful journeys; Natural necessities; Awesome archaeology; Political powerhouse; Military madness; Tantalizing tidbits; Fickle finances; Fantastic foreigners

"The entries in this book discuss the meanings and derivations of 750 words and phrases. . . . While exploring word origins, Baker also touches on interesting facets of European history and Greek mythology. The jaunty illustrations are reproduced in black and shades of gray. . . . This informative book fosters an appreciation for the richness of the English language." Booklist

423 Dictionaries of standard English

The **American** Heritage Children's Dictionary; by the editors of the American Heritage dictionaries. updated ed. Houghton Mifflin 2004 c2003 856p il map $17.95 (3-6) **423**

1. English language—Dictionaries

ISBN 0-618-28002-2

First published 1986

An illustrated reference book including an A-Z vocabulary listing, a thesaurus, and special sections on synonyms, word histories, vocabulary builders, and phonics

The **American** Heritage picture dictionary; by the editors of the American Heritage Dictionaries. Houghton Mifflin 2003 138p il $14.95 (k-1) **423**

1. Picture dictionaries 2. English language—Dictionaries

ISBN 0-618-28004-9

LC 2003-270591

A dictionary for preschool and early elementary grades, with each word defined by a sentence using the word to describe the object or activity portrayed in the accompanying illustration.

Bollard, John K.

Scholastic children's thesaurus; illustrated by Mike Reed. Scholastic Ref. 1998 256p il $15.95 (4 and up) **423**

1. English language—Synonyms and antonyms

ISBN 0-590-96785-1

LC 97-25049

This work contains more than 500 headwords and 2,500 synonyms. Each entry includes part of speech, a definition, and sample sentences. Information boxes and full-color illustrations accompany the text

The **Cat** in the Hat beginner book dictionary; by the Cat himself and P. D. Eastman. Beginner Bks. 1964 133p il $14.95 (k-3) **423**

1. Picture dictionaries 2. English language—Dictionaries

ISBN 0-394-81009-0

Also available Spanish-English edition

"This alphabetically arranged dictionary, illustrated with rollicking funny drawings, explains word meanings with sentences and pictures. It intends to help preschoolers 'recognize, remember, and really enjoy a basic vocabulary of 1,350 words.' Despite its age, this book will still appeal to young children." Peterson. Ref Books for Child. 4th edition

Delahunty, Andrew

Barron's first thesaurus; compiled by Andrew Delahunty; illustrated by Steve Cox. Barron's Educational Series 2005 il pa $12.95 (1-5) **423**

1. English language—Synonyms and antonyms

ISBN 0-7641-3159-1

This "volume presents more than 100 headwords—one headword to a page—then provides a short definition that includes synonyms an example sentence, a separate list of synonyms, and where appropriate, an antonym. Young readers will find a total of more than 1,000 synonyms." Publisher's note

An "excellent, easy-to-use resource. . . . The relevant, color cartoon illustrations are eye-catching." SLJ

DK illustrated Oxford dictionary. rev ed. Dorling Kindersley; Oxford University Press 2003 1008p il map $50 (5 and up) **423**

1. Picture dictionaries 2. English language—Dictionaries

ISBN 0-7894-9359-4

LC 2003-276099

First published 1998

DK illustrated Oxford dictionary—*Continued*

Over 4,500 full-color images accompany the 187,000 definitions and entries covering general English vocabulary from around the world. Grammar, style, and usage notes are provided. New words and phrases as well as specialized, technical, and rare words are covered

DK Merriam-Webster children's dictionary. rev ed. Dorling Kindersley 2005 911p il map $19.99 (3-6)   **423**
1. English language—Dictionaries
ISBN 0-7566-1143-1
First published 2000
Presents definitions for over 32,000 entries and includes some 3,000 illustrations interspersed throughout the text

The **Harcourt** Brace student thesaurus. 2nd ed. Harcourt Brace & Co. 1994 312p il $18 (4 and up)   **423**
1. English language—Synonyms and antonyms
ISBN 0-15-200186-7   LC 94-15603
Replaces The HBJ student thesaurus, published 1991
Editor, Christopher Morris
"The 800 main entries are all given part-of-speech, one-line definitions, and four to six synonyms, each of which is used in a sentence. Full-color illustrations in a variety of cartoon styles appear with about 150 of the entries." SLJ

Hellweg, Paul
The American Heritage children's thesaurus; by Paul Hellweg with the editors of American Heritage dictionaries. Houghton Mifflin 2006 $17.95 (4-6)   **423**
1. English language—Synonyms and antonyms
ISBN 0-618-70166-4
First published 1997
Presents over than 4,000 alphabetically arranged words with several synoyms and an illustrative sentence for each

Macmillan dictionary for children; Robert B. Costello, editor in chief. 4th rev ed. Simon & Schuster Books for Young Readers 2001 32, 880p il map $17.95 (4-6)   **423**
1. English language—Dictionaries
ISBN 0-689-84323-2   LC 2001-31084
First published 1975
"Approximately 35,000 entries provide easy-to-understand definitions along with pronunciation guides, syllable division, parts of speech, and plural forms. Some entries also contain verb forms, example sentences, homophones, synonyms, and photographs or illustrations. . . . After the dictionary portion of the work, students will find a valuable reference section. . . . This dictionary is highly recommended for all juvenile reference collections." Amer Ref Books Annu, 2002

Macmillan first dictionary; Judith S. Levey, editor in chief. Macmillan 1990 402p il $16.95 (1-3)   **423**
1. English language—Dictionaries
ISBN 0-02-761731-9   LC 90-6062

Replaces Macmillan very first dictionary, published 1983
"This work focuses on the most common words in the English language. An introduction outlines the development of words and explains how to use a dictionary. Simple definitions for each of the 2,200 words are often supported by illustrative sentences. Nearly 550 pictures in color explain concepts and abstract words." Nichols. Guide to Ref Books for Sch Media Cent. 4th edition

The **McGraw-Hill** children's dictionary; by the Wordsmyth Collaboratory. McGraw-Hill Children's Pub. 2003 various paging il (Wordsmyth reference series) $24.95 (4 and up)   **423**
1. English language—Dictionaries
ISBN 1-57768-298-X   LC 2002-18796
A dictionary with word histories, synonyms, illustrations, and spelling, grammar, and usage features
"The more than 30,000 entries are easy to read, with definitions arranged in three columns. 'Word History,' 'Homophone Note,' and 'Synonyms' boxes give extra information about some words. . . . This attractive dictionary is a fine work." Booklist

The **McGraw-Hill** children's thesaurus; by the Wordsmyth Collaboratory. McGraw-Hill Children's Pub. 2003 various paging il (Wordsmyth reference series) $19.95 (4 and up)   **423**
1. English language—Synonyms and antonyms
ISBN 1-57768-296-3   LC 2002-18797
Presents an alphabetical list of more than 3000 entries, with explanations of the different meanings of each headword and its synonyms
This is "a valuable addition to the upper elementary classroom, library, or any place where children write or do homework." Am Ref Books Annu, 2003

Merriam-Webster's elementary dictionary. Merriam-Webster 1994 20a, 587p il $15.95 (4-6)   **423**
1. English language—Dictionaries
ISBN 0-87779-575-4   LC 93-41502
Replaces Webster's elementary dictionary, published 1986
This illustrated dictionary for grades four to six includes some 32,000 entries; a color-keyed guide to using the dictionary; word history and synonym paragraphs; abbreviations; signs and symbols; U.S. presidents and vice-presidents; and geographical names

Merriam-Webster's intermediate dictionary. Merriam-Webster 2004 18a, 1005p il $17.95 (5 and up)   **423**
1. English language—Dictionaries
ISBN 0-87779-579-7   LC 2004-45792
First published 1994 as a replacement for Webster's intermediate dictionary (1986)
This dictionary includes over 70,000 words and more than 1,000 illustrations, providing definitions, pronunciation, etymology, part of speech designation, and other appropriate information.

Merriam-Webster's primary dictionary; with illustrations by Ruth Heller. Merriam-Webster 2005 436p il $16.95 (k-3) **423**
1. English language—Dictionaries
ISBN 0-87779-174-0

"A beginner's dictionary. . . . Nearly 1,000 entries include definitions, example sentences, and word histories. Introduces basic dictionary skills such as alphabetization, spelling, pronunciations, use of synonyms and antonyms, and using words in context. [Includes] jokes, poems, and fun facts." Publisher's note

This work "displays an extraordinary level of care in its presentation. . . . A gift to budding wordsmiths." SLJ

Roget's children's thesaurus. Scott, Foresman 2000 240p il $16 (3-5) **423**
1. English language—Synonyms and antonyms
ISBN 0-673-65137-1

First published 1977 with title: in other words

Under alphabetically arranged entries are more than a thousand words with illustrative sentences to help the middle grader in choosing the exact word from several synonyms

Roget's student thesaurus. Scott, Foresman/Addison Wesley 2000 536p il $17 (5 and up) **423**
1. English language—Synonyms and antonyms
ISBN 0-673-65138-X

First published 1991

This thesaurus features illustrative sentences, phrases from other cultures, idioms, and exercises for improving writing skills

Scholastic children's dictionary. new and updated. Scholastic Ref. 2002 648p il map $17.95 (3-5) **423**
1. English language—Dictionaries
ISBN 0-439-36563-5 LC 2001-42844

First published 1996

A dictionary that includes pronunciations, definitions, parts of speech, sample sentences, etymologies, synonyms, cross-references, and illustrations. The reference section includes the Braille and American sign language alphabets, a map of the world and of the U.S., flags of the world, and facts about the 50 states and U.S. presidents

Scholastic first dictionary; Judith S. Levey, editor in chief. Scholastic Ref. 1998 224p il $14.95 (1-3) **423**
1. English language—Dictionaries
ISBN 0-590-96786-X LC 97-25050

Entries include pronunciations, simple definitions, sentences, and plurals and other forms of the words

"With a crisp layout, bright colors, and a large typeface, this dictionary is appealing and accessible. The 1500 main entries are well suited to use by young readers and writers. There are at least two full-color photographs on each page." SLJ

Terban, Marvin
Mad as a wet hen! and other funny idioms; illustrated by Giulio Maestro. Clarion Bks. 1987 64p il pa $7.95 hardcover o.p. (3-5) **423**
1. English language—Idioms 2. English language—Terms and phrases
ISBN 0-89919-479-6 LC 86-17575

Illustrates and explains over 100 common English idioms, in categories including animals, body parts, and colors

"Maestro's two-color cartoonlike illustrations are amusing and informative themselves, providing visual clues that support the textual explanations. . . . Although some of the expressions included are dated, the alphabetical index enables teachers and librarians to pick and choose. This book might be particularly beneficial in schools having a large ESL program, especially for older, more advanced students." SLJ

Scholastic dictionary of idioms. Scholastic 1996 245p il pa $8.95 hardcover o.p. (4 and up) **423**
1. English language—Idioms
ISBN 0-590-38157-1 (pa) LC 95-16593

"Terban explains the meanings and origins (if known) of more than 600 idioms and proverbs. . . . Each page includes one lightly comical line drawing of a child expressing feelings such as quizzical, annoyed, amused, or distressed. Not only is this a good resource for teachers who discuss idioms in the classroom but it also has some appeal for browsers." Booklist

Webster's New World children's dictionary; editor in chief, Michael Agnes. 2nd ed. Macmillan 1999 16, 928p il map $17.95 (3-5) **423**
1. English language—Dictionaries
ISBN 0-02-862766-0 LC 99-21174

Also available with CD-ROM $24.95 (ISBN 0-02-863125-0)

First published 1991

This dictionary contains approximately 33,000 entries and 750 illustrations. "Bright colors highlight boxes providing synonyms, word histories, spelling tips, and similar features. . . . Material at the back of the book includes a thesaurus, a basic atlas, and information about American history, presidents, states, and weights and measures." Booklist

427 English language variations

O'Reilly, Gillian
Slangalicious; where we got that crazy lingo; text by Gillian O'Reilly; illustrations by Krista Johnson. Annick Press 2004 84p il $24.95; pa $12.95 (4 and up) **427**
1. English language—Slang 2. English language—Etymology
ISBN 1-55037-765-5; 1-55037-764-7 (pa)

"This volume explores the origins and meanings of slang words by tracing the efforts of a fictional student doing an assignment. . . . After a general introduction to slang, succeeding chapters explore the colorful terminology used in the food industry, in different types of work,

O'Reilly, Gillian—*Continued*

and in the world of sports. Also discussed are words used for money, musical terms, criminal jargon, and slang used during wartime and in different countries. . . . This is a clever way for younger students to learn about the topic. . . . Colorful, amusing illustrations appear throughout." SLJ

Includes bibliographical references

428 Standard English usage

Cleary, Brian P.

Hairy, scary, ordinary; what is an adjective? illustrated by Jenya Prosmitsky. Carolrhoda Bks. 2000 32p il (Words are categorical) $12.95; pa $5.95 (2-4)   **428**

1. English language—Grammar
ISBN 1-57505-401-9; 1-57505-419-1 (pa)
LC 98-32132

"Descriptive words of many kinds are presented in bouncy, rhyming text. . . . The adjectives are colorfully highlighted and readers will see their function demonstrated in a wide variety of contexts. Little round cats and quirky humans, both with fat noses and wide eyes, humorously illustrate the meanings." SLJ

How much can a bare bear bear? what are homonyms and homophones? by Brian P. Cleary; illustrated by Brian Gable. Millbrook Press 2005 unp il (Words are categorical) lib bdg $15.95 (2-4)   **428**

1. English language—Homonyms
ISBN 1-57505-824-3   LC 2004031106

"Through rhyming wordplay, Cleary explains two parts of speech that are often difficult to understand. . . . Gable took ample advantage of the pairings to create zany cartoons that provide visual clues for readers. The grouping of each set of homophones and homonyms by color is also a helpful tool." SLJ

I and you and don't forget who; what is a pronoun? illustrated by Brian Gable. Carolrhoda Books 2004 unp il (Words are categorical) lib bdg $14.95 (2-4)   **428**

1. English language—Grammar
ISBN 1-57505-596-1   LC 2003-1712

Rhyming text and illustrations of comical cats present numerous examples of pronouns and their functions, from "he" and "she" to "anyone," "neither," and "which."

The "text presents the major uses of pronouns with precision, brevity, and wit. The cartoon-style ink drawings brim with irrepressible humor, while the bold use of color in the artwork adds to the high-spirited look of the pages." Booklist

Heller, Ruth

Behind the mask; a book about prepositions; written and illustrated by Ruth Heller. Grosset & Dunlap 1995 unp il $17.99; pa $6.99 (k-2)   **428**

1. English language—Grammar
ISBN 0-448-41123-7; 0-698-11698-4 (pa)
LC 95-9535

Explores through rhyming text the subject of prepositions and how they're used

"Large, colorful drawings illustrate the words imaginatively." Booklist

A cache of jewels and other collective nouns; written and illustrated by Ruth Heller. Grosset & Dunlap 1987 unp il $17.99; pa $6.99 (k-2)   **428**

1. English language—Grammar
ISBN 0-448-19211-X; 0-698-11354-3 (pa)
LC 87-80254

"In light verse and brightly colored pictures, Heller provides an introduction to a specialized part of speech, the collective noun. She lists and depicts more than 25, including such familiar terms as 'batch of bread' and 'bunch of bananas,' as well as more unusual phrases. . . . The concept will stimulate the curiosity and imaginations of children with an ear for language. The illustrations, containing large, bold objects in simple yet striking compositions, ensure a visually inspiring exploration as well." Publ Wkly

Fantastic! wow! and unreal! a book about interjections and conjunctions; written and illustrated by Ruth Heller. Grosset & Dunlap 1998 unp il lib bdg $17.99; pa $6.99 (k-2)   **428**

1. English language—Grammar
ISBN 0-448-41862-2; 0-698-11875-8 (pa)
LC 98-36361

Rhyming text and illustrations introduce and explain various interjections and conjunctions, including "awesome," "alas," and "yet."

Kites sail high: a book about verbs; written and illustrated by Ruth Heller. Grosset & Dunlap 1988 unp il $17.99; pa $6.99 (k-2)   **428**

1. English language—Grammar
ISBN 0-448-10480-6; 0-698-11389-6 (pa)
LC 87-82718

This "book explicates and celebrates verbs of all kinds, in ebullient verses which themselves sail and soar. . . . The verses are accompanied by bold, gaily colored graphics that are especially striking for their skillful use of pattern and design." Publ Wkly

Many luscious lollipops: a book about adjectives; written and illustrated by Ruth Heller. Grosset & Dunlap 1989 unp il lib bdg $17.99; pa $6.99 (k-2)   **428**

1. English language—Grammar
ISBN 0-448-03151-5 (lib bdg); 0-698-11641-0 (pa)
LC 88-83045

"The text begins: 'An adjective's terrific/when you want to be specific/It easily identifies/by number, color or by size/TWELVE LARGE, BLUE, GORGEOUS butterflies.' And there they are, blue and yellow, filling a double-page spread. . . . There is great diversity and technical brilliance in the art work, and the text has rhyme, rhythm, humor, and a very clear presentation of the concepts of different kinds of adjectives and what they do." Bull Cent Child Books

Heller, Ruth—*Continued*
Merry-go-round; a book about nouns; written and illustrated by Ruth Heller. Grosset & Dunlap 1990 unp il $17.99; pa $6.99 (k-2) **428**
  1. English language—Grammar
  ISBN 0-448-40085-5; 0-698-11642-9 (pa)
                    LC 90-80645
Rhyming text and illustrations present explanations of various types of nouns and rules for their usage
"While the text will be helpful to children struggling with noun usage, the large, bountiful illustrations will appeal to everyone." Horn Book Guide

Mine, all mine; a book about pronouns; written and illustrated by Ruth Heller. Grosset & Dunlap 1997 unp il $17.99; pa $6.99 (k-2) **428**
  1. English language—Grammar
  ISBN 0-448-41606-9; 0-698-11797-2 (pa)
                    LC 97-10051
Introduces various types of pronouns, explains how and when to use them, and provides whimsical glimpses of what our language would be without them
"Heller has taken a part of speech and made its function perfectly and entertainingly clear. . . . The stylishly drawn, brilliantly colored, double-paged illustrations grab readers and don't let go. The exceptionally fluent, rhythmic text is printed in an unobtrusive font with pronouns highlighted in bright blue." SLJ

Up, up and away; a book about adverbs; written and illustrated by Ruth Heller. Grosset & Dunlap 1991 unp il $17.99; pa $6.99 (k-2) **428**
  1. English language—Grammar
  ISBN 0-448-40249-1; 0-698-11663-1 (pa)
                    LC 91-70668
"Here the author explains concisely how adverbs answer precisely the questions of How? How often? When? and Where? The adverbs, in capital letters, stand out boldly and cannot be missed. . . . In the large, appealing illustrations, her penguins stand proudly, her pandas eat daintily, and her cat stares piercingly. . . . The cheerful volume . . . offers a clever introduction to kinds of words." Booklist

Leedy, Loreen
There's a frog in my throat; 440 animal sayings a little bird told me; written by Loreen Leedy & Pat Street; illustrated by Loreen Leedy. Holiday House 2003 48p il $16.95 (2-5) **428**
  1. English language—Terms and phrases 2. Animals—Folklore
  ISBN 0-8234-1774-3   LC 2002-68920
"The sayings are loosely grouped by types of animals—domestic, barnyard, winged, etc.—and each adage is accompanied by a short definition. For example, 'It's raining cats and dogs. *It's raining hard.*' . . . Children will pore over the pages. The collaboration of text and art makes the volume lively and humorous." SLJ

Roy, Jennifer Rozines
You can write using good grammar; [by] Jennifer Rozines Roy. Enslow 2004 64p il (You can write) lib bdg $22.60 (4-6) **428**
  1. English language—Grammar
  ISBN 0-7660-2084-3   LC 2002-156035

Contents: Why learn grammar?; Parts of speech; Sentences and paragraphs; Using parts of speech; Punctuation, proofreading, and other word forms; Common grammar goofs
This "discusses parts of speech, punctuation, and proofreading. A list of 'Common Grammar Goofs' is appended. . . . Students will find [this book] useful." Horn Book Guide
Includes glossary and bibliographical references

Terban, Marvin
Building your vocabulary. Scholastic Ref. 2002 188p il (Scholastic guides) $12.95; lib bdg $16.95; pa $7.95 (4 and up) **428**
  1. Vocabulary
  ISBN 0-439-28561-5; 0-439-55498-5 (lib bdg); 0-439-28562-3 (pa)   LC 2001-20838
"Chapters are devoted to prefixes, roots, and suffixes; word families; homonyms and homographs; understanding the meaning of words using context clues; how to use a dictionary and thesaurus; and how to increase one's vocabulary using techniques such as games. . . . Explanations and examples are clear and often amusing. . . . This easy-to-read, enjoyable guide says a great deal about language." SLJ

Punctuation power! Scholastic 2000 96p il (Scholastic guides) $12.95 (4 and up) **428**
  1. Punctuation
  ISBN 0-590-38673-5   LC 99-19179
Explains the purpose and importance of punctuation and how it is used, covering apostrophes, colons, commas, exclamation points, hyphens, parentheses, slashes, and more
"Children will find this book helpful as they try to craft writing assignments. The examples and the pictures help keep the tone light." SLJ

Scholastic dictionary of spelling; over 15,000 words. Scholastic Ref. 1998 223p il $15.95; pa $8.95 (4 and up) **428**
  1. Spellers
  ISBN 0-590-30697-9; 0-439-14496-5 (pa)
                    LC 97-18020
The words in this speller are "arranged alphabetically (i.e., ladies comes before lady) broken into syllables with the accented syllables in boldface, on attractively laid-out pages, with occasional cartoonish illustrations. Homophones include pronunciation help, and a parenthetical sentence illustrates proper use. The first 26 pages are a treasure trove of helpful hints. . . . The book concludes with the 'Misspeller's Dictionary,' 600 words with tricky beginnngs listed in matched pairs of the common misspelling and the correct one." Book Rep

463 Dictionaries of standard Spanish

Elya, Susan Middleton
Say hola to Spanish, otra vez; illustrated by Loretta Lopez. Lee & Low Bks. 1997 unp il $15.95 (1-4) **463**
  1. Spanish language
  ISBN 1-880000-59-8   LC 97-6851

Elya, Susan Middleton—*Continued*

Also available: Say hola to Spanish $15.95 (ISBN 1-880000-29-6); pa $6.95 (ISBN 1-880000-64-4) and Say hola to Spanish at the circus $15.95 (ISBN 1-880000-92-X)

"A rhyming text and bright cartoon illustrations introduce 72 Spanish words." SLJ

"The playful design scatters the text throughout Lopez's gouache and colored-pencil two-page spreads; the most effective scenes group the words thematically. . . . Lopez provides images bound to aid early elementary students' retention and recall of these Spanish words." Publ Wkly

Includes glossary

492.4   Hebrew language

Groner, Judyth Saypol

My first Hebrew word book; [by Judye Groner and Madeline Wikler]; pictures by Pepi Marzel. Kar-Ben Pub 2005 32p il lib bdg $17.95 (k-2)
492.4

1. Hebrew language
ISBN 1-58013-126-3   LC 2004-13504

Contents: Me; My family; House; Kitchen; Bedroom; Bathroom; Living room; School; Playground; Community; People in neighborhood; Food; Meals; Transportation; Zoo; Farm; Beach; Park; Birthday party; Clothing; Weather; Seasons; Synagogue; Holidays; Verbs

"Basic Hebrew words . . . are included. All are written in block letters with English transliteration and translation. Each spread includes a large, detailed illustration with the individual items clearly identified along the bottom. The color cartoon art is cheerful and contemporary. At the back of the book, a word list is organized alphabetically in English and includes the Hebrew words and corresponding page numbers. All in all, this is a wonderful resource." SLJ

493   Non-Semitic Afro-Asiatic languages

Donoughue, Carol

The mystery of the hieroglyphs; the story of the Rosetta stone and the race to decipher Egyptian hieroglyphs. Oxford Univ. Press 1999 48p il lib bdg hardcover o.p.; pa $12.95 (4 and up)
493

1. Rosetta stone   2. Egyptian language
3. Hieroglyphics
ISBN 0-19-521553-2 (lib bdg); 0-19-521850-7 (pa)

This is a history of the discovery and deciphering of the Rosetta stone which led to the understanding of Egyptian hieroglyphics

"What makes this book so involving is that readers must do their own learning, translating, and reading of hieroglyphics. . . . Crisp color photos, reproductions, and sidebars enrich the text. An enticing volume." SLJ

Includes glossary and bibliographical references

Giblin, James

The riddle of the Rosetta Stone; key to ancient Egypt; [by] James Cross Giblin. Crowell 1990 85p il pa $7.99 hardcover o.p. (5 and up)   **493**

1. Rosetta stone   2. Egyptian language
3. Hieroglyphics
ISBN 0-06-446137-8 (pa)   LC 89-29289

Describes how the discovery and deciphering of the Rosetta Stone unlocked the secret of Egyptian hieroglyphics

"Suspense keeps the reader glued to this fine piece of nonfiction as the mystery of hieroglyphs is slowly unraveled. . . . The author has done a masterful job of distilling information, citing the highlights, and fitting it all together in an interesting and enlightening look at a puzzling subject." Horn Book

Includes bibliographical references

495.1   Chinese language

Lee, Huy Voun

1, 2, 3 go! Holt & Co. 2000 unp il $16 (k-3)
495.1

1. Chinese language   2. Counting
ISBN 0-8050-6205-X   LC 99-48326

Parallel title on cover in Chinese characters

An introduction to Chinese writing describing the construction, meaning, and pronunciation of simple characters used for a variety of words and the numbers one through ten

"Lee effectively displays boldly contrasted cut-paper shapes on stark white backgrounds. . . . With masterful simplicity, Lee leads readers to a preliminary appreciation of Chinese culture." Booklist

At the beach; written and illustrated by Huy Voun Lee. Holt & Co. 1994 unp il $16.95; pa $6.95 (k-3)
495.1

1. Chinese language
ISBN 0-8050-2768-8; 0-8050-5822-2 (pa)
LC 93-25462

A mother amuses her young son at the beach by drawing in the sand Chinese characters, many of which resemble the objects they stand for

"The intricate, visually captivating cut-paper collages have borders with sea motifs. Useful for beginning language study and interesting due to its artistic innovation, the book includes a pronunciation guide." Horn Book Guide

Other titles in this series are:
In the leaves (2005)
In the park (1998)
In the snow (1995)

497 North American native languages

Coulter, Laurie

Secrets in stone; all about Maya hieroglyphs; illustrations by Sarah Jane English; historical consultation by Elizabeth Graham and Simon Martin. Little, Brown 2001 48p il $17.95

497

1. Mayan languages 2. Hieroglyphics 3. Mayas—Antiquities

ISBN 0-316-15883-6   LC 00-54963

"Coulter leads readers through historical background on Mexican site discoveries, extant codices, early efforts to make sense of the intricate pictograms, and ongoing problems in translation." Bull Cent Child Books

"Combining historical information with activity-based ideas, this attractive volume may reach a larger audience than the usual history title." SLJ

Includes glossary and bibliographical references

500 SCIENCE

Schwartz, David M.

Q is for quark; a science alphabet book; written by David M. Schwartz; illustrated by Kim Doner. Tricycle Press 2001 64p il $15.95 (4 and up)

500

1. Science 2. Alphabet

ISBN 1-58246-021-3   LC 00-10659

Explains the meaning of scientific terms which begin with the different letters of the alphabet such as atom, black hole, and clone

"The text is filled with readable and clear explanations for some very complex concepts. . . . [Readers] will enjoy browsing through this funny and informative book." SLJ

Swanson, Diane

Nibbling on Einstein's brain; the good, the bad & the bogus in science; illustrated by Warren Clark. Annick Press 2001 104p il $24.95; pa $14.95 (5 and up)

500

1. Science—Methodology

ISBN 1-55037-687-X; 1-55037-686-1 (pa)

The author "discusses topics such as the difference between correlation and cause-and-effect relationships, the importance of asking the right questions about advertisers' claims, and the links between superstition, coincidence, and probability. With a highly readable text and jaunty line illustrations, the book encourages critical thinking and skepticism when evaluating science reporting and media hype." Booklist

Thimmesh, Catherine

The sky's the limit; stories of discovery by women and girls; illustrated by Melissa Sweet. Houghton Mifflin 2002 73p il $16; pa $7.95 (5 and up)

500

1. Science 2. Women scientists

ISBN 0-618-07698-0; 0-618-49489-8 (pa)

LC 2001-39111

"This collection highlights a variety of women discoverers from the well known, including Jane Goodall and Mary Leakey, to budding pioneers, such as eleven-year-old science-lover Katie Murray." Voice Youth Advocates

"The lively design and the mixed-media collage artwork is a creative delight, and the intricate ink-and-watercolor borders, inventive paintings, and childlike pictures will draw readers in. The best thing about the book, however, is Thimmesh's sparkling writing style. . . . Report writers will appreciate this, but the book will also charm browsers." Booklist

Includes bibliographical references

500.5 Space sciences

Space science. Grolier 2004 8v il map set $289 (5 and up)

500.5

1. Space sciences

ISBN 0-7172-5825-4   LC 2003-61836

Contents: v1 How the universe works; v2 Sun and solar system; v3 Earth and Moon; v4 Rocky planets; v5 Gas giants; v6 Journey into space; v7 Shuttle to space station; v8 What satellites see

This set "provides general coverage of astronomy and cosmology, . . . [discusses] the technology and engineering aspects of understanding and exploring space, and [covers] the solar system and its central star. . . . The books all make excellent use of fantastic photographs and drawings. . . . The text is well-written and complete. . . . [This is] a must-have set." Sci Books Films

502.8 Science--Auxiliary techniques and procedures; apparatus, equipment, materials

Kramer, Stephen

Hidden worlds: looking through a scientist's microscope; photographs by Dennis Kunkel. Houghton Mifflin 2001 57p il (Scientists in the field) $16; pa $5.95 (4 and up)

502.8

1. Kunkel, Dennis 2. Microscopes

ISBN 0-618-05546-0; 0-618-35405-0 (pa)

LC 00-58083

This book takes a "look at the work of a microscopist. Kunkel works with microscopes to explore science. . . . This book contains many of his photos, most taken with electron microscopes. . . . Several opening pages, along with the front and back endpapers, are visually dazzling. The heart of the book, though, is what readers learn about how Kunkel produces these images, and to what uses scientists put them. . . . This title offers a wealth of scientific information along with an insightful look at the world of an individual scientist." SLJ

Includes bibliographical references

Simon, Seymour

Out of sight; pictures of hidden worlds. SeaStar Bks. 2000 unp il lib bdg $16.50; pa $6.95 (4 and up) **502.8**

1. Science—Pictorial works 2. Photography—Scientific applications

ISBN 1-58717-012-4 (lib bdg); 1-58717-149-X (pa)

LC 00-25684

Shows pictures of objects which are too small, too far away, or too fast to see without mechanical assistance such as microscopes, telescopes, X-rays, and other techniques

"The text serves primarily as extended captions to the photos, providing information on the ways the pictures were taken and a basic explanation of what the images represent. The large, bright illustrations are beautifully reproduced and present some fascinating views of the world." SLJ

Stewart, Gail

Microscopes; by Gail B. Stewart. KidHaven Press 2003 48p il (Kidhaven science library) lib bdg $23.70 (4-6) **502.8**

1. Microscopes

ISBN 0-7377-0945-6   LC 2002-15269

First published 1992 by Lucent Books

Contents: The first microscopes; Beyond details; New kinds of microscopes; A microscopic future

"A general overview of microscopes from the discovery and use of early lenses to their many uses today. . . . The layout is simple and appealing and includes large, color photographs on nearly every page." SLJ

Includes glossary and bibliographical references

503 Science--Encyclopedias and dictionaries

The **American** Heritage children's science dictionary. Houghton Mifflin 2003 280p il $17.95 (5 and up) **503**

1. Science—Dictionaries

ISBN 0-618-35401-8   LC 2003-10476

"The 2,600 entries were selected to represent different areas of science such as astronomy, biology, and physics as well as areas like weather and computer technology. . . . One nice feature is the 'Did You Know?' boxes that are interspersed throughout the book and contain extra information. . . . School and public libraries that serve upper-elementary and middle-school patrons will find this a useful addition to their reference collections. It is well bound, attractive, and accessible and has the types of definitions a young patron needs." Booklist

The **DK** science encyclopedia. new rev ed. DK Pub. 1998 448p il map $39.99; pa $9.99 (5 and up) **503**

1. Science—Encyclopedias

ISBN 0-7894-2190-9; 0-7894-2871-7 (pa)

LC 97-20881

First published 1993 with title: The Dorling Kindersley science encyclopedia

"Entries are grouped into 12 topical sections ('Weather,' 'Ecology,' 'Reactions,' etc.). Each one-to-two page article is drizzled with small, clipped color photos and paintings supplemented by boxed capsule biographies, brief side excursions, and see-also references. The book concludes with a relatively dense 'Fact Finder Section' into which are gathered charts, statistics, and specialized terms." SLJ

Growing up with science. 3rd ed. Marshall Cavendish 2006 17v il set $429.95 (5 and up) **503**

1. Science—Encyclopedias 2. Technology—Encyclopedias

ISBN 0-7614-7505-2   LC 2004049962

First published 1987

This set "explains many of the most complicated aspects of science and technology, such as how laser disks and computers work, in clear and precise language with the help of beautiful color photographs and drawings. . . . More than 500 articles are arranged in alphabetical order. . . . What is covered is important, current, and well presented." Booklist

The **New** book of popular science. Grolier 2006 6v il set $279 (5 and up) **503**

1. Science—Encyclopedias 2. Technology—Encyclopedias

ISBN 0-7172-1225-4   LC 2005029898

First published 1924 with title: The Book of popular science. Frequently revised

Cotents: v1 Astronomy, space science, mathematics, past and future; v2 Earth sciences, energy, environmental sciences; v3 Chemistry, physics, biology; v4 Plant life, animal life; v5 Mammals, human sciences; v6 Technology

The information in this set is classified under such broad categories as astronomy and space science, computers and mathematics, earth sciences, energy, environmental sciences, physical sciences, general biology, plant life, animal life, mammals, human sciences and technology

Includes bibliographical references

Visual science encyclopedia. Grolier Educ. 2001 12v set $279 (5 and up) **503**

1. Science—Encyclopedias

ISBN 0-7172-5595-6   LC 2001-23704

Contents: v1 Weather; v2 Elements; v3 Rocks, minerals, and soil; v4 Forces; v5 Light and sound; v6 Water; v7 Plants; v8 Electricity and magnetism; v9 Earth and space; v10 Computers and the Internet; v11 Volcano [sic] and earthquakes; v12 Heat and energy

This set defines main terms and concepts in science with over 500 full color illustrations and cross references

"This is a useful resource for students seeking quick definitions and clear illustrations that help explain terms." Booklist

507 Science--Education and related topics

Junior science diagrams on file; [by] the Diagram Group. Facts on File 2003 2v loose-leaf set $330 **507**

1. Science—Study and teaching

ISBN 0-8160-4963-7   LC 2002-45217

Junior science diagrams on file—*Continued*

Also available CD-ROM version

"Facts on File science library"

Contents: v1 The physical world; v2 The natural world

"This three-ring binder set serves as a valuable visual resource to the elementary science curriculum. Vol. 1— *The Physical World* cover topics from air and water, the earth and universe, properties of matter, energy, forces and motion. Vol. 2—*The Natural World* is comprised of structure and functioning of living things, the human body, ecosystems, diversity of life, and reproduction and heredity. . . . Each volume features a glossary of relevant terms, Internet resources, and a full index. All material may be reproduced and used as handouts or as transparencies for instruction." Libr Media Connect

Includes bibliographical references

Kramer, Stephen

How to think like a scientist; answering questions by the scientific method; [by] Stephen P. Kramer; illustrated by Felicia Bond. Crowell 1987 44p il lib bdg $15.89 (3-5) **507**

1. Science—Methodology

ISBN 0-690-04565-4　　　　　　　LC 85-43604

An "exploration of the ways questions are asked and how scientists try to make sure that the questions are answered correctly. Relying on concrete story examples, Kramer shows how observed information can result in different or incorrect conclusions. Examples are also used to explain the principles of the scientific method." Booklist

"This is a pleasant book with an open format; an amusing halftone cartoon on almost every page illustrates the child oriented experiments and supports the light tone of the book." SLJ

507.8　Science--Use of apparatus and equipment in study and teaching

Bazler, Judith A.

More science projects for all students. Facts on File 2002 various paging il (Facts on File science library) loose-leaf $185 **507.8**

1. Science—Experiments 2. Science projects

ISBN 0-8160-4518-6　　　　　　LC 2002-1463

Also available CD-ROM version

Companion volume to Science projects for all students by Marty Berda and Mary Jean Blaisdell, published 1998

"More than 55 large-print experiments are presented in binder format and illustrated with clear, accurate pen-and-ink drawings. . . . Changes in equipment and presentation have been made so that children with learning disabilities or visual or motor impairment can be successful. Areas covered include earth science, weather, space science, life science, and physical science." SLJ

Includes glossary and bibliographical references

Chahrour, Janet

Zap! blink! taste! think! exciting life science for curious minds; illustrated by Abe Gurvin. Barron's Educ. Ser. 2003 211p il $14.95 (5 and up) **507.8**

1. Science—Experiments 2. Science projects

ISBN 0-7641-1912-5　　　　　　LC 2002-28036

Contents: Your senses; Food science; Create your own; Inspections and dissections; Psychology and beliefs

Presents the procedures and concepts involved in twenty-four science experiments that can be done at home with readily available materials, exploring psychology, food chemistry, crime-solving, and horoscopes

"This volume is an excellent book for any elementary school, junior high, or home library. The colorful illustrations, large print, and clear directions make it easy to use and a pleasure to look at. . . . Goofy jokes and inspiring quotes are scattered throughout the book." Sci Books Films

Includes bibliographical references

Cobb, Vicki

Science experiments you can eat; illustrated by David Cain. rev & updated. HarperCollins Pubs. 1994 214p il lib bdg $15.89; pa $5.95 (5 and up) **507.8**

1. Science—Experiments 2. Cooking

ISBN 0-06-023551-9 (lib bdg); 0-06-446002-9 (pa)
　　　　　　　　　　　　　　　LC 93-13679

First published 1972

Experiments with food demonstrate various scientific principles and produce an eatable result. Includes rock candy, grape jelly, cupcakes, and popcorn

Includes glossary

Squirts and spurts; science fun with water; illustrated by Steve Haefele. Millbrook Press 2000 48p il lib bdg $24.90 (3-6) **507.8**

1. Science—Experiments 2. Water

ISBN 0-7613-1572-1　　　　　　LC 00-22113

Explains the physics of water pressure, showing how it makes everyday products such as faucets, spray bottles, and water pistols work. Includes experiments

"The text succeeds in conveying sophisticated concepts through accessible language, and Steve Haefele's drawings of an exuberant, grinning narrator and her robot sidekick clearly illustrate both the broad, abstract concepts and the concrete activity steps." Booklist

You gotta try this! absolutely irresistible science; by Vicki Cobb and Kathy Darling; illustrated by True Kelley. Morrow Junior Bks. 1999 144p il $15.99 (4 and up) **507.8**

1. Science—Experiments 2. Scientific recreations

ISBN 0-688-15740-8　　　　　　LC 98-29556

A collection of science experiments and activities, arranged in such categories as "Physical Attractions," "Curious Chemistry," and "Freaky Fluids"

"True Kelley's line-and-gray-wash illustrations clarify the directions and add their own good-natured visual appeal. A fine addition to science collections." Booklist

Haduch, Bill

Science fair success secrets; how to win prizes, have fun, and think like a scientist; illustrated by Philip Scheuer. Dutton 2002 134p il pa $10.99 (5 and up)   **507.8**

1. Science projects 2. Science—Experiments

ISBN 0-525-46534-0   LC 2002-23536

Explains the scientific method and describes a variety of actual science fair projects in such fields as engineering, botany, behavioral science, and chemistry

"The often jaunty tone of the text and the cartoon-style drawings make this an unusually appealing book on the topic, while the respect for science and the solid presentation make it a highly useful book as well." Booklist

Includes bibliographical references

Hands-on science; [by] John Graham [et al.]; illustrated by David Le Jars. Kingfisher (NY) 2002 160p il pa $10.95 (4-6)   **507.8**

1. Science—Experiments

ISBN 0-7534-5440-8

First published 2001 in the United Kingdom

This includes 150 "experiments about forces and motion, sound and light, electricity and magnets, and matter and materials. . . . The experiments are carefully selected to illustrate basic concepts. . . . Colorful computer-generated illustrations and photographs accompany each observation. . . . These experiments are accessible, easy to perform, and interesting." SLJ

Includes glossary

Hauser, Jill Frankel

Super science concoctions; 50 mysterious mixtures for fabulous fun; illustrations by Michael Kline. Williamson 1997 160p il pa $12.95 (3-5)   **507.8**

1. Science—Experiments 2. Scientific recreations

ISBN 1-885593-02-3   LC 95-47894

"A Williamson kids can! book"

Over 75 science experiments with mixtures that illustrate changes in form and chemical composition

"The sequential logic of the text make[s] this title valuable for teaching basic chemistry principles. Pen-and-ink cartoon illustrations are well placed, informative, and humorous. Safety precautions are emphasized." SLJ

Junior science experiments on file. Facts on File il each volume $185 (3-5)   **507.8**

1. Science—Experiments

Also available CD-ROM version

First published 2004

"Experiments in this loose-leaf collection range from folding a simple mobius strip to creating a gravity gauge. Each experiment is clearly marked with a biker riding up a hill (hard), down a hill (easy), or on a flat surface (intermediate). The print is large and the text is concise, giving readers information on how long the experiment will take, what materials are necessary, safety precautions, clearly written instructions, and questions to consider during observations. . . . Clear line drawings and sample data tables complement the text. A fine collection for young scientists." SLJ

Levine, Shar

Backyard science; [by] Shar Levine & Leslie Johnstone; illustrated by Dave Garbot. Sterling Pub. 2005 80p il $19.95 (3-5)   **507.8**

1. Science—Experiments

ISBN 1-4027-1519-6   LC 2004-26753

"Projects include building a home for ladybugs, making bird nests and looking closely at those that might be found, . . . and identifying footprints. The attractive layout includes full-color photos and drawings. The text clearly outlines what is needed for each experiment, and the concise explanations will satisfy budding scientists." SLJ

Bathtub science; [by] Shar Levine & Leslie Johnstone; illustrations by Dave Garbot; photography by Jeff Connery. Sterling 2000 80p il $19.95 (3-5)   **507.8**

1. Science—Experiments 2. Water

ISBN 0-8069-7185-1   LC 2001-273784

"From a simple, familiar sink-and-float experiment to the more complicated construction of a miniature diving bell, this book covers a wide array of science experiments that can be performed in water. Clear descriptions of how to perform and understand the experiments, as well as photos of the different steps involved, make the book particularly easy to use." Horn Book Guide

Includes glossary

Kitchen science; [by] Shar Levine & Leslie Johnstone; illustrated by Dave Garbot. Sterling Pub. 2004 c2003 80p il $19.95; pa $9.95 (3-5)   **507.8**

1. Science—Experiments

ISBN 1-4027-0332-5; 1-4027-2232-X (pa)

         LC 2003-8841

"This title features 33 activities that use commonly found materials. . . . Safety is emphasized. . . . Although many of them could be done as demonstrations in primary-grade classrooms, the clean and colorful format, cleverly boxed lists of supplies, and cartoon characters will encourage youngsters to try these activities on their own." SLJ

Muller, Eric Paul

While you're waiting for the food to come; a tabletop science activity book: experiments and tricks that can be done at a restaurant or wherever food is served; by Eric Muller; illustrated by Eldon Doty. Orchard Bks. 1999 84p il $15.95; pa $8.95 (3-6)   **507.8**

1. Science—Experiments

ISBN 0-531-30199-0; 0-531-07144-8 (pa)

         LC 99-17168

A collection of science experiments and activities that can be done where food is served, exploring such topics as the senses, gravity, and water

"A delightful book. . . . An 'Attention-Attraction Factor Key' indicates whether people at other tables will notice what you're up to. The black-and-white cartoons provide information and entertainment. A winner." SLJ

Includes glossary and bibliographical references

Pentland, Peter

Party science; [by] Peter Pentland and Pennie Stoyles. Chelsea House 2003 c2002 32p il (Science and scientists) lib bdg $18.95 (4 and up)
507.8

1. Science
ISBN 0-7910-7015-8   LC 2002-1281
First published 2002 in Australia
Contents: Have you ever wondered ...?; Where do soft drink bubbles come from?; Party food that pops and fizzes; Making an insulated cake; How cool is ice cream?; What makes ice cream taste good?; Gelatin: wobbly, foamy and chewy; Balloons; Candles; What is your star sign?; Party lights; Fireworks; Meet a science communicator; Party noise; Party tricks and illusions; Laughter; Too much fun; Party science timeline
Discusses the scientific principles behind various objects and activities at a party including balloons, fireworks, magic, and laughter
"These authors have a knack for offering concise, easy-to-understand explanations of common phenomena. . . . [This book is] sound, highly educational, and entertaining." SLJ
Includes glossary

Pilger, Mary Anne

Science experiments index for young people. 4th ed. Libraries Unlimited 2005 184p $60
507.8

1. Science—Experiments—Indexes
ISBN 1-59158-237-7
This is a guide to science books that contain elementary and intermediate-level projects and experiments. Organized alphabetically by subject and including a list of headings, the book has 7000 entries that consist of a brief description, book and page numbers, and cross-references.

Rhatigan, Joe

Prize-winning science fair projects for curious kids; [by] Joe Rhatigan & Rain Newcomb. 1st ed. Lark Books 2004 112p il $19.95; pa $7.97 (5 and up)
507.8

1. Science projects 2. Science—Experiments
ISBN 1-57990-478-5; 1-57990-750-4 (pa)
LC 2003-24957
"Fifty experiments in biology, the physical sciences, and chemistry are presented in an attractive and easy-to-follow format and illustrated with sharp photographs of children and of the materials needed. One of the book's strengths is the first chapter about choosing and doing a project. Ideas include checking out the validity of horoscopes, mummifying fish, testing the effectiveness of sunscreens, and testing spray-on water repellents." SLJ

Sure-to-win science fair projects; [by] Joe Rhatigan with Heather Smith. Lark Bks. 2001 128p il $21.95; pa $14.95 (5 and up)
507.8

1. Science projects 2. Science—Experiments
ISBN 1-57990-238-3; 1-57990-374-6 (pa)
LC 2001-16505

The authors give "directions for choosing a topic and an . . . assessment of the time and effort a good experiment will take, along with . . . instructions for record keeping, the use of constant and variable controls, and the successful presentation of results. A variety of research venues is suggested, including interviews, print, and the Internet." SLJ
Students "will find a gold mine of instructions in this well-written, easy-to-grasp volume that includes nearly 60 amusing, sometimes ingenious biology, physical science, and chemistry projects." Booklist

Science activities. Grolier Educ. 2002 10v set $399 (4 and up)
507.8

1. Science—Experiments
ISBN 0-7172-5608-1   LC 2001-40519
Contents: v1 Electricity and magnetism; v2 Everyday chemistry; v3 Force and motion; v4 Heat and energy; v5 Inside matter; v6 Light and color; v7 Our environment; v8 Sound and hearing; v9 Using materials; v10 Weather and climate
Each volume in this set presents 10 experiments, each with an introduction, step-by-step instructions, follow-up activities, and analysis

VanCleave, Janice Pratt

Janice VanCleave's 201 awesome, magical, bizarre & incredible experiments. Wiley 1994 118p il pa $12.95 (4 and up)
507.8

1. Science—Experiments
ISBN 0-471-31011-5   LC 93-29807
The experiments in this book "are organized by field: astronomy, biology, chemistry, earth science, and physics; the purpose, materials needed, procedure, results, and an explanation are included for each demonstration. The author writes in a clear, easy-to-understand style. . . . The book will be especially useful to teachers looking for ideas that can be adapted as hands-on activities." SLJ
Includes glossary

Janice VanCleave's 202 oozing, bubbling, dripping & bouncing experiments. Wiley 1996 120p il pa $12.95 (4 and up)
507.8

1. Science—Experiments
ISBN 0-471-14025-2   LC 95-46398
Provides instructions for over 200 short experiments in astronomy, biology, chemistry, earth science, and physics
"Some activities consist merely of observation, such as 'To study parts of a feather.' Some are more complex, but all are clearly and concisely explained. Many are repeats from prior VanCleave books, but 40 are supposedly new." SLJ
Includes glossary

Janice VanCleave's 203 icy, freezing, frosty, cool & wild experiments. Wiley 1999 122p pa $12.95 (4 and up)
507.8

1. Science—Experiments
ISBN 0-471-25223-9   LC 98-49721
This includes "experiments in astronomy, biology, chemistry, earth science, and physics. . . . Each activity includes a purpose, a list of materials, a step-by-step procedure, results, and an explanation. Experiments address such topics as the Moon's 'changing' size, how environment affects body temperature, and why ice pops are softer than ice. An excellent resource." SLJ

VanCleave, Janice Pratt—*Continued*

Janice VanCleave's guide to more of the best science fair projects. Wiley 2000 156p il pa $14.95 (4 and up)   **507.8**

1. Science projects 2. Science—Experiments

ISBN 0-471-32627-5   LC 99-25575

This volume includes "fifty experiments . . . in the areas of astronomy, biology, earth science, engineering, physical science, and mathematics. . . . A valuable addition to science collections." SLJ

Includes bibliographical references

Janice VanCleave's guide to the best science fair projects; [by] Janice VanCleave. Wiley 1997 156p il pa 14.95 (4 and up)   **507.8**

1. Science projects 2. Science—Experiments

ISBN 0-471-14802-4   LC 96-27512

"In the first section, VanCleave discusses scientific methodology: how to organize a project from selecting a topic through the investigatory process, the importance of keeping records, writing a final report, and the value of a nicely crafted presentation. . . . The next section—the largest by far—presents a number of double-page projects in a variety of fields. . . . A clear and informative addition." SLJ

Includes glossary and bibliographical references

Janice VanCleave's science around the year. Wiley 2000 122p il pa $12.95 (4 and up)

     507.8

1. Science—Experiments

ISBN 0-471-33096-5   LC 99-53778

Presents experiments and activities in such fields as astronomy, biology, chemistry, earth science, and physics that are in some way related to one of the four seasons

Walker, Pamela

Science experiments on file; [by] Pamela Walker and Elaine Wood. Facts on File 2004-2005 2v unp il loose-leaf ea $185 (5 and up)

     507.8

ISBN 0-8160-5734-6   LC 2004-47230

Also available CD-ROM version

First published 1988

This offers 120 science experiments with over 250 illustrations, tables, and diagrams, listing time required, safety precautions, materials, procedure, principles illustrated, data tables, connections, and additional activities, which may be reproduced for classroom use

Includes glossaries and bibliographical references

508   Natural history

Arnosky, Jim

Crinkleroot's nature almanac. Simon & Schuster Bks. for Young Readers 1999 64p il $16 (k-3)

     508

1. Seasons 2. Animals 3. Nature study

ISBN 0-689-80534-9   LC 98-27191

Crinkleroot the forest dweller describes the changes that take place in animals and plants throughout the four seasons

"The book combines chatty prose sprinkled with facts and watercolor illustrations—some of which are realistic (like the wildflowers) and others, like Crinkleroot himself, that are more cartoonlike." SLJ

Field trips; bug hunting, animal tracking, bird-watching, shore walking with Jim Arnosky. HarperCollins Pubs. 2002 96p il $15.95; lib bdg $15.89 (3-6)   **508**

1. Natural history 2. Nature study

ISBN 0-688-15172-8; 0-688-15173-6 (lib bdg)

     LC 00-69721

"Information on planning outdoor experiences is woven through four chapters filled with detailed sketches of bugs, animal tracks, birds, and the plants and animals at the water's edge. The book's annotated descriptions introduce readers to the conventions of plant and animal classification and infuse the text with Arnosky's friendly encouragement." Horn Book Guide

Björk, Christina

Linnea's almanac; text [by] Christina Björk; drawings [by] Lena Anderson. R & S Bks. 1989 61p il $13 (2-5)   **508**

1. Nature study

ISBN 91-29-59176-7   LC 89-83540

Original Swedish edition, 1982

Linnea, featured in Linnea in Monet's garden and Linnea's windowsill garden, "is inspired by the *Old Farmer's Almanac* to track the growing things in her city world. Month by month, the round-faced girl with stick-straight hair never lacks for activities, whether making flower garlands, identifying birds or creating a Christmas-present collage out of beach debris." Publ Wkly

"The book is unusually fresh and charming in its approach; the many facts are presented agreeably and lightened by the child's pleasure in activities which young readers could copy." Grow Point

Burnie, David

The Kingfisher illustrated nature encyclopedia; [by] David Burnie. Kingfisher 2004 320p il $24.95 (5 and up)   **508**

1. Natural history 2. Nature

ISBN 0-7534-5576-5   LC 2003-61914

"Three major sections discuss the formation of the Earth, the biosphere, and climate change; focus on life from microscopic plants through the shapes, senses, and categories of animals, including habitats; and consider biomes. Highly detailed color photography, including many full-page, spectacular spreads, illuminates the concepts and discussions. Clear, colorful diagrams explain the unseen processes of nature." SLJ

DK nature encyclopedia. DK Pub. 1998 304p il map $29.99   **508**

1. Natural history—Encyclopedias

ISBN 0-7894-3411-3   LC 98-16657

"The book is divided into six sections. 'The Natural World' describes the origins and evolution of life on

DK nature encyclopedia—*Continued*

earth. 'How Living Things Work' examines the basic characteristics shared by all living things—respiration, reproduction, life cycles, etc. 'Ecology' surveys the major types of habitats around the world and discusses topics such as food chains and endangered species. A short section explains 'How Living Things Are Classified,' while the final chapters look at specific groups of plants. . . . Well organized, clearly written, and with an amazing scope, this encyclopedia makes a valuable guide to nature." SLJ

McMillan, Bruce

Summer ice; life along the Antarctic peninsula; written and photo-illustrated by Bruce McMillan. Houghton Mifflin 1995 48p il map $16 (3-6)
508

1. Natural history—Antarctica 2. Antarctica
ISBN 0-395-66561-2   LC 93-38831
"This photo-essay introduces readers to the animals and plants of the Antarctic Peninsula. . . . After showing the landforms and glacial iceforms there, McMillan turns to the unexpected wealth of summer wildlife: algae and moss, plankton and krill, humpback whales and orcas, skuas and shags, seals and (of course) penguins." Booklist
"The full-color photography is brilliant in its beauty and attention to detail. However, the text is lively and knowledgeable, and could stand alone and still catch readers' interest." SLJ
Includes glossary and bibliographical references

Morrison, Gordon

Nature in the neighborhood; [by] Gordon Morrison. Houghton Mifflin Company 2004 32p il $16 (3-6)
508

1. Natural history 2. Seasons
ISBN 0-618-35215-5   LC 2004-2354
"Walter Lorraine books"
The author "focuses on plants and animals in a single neighborhood in an unnamed North American city, beginning in spring as the snow melts and following them through the seasons." SLJ
"Morrison offers another quiet, layered view of a natural world that is familiar to many children. . . . His precise, pencil-and-watercolor artwork encourages viewers to look closely at common neighborhood scenes." Booklist

Potter, Jean

Nature in a nutshell for kids; over 100 activities you can do in ten minutes or less. Wiley 1995 136p il pa $12.95 (2-4)
508

1. Nature study
ISBN 0-471-04444-X   LC 94-28953
"Each of the 102 experiments is easy, uses safe and mostly readily available household supplies, and is fun at the same time. Divided into seasonal sections, the activities have catchy titles, state hypotheses, list materials, lay out procedures, and finish with clear explanations. Among the noteworthy investigations are: how duck feathers react to water, how mountains are formed, what keeps a seal from freezing in icy weather, whether ants prefer sugar or aspertame, and more." SLJ
Includes glossary and bibliographical references

Weber, Sandra

Two in the wilderness; adventures of a mother and daughter in the Adirondack Mountains; photographs by Carl E. Heilman II. Boyds Mills Press 2005 48p lib bdg $19.95 (4 and up)
508

1. Natural history—New York (State) 2. Adirondack Mountains (N.Y.) 3. Hiking 4. Outdoor life
ISBN 1-59078-182-1
The author "recounts with vivid detail a 12-day journey with her 11-year-old daughter, Marcy, in the Adirondack Mountains. . . . The narrative weaves together the history of the mountains, both geological and cultural, with a here-and-now account of their ups and downs through this rugged landscape. . . . Sidebars from Marcy's own journal of the trip offer up a humorous counterpoint to her mother's poetic descriptions of the environment. Color photographs . . . document most of the outing." SLJ

Wright-Frierson, Virginia

An island scrapbook; dawn to dusk on a barrier island; written and illustrated by Virginia Wright-Frierson. Simon & Schuster 1998 unp $16 (3-5)
508

1. Natural history—North Carolina 2. Barrier islands 3. Ecology
ISBN 0-689-81563-8   LC 97-17998
An artist and her daughter explore a North Carolina barrier island and tell of all they observe during the course of a September day
"The accurately rendered, muted watercolors and pencil drawings on glossy paper present a vivid portrait of island ecology and convey the author's keen sense of observation. . . . A carefully detailed look at a unique ecosystem, sensitively described and beautifully rendered." SLJ

508.2   Seasons

Branley, Franklyn Mansfield

Sunshine makes the seasons; illustrated by Michael Rex. Newly illustrated ed. HarperCollins Pub. 2005 31p il (Let's-read-and-find-out science) $15.99; pa $4.99 (k-3)
508.2

1. Seasons
ISBN 0-06-059203-6; 0-06-059205-2 (pa)
LC 2003-25457
First published 1974; this is a newly illustrated edition of the text revised for the 1985 edition
Describes how sunshine and the tilt of the earth's axis are responsible for the changing seasons.
Includes bibliographical references

Maass, Robert

When spring comes. Holt & Co. 1994 unp il pa $6.95 hardcover o.p. (k-2)
508.2

1. Spring
ISBN 0-8050-4705-0 (pa)   LC 93-29816
Companion volumes: When autumn comes (1990), When summer comes (1993), When winter comes (1993)

Maass, Robert—*Continued*

Color photographs and brief text introduce activities of the spring season

"The spirit of hope and renewal unfolds in the uncomplicated text, which is accompanied by large and small photographs warmly expressing the feelings of this special time of year." Booklist

509   Science--Historical and geographic treatment

Beshore, George W.

Science in ancient China; [by] George Beshore. Watts 1998 63p il map (Science of the past) lib bdg $26; pa $8.95 (4 and up)   **509**

1. Science—China—History 2. Science and civilization

ISBN 0-531-11334-5 (lib bdg); 0-531-15914-0 (pa)
                 LC 97-3519

First published 1988 in the First book series

Surveys the achievements of the ancient Chinese in science, medicine, astronomy, and cosmology, and describes such innovations as rockets, wells, the compass, water wheels, and movable type

Includes glossary and bibliographical references

Science in early Islamic culture; [by] George Beshore. Watts 1998 64p il maps (Science of the past) lib bdg $26; pa $8.95 (4 and up)
                 509

1. Science—History 2. Science and civilization 3. Islamic countries—Civilization

ISBN 0-531-20355-7 (lib bdg); 0-531-15917-5 (pa)
                 LC 97-5012

First published 1988 in the First book series

Discusses the extraordinary scientific discoveries and advancements in the Islamic world after the birth of Mohammed in 570 and their impact on Western civilization in subsequent centuries and today

"The writing is crisp and lively. . . . Numerous full-color and black-and-white photographs, reproductions, and drawings illuminate the text." SLJ

Includes glossary and bibliographical references

Fradin, Dennis B.

With a little luck; surprising stories of amazing discoveries; [by] Dennis Brindell Fradin. 1st ed. Dutton Children's Books 2006 183p il $17.99 (5 and up)   **509**

1. Science—History

ISBN 0-525-47196-0   LC 2005-04798

This describes 11 scientific discoveries, including gravity, fossils, rubber, anesthesia, hygienic medicine, prehistoric cave paintings, penicillin, the planet Pluto, nuclear fission, the Dead Sea Scrolls, and pulsars.

The author "smoothly combines personal stories . . . with fascinating science, technology, and history. His style is open and chatty, and the book design is very attractive." Booklist

Includes bibliographical references

Gay, Kathlyn

Science in ancient Greece. Watts 1998 64p il (Science of the past) lib bdg $26; pa $8.95 (4 and up)   **509**

1. Science—Greece—History 2. Science and civilization

ISBN 0-531-20357-3 (lib bdg); 0-531-15929-9 (pa)
                LC 97-24029

First published 1988 in the First book series

Discusses the theories of ancient Greek philosopher-scientists such as Ptolemy, Pythagoras, Hippocrates, and Aristotle, and describes some of the scientific discoveries attributed to the Greeks and their impact on modern science

"Useful for reports, and there's also much to interest science students." SLJ

Includes glossary and bibliographical references

Harris, Jacqueline L.

Science in ancient Rome. Watts 1998 64p il map (Science of the past) lib bdg $26; pa $8.95 (4 and up)   **509**

1. Science—Rome—History 2. Science and civilization

ISBN 0-531-20354-9 (lib bdg); 0-531-15916-7 (pa)
                LC 97-1901

First published 1988 in the First book series

Describes how the Romans put to use and expanded the scientific achievements of earlier civilizations

This "includes clear, easy-to-read text; simple yet effective topic headings; excellent-quality, full-color photographs and reproductions; and Internet sites." SLJ

Includes glossary and bibliographical references

January, Brendan

Science in colonial America. Watts 1999 64p il (Science of the past) lib bdg $26; pa $8.95 (4 and up)   **509**

1. Science—United States—History 2. Science and civilization

ISBN 0-531-11525-9 (lib bdg); 0-531-15940-X (pa)
                LC 98-10450

Describes the scientific contributions made by people in colonial America, including natural history, medicine, astronomy, and electricity

"Attractive and accessible. . . . Plentiful, accurate material." SLJ

Includes glossary and bibliographical references

Science in the Renaissance. Watts 1999 64p il (Science of the past) lib bdg $25 (4 and up)
                 509

1. Science—History 2. Science and civilization 3. Renaissance

ISBN 0-531-11526-7   LC 97-38633

Describes advances in scientific knowledge that occurred during the Renaissance in Europe during the 15th and 16th centuries

"Many colorful photographs as well as reproductions of period art illustrate [this] attractive and interesting [book]." Booklist

Includes glossary and bibliographical references

McCutcheon, Marc

The kid who named Pluto; and the stories of other extraordinary young people in science; illustrated by Jon Cannell. Chronicle Books 2004 85p il $15.95 (4-6) **509**

1. Scientists

ISBN 0-8118-3770-X   LC 2003-3662

Contents: The boy who dreamed of Mars; The girl who named Pluto; The bookworm who became a science fiction writer; The teenager who invented television; The curious girl who discovered sea-monster skeletons; The high schooler who created an incredible secret code; The math whiz who calculated the movement of the moon; The fourth-grader who outsmarted medical experts; The blind boy who developed a new way to see

"This book profiles nine people who made significant contributions to science while still quite young. Louis Braille and Robert Goddard are among the more famous, while others, such as television pioneer Philo Farnsworth and Venetia Burney, the girl who named Pluto, are less well known. . . . The lively and lighthearted text conveys a sense of the excitement of discovery, with an appropriate amount of background information, along with the biographical facts. . . . Lively cartoon pen-and-ink illustrations, all in greens and grays, help to unify the individual chapters. " Booklist

Moss, Carol (Carol Marie)

Science in ancient Mesopotamia. Watts 1998 63p il (Science of the past) pa $8.95 hardcover o.p. (4 and up) **509**

1. Science—Iraq—History 2. Science and civilization

ISBN 0-531-15930-2 (pa)   LC 97-24030

First published 1988 in the First book series

Describes the enormous accomplishments of the Sumerians and Babylonians of ancient Mesopotamia in every scientific area, a heritage which affects our own everyday lives

"Clearly written. . . . Black-and-white and full-color photographs and reproductions . . . are well captioned." SLJ

Includes glossary and bibliographical references

Popular science: science year by year; discoveries and inventions from the last century that shape our lives. Scholastic Ref. 2001 240p il $19.95 **509**

1. Science—History 2. Technology—History

ISBN 0-439-28438-4   LC 00-50476

One illustrated page per each year from 1900 to 2000 chronicles important discoveries and inventions in such fields as medicine, earth sciences, space exploration, computers, mathematics, and biology

Stewart, Melissa

Science in ancient India. Watts 1999 64p il map (Science of the past) lib bdg $26 (4 and up) **509**

1. Science—India—History 2. Science and civilization

ISBN 0-531-11626-3   LC 98-18536

An overview of the scientific contributions of ancient India including Arabic numerals, ayurveda, basic chemistry and physics, and celestial observations

"A useful and unique resource." SLJ

Includes glossary and bibliographical references

Woods, Geraldine

Science in ancient Egypt. Watts 1998 64p il (Science of the past) lib bdg $26; pa $8.95 (4 and up) **509**

1. Science—Egypt—History 2. Science and civilization

ISBN 0-531-20341-7 (lib bdg); 0-531-15915-9 (pa)
          LC 97-649

First published 1988 in the First book series

Discusses the achievements of the ancient Egyptians in science, mathematics, astronomy, medicine, agriculture, and technology

"Well-researched and easy-to-understand. . . . Woods offers a fascinating look at the ancient Egyptians' accomplishments." SLJ

Includes glossary and bibliographical references

Science of the early Americas. Watts 1999 64p il (Science of the past) lib bdg $26; pa $8.95 (4 and up) **509**

1. Science—History 2. Science and civilization 3. Native Americans

ISBN 0-531-11524-0 (lib bdg); 0-531-15941-8 (pa)
          LC 97-44047

Discusses the scientific accomplishments in such fields as medicine, mathematics, engineering, and astronomy of various groups of American Indians

Includes glossary and bibliographical references

510 Mathematics

Merriam, Eve

12 ways to get to 11; written by Eve Merriam; illustrated by Bernie Karlin. Simon & Schuster Bks. for Young Readers 1993 unp il pa $6.99 hardcover o.p. (k-3) **510**

1. Mathematics 2. Counting

ISBN 0-689-80892-5 (pa)   LC 91-25810

Uses ordinary experiences to present twelve combinations of numbers that add up to eleven. Example: At the circus, six peanut shells and five pieces of popcorn

"Some of the double-page spreads are simpler to solve than others, which allows children to progress as they learn more about counting. The huge, vibrant cut-paper and colored-pencil pictures make the book fun, lively, and painlessly educational." Horn Book Guide

Schwartz, David M.

G is for googol; a math alphabet book; written by David M. Schwartz; illustrated by Marissa Moss. Tricycle Press 1998 57p il $15.95 (4 and up) **510**

1. Mathematics 2. Alphabet

ISBN 1-883672-58-9   LC 98-15162

Explains the meaning of mathematical terms which begin with the different letters of the alphabet from abacus, binary, and cubit to zillion

"The text is lively and clear and will appeal to even those who think math is as dull as the kitchen floor. . . . The cartoon illustrations are colorful, amusing, and informative." SLJ

Includes glossary

Tang, Greg

Math-terpieces; the art of problem-solving; illustrated by Greg Paprocki. Scholastic Press 2003 31p il $16.95 (2-4)   **510**

1. Set theory 2. Counting 3. Art appreciation

ISBN 0-439-44388-1   LC 2002-5361

A series of rhymes about artists and their works introduces counting and grouping numbers, as well as such artistic styles as cubism, pointillism, and surrealism

"Clearly written solutions to these exercises are given at the end of the book along with art definitions and brief explanations. This math-concept book is far more appealing than most." SLJ

Wyatt, Valerie

The math book for girls and other beings who count; written by Valerie Wyatt; illustrated by Pat Cupples. Kids Can Press 2000 64p il $14.95; pa $9.95 (3-6)   **510**

1. Mathematics

ISBN 1-55074-830-0; 1-55074-584-0 (pa)

This offers activities to entice "girls to stretch their math skills in measurement and probability, geometric construction and graphing, using a calculator and changing scale. . . . Activity directions are clear and simple, and cheerful line-and-watercolor cartoons keep the presentation breezy." Bull Cent Child Books

Includes glossary

511   General principles of mathematics

Murphy, Stuart J.

The sundae scoop; illustrated by Cynthia Jabar. HarperCollins Pubs. 2003 33p il (Mathstart) $15.99; lib bdg $16.89; pa $4.99 (1-3)   **511**

1. Mathematics

ISBN 0-06-028924-4; 0-06-028925-2 (lib bdg); 0-06-446250-1 (pa)   LC 2001-24322

This "presents the concept of combinations in a story about a group of children who host an ice-cream booth at their school picnic. With two flavors of ice cream, two sauces, and two choices of toppings, the children are surprised that eight different sundaes are available. . . . Murphy easily folds the math concepts into a lively story that will capture young readers, and Jabar reinforces the lesson with colorful, whimsical drawings of delectable ice-cream scoops." Booklist

Nagda, Ann Whitehead

Tiger math; learning to graph from a baby tiger; by Ann Whitehead Nagda and Cindy Bickel. Holt & Co. 2000 unp il $16 (2-4)   **511**

1. Graphic methods 2. Tigers

ISBN 0-8050-6248-3   LC 99-46686

Describes the growth of an orphan Siberian tiger cub, by means of words and graphs

"Easy-to-understand picture, pie or circle, bar, or line graphs, all with explanations, appear on the left; facing pages of text and clear full-color photographs are on the right." SLJ

511.3   Mathematical logic (Symbolic logic)

Murphy, Stuart J.

Dave's down-to-earth rock shop; illustrated by Cat Bowman Smith. HarperCollins Pubs. 2000 33p il (MathStart) $15.95; lib bdg $15.89; pa $4.95 (k-3)   **511.3**

1. Set theory 2. Rocks—Collectors and collecting

ISBN 0-06-028018-2; 0-06-028019-0 (lib bdg); 0-06-446729-5 (pa)   LC 98-32128

"MathStart. Classifying; Level 3."

As they consider sorting their rock collection by color, size, type, and hardness, Josh and Amy learn that the same objects can be organized in many different ways

"Murphy's forte is explaining complex topics in a down-to-earth manner, and that's just what he's done here. Along the way, he also includes a good deal of information about rocks, minerals, and the scientific method. Smith's full-color illustrations capture the excitement of rock hunting and include many geological and equipment details." Booklist

Seaweed soup; by Stuart Murphy; illustrated by Frank Remkiewicz. HarperCollins Pubs. 2001 31p il (MathStart) $15.95; lib bdg $15.89; pa $4.95 (k-3)   **511.3**

1. Set theory

ISBN 0-06-028032-8; 0-06-028033-6 (lib bdg); 0-06-028036-8 (pa)   LC 99-87634

As he asks more and more friends to join him for lunch, Turtle must make up sets of dishes to accommodate them

"A graph will help children review what they've learned, and two pages of ideas for extending the book are appended. Remkiewicz's appealing illustrations encourage children to match sets and count items in each set." Booklst

512   Algebra

Anno, Masaichiro

Anno's mysterious multiplying jar; [by] Masaichiro and Mitsumasa Anno; illustrated by Mitsumasa Anno. Philomel Bks. 1983 unp il $19.99; pa $7.99 (2-5)   **512**

1. Factorials 2. Mathematics

ISBN 0-399-20951-4; 0-698-11753-0 (pa)

     LC 82-22413

Simple text and pictures introduce the mathematical concept of factorials

This book "begins with a painting of a handsome blue and white lidded jar, moves into fantasy with pictures of the water in the jar becoming a sea on which an old sailing ship is moving, transfers to an island on the sea, and goes on to describe the rooms in the houses in the kingdoms on the mountains in the countries on the island. Each time the number grows: one island, two countries, three mountains, etc. How many jars, then, were in the boxes that were in the cupboards in the rooms? . . . The explanation is in itself clear, and is expanded by other examples of factorials." Bull Cent Child Books

Murphy, Stuart J.
Safari Park; illustrated by Steve Björkman.
HarperCollins Pubs. 2002 31p il (Mathstart)
$15.95; lib bdg $15.89; pa $4.99 (2-4)

512

1. Equations
ISBN 0-06-028914-7; 0-06-028915-5 (lib bdg);
0-06-446245-5 (pa) LC 00-63201
"Finding unknowns, level 3."
"At the new amusement park, Grandpa gives his
grandkids twenty tickets each. With a little help, the kids
add up the cost in tickets for rides and figure out the
'unknowns,' the number of tickets left over for snacks
and games. Cartoony watercolors keep up the carnival atmosphere, while a plot about Paul's lost tickets and the
Terrible Tarantula ride adds a hint of suspense. Related
activities are appended." Horn Book Guide

513 Arithmetic

Adler, David A.
Fraction fun; illustrated by Nancy Tobin.
Holiday House 1996 unp il $16.95; pa $6.95 (2-4)

513

1. Fractions
ISBN 0-8234-1259-8; 0-8234-1341-1 (pa)
LC 96-10773
"Adler presents the concept of fractions with the tried-
and-true example of dividing a pie (pizza pie, in this
case), then directs readers to draw lines across paper
plates and color the eight resultant wedges in various
color combinations. . . . Adler doesn't shy away from
correct terminology—numerators and denominators—in
this primary-grade introduction. Next he launches into
some hands-on experimentation. . . . Tobin supplies a
jazzy, eye-popping color scheme and diagrams of exceptional clarity to illuminate the straightforward text." Bull
Cent Child Books

Roman numerals; illustrated by Byron Barton.
Crowell 1977 33p il lib bdg $15.89 (2-4)

513

1. Numerals
ISBN 0-690-01302-7 LC 77-2270
"Adler provides exercises on how to write Roman numerals and handle the subscription principle involved in
writing the symbols representing four and nine. He also
explains the historical origins of the symbols for five and
ten plus the uses and development of Roman numerals."
SLJ
"A simple demonstration with labeled cards clearly
explains how the symbols are ordered; another practice
lesson tests readers' comprehension of when to use subtraction symbols. . . . A jaunty cartoon figure acts out
textual descriptions against an orange-and-brown backdrop. It's a light, lucid, good-humored lesson." Booklist

Anno, Mitsumasa
Anno's magic seeds; written and illustrated by
Mitsumasa Anno. Philomel Bks. 1995 unp il
$19.99; pa $6.99 (k-3) **513**
1. Mathematics
ISBN 0-399-22538-2; 0-698-11618-6 (pa)
LC 92-39309

The reader is asked to perform a series of mathematical operations integrated into the story of a lazy man
who plants magic seeds and reaps an increasingly abundant harvest
"Anno has succeeded in combining both the moral issue of conservation of resources and arithmetical games
in a charming story for young readers. A tour de force
from a most original author-illustrator." Horn Book

Burns, Marilyn
The I hate mathematics! book; illustrated by
Martha Hairston. Little, Brown 1975 127p il pa
$13.95 hardcover o.p. (4 and up) **513**
1. Mathematics
ISBN 0-316-11741-2 (pa)
"A Brown paper school book"
"This lively collection of puzzles, riddles, magic
tricks, and brain teasers provides a painless introduction
to mathematical concepts and terms through the process
of experimentation and discovery. The cartoon-like illustration and breezy titles . . . should appeal to the not-so-
mathematically inclined as well as to puzzle devotees.
Required materials are readily available and inexpensive;
the techniques described are educationally sound and exciting. An excellent resource for parents, teachers, and
children." Horn Book

Clements, Andrew
A million dots; illustrated by Mike Reed. Simon
& Schuster Books for Young Readers 2006 unp il
$16.95 (k-3) **513**
1. Million (The number)
ISBN 0-689-85824-8 LC 2004-05349
"With one million dots printed on its pages, this large-
format picture book shows how big a million really is.
Along the way, the text and illustrations offer plenty to
look at and think about besides the rows and rows of
tiny dots. On each page, Clements selects one number
and connects it to a numerical fact." Booklist

Geisert, Arthur
Roman numerals I to MM; Numerabilia romana
uno ad duo mila: liber de difficillimo computando
numerum. Houghton Mifflin 1996 xxxiip $16 (k-3)
513
1. Roman numerals 2. Counting
ISBN 0-395-74519-5 LC 95-36247
"Seven Roman numerals are introduced, accompanied
by very detailed illustrations of . . . pigs engaged in a
variety of activities. What little text there is . . . explains
the concept of Roman numerals and how they build on
one another." Child Book Rev Serv
"Geisert's detailed etchings reward extended perusal,
and children will revel in the sheer abundance of pigs.
A great lesson in Roman numerals." Publ Wkly

Leedy, Loreen
2 x 2 = boo! a set of spooky multiplication
stories; written and illustrated by Loreen Leedy.
Holiday House 1995 32p il $15.95 (k-3)
513
1. Multiplication
ISBN 0-8234-1190-7 LC 94-46711

Leedy, Loreen—*Continued*

This is an "introduction to basic multiplication, with witches, cats, and monsters demonstrating the consequences of multiplying numbers from 0 to 5. The illustrations are done in muted, autumnal tones of black, blue, orange, and mustard, and arranged in a comic-strip format. . . . The concepts are clear and understandable. . . . Leedy's book presents an entertaining alternative to rote memorization." SLJ

Fraction action; written and illustrated by Loreen Leedy. Holiday House 1994 31p il $16.95; pa $6.95 (k-3) **513**
1. Fractions
ISBN 0-8234-1109-5; 0-8234-1244-X (pa)
LC 93-22800
Miss Prime and her animal students explore fractions by finding many examples in the world around them
"Thickly pigmented paintings loaded with sporty animal figures add to the humorous presentation, which should make fractions not only more understandable, but also more fun for young children." Bull Cent Child Books

Mission: addition; written and illustrated by Loreen Leedy. Holiday House 1997 unp il $16.95; pa $6.95 (k-3) **513**
1. Addition
ISBN 0-8234-1307-1; 0-8234-1412-4 (pa)
LC 96-37149
Miss Prime and her animal students explore addition by finding many examples in the world around them
"Flat chalk-box colors predominate in the illustrations, which will please kids with their liveliness, their informality, and their cartoonlike speech balloons. . . . An attractive picture book to support the math curriculum." Booklist

Subtraction action. Holiday House 2000 32p il $16.95; pa $6.95 (k-3) **513**
1. Subtraction
ISBN 0-8234-1454-X; 0-8234-1244-X (pa)
LC 99-49803
Introduces subtraction through the activities of animal students at a school fair. Includes problems for the reader to solve
This is "an action-packed volume that is perfectly suited to its audience. The softly hued cartoon animals and dialogue balloons are skillfully combined on pages divided into framed sequences." SLJ

Lewis, J. Patrick

Arithme-tickle; an even number of odd riddle-rhymes; illustrated by Frank Remkiewicz. Harcourt 2002 32p il $16 (2-4) **513**
1. Arithmetic 2. Mathematical recreations
ISBN 0-15-216418-9
LC 2001-3228
"Silver Whistle"
"Wordplay, riddles, and math problems test readers' skill at addition, subtraction, multiplication, division, telling time, logic, and even general knowledge in this colorfully illustrated collection. Clearly meant to make math more approachable and enjoyable, this compilation includes enough genuinely complex puzzles to keep hardcore young math buffs entertained." Booklist

Long, Lynette

Fabulous fractions; games and activities that make math easy and fun. Wiley 2001 122p il (Magical math) pa $12.95 (3-6) **513**
1. Fractions
ISBN 0-471-36981-0
LC 00-43386
This introduction to fractions includes activities using such materials as sandwiches, paper plates, cards, and dominoes
This book includes "lists of the required materials, clear and complete procedures, and a black-and-white illustration." SLJ

Marvelous multiplication; games and activities that make math easy and fun. Wiley 2000 122p il (Magical math) pa $12.95 (3-6) **513**
1. Multiplication
ISBN 0-471-36982-9
LC 00-20473
Presents a series of activities, arranged in order of difficulty, that teach the operation of multiplication
"The cheerful ink drawings help make the [book] more inviting." Booklist

Murphy, Stuart J.

Divide and ride; illustrated by George Ulrich. HarperCollins Pubs. 1997 32p il (MathStart) $14.95; lib bdg $15.89; pa $4.95 (1-3) **513**
1. Division
ISBN 0-06-026776-3; 0-06-026777-1 (lib bdg); 0-06-446710-4 (pa)
LC 95-26134
"Eleven friends climb aboard the Dare-Devil roller coaster and three other rides, but before each ride can begin, all of the seats must be filled. Readers follow the children as they solve each problem by dividing and then filling the empty seats with new friends. Watercolor, pen, and ink illustrations and follow-up activities accompany the story." Horn Book Guide

Double the ducks; illustrated by Valeria Petrone. HarperCollins Pubs. 2003 31p il (MathStart) $15.99; lib bdg $16.89; pa $4.99 (k-1) **513**
1. Multiplication
ISBN 0-06-028922-8; 0-06-028923-6 (lib bdg); 0-06-446249-8 (pa)
LC 2001-24321
"Level 1."; "Doubling numbers."
"A young cowboy cares for his five little ducks, and he scurries around to bring them three sacks of food and four bundles of hay with his two hands. When each duck brings a friend, the boy has double the ducks, so he needs to double the hay and double the food. . . . In a double-page spread at the back of the book, Murphy suggests lots of activities and games for parents to use in the kitchen and at play to make preschoolers' first steps into addition and multiplication more fun." Booklist

Earth Day-hooray! illustrated by Renee Andriani. HarperCollins Pub. 2004 32p il (MathStart) $15.99; pa $4.99 (1-3) **513**
1. Place value (Mathematics) 2. Recycling
ISBN 0-06-000127-5; 0-06-000129-1 (pa)
LC 2002-155234
"Place value."; "Level 3."

Murphy, Stuart J.—*Continued*

A drive to recycle cans on Earth Day teaches the children of the Maple Street School Save-the-Planet Club about place value.

"Andriani's cheerful illustrations fairly teem with information about recycling and add humor and human interest to the story." SLJ

Includes bibliographical references

Elevator magic; illustrated by G. Brian Karas. HarperCollins Pubs. 1997 32p il (MathStart) lib bdg $15.89; pa $4.95 (k-2)   **513**
1. Subtraction
ISBN 0-06-026775-5 (lib bdg); 0-06-446709-0 (pa)
LC 96-5672

"A boy meets his mother on the 10th floor of a high rise. On the way down, Mom needs to do some errands. The first stop, two floors down, is to cash a check at the Farm Bank and Trust, which is (lo and behold!) filled with horses, barns, and hay fields. Farther down is the Hard Rock Candy Store, which is not only full of candy but also the sounds and lights of a heavy metal band. Karas's zany illustrations support the main concept being taught, while picking up on the humor in the word play." SLJ

The Grizzly Gazette; illustrated by Steve Björkman. HarperCollins Pubs. 2003 31p il (MathStart) $15.99; lib bdg $16.89; pa $4.99 (1-3)   **513**
1. Percentage
ISBN 0-06-000027-9; 0-06-000025-2 (lib bdg); 0-06-000026-0 (pa)   LC 2001-24633
"Percentages. Level 2."

At Camp Grizzly the camp newspaper takes a poll each day to see who has the greatest percentage of the vote so far in the election to chose a mascot. Includes activities for learning about percentages.

Henry the fourth; illustrated by Scott Nash. HarperCollins Pubs. 1999 33p il (MathStart) $15.95; lib bdg $15.89; pa $4.95 (k-1)   **513**
1. Numbers
ISBN 0-06-027610-X; 0-06-027611-8 (lib bdg); 0-06-446719-8 (pa)   LC 98-4960

A simple story about four dogs at a dog show introduces the ordinal numbers: first, second, third, and fourth

"The numerical concepts are sequential and simple enough for young children to follow. The watercolor cartoons fill the pages with action." SLJ

Jack the builder; illustrated by Michael Rex. HarperCollins Pubs. 2006 33p il (MathStart) $15.99; pa $4.99 (k-1)   **513**
1. Counting
ISBN 0-06-055774-5; 0-06-055775-3 (pa)
"Jack stacks 2 blocks taken from a big pile. Turn the page, and a wild, colorful double-page spread shows what his simple stack becomes with the addition of a little imagination—a robot. A third block makes a hot-dog stand . . . and 2 more build 'a ferryboat out on the sea.' Eight blocks become a lookout tower, and, using 17, Jack creates a rocket ship. . . . Murphy begins and ends with simple hands-on activities for adults to help bring

the math into kids' everyday life. Rex's bright illustrations will encourage even young preschoolers to point at shapes and colors as they count and add on." Booklist

Jump, kangaroo, jump! illustrated by Kevin O'Malley. HarperCollins Pubs. 1999 unp il (MathStart) $15.95; pa $4.95 (1-3)   **513**
1. Division 2. Fractions
ISBN 0-06-027614-2; 0-06-446721-X (pa)
LC 97-45814

Kangaroo and his Australian animal friends divide themselves up into different groups for the various field day events at camp

"The simple story line presents a real-world application of fractions and division, neatly reinforced by O'Malley's expressive illustrations. Related activities are suggested." Horn Book Guide

Just enough carrots; illustrated by Frank Remkiewicz. HarperCollins Pubs. 1997 31p il (MathStart) $14.95; lib bdg $15.89; pa $4.95 (k-1)   **513**
1. Counting
ISBN 0-06-026778-X; 0-06-026779-8 (lib bdg); 0-06-446711-2 (pa)   LC 96-19495
"Level 1, comparing amounts."

While a bunny and his mother shop in a grocery store for lunch guests, the reader may count and compare the amounts of carrots, peanuts, and worms in the grocery carts of other shoppers

"Bright, colorful illustrations, a surprise ending, and two pages of activities for adults and children extend and enhance the book's appeal." SLJ

Less than zero; illustrated by Frank Remkiewicz. HarperCollins Pubs. 2003 33p il (MathStart) $15.99; pa $4.99 (k-3)   **513**
1. Arithmetic 2. Zero (The number)
ISBN 0-06-000124-0; 0-06-000126-7 (pa)
LC 2002-20732
"Dollars and cents."; "Level 3."

While trying to save enough money to buy a new ice scooter, Perry the Penguin learns about managing his money and about negative numbers

Includes bibliographical references

Mall mania; illustrated by Renée Andriani. HarperCollins 2006 33p il (MathStart) $15.99; pa $4.99 (k-2)   **513**
1. Addition 2. Counting
ISBN 0-06-055776-1; 0-06-055776-X (pa)
"The 100th person to enter Parkside Mall will get lots of promotional gifts, and four kids from Wilson Elementary School's chess club are on hand to count up the shoppers and add the numbers together. . . . The counters use a variety of addition strategies and activities, as always, Murphy adds greatly to the math lesson by making it seem a part of daily life. Suggestions for follow-up activities, both complex and easy . . . are appended." Booklist

Includes bibliographical references

Murphy, Stuart J.—*Continued*

More or less; illustrated by David T. Wenzel. 1st ed. HarperCollinsPublishers 2005 33p il (MathStart) $15.99; pa $4.99 (k-3) **513**

1. Arithmetic

ISBN 0-06-053165-7; 0-06-053167-3 (pa)

LC 2003-27847

"In this story, Eddie works the 'guess the age' booth at the fair. . . . The way Eddie progresses . . . leads children into the world of logical, educated guesses. . . . Youngsters who need to understand the math concept in more depth will find several activities at the conclusion of the book. . . . Sprightly watercolor artwork makes math look like fun. " Booklist

Sluggers' car wash; illustrated by Barney Saltzberg. HarperCollins Pubs. 2002 33p il (MathStart) $15.99; lib bdg $17.89; pa $4.99 (1-3) **513**

1. Addition

ISBN 0-06-028920-1; 0-06-028921-X (lib bdg); 0-06-446248-X (pa) LC 00-54062

"Dollars and sense."; "Level 3."

When the 21st Street Sluggers, a baseball team, have a car wash to raise money, they learn to keep careful track of their dollars and cents

"Colorful illustrations both enhance the story line and elucidate the math lesson with clear tabulations for the money counting and change." SLJ

Nagda, Ann Whitehead

Polar bear math; learning about fractions from Klondike and Snow; by Ann Whitehead Nagda and Cindy Bickel. H. Holt and Co 2004 29p il $16.95 (2-4) **513**

1. Fractions 2. Polar bear

ISBN 0-8050-7301-9 LC 2003-20996

"Following the lives of two cubs that were born at the Denver Zoo and abandoned by their mother, this book provides information about polar bears and fractions. Right-hand pages tell the story of Snow and Klondike, with excellent, full-color photos showing how zoo personnel raised them from newborns until their first birthday. . . . The explanations, which combine text with pictographs, are clear and well formulated." SLJ

Packard, Edward

Big numbers; and pictures that show just how big they are! illustrated by Salvatore Murdocca. Millbrook Press 2000 unp il $14.95; lib bdg $22.40 (k-3) **513**

1. Numbers

ISBN 0-7613-1280-3; 0-7613-1570-5 (lib bdg)

LC 99-32242

Uses illustrations of exponentially increasing peas to present the concept of numbers from one to a million, billion, trillion

"A rollicking, cartoon-style expression of big numbers shown in different ways. . . . Bright and sassy, Murdocca's line-and-wash illustrations create an atmosphere of fun that could break through all but the strongest math anxiety." Booklist

Schmandt-Besserat, Denise

The history of counting; illustrated by Michael Hays. Morrow Junior Bks. 1999 45p il $17; lib bdg $16.93 (4 and up) **513**

1. Counting 2. Mathematics

ISBN 0-688-14118-8; 0-688-14119-6 (lib bdg)

LC 96-35316

"Beginning with a look at primitive expressions of numbers, the text goes on to explain abstract counting and the methods used by the Sumerians, the Phoenicians, the Greeks, the Romans, and finally the Arabs, who brought Hindu numerals from India to Europe about 1,000 years ago. . . . Imaginatively conceived and well composed, Hays' acrylic paintings feature warm, harmonious colors and delicate plays of light and shadow against textured-linen backings. Cogently written and beautifully made." Booklist

Includes glossary

Schwartz, David M.

On beyond a million; an amazing math journey; illustrated by Paul Meisel. Doubleday Bks. for Young Readers 1999 unp il $15.95 (2-4) **513**

1. Counting

ISBN 0-385-32217-8 LC 98-52990

"Schwartz helps youngsters conceptualize enormous numbers by introducing them to counting by powers of ten. Professor X, along with his dog Y, comes to the rescue of some children with an out-of-control popcorn popper as they futilely attempt to count the kernels." SLJ

"The design is busy, with sidebars and balloon comments. Each double-page spread is clearly meant to be talked about, and the discussions aren't overwhelming. . . . Awesome and yet accessible." Booklist

Tang, Greg

The best of times; math strategies that multiply; illustrated by Harry Briggs. Scholastic Press 2002 unp il $16.95 (2-4) **513**

1. Multiplication

ISBN 0-439-21044-5 LC 2002-23043

Simple rhymes offer hints on how to multiply any number by zero through ten without memorizing the multiplication tables

"Encouraging rhymes and colorful, jaunty illustrations bolster the multiplication lesson." Booklist

Math fables; lessons that count; illustrated by Heather Cahoon. Scholastic Press 2004 unp il $16.95 (k-1) **513**

1. Counting

ISBN 0-439-45399-2 LC 2002-5360

A series of rhymes about animals introduces counting and grouping numbers, as well as examples of such behaviors as cooperation, friendship, and appreciation.

"The text and perky, computer-generated cartoons show youngsters that there are many different ways of putting numbers together. . . . The enriching vocabulary is an added bonus. A fine addition to math shelves." SLJ

VanCleave, Janice Pratt
Janice VanCleave's play and find out about math; easy activities for young children. Wiley 1998 122p il $29.95; pa $12.95 (k-2)   **513**
1. Mathematics
ISBN 0-471-12937-2; 0-471-12938-0 (pa)
LC 96-53002
"Fifty simple activities that involve basic arithmetic such as using one's fingers to do simple addition and subtraction. . . . Most procedures are between four and eight steps and are clearly written and accompanied by pencil drawings." SLJ

515   Analysis

Murphy, Stuart J.
Beep beep, vroom vroom! illustrated by Chris Demarest. HarperCollins Pubs. 2000 33p il (MathStart) $15.93; lib bdg $15.89; pa $4.95 (k-1)   **515**
1. Patterns (Mathematics)
ISBN 0-06-028016-6; 0-06-028017-4 (lib bdg);
0-06-446728-7 (pa)   LC 98-51907
"Molly loves playing with cars, but her brother, Kevin, tells her she's too young. He lines up his 12 cars—four red, four green, four yellow—in special order on the shelf and tells her not to touch them while he's gone. . . . At the back are practical suggestions for adults and kids to find patterns on the pages and make their own patterns with pebbles, buttons, coins, and kitchen utensils. Demarest's clear, simple pastel pictures express the fun of playing with cars as the vrooming action reveals the patterns in everyday things." Booklist
Includes bibliographical references

516   Geometry

Adler, David A.
Shape up! illustrated by Nancy Tobin. Holiday House 1998 unp il $16.95; pa $6.95 (2-4)   **516**
1. Geometry 2. Shape
ISBN 0-8234-1346-2; 0-8234-1638-0 (pa)
LC 97-22236
Uses cheese slices, pretzel sticks, a slice of bread, graph paper, a pencil, and more to introduce various polygons, flat shapes with varying numbers of straight sides
"Tobin's colorful diagrams and lanky, baseball-capped tour guide make each definition and direction crystal clear, making this a useful and appealing title for extending classroom lessons or encouraging beginners to charge beyond circle-square-triangle." Bull Cent Child Books

Murphy, Stuart J.
Bigger, Better, BEST! illustrated by Marsha Winborn. HarperCollins Pubs. 2002 33p il (MathStart) $15.99; lib bdg $17.89; pa $4.99 (k-3)   **516**
1. Size 2. Measurement
ISBN 0-06-028918-X; 0-06-028919-8 (lib bdg);
0-06-446247-1 (pa)   LC 00-54034
"Area."; "Level 2."
"Jeff and Jenny are always fighting about who has something bigger or better, while Jill just ignores them. When the family moves to a bigger house with a separate room for each child, the two start arguing about whose room and windows are bigger. Mom then has them measure the windows with sheets of paper and the floor with newspaper. . . . [The story] carefully incorporates math without being overwhelming. The colorful and humorous illustrations add to the story." SLJ

Captain Invincible and the space shapes; illustrated by Rémy Simard. HarperCollins Pubs. 2001 33p il (MathStart) $15.95; lib bdg $15.89; pa $4.95 (k-3)   **516**
1. Geometry 2. Shape
ISBN 0-06-028022-0; 0-06-028023-9 (lib bdg);
0-06-446731-7 (pa)   LC 00-39609
"Level 2."
While piloting his spaceship through the skies, Captain Invincible encounters three-dimensional shapes, including cubes, cylinders, and pyramids
"An excellent tool for introducing a unit on three-dimensional shapes. . . . The bold cartoon art in deep, bright colors draws readers into this fun and exciting story. . . . The concluding reinforcement strategies and activities are very good." SLJ

Hamster champs; by Stuart J. Murphy; illustrated by Pedro Martin. 1st ed. HarperCollins 2005 31p il (MathStart) $15.99; pa $4.99 (1-3)   **516**
1. Angles 2. Hamsters—Fiction 3. Cats—Fiction
ISBN 0-06-055772-9; 0-06-055773-7 (pa)
LC 2004-22471
"Level 3: angles."
This "book offers a lesson on angles. Three rodents that are racing-car enthusiasts create a series of ramps in an attempt to get the feisty house cat with attitude to stop bothering them." SLJ
"The humorous cartoonlike characters are fun, and plenty of good-natured banter between the hamsters and the cat helps make the concept clear." Booklist

Let's fly a kite; illustrated by Brian Floca. HarperCollins Pubs. 2000 33p il (MathStart) $15.95; lib bdg $15.89; pa $4.95 (k-3)   **516**
1. Symmetry 2. Kites
ISBN 0-06-028034-4; 0-06-028035-2 (lib bdg);
0-06-446737-6 (pa)   LC 99-26550
"Level 2."; "Symmetry."
Two squabbling siblings learn about symmetry when their babysitter helps them build and fly a kite
"Floca's watercolor-and-inkline cartoons enhance the story and ably depict the method used to divide everyday objects into two equal parts." SLJ

Polly's pen pal; illustrated by Remy Simard. HarperCollins 2005 30p il (MathStart) $15.99; pa $4.99 (k-3)   **516**
1. Metric system 2. Measurement
ISBN 0-06-053168-1; 0-06-053170-3 (pa)
LC 2003-27526

Murphy, Stuart J.—*Continued*

"Polly has an e-mail pen pal in Montreal. As Ally uses metrics to discuss height, weight, and distances, Polly learns what they mean. No comparisons to English measurements are made but the metric measurements are likened to common objects that kids will recognize. This title features colorful . . . computer-generated cartoons." SLJ

VanCleave, Janice Pratt

Janice VanCleave's geometry for every kid; easy activities that make learning geometry fun; [by] Janice VanCleave. Wiley 1994 221p il $29.95; pa $12.95 (4 and up)   **516**

1. Geometry
ISBN 0-471-31142-1; 0-471-31141-3 (pa)
             LC 93-43049

This "introductory text covers many topics in geometry, from lines, optical illusions, and art-related activities to applications with protractors and the construction of basic solids. Terms are presented in a simplified fashion and are easily understood. Graphics are clear. The hands-on activities encourage learning, creativity, and excitement." Sci Books Films

Includes glossary

519   Probabilities and applied mathematics

Murphy, Stuart J.

Coyotes all around; illustrated by Steve Björkman. HarperCollins Pubs. 2003 31p il (MathStart) $15.99; pa $4.99 (1-3)   **519**

1. Approximate computation 2. Coyotes 3. Roadrunners 4. Counting
ISBN 0-06-051529-5; 0-06-051531-7 (pa)
             LC 2002-151776

A pack of coyotes tries to determine how many roadrunners and other creatures are in their vicinity, and while some count different groups and add their totals together, Clever Coyote rounds off and estimates

"Humorous watercolor cartoons depict the action and clarify the concept. . . . Factoids about coyotes and other desert creatures appear throughout, so readers learn not only math, but also get their fair share of science sprinkled into the mix." SLJ

519.2   Probabilities

Murphy, Stuart J.

Probably pistachio; illustrated by Marsha Winborn. HarperCollins Pubs. 2001 30p il (MathStart) $15.95; lib bdg $15.89; pa $4.95 (k-3)   **519.2**

1. Probabilities
ISBN 0-06-028028-X; 0-06-028029-8 (lib bdg); 0-06-446734-1 (pa)   LC 99-27695
"Level 2."

Readers are introduced to the concept of probability in a story about a boy who has a day in which nothing goes right

"Winborn's watercolors playfully depict Jack's misery as things go from bad to worse. . . . A closing section has follow-up activities to extend and enrich the lesson, as well as a short list of books with related themes." Booklist

519.5   Statistical mathematics

Murphy, Stuart J.

Betcha! illustrated by S.D. Schindler. HarperCollins Pubs. 1997 33p il (MathStart) $15.95; lib bdg $15.89; pa $4.95 (1-3)
            519.5

1. Approximate computation 2. Arithmetic
ISBN 0-06-026768-2; 0-06-026769-0 (lib bdg); 0-06-446707-4 (pa)   LC 96-15486
"estimating; level 3"

"On their way to a store sponsoring a contest that involves guessing the number of jellybeans in a jar, two friends encounter situations that involve numerical determinations. . . . One boy counts one by one to obtain the answers, whereas the other one uses simple techniques to come up with near estimations. The easy-to-read picture-book format with only one or two sentences per page will appeal to reluctant readers. . . . The uncomplicated drawings show how the boy's brain is processing data and the skills he employs to arrive at an educated guess." SLJ

520   Astronomy and allied sciences

Campbell, Ann

The New York Public Library amazing space; a book of answers for kids; [by] Ann-Jeanette Campbell; illustrated by Jessica Wolk-Stanley. Wiley 1997 186p il pa $12.95 (5 and up)
              520

1. Astronomy 2. Outer space
ISBN 0-471-14498-3   LC 96-29785
"A Stonesong Press book"

"Arranged in chapters by major topics, the author states and then addresses questions on general astronomy, celestial objects, our solar system, and space exploration. . . . The material is up to date and presented clearly, with simple illustrations sprinkled in that are sure to catch a child's attention." Sci Books Films

Includes glossary and bibliographical references

Love, Ann

The kids book of the night sky; by Ann Love & Jane Drake; illustrated by Heather Collins. Kids Can Press 2004 144p il $19.95; pa $12.95 (3-6)
              520

1. Astronomy
ISBN 1-55337-357-X; 1-55337-128-3 (pa)

"Using a lively combination of clearly written text, myths and legends, jokes, and activities, the authors present an excellent introduction to the many wonders of the night sky throughout the seasons." SLJ

Mechler, Gary

National Audubon Society first field guide: night sky; sky maps by Wil Tirion. Scholastic 1999 159p il maps $17.95; pa $8.95 (4 and up)
520

1. Astronomy
ISBN 0-590-64085-2; 0-590-64086-0 (pa)
LC 98-51876

A field guide to the night sky, explaining through text and maps how to locate and identify stars, planets, meteors, comets, and constellations

Includes bibliographical references

Reed, George

Eyes on the universe. Benchmark Bks. 2001 80p il (Story of science) lib bdg $29.93 (5 and up)
520

1. Astronomy
ISBN 0-7614-1150-X
LC 00-31527

This survey examines the history of astronomy from ancient times to the present. Aristotle, Ptolemy, Galileo, Newton, Copernicus, William Hubble and Karl Jansky are among the major figures discussed

Includes glossary and bibliographical references

Rhatigan, Joe

Out-of-this-world astronomy; 50 amazing activities & projects; [by] Joe Rhatigan & Rain Newcomb; with Gregg Doppmann, special consultant. Lark Books 2003 128p il $19.95 (5 and up)
520

1. Astronomy
ISBN 1-57990-410-6
LC 2003-5196

Contents: The view from here; The Moon; The Sun; The solar system; The stars and beyond

Introduces the study of "stuff in space," providing statistics, quizzes, activities, and experiments about the stars and planets

"An excellent introduction to astronomy. . . . Most [of the projects] are interesting, informative, and well within the abilities of the intended audience. . . . Spectacular color photos and other graphics, useful charts, and graphs augment the text." SLJ

Includes glossary

Scagell, Robin

Children's night sky atlas; written by Robin Scagell. Dorling Kindersley Pub 2004 96p il spiral bdg $19.99 (5 and up)
520

1. Astronomy
ISBN 0-7566-0284-X
LC 2004-131

"This atlas illustrates . . . constellations, the evolution of stars and galaxies, and the planets in the solar system. Acetate overlays highlight special points of interest." Publisher's note

"A visually stunning and informative introduction to astronomy and stargazing." SLJ

Inlcudes glossary

Simon, Seymour

Destination: space. HarperCollins Pubs. 2002 unp il $15.99; lib bdg $16.89; pa $6.99 (4 and up)
520

1. Astronomy 2. Hubble Space Telescope
ISBN 0-688-16289-4; 0-688-16290-8 (lib bdg); 0-06-059681-3 (pa)
LC 2001-24773

Explains new discoveries about the universe made possible by the Hubble Telescope

This book is "handsome and fascinating. . . . On each spread, the large-print, easy-to-understand text is supported by a stunning, full-page color photograph. The author explains what discovery each image produced and how the information fits into our existing knowledge. His enthusiastic descriptions create vivid pictures in and of themselves." SLJ

522 Techniques, equipment, materials of astronomy

Carruthers, Margaret W.

The Hubble Space Telescope; [by] Margaret W. Carruthers. Franklin Watts 2003 64p il (Watts library) lib bdg $25.50; pa $8.95 (5 and up)
522

1. Hubble Space Telescope
ISBN 0-531-12279-4 (lib bdg); 0-531-16372-5 (pa)
LC 2003-5816

Contents: A new eye on the universe; How a telescope got to space; The guts of the Hubble Space Telescope; Hubble's universe; The future; Timeline of the Hubble Space Telescope

A comprehensive look at the Hubble Space Telescope which has, since 1990, collected information about our solar system, star clusters in the Milky Way galaxy, and even other galaxies as it orbits the Earth.

This is "full of large, sharp, and clear photographs. . . . [This book] will satisfy students looking for introductory research material . . . as well as those with a general interest in the subject." SLJ

Includes bibliographical references

Cole, Michael D.

Hubble Space Telescope; exploring the universe. Enslow Pubs. 1999 48p il (Countdown to space) lib bdg $23.93 (4 and up)
522

1. Astronomy 2. Hubble Space Telescope 3. Astronautics
ISBN 0-7660-1120-8
LC 98-3298

Details the initiation of the Hubble Space Telescope in April 1990 and the repair and servicing missions which followed; explains the telescope's role in answering questions about the universe

"Illustrated with color photographs, the book provides solid basic information." Horn Book

Includes glossary and bibliographical references

Nardo, Don

Telescopes. Kidhaven Press 2005 48p il (Kidhaven science library) $23.70 (4 and up)
522

1. Telescopes
ISBN 0-7377-3060-9
This "volume explains how telescopes work and traces their history, along with the major discoveries they made possible, from Galileo's time to the present. The final chapter deals with present and planned space telescopes." Publisher's note
Includes glossary and bibliographical references

523   Specific celestial bodies and phenomena

Berger, Melvin

Do stars have points? questions and answers about stars and planets; [by] Melvin and Gilda Berger; illustrated by Vincent Di Fate. Scholastic Ref. 1998 48p il (Scholastic question and answer series) lib bdg $12.95; pa $5.95 (2-4)
523

1. Astronomy 2. Stars 3. Solar system
ISBN 0-590-13080-3 (lib bdg); 0-590-13087-0 (pa)
LC 97-36005
Questions and answers explore various aspects of stars and our solar system, including the sun, planets, moons, comets, and asteroids
This book "organizes the material well, it asks questions that children may actually have posed, and the answers are clear and precise. . . . Often dramatic and beautiful, the paintings illustrate the text quite effectively." Booklist

Cole, Joanna

The magic school bus, lost in the solar system; illustrated by Bruce Degen. Scholastic 1990 unp il pa $4.99 hardcover o.p. (2-4)
523

1. Astronomy 2. Outer space—Exploration 3. Planets
ISBN 0-590-4429-1 (pa)
LC 89-10185
Also available Spanish language edition
"The planetarium is closed for repairs, so the Magic School Bus blasts off on a real tour of the solar system. After their previous field trips, the children in Ms. Frizzle's class are all blasé about such things; as they land on the Moon, Venus, and Mars, and fly by the other planets and the Sun, they comment on what they see, generate a blizzard of one- or two-sentence reports on special topics and—even while Ms. Frizzle is temporarily left behind in the asteroid belt—crack terrible jokes." SLJ

Simon, Seymour

The universe. Morrow Junior Bks. 1998 unp il $16.95; pa $6.99 (4 and up)
523

1. Cosmology
ISBN 0-688-15301-1; 0-06-443752-3 (pa)
LC 97-20489
"Matching full-color, full- and double-page-spread-sized light and radio photographs of nebulas, galaxies, and sundry deep-space phenomena with two or three paragraphs of explanatory text [Simon] covers a wide range of topics, from the Big Bang to quasars, from star formation to extrasolar planets. . . . The choice of detail is guaranteed to whet youngster's appetites for a more thorough, narrowly focused treatment." SLJ

523.1   The universe, galaxies, quasars

Asimov, Isaac

The Milky Way and other galaxies; by Isaac Asimov; with revisions and updating by Richard Hantula. Gareth Stevens Pub 2005 32p (Isaac Asimov's 21st century library of the universe) lib bdg $24.67 (4-6)
523.1

1. Galaxies 2. Milky Way
ISBN 0-8368-3968-4   LC 2004-58313
First published 1995 with title: Our vast home
This "examines various galactic types, structures, and superstructures, as observed by a wide array of specialized telescopes. . . . The pictures . . . are striking. . . . [An] excellent collection [enhancer]." SLJ
Includes bibliographical references

Rau, Dana Meachen

The Milky Way and other galaxies; by Dana Meachen Rau. Compass Point Books 2005 32p il (Our solar system) $22.60 (3-5)
523.1
1. Galaxies 2. Milky Way
ISBN 0-7565-0853-3   LC 2004-15571
Contents: A milky path of stars; A spinning pinwheel; Where in the galaxy are we?; Parts of the Milky Way; Types of galaxies; Groups of galaxies; Always on the move
The author "describes the nature of our own galaxy, then presents a gallery of other types, along with brief mentions of quasars, clusters, and superclusters. [The book is] illustrated with a mix of photos and digital art. . . . [This earns] high marks for visual appeal, and for clear, specific presentation of material." SLJ
Includes glossary and bibliographical references

Simon, Seymour

Galaxies. Morrow Junior Bks. 1988 unp il $18; pa $6.95 (3-6)
523.1
1. Galaxies
ISBN 0-688-08002-2; 0-688-10992-6 (pa)
LC 87-23967
"This is a step-by-step introduction to and description of the many galaxies in the universe. . . . He includes discussions of the ways in which astronomers classify galaxies, black holes, smaller satellite galaxies such as the Magellanic Clouds and supernovas. The terms are explained within the text." Publ Wkly
"This fine introduction to an awe-inspiring subject will surely stimulate interest in stargazing, further reading, and investigation." Horn Book

523.2 Planetary systems

Ride, Sally K.
Exploring our solar system; [by] Sally Ride and Tam O'Shaughnessy. Crown 2003 110p il $19.95 (4 and up)   **523.2**
1. Solar system 2. Planets
ISBN 0-375-81204-0   LC 2002-17471
Describes what we have learned about our solar system from telescopes and spacecraft, focusing on the characteristics of the planets and their moons
"In this copiously illustrated volume, astronaut Ride and educator O'Shaughnessy offer a thrilling introduction to our solar system. . . . Visually arresting and clearly presented." Booklist
Includes glossary

Simon, Seymour
Our solar system. Morrow Junior Bks. 1992 64p il $19.95; lib bdg $19.93 (3-6)   **523.2**
1. Solar system
ISBN 0-688-09992-0; 0-688-09993-9 (lib bdg)
                                      LC 91-36665
"With a variety of full-color photographs, the solar system and its characteristics are described, including the sun, asteroids, meteoroids, and comets. This book is a wonderful introduction into the mysteries surrounding the solar system." Sci Child

VanCleave, Janice Pratt
Janice VanCleave's solar system; mind-boggling experiments you can turn into science fair projects. Wiley 2000 90p il map pa $10.95 (4 and up)
                                      523.2
1. Solar system 2. Science projects 3. Science—Experiments
ISBN 0-471-32204-0   LC 99-15479
Provides instructions for a variety of experiments and science fair projects exploring the solar system, including the sun, moon, planets, comets, and meteorites
"Welcome and valuable." SLJ
Includes glossary

523.3 Moon

Branley, Franklyn Mansfield
The moon seems to change; by Franklyn M. Branley; illustrations by Barbara and Ed Emberley. rev ed. Crowell 1987 29p il (Let's-read-and-find-out science book) pa $4.95 hardcover o.p. (k-3)   **523.3**
1. Moon
ISBN 0-06-445065-1 (pa)   LC 86-47747
A revised and newly illustrated edition of the title first published 1960
The author "explains the waxing and waning of the moon and compares the length of a day on earth and on the moon. Each page has colorful explanatory illustrations. . . . Branley's brief-easy-to-read text and the Emberleys' diagrams make this book a welcome addition to science collections for young children or the picture book section." SLJ

What the moon is like; by Franklyn M. Branley; illustrated by True Kelley. Newly illustrated ed. HarperCollins Pubs. 2000 30p il (Let's-read-and-find-out science) $15.95; lib bdg $15.89; pa $4.95 (k-3)   **523.3**
1. Moon
ISBN 0-06-027992-3; 0-06-027993-1 (lib bdg); 0-06-445185-2 (pa)   LC 98-54072
A revised and newly illustrated edition of the title first published 1963 by Crowell
This book "invites readers simply to observe the moon from Earth before it delves into facts. . . . The following pages, all illustrated with clear, colorful pictures of astronauts and the lunar landscape, explore the moon's actual surface, climate, and temperature; briefly discuss lunar landings (with a map); and draw comparisons between the moon and Earth." Booklist

Bredeson, Carmen
The moon. Watts 1998 63p il pa $6.95 hardcover o.p. (4 and up)   **523.3**
1. Project Apollo 2. Moon 3. Apollo project
ISBN 0-531-15911-6 (pa)   LC 96-40226
"A First book"
Describes what people have believed about the moon and what has been learned over time and presents an overview of the Apollo space program
"Clear, effective illustrations, most in color, appear throughout the book. . . . A good resource for science collections." Booklist
Includes glossary and bibliographical references

Gibbons, Gail
The moon book. Holiday House 1997 unp il $16.95; pa $6.95 (k-3)   **523.3**
1. Moon
ISBN 0-8234-1297-0; 0-8234-1364-0 (pa)
                                      LC 96-36826
Identifies the moon as our only natural satellite, describes its movement and phases, and discusses how we have observed and explored it over the years
"Gibbons presents a great deal of information in a deceptively simple format by combining inviting illustrations with clear writing." Horn Book Guide

Simon, Seymour
The moon. [rev ed] Simon & Schuster Bks. for Young Readers 2003 unp il $17.95 (4 and up)
                                      523.3
1. Moon
ISBN 0-689-83563-9   LC 2001-31303
First published 1984 by Four Winds Press
A basic introduction to Earth's closest neighbor, its composition, and man's missions to it
"The digitally remastered color photographs in this update are incredible. . . . The text has undergone minimal change. . . . The facts remain true and relevant, and the writing reflects the graphics: beautiful. This is a must-have for astronomy sections." SLJ

Tomecek, Steve

Moon; illustrated by Liisa Chauncy Guida. National Geographic 2005 31p il (Jump into science) $16.95; lib bdg $25.90 (k-2)

523.3

1. Moon

ISBN 0-7922-5123-7; 0-7922-8304-X (lib bdg)

LC 2004-8761

"A cartoon cat and bug explain scientific history and concepts regarding the Earth's moon: its ever-changing appearance, composition, comparisons to Earth and the sun, Galileo's observations and discoveries in 1609, astronauts, orbits, and other topics." SLJ

"Guida's artwork, in bright, saturated colors, will easily draw children into the science. . . . Tomecek's words encourage a sense of awe and wonder." Booklist

523.4   Planets

Bortolotti, Dan

Exploring Saturn. Firefly Bks. 2003 64p il $19.95; pa $9.95 (5 and up)   **523.4**

1. Saturn (Planet)

ISBN 1-55297-766-8; 1-55297-765-X (pa)

This "introduction to the sixth planet [describes] . . . what we know, don't know, and hope to find out soon. The author . . . lays out Saturn's probable origins and inner structure, provides . . . glimpses of [its] rings, and describes each moon in turn—including one, as yet unnamed, discovered in 2003. He then covers the Cassini-Huygens mission in detail." SLJ

"This appealing presentation features a well-organized and engaging text as well as many exceptionally clear, colorful illustrations: photographs, space-telescope images, paintings, and drawings." Booklist

Branley, Franklyn Mansfield

The planets in our solar system; by Franklyn M. Branley; illustrated by Kevin O'Malley. HarperCollins Pubs. 1998 31p il (Let's-read-and-find-out science) $15.95; lib bdg $15.89; pa $4.95 (k-3)   **523.4**

1. Planets 2. Solar system

ISBN 0-06-027769-6; 0-06-027770-X (lib bdg); 0-06-445178-X (pa)   LC 97-1174

First published 1981

Describes the nine planets and other bodies of the solar system; includes directions for making models showing the size of the planets and their distance from the sun

"Branley makes his points briefly and precisely." SLJ

Croswell, Ken

Ten worlds; everything that orbits the sun; [by] Ken Croswell. 1st ed. Boyds Mills Press 2006 56p il $19.95 (5 and up)   **523.4**

1. Planets 2. Solar system

ISBN 1-59078-423-5   LC 2005035316

This describes the planets of our solar system and their moons, plus comets, meteors, and asteroids.

"On the basis of its striking design and photographs,

this handsome, large-format volume is well worthy of praise. And astronomer Crosswell's . . . concise yet conversational, information-packed text wins it sky-high accolades in the narrative sphere as well." Publ Wkly

Dussling, Jennifer

Planets; illustrated by Denise Ortakales. Grosset & Dunlap 2000 unp il lib bdg $13.89; pa $3.99 (1-3)   **523.4**

1. Planets

ISBN 0-448-42416-9 (lib bdg); 0-448-42406-1 (pa)

LC 00-59601

"All aboard reading"

This "title offers basic information on the solar system, including some mention of historical beliefs about the planets." Booklist

This offers "simple, informative text and clearly labeled cut-paper illustrations." Horn Book Guide

Fradin, Dennis B.

The planet hunters; the search for other worlds; [by] Dennis Brindell Fradin. Margaret K. McElderry Bks. 1997 148p il $19.95 (5 and up)   **523.4**

1. Astronomers 2. Astronomy 3. Planets

ISBN 0-689-81323-6   LC 96-29721

Provides historical information on astronomy, the discovery of the planets, and the people who have made such discoveries

This is "a well-researched book. . . . Black-and-white photographs appear throughout the book, with a section of color plates inserted in the middle. . . . The immediacy of the writing will carry readers along in the narrative flow of this often dramatic story." Booklist

Includes bibliographical references

Gibbons, Gail

The planets. rev ed. Holiday House 2005 unp il $16.95 (k-3)   **523.4**

1. Planets

ISBN 0-8234-1957-6

First published 1993

Discusses the movements, location, and characteristics of the nine known planets of our solar system

"The bright colors, simplified shapes, and spacious, uncomplicated page design make this an inviting gateway to the subject." SLJ [review of 1993 edition]

Miller, Ron

Mercury and Pluto; [by] Ron Miller. Twenty-First Century Books 2003 80p il (Worlds beyond) lib bdg $27.90 (5 and up)   **523.4**

1. Mercury (Planet) 2. Pluto (Planet)

ISBN 0-7613-2361-9   LC 2002-14099

Contents: The limits of the solar system; New worlds; The planet hunt; Worlds of fire and ice; Pluto

Contrasts the discovery, creation, orbit, atmosphere, composition, surface features, and rotation of the nearest and farthest planets from the sun.

"Concepts are explained clearly, and helpful diagrams and carefully chosen illustrations assist understanding." SLJ

Includes bibliographical references

Miller, Ron—*Continued*

Saturn. Twenty-First Century Books 2003 80p il (Worlds beyond) lib bdg $27.90 (5 and up)

523.4

1. Saturn (Planet)
ISBN 0-7613-2360-0   LC 2002-14098
Contents: Lord of the rings; Exploring Saturn; The crown jewel of the solar system; Moons, moons, and more moons; The future of Saturn
Chronicles the discovery and exploration of the planet Saturn and discusses its rings and moons, its place in the solar system, and more.
"Concepts are explained clearly, and helpful diagrams and carefully chosen illustrations assist understanding." SLJ
Includes bibliographical references

Simon, Seymour
Destination: Jupiter. rev ed. Morrow Junior Bks. 1998 unp il $16.89; pa $6.99 (3-6)   **523.4**
1. Jupiter (Planet)
ISBN 0-688-15620-7; 0-06-443759-0 (pa)
LC 97-20488
First published 1985 with title: Jupiter
This is a "guide to the planet and its four Galilean moons, Io, Europa, Ganymede, and Callisto. The complete planetary portrait is achieved by combining classic *Voyager* spacecraft images and more recent *Galileo* mission photographs." Horn Book Guide
"Expertly balancing the verbal and visual presentation, Simon . . . demonstrates his ability to inform and entertain simultaneously." SLJ

Destination: Mars. HarperCollins Pubs. 2000 unp il $15.95; lib bdg $15.89 (3-6)   **523.4**
1. Mars (Planet)
ISBN 0-688-15770-X; 0-688-15771-8 (lib bdg)
LC 99-15523
First published 1987 by Morrow with title: Mars
"The descriptions and explanations of Mars—its geological and meteorological features, and historical speculation about them—present a coherent picture of what scientists know about the planet. Also included within the text are vital statistics, such as Mars's distance from the earth and sun, orbit position, and gravity. . . . [Includes] remarkable new color photographs from the Global Surveyor and Pathfinder missions . . . and from the Hubble telescope. . . . *Destination Mars* presents a comprehensive and informative survey of the planet." Horn Book

523.6   Comets

Bonar, Samantha
Comets. Watts 1998 63p il pa $6.95 hardcover o.p. (4 and up)   **523.6**
1. Comets
ISBN 0-531-15907-8 (pa)   LC 96-53502
"A First book"
Describes what has been learned about the composition, orbits, and the existence of several well-known comets
"Attractive, colorful illustrations are numerous and complement the text. . . . An excellent reference book for young readers." Sci Books Films
Includes glossary and bibliographical references

Cole, Michael D.
Comets and asteroids; ice and rocks in space. Enslow Pubs. 2003 48p il (Countdown to space) lib bdg $18.95 (4 and up)   **523.6**
1. Comets
ISBN 0-7660-1954-3   LC 2002-8520
Explores what comets and asteroids are, how scientists have studied them throughout history, and the effects of space debris on the Earth when it enters our atmosphere
Includes glossary and bibliographical references

Marsh, Carole S.
Asteroids, comets, and meteors; [by] Carole Marsh. 21st Cent. Bks. (NY) 1996 64p il (Secrets of space) lib bdg $23.90 (4-6)   **523.6**
1. Comets 2. Meteors 3. Asteroids
ISBN 0-8050-4473-6   LC 96-8882
This "discusses the discovery of the nature of comets, asteroids, and meteors, from the observations and beliefs of ancient Greek and Chinese astronomers to the first sighting of comet Hyakutake. . . . Many colorful illustrations, photographs as well as diagrams and paintings, complement the succinctly written [text]." Booklist
Includes glossary and bibliographical references

Simon, Seymour
Comets, meteors, and asteroids. Morrow Junior Bks. 1994 unp il pa $6.95 hardcover o.p. (3-6)
523.6
1. Comets 2. Meteors 3. Asteroids
ISBN 0-688-15843-9 (pa)   LC 93-51251
"Simon presents basic information about comets, meteors, and asteroids in an attractive oversize book. . . . Blocks of text appear in fairly large type, usually facing a full-page illustration. . . . Simon writes in plain language, without talking down to his audience. The intriguing photographs include shots of comets and meteor showers in the sky, a meteorite in Antarctica, and an enormous impact crater in Arizona." Booklist

Vogt, Gregory
Asteroids, comets, and meteors; [by] Gregory L. Vogt. Millbrook Press 1996 31p il (Gateway solar system) lib bdg $20.90 (2-4)   **523.6**
1. Comets 2. Asteroids 3. Meteors
ISBN 1-56294-601-3   LC 95-19735
Presents information on the different types of celestial matter known as asteroids, comets, and meteors and on what scientists learned from the impact of a comet on the surface of Jupiter
This "is a relatively thorough, reliable introduction to its subject. . . . [It features] plenty of clear full-color photos and art from NASA." SLJ
Includes glossary and bibliographical references

523.7   Sun

Branley, Franklyn Mansfield
The sun, our nearest star; by Franklyn M.
Branley; illustrated by Edward Miller.
HarperCollins Pubs. 2002 25p il
(Let's-read-and-find-out science) $15.95; lib bdg
$15.89; pa $4.95 (k-2)   **523.7**
  1. Sun
  ISBN 0-06-028534-6; 0-06-028535-4 (lib bdg);
0-06-445202-6 (pa)   LC 2001-24951
  A revised and newly illustrated edition of the title first
published 1961
  Describes the sun and how it provides the light and
energy which allow plant and animal life to exist on the
earth
  "This edition marks the third incarnation of an old
standby. . . . The gently edited text reads better than the
old one. The new design features a larger format, bolder
typography, and eye-catching artwork." Booklist

Gibbons, Gail
Sun up, sun down; written and illustrated by
Gail Gibbons. Harcourt Brace Jovanovich 1983
unp il $16; pa $6 (k-3)   **523.7**
  1. Sun
  ISBN 0-15-282781-1; 0-15-282782-X (pa)
         LC 82-23420
  The author explains "the sun and its effect on the
earth. Narrated by a little girl who notices the sun shining when she wakes up one morning, this . . . [book
covers] what the sun does, what makes shadows, how the
sun helps form rain clouds, and how it keeps the planet
warm." Booklist
  "The illustrations clarify the text with bold, clear
drawings in full color." SLJ

523.8   Stars

Asimov, Isaac
The life and death of stars; by Isaac Asimov.
rev and updated ed, with revisions and updating by
Richard Hantula. Gareth Stevens Pub 2005 32p il
lib bdg $24.67 (4-6)   **523.8**
  1. Stars
  ISBN 0-8368-3967-6   LC 2004-57842
  First published 1995 with title: Star cycles
  This "begins with the birth of stars in dust cloud nur-
series; goes on to profile the different types of stars; describes supernovas, neutron stars, and other late-stage developments; then closes with an account of our Sun's
probable fate. . . . [This is an] excellent collection
[enhancer]." SLJ
  Includes bibliographical references

Branley, Franklyn Mansfield
The Big Dipper; by Franklyn M. Branley;
illustrated by Molly Coxe. rev ed. HarperCollins
Pubs. 1991 32p il (Let's-read-and-find-out science
book) pa $4.95 hardcover o.p. (k-1)   **523.8**
  1. Ursa Major
  ISBN 0-06-445100-3 (pa)   LC 90-31199

  A revised and newly illustrated edition of the title first
published 1962
  Explains basic facts about the Big Dipper, including
which stars make up the constellation, how its position
changes in the sky, and how it points to the North Star

Mitton, Jacqueline
Once upon a starry night; a book of
constellations; [illustrated by] Christina Balit.
National Geographic 2004 c2003 unp il $16.95
(k-3)   **523.8**
  1. Constellations 2. Classical mythology
  ISBN 0-7922-6332-4   LC 2003-10993
  Companion volume to Zoo in the sky (1998)
  First published 2003 in the United Kingdom
  Presents facts about stars, nebulas, galaxies, and constellations and recounts the Greek myths that provided
widely-known names for ten constellations, from An-
dromeda to Pegasus.
  "Although the stories are quite short, Mitton's vivid
word choices make the text as dynamic as Balit's striking pictures. Partly abstract and partly representational,
the artwork features bold figures of mythological characters with silver-foil stars highlighting the points of light
that make up the constellations." Booklist

Rau, Dana Meachen
Black holes; by Dana Meachen Rau. Compass
Point Books 2005 32p il (Our solar system) $22.60
(3-5)   **523.8**
  1. Black holes (Astronomy)
  ISBN 0-7565-0849-5   LC 2004-15567
  Contents: Invisible spots in outer space; Imagining a
visit; The life of stars; Types of black holes; Thinking
about black holes; Studying black holes
  "Rightly noting . . . that black holes by their very nature can neither be seen nor directly measured, [the au-
thor] discusses what we can infer and theorize from indi-
rect observations, then closes with a revealing 2004 discovery. . . . [This earns] high marks for visual appeal,
and for clear, specific presentation of material." SLJ
  Includes glossary and bibliographical references

Rey, H. A. (Hans Augusto)
Find the constellations. rev ed. Houghton
Mifflin 1976 72p il $20; pa $9.95 (3-6)
     523.8
  1. Constellations
  ISBN 0-395-24509-5; 0-395-24418-8 (pa)
  First published 1954
  "Constellation diagrams are presented with and without connecting lines and are drawn for 40° N. Latitude
to cover the continental United States. . . . Scientific accuracy is stressed, stellar magnitudes are indicated on the
diagrams, and the concept of light year is discussed.
Some of the myths surrounding the names of the constellations are given." Sci Books Films
  "This is unquestionably a readable, enjoyable, and informative guide." SLJ

Rockwell, Anne F.

Our stars; written and illustrated by Anne Rockwell. Silver Whistle Bks. 1999 unp il $13 (k-2) **523.8**

1. Stars 2. Planets 3. Outer space

ISBN 0-15-201868-9 LC 97-49518

A simple introduction to the stars, planets, and outer space

"This book clearly explains many science facts without 'talking down' to youngsters. The storybook-style illustrations, . . . invite children to look at the night sky and think about the information presented in the text." Sci Books Films

VanCleave, Janice Pratt

Janice VanCleave's constellations for every kid; easy activities that make learning science fun. Wiley 1997 247p il maps $29.95; pa $12.95 (4 and up) **523.8**

1. Constellations 2. Astronomy

ISBN 0-471-15981-6; 0-471-15979-4 (pa)

LC 96-35309

Describes twenty of the most prominent constellations, including the Big Dipper, Orion, and Cancer, explains how to locate them, and provides instructions for related activities

"Much more than a connect-the-dots stargazer guide, this comprehensive book is packed with information on locating constellations that goes far beyond what is found in most books on the subject." Booklist

Includes glossary

525 Earth (Astronomical geography)

Bailey, Jacqui

Sun up, sun down; the story of day and night; written by Jacqui Bailey; illustrated by Matthew Lilly. 1st American ed. Picture Window Books 2004 31p il (Science works) lib bdg $23.93 (2-4) **525**

1. Day 2. Night 3. Sun 4. Earth 5. Moon

ISBN 1-4048-0567-2 LC 2003-20119

Follows the sun from dawn to dusk to explain how light rays travel, how shadows are formed, how the moon lights up the night sky, and more.

This "excellent science [book explains its subject] lucidly and sometimes amusingly. . . . Children will be illuminated and engaged." SLJ

Includes bibliographical references

Gallant, Roy A.

Earth's place in space. Benchmark Bks. 1999 80p il (Story of science) lib bdg $28.50 (5 and up) **525**

1. Earth 2. Universe

ISBN 0-7614-0963-7 LC 98-28043

Relates the history of the struggle to understand earth's place in the universe, from earliest mythmaking to today's discoveries via the Hubble telescope

This book is "highly useful. . . . [It is] richly illustrated with color photos, drawings, and charts." Booklist

Includes glossary and bibliographical references

Gibbons, Gail

The reasons for seasons. Holiday House 1995 unp il $16.95; pa $6.95 (k-3) **525**

1. Seasons 2. Earth

ISBN 0-8234-1174-5; 0-8234-1238-5 (pa)

LC 94-32904

"Gibbons uses simple words and clear, colorful pictures to explain the seasons, the solstices, and the equinoxes. Besides discussing the earth's tilt and orbit, she also comments on what people and animals do in each season of the year." Booklist

Karas, G. Brian

On Earth; written and illustrated by G. Brian Karas. Putnam 2005 unp il $16.99 (k-2) **525**

1. Earth

ISBN 0-399-24025-X LC 2004-18204

"Karas covers the earth's rotation and revolution, space and time, hemispheres, and gravity. The spare text alternates between technical descriptions and personal experiences. Artistic renderings of the earth and its cycles introduce diagrams and offer concrete images showing what happens as day turns to night, seasons change, and the earth rotates on its axis." Horn Book Guide

Miller, Ron

Earth and the moon. 21st Cent. Bks. (Brookfield) 2003 96p il (Worlds beyond) lib bdg $25.90 (5 and up) **525**

1. Earth 2. Moon

ISBN 0-7613-2358-9 LC 2001-8479

Contents: Discovering a planet; The beginning; The story of the moon; Earth, air, fire, and water; The birth of life; The first animals; Earth takes shape; The rise and fall of the dinosaurs; Earth today; Earth around us; A planet on the move; A visit to the moon; The end of the world

Chronicles the origin, evolution, and exploration of the Earth and the Moon, and discusses their composition, their place in our solar system, and more

This is illustrated "with a mix of NASA photos and wide-angle, computer-generated art. . . . Students with a serious interest in the physical history of the Earth and its moon will be engrossed by his account of our planet's first few billion years, the Moon's probable origin, and the rise of life." SLJ

Includes glossary and bibliographical references

Ross, Michael Elsohn

Earth cycles; illustrated by Gustav Moore. Millbrook Press 2001 unp il (Cycles) lib bdg $22.40 (k-3) **525**

1. Earth

ISBN 0-7613-1815-1 LC 00-41860

"Ross discusses Earth's daily cycle of light and dark, the thirteen lunar cycles, and Earth's yearly trip around the sun. The simple text provides very basic information about periodicity and uses familiar examples to introduce new concepts. . . . Pleasing watercolors expand the text." Horn Book Guide

Simon, Seymour
Earth: our planet in space. [rev ed] Simon & Schuster Bks. for Young Readers 2003 unp il $17.95 (4 and up)   **525**
1. Earth
ISBN 0-689-83562-0   LC 2001-31304
First published 1984 by Four Winds Press
This describes the relationship between the Earth, the sun, and the moon and explains the seasons, day and night, the atmosphere, and changes in the planet's surface. Illustrated with photographs taken from space

526   Mathematical geography

Borden, Louise
Sea clocks; the story of longitude; illustrated by Erik Blegvad. Margaret K. McElderry Bks. 2003 unp il $18.95 (3-6)   **526**
1. Harrison, John, 1693-1776 2. Clocks and watches 3. Longitude
ISBN 0-689-84216-3   LC 00-45599
This "picture book introduces John Harrison, the 18th-century English carpenter turned clockmaker who spent more than 40 years perfecting a device that solved the centuries-old problem of determining longitude. . . . The writing has a measured pace that helps readers to keep the details straight and the scientific concepts are clearly explained and smoothly incorporated into the text. Blegvad's precise illustrations create a strong sense of time and place." SLJ

Lasky, Kathryn
The man who made time travel; pictures by Kevin Hawkes. Farrar, Straus & Giroux 2003 unp il $17 (3-5)   **526**
1. Harrison, John, 1693-1776 2. Clocks and watches 3. Longitude 4. Navigation
ISBN 0-374-34788-3   LC 2001-33266
"Melanie Kroupa books"
Describes the need for sailors to be able to determine their position at sea and the efforts of John Harrison, an eighteenth century man who spent his life refining instruments to enable them to do this
"With Hawkes's luminous full-color paintings on every page, its clear science, and its compelling social commentary, this title is not to be missed." SLJ
Includes bibliographical references

529   Chronology

Gardner, Robert
It's about time! Science projects; How long does it take? Enslow Pubs. 2003 48p il (Sensational science experiments) $18.95 (3-6)   **529**
1. Time 2. Clocks and watches 3. Science—Experiments 4. Science projects
ISBN 0-7660-2012-6   LC 2002-4621
Contents: Time before clocks; Measuring time with the sun; A water clock; A problem with water clocks; A

sand clock; A candle clock; Heart time; From heart clock to pendulum clock; A pendulum clock; Running time; Time to breathe; Quick as a wink or a squeeze; Time to fall; How fast can you react?; Decay time; Estimating time; Using time to stop motion; A year of change
This offers 18 experiments in time measurement
This is an "approachable, hands-on-book. . . . This volume is not casual reading; it deserves and requires some attention as well as adult guidance and will be rewarding to those who make the effort." Sci Books Films
Includes bibliographical references

Koscielniak, Bruce
About time; a first look at time and clocks; by Bruce Koscielniak. Houghton Mifflin 2004 unp il map $16 (3-5)   **529**
1. Time 2. Clocks and watches
ISBN 0-618-39668-3   LC 2003-17469
Describes the concept of time and how it has been measured throughout history, using water clocks, sundials, calendars, and atomic vibrations.
"Koscielniak gives an instructive yet entertaining march through the ages. . . . Attractive watercolor illustrations in green and tan tones enhance the text." SLJ

Kummer, Patricia K.
The calendar; by Patricia K. Kummer. Franklin Watts 2005 80p il (Inventions that shaped the world) $30.50; pa $9.95 (4 and up)   **529**
1. Calendars
ISBN 0-531-12340-5; 0-531-16720-8 (pa)
    LC 2004-6914
This "book presents the origins and history of the calendar. . . . The illustrations include clear reproductions of period paintings, engravings, and drawings as well as photos of artifacts, sculpture, and contemporary scenes. . . . A good basic introduction." Booklist
Includes bibliographical references

Maestro, Betsy
The story of clocks and calendars; marking a millennium; illustrated by Giulio Maestro. Lothrop, Lee & Shepard Bks. 1999 48p il $16; lib bdg $15.89 (3-6)   **529**
1. Calendars 2. Clocks and watches 3. Time
ISBN 0-688-14548-5; 0-688-14549-3 (lib bdg)
    LC 98-21305
"This overview of timekeeping begins with prehistoric 'calendar sticks' and stone structures, and continues through today's ultra-precise atomic clocks. The text takes a broad multicultural approach, showing how science, history, and societal differences have influenced the calendar; the color illustrations are executed in styles that match the eras and cultures discussed in the volume." Horn Book Guide

Murphy, Stuart J.
It's about time! illustrated by John Speirs. HarperCollins Publishers 2005 33p il (MathStart) $15.99; pa $4.99 (k-2)   **529**
1. Time 2. Day 3. Night
ISBN 0-06-055768-0; 0-06-055769-9 (pa)
    LC 2003-27524

Murphy, Stuart J.—*Continued*

"Each page shows an analog clock and a digital clock displaying the time, from seven o'clock one morning through the day and night to seven the next morning. The illustrations show the child's activities and, in the night, his dreams. . . . Soft pencil drawings deliniate the rounded forms of children engaged in their daily activities. The rich colors of the washes glow against the white backgrounds." Booklist

Nagda, Ann Whitehead

Chimp math; learning about time from a baby chimpanzee; by Ann Whitehead Nagda and Cindy Bickel. Holt & Co. 2002 29p il $16.95 (2-4)

529

1. Time 2. Chimpanzees
ISBN 0-8050-6674-8   LC 00-57529
Companion volume to Tiger math

The authors "integrate the elementary-level mathematical skills of telling and representing time with the story of [a] . . . chimp, Jiggs. . . . Jiggs's growth and feeding are shown through representations of time: timelines, graphs of variables over time, calendars, and daily charts." Horn Book

"The details of the chimp's young life will fascinate readers. . . . The time lines, in particular, illuminate the narrative and can lead to classroom projects." SLJ

Older, Jules

Telling time; how to tell time on digital and analog clocks! written by Jules Older; illustrated by Megan Halsey. Charlesbridge Pub. 2000 unp il $16.95; pa $6.95 (k-3)   **529**

1. Time 2. Clocks and watches
ISBN 0-88106-396-7; 0-88106-397-5 (pa)
                                         LC 99-18764
Humorous text explains the concept of time, from seconds to hours on both analog and digital clocks, from years to millennia on the calendar

"The cartoon illustrations, showing children and many, many types of clocks are colorful, plentiful, and inviting. . . . This jovial look at time and time telling is as handy as they come." SLJ

Skurzynski, Gloria

On time; from seasons to split seconds. National Geographic Soc. 2000 41p il $17.95 (4 and up)

529

1. Time
ISBN 0-7922-7503-9   LC 99-33927
Examines the ways humans have measured time throughout history and discusses the various units that are used to keep track of it

"This attractive offering is brimming with information. . . . The conversational tone helps readers get through the more difficult concepts. . . . The book is heavily illustrated with full-color drawings, photographs, and diagrams." SLJ

530   Physics

Gardner, Robert

Science projects about physics in the home. Enslow Pubs. 1999 112p il (Science projects) lib bdg $26.60 (5 and up)   **530**

1. Physics 2. Science—Experiments 3. Science projects
ISBN 0-89490-948-7   LC 98-6822
Presents instructions for physics projects and experiments that can be done at home and exhibited at science fairs

"This volume is well organized with lots of hands-on activities that use relatively simple pieces of equipment. . . . A good starting point in the understanding of the physics of objects and events in our daily life." Sci Books Films

Includes bibliographical references

Ross, Michael Elsohn

Toy lab; illustrations by Tim Seeley. Carolrhoda Bks. 2003 48p il (You are the scientist) lib bdg $23.29 (3-6)   **530**

1. Toys 2. Physics 3. Science—Experiments
ISBN 0-87614-456-3   LC 2001-5456
"Using the scientific method, youngsters are encouraged to experiment with toys like Slinkies, Silly Putty, Frisbees, and blocks to learn about flight, gravity, matter, pressure and waves, and objects in motion. . . . Toy Lab should pique youngsters' interest, even those who are not usually drawn to scientific experiments, and will give students some ideas for science fair projects as well." SLJ

Includes glossary

530.4   States of matter

Bradley, Kimberly Brubaker

Pop! a book about bubbles; photographs by Margaret Miller. HarperCollins Pubs. 2001 33p il (Let's-read-and-find-out science) $15.95; lib bdg $15.89; pa $4.95 (k-1)   **530.4**

1. Bubbles
ISBN 0-06-028700-4; 0-06-028701-2 (lib bdg);
0-06-445208-5 (pa)   LC 99-57794
Simple text explains how soap bubbles are made, why they are always round, and why they pop

"A simple, accurate text that is also fun to read. . . . Delightful color photographs of charming children making bubbles and of bubbles floating freely reinforce and extend the text. . . . This is science learning at its best." SLJ

Hewitt, Sally

Solid, liquid, or gas? Children's Press 1998 30p il (It's science!) lib bdg $20.50; pa $6.95 (k-3)
                                         530.4

1. Matter
ISBN 0-516-20794-6 (lib bdg); 0-516-26393-5 (pa)
                                         LC 97-5308
Presents information about the properties of solids, liquids, and gases, using observation and activities

Mason, Adrienne

Touch it! materials, matter and you; written by Adrienne Mason; illustrated by Claudia Dávila. Kids Can Press 2005 32p il (Primary physical science) $12.95; pa $5.95 (k-2)   **530.4**

1. Materials 2. Matter

ISBN 1-55337-760-5; 1-55337-761-3 (pa)

"Large-scale digital illustrations show children, animals, and adults commenting on and exploring the properties of matter. Some sections discuss ideas such as mass, buoyancy, or magnetism, while others suggest informal activities, for example describing different foods. Five double-page spreads present very simple science projects, beginning with a question-and-answer section followed by a short list of materials, a few steps to follow, and a brief concluding paragraph. . . . This colorful beginning science series is suitable for primary-grade students in groups and even younger children one-on-one." Booklist

Includes glossary

Zoehfeld, Kathleen Weidner

What is the world made of? all about solids, liquids, and gases; illustrated by Paul Meisel. HarperCollins Pubs. 1998 32p il (Let's-read-and-find-out science) $15.95; lib bdg $15.89; pa $4.95 (k-3)   **530.4**

1. Matter

ISBN 0-06-027143-4; 0-06-027144-2 (lib bdg); 0-06-445163-1 (pa)   LC 97-30658

In simple text, presents the three states of matter, solid, liquid, and gas, and describes their attributes

"The explanations are clear with a simple, informal text for the new reader, and the lively line-and-watercolor pictures bring in humor and common-sense." Booklist

530.8   Measurement

Adler, David A.

How tall, how short, how faraway; illustrated by Nancy Tobin. Holiday House 1999 unp il $16.95; pa $6.95 (k-3)   **530.8**

1. Measurement

ISBN 0-8234-1375-6; 0-8234-1632-1 (pa)
          LC 98-18802

Introduces several measuring systems such as the Egyptian system, the inch-pound system, and the metric system

"In this wonderful hands-on concept book, easy technological measuring tools are superbly introduced and explained. . . . The informative text and colorful illustrations clearly explain the difference between customary and metric systems." Sci Child

Gardner, Robert

Far-out science projects with height and depth; How high is up? How low is down? Enslow Pubs. 2003 48p il (Sensational science experiments) lib bdg $18.95 (3-6)   **530.8**

1. Measurement 2. Science—Experiments 3. Science projects

ISBN 0-7660-2016-9   LC 2002-4619

Contents: Introduction; How to measure; Safety first; How tall are you?; How high is your ceiling?; How high are your stairs?; How high is your roof?; How high is a flagpole?; How high is a tall tree?; How high is a skyscraper?; How high is a mountain?; How high are low clouds?; How high are high clouds?; How do we know cloud heights?; How deep is this book?; How deep is one page?; How deep is your bathtub?; How deep is your basement?; How deep is a pond or lake?; What is the farthest "down"?

"Following a brief introduction to measurement, a review of units (metric and English standard), and a list of safety tips, Gardner presents a series of 17 measurement activities for readers. . . . The colorful illustrations provide additional clarity for the narrative directions. . . . The activities provide hands-on, mind-on measurement experiences with real-world applications." Sci Books Films

Includes glossary and bibliographical references

Heavy-duty science projects with weight; how much does it weigh? Enslow Pubs. 2003 48p il (Sensational science experiments) lib bdg $18.95 (3-6)   **530.8**

1. Gravitation 2. Measurement 3. Science—Experiments 4. Science projects

ISBN 0-7660-2013-4   LC 2002-8460

Contents: Safety first; Weighing in; More weighing in; Weight and position; Gravity and different weights; Measuring weight: a "spring" scale; Weight and friction; Becoming weightless; Seesaws, weights, distances, and levers; Levers to lift weights; An inclined plane; Measuring weight with a balance; Can you weigh air?; Weighing air; Some effects of air's weight; Defying gravity; Defying gravity again; Using a siphon to defy gravity; Forces other than gravity

This "includes a variety of hands-on activities that use everyday cheap materials to introduce students to many significant physics concepts related to gravity. . . . While challenging, the activities are accessible and interesting to all students. . . . The language used in the volume is simple, accurate, and scientific." Sci Books Films

Includes glossary and bibliographical references

Super-sized science projects with volume; how much space does it take up? Enslow Pubs. 2003 48p il (Sensational science experiments) lib bdg $18.95 (3-6)   **530.8**

1. Volume (Cubic content) 2. Measurement 3. Science—Experiments 4. Science projects

ISBN 0-7660-2014-2   LC 2002-153850

Contents: Measuring—how big is it?; Safety first; Measuring with cubes; Cubic friends; Inch, foot, and yard; Cup, pint, quart, and gallon; Liter vs. quart and milliliter; Volume of a drop; Air takes up space; Underwater mystery; Displacing water; Seeds and water; How much air is in sand?; What fraction of air is oxygen?; Temperature and the volume of a gas; Temperature and the volume of a liquid; Freezing and the volume of water; The volume of a breath; Volume of a deep breath; Testing paper towels; Words to know

This "explores topics ranging from determining the volume of a quart and a liter to the amount of air in a container of sand. Gardner's clear, informal explanations are echoed in LaBaff's colorful illustrations." Booklist

Includes glossary and bibliographical references

Leedy, Loreen

Measuring Penny; written and illustrated by Loreen Leedy. Holt & Co. 1997 unp il $16.95; pa $6.95 (1-3) **530.8**

1. Measurement

ISBN 0-8050-5360-3; 0-8050-6572-5 (pa)

LC 97-19108

"For a measuring project, Lisa decides to measure her dog, Penny, and a cast of other dogs at the park. Noses, tails, ears, paws—nothing escapes her measuring zeal. Also, time, temperature, cost, and even value are creatively calculated throughout a day spent caring for Penny. Leedy cleverly incorporates Lisa's notebook recordings into the illustrations, which depict a wide range of shapes and sizes for easy visual comparison." Horn Book Guide

Long, Lynette

Measurement mania; games and activities that make math easy and fun. Wiley 2001 122p il (Magical math) pa $12.95 (3-6) **530.8**

1. Measurement

ISBN 0-471-36980-2

LC 00-43383

In this introduction to measurement "the activities range from using hands and feet to measure distance to making a sundial. . . . [This book provides] valuable activities and games to help children learn about the concepts." SLJ

Murphy, Stuart J.

Room for Ripley; illustrated by Sylvie Wickstrom. HarperCollins Pubs. 1999 33p il (MathStart) lib bdg $15.89; pa $4.95 (1-3) **530.8**

1. Measurement 2. Aquariums

ISBN 0-06-027621-5 (lib bdg); 0-06-446724-4 (pa)

LC 98-26109

Uses a story about a young boy who is getting a fish bowl ready for his new pet to introduce various units of liquid measure

"The writing is breezy and reads like a story about a boy who wants a pet, but the text constantly reinforces the mathematical concepts (how many cups in a pint, a quart, etc.). The illustrations are painted in muted primary colors against a lot of white space. . . . A fun, painless math lesson." SLJ

Schwartz, David M.

Millions to measure; pictures by Steven Kellogg. HarperCollins Pubs. 2003 unp il $16.99; lib bdg $17.89 (2-4) **530.8**

1. Measurement 2. Weights and measures

ISBN 0-688-12916-1; 0-06-623784-X (lib bdg)

LC 2001-39683

Marvelosissimo the Magician explains the development of standard units of measure, and shows the simplicity of calculating length, height, weight, and volume using the metric system

"Schwartz not only manages to impart a good deal of basic information . . . but also entertains the reader. He receives ample support from illustrator Kellogg, who contributes enough merry madness to make learning fun.

Bright with shining colors, the large, detailed pictures brim with action and humor as well as history and math." Booklist

531 Classical mechanics. Solid mechanics

Bradley, Kimberly Brubaker

Energy makes things happen; illustrated by Paul Meisel. HarperCollins Pubs. 2003 33p il (Let's-read-and-find-out science) $15.99; lib bdg $16.89; pa $4.99 (k-3) **531**

1. Force and energy

ISBN 0-06-028908-2; 0-06-028909-0 (lib bdg); 0-06-445213-1 (pa) LC 2001-39520

This book shows how energy comes originally from the sun and can be transferred from one thing to another

"This worthy title uses familiar examples and a clear focus to introduce basic scientific concepts. . . . Meisel's color illustrations of cheerful multiethnic children match the level and tone of the text perfectly, make it more comprehensible, and add to the book's appeal." SLJ

Forces make things move; illustrated by Paul Meisel. 1st ed. HarperCollins 2005 33p il (Let's-read-and-find-out science) $15.99; lib bdg $16.89; pa $4.99 (k-3) **531**

1. Force and energy 2. Gravity

ISBN 0-06-028906-6; 0-06-028907-4 (lib bdg); 0-06-445214-X (pa) LC 2002-14763

Simple language and humorous illustrations show how forces make things move, prevent them from starting to move, and stop them from moving.

"Colorful line-and-watercolor-wash illustrations brighten the pages. . . . A practical starting place for understanding forces." Booklist

Cobb, Vicki

I fall down; illustrated by Julia Gorton. HarperCollins Publishers 2004 unp il (Science play) $15.99; lib bdg $16.89 (k-2) **531**

1. Gravity 2. Science—Experiments

ISBN 0-688-17842-1; 0-688-17843-X (lib bdg)

LC 2003-1822

Simple experiments introduce the basic concept of gravity and its relationship to weight.

"The digital illustrations offer clearly defined images with a distinctive, retro look. Their eye-catching pizzazz will help hold the attention of the audience. . . . Attuned to the learning style of young children, Cobb's questions and suggestions offer kids the experience of the scientific process." Booklist

Gardner, Robert

Split-second science projects with speed; how fast does it go? Enslow Pubs. 2003 48p il (Sensational science experiments) lib bdg $18.95 (3-6) **531**

1. Speed 2. Science—Experiments 3. Science projects

ISBN 0-7660-2017-7 LC 2002-4618

Gardner, Robert—*Continued*

Contents: Introduction; Speedometer readings; An odometer and a clock; Walking speeds; Running speeds; Animals: fast and slow; Wind speeds by observation; Wind speeds by meter; Wind direction and velocity; The speed of falling leaves; Speed and parachutes; Growth speed; How fast do your fingernails grow?; How fast do you read?; Speed of melting; Speed of dissolving; Speed while falling; Speed of a chemical reaction

This serves as an "introduction to speed and velocity by providing introductory explanations and step-by-step instructions on how to set up and conduct different simple experiments. . . . Perhaps the book's strongest point is its readability. . . . The book is nicely illustrated and appealing." Sci Books Films

Includes glossary and bibliographical references

Mason, Adrienne

Move it! motion, forces and you; written by Adrienne Mason; illustrated by Claudia Dávila. Kids Can Press 2005 32p il (Primary physical science) $12.95; pa $5.95 (k-2)   **531**

1. Motion 2. Force and energy
ISBN 1-55337-758-3; 1-55337-759-1 (pa)

This explores the physics of why and how things move with simple activities such as pushing, pulling or lifting objects.

Includes glossary

Parker, Barry R.

The mystery of gravity. Benchmark Bks. 2003 78p il (Story of science) lib bdg $28.50 (5 and up)   **531**

1. Gravitation
ISBN 0-7614-1428-2   LC 2002-970

Defines gravity and discusses how our knowledge of the natural force has broadened and evolved

"Readers will find accurate, readable explanations for the phenomenon of gravity. The text moves from classical attempts to understand why and how objects fall to the work of Kepler, Galileo, Newton, and Einstein's general theory of relativity. The book is ably illustrated by well-captioned photos and clear diagrams, such as the wormhole of a black hole." Horn Book Guide

Includes glossary and bibliographical references

Pentland, Peter

Toy and game science; [by] Peter Pentland and Pennie Stoyles. Chelsea House 2003 c2002 32p il (Science and scientists) lib bdg $18.95 (4 and up)   **531**

1. Mechanics 2. Toys
ISBN 0-7910-7013-1   LC 2002-1285

First published 2002 in Australia

Contents: Have you ever wondered . . . ?; How do toys balance?; Construction toys; Meet the K'Nex events coordinator; Why do toy cars move the way they do?; Spinning toys; How can air move toys?; Why can some toys fly?; Why do some toys float and others sink?; Toys with springs; Toys that make noise; What is the difference between noise and music?; Toys that use light; Magnetic toys; Electric toys; Toy science timeline

Describes different kinds of toys and the scientific principles that explain how they work

"These authors have a knack for offering concise, easy-to-understand explanations of common phenomena. . . . [This book is] sound, highly educational, and entertaining." SLJ

Includes glossary

532   Fluid mechanics

Cobb, Vicki

I get wet; illustrated by Julia Gorton. HarperCollins Pubs. 2002 unp il $15.99; lib bdg $17.89 (k-2)   **532**

1. Water 2. Science—Experiments
ISBN 0-688-17838-3; 0-688-17839-1 (lib bdg)
LC 00-49882

In this book "a boy learns some of the properties of water through pouring it into different containers, observing it drip and flow, and trying to absorb it with waxed paper and paper toweling." Booklist

"The simple yet well-conceived activities engage children in more than just observations—the questions and explanations are constructed to help young kids draw conclusions from their observations. Remarkably, all this is accomplished in a child-friendly, straightforward text. The illustrations are bright and energetic." Horn Book

Farndon, John

Water. Benchmark Bks. 2001 32p il (Science experiments) lib bdg $16.95 (3-6)   **532**

1. Water 2. Science—Experiments
ISBN 0-7614-1087-2   LC 00-60187

A collection of experiments exploring the properties of water, including ice, water, and steam, floating and sinking, heavy water, and surface tension

Includes glossary

Meiani, Antonella

Water. Lerner Publs. 2003 40p il (Experimenting with science) lib bdg $23.93 (4 and up)   **532**

1. Water 2. Science—Experiments
ISBN 0-8225-0083-3   LC 2001-50773

Contents: The force of water; To float or not to float?; The transformation of water; Water solutions; The force of water; Fact finder; Metric conversion chart

Describes experiments with water which answer such questions as "Why are water droplets round?" and "Why do some things, like salt, dissolve in water and other things, like fish, don't?"

This offers "straightforward, well-designed experiments. . . . Numerous clear diagrams, some photos, and occasional historical sidebars extend this material, which is notable for its substance." Horn Book Guide

Includes glossary and bibliographical references

Parker, Steve

The science of water; projects with experiments with water and power; [by] Steve Parker. Heinemann Library 2005 32p il (Tabletop scientist) lib bdg $29.29; pa $7.85 (4 and up)

532

1. Water 2. Science—Experiments
ISBN 1-4034-7282-3 (lib bdg); 1-4034-7289-0 (pa)
LC 2005007027

This "has experiments on the water cycle, water density, water as a solvent, surface tension, capillary action, buoyancy, water power, and water propulsion. . . . The colorful illustrations, organization, and ease of use of [this title makes it an] excellent [addition]." SLJ

Includes glossary

Simon, Seymour

Let's try it out in the water; by Seymour Simon and Nicole Fauteux; illustrated by Doug Cushman. Simon & Schuster Bks. for Young Readers 2000 unp il $15 (k-2)

532

1. Water 2. Science—Experiments
ISBN 0-689-82919-1
LC 99-20371

Presents simple activities and experiments that demonstrate buoyancy by observing why some things sink and others float in water

This does "a great job of using hands-on activities in daily life to explain basic science to young children. . . . The writers include helpful information for adults about how to teach the science as an active part of the child's ordinary experience. The exuberant, colorful pictures add to the fun." Booklist

533 Gas mechanics (Pneumatics)

Meiani, Antonella

Air. Lerner Publs. 2003 40p il (Experimenting with science) lib bdg $23.93 (4 and up)

533

1. Air 2. Science—Experiments
ISBN 0-8225-0082-5
LC 2001-37730

Explains the properties of air through experiments which feature such topics as what air is, how much force wind has, what shape is best for flying, and how sound travels

This offers "straightforward, well-designed experiments. . . . Numerous clear diagrams, some photos, and occasional historical sidebars extend this material, which is notable for its substance." Horn Book Guide

Includes glossary and bibliographical references

Parker, Steve

The science of air; projects and experiments on air and flight; [by] Steve Parker. Heinemann Library 2005 32p il (Tabletop scientist) lib bdg $29.29; pa $7.85 (4 and up)

533

1. Air 2. Science—Experiments
ISBN 1-4034-7280-7 (lib bdg); 1-4034-7287-4 (pa)
LC 2005006940

"The 12 experiments in [this] book have a materials list and step-by-step photo instructions. Boxed text explains the scientific ideas in each project and the processes that make it work, and offer ideas for further experimentation. The activities are followed by a history of the topic. . . . [This] title introduces air movement, air pressure, wind resistance, lift, flight, and energy from the wind. . . . The colorful illustrations, organization, and ease of use [this title makes it an] excellent [addition]." SLJ

Includes glossary

Simon, Seymour

Let's try it out in the air; hands-on early-learning science activities; by Seymour Simon and Nicole Fauteux; illustrated by Doug Cushman. Simon & Schuster Bks. for Young Readers 2001 unp il $15 (k-2)

533

1. Air 2. Science—Experiments
ISBN 0-689-82918-3
LC 99-20370

Presents simple activities and experiments that demonstrate the properties of air by observing the presence of air and the pressure it exerts

This does "a great job of using hands-on activities in daily life to explain basic science to young children. . . . The writers include helpful information for adults about how to teach the science as an active part of the child's ordinary experience. The exuberent, colorful pictures add to the fun." Booklist

534 Sound and related vibrations

Farndon, John

Sound and hearing. Benchmark Bks. 2001 32p il (Science experiments) lib bdg $16.95 (3-6)

534

1. Sound 2. Hearing 3. Science—Experiments
ISBN 0-7614-1091-0
LC 99-89262

A collection of experiments that explore the nature of sound and how we hear it. Activities include making a string telephone, a megaphone, and a bottle organ

Includes glossary

Gardner, Robert

Jazzy science projects with sound and music; [by] Robert Gardner. 1st ed. Enslow Publishers 2006 48p il (Fantastic physical science experiments) $23.93 (4-6)

534

1. Sound 2. Science—Experiments
ISBN 0766025888
LC 2005018729

This offers science experiments illustrating such concepts as pitch, vibration, how sound travels and how it is perceived.

Includes glossary and bibliographical references

Levine, Shar

The science of sound & music; [by] Shar Levine & Leslie Johnstone. Sterling 2000 80p il $19.95 (4 and up)

534

1. Sound 2. Science—Experiments
ISBN 0-8069-7183-5
LC 00-58318

Levine, Shar—*Continued*

"This book explores the physics of sound through a series of activities using fairly common materials, such as drinking glasses, metal coat hangers, rubber bands, and wooden dowels." Booklist

"The many colorful illustrations and photographs contribute to the educational experience by visually engaging the reader. . . . Both enjoyable and stimulating." Voice Youth Advocates

Includes glossary

Parker, Steve

The science of sound; projects with experiments with music and sound waves; [by] Steve Parker. Heinemann Library 2005 32p il (Tabletop scientist) lib bdg $29.29; pa $7.85 (4 and up)

    534

1. Sound 2. Music 3. Science—Experiments
ISBN 1-4034-7281-5 (lib bdg); 1-4034-7288-2 (pa)

    LC 2005006960

This book of experiments "covers sound waves as they travel through air and underwater, high and low sounds, how we hear, the Doppler effect, soundproofing, and recorded sound. . . . The colorful illustrations, organization, and ease of use of [this title makes it an] excellent [addition]." SLJ

Includes glossary

Pfeffer, Wendy

Sounds all around; illustrated by Holly Keller. HarperCollins Pubs. 1999 32p il (Let's-read-and-find-out science) $15.95; lib bdg $15.89 (k-3)

    534

1. Sound
ISBN 0-06-027711-4; 0-06-027712-2 (lib bdg)

    LC 97-17993

This "surveys the topic of sound by discussing vibration, communication, echolocation, radar, and the measurement of loudness by decibels. . . . The last three pages offer instructions for activities and games related to sound. Like the writing, the attractive line-and-watercolor illustrations are clear and simple." Booklist

535   Light and infrared and ultraviolet phenomena

Branley, Franklyn Mansfield

Day light, night light; where light comes from; by Franklyn M. Branley; illustrated by Stacey Schuett. Newly il ed. HarperCollins Pubs. 1998 32p col il (Let's-read-and-find-out science) $14.95; lib bdg $15.89; pa $4.95 (k-3)

    535

1. Light
ISBN 0-06-027294-5; 0-06-027295-3 (lib bdg); 0-06-445171-2 (pa)   LC 96-33316

First published 1975 with title: Light and darkness

Discusses the properties of light, particularly its source in heat

"This is a beautifully illustrated children's book about a basic concept in science. The pictures add to the clearly written text." Sci Books Films

Bulla, Clyde Robert

What makes a shadow? illustrated by June Otani. rev ed. HarperCollins Pubs. 1994 32p il (Let's-read-and-find-out science) lib bdg $15.89 (k-1)

    535

1. Shades and shadows
ISBN 0-06-022916-0   LC 92-36350

A revised and newly illustrated edition of the title first published 1962 by Crowell

"Using short sentences and developmentally appropriate language, the author explains how shadows are formed, gives numerous examples of shadows, and describes how to make shadow pictures on the wall. Each page is illustrated with bright, colorful drawings, and the gender and cultural representation is excellent." Sci Books Films

Burnie, David

Light. Dorling Kindersley 1992 64p il (Eyewitness science) $15.95; lib bdg $19.99 (4 and up)

    535

1. Light
ISBN 0-7894-4885-8; 0-7894-6709-7 (lib bdg)

    LC 92-7661

A guide to the origins, principles, and historical study of light

"Each double-page spread is lavishly illustrated with full-color photographs and diagrams, and each contains a wealth of information." Booklist

Cobb, Vicki

I see myself; illustrated by Julia Gorton. HarperCollins Pubs. 2002 unp il (Science play) $15.99; lib bdg $17.89 (k-2)

    535

1. Optics 2. Light
ISBN 0-688-17836-7; 0-688-17837-5 (lib bdg)

    LC 00-57220

This book "features a girl who finds out a little about vision, light, and reflection by playing with a mirror, a flashlight, and a bouncing ball." Booklist

"The simple yet well-conceived activities engage children in more than just observations—the questions and explanations are constructed to help young kids draw conclusions from their observations. Remarkably, all this is accomplished in a child-friendly, straightforward text. The illustrations are bright and energetic." Horn Book

Farndon, John

Light and optics. Benchmark Bks. 2000 32p il (Science experiments) lib bdg $16.95 (3-6)

    535

1. Light 2. Optics 3. Science—Experiments
ISBN 0-7614-1090-2   LC 99-89898

A collection of experiments that explore the nature of light and how it is measured and perceived. Activities include making a shadow theater, a periscope, a microscope, a telescope, and a pinhole camera

Includes glossary

Gardner, Robert

Dazzling science projects with light and color. Enslow Elementary 2006 48p il (Fantasic physical science experiments) $23.93 (4-6)   **535**

1. Light 2. Color 3. Science—Experiments

ISBN 0-7660-2587-X   LC 2005-09498

This "title is devoted to light and seeing, mixing colors, and more. Each of 10 chapters includes an experiment, followed by an explanation of why it works, and offers ideas for devising projects to present at a science fair. . . . Large colorful, cartoonlike drawings complement the [text]. . . . [This offers] solid information." SLJ

Includes glossary and bibliographical references

Lauw, Darlene

Light; [by Darlene Lauw & Lim Cheng Puay; series illustrator, Roy Chan Yoon Loy] Crabtree 2002 31p il (Science alive!) lib bdg $21.28; pa $7.95 (3-6)   **535**

1. Light 2. Optics 3. Science—Experiments

ISBN 0-7787-0560-9 (lib bdg); 0-7787-0606-0 (pa)   LC 2001-42423

Presents activities that demonstrate how light works in our everyday lives. History boxes feature the scientists who made significant discoveries in the field of light

This book explains its subject matter "in a colorful and easy to understand format. . . . All experiments use easily obtainable parts and in some cases actual household items." Sci Books Films

Includes glossary

Levine, Shar

The optics book; fun experiments with light, vision & color; [by] Shar Levine & Leslie Johnstone; illustrated by Jason Coons. Sterling 1998 80p il lib bdg $21.95; pa $10.95 (4 and up)   **535**

1. Optics 2. Color 3. Science—Experiments

ISBN 0-8069-9947-0 (lib bdg); 0-8069-9942-X (pa)   LC 98-26732

Explores the properties of light and color by means of experiments and analysis of various optical instruments including periscopes, and telescopes

"Illustrated in full color with cartoon-like drawings and diagrams as well as photographs of equipment and results, the pages have a more inviting look than most books of science projects." Booklist

Includes glossary

Meiani, Antonella

Light. Lerner Publs. 2003 40p il (Experimenting with science) lib bdg $23.93 (4 and up)   **535**

1. Light 2. Science—Experiments

ISBN 0-8225-0084-1   LC 2001-38947

Experiments with light explain shadows and colors, and demonstrate such concepts as reflection and refraction

This offers "straightforward, well-designed experiments. . . . Numerous clear diagrams, some photos, and occasional historical sidebars extend this material, which is notable for its substance." Horn Book Guide

Includes glossary and bibliographical references

535.6   Color

Farndon, John

Color. Benchmark Bks. 2000 32p il (Science experiments) lib bdg $16.95 (3-6)   **535.6**

1. Color 2. Science—Experiments

ISBN 0-7614-1092-9   LC 99-86994

A collection of experiments that explore the nature of color and how it is created and perceived

"Activities include creating a spectrum using a bottle of water and a piece of black cardboard, and making a color wheel. . . . The clearly illustrated, step-by-step directions for the science activities will make this a useful addition to many libraries." Booklist

Includes glossary

536   Heat

Gardner, Robert

Really hot science projects with temperature; how hot is it? how cold is it? Enslow Pubs. 2003 48p il (Sensational science experiments) lib bdg $18.95 (3-6)   **536**

1. Temperature 2. Heat 3. Cold 4. Science—Experiments 5. Science projects

ISBN 0-7660-2015-0   LC 2002-153849

Contents: Introduction; Thermometer liquid rises and falls; Go on a temperature hunt; Moving liquids by temperature difference; What is your temperature?; Temperature and evaporation; Temperatures all day long!; Temperatures above and below ground; Sun, color, and temperature; Sun and seasonal temperatures; Earth, sun, and temperature; Diffusion and temperature; Temperature and chemistry; Temperature and speed of a chemical reaction; How cold can you make water ice?; Temperature of melting ice or snow; Make your own thermometer; Measuring dew point; Temperature and the greenhouse effect

"Includes such experiments as observing diffusion in hot and cold water and measuring the dew point. . . . Gardner's clear, informal explanations are echoed in LaBaff's colorful illustrations." Booklist

Includes glossary and bibliographical references

537   Electricity and electronics

Berger, Melvin

Switch on, switch off; illustrated by Carolyn Croll. Crowell 1989 32p il (Let's-read-and-find-out science book) lib bdg $15.89; pa $4.95 (k-3)   **537**

1. Electricity

ISBN 0-690-04786-X (lib bdg); 0-06-445097-X (pa)   LC 88-17638

"This book presents rudimentary exploration of electricity and how electrical current flows to the light switch in a child's room. Follow the current from the generator to a power plant to the switch on the wall. Includes instructions for a simple generator. A good, first look at a topic that mystifies young scientists." Sci Child

Farndon, John

Electricity. Benchmark Bks. 2001 32p il (Science experiments) lib bdg $16.95 (3-6)
    537

1. Electricity 2. Science—Experiments

ISBN 0-7614-1086-4   LC 00-39752

A collection of activities that explore electricity "discussing charges, circuits, conductors, and insulators. Activities include creating a Xerox effect and making an electroscope." SLJ

Includes glossary

Gardner, Robert

Energizing science projects with electricity and magnetism; [by] Robert Gardner. 1st ed. Enslow Elementary 2006 48p il (Fantastic physical science experiments) $23.93 (4-6)   **537**

1. Electricity 2. Magnetism 3. Science—Experiments

ISBN 0-7660-2584-5   LC 2005018730

This offers science experiments concerning electric charges, magnetism and compasses, batteries, electric bulbs, and wires, and electromagnets.

Includes glossary and bibliographical references

Lauw, Darlene

Electricity; [by Darlene Lauw, Lim Cheng Puay; series illustrator, Roy Chan Yoon Loy] Crabtree 2002 31p il lib bdg $21.95; pa $7.95 (3-6)
    537

1. Electricity 2. Science—Experiments

ISBN 0-7787-0561-7 (lib bdg); 0-7787-0607-9 (pa)
     LC 2001-42421

Presents activities that demonstrate how electricity works in our everyday lives. History boxes feature the scientists who made significant discoveries in the field of electricity

This is "easy to use, read and understand." Sci Books Films

Includes glossary

Levine, Shar

Shocking science; fun & fascinating electrical experiments; [by] Shar Levine & Leslie Johnstone; illustrated by Emily S. Edliq. Sterling 1999 80p il $19.95; pa $10.95 (5 and up)   **537**

1. Electricity 2. Science—Experiments

ISBN 0-8069-3946-X; 0-8069-2271-0 (pa)
     LC 99-43501

Suggested experiments studying static electricity and electrical circuits, with easily obtained supplies. Includes historical information and glossary

"The organization and writing as a whole is clear and purposeful. . . . Small color photographs illustrate the text in a useful and attractive manner. . . . A practical and informative book of science experiments." Booklist

Meiani, Antonella

Electricity. Lerner Publs. 2003 40p il (Experimenting with science) lib bdg $23.93 (4 and up)   **537**

1. Electricity 2. Science—Experiments

ISBN 0-8225-0086-8   LC 2001-50517

Experiments and text illustrate characteristics of static electricity, circuits and switches, and electrical currents

This offers "straightforward, well-designed experiments. . . . Numerous clear diagrams, some photos, and occasional historical sidebars extend this material, which is notable for its substance." Horn Book Guide

Includes glossary and bibliographical references

Parker, Steve

Electricity; written by Steve Parker. rev ed. DK Pub. 2005 64p il (DK eyewitness books) $15.99 (4 and up)   **537**

1. Electricity

ISBN 0-7566-1388-4

First published 1992

Discusses the properties of electricity and describes how it is made and used

VanCleave, Janice Pratt

Janice VanCleave's electricity; mind-boggling experiments you can turn into science fair projects; [by] Janice VanCleave. Wiley 1994 89p il $10.95 (4 and up)   **537**

1. Electricity 2. Science projects 3. Science—Experiments

ISBN 0-471-31010-7   LC 93-40913

"The experiments move from the simple, which do not require the use of batteries, to those that require small batteries, sizes AA, AAA, C, or D. An appendix shows how to make strips of aluminum foil that can be used to form the electrical circuits that are part of some of the experiments. By encouraging students to move beyond the basic problems (with adult supervision), the author encourages them to be creative in designing science fair projects." Booklist

Includes glossary

Woodford, Chris

Electricity; [by] Chris Woodford. Blackbirch Press 2004 40p il (Routes of science) $23.70; pa $18.70 (5 and up)   **537**

1. Electricity

ISBN 1-4103-0165-6; 1-4103-0304-7 (pa)
     LC 2004-301790

Contents: The mysteries of electric fluid; From frogs' legs to batteries; Electricity meets magnetism; The power of electricity; Electricity makes waves; The electronic age; Into the future

"This book traces the history of electrical discovery from ancient Greek experiments with static electricity to Benjamin Franklin's famous kite experiment to today's work with superconductivity." Publisher's note

This "volume contains color photographs, illustrations, and diagrams to help explain the important concepts and discoveries. [This volume] would be [an] excellent [supplement] to the science curriculum." SLJ

Includes glossary and bibliographical references

538 Magnetism

539.7 Atomic and nuclear physics

Branley, Franklyn Mansfield
What makes a magnet? by Franklyn M. Branley; illustrated by True Kelley. HarperCollins Pubs. 1996 31p il (Let's-read-and-find-out science) $15.95; pa $4.95 (k-3)　**538**
1. Magnets
ISBN 0-06-026441-1; 0-06-445148-8 (pa)
　　　　　　　　　　　　　　　LC 95-32181
Describes how magnets work and includes instructions for making a magnet and a compass
"Kelley's happy line drawings incorporate a humorous mouse to add safety warnings and goofy side comments. The clear diagrams and lucid explanations are both informative and engaging." Horn Book

Farndon, John
Magnetism. Benchmark Bks. 2001 32p il (Science experiments) lib bdg $16.95 (3-6)
　　　　　　　　　　　　　　　　　538
1. Magnetism 2. Science—Experiments
ISBN 0-7614-1343-X　　　　LC 2001-25168
A collection of activities that explore magnetism, discussing magnetic materials, magnetic poles, electricity and magnetism, Earth's magnetism, and magnetism in space
Includes glossary

Meiani, Antonella
Magnetism. Lerner Publs. 2003 40p il (Experimenting with science) lib bdg $23.93 (4 and up)　　　　　　　　　　　**538**
1. Magnetism 2. Science—Experiments
ISBN 0-8225-0085-X　　　　LC 2001-50464
Describes a variety of experiments that explore the world of magnets and magnetism, arranged in the categories "Magnets," "Magnetic Poles," "Magnetic Force," and "Magnetism and Electricity"
This offers "straightforward, well-designed experiments. . . . Numerous clear diagrams, some photos, and occasional historical sidebars extend this material, which is notable for its substance." Horn Book Guide
Includes glossary and bibliographical references

Souza, D. M. (Dorothy M.)
Northern lights. Carolrhoda Bks. 1994 48p il (Nature in action) lib bdg $21.27 (4-6)
　　　　　　　　　　　　　　　　　538
1. Auroras
ISBN 0-87614-799-6　　　　　LC 93-3027
Discusses the origins, characteristics, and lore of the Northern and Southern Lights known as auroras
This "is written in a clear, concise style and is illustrated with magnificent color photographs and accurate paintings." Sci Books Films
Includes glossary

Gallant, Roy A.
The ever changing atom. Benchmark Bks. 1999 80p il (Story of science) lib bdg $29.93 (5 and up)
　　　　　　　　　　　　　　　　539.7
1. Atoms 2. Atomic theory 3. Nuclear physics
ISBN 0-7614-0961-0　　　　　LC 98-35420
Introduces atoms, the tiny particles which make up everything in the world, discussing their different parts, how they were discovered, and how they can be used as a source of energy
Includes glossary and bibliographical references

Nardo, Don
Atoms. KidHaven Press 2002 48p il (Kidhaven science library) lib bdg $23.70 (3-5)
　　　　　　　　　　　　　　　　539.7
1. Atoms 2. Nuclear energy 3. Radioactivity
ISBN 0-7377-0942-1　　　　　LC 2001-2963
Discusses the discovery of atoms and how they work, nuclear energy and weapons, nuclear radiation and its medical uses, atomic clocks, and other applications
"The appealing layout includes large fonts, many color photographs, and simple diagrams." SLJ

540 Chemistry & allied sciences

Baxter, Roberta
Chemical reaction. Kidhaven Press 2005 48p il (Kidhaven science library) $23.70 (4 and up)
　　　　　　　　　　　　　　　　540
1. Chemistry
ISBN 0-7377-2072-7
"Baxter defines her subject and describes many different types of reactions, including acid-base reactions, oxidation, and photosynthesis. The explanations are clear and succinct. The final chapter presents some potential uses for chemical reactions, citing the development of molecular computers." SLJ
Includes glossary and bibliographical references

Juettner, Bonnie
Molecules. Kidhaven Press 2005 48p il (Kidhaven science library) $23.70 (4 and up)
　　　　　　　　　　　　　　　　540
1. Molecules 2. Chemistry
ISBN 0-7377-2076-X
"Juettner gives an overview of the building blocks of elements and compounds, including atoms, molecules, and the various states of matter, and describes their characteristics. The last chapter offers information on some extreme materials, such as plasma and the recently discovered Bose-Einstein condensates (BEC)." SLJ

Newmark, Ann

Chemistry; written by Ann Newmark. rev ed. DK Pub. 2005 72p il (DK eyewitness books) $15.99 (4 and up) **540**

1. Chemistry
ISBN 0-7566-1385-X
First published 1993

Explores the world of chemical reactions and shows the role that chemistry plays in our world.

Woodford, Chris

Atoms and molecules; [by] Chris Woodford [and] Martin Clowes. Blackbirch Press 2004 40p il (Routes of science) $23.70; pa $18.70 (5 and up) **540**

1. Atoms 2. Molecules
ISBN 1-4103-0295-4; 1-4103-0324-1 (pa)

Contents: Philosophers and alchemists; Discovering the elements; The periodic table; Molecules, matter, and motion; Inside the atom; Into the future

"This book traces the history of atomic discovery from ancient Greek theories about four basic elements to today's research into nanotechnology." Publisher's note

This "volume contains color photographs, illustrations, and diagrams to help explain the important concepts and discoveries. [This] up-to-date [volume] would be [an] excellent [supplement] to the science curriculum." SLJ

540.7 Chemistry--Education and related topics

Gardner, Robert

Science project ideas about kitchen chemistry. rev ed. Enslow Publishers 2002 128p il lib bdg $26.60 (5 and up) **540.7**

1. Chemistry 2. Science projects 3. Science—Experiments
ISBN 0-7660-1706-0 LC 2001-704
First published 1988 with title: Kitchen chemistry

Presents experiments suitable for science fair projects, dealing with the chemistry involved with foods and activities related to the kitchen

Includes bibliographical references

Meiani, Antonella

Chemistry. Lerner Publs. 2003 40p il (Experimenting with science) lib bdg $23.93 (4 and up) **540.7**

1. Chemistry 2. Science—Experiments
ISBN 0-8225-0087-6 LC 2001-50503

Uses experiments to explore such topics as how heat changes a substance, the purpose of chemical analysis, and how the human stomach digests food

"This book makes chemistry both accessible and exciting." Sci Books Films

Includes glossary and bibliographical references

Rhatigan, Joe

Cool chemistry concoctions; 50 formulas that fizz, foam, splatter & ooze; [by] Joe Rhatigan & Veronika Gunter; illustrated by Tom LaBaff. 1st ed. Lark Books 2005 80p il $14.95 (3-6) **540.7**

1. Chemistry 2. Science—Experiments
ISBN 1-57990-620-6 LC 2004-13287

This describes such experiments as how to make slime, volcanoes, stalactites, water bombs, and shrunken heads (using apples and Epsom salts)

"This lively book offers an engaging introduction to science experiments. The projects . . . are simple and require household materials. . . . The zany cartoon illustrations are the perfect accompaniment to the text, which is fun and informative." SLJ

546 Inorganic chemistry

Elements. Grolier Educ. 1996-2002 18v il set $329 (5 and up) **546**

1. Chemical elements
ISBN 0-7172-7572-8 LC 95-82222

Contents: v1 Hydrogen and the noble gases; v2 Sodium and potassium; v3 Calcium and magnesium; v4 Iron, chromium, and manganese; v5 Copper, silver, and gold; v6 Zinc, cadmium, and mercury v7 Aluminum; v8 Carbon; v9 Silicon; v10 Lead and tin; v11 Nitrogen and phosphorus; v12 Oxygen; v13 Sulfur; v14 Chlorine, fluorine, bromine, and iodine; v15 Uranium and other radioactive elements; v16 Actinium-Fluorine; v17 Francium-Polonium; v18 Potassium-Zirconium

This set "discusses each element's discovery, forms, extraction, industrial uses, and unique character. In a one-topic-per-spread format, text blocks surround several large, clear, full-color photos or, more rarely, schematics. . . . This resource will strengthen both school labs and library collections." SLJ

The **Elements**. Benchmark Bks. 1999-2006 36v il ea $25.64 (5 and up) **546**

1. Chemical elements

Contents: Aluminum, by J. Farndon; Arsenic by C. Cooper; Boron by R. Beatty; Calcium, by J. Farndon; Carbon, by G. Sparrow; Chlorine, by S. Watt; Chormium by T. Jackson; Cobalt by S. Watt; Copper, by R. Beatty; Flourine by T. Jackson; Gold, by S. Angliss; Hydrogen, by J. Farndon; Iodine by L. Gray; Iron, by G. Sparrow; Lead by S. Watt; Lithium by T. Jackson; Magnesium, by C. Uttley; Manganese by R. Beatty; Mercury by S. Watt; Molybdenum by N. Lepora; Nickel by G. Sparrow; Nitrogen, by J. Farndon; Noble gases, by J. Thomas; Oxygen, by J. Farndon; Phosphorus, by R. Beatty; Platinum by I. Wood; Potassium, by C. Woodford; Radioactive elements by T. Jackson; Silicon, by A. O'Daly; Silver, by S. Watt; Sodium, by A. O'Daly; Sulfur, by R. Beatty; Tin, by L. Gray; Titanium, by C. Woodford; Tungsten by K. Turrell; Zinc by L. Gray

These "titles cover where these substances are found, how they were discovered, their characteristics and reactions, and their importance in the human body and the environment. Each volume includes a double-page spread on the element's position in the periodic table. The captioned, full-color drawings, photographs, and diagrams clarify the text while boxed 'Did you Know?' items offer

The Elements—*Continued*

interesting extensions to it. . . . Informative, accessible science books that will be of interest for both general reading and report writing." SLJ

Includes glossaries

548 Crystallography

Stangl, Jean

Crystals and crystal gardens you can grow. Watts 1990 64p il lib bdg $23 (4 and up)
548

1. Crystals 2. Science—Experiments

ISBN 0-531-10889-9   LC 89-38999

"A First book"

The author discusses the nature and structure of crystals and presents experiments in crystal formation

With "clear explanatory background on crystal formations, and easy directions for experiments, this will meet a real need in every classroom and public library collection." Bull Cent Child Books

Includes bibliographical references

Symes, R. F.

Crystal & gem; written by R. F. Symes and R. R. Harding. rev ed. DK Pub. 2004 72p il (DK eyewitness books) $15.99 (5 and up)   **548**

1. Crystals 2. Precious stones

ISBN 0-7566-0664-0

First published 1991

Describes how crystals form in nature, how crystals are grown artificially, and how crystals are used in industry. Numerous color photos with text identify the various gemstones.

549 Mineralogy

Farndon, John

Rocks and minerals. Benchmark Bks. 2003 32p il (Science experiments) lib bdg $25.64 (4 and up)
549

1. Rocks 2. Minerals 3. Science—Experiments

ISBN 0-7614-1468-1   LC 2002-908

Discusses the physical properties of various rocks and minerals and gives instructions for experiments that identify their unique characteristics

Includes glossary

Symes, R. F.

Eyewitness rocks & minerals; written by R. F. Symes and the staff of the Natural History Museum, London. rev ed. DK Pub. 2004 72p il (DK eyewitness books) $15.99 (5 and up)
549

1. Rocks 2. Minerals

ISBN 0-756-0719-1

First published 1988

Text and photographs examine the creation, importance, erosion, mining, and uses of rocks and minerals

550 Earth sciences

Gibbons, Gail

Planet earth/inside out. Morrow Junior Bks. 1995 unp il maps lib bdg $16.89; pa $4.95 (k-3)
550

1. Earth 2. Geology

ISBN 0-688-09681-6 (lib bdg); 0-688-15849-8 (pa)
LC 94-41926

"From Pangaea to recycling, Gibbons skims the surface of geology, touching on plate tectonics, volcanoes, earthquakes, and climates." SLJ

Gibbons' "explanations of the earth's interior are enlivened by comparisons . . . and her plentiful pictures, with their sharp outlines and broad blocks of color, will help clarify the concepts for the youngest learners." Booklist

Lauber, Patricia

You're aboard Spaceship Earth; illustrated by Holly Keller. HarperCollins Pubs. 1996 32p il (Let's-read-and-find-out science) pa $4.95 hardcover o.p. (k-3)   **550**

1. Earth sciences

ISBN 0-06-445159-3 (pa)   LC 94-18704

In this book "life on our planet is compared with a manned shuttle mission that must take special care to insure the health and safety of its crew. . . . Once that concept is established, youngsters learn interesting facts about the supplies needed to survive—food, air with oxygen, and water. Lauber is adept at writing for this audience, using simple vocabulary and straightforward sentences. . . . Keller's bright and colorful drawings further explain complicated concepts such as the water cycle." SLJ

Patent, Dorothy Hinshaw

Shaping the earth; photographs by William Muñoz. Clarion Bks. 2000 88p il maps $18 (4 and up)   **550**

1. Geology

ISBN 0-395-85691-4   LC 99-37093

Explains the forces that have created the geological features on the earth's surface

"This concise, attractive volume succeeds in a daunting task—to present the history of Earth in 88 pages of compelling, age-appropriate text. . . . William Muñoz's full-color photographs, well-chosen and reproduced, will draw young readers into the text. . . . A glossary and a list of further references, including Web sites, are appended." Booklist

Includes bibliographical references

VanCleave, Janice Pratt

Janice VanCleave's earth science for every kid; 101 easy experiments that really work. Wiley 1991 231p il pa $12.95 hardcover o.p. (4 and up)
550

1. Earth sciences 2. Science—Experiments

ISBN 0-471-53010-7 (pa)   LC 90-42724

VanCleave, Janice Pratt—*Continued*

Instructions for experiments, each introducing a different earth science concept

"An entertaining, educational, and nonthreatening aid to understanding earth science. The easy experiments are carefully organized." SLJ

551 Geology, hydrology, meteorology

Blobaum, Cindy

Geology rocks! 50 hands-on activities to explore the earth; illustrations by Michael Kline. Williamson 1999 96p il pa $10.95 (4-6) **551**

1. Geology 2. Science—Experiments
ISBN 1-88559-329-5   LC 98-53299

Presents fifty hands-on activities to introduce the science of geology and explain the formation and history of the earth

"The text is witty but conveys much factual material. The experiments can be done easily with household items and include safety precautions. . . . The book is illustrated with red-and-purple tinted cartoons and photographs." SLJ

Includes bibliographical references

551.1 Gross structure and properties of the earth

Cole, Joanna

The magic school bus inside the Earth; illustrated by Bruce Degen. Scholastic 1987 40p il $15.95; pa $4.95 (2-4) **551.1**

1. Earth—Internal structure 2. Geology
ISBN 0-590-40759-7; 0-590-40760-0 (pa)
          LC 87-4563

Also available Spanish language edition

In this book Ms. Frizzle teaches "geology via a field trip through the center of the earth. As her class learns about fossils, rocks, and volcanoes, so will readers, absorbing information painlessly as they vicariously travel through the caves, tunnels, and up through the cone of a volcanic island shortly before it erupts. . . . Degen's bright, colorful artwork includes many witty details to delight observant children. Carried in cartoonlike balloons, the schoolmates' thoughts, banter, and asides add spice to the geology lesson. Bright, sassy, and savvy, the magic school bus books rate high in child appeal." Booklist

Gallant, Roy A.

Dance of the continents. Benchmark Bks. 2000 80p il (Story of science) lib bdg $29.93 (5 and up) **551.1**

1. Plate tectonics 2. Geology
ISBN 0-7614-0962-9   LC 98-28046

Describes the development of geological theory from the ancient Greek philosophers to the discovery of plate tectonics, which explains the forming of geological structures

"This book is a good brief description of continental drift as it is now perceived by most geologists." Sci Books Films

Includes glossary and bibliographical references

Plates; restless earth. Benchmark Bks. 2002 c2003 80p il map (Earthworks) lib bdg $29.93 (5 and up) **551.1**

1. Plate tectonics
ISBN 0-7614-1370-7   LC 2002-915

Discusses plate tectonics, the theory that the surface of the earth is always moving, and the connection of this phenomenon to earthquakes and volcanoes

Includes glossary and bibliographical references

Structure; exploring the earth's interior. Benchmark Bks. 2002 c2003 80p il map (Earthworks) lib bdg $29.93 (5 and up) **551.1**

1. Geology 2. Earth—Internal structure
ISBN 0-7614-1368-5   LC 2001-43858

Describes the formation of the earth, the composition of its surface and interior, and the effects of earthquakes and volcanoes

Includes glossary and bibliographical references

Silverstein, Alvin

Plate tectonics; [by] Alvin Silverstein, Virginia Silverstein [and] Laura Silverstein Nunn. 21st Cent. Bks. (Brookfield) 1998 64p il maps (Science concepts) lib bdg $26.90 (5 and up) **551.1**

1. Plate tectonics 2. Earthquakes 3. Volcanoes
ISBN 0-7613-3225-1   LC 98-24934

Discusses plate tectonics, the theory that the surface of the earth is always moving, and the connection of this phenomenon to earthquakes and volcanoes

"The inviting layout includes many colorful photographs, maps, and diagrams, as well as some interesting informational sidebars." Booklist

Includes glossary and bibliographical references

551.2 Volcanoes, earthquakes, thermal waters and gases

Branley, Franklyn Mansfield

Earthquakes; by Franklyn M. Branley; illustrated by Megan Lloyd. Newly il ed. HarperCollinsPublishers 2005 33p il (Let's-read-and-find-out science) $15.99; lib bdg $16.89; pa $4.99 (k-3) **551.2**

1. Earthquakes
ISBN 0-06-028008-5; 0-06-028009-3 (lib bdg); 0-06-445188-7 (pa)   LC 2003-25458

A newly illustrated edition of the title first published 1990

This "introduction to earthquakes explores what causes them, how they are measured, and what to do when you are in one." Publisher's note

"The most effective pictures are those that show the

Branley, Franklyn Mansfield—*Continued*

unseen and unseeable, such as cross-sections of mountains, volcanoes, and faults in the earth's moving crust." Booklist

Burleigh, Robert

Volcanoes; journey to the crater's edge; photographs by Philippe Bourseiller; adapted by Robert Burleigh; text by Helene Montardre; drawings by David Giraudon. H.N. Abrams 2003 75p il map $14.95 (4 and up) **551.2**

1. Volcanoes

ISBN 0-8109-4590-8   LC 2003-971

Over thirty photographs and accompanying text reveal the facts about the world's volcanoes

"Photographer Bourseiller takes young readers to the crater's edge with truly spectacular full-color photographs. . . . The book does an excellent job of documenting the effect of volcanoes on the lives of those who live close to them, and small watercolor paintings further enliven the sense of human history." Booklist

Donovan-O'Meara, Donna

Into the volcano; photographs by Stephen and Donna O'Meara. Kids Can Press 2005 56p il $16.95 (4-6) **551.2**

1. Volcanoes

ISBN 1-55337-692-7

"Donna O'Meara and her husband, Steve, explore active volcanoes, gather data about them, and photograph volcanic eruptions. . . . Following a description of her early life, O'Meara vividly describes her visits to observe volcanoes in Hawaii, Costa Rica, Guatemala, and Italy. . . . Illustrating the text are exceptionally fine photos of volcanic landscapes and members of the expeditions." Booklist

Includes glossary

Grace, Catherine O'Neill

Forces of nature; the awesome power of volcanoes, earthquakes, and tornadoes; by Catherine O'Neill Grace. National Geographic Society 2004 62p il $17.95 (4 and up) **551.2**

1. Stein, Ross S. 2. Wurman, Joshua 3. Edmonds, Marie 4. Herd, Richard 5. Volcanoes 6. Earthquakes 7. Tornadoes

ISBN 0-7922-6328-6   LC 2003-18929

Contents: On the rim of a volcano; In an earthquake zone; In the path of a storm

"A companion volume to the National Geographic film of the same title, this book presents the basics of these phenomena with a focus on the work of four scientists who study them: Richard Herd, Marie Edmonds, Ross Stein, and Joshua Wurman. . . . Outstanding color and black-and-white photos and diagrams augment the very readable text." SLJ

Harrison, David L. (David Lakin)

Volcanoes: nature's incredible fireworks; illustrated by Cheryl Nathan. Boyds Mills Press 2002 unp il (Earthworks) $15.95 (1-3) **551.2**

1. Volcanoes

ISBN 1-56397-996-9   LC 2001-94536

"The author and illustrator offer a look at volcanoes and the forces at work deep beneath the earth. The book addresses basic questions such as how rocks get so hot that they melt and what causes a volcano." SLJ

"The surprisingly graceful text is illuminated with dynamic artwork. . . . The expressive compositions, rich in color and subtle texture, serve as literal scenes of what's happening on the earth, and there are plenty of cross sections and diagrams of what's happening beneath the earth's crust." Booklist

Includes bibliographical references

Lauber, Patricia

Volcano: the eruption and healing of Mount St. Helens. Bradbury Press 1986 60p il $17.99; pa $8.99 (4 and up) **551.2**

1. Mount Saint Helens (Wash.) 2. Volcanoes

ISBN 0-02-754500-8; 0-689-71679-6 (pa)

           LC 85-22442

A Newbery Medal honor book, 1987

"A clearly written account of the volcano's 1980 eruption in Washington State, with handsome color photographs of every phase of the eruption and its aftermath. Perhaps most interesting is the detailed description of the healing process—what flora and fauna survived and how." N Y Times Book Rev

Lindop, Laurie

Probing volcanoes. Twenty-First Century Books 2003 80p il map (Science on the edge) lib bdg $26.90 (5 and up) **551.2**

1. Volcanoes

ISBN 0-7613-2700-2   LC 2002-14251

Contents: Predicting eruptions; Eruption! Volcanologists on the edge; History of volcano monitoring; Looking to the future; Becoming a volcanologist

This "examines the work of volcanologists, whose main goal is to determine how to predict volcanic eruptions. A great deal of scientific information is included, beginning with a basic explanation of the subject and what the scientists are trying to discover. . . . [The book is] profusely illustrated with well-placed color photographs." SLJ

Includes bibliographical references

Reed, Jennifer

Earthquakes; disaster & survival; [by] Jennifer Bond Reed. Enslow Publishers 2004 48p il map (Deadly disasters) $23.93 (4 and up) **551.2**

1. Earthquakes

ISBN 0-7660-2381-8   LC 2004-11698

Contents: Living dangerously; What is an earthquake?; Devastation in Central and South America; Asia and the Middle East; On shaky ground: North America; Saving lives; Top ten deadliest earthquakes ever

Reed, Jennifer—*Continued*

This explains the causes of earthquakes, tells stories of survivors and rescuers, and offers safety advice

This is an "attractive and straightforward volume. . . . Illustrations include dramatic full-color photos, as well as maps and diagrams." SLJ

Includes glossary and bibliographical references

Simon, Seymour

Earthquakes. Morrow Junior Bks. 1991 unp il maps $16.95; pa $6.95 (3-6) **551.2**

1. Earthquakes

ISBN 0-688-09633-6; 0-688-14022-X (pa)

LC 90-19328

Examines the phenomenon of earthquakes, describing how and where they occur, how they can be predicted, and how much damage they can inflict

"This makes a lasting impression with its combination of direct text and sharp color photos and drawings. . . . This informational treasure will draw science enthusiasts and browsers alike." Booklist

Volcanoes. Morrow Junior Bks. 1988 unp il $15.95; lib bdg $15.88; pa $5.95 (3-6)

551.2

1. Volcanoes

ISBN 0-688-07411-1; 0-688-07412-X (lib bdg); 0-688-14029-7 (pa) LC 87-33316

"Using examples like St. Helens and the volcanoes of Iceland and Hawaii, the author is able to address all aspects of his subject: the history, nature and causes of volcanoes." Publ Wkly

"The photographs are large, informative, and spectacular, reproduced in brilliant color. Aside from one confusing map of the earth's tectonic plates, this is a solid introduction." Bull Cent Child Books

Walker, Sally M.

Earthquakes. Carolrhoda Bks. 1996 48p il (Carolrhoda earth watch book) lib bdg $21.27 (3-6) **551.2**

1. Earthquakes

ISBN 0-87614-888-7 LC 94-36178

The author offers "explanations for how and where earthquakes occur, how scientists are working to predict them, and how to survive if one strikes. In addition to photographs, a number of informative charts and graphs extend the text. . . . This book is informative enough for reports, yet readable and visually appealing to browsers." SLJ

Includes glossary

551.3 Surface and exogenous processes and their agents

Harrison, David L. (David Lakin)

Glaciers; nature's icy caps; [by] David L. Harrison; illustrated by Cheryl Nathan. 1st ed. Boyds Mills Press 2006 unp il (Earthworks) $15.95 (k-3) **551.3**

1. Glaciers

ISBN 1-59078-372-7 LC 2005024988

The author "provides a straightforward introduction to glaciers. Opening with the sinking of the *Titanic*, he explains how they form, move, and drop icebergs into the sea, going on to discuss where glaciers can be found and how their range shifts as Earth cycles in and out of ice ages. . . . The text reads like clear, informational prose. Nathan's digital illustrations vary in quality, but the best double-page spreads . . . are exceptionally fine." Booklist

Simon, Seymour

Icebergs and glaciers. Morrow 1987 unp il pa $5.95 hardcover o.p. (3-6) **551.3**

1. Glaciers 2. Icebergs

ISBN 0-688-16705-5 (pa) LC 86-18142

"After an explanation of the consistency of snowflakes, packed snow, and ice fields, the text describes the movement of glaciers by sliding or creeping, various processes of measurement, landscape alteration, geological effects of glacial movement, and the formation of icebergs." Bull Cent Child Books

The author "chronicles the development of glaciers and icebergs with a wonderfully clear, almost Spartan text that receives all of the support necessary from the magnificent color photographs which accompany it. . . . This book would be an excellent addition to any elementary school library or any personal juvenile collection." Appraisal

551.4 Geomorphology and hydrosphere

Brimner, Larry Dane

Caves. Children's Press 2000 47p il lib bdg $23; pa $6.95 (2-4) **551.4**

1. Caves

ISBN 0-516-21567-1 (lib bdg); 0-516-27189-X (pa)

LC 99-58037

"A True book"

Describes the different kinds of caves, how they are formed, and the wildlife that lives within them

Includes bibliographical references

Kaplan, Elizabeth

The tundra. Marshall Cavendish 1995 64p il (Biomes of the world) lib bdg $25.64 (4-6)

551.4

1. Tundra ecology 2. Arctic regions

ISBN 0-7614-0080-X LC 95-2192

This book "concerns life in 'the earth's coldest biome,' including seasonal changes in the arctic tundra, the fragile ecosystem of the alpine tundra, wildlife from algae to musk oxen, and environmental hazards." Booklist

Includes bibliographical references

Kramer, Stephen
Caves; photographs by Kenrick L. Day. Carolrhoda Bks. 1995 48p il (Nature in action) lib bdg $21.27; pa $7.95 (4-6)   **551.4**
1. Caves
ISBN 0-87614-447-4 (lib bdg); 0-87614-896-8 (pa)
LC 93-42136
The author "explains many aspects of speleology. He discusses various kinds of caves but focuses on limestone caves, describing the creation of stalactites, stalagmites, and other speleothems, giving an overview of cave flora and fauna, and offering guidelines for those interested in exploring caves themselves." Bull Cent Child Books
"Through an enticing introduction, full-color photographs of spectacular sites and features, and a generally accurate and useful text, this book provides readers with a glimpse of the alluring world of caving." SLJ
Includes glossary

Simon, Seymour
Mountains. Morrow Junior Bks. 1994 unp il pa $6.99 hardcover o.p. (3-6)   **551.4**
1. Mountains
ISBN 0-688-15477-8 (pa)   LC 93-11398
Introduces various mountain ranges, how they are formed and shaped, and how they affect vegetation and animals, including humans
"The striking color photographs work well with the clear text to illustrate key points and highlight the diversity among the Earth's mountain ranges." Horn Book Guide

Zoehfeld, Kathleen Weidner
How mountains are made; illustrated by James Graham Hale. HarperCollins Pubs. 1995 29p il maps (Let's-read-and-find-out science) lib bdg $15.89; pa $4.95 (k-3)   **551.4**
1. Mountains 2. Geology
ISBN 0-06-024510-7 (lib bdg); 0-06-445128-3 (pa)
LC 93-45436
"Four children and a dog climbing a forest trail provide the framework for this discussion of mountains. Along the way, the knowledgeable characters explain the earth's structure and tectonic plates as well as the different types of mountains and how they are formed." Booklist
"The text and illustrations work together well in this sequential, well-organized book. Much credit goes to Hale's engaging watercolor illustrations done in cheery colors; they are simply drawn but add effective examples and diagrams." SLJ

551.46 Hydrosphere and submarine geology. Oceanography

Adamson, Thomas K.
Tsunamis; with Walter C. Dudley, consultant. Capstone Press 2005 c2006 24p il $22.26 (2-4)
551.46
1. Tsunamis
ISBN 0-7368-5248-4   LC 2005-01640
"Bridgestone books"

"Adamson explains how tsunamis are caused and how they move through the ocean and grow in height as they approach the shore. He describes the damage they cause, the kinds of warning systems used to detect them, and the impact of the 2004 Indian Ocean disaster. The writing is concise but clear, and the layout features a full-page illustration facing each page of easy-to-read text. Excellent photos of the 2004 tsunami are featured, and the diagrams of the earth's plates and earthquakes are simple but informative." SLJ
Includes bibliographical references

Burleigh, Robert
The sea; exploring life on an ocean planet; photographs by Philip Plisson; adapted by Robert Burleigh; text by Yvon Mauffret; drawings by Emmanuel Cerisier. Harry N. Abrams 2003 79p il $14.95 (5 and up)   **551.46**
1. Ocean
ISBN 0-8109-4591-6
Originally published in French
Text and photographs of storms, ports, pollution, diving, rescues, surfing, lighthouses, tides, and many kinds of boats, plants, and animals reveal the world's oceans and the people who live on or near them
"Each photograph is a work of art. Plisson's innate love the the sea is obvious, and he shares this feeling with his audience. . . . Text explains the significance of each photograph. . . . This book is a deep-sea treasure chest." Libr Media Connect

Earle, Sylvia A.
Dive! my adventures in the deep frontier. National Geographic Soc. 1999 64p il map $18.95 (4-6)   **551.46**
1. Underwater exploration 2. Submarine diving
ISBN 0-7922-7144-0   LC 98-11480
The author relates some of her adventures studying and exploring the world's oceans, including tracking whales, living in an underwater laboratory, and helping to design a deep water submarine
"In this extraordinary photo-essay, an eminent marine biologist and ocean explorer combines personal adventure and scientific fact with glorious color action pictures." Booklist
Includes glossary

Gibbons, Gail
Exploring the deep, dark sea. Little, Brown 1999 unp il $14.95; pa $5.95 (k-3)
551.46
1. Underwater exploration 2. Ocean bottom 3. Marine biology
ISBN 0-316-30945-1; 0-316-75549-4 (pa)
LC 98-14443
"From the sunlight zone to the abyss, Gibbons follows the crew of a deep-diving submersible craft into the ocean depths, noting the changes in terrain and animal life at the various levels. Labels identify parts of the craft and the many animals, and explanations of the differing ecologies of the many levels are brief. Thoughtful attention to page design and narrative produce an account that is both spare and surprisingly rich." Horn Book Guide

Hamilton, John

Tsunamis; [by] John Hamilton. Abdo Pub. Co. 2006 32p il map $24.21 (2-4)   **551.46**

1. Tsunamis

ISBN 1-59679-333-3   LC 2005040427

"Hamilton describes the 2004 Indian Ocean disaster and explains the causes and nature of tsunamis. . . . The brief but readable text adequately presents the phenomenon and the specific events. Excellent, informative color photos include several that are not common to many of the other recent books on the topic." SLJ

Includes bibliographical references

Littlefield, Cindy A.

Awesome ocean science! investigating the secrets of the underwater world; illustrations by Sarah Rakitin. Williamson 2003 120p il pa $12.95 (3-5)   **551.46**

1. Ocean 2. Marine ecology 3. Science—Experiments

ISBN 1-88559-371-6   LC 2002-33077

"A Williamson kids can! book"

Contents: You and the ocean; Water world; Currents & waves; Shorelines & tide pools; Sea life; The ocean floor

Explores the wonders of the ocean, its floor, and the plants and animals that dwell in it, teaches how to protect these resources, and provides hands-on activities for further investigation

"Activities that illustrate the concepts . . . are mostly creative, illuminating, and easy to follow. Lighthearted cartoon art adds to the appeal of this fact-packed title." Booklist

Includes bibliographical references

Matsen, Bradford

The incredible record-setting deep-sea dive of the bathysphere; [by] Brad Matsen. Enslow Pubs. 2003 48p il map (Incredible deep-sea adventures) lib bdg $18.95 (4 and up)   **551.46**

1. Beebe, William, 1877-1962 2. Barton, Otis 3. Underwater exploration 4. Ocean bottom

ISBN 0-7660-2188-2   LC 2002-13822

Contents: Heroes of the deep; The voyage into the depths; A record is broken, a record is set; Explorers of the abyss; The ultimate dive to the bottom of the sea

Describes the 1934 dive of a bathysphere, or "sphere of the deep," in which two explorers, William Beebe and Otia Barton, set the world depth record and saw mysterious creatures of the deep ocean

"Attractive color photos contribute to the content." SLJ

Includes glossary and bibliographical references

Scholastic atlas of oceans. Scholastic Reference 2004 96p il map $18.95 (4 and up)   **551.46**

1. Ocean

ISBN 0-439-56128-0

This presents an "overview of the origins and workings of [ocean] ecosystems and examines some of the unique characteristics and features of the five oceans and the five major seas. Marine inhabitants and their activities are included as are humankind's effects on these fragile resources. . . . The illustrations are eye-catching and appealing for browsing. The organization and factual approach make the title useful for reports." SLJ

Simon, Seymour

Oceans. Morrow Junior Bks. 1990 unp il $16 (3-6)   **551.46**

1. Ocean

ISBN 0-688-09453-8   LC 89-28452

This book "covers the geography of the ocean floor, major currents, and El Nino (a shift in the prevailing currents that causes severe climactic changes). Tides, tsunami, waves, coastal erosion, and marine life are also touched upon." Booklist

"Simon presents clear, simplified explanations of natural phenomena with well-chosen full-color photographs that go beyond decoration. He includes good black-and-white diagrams of how tides work and how waves form and transfer energy. The endpapers are maps of the world showing how and where the major currents flow." SLJ

Stille, Darlene R.

Oceans. Children's Press 1999 47p il maps $22; pa $6.95 (2-4)   **551.46**

1. Ocean

ISBN 0-516-21510-8; 0-516-26768-X (pa)

     LC 98-53857

"A True book"

An introduction to the ocean describing its physical characteristics, the plants and animals that live in or near it, and its importance to life on Earth

Includes bibliographical references

VanCleave, Janice Pratt

Janice VanCleave's oceans for every kid; easy activities that make learning science fun. Wiley 1996 245p il maps (Science for every kid series) pa $12.95 hardcover o.p. (4 and up)

     551.46

1. Oceanography

ISBN 0-471-12453-2 (pa)   LC 95-9201

Includes information on techniques and technologies of oceanography, the topology of the ocean floor, movement of the sea, properties of sea water, and life in the sea

"An engaging overview of marine sciences. Each chapter explores a topic in two to four pages, then poses questions accompanied by lucid explanations." SLJ

Includes glossary

551.48 Hydrology

Cole, Joanna

The magic school bus at the waterworks; illustrated by Bruce Degen. Scholastic 1986 39p il $15.95; pa $4.95 (2-4)   **551.48**

1. Water 2. Water supply

ISBN 0-590-43739-9; 0-590-40360-5 (pa)

     LC 86-6672

Also available Spanish language edition

Cole, Joanna—*Continued*

The author presents "specific facts about water and a memorable image of the water cycle process. The story involves a 'strange' teacher who takes her class on a magical trip: up to the clouds—down to earth in raindrops—down a stream into a reservoir where the water is purified—finally into the underground pipes leading back to school. The illustrations both enhance the humor and provide visual presentation of the water cycle." Appraisal

Dorros, Arthur

Follow the water from brook to ocean; written and illustrated by Arthur Dorros. HarperCollins Pubs. 1991 32p il (Let's-read-and-find-out science book) $13.95; lib bdg $13.89 (k-3)

551.48

1. Water

ISBN 0-06-021598-4; 0-06-021599-2 (lib bdg)

LC 90-1438

Explains how water flows from brooks, to streams, to rivers, over waterfalls, through canyons and dams, to eventually reach the ocean

"An excellent presentation of introductory material about water. . . . The illustrations are simple, almost childlike, in soft colors." SLJ

Gallant, Roy A.

Water. Benchmark Bks. 2001 48p il (Kaleidoscope) lib bdg $15.95 (3-5)

551.48

1. Water

ISBN 0-7614-1040-6   LC 99-49627

Explains why water, although common, has characteristics which make it an unusual substance

"The large-print [text is] easy to read, and the explanations are clear and concise. Outstanding full-page, full-color photographs appear throughout." SLJ

Includes glossary and bibliographical references

Hiscock, Bruce

The big rivers; the Missouri, the Mississippi, and the Ohio; written and illustrated by Bruce Hiscock. Atheneum Bks. for Young Readers 1997 unp il maps $16 (2-4)   **551.48**

1. Floods 2. Mississippi River valley

ISBN 0-689-80871-2   LC 96-2435

Describes the conditions that led up to the severe flooding in the Mississippi River Valley in 1993

"Hiscock's well-conceived and appealing watercolor paintings, some in double-page spreads, demonstrate clearly what is happening. His time line of rainfall and flood levels in 1993 is particularly effective. An excellent resource for an increasingly timely topic." Booklist

Lauber, Patricia

Flood; wrestling with the Mississippi. National Geographic Soc. 1996 63p il maps $18.95 (4 and up)   **551.48**

1. Floods 2. Mississippi River

ISBN 0-7922-4141-X   LC 95-47338

This provides a "description of the Mississippi River: its modern history as a mighty natural force, as enemy and ally; and how it has impacted the lives of people who depend on it for better and for worse. Lauber looks at the 1927 and 1993 floods and highlights what has been learned about harnessing and controlling the Mississippi. Each page is well balanced with text and informative, well-chosen full-color photographs or drawings." SLJ

Rauzon, Mark J.

Water, water everywhere; [by] Mark J. Rauzon and Cynthia Overbeck Bix. Sierra Club Bks. for Children 1994 32p il $14.95; pa $6.95 (k-3)

551.48

1. Water

ISBN 0-87156-598-6; 0-87156-383-5 (pa)

LC 92-34521

Describes the forms water takes, how it has shaped Earth, and its importance to life

"Water's vital role in the life of our planet is vividly portrayed in a crisp, economical text that cultivates respect for the environment. . . . Striking, often full-page, color photographs will engage the imagination of young readers." Horn Book Guide

Waldman, Neil

The snowflake; a water cycle story; [by] Neil Waldman. Millbrook Press 2003 unp il $14.95 (k-3)   **551.48**

1. Water 2. Snow

ISBN 0-7613-2347-3   LC 2003-4806

Follows the journey of a water droplet through the various stages of the water cycle, from precipitation to evaporation and condensation

"The clear text is undeniably lyrical. . . . The real stunners here, though, are the dazzling, cool-toned paintings that convey the wonders of nature with delicate precision." SLJ

551.5 Meteorology

Branley, Franklyn Mansfield

Air is all around you; by Franklyn M. Branley; illustrated by Holly Keller. rev ed. Crowell 1986 31p il (Let's-read-and-find-out science book) pa $4.95 hardcover o.p. (k-1)   **551.5**

1. Air

ISBN 0-06-445048-1 (pa)   LC 85-47884

A revised and newly illustrated edition of the title first published 1962

Describes the various properties of air and shows how to prove that air takes up space and that there is air dissolved in water

"Illustrations in both bold and pastel colors are coordinated with the easy-to-read text and make this an eye-pleasing and informative book." SLJ

Kahl, Jonathan D.

National Audubon Society first field guide: weather. Scholastic 1998 159p il pa $10.95 hardcover o.p. (4 and up) **551.5**

1. Weather 2. Meteorology

ISBN 0-590-05488-0 (pa)   LC 98-2938

Provides an overview of various weather conditions, how they develop, and how they are studied

Includes glossary and bibliographical references

Lauw, Darlene

Weather; [by Darlene Lauw and Lim Cheng Puay] Crabtree 2003 29p il (Science alive!) lib bdg $21.28; pa $7.95 (3-6)   **551.5**

1. Weather 2. Science—Experiments

ISBN 0-7787-0565-X (lib bdg); 0-7787-0611-7 (pa)
    LC 2002-11641

Contents: The power of the sun!; The weight of air affects weather!; Windy days are fun!; Water, water everywhere!; Light rain, heavy rain; What a muggy day!; Flash, crash, boom!

Introduces concepts related to weather through various activities and projects

"The directions are kid friendly, and the graphics that support them are very helpful. . . . The science content is within the range of understanding of an upper elementary school student." Sci Books Films

Includes glossary

Levine, Shar

Wonderful weather; [by] Shar Levine and Leslie Johnstone; illustrated by Steve Harpster. Sterling Pub 2003 48p il (First science experiments) $12.95 (2-4)   **551.5**

1. Weather 2. Science—Experiments

ISBN 0-8069-7249-1   LC 2002-15330

This "book provides answers to the questions children tend to ask about the weather, such as 'Why is the sky blue?' and 'Why does my shirt sometimes stick to me on hot days?' Each answer is demonstrated by a simple experiment that includes an explanation of what happened." SLJ

This "is an excellent volume that provides the reader with accurate information on weather phenomena." Sci Books Films

Scholastic atlas of weather. Scholastic Reference 2004 80p il $17.95 (5 and up)   **551.5**

ISBN 0-439-41902-6   LC 2002-26915

Contents: The ABCs of weather; When weather runs wild; A planet under many influences; Predictions . . . for better or worse

A guide to weather phenomena and climate which explains precipitation, ocean currents, weather prediction, pollution, and global warming, plus activities, weather facts, records, and statistics.

"Replete with a multitude of colorful illustrations and diagrams (and data-packed captions) and a plethora of sidebars, the conversational text is limited to a paragraph or so on each topic. . . . This offering presents a fresh face in the weather lineup." SLJ

Includes glossary

Simon, Seymour

Weather. Morrow Junior Bks. 1993 unp il $15.95; lib bdg $14.93; pa $6.95 (3-6)
    551.5

1. Weather 2. Meteorology

ISBN 0-688-10546-7; 0-688-10547-5 (lib bdg); 0-688-17521-X (pa)   LC 92-31069

Explores the causes, changing patterns, and forecasting of weather

"Gorgeous full-page color photos, helped by a few cogent diagrams, illustrate Simon's outline of how weather works. . . . The organization is clear and logical." Bull Cent Child Books

VanCleave, Janice Pratt

Janice VanCleave's weather; mind-boggling experiments you can turn into science fair projects; [by] Janice VanCleave. Wiley 1995 89p il (Spectacular science projects series) pa $10.95 (4 and up)   **551.5**

1. Weather 2. Science projects 3. Science—Experiments

ISBN 0-471-03231-X   LC 94-25646

"Using everyday household items, the reading audience can demonstrate to itself such phenomena as differences in climate at different points on the Earth, lightning, wind direction and intensity, clouds, rain, fronts, etc. Through excellent directions and adequate illustrations, the reader can do 20 simple experiments at little or no cost that demonstrate many aspects of the weather." Sci Books Films

Includes glossary

551.51 Composition, regions, dynamics of atmosphere

Bauer, Marion Dane

Wind; illustrated by John Wallace. Aladdin 2004 32p il lib bdg $11.89; pa $3.99 (k-2)
    551.51

1. Winds

ISBN 0-689-85442-0 (lib bdg); 0-689-85443-9 (pa)
    LC 2002-9656

"Ready-to-read"

Illustrations and simple text explain what wind is, how it is used by plants, birds, and people, and how wind can become a storm.

Cobb, Vicki

I face the wind; illustrated by Julia Gorton. HarperCollins Pubs. 2003 unp il (Science play) $15.99; lib bdg $16.89 (k-2)   **551.51**

1. Winds 2. Science—Experiments

ISBN 0-688-17840-5; 0-688-17841-3 (lib bdg)
    LC 2001-26480

Introduces the characteristics and actions of the wind through simple hands-on activities

"All demonstrations . . . are conducted with readily available materials. . . . Streamlined and jargon-fee though the text may be, it gets the basics across in kid-friendly terms. . . . Gorton's strong, angular graphics

Cobb, Vicki—*Continued*
feature a redheaded little gal with wide-set eyes and a powerful curiosity who alternately serves as wind-tousled subject of forces real but unseen and as demonstrator for each experiment." Bull Cent Child Books

Dorros, Arthur
Feel the wind; written and illustrated by Arthur Dorros. Crowell 1989 32p il (Let's-read-and-find-out science book) $12.95; lib bdg $12.89 (k-3)   551.51
1. Winds
ISBN 0-690-04739-8; 0-690-04741-X (lib bdg)
LC 88-18961
"The motion of air in the form of wind is discernible in many ways. Simple text accompanied by bright illustrations explains the causes, power, effects, and uses of wind. Encourages outdoor experimentaton." Sci Child

Friend, Sandra
Earth's wild winds. 21st Cent. Bks. (Brookfield) 2002 32p il maps (Exploring planet earth) lib bdg $24.90 (5 and up)   551.51
1. Winds
ISBN 0-7613-2673-1   LC 2001-6515
Examines different aspects of the wind, including its measurement, effects on weather, potential destructiveness, and uses
"This attractive and fact-filled book will be useful for earth-science reports. . . . The full-color charts, maps, and photos contribute immeasurably to the success of the presentation." SLJ
Includes bibliographical references

Gallant, Roy A.
Atmosphere; sea of air. Benchmark Bks. 2002 79p il (Earthworks) lib bdg $19.95 (5 and up)
551.51
1. Atmosphere 2. Meteorology
ISBN 0-7614-1366-9   LC 2001-43301
Describes the atmosphere which makes life on earth possible, explores its effects on weather and climate, and examines what causes air pollution and what can be done it
"Gallant's prose is nearly conversational in its easy delivery, but his facts are always thorough and his ideas clearly explained. . . . Crisp graphs, maps, and excellent color photos illustrate [this] fine [volume]." Booklist
Includes glossary and bibliographical references

Sayre, April Pulley
Stars beneath your bed; the surprising story of dust; pictures by Ann Jonas. 1st ed. Greenwillow Books 2005 unp il $15.99; lib bdg $16.89 (k-3)
551.51
1. Dust
ISBN 0-06-057188-8; 0-06-057189-6 (lib bdg)
LC 2004-2108
"Dust gets a poetic treatment in a picture book that tells all about dust's what and where, and sometimes its why. Using free verse, Sayre explains how dust is made

everywhere. . . . The watercolors in the well-composed two-page spreads sometimes soar . . . but there are also smaller images . . . that are equally effective." Booklist

551.55 Atmospheric disturbances and formations

Branley, Franklyn Mansfield
Flash, crash, rumble, and roll; by Franklyn M. Branley; illustrated by True Kelley. newly il ed. HarperCollins Pubs. 1999 32p il (Let's-read-and-find-out science) $15.95; lib bdg $15.89; pa $4.95 (k-3)   551.55
1. Thunderstorms 2. Lightning
ISBN 0-06-027858-7; 0-06-027859-5 (lib bdg); 0-06-445179-8 (pa)   LC 97-43599
A revised and newly illustrated edition of the title first published 1964 by Crowell
Explains how and why a thunderstorm occurs and gives safety steps to follow when lightning is flashing
This offers "clear and informative explanations . . . [and] colorful cartoonlike pictures." Horn Book Guide

Ceban, Bonnie J.
Hurricanes, typhoons, and cyclones; disaster & survival; [by] Bonnie J. Ceban. Enslow Pubs. 2005 48p il map (Deadly disasters) lib bdg $31.93 (4 and up)   551.55
1. Hurricanes 2. Typhoons 3. Cyclones
ISBN 0-7660-2388-5
This briefly explains the science of hurricanes, typhoons, and cyclones; describes Cyclone Tracy in Australia in 1974, Hurricanes Andrew and Floyd in Florida in 1991 and 1999 respectively, and Typhoon Tokage in Japan in 2004; and suggests safety precautions.
Includes glossary and bibliographical references

Tornadoes; disaster & survival; [by] Bonnie J. Ceban. Enslow Publishers 2005 48p il map (Deadly disasters) $23.93 (4 and up)
551.55
1. Tornadoes
ISBN 0-7660-2383-4   LC 2004-11700
This explores the causes of tornadoes, how people survive these storms, and how they are predicted.
Includes glossary and bibliographical references

Challoner, Jack
Hurricane & tornado; written by Jack Challoner. Dorling Kindersley 2000 61p il maps (DK eyewitness books) $15.95; lib bdg $19.99 (4 and up)   551.55
1. Weather 2. Natural disasters
ISBN 0-7894-5242-1; 0-7894-6804-2 (lib bdg)
LC 99-44160
Describes dangerous and destructive weather conditions around the world, such as thunderstorms, tornadoes, hurricanes, lightning, hail, and drought with photographs, historical background, and legends

Cole, Joanna

The magic school bus inside a hurricane; illustrated by Bruce Degen. Scholastic 1995 unp il $15.95; pa $4.99 (2-4)   **551.55**
1. Hurricanes 2. Weather 3. Meteorology
ISBN 0-590-44686-X; 0-590-44687-8 (pa)
                  LC 94-34703
Also available Spanish language edition
"The magic school bus changes into a weather balloon and then into an airplane as the class experiences the hurricane and a spin-off tornado firsthand. As usual, Ms. Frizzle's wardrobe is as changeable as the weather. The familiar format features lots of weather information delivered via students' written reports and spoken comments." SLJ
"Cole presents the science in easy-to-understand terms, with Degen clarifying the concepts and adding comic relief through double-page-spread pictures that brim with details." Booklist

Demarest, Chris L.

Hurricane hunters! riders on the storm; [by] Chris L. Demarest. 1st ed. Margaret K. McElderry Books 2006 unp il $17.95 (k-3)   **551.55**
1. Hurricanes 2. Weather forecasting
ISBN 978-0-689-86168-0   LC 2005011292
This "picture book explains the work of the large converted cargo planes that fly into hurricanes to collect weather data. . . . The pastels are particularly effective at capturing the look and feel of the powerful winds and swirling water caused by a hurricane at its height." SLJ
Includes bibliographical references

Simon, Seymour

Hurricanes. HarperCollins Pubs. 2003 unp il $15.99; lib bdg $16.89 (4 and up)   **551.55**
1. Hurricanes
ISBN 0-688-16291-6; 0-688-16292-4 (lib bdg)
                  LC 2002-151603
Discusses where and how hurricanes are formed, the destruction caused by legendary storms, and the precautions to take when a hurricane strikes
"Pairing a simply phrased narrative with arresting, eye-catching color photos, Simon explains what hurricanes are and imparts a vivid sense of their destructive potential." Booklist

Storms. Morrow Junior Bks. 1989 unp il pa $5.95 hardcover o.p. (4 and up)   **551.55**
1. Storms
ISBN 0-688-11708-2 (pa)   LC 88-22045
This book describes the atmospheric conditions which create thunderstorms, hailstorms, lightning, tornadoes, and hurricanes and how violent weather affects the environment and people
"The half- to full-page glossy color photographs are sure to attract young readers as will the subject. *Storms* is an excellent way to introduce the science of meteorology to children." Sci Books Films

Tornadoes. Morrow Junior Bks. 1999 unp il map $16.95; pa $6.99 (4 and up)   **551.55**
1. Tornadoes
ISBN 0-688-14646-5; 0-06-443791-4 (pa)
                  LC 98-27953

Describes the location, nature, development, measurement, and destructive effects of tornadoes, as well as how to stay out of danger from them
"Incredible full-color photographs and diagrams, clearly portraying the different formations and devastating power of the windstorms, complement the text perfectly." Booklist

551.56   Atmospheric electricity and optics

Kramer, Stephen

Lightning; photographs by Warren Faidley. Carolrhoda Bks. 1992 48p il (Nature in action) lib bdg $21.27; pa $7.95 (4-6)   **551.56**
1. Lightning
ISBN 0-87614-659-0 (lib bdg); 0-87614-617-5 (pa)
                  LC 91-21793
This introduction to lightning "explains how a thunderhead develops, how lightning results from negatively and positively charged electrons, kinds of lightning, and [includes] safety information." Bull Cent Child Books
"Diagrams supplement the well-written narrative in describing scientific concepts. Exceptionally fine, full-color photographs—each a work of art—perfectly illustrate the text, powerfully and spectacularly showing the majesty and might of this phenomenon." SLJ
Includes glossary

Simon, Seymour

Lightning. Morrow Junior Bks. 1997 unp il $16; pa $6.99 (4 and up)   **551.56**
1. Lightning
ISBN 0-688-14638-4; 0-688-16706-3 (pa)
                  LC 96-16962
Photographs and text explore the natural phenomenon of lightning
"The subject is exciting, the information is amazing, and the full-color photographs are riveting. . . . Simon's explanations are concise but thorough." Booklist

551.57   Hydrometeorology

Branley, Franklyn Mansfield

Down comes the rain; by Franklyn M. Branley; illustrated by James Graham Hale. HarperCollins Pubs. 1997 31p il (Let's-read-and-find-out science) lib bdg $15.89; pa $4.95 (k-3)   **551.57**
1. Rain 2. Clouds
ISBN 0-06-025338-X (lib bdg); 0-06-445166-6 (pa)
                  LC 96-3519
A revised and newly illustrated edition of Rain & hail published 1983 by Crowell
The author explains "how water is recycled, how clouds are formed, and why rain and hail occur. A few easy science activities are included. . . . The pen-and-ink with watercolor wash paintings clearly interpret the concepts presented on each page." SLJ

Branley, Franklyn Mansfield—*Continued*
Snow is falling; by Franklyn M. Branley; illustrated by Holly Keller. HarperCollins Pubs. 2000 33p il (Let's-read-and-find-out science) $15.95; lib bdg $15.89; pa $4.95 (k-1)
551.57
1. Snow
ISBN 0-06-027990-7; 0-06-027991-5 (lib bdg); 0-06-445186-0 (pa)   LC 98-23106
A revised and newly illustrated edition of the title first published 1963 by Crowell
Describes snow's physical qualities and how quantities of it can be fun as well as dangerous
"Keller's new illustrations are a good match for the spare, informative text. A few easy activities explore snow's different properties, and a list of websites is appended." Horn Book Guide

De Paola, Tomie
The cloud book; words and pictures by Tomie de Paola. Holiday House 1975 30p il lib bdg $16.95; pa $6.95 (k-3)   **551.57**
1. Clouds
ISBN 0-8234-0259-2 (lib bdg); 0-8234-0531-1 (pa)
The author instructs "young readers about the ten most common types of clouds, how they were named, and what they mean in terms of changing weather. Actually a very good text to use for early science instruction. Includes a scattering of traditional myths that have clouds as a basis." Adventuring with Books

551.6   Climatology and weather

Arnold, Caroline
El Niño; stormy weather for people and wildlife. Clarion Bks. 1998 48p il $16; pa $5.95 (4 and up)
551.6
1. El Niño Current 2. Climate
ISBN 0-395-77602-3; 0-618-55110-7 (pa)
LC 98-4826
Explores the nature of the El Niño current and its effects on people and wildlife
This book has a "readable, informative text. . . . Full-color photos, a computer-image series, diagrams, and Internet sources bolster the narrative." SLJ
Includes glossary and bibliographical references

Gibbons, Gail
Weather words and what they mean. Holiday House 1990 unp il $16.95; pa $6.95 (k-3)
551.6
1. Weather
ISBN 0-8234-0805-1; 0-8234-0952-X (pa)
LC 89-39515
The author discusses the meaning of meteorological terms such as temperature, air pressure, thunderstorm and moisture
"Gibbons' easily identifiable artistic style works well with her explanations of sometimes misunderstood weather-related terms. Drawings are appealing, attractively arranged, and closely matched to the textual information. . . . An attractive introduction for weather units in the primary grades." SLJ

Rupp, Rebecca
Weather; with journal illustrations by Melissa Sweet and experiment illustrations by Dug Nap. Storey Kids 2003 136p il map $21.95; pa $14.95 (4 and up)   **551.6**
1. Weather
ISBN 1-58017-469-8; 1-58017-420-5 (pa)
LC 2002-152310
Contents: The atmosphere: what's up?; Wind: huffs, puffs, & hurricanes; Sunshine: beams, burns, & blue skies; Clouds: white sheep & little cat feet; Rain: drops, drizzles, & downpours; Thunder & lightning: Thor's hammer & Zeus's spear; Snow & ice: frost, flurries, and blizzards; Predicting the weather: reading the skys
This includes facts about weather with instructions for 22 science projects
"A lively, upbeat presentation. Chock-full of solid information, this compendium includes lots of slightly offbeat, appealing observations. . . . Numerous, attention-grabbing visuals illustrate experiments." SLJ
Includes glossary

Singer, Marilyn
On the same day in March; a tour of the world's weather; illustrated by Frané Lessac. HarperCollins Pubs. 2000 unp il $15.95; lib bdg $15.89 (k-3)   **551.6**
1. Weather
ISBN 0-06-028187-1; 0-06-028188-X (lib bdg)
LC 98-52797
Highlights a wide variety of weather conditions by taking a tour around the world and examining weather in different places on the same day in March
"For each setting, singer provides a few lines of lyrical text that vividly create the climate . . . as Lessac's single-and double-page spreads colorfully show us the way the weather and the world look. An appended author's note adds factual information to the mix, an endpaper map puts the places readers will visit in a global context. The book doubles as a delightfully agreeable introduction to both climatology and geography." Booklist

551.63   Weather forecasting and forecasts, reporting and reports

Breen, Mark
The kids' book of weather forecasting; build a weather station, "read" the sky & make predictions; with meteorologist Mark Breen and Kathleen Friestad; illustrations by Michael Kline. Williamson 2000 140p il maps music pa $12.95 (4 and up)   **551.63**
1. Weather forecasting 2. Science—Experiments
ISBN 1-88559-339-2   LC 99-89954
"A Williamson kids can! book"
A hands-on introduction to the science of meteorology, explaining how to make equipment to measure rainfall, wind direction, and humidity, record measurements and observations in a weather log, make weather predictions, and perform other weather related activities
"A useful, accessible book illustrated with black-and-white diagrams and cartoons." SLJ
Includes bibliographical references

Gibbons, Gail

Weather forecasting. Four Winds Press 1987
unp il pa $5.99 hardcover o.p. (k-3)

                                 551.63

1. Weather forecasting

ISBN 0-689-71683-4 (pa)   LC 86-7602

"The book is divided into four sections, one per season, which treat different kinds of weather as they're observed, recorded, and reported at a weather station." Bull Cent Child Books

"Any child can learn the basic concepts from the text at the bottom of each page, while the precocious can garner an impressive weather vocabulary by absorbing the terms labeled and defined within the artwork. Brightly illustrated with the artist's usual bold, flat colors, this book will serve as an appealing introduction to weather forecasting for young children." Booklist

552   Petrology

Christian, Peggy

If you find a rock; written by Peggy Christian; photographs by Barbara Hirsch Lember. Harcourt 2000 unp il $16 (k-3)   **552**

1. Rocks

ISBN 0-15-239339-0   LC 98-48938

Celebrates the variety of rocks that can be found, including skipping rocks, chalk rocks, and splashing rocks

"Poetic text and thoughtfully composed, hand-tinted photographs combine to explore the variety and purposes of rocks. . . . Lember's intriguing artwork is especially suited to the quiet text. . . . A good story hour selection, especially for introducing primary geology units or setting the mood for creative writing." Booklist

De Paola, Tomie

The quicksand book. Holiday House 1977 unp il lib bdg $16.95; pa $6.95 (k-3)   **552**

1. Quicksand

ISBN 0-8234-0291-6 (lib bdg); 0-8234-0532-X (pa)
                                LC 76-28762

Also available Spanish language edition

"Jungle Girl, swinging on a vine from her treehouse, falls into a patch of . . . [quicksand] but, fortunately, is observed by Jungle Boy. As she slowly sinks, her scholarly bespectacled young Tarzan delivers a long but interesting lecture on the properties of and useful means of rescue from quicksand." Horn Book

De Paola "uses a picture-book format to present basic science information in an utterly appealing, humorous way. . . . Very funny and very sensible." SLJ

Gans, Roma

Let's go rock collecting; illustrated by Holly Keller. newly il ed. HarperCollins Pubs. 1997 31p il (Let's-read-and-find-out science) $15.95; lib bdg $15.89 (k-2)   **552**

1. Rocks—Collectors and collecting

ISBN 0-06-027282-1; 0-06-027283-X (lib bdg)
                                LC 95-44999

A revised and newly illustrated edition of Rock collecting, published 1984 by Crowell

Describes the formation and characteristics of igneous, metamorphic, and sedimentary rocks and how to recognize and collect them

"The excellent diagrams, full-color photographs of specimens, and minor textual changes clarify the concepts (for example, Mohs' scale of hardness) and extend the presentation. . . . The pair of youngsters featured in Keller's brightly colored illustrations . . . convey the joys of being a rock hound." SLJ

Hynes, Margaret

Rocks & fossils; [by] Margaret Hynes; foreword by Professor Jack Horner. 1st ed. Kingfisher 2006 63p il map (Kingfisher knowledge) $12.95 (5 and up)   **552**

1. Rocks 2. Fossils

ISBN 9780753459744   LC 2005023897

Includes index

This covers "the history of rock, . . . the minerals that make them, and . . . their different uses, from building materials to pigments for paints and dyes. The formation of fossils is also explained." Publisher's note

This is a "lavishly illustrated book. . . . The well-written text is pithy and comprehensible." Voice Youth Advocates

Includes glossary and bibliographical references

Trueit, Trudi Strain

Rocks, gems, and minerals. Watts 2003 63p il $24; pa $8.95 (4 and up)   **552**

1. Rocks 2. Minerals 3. Precious stones

ISBN 0-531-12195-X; 0-531-16241-9 (pa)
                                LC 2001-7222

"Watts library"

Contents: World of wonders; Mineral magic; The circle of stone; A rocky road; Where do you stand?

"The formation of basic rocks— sedimentary, igneous, and metamorphic—are covered, as are rock crystals and crystallization. Chemical symbols for elements, charts such as the Mohs scale and the geographic location of major gem finds, and fun facts are included." SLJ

This includes "attention-grabbing photography, excellent charts and diagrams, short articles with or without photographs, and vocabulary terms that appear in bold and are explained in context." Sci Books Films

Includes glossary and bibliographical references

VanCleave, Janice Pratt

Janice VanCleave's rocks and minerals; mind-boggling experiments you can turn into science fair projects. Wiley 1996 90p il (Spectacular science projects series) pa $10.95 (4 and up)   **552**

1. Rocks 2. Minerals 3. Science projects 4. Science—Experiments

ISBN 0-471-10269-5   LC 95-10324

"The experiments lead the investigator through a range of topics such as crystal shapes; mineral characteristics . . . magnetism in minerals; sedimentary, metamorphic, and igneous rock formation; rock weathering; fossil types and formation; and how to put together a mineral, rock, or fossil collection." Sci Books Films

VanCleave, Janice Pratt—*Continued*

"VanCleave presents stunningly clear, direct, and informative projects. They are generally simple enough for self-directed students to do on their own, but a teacher's guidance would be helpful." SLJ

Includes glossary

553.6 Other economic materials

Dewey, Jennifer

Mud matters; written and illustrated by Jennifer Owings Dewey; photographs by Stephen Trimble. Marshall Cavendish 1998 72p il $15.95 (4-6)

553.6

1. Clay

ISBN 0-7614-5014-9   LC 97-32929

A personal account describing various uses of mud in such activities as ritual dancing, making pottery, building villages, contructing nests, playing games, and celebrating customs

"Dewey's lively account includes rich descriptions of the mucky stuff, interesting information, and episodes from her own childhood. . . . The four chapters are accompanied by striking full-page photos and Dewey's own characteristically fine pencil drawings." Horn Book Guide

Includes glossary

Kurlansky, Mark

The story of salt; [by] Mark Kurlansky; [illustrated by] S. D. Schindler. G.P. Putnam's Sons 2006 48p il map $16.99 (3-6)   **553.6**

1. Salt

ISBN 0-399-23998-7   LC 2005032629

An adaptation of the author's title for adults: Salt: a world history (2002)

"The informal narrative and the exquisitely detailed, sometimes playful ink-and-watercolor illustrations dramatize the sweeping world history of salt's essential role in human life—from prehistoric times and the early voyages of discovery through the breakthrough of refrigeration and the latest drilling technology." Booklist

Includes bibliographical references

553.7 Water

Gallant, Roy A.

Water; our precious resource. Benchmark Bks. 2002 c2003 79p il map (Earthworks) lib bdg $29.93 (5 and up)   **553.7**

1. Water

ISBN 0-7614-1365-0   LC 2001-43290

Contents: What is water?; Some properties of water; Where is all the water?; Our needs for water; Water pollution and purification; Whose water is it?

An in-depth look at Earth's waters and mankind's uses of water throughout history which includes ideas about planning better use of this critical resource in the future

"Gallant's prose is nearly conversational in its easy delivery, but his facts are always thorough and his ideas

clearly explained. Best of all, he raises informed points that will help readers rethink their habits and realize the complexity of the issues. . . . Crisp graphs, maps, and excellent color photos illustrate [this] fine [volume]." Booklist

Includes glossary and bibliographical references

Lauw, Darlene

Water; [by Darlene Lauw and Lim Cheng Puay] Crabtree 2003 31p il (Science alive!) lib bdg $21.28; pa $7.95 (3-6)   **553.7**

1. Water 2. Science—Experiments

ISBN 0-7787-0567-6 (lib bdg); 0-7787-0613-3 (pa)

LC 2002-11640

Contents: What is water made of?; Solid, liquid, gas; Keeping cool; Water pressure; Water seeks its own level; Water flows up!; Water pollution and water treatment

Uses simple experiments to demonstrate the properties of water

"The directions are kid friendly, and the graphics that support them are very helpful. . . . The science content is within the range of understanding of an upper elementary school student." Sci Books Films

Includes glossary

Royston, Angela

Water; let's look at a puddle. Heinemann Library 2005 24p il (Material detectives) lib ed $21.36 (k-3)   **553.7**

1. Water

ISBN 1-4034-7676-4

Contents: What is a puddle?; What is water?; What shape are puddles?; Can puddles get bigger or smaller?; What happens when you jump into a puddle?; What happens when a puddle gets very cold?

"With clear color photos and a simple, lively, interactive text, this title . . . makes science fun for young readers. . . . An excellent title that brings science into daily life." Booklist

Wick, Walter

A drop of water; a book of science and wonder; written and photographed by Walter Wick. Scholastic 1997 40p il $16.95 (4-6)   **553.7**

1. Water

ISBN 0-590-22197-3   LC 95-30068

The author "uses simple techniques to show water properties such as surface tension, adhesion, capillary attraction, molecular motion, freezing, evaporation, and condensation." Booklist

"This title is an elegant synthesis of science and art. . . . The close-up photographs are breathtakingly distinct; and the clarity provided by the combination of concept, text, and photography of this quality is noteworthy." Bull Cent Child Books

553.8 Gems

Kallen, Stuart A.

Gems. KidHaven Press 2003 48p il (Wonders of the world) $23.70 (4 and up)   **553.8**

1. Precious stones

ISBN 0-7377-1028-4   LC 2002-6025

Kallen, Stuart A.—*Continued*

Contents: Gems from rocks; Gems from plants and animals; History of gem mining; Amazing gems

This "explains how mineral (diamonds, rubies) and organic (amber, pearls) precious materials are formed. Later chapters introduce legends behind famous stones such as the Hope Diamond and describe how gems are mined. . . . There's plenty of information to support reports, all of which is presented in . . . Kallen's straightforward, sometimes lively language." Booklist

557 Earth sciences--North America

Weintraub, Aileen

The Grand Canyon; the widest canyon. PowerKids Press 2001 24p il (Great record breakers in nature) lib bdg $18.75 (2-4)

557

1. Geology 2. Natural history—Arizona 3. Grand Canyon (Ariz.)
ISBN 0-8239-5641-5 LC 00-39165

This describes how the Grand Canyon was formed and how it functions today

This book has "a breath-taking, full-page color photograph on every spread with informative captions. In [this] easy-to-understand, information-rich [title] readers will discover many interesting facts." SLJ

560 Paleontology. Paleozoology

Aliki

Fossils tell of long ago. rev ed. Crowell 1990 32p il (Let's-read-and-find-out science book) pa $4.95 hardcover o.p. (k-3)

560

1. Fossils
ISBN 0-06-445093-7 (pa) LC 89-17247

Also available Spanish language edition

First published 1972

"Information about how fossils are formed and discovered is presented in simple text and an appealing variety of colorful illustrations. Includes directions for creating a fossil." Sci Child

Bonner, Hannah

When bugs were big, plants were strange, and tetrapods stalked the earth; a cartoon prehistory of life before dinosaurs; written and illustrated by Hannah Bonner. National Geographic 2004 c2003 44p il $16.95 (3-6)

560

1. Prehistoric animals 2. Fossils
ISBN 0-7922-6326-X LC 2003-7818

"The Carboniferous and Permian periods spanned 100 million years or so just before the better-known Mesozoic Era. The author describes many of the unusual plant and animal species from those times." SLJ

The information is "presented with verve and humor that don't shortchange the young natural historian's quest for good explanations of the earth's distant past. . . . An exemplary curriculum support resource, but kids who dig dinosaurs will read the book purely for pleasure." Booklist

Camper, Cathy

Bugs before time; prehistoric insects and their relatives; illustrated by Steve Kirk. Simon & Schuster Bks. for Young Readers 2002 unp il $16.95 (4 and up)

560

1. Insects 2. Fossils
ISBN 0-689-82092-5 LC 98-22872

Describes the physical characteristics, habits, and natural environment of various prehistoric insects some of which, including cockroaches, centipedes, and dragonflies, have survived into the present day

"A handsome introduction to prehistoric insects and other arthropods. . . . [Includes] up-to-date, conversational text and informative captions and date boxes. . . . Kirk's eye-catching, realistic watercolors portray a fascinating array of creatures." SLJ

Includes glossary and bibliographical references

Gallant, Jonathan R.

The tales fossils tell. Benchmark Bks. 2000 80p il (Story of science) lib bdg $29.93 (5 and up)

560

1. Fossils 2. Prehistoric animals
ISBN 0-7614-1153-4 LC 00-20077

Describes fossils, how they are formed, and what they can tell us about life in the past

This "will strengthen any science collection." SLJ

Includes glossary and bibliographical references

Gallant, Roy A.

Fossils. Benchmark Bks. 2000 48p il map (Kaleidoscope) lib bdg $15.95 (3-5)

560

1. Fossils
ISBN 0-7614-1041-4 LC 99-47494

Describes what fossils are, how they are formed, and what they tell scientists about the earth's past

"The easy-to-read text offers clear explanations. . . . Well-selected, beautifully reproduced photographs and computer graphics." SLJ

Includes glossary and bibliographical references

Jenkins, Steve

Prehistoric actual size. Houghton Mifflin Co 2005 unp il $16 (k-3)

560

1. Prehistoric animals
ISBN 0-618-53578-0 LC 2004-25124

Illustrated with cut-paper artwork, "the animals pictured here include the minuscule protozoa; . . . the eight-foot-tall 'terror bird'; and the Giganotosaurus. . . . The most arresting spreads are those in which the animal is too large to picture in its entirety. . . . Information about and an illustration of the entire creature (not to scale) completes this colorful volume." Booklist

Larson, Peter L.

Bones rock! everything you need to know to be a paleontologist; [by] Peter Larson and Kristin Donnan. 1st ed. Invisible Cities Press 2004 204p il pa $19.95 (5 and up)

560

1. Fossils
ISBN 1-93122-935-X LC 2004-413

Larson, Peter L.—*Continued*

"Revealing true stories about kids who have made paleo-discoveries and providing young readers with the tools necessary to make the next big discovery, this book shows kids how to collect, clean, and study fossil samples in order to develop and further their own research interests." Publisher's note

"Illustrations include high-quality color photographs and helpful diagrams and drawings. There's fascinating information here, and Larson's enthusiasm and sound advice give plenty of encouragement to young scientists." SLJ

Includes bibliographical references

Sabuda, Robert

Sharks and other sea monsters; encyclopedia prehistorica; [by] Robert Sabuda & Matthew Reinhart. 1st ed. Candlewick Press 2006 unp il $27.99 **560**

1. Prehistoric animals

ISBN 0-7636-2229-X   LC 2005044866

This pop-up book introduces such prehistoric creatures as giant sharks, sea scorpions, and squids.

"Gatefolds and inset minibooks expand the capacity of the book's seven spreads. . . . The sheer wonder generated by the collaborators' dimensional sleight-of-hand will more than justify purchase." Booklist

Taylor, Paul D.

Fossil; written by Paul D. Taylor. rev ed. DK Pub. 2004 72p il map (DK eyewitness books) $15.99; lib bdg $19.99 (4 and up) **560**

1. Fossils

ISBN 0-7566-0682-9; 0-7566-0681-0 (lib bdg)

First published 1990 by Knopf

This book describes different types of fossils, from algae to birds and mammals.

Thompson, Sharon Elaine

Death trap; the story of the La Brea Tar Pits. Lerner Publs. 1995 72p il lib bdg $23.95 (4 and up) **560**

1. Fossils 2. California—Antiquities

ISBN 0-8225-2851-7   LC 93-39583

Thompson "begins at Hancock Park in Los Angeles, California, the site of the La Brea Tar Pits. She describes the unique conditions 25 million years ago that caused the formation of the asphalt pools where thousands of Ice Age animals were trapped, their bones preserved in the oily asphalt. . . . [She also] discusses how scientists use the fossil findings to learn more about Ice Age animal populations, migration patterns, climate, vegetarian and animal extinctions." Appraisal

"Excellent artist's re-creations of the prehistoric bring extra life to a fascinating story." Booklist

Includes glossary

567   Fossil cold-blooded vertebrates

Arnold, Caroline

Giant shark: megalodon, prehistoric super predator; illustrated by Laurie Caple. Clarion Bks. 2000 32p il $15 (3-6) **567**

1. Sharks 2. Prehistoric animals 3. Fossils

ISBN 0-395-91419-1   LC 99-86991

Describes Megalodon, an extinct shark that was more than fifty feet long and could swallow an object the size of a small car

"This book's glowing artwork, clearly accessible text, and engrossing subject will attract readers." SLJ

O'Brien, Patrick

Megatooth! Holt & Co. 2001 unp il $16.95 (k-3) **567**

1. Sharks 2. Prehistoric animals 3. Fossils

ISBN 0-8050-6214-9   LC 00-28135

"Megatooth, or Megalodon, was an ancient shark three times as large as today's great white shark. O'Brien supplies . . . several interesting facts that scientists have surmised about this fascinating creature from the huge teeth that have been found. . . . The brief text is accompanied by oversized watercolor-and-gouache illustrations." SLJ

567.9   Fossil reptiles. Dinosaurs

Arnold, Caroline

Dinosaur mountain; graveyard of the past; photographs by Richard Hewett. Clarion Bks. 1989 48p il $16 (4 and up) **567.9**

1. Dinosaurs 2. Dinosaur National Monument (Colo. and Utah)

ISBN 0-89919-693-4   LC 88-30218

This book describes the work of paleontologists in learning about dinosaurs, especially the discoveries made at Dinosaur National Monument

"Arnold seamlessly blends general information about paleontology with facts about specific finds near the Monument and additionally offers intriguing descriptions of ongoing work. . . . Lively writing, a dramtic subject, and a sure-fire hit with young readers." Horn Book

Dinosaurs all around; an artist's view of the prehistoric world; photographs by Richard Hewett. Clarion Bks. 1993 48p il $14.95; pa $7.95 (4 and up) **567.9**

1. Dinosaurs

ISBN 0-395-62363-4; 0-395-86620-0 (pa)

LC 92-5726

On a visit to the workshop of Stephen and Sylvia Czerkas where a life-size dinosaur model is being constructed, the reader learns much information about dinosaurs and how conclusions are made from fossil remains

"The meticulous work involved in creating the sculptures is pictured and described in clear photographs and a direct, concise text." Horn Book

Arnold, Caroline—*Continued*

Pterosaurs; rulers of the skies in the dinosaur age; illustrated by Laurie Caple. Clarion Books 2004 40p il map $16 (3-6)   **567.9**

1. Pterosaurs 2. Fossils

ISBN 0-618-31354-0   LC 2003-27698

Contents: Wing lizards; The age of reptiles; The first pterosaurs; The "wing fingers;" Bodies built for flight; Mealtime for pterosaurs; Baby pterosaurs; Discovering pterosaur fossils; Pterodactyl; A Jurassic lagoon; In the air over western Kansas; The Brazilian pterosaurs; A "hairy" pterosaur; The last of the pterosaurs; Where you can see pterosaur fossils

This "covers pterosaurs' ancestry, their peculiar physiology, theories about their behavior, and major fossil discoveries, frequently making abstract facts concrete through vivid comparisons. . . . Caple's neatly labeled watercolors emphasize clarity over drama, but her subjects' exotic physical oddities . . . will draw kids into the diorama-like tableaus." Booklist

Ashby, Ruth

Pteranodon; the life story of a pterosaur; by Ruth Ashby; art by Phil Wilson. Harry N. Abrams 2005 unp il map $14.95 (1-3)   **567.9**

1. Pterosaurs

ISBN 0-8109-5778-7   LC 2004-15612

"Ashby imagines the life of a Pteranodon from its hatching to its successful mating years later. . . . Wilson's colorful interpretations of the fossil record provide eye-catching images to enhance the narrative. Appended notes provide the reasoning behind the author's extrapolations on the pterosaur's life cycle and behaviors and the artist's bright palette. . . . this is an attractive and a rewarding look at the possibilities in a long-lost life history." SLJ

Includes bibliographical references

Bailey, Jacqui

Monster bones; the story of a dinosaur fossil; written by Jacqui Bailey; illustrated by Matthew Lilly. Picture Window Books 2004 31p il (Science works) lib bdg $23.93 (2-4)   **567.9**

1. Dinosaurs 2. Fossils

ISBN 1-4048-0565-6   LC 2003-20117

Describes how the bones of a dinosaur became fossilized, were discovered by a paleontologist, and were ultimately displayed in a museum.

This "excellent science [book explains its subject] lucidly and sometimes amusingly. . . . Children will be illuminated and engaged." SLJ

Bergen, David

Life-size dinosaurs. Sterling Pub. 2004 48p il $9.95 (3-6)   **567.9**

1. Dinosaurs

ISBN 1-4027-1755-X

This includes life-size illustrations of such dinosaurs as Atreipus, Oviraptor, and Therizinosaurus in three 8-page-long gatefolds and four 6-page ones.

"This slim, oversize title will be eye candy indeed to dinophiles. . . . These vivid color illustrations are surrounded by chatty explanatory paragraphs and information boxes." SLJ

Bishop, Nic

Digging for bird-dinosaurs; an expedition to Madagascar. Houghton Mifflin 2000 48p il $16; pa $4.95 (4 and up)   **567.9**

1. Forster, Cathy 2. Dinosaurs 3. Birds 4. Fossils 5. Madagascar

ISBN 0-395-96056-8; 0-618-1982-X (pa)

                  LC 99-36145

The story of Cathy Forster's experiences as a member of a team of paleontologists who went on an expedition to the island of Madagascar in 1998 to search for fossil birds

"Throughout the engaging, personal story, Bishop presents a great deal of information in highly readable, age-appropriate language, well matched by exceptional full-color images of scientists at work and the Malagasy landscape and people." Booklist

Includes bibliographical references

Cole, Joanna

The magic school bus: in the time of the dinosaurs; illustrated by Bruce Degen. Scholastic 1994 unp il $15.95; pa $4.99 (2-4)   **567.9**

1. Dinosaurs

ISBN 0-590-44688-6; 0-590-44639-4 (pa)

                  LC 93-5753

Also available Spanish language edition

"The fashionable Ms. Frizzle warps her students back to the late Triassic period, where they begin a journey forward through time in search of Maiasaura eggs for Jeff, the Friz's paleontologist friend from high school." Bull Cent Child Books

"An eye-catching, humorous book with bright, busy illustrations . . . packed with information." Sci Books Films

Cooley, Brian

Make-a-saurus; my life with raptors and other dinosaurs; by Brian Cooley and Mary Ann Wilson. Annick Press 2000 58p il lib bdg $24.95; pa $14.95 (4 and up)   **567.9**

1. Dinosaurs 2. Models and modelmaking

ISBN 1-55037-645-4 (lib bdg); 1-55037-644-6 (pa)

This "book informs readers about new discoveries in paleontology, how museum artists work, how to make non-carved sculptures, and how to adapt these techniques at home." SLJ

"This is a great how-to book with wonderful insight into the twin worlds of art and science." Sci Books Films

Dinosaurs of the world; with an introduction by Mark Norell; consultants, Michael Benton, Tom Holtz; edited by Chris Marshall. Marshall Cavendish 1998 11v 704p il map lib bdg set $471.36 (5 and up)   **567.9**

1. Dinosaurs—Encyclopedias

ISBN 0-7614-7072-7   LC 97-43365

"The first 10 volumes contain more than 200 articles on dinosaurs and related topics. Volume 11 has been designated the 'reference' volume, and features a brief history of the earth, time lines, a list of famous fossil sites and digs, dinosaur family trees, brief biographies of 24 dinosaur hunters, museums with pertinent collections,

Dinosaurs of the world—*Continued*

and a section called 'Things to Do,' which lists resources and activities." Booklist

"This superb set is current, well organized, and provides interesting and comprehensive coverage of life in prehistoric times." SLJ

Includes bibliographical references

Dixon, Dougal

Dougal Dixon's amazing dinosaurs; the fiercest, the tallest, the smallest. Boyds Mills Press 2000 128p il lib bdg $17.95 (3-6)   **567.9**

1. Dinosaurs

ISBN 1-56397-773-7

"Divided into four sections representing meat eaters, long-necked plant eaters, armored dinosaurs, and two-footed plant eaters, this book provides information on these prehistoric creatures. Each double-page spread contains copious color illustrations and fact boxes that include helpful pronunciation guides." Horn Book Guide

"Dixon has compiled an impressive amount of information and organized it into an eye-catching, manageable format." Booklist

Includes bibliographical references

Dougal Dixon's dinosaurs. 2nd ed. Boyds Mills Press 1998 160p il $19.95 (4 and up)   **567.9**

1. Dinosaurs

ISBN 1-56397-722-2   LC 98-180620

First published 1993

The life and times of dinosaurs, from their evolution to the present-day discovery of their fossils

This "is a wonderful introduction to the most popular beasts of the ancient world. Loaded with full color illustrations and a wealth of dinosaur facts, it's sure to inspire young dinosaur enthusiasts to explore more fully this begone world." Appraisal

Farlow, James Orville

Bringing dinosaur bones to life; how do we know what dinosaurs were really like? [by] James O. Farlow; with illustrations by James E. Whitcraft. Watts 2001 63p il lib bdg $25 (5 and up)   **567.9**

1. Dinosaurs 2. Fossils

ISBN 0-531-11403-1   LC 00-38150

This "describes how paleontologists draw conclusions from the dinosaur fossils they study. Separate chapters examine physical appearance, diet, fighting, and reproduction." SLJ

"Clearly written and well organized, this book will interest children intrigued by the process of scientific thinking as well as its results." Booklist

Includes glossary and bibliographical references

Floca, Brian

Dinosaurs at the ends of the earth; the story of the Central Asiatic Expeditions. DK Ink 2000 unp il $15.95 (3-5)   **567.9**

1. Andrews, Roy Chapman, 1884-1960 2. Dinosaurs 3. Fossils

ISBN 0-7894-2539-4   LC 99-43071

"A Richard Jackson book"

Describes the expeditions led by Roy Chapman Andrews for New York's American Museum of Natural History to the Gobi Desert in Mongolia in an effort to uncover dinosaur fossils

"The upbeat dialogue feels historically appropriate, a tone that is reflected in the illustrations careful attention to period details, and the attention to scientific detail is also excellent." Horn Book Guide

Halls, Kelly Milner

Dinosaur mummies; beyond bare-bone fossils; illustrated by Rick Spears. Darby Creek 2003 48p il $17.95 (5 and up)   **567.9**

1. Dinosaurs 2. Fossils

ISBN 1-58196-000-X

After "explaining the fossilization process, the book spotlights six significant dinosaur mummies. . . . Halls' enthusiasm shines through in this well-researched and clearly written book. Drawings washed with color show how the dinosaurs might have looked, while many excellent color photos illustrate the fossilized finds, and dinosaur diggers and paleontologists at work." Booklist

Includes bibliographical references

Henderson, Douglas

Asteroid impact. Dial Bks. for Young Readers 2000 40p il map $16.99 (3-5)   **567.9**

1. Dinosaurs 2. Asteroids

ISBN 0-8037-2500-0   LC 99-38263

Text and illustrations explore the theory that the collision of an asteroid with the Earth ended the Cretaceous Period and caused the extinction of the dinosaurs

"Through vivid words and pictures, Henderson makes this lesson in Earth's history into a you-were-there experience that will captivate both children and adults. . . . Words and pictures work exceedingly well together. The illustrations, apparently acrylic paintings, are beautifully composed." Booklist

Kudlinski, Kathleen V.

Boy, were we wrong about dinosaurs! illustrated by S. D. Schindler. Dutton Children's Books 2005 unp il $15.99 (k-3)   **567.9**

1. Dinosaurs

ISBN 0-525-46978-8   LC 2003-53140

Examines what is known about dinosaur bones, behavior, and other characteristics and how different the facts often are from what scientists, from ancient China to the recent past, believed to be true.

"Intelligently designed and imaginatively conceived, the artwork makes the text more understandable and the whole book more beautiful. . . . Best of all, the closing paragraph acknowledges that the search is not over yet." Booklist

Includes bibliographical references

Lessem, Don

The fastest dinosaurs; by Don Lessem; illustrations by John Bindon. Lerner Publications 2005 32p il (Meet the dinosaurs) lib bdg $23.93; pa $6.95 (2-4)   **567.9**

1. Dinosaurs

ISBN 0-8225-1422-2 (lib bdg); 0-8225-2620-4 (pa)

LC 2004-7055

This "looks at how paleontologists determine living speed when only the fossil record remains, and cites some prime examples of dinosprinters, such a Gallimimus and Troodon. The realistic, soft illustrations . . . are lively enough to please budding paleontologists. Simple, eye-catching, and informative." SLJ

Feathered dinosaurs; by Don Lessem; illustrations by John Bindon. Lerner Publications 2005 32p il (Meet the dinosaurs) lib bdg $23.93; pa $6.95 (2-4)   **567.9**

1. Dinosaurs 2. Birds

ISBN 0-8225-1423-0 (lib bdg); 0-8225-2621-2 (pa)

LC 2004-19651

This covers the "links between dinosaurs and birds. . . . Lessem writes in simple language and short sentences appropriate for children transitioning out of early readers. But the brief text . . . will also read well to younger dino fans. . . . Bindon's detailed illustrations imagine the creatures in dramatic settings that will bring the drama of the ancient age alive." Booklist

Flying giants of dinosaur time; by Don Lessem; illustrations by John Bindon. Lerner Publications Co 2005 32p il map (Meet the dinosaurs) lib bdg $23.93; pa $6.95 (2-4)   **567.9**

1. Pterodactyls 2. Pterosaurs

ISBN 0-8225-1424-9 (lib bdg); 0-8225-2622-0 (pa)

LC 2004-17918

Contents: Meet the flying reptiles; The world of flying reptiles; Wings, necks, and tails; The lives of pterosaurs; Mysteries of the flying giants

This "covers the pterosaurs and pterodactyls, extrapolating some behaviors using modern birds as models, and speculates on beak shapes and sizes in the food-gathering process. . . . The realistic, soft illustrations . . . are lively enough to please budding paleontologists. Simple, eye-catching, and informative." SLJ

Scholastic dinosaurs A to Z; the ultimate dinosaur encyclopedia; illustrated by Jan Sovak. Scholastic 2003 224p il $22.95 (4 and up)

567.9

1. Dinosaurs

ISBN 0-439-16591-1   LC 00-41304

This reference "lists dinosaurs in alphabetical order and gives their pronunciation. Other information includes what each dinosaur's name means, its complete taxonomic classification, length, time period, place, diet, and other details. Icons beside each name tell the reader to which class of dinosaur it belongs. . . . The text is thorough and interesting. . . . This is an excellent purchase for every school and public library, and many children will want their own copies." Booklist

Includes glossary and bibliographical references

Sea giants of dinosaur time; by Don Lessem; illustrations by John Bindon. Lerner Publications Co 2005 32p il map (Meet the dinosaurs) lib bdg $23.93; pa $6.95 (2-4)   **567.9**

1. Dinosaurs

ISBN 0-8225-1425-7 (lib bdg); 0-8225-2623-9 (pa)

LC 2004-17916

Contents: Meet the sea giants; Water wonders; Life in the sea; What happened to the sea giants?

"A quick glimpse at eight of the larger prehistoric marine reptiles, ranging in eras from 220 million to 65 million years ago. The simple text presents a time line for these creatures, a global map of fossil finds, and some details of their physiology and distribution. The colorful double-page illustrations on blue backgrounds are accompanied by a paragraph or two of particulars." SLJ

The smartest dinosaurs; by Don Lessem; illustrations by John Bindon. Lerner Publications 2005 32p il (Meet the dinosaurs) lib bdg $23.93; pa $6.95 (2-4)   **567.9**

1. Dinosaurs

ISBN 0-8225-1373-0 (lib bdg); 0-8225-2618-2 (pa)

LC 2004-11152

Contents: Meet the smartest dinosaurs; How smart were dinosaurs?; Big brains; Which dinosaurs were the smartest?

"After a discussion of brain/body-size ratios, Lessem goes on to describe the importance of fossil finds in determining intelligence possibilities, leading to brief descriptions of seven dinosaurs that scientists feel may have been brighter than their contemporaries. . . . This is a clear look at a facet of dinosaur makeup not often touched on in other works." SLJ

Markle, Sandra

Outside and inside dinosaurs. Atheneum Bks. for Young Readers 2000 40p il $16 (2-4)

567.9

1. Dinosaurs 2. Fossils

ISBN 0-689-82300-2   LC 99-45808

Describes the inner and outer workings of dinosaurs, discussing what has been learned about their anatomy, diet, and behavior from fossils

"Excellent, large color photos march hand in hand with Markle's readable, informative text." SLJ

Includes glossary

Relf, Patricia

A dinosaur named Sue: the story of the colossal fossil: the world's most complete T. rex; by Pat Relf; with the SUE Science Team of The Field Museum. Scholastic 2000 64p il $15.95 (5 and up)

567.9

1. Fossils 2. Dinosaurs

ISBN 0-439-09985-4   LC 00-38038

"Sue, named after discoverer Susan Hendrickson, is the most complete *Tyrannosaurus Rex* in existence. The reader follows the scientific journey from the fossil excavation in 1990 to its display at Chicago's Field Museum." Sci Child

"Readers will get a real sense of the team effort that science can be. . . . Many color photographs, as well as diagrams and paintings, appear throughout the book." Booklist

Sabuda, Robert

Dinosaurs; encyclopedia prehistorica; by Robert Sabuda and Matthew Reinhart. 1st ed. Candlewick Press 2005 unp il $26.99 **567.9**

1. Dinosaurs

ISBN 0-7636-2228-1 LC 2004-51899

"With Sabuda lending deft paper engineering to artwork rendered by Reinhart, who also wrote this book's text, the Mesozoic's major players leap into three dimensions. Pop-ups featured on the six spreads include a gargantuan brachiosaurus; an anklyosaurus studded with paper spikes; and, perhaps most impressive from a technical standpoint, a minutely detailed T. rex skeleton." Booklist

Schomp, Virginia

Prehistoric world [series] Benchmark Bks. 2003-2005 15v il (3-6) **567.9**

1. Dinosaurs

Group 1 (ISBN 0-7614-1021-X); Group 2 (ISBN 0-7614-1514-6); Group 3 (ISBN 0-7614-2004-5) each group $128.21; titles also available individually for $25.64 each

Contents: [Group 1]: Ankylosaurus and other armored plant-eaters; Apatosaurus and other giant long-necked plant-eaters; Triceratops and other horned plant-eaters; Tyrannosaurus and other giant meat-eaters; Velociraptor and other small, speedy meat-eaters; [Group 2]: Archaeopteryx and other flying dinosaurs; Kronosaurus and other sea creatures; Maiasaura and other duck-billed plant eaters; Pachycephalosaurus and other bone-headed plant eaters; Stegosaurus and other plate-backed plant-eaters; [Group 3] Ceratosaurus and other horned meat-eaters; Iguanodon and other spiky-thumbed plant eaters; Ornithomimus and other speedy "ostrich dinosaurs;" Plateosaurus and other early long-necked plant-eaters; Therizinosaurus and other colossal-clawed plant-eaters

"Each book features a different type of dinosaur, focusing on a well-known member of a particular group but also discussing its relatives and other similar creatures. Coverage includes the animal's physical characteristics, the world in which it lived, how it lived, and the secrets of its daily survival." Publisher's note

"There is an impressive amount of science packed into the . . . pages of each of these books. . . . The artwork is superb throughout the series." Sci Books Films

Includes glossaries and bibliographical references

Sloan, Christopher

Feathered dinosaurs; introduction by Philip J. Currie. National Geographic Soc. 2000 64p il $17.95 (5 and up) **567.9**

1. Dinosaurs 2. Birds 3. Fossils

ISBN 0-7922-7219-6 LC 00-27001

Looks at the evidence of dinosaurs with skeletal structures and feathers so similar to birds and why that is convincing many scientists that birds evolved from dinosaurs

"This exciting title combines an accurate, readable text and excellent drawings, photos, and diagrams." SLJ

How dinosaurs took flight; the fossils, the science, what we think we know, and the mysteries yet unsolved; foreword by Dr. Xu Xing. National Geographic 2005 64p il $17.95 (5 and up) **567.9**

1. Dinosaurs 2. Birds 3. Fossils

ISBN 0-7922-7298-6

This explains the evolutionary relationships between dinosaurs and birds, based on fossils and the latest research.

Includes glossary and bibliographical references

Supercroc and the origin of crocodiles; introduction by Paul Sereno. National Geographic Soc. 2002 55p il map $18.95 (5 and up) **567.9**

1. Fossil reptiles 2. Crocodiles

ISBN 0-7922-6691-9 LC 2001-3976

Discusses prehistoric crocodiles, including the discovery of SuperCroc in the Sahara Desert, and the lifestyles, habitats, and conservation of modern crocodiles

"Fans of paleontology or of crocodiles will find a great deal of information clearly explained. The illustrations are up to the high National Geographic standard." Booklist

Includes glossary

Tanaka, Shelley

New dinos; The latest finds! The coolest dinosaur discoveries! written by Shelley Tanaka; illustrated by Alan Barnard. Atheneum Bks. for Young Readers 2003 48p il maps $16.95 (3-6) **567.9**

1. Dinosaurs 2. Fossils

ISBN 0-689-85183-9 LC 2002-9809

"Madison Press book"

Describes some of the newly discovered dinosaurs and what paleontologists have learned about these prehistoric creatures in recent years

"Vivid, dramatic illustrations are a sure draw to an already hot topic. . . . Tanaka's lively, brief text provides enough data to satisfy many readers, including true aficionados." SLJ

Includes glossary and bibliographical references

Wallace, Karen

I am an ankylosaurus; written by Karen Wallace; illustrated by Mike Bostock. 1st U.S. ed. Atheneum Books for Young Readers 2005 c2003 unp il $15.95 (k-2) **567.9**

1. Dinosaurs

ISBN 0-689-87318-2 LC 2004-6152

First published 2003 in the United Kingdom

"The book presents the mother ankylosaurus laying her eggs, smashing an egg-stealing troodon with her clublike tail, foraging for food, and, months later, watching her eggs hatch. Bostock's clear, simple drawings with sunlit washes offer an imaginative vision of peaceful interludes in desert and forest habitats as well as tooth-and-claw dinosaur fights." Booklist

Another title in this series is:

I am a tyrannosaurus (2004)

Zoehfeld, Kathleen Weidner

Dinosaur babies; illustrated by Lucia Washburn. HarperCollins Pubs. 1999 33p il (Let's-read-and-find-out science) $15.95; lib bdg $15.89; pa $4.95 (k-3)   **567.9**

1. Dinosaurs

ISBN 0-06-027141-8; 0-06-027142-6 (lib bdg); 0-06-445162-3 (pa)   LC 98-43594

Describes the parenting habits of the Maiasaura, a dinosaur whose way of raising children bore similarities to that of birds

"Washburn's beautifully shaded pastel illustrations, using glowing other-worldly colors, create eye-catching scenes. The title is catchy and the presentation is good; a fine book for dinosaur fans." Booklist

Dinosaur parents, dinosaur young; uncovering the mystery of dinosaur families; with full-color paintings by Paul Carrick and line drawings by Bruce Shillinglaw. Clarion Bks. 2001 58p il map $17 (4 and up)   **567.9**

1. Dinosaurs 2. Fossils

ISBN 0-395-91338-1   LC 00-43101

The author "guides readers through the complex historical trail of evidence collection and theory development that make up what we currently believe we know about dinosaur family life." Horn Book Guide

"High-quality, color photographs of fossils of eggs and embryos and of paleontologists at work as well as line drawings and full-color paintings add to this inviting, thought-provoking book." SLJ

Includes glossary and bibliographical references

568   Fossil birds

Arnold, Caroline

Dinosaurs with feathers; the ancestors of modern birds; illustrated by Laurie Caple. Clarion Bks. 2001 32p il $15 (3-6)   **568**

1. Dinosaurs 2. Birds 3. Fossils 4. Archaeopteryx

ISBN 0-618-00398-3   LC 00-52308

"Starting with the discovery of the first *Archaeopteryx* fossil in 1861, Arnold traces the relationship between dinosaurs and modern birds. Along the way she shares a wealth of information about how and why scientists classify ancient species. . . . Caple's watercolors are clear and lively, and not overly dramatic." SLJ

Includes bibliographical references

Zoehfeld, Kathleen Weidner

Did dinosaurs have feathers? illustrated by Lucia Washburn. HarperCollins Publishers 2004 33p il (Let's-read-and-find-out science) $15.99; lib bdg $16.89; pa $4.99 (k-3)   **568**

1. Dinosaurs 2. Birds 3. Fossils 4. Archaeopteryx

ISBN 0-06-029026-9; 0-06-029027-7 (lib bdg); 0-06-029027-7 (pa)   LC 2002-10585

Discusses the discovery and analysis of Archaeopteryx, a feathered dinosaur which may have been an ancestor of modern birds.

"Using short sentences and simple words, Zoehfeld clearly explains what we know about dinosaurs with

feathers. . . . Iridescent shades of blue and orange give the theropods and their settings an appealing glow." Horn Book Guide

569   Fossil mammals

Aliki

Wild and woolly mammoths; written and illustrated by Aliki. rev ed. HarperCollins Pubs. 1996 32p il pa $6.95 hardcover o.p. (k-3)   **569**

1. Mammoths

ISBN 0-06-446179-3 (pa)   LC 94-48217

A revised and newly illustrated edition of the title first published 1977

An easy-to-read account of the woolly mammoth, a giant land mammal which has been extinct for over 11,000 years

"With concise text and informative art, Aliki illuminates the timeless appeal of these long-gone animals—and drops a gentle warning about the possible fate of tusked decendants." Publ Wkly

Arnold, Caroline

When mammoths walked the earth; illustrated by Laurie Caple. Clarion Bks. 2002 40p il $16 (3-6)   **569**

1. Mammoths

ISBN 0-618-09633-7   LC 2001-47192

Describes the physical characteristics, known habits, and fossil sites of mammoths, prehistoric animals closely related to the elephant

"The information is brief but thorough, with realistic watercolor illustrations depicting the giant animals and their surroundings." Booklist

Chorlton, Windsor

Woolly mammoth; life, death, and rediscovery. Scholastic Ref. 2001 40p il $15.95 (4 and up)   **569**

1. Mammoths

ISBN 0-439-24134-0   LC 00-59508

"Along with considerable data about woolly mammoths, this book recounts the 1999 expedition to excavate a woolly mammoth preserved whole in Siberian permafrost." Horn Book Guide

"Youngsters get an involving look at current scientists in action, along with enough background information to gain context." SLJ

Includes bibliographical references

Giblin, James

The mystery of the mammoth bones; and how it was solved. HarperCollins Pubs. 1999 97p il lib bdg $16.89 (4 and up)   **569**

1. Peale, Charles Willson, 1741-1827 2. Mastodon 3. Fossil mammals

ISBN 0-06-027494-8   LC 98-6701

Describes the efforts of the artist, museum curator, and self-taught paleontologist, Charles Willson Peale, to

Giblin, James—*Continued*

excavate, study, and display the bones of a prehistoric creature that is later named "mastodon"

"Giblin's research is superb, and he turns to Peale's actual notes for details. He also includes recent information about the mammoth (and mastodon)." SLJ

Includes bibliographical references

Hehner, Barbara

Ice Age cave bear; the giant beast that terrified ancient humans; illustrations by Mark Hallett; scientific consultation by Mark Engstrom and Kevin Seymour. Crown 2002 32p il lib bdg $18.99 hardcover o.p. (5 and up)   **569**

1. Bears 2. Fossil mammals

ISBN 0-375-91329-7   LC 2001-52953

"A Madison Press book"

Describes how and where cave bears lived, possible reasons for their extinction, and what kind of relationship might have existed between these huge creatures and prehistoric man

"Accompanied by full-color photographs and Hallett's rich, realistic illustrations, the book is eye-catching and informative." SLJ

Includes glossary and bibliographical references

Ice Age mammoth; will this ancient giant come back to life? illustrated by Mark Hallett. Crown 2001 32p il pa $8.99 hardcover o.p. (5 and up)   **569**

1. Mammoths

ISBN 0-375-82192-9 (pa)   LC 00-66023

"A Madison Press book"

Beginning with the "find in 1997 of the Jarkov Mammoth frozen into the Siberian permafrost, Hehner presents what is positively known about such Ice Age creatures and what is surmised by studies of their modern-day cousins, the elephants. . . . The author discusses the possibility of cloning a mammoth should the Jarkov find provide usable DNA or even undamaged frozen sperm. . . . The brief, readable text is larded with information boxes, maps, and color photos." SLJ

Includes glossary and bibliographical references

Ice Age sabertooth; the most ferocious cat that ever lived; illustrations by Mark Hallett; scientific consultation by Mark Engstrom and Kevin Seymour. Crown 2002 32p il pa $8.99 hardcover o.p. (5 and up)   **569**

1. Saber-toothed tigers

ISBN 0-375-82193-7 (pa)   LC 2001-28539

"A Madison Press book"

The "text presents what is known about these big cats from their fossilized remains, and discusses what paleontologists surmise about their outward appearance, behavior, and hunting techniques." SLJ

"The dramatic pictures grab attention and the detailed, straightforward text fills in the astonishing facts." Booklist

Includes glossary and bibliographical references

Turner, Alan

National Geographic prehistoric mammals; illustrated by Mauricio Antón. National Geographic 2004 192p il map $29.95; lib bdg $49.90 (5 and up)   **569**

1. Fossil mammals

ISBN 0-7922-7134-3; 0-7922-6997-7 (lib bdg)

LC 2004-1189

This describes the Age of Mammals and profiles over 100 prehistoric mammals, including time lines, fact boxes, distribution maps, photos of fossils, and illustrations

"Dramatic full-color pictures . . . and captions enhance the brief, informative text." SLJ

570   Life sciences. Biology

Biology matters! Grolier 2004 10v il set $389 (5 and up)   **570**

1. Biology

ISBN 0-7172-5979-X   LC 2003-56942

Contents: v1 Introduction to biology; v2 Cell biology; v3 Genetics; v4 Microorganisms; v5 Plants; v6 Animals; v7 The human body; v8 Reproduction; v9 Evolution; v10 Ecology

"This set presents the fundamentals of the life sciences in a clear format. . . . Volumes contain between six and eight articles in 80 pages . . . introducing its subject, presenting a brief history, and covering many aspects of its current study and applications. . . . The text is large and easy to read, and the writing is straightforward. . . . This title . . . would be a useful addition for public and school libraries." Booklist

Exploring life science. Marshall Cavendish 2000 11v set $329.95 (4-6)   **570**

1. Life sciences—Encyclopedias

ISBN 0-7614-7135-9   LC 98-52925

Based on the high school level Encyclopedia of life sciences (1966)

"Arranged into a single alphabet, these more than 300 specific, easily digestible articles cover living things, the environment, and the life sciences themselves. Entries are enhanced by numerous crisply detailed photos, full-color drawings, and boxed closer looks at special issues or topics." SLJ

VanCleave, Janice Pratt

Janice VanCleave's play and find out about nature; easy experiments for young children. Wiley 1997 122p il $29.95; pa $12.95 (k-2)   **570**

1. Biology 2. Nature 3. Science—Experiments

ISBN 0-471-12939-9; 0-471-12940-2 (pa)

LC 96-2865

Provides instructions for fifty nature experiments and activities involving both plants and animals

"VanCleave's explanations are straightforward and concise. The book has a clear and uncluttered look." SLJ

Includes glossary

571.8   Reproduction, development, growth

Collard, Sneed B., III
Making animal babies; [by] Sneed B. Collard III; illustrated by Steve Jenkins. Houghton Mifflin 2000 unp il $16 (k-3)   **571.8**
1. Reproduction 2. Animal courtship
ISBN 0-395-95317-0   LC 99-35797
Describes the mating rituals and reproductive methods of a variety of animals, including flatworms, jellyfish, chameleons, and walruses
"On each page, Collard pairs a line or two of large-type text with a paragraph in smaller type that covers similar ground in more detail. . . . Jenkins creates beautiful, evocative, sometimes astonishingly realistic paper collages for this two-level survey of animal reproduction." Booklist
Includes glossary

572   Biochemistry

Collard, Sneed B., III
In the deep sea; by Sneed B. Collard III. Marshall Cavendish Benchmark 2005 43p il (Science adventures) lib bdg $25.64 (4-6)   **572**
1. Widder, Edith 2. Bioluminescence 3. Ocean bottom
ISBN 0-7614-1952-7   LC 2004026489
"Describes the work of Dr. Edith Widder and other biologists in the field of bioluminescence research." Publisher's note
Includes glossary and bibliographical references

573.4   Endocrine and excretory systems

Davies, Nicola
Poop; a natural history of the unmentionable; illustrated by Neal Layton. Candlewick 2004 il $12.99 (2-5)   **573.4**
1. Feces 2. Animal behavior
ISBN 0-7636-2437-3
"Davies begins with a 'tour of poop' that illustrates the wide variety of feces. . . . She then goes on to discuss how it's produced, what animals do with it . . . and what humans occasionally do with animal feces. . . . The very informative text uses humor but mostly plays it straight. The clever ink-and-watercolor cartoons go for big laughs." Booklist

Goodman, Susan
The truth about poop; by Susan E. Goodman; illustrated by Elwood H. Smith. Viking 2004 40p il $15.99 (2-5)   **573.4**
1. Feces 2. Animal behavior
ISBN 0-670-03674-9   LC 2003-22547

"Chock-full of . . . facts about animal and human excrement, Goodman's free-range text discusses everything from Tyrannosaurus rex dung to the evolution of toilet paper. The three main sections outline animal elimination practices, the processes of human excretion and plumbing, and helpful uses for poop (e.g., for fertilizer or scientific research)." SLJ
This book is "very readable, appropriately visual, and exceedingly encompassing. . . . The well-executed cartoon artwork successfully goes for the clever" Booklist

573.8   Nervous and sensory systems

Jenkins, Steve
What do you do with a tail like this? [by] Steve Jenkins & Robin Page. Houghton Mifflin 2003 unp il $15 (k-3)   **573.8**
1. Senses and sensation
ISBN 0-618-25628-8   LC 2002-11673
A Caldecott Medal honor book, 2004
"Tandem spreads treat each body part, with the first posing the question ('What do you do with a nose like this?') and offering five examples . . . positioned on the page so as to obscure the rest of their owners. A turn of the page not only reveals the animals in question . . . but also offers brief answers to the question for each, outlining the special functions of each variant of the featured body part." Bull Cent Child Books
"Jenkins' handsome paper-cut collages are both lovely and anatomically informative. . . . This is a striking, thoughtfully created book with intriguing facts made more memorable through dynamic art." Booklist

576.5   Genetics

Gallant, Roy A.
The treasure of inheritance. Benchmark Bks. 2003 78p il (Story of science) lib bdg $19.95 (5 and up)   **576.5**
1. Genetics 2. Heredity
ISBN 0-7614-1426-6   LC 2002-10
Discusses how living things inherit traits, chronicles the history of the study of heredity, and examines current research on genetic engineering and mapping the human gene
"Readers will find accurate, readable explanations for the scientific principles here addressed. . . . Up-to-date controversies and predictions conclude the [book] . . . illustrated with well-captioned photos." Horn Book Guide
Includes glossary and bibliographical references

Johnson, Rebecca L.
Genetics. Twenty-First Century Books 2005 80p il (Great ideas of science) $27.93 (5 and up)   **576.5**
1. Genetics
ISBN 0-8225-2910-6   LC 2004-28212
"The history of genetics is introduced, beginning with Gregor Mendel's studies of pea-plant cross-pollination. The book skillfully explains the discovery of DNA and the emergence of modern biotechnology, including how

Johnson, Rebecca L.—*Continued*
DNA is replicated, how genes are expressed and translated as cell proteins, and how the human genome is being mapped. Thirty color photos, informational sidebars, and detailed diagrams complement the text." SLJ
Includes bibliographical references

Walker, Richard
Genes & DNA; foreword by Steve Jones. Kingfisher 2003 63p il (Kingfisher knowledge) $11.95 (5 and up) **576.5**
1. Genetics
ISBN 0-7534-5621-4   LC 2004-269108
This briefly discusses such topics as the role of genes in inheritance, the structure of the DNA molecule, mutations, The Human Genome Project, and genetic technology such as DNA fingerprinting, gene therapy, genetic engineering, and cloning
Includes glossary and bibliographical references

576.8   Evolution

Branley, Franklyn Mansfield
Is there life in outer space? by Franklyn M. Branley; illustrated by Edward Miller. HarperCollins Pubs. 1999 31p il (Let's-read-and-find-out science) $15.95; lib bdg $15.89; pa $4.95 (k-3) **576.8**
1. Life on other planets 2. Outer space—Exploration
ISBN 0-06-028146-4; 0-06-028145-6 (lib bdg); 0-06-445192-5 (pa)   LC 99-10904
A newly illustrated edition of the title first published 1984 by Crowell
Discusses some of the ideas and misconceptions about life in outer space and speculates on the existence of such life in light of recent space explorations
"Children curious about the possibility of life on distant planets will find much to think about in this speculative yet scientifically accurate text. The new illustrations, which incorporate photographs of planets, are bright and colorful." Horn Book Guide

Gallant, Roy A.
The origins of life. Benchmark Bks. 2001 80p il (Story of science) lib bdg $29.93 (5 and up) **576.8**
1. Life—Origin
ISBN 0-7614-1151-8   LC 99-86435
Explores the many different myths, theories, and experiments which explain the origin of life, including spontaneous generation, the development of planets, chemical evolution of matter, and the various places in the solar system where life exists or may exist
Includes glossary and bibliographical references

Gamlin, Linda
Evolution; written by Linda Gamlin. Dorling Kindersley 2000 64p il (DK eyewitness books) $15.99 (4 and up) **576.8**
1. Evolution
ISBN 0-7894-5579-X
First published 1993

Text about and photography of experiments, animals, plants, bones, and fossils reveal the ideas and discoveries that have changed our understanding of the natural world and how life began.

Jackson, Ellen B.
Looking for life in the universe; the search for extraterrestrial intelligence; by Ellen Jackson; with photographs by Nic Bishop. Houghton Mifflin 2002 57p il (Scientists in the field) $16 (4 and up) **576.8**
1. Tarter, Jill Cornell, 1944- 2. Life on other planets
ISBN 0-618-12894-8   LC 2001-51312
Investigates how scientists, particularly Jill Tarter, Director of the SETI Institute in Mountain View, California, use twenty-first century technology to investigate whether life exists on other planets
"An exciting, visually awesome look at frontier science." SLJ
Includes glossary and bibliographical references

Jenkins, Steve
Life on earth: the story of evolution. Houghton Mifflin 2002 unp il $16 (3-6) **576.8**
1. Evolution
ISBN 0-618-16476-6   LC 2002-472
Provides an overview of the origin and evolution of life on earth and of what has been learned from the study of evolution
"Jenkins presents a superb introduction to evolution. . . . His signature cut-paper illustrations placed on white backgrounds work well. . . . Jenkins's explanations of science concepts are comprehensive and comprehensible. . . . Particularly admirable is his avoidance of any oversimplifications." Horn Book
Includes bibliographical references

Skurzynski, Gloria
Are we alone? scientists search for life in space. National Geographic Society 2004 92p il $18.95 (5 and up) **576.8**
1. Life on other planets
ISBN 0-7922-6567-X   LC 2003-17732
The author begins with a "history of how the idea of flying saucers and extraterrestrials became part of the American consciousness. Later chapters trace specific quests . . . for signs of life beyond earth. . . . The text remains readable even while explaining intricate scientific concepts and complex . . . ideas. The vibrant full-color photos enhance the work impressively." Booklist
Includes glossary and bibliographical references

577   Ecology

Batten, Mary
Aliens from Earth; when animals and plants invade other ecosystems; written by Mary Batten; illustrated by Beverly Doyle. Peachtree Pubs. 2003 unp il $15.95 (3-6) **577**
1. Biological invasions 2. Animal introduction 3. Plant introduction
ISBN 1-56145-236-X   LC 2002-13170

Batten, Mary—*Continued*

Explores how and why plants and animals enter ecosystems to which they are not native, as well as the consequences of these invasions for other animals, plants, and humans

"From the book title and first line of text . . . to the information-packed, full-page color illustrations, this overview of ecological missteps is nonstop intriguing." Booklist

Habitats of the world. Marshall Cavendish 2005 c2006 11v il map set $329.95 (5 and up)

577

1. Habitat (Ecology)

ISBN 0-7614-7523-0   LC 2004-52782

Contents: v1 Abbey-Badlands; v2 Baikal-coral reef; v3 Cousteau-estuary and delta; v4 Etosha-Great Barrier Reef; v5 Habitat-island; v6 Kilimanjaro-Muir; v7 Nile River-pollution; v8 Pond-severe weather; v9 Shrubland-tree; v10 Tropical ocean-Yellowstone National Park; v11 Index

"This encyclopedia informs students about ecology and the connections between people and the natural environment. Emphasizing how humans make a difference, articles on particular habitats draw attention to the threat of species extinction, the promise of sustainability, and personal responsibilities for stewardship of the earth. Biographies of ecologists and articles discussing broad environmental concerns contribute to students' knowledge of concepts central to the science curriculum." Publisher's note

Lauber, Patricia

Who eats what? food chains and food webs; illustrated by Holly Keller. HarperCollins Pubs. 1995 32p il (Let's-read-and-find-out science) $15.95; lib bdg $15.89; pa $4.95 (k-3)

577

1. Food chains (Ecology)

ISBN 0-06-022981-0; 0-06-022982-9 (lib bdg); 0-06-445130-5 (pa)   LC 93-10609

The author "demonstrates the interconnectedness of nature by showing how creatures form chains through the foods they eat. . . . Lauber gives several examples, from short chains (apple to child) to the web of connections between sea creatures. She uses sea otters to show how the disappearance of one link in the chain can disrupt the flow of food both up and down." Bull Cent Child Books

"Clear, simple ink-and-watercolor drawings illustrate the clear, simple text. Informative and intriguing, this basic science book leads children to think about the complex and interdependent web of life on Earth." Booklist

Lorbiecki, Marybeth

Planet patrol; a kids' action guide to earth care; by Marybeth Lorbiecki; illustrated by Nancy Meyers. Two-Can Pub. 2005 48p il $15.95; pa $8.95 (3-5)

577

1. Ecology 2. Environmental sciences

ISBN 1-58728-514-2; 1-58728-518-5 (pa)

LC 2005012476

"An introduction to ecology that uses examples of real-life human endeavors, action tips and factoids to show how environmental problems can be slowed or reversed." Publisher's note

"The amazing facts . . . the immediate action tips . . . the chatty, interactive style . . . and the urgent message about global warming and pollution will draw young readers to this lively, browsable conservation manual." Booklist

Includes bibliographical references

Pollock, Steve

Ecology; written by Steve Pollock. rev. ed. DK Pub. 2005 72p il (DK eyewitness books) $15.99; lib bdg $19.99 (4 and up)

577

1. Ecology

ISBN 0-7556-1387-6; 0-7556-1396-5 (lib bdg)

First published 1993

Illustrations and text provide information about ecology in general, specific ecosystems, and our changing understanding of life around us.

Toft, Kim Michelle

The world that we want; [by] Kim Michelle Toft. Charlesbridge 2005 unp il $16.95 (k-3)

577

1. Habitat (Ecology)

ISBN 1-58089-114-4   LC 2004-20717

"This book offers two-page vistas that incorporate animals found in a variety of habitats, including a mangrove, a tide pool, and a reef. As viewers move from flying pelican to gliding barracuda, Toft creates ever-widening perspectives to reveal how various ecosystems relate to one another. . . . This process culminates in an impressive four-page, foldout panorama that includes all 45 animals. The minimal text cumulates as well. . . . The arresting, brilliantly hued illustrations were drawn and painted on silk." SLJ

VanCleave, Janice Pratt

Janice Vancleave's ecology for every kid; easy activities that make learning science fun. Wiley 1996 219p il maps (Science for every kid series) $32.50; pa $10.95 (4 and up)   577

1. Ecology 2. Habitat (Ecology) 3. Science—Experiments

ISBN 0-471-10100-1; 0-471-10086-2 (pa)

LC 95-6112

This book of science activities covers "25 topics, ranging from plant and animal food chains to the effect of plastics on the environment. Subjects are introduced in a 'What You Need to Know' section that gives explanation of the scientific principles, plus plenty of everyday examples. A brief preparatory exercise follows, usually in the form of an imaginative game. . . . Simple black-line drawings are crisp, uncluttered, and well placed. . . . Solid information and a generous portion of fun are combined to elevate this selection above the standard collection of experiments." SLJ

Includes glossary

577.2 Specific factors affecting ecology

Patent, Dorothy Hinshaw
Fire: friend or foe; photographs by William Muñoz. Clarion Bks. 1998 80p il $16 (4 and up)
577.2
1. Forest fires 2. Forest ecology
ISBN 0-395-73081-3   LC 98-11754
Discusses forest fires and the effect that they have on both people and the natural world
"The text offers rich science support. . . . Muñoz's full-color photographs are a nice complement to the text." Booklist

Simon, Seymour
Wildfires. Morrow Junior Bks. 1996 unp il pa $6.99 hardcover o.p. (3-6)   **577.2**
1. Forest fires 2. Forest ecology
ISBN 0-688-17530-9 (pa)   LC 95-12653
"Exploring the place of fire in nature, Simon explains that . . . forest fires have important functions in the ecosystem. With a brilliantly clear and colorful photograph facing each page of text, the book describes the causes and the progression of the wildfires that burned areas of Yellowstone National Park in 1988, explains how the fires were beneficial in many ways. . . . Lucid writing and excellent book design." Booklist

577.3 Forest ecology

Brenner, Barbara
One small place in a tree; illustrated by Tom Leonard. HarperCollins Publishers 2004 unp il $15.99; lib bdg $16.89 (2-4)   **577.3**
1. Forest ecology
ISBN 0-688-17180-X; 0-688-17181-8 (lib bdg)
LC 2002-1181
A child visitor observes as one tiny scratch in a tree develops into a home for a variety of woodland animals over many years, even after the tree has fallen.
"Brenner makes the science enjoyable and understandable, and Leonard's highly detailed, realistic illustrations provide great visual aid." Booklist

Burnie, David
Shrublands. Raintree Steck-Vaughn Pubs. 2003 64p il map (Biomes atlases) lib bdg $31.42 (5 and up)   **577.3**
1. Forest ecology
ISBN 0-7398-5514-X   LC 2002-68093
A comprehensive look at the shrubland biome, describing the climate, plants, animals, people, and future of these areas, and providing detailed views of some major shrubland regions
"Especially effective are the maps. Brief notes for 10 to 12 highlights appear on each one, commenting on the diversity of flora, fauna, and landforms that occurs. . . . [The book includes] excellent-quality, full-color photographs and related sidebars." SLJ
Includes glossary and bibliographical references

Collard, Sneed B., III
Forest in the clouds; by Sneed Collard III; illustrated by Michael Rothman. Charlesbridge Pub. 2000 unp il map $16.95; pa $7.95 (2-4)
577.3
1. Forest ecology 2. Cloud forests 3. Natural history—Costa Rica
ISBN 0-88106-985-X; 0-88106-986-8 (pa)
LC 98-6150
Describes some of the exotic plants and animals that live in the cloud forest of Costa Rica, and discusses some environmental threats faced by this region
"Rothman's detailed acrylic paintings, dominated by rich greens and browns, cover the better part of each spread. . . . Although valuable for reports, Collard's book will interest browsers as well." SLJ

Fusco Castaldo, Nancy
Rainforests; an activity guide for ages 6-9; [by] Nancy F. Castaldo. Chicago Review Press 2003 133p il $14.95 (2-5)   **577.3**
1. Rain forest ecology
ISBN 1-55652-476-5   LC 2002-152661
Provides facts and activities that explore tropical and temperate ancient forests, discusses how individuals can help preserve them, and describes well-known and unfamiliar creatures of the rain forest
"The activities are varied and interesting, ranging from science projects to crafts to recipes. . . . The book would serve as a valuable resource." SLJ
Includes bibliographical references

Gibbons, Gail
Nature's green umbrella; tropical rain forests. Morrow Junior Bks. 1994 unp il maps $15.95; lib bdg $15.93; pa $5.95 (k-3)   **577.3**
1. Rain forest ecology
ISBN 0-688-12353-8; 0-688-12354-6 (lib bdg); 0-688-15411-5 (pa)   LC 93-17569
Describes the climatic conditions of the rain forest as well as the different layers of plants and animals that comprise the ecosystem
The language is "simple, yet poetic and evocative. . . . Colorful maps pinpoint the locations of these global resources. Green vines entwine around the borders of each page and enclose the text and bright illustrations." Sci Books Films

Greenaway, Theresa
Jungle; written by Theresa Greenaway; photographed by Geoff Dann. rev ed. DK Pub. 2004 71p il map (DK eyewitness books) $15.99 (4 and up)   **577.3**
1. Rain forest ecology
ISBN 0-7566-0694-2   LC 2004558978
First published 1994
Color photographs, drawings, and brief text describe the animals, plants, and ecology of tropical forests of the world

Grupper, Jonathan

Destination: rain forest. National Geographic Soc. 1997 31p il $16 (3-6)   **577.3**

1. Rain forests 2. Rain forest ecology

ISBN 0-7922-7018-5   LC 97-68

Describes the unique environment of and the varied animal and plant life found in the world's tropical rain forests

"Excellent photographs provide close-up views of the creatures, most from Central and South America and the rest from Southeast Asia and Africa. . . . Though too generalized for research, this still provides vivid glimpses of the rain forest and its inhabitants." Booklist

Guiberson, Brenda Z.

Rain, rain, rain forest; illustrated by Steve Jenkins. Henry Holt 2004 unp il $16.95 (k-3)   **577.3**

1. Rain forest ecology

ISBN 0-8050-6582-2   LC 2003-12250

"Vibrant words and sensory impressions bring the creatures' noisy cacophony and slithering, swooping motions up close, while gracefully incorporated facts convey a surprising amount of information. . . . The artist's colorful, textured images create a rich sense of atmosphere, and the precise details and lively compositions will easily draw children back to the text." Booklist

Jackson, Tom

Tropical forests. Raintree Steck-Vaughn Pubs. 2003 64p il maps (Biomes atlases) lib bdg $31.42 (5 and up)   **577.3**

1. Rain forest ecology

ISBN 0-7398-5250-7   LC 2002-68094

A comprehensive look at the tropical forest biome, examining its climate, plants, animals, people, and future, plus detailed views of some particular tropical forest locations

"Especially effective are the maps. Brief notes for 10 to 12 highlights appear on each one, commenting on the diversity of flora, fauna, and landforms that occurs. . . . [The book includes] excellent-quality, full-color photographs and related sidebars." SLJ

Includes glossary and bibliographical references

Johansson, Philip

The forested Taiga; a web of life. Enslow Pubs. 2004 48p il map (World of biomes) lib bdg $18.95 (3-5)   **577.3**

1. Forest ecology

ISBN 0-7660-2197-1   LC 2003-4436

Contents: A wolf's dining room; The Taiga biome; Biome communities; Taiga plants; Taiga animals

This describes the ecology of dark evergreen forests of northern Europe, Asia and North America

This book is "extremely well written, and [it contains] ample information presented in a way that is easy to understand." Sci Books Films

Includes glossary and bibliographical references

The temperate forest; a web of life. Enslow Pubs. 2004 48p il map (World of biomes) lib bdg $18.95 (3-5)   **577.3**

1. Forest ecology

ISBN 0-7660-2198-X   LC 2003-3614

Contents: A forest for bears; The temperate forest biome; Forest communities; Temperate forest plants; Temperate forest animals

This describes the ecology of temperate forests.

This book is "extremely well written, and [it contains] ample information in a way that is easy to understand." Sci Books Films

Includes glossary and bibliographical references

The tropical rain forest; a web of life. Enslow Pubs. 2004 48p il map (World of biomes) lib bdg $18.95 (3-5)   **577.3**

1. Rain forest ecology

ISBN 0-7660-2199-8   LC 2003-6481

Contents: The eating machines; The rain forest biome; Tropical rain forest communities; Tropical rain forest plants; Tropical rain forest animals

This describes the ecology of the tropical rain forests

This book is "extremely well written, and [it contains] ample information presented in a way that is easy to understand." Sci Books Films

Includes glossary and bibliographical references

Johnson, Rebecca L.

A walk in the boreal forest; with illustrations by Phyllis V. Saroff. Carolrhoda Bks. 2001 48p il map (Biomes of North America) lib bdg $23.93 (3-6)   **577.3**

1. Forest ecology

ISBN 1-57505-156-7   LC 00-8240

Describes the climate, seasons, plants, animals, and soil of the boreal forest, a biome or land zone, which stretches across the northern parts of North America, Europe, and Asia

"A fine overview of the plant and animal life of the boreal forest. . . . Excellent full-color photographs." SLJ

Includes glossary and bibliographical references

A walk in the deciduous forest; with illustrations by Phyllis V. Saroff. Carolrhoda Bks. 2001 48p il map (Biomes of North America) lib bdg $23.93 (3-6)   **577.3**

1. Forest ecology

ISBN 1-57505-155-9   LC 00-8243

Takes readers on a walk through a forest of trees that lose their leaves in the fall, showing examples of how the animals and plants depend on each other and their environment to survive

"The simple design and clearly written, informative text will appeal to readers who enjoy nature." Horn Book Guide

Includes glossary and bibliographical references

Lasky, Kathryn

The most beautiful roof in the world; exploring the rainforest canopy; photographs by Christopher G. Knight. Harcourt Brace & Co. 1997 unp il $18; pa $9 (4 and up)   **577.3**

1. Lowman, Margaret 2. Rain forest ecology
ISBN 0-15-200893-4; 0-15-200897-7 (pa)
LC 95-48193

"Gulliver Green"

Describes the work of Meg Lowman in the rainforest canopy, an area unexplored until the last ten years and home to previously unknown species of plants and animals

"Fresh in out-look and intriguing in details, this memorable book features colorful photographs that reflect the you-are-there quality of the text." Booklist

Includes glossary

Pfeffer, Wendy

A log's life; illustrations by Robin Brickman. Simon & Schuster Bks. for Young Readers 1997 various paging il $16 (k-3)   **577.3**

1. Oak 2. Forest ecology
ISBN 0-689-80636-1   LC 95-30020

This is an "introduction to the life, death, and decay of an oak tree. The simple, informative text presents the complex cast of characters residing in or on the living tree as well as the decomposing log. . . . The verbal descriptions of this rich ecosystem are enhanced by striking illustrations of three-dimensional paper sculptures, often so realistic as to seem to be preserved natural specimens." SLJ

Stille, Darlene R.

Tropical rain forest. Children's Press 1999 47p il lib bdg $22 (2-4)   **577.3**

1. Rain forest ecology
ISBN 0-516-21511-6   LC 98-50753

"A True book"

Differentiates a tropical rain forest from all others, and describes its typical plant and animal life

"The plain style, accessible design, and beautiful photographs of landscapes and wildlife make this a good [title] for children's first research presentations." Booklist

Includes glossary and bibliographical references

577.4 Grassland ecology

Collard, Sneed B., III

The prairie builders; reconstructing America's lost grasslands; written and photographed by Sneed B. Collard III. Houghton Mifflin Co 2005 66p il (Scientists in the field) $17 (4 and up)
577.4

1. Prairies 2. Nature conservation
ISBN 0-618-39687-X   LC 2004-13201

This describes an effort to restore part of the native tallgrass prairie in the the 8,000-acre Neal Smith National Wildlife Refuge in Iowa.

"The engaging text is accompanied by large, inviting color photographs. . . . An essential purchase for libraries in prairie regions and a worthwhile choice for others." SLJ

Includes bibliographical references

Dunphy, Madeleine

Here is the African savanna; illustrated by Tom Leonard. Hyperion Bks. for Children 1999 unp il $14.99; lib bdg $15.99 (k-3)   **577.4**

1. Grassland ecology 2. Natural history—Africa
ISBN 0-7868-0162-X; 0-7868-2134-5 (lib bdg)
LC 98-30007

Cumulative text describes the interdependence among the plants and animals of an African savanna

"The acrylic illustrations are rich with detail and gold-toned radiance. An endnote provides some additional information about conservation. This is an attractive, effective way to introduce ecology to young readers." Horn Book Guide

Hoare, Ben

Temperate grasslands. Raintree Steck-Vaughn Pubs. 2003 64p il map (Biomes atlases) lib bdg $31.42 (5 and up)   **577.4**

1. Grassland ecology
ISBN 0-7398-5249-3   LC 2002-12818

Contents: Biomes of the world; Temperate grasslands of the world; Grassland climate; Grassland plants; Grassland animals; People and grasslands; The future

This offers a look at temperate grasslands of the world describing their climate, plants, animals, people, and future

"Especially effective are the maps. Brief notes for 10 to 12 highlights appear on each one, commenting on the diversity of flora, fauna, and landforms that occurs. . . . [The book includes] excellent-quality, full-color photographs and related sidebars." SLJ

Includes glossary and bibliographical references

Johansson, Philip

The wide open grasslands; a web of life. Enslow Publishers 2004 48p il (World of biomes) lib bdg $18.95 (3-5)   **577.4**

1. Grassland ecology
ISBN 0-7660-2201-3 (lib bdg)   LC 2003-25433

Contents: Life in the grasslands; The grassland biome; Grassland communities; Grassland plants; Grassland animals

This describes the plants, animals, and ecology of the grasslands of the world

Includes glossary and bibliographical references

Johnson, Rebecca L.

A walk in the prairie; with illustrations by Phyllis V. Saroff. Carolrhoda Bks. 2001 48p il map (Biomes of North America) lib bdg $23.93 (3-6)   **577.4**

1. Prairie ecology
ISBN 1-57505-153-2   LC 00-8252

Describes the climate, soil, seasons, plants, and animals of the North American prairie and the ways in which the plants and animals depend on each other and their environment to survive

Includes glossary and bibliographical references

Patent, Dorothy Hinshaw

Life in a grassland; photographs by William Muñoz. Lerner Publs. 2003 72p il maps (Ecosystems in action) lib bdg $26.60 (4 and up)　　　**577.4**

1. Grassland ecology

ISBN 0-8225-2139-3　　　　LC 2002-952

Contents: What is an ecosystem?; A world of grass and sun; Among the grasses; Life underground; Living on the edge; Biodiversity; People and the prairie; What you can do

Examines the physical features, processes, and many different species of plants and animals that make up the ecosystem of the American tallgrass prairie

"The readable text is enhanced by colorful photographs and text boxes." Soc Educ

Includes glossary and bibliographical references

Prairies; photographs by William Muñoz. Holiday House 1996 40p il map $15.95 (4 and up)　　　**577.4**

1. Prairie ecology

ISBN 0-8234-1277-6　　　　LC 96-14125

Describes the characteristics of the North American prairie, the plants and animals found there, and the efforts made to preserve and restore the landscape

"Large, clear, full-color photos on almost every page vividly capture the prairies and their natural wildlife. . . . *Prairies* provides a well-balanced amount of information that will give children a clear understanding of grassland regions." SLJ

Includes glossary

Stille, Darlene R.

Grasslands. Children's Press 1999 47p il lib bdg $22; pa $6.95 (2-4)　　　**577.4**

1. Grassland ecology

ISBN 0-516-21509-4 (lib bdg); 0-516-26762-0 (pa)

LC 98-49728

"A True book"

Examines the different types of grasslands and the plant and animal life they support

Includes glossary and bibliographical references

Toupin, Laurie

Life in the temperate grasslands; [by] Laurie Peach Toupin. 1st ed. Franklin Watts 2005 63p il map (Biomes and habitats) $25.50 (4 and up)　　　**577.4**

1. Grassland ecology

ISBN 0-531-12385-5　　　　LC 2004-13282

"Watts library"

Contents: No trees, no problem; Tough as grass; Grazers big and small; Predators feathery, furry, and slippery; Giving mother nature a hand; In your hands

This describes the ecology of grasslands such as the North American prairie, the South American pampas, the African veldt and the European steppes.

This is "written in an accessible and interesting, conversational style. The [author conveys] a good deal of information about topics such as adaptation, environmental threats, seasonal changes, and other essentials important to report writers and general readers." SLJ

Includes bibliographical references

Savannas; life in the tropical grasslands; [by] Laurie Peach Toupin. 1st ed. Franklin Watts 2005 63p il map (Biomes and habitats) $25.50 (4 and up)　　　**577.4**

1. Grassland ecology

ISBN 0-531-12386-3　　　　LC 2004-13281

"Watts library"

Contents: Too dry, too wet . . . ah, home!; Grasses rule; Landscapers and gardeners; Hoofed vegetarians; Tooth and claw; People and the grasslands

This introduces "readers to the climate characteristics as well as plants and animals of [tropical grasslands. It is] written in an accessible and interesting, conversational style. The authors convey a good deal of information about topics such as adaptation, environmental threats, seasonal changes, and other essentials important to report writers and general readers." SLJ

Includes bibliographical references

577.5　Ecology of miscellaneous environments

Baylor, Byrd

The desert is theirs; illustrated by Peter Parnall. Scribner 1975 unp il lib bdg $16; pa $5.95 (1-4)　　　**577.5**

1. Desert ecology 2. Papago Indians

ISBN 0-684-14266-X (lib bdg); 0-689-71105-X (pa)

LC 74-24417

"Poetic interpretations of Papago Indians' ecological and spiritual relationships with desert resources. . . . Illustrations add to the usefulness of this mood piece for sensitizing children to respect for nature, reading aloud, studying Indian cultures and techniques of using line, space and color." Read Teach

Bial, Raymond

A handful of dirt. Walker & Co. 2000 32p il $16.95; lib bdg $17.85 (3-6)　　　**577.5**

1. Soils 2. Soil ecology

ISBN 0-8027-8698-7; 0-8027-8699-5 (lib bdg)

LC 99-53632

The author "discusses how plant, animal, and mineral matter are broken down to create soil, as well as the vast amount of life forms soil supports, such as protozoa, earthworms, insects, moles, snakes, and prairie dogs. Tips on how to compost are included. The book is illustrated with crisp color photos, including several using an electron microscope." Horn Book Guide

Includes bibliographical references

Johansson, Philip

The dry desert; a web of life. Enslow Publishers 2004 48p il (World of biomes) lib bdg $18.95 (3-5)　　　**577.5**

1. Desert ecology

ISBN 0-7660-2200-5　　　　LC 2003-20443

Contents: Life in the slow lane; The desert biome; Desert communities; Desert plants; Desert animals

This describes the plants, animals, and ecology of deserts of the world

Includes glossary and bibliographical references

Johansson, Philip—Continued

The frozen tundra; a web of life. Enslow Pubs. 2004 48p il map (World of biomes) lib bdg $18.95 (3-5)   **577.5**
1. Tundra ecology
ISBN 0-7660-2176-9   LC 2003-2271
Contents: Learning the bear facts; The Tundra biome; Biome communities; Tundra plants; Tundra animals
This describes the ecology of the arctic tundra
This book is "extremely well written, and [it contains] ample information presented in a way that is easy to understand." Sci Books Films
Includes glossary and bibliographical references

Johnson, Rebecca L.
A walk in the desert; with illustrations by Phyllis V. Saroff. Carolrhoda Bks. 2001 48p il map (Biomes of North America) lib bdg $23.93 (3-6)   **577.5**
1. Desert ecology
ISBN 1-57505-152-4   LC 00-8251
Describes the climate, soil, plants, and animals of North American deserts and the ways in which the plants and animals depend on each other and their environment to survive
"The many full-color, close-up photographs and black-and-white drawings are sure to engage readers' interest." SLJ
Includes glossary and bibliographical references

A walk in the tundra; with illustrations by Phyllis V. Saroff. Carolrhoda Bks. 2001 48p il map (Biomes of North America) lib bdg $23.93 (3-6)   **577.5**
1. Tundra ecology
ISBN 1-57505-157-5   LC 00-8245
Takes readers on a walk in the tundra, showing examples of how the animals and plants of the tundra are connected and dependent on each other and the tundra's soil and climate
"A visually pleasing title with plenty of clear, colorful photographs of the biome's flora and fauna throughout the year." SLJ
Includes glossary and bibliographical references

Lesser, Carolyn
Storm on the desert; written by Carolyn Lesser; illustrated by Ted Rand. Harcourt Brace & Co. 1997 unp il $16 (2-4)   **577.5**
1. Desert ecology 2. Thunderstorms
ISBN 0-15-272198-3   LC 95-44923
Describes the animal and plant life in a desert in the American Southwest and the effects of a short but violent thunderstorm
"The poetic prose is rich with terms and images of the plants and animals that have adapted to desert life. Illustrations done in pencil, pastel, chalk, and watercolor impart character to the animals and the storm itself." Horn Book Guide

Levinson, Nancy Smiler
Death Valley; a day in the desert; illustrated by Diane Dawson Hearn. Holiday House 2001 29p il $14.95 (1-3)   **577.5**
1. Desert ecology
ISBN 0-8234-1566-X   LC .00-23305
"A Holiday House reader"
Describes the desert habitat of Death Valley and the plants and animals that live there
"Newly independent readers will appreciate the simple text of this nonfiction easy reader. . . . The illustrations are clear and attractive." Horn Book Guide

Pascoe, Elaine
Soil; text by Elaine Pascoe; photographs by Dwight Kuhn. Blackbirch Press 2005 24p il (Nature close-up juniors) $21.20 (k-3)
                                            577.5
1. Soil ecology
ISBN 1-4103-0311-X   LC 2004-13975
"This book introduces young readers to the wildlife lurking in the soil right under their feet and to the role of soil in plant growth. Activities include starting plants from seed and watching earthworms tunnel." Publisher's note
Includes bibliographical references

Stille, Darlene R.
Deserts. Children's Press 1999 47p il lib bdg $22; pa $6.95 (2-4)   **577.5**
1. Desert ecology
ISBN 0-516-21508-6 (lib bdg); 0-516-26760-4 (pa)
                                    LC 98-53856
"A True book"
Presents a general description of deserts and describes specific desert plants, animals, people, and activities
Includes glossary and bibliographical references

Tocci, Salvatore
Alpine tundra; life on the tallest mountain; [by] Salvatore Tocci. 1st ed. Franklin Watts 2005 63p il (Biomes and habitats) $25.50 (4 and up)
                                            577.5
1. Tundra ecology
ISBN 0-531-12365-0   LC 2004-13583
"Watts library"
Contents: A land high up; The season to grow; The season to prepare; The season to hide; The season to reappear; People of the tundra
This introduces "readers to the climate characteristics as well as plants and animals of [the Alpine tundra. It is] written in an accessible and interesting, conversational style. The authors convey a good deal of information about topics such as adaptation, environmental threats, seasonal changes, and other essentials important to report writers and general readers." SLJ
Includes bibliographical references

Arctic tundra; life at the North Pole; [by] Salvatore Tocci. 1st ed. Franklin Watts 2005 63p il map (Biomes and habitats) $25.50 (4 and up)
                                            577.5
1. Tundra ecology
ISBN 0-531-12366-9   LC 2004-13283

Tocci, Salvatore—*Continued*

"Watts library"

This introduces "readers to the climate characteristics as well as plants and animals of [the Arctic tundra. It is] written in an accessible and interesting, conversational style. The [author conveys] a good deal of information about topics such as adaptation, environmental threats, seasonal changes, and other essentials important to report writers and general readers." SLJ

Includes bibliographical references

Wright-Frierson, Virginia

A desert scrapbook; dawn to dusk in the Sonoran Desert. Simon & Schuster Bks. for Young Readers 1996 unp il $16 (3-5)   **577.5**

1. Desert ecology 2. Sonoran Desert

ISBN 0-689-80678-7   LC 95-19629

"Wright-Frierson invites readers to spend a day in her company, savoring the Sonoran Desert of the American Southwest. She presents a dawn to dusk panorama in a profusion of watercolor sketches and a brief, conversational text." SLJ

577.6 Aquatic ecology. Freshwater ecology

Brenner, Barbara

One small place by the sea; illustrated by Tom Leonard. HarperCollins Publishers 2004 unp il $15.99; lib bdg $16.89 (2-4)   **577.6**

1. Tide pool ecology

ISBN 0-688-17182-6; 0-688-17183-4 (lib bdg)
          LC 2002-1180

For one afternoon, a child visitor observes the cycle of change within a tidepool, a small place at the edge of the sea that is home to many plants and animals.

"The contents of the book are well organized, current, and accurate. The content is well illustrated, with colored pictures of the organisms, as well as many of their life habits, discussed." Sci Books Films

Gibbons, Gail

Marshes & swamps. Holiday House 1998 unp il $16.95; pa $6.95 (k-3)   **577.6**

1. Wetlands 2. Ecology

ISBN 0-8234-1347-0; 0-8234-1515-5 (pa)
          LC 97-17995

Defines marshes and swamps, discusses how conditions in them may change, and examines the life found in and around them

"Gibbons balances a succinct, informative text with well-labeled watercolors." Horn Book Guide

Marx, Trish

Everglades forever; restoring America's great wetland; photographs by Cindy Karp. 1st ed. Lee & Low Books 2004 40p il map $17.95 (3-6)
          577.6

1. Everglades (Fla.)

ISBN 1-58430-164-3   LC 2004-2934

The author offers an "introduction to the natural history and environment of the Everglades by documenting the studies of a fifth-grade class. . . . Complementing the excellent, informative text are high-quality color photographs and maps." Booklist

Miller, Debbie S.

River of life; illustrated by Jon Van Zyle. Clarion Bks. 2000 32p il $15 (k-3)   **577.6**

1. River ecology 2. Natural history—Alaska

ISBN 0-395-96790-2   LC 99-38350

Describes a river in Alaska and the life that it supports, emphasizing how the living things around it are connected and dependent upon it for their survival

"Rich in word choice, this book develops strong images of the life cycle that unfolds along a river, as winter melts into spring and spring becomes the warm days of summer. Inviting illustrations help tell this story of a river ecosystem." Sci Child

Includes glossary

Morrison, Gordon

Pond. Houghton Mifflin 2002 30p il $16 (2-4)
          577.6

1. Pond ecology

ISBN 0-618-10271-X   LC 2002-3494

Observes how a glacial pond and the abundance of plants and animals that draw life from it change over the course of a year

"Lovely, realistic watercolor paintings illustrate the text; small, detailed pencil drawings and diagrams accompany each note. . . . This lovingly crafted sketchbook has the potential to awaken in readers an awareness of the workings of nature." SLJ

577.7 Marine ecology

Cerullo, Mary M.

Coral reef; a city that never sleeps; text by Mary M. Cerullo; photographs by Jeffrey L. Rotman. Cobblehill Bks. 1996 58p il $18.99 (4 and up)   **577.7**

1. Coral reefs and islands 2. Marine ecology

ISBN 0-525-65193-4   LC 95-6635

This describes the ecosystem of coral reefs and their inhabitants

"As fascinatingly fact-filled as the text is, it's even more outstanding because of Rotman's spectacular, full-color photographs." SLJ

Includes glossary and bibliographical references

Collard, Sneed B., III

On the coral reefs; by Sneed B. Collard III. Marshall Cavendish Benchmark 2005 43p il (Science adventures) lib bdg $25.64 (4-6)
          577.7

1. Grutter, Alexandra 2. Coral reefs and islands 3. Marine ecology

ISBN 0-7614-1953-5   LC 2004030316

This describes the ecology of coral reefs and the research of marine biologist Dr. Alexandra Grutter.

Includes glossary and bibliographical references

Crenson, Victoria

Horseshoe crabs and shorebirds; the story of a food web; illustrated by Annie Cannon. Marshall Cavendish 2003 unp il lib bdg $16.95 (2-4)

577.7

1. Food chains (Ecology) 2. Crabs 3. Delaware Bay (Del. and N.J.)

ISBN 0-7614-5115-3   LC 2002-156473

Presents a portrait of the Delaware Bay in the spring when a wide variety of animals, including minnows, mice, turtles, raccoons, and especially migrating shorebirds, come to feed on the billions of eggs laid by horseshoe crabs

"Crenson's text is highly descriptive and reads like an adventure story, conveying the action and excitement of nature. Cannon's watercolors fill the pages with atmosphere and motion." SLJ

Parker, Steve

Seashore; written by Steve Parker. rev ed. DK Pub. 2004 72p il (DK eyewitness books) $15.99; lib bdg $19.99 (4 and up)   **577.7**

1. Seashore 2. Marine animals 3. Marine plants

ISBN 0-7566-0721-3; 0-7566-0720-5 (lib bdg)

First published 1989 by Knopf

Brief text and photos introduce the animal inhabitants of the seashore, including fish, crustaceans, snails, and shorebirds.

Patent, Dorothy Hinshaw

Colorful, captivating coral reefs; illustrations by Kendahl Jan Jubb. Walker 2003 unp il $17.95; lib bdg $18.85 (2-4)   **577.7**

1. Coral reefs and islands

ISBN 0-8027-8862-9; 0-8027-8863-7 (lib bdg)

LC 2003-43258

Provides an overview of coral reefs as ecosystems, describing different types of corals and how they reproduce and discussing the variety of fishes and other animals that depend on coral reefs to sustain them.

"This beautifully illustrated, informative title takes readers on a journey through the fascinating undersea world of coral reefs. . . . An attractive, fascinating introduction." Booklist

Pringle, Laurence P.

Come to the ocean's edge; a nature cycle book; illustrated by Michael Chesworth. Boyds Mills Press 2003 32p il $15.95 (k-3)   **577.7**

1. Seashore ecology

ISBN 1-56397-779-6

"Spanning sunrise to sunset, Pringle gives [an] . . . account of a coastline environment." Horn Book Guide

This offers "a poetic text and beautifully composed watercolor paintings. . . . While providing a realistic view of this environment, the artwork also echoes the expressive tone of the narrative." SLJ

577.8 Synecology and population biology

Aruego, Jose

Weird friends; unlikely allies in the animal kingdom; [by] Jose Aruego and Ariane Dewey. Harcourt 2002 unp il $16 (k-3)   **577.8**

1. Symbiosis

ISBN 0-15-202128-0   LC 2001-1154

"Gulliver books"

"This book offers an overview of fourteen symbiotic animal relationships, such as that between rhinos and cattle egrets. . . . The brief text provides a short description of the animals, what their functions are, and how they cooperate with their allies. The brightly colored illustrations feature anthropomorphized creatures, which may attract younger naturalists." Horn Book Guide

578 Natural history of organisms and related subjects

Arnosky, Jim

Under the wild western sky; [by] Jim Arnosky. 1st ed. HarperCollins 2005 unp il $15.99; lib bdg $16.89 (2-4)   **578**

1. Natural history—Southwestern States

ISBN 0-688-17121-4; 0-688-17122-2 (lib bdg)

LC 2004-14509

"Based on Arnosky's personal observations, this . . . sampler describes birds, snakes and lizards, long-horned cattle, buffalo, and common varieties of cactus of the American West. . . . A combination of luminous acrylic paintings and detailed, soft pencil drawings conveys both the scale of the land and the more intricate details of nature. The illustrations are labeled throughout, with additional information presented in sidebars." SLJ

Collard, Sneed B., III

In the rain forest canopy; by Sneed B. Collard III. Marshall Cavendish Benchmark 2005 43p il (Science adventures) lib bdg $25.70 (4-6)

578

1. Nadkarni, Nalini, 1954- 2. Rain forests 3. Natural history—Costa Rica

ISBN 0-7614-1954-3   LC 2004027940

This describes the rain forest canopy and the research of Dr. Nalini Nadkarni in Monteverde, Costa Rica.

Includes glossary and bibliographical references

Kelsey, Elin

Strange new species; astonishing discoveries of life on earth. Maple Tree Press 2005 96p il $24.95

578

1. Natural history 2. Biology 3. Scientists

ISBN 1-897066-31-7; 1-897066-32-5 (pa)

"This large-format book showcases new species . . . and the scientists who have discovered them. . . . The discussion ends with information on cloning, genetically modified food, and the future of life. . . . With many

Kelsey, Elin—*Continued*

excellent photos, this introductory book on new species will be an intriguing addition to classroom units on classification or biology." Booklist

Strauss, Rochelle

Tree of life; the incredible biodiversity of life on Earth. Kids Can Press 2004 40p il $16.95 (5 and up)   **578**

1. Biology—Classification 2. Biological diversity
ISBN 1-55337-669-2

The "text first introduces the concept of a family tree for all living things, then goes on to name the five kingdoms of scientific classification. . . . The author describes the life-forms included in each species, with specific examples shown in the softly colorful illustrations accompanied by informative captions. . . . Striking, lucid, and deceptively simple." SLJ

578.7   Organisms characteristic of specific kinds of environments

Aquatic life of the world. Marshall Cavendish 2001 11v set $471.36 (4 and up)   **578.7**

1. Marine biology 2. Freshwater animals
ISBN 0-7614-7170-7   LC 99-86128

Arranged alphabetically, the more than 200 articles in volumes 1-10 cover mammals, fish, amphibians reptiles, birds, plants and their habitats. Biogeography, global warming and scuba diving are among the general topics discussed. Volume II contains a comprehensive index and nine subject indexes. Over 900 full-color photographs, illustrations and maps accompany the text

Arnold, Caroline

A walk on the Great Barrier Reef; photographs by Arthur Arnold; with additional photographs by Marty Snyderman [et al.] Carolrhoda Bks. 1988 47p il (Carolrhoda nature watch book) lib bdg $23.93 (3-5)   **578.7**

1. Coral reefs and islands 2. Marine animals 3. Great Barrier Reef (Australia)
ISBN 0-87614-285-4   LC 87-27746

The author leads "the reader on a tour of discovery that explores the structure of the reef and the life cycles and habits of its various inhabitants. Following a discussion of how the reef was formed, the book includes diagrams of the three types of coral reef formations (fringing, barrier, and atoll)." Sci Child

"The fascinating plants and animals of Australia's Great Barrier Reef are described in a straightforward way and illustrated with stunning, clear full-color photographs." SLJ

Includes glossary

Arnosky, Jim

Beachcombing; exploring the seashore. Dutton Children's Bks. 2004 unp il $15.99 (k-3)   **578.7**

1. Seashore
ISBN 0-525-47104-9

Illustrations and text describe some of the many things that can be found on a walk along a beach, including coconuts, shark teeth, jellyfish, crabs and different kinds of shells.

"Young beachcombers will discover old and new ideas about collecting or just identifying their finds, and the book will appeal to those children who are looking for relaxing fun." SLJ

Cerullo, Mary M.

Life under ice; photography by Bill Curtsinger. Tilbury House 2003 37p il map $16.95 (3-5)   **578.7**

1. Marine animals 2. Marine plants 3. Natural history—Antarctica
ISBN 0-88448-246-4   LC 2002-154451

Follows marine photographer Bill Curtsinger as he dives under the ice at Antarctica to learn about the plants and animals that thrive in this extreme habitat

"Illustrated with stunning color undersea photographs, this offers a fascinating look at the many creatures living near and beneath the waters of Antarctica. . . . The text is clear and well written, but it is the wonderful photography that distinguishes the book." Booklist

Includes glossary and bibliographical references

Conlan, Kathy

Under the ice. Kids Can Press 2002 55p il $16.95; pa $8.95 (4 and up)   **578.7**

1. Marine biology 2. Marine pollution 3. Polar regions
ISBN 1-55337-001-5; 1-55337-060-0 (pa)

"A Canadian Museum of Nature book."

"In this photo-essay, Conlan details her three-month stay in Antarctica, highlighting some of her experiences and her involvement in ongoing experiments relating to the effects of human waste on marine life." SLJ

"The first-person text creates a feeling of immediacy. . . . Well-captioned, color photos appear throughout the book. . . . Conlan . . . offers readers an engaging account of her adventurous career in scientific field research." Booklist

Pandell, Karen

Journey through the northern rainforest; photographs by Art Wolfe; illustrations by Denise Y. Takahashi. Dutton Children's Bks. 1999 unp il $17.99 (4 and up)   **578.7**

1. Rain forest ecology 2. Pacific Northwest
ISBN 0-525-45804-2   LC 99-31646

"The text combines discussion of the interdependence of plants, animals, and environments in the temperate rainforest ecosystem with a strong message against the irreversible devastation caused by logging. Color photographs and illustrations from an eagle's point of view accompany the informative text." Horn Book Guide

579 Microorganisms, fungi, algae

Maynard, Christopher
Micromonsters; life under the microscope; written by Chris Maynard. DK Pub. 1999 48p il (Eyewitness readers) $12.95; pa $3.95 (2-4)
579
1. Microorganisms
ISBN 0-7894-4757-6; 0-7894-4756-8 (pa)
LC 99-20401
Explores the hidden world of very small creatures that live around us and even inside us, including fleas, bedbugs, itch mites, and more
"Maynard supplies lots of interesting facts in this accessible, nicely designed Eyewitness Reader that is loaded with fairly good magnified photos and sidebars with related facts." Booklist

Nye, Bill
Bill Nye the science guy's great big book of tiny germs; with additional writing by Kathleen W. Zoehfeld; illustrated by Bryn Barnard. Hyperion Books for Children 2005 47p il $16.99 (3-5)
579
1. Microorganisms
ISBN 0-7868-0543-9
"Nye covers bacteria, viruses, how germs travel and attack humans, the immune system, and the history of the pox, plagues, and other little diseases. He touches on how germs were discovered, vaccinations, antibiotics, HIV and AIDs, keeping safe and germ free, and why we love and hate germs. Activities are included at the end of each chapter. . . . The author is a natural teacher and writes in an easygoing, smoothly flowing style. Fun and inviting cartoons and full-color photos appear throughout." SLJ

Zabludoff, Marc
The protoctist kingdom. Benchmark Books 2006 95p il (Family trees) lib bdg $29.92
579
1. Protoctista
ISBN 0-7614-1818-0 (lib bdg)
LC 2004-21821
This examines the physical traits, adaptations, diets, habitats, and life cycles of such life forms as bacteria, amoebas, slime nets, molds, algae, coccoliths, forams, and diatoms.
"Fact-filled, yet surprisingly readable. . . . [This] title contains a wide variety of excellent-quality, full-color photographs; interesting sidebars; and diagrams." SLJ

579.5 Fungi

Pascoe, Elaine
Slime, molds, and fungi; text by Elaine Pascoe; photographs by Dwight Kuhn. Blackbirch Press 1999 48p il (Nature close-up) lib bdg $23.70 (4 and up)
579.5
1. Fungi
ISBN 1-56711-182-3
LC 97-36751

Using hands-on natural science projects, explores and explains different types and characteristics of fungi
This is "clearly written and well organized, and the photographs are outstanding in their clarity and composition." SLJ
Includes glossary and bibliographical references

Souza, D. M. (Dorothy M.)
What is a fungus? Watts 2002 63p il lib bdg $24.50; pa $8.95 (5 and up)
579.5
1. Fungi
ISBN 0-531-11979-3 (lib bdg); 0-531-16223-0 (pa)
LC 2001-17565
"Watts library"
This explains "how a fungus lives, what it eats, and how it reproduces. The writing is accessible and entertaining enough to keep readers engaged." SLJ
Includes glossary and bibliographical references

579.6 Mushrooms

Royston, Angela
Life cycle of a mushroom. Heinemann Lib. 2000 32p il lib bdg $13.95 (k-3)
579.6
1. Mushrooms
ISBN 1-57572-210-0
LC 99-46105
Introduces the life cycle of a mushroom, from formation of spores through underground growth of the mycelia to formation of mature mushrooms
This is an "excellent first book about mushrooms. . . . Photographs on each page are lovely and enhance the text, which is clear and contains a lot of factual information." Sci Books Films
Includes bibliographical references

580 Plants

Armentrout, David
50 words about plants; [by] David and Patricia Armentrout. Rourke Publs. 2002 32p il $26.60 (3-5)
580
1. Plants
ISBN 1-58952-345-8
LC 2002-2375
Provides simple definitions for fifty words related to plants along with sample sentences using each word
"The authors got it right! . . . The definitions are straightforward, the pictures are germane, and the sentences relate well." Sci Books Films
Includes glossary and bibliographical references

Pascoe, Elaine
Plants with seeds; photographs by Dwight Kuhn. PowerKids Press 2003 32p il (Kid's guide to the classification of living things) lib bdg $20.65 (2-5)
580
1. Plants 2. Seeds
ISBN 0-8239-6314-4
LC 2001-7793
Details the life cycles and characteristics of plants that use seeds to reproduce

Pascoe, Elaine—*Continued*

This "slim, well-organized . . . [introduction is] a must for schools in which plant studies are a part of the curriculum. . . . Useful for reports, with browsing appeal as well." SLJ

Includes glossary and bibliographical references

580.7 Plants--Education, research, related topics

VanCleave, Janice Pratt

Janice VanCleave's plants; mind-boggling experiments you can turn into science fair projects. Wiley 1997 90p il (Spectacular science projects series) pa $10.95 (5 and up) **580.7**
1. Botany 2. Plants 3. Science projects 4. Science—Experiments
ISBN 0-471-14687-0 LC 96-2744
Presents facts about plants and includes experiments, projects, and activities related to each topic
This book "is inspiring without being flashy. . . . The black-and-white line drawings are sketchy but helpful. . . . This is a fine example of helpful information that is neither academically dry nor ingratiatingly slangy." SLJ
Includes glossary

581.4 Adaptation

Goodman, Susan

Seeds, stems, and stamens; the ways plants fit into their world; by Susan E. Goodman; photographs by Michael Doolittle. Millbrook Press 2001 48p il $22.90 (2-4) **581.4**
1. Adaptation (Biology) 2. Plants 3. Ecology
ISBN 0-7613-1874-7 LC 00-68367
The author describes "a variety of ways plants adapt to their environment in order to survive. . . . The text is clearly and concisely written, and Doolittle's color photography is outstanding." Booklist

Richards, Jean

A fruit is a suitcase for seeds; illustrated by Anca Hariton. Millbrook Press 2002 unp il lib bdg $21.90 (k-2) **581.4**
1. Seeds 2. Fruit
ISBN 0-7613-1622-1 LC 2001-32959
Provides an illustrated description of seed dispersal by which plants, most specifically fruits, travel from one place to another
"Richard's carefully worded information provides an excellent introduction to seeds, their purpose, and growth that should be easy for young children to grasp. . . . Hariton's use of bright watercolors adds sensual appeal to her illustrations." SLJ

Robbins, Ken

Seeds; text and pictures by Ken Robbins. Atheneum Books for Young Readers 2005 unp il $15.95 (k-3) **581.4**
1. Seeds
ISBN 0-689-85041-7
This "book focuses on seed basics: differences in shapes and sizes, and links between structure and function. . . . Seeds are show alongside the whole plants and fruits they come from. . . . The superb photographs lend themselves to scientific scrutiny: the details are sharp and clear." Horn Book

581.6 Miscellaneous nontaxonomic kinds of plants

Souza, D. M. (Dorothy M.)

Plant invaders; [by] D. M. Souza. F. Watts 2003 63p il lib bdg $25.50; pa $8.95 (3-5) **581.6**
1. Plant ecology
ISBN 0-531-12211-5 (lib bdg); 0-531-16247-8 (pa) LC 2002-8887
Discusses nonnative plants, such as the kudzu vine and the tree-of-heaven, which were imported from other countries and now pose a significant threat to the ecosystems of North America
"Large, brightly colored closeup photos ranging from beautiful to bizarre are nicely placed to support the well-written [narrative.]" SLJ

582 Plants notable for specific vegetative characteristics and flowers

Schaefer, Lola M.

Pick, pull, snap! where once a flower bloomed; illustrated by Lindsay Barrett George. Greenwillow Bks. 2003 unp il $15.99 (k-3) **582**
1. Plants 2. Flowers 3. Fruit 4. Seeds
ISBN 0-688-17834-0 LC 2002-66818
Describes how raspberries, peanuts, corn, and other foods are produced as various plants flower, create seeds, and finally bear fruit
"On each spread, rhythmic, poetic text describes a plant's flower or husk and shows a cross section that reveals the seeds inside. A few lines of text explain a plant's growth, and then the page folds out to reveal the mature plant. . . . George's inviting, realistic color art brings youngsters up close to plants that produce familiar foods." Booklist
Includes glossary

582.13 Plants noted for their flowers

582.16 Trees

Pascoe, Elaine

Flowers; text by Elaine Pascoe; photographs by Dwight Kuhn. Blackbirch Press 2003 48p il lib bdg $23.70 (3-5) **582.13**

1. Flowers

ISBN 1-56711-432-6   LC 2002-151824

Describes the parts of different flowers, their role in the plants' reproduction, how to grow flowers, and how to press them. Includes activites and experiments related to flowers.

This is "well organized. . . . Different-sized, sharply focused pictures complement the text on almost every page; many are remarkably detailed, extreme closeups." SLJ

Includes bibliographical references

Ryden, Hope

Wildflowers around the year; photographs and text by Hope Ryden. Clarion Bks. 2001 90p il $17 (5 and up) **582.13**

1. Wild flowers

ISBN 0-395-85814-3   LC 00-43011

"Ryden introduces the reader to 38 species of wildflowers. . . . The flowers are identified by both their common names and the genus-species nomenclature. The months during which they are expected to be in full bloom are given as well." Sci Books Films

"Accompanied by exquisite, sharply focused photos. . . . Filled with interesting tidbits, Ryden's lyrical text meanders appealingly through moments of wonder, experience, explanation, and speculation." Horn Book Guide

Includes bibliographical references

Souza, D. M. (Dorothy M.)

Freaky flowers. Watts 2002 63p il lib bdg $24.50; pa $8.95 (5 and up) **582.13**

1. Flowers

ISBN 0-531-11981-5 (lib bdg); 0-531-16221-4 (pa)
          LC 2001-17573

"Watts library"

"The book begins with a short course in botany that stresses vocabulary and processes. Subsequent chapters discuss different ways plants attract pollinators through colors, odors, and habitats. The last chapter acts as a warning that many plants are endangered because their pollinators are threatened, emphasizing the balance of nature. The outstanding full-color photos feature some of the most spectacular flowers found anywhere. Small sidebars offer interesting bits of trivia about similar plants. The text is packed with biological information and pertinent vocabulary." SLJ

Includes bibliographical references

Bulla, Clyde Robert

A tree is a plant; illustrated by Stacey Schuett. HarperCollins Pubs. 2001 31p il (Let's-read-and-find-out science) $15.95; lib bdg $15.89; pa $4.95 (k-2) **582.16**

1. Trees 2. Apples

ISBN 0-06-028171-5; 0-06-028172-3 (lib bdg); 0-06-445196-8 (pa)   LC 00-40797

A newly illustrated edition of the title first published 1960 by Crowell

The text "follows an apple plant from seed to sprout to tree, including the development of blossoms, leaves, and fruit. The functions of roots, trunk, branches, and leaves are also discussed, as well as the seasonal changes in the tree. Schuett's colorful paintings clearly illustrate topics explained in the text, while their pleasing colors, rounded forms, and small, playful animals will help keep children involved in the topic." Booklist

Burnie, David

Tree; written by David Burnie. rev ed. DK Pub. 2005 72p il (DK eyewitness books) $15.99; lib bdg $19.99 (4 and up) **582.16**

1. Trees

ISBN 0-7566-1094-X; 0-7566-1093-1 (lib bdg)

First published 1988 by Knopf

Photographs and text explore the anatomy and life cycle of trees, examining the different kinds of bark, seeds, and leaves, the commercial processing of trees to make lumber, and the creatures that live in trees.

Ehlert, Lois

Red leaf, yellow leaf. Harcourt Brace Jovanovich 1991 unp il $16 (k-3) **582.16**

1. Trees

ISBN 0-15-266197-2   LC 90-21195

"In a quiet, first-person narrative, a young child details the life cycle of a sugar maple tree. . . . The story is quite brief, and the choice of a very large typeface makes the main portion of the book accessible to beginning readers. The concluding section offers more detailed and concrete botanical information and provides hints on selecting and planting one's own tree. . . . Ehlert has combined many media to create the book's dazzling illustrations." Horn Book

Gardner, Robert

Science project ideas about trees. Enslow Pubs. 1997 96p il (Science project ideas) lib bdg $25.26 (5 and up) **582.16**

1. Trees 2. Science projects 3. Science—Experiments

ISBN 0-89490-846-4   LC 97-6515

Contains many experiments introducing the processes that take place in plants and trees

The directions "are easy to understand, and the vocabulary is fairly accessible. The accompanying diagrams are particularly sharp and clear." SLJ

Includes bibliographical references

Gibbons, Gail

Tell me, tree; all about trees for kids. Little, Brown 2002 unp il $15.95 (k-3) **582.16**

1. Trees

ISBN 0-316-30903-6 LC 00-64967

"Gibbons discusses the parts of the tree and their functions, types of fruits and seeds, kinds of bark, and uses for trees. She includes a discussion of photosynthesis and gives directions for students to make their own tree identification books." SLJ

"The bright, watercolor illustrations show cheerful children and adults observing, planting, using, and enjoying many kinds of trees. In this simple, informative book, Gibbons provides a basic guide that is sure to please parents and teachers as well as children." Booklist

Lauber, Patricia

Be a friend to trees; illustrated by Holly Keller. HarperCollins Pubs. 1994 32p il (Let's-read-and-find-out science) lib bdg $15.89; pa $4.95 (k-3) **582.16**

1. Trees

ISBN 0-06-021529-1 (lib bdg); 0-06-445120-8 (pa) LC 92-24082

In this book "photosynthesis is explained, as well as the beauty and usefulness of trees. Easy conservation suggestions are also offered." Horn Book Guide

"This conveys a lot of information in a simple text with clear line-and-watercolor illustrations." Booklist

Maestro, Betsy

Why do leaves change color? illustrated by Loretta Krupinski. HarperCollins Pubs. 1994 32p il (Let's-read-and-find-out science) lib bdg $15.89; pa $4.95 (k-3) **582.16**

1. Leaves 2. Autumn

ISBN 0-06-022874-1 (lib bdg); 0-06-445126-7 (pa) LC 93-9611

Explains how leaves change their colors in autumn and then separate from the tree as the tree prepares for winter

"This is an informative concept book. . . . Krupinski's bright gouache-and-colored pencil illustrations show a boy and a girl playing in a country landscape that changes with weather and light. There are also detailed pictures of leaves in different sizes, shapes, and colors. Maestro includes simple instructions for making a leaf rubbing and for pressing leaves, as well as suggestions for places to visit where the fall foliage is special." Booklist

Robbins, Ken

Autumn leaves. Scholastic Press 1998 39p il $15.95 (3-6) **582.16**

1. Leaves 2. Autumn

ISBN 0-590-29879-8 LC 97-43895

Examines the characteristics of different types of leaves and explains how and why they change colors in the autumn

"Nicely produced, this attractive and instructive book employs full-color photos, most set against stark white backgrounds, to introduce children to a bounty of autumn

leaves. . . . This is a sure bet for classroom use and will also be wonderful for parent-child and school outdoor expeditions." Booklist

583 Dicotyledons

Bash, Barbara

Desert giant; the world of the saguaro cactus. Sierra Club Bks. 1989 unp il pa $6.95 hardcover o.p. (3-5) **583**

1. Cactus 2. Desert ecology

ISBN 0-316-68307-0 (pa) LC 88-4706

"Animals find food and shelter in the towering plant of the Sonoran desert, and the local Tohono O'odom Indians have multiple uses for it. The cactus's 200-year life cycle is depicted as part of the ecosystem with colorful illustrations and clear text." Sci Child

In the heart of the village; the world of the Indian Banyan tree. Sierra Club Bks. 1996 unp il $16.95 (3-5) **583**

1. Banyan tree 2. India—Social life and customs

ISBN 0-87156-575-7 LC 95-51345

"In a small village in India, the sacred banyan tree is the center and heart of life, and it is protected and worshipped by the people. . . . This day in the life of a banyan is presented in lilting text that effectively captures the activities of a community and shows how its people revolve around this majestic tree. The rich, full-page watercolor illustrations make the book a natural for reading aloud." SLJ

Guiberson, Brenda Z.

Cactus hotel; illustrated by Megan Lloyd. Holt & Co. 1991 unp il $16.95; pa $6.95 (k-3) **583**

1. Cactus 2. Desert ecology

ISBN 0-8050-1333-4; 0-8050-2960-5 (pa) LC 90-41748

Describes the life cycle of the giant saguaro cactus, with an emphasis on its role as a home for other desert dwellers

"Guiberson's simple, understandable text gives an enjoyable lesson in desert ecology. Crisply attractive illustrations in color pencil and watercolor show the beauty of the desert landscape and its variety of wildlife." Booklist

Hughes, Meredith Sayles

Spill the beans and pass the peanuts: legumes. Lerner Publs. 1999 80p il lib bdg $26.60 (4 and up) **583**

1. Legumes

ISBN 0-8225-2834-7 LC 98-29663

Presents information on the history, production, and uses of several popular members of the legume family: peanuts, lentils, peas, and beans, particularly soybeans. Includes recipes

"Chapters are illustrated with clear color and black-and-white photographs, reproductions, and drawings. Various cooking methods around the world are discussed

Hughes, Meredith Sayles—*Continued*

and one recipe for each legume is provided. The tone is lively and the information is scientifically correct and thorough. . . . A rich presentation about these common but important foods." SLJ

Morrison, Gordon

Oak tree. Houghton Mifflin 2000 30p il $16 (3-6) **583**

1. Oak 2. Forest ecology

ISBN 0-395-95644-7 LC 98-55148

"Walter Lorraine books"

Describes the impact of the changing seasons on an old oak tree and the life that surrounds it

"Each phase of the tree's development is lovingly depicted in language and pictures that are scientific as well as colorful and accessible. . . . This book is equally engaging as reference or personal-interest reading for the science-minded child." Booklist

Pascoe, Elaine

Carnivorous plants; text by Elaine Pascoe; photographs by Dwight Kuhn. Blackbirch Press 2005 48p il (Nature close-up) $23.70 (4 and up) **583**

1. Carnivorous plants

ISBN 1-4103-0309-8 LC 2005-276141

This describes such plants as venus flytraps, pitcher plants, cobra plants, and blatterworts, with instructions for growing and investigating them.

Includes glossary and bibliographical references

Pfeffer, Wendy

From seed to pumpkin; illustrated by James Graham Hale. HarperCollins 2004 33p il (Let's-read-and-find-out science) $15.99; lib bdg $16.89; pa $4.99 (k-1) **583**

1. Pumpkin

ISBN 0-06-028038-7; 0-06-028039-5 (lib bdg); 0-06-445190-9 (pa) LC 00-54039

This explains the stages in the development of a seed into a pumpkin.

Written "in simple, clear language. . . . A couple of easy recipes and experiments are appended. Appealing watercolor-and-pencil illustrations show children involved in planting and tending the pumpkins, and help make the process and the passage of time understandable to this audience. " SLJ

Posada, Mia

Dandelions; stars in the grass. Carolrhoda Bks. 2000 unp il lib bdg $15.95 (2-4) **583**

1. Dandelions

ISBN 1-57505-383-7 LC 98-53000

Rhyming text presents the dandelion, not as a weed, but as a flower of great beauty. Includes information about the flower, a recipe, and science activities

"This cheerful book is a nice combination of rhyme and information. . . . Bright and pleasing acrylic illustrations extend the text. . . . Posada includes just enough botanical detail for beginning dandelion pickers." SLJ

Includes bibliographical references

Royston, Angela

Life cycle of an oak tree. Heinemann Lib. 2000 32p il lib bdg $13.95 (k-3) **583**

1. Oak

ISBN 1-57572-211-9 LC 99-46855

Introduces the life cycle of an oak tree, from the sprouting of an acorn through its more than 100 years of growth

"Easy enough for primary-grade students, the book contains concepts appropriate for all elementary school students." Sci Books Films

Includes glossary and bibliographical references

Winner, Cherie

The sunflower family; photographs by Sherry Shahan. Carolrhoda Bks. 1996 48p il (Carolrhoda nature watch book) $23.93; pa $7.95 (3-6) **583**

1. Wild flowers

ISBN 1-57505-007-2; 1-57505-029-3 (pa) LC 95-46110

The topic of this "book is the varied and adaptable Compositae family rather than just its namesake member, the sunflower. . . . This volume describes the distinct characteristics of the composites. . . . The making and dispersal of seeds is discussed and dazzlingly illustrated with full-color photos and diagrams. . . . The many uses of composites as food, lubricant, and pesticide are discussed. This is an excellent introduction to plant function and the concept of scientific grouping." SLJ

Includes glossary

585 Gymnosperms. Conifers

Bash, Barbara

Ancient ones; the world of the old-growth Douglas fir. Sierra Club Bks. for Children 1994 unp il (Tree tales) $16.95 (3-5) **585**

1. Douglas fir 2. Forest ecology

ISBN 0-87156-561-7 LC 93-45251

"Boxes of text set into double-page paintings sketch the activities of animals occupying a Pacific Northwest forest of mixed trees. Striking scenes of the skyward view, the lush canopy, dead and fallen trees, night and winter, and even a forest ablaze offer a broad view of life in this ecosystem, with special focus on the 'mighty Douglas fir.'" Horn Book Guide

586 Seedless plants

Pascoe, Elaine

Plants without seeds; photography by Dwight Kuhn. PowerKids Press 2003 32p il (Kid's guide to the classification of living things) $20.65 (2-5) **586**

1. Mosses 2. Ferns

ISBN 0-8239-6315-2 LC 2001-7794

An introduction to the life cycles and characteristics of bryophytes, or plants without seeds, such as mosses and ferns

Pascoe, Elaine—*Continued*

This "slim, well-organized . . . [introduction is] a must for schools in which plant studies are a part of the curriculum. . . . Useful for reports, with browsing appeal as well." SLJ

Includes glossary and bibliographical references

590   Animals

DuQuette, Keith

They call me Woolly; what animal names can tell us; written and illustrated by Keith DuQuette. Putnam 2002 31p il $15.99 (k-3)   **590**
1. Animals 2. Vocabulary
ISBN 0-399-23445-4   LC 00-55356

The author "invites children to learn something about a species just by paying attention to its names. DuQuette's handsome, realistically detailed illustrations pair with brief examples of names that give information about an animal's habitat ('polar bear'), how it moves ('grasshopper'), what it sounds like ('howler monkey'), and so on. . . . Quirky and informative, this offers a satisfying combination of wordplay and breezy animal facts for zoologists in the making." Booklist

Jenkins, Steve

Biggest, strongest, fastest. Ticknor & Fields Bks. for Young Readers 1995 unp il $16; pa $5.95 (k-2)   **590**
1. Animals
ISBN 0-395-69701-8; 0-395-86136-5 (pa)
      LC 94-21804

"Here are 14 creatures of distinction, including elephants, ants, jellyfish, cheetahs and fleas. The collage illustrations show them at work, and silhouette graphics with captions provide scientific information about comparative achievement." N Y Times Book Rev

"A helpful chart at the end contains further information about each creature, such as diet and habitat. An all-round superlative effort." SLJ

Lewin, Ted

Tooth and claw; animal adventures in the wild. HarperCollins Pubs. 2003 97p il maps $15.99; lib bdg $16.89 (4 and up)   **590**
1. Wildlife 2. Dangerous animals
ISBN 0-688-14105-6; 0-688-14106-4 (lib bdg)
      LC 2002-4588

Contents: Beach master; Grizzly; Macaco meojor; Waiting for puff adder; Bears, bears, bears; Roar; The meat eaters of Kibale; Barnstorming; Sleeping with bison; Rattler; Deputy Dawg; Downwind of a dung beetle; The joker; Garbage elephants

Author/illustrator Ted Lewin relates fourteen of his experiences with wild animals while travelling the world, following each anecdote with facts about the featured animal and its habitat

"This is outstanding nature storytelling, related in a distinctive voice imbued with humor and personality; it's even better when read aloud." Horn Book

Includes glossary

590.3   Animals--Encyclopedias and dictionaries

Dorling Kindersley animal encyclopedia. Dorling Kindersley 2000 376p il $29.95 (4 and up)
      590.3
1. Animals—Encyclopedias
ISBN 0-7894-6499-3   LC 00-23782

Provides information about the physical characteristics, habits, and behavior of such animals as hedgehogs, peacocks, penguins, salamanders, and snakes

"The art, a richly informative blend of painted or photographic close-ups, action shots, and isolated portraits, is up to DK's usual standards for sharpness of detail, brilliance of color, and dramatic impact. . . . This book will reward both browsers and focused inquirers and enhance any reference collection." SLJ

National Geographic animal encyclopedia. National Geographic Soc. 2000 262p il $29.95 (3-6)   **590.3**
1. Animals—Encyclopedias
ISBN 0-7922-7180-7   LC 99-48020

First published 1999 in the United Kingdom with title: The Marshall children's animal encyclopedia

A comprehensive look at the world of animals, their features, behavior, and life cycles, arranged by the categories "Mammals," "Birds," "Reptiles," "Amphibians," "Fish," and "Insects, Spiders, and Other Invertebrates"

This is an "excellent introduction to animal life. . . . The book is generously illustrated with attractive full-color drawings and clear photographs." SLJ

590.73   Collections and exhibits of living animals

Aliki

My visit to the zoo. HarperCollins Pubs. 1997 33p il $14.95; lib bdg $15.89; pa $6.95 (k-3)
      590.73
1. Zoos 2. Animals
ISBN 0-06-024939-0; 0-06-024943-9 (lib bdg); 0-06-446217-X (pa)   LC 96-9897

A day at the zoo introduces the different animals that exist in the world, where they come from, what their natural habitats are like, and whether or not they are endangered

"Aliki's accessible text and lush illustrations bring the animal world to life." SLJ

Zoehfeld, Kathleen Weidner

Wild lives; a history of the people & animals of the Bronx Zoo; with photographs from the Wildlife Conservation Society. Alfred A. Knopf 2006 86p il $18.95; lib bdg $20.99 (5 and up)
      590.73
1. Bronx Zoo 2. Zoos 3. Animals
ISBN 0-375-80630-X; 0-375-90630-4 (lib bdg)
      LC 2005-18943

"Zoehfeld tells the story of the Bronx Zoo, from the preparations for its opening in 1899 to its current efforts

Zoehfeld, Kathleen Weidner—*Continued*
in the areas of conservation and education. Along with information on the zoo, she discusses trends in thinking about wildlife, the ethics of removing animals from their habitats for their safety or for public display, and ongoing threats to the existence of many species. . . . The many photos, attractive layout, and use of color contribute to the visual appeal of this informative zoo story." Booklist
Includes bibliographical references

591.3 Genetics, evolution, young of animals

Bauer, Marion Dane
If you were born a kitten; illustrated by JoEllen McAllister Stammen. Simon & Schuster Bks. for Young Readers 1997 unp il $16; pa $6.99 (k-1)
591.3
1. Animal babies 2. Childbirth
ISBN 0-689-80111-4; 0-689-84212-0 (pa)
LC 96-7408
Simply describes how various baby animals come into the world and what happens when a human baby is born
"Stammen's large pastel illustrations will be as good for small groups as for lap sharing, and Bauer's simple words are quiet and graceful, drawing intensity from references to the senses." Booklist

Rose, Deborah Lee
Ocean babies; illustrations by Hiroe Nakata. National Geographic 2005 unp il $16.95; lib bdg $25.90 (k-2)
591.3
1. Marine animals 2. Animal babies
ISBN 0-7922-6669-2; 0-7922-8312-0 (lib bdg)
LC 2003-14075
Describes baby animals that live in the ocean, pointing out their many differences as well as the most important similarity.
"Nakata's cheerful watercolor paintings clearly illustrate the book's ideas while creating a beautiful undersea setting, bright with colors, teeming with varied creatures, and studded with intriguing details. Many books present information in this format, but few manage to stay as focused on the topic and sensitive to the intended audience as this one." Booklist

Ruurs, Margriet
Wild babies; paintings by Andrew Kiss. Tundra Bks. 2003 32p il $14.95 (k-3)
591.3
1. Animal babies
ISBN 0-88776-627-7
LC 2002-111645
"A descriptive sentence accompanies each of a dozen . . . paintings introducing a variety of young mammals and birds native to a North American forest." SLJ
"Exceptionally lifelike wildlife paintings will draw young nature lovers to this attractive book. . . . A high-quality book well worth purchasing." Booklist

591.4 Physical adaptation

Aston, Dianna Hutts
An egg is quiet; by Diana Aston; illustrated by Sylvia Long. Chronicle Books 2006 unp il $16.95 (k-3)
591.4
1. Eggs
ISBN 978-0-8118-4428-4
LC 2005012090
"An exceptionally handsome book on eggs, from the delicate ova of the green lacewing to the rosy roe of the Atlantic salmon to the mammoth bulk of an ostrich egg. Aston's simple, readable text celebrates their marvelous diversity, commenting on size, shape, coloration, and where they might be found." SLJ

Goodman, Susan
Claws, coats, and camouflage; the ways animals fit into their world; photographs by Michael Doolittle. Millbrook Press 2001 48p il lib bdg $22.90 (2-4)
591.4
1. Adaptation (Biology) 2. Animals
ISBN 0-7613-1865-5
LC 00-48167
"After a short introduction about adaptation, the photographs and text demonstrate how animals fit into their environment, stay safe, obtain food, and reproduce. . . . Both narrative and photographs are understandable, engaging, and informative." Booklist

Heller, Ruth
Chickens aren't the only ones. Grosset & Dunlap 1981 unp il $16.99; pa $6.99 (k-1)
591.4
1. Eggs 2. Reproduction 3. Animal babies
ISBN 0-448-01872-1; 0-698-71778-6 (pa)
LC 80-85257
A pictorial introduction to the animals that lay eggs, including chickens as well as other birds, reptiles, amphibians, fishes, insects, and even a few mammals
The animals "are displayed in buoyant but realistic full-color drawings that sing out from the page. It's unusual to see a science lesson so festively done for such a young audience; in fact this has the fun of pure fiction, though it is straight fact." Booklist

Jenkins, Steve
Actual size. Houghton Mifflin 2004 unp il $16 (k-3)
591.4
1. Animals 2. Size
ISBN 0-618-37594-5
LC 2003-17462
In "torn-and-cut paper collages, Jenkins depicts 18 animals and insects—or a part of their body—in actual size. . . . The end matter offers full pictures of the creatures and more details about their habitats and habits. Mixing deceptive simplicity with absolute clarity, this beautiful book is an enticing way to introduce children to the glorious diversity of our natural world, or to illustrate to budding scientists the importance of comparison, measurement, observation, and record keeping. A thoroughly engaging read-aloud and a must-have for any collection." SLJ

Jenkins, Steve—*Continued*

Big & little. Houghton Mifflin 1996 unp il $14.95 (k-2)   **591.4**

1. Animals 2. Shape

ISBN 0-395-72664-6   LC 95-41162

Jenkins "points out the differences in size between animals who are similar in other ways. The artwork combines cuttings of colored, textured papers to form animals that stand out strikingly against white backgrounds. . . . One line of text comments on the two animals' sizes, habits, or habitats. The final pages include a presentation of the comparative sizes of all the animals, [and] a paragraph of additional information about each species." Booklist

Includes bibliographical references

Miller, Debbie S.

Arctic lights, arctic nights; illustrations by Jon Van Zyle. Walker & Co. 2003 unp il map $16.95; lib bdg $17.85 (2-4)   **591.4**

1. Animals—Arctic regions 2. Natural history—Alaska

ISBN 0-8027-8856-4; 0-8027-8857-2 (lib bdg)

     LC 2002-191047

Describes the unique light phenomena of the Alaskan Arctic and the way animals adapt to the temperature and daylight changes each month of the year

The "brief text includes not only lyrical messages about light and its partner, darkness, but also references to the reaction of wildlife to the waxing and waning. . . . Wrapped about this unfamiliar (to many of us) swirl of seasons of light are Van Zyle's superb and quietly beautiful acrylic paintings, which capture both light and dark in perfect harmony with the text." SLJ

Includes glossary

Zoehfeld, Kathleen Weidner

What lives in a shell? illustrated by Helen K. Davie. HarperCollins Pubs. 1994 32p il (Let's-read-and-find-out science) pa $4.95 hardcover o.p. (k-1)   **591.4**

1. Shells 2. Animal defenses

ISBN 0-06-445124-0 (pa)   LC 93-12428

Describes such animals as snails, turtles, and crabs, which live in shells and use these coverings as protection

This book uses "interesting and accurate illustrations and just the right words. . . . The science here is good, and the explanations should cause young readers to want to learn more." Sci Books Films

591.47   Protective and locomotor adaptations, color

Bishop, Nic

The secrets of animal flight. Houghton Mifflin 1997 31p il $16 (3-6)   **591.47**

1. Flight 2. Animal behavior

ISBN 0-395-77848-4   LC 96-23131

"The mechanics of birds' flight are explored first; the author then turns his attention to bats, and, finally, to insects. In conclusion, he discusses unanswered questions that are still being researched." SLJ

"The many colorful photographs (bolstered by a few diagrams) expand the text with precision and beauty. . . . A good choice for curious browsers as well as information seekers." Booklist

Includes bibliographical references

Hickman, Pamela M.

Animals in motion; how animals swim, jump, slither and glide; written by Pamela Hickman; illustrations by Pat Stephens. Kids Can Press 2000 40p il $10.95; pa $5.95 (3-5)   **591.47**

1. Animal locomotion

ISBN 1-55074-573-5; 1-55074-575-1 (pa)

"The chapters are organized according to method of locomotion ('Swimmers and floaters,' 'Hoppers and jumpers,' 'Runners and walkers,' etc.). There's a lot of information to be found here, but what gives this book a different twist is that it encourages kids to think about the ways animals move and compare them to their own means of locomotion." SLJ

Jenkins, Steve

What do you do when something wants to eat you? Houghton Mifflin 1997 unp il $16 (k-3)

    591.47

1. Animal defenses

ISBN 0-395-82514-8   LC 96-44993

Describes how various animals, including an octopus, a bombadier beetle, a puff adder, and a gliding frog, escape danger

"Jenkins achieves remarkable anatomical detail in his boldly textured cut-paper collages; simple backgrounds keep attention tightly focused on the animals and their survival strategies." Bull Cent Child Books

591.5   Behavior

Fraser, Mary Ann

Where are the night animals? HarperCollins Pubs. 1999 29p il (Let's-read-and-find-out science) $15.95; lib bdg $15.89; pa $4.95 (k-1)

    591.5

1. Animal behavior

ISBN 0-06-027717-3; 0-06-027718-1 (lib bdg); 0-06-445176-3 (pa)   LC 97-34683

Describes various nocturnal animals and their nighttime activities, including the opossum, brown bat, and tree frog

"The narrative approach and affable, realistic paintings make this basic science lesson accessible and engaging to the preschool audience." Horn Book Guide

Kaner, Etta

Animals migrating; how, when, where and why animals migrate; written by Etta Kaner; illustrated by Pat Stephens. Kids Can Press 2005 40p il $12.95; pa $5.95 (2-4)   **591.5**

1. Animals—Migration

ISBN 1-55337-547-5; 1-55337-548-3 (pa)

This briefly describes the migration of mammals, birds, insects, sea life, and reptiles and amphibians.

Kaner, Etta—*Continued*

"Packed with fascinating facts about a wide range of migrating animals and relayed in chatty style, this attractive picture book is illustrated with handsome line-and-watercolor pictures." Booklist

Krautwurst, Terry

Night science for kids; exploring the world after dark; by Terry Krautwurst. 1st ed. Lark Books 2003 144p il $19.95 (4-6)   **591.5**
1. Animals 2. Night
ISBN 1-57990-411-4   LC 2003-4388
Contents: Into the night; Becoming a night explorer; Night animals; The fly-by-nights; Insects in the night; Eyes to the sky; The edges of night
Provides ideas and activities for discovering what changes in the world after dark, including the arrival of moths and owls, fog, and the stars
"The writing is clear and readable, with a light and sometimes humorous tone. Outstanding full-color photos illustrate the projects well." SLJ

Selsam, Millicent Ellis

Big tracks, little tracks; following animal prints; by Millicent E. Selsam; illustrated by Marlene Hill Donnelly. rev ed. HarperCollins Pubs. 1999 31p il (Let's-read-and-find-out science) lib bdg $15.89; pa $4.95 (k-3)   **591.5**
1. Animal tracks 2. Tracking and trailing
ISBN 0-06-028209-6 (lib bdg); 0-06-445194-1 (pa)
                                         LC 98-18315
"An I can read book"
First published with this title 1995; originally published with title How to be a nature detective
This book "teaches young readers how to track animals by finding footprints and other clues. . . . Included is a new Find Out More page with lots of hands-on activites." Publisher's note

Settel, Joanne

Exploding ants; amazing facts about how animals adapt. Atheneum Bks. for Young Readers 1999 40p il $16.95 (4 and up)   **591.5**
1. Animal behavior
ISBN 0-689-81739-8   LC 97-35395
Describes examples of animal behavior that may strike humans as disgusting, including the "gross" ways animals find food, shelter, and safety in the natural world
"This attractive volume presents its material as wondrous science instead of sensational effect." Booklist
Includes glossary and bibliographical references

591.56   Behavior relating to life cycle

Bancroft, Henrietta

Animals in winter; by Henrietta Bancroft and Richard G. Van Gelder; illustrated by Helen K. Davie. rev ed. HarperCollins Pubs. 1997 32p il (Let's-read-and-find-out science) lib bdg $15.89; pa $4.95 (k-1)   **591.56**
1. Animal behavior 2. Winter
ISBN 0-06-027158-2 (lib bdg); 0-06-445165-8 (pa)
                                         LC 95-36246
First published 1963
Describes the many different ways animals cope with winter, including migration, hibernation, and food storage
"The words are immediate . . . and the clear, active illustrations will draw new readers to a popular subject." Booklist

Collard, Sneed B., III

Animal dads; [by] Sneed B. Collard III; illustrated by Steve Jenkins. Houghton Mifflin 1997 unp il $15.95; pa $5.95 (k-3)
                                         591.56
1. Animal behavior
ISBN 0-395-83621-2; 0-618-03299-1 (pa)
                                         LC 96-22171
"The text highlights the roles and responsibilities of male parents in the wild, primarily the protection and care of their young." Horn Book Guide
"Each father and his offspring are presented on a single or double-page spread, illustrated with striking, cut-paper collage figures. The large, lifelike creatures are set against backgrounds that are true to each animal's natural habitat." SLJ

Animals asleep; illustrated by Anik McGrory. Houghton Mifflin 2004 unp il $15 (k-3)
                                         591.56
1. Animal behavior 2. Sleep
ISBN 0-618-27697-1
Provides a look at the many different ways in which animals sleep, from a snoozing orangutan to a sleeping whale, as well as facts about each animal pictured.
"A parent or child could read just a few words appearing in large type or dip into the smaller-print paragraph of related information below. . . . McGrory's paintings offer graceful, well-composed depictions of beasts, birds, and butterflies in a series of beautifully lit settings." Booklist

Fraser, Mary Ann

How animal babies stay safe. HarperCollins Pubs. 2002 33p il (Let's-read-and-find-out science) $15.95; lib bdg $15.89; pa $4.95 (k-1)
                                         591.56
1. Animal babies
ISBN 0-06-028803-5; 0-06-028804-3 (lib bdg);
0-06-445211-5 (pa)   LC 00-57267
The author "describes how animal babies are cared for by their parents, including alligator babies who are car-

Fraser, Mary Ann—*Continued*

ried about in their mother's mouth and young elephants who are placed in the middle of the herd for protection. Watercolor illustrations in muted colors help expand the simple text." Horn Book Guide

Hickman, Pamela M.

Animals and their mates; how animals attract, fight for and protect each other; written by Pamela Hickman; illustrated by Pat Stephens. Kids Can Press 2004 40p il $10.95; pa $5.95 (3-5)

591.56

1. Animal behavior

ISBN 1-55337-545-9; 1-55337-546-7 (pa)

"From insects and worms to birds and mammals, this colorfully illustrated introduction considers the who, what, when, where and how of mating. Though not detailed about the mechanics of reproduction, the book discusses matters such as amusing, bizarre, or aggressive courtship behaviors and the reasons certain animals mate at specific times of the year. . . . Tinted with colorful washes, the attractive artwork shows many different animals in a variety of habitats." Booklist

Animals and their young; how animals produce and care for their babies; written by Pamela Hickman; illustrated by Pat Stephens. Kids Can Press 2003 40p il $10.95; pa $5.95 (3-5)

591.56

1. Animal babies

ISBN 1-55337-061-9; 1-55337-062-7 (pa)

The author compares "human babies and animals such as an Atlantic puffin chick, branching out to show how creatures that lay eggs are similar and different, and then . . . [discusses] mammals and marsupials." SLJ

"Young naturalists will appreciate this picture-book-size take on animals' habits. . . . [It is a] clear, colorfully illustrated exposition of animals' reproductive habits." Booklist

Rylant, Cynthia

The journey; stories of migration; illustrated by Lambert Davis. Blue Sky Press 2006 unp il $16.99 (2-4)

591.56

1. Animals—Migration

ISBN 0-590-30717-7   LC 2004-20762

"This large-format book begins with a brief introduction to animal migration before relating six tales of migration. These are . . . narratives relating the migratory habits of six species: the desert locust, the blue whale, the American silver eel, the monarch butterfly, the caribou, and the Arctic tern. . . . Well matched with Rylant's measured prose, Davis' paintings offer clearly delineated, well-composed views of the animals in different stages of growth and habitats." Booklist

Simon, Seymour

Ride the wind; airborne journeys of animals and plants; illustrated by Elsa Warnick. Browndeer Press 1997 unp il $15 (4-6)

591.56

1. Animals—Migration 2. Flight

ISBN 0-15-292887-1   LC 94-29052

"Simon concentrates on the travels of birds in these brief, factual nature stories, but also includes the migration of several insects, spiders, bats, and seeds. . . . The strength of this book is in the lovely paintings, which range from fairly detailed to suggestive, using shapes and colors to impart information." SLJ

Stockdale, Susan

Carry me! animal babies on the move; written and illustrated by Susan Stockdale. 1st ed. Peachtree Publishers 2005 unp il $15.95 (k-2)

591.56

1. Animal behavior

ISBN 1-56145-328-5   LC 2004-16585

"The facts of zoology are both exciting and cuddly in this science picture book with clear, bright acrylic illustrations that show how various animals carry their babies. The settings give the big picture—from the African savannah and Antarctica to South America. Then children can look closely and find animal babies tucked into pouches, clinging to bellies, propped on shoulders, perched on feet, gripped between teeth." Booklist

Includes bibliographical references

Swinburne, Stephen R.

Safe, warm, and snug; illustrated by Jose Aruego and Ariane Dewey. Harcourt Brace & Co. 1999 unp il $16 (k-3)

591.56

1. Animal behavior 2. Animal babies

ISBN 0-15-201734-8   LC 98-9978

"Gulliver books"

Describes how a variety of animals, including kangaroos cockroaches, and pythons, protect their unhatched eggs and young offspring from predators

"Swinburne's informative verses combine with Aruego and Dewey's delightful artwork. . . . Appended with notes offering additional details for each species, this will be useful for primary science units and story hours." Booklist

591.59   Animal communication

Sayre, April Pulley

Secrets of sound; studying the calls and songs of whales, elephants, and birds. Houghton Mifflin 2002 63p il (Scientists in the field) $16 (4 and up)

591.59

1. Animal communication

ISBN 0-618-01514-0   LC 2001-51877

Examines the work of several bioacousticians, scientists who study the sounds made by living creatures, discussing the results and importance of their research

"This fascinating title shows the thrill of scientific discovery up close. . . . Lots of well-edited quotes from the scientists convey their contagious enthusiasm for what they do, and sharp color photos, sound charts, and activity boxes break up the text, making it even more readable." Booklist

Includes glossary and bibliographical references

591.6 Miscellaneous nontaxonomic kinds of animals

Wilkes, Angela
Dangerous creatures; foreword by Steve Leonard. Kingfisher 2003 63p il (Kingfisher knowledge) $11.95 (5 and up) **591.6**
1. Dangerous animals
ISBN 0-7534-5622-2 LC 2003-40063
Describes various kinds of dangerous animals, such as lions, piranhas, killer bees, and vampire bats

591.68 Rare and endangered animals

Collard, Sneed B., III
In the wild; by Sneed B. Collard III. Marshall Cavendish Benchmark 2006 43p il (Science adventures) lib bdg $25.64 (4-6) **591.68**
1. Endangered species 2. Zoos 3. Primates 4. Wildlife conservation
ISBN 0-7614-1955-1
This "explains the vital role zoos are playing in the world by sending their scientists out into the field to save animals such as Africa's great apes and Brazil's golden lion tamarins." Publisher's note
Includes glossary and bibliographical references

Jenkins, Steve
Almost gone; the world's rarest animals. HarperCollins Pubs. 2006 33p il (Let's-read-and-find-out science) $16.99; pa $5.99 **591.68**
1. Rare animals 2. Endangered species
ISBN 0-06-053598-9; 0-06-053600-4 (pa)
LC 2004-30199
The author "shows 21 endangered species, accompanying each image with a few sentences about the animal's habitat, a particular characteristic, and, sometimes, the reason for its endangered status." Booklist
"This engaging title is informative as well as visually stunning." SLJ

Miles, Victoria
Wild science; amazing encounters between animals and people who study them. Raincoast Books 2004 168p il pa $18.95 (5 and up) **591.68**
1. Zoologists 2. Endangered species
ISBN 1-55192-618-0
This offers a "look at 10 wildlife biologists and their work. Each chapter contains sections describing a field experience, biographical data on the scientist, goals set and procedures followed, and pertinent facts on the animals themselves (including classification, habitat, food, and so on). . . . The readable text is conversational in tone, with frequent quotes from the scientists themselves, and is spiced with full-color photos of both animals and biologists." SLJ

Pringle, Laurence P.
Strange animals, new to science; [by] Laurence Pringle. Marshall Cavendish 2002 64p il $16.95 (4 and up) **591.68**
1. Rare animals
ISBN 0-7614-5083-1 LC 2001-28185
"Text covers seventeen unusual animals that have been newly discovered or previously thought to be extinct. Pringle describes their habitats, which are often in remote and inaccessible places, as well as how the animals came to be discovered." Horn Book Guide
"Many of the animals discussed in the short chapters are shown in intriguing color photos. An informative book on an unusual topic that will open kids' minds." Booklist

591.7 Animal ecology, animals characteristic of specific environments

Arnosky, Jim
Crinkleroot's guide to knowing animal habitats. Simon & Schuster Bks. for Young Readers 1997 unp il $14; pa $5.99 (k-3) **591.7**
1. Habitat (Ecology) 2. Animals
ISBN 0-689-80583-7; 0-689-83538-8 (pa)
LC 96-19226
"The white-bearded Crinkleroot and his snake friend take a . . . tour of a series of wildlife habitats including wetlands, grasslands, and woodlands. For each habitat, numerous species of animals are portrayed." Horn Book Guide
"The facts are accurate, and the attractive pictures are clearly labeled." Booklist

Watching desert wildlife. National Geographic Soc. 1998 unp il $15.95 (3-6) **591.7**
1. Desert animals
ISBN 0-7922-7304-4 LC 98-13189
Illustrations and text describe some of the animals the author encountered in the deserts of the American Southwest
"An informative and well-illustrated addition to science units on desert wildlife." Booklist

Wild and swampy; exploring with Jim Arnosky. Morrow Junior Bks. 2000 unp il lib bdg $16.89 (2-4) **591.7**
1. Swamp animals
ISBN 0-688-17120-6 LC 99-52381
Describes and portrays the birds, snakes, and other animals that can be seen in a swamp
"The descriptive language combines nicely with the attractive pictures, making this a wonderful read-aloud. . . . Youngsters are sure to come away from this tour with a new appreciation for swamps and a desire to do some exploring on their own." SLJ

Berger, Melvin

Penguins swim but don't get wet; and other amazing facts about polar animals; [by] Melvin and Gilda Berger. Scholastic 2004 48p il (Speedy facts) pa $7.99 (2-4)   **591.7**

1. Animals—Arctic regions 2. Animals—Antarctica

ISBN 0-439-62535-1

Introduction to polar animals.

"The facts are amazing and entertaining in this title . . . and a wealth of information is presented with clarity and excitement in pages that are packed with color photos and lots of boxed facts." Booklist

Cerullo, Mary M.

The truth about dangerous sea creatures; written by Mary M. Cerullo; photographs by Jeffrey L. Rotman; illustrated by Michael Wertz. Chronicle Books 2003 46p il $15.95 (3-5)   **591.7**

1. Marine animals

ISBN 0-8118-4050-6   LC 2003-828

Contents: Giant squid; Giant octopus; Blue-ringed octopus; Giant clam; Spiny sea urchin; Crown-of-thorns sea star; Jellies; Sea wasp; Surgeonfish; Cone shel; Stonefish; Lionfish; Coral reefs; Damselfish; Sea anemone; Sea snake;- Barracuda; Giant grouper; Puffer fish; Manta ray; Stingray; Torpedo ray; Basking shark and whale shark; Tiger shark; Bull shark; Great white shark

"This book looks at a variety of 'dangerous' sea animals, such as sharks, jellies, and a giant squid, and provides readers with solid information. . . . The amount of text is brief enough to keep the material accessible. Fullcolor photos and childlike drawings add a lot of visual appeal." SLJ

Includes bibliographical references

Cole, Joanna

The magic school bus on the ocean floor; illustrated by Bruce Degen. Scholastic 1992 unp il $15.95; pa $4.99 (2-4)   **591.7**

1. Ocean 2. Marine animals

ISBN 0-590-41430-5; 0-590-41431-5 (pa)

LC 91-17695

Also available Spanish language edition

On another special field trip on the magic school bus, Ms. Frizzle's class learns about the ocean and the different creatures that live there

"Cole's straightforward text explains the main action while energetic (but never hectic), colorful doublespread pictures supply a wealth of detail. . . . A perfect match of text and art, this is another first-class entry in a stellar series that makes science fascinating and fun." Booklist

Earle, Sylvia A.

Sea critters; with photographs by Wolcott Henry. National Geographic Soc. 2000 31p il $16.95 (k-3)   **591.7**

1. Marine animals

ISBN 0-7922-7181-5   LC 00-26875

Examines a variety of animals found in the sea, including jellyfish, worms, scallops, and squids

The author's "style is lively, clear, and sometimes lyrical. . . . Henry's full-page, brilliantly colored photos are astonishing and exquisitely reproduced." Booklist

Grupper, Jonathan

Destination: deep sea. National Geographic Soc. 2000 31p il $16.95 (3-6)   **591.7**

1. Marine animals

ISBN 0-7922-7693-0   LC 00-27643

Describes the physical characteristics, behavior, and habitat of various sea creatures, from familiar crabs to giant whales to tube worms

"Every stunning photograph is a celebration of ocean life." SLJ

Jenkins, Steve

I see a kookaburra! discovering animal habitats around the world; [by] Steve Jenkins & Robin Page. Houghton Mifflin Co 2005 unp il map $16 (k-3)   **591.7**

1. Habitat (Ecology) 2. Animals

ISBN 0-618-50764-7   LC 2004-13188

A pictorial introduction to desert, tide pool, jungle, savana, forest, and pond habitats, with examples of the animals that live in each

"Filled with vibrant colors and palpable textures, the illustrations are breathtaking and give a real sense of the vitality, diversity, and beauty of nature. A first-rate foray into ecology that will encourage readers to explore the world around them." SLJ

Includes bibliographical references

Johnson, Jinny

Simon & Schuster children's guide to sea creatures. Simon & Schuster Bks. for Young Readers 1998 80p il $21.95 (4 and up)

     591.7

1. Marine animals

ISBN 0-689-81534-4   LC 97-8227

Describes the major groups of marine animals, including fish, birds, mammals, and crustaceans

"A beautifully illustrated guide, with a full-color drawing of each animal. . . . The book has enough information to be a useful research tool in the library. The organization, by habitat, is outstanding." Book Rep

Includes glossary

Kratter, Paul

The living rain forest; an animal alphabet. Charlesbridge 2004 unp il $17.95 (k-3)

     591.7

1. Rain forest animals 2. Alphabet

ISBN 1-57091-603-9   LC 2003-3761

Introduces twenty-six rain forest animals from A to Z, providing the name, favorite foods, and unique characteristics of each.

"The uncluttered layouts position the text blocks and the exquisite, photorealistic paintings of the animals against lots of white space. . . . With eye-catching visuals, an engaging theme, and basic information, the book will appeal to a wide age range." Booklist

Lavies, Bianca

Compost critters; text and photographs by Bianca Lavies. Dutton Children's Bks. 1993 unp il $15.99 (4 and up)   **591.7**

1. Compost 2. Soil ecology
ISBN 0-525-44763-6   LC 92-35651

Examines how creatures, from bacteria and mites to millipedes and earthworms, aid in the process of turning compost into humus

"The author is to be commended for her excellent use of basic taxonomy in reference to animals. . . . The writing is very well done, and almost every page has a beautiful full-color photograph." Sci Books Films

Rose, Deborah Lee

Into the A, B, sea; an ocean alphabet; pictures by Steve Jenkins. Scholastic Press 2000 unp il $15.95 (k-3)   **591.7**

1. Marine animals 2. Alphabet
ISBN 0-439-09696-0   LC 99-50034

An alphabet book featuring twenty-six animals found in the ocean and including endnotes giving additional details about each of these sea creatures

"The text reads aloud smoothly, with natural-sounding rhymes and an even pace. The collage artwork is breathtaking. Using a variety of textures and a palette of deep blues and purples, Jenkins captures the grace and vitality of his subjects." SLJ

Swinburne, Stephen R.

The woods scientist; with photographs by Susan C. Morse. Houghton Mifflin 2002 41p il map (Scientists in the field) $16 (4 and up)   **591.7**

1. Morse, Susan 2. Forest animals
ISBN 0-618-04602-X   LC 2002-302

A devoted nature lover and animal tracker, Sue Morse shares her knowledge and love of some of the creatures that inhabit America's woodlands

"The language is immediate, clear, and filled with moment-by-moment observations and well-presented facts. . . . Readers will come away with a much more informed view of wildlife at risk, enriched by Morse's superb color photographs." Booklist

Includes glossary and bibliographical references

Vogel, Carole Garbuny

Ocean wildlife. Franklin Watts 2003 95p il $29.50; pa $12.95 (5 and up)   **591.7**

1. Marine animals
ISBN 0-531-12324-3; 0-531-16681-3 (pa)
                    LC 2003-5302

Discusses how various underwater creatures have adapted to their environment in order to keep themselves safe from dangerous predators

This offers "magnificent, full-color photographs. . . . The clearly written narrative introduces the many creatures that have adapted to the harsh conditions of the ocean. The disastrous effects of overfishing, contamination, and pollution are briefly examined." SLJ

591.9 Treatment of animals by continents, countries, localities

Arnold, Caroline

African animals. Morrow Junior Bks. 1997 48p il $16.95 (k-3)   **591.9**

1. Animals—Africa
ISBN 0-688-14115-3   LC 96-16964

Describes animals of the African plains, forests, jungles, and deserts, and explains how each is able to adapt to its special environment

This offers "superb full-color photography, simple but intelligent language, and excellent organization." SLJ

Australian animals. HarperCollins Pubs. 2000 48p il $15.95; lib bdg $15.89 (k-3)   **591.9**

1. Animals—Australia
ISBN 0-688-16766-7; 0-688-16767-5 (lib bdg)
                    LC 99-52378

Depicts the many animals that live in the diverse habitats of Australia, including forest, grassland, desert, and seacoast

"Well-organized. . . . Koalas, quolls, echidnas, dingoes, bilbies, and penguins are some of the animals introduced. Striking, close-up photos complement the author's comments." SLJ

South American animals. Morrow Junior Bks. 1999 48p il maps $16 (k-3)   **591.9**

1. Animals—South America
ISBN 0-688-15564-2   LC 98-7669

Discusses the variety of animals found in the rainforests, mountains, grasslands, and coastal regions of South America, including the birds, mammals, reptiles, and amphibians

"The photography is exceptional, with many wonderful close-ups, and the text is nicely written." Booklist

Grupper, Jonathan

Destination: Australia. National Geographic Soc. 2000 31p il map $16.95 (3-6)   **591.9**

1. Animals—Australia
ISBN 0-7922-7143-2   LC 99-29944

Describes the characteristics of some of Australia's unusual animals, including the kangaroo, numbat, Perentie lizard, echidna, and lyrebird

"This concise book is made invaluable by its exceptional color photographs and informative text." Sci Books Films

Hooper, Meredith

Antarctic journal; the hidden worlds of Antarctica's animals; illustrated by Lucia deLeiris. National Geographic Soc. 2000 35p il maps $16.95 (3-6)   **591.9**

1. Animals—Antarctica 2. Antarctica
ISBN 0-7922-7188-2   LC 00-35496

"Hooper describes the three-and-a-half months she and deLeiris spent at Palmer Station, Antarctica, observing marine life. . . . The realistic watercolors and black-and-white sketches work well with the detailed text." Horn Book Guide

Lewin, Ted

Elephant quest; [by] Ted & Betsy Lewin. HarperCollins Pubs. 2000 47p il $15.95; lib bdg $15.89 (3-6)   **591.9**

1. Animals—Africa

ISBN 0-688-14111-0; 0-688-14112-9 (lib bdg)

LC 99-55369

Recounts an expedition through the Moremi Wildlife Reserve in Botswana, describing the vegetation and wildlife, and culminating in the sighting of an African elephant herd

"Each encounter is accompanied by glorious watercolors—Betsy Lewin's humorous, emotive sketches and Ted Lewin's full-page paintings. . . . Throughout, a cheerful, humorous tone combines with reverence for the beauty and variety of nature." Horn Book

592   Invertebrates

Blaxland, Beth

Earthworms, leeches, and sea worms; annelids; [by] Beth Blaxland for the Australian Museum. Chelsea House 2003 c2002 32p il (Invertebrates) $18.95 (3-6)   **592**

1. Worms

ISBN 0-7910-6993-1   LC 2002-3182

First published 2002 in Australia

Defines annelids, such as blood-sucking leeches and earthworms, and describes their physical characteristics, life cycles, habitats, senses, food, and means of self-defense

This offers "basic report-worthy information, mesmerizing photographs, and a layout that will please young readers." Booklist

Includes glossary

Dixon, Norma

Lowdown on earthworms. Fitzhenry & Whiteside 2005 32p il $16.95 (3-5)   **592**

1. Worms

ISBN 1-55041-114-8

"This project-oriented study combines basic facts about worm anatomy and behavior with general instructions for building, maintaining, and performing simple experiments with both a 'plastic-bottle wormery'; and a more ambitious compost bin. A mix of color photos and simple paintings offer cutaways views of worms and their burrows, representations of several types of earthworms, and pictures of finished projects." Booklist

Includes bibliographical references

Pfeffer, Wendy

Wiggling worms at work; illustrated by Steve Jenkins. HarperCollins Publishers 2004 33p (Let's-read-and-find-out science) $15.99; lib bdg $16.89; pa $4.99 (k-3)   **592**

1. Worms

ISBN 0-06-028448-X; 0-06-028449-8 (lib bdg); 0-06-445199-2 (pa)

"This book is filled with clear explanations. . . . The concluding activities . . . are important because Jenkins's cut-paper illustrations, while lovely, include only a few anatomical details." Horn Book Guide

593.4   Sponges

Esbensen, Barbara Juster

Sponges are skeletons; illustrated by Holly Keller. HarperCollins Pubs. 1993 32p il (Let's-read-and-find-out science book) $15.95; lib bdg $15.89; pa $4.95 (k-3)   **593.4**

1. Sponges

ISBN 0-06-021034-6; 0-06-021037-0 (lib bdg); 0-06-445184-4 (pa)   LC 92-9740

Explains how sponges are animals that live in the ocean and how they are harvested and used by humans

"The presentation is both lively and informative. . . . The text is simple and thought provoking, and the illustrations are bright and animated." Booklist

593.5   Coelenterates

George, Twig C.

Jellies; the life of jellyfish. Millbrook Press 2000 unp il lib bdg $21.90 (2-4)   **593.5**

1. Jellyfishes

ISBN 0-7613-1659-0   LC 99-48390

Describes the physical characteristics, habits, and natural environment of many species of jellyfish

"Gorgeous full-color underwater photos and a simple, readable text provide a fascinating introduction to some little-known and often unheralded marine organisms." SLJ

King, David C.

Jellyfish; by David C. King. Marshall Cavendish Benchmark 2006 48p il map (Animals, animals) lib bdg $23.64 (3-6)   **593.5**

1. Jellyfishes

ISBN 0-7614-1867-9   LC 2004-21441

Describes the physical characteristics, behavior, and habitat of jellyfish

Includes glossary and bibliographical references

593.6   Anthozoa

Collard, Sneed B., III

One night in the Coral Sea; [by] Sneed B. Collard III; illustrated by Robin Brickman. Charlesbridge 2005 32p il $15.95; pa $6.95 (3-5)   **593.6**

1. Corals 2. Coral reefs and islands

ISBN 1-57091-389-7; 1-57091-390-0 (pa)

LC 2004-3307

"On a single spring night . . . the coral in the Great Barrier Reef releases millions of eggs into the ocean. . . . Collard explains the unique spawning event and provides some background about coral and the sea creatures that share the reef. . . . Whether or not children understand the specifics of fertilization, they will be captivated by Brickman's realistic, astonishingly detailed colored-paper collages of the brilliant underwater world." Booklist

Includes glossary and bibliographical references

593.9 Echinoderms and hemichordates

Blaxland, Beth
Sea stars, sea urchins, and their relatives; echinoderms; [by] Beth Blaxland for the Australian Museum. Chelsea House 2003 c2002 32p il (Invertebrates) $18.95 (3-6)   **593.9**
1. Echinoderms
ISBN 0-7910-6996-6   LC 2002-3177
First published 2002 in Australia
Defines echinoderms, such as sand dollars and crown-of-thorns sea stars, and describes their physical characteristics, life cycles, habitats, sense, food, and means of self-defense
"One or two clear, color photographs complement the text on almost every page; many are close-ups of body parts, with labels. . . . [The text is] well organized." SLJ
Includes glossary

594 Mollusks and mollusk-like animals

Blaxland, Beth
Octopuses, squids, and their relatives; cephalopods; [by] Beth Blaxland for the Australian Museum. Chelsea House 2003 c2002 32p il (Invertebrates) $18.95 (3-6)   **594**
1. Cephalopods
ISBN 0-7910-6992-3   LC 2002-3181
First published 2002 in Australia
Defines cephalopods, such as blue-ringed octopuses and giant squids, and describes their physical characteristics, life cycles, habitats, senses, food, and means of self-defense
This offers "basic report-worthy information, mesmerizing photographs, and a layout that will please young readers." Booklist
Includes glossary

Snails, clams, and their relatives; mollusks; [by] Beth Blaxland for the Australian Museum. Chelsea House 2003 c2002 32p il (Invertebrates) $18.95 (3-6)   **594**
1. Mollusks
ISBN 0-7910-6997-4   LC 2002-3176
First published 2002 in Australia
Defines mollusks, such as land snails and pearl oysters, and describes their physical features, life cycles, habitats, sense, food, and means of self-defense
Includes glossary

Jango-Cohen, Judith
Octopuses. Marshall Cavendish 2004 47p il map (Animals, animals) lib bdg $17.95 (3-6)
                594
1. Octopuses
ISBN 0-7614-1614-5   LC 2003-739
Contents: Introducing octopuses; Dodging danger; A cunning hunter; Batches of hatchlings; Octopuses and us

Describes the physical characteristics, behavior, and habitat of octopuses
This has "excellent, full-color photographs and lively [text] that [brings] these animals to life." SLJ
Includes glossary and bibliographical references

Markle, Sandra
Outside and inside giant squid. Walker & Co. 2003 35p il $16.95; lib bdg $17.85 (2-4)
                594
1. Squids
ISBN 0-8027-8872-6; 0-8027-8873-4 (lib bdg)
                LC 2002-191044
Describes the inner and outer workings of giant squids, enormous deep-sea creatures that have never been seen alive, discussing their diet, anatomy, and reproduction
The book "benefits from its color photos. The volume is a treasure trove of facts sure to intrigue budding biologists and the merely curious to an equal degree." Booklist
Includes glossary

Redmond, Shirley-Raye
Tentacles! tales of the giant squid; illustrated by Bryn Barnard. Random House 2003 44p il $11.99; pa $3.99 (1-3)   **594**
1. Squids
ISBN 0-375-91307-6; 0-375-81307-1 (pa)
                LC 2002-10238
"Step into reading"
Describes some of the exaggerated stories that have been told about giant squids and also what scientists have learned about their real physical characteristics and behavior
"An excellent choice to introduce early elementary students to nonfiction titles." Booklist

595.3 Crustaceans

Blaxland, Beth
Crabs, crayfishes, and their relatives; crustaceans; [by] Beth Blaxland for the Australian Museum. Chelsea House 2003 c2002 32p il (Invertebrates) $18.95 (3-6)   **595.3**
1. Crustaceans
ISBN 0-7910-6994-X   LC 2002-3178
First published 2002 in Australia
Defines crustaceans, such as slaters and freshwater crayfishes, and describes their physical characteristics, life cycles, habitats, senses, food and means of self-defense
"One or two clear, color photographs complement the text on almost every page. . . . [The text is] well organized." SLJ
Includes glossary

Greenaway, Theresa
Crabs; [illustrated by Colin Newman] Raintree Steck-Vaughn Pubs. 2001 48p il (Secret world of) lib bdg $18.98 (4 and up)   **595.3**
1. Crabs
ISBN 0-7398-3506-8   LC 00-62833

Greenaway, Theresa—*Continued*

This describes the anatomy, habits, and life cycle of crabs and their place in the ecosystem

"The well-designed pages consist of text broken up with blocks of related facts and colorful, close-up photographs and labeled drawings. . . . [This offers] a balance of research material and interest-piquing detail." SLJ

Includes glossary and bibliographical references

Himmelman, John

A pill bug's life; written and illustrated by John Himmelman. Children's Press 1999 unp il (Nature upclose) lib bdg $24; pa $6.95 (k-2)

595.3

1. Woodlice

ISBN 0-516-21165-X (lib bdg); 0-516-26798-1 (pa)

LC 99-30137

Describes the daily activities and life cycle of a pill bug or wood louse

"Each page offers a large, appealing illustration, drawing youngsters into the action." SLJ

Includes glossary

Pascoe, Elaine

Crabs; text by Elaine Pascoe; photographs by Dwight Kuhn. Blackbirch Press 2005 48p (Nature close-up) $23.70 (4 and up)   **595.3**

1. Crabs

ISBN 1-4103-0535-X

Describes the characteristics, habitat and life cycle of crabs, and includes learning activites

Includes glossary and bibliographical references

Sill, Cathryn P.

About crustaceans; a guide for children; written by Cathryn Sill; illustrated by John Sill. 1st ed. Peachtree Publishers 2004 unp il $15.95 (k-2)

595.3

1. Crustaceans

ISBN 1-56145-301-3   LC 2003-16838

Describes the anatomy, behavior, and habitat of various crustaceans, including the lobster, crab, and shrimp.

"Done in bright watercolors, the illustrations give a sense of these creatures' different habitats. . . . This is an excellent example of easy nonfiction, perfect for beginning readers or for sharing aloud with budding naturalists." SLJ

Tokuda, Yukihisa

I'm a pill bug; written by Yukihisa Tokuda; illustrated by Kiyoshi Takahashi. Kane/Miller 2006 unp il pa $7.95 (k-2)   **595.3**

1. Woodlice

ISBN 1-929132-95-6

"In this picture book, a pill bug narrates a fascinating account of life among his humble yet admirable fellow crustaceans. In an easy-to-follow, conversational style, he explains what pill bugs eat and excrete, why they live near people, how they protect themselves against predators, why they shed and then eat their shells . . . how they reproduce, and more. . . . The lucid, matter-of-fact text answers the main questions children may have about the critters as well as some they might not have thought to ask. Meanwhile, handsome cut-paper collages recreate the pill bugs' world in realistic yet simplified terms." Booklist

595.4　Chelicerates. Arachnids

Allman, Toney

From spider webs to man-made silk. KidHaven 2005 48p il (Imitating nature) lib bdg $17.96 (4 and up)   **595.4**

1. Spiders 2. Silk

ISBN 0-7377-3124-9

"An introductory chapter gives background on spider physiology and web building. Later chapters describe how scientists' efforts have resulted in a silk approximation that is better described as goat-made than man-made. By successfully splicing spider silk-producing genes into goats, researchers have created an animal whose milk contains a substance similar to spider silk's raw material. . . . A final section discusses the uses for stronger-than-steel spider silk. The picture-book format features diagrams and photos, sometimes microscopic views to illustrate the science. . . . [An] intriguing, useful volume." Booklist

Includes glossary and bibliographical references

Berger, Melvin

Spinning spiders; illustrated by S.D. Schindler. HarperCollins Pubs. 2003 33p il (Let's-read-and-find-out science) $15.99; lib bdg $16.89; pa $4.99 (k-3)   **595.4**

1. Spiders

ISBN 0-06-028696-2; 0-06-028697-0 (lib bdg); 0-06-445207-7 (pa)   LC 2001-39507

Describes the characteristics of spiders and the methods they use to trap their prey in webs

Written "in a clear, easy-to-read style. . . . Detailed, full-color illustrations, often on spreads, highlight the well-organized text." SLJ

Facklam, Margery

Spiders and their web sites; illustrated by Alan Male. Little, Brown 2001 32p il $15.95 (3-6)

595.4

1. Spiders

ISBN 0-316-27329-5   LC 97-43822

Illustrations and text provide a close-up look at the physical characteristics and habits of twelve different spiders and daddy-longlegs

The author "briskly introduces a wealth of information on the architectronics and psychology of web design and the physical characteristics of spiders, never losing sight of her target audience. . . . Male's full-color illustrations add lavish, sometimes chilling details." Booklist

Includes glossary and bibliographical references

Kallen, Stuart A.

Spiders. KidHaven Press 2002 48p il (Nature's predators) $23.70 (4 and up)   **595.4**

1. Spiders

ISBN 0-7377-0630-9   LC 00-12810

Kallen, Stuart A.—*Continued*

This describes how spiders hunt, catch, and devour food

This is "well-written, well-organized, [and] thorough." Booklist

Includes bibliographical references

Markle, Sandra

Spiders; biggest! littlest! photographs by Simon Pollard. 1st ed. Boyds Mills Press 2004 unp il $15.95 (k-3)   **595.4**
1. Spiders
ISBN 1-59078-190-2   LC 2003-26794

This "focuses on seven spiders and explains why their size gives them an edge over other species. . . . The book also incorporates information about the arachnid's role as predator, its use of venom, molting, feeding methods, reproduction, etc. . . . Amazingly detailed, closeup, color photographs appear on every spread. . . . Well organized and clearly written, this engaging work offers important insights into spider physiology not present in many other overviews." SLJ

Montgomery, Sy

The tarantula scientist; text by Sy Montgomery; photographs by Nic Bishop. Houghton Mifflin Co 2004 80p il map (Scientists in the field) $18 (4 and up)   **595.4**
1. Marshall, Samuel D. 2. Tarantulas
ISBN 0-618-14799-3   LC 2003-20125

Describes the research that Samuel Marshall and his students are doing on tarantulas, including the largest spider on earth, the Goliath birdeating tarantula

"Enthusiasm for the subject and respect for both Marshall and his eight-legged subjects come through on every page of the clear, informative, and even occasionally humorous text. Bishop's full-color photos . . . are amazing." Booklist

Includes glossary and bibliographical references

Murawski, Darlyne

Spiders and their webs; [by] Darlyne A. Murawski. National Geographic 2004 31p il $16.95 (2-5)   **595.4**
1. Spiders
ISBN 0-7922-6979-9   LC 2004-397

This describes nine species of spiders and how they make and use webs

"Even fainthearted arachnophobes will appreciate this gallery of spider profiles featuring full-color, telephoto views. . . . Murawski writes about her subjects with an awe and a reverence that will encourage reluctant children to move beyond spiders' creepy reputation to their fascinating features." Booklist

Includes bibliographical references

Ross, Michael Elsohn

Spiderology; photographs by Brian Grogan; illustrations by Darren Erickson. Carolrhoda Bks. 2000 48p il (Backyard buddies) lib bdg $19.93; pa $6.95 (3-6)   **595.4**
1. Spiders
ISBN 1-57505-387-X (lib bdg); 1-57505-438-8 (pa)
LC 98-51406

Describes the physical characteristics and habits of spiders and provides instructions for finding, collecting, and keeping spiders

"Clear color photographs and black-and-white diagrams enhance the text. . . . The experiments . . . are creative and easily replicable for a classroom demonstration or science fair project." Booklist

Includes glossary

Sill, Cathryn P.

About arachnids; a guide for children; illustrated by John Sill. Peachtree Pubs. 2003 unp il $15.95 (k-3)   **595.4**
1. Spiders
ISBN 1-56145-038-3   LC 2002-11739

An introduction to the physical characteristics, behavior, and life cycle of arachnids

"This clearly written presentation offers the basic facts about arachnids in very simple language, enhanced by excellent, large-scale paintings." Booklist

Simon, Seymour

Spiders. HarperCollins 2003 unp il $15.99; lib bdg $16.89 (4 and up)   **595.4**
1. Spiders
ISBN 0-06-028391-2; 0-06-028392-0 (lib bdg)
LC 2002-14922

An introduction to the physical characteristics, behavior, and life cycle of different kinds of spiders

"In his now familiar picture-book format that pairs incredible photographs with graceful, clear prose, Simon provides a wealth of information." Booklist

595.6   Myriapods

Blaxland, Beth

Centipedes, millipedes, and their relatives; myriapods; [by] Beth Blaxland for the Australian Museum. Chelsea House 2003 c2002 32p il (Invertebrates) $18.95 (3-6)   **595.6**
1. Millipedes 2. Centipedes
ISBN 0-7910-6995-8   LC 2002-3179

First published 2002 in Australia

Defines myriapods, such as centipedes and three groups of millipedes, and describes their physical characteristics, life cycles, habitats, senses, food, and means of self-defense

"One or two clear, color photographs complement the text on almost every page. . . . [The text is] well organized." SLJ

Includes glossary

Povey, Karen D.

Centipede; [by] Karen Povey. KidHaven Press 2004 32p il (Bugs) $22.45 (3-5) **595.6**

1. Centipedes

ISBN 0-7377-1766-1   LC 2003-15274

Describes the physical characteristics, behavior, and habitat of centipedes.

Ross, Michael Elsohn

Millipedeology; photographs by Brian Grogan; illustrations by Darren Erickson. Carolrhoda Bks. 2000 48p il (Backyard buddies) lib bdg $19.93; pa $6.95 (3-6) **595.6**

1. Millipedes

ISBN 1-57505-398-5 (lib bdg); 1-575505-436-1 (pa)   LC 99-35398

Describes the physical characteristics and behavior of the millipede and presents millipede-related activities

"Illustrated with diagrams, cartoons, and color photos." Horn Book Guide

Includes glossary

595.7   Insects

Berger, Melvin

Chirping crickets; illustrated by Megan Lloyd. HarperCollins Pubs. 1998 32p il (Let's-read-and-find-out science) $15.95; lib bdg $15.89; pa $4.95 (k-3) **595.7**

1. Crickets

ISBN 0-06-024961-7; 0-06-024962-5 (lib bdg); 0-06-445180-1 (pa)   LC 96-51661

Describes the physical characteristics, behavior, and life cycle of crickets while giving particular emphasis to how they chirp

"Clear and detailed, the ink-and-watercolor artwork is often visually striking as well as educationally sound. . . . A well-rounded introduction." Booklist

How do flies walk upside down? questions and answers about insects; by Melvin and Gilda Berger; illustrated by Jim Effler. Scholastic Ref. 1999 48p il (Scholastic question and answer series) $12.95; pa $5.95 (3-5) **595.7**

1. Insects

ISBN 0-590-13089-7; 0-439-08572-1 (pa)   LC 98-18457

A series of questions and answers provides information about the physical characteristics, senses, eating habits, life cycles, and behavior of different insects

"The colorful illustrations are detailed, vivid, and well conceived. . . . Attractive enough for browsers, yet solid enough to help support the curriculum." Booklist

Blobaum, Cindy

Insectigation! 40 hands-on activities to explore the insect world; [by] Cindy Blobaum. Chicago Review Press 2005 133p il pa $12.95 (3-6) **595.7**

1. Insects

ISBN 1-55652-568-0

"Raising mealworms, testing the visual acuity of bees, setting up a watering hole for butterflies—these are just a few of the 40 activities included in this earnest introduction to entomology. Each of eight chapters focuses on a different topic, such as physical and behavioral characteristics; metamorphosis; communication; methods to attract, collect and keep insects, etc. . . . Clear line drawings, diagrams of body parts and project materials, plus the occasional black-and-white photograph are found on almost every page. . . . The text is clearly written and well organized." SLJ

Includes bibliographical references

Cole, Joanna

The magic school bus inside a beehive; illustrated by Bruce Degen. Scholastic 1996 47p $15.95; pa $4.99 (2-4) **595.7**

1. Bees

ISBN 0-590-44684-3; 0-590-025721-8 (pa)   LC 95-38288

Ms. Frizzle "introduces her class to the insect kingdom via an excursion through a honeybee hive. Garbed in bee costumes complete with antennae, and sprayed with the proper pheromones, the students are accepted by the workers and allowed to perform such chores as foraging for nectar and pollen, building honeycombs, making honey, and feeding larvae. . . . A plethora of pseudo school reports provide additional information on the topic. Degen's colorful and amusing cartoons heighten the adventures. Clearly written and well organized." SLJ

Collard, Sneed B., III

A firefly biologist at work; [by] Sneed B. Collard III. Watts 2001 48p il map lib bdg $22.50; pa $6.95 (4-6) **595.7**

1. Case, James F., 1926- 2. Biologists 3. Fireflies

ISBN 0-531-11798-7 (lib bdg); 0-531-16568-X (pa)   LC 00-29622

"A Wildlife Conservation Society book"

"Collard follows the career of a biologist, sharing . . . information about fireflies as well as some of the difficulties of field research and the personality traits (curiosity, passion, etc.) common to most successful scientists." Booklist

"The simply written text is both entertaining and informative." Sci Books Films

Includes glossary and bibliographical references

Derzipilski, Kathleen

Beetles; by Kathleen Derzipilski. Benchmark Books 2004 46p il map (Animals, animals) lib bdg $25.64 (3-6) **595.7**

1. Beetles

ISBN 0-7614-1751-6   LC 2003-24841

Contents: What is a beetle; The beetle's body; How beetles grow; How beetles live; Beetles and people

Derzipilski, Kathleen—*Continued*
This describes the life cycles and characteristics of beetles, illustrated with color photographs
Includes glossary and bibliographical references

Dorros, Arthur
Ant cities; written and illustrated by Arthur Dorros. Crowell 1987 28p il (Let's-read-and-find-out science book) $11.50; lib bdg $11.89 (k-3)   **595.7**
1. Ants
ISBN 0-690-04568-9; 0-690-04570-0 (lib bdg)
LC 85-48244
"Using harvester ants as a basic example, Dorros shows how the insects build tunnels with rooms for different functions and how workers, queens, and males have distinct roles in the ant hill. Along the way, she works in details of food and reproduction, ending with descriptions of other kinds of ants and suggestions for ways to observe them (including instructions for making an ant farm). The text is simple without becoming choppy, the full-color illustrations are inviting as well as informative." Bull Cent Child Books

Froman, Nan
What's that bug? illustrated by Julian Mulock. Little, Brown 2001 31p il $16.95 (4-6)
595.7
1. Insects
ISBN 0-316-29692-9
"A Madison Press book"
"Nine familiar orders of insects are depicted in this overview. Each order of insect appears on a double-page spread that contains detailed illustrations and important facts." Horn Book Guide
"Excellent scientific illustrations by Julian Mulock are what kids will see first. Their extraordinary details will attract not only children curious about bugs but also budding entomologists. . . . The text is both informal and informative." Booklist
Includes bibliographical references

Gibbons, Gail
Monarch butterfly. Holiday House 1989 unp il $16.95; pa $6.95 (k-3)   **595.7**
1. Butterflies
ISBN 0-8234-0773-X; 0-8234-0909-0 (pa)
LC 89-1880
"Large-scale paintings, clearly detailed, and a simply written, sequential text describe the life cycle of the monarch butterfly and its migratory patterns. This is Gibbons at her best, providing information in a text that is cohesive and comprehensible." Bull Cent Child Books

Glaser, Linda
Brilliant bees; illustrated by Gay W. Holland. Millbrook Press 2003 unp il lib bdg $22.90; pa $8.95 (k-3)   **595.7**
1. Bees
ISBN 0-7613-2670-7 (lib bdg); 0-7613-1943-3 (pa)
LC 2001-8630

Simple text and illustrations describe the physical characteristics, habits, and life cycle of the honey bee.
This "features excellent, large-scale pictures in colored pencil. Printed in uneven lines that look like verse, the first-person, large-type text frequently includes poetic rhythm and rhyme." Booklist

Heiligman, Deborah
From caterpillar to butterfly; illustrated by Bari Weissman. HarperCollins Pubs. 1996 31p il (Let's-read-and-find-out science) $15.95; lib bdg $15.89; pa $4.95 (k-1)   **595.7**
1. Butterflies 2. Caterpillars
ISBN 0-06-024264-7; 0-06-024268-X (lib bdg); 0-06-445129-1 (pa)   LC 93-39055
Young children observe the metamorphosis of a caterpillar into a butterfly in a jar in their classroom
"Pen-and-ink and watercolor illustrations create a cheerful setting. . . . A small collection of butterflies commonly found in most parts of the U.S. and a list of addresses of butterfly centers are appended. An inviting book that young children can relate to and one that teachers will find valuable to support nature-study projects." SLJ

Honeybees; illustrated by Carla Golembe. National Geographic Soc. 2002 31p il (Jump into science) $16.95 (k-3)   **595.7**
1. Bees
ISBN 0-7922-6678-1   LC 2001-1717
"Heiligman focuses on metamorphosis and the roster of sequential duties that a worker bee experiences in her six-week life—cleaning her cell, nursing larva, tending the honeycomb, grooming the queen, guarding the hive, foraging for nectar and pollen." Bull Cent Child Books
"This well-written, detailed description of the honeybee is given added appeal by the colorful, full-page gouache illustrations." Horn Book Guide

Hipp, Andrew
Orchid mantises; by Andrew Hipp. 1st ed. PowerKids Press 2003 24p il (Really wild life of insects) lib bdg $18.75 (3-5)   **595.7**
1. Insects
ISBN 0-8239-6239-3   LC 2001-4847
Describes the physical characteristics, behavior, life cycle, protective devices, and relatives of the orchid mantis.
"In most sections, a full-page, sharp, color closeup photograph of the insect appears opposite the text. . . . well organized and clearly written." SLJ
Includes bibliographical references

Peanut-head bugs; [by] Andrew Hipp. PowerKids Press 2003 24p il (Really wild life of insects) lib bdg $18.75 (3-5)   **595.7**
1. Insects
ISBN 0-8239-6242-3   LC 2001-6656
Contents: A bug with many names; Throat-beaked bugs; Plantsuckers and prey; What's in that head?; Lizard or lunch?; Surprise!; Young bugs; Growing up; Mating and laying eggs; Peanut-head myths

Hipp, Andrew—Continued

Introduces the insects of the Fulgoridae family, which live on the sap of Central and South American simaruba trees and are sometimes called peanut-head bugs.

"In most sections, a full-page, sharp, color closeup photograph of the insect appears opposite the text. . . . [This is] well organized and clearly written." SLJ

Includes bibliographical references

Insects and spiders of the world. Marshall Cavendish 2003 11v il map set $329.95 (5 and up)   **595.7**

1. Insects 2. Spiders

ISBN 0-7614-7334-3   LC 2001-28882

"Nearly 200 entries are arranged alphabetically and range in length from one to six pages. Each entry is color coded into one of four categories: insects (Ant, Bedbug, Termite); spiders (Black widow, House spider, Tarantula); other arthropods (Centipede, Millipede, Scorpion); and overview (Arachnology, Communication, Metamorphosis). Many articles include a 'Key Facts' box with basic details concerning habitat, breeding, and so on as well as a distribution map that indicates where the insect or spider lives in the world. . . . Entries are further enhanced by diagrams, illustrations, and vivid color photographs." Booklist

Includes bibliographical references

Jackson, Donna M.

The bug scientists; by Donna M. Jackson. Houghton Mifflin 2002 48p il (Scientists in the field) $16 (4 and up)   **595.7**

1. Insects

ISBN 0-618-10868-8   LC 2001-39256

Bug scientists, called entomologists, present information on insects and explain how they use that information in their work

"The much-maligned world of insects becomes fascinating in this . . . entry in the excellent Scientists in the Field series. . . . The highly readable text weaves in plenty of science. . . . With its crisp photos and lively story angles and language, this is sure to attract young readers." Booklist

Includes glossary and bibliographical references

Johnson, Jinny

Simon & Schuster children's guide to insects and spiders. Simon & Schuster Bks. for Young Readers 1996 80p il $19.95 (4 and up)

595.7

1. Insects 2. Spiders

ISBN 0-689-81163-2   LC 96-27600

Provides an introduction to more than 100 insects and arachnids, giving general information about family characteristics and habits, and more specific facts about some species

"Crisp and well-designed, this is an inviting visual introduction to insects and arachnids." Booklist

Includes glossary

Kite, L. Patricia

Insect facts and folklore. Millbrook Press 2001 80p il lib bdg $27.90 (4 and up)   **595.7**

1. Insects

ISBN 0-7613-1822-4   LC 00-50074

The author investigates "various insects ranging from beetles to butterflies, fleas to fireflies." SLJ

"Packed with more than standard statistics about size, food, and nests, this volume offers a bounty of fascinating facts and intriguing lore." Booklist

Includes bibliographical references

Latimer, Jonathan P.

Butterflies; [by] Jonathan P. Latimer, Karen Stray Nolting; illustrations by Amy Bartlett Wright; foreword by Virginia Marie Peterson. Houghton Mifflin 2000 48p il (Peterson field guides for young naturalists) $15; pa $5.95 (4 and up)   **595.7**

1. Butterflies

ISBN 0-395-97943-9; 0-395-97944-7 (pa)

LC 99-38605

A guide to help identify various butterflies, using the Peterson System of identification

Caterpillars; [by] Jonathan P. Latimer, Karen Stray Nolting; illustrations by Amy Bartlett Wright; foreword by Virginia Marie Peterson. Houghton Mifflin 2000 48p il (Peterson field guides for young naturalists) $15; pa $5.95 (4 and up)   **595.7**

1. Caterpillars

ISBN 0-395-97942-0; 0-395-97945-5 (pa)

LC 99-38944

Describes the physical characteristics, behavior, and habitat of a variety of caterpillars, arranged by the categories "Smooth," "Bumpy," "Sluglike," "Horned," "Hairy," "Bristly," and "Spiny"

Lerner, Carol

Butterflies in the garden. HarperCollins Pubs. 2002 29p il $16.95; lib bdg $16.89 (k-3)

595.7

1. Butterflies

ISBN 0-688-17478-7; 0-688-17479-5 (lib bdg)

LC 00-61408

The "text describes how butterflies eat, introduces distinguishing characteristics of a few species, gives a basic overview of the life cycle from caterpillar to butterfly, and describes plants that attact butterflies to the garden." Booklist

This "is very attractive. Watercolors done in spring shades rest neatly in precise outlines of lovely butterflies and flowers. . . . The text . . . is lively and clear." SLJ

Llewellyn, Claire

Butterfly; illustrated by Simon Mendez. NorthWord Press 2003 23p il (Starting life) $16.95 (k-3)   **595.7**

1. Butterflies

ISBN 1-55971-868-4   LC 2003-40974

Llewellyn, Claire—*Continued*
Describes the physical characteristics and behavior of butterflies, including their development from egg to caterpillar to adult
This has "bold, bright, full-page paintings throughout. . . . The interesting page sizes and full-page illustrations will appeal to young naturalists." SLJ
Includes glossary

Markle, Sandra
Outside and inside killer bees; [by] Sandra Markle. Walker & Company 2004 37p il $17.95; lib bdg $18.85 (2-4)   **595.7**
1. Bees
ISBN 0-8027-8906-4; 0-8027-8907-2 (lib bdg)
                                LC 2003-70500
The author presents "factual information about bee anatomy, social behavior, honey production, and the like. . . . She imbeds these facts in a deeper examination of the greater ecological topic of invasive species." Horn Book
"The subject of this photo-essay . . . is highly dramatic, and the [book has an] attractive design, with big, clear, full-color pictures and spacious type. . . . This is . . . an excellent introduction to the excitement of entomology." Booklist

Merrick, Patrick
Cockroaches. Child's World 2003 32p il (Naturebooks) lib bdg $25.64 (1-4)   **595.7**
1. Cockroaches
ISBN 1-56766-206-4   LC 2002-151471
Describes the physical characteristics, behavior, habitat, and life cycle of cockroaches
This gives "children a firm grasp of the basics. . . . Most pages of text alternate with large, sharp, color closeup photographs . . . [The text is] succinctly written and well organized." SLJ

Micucci, Charles
The life and times of the ant. Houghton Mifflin 2003 32p il $16 (2-4)   **595.7**
1. Ants
ISBN 0-618-00559-5   LC 2002-478
Describes the evolution, physical characteristics, behavior, and social nature of ants
This "offers succinct text and an impressive amount of information presented in an attractive, picture-book format." Booklist
Includes bibliographical references

The life and times of the honeybee. Ticknor & Fields Bks. for Young Readers 1995 32p il pa $5.95 hardcover o.p. (2-4)   **595.7**
1. Bees 2. Honey
ISBN 0-395-86139-X (pa)   LC 93-8135
The author "covers everything from distribution, reproduction, behavior, and honey manufacture to the honeybee's niche in history." Booklist
"The multitude of original watercolors bring the subject to life, provide a sense of scale and amplify the text. . . . A must acquisition for a library." Appraisal

Miller, Sara Swan
Ants, bees, and wasps of North America. Watts 2003 47p il (Animals in order) lib bdg $25; pa $6.95 (4-6)   **595.7**
1. Ants 2. Bees 3. Wasps
ISBN 0-531-12244-1 (lib bdg); 0-531-16658-9 (pa)
                                LC 2002-1731
Introduces the different animals in the hymenoptra order, their similarities and differences, environments in which they live, and how to observe them
This book makes "fascinating reading. . . . Photographs are glorious." Libr Media Connect
Includes glossary and bibliographical references

Noonan, Diana
The butterfly. Chelsea House 2003 32p il (Life cycles) $13.95 (2-4)   **595.7**
1. Butterflies
ISBN 0-7910-6963-X   LC 2002-28
An introduction to the physical characteristics, behavior, and life cycle of the insect that changes from an egg to a caterpillar to a butterfly
"Clear, colorful, and striking photographs accompany the simple yet educational text." Libr Media Connect
Includes glossary

Pascoe, Elaine
Bugs; text by Elaine Pascoe; photographs by Dwight Kuhn. Blackbirch Press 2004 48p il (Nature close-up) $23.70 (4 and up)
                                595.7
1. Insects
ISBN 1-56711-458-X   LC 2003-7098
Contents: The Bug Club: X marks the bug, A bug's life, Plant eaters and predators, Water dwellers, Bugs and people, Bogus bugs; Collecting and caring for bugs: Milkweed bugs, A home for bugs, Raising Milkweed bugs; Investigating bugs: Do Ambush bugs like their prey dead or alive? Do Milkweed bugs grow faster in warm or cold temperatures? How picky are wild Milkweed bugs about their food? Will mail-order Milkweed bugs eat Milkweed or other plant foods? More activities with bugs, Results and conclusions
This describes such insects as milkweed bugs, water bugs, squash bugs, bed bugs, stink bugs, and assassin bugs, with suggestions for collecting and investigating them
Includes glossary and bibliographical references

Posada, Mia
Ladybugs; red, fiery, and bright; written and illustrated by Mia Posada. Carolrhoda Bks. 2002 unp il $15.95 (k-2)   **595.7**
1. Ladybugs
ISBN 0-87614-334-6
"The description of the life cycle of ladybugs begins with fully developed insects . . . and progresses through a . . . study of behavior, birth, and development." SLJ
"A colorful description of the ladybug's life cycle, depicted in beautiful illustrations and expressed in poetic verse." Soc Educ

Pringle, Laurence P.

An extraordinary life; the story of a monarch butterfly; by Laurence Pringle; paintings by Bob Marstall. Orchard Bks. 1997 64p il $18.95 (5 and up)   **595.7**

1. Butterflies

ISBN 0-531-30002-1   LC 96-31482

Introduces the life cycle, feeding habits, migration, predators, and mating of the monarch butterfly through the observation of one particular monarch named Danaus

"The narrative is scientifically sound and includes information from the most recent research. . . . The attractive, oversized book is lavished with realistic, full-color paintings." SLJ

Includes bibliographical references

Rockwell, Anne F.

Becoming butterflies; by Anne Rockwell; pictures by Megan Halsey. Walker & Co. 2002 unp il map $15.95; lib bdg $16.85 (k-2)   **595.7**

1. Butterflies

ISBN 0-8027-8797-5; 0-8027-8798-3 (lib bdg)
      LC 2001-26935

A class observes the various stages caterpillars go through to become butterflies

"Without an unneccessary word of explanation, the text makes clear the science of metamorphosis, and leavens the story with the humor of the children's comments. The illustrations are watercolors with pieces of cut paper layered to give depth." SLJ

Bugs are insects; by Anne Rockwell; illustrated by Steve Jenkins. HarperCollins Pubs. 2001 29p il (Let's-read-and-find-out science) $15.95; lib bdg $15.89; pa $4.95 (k-3)   **595.7**

1. Insects

ISBN 0-06-028568-0; 0-06-028569-9 (lib bdg);
0-06-445203-4 (pa)   LC 99-39846

Introduces common backyard insects and explains the basic characteristics of these creatures

This is a "well-written and informative book. . . . The collage illustrations are beautifully rendered with layered colored papers of a variety of textures that add both depth and details to the creatures." SLJ

Honey in a hive; by Anne Rockwell; illustrated by S. D. Schindler. HarperCollinsPublishers 2005 33p il (Let's-read-and-find-out science) $15.99; lib bdg $16.89; pa $4.99 (k-3)   **595.7**

1. Bees 2. Honey

ISBN 0-06-028566-4; 0-06-028567-2 (lib bdg);
0-06-445204-2 (pa)   LC 2003-10357

An introduction to the behavior and life cycle of honeybees, with particular emphasis on the production of honey.

"Schindler's realistic artwork is both colorful and nicely matched to the text. . . . This attractive introduction to honey production will serve students well." Booklist

Sayre, April Pulley

Army ant parade; illustrated by Rick Chrustowski. Holt & Co. 2002 unp il $16.95 (k-3)   **595.7**

1. Ants

ISBN 0-8050-6353-6   LC 2001-285

This book describes a swarm of army ants in the Panamanian rain forest

"Chrustowski's close-up, realistic illustrations, comprised of multiple layers of colored pencil over watercolor wash, are vivid and effective. . . . Eye-catching and clearly written." SLJ

The bumblebee queen; illustrated by Patricia J. Wynne. Charlesbridge Pub 2005 unp il $14.95 (1-3)   **595.7**

1. Bees

ISBN 1-57091-362-5   LC 2004-3305

This "describes the life of a typical North American bumblebee queen." Publisher's note

"Engaging watercolors keep time with a simple, easy-to-read text. . . . Gentle, informative, and appealing." SLJ

Includes bibliographical references

Schwabacher, Martin

Butterflies. Benchmark Bks. 2004 45p il map (Animals, animals) lib bdg $17.95 (3-6)   **595.7**

1. Butterflies

ISBN 0-7614-1618-8   LC 2003-3627

Contents: Beautiful butterflies; The butterfly family; The big change; Butterfly enemies; Butterflies and people

This describes the life cycles and characteristics of butterflies, illustrated with color photographs

Includes glossary and bibliographical references

Siy, Alexandra

Mosquito bite; [by] Alexandra Siy & Dennis Kunkel. Charlesbridge 2005 32p il $15.95; pa $6.95 (3-5)   **595.7**

1. Mosquitoes

ISBN 1-57091-591-1 (lib bdg); 1-57091-592-X (pa)
      LC 2004-18959

"Black-and-white photographs of an evening game of hide-and-seek are interspersed with stunning color-enhanced microphotographs that record the life cycle of another seeker: a female Culex pipiens mosquito looking for a meal. . . . This title is fascinating for its photography and the informative text and captions." SLJ

Stewart, Melissa

Maggots, grubs, and more; the secret lives of young insects; [by] Melissa Stewart. Millbrook Press 2003 63p il lib bdg $24.90 (4-6)   **595.7**

1. Insects

ISBN 0-7613-2658-8   LC 2002-13965

Contents: Two kinds of young insects; A closer look at nymphs; Dragonflies and damselflies; Grasshoppers and crickets; Mantids and walkingsticks; Cockroaches

Stewart, Melissa—*Continued*

and termites; True bugs; Cicadas and aphids; A closer look at larvae; Flies and mosquitoes; Beetles; Bees, wasps, and ants

"The life cycles of close to two dozen kinds of insects are examined here. . . . The text is meticulous in its descriptions of individual species' life cycles. . . . Sharp color photographs accompany the text on about every other page. . . . This [is a] lucid, well-organized introduction." SLJ

Includes bibliographical references

Swinburne, Stephen R.

Wings of light; the migration of the yellow butterfly; [by] Stephen R. Swinburne; illustrated by Bruce Hiscock. 1st ed. Boyds Mills Press 2006 unp il map $15.95 (k-3)   595.7

1. Butterflies—Migration

ISBN 1-59078-082-5   LC 2005021140

"A yellow butterfly joins others of its species in a migratory flight. Beginning in a rain forest on the Yucatan Peninsula, the butterflies (cloudless sulphurs) cross the Gulf of Mexico and scatter throughout the southern states, with the featured butterfly, along with a few others, continuing up the East Coast to Vermont. . . . Swinburne makes the story compelling by weaving sensory details into the facts. Hiscock's large-scale watercolor paintings capture the qualities of light in different environments as well as the beauty of nature. . . . An excellent map shows the migratory path. A well-written and beautifully illustrated picture book." Booklist

VanCleave, Janice Pratt

Janice VanCleave's insects and spiders; mind-boggling experiments you can turn into science fair projects. Wiley 1998 92p il (Spectacular science projects series) pa $10.95 (4 and up)   595.7

1. Insects 2. Spiders 3. Science projects 4. Science—Experiments

ISBN 0-471-16396-1   LC 97-12595

Presents facts about insects and spiders and includes experiments, projects, and activities related to each topic

"This title is chock-full of meaningful, but not difficult, projects. . . . Clear line drawings illustrate the text on almost every page. . . . The lucid text is well organized and liberally sprinkled with safety warnings." SLJ

Includes glossary and bibliographical references

Janice VanCleave's play and find out about bugs; easy experiments for young children; [by] Janice VanCleave. Wiley 1999 121p il $29.95; pa $12.95 (k-2)   595.7

1. Insects 2. Science—Experiments

ISBN 0-471-17664-8; 0-471-17663-X (pa)
LC 97-52088

Presents simple experiments answering such questions about insects as "Are spiders insects?" "Where do butterflies come from?" and "Why do fireflies light up?"

"Each project leads seamlessly to the next with a child wondering about some aspect of these animals. . . . The black-and-white illustrations with purple highlights are flat and childlike, but clear and informative." SLJ

Includes glossary

Walker, Sally M.

Fireflies. Lerner Publs. 2001 47p il (Early bird nature books) lib bdg $22.60 (k-3)   595.7

1. Fireflies

ISBN 0-8225-3047-3

Describes the physical characteristics, behavior and life cycle of fireflies

"The text is well organized and clearly written. . . . One or two good-quality color photographs or diagrams with informative captions appear on almost every page." SLJ

Whalley, Paul Ernest Sutton

Butterfly & moth; written by Paul Whalley; [special photography, Colin Keates, Kim Taylor, and Dave King] Dorling Kindersley 2000 63p il (DK eyewitness books) $15.99 (4 and up)
595.7

1. Butterflies 2. Moths

ISBN 0-7894-5832-2

First published 1988 by Knopf

Photographs and text explore the behavior and life cycles of butterflies and moths, examining mating rituals, camouflage, habitat, growth from pupa to larva to adult, and other aspects.

Zabludoff, Marc

The insect class. Benchmark Books 2006 95p il (Family trees) lib bdg $29.93 (5 and up)
595.7

1. Insects

ISBN 0-7614-1819-9 (lib bdg)   LC 2004-21819

This examines physical traits, adaptations, diets, habitats, and life cycles of insects.

"Fact-filled, yet surprisingly readable. . . . [This] title contains a wide variety of excellent-quality, full-color photographs; interesting sidebars; and diagrams." SLJ

Includes glossary and bibliographical references

Zemlicka, Shannon

From egg to butterfly. Lerner Publs. 2003 24p il (Start to finish) lib bdg $18.60 (k-2)
595.7

1. Butterflies

ISBN 0-8225-0713-7   LC 2001-4652

Follows the development of a butterfly from the egg its mother lays on a plant to the fully developed insect that flies away

"Readers will be transfixed by the incredibly crisp and clear photographs accompanying the text. This up-close and intimate look at the life stages of a monarch butterfly will be an asset to any young entomologist's library." Sci Teach

597 Cold-blooded vertebrates. Fishes

Arnosky, Jim

All about sharks. Scholastic Press 2003 unp il $15.95 (k-3)   597

1. Sharks

ISBN 0-590-48166-5   LC 2002-67004

Arnosky, Jim—*Continued*

Describes the physical characteristics, behavior, and survival techniques of different kinds of sharks

"Different species and families are illustrated in simple drawings, and the various parts of a shark's body are labeled and explained in a basic, easy-to-read text." SLJ

Berman, Ruth

Sharks; photographs by Jeffrey L. Rotman. Carolrhoda Bks. 1995 47p il (Carolrhoda nature watch book) lib bdg $23.93; pa $7.95 (3-6)

597

1. Sharks
ISBN 0-87614-870-4 (lib bdg); 0-87614-897-6 (pa)
LC 94-21468

The author introduces shark physiology "through brief but detailed descriptions. Full-color photographs show the variety of sharks, and colorful diagrams amplify the easy-to-understand explanations of their behavior and anatomy. Unfamiliar terms are highlighted in bold print and defined in context; a photograph and caption further explicate them." SLJ

Includes glossary

Butterworth, Christine

Sea horse; the shyest fish in the sea; [by] Chris Butterworth; illustrated by John Lawrence. 1st U.S. ed. Candlewick Press 2006 27p il $16.99 (k-2)

597

1. Sea horses
ISBN 0-7636-2989-8
LC 2005050755

First published 2005 in the United Kingdom with title: Sea-steady sea horse

"Pairing a central narrative about a male Barbour's sea horse with facts in smaller type, Butterworth first pinpoints the creatures' most immediately appealing attributes . . . then goes on to discuss the males' gestational role in reproduction and survival tactics of newly independent offspring. . . . Butterworth has a flair for dynamic writing. . . . Lawrence has created vinyl engravings that masterfully capture the delicate textures of sea horses' graceful, spiny bodies and of their undersea habitats." Booklist

Cerullo, Mary M.

The truth about great white sharks; written by Mary M. Cerullo; photographs by Jeffrey L. Rotman; illustrations by Michael Wertz. Chronicle Bks. 2000 48p il $14.95 (4 and up)

597

1. Sharks
ISBN 0-8118-2467-5
LC 00-31506

This provides information "about shark anatomy, senses, eating habits, and their relationships with humans. . . . The book also contains unusual information such as how these fish are measured and photographed and why they are not able to survive in an aquarium. The attractive layout blends line drawings, full-color photographs, varied typefaces, and eye-catching graphics. Rotman's pictures are clear and informative. . . . This title will be accessible to reluctant readers and is a must for most collections." SLJ

Includes bibliographical references

Davies, Nicola

Surprising sharks; illustrated by James Croft. Candlewick Press 2003 29p il $15.99 (k-3)

597

1. Sharks
ISBN 0-7636-2185-4
LC 2003-40943

Introduces many different species of sharks, pointing out such characteristics as the small size of the dwarf lantern shark and the physical characteristics and behavior that makes sharks killing machines

"Davies manages to impart a remarkable amount of information about sharks in this picture-book science volume. . . . Croft's bright, humorous artwork . . . and the clever layout will make this a first choice for many young children." Booklist

George, Twig C.

Seahorses. Millbrook Press 2003 31p il lib bdg $24.90 (k-3)

597

1. Sea horses
ISBN 0-7613-2869-6
LC 2003-10124

Describes the physical characteristics, behavior, and habitats of different species of seahorses, sea dragons, and pipefish, through simple text and photographs

"Some of the photographs are simply quite beautiful. Others stand out for their subjects. . . . The text is well cadenced and informative." Booklist

Gibbons, Gail

Sharks. Holiday House 1992 unp il $16.95; pa $6.95 (k-3)

597

1. Sharks
ISBN 0-8234-0960-0; 0-8234-1068-4 (pa)
LC 91-31524

Describes shark behavior and different kinds of sharks

The author's "bold, appealing illustrations (many of them labeled and explained) are the strength of the presentation. An excellent choice for even the youngest shark fan, this will be useful for simple reports as well." Booklist

Landau, Elaine

Electric fish. Children's Press 1999 47p il lib bdg $22; pa $6.95 (2-4)

597

1. Eels 2. Fishes
ISBN 0-516-20666-4 (lib bdg); 0-516-26491-5 (pa)
LC 98-16122

"A True book"

An introduction to various species of electric fish, particularly the electric eel, explaining how they generate and discharge electricity

Includes glossary and bibliographical references

Macquitty, Miranda

Shark; written by Miranda MacQuitty. rev ed. DK Pub. 2004 72p il (DK eyewitness books) $15.99; lib bdg $19.99 (4 and up)

597

1. Sharks
ISBN 0-7566-0725-6; 0-7566-0724-8 (lib bdg)

First published 1992 by Knopf

Describes, in text and photographs, the physical characteristics, behavior, and life cycle of various types of sharks.

Mallory, Kenneth

Swimming with hammerhead sharks. Houghton Mifflin 2001 48p il (Scientists in the field) $16 (4 and up)   597

1. Klimley, A. Peter 2. Sharks

ISBN 0-618-05543-6   LC 00-61401

"A New England Aquarium book"

Published "in association with the New England Aquarium."

This book follows "marine biologist Pete Klimley and an IMAX film team to seamounts off Cocos Island in the Pacific Ocean to observe and film schooling hammerhead sharks. . . . A fascinating record of research and investigation, this inviting book is larded with numerous dramatic color photos." SLJ

Includes bibliographical references

Markle, Sandra

Great white sharks; by Sandra Markle. Carolrhoda Books 2004 40p il (Animal predators) lib bdg $25.26; pa $7.95 (3-6)   597

1. Sharks

ISBN 1-57505-731-X (lib bdg); 1-57505-747-6 (pa)

LC 2003-23180

"Markle observes great whites' hunting techniques and includes information about their physical characteristics, physiology, habitats, and care of young." Horn Book Guide

"The role of camouflage is aptly explained in flowing text and illustrated in clear photography. . . . The full-color photography bedazzles on almost every page." SLJ

Includes bibliographical references

Outside and inside sharks. Atheneum Bks. for Young Readers 1996 40p il $16; pa $5.99 (2-4)

597

1. Sharks

ISBN 0-689-80348-6; 0-689-82683-4 (pa)

LC 95-30245

"The book gives a basic overview of the physiology of the species (including the shark's senses, its digestive habits, and its reproduction), which is aided by photographs not only of sharks but also bits of shark interiors." Bull Cent Child Books

"The full-color photographs are striking, giving readers close-up looks at different species and body parts. Children fascinated by these creatures should be thrilled with Markle's offering." SLJ

Includes glossary

Pfeffer, Wendy

What's it like to be a fish? illustrated by Holly Keller. HarperCollins Pubs. 1996 32p il (Let's-read-and-find-out science) lib bdg $15.89; pa $4.95 (k-1)   597

1. Fishes

ISBN 0-06-024429-1 (lib bdg); 0-06-024429-1 (pa)

LC 94-6543

"By comparing goldfish to wild fish and human beings, this book describes the basic physiology of fish. The colorful illustrations are done in watercolors and pastels. . . . In a very accessible narrative that flows from point to point, the basic external anatomy of fish and such behaviors as movement, breathing, eating, and maintenance of temperature are defined in terms of caring for a goldfish in a bowl." Sci Books Films

Pringle, Laurence P.

Sharks!: strange and wonderful; by Laurence Pringle; illustrated by Meryl Henderson. Boyds Mills Press 2001 32p il $15.95 (3-5)   597

1. Sharks

ISBN 1-56397-863-6

"Basic information about sharks—including physical characteristics, feeding habits, and their role in the chain of ocean life—is presented in clear, accessible prose. The acrylic paintings serve as a veritable catalog showcasing the variety of known sharks." Horn Book Guide

Rockwell, Anne F.

Little shark; [by] Anne Rockwell; pictures by Megan Halsey. Walker & Company 2005 unp il $15.95; lib bdg $16.85 (k-2)   597

1. Sharks

ISBN 0-8027-8955-2; 0-8027-8956-0 (lib bdg)

LC 2004-52611

"Rockwell invites her readers to follow a newborn shark pup as it grows, explores its ocean home on its own, and develops at last into an adult blue shark. Strung throughout the narrative . . . are interesting facts about shark physiology, behaviors, and deep-sea dangers. . . . The whole is decorated with soft watercolor-and-pencil collage illustrations that are both attractive and . . . informative." SLJ

Simon, Seymour

Sharks. HarperCollins Pubs. 1995 unp il $16.95; pa $6.95 (2-4)   597

1. Sharks

ISBN 0-06-023029-0; 0-06-446187-4 (pa)

LC 95-1593

The author "explores the fascinating undersea life of sharks, examining the truths and myths about these amazing creatures. Astounding close-up photographs enhance the informative and exciting text." Sci Child

Troll, Ray

Sharkabet; a sea of sharks from A to Z. West Wind Press 2002 39p il $16.95; pa $8.95 (k-3)

597

1. Sharks 2. Alphabet

ISBN 1-55868-518-9; 1-55868-519-7 (pa)

LC 2001-46528

"Both modern and extinct sharks are included in this alphabet book, some listed by common name (angel sharks, cookie-cutter sharks), others identified by scientific name." Horn Book Guide

This provides "enough information for the merely curious and a sturdy launching platform for further investigations. However, the book's greatest asset is the brilliant art bursting from the pages like jewels. . . . The images glow on the pages like mixed-media gems." SLJ

Walker, Sally M.

Fossil fish found alive; discovering the coelacanth. Carolrhoda Bks. 2002 72p il map lib bdg $17.95 (5 and up) **597**

1. Coelacanth

ISBN 1-57505-536-8   LC 2001-3815

Describes the 1938 discovery of the coelacanth, a fish previously believed to be extinct, and subsequent research about it

"Walker writes well, making this relatively unknown area of science history an exciting story of exploration and discovery. Excellent, full-color photos illustrate the text." Booklist

Includes bibliographical references

Rays. Carolrhoda Bks. 2003 48p il (Carolrhoda nature watch book) lib bdg $23.93 (3-6)
    597

1. Rays (Fishes)

ISBN 1-57505-172-9   LC 2001-6586

Describes the physical characteristics, behavior, life cycle, and endangered status of rays

"The crisp, well-captioned color photos highlight the many varieties of this unusual fish. Information is presented clearly." Horn Book Guide

Includes glossary

597.8 Amphibians

Arnosky, Jim

All about frogs. Scholastic Press 2002 unp il $15.95 (k-3)   **597.8**

1. Frogs

ISBN 0-590-48164-9   LC 2001-20680

"Beginning with a discussion of amphibians, the book goes on to talk specifically about frogs: their distinctive characteristics, habits, habitats, range, life cycle, diet, and the threats to their existence. The attractive acrylic paintings, well designed to illustrate particular points, zoom in for details. . . . Always informative, yet casual in tone, the text will engage young readers without talking down to them." Booklist

Clarke, Barry

Amphibian; written by Barry Clarke; photographed by Geoff Brightling and Frank Greenaway. rev ed. DK Pub. 2005 72p il (DK eyewitness books) $15.99; lib bdg $19.99 (4 and up)   **597.8**

1. Amphibians

ISBN 0-7566-1380-9; 0-7566-1381-7 (lib bdg)

First published 1993

Examines the evolution, behavior, physical characteristics, and life cycle of various types of amphibians.

Dewey, Jennifer

Poison dart frogs; [by] Jennifer Owings Dewey. Boyds Mills Press 1998 unp il $15.95; pa $8.95 (3-5)   **597.8**

1. Frogs

ISBN 1-56397-655-2; 1-56397-945-4 (pa)
    LC 97-74194

A variety of colorful and tiny poison dart frogs living in the rain forests of Central and South America are pictured in their natural habitat. Topics covered include mating habits, natural predators, methods to extract the frog's poison, and their unique nurturing habits

"Dewey's straightforward text is clear and concise, providing enough fascinating details to interest young readers and listeners without overwhelming them." Booklist

French, Vivian

Growing frogs; illustrated by Alison Bartlett. Candlewick Press 2000 32p il $15.99 (k-3)
    597.8

1. Frogs

ISBN 0-7636-0317-1   LC 99-43695

A mother and child watch as tadpoles develop and grow into frogs

"The illustrations . . . are just right for a first encounter with tadpole mysteries. The text presents all of the essential tips in such a lively manner that readers will want to become involved." SLJ

Fridell, Ron

The search for poison-dart frogs. Watts 2001 48p il map lib bdg $23.50; pa $6.95 (4-6)
    597.8

1. Frogs 2. Wildlife conservation 3. Suriname

ISBN 0-531-11888-6 (lib bdg); 0-531-16570-1 (pa)
    LC 00-36507

"Wildlife Conservation Society books"

This describes a scientific "expedition as a team travels to Suriname to study the electric blue amphibians. Written with vivid detail, the text explains environmental issues and shows why preservation of the area is so crucial." Booklist

Includes glossary and bibliographical references

Gibbons, Gail

Frogs. Holiday House 1993 unp il $16.95; pa $6.95 (k-3)   **597.8**

1. Frogs

ISBN 0-8234-1052-8; 0-8234-1134-6 (pa)
    LC 93-269

An introduction to frogs, discussing their tadpole beginnings, noises they make, their hibernation, body parts, and how they differ from toads

"Gibbons' distinctive, labeled drawings identify the features described in the text, and her subjects float, swim, jump, and dive in colorful, lifelike illustrations. . . . This attractive book will appeal to prereaders, beginning readers, and the adults who read to those groups." Booklist

Hamilton, Garry

Frog rescue; changing the future for endangered wildlife. Firefly Books 2004 64p il (Firefly animal rescue series) $19.95; pa $9.95 (5 and up)

597.8

1. Frogs 2. Endangered species 3. Wildlife conservation

ISBN 1-55297-597-5; 1-55297-506-7 (pa)

This describes endangered species of frogs, how and why they are in danger, and explains what efforts are being made to protect them.

This is "well-written. . . . Stunning, full-color photographs bring each species to life and depict a number of individuals in the field and laboratory working to save these animals." SLJ

Llewellyn, Claire

Frog; illustrated by Simon Mendez. NorthWord Press 2003 23p il (Starting life) $16.95 (k-3)

597.8

1. Frogs

ISBN 1-55971-869-2   LC 2002-45505

Describes the physical characteristics and behavior of frogs, including their development from egg to tadpole to adult.

This has "bold, bright, full-page paintings throughout. . . . The interesting page sizes and full-page illustrations will appeal to young naturalists." SLJ

Includes glossary

Magloff, Lisa

Frog. Dorling Kindersley 2003 24p il (Watch me grow) $7.99 (k-2)   **597.8**

1. Frogs

ISBN 0-7894-9629-1   LC 2003-1578

Shows the frog as it grows up in its natural environment

"The full-color photographs . . . are not only exceptionally well chosen but downright dynamic. . . . Outstanding for browsing, with solid content for animal reports." Booklist

Includes glossary

Noonan, Diana

The frog. Chelsea Clubhouse Bks. 2003 32p il (Life cycles) lib bdg $14.95 (2-4)   **597.8**

1. Frogs

ISBN 0-7910-6966-4   LC 2002-34

An introduction to the physical characteristics, behavior, and development from egg to adult of frogs, amphibians that hibernate in the cold

"Clear, colorful, and striking photographs accompany the simple yet educational text." Libr Media Connect

Includes glossary

Patent, Dorothy Hinshaw

Flashy fantastic rain forest frogs; illustrations by Kendahl Jan Jubb. Walker & Co. 1997 31p il maps $15.95; pa $6.95 (k-3)   **597.8**

1. Frogs 2. Rain forests

ISBN 0-8027-8615-4; 0-8027-7536-5 (pa)

LC 96-29060

Describes the physical characteristics, behavior, reproduction, and habitat of frogs that live in the rain forest

"The pictures are dense with color and line. . . . The book's well-written text is right on the mark for the age group." Booklist

Pfeffer, Wendy

From tadpole to frog; illustrated by Holly Keller. HarperCollins Pubs. 1994 32p il (Let's-read-and-find-out science) $15.95; pa $4.95 (k-1)   **597.8**

1. Frogs

ISBN 0-06-023044-4; 0-06-445123-2 (pa)

LC 93-3135

This "introduction sketches the most basic aspects of frog life—the laying and hatching of eggs, the stages of growth, eating and the danger of being eaten, and hibernation." Horn Book Guide

"The illustrations are simple, interesting, and just right for young children. The science is accurate and presented in a way to excite young readers to get outside and look for some frogs and tadpoles." Sci Books Films

Schwabacher, Martin

Frogs. Benchmark Bks. 2004 47p il map (Animals, animals) lib bdg $17.95 (3-6)

597.8

1. Frogs

ISBN 0-7614-1619-6   LC 2003-13124

Contents: Introducing frogs; Many kinds of frogs; Frog bodies; A frog's life; Frogs and people

Describes the physical characteristics, behavior, habitat, and endangered status of the frog

This has "excellent, full-color photographs and lively [text] that [brings] these animals to life." SLJ

Includes glossary and bibliographical references

Wallace, Karen

Tale of a tadpole. DK Pub. 1998 32p il (Eyewitness readers) $12.95; pa $3.95 (k-1)

597.8

1. Frogs

ISBN 0-7894-3761-9; 0-7894-3437-7 (pa)

LC 98-14976

Describes the development of a tadpole

This is "heavily illustrated with striking full-color photographs and insets that invite a close inspection of features that might normally be overlooked, such as the creature's delicate fingers, tiny nostrils, or long tongue. The photographs are well chosen to illustrate this lively, carefully written narrative." SLJ

Winer, Yvonne

Frogs sing songs; written by Yvonne Winer; illustrated by Tony Oliver. Charlesbridge Pub. 2003 unp il $16.95; pa $6.95 (k-3)   **597.8**

1. Frogs 2. Animal communication

ISBN 1-57091-548-2; 1-57091-549-0 (pa)

LC 2002-6234

First published 2002 in the United Kingdom

Winer, Yvonne—*Continued*

Describes how, when, where, and why frogs sing songs. Includes frog identification guide

"One of Winer's short, simple poems appears under a spot illustration of a frog. Opposite is a full-page, vivid, realistic watercolor illustration of that particular species in its natural habitat." Booklist

597.9 Reptiles

McCarthy, Colin

Reptile; written by Colin McCarthy; [special photography, Karl Shone . . . [et al.]] Dorling Kindersley 2000 63p il (DK eyewitness books) $15.99; lib bdg $19.99 (4 and up)   **597.9**

1. Reptiles
ISBN 0-7894-5786-5; 0-7894-6575-2 (lib bdg)

First published 1991 by Knopf

Photographs and text depict the many different kinds of reptiles, their similarities and differences, habitats, and behavior.

Zabludoff, Marc

The reptile class. Benchmark Books 2005 95p il (Family trees) lib bdg $29.92   **597.9**

1. Reptiles
ISBN 0-7614-1820-2   LC 2004-21820

This examines physical traits, adaptations, diets, habitats, and life cycles of reptiles.

"Fact-filled, yet surprisingly readable. . . . [This] title contains a wide variety of excellent-quality, full-color photos; interesting sidebars; and diagrams." SLJ

597.92 Turtles

Berger, Melvin

Look out for turtles! illustrated by Megan Lloyd. HarperCollins Pubs. 1992 32p il (Let's-read-and-find-out science book) lib bdg $15.89; pa $4.95 (k-3)   **597.92**

1. Turtles
ISBN 0-06-022540-8 (lib bdg); 0-06-445156-9 (pa)
LC 90-36894

"This simple introductory resource provides an overview of the different types of turtles and their characteristics and habits. It is a good resource for young children to use independently." Sci Child

Cerullo, Mary M.

Sea turtles: ocean nomads; photographs by Jeffrey L. Rotman. Dutton 2003 unp il $17.99 (4 and up)   **597.92**

1. Sea turtles
ISBN 0-525-46649-5   LC 2002-74150

Presents information on the physical characteristics, behavior, habitat, various species, and life cycle of sea turtles, along with a discussion of their endangered status and the efforts being made to study and conserve them

"Spectacular close-up pictures showing a variety of

sea turtles in the wild and an informative, spirited text combine for a dynamic photo-essay on these ancient, endangered animals." SLJ

Includes glossary and bibliographical references

Davies, Nicola

One tiny turtle; illustrated by Jane Chapman. Candlewick Press 2001 29p il $15.99 (k-3)
597.92

1. Turtles
ISBN 0-7636-1549-8   LC 00-52326

"This story follows one female loggerhead turtle from infancy to adulthood, when she lays her own eggs." Horn Book Guide

This offers "simple, lyrical words and bright, acrylic double-page pictures. . . . Without condescension, this tells a powerful nature story for a young audience." Booklist

Gibbons, Gail

Sea turtles. Holiday House 1995 unp il $16.95; pa $6.95 (k-3)   **597.92**

1. Sea turtles
ISBN 0-8234-1191-5; 0-8234-1373-X (pa)
LC 94-48579

This book examines "the size, habitat, and diet of the eight kinds of sea turtles and efforts environmentalists are making to protect them." Sci Child

This is "a very appealing book. . . . The illustrations are lovely paintings, highlighted with black outlines and clear labels. Children should find the diagram that shows differences between sea turtles and other turtles fascinating because they are often familiar only with the latter." Sci Books Films

Guiberson, Brenda Z.

Into the sea; illustrated by Alix Berenzy. Holt & Co. 1996 unp il $16.95; pa $6.95 (k-3)
597.92

1. Sea turtles
ISBN 0-8050-2263-5; 0-8050-6481-8 (pa)
LC 95-46757

The author "recounts the life of a sea turtle from its days as a hatchling on a sandy beach through its return to the same island as an egg-laying adult many years later." Booklist

"Guiberson uses italicized sound words such as *tap*, *tap*, and *scritch* to draw readers into the story. Berenzy captures the essence of the text with her colored-pencil and gouache illustr- ations that alternate from dark to light, reflecting the various habitats." SLJ

Lockwood, Sophie

Sea turtles; by Sophie Lockwood. Child's World 2006 40p il map (World of reptiles) lib bdg $29.93 (4 and up)   **597.92**

1. Sea turtles
ISBN 1-59296-550-4   LC 2005024792

"Conservation is the dominant theme of this attractive photo-essay. . . . which has beautiful full-page color photos that bring readers close to the subject. Fast-fact

Lockwood, Sophie—*Continued*
boxes focus on particular species, providing spot statistics on weight, length, color, habitat, threatened or endangered status, and more." Booklist
Includes glossary and bibliographical references

Noonan, Diana
The green turtle. Chelsea Clubhouse Bks. 2003
32p il (Life cycles) lib bdg $14.95 (2-4)
597.92
1. Turtles
ISBN 0-7910-6967-2   LC 2002-32
An introduction to the physical characteristics, behavior, and development from egg to adult of the green turtle, a reptile that is endangered
"Clear, colorful, and striking photographs accompany the simple yet educational text." Libr Media Connect
Includes glossary

Swinburne, Stephen R.
Turtle tide; the ways of sea turtles; illustrated by
Bruce Hiscock. 1st ed. Boyds Mills Press 2005
unp il $15.95 (2-4)   **597.92**
1. Sea turtles
ISBN 1-59078-081-7   LC 2004-16856
"A mother loggerhead crawls onto an Atlantic beach, lays a hundred eggs in a deep nest, and heaves her way back to the sea. . . . Predators quickly reduce the clutch to a solitary hatchling. . . . [The book] closes with a view of the lone survivor, intrepidly paddling off into the wide, sunrise-lit sea." Booklist
"Simple, lyrical prose accompanies brilliant watercolors in this account." SLJ

597.95 Lizards

Cowley, Joy
Chameleon chameleon; story by Joy Cowley; illustrated with photographs by Nic Bishop. 1st ed. Scholastic Press 2005 unp il $16.95 (k-2)
597.95
1. Chameleons
ISBN 0-439-66653-8   LC 2004-7291
A chameleon creeps through the rain forest avoiding danger and searching for food
This is a "stunning photo-essay. . . . Crisp, clear, full-color photos portray this reptile and its habitat. . . . An informative, thoughtfully produced science book that will be popular with a wide range of animal lovers. Excellent for browsing as well as learning." Booklist

Facklam, Margery
Lizards: weird and wonderful; illustrated by
Alan Male. Little, Brown 2003 unp il $15.95 (3-6)
597.95
1. Lizards
ISBN 0-316-17346-0   LC 2002-19173
This offers "page-long profiles of 13 types of lizards—among them, Komodo dragons, anoles, and skinks—heightened by crisp, colorful illustrations. Facklam packs a great deal of scientific information into her chatty descriptions." Booklist

597.96 Snakes

Holub, Joan
Why do snakes hiss? and other questions about snakes, lizards, and turtles; illustrations by Anna DiVito. Dial Books for Young Readers 2004 46p il $14.99; pa $3.99 (k-2)   **597.96**
1. Reptiles 2. Snakes
ISBN 0-8037-3000-4; 0-14-240105-6 (pa)
LC 2003-64948
"Dial easy-to-read"
Questions and answers present information about the behavior and characteristics of snakes, lizards, and turtles
"The photos and attractive ink drawings with color washes that come two to three to a page result in a colorful presentation with illustrations in different styles from many sources." Booklist

Markle, Sandra
Outside and inside snakes. Macmillan Bks. for Young Readers 1995 40p il $17; pa $5.99 (2-4)
597.96
1. Snakes
ISBN 0-02-762315-7; 0-689-81998-6 (pa)
LC 94-20647
This volume "discusses how snakes capture their food, how they move, and how their sensory, digestive, musculo-skeletal, and reproductive systems function. The text is conversational, leading the young reader to each important question and its answer." Sci Books Films
"The photographs are particularly strong in this title, depicting unfamiliar snakes and showing close-ups of amazing snake activity. A fine addition to reptile collections." Horn Book
Includes glossary

Snakes; biggest! littlest! photographs by Joe McDonald. 1st ed. Boyds Mills Press 2004 unp il $15.95 (k-3)   **597.96**
1. Snakes
ISBN 1-59078-189-9   LC 2004-14576
This describes the anatomy and behavior of various species of snakes.
"Bright, crisp color photos illuminate Markle's staccato text that is just right for younger readers. . . . The book is not merely a litany of factoids, but a cogent look at commonalities or disparate evolutions that are advantageous for these sleek reptiles in their specific habitats." SLJ
Includes glossary

Montgomery, Sy
The snake scientist; photographs by Nic Bishop.
Houghton Mifflin 1999 48p il map $16; pa $5.95
(4 and up)   **597.96**
1. Mason, Bob 2. Snakes
ISBN 0-395-87169-7; 0-618-11119-0 (pa)
LC 98-6124
Discusses the work of Bob Mason and his efforts to study and protect snakes, particularly red-sided garter snakes
"The lively text communicates both the meticulous

Montgomery, Sy—*Continued*

measurements required in this kind of work and the thrill of new discoveries. Large, full-color photos of the zoologist and young students at work, and lots of wriggly snakes, pull readers into the presentation." SLJ

Includes bibliographical references

Patent, Dorothy Hinshaw

Slinky, scaly, slithery snakes; illustrations by Kendahl Jan Jubb. Walker & Co. 2000 32p il $16.95; lib bdg $17.85; pa $6.95 (k-3)

597.96

1. Snakes

ISBN 0-8027-8743-6; 0-8027-8744-4 (lib bdg); 0-8027-7652-3 (pa)   LC 00-28099

"Patent discusses camouflage and predatory skills as well as how snakes move, where they live, how they can devour animals larger than themselves. . . . Surrounding and sometimes underlying the text are vibrant paintings that offer close-up views of snakes in the wild. An inviting look at snakes." Booklist

Pringle, Laurence P.

Snakes! strange and wonderful; by Laurence Pringle; illustrated by Meryl Henderson. Boyds Mills Press 2004 31p il $15.95 (3-5)

597.96

1. Snakes

ISBN 1-59078-003-5   LC 2003-26418

"Short paragraphs describe [snakes'] major physical and behavioral characteristics and highlight some distinctive traits of several different species. . . . More than three dozen species from around the world are depicted in the realistic watercolors. . . . The narrative is well organized and clearly written." SLJ

Schlaepfer, Gloria G.

Pythons and boas; squeezing snakes; [by] Gloria G. Schlaepfer and Mary Lou Samuelson. Watts 2002 63p il $24 (4 and up)   **597.96**

1. Pythons 2. Boa constrictors

ISBN 0-531-13954-9   LC 2001-5900

"Watts library"

First published 1999 by Dillon Press

Discusses the physical characteristics and behavior of various species of constrictor snakes, their relationship with humans, and how to keep one as a pet.

"This volume is an exceptionally well-written and superbly illustrated book for young readers." Sci Books Films

Includes glossary and bibliographical references

597.98   Crocodilians

Markle, Sandra

Crocodiles; by Sandra Markle. Carolrhoda Books 2004 39p il (Animal predators) lib bdg $25.26; pa $7.95 (3-6)   **597.98**

1. Crocodiles

ISBN 1-57505-726-3 (lib bdg); 1-57505-742-5 (pa)   LC 2003-15402

"Markle observes Nile crocodiles' hunting techniques and includes information about their physiology, habitats, and care of young." Horn Book Guide

"The straightforward, descriptive text and superb photos give [this title] surefire appeal to middle readers." Booklist

Includes glossary and bibliographical references

Outside and inside alligators. Atheneum Bks. for Young Readers 1998 40p il lib bdg $16 (2-4)

597.98

1. Alligators

ISBN 0-689-81457-7   LC 97-39804

Describes the external and internal physical characteristics of alligators and how they find their food, mate, and raise their young

This is an "accessible and visually appealing introduction. . . . Large, full-color photographs abound, enhancing every page." SLJ

Includes glossary

Simon, Seymour

Crocodiles & alligators. HarperCollins Pubs. 1999 unp il $15.95; lib bdg $16.89; pa $6.99 (4 and up)   **597.98**

1. Crocodiles 2. Alligators

ISBN 0-06-027473-5; 0-06-027474-3 (lib bdg); 0-06-443829-5 (pa)   LC 98-34705

Describes the physical characteristics and behavior of various members of the family of animals known as crocodilians

"The book is filled with interesting information, and the vivid, well-composed, full-color photographs and entertaining text will draw in browsers." SLJ

598   Birds

Arnold, Caroline

Birds; nature's magnificent flying machines; illustrated by Patricia J. Wynne. Charlesbridge Pub. 2003 32p il $16.95; pa $6.95 (3-6)

598

1. Birds—Flight

ISBN 1-57091-516-4; 1-57091-572-5 (pa)

     LC 2002-10441

An introduction to the science that explains how birds fly

"A clear, interesting book. . . . Each spread contains one or two paragraphs with a large, full-color illustration as well as smaller, captioned pictures that cover such topics as bone structure and preening. The colorful artwork consistently clarifies the concepts being discussed." SLJ

Includes glossary and bibliographical references

A penguin's world; written and illustrated by Caroline Arnold. Picture Window Books 2005 24p il $23.93 (k-3)   **598**

1. Penguins

ISBN 1-4048-1323-3   LC 2005023159

"This title follows an Adelie penguin family from scenes in which the parents build a nest and warm their

Arnold, Caroline—*Continued*

eggs to final pages showcasing the four-month-old, newly independent chicks. The simple, well-paced text weaves basic concepts into the captivating narrative, and the artwork's strong colors and bold, uncluttered compositions capture the expression and movement of the birds." Booklist

Includes glossary and bibliographical references

Arnosky, Jim

Watching water birds. National Geographic Soc. 1997 unp il $16 (2-4) **598**

1. Water birds

ISBN 0-7922-7073-8   LC 97-7594

Provides a personal look at various species of fresh- and saltwater birds, including loons and grebes, mergansers, mallards, wood ducks, Canada geese, gulls, and herons

Arnosky "weaves facts and many personal observations in the breezy conversational blocks of text and informative captions that surround the naturalistic, almost photoreal, watercolor paintings. . . . He offers marvelous anatomical detail and captures close-up views of that casual observers rarely get to see." SLJ

Bash, Barbara

Urban roosts: where birds nest in the city. Sierra Club Bks. 1990 unp il pa $6.95 hardcover o.p. (1-4) **598**

1. Birds—Nests

ISBN 0-316-08312-7 (pa)   LC 89-70187

"Excellent treatment of an unusual subject reveals that human-made places of steel, stone, and concrete are home to a variety of birds. Includes information on sparrows, finches, barn and snowy owls, swallows, swifts, nighthawks, killdeers, pigeons, wrens, crows, starlings, and falcons that have successfully adapted to city life." Sci Child

Brenner, Barbara

Chibi; a true story from Japan; by Barbara Brenner and Julia Takaya; illustrated by June Otani. Clarion Bks. 1996 63p il lib bdg $14.95; pa $5.95 (k-3) **598**

1. Ducks 2. Japan—Social life and customs

ISBN 0-395-69623-2 (lib bdg); 0-395-72088-5 (pa)   LC 94-31082

This is a "true story about a duck who built her nest in a busy office park and then decided to take her brood across eight lanes of traffic to live in the moat of the Imperial Gardens. The ducks became an obsession of the Japanese in general and a photojournalist named Sato in particular, who made a media star out of the smallest and weakest duckling, Chibi, and who led the search when Chibi was lost in a typhoon." Bull Cent Child Books

The story "is told in a crisp, straightforward style and illustrated with uncluttered, realistic watercolor and ink artwork that has captured a sense of traditional Japanese painting." Horn Book Guide

Includes glossary

Burnie, David

Bird; written by David Burnie. rev ed. DK Pub. 2004 72p il (DK eyewitness books) $15.99; lib bdg $19.99 (4 and up) **598**

1. Birds

ISBN 0-7566-06586; 0-7566-0657-8 (lib bdg)

First published 1988 by Knopf

A photo essay on the world of birds examining such topics as body construction, feathers and flight, the adaptation of beaks and feet, feeding habits, courtship, nests and eggs, and bird watching.

Cherry, Lynne

Flute's journey; the life of a wood thrush; written and illustrated by Lynne Cherry. Harcourt Brace & Co. 1997 unp il $15 (2-4) **598**

1. Wood thrush

ISBN 0-15-292853-7   LC 96-17024

"A Gulliver green book"

A young wood thrush makes his first migration from his nesting ground in a forest preserve in Maryland to his winter home in Costa Rica and back again

This features "detailed watercolors. . . . The story and illustrations contain much useful information." Horn Book Guide

Collard, Sneed B., III

Beaks! illustrated by Robin Brickman. Charlesbridge Pub. 2002 unp il $16.95; pa $6.95 (k-3) **598**

1. Birds

ISBN 1-57091-387-0; 1-57091-388-9 (pa)   LC 2001-4362

Simple text describes various bird beaks and how birds use them to eat, hunt, and gather food. Includes a quiz

"The intricate characteristics of a variety of birds' beaks are presented skillfully through words and vividly painted, cut-and-sculpted-paper illustrations. . . . The clear text is easy to follow." SLJ

Includes bibliographical references

Dewey, Jennifer

Paisano, the roadrunner; [by] Jennifer Owings Dewey; photographs by Wyman Meinzer. Millbrook Press 2002 48p il lib bdg $23.90 (k-3) **598**

1. Roadrunners

ISBN 0-7613-1250-1   LC 2001-44427

The author describes her experiences with a family of roadrunners who come to live near her house

"Well-observed sketches and well-integrated color photos accompany Dewey's story. . . . Scientific detail is skillfully woven throughout the text." Horn Book Guide

Dubois, Philippe J.

Birds; photographs by Gilles Martin; text by Philippe J. Dubois and Valerie Guidoux; drawings by Jean Chevallier. H.N. Abrams 2005 70p il $18.95 (5 and up) **598**

1. Birds

ISBN 0-8109-5878-3   LC 2004-22214

Dubois, Philippe J.—*Continued*

"This oversize album centers on Martin's knockout color photographs, enhanced by smaller watercolor sketches and illuminating commentary contributed by Philippe Dubois and Valerie Guidoux. . . . Martin not only captures such rare moments as egg laying in the wild and a face-off between a jackal and a nesting crane but also shows a gift for making even the most inconspicuous of birds as visually arresting as their more spectacular tropical cousins." Booklist

DuTemple, Lesley A.

North American cranes. Carolrhoda Bks. 1999 48p il (Carolrhoda nature watch book) $25.26 (3-6) **598**

1. Cranes (Birds)

ISBN 1-57505-302-0   LC 98-4519

"A Carolrhoda nature watch book."

Describes the physical characteristics, diet, natural habitat, and life cycle of these large wading birds, and tells about the efforts of scientists to establish resident flocks

"Colorful and informative. . . . Illustrated with many excellent, full-color photos." Booklist

Esbensen, Barbara Juster

Tiger with wings; the great horned owl; illustrated by Mary Barrett Brown. Orchard Bks. 1991 unp il $16.95; lib bdg $17.99; pa $5.95 (2-4) **598**

1. Owls

ISBN 0-531-05940-5; 0-531-08540-6 (lib bdg); 0-531-07071-9 (pa)   LC 90-23034

Describes the hunting technique, physical characteristics, mating ritual, and nesting and child-rearing practices of the great horned owl

"The watercolor paintings in mainly grays, brown, and blues beautifully convey information, mood, and sometimes humor. . . . The writing is clean and clear, with an occasional colorful simile or metaphor." SLJ

Evert, Laura

Birds of prey; explore the fascinating worlds of eagles, falcons, owls, vultures; by Laura Evert and Wayne Lynch; illustrations by Sherry Neidigh and John F. McGee. NorthWord 2005 191p il (Our wild world) $16.95 (3-6) **598**

1. Birds of prey

ISBN 1-55971-925-7   LC 2005000189

This "volume is divided into four sections, each addressing one of the major groups of raptors: eagles, falcons, owls, and vultures. The chapters, which have color-coded pages for quick reference, are similarly organized, making for easier reading, and deal with all aspects of the birds' life cycles and habits. Plentiful, high-quality photographs . . . and clear illustrations elucidate the narrative." SLJ

Gibbons, Gail

Gulls—gulls—gulls. Holiday House 1997 unp il $15.95 (k-3) **598**

1. Gulls

ISBN 0-8234-1323-3   LC 97-1266

Describes the life cycle, behavior patterns, and habitat of various species of gulls, focusing on those found in North America

"Both illustration and text provide basic, easy-to-understand facts. . . . The format is attractive with framed, simply drawn watercolor illustrations showing the birds in the foreground against bright colorful seashore or seascape backgrounds of dominant blues and greens." SLJ

Owls; [by] Gail Gibbons. 1st ed. Holiday House 2005 32p il $16.95 (k-3) **598**

1. Owls

ISBN 0-8234-1880-4   LC 2004-48225

A "factual look at raptors of the night, full of information tied specifically to the owls of North America. General facts on physiology, hunting tactics, digestion, habitats, and communication are offered, as is a section on mating, egg laying and incubation, and owlet development. . . . Gibbons's trademark watercolors provide lively renditions of a variety of these silent hunters. . . . This is a bright addition to owl lore for younger readers." SLJ

Penguins! Holiday House 1998 unp il maps $16.95; pa $6.95 (k-3) **598**

1. Penguins

ISBN 0-8234-1388-8; 0-8234-1516-3 (pa)

LC 98-5194

Describes the habitat, physical characteristics, and behavior of different kinds of penguins

This book has "simply written, clear text. . . . The oversized format, brightly colored illustrations, and large type font result in an eye-catching appearance that will attract young researchers and the curious minded alike." SLJ

The puffins are back! HarperCollins Pubs. 1991 unp il $15.95 (k-3) **598**

1. Puffins

ISBN 0-06-021603-4   LC 90-30525

A simple introduction to the physical characteristics, life cycle, and natural environment of the puffins living off the coast of Maine

"Gail Gibbons tells the story of the endangered puffin colony in a clear, direct text, weaving facts about puffin characteristics and behavior throughout her dramatic narrative. Her rich palette of blues and greens gives life and depth to the island setting and contrasts with the clean black and white of the puffins." Horn Book

Soaring with the wind; the bald eagle. Morrow Junior Bks. 1998 unp il $16.95; lib bdg $16.89 (k-3) **598**

1. Bald eagle

ISBN 0-688-13730-X; 0-688-13731-8 (lib bdg)

LC 97-20497

Describes the characteristics, behavior, and life cycle of the bald eagle

"Appealing watercolor illustrations, labeled diagrams, definitions, and well-researched facts come together to form a perfect connection for teachers seeking to expand science units." SLJ

Goldin, Augusta R.

Ducks don't get wet; by Augusta Goldin; illustrated by Helen K. Davie. newly il ed. HarperCollins Pubs. 1999 32p il (Let's-read-and-find-out science) $15.95; lib bdg $15.89; pa $4.95 (k-3)   **598**

1. Ducks
ISBN 0-06-027881-1; 0-06-027882-X (lib bdg); 0-06-445187-9 (pa)   LC 97-43597
A newly illustrated edition of the title first published 1965 by Crowell
Describes the behavior of different kinds of ducks and, in particular, discusses how all ducks use preening to keep their feathers dry
"The text is well focused throughout. . . . Notable for its clarity, subtlety, and beauty, the artwork illustrates the text with precision and imagination." Booklist

Guiberson, Brenda Z.

The emperor lays an egg; illustrated by Joan Paley. Holt & Co. 2001 unp il $16.95 (k-3)
                    598

1. Penguins
ISBN 0-8050-6204-1   LC 00-40980
"Beginning with the laying of an egg, Guiberson describes the care given to a baby emperor penguin by both parents from the time it hatches until it is on its own." SLJ
"Guiberson's vivid prose fleshes out the bare bones of the penguin's life cycle. . . . Paley's collages of painted and cut papers provide exceptionally beautiful scenes of the birds." Booklist

Mud city; a flamingo story; [by] Brenda Z. Guiberson. 1st ed. Henry Holt and Co 2005 unp il $16.95 (2-4)   **598**

1. Flamingos
ISBN 0-8050-7177-6   LC 2004-9199
On a muddy mound in a salty lake, a mother and father flamingo take turns shading their egg from the blistering sun. Soon a fluffy white chick hatches in the nest by the mangrove shrub. Thus begins a life cycle of a baby flamingo.
"Guiberson's brightly colored watercolor/gouache illustrations are a perfect complement for her informative, conversational text." SLJ

Holub, Joan

Why do birds sing? illustrations by Anna DiVito. Dial Books for Young Readers 2004 47p il $14.99; pa $3.99 (k-2)   **598**

1. Birds
ISBN 0-8037-2999-5; 0-14-240106-4 (pa)
                    LC 2003-64945
"Dial easy-to-read"
Questions and answers present information about the behavior and characteristics of birds
"The photos and attractive ink drawings with color washes that come two to three to a page result in a colorful presentation with illustrations in different styles from many sources." Booklist

Jenkins, Martin

The emperor's egg; illustrated by Jane Chapman. Candlewick Press 1999 29p il $16.99 (k-3)   **598**

1. Penguins
ISBN 0-7636-0557-3   LC 98-46839
Describes the parental behavior of Emperor penguins, focusing on how the male keeps the egg warm until it hatches and how the parents care for the chick after it is born
"Chapman's acrylics reflect the gleeful tone of the text without anthropomorphizing the subject, relying on the odd perspective and occasional close-up of the penguins' naturally comic visage to do the trick. . . . Beginning readers will get a charge out of something that's interesting, accurate, and theirs." Bull Cent Child Books

Johnson, Sylvia A.

Crows; by Sylvia A. Johnson. Carolrhoda Books 2005 48p il (Carolrhoda nature watch book) lib bdg $25.26 (3-6)   **598**

1. Crows
ISBN 1-57505-628-3   LC 2004-564
Contents: Crows all around us; The crow family tree; Country birds, city birds; Studying crows; Crows and people
This "book introduces the American crow, its broader family of corvids, and its range, habitats, cooperative breeding system, life cycle, winter migration, roosting behavior, language, and relations with people. . . . Though the clear, color photographs take up most of the space on the pages, the text offers a well-organized, informative discussion of the species." Booklist

Songbirds; the language of song. Carolrhoda Bks. 2001 48p il (Carolrhoda nature watch book) lib bdg $23.93 (3-6)   **598**

1. Birdsongs 2. Birds
ISBN 1-57505-483-3   LC 99-50533
Introduces the phenomenon of bird song, explains how and why birds sing, describes how scientists learn about bird communication, and indicates the dangers to songbirds due to changes in their habitats
This "is a beautifully written book with excellent photographs." Sci Books Films

Kelly, Irene

It's a hummingbird's life. Holiday House 2003 unp il $16.95 (k-3)   **598**

1. Hummingbirds
ISBN 0-8234-1658-5   LC 00-53544
"Kelly follows the activities of the ruby-throated hummingbird throughout the seasons, relating facts and bits of trivia. . . . The tiny pen-and-ink and watercolor illustrations effectively show the features described and comparisons drawn in the narrative." SLJ

Laubach, Christyna M.

Raptor! a kid's guide to birds of prey; by Christyna & René Laubach and Charles W.G. Smith. Storey Bks. 2002 118p il maps $21.95; pa $14.95 (4 and up)   **598**

1. Birds of prey

ISBN 1-58017-475-2; 1-58017-445-0 (pa)

LC 2001-54980

This is an "overview of North American raptors. . . . After describing their characteristics and behavior, the book introduces individual species within family groups: vultures, hawks, falcons, barn owls, and true owls. . . . There is also advice on bird-watching and efforts to save endangered species. Well-designed projects . . . are followed by a glossary and extensive lists of hawk-watching sites, raptor centers, banding demonstration sites, books, videos, organizations, and Web sites related to birds in general and raptors in particular." Booklist

Lynch, Wayne

Penguins! text and photographs by Wayne Lynch. Firefly Bks. (Willowdale) 1999 64p il map $19.95; pa $9.95 (4 and up)   **598**

1. Penguins

ISBN 1-55209-421-9; 1-55209-424-3 (pa)

In a "first-person narrative, peppered with journal excerpts, personal observations, and anecdotes, Lynch discusses penguins' evolution, varied habitats, physical and behavioral adaptations, diet, predators, mating and nesting habits, and chick development." Horn Book Guide

This "is a delightful book. . . . The beautiful color photographs and the text tell a fascinating, exciting, and revealing story." Sci Books Films

Magloff, Lisa

Duckling. Dorling Kindersley 2003 24p il (Watch me grow) $7.99 (k-2)   **598**

1. Ducks

ISBN 0-7894-9628-3   LC 2003-1577

Shows the duck as it grows up in its natural environment

"The full-color photographs . . . are not only exceptionally well chosen but downright dynamic. . . . Outstanding for browsing, with solid content for animal reports." Booklist

Markle, Sandra

A mother's journey; illustrated by Alan Marks. Charlesbridge 2005 32p il $15.95; pa $6.95 (k-3)   **598**

1. Penguins

ISBN 1-57091-621-7; 1-57091-622-5 (pa)

LC 2004-18954

"A simple, lyrical text follows the fortunes of an Emperor penguin from laying her first egg through her epic journey to open sea seeking food and culminating in her timely return with a belly full to regurgitate for her newly hatched chick. The whole is perfectly accompanied by Marks's luminous blue-toned watercolors." SLJ

Owls. Carolrhoda 2004 39p il (Animal predators) lib bdg $25.26; pa $7.95 (3-6)

598

1. Owls

ISBN 1-57505-729-8 (lib bdg); 1-57505-745-X (pa)

"Markle observes owls' hunting techniques and includes information about their physical characteristics, physiology, habitats, and care of young." Horn Book Guide

"The full-color photography bedazzles on almost every page." SLJ

Includes glossary and bibliographical references

Vultures. Lerner 2005 40p il (Animal scavengers) lib ed $25.26 (3-5)   **598**

1. Vultures

ISBN 0-8225-3195-X

Talks about vultures, their habitats, feeding habits, how they grow and how they protect themselves.

"Astonishing color photos of action in the wild share space with clear, dramatic zoological facts and connections." Booklist

Includes bibliographical references

McMillan, Bruce

Days of the ducklings; written and photo-illustrated by Bruce McMillan. Houghton Mifflin 2001 32p il $16 (2-4)   **598**

1. Ducks

ISBN 0-618-04878-2   LC 00-13258

"Walter Lorraine books"

The author focuses on a remote island off the coast of Iceland "and its eider duck population. . . . A girl named Drifa, daughter of one of the island's new owners, takes on the task of fostering the ducklings and ensuring their safety until their return to the wild." Bull Cent Child Books

"McMillan's photographs are of extremely high quality, a wonderful blend of artistry and emotion, and his text flows well." Booklist

Includes bibliographical references

Nights of the pufflings; written and photo-illustrated by Bruce McMillan. Houghton Mifflin 1995 32p il $16; pa $5.95 (2-4)

598

1. Puffins

ISBN 0-395-70810-9; 0-395-85693-0 (pa)

LC 94-14808

"For two weeks every year, the children of Heimaey Island, Iceland, stay out late rescuing hundreds of stranded pufflings. Many of the birds are confused by the village lights and need help flying toward the sea." Sci Child

"This fascinating story, combined with gorgeous color photographs, a simple, clear text, and handsome book design, makes an appealing package. McMillan includes the pronunciation of unfamiliar Icelandic names and words within the text and follows his story with an afterwood about the North Atlantic puffins." Horn Book

Includes bibliographical references

McMillan, Bruce—*Continued*

Penguins at home; gentoos of Antarctica; written and photo-illustrated by Bruce McMillan. Houghton Mifflin 1993 32p il $17 (2-4)

598

1. Penguins
ISBN 0-395-66560-4   LC 92-34769

Describes the physical characteristics, behavior, and life cycle of the timid gentoo penguin

"First-rate photographs illustrate a text that supplies interesting information. . . . Large captions summarize important facts and detailed descriptions are provided to enrich the volume." Sci Child

Includes bibliographical references

Wild flamingos; written and photo-illustrated by Bruce McMillan. Houghton Mifflin 1997 32p il $17 (2-4)   **598**

1. Flamingos
ISBN 0-395-84545-9   LC 97-1521

A photo essay describing the physical characteristics, natural habitat, and behavior of the flamingos of Bonaire, Netherlands Antilles

"Children can learn a great deal from the readable text. . . . The striking full-color photographs capture the birds in a variety of interesting poses." SLJ

Includes bibliographical references

Miller, Sara Swan

Woodpeckers, toucans, and their kin. Watts 2003 47p il (Animals in order) lib bdg $25; pa $6.95 (4-6)   **598**

1. Woodpeckers 2. Toucans 3. Honeyguides (Birds)
ISBN 0-531-12243-3 (lib bdg); 0-531-16661-9 (pa)
LC 2002-1732

Introduces the different animals in the piciform order, their similarities and differences, environments in which they live, and how to observe them

This book makes "fascinating reading. . . . Photographs are glorious." Libr Media Connect

Includes glossary and bibliographical references

Morrison, Gordon

Bald eagle. Houghton Mifflin 1998 30p il $16 (2-4)   **598**

1. Bald eagle
ISBN 0-395-87328-2   LC 97-42007

"Walter Lorraine books"

"Large watercolor and black-ink drawings illustrate the life cycle of the American bald eagle." SLJ

This "works on several levels. . . . Without anthropomorphizing, Morrison offers an elegant, scientific look at the way eagles live in the wild." Booklist

Mudd-Ruth, Maria

Hawks & falcons. Benchmark Bks. 2004 47p il map (Animals, animals) lib bdg $17.95 (3-6)
598

1. Hawks 2. Falcons
ISBN 0-7614-1616-1   LC 2003-1435

Contents: Introducing hawks and falcons; Hawk or falcon?; Life cycle; The great migration; Masters of the sky

Describes the physical characteristics, behavior, habitat, and endangered status of hawks and falcons

Includes glossary and bibliographical references

Owls; by Maria Mudd Ruth. Benchmark Books 2004 46p il map (Animals, animals) lib bdg $25.64 (3-6)   **598**

1. Owls
ISBN 0-7614-1752-4   LC 2004-364

Contents: Introducing owls; Who's an owl; The silent hunters; Life cycle; A promising future?

This describes the life cycles and characteristics of owls, illustrated with color photographs

Includes glossary and bibliographical references

Noonan, Diana

The emperor penguin. Chelsea Clubhouse Bks. 2003 32p il (Life cycles) lib bdg $14.95 (2-4)
598

1. Penguins
ISBN 0-7910-6965-6   LC 2002-30

An introduction to the physical characteristics, behavior, and development from egg to adult of the emperor penguin, birds who live in Antarctica

"Clear, colorful, and striking photographs accompany the simple yet educational text." Libr Media Connect

Includes glossary

Osborn, Elinor

Project UltraSwan; written and photographed by Elinor Osborn. Houghton Mifflin 2002 64p il map (Scientists in the field) $16 (4 and up)
598

1. Swans
ISBN 0-618-14528-1   LC 2002-223

Describes the life of large trumpeter swans, how they nearly became extinct, and efforts to reintroduce them to the Northeastern United States and to help them relearn migration routes

"Beautifully illustrated with crisp, colorful photographs and maps, *Project UltraSwan* describes in clear, succinct language all that the scientists must take into account in their work, as well as what they have learned about their subject so far." Booklist

Patent, Dorothy Hinshaw

The bald eagle returns; [by] Dorothy Hinshaw Patent; [photographs by] William Muñoz. Clarion Bks. 2000 68p il map $15 (4 and up)
598

1. Bald eagle 2. Birds—Protection
ISBN 0-395-91416-7   LC 00-21751

"A revised version of the author's and photographer's earlier book *Where the Bald Eagles Gather*." Title page

Describes how bald eagles have recovered from the threat of extinction, how they raise their families, and why they are the national bird of the United States

This offers "exciting new information about the status of our national bird; and crisp, beautiful, full-color photos." SLJ

Patent, Dorothy Hinshaw—*Continued*

Pigeons; photographs by William Muñoz. Clarion Bks. 1997 78p il $16 (4 and up)

       598

1. Pigeons

ISBN 0-395-69848-0   LC 96-42072

Describes the physical characteristics, behavior, and usefulness of these birds, which have lived with people since prehistoric times

"This informative book offers a well-researched and readable text illustrated with clear, full-color photographs." Booklist

Includes glossary

Penny, Malcolm

Golden eagle; habitats, life cycles, food chains, threats. Raintree Steck-Vaughn Pubs. 2001 48p il (Natural world) $27.12 (k-3)   **598**

1. Eagles

ISBN 0-7398-4437-7   LC 2001-19207

A look at "the life of the golden eagle. Brief descriptions give information on mating, incubating eggs, eaglets learning how to fly, and leaving the nest. Loss of habitat and threats to the golden eagle are also addressed." Horn Book Guide

This "title has an abundance of excellent color photographs. . . . The writing style is quick flowing, fact filled, and likely to keep the attention of the intended audience." Sci Books Films

Includes glossary and bibliographical references

Peterson, Roger Tory

A field guide to the birds of eastern and central North America; by Roger Tory Peterson and Virginia Marie Peterson. 5th ed. Houghton Mifflin 2002 xxii, 427p il maps $30 (5 and up)

       598

1. Birds—North America

ISBN 0-395-74047-9   LC 2001-51879

Also available large print edition $24 (ISBN 0-395-96371-0)

"The Peterson field guide series"

First published 1934 with title: A field guide to the birds

"Sponsored by the National Audubon Society, the National Wildlife Federation, and the Roger Tory Peterson Institute"

This guide to birds found east of the Rocky Mountains contains colored illustrations painted by the author, with a description of each species on the facing page. Views of young birds and seasonal variations in plumage are included. Birds are arranged in eight major groups of body shape

A field guide to western birds; text and illustrations by Roger Tory Peterson; maps by Virginia Marie Peterson. 3rd ed, completely rev and enl. Houghton Mifflin 1998 432p il maps $27; pa $18 (5 and up)   **598**

1. Birds—West (U.S.)

ISBN 0-395-91174-5; 0-395-91173-7 (pa)

       LC 89-31517

Also available vinyl-bound edition (ISBN 0-618-13218-X) $20

"The Peterson field guide series"

First published 1941

"Sponsored by the National Audubon Society, the National Wildlife Federation, and the Roger Tory Peterson Institute"

"A completely new guide to field marks of all species found in North America west of the 100th meridian and north of Mexico." Title page

This guide illustrates over 1,000 birds (700 species) on 165 color plates. In addition, over 400 distribution maps are included

Pringle, Laurence P.

Crows!: strange and wonderful; illustrated by Bob Marstall. Boyds Mills Press 2002 32p il $15.95 (2-4)   **598**

1. Crows

ISBN 1-56397-899-7   LC 2001-92591

"The book provides basic information about various members of the crow family but focuses mainly on the well-known common crow and its behavior, covering vocalizations, nesting habits, defense against predators, and food acquisition." Bull Cent Child Books

"The text is vividly written and easy to understand, and the detailed color illustrations are striking." SLJ

Sattler, Helen Roney

The book of North American owls; illustrated by Jean Day Zallinger. Clarion Bks. 1995 64p il maps $17; pa $7.95 (4 and up)   **598**

1. Owls

ISBN 0-395-60524-5; 0-395-90017-4 (pa)

       LC 91-43626

This volume "includes owl classification and history, hunting and habitat, courtship and nesting, and the complex relationship between owls and humans. The comprehensive glossary includes all of the 21 North American species." Sci Child

This "is a superb ornithological primer. . . . The book is lavishly illustrated." Appraisal

Includes bibliographical references

Sayre, April Pulley

The hungry hummingbird; illustrated by Gay W. Holland. Millbrook Press 2001 unp il $22.90 (k-3)

       598

1. Hummingbirds

ISBN 0-7613-1951-4   LC 00-50064

The text and illustrations describe a young hummingbird's day in the hot summer focusing on how the bird learns what is good to eat. In a factual afterword, the author offers some advice on the proper preparation and care of a hummingbird feeder

"Appealing artwork and factual information laid out in an easy-to-understand format make this book a winner. . . . Holland's soft, predominantly pastel art done in colored pencils features birds and insects that have been precisely drawn with exquisite detail." SLJ

Swan, Erin Pembrey

Penguins: from emperors to macaronis. Watts 2003 47p il (Animals in order) $25 (4-6)

598

1. Penguins

ISBN 0-531-12264-6   LC 2002-8886

Contents: Penguins in Antarctica and sub-Antarctic Islands; Penguins in South America; Penguins in South Australia and New Zealand; Penguins in Africa; Penguins and people

Describes the general physical characteristics and behavior of penguins and takes an indepth look at fourteen different species

This book makes "fascinating reading. . . . Photographs are glorious." Libr Media Connect

Includes glossary and bibliographical references

Tatham, Betty

Penguin chick; illustrated by Helen K. Davie. HarperCollins Pubs. 2002 33p il (Let's-read-and-find-out science) $15.95; lib bdg $15.89; pa $4.95 (k-3)   **598**

1. Penguins

ISBN 0-06-028594-X; 0-06-028595-8 (lib bdg); 0-06-445206-9 (pa)   LC 00-59696

This book "follows the growth of one penguin chick from egg to adulthood. The story has been told before, but the clear, simple text provides intriguing details and inherent drama that will keep young children involved straight through till the end." Booklist

Watts, Barrie

Duck. Smart Apple Media 2003 32p il (Watch it grow) lib bdg $24.25 (k-3)   **598**

1. Ducks

ISBN 1-58340-197-0   LC 2002-17032

First published 2002 by Franklin Watts

A simple introduction to the physical characteristics and behavior of ducks, emphasizing the birth and development of ducklings

The text is "easy without being oversimplified or overly anthropomorphized. . . . The full-color photograph cutouts on white backgrounds reflect clearly the information in the text. Additionally, each double-page spread has borders of full-color drawings of the featured animal engaging in natural activities." SLJ

Webb, Sophie

Looking for seabirds; journal from an Alaskan voyage. Houghton Mifflin Co 2004 48p il $16 (4 and up)   **598**

1. Birds 2. Alaska

ISBN 0-618-21235-3   LC 2003-12420

A journal of the author's observations and adventures while working on a research vessel counting seabirds through Alaska's Aleutian Island chain.

The "immediacy of the narrative . . . and the clear and colorful watercolor-and-gouache landscapes and drawings of the birds form an appealing travelogue that is as exciting as it is informative." SLJ

My season with penguins; an Antarctic journal. Houghton Mifflin 2000 48p il map $15; pa $5.95 (4 and up)   **598**

1. Penguins 2. Antarctica

ISBN 0-395-92291-7; 0-618-43234-5 (pa)

LC 99-54781

Describes the author's two-month stay in Antarctica to study and draw penguins

"Webb presents a great deal of scientific information through an effective blend of journal entries and illustrations. . . . Done in gouache and watercolor, the paintings range from scenes of mountains and moving ice to depictions of penguins engaged in typical behaviors. . . . Webb offers a fine look at the scientific method in action." SLJ

Includes glossary

Wilcox, Charlotte

Bald eagles; photographs by Jerry Boucher. Carolrhoda Bks. 2003 48p il (Carolrhoda nature watch book) lib bdg $25.26 (3-6)   **598**

1. Bald eagle

ISBN 1-57505-170-2   LC 2001-6803

Describes the physical characteristics, life cycle, and behavior of bald eagles, as well as efforts to protect them

Winer, Yvonne

Birds build nests; written by Yvonne Winer; illustrated by Tony Oliver. Charlesbridge Pub. 2002 unp il $16.95; pa $6.95 (k-3)   **598**

1. Birds—Nests

ISBN 1-57091-500-8; 1-57091-501-6 (pa)

LC 2001-28998

Rhyming text and illustrations describe how, where, why, and when birds around the world build nests

"The common refrain 'birds build nests' helps create an enticing, rolling rhythm that will draw young ones into the simply phrased lyrical text. Oliver's beautiful, highly detailed paintings show species and their nests in near-photographic detail." Booklist

Includes bibliographical references

599.2   Marsupials and monotremes

Burt, Denise

Kangaroos; photographs by Neil McLeod; edited by Sylvia A. Johnson. Carolrhoda Bks. 2000 48p il (Carolrhoda nature watch book) $23.93 (3-6)

599.2

1. Kangaroos

ISBN 1-57505-388-8   LC 99-26680

"What makes a kangaroo distinct? What is a kangaroo, large or small? How does a kangaroo live, and what is its family life like? The book answers such questions superbly and concisely. Excellent photos support the text and vice versa." Sci Books Films

Includes glossary

Collard, Sneed B.
Platypus, probably; [by] Sneed B. Collard III;
illustrated by Andrew Plant. Charlesbridge 2005
unp il   **599.2**
1. Platypus
ISBN 1-57091-583-0; 1-57091-584-9 (pa)
LC 2004-18957
This "introduces the platypus, which lives only in
Australia, and describes the physical characteristics and
behaviors of this unusual animal. . . . Richly detailed
and atmospheric, the acrylic-and-gouache paintings illustrate the text with many large-scale, horizontal spreads."
Booklist

Jango-Cohen, Judith
Kangaroos; by Judith Jango-Cohen. 1st ed.
Benchmark Books 2006 48p il (Animals, animals)
lib bdg $25.64 (3-6)   **599.2**
1. Kangaroos
ISBN 0-7614-1869-5   LC 2004-21621
Describes the physical characteristics, behavior, and
habitat of kangaroos
Includes glossary and bibliographical references

Lang, Aubrey
Baby koala; text by Aubrey Lang; photography
by Wayne Lynch. Fitzhenry & Whiteside 2004
36p il (Nature babies) $11.95; pa $6.95 (k-3)
599.2
1. Koalas
ISBN 1-55041-874-2; 1-55041-876-9 (pa)
This describes the behavior of a mother and baby koala in the Australian eucalyptus forest.
"This photo-essay combines a clear, informal text with
full-color closeup pictures." Booklist

Noonan, Diana
The kangaroo. Chelsea Clubhouse Bks. 2003
32p il (Life cycles) lib bdg $14.95 (2-4)
599.2
1. Kangaroos
ISBN 0-7910-6968-0   LC 2002-36
An introduction to the physical characteristics, behavior, and birth and development of kangaroos, marsupials
that live in Australia
"Clear, colorful, and striking photographs accompany
the simple yet educational text." Libr Media Connect
Includes glossary

Sill, Cathryn P.
About marsupials; a guide for children; [by]
Cathryn Sill; illustrated by John Sill. Peachtree
2006 unp il $15.95 (k-2)   **599.2**
1. Marsupials
ISBN 1-56145-358-7   LC 2005020582
This introduces the characteristics and behavior of 17
marsupials, such as the marsupial mole, the red kangaroo, the numbat, the spotted cuscus, the koala and tasma-
nian devil.
"Written with simplicity and dignity. . . . Well-suited
to classroom sharing, the paintings are attractively composed and clearly delineated." Booklist
Includes glossary and bibliographical references

599.3 Miscellaneous orders of placental mammals

Gibbons, Gail
Rabbits, rabbits, & more rabbits! Holiday House
2000 unp il $16.95; pa $6.95 (k-3)   **599.3**
1. Rabbits
ISBN 0-8234-1486-8; 0-8234-1660-7 (pa)
LC 99-16765
Describes different kinds of rabbits, their physical
characteristics, behavior, where they live, and how to
care for them
"Colored washes and crayon shading enliven the clearly delineated ink drawings." Booklist

Jango-Cohen, Judith
Armadillos. Benchmark Bks. 2004 47p il map
(Animals, animals) lib bdg $25.64 (3-6)
599.3
1. Armadillos
ISBN 0-7614-1617-X   LC 2003-3824
Contents: Introducing armadillos; Digging up dinner;
Little pink pups; Armadillo defenses; Armadillos and
people
Describes the physical characteristics, behavior, and
habitat of armadillos
Includes glossary and bibliographical references

Lang, Aubrey
Baby sloth; text by Aubrey Lang; photography
by Wayne Lynch. Fitzhenry & Whiteside 2005
c2004 36p il (Nature babies) $11.95; pa $6.95
(k-3)   **599.3**
1. Sloths 2. Panama 3. Rain forests
ISBN 1-55041-825-4; 1-55041-827-0 (pa)
This describes the author and illustrator's journey to
Panama's rainforests and their observations of sloth behavior.
This title pairs "excellent-quality, never-before-
published photos with simple [text]. . . . Appealing and
useful." SLJ

Rounds, Glen
Beaver. Holiday House 1999 unp il $16.95 (k-3)
599.3
1. Beavers
ISBN 0-8234-1440-X   LC 98-28803
Describes the physical characteristics, diet, and nighttime activities of the beaver, an expert swimmer and
builder
"Round's rough, scribbly lines are especially suited to
these evocative pictures of beavers at rest and at work.
. . . The text, outlining the beaver's daily habits and
modus vivendi, is a model of how to convey a wealth of
information in just a few clear, well-phrased statements."
Horn Book Guide

Stewart, Melissa

Sloths. Carolrhoda Books 2005 48p il map (Carolrhoda nature watch book) lib bdg $25.26 (3-6)   **599.3**

1. Sloths

ISBN 1-57505-577-5   LC 2003-23223

Contents: Sloths through time; At home in the tropical forest; Food facts; Avoiding enemies; Raising a family; Can sloths survive?

In this "book, two and three-toed sloths' physical features, habitat, and environmental issues are featured. The well-composed text traces their evolution from prehistoric progenitors' to the current day. . . . With its well-captioned, full-color photos on every page and informative text, Sloths offers enough information for solid reports and general interest." SLJ

Tagholm, Sally

The rabbit; illustrated by Bert Kitchen; written by Sally Tagholm. Kingfisher (NY) 2000 32p il (Animal lives) $9.95 (2-4)   **599.3**

1. Rabbits

ISBN 0-7534-5214-6   LC 99-45787

Describes how the European rabbit, now found on every continent, burrows, breeds, feeds, plays, and lives

"Charming illustrations and an attractive layout support the lyrical and engaging text." Sci Child

Includes glossary

599.35   Rodents

Conniff, Richard

Rats! the good, the bad, and the ugly. Crown 2002 35p il $15.95; lib bdg $17.99 (3-6)
                                       599.35

1. Rats

ISBN 0-375-81207-5; 0-375-91207-X (lib bdg)
                              LC 2002-67355

Discusses the physical characteristics, behavior, origins, various types, interaction with humans, and more of rats

"Informative color photographs and a stylish design accompany many facts and anecdotes about rats in this lively book." Booklist

Jango-Cohen, Judith

Porcupines; by Judith Jango-Cohen. 1st ed. Benchmark Books 2005 48p il (Animals, animals) lib bdg $25.64 (3-6)   **599.35**

1. Porcupines

ISBN 0-7614-1868-7   LC 2004-21443

Describes the physical characteristics, behavior, and habitat of porcupines

This is "eye-catching . . . smoothly written and informative . . . [This includes] numerous clear, closeup color photographs." SLJ

Includes glossary and bibliographical references

Markle, Sandra

Outside and inside rats and mice. Atheneum Bks. for Young Readers 2001 39p il $16 (2-4)
                                       599.35

1. Rats 2. Mice

ISBN 0-689-82301-0   LC 00-29290

Describes the external and internal physical characteristics of mice and rats and their behavior

"Markle skillfully draws readers into careful observation of outstanding close-up photographs of mice and rats. . . . The friendly text maintains its scientific rigor." Horn Book

Includes glossary

Pascoe, Elaine

Mice; text by Elaine Pascoe; photographs by Dwight Kuhn. Blackbirch Press 2005 48p il (Nature close-up) $23.70 (4 and up)
                                       599.35

1. Mice

ISBN 1-4103-0537-6   LC 2005007650

This introduces mouse breeds, physical characteristics, and life cycles, and offers tips on keeping mice as pets, and activities for studying them, and information on scientific research.

"Clear photographs that show every mouse whisker and toe will attract browsers as well as report writers. . . . The language presents concepts in easily understood, straightforward language, and the surprising facts . . . are sure to illicit newfound appreciation." Booklist

Includes glossary and bibliographical references

599.4   Bats

Dornfeld, Margaret

Bats; [by] Margaret Dornfeld. Benchmark Books 2004 46p il map (Animals, animals) lib bdg $25.64 (3-6)   **599.4**

1. Bats

ISBN 0-7614-1754-0   LC 2004-9342

Contents: Introducing bats; Bat basics; Calling all bats; Living upside down; Bats at risk

This describes the life cycles and characteristics of bats, illustrated with color photographs.

Includes glossary and bibliographical references

Earle, Ann

Zipping, zapping, zooming bats; illustrated by Henry Cole. HarperCollins Pubs. 1995 32p il (Let's-read-and-find-out science) lib bdg $15.89; pa $4.95 (k-3)   **599.4**

1. Bats

ISBN 0-06-023480-6 (lib bdg); 0-06-445133-X (pa)
                              LC 93-11052

"Brown bats are introduced as fliers, hunters, and contributors to good ecology in this simple discussion of the flying mammals' physical characteristics and behavior. The illustrations include realistic close-ups, informative diagrams, and scenes incorporating children. Instructions for building a bat house are included." Horn Book Guide

Gibbons, Gail

Bats. Holiday House 1999 unp il $16.95; pa
$6.95 (k-3)   **599.4**

1. Bats

ISBN 0-8234-1457-4; 0-8234-1637-2 (pa)

LC 99-12051

Describes different kinds of bats, their physical characteristics, habits and behavior, and efforts to protect
them

"The occasional splashes of color light up brilliantly
against the dark backgrounds. Well suited for classroom
use, this book makes a good case for bats as an admirable part of the natural world." Booklist

Markle, Sandra

Little lost bat; [by] Sandra Markle; illustrated by
Alan Marks. Charlesbridge 2006 unp il lib bdg
$15.95; pa   **599.4**

1. Bats

ISBN 9781570916564 (lib bdg); 9781570916571

LC 2005019619

"Chronicles the early life of an orphaned Mexican
free-tailed bat, from its birth to its adoption by a new
mother. Includes back matter about bats." Publisher's
note

"The lucid free verse tells the elemental nature drama,
and Marks' beautiful double-page watercolors with delicate ink details are equally effective at depicting the expansive blue sky and the tiny, furry brown baby, alone
and then cuddled up safely at last." Booklist

Outside and inside bats. Atheneum Bks. for
Young Readers 1997 40p il $16 (2-4)

       599.4

1. Bats

ISBN 0-689-81165-9   LC 96-48291

Describes the inner and outer workings of bats, discussing their diet, anatomy, and reproduction

"The photographs are excellent, clearly described and
labeled. . . . The author presents a particularly felicitous
accord of words and pictures in an outstanding science
book." Horn Book

Includes glossary

Pringle, Laurence P.

Bats! strange and wonderful; by Laurence
Pringle; illustrated by Meryl Henderson. Boyds
Mills Press 2000 32p il $15.95 (3-5)

       599.4

1. Bats

ISBN 1-56397-327-8

This "describes some general physical and behavioral
characteristics common to all types of bats. The ways in
which these flying mammals benefit world ecosystems
. . . are emphasized. Vibrant, realistic watercolors of
representative species extend the text on every page."
SLJ

599.5   Cetaceans and sea cows

Becker, John E.

Gray whales. KidHaven Press 2005 48p il map
(Returning wildlife) $23.70 (4-6)   **599.5**

1. Whales

ISBN 0-7377-2293-2   LC 2004-02669

Discusses the history, characteristics, behavior, and
habitat of gray whales including population decline and
recovery and conservation efforts.

Berger, Melvin

Do whales have belly buttons? questions and
answers about whales and dolphins; [by] Melvin
and Gilda Berger; illustrated by Higgins Bond.
Scholastic Ref. 1999 48p il (Scholastic question
and answer series) lib bdg $12.95; pa $5.95 (2-4)

       599.5

1. Whales 2. Dolphins

ISBN 0-590-13081-1 (lib bdg); 0-439-08571-3 (pa)

LC 98-13430

Provides answers to such questions as "Do all whales
have teeth?", "How long do most whales live?", "Why
do dolphins whistle?", and "Can dolphins save humans?"

"Basic up-to-date information presented in a chatty,
readable style." SLJ

Davies, Nicola

Big blue whale; illustrated by Nick Maland.
Candlewick Press 1997 27p il $15.99 (k-3)

       599.5

1. Whales

ISBN 1-56402-895-X   LC 96-42327

Also available Big book edition

Examines the physical characteristics, habits, and habitats of the blue whale

"Davies's brief overview offers young readers exactly
what they want to know about this magnificent animal,
and her judicious use of comparison makes the abstract
more understandable. . . . Maland's cross-hatched pen-
and-ink drawings rest on blue watercolor wash backgrounds." Horn Book Guide

Dudzinski, Kathleen

Meeting dolphins; my adventures in the sea.
National Geographic Soc. 2000 64p il $17.95 (4
and up)   **599.5**

1. Dolphins 2. Animal communication

ISBN 0-7922-7129-7   LC 99-39069

The author describes her work studying dolphin communication and her invention of a listening device that
allows researchers to tell which of a group of dolphins
is vocalizing underwater

"The lively, first-person narrative incorporates abundant facts and entertaining anecdotes, infused with
Dudzinski's infectious enthusiasm for her subjects and
her work. Beautiful, full-color photos are breathtaking
and well chosen for explication." Booklist

Esbensen, Barbara Juster

Baby whales drink milk; illustrated by Lambert Davis. HarperCollins Pubs. 1994 32p il (Let's-read-and-find-out science) pa $4.95 hardcover o.p. (k-1)   **599.5**
1. Whales 2. Mammals
ISBN 0-06-445119-4 (pa)   LC 92-30375
Describes the behavior of the humpback whale, with an emphasis on the fact that it is a mammal and shares the characteristics of other mammals
"Full-color paintings, mainly in watery greens and blues, show the animals in their habitat, along with a scene of a whale model in a museum and a map of migration. The book's strong point, though, is Esbensen's simple, informative text, which keeps its young audience clearly in view." Booklist

Greenaway, Theresa

Whales; [illustrated by Colin Newman] Raintree Steck-Vaughn Pubs. 2001 48p il (Secret world of) lib bdg $18.98 (4 and up)   **599.5**
1. Whales
ISBN 0-7398-3508-4   LC 00-62828
This describes the anatomy, habits, and life cycle of whales and their place in the ecosystem
"The accessible presentation and clear writing style combined with a high level of detail make . . . [this] valuable for simple reports." Booklist
Includes glossary and bibliographical references

Hoyt, Erich

Whale rescue; changing the future for endangered wildlife. Firefly 2005 64p il $19.95; pa $9.95 (5 and up)   **599.5**
1. Whales 2. Wildlife conservation
ISBN 1-55297-601-7; 1-55297-600-9 (pa)
"Hoyt examines the impact of commercial whaling on global whale populations and the efforts being made by scientists, environmentalists, and some governments to protect these endangered mammals. Crisp, color photos portray these leviathans in their natural habitat and also show scientists hard at work on cetacean projects, whaling ships and their harvest on the high seas, and seagoing environmentalists in action." SLJ

Markle, Sandra

Killer whales; [by] Sandra Markle. Carolrhoda Books 2004 39p il (Animal predators) lib bdg $25.26; pa $7.95 (3-6)   **599.5**
1. Whales
ISBN 1-57505-728-X (lib bdg); 1-57505-743-3 (pa)
                                          LC 2003-25944
The author observes killer whales' "hunting techniques and includes information about their physical characteristics, physiology, habitats, and care of young." Horn Book Guide
"Dramatic, large color photos keep step with informative, readable [text]." SLJ
Includes glossary and bibliographical references

Montgomery, Sy

Encantado; pink dolphin of the Amazon; with photographs by Dianne Taylor-Snow. Houghton Mifflin 2002 73p il $18 (4 and up)   **599.5**
1. Dolphins 2. Amazon River valley
ISBN 0-618-13103-5   LC 2001-39251
Introduces the world of the freshwater dolphins called Encantados, or Enchanted, by the people who live near them in the region of the Amazon and Orinoco rivers in South America
"The book contains remarkable descriptions and color photos of the Amazonian rainforest and its inhabitants." Horn Book Guide
Includes bibliographical references

Pfeffer, Wendy

Dolphin talk; whistles, clicks, and clapping jaws; illustrated by Helen K. Davie. HarperCollins Pubs. 2003 33p il (Let's-read-and-find-out science) $15.99; lib bdg $16.89; pa $4.99 (k-2)
                                                599.5
1. Dolphins 2. Animal communication
ISBN 0-06-028801-9; 0-06-028802-7 (lib bdg); 0-06-445210-7 (pa)   LC 2001-39518
Describes how dolphins communicate with each other in squeaks, whistles, and pops
"Pfeffer does a great job of keeping the concept understandable and comparing human and animal communication. . . . Davie's watercolor illustrations are pleasant and upbeat." SLJ

Pringle, Laurence P.

Whales! strange and wonderful; by Laurence Pringle; illustrated by Meryl Henderson. Boyds Mills Press 2003 32p il $15.95 (3-5)
                                                599.5
1. Whales
ISBN 1-56397-439-8   LC 2002-105798
"This volume introduces the varieties, physical features, and behaviors of whales. . . . Pringle's succinct text provides a surprising amount of information in an interesting manner. The clearly delineated and often beautiful illustrations, apparently paintings, help readers visualize the animals and their activities." Booklist

Thomson, Sarah L.

Amazing whales! written by Sarah L. Thomson; photographs provided by the Wildlife Conservation Society. HarperCollins 2004 27p il $15.99; lib bdg $16.89 (1-3)   **599.5**
1. Whales
ISBN 0-06-054465-1; 0-06-054466-X (lib bdg)
                                          LC 2004-2473
"An I can read book"
"Thomson takes a look at blue whales, killer whales, sperm whales, dolphins, and porpoises, describing common physical characteristics of the group as well as hunting and feeding habits, methods of communication, and endangered status." Booklist
"Thomson's superior text sustains readers' attention with interesting facts and apt comparisons. . . . Spectacular color photographs add detail and drama." SLJ

599.63 Even-toed ungulates

Anderson, Jill

Giraffes; by Jill Anderson. NorthWord 2005 unp il (Wild ones) $12.95; pa $6.95 (k-2)

599.63

1. Giraffes

ISBN 1-55971-928-1; 1-55971-929-X (pa)

LC 2004031117

This describes the physiology, habitat, and life cycle of giraffes.

"With simple, direct words and clear, closeup color photo images, this . . . does an excellent job of introducing preschoolers to basic facts about giraffe physiology and habitat, and, especially, how the animals get their food and digest it, and how they care for their young." Booklist

Hatkoff, Isabella

Owen & Mzee; the true story of a remarkable friendship; told by Isabella Hatkoff, Craig Hatkoff, and Paula Kahumbu; photographs by Peter Greste. Scholastic Press 2006 unp il $16.99 (k-3)

599.63

1. Hippopotamus 2. Turtles 3. Indian Ocean earthquake and tsunami, 2004 4. Kenya

ISBN 0-439-82973-9

LC 2005-21341

The "true story of two great friends, a baby hippo named Owen and a 130-yr-old giant tortoise named Mzee (Mm-ZAY). When Owen was stranded after the Dec 2004 tsunami, villagers in Kenya worked tirelessly to rescue him. Then, to everyone's amazement, the orphan hippo and the elderly tortoise adopted each other." Publisher's note

"The text and the back matter are brimming with information about the animals, their caregivers, and the locale. This touching story of the power of a surprising friendship to mitigate the experience of loss is full of heart and hope." SLJ

Jango-Cohen, Judith

Camels; [by] Judith Jango-Cohen. Benchmark Books 2004 c2005 47p il map (Animals, animals) lib bdg $25.64 (3-6)

599.63

1. Camels

ISBN 0-7614-1750-8

LC 2003-24842

Contents: Introducing camels; A camel's diet; Blasting sand and blazing sun; Birth and growth; From caravan to race track

This describes the life cycle and behavior of camels, and their relationships to humans

This "beautifully crafted [book presents] information in a lively, readable manner. [It includes] excellent-quality, candid full-color photographs." SLJ

Includes glossary and bibliographical references

Leach, Michael

Giraffe; habitats, life cycles, food chains, threats. Raintree Steck-Vaughn Pubs. 2001 48p il (Natural world) $18.98 (3-5)

599.63

1. Giraffes

ISBN 0-7398-4435-0

LC 2001-18573

This describes the life cycle of the giraffe, how it evades predators, and its habitat

This book "has an abundance of excellent color photographs. . . . The writing style is quick flowing, fact filled, and likely to keep the attention of the intended audience." Sci Books Films

Includes glossary and bibliographical references

Walker, Sally M.

Hippos; photographs by Gerry Ellis. Carolrhoda Bks. 1998 48p il (Carolrhoda nature watch book) lib bdg $19.93 (3-6)

599.63

1. Hippopotamus

ISBN 1-57505-078-1

LC 96-38135

An introduction to the physical characteristics, habits, and natural environment of the common and the pygmy hippopotamus

This offers "a straightforward text and lots of excellent, well-chosen pictures of hippos in the wild." Booklist

Includes glossary

599.64 Bovids

Berman, Ruth

American bison; photographs by Cheryl Walsh Bellville. Carolrhoda Bks. 1992 48p il map (Carolrhoda nature watch book) lib bdg $23.95 (3-6)

599.64

1. Bison

ISBN 0-87614-697-3

LC 91-25852

Discusses the life cycle of the bison, its role in the settlement of the American West, and its near extinction

"Readers will learn many interesting facts about this, the largest native American mammal. The book is replete with excellent color photos." Sci Books Films

Includes glossary

Perry, Phyllis J.

Buffalo; by Phyllis J. Perry. Benchmark Books 2005 48p il (Animals, animals) lib bdg $25.64 (3-6)

599.64

1. Bison

ISBN 0-7614-1866-0

LC 2004-21438

Contents: The buffalo; What are buffalo?; A native species; The herd; Saving the buffalo

Describes the physical characteristics, behavior, and habitat of buffalo

This is "eye-catching . . . smoothly written and informative. . . . [It includes] numerous clear, closeup color photographs." SLJ

Includes glossary and bibliographical references

599.65 Deer

DuTemple, Lesley A.

North American moose. Carolrhoda Bks. 2000 48p il maps (Carolrhoda nature watch book) lib bdg $23.93 (3-6)

599.65

1. Moose

ISBN 1-57505-426-4

LC 99-37091

DuTemple, Lesley A.—*Continued*
Describes the physical characteristics, life cycle, and behavior of North American moose

Estigarribia, Diana
Moose; by Diana Estigarribia. 1st ed. Benchmark Books 2006 48p il (Animals, animals) lib bdg $25.64 (3-6) **599.65**
1. Moose
ISBN 0-7614-1870-9 LC 2004-21444
Describes the physical characteristics, behavior, and habitat of moose
This is "eye-catching . . . smoothly written and informative. . . . [It includes] numerous clear, closeup color photographs." SLJ
Includes glossary and bibliographical references

Patent, Dorothy Hinshaw
White-tailed deer; photographs by William Muñoz. Lerner Publications Co 2005 47p il map (Early bird nature books) lib bdg $25.26 (2-4) **599.65**
1. Deer
ISBN 0-8225-3052-X LC 2004-2381
Contents: Deer around the world; The whitetail; Raising a family; Life in fall and winter; Whitetails and people
"Short chapters introduce children first to the larger deer family, then provide information on whitetails' life cycles, adaptations for survival, and interactions with humans. . . . A solid offering." Booklist

Quinlan, Susan E.
Caribou. Carolrhoda Books 2005 48p il (Carolrhoda nature watch book) lib bdg $25.26 (3-6) **599.65**
1. Caribou
ISBN 1-57505-579-1 LC 2003-27201
Contents: Nomads of the northlands; Land of winter; In search of food; On the move; Season of calving; The insect tormenters; Return to winter; The rise and fall of great herds; Of caribou and humans; Caribou for the future
Describes the physical characteristics, habitat, behavior, and life cycle of the caribou
"Clearly written. . . . Crisp color photographs appear throughout." Horn Book Guide
Includes glossary

599.66 Odd-toed ungulates

Jango-Cohen, Judith
Rhinoceroses. Benchmark Books 2004 c2005 47p il map (Animals, animals) lib bdg $25.64 (3-6) **599.66**
1. Rhinoceros
ISBN 0-7614-1753-2 LC 2004-839
Contents: Introducing rhinoceroses; Horns, hides, and hooves; Mud baths and back scratches; Rhino reproduction; Rhino survival

This describes the life cycle and behavior of rhinoceroses
This "beautifully crafted [book presents] information in a lively, readable manner. [It includes] excellent-quality, candid full-color photographs." SLJ
Includes glossary and bibliographical references

Noble-Goodman, Katherine
Zebras; by Katherine Noble-Goodman. Benchmark Books 2006 48p il (Animals, animals) lib bdg $25.64 (3-6) **599.66**
1. Zebras
ISBN 0-7614-1871-7
Describes the physical characteristics, behavior, and habitat of zebras
Includes glossary and bibliographical references

Peterson, Cris
Wild horses; Black Hills Sanctuary; photographs by Alvis Upitis. Boyds Mills Press 2003 unp il $16.95 (3-6) **599.66**
1. Hyde, Dayton O., 1925- 2. Horses 3. Wildlife conservation
ISBN 1-56397-745-1 LC 2002-110799
"In the early 1980s, rancher Dayton Hyde purchased land in the Black Hills of South Dakota and created the Wild Horse Sanctuary, which is now home to about 300 horses. In this engaging photo-essay, Peterson tells the history of Hyde and his horses. . . . The color photographs will captivate readers most. . . . This is an informative, also inspiring look at the results of one man's conservation efforts." Booklist

Ryden, Hope
Wild horses I have known. Clarion Bks. 1999 90p il $18 (4 and up) **599.66**
1. Horses
ISBN 0-395-77520-5 LC 97-49021
Text and photographs depict mustang social behavior observed by the author, as well as an account of how the mustang established itself and adapted to being a wild horse in the American West
"A carefully crafted book that features abundant use of strikingly beautiful photographs. . . . A nice combination of elegance and sound information." Horn Book
Includes bibliographical references

599.67 Elephants

Arnold, Katya
Elephants can paint, too! pictures and text by Katya Arnold. Atheneum Books for Young Readers 2005 unp il $16.95 (k-3) **599.67**
1. Elephants 2. Painting
ISBN 0-689-86985-1 LC 2004-17387
"An Anne Schwartz book"
The author "tells how she trains elephants to paint and compares the work of her human and elephant pupils. The spare narrative is easy to understand and reads like a picture book. . . . Arnold's amusing and colorful photographs—of elephants and children at work—will have readers laughing as they view them side-by-side." SLJ

Morgan, Jody

Elephant rescue; changing the future for endangered wildlife. Firefly Books 2004 64p il $19.95; pa $9.95 (5 and up) **599.67**

1. Elephants 2. Wildlife conservation

ISBN 1-55297-595-9; 1-55297-594-0 (pa)

This "photo-essay . . . combines an urgent message about conservation with a closeup view of elephant physiology, behavior, and habitat in Africa and Asia." Booklist

This is "well-written. . . . Stunning, full-color photographs bring [these animals] to life." SLJ

599.7 Carnivores. Land carnivores

North, Sterling

Rascal; illustrated by John Schoenherr. Dutton 1984 c1963 189p il $16.99; pa $5.99 (5 and up) **599.7**

1. Raccoons

ISBN 0-525-18839-8; 0-14-034445-4 (pa)

LC 84-10292

Also available Spanish language edition

A Newbery Award honor book, 1964

First published 1963 with subtitle: A memoir of a better era

A book about Rascal "a young raccoon, Sterling North's pet the year he was eleven, in rural Wisconsin. . . . The book calls up a series of marvelous pictures; boy fishing in peaceful company of raccoon, boy riding on bike with raccoon (a demon for speed) standing up in the bike basket, raccoon with friend, a prize trotting horse, raccoon helping boy to win a pie-eating contest. A central episode is about an idyllic camping trip." Publ Wkly

Tatham, Betty

Baby sea otter; illustrated by Joan Paley. Holt & Co. 2005 unp il $16.95 (k-2) **599.7**

1. Otters

ISBN 0-8050-7504-6 (lib bdg) LC 2004-23393

"A baby sea otter is born and cared for by her mother, who grooms her, hunts for food, feeds her, and saves her from a hungry eagle. . . . The clear, simple paragraphs of text, interspersed with the drama that the otters face daily, will keep young readers interested. Paley's lush blue and aqua-toned collages add texture and richness." SLJ

599.75 Cat family

Clutton-Brock, Juliet

Cat; written by Juliet Clutton-Brock. rev ed. Dorling Kindersley 2004 72p il (DK eyewitness books) $15.99 (4 and up) **599.75**

1. Wild cats 2. Cats

ISBN 0-7566-0662-4

First published 1991

Text and photographs present the anatomy, behavior, habitats, and other aspects of wild and domestic cats

Darling, Kathy

Lions; photographs by Tara Darling-Lyon. Carolrhoda Bks. 2000 48p il (Carolrhoda nature watch book) lib bdg $23.93 (3-6) **599.75**

1. Lions

ISBN 1-57505-404-3 LC 99-32632

Describes the physical characteristics and behavior of lions, as well as some of the threats they face

"Strong writing and animal photography work together to create [a book] that will be sought out for school assignments and recreational reading." Horn Book Guide

Includes glossary

Estigarribia, Diana

Cheetahs; by Diana Estigarribia. Benchmark Books 2004 c2005 46p il map (Animals, animals) lib bdg $25.64 (3-6) **599.75**

1. Cheetahs

ISBN 0-7614-1749-4 LC 2003-22600

Contents: Introducing cheetahs; Built for speed; A cheetah's life; The hunter; Cheetahs and us

Describes the physical characteristics, behavior, hunting methods, and habitat of cheetahs.

This "beautifully crafted [book presents] information in a lively, readable manner. [It includes] excellent-quality, candid full-color photographs." SLJ

Includes glossary and bibliographical references

Markle, Sandra

Lions; by Sandra Markle. Carolrhoda 2004 39p il (Animal predators) lib bdg $25.26; pa $7.95 (3-6) **599.75**

1. Lions

ISBN 1-57505-727-1 (lib bdg); 1-57505-744-1 (pa)

LC 2003-11198

The author observes lions' "hunting techniques and includes information about their physical characteristics, physiology, habitats, and care of young." Horn Book Guide

"The straightforward, descriptive text and superb photos give [this title] surefire appeal to middle readers." Booklist

Includes glossary and bibliographical references

Outside and inside big cats. Atheneum Bks. for Young Readers 2003 39p il $16.95 (2-4) **599.75**

1. Wild cats

ISBN 0-689-82299-5 LC 2001-46368

The author "gives readers a close-up view of a variety of cat species, including lions and tigers and cheetahs and panthers. She guides animal enthusiasts through the basics of organism structure and function, anatomy, and animal behavior. . . . Excellent color photographs capture all aspects of big cats, from cuddly views of baby animals to detailed pictures of interior organs to grisly scenes of feeding frenzies." Horn Book

Includes glossary

Montgomery, Sy

The man-eating tigers of Sundarbans; with photographs by Eleanor Briggs. Houghton Mifflin 2001 57p il map $16; pa $6.95 (4 and up)

599.75

1. Tigers
ISBN 0-618-07704-9; 0-618-49490-1 (pa)

LC 00-32031

"The author introduces readers to the geography of India and the ecology of Sundarbans, gives a brief overview of tiger behavior . . . discusses the man-eating habits of the tigers of Sundarbans, and puts forth some possible explanations for their unusual behavior." Bull Cent Child Books

"To draw readers into this scientific puzzle, Montgomery integrates science, storytelling, anthropology, and adventure in a unique treatment, illustrated with excellent color photos and diagrams." Horn Book Guide

Includes bibliographical references

Patent, Dorothy Hinshaw

Big cats; illustrations by Kendahl Jan Jubb. Walker & Co. 2005 unp il map $17.95 (2-4)

599.75

1. Wild cats
ISBN 0-8027-8968-4
"After mentioning the physical features and behaviors common to all or most big cats, the book looks more closely at the lion, leopard, cheetah, tiger, snow leopard, cougar, and jaguar. Patent writes with clarity, economy, and a knack for finding apt descriptions. . . . The watercolor paintings clearly represent the animals in their habitats." Booklist

Simon, Seymour

Big cats. HarperCollins Pubs. 1991 unp il lib bdg $17.89; pa $6.95 (3-6)

599.75

1. Wild cats
ISBN 0-06-021647-6 (lib bdg); 0-06-446119-X (pa)

LC 90-36374

Simon "begins with a general overview of the big cats, and then presents details on the tiger, lion, leopard, jaguar, puma, cheetah and snow leopard. . . . The author also discusses concerns about wildlife conservation." Appraisal

The author "offers a clear, succinct text illuminated with stunning, large color photographs." Booklist

Squire, Ann

Cheetahs; by Ann O. Squire. Children's Press 2005 47p il lib bdg $25; pa $6.95 (2-4)

599.75

1. Cheetahs
ISBN 0-516-22792-0 (lib bdg); 0-516-27932-7 (pa)

LC 2003-5174

"A True book"

Contents: Meet a cheetah; Built for speed; What's for dinner?; Cheetah cubs

"Beginning with cheetahs' best-known quality, their speed, this very readable volume goes on to discuss their prowess and limitations as hunters as well as their prey, social habits, life cycle, and use of camouflage. . . . Re-markably clear, often-dramatic color photos of cheetahs in the wild offer unusually good views of the animals." Booklist

Includes bibliographical references

Stone, Lynn M.

Tigers; written and photographed by Lynn M. Stone. Carolrhoda Books 2005 48p il map (Carolrhoda nature watch book) lib bdg $25.26 (3-6)

599.75

1. Tigers
ISBN 1-57505-578-3

LC 2003-23230

Contents: Tigers are cats; Tiger country; Becoming a tiger; Born to kill; Tracking tigers; Saving the perfect predator

An introduction to the physical characteristics, habits, natural habitat, relationship to humans, and future of the tiger, one of the largest meat-eating animals in the world.

Includes glossary

Swinburne, Stephen R.

Bobcat: North America's cat. Boyds Mills Press 2001 32p il map $15.95 (4 and up)

599.75

1. Bobcats
ISBN 1-56397-843-1
The author "weaves together information about bobcats' physical features, habitat, diet, and behaviors with his personal experiences tracking them on various outings and observing them in captivity. His first-person narrative has an easy, intimate tone and is filled with the insights and fascination of a true and passionate naturalist. Sidebars and a variety of photos round out this absorbing book." Horn Book Guide

Thapar, Valmik

Tiger; habitats, life cycles, food chains, threats. Raintree Steck-Vaughn Pubs. 2000 48p il (Natural world) $27.12; pa $9.95 (3-5)

599.75

1. Tigers 2. Endangered species
ISBN 0-7398-1055-3; 0-7398-0946-6 (pa)

LC 98-53279

Explains the physical characteristics, life cycle, habits, habitat, and endangered status of the tiger

"The writing . . . is clear and lively. . . . The color photographs . . . demand attention." Booklist

Includes glossary and bibliographical references

Thompson, Sharon Elaine

Built for speed; the extraordinary, enigmatic cheetah. Lerner Publs. 1998 88p il lib bdg $27.93 (5 and up)

599.75

1. Cheetahs
ISBN 0-8225-2854-1

LC 96-51094

Describes the habitat, physical characteristics, and behavior of the cheetah, as well as efforts to ensure the continued existence of this fastest land mammal

This "includes and explains many fascinating details of the animals' lives in a comprehensive, well-organized, and attractive way." Sci Books Films

Includes glossary and bibliographical references

599.77 Dog family

Brandenburg, Jim

To the top of the world; adventures with Arctic wolves; edited by JoAnn Bren Guernsey. Walker & Co. 1993 44p il $16.95; pa $7.95 (4 and up)

599.77

1. Wolves

ISBN 0-8027-8219-1; 0-8027-7462-8 (pa)

LC 93-12105

A wildlife photographer records in text and photographs two visits to Ellesmere Island, Northwest Territories, where he filmed a pack of Arctic wolves over several months

"Captivating pictures combine with an informal narrative to create a topnotch, firsthand view of a much-maligned animal." SLJ

George, Michael

Wolves. Child's World 2000 32p il (Nature books) lib bdg $24.21 (1-3) **599.77**

1. Wolves

ISBN 1-56766-584-5

LC 98-36871

Describes the physical characteristics, behavior, habitat, and life cycle of wolves

"The gorgeous, full-color photographs are big, clear, and detailed." SLJ

Gibbons, Gail

Wolves. Holiday House 1994 unp il $16.95; pa $6.95 (k-3) **599.77**

1. Wolves

ISBN 0-8234-1127-3; 0-8234-1202-4 (pa)

LC 94-2108

"A simply written introduction that focuses on the gray, or timber, wolf. . . . Material covered includes physical characteristics, behavior within a pack, and communication by howling and body language. . . . The format is open and spacious, the print is large, and the realistic, watercolor illustrations are set against backgrounds of white and deep blues." SLJ

Greenaway, Theresa

Wolves, wild dogs, and foxes; illustrated by Robert Morton. Raintree Steck-Vaughn Pubs. 2001 48p il (Secret world of) lib bdg $18.98 (4 and up) **599.77**

1. Wolves 2. Wild dogs 3. Foxes

ISBN 0-7398-3507-6

LC 00-62829

This describes the anatomy, habits, and life cycles of wolves, wild dogs, and foxes and their place in the ecosystem

"The accessible presentation and clear writing style combined with a high level of detail make . . . [this] valuable for simple reports." Booklist

Includes glossary and bibliographical references

Halls, Kelly Milner

Wild dogs; past and present. Darby Creek Pub. 2005 64p il (World of animals) $18.95 (5 and up)

599.77

1. Wild dogs

ISBN 1-58196-027-1

This "book explains how fossils and DNA are used to show the evolutionary lines from prehistoric canids to the dogs we live with today. . . . The author presents a wealth of detail through the accessible text; the informative captions, charts, sidebars; and the simple but clear maps." SLJ

Includes bibliographical references

Markle, Sandra

Growing up wild: wolves. Atheneum Bks. for Young Readers 2001 31p il $16 (2-4)

599.77

1. Wolves

ISBN 0-689-81886-6

LC 99-54145

Text and color photographs show how gray wolf cubs are born and grow up in the wild

"The brief narrative is written in fairly simple language and is interesting enough to share with young children. . . . Excellent color photos show the canine family close up." SLJ

Includes glossary

Wolves; by Sandra Markle. Lerner Publications 2004 40p il (Animal predators) lib bdg $25.26; pa $7.95 (3-6) **599.77**

1. Wolves

ISBN 1-57505-732-8 (lib bdg); 1-57505-748-4 (pa)

LC 2003-11197

The author "describes the birth, physical growth, and education of three gray wolf cubs during the several seasons that it takes them to mature to adulthood." SLJ

"The text works well with the often striking full-color photos that illustrate the book." Booklist

Includes glossary and bibliographical references

Swinburne, Stephen R.

Coyote; North America's dog. Boyds Mills Press 1999 32p il $15.95 (4-6) **599.77**

1. Coyotes

ISBN 1-56397-765-6

The author describes the lifestyles of this "canine, its place in Native American folklore, the conflict between ranchers/farmers and this elusive predator, and the problems the animal faces as it struggles to thrive in pristine wilderness areas and in congested suburbs." SLJ

This book "packs a lot of information about North American coyotes into a small space. The author, a veteran park ranger, knows his subject well and succeeds in making it interesting to his audience. . . . The full-color photographs are clean and clear and enliven the text." Booklist

599.78 Bears

Davies, Nicola

Ice bear; in the steps of the Polar Bear; illustrated by Gary Blythe. Candlewick Press 2005 27p il $16.99 (k-3) **599.78**

1. Polar bear

ISBN 0-7636-2759-3

Describes how the polar bear, also called Nanuk, thrives in the Arctic and explains the lessons that the Inuit people have learned from watching the creature.

"This inviting picture book delivers facts about polar bears and conveys respect for their adaptive success. . . . Children will be fascinated by the impressionistic oil paintings of stunning polar settings and bears at play, tenderly nursing young, and, yes, hunting seals, an activity represented by a stark image of a bear's crimson-stained muzzle that may startle the youngest readers." Booklist

Gibbons, Gail

Giant pandas. Holiday House 2002 unp il $16.95 (k-3) **599.78**

1. Giant panda

ISBN 0-8234-1761-1 LC 2002-19057

An introduction to the physical characteristics, behavior, life cycle, and habitat of giant pandas

"Fascinating panda facts abound. . . . Gibbons encourages early readers by sticking to the facts and keeping her sentence structure simple. Stylized, instructive watercolor paintings convey a genuine affection for this appealing animal." Booklist

Polar bears. Holiday House 2001 unp il map $16.95 (k-3) **599.78**

1. Polar bear

ISBN 0-8234-1593-7 LC 00-54075

An introduction to polar bear behavior discussing "where it lives, what it eats, how it gets its food, when it mates, how it rears its young, and the dangers it faces." SLJ

"Written in brief, engaging sentences with facts that inform but don't overwhelm, this is a good selection for beginning report writers; it will also work well as nonfiction read-aloud for young ones." Booklist

Hirschi, Ron

Searching for grizzlies; photographs by Thomas D. Mangelsen; drawings by Deborah Cooper. Boyds Mills Press 2005 unp il $15.95 (3-5) **599.78**

1. Bears

ISBN 1-59078-014-0

Describes the physical characteristics, behavior, and habitat primarily of grizzly bears, with some comparisons to black bears and polar bears.

"Mangelsen's fine photos and Cooper's attractive sketches accompany Hirschi's readable text bursting with the bear facts." SLJ

Lockwood, Sophie

Polar Bears. Child's World 2005 40p il (World of mammals) lib bdg $29.93 (5 and up) **599.78**

1. Polar bear

ISBN 1-59296-501-6

"The first chapter of *Polar Bears* discusses the bond between the animal and the Inuit people, who have depended on hunting the bears for survival. Then the discussion turns to the bears themselves: their physical features, behaviors, and relatives as well as the threats to their survival." Booklist

Includes bibliographical references

Markle, Sandra

Polar bears; [by] Sandra Markle. Carolrhoda Books 2004 40p il (Animal predators) lib bdg $25.26; pa $7.95 (3-6) **599.78**

1. Polar bear

ISBN 1-57505-730-1 (lib bdg); 1-57505-746-8 (pa)
LC 2003-19515

The author observes polar bears' "hunting techniques and includes information about their physical characteristics, physiology, habitats and care of young." Horn Book Guide

Includes glossary and bibliographical references

Miller, Debbie S.

A polar bear journey; pictures by Jon Van Zyle. Little, Brown 1997 unp il $15.95 (2-4) **599.78**

1. Polar bear

ISBN 0-316-57244-6 LC 96-42284

Details the life cycle of a mother polar bear and her two cubs, from their birth to their learning of survival lessons

"Lovely acrylic paintings accompany this informative and lyrical text." SLJ

Montgomery, Sy

Search for the golden moon bear; science and adventure in the Asian tropics. Houghton Mifflin 2004 80p il $17 (5 and up) **599.78**

1. Bears

ISBN 0-618-35650-9 LC 2004-5236

The author reports on an expedition into Laos and Thailand in search of a rare species of bear

"The exciting narrative is complemented by an array of full-color photos. . . . This attractive and informative offering is an intelligent reportage of science as it happens." SLJ

Includes bibliographical references

Patent, Dorothy Hinshaw

Garden of the spirit bear; illustrated by Deborah Milton. Clarion Books 2004 40p il $16 (3-5) **599.78**

1. Bears 2. Rain forest ecology 3. Pacific Northwest

ISBN 0-618-21259-0 LC 2003-27779

Contents: Garden of the bears; Home of the spirit bear; The many colors of black bears; Trees of the for-

Patent, Dorothy Hinshaw—*Continued*
est; How bears use the trees; First nations and bears;
From canopy to forest floor; Bears use the varied landscape; Nature's recycling; The life of the salmon; The
importance of salmon; Logging the forests; Protecting the
spirit bear's realm; Gifts of the forest
"Patent introduces readers to the area of British Columbia's coastal rainforest that is home to Kermode
bears (sometimes called spirit bears). . . . Milton's watercolor illustrations depict vast, unspoiled landscapes
and show the animals at home in the forest. . . . Patent's
work highlights the threat to one irreplaceable stretch of
wilderness and the creatures that live there." SLJ

A polar bear biologist at work. Watts 2001 48p
il map lib bdg $23.50 (4 and up)   **599.78**
1. Jonkel, Charles 2. Polar bear
ISBN 0-531-11850-9   LC 00-38151
"A Wildlife Conservation Society book"
Describes the work of Charles Jonkel, a biologist who
studied polar bears in the Arctic and primarily in Churchill, Manitoba
"Patent's lucid text is brimming with enough data on
habitat, physiology, and behavior to satisfy the needs of
report writers. . . . Patent's book is important not only
for the basic 'critter data' it contains, but also for its picture of a scientist at work in the field. . . . Approachable
and appealing." SLJ
Includes glossary and bibliographical references

Polar bears; photographs by William Munõz.
Carolrhoda Bks. 2000 48p il map (Carolrhoda
nature watch book) lib bdg $23.93 (3-6)
                                          599.78
1. Polar bear
ISBN 1-57505-020-X   LC 99-29601
Describes the physical characteristics, diet, natural
habitat, and life cycle of polar bears
"Each page includes a large, color photograph. . . .
The lively writing style combined with many interesting
facts make this a solid resource for reports and an excel-
lent choice for young nature lovers." SLJ
Includes glossary

Ryder, Joanne
Little panda; the world welcomes Hua Mei at
the San Diego Zoo. Simon & Schuster 2001 unp
il $16.95 (k-3)   **599.78**
1. Giant panda
ISBN 0-689-84310-0
"Ryder's photo-essay chronicles the life of Hua Mei,
born at the World Famous San Diego Zoo in 1999. . . .
Ryder's brief, almost haiku-like text is bolstered by informative paragraphs set in smaller type. The crisp, engaging photos were provided by the zoo." Booklist

A pair of polar bears; twin cubs find a home at
the San Diego Zoo; by Joanne Ryder; photos by
the world-famous San Diego Zoo. 1st ed. Simon &
Schuster Books for Young Readers 2006 unp il
$16.95 (k-2)   **599.78**
1. Polar bear
ISBN 0-689-85871-X   LC 2005014013

"This photo-essay introduces children to an engaging,
true story from the San Diego Zoo. . . . The stars are
rescued polar bear twins Tatqiq and Kalluk, who progress through the photo-rich pages from needy, quaran-
tined cubs to fully acclimated adults with mastery over
their outdoor habitat. The images, all provided by the
zoo and most sharply focused and closeup, will elicit
coos from readers." Booklist

Swinburne, Stephen R.
Black bear; North America's bear. Boyds Mills
2003 32p il map $15.95 (3-5)   **599.78**
1. Bears
ISBN 1-59078-023-X
An examination of black bears, their behavior and
habitat.
"Stunning, full-color photos and a lively text make for
an intriguing introduction to these fascinating animals."
SLJ

599.8   Primates

Bow, Patricia
Chimpanzee rescue; changing the future for
endangered wildlife. Firefly Books 2004 64p il
(Firefly animal rescue series) $19.95; pa $9.95 (5
and up)   **599.8**
1. Chimpanzees 2. Wildlife conservation
ISBN 1-55297-909-1; 1-55297-908-3 (pa)
This introduces chimpanzees, how and why they are
in danger, and explains what efforts are being made to
protect them.
This is "well-written. . . . Stunning, full-color photographs bring [this] species to life and depict a number of
individuals in the field and laboratory working to save
these animals." SLJ

Costa-Prades, Bernadette
Little gorillas; [by] Bernadette Costa-Prades.
Gareth Stevens Pub 2005 23p il (Born to be wild)
lib bdg $22 (3-5)   **599.8**
1. Gorillas
ISBN 0-8368-4437-8   LC 2004-59721
Originally published in French
"The text introduces a variety of facts, beginning with
the lives of gorilla babies. Children will be fascinated by
the clearly drawn parallels between the behaviors of gorillas and humans. . . . The concise, simply worded
paragraphs are written at a suitable level for elementary-
school report writers." Booklist

Goodall, Jane
The chimpanzees I love; saving their world and
ours. Scholastic Press 2001 80p il map $17.95 (4
and up)   **599.8**
1. Chimpanzees
ISBN 0-439-21310-X   LC 00-47080
"A Byron Preiss book"
"Goodall presents her long involvement with the
chimpanzees of Gombe, describing the amazing discover-

Goodall, Jane—*Continued*
ies she has made over 40 years." SLJ
"Striking an admirable balance between scientific reporting and deep affection, Goodall's . . . impassioned introduction to the creatures to whom she's dedicated her life's work may well ignite in readers a similar appreciation." Publ Wkly
Includes bibliographical references

With love; illustrated by Alan Marks. North-South Bks. 1998 unp il $15.95; lib bdg $15.88 (4 and up)   **599.8**
1. Chimpanzees
ISBN 1-55858-911-2; 1-55858-912-0 (lib bdg)
LC 97-49948
First published 1994 by the Jane Goodall Institute
A collection of stories based on the author's experiences with chimpanzees in Gombe Stream National Park in Tanzania over a period of almost forty years
"Children will love these stories because they are sometimes silly or gross and because they are always tender, and young humans will recognize aspects of themselves in the younger chimps. . . . Marks' watercolor-and-ink paintings capture both action and stasis beautifully and without affectation or sentimentality." Booklist

Lewin, Ted
Gorilla walk; [by] Ted & Betsy Lewin. Lothrop, Lee & Shepard Bks. 1999 48p il map lib bdg $16.89 (4 and up)   **599.8**
1. Gorillas
ISBN 0-688-16510-9   LC 98-44727
Describes an expedition into the field in southern Uganda to observe mountain gorillas in their native habitat
"Briefly captioned, thumbnail watercolors picture the jungle trek, and magnificent double-page spreads replicate the exotic surroundings and show the animals close up." Booklist

McDaniel, Melissa
Monkeys. Benchmark Bks. 2004 47p il map (Animals, animals) lib bdg $25.64 (3-6)
599.8
1. Monkeys
ISBN 0-7614-1615-3   LC 2003-1837
Contents: Introducing monkeys; A monkey's world; Family life; Monkey food; Monkeys and man
Describes the life of monkeys, including social structure, reproduction and child rearing, diet, interaction with humans, and loss of habitat
Includes glossary and bibliographical references

Redmond, Ian
Gorilla, monkey & ape; written by Ian Redmond; photographed by Peter Anderson & Geoff Brightling. Dorling Kindersley 2000 63p il (DK eyewitness books) $15.99; lib bdg $19.99 (4 and up)   **599.8**
1. Primates
ISBN 0-7894-6036-X; 0-7894-6613-9 (lib bdg)
First published 1995 by Knopf with title: Gorilla

An illustrated look at primates, including lemurs, monkeys, and apes.

Simon, Seymour
Gorillas. HarperCollins Pubs. 2000 unp il $15.95; lib bdg $15.89 (3-6)   **599.8**
1. Gorillas
ISBN 0-06-023035-5; 0-06-023036-3 (lib bdg)
LC 99-87161
Describes the physical characteristics and behavior of various kinds of gorillas
"A clear, concise picture of these endangered creatures and their lifestyle. . . . The extremely handsome, oversized color photos enhance the readable text and complement it perfectly." SLJ

Stefoff, Rebecca
The primate order. Benchmark Books 2005 92p il (Family trees) lib bdg $29.93 (5 and up)
599.8
1. Primates
ISBN 0-7614-1816-4   LC 2004-21404
This examines physical traits, adaptations, diets, habitats, and life cycles of primates.
"Fact-filled, yet suprisingly readable. . . . [This] title contains a wide variety of excellent-quality, full-color photographs; interesting sidebars; and diagrams." SLJ

599.93 Genetics, sex and age characteristics, evolution

Gallant, Roy A.
Early humans. Benchmark Bks. 1999 c2000 80p il maps (Story of science) lib bdg $29.93 (5 and up)   **599.93**
1. Fossil hominids 2. Human origins 3. Evolution
ISBN 0-7614-0960-2   LC 98-28037
Discusses human evolution and the search for the earliest forms of humans, examining the Neanderthals, Homo erectus, the variety of fossils found in Africa, and the early apelike hominids
"Richly illustrated with color photos, drawings, and charts. . . . Gallant writes clearly and provides readers with balanced, informative discussions." Booklist
Includes glossary and bibliographical references

600 TECHNOLOGY

Macaulay, David
The new way things work; [by] David Macaulay with Neil Ardley. Houghton Mifflin 1998 400p il $35 (4 and up)   **600**
1. Technology 2. Machinery 3. Inventions
ISBN 0-395-93847-3   LC 98-14224
First published 1988 with title: The way things work
Arranged in five sections this volume provides information on "the workings of hundreds of machines and devices—holograms, helicopters, airplanes, mobile

Macaulay, David—*Continued*
phones, compact disks, hard disks, bits and bytes, cash machines. . . . Explanations [are also given] of the scientific principles behind each machine—how gears make work easier, why jumbo jets are able to fly, how computers actually compute." Publisher's note

Romanek, Trudee
The technology book for girls and other advanced beings; written by Trudee Romanek; illustrated by Pat Cupples. Kids Can Press 2001 56p il $14.95 (4 and up)   **600**
1. Technology
ISBN 1-55074-936-6
"When Gina is assigned a science-project topic, Advanced Technology in Our Everyday Lives, she explores the inner workings of remote controls, smoke detectors, automatic doors, bar codes, and many other mysterious modern conveniences. . . . Simple experiments are described throughout, and a compendium of further experiments is offered in the back of the book. Even young readers who don't fancy themselves science aficionados will have trouble putting this book down." Bull Cent Child Books

603   Technology--Encyclopedias and dictionaries

Exploring technology. Marshall Cavendish 2004 11v il set $329.95 (5 and up)   **603**
1. Technology—Encyclopedias
ISBN 0-7614-7406-4   LC 2002-71510
"The set offers 280 articles pertaining to all facets of technology. . . . The history of invention and innovation are also included in the coverage. . . . The colorful and eye-catching presentation, featuring many color photographs and diagrams as well as the boxed features, will especially appeal to casual browsers. . . . The articles contain enough information to meet the needs of most upper-elementary and middle-school students." Booklist

608   Inventions and patents

Erlbach, Arlene
The kids' invention book. Lerner Publs. 1997 64p il lib bdg $22.60; pa $9.95 (4 and up)
     608
1. Inventions
ISBN 0-8225-2414-7 (lib bdg); 0-8225-9844-2 (pa)
     LC 96-27105
Profiles eleven inventors between the ages of eight and fourteen, describes the steps involved in inventing a new product, and discusses contests, patents, lawyers, and clubs
"Readers will enjoy the stories behind such clever creations as an edible pet-food spoon, an adjustable jump-rope belt, and a portable wheelchair ramp; and the accounts serve as wonderful encouragement for kids who want to pursue ideas of their own." Booklist
Includes bibliographical references

609   Technology--Historical and geographic treatment

Bender, Lionel
Invention; written by Lionel Bender. rev ed. DK Pub. 2005 72p il (DK eyewitness books) $15.99; lib bdg $19.99 (4 and up)   **609**
1. Inventions
ISBN 0-7566-1076-1; 0-7566-1075-3 (lib bdg)
First published 1991 by Knopf
Photographs and text explore such inventions as the wheel, gears, levers, clocks, telephones, and rocket engines.

Bridgman, Roger Francis
1,000 inventions & discoveries; written by Roger Bridgman. DK Pub. 2002 256p il $24.99 (5 and up)   **609**
1. Inventions—History
ISBN 0-7894-8826-4   LC 2002-23742
Summarizes 1000 notable inventions and discoveries of ancient and modern times, from 3,000,000 B.C. to the beginning of the twenty-first century A.D
This offers "color photos, highly informative and readable text, and easy-to-read layouts." ALAN

Harper, Charise Mericle
Imaginative inventions; the who, what, where, when, and why of roller skates, potato chips, marbles, and pie and more! Little, Brown 2001 32p il $14.95 (k-3)   **609**
1. Inventions
ISBN 0-316-34725-6   LC 00-62443
"Megan Tingley books"
This "volume explains how such everyday items as gum, roller skates and potato chips came to be, describing each item in doggerel verse. With its crazy-quilt visual patterns, bouncy stanzas and fun facts, this collection of miscellany zigzags between informational and whimsical." Publ Wkly

Landau, Elaine
The history of everyday life. 21st Century Bks. 2005 56p il (Major inventions through history) $26.60 (5 and up)   **609**
1. Inventions—History
ISBN 0-8225-3808-3
This "explores fireplaces and central heating, indoor plumbing, the washing machine, food and clothing production, and microwave ovens. . . . [It] presents information about daily living from ancient times to the present. . . . The text . . . is breezy but informative. . . . Illustrations are a mixture of period black-and-white and color photos." SLJ
Includes bibligraphical references

Platt, Richard

Eureka! great inventions and how they happened. Kingfisher 2003 95p il $18.95 (4 and up)   **609**

1. Inventions—History

ISBN 0-7534-5580-3   LC 2002-34029

"Platt organizes his introductions to inventors and inventions around 'eureka moments' when scientific breakthroughs occurred. Two-page topical entries include a brief biography of the scientist, an account of the pivotal event, and an explanation of what happened next." SLJ

This is a "most excellent work." Sci Books Films

Includes glossary

Rossi, Ann

Bright ideas; the age of invention in America, 1870-1910; [by] Ann Rossi. National Geographic 2005 40p il (Crossroads America) $12.95 (4-6)   **609**

1. Inventions—History

ISBN 0-7922-8276-0   LC 2003-19834

This describes the history of late 19th and early 20th century inventions such as the light bulb, the telegraph, the telephone, and the automobile.

This "solid [title] for report writers may even pull in a few curious browsers because of [its] plentiful, full-color photos and reproductions. The [layout is] inviting, and the [text is] clear, informative, and readable." SLJ

Includes glossary

St. George, Judith

So you want to be an inventor? illustrated by David Small. Philomel Bks. 2002 53p il $16.99 (3-6)   **609**

1. Inventors 2. Inventions

ISBN 0-399-23593-0   LC 2001-55447

Presents some of the characteristics of inventors by describing the inventions of people such as Alexander Graham Bell, Thomas Edison, and Eli Whitney.

"St. George and Small take a skewed, funny, and informative look at the history of inventions and their inventors and what it takes to become one. . . . Small's lively, fluid caricatures make for a winning collaboration." SLJ

Includes bibliographical references

Tomecek, Steve

What a great idea! inventions that changed the world; [by] Stephen M. Tomecek; illustrated by Dan Stuckenschneider. Scholastic Ref. 2003 112p il $18.95 (4 and up)   **609**

1. Inventions—History

ISBN 0-590-68144-3   LC 2001-20937

"Tomecek puts significant inventions and discoveries in a historical context. Dividing the text into five broad time periods, he offers a series of essays on important advances that occurred in each 'age'. . . . What emerges is a sense of interconnectedness that other books often lack. . . . Full-color diagrams and illustrations are well integrated into each spread." SLJ

Includes bibliographical references

Tucker, Tom

Brainstorm! the stories of twenty American kid inventors; with drawings by Richard Loehle. Farrar, Straus & Giroux 1995 148p il pa $6.95 hardcover o.p. (5 and up)   **609**

1. Inventors 2. Inventions

ISBN 0-374-40928-5 (pa)   LC 94-38780

The author looks at inventions devised by children since the 18th century. Ear muffs, water skis, the popsicle, colored car wax and the electronic television are among the products discussed. Includes a discussion of how the Patent Office works

Includes glossary and bibliographical references

Williams, Marcia

Hooray for inventors! Candlewick Press 2005 37p il $16.99 (3-5)   **609**

1. Inventors 2. Inventions

ISBN 0-7636-2760-7   LC 2005-46915

"Williams takes a light look at inventors. . . . Eight inventions receive the bulk of her attention in a series of breezy comic strips. Narrative captions under each frame relate historical information. This addictive browsing item offers an enthusiastic approach to the subject." Horn Book Guide

Wulffson, Don L.

The kid who invented the popsicle and other surprising stories about inventions. Cobblehill Bks. 1997 114p $13.99; pa $4.99 (4 and up)   **609**

1. Inventions

ISBN 0-525-65221-3; 0-14-130204-6 (pa)

LC 96-31148

"Beginning with animal crackers and ending with the zipper, this book alphabetically lists a number of 'inventions' and briefly describes how they came into being. Among the items noted are blue jeans, doughnuts, matches, miniature golf, and Scrabble." Booklist

This book is "very entertaining. . . . It would be a useful starting point for class projects." Sci Books Films

610.3 Medical sciences-- Encyclopedias and dictionaries

Encyclopedia of health. 3rd ed. Marshall Cavendish 2003 16v il set $329.95 (4 and up)   **610.3**

1. Medicine—Encyclopedias

ISBN 0-7614-7347-5   LC 2001-28883

Replaces The Marshall Cavendish encyclopedia of health published 1995 in 14 volumes

"This reference features entries on body function, fitness, diet, disease, hygiene, medicine and drugs." Publisher's note

This "combines compelling text with remarkable illustrations. Sixteen attractive, slim volumes offer . . . easy-to-read articles on a vast array of specific topics related to physical and emotional health." SLJ

610.9   Medical sciences--Historical and geographic treatment

Fisher, Leonard Everett
The doctors; written & illustrated by Leonard Everett Fisher. Benchmark Bks. 1997 47p il (Colonial craftsmen) $21.36 (4 and up)
           610.9
1. Medicine—History 2. Physicians 3. United States—History—1600-1775, Colonial period
ISBN 0-7614-0481-3   LC 96-13081
A reissue of the title first published 1968 by Watts
Traces the early development of medicine in colonial America and discusses some of the methods and medications used at that time for treating illness

Green, Jen
Medicine; by Jen Green. Blackbirch Press 2004 40p il (Routes of science) $23.70; pa $18.70 (5 and up)
           610.9
1. Medicine—History
ISBN 1-4103-0168-0; 1-4103-0305-5 (pa)
           LC 2003-12999
Contents: Ancient medicine; Eastern medicine; Greece and Rome; The Dark Ages and the Renaissance; A scientific approach; Modern medicine
"This book traces the history of medical discovery from trepanning (the ancient practice of drilling holes in the skull to release evil spirits) to today's . . . advances in transplants and vaccines." Publisher's note
This "volume contains color photographs, illustrations, and diagrams to help explain the important concepts and discoveries. [This] up-to-date [volume] would be [an] excellent [supplement] to the science curriculum." SLJ
Includes glossary and bibliographical references

Lindsay, Judy
The story of medicine; from acupuncture to x rays. Oxford Univ. Press 2003 40p il lib bdg $21.95 (4-6)
           610.9
1. Medicine—History
ISBN 0-19-521984-8
"A trip through time tracing the history of modern medicine (including alternative therapies) from the practices of healers in ancient times up through the present." Publisher's note
"This book will delight both seekers of gross-out trivia and students working on reports. Filled with crisply rendered reproductions from The British Museum's archives, the text balances a lively, conversational tone with historical information." SLJ
Includes glossary and bibliographical references

Woolf, Alex
Death and disease; [by] Alex Woolf. Lucent Books 2004 48p il map (Medieval realms) $28.70 (5 and up)
           610.9
1. Medicine—History 2. Medieval civilization
ISBN 1-59018-533-1   LC 2003-61797

This "discusses topics such as medieval theories about the body and disease, the influence of the Church on health practices, the causes and effects of bubonic plague, and the emergence of modern medicine as the medieval era drew to an end." Booklist
"Clear, well-organized [text] along with full-color reproductions of art and artifacts and photos of period structures immerse readers in . . . medieval life and offer sufficient information for reports." SLJ
Includes glossary and bibliographical references

611   Human anatomy, cytology, histology

Barner, Bob
Dem bones; [illustrations and informational bone text by] Bob Barner. Chronicle Bks. 1996 unp il $14.95 (k-3)
           611
1. Skeleton 2. Bones
ISBN 0-8118-0827-0   LC 95-29
An "introduction to the human skeleton, this picture book is based on the African American spiritual 'Dem bones.'. . . Each double-page spread illustrates one phrase from the song, which dances through the spread, while in smaller letters Barner discusses one of the 10 bones named in the song in a few lines of simple, informative text." Booklist
"A rollicking read-aloud, sing-along treat for children as they learn anatomy, rhyme, and language. . . . Scientific facts and names combined with lyrics make this a fascinating book." Exploring Sci in the Libr

Jackson, Donna M.
In your face; the facts about your features. Viking 2004 42p il $17.99 (3-6)
           611
1. Face
ISBN 0-670-03657-9   LC 2003-26331
"Jackson explains the physiology of facial features, their evolution, and their roles in survival and communication. . . . With its well-captioned and colorful photos, logical organization, interesting topics, and profusion of ideas and information, this thin volume offers an unusual array of scientific and cultural concepts." SLJ
Includes glossary and bibliographical references

Sweeney, Joan
Me and my amazing body; illustrated by Annette Cable. Crown 1999 unp il $13; lib bdg $14.99; pa $6.99 (k-2)
           611
1. Human anatomy
ISBN 0-517-80053-5; 0-517-80054-3 (lib bdg); 0-375-80623-7 (pa)   LC 98-34628
A girl describes how her skin, bones, muscles, brain, blood, heart, lungs, and stomach receive energy and function as parts of her body
With "lively text and simple, colorful illustrations, this picture book explains a lot of human anatomy and physiology." Booklist

Walker, Richard

Body. DK Pub. 2005 96p il $19.99 (4 and up)
611

1. Human anatomy
ISBN 0-7566-1371-X

Subtitle on cover: an amazing tour of human anatomy

"This book features eye-catching views of the human body. The computer-generated, three-dimensional images were created by scanning successive horizontal slices of a specially treated human cadaver. . . . The accompanying CD allows users to examine interactive, 360-degree animations of the images. Suitable as a ready-reference source as well as for casual browsers, this informative title does a magnificent job of showing just how complicated and elaborate the human body is." SLJ

612 Human physiology

Aliki

My feet. Crowell 1990 31p il (Let's-read-and-find-out science book) lib bdg $15.89; pa $4.99 (k-1)
612

1. Foot
ISBN 0-690-04815-7 (lib bdg); 0-06-445106-2 (pa)
LC 89-49357

"An extensive discussion of feet, through simple text and playful illustration, demonstrates their parts, relative sizes, what they do, and what they wear in different seasons. Includes a handicapped child whose crutches supplement feet." Sci Child

My hands. rev ed. Crowell 1990 32p il (Let's-read-and-find-out science book) lib bdg $15.89; pa $4.99 (k-1)
612

1. Hand
ISBN 0-690-04880-7 (lib bdg); 0-06-445096-1 (pa)
LC 89-49158

First published 1962

The author "calls attention to hand structure—fingers, nails, an opposable thumb—and the special ways we use our hands to carry on everyday activities. . . . The jaunty illustrations and simple but efficient text combine for a fresh take on some very basic information." Booklist

Berger, Melvin

Why don't haircuts hurt? questions and answers about the human body; [by] Melvin and Gilda Berger; illustrated by Karen Barnes. Scholastic Ref. 1999 48p il (Scholastic question and answer series) $12.95; pa $5.95 (2-4)
612

1. Human anatomy 2. Physiology
ISBN 0-590-13079-X; 0-439-08569-1 (pa)
LC 97-45874

Provides answers to a variety of questions about the human body including "Why do you blush?", "Why do you need two ears?", "How strong is hair?", and "What are goosebumps?"

"The student-friendly question-and-answer format is appealing, with simple and concise one or two paragraph answers and attractive, colorful illustrations." SLJ

Cole, Joanna

The magic school bus inside the human body; illustrated by Bruce Degen. Scholastic 1989 unp il lib bdg $15.95; pa $5.99 (2-4)
612

1. Physiology 2. Human anatomy
ISBN 0-590-41426-7 (lib bdg); 0-590-41427-5 (pa)
LC 88-3070

Also available Spanish language edition

"Ms. Frizzle's class leaves on a trip to the science museum, but stops for a snack along the way. Arnold is left behind when his classmates reboard the bus. Meanwhile, Ms. Frizzle has miniaturized the bus and its riders. Unwittingly, Arnold swallows it. Traveling through Arnold's insides, the class visits his digestive system, arteries, lungs, heart, brain, and muscles, finally departing through his nostrils when he sneezes." Booklist

"This is an enjoyable look at factual material painlessly packaged with the ribbons and balloons of jokes and asides meant to appeal to kids. Degen's zany, busy, full-color drawings fill the pages with action and information far beyond the text." SLJ

Gray, Susan Heinrichs

The human body [series] Child's World 2004 6v il (3-6)
612

1. Physiology 2. Human anatomy

Set $162.42. Also available as separate volumes $27.07 each

Contents: The circulatory system (1-59296-036-7); The digestive system (1-59296-037-5); The muscular system (1-59296-038-3); The nervous system (1-59296-039-1); The respiratory system (1-59296-040-5); The skeletal system (1-59296-041-3)

This series introduces the systems of the human body

These titles "provide an unusually sound overview of a topic represented in most upper-elementary science curricula. Each book opens with a child performing a familiar activity . . . that introduces the featured system in a concrete way. This tactic reflects Gray's consistently child-centered approach, which is reinforced by clear, vivid explanations." Booklist

Includes glossaries and bibliographical references

Rau, Dana Meachen

What's inside me? [series] Benchmark Books 2005 6v il set $128.14 (k-3)
612

1. Human body
ISBN 0-7614-1776-1

Also available as separate volumes $21.36 each

Contents: My bones and muscles; My brain; My heart and blood; My lungs; My skin; My stomach

"These titles provide descriptions, photographs, and illustrations of the body and some of its systems. . . . The photographs in each book depict a diverse group of children, and diagrams, illustrations, and X-rays provide age-appropriate and specific details. The books are written for proficient readers and make excellent additions to most collections." SLJ

Rockwell, Lizzy
The busy body book; a kid's guide to fitness. Crown 2004 unp il $15.95; lib bdg $17.99 (k-1)
612
1. Physiology 2. Exercise
ISBN 0-375-82203-8; 0-375-92203-2 (lib bdg)
An introduction to the human body, how it functions, and its need for exercise.
"The text is purposely motivating, yet easy to understand and informative. The age-appropriate artwork is colorful and lively, and provides just the right amount of detail." SLJ

VanCleave, Janice Pratt
Janice VanCleave's the human body for every kid; easy activities that make learning science fun. Wiley 1995 223p il $32.50; pa $12.95 (4 and up)
612
1. Physiology 2. Human anatomy 3. Science—Experiments
ISBN 0-471-02413-9; 0-471-02408-2 (pa)
LC 94-20862
"The book's 23 chapters cover cells, skin, the brain, the senses, lungs, blood and the heart, the digestive system, bones, muscles, and genetics. Each chapter includes . . . background information, problem-solving strategies, and simple activities." Sci Child
"The activities described are easy to follow, are inexpensive, use readily obtainable supplies, and, most importantly, make the learning of human anatomy and physiology fun and exciting. Moreover, the material is presented in an organized, clear, and accurate manner." Sci Books Films

Walker, Richard
The Kingfisher first human body encyclopedia. Kingfisher (NY) 1999 112p il $16.95 (3-5)
612
1. Human anatomy 2. Physiology
ISBN 0-7534-5177-8
LC 98-53275
An illustrated introduction to the different parts of the human body and how they work
"With stark white pages providing the backdrop for more than 500 vivid, full-color photographs, diagrams, and illustrations, *The Kingfisher First Human Body Encyclopedia* . . . is a visual delight for curious young minds." Booklist
Includes glossary

612.1   Blood and circulation

Showers, Paul
A drop of blood. HarperCollins Pub. 2004 32p il (Let's-read-and-find-out science) $15.99; lib bdg $16.89; pa $4.99 (k-3)
612.1
1. Blood
ISBN 0-06-009108-8; 0-06-009109-6 (lib bdg); 0-06-009110-x (pa)
A newly illustrated edition of the title first published 1967 and revised in 1989

A simple introduction to the composition and functions of blood.
"Showers's classic introduction to this vital fluid is cleverly updated by Miller's amusing illustrations featuring a Dracula-like vampire and his Igorish friend. . . . High-quality, closeup photographs of blood cells, platelets, and fibrin under the microscope are well placed within the illustrations, and science concepts are presented with just the right amount of detail for the intended audience." SLJ

Hear your heart; illustrated by Holly Keller. HarperCollins Pubs. 2001 33p il (Let's-read-and-find-out science) $15.95; lib bdg $15.89; pa $4.95 (k-3)
612.1
1. Heart
ISBN 0-06-025410-6; 0-06-025411-4 (lib bdg); 0-06-445139-9 (pa)
LC 99-41336
A revised and newly illustrated edition of the title first published 1968
A simple explanation of the structure of the heart and how it works
"This is an excellent introduction to the heart and how it works. . . . The open, informal design brings the physiology right into daily life. Factual, accurate, and fun." Booklist

Simon, Seymour
The heart. Morrow Junior Bks. 1996 unp lib bdg $18.89; pa $6.99 (4 and up)
612.1
1. Cardiovascular system 2. Heart
ISBN 0-688-11407-5 (lib bdg); 0-688-17059-5 (pa)
LC 95-38021
This "introduces the human circulatory system: the heart, the blood, the arteries and veins, the transfer of oxygen and carbon dioxide, the functions of various blood cells, and heart problems and their solutions. The text is succinct and direct, making the details understandable without losing the sense that the whole process of circulation is 'strange and wonderful.' . . . The often striking pictures include many computer-enhanced photographs as well as diagrams and highly enlarged images made possible by electron microscopes. Handsome and well-conceived in every way." Booklist

612.2   Respiration

Parker, Steve
The lungs and respiratory system. Raintree Steck-Vaughn Pubs. 1997 48p il (Human body) lib bdg $16.98 (5 and up)
612.2
1. Lungs 2. Respiratory system
ISBN 0-8172-4803-X (lib bdg)
LC 96-43516
Examines the different parts and functions of the lungs and respiratory system
The information in this book "is especially well organized and well coordinated with colorful illustrations and photographs." SLJ
Includes glossary and bibliographical references

612.3 Digestion

Showers, Paul

What happens to a hamburger? illustrated by Edward Miller. HarperCollins Pubs. 2001 33p il (Let's-read-and-find-out-science) $15.95; lib bdg $15.89; pa $4.99 (k-3) **612.3**

ISBN 0-06-027947-8; 0-06-027948-6 (lib bdg); 0-06-445183-6 (pa)   LC 97-39007

A newly illustrated edition of the title first published 1970

Explains the processes by which a hamburger and other foods are used to make energy, strong bones, and solid muscles as they pass through the digestive system

This edition offers "attractive new illustrations, enhanced in a few places with photos that show body parts such as the epiglottis and the stomach lining. . . . Miller's digital artwork has a jaunty, retro look." Booklist

Simon, Seymour

Guts; our digestive system; [by] Seymour Simon. 1st ed. HarperCollins 2005 unp il $15.99; lib bdg $16.89 (4 and up) **612.3**

1. Digestion

ISBN 0-06-054651-4; 0-06-054652-2 (lib bdg)   LC 2004-14508

This "explains how the digestive system works. . . . [The author] describes the complex facts and processes of the physiology, from the time food enters the mouth until all the various organs transform it into energy, nutrients, and waste." Booklist

"Simon's specialty of drawing in readers through large, detailed, breathtaking photos and then entertaining them with facts is again in evidence. . . . The text is enhanced with detailed colored X rays, computer-generated pictures, and microscopic photos." SLJ

612.6 Reproduction, development, maturation

Butler, Dori Hillestad

My mom's having a baby! illustrated by Carol Thompson. Albert Whitman & Co 2005 unp il $15.95 (2-4) **612.6**

1. Pregnancy 2. Childbirth 3. Sex education

ISBN 0-8075-5344-1   LC 2004-18585

"Elizabeth describes the month-by-month development of the baby as well as the changes in Mom's body. . . . Through very direct language and clear illustrations, children will learn about a man's testicles where sperm are made and the fallopian tube where an egg is fertilized. . . . Mom answers Elizabeth's big question, 'how do Dad's sperm and your egg get together?' . . . Details are not spared when the birth is described. The playful and colorful illustrations add exuberance to the text, combining full-page paintings, cartoon panels, word balloons, and free-floating images. The joy and love felt by all of the family members is palpable. This volume is an excellent choice for those readers who are ready to ask and be told some of life's basic facts." SLJ

Cole, Joanna

How you were born; photographs by Margaret Miller. rev & expanded ed. Morrow Junior Bks. 1993 48p il $15.95; pa $6.99 (k-2) **612.6**

1. Pregnancy 2. Childbirth 3. Infants

ISBN 0-688-12059-8; 0-688-12061-X (pa)   LC 92-23970

A revised and newly illustrated edition of the title first published 1984

"Illustrated with photographs of culturally diverse families, Cole's text explains conception, the development of the fetus, and the birth process. A note to parents and a suggested reading list are included." J Youth Serv Libr

When you were inside Mommy; illustrated by Maxie Chambliss. HarperCollins Pubs. 2001 unp il $5.95 (k-1) **612.6**

1. Pregnancy 2. Childbirth 3. Infants

ISBN 0-688-17043-9   LC 00-40890

This "begins with a simple explanation of a baby's development in the mother's uterus. It goes on to show the baby's birth, followed by his growth to a child of perhaps three or four years old. An appended 'Note to Parents' offers a sound approach to talking with children. . . . The simplicity and sensitivity of the writing is well matched by Chambliss' line and watercolor wash illustrations." Booklist

Gravelle, Karen

The period book; everything you don't want to ask (but need to know); by Karen Gravelle & Jennifer Gravelle; illustrations by Debbie Palen. Walker & Co. 1996 117p il pa $8.95 hardcover o.p. (4 and up) **612.6**

1. Menstruation

ISBN 0-8027-7478-4 (pa)   LC 95-31101

"An aunt and her fifteen-year-old niece provide forthright information about tampon insertion, pelvic exams, body changes during puberty, and other topics adolescent girls might feel uncomfortable discussing with parents and friends. The cartoonlike illustrations and conversational tone make this a friendly, reassuring resource as well as a thorough one." Horn Book Guide

Harris, Robie H.

Go! Go! Maria! What it's like to be 1; illustrated by Michael Emberley. Margaret K. McElderry Bks. 2003 unp il (Growing up stories) $16.95 (k-3) **612.6**

1. Infants 2. Growth

ISBN 0-689-83258-3   LC 2002-14637

One-year-old Maria learns to do new things almost every day. Includes secondary text which describes the characteristics of toddlers

"The dynamic combination of Harris' text and Emberley's sweepingly energetic cartoon-style art depicts Maria always on the move. . . . It's fun and fact in a lively package." Booklist

Harris, Robie H.—*Continued*

Hello Benny! What it's like to be a baby; illustrated by Michael Emberley. Margaret K. McElderry Bks. 2002 unp il (Growing up stories) $16.95 (k-3)   **612.6**

1. Infants 2. Growth

ISBN 0-689-83257-5   LC 00-58741

"This book follows Benny from the day he is born to his first birthday. The large-type text includes anecdotal incidents and the things that he's learning to do; inset boxes, printed in blue, offer more general, factual information." SLJ

"Both the story and the informative sections of the text flow easily and blend well. Emberley's large-scale artwork, rendered in watercolor, pastel, and ink, brims with warmth." Booklist

It's not the stork! a book about girls, boys, babies, bodies, families, and friends; [by] Robie H. Harris; illustrated by Michael Emberley. Candlewick Press 2006 59p il $16.99 (k-3)   **612.6**

1. Sex education 2. Childbirth 3. Pregnancy

ISBN 0-7636-0047-4   LC 2005054280

"Harris opens by introducing two cartoon characters—a green-feathered bird clad in a purple shirt and blue hightop sneakers and his spike-haired friend, a bee. They wonder, 'So where DO babies come from?' Their conversational commentary, given in word balloons, is a lighthearted supplement to a more focused narrative. Told in the second person, the text is straightforward, informative, and personable. Facts are presented step-by-step, starting from the similarities and differences between boys' and girls' bodies, moving to a baby's conception, growth in the womb, and birth, ending with an exploration of different configurations of families as well as a section on 'okay' versus 'not okay' touches." SLJ

It's so amazing! a book about eggs, sperm, birth, babies, and families; illustrated by Michael Emberley. Candlewick Press 1999 81p il $21.99; pa $10.99 (2-4)   **612.6**

1. Pregnancy 2. Childbirth 3. Sex education

ISBN 0-7636-0051-2; 0-7636-1321-5 (pa)

LC 98-33119

Uses bird and bee cartoon characters to present straightforward explanations of topics related to sexual development, love, reproduction, adoption, sexually transmitted diseases, and more

"While the illustrations are engaging and often hilarious, factual information is effectively presented in a clear, nonjudgmental tone that will inform and assure readers." SLJ

Sweet Jasmine, nice Jackson; what it's like to be 2--and to be twins! illustrated by Michael Emberley. Margaret K. McElderry Books 2004 unp il (Growing up stories) $16.95 (k-3)   **612.6**

1. Toddlers 2. Twins

ISBN 0-689-83259-1   LC 2002-152902

Jasmine and Jackson celebrate the year they are two by learning to do new things and showing their independence. Includes nonfiction information about two-year-olds and twins.

"This book presents a delightful mix of story, factual text, and endearing artwork. . . . The paintings are filled with action, homey details, and many interesting faces." SLJ

Jukes, Mavis

Growing up: it's a girl thing; straight talk about first bras, first periods, and your changing body; illustrations by Debbie Tilley. Knopf 1998 72p il pa $10 hardcover o.p. (4 and up)   **612.6**

1. Adolescence 2. Girls 3. Menstruation

ISBN 0-679-89027-0 (pa)   LC 98-18113

This "covers body hair and shaving, perspiration and deodorant, and how to buy your first bra. The second half of the book is devoted to what to expect and how to plan for your first period. . . . The narration has an easy, comfortable voice and imparts accurate and important information." SLJ

Movsessian, Shushann

Puberty girl. Allen & Unwin 2005 128p $15.95 (4 and up)   **612.6**

1. Puberty 2. Girls

ISBN 1-74114-104-4

"In addition to chapters about the basic body changes during female puberty, including one about menstruation and the necessary equipment, the author offers helpful suggestions for conflict resolution, listening to one's feelings, and understanding personal boundaries (and when they are breached). She also includes a brief list of boys' puberty changes, and a closing chapter mentions homosexuality. The glossy, girl-magazine design, with lots of color photos of attractive preteens, is matched by the bubbly, girl-power tone." Booklist

Parker, Steve

Reproduction. Raintree 2004 48p il (Our bodies) lib bdg $31.43 (5 and up)   **612.6**

1. Reproduction 2. Sex education 3. Growth

ISBN 0-7398-6623-0   LC 2003-10547

Contents: Female reproductive organs; The menstrual cycle; Egg production; Male reproductive organs; Sperm production; The reproductive process; The first week; Reproductive problems; The early embryo; Growth in the uterus; Life support in the uterus; Toward birth; The day of birth; A new baby; Birth problems; Growing up; The young child; The older child; Child to adult; The next generation

This "discusses the male and female reproductive organs and how they work, the process of fertilization, growth of the embryo and fetus, birth, and stages of life from infancy to adulthood. . . . The anatomy is accurate, and the format, with plenty of pictures, diagrams, and magnified photos, is very accessible. There are also lots of lively boxed facts." Booklist

Includes bibliographical references

Pringle, Laurence P.

Everybody has a bellybutton; your life before you were born; by Laurence Pringle; illustrated by Clare Wood. Boyds Mills Press 1997 unp il $14.95 (k-3)   **612.6**

1. Fetus 2. Pregnancy 3. Childbirth

ISBN 1-56397-009-0   LC 95-83168

Pringle, Laurence P.—*Continued*

Pringle "offers a gently phrased, solidly scientific look at the growth of a baby. . . . The narrative gives specific, sensorial details that will keep even young children engaged, and the description of childbirth is matter-of-fact and undisturbing. . . . Illustrations are softly realistic pencil drawings on pink and blue backgrounds." Booklist

Includes bibliographical references

Saltz, Gail

Amazing you; getting smart about your private parts; illustrated by Lynn Cravath. 1st ed. Dutton Children's Books 2005 unp il $15.99 (k-1)

612.6

1. Sex education 2. Reproduction 3. Growth

ISBN 0-525-47389-0   LC 2004-22014

"This upbeat picture book, illustrated with sunny cartoon drawings, introduces kids to basic reproductive physiology. Saltz offers simple, accessible definitions of terms, accompanied by pictures of unclothed kids and labeled diagrams of internal organs. Subsequent drawings show three stages of body development from baby to young adult, followed by an abbreviated explanation, illustrated with a heart-shaped drawing of a smiling egg and sperm, of reproduction. . . . Saltz presents the information clearly in a cheerful, positive tone." Booklist

Sears, William

Baby on the way; [by] William Sears, Martha Sears, and Christie Watts Kelly; illustrated by Renée Andriani. Little, Brown 2001 unp il (Sears children's library) $12.95 (k-2)

612.6

1. Pregnancy 2. Childbirth 3. Infants

ISBN 0-316-78767-1   LC 00-38451

This book describes how a family prepares for the arrival of a new baby and explains pregnancy and childbirth to an older sibling

"Andriani's brightly colored, cartoon-style illustrations help create the books' upbeat, yet realistic tone." Booklist

Includes bibliographical references

612.7   Musculoskeletal system, integument

Ballard, Carol

The skeleton and muscular system. Raintree Steck-Vaughn Pubs. 1998 48p il (Human body) lib bdg $27.12 (5 and up)

612.7

1. Musculoskeletal system 2. Skeleton

ISBN 0-8172-4805-6   LC 96-29688

Explains the various parts of the human skeleton and different types of muscles and their functions

The text is "well organized and well written. The full-color photos, diagrams, and illustrations are clear and complement the text." SLJ

Includes glossary and bibliographical references

Berger, Melvin

Why I sneeze, shiver, hiccup, and yawn; illustrated by Paul Meisel. HarperCollins Pubs. 2000 unp il (Let's-read-and-find-out science) pa $4.99 hardcover o.p. (k-3)

612.7

1. Reflexes 2. Nervous system

ISBN 0-06-445193-3 (pa); 0-06-028144-8 (hc)

     LC 98-55542

A revised and newly illustrated edition of Why I cough, sneeze, shiver, hiccup & yawn, published 1983 by Crowell

An introduction to reflex acts that explains why we sneeze, shiver, hiccup, and yawn

"The writing is simple but effective, and the charming, colorful pen-and-ink and watercolors are [detailed]. . . . Attractive introductory nonfiction." SLJ

Macnair, Patricia Ann

Movers & shapers; bones, muscles, and joints; consultant, Richard Walker. Kingfisher 2004 40p il (Bodyscope) $9.95 (3-5)

612.7

1. Musculoskeletal system

ISBN 0-7534-5791-1   LC 2003-27315

Contents: Bony framework; Where the bones meet: joints; Cartilage; Muscles that get us moving; The skull; From a smile to a frown: the face; The secrets of skeletons; The ribs and spine; Legs and feet; Artificial limbs; Arms and hands; The story of a broken bone; Health and exercise

This describes the musculoskeletal system including how limbs move, the importance of exercise, and how bones heal.

The author has "a flair for kid-friendly trivia. . . . Macnair is . . . adept at describing complex processes for young readers without too much distracting detail." Booklist

Includes glossary

Parker, Steve

The skeleton and muscles; [by] Steve Parker. Raintree 2004 48p il (Our bodies) lib bdg $29.93 (5 and up)

612.7

1. Musculoskeletal system

ISBN 0-7398-6622-2   LC 2003-6594

Contents: The skeleton; Inside bones; The growing skeleton (case study); Bones of the skull and face; Healthy bones (focus on health); The muscle system; More muscles; Tendons; Inside a muscle; Making movements (case study); Controlling muscles; Muscles of the face and head; Bone and muscle disorders (focus on health); How joints work; Keeping joints healthy (case study); How the hands work; The shoulder and arm (case study); The leg and foot; The back joints and muscles; Joint problems

This "takes a look at bones, muscles, and joints; how they are connected and function; and how to keep them healthy. The anatomy is accurate, and the format, with plenty of pictures, diagrams, and magnified photos, is very accessible. There are also lots of lively boxed facts." Booklist

Includes bibliographical references

Showers, Paul

Your skin and mine; illustrated by Kathleen Kuchera. rev ed. HarperCollins Pubs. 1991 32p il (Let's-read-and-find-out science book) pa $5.99 hardcover o.p. (k-3)   **612.7**

1. Skin

ISBN 0-06-445102-X (pa)   LC 90-37430

A revised and newly illustrated edition of the title first published 1965 by Crowell

Explains the basic properties of skin, how it protects the body, and how it can vary in color

"This book proves far superior to its predecessor. . . . Ink-and-watercolor illustrations are lively and vibrant." SLJ

Simon, Seymour

Bones; our skeletal system. Morrow Junior Bks. 1998 unp il lib bdg $16.89 hardcover o.p.; pa $6.99 (4 and up)   **612.7**

1. Bones 2. Skeleton

ISBN 0-688-14645-7 (lib bdg); 0-688-17721-2 (pa)
                                    LC 97-44751

Describes the skeletal system and outlines the many important roles that bones play in the healthy functioning of the human body

"Simon once again proves his remarkable facility for making complicated science clear and understandable." Booklist

Muscles; our muscular system. Morrow Junior Bks. 1998 unp il $15.89 hardcover o.p.; lib bdg $16.99; pa $6.99 (4 and up)   **612.7**

1. Muscles

ISBN 0-688-14642-2; 0-688-14643-0 (lib bdg); 0-688-17720-4 (pa)   LC 97-44758

Describes the nature and work of muscles, the different kinds, and the effects of exercise and other activities on them

"The full-paged illustrations are great and include full-color photographs, MRI scans, X rays, and excellent drawings." SLJ

612.8   Nervous functions. Sensory functions

Aliki

My five senses. rev ed. Crowell 1989 31p il (Let's-read-and-find-out science book) pa $4.99 hardcover o.p. (k-1)   **612.8**

1. Senses and sensation

ISBN 0-06-445083-X (pa)   LC 88-35350

First published 1962

The faculties of touch, hearing, sight, smelling and taste are introduced in relation to everyday experiences

"Each sense is used independently to observe common phenomena. Next, the author demonstrates more than one sense being used. . . . The book effectively introduced the five senses to young people." Appraisal

Cobb, Vicki

Feeling your way; discover your sense of touch; illustrations by Cynthia C. Lewis. Millbrook Press 2001 unp il lib bdg $22.90 (2-4)   **612.8**

1. Touch

ISBN 0-7613-1657-4   LC 00-32916

"A look at over a dozen ways to explore this sense. . . . The experiments are simple to carry out and include little or no equipment. The illustrations include photographed heads superimposed on drawings and simple cartoons with dialogue balloons." SLJ

Follow your nose; discover your sense of smell; illustrated by Cynthia C. Lewis. Millbrook Press 2000 unp il lib bdg $22.60; pa $7.95 (2-4)
                                    612.8

1. Smell

ISBN 0-7613-1521-7 (lib bdg); 0-7613-1978-6 (pa)
                                    LC 99-47872

Examines the sense of smell, how the nose detects different odors, and how we react to different smells. Includes simple experiments to test the sense of smell

An "entertaining and colorful book. . . . The science is accurate, and the pictorial and written anecdotes are cleverly directed toward advanced elementary school . . . students." Sci Books Films

Your tongue can tell; discover your sense of taste; illustrations by Cynthia C. Lewis. Millbrook Press 2000 unp il lib bdg $22.60; pa $7.95 (2-4)
                                    612.8

1. Taste

ISBN 0-7613-1473-3 (lib bdg); 0-7613-1979-4 (pa)
                                    LC 99-47873

Text and suggested activities explore the sense of taste, how it works, and how it can help us detect which foods are sweet, sour, salty, or spicy

Cole, Joanna

The magic school bus explores the senses; illustrated by Bruce Degen. Scholastic Press 1999 47p il pa $5.99 hardcover o.p. (2-4)
                                    612.8

1. Senses and sensation

ISBN 0-590-44698-3 (pa); 0-590-44697-5 (hc)
                                    LC 98-18662

Ms. Frizzle and her class explore the senses by traveling on the magic school bus in and out of an eye, ear, mouth, nose, and other parts of both human and animal bodies

"Along the margins are snippets of information in the form of Frizzle Facts and excerpts from kids' school reports. Degen's clever illustrations are both humorous and informative, acting as excellent visual aids for little learners." Booklist

Funston, Sylvia

It's all in your head; a guide to your brilliant brain; [by] Sylvia Funston, Jay Ingram; illustrated by Gary Clement. 2nd ed. Maple Tree Press 2005 64p il $16.95; pa $9.95 (3-6)   **612.8**

1. Brain 2. Psychology

ISBN 1-897066-43-0; 1-897066-44-9 (pa)

First published 1994 with title: A kid's guide to the brain

Funston, Sylvia—Continued

This "explains how the brain controls our senses, emotions, memory, and thinking. Each chapter includes experiments, with easy-to-find items such as buttons and jelly beans, brain teasers, . . . historical information, and current theories on brain function. . . . Color photographs and whimsical illustrations make the presentation appealing." SLJ

Newquist, H. P. (Harvey P.)

The great brain book; an inside look at the inside of your head; illustrations by Keith Kasnot and Eric Brace. Scholastic Reference 2005 c2004 160p il $18.95 (5 and up)   **612.8**

1. Brain

ISBN 0-439-45895-1   LC 2004-42955

This describes the anatomy and physiology of the brain and covers such topics as the history of brain research, neurons, learning and memory, brain diseases and mental illness, and the possible future of brain research.

"With an appealing, colorful design and a flashy cover, this in-depth introduction to the human brain and its remarkable powers will attract browsers, but strong readers are its best audience. . . . The clever, kid-friendly anecdotes amid the anatomy lessons . . . enhance accessibility." Booklist

Romanek, Trudee

Zzz...: the most interesting book you'll ever read about sleep; written by Trudee Romanek; illustrated by Rose Cowles. Kids Can Press 2002 40p il (Mysterious you) $14.95 (3-6)

612.8

1. Sleep

ISBN 1-55074-944-7

This covers "topics such as REM sleep, nightmares, sleepwalking, dreams, hibernation, and sleep disorders." SLJ

The information "is presented via colloquial prose and colorful comic illustrations. . . . The book . . . serves as a solid introduction, accessibly explaining the science of sleep and including seven 'You Try It' activities that demonstrate these concepts." Horn Book Guide

Showers, Paul

Sleep is for everyone; illustrated by Wendy Watson. HarperCollins Pubs. 1997 32p il (Let's-read-and-find-out science) $15.89 hardcover o.p.; pa $4.99 (k-2)   **612.8**

1. Sleep

ISBN 0-06-025392-4; 0-06-445141-0 (pa)

LC 96-49375

A newly illustrated edition of the title first published 1974 by Crowell

This volume examines "how different animals sleep, why we sleep, and what happens while we sleep and when we don't sleep enough. Colorful paper cut-out illustrations are simple and light-hearted with mottled paper as background creating a restful, gentle feeling." Horn Book Guide

Silverstein, Alvin

Sleep; [by] Alvin Silverstein, Virginia Silverstein, and Laura Silverstein Nunn. Watts 2000 48p il (My health) lib bdg $24.50; pa $6.95 (3-5)   **612.8**

1. Sleep

ISBN 0-531-11636-0 (lib bdg); 0-531-16452-7 (pa)

LC 98-53647

Discusses the activities of the body during sleep, the importance of sleep, common sleep disorders, and the phenomenon of dreams

Includes bibliographical references

Simon, Seymour

The brain; our nervous system. Morrow Junior Bks. 1997 unp il $17.89 hardcover o.p.; pa $6.99 (4 and up)   **612.8**

1. Brain 2. Nervous system

ISBN 0-688-14641-4; 0-688-17060-9 (pa)

LC 96-36801

Describes the various parts of the brain and the nervous system and how they function to enable us to think, feel, move, and remember

Simon's "clear, concise writing style is complemented by stunning color images taken with radiological scanners, such as CAT scans, MRIs, and SEMs (scanning electron microscopes.)" SLJ

Eyes and ears. HarperCollins Pubs. 2003 unp il $15.99; lib bdg $16.89 (4 and up)   **612.8**

1. Eye 2. Ear 3. Vision 4. Hearing

ISBN 0-688-15303-8; 0-688-15304-6 (lib bdg)

LC 2002-19060

Describes the anatomy of the eye and ear, how those organs function and some ways in which they may malfunction, and how the brain is also involved in our seeing and hearing

"Simon is at his very best here. . . . The large, exquisitely reproduced photographs from a number of sources look like fiery planets, galaxies, and monster creatures. . . . The anatomy and physiology are detailed and accurate, with clear diagrams." Booklist

613   Personal health and safety

Cheung, Lilian W. Y.

Be healthy! it's a girl thing; food, fitness, and feeling great; [by] Lilian Cheung and Mavis Jukes. Crown Publishers 2003 117p il lib bdg $18.99; pa $12.95 (5 and up)   **613**

1. Girls—Health and hygiene 2. Nutrition 3. Physical fitness

ISBN 0-679-99029-1 (lib bdg); 0-679-89029-7 (pa)

LC 2003-10114

This "offers girls going through puberty advice on nutrition, fitness, self-image, and appearance." SLJ

"Given the alarmingly high rates of eating disorders, girls definitely need to hear some of the straight talk more often. . . . A chapter devoted to advertising is also helpful in countering the unrealistic images portrayed in the media." Booklist

613.2 Dietetics

King, Hazel

Carbohydrates for a healthy body; [by] Hazel King. Heinemann Library 2003 48p il (Body needs) $29.93; pa $8.50 (4-6)   **613.2**
1. Carbohydrates 2. Nutrition
ISBN 1-4034-0756-8; 1-4034-3310-0 (pa)
LC 2002-12642

Describes what carbohydrates are, what types of foods contain them, how they are digested and used to produce energy, and their role in a healthy diet.

This is "written in a clear, organized style and the full-color illustrations and photos complement the [text]." SLJ

Includes bibliographical references

Rockwell, Lizzy

Good enough to eat; a kid's guide to food and nutrition. HarperCollins Pubs. 1999 unp il $15.99; lib bdg $16.89 (k-3)   **613.2**
1. Nutrition 2. Food
ISBN 0-06-027434-4; 0-06-027435-2 (lib bdg)
LC 97-32145

Describes the six categories of nutrients needed for good health, how they work in the body, and what foods provide each. Includes five recipes

"There's an amazing amount of information packed into this inviting, clear, and valuable book." SLJ

Royston, Angela

Proteins for a healthy body; [by] Angela Royston. Heinemann Library 2003 48p il (Body needs) $29.93; pa $8.50 (4-6)   **613.2**
1. Proteins 2. Nutrition
ISBN 1-4034-0759-2; 1-4034-3312-7 (pa)
LC 2002-12644

Contents: Why do we need to eat?; Protein; What is protein?; Protein from food; Vegetable protein; How your body digests protein; Enzymes; Absorbing; Using protein; Proteins on the move; Growing new cells; Protein as a source of energy

"Royston looks at different kinds of proteins—antibodies, hormones, enzymes—and how vegetarians and vegans can get enough of them. . . . [This is] written in a clear, organized style and the full-color illustrations and photos complement the [text]." SLJ

Includes bibliographical references

Vitamins and minerals for a healthy body. Heinemann Library 2003 48p il (Body needs) lib bdg $29.93; pa $8.50 (4-6)   **613.2**
1. Vitamins 2. Minerals 3. Nutrition
ISBN 1-4034-0758-4 (lib bdg); 1-4034-3313-5 (pa)
LC 2002-12645

Contents: Fueling the body machine; Vitamins and minerals; What are vitamins?; What are minerals?; Digesting vitamins and minerals; Absorbing vitamins and minerals; How the body uses vitamins; Using B vitamins and vitamin C; Using Vitamins D, E and K; How the body uses minerals; Minerals in body fluids; Minerals in enzymes; Too much of a good thing; Too much salt and other minerals; Deficiency diseases; Vitamin deficiencies; Mineral deficiencies; Healthy eating; Special requirements; Recommended daily amounts

Discusses what vitamins and minerals are, how they are digested, absorbed, and used by the body, and the role of these substances in a healthy diet.

This volume is "written in a clear, organized style and the full-color illustrations and photos complement the [text]." SLJ

Includes bibliographical references

VanCleave, Janice Pratt

Janice VanCleave's food and nutrition for every kid; easy activities that make learning science fun. Wiley 1999 232p il (Science for every kid series) $32.50; pa $12.95 (4 and up)   **613.2**
1. Nutrition 2. Food
ISBN 0-471-17666-4; 0-471-17665-6 (pa)
LC 98-53677

VanCleave instructs "about food groups, vitamins and minerals, the relationship between energy and food, how to read nutrition labels, and more. The text is straightforward, with good use of scientific terms. . . . The heart of this book is the array of activities that relate to real-life situations." SLJ

Includes glossary

613.6 Personal safety and special topics of health

Raatma, Lucia

Safety in your neighborhood. Child's World 2005 32p il (Living well) lib bdg $25.64 (4 and up)   **613.6**
1. Crime prevention 2. Safety education
ISBN 1-59296-240-8   LC 2003-27214

Contents: Who is that man?; Your home and neighborhood; Knowing your neighbors; Strangers on your street; Someone's at your door; Keeping your neighborhood safe; Glossary; Questions and answers about neighborhood safety; Helping a friend learn about neighborhood safety; Did you know?; How to learn more about neighborhood safety

This book teaches young readers how to keep their neighborhood a safe place and what to do if that safety is compromised.

This "clearly written [title has] an appealing layout with plenty of full-color photos and a triple-spaced text. . . . [It] provides solid tips." SLJ

Includes glossary and bibliographical references

613.7 Physical fitness

Chryssicas, Mary Kaye

I love yoga; written by Mary Kaye Chryssicas; photography by Angela Coppola. DK Pub. 2005 47p il $12.99 (3-5)   **613.7**
1. Yoga
ISBN 0-7566-1400-7

The author "offers a vicarious tour of a typical [yoga] class. Opening spreads discuss equipment, clothing, and

Chryssicas, Mary Kaye—*Continued*

camaraderie among the young learners. Later spreads showcase poses. . . . The mostly sharp, clear photos of accomplished kids having fun . . . may inspire some children to dip into their first 'Downward Dog,' while others will marvel at yoga's mental benefits." Booklist

Miller, Edward

The monster health book; a guide to eating healthy, being active, & feeling great for monsters & kids! [by] Edward Miller. Holiday House 2006 40p il $16.95 (2-4) **613.7**

1. Nutrition 2. Health

ISBN 0-8234-1956-8   LC 2005046383

"Featuring a friendly, rotund, green monster determined to make healthy choices, this book presents basic information about food, exercise, and health. . . . Subjects include food nutrients, counting calories and understanding food labels, tips for making healthy lunches and snacks, the benefits of getting enough sleep and exercise, and ways to improve self-esteem. Miller's retro-style illustrations fill the pages with color, shapes, and humorous details, and silly jokes are tucked everywhere. . . . This lively, visually appealing book . . . belongs in children's hands." SLJ

Silverstein, Alvin

Physical fitness; [by] Alvin Silverstein, Virginia Silverstein, and Laura Silverstein Nunn. Watts 2002 48p il (My health) lib bdg $24; pa $6.95 (3-5) **613.7**

1. Physical fitness

ISBN 0-531-11860-6 (lib bdg); 0-531-15563-3 (pa)
LC 2001-17577

Discusses the importance of physical fitness, different types of exercise, eating right, and getting enough sleep

Includes glossary and bibliographical references

Whitford, Rebecca

Little yoga; a toddler's first book of yoga; [by] Rebecca Whitford & Martina Selway. Holt & Co. 2005 unp il $9.95 (k-1) **613.7**

1. Yoga

ISBN 0-8050-7879-7

"This small, square book offers a simple sequence of yoga poses designed especially for toddlers. On each cheerfully designed spread, a simple, black-outlined illustration shows a smiling toddler in a pose; on the opposite page, an animal mimics the same motion. . . . Appended material includes tips for adults to help guide children through the motions and photos of toddlers performing the poses." Booklist

613.9 Birth control, reproductive technology, sex hygiene

Brown, Laurene Krasny

What's the big secret? talking about sex with girls and boys; [by] Laurie Krasny Brown and Marc Brown. Little, Brown 1997 31p il $15.95; pa $5.95 (k-3) **613.9**

1. Sex education

ISBN 0-316-10915-0; 0-316-10183-4 (pa)
LC 96-15521

This "picture book's subject is sex and sexuality: not simply physical differences but also gender roles, the issue of privacy, and reproduction. . . . The Browns do an outstanding and very responsible job of introducing a wide variety of terms (everything from the expected, *umbilical cord*, to the unexpected, *masturbation*, which is handled with honesty but restraint), synthesizing a great deal of information kids want to know at this age, and presenting facts in a nonthreatening but forthright context. They even manage a good deal of humor along the way. . . . The words and illustrations work extremely well together, with the busy, bright cartoon art and balloon dialogue conveying as much of the information as the text." Booklist

Harris, Robie H.

It's perfectly normal; a book about changing bodies, growing up, sex, and sexual health; illustrated by Michael Emberley. 10th anniversary edition. Candlewick Press 2004 89p il $19.99; pa $10.99 (4 and up) **613.9**

1. Sex education

ISBN 0-7636-2610-4; 0-7636-2433-0 (pa)

First published 1994

The author "explains the physical, psychological, emotional and social changes that occur during puberty—and the implications of these changes." Publ Wkly

"This caring, conscientious, and well-crafted book will be a fine library resource as well as a marvelous adjunct to the middle-school sex-education curriculum. . . . The bold color cartoon drawings are very candid: a double-page spread of nudes, which beautifully demonstrates the varied shapes and sizes humans come in; a picture of a couple making love; one of a boy masturbating as he sits on his bed; another of a girl examining her genitals with a mirror. . . . Harris' text, as forthright as Emberley's art, encompasses . . . (the structure of the reproductive system and puberty) . . . intercourse, birth, abortion, sexual responsibility and respect." Booklist

Madaras, Lynda

Ready, set, grow! a "what's happening to my body?" book for younger girls; illustrations by Linda Davick. Newmarket Press 2003 127p il $22; pa $12 (3-6) **613.9**

1. Puberty

ISBN 1-55704-587-9; 1-55704-565-8 (pa)
LC 2003-9489

Contents: A note from the author: Hi, I'm Lynda Madaras; What's happening to me? puberty is about

Madaras, Lynda—*Continued*

change; Buds, boobs, and bras: your growing breasts;
Hair, there and everywhere: all about body hair; You
grow, girl! the height spurt; Bigger Is beautiful: the
weight spurt; BO and zits: a survival guide; What's up
down there? a look at your private parts; The inside story: changes you can't see; That time of the month: all
about getting your period; Yours alone: respecting and
protecting your body

This "introduces the basics of puberty and the physical
changes that come with it." Publ Wkly

This "is a timely and important book. In a consistently
sensitive and encouraging tone, Madaras reassures pread-
olescents that the changes they know are approaching or
they are beginning to experience are normal, natural, and
cause for celebration. Humorous sketches illustrate the
emotions and stages of puberty, and keep the tone light."
SLJ

The "what's happening to my body?" book for
boys; a growing-up guide for parents and sons;
[by] Lynda Madaras, with Dane Saavedra;
drawings by Jackie Aher. 3rd ed. Newmarket Press
2000 xxxii, 238p il $22.95; pa $12.95 (4 and up)
613.9

1. Adolescence 2. Hygiene 3. Sex education 4. Boys
ISBN 1-55704-447-3; 1-55704-443-0 (pa)

LC 00-31873

First published 1984

Discusses the changes that take place in a boy's body
during puberty, including information on the body's
changing size and shape, the growth spurt, reproductive
organs, pubic hair, beards, pimples, voice changes, wet
dreams, and puberty in girls

Includes bibliographical references

The "what's happening to my body" book for
girls; a growing-up guide for parents and
daughters; [by] Lynda Madaras, with Area
Madaras; drawings by Claudia Ziroli and Jackie
Aher. 3rd ed. Newmarket Press 2000 xxxvii, 263p
il $22.95; pa $12.95 (4 and up)   **613.9**

1. Adolescence 2. Hygiene 3. Sex education 4. Girls
ISBN 1-55704-448-1; 1-55704-444-9 (pa)

LC 00-39412

First published 1983 with title: What's happening to
my body? a growing up guide for mothers and daughters

Discusses the changes that take place in a girl's body
during puberty, including information on the menstrual
cycle, reproductive organs, breasts, pimples, eating disorders, nutrition, exercise, sexually transmitted diseases,
birth control, and puberty in boys

Includes bibliographical references

614   Forensic medicine, incidence & prevention of disease

Jackson, Donna M.

The bone detectives; how forensic
anthropologists solve crimes and uncover mysteries
of the dead; by Donna M. Jackson; photographs by
Charlie Fellenbaum. Little, Brown 1996 48p il lib
bdg $17.95 (5 and up)   **614**

1. Forensic sciences 2. Criminal investigation
ISBN 0-316-82935-8   LC 95-19051

"Jackson follows forensic anthropologist Dr. Michael
Charney and his colleagues as they solve an actual case
by developing a physical profile from bones and teeth,
reconstructing the victim's skull, and using clues from fi-
bers and other material to make further identification."
Booklist

"Laced with eye-catching full-color photos, this readable book is a fine example of the application of scientific knowledge to the 'real' world." SLJ

Includes glossary

614.4   Incidence of and public measures to prevent disease

Barnard, Bryn

Outbreak; plagues that changed history; written
and illustrated by Bryn Barnard. Crown Publishers
2005 47p il maps $17.95 (5 and up)
614.4

1. Epidemics 2. Diseases
ISBN 0-375-82986-5   LC 2005-15086

This "volume explores specific plagues that have impacted society. Barnard begins with an introduction to
microbes and the positive and negative effects that they
can have on humans. A history of the study of microorganisms follows. The bulk of the book then focuses on
specific plagues with a chapter devoted to each, including the Black Death, smallpox, yellow fever, cholera, tu-
berculosis, and influenza. The final chapter discusses the
modern struggle against disease. . . . The evocative
paintings help to clarify the text. Browsers and report
writers alike will find this to be a fascinating and informative resource." SLJ

614.5   Incidence & prevention of specific diseases

Marrin, Albert

Dr. Jenner and the speckled monster; the search
for the smallpox vaccine. Dutton Children's Bks.
2002 120p il $17.99 (5 and up)   **614.5**

1. Jenner, Edward, 1749-1823 2. Smallpox
ISBN 0-525-46922-2   LC 2002-2698

This is a "social history of smallpox, with an emphasis on Dr. Edward Jenner's contributions to eradicate the
disease. . . . Marrin's writing is direct and succinct, and
his scientific explanations are lucid and well detailed.
Numerous black-and-white period illustrations (some ap-

Marrin, Albert—*Continued*
propriately gruesome) appear in most chapters, adding interest to the text." Booklist
Includes bibliographical references

Murphy, Jim
An American plague; the true and terrifying story of the yellow fever epidemic of 1793. Clarion Bks. 2003 165p il maps $17 (5 and up)
614.5
1. Yellow fever 2. Philadelphia (Pa.)—History
ISBN 0-395-77608-2   LC 2002-151355
A Newbery Medal honor book, 2004
Contents: No one noticed; "All was not right"; Church bells tolling; Confusion, distress, and utter desolation; "It was our duty"; The prince of bleeders; "By twelve only"; "This unmerciful enemy"; "A delicate situation"; Improvements and the public gratitude; "A modern-day time bomb"
"Murphy culls from a number of historical records the story of the yellow fever epidemic that swept Philadelphia in 1793, skillfully drawing out from these sources the fear and drama of the time and making them immediate to modern readers. . . . Thoroughly documented, with an annotated source list, the work is both rigorous and inviting." Horn Book

Ramen, Fred
SARS; severe acute respiratory syndrome; [by] Fred Ramen. 1st ed. Rosen Pub. Group 2005 64p il (Epidemics! Deadly diseases throughout history) lib bdg $26.50 (4-6)
614.5
1. SARS (Disease)
ISBN 1-4042-0258-7   LC 2004017294
Contents: The first outbreak; The Hong Kong outbreak; The search for the killer; The global outbreak
This addresses "the first outbreaks of [SARS], with additional chapters covering symptoms, research, and treatment. The writing is complete and accurate." SLJ
Includes bibliographical references

615   Pharmacology and therapeutics

Silverstein, Alvin
Vaccinations; [by] Alvin Silverstein, Virginia Silverstein, and Laura Silverstein Nunn. Watts 2002 48p il (My health) lib bdg $25.50; pa $6.95 (3-5)
615
1. Vaccination
ISBN 0-531-11874-6 (lib bdg); 0-531-15564-1 (pa)
LC 2001-17765
This "describes how the common childhood communicable diseases are transmitted, their signs, and their symptoms. Background material includes how vaccines were developed, how they work, why they are necessary, and their public-health aspect. [This book has] succinct, easy-to-understand [text]; well-placed, informative color graphics; and activities." SLJ
Includes glossary and bibliographical references

615.9   Toxicology

Bjorklund, Ruth
Food-borne illnesses. Marshall Cavendish Benchmark 2006 . 64p il (Health alert) $19.95 (4 and up)
615.9
1. Food contamination 2. Diseases
ISBN 0-7614-1917-9
"Discusses food-borne illnesses and their effects on people and society." Publisher's note
"Children seeking up-to-date and reliable information about the many kinds of food-borne illnesses, treatments, preventions, and coping strategies, as well as a historical overview of food-safety efforts in the United States, will appreciate this easy-to-use and information-rich resource. . . . Useful features include color photos, diagrams, and sidebars." SLJ
Includes glossary and bibliographical references

616   Diseases

Dendy, Leslie A.
Guinea pig scientists; bold self-experimenters in science and medicine; [by] Leslie Dendy and Mel Boring; with illustrations by C. B. Mordan. Henry Holt & Co. 2005 213p il $19.95 (5 and up)
616
1. Medicine—Research 2. Scientists
ISBN 0-8050-7316-7   LC 2004-52364
"The authors offer 10 . . . case studies of scientists from the past several centuries who became their own test subjects. . . . The accounts are lively, compelling, and not always for the squeamish. . . . The authors cogently discuss each experiment's significance in advancing our understanding of science and medicine. Illustrated with a mix of period black-and-white photos and Mordan's nineteenth-century-style portraits . . . the episodes make riveting reading." Booklist
Includes bibliographical references

Tesar, Jenny
Stem cells; written by Jenny Tesar. Blackbirch Press 2003 48p il (Science on the edge) lib bdg $23.70 (5 and up)
616
1. Stem cell research
ISBN 1-56711-787-2
Examines the very promising but controversial use of human stem cells in treating medical conditions ranging from burned skin to damaged spinal cords to various diseases.
This "uses remarkably clear language to explain what stem cells are and to distill the arguments on both sides of the ethical debates. . . . Illustrated with sharp microscopic images as well as color photos of scientists at work. Very accessible and informative." Booklist
Includes bibliographical references

616.1 Diseases of the cardiovascular system

Baldwin, Carol

Sickle cell disease. Heinemann Lib. 2003 32p il (Health matters) lib bdg $22.79 (4-6)

616.1

1. Sickle cell anemia

ISBN 1-4034-0252-3   LC 2001-7975

Contents: What is sickle cell disease?; What causes sickle cell disease?; Diagnosing sickle cell disease; Treating sickle cell disease; Classmates with sickle cell disease; How you can help; Visiting friends with sickle cell disease; Sickle cell success stories

This "inviting, colorful [book] will attract students who need a clear, readable introduction to [sickle cell disease]." SLJ

Includes glossary and bibliographical references

Gold, Susan Dudley

Sickle cell disease. Enslow Pubs. 2001 48p il (Health watch) lib bdg $23.93 (4 and up)

616.1

1. Sickle cell anemia

ISBN 0-7660-1662-5   LC 00-12883

"Sickle cell disease, also called sickle cell anemia, is explained through the life story of one boy. . . . Through Keone's experience, readers learn about the disease: its symptoms, diagnosis, and treatment. Color photographs and diagrams illustrate the text." SLJ

Includes glossary and bibliographical references

616.2 Diseases of the respiratory system

Baldwin, Carol

Asthma. Heinemann Lib. 2003 32p il (Health matters) lib bdg $22.79 (4-6)   **616.2**

1. Asthma

ISBN 1-4034-0248-5   LC 2001-7972

Contents: What is asthma?; What causes asthma attacks?; Diagnosing asthma; Treating asthma; Classmates with asthma; How you can help; Visiting a friend with asthma; Asthma success stories; Learning more about asthma

This "inviting, colorful [book] will attract students who need a clear, readable introduction to [asthma]." SLJ

Includes glossary and bibliographical references

Bjorklund, Ruth

Asthma. Benchmark Books 2005 64p il (Health alert) $28.50 (4 and up)   **616.2**

1. Asthma

ISBN 0-7614-1803-2   LC 2004-5976

The author explains "the causes, physiology, treatments, and complications associated with [asthma]. The [book is] well organized. . . . The photos are colorful and . . . some are startling." SLJ

Includes bibliographical references

Gray, Shirley W.

Living with asthma; by Shirley Wimbish Gray. Child's World 2002 32p il (Living well) lib bdg $25.64 (4 and up)   **616.2**

1. Asthma

ISBN 1-56766-100-9   LC 2002-2866

Contents: Do you know someone who has asthma?; What is asthma?; What's it like to have asthma?; Who gets asthma?; What can we do about asthma?; Will we ever cure asthma?

This begins with "anecdotes about young people who suffer from [asthma]. [It] explains the condition and what happens in the body when an attack occurs. Also covered are causes of asthma, medications, and prospects for a cure. . . . [The volume has] clear, well-chosen color photos." Booklist

Includes bibliographical references

Lennard-Brown, Sarah

Asthma. Raintree Steck-Vaughn Pubs. 2002 64p il (Health issues) lib bdg $28.54 (5 and up)

616.2

1. Asthma

ISBN 0-7398-5218-3   LC 2002-16375

Examines the causes and treatment of asthma and discusses how to deal with the environmental triggers that may stimulate an attack

The book is "comprehensive and not written down for young people. The color photographs and the bright design help make the [text] more accessible." Booklist

Includes glossary and bibliographical references

Silverstein, Alvin

Common colds; [by] Alvin Silverstein, Virginia Silverstein and Laura Silverstein Nunn. Watts 1999 48p il (My health) lib bdg $24.50; pa $6.95 (3-5)   **616.2**

1. Cold (Disease)

ISBN 0-531-11579-8 (lib bdg); 0-531-16410-1 (pa)   LC 98-22025

Explains how people catch colds, how the body fights the germs, how colds are spread, and what precautions people can take against them

This is "attractively designed, with plenty of sidebars containing fascinating facts and color photographs." Booklist

Includes glossary and bibliographical references

The flu and pneumonia update; [by] Alvin and Virginia Silverstein, and Laura Silverstein Nunn. 1st ed. Enslow Publishers 2006 104p il (Disease update) lib bdg $31.93 (5 and up)   **616.2**

1. Influenza 2. Pneumonia

ISBN 0-7660-2480-6   LC 2005005988

This "provides a clear idea of the etiology, common symptoms, and treatment of both influenza and its secondary bacterial infection, pneumonia. The tone is serious but reassuring as the authors discuss the great flu epidemic of 1918, then go on to consider the nature of both illnesses and what readers can do to prevent or minimize effects." Booklist

Includes glossary and bibliographical references

616.3 Diseases of the digestive system

Gold, Susan Dudley
Cystic fibrosis. Enslow Pubs. 2000 48p il (Health watch) lib bdg $18.95 (4 and up)
616.3
1. Cystic fibrosis
ISBN 0-7660-1655-2   LC 98-48581
This discusses the effects of cystic fibrosis on the body, its diagnosis and treatments, research, and living with the disease
Includes glossary and bibliographical references

616.4 Diseases of endocrine system

Carter, Alden R.
I'm tougher than diabetes! photographs by Carol Shadis Carter. Whitman, A. 2001 unp il $15.95 (2-4)
616.4
1. Diabetes
ISBN 0-8075-1572-8   LC 2001-891
"Natalie, who appears to be 9 or 10, introduces readers to her diabetes kit that she calls Philomena. Then . . . she proceeds to explain the disease—its symptoms, testing, treatment, diet—and how she and her family manage her condition at home and at school. . . . The book concludes with 13 frequently asked questions and answers about diabetes." SLJ
This title is "upbeat and informative." Booklist

Haney, Johannah
Juvenile diabetes. Benchmark Books 2005 63p il (Health alert) lib bdg $28.50 (4 and up)
616.4
1. Diabetes
ISBN 0-7614-1798-2   LC 2004-5969
The author explains "the causes, physiology, treatments, and complications associated with [juvenile diabetes]. The [book is] well organized. . . . The photos are colorful and . . . some are startling." SLJ
Includes bibliographical references

Pirner, Connie White
Even little kids get diabetes; pictures by Nadine Bernard Westcott. Whitman, A. 1991 unp il $13.95; pa $5.95 (k-1)
616.4
1. Diabetes
ISBN 0-8075-2158-2; 0-8075-2159-0 (pa)
LC 90-12738
A young girl who has had diabetes since she was two years old describes her adjustments to the disease
"Language is simple, age appropriate, and effectively gets the point across. The ink-and-watercolor drawings are lively and often upbeat. . . . Perhaps the most valuable part of the book is the 'note for parents,' which relates Pirner's personal experience over the last three years in caring for a diabetic child." SLJ

Semple, Carol McCormick
Diabetes. rev ed. Enslow Pubs. 2000 48p il (Health watch) lib bdg $18.95 (4 and up)
616.4
1. Diabetes
ISBN 0-7660-1660-9   LC 00-8400
First published 1996 by Crestwood House
Discusses the different kinds of diabetes, their symptoms and proper treatment, as well as medical complications connected with this lifetime disease
Includes glossary and bibliographical references

Silverstein, Alvin
Diabetes; by Alvin Silverstein, Virginia Silverstein, and Laura Silverstein Nunn. Watts 2002 48p il (My health) lib bdg $24 (3-5)
616.4
1. Diabetes
ISBN 0-531-12049-X   LC 2001-4965
Contents: The sugar disease; What is diabetes?; Types of diabetes; What causes it?; Testing for diabetes; Treating diabetes; Living with diabetes
This title is "well-organized. The full-color cartoons and photos . . . complement the [text]." SLJ
Includes glossary and bibliographical references

616.5 Diseases of integument

Caffey, Donna
Yikes-lice! illustrations by Patrick Girouard. Whitman, A. 1998 unp il $14.95; pa $5.95 (k-3)
616.5
1. Lice
ISBN 0-8075-9374-5; 0-8075-9375-3 (pa)
LC 97-30679
Rhyming text describes what happens when a family discovers lice in the home and fights against them. Includes factual information about how lice live, spread, and can be eradicated

DerKazarian, Susan
You have head lice! by Susan Derkazarian. 1st ed. Children's Press 2005 31p il (Rookie read-about health) $19.50; pa $5.95 (k-2)
616.5
1. Lice
ISBN 0-516-25879-6; 0-516-27920-3 (pa)
LC 2004-15308
This "approaches the sometimes-touchy subject of head lice in a straightforward, reassuring manner. . . . Adults wanting to explain head lice to children will find this a helpful source of basic information." Booklist

Hirschmann, Kris
Lice; by Kris Hirschmann. KidHaven Press 2004 32p il (Parasites) $22.45 (4-6)
616.5
1. Lice
ISBN 0-7377-1782-3   LC 2003-12157
Contents: Human-loving parasites; Infestation; Lice in action; The fight against lice

Hirschmann, Kris—*Continued*

"Several short chapters briefly describe the distinctive physical and behavioral characteristics of [lice] and special characteristics of particular species. [The book] also [highlights] the symptoms, victims' experiences, the organisms' potential threats as disease vectors, current treatments, and prevention methods. . . . Clear, color photographs illustrate the [text]. . . . Well organized and clearly written. " SLJ

Includes bibliographical references

Silverstein, Alvin

Is that a rash? Watts 2000 48p il (My health) lib bdg $24.50; pa $6.95 (3-5) **616.5**

1. Skin—Diseases

ISBN 0-531-11637-9 (lib bdg); 0-531-16451-9 (pa)

LC 98-53648

Describes various types of rashes with information on how they affect people, how they spread, and how to treat them, including some rashes associated with childhood diseases

Includes bibliographical references

616.7 Diseases of the musculoskeletal system

Burnett, Gail Lemley

Muscular dystrophy. rev ed. Enslow Pubs. 2000 48p il (Health watch) lib bdg $18.95 (4 and up)

616.7

1. Muscular dystrophy 2. Heart diseases

ISBN 0-7660-1651-X   LC 00-8401

First published 1995 by Crestwood House

Discusses the cause, symptoms, and treatment of muscular dystrophy and examines research into treatment and a possible cure

Includes glossary and bibliographical references

Gray, Susan Heinrichs

Living with juvenile rheumatoid arthritis. Child's World 2003 32p il (Living well) lib bdg $25.64 (4 and up) **616.7**

1. Arthritis

ISBN 1-56766-104-1   LC 2002-2870

This title "leads off with an introduction to a young person who has [juvenile rheumatoid arthritis]. Subsequent chapters explain the physiology of the illness, what causes it, and what it's like to live with it. [The concluding section looks] at possible treatments and potential cures. [The text is] clear and simple, double spaced, and punctuated by colorful exemplary photos of kids dealing with the disease." SLJ

Includes glossary and bibliographical references

Silverstein, Alvin

Scoliosis; [by] Alvin Silverstein, Virginia Silverstein, and Laura Silverstein Nunn. Watts 2002 48p il (My health) lib bdg $24; pa $6.95 (3-5) **616.7**

1. Scoliosis

ISBN 0-531-12046-5 (lib bdg); 0-531-16639-2 (pa)

LC 2002-7389

Discusses the medical condition known as scoliosis, its detection and treatment, and how to live with it

Includes glossary and bibliographical references

616.8 Diseases of the nervous system and mental disorders

Ali-Walsh, Rasheda

I'll hold your hand so you won't fall; a child's guide to Parkinson's disease; [by] Rasheda Ali; foreword for Muhammad Ali. Merit 2005 40p il $19.95 (2-4) **616.8**

1. Parkinson's disease

ISBN 1-873413-13-0

"Ali's father, Muhammad Ali, suffers from Parkinson's disease, and she answers questions children may have about the illness. . . . The text is well written and basic, without being oversimplified. . . . A short CD-ROM of the author introducing the book and its contents is included. An excellent overview written in an approachable style that will be reassuring to young readers." SLJ

Brill, Marlene Targ

Alzheimer's disease. Benchmark Books 2005 64p il (Health alert) $28.50 (4 and up)

616.8

1. Alzheimer's disease

ISBN 0-7614-1799-0   LC 2004-6528

Contents: What is it like to have Alzheimer's disease; Defining the disease; The history of Alzheimer's disease; Coping with Alzheimer's disease; What treatments help slow Alzheimer's disease

The author explains "the causes, physiology, treatments, and complications associated with [Alzheimer's disease]. The [book is] well organized. . . . The photos are colorful and . . . some are startling, including the brain scans of a patient with Alzheimer's." SLJ

Includes bibliographical references

Burnfield, Alexander

Multiple sclerosis; [by] Alexander Burnfield. Heinemann Library 2003 56p il (Just the facts) lib bdg $31.36 (5 and up) **616.8**

1. Multiple sclerosis

ISBN 1-4034-4602-4   LC 2003-10913

Contents: Multiple sclerosis; What is MS?; History of MS; Types of MS; Diagnosis and investigations; Symptoms of MS; Who gets MS?; How does MS develop?; Managing MS; Treating MS; Living with MS; MS fatigue; Other problems; MS and the family; MS and society; Will a cure be found?; Information and advice

Describes the different types of MS, their symptoms, why this disease can be difficult to diagnose, various types of treatment, and other issues related to multiple sclerosis.

This is "well written and organized, and [includes] factual information without overwhelming readers." SLJ

Includes bibliographical references

Draper, Allison Stark
Polio; by Allison Draper. Rosen Pub. Group 2001 64p il (Epidemics! Deadly diseases throughout history) lib bdg $19.95 (5 and up)
616.8
1. Poliomyelitis
ISBN 0-8239-3348-2   LC 00-9371
This book discusses "the history and social and political consequences of [polio] as well as [its] causes, symptoms, prevention, treatment, and current research." SLJ
Includes glossary and bibliographical references

Gold, John Coopersmith
Cerebral palsy. Enslow Pubs. 2001 48p il (Health watch) lib bdg $23.93 (4 and up)
616.8
1. Cerebral palsy
ISBN 0-7660-1663-3   LC 00-12882
This discusses what cerebral palsy is, its causes, diagnosis, and treatment, and living with the disease
Includes glossary and bibliographical references

Gold, Susan Dudley
Multiple sclerosis. rev ed. Enslow Pubs. 2001 48p (Health watch) lib bdg $23.93 (4 and up)
616.8
1. Multiple sclerosis
ISBN 0-7660-1658-7   LC 00-10515
First published 1997 by Crestwood House
This discusses what multiple sclerosis is, its causes, diagnosis, and treatment
Includes glossary and bibliographical references

Routh, Kristina
Meningitis; [by] Kristina Routh. Heinemann Library 2004 56p il (Just the facts) $23 (5 and up)
616.8
1. Meningitis
ISBN 1-4034-5146-X   LC 2003-22569
Provides an overview of meningitis, describing what it is, the history of the disease, what it is like to live with meningitis, and some of the available treatments.
This is "well written and substantive without being overly technical." SLJ
Includes bibliographical references

616.85 Neuroses; speech and language disorders; disorders of personality, intellect, impulse control

Gold, Susan Dudley
Attention deficit disorder. Enslow Pubs. 2000 48p il (Health watch) lib bdg $18.95 (4 and up)
616.85
1. Attention deficit disorder
ISBN 0-7660-1657-9   LC 00-8383
Describes the causes, symptoms, diagnosis, and treatment of attention deficit disorder, as well as ways in which people live with it
Includes glossary and bibliographical references

Landau, Elaine
Dyslexia; by Elaine Landau. Franklin Watts 2004 79p (Life balance) lib bdg $19.50; pa $6.95 (5 and up)
616.85
1. Dyslexia
ISBN 0-531-12217-4 (lib bdg); 0-531-16612-0 (pa)
LC 2003-7142
Contents: Being dyslexic; Dyslexia; Getting help; Questions and answers about dyslexia
"Narration by dyslexics combines with an overview of the disorder to give readers an informative and thought-provoking look at this often misunderstood condition. Beginning with the struggles of a young student to cover for his difficulties, the book goes on to describe the various manifestations of dyslexia, therapies, and outcomes." SLJ
Includes glossary and bibliographical references

Pigache, Philippa
ADHD; [by] Philippa Pigache. Heinemann Library 2004 56p il (Just the facts) $23 (5 and up)
616.85
1. Attention deficit disorder
ISBN 1-4034-5142-7   LC 2003-22566
Provides an overview of attention-deficit hyperactivity disorder, describing what it is, the history of the disorder, what it is like to live with ADHD, and some of the available treatments.
"The well-organized information provides a good overview and a hopeful outlook." SLJ
Includes bibliographical references

Routh, Kristina
Down syndrome; [by] Kristina Routh. Heinemann Library 2004 56p il (Just the facts) $23 (5 and up)
616.85
1. Down syndrome
ISBN 1-4034-5145-1   LC 2003-22568
Provides an overview of Down's syndrome, describing what it is, the history of this disorder, what it is like to live with Down's syndrome, and some of the available treatments
This is "well written and substantive without being overly technical." SLJ

Roy, Jennifer Rozines
Depression. Benchmark Books 2005 64p il (Health alert) lib bdg $28.50 (4 and up)
616.85
1. Depression (Psychology)
ISBN 0-7614-1800-8   LC 2004-5970
Contents: What depression is like; Defining the disease; The history of depression; Living with depression; Coping with depression; Conclusion
The author explains "the causes, physiology, treatments, and complications associated with [depression]. The [book is] well organized. . . . The photos are colorful and . . . some are startling, including the brain scans of a patient . . . who suffers from depression." SLJ
Includes bibliographical references

Trueit, Trudi Strain

ADHD. Franklin Watts 2004 79p il (Life balance) $19.55 (5 and up)   **616.85**

1. Attention deficit disorder

ISBN 0-531-12261-1   LC 2003-7154

The author "examines the controversy surrounding ADHD, as well as the symptoms, possible causes, and methods of treatment." Publisher's note

"Trueit explains ADHD well. . . . [This book offers] solid, easy-to-understand information." SLJ

Wiltshire, Paula

Dyslexia. Raintree Steck-Vaughn Pubs. 2003 64p il (Health issues) lib bdg $28.54 (5 and up)   **616.85**

1. Dyslexia

ISBN 0-7398-5221-3   LC 2002-16377

Contents: The dyslexic brain: what makes someone dyslexic?; Diagnosing dyslexia: when and how to get assessed; Reading and writing: cracking the code; Math, music and maps: other effects of dyslexia; The dyslexic student: techniques for success

A comprehensive look at dyslexia, a learning disability that affects up to ten percent of the population of the Western world, covering its definitions, causes, assessment, and treatments

The book is "comprehensive and not written down for young people. The color photographs and the bright design help make the [text] more accessible." Booklist

Includes glossary and bibliographical references

616.89   Mental disorders

Baldwin, Carol

Autism. Heinemann Lib. 2003 32p il (Health matters) lib bdg $22.79 (4-6)   **616.89**

1. Autism

ISBN 1-4034-0250-7   LC 2001-7973

Contents: What is autism?; What causes autism?; Diagnosing autism; Treating autism; Classmates with autism; How you can help; Visiting friends with autism; Autism success stories

This "inviting, colorful [book] will attract students who need a clear, readable introduction to [autism]." SLJ

Includes glossary and bibliographical references

Gold, Susan Dudley

Bipolar disorder and depression. Enslow Pubs. 2000 48p il (Health watch) lib bdg $18.95 (4 and up)   **616.89**

1. Manic-depressive illness 2. Depression (Psychology)

ISBN 0-7660-1654-4   LC 00-8384

Discusses the symptoms, diagnosis, cause, and treatment of bipolar disorder, also known as manic depression, a mental illness that causes a person's moods to swing from happy and energized to extremely sad

Includes glossary and bibliographical references

Rashkin, Rachel

Feeling better; a kid's book about therapy; by Rachel Rashkin; illustrated by Bonnie Adamson. Magination Press 2005 48p il $14.95; pa $8.95 (4 and up)   **616.89**

1. Psychotherapy

ISBN 1-59147-237-7; 1-59147-238-5 (pa)

    LC 2004022727

"Using a journal format, 12-year-old Maya chronicles her emotional ups and downs and describes the process of psychotherapy." Publisher's note

"Clearly written and well-organized. . . . Animated black-and-white sketches portray the girl's various emotions. This title gently encourages kids who are struggling with issues to seek help." SLJ

616.9   Other diseases

Berger, Melvin

Germs make me sick! illustrated by Marylin Hafner. rev ed. HarperCollins Pubs. 1995 32p il (Let's-read-and-find-out science) lib bdg $16.89 hardcover o.p.; pa $4.99 (k-3)   **616.9**

1. Bacteria 2. Viruses

ISBN 0-06-024250-7 (lib bdg); 0-06-445154-2 (pa)

    LC 93-27059

First published 1985

Explains how bacteria and viruses affect the human body and how the body fights them

This features "Hafner's lively color cartoon illustrations. . . . [It offers a] lively combination of fact and narrative that has made this a great title for easy reading and for sharing aloud." Booklist

Bueche, Shelley

The Ebola virus; by Shelley Bueche. KidHaven Press 2004 32p il map (Parasites) $22.45 (4-6)   **616.9**

1. Ebola virus

ISBN 0-7377-1780-7   LC 2003-9613

Contents: The ebola virus as a parasite; The ebola virus attacks; Stories in the "hot zone;" Prevention and hope for a cure

"Bueche discusses the nature of viruses in general and Ebola in particular, the pathogen's usually deadly method of attack, ways to prevent the spread of this highly contagious disease, and current efforts to develop a vaccine. . . . Clear, color photographs illustrate the [text]. . . . Well organized and clearly written." SLJ

Includes glossary and bibliographical references

Casil, Amy Sterling

Hantavirus; [by] Amy Sterling Casil. 1st ed. Rosen Pub. Group 2005 64p il (Epidemics! Deadly diseases throughout history) lib bdg $26.50 (4-6)   **616.9**

1. Hantavirus infections

ISBN 1-4042-0254-4   LC 2004013897

Contents: The discovery of the sin nombre virus; Other outbreaks of hantavirus; The science of epidemiology; Hantavirus carriers, symptoms, and prevention; Bioterrorism and the future of hantavirus

Casil, Amy Sterling—*Continued*
This addresses "the first outbreaks of [hantavirus infections], with additional chapters covering symptoms, research, and treatment. The writing is complete and accurate." SLJ
Includes bibliographical references

Hoffmann, Gretchen
Mononucleosis; [by] Gretchen Hoffmann. Marshall Cavendish Benchmark 2006 64p il (Health alert) lib bdg $28.50 (4 and up)
616.9
1. Mononucleosis
ISBN 0-7614-1915-2   LC 2005005001
This describes the symptoms and causes of mononucleosis, its history, diagnosis and treatment.
This is "well-designed and easy-to-use . . . with accurate and reliable information. Colorful photos, micrographs, and sidebars appear throughout." SLJ
Includes glossary and bibliographical references

Isle, Mick
Malaria. Rosen Pub. Group 2001 64p il (Epidemics! Deadly diseases throughout history) lib bdg $19.95 (5 and up)   **616.9**
1. Malaria
ISBN 0-8239-3342-3   LC 00-9488
This book about malaria covers "the history of the disease, the search for the cause, and the search for a cure." Book Rep
"The attractive format of [this] introductory [title] will entice young report writers. . . . Well-researched." SLJ
Includes glossary and bibliographical references

Jarrow, Gail
Chiggers; [by] Gail Jarrow. KidHaven Press 2004 32p il (Parasites) $22.45 (4-6)   **616.9**
1. Mites
ISBN 0-7377-1778-5   LC 2003-9614
Contents: The chigger: a young mite; Attack on humans; The chigger disease; Avoiding chigger bites
"Several short chapters briefly describe the distinctive physical and behavioral characteristics of [chiggers] and special characteristics of particular species. [The book] also [highlights] the symptoms, victims' experiences, the organisms' potential threats as disease vectors, current treatments, and prevention methods. . . . Clear, color photographs illustrate the [text]. . . . Well organized and clearly written." SLJ

Margulies, Phillip
Diphtheria; [by] Phillip Margulies. 1st ed. Rosen Publishing Group 2005 64p il (Epidemics! Deadly diseases throughout history) lib bdg $26.50 (4-6)
616.9
1. Diphtheria
ISBN 1-4042-0253-6   LC 2004013395
This addresses "the first outbreaks of [diphtheria], with additional chapters covering symptoms, research, and treatment. The writing is complete and accurate." SLJ
Includes bibliographical references

616.97　Diseases of the immune system

Bardhan-Quallen, Sudipta
AIDS; [by] Sudipta Bardhan-Quallen. KidHaven Press 2005 48p il (Understanding diseases and disorders) $23.70 (4-6)   **616.97**
1. AIDS (Disease)
ISBN 0-7377-2638-5   LC 2004-23003
Contents: What is AIDS?; What is HIV and how does it spread?; Treating HIV and AIDS; Living with HIV and AIDS
This "defines HIV and AIDS, explains the spread of HIV and the treatment of both HIV and AIDS, and discusses related scientific and humanitarian efforts around the world. Medical descriptions are clear . . . and statistics are current and startling. Well-chosen quotations from patients put a human face on the disease." Booklist
Includes glossary and bibliographical references

Hicks, Terry Allan
Allergies. Marshall Cavendish Benchmark 2006 64p il (Health alert) lib bdg $28.50 (4 and up)
616.97
1. Allergy
ISBN 0-7614-1918-7 (lib bdg)   LC 2005-05000
This describes the causes of allergies, their history, and how to live with them.
This is "well-designed and easy-to-use . . . with accurate and reliable information. Colorful photos, micrographs, and sidebars appear throughout." SLJ
Includes glossary and bibliographical references

McPhee, Andrew T.
AIDS. Watts 2000 63p il lib bdg $24.50; pa $8.95 (5 and up)   **616.97**
1. AIDS (Disease)
ISBN 0-531-11779-0 (lib bdg); 0-531-16528-0 (pa)
          LC 99-45288
"Watts library"
Discusses how AIDS is spread, diagnosed, and treated. Methods of protecting oneself from the disease are presented
Includes bibliographical references

Parker, Steve
Allergies; [by] Steve Parker. Heinemann Library 2004 56p il (Just the facts) lib bdg $32.86 (5 and up)
616.97
1. Allergy
ISBN 1-4034-4598-2   LC 2003-10872
Contents: Allergies; Early history of allergies; Recent history of allergies; What is an allergy?; Different types of allergies; Who is affected?; More and more allergies; Allergies in the nose; Hay fever and similar allergies; Skin allergies; Food allergies; Drug and microbe allergies; Allergies to bites and stings; Allergy can be deadly=anaphylaxis; Is it an allergy?; Tackling an allergy; Living with an allergy; Allergy out and about; Prevention and treatment; Medical science and allergies; Complementary therapies; Can allergies be cured?; Hopes for the future; Allergies: same but different

Parker, Steve—*Continued*

Defines what an allergy is, various types of allergies, some prevention and treatment methods, and other issues related to allergic conditions

This is "well written and organized." SLJ

Includes bibliographical references

Silverstein, Alvin

Allergies; [by] Alvin Silverstein, Virginia Silverstein and Laura Silverstein Nunn. Watts 1999 48p il (My health) lib bdg $24.50; pa $6.95 (3-5)   **616.97**

1. Allergy

ISBN 0-531-11581-X (lib bdg); 0-531-16409-8 (pa)

LC 98-26033

Discusses the nature and effects of allergies, who gets them, how they develop, the different kinds, and how they are treated

This is "well written and complete, without being overly technical. The occasional cartoon illustrations are clear and informative, and the frequent close-up color photographs . . . are an added bonus." SLJ

Includes glossary and bibliographical references

616.99   Tumors and cancers

Gillie, Oliver

Cancer; [by] Oliver Gillie. Heinemann Library 2004 56p il (Just the facts) $23 (5 and up)

616.99

1. Cancer

ISBN 1-4034-5144-3   LC 2003-22508

Provides an overview of cancer, describing what it is, what the various forms are that it takes, what it is like to live with this disease, and some of the available treatments.

This is "well written and substantive without being overly technical." SLJ

Includes bibliographical references

Watters, Debbie

Where's Mom's hair? a family's journey through cancer; by Debbie Watters; with Haydn and Emmett Watters; photographs by Sophie Hogan. Second Story Press; distributed by Orca 2005 31p il pa $10.95 (2-4)   **616.99**

1. Cancer 2. Hair

ISBN 1-896764-94-0

"When the author underwent chemotherapy following cancer surgery, she faced the loss of her hair with courage and humor. Family and friends gathered for a 'hair-cutting party,' where her husband and two young sons . . . joined her in getting buzz cuts. . . . The gentle kindness conveyed in the often-humorous writing will reassure young children facing similar circumstances." SLJ

617.1   Injuries and wounds. Sports medicine

Silverstein, Alvin

Burns and blisters; [by] Alvin Silverstein, Virginia Silverstein, and Laura Silverstein Nunn. Watts 2002 48p il (My health) lib bdg $23; pa $6.95 (3-5)   **617.1**

1. Burns and scalds 2. Wounds and injuries 3. First aid

ISBN 0-531-11871-1 (lib bdg); 0-531-15561-7 (pa)

LC 2001-17571

This "discusses the function of skin, what happens when burns or blisters damage it, types of injuries, their treatment, and why protection from the sun is important. . . . [This book has] succinct, easy-to-understand [text]; well-placed, informative color graphics; and activities." SLJ

Includes glossary and bibliographical references

Cuts, scrapes, scabs, and scars; [by] Alvin Silverstein, Virginia Silverstein and Laura Silverstein Nunn. Watts 1999 48p il (My health) lib bdg $24.50; pa $6.95 (3-5)   **617.1**

1. Wounds and injuries 2. First aid

ISBN 0-531-11582-8 (lib bdg); 0-531-16411-X (pa)

LC 98-36479

Describes how the body responds to wounds and heals itself when the skin is broken and discusses how to care for minor abrasions

Includes bibliographical references

617.6   Dentistry

Keller, Laurie

Open wide; Tooth School inside. Holt & Co. 2000 unp il lib bdg $16.95 (k-3)   **617.6**

1. Dentistry 2. Teeth

ISBN 0-8050-6192-4   LC 99-27965

Through a classroom setting in which teeth are the students, presents information about the structure and care of teeth and the services provided by dentists

"The sprawling comic art, featuring acrylics and collage, is busy with unruly figures riding on a 'molar coaster,' jumping rope made with floss, and engaging in food fights. . . . Consistently humorous, the book is instructive throughout." Horn Book

Silverstein, Alvin

Tooth decay and cavities; [by] Alvin Silverstein, Virginia Silverstein and Laura Silverstein Nunn. Watts 1999 48p il (My health) lib bdg $24.50; pa $6.95 (3-5)   **617.6**

1. Teeth

ISBN 0-531-11580-1 (lib bdg); 0-531-16412-8 (pa)

LC 98-22024

Describes the structure and function of teeth and discusses how cavities form and how to prevent them

Includes bibliographical references

617.7 Ophthalmology

Silverstein, Alvin
Can you see the chalkboard? [by] Alvin Silverstein, Virginia Silverstein, and Laura Silverstein Nunn. Watts 2001 48p il (My health) lib bdg $22.50 (3-5)   **617.7**
1. Eye 2. Vision
ISBN 0-531-11783-9   LC 00-28983
Describes the human eye and how it functions, various visual problems and how they are corrected, and how to take care of one's eyes
The text is "easy to read and [contains] a lot of information. The illustrations, sharp and in bright colors, are a combination of well-placed photographs, cartoons, and diagrams." SLJ
Includes glossary and bibliographical references

617.9 Transplantation of tissue and organs

Fullick, Ann
Rebuilding the body; organ transplantation. Heinemann Lib. 2002 64p il (Science at the edge) lib bdg $32.79; pa $9.50 (5 and up)
                    617.9
1. Transplantation of organs, tissues, etc.
ISBN 1-58810-700-0 (lib bdg); 1-4034-4122-7 (pa)
                    LC 2001-6082
Contents: The organs of the body; Organ failure; New parts for old; How is it done?; Rejection; Life from death; Lucy's story; Pushing the boundaries; Xenotransplantation; The cutting edge; Stem cell research
This "sets the stage for understanding complex transplant procedures by first explaining how the major organs function and some of the causes of organ failure, then discussing issues related to compatibility, organ preservation, rejection, and the ethics of organ donation and transplant research. . . . [This title is] nicely written, well organized, and filled with lots of visuals." Booklist
Includes glossary and bibliographical references

Rosaler, Maxine
Bionics. Blackbirch Press 2003 48p il (Science on the edge) lib bdg $23.70 (5 and up)
                    617.9
1. Bionics
ISBN 1-56711-784-8   LC 2002-15970
Discusses the history of replacement body parts, current accomplishments in the field, and visions of future technology.
Includes glossary and bibliographical references

618.1 Gynecology

Orr, Tamra
Test tube babies; written by Tamra B. Orr. Blackbirch Press 2003 48p il (Science on the edge) lib bdg $23.70 (5 and up)   **618.1**
1. Fertilization in vitro 2. Infertility 3. Reproduction
ISBN 1-56711-788-0   LC 2002-11928

Contents: In the beginning; The current picture; A future of possibilities
Examines the causes of infertility, the history of in vitro fertilization, the steps involved in creating a 'test tube baby,' and ethical questions the technology has raised
Includes bibliographical references

618.2 Obstetrics

Jackson, Donna M.
Twin tales; the magic and mystery of multiple birth; by Donna M. Jackson. Little, Brown 2001 48p il $16.95 (4 and up)   **618.2**
1. Multiple birth 2. Twins
ISBN 0-316-45431-1   LC 99-44741
"Megan Tingley books"
Explores aspects of the topic of twins, including why and how they are born, twin telepathy, identical and fraternal twins, and separation of twins
"Jackson blends scientific facts with interesting personal anecdotes to create an informative and intriguing look at twins. The text is clearly written, and the tone remains lively throughout." SLJ
Includes glossary

621.3 Electrical, magnetic, optical, communications, computer engineering; electronics, lighting

Cole, Joanna
The magic school bus and the electric field trip; illustrated by Bruce Degen. Scholastic 1997 48p il $15.95 hardcover o.p.; pa $5.99 (2-4)
                    621.3
1. Electricity 2. Electric power
ISBN 0-590-44682-7; 0-590-44683-5 (pa)
                    LC 97-2080
Also available Spanish language edition
Ms. Frizzle takes her class on a field trip through the town's electrical wires so they can learn how electricity is generated and how it is used
"Spiced with plenty of puns and jokes, the writing and the colorful artwork continue the series' unbeatable combination of clearly presented information and plenty of fun." Booklist

621.31 Generation, modification, storage, transmission of electric power

Bartholomew, Alan

Electric mischief; battery-powered gadgets kids can build; written by Alan Bartholomew; illustrated by Lynn Bartholomew. Kids Can Press 2002 48p il (Kids can do it) $12.95; pa $5.95 (4-6)   **621.31**

1. Electric apparatus and appliances 2. Electricity

ISBN 1-55074-923-4; 1-55074-925-0 (pa)

This provides instructions for building 10 electric gadgets such as a bumper car, electric dice, and a robot hand

"Projects are clearly explained and easy to follow; colorful illustrations aid understanding. Materials required . . . are readily available at hardware stores." SLJ

621.36 Optical engineering

Boekhoff, P. M.

Lasers; by P.M. Boekhoff and Stuart A. Kallen. KidHaven Press 2002 48p il (Kidhaven science library) lib bdg $23.70 (3-5)   **621.36**

1. Lasers

ISBN 0-7377-0944-8   LC 2001-2184

The authors "discuss lasers from Einstein's description of their basic principles to today's pervasive devices, tallying their uses in medicine, recreation, military endeavors, and heavy and fine industry." Booklist

"The appealing layout includes large fonts, many color photographs, and simple diagrams." SLJ

Includes glossary and bibliographical references

621.47 Solar-energy engineering

Bang, Molly

My light. Blue Sky Press 2004 unp il $16.95 (1-3)   **621.47**

1. Solar energy 2. Electricity

ISBN 0-439-48961-X

"Writing in the voice of the sun, the first-person narrative investigates various forms of energy on Earth, all derived in one way or another from the light and heat of this solar system's major star." SLJ

"Bang's strong design sense comes through in compositions that gracefully incorporate diagrams and strike a balance between graphic forms and delicate, decorative patterns. A lovely and illuminating book that presents sound science while expressing the wonder of flipping a switch and flooding a room with light." Booklist

621.8 Machine engineering

Bingham, Caroline

Monster machines. DK Pub. 1998 32p il $14.99 (k-3)   **621.8**

1. Machinery

ISBN 0-7894-2796-6   LC 97-39624

Photographs and text examine the parts and functions of such large machines as trucks, jets, supertankers, tractors, bulldozers, and fire engines

"It is the sheer visual bigness (including two double-spread foldouts) of this oversized book that will captivate mechanically minded audiences." Horn Book Guide

Includes glossary

Gardner, Robert

Sensational science projects with simple machines; [by] Robert Gardner. Enslow Elementary 2006 48p il (Fantastic physical science experiments) $23.93 (4-6)   **621.8**

1. Simple machines 2. Science—Experiments

ISBN 0-7660-2585-3   LC 2005008974

"The first chapter of [this book] explains force, friction, distance, and work. The book then introduces levers, inclined planes, pulleys, etc. . . . Large colorful, cartoonlike drawings complement the [text]. . . . [This offers] solid information." SLJ

Includes glossary and bibliographical references

Hoban, Tana

Construction zone. Greenwillow Bks. 1997 unp il $16.99 (k-2)   **621.8**

1. Machinery

ISBN 0-688-12284-1   LC 96-5696

Hoban uses "full-color photographs to introduce construction equipment. Each of the 13 machines presented is given a two-page spread, one picture taken at middle distance, the other close up. The final two pages match thumbnail photos with explanatory text." SLJ

The "photos have extraordinary depth and detail." Booklist

Solway, Andrew

Castle under siege! simple machines; [by] Andrew Solway. Raintree 2005 32p il lib bdg $28.21; pa $7.85 (3-5)   **621.8**

1. Simple machines 2. Castles

ISBN 1-4109-1918-8 (lib bdg); 1-4109-1949-8 (pa)   LC 2005014549

"Raintree fusion"

"The author leads readers through the construction of a castle, the workings of the drawbridge, the execution of a siege and how the inhabitants would protect the castle from attack, methods the invaders might use, and what would happen afterward to repair the damage. While readers are drawn into the action, they are also introduced to the simple machines used during this period of time. . . . Detailed, easily interpreted diagrams are included for added understanding of concepts. Vivid and realistic photos add to the appeal. An excellent choice for research or for general interest." SLJ

621.9 Tools

Clements, Andrew
Workshop; illustrated by David Wisniewski. Clarion Bks. 1998 unp il $16 (k-2)　　**621.9**
1. Tools 2. Workshops
ISBN 0-395-85579-9　　LC 97-48534
"From ruler to wrench, 13 basic tools are described in short text and bright, bold cut-paper illustrations. In each large-scale, double-page spread, a young apprentice watches a different craftsman at work with saw, chisel, grinder, or knife." SLJ
"Wisniewski's cut-paper illustrations and collage ably illustrate Clements' spare, poetic text. . . . A unique introduction to the world of wood and art for budding artisans." Bull Cent Child Books

623.4 Ordnance

Gurstelle, William
The art of the catapult; build Greek ballistae, Roman onagers, English trebuchets, and more ancient artillery. Chicago Review Press 2004 172p il map $16.95 (5 and up)　　**623.4**
1. Catapult
ISBN 1-55652-526-5
"This collection of 10 working catapult projects offers a fascinating look at world history, military strategy, and physics, related with an engaging yet lighthearted touch. . . . Instructions are clear, with full materials lists, helpful diagrams, and no skipped steps. . . . There's excellent booktalk potential here, and lively reading even for those who never get around to constructing a catapult." SLJ
Includes bibliographical references

623.8 Nautical engineering and seamanship

Kovacs, Deborah
Dive to the deep ocean; voyages of exploration and discovery. Raintree Steck-Vaughn Pubs. 2000 64p il maps (Turnstone ocean explorer book) lib bdg $28.55; pa $10.80 (4 and up)　　**623.8**
1. Alvin (Submersible) 2. Underwater exploration 3. Submersibles
ISBN 0-7398-1234-3 (lib bdg); 0-7398-1235-1 (pa)
　　LC 99-17877
Relates the history of deep sea research, explaining how the development of submersibles, particularly the Alvin, has led to many fascinating discoveries
"The plentiful photographs and occasional diagram are well placed and present clear, concise information that reinforces what is read in the text." Sci Books Films
Includes glossary and bibliographical references

623.89 Navigation

Morrison, Taylor
The coast mappers. Houghton Mifflin Co 2004 45p il map $16 (5 and up)　　**623.89**
1. Davidson, George 2. Maps 3. Surveying 4. Pacific Coast (North America)
ISBN 0-618-25408-0　　LC 2003-13534
Chronicles the difficulties encountered by George Davidson and others as they attempted to create nautical charts to complete the U.S. Coast Survey of the West Coast in the mid-nineteenth century.
"Cartographic methods are clearly explained through both the carefully researched text and the precise illustrations. . . . The artwork clarifies the text, depicts the breathtaking beauty of the coastline, and adds a sense of adventure. " SLJ
Includes glossary and bibliographical references

624 Civil engineering

Kent, Peter
Great building stories of the past. Oxford Univ. Press 2001 45p il map lib bdg $18.95 (4 and up)
　　624
1. Architecture
ISBN 0-19-521846-9　　LC 2001-36557
Explains the stories and principles behind some of the world's greatest structures, including the Great Pyramid at Giza, the Great Wall of China, the Eiffel Tower, and the Brooklyn Bridge
"The text is concise, yet informative, describing each project's construction in a few pages. The illustrations are clear, crisp, and frequently humorous." Booklist
Includes bibliographical references

Macaulay, David
Underground. Houghton Mifflin 1976 109p il $19; pa $9.95 (5 and up)　　**624**
1. Civil engineering
ISBN 0-395-24739-X; 0-395-34065-9 (pa)
In this "examination of the intricate support systems that lie beneath the street levels of our cities, Macaulay explains the ways in which foundations for buildings are laid or reinforced, and how the various utilities or transportation services are constructed." Bull Cent Child Books
"Introduced by a visual index—a bird's eye view of a busy, hypothetical intersection with colored indicators marking the specific locations analyzed in subsequent pages—detailed illustrations are combined with a clear, precise narrative to make the subject comprehenssible and fascinating." Horn Book
Includes glossary

Sullivan, George
Built to last; building America's amazing bridges, dams, tunnels, and skyscrapers. Scholastic Nonfiction 2005 128p il maps $18.99 (5 and up)
　　624
1. Civil engineering
ISBN 0-439-51737-0　　LC 2004-60996

Sullivan, George—*Continued*

This is a "survey of American building—from the Erie Canal to Boston's current 'Big Dig.' Chronological chapters describe the historical forces that helped drive each project as well as the specific technological feats linked to each pioneering structure. . . . The wide selection of captivating illustrations includes archival photos and engravings, architectural drawings, and color photos. . . . Sullivan's skillful integration of social and economic history distinguishes this clear, well-designed title." Booklist

624.1 Structural engineering and underground construction

Fantastic feats and failures; by the editors of YES magazine. Kids Can Press 2004 52p il $15.95; pa $7.95 (4 and up) **624.1**
1. Civil engineering
ISBN 1-55337-633-1; 1-55337-634-X (pa)

This "book spotlights 20 notable highs and lows in engineering. The 'feats' celebrated include the Sydney Opera House, the Brooklyn Bridge, and Canadarm (a huge, Canadian-built robotic arm used for repairs in space). Among the 'failures' are the space shuttle Challenger, the Tacoma Narrows Bridge, and the Chernobyl nuclear power plant. . . . Well organized and engagingly written. . . . Excellent photos . . . illustrate the places and events discussed, while colorful drawings visually represent concepts " Booklist

Simon, Seymour

Let's try it out with towers and bridges; by Seymour Simon and Nicole Fauteux. Simon & Schuster Bks. for Young Readers 2003 unp il $14.95 (k-2) **624.1**
1. Structural engineering 2. Bridges 3. Models and modelmaking
ISBN 0-689-82923-X LC 2001-20802

This describes activities for learning about structural engineering using such materials as modeling clay, building blocks, corrugated cardboard, tape, and drinking straws

"Lively illustrations in pen-and-ink, watercolor, and gouache show children experimenting with . . . building materials and having *fun*." Booklist

624.2 Bridges

Adkins, Jan

Bridges; from my side to yours; written & illustrated by Jan Adkins. Roaring Brook Press 2002 96p il $18.95; lib bdg $25.90 (4 and up) **624.2**
1. Bridges
ISBN 0-7613-2510-7; 0-7613-1542-X (lib bdg)
LC 2001-48297

A look at bridges throughout history, from simple arrangements of stepping stones, to famous landmarks such as London Bridge, to marvels of engineering such as New York's Brooklyn Bridge

"Varying perspectives are used to explain technologi-cal concepts, rendering them clear and understandable. . . . The author's fascination with his subject is well communicated, and his knowledge of history is as dazzling as his understanding of engineering principles. . . . An outstanding book for reference and or enjoyment." Horn Book

Includes glossary

Curlee, Lynn

Brooklyn Bridge. Atheneum Bks. for Young Readers 2001 35p il map $18 (3-6) **624.2**
1. Roebling, John Augustus 2. Roebling, Washington Augustus, 1837-1926 3. Brooklyn Bridge (New York, N.Y.) 4. Bridges
ISBN 0-689-83183-8 LC 99-43771

This book "tells the history behind the bridge and its construction . . . explains the financing and final decision to build the bridge, and describes the roles of John A. Roebling and, later, his son, Washington, as Chief Engineer." SLJ

"Biography, social history, and introductory engineering are . . . precisely balanced, with human-interest angles. . . . This is a grand yet practical tribute to a grand yet practical edifice." Bull Cent Child Books

Includes bibliographical references

Johmann, Carol

Bridges! amazing structures to design, build & test; [by] Carol Johmann & Elizabeth Rieth; illustrations by Michael Kline. Williamson 1999 96p il pa $10.95 (4 and up) **624.2**
1. Bridges
ISBN 1-88559-330-9 LC 98-53272

"A Williamson Kaleidoscope Kids book"

Describes different kinds of bridges, their history, design, construction, and effects on populations, environmental dilemmas, safety, and more

"Eye-catching photographs and cartoon illustrations in blue and orange tones abound; clear organization of text and unifying page borders create an attractive graphic package. The volume includes a list of notable bridges by state and country." SLJ

Sturges, Philemon

Bridges are to cross; illustrated by Giles Laroche. Putnam 1998 unp il paperback o.p. $15.99 (2-4) **624.2**
1. Bridges
ISBN 0-399-23174-9; 0-698-11874-X
LC 97-13775

Discusses different kinds of bridges, from train bridges to fortified castle bridges, and provides an example of each

"The pictures, a combination of paint and cut paper, show the bridges at their elegant best and reflect the surroundings, whether modern or ancient, beautifully. . . . This is guaranteed to make most readers look at bridges with new eyes." Booklist

625.1 Railroads

Barton, Byron
Trains. Crowell 1986 unp il lib bdg $16.89 (k-1)
625.1
1. Railroads
ISBN 0-690-04534-4   LC 85-47898
Brief text and illustrations present a variety of trains
and what they do
"The concepts are simple and Barton's illustrations are
just enough, and no more." Publ Wkly

Big book of trains; [by] National Railway
Museum, York, England. DK Pub. 1998 32p il
$14.99 (4-6)   **625.1**
1. Railroads
ISBN 0-7894-3436-9   LC 98-18830
Describes the locomotives, cars, tunnels, stations, and
functions of such trains as freight trains, channel tunnel
trains, bullet trains, mountain trains, and snow trains
Includes glossary

Simon, Seymour
Seymour Simon's book of trains. HarperCollins
Pubs. 2002 unp il $16.99; lib bdg $17.89; pa $6.99
(k-3)   **625.1**
1. Railroads
ISBN 0-06-028475-7; 0-06-028476-5 (lib bdg);
0-06-446223-4 (pa)   LC 2001-24020
"Each double-page spread in this picture book sets a
dramatic close-up photo of a moving train opposite a few
sentences about the train's source of power (steam, die-
sel, electric) and how it works. The full-color, close-up
pictures by a number of photographers will grab even
young preschoolers. . . . The astonishing facts will interest older train buffs." Booklist

625.4 Rapid transit systems

McKendry, Joe
Beneath the streets of Boston; building
America's first subway; written & illustrated by
Joe McKendry. David R. Godine 2005 unp il maps
$19.95 (4-6)   **625.4**
1. Subways 2. Boston (Mass.)—History
ISBN 1-56792-284-8   LC 2004-16418
This book covers over twenty years of the early histo-
ry of the Boston subway system
"The text is clear and well written. . . . The paintings
convey the sense of story, while the drawings provide
specific details. Both are equally well executed and contribute to the overall understanding of the text." SLJ

Weitzman, David L.
A subway for New York; [by] David Weitzman.
Farrar, Straus and Giroux 2005 unp il map $17 (4
and up)   **625.4**
1. Subways 2. New York (N.Y.)—History
ISBN 0-374-37284-5   LC 2004-56286

"Weitzman recounts the construction of [New York's]
first subterranean train system, beginning above ground
with descriptions of [the city's] crowded streets in 1904.
. . . The text and captivating images convey the awe-
inspiring scope of the project and the engineering feats
that produced what remains the fastest method of navigating the city." Booklist
Includes bibliographical references

625.7 Roads

Hennessy, B. G. (Barbara G.)
Road builders; pictures by Simms Taback.
Viking 1994 unp il $16.99; pa $5.99 (k-2)
625.7
1. Roads 2. Trucks
ISBN 0-670-83390-8; 0-14-054276-0 (pa)
LC 93-42248
This book introduces "children to the process of building a road. The focus is on the vehicles involved, depicting them all together and then individually or in pairs as
the project unfolds. Taback's cartoon illustration show
the multiethnic crew at work and a flatbed truck carrying
them to the next job when the highway is completed.
This book is a good choice for both beginning readers
and preschool construction buffs." SLJ

627 Hydraulic engineering

Mann, Elizabeth
Hoover Dam; with illustrations by Alan
Witschonke. Mikaya Press 2001 unp il (Wonders
of the world) $19.95 (4 and up)   **627**
1. Hoover Dam (Ariz. and Nev.)
ISBN 1-931414-02-5   LC 2001-34520
Describes the engineering, construction, and social and
historical contexts of the Hoover Dam.
"A wonderfully readable, well-organized book filled
with fascinating detail." SLJ

628.9 Fire-fighting technology

Beil, Karen Magnuson
Fire in their eyes; wildfires and the people who
fight them. Harcourt Brace & Co. 1999 64p il pa
$11 hardcover o.p. (4 and up)   **628.9**
1. Fire fighters 2. Forest fires 3. Forest ecology
ISBN 0-15-201042-4 (pa)   LC 98-6378
Depicts in text and photographs the training, equipment, and real-life experiences of people who risk their
lives to battle wildfires, as well as people who use fire
for ecological reasons
"The ferocity of fire is forcefully depicted in both narrative and well-chosen photographs." Horn Book Guide
Includes glossary

Bingham, Caroline

Fire truck. DK Pub. 2003 29p il (Machines at work) $8.99 (k-3) **628.9**

1. Fire engines 2. Fire fighting

ISBN 0-7894-9221-0

Introduces fire engines and the work that they help firefighters do in all kinds of settings

"Bingham immediately grabs the reader's attention with brilliantly colored pictures. . . . An excellent stimulant for a child's imagination." Sci Books Films

Includes glossary

Demarest, Chris L.

Firefighters A to Z. Margaret K. McElderry Bks. 2000 unp il lib bdg $16.95 (k-1)

628.9

1. Fire fighters 2. Alphabet

ISBN 0-689-83798-4 LC 99-56382

An alphabetic look at a firefighter's day

"There's nothing babyish or cute about the robust, action-oriented pastel artwork in *Firefighters A to Z*. . . . Permeated with intense primary colors, the images build on one another to convey the physical nature of this dramatic but serious job. The firefighters themselves, in their bulky yellow suits and oxygen masks, appear straight out of science fiction, but the smoothly rhyming text grounds their activities in reality." Horn Book

Gibbons, Gail

Fire! Fire! Crowell 1984 unp il lib bdg $15.89; pa $6.95 (k-3) **628.9**

1. Fire fighting

ISBN 0-690-04416-X (lib bdg); 0-06-446058-4 (pa)
LC 83-46162

This book "depicts fire fighting in the city, forest, and on the water, and integrates some points on fire safety." Child Book Rev Serv

The author/illustrator "uses bright colors and simplified diagrams to convey the excitement and teamwork necessary in firefighting. There are details for children to pore over and the equipment in the illustrations is clearly labeled." SLJ

Landau, Elaine

Smokejumpers; photographs by Ben Klaffke. Millbrook Press 2002 48p il lib bdg $23.90 (3-6)

628.9

1. Fire fighters 2. Forest fires

ISBN 0-7613-2324-4 LC 2001-30974

"The first half explains the physical training smokejumpers undergo and the fire-fighting theory they must learn. The second half shows what happens when a fire call comes in. . . . The pictures and text work together beautifully. . . . This is a must-purchase for libraries in places where forest fires occur, and the true-life-adventure aspect will make it popular in other libraries as well." Booklist

Includes glossary and bibliographical references

Masoff, Joy

Fire! principal photography by Jack Reznicki and Barry D. Smith. Scholastic Ref. 1998 48p il pa $6.95 hardcover o.p. (4 and up) **628.9**

1. Fire fighters

ISBN 0-439-47217-2 LC 97-10928

Presents the work done by fire fighters, including the equipment they use, the fires they fight, the rescues and investigations they perform, and the history and future of fire fighting

"Masoff's personal enthusiasm for her subject along with her attention to detail and clear, lively writing set this far above the common run of razzle-dazzle, photo-filled compendia." Horn Book Guide

Includes bibliographical references

629.04 Transportation engineering

Bingham, Caroline

Big book of rescue vehicles. Dorling Kindersley 2000 31p il $14.95 (k-3) **629.04**

1. Vehicles 2. Rescue work

ISBN 0-7894-5454-8 LC 99-42517

Text and detailed photographs explain how various emergency vehicles work, including the fire engine, rescue hovercraft, and snow mobile and rescue sled

629.13 Aeronautics

Brown, Don

Ruth Law thrills a nation; story and pictures by Don Brown. Ticknor & Fields 1993 unp il $16; pa $5.95 (k-3) **629.13**

1. Law, Ruth, b. 1887 2. Women air pilots

ISBN 0-395-66404-7; 0-395-73517-3 (pa)
LC 92-45701

Describes the record-breaking flight of a daring woman pilot, Ruth Law, from Chicago to New York in 1916

"Using a simple text and effective watercolors, Brown successfully re-creates the remarkable flying feat. He sets Law in her historical context with humor and precision." Booklist

Carson, Mary Kay

The Wright Brothers for kids; how they invented the airplane: 21 activities exploring the science and history of flight; illustrations by Laura D'Argo. Chicago Review Press 2003 146p il pa $14.95 (4 and up) **629.13**

1. Wright, Orville, 1871-1948 2. Wright, Wilbur, 1867-1912 3. Aeronautics 4. Science—Experiments

ISBN 1-55652-477-3 LC 2002-155449

This account of the Wright brothers' invention of the airplane, explains the forces of flight-lift, thrust, gravity, and drag and includes such activities as making a Chinese flying top, building a kite, bird watching, making a paper glider and a rubber-band-powered flyer

"A treasure trove of activities awaits readers of this wonderfully executed survey of the Wright brothers and their invention. The narrative flows easily and is comple-

Carson, Mary Kay—*Continued*

mented by numerous photographs that give a sense of history and this event. . . . This is a valuable resource for student reports and projects, and for classroom units." SLJ

Includes glossary and bibliographical references

Haskins, James

Black eagles; African Americans in aviation. Scholastic 1995 196p il pa $4.50 hardcover o.p. (5 and up)   **629.13**

1. African American pilots
ISBN 0-590-45913-9 (pa)   LC 94-18623

"Haskins presents the . . . achievements of African-American aviators from the beginning of the twentieth century to the present." Horn Book Guide

"In addition to introducing the people involved, Haskins ably sets the background scene, revealing a social context of discrimination. . . . An excellent job of dealing with the particular and the more general aspects of 'what it was like.'" Booklist

Includes bibliographical references

Hunter, Ryan Ann

Take off! illustrated by Edward Miller. Holiday House 2000 unp il lib bdg $15.95 (k-3)
                                              629.13

1. Aeronautics 2. Airplanes
ISBN 0-8234-1466-3   LC 98-45423

"Traces flight from wing-flapping and balloons through Kitty Hawk and the twentieth-century flying boom, then examines the breadth of current aviation and some future possibilities." Bull Cent Child Books

"Bright, colorful illustrations offer youngsters plenty of airplanes and other flying machines to inspect. . . . Best perhaps are the endpapers showing 26 planes of different sizes from different periods in history, which offer children a chance to study the many variations in airplane shape and wing construction throughout the years." Booklist

629.133   Aircraft types

Bingham, Caroline

Airplane. DK Pub. 2003 30p il (Machines at work) $8.99 (k-3)   **629.133**

1. Airplanes
ISBN 0-7894-9222-9   LC 2002-14866

Contents: How big is a jumbo?; What's the tug for?; What a monster!; What's that?; How does it fly?; Where's the engine?; Thirsty beasts; How does a helicopter fly?; Air acrobatics; Little flyers; It's a record holder; A watery landing; Blast off!; Picture gallery

Introduces assorted airplanes and other flying machines, including gliders, helicopters, and space shuttles

"Bingham immediately grabs the reader's attention with brilliantly colored pictures. . . . An excellent stimulant for a child's imagination." Sci Books Films

Includes glossary

Englart, Mindi Rose

Helicopters; from start to finish; photographs by Peter Casolino. Blackbirch Press 2003 c2002 32p il (Made in the U.S.A.) $19.95 (2-4)
                                              629.133

1. Helicopters
ISBN 1-56711-478-4   LC 2002-4578

Describes, in text and illustrations, the design, construction, and uses of various types of helicopters

"Excellent photos, a picture-book format, and clear, informative text distinguish [this title]." Booklist

Includes glossary and bibliographical references

Hosking, Wayne

Asian kites. Tuttle 2005 63p il (Asian arts & crafts for creative kids) $12.95 (3-6)
                                              629.133

1. Kites 2. Handicraft
ISBN 0-8048-3545-4

"This survey offers brief anecdotes and legends along with carefully annotated construction diagrams for 15 simple kites commonly flown in Asia. . . . Closing with notes on running a kite-making workshop for children, lists of associations and sources of supplies, and a relatively extensive bibliography, this title merits, and will find, a wide audience in libraries large or small." SLJ

Murdico, Suzanne J.

Concorde. Children's Press 2001 48p il (Built for speed) lib bdg $22; pa $6.95 (4 and up)
                                              629.133

1. Jet planes
ISBN 0-516-23158-8 (lib bdg); 0-516-23261-4 (pa)
                                          LC 00-63896

This describes a flight on the Concorde and gives a brief history of the jet aircraft

This "is excellent for upper elementary students, older reluctant readers, and ESL students. . . . The pictures enhance the text." Book Rep

Includes glossary and bibliographical references

Nahum, Andrew

Flying machine; written by Andrew Nahum. rev ed. DK Pub. 2004 72p il (DK eyewitness books) $15.99; lib bdg $19.99 (4 and up)
                                              629.133

1. Aeronautics—History
ISBN 0-7566-0680-2; 0-7566-0679-9 (lib bdg)

First published 1990 by Knopf

A photo essay tracing the history and development of aircraft from hot-air balloons to jetliners. Includes information on the principles of flight and the inner workings of various flying machines.

O'Brien, Patrick

The Hindenburg. Holt & Co. 2000 unp il map $17 (4 and up)   **629.133**

1. Hindenburg (Airship) 2. Airships
ISBN 0-8050-6415-X   LC 99-46687

Describes the development and early flights of airships and the disastrous crash of the Hindenburg at an airfield

O'Brien, Patrick—*Continued*

in New Jersey in 1937

"In both pictures and text, this beautiful, fact-filled book truly makes history come alive." Booklist

629.2 Motor land vehicles, and cycles

Mitchell, Joyce Slayton

Crashed, smashed, and mashed; a trip to junkyard heaven; photographs by Steven Borns. Tricycle Press 2001 unp il pa $7.95 hardcover o.p. (3-6)   **629.2**

1. Automobiles 2. Salvage

ISBN 1-58246-156-2 (pa); 1-58246-034-5 (hc)

LC 00-10713

This describes an automobile junkyard where old cars are salvaged for parts and scrap metal

This book offers "excellent, clear, close-up photographs and a wealth of facts." Booklist

Includes glossary

629.224 Trucks

Barton, Byron

Trucks. Crowell 1986 unp il lib bdg $15.89 (k-1)   **629.224**

1. Trucks

ISBN 0-690-04530-1   LC 85-47901

Also available Board book edition

Brief text and illustrations present a variety of trucks from cement trucks to ice-cream trucks, and what they do

"A tightly focused (book) . . . featuring Barton's trademark bright, blocky graphics and spare text." Publ Wkly

Robbins, Ken

Trucks; giants of the highway; text and pictures by Ken Robbins. Atheneum Bks. for Young Readers 1999 unp il $16 (k-2)   **629.224**

1. Trucks

ISBN 0-689-82664-8   LC 98-47640

Describes different kinds of tractor trailers, or big rigs, and the loads they haul

"Young truck enthusiasts will enjoy this well-written, attractive photo-essay." Booklist

Simon, Seymour

Seymour Simon's book of trucks. HarperCollins Pubs. 2000 unp $15.95; lib bdg $15.89 (k-3)   **629.224**

1. Trucks

ISBN 0-06-028473-0; 0-06-028481-1 (lib bdg)

LC 99-14602

Describes various kinds of trucks and their functions, including a log truck, cement mixer truck, and sanitation truck

"The exciting photographs, many of them close-ups, will captivate youngsters. . . . The visual appeal of this book is very high and the information is clear and equally engaging." SLJ

Stille, Darlene R.

Trucks. Children's Press 1997 47p il lib bdg $22; pa $6.95 (2-4)   **629.224**

1. Trucks

ISBN 0-516-20343-6 (lib bdg); 0-516-26179-7 (pa)

LC 96-25727

"A True book"

Describes different kinds of trucks, including tractor trailers and tank trucks, pick-ups, tow trucks, fire trucks, garbage trucks, vans, and recreational vehicles

Includes bibliographical references

629.227 Cycles

Gibbons, Gail

Bicycle book. Holiday House 1995 unp il $16.95; pa $6.95 (k-3)   **629.227**

1. Bicycles 2. Cycling

ISBN 0-8234-1199-0; 0-8234-1408-6 (pa)

LC 95-5911

"The history of bicycles, the science behind their design, descriptions of different types, their care, and safety rules are all clearly and simply presented in Gibbons's typical, inimitable style. Lots of color, accurate explanations, and interesting facts make this a winning choice." SLJ

Haduch, Bill

Go fly a bike! the ultimate book about bicycle fun, freedom & science; illustrated by Chris Murphy. Dutton Children's Books 2004 83p il $16.99 (4-6)   **629.227**

1. Bicycles

ISBN 0-525-47024-7

Gives the history, science, types of cycles, safety and the basics and maintenance of bicycles

"Halftone cartoonlike illustrations are scattered throughout, and a funny fact or joke appears in an inset on most pages. . . . This is a versatile, fact-packed book that can work for both research and recreational reading." Booklist

629.228 Racing cars

Rex, Michael

My race car. Holt & Co. 2000 unp il lib bdg $15.95 (k-1)   **629.228**

1. Automobile racing 2. Automobiles

ISBN 0-8050-6101-0   LC 99-31773

"'I have a race car. I drive it all the time,' says a boy sitting on the floor with his toy cars. As the pages turn, the toy world becomes reality: the boy finds himself on the track with his crew, checking his car engine, and then driving his laps. . . . Short, simple sentences create excitement . . . and Rex's bright, thick-lined cartoon drawings are appealingly energetic and clear. A great choice for young race car enthusiasts who are beginning to read on their own." Booklist

629.4   Astronautics

Bredeson, Carmen
John Glenn returns to orbit; life on the space shuttle. Enslow Pubs. 2000 48p il (Countdown to space) $18.95 (4 and up)   **629.4**
1. Glenn, John, 1921- 2. Space flight 3. Space shuttles 4. Astronauts
ISBN 0-7660-1304-9   LC 99-12490
Describes the activities aboard the space shuttle Discovery during its historic flight in 1998 when John Glenn, at age seventy-seven, returned to space
"The accessible [text is] accompanied by plenty of well-captioned photos and diagrams." Horn Book Guide
Includes glossary and bibliographical references

Cole, Michael D.
Moon base; first colony in space. Enslow Pubs. 1999 48p il (Countdown to space) lib bdg $23.93 (4 and up)   **629.4**
1. Lunar bases 2. Moon—Exploration
ISBN 0-7660-1118-6   LC 98-13126
Describes the Apollo 11 mission to the moon, explains the need for establishing a moon base, and speculates about future situations in which the base would be used
Includes glossary and bibliographical references

Space launch disaster; when liftoff goes wrong. Enslow Pubs. 2000 48p il (Countdown to space) lib bdg $18.95 (4 and up)   **629.4**
1. Space vehicle accidents
ISBN 0-7660-1309-X   LC 99-32179
Describes the dangers of launching spacecraft, covering the Russian Mars space probe explosion, the Apollo 1 fire, the Apollo 12 lightning strike, and the Challenger explosion
Includes glossary and bibliographical references

Stott, Carole
Space exploration; written by Carole Stott; photographed by Steve Gorton. rev ed. DK Pub. 2004 72p il (DK eyewitness books) $15.99; lib bdg $19.99 (4 and up)   **629.4**
1. Astronautics 2. Outer space—Exploration
ISBN 0-7566-0731-0; 0-7566-0730-2 (lib bdg)
First published 1997 by Knopf
Describes rockets, exploratory vehicles, and other technological aspects of space exploration, satellites, space stations, and the life and work of astronauts.

629.43   Unmanned flight

Kerrod, Robin
Space probes; [by] Robin Kerrod. World Almanac Library 2005 48p il (History of space exploration) lib bdg $30; pa $11.95 (5 and up)
629.43
1. Space probes
ISBN 0-8368-5708-9 (lib bdg); 0-8368-5715-1 (pa)
LC 2004-48207

Discusses how technology has changed the way we look at the celestial bodies of our Solar System, and examines how the space probes have helped discover black holes, star clusters, and nebulae
This "is profusely illustrated with sharply reproduced space photos and artists' conceptions. . . . [This] makes an important addition for any collection supporting avid young scientists or strong science curricula." SLJ
Includes bibliographical references

629.44   Auxiliary spacecraft

Branley, Franklyn Mansfield
The International Space Station; by Franklyn M. Branley; illustrated by True Kelley. HarperCollins Pubs. 2000 32p il (Let's-read-and-find-out science) $16.95; lib bdg $16.89; pa $5.95 (k-3)
629.44
1. Space stations 2. Astronauts
ISBN 0-06-028702-0; 0-06-028703-9 (lib bdg); 0-06-445209-3 (pa)   LC 99-31897
Explains the construction and purpose of the International Space Station and the life of the astronauts on board
"The facts, including a history and background of the station and descriptions of life in space, are presented in a clear, easy-to-read manner. . . . Kelley's clearly labeled drawings and configurations reinforce the concepts presented, and the watercolor illustrations add dimension to the presentation." SLJ

Cole, Michael D.
The Columbia space shuttle disaster; from first liftoff to tragic final flight. Enslow Pubs. 2003 48p il (Countdown to space) lib bdg $18.95 (4 and up)
629.44
1. Columbia (Space shuttle) 2. Space vehicle accidents
ISBN 0-7660-2295-1   LC 2003-4823
First published 1995 with title: Columbia
Contents: A new kind of spaceship; Columbia in orbit; Flight and reentry; Welcome home, Columbia!; Columbia's last mission
Details the first flight of the space shuttle Columbia, as well as its tragic final flight
"The account offers a lot of information, helping to make sense of a highly complicated subject. . . . The color and b&w photographs complement the story." Libr Media Connect
Includes glossary and bibliographical references

NASA space vehicles; capsules, shuttles, and space stations. Enslow Pubs. 2000 48p il (Countdown to space) lib bdg $18.95 (4 and up)
629.44
1. Space vehicles 2. Outer space—Exploration
ISBN 0-7660-1308-1   LC 99-35533
Describes American space vehicles and their uses, including various space probes, the Mercury, Gemini, and Apollo capsules, Skylab, the space shuttles, and the International Space Station
Includes glossary and bibliographical references

Gallant, Roy A.

Space stations. Benchmark Bks. 2000 48p il (Kaleidoscope) $15.95 (3-5) **629.44**

1. Space stations 2. Astronauts

ISBN 0-7614-1035-X LC 99-53511

Explains what a space station is, how it is put into orbit, and what experiments and living conditions are like there

"The text is well written and filled with interesting discussions. . . . The visual appeal of this book . . . should aid in attracting young readers." Sci Books Films

Includes glossary and bibliographical references

Kerrod, Robin

Space shuttles; [by] Robin Kerrod. World Almanac Library 2005 48p il (History of space exploration) lib bdg $30; pa $11.95 (5 and up) **629.44**

1. Space shuttles

ISBN 0-8368-5709-7 (lib bdg); 0-8368-5716-X (pa) LC 2004-49217

Explores the successes of the shuttle program, including the daring recovery and repair of satellites by spacewalking astronauts, and examines the human and technological costs of its tragic failures, such as the losses the Challenger and Columbia

This "is profusely illustrated with sharply reproduced space photos and artists' conceptions. . . . [This] makes an important addition for any collection supporting avid young scientists or strong science curricula." SLJ

Includes bibliographical references

Space stations; [by] Robin Kerrod. World Almanac Library 2005 48p il (History of space exploration) lib bdg $30; pa $11.95 (5 and up) **629.44**

1. Space stations

ISBN 0-8368-5710-0 (lib bdg); 0-8368-5717-8 (pa) LC 2004-49071

Explores the history of space homes such as the Soviet's Salyut 1, Mir, the United States's Skylab, and the International Space Station, a truly international venture between several countries and scheduled for completion in 2008

This "is profusely illustrated with sharply reproduced space photos and artists' conceptions. . . . [This] makes an important addition for any collection supporting avid young scientists or strong science curricula." SLJ

Includes bibliographical references

629.45 Manned space flight

Branley, Franklyn Mansfield

Floating in space; by Franklyn M. Branley; illustrated by True Kelley. HarperCollins Pubs. 1998 32p il (Let's-read-and-find-out science) lib bdg $15.89; pa $4.95 (k-3) **629.45**

1. Astronauts 2. Space stations

ISBN 0-06-025433-5 (lib bdg); 0-06-445142-9 (pa) LC 97-13052

Examines life aboard a space shuttle, describing how astronauts deal with weightlessness, how they eat and exercise, some of the work they do, and more

"This is a beautifully illustrated children's book. . . . The textual information is clearly written, easy to read, and well organized." Sci Books Films

Mission to Mars; by Franklin M. Branley; illustrated by True Kelley; foreword by Neil Armstrong. HarperCollins Pubs. 2002 33p il (Let's-read-and-find-out science) $15.99; lib bdg $17.89; pa $4.99 (k-3) **629.45**

1. Space flight to Mars 2. Mars (Planet)—Exploration

ISBN 0-06-029807-3; 0-06-029808-1 (lib bdg); 0-06-445233-6 (pa) LC 00-54036

The author invites readers to envision "themselves as members of the first Mars Mission's crew. . . . Along with a sprinkling of black-and-white and full-color photos, the illustrations mix clearly drawn schematics with scenes of crew members working busily inside the Mars Station or outside in heavy protective suits. An informative, inspirational introduction." SLJ

Cole, Michael D.

Space emergency; astronauts in danger. Enslow Pubs. 2000 48p il (Countdown to space) lib bdg $18.95 (4 and up) **629.45**

1. Astronautics 2. Space vehicle accidents

ISBN 0-7660-1307-3 LC 99-26855

Describes emergencies that occurred during several space missions, including Apollo 13, Friendship 7, Gemini 8, and Mir

Includes glossary and bibliographical references

Dyson, Marianne J.

Home on the moon; living on a space frontier. National Geographic Soc. 2003 64p il $18.95 (4 and up) **629.45**

1. Moon

ISBN 0-7922-7193-9 LC 2002-5280

Considers the moon as a frontier that has been only partially explored, looking at its history, geography, and weather, as well as what people would require to live and work there. Includes activities

"Clear writing, vivid images, interesting details, and quotes from astronauts and scientists make this a lively, fact-filled introduction." Booklist

Includes glossary and bibliographical references

Goodman, Susan

Ultimate field trip 5; blasting off to Space Academy; by Susan E. Goodman; photographs by Michael J. Doolittle. Atheneum Bks. for Young Readers 2001 41p il $17; pa $6.99 (4 and up) **629.45**

1. U.S. Space Camp (Huntsville, Ala.) 2. Astronauts 3. Space flight

ISBN 0-689-83044-0; 0-689-84863-3 (pa) LC 00-38082

"This book follows student trainees through a weeklong session at the U.S. Space Academy in Huntsville, AL, as they are exposed to what it takes to become an astronaut and to the inner workings of the entire space program. . . . Varied-colored pages, replete with

Goodman, Susan—_Continued_
outstanding full-color, captioned photos, are artistically appealing as well as informative." SLJ
Includes glossary and bibliographical references

Hehner, Barbara
First on the moon; what it was like when man landed on the moon; illustrations by Greg Ruhl. Hyperion Bks. for Children 1999 48p il $16.99; pa $7.99 (4 and up)   **629.45**
1. Apollo 11 (Spacecraft) 2. Space flight to the moon
ISBN 0-7868-0489-0; 0-7868-1538-8 (pa)
                                        LC 98-42651
"An I was there book"
An account of the first moon landing by Apollo 11 in 1969
"The informative and entertaining text is illustrated with an abundance of full-color and black-and-white photographs as well as paintings." SLJ
Includes glossary and bibliographical references

McNulty, Faith
If you decide to go to the moon; illustrated by Steven Kellogg. Scholastic Press 2005 unp il $16.99 (k-3)   **629.45**
1. Space flight to the moon 2. Moon
ISBN 0-590-48359-5   LC 2004-27755
In this "picture book, readers accompany a boy on a fascinating excursion to the moon. The lyrical text provides tips on what to pack and describes the distance to be covered. After blastoff, facts about space travel are mingled with descriptions of what the journey might be like. . . . Rich artwork complements the strong text." SLJ

Thimmesh, Catherine
Team moon; how 400,000 people landed Apollo 11 on the moon. Houghton Mifflin Company 2006 80p il $19.95 (5 and up)   **629.45**
1. Apollo 11 (Spacecraft) 2. Space flight to the moon
ISBN 0-618-50757-4
"Thimmesh retraces the course of the space mission that landed an actual man, on the actual Moon. It's an oft-told tale, but the author tells it from the point of view not of astronauts or general observers, but of some of the 17,000 behind-the-scenes workers at Kennedy Space Center, the 7500 Grumman employees who built the lunar module, the 500 designers and seamstresses who actually constructed the space suits, and other low-profile contributors who made the historic flight possible. . . . This dramatic account will mesmerize even readers already familiar with the event. . . . This stirring, authoritative tribute to the collective effort . . . belongs in every collection." SLJ
Includes glossary and bibliographical references

Vogt, Gregory
Apollo moonwalks; the amazing lunar missions. Enslow Pubs. 2000 48p il (Countdown to space) lib bdg $18.95 (4 and up)   **629.45**
1. Project Apollo 2. Space flight to the moon 3. Moon—Exploration
ISBN 0-7660-1306-5   LC 99-16921

Discusses the six Apollo missions that landed on the moon, describing the work performed there, what it is like to walk on the moon, and the collection of moon rocks
Includes glossary and bibliographical references

Spacewalks; the ultimate adventure in orbit; [by] Gregory L. Vogt. Enslow Pubs. 2000 48p il (Countdown to space) lib bdg $18.95 (4 and up)   **629.45**
1. Extravehicular activity (Space flight) 2. Space flight
ISBN 0-7660-1305-7   LC 99-37094
Describes the training and preparation for spacewalking, the hazards faced by astronauts, as well as the construction of spacesuits
Includes glossary and bibliographical references

629.8   Automatic control engineering

Domaine, Helena
Robotics. Lerner 2005 48p il lib bdg $25.26 (4-6)   **629.8**
1. Robots
ISBN 0-8225-2112-1   LC 2004-13938
This "offers a brief history of efforts to create machines that can perform functions in place of humans, then brings readers up-to-date on applications of robotic technology in exploration, industry, and medicine." Booklist
This has "an attractive, colorful layout that will appeal to readers. Each spread includes captioned, color photographs and/or illustrations; text boxes; and, often, a fun fact. . . . The content is sound and should be accessible to most students." SLJ

Jones, David
Mighty robots; mechanical marvels that fascinate and frighten. Annick Press 2006 126p il $24.95; pa $14.95 (5 and up)   **629.8**
1. Robots
ISBN 1-55037-929-1; 1-55037-928-3 (pa)
"From the development of robotic technology to the history of robots in books and films, this informative offering surveys the field broadly but zeroes in with detailed accounts of many topics. . . . Many clear color photos and detailed sidebars expand the text. . . . Jones presents a great deal of information in a well-organized, accessible manner." Booklist

Sonenklar, Carol
Robots rising; with illustrations by John Kaufmann. Holt & Co. 1999 103p il $15.95 (3-5)   **629.8**
1. Robots
ISBN 0-8050-6096-0   LC 99-19717
Simple text and illustrations describe technological advancements in the field of robotics
"Short chapters, large print, and frequent black-and-white illustrations make the format appealing, and the lively text will attract browsers as well as young researchers." Booklist
Includes glossary and bibliographical references

630.1 Agriculture--Philosophy and theory. Country and farm life

Bial, Raymond

Portrait of a farm family. Houghton Mifflin 1995 48p il $17 (4 and up)   **630.1**

1. Farm life 2. Agriculture

ISBN 0-395-69936-3   LC 94-38201

In this photo essay about the Steidinger family farm in Illinois "Bial explores the specifics of milking, raising feed-lot calves, and cutting silage and discusses the factors to be weighed before buying expensive equipment or choosing a particular kind of animal to raise. . . . Bial brings the Steidingers' everyday world to life, fitting it neatly into an excellent discussion of family-farm-based agriculture and the U.S. economy." Booklist

Includes bibliographical references

Halley, Ned

Farm. Dorling Kindersley 2000 63p il (DK eyewitness books) $15.99; lib bdg $19.99 (4 and up)   **630.1**

1. Agriculture 2. Farms

ISBN 0-7894-6040-8; 0-7894-6615-5 (lib bdg)

First published 1996 by Knopf

Text and photographs depict different aspects of farming through the ages including the equipment, domestic animals, crops, and the future of farming.

Peterson, Cris

Century farm; one hundred years on a family farm; with photographs by Alvis Upitis. Boyds Mills Press 1999 unp il $16.95 (k-3)

                    630.1

1. Farm life

ISBN 1-56397-710-9

"Peterson crafts a warmly personal look at their family farm, noting both constants and changes over the farm's hundred-year history. Family album photographs, reproduced in soft-edged sepia, give descriptions of the past a nostalgic yet immediate appeal and contrast well with the sharp-edged full-color contemporary shots." Horn Book Guide

Splear, Elsie Lee

Growing seasons; paintings by Ken Stark. Putnam 2000 unp il $15.99 (3-5)   **630.1**

1. Farm life 2. Seasons

ISBN 0-399-23460-8   LC 99-23586

Born into an Illinois farm family in 1906, Elsie Lee Splear describes how she, her parents, and her sisters lived in the early years of the twentieth century and how the changing seasons shaped their existence

"In this exceptionally well-designed book, life on a Midwestern farm at the turn of the century is exquisitely portrayed. . . . Stark's evocative paintings are filled with motion, life, and homey details." SLJ

631.3 Tools, machinery, apparatus, equipment

Peterson, Cris

Fantastic farm machines; photographs by David R. Lundquist. Boyd Mills Press 2006 unp il $17.95 (k-3)   **631.3**

1. Agricultural machinery

ISBN 1-59078-271-2   LC 2005-33561

"Peterson gives readers an accurate firsthand view of modern, often computerized equipment used on today's farms. Her easy-to-understand text describes both the machines and their functions. . . . The short, informative paragraphs are surrounded by excellent color photographs that extend the text." SLJ

633.1 Cereals

Aliki

Corn is maize; the gift of the Indians; written and illustrated by Aliki. Crowell 1976 33p il (Let's-read-and-find-out science book) lib bdg $15.89; pa $4.95 (k-3)   **633.1**

1. Corn

ISBN 0-690-00975-5 (lib bdg); 0-06-445026-0 (pa)

In this book, the author provides a history of corn, or maize, and "also the life cycle of the plant itself, its growth and reproductive patterns, and its many uses. Excellent illustrations by the author help convey both cultural aspects and technological uses of corn." Sci Child

Landau, Elaine

Corn. Children's Press 1999 47p il lib bdg $22; pa $6.95 (2-4)   **633.1**

1. Corn

ISBN 0-516-21026-2 (lib bdg); 0-516-26759-0 (pa)

                    LC 98-47332

"A True book"

Examines the history, cultivation, and uses of corn

"Landau does her usual fine job of explaining a topic so that it is understandable to kids." Booklist

Includes glossary and bibliographical references

Wheat. Children's Press 1999 47p il lib bdg $22; pa $6.95 (2-4)   **633.1**

1. Wheat

ISBN 0-516-21029-7 (lib bdg); 0-516-26792-2 (pa)

                    LC 98-47333

"A True book"

Examines the history, cultivation, and uses of wheat

Includes glossary and bibliographical references

634 Orchards, fruits, forestry

Burns, Diane L.

Cranberries: fruit of the bogs; photographs by Cheryl Walsh Bellville. Carolrhoda Bks. 1994 48p il (Photo books) lib bdg $22.60; pa $7.95 (3-5)

634

1. Cranberries

ISBN 0-87614-822-4 (lib bdg); 0-87614-964-6 (pa)

LC 93-29620

"After a brief history of the cranberry in North America, the photo-essay focuses on the planting, growing, harvesting, and processing of the fruit known as the 'bog ruby.' An interesting account of a fruit with historical importance is accompanied by color photographs as clear as the autumn days needed for harvesting the cranberries." Horn Book Guide

Includes glossary

Gibbons, Gail

Apples. Holiday House 2000 unp il $16.95 (k-3)

634

1. Apples

ISBN 0-8234-1497-3 LC 99-54246

Explains how apples were brought to America, how they grow, their traditional uses and cultural significance, and some of the varieties grown

"With its cheerful, bright illustrations and clear, simple presentation, this title will be the perfect pick for the perennial fall apple-book requests." SLJ

The berry book. Holiday House 2002 unp il $16.95 (k-3)

634

1. Berries

ISBN 0-8234-1697-6 LC 2001-40602

Describes different types of berries and how they grow. Includes recipes with berry ingredients

This is a "brief, informative account. . . . Cheerful illustrations with clear labels enliven the accessible text." Horn Book Guide

Hall, Zoe

The apple pie tree; illustrated by Shari Halpern. Blue Sky Press (NY) 1996 unp il $15.95 (k-1)

634

1. Apples

ISBN 0-590-62382-6 LC 95-31134

"From bud to fruit, two children follow the cycle of an apple tree as it is nurtured through the seasons. . . . The story ends with a nice, warm apple pie being taken from the oven. The large pictures and text are suitable for young children. The colorful, clear-cut illustrations use a paint and paper collage technique. An end note shows how bees pollinate the tree's flowers and offers a recipe for apple pie." SLJ

Hughes, Meredith Sayles

Yes, we have bananas; fruits from shrubs & vines. Lerner Publs. 1999 80p il lib bdg $26.60 (4 and up)

634

1. Fruit 2. Fruit culture

ISBN 0-8225-2836-3 LC 98-45738

Describes the historical origins, domestication, uses, growing requirements, harvesting, and shipping of bananas, pineapples, berries, grapes, and melons

"In addition to the substantive text, many color illustrations depict the historical origins of each fruit, beautiful color photographs show the fruits themselves. Nutritional values and recipes are included for each fruit. A glossary of terms, a list of further readings, and an index are provided at the end of the text." Sci Books Films

Landau, Elaine

Apples. Children's Press 1999 47p il lib bdg $22; pa $6.95 (2-4)

634

1. Apples

ISBN 0-516-21024-6 (lib bdg); 0-516-26571-7 (pa)

LC 98-47327

"A True book"

Surveys the history, cultivation, and uses of apples and describes the different kinds

This "will fill a need for young report writers." Booklist

Includes glossary and bibliographical references

Bananas. Children's Press 1999 47p il lib bdg $22; pa $6.95 (2-4)

634

1. Banana

ISBN 0-516-21025-4 (lib bdg); 0-516-26574-1 (pa)

LC 98-47328

"A True book"

Examines the history, cultivation, and uses of bananas

Includes glossary and bibliographical references

Maestro, Betsy

How do apples grow? illustrated by Giulio Maestro. HarperCollins Pubs. 1992 32p il (Let's-read-and-find-out science book) lib bdg $14.89; pa $4.95 (k-3)

634

1. Apples

ISBN 0-06-020056-1 (lib bdg); 0-06-445117-8 (pa)

LC 91-9468

Describes the life cycle of an apple from its initial appearance as a spring bud to that point in time when it becomes a fully ripe fruit

"Clear, complete. . . . Inquisitive children will find simple yet scientifically accurate answers to their questions about apple trees and their fruit. Large illustrations and limited text facilitate group-reading. The endearing, soft-toned drawings are clearly labelled, providing an excellent teaching tool or reference point for the science teacher." Sci Child

Robbins, Ken

Apples; text and pictures by Ken Robbins. Atheneum Bks. for Young Readers 2002 32p il $15.95 (k-3)

634

1. Apples

ISBN 0-689-83024-6 LC 2001-33764

Describes how apples are grown, harvested, and used, and details facts about apples in history, literature, and our daily lives

"Robbins wraps his tribute to the popular fruit in a slim package of simple text and artistically rendered photographs." SLJ

634.9 Forestry

Appelbaum, Diana Karter
Giants in the land; [by] Diana Appelbaum;
illustrated by Michael McCurdy. Houghton Mifflin
1993 unp il $17; pa $6.95 (2-4)   **634.9**
1. Trees 2. Lumber and lumbering 3. Shipbuilding—
History
ISBN 0-395-64720-7; 0-618-03305-X (pa)
                                    LC 92-26526
Describes how giant pine trees in New England were
cut down during the colonial days to make massive
wooden ships for the King's Navy
"The prose is restrained and lyrical. . . . McCurdy's
dramatic black-and-white scratchboard drawings, many
spread across two pages, capture the sweep and detail of
the landscape." Booklist

Morrison, Taylor
Wildfire; [by] Taylor Morrison. Houghton
Mifflin Co. 2006 48p il $17 (4-6)   **634.9**
1. Wildfires 2. Forest fires
ISBN 978-0-618-50900-3   LC 2005030483
"Walter Lorraine books"
This is an "overview of the people involved in fight-
ing wildfires and the techniques and equipment they use.
Detailed paintings aid in explaining how firefighters
work and in describing the natural conditions that lead to
initial fires and more dangerous developments. . . . The
pages are packed with visual and textual information."
SLJ
Includes glossary and bibliographical references

635 Garden crops (Horticulture)

Creasy, Rosalind
Blue potatoes, orange tomatoes; illustrations by
Ruth Heller. Sierra Club Bks. for Children 1994
40p il $15.95; pa $6.95 (3-5)   **635**
1. Vegetable gardening 2. Vegetables
ISBN 0-87156-576-5; 0-87156-919-1 (pa)
                                    LC 92-38800
Describes how to plant and grow a variety of colorful
vegetables, including red corn, yellow watermelons, and
multicolored radishes, and includes recipes
"With interesting and authentic information about gardening accompanied by brilliant, life-like illustrations,
this book will not only promote the delight in growing
plants but enhance the wonder in the natural world right
in your own backyard." Appraisal

Gibbons, Gail
The pumpkin book. Holiday House 1999 unp il
$16.95; pa $6.95 (k-3)   **635**
1. Pumpkin
ISBN 0-8234-1465-5; 0-8234-1636-4 (pa)
                                    LC 98-45267
Describes how pumpkins come in different shapes and
sizes, how they grow, and their traditional uses and cultural significance. Includes instructions for carving a

pumpkin and drying the seeds
"Bold, clear watercolor illustrations and a concise text
work together. . . . Gibbons succeeds once again at covering a topic in a useful way at just the right level for
beginning readers." SLJ

Morris, Karyn
The Kids Can Press jumbo book of gardening;
written by Karyn Morris; illustrated by Jane
Kurisu. Kids Can Press 2000 240p il pa $14.95
(3-6)   **635**
1. Gardening
ISBN 1-55074-690-1
"Sections cover general information; fruit, vegetable,
and flower gardens; noninvasive native plants; gardens
that attract wildlife; and group projects. Projects range
from a few annuals in a container and thickets designed
with native wildlife in mind to community gardens. Directions are clear, with plenty of diagrams and illustrations." Booklist

Rockwell, Anne F.
One bean; pictures by Megan Halsey. Walker &
Co. 1998 unp il $14.95; pa $5.95 (k-2)
                                    635
1. Beans
ISBN 0-8027-8648-0; 0-8027-7572-1 (pa)
                                    LC 97-36249
"An easy-to-read text combines with lively illustra-
tions to create the story of what happens to one small
bean when it interacts with some soil, just a little water,
a lot of sunlight, and a young child's tender care." Sci
Child

636.088 Animals for specific purposes

Kent, Deborah
Animal helpers for the disabled. Watts 2003 63p
il $24; pa $8.95 (4 and up)   **636.088**
1. Animals and the handicapped 2. Animals—Training
3. Guide dogs
ISBN 0-531-12017-1; 0-531-16663-5 (pa)
                                    LC 2002-8885
"Watts library"
Explores the history of guide dogs, service animals,
and assistance dogs, and discusses the process of training
them to help people who have physical disabilities
This is an "informative, often inspirational and
thought-provoking [book]." Booklist
Includes bibliographical references

636.089 Veterinary sciences. Veterinary medicine

Jackson, Donna M.
ER vets; life in an animal emergency room. Houghton Mifflin 2005 88p il $17 (5 and up)
636.089
1. Veterinary medicine
ISBN 0-618-43663-4
"With plentiful, excellent-quality photographs, this highly visual book offers a behind-the-scenes look at an emergency animal hospital in Colorado. . . . A section on grief counseling for families with critically ill pets and a spread on how to put together a pet first-aid kit are included. Well-researched and well-written, ER Vets is an engaging book on a hot topic." SLJ

636.1 Equines. Horses

Budiansky, Stephen
The world according to horses; how they run, see, and think. Holt & Co. 2000 101p il $17.95 (4 and up)
636.1
1. Horses
ISBN 0-8050-6054-5
LC 99-31778
Discusses the interaction between people and horses, the horse as a social animal, its intelligence, abilities to communicate, athletic abilities, and physical evolution
"Intriguing premises are explained here in a straightforward and thought-provoking manner. . . . This title also will serve as a valuable resource for a beginning basic science reasoning study." Voice Youth Advocates
Includes glossary and bibliographical references

Draper, Judith
My first horse and pony book. Kingfisher 2005 47p il $9.95 (k-3)
636.1
1. Horses 2. Horsemanship
ISBN 0-7534-5878-0
This "guide covers the basics about horses and ponies, including physical characteristics, care and feeding, grooming, and stabling. After discussing proper clothing and tacking up, the author takes a look at English and Western riding. . . . The photos are excellent—bright and clear—and precisely illustrate what the text is describing." SLJ

Gibbons, Gail
Horses! Holiday House 2003 unp il $17.95; pa $6.95 (k-3)
636.1
1. Horses 2. Horsemanship
ISBN 0-8234-1703-4; 0-8234-1875-8 (pa)
LC 2003-41683
Presents information on horses, including their physical characteristics, behavior, and how to ride a horse.
"Attractive, full-color labeled illustrations fill every page, with many expanding on a particular point in the main text. . . . The book's accessible format will attract browsers as well as legions of young would-be equestrians." Booklist

Holub, Joan
Why do horses neigh? illustrations by Anna DiVito. Dial Bks. for Young Readers 2003 46p il lib bdg $13.99; pa $3.99 (k-2)
636.1
1. Horses
ISBN 0-8037-2770-4 (lib bdg); 0-14-230119-1 (pa)
LC 2001-47476
"Dial easy-to-read"
Questions and answers present information about the behavior and characteristics of horses and their interactions with humans
The book has "a bright, appealing format that combines jaunty original art and well-chosen photos." Booklist

Jeffrey, Laura S.
Horses; how to choose and care for a horse. Enslow Publishers 2004 48p il (American Humane pet care library) lib bdg $23.93 (3-5)
636.1
1. Horses
ISBN 0-7660-2519-5
LC 2003-22970
Provides information on owning a horse, including how to choose among different breeds and how to groom, house, feed, and keep a horse healthy.
This offers "children solid information . . . at a level they can understand. Many endearing photos . . . make [this book] fun to look at." Booklist
Includes glossary and bibliographical references

Lauber, Patricia
The true-or-false book of horses; illustrated by Rosalyn Schanzer. HarperCollins Pubs. 2000 32p il $15.95; lib bdg $15.89 (k-3)
636.1
1. Horses
ISBN 0-688-16919-8; 0-688-16920-1 (lib bdg)
LC 99-30763
Through a true-or-false format, presents statements about the history, uses, and behavior of horses
This "book combines a crowd-pleasing topic with generous measures of historical and behavioral information." Booklist

Peterson, Cris
Horsepower; the wonder of draft horses; photographs by Alvis Upitis. Boyds Mills Press 1997 unp il $16.95; pa $9.95 (k-3)
636.1
1. Horses
ISBN 1-56397-626-9; 1-56397-943-8 (pa)
LC 96-84679
"This book focuses on three popular breeds of draft horses, commonly known as work horses: Belgians, Percherons, and Clydesdales. Peterson introduces the families who raise and care for the horses and discusses some horse-training procedures." Horn Book Guide
"Crisp, full-color photographs accompany the short, smoothly written text." SLJ

Ransford, Sandy

Horse & pony breeds; written by Sandy Ransford; photographed by Bob Langrish. Kingfisher (NY) 2003 64p il (Kingfisher riding club) $14.95 (4 and up) **636.1**

1. Horses

ISBN 0-7534-5575-7   LC 2003-272944

An "overview of an international array of horse and pony breeds including many that may be unfamiliar to American children. The book covers the majority of breeds in half-page treatments that feature at least a paragraph of commentary and a captioned side body, and a full-color photograph that points out conformation differences particular to each breed. . . . An attractive, informative book that is sure to please both readers and browsers." SLJ

Includes glossary

Horse & pony care; written by Sandy Ransford; photographed by Bob Langrish. Kingfisher (NY) 2002 64p il $14.95; pa $8.95 (4 and up) **636.1**

1. Horses

ISBN 0-7534-5439-4; 0-7534-5744-X (pa)

This offers instructions on such topics as washing and clipping a pony, exercise routines and caring for pastureland, and includes information about types of feed and how much feed a pony needs

"Children who have a horse or want one will find a good deal of information in this attractive, photo-rich book. There are clear instructions. . . . The full-color photos are well composed, fully captioned, and quite thorough." Booklist

The Kingfisher illustrated horse & pony encyclopedia; written by Sandy Ransford; photographed by Bob Langrish. Kingfisher 2004 224p il $24.95 (4 and up) **636.1**

1. Horses 2. Horsemanship

ISBN 0-7534-5781-4   LC 2003-27293

"The first part of the book covers the life cycle, domestication, and types of horses and ponies. . . . The second part deals with how to care for these animals and discusses horsemanship from taking riding lessons to training and driving a horse. . . . Filled with appealing photos of young people interacting with their four-legged friends, this title is an extremely useful addition to any collection." SLJ

Simon, Seymour

Horses. HarperCollins Pubs. 2006 unp il $15.99; lib bdg $16.89 (2-4) **636.1**

1. Horses

ISBN 0-06-028944-9; 0-06-028945-7 (lib bdg)

LC 2004-30392

"Simon provides the basic facts, which include the importance of horses to humans throughout history, their evolution, physical traits, interactions among themselves, and the various breeds. The information is clear and accurate. The striking color photos will capture readers attention." SLJ

636.2   Ruminants. Bovines. Cattle

Freedman, Russell

In the days of the vaqueros; America's first true cowboys. Clarion Bks. 2001 70p il $18 (4 and up) **636.2**

1. Cowhands 2. Mexican Americans 3. Ranch life 4. Southwestern States

ISBN 0-395-96788-0   LC 2001-17357

"Freedman explores the often-overlooked role of the Central American cowherders who preceded by centuries the cowboys of popular lore and legend." SLJ

The author "tells the story with depth, clarity, and a vigor that conveys the thrilling excitement of the work and the macho swagger of the culture. . . . The book's design is beautiful, with spacious type on thick paper, and the dazzling illustrations—prints, paintings, and photos on almost every page." Booklist

Includes glossary and bibliographical references

636.3   Sheep and goats

Urbigkit, Cat

A young shepherd. Boyd Mills Press 2006 unp il $15.95 (k-3) **636.3**

1. Sheep 2. Shepherds

ISBN 1-59078-364-6

"This photo-essay features a 12-year-old 4H member (Urbigkit's son) who tends his own flock of sheep. Urbigkit . . . communicates Cass' commitment to his task in compelling photos that showcase the gamboling baby animals. . . . The closeup look at a fascinating, animal-focused activity will appeal even to readers who rarely rub shoulders with livestock." Booklist

636.4   Swine

Gibbons, Gail

Pigs. Holiday House 1999 unp il $16.95; pa $6.95 (k-3) **636.4**

1. Pigs

ISBN 0-8234-1441-8; 0-8234-1554-6 (pa)

LC 98-28807

Examines the basic characteristics, common breeds, intelligence, behavior, life cycle, and uses of pigs

"Bright with spring greens and yellows, this attractive book introduces pigs through simple sentences and many colorful pictures." Booklist

King-Smith, Dick

All pigs are beautiful; illustrated by Anita Jeram. Candlewick Press 1993 unp il pa $5.99 hardcover o.p. (k-3) **636.4**

1. Pigs

ISBN 1-56402-431-8 (pa)   LC 92-53136

"Read and wonder"

The author "interlards fond reminiscences of porkers he has known with interesting facts about them that are sure to keep children absorbed. His tone is affectionate,

King-Smith, Dick—*Continued*
amusing, and informative. Jeram's pen-and-ink and watercolor illustrations, done in soft, earthy colors, are a warm match for the text." SLJ

636.5   Poultry. Chickens

Gibbons, Gail
Chicks & chickens. Holiday House 2003 unp il $17.95; pa $6.95 (k-3)   **636.5**
1. Chickens
ISBN 0-8234-1700-X; 0-8234-1939-8 (pa)
LC 2002-27472
An introduction to the physical characteristics, behavior, and life cycle of chickens, as well as a discussion of how chickens are raised on farms
The author "offers lots of solid information as well as bits of trivia that will be of interest to this audience. Cartoon illustrations are large, colorful, and plentiful." SLJ

Sklansky, Amy E.
Where do chicks come from? illustrated by Pam Paparone. HarperCollins Publishers 2005 unp il (Let's-read-and-find-out science) $15.99; lib bdg $16.89; pa $4.99 (k-2)   **636.5**
1. Chickens 2. Eggs
ISBN 0-06-028892-2; 0-06-028893-0 (lib bdg); 0-06-445212-3 (pa)   LC 2003-7711
Describes what happens day-by-day for the three weeks from the time a hen lays an egg until the baby chick hatches.
This offers "clear and accurate text. . . . The illustrations are soft and friendly, but retain enough realism for children to understand the subject matter. . . . This is an enjoyable and informative introduction to scientific information." SLJ

636.6   Birds other than poultry

Altman, Linda Jacobs
Parrots. Benchmark Bks. 1999 32p il (Perfect pets) lib bdg $15.95 (3-6)   **636.6**
1. Parrots
ISBN 0-7614-1102-X   LC 99-49672
Provides information about the history, physical characteristics, choosing, and care of all kinds of parrots
"The writing is clear and informative. . . . Colorful, nicely detailed, framed photographs and reproductions of the animals are interspersed throughout." SLJ
Includes glossary and bibliographical references

Jeffrey, Laura S.
Birds; how to choose and care for a bird. Enslow Publishers 2004 48p il (American humane pet care library) lib bdg $23.93 (3-5)
636.6
1. Birds
ISBN 0-7660-2515-2   LC 2003-22966
Provides information on keeping birds as pets, including how to choose and care for a bird

636.7   Dogs

Altman, Linda Jacobs
Big dogs. Benchmark Bks. 2001 32p il (Perfect pets) lib bdg $15.95 (3-6)   **636.7**
1. Dogs
ISBN 0-7614-1101-1   LC 99-49674
Provides information about the history, physical characteristics, choice, training and care of various breeds of large dogs
Includes glossary and bibliographical references

Calmenson, Stephanie
Rosie; a visiting dog's story; photographs by Justin Sutcliffe. Clarion Bks. 1994 47p il $15.95; pa $5.95 (k-3)   **636.7**
1. Dogs
ISBN 0-395-65477-7; 0-395-92722-6 (pa)
LC 93-21243
"Rosie is the true story of an endearing Tibetan terrier who works as a therapy dog with Delta Society's Pet Partners Program of New York City. Rosie's tenderness and enthusiasm come through in Sutcliffe's fantastic photos that chronicle Rosie's training and first visit to a children's hospital and a nursing home." Child Book Rev Serv

The **Complete** dog book for kids; official publication of the American Kennel Club. Howell Bk. House; distributed by Hungry Minds 1996 274p il maps pa $22.95 hardcover o.p. (4 and up)   **636.7**
1. Dogs
ISBN 0-87605-460-2 (pa)   LC 96-29228
This "begins with a general section that advises readers on buying a dog, responsibilities, rewards, and how to match a dog with one's situation. . . . More than 100 dogs are profiled, with information on history, appearance, health, and 'fun facts.' Crisp color photographs accompany each article. . . . A final section gives good advice about nutrition and health issues." Booklist

George, Jean Craighead
How to talk to your dog; illustrated by Sue Truesdell. HarperCollins Pubs. 2000 26p il $9.95 (2-4)   **636.7**
1. Dogs
ISBN 0-06-027092-6   LC 98-41515
Describes how dogs communicate with people through their behavior and sounds and explains how to talk back to them using sounds, behavior, and body language
"The mixed photography (of George, representing the humans) and illustration (an endearingly scruffy yellow mutt is the main canine representative) is . . . effective. . . . This will be an accessible and perhaps paradigm-shifting introduction for young readers." Bull Cent Child Books

Gibbons, Gail

Dogs. Holiday House 1996 32p il $16.95; pa
$6.95 (k-3)   **636.7**
1. Dogs
ISBN 0-8234-1226-1; 0-8234-1335-7 (pa)
                              LC 95-24966
An introduction to dogs including their history, types
of breeds, senses, and ways of communication
"There is something for all dog enthusiasts here. A
good choice for both reports and pleasure reading." SLJ

Gorrell, Gena K. (Gena Kinton)

Working like a dog; the story of working dogs
through history. Tundra 2003 156p il pa $16.95 (4
and up)   **636.7**
1. Working dogs
ISBN 0-88776-589-0
"Gorrell begins by tracing the evolution of 'household
canids' from the wild into the civilized world. Other
chapters delve into the many ways in which these animals have been viewed throughout history, what makes
particular breeds right for certain jobs, dogs at war, famous pooches, etc. . . . The well-captioned, black-and-
white photographs and reproductions add greatly to a
narrative that's packed with intriguing details." SLJ
Includes bibliographical references

Holub, Joan

Why do dogs bark? Dial Bks. for Young
Readers 2001 48p il $13.99 (k-2)   **636.7**
1. Dogs
ISBN 0-8037-2504-3   LC 00-23984
"Dial easy-to-read"
Questions and answers present information about the
origins, behavior, and characteristics of dogs and their in-
teraction with humans
This book combines "appealing color photos and
sprightly cartoons with an informative, easy-to-read text."
Booklist

Jeffrey, Laura S.

Dogs; how to choose and care for a dog.
Enslow Publishers 2004 48p il (American humane
pet care library) lib bdg $23.93 (3-5)
                                 636.7
1. Dogs
ISBN 0-7660-2520-9   LC 2003-22971
Explains who to consult, where to go to pick the right
dog, and how to keep them happy and healthy
Includes glossary and bibliographical references

Kehret, Peg

Shelter dogs; amazing stories of adopted strays.
Whitman, A. 1999 unp il $14.95 (3-5)
                                 636.7
1. Dogs
ISBN 0-8075-7334-5   LC 98-34760
Tells the stories of eight stray dogs that were adopted
from animal shelters and went on to become service
dogs, actors, and heroes
"The writing is clear and straightforward, letting the
drama and pathos of the dogs' triumphs, and the owners'
dedication, carry the stories." SLJ

Kimmel, Elizabeth Cody

Balto and the great race; illustrated by Nora
Koerber. Random House 1999 99p il map lib bdg
$11.99; pa $3.99 (3-5)   **636.7**
1. Sled dog racing 2. Nome (Alaska) 3. Diphtheria
ISBN 0-679-99198-0 (lib bdg); 0-679-89198-6 (pa)
                              LC 98-35753
"A Stepping Stone book"
Recounts how the sled dog Balto saved Nome, Alaska,
in 1925 from a diphtheria epidemic by delivering medicine through a raging snowstorm
"Kimmel's writing deftly combines geography, sled
racing, and historical background with the gripping adventure of Balto's race to save lives. In many ways, the
book reads like fast-paced fiction. Koerber's serviceable
black-and-white illustrations appear throughout and reflect the action. Sure to appeal to beginning chapter-book
readers." SLJ

Lauber, Patricia

The true-or-false book of dogs; illustrated by
Rosalyn Schanzer. HarperCollins Pubs. 2003 28p
il $15.99; lib bdg $16.89 (k-3)   **636.7**
1. Dogs
ISBN 0-06-029767-0; 0-06-029768-9 (lib bdg)
                             LC 2001-51911
The author "opens with a brief discussion of the relationship between wolves and early humans, and describes
how all dogs descended from the first domesticated
wolves. Thirteen true-or-false statements follow, along
with the information that allows readers to determine the
answers. The topics addressed here are high interest and
kid friendly. . . . A lively look at an ever-popular topic."
SLJ

Simon, Seymour

Dogs. HarperCollinsPub. 2004 unp il $15.99; lib
bdg $16.89 (1-4)   **636.7**
1. Dogs
ISBN 0-06-028942-2; 0-06-028943-0 (lib bdg)
                           LC 2003-12484
Provides a basic introduction to the physical characteristics and behavior of dogs.
"The striking color photos, including many closeups,
create a feeling of intimacy. . . . Simon succeeds in addressing his topic in clear, easily understood vocabulary
without writing down to children." SLJ

Singer, Marilyn

A dog's gotta do what a dog's gotta do; dogs at
work. Holt & Co. 2000 86p il $16 (3-6)
                                 636.7
1. Working dogs
ISBN 0-8050-6074-X
Describes how dogs use their physical abilities, intelligence, and training by humans to perform a variety of
jobs, including working in the movies, catching burglars,
delivering messages, and cheering up children in hospitals
"Dog lovers will appreciate this readable, informative
look at canines and the work they do." Booklist

Urbigkit, Cat

Brave dogs, gentle dogs; how they guard sheep; by Cat Urbigkit. 1st ed. Boyds Mills Press 2005 32p il $15.95 (k-3)   **636.7**

1. Sheep dogs

ISBN 1-59078-317-4   LC 2004-16855

A "photo-essay on guardian dogs. Accompanied by clear, full-color photos, the simple, informative text describes the raising of these sheepdogs and their natural proclivity for guarding 'their' flocks." SLJ

636.8   Cats

George, Jean Craighead

How to talk to your cat; illustrated by Paul Meisel. HarperCollins Pubs. 2000 28p il $9.95 (2-4)   **636.8**

1. Cats

ISBN 0-06-027968-0   LC 98-41517

Describes how cats communicate with people through their behavior and sounds and explains how to talk back to them using sounds, behavior, and body language

"The writing style is breezy, conversational, and amusing, and is helped along by the many color illustrations. The photographs of the author are cleverly combined with humorous cartoon drawings of cats that display a great deal of intelligence and comedic personality. . . . A useful and readable addition to any pet collection." SLJ

Gibbons, Gail

Cats. Holiday House 1996 unp il $16.95; pa $6.95 (k-3)   **636.8**

1. Cats

ISBN 0-8234-1253-9; 0-8234-1410-8 (pa)

LC 96-3953

Presents information about the physical characteristics, senses, and behavior of cats, as well as how to care for these animals and some general facts about them

"This easy-to-read picture book will appeal to lovers of the popular pet. Brightly colored illustrations identify different breeds, while the informative . . . text describes physical and behavioral traits of kittens and cats." Horn Book Guide

Holub, Joan

Why do cats meow? illustrations by Anna DiVito. Dial Bks. for Young Readers 2001 46p il $13.99 (k-2)   **636.8**

1. Cats

ISBN 0-8037-2503-5   LC 00-23985

"Dial easy-to-read"

Questions and answers present information about the history, behavior, and characteristics of cats and their interaction with humans

"Packed with interesting information and illustrated with an abundance of cartoon artwork and color photographs." Horn Book Guide

Jeffrey, Laura S.

Cats; how to choose and care for a cat. Enslow Publishers 2004 48p il (American humane pet care library) lib bdg $23.93 (3-5)   **636.8**

1. Cats

ISBN 0-7660-2516-0   LC 2003-22967

Provides information on cats as pets, including how to choose among different breeds, find a cat to buy or adopt, and how to feed and keep a cat healthy

This offers "children solid information about pet selection and care at a level they can understand." SLJ

Includes glossary and bibliographical references

Lauber, Patricia

The true-or-false book of cats; illustrated by Rosalyn Schanzer. National Geographic Soc. 1998 31p il $15.95 (k-3)   **636.8**

1. Cats

ISBN 0-7922-3440-5   LC 97-11144

Discusses the truth behind such beliefs as "Cats can see in total darkness," "Cats have nine lives," and "A cat signals its feelings with its tail"

The author "attends to each question in a lucid, nicely detailed yet concise fashion, with Rosalyn Schanzer's colorful, lively artwork adding humorous details that help the facts slide down easily. The illustrations make this look like a picture book for younger readers, but the text is keyed to older ones." Booklist

Simon, Seymour

Cats. HarperCollins Pub. 2004 unp il $15.99; lib bdg $16.89 (1-4)   **636.8**

1. Cats

ISBN 0-06-028940-6; 0-06-028941-4 (lib bdg)

LC 2003-8337

Discusses the history, physical characteristics, behavior, and various breeds of cats, and provides basic information on caring for one as a pet.

"The striking color photos, including many closeups, create a feeling of intimacy. . . . Simon succeeds in addressing his topic in clear, easily understood vocabulary without writing down to children." SLJ

Tildes, Phyllis Limbacher

Calico's cousins; cats from around the world. Charlesbridge Pub. 1999 unp il lib bdg $15.95; pa $6.95 (k-3)   **636.8**

1. Cats

ISBN 0-88106-648-6 (lib bdg); 0-88106-649-4 (pa)

LC 98-4011

"Calico, a domestic longhair cat, introduces various breeds by describing both their origin and common traits. Each double-page spread features realistic illustrations of several cats in an environment appropriate to their origin, and a map at the end provides geographical reference." Horn Book Guide

636.9   Other mammals

Hansen, Elvig

Guinea pigs. Carolrhoda Bks. 1992 48p il (Carolrhoda nature watch book) lib bdg $23.93; pa $6.95 (3-6)   **636.9**

1. Guinea pigs

ISBN 0-87614-681-7; 0-87614-613-2 (pa)

                           LC 91-30694

Original German edition published 1988 in Switzerland

Describes the physical characteristics, habitat, and life cycle of the guinea pig

"Though uncaptioned, the pictures (featuring Hansen's own animals) are marvelous. . . . But the photos are more than simply bright, clear shots. They're informative and carefully keyed to the text. . . . It supplies plenty for both student researchers and prospective pet owners, all of whom will join browsers in eagerly thumbing through the wonderful pictures." Booklist

Includes glossary

Hinds, Kathryn

Hamsters and gerbils. Benchmark Bks. 2001 32p il (Perfect pets) lib bdg $15.95 (3-6)

                                 636.9

1. Hamsters 2. Gerbils

ISBN 0-7614-1104-6   LC 99-58089

Describes the characteristics, habits, habitat, and history of gerbils and hamsters and how to raise them as pets

"The full-color photos are winning. . . . [The text is] very accessible, with enough to get young pet keepers off to a good start." Booklist

Includes glossary and bibliographical references

Holub, Joan

Why do rabbits hop? and other questions about rabbits, guinea pigs, hamsters, and gerbils; illustrations by Anna DiVito. Dial Bks. for Young Readers 2002 46p il lib bdg $13.99; pa $3.99 (k-2)

                                 636.9

1. Rabbits 2. Guinea pigs 3. Hamsters 4. Gerbils

ISBN 0-8037-2771-2 (lib bdg); 0-14-230120-5 (pa)

                          LC 2001-47477

"Dial easy-to-read"

Questions and answers present information about the behavior and characteristics of rabbits, guinea pigs, hamsters, and gerbils and their interaction with humans

"The text is both interesting and informative. . . . [The book has] a bright, appealing format that combines jaunty original art and well-chosen photos." Booklist

Jeffrey, Laura S.

Hamsters, gerbils, guinea pigs, rabbits, ferrets, mice, and rats; how to choose and care for a small mammal. Enslow Publishers 2004 48p il (American humane pet care library) lib bdg $23.93 (3-5)   **636.9**

1. Hamsters 2. Guinea pigs 3. Rabbits 4. Ferrets 5. Mice 6. Rats

ISBN 0-7660-2518-7   LC 2003-22969

Explains the different personalities of several small mammals, where to go to pick the right one, and how to keep them happy and healthy

Includes glossary and bibliographical references

Johnson, Sylvia A.

Ferrets. Carolrhoda Bks. 1996 48p il (Carolrhoda nature watch book) lib bdg $23.95 (3-6)   **636.9**

1. Ferrets

ISBN 1-57505-014-5   LC 96-7068

Presents information about the physical characteristics, behavior, and history of ferrets and discusses keeping and caring for these animals as pets

"In her coverage of both wild ferrets and their domesticated cousins, Johnson uses a nice balance of sharp photos and explanatory text." Booklist

King-Smith, Dick

I love guinea pigs; illustrated by Anita Jeram. Candlewick Press 1995 c1994 unp il pa $5.99 hardcover o.p. (k-3)   **636.9**

1. Guinea pigs

ISBN 0-7636-0150-0 (pa)   LC 94-4880

"Read and wonder"

First published 1994 in the United Kingdom

"King-Smith provides a bit of history and some general information about physical characteristics, concentrating most fully on the care of these responsive animals as pets. He mentions the rudiments of handling, housing, feeding, and watering, explaining that guinea pigs can live for several years and describing their repertoire of sounds. King-Smith's advice is interspersed with anecdotes about favorite guinea pigs he has owned." Horn Book

"Jeram's line-and-watercolor illustrations transform fuzzy lumps into curious, cuddly, thoroughly engaging creatures." SLJ

McNicholas, June

Rats. Heinemann Lib. 2003 48p il (Keeping unusual pets) $24.22 (4 and up)   **636.9**

1. Rats

ISBN 1-4034-0283-3   LC 2002-3164

Contents: What is a rat?; Ratty facts; Is a rat for you?; What do I need?; Routine care; Handling and play; Health issues; Major problems; A record of your rat

Describes how to select a pet rat, what to feed it, and when to take it to the vet, as well as how to keep a pet scrapbook

"A valuable, accessible resource." Booklist

Includes bibliographical references

Rockwell, Anne F.

My pet hamster; by Anne Rockwell; illustrated by Bernice Lum. HarperCollins Pubs. 2002 33p il (Let's-read-and-find-out science) $15.99; lib bdg $17.89; pa $4.99 (k-2)   **636.9**

1. Hamsters

ISBN 0-06-028564-8; 0-06-028565-6 (lib bdg); 0-06-445205-0 (pa)   LC 2001-26481

Rockwell, Anne F.—*Continued*

Describes what pet hamsters are like, what they eat, and how they act, and explains the difference between wild and domestic animals

"The large, bold illustrations resemble a child's drawings . . . A useful title for reading aloud or independently, for enjoyment, or in beginning research." SLJ

Sobol, Richard

An elephant in the backyard; text and photographs by Richard Sobol. Dutton Children's Books 2004 unp il $17.99 (k-3)   **636.9**

1. Elephants 2. Thailand

ISBN 0-525-47288-6   LC 2003-52492

Describes how special elephants are in the village of Tha Kleng in Thailand and looks at the life of one particular young elephant named Wan Pen.

This is an "engaging photo-essay. Large, colorful photographs enhance the text. . . . The text is packed with interesting tidbits about these large mammals." SLJ

637 Processing dairy and related products

Aliki

Milk from cow to carton. rev ed. HarperCollins Pubs. 1992 31p il (Let's-read-and-find-out science book) pa $5.95 hardcover o.p. (k-3)   **637**

1. Dairying 2. Milk 3. Cattle

ISBN 0-06-445111-9 (pa)   LC 91-23807

First published 1974 by Crowell with title: Green grass and white milk

Briefly describes how a cow produces milk, how the milk is processed in a dairy, and how various other dairy products are made from milk

This features "full-color artwork. . . . An excellent primary-level introduction to dairy science." Booklist

Cooper, Elisha

Ice cream. Greenwillow Bks. 2002 unp il $15.95; lib bdg $15.89 (k-3)   **637**

1. Ice cream, ices, etc.

ISBN 0-06-001423-7; 0-06-001424-5 (lib bdg)
    LC 2001-40495

A step-by-step exploration of how ice cream is made, beginning with the healthy foods cows eat to produce good milk, and ending with a carton of frozen treat

"Cooper balances the relevant facts with his folksy, child-centered descriptions of minutiae. . . . Throughout, Cooper's relaxed pencil and watercolor drawings imply as much as they show, while the text keeps the atmosphere playful with a design that maximizes Cooper's sense of visual rhythm." Horn Book

Gibbons, Gail

The milk makers. Macmillan 1985 unp il $16; pa $5.99 (k-3)   **637**

1. Dairying 2. Milk 3. Cattle

ISBN 0-02-736640-5; 0-689-71116-6 (pa)
    LC 84-20081

Explains how cows produce milk and how it is processed before being delivered to stores

"Starting with dairy cows grazing at pasture, nothing is overlooked in the procedure, from the role of the calf to winter feed and shelter, the function of four stomachs, milking, milk handling, and the operation of a dairy. Diagrams of the cow stomachs as well as the machines used at farm and dairy leave no question unanswered, although city children will be unfamiliar with what it means to breed a cow. Finally, there is a pictorial list of the many other dairy products found in most homes." Sci Books Films

Greenstein, Elaine

Ice cream cones for sale! Arthur A. Levine Bks. 2003 unp il $15.95 (k-3)   **637**

1. Ice cream, ices, etc.

ISBN 0-439-32728-8   LC 2002-12556

Reveals who really invented the ice cream cone, even before the 1904 St. Louis World's Fair where five people claim they did so

"This looks and sounds just right for the age group. The monoprints overpainted with gouache feature appealing close-ups, bright colors, and lots of ice cream." Booklist

Includes bibliographical references

Kreger, Claire

Cheese; from start to finish; photographs by Patrick Carney. Blackbirch Press 2003 c2002 32p il (Made in the U.S.A.) $19.95 (2-4)   **637**

1. Cheese

ISBN 1-56711-380-X   LC 2002-151685

Explains how cheese is made at the Hilmar Cheese Company in California, from milking the cows to pasteurizing, processing, aging, and shipping the cheese

"Excellent photos, a picture-book format, and clear, informative text distinguish [this title]." Booklist

Includes glossary and bibliographical references

Peterson, Cris

Extra cheese, please! mozzarella's journey from cow to pizza; photographs by Alvis Upitis. Boyds Mills Press 1994 unp il $15.95 (k-3)   **637**

1. Dairying 2. Cheese

ISBN 1-56397-177-1   LC 93-70876

In photographs and text, this book introduces "dairying and cheese making. Using her own farm as an example, Peterson describes the care and feeding of dairy cattle, the milking process, and the steps involved in producing mozzarella cheese." Booklist

"Nicely balanced pages contain brief blocks of clearly written text and many full-color photographs." SLJ

Includes glossary and bibliographical references

639.2　Commercial fishing, whaling, sealing

Carrick, Carol

Whaling days; woodcuts by David Frampton. Clarion Bks. 1993 40p il $15.95; pa $6.95 (3-6)

639.2

1. Whaling 2. Whales

ISBN 0-395-50948-3; 0-395-76480-7 (pa)

LC 91-22483

Surveys the whaling industry, ranging from hunting in colonial America to modern whaling regulations and conservation efforts

"Frampton's strong woodcuts, tinted with muted tones of tan and blue, give the book a period look and a sense of drama. An informative and visually striking picture book for older children." Booklist

Includes glossary and bibliographical references

Kurlansky, Mark

The cod's tale; illustrated by S.D. Schindler. Putnam 2002 43p il map $16.99 (3-6)

639.2

1. Codfish 2. Commercial fishing

ISBN 0-399-23476-4　　　　　　　LC 00-68412

"Kurlansky traces the role that the once plentiful Atlantic cod has played in the history of North America and Europe." Publ Wkly

"Schindler's line-and-watercolor scenes are rendered with the delicate hatching of fine engraving and suffused with gentle humor. . . . This is a classic example of an unlikely subject made not only likely but fascinating and informative through authorial and illustrative craftsmanship." Bull Cent Child Books

Includes bibliographical references

McKissack, Patricia C.

Black hands, white sails; the story of African-American whalers; [by] Patricia C. McKissack & Fredrick L. McKissack. Scholastic Press 1999 xxiv, 152p il $17.95 (5 and up)

639.2

1. Whaling 2. African Americans

ISBN 0-590-48313-7　　　　　　　LC 99-11439

A Coretta Scott King honor book for text, 2000

A history of African-American whalers between 1730 and 1880, describing their contributions to the whaling industry and their role in the abolitionist movement

"A well-researched and detailed book." SLJ

Includes bibliographical references

McMillan, Bruce

Salmon summer; written and photo-illustrated by Bruce McMillan. Houghton Mifflin 1998 32p il $16 (2-4)

639.2

1. Salmon 2. Fishing 3. Alaska

ISBN 0-395-84544-0　　　　　　　LC 97-29679

A photo essay describing a young native Alaskan boy fishing for salmon on Kodiak Island as his ancestors have done for generations

"McMillan documents the goings on with his trademark crystal-clear color photographs and an engaging text." Booklist

Includes glossary and bibliographical references

Sandler, Martin W.

Trapped in ice! an amazing true whaling adventure. Scholastic Nonfiction 2006 168p il $16.99 (5 and up)

639.2

1. Whaling

ISBN 0-439-74363-X　　　　　　　LC 2005-42644

"In 1871, people aboard 32 whaling ships discovered just how dangerous Arctic waters could be after they ignored warnings of an early winter. As conditions worsened, the ships were trapped by ice, forcing the 1,219 people to abandon the vessels or die. Sandler's account of this true story is both informative and absorbing. . . . Well-chosen illustrations and side notes on such topics as life aboard ship and women at sea extend readers' understanding." Booklist

Includes glossary and bibliographical references

639.3　Fish culture

Cone, Molly

Come back, salmon; how a group of dedicated kids adopted Pigeon Creek and brought it back to life; photographs by Sidnee Wheelwright. Sierra Club Bks. for Children 1992 48p il pa $7.95 hardcover o.p. (3-6)

639.3

1. Salmon 2. Wildlife conservation

ISBN 0-87156-489-0 (pa)　　　　LC 91-29023

Describes the efforts of the Jackson Elementary School in Everett, Washington, to clean up a nearby stream, stock it with salmon, and preserve it as an unpolluted place where the salmon could return to spawn

"The photographs are superb. . . . Personal and inspiring, the text alternates between descriptions of the project, background information about pollution and renewal, and dialogue of the students recorded; additional scientific information is displayed in panels set off from the main text." Horn Book

Includes glossary

Hernandez-Divers, Sonia

Geckos. Heinemann Lib. 2003 48p il (Keeping unusual pets) lib bdg $24.22 (3-6)　　**639.3**

1. Geckos

ISBN 1-4034-0282-5　　　　　　　LC 2002-3163

This offers information about geckos and advice about keeping them as pets

"Lively and informative, with photos scattered across and around the pages . . . [this offers] a wealth of valuable advice." SLJ

Includes glossary and bibliographical references

Schafer, Susan

Lizards. Benchmark Bks. 2001 32p il (Perfect pets) lib bdg $15.95 (3-6)　　**639.3**

1. Lizards

ISBN 0-7614-1103-8　　　　　　　LC 99-58088

Schafer, Susan—*Continued*

Describes various kinds of lizards while focusing on those which could best serve as pets by indicating the food they need and the care they require

Includes glossary and bibliographical references

639.34   Aquariums

Aliki

My visit to the aquarium. HarperCollins Pubs. 1993 unp il $15.95; pa $6.95 (k-3)

639.34

1. Marine aquariums 2. Marine animals 3. Freshwater animals

ISBN 0-06-021458-9; 0-06-446186-6 (pa)

LC 92-18678

During his visit to an aquarium, a boy finds out about the characteristics and environments of many different marine and freshwater creatures

"Fish facts, selected for their child-appeal and delivered in a brisk, conversational tone, are neatly organized by marine environment. . . . The dominant blues and greens of Aliki's watercolors are not only cool and inviting; they also provide visual continuity amid the riot of brightly colored fish." Booklist

Jeffrey, Laura S.

Fish; how to choose and care for a fish. Enslow Publishers 2004 48p il (American humane pet care library) lib bdg $23.93 (3-5)   **639.34**

1. Fishes 2. Aquariums

ISBN 0-7660-2517-9   LC 2003-22968

Explains how to set up a personalized aquarium, pick the right fish, and how to keep them happy and healthy

Includes glossary and bibliographical references

639.9   Conservation of biological resources

Bortolotti, Dan

Panda rescue; changing the future for endangered wildlife. Firefly 2003 64p il map lib bdg $19.95; pa $9.95 (4 and up)   **639.9**

1. Wildlife conservation 2. Giant panda

ISBN 1-55297-598-3 (lib bdg); 1-55297-557-6 (pa)

This describes the panda's "natural habitat, habits, physiology, and behavior in captivity. [It also includes] a time line of conservation efforts, profiles of conservationists in the field, and forecasts of the animals' future. Throughout, the author makes clear the factors that can threaten animal populations, and discusses human attitudes toward the animals throughout history. . . . Written in accessible, lively language and nicely illustrated with exciting color photos, [this] will be useful for reports and browsing." Booklist

Fleming, Denise

Where once there was a wood. Holt & Co. 1996 unp il $16.95; pa $6.95 (k-2)   **639.9**

1. Habitat (Ecology) 2. Wildlife conservation

ISBN 0-8050-3761-6; 0-8050-6482-6 (pa)

LC 95-18906

"Fleming's brief text describes the many creatures who once lived in a wild area but whose homes have been destroyed by a new housing development. Fleming includes an afterword that describes the things families can do to create new backyard habitats for birds and animals." Horn Book Guide

"Lush, textured collage artwork features a stunning combination and arrangement of colors with brilliant hues juxtaposed against muted earth tones. . . . The gentle, poetic narration is never overpowered by the pictures." SLJ

Includes bibliographical references

Lasky, Kathryn

Interrupted journey; illustrated by Christopher Knight. Candlewick Press 2001 unp il $16.99 (3-6)   **639.9**

1. Sea turtles 2. Rare animals 3. Wildlife conservation

ISBN 0-7636-0635-9   LC 99-57126

Describes efforts to protect sea turtles, particularly Kemp's ridley turtles, and help them reproduce and replenish their once-dwindling numbers

"There's a sense of wonder in the simple words and the huge, thrilling color pictures in this photo-essay." Booklist

Stetson, Emily

Kids' easy-to-create wildlife habitats; [by] Emily Stetson. Williamson Books 2004 128p il map (Quick starts for kids!) pa $12.95 (2-4)

639.9

1. Wildlife conservation 2. Habitat (Ecology)

ISBN 0-8249-8665-2   LC 2004-40871

This "book shows children how to observe and support wildlife around their homes, schools, and communities. Packed with useful information. . . . With sound advice and many helpful illustrations, precisely drawn in blue and gray ink, this offers children small ways to support wildlife close to home." Booklist

Thomas, Peggy

Marine mammal preservation. 21st Cent. Bks. (Brookfield) 2000 64p il lib bdg $25.90 (5 and up)

639.9

1. Marine mammals 2. Wildlife conservation

ISBN 0-7613-1458-X   LC 00-30223

This title explains "how scientific studies of animal behavior combined with public awareness can help to save lives of marine mammals. Research and rehabilitation techniques for whales, manatees, seals, and sea otters are featured." Sci Child

"Illustrated with good-quality color photographs. . . . A highly readable and informative title." SLJ

Includes glossary and bibliographical references

641.3 Food

Burleigh, Robert

Chocolate; riches from the rainforest. Abrams 2002 unp il $16.95 (3-6) **641.3**

1. Chocolate

ISBN 0-8109-5734-5 LC 2001-3744

Traces the history of chocolate from a drink of the Olmec and Maya and later in Europe to its popularity around the world today

"Chocolate's fascinating story pairs with mouth watering photos in this handsome, picture-book-size overview." Booklist

Includes glossary and bibliographical references

D'Amico, Joan

The science chef; 100 fun food experiments and recipes for kids; [by] Joan D'Amico, Karen Eich Drummond; illustrations by Tina Cash-Walsh. Wiley 1995 180p il $12.95 (4-6) **641.3**

1. Food 2. Cooking 3. Science—Experiments

ISBN 0-471-31045-X LC 94-9045

This includes facts about food, recipes, and experiments with food

"Attractively illustrated with black-and-white line drawings, easy and interesting to read, and filled with tidbits of information." SLJ

Includes glossary

De Paola, Tomie

The popcorn book. Holiday House 1978 unp il lib bdg $16.95; pa $6.95 (k-3) **641.3**

1. Popcorn

ISBN 0-8234-0314-9 (lib bdg); 0-8234-0533-8 (pa)
LC 77-21456

"While one twin prepares the treat, the other stays close-by and reads aloud what popcorn is, how it's cooked, stored, and made, how the Indians of the Americas discovered it, and who eats the most. . . . The best thing about popcorn, the twins decide, is eating it. Two recipes are included." Babbling Bookworm

The author-artist's "amusing soft-color pictures—each bordered with a lavender frame—show action in the past or the present while a few lines of text or balloon speeches describe what is happening." Horn Book

Jango-Cohen, Judith

The history of food; [by] Judith Jango-Cohen. Twenty-First Century Books 2006 56p il (Major inventions through history) lib bdg $26.60 (5 and up) **641.3**

1. Food—History

ISBN 0-8225-2484-8 LC 2004-23022

This history of food "discusses canning, pasteurization, refrigeration, supermarkets, and genetically modified foods. . . . The text . . . is breezy but informative; unfamiliar terms are defined. Illustrations are a mixture of period black-and-white and color photos." SLJ

Includes bibliographical references

Landau, Elaine

Popcorn; illustrated by Brian Lies. Charlesbridge Pub. 2003 32p il lib bdg $16.95; pa $6.95 (2-4) **641.3**

1. Popcorn

ISBN 1-57091-442-7 (lib bdg); 1-57091-443-5 (pa)
LC 2002-2271

Provides a history of one of America's favorite snack foods, presenting its origins, nutritional information and recipes

"Lies' brightly colored acrylic illustrations enhance the humor of the text. . . . This will be useful for classroom projects and report writers as well as entertaining reading." Booklist

Includes bibliographical references

Llewellyn, Claire

Oranges. Children's Press 1999 32p il (What's for lunch?) lib bdg $20.50 (k-3) **641.3**

1. Oranges

ISBN 0-516-21548-5 LC 99-28942

Presents facts about oranges, including how they are grown, harvested, and marketed, as well as turned into juice and flavoring for other foods

Includes glossary

Micucci, Charles

The life and times of the peanut. Houghton Mifflin 1997 31p il music $15.95; pa $5.95 (2-4) **641.3**

1. Peanuts

ISBN 0-395-72289-6; 0-618-03314-9 (pa)
LC 96-1290

"The author presents information on how peanuts grow, how they are farmed, where they are produced . . . and how they are used worldwide. What sets this book apart is Micucci's amusing and creative techniques for bringing statistics to life. . . . The artwork is attractive . . . with great attention to line, movement, and color, all carefully placed on the pages." Booklist

Pentland, Peter

Kitchen science; [by] Peter Pentland and Pennie Stoyles. Chelsea House 2003 c2002 32p il (Science and scientists) lib bdg $18.95 (4 and up) **641.3**

1. Food 2. Science 3. Cooking

ISBN 0-7910-7014-X LC 2002-1280

First published 2002 in Australia

Surveys some of the scientific principles related to foods and their preparation

This title has "colorful illustrations and [uses] sidebars to present interesting tidbits of relevant information." SLJ

Includes glossary

Solheim, James

It's disgusting—and we ate it! true food facts from around the world—and throughout history! illustrated by Eric Brace. Simon & Schuster Bks. for Young Readers 1998 37p il $16.95; pa $6.99 (4 and up)   **641.3**

1. Food 2. Eating customs

ISBN 0-689-80675-2; 0-689-84393-3 (pa)

LC 96-7406

This "look at culinary culture is divided into three sections, the first discussing the global breadth of tastes, the second describing some startling dishes of history, and the third revealing some of the colorful truths behind contemporary American favorites." Bull Cent Child Books

Includes bibliographical references

641.5   Cooking

Braman, Arlette N.

Kids around the world cook! the best foods and recipes from many lands. Wiley 2000 116p il pa $12.95 (4-6)   **641.5**

1. Cooking

ISBN 0-471-35251-9   LC 99-46110

Presents information on and recipes for a variety of foods from many countries, including Sweet Lassi from India, Challah from Israel, Strawberry Soup from Poland, Kushiyaki from Japan, and Prairie Berry Cake from Canada

Crespo, Clare

The secret life of food; photographs by Eric Staudenmaier. Hyperion 2002 108p il $19.99 (4 and up)   **641.5**

1. Cooking

ISBN 0-7868-0846-2

This includes "recipes for dishes that look remarkably like spiders, roses, fingers, footballs, ponds, shoes—even a chocolate moose. . . . Younger readers will need adult help to re-create Crespo's culinary delights. The stunning full-page color photos of each dish, posed in clever context, lend great 'ooh and aah' motivation, making this useful for groups as well as for kids planning parties at home." SLJ

D'Amico, Joan

The coming to America cookbook; delicious recipes and fascinating stories from America's many cultures; [by] Joan D'Amico, Karen Eich Drummond. Wiley 2005 180p il pa $14.95 (5 and up)   **641.5**

1. Cooking 2. United States—Immigration and emigration

ISBN 0-471-48335-4   LC 2004-14947

The authors "provide information about American immigrants from 18 nations as well as recipes representing each group. . . . Accompanied by line drawings of ethnic families choosing, preparing, and eating food, . . . chapters discuss each country's climate, history, major waves of emigration, and traditional foods. Typically,

three recipes follow. . . . Teachers and students looking for recipes from American immigrant cultures will make good use of this handy resource." Booklist

The healthy body cookbook; over 50 fun activities and delicious recipes for kids; [by] Joan D'Amico, Karen Eich Drummond; illustrations by Tina Cash-Walsh. Wiley 1999 184p il pa $12.95 (4 and up)   **641.5**

1. Cooking 2. Nutrition

ISBN 0-471-18888-3   LC 98-2776

Discusses the various parts of the human body and what to eat to keep them healthy. Includes recipes that contain nutrients important for the heart, muscles, teeth, skin, nerves, and other parts of the body

"The line drawings are helpful and the writing is informal but straightforward. The recipes are clear, thoroughly explained, and tasty." SLJ

The math chef; over 60 math activities and recipes for kids; [by] Joan D'Amico, Karen Eich Drummond; illustrations by Tina Cash-Walsh. Wiley 1997 180p il pa $12.95 (4-6)   **641.5**

1. Cooking 2. Mathematics

ISBN 0-471-13813-4   LC 96-22143

Relates math and cookery by presenting math concepts and reinforcing them with recipes. Provides practice in converting from English to metric system, multiplying quantities, measuring area, estimating, and more

"The instructional value of this book is excellent. . . . The illustrations and content are accurate and very well depicted." Sci Books Films

Includes glossary

Easy menu ethnic cookbooks. rev ed. Lerner Publs. 2002-2005 37v ea $25.26 (5 and up)   **641.5**

1. Cooking

Some titles also available in paperback

Series first published 1982-1995

Available volumes in the revised series are: Cooking the Australian way by E. Germaine & A. L. Burchhardt; Cooking the Austrian way by H. Hughes; Cooking the Brazilian way by A. Behnke & K. L. Duro; Cooking the Caribbean way, by C. D. Kaufman; Cooking the Central American way by A. Behnke; Cooking the Chinese way, by L. Yu; Cooking the Cuban way by A. Behnke & V. M. Valens; Cooking the East African way, by C. Nabwire & B. V. Montgomery; Cooking the English way, by B. W. Hill; Cooking the French way, by L. M. Waldee; Cooking the German way, by H. Parnell; Cooking the Greek way, by L. W. Villios; Cooking the Hungarian way, by M. Hargittai; Cooking the Indian way, by V. Madavan; Cooking the Indonesian way by M. Anwar & K. Cornell; Cooking the Israeli way, by J. Bacon; Cooking the Italian way, by A. Bisignano; Cooking the Japanese way, by R. Weston; Cooking the Korean way, by O. Chung and J. Monroe; Cooking the Lebanese way, by S. Amari; Cooking the Mediterranean way by A. Behnke; Cooking the Mexican way, by R. Coronado; Cooking the Middle Eastern Way by A. Behnke; Cooking the North African way by M. Winget & H. Cahlbi; Cooking the Norwegian way, by S. Munsen; Cooking the Polish way, by D. Zamojska-Hutchins; Cooking the Rus-

Easy menu ethnic cookbooks—*Continued*

sian way, by G. & R. Plotkin; Cooking the Southern American way by H. Parnell; Cooking the Southern African way by K. Cornell & P. Thomas; Cooking the Spanish way, by R. Christian; Cooking the Thai way, by S. Harrison & J. Monroe; Cooking the Turkish way by K. Cornell & N. Turkoglu; Cooking the Vietnamese way, by C. Nguyen & J. Monroe; Cooking the West African way, by C. Nabwire & B. V. Montgomery; Desserts aroung the world by L. Engfer; Holiday cooking around the world, by R. Wolfe & D. Wolfe; Vegetarian cooking around the world, by A. Behnke

"In each volume, the front matter comprises close to half the book. Geography, history, holidays, and festivals, typical ingredients, and sample menus are all covered. . . . Each book presents about 20 recipes, mostly focusing on lunch, dinner, and holiday foods. . . . The narrative pieces are smoothly written and offer some interesting tidbits. . . . The pages are a warm buff color, and the design allows plenty of space on the pages for the text and the nicely reproduced color photos." SLJ

Gillies, Judi

The jumbo vegetarian cookbook; written by Judi Gillies and Jennifer Glossop; illustrated by Louise Phillips. Kids Can Press 2002 256p il pa $14.95 (4 and up)   **641.5**
1. Vegetarian cooking
ISBN 1-55074-977-3

"Much more than just a cookbook, this sprawling title introduces basic nutrition and how to achieve it with a vegetarian diet. Beginning sections cover safety tips and culinary basics . . . as well as types of vegetarianism, the environmental and health reasons that have led many to a meatless diet, and a list of common vegetarian ingredients. The recipe sections are extensive, with well-chosen dishes from breakfast foods through entrées and desserts." Booklist

The Kids Can Press jumbo cookbook; written by Judi Gillies and Jennifer Glossop; illustrated by Louise Phillips. Kids Can Press 2000 256p il pa $14.95 (4 and up)   **641.5**
1. Cooking
ISBN 1-55074-621-9

A "collection of over 100 recipes, arranged by categories such as 'Soups and Chilis'; 'Salads and Vegetables'; 'Pasta, Noodles, Rice and Grains'; etc. All have simple, step-by-step instructions, call for commonly available ingredients, and range in difficulty from boiled rice to sushi and shepherd's pie." SLJ

"The book's format is kid-friendly, with large print and cartoon art, but many of the numerous recipes are quite grown-up." Booklist

Hopkinson, Deborah

Fannie in the kitchen; the whole story from soup to nuts of how Fannie Farmer invented recipes with precise measurements; pictures by Nancy Carpenter. Atheneum Bks. for Young Readers 2001 unp il $16 (k-3)   **641.5**
1. Farmer, Fannie Merritt, 1857-1915 2. Cooking
ISBN 0-689-81965-X   LC 97-46712
"An Anne Schwartz book"

Fannie Farmer is a mother's helper in the Shaw house, where the daughter gives her the idea of writing down precise instructions for measuring and cooking, which eventually became one of the first modern cookbooks

"A clever introduction to the renowned nineteenth century cook. . . . The collage artwork is exceptional—elegant as well as whimsical. Carpenter brings together original pen-and-ink artwork and engravings, all washed in watercolor, to create a houseful of expressive characters and abundant, often witty details." Booklist

Ichord, Loretta Frances

Skillet bread, sourdough, and vinegar pie; cooking in pioneer days; illustrated by Jan Davey Ellis. Millbrook Press 2003 64p il maps lib bdg $24.90 (3-5)   **641.5**
1. Cooking 2. Frontier and pioneer life—West (U.S.)
ISBN 0-7613-1864-X   LC 2002-8157

Presents a look at what was eaten in the American West by pioneers on the trail, cowboys on cattle drives, and gold miners in California camps, with available ingredients, cooking methods, and equipment. Includes recipes and appendix of classroom cooking directions

"This unique title effectively combines recipes with history, a must for any collection needing information on the old West." Libr Media Connect

Includes bibliographical references

Katzen, Mollie

Honest pretzels; and 64 other amazing recipes for cooks ages 8 & up. Tricycle Press 1999 177p il $19.95 (4-6)   **641.5**
1. Vegetarian cooking
ISBN 1-88367-288-0   LC 99-20184

Provides step-by-step instructions for a variety of vegetarian recipes, arranged in such categories as "Breakfast Specials," "Soups, Sandwiches & Salads for Lunch or Supper," and "Desserts and a Few Baked Things"

"Small, colorful drawings illustrate most of the cooking instructions and brighten many of the other pages as well." Booklist

Salad people and more real recipes; a new cookbook for preschoolers and up. Tricycle Press 2005 93p il $17.95 (k-3)   **641.5**
1. Cooking
ISBN 1-58246-141-4

"Katzen offers a range of vegetarian, kid-friendly recipes in an artistic, innovative format. Each recipe receives two spreads. The first contains detailed, step-by-step instructions for adults; the second, directed to children, illustrates stages of preparation in a series of clear, boxed drawings. Katzen's whimsical color pictures of dancing produce and animals decorate the pages. . . . These detailed, practical, and inspired ideas may extend far beyond the kitchen, helping adults approach parenting in new ways and helping kids develop a lifelong interest and confidence in healthy food." Booklist

Kids' first cookbook; delicious-nutritious treats to make yourself. American Cancer Soc. 2000 88p il $13.95 (k-3)   **641.5**

1. Cooking

ISBN 0-944235-19-0

A collection of easy-to-make recipes for breakfast foods, snacks, main dishes, drinks, and desserts

"A cookbook with a contemporary look filled with nutrition information. . . . A solid effort that will encourage healthy eating habits." SLJ

Lagasse, Emeril

Emeril's there's a chef in my family! recipes to get everybody cooking; illustrated by Charles Yuen; photographs by Quentin Bacon. HarperCollins Publishers 2004 209p il $22.99 (5 and up)   **641.5**

1. Cooking

ISBN 0-06-000439-8   LC 2003-5612

Provides tips for having fun and keeping safe in the kitchen, along with dozens of world-famous chef Emeril Lagasse's favorite recipes that families can make and eat together

"The step-by-step directions are clearly laid out, and most of the dishes look delicious. The fresh and attractive design includes a mix of simple paintings (for the food) and photos (for the people). Emeril himself is shown throughout, conveying his enthusiasm and sense of play." SLJ

Locricchio, Matthew

The international cookbook for kids; by Matthew Locricchio; photographs by Jack McConnell. Marshall Cavendish 2004 175p il $18.95 (5 and up)   **641.5**

1. Cooking

ISBN 0-7614-5185-4   LC 2004-5894

This includes "60 classic recipes from Italy, France, China, and Mexico, . . . chef's tips discussing ingredients, nutrition, and technique, safety section discussing basic kitchen precautions, cooking terms and definitions." Publisher's note

"This is a strong collection of popular dishes attractively presented." SLJ

Walker, Barbara Muhs

The Little House cookbook; frontier foods from Laura Ingalls Wilder's classic stories; by Barbara M. Walker; illustrated by Garth Williams. Harper & Row 1979 240p il $16.95; pa $9.95 (5 and up)   **641.5**

1. Wilder, Laura Ingalls, 1867-1957 2. Cooking 3. Frontier and pioneer life

ISBN 0-06-026418-7; 0-06-446090-8 (pa)

     LC 76-58733

Recipes based on the pioneer food written about in the "Little House" books of Laura Ingalls Wilder, along with quotes from the books and descriptions of the food and cooking of pioneer times

"Illustrated by Williams's familiar warm drawings, the adaptations of menus from pioneer days include paragaphs describing the Wilder and Ingalls families

working together, preparing holiday meals, individual foods, special treats and staple fare." Publ Wkly

Includes bibliographical references

Warshaw, Hallie

The sleepover cookbook; photography by Julie Brown; including healthy recipes by Diane Nepa. Sterling 2000 126p il $19.95 (4 and up)

     641.5

1. Cooking

ISBN 0-8069-4497-8   LC 2001274608

A collection of kid-tested recipes, suitable for a sleepover or any time. Includes recipes, using readymade ingredients, for desserts, snacks, lunch, supper and breakfast dishes, soups, and salads

"The treats are easy to prepare. . . . Bold color photographs highlight almost every spread, with sleepovers pictured for boys and for girls." SLJ

Webb, Lois Sinaiko

Holidays of the world cookbook for students. Oryx Press 1995 xxxiv, 297p il maps pa $36.95 (5 and up)   **641.5**

1. Cooking 2. Holidays

ISBN 0-89774-884-0   LC 95-26019

In this cookbook "more than 136 countries are represented, with 388 recipes. The U.S. is divided into six sections with 10 recipes for regional celebrations. History behind the holiday is included where possible, as is pertinent background information on the culture represented. . . . A discussion of different calendars used around the world is an interesting inclusion. The recipes' directions are clear and include equipment lists." SLJ

Includes glossary and bibliographical references

641.6 Cooking specific materials

MacLeod, Elizabeth

Chock full of chocolate; written by Elizabeth MacLeod; illustrated by June Bradford. Kids Can Press 2005 40p il (Kids can do it) $12.95 (4-6)

     641.6

1. Chocolate 2. Cooking

ISBN 1-55337-762-1

This includes recipes for chocolate cookies, cakes, and other desserts.

641.8 Cooking specific kinds of dishes, preparing beverages

Fleisher, Paul

Ice cream treats; the inside scoop; photographs by David O. Saunders. Carolrhoda Bks. 2001 48p il lib bdg $23.93 (4 and up)   **641.8**

1. Ice cream, ices, etc.

ISBN 1-57505-268-7   LC 00-9229

"Focusing on the production of ice cream novelties at a Good Humor-Breyers factory, this . . . describes the

Fleisher, Paul—*Continued*

process from pasteurization of raw milk to the formation of ice cream bars to the trip through the wrapping machine. . . . The book includes several recipes for homemade ice cream." Horn Book Guide

"An appealing and instructive book." SLJ

Goss, Gary

Blue moon soup; a family cookbook; recipes by Gary Goss; illustrated by Jane Dyer. Little, Brown 1999 60p il $16.95 (4-6)   **641.8**

1. Soups 2. Cooking

ISBN 0-316-32991-6   LC 98-19458

This "cookbook includes eight to ten soup recipes for each season of the year as well as several related recipes for bread, salads, snacks, and croutons." Booklist

"The tone is lighthearted and full of quirky humor. . . . The recipes are clear. . . . Dyer's outstanding watercolors echo the tone of the text; there are 14 fanciful full-page illustrations, and whimsical spot art is scattered throughout." SLJ

Jones, Judith

Knead it, punch it, bake it! the ultimate breadmaking book for parents and kids; [by] Judith and Evan Jones; illustrations by Mitra Modarressi. 2nd ed. Houghton Mifflin 1998 144p il spir $16 (3-6)   **641.8**

1. Bread

ISBN 0-395-89256-2   LC 98-27319

First published 1981 by Crowell

Presents more than forty recipes for baking all kinds and shapes of bread from French bread to peanut butter muffins to pizza

Kreger, Claire

Jelly beans; from start to finish; photographs by Patrick Carney. Blackbirch Press 2003 c2002 31p il (Made in the U.S.A.) $19.95 (2-4)   **641.8**

1. Confectionery

ISBN 1-56711-477-6   LC 2002-5757

Looks at how the candy Jelly Belly is made, including adding sugars, coloring, and packaging

Includes glossary and bibliographical references

MacLeod, Elizabeth

Bake and make amazing cakes; written by Elizabeth MacLeod; illustrated by June Bradford. Kids Can Press 2001 40p il (Kids can do it) $12.95; pa $5.95 (4-6)   **641.8**

1. Cake

ISBN 1-55074-849-1; 1-55074-848-3 (pa)

In this book "there are four cake recipes; three icing recipes; and 19 different creations, including cakes in the shape of a mouse, a house, a butterfly, and a bus. . . . The directions are clear and the format is clean." SLJ

Bake and make amazing cookies; written by Elizabeth MacLeod; illustrated by June Bradford. Kids Can Press 2004 40p il (Kids can do it) $12.95; pa $6.95 (4-6)   **641.8**

1. Cookies

ISBN 1-55337-631-5; 1-55337-632-3 (pa)

This offers "32 recipes under four headings 'Holidays,' 'For Special People,' 'Seasons,' and 'Just for Fun.' This book is sure to please bakers. The step-by-step instructions . . . are easy to follow, and the ingredients/tools listed are readily available or easily obtainable. . . . Each recipe is accompanied by precise, softly colored illustrations." SLJ

Morris, Ann

Bread, bread, bread; photographs by Ken Heyman. Lothrop, Lee & Shepard Bks. 1989 unp il $15.93; lib bdg $16; pa $5.95 (k-1)   **641.8**

1. Bread

ISBN 0-688-06335-7; 0-688-06334-9 (lib bdg); 0-688-12275-2 (pa)   LC 88-26677

Also available Big book edition

This photo essay shows different kinds of bread around the world from baguettes to challah

"Each picture offers a strong ethnic identity or a thought-provoking human interaction, with captions of only a few words in large print. An unusual index . . . gives background information about the pictures, citing the countries of origin and a few facts about each type of bread." SLJ

Paulsen, Gary

The tortilla factory; paintings by Ruth Wright Paulsen. Harcourt Brace & Co. 1995 unp il $16; pa $7 (k-3)   **641.8**

1. Tortillas

ISBN 0-15-292876-6; 0-15-201698-8 (pa)

     LC 93-48590

Also available Spanish language edition

"Paulsen traces the journey of the corn, from harvest and grinding, to the tortilla factory, where people turn the corn flour into tortillas that, filled with beans, 'give strength to the brown hands that work the black earth to plant yellow seeds.' . . . Replete with the lush greens of healthy plants, the rich browns of adobe buildings and fertile soil, and the vibrant gold of ears of corn, the highly satisfying illustrations reinforce the reverential mood established by the spare poetic narrative." Horn Book

646　Sewing, clothing, personal living

Fisher, Leonard Everett

The hatters. Benchmark Bks. 2001 48p il (Colonial craftsmen) lib bdg $14.95 (4 and up)   **646**

1. Hats 2. Fur 3. United States—Social life and customs—1600-1775, Colonial period

ISBN 0-7614-1146-1   LC 00-45160

A reissue of the title first published 1965 by Watts

Fisher, Leonard Everett—*Continued*
"Leonard Everett Fisher here gives some of the historical background of the beaver hat [in colonial America] and describes and illustrates how a beaver pelt was made into felt and fashioned into a variety of hat shapes." Publisher's note
Includes glossary

646.2 Sewing and related operations

Sadler, Judy Ann
Simply sewing; written by Judy Ann Sadler; illustrated by Jane Kurisu. Kids Can Press 2004 48p il (Kids can do it) $12.95; pa $6.95 (4-6) **646.2**
1. Sewing
ISBN 1-55337-659-5; 1-55337-660-9 (pa)
This "book opens with a section on sewing supplies. . . . Subsequent chapters discuss fabric and the basics of hand and machine stitching. . . . Each of the 12 projects is accompanied by a color photo, step-by-step color illustrations, and a list of supplies needed. . . . This attractive book has a wide assortment of ideas to spark interest." SLJ

646.4 Clothing and accessories construction

Schwarz, Renée
Making masks; written and illustrated by Renée Schwarz. Kids Can Press 2002 40p il (Kids can do it) $12.95; pa $5.95 (4-6) **646.4**
1. Masks (Facial) 2. Handicraft
ISBN 1-55074-929-3; 1-55074-931-5 (pa)
This offers instructions for creating a variety of masks using such materials as cardboard, felt, paper, and pipe cleaners
This includes "appealing projects and easy-to-follow directions. . . . Schwarz does a good job constructing and illustrating a variety of masks." SLJ

649 Child rearing & home care of persons

Raatma, Lucia
Safety for babysitters. Child's World 2005 32p il (Living well) lib bdg $25.64 (4 and up) **649**
1. Babysitting 2. Safety education
ISBN 1-59296-239-4 LC 2003-27213
Contents: An evening at the Martins' house; Getting ready to babysit; Being in charge; How to have fun and be safe; What to do in an emergency; When the parents come home; Glossary; Questions and answers about babysitting safety; Helping a friend learn about babysitting safety; Did you know?; How to learn more about babysitting safety

The offers advice on how to prepare for a babysitting job, what kinds of questions to ask the parents, what to do in emergencies
This has "an appealing layout with plenty of full-color photos and a triple-spaced text. . . . An excellent, easy-to-understand overview." SLJ
Includes glossary and bibliographical references

Sears, William
What baby needs; [by] William Sears, Martha Sears and Christie Watts Kelly; illustrated by Renée Andriani. Little, Brown 2001 unp il (Sears children's library) $12.95 (k-2) **649**
1. Infants 2. Siblings
ISBN 0-316-78828-7 LC 00-37529
This "is a warm look at how life in the family changes to accommodate the needs of a newborn, and the care an infant requires. . . . The lighthearted, full-color cartoons bring some welcome new images to baby books: breastfeeding, babywearing (including both a dad and a mom with an infant in a baby sling), and the newborn snoozing near the parents' bed." SLJ
Includes bibliographical references

650.1 Personal success in business

Kiefer, Jeanne
Jobs for kids; a smart kid's Q & A guide; illustrations by Carol Nicklaus. Millbrook Press 2003 112p il lib bdg $25.90 (4 and up) **650.1**
1. Money-making projects for children 2. Entrepreneurship
ISBN 0-7613-2611-1 LC 2002-8353
Answers questions about the five most popular jobs for young people, as well as about other ways they can make money, with advice on the planning and marketing involved
"Packed with information, forms, and ideas, this is an ideal guide for young people looking to make money and have fun at the same time." SLJ

652 Processes of written communication

Janeczko, Paul B.
Top secret; a handbook of codes, ciphers and secret writing; illustrated by Jenna LaReau. Candlewick Press 2004 136p il $16.99 (4 and up) **652**
1. Cryptography 2. Ciphers
ISBN 0-7636-0971-4
This is a "guide to secret writing. Janeczko relates how different codes came to be and why they were needed, and gives some historical examples. The book also contains information and exercises (with answers) on deciphering codes and provides children with the tools to make their own field kit. . . . Humorous black-and-white sketches . . . are found throughout the book. The author's upbeat, positive tone is refreshing and his enthusiasm about his topic is contagious." SLJ

659.1 Advertising

Graydon, Shari
Made you look; how advertising works and why you should know; illustrations by Warren Clark. Annick Press 2003 115p il $24.95; pa $14.95 (5 and up)   **659.1**
1. Advertising
ISBN 1-55037-815-5; 1-55037-814-7 (pa)
This "analysis seeks to raise preteens' awareness of themselves as targets and vectors of advertising messages. Brimming with anecdotes, facts, and quotes . . . the text covers controversial programs that bring ads into the schools, and describes traditional marketing methods as well as 'stealth' techniques. . . . Graydon . . . often ends sections with a provocative question . . . and she helpfully includes addresses of watchdog organizations, tips for writing effective complaints, and an impressive set of endnotes." Booklist
Includes bibliographical references

Hoban, Tana
I read signs. Greenwillow Bks. 1983 unp il $18; lib bdg $15.93; pa $4.95 (k-2)   **659.1**
1. Signs and signboards
ISBN 0-688-02317-7; 0-688-02318-5 (lib bdg); 0-688-07331-X (pa)   LC 83-1482
In this book "30 verbal and 27 symbolic street signs have been caught on location in close-ups with a minimum of background to give just a soupçon of milieu (city, sky or apple tree) or hint of meaning ('Beware of dog' on chain link fence). Design is bold; primary colors are emphasized. The familiar predominates; more unusual signs . . . add interest." SLJ

660.6 Biotechnology

Nardo, Don
Cloning. Blackbirch Press 2003 48p il (Science on the edge) $20.95 (5 and up)   **660.6**
1. Cloning
ISBN 1-56711-782-1   LC 2002-10369
Contents: Cloning is Nothing New; Potential Benefits of Animal Cloning; The Promise of Human Cloning
Discusses the history of the concept of cloning and the pros and cons of cloning animals and humans
"Very accessible and informative . . . exemplary." Booklist

662 Technology of explosives, fuels, related products

Cobb, Vicki
Fireworks; photographs by Michael Gold. Millbrook Press 2005 48p il (Where's the science here?) $23.93 (3-5)   **662**
1. Fireworks
ISBN 0-7613-2771-1   LC 2004-29823

"From pictures of different types of display formations to those of chemicals being loaded into mortar tubes, readers will find interesting illustrations that support the text in *Fireworks*. They will learn about the science of pyrotechnics and be exposed to words like chemical reaction, combustion, and lift charges. Sections offer a historical overview of the evolution of the study of fire, the mechanics of building fireworks . . . how explosions are timed, and how pyrotechnicians avoid nasty surprises." SLJ

664 Food technology

Bledsoe, Karen E.
Genetically engineered foods; written by Karen E. Bledsoe. Blackbirch Press 2006 48p il (Science on the edge) $23.70 (5 and up)   **664**
1. Food—Biotechnology 2. Genetic engineering
ISBN 1-4103-0602-X
This offers a brief summary of Mendel's discoveries and the discovery of DNA, then discusses how foods are modified by genetics and the issues associated with genetic engineering of foods.
Includes glossary and bibliographical references

Cobb, Vicki
Junk food; photographs by Michael Gold. Millbrook 2005 48p il (Where's the science here?) lib bdg $23.93 (3-5)   **664**
1. Food industry 2. Food—Composition
ISBN 0-7613-2773-8
The author "focuses on food chemistry, not nutrition, in examinations of six seductive snack foods (popcorn, corn chips, chocolate, candy, potato chips, and soda). Well-digested explanations and low-tech projects reinforce Cobb's reputation for snappy hands-on science writing for children. . . . Gold's photos stand well above those in most nonfiction science series and directly support Cobb's intentions." Booklist

668 Technology of other organic products

Rhatigan, Joe
Soapmaking; 50 fun & fabulous soaps to melt & pour. Lark Books 2003 112p il (Kids' crafts) $19.95 (3-6)   **668**
1. Soap 2. Handicraft
ISBN 1-57990-416-5   LC 2003-883
This describes soapmaking projects beginning with choosing a soap base and selecting molds, adding fragrance, color, or other extras. Projects include eyeball soaps, making soap popsicles, smiley faces, a soapasaurus, alphabet soap, a soap bracelet and a clear bar with an embedded photo.
"This book has a wonderful, 'squeaky-clean' appearance and a perfect combination of text, color photography, design, and child models." SLJ

Wagner, Lisa
Cool melt & pour soap; [by] Lisa Wagner. Abdo Pub. 2005 32p il (Cool crafts) lib bdg $22.78 (4-6) **668**
1. Soap 2. Handicraft
ISBN 1-59197-741-X   LC 2004-46291
This guide to soap crafting "discusses premade bases, coloring and fragrance, layered soaps, treasure-packed soaps, relief soaps, and packaging ideas." SLJ

670 Manufacturing

Slavin, Bill
Transformed; how everyday things are made; written by Bill Slavin with Jim Slavin; illustrated by Bill Slavin. Kids Can Press 2005 160p il $24.95 (4 and up) **670**
1. Manufactures
ISBN 1-55337-179-8
This describes the manufacture of such items "as baseballs, plastic dinosaurs, toothpaste, cereal, paper, and bricks. Each two-page spread covers the making of one of the 69 items in numbered paragraphs. The pictures are the best part—clear watercolor and ink images, made all the more engaging by folks in overalls directing the action." Booklist
Includes glossary and bibliographical references

675 Leather and fur processing

Fisher, Leonard Everett
The tanners; written & illustrated by Leonard Everett Fisher. Benchmark Bks. 2001 43p (Colonial craftsmen) $21.36 (4 and up) **675**
1. Tanning 2. Leather work 3. United States—Social life and customs—1600-1775, Colonial period
ISBN 0-7614-1148-8   LC 00-45159
A reissue of the title first published 1966 by Watts
This describes the development of leather making in Colonial America
Includes glossary

676 Pulp and paper technology

Fisher, Leonard Everett
The papermakers; written & illustrated by Leonard Everett Fisher. Benchmark Bks. 2001 46p il (Colonial craftsmen) $14.95 (4 and up) **676**
1. Papermaking 2. United States—Social life and customs—1600-1775, Colonial period
ISBN 0-7614-1147-X   LC 00-45158
A reissue of the title first published 1965 by Watts
Describes the history and technique of papermaking in colonial America

677 Textiles

Fisher, Leonard Everett
The weavers; written & illustrated by Leonard Everett Fisher. Marshall Cavendish 1998 45p il (Colonial craftsmen) $14.95 (4 and up) **677**
1. Weaving 2. United States—Social life and customs—1600-1775, Colonial period
ISBN 0-7614-0509-7   LC 96-36135
A reissue of the title first published 1966 by Watts
Presents background information on cloth making in the colonies and describes the various techniques involved

680 Manufacture of products for specific uses

Tunis, Edwin
Colonial craftsmen and the beginnings of American industry; written and illustrated by Edwin Tunis. Johns Hopkins Univ. Press 1999 159p pa $18.95 (4 and up) **680**
1. Decorative arts 2. United States—Social life and customs—1600-1775, Colonial period 3. Handicraft
ISBN 0-8018-6228-0   LC 99-20398
A reprint of the edition published 1965 by World Pub. Co.
The author describes the working methods and products, houses and shops, town and country trades, individual and group enterprises by which the early Americans forged the economy of the New World. He discusses such trades as papermaking, glassmaking, shipbuilding, printing, and metalworking
"An oversize book that is impressively handsome and that should be tremendously useful; well-organized and superbly illustrated, the text is comprehensive, lucid, and detailed. . . . An extensive index is appended." Chicago. Children's Book Center

681.1 Instruments for measuring time

Duffy, Trent
The clock; fold out illustration by Toby Willes. Atheneum Bks. for Young Readers 2000 80p il (Turning point inventions series) lib bdg $17.95 (4 and up) **681.1**
1. Clocks and watches 2. Time
ISBN 0-689-82814-4   LC 99-65242
A history of time measurement, including a short biography of John Harrison, inventor of the chronometric clock, and the effect of the clock on the Industrial Revolution
"This accessible and thorough treatment should be welcomed by students in search of an unusual topic for the ubiquitous 'invention report.'" Bull Cent Child Books
Includes bibliographical references

682 Small forge work (Blacksmithing)

Fisher, Leonard Everett
The blacksmiths; written & illustrated by
Leonard Everett Fisher. Marshall Cavendish 1999
47p il (Colonial craftsmen) lib bdg $21.36 (4 and
up) **682**
1. Blacksmithing 2. United States—History—1600-
1775, Colonial period
ISBN 0-7614-0930-0 LC 99-33360
A reissue of the title first published 1976 by Watts
Introduces the history of blacksmithing and discusses
the techniques, products, well-known blacksmiths, and
commercial importance of this trade in colonial America
Includes bibliographical references

684.1 Furniture

Fisher, Leonard Everett
The cabinetmakers; written and illustrated by
Leonard Everett Fisher. Benchmark Bks. 1997 47p
il (Colonial craftsmen) $21.36 (4 and up)
684.1
1. Cabinetwork 2. American furniture 3. United
States—Social life and customs—1600-1775, Colonial
period
ISBN 0-7614-0479-1 LC 96-16606
A reissue of the title first published 1966 by Watts
The author explains that colonial American furniture
is a reflection of the social life of the times and of the
history of the craftsmen who designed it. He also discusses how cabinetmakers worked, what tools they used,
and what skills were employed to bring about the final
product
"Partly because Mr. Fisher's distinctive illustrative
style lends itself well to the graining of wood, the pictures seem unusually handsome. [Includes] two pages of
photographs of colonial furniture." Bull Cent Child
Books

685 Leather and fur goods, and related products

Cobb, Vicki
Sneakers; photographs by Michael Gold.
Millbrook Press 2006 48p il (Where's the science
here?) $23.93 (3-5) **685**
1. Sneakers
ISBN 0-7613-2772-X LC 2004-29816
"From photographs of the inside of a sneaker factory
to X-rays of the foot to a picture of how rubber is ex-
tracted from a rubber tree, readers will find a new angle
to spark their interest in *Sneakers*. They will learn about
how sneakers are designed and made, and even how to
test their fit. [An] attractive [choice] that [relates] science
to [a topic] that fascinate kids." SLJ

Fisher, Leonard Everett
The shoemakers; written & illustrated by
Leonard Everett Fisher. Benchmark Bks. 1998 44p
il (Colonial craftsmen) $14.95 (4 and up)
685
1. Shoemakers 2. United States—Social life and customs—1600-1775, Colonial period
ISBN 0-7614-0510-0 LC 96-40975
A reissue of the title first published 1967 by Watts
The author tells the history of the American shoemakers and gives an account of how they went about their
work
Written in a "lucid, graphic manner. . . . A glossary
of terms is included and the book is illustrated with carefully drawn, detailed pictures on every other page."
Booklist

686.2 Printing

Fisher, Leonard Everett
The printers; written & illustrated by Leonard
Everett Fisher. Marshall Cavendish 1999 46p il
(Colonial craftsmen) lib bdg $21.36 (4 and up)
686.2
1. Printing—History 2. United States—History—1600-
1775, Colonial period
ISBN 0-7614-0929-7 LC 99-33361
A reissue of the title first published 1965 by Watts
Surveys the history of printing in colonial America,
describing the work of the early printers, the develop-
ment of the free press, and the printer's craft and tech-
nique
Includes bibliographical references

Koscielniak, Bruce
Johann Gutenberg and the amazing printing
press. Houghton Mifflin Co 2003 unp il $16 (2-4)
686.2
1. Gutenberg, Johann, 1397?-1468 2. Printing—History
ISBN 0-618-26351-9 LC 2002-151176
"The pleasing line drawings and the subtle hues of
Boscielniak's watercolors give the illustrations an informal look that makes their informative content all the
more accessible." Booklist

688.7 Recreational equipment

Markel, Michelle
Cornhusk, silk, and wishbones; a book of dolls
from around the world. Houghton Mifflin 2000
48p il map $15 (3-6) **688.7**
1. Dolls
ISBN 0-618-05487-1 LC 99-89789
Examines a variety of dolls throughout the world, discussing how they have been used at different times and
how they reflect the cultures that created them
"The type of doll appears in boldly colored typeface
along with a stunning, full-color photograph. . . . The
text is lively and engaging and imparts solid cultural and
historical information." SLJ
Includes bibliographical references

Wulffson, Don L.

Toys! amazing stories behind some great inventions; [by] Don Wulffson; with illustrations by Laurie Keller. Holt & Co. 2000 137p il $16.95 (4 and up) **688.7**

1. Toys 2. Inventions

ISBN 0-8050-6196-7 LC 99-58440

Describes the creation of a variety of toys and games, from seesaws to Silly Putty and toy soldiers to Trivial Pursuit

"Each of the 25 chapters is illustrated with small, humorous drawings and discusses a particular toy or game's origin and development. The book ends with a bibliography and a list of Web sites. Good, readable fare for browsing or light research." Booklist

Includes bibliographical references

690 Buildings

Barton, Byron

Building a house. Greenwillow Bks. 1981 unp il pa $5.95 hardcover o.p. (k-1) **690**

1. Building 2. Houses

ISBN 0-688-09356-6 (pa)

"In the simplest possible book on building a house, a step-by-step, one-line description is given of the major factors in construction. Such workers as bricklayers, carpenters, plumbers, electricians, and painters do their own jobs until the small, bright red-and-green house is completed and a family moves in. Flat drawings in brilliant primary colors enable the very young to visualize the methods of housebuilding." Horn Book

Machines at work. Crowell 1987 unp il $15.95; lib bdg $15.89; pa $6.95 (k-1) **690**

1. Building

ISBN 0-694-00190-2; 0-690-04573-5 (lib bdg); 0-694-01107-X (pa) LC 86-24221

"Double-page illustrations depict a busy day at a construction site as workers (with the positive inclusion of women) knock down a building and start a new one." SLJ

"The short, punchy narrative reinforces the dynamics of the illustrations. . . . This should be a popular read-aloud for preschoolers and satisfying read-alone for beginners." Publ Wkly

Gibbons, Gail

How a house is built. Holiday House 1990 unp il $16.95; pa $6.95 (k-3) **690**

1. Building 2. Houses

ISBN 0-8234-0841-8; 0-8234-1232-6 (pa) LC 90-55107

This book describes how the surveyor, heavy machinery operators, carpenter crew, plumbers, and other workers build a house

"With her customary bright illustrations, Gibbons gives a fine introduction to the construction of a wood-frame house. . . . Construction machines and materials as well as parts of the house are identified, and each stage of construction logically follows the others. Workers are drawn in both sexes and several skin tones." Booklist

Hudson, Cheryl Willis

Construction zone; photographs by Richard Sobol; text by Cheryl Willis Hudson. Candlewick Press 2006 unp il $15.99 (2-4) **690**

1. Building

ISBN 0-7636-2684-8

"Large photographs of the construction of the MIT Stata Center in Cambridge, MA, are the core of this book. The simple text explains the process from the design by Frank O. Gehry to the completed building. Construction-zone activity, equipment, and jargon are pictured and explained. . . . Words in bold . . . are defined and explained at the bottom of the page on which they appear. . . . Children will be fascinated by both the picture story and the informative text." SLJ

Macaulay, David

Mill. Houghton Mifflin 1983 128p il $18; pa $9.95 (4 and up) **690**

1. Mills 2. Textile industry—History

ISBN 0-395-34830-7; 0-395-52019-3 (pa) LC 83-10652

This is an "account of the development of four fictional 19th-Century Rhode Island cotton mills. In explaining the construction and operation of a simple water-wheel powered wooden mill, as well as the more complex stone, turbine and steam mills to follow, the author also describes the rise and decline of New England's textile industry." SLJ

Unbuilding. Houghton Mifflin 1980 78p il $18; pa $9.95 (4 and up) **690**

1. Empire State Building (New York, N.Y.) 2. Building 3. Skyscrapers

ISBN 0-395-29457-6; 0-395-45425-5 (pa) LC 80-15491

This fictional account of the dismantling and removal of the Empire State Building describes the structure of a skyscraper and explains how such an edifice would be demolished

"Save for the fact that one particularly stunning double-page spread is marred by tight binding, the book is a joy: accurate, informative, handsome, and eminently readable." Bull Cent Child Books

Schwarz, Renée

Birdfeeders. Kids Can Press 2005 40p il (Kids can do it) $12.95; pa $6.95 (4-6) **690**

1. Bird feeders

ISBN 1-55337-699-4; 1-55337-700-1 (pa)

This offers instructions for constructing nine types of bird feeders composed of recycled or common household materials such as flowerpots, juice cans, Frisbees and ketchup bottles.

Birdhouses. Kids Can Press 2005 40p il (Kids can do it) $12.95; pa $6.95 (4-6) **690**

1. Birdhouses 2. Woodwork

ISBN 1-55337-549-1; 1-55337-550-5 (pa)

This "shows and tells how to build nine birdhouses using inexpensive materials such as wood, plastic drainage pipes, flower pots, and even an old boot. . . . Small, clear pictures illustrate the step-by-step directions." Booklist

693 Construction in specific types of materials and for specific purposes

Rounds, Glen

Sod houses on the Great Plains; written and illustrated by Glen Rounds. Holiday House 1995 unp il $16.95; pa $6.95 (k-3)   **693**

1. Houses 2. Frontier and pioneer life

ISBN 0-8234-1162-1; 0-8234-1263-6 (pa)

LC 94-27390

"The author explains plainly and clearly just how the homesteaders built their warm, dry, fireproof, ecologically sound sod dwellings on the prairies more than a century ago. His spare but evocative crayon illustrations detail the text and add sly wit." N Y Times Book Rev

694 Wood construction. Carpentry

Robertson, J. Craig

The kids' building workshop; 15 woodworking projects for kids and parents to build together; [by] J. Craig and Barbara Robertson, with their daughters Camille and Allegra. Storey Kids 2004 136p il $22.96; pa $12.95 (3-6)   **694**

1. Woodwork

ISBN 1-58017-572-4; 1-58017-488-4 (pa)

LC 2004-1521

"The first section, 'Setting Up Shop: Getting to Know Your Tools,' includes a basic introduction to hammering, sawing, drilling, block planing, and measuring. Next, 'Down to Business: Building Your Own Projects' puts these tools and techniques to work in simple, yet cleverly designed, kid-friendly projects that increase in complexity. . . . Clear instructions, black-and-white photos, and cutting diagrams are included for each one. . . . Practical and enjoyable introduction to the subject." SLJ

Walker, Lester

Carpentry for children; preface by David Macaulay. Overlook Press 1982 208p il pa $14.95 hardcover o.p. (4 and up)   **694**

1. Carpentry 2. Handicraft

ISBN 0-87951-990-8 (pa)

LC 82-3469

A step-by-step guide to carrying out such carpentry projects as a birdhouse, candle chandelier, doll cradle, puppet theater, and coaster car

700 ARTS & RECREATION

Ajmera, Maya

To be an artist; [by] Maya Ajmera & John D. Ivanko; foreword by Jacques d'Amboise. Charlesbridge 2004 unp il $15.95 (k-3)   **700**

1. Arts

ISBN 1-57091-503-2   LC 2003-8154

"Shakti for Children"

This includes "photographs of youngsters from many different countries engaged in a variety of art forms, including dancing, singing, writing, and painting. The bold text introduces each discipline and is supported with more extensive descriptions of the individual endeavors and the nature of artistic expression in general. . . . This vibrant book pulsates with the energy and sense of accomplishment that accompanies participation in the arts." SLJ

Rubin, Susan Goldman

Art against the odds; from slave quilts to prison paintings. Crown Publishers 2004 48p il $19.95; lib bdg $21.99 (5 and up)   **700**

1. Art

ISBN 0-375-82406-5; 0-375-92406-X (lib bdg)

LC 2003-12139

Contents: Outsider art; Captured; Pattern for freedom: women's quilts as art; Kids create art against the odds

This is a "survey of outsider art, encompassing the works of patients, slaves, concentration and internment-camp prisoners, and disadvantaged children living in modern blighted urban areas and developing nations. . . . The vivid, resilient life force radiating from these works contrasts sharply with the unimaginably bleak conditions under which they were created. . . . This unique offering is a top priority for most libraries." SLJ

Includes bibliographical references

701 Art--Philosophy and theory

Micklethwait, Lucy

A child's book of art: great pictures, first words; selected by Lucy Micklethwait. Dorling Kindersley 1993 64p il $16.95 (k-2)   **701**

1. Art appreciation 2. Vocabulary

ISBN 1-56458-203-5   LC 92-54320

An introduction to art that uses well-known works of art to illustrate familiar words

"Micklethwait wisely includes an abundance of paintings featuring children, action scenes and vibrant colors—all elements guaranteed to snare a youngster's attention. The thematic arrangement of the works of art places them in contexts familiar to kids." Publ Wkly

702.8 Art--Technique, procedures, apparatus, equipment, materials

Gibbons, Gail

The art box. Holiday House 1998 unp il $16.95; pa $6.95 (k-1)   **702.8**

1. Artists' materials

ISBN 0-8234-1386-1; 0-8234-1556-2 (pa)

LC 97-44171

Describes the many different kinds of tools and supplies which artists use to produce their work

This offers "Illustrations with clean lines and bright colors set against textured handmade papers. . . . The straightforward text combines boldface headings, captions, and succinct descriptions." Booklist

Luxbacher, Irene

The jumbo book of art; written and illustrated by Irene Luxbacher. Kids Can Press 2003 208p il pa $14.95 (4 and up)   **702.8**

1. Art—Study and teaching
ISBN 1-55074-762-2

"Each of the four chapters is devoted to instructing readers in the basics of one technique—drawing, creating with color, sculpture, and mixed-media projects, respectively—and then inspires those readers to let loose and have fun making something beautiful. . . . The book features clear layouts, well-written definitions of terms, full-color illustrations, and more than 90 projects. . . . This practical, lively, and smart package is a must-have for every art and elementary school classroom, and a welcome addition to most library collections." SLJ

Includes glossary

704   Art--Special topics

Barber, Nicola

Islamic empires; [by] Nicola Barber. Raintree 2005 48p il map (History in art) $31.43 (4 and up)
                                                      704

1. Islamic art 2. Islam
ISBN 1-4109-0522-5   LC 2004-7527

Contents: Art as evidence; The spread of Islam; The great empires; Life in the Islamic empires; Religion

This is an introduction to the art, culture, and history of Islamic empires.

This book has "a depth of content that is unusual in art-history books for this age group. . . . [It] is amply illustrated with full-color photographs and reproductions. . . . Well-written, informative." SLJ

Includes bibliographical references

Coyne, Jennifer Tarr

Come look with me: discovering women artists for children; [by] Jennifer Tarr Coyne. Lickle 2005 32p il $15.95 (3-5)   **704**

1. Women artists 2. Art appreciation
ISBN 1-890674-08-7

Introduces twelve women artists, including Faith Ringgold, Mary Cassatt, Frida Kahlo, and Grandma Moses, each with a short biography, a full-page color plate, a description of the image, and a set of discussion questions.

"This offering encourages children to learn biographical facts about artists and to look closely at the images and think about artistic decisions. . . . Each spread features a beautifully reproduced image." Booklist

Rolling, James Haywood, Jr.

Come look with me: discovering African American art for children; [by] James Haywood Rolling, Jr. Lickle 2005 32p il $15.95 (3-5)
                                                      704

1. African American art 2. Art appreciation
ISBN 1-890674-07-9

This volume presents 12 works of African American art "reproduced in full color and accompanied by descriptive information; the facing page contains several questions designed to engage young viewers and an adult in conversation as well as a few paragraphs of background. . . . Artists . . . include . . . Palmer Hayden and Clementine Hunter . . . Henry Ossawa Tanner, Romare Bearden, and Jacob Lawrence." SLJ

704.9   Iconography

Thomson, Ruth

Creatures. Chelsea Clubhouse 2004 c2003 32p il (First look at art) $14.95 (2-5)   **704.9**

1. Animals in art 2. Art appreciation
ISBN 0-7910-7945-7   LC 2003-14427

Contents: Animals in art; Texture and mood; Making marks; Nature's patterns; Decorative displays; Creatures in motion; Modeling movement; Color and camouflage; In the wild; A mythical beast; Making monsters; Imaginary creatures; Just imagine; Artists and answers

This describes various ways in which animals, real and imaginary, are depicted in art, and includes related art activities

"Teachers will find easy-to-understand art lessons and projects and students will find inspiration in [this] well-organized, attractive [title]." SLJ

Includes glossary

Families. Chelsea Clubhouse 2004 c2003 32p il (First look at art) $14.95 (2-5)   **704.9**

1. Family in art 2. Art appreciation
ISBN 0-7910-7946-5   LC 2003-16004

Contents: Families forever; Family fortunes; Family matters; A family tree; Family ties; Model families; Sculpting the family; Family feelings; In the mood; Two of a kind; Me and you; Family album; Family snapshots; Artists and answers

This describes various ways in which families are depicted in painting, sculpture, and photography, and includes related art activities

"Teachers will find easy-to-understand art lessons and projects and students will find inspiration in [this] well-organized, attractive [title]." SLJ

Includes glossary

Places. Chelsea Clubhouse 2004 32p il (First look at art) $14.95 (2-5)   **704.9**

1. Landscape painting 2. Art appreciation
ISBN 0-7910-7947-3   LC 2003-16035

Contents: Picture a place; A country scene; Looking at landscapes; Personal place; Your room and view; A place of excitement; Capture the feeling; Bright city lights; Night sights; Sunshine and snow; Feel the heat; An imaginary place; In your dreams; Artists and answers

This describes various ways in which indoor, outdoor, and imaginary places are depicted in art, and includes related art activities

"Teachers will find easy-to-understand art lessons and projects and students will find inspiration in [this] well-organized, attractive [title]." SLJ

Includes glossary

708   Art--Galleries, museums private collections

Brown, Laurene Krasny

Visiting the art museum; [by] Laurene Krasny Brown and Marc Brown. Dutton 1986 32p il pa $6.99 hardcover o.p. (k-3)   **708**

1. Art museums 2. Art appreciation

ISBN 0-14-054820-3 (pa)   LC 85-32552

As a family wanders through an art museum, they see examples of various art styles from primitive through twentieth-century pop art

"A lively, fact-filled introduction to the art museum for the whole family, with animated drawings and full-color reproductions of art from all over the world. . . . All of the paintings are identified, both in the text and in the back, and all possible periods of art—from primitive to modern—are shown." Publ Wkly

709   Art--Historical and geographic treatment

Sayre, Henry M.

Cave paintings to Picasso; the inside scoop on 50 art masterpieces; by Henry Sayre. Chronicle Books 2004 93p il $22.95 (5 and up)   **709**

1. Art—History

ISBN 0-8118-3767-X   LC 2002-15583

Introduces fifty celebrated works of art, including King Tut's sarcophagus and Andy Warhol's paintings of Campbell's soup cans, with historical and interpretive information for each piece.

"The author's breezy style captures interest early on. . . . Many of the world's cultures are represented and a variety of techniques are explained. . . . A dazzling and accessible introduction to art history." SLJ

Includes glossary

709.01   Arts of nonliterate peoples, and earliest times to 499

Arnold, Caroline

Stories in stone; rock art pictures by early Americans; photographs by Richard Hewett. Clarion Bks. 1996 48p il map $16 (4 and up)   **709.01**

1. Native Americans—Antiquities 2. Rock drawings, paintings, and engravings

ISBN 0-395-72092-3   LC 96-387

This focuses "on the rock art found in the Coso Range of eastern California. . . . Arnold describes the various methods that were used to create the designs. She also discusses climatic changes in the area, beginning with the last Ice Age, and surmises what life might have been like for those ancient people." Booklist

"This is a crisply written, richly photographed account of the oldest known art in the world. . . . Hewett's color photographs are finely detailed, clear, and well com-

posed, and they enrich the text enormously." Bull Cent Child Books

Includes glossary

Curlee, Lynn

Seven wonders of the ancient world. Atheneum Bks. for Young Readers 2002 33p il map $17 (3-6)   **709.01**

1. Curiosities and wonders 2. Ancient civilization

ISBN 0-689-83182-X   LC 00-46919

"Curlee discusses how the list of the seven 'ancient wonders' originated, then devotes four pages each to the Great Pyramid, the Hanging Gardens, the Temple of Artemis, the Statue of Zeus, the Mausoleum, the Colossus of Rhodes, and the Pharos." Horn Book Guide

Curlee "offers an informative, richly descriptive text and artwork that enables readers to envision the wonders for themselves." Booklist

709.04   Art--20th century, 1900-1999

Raimondo, Joyce

Express yourself! activities and adventures in expressionism. Watson-Guptill Pub. 2005 48p il (Art explorers) $12.95 (1-5)   **709.04**

1. Expressionism (Art) 2. Art appreciation

ISBN 0-8230-2506-3

An introduction to Expressionism which includes guidance for related activities as well as brief biographies of six artists: Edvard Munch, Vincent van Gogh, Ernst Ludwig Kirchner, Visily Kandinsky, Willem de Kooning, and Jackson Pollock

"The layout is particularly attractive, with crisp, full-color photos and drawings set against brightly colored borders; the text and captions are easy to read. . . . This book will be welcomed by teachers, parents, and would-be artists." Booklist

Imagine that! activities and adventures in surrealism. Watson-Guptill 2004 48p il (Art explorers) $12.95 (1-5)   **709.04**

1. Surrealism 2. Art appreciation

ISBN 0-8230-2502-0   LC 2003-19487

An introduction to Surrealism which includes guidance for related activities as well as brief biographies of six artists: Salvador Dali, Rene Magritte, Max Ernst, Joan Mir, Merit Oppenheim, and Frida Kahlo

"One of the strengths of this book is the inclusion of artwork produced by children. . . . It offers a wealth of intriguing and easy-to-do activities." SLJ

709.37   Ancient Italian art. Roman art

Chrisp, Peter

Ancient Rome. Raintree 2005 48p il (History in art) $29.93 (4 and up)   **709.37**

1. Roman art 2. Rome—Civilization

ISBN 1-4109-0520-9   LC 2004-7567

Contents: The Roman empire; The story of Rome; The city of Rome; Family life; Roman religion; Timeline

Chrisp, Peter—*Continued*

While telling about her life in ancient Rome, eight-year-old Flavia includes information about the homes, families, clothing, food, gods, sports, goods traded, and things the people build.

The book follows "a well-organized format that makes the history accessible for reports, but the [author takes the book] beyond a reports-only status. Captions for the two or three illustrations per spread are clear." SLJ

Includes glossary and bibliographical references

709.38   Ancient Greek art

Langley, Andrew

Ancient Greece. Raintree 2005 48p il (History in art) $29.93 (4 and up)   **709.38**

1. Greek art 2. Greece—Civilization

ISBN 1-4109-0517-9   LC 2004-7523

Contents: Art as evidence; The story of ancient Greece; Inside the city-state; Everyday life; Religion and mythology; Time line

The author shows "how art provides primary-source information about everyday and family life, beliefs and religion, and philosophy and mythology in . . . ancient [Greece]. . . . The [book follows] a well-organized format that makes the history accessible for reports, but the [author takes the book] beyond a reports-only status. Captions for the two or three illustrations per spread are clear." SLJ

Includes glossary and bibliographical references

709.51   Chinese art

Anderson, Dale

Ancient China; [by] Dale Anderson. Raintree 2005 48p il map (History in art) $29.93 (4 and up)   **709.51**

1. Chinese art 2. China—Civilization

ISBN 1-4109-0519-5   LC 2004-7587

Contents: Art as evidence; The story of ancient China; Imperial government; Daily life in ancient China; Beliefs and philosophies; Timeline

The author shows "how art provides primary-source information about everyday and family life, beliefs and religion, and philosophy and mythology in . . . ancient [China]. . . . The [book follows] a well-organized format that makes the history accessible for reports, but the [author takes the book] beyond a reports-only status. Captions for the two or three illustrations per spread are clear." SLJ

Includes glossary and bibliographical references

709.7   North American art

January, Brendan

Native Americans; [by] Brendan January. Raintree 2005 48p il map (History in art) $31.43 (4 and up)   **709.7**

1. Native American art 2. Native Americans

ISBN 1-4109-0523-3   LC 2004-7526

Contents: The Native Americans; A chronological history; Traditional ways; Everyday life; Beliefs and mythology

This book has "a depth of content that is unusual in art-history books for this age group. . . . [It] is amply illustrated with full-color photographs and reproductions. . . . Well-written, informative." SLJ

Includes bibliographical references

711   Area planning

Macaulay, David

City: a story of Roman planning and construction. Houghton Mifflin 1974 112p il $18; pa $7.95 (4 and up)   **711**

1. City planning—Rome 2. Civil engineering 3. Roman architecture

ISBN 0-395-19492-X; 0-395-34922-2 (pa)

LC 74-4280

"By following the inception, construction, and development of an imaginary Roman city, the account traces the evolution of Verbonia from the selection of its site under religious auspices in 26 B.C. to its completion in 100 A.D." Horn Book

Includes glossary

720   Architecture

Arbogast, Joan Marie

Buildings in disguise; architecture that looks like animals, food, and other things; by Joan Marie Arbogast. 1st ed. Boyds Mills Press 2004 48p il $16.95 (4 and up)   **720**

1. Architecture 2. Buildings

ISBN 1-59078-099-X   LC 2003-26793

A "look at examples of memetic architecture. . . . One chapter is devoted to gas stations shaped like a teepee, a teapot, a pagoda, etc. . . . The full color photos are bright and striking. . . . A fun browsing title that reveals the vitality and spirit of inventive architecture." SLJ

Goodman, Susan

Skyscraper; from the ground up; [by] Susan E. Goodman; [photographs by] Michael J. Doolittle. A.A. Knopf 2004 unp il map $16.95; lib bdg $18.99 (2-5)   **720**

1. Skyscrapers 2. Design and construction

ISBN 0-375-81309-8; 0-375-91309-2 (lib bdg)

LC 2003-27925

"Following the construction of the new Random House Building in New York City, Doolittle and Goodman have created a visual time line with photographs and personal interviews." SLJ

This offers "graceful, clear text and exciting color photos. . . . [This is a] thoughtful, well-composed offering." Booklist

Macaulay, David

Building big. Houghton Mifflin 2000 192p il $30; pa $12.95 (5 and up)   **720**

1. Architecture 2. Engineering

ISBN 0-395-96331-1; 0-618-46527-8 (pa)

LC 00-28116

"Walter Lorraine books"

This companion to the PBS series examines the architecture and engineering of "bridges, tunnels, dams, domes, and skyscrapers. Each section offers an implicitly chronological analysis as it focuses on several significant examples of that particular kind of structure." Bull Cent Child Books

"Macaulay combines his detailed yet vaguely whimsical illustrations with simple, straightforward prose that breaks down complex architectural and engineering accomplishments into easily digestible tidbits that don't insult the intelligence of the reader of any age." N Y Times Book Rev

Includes glossary

720.9   Architecture--Historical and geographic treatment

Fisher, Leonard Everett

The architects; written & illustrated by Leonard Everett Fisher; with additional photographs. Benchmark Bks. 1999 48p il (Colonial craftsmen) lib bdg $24.36 (4 and up)   **720.9**

1. Architecture 2. United States—Social life and customs—1600-1775, Colonial period

ISBN 0-7614-0931-9   LC 99-33370

A reissue of the title first published 1970 by Watts

Traces the history of architecture in the American colonies, describing the influence of existing styles and the needs of environment

"Illustrated with strong, informative, distinctive scratchboard drawings." Horn Book Guide

Includes bibliographical references

Ross, Stewart

Art and architecture; by Stewart Ross. Lucent Books 2004 48p il (Medieval realms) $28.70 (5 and up)   **720.9**

1. Medieval architecture 2. Medieval art

ISBN 1-59018-534-X   LC 2004-11491

Contents: Romanesque architecture; Romanesque art: painting; Romanesque art: tapestry; The Gothic revolution: architecture; The Gothic revolution: art; Gothic glory; High Gothic architecture; Islamic architecture; Islamic art; Picture windows; Sculpture: decoration; Sculpture: tombs and monuments; Parish churches; The monastery; Manuscript illumination; Early castles: motte and bailey; Later castles; Manors and halls; The houses of the poor; Town architecture; Towards the Renaissance; Timeline

This "discusses the role of the church in medieval art; prominent cathedrals of the Romanesque and Gothic periods; Moorish and Islamic influences in Eastern Europe; manuscript illumination; and castles, manors, and more. . . . Distinctive borders surround the top and sides of the beautifully designed spreads, and the [text is] presented in small, accessible sections with glossary words in bold, cross-references, captions, and sidebars." SLJ

Includes glossary and bibliographical references

Zaunders, Bo

Gargoyles, girders, & glass houses; magnificent master builders; illustrated by Roxie Munro. Dutton Children's Books 2004 48p il $17.99 (3-6)   **720.9**

1. Architecture—History 2. Architects

ISBN 0-525-47284-3   LC 2003-28192

The author and illustrator "tell the stories of Brunelleschi's dome of Santa Maria del Fiore, the mosques of Mimar Koca Sinan, the sculpture and architecture of Brazil's Lisboa, the Roeblings' Brooklyn Bridge, Eiffel's tower in Paris, the buildings of Barcelona's Gaudi, and Van Alen's Chrysler Building in New York City. Zaunders' narrative approach to nonfiction adds an appealing dimension to these artistic and engineering feats. Munro's often-beautiful ink drawings with color washes capture the special qualities of each construction." Booklist

Includes bibliographical references

725   Public structures

Nardo, Don

Roman amphitheaters. Watts 2002 63p il lib bdg $24; pa $8.95 (5 and up)   **725**

1. Colosseum (Rome, Italy) 2. Roman architecture

ISBN 0-531-12036-8 (lib bdg); 0-531-16224-9 (pa)

LC 2001-17769

"Watts library"

The author discusses the Colosseum in Rome as an example of how amphitheaters were constructed and "provides a brief cultural context; a history of the development of the building type; and a history of the . . . [Colosseum] including how it was built, what it was used for, and what happened after the society that created it lost prominence. . . . The writing is informative and engaging and not oversimplified. The illustrations are mainly clear, high-quality, full-color photographs." SLJ

Includes glossary and bibliographical references

726   Buildings for religious and related purposes

Curlee, Lynn

Parthenon. Atheneum Books for Young Readers 2004 unp il $17.95 (3-6)   **726**

1. Parthenon (Athens, Greece)

ISBN 0-689-84490-5   LC 2003-2615

A detailed history of the Parthenon exploring its construction and restoration.

This is a "splendid introduction to Greece's most renowned monument. . . . [The author's] examination of the architectural details is particularly accurate and absorbing. . . . The limpid, forthright prose matches artwork of similar clarity and elegant simplicity. The acrylic paintings balance areas of flat color with finely controlled line." SLJ

DuTemple, Lesley A.
The Pantheon. Lerner Publs. 2003 72p il (Great building feats) lib bdg $27.93 (5 and up)
726
1. Pantheon (Rome, Italy) 2. Temples 3. Roman architecture
ISBN 0-8225-0376-X   LC 2001-05694
Describes the building of the Pantheon, discussing the role of the Roman emperor Hadrian and the significance of the Pantheon in the fields of history and architecture
This offers a "clear and straightforward text. . . . There are numerous color photographs, clear diagrams, and architectural drawings of the building and its interior." SLJ
Includes bibliographical references

Hyman, Teresa L.
Pyramids; [by] Teresa Hyman. KidHaven Press 2004 48p il (Wonders of the world) lib bdg $23.70 (3-6)
726
1. Pyramids
ISBN 0-7377-2055-7   LC 2004-12063
Contents: Pyramids of treasure; Pyramids of power; Pyramids of enlightenment; Pyramids of sacrifice
This "introduces structures in ancient Egypt, Africa, Cambodia, and Mexico and is full of large, colorful photos and illustrations. . . . Attractive, readable." SLJ
Includes bibliographical references

Macaulay, David
Building the book Cathedral. Houghton Mifflin 1999 112p il $29.95 (4 and up)
726
1. Cathedrals 2. Gothic architecture
ISBN 0-395-92147-3   LC 99-17975
"Walter Lorraine books"
"On its twenty-fifth anniversary, the author recounts the origins of his first book and suggests revisions he'd make in light of what he's learned. . . . Most of the original *Cathedral: the story of it's construction* is reproduced in this oversized celebratory volume, along with lots of preliminary sketches, new commentary, and revised, or newly deployed, art. . . . Touches of informal humor further enliven a book that's already mesmerizing for both its original content and its insights into this author-illustrator's incisive, ebulliently creative mind." Horn Book

Cathedral: the story of its construction. Houghton Mifflin 1973 77p il $18; pa $8.95 (4 and up)
726
1. Cathedrals 2. Gothic architecture
ISBN 0-395-17513-5; 0-395-31668-5 (pa)
LC 73-6634
This is a description, illustrated with black-and-white line drawings, of the construction of an imagined representative Gothic cathedral "in southern France from its conception in 1252 to its completion in 1338. The spirit that motivated the people, the tools and materials they used, the steps and methods of constructions, all receive . . . attention." Booklist
Includes glossary

Mosque. Houghton Mifflin 2003 96p il $18 (4 and up)
726
1. Mosques—Design and construction
ISBN 0-618-24034-9   LC 2003-177
"Walter Lorraine books"
Using "a fictional framework to hold his nonfictional material, the author introduces readers to Admiral Suha Mehmet Pasa, a wealthy aristocrat living in Istanbul, who decides in his declining years to fund the building of a mosque and its associated buildings—religious school, soup kitchen, public baths, public fountain, and tomb. Detailing the activities of the architect and workers, Macaulay creates a from-the-ground-up look not only at the actual construction, but also at the uses of the various buildings." SLJ
"Once again Macaulay uses clear words and exemplary drawings to explore a majestic structure's design and construction. . . . In his respectful, straightforward explanation of the mosque's design, Macaulay offers an unusual, inspiring perspective into Islamic society." Booklist
Includes glossary

Pyramid. Houghton Mifflin 1975 80p il $18; pa $9.95 (4 and up)
726
1. Pyramids 2. Egypt—Civilization
ISBN 0-395-21407-6; 0-395-32121-2 (pa)
LC 75-9964
The construction of a pyramid in 25th century B.C. Egypt is described. "Information about selection of the site, drawing of the plans, calculating compass directions, clearing and leveling the ground, and quarrying and hauling the tremendous blocks of granite and limestone is conveyed as much by pictures as by text." Horn Book
Includes glossary

Nardo, Don
Greek temples. Watts 2002 63p il lib bdg $24; pa $8.95 (5 and up)
726
1. Parthenon (Athens, Greece) 2. Greek architecture
ISBN 0-531-12035-X (lib bdg); 0-531-16225-7 (pa)
LC 2001-22033
"Watts library"
The author discusses the Parthenon in Athens as an example of Ancient Greek temple architecture and "provides a brief cultural context; a history of the development of the building type; and a history of the . . . [Parthenon] including how it was built, what it was used for, and what happened after the society that created it lost prominence. . . . The writing is informative and engaging and not oversimplified. The illustrations are mainly clear, high-quality, full-color photographs." SLJ
Includes glossary and bibliographical references

728 Residential and related buildings

Steltzer, Ulli
Building an igloo; text and photographs by Ulli Steltzer. Holt & Co. 1995 c1981 unp il $15.95; pa $6.95 (3-6)
728
1. Igloos 2. Inuit
ISBN 0-8050-3753-5; 0-8050-6313-7 (pa)
LC 95-5893

Steltzer, Ulli—*Continued*

First published 1981 in Canada

"Steltzer follows Tookillkee Kiguktak, an Inuit, as he builds an igloo to use while on a hunting trip. The brief, clear text, thorough introduction, and brilliant black-and-white photographs make the book an exceptionally fascinating and respectful glimpse of a traditional art." Horn Book Guide

Yue, Charlotte

The igloo; [by] Charlotte and David Yue. Houghton Mifflin 1988 117p il $16; pa $7.95 (4 and up) **728**

1. Igloos 2. Inuit

ISBN 0-395-44613-9; 0-395-62986-1 (pa)

LC 88-6154

Describes how an igloo is constructed and the role it plays in the lives of the Eskimo people. Also discusses many other aspects of Eskimo culture that have helped them adapt to life in the Arctic

"This book is a tidy source of reference information, curriculum support, and just plain compelling reading." SLJ

Includes bibliographical references

728.8 Large and elaborate private dwellings

Cole, Joanna

Ms. Frizzle's adventures: medieval castle; illustrated by Bruce Degen. Scholastic Press 2003 unp il $15.95 (2-4) **728.8**

1. Castles 2. Medieval civilization

ISBN 0-590-10820-4 LC 2002-5257

When Ms. Frizzle and her student Arnold follow an underground passage beneath Craig's Castle Shop and find themselves in the middle of a siege of a 12th century English castle, they learn a great deal about both castles and the Middle Ages

"There's plenty of action and comic byplay, but along the way children will learn a good deal. . . . The pictures are brightly colored and the graphic design is reminiscent of comic books, with small panels and speech balloons in addition to narrative text and larger illustrations." Booklist

Gravett, Christopher

Castle; written by Christopher Gravett; photographed by Geoff Dann. rev ed. DK Pub. 2004 72p il (DK eyewitness books) $15.99 (4 and up) **728.8**

1. Castles 2. Fortification

ISBN 0-7566-0660-8 LC 2004558977

First published 1994 by Knopf

This is a "guide to the castles of the Middle Ages and the lives of the people who lived in them. . . . [It includes] full-color photographs of castles around the world, plus specially built models." Publisher's note

Macaulay, David

Castle. Houghton Mifflin 1977 74p il $18; pa $9.95 (4 and up) **728.8**

1. Castles 2. Fortification

ISBN 0-395-25784-0; 0-395-32920-5 (pa)

LC 77-7159

Macaulay depicts "the history of an imaginary thirteenth-century castle—built to subdue the Welsh hordes—from the age of construction to the age of neglect, when the town of Aberwyfern no longer needs a fortified stronghold." Economist

Includes glossary

Scarre, Christopher

The Palace of Minos at Knossos; [by] Chris Scarre and Rebecca Stefoff. Oxford University Press 2003 47p il map (Digging for the past) $21.95 (4 and up) **728.8**

1. Evans, Sir Arthur John, 1851-1941 2. Palace of Knossos 3. Excavations (Archeology)—Greece 4. Crete (Greece)

ISBN 0-19-514272-1 LC 2003-3712

Contents: An unexplored world; Discovering a lost palace; In search of the Minoans; Knossos today; Interview with Chris Scarre

Discusses the ancient Minoan civilization of Knossos, Crete, as manifested by the excavations of that city by the archaeologist Sir Arthur Evans.

"Many excellent photos and diagrams, mainly in color; time lines . . . and explanations of archaeological stratigraphy and of the mysterious Linear B writing are included. The book is concise, clear, entertaining, and factual." SLJ

Includes bibliographical references

Steele, Philip

Castles. Kingfisher (NY) 1995 63p il $16.95; pa $10.95 (4 and up) **728.8**

1. Castles

ISBN 1-85697-547-9; 0-7534-5258-8 (pa)

LC 94-29366

An "overview of medieval European (and a few Near Eastern) castles. The book's strengths are its well-organized format and careful balance of text and illustrations. Steele touches on almost every facet of castle construction, inhabitants, celebrations, and rituals, as well as more mundane topics such as sanitation and the kitchen." SLJ

Includes glossary

730.9 Sculpture--Historical and geographic treatment

Fritz, Jean

Leonardo's horse; illustrated by Hudson Talbott. Putnam 2001 unp il $16.99 (4 and up) **730.9**

1. Leonardo, da Vinci, 1452-1519 2. Dent, Charlie, 1919-1994 3. Bronzes

ISBN 0-399-23576-0 LC 00-41550

Fritz, Jean—*Continued*

"In 1482, Leonardo da Vinci began work on a mammoth bronze horse. But though he completed a twenty-four-foot clay model, it was never cast. . . . Half a millennium later, retired pilot Charles Dent dedicated himself to re-creating Leonardo's dream, a venture eventually realized with the help of sculptor Nina Akamu." Horn Book

"Combining biography, history, and art, Fritz's absorbing text is both a lively introduction to Leonardo and a tribute to Dent." Booklist

731.4 Sculpture--Techniques and procedures

Scheunemann, Pam

Cool clay projects; [by] Pam Scheunemann. Abdo Pub 2005 32p il (Cool crafts) $22.78 (4-6)
731.4

1. Clay 2. Handicraft
ISBN 1-59197-740-1   LC 2004-53119

This "explores polymer-clay conditioning, color mixing, millefiori, and bead making. It also includes clear directions for making a pen, a picture frame, and decorating a purchased clay pot." SLJ

736 Carving and carvings. Paper cutting and folding

Diehn, Gwen

Making books that fly, fold, wrap, hide, pop up, twist, and turn; books for kids to make. Lark Bks. 1998 96p il $19.95 (4 and up)   **736**

1. Paper crafts 2. Handicraft
ISBN 1-57990-023-2   LC 97-41037

Presents instructions for making various kinds of books including those that carry messages across space and time as well as those that save words, ideas, and pictures

"Clear directions and diagrams and attractive full-color photographs of completed projects will make it easy for readers to duplicate 18 different folded, wrapped, and pop-up books." Booklist

Includes glossary

Garza, Carmen Lomas

Making magic windows; creating papel picado/cut-paper art with Carmen Lomas Garza. Children's Bk. Press 1999 61p il pa $9.95 (3-6)
736

1. Paper crafts
ISBN 0-89239-159-6   LC 98-38518

Provides instructions for making paper banners and more intricate cut-outs. Includes diagrams for creating specific images

"Based on workshops conducted by the artist, the step-by-step instructions and illustrations have been fine-tuned and are clear and easy to follow. . . . Multiculturally authentic and a guaranteed kid-crowd pleaser, this workbook is enthusiastically recommended for all craft collections." Booklist

Irvine, Joan

How to make holiday pop-ups; illustrated by Linda Hendry. Morrow Junior Bks. 1996 64p il pa $6.95 hardcover o.p. (3-6)   **736**

1. Paper crafts 2. Handicraft 3. Holidays
ISBN 0-688-13610-9 (pa)   LC 95-35174

First published 1995 in Canada

This "craft book suggests designs and provides detailed instructions for making holiday cards with pop-up pictures. . . . The line-and-watercolor illustrations reinforce the directions and show the finished product. This attractive addition to craft collections will be useful throughout the year." Booklist

738.1 Ceramic arts--Techniques, equipment, materials

Ellis, Mary

Ceramics for kids; creative clay projects to pinch, roll, coil, slam & twist. Lark Bks. 2002 144p il $24.95 (3-6)   **738.1**

1. Ceramics
ISBN 1-57990-198-0   LC 2002-19059

Provides an introduction to clay and pottery, plus instructions for twenty-five projects using various methods, such as a pinch and coil Japanese tea bowl and a press-molded hanging bird bath

"A collection of appealing hand-built, low-fired clay projects, organized by technique and increasing levels of complexity. Ellis provides clear directions, uses simple procedures, suggests inexpensive tools and safety guidelines, and usually offers several photo examples of completed projects." SLJ

Includes glossary

739.2 Work in precious metals

Fisher, Leonard Everett

The silversmiths; written & illustrated by Leonard Everett Fisher. Benchmark Bks. 1997 46p il (Colonial craftsmen) lib bdg $21.36 (4 and up)
739.2

1. Silverwork 2. United States—Social life and customs—1600-1775, Colonial period
ISBN 0-7614-0478-3   LC 96-16607

A reissue of the title first published 1964 by Watts

This is a story of early colonial silversmiths and how they worked to create beautiful and useful objects of art

"Respect for . . . achievement is reflected in striking full-page scratchboard illustrations and in concise, informative text." Horn Book

741.2 Drawing--Techniques, equipment, materials

Emberley, Ed

Ed Emberley's big green drawing book. Little, Brown 1979 91p il pa $10.99 hardcover o.p. (2-5)
741.2

1. Drawing
ISBN 0-316-23596-2 (pa)   LC 79-16247

Emberley, Ed—*Continued*

The author "combines basic shapes (circles, triangles, lines, squiggles) to create a variety of cartoon people and animals. The crisp green-and-black illustrations on a white background are large and well spaced. . . . As in his other drawing books, Emberley's wordless step-by-step method is easy to follow; even very young children can successfully reproduce the simple but appealing figures." SLJ

Ed Emberley's big red drawing book. Little, Brown 1987 unp il pa $10.99 hardcover o.p. (2-5)

                                  741.2

1. Drawing

ISBN 0-316-23435-4 (pa)   LC 87-3091

The author explains "how to create objects and figures by building up a series of simple lines and squiggles into a more complicated and complete whole. The color red suggests most of the subjects, among them a U.S. flag, a fire engine, and assorted red-and-green Christmas items." Booklist

Ed Emberley's drawing book: make a world. Little, Brown 1972 unp il pa $6.99 hardcover o.p. (2-5)   **741.2**

1. Drawing

ISBN 0-316-78972-0 (pa)

"Emberley gives directions for drawing, among a myriad of other things, 10 different kinds of cars, 16 varieties of trucks, and animals of all species including anteaters and dinosaurs." Book World

"The final three pages, which supply suggestions for making comic strips, posters, mobiles and games, help make the volume particularly appealing. For all developing artists and even plain scribblers." Horn Book

Ed Emberley's fingerprint drawing book. Little, Brown 2000 unp il $15.95; pa $7.95 (2-5)

                                    741.2

1. Drawing

ISBN 0-316-23215-7; 0-316-23319-6 (pa)

                                  LC 00-31026

"A step-by-step approach to drawing for beginners and those who are artistically challenged. Each figure introduced can be made with a basic fingerprint or more, and then lines and dots are placed beneath the form to take budding artists to a complete picture. It is so easy to do that even very young children can enjoy a simple art adventure." SLJ

Ed Emberley's great thumbprint drawing book. Little, Brown 1977 37p il lib bdg $15.95; pa $6.95 (2-5)   **741.2**

1. Drawing

ISBN 0-316-23613-6 (lib bdg); 0-316-23668-3 (pa)

                                  LC 76-57346

"The artist shows how to combine thumbprints and simple lines to create a multitude of animals, people, birds, and flowers." Booklist

"There is little text; most of the book consists of illustrations, step-by-step, of making pictures out of thumbprints. A few Emberley embellishments and a page that suggests other ways of making prints (carrot or potato) are included." Bull Cent Child Books

Temple, Kathryn

Drawing; the only drawing book you'll ever need to be the artist you've always wanted to be; [by] Kathryn Temple. 1st ed. Lark Books 2005 112p il (Art for kids) $17.95 (5 and up)

                                    741.2

1. Drawing

ISBN 1-57990-587-0   LC 2004-17909

Contents: Drawing basics; Line drawing; Light & shadow; Scale & proportion; Perspective; Faces & bodies; Still life and drawing nature; Drawing on the imagination; Composition

This "introduction to essential drawing techniques builds from the starting points of lines and simple shapes. . . . Eight concise chapters explore seeing with artist's eyes, line drawing, light and shadow, proportion and scale, perspective, drawing faces, drawing bodies, and using imagination. The succinct text reads smoothly and is written in a clear, understandable style. Sample sketches and crisp, color photographs extend the text." SLJ

Zemke, Deborah

2 is for Toucan; oodles of doodles from 0 to 42: a step-by-step drawing book. Blue Apple Books; distributed by Chronicle Books 2005 unp il spiral $12.95 (3-5)   **741.2**

1. Drawing

ISBN 1-59354-075-2

"This book presents simple to intermediate art activities that children will enjoy. . . . The drawings have numbers as their base, e.g., two swans are formed from 21. . . . A brief introduction explains that numerals are made up of curves and lines, and introduces the shapes used in the book (zigzag, waves, arch, curve, curl, and more). Drawing activities include a variety of animals and various other subjects. . . . Print is large and the design combines illustrations, color, and humorous touches that will appeal to budding artists." SLJ

741.5   Cartoons, caricatures, comics

Avery, Ben

Lullaby: Wisdom seeker; [by] Ben Avery, Mike S. Miller, and Hector Sevilla. Alias Enterprises 2005 96p il pa $9.99 (4-6)   **741.5**

1. Graphic novels

ISBN 1-933428-62-7

In this book, Alice never left Wonderland, she grew up to become the Queen's warrior. When dark magic threatens the world, Alice, haunted by vague memories of another life, sets out to discover the cause, and on the way she encounters the Pied Piper, Little Red Riding Hood (who is a werewolf), Jim Hawkins (from Treasure Island), and Pinocchio, as they all travel to Oz.

Azuma, Kiyohiko

Yotsuba&! volume 1; translated from Japanese by Javier Lopez. ADV Manga 2005 232p il pa $9.99 (2-4) **741.5**

1. Graphic novels

ISBN 1-4139-0317-7

The title is pronounced "yoh-tsoo-bah-toe" and means "Yotsuba and." There are currently three volumes available.

"In seven stories, the green-haired four-year-old discovers air conditioners, doorbells, cicadas, swings and more, and does it all with the energy of a small hurricane." Publ Wkly

Big fat Little Lit; [edited by] Art Spiegelman and Francoise Mouly. Puffin 2006 144p il pa $14.99 (2-4) **741.5**

1. Graphic novels

ISBN 0-14-240706-2

This volume collects all three previously published Little Lit books: *Little Lit: Once Upon a Time, Little Lit: Strange Stories for Strange Kids,* and *Little Lit: It Was a Dark and Silly Night.* Many comics creators and children's book writers and illustrators contributed stories, including Ian Falconer, Daniel Clowes, Maurice Sendak, David Sedaris, Chris Ware, Jules Feiffer, Barbara McClintock, Crockett Johnson, J. Otto Siebold, Neil Gaiman, Art Spiegelman, and Lemony Snicket.

Brennan, Michael

Electric Girl. AiT/PlanetLar 2000 168p il pa $9.95 (5 and up) **741.5**

1. Graphic novels

ISBN 0-9703555-0-5

Virginia is an average suburban girl except for her electric powers, which cause her to zap things all the time, and except for her invisible gremlin "friend" Oogleeoog, who has been with her since she was born. The stories go back and forth in time from her early childhood to her teen years and back again as the reader learns about Virginia's powers and how they affect her life.

"Facial expressions and body postures are fluid and evocative, while the verbal text is easy to read." SLJ

Other titles is this series are:

Electric Girl vol. 2 (2002)

Electric Girl vol. 3 (2005)

Bullock, Mike

Lions, tigers, and bears, vol. 1: Fear and pride; [by] Mike Bullock and Jack Lawrence. Image Comics 2006 128p il pa $12.99 (2-4) **741.5**

1. Graphic novels

ISBN 1-58240-657-X

When Joey Price has to move away from his grandmother, she gives him a new set of stuffed animals that she says will guard him from nightmares. And one night, he discovers that the stuffed animals are real, and unfortunately, so are the Beasties, the nightmares in his closet

Caldwell, Ben

Fantasy! cartooning; [by] Ben Caldwell. Sterling Pub. Co. 2005 95p il pa $9.95 (5 and up) **741.5**

1. Cartoons and comics 2. Drawing 3. Fantasy in art

ISBN 1-4027-1612-5 LC 2005041676

Caldwell's "drawing style is . . . a blend of modern Disney (Hercules, Mulan), Don Bluth (Dragon's Lair), and the Cartoon Network (Powderpuff Girls, Samurai Jack, Star Wars: Clone Wars). . . . Caldwell shows original thinking, and his technique is exciting, modern, and unique." SLJ

Crane, Jordan

The clouds above. Fantagraphics 2005 216p il $18.95 (3-5) **741.5**

1. Graphic novels

ISBN 1-560976-27-6

Simon and his cat Jack embark on an adventure among the clouds one day when Simon skips school and finds a rickety stairway leading skyward. They find a friendly cloud, flee thunderstorms and trick a flock of belligerent birds, only to find themselves back at school.

"Everything's exciting . . . and the dialogue is witty and bubbly. . . . The book is a joy to look at—Crane's loose, gliding lines burst with character, and his compositional gifts make every panel worth contemplating on its own." Publ Wkly

Crilley, Mark

Akiko pocket-size, vol. 1. Sirius Entertainment 2004 192p il pa $11.95 (3-5) **741.5**

1. Graphic novels

ISBN 1-579890-67-9

Fourth-grader Akiko travels to the planet Smoo, on a mission to rescue King Froptoppit's son from the evil Alia Rellapor. Teamed up with the scruffy adventurer Spuckler, bookish Mr. Beeba, Spuckler's robot Gax, and the floating alien known as Poog, Akiko faces sea monsters, Sky Pirates, Sleeslup worms, and other dangers as they travel around the planet on their quest. This is the first volume in an ongoing series of graphic novels. Crilley also has written a series of prose fiction featuring Akiko and her friends.

Czekaj, Jef

Grampa & Julie: Shark hunters. Top Shelf 128p il pa $14.95 (2-4) **741.5**

1. Graphic novels

ISBN 1-891830-52-X

"In this full-color graphic novel, Julie and her grampa spend summer vacation looking for the largest shark in the world, Stephen. Meeting Stephen leads to even more exciting adventures, including a quest to find Stephen's mom. The shark hunters meet monkeys at the bottom of the ocean, pirates, and even aliens. Gramma has to rescue them from a couple of scrapes." Booklist

"Taken from the pages of Nickelodeon magazine, this charming children's comic overflows with humor, adventure and whimsy." Publ Wkly

De Campi, Alex

Kat & Mouse: Teacher torture; [by] Alex de Campi; art by Frederica Manfredi. Tokyopop 2006 96p il pa $5.99 (4-6)   **741.5**

1. Graphic novels 2. Mystery fiction

ISBN 1-59816-548-8

Middle schooler Kat starts at a posh school where her father has been hired as the new science teacher, but all is not well. Accidents happen in the science lab, and an anonymous student threatens worse unless Kat's dad passes all the rich, popular students. Kat decides to investigate, aided by her one new friend, Mouse, the rebellious computer nerd and would-be CSI investigator.

Di Fiori, Lawrence

Jackie and the Shadow Snatcher; [by] Lawrence DiFiori. 1st ed. Alfred A. Knopf for Young Readers 2006 32p il $15.95; lib bdg $17.99 (k-3)   **741.5**

1. Graphic novels

ISBN 0-375-87515-8; 0-375-97515-2 (lib bdg)

                LC 2005018290

"In this picture-book-size graphic novel, Di Fiori uses black-and-white illustrations to tell the story of Jackie, a boy who has lost his lunch pail, his math book, and his shadow. Wise Mr. Socrates tells Jackie that the evil Shadow Snatcher is the thief, and Jackie must confront him to get his shadow back. . . . The scenery is beautifully detailed without overwhelming the panels. Children will care less about that, however, than about the rollicking, old-fashioned adventure." Booklist

Espinosa, Rod

The courageous princess. Antarctic Press 2004 c2003 240p il pa $24.95; pa $15.95 (3-5)   **741.5**

1. Graphic novels

ISBN 0-9728978-6-0; 1-9324533-6-9 (pa)

Plain Princess Mabelrose doesn't get along with the other, prettier princesses, but her intelligence helps her when a dragon kidnaps her. Instead of waiting for rescue, Mabelrose escapes, taking a friendly hedgehog and a few useful-looking items (a pouch, a length of rope) that she doesn't know are magic.

Giarrano, Vince

Comics crash course; [by] Vincent Giarrano. Impact Books 2004 127p il pa $19.99 (5 and up)   **741.5**

1. Cartoons and comics 2. Drawing

ISBN 1-58180-533-0   LC 2004-43969

This is a guide to creating comic book stories and characters.

This offers "plenty of great art advice, striking imagery, and just enough edginess to satisfy most aspiring comic-book artists. . . . An excellent introduction to comic drawing, composition, and graphic storytelling." SLJ

Goscinny

Asterix the Gaul; [by] René Goscinny and Albert Uderzo. Orion Media 2004 48p il map $12.95; pa $9.95 (4 and up)   **741.5**

1. Graphic novels

ISBN 0-7528-6604-4; 0-7528-6605-2 (pa)

Translated from the French

Meet Asterix, a diminutive but extremely strong Gaul living in ancient France during the time of the Roman Republic. Together with his friend Obelix, Asterix continually outwits the Roman Legionnaires sent to conquer Gaul for Julius Caesar. Full of puns and outrageous humor, the books also manage to teach a lot of history. This is the first in a long-running series of graphic novels translated from the original French.

  Other titles in this series are:

Asterix and Caesar's Gift

Asterix and Cleopatra

Asterix and the actress

Asterix and the banquet

Asterix and the big fight

Asterix and the cauldron

Asterix and the Goths

Asterix and the Great Crossing

Asterix and the laurel wreath

Asterix the legionary

Asterix and the Normans

Asterix and the Roman Agent

Asterix and the soothsayer

Asterix at the Olympic Games

Asterix in Belgium

Asterix in Britain

Asterix in Corsica

Asterix in Spain

Asterix in Switzerland

Asterix Obelix and Co.

Asterix the gladiator

Asterix The Mansions of the Gods

Gownley, Jimmy

Amelia rules! the whole world's crazy! ibooks 2003 176p il pa $14.95 (4 and up)   **741.5**

1. Graphic novels

ISBN 0-7434-7503-8

Also available self-published Renaissance Press edition 2006 through Diamond Press Distributors $24.95; pa $14.95 (ISBN 0-9712169-3-2; pa 0-9712169-2-4)

"Amelia . . . is getting used to life with her newly divorced mom and her hip, young aunt Tanner; settling in at a strange new school; and finding a group of friends. Amelia is no sweet innocent, nor are her three G.A.S.P (Gathering of Awesome Superpals) buddies: Reggie, superhero in the making; Rhonda, Amelia's tough bete noire with a fourth-grade 'thing' for Reggie; and quiet, mysterious Pajamaman. Jealousy, meanness, sadness, and confusion, as well as surprising generosity, and love crisscross the pages in energetic, freewheeling, full-color cartoon art that unwraps a kid'seye view of life honestly, poignantly, and with a hefty dollop of melodrama." Booklist

  Other titles in this series are:

Amelia rules!: What makes you happy? (2004)

Amelia rules! Superheroes (2005)

Guibert, Emmanuel

Sardine in outer space; [by] Emmanuel Guibert; illustrated by Joann Sfar; translated by Sasha Watson; colorist, Walter Pezzali. 1st American ed. First Second 2006 128p il pa $12.95 (3-5)

741.5

1. Graphic novels

ISBN 978-1-59643-126-3　　　　LC 2005021790

In this volume of twelve interconnected stories, little space pirate Sardine cruises in the spaceship Huckleberry with Uncle Yellow Shoulder and Little Louie. They do battle with Supermuscleman, who runs a tough space orphanage where children are taught "good behavior."

"Sfar's off-kilter, slightly uglified art, reminiscent of a toned-down Beavis and Butthead, gives the simple fun an unusual punch." Booklist

Hart, Christopher

Kids draw anime. Watson-Guptill 2002 64p il (Kids draw) pa $10.95 (3-6)　　　　741.5

1. Cartoons and comics 2. Drawing

ISBN 0-8230-2690-6　　　　LC 2002-6799

Provides step-by-step instructions for drawing a variety of human, animal, and other figures in the style of Japanese anime, covering general tips, details of specific features, and how to show action

"Though this book never gets beyond the drawing of single figures, it makes a good start for serious beginners." SLJ

Kids draw Manga Shoujo; [by] Christopher Hart. Watson Guptill Pub. 2005 54p il (Kids draw) pa $10.95 (1-4)　　　　741.5

1. Cartoons and comics 2. Drawing

ISBN 0-8230-2622-1　　　　LC 2004-19367

"Each page takes a character, then shows a step-by-step rendering starting with simple shapes and adding more detailed lines until the final figure is realized. *Manga Shoujo* is full of clean, bold colors and lines. . . . Hart's books are designed for young, casual fans who will appreciate the simplicity of the drawing style and will use these titles as an easy introduction to this art." SLJ

Mecha mania; how to draw the battling robots, cool spaceships, and military vehicles of Japanese comics. Watson-Guptill 2002 128p il pa $19.95 (5 and up)　　　　741.5

1. Cartoons and comics 2. Drawing

ISBN 0-8230-3056-3　　　　LC 2002-6402

"Hart offers budding cartoonists a mix of basic instructions and savvy technical advice for creating a wide variety of generic giant robots, robotlike craft, cyborgs of both sexes, and bad-guy types . . . then posing them for maximum visual effect. . . . His 'can-do!' tone and cogent instructions, as well as the gallery of chiseled, heavily armed, hypercomplicated machines, will make this volume appealing to both casual browsers and serious young artists." SLJ

Hastings, Jon

Terrabella Smoot and the unsung monsters. SLG Publishing 2005 48p il $10.95 (k-3)

741.5

1. Graphic novels 2. Monsters—Fiction

ISBN 1-59362-017-9

When she becomes separated from her family on the way to the Monster of the Year celebration, young monster Terrabella meets up with a loose-lipped dip and other creatures as she makes her way to Lord Thonk's castle. There, she discovers that Lord Thonk, the Monster of the Year, has imprisoned all the monster servants who actually performed the monstrous deeds, and she finds a way to bring justice to the celebration.

Hergé

The adventures of Tintin, vol. 1; Tintin in America, Cigars of the Pharaoh, The Blue Lotus. Little, Brown 1994 192p il $18.99 (4 and up)

741.5

1. Graphic novels

ISBN 0-316-35940-8

Tintin, the heroic boy reporter from France, travels to America where he outwits gangsters in Chicago of the 1930s and adventures in the wild West; sails the Mediterranean Sea with faithful dog Snowy and finds himself in a mystery involving a movie tycoon, drugs, and cigars in an ancient Egyptian tomb; then he travels to India to finally solve the mystery. This Little, Brown edition reprints some of the early Tintin adventures published in the 1930s in a 3-in-1 volume. This is the first in a series that reprints most of the Tintin stories by Herge. Librarians and teachers should note that the books retain some stereotypical depictions of people of other cultures and remember that these were acceptable and expected at the time of original publication.

Holm, Jennifer L.

Babymouse; queen of the world! [by] Jennifer Holm and Matthew Holm. Random House Books for Young Readers 2005 96p il lib bdg $12.99; pa $5.95 (3-5)　　　　741.5

1. Graphic novels 2. Mice—Fiction

ISBN 0-375-93229-1 (lib bdg); 0-375-83229-7 (pa)

LC 2004051166

"In this energetic comic . . . Babymouse, a wisecracking rodent stand-in for your average, adventure-seeking nine-year-old, strives to capture popular Felicia's goodwill, finally achieving her end at the expense of Wilson Weasel, truest of friends. But, wouldn't you know it, Felicia's world has little to offer a smart, fun-loving mouse, after all." Booklist

Other titles in this series are:

Babymouse: beach babe (2006)

Babymouse: our hero (2005)

Babymouse: rock star (2006)

Huey, Debbie

Bumperboy loses his marbles. Adhouse Books 2005 96p il pa $7.95 (2-4)   741.5

1. Graphic novels

ISBN 0976661004

Bumperboy is all set to play in the big Marble Tournament, but on his way to the park, he trips on a rock and his marbles including Grandma's prize shooter fall into a Borp Hole! Borp Holes are short cuts through many different lands, and Bumperboy must go through the Borp Hole and search as many of the lands as he can to find his marbles in time for the tournament.

Another title about Bumperboy is:

Bumperboy and the Loud Loud Mountain (2006)

Kochalka, James

Peanutbutter & Jeremy's best book ever. Alternative Comics 2003 280p il pa $14.95 (4 and up)   741.5

1. Graphic novels

ISBN 1-891867-46-6

Peanutbutter is a sweet cat who acts like a hardworking office cat but usually naps on top of the paperwork, and Jeremy is a troublemaking crow; and they are friends. Jeremy may seem spiteful and sometimes does very mean things to Peanutbutter, such as pretending to threaten the cat with a pistol, but most of the stories are silly and fun.

Kunkel, Mike

Herobear and the Kid, vol. 1: The Inheritance. Astonish Factory 2003 220p il pa $19.95 (3-5)   741.5

1. Graphic novels

ISBN 0-972125-91-4

Tyler's beloved grandfather died, leaving him an old stuffed bear and a broken pocket watch. It seems like a lousy inheritance, until the day Tyler learns that the toy bear becomes Herobear when he's in trouble, and that the pocket watch has a few cool tricks of its own. The real inheritance is that Tyler is supposed to take over his grandfather's job, which is still a secret.

Land of Sokmunster; [by] Mike Kunkel and Randy Heuser. Astonish Factory 2003 60p il $14.95 (2-4)   741.5

1. Graphic novels

ISBN 0-972125-92-2

Sam dives into the family dryer's lint trap when a sock comes out and steals a rare nickel then dives back in. He finds himself in a land where the lost socks go and learns that the sokmunsters don't care much for humans. When he and a sokmunster named Spike set out to rescue King Jacque's daughter from the evil Moth King, Sam starts to learn about friendship, trust, and forgiveness.

Lepp, Royden

David: Shepard's song, vol. 1. Cross Culture Entertainment/Alias Enterprises 2005 72p il pa $8.99 (3-5)   741.5

1. David, King of Israel—Fiction 2. Samuel (Biblical figure)—Fiction 3. Graphic novels 4. Bible stories

ISBN 1-933428-82-1

Anointed by the prophet Samuel as a young boy and mocked by his family, young David is hunted even by King Saul himself. While hiding in a cave, David looks back on the day that Samuel found him tending the sheep and anointed him to become the next King of Israel. This retelling can be exciting for any young reader.

Martin, Ann M.

The Baby-sitter's Club: Kristy's great idea; a graphic novel. Scholastic Graphix 2006 192p il $16.99; pa $8.99 (3-5)   741.5

1. Graphic novels

ISBN 0-439-80241-5; 0-439-73933-0 (pa)

LC 2005037749

Follows the adventures of Kristy and the other members of the Baby-sitters Club as they deal with crank calls, uncontrollable two-year-olds, wild pets, and parents who do not always tell the truth. A graphic novel based on the 1988 book by the same name.

"Comics artist Telgemeier's clean-lined, black-and-white art with stark black details nicely differentiates the four personable seventh-graders who parlay their babysitting experience into a business." Booklist

Mayne, Don

Draw your own cartoons! Williamson 2000 64p il (Quick starts for kids!) pa $7.95 (3-6)   741.5

1. Cartoons and comics 2. Drawing

ISBN 1-88559-376-7   LC 00-43484

This book offers instructions in drawing cartoons with emphasis on human figures and facial expressions

"Mayne covers the basics of creating a cartoon character well. . . . The kid-friendly tone, accessible format, and popular subject matter will make this one a winner with aspiring young cartoonists." SLJ

Medley, Linda

Castle waiting. Fantagraphics 2006 456p il $29.95 (5 and up)   741.5

1. Graphic novels 2. Fairy tales

ISBN 1-56097-747-7

All of Medley's previously self-published comics are collected here in one volume for the first time. The titular castle was the home of Sleeping Beauty, whose story is retold from the viewpoint of the flibbertigibbet ladies in waiting. After the flighty princess awakens with the kiss of a handsome but not too bright prince, the castle becomes a sanctuary for various misfits. Readers will find references to many fairy tales, folk tales, and nursery rhymes in Medley's book, and her clean, clear black-and-white art reflects the works of classic illustrators such as Arthur Rackham.

Oakley, Mark
Thieves & kings; [by Mark Oakley] I Box Pub 1998 154p il pa $18.95 (4 and up)   **741.5**
1. Graphic novels
ISBN 0-9681025-0-6   LC 2003-446777
Originally published as individual issues of the Thieves & kings comic series, beginning in 1994
In a story that mixes pages of text with pages of comic book art, the reader meets the young thief Rubel, who has returned home from a long voyage to find things no longer as they were. He has to deal with soldiers and pirates, princes and princesses, a strange young wizard, and a mysterious Shadow Lady.

O'Brien, Anne Sibley
The legend of Hong Kil Dong, the Robin Hood of Korea; [by] Anne Sibley O'Brien. Charlesbridge 2006 48p il $14.95 (3-5)   **741.5**
1. Graphic novels 2. Korea—Fiction
ISBN 978-1-58089-302-2   LC 2005056941
Based on a classic tale from early 17th century Korea. Hong Kil Dong is the son of a powerful government minister and one of his servants; this means the father will not recognize his son as his own. The boy grows up with great intelligence and wit, and leaves home to find his fortune. He learns martial arts and magic, and when he encounters thieves who rob only because corrupt government officials have ruined them, he turns the thieves into an army to right the wrongs. This story is based on a seventeenth century Korean legend.
Includes bibliographical references

Pellowski, Michael
The art of making comic books; [by] Michael Morgan Pellowski; with illustrations by Howard Bender. Lerner Publs. 1995 80p il (Media workshop) $21.27 (5 and up)   **741.5**
1. Cartoons and comics
ISBN 0-8225-2304-3; 0-8225-9672-5
                                LC 94-27589
"After a brief overview of comic-book history, the text describes the making of a comic book, explaining the various jobs people hold and the various stages books must go through. . . . Serious comic fans will relish Pellowski's detail-oriented and knowledgeable pragmatism." Bull Cent Child Books
Includes glossary and bibliographical references

Renier, Aaron
Spiral-bound. Top Shelf Production 2005 144p il pa $14.95 (4-6)   **741.5**
1. Graphic novels
ISBN 1-891830-50-3
"Turnip the elephant is using the summer to find his artistic voice through sculpture, his friend Stucky the dog is building a submarine, and Ana the rabbit is working on the town's underground newspaper. Their stories all wind around the town's deep, dark secret about the monster that lives in the pond. . . . The characters seem like real children, wholesome without being too sweet, and Renier's art is light and fun, a sort of Babar meets underground comix." Booklist

Roberts, Scott
Patty-cake and friends: color collection. SLG Publishing 2006 104p il pa $12.95 (4 and up)   **741.5**
1. Graphic novels
ISBN 1-59362-030-6
Patty-Cake (real name Patricia Bakerman), her family and her neighborhood friends star in a series of true-to-life everyday adventures and misadventures, including getting even with her older sister at the pool, helping her best friend Irving get even with his pesky older brother, going on her first train ride with her dad, and more. Roberts' exaggerated cartoon style is reminiscent of old Tex Avery cartoons, as characters fully express their emotions particularly anger and surprise. Some use of frank language may keep this book in public library collections.

Roche, Art
Cartooning; the only cartooning book you'll ever need to be the artist you've always wanted to be. Lark Books 2005 111p il (Art for kids) $17.95 (3-6)   **741.5**
1. Cartoons and comics 2. Drawing
ISBN 1-57990-623-0
Contents: Cartoons everywhere!; Cartooning materials; Making faces; Drawing bodies; Drawing stuff; Drawing animals; Writing jokes; Putting it all together; Publishing your cartoons; Draw, draw, draw!
"This how-to guide is a step above the average cartooning instruction book. The glossy, full-color pages are visually attractive. . . . Roche's engaging writing style is informative and fun. . . . His loose, spacious cartooning style is perfect for beginners or kids who might be intimidated by more detail-oriented techniques." SLJ

Runton, Andy
Owly: The way home and The bittersweet summer; [by] Andy Runton. Top Shelf 2004 160p il pa $10 (1-3)   **741.5**
1. Graphic novels 2. Owls—Fiction
ISBN 1-891830-62-7   LC 2005298860
Rotund little Owly befriends Wormy despite their differences, and together they help a couple of hummingbirds and learn that friendship doesn't end with separation.
"The whimsical black-and-white art is done with great facility for expressing emotion, and Runton's reliance on icons and pictures in lieu of the usual dialogue makes the story perfect for give-and-take between children and their parents." Booklist
Other titles in this series are:
Owly vol. 2: Just a little blue (2005)
Owly vol. 3: Flying lessons (2005)

Sava, Scott Christian
Ed's terrestrials. Alias Enterprises 2005 80p il $19.95 (2-4)   **741.5**
1. Graphic novels
ISBN 1-933428-64-3
Aliens have escaped from the Intergalactic Food Court, where they worked as slaves, and crashland into

Sava, Scott Christian—*Continued*
Ed's tree house. They all become friends, and the aliens want to help their fellow slaves come to Earth. But the Intergalactic Mall security officer, Maximus Obliterus, has come to send them back, and he has teamed up with Ed's school nemesis, Natalie.

Sfar, Joann

Little Vampire goes to school; stories and drawings by Joann Sfar; colors by Walter; translated by Mark and Alexis Siegel. Simon & Schuster Bks. for Young Readers 2003 40p il $12.95 (2-4)　　　　　**741.5**
1. Vampires—Fiction 2. Graphic novels
ISBN 0-689-85717-9　　　　　LC 2002-152656
A lonely little vampire, yearning for a friend, gets permission from the other monsters to go to school and makes the acquaintance of a boy who does not believe that vampires are real
Another title about Little Vampire is:
Little Vampire does kung fu! (2003)

Siegel, Siena Cherson

To dance: a ballerina's graphic novel; [by] Siena Cherson Siegel; illustrated by Mark Siegel. Simon & Schuster 2006 60p il pa $9.99 (4 and up)
　　　　　741.5
1. Ballet 2. Graphic novels 3. Puerto Ricans—Biography
ISBN 1-4169-2687-9
"Aladdin paperbacks"
In this memoir of her youth in dance from ages six to eighteen, Siegel tells what it was like to be totally involved in dance, in ballet—all the joys and the physical pain. She worked as a young dancer with George Ballanchine. Her absolute desire to be a dancer took her from her native Puerto Rico to New York City to study. Her simple but heartfelt narration is ably illustrated by her husband Mark Siegel.

Stanley, John

Little Lulu, vol. 1: My dinner with Lulu; [by] John Stanley and Irving Tripp. Dark Horse Comics 2005 200p il pa $9.95 (4 and up)　　　　　**741.5**
1. Graphic novels
ISBN 1-59307-318-6
Lulu Moppet plays with best friend Tubby, except when he hangs out with the other neighborhood boys and tries to keep girls out of their clubhouse; she deals with terrible toddler Alvin by weaving extravagant tales featuring herself; and other everyday adventures. This is the first volume of a series that will eventually reprint every Little Lulu comic for new young readers.
Other titles in this series are:
Little Lulu vol. 2: Sunday afternoon
Little Lulu vol. 3: Lulu in the doghouse
Little Lulu vol. 4: Lulu goes shopping
Little Lulu vol. 5: Lulu takes a trip
Little Lulu vol. 6: Letters to Santa
Little Lulu vol. 7: Lulu's umbrella
Little Lulu vol. 8: Late for school
Little Lulu vol. 9: Lucky Lulu

Little Lulu vol. 10: All dressed up
Little Lulu vol. 11: April fools
Little Lulu vol. 12: Leave it to Lulu
Little Lulu vol. 13: Too much fun

Thompson, Jill

Scary Godmother; written and illustrated by Jill Thompson. Sirius Entertainment 1997 48p il $19.95 (k-3)　　　　　**741.5**
1. Graphic novels 2. Halloween—Fiction
ISBN 1-57989-015-6　　　　　LC 99-196363
On Hannah Marie's first Halloween, her mean cousin Jimmy and his friends leave her at the haunted house, but instead of being scared, she meets Scary Godmother and the other inhabitants of the Night Side and has fun.
Other titles in this series are:
Scary Godmother: The boo flu (2000)
Scary Godmother: The mystery date (2006)
Scary Godmother: Ghoul's out for summer (2002)
Scary Godmother: Spooktacular stories (2006)
Scary Godmother: Wild about Harry (2001)

Varon, Sara

Sweaterweather. 2nd ed. Alternative Comics 2006 96p il pa $14.95 (3-5)　　　　　**741.5**
1. Graphic novels 2. Animals—Fiction 3. Stories without words
ISBN 1-891867-93-8
First published 2003
A turtle, a rabbit, and other creatures venture out on a wordless snowy journey full of friendship and sweetness. Varon includes interactive bits to the book, such as paper dolls, postcards, and stamps.

741.6　Graphic design, illustration and commercial art

The **art** of reading; forty illustrators celebrate RIF's 40th anniversary; with a foreword by Leonard S. Marcus. Dutton Bks. 2005 96p il lib bdg $19.99　　　　　**741.6**
1. Illustration of books 2. Illustrators
ISBN 0-525-47484-6
"Forty well-known, well-loved children's book illustrators share memories of a book . . . seminal to their development as readers and artists, and offer accompanying pieces of art—reimagined from those books. . . . This is a lovingly conceived, cohesive, and distinctively designed treasure. . . . Leonard S. Marcus's insightful and affecting foreword sets just the right anticipatory tone for readers who will be treated to spectacular pictures and often-moving personal statements." SLJ

Carle, Eric

The art of Eric Carle. Philomel Bks. 1996 125p il $35　　　　　**741.6**
1. Picture books for children 2. Illustration of books
ISBN 0-399-22937-X　　　　　LC 95-24940
This is "both a textual and visual anthology: in addition to Carle's autobiographical chapter and the text of his 1990 speech at the Library of Congress, chapters in-

Carle, Eric—*Continued*

clude accolades from Ann Beneduce (Carle's U.S. editor) and from Dr. Viktor Christen (Carle's German editor). A photoessay on the artist's collage technique rubs shoulders with a forty-page gallery of his illustrations over the last quarter of a century, which precedes a look at some of his quick sketches and an illustrated bibliography of his oeuvre. The book's inviting layout may appeal to artistic youngsters as well as grown Carle fans, and the information about his working process, particularly the technical details, is absorbing." Bull Cent Child Books

Christelow, Eileen

What do illustrators do? written and illustrated by Eileen Christelow. Clarion Bks. 1999 40p il $15 (1-3)   **741.6**

1. Illustration of books
ISBN 0-395-90230-4   LC 98-8297

Shows two illustrators going through all the steps involved in creating new picture books of "Jack and the Beanstalk," including layout, scale, and point-of-view

"Christelow gives readers a great deal of insight into the creative process while entertaining them. . . . The pen-and-ink and watercolor drawings are expressive and engaging throughout." SLJ

Cox, Sarah Mayor

Pictures telling stories; the art of Robert Ingpen; commentary by Sarah Mayor Cox. 1st American ed. Minedition 2005 c2004 112p il $35
                                                        741.6

1. Ingpen, Robert R. 2. Illustration of books
ISBN 0-698-40011-9   LC 2004-58784
First published 2004 in Hong Kong

"This Australian artist has illustrated over 100 books, fiction and nonfiction, in a career that spans over 40 years. His representational style is evocative as well as narrative. [This book] showcases some of his work and includes his commentaries about the selections in detailed captions. . . . Though the reproductions are the obvious stars of this book, there is a surprising amount of information in the captions and Sarah Mayor Cox's analytical commentaries on both the illustrations and Ingpen's working process." SLJ

Kushner, Tony

The art of Maurice Sendak; 1980 to present; text by Tony Kushner. Abrams 2003 223p il $60
                                                        741.6

1. Sendak, Maurice
ISBN 0-8109-4448-0   LC 2003-9293
Companion volume to The art of Maurice Sendak by Selma Lanes, published 1981 by Harry Abrams

This "collection presents 350 illustrations, many of which are drawings for set and costume design work, . . . others of which are posters for plays and for events such as the New York is Book Country fair. . . . Sendak's precise, intensely shaded yet welcoming shapes and figures have lost none of their luster. They would ordinarily be enough in themselves in a survey like this, but Kushner's lovely, funny, partisan text . . . lifts the book to another level." Publ Wkly
Includes bibliographical references

Marcus, Leonard S.

A Caldecott celebration; six artists and their paths to the Caldecott medal. Walker & Co. 1998 49p il $18.95   **741.6**

1. Caldecott Medal 2. Illustrators 3. Illustration of books
ISBN 0-8027-8656-1   LC 98-6616

Profiles six Caldecott award winning books and their authors, including Robert McCloskey's "Make Way for Ducklings," Marcia Brown's "Cinderella," Maurice Sendak's "Where the Wild Things Are," William Steig's "Sylvester and the Magic Pebble," Chris Van Allsburg's "Jumanji," and David Wiesner's "Tuesday"

"Marcus, who interviewed each artist, provides a lively, informative introduction to each book and its maker. A beautifully made book, this will serve as a fine resource for children interested in illustration and for teachers researching author/illustrator studies." Booklist
Includes glossary

Ways of telling; conversations on the art of the picture book. Dutton Children's Bks. 2002 247p il $29.99   **741.6**

1. Picture books for children 2. Illustrators 3. Authors
ISBN 0-525-46490-5   LC 2002-67499

Contents: Mitsumasa Anno; Ashley Brian; Eric Carle; Tana Hoban; Karla Kuskin; James Marshall; Robert McCloskey; Iona Opie; Helen Oxenbury; Jerry Pinkney; Maurice Sendak; William Steig; Rosemary Wells; Charlotte Zolotow

"This engaging volume offers insight into the creative process of each author and illustrator as well as the social and political contexts from which their work emerged." Publ Wkly

Stevens, Janet

From pictures to words; a book about making a book; written and illustrated by Janet Stevens. Holiday House 1995 unp il $16.95 (k-3)
                                                        741.6

1. Picture books for children 2. Authorship
ISBN 0-8234-1154-0   LC 94-18976

"Stevens, appearing as herself sketched in black-and-white, is the main character in her story. She's surrounded by . . . animal characters who encourage her to write a book starring them. With help from Cat, Koala Bear, and Rhino, she does, explaining as she goes along the basic elements of writing and illustrating—setting, plot, tension, and characterization." Booklist

"The straightforward text carefully presents information while maintaining the narrative flow. Dialogue balloons and funny asides from the characters keep the presentation lively." SLJ

Talking with artists [I-III]; compiled and edited by Pat Cummings. Bradbury Press 1992-1999 3v il v1 $22.95; v2-3 ea $22   **741.6**

1. Illustrators 2. Illustration of books
ISBN 0-02-724245-5 (v1); 0-689-80310-9 (v2 Simon & Schuster); 0-395-89132-9 (v3 Houghton Mifflin)
                                                        LC 91-9982

Volume two published by Simon & Schuster Bks. for Young Readers; volume 3 published by Clarion Bks.

Talking with artists [I-III]—*Continued*

Each volume presents interviews with illustrators, who discuss their lives and works. Among the 14 artists in the first volume are Victoria Chess, Leo and Diane Dillon, Amy Schwartz, Tom Feelings, and Steven Kellogg. The 13 artists represented in the second volume include Brian Pinkney, Denise Fleming, Floyd Cooper, Maira Kalman, and David Wisniewski. Samples of each illustrator's work are included

Under the spell of the moon; art for children from the world's great illustrators; [edited by Patricia Aldana; texts translated by Stan Dragland] Groundwood Books 2004 80p il $25

741.6

1. Illustration of books 2. Illustrators
ISBN 0-88899-559-8

This "collection features the artwork of children's book illustrators who, together, represent more than 25 countries. Each double-page spread includes a different artist's image accompanied by a poem, nursery rhyme, song, or bit of nonsense that appears in both English and the illustrator's native language. . . . Katherine Paterson offers a stirring introduction that discusses IBBY (The International Board on Books for Young People)." Booklist

Wings of an artist; children's book illustrators talk about their art; introduction by Julie Cummins; activity guide by Barbara Kiefer. Abrams 1999 31p il $17.95 **741.6**

1. Illustrators 2. Illustration of books
ISBN 0-8109-4552-5 LC 99-25906

More than twenty illustrators of children's books, including James Ransome, Robert Sabuda, Maira Kalman, and Maurice Sendak, talk about their work

"Aspiring artists, young and old, will be drawn to this collection. . . . It will serve as a useful art-education tool and as a stepping stone to discussions of fine art. An introduction and an idea-rich activity guide are also included." SLJ

741.9 Collections of drawings

—**I** never saw another butterfly—; children's drawings and poems from Terezin concentration camp, 1942-1944; edited by Hana Volavková; foreword by Chaim Potok; afterword by Vaclav Havel. expanded 2nd ed, by U.S. Holocaust Memorial Mus. Schocken Bks. 1993 xxii, 106p il pa $17.50 hardcover o.p. **741.9**

1. Child artists 2. Children's writings 3. Terezin (Czechoslovakia: Concentration camp)
ISBN 0-8052-1015-6 LC 92-50477

Original Czech edition, 1959; first American edition published 1964 by McGraw-Hill

"Of the 15,000 children who passed through Terezin before going to Auschwitz, only 100 lived. This book is a collection of poems and drawings by some of them. . . . This touching book adds another facet to library collections on the Holocaust." SLJ

Pericoli, Matteo

See the city; the journey of Manhattan unfurled; [by] Matteo Pericoli. 1st ed. Alfred A. Knopf 2004 unp il $15.95 (4 and up) **741.9**

1. Drawing 2. Manhattan (New York, N.Y.)
ISBN 0-375-82469-3 LC 2003-25881

"This depiction of Manhattan began as two continuous scrolls, one of the East Side, one of the West Side, each 37 feet long, which were published in 2001 (Random). The drawings in pen and ink depict the city skyline from the perspective of a boat tour taken around the island by Pericoli. . . . A personal narrative accompanies the drawings, affording insight into the creative processes of writing and illustrating. This is a fascinating work." SLJ

743 Drawing and drawings by subject

Ames, Lee J.

[Draw 50 series] Doubleday 1974-2003 21v pa each $8.95 (4 and up) **743**

1. Drawing

Available titles are: Draw 50 Airplanes, aircraft, and spacecraft; Draw 50 aliens; Draw 50 animal toons; Draw 50 animals; Draw 50 athletes; Draw 50 baby animals; Draw 50 beasties; Draw 50 birds; Draw 50 boats, ships, trucks, & trains; Draw 50 buildings and other structures; Draw 50 cats; Draw 50 dinosaurs and other prehistoric animals; Draw 50 dogs; Draw 50 endangered animals; Draw 50 famous faces; Draw 50 flowers, trees, and other plants; Draw 50 holiday decorations; Draw 50 horses; Draw 50 monsters; Draw 50 people; Draw 50 people from the Bible

Each volume presents step-by-step instructions for drawing a variety of animals, people, or objects

Court, Rob

How to draw cars and trucks; [by] Rob Court. Child's World 2005 32p il (Scribbles Institute) lib bdg $21.36 (4-6) **743**

1. Drawing 2. Automobiles 3. Trucks
ISBN 1-59296-148-7 LC 2004-3729

Contents: Drawing cars and trucks; Drawing with shapes; Drawing with lines; Freehand drawing; Three-dimensional form; Light and shadows; Drawing ideas; Patterns; Space and composition; Drawing with color; The artist's studio

This volume does "more than deconstruct objects into basic shapes then reconstruct them to show budding artists how to draw. [It] also [provides] information about select information of what's being drawn . . . which makes artists look harder at details and helps them better understand what they are creating. . . . [The author] introduces a few drawing fundamentals—perspective, shading, and composition—and supplies tips on choosing drawing pencils and using color to enliven a picture. . . . There's a lot more than just drawing practice here." Booklist

Emberley, Ed
Ed Emberley's drawing book of faces. Little, Brown 1975 32p il pa $6.95 hardcover o.p. (2-5)
743
1. Drawing 2. Face in art
ISBN 0-316-23655-1 (pa)
Provides step-by-step instructions for drawing a wide variety of faces reflecting various emotions and professions

745.4   Pure and applied design and decoration

Gonyea, Mark
A book about design; complicated doesn't make it good. Henry Holt 2005 unp il $18.95 (3-5)
745.4
1. Design
ISBN 0-8050-7575-5   LC 2004-08982
"This stylish, square volume delivers a cheerful manifesto on graphic design. . . . Chatty, brief chapters present principles of composition, line, color, and contrast, as well as techniques for drawing attention to 'what's important' on a page. . . . The text, set against pure white backdrops, is easy to read, and the artwork's elemental shapes and bright colors illustrate the theories in ways that children will readily grasp." Booklist

745.5   Handicrafts

Bruder, Mikyla
Button girl; more than 20 cute-as-a-button projects; photographs by Scott Nobles. Chronicle Books 2005 60p il spiral bdg $12.95 (5 and up)
745.5
1. Handicraft 2. Buttons
ISBN 0-8118-4553-2   LC 2004-8944
This offers instructions for creating 20 accessories including Button Barrettes and Bobbies, Hip Ribbon Button Belts, Crazy Coasters, and more.

Cano-Murillo, Kathy
The crafty diva's lifestyle makeover; awesome ideas to spice up your life; by Kathy Cano Murillo; illustrated by Carrie Wheeler; photography by John Samora. Watson-Guptill Pub. 2005 144p il pa $12.95 (5 and up)   **745.5**
1. Handicraft
ISBN 0-8230-1008-2
"Chapters include Redo Your Room, Wake Up Your Workout, and Get a Passion for Fashion. Complete with media references, each chapter includes three crafts with instructions, a difficulty meter for each one, and a list of needed supplies. A picture of the finished item, more ideas, and illustrations of supplies and the more difficult steps are included. The result is [a] fun, imaginative book." SLJ

Check, Laura
Create your own candles; 30 easy-to-make designs; illustrations by Norma Jean Martin-Jourdenais. Williamson Books 2004 62p il (Quick starts for kids!) pa $8.95 (5 and up)
745.5
1. Candles
ISBN 1-88559-352-X   LC 2004-40870
"Check begins this useful resource with 'Ten Hot Safety Tips.' . . . Next, she lists and describes basic equipment. . . . The projects range from simple beeswax candles to molded candles, hand-dipped candles, and gel candles." SLJ

Cook, Deanna F.
Kids' pumpkin projects; planting & harvest fun; illustrated by Kate Flanagan. Williamson 1998 98p il pa $8.95 (2-4)   **745.5**
1. Handicraft 2. Pumpkin
ISBN 1-885593-21-X   LC 97-48366
"A Williamson good times! book"
Provides instructions for fifty projects and activities involving pumpkins, including growing them, using them in recipes, and making things out of them

Dall, Mary Doerfler
Little Hands create! art & activities for kids ages 3 to 6; [by] Mary Dall; illustrations by Sarah Rakitin. Williamson Books 2004 118p il pa $9.95 (k-2)   **745.5**
1. Handicraft
ISBN 1-88559-365-1   LC 2004-40872
"A Williamson Little Hands book"
"Although Dall's text is addressed to the little ones who will be making these projects . . . it's really for adult helpers, who can read the instructions aloud as they shepherd their charges through a wealth of crafts activities—from twisted-paper jewelry to pictures and sculptures. Most of the projects depend on readily available materials. . . . The directions are clear. . . . Dall extends the fun with some bright, silly poems and occasional suggestions of simple games to play or picture books that dovetail nicely with the craft. . . . Great for teachers, daycare providers, or anyone looking for rainy-day activities for the very young." Booklist

Diehn, Gwen
Nature smart; awesome projects to make with mother nature's help; [by] Gwen Diehn, Terry Krautwurst, & Bobbie Needham. Main Street 2003 398p il pa $19.95 (3-6)   **745.5**
1. Nature craft 2. Outdoor recreation 3. Natural history
ISBN 1-4027-0515-8   LC 2004-296262
More than 150 nature crafts, including: wind vanes, beach baskets, bird feeders, scented soap, barometers, egg shell mosaics, etc.
"The directions are given in readable prose, accompanied by instructive and attractive photographs. . . . The science snippets scattered throughout the book give fascinating and accurate factual information. . . . This is a wonderful and practical book." Sci Books Films

Haab, Sherri

Dangles and bangles; 25 funky accessories to make and wear; by Sherri Haab and Michelle Haab; with illustrations by Barbara Pollak. Watson-Guptill Pub. 2005 96p il pa $9.95 (5 and up)   **745.5**

   1. Jewelry 2. Handicraft

   ISBN 0-8230-0064-8

This describes "jewelry hardware, . . . tools, glues and adhesives, and . . . craft supplies, as well as ideas about where to purchase these materials. A spread on basic techniques explains how to work with cord and elastic, glue, rings/pins, etc. The projects . . . range from necklaces to key chains to hair accessories. . . . The mix of colorful photographs, full-page paintings of stylishly dressed youngsters, and varied typefaces makes for an attractive layout. Packed full of wonderful ideas, this irresistible title will be popular with young crafters as well as with adults who plan craft programs." SLJ

Hauser, Jill Frankel

Kids' crazy concoctions; 50 mysterious mixtures for art & craft fun; illustrated by Loretta Trezzo Braren. Williamson 1995 156p il pa $12.95 (3-6)
745.5

   1. Handicraft

   ISBN 0-913589-81-0   LC 94-4633

"A Williamson kids can! book"

"Hauser includes recipes for homemade papers, glues, paints, molding doughs and clay; they are followed by directions for making decorator boxes, stationery, books, bookmarks, gift tags, mobiles, sand paintings, ornaments, toys, stained-glass art, and jewelry. Illustrated with pen-and-ink sketches, each project begins with a 'What You Need' list and numbered steps of 'What You Do.'. . . An outstanding practical resource for classrooms." SLJ

Hendry, Linda

Cat crafts; written and illustrated by Linda Hendry. Kids Can Press 2002 40p il (Kids can do it) $12.95; pa $5.95 (4-6)   **745.5**

   1. Handicraft 2. Cats

   ISBN 1-55074-964-1; 1-55074-921-8 (pa)

This includes instructions for 17 craft projects including a spider cat toy, a scratch pad, a catnip fish, and decorated placemats, earrings, and bookends

"Nicely designed, double-page spreads show the project step-by-step, each one clearly and succinctly described and illustrated with a color drawing." Booklist

Dog crafts; written and illustrated by Linda Hendry. Kids Can Press 2002 40p il (Kids can do it) $12.95; pa $5.95 (4-6)   **745.5**

   1. Handicraft 2. Dogs

   ISBN 1-55074-960-9; 1-55074-962-5 (pa)

This includes instructions for 17 craft projects including decorated jars, picture frames, placemats, jewelry, and bookends

"Nicely designed, double-page spreads show the project step-by-step, each one clearly and succinctly described and illustrated with a color drawing." Booklist

Horse crafts; written and illustrated by Linda Hendry. Kids Can Press 2006 40p il (Kids can do it) $12.95; pa $6.95 (4-6)   **745.5**

   1. Handicraft 2. Horses

   ISBN 1-55337-646-3; 1-55337-647-1 (pa)

This includes instructions for craft projects including drawing a horse, making a silhouette, a pencil top, a lampshade, a pin, a browband cover, a mirror, a plaque, a clipboard, a pillow, a keepsake box, a blue jean bag, bookends, a CD box, and a sock horse.

Irvin, Christine M.

Egg carton mania. Children's Press 2002 32p il (Craft mania) lib bdg $22; pa $6.95 (k-2)
745.5

   1. Handicraft

   ISBN 0-516-22277-5 (lib bdg); 0-516-27758-8 (pa)

                     LC 00-65647

"Projects include making a collection box, finger puppets, and a game board. . . . Each project is presented on a double-page spread with a list of materials, simple directions, 'Other Ideas' for variations on the theme, and a number of brightly colored illustrations." Booklist

Martin, Laura C.

Nature's art box; from t-shirts to twig baskets: 65 cool projects for crafty kids to make with natural materials you can find anywhere; written by Laura C. Martin; with drawings by David Cain. Storey Bks. 2003 215p il $23.95; pa $16.95 (4 and up)   **745.5**

   1. Nature craft

   ISBN 1-58017-503-1; 1-58017-490-6 (pa)

                LC 2002-154374

"Each chapter includes information about historical and ethnic uses for the natural substances. Activities are rated by level of difficulty; all have easy-to-follow instructions. Projects range from baskets, picture frames, wreaths, necklaces, and gift wrap to body paint, amulet bags, and painted stones. . . . The projects display a respect for nature and art, and a simple, subtle beauty." SLJ

Includes bibliographical references

Press, Judy

Around-the-world art & activities; visiting the 7 continents through craft fun; illustrations by Betsy Day. Williamson 2001 128p il (Williamson Little Hands book) pa $12.95 (k-2)   **745.5**

   1. Handicraft

   ISBN 1-88559-345-7   LC 00-60030

"North American totem poles, Hawaiian leis, Aboriginal bark painting, Japanese dolls in kimonos, Korean drums, egg-carton camels, Masai beaded necklaces, nesting Russian dolls, and South American gaucho belts are among the projects. While the ideas will not be new to veteran crafters, they are basic and solid for the intended audience." SLJ

Press, Judy—*Continued*

ArtStarts for little hands! fun & discoveries for 3- to 7-year olds; illustrations by Karol Kaminski. Williamson 2000 118p il (Williamson Little Hands book) pa $12.95 (k-2) **745.5**
1. Handicraft
ISBN 1-88559-337-6 LC 99-89956
Presents a variety of art projects and related activities grouped around such themes as the family, animals, nature, transportation, color, and more

"These simple activities use easy-to-find materials such as egg cartons, paper plates, craft sticks, and paper-towel tubes. The directions are easy to follow and are supplemented with clear, black-line drawings of almost every step." SLJ

The kids' natural history book; making dinos, fossils, mammoths & more! illustrations by Michael Kline. Williamson 2000 132p il pa $12.95 (3-5) **745.5**
1. Handicraft 2. Natural history
ISBN 1-88559-324-4 LC 98-30052
"A Williamson kids can! book"
Arts, crafts, and nature activities explore various elements of the natural world, including ocean life, insects, dinosaurs, amphibians and reptiles, birds, mammals, and early man

"The light yet informative tone is reflected in the illustrations, which include jaunty, cartoonlike figures of people and animals as well as scientifically accurate drawings." Booklist

The little hands big fun craft book; creative fun for 2- to 6-year-olds; illustrated by Loretta Trezzo Braren. Williamson 1996 142p il (Williamson Little Hands book) pa $12.95 **745.5**
1. Handicraft
ISBN 0-913589-96-9 LC 95-17574
This includes "seventy five simple arts-and-crafts projects. . . . In the introduction, the author explains the 'whole learning' concept on which the activities are based and gives safety tips for working with young children. The crafts are organized under general headings, such as 'Animals and Trees,' 'Friendship,' and 'Family Fun.' . . . Of special interest to teachers and childcare providers is the section called 'Big Fun in Special Places,' which includes great pre- or post field trip projects relating to the zoo, circus, museum, library, aquarium, etc. Black-and-white cartoon drawings make the directions even easier to understand." SLJ

Sattler, Helen Roney

Recipes for art and craft materials; with new illustrations by Marti Shohet. rev ed. Lothrop, Lee & Shepard Bks. 1987 144p il pa $4.95 hardcover o.p. (4 and up) **745.5**
1. Handicraft—Equipment and supplies 2. Artists' materials
ISBN 0-688-13199-9 (pa) LC 86-34271
First published 1973
The author explains "how to make pastes and glues, modeling compounds, papier-mâché, casting compounds, paints, inks, flower preservatives, recycled paper, and more. Activities are studies in applied science that can

provoke questions that invite investigations, encourage careful observation, and celebrate the cleverness of hands as well as brain." Sci Child

Schwarz, Renée

Funky junk; cool stuff to make with hardware. Kids Can Press 2003 40p il (Kids can do it) $12.95; pa $5.95 (4-6) **745.5**
1. Handicraft
ISBN 1-55337-387-1; 1-55337-388-X (pa)
This offers ideas for craft projects using materials found "at the hardware store. Directions are given for turning nuts, bolts, corner braces, and so on into jewelry, a chess set, and more." SLJ

Silver, Patricia

Face painting; written by Patricia Silver (Patty the clown); illustrated by Louise Phillips. Kids Can Press 2000 40p il (Kids can do it) $12.95; pa $5.95 (4-6) **745.5**
1. Face painting
ISBN 1-55074-845-9; 1-55074-689-8 (pa)
The author "includes step-by-step instructions for 16 of the most commonly requested faces, rules for safety, and the all-important cleanup tips. Clear, full-color photographs and drawings of children in the makeup accompany the instructions. These simple illustrations are charming and helpful." SLJ

St. Pierre, Stephanie

The Muppets' big book of crafts; by The Muppet Workshop and Stephanie St. Pierre; illustrations by Stephanie Osser; photographs by John E. Barrett. Workman 1999 322p il pa $18.95 (2-5) **745.5**
1. Handicraft
ISBN 0-7611-0526-3 LC 99-38606
Includes instructions for creating all kinds of craft projects, including rugs, placemats, costumes, masks, jewelry, models, puppets, and more

"A fun-filled, delightful book. . . . The directions are clear and complete, yet children will feel free to improvise. A sense of joy prevails in the instructions for the wildly funny as well as the more useful activities. Witty illustrations are populated by Muppet characters." SLJ

Temko, Florence

Traditional crafts from Africa; with illustrations by Randall Gooch; and photographs by Robert L. and Diane Wolfe. Lerner Publs. 1996 64p il maps (Culture crafts) lib bdg $23.93 (4 and up) **745.5**
1. Handicraft 2. Africa—Social life and customs
ISBN 0-8225-2936-X LC 95-8109
"Each chapter focuses on one craft technique and includes a project from a specific African region. Vivid maps of each region show its climate and the culture of its people. . . . Bright, full-color photographs accompany descriptions of technique. Clear diagrams demonstrate how to make reproductions of the crafts with readily available materials." SLJ
Includes glossary and bibliographical references

Temko, Florence—_Continued_

Traditional crafts from China; with illustrations by Randall Gooch. Lerner Publs. 2001 64p il (Culture crafts) lib bdg $23.93 (4 and up)

745.5

1. Handicraft 2. China—Social life and customs
ISBN 0-8225-2939-4   LC 99-50692

Explains the meaning of Chinese culture which is found in eight traditional handicrafts and provides instructions for creating them

The author's "clear and consistent, step-by-step directions are easy to follow and the required materials are easily obtainable." SLJ

Includes glossary and bibliographical references

Traditional crafts from Japan; with illustrations by Randall Gooch. Lerner Publs. 2001 64p il (Culture crafts) lib bdg $23.93 (4 and up)

745.5

1. Handicraft 2. Japan—Social life and customs
ISBN 0-8225-2938-6   LC 99-50690

Explains the meaning of Japanese culture which is found in eight traditional handicrafts and provides instructions for creating them

Includes glossary and bibliographical references

Traditional crafts from Mexico and Central America; with illustrations by Randall Gooch and photographs by Robert L. and Diane Wolfe. Lerner Publs. 1996 63p il (Culture crafts) lib bdg $23.93 (4 and up)

745.5

1. Handicraft 2. Mexico—Social life and customs
ISBN 0-8225-2935-1   LC 95-46583

Provides instructions on how to make traditional Mexican and Central American handicraft such as metal ornaments, tissue paper banners, and Guatemalan worry dolls

"The directions and pictures are clear and enticing; there are full-color photographs of the completed projects as well as of the original handiwork that inspired them." SLJ

Includes glossary and bibliographical references

Traditional crafts from native North America; with illustrations by Randall Gooch; and photographs by Robert L. and Diane Wolfe. Lerner Publs. 1997 64p il map (Culture crafts) lib bdg $23.93 (4 and up)

745.5

1. Handicraft 2. Native American art
ISBN 0-8225-2934-3   LC 96-4973

Provides instructions for making such traditional North American Indian crafts as dreamcatchers, beadwork, and cornhusk dolls

Includes glossary and bibliographical references

Traditional crafts from the Caribbean; with illustrations by Randall Gooch. Lerner Publs. 2001 64p il (Culture crafts) lib bdg $23.93 (4 and up)

745.5

1. Handicraft 2. Caribbean region—Social life and customs
ISBN 0-8225-2937-8   LC 00-8968

Provides instructions on how to make traditional Caribbean Island handicrafts such as Jamaican woven fish, Puerto Rican vejigante masks, and tap-tap trucks

Includes glossary and bibliographical references

Torres, Laura

Best friends forever! 199 crafts to make and share; . Workman Pub. 2004 148p il pa $13.95 (5 and up)

745.5

1. Handicraft
ISBN 0-7611-3274-0   LC 2004-45635

"These projects are organized into seven categories: 'Photo Fun,' 'Cool Notes,' 'Gifts to Make Together,' 'Home and School,' 'Fashions,' 'Fun and Games,' and 'Jewelry.' . . . Using clear language, detailed directions, and bright color photos of the finished products, Torres has pulled together a wealth of craft ideas." SLJ

745.54   Paper handicrafts

Boursin, Didier

Easy origami. Firefly 2005 64p il $19.95; pa $9.95 (4 and up)

745.54

1. Origami 2. Paper crafts
ISBN 1-55297-928-8; 1-55297-939-3 (pa)

This guide provides step-by-step instructions for 24 origami projects, ranked as very easy, easy, and detailed, and the book includes tips for best results.

"Paper-folding novices in particular may be drawn to this collection by its unusually clean design and bright, inviting colors." SLJ

Check, Laura

Little Hands paper plate crafts; creative art fun for 3- to 7-year-olds; illustrations by Norma Jean Martin-Jourdenais. Williamson 2000 128p il (Williamson Little Hands book) pa $12.95 (k-2)

745.54

1. Paper crafts
ISBN 1-88559-343-0   LC 00-43483

This "gives suggestions for creating sea animals, insects, frogs, turkeys, lions, tigers, and other animals. Instructions are also given for making masks, hats, and seasonal crafts. The instructions are very simple." SLJ

Includes bibliographical references

Henry, Sandi

Cut-paper play! dazzling creations from construction paper; illustrations by Norma Jean Jourdenais. Williamson 1997 160p il pa $12.95

745.54

1. Paper crafts
ISBN 1-88559-305-8   LC 96-33183

"A Williamson kids can! book"

Contains instructions for more than eighty two- and three-dimensional construction paper creations, including a Matisse cut-out, a hanging snake mobile, and a personal desk top robot

"Black-line drawings accompany the easy-to-follow directions and most projects do not need more than construction paper, scissors, and glue to complete." SLJ

Irvin, Christine M.

Paper cup mania. Children's Press 2002 32p il (Craft mania) lib bdg $22; pa $6.95 (k-2)

745.54

1. Paper crafts

ISBN 0-516-22278-3 (lib bdg); 0-516-27760-X (pa)

LC 00-65644

This offers instructions for craft projects made from paper cups including a pyramid, ghost, telephone, robot, and windmill

"The steps are clearly numbered, and the directions are easy to understand. . . . The bright, color illustrations of the completed objects and steps are realistic and precise." SLJ

Paper plate mania. Children's Press 2002 31p il (Craft mania) lib bdg $22; pa $6.95 (k-2)

745.54

1. Paper crafts

ISBN 0-516-21675-9 (lib bdg); 0-516-27761-8 (pa)

LC 00-46604

This offers instructions for craft projects made from paper plates including Halloween pumpkin masks, string art, necklaces, a snake, and a sun catcher

"The steps are clearly numbered, and the directions are easy to understand. . . . The bright, color illustrations of the completed objects and steps are realistic and precise." SLJ

Johnson, Ginger

Paper-folding fun! 50 awesome crafts to weave, twist & curl; illustrations by Betsy Day. Williamson 2002 128p il pa $12.95 (3-5)

745.54

1. Paper crafts

ISBN 1-88559-367-8

LC 2002-16825

"A Williamson kids can! book"

Provides step-by-step instructions for creating fifty paper crafts, including pop-up greeting cards, stacking boxes, folded journals, and three-dimensional creatures, plus "magic" paper tricks

"Each project begins with a picture of the finished product, a list of materials, and good, step-by-step directions. . . . This shows how to make a number of appealing projects using inexpensive and readily available materials." Booklist

Lewis, Amanda

The jumbo book of paper crafts; written by Amanda Lewis; illustrated by Jane Kurisu. Kids Can Press 2002 160p il pa $14.95 (3-6)

745.54

1. Paper crafts

ISBN 1-55074-940-4

This "book presents craft projects from five paper-art categories: folding, cutting, weaving, paper gluing, and papermaking." Booklist

"Each craft has a full page or spread with clear, easy-to-understand, full-color illustrations and clear step-by-step instructions." SLJ

Rhatigan, Joe

Paper fantastic; 50 creative projects to fold, cut, glue, paint & weave; [by] Joe Rhatigan & Rain Newcomb. Lark Bks. 2004 111p $19.95 (3-6)

745.54

1. Paper crafts

ISBN 1-57990-476-9

LC 2003-15802

Provides step-by-step instructions for creating fifty objects from paper, as well as an explanation of the various tools required to make these and many other decorative or fun paper products.

The author and illustrator provide "concise, clear instructions and full-color photographs to show how each step progresses to the finished product. [The book presents] interesting projects that are easy to complete and will appeal to this audience." SLJ

745.58 Handicrafts from beads, found and other objects

Scheunemann, Pam

Cool beaded jewelry; [by] Pam Scheunemann. Abdo Pub 2005 32p il (Cool crafts) $22.78 (4-6)

745.58

1. Beadwork 2. Jewelry

ISBN 1-59197-739-8

LC 2004-46292

This "has an extensive section on bead history, sizes, shapes, types, and metal findings (clasps, etc.). Projects include a memory wire bracelet, a beaded necklace and bracelet, daisy chain necklace, and beaded rings." SLJ

745.59 Making specific objects

Hufford, Deborah

Greeting card making; send your personal message; by Deborah Hufford. Capstone Press 2006 32p il (Snap books crafts) $25.26 (3-5)

745.59

1. Greeting cards 2. Handicraft

ISBN 0-7368-4385-X

LC 2005006899

"A pop-up birthday cake, a dried flower-petal design, and a lacey valentine are among the homemade card ideas featured in this simple, easy-to-follow title. . . . Introductory pages cover basic paper folds and materials; later spreads present mostly clear, step-by-step instructions." Booklist

Includes glossary and bibliographical references

745.592 Toys, models, miniatures, related objects

Kelly, Emery J.

Paper airplanes; models to build and fly; illustrations by Darren Erickson; photographs by Richard Trombley. Lerner Publs. 1997 64p il lib bdg $23.93 (4 and up)

745.592

1. Airplanes—Models 2. Paper crafts

ISBN 0-8225-2401-5

LC 96-10909

Kelly, Emery J.—*Continued*

Presents information on aerodynamic principles and flying techniques along with instructions for making twelve different paper airplanes

"The photos of the finished planes will have kids itching to make and fly them. Fortunately, the materials (paper, paperclips, tape) are readily available, and the instructions and patterns are clear." Booklist

Mahren, Sue

Make your own teddy bears & bear clothes! illustrations by Stan Jaskiel. Williamson 2001 63p il (Quick starts for kids!) pa $7.95 (3-6)

745.592

1. Teddy bears 2. Sewing 3. Handicraft
ISBN 1-88559-375-9   LC 00-47718

"Instructions for making a 6-inch minibear and a 16-inch hugging bear require such standard items as scissors, needle and thread, and paper for tracing patterns. Neither a sewing machine nor a sewing background is needed. . . . The patterns are clearly drawn and easily traced. . . . The patterns for the articles of clothing are also no-sew or sew-easy." SLJ

Includes glossary

Pinchuk, Amy

Make amazing toy and game gadgets; illustrated by Allan Moon and Tina Holdcroft. HarperCollins Pubs. 2001 64p il (Popular mechanics for kids) $21.95; pa $12.95 (4 and up)   **745.592**

1. Toys 2. Mechanics
ISBN 1-894379-13-6; 1-894379-14-4 (pa)

This book offers instructions on creating a light box, battery-powered flash jewelry, a pinhole camera, a buzzer game and flashing sunglasses

Includes glossary

Simon, Seymour

The paper airplane book; illustrated by Byron Barton. Viking 1971 48p il pa $6.99 (3-5)

745.592

1. Airplanes—Models 2. Paper crafts
ISBN 0-14-030925-X

Step-by-step instructions for making paper airplanes with suggestions for experimenting with them

745.593   Useful objects

Price, Pamela S.

Cool scrapbooks; [by] Pam Price. Abdo Pub 2005 32p il (Cool crafts) $22.78 (4-6)

745.593

1. Scrapbooks
ISBN 1-59197-744-4   LC 2004-46290

This guide to scrapbooks "addresses the use of photos, embellishments, adding words, computer possibilities, and more. . . . [This book lists] required materials, [has] small color photos, and [includes] clearly explained, numbered steps." SLJ

745.594   Decorative objects

Ancona, George

The piñata maker: El piñatero. Harcourt Brace & Co. 1994 unp il $17; pa $9 (k-3)

745.594

1. Paper crafts 2. Bilingual books—English-Spanish 3. Mexico—Social life and customs
ISBN 0-15-261875-9; 0-15-200060-7 (pa)

      LC 93-2389

Describes how Don Ricardo, a craftsman from Ejutla de Crespo in southern Mexico, makes piñatas for all the village birthday parties and other fiestas

"Ancona tells his story in both English and Spanish, with both languages on every page. His clear, bright, full-color photographs complement the detailed text, giving the reader much additional information." Horn Book

Bledsoe, Karen E.

Chinese New Year crafts; [by] Karen E. Bledsoe. 1st ed. Enslow Publishers 2005 32p il (Fun holiday crafts kids can do) lib bdg $22.60 (2-4)   **745.594**

1. Handicraft 2. Chinese New Year
ISBN 0-7660-2347-8   LC 2004-9622

This includes directions for ten craft projects related to Chinese New Year including a dragon-streamer puppet, a ribbon lantern, and Chinese zodiac pictures.

This is "aesthetically pleasing with . . . bright colorful pages, clear concise instructions on the left side and photographs of various stages of the final product on the right. . . . Use of everyday items such as paper cups, cupcake liners, and construction paper makes these activities practical for both students and teachers." SLJ

Includes bibliographical references

Gnojewski, Carol

Cinco de Mayo crafts; [by] Carol Gnojewski. 1st ed. Enslow Publishers 2004 32p il (Fun holiday crafts kids can do) lib bdg $22.66 (2-4)

745.594

1. Handicraft 2. Cinco de Mayo
ISBN 0-7660-2344-3   LC 2004-9624

This includes instructions for ten craft projects related the Cinco de Mayo including a peace votive, sombrero, and paper poncho.

This is "aesthetically pleasing with . . . bright colorful pages, clear concise instructions on the left side and photographs of various stages of the final product on the right. . . . Use of everyday items such as paper cups, cupcake liners, and construction paper makes these activities practical for both students and teachers." SLJ

Includes bibliographical references

Levine, Shar

The ultimate balloon book; 46 projects to blow up, bend & twist; [by] Shar Levine and Michael Ouchi. Sterling 2000 96p il pa $9.95 (5 and up)

745.594

1. Balloons 2. Handicraft
ISBN 0-8069-2959-6   LC 00-61899

Levine, Shar—*Continued*

The authors "explore the possibilities and the methods of making animals, bracelets, hats, costumes, and even playhouses from balloons. . . . Beginning with information about materials, techniques, and safety, the book goes on to explain how to make a wide variety of projects, which are clearly illustrated with step-by-step line drawings as well as colorful photos of the evolving shapes. An appealing and practical guide." Booklist

Newcomb, Rain

The Girls' World book of jewelry: 50 cool designs to make. Lark Books 2004 127p il pa $14.95 (5 and up)   **745.594**

1. Jewelry 2. Handicraft

ISBN 1-57990-473-4   LC 2004-4990

This offers instructions for jewelry making projects such as bracelets made of copper washers or from old wooden game pieces, or chokers made from small metal flower embellishments to a ribbon.

"This exciting collection contains clear directions, sharp photos, and precise illustrations." SLJ

Sadler, Judy Ann

Christmas crafts from around the world; written by Judy Sadler; illustrated by June Bradford. Kids Can Press 2003 40p il (Kids can do it) $12.95; pa $6.95 (4-6)   **745.594**

1. Handicraft 2. Christmas decorations

ISBN 1-55337-427-4; 1-55337-428-2 (pa)

"From cranberry and popcorn garlands (U.S.) to woven hearts (Denmark) to a piñata (Mexico) to a crinkle-paper chain (South Africa), these 17 projects for craft-confident readers also include snippets of information on how and why the holiday is celebrated in a variety of countries. A photograph of each finished product is provided, along with a list of materials needed and succinct but clear instructions. Small but clear illustrations guide reader through each step." SLJ

745.7   Decorative coloring

Souter, Gillian

Paints plus. Stevens, G. 2001 48p il (Handy crafts) lib bdg $22.60 (2-5)   **745.7**

1. Painting 2. Handicraft

ISBN 0-8368-2821-6   LC 00-52243

The book describes painting tools including sponges, toothbrushes, and cotton swabs, and gives instructions on decorating book covers, pillowcases, place mats, flowerpots, gift wrap, and stationery

This book gets high marks for its "simplicity and practicality. . . . Colorful drawings and clear photos leave little doubt about how to complete each step." SLJ

Includes bibliographical references

Wagner, Lisa

Cool painted stuff; [by] Lisa Wagner. Abdo Pub 2005 32p il (Cool crafts) $22.78 (4-6)

745.7

1. Painting 2. Handicraft

ISBN 1-59197-742-8   LC 2004-53117

This guide to painted crafts "includes four projects (in six or seven steps): a flowered mini-tote, checkered frame, treasure box, and fancy flowerpot. [This book lists] required materials, [has] small color photos, and [includes] clearly explained, numbered steps." SLJ

746   Textile arts

Sadler, Judy Ann

Making fleece crafts; written by Judy Ann Sadler; illustrated by June Bradford. Kids Can Press 2000 40p il (Kids can do it) $12.95; pa $5.95 (4-6)   **746**

1. Sewing 2. Handicraft

ISBN 1-55074-847-5; 1-55074-739-8 (pa)

"Mittens, a scarf, a jester's hat, a beanbag animal, and a pillow are a few of the 15 . . . projects included. There are further instructions for stitched-on and iron-on appliqués and actual traceable patterns for several of the crafts. A mix of full-color photographs and drawings results in an attractive and effective presentation." SLJ

746.4   Needlework and handwork

The **jumbo** book of needlecrafts; written by Judy Ann Sadler [et al]; illustrated by Esperaça Melo [et al.] Kids Can Press 2005 208p il $16.95 (4-6)   **746.4**

1. Needlework

ISBN 1-55337-793-1

A compilation with a new introduction of 5 books previously published: Knitting by Judy Ann Sadler (2002); Crocheting by Gwen Blakely Kinsler (2003); Simply sewing by Judy Ann Sadler (2004); Embroidery by Judy Ann Sadler (2004); Quilting by Biz Storms (2001)

This is a "how-to guide to the basics of knitting, crocheting, embroidery, quilting, and sewing. . . . The volume begins with helpful suggestions on gathering supplies, measuring, selecting fabric, and stitching. The rest of the book presents detailed, step-by-step directions on basic techniques for projects that range from very simple to intricate. . . . Color drawings and photographs are appealing as well as instructive. . . . An excellent addition to needlework collections." SLJ

746.41   Weaving, braiding, matting unaltered vegetable fibers

Monaghan, Kathleen

You can weave! projects for young weavers; [by] Kathleen Monaghan and Hermon Joyner. Davis Publs. (Worcester) 2000 96p il $19.95 (4 and up)   **746.41**

1. Weaving

ISBN 0-87192-493-5   LC 2001-270107

This is a "collection of 18 step-by-step weaving projects. . . . Divided into five chapters, the text explores the basics of weaving (with photos and step-by-step instructions), loom construction (cardboard, strap looms,

Monaghan, Kathleen—_Continued_
and more), and potential mediums. From very simple paper placemats to complex beaded designs, Monaghan tackles each project clearly." Booklist

Includes bibliographical references

746.42 Nonloom weaving and related techniques

Sadler, Judy Ann

Hemp jewelry; written by Judy Ann Sadler; illustrated by June Bradford. Kids Can Press 2005 40p il (Kids can do it) $12.95; pa $6.96 (4-6)
746.42

1. Macramé 2. Beadwork 3. Jewelry
ISBN 1-55337-774-5; 1-55337-775-3 (pa)

This "provides instructions for making jewelry from strands of hemp that are woven in various patterns while incorporating beads, clasps, and other findings. . . . Attractive and easy to follow. . . . Detailed, step-by-step instructions, . . . are clearly illustrated with large-scale, colorful ink-and-wash drawings." Booklist

746.43 Knitting, crocheting, tatting

Blakley Kinsler, Gwen

Crocheting; written by Gwen Blakley Kinsler and Jackie Young; illustrated by Esperança Melo. Kids Can Press 2002 40p il (Kids can do it) $12.95; pa $5.95 (4-6)
746.43

1. Crocheting
ISBN 1-55337-176-3; 1-55337-177-1 (pa)

This describes basic crochet techniques and projects including a fashion scarf, bookmarks, headbands, and purses

"Clearly written instructions and ideas, illustrated with color diagrams and photographs." SLJ

Blanchette, Peg

Kids' easy knitting projects; illustrations by Mark Nadel. Williamson 2001 64p il (Quick starts for kids!) pa $7.95 (3-6)
746.43

1. Knitting
ISBN 1-88559-348-1   LC 00-43496

This book "has instructions for making coasters, a wool scarf, slippers, stuffed animals, a purse, socks, and a hat. . . . Black-and-white line drawings clearly illustrate the step-by-step directions." SLJ

Includes glossary

Bradberry, Sarah

Kids knit! simple steps to nifty projects; [by] Sarah Bradberry. Sterling Pub. Co 2004 96p il $14.95 (5 and up)
746.43

1. Knitting
ISBN 0-8069-7733-7   LC 2004-19375

Presents basic knitting techniques and instructions for making a backpack, pillow, doll, and other simple projects.

This "book works equally well for beginners and experienced knitters. . . . Besides the requisite information on knitting and purling, there are invaluable tips about finishing garments, fixing mistakes, and adding embellishments. The projects have been chosen with an eye toward simplicity, yet they have real appeal." Booklist

Clewer, Carolyn

Kids can knit; fun and easy projects for your small knitter. Barron's 2003 128p il pa $16.95 (4 and up)
746.43

1. Knitting
ISBN 0-7641-2718-7

"A Quarto book"

This "book begins by discussing types of yarn, needles, and other knitting equipment. The author explains the basic techniques of finger knitting and spool knitting, casting on, knit and purl stitches, combining stitches to create patterns, increasing and decreasing, binding off, and picking up dropped stitches. Instructions on how to make pompoms, fringes, and braiding are also provided. The 16 eye-catching projects are arranged in an orderly progression of difficulty. . . . [This is a] useful and attractive resource." SLJ

Davis, Jane

Crochet; fantastic jewelry, hats, purses, pillows & more. Lark Books 2005 112p il (Kids' crafts) $19.95 (5 and up)
746.43

1. Crocheting
ISBN 1-57990-477-7   LC 2004-13288

Contents: Introduction; Getting started; The projects; Ready, begin! -easy accessories and game; Shoe laces; String game; Key chain; Circle games; Scrunchies; Shape it up -rectangles, triangles, and squares; Comfy slippers; Juggling blocks; Purse; Pencil case; Phone carrier; Get around-circles and balls; Hacky sack; Large indoor ball; Space balls; Felted hat; Roly poly pig; Work fast-netting; Corner shelf; Shawl; Basic net bag; Large bag; Small lace-edged bag; Challenge yourself! -longer projects; Chemistry pillows; Pocket scarf and matching hat; Case; Zippered front summer top; Felted backpack; Shine and dazzle -beads and cord crochet; Barrette; Amulet bag; Corner bookmark; Shirt edging; Bead crochet necklace and bracelet

This describes basic crochet techniques and includes instructions for 50 projects.

"The book is a pleasure to look at. . . . Photographs are large and crisp. . . . Davis clearly knows what kids like. . . . Both visual and text explanations are very clear. . . . This is a must for your craft shelves." Booklist

Ronci, Kelli

Kids crochet; projects for kids of all ages; photographs by John Gruen; illustrations by Lena Corwin. Stewart, Tabori & Chang 2005 128p il $19.95 (4 and up)
746.43

1. Crocheting
ISBN 1-58479-413-5   LC 2004-17477

Contents: Introduction; Getting started; Crochet with a hook; Color; Texture; Shape; Crochet in a circle; Stuffed shapes; Your first sweater

Ronci, Kelli—*Continued*

This offers instructions for "15 projects. All aspects of crocheting are covered. . . . Handcrafted items include a neck cozy, tool pouch, friendship cuffs, patchwork poncho, triangle-square quilt and pillow, and critter cushions." SLJ

This "has projects that kids will really enjoy making. . . . What will especially entice children are the sharply reproduced color photographs. . . . Also excellent are the attractive drawings." Booklist

Sadler, Judy Ann

Knitting; written by Judy Ann Sadler; illustrated by Esperança Melo. Kids Can Press 2002 40p il (Kids can do it) $12.95; pa $5.95 (4-6)

746.43

1. Knitting
ISBN 1-55337-050-3; 1-55337-051-1 (pa)

This "book discusses yarn, needles and other supplies. Beyond instruction in the basic techniques of casting on, knit and purl stitches, increasing and decreasing, and binding off, it shows how to make fringe, pom-poms, and tassels, and how to combine stitches to create patterns. . . . There are complete instructions for a headband, a rolled-brim hat, slipper socks, a book bag, and more. The step-by-step instructions are easy to follow, and the large, softly colored, superior-quality diagrams show exactly how to perform each step in the process." SLJ

746.44   Embroidery

Cobb, Mary

A sampler view of colonial life; illustrated by Jan Davey Ellis. Millbrook Press 1999 64p il lib bdg $24.90; pa $8.95 (2-5)   **746.44**

1. Embroidery 2. United States—Social life and customs—1600-1775, Colonial period
ISBN 0-7613-0372-3 (lib bdg); 0-7613-0382-0 (pa)
LC 98-2873

Describes the samplers stitched by girls in colonial America and explains what these samplers tell about the lives of their makers. Includes simple projects

"Many decorative watercolor illustrations make this an attractive choice." Booklist

Nicholas, Kristin

Kids embroidery; projects for kids of all ages; [by] Kristin Nicholas; photographs by John Gruen. Stewart, Tabori & Chang 2004 144p il $19.95 (3-6)   **746.44**

1. Embroidery
ISBN 1-58479-366-X   LC 2004-6106

This "shows how 'drawing with yarn' can add a funky personal touch to decor, clothes, and accessories. Nicholas opens with sample stitches on plastic mesh, then introduces more advanced, freestyle techniques; her own watercolor-and-ink diagrams make mastering even the whimsical 'lazy daisy' a snap." Booklist

Sadler, Judy Ann

Embroidery; written by Judy Ann Sadler; illustrated by June Bradford. Kids Can Press 2004 40p il (Kids can do it) $12.95; pa $6.95 (4-6)

746.44

1. Embroidery
ISBN 1-55337-616-1; 1-55337-617-X (pa)

This describes materials and techniques for simple embroidery stitches and includes instructions for creating such objects as a pincushion, a stitched greeting card, a beaded star ornament, and embroidered clothing.

"With an attractively designed cover featuring photos of sample projects, this book is sure to encourage interest in needlework." SLJ

746.46   Patchwork and quilting

Bial, Raymond

With needle and thread; a book about quilts. Houghton Mifflin 1996 48p il $16 (4 and up)

746.46

1. Quilting 2. Quilts
ISBN 0-395-73568-8   LC 95-16416

"With illustrated examples of traditional patchwork patterns . . . Bial describes the processes of marking, piecing, and quilting. An historical overview ranges from the Colonial period to the famous AIDS Memorial Quilt. Highlighting the multicultural scope of this art form, Bial shows work by Amish, African-American, and Hmong quilters. The narrative is accessibly simple, the photography is clear and colorful." Bull Cent Child Books

Includes bibliographical references

Stapleton, Dorothy

Kids can quilt; fun and easy projects for your small quilter. Barron's Educational Series 2004 128p il pa $16.95 (5 and up)   **746.46**

1. Quilting
ISBN 0-7641-2770-5

"This large-format book of advice and 23 projects for aspiring and experienced quilters introduces sewing tools and offers detailed instructions for cutting, piecing, and hand and machine-sewing. Illustrated step-by-step directions and several colorful photos and drawings per page make the projects look inviting. . . . A good source of ideas, though beginners may need help." Booklist

Storms, Biz

Quilting; written by Biz Storms; illustrated by June Bradford. Kids Can Press 2001 40p il (Kids can do it) $12.95; pa $5.95 (4-6)   **746.46**

1. Quilting
ISBN 1-55074-967-6; 1-55074-805-X (pa)

"*Quilting* uses step-by-step instructions keyed to excellent color illustrations to present basics. Ten kid-pleasing projects of increasing difficulty follow—from an appliquéd tee shirt to a full-size quilt—each as appealingly and clearly presented as the last." Booklist

Thibault, Terri

Kids' easy quilting projects; illustrations by Heather Barberie. Williamson 2000 64p il (Quick starts for kids!) pa $7.95 (3-6)   **746.46**

1. Quilting

ISBN 1-88559-349-X   LC 00-43495

This book of quilting projects "includes a butterfly pincushion, a tic-tac-toe board, wall nesters, a moon and stars mobile, a friendship pillow, and a doll quilt. Black-and-white line drawings clearly illustrate the step-by-step directions." SLJ

Includes glossary

750   Painting and paintings

Blake, Quentin

Tell me a picture. Millbrook Press 2003 unp il lib bdg $29.90; pa $17.95   **750**

1. National Gallery (Great Britain) 2. Art appreciation

ISBN 0-7613-2748-7 (lib bdg); 0-7613-1893-3 (pa)

LC 2002-13827

Published to accompany an exhibition at the National Gallery, London, Feb. 14-June 17, 2001

Provides guidance for studying paintings and illustrations from the National Gallery in London to find the story within each

"Blake's signature caricatures cavort and converse before and after each of the 26 pictures, modeling responses that invite imitation. . . . Blake's approach is an engaging path to art appreciation, with plenty of child appeal." SLJ

Cressy, Judith

Can you find it? Abrams 2002 40p il $15.95 (2-5)   **750**

1. Painting 2. Art appreciation

ISBN 0-8109-3279-2   LC 2002-18358

"Nineteen paintings from New York City's Metropolitan Museum of Art were chosen for careful scrutiny in this book. Next to each striking, full-color reproduction is a list of items to search for: e.g., '2 cats, 6 lotus blossoms, 3 eye amulets,' etc., for a painting from ancient Egypt. The works of art are from around the globe and range from illuminated manuscripts to 20th-century canvases. Designed to encourage discovery, the tiny, sometimes indistinct details will keep children engrossed for hours." SLJ

Raczka, Bob

More than meets the eye; seeing art with all five senses; by Bob Raczka. Millbrook Press 2003 32p il lib bdg $23.90; pa $9.95 (k-3)   **750**

1. Painting 2. Art appreciation

ISBN 0-7613-2797-5; 0-7613-1994-8 (pa)

LC 2003-343

Provides images of paintings and new, sensory ways to experience them, such as tasting the milk in Vermeer's "The Milkmaid," hearing the music in Tanner's "The Banjo Lesson," or feeling the fur in da Vinci's "Lady with an Ermine."

"Raczka's short, rhyming text gives structure to the book, but the color reproductions of well-chosen, vivid paintings steal the show. This art book rests on a simple concept, beautifully executed." Booklist

Unlikely pairs; fun with famous works of art; [by] Bob Raczka. Millbrook Press 2006 31p il lib bdg $23.93; pa $9.95 (4 and up)   **750**

1. Art appreciation 2. Painting

ISBN 0-7613-2936-6 (lib bdg); 0-7613-2378-3 (pa)

LC 2003-14078

Invites the reader to discover fourteen funny stories produced by pairing twenty-eight paintings from different eras and styles.

"Raczka deserves an A+ for cleverness. . . . Rodin's *The Thinker* is juxtaposed with Klee's modernistic painting of a chessboard so that the statue looks as if it is contemplating the next move. Siméon-Chardin's picture of a boy blowing soap bubbles seems to be creating Kandinsky's *Several Circles*. Each selection takes up a page and is reproduced in crisp color. . . . This book is an amusing way to introduce children to famous works of art." SLJ

751   Techniques, procedures, apparatus, equipment, materials, forms

Ancona, George

Murals; walls that sing. Marshall Cavendish 2003 48p il $17.95 (3-6)   **751**

1. Mural painting and decoration

ISBN 0-7614-5131-5   LC 2002-10114

Presents a photo essay about murals, a form of art the photographer, George Ancona, regards as authentically for the people or "para el pueblo"

"Ancona's brief, enthusiastic text provides sufficient introduction to the murals' symbols. . . . The beautiful, sharp color photos and the unusual subject will attract plenty of browsers, and the book is a great choice for starting classroom discussions about community." Booklist

757   Human figures

Thomson, Ruth

Portraits. Chelsea Clubhouse 2004 c2003 32p il (First look at art) $14.95 (2-5)   **757**

1. Portraits 2. Art appreciation

ISBN 0-7910-7948-1   LC 2003-14428

First published 2003 in the United Kingdom

Contents: What is a portrait?; People in profile; Looking sideways; Self-portraits; Picturing yourself; A magnificent queen; Portraying royalty; Multiple faces; Repeating portraits; Portraits of a hero; A heroic you!; A made-up face; Collage portraits; Artists and answers

This describes various types of portraits including profiles and silhouettes, self-portraits, depictions of royalty, multiple faces, heroic portraits, and collage portraits, and includes related art activities.

"Teachers will find easy-to-understand art lessons and projects and students will find inspiration in [this] well-organized, attractive [title]." SLJ

Includes glossary

759.05   Painting--1800-1899

Raimondo, Joyce
Picture this! activities and adventures in impressionism. Watson-Guptill 2004 48p il (Art explorers) $12.95 (1-5)   **759.05**
1. Impressionism (Art) 2. Art appreciation
ISBN 0-8230-2503-9   LC 2004-7356
"With step-by-step activities, full-color reproductions, and examples of children's imitative art, this slim volume provides a creative and simple introduction to the Impressionists. . . . Brief biographies of the painters are appended. A highly useful and entertaining book." SLJ

Sabbeth, Carol
Monet and the impressionists for kids; their lives and ideas, 21 activities. Chicago Review Press 2002 140p il pa $17.95 (5 and up)
759.05
1. Impressionism (Art) 2. Art appreciation
ISBN 1-55652-397-1   LC 2001-47191
Discusses the nineteenth-century French art movement known as Impressionism, focusing on the works of Monet, Renoir, Degas, Cassatt, Cezanne, Gauguin, and Seurat
"A beautifully designed introduction to Impressionism. . . . Sabbeth also includes 21 appealing extension activities such as recipes, crafts, games, and writing suggestions. Quality color reproductions on glossy pages, and varied, attractive layouts add to the book." SLJ
Includes glossary and bibliographical references

759.06   Painting--1900-1999

Raczka, Bob
No one saw; ordinary things through the eyes of an artist. Millbrook Press 2002 32p il lib bdg $23.90 (k-3)   **759.06**
1. Modern painting 2. Art appreciation
ISBN 0-7613-2370-8   LC 2001-30006
"Reproductions of sixteen famous paintings, set against complementary backgrounds, reflect their creators' unique viewpoints, while a gentle rhyming text comments on the masterpieces ('No one saw mothers like Mary Cassatt. / No one saw Sunday like Georges Seurat'). The selections serve the impressionist through modern works well and conclude that 'nobody sees the world like you.' " Horn Book Guide

759.13   American painting

Fisher, Leonard Everett
The limners; America's earliest portrait painters; written & illustrated by Leonard Everett Fisher. Benchmark Bks. 1999 47p il (Colonial craftsmen) lib bdg $21.36 (4 and up)   **759.13**
1. Portrait painting 2. American art 3. United States—Social life and customs—1600-1775, Colonial period
ISBN 0-7614-0932-7   LC 99-33369

A reissue of the title first published 1969 by Watts
Discusses the motivation, materials, and techniques of the first "artists" in colonial America—the sign painters who expanded their profession to include portrait painting—and how their works contribute to a better understanding of early American history and society
Includes bibliographical references

Honoring our ancestors; stories and pictures by fourteen artists; edited by Harriet Rohmer. Children's Bk. Press 1999 31p il $15.95 (3-6)
759.13
1. Artists—United States
ISBN 0-89239-158-8   LC 98-38686
Fourteen artists and picture book illustrators present paintings with descriptions of ancestors or other sources of inspiration that have inspired them
This is "rewarding in its breadth and vivacity. The portraits are thematically rich yet accessible; generally, the texts are cheerful and resist sentimentality." Horn Book Guide

Lawrence, Jacob
The great migration; an American story; paintings by Jacob Lawrence; with a poem in appreciation by Walter Dean Myers. HarperCollins Pubs. 1993 unp il pa $8.99 hardcover o.p.
759.13
1. African Americans in art
ISBN 0-06-443428-1 (pa)   LC 93-16788
Published by The Museum of Modern Art, The Phillips Collection, and HarperCollins Pubs.
"A noted African-American artist chronicles the 1916-1919 migration of blacks from the South through a sequence of 60 paintings and accompanying narrative captions." SLJ
"Lawrence is a storyteller with words as well as pictures: his captions and his own 1992 introduction to this book are the best commentary on his work." Booklist

759.4   French painting

Burleigh, Robert
Seurat and La Grande Jatte; connecting the dots. H.N. Abrams 2004 31p il $17.95 (3-6)
759.4
1. Seurat, Georges Pierre, 1859-1891
ISBN 0-8109-4811-7   LC 2003-14256
An analysis of Georges Seurat's famous painting, A Sunday on La Grande Jatte, including where and when it was made, interesting details, and the techniques used to create a sense of stillness.
"Throughout, the author does a thorough job of explaining Seurat's invention of pointillism without using technical terms. Easy-to-read, with large reproductions, this is a grand introduction." SLJ
Includes glossary and bibliographical references

Rubin, Susan Goldman

The yellow house; Vincent van Gogh & Paul Gauguin side by side; illustrations by Jos. A. Smith. Abrams 2001 unp il $17.95 (2-4)

759.4

1. Gogh, Vincent van, 1853-1890 2. Gauguin, Paul, 1848-1903

ISBN 0-8109-4588-6   LC 2001-455

Published in association with The Art Institute of Chicago

This book "focuses on the two months in 1888 that Gauguin shared van Gogh's studio in the south of France. . . . Juxtaposed images showing both artists' interpretations of the same subject offer a basic introduction to the artists' styles, techniques, and mutual influences." Booklist

"The illustrations include reproductions of the artists' paintings and excellent pictures of the men at work and home. . . . This book provides an excellent introduction to the study of these painters and their styles." SLJ

Includes bibliographical references

759.9492   Dutch painting

Gogh, Vincent van

Vincent's colors; words and pictures by Vincent van Gogh. Chronicle Books 2005 unp il $14.95 (k-3)

759.9492

1. Color in art 2. Artists, Dutch

ISBN 0-8118-5099-4

"This text is pulled directly from the letters Van Gogh wrote about his paintings to his brother, Theo. Each line of the rhyming stanzas is accompanied by a rich, full-color reproduction of one of the artist's key works. . . . Van Gogh's poetic descriptions will hold the attention of young readers; even preschoolers will enjoy the simple text and vibrant pictures. The brilliant colors and brush strokes are reproduced faithfully." SLJ

761   Relief processes (Block printing)

Price, Pamela S.

Cool rubber stamp art; [by] Pam Price. Abdo Pub. Co. 2005 32p il (Cool crafts) lib bdg $22.78 (4-6)

761

1. Rubber stamp printing

ISBN 1-59197-743-6   LC 2004-53123

This describes five rubber stamp art projects : "a terra-cotta flowerpot, spring greeting card, wrapping paper, canvas beach bag, and homemade stamps (sponge, string, leaf). . . . [This book lists] required materials, [has] small color photos, and [includes] clearly explained, numbered steps. . . . [It will] will appeal to children." SLJ

Rhatigan, Joe

Stamp it! 50 amazing projects to make; [by] Joe Rhatigan & Rain Newcomb. Lark Books 2004 112p (Kids' crafts) $19.95 (3-6)

761

1. Rubber stamp printing

ISBN 1-57990-504-8   LC 2003-10177

Provides step-by-step instructions for using stamps to decorate clothing, party decorations, gifts, and much more, as well as for making one's own stamps

The author and illustrator "provide concise, clear instructions and full-color photographs to show how each step progresses to the finished product. . . . [The book presents] interesting projects that are easy to complete and will appeal to this audience." SLJ

769.5   Forms of prints

Parker, Nancy Winslow

Money, money, money; the meaning of the art and symbols on United States paper currency. HarperCollins Pubs. 1995 32p il map $16.95; lib bdg $16.89 (3-5)

769.5

1. Paper money 2. Signs and symbols

ISBN 0-06-023411-3; 0-06-023412-1 (lib bdg)

LC 93-43534

"The text provides information regarding the graphics of our money. Brief snippets about the various U.S. presidents, the decorations, and other related facts are supplied. The illustrations of the bills in question are small and blurred, but pertinent details on the bills are shown enlarged." Horn Book Guide

770   Photography, photographs, computer art

Friedman, Debra

Picture this; fun photography and crafts. Kids Can Press 2003 40p il (Kids can do it) $12.95; pa $5.95 (4-6)

770

1. Photography 2. Handicraft

ISBN 1-55337-046-5; 1-55337-047-3 (pa)

This focuses "on composition and presentation techniques adaptable for 35mm, disposable, and, to a more limited extent, digital cameras. Novices and enthusiasts will find hints on capturing shadows and motion, creating montaged panoramas and simple optical illusions, and adding interest to portraits with before/after, bug's-eye, and bird's-eye views. Suggestions for cropping, grouping, and sequencing raise the bar from simple scrapbook-style mounting." Bull Cent Child Books

"Clearly written instructions and ideas, illustrated with color diagrams and photographs . . . explores such concepts as light and shadow, action, and point of view. The crafts include framing and matting as well as suggestions for arranging pictures in a scrapbook." SLJ

Includes glossary

770.9   Photography--Historical and geographic treatment

Czech, Kenneth P.

Snapshot; America discovers the camera. Lerner Publs. 1996 88p il $26.60 (5 and up)

770.9

1. Photography—History

ISBN 0-8225-1736-1   LC 95-51136

Czech, Kenneth P.—*Continued*

"A history of photography from its inception to its many influences in American history. . . . The author explains complex photographic inventions and processes in easy-to-understand language. . . . A profusion of excellent black-and-white photographs are distributed throughout and complement the text. Well-placed quotes, historical diagrams, anecdotes, and advertisements enhance and accent topics discussed." SLJ

Includes bibliographical references

771 Photography--Techniques, equipment, materials

Price, Susanna

Click! fun with photography; [by] Susanna Price & Tim Stephens. Sterling 1997 48p il pa $7.95 hardcover o.p. (4 and up) **771**

1. Photography 2. Cameras

ISBN 0-8069-9652-8 (pa) LC 96-37211

First published 1995 in the United Kingdom

Presents the basics of photography, from choosing a camera to making the most of the flash

"With numerous full-color photos and a brief, clearly written text, this book exposes more than just the basics. The authors include frequent checklists that summarize major points and an extensive glossary. . . . A multitude of activities complete this useful introduction." SLJ

775 Digital photography

Bidner, Jenni

The kids' guide to digital photography; how to shoot, save, play with & print your digital photos. Lark Books 2004 96p il $14.95; pa $9.95 (5 and up) **775**

1. Digital photography

ISBN 1-57990-604-4; 1-57990-643-5 (pa)

LC 2004-14465

"Beginning chapters address basics, including understanding camera features, using focus and flash functions, capturing motion, and so on. Bidner then delves into picture-editing software and even how to set up a Web site. . . . Final sections offer ideas for projects. . . . Bidner introduces sophisticated technical material in enthusiastic language that is kid-friendly without being condescending." Booklist

Includes glossary

778.59 Video production (Television photography)

Shulman, Mark

Attack of the killer video book; tips and tricks for young directors; by Mark Shulman and Hazlitt Krog; art by Martha Newbigging. Annick Press 2004 64p il $24.95; pa $12.95 (5 and up) **778.59**

1. Video recording

ISBN 1-55037-841-4; 1-55037-840-6 (pa)

This "guide explores every stage of video production, from brainstorming, to organizing a shoot, to finally piecing it all together." Publisher's note

"This lighthearted primer uses lots of humor and colorful, cartoon-style illustrations. . . . A good choice for collections in need of an updated video-production guide that won't become dated too quickly." SLJ

778.9 Photography of specific subjects

Aaseng, Nathan

Wild shots; the world of the wildlife photographer. Millbrook Press 2001 79p il lib bdg $29.90 (5 and up) **778.9**

1. Photography of animals

ISBN 0-7613-1551-9 LC 00-45089

In this "introduction to wildlife photography, Aaseng discusses different facets of the subject, introduces many photographers and relates their experiences in the wild. . . . Illustrating the intriguing text are many outstanding, well-captioned photos of wild animals." Booklist

Includes bibliographical references

779 Photographs

Arthus-Bertrand, Yann

Earth from above for young readers; concept and photographs by Yann Arthus-Bertrand; text by Robert Burleigh; illustrations by David Giraudon. Abrams 2002 77p il $12.95 (4 and up) **779**

1. Aerial photography 2. Human geography

ISBN 0-8109-3486-8 LC 2002-4259

Original French edition 2001

Presents aerial photographs of various scenes from around the world including fishermen in Morocco, a farm on the island of Crete, and a mangrove forest in New Caledonia

"The 34 stunning aerial views from all over the world were snapped by photographer Arthus-Bertrand while leaning out of a helicopter. The images appeared in his earlier book for adults, Earth from Above: 365 Days (Abrams, 2001), but here they are larger and even more gorgeous. . . . Burleigh's interesting and informative text expands on each photo, explaining natural phenomena, human impact, and wildlife and human adaptations." SLJ

780 Music

Aliki

Ah, music! written and illustrated by Aliki. HarperCollins Pubs. 2003 47p il $16.99; lib bdg $17.89 (k-3)   **780**
1. Music
ISBN 0-06-028719-5; 0-06-028727-6 (lib bdg)
                                    LC 2001-26476
This introduction to music defines such terms as rhythm, melody, pitch, and volume, gives a brief description of written music, instruments of the orchestra, vocal parts, harmony, dynamics, and tempo, cultural diversity in dance and music, and gives a brief outline of musical history

"Terms are explained in an easy, child-friendly manner. . . . Aliki's love of her subject shines through. This enjoyable title is best shared one-on-one and its format makes it ideal for browsing." SLJ

Ardley, Neil

A young person's guide to music; with music by Poul Ruders. DK Pub. 2004 80p il $24.99 (5 and up)   **780**
1. Music 2. Orchestra
ISBN 0-7566-0549-7
A reissue of the title first published 1995
"In association with the BBC Symphony Orchestra conducted by Andrew Davis." Title page
This "interactive guide to the orchestra is a combination of book and compact disk. The CD features a new work by the Dutch composer Poul Ruder. . . . The text itself has facts on the orchestra as a whole, the conductor, composer, and each instrument. . . . A history section features a timeline, names of musicians and composers, definitions of musical forms with examples, and a glossary." SLJ

"A rich resource for young people who want to understand orchestral music." Booklist

Nathan, Amy

Meet the musicians; from prodigy (or not) to pro. 1st ed. Henry Holt and Co. 2006 168p il $17.95 (5 and up)   **780**
1. Musicians 2. Music
ISBN 9780805077438   LC 2005026508
The author "interviewed 13 of the New York Philharmonic's members, representing 11 different instruments, and spun their articulate comments into brief, readable profiles, supplemented by various sidebars—among them, an invaluable feature outlining pros and cons of individual instruments. . . . The practical advice mixed with inspirational words strikes just the right note for children at many different stages in their musical education." Booklist

Includes bibliographical references

780.3 Music--Encyclopedias and dictionaries

Barber, Nicola

Music: an A-Z guide; written by Nicola Barber. Watts 2001 128p il (Watts reference) lib bdg $34; pa $19.95 (4 and up)   **780.3**
1. Music—Dictionaries
ISBN 0-531-1898-3 (lib bdg); 0-531-15450-5 (pa)
                                    LC 00-51325
"Subjects range from performers to instruments, elements to musical forms, and pop to classical. Topics are covered in one to several pages, with a brief explanation, definition, or background for the term followed by more detailed information on ancillary areas. Each page has bright, colorful photos and reproductions that aid in clarifying, creating interest in, and helping to understand the text. . . . Without getting too complicated, the book succeeds in explaining each subject well enough for readers to acquire a basic understanding of it." SLJ

Includes bibliographical references

780.89 Music of racial, ethnic, national groups

Igus, Toyomi

I see the rhythm; paintings by Michele Wood; text by Toyomi Igus. Children's Bk. Press 1998 32p il $15.95 (4 and up)   **780.89**
1. African American music
ISBN 0-89239-151-0   LC 97-29310
Coretta Scott King award for illustration, 1999
Chronicles and captures poetically the history, mood, and movement of African American music

"The text, made up of free verse and music lyrics, incorporates different font sizes, shapes, and colors to underline the mood of each genre. . . . The colors of each full-page scenario underline the mood. . . . This book celebrates music with art and words and successfully blends all three." SLJ

781 Music--General principles and musical forms

Sabbeth, Alex

Rubber-band banjos and a java jive bass; projects and activities on the science of music and sound; project illustrations by Laurel Aiello. Wiley 1997 102p il pa $12.95 (4 and up)   **781**
1. Music 2. Sound 3. Musical instruments
ISBN 0-471-15675-2   LC 96-22144
This "presentation explores the world of sound and provides instructions for making musical instruments. Along the way, readers will learn about famous scientists who had musical inclinations. . . . Numerous, clear, pen-and-ink drawings illustrate the construction of instruments from a glass harmonica, to a violin, drums, and a foot-powered organ. . . . The scientific principles behind the creation of all the wonderful noises are explained, as is basic music notation." SLJ

Includes glossary

781.65 Jazz music

Marsalis, Wynton
Jazz A-B-Z; [by] Wynton Marsalis and Paul Rogers; with biographical sketches by Phil Schaap. Candlewick Press 2005 unp il $24.99 (5 and up)
781.65

1. Jazz music 2. Jazz musicians
ISBN 0-7636-2135-8   LC 2005-48448
This is an illustrated alphabetically arranged introduction to jazz musicians.
This is a "witty, stunningly designed alphabet catalog. . . . The biographical sketches and notes on poetic forms by Phil Schaap are concise and genuinely informative. . . . Rogers's pastiche full-page portraits, his use of expressive typography and the smaller vignettes he sprinkles throughout are bound to heighten any reader's appreciation of both the musicians and the music. . . . [Marsalis offers] clever . . . poems, wordplays, odes and limericks." N Y Times Book Rev

782.25 Sacred songs

All night, all day; a child's first book of African-American spirituals; selected and illustrated by Ashley Bryan; musical arrangements by David Manning Thomas. Atheneum Pubs. 1991 48p il music $16
782.25

1. Spirituals (Songs)
ISBN 0-689-31662-3   LC 90-753145
This is a "selection of 20 well-known spirituals." SLJ
"An exuberance of warm color and great variety in pattern and design distinguish the illustrations. . . . Excellent piano accompaniments and guitar chords further enrich the beautiful, wholly gratifying book." Horn Book

Nelson, Kadir
He's got the whole world in his hands; . Dial Books for Young Readers 2005 unp il $16.99 (k-2)
782.25

1. Spirituals (Songs)
ISBN 0-8037-2850-6   LC 2004-23075
An illustrated version of the well-known spiritual song
"Nelson uses pencils, oils, and watercolors to create a series of striking, beautifully composed pictures. . . . Nelson envisions the song in a highly personal and involving manner while embodying its strength and spirit." Booklist

This little light of mine; illustrated by E. B. Lewis. Simon & Schuster Books for Young Readers 2005 unp il $16.95 (k-3)
782.25

1. Spirituals (Songs)
ISBN 0-689-83179-X
"A visual interpretation of an African-American spiritual. It is morning when the book opens, and readers are greeted by a smiling boy. Throughout the day, he spreads his own special brand of joy wherever he goes. . . . Lewis's watercolor illustrations across double pages effectively convey emotions of happiness and the giving and sharing of oneself." SLJ

782.28 Carols

Neale, J. M. (John Mason)
Good King Wenceslas; [by] John M. Neale; [illustrations by] Tim Ladwig. Eerdmans Books for Young Readers 2005 unp $16 (k-3)
782.28

1. Carols
ISBN 0-8028-5209-2   LC 2004-10237
"In this rhythmic Christmas ballad, a good king looks out of his castle and sees a poor man gathering fuel. 'Yonder peasant, who is he?' he asks his page. The king makes his way through the snow, loaded with gifts, to share his wealth with the poor man. Henterly's majestic illustrations, in opulent colors, convey the difficulties of the peasant's search for fuel as well as the generous measures of the king. The carol's delicate text is left intact, and the melody appears on the end page." SLJ

O holy night; Christmas with the Boys Choir of Harlem; pictures by Faith Ringgold. HarperCollins Publishers 2004 unp il $18.99; lib bdg $19.89 (k-3)
782.28

1. Carols
ISBN 0-06-000979-9; 0-06-051819-7 (lib bdg)
LC 2003-1820

"Amistad"
Presents the Christmas story according to Luke plus the words to five popular Christmas carols—"Silent Night," "O Come All Ye Faithful," "O Holy Night," "Hark! the Herald Angels Sing," and "Joy to the World," sung on the accompanying CD by the Boys Choir of Harlem
"Ringgold's paintings, set against backgrounds of sky blue and ruby red and decorated with touches of gold, feature an African American Holy Family who are visited by dark-skinned wise men and shepherds, and angels of all races and colors. The folk-art style imbues the characters with a humanity that brings them close to readers." Booklist

Thuswaldner, Werner
Silent night holy night; a song for the world; [by] Werner Thuswaldner and Patricia Crampton; pictures by Robert Ingpen. Minedition 2005 unp il $16.99 (k-3)
782.28

1. Gruber, Franz Xaver, 1787-1863 2. Silent night (Song)
ISBN 0-698-40032-1   LC 2005-47201
"The history of the internationally known Christmas carol, Silent Night—how it was composed and first sung, and its connections across time and place—is celebrated in this handsome, oversize picture book. . . . Ingpen . . . evokes the old European masters in moving portraits as well as crowded candlelit interiors." Booklist

The **Twelve** days of Christmas   **782.28**
1. Carols
Some editions are:
Boyds Mills Press $14.95 Illustrated by John O'Brien (ISBN 1-56397-142-9)
Godine $17.95 Illustrated by Ilse Plume (ISBN 1-56792-300-3)

The Twelve days of Christmas—*Continued*

Little Simon $21.95 A pop-up celebration illustrated by Robert Sabuda (ISBN 0-689-80865-8)

Putnam pa $6.99 Illustrated by Jan Brett (ISBN 0-698-11569-4)

Illustrated versions of The Christmas carol in which a young woman's true love sends her extravagant gifts on each of the twelve days of Christmas

782.42 Songs

All the pretty little horses; a traditional lullaby; illustrated by Linda Saport. Clarion Bks. 1999 32p il music $15 (k-2)   **782.42**

1. Lullabies 2. Folk songs—United States

ISBN 0-395-93097-9   LC 98-32129

A traditional lullaby presented with music, a note on the origin of the song, and pastel illustrations which reflect its possible connection to slaves in the American South

The "dreamy pastel illustrations in gorgeous color show an African American woman rocking her baby on the porch in the rural South long ago. . . . The magical realism is glowing and gentle. . . . With the music on the back page, this is sure to become a favorite version of a beautiful song." Booklist

Arroz con leche; popular songs and rhymes from Latin America; selected and illustrated by Lulu Delacre; English lyrics by Elena Paz; musical arrangements by Ana-María Rosado. Scholastic 1989 32p il music pa $4.99 hardcover o.p. (k-3)   **782.42**

1. Folk songs 2. Folklore—Latin America 3. Bilingual books—English-Spanish

ISBN 0-590-041886-6 (pa)

A Lucas/Evans Bk.

This is a bilingual collection of twelve folk songs and rhymes from Puerto Rico, Mexico and Argentina. Instructions for fingerplays and games accompany some of the songs. Musical arrangements for nine of the entries are included at the end of the book

"Delacre has selected lilting verses that are pleasing to the ear—ones likely to encourage non-Spanish-speakers to join in the fun. . . . Fresh, springlike colors brighten the pictures. . . . An author's note explains that many of the scenes depict real places." Booklist

Bates, Ivan

Five little ducks; illustrated by Ivan Bates. Scholastic 2006 unp il $12.99 (k-2)   **782.42**

1. Ducks—Songs 2. Songs 3. Counting

ISBN 0-439-74693-0   LC 2005000112

"Orchard books"

One by one, five little ducks wander away from their mother until her lonely quack brings them all waddling back

"Bates's muted watercolors bring a lively energy . . . to this beloved song. The artist's sweet and nostalgic adaptation is unique for its gentle and warm tone." SLJ

Boynton, Sandra

Dog train; deluxe illustrated lyrics book of the unpredictable rock-and-roll journey; music by Sandra Boynton & Michael Ford; lyrics and drawings by Sandra Boynton. Workman Pub. 2005 64p il $17.95 (k-3)   **782.42**

1. Songs 2. Rock music

ISBN 0-7611-3966-4   LC 2005051801

"This collection of songs erupts with energy, humor, and a strong dose of rock n roll. . . . The book has a spread for each song – a colorful, cheerful illustration and excerpts of lyrics – followed by complete lyrics and musical scores at the end. An About the Artists section includes a photo and biographical sketch of each artist who performs on the accompanying CD." SLJ

Philadelphia chickens; a too-illogical zoological musical revue: deluxe illustrated lyrics book of the original cast recording of the unforgettable (though completely imaginary) stage spectacular; music by Sandra Boynton & Michael Ford; lyrics and drawings by Sandra Boynton. Workman Pub. 2002 64p il $16.95 (k-3)   **782.42**

1. Musicals 2. Songs

ISBN 0-7611-2636-8   LC 2002-27049

This is "a book-and-CD package billed as an 'imaginary musical revue.' The first 32 pages contain lyrics and illustrations, the second half of the book includes musical notation and additional lyrics for each song. An all-star cast, including Meryl Streep, Laura Linney, Eric Stoltz and the Bacon Brothers, headlines the musical recording, which features a variety of original show tunes." Publ Wkly

Carle, Eric

Today is Monday; pictures by Eric Carle. Philomel Bks. 1993 unp il music $16.99; pa $6.99 (k-3)   **782.42**

1. Songs 2. Food—Songs 3. Animals—Songs

ISBN 0-399-21966-8; 0-698-11563-5 (pa)

LC 91-45866

Each day of the week brings a new food, until on Sunday all the world's children can come and eat it up

This song "gets new life in a picture book bursting with food, animals, and lots of energy. Beginning with the grinning cat on the cover . . . a zooful of animals act out the lyrics: snakes get tangled in spaghetti, elephants use their trunks to slurp 'Zoooop,' and pelicans catch fish on Friday. With text at a minimum, Carle's always innovative artwork steps center stage in an oversize format that allows gloriously colored collages to spread over two pages." Booklist

The **Children's** song index, 1978-1993; compiled by Kay Laughlin, Pollyanne Frantz, Ann Branton. Libraries Unlimited 1996 153p $40   **782.42**

1. Songs—Indexes

ISBN 1-56308-332-9   LC 95-40236

"This book indexes more than 2,500 songs from 77 song books listed in *Cumulative Book Index*, 1977-1994. . . . [Songs are indexed] by song title, first line, or subject. . . . A quick-reference tool for those who need to locate in which songbook a particular song can be found,

The Children's song index, 1978-1993—*Continued*
this index encompasses songs appealing to children pre-kindergarten through middle school." Booklist
   Includes bibliographical references

Coots, John Frederick
   Santa Claus is comin' to town; written by J. Fred Coots & Haven Gillespie; illustrated by Steven Kellogg. HarperCollins 2004 unp il $15.99; lib bdg $16.89 (k-3)   **782.42**
   1. Songs 2. Santa Claus—Songs 3. Christmas—Songs
   ISBN 0-688-14938-3; 0-06-623849-8 (lib bdg)
                                              LC 2003-1821
   "A little bear has just returned from visiting Santa at the North Pole. Armed with insider information, he uses the familiar words of this upbeat Christmas standard to warn the children that they had best behave themselves." SLJ
   This "manages to get the rhythm of the music right onto the page. . . . The pictures are packed, and the design is witty." Horn Book

De colores and other Latin-American folk songs for children. Dutton Children's Bks. 1994 56p $17.99; pa $6.99 (k-3)   **782.42**
   1. Folk songs 2. Bilingual books—English-Spanish 3. Folklore—Latin America
   ISBN 0-525-45260-5; 0-14-056548-5 (pa)
   "Each of the 27 songs is presented with background notes; lyrics in both Spanish and English; simple arrangements for the voice, piano, and guitar; and suggestions for group sing-alongs and musical games. . . . The book is a delight for the eyes as well as the ear. . . . Kleven provides bountiful illustrations—the endpapers are sunshine bright with a crisp quilt of yellow flowers, and playful borders that ripple with colorful patterns and miniature pictures line the edge of every page." Booklist

Diez deditos. Ten little fingers & other play rhymes and action songs from Latin America; selected, arranged, and translated by José-Luis Orozco; illustrated by Elisa Kleven. Dutton Children's Bks. 1997 56p il music $18.99 (k-3)
                                                 782.42
   1. Songs 2. Folklore—Latin America 3. Finger play 4. Bilingual books—English-Spanish
   ISBN 0-525-45736-4
   "This collection of fingerplays and action songs in Spanish and English comes with clear instructions for physical movements and simple musical notation. A brief sentence or paragraph introduces each entry. . . . Orozco's selections, some traditional, some written by himself, include versifications on such child-appealing subjects as dancing, singing, animals, weather, and food. . . . Kleven's collage illustrations practically pop off the pages with flashy colors and rich details that make each bustling composition a viewer's delight." Bull Cent Child Books

The Farmer in the dell; illustrated by Alexandra Wallner. Holiday House 1998 unp il music $15.95 (k-1)   **782.42**
   1. Folk songs—United States
   ISBN 0-8234-1382-9   LC 97-44206

An illustrated version of the traditional game song accompanied by music
   "Wallner's primitive folk art sparkles with life, action, and energy. The colored pen-and-ink illustrations are packed with details." SLJ

Fiestas: a year of Latin American songs of celebration; selected, arranged, and translated by José-Luis Orozco; illustrated by Elisa Kleven. Dutton Children's Bks. 2002 48p il music $17.99 (k-3)   **782.42**
   1. Songs 2. Festivals 3. Latin America—Social life and customs 4. Bilingual books—English-Spanish
   ISBN 0-525-45937-5
   "Orozco presents 22 songs that center around holidays. . . . Arranged by month, each song is presented with a paragraph of background, the music for the melody (with guitar chords), and the lyrics in both Spanish and English. . . . Kleven's bright borders and busy illustrations . . . make this not only an exemplary songbook, but also a stunning visual experience." SLJ

Fishing for a dream; ocean lullabies and night verses; collected and illustrated by Kate Kiesler. Clarion Bks. 1999 29p il $16   **782.42**
   1. Lullabies 2. Sea poetry 3. Poetry—Collections
   ISBN 0-395-94149-0   LC 99-11182
   A collection of lullabies centered on a theme of the sea, ships, and fishes
   "This enchanting collection includes traditional lullabies such as 'Dance to Your Daddy' and classic poems such as Robert Louis Stevenson's 'My Bed Is a Boat', as well as more recent playful creations by Eve Merriam and Dahlov Ipcar. The gentle, muted colors in Kiesler's illustrations reinforce the calm, restful mood of the verses." SLJ

The Fox went out on a chilly night; an old song; illustrated by Peter Spier. Doubleday 1961 unp il music hardcover o.p. pa $6.95 (k-3)
                                                 782.42
   1. Folk songs—United States 2. Foxes—Songs
   ISBN 0-385-07990-7; 0-440-40829-6 (pa)
   Set in New England, this old song tells about the trip the fox father made to town to get some of the farmer's plump geese for his family's dinner, and how he manages to evade the farmer who tries to shoot him
   "A true picture book in the Caldecott-Brooke tradition. Fine drawings, lovely colors, and pictures so full of amusing details that young viewers will make fresh discoveries every time they . . . scrutinize these beautiful, action-filled pages." Horn Book

Guthrie, Woody
   This land is your land; words and music by Woody Guthrie; paintings by Kathy Jakobsen; with a tribute by Pete Seeger. Little, Brown 1998 unp il music $15.95 (k-3)   **782.42**
   1. Songs 2. United States—Songs
   ISBN 0-316-39215-4   LC 96-54628
   Includes musical notation
   "The song is a paean to America's beautiful geography and landscapes, the diversity of its inhabitants, and the indomitable spirit of the American people. Here the

Guthrie, Woody—*Continued*

complete lyrics serve as the book's main text and are brought to life by stunning, vibrant folk-art illustrations of the people and places of America, coast to coast and past to present. . . . A complete musical notation is included, as is a tribute to Guthrie written by folksinger Pete Seeger. The biographical scrapbook at the book's end is both fascinating and informative." Booklist

Hillenbrand, Will

Down by the station. Harcourt Brace & Co. 1999 unp il music $15 (k-2)   **782.42**
1. Songs 2. Animals—Songs 3. Railroads—Songs
ISBN 0-15-201804-2   LC 98-41770
"Gulliver books"
In this version of a familiar song, baby animals ride to the children's zoo on the zoo train
"This twist on an old favorite combines sunny illustrations, playful humor, and appealing animals." SLJ

Fiddle-i-fee. Harcourt 2002 unp il music $16 (k-3)   **782.42**
1. Folk songs—United States 2. Animals—Songs
ISBN 0-15-201945-6   LC 2001-1382
"Gulliver Books"
In this adaptation of a traditional folk song, a farmer and his wife prepare for a new baby as their animals secretly meet at night to plan a surprise of their own
"The pastel-colored artwork shows the farm throughout the seasons and includes plenty of visual humor and hints of what's ahead. With its pleasing repetition, animal and musical sounds, farmyard setting, and playful surprise, this picture book will have listeners clamoring for an encore." Horn Book

Hinojosa, Tish

Cada niño/Every child; a bilingual songbook for kids; illustrated by Lucia Angela Perez. Cinco Puntos Press 2002 56p il music $18.95; pa $9.95 (k-3)   **782.42**
1. Songs 2. Bilingual books—English-Spanish
ISBN 0-9383-1760-1; 0-9383-1779-2 (pa)
"Hinojosa has gathered 11 traditional, original, and adapted songs to celebrate both Hispanic culture and universal experiences and feelings. A brief author's note in English and Spanish prefaces the music, with chords and melody, and verses in both languages. . . . Lovely, bright, folk-art illustrations, brimming with pattern play and whimsical details, create magical worlds of familiar objects and experiences as they incorporate cultural elements. . . . A CD is available for separate purchase." Booklist

Hoberman, Mary Ann

Bill Grogan's goat; adapted by Mary Ann Hoberman; illustrated by Nadine Bernard Westcott. Little, Brown 2002 unp il $14.95 (k-3)   **782.42**
1. Songs 2. Goats—Songs
ISBN 0-316-36232-8   LC 00-50008
"Megan Tingley books"

Presents the familiar rhyme about a pesky goat that gets in trouble for eating shirts off the clothesline
"The rhyme moves merrily along, succinctly describing the comic scenes that unfold. The zany cartoon illustrations capture the spirit of the story and draw readers into the action." SLJ

The eensy-weensy spider; adapted by Mary Ann Hoberman; illustrated by Nadine Bernard Westcott. Little, Brown 2000 unp il music $12.95 (k-3)   **782.42**
1. Songs 2. Finger play 3. Spiders—Songs
ISBN 0-316-36330-8   LC 99-25701
An expanded version of the familiar children's finger-play rhyme describing what the little spider does after being washed out of the water-spout
"Whimsical, watercolor cartoons capture the light-hearted tone of the verse. . . . This sprightly adaptation lends itself to singing aloud and is sure to be a hit." SLJ

Mary had a little lamb; adapted by Mary Ann Hoberman; illustrated by Nadine Bernard Westcott. 1st ed. Little, Brown 2003 unp il (Sing-along stories) $15.95 (k-2)   **782.42**
1. Songs 2. Sheep—Songs
ISBN 0-316-60687-1   LC 2002-72478
"Megan Tingley books"
This expanded version of the traditional rhyme shows what happens after the lamb gets to school. Includes music on the last page.
"This playful extension of the original nursery rhyme adds to the nonsense with simple words and clear, slapstick watercolor-and-ink illustrations." Booklist

There once was a man named Michael Finnegan; adapted by Mary Ann Hoberman; illustrated by Nadine Bernard Westcott. Little, Brown 2001 unp il music $14.95 (k-3)   **782.42**
1. Songs
ISBN 0-316-36301-4   LC 99-57266
"Megan Tingley books"
An elaborated version of the repetitive children's song about a man who creates quite a "din-igan" playing the "violin-igan"
"Kids will delight in the silly word play, the wild slapstick details of the big, bright line-and-watercolor pictures, and the cozy, sloppy ending, when the dog kisses Michael on his chin-igan." Booklist

Hort, Lenny

The seals on the bus; illustrated by G. Brian Karas. Holt & Co. 2000 unp il $15.95 (k-2)   **782.42**
1. Songs 2. Animals—Songs
ISBN 0-8050-5952-0   LC 99-33612
Different animals—including seals, tigers, geese, rabbits, monkeys, and more—make their own sounds as they ride all around the town on a bus
"Karas' artwork combines cut paper, gouache, acrylic, and pencil to create a series of pleasingly varied scenes of cheerful chaos. A good story hour choice." Booklist

Hush, little baby; a folk song; with pictures by Mark Frazee. Harcourt Brace & Co. 1999 unp il music $15 (k-2) **782.42**
1. Folk songs—United States 2. Lullabies
ISBN 0-15-201429-2   LC 98-9608
In an old lullaby a baby is promised an assortment of presents from its adoring parent
"True to the song's Appalachian roots, Frazee sets the traditional lullaby in the hills of West Virginia, with big, detailed pictures that add character and exaggerated sibling rivalry to the nonsense story. . . . The music is on the last page, and Frazee's clear narrative pictures in acrylics and pencil capture the rhythm of the words, the historic particulars of the place, the nighttime farce, and the universal family scenarios of jealousy and love." Booklist

I hear America singing! folk songs for American families; collected and arranged by Kathleen Krull; illustrated by Allen Garns; introductory note by Arlo Guthrie. Knopf 2003 145p il $24.95 **782.42**
1. Folk songs—United States
ISBN 0-375-82527-4
Includes audio CD
First published 1992 without CD with title: Gonna sing my head off!
"Work songs, love songs, ballads and blues, lullabies, spirituals, protest songs, and sheer nonsense make up this entertaining collection of 62 traditional and contemporary favorites. For each song, Krull provides the simplest piano and guitar arrangements in a clear double-page spread design that includes the words to all the verses. . . . The exuberant illustrations, mostly in bright pastels, manage to be both familiar and dramatic. . . . Informal notes at the head of each song give something about history, origin, performance, and possibilities for variation." Booklist

In the hollow of your hand; slave lullabies; collected by Alice McGill; pictures by Michael Cummings. Houghton Mifflin 2000 unp il music $18 **782.42**
1. Lullabies 2. African Americans—Poetry 3. Slavery—Poetry
ISBN 0-395-85755-4   LC 97-20269
A collection of lullabies orally transmitted by African-American slaves revealing their hardships and sorrows as well as soothing notes of well-being and belief in a better time to come
"This moving collection of 13 folk lullabies is a powerful way to communicate what family life was like under slavery. . . . Opposite each song is a handsome full-page quilt collage contributed by Michael Cummings. . . . There's full musical notation at the back, and a CD of the songs, sung by McGill, is included. The people's words are achingly beautiful, and the combination with history and personal experience makes this an enduring collection." Booklist

Johnson, James Weldon
Lift every voice and sing; illustrations by Elizabeth Catlett; introductions by Jim Haskins. Walker & Co. 1993 unp il $15.95 **782.42**
1. African American music 2. Songs
ISBN 0-8027-8250-7   LC 92-27333
Includes music for voice and piano
Illustrated version of the song that has come to be considered the African American national anthem
"Ms Catlett's woodcuts, done in the 1940's, are a perfect complement to the text and help make this a book to be treasured for generations to come." Child Book Rev Serv

Katz, Alan
Take me out of the bathtub and other silly dilly songs; illustrated by David Catrow. Margaret K. McElderry Bks. 2001 unp il $15 (k-3) **782.42**
1. Songs
ISBN 0-689-82903-5   LC 99-89390
Well-known songs, including "Oh Susannah" and "Row Row Row Your Boat," are presented with new words and titles, such as "I'm So Carsick" and "Go Go Go to Bed"
"Catrow's animated double-spread pictures are at least as silly as the song lyrics, offering action-filled scenes bursting with odd-looking creatures." Booklist

Kellogg, Steven
Give the dog a bone. SeaStar 2000 33p il music $15.95; lib bdg $15.88 (k-3) **782.42**
1. Folk songs 2. Dogs—Songs 3. Counting
ISBN 1-58717-001-9; 1-58717-002-7 (lib bdg)
                                      LC 00-25203
A variation on the familiar song, "This Old Man," in which an increasing number of dogs look for treats
Kellogg's "busy and buoyant art—rendered in colored ink, colored pencil, acrylic and watercolor—typifies his appealing style and kid-targeted humor." Publ Wkly

Key, Francis Scott
The Star-Spangled Banner il **782.42**
1. Star spangled banner (Song) 2. National songs—United States
Some editions are:
Applewood Bks. $14.95 Illustrated by Ingri and Edgar Parin D'Aulaire (ISBN 1-55709-390-3)
Dell pa $10.95 Illustrated by Peter Spier (ISBN 0-440-40697-6)
Illustrated versions of Frances Scott Key's text for our national anthem

Kroll, Steven
By the dawn's early light; the story of the Star spangled banner; illustrated by Dan Andreasen. Scholastic 1994 40p il maps music pa $5.99 hardcover o.p. (3-5) **782.42**
1. Key, Francis Scott, 1779-1843 2. Star spangled banner (Song) 3. War of 1812
ISBN 0-590-45055-7 (pa)   LC 92-27101

Kroll, Steven—*Continued*

This is an account of the events that led Francis Scott Key to compose the United States national anthem, during the War of 1812

"Handsome full-page oil paintings in warm golden tones blend nineteenth-century romance with twentieth-century realism. . . . Kroll's details of this dramatic story match those told at Fort McHenry today; judicious use of dialogue moves the story along while remaining true to the facts." Bull Cent Child Books

Includes bibliographical references

Langstaff, John M.

Frog went a-courtin'; retold by John Langstaff; with pictures by Feodor Rojankovsky. Harcourt Brace Jovanovich 1955 unp il music $16; pa $7 (k-3)   **782.42**

1. Folk songs 2. Frogs—Songs 3. Mice—Songs
ISBN 0-15-230214-X; 0-15-633900-5 (pa)
Awarded the Caldecott Medal, 1956

"Retelling of a merry old Scottish ballad with many-colored illustrations about the marriage between Mr. Frog and Miss Mouse. A composite American version set to Appalachian mountain music." Chicago Public Libr

Oh, a-hunting we will go; [by] John Langstaff; pictures by Nancy Winslow Parker. Atheneum Pubs. 1974 unp il music pa $6.99 hardcover o.p. (k-2)   **782.42**

1. Folk songs 2. Animals—Songs
ISBN 0-689-71503-X (pa)

"A Margaret K. McElderry book"

The nonsense verses of this folk song trace the hunt for such animals as an armadillo, a fox, and a snake, and describe the imagined treatment of each animal once it is caught

"The 12 stanzas are complemented by Parker's droll crayon illustrations (the fox caught in the box is watching TV), and a score for guitar and piano is appended. An amusing addition to 'song' picture books." SLJ

Over in the meadow; with pictures by Feodor Rojankovsky. Harcourt Brace & Co. 1957 unp il music $16; pa $7 (k-2)   **782.42**

1. Folk songs 2. Counting 3. Animals—Songs
ISBN 0-15-258854-X; 0-15-670500-1 (pa)

"This old counting rhyme tells of ten meadow families whose mothers advise them to dig, run, sing, play, hum, build, swim, wink, spin and hop. The illustrations, half in full color, show the combination of realism and imagination which little children like best. The tune, arranged simply, is on the last page, and children will have fun acting the whole thing out." Horn Book

Leodhas, Sorche Nic

Always room for one more; illustrated by Nonny Hogrogian. Holt & Co. 1965 unp il music $14.95; pa $5.95 (k-3)   **782.42**

1. Folk songs
ISBN 0-8050-0331-2; 0-8050-0330-4 (pa)
Awarded the Caldecott Medal, 1966

"A picture book based on an old Scottish folk song about hospitable Lachie MacLachlan, who invited in so

many guests that his little house finally burst. Rhymed text . . . a glossary of Scottish words, and music for the tune are combined into an effective whole." Hodges. Books for Elem Sch Libr

MacDonald, Margaret Read

The round book; rounds kids love to sing; by Margaret Read MacDonald and Winifred Jaeger; illustrated by Yvonne LeBrun Davis. Linnet Bks. 1999 121p il music $22.50; pa $16.50

782.42

1. Songs
ISBN 0-208-02441-7; 0-208-02472-7 (pa)

"Eighty rounds for choral singing from the sixteenth to twentieth centuries are presented in this easy-to-follow resource book. . . . If you can already read music this is a handy source, and even novice sight readers will have little difficulty with these selections. The musical notation is beginner-basic, with the times clearly marked." Bull Cent Child Books

Mallett, David

Inch by inch; the garden song; pictures by Ora Eitan. HarperCollins Pubs. 1995 unp il music pa $5.95 hardcover o.p. (k-2)   **782.42**

1. Songs 2. Gardens—Songs
ISBN 0-06-443481-8 (pa)   LC 93-38352

"In this picture-book version of the song first published in 1975 . . . a young child plants seeds . . . weeds and tends them, and finally, gleans a bountiful harvest. . . . Employing a variety of media including cut paper, Eitan uses color and space to create a striking effect." SLJ

Old MacDonald had a farm (k-2)   **782.42**

1. Folk songs—United States 2. Farm life—Songs
Some editions are:

Houghton Mifflin pa $5.95 Illustrated by Carol Jones (ISBN 0-395-90125-1)
North-South Bks. pa $6.95 Illustrated by Holly Berry (ISBN 1-55858-703-9)

Illustrated versions of the American folk song in which the inhabitants of Old MacDonald's farm are described, verse by verse

Pinkney, Brian

Hush, little baby; adapted and illustrated by Brian Pinkney. 1st ed. Greenwillow Books 2006 unp il $15.99; lib bdg $16.89 (k-2)

782.42

1. Folk songs—United States 2. Lullabies
ISBN 0-06-055993-4; 0-06-055994-2 (lib bdg); 9780060559939 (13-digit lib. bdg.); 9780060559946 (13-digit)   LC 2005008216

"Pinkney sets his version of the traditional Appalachian folksong in an African American household of the early 1900s. . . . Ink-on-clayboard scenes show a distraught toddler girl comforted by a playful father and older brother, who sing, dance, and, of course, offer a series of whimsical gifts. . . . An appended musical arrangement gives the tune a jazzy beat to match the wheeling, undulating figures in the story." Booklist

Raffi

Baby Beluga; illustrated by Ashley Wolff. Crown 1990 unp il music (Raffi songs to read) pa $5.99 hardcover o.p. (k-2)   **782.42**
1. Songs 2. Whales—Songs
ISBN 0-517-58362-3 (pa)   LC 89-49367
Also available Board book edition
Presents the illustrated text to the song about the little white whale who swims wild and free
"Wolff's striking double-page spreads show the young whale among its fellow Arctic Sea inhabitants. Diversifying her views, the illustrator eyes Baby Beluga and mother swimming together underwater; takes an aerial angle, looking down on the whales from a puffin's perspective; and observes the icy yet welcoming formations where seals, polar bears, and an Eskimo find shelter. . . . An inviting approach to reading encouragement." Booklist

Down by the bay; illustrated by Nadine Bernard Westcott. Crown 1987 unp il music (Raffi songs to read) pa $5.99 hardcover o.p. (k-2)   **782.42**
1. Songs
ISBN 0-517-56645-1 (pa)   LC 87-750291
Also available Board book edition
This illustrated version of one of Raffi's songs depicts a variety of unusual sights to be seen "down by the bay"
The "cheerful nonsense verses are illustrated with equal cheer. Westcott's scraggly lines and bright, clear colors humorously portray the busy children, jolly animals, and frantic mothers that populate the song." SLJ

Five little ducks; illustrated by Jose Aruego and Ariane Dewey. Crown 1989 unp il (Raffi songs to read) hardcover o.p. pa $5.99 (k-2)   **782.42**
1. Songs 2. Ducks—Songs
ISBN 0-517-58360-7; 0-517-56945-0 (pa)
LC 88-3752
Also available Board book edition
When her five little ducks disappear one by one, Mother Duck sets out to find them

Reid, Rob

Children's jukebox; a subject guide to musical recordings and programming ideas for songsters ages one to twelve. American Lib. Assn. 1995 225p il pa $25   **782.42**
1. Songs—Indexes 2. Children's libraries
ISBN 0-8389-0650-8   LC 95-6163
"Arranging selections into 35 categories reflecting 'popular themes for story programs and classroom use,' Reid has assembled 300 recordings, graded (preschool, primary, intermediate, all) for children ages 2 through 12. An alphabetically arranged discography and a selection of Reid's 'top twenty' suggestions for a core collection precede the thematic listings. . . . The annotations, which are arranged by broad subject—for example, animals, bath time, growing up, imagination—are short, informal, and spunky." Booklist
Includes bibliographical references

Roth, Susan L.

Hanukkah, oh Hanukkah; [by] Susan L. Roth. Dial Books for Young Readers 2004 unp il $10.99 (k-2)   **782.42**
1. Hanukkah—Songs 2. Songs
ISBN 0-8037-2843-3   LC 2003-13165
A family of mice celebrates the eight days of Hannukah with friends in this illustrated version of the holiday song.
"Cloth and paper collages done in many different patterns and textures add interest to the cozy tableaux. . . . The lovely colors and the appealing tune make this a good holiday choice." SLJ

Seeger, Pete

One grain of sand; a lullaby; words & music by Pete Seeger; paintings by Linda Wingerter. Little, Brown 2002 unp il $15.95 (k-1)   **782.42**
1. Lullabies
ISBN 0-316-78140-1   LC 00-50687
A lullaby celebrating the fragility of the environment, the innocence of childhood, and the sense that we all are connected and part of the world's family
"Gentle, lyrical verses enfold young listeners in a wide, wonderful world, united by love and family. The concept is echoed and enhanced by Wingerter's luminescent, realistic art." Booklist

Sturges, Philemon

She'll be comin' 'round the mountain; illustrated by Ashley Wolff. Little, Brown 2004 unp il $15.95 (k-3)   **782.42**
1. Songs
ISBN 0-316-82256-6
New words to the traditional tune describe a camper-driving, "hootin' " and "shoutin' " guest and the party that will begin when she arrives.
"The action is set in a little town in the Southwest where an array of animals awaits a visitor's arrival. . . . Wolff's festive and funny illustrations, done in gouache and pastels, enhance the merriment of Sturges's rhythmic verses." SLJ

Taback, Simms

There was an old lady who swallowed a fly. Viking 1997 unp il $16.99   **782.42**
1. Folk songs 2. Animals—Songs
ISBN 0-670-86939-2
Also available Little, Brown paperback edition by Nadine Bernard Westcott with title: I know an old lady who swallowed afly
A Caldecott Medal honor book, 1998
Simms Taback's illustrated version of the folk song in which an old lady swallows a variety of progressively larger animals
"Each page is full of details and humorous asides. . . . A die-cut hole allows readers to see inside [the old lady's] belly, first the critters already devoured and, with the turn of the page, the new animal that will join the crowd in her ever-expanding stomach. . . . The text is handwritten on vivid strips of paper that are loosely placed on the patterned page, thus creating a lively interplay between the meaning of the words and their visual power." SLJ

Trapani, Iza

Mary had a little lamb; as told and illustrated by Iza Trapani. Whispering Coyote Press 1998 unp il $16.95; pa $6.95 (k-2) **782.42**

1. Songs 2. Nursery rhymes 3. Sheep—Songs
ISBN 1-58089-009-1; 1-58089-090-3 (pa)
LC 98-14728

Also available board book edition

This expanded version of the traditional rhyme shows what happens when the lamb decides to go off alone. Includes music on the last page

"The bright and lively watercolor illustrations are sweet. . . . Preschoolers will find it both humorous and reassuring." SLJ

A **treasury** of children's songs; forty favorites to sing and play. Holt/Metropolitan Museum of Art 2003 unp il $19.95 (k-3) **782.42**

1. Songs
ISBN 0-8050-7445-7

A collection of forty traditional songs such as "London Bridge," "Pop Goes the Weasel," and "The Mulberry Bush," illustrated with works of art from the Metropolitan Museum of Art. Includes commentary on the art works.

"A beautifully produced abridgment of Go in and out the Window (Holt, 1987), which included 61 selections. . . . The art on the front cover and typeface, as attractive and lavish as in the first book, suggest a younger audience." SLJ

Weave little stars into my sleep; Native American lullabies; edited by Neil Philip; photographs by Edward S. Curtis. Clarion Bks. 2001 unp il $16 (2-4) **782.42**

1. Lullabies 2. Native American literature
ISBN 0-618-08856-3
LC 00-60324

Published in the United Kingdom with title: Where did you fall from?

This is a "book of 15 lullabies, selected, adapted, and, in some cases, reworked from original Native American material. Striking, carefully chosen photographs, originally published in the early 1900s, portray the spirit of the words." Booklist

Includes bibliographical references

Whippo, Walt

Little white duck; lyrics by Walt Whippo; music by Bernard Zaritzky; illustrations by Joan Paley. Little, Brown 2000 unp il music $15.99 (k-2) **782.42**

1. Songs 2. Ducks—Songs
ISBN 0-316-03227-1
LC 99-13661

Also available board book edition

Based on the song of the same title, a little white duck causes a commotion in its pond

This song "gets a modern update courtesy of vibrant collage illustrations. Each verse of the song is sung by a small, brown mouse troubadour. . . . The illustrations are done in bright and beautiful shades of red, blue, and green." Booklist

Yolen, Jane

Apple for the teacher; thirty songs for singing while you work; collected and introduced by Jane Yolen; music arranged by Adam Stemple; art edited by Eileen Michaelis Smiles. Harry N. Abrams, Inc 2005 117p il $24.95 (4 and up) **782.42**

1. Songs 2. Work—Songs
ISBN 0-8109-4825-7
LC 2004-24404

Contents: Astronaut: Fire in the sky; Barber: Barber, spare those hairs; Bargee: The Erie Canal; Chimney sweeper: Chimney sweeper; Cowboy: Git along, little dogies; Doctor: The doctor song; Farmer: The farmer is the man; Field hand: Cotton needs pickin'; Fisherman: Boston come-all-ye; Housewife: Old grumble; Hunter: Let's go a-hunting; Jockey: Stewball; Laundry worker: Dashing away with the smoothing iron; Logger: The frozen logger; Girls: Cotton mill girls; Miner: Down in a coal mine; Musician (orchestra): The orchestra; Programmer: My father is a programmer; Railroad engineer: Casey Jones; Railway worker: Pat works on the railway; Reaper: The reaper on the plain; Rescue workers: Bodies on the line; Shoemaker: Peg an' awl; Street vendor: Chairs to mend; Tarrier: Drill ye tarriers, drill; Teacher: In the good old days; Teamsters: The oxen song; Telephone operator: Long distance blues; Wait staff: Stand and wait; Weavers: Weave-room blues.

"Yolen has brought together a collection of 30 work songs . . . which represent a wide variety of occupations. . . . She introduces each job, explaining unusual vocabulary and references in the songs. . . . The artwork . . . is elegant. Ranging from sculpture to paintings to needlework, each selection of Americana has been carefully matched to the occupation, beautifully reproduced on high-quality paper, and meticulously identified." Booklist

Zelinsky, Paul O.

Knick-knack paddywhack! a moving parts book; adapted from the counting song and illustrated by Paul O. Zelinsky; paper engineering by Andrew Baron. Dutton 2002 unp il $18.99 (k-3) **782.42**

1. Counting 2. Songs
ISBN 0-525-46908-7

A young boy sets out on a walk—pull the tabs and tiny old men from One to Ten act out the familiar refrain of the traditional counting song on and all around him.

"This glorious title is a paper-engineering and bookmaking marvel as well as a freewheeling romp." SLJ

784.19 Musical instruments

Ardley, Neil

Music; written by Neil Ardley. rev ed. DK Pub. 2004 72p il (DK eyewitness books) $15.99; lib bdg $19.99 (4 and up) **784.19**

1. Musical instruments
ISBN 0-7566-0790-4; 0-7566-0708-6 (lib bdg)

First published 1989 by Knopf

Text and pictures introduce musical instruments from early times to the present—from pipes and flutes to electronic synthesizers.

Wiseman, Ann Sayre

Making music; [by] Ann Sayre Wiseman and John Langstaff; illustrations by Ann Sayre Wiseman. Storey Bks. 2003 96p il $19.95; pa $9.95 (3-6)   **784.19**

1. Musical instruments 2. Handicraft
ISBN 1-58017-513-9; 1-58017-512-0 (pa)
                                        LC 2003-54218

First published 1979 by Scribner with title: Making musical things

Includes instructions for making a variety of simple musical instruments from ordinary household items

Includes glossary and bibliographical references

784.2 Full orchestra (Symphony orchestra)

Ganeri, Anita

The young person's guide to the orchestra; Benjamin Britten's composition on CD narrated by Ben Kingsley; book written by Anita Ganeri. Harcourt Brace & Co. 1996 56p il $25 (4 and up)
                                        784.2

1. Orchestra 2. Musical instruments 3. Music appreciation
ISBN 0-15-201304-0   LC 95-41478

"Accompanying this book on orchestral music is a CD featuring Britten's *A Young Person's Guide to the Orchestra* . . . as well as Dukas' *The Sorcerer's Apprentice*. The book begins with an overview of the orchestra and then centers around groups of instruments, explaining a bit of their history and their sound's distinctive quality. . . . The book also introduces eight famous composers, world music, Benjamin Britten, and the background of *The Young Person's Guide to the Orchestra*. . . . Handsome and useful." Booklist

Includes glossary

Hayes, Ann

Meet the orchestra; written by Ann Hayes; illustrated by Karmen Thompson. Harcourt Brace Jovanovich 1990 unp il $16; pa $6 (k-3)
                                        784.2

1. Orchestra 2. Musical instruments
ISBN 0-15-200526-9; 0-15-200222-7 (pa)
                                        LC 89-32959

Also available Spanish language edition
"Gulliver books"

Describes the features, sounds, and role of each musical instrument in the orchestra

"Spacious watercolors depicting animal musicians in formal evening dress enhance this charming introduction to the orchestra. . . . The descriptive writing has immediacy . . . while the artwork has a subtle sense of color and humor that increases the fun." Booklist

Koscielniak, Bruce

The story of the incredible orchestra; an introduction to musical instruments and the symphony orchestra. Houghton Mifflin 2000 unp il $15 (2-4)   **784.2**

1. Orchestra 2. Musical instruments
ISBN 0-395-96052-5   LC 98-43933

Describes the orchestra, the families of instruments of which it is made, and the individual instruments in each family

"The illustrations are dense with gentle color and filled with scenes of musicians at play and pictures of instruments, with banner labels adding more information. . . . A lot of information about who invented what and how it's played is packed into these engaging pages." Booklist

790.1 General kinds of recreational activities

Blakey, Nancy

Go outside! over 130 activities for outdoor adventures; photographs by Dana Dean Doering. Tricycle Press 2002 134p il pa $13.95 (3-6)
                                        790.1

1. Outdoor recreation 2. Amusements
ISBN 1-58246-064-7   LC 2001-5914

Presents outdoor activities and creative projects, organized by the seasons

"Few activity books for children present ideas that look and sound as appealing as the ones described in these pages. . . . Some of the projects explore science, others bring in nature lore or outdoor cooking skills, while many more are simply fun. . . . Throughout this treasure trove black-and-white photos focus on procedures indicated in the directions and, more notably, on children happily engaged in the activities discussed." Booklist

Drake, Jane

The kids winter handbook; [by] Jane Drake & Ann Love; illustrated by Heather Collins. Kids Can Press 2001 127p il $18.95; pa $12.95 (4 and up)   **790.1**

1. Recreation 2. Handicraft 3. Nature craft
ISBN 1-55337-033-3; 1-55074-969-2 (pa)

Companion volume to The kids' summer handbook

This offers ideas for winter activities such as sewing, observing the night sky, identifying animal tracks, storytelling, cooking, crafts, and games

"Most of the projects are inexpensive to make, and supplies are easy to obtain, making these interesting alternatives to holiday boredom or too much TV. Many of the activities, especially those that are science related, are also suitable for the classroom." SLJ

Love, Ann

Kids and grandparents: an activity book; written by Ann Love & Jane Drake; illustrated by Heather Collins. Kids Can Press 2000 160p il $17.95; pa $10.95 (3-6)   **790.1**

1. Amusements

ISBN 1-55074-784-3; 1-55074-492-5 (pa)

First published 1999 in Canada

"A collection of more than 90 games, crafts, recipes, and activities for children to do with their grandparents. . . . A good choice for old-fashioned fun." SLJ

Warshaw, Hallie

Get out! outdoor activities kids can enjoy everywhere (except indoors); [by] Hallie Warshaw with Jake Miller; photography by Julie Brown. Sterling 2001 125p il $19.95 (3-6)   **790.1**

1. Outdoor recreation

ISBN 0-8069-9091-0   LC 2001-277024

This is a "collection of creative activities that will keep youngsters busy outside when the weather is nice. Seven chapters offer suggestions for various games, group events, nature projects, community service, and kid businesses. The activities include staging a balloon Olympics, playing broom ball, creating a spy journal, building a sundial, helping a neighbor, or having a yard sale. . . . The fun, engaging text is well written and speaks directly to children. Bold colors, various fonts, whimsical illustrations, and a superb layout add to the appeal in this well-organized title." SLJ

Williamson, Susan

Summer fun! 60 activities for a kid-perfect summer; illustrations by Michael Kline. Williamson 1999 138p il pa $12.95   **790.1**

1. Amusements 2. Games 3. Handicraft

ISBN 1-88559-333-3   LC 98-53269

"A Williamson kids can! book"

Suggests a variety of activities for summertime, including nature study, cooking, crafts, games, creative activities, and more

"The 60 activities promised in the title hark back to a slower, quieter time. . . . The black-and-white cartoons that appear on each page add to the fun." SLJ

791.3   Circuses

Burgess, Ron

Be a clown! techniques from a real clown; [by] Ron Burgess, aka "Silly Willy"; illustrations by Heather Barberie. Williamson 2001 63p il (Quick starts for kids!) pa $7.95 (3-6)   **791.3**

1. Clowns

ISBN 1-88559-357-0   LC 2001-17370

"From name choices to costumes to makeup, actions, gags, and simple magic tricks, everything is here for would-be clowns. Burgess offers plenty of practical tips on creating laughter through clothing, joking, and pantomime, but he also explores some of the basic philosophy of clowning in its traditional styles. . . . The directions are clear and easy to follow. The shaded-line drawings are helpful, as are the several black-and-white photos of the author in costume." SLJ

Helfer, Ralph

The world's greatest elephant; illustrated by Ted Lewin. Philomel Books 2006 unp il $16.99 (1-3)   **791.3**

1. Circus 2. Elephants

ISBN 0-399-24190-6   LC 2005-06490

The true story of the lives and travels of the circus elephant Modoc who travelled widely and experienced dangerous adventures with his owner and trainer Bram Gunterstein.

"The large picture-book format is the typical choice for Lewin's fine watercolors, boldly portraying the dramatic episodes of the elephants life and the story of friendship, separation, and reunion. This bold and heartwarming adventure tale should have wide appeal." SLJ

791.43   Motion pictures

Reynolds, David West

Star wars: incredible cross sections; illustrated by Hans Jenssen & Richard Chasemore. DK Pub. 1998 32p il $19.95   **791.43**

1. Star Wars films

ISBN 0-7894-3480-6   LC 98-22878

This book "includes diagrams for the *Millennium Falcon*, T-65 X-wing, Blockade Runner, Tie Fighters, Sandcrawler, and BLT-A4 Y-wing, among others. An elaborate four-page fold-out analyzes the Death Star in minute detail. . . . AT-AT Walkers, AT-STs, snowspeeders, and speeder bikes are also included. Diagrams are surrounded by inserts of fascinating trivia, history, and technical notes." Voice Youth Advocates

Star wars: the visual dictionary; written by David West Reynolds; special fabrications by Don Bies and Nelson Hall; new photography by Alexander Ivanov. DK Pub. 1998 64p il $19.95   **791.43**

1. Star Wars films

ISBN 0-7894-3481-4   LC 98-22877

"This oversized volume is packed with full-color photographs of the characters and costumes, equipment, weaponry, mechanical droids, and assorted creatures from the Star Wars universe. . . . 'Data Files' provide additional, often fascinating, and personal tidbits about the inhabitants of this fantasy world. . . . It is a visual treat." SLJ

791.44   Radio

Krull, Kathleen

The night the Martians landed; just the facts (plus the rumors) about invaders from Mars; illustrations by Christopher Santoro. HarperCollins Pubs. 2003 74p il lib bdg $15.89; pa $4.25 (3-6)   **791.44**

1. War of the worlds (Radio program)

ISBN 0-688-17247-4 (lib bdg); 0-688-17246-6 (pa)

LC 2003-11365

Krull, Kathleen—*Continued*

Recounts the night before Halloween in 1938 when a play in the form of a news broadcast invading Martians sent radio listeners around the country into a panic, and examines why so many people confused entertainment with reality

This is written "in simple, informal prose and large text. . . . The whimsical cover art and cartoon illustrations featuring octopuslike martians will no doubt draw in readers and help sustain their attention. . . . Krull introduces some timelessly relevant points about media literacy and critical thinking." SLJ

McCarthy, Meghan

Aliens are coming! the true account of the 1938 War of the worlds radio broadcast. Knopf 2006 unp il $16.95; lib bdg $18.99 (1-3)

791.44

1. War of the worlds (Radio program)
ISBN 0-375-83518-0; 0-375-93518-5 (lib bdg)

LC 2005-08941

"In an average American living room of 1938, folks gather around the radio for a night's entertainment, when there's a new bulletin: 'Aliens are coming!' Orson Welles' infamous Halloween trick, his October 30 broadcast of H. G. Wells' War of the Worlds, is greatly excerpted and put together with quirky, imaginative artwork that reinforces the fantasy. . . . Using a 1930's art style, and a palette comprising mostly muted grays and reds, McCarthy evokes an era gone by. . . . This is packed with age-appropriate thrills and scares." Booklist

791.5 Puppetry and toy theaters

Exner, Carol R.

Practical puppetry A-Z; a guide for librarians and teachers; [by] Carol R. Exner. McFarland 2005 267p il pa $39.95

791.5

1. Puppets and puppet plays
ISBN 0-7864-1516-9

LC 2005010590

"Exner presents the art of puppetry as a creative and engaging way to snag the interests of both adults and children. Presented in alphabetical order, approximately 135 entries cover everything from starting a puppetry business to puppetry history to creating numerous kinds of puppets: glove, sponge, life-size, even marionettes. . . . This is an excellent resource for school or public libraries." Booklist

Includes bibliographical references

Minkel, Walter

How to do "The three bears" with two hands; performing with puppets. American Lib. Assn. 2000 154p il pa $28

791.5

1. Puppets and puppet plays 2. Children's libraries
ISBN 0-8389-0756-3

LC 99-28228

This guide to performing puppet plays in libraries offers advice on such topics as voice control and manipulation technique, script writing and adaptation, puppets, stages, scenery and props, and includes five puppet show scripts and stage-building plans

Includes bibliographical references

791.8 Animal performances

Schubert, Leda

Ballet of the elephants; illustrated by Robert Andrew Parker. 1st ed. Roaring Brook Press 2006 unp il $17.95

791.8

1. Circus 2. Ballet 3. Elephants
ISBN 1-59643-075-3

LC 2005-02670

"A Deborah Brodie Book"

The story of how "Circus polka" a dance of 50 elephants and 50 ballerinas, conceived by John Ringling North, choreographed by George Balanchine to music written by Igor Stravinsky, was created.

"Schubert's book tells an astonishing true story. . . . The words are simple and lyrical . . . and the beautiful, freely sketched double-page ink-and-watercolor art celebrates the excitement of the animals' dance. " Booklist

792 Stage presentations

Becker, Helaine

Funny business; clowning around, practical jokes, cool comedy, cartooning, and more. . . .; illustrated by Claudia Dávila. Maple Tree 2005 160p il $21.95; pa $9.95 (5 and up)

792

1. Wit and humor 2. Clowns 3. Cartoons and comics
ISBN 1-897066-40-6; 1-897066-41-4 (pa)

"Becker offers funny facts, an informative diagram showing what goes on in the body when you laugh, brief discussions of different types of humor (situation comedy, parody, farce, riddles, puns), a How Funny Are You? quiz, tips and timing for standup routines, body lingo, props, six improvisation games, clowning material, and more. For kids who want to learn how to juggle, tell jokes, or use sight-gag items, it's all here. Cartooning is explained as well." SLJ

Dunleavy, Deborah

The jumbo book of drama; illustrations by Jane Kurisu. Kids Can Press 2004 208p il $14.95 (4 and up)

792

1. Theater—Production and direction
ISBN 1-55337-008-2 (pa)

"In Act I (the first chapter), Dunleavy focuses on body movement (mime, clowning, dance). In Act II, she concentrates on voice (readers' theater, puppetry, radio plays). She explains melodrama, comedy, and tragedy in Act III, and rounds out Act IV with 'behind-the-scenes stuff' about directing, staging, special effects, lighting, props, and costumes." Booklist

"This concise introduction is sure to motivate young actors and give them the chance to explore both the performance and design elements of the theater. . . . The delightful watercolor cartoons are both decorative and informative and add much to the text's light tone." SLJ

Friedman, Lise

Break a leg! the kids' guide to acting and stagecraft; photographs by Mary Dowdle. Workman 2002 222p il pa $14.95 hardcover o.p. (4 and up)   **792**

1. Acting 2. Theater—Production and direction

ISBN 0-7611-2590-6 (pa)   LC 2001-26986

A comprehensive manual for acting and theater, discussing improvisation, voice projection, breathing exercises, script analysis, and technical aspects of theater production

"The information is solid and presented well, and the sidebars, in which young actors offer comments and tips, add life to the text." Booklist

792.5   Opera

Ganeri, Anita

The young person's guide to the opera; with music from the great operas on CD; book written by Anita Ganeri and Nicola Barber. Harcourt 2001 55p il $25 (4 and up)   **792.5**

1. Opera

ISBN 0-15-216498-7   LC 00-54105

"In association with the Royal Opera House and the San Diego Opera." Title page

The authors cover "opera, from the origins of the form to the stories behind the great works to the most famous opera singers and the venues in which they perform. . . . The accompanying CD is an excellent complement to the book. It contains an enticing mix of vocal and instrumental tracks. . . . The book and CD are an attractive and effective package that will make this often-intimidating art form more accessible." SLJ

Includes glossary

Rosenberg, Jane

Sing me a story; the Metropolitan Opera's book of opera stories for children; introduction by Luciano Pavarotti. Thames & Hudson 1989 158p il pa $15.95 hardcover o.p. (4-6)   **792.5**

1. Opera—Stories, plots, etc.

ISBN 0-500-27873-3 (pa)   LC 88-51929

"Alongside the so-called ABC's—*Aida, La Boheme and Carmen*—are less often performed works such as *L'Enfant et les Sortileges, Porgy and Bess* and *The Love for Three Oranges*. The author skillfully refers to specific musical passages and uses dialogue drawn from the libretto to link each story to an actual performance. . . . Although brief accounts in cannot do justice to the deep emotion and psychological insight of *Pagliacci* or *The Magic Flute*, these failings are more than redeemed by Rosenberg's handsomely detailed watercolors, which convey the opulent sensuality of opera at its most sublime." Publ Wkly

Siberell, Anne

Bravo! brava! a night at the opera; behind the scenes with composers, cast, and crew; introduction by Frederica von Stade. Oxford Univ. Press 2001 64p il $19.95 (4 and up)   **792.5**

1. Opera

ISBN 0-19-513966-6   LC 2001-21206

This "book introduces all features of the opera, including stars, stagehands, set designers, conductors, and supernumeraries. . . . Cartoon artwork illustrates the text, and a world map highlighting the settings of well-known operas is also included, as are curtain diagrams, plot summaries of favorite operas, and sample costumes." Horn Book Guide

"An excellent resource for reports, this unusual book has an exceptional range of topics for younger students and is an essential purchase for upper elementary and middle school music programs." SLJ

Includes glossary and bibliographical references

Verdi, Giuseppe

Aïda; as told by Leontyne Price; illustrated by Leo and Diane Dillon. Harcourt Brace Jovanovich 1990 unp il $19; pa $8 (4 and up)   **792.5**

1. Opera—Stories, plots, etc.

ISBN 0-15-200405-X; 0-15-200987-6 (pa)

     LC 89-36481

Coretta Scott King Award for illustration, 1990

"Gulliver books"

"Based on the opera by Giuseppi Verdi"

Tragedy results when an enslaved Ethiopian princess falls in love with an Egyptian general

"The text appears on the left surmounted by a friezelike series of figures which interpret the action; on the right, a full-page illustration focuses on a particular character or grouping. A worthy introduction to the opera for a varied audience." Horn Book Guide

792.6   Musical plays

Amendola, Dana

A day at the New Amsterdam Theatre; photos by Gino Domenico; written by Dana Amendola. Disney Editions 2004 125p il $24.95 (4 and up)   **792.6**

1. New Amsterdam Theatre (New York, N.Y.)
2. Theater

ISBN 0-7868-5438-3

"This title covers a day in the life of Disney's *The Lion King*, the long-running Broadway musical. . . . A clock in a corner of each spread guides readers through the day as box-office personnel, makeup designers, dancers, actors, cleaning staff, and others do their jobs. Each spread includes several full-color photos that are often gritty, sometimes glamorous. . . . This unique volume provides an honest, realistic, eye-opening look at the behind-the-scenes work that goes into the running of a Broadway show." SLJ

792.8 Ballet and modern dance

Augustyn, Frank

Footnotes; dancing the world's best-loved ballets; [by] Frank Augustyn and Shelley Tanaka. Millbrook Press 2001 94p il lib bdg $24.90; pa $17.95 (5 and up)   **792.8**

1. Ballet

ISBN 0-7613-2323-6 (lib bdg); 0-7613-1646-9 (pa)

LC 00-50075

"*Footnotes* uses seven classical ballets as a jumping-off point to talk about the evolution of this unique art form, partnering, dancer as actor, training, costumes, choreography, and some of the world's most well-known performers." SLJ

"Fine photographs, most in color, add enormously to the book's appeal. A well-crafted, readable volume." Booklist

Cooper, Elisha

Dance! Greenwillow Bks. 2001 unp il $15.95; lib bdg $15.89 (2-4)   **792.8**

1. Dance

ISBN 0-06-029418-3; 0-06-029419-1 (lib bdg)

LC 00-41102

This book follows "dancers who bring a show through four grueling weeks of rehearsal to the opening curtain of a debut. " Bull Cent Child Books

"The text is keenly observant, describing scenes that are completely authentic yet will also strike a familiar chord with young children. . . . With an economy of line and color, Cooper conjures up pain and grace, hard work and camaraderie, stillness and velocity." Horn Book

Frith, Margaret

Hooray for ballet! illustrated by Amanda Haley. Grosset & Dunlap 2003 unp il (Smart about the arts) lib bdg $14.89; pa $5.99 (2-4)   **792.8**

1. Ballet

ISBN 0-448-43155-6 (lib bdg); 0-448-42884-9 (pa)

LC 2002-151250

Presents the history of ballet and a look at one particular ballet, Swan Lake, in the form of a child's school report

"This lighthearted, clever look at the world of ballet is a fine introduction for those who enjoy some humor with their art. . . . Childlike, colorful illustrations and dramatic color photos depict theatrical moments. Interspersed throughout are interesting facts about the history of this dance." SLJ

Grau, Andrée

Dance; written by Andrée Grau. rev ed. DK Pub. 2005 72p il (DK eyewitness books) $15.99; lib bdg $19.99 (4 and up)   **792.8**

1. Dance

ISBN 0-7566-1065-6; 0-7566-1066-4 (lib bdg)

First published 1998 by Knopf

Surveys all forms of dance throughout the world, discussing its cultural and social significance, its costume, its history, and noted dancers and choreographers

Jones, Bill T.

Dance; written by Bill T. Jones and Susan Kuklin; photographed by Susan Kuklin. Hyperion Bks. for Children 1998 unp il $14.95; lib bdg $15.49 (k-3)   **792.8**

1. Dance

ISBN 0-7868-0362-2; 0-7868-2307-0 (lib bdg)

LC 97-32375

Introduces basic concepts of dance through poetic text and photographs

"This celebration of dance combines Kuklin's luminous photography with Jones' spare but lyrical first-person narrative to create a sense of three-dimensional movement arrested in space." Bull Cent Child Books

Schorer, Suki

Put your best foot forward; a young dancer's guide to life; by Suki Schorer and the School of American Ballet; illustrations by Donna Ingemanson. Workman Publishing 2005 96p il pa $9.95 (4 and up)   **792.8**

1. Ballet

ISBN 9780761137955; 0761137955

LC 2005051428

"The words of counsel proffered by the author, who was a principal dancer for the New York City Ballet and is a teacher at the School of American Ballet, are engaging, imaginative, and right on target. . . . Practical tips such as essentials that need to be in your bag and behavioral advice such as being grateful for criticism are nicely woven into the book. The photographs, mainly of female dancers, are clear and colorful. These words of wisdom will keep dancers on their toes and stretching their minds and hearts." SLJ

Varriale, Jim

Kids dance; the students of Ballet Tech; text and photographs by Jim Varriale; with a foreword by Eliot Feld. Dutton Children's Bks. 1999 unp il $15.99 (4 and up)   **792.8**

1. Ballet Tech School (New York, N.Y.) 2. Ballet

ISBN 0-525-45536-1   LC 98-55905

Explains the rules, admissions process, academic classes, training exercises, and performances of Ballet Tech, America's first public school offering free ballet lessons for children

"The full-color and black-and-white photos depict ethnically and racially diverse groups of children and a broad range of ages. The young dancers are seen at practice, in performance, and at rest. Their enthusiasm for their art comes through clearly, in the pictures and in the lively prose." Horn Book

793   Indoor games and amusements

Becker, Helaine

Boredom blasters; brain bogglers, awesome activities, cool comics, tasty treats, and more; written by Helaine Becker; illustrated by Claudia Dávila. Maple Tree Press 2004 160p il $21.95; pa $9.95 (4-6)   **793**

1. Games 2. Amusements

ISBN 1-897066-02-3; 1-897066-03-1 (pa)

"This kid-friendly book is chock-full of amusing things to do, including tricks readers can play on their friends, yummy concoctions to make and eat, brain teasers, and some unusual games. . . . Each suggestion has clear, step-by-step directions. . . . The attractive layout features helpful diagrams and colorful illustrations." SLJ

Glenn, Jim

The treasury of family games; hundreds of fun games for all ages, complete with rules and strategies; [by] Jim Glenn and Carey Denton. Reader's Digest Association 2003 256p il $29.95 (5 and up)   **793**

1. Games

ISBN 0-7621-0431-7   LC 2003-46602

"This compendium is divided into categories: board games, card games, party games, games to play anywhere, indoor games, and outdoor games, and then subdivided into more focused categories within each color-coded section. Each entry includes step-by-step instructions, full-color photos, and clipart decorations. . . . The authors also provide the background and history of many of the games. . . . A useful and fun-packed volume." SLJ

Gunter, Veronika Alice

The ultimate indoor games book; the 200 best boredom busters ever! [by] Veronika Alice Gunter. 1st ed. Lark Books 2005 128p il $19.95 (3-6)
                                793

1. Indoor games

ISBN 1-57990-625-7   LC 2005006054

Includes index

"This compilation of brain games, ball games, pen-and-paper games, etc., provides a good supply of ideas that will appeal to most any player in a variety of circumstances. The activities are suitable for individuals or two or more players. Most of the suggestions require little or no equipment." SLJ

Ripoll, Oriol

Play with us; 100 games from around the world. Chicago Review Press 2005 128p il pa $16.95 (3-5)   **793**

1. Games

ISBN 1-55652-594-X

Originally published in Spain

"This sturdy, large-format paperback provides a bountiful selection of games from around the world. Typically, a section begins with an introduction to a type of game, such as games of strength or ball games, followed by several variations, each game identified by its name and place of origin as well as the rules that govern play. Colorful and playful illustrations brighten every page." Booklist

Includes bibliographical references

Warshaw, Hallie

Zany rainy days; indoor ideas for active kids; [by] Hallie Warshaw with Mark Shulman; photography by Morten Kettel. Sterling 2000 122p il $19.95 (2-5)   **793**

1. Indoor games

ISBN 0-8069-6623-8   LC 00-48264

This offers ideas for activities such as games, arts and crafts, cooking, creative writing, storytelling, singing, and puppetry

"An appealing, creative collection of activity ideas. . . . The animated text speaks directly to children. . . . Clear color photos and drawings, lots of white space and bright backgrounds, and varying layouts and fonts make this an engaging book." SLJ

793.2   Parties and entertainments

Griffin, Margot

The sleepover book; written by Margot Griffin; illustrated by Jane Kurisu. Kids Can Press 2001 144p il pa $14.95 (3-6)   **793.2**

1. Parties

ISBN 1-55074-522-0

This book offers "ideas for sleepover (or birthday party) themes, invitations, decorations, and favors. There are chapters on games and things to do, crafts, and 'beauty fun.'. . . The chapter on cooking is subdivided into dinners, desserts, midnight snacks, and breakfasts. . . . The illustrations, done in blue and yellow and all featuring girls, are lively and engaging." SLJ

Ross, Kathy

The best birthday parties ever! a kid's do-it-yourself guide; art by Sharon Lane Holm. Millbrook Press 1999 78p il lib bdg $24.90; pa $9.95 (2-4)   **793.2**

1. Parties 2. Birthdays

ISBN 0-7613-1410-5 (lib bdg); 0-7613-0989-6 (pa)
                                LC 98-27503

Provides instructions for the invitations, games, crafts, table decorations, and cakes for a dozen birthday parties based on such themes as outer space, puppets, and dinosaurs

"The book is appealing. The illustrations are colorful and plentiful." SLJ

Souter, Gillian

Perfect parties. Stevens, G. 2001 48p il (Handy crafts) lib bdg $22.60 (2-5)   **793.2**

1. Parties

ISBN 0-8368-2822-4   LC 00-52244

Souter, Gillian—*Continued*

This "title opens with a checklist for party givers to consider: theme, invitations, decorations, games and activities, prizes, food and favors. The subsequent sections address all of these details. Suggested crafts include bi-colored crepe-paper chains for decorations and games such as a piñata, indoor ball toss, tambourines, and a math fishing game. The personalized cookies and pizzas are sure to be a hit with young party goers and givers." SLJ

Includes bibliographical references

793.7 Games not characterized by action

Wise, Leonard

The way cool license plate book. Firefly Bks. 2002 64p il $19.95; pa $9.95 (4 and up)

793.7

1. Games

ISBN 1-55297-686-6; 1-55297-563-0 (pa)

LC 2003-279447

"The introduction explains what vanity license plates are and how to read them. A short history discusses the origin of license plates, the various kinds of materials that have been used to manufacture them, and collecting as a hobby, followed by six pages of directions for various license-plates-related games that can be played while traveling. . . . This is one of those titles that libraries should have just because." SLJ

793.73 Puzzles and puzzle games

Agee, Jon

Elvis lives! and other anagrams; collected and illustrated by Jon Agee. Farrar, Straus & Giroux 2000 unp il $15

793.73

1. Word games

ISBN 0-374-32127-2

LC 99-38139

Agee "demonstrates how letters can be rearranged to produce new meanings. . . . 'Astronomer' converts to 'moonstarer', and a pig pronounces a 'dormitory' chamber a 'dirty room.'" Publ Wkly

"Agee's cartoonlike drawings bring out the most in every phrase. . . . An entertaining introduction to anagrams." Booklist

Jon Agee's palindromania! Farrar, Straus & Giroux 2002 unp il $15.51

793.73

1. Palindromes

ISBN 0-374-35730-7

LC 2002-101771

In this collection "the pages are filled with whimsical black-and-white drawings of absurd or nonsensical situations. Some of the approximately 170 palindromes are monologues, some are comic-strip stories, and others are simply descriptive situations. From 'How Palindromes Are Formed in the Atmosphere' to 'AIBOHPHOBIA: Unusual Fear of Palindromes.'" SLJ

This "book on word play is a creative, comedic gem." Booklist

Sit on a potato pan, Otis! more palindromes. Farrar, Straus & Giroux 1999 unp il $14.41

793.73

1. Palindromes

ISBN 0-374-31808-5

LC 98-31783

"This volume collects more than sixty palindromes and displays them in witty cartoon drawings, notable for their off-center deadpan humor. Most of the entries will have readers chuckling aloud and trying to concoct their own palindromes." Horn Book Guide

So many dynamos! and other palindromes. Farrar, Straus & Giroux 1994 80p il pa $6.96 hardcover o.p.

793.73

1. Palindromes

ISBN 0-374-46905-9 (pa)

LC 94-73749

"This book features one palindromic phrase per page or spread. . . . Even children who have never heard of a palindrome will be drawn to the cartoons, while readers fascinated by concept may want to try writing (and illustrating) their own." Booklist

Cerf, Bennett

Riddles and more riddles! illustrated by Debbie Palen. Random House 1999 unp il $7.99; lib bdg $11.99

793.73

1. Riddles 2. Jokes

ISBN 0-679-88970-1; 0-679-98970-6 (lib bdg)

LC 99-20133

"Beginner books"

This volume combines Book of riddles (1960) and More riddles (1961)

A collection of riddles, such as "When is a cook bad? When she beats an egg." and "What kind of coat should be put on when it is wet? A coat of paint"

Cole, Joanna

Why did the chicken cross the road? and other riddles, old and new; compiled by Joanna Cole and Stephanie Calmenson; illustrated by Alan Tiegreen. Morrow Junior Bks. 1994 64p il pa $7.95 hardcover o.p. (3-5)

793.73

1. Riddles

ISBN 0-688-12204-3 (pa)

LC 94-2582

The authors "begin with a brief explanation about the origin of riddles and proceed with a collection of over two hundred, classic and new. Though many of the riddles appear in other collections, the book, illustrated with black-and-white line drawings, will be useful for its short bibliography and subject index." Horn Book Guide

Hall, Katy

Creepy riddles; [by] Katy Hall and Lisa Eisenberg; pictures by S.D. Schindler. Dial Bks. for Young Readers 1998 48p il $13.99; pa $3.99 (k-2)

793.73

1. Riddles

ISBN 0-8037-1684-2; 0-14-130988-1 (pa)

LC 94-37524

"Dial easy-to-read"

Hall, Katy—*Continued*

"A collection of riddles about vampires, ghosts, ghouls, and assorted monsters. . . . The illustrations are a scream. Schindler uses a find-nibbed pen to include lots of subtle details before adding vivid watercolor washes. . . . A superior choice for most joke or beginning-to-read collections." SLJ

Dino riddles; by Katy Hall and Lisa Eisenberg; pictures by Nicole Rubel. Dial Bks. for Young Readers 2002 40p il $13.99 (k-2)   **793.73**
1. Riddles
ISBN 0-8037-2239-7   LC 97-49947
"Dial easy-to-read"

A collection of riddles relating to dinosaurs, such as "What do you get if you cross a dinosaur with a rabbit? Tricerahops!" and "What did dinosaur campers cook over the fire? Dino-s'mores!"

"Rubel's informal ink-and-marker illustrations are suitably silly. . . . This will be just right for joke-book junkies, beginning readers, and teachers looking to breathe new life into staid dinosaur units." Bull Cent Child Books

Mummy riddles; [by] Katy Hall and Lisa Eisenberg; pictures by Nicole Rubel. Dial Bks. for Young Readers 1997 48p il $13.99; pa $3.99 (k-2)   **793.73**
1. Riddles
ISBN 0-8037-1846-2; 0-14-130364-6 (pa)
       LC 94-37525
"Dial easy-to-read"

In this riddle book "the droll and grisly wordplay will appeal to new readers. . . . The bright, detailed illustrations are as deadpan and silly as the words." Booklist

Ribbit riddles; by Katy Hall and Lisa Eisenberg; pictures by Robert Bender. Dial Bks. for Young Readers 2001 40p il $13.99 (k-2)   **793.73**
1. Riddles 2. Jokes
ISBN 0-8037-2525-6   LC 99-89174
"Dial easy-to-read"

A collection of riddles and jokes about frogs. Example: What do little frogs like to eat on a hot summer day? Hopsicles!

"The distinctive art, cell-vinyl on layers of acetate, has a shimmery, almost fuzzy look that catches the eye—and the jokes." Booklist

Snakey riddles; by Katy Hall and Lisa Eisenberg; pictures by Simms Taback. Dial Bks. for Young Readers 1990 48p il pa $3.99 hardcover o.p. (k-2)   **793.73**
1. Riddles
ISBN 0-14-054588-3   LC 88-23687
"Dial easy-to-read"

An illustrated collection of riddles about snakes

"Riddle lovers will groan with delight at some of these riddles. . . . The best thing about the book is the cleverly drawn, lively cartoon illustrations. Long, colorful snakes form borders framing the text and picture for each riddle." SLJ

Stinky riddles; by Katy Hall and Lisa Eisenberg; pictures by Renée Andriani. Dial Books for Young Readers 2005 40p il $14.99 (k-2)   **793.73**
1. Riddles
ISBN 0-8037-2928-6   LC 2003-14420
"Dial easy-to-read"

A collection of jokes, puns, and riddles about skunks.

"Readers will find scent-sational artwork and some really funny riddles in this appealing easy reader. . . . A well-thought-out and well-crafted riddle book" SLJ

Turkey riddles; by Katy Hall and Lisa Eisenberg; pictures by Kristin Sorra. Dial Bks. for Young Readers 2002 40p il $13.99 (k-2)   **793.73**
1. Riddles
ISBN 0-8037-2530-2   LC 2001-47475
"Dial easy-to-read"

A collection of nearly three dozen riddles featuring turkeys, such as "What happened when Tom Turkey stepped up to the plate? He hit a fowl ball"

"The art, with cross-hatched details, is bright and appealing. . . . Great for a good time alone, with friends, or even in a classroom." Booklist

Kessler, Leonard P.

Old Turtle's 90 knock-knocks, jokes, and riddles; [by] Leonard Kessler. Greenwillow Bks. 1991 48p il $15.95 (1-3)   **793.73**
1. Jokes 2. Riddles
ISBN 0-688-09585-2   LC 89-77505

An illustrated collection of animal jokes and riddles

This book includes "a string of jokes and riddles silly enough to please kids this age and usually simple enough not to baffle them. . . . Kessler's cartoonlike drawings, bright with watercolor washes, give the book a fresh, funny look that makes the verbal humor twice as effective." Booklist

Lupton, Hugh

Riddle me this! riddles and stories to challenge your mind; retold by Hugh Lupton; illustrated by Sophie Fatus. Barefoot Books 2003 64p il $19.99 (2-4)   **793.73**
1. Riddles 2. Folklore
ISBN 1-84148-169-6

A whimsical collection of riddles and riddling stories from all over the world. The illustrations offer clues that will help children to solve the riddles.

"Lupton's blend of puzzle, trick, and joke is a winning combination, and Fatus' clear, bright ink-and-watercolor pictures in folk-art style are playful and clever." Booklist

Maestro, Giulio

Riddle roundup. Clarion Bks. 1989 64p il pa $6.95 hardcover o.p. (2-4)   **793.73**
1. Riddles 2. Word games
ISBN 0-8991-9537-7 (pa)   LC 86-33403

A collection of sixty-one riddles based on different kinds of word play such as puns, homonyms, and homographs

Maestro, Marco

Geese find the missing piece; school time riddle rhymes; by Marco and Giulio Maestro; pictures by Giulio Maestro. HarperCollins Pubs. 1999 48p il $14.95; lib bdg $14.89; pa $3.95 (k-2)

793.73

1. Riddles
ISBN 0-06-026220-6; 0-06-026221-4 (lib bdg); 0-06-443707-8 (pa)   LC 98-41513
"An I can read book"

Rhyming riddles answer questions about a variety of animals at school

"The simple text and structure of the riddles are just right for the target audience. The book is populated by a colorful assortment of birds and animals that provide visual clues." SLJ

What do you hear when cows sing? and other silly riddles; by Marco and Giulio Maestro; pictures by Giulio Maestro. HarperCollins Pubs. 1996 48p il pa $3.95 hardcover o.p. (k-2)

793.73

1. Riddles
ISBN 0-06-444227-6 (pa)   LC 94-18686
"An I can read book"

"The subjects of the riddles will be familiar to most readers—trains, bugs, mice, fish, boats. . . . Most of the selections involve plays on words, but some are relatively straightforward. . . . Children will love the silly pictures, laugh at the riddles, enjoy sharing them with others, and expand their vocabularies all at the same time." SLJ

Mignon, Philippe

Labyrinths; can you escape from the 26 letters of the alphabet? Firefly Bks. 2002 59p il $14.95; pa $9.95 (3-5)   **793.73**

1. Maze puzzles 2. Alphabet
ISBN 1-55297-559-2; 1-55297-479-7 (pa)
LC 2003-267758

"In this title, the right side of each spread portrays a letter of the alphabet as an intricate puzzle maze, each one a symbol of myth or nature. The left side features a short, open-ended poem based on the theme. The mazes, done in watercolor, are complex, varied, and beautiful, and they change in style to reflect each subject." Booklist

Munro, Roxie

Amazement park; by Roxie Munro. Chronicle Books 2005 37p il $16.95 (k-3)   **793.73**

1. Maze puzzles
ISBN 0-8118-4581-8   LC 2004-8482

This book includes "12 . . . mazes to navigate. . . . All mazes lead from one page to the next and then back again to the first one. . . . The mazes do get tricky and sometimes completely confusing, but an answer key is included for those who get stuck. The cartoon art is eye-catching and colorful." SLJ

Another book of maze puzzles by this author is: Mazescapes (2001)

Steig, William

C D B. Simon & Schuster Bks. for Young Readers 2000 c1968 47p il $16; pa $4.99
793.73

1. Word games
ISBN 0-689-83160-9; 0-671-66689-4 (pa)
LC 99-32720

First published 1968 by Windmill Bks.

Letters and numbers are used to create the sounds of words and simple sentences 4 u 2 figure out with the aid of illustrations

Readers "will delight in puzzling out the letter-and-number messages, aided by the simple, thickly outlined drawings and an answer key." Booklist

C D C? Farrar, Straus & Giroux 2003 c1984 57p il $16   **793.73**

1. Word games
ISBN 0-374-31233-8   LC 2002-111704

Also available in paperback with black & white illustrations

A color illustrated edition of the title first published 1984

Letters, numbers, and symbols are used to create the sounds of words and simple sentences which U R expected to figure out with the aid of illustrations. Includes an answer key

"Flawlessly executed, purely pleasurable, the book is definitely 'D-Q-R' for doldrums at any season." Horn Book

Terban, Marvin

The dove dove; funny homograph riddles; illustrated by Tom Huffman. Clarion Bks. 1988 64p il pa $7.95 hardcover o.p. (3-5)

793.73

1. Riddles 2. Word games
ISBN 0-89919-810-4 (pa)   LC 88-2611

"An introduction to the sometimes confusing world of homographs—words that are spelled alike, but are pronounced differently and have different meanings. Using the general pattern of riddle and accompanying illustration, Terban leads readers through a variety of homographs. . . . The book will prove of interest to those students who enjoy the challenge of, and appreciate, word play." SLJ

Funny you should ask; how to make up jokes and riddles with wordplay; illustrated by John O'Brien. Clarion Bks. 1992 64p il pa $7.95 hardcover o.p. (3-5)   **793.73**

1. Riddles 2. English language—Homonyms 3. Puns
ISBN 0-395-58113-3 (pa)   LC 91-19509

The author "introduces four kinds of wordplay—homonyms, 'almost-sound-alike words,' homographs, and idioms. In a laid-back fashion that won't put off readers, he shows clearly how each type of wordplay works, provides numerous examples to illustrate . . . and suggests some words to use when making up jokes and riddles of one's own. O'Brien's black-and-white cartoon sketches, liberally scattered throughout, add the perfect visual touch. Great for classroom use and for aspiring comedians—of any age." Booklist

Includes bibliographical references

Thomas, Lyn

Ha! Ha! Ha! 1000+ jokes, riddles, facts, and more; written by Lyn Thomas; illustrated by Dianne Eastman. Firefly Bks. (Willowdale) 2001 128p il $19.95; pa $9.95 (3-6)   **793.73**

1. Jokes 2. Riddles 3. Word games

ISBN 1-89437-915-2; 1-89437-916-0 (pa)

"Word puzzles, 'Knock! Knock!' jokes, computer jokes, puns, optical illusions, and more are presented on pages illustrated with black-and-white cartoons, many with dialogue balloons. . . . A fact box appears on each spread, giving interesting information about the subjects on the page. The design, layout, and very funny art all command attention." SLJ

Wick, Walter

Can you see what I see? picture puzzles to search and solve. Scholastic 2002 35p il $13.95   **793.73**

1. Puzzles

ISBN 0-439-16391-9   LC 2001-49032

"Cartwheel books"

Presents twelve brain-teasing hidden picture puzzles to solve

"With its range of activities and perspective-shifting challenges, this is sure to appeal to a wide age group of children, who won't be satisfied until they've solved the last puzzle." Booklist

Other titles in this series are:

Can you see what I see?: Cool collections (2004)

Can you see what I see?: Dream machine (2003)

Can you see what I see?: Seymour and the juice box boat (2004)

Can you see what I see: Seymour makes new friends (2006)

Can you see what I see?: The night before Christmas (2005)

I spy; a book of picture riddles; photographs by Walter Wick; riddles by Jean Marzollo; design by Carol Devine Carson. Scholastic 1992 33p il $13.95   **793.73**

1. Puzzles

ISBN 0-590-45087-5   LC 91-28268

Also available I spy board books for younger readers and I spy easy readers

"Cartwheel books"

This visual game book consists of "a series of rhymed riddles listing objects that children must locate in the accompanying photographs. Each double-page spread features crisp, full-color shots featuring an abundance of familiar items. The objects range from large and easy-to-spot to tiny and partially hidden. . . . An appealing book for children and adults to share and enjoy together." SLJ

Other titles in this series are:

I spy Christmas (1992)

I spy extreme challenger! (2000)

I spy fantasy (1994)

I spy fun house (1993)

I spy gold challenger! (1998)

I spy mystery (1993)

I spy school days (1995)

I spy spooky night (1996)

I spy super challenger! (1997)

I spy treasure hunt (1999)

I spy ultimate challenger! (2003)

I spy year-round challenger! (2003)

793.74   Mathematical games and recreations

Adler, David A.

Easy math puzzles; illustrated by Cynthia Fisher. Holiday House 1997 unp il $15.95 (2-4)   **793.74**

1. Mathematical recreations 2. Riddles

ISBN 0-8234-1283-0   LC 96-30921

A collection of mathematical riddles involving people, animals, coins, or food

These problems "stimulate and challenge children to use critical thinking skills to determine solutions—and they're fun. Adler's puzzles require clear reasoning more than sophisticated mathematics know-how or scratch paper. . . . Fisher's cartoon-style illustrations are cheerful and lively." SLJ

Ball, Johnny

Go figure! DK Pub. 2005 96p il map $15.99 (4 and up)   **793.74**

1. Mathematical recreations 2. Mathematics

ISBN 0-7566-1374-4

A collection of math activities that include brainteasers, magic tricks, and mind-reading games

"A dynamic book. . . . Blocks of color, diagrams, and photo collages contribute to the exciting layout. . . . A fun romp for number and puzzle lovers." SLJ

Math for the very young; a handbook of activities for parents and teachers; [by] Lydia Plonsky [et al.]; illustrated by Marcia Miller. Wiley 1995 210p il $29.95; pa $14.95   **793.74**

1. Mathematical recreations

ISBN 0-471-01671-3; 0-471-01647-0 (pa)

LC 94-20861

"This guide suggests ways to introduce math to children through everyday activities. Sections include making a record book about the child and the family as well as activities for each month of the year, geometric crafts, math games, counting rhymes and stories, and ways to use math in the home and on the road." Booklist

Includes bibliographical references

Tang, Greg

The grapes of math; mind-stretching math riddles; illustrated by Harry Briggs. Scholastic Press 2001 unp il $16.95 (2-4)   **793.74**

1. Mathematical recreations

ISBN 0-439-21033-X   LC 00-30062

Illustrated riddles introduce strategies for solving a variety of math problems in using visual clues

"This clever collection of puzzles could spark the interest of even the mathematically challenged. . . . The simple, staccato rhymes and crisp lines of the artwork keep attention focused, while those who find themselves stumped can consult the 'Answers' section at the back of the book." Publ Wkly

Tang, Greg—*Continued*

Math appeal; mind-stretching math riddles; illustrated by Harry Briggs. Scholastic Press 2003 unp il $16.95 (2-4)   **793.74**
1. Mathematical recreations
ISBN 0-439-21046-1   LC 2002-5354
Rhyming anecdotes present opportunities for simple math activities and hints for solving

"Bright, whimsical illustrations and clever rhymes introduce challenging exercises. . . . In a note, Tang states that his goal is 'to encourage clever, creative thinking,' and the questions posed do that." SLJ

Math potatoes; mind-stretching brain food; illustrated by Harry Briggs. 1st ed. Scholastic Press 2005 unp $16.95 (2-4)   **793.74**
1. Mathematical recreations
ISBN 0-439-44390-3   LC 2004-16638
"This picture book uses all kinds of visual tricks to demonstrate how to make arithmetic faster and easier. On each double-page spread, a rhyming verse has fun with a variety of subjects. Most rhymes are about foods . . . and the bright, computer-generated pictures are as playful as the words. . . . The games are complex, the visuals are tricky, and although the rhyme seems straightforward . . . readers must think carefully about adding, subtracting, and multiplying." Booklist

793.8 Magic and related activities

Broekel, Ray
Hocus pocus: magic you can do; [by] Ray Broekel and Laurence B. White, Jr; illustrated by Mary Thelen. Whitman, A. 1984 48p il $13.95 (3-5)   **793.8**
1. Magic tricks
ISBN 0-8075-3350-5   LC 83-26096
Step-by-step instructions for twenty simple magic tricks, together with tips on patter, timing, slight-of-hand, and misdirection for the beginning magician

"Most children, if they read carefully, will be able to figure out the tricks. The black-and-white illustrations dabbed with purple are clearly marked, and the jokes that accompany them add a spot of humor." Booklist

Burgess, Ron
Kids make magic! the complete guide to becoming an amazing magician; illustrations by Marie Ferrante-Doyle and Sarah Rakitin. Williamson Pub. 2004 127p il (Kids can!) pa $12.95   **793.8**
1. Magic tricks
ISBN 1-88559-387-2
"A Williamson's kids can! book"
Offers guidelines and tips for putting together a magic act including selecting a wand, mastering official terminology, developing a stage personality, and selecting and performing tricks.

This is an "inviting, easy-to-use resource. . . . Cartoons done in blue ink show enthusiastic youngsters practicing their skills." SLJ
Includes bibliographical references

White, Laurence B.
Shazam! simple science magic; [by] Laurence B. White, Jr., & Ray Broekel; illustrated by Meyer Seltzer. Whitman, A. 1990 48p il pa $4.95 hardcover o.p. (3-6)   **793.8**
1. Scientific recreations 2. Magic tricks
ISBN 0-8075-7333-7 (pa)   LC 90-42441
"Section titles such as 'How to Hypnotize a Potato' or 'The Uncanny Can That Can' will entice young readers to investigate nineteen simple science 'tricks.' Humorous illustrations in simple black line, highlighted with orange, add appeal and clarity. Directions are given in short paragraphs rather than prescriptive 'steps,' and each bit of magic is explained scientifically in a highly readable style." Adventuring with Books

Wyler, Rose
Magic secrets; by Rose Wyler and Gerald Ames; pictures by Arthur Dorros. rev ed. Harper & Row 1990 63p il pa $3.99 hardcover o.p. (k-2)   **793.8**
1. Magic tricks
ISBN 0-06-444153-9 (pa)   LC 89-35841
"An I can read book"
A revised and newly illustrated edition of the title first published 1967
Easy magic tricks for the aspiring young magician
"Most of the magic tricks presented here are easily understood and appear to be simple to learn and to execute with ample practice." SLJ

794 Indoor games of skill

King, Daniel
Games; learn to play, play to win. Kingfisher 2003 64p il $16.95 (5 and up)   **794**
1. Card games 2. Board games
ISBN 0-7534-5581-1   LC 2002-35660
Contents: Board games: Ancient games I; Ancient games II; Nine men's morris; Fox and geese; Backgammon; Go; Chess; Mancala; Checkers; Card games: The pack; First card games; Rummy; Cribbage; Whist; Spades; Hearts; Blackjack; Poker
Provides instructions on how to play a range of card and board games, as well as strategy and history of the games.
This is a "visually appealing book. . . . Great for beginners as well as seasoned players." SLJ

794.1 Chess

Basman, Michael
Chess for kids; written by Michael Basman. Dorling Kindersley 2001 45p il $12.99 (4 and up)   **794.1**
1. Chess
ISBN 0-7894-6540-X   LC 00-59018
This guide to chess explains the rudiments of the game, techniques and winning strategies
"A solid introduction for novices and good for skilled players wanting to develop their strategies and find out about chess clubs and tournaments." Booklist

795.3　Games dependent on drawing numbers or counters

Lankford, Mary D.

Dominoes around the world; illustrated by Karen Dugan. Morrow Junior Bks. 1998 40p il $16; lib bdg $15.93 (3-5)　　　**795.3**

1. Dominoes

ISBN 0-688-14051-3; 0-688-14052-1 (lib bdg)

LC 97-20975

Examines the history and basic rules of the game of dominoes and describes how it can vary from country to country

"While perhaps best used as a domino-instruction aid, the information may be useful for reports and the clean, attractive layout invites browsing." SLJ

Includes glossary and bibliographical references

795.4　Card games

Cole, Joanna

Crazy eights and other card games; by Joanna Cole and Stephanie Calmenson; illustrated by Alan Tiegreen. SeaStar Bks. 2002 c1994 76p il $14.95; pa $5.95 (3-5)　　　**795.4**

1. Card games

ISBN 1-58717-950-4; 1-58717-951-2 (pa)

LC 2002-70574

A reissue of the title first published 1994 by Morrow Junior Bks.

Introduces the different suits and face cards in a deck of cards, explains how to hold, shuffle, and deal them, and provides instructions for such games as Aces Up, Go Fish, and Spit

This offers "well-thought-out instructions, which are illustrated with card diagrams . . . and Tiegreen's comic cartoon-style drawings. A must for the recreation shelf." Booklist

Includes bibliographical references

Street, Michael

Lucky 13; solitaire games for kids; illustrated by Alan Tiegreen. SeaStar Bks. 2001 128p il $14.95; pa $6.95 (4 and up)　　　**795.4**

1. Solitaire (Game)

ISBN 1-58717-013-2; 1-58717-014-0 (pa)

LC 00-63764

This offers instructions for solitary card games, with historical comments on some of the games and strategies to improve one's playing

"Street's easy-to-understand directions and Tiegreen's clear, informative illustrations will have just about anyone playing like a pro in no time." SLJ

Includes glossary

Ward, Adam

Card games for kids; 50 fun games for your children; [by] Adam Ward. Hamlyn; distributed by Sterling 2004 128p il (Hamlyn reference) pa $7.95 (3-6)　　　**795.4**

1. Card games

ISBN 0-600-61074-8

"A collection of 50 easy games. . . . Sectioned into games for one player, two players or more, for parties, and for prizes, there is something for everyone. An index sorts the games by age appropriateness and another organizes them by skill levels. . . . This [book] is particularly kid-friendly, with cartoon illustrations and easy-to-follow instructions." SLJ

796　Athletic and outdoor sports and games

Ajmera, Maya

Let the games begin! [by] Maya Ajmera, Michael Regan; with a foreword by Bill Bradley. Charlesbridge Pub. 2000 unp il $16.95; pa $6.95 (3-5)　　　**796**

1. Sports

ISBN 0-88106-067-4; 0-88106-068-2 (pa)

LC 99-24032

Text and photographs of children from around the world focus on various aspects of sports, including physical benefits, the importance of practice, overcoming obstacles, teamwork, and more

"In addition to illustrating how children all over the world love sports, this book will inspire youngsters to get involved in athletics and teach them about sportsmanship." SLJ

Blumenthal, Karen

Let me play; the story of Title IX, the law that changed the future of girls in America; [by] Karen Blumenthal. 1st ed. Atheneum Books for Young Readers 2005 152p il $17.95 (6 and up)　　　**796**

1. Women athletes 2. Sex discrimination

ISBN 0-689-85957-0　　　LC 2004-1450

"The author looks at American women's evolving rights by focusing on the history and future of Title IX, which bans sex discrimination in U.S. education. . . . The images are . . . gripping, and relevant political cartoons and fact boxes add further interest. Few books cover the last few decades of American women's history with such clarity and detail" Booklist

Includes bibliographical references

Rhatigan, Joe

Run, jump, hide, slide, splash; the 200 best outdoor games ever; [by] Joe Rhatigan & Rain Newcomb. 1st ed. Lark Books 2004 128p il $19.95; pa $9.95 (2-6)　　　**796**

1. Games

ISBN 1-57990-509-9; 1-57990-754-7 (pa)

LC 2003-22186

Rhatigan, Joe—*Continued*
Provides directions, equipment lists, and variations for 150 outdoor games.

"From amusements for one or two participants to those appropriate for a crowd, there is something here for everyone. . . . The easy-to-follow instructions also include variations. The action-packed, full-color photographs show children participating in the activities, while occasional line drawings help explain equipment or setup." SLJ

Sierra, Judy
Children's traditional games; games from 137 countries and cultures; by Judy Sierra, Robert Kaminski. Oryx Press 1995 232p il pa $35

796

1. Games
ISBN 0-89774-967-7   LC 95-35623
The authors "describe popular games from 137 countries and cultures, including over 20 games from Native American groups. Each game . . . can be played by small groups in the classroom or on the playground." Publisher's note
Includes bibliographical references

796.03   Sports--Encyclopedias and dictionaries

Scholastic visual sports encyclopedia. Scholastic Ref. 2003 224p il $19.95 (4 and up)

796.03

1. Sports—Encyclopedias
ISBN 0-439-31721-5   LC 2001-49507
Text and drawings explain the equipment and rules for approximately one hundred sports, including track and field, ball sports, and motor sports
"The book is well organized, clearly written, and effectively illustrated." Booklist

796.1   Miscellaneous games

Brown, Marc Tolon
Play rhymes; collected and illustrated by Marc Brown. Dutton 1987 32p il music pa $5.99 hardcover o.p.   **796.1**
1. Finger play 2. Nursery rhymes
ISBN 0-14-054936-6 (pa)   LC 87-13537
A collection of twelve play rhymes with illustrations to demonstrate the accompanying finger plays or physical activities. Includes music for the six rhymes which are also songs
"The illustrations are full-color pastels with many small details and humorous elements to appeal to children. This is a good choice for program planning or for a rainy afternoon with a favorite child." SLJ

The **Eentsy,** weentsy spider: fingerplays and action rhymes; compiled by Joanna Cole and Stephanie Calmenson; illustrated by Alan Tiegreen. Morrow Junior Bks. 1991 64p il music pa $6.95 hardcover o.p.   **796.1**
1. Finger play 2. Songs
ISBN 0-688-10805-9 (pa)   LC 90-44594

"This collection of 38 fingerplays and action rhymes ranges from the familiar 'I'm a Little Teapot,' to the older 'Two Fat Gentlemen.' Simple musical arrangements are included where appropriate." SLJ
"Tiegreen uses a few simple lines to create a cast of multicultural characters whose enthusiasm is infectious. . . . An attractive, upbeat addition to the finger-play collection." Booklist
Includes bibliographical references

Erlbach, Arlene
Sidewalk games around the world; illustrated by Sharon Lane Holm. Millbrook Press 1997 64p il map pa $8.95 hardcover o.p. (3-5)   **796.1**
1. Games
ISBN 0-7613-0178-X (pa)   LC 96-8715
Describes various games played by children in 26 countries around the world
"Equipment needs are simple, varying from chalk to jump ropes to jacks or stones. Directions are clearly and succinctly written. Each double-page spread includes a brief note about the country of origin, a world map showing its location, and a description of the game with illustrations. An added treat is the occasional language boxes giving common phrases . . . in that nation's language." SLJ
Includes bibliographical references

Miss Mary Mack and other children's street rhymes; compiled by Joanna Cole and Stephanie Calmenson; illustrated by Alan Tiegreen. Morrow Junior Bks. 1990 64p pa $7.95 hardcover o.p.   **796.1**
1. Games 2. Nursery rhymes
ISBN 0-688-09749-9 (pa)   LC 89-37266
This is a collection of over 100 traditional childhood hand-clapping and street rhymes
"Tiegreen's lighthearted pen-and-ink illustrations are sure to tickle the fancy of young readers. . . . A book that's sure to produce smiles in any story hour or program." SLJ

796.2   Active games requiring equipment

Chambers, Veronica
Double dutch; a celebration of jump rope, rhyme, and sisterhood. Jump at the Sun/Hyperion Bks. for Children 2002 64p il $18.99 (4 and up)
796.2
1. Rope skipping 2. Jump rope rhymes
ISBN 0-7868-0512-9
"Chambers introduces readers to the world of jump roping through personal reminiscences, wonderful action photos, and factual narratives. The book looks like a vibrant collage, a clean typeface is interspersed with pictures and inserts of the rhymes themselves. From it, readers learn not only the history of double Dutch . . . and its current state, but also experience some of the joy of jumping." SLJ

Lankford, Mary D.

Hopscotch around the world; illustrated by Karen Milone. Morrow Junior Bks. 1992 47p il map pa $6.95 hardcover o.p. (3-5)　　**796.2**

1. Hopscotch

ISBN 0-688-14745-3 (pa)　　　　LC 91-17152

The author "presents 19 variations of hopscotch played in 16 countries around the world. Each double-page spread contains a diagram of the pattern to be scratched or chalked on the ground, a description of the game, step-by-step directions, and a large illustration showing how it is played. Lankford's research, briefly described in the text, brings in history as well as geography, language, and cultural differences. . . . A handsomely designed book on an unusual topic." Booklist

Includes bibliographical references

Thomas, Keltie

Blades, boards & scooters; illustrated by Steve Attoe and Allan Moon. Maple Tree Press; distributed by Firefly Books 2003 64p il (Popular mechanics for kids) $21.95; pa $12.95 (5 and up)　　**796.2**

1. In-line skating 2. Skateboarding 3. Snowboarding

ISBN 1-89437-945-4; 1-89437-946-2 (pa)

This "volume introduces scooters, in-line skates, skateboards, and snowboards. Thomas combines sound advice for beginners with glimpses of the 'X-treme scene,' showcasing the amazing feats performed by the pros and other experienced riders. . . . Throughout the book, colorful photographs show action scenes, while very clear pictures, evidently digital, illustrate the gear and some of the moves used in the sports." Booklist

796.22　Skateboarding

Spencer, Russ

Skateboarding; by Russ Spencer. Child's World 2005 32p il (Kids' guides) lib bdg $24.21 (4-6)　　**796.22**

1. Skateboarding

ISBN 1-59296-210-6　　　　LC 2003-27370

Contents: Go rip!; Into the great wide open; Gear up!; In action; Stars and competition

This "opens with an explanation of the sport and gives reasons why people enjoy it. The four chapters that follow cover background and development, equipment, technique, and stars and competitions. The excellent color photos are clear and exciting." SLJ

Includes bibliographical references

796.323　Basketball

Gibbons, Gail

My basketball book. HarperCollins Pubs. 2000 unp il $5.95 (k-2)　　**796.323**

1. Basketball

ISBN 0-688-17140-0　　　　LC 99-87902

Introduces the basics of the game of basketball, describing the players, court, techniques, and rules of play

Includes glossary

Kuklin, Susan

Hoops with Swoopes; words and photographs by Susan Kuklin. Jump at the Sun 2001 unp il $15.99 (k-3)　　**796.323**

1. Swoopes, Sheryl, 1971- 2. Basketball

ISBN 0-7868-2477-8　　　　LC 00-63887

"Sheryl Swoopes, WNBA basketball star, is featured in this photo-essay that describes the basics of the game." SLJ

"The streaming narrative, one-word labels, and stunning photographs of a solo Swoopes in action work together to replicate the stop-and-go rhythm of players on the court." Bull Cent Child Books

Thomas, Keltie

How basketball works. Maple Tree Press 2005 64p il $16.95; pa $6.95 (5 and up)　　**796.323**

1. Basketball

ISBN 1-89706-618-X; 1-89706-619-8 (pa)

This guide to basketball offers information about the game's origins, history, and equipment as well as positions, training, skills, stats, & rules of the game. It also offers tips and fascinating factoids.

"The writing style is razzle-dazzle energetic. . . . The layout features numerous sidebars and brightly colored photos and digital drawings. Even longtime fans will learn something from this engaging, enthusiastic book." Booklist

796.325　Volleyball

Jensen, Julie

Fundamental volleyball; photographs by Andy King. Lerner Publs. 1995 63p il (Fundamental sports) lib bdg $22.60 (5 and up)　　**796.325**

1. Volleyball

ISBN 0-8225-3452-5　　　　LC 94-5743

This book begins with a brief history of the sport. The following chapters describe how to play the game; the importance of conditioning and practicing; advanced moves; and variations on the game

Includes glossary and bibliographical references

796.332　American football

Gibbons, Gail

My football book. HarperCollins Pubs. 2000 unp il $5.95 (k-2)　　**796.332**

1. Football

ISBN 0-688-17139-7　　　　LC 99-87202

Introduces the basics of the game of football, describing the players, field, and how the game is played

"What shines through [in this book] is Gibbons's dedication to presenting the game as fun. . . . The illustrations, especially those of the players, clearly reflect the action." SLJ

Includes glossary

796.334   Soccer

Blackstone, Margaret

This is soccer; illustrated by John O'Brien. Holt & Co. 1999 unp il $15.95 (k-2)   **796.334**

1. Soccer

ISBN 0-8050-2801-3   LC 98-23474

A simple introduction to the game of soccer, covering its equipment, players, and basic plays and depicting a game in progress

"The humorous illustrations, in watercolor and pen, convey plenty of action, with swirling lines and jagged marks showing lots of movement and kicks. . . . The book provides an appropriate starting point for beginners." Booklist

Coleman, Lori

Fundamental soccer; photographs by Andy King. Lerner Publs. 1995 64p il (Fundamental sports) lib bdg $22.60 (5 and up)   **796.334**

1. Soccer

ISBN 0-8225-3451-7   LC 94-11907

This "book covers the history of the sport, positions, equipment, basic and more advanced moves, rules, the merits of practice, and variations in the game. . . . King's colorful, clear, informative photographs enhance the text." SLJ

Includes glossary and bibliographical references

Gibbons, Gail

My soccer book. HarperCollins Pubs. 2000 unp il $5.95 (k-2)   **796.334**

1. Soccer

ISBN 0-688-17138-9   LC 99-34514

Briefly describes the equipment, terminology, rules, positions, and plays of one of the world's most popular games

This "small, snappily designed book [is] attractive, accessible. . . . Diverse groups of children, drawn in Gibbons' typically bright colors and cheery style, demonstrate sports equipment and game plays." Booklist

Includes glossary

Hornby, Hugh

Soccer; written by Hugh Hornby; photographed by Andy Crawford. rev ed. DK Pub. 2005 72p il (DK eyewitness books) $15.99; lib bdg $19.99 (4 and up)   **796.334**

1. Soccer

ISBN 0-7566-1091-5; 0-7566-1092-3 (lib bdg)

First published 2000

Examines all aspects of the game of soccer: its history, rules, techniques, tactics, equipment, playing fields, competitive play, and more.

796.342   Tennis

Ditchfield, Christin

Tennis. Children's Press 2003 47p il lib bdg $23.50 (2-4)   **796.342**

1. Tennis

ISBN 0-516-22589-8   LC 2001-8504

"A True book"

This examines the history, basic rules, terminology, and major events of the sport of tennis

This book is "just the thing for eager young sports fans. Brief, yet quite thorough. . . . Good-quality photos, most in color, appear on almost every page, and deftly illustrate the text." SLJ

Includes glossary and bibliographical references

Miller, Marc

Fundamental tennis; photographs by Andy King. Lerner Publs. 1995 64p il (Fundamental sports) lib bdg $22.60 (5 and up)   **796.342**

1. Tennis

ISBN 0-8225-3450-9   LC 94-21107

This book presents a brief history of the game, the basics (including rackets, clothes, strokes, grips, serves, and stance), rules for singles play and rules for doubles, practice drills, and advanced shots. Color photographs show young tennis players in action

Includes glossary and bibliographical references

Williams, Venus

How to play tennis; learn to play tennis with the Williams sisters; [by Venus and Serena Williams]; text editor, Laura Buller; photographer, Russell Sadur. DK Pub. 2004 95p il $19.99 (5 and up)   **796.342**

1. Tennis

ISBN 0-7566-0582-2   LC 2004-7187

Tennis champions "Venus and Serena Williams host this how-to book about the game of tennis, teaching readers essential rules, swings, shots, and other must-knows for winning." Publisher's note

796.352   Golf

Ditchfield, Christin

Golf. Children's Press 2003 47p il lib bdg $23.50 (2-4)   **796.352**

1. Golf

ISBN 0-516-22590-1   LC 2002-5896

"A True book"

Contents: Tigermania; Years ago; The equipment; The rules; On the course; The professional tour

This examines the history, basic rules, terminology, and major events of the sport of golf

This book is "just the thing for eager young sports fans. Brief, yet quite thorough. . . . Good-quality photos, most in color, appear on almost every page, and deftly illustrate the text." SLJ

Includes glossary and bibliographical references

Gordon, John

The kid's book of golf. Kids Can Press 2001
48p il $14.95; pa $7.95 (3-6)   **796.352**
1. Golf
ISBN 1-55337-017-1; 1-55074-617-0 (pa)

This "book provides a quick history of the sport, followed by short chapters on equipment, swings, rules, and golf courses. . . . The clear, interesting, and engaging text includes 'amazing' and 'strange but true' facts. The attractive, full-color photographs of children and famous golfers executing the skills add to the book's utility as do the strategically placed diagrams." SLJ

Includes glossary

Krause, Peter

Fundamental golf; photographs by Andy King. Lerner Publs. 1995 64p il (Fundamental sports) lib bdg $22.60 (5 and up)   **796.352**
1. Golf
ISBN 0-8225-3454-1   LC 94-23166

This book presents a brief history of the game; the basics, including the function of each type of golf club; rules and etiquette; and skill shots. Photographs of young golfers illustrate proper stance and swing motion

Includes glossary and bibliographical references

Simmons, Richard

Golf; written by Richard Simmons; foreword by Nick Faldo. Dorling Kindersley 2001 48p il $9.95 (4 and up)   **796.352**
1. Golf
ISBN 0-7894-7390-9   LC 00-57060

"DK superguides"

Replaces The young golfer, published 1999

This "includes an introduction to golf with information about the history of the game, expert instruction on playing the game, golf course layouts, and steps for taking your game to the next level." Publisher's note

796.357   Baseball

Buckley, James, Jr.

Play ball! by James Buckley, Jr.; photography by Mike Eliason. DK Pub. 2002 48p il $12.95 (3-6)   **796.357**
1. Baseball
ISBN 0-7894-8509-5   LC 2001-47620

Photographs and text, including tips from professional players, show how to warm up, select the right equipment, and play baseball

"Vivid photographs and clear, straightforward texts are the hallmarks of DK, and this fine guide to baseball fits well into that tradition." Booklist

Coleman, Janet Wyman

Baseball for everyone; stories from the great game; by Janet Wyman Coleman with Elizabeth V. Warren. Abrams 2003 48p il $16.95 (4-6)   **796.357**
1. Baseball
ISBN 0-8109-4580-0   LC 2002-155971

Partial contents: Batter up! A single or a walk? 1826-1900. Baseball's beginnings; No more "soaking"; Measuring the heroes; A game for everyone; Baseball near the battlefield; "Slide, Kelly, Slide"; A profit of $1.39; Who's that on first?; Signs of the game; Going for a double 1900-1930. The ball player who made more money than the President; Baseball's silent heroes; Native Americans and the American pastime; A rookie decides not to run to second base; "Katie Casey was Baseball Mad"; Baseball leaves home; Shadow Ball, "Satchel" and the segregated game; Rounding second, headed for third 1930-1960

An illustrated history of baseball, covering the origins of the game, some of its best-known players, and significant changes in rules and practices throughout the nineteenth and twentieth centuries

"Drawing on The Perfect Game, Warren's adult book and exhibit of the same name at New York's American Folk Art Museum, . . . this elegant volume may well be irresistible to fans of America's favorite pastime. . . . [This offers] lively, informative text . . . enticingly packaged with a plethora of photographs, memorabilia and often astonishing folk art." Publ Wkly

Curlee, Lynn

Ballpark; the story of America's baseball fields. Atheneum Books for Young Readers 2005 41p il $17.95 (3-6)   **796.357**
1. Baseball 2. Stadiums
ISBN 0-689-86742-5   LC 2003-23144

This is a "history of baseball parks in words and pictures. The text briefly recaps the history of the game, mentioning star players through the years . . . but emphasizing the game's growth through the evolution of its playing fields." Booklist

This is a "succinct and thoughtful overview. . . . Stylized, full-page acrylic paintings add to the nostalgic tone of the book." SLJ

Geng, Don

Play-by-play baseball; photographs by Andy King. Lerner Publs. 2001 80p il pa $7.95 (5 and up)   **796.357**
1. Baseball
ISBN 0-8225-9880-9   LC 00-8879

First published 1995 with title: Fundamental baseball

Presents information on the history of baseball and the equipment used, demonstrates the basic skills involved in fielding, throwing, hitting, and baserunning, and describes how these skills are used in a game

"Not only does it have kid appeal, but there's a wealth of clearly written information in a logical format enhanced by action-packed photos." Book Rep

Includes bibliographical references

Gibbons, Gail

My baseball book. HarperCollins Pubs. 2000 unp il $5.95 (k-2)   **796.357**
1. Baseball
ISBN 0-688-17137-0   LC 99-32945

An introduction to baseball, describing the equipment, playing field, rules, players, and process of the game

"The information is well augmented by clearly labeled, colorful drawings." SLJ

Includes glossary

Isadora, Rachel

Nick plays baseball. Putnam 2001 unp il $15.99 (k-3)   **796.357**

1. Baseball

ISBN 0-399-23231-1   LC 00-38228

Uses the story of Nick and his teammates' championship baseball game to provide an introduction to aspects of the game of baseball including equipment, player positions, and rules

"Isadora's pictures are bright and sunny, perfectly evocative of a day playing ball. . . . Lots of fun and plenty of good advice, especially for the baseball newbie." Booklist

Kennedy, Mike

Baseball; [by] Mike Kennedy. Franklin Watts 2003 63p il $25.50; pa $8.95 (4 and up)   **796.357**

1. Baseball

ISBN 0-531-12271-9; 0-531-15588-9 (pa)

LC 2003-124

"Watts library"

Discusses the sport of baseball including its history, rules and regulations, statistics, and some outstanding players.

This is "well-organized. . . . [It includes] an abundance of excellent, captioned photos, mainly in color." SLJ

Kisseloff, Jeff

Who is baseball's greatest pitcher? Cricket Bks. 2003 181p il $15.95 (5 and up)   **796.357**

1. Baseball

ISBN 0-8126-2685-0   LC 2003-1245

Also available: Who is baseball's greatest hitter? (2000)

"A Marcato book"

Contents: So who's the best?; Grover Cleveland Alexander; Mordecai Brown; Steve Carlton; John Clarkson; Roger Clemens; Dizzy Dean; Bob Feller; Whitey Ford; James Galvin; Bob Gibson; Lefty Grove; Carl Hubbell; Randy Johnson; Walter Johnson; Addie Joss; Tim Keefe; Sandy Koufax; Greg Maddux; Juan Marichal; Pedro Martinez; Christy Mathewson; Joe McGinnity; Kid Nichols; Satchel Paige; Jim Palmer; Eddie Plank; Charles Radbourn; Amos Rusie; Nolan Ryan; Tom Seaver; Warren Spahn; Ed Walsh; Cy Young; Who's it gonna be?

Asks the reader to compare the statistics for thirty-three of baseball's greatest starting pitchers and decide who is the best

"Accomplishments and anecdotes are related in an informative and entertaining manner. . . . Anyone who enjoys baseball will be delighted with this information-packed, informal book." SLJ

Includes bibliographical references

Krasner, Steven

Play ball like the hall of famers; the inside scoop from 19 baseball greats; written by Steven Krasner; illustrations by Keith Neely. Peachtree 2005 221p $14.95 (5 and up)   **796.357**

1. Baseball

ISBN 1-56145-339-0

"Krasner assembles an impressive group of subjects, from Johnny Bench and Gary Carter on catching, to Don Sutton, Phil Niekro, and Tom Seaver on aspects of pitching. . . . Each entry includes anecdotes, a glossary of key terms, and mention of how the advice can be put into action. Black-and-white photos and line drawings appear throughout the succinct and readable interviews, and the perspectives are both detailed and insightful." SLJ

Play ball like the pros; tips for kids from 20 big league stars; written by Steven Krasner. Peachtree Pubs. 2002 181p il pa $12.95 (5 and up)   **796.357**

1. Baseball

ISBN 1-56145-261-0   LC 2001-7342

Nearly two dozen professional baseball players, such as Pedro Martinez and Derek Jeter, provide insights into how they prepare for and play the game.

"This title is just the sort of finely tuned analysis of baseball that many young players are looking for. . . . The tips given are detailed and insightful. . . . This is a good reference for young people working to improve their skills." Booklist

Lipsyte, Robert

Heroes of baseball; the men who made it America's favorite game; [by] Robert Lipsyte. Atheneum Books for Young Readers 2006 92p il $19.95 (4 and up)   **796.357**

1. Baseball—Biography

ISBN 0-689-86741-7   LC 2005010841

"Using as a focus some of baseball's greats—Big Al Spalding, Babe Ruth, Mickey Mantle, Jackie Robinson, Curt Flood . . . —Lipsyte offers a strong history of the game and its place in American culture. . . . Although much of this material, including the pictures, might be familiar to young readers already absorbed in the game, it is nicely laid out and colorfully formatted. Lipsyte has a clear, vivid style." Booklist

Includes glossary and bibliographical references

McKissack, Patricia C.

Black diamond; the story of the Negro baseball leagues; [by] Patricia C. McKissack and Fredrick McKissack, Jr. Scholastic 1994 184p il pa $5.99 hardcover o.p. (6 and up)   **796.357**

1. Baseball 2. African American athletes

ISBN 0-590-68213-X (pa)   LC 93-22691

Traces the history of baseball in the Negro Leagues and its great heroes, including Monte Irwin, Buck Leonard, and Cool Papa Bell

This is "an engaging account. . . . It includes a chronology, player profiles and wonderful photographs from the Negro Leagues." N Y Times Book Rev

Includes bibliographical references

Ritter, Lawrence S.

Leagues apart; the men and times of the Negro baseball leagues; illustrations by Richard Merkin. Morrow Junior Bks. 1995 unp il pa $5.95 hardcover o.p. (2-4)   **796.357**

1. Baseball 2. African American athletes

ISBN 0-688-16693-8   LC 94-17512

"Beginning with a brief history of the Negro Leagues, the text provides short biographies of twenty-two baseball players of color, interspersed with information about segregation and the racism of the 1920s through the 1940s. . . . Most of the players' biographies are accompanied by large stylized portraits in oil pastel." Horn Book

This "is a fine melding of text and illustration that makes accessible an important part of baseball history." SLJ

Smith, Charles R.

Diamond life; baseball sights, sounds, and swings. Orchard Bks. 2004 28p il $15.95 (2-4)   **796.357**

1. Baseball

ISBN 0-439-43180-8

"A celebration of America's pastime that . . . utilizes a jazzed layout, multiple fonts, and enhanced photography." Booklist

"Smith captures the colorful language and vivid images of the game. . . . The energetic, playful language begs to be read aloud. Combined with bright colors, bold print in a variety of fonts, and exceptional photography, this book is a winner." SLJ

Smyth, Ian

The young baseball player; written by Ian Smyth; with a foreword by Eduardo Perez. DK Pub. 1998 37p il (Young enthusiast) $15.99 (4 and up)   **796.357**

1. Baseball

ISBN 0-7894-2825-3   LC 97-41728

Provides information on the offensive and defensive techniques of baseball as well as on the history and equipment of the game, with step-by-step instructions on individual positions

This is "filled with beautifully-reproduced full-color photos. . . . Smyth provides solid, basic information in an attractive format." SLJ

Includes glossary

Stewart, Mark

Long ball; the legend and lore of the home run; [by] Mark Stewart and Mike Kennedy. Millbrook Press 2006 64p il lib bdg $22.60 (4 and up)   **796.357**

1. Baseball

ISBN 9780761327790 (lib bdg); 0761327797 (lib bdg)   LC 2005015041

"Stewart and Kennedy offer an overview of the history and significance of the long ball." SLJ

"The highly readable text is extended by excellent graphics, photographs, and reproductions of baseball cards and magazine covers." Booklist

Includes bibliographical references

Weatherford, Carole Boston

A Negro league scrapbook; foreword by Buck O'Neil. 1st ed. Boyds Mills Press 2005 48p il $19.95 (4 and up)   **796.357**

1. Baseball 2. Negro leagues 3. African American athletes

ISBN 1-59078-091-4   LC 2004-19324

"Weatherford's text covers . . . a summation of the history of the Negro Leagues and sections on the pitchers, hitters, utility men, various teams, and so forth. Each topic is briefly covered on a spread of text with black-and-white photos and full-color realia designed to look like a scrapbook. Topics are introduced with a few lines of verse. . . . The book is especially successful in conveying the significance of the Negro Leagues to the black community, and in detailing the realities of segregation. . . . This title succeeds as a thoughtful introduction." SLJ

796.41 Weight lifting

Knotts, Bob

Weightlifting. Children's Press 2000 47p il lib bdg $22; pa $6.95 (2-4)   **796.41**

1. Weight lifting

ISBN 0-516-21067-X (lib bdg); 0-515-20732-X (pa)   LC 99-15089

"A True book"

Describes the history of the sport of weight lifting, as well as the training, equipment, rules, and techniques involved

Includes bibliographical references

796.42 Track and field

Knotts, Bob

Track and field. Children's Press 2000 47p il lib bdg $22; pa $6.95 (2-4)   **796.42**

1. Track athletics

ISBN 0-516-21066-1 (lib bdg); 0-516-27031-1 (pa)   LC 99-15088

"A True book"

Describes the history of track competitions, the various events involved, as well as several of the stars in this sport

Includes bibliographical references

796.44 Sports gymnastics

Bragg, Linda Wallenberg

Fundamental gymnastics; photographs by Andy King. Lerner Publs. 1995 80p il (Fundamental sports) lib bdg $22.60 (5 and up)   **796.44**

1. Gymnastics

ISBN 0-8225-3453-3   LC 94-40770

"Four chapters provide a brief history of gymnastics, descriptions of the six events for boys and the four events for girls, the basic moves, the general workout, and competition. The events and some of the skills are

Bragg, Linda Wallenberg—_Continued_
shown in excellent-quality full-color photographs on each page. Interesting facts in orange boxes appear throughout." SLJ
Includes glossary and bibliographical references

Bray-Moffatt, Naia
Gymnastics school; written by Naia Bray-Moffatt; photography by David Handley. DK Pub. 2005 48p $12.99 (k-3)   **796.44**
1. Gymnastics
ISBN 0-7566-1011-7
Cover title: I love gymnastics
This "invites readers inside a British gymnastics training center. Variations in experience are accommodated through an upbeat narrative that brings an absolute beginner, a girl of about seven, to class with her more advanced friend. . . . Members of the book's target audience . . . will appreciate the attractive, up-to-date coverage." Booklist

Jackman, Joan
Gymnastics. Dorling Kindersley 2000 45p il $9.95 (4 and up)   **796.44**
1. Gymnastics
ISBN 0-7894-5430-0   LC 99-50026
"DK superguides"
Replaces The young gymnast, published 1995
Explores every aspect of gymnastics including clothing, warming up, apparatuses, balances, rolls and rolling, headstands and handstands, tumbling, and vaulting

796.48   Olympic games

Fischer, David
The encyclopedia of the Summer Olympics; written by David Fischer. F. Watts 2003 160p il (Watts reference) $19.95 (4 and up)
                796.48
1. Olympic games
ISBN 0-531-11886-X   LC 2002-38024
Explores the history and traditions of the Olympics and the various events included in the competitions held every four years.
"A good assortment of full-color and archival black-and-white photos elucidates the text. With the plethora of books to choose from on the topic, this title is a worthy one." SLJ
Includes bibliographical references

Knotts, Bob
The Summer Olympics. Children's Press 2000 48p il lib bdg $22; pa $6.95 (2-4)   **796.48**
1. Olympic games
ISBN 0-516-21064-5 (lib bdg); 0-516-27029-X (pa)
                LC 99-15090
"A True book"
Describes the history, ideals, events, and heroes of the Olympic Games, with an emphasis on the Summer Olympics
"Large print and informative texts are the hallmarks of the series. The color photographs are plentiful." Booklist
Includes bibliographical references

Macy, Sue
Swifter, higher, stronger; a photographic history of the Summer Olympics; foreword by Bob Costas. National Geographic Society 2004 96p il $18.95; lib bdg $28.90 (4 and up)   **796.48**
1. Olympic games
ISBN 0-7922-6667-6; 0-7922-6980-2 (lib bdg)
                LC 2003-14079
A detailed look at the history of the Olympic Games, from their origins in Ancient Greece, through their rebirth in nineteenth century France, to the present, highlighting the contributions of individuals to the Games' success and popularity.
"While other books on the topic go into more depth on specific sports, athletes, or historical events, none are as enthusiastically broad or as enjoyable to read as this one. And, it's superbly illustrated with colorful, well-chosen, and enticing photographs." SLJ
Includes bibliographical references

Woff, Richard
The ancient Greek Olympics. Oxford Univ. Press 2000 c1999 32p il $16.95 (4 and up)
                796.48
1. Olympic games 2. Greece—Civilization
ISBN 0-19-521581-8   LC 99-87603
First published 1999 in the United Kingdom
Describes the history, traditions, and competitive events connected with the Olympic games held in ancient Greece
"The text brings to life the sights and sounds of the spectacle, Woff provides the sort of juicy information that students will find invaluable for research. Illustrations, including photographs of Greek art and statuary, are plentiful." Booklist
Includes bibliographical references

796.5   Outdoor life

Drake, Jane
The kids campfire book; [by] Jane Drake & Ann Love; illustrated by Heather Collins; songs arranged by Matthew Dewar. Kids Can Press 1998 128p il music $17.95 (4-6)   **796.5**
1. Outdoor life
ISBN 0-55074-539-5
First published 1996 in Canada
Topics include "how to select the right wood for the specific type of fire that is being built; recipes for food to cook over an open fire; games to play; songs, complete with the music and lyrics, to sing; ghost stories for spine-tingling telling; helpful hints for interacting—or not—with wildlife and insects; guides to viewing the night sky; and the appropriate gear for sleeping under the stars. Black-and-white illustrations are scattered throughout the lively, readable text." Booklist

Rhatigan, Joe
The kids' guide to nature adventures; 80 great activities for exploring the outdoors. Lark Bks. 2003 128p il pa $17.95 (3-6)   **796.5**
1. Outdoor life 2. Natural history 3. Nature study
ISBN 1-57990-373-8   LC 2002-41102

Rhatigan, Joe—*Continued*
Contents: Take a hike; Camp out!; Wildlife; Mini-wildlife; Plant life; Explore the shore; Night life

Provides ideas for exploring nature to learn the answers to such questions as when a chrysalis will open, why a wolf howls, or how the tide goes out, and gives advice about equipment and safety

"Both casual and wildly enthusiastic, this readable guide is packed with practical detail about how to have fun exploring the natural world." Booklist

796.52 Walking and exploring by kind of terrain

Jenkins, Steve
The top of the world; climbing Mount Everest. Houghton Mifflin 1999 unp il $16 (2-4)
796.52
1. Mountaineering 2. Mount Everest (China and Nepal)
ISBN 0-395-94218-7   LC 98-42748
"Jenkins' papercut illustrations are extraordinary—feathery light to catch the effect of fog radiating off the mountains, mottled and striated to replicate rocky plateaus, pebbled to look like ice flowers. . . . A very attractive book, with plenty of substance for curious children." Booklist
Includes bibliographical references

Skreslet, Laurie
To the top of Everest; [by] Laurie Skreslet with Elizabeth MacLeod. Kids Can Press 2001 56p il $16.95; pa $8.95 (4 and up)   **796.52**
1. Mountaineering 2. Mount Everest (China and Nepal)
ISBN 1-55074-721-5; 1-55074-814-9 (pa)
This is an account of Skreslet's "1982 trek up Everest when he became one of the first Canadians to make it to the top. Skreslet takes readers through every exciting, excruciating element of the climb. Beautiful color photographs abound." Booklist
Includes glossary

Venables, Stephen
To the top; the story of Everest. Candlewick Press 2003 96p il map $17.99 (5 and up)
796.52
1. Mountaineering 2. Mount Everest (China and Nepal)
ISBN 0-7636-2115-3   LC 2002-41110
Describes many of the attempts to scale Mount Everest, including the author's own experiences
"Drawing on the Royal Geographic Society's archives, familiar photos are mixed with some haunting, never-before-published images to illustrate the informed and evocative text." SLJ

796.6 Cycling and related activities

Schoenherr, Alicia
Mountain biking; by Alicia and Rusty Schoenherr. Child's World 2005 32p il (Kids' guides) lib bdg $24.21 (4-6)   **796.6**
1. Mountain biking
ISBN 1-59296-209-2   LC 2003-27371
Contents: From street to trail; The klunkers; Gearing up to ride; Mountain biking in action; Superstars of the mountains
This "opens with an explanation of the sport and gives reasons why people enjoy it. The four chapters that follow cover background and development, equipment, technique, and stars and competitions. The excellent color photos are clear and exciting." SLJ
Includes bibliographical references

796.72 Automobile racing

Buckley, James, Jr.
NASCAR; written by James Buckley Jr. DK Pub. 2005 72p il (DK eyewitness books) $15.99; lib bdg $19.99 (4 and up)   **796.72**
1. National Association for Stock Car Auto Racing 2. Automobile racing
ISBN 0-7566-1194-6; 0-7566-1193-8 (lib bdg)
This offers information about NASCAR stock car racing and its stars, including such topics as history, car construction, driving gear, the meaning of flag colors, track layouts, and race-day routines.
This is a "first-rate introduction to a hugely popular sport. Guaranteed to please both the simply curious and the avid fan." Booklist

Dooling, Michael
The great horseless carriage race. Holiday House 2002 unp il $16.95 (2-4)   **796.72**
1. Duryea, J. Frank, 1869-1967 2. Automobile racing
ISBN 0-8234-1640-2   LC 2001-16589
"In 1895, a Chicago newspaper sponsored the first automobile race, a 52-mile 'dash' across the city's environs. . . . [Frank] Duryea crossed the finish line after 10 hours and 23 minutes. . . . In 1896, he and his brother went on to start the Duryea Motor Company. Dooling has lovingly re-created an era in sepias and watercolor washes." SLJ

796.8 Combat sports

Ditchfield, Christin
Wrestling. Children's Press 2000 47p il lib bdg $22; pa $6.95 (2-4)   **796.8**
1. Wrestling
ISBN 0-516-21611-2 (lib bdg); 0-516-27033-8 (pa)
LC 99-28191
"A True book"
Describes the history, rules, and styles of wrestling
Includes bibliographical references

Knotts, Bob
Martial arts. Children's Press 2000 47p il lib bdg $22; pa $6.95 (2-4)   **796.8**
1. Martial arts
ISBN 0-516-21609-0 (lib bdg); 0-516-27028-1 (pa)
LC 99-15091
"A True book"
Introduces judo, karate, and several other martial arts, highlighting safety and the mental discipline involved
Includes bibliographical references

Rielly, Robin L.
Karate for kids; [by] Robin Rielly. 1st ed. Tuttle Pub 2004 48p il $11.95 (4 and up)   **796.8**
1. Karate
ISBN 0-8048-3534-9   LC 2003-27610
Contents: What is karate?; The uniform; The dojo; The class; Warming up; Practicing karate; Advancing in karate; Is karate good for me?
"Rielly begins with a history of karate before going on to information about the uniform, including the meaning of the belt colors, the rules and etiquette of the dojo, and the interaction between student and teacher. The actual stances are clearly portrayed in watercolor-and-ink artwork that features both boys and girls in a number of stances and practicing thrusts and kicks. The book ends with advice for advancing in karate." Booklist

796.9   Ice and snow sports

Woods, Bob
Snowboarding; by Bob Woods. Child's World 2005 32p il (Kids' guides) lib bdg $24.21 (4-6)   **796.9**
1. Snowboarding
ISBN 1-59296-211-4   LC 2003-27365
Contents: Get on board; Snowboarding's cold, hard history; Gear up and go; Hit the slippery slopes; Snowboarding stars
This "opens with an explanation of the sport and gives reasons why people enjoy it. The four chapters that follow cover background and development, equipment, technique, and stars and competitions. The excellent color photos are clear and exciting." SLJ
Includes bibliographical references

796.91   Ice skating

Gutman, Dan
Ice skating; from axels to Zambonis. Viking 1995 176p il $14.99; pa $6.99 (5 and up)   **796.91**
1. Ice skating
ISBN 0-670-86013-1; 0-14-037501-5 (pa)
LC 95-14598
"This book is actually a narrative discussion of figure skating. The first chapter describes the sport's history, beginning with skating's prehistoric origins. Remaining chapters discuss the evolution of ice skating as a sport, stars of the past and present, a day in the life of a young

skater, terminology, and trivia. A complete glossary and charts listing world, Olympic and U.S. skating champions make this a handy reference work as well." Voice Youth Advocates

Isadora, Rachel
Sophie skates. Putnam 1999 unp il $15.99 (k-3)   **796.91**
1. Ice skating
ISBN 0-399-23046-7   LC 98-21930
Uses a story about a young girl who loves to ice skate to introduce the sport: the parts and care of skates, the techniques of different skating moves, and ice skating competitions
"On the large, white pages are graceful watercolors depicting all sorts of specific details. . . . This provides an excellent balance between information (the pictures of equipment and moves are labeled) and a profile of a believable little Asian American girl." Booklist

Wilkes, Debbi
The figure skating book; a young person's guide to figure skating. Firefly Bks. (Buffalo) 2000 116p il $19.95; pa $12.95 (4 and up)   **796.91**
1. Ice skating
ISBN 1-55209-444-8; 1-55209-445-6 (pa)
The author "gives specific advice on which skates to buy (expensive), how to find a skating club, and skating technique—from the most basic glide to complicated maneuvers." Booklist

796.962   Ice hockey

Foley, Mike
Fundamental hockey; photographs by Andy King. Lerner Publs. 1996 80p il (Fundamental sports) lib bdg $22.60 (5 and up)   **796.962**
1. Hockey
ISBN 0-8225-3456-8   LC 95-7077
"A brief history of the sport is followed by an explanation of what players do during hockey practice and what occurs during a game. Finally, readers see some of the drills and variations of the game, such as broomball and sledge hockey, which is played by players with lower-body disabilities. A substantial glossary and list of places to write for more information are appended." SLJ
Includes glossary and bibliographical references

Kennedy, Mike
Ice hockey. Franklin Watts 2003 63p il lib bdg $25.50; pa $8.95 (4 and up)   **796.962**
1. Hockey
ISBN 0-531-12273-5 (lib bdg); 0-531-15590-0 (pa)
LC 2002-15340
"Watts library"
Contents: Out of the wilderness; Goal oriented; Outside the box; Fast & furious; Power players; Timeline
Reviews the history of ice hockey, how it is played, the rules of the game, and introduces readers to some of

Kennedy, Mike—*Continued*
hockey's greatest players.
This is "well-organized. . . . [It includes] an abundance of excellent, captioned photos, mainly in color."
SLJ
Includes bibliographical references

Thomas, Keltie
How hockey works; illustrations by Greg Hall.
Maple Tree Press 2002 64p il $19.95; pa $9.95
(3-6)   **796.962**
1. Hockey
ISBN 1-894379-35-7; 1-894379-36-5 (pa)
This "book for beginning and experienced players features tips to perfect an athlete's game, the science behind each activity, quick-shot facts, and stories from former and current pros. Numerous solutions to questions such as why ice is slippery and what makes a hockey stick feel right are offered. Attractive full-color photos, cartoons, and diagrams appear on every spread. . . . An appealing presentation that's chock-full of information."
SLJ
Includes glossary

796.98   Winter Olympic games

Macy, Sue
Freeze frame; a photographic history of the Winter Olympics. National Geographic 2006 96p il map $18.95 (5 and up)   **796.98**
1. Olympic games 2. Winter sports
ISBN 0-7922-7887-9
Highlights in the history of the Winter Olympics from their inception in 1924 to today, including profiles of the Olympic athletes and information on the lesser-known winter sports. Also includes an Olympic almanac with information about each Olympiad.
This "has spectacular photographs and clear, captivating prose." SLJ
Includes bibliographical references

797.1   Boating

Bass, Scott
Kayaking; by Scott Bass. Child's World 2005
32p il (Kids' guides) lib bdg $24.21 (4-6)
          797.1
1. Kayaks and kayaking
ISBN 1-59296-208-4   LC 2003-27372
Contents: The freedom of kayaking; Climb in a kayak; Gear and events; Kayaks in action; Kayaking stars
This "opens with an explanation of the sport and gives reasons why people enjoy it. The four chapters that follow cover background and development, equipment, technique, and stars and competitions. The excellent color photos are clear and exciting." SLJ
Includes bibliographical references

797.2   Swimming and diving

Lourie, Peter
First dive to shark dive. Boyds Mills Press 2006
48p il $17.95   **797.2**
1. Scuba diving 2. Bahamas
ISBN 1-59078-068-X   LC 2005-24987
"In this photo-essay, a father and his 12-year-old daughter, Suzanna, fly to Andros, in the Bahamas, so Suzanna can learn to scuba dive. During an intense seven days, she becomes certified and makes four dives. The narrative . . . also covers information about the island . . . the ocean and its inhabitants . . . and the old Andros traditions. . . . Stunning color photographs . . . reveal why Suzanna wanted to be certified to dive."
Booklist

798.2   Horsemanship

Hayden, Kate
Horse show; written by Kate Hayden. DK Pub.
2001 32p il $12.95; pa $3.95 (1-3)   **798.2**
1. Horsemanship
ISBN 0-7894-7372-0; 0-7894-7371-2 (pa)
          LC 00-56975
"Dorling Kindersley readers"
"As three children prepare for a show, readers are introduced to the horses at White Lane Farm, the preparations, and the basic events. . . . Ample white space and compelling color photographs of young equestrians competing in English-style riding are appealing and encouraging." SLJ

Kimball, Cheryl
Horse show handbook for kids; everything a young rider needs to know to prepare, train, and compete in English or Western events: plus getting-ready checklists and show diary pages; [by] Cheryl Kimball. Storey Pub 2004 151p il $26.95; pa $16.95 (4 and up)   **798.2**
1. Horsemanship
ISBN 1-58017-573-2; 1-58017-501-5 (pa)
          LC 2003-21732
Paperback edition has title: Horse showing for kids
Contents: Types of shows; Types of classes; Show personnel; Choosing the right horse; Conditioning and training; Trailering; Grooming; Attire and equipment (you & your horse); Planning for a show; On the big day; After the show; Moving up the competitive ladder
"For kids who have ever wondered if there is a certain color that complements their horse more than another, what last-minute checks they need to do before entering a show ring, how to dress for success, and much more, this handbook is invaluable. Presenting a wealth of information in a well-organized and enthusiastic manner, the author also addresses the more serious issues such as safety and good sportsmanship. The format is appealing, with lots of colorful photos." SLJ

Richter, Judy

Riding for kids. Storey Bks. 2003 128p il $23.95; pa $16.95 (3-5)   **798.2**

1. Horsemanship

ISBN 1-58017-511-2; 1-58017-510-4 (pa)

LC 2003-45842

Provides abundant photographs and detailed information describing how to ride a horse, from dress and equipment to jumping and competition

"Beginning equestrians will appreciate this comprehensive guide. . . . Well written and handsomely illustrated." Booklist

Includes glossary and bibliographical references

798.4   Horse racing

Dubowski, Cathy East

A horse named Seabiscuit; by Mark and Cathy Dubowski; illustrated by Mark Rowe. Grosset & Dunlap 2003 47p il $12; pa $3.99 (2-4)

798.4

1. Seabiscuit (Race horse) 2. Horse racing

ISBN 0-448-43343-5; 0-448-43342-7 (pa)

LC 2003-16839

"All aboard reading"

This "account focuses on the racehorse's rise from 'a big disappointment' . . . to a great champion and symbol of hope during the Great Depression. . . . The lively text will keep readers' interest. . . . The soft-toned realistic illustrations and occasional black-and-white photographs nicely complement the story." SLJ

798.8   Dog racing

Miller, Debbie S.

The great serum race; blazing the Iditarod Trail; illustrations by Jon van Zyle. Walker & Co. 2002 unp il map $17.95; lib bdg $18.85 (3-5)

798.8

1. Dogs 2. Alaska 3. Iditarod Trail Sled Dog Race, Alaska

ISBN 0-8027-8811-4; 0-8027-8812-2 (lib bdg)

LC 2001-56777

The story of the heroic role played by sled dogs, including the Siberian husky Togo, in the delivery of antitoxin serum to those stricken with diphtheria in 1925 Nome. Includes historical notes about the event as well as about the Iditarod Sled Dog Race which commemorates it

"Zyle, official artist of the Iditarod and a musher himself, has created vivid, full-spread paintings to bring the story to life. . . . This is an excellent account told with lots of detail and drama." SLJ

Includes bibliographical references

Wood, Ted

Iditarod dream; Dusty and his sled dogs compete in Alaska's Jr. Iditarod. Walker & Co. 1996 48p il map $17.95; pa $8.95 (4 and up)

798.8

1. Sled dog racing

ISBN 0-8027-8406-2; 0-8027-7535-7 (pa)

LC 95-31084

This "photo essay follows 15-year-old Dusty Whittemore of Cantwell, AK, through the 1995 Jr. Iditarod Sled Dog Race—158 miles from Lake Lucille to Yentna and back." SLJ

"Clear, close-up color photographs portray every stage of the event and offer interesting information about the difficulties and hazards of this two-day competition." Booklist

799.1   Fishing

Arnosky, Jim

Hook, line, & seeker; a beginner's guide to fishing, boating, and watching water wildlife; with photographs and illustrations by the author. Scholastic Nonfiction 2005 192p il $12.95 (4 and up)

799.1

1. Fishing 2. Boats and boating 3. Marine animals

ISBN 0-439-45584-7   LC 2004-52501

.

"Distilling experiences garnered from a lifetime of fishing, boating and wildlife observation, naturalist Arnosky offers outdoorsy readers a handbook that is as much memoir as vademecum. . . . Illustrated with finished paintings, quick sketches from his notebooks . . . and small but very sharp color photos, this fills in the basics on diverse topics from boating safety to artificial flies to sport fish and shore birds." Booklist

800   LITERATURE

803   Literature--Encyclopedias and dictionaries

Brewer's dictionary of phrase and fable $55

803

1. Literature—Dictionaries 2. Allusions

First published 1870. (17th edition 2006) Periodically revised

Current editor: John Ayto

"Over 15,000 brief entries give the meanings and origins of a broad range of terms, expressions, and names of real, fictitious and mythical characters from world history, science, the arts and literature." N Y Public Libr. Ref Books for Child Collect. 2d edition

808 Rhetoric

Christelow, Eileen

What do authors do? Clarion Bks. 1995 32p il $15; pa $5.95 (1-3)   **808**
1. Authorship 2. Authors 3. Illustrators 4. Publishers and publishing
ISBN 0-395-71124-X; 0-395-86621-9 (pa)
LC 94-19725

The author "follows two next-door neighbors as they independently develop stories about their pets—the scruffy sheepdog, Rufus; and Max, his energetic feline adversary. Dialogue in cartoon balloons and brief text describe the writing process and the mechanics of publishing." SLJ

"Christelow packs a great deal of humor as well as information into her attractive pages. Best of all, she infuses the whole with a sense of the zest and love that writers feel for their work." Booklist

Fletcher, Ralph

How writers work; finding a process that works for you. HarperTrophy 2000 114p pa $4.99 (4 and up)   **808**
1. Authorship 2. Creative writing
ISBN 0-380-79702-X   LC 00-27573

Focuses on the skills and techniques necessary for good writing, with excerpts from established writers and samples of young people's work as examples

"The book makes youngsters feel good about their writing without making light of the work involved. . . . This is a useful resource." SLJ

Includes bibliographical references

James, Elizabeth

How to write terrific book reports; [by] Elizabeth James and Carol Barkin. rev ed. Lothrop, Lee & Shepard Bks. 1998 80p (School survival guide) pa $4.95 hardcover o.p. (4 and up)   **808**
1. Report writing 2. Books—Reviews
ISBN 0-688-16140-5   LC 98-9198

First published 1986 with title: How to write your best book report

"The authors explore what a book report is, how to choose a title, writing preliminary and final drafts, giving an oral presentation, the importance of the library in finding material, and other aspects of this common assignment." SLJ

Leedy, Loreen

Look at my book; how kids can write & illustrate terrific books; written and illustrated by Loreen Leedy. Holiday House 2004 32p il $16.95 (k-3)   **808**
1. Authorship 2. Illustration of books 3. Bookbinding
ISBN 0-8234-1590-2   LC 2003-41713

Provides ideas and simple directions for writing, illustrating, designing, and binding books.

"Following the writing process fairly closely . . . [the author] takes readers through a step-by-step formula that almost guarantees a successful product. . . . Lively, colorful illustrations expand and interpret the text." SLJ

Messages in the mailbox; how to write a letter; written and illustrated by Loreen Leedy. Holiday House 1991 unp il $16.95; pa $5.95 (k-3)
808
1. Letter writing
ISBN 0-8234-0889-2; 0-8234-1079-X (pa)
LC 91-8718

Discusses the different kinds of letters, the parts of a letter, and who can be a potential correspondent, and provides examples

"Leedy's softly colored realistic illustrations feature both animal characters and people from a variety of cultures. The partnership of text and illustration gives a lively and interesting perspective to an otherwise dull topic. . . . A superb book that shouldn't be missed." SLJ

Trueit, Trudi Strain

Keeping a journal; [by] Trudi Strain Trueit. F. Watts 2004 80p (Life balance) $19.50 (5 and up)
808
1. Diaries 2. Authorship
ISBN 0-531-12262-X   LC 2003-25290

Contents: Navigating the journey; Why journal?; Time travel; Getting started; Write now! A 30-day journal

"Trueit features examples . . . to spark the imaginations of young people eager to express their unique views. Tips on how to begin, exercises designed to help overcome writer's block, and a 30-day calendar of creative ideas to get started are included. . . . The enthusiastic tone, inspirational examples, and writing prompts will help even those reluctant to express themselves to pick up a pen or pencil." SLJ

Includes bibliographical references

Young, Sue

Writing with style. Scholastic Ref. 1997 143p (Scholastic guides) pa $8.95 hardcover o.p. (5 and up)   **808**
1. Authorship 2. Creative writing
ISBN 0-590-25424-3 (pa)   LC 96-8772

Presents tips for writing interesting stories, passionate essays, and exciting reports, focusing on the elements of sentence structure, paragraph organization, grammar, usage, punctuation, and footnotes

"The book is easy to comprehend, upbeat, and relevant. A must for library shelves and classrooms." SLJ

Includes bibliographical references

808.1 Rhetoric of poetry

Fletcher, Ralph

Poetry matters; writing a poem from the inside out. HarperCollins Pubs. 2002 142p lib bdg $15.89; pa $4.99 (4 and up)   **808.1**
1. Poetics
ISBN 0-06-623599-5 (lib bdg); 0-380-79703-8 (pa)
LC 2001-24640

"Chapters deal with images; creating 'music,' or sounds and rhythms; how to generate ideas for poems; the construction of the words on the page; and more. Tips on fine-tuning are also given. . . . Major poetic

Fletcher, Ralph—*Continued*
forms are defined, including haiku, ode, and free verse, and there is a section on ways to share your work. Interspersed are Fletcher's personal insights and interviews with three poets—Kristine O'Connell George, Janet S. Wong, and J. Patrick Lewis. . . . Since this thought-provoking book covers more of the internal, less-tangible aspects of poetry, it may be more suited for readers who have some experience with the genre." SLJ

Includes bibliographical references

Poetry from A to Z; a guide for young writers; compiled by Paul B. Janeczko; illustrated by Cathy Bobak. Bradbury Press 1994 131p il $16.95 (5 and up) **808.1**
1. Poetics 2. American poetry—Collections
ISBN 0-02-747672-3   LC 94-10528
"In his guide, Janeczko gives many examples and ideas to get young writers started writing poetry. The book is organized alphabetically with seventy-two poems on almost any topic you could imagine. In addition, fourteen exercises labeled 'Try This' explain how to write different types of poems and help a young writer get started." Voice Youth Advocates

Includes bibliographical references

808.3   Rhetoric of fiction

Bauer, Marion Dane
What's your story? a young person's guide to writing fiction. Clarion Bks. 1992 134p pa $7.95 hardcover o.p. (5 and up)   **808.3**
1. Authorship 2. Creative writing
ISBN 0-395-57780-2   LC 91-3816
Discusses how to write fiction, exploring such aspects as character, plot, point of view, dialogue, endings, and revising
"Bauer reveals the somber reality that writing can be hard work, though worth the effort for those who persevere. What follows is a clear, concise elucidation on the elements of fiction. . . . Bauer has taken a thorough, clear, and functional approach to this topic." Horn Book

Harrison, David L. (David Lakin)
Writing stories; fantastic fiction from start to finish. Scholastic Reference 2004 126p (Scholastic guides) $16.95; pa $7.99 (4 and up)   **808.3**
1. Authorship 2. Creative writing
ISBN 0-439-51914-4; 0-439-51915-2 (pa)
"Harrison begins by breaking down the elements of a story and giving concrete examples for young writers to make their own. He offers basic descriptions and tools for genre writing and careful instructions on revision and rewriting. . . . Expect children to begin their writer's journal . . . immediately." Booklist

Otfinoski, Steven
Extraordinary short story writing; by Steven Otfinoski. Franklin Watts 2005 128p il (F.W. prep) lib bdg $30.50; pa $9.95 (5 and up)   **808.3**
1. Short story 2. Authorship
ISBN 0-531-16760-7 (lib bdg); 0-531-17578-2 (pa)
          LC 2005006650
"In this excellent resource, specific ways to write different types of stories, project ideas, and resources are presented in such a way as to make short story assignments enjoyable. Readers are given many tips and practice activities in chapters that progress from gathering ideas to the final revision. Each section includes quotes from wellknown authors such as Edgar Allan Poe, Richard Peck, and Louis Sachar." SLJ

Includes bibliographical references

808.5   Rhetoric of speech

Otfinoski, Steven
Speaking up, speaking out; a kid's guide to making speeches, oral reports, and conversation; illustrated by Carol Nicklaus. Millbrook Press 1996 79p il lib bdg $24.90 (5 and up)   **808.5**
1. Public speaking
ISBN 1-56294-345-6 (lib bdg)   LC 96-509
Provides strategies and encouraging tips for speaking in social situations, reading aloud, presenting oral reports, and making speeches of all kinds
"This appealing handbook provides youngsters with just about everything they need to know about oral communication. . . . Nicklaus's cartoon illustrations are appropriately lighthearted, adding touches of humor to the text." SLJ

Includes glossary and bibliographical references

808.8   Literature--Collections

Bauer, Caroline Feller
Celebrations; read-aloud holiday and theme book programs; drawings by Lynn Gates Bredeson. Wilson, H.W. 1985 301p il $55   **808.8**
1. Holidays 2. Literature—Collections 3. Books and reading 4. Children's libraries
ISBN 0-8242-0708-4   LC 85-714
"Aimed at librarians and other adults who work with middle-grade children, this book offers a potpourri of ideas and suggestions for planning holiday programs. Each chapter focuses on a holiday—some well known, some concocted by Bauer—and includes prose [and poetry] selections, activities, and a booklist." Booklist

Beware!; R.L. Stine picks his favorite scary stories. HarperCollins Pubs. 2002 214p il $11.99; lib bdg $14.89; pa $5.99 (4 and up)   **808.8**
1. Horror fiction 2. Literature—Collections
ISBN 0-06-623842-0; 0-06-623843-9 (lib bdg); 0-06-055547-5 (pa)   LC 2002-18938

Beware!—*Continued*

"A Parachute Press book"

Stine "brings together 19 brief stories, folktales, poems, and cartoons from the likes of Ray Bradbury, William Sleator, Robert W. Service . . . Gahan Wilson, and Alvin Schwartz. . . . There's something in this diverse literary buffet for every taste—including enough genuine eeriness to make it a discomfiting choice for under-the-covers reading." Booklist

Celebrate Cricket; 30 years of stories and art; edited by Marianne Carus. Cricket Bks. 2003 262p il $24.95   **808.8**
1. Cricket (Periodical) 2. Literature—Collections
ISBN 0-8126-2695-8   LC 2003-10284

A treasury of stories, poems, and illustrations from Cricket, along with reminiscences about the magazine and color reproductions of Cricket cover art

"The selections flow well, and most of them are enjoyable at least and remarkable at best. . . . This is primarily a book for adults, and it deserves a place in collections where there's an interest in children's literature." SLJ

A **Christmas** treasury; very merry stories and poems; [illustrated by Kevin Hawkes] Lothrop, Lee & Shepard Bks. 2000 33p il $16.95; lib bdg $16.89 (2-4)   **808.8**
1. Christmas 2. Literature—Collections
ISBN 0-688-12039-3; 0-688-12039-3 (lib bdg)
          LC 00-53513

This is a "collection for fireside reading which includes excerpts from 'The Wind in the Willows,' 'A Visit From St. Nicholas,' 'Christmas at the Hollow Tree Inn,' by Albert Bigelow Paine, and two carols, 'Jolly Old St. Nicholas' and 'The Friendly Beasts.'" N Y Times Book Rev

"Hawkes adds delightful decoration to this appealing selection of poetry and story. . . . Hawkes' artwork brings vibrant life to the familiar words." Booklist

Hudson, Wade

Powerful words; more than 200 years of extraordinary writing by African Americans; illustrated by Sean Qualls; foreword by Marian Wright Edelman. Scholastic Nonfiction 2004 178p il $19.95 (5 and up)   **808.8**
1. American literature—African American authors 2. African Americans—Biography 3. African Americans—History
ISBN 0-439-40969-1   LC 2003-42792

A collection of speeches and writings by African Americans, with commentary about the time period in which each person lived, information about the speaker/writer, and public response to the words.

"Short enough to hold attention, the selections . . . are also long enough to show the writers' tone and style. Many sensitive full-page portraits are included. . . . This well-designed volume will be an excellent addition to many library collections." Booklist

Includes bibliographical references

I can make a difference; a treasury to inspire our children; selected by Marian Wright Edelman; illustrations by Barry Moser. 1st ed. HarperCollins Pub. 2005 112p il $19.99; lib bdg $20.89   **808.8**
1. Conduct of life—Literary collections
ISBN 0-06-028051-4; 0-06-028052-2 (lib bdg)
          LC 2004-24884

"Edelman takes that sturdy statement and breaks it down into 12 components, easily understandable by kids, and then decorates each with meaningful poems, stories, and memorable art. . . . An oversize format allows Moser to mix full-size paintings, portraits, and spot art in artwork that ranges from utilitarian to effective to stunning." Booklist

Joy to the world; a family Christmas treasury; selected, edited, and introduced by Ann Keay Beneduce; illustrated by Gennady Spirin. Atheneum Bks. for Young Readers 2000 179p il $25 (4 and up)   **808.8**
1. Christmas 2. Literature—Collections
ISBN 0-689-82113-1   LC 99-40002

A collection of stories, poems, and plays about Christmas, arranged in the categories of "The Star," "The Manger," "The Gift-givers," "The Tree," and "Christmas Around the World"

"Beneduce offers a fine selection of traditional Christmas stories, carols, and poems in this handsome volume, which is accessible to a wide age range. . . . Spirin's graceful paintings, with their gold tones and look of bygone days, create a richly detailed and dignified setting for the writing." Booklist

The **Norton** anthology of children's literature; the traditions in English; Jack Zipes, general editor [et al.] W.W. Norton 2005 xxxviii, 2471p il pa $65   **808.8**
1. Literature—Collections 2. Children's literature—History and criticism
ISBN 0-393-97538-X   LC 2004-54172

A collection of fairy tales, picture books, nursery rhymes, fantasy, alphabets, chapbooks, and comics published in English since 1659, representing 170 authors and illustrators, and including more than ninety complete works and excerpts from others

"The delights are abundant. . . . A mile wide and very deep, this is an invaluable resource for professionals, but fun for casual perusing, too." Publ Wkly

Includes bibliographical references

Snowy day: stories and poems; edited by Caroline Feller Bauer; illustrated by Margot Tomes. Lippincott 1986 68p il lib bdg $16.89 (2-4)   **808.8**
1. Literature—Collections
ISBN 0-397-32177-5   LC 85-45858

This collection "features three short stories—Uchida's Japanese 'New Year's Hats for the Statues,' Singer's Jewish 'The Snow in Chelm,' and Bauer's adaptation of the Russian 'Marika the Snowmaiden.' The 28 poems include selections by X. J. Kennedy, Gwendolyn Brooks, David McCord, Lilian Moore, Dennis Lee, Kaye Starbird, John Ciardi, Myra Cohn Livingston, Karla Kuskin, and others." Bull Cent Child Books

Snowy day: stories and poems—*Continued*
"Margot Tomes's charming, evocative, black-and-white illustrations of snowflakes and leafless trees, sleds, and snowballs add the perfect touch to a wintry treat." Horn Book
Includes bibliographical references

Wiggle waggle fun; stories and rhymes for the very, very young; [collected by] Margaret Mayo. Knopf 2002 c2000 62p il $16.95; lib bdg $18.99 (k-1)   **808.8**
1. Literature—Collections
ISBN 0-375-81529-5; 0-375-91529-X (lib bdg)
                                                         LC 2001-29568
First published 2000 in the United Kingdom with title: Plum pudding
A collection of poems, songs, traditional verses, action rhymes, and stories, illustrated by twenty-four different artists
"The infectious rhythm and action in the words and the appealing visuals will keep kids asking for this treasury." Booklist

808.81   Poetry--Collections

The **baby's** bedtime book; [compiled and illustrated by] Kay Chorao. Dutton Children's Books 2004 c1984 64p il $16.99
                                                            808.81
1. Poetry—Collections 2. Nursery rhymes 3. Lullabies
ISBN 0-525-47327-0
A reissue of the title first published 1984
This collection includes traditional rhymes, lullabies and prayers and poems by authors including Blake, Kipling, Tennyson, Rossetti and Robert Louis Stevenson
"Luminous cross-hatched illustrations create magic for the 27 poems collected here. Each poem is adorned with Chorao's softly-colored full-page illustrations, bordered in tranquil blue." SLJ

The **baby's** book of baby animals; [compiled and illustrated by] Kay Chorao. Dutton Children's Bks. 2004 40p il $16.99   **808.81**
1. Animals—Poetry 2. Nursery rhymes 3. Poetry—Collections
ISBN 0-525-47199-5
This is a collection of poems and nursery rhymes including selections such as "Baa, Baa, Black Sheep" and excerpts from the work of William Wordsworth, Alfred, Lord Tennyson, and William Blake.
"This delightful collection . . . is an absolute must for all libraries. . . . All of the selections feature rhythmic language that will appeal to preschoolers. The colorful illustrations are filled with sweet-faced youngsters and baby animals romping through the countryside and engaged in a multitude of activities." SLJ

The **baby's** good morning book; [compiled and illustrated by] Kay Chorao. Dutton 1986 64p il $16.99   **808.81**
1. Poetry—Collections 2. Nursery rhymes
ISBN 0-525-44257-X   LC 86-6415

A selection of poems and rhymes by a variety of English and American poets
"Cheerful, brilliantly colored illustrations spread through the pages like the first rays of summer sun in this refreshing collection of short poems for children. Chorao's selections are a veritable bouquet—authors include Dickinson, Stevenson, Milne, Farjeon, Mother Goose, Walter Crane, and Frank Asch, so that 'classic' pieces are warmly arranged among newer poems." SLJ

Christmas poems; selected by Myra Cohn Livingston; illustrated by Trina Schart Hyman. Holiday House 1984 32p il lib bdg $15.95
                                                            808.81
1. Christmas—Poetry 2. Poetry—Collections
ISBN 0-8234-0508-7   LC 83-18559
The selections "range from the Nativity to John Ciardi's speculations about how Santa gets down to Key West to a nice limerick applauding Mrs. S. Claus. The collection gets its unity from Trina Schart Hyman's drawings, placing all the figures in the vicinity of a Christmas tree supervised by the family cat." Read Teach

Driscoll, Michael
A child's introduction to poetry; listen while you learn about the magic words that have moved mountains, won battles and made us laugh and cry; illustrated by Meredith Hamilton. Black Dog & Leventhal 2003 90p il $19.95 (4 and up)
                                                            808.81
1. Poetry—Collections 2. Poetry—History and criticism
ISBN 1-57912-282-5
"The first section discusses the different forms the genre takes: nursery rhyme, narrative verse, ballad, free verse, pastoral, etc. Driscoll offers a clear explanation of each type and defines any difficult, associated vocabulary. Commentary on each example and a note on where to find the recording on the accompanying CD is provided for each selection. The second section covers individual poets from Homer to Maya Angelou and offers at least one example or excerpt from each writer's work. The brief introductions to the forms and poets are lively and often amusing. Readers will find the varied layouts and warm cartoon watercolors inviting." SLJ
Includes glossary and bibliographical references

Eric Carle's animals, animals; poems compiled by Laura Whipple. Philomel Bks. 1989 82p il $21.99; pa $7.99   **808.81**
1. Animals—Poetry 2. Poetry—Collections
ISBN 0-399-21744-4; 0-698-11855-3 (pa)
                                                         LC 88-31646
"Illustrations take center stage in *Eric Carle's Animals Animals* . . . compiled by Laura Whipple. The well-chosen poems are from a variety of sources—the Bible, Shakespeare, Japanese Haiku, Pawnee Indian, weather sayings and contemporary poets like Judith Viorst, Ogden Nash, and Jack Prelutsky. On many pages the poem may be only two or three lines but the pictures are full-page spreads in Mr. Carle's familiar vividly colored, collage style." Kobrin Letter

Eric Carle's dragons dragons and other creatures that never were; compiled by Laura Whipple. Philomel Bks. 1991 69p il $19.99; pa $8.99   **808.81**

1. Mythical animals—Poetry 2. Poetry—Collections
ISBN 0-399-22105-0; 0-399-22837-3 (pa)

                                LC 91-11986

An illustrated collection of poems about dragons and other fantastic creatures by a variety of authors

"The collection offers a sumptuous viewing of Carle's rich blend of tissue-paper and paint collages and a grand introduction to the imaginary beasts. Laura Whipple concludes this adroit compilation with a brief commentary on the fabulous animals as 'a magical part of our human heritage.'" Horn Book

Includes glossary

A **family** of poems; my favorite poetry for children; [selected by] Caroline Kennedy; paintings by Jon J. Muth. Hyperion Books for Children 2005 143p il $19.95   **808.81**
1. Poetry—Collections
ISBN 0-7868-5111-2

An anthology of over 100 poems divided into categories such as "About Me," "Animals," "Adventure" and "Bedtime," including works by such poets as A.A. Milne, Robert Louis Stevenson, Jack Prelutsky, Edward Lear, Robert Frost, William Wordsworth, T.S. Eliot, Carl Sandberg, William Shakespeare.

"From the cover photograph of Kennedy as a toddler reading to her teddy to the red linen-textured endpapers; from her thoughtful introduction and words of encouragement to children at the beginning of each section of carefully chosen poems to Muth's beautifully executed watercolors, this volume is a treasure." SLJ

Index to children's poetry; a title, subject, author, and first line index to poetry in collections for children and youth; compiled by John E. and Sara W. Brewton. Wilson, H.W. 1942-1965 3v
                                 808.81
1. Poetry—Indexes

Basic volume published 1942 $75 (ISBN 0-8242-0021-7); first supplement published 1954 $80 (ISBN 0-8242-0022-5); second supplement published 1965 $80 (ISBN 0-8242-0023-3)

The main volume indexes 15,000 poems by 2,500 authors in 130 collections. The two supplements analyze another 15,000 poems by 2700 authors in 151 collections

"This tool is an invaluable reference source." Peterson. Ref Books for Child

Index to poetry for children and young people; a title, subject, author, and first line index to poetry in collections for children and young people. Wilson, H.W. 1972-1998 6v
                                 808.81
1. Poetry—Indexes

A continuation of Index to children's poetry

The volume published 1972 covering 1964-1969 compiled by John E. and Sara W. Brewton and G. Meredith Blackburn III $100 (ISBN 0-8242-0435-2); 1970-1975 published 1978 compiled by John E. Brewton, G. Meredith Blackburn III and Lorraine A. Blackburn $100 (ISBN 0-8242-0621-5); 1976-1981 published 1984 com-

piled by John E. Brewton, G. Meredith Blackburn III and Lorraine A. Blackburn $100 (ISBN 0-8242-0681-9); 1982-1987 compiled 1989 compiled by G. Meredith Blackburn III and Lorraine A. Blackburn $105 (ISBN 0-8242-0773-4); 1988-1992 published 1994 compiled by G. Meredith Blackburn III $105 (ISBN 0-8242-0861-7); 1993-1997 published 1998 compiled by G. Meredith Blackburn III $110 (ISBN 0-8242-0939-7)

Each volume analyzes approximately 10,000 poems by some 2,000 authors in more than 110 collections. Over 2,000 subject headings are used in each volume

My first Oxford book of animal poems; compiled by John Foster. Oxford Univ. Press 2001 94p il lib bdg $19.95; pa $14.67 (1-4)   **808.81**
1. Animals—Poetry 2. Poetry—Collections
ISBN 0-19-276269-9; 0-19-276326-1 (pa)

                               LC 2001-283482

"Sections such as 'Around the House and in the Garden' and 'Beside the Sea, Beneath the Waves,' include more than 90 poems by writers as diverse as Dylan Thomas, Emily Bronte, Jane Yolen and Margaret Wise Brown." Publ Wkly

"Seven artists contributed illustrations in a range of styles, from naive scrawls to dreamy watercolors. Overall, their bright-hued pictures provide a fine complement to this lively compendium." SLJ

The **New** Oxford treasury of children's poems; [compiled by] Michael Harrison and Christopher Stuart-Clark. Oxford Univ. Press 1997 165p il $25 (3-5)   **808.81**
1. Poetry—Collections
ISBN 0-19-276137-4

Companion volume to The Oxford treasury of children's poems (1988)

"This anthology features primarily English and American poets, from W. B. Yeats and William Blake to Eve Merriam and Nikki Giovanni. While the focus is on older rhyming poems with playful subjects, there is a smattering of modern poetry, free verse, and serious themes." SLJ

"Large-format anthology features excellent poems illustrated in full color. . . . Eleven artists contributed illustrations that interpret the poetry with wit, verve, and delicacy." Booklist

Includes indexes

Once upon a poem; favorite poems that tell stories; foreword by Kevin Crossley-Holland; illustrated by Peter Bailey, Siân Bailey, Carol Lawson, Chris McEwan. The Chicken House 2004 124p il $18.95 (3-6)   **808.81**
1. Poetry—Collections
ISBN 0-439-65108-5

"This collection of 15 story-poems ranges widely, from Eugene Field's 'Wynken Blynken, and Nod' to Alfred Noyes's 'The Highwayman.' . . . The illustrations . . . are well matched to each piece, rendered in a variety of mediums. . . . The selections are well suited for read-alouds, with plenty of dense, sophisticated language. . . . This is a collection to grow on and to treasure over the years." SLJ

Sing a song of popcorn; every child's book of poems; illustrated by nine Caldecott Medal artists, Marcia Brown [et al.]; selected by Beatrice Schenk de Regniers [et al.] Scholastic 1988 142p il $18.95 **808.81**

1. Poetry—Collections
ISBN 0-590-43974-X   LC 87-4330

Revised edition of Poems children will sit still for, published 1969

A collection of 128 poems by a variety of well-known authors with illustrations by nine Caldecott medalists

"A pleasant book, still a useful if conservative anthology, this has title, author, and first line indexes, and brief notes on the illustrators." Bull Cent Child Books

Talking to the sun: an illustrated anthology of poems for young people; selected and introduced by Kenneth Koch and Kate Farrell. Metropolitan Mus. of Art 1985 112p il $14.95 **808.81**

1. Poetry—Collections
ISBN 0-87099-436-0   LC 85-15428

Also available from Holt & Co. for $19.95 (ISBN 0-8050-0144-1)

"Poems from a wide variety of times and cultures and reproductions from the Metropolitan Museum of Art are organized by themes that include spring, love, nonsense, animals, and the secrets beneath the ordinary. The combination works well . . . but sometimes this anthology crams in too much, leaving a design that is cluttered and confusing." Booklist

War and the pity of war; edited by Neil Philip; illustrated by Michael McCurdy. Clarion Bks. 1998 96p il $20 (5 and up) **808.81**

1. War poetry 2. Poetry—Collections
ISBN 0-395-84982-9   LC 97-32897

"The selections, covering conflicts from ancient Persia to modern-day Bosnia, are by a wide variety of poets, from the well known (Tennyson, Whitman, Sandburg, Auden), to the obscure (Anakreon from ancient Greece and 11th-century Chinese poet Bunno). . . . The stark and simple scratchboard drawings are reminiscent of the Ernie Pyle illustrations from World War II and are as memorable as the best propaganda." SLJ

Winter poems; selected by Barbara Rogasky; illustrated by Trina Schart Hyman. Scholastic 1994 40p il $15.95; pa $5.99 **808.81**

1. Winter—Poetry 2. Poetry—Collections
ISBN 0-590-42872-1; 0-590-42873-X (pa)
LC 91-24419

"Rogasky has selected a wide range of poems—25 in all—dating from 10th-century Japan to the contemporary U.S. The best of the ages is represented, with familiar favorites from Shakespeare, Thomas Hardy, Robert Frost, Emily Dickinson, Carl Sandburg, etc. . . . Hyman's illustrations perfectly capture the spirit of that season, with acrylics in deep, chilling shades. . . . A beautiful presentation of outstanding quality." SLJ

A **Zooful** of animals; selected by William Cole; illustrated by Lynn Munsinger. Houghton Mifflin 1992 88p il $17.95; pa $8.95 **808.81**

1. Animals—Poetry 2. Poetry—Collections
ISBN 0-395-52278-1; 0-395-77873-5 (pa)
LC 91-21885

A collection of animal poems by authors including Rachel Field, Shel Silverstein, and John Ciardi

"Not your usual zoo, this happy gathering of poetry and verse is broadly inclusive of its denizens, who live in unfettered joy within handsomely designed pages. . . . Lynn Munsinger's full-color illustrations contribute to making this book outstanding. She has a wonderfully expressive yet delicate line, the ability to be elegant and humorous at the same time." Horn Book

808.82   Drama--Collections

Play index. Wilson, H.W. 1953-2003 10v **808.82**

1. Drama—Indexes
ISSN 0554-3037

Also available on-line version

First published 1953 covering the years 1949-1952, and edited by Dorothy Herbert West and Dorothy Margaret Peake $80. Additional volumes: 1953-1960 $80 edited by Estelle A. Fidell and Dorothy Margaret Peake; 1961-1967 $70 edited by Estelle A. Fidell; 1968-1972 $80 edited by Estelle A. Fidell; 1973-1977 $80 edited by Estelle A. Fidell; 1978-1982 $80 edited by Juliette Yaakov; 1983-1987 $240 edited by Juliette Yaakov and John Greenfieldt; 1988-1992 $240 edited by Juliette Yaakov and John Greenfieldt; 1993-1997 edited by Juliette Yaakov and John Greenfieldt $240; 1998-2002 edited by John Greenfieldt $240

Play index indexes plays in collections and single plays; one-act and full-length plays; radio, television, and Broadway plays; plays for amateur production; plays for children, young adults, and adults. It is divided into four parts. Part I is an author, title, and subject index; the author or main entry includes the title of the play, brief synopsis of the plot, number of acts and scenes, size of cast, number of sets, and bibliographic information. Part II is a list of collections indexed, and Part III, a cast analysis, lists plays by the type of cast and number of players required

"This index is an excellent source for locating published plays." Safford. Guide to Ref Materials for Sch Media Cent. 5th edition

808.88   Collections of miscellaneous writings

Bartlett, John

Familiar quotations. Little, Brown $50 **808.88**

1. Quotations

First published 1855. (17th edition 2003) Periodically revised. Editors vary

"Arranged chronologically by author, with exact references. Includes many interesting footnotes, tracing histo-

Bartlett, John—*Continued*
ry or usage of analogous thoughts, the circumstances under which a particular remark was made, etc. Author and keyword indexes. One of the best books of quotations with a long history." Guide to Ref Books. 11th edition

Schwartz, Alvin
Busy buzzing bumblebees and other tongue twisters; illustrated by Paul Meisel. HarperCollins Pubs. 1992 61p il lib bdg $15.89; pa $4.50 (k-2)
808.88
1. Tongue twisters
ISBN 0-06-025269-3 (lib bdg); 0-06-444036-2 (pa)
LC 91-4799
"An I can read book"
First published 1982 with different illustrations
This book "contains 46 easy-to-read tongue twisters." SLJ
"Illustrated in wild, cheerful watercolors and with a multicultural cast, this . . . collection of tongue twisters is perfect for beginning readers." Booklist

809　Literary history and criticism

Carpenter, Humphrey
The Oxford companion to children's literature; [by] Humphrey Carpenter and Mari Prichard. Oxford Univ. Press 1984 586p il $49.95
809
1. Children's literature—Dictionaries
ISBN 0-19-211582-0　　　LC 83-15130
"One volume work with brief critiques of authors, illustrators, books, characters, and radio and television programs. Largely British in coverage of materials but does include most Newbery winners as well as well-known American, Australian and Canadian authors. Contemporary and historical subjects related to children's literature are examined." N Y Public Libr. Ref Books for Child Collect. 2d edition

810.3　American literature-- Encyclopedias and dictionaries

McElmeel, Sharron L.
100 most popular children's authors; biographical sketches and bibliographies. Libraries Unlimited 1999 xxxi, 493p il (Popular authors series) $55
810.3
1. Children's literature—Bio-bibliography
ISBN 1-56308-646-8　　　LC 98-41942
"Based on a 1997 survey of both teachers and students, this volume includes such well-known authors as Beverly Clearly (most recognized by the survey respondents) and classic writers like Lewis Carroll and C. S. Lewis. Each entry provides several pages about the author and his or her writings followed by a section called 'Books and Notes,' which has details about specific books and their themes, including bibliographic information. A list of additional material about or by the author completes each entry." Booklist

100 most popular picture book authors and illustrators; biographical sketches and bibliographies. Libraries Unlimited 2000 xxix, 579p (Popular authors series) $55
810.3
1. Children's literature—Bio-bibliography
ISBN 1-56308-647-6　　　LC 00-23181
The 100 profiles "are accompanied by photographs, reading lists, and lists of related information sources (such as Web pages). Contemporary authors and illustrators whose works are still in print provide the focus." Publisher's note

810.8　American literature-- Collections

Girls got game; sports stories and poems; edited by Sue Macy. Holt & Co. 2001 152p $17.95 (5 and up)
810.8
1. Sports 2. Women athletes 3. American literature—Collections
ISBN 0-8050-6568-7　　　LC 00-47297
A collection of short stories and poems written by and about young women in sports
"The lineup of authors includes heavy hitters such as Virginia Euwer Wolff and Jacqueline Woodson as well as some lesser-known talents. . . . This earnest and high-minded anthology can be dipped into or devoured in one sitting; however it is read, it should empower girls and guide them along their paths toward becoming strong, independent women." SLJ

Rising voices; writings of young Native Americans; selected by Arlene B. Hirschfelder and Beverly R. Singer. Scribner 1992 115p $13.95 (5 and up)
810.8
1. American literature—Native American authors—Collections 2. Native Americans 3. Children's writings
ISBN 0-684-19207-1　　　LC 91-32083
Also available in paperback from Ivy Bks.
A collection of poems and essays in which young Native Americans speak of their identity, their families and communities, rituals, and the harsh realities of their lives
"These 'rising voices' speak eloquently in this important collection. . . . Some pieces are over 100 years old; some are quite current. Some were written by elementary school students, and others by high schoolers. All are poignant and haunting." Voice Youth Advocates

Scared silly! a book for the brave; [compiled and illustrated by] Marc Brown. Little, Brown 1994 61p il music $18.95; pa $7.95 (k-3)
810.8
1. American literature—Collections
ISBN 0-316-11360-3; 0-316-10372-1 (pa)
LC 93-13501
An illustrated collection of spooky stories, poems, and riddles including a humorous array of ghosts, monsters, ghouls, and witches
This is "shivery enough to awe a young audience, yet silly enough for them to giggle their apprehensions away. Selections by such well-known authors as Ogden Nash, Jack Prelutsky, and Judith Viorst are included, as well as several original pieces by Brown. . . . Brown scores again with his own brand of warm, engaging watercolor

Scared silly!—*Continued*

art. . . . Brilliant colors, attention to detail, and the excellent balance of text and art provide a feast for the eye." SLJ

Wáchale! poetry and prose on growing up Latino in America; edited by Han Stavans. Cricket Publs. 2001 146p $16.95 (5 and up)

810.8

1. Hispanic Americans 2. American literature—Hispanic American authors—Collections 3. Bilingual books—English-Spanish
ISBN 0-8126-4750-5   LC 2001-47189

A bilingual collection of poems, stories, and other writings which celebrates diversity among Latinos.

"This collection would make a fine classroom text, great for reading aloud and for stimulating students from everywhere to write about their roots and celebrate their shifting places across borders." Booklist

Includes glossary and bibliographical references

Yolen, Jane

Here there be dragons; illustrated by David Wilgus. Harcourt Brace & Co. 1993 149p il pa $10 hardcover o.p. (5 and up)   **810.8**

1. Dragons—Fiction 2. American literature—Collections
ISBN 0-15-201705-4 (pa)   LC 92-23194

"Yolen has compiled a collection of her poetry and prose about dragons of all sizes, shapes and dispositions. She introduces each piece with a brief description including the circumstances surrounding its writing. . . . The poetry, like the prose, varies in length but will enthrall readers. David Wilgus' pen and ink drawings further enhance the book." Book Rep

810.9 American literature--History and criticism

Day, Frances Ann

Latina and Latino voices in literature; lives and works. Updated and expanded. Greenwood Press 2003 xx, 353p il por $57.95   **810.9**

1. Children's literature—Bibliography 2. Young adult literature—Bibliography
ISBN 0-313-32394-1   LC 2002-28439

"Thirty-five Latina and Latino authors of books for children and young adults are profiled in this work. . . . Entries are arranged alphabetically by author and begin with a photograph, essential biographical data, and a contact address. There are also quotations that summarize the person's philosophy of writing. Following this introductory information are lists of works, a biographical profile, and a list of resources for additional information. Selected works are then discussed in entries that range in length from a few lines to two pages. Also provided for each title are grade levels, subject headings, and a list of awards. . . . [This] is an essential reference tool for any library interested in serving this fast-growing population." Booklist

Includes bibliographical references

Wilkinson, Brenda Scott

African American women writers; [by] Brenda Wilkinson. Wiley 2000 166p il (Black stars) $22.95 (4 and up)   **810.9**

1. African American authors—Bio-bibliography
ISBN 0-471-17580-3   LC 99-25552

Discusses the lives and work of such notable African American women authors as: Phillis Wheatley, Ida B. Wells-Barnett, Zora Neale Hurston, Gwendolyn Brooks, Nikki Giovanni, and Terry McMillan

Includes bibliographical references

811 American poetry

Ada, Alma Flor

Gathering the sun; an alphabet in Spanish and English; English translation by Rosa Zubizarreta; illustrated by Simón Silva. Lothrop, Lee & Shepard Bks. 1997 unp il $16.95 (2-4)

811

1. Mexican Americans—Poetry 2. Alphabet 3. Bilingual books—English-Spanish
ISBN 0-688-13903-5

"Using the Spanish alphabet as a template, Ada has written 27 poems that celebrate both the bounty of the harvest and the Mexican heritage of the farmworkers and their families. The poems, presented in both Spanish and English, are short and simple bursts of flavor. . . . Silva's sun-drenched gouache paintings are robust, with images sculpted in paint." Booklist

Adoff, Arnold

Love letters; illustrated by Lisa Desimini. Blue Sky Press (NY) 1997 unp il $15.95 (3-6)

811

1. Love poetry
ISBN 0-590-48478-8   LC 96-19982

"This collection of twenty poems, written in letter form, celebrates love (and occasionally not-quite-love) for friends, teachers, family, pets, and even oneself. Adoff blends everyday images with humor and pays special attention to the visual appearance of each poem. Desimini's intriguing illustrations use a variety of techniques, including collage, sculpture, photographs, and paintings." Horn Book Guide

Touch the poem; poems by Arnold Adoff; pictures by Lisa Desimini. Blue Sky Press (NY) 2000 unp il $16.95 (k-3)   **811**

1. Touch—Poetry
ISBN 0-590-47970-9

A collection of poems about the sense of touch including a baby's foot in one's palm, peach fuzz on the lip, and the forehead against a cold window

"The solid imagery of Adoff's poetry takes on a visual dimension when paired with Desimini's bold photographs." Booklist

Alarcón, Francisco X.

From the bellybutton of the moon and other
summer poems; poems, Francisco X. Alarcón;
illustrations, Maya Christina Gonzalez. Children's
Bk. Press 1998 31p il $15.95 (2-4)   **811**
  1. Summer—Poetry 2. Bilingual books—English-
Spanish
ISBN 0-89239-153-7   LC 97-37457
A bilingual collection of poems in which the renowned Mexican American poet revisits and celebrates
his childhood memories of summers, Mexico, and nature
"Responding to and expanding on the poetry, Gonzalez's happy paintings weave rich waves of color in an
exuberant dance between text and design." Booklist

Iguanas in the snow and other winter poems;
poems, Francisco X. Alarcón; illustrations, Maya
Christina Gonzalez. Children's Bk. Press 2001 31p
il $15.95 (2-4)   **811**
  1. Winter—Poetry 2. Bilingual books—English-
Spanish
ISBN 0-89239-168-5   LC 00-65667
Text and title page in English and Spanish
"Eighteen verses in Spanish and English offer homage
not just to winter but to the year-round delights of San
Francisco and the rest of northern California." Bull Cent
Child Books
"Brief, zippy verses express delight in such simple
things as a family frolic in the snow and the wonder of
giant redwoods. . . . The selections are short of line and
long on meter, with a rhythmic roll that begs reading
aloud. . . . Gonzalez's illustrations are bright and busy,
catching the playful cadence of the words." SLJ

Laughing tomatoes and other spring poems;
illustrations, Maya Christina Gonzalez. Children's
Bk. Press 1997 32p il $15.95 (2-4)   **811**
  1. Spring—Poetry 2. Bilingual books—English-
Spanish
ISBN 0-89239-139-1   LC 96-7459
Title page and text in English and Spanish
"This bilingual collection of poems by Chicano poet
Alarcón celebrates spring and the fruits of family and
sunshine. . . . The poems are short and simple imagistic
reflections exuberantly expanded by Gonzalez in colorful
double-page illustrations." Booklist

Poems to dream together; Poemas para soñar
juntos; illustrations by Paula Barragán. 1st ed. Lee
& Low Books 2005 unp il $16.95 (3-5)
   811
  1. Mexican Americans—Poetry 2. Bilingual books—
English-Spanish
ISBN 1-58430-233-X   LC 2004-20963
In a "bilingual collection of short poems, Alarcon
shares his dreams of peace, community building, and a
bright future for children of all cultures. . . . The rhythm
and cadence work well in both the Spanish and the English entries, and Barragan's illustrations are a fine complement to the text. Flat, bright colors and simple shapes
give them the look of classroom paper cutouts, but the
compositions are as intricate as Mexican mural paintings." Booklist

Behn, Harry

Halloween; illustrated by Greg Couch.
North-South Bks. 2003 unp il $15.95; lib bdg
$16.50 (1-3)   **811**
  1. Halloween—Poetry
ISBN 0-7358-1609-3; 0-7358-1766-9 (lib bdg)
      LC 2002-43238
"A Cheshire Studio book"
"A skeleton, a witch, and a devil go out to trick-or-
treat, but are frightened by every sound they hear and
everything they see. Larger-than-life, vivid illustrations
bring this simple rhyming verse to life on each haunting
spread." SLJ

Bernier-Grand, Carmen T.

César; si, se puede! yes, we can! illustrated by
David Diaz. Marshall Cavendish 2004 48p il
$16.95 (3-6)   **811**
  1. Chavez, Cesar, 1927-1993 2. Mexican Americans—
Poetry
ISBN 0-7614-5172-2   LC 2003-26866
Also available Spanish language edition
"A sequence of free-verse poems surveys the life and
the work of Mexican-American activist Cesar Chavez."
Bull Cent Child Books
"The lyrical language describes events and paints
evocative pictures to which children will relate. Diaz's
stylized, computer-drawn, folk-art illustrations capture the
subject's private and public life." SLJ
Inlcudes glossary and bibligraphical references

Bolden, Tonya

Rock of ages; a tribute to the Black church;
illustrated by R. Gregory Christie. Knopf 2002 unp
il $16.95; lib bdg $18.99 (3-5)   **811**
  1. African Americans—Religion 2. African Americans—Poetry
ISBN 0-679-89485-3; 0-679-99485-8 (lib bdg)
      LC 2001-38534
A poem celebrating the role of church in the lives and
history of African Americans, from the time of slavery
through the struggle for civil rights to the well-
established churches of today
"The imagery is vivid, the rhythmic text is inspiring,
and the art sweeps across the pages." Booklist

Boling, Katharine

New year be coming! a Gullah year; written by
Katharine Boling; illustrated by Daniel Minter.
Whitman, A. 2002 unp il $15.95 (k-3)
   811
  1. Months—Poetry 2. Gullahs—Poetry
ISBN 0-8075-5590-8   LC 2002-1952
Verses written in the Gullah dialect of the southeastern seacoast describe the months of the year and activities that characterize each
"Boling provides an introduction to the history, language, and culture of the Gullahs. . . . A glossary defines any words that remain puzzling. The large linoleum
block prints are strong in composition, rhythmic in their
use of pattern, and bright with color washes." Booklist

Booth, Philip

Crossing; illustrations by Bagram Ibatoulline. Candlewick Press 2001 unp il $16.99; pa $6.99 (k-3) **811**

1. Railroads—Poetry

ISBN 0-7636-1420-3; 0-7636-2434-9 (pa)

LC 00-39781

"In 1953 Booth published a propulsive, almost onomatopoeic rhymed poem, re-creating the experience of witnessing a huge freight train at a rural crossing in sound and rhythm. . . . This verse, which almost reads itself aloud as it runs along the bottom of each page, is paired in this new picture book with gouache paintings that fill the pages to the very edge." Booklist

Brand, Dionne

Earth magic; poems by Dionne Brand; with illustrations by Eugenie Fernandes. KCP Poetry 2006 30p il $14.95 (4 and up) **811**

1. Trinidad—Poetry

ISBN 1-55337-706-0

"Brand celebrates Trinidad, her birthplace, in her debut collection [of poetry] for youth. The rhythmic selections, seemingly narrated by a girl, are filled with a child's view of island life, and the natural world appears as characters capable of powerful action. . . . Fernandes' striking, acrylic collage artwork beautifully extends the moods and metaphors in vibrantly colored scenes that amplify the sense of mysticism while reinforcing the poems' concrete images." Booklist

Brown, Calef

Dutch sneakers and flea keepers; 14 more stories. Houghton Mifflin 2000 unp il $15 (2-4) **811**

1. Humorous poetry

ISBN 0-618-05183-X

LC 99-53722

Also available companion volume Polkabats and octopus slacks: 14 stories (1998)

This "collection is more a gallery of odd characters and their bizarre worlds than it is a book of tales. In zany, ebullient verse and stylish, wildly angled paintings, Brown presents an irresistible roundup of eccentrics. . . . Brown's paintings combine elements of folk art with swirling, energetic designs and ultrahip colors and details that match the text's irreverent wit and fantastic scenarios." Booklist

Bruchac, Joseph

Thirteen moons on a turtle's back; a Native American year of moons; by Joseph Bruchac and Jonathan London; illustrated by Thomas Locker. Philomel Bks. 1992 unp il $16.95; pa $5.99 **811**

1. Native Americans—Folklore 2. Native Americans—Poetry 3. Seasons—Poetry

ISBN 0-399-22141-7; 0-698-11584-8 (pa)

LC 91-3961

"Native American stories are retold as poems that capture the cycles of the moon. Months slip by as the oil paintings show each moon in the shell of the turtle's back." Child Book Rev Serv

"Locker . . . has created a dramatic oil painting for each short tale. His artwork portrays seasonal changes in the land as well as the specific seasonal activities of humans and animals. The large format with minimal text will appeal to younger children, while the alternative calendar, based on changes in nature, will interest middle readers. An unusual, easy-to-use resource for librarians, teachers, and others wishing to incorporate multicultural activites throughout the year." Booklist

Bryan, Ashley

Sing to the sun; poems and pictures by Ashley Bryan. HarperCollins Pubs. 1992 unp il pa $6.95 **811**

ISBN 0-06-443437-0

LC 91-38359

A collection of poems and paintings celebrating the ups and downs of life

"With an energetic beat that's hard to resist, Bryan drums out poetry with a Caribbean sway. These short poems that sing the praises of everyday joys are further charged by the riotous primary colors Bryan splashes around." Booklist

Bunting, Eve

Sing a song of piglets; a calendar in verse; pictures by Emily Arnold McCully. Clarion Bks. 2002 32p il $16 (k-2) **811**

1. Pigs—Poetry 2. Months—Poetry

ISBN 0-618-01137-4

LC 2001-55267

From skiing in January to surfing in July, two energetic piglets romp through the months of the years in this calendar in verse

"There's a delightful exuberance to the artwork, and children will enjoy looking at the pictures to catch more of the details. A charming choice, too, for beginning readers." Booklist

Burg, Brad

Outside the lines; poetry at play; [illustrated by] Rebecca Gibbon. Putnam 2002 32p il $15.99 (k-3) **811**

1. Play—Poetry

ISBN 0-399-23446-2

LC 00-51726

The poems in this "collection mimic the shapes and forms of the children's games they celebrate. A poem about a girl on a swing follows her arc as she flies through the air, leaving a trail of words across the page. . . . Gibbon's understated watercolor spreads and vignettes accent Burg's whimsy without overshadowing it." Publ Wkly

Burleigh, Robert

Goal; illustrated by Stephen T. Johnson. Silver Whistle Bks. 2001 unp il $16 (k-3) **811**

1. Soccer—Poetry

ISBN 0-15-201789-5

LC 98-33181

Illustrations and poetic text describe the movement and feel of a fast-paced game of soccer

"The poetry, expertly complemented by Johnson's blurry pastel illustrations of children on the field, mirrors the dizzy rush of winning—and the thrill of giving one's all." Booklist

Burleigh, Robert—*Continued*

Hoops; illustrated by Stephen T. Johnson.
Harcourt Brace & Co. 1997 unp il $16; pa $6
                                                811
1. Basketball—Poetry
ISBN 0-15-201450-0; 0-15-216380-8 (pa)
                                         LC 96-18440
"Silver Whistle"
Illustrations and poetic text describe the movement
and feel of the game of basketball
"Burleigh's staccato text is well matched by Johnson's
dynamic pastels. Muted colors and a strong sense of motion as bodies leap and lift, pounce and poke, aptly complement the words." SLJ

Calmenson, Stephanie

Good for you! toddler rhymes for toddler times;
original rhymes by Stephanie Calmenson; pictures
by Melissa Sweet. HarperCollins Pubs. 2001 64p
il $16.95; lib bdg $16.89 (k-1)   **811**
ISBN 0-688-17737-9; 0-06-029811-1 (lib bdg)
                                         LC 00-40891
"This collection includes verses about colors, riddles
about the playground, poems about manners, and bits on
other topics of concern to toddlers. Sweet's vibrant illustrations with bright backgrounds pick up where the
rhymes leave off, giving the audience a nice view of the
diverse world of children." SLJ

Kindergarten kids; riddles, rebuses, wiggles,
giggles, and more! original rhymes by Stephanie
Calmenson; pictures by Melissa Sweet.
HarperCollins 2005 32p il $15.99; lib bdg $16.89
(k-1)   **811**
1. Schools—Poetry
ISBN 0-06-000713-3; 0-06-000714-1 (lib bdg)
                                         LC 2004-04175
This "collection of original rhymes and riddles focuses
on activities that are part of the kindergarten experience,
such as attendance, show-and-tell, and classroom pets.
. . . The simple, interactive rhymes . . . provide a light,
accessible introduction for new students. Sweet's delightful illustrations bring color, energy, and information to
each page." SLJ

Welcome, baby! baby rhymes for baby times;
original rhymes by Stephanie Calmenson; pictures
by Melissa Sweet. HarperCollins Pubs. 2002 64p
il $16.99; lib bdg $18.89 (k-1)   **811**
1. Infants—Poetry
ISBN 0-688-17736-0; 0-06-000492-4 (lib bdg)
                                         LC 2001-24634
Companion volume to Good for you!
This "offers very young children 33 short poems to
match to their own perspective of the world. . . . Colorful and childlike Sweet's appealing artwork is a wonderful complement to the simple language and early childhood topics." Booklist

Cameron, Eileen

Canyon; photographs by Michael Collier.
Mikaya Press 2002 unp il $16.95 (3-5)
                                                811
1. Canyons—Poetry
ISBN 1-931414-03-3   LC 2001-52180
"Colorful landscapes accompany a short poem about
water and the path it takes from clouds, over canyon
walls, and into a river. The poetry is at times quite vivid
. . . but it's the artwork that's the star. From rivulets
streaming down rocks to sculpted pools of mud, Collier's
photography touches the imagination." Booklist

Carlstrom, Nancy White

Thanksgiving Day at our house; Thanksgiving
poems for the very young; written by Nancy
White Carlstrom; illustrated by R.W. Alley. Simon
& Schuster Bks. for Young Readers 1999 31p il
$15 (k-2)   **811**
1. Thanksgiving Day—Poetry
ISBN 0-689-80360-5   LC 98-49254
A collection of poems about one family's activities on
Thanksgiving Day, including pondering the history behind the holiday, welcoming visiting relatives, praying
for others, enjoying the good food, and giving thanks at
the end of the day
"Sometimes humorous, sometimes tender, the lively
details in Alley's illustrations make each turn of the page
a delight." Booklist

Who said boo? Halloween poems for the very
young; written by Nancy White Carlstrom;
illustrated by R.W. Alley. Simon & Schuster Bks.
for Young Readers 1995 32p il pa $5.99 hardcover
o.p. (k-3)   **811**
1. Halloween—Poetry
ISBN 0-689-83151-X (pa)   LC 94-33577
A collection of poems celebrating such Halloween
phenomena as monsters, witches, haunted houses, and
jack-o-lanterns
"The verse is simple, full of action, rhyme, and physicality that small kids will love. The watercolor pictures
are very bright and very detailed." Booklist

Chaikin, Miriam

Don't step on the sky; a handful of haiku;
illustrated by Hiroe Nakata. Holt & Co. 2002 unp
il $16.95 (k-3)   **811**
1. Haiku 2. Nature poetry
ISBN 0-8050-6474-5   LC 2001-1469
"In this group of haiku, the world of nature is observed from a child's perspective." Horn Book Guide
"Nakata successfully uses cheerful watercolor to create
concrete images from obscure words and to extend the
speaker's shifting perspective. . . . Simple, elegant, and
playful, this is poetry that children will enjoy in and out
of the classroom." Booklist

Child, Lydia Maria Francis

Over the river and through the wood (k-2)
                                                811
1. Thanksgiving Day—Poetry 2. Songs
Some editions are:

Child, Lydia Maria Francis—*Continued*

Holt & Co. pa $7.95 Illustrated by David Catrow (ISBN 0-8050-6311-0)

North-South Bks. pa $6.95 Illustrated by Christopher Manson (ISBN 1-55858-959-7)

Text originally published in volume 2 of the author's Flowers for children, 1844, under title: A boy's Thanksgiving Day

Illustrated versions of a poem about a family's visit to their grandparents for Thanksgiving

Ciardi, John

You read to me, I'll read to you; drawings by Edward Gorey. Lippincott 1962 64p il pa $7.95 hardcover o.p. **811**

1. Humorous poetry

ISBN 0-06-446060-6 (pa)

Thirty-five "imaginative and humorous poems for an adult and a child to read aloud together. Written in a basic first-grade vocabulary, the poems to be read by the child alternate with poems to be read by the adult." Booklist

Cox, Kenyon

Mixed beasts; or, A miscellany of rare and fantastic creatures; compiled by Professor Julius Duckworth O'Hare, Esq.; illustrations by Wallace Edwards; verses by Kenyon Cox. Kids Can Press 2005 unp il $17.95 (3-5) **811**

1. Nonsense verses 2. Animals—Poetry

ISBN 1-55337-796-6

"Inspired by Kenyon Cox's Mixed beasts published in 1904"

"These original nonsense poems about a miscellany of odd beasts comprised of a mixture of two species, such as a Rhinocerostrich, a Bumblebeaver, a Kangarooster, and a Camelelephant, are clever and funny. Full-page, detailed illustrations of exotic flora and fauna as well as preposterous creatures are rendered in watercolor, colored pencil, and gouache. The humor of the selections is carried out in the art." SLJ

Crawley, Dave

Cat poems; illustrations by Tamara Petrosino. Wordsong/Boyds Mills Press 2005 32p il $15.95 (2-4) **811**

1. Cats—Poetry

ISBN 1-59078-287-9 LC 2004-20095

"These playful poems muse about why cats do what they do. The cheerful, mostly rhymed couplets describe scenes that kids who know cats will immediately recognize. . . . Petrosino's lively, cartoon-style, and pen-and-ink and watercolor illustrations match the buoyant, affectionate tone of the poems." Booklist

Cyrus, Kurt

Hotel deep; light verse from dark water; [by] Kurt Cyrus. Harcourt 2005 unp il $16 (3-5) **811**

1. Marine animals—Poetry 2. Ocean—Poetry

ISBN 0-15-216771-4 LC 2003-25999

Twenty-one poems tell the story of a lone sardine separated from his school within a huge coral reef and the creatures he meets as he searches for the way back.

"Cyrus' lavishly colored, detailed paintings show the creatures that lurk in the gorgeous underworld. . . . The sounds of the poetry are as much fun as the exciting action in the wild setting, making this a great read-aloud for sharing." Booklist

Dakos, Kalli

Put your eyes up here; and other scool poems; illustrated by G. Brian Karas. Simon & Schuster Bks. for Young Readers 2003 63p il $16.95 (2-4) **811**

1. Schools—Poetry

ISBN 0-689-81117-9 LC 2001-20543

"This collection of forty-nine poems celebrates humorous, poignant, and challenging events at school. The poems . . . aptly reflect a child's view and growing appreciation of a teacher who brings a special magic to her classroom. Kara's simple black-and-white illustrations add to the generally lighthearted mood." Horn Book Guide

Dawes, Kwame Senu Neville

I saw your face; [drawings by] Tom Feelings; text by Kwame Dawes; afterword by Jerry Pinkney. Dial Books 2004 unp il $16.99 (3-5) **811**

1. Blacks—Poetry 2. Face in art

ISBN 0-8037-1894-2 LC 2004-00241

A poem and portraits of children illustrate the shared beauty and heritage of people of African descent living throughout the world.

"Accompanied by Dawes's celebratory verses, page after page of evocative drawings are set in Africa, the Caribbean, England, and the American South." Horn Book Guide

Di Pasquale, Emanuel

Cartwheel to the moon; my Sicilian childhood: poems; by Emanuel di Pasquale; selected and arranged by Marianne Carus; introduction by X.J. Kennedy; illustrated by K. Dyble Thompson. Cricket Bks. 2003 64p il $16.95 (3-6) **811**

1. Sicily (Italy)—Poetry

ISBN 0-8126-2679-6 LC 2002-152826

An illustrated collection of poems celebrating the landscape, people, plants and animals, customs, and traditions of the Italian island of Sicily

"These glimpses of the author's Mediterranean childhood are extremely tangible. . . . Thompson's softly washed blue-and-white watercolor images are like picture postcards, amplifying the scenic words as they trace the seasons in Sicily." SLJ

Dickinson, Emily

I'm nobody! who are you? poems of Emily Dickinson for children; illustrated by Rex Schneider; with an introduction by Richard B. Sewall. Stemmer House 1978 84p il $21.95 (3-6)
811

ISBN 0-916144-21-6   LC 78-6828

"A Barbara Holdridge book"

This collection of Emily Dickinson's poetry is illustrated with full color drawings depicting life in nineteenth century New England

Includes glossary

Dotlich, Rebecca Kai

Over in the pink house. Wordsong/Boyds Mills Press 2004 30p il $15.95 (k-3)   **811**

1. Jump rope rhymes

ISBN 1-59078-027-2

"These 32 original rhymes are infused with fresh, colorful imagery and toe-tapping rhythm. Appropriate for reading or chanting aloud while jumping rope, each one has a lighthearted, whimsical quality. The vibrantly colored illustrations are equally playful." SLJ

Esbensen, Barbara Juster

Swing around the sun; poems; art by Cheng-Khee Chee {et al.}. Carolrhoda Bks. 2003 unp il lib bdg $16.95 (2-4)   **811**

1. Seasons—Poetry

ISBN 0-87614-143-2   LC 2002-7980

A newly illustrated edition of the title first published 1965 by Lerner

A collection of poems that celebrates the seasons, with illustrations for each season by a different Minnesota artist

"A rich, vibrant reading and viewing experience. . . . The poetry's impact is heightened by masterful new illustrations from four distinguished artists. . . . Cheng-Khee Chee's textured watercolors sprout and bloom across the pages of 'Spring.' Janice Lee Porter's 'Summer' oil pastels hum with energetic color and sinuous shapes. Mary GrandPré ushers in fall with a warmer palette of pastels. . . . Finally, Stephen Gammell's snowscapes, spattered in icy grays and blue capture winter's wild spirit." SLJ

Evans, Lezlie

Rain song; illustrated by Cynthia Jabar. Houghton Mifflin 1995 unp il $16; pa $5.95 (k-1)
811

1. Rain—Poetry

ISBN 0-395-69865-0; 0-395-85077-0 (pa)

LC 94-17368

"A playful rhyming poem and energetic, lighthearted illustrations show two girls relishing the delights of a rainstorm." Booklist

Field, Eugene

Wynken, Blynken, and Nod; written by Eugene W. Field; illustrated by David McPhail. Scholastic 2004 unp il $15.95   **811**

1. Sleep—Poetry

ISBN 0-439-54303-7   LC 2003-7706

"Cartwheel books"

A classic lullaby poem about three fishermen who try to catch the stars in nets of silver and gold.

"McPhail's interpretation sends three bunnies, clothed as sailors, off in the wooden shoe that sails through a dreamy version of the night sky and into the bedroom of a little girl. . . . Rich with deep, soft colors, the illustrations sweep broadly across the double-page spreads. . . . The pictures suggest rhythm, grace, and mystery." Booklist

Fleischman, Paul

Big talk; poems for four voices; illustrated by Beppe Giacobbe. Candlewick Press 2000 44p il $17.99 (4 and up)   **811**

ISBN 0-7636-0636-7   LC 99-46882

A collection of poems to be read aloud by four people, with color-coded text to indicate which lines are read by which readers

"Each poem is more demanding, and more rewarding, than the last. Giacobbe highlights the humor in strips of vignettes that run along the bottom of the page. This is 'toe-tapping, tongue-flapping fun.'" Horn Book Guide

I am phoenix: poems for two voices; illustrated by Ken Nutt. Harper & Row 1985 51p il pa $5.99 hardcover o.p. (4 and up)   **811**

1. Birds—Poetry

ISBN 0-06-446092-4 (pa)   LC 85-42615

"A Charlotte Zolotow book"

A collection of poems about birds to be read aloud by two voices

"Devotés of the almost lost art of choral reading should be among the first to appreciate this collection. . . . Printed in script form, the selections . . . have a cadenced pace and dignified flow; their combination of imaginative imagery and realistic detail is echoed by the combination of stylized fantasy and representational drawings in the black and white pictures, all soft line and strong nuance." Bull Cent Child Books

Joyful noise: poems for two voices; illustrated by Eric Beddows. Harper & Row 1988 44p il $15.99; lib bdg $16.89; pa $5.99 (4 and up)
811

1. Insects—Poetry

ISBN 0-06-021852-5; 0-06-021853-3 (lib bdg); 0-06-446093-2 (pa)   LC 87-45280

Awarded the Newbery Medal, 1989

"A Charlotte Zolotow book"

"This collection of poems for two voices explores the lives of insects. Designed to be read aloud, the phrases of the poems are spaced vertically on the page in two columns, one for each reader. The voices sometimes alternate, sometimes speak in chorus, and sometimes echo each other." Booklist

"There are fourteen poems in the handsomely designed volume, with stylish endpapers and wonderfully interpretive black-and-white illustrations. Each selection is a gem, polished perfection." Horn Book

Fletcher, Ralph

A writing kind of day; poems for young poets; illustrations by April Ward. Wordsong/Boyds Mills Press 2005 32p il $17.95; pa $9.95 (3-5)

811

ISBN 1-59078-276-3; 1-59078-353-0 (pa)

"A young writer's daily experiences and concerns are folded into poems to which many readers can relate. . . . Varied in mood and tone, the offerings entertain as they celebrate words and language. . . . Ward's black-and-white illustrations use a variety of mediums, including pencil, photography, computer-generated images, and ink." SLJ

Florian, Douglas

Autumnblings; poems and paintings by Douglas Florian. Greenwillow Bks. 2003 48p il $15.99; lib bdg $16.89

811

1. Autumn—Poetry

ISBN 0-06-009278-5; 0-06-009279-3 (lib bdg)

LC 2002-29780

A collection of poems that portray the essence of the season between summer and winter

"Short verse lines make the entries particularly suitable for reading aloud or reciting. . . . The illustrations, luminous watercolors touched with colored pencils, often move beyond the decorative to witty visual commentary or elegant, streamlined scenes." Bull Cent Child Books

Beast feast; poems and paintings by Douglas Florian. Harcourt Brace & Co. 1994 48p il $16; pa $7

811

1. Animals—Poetry

ISBN 0-15-295178-4; 0-15-201737-2 (pa)

LC 93-10720

A collection of humorous poems about such animals as the walrus, anteater, and boa

"Most verses are rhymed and employ standard poetic schemes, but clever wordplay, good rhythm, and liberal humor in word and illustrations make a fine poetic feast." Horn Book Guide

Bing bang boing; poems and drawings by Douglas Florian. Harcourt Brace & Co. 1994 144p il $16

811

1. Nonsense verses

ISBN 0-15-233770-9

LC 94-3894

Also available in paperback from Penguin Bks.

An illustrated collection of more than 150 nonsense verses

"The author's spare, pen-and-ink drawings, like the poems themselves, deftly explore the comic potential in each combination of words. With a few clean lines, he creates an original, funny vision." SLJ

Bow wow meow meow; it's rhyming cats and dogs; poems and paintings by Douglas Florian. Harcourt 2003 47p il $17

811

1. Cats—Poetry 2. Dogs—Poetry

ISBN 0-15-216395-6

LC 2002-6309

Contents: Dog log; The Chihuahua; The bloodhound; The bulldog; The poodles; The pointers; The sheepdog; The Dalmatian; The whippet; The wolf; The dachshund; Cat chat; The Persian; The cheetah; The ocelot; The Siamese; The lion; The Manx; The leopard; The jaguarundi; The black panther

"Twenty-one humorous poems and paintings about dogs, cats, the wolf, and a few large felines. . . . The watercolor paintings in primarily pastel colors are great fun, revealing an attribute or the character of each animal. This is a delightful selection to read aloud to younger children, and it offers older students models of simple poems that really work." SLJ

Handsprings; poems & paintings by Douglas Florian. Greenwillow Books 2006 48p il $15.99; lib bdg $16.89

811

1. Spring—Poetry

ISBN 0-06-009280-7; 0-06-009281-5 (lib bdg)

LC 2005-04567

A collection of short poems about spring

This includes "twenty-nine exuberant poems coupled with whimsical paintings distinguished for their warm colors, spare imagery, and a peculiar, sweet grace." Horn Book

In the swim; poems and paintings by Douglas Florian. Harcourt Brace & Co. 1997 unp il $16

811

1. Marine animals—Poetry 2. Humorous poetry

ISBN 0-15-201307-5

LC 95-52616

"This collection of 21 original short poems features fresh-and saltwater critters such as the piranha, manatee, and rainbow trout." Booklist

"These clipped verses splash with mischief and wit. The watercolor paintings, one per poem, also connect the silly and sublime." Horn Book Guide

Insectlopedia; poems and paintings by Douglas Florian. Harcourt Brace & Co. 1998 47p il $16

811

1. Insects—Poetry

ISBN 0-15-201306-7

LC 96-23029

Presents twenty-one short poems about such insects as the inchworm, termite, cricket, and ladybug

"The artwork consists of collages of drawn and painted images and printed letters on paper that is cut and juxtaposed for effect. The clever artwork, deftly constructed, and the entertaining collection of insect and arachnid verse it illustrates will delight readers." Booklist

Laugh-eteria; poems and drawings by Douglas Florian. Harcourt Brace & Co. 1999 157p il $17

811

1. Humorous poetry

ISBN 0-15-202084-5

LC 98-20047

Also available in paperback from Puffin Bks.

A collection of more than 100 humorous poems on such topics as ogres, pizza, fear, school, dragons, trees, and hair

"Florian's pithy poems echo playground chants (and sometimes, better yet, jeers) in their rhythmic recitability . . . and his focus on orality and absurdity makes them thematically irresistible. The line drawings have a sophisticated quirkiness." Bull Cent Child Books

Lizards, frogs, and pollywogs; poems and paintings by Douglas Florian. Harcourt 2001 46p il $16

811

1. Reptiles—Poetry 2. Amphibians—Poetry

ISBN 0-15-202591-X

LC 99-50830

Florian, Douglas—*Continued*

A collection of humorous poems about such reptiles and amphibians as the glass frog, the gecko, and the rattlesnake

"This volume contains witty poems filled with comic word play. . . . Florian uses watercolors and collage elements atop brown paper bags. The warm, familiar tones and soft lines belie the idiosyncrasy of the compositions." Publ Wkly

Mammalabilia; poems and paintings by Douglas Florian. Harcourt 2000 47p il $16   **811**
1. Mammals—Poetry
ISBN 0-15-202167-1   LC 99-10702

A collection of humorous poems about mammals such as the tiger, gorilla, and rhebok

"This collection of 21 short light verse brims with whimsy and fun. . . . The artwork taps into childlike qualities without being simplistic; the animal portraits are clever yet appropriate. An irresistible homage to mammal memorabilia." Publ Wkly

Omnibeasts; animal poems and paintings by Douglas Florian. Harcourt 2004 95p il $18
                                              811
1. Animals—Poetry
ISBN 0-15-205038-8   LC 2003-18823

A compilation of animal poems selected from the author's previously published collections.

This "is a treasure chest of wit and charm. The author weaves information into each poem, combining fun and fact. Combined with Florian's signature watercolors . . . each short offering occupies its own spread. This book has enormous appeal for readers of many ages" SLJ

On the wing; bird poems and paintings by Douglas Florian. Harcourt Brace & Co. 1996 47p il $16; pa $6   **811**
1. Birds—Poetry
ISBN 0-15-200497-1; 0-15-202366-6 (pa)
                                        LC 95-9976

This "collection features 21 poems about a variety of birds, from hummingbird to vulture, roadrunner to emperor penguin. The imagery in these short poems finds visual expression in the full-page, watercolor paintings, illustrating verse with high spirits and ingenuous charm." Booklist

Summersaults; poems & paintings by Douglas Florian. Greenwillow Bks. 2002 48p il $15.95; lib bdg $15.89   **811**
1. Summer—Poetry
ISBN 0-06-029267-9; 0-06-029268-7 (lib bdg)
                                     LC 2001-23619

"Florian examines the joys of summer in twenty-eight brief verses." Bull Cent Child Books

"Florian ably captures the freedom and exuberance of the season in bright, new greens, sun-baked browns, and images of leaping, grinning figures. The gleeful puns, wordplay, and creative grammar will charm youngsters." Booklist

Winter eyes; poems & paintings by Douglas Florian. Greenwillow Bks. 1999 48p il $16
                                              811
1. Winter—Poetry
ISBN 0-688-16458-7   LC 98-19483

A collection of poems about winter, including "Sled," "Icicles," and "Ice Fishing"

"The short rhyming lines are clear and will be easy to read aloud, and the softly toned watercolor-and-colored-pencil pictures show snowy winter scenes, some realistic, some playful." Booklist

Zoo's who; poems and paintings by Douglas Florian. Harcourt 2005 47p il $17 (k-3)
                                              811
1. Animals—Poetry
ISBN 0-15-204639-9   LC 2004-4576

A collection of short poems about animals

"There's plenty of humor throughout. . . . The artwork . . . always has unexpected bits. . . . The more astute the reader, the better the time he or she will have with this." Booklist

Franco, Betsy

Mathematickles; poems by Betsy Franco + illustrations by Steven Salerno. Margaret K. McElderry Bks. 2003 unp il $17.95 (2-4)
                                              811
1. Mathematics—Poetry
ISBN 0-689-84357-7   LC 2001-55844

A collection of poems written in the form of mathematical problems and grouped according to seasonal themes

"Franco's clever mathcapades are boldly partnered by the strong, fluid lines and splashy palette of the appealingly retro artwork. . . . This book's jazzy, wholly original approach elevates basic mathematical concepts plus wordplay to the level of inspiration." Publ Wkly

Frost, Robert

Birches; illustrated by Ed Young. Holt & Co. 1988 unp il pa $5.95 hardcover o.p.   **811**
1. Trees—Poetry
ISBN 0-8050-1316-4 (pa)   LC 86-4787

An illustrated version of the well-known poem written in 1916, about birch trees and the pleasures of climbing them

"The freedom called for in the sweep and depth of Frost's words should not be hemmed in by rigidly defined illustrations, and Young allows this license, giving the viewer ample opportunity to absorb and be absorbed by the imagery. The text is set two to three lines to a page, with the poem repeated in its entirety at the end." Booklist

Robert Frost; edited by Gary D. Schmidt; illustrated by Henri Sorensen. Sterling 1994 48p il (Poetry for young people) $14.95 (4 and up)
                                              811
ISBN 0-8069-0633-2   LC 94-11161

"A Magnolia Editions book"

This volume "contains a three-page overview of the poet's life, 29 poems selected and arranged around the seasons of the year, brief and apt commentaries on each, and a useful index of titles and subject matter. The realistic watercolor illustrations capture the delicate beauty of a New England spring and the glory of fall while still suggesting the around-the-corner chill of winter, a disquiet echoing throughout much of Frost's poetry." SLJ

George, Kristine O'Connell

Fold me a poem; illustrated by Lauren Stringer. Harcourt 2005 unp il $16 (k-3) **811**

1. Origami—Poetry

ISBN 0-15-202501-4   LC 2003-19382

"George's 32 brief poems focus on a boy as he folds a series of origami animals and imagines their thoughts and possible activities. . . . The vividly colored acrylics depict the boy actively engaged in play with his creations, and the details that Stringer provides infuse the verses with both energy and humor." SLJ

Includes bibliographical references

The great frog race and other poems; pictures by Kate Kiesler; with an introduction by Myra Cohn Livingston. Clarion Bks. 1997 40p il $15 (3-5) **811**

ISBN 0-395-77607-4   LC 95-51090

A collection of poems about frogs and dragonflies, wind and rain, a visit to the tree farm, the garden hose, and other aspects of country life

"George's astute imagery pairs beautifully with Kiesler's rich, warm-toned oil paintings to impart a strong sense of the pleasures of rural landscape." Booklist

Little Dog and Duncan; poems by Kristine O'Connell George; illustrated by June Otani. Clarion Bks. 2002 40p il $12 (k-2) **811**

1. Dogs—Poetry

ISBN 0-618-11758-X   LC 2001-28481

"Little Dog hosts a sleepover when big dog Duncan, a rangy Irish wolfhound, comes for a visit. . . . The verses themselves could hardly be shorter, but they are just the right size for Litte Dog and little kids. The layout of the poems is harmoniously designed both for sense and for interplay with Otani's beguilingly casual watercolor sketches." Horn Book Guide

Little dog poems; illustrated by June Otani. Clarion Bks. 1999 40p il $12 (k-2) **811**

1. Dogs—Poetry

ISBN 0-395-82266-1   LC 97-46678

"Thirty short poems about a lively terrier, narrated by the dog's young mistress." SLJ

"The language is simple and concrete enough for the youngest listeners. Otani's pen and watercolor illustrations make a fine complement to the verse." Horn Book Guide

Old Elm speaks; tree poems; illustrated by Kate Kiesler. Clarion Bks. 1998 48p il $15 (2-4) **811**

1. Trees—Poetry

ISBN 0-395-87611-7   LC 97-49333

A collection of short, simple poems which present images relating to trees in various circumstances and throughout the seasons

"George conveys a deep understanding of nature, here particularly of trees, in a way that is readily accessible to children. Kiesler's warm oil paintings beautifully complement the poems." Booklist

Toasting marshmallows; camping poems; illustrated by Kate Kiesler. Clarion Bks. 2001 48p il $15 (3-5) **811**

1. Camping—Poetry

ISBN 0-618-04597-X   LC 00-56984

"Thirty poems, mostly unrhymed, treat the splendors of camping in the woods." Bull Cent Child Books

"All of the selections convey a child-focused sense of wonder. . . . The poems are varied and inventive, replete with marvelous images and universal truths. . . . Each one is accompanied by a well-executed and evocative acrylic painting." SLJ

Giovanni, Nikki

Ego-tripping and other poems for young people; illustrations by George Ford; foreword by Virginia Hamilton. 2nd ed. Hill Bks. 1993 52p il pa $10.95 hardcover o.p. (5 and up) **811**

1. African Americans—Poetry

ISBN 1-55652-189-8 (pa)   LC 93-29578

First published 1974

Giovanni has added 10 new poems to her earlier "collection of 23 poems for young people. Ford's illustrations in sepia shades are bold and full of character and dreaming. As Virginia Hamilton says in her foreword, Giovanni's voice is personal and warm, she 'celebrates ordinary folks' and writes of struggle and liberation. She's upbeat and celebratory without minimizing hard times." Booklist

Spin a soft black song: poems for children; illustrated by George Martins. rev ed. Hill & Wang 1985 57p il pa $4.95 hardcover o.p. (3-6) **811**

1. African Americans—Poetry

ISBN 0-374-46469-3 (pa)   LC 84-19287

First published 1971

A poetry collection which recounts the feelings of black children about their neighborhoods, American society, and themselves

"A beautifully illustrated book of poems about black children for children of all ages. . . . Simple in theme but a very moving collection nonetheless." Read Ladders for Hum Relat. 5th edition

The sun is so quiet; poems; illustrations by Ashley Bryan. Holt & Co. 1996 31p il $14.95 (k-3) **811**

1. Nature poetry

ISBN 0-8050-4119-2   LC 95-39357

A collection of poems primarily about nature and the seasons but also concerned with chocolate and scary movies

"Of the 13 poems presented here, 12 appeared in books published between 1973 and 1993. The new poem, entitled 'Connie,' represents the best of Giovanni: a series of quicksilver images that capture a mood to perfection. Painted in Bryan's signature style, the illustrations fill the pages with sunny colors and bold patterns." Booklist

Godwin, Laura

Barnyard prayers; illustrated by Brian Selznick. Hyperion Bks. for Children 2000 unp il $14.99; lib bdg $15.49 (k-2)   **811**
1. Domestic animals—Poetry 2. Prayers
ISBN 0-7868-0355-X; 0-7868-2302-X (lib bdg)
                              LC 99-40918
A boy's toy farm animals come to life and talk to God in a series of prayers
"Gentle humor lightens the reverence in Godwin's poetry and also in Selznick's peaceful, twilit paintings." Booklist

Gottfried, Maya

Good dog; poems by Maya Gottfried; paintings by Robert Rahway Zakanitch. 1st ed. Alfred A. Knopf 2005 unp il $15.95; lib bdg $17.99 (k-3)
                                        811
1. Dogs—Poetry
ISBN 0-375-83049-9; 0-375-93049-3 (lib bdg)
                              LC 2004-15098
In this "book, free-verse poems that present the inner musings of 16 dogs are combined with painterly, full-page portraits. The verses capture distinct canine personalities. . . . Pencil sketches of the canines are scattered around the text. On the facing pages, Zakanitch's stunning oil paintings of the pets are set against shiny black backgrounds." SLJ

Graham, Joan Bransfield

Flicker flash; poems by Joan Bransfield Graham; illustrated by Nancy Davis. Houghton Mifflin 1999 unp il $15   **811**
1. Light—Poetry
ISBN 0-395-90501-X   LC 98-12956
A collection of poems celebrating light in its various forms, from candles and lamps to lightning and fireflies
"A vivid fusion of ingenious concrete poetry and boldly colored graphics." SLJ

Splish splash; illustrated by Steven M. Scott. Ticknor & Fields 1994 unp $16   **811**
1. Water—Poetry
ISBN 0-395-70128-7   LC 94-1237
A collection of poems celebrating water in its various forms, from ice cubes to the ocean
"The variety of text styles, colors and formats is fascinating for young and older readers, and invites aspiring writers to experiment with their own poetry. The graphics are bright, crisp and inviting." Child Book Rev Serv

Grandits, John

Technically, it's not my fault; concrete poems; by John Grandits. Clarion Books 2004 unp il $15; pa $5.95 (4 and up)   **811**
ISBN 0-618-42833-X; 0-618-50361-7 (pa)
                              LC 2004-231
A collection of concrete poems on such topics as roller coasters, linguini, basketball, and sisters
"Grandits combines technical brilliance and goofy good humor to provide an accessible, fun-filled collection of poems, dramatically brought to life through a brilliant book design." SLJ

Greenfield, Eloise

Honey, I love; illustrations by Jan Spivey Gilchrist. HarperCollins 2003 unp il $15.95; lib bdg $16.89 (k-2)   **811**
1. African Americans—Poetry
ISBN 0-06-009123-1; 0-06-009124-X (lib bdg)
                              LC 2002-1464
"A young African-American girl describes her favorite things: going for rides in the car, laughing, the way her Southern cousin talks. This sunny poem from Greenfield's 1978 collection of the same title . . . features new illustrations—warm realistic artwork of the girl's family scenes." Horn Book Guide

Honey, I love, and other love poems; pictures by Diane and Leo Dillon. Crowell 1978 unp il $14.95; pa $5.95 (2-4)   **811**
1. African Americans—Poetry 2. Love poetry
ISBN 0-690-01334-5; 0-06-443097-9 (pa)
                              LC 77-2845
"These 16 poems explore facets of warm, loving relationships with family, friends and schoolmates as experienced by a young Black girl. Central to the theme of the book is the idea that the child loves herself and is very confident in expressing that love." Interracial Books Child Bull
"The Dillons transform this quiet book into magic with soft, grey charcoal renderings of the young girl and her friends, overlaid with child-like brown scratchboard pictures embodying the images in the poems." SLJ

Nathaniel talking; illustrated by Jan Spivey Gilchrist. Black Butterfly Children's Bks. 1989 c1988 unp il $12.95; pa $6.95 (2-4)   **811**
1. African Americans—Poetry
ISBN 0-86316-200-2; 0-86316-201-0 (pa)
                              LC 88-51011
Coretta Scott King Award for illustration, 1990
"The rhythm of Greenfield's text is infectious from a very early line: 'It's Nathaniel talking/and Nathaniel's me/I'm talking about/My philosophy/About the things I do/And the people I see/All told in the words/Of Nathaniel B. Free/That's me.' Her sentiments are equally affecting, but in a more sobering way; Nathaniel wonders when he'll ever be old enough not to have to answer a question 'I don't know,' and he remembers his mother, who has died. . . . His experiences are warmly universal, as are Gilchrist's depictions of his joyful and sorrowful moments." Publ Wkly

Under the Sunday tree; paintings by Amos Ferguson; poems by Eloise Greenfield. Harper & Row 1988 38p il pa $10.95 hardcover o.p. (2-4)
                                        811
1. Bahamas—Poetry
ISBN 0-06-443257-2 (pa)   LC 87-29373
"This collection of poems and paintings present a vivid picture of life in the Bahamas. The poems cover a variety of subjects and occasionally seem to have been written to go with a painting. The folk-art styled paintings are detailed, vibrant and certainly evoke a picture of island life." Child Book Rev Serv

Grimes, Nikki

At Jerusalem's gate; poems of Easter; with woodcuts by David Frampton. Eerdmans Books for Young Readers 2005 unp il $20 (5 and up)
811

1. Jesus Christ—Poetry 2. Easter—Poetry
ISBN 0-8028-5183-5   LC 2003-1089
A collection of poems which tells the story of the first Easter.

"Each poem is preceded by a brief synopsis of the event, often accompanied by the author's own musings and queries, which prompt readers to think and ask questions of their own. . . . Bold, handsome woodcuts reinforce the powerful drama depicted in poetry. An outstanding effort." SLJ

Come Sunday; written by Nikki Grimes; illustrated by Michael Bryant. Eerdmans 1996 unp il $15; pa $7.50 (k-3)
811

1. African Americans—Poetry
ISBN 0-8028-5108-8; 0-8028-5134-7 (pa)
                                     LC 95-33067
"In fourteen poems, a young girl named LaTasha describes a typical Sunday of worship at the Paradise Baptist Church. From the joyful rhythms of singing and swaying and the spiritual plunge of baptism to church suppers and visiting preachers, the conversational verse evokes both solemn and joyous moods. Loose-lined watercolors burst with life, aptly conveying a community gathered in worship." Horn Book Guide

A dime a dozen; pictures by Angelo. Dial Bks. for Young Readers 1998 54p il $17.99 (5 and up)
811

1. African Americans—Poetry
ISBN 0-8037-2227-3   LC 97-5798
A collection of poems about an African-American girl growing up in New York

"Free-flowing and very accessible, the poetry may inspire readers to distill their own life experiences into precise, imaginative words and phrases." Booklist

Hopscotch love; a family treasury of love poems; illustrated by Melodye Benson Rosales. Lothrop, Lee & Shepard Bks. 1999 39p il $16.99 (4 and up)
811

1. Love poetry 2. African Americans—Poetry
ISBN 0-688-15667-3   LC 98-21310
A collection of more than twenty poems speaking of different kinds of love

"All of the poetry is simple, written with everyday language in a straightforward style that needs no analysis or search for symbolism. . . . This small treasury will lift readers' spirits and touch their hearts." SLJ

Meet Danitra Brown; illustrated by Floyd Cooper. Lothrop, Lee & Shepard Bks. 1994 unp il pa $6.99 hardcover o.p. (2-4)
811

1. African Americans—Poetry 2. Friendship—Poetry
ISBN 0-688-15471-9 (pa)   LC 92-43707
"A collection of 13 original poems that stand individually and also blend together to tell a story of feelings and friendship between two African-American girls. . . . Cooper's distinguished illustrations in warm dusty tones convey the feeling of closeness. The poignant text and lovely pictures are an excellent collaboration." SLJ

Other titles about Danitra Brown are:
Danitra Brown, class clown (2005)
Danitra Brown leaves town (2002)

My man Blue; poems; pictures by Jerome Lagarrigue. Dial Bks. for Young Readers 1999 il $16.99; pa $6.99 (2-5)
811

1. African Americans—Poetry
ISBN 0-8037-2326-1; 0-14-230197-3 (pa)
                                     LC 98-28229
A collection of poems describes a young boy's life with his working mother as he establishes his own identity and develops a close relationship with his mother's friend, Blue

"The poems are accessible and filled with imagery, and the intergenerational friendship is believable. . . . The unsentimental acrylic paintings aptly reflect the poems." Horn Book Guide

A pocketful of poems; illustrated by Javaka Steptoe. Clarion Bks. 2001 30p il $15 (k-3)
811

1. City and town life—Poetry 2. Haiku
ISBN 0-395-93868-6   LC 00-24232
"Tiana has round glasses, a wide mouth, and long braids; she opens her hands full of letters and her pocket full of words. Each page has two facing poems, both in Tiana's voice: one is short and bracing, the other is a haiku in the standard five-seven-five syllable configuration. . . . The first poem in a pair is set in standard type; the haiku usually floats or sways or sashays amidst the illustrations. . . . Steptoe is a fabulously inventive collagist. He does amazing things not only with cut and torn paper and string but also with drinking straws, aluminum plates, and stray beads." Booklist

Tai chi morning; snapshots of China; [illustrated by] Ed Young. Cricket Books 2004 51p il $15.95 (5 and up)
811

1. China—Poetry
ISBN 0-8126-2707-5   LC 2003-16506
"In 1988, Grimes traveled to China . . . and recorded her impressions of the country. . . . She paints her personal visions of a particular area or experience in a narrative paragraph, and then knits the ideas together into a poem on the facing page. . . . Young's simple artwork complements Grimes's eloquent images. The reedy pen-and-ink drawings deftly capture the exotic and ancient culture of the country." SLJ

Thanks a million; poems by Nikki Grimes; pictures by Cozbi A. Cabrera. 1st ed. Greenwillow Books 2006 31p il $15.99; lib bdg $16.89 (k-3)
811

ISBN 0-688-17292-X; 0-688-17293-8 (lib bdg)
                                     LC 2004-54158
"Sixteen thoughtful poems about being thankful for everyday things. Grimes uses a variety of forms that include haiku, a riddle, and a rebus in selections that speak directly to the experiences of young children. . . . Cabreras acrylic illustrations are distinctive, folksy, and effective." SLJ

Grimes, Nikki—*Continued*

Under the Christmas tree; illustrated by Kadir Nelson. HarperCollins Pubs. 2002 unp il $15.99; lib bdg $17.89 (k-3)   **811**

1. Christmas—Poetry 2. African Americans—Poetry

ISBN 0-688-15999-0; 0-688-16000-X (lib bdg)

LC 2001-24330

This is a "celebration of the sights, sounds, and feelings of Christmas from a child's point of view. Twenty-three poems take readers through the season, focusing on the life of an urban African-American family. . . . Nelson's realistic paintings in rich, muted colors and soft textures masterfully portray the warmth and joy of the selections." SLJ

What is goodbye? illustrations by Raúl Colón. Hyperion Books for Children 2004 unp il $15.99 (4 and up)   **811**

1. Death—Poetry 2. Family life—Poetry

ISBN 0-7868-0778-4   LC 2002-72987

Alternating poems by a brother and sister convey their feelings about the death of their older brother and the impact it had on their family.

"Grimes handles these two voices fluently and lucidly, shaping her characters through her form. Colón's paintings in muted colors combine imagism with realism to create an emotional dreamscape on nearly every page." SLJ

Havill, Juanita

I heard it from Alice Zucchini; poems about the garden; by Juanita Havill; illustrated by Christine Davenier. Chronicle Books 2006 29p il $15.95   **811**

1. Gardens—Poetry 2. Gardening—Poetry

ISBN 0-8118-3962-1   LC 2004013365

"Havill's collection of verse captures the science and backyard magic of growing things. . . . Davenier extends the fanciful imagery in scenes of lively, gossiping plants and animals, rendered in her signature watercolor-washed ink sketches." Booklist

Herrera, Juan Felipe

Laughing out loud, I fly; poems in English and Spanish; drawings by Karen Barbour. HarperCollins Pubs. 1998 unp il $15.99   **811**

1. Bilingual books—English-Spanish

ISBN 0-06-027604-5   LC 96-45476

"Joanna Cotler books"

A collection of poems in Spanish and English about childhood, place, and identity

"Barbour's black-and-white drawings accompany each poem, delicately underlining its images but allowing the strong sensuality of the words to seep into readers' minds." SLJ

Hines, Anna Grossnickle

Pieces; a year in poems & quilts. Greenwillow Bks. 2001 unp il $15.95; lib bdg $15.89 (k-3)   **811**

1. Nature poetry 2. Quilts

ISBN 0-688-16963-5; 0-688-16964-3 (lib bdg)

LC 99-86463

Poems about the four seasons, as reflected in the natural world, are accompanied by photographs of quilts made by the author

"An appendix explains Hines's meticulous quilting process. . . . Hines takes her quilter's stash of fabric swatches and her wordsmith's metaphors for memories of the seasons, and pieces together a unified, artistic whole. An outstanding book for aspiring quilters or anyone at all." Publ Wkly

Includes bibliographical references

Winter lights; a season in poems & quilts. Greenwillow Bks. 2005 unp il $16.99; lib bdg $17.89 (k-3)   **811**

1. Winter—Poetry 2. Holidays—Poetry 3. Quilts

ISBN 0-06-000817-2; 0-06-000818-0 (lib bdg)

"Winter is the time of lights, and Hines celebrates the season in thoughtful poems and pictures of gorgeous quilts full of bright, beautiful colors. Christmas is only one of the light-producing celebrations that Hines illuminates. The feast of Santa Lucia, Hanukkah, Kwanzaa, and the Chinese New Year are spectacularly introduced with short bursts of poetry and quilts that capture the spirit of the day." Booklist

Hoberman, Mary Ann

You read to me, I'll read to you; very short Mother Goose tales to read together; illustrated by Michael Emberley. 1st ed. Little, Brown 2005 32p il $16.99 (k-3)   **811**

1. Nursery rhymes—Fiction

ISBN 0-316-14431-2   LC 2004-7569

"Megan Tingley books"

Contents: Humpty dumpty; Jack, be nimble; Jack and Jill; Jack Sprat; Little Boy Blue and Little Bo Peep; Little Jack Horner and Little Tommy Tucker; Little Miss Muffet; Old King Cole and The cat and the fiddle; Old Mother Hubbard; Peter, Peter, pumpkin eater; Pussycat, pussycat, where have you been?; Simple Simon

"Hoberman and Emberley introduce shared reading experiences that retell and elaborate on Mother Goose rhymes. Consisting of 14 short tales, each story is designed to be read by two voices that, at times, come together for shared lines. . . . Told in verse, these stories will appeal to readers who are familiar with the original rhymes. . . . The careful word choices are ideal for beginning and reluctant readers. . . . The bright and cheery artwork captures the humor." SLJ

You read to me, I'll read to you; very short stories to read together; illustrated by Michael Emberley. Little, Brown 2001 unp il $15.95 (k-3)   **811**

ISBN 0-316-36350-2   LC 00-35230

"Megan Tingley books"

"Hoberman offers 13 rhymed variations on the theme of getting together to read. The short poems are designed to be read aloud by two voices, with occasional parts to share. . . . The energy never flags, neither in Hoberman's trademark bouncy rhythms nor in Emberley's exuberant illustrations, which picture a wonderful array of children and animals tumbling across the pages." Booklist

Hoce, Charley

Beyond Old MacDonald; funny poems from down on the farm; illustrated by Eugenie Fernandes. Wordsong/Boyds Mills Press 2005 31p il $16.95 (k-3)   **811**

1. Farm life—Poetry

ISBN 1-59078-312-3

"Hoce employs wordplay in many of these 30 selections. . . . The humor is age appropriate and poems about 'ants in my plants' and a hoarse horse will appeal to children who are beginning to enjoy playing with language. . . . This book is fun, but it's also excellent for classroom use; a 'Wordplay Guide' that indicates language skills, such as identifying homophones, personification, and idioms, is appended." SLJ

Hopkins, Lee Bennett

Been to yesterdays: poems of a life; illustrations by Charlene Rendeiro. Wordsong 1995 64p il $15.95; pa $9.95 (4 and up)   **811**

ISBN 1-56397-467-3; 1-56397-808-3 (pa)

LC 94-73320

"Hopkins distills the experience of his middle-grade years into 28 poems of poignant clarity. . . . Good reading and an excellent, unconventional choice for teachers doing units on poetry and autobiography." Booklist

Hovey, Kate

Arachne speaks; with paintings by Blair Drawson. Margaret K. McElderry Bks. 2000 unp il $17.95 (4 and up)   **811**

1. Arachne (Greek mythology)—Poetry

ISBN 0-689-82901-9   LC 99-46926

A poem about Arachne, who challenged the goddess Athena to a weaving contest and was changed into a spider

"In lyrical language that invites oral interpretation, Hovey offers an interesting psychological twist that enlivens a traditional tale. At the same time, Blair Drawson's acrylic paintings, which have the weight and texture of a formal sculpture garden, add a necessary *gravitas* to the classical setting and characters." Booklist

Hughes, Langston

Carol of the brown king; nativity poems; illustrated by Ashley Bryan. Atheneum Bks. for Young Readers 1998 unp il $16   **811**

1. Jesus Christ—Poetry

ISBN 0-689-81877-7   LC 97-30814

"A Jean Karl book"

"Six poems, five by Hughes and one from a Puerto Rican Christmas card that he translated from the Spanish, have been appealingly illustrated in glowing colors." N Y Times Book Rev

The dream keeper and other poems; including seven additional poems; illustrated by Brian Pinkney. Knopf 1994 83p il $14.99; pa $8.99 (5 and up)   **811**

1. African Americans—Poetry

ISBN 0-679-94421-4; 0-679-88347-9 (pa)

LC 92-10240

First published 1932

"Langston Hughes's poems range from the romantic to the poignant, from the spiritual to the challenging. His lyrical voice asks for recognition of the Negro, offers encouragement, and reminds his African-American brothers of their glorious past. Although the pieces in *The Dream Keeper* were written over a half-century ago . . . the words have the same strength of meaning and power as if they had been written today." Horn Book

Langston Hughes; edited by Arnold Rampersad & David Roessel; illustrations by Benny Andrews. Sterling Pub. 2006 48p il (Poetry for young people) $14.95 (5 and up)   **811**

1. African Americans—Poetry

ISBN 1-4027-1845-4; 978-1-4027-1845-8

LC 2005025369

A brief profile of African American poet Langston Hughes accompanies some of his better known poems for children.

"This charming collection of 26 poems is vibrantly illustrated with depictions of African Americans in varied settings. . . . This will be a welcome introduction to Hughes's poetry for elementary students, and it includes sufficient detail to make it useful and enjoyable for older students." SLJ

Jackson, Robert B.

Animal mischief; poems by Rob Jackson; illustrated by Laura Jacobsen. Wordsong 2006 32p il $15.95 (2-4)   **811**

1. Animals—Poetry

ISBN 1-59078-254-2

"Biologist Rob Jackson shares both his knowledge of animals and his way with words in this collection of 18 short, witty poems. A typical selection zeroes in on a particular species and comments on some aspect of its appearance or behavior. . . . Appealing colored-pencil artwork reflects the light tone of the verse." Booklist

Janeczko, Paul B.

Wing nuts; screwy haiku; by Paul B. Janeczko and J. Patrick Lewis; illustrated by Tricia Tusa. 1st ed. Little, Brown 2006 unp il $15.99 (2-4)   **811**

ISBN 0-316-60731-2   LC 2005-07970

"This book introduces senryu, a Japanese verse form that can involve the evasive, the punny, the parodic, and the slapstick. . . . The highly spirited verses feature witty wordplay and puns. . . . This book fulfills its purpose to revive and invigorate the language, and does so with humor. In her ink-and-watercolor cartoons, Tusa uses a soft palette, strong lines, and abundant white space to define the comical characters." SLJ

Johnson, Angela

The other side; Shorter poems. Orchard Bks. 1998 44p il pa $6.95 hardcover o.p.   **811**

1. African Americans—Poetry

ISBN 0-531-07167-7 (pa)   LC 98-13736

A Coretta Scott King honor book for text, 1999

A collection of poems reminiscent of growing up as an African-American girl in Shorter, Alabama

"Photographs of the author as a child emphasize the personal nature of this captivating narrative." Horn Book

Johnston, Tony

It's about dogs; poems by Tony Johnston; paintings by Ted Rand. Harcourt 2000 48p il $16 (2-4)   **811**

1. Dogs—Poetry
ISBN 0-15-202022-5   LC 98-53783

Presents poems about dogs and their attributes, including their loyalty to people, their love of food and smells, and their varied appearances and personalities

"Rand's versatile paintings capture the dog denizens and the poetic moods with verve. . . . There are poignant moments as well as funny in this richly rendered tribute to be read and savored." SLJ

Katz, Bobbi

Once around the sun; poems by Bobbi Katz; illustrated by LeUyen Pham. Harcourt 2006 unp il $16 (k-3)   **811**

1. Months—Poetry
ISBN 0-15-216397-2   LC 2004-22500

"In joyful poems, one for each month of the year, a young boy has fun during the changing seasons in his city neighborhood. . . . Pham's paintings of an African American boy and his younger sister are brightly colored and full of energy, and the simple words in short lines will be great for reading aloud." Booklist

We the people; poems; illustrations by Nina Crews. Greenwillow Bks. 2000 102p il $15.95 (5 and up)   **811**

1. United States—History—Poetry
ISBN 0-688-16531-1   LC 99-50009

A collection of sixty-five original poems that depict people and events throughout the history of the United States

"Giving voice to the diversity of American experience, the poems are vividly imagined from the point of view of pioneers, presidents, suffragettes, soldiers, and more. Handsome collage pictures capture the spirit of each century's history." Horn Book Guide

Includes bibliographical references

Katz, Susan

A revolutionary field trip; poems of colonial America; pictures by R.W. Alley. Simon & Schuster Books for Young Readers 2004 37p il $16.95 (2-4)   **811**

1. United States—History—1600-1775, Colonial period—Poetry
ISBN 0-689-84004-7   LC 2002-09771

Nineteen poems reveal life in colonial America as seen through the eyes of a teacher and her class when they go on field trips to historic sites from the Revolutionary War era.

"Alley's animated watercolor illustrations portray exuberant, engaged students experiencing history. . . . Young readers will absorb much of the characters' excitement about history from this worthwhile offering." SLJ

Kuskin, Karla

Moon, have you met my mother? the collected poems of Karla Kuskin; illustrations by Sergio Ruzzier. Laura Geringer Bks. 2003 322p il $16.99; lib bdg $17.89 (2-4)   **811**

ISBN 0-06-027173-6; 0-06-027174-4 (lib bdg)
LC 2001-24620

"This collection brings together more than 40 years of Kuskin's poetry, as well as several newly published selections. Divided thematically rather than chronologically, the poems focus on Kuskin's favorite topics: animals and other creatures, the seasons, food, day and night, and our secret selves. . . . Kuskin's sounds and playful nonsense are irresistible. . . . The book's handsome design . . . [features] small ink drawings—subtle, funny, and wild— on spacious cream-colored pages." Booklist

Toots the cat; illustrated by Lisze Bechtold. Holt 2005 unp il $16.95 (k-3)   **811**

1. Cats—Poetry
ISBN 0-8050-6841-4   LC 2004-26770

"In this story in poems, readers are introduced to Toots—a calico—who saunters inside a house, claims the best chair as her own, and decides that she is home." SLJ

"The verses . . . are elegantly, appealingly feline. Entries are succinct, with flexible rhyme schemes and meters, neat yet sinewy in their patterns of imagery and sound. . . . The cats, watercolor and gouache touched with pencil, are fluid yet perky." Bull Cent Child Books

Larios, Julie Hofstrand

Have you ever done that? [by] Julie Larios; pictures by Anne Hunter. Front St. 2001 unp il $15.95 (k-3)   **811**

1. Nature poetry
ISBN 1-88691-049-9   LC 00-59326

"In each verse of this . . . poem, the speaker describes an experience—sleeping outside, holding a snake, nursing a baby bird—and ends with the question, 'Have you ever done that?' The next speaker responds with a different experience, until the poem ends with an invitation to participate in nature's wonders. Hunter's illustrations, their simple shapes accented by crosshatching, add mystery and drama." Horn Book Guide

Yellow elephant; a bright bestiary; poems by Julie Larios; paintings by Julie Paschkis. Harcourt 2006 31p il $16   **811**

1. Animals—Poetry 2. Color—Poetry
ISBN 0-15-205422-7   LC 2004-25163

"The animals featured in these well-crafted poems flash with color and emotion. Each spread features a picture of a brightly hued animal, and Larios' rhythms and sounds skillfully reinforce the memorable, evocative images. . . . Together with Paschkis' vibrant, patterned, gouache paintings, the poems beautifully show how color and sound create mood and imagery." Booklist

Lawrence, Jacob

Harriet and the Promised Land. Simon & Schuster Bks. for Young Readers 1993 unp il $18; pa $6.99   **811**
   1. Tubman, Harriet, 1815?-1913—Poetry
   2. Underground railroad—Poetry
   ISBN 0-671-86673-7; 0-689-80965-4 (pa)
                        LC 92-33740
A newly illustrated edition of the title first published 1968 by Windmill Books
"Simple rhymes tell the story of Harriet Tubman, the slave who led many of her people North to freedom." Adventuring with Books
"The strength of this volume is in the forceful, stylized paintings by the famous black artist, which capture the degradation of slavery." Brooklyn. Art Books for Child

Levy, Constance

Splash! poems of our watery world; illustrations by David Soman. Orchard Bks. 2002 39p il $16.95 (3-6)   **811**
   1. Water—Poetry
   ISBN 0-439-29318-9   LC 2001-34004
More than thirty poems celebrate water in its myriad forms, from the ocean to a droplet of dew
"This is an accessible, charming collection with imaginative, kid-friendly similes and metaphors and poems that run the gamut from lyrical to playful." Booklist

Lewin, Betsy

Animal snackers; by Betsy Lewin. 1st Henry Holt ed. H. Holt 2004 unp il $15.95 (k-3)
                              811
   1. Animals—Poetry 2. Food—Poetry
   ISBN 0-8050-6748-5   LC 2003-22501
A revised and newly illustrated edition of the title first published 1980 by Dodd, Mead
Short poems describe the eating habits of gorillas, ostriches, koalas, tickbirds, sea otters, and other animals.
"Lewin uses humor in language and large, loose ink and watercolor paintings to give preschoolers a first, very basic natural history lesson." Horn Book Guide

Lewis, J. Patrick

Doodle dandies; poems that take shape; J. Patrick Lewis, words; Lisa Desimini, images; with design and typography by Ann Bobco and Lisa Desimini. Atheneum Bks. for Young Readers 1998 unp il $16   **811**
   ISBN 0-689-81075-X   LC 96-1920
"An Anne Schwartz book"
A collection of poems each of which appears on the page in the shape of its subject so that the poem looks like whatever it's about
"Every page of this book is well designed, creating words and images that work together in harmony. . . . *Doodle Dandies* captures the joy that wordplay can bring." SLJ

Freedom like sunlight; praisesongs for Black Americans; [illustrated by] John Thompson. Creative Eds. 2000 40p il $17.95; pa $7.95 (5 and up)   **811**
   1. African Americans—Poetry
   ISBN 1-56846-163-1; 0-89812-382-8 (pa)
                        LC 98-50909
Presents poems and brief biographical notes about such well-known African Americans as: Arthur Ashe, Harriet Tubman, Sojourner Truth, Louis Armstrong, Martin Luther King, Jr., "Satchel" Paige, Rosa Parks, Langston Hughes, Jesse Owens, Marian Anderson, Malcolm X, Wilma Rudolph, and Billie Holiday
"Stunning illustrations by John Thompson take center stage in this attractively designed poetry collection. . . . Using a range of styles and meter, the mostly rhyming poems are dramatic and reverential." Booklist

Monumental verses. National Geographic 2005 31p il $16.95; lib bdg $25.90 (5 and up)
                              811
   1. Monuments—Poetry
   ISBN 0-7922-7135-1; 0-7922-7139-4 (lib bdg)
"Lewis offers 14 poems celebrating monumental structures. From the remnants of civilizations at Stonehenge, Easter Island, and Machu Picchu to the more modern achievements of the Taj Mahal, the Eiffel Tower, and the Statue of Liberty, the subjects are varied and the accompanying photos are striking." Booklist

Please bury me in the library; illustrated by Kyle M. Stone. Harcourt 2005 32p il $16 (3-5)
                              811
   1. Books and reading—Poetry
   ISBN 0-15-216387-5   LC 2003-26983
"Gulliver books"
A "collection of 16 poems celebrating books, reading, language, and libraries. . . . The brief selections encompass various forms, from an eight-word acrostic to haiku to rhyming quatrains and couplets. . . . The poems are accompanied by richly dark artwork. The thickly applied acrylic paint and mixed-media illustrations . . . [have] a comically grotesque air, and add comprehension to the verses." SLJ

Scien-trickery; riddles in science; illustrated by Frank Remkiewicz. Silver Whistle/Harcourt 2004 32p il $16 (2-4)   **811**
   1. Science—Poetry 2. Riddles
   ISBN 0-15-216681-5   LC 2002-153962
A collection of riddle poems that describe people, places, and things associated with science, including oxygen, the ocean, and germs
"The jokes are lively, entertaining, and moderately challenging. . . . The text and illustrations reinforce the atmosphere of learning while having fun." SLJ

A world of wonders; geographic travels in verse and rhyme; pictures by Alison Jay. Dial Bks. for Young Readers 2002 unp il $16.99 (3-5)
                              811
   1. Geography—Poetry 2. Voyages and travels—Poetry
   ISBN 0-8037-2579-5   LC 00-45181
"Terse verse, doggerel, and other rhymes ponder places and climes in this slim collection." SLJ

Lewis, J. Patrick—*Continued*

The poet offers "enough odd places and names to intrigue and tickle young readers. . . . Lewis's verbal somersaults, both whimsical and plentiful, pepper the volume. . . . The artist's many bird's-eye views brim with easy-to-recognize landmarks. She overlays each illustration with a crackle-glass web of lines." Publ Wkly

Lillegard, Dee

Wake up house! rooms full of poems; illustrated by Don Carter. Knopf 2000 unp il $12.95; lib bdg $14.99 (k-2) **811**

1. Houses—Poetry
ISBN 0-679-88351-7; 0-679-98351-1 (lib bdg)
LC 99-33420

Short poems which personify household objects from the bedroom window that greets the sun's morning rays to the nightlight that watches over sleeping dreamers

"Carter's clear, beautiful three-dimensional illustrations use foam board, plaster, and bold acrylic paints to produce art as tactile and immediate as the words." Booklist

Lindbergh, Reeve

Johnny Appleseed; a poem; paintings by Kathy Jakobsen. Little, Brown 1990 unp il pa $5.95 hardcover o.p. (k-3) **811**

1. Appleseed, Johnny, 1774-1845—Poetry 2. Frontier and pioneer life—Poetry
ISBN 0-316-52634-7 (pa)
LC 89-35192

"Joy Street books"

Rhymed text and illustrations relate the life of John Chapman, whose distribution of appleseeds and trees across the Midwest made him a legend and left a legacy still enjoyed today

"The folk art paintings add a dimension that enhances the lyrical, moving poem. Together they combine to capture daily pioneer life and the legend." Child Book Rev Serv

Livingston, Myra Cohn

Celebrations; [by] Myra Cohn Livingston, poet; Leonard Everett Fisher, painter. Holiday House 1985 unp il lib bdg $16.95; pa $6.95 **811**

1. Holidays—Poetry
ISBN 0-8234-0550-8 (lib bdg); 0-8234-0654-7 (pa)
LC 84-19216

"Sixteen short, mainly rhymed verses celebrate major holidays beginning with New Year's and ending with Christmas. A final page recalls that special event, 'birthday.' The book exhibits a fine variety of moods; all the poems would work with the intended audience. . . . Visually dramatic, the illustrations pack a punch. All but three of the poems appear on double-page spreads with text on one side, the painting encompassing both. In addition, the large page size, lack of margins, brilliant colors and surprising compositions all add a great sense of excitement." SLJ

Festivals; [by] Myra Cohn Livingston, poet; Leonard Everett Fisher, painter. Holiday House 1996 32p il $16.95 **811**

1. Festivals—Poetry
ISBN 0-8234-1217-2
LC 95-31055

"An eclectic collection of 14 poems celebrating festivals from around the world. The book begins in January with the Chinese New Year, ends in December with Kwanzaa, and includes the Vietnamese*Tet Nguyen-Dan,* Iranian *Now-Ruz,* Jewish Purim, Muslim Ramadan and *Id-Ul-Fitr,* Hindu *Diwali,* and Mexican Day of the Dead. . . . What makes the volume special, . . . is the inspired paring of text and artwork. . . . The words plus the accompanying illustration—purple pumpkins, orange moon, black sky—elicit a shiver of mystery and delight." SLJ

Includes glossary

Keep on singing; a ballad of Marian Anderson; illustrated by Samuel Byrd. Holiday House 1994 unp il $15.95 (k-3) **811**

1. Anderson, Marian, 1897-1993—Poetry
ISBN 0-8234-1098-6
LC 93-46909

"In this ballad, Myra Cohn Livingston narrates the story of Marian Anderson's life, from her humble beginnings in Philadelphia in the early 1900s to her triumphant career as a world-renowned singer, despite racial barriers." Publisher's note

"The large illustrations, often based on photographs, use details sparingly and employ sweeping backgrounds to lend a feeling of significance to a scene. Adults may want to review Livingston's closing biographical notes before reading the book to children, but the ballad itself still catches the inspiring outlines of Anderson's life and makes her story accessible to a young audience." Booklist

Longfellow, Henry Wadsworth

Hiawatha; pictures by Susan Jeffers. Dial Bks. for Young Readers 1983 unp il pa $6.99 hardcover o.p. **811**

1. Native Americans—Poetry 2. Native Americans—Folklore
ISBN 0-14-055882-9 (pa)
LC 83-7225

Verses excerpted from the poem first published 1855 with title: Song of Hiawatha

"Jeffers has captured the essence of this brief section from the classic poem. . . . The pale tints of the pictures are in complete harmony with nature and with the text and show in detail how Hiawatha might have seen his world. A fine first exposure to the poem for children and a beautiful artistic experience." SLJ

Paul Revere's ride **811**

1. Revere, Paul, 1735-1818—Poetry 2. Lexington (Mass.), Battle of, 1775—Poetry

Some editions are:

Dutton pa $6.99 Illustrated by Ted Rand (ISBN 0-14-055612-5)

Handprint Pubs. $17.95 illustrated by Christopher Bing. Has title: The midnight ride of Paul Revere (ISBN 1-929766-13-0)

HarperCollins Pub. $16.99 Illustrated by Charles Santore (ISBN 0-688-16552-4)

National Geographic Soc. $17.95 Illustrated by Jeffrey Thompson. Has title: The midnight ride of Paul Revere (ISBN 0-7922-7674-4)

The famous narrative poem recreating Paul Revere's midnight ride in 1775 to warn the people of the Boston countryside that the British were coming

Medina, Tony

Love to Langston; illustrated by R. Gregory Christie. Lee & Low Bks. 2002 unp il $16.95 (3-5)   **811**

    1. Hughes, Langston, 1902-1967—Poetry

    ISBN 1-58430-041-8   LC 2001-38140

A series of poems written from the point of view of the poet Langston Hughes, offering an overview of key events and themes in his life

"The twists that the poet's life took, the people (both good and bad) whom he met, and the important places he visited are vividly brought to life. . . . Christie's full-page, vibrant illustrations with broad expanses of bold, flat colors and stylized figures invite readers into the world of sharecroppers, ocean liners, and libraries." SLJ

Merriam, Eve

Spooky A B C; [illustrated by] Lane Smith. Simon & Schuster Bks. for Young Readers 2002 unp il $16.95 (3-6)   **811**

    1. Halloween—Poetry 2. Alphabet

    ISBN 0-689-85356-4   LC 2002-5564

First published 1987 by Macmillan with title: Halloween ABC

In this book a poem for each letter of the alphabet introduces a different, spooky aspect of Halloween

"Richly atmospheric and downright scary. . . . A handsome showcase for Merriam's poems and Smith's artwork." Booklist

Moore, Clement Clarke

The night before Christmas (k-3)   **811**

    1. Santa Claus—Poetry 2. Christmas—Poetry

Some editions are:

Little, Brown $15.95 illustrated by Tasha Tudor 0-316-85579-0)

Minedition $15.99 with pictures by Lisbeth Zwerger (ISBN 0-698-40030-5)

Putnam $16.99 illustrated by Jan Brett (ISBN 0-399-23190-0)

Little, Simon (A classic collectible pop-up) $24.95 illustrated by Robert Sabuda (ISBN 0-689-83899-9)

Text first published 1823 with title: A visit from St. Nicholas

This popular Christmas poem has been a favorite with American children ever since the author wrote it for his children in 1822. It is from this poem that we get the names for the Christmas reindeer

Moore, Lilian

I'm small and other verses; illustrated by Jill McElmurry. Candlewick Press 2001 unp il $13.99 (k-2)   **811**

    ISBN 0-7636-1169-7   LC 99-57130

A collection of very short poems, including "Snowsuit," "Alone," and "I Like Peanut Butter"

"This collection of poems is brought to vibrant life by McElmurry's gouache artwork. The verses focus on typical childhood concerns and pleasures. . . . These selections will work well for storytime and one-on-one sharing." SLJ

Mural on Second Avenue, and other city poems; illustrated by Roma Karas. 1st ed. Candlewick Press 2005 unp il $16.99 (k-3)   **811**

    1. City and town life—Poetry

    ISBN 0-7636-1987-6   LC 2002-73702

"These 17 poems, all but one of which were chosen from Moore's previous collections, celebrate life in the city. . . . The poems appear on pages covered in bright oil paintings. . . . These poems speak loudly to children." SLJ

Mordhorst, Heidi

Squeeze; poems for a juicy universe; [by] Heidi Mordhorst; photographs by Jesse Torrey. Wordsong/Boyds Mills Press 2005 32p il $16.95 (2-4)   **811**

    ISBN 1-59078-292-5   LC 2004030659

"Familiar elements of a child's world are explored in these sensitive, free-form verses. The 24 original poems capture an imaginative view of commonplace things and happenings. . . . Artistic, full-page color photos add to the attractiveness of the book." SLJ

Myers, Tim

Dark sparkle tea; and other bedtime poems; illustrated by Kelley Cuningham. Wordsong 2006 31p il $16.95 (2-4)   **811**

    1. Bedtime—Poetry

    ISBN 1-59078-288-7

"The subject is bedtime, but these aren't sleepy-time rhymes. Many poems describe rambunctious prebedtime preparations. . . . The pastel illustrations ably extend both the family coziness and the outside world's quiet starlight." Booklist

Myers, Walter Dean

Blues journey; illustrated by Christopher Myers. Holiday House 2003 unp il $18.95   **811**

    1. Blues music—Poetry 2. African Americans—Poetry

    ISBN 0-8234-1613-5   LC 2001-16645

"In this picture book for older readers, Myers offers blues-inspired verse that touches on the black-and-blue moments of individual lives. . . . Much of Myers' poetry here is terrific, by turn, sweet, sharp, ironic, but it's the memorable collage artwork, executed in the bluest of blue ink and brown paper, that will draw readers first." Booklist

Brown angels; an album of pictures and verse. HarperCollins Pubs. 1993 unp il $16.95; pa $6.95   **811**

    1. African Americans—Poetry

    ISBN 0-06-022917-9; 0-06-443455-9 (pa)

                    LC 92-36792

A collection of poems, accompanied by antique photographs, about African American children living around the turn of the century

"Myers has created an exquisite album. The 42 superbly sepia prints radiate intensely with the personalities of their subjects. The author's 11 original poems are in various forms and range from humorous to elegiac. The language is simple and reads aloud well." SLJ

Myers, Walter Dean—*Continued*

Harlem; a poem; pictures by Christopher Myers. Scholastic 1997 unp il $16.95   **811**

1. African Americans—Poetry 2. Harlem (New York, N.Y.)—Poetry

ISBN 0-590-54340-7   LC 96-8108

A Caldecott Medal honor book, 1998

A poem celebrating the people, sights, and sounds of Harlem

"Myers's paean to Harlem sings, dances, and swaggers across the pages, conveying the myriad sounds on the streets. . . . Christopher Myers's collages add an edge to his father's words, vividly bringing to life the sights and scenes of Lenox Avenue." Horn Book Guide

Numeroff, Laura Joffe

Sometimes I wonder if poodles like noodles; written by Laura Numeroff; illustrated by Tim Bowers. Simon & Schuster Bks. for Young Readers 1999 unp il $15 (k-3)   **811**

1. Humorous poetry

ISBN 0-689-80563-2   LC 96-44988

An illustrated collection of humorous verses about a child's day-to-day experiences and other topics

"A light, playful tone permeates these twenty-one mostly brief rhyming poems told from an imaginative young girl's point of view. . . . Oil paintings rendered in a warm palette of colors capture the collection's affectionate humor." Horn Book Guide

Nye, Naomi Shihab

Come with me; poems for a journey; images by Dan Yaccarino. Greenwillow Bks. 2000 32p il $15.95; lib bdg $15.89 (3-6)   **811**

ISBN 0-688-15946-X; 0-688-15947-8 (lib bdg)

LC 99-34164

"Sixteen poems depict different aspects of going places: subjects include imaginary voyages, the pace of travel, arrival in new places, the trajectory of words, and personal journeys of growth. . . . Nye uses sophisticated metaphor and oblique evocations of emotion in simple and concrete phraseology, making the poems conceptually challenging yet literarily accessible. The visuals are bold and dramatic, making excellent use of collage and mixed media." Bull Cent Child Books

O'Neill, Mary Le Duc

Hailstones and halibut bones; adventures in color; newly illustrated by John Wallner. Doubleday 1989 unp il $15.95; pa $9.95 (k-3)

    811

1. Color—Poetry

ISBN 0-385-24484-3; 0-385-41078-6 (pa)

LC 88-484

A newly illustrated edition of the title first published 1961

Twelve poems reflect the author's feelings about various colors

"Wallner has created montages of each poem's images and colored them with various hues of the featured color. The results do complement the moods of the poems." SLJ

Paolilli, Paul

Silver seeds; a book of nature poems; by Paul Paolilli and Dan Brewer; paintings by Steve Johnson and Lou Fancher. Viking 2001 unp il $15.99 (k-3)   **811**

1. Nature poetry

ISBN 0-670-88941-5   LC 00-9469

"Paolilli and Brewer have selected 15 . . . words on which to build nature poems. The first letter of the first word in each line of a poem is part of another word that is the title (or subject) of the poem." Booklist

Patz, Nancy

Who was the woman who wore the hat? written and illustrated by Nancy Patz. Dutton 2003 unp il $14.99 (3-5)   **811**

1. Jews—Poetry

ISBN 0-525-46999-0   LC 2003-545123

"When author Patz saw an unlabeled woman's hat in a glass case in the Jewish Historical Museum in Amsterdam, she wondered whose it could be. . . . She drew the hat in her sketchbook and eventually created this quiet tribute to the woman—any Jewish woman—who might have been forced to leave her home in Amsterdam for a cruel fate in the Nazi extermination camps. Patz combines an accessible prose poem . . . with collages that blend historical photographs with her own sketches. A chronology of the Holocaust completes the book." Booklist

Peters, Lisa Westberg

Earthshake; poems from the ground up; pictures by Cathie Felstead. Greenwillow Bks. 2003 32p il $16.99; lib bdg $17.89 (3-5)   **811**

1. Geology—Poetry

ISBN 0-06-029265-2; 0-06-029266-0 (lib bdg)

LC 2002-32177

Presents twenty-two poems about geology. End notes provide information about the earth's surface and interior, types of rocks, and how volcanoes, glaciers, and erosion modify the landscape

"Exuberant, silly, and serious by turns, the selections engage imagination with often-humorous wordplay. The simple yet clever collages, many of which incorporate clip-art elements, deepen the intellectual and emotional content, yet keep a light tone." SLJ

Podwal, Mark H.

Jerusalem sky; stars, crosses, and crescents. Doubleday Book for Young Readers 2005 unp $15.95; lib bdg $17.99 (3-5)   **811**

1. Jerusalem—Poetry 2. Religious poetry

ISBN 0-385-74689-x; 0-385-90927-6 (lib bdg)

A series of illustrated poems about the city of Jerusalem and its importance to Jews, Christians, and Muslims

"With beautiful poems and vivid, impressionistic artwork, Podwal captures the hope and tears the city evokes among followers of the three monotheistic religions of the world." Booklist

Pollock, Penny

When the moon is full; illustrated by Mary Azarian. Little, Brown 2001 unp il $15.95 (k-3)

811

1. Moon—Poetry

ISBN 0-317-71317-1   LC 00-28238

This "collection of poems offers a . . . look at a year's worth of full moons. The Native American name for each moon is given, along with brief facts about it. . . . Short and simple selections convey a variety of moods. . . . Azarian's woodcuts are bathed in soothing blues, greens, and buttery yellows." SLJ

Prelutsky, Jack

Awful Ogre's awful day; poems by Jack Prelutsky; pictures by Paul O. Zelinsky. Greenwillow Bks. 2001 39p il $15.95; lib bdg $15.89 (2-5)   **811**

1. Monsters—Poetry

ISBN 0-688-07778-1; 0-688-07779-X (lib bdg)

LC 99-54323

In a series of poems, Awful Ogre rises, grooms himself, dances, pens a letter, and goes through other activities as the day passes

"Awful Ogre proves an ideal agent for Prelutsky's oversize humor. . . . Zelinsky presents Awful Ogre as a grotesque but goofy innocent, sillier than he is sinister. . . . A virtuoso performance by two master funny-bone-ticklers." Publ Wkly

Beneath a blue umbrella: rhymes; pictures by Garth Williams. Greenwillow Bks. 1990 64p il lib bdg $15.95 (k-3)   **811**

1. Nonsense verses 2. Nursery rhymes

ISBN 0-688-06429-9   LC 86-19406

A collection of illustrated humorous poems in which a hungry hippo raids a melon stand, a butterfly tickles a girl's nose, and children frolic in a Mardi Gras parade

"Prelutsky has an unerring sense of popular appeal; these verses bounce as rhythmically as children do on a bed or jumping rope. They also feature plenty of reassurance and humor, staples for chanting. Garth Williams' homey pen drawing and luminous colors enliven each full-page illustration with a dramatic simplicity set off by spacious book design." Bull Cent Child Books

The dragons are singing tonight; pictures by Peter Sis. Greenwillow Bks. 1993 39p il $16; lib bdg $15.93; pa $6.95 (2-5)   **811**

1. Dragons—Poetry

ISBN 0-688-09645-X; 0-688-12511-5 (lib bdg); 0-688-16162-6 (pa)   LC 92-29013

"Dragons are verbally and visually portrayed in this collection with wonder, whimsy, and a touch of wistfulness. . . . The oil and gouache paintings on a gesso background have marvelous details and unexpected bursts of humor." SLJ

The frogs wore red suspenders; rhymes by Jack Prelutsky; pictures by Petra Mathers. Greenwillow Bks. 2002 63p il $16.95; lib bdg $16.89 (k-3)

811

1. Nonsense verses 2. Nursery rhymes

ISBN 0-688-16719-5; 0-688-16720-9 (lib bdg)

LC 00-68128

A collection of 28 "lighthearted poems, many of which invoke place names in the United States. . . . The mild humor lies not in the action but in Prelutsky's deft use of language, particularly effective shared aloud. The result is enjoyable, but it is Petra Mathers's illustrations that make the book memorable. Demurely naive, her cheerful, delicately delineated human and animal characters focus on their activities with becoming modesty and grace." Horn Book

The gargoyle on the roof; poems by Jack Prelutsky; pictures by Peter Sis. Greenwillow Bks. 1999 39p il $15.89; lib bdg $16 (2-5)

811

1. Monsters—Poetry

ISBN 0-688-16553-2; 0-688-09643-3 (lib bdg)

LC 99-10578

Presents poems about gargoyles, vampires, the bogeyman, gremlins, and other monsters

"Prelutsky achieves a masterful range in tone here. He evokes the traditional attributes of the monsters but gives children insight into what it would be like to be a monster. . . . Sis' cross-hatched oil-and-gouache paintings extend the poems, working especially well to catch the sinister and frightening mood." Booklist

The Headless Horseman rides tonight; more poems to trouble your sleep; illustrated by Arnold Lobel. Greenwillow Bks. 1980 38p il pa $4.95 hardcover o.p. (2-5)   **811**

1. Monsters—Poetry

ISBN 0-688-11705-8 (pa)   LC 80-10372

"In addition to the perambulating mummy, the author deals with, among others, a writhing specter on a misty moor, a zombie, a sorceress, a baleful banshee . . . the abominable snowman and a headless horseman." Horn Book

The author's "rhymes are as lethal, lithe, and literate as ever and Lobel wrings every atmospheric ounce out of them." SLJ

If not for the cat; haiku by Jack Prelutsky; paintings by Ted Rand. Greenwillow Books 2004 40p il $16.99; lib bdg $17.89 (1-4)   **811**

1. Animals—Poetry 2. Haiku

ISBN 0-06-059677-5; 0-06-059678-3 (lib bdg)

LC 2003-17064

"Each of the 17 haiku in this collection explores the essence of an animal, the words forming a sort of riddle answered in Rand's accompanying double-page illustration. . . . Prelutsky shows his command of word choice through a minimalist form that is perfectly matched by Rand's control of his mixed-media artwork to create a wonderful celebration of the art of haiku." SLJ

It's Christmas; pictures by Marylin Hafner. Greenwillow Bks. 1981 46p il pa $5.95 hardcover o.p. (1-3)   **811**

1. Christmas—Poetry

ISBN 0-688-14393-8 (pa)   LC 81-1100

"A Greenwillow read-alone book"

"The poems cover subjects of interest to children—making a Christmas list, performing in the school assembly, cutting a Christmas tree . . . [and dealing] with the disappointments that sometimes occur: being sick on

Prelutsky, Jack—*Continued*

Christmas, getting underwear as a gift and having a new sled but no snow. Marilyn Hafner's cartoonlike drawings add to the fun." SLJ

It's raining pigs & noodles; poems by Jack Prelutsky; drawings by James Stevenson. Greenwillow Bks. 2000 159p il $17.95; lib bdg $17.89 (3-6)   **811**

1. Humorous poetry

ISBN 0-06-029194-X; 0-06-029195-8 (lib bdg)

               LC 00-24707

A collection of humorous poems such as "The Dancing Hippopotami," "You Can't Make Me Eat That," "My Father's Name is Sasquatch," and "Dear Wumbledeedumble"

"The verse is fresh and catchy with sparkling wordplay and unexpected rhymes, and Stevenson's line drawings project the humor with verve." SLJ

It's snowing! it's snowing! winter poems; illustrated by Yossi Abolafia. HarperCollins Pubs. 2006 48p il $15.99; lib bdg $16.89 (1-3)

                               811

1. Winter—Poetry

ISBN 0-06-053715-9; 0-06-053716-7 (lib bdg)

"An I can read book"

A newly illustrated edition of the title first published 1984 by Greenwillow Bks.

A collection of short poems about winter.

"The sounds of the rhyming words are as much fun as the snow action in these 16 poems . . . accompanied by exuberant line-and-watercolor illustrations that capture all the play in the cold." Booklist

It's Thanksgiving; pictures by Marylin Hafner. Greenwillow Bks. 1982 47p il lib bdg $16; pa $5.95 (1-3)   **811**

1. Thanksgiving Day—Poetry

ISBN 0-688-00442-3 (lib bdg); 0-688-14729-1 (pa)

               LC 81-1929

"A Greenwillow read-alone book"

This "collection of poems about Thanksgiving has rhyme, rhythm, and humor as well as a variety of topics: helping Grandma with the meal, watching Daddy watch a football game, seeing a Thanksgiving Day parade, working on school projects, not being able to eat any of the holiday treats because of braces, and the Pilgrim Thanksgiving. The poems are illustrated by brisk, often comic drawings, line and wash. This isn't great poetry, but it has a bouncy quality that's appealing." Bull Cent Child Books

It's Valentine's Day; pictures by Yossi Abolafia. Greenwillow Bks. 1983 47p il pa $5.95 hardcover o.p. (1-3)   **811**

1. Valentine's Day—Poetry

ISBN 0-688-14652-X (pa)   LC 83-1449

"A Greenwillow read-alone book"

"The 14 poems here range from the genuine joy of 'It's Valentine's Day' . . . to the giddy goofiness of 'I love you more than applesauce' or 'Jelly Jill loves Weasel Will'. . . . The rhymes are generally simple but clever and the line drawings in red and blue, with their expressive faces and explanatory vignettes, add tremendously to the enjoyment of the poetry." SLJ

Monday's troll; poems by Jack Prelutsky; pictures by Peter Sis. Greenwillow Bks. 1996 39p il $16; lib bdg $15.93; pa $5.95 (2-5)

                               811

1. Supernatural—Poetry

ISBN 0-688-09644-1; 0-688-14373-3 (lib bdg); 0-688-17529-5 (pa)   LC 95-7085

A collection of seventeen poems about such unsavory characters as witches, ogres, wizards, trolls, giants, a yeti, and seven grubby goblins

This "collection overflows with energy, tongue-in-cheek wit, rich vocabulary, and rollicking rhyme and meter. The oil and gouache paintings on gesso backgrounds are equally playful, as each gold-bordered, double-page spread adds more layers of meaning to the words." SLJ

My parents think I'm sleeping: poems; pictures by Yossi Abolafia. Greenwillow Bks. 1985 47p il $16; lib bdg $14.93; pa $6.95 (2-4)   **811**

1. Sleep—Poetry

ISBN 0-688-04018-7; 0-688-04019-5 (lib bdg); 0-688-14028-9 (pa)   LC 84-13640

This is a collection of humorous poems about bedtime

"Sometimes humorous, sometimes thoughtfully quiet, the poems reflect an interesting range of reactions to the night. . . . Illustrations, done for the most part in appropriate shades of gray and blue with occasional glints of yellow light, extend the nuances of the poetry." Horn Book

The new kid on the block: poems; drawings by James Stevenson. Greenwillow Bks. 1984 159p il $17.95; lib bdg $17.93 (3-6)   **811**

1. Humorous poetry

ISBN 0-688-02271-5; 0-688-02272-3 (lib bdg)

               LC 83-20621

"Most of the 100-plus poems here are mini-jokes, wordplay, and character sketches . . . with liberal doses of monsters and meanies as well as common, garden-variety child mischief." Booklist

"The author's rollicking, silly poems bounce and romp with fun; Stevenson's cartoon-like sketches capture the hilarity with equal skill. A book everyone will enjoy dipping into." Child Book Rev Serv

Nightmares: poems to trouble your sleep; illustrated by Arnold Lobel. Greenwillow Bks. 1976 38p il lib bdg $13.93 (2-5)   **811**

1. Monsters—Poetry

ISBN 0-688-84053-1   LC 76-4820

This "collection of poems is calculated to evoke icy apprehension, and the poems about wizards, bogeymen, ghouls, ogres (well, one poem apiece to each or to others of their ilk) are exaggerated just enough to bring simultaneous grins and shudders. Prelutsky uses words with relish and his rhyme and rhythm are, as usual, deft. Lobel's illustrations are equally adroit, macabre yet elegant." Bull Cent Child Books

A pizza the size of the sun; poems by Jack Prelutsky; drawings by James Stevenson. Greenwillow Bks. 1996 159p il $18; lib bdg $17.93 (3-6)   **811**

1. Humorous poetry

ISBN 0-688-13235-9; 0-688-13236-7 (lib bdg)

               LC 95-35930

Prelutsky, Jack—*Continued*

This collection of humorous poems is "filled with zany people, improbable creatures, and rhythm and rhyme galore, all combining to celebrate the unusual, the mundane, and the slightly gruesome. . . . Each page is brimming with Stevenson's complementary, droll water-colors, reproduced here in black and white." SLJ

Ride a purple pelican; pictures by Garth Williams. Greenwillow Bks. 1986 64p il $17.95; pa $7.95 (k-3) **811**
1. Nonsense verses 2. Nursery rhymes
ISBN 0-688-04031-4; 0-688-15625-8 (pa)
LC 84-6024
A collection of short nonsense verses and nursery rhymes
"Prelutsky has caught the rhythm and spirit of nursery rhymes in 29 short poems about drum-beating bunnies, bullfrogs on parade, Chicago winds, giant sequoias and other wondrous things. Many of these easy-to-remember poems are filled with delicious sounding American and Canadian place names. Garth Williams' full-color, full-page illustrations are good complements to the poems. Highly recommended." Child Book Rev Serv

Rolling Harvey down the hill; illustrated by Victoria Chess. Greenwillow Bks. 1980 30p il $16; lib bdg $15.93; pa $4.95 (1-3) **811**
1. Friendship—Poetry 2. Humorous poetry
ISBN 0-688-80258-3; 0-688-84258-5 (lib bdg); 0-688-12270-1 (pa) LC 79-18236
"Fifteen contemporary poems describe the mischievous antics of five apartment-house buddies." Child Book Rev Serv
"Chess' puckish black-and-white scenes cash in on all the text's mischief. The motley cast is suitably dishev-eled and just bizarre enough in expression. This is fresh, funny, and quite in tune with scampish concerns." Booklist

Scranimals; poems by Jack Prelutsky; pictures by Peter Sis. Greenwillow Bks. 2002 40p il $16.99; lib bdg $18.89 (2-5) **811**
1. Nonsense verses
ISBN 0-688-17819-7; 0-688-17820-0 (lib bdg)
LC 2001-23620
"Prelutsky introduces the curious inhabitants of Scranimal Island through his . . . poems. The creatures, such as the Mangorilla and Orangutanerine, are each a cross between an animal and a fruit, vegetable, or flower, and behave accordingly." SLJ
"The verse sparkles with wit and mad invention. . . . Sis' art picks up on the strange and otherworldly aspects of the poems, evincing a surreal and haunting edge to its intricately lined visions." Bull Cent Child Books

Something big has been here; drawings by James Stevenson. Greenwillow Bks. 1990 160p il $17.95 (3-5) **811**
1. Humorous poetry
ISBN 0-688-06434-5 LC 89-34773
An illustrated collection of humorous poems on a vari-ety of topics
"Puns and verbal surprises abound. Clever use of allit-eration and abundant variety in the sound and texture of words add to the pleasure. . . . Stevenson's small car-toons of snaggle-toothed animals and deadpan children extend and expand the mad humor of the poems, sup-porting but never overwhelming their good-natured fun. A fine prescription against the blues at any time of year." Horn Book

Tyrannosaurus was a beast; illustrated by Arnold Lobel. Greenwillow Bks. 1988 31p il lib bdg $15.93; pa $4.95 (2-5) **811**
1. Dinosaurs—Poetry
ISBN 0-688-06443-4 (lib bdg); 0-688-11569-1 (pa)
LC 87-25131
A collection of humorous poems about dinosaurs
"Fourteen dinosaurs meet their match in this outstand-ing author/illustrator team. While Prelutsky's short, pithy, often witty verses sum up their essential characters, Lobel's line and watercolor portraits bring the beasts to life, enormous yet endearingly vulnerable." Booklist

Quattlebaum, Mary

Winter friends; illustrated by Hiroe Nakata. Doubleday Books for Young Readers 2005 unp il $15.95; lib bdg $17.99 (k-2) **811**
1. Snow—Poetry 2. Friendship—Poetry 3. Winter—Poetry
ISBN 0-385-74626-1; 0-385-90868-7 (lib bdg)
LC 2004-30937
"In 16 brief poems, a girl . . . describes a day spent making snow angels, watching—and listening to—icicles drip, finding a lost mitten, and making a new friend. . . . The child's voice is clear and believable. Nakata's inspired illustrations perfectly complement the effortless verse." SLJ

Ross, Mandy

Wake up sleepy head! early morning poems; [by] Mandy Ross; illustrated by Dubravka Kolanovic. Child's Play 2005 unp il pa $7.99 (k-1) **811**
1. Animals—Poetry
ISBN 1-904550-33-9 LC 2004-58262
"These deceptively simple poems, sometimes silly and consistently sweet, are perfect for infants and toddlers. A pig dreams of slops for breakfast. Pandas look forward to bamboo. Peacock can't wait for the sun to highlight its gorgeous feathers, and the owls are getting ready for a good day's sleep. . . . Kolanovic's watercolor illustra-tions depict the action and enhance the warm and friend-ly tone of the verses with soft yellows, greens, and light blues." SLJ

Rosten, Norman

A city is; collected and edited by Patricia Rosten Filan; illustrated by Melanie Hope Greenberg. Henry Holt 2004 unp il $16.95 (k-3) **811**
1. New York (N.Y.)—Poetry 2. City and town life—Poetry
ISBN 0-8050-6793-0 LC 2003-12247
An illustrated collection of poems about New York City.

Rosten, Norman—*Continued*

"These very simple poems . . . celebrate both the big picture and the closeup, tiny detail. . . . Greenberg's clear, collage-style gouache illustrations on watercolor paper show the city through the day and night and through the seasons." Booklist

Sandburg, Carl

Carl Sandburg; edited by Frances Schoonmaker Bolin; illustrated by Steve Arcella. Sterling 1995 48p il (Poetry for young people) $14.95 (4 and up)

        811

ISBN 0-8069-0818-1   LC 94-30777

"A Magnolia Editions book"

"The 33 poems in *Sandburg* vary in length and theme, but most are the staples of anthologies, e.g., 'Fog,' 'Arithmetic,' and 'We Must Be Polite.' The surrealistic illustrations, which appear to be rendered in pastels, are appealing; the soft edges and warm tones work well with Sandburg's imagery." SLJ

Rainbows are made: poems; selected by Lee Bennett Hopkins; wood engravings by Fritz Eichenberg. Harcourt Brace Jovanovich 1982 81p il pa $13 hardcover o.p. (5 and up)   **811**

ISBN 0-15-265481-X (pa)   LC 82-47934

This book "offers some 70 short poems by Carl Sandburg and groups them by theme: the seasons, the sea, the imaginative mind, etc. Each theme explores different aspects of poetic creativity as envisioned by Sandburg and illustrated by Fritz Eichenberg's wood engravings. Eichenberg has truly captured the power and vigorousness of Sandburg's verse." SLJ

Scieszka, Jon

The book that Jack wrote; illustrated by Daniel Adel. Viking 1994 unp $14.99; pa $5.99 (2-4)

        811

1. Nursery rhymes

ISBN 0-670-84330-X; 0-14-055385-1 (pa)

        LC 94-10932

"An updated version of 'This Is the House That Jack Built,' this cumulative tale tells of a blind rat who falls into a picture in the book that Jack wrote, thus setting off a chain of events in which the players are done in one by one until nothing is left but the book itself. . . . The dark tones of Adel's full-page oil paintings are a fine match for the irreverent mood of the piece." SLJ

Service, Robert W.

The cremation of Sam McGee; by Robert W. Service; paintings by Ted Harrison; introduction by Pierre Berton. 20th anniversary ed. Kids Can Press 2006 unp il $17.95 (4 and up)   **811**

1. Yukon Territory—Poetry

ISBN 978-1-55453-092-2

Text first published 1907. This is a reissue of the edition first published 1986 in Canada and 1987 in the United States by Greenwillow Bks.

"Pledged to cremate his friend Sam, the narrator tells how, after carting the frozen body for miles, he stuffs it into a ship's roaring furnace. To his surprise, when he later opens the door he discovers Sam alive . . . and warm for the first time 'since he left Tennessee.'" Publ Wkly

This poem "has gripped readers and listeners for decades. . . . [The illustrator] obviously appreciates the humor inherent in the text. . . . As Pierre Berton observes in his introduction, [Harrison's] 'style is unique: part Oriental, part native American, part Ted Harrison.'" Horn Book

The shooting of Dan McGrew; paintings by Ted Harrison. Godine 1988 unp il pa $10.95 hardcover o.p. (4 and up)   **811**

1. Yukon Territory—Poetry

ISBN 0-567-92065-9 (pa)   LC 88-6124

Text first published 1907

A narrative poem set in the Yukon describing the shoot-out in a saloon between a trapper and the man who stole his girl

"While the action of the poem is intense and demanding, the painterly illustrations by Harrison are overwhelmingly powerful; they seem to take on a life of their own, drawing readers' attentions away from the text and toward the surrealistic interpretation of events. . . . Harrison creates a pulsating world of hate and destruction; it's a fascinating interpretation of a well-known poem." Publ Wkly

Shannon, George

Busy in the garden; poems by George Shannon; pictures by Sam Williams. Greenwillow Books 2006 36p il $15.99; lib bdg $16.89 (k-2)

        811

1. Gardening—Poetry

ISBN 0-06-000464-9; 0-06-000465-7 (lib bdg)

        LC 2003-56863

A collection of short poems and riddles about planting seeds, watching garden vegetables dance, and growing jack-o-lanterns.

"The best selections are immediately accessible and bounce with humor and an irresistible beat. Williams' lively watercolor-and-pencil illustrations of children and animals digging in the rows shine with the colors of spring." Booklist

Shields, Carol Diggory

Almost late to school and more school poems; illustrated by Paul Meisel. Dutton Children's Bks. 2003 40p il $15.99 (2-4)   **811**

1. Schools—Poetry 2. Humorous poetry

ISBN 0-525-45743-7

Companion volume to Lunch money and other poems about school

"The 22 energetic selections reflect the typical day-to-day activities and problems including being late for school, the first day, having to go to the bathroom, fundraising, and other events. Shields utilizes a variety of forms including a concrete poem, poems for two voices, and a jump-rope rhyme. Meisel's vibrant cartoon illustrations are lively and fun and capture the poems' humor and insight." SLJ

Shields, Carol Diggory—*Continued*

English, fresh squeezed! 40 thirst-for-knowledge-quenching poems; by Carol Diggory Shields; illustrations by Tony Ross. 1st ed. Handprint Books 2004 80p il $14.95 (4 and up) **811**

1. English language—Poetry
ISBN 1-59354-053-1   LC 2004-53905

"Shields presents humorous poems both celebrating and bemoaning parts of speech, grammatical rules, and other annoyances of English class. Her rhyming verse is generally snappy and pointed. . . . Ross's spot illustrations in black and white with a blue tone add visual amusement without overwhelming." SLJ

Lunch money and other poems about school; written by Carol Diggory Shields; illustrated by Paul Meisel. Dutton Children's Bks. 1995 40p il $15.99; pa $5.99 (2-4) **811**

1. Schools—Poetry 2. Humorous poetry
ISBN 0-525-45345-8; 0-14-055890-X (pa)
                                   LC 95-7332

A "collection of 24 childlike perceptions of the zanier happenings during a school day. The poems' appeal relies on irreverent topics, robust action, sing-song rhythms, and rhyming couplets. The bright, expresssive cartoonstyle illustrations highlight the rollicking nature of most of the selections." SLJ

Shore, Diane ZuHone

This is the dream; by Diane Z. Shore and Jessica Alexander; illustrated by James Ransome. 1st ed. HarperCollinsPublishers 2006 unp il $15.99; lib bdg $16.89 (2-4) **811**

1. African Americans—Civil rights—Poetry
ISBN 0-06-055519-X; 0-06-055520-3 (lib bdg)
                                   LC 2003-26554

"A chronicle of the Civil Rights movement presented through lyrical verses and distinguished illustrations. Ransome juxtaposes collaged archival photographs and newspaper clippings with his paintings. . . . Each succinct and evocative verse is accompanied by a double-page image." SLJ

Sidman, Joyce

Eureka! poems about inventors; illustrated by K. Bennett Chavez. Millbrook Press 2002 48p il lib bdg $24.90 (4-6) **811**

1. Inventors—Poetry
ISBN 0-7613-1665-5   LC 00-56620

"In 16 poems, mostly free verse, Sidman commemorates the best-known achievements of dozens of inventors, from the World Wide Web's Tim Berners-Lee to the prehistoric person—a woman, Sidman supposes—who first shaped clay into a bowl." Booklist

"Chavez's full-color, surrealistic illustrations add depth, character, and feeling to the selections. . . . The entire book reads beautifully." SLJ

Meow ruff; a story in concrete poetry; written by Joyce Sidman; illustrated by Michelle Berg. Houghton Mifflin 2006 unp il $16 (1-3) **811**

1. Cats—Poetry 2. Dogs—Poetry 3. Rain—Poetry
ISBN 0-618-44894-2

"Sidman develops a simple tale about a cat and dog trapped in a rainstorm, coding much of the substance right into the physical landscape. . . . Berg, who created the pictures digitally and is also the book's graphic designer, intelligently showcases the concept of words as building blocks in a stylized landscape of flat colors, two-dimensional forms, and wildly mutating typefaces." Booklist

Song of the water boatman; & other pond poems; written by Joyce Sidman; illustrated by Beckie Prange. Houghton Mifflin 2005 unp il $16 (3-5) **811**

1. Ponds—Poetry
ISBN 0-618-13547-2

A Caldecott Medal honor book, 2006

A collection of poems that provide a look at some of the animals, insects, and plants that are found in ponds, with accompanying information about each.

"In this strikingly illustrated collection, science facts combine with vivid poems about pond life through the seasons. . . . Throughout, plants and animals come alive in the bold woodcut prints." Booklist

Siebert, Diane

Tour america; a journey through poems and art; by Diane Siebert; illustrated by Stephen T. Johnson. Chronicle Books 2006 unp il map $17.95 (3-6) **811**

1. United States—Poetry
ISBN 9780811850568; 0-8118-5056-0
                                   LC 2005027125

"This stunning tour of America highlights 26 of the poet's favorite sights . . . Siebert's striking word choices and images reflect the essence of each subject. . . . A double-page map at the beginning of the book alerts readers to the exciting destinations they will experience, and a smaller map and inset box of additional information for each sight increase the educational value. Johnson masterfully varies his medium and art style to reflect the mood of each locale. There are quiet watercolors . . . and dynamic collages . . . as well as pastels, oils, acrylics, and photos." SLJ

Sierra, Judy

Antarctic antics; a book of penguin poems; written by Judy Sierra; illustrated by Jose Aruego & Ariane Dewey. Harcourt Brace & Co. 1998 unp il $16 (k-3) **811**

1. Penguins—Poetry
ISBN 0-15-201006-8   LC 96-41041

"Gulliver books"

A collection of poems celebrating the habits and habitat of Emperor penguins

"Kids will love these high-energy, humorous poems, with some factual information about penguin life woven in. Aruego and Dewey do a nice job of giving readers a feel for the penguins' beautiful but chilly habitat." Booklist

Sierra, Judy—*Continued*

Monster Goose; illustrated by Jack E. Davis. Harcourt 2001 unp il $16 (2-5)   **811**
  1. Monsters—Poetry
  ISBN 0-15-202034-9   LC 00-8808
  "Gulliver books"
A collection of parodies of Mother Goose rhymes featuring monsters
"Davis, working in acrylics and colored pencil, crowds his illustrations with monsters, vermin and gross gags. . . . This volume strikes a nice balance between goofy and ghastly." Publ Wkly

Silverstein, Shel

Falling up; poems and drawings by Shel Silverstein. HarperCollins Pubs. 1996 171p il $17.99; lib bdg $18.89   **811**
  1. Humorous poetry 2. Nonsense verses
  ISBN 0-06-024802-5; 0-06-024803-3 (lib bdg)
    LC 96-75736
This "collection includes more than 150 poems. . . . As always, Silverstein has a direct line to what kids like, and he gives them poems celebrating the gross, the scary, the absurd, and the comical. The drawings are much more than decoration. They often extend a poem's meaning and, in many cases, add some great comedy." Booklist

A light in the attic. Harper & Row 1981 167p il lib bdg $18.89   **811**
  1. Humorous poetry 2. Nonsense verses
  ISBN 0-06-025674-5   LC 80-8453
Also available book with audio CD $22.99 (ISBN 0-06-623617-7)
This collection of more than one hundred poems "will delight lovers of Silverstein's raucous, rollicking verse and his often tender, whimsical, philosophical advice. . . . The poems are tuned in to kids' most hidden feelings, dark wishes and enjoyment of the silly. . . . The witty line drawings are a full half of the treat of this wholly satisfying anthology by the modern successor to Edward Lear and Hilaire Belloc." SLJ

Runny Babbit; a billy sook. HarperCollins Pub. 2005 89p il $17.99; lib bdg $18.89   **811**
  1. Humorous poetry
  ISBN 0-06-025653-2; 0-06-028404-8 (lib bdg)
In this book "readers are introduced to Runny Babbit and his friends . . . and are encouraged to plunge headlong into this phonemic flipflop world of funny poems. . . . Complete with signature comical bold line drawings that provide visual clues, the poems require concentration to translate the silly phrases. . . . Children will love these clever poems and without prompting will probably create their own." SLJ

Where the sidewalk ends; the poems & drawings of Shel Silverstein. 30th anniversary special ed. HarperCollins 2004 183p il $17.99; lib bdg $18.89   **811**
  1. Humorous poetry 2. Nonsense verses
  ISBN 0-06-057234-5; 0-06-058653-2 (lib bdg)
    LC 2004-269335
First published 1974

This edition contains 12 new poems
"There are skillful, sometimes grotesque line drawings with each of the 127 poems, which run in length from a few lines to a couple of pages. The poems are tender, funny, sentimental, philosophical, and ridiculous in turn, and they're for all ages." Sat Rev

Singer, Marilyn

Central heating; poems about fire and warmth; illustrated by Meilo So. 1st ed. Alfred A. Knopf 2005 41p il $15.95; lib bdg $17.99 (4 and up)   **811**
  1. Fire—Poetry 2. Heat—Poetry
  ISBN 0-375-82912-1; 0-375-92912-6 (lib bdg)
    LC 2004-4274
"The complicated nature of fire is explored in Singer's energetic short poems and So's deceptively simple single-color illustrations. . . . This title . . . belongs on library shelves everywhere." SLJ

Creature carnival; illustrations by Gris Grimly. Hyperion Bks. for Children 2004 40p il $15.99 (2-4)   **811**
  1. Mythical animals—Poetry
  ISBN 0-7868-1877-8
"In this picture-book collection of poems, a creepy Victorian carnival barker . . . draws a motley crew of kids into the Creature Carnival. In each poem, the barker introduces a new fantastic being from mythology and literature. . . . The rhymed couplets bounce with rhythm and gleefully sinister words that will appeal to children, and Grimly's scribbly ink-and-watercolor illustrations create a gruesome menagerie of characters that are as buffoonish and appealing as they are grotesque." Booklist

Family reunion; illustrated by R.W. Alley. Macmillan 1994 unp il $14.95 (k-3)   **811**
  1. Family life—Poetry
  ISBN 0-02-782883-2   LC 92-40336
"Read in sequence, this collection of 14 free-verse poems tells the story of a great day at a family reunion. Read alone each selection stands on its own. Outrageous, silly fun is the theme; and this gathering is full of gregarious, entertaining types. . . . Alley 's watercolor and pen illustrations help to reinforce the free-spirited mood of the day." SLJ

Fireflies at midnight; pictures by Ken Robbins. Atheneum Bks. for Young Readers 2003 unp il $16.95 (2-4)   **811**
  1. Insects—Poetry 2. Animals—Poetry
  ISBN 0-689-82492-0   LC 00-54282
"Singer's poems give glimpses into the lives of several creatures during one summer day. The various rhythms and unique 'voices' masterfully capture the nature of the beasts. . . . Robbins's 'photographic treatments' use full-color, graphically enhanced photos and photo collage for an almost painterly effect." SLJ

Footprints on the roof; poems about the earth; illustrated by Meilo So. Knopf 2002 41p il $14.95; lib bdg $16.99 (4 and up)   **811**
  1. Earth—Poetry 2. Nature poetry
  ISBN 0-375-81094-3; 0-375-91094-8 (lib bdg)
    LC 2001-29407

Singer, Marilyn—*Continued*

A collection of 19 poems on such topics as caves, mud, ice, deserts, and dunes

"This elegantly presented collection of free-verse poems focuses primarily on the young narrator's emotional response to nature—its bounties, mysteries, and delights. Like the poems themselves, the black-and-white ink drawings are spare and finely crafted." Horn Book Guide

How to cross a pond; poems about water; illustrated by Meilo So. Knopf 2003 41p il $16.99 (3-6) **811**

1. Water—Poetry

ISBN 0-375-92376-4   LC 2002-34210

Such poems as "Babbling Brook," "Spring in the Garden," "Watercolors," "City River," and "Ocean Checklist" present some of the many facets of water

"Singer's clear words and flowing sounds combine the universal and the immediate to reveal the wonder of what is all around us. . . . The small, narrow book design is inviting; the clear blue type and splashy, blurry double-page watercolors extend the music of the words." Booklist

Monster museum; illustrations by Gris Grimly. Hyperion Bks. for Children 2001 40p il $14.99; lib bdg $15.49 (2-4) **811**

1. Monsters—Poetry

ISBN 0-7868-0520-X; 0-7868-2457-3 (lib bdg)
          LC 00-46169

"Singer describes an array of scary apparitions and frightful figures in this . . . collection of poems. . . . Grimly's colorful caricatures add to the madcap fun. . . . The humor and wordplay running rampant adds to the delight." SLJ

Smith, Charles R.

Hoop kings; poems. Candlewick Press 2004 37p il $14.99 **811**

1. Basketball—Poetry

ISBN 0-7636-1423-8   LC 2003-55340

A collection of twelve poems that celebrate contemporary basketball stars, including Shaquille O'Neal, Allen Iverson, and Kobe Bryant.

"Combining dynamic illustrations and full-bodied language, Smith's latest collection of poems enthusiastically conveys both love for and knowledge of the game. . . . This book will have enormous appeal for all ages; basketball fans will love it, but so will others who respond to color, lively language, and energy." SLJ

Hoop queens; poems. Candlewick Press 2003 35p il $14.99 **811**

1. Basketball—Poetry 2. Women athletes—Poetry

ISBN 0-7636-1422-X   LC 2002-41111

A collection of twelve poems that celebrate contemporary women basketball stars, including Yolanda Griffith, Chamique Holdsclaw, and Natalie Williams

"Action photos of the athletes are pasted large on colorful, dynamic backgrounds that barely hold the motion-filled poems to the page. Notes about each player and poem communicate the joy Smith finds both in watching the game and writing poetry. Pure pleasure for basketball fans and inspiration for kids who doubted poetry was alive." SLJ

Perfect harmony; a musical journey with the Boys Choir of Harlem; poems and photographs by Charles R. Smith, Jr. Jump at the Sun 2002 32p il $15.99 (4 and up) **811**

1. Boys Choir of Harlem 2. Music—Poetry

ISBN 0-7868-0758-X   LC 2001-42277

A collection of poems that capture the feelings and expression of music in some of its forms

This is "illustrated with striking color photos of the Boys Choir of Harlem. . . . Children will be educated as well as energized by these strong, playful poems that may inspire them to find their own sounds in poetry or music." Booklist

Includes glossary

Smith, Hope Anita

The way a door closes; [by] Hope Anita Smith; with illustrations by Shane W. Evans. Holt & Co. 2003 52p il $18.95 (4 and up) **811**

1. Fathers—Poetry 2. Family life—Poetry 3. African Americans—Poetry

ISBN 0-8050-6477-X   LC 2002-67884

In these "poems, readers are drawn into the thoughts and feelings of a 13-year-old African American as he tries to understand and cope with a parent's departure from the family. . . . In carefully chosen, straightforward language, Smith conveys the boy's roller-coaster emotions with pinpoint accuracy. The results are poems that are heartbreaking, angry, and tender. Done in warm shades of mostly brown, blue, and gold, Evans's color spot and full-page paintings have a realistic, slightly sculptural appearance and are a perfect complement to the poems." SLJ

Smith, William Jay

Around my room; poems by William Jay Smith; illustrations by Erik Blegvad. Farrar, Straus & Giroux 2000 31p il $16 (k-3) **811**

ISBN 0-374-30406-8   LC 99-23556

"Smith's collection is for children who are in the mood for silliness. While there is plenty of strong new material, many of the 29 poems previously appeared in his 'Laughing Time: Nonsense Poems' (1955). 'Around My Room' successfully reaches out to a younger audience. Erik Blegvad's illustrations nicely ground the verbal shenanigans with his crisp, consistently lovely, whimsical watercolors." N Y Times Book Rev

Soto, Gary

Canto familiar; [illustrated by Annika Nelson] Harcourt Brace & Co. 1995 79p il $18 (4-6) **811**

1. Mexican Americans—Poetry

ISBN 0-15-200067-4   LC 94-24218

"This collection of simple free verse captures common childhood moments at home, at school, and in the street. Many of the experiences are Mexican American . . . and occasional Spanish words are part of the easy, colloquial, short lines. . . . The occasional full-page, richly colored woodcuts by Annika Nelson capture the child's imaginative take on ordinary things." Booklist

Soto, Gary—*Continued*

Fearless Fernie; hanging out with Fernie & me; poems by Gary Soto; illustrated by Regan Dunnick. Putnam 2002 64p il $14.99 (4-6)

811

1. Friendship—Poetry
ISBN 0-399-23615-5   LC 2001-19712

This is "a collection of 41 short poems. . . . The narrator and his friend Fernie are sixth graders with lots on their minds: sports, girls, school, family. Strongly rhythmic, with vivid imagery, the mostly unrhymed selections are universal yet wonderfully particular. . . . The simple, dynamic sketches sprinkled throughout are just right, providing some humorous and rueful grace notes for this little gem." SLJ

Another title about Fernie is:
Worlds apart: traveling with Fernie and me (2005)

Neighborhood odes; illustrated by David Diaz. Harcourt Brace Jovanovich 1992 68p il $17; pa $5.95 (4-6)

811

1. Hispanic Americans—Poetry
ISBN 0-15-256879-4; 0-15-205364-6 (pa)
LC 91-20710

Also available in paperback from Scholastic

"Twenty-one poems, all odes, celebrate life in a Hispanic neighborhood. Other than the small details of daily life—peoples' names or the foods they eat—these poems could be about any neighborhood. With humor, sensitivity, and insight, Soto explores the lives of children. . . . David Diaz's contemporary black-and-white illustrations, which often resemble cut paper, effortlessly capture the varied moods—happiness, fear, longing, shame, and greed—of this remarkable collection. With a glossary of thirty Spanish words and phrases." Horn Book

Stevenson, James

Candy corn; poems. Greenwillow Bks. 1999 55p il $15

811

ISBN 0-688-15837-4   LC 98-2965

A collection of short poems with titles such as "The Morning After Halloween," "Dumpsters," and "What Frogs Say To Each Other"

"Stevenson's images range from junkyard jumble to fragile blossoms. With minute particulars of ordinary life, his casual words and wonderful, scribbly ink-and-watercolor pictures work together to make you feel love and longing, mystery and wonder." Booklist

Corn chowder; poems by James Stevenson with illustrations by the author. Greenwillow Bks. 2003 48p il $15.99; lib bdg $16.89

811

ISBN 0-06-053059-6; 0-06-053060-X (lib bdg)
LC 2002-9111

A collection of short poems with titles such as "In the Morning at the National Zoo," "Cell Phone," and "Backpack Mystery"

"This lovable collection of poems and whimsical watercolors will bring smiles and a new perspective to the common things around us." SLJ

Corn-fed; poems by James Stevenson; with illustrations by the author. Greenwillow Bks. 2002 48p il $15.95; lib bdg $15.89

811

ISBN 0-06-000597-1; 0-06-000598-X (lib bdg)
LC 2001-33261

A collection of short poems with such titles as "Coney Island movie," "Why bicycles are locked up," and "Aquarium"

"These musings are shot through with Stevenson's wry scrutiny of and appreciation for, the world around him. . . . Spare but appealing, these poetic ponderings render the ordinary fresh." Horn Book Guide

Cornflakes; poems by James Stevenson; with illustrations by the author. Greenwillow Bks. 2000 47p il $14.95

811

ISBN 0-688-16718-7   LC 99-29846

A collection of short poems with such titles as "I Can't Move Mountains," "Junkyard," and "Greenhouse in March"

Stevenson "disarms readers with his choice of subjects, his offhand ink-and-watercolor art and his wryly comic verse offering sharp new takes on objects or actions so familiar that they usually escape notice altogether." Publ Wkly

Just around the corner; poems by James Stevenson; with illustrations by the author. Greenwillow Bks. 2001 55p il $14.95; lib bdg $14.89

811

ISBN 0-688-17303-9; 0-06-029189-3 (lib bdg)
LC 00-22547

A collection of short poems on a variety of topics, including "Classroom," "After the Storm," and "Tow Truck"

"A delightful collection. . . . The small format, attractive layouts, varied type sizes and colors, and accomplished pen-and-ink and watercolor illustrations add to the appeal. A charming partnership of inspired language and design." SLJ

Popcorn; poems by James Stevenson; with illustrations by the author. Greenwillow Bks. 1998 64p il $15

811

ISBN 0-688-15261-9   LC 97-6320

A collection of short poems with such titles as "Popcorn," "Driftwood," and "My new bird book"

"With a physical immediacy and a casual voice, Stevenson's poems capture quiet, intensely moving moments of daily life in a small seaside town, and his exquisite, understated watercolors extend the concrete particulars of the words." Booklist

Sturges, Philemon

Down to the sea in ships; illustrated by Giles Laroche. Putnam's 2005 unp il $16.99 (3-5)

811

1. Boats and boating—Poetry
ISBN 0-399-23464-0   LC 2002-67957

Poems describe a variety of watercraft, from birch bark canoes to cruise ships, and reveal their impact on the world.

"A seamless collection of finely honed but telling histories of important ships in fully realized poems. . . . Laroche's boats, made of cut paper and paint, appear to lift from the waves and float in their pictorial waters. This author and illustrator work wonders together." SLJ

Testa, Maria
Becoming Joe DiMaggio; with illustrations by Scott Hunt. Candlewick Press 2002 51p il $14.99; pa $5.99 (4 and up)   **811**
1. Italian Americans—Poetry 2. Grandfathers—Poetry
ISBN 0-7636-1537-4; 0-7636-2444-6 (pa)
LC 2001-25886
"Growing up in New York City during the 1940s and 1950s, Joseph Paul, an Italian boy, finds solace from a difficult life by listening to baseball games with his beloved grandfather. This powerful story, told in 24 poems, describes their relationship and their love of listening to another Italian, Joe DiMaggio, achieve success. . . . The beauty and the charm of the poetry—its concise language, its flow and descriptive power—add to the intensity of the experiences described. Hunt's charcoal-and-pastel spot illustrations are scattered throughout." SLJ

Thayer, Ernest Lawrence
Casey at the bat   **811**
1. Baseball—Poetry
Some editions are:
Godine pa $10.95 Illustrations by Barry Moser; afterword by Donald Hall (ISBN 1-56792-072-1)
Handprint $17.95 illustrated by Christopher Bing (ISBN 1-92976-600-9)
Putnam pa $5.95 With additional text and illustrations by Patricia Polacco (ISBN 0-698-11557-0)
Simon & Schuster Books for Young Readers $16.95 illustrated by C. F. Payne (ISBN 0-689-85494-3)
First published 1888
A narrative poem about the celebrated baseball player who strikes out at the crucial moment of a game

Thomas, Joyce Carol
Brown honey in broomwheat tea; poems by Joyce Carol Thomas; illustrated by Floyd Cooper. HarperCollins Pubs. 1993 unp il $16.95; pa $4.95 (k-3)   **811**
1. African Americans—Poetry
ISBN 0-06-021087-7; 0-06-443439-7 (pa)
LC 91-46043
"A dozen poems rooted in home, family, and the African American experience combine with a series of warm and evocative watercolors in this highly readable and attractive picture book." Booklist

Crowning glory; poems; illustrated by Brenda Joysmith. HarperCollins Pubs. 2002 unp il $15.95; lib bdg $15.89 (k-3)   **811**
1. African Americans—Poetry 2. Hair—Poetry 3. Family life—Poetry
ISBN 0-06-023473-3; 0-06-023474-1 (lib bdg)
LC 96-26690
"Joanna Cotler books"
"Fourteen poems describe the beauty of African-American hairstyles across generations—from Grandma's wigs to the art of draping with colorful wraps." Horn Book Guide
"Joysmith's full-page pastels present an intimate look into the life of this African-American family and are a perfect complement to the poetry. These selections have the makings for read-aloud magic." SLJ

Unobagha, Uzoamaka Chinyelu
Off to the sweet shores of Africa and other talking drum rhymes; illustrated by Julia Cairns. Chronicle Bks. 2000 unp il $16.95 (k-3)   **811**
1. Africa—Poetry
ISBN 0-8118-2378-4   LC 00-8933
A collection of poems featuring the animals, people, and cultures of Africa
"The playful, joyful rhymes brim with African words and shed light on culture and customs, and a helpful glossary at the end of the book explains unfamiliar terms. Cairns's watercolors burst with energy." Publ Wkly

Updike, John
A child's calendar; illustrations by Trina Schart Hyman. Holiday House 1999 unp il $16.95   **811**
1. Months—Poetry
ISBN 0-8234-1445-0   LC 98-46166
A Caldecott Medal honor book, 2000
A newly illustrated edition of the title first published 1965 by Knopf
"Hyman's colorful illustrations portray a multiracial family living in rural New Hampshire. . . . Each evocative illustration has its own story to tell, celebrating the small moments in children's lives with clarity and sensitivity, with empathy and joy." Booklist

Viorst, Judith
If I were in charge of the world and other worries; poems for children and their parents; illustrated by Lynne Cherry. Atheneum Pubs. 1981 56p il lib bdg $16.95; pa $4.95 (3-6)   **811**
ISBN 0-689-30863-9 (lib bdg); 0-689-70770-3 (pa)
LC 81-2342
"Forty-one lively, funny poems written from a wry, self-deprecating point of view. Some poems verge on adult feelings—such as a broken heart or a lyrical appreciation of spring—but most of them deal with children's worries, to which the author seems to be specially attuned." Horn Book

Sad underwear and other complications; poems; illustrated by Richard Hull. Atheneum Pubs. 1995 78p $16; pa $4.99 (3-6)   **811**
1. Humorous poetry
ISBN 0-689-31929-0; 0-689-83376-8 (pa)
LC 94-3357
"From 'The Seventh Swimming Lesson,' in which Sally finally puts her face in the water, to a practical version of 'Sleeping Beauty,' this is an inspired book of verse guaranteed to tickle the humerus again and again. Yet, poignancy is present, too. . . . Both humorous and dreamlike pen-and-ink illustrations are scattered throughout." SLJ

Weatherford, Carole Boston
Remember the bridge; poems of a people; designed by Semador Megged. Philomel Bks. 2002 53p il $17.99   **811**
1. African Americans—Poetry
ISBN 0-399-23726-7   LC 2001-36161

Weatherford, Carole Boston—*Continued*

"Twenty-nine poems trace African-American history and include observations about Harriet Tubman, Marian Anderson, and Martin Luther King, Jr." Horn Book Guide

"The author evokes imagined and actual individual experiences of the people . . . in the historical black-and-white photos, drawings, and etchings. . . . This celebratory, visually striking book will be appreciated in most collections." SLJ

Whipple, Laura

If the shoe fits; voices from Cinderella; illustrations by Laura Beingessner. Margaret K. McElderry Bks. 2002 67p il $17.95 (5 and up)
                                                    811

1. Cinderella—Poetry 2. Fairy tales—Poetry
ISBN 0-689-84070-5   LC 2001-30778

In this version of the fairy tale "the characters tell the story in blank verses. . . . The story unfolds just as it always does, but the multiple points of view—from Cinderella's to the prince's to the rat's to the queen's—enlarge and enrich the familiar tale to win a more sophisticated audience. . . . Paintings by Beingessner achieve just the right mixture of sorrow, beauty, and humor." Booklist

Wilbur, Richard

The disappearing alphabet; illustrated by David Diaz. Harcourt Brace & Co. 1998 unp il $16 (3-5)
                                                    811

1. Alphabet
ISBN 0-15-201470-5   LC 97-24617

A collection of twenty-six short poems pondering what the world would be like if any letters of the alphabet should disappear

"The poems presented here were first printed in *The Atlantic Monthly* magazine. A series of rhyming couplets of varying lengths, they range from the innocently whimsical to the cleverly sophisticated. Diaz uses computer-generated illustrations to add just the right touches to the verses; the images are lush and playful at the same time." SLJ

Willard, Nancy

Pish, posh, said Hieronymus Bosch; illustrations by the Dillons. Harcourt Brace Jovanovich 1991 unp il $22 (2-5)   811

1. Bosch, Hieronymus, d. 1516—Poetry
ISBN 0-15-262210-1   LC 86-3173

In this poem, the housekeeper for medieval Dutch artist Hieronymus Bosch complains about the weird creatures which inhabit his home

"Once again, the Dillons have tailored their style to perfectly suit—and here, lend waggish twists to—their subject. Rendered in the opulent tones and peculiar, wild spirit of Bosch's works, their parade of fantastical creatures would make the master proud: animate cucumbers, an armor-plated, two-headed dragon, a flying fish with wings of pickles. . . . This eccentric work may not be for youngest children, but anyone with unusual vision and an affinity for the quirkiest corners of the imagination will find it a source of endless fascination." Publ Wkly

A visit to William Blake's inn; poems for innocent and experienced travelers; illustrated by Alice and Martin Provensen. Harcourt Brace Jovanovich 1981 44p il $16; pa $7 (2-5)
                                                    811

1. Nonsense verses
ISBN 0-15-293822-2; 0-15-293823-0 (pa)
                             LC 80-27403

Awarded the Newbery Medal, 1982 and also a Caldecott Medal honor book for the same year

This "collection of sixteen nonsense verses describes the lively goings-on among several incongruous travelers who put up at an imaginary inn run by the English poet William Blake." Child Book Rev Serv

"Nancy Willard's fantasy is pure pleasure, and her joy is expressed in the juxtaposition of sense and nonsense. . . . Done chiefly in glowing tawny colors, the pictures are highly decorative, and the whole book, printed on buff paper speckled to simulate an antique look, presents an elegant appearance." Horn Book

Williams, Vera B.

Amber was brave, Essie was smart; the story of Amber and Essie told here in poems and pictures by Vera B. Williams. Greenwillow Bks. 2001 unp il $15.95; lib bdg $15.89 (3-5)   811

1. Sisters—Poetry
ISBN 0-06-029460-4; 0-06-029461-2 (lib bdg)
                             LC 00-48438

Two sisters help each other deal with life while their mother is working and their father has been sent to jail

"An engaging, affecting view of the bonds between sisters, this balances reality with hope and love as it shows how small moments tell a big story." Booklist

Winter, Jeanette

Emily Dickinson's letters to the world; story and pictures by Jeanette Winter. Foster Bks. 2002 unp il $16 (k-3)   811

1. Dickinson, Emily, 1830-1886
ISBN 0-374-32147-7   LC 2001-33277

Includes selections from the poetry of Emily Dickinson

"Written from the point of view of Dickinson's sister after the reclusive poet has died, this brief volume blends a few biographical tidbits with twenty-one of Dickinson's poems." Horn Book Guide

"Dickinson's poetry is both magnificent and intimate. . . . Winter artfully mirrors this mix of grand and personal: the book's small size, its delicate star- and flower-filled inner margins, the graceful handwritten script of the poems have a feeling of intimacy, while the paintings, bold in color and shape, convey the strength and sharpness of the poet's vision." N Y Times Book Rev

Wise, William

Dinosaurs forever; pictures by Lynn Munsinger. Dial Bks. for Young Readers 2000 unp il $15.99 (k-3)   811

1. Dinosaurs—Poetry
ISBN 0-8037-2114-5   LC 99-34702

Wise, William—*Continued*

A collection of humorous poems about dinosaurs
This book offers "zippy poems and hilarious art that together humanize the extinct yet undyingly popular creatures." Booklist

Zany zoo; [by] William Wise; illustrated by Lynn Munsinger. Houghton Mifflin Company 2006 32p il $16 (k-3) **811**
1. Animals—Poetry 2. Humorous poetry
ISBN 0-618-18891-6 LC 2005020058
An illustrated, pun-filled collection of short rhymes about a variety of animals, including Gertrude the good agouti and Sabrina the carefree snake.
"Exuberant wordplay fuels this animal-themed collection of light verse. . . . Munsinger will keep kids riveted with her goofy, anthropomorphic illustrations, and the chanting rhythms and spot-on rhymes will perk up listeners." Booklist

Wong, Janet S.

Knock on wood; poems about superstitions; written by Janet S. Wong; illustrated by Julie Paschkis. Margaret K. McElderry Bks. 2003 33p il $17.95 (3-5) **811**
1. Superstition—Poetry
ISBN 0-689-85512-5 LC 2002-8319
Contents: Cat; Clover; Ears; Garlic; Hair; Hat; Horseshoe; Key; Ladybug; Mirror; Potatoes; Rooster; Salt; Thirteen; Umbrellas; Wood
A collection of seventeen original poems about superstitions, including walking under a ladder, breaking a mirror, and knocking on wood. Includes notes about the superstitions
"Some selections are haunting, and some humorous. . . . Paschkis creates an exquisite backdrop for the verses. Presented on a panoramic spread, each poem and facing watercolor scene have matching frames, anchoring them as reflections of one another. . . . There is much to ponder in both words and pictures." SLJ

Night garden; poems from the world of dreams; illustrated by Julie Paschkis. Margaret K. McElderry Bks. 2000 28p il $16 (3-6)
811
1. Dreams—Poetry
ISBN 0-689-82617-6 LC 98-46302
A collection of poems describing a variety of dreams, some familiar, some strange, some beautiful, and some on the darker side
"The combination of the impressionistic and the prosaic in these vivid poems invites rereading just as the fabulous images of the illustrations and the dreamy monochromatic backgrounds invite re-viewing." Bull Cent Child Books

The rainbow hand; poems about mothers and children; illustrations by Jennifer Hewitson. Margaret K. McElderry Bks. 1999 22p il $15 (4-6)
811
1. Mothers—Poetry
ISBN 0-689-82148-4 LC 97-50554
"Eighteen free verse poems about mothers and the experience of motherhood are told from the perspectives of both parent and child. The author's mother inspired the poems, but they transcend any particular relationship to become an honest portrayal of mother/child universalities. Stylized scratchboard and watercolor illustrations complement the poems." Horn Book Guide

Woodson, Jacqueline

Locomotion. Putnam 2003 100p $15.99 (4 and up) **811**
1. African Americans—Poetry 2. Foster home care—Poetry
ISBN 0-399-23115-3 LC 2002-69779
In a series of poems, eleven-year-old Lonnie writes about his life, after the death of his parents, separated from his younger sister, living in a foster home, and finding his poetic voice at school
"In a masterful use of voice, Woodson allows Lonnie's poems to tell a complex story of loss and grief and to create a gritty, urban environment. Despite the spare text, Lonnie's foster mother and the other minor characters are three-dimensional, making the boy's world a convincingly real one." SLJ

Worth, Valerie

All the small poems and fourteen more; pictures by Natalie Babbitt. Farrar, Straus & Giroux 1994 194p il pa $6.95 hardcover o.p. **811**
ISBN 0-374-40345-7 (pa) LC 94-8810
"As the title implies, all the original collaborations between this poet and artist are collected in this volume, which includes ninety-nine poems and an additional fourteen new ones. The earlier works have been widely praised, for good reason, and the new verses are every bit as worthy as their predecessors." Horn Book

Peacock and other poems; pictures by Natalie Babbitt. Farrar, Straus & Giroux 2002 40p il $15
811
ISBN 0-374-35766-8 LC 2001-23828
A collection of short blank verse about common sights and objects such as "umbrella," "pencil," "crayons"
"The illustrations, minimalist in form but not in impact, match the incisive delicacy of the poems, twenty-six in all—and each is a delight." Horn Book

Yolen, Jane

The ballad of the pirate queens; illustrated by David Shannon. Harcourt Brace & Co. 1995 unp il $16; pa $6 (3-5) **811**
1. Bonny, Anne, b. 1700—Poetry 2. Read, Mary, 1680-1721—Poetry 3. Pirates—Poetry
ISBN 0-15-200710-5; 0-15-201885-9 (pa)
LC 94-7874
"A poem about Anne Bonney and Mary Reade, who were real pirates and who sailed on the sloop Vanity and fought the man-of-war Albion. They were tried in Jamaica in 1720 but, some say, were released because they were pregnant. Dramatic seafaring illustrations." N Y Times Book Rev

Yolen, Jane—*Continued*

Color me a rhyme; nature poems for young people; photographs by Jason Stemple. Boyds Mills Press 2000 unp il $19.95; pa $9.95 (3-5)
811

1. Nature poetry
ISBN 1-56397-892-X; 1-59078-172-4 (pa)
LC 99-68893

"Thirteen poems, each a study of a different color found in nature, accompanied by gorgeous photographs, beautifully reproduced and artfully presented. . . . There's playful yet elegant mood in the way the words and pictures merge on many of the pages. This is a visual delight." SLJ

Count me a rhyme; animal poems by the numbers; [by] Jane Yolen; photographs by Jason Stemple. Wordsong/Boyds Mills Press 2006 32p il $17.95 (3-5)
811

1. Animals—Poetry 2. Counting
ISBN 1-59078-345-X   LC 2004030656

"Stemple's color photos of animals in the wild represent the numbers from 1 to 10 and the concept 'many.' Each photo fills a wide, double-page spread, forming the backdrop as well as the inspiration for the poems, which are succinct, sometimes witty, and well suited to reading aloud. Words and symbols and numerals related to the number enrich each spread." Booklist

Fine feathered friends; poems for young people; photographs by Jason Stemple. 1st ed. Wordsong/Boyds Mills Press 2004 31p il $17.95 (3-5)
811

1. Birds—Poetry
ISBN 1-59078-193-7   LC 2003-26791

"Each spread consists of a large, clear full-color photo of a single bird in the wild and a poem that describes its appearance, habits, or eccentricities. . . . Yolen has successfully used a variety of poetic styles. Her words are carefully chosen; her phrases often create clever images." SLJ

How beastly! a menagerie of nonsense poems; pictures by James Marshall. Wordsong 1994 46p il $14.95 (3-5)
811

1. Mythical animals—Poetry 2. Nonsense verses
ISBN 1-56397-086-4   LC 92-85036

A reissue of the title first published 1980 by Collins
This is a collection of nonsense verses on such imaginary creatures as the alligate, the tuner fish and the canterpillar

"For each of the twenty-two verses, a full-page line drawing washed with gray illuminates and comments on the fanciful fauna." Horn Book

The three bears holiday rhyme book; written by Jane Yolen; illustrated by Jane Dyer. Harcourt Brace & Co. 1995 32p il $15 (k-2)
811

1. Holidays—Poetry
ISBN 0-15-200932-9   LC 93-17252

"Baby Bear, joined by Mother, Father, or their friend Goldilocks, celebtrates 15 special days throughout the year. Each occasion is featured in a splendid two-page water-color illustration with a short poem honoring the event." SLJ

Wild wings; poems for young people; photographs by Jason Stemple. Wordsong/Boyds Mills Press 2002 32p il $17.95 (3-6)
811

1. Birds—Poetry
ISBN 1-56397-904-7

Yolen "wrote the poems in this book to accompany her son's color photos of various birds, such as a heron, a warbler, and swallows, in their natural habitat." Horn Book Guide

The photos "are themselves a sort of visual poetry. . . . Yolen's poetry is elegantly spare, with a purity of thought and language that will send readers back to the photo with new eyes, which in turn will inspire them to read the poem again." Booklist

Young, Ed

Beyond the great mountains; a visual poem about China. Chronicle Books 2005 unp $17.95 (4 and up)
811

1. China—Poetry
ISBN 0-8118-4343-2

"The book is comprised of 14 lines, each of which is accompanied by its own double-page illustration, done in cut and torn-paper collage. Young also provides the ancient characters for the images he presents. . . . Designed to be read vertically, each page is flipped up to reveal the accompanying illustration. In this way, the entire book becomes a piece of art, a visual treat of sublime colors and textures that joins with text and characters to describe the vastness and beauty of China." SLJ

Zolotow, Charlotte

Seasons; a book of poems; illustrated by Erik Blegvad. HarperCollins Pubs. 2002 64p il $14.95; lib bdg $14.89 (k-3)
811

1. Seasons—Poetry 2. Nature poetry
ISBN 0-06-026698-8; 0-06-026699-6 (lib bdg)
LC 00-61409

"An I can read book"
"Divided into the four seasons, Zolotow's 40 poems . . . are brief . . . evocative reflections on and responses to the natural world, but they also tap feelings that children experience regardless of the season. . . . Featuring youngsters in charming country settings, Blegvad's precise ink drawings are washed with a delicate full-color palette and reinforce the quiet, thoughtful mood of the selections." SLJ

811.008   American poetry-- Collections

The **20th** century children's poetry treasury; selected by Jack Prelutsky; illustrated by Meilo So. Knopf 1999 87p il $19.95; lib bdg $21.99
811.008

1. American poetry—Collections
ISBN 0-679-89314-8; 0-679-99314-2 (lib bdg)
LC 99-23988

A collection of more than 200 poems by such modern poets as Nikki Grimes, John Ciardi, Karla Kuskin, Ted Hughes, e.e. cummings, Eve Merriam, Deborah Chandra, Arnold Adoff, and more than 100 others

The 20th century children's poetry treasury—
Continued

"While all of these selections have been published elsewhere, the format and illustrations in this collection give them new life. . . . So's watercolor illustrations are, by turn, impressionistic, childlike, silly, and serious, as called for by the tone of the poems featured. . . . A splendid collection." SLJ

Ashley Bryan's ABC of African-American poetry. Atheneum Bks. for Young Readers 1997 unp il $16; pa $5.99 (k-3) **811.008**
1. African Americans—Poetry 2. American poetry—African American authors—Collections 3. Alphabet
ISBN 0-689-81209-4; 0-689-84045-4 (pa)
LC 96-25148
"A Jean Karl book"
Each letter of the alphabet is represented by a line from a poem by a different African American poet, describing an aspect of the black experience
This book is illustrated "by Bryan's vivid tempera and gouache paintings. . . . The selections . . . display a loving acquaintance with poets from James Weldon Johnson to Rita Dove. While there is a full range of emotions, joy and pride predominate." SLJ

The baby's playtime book; [compiled by] Kay Chorao. 1st ed. Dutton Children's Books 2006 40p il $16.99 (k-1) **811.008**
1. American poetry—Collections 2. Nursery rhymes
ISBN 0-525-47576-1
LC 2005009906
Chorao "skillfully combines traditional verses, modern poems, and songs with color illustrations of animals and children in a book that begs to be read aloud. Her drawings are sweet and endearing, but the sentimentality is cut by a deft choice of words." SLJ

The Beauty of the beast; poems from the animal kingdom; selected by Jack Prelutsky; illustrated by Meilo So; opening poems for each section especially written for this anthology by Jack Prelutsky. Knopf 1997 101p il $19.95 (4-6) **811.008**
1. Animals—Poetry 2. Poetry—Collections
ISBN 0-679-87058-X
LC 96-14423
This collection includes "more than 200 animal poems by twentieth-century writers, loosely arranged into five sections—insects and worms, fish, reptiles, birds, and mammals. . . . The poets include Hoberman, Lawrence, Worth, Jarrell, Roethke, and many more." Booklist
"Prelutsky has selected a remarkable array of poems full of movement and sound. . . . Each page has several poems and bright watercolors that writhe with texture." SLJ
Includes bibliographical references

Big, bad, and a little bit scary; poems that bite back! [compiled and illustrated by] Wade Zahares. Viking 2001 unp il $15.99 (k-3) **811.008**
1. Animals—Poetry 2. American poetry—Collections
ISBN 0-670-03513-0
LC 2001-416
A collection of "15 poems about 'big, bad, and a little bit scary' land and sea creatures. . . . Authors of the . . . verse range from John Gardner, D. H. Lawrence,

and Maxine Kumin to Mary Ann Hoberman and Dick King-Smith." Booklist
"The entertaining, humorous poems will appeal to readers who think that poetry is drab and dull, and the selections are easy and fun to read aloud. The double-page spreads come to life with large, lush paintings of grimacing eels and curious vultures." SLJ

The Blackbirch treasury of American poetry. Blackbirch Press 2001 288p il $46.20 (5 and up) **811.008**
1. American poetry—Collections
ISBN 1-56711-472-5
LC 00-52899
This treasury combines volumes previously published in Sterling Publications Poetry for young people series
Contents: Carl Sandburg, illustrated by Steven Arcella; Robert Frost, illustrated by Henri Sorensen; Emily Dickinson, illustrated by Chi Chung; Edgar Allan Poe, illustrated by Carolynn Cobleigh; Walt Whitman, illustrated by Jim Burke; Henry Wadsworth Longfellow, illustrated by Chad Wallace
"This is an attractive book that will be of interest to students who are learning about American poets." Book Rep

Carnival of the animals; poems inspired by Saint-Saëns' music; by James Berry [et al]; edited by Judith Chernaik; illustrated by Satoshi Kitamura. Candlewick Press 2006 unp il $16.99 **811.008**
1. Animals—Poetry 2. Music—Poetry 3. American poetry—Collections
ISBN 0-7636-2960-X
LC 2005-48445
"Chernaik commissioned 13 poets to respond to the musical animal portraits in Saint-Saens' kid-friendly *Carnival of the Animals* . . . Their concise, vibrant word painting will forge an instant connection with children. . . . The poems . . . can be appreciated with or without the accompanying 55-minute CD of music and readings. . . . Having said that, separating this from its inspirational basis would miss the point; children will find it fascinating to see how their own impressions of the original works match the poets'—not to mention illustrator Kitamura's, whose engaging watercolors shift fluidly among the poems' many moods while lending the whole a welcome cohesion." Booklist

Christmas presents; holiday poetry; selected by Lee Bennett Hopkins; pictures by Melanie Hall. HarperCollins 2004 32p il $15.99; lib bdg $16.89 (k-3) **811.008**
1. Christmas—Poetry 2. American poetry—Collections
ISBN 0-06-008054-X; 0-06-008055-8 (lib bdg)
LC 2003-49513
"An I can read book"
A collection of poems by a variety of authors celebrating the various aspects of Christmas
This collection is "just right for beginning readers. . . . The poems are simple, evocative, and rhythmic. . . . Hall's expressive artwork creates an appealing contemporary tone with vivid pastels and a smattering of collage." SLJ

Cool salsa; bilingual poems on growing up Latino in the United States; edited by Lori M. Carlson; introduction by Oscar Hijuelos. Holt & Co. 1994 xx, 123p il $16.95 (5 and up)   **811.008**
1. American poetry—Hispanic American authors—Collections 2. Bilingual books—English-Spanish
ISBN 0-8050-3135-9   LC 93-45798
Also available in paperback from Fawcett Bks.
"This collection presents poems by 29 Mexican-American, Cuban-American, Puerto Rican, and other Central and South American poets, including Sandra Cisneros, Luis J. Rodriguez, Pat Mora, Gary Soto, Ana Castillo, Oscar Hijuelos, Ed J. Vega, Judith Ortiz-Cofer, and other Latino writers both contemporary and historical. Brief biographical notes on the authors are provided. All the poems deal with experiences of teenagers." Book Rep

Days like this; a collection of small poems; selected and illustrated by Simon James. Candlewick Press 2000 45p il $17.99   **811.008**
ISBN 0-7636-0812-2   LC 99-11363
First published 1999 in the United Kingdom
A collection of short poems by such authors as Eve Merriam, Ogden Nash, and Charlotte Zolotow
"Pen-and-ink and watercolor cartoons reflect the everyday world. . . . A lively variety of perspectives and flashes of humor make this book worth many returns." SLJ

Dinosaurs: poems; selected by Lee Bennett Hopkins; illustrated by Murray Tinkleman. Harcourt Brace Jovanovich 1987 46p il $12.95; pa $6 (3-5)   **811.008**
1. Dinosaurs—Poetry 2. American poetry—Collections
ISBN 0-15-223495-0; 0-15-223496-9 (pa)
       LC 86-14818
"In this volume of 18 poems, Hopkins invites us to 'Reflect upon the dinosaur,/A giant that exists no more.' With poems by Myra Cohn Livingston, Lilian Moore, Valerie Worth and others, the collection explores fossils . . . and the museums that house [them]." Publ Wkly
"The collection will offer a spur to the imagination which more scientific material may lack. Minutely cross-hatched, black-and-white illustrations effectively recreate the nubbly, grainy skins of the mysterious, ponderous creatures and the swamps and savannas of their remote and shadowy world." Horn Book

The **entrance** place of wonders; poems of the Harlem Renaissance; edited by Daphne Muse; illustrated by Charlotte Riley-Webb. Abrams 2006 unp il $15.95 (3-5)   **811.008**
1. American poetry—African American authors—Collections 2. Harlem Renaissance
ISBN 0-8109-5997-6
"Twenty poems written during the Harlem Renaissance are perfectly paired with exuberant oil paintings. Familiar poets such as Countee Cullen, Langston Hughes, James Weldon Johnson, and Claude McKay are joined by less immediately recognized names such as Effie Lee Newsome, Dorothy Vena Johnson, and Gladys May Caseley-Hayford. Their collective work, firmly grounded in this exciting explosion of African-American culture, affirms the joy of life and of personal growth and discovery." SLJ

Extra innings; baseball poems; selected by Lee Bennett Hopkins; illustrated by Scott Medlock. Harcourt Brace Jovanovich 1993 40p il $16 (4 and up)   **811.008**
1. Baseball—Poetry 2. American poetry—Collections
ISBN 0-15-226833-2   LC 92-13013
"A collection of 19 poems about baseball, bolstered by vibrant oil-on-paper illustrations that are sure to attract attention, even from reluctant readers. Poets include May Swenson, Lillian Morrison, Ernest Thayer, and Lee Bennett Hopkins." Booklist

The **Fish** is me; bathtime rhymes; selected by Neil Philip; illustrated by Claire Henley. Clarion Bks. 2002 unp il $16 (k-2)   **811.008**
1. Baths—Poetry 2. American poetry—Collections
ISBN 0-618-15939-8   LC 2001-42094
A collection of poems about bathtime, by such authors as Aileen Fisher, Martin Gardner, Caryl Brahms, and John Drinkwater
"Like the Mother Goose rhymes, these will hook children with the sounds of the words and the rhythm of the action. . . . Big, brightly colored pictures on every page express the universal delight of not being clean as well as the comfort of 'steaming and dreaming' in the water." Booklist

For laughing out loud; poems to tickle your funnybone; selected by Jack Prelutsky; illustrated by Marjorie Priceman. Knopf 1991 84p il $17   **811.008**
1. American poetry—Collections 2. Humorous poetry
ISBN 0-394-82144-0   LC 90-33010
A collection of humorous poems by writers including Ellen Raskin, Karla Kuskin, Ogden Nash, and Arnold Lobel
"These nonsense verses by a wide variety of poets combine the domestic and the gross, deadpan and slapstick, with a lilting rhythm and satisfying rhyme. . . . The design is ebullient, often with several poems appearing on a double-page spread surrounded by wildly energetic wash-and-line illustrations." Booklist

Good books, good times! selected by Lee Bennett Hopkins; pictures by Harvey Stevenson. Harper & Row 1990 31p il lib bdg $16.89; pa $5.95 (1-3)   **811.008**
1. Books and reading—Poetry 2. American poetry—Collections
ISBN 0-06-022528-9 (lib bdg); 0-06-446222-6 (pa)
       LC 89-49108
"A Charlotte Zolotow book"
An anthology of poems about the joys of books and reading. Includes selections by David McCord, Karla Kuskin, Myra Cohn Livingston, and Jack Prelutsky
"The tone of the poems . . . ranges from exuberant to meditative. The collection will excite any parent, teacher, or librarian looking for brief, accessible poems on the subject of books and reading. Stevenson's lighthearted watercolors perfectly capture the jubilant mood of the book." Horn Book

Got geography! poems; selected by Lee Bennett Hopkins; pictures by Philip Stanton. Greenwillow Books 2006 32p il $15.99; lib bdg $16.89 (3-5)   **811.008**
1. Geography—Poetry
ISBN 0-06-055601-3; 0-06-055602-1 (lib bdg)
LC 2004-59662
"Sixteen selections from a variety of poets explore the curiosity piqued by maps, globes, the land we live on, and places far away. The gentle, often-moving verses cover a wide spectrum of ways to explore the Earth from mapping the world to examining its surface to finding one's place within it. . . . . The bright acrylic-and-watercolor illustrations bring energy to the pages and set the mood for each poem." SLJ

Grandad's tree; poems about families; compiled by Jill Bennett; illustrated by Julia Cairns. Barefoot Bks. (NY) 2003 32p il $16.99 (k-3)
811.008
1. Family life—Poetry 2. American poetry—Collections
ISBN 1-84148-541-1
"Included are poems that show the various sentiments of family life: humor, affection, sorrow, sibling rivalry, and intergenerational love. The collection is decidedly multicultural, featuring work from such notable contemporary children's poets as Arnold Adoff, Grace Nichols, Michael Rosen, and Eve Merriam, among others, as well as classics from Christina Rossetti and Carl Sandburg." Bull Cent Child Books
"Readers will find significant differences in subject matter, voice, and emotion. Each selection is enhanced by Cairns' appealing watercolor illustrations with their stylized shapes, rich colors, and pleasing patterns." Booklist

Halloween howls; holiday poetry; selected by Lee Bennett Hopkins; pictures by Stacey Schuett. 1st ed. HarperCollins Publishers 2005 24p il $15.99; lib bdg $16.89 (k-3)   **811.008**
1. Halloween—Poetry 2. American poetry—Collections
ISBN 0-06-008060-4; 0-06-008061-2 (lib bdg)
LC 2004-22513
"An I can read book"
A collection of 12 illustrated easy-to-read poems about Halloween
"The simple yet evocative language will delight beginning readers. . . . Schuett's illustrations show a friendly suburban neighborhood, feature a mix of multicultural characters, and reflect all of the fun of this special night." SLJ

Hanukkah lights; holiday poetry; selected by Lee Bennett Hopkins; pictures by Melanie Hall. HarperCollins 2004 28p il $15.99; lib bdg $16.89 (k-3)   **811.008**
1. Hanukkah—Poetry 2. American poetry—Collections
ISBN 0-06-008051-5; 0-06-008052-3 (lib bdg)
LC 2003-18901
"An I can read book"
A collection of poems that celebrate the activities and experiences of Hanukkah
"The poems are simple, evocative, and rhythmic with-

out lapsing into a singsong cadence. Hall's expressive artwork creates an appealing contemporary tone with vivid pastels and a smattering of collage." SLJ

Heart to heart; new poems inspired by twentieth-century American art; edited by Jan Greenberg. Abrams 2001 80p il map $19.95 (5 and up)   **811.008**
1. American poetry—Collections 2. American art 3. Art—20th century
ISBN 0-8109-4386-7   LC 99-462335
A compilation of poems by Americans writing about American art in the twentieth century, including such writers as Nancy Willard, Jane Yolen, and X. J. Kennedy
"From a tight diamante and pantoum to lyrical free verse, the range of poetic styles will speak to a wide age group. . . . Concluding with biographical notes on each poet and artist, this rich resource is an obvious choice for teachers, and the exciting interplay between art and the written word will encourage many readers to return again and again to the book." Booklist

Hello sunshine, good night moonlight; illustrated by John Wallace. Harry N. Abrams 2004 32p il $14.95 (k-3)   **811.008**
1. Poetry—Collections
ISBN 0-8109-4834-6   LC 2003-14243
First published 2003 in the United Kingdom
A collection of short poems highlighting different moments of the day by such poets as Eleanor Farjeon, Molly Bang, Robert Louis Stevenson, and Margaret Wise Brown.
"In most of the selections, the verses rhyme, the tone is light, and the point of view is childlike. . . . Wallace's cheerful watercolor illustrations look fresh and appealing." Booklist
Includes bibliographical references

Home to me; poems across America; selected by Lee Bennett Hopkins; illustrated by Stephen Alcorn. Orchard Bks. 2002 44p il $17.95 (3-5)
811.008
1. Home—Poetry 2. American poetry—Collections
ISBN 0-439-34096-9   LC 2001-36975
A collection of fifteen poems by various authors about home, whether it is on a boat, in a trailer park, on a reservation, or in a small town
"Imaginatively stylized illustrations—some earthy and concrete, some more fanciful—make fitting partners for the poetry, which gives children a nostalgic feel for the American experience." Booklist

Hoofbeats, claws, & rippled fins; creature poems; edited by Lee Bennett Hopkins; art by Stephen Alcorn. HarperCollins Pubs. 2002 30p il $15.95; lib bdg $16.89 (3-6)   **811.008**
1. Animals—Poetry 2. American poetry—Collections
ISBN 0-688-17942-8; 0-688-17943-6 (lib bdg)
LC 2001-24018
"Fourteen poems (four appearing for the first time here) from as many poets treat creatures from the lowly iguana to the lofty owl, the common cat to the exotic anteater." Bull Cent Child Books
These "poems accent the creatures' physicality, inspired by Stephen Alcorn's impressive, bold woodblock

Hoofbeats, claws, & rippled fins—*Continued*

prints. . . . Despite the verbal muscularity of many of the poems, it is Alcorn's powerful visual imagery that underpins and binds together this striking tribute to the grandeur of nature's creatures." Horn Book

Hot potato; mealtime rhymes; selected by Neil Philip; illustrated by Claire Henley. Clarion Books 2004 unp il $16 (k-2)　　　**811.008**

1. Food—Poetry 2. Poetry—Collections

ISBN 0-618-31554-3　　　　　LC 2003-14167

An anthology of short poems inspired by food, from soup to dessert, and written by such poets as Lewis Carroll, Douglas Florian, A.A. Milne, and Edward Lear.

"The acrylic paintings—in bright, almost garish hues and with the sugary, glossy texture of cake icing—illustrate the action and extend the giddy, playful sense in the words." Booklist

I am the darker brother; an anthology of modern poems by African Americans; edited and with an afterword by Arnold Adoff; drawings by Benny Andrews; introduction by Rudine Sims Bishop; foreword by Nikki Giovanni. rev ed. Simon & Schuster Bks. for Young Readers 1997 208p il $17; pa $5.99　　　**811.008**

1. American poetry—African American authors—Collections

ISBN 0-689-81241-8; 0-689-80869-0 (pa)

　　　　　　　　　　　　　　LC 97-144181

First published 1968

This anthology presents "the African-American experience through poetry that speaks for itself. . . . Because of the historical context of many of the poems, the book will be much in demand during Black History Month, but it should be used and treasured as part of the larger canon of literature to be enjoyed by all Americans at all times of the year. An indispensable addition to library collections." SLJ

I, too, sing America; three centuries of African American poetry; [selected and annotated by] Catherine Clinton; illustrated by Stephen Alcorn. Houghton Mifflin 1998 128p il $21 (6 and up)　　　**811.008**

1. African Americans—Poetry 2. American poetry—African American authors—Collections

ISBN 0-395-89599-5　　　　　LC 97-46137

"For each poet, Clinton provides a biography and a brief, insightful commentary on the poem(s) she has chosen, including a discussion of political as well as literary connections. Alcorn's dramatic, full-page, full-color illustrations opposite each poem evoke the quiltlike patterns and rhythmic figures of folk art." Booklist

If you ever meet a whale; poems selected by Myra Cohn Livingston; illustrated by Leonard Everett Fisher. Holiday House 1992 32p il $14.95 (3-5)　　　**811.008**

1. Whales—Poetry 2. American poetry—Collections

ISBN 0-8234-0940-6　　　　　LC 91-36265

A collection of poems about whales, by such authors as Jane Yolen, Theodore Roethke, and John Ciardi

"Fisher's majestic full-color paintings depict the underwater world in deep, cool hues shot with warmer or

whiter highlights. . . . The spacious design, a necessity for displaying such mammoth creatures, is a fine counterpoint to the pithy poems." Booklist

In daddy's arms I am tall; African Americans celebrating fathers; illustrated by Javaka Steptoe. Lee & Low Bks. 1997 unp il $15.95; pa $6.95　　　**811.008**

1. Fathers—Poetry 2. African Americans—Poetry 3. American poetry—Collections

ISBN 1-880000-31-8; 1-58430-016-7 (pa)

　　　　　　　　　　　　　　LC 97-7311

Coretta Scott King award for illustration, 1998

A collection of poems celebrating African-American fathers by Angela Johnson, E. Ethelbert Miller, Carole Boston Weatherford, and others

"Certain poems . . . elevate this collection above the mundane, but it is the illustrations that set this volume apart. Steptoe uses a variety of materials and techniques and art forms to enhance the language of the poems, including torn paper, collages, realia, paintings, and drawings." Horn Book

It rained all day that night; autographs, rhymes & inscriptions; compiled by Lillian Morrison; illustrated by Christy Hale. August House 2003 80p il $16.95; pa $9.95 (3-6)　　　**811.008**

1. American poetry—Collections

ISBN 0-87483-735-9; 0-87483-726-X (pa)

　　　　　　　　　　　　　　LC 2003-51987

An illustrated compilation of short poems and other inscriptions from autograph albums, arranged by such themes as friendship, school, and nonsense.

"Morrison has created a stunning collection of autograph verses. . . . Hale's ink-and-watercolor paintings dance across each page, extending the sentiment . . . implicit in each verse." SLJ

A kick in the head; selected by Paul B. Janeczko; illustrated by Chris Raschka. 1st ed. Candlewick Press 2005 61p il $17.99　　　**811.008**

1. Poetry—Collections

ISBN 0-7636-0662-6　　　　　LC 2004-48508

This collection offers examples of poetic forms "building from a couplet, tercet, and quatrain to the less familiar and more complex persona poem, ballad, and pantoum." SLJ

"Raschka's high-spirited, spare torn-paper-and-paint collages ingeniously broaden the poems' wide-ranging emotional tones. . . . Clear, very brief explanations of poetic forms . . . accompany each entry; a fine introduction and appended notes offer further information. . . . This is the introduction that will ignite enthusiasm." Booklist

Knock at a star; a child's introduction to poetry; [compiled by] X. J. Kennedy and Dorothy M. Kennedy; illustrated by Karen Lee Baker. rev ed. Little, Brown 1999 180p il $17.95; pa $10.95　　　**811.008**

1. American poetry—Collections 2. English poetry—Collections

ISBN 0-316-48436-9; 0-316-48800-3 (pa)

　　　　　　　　　　　　　　LC 98-21572

A revised and newly illustrated edition of the title first published 1982

Knock at a star—*Continued*

An anthology of mostly very short poems by standard, contemporary, and anonymous poets, intended to stimulate interest in reading and writing poetry

"Karen Lee Baker's small, shaded-pencil drawings capture the many moods of the verse." Booklist

Lives: poems about famous Americans; selected by Lee Bennett Hopkins; illustrated by Leslie Staub. HarperCollins Pubs. 1999 31p il $15.99; lib bdg $16.89 (4 and up) **811.008**
1. United States—Biography—Poetry 2. American poetry—Collections
ISBN 0-06-027767-X; 0-06-027768-8 (lib bdg)
LC 98-29851

A collection of poetic portraits of sixteen famous Americans from Paul Revere to Neil Armstrong, by such authors as Jane Yolen, Nikki Grimes, and X. J. Kennedy

"Hopkins's eloquent introduction praises the power of poetry. Concluding 'Notes on the Lives' give readers useful biographical information. Full-page portraits feature Staub's distinctive, flat, primitive style, and their backgrounds have details particular to the subject. . . . A winning combination of poems and illustrations." SLJ

Love to mamá; a tribute to mothers; edited by Pat Mora; illustrated by Paula Barragán. Lee & Low Bks. 2001 unp il $16.95 (3-6) **811.008**
1. Mothers—Poetry 2. Grandmothers—Poetry 3. Hispanic Americans—Poetry 4. American poetry—Collections
ISBN 1-58430-019-1
LC 00-47787
English and Spanish

"Thirteen poems by thirteen Latino authors (Francisco X. Alarcón, Mora herself, and others) provide a variety of views on mothers and mothering." Bull Cent Child Books

"The offerings . . . are narrative and impressionistic, speckled with Spanish, and by turns romantic, nostalgic, sentimental, heartbreaking, and humorous in mood. . . . The mixed-media illustrations by Ecuadorian artist Barragán are mural-like in scale and drenched with color. . . . The result is a visual feast of textures, patterns, and hues." Horn Book

Marvelous math; a book of poems; selected by Lee Bennett Hopkins; illustrated by Karen Barbour. Simon & Schuster Bks. for Young Readers 1997 31p il $17; pa $6.99 (4 and up) **811.008**
1. Mathematics—Poetry 2. American poetry—Collections
ISBN 0-689-80658-2; 0-689-84442-5 (pa)
LC 96-21597

Presents such poems as "Math Makes Me Feel Safe," "Fractions," "Pythagoras," and "Time Passes," by such writers as Janet S. Wong, Lee Bennett Hopkins, and Ilo Orleans

"Rhymed and open verse styles are represented, as are a variety of tones. . . . Barbour's lively illustrations dance and play around the poems. Her boldly outlined watercolor figures, often wearing ill-fitting hats, fill the pages with childlike whimsy." SLJ

More spice than sugar; poems about feisty females; compiled by Lillian Morrison; illustrated by Ann Boyajian. Houghton Mifflin 2001 80p il $15 (4 and up) **811.008**
1. Women—Poetry 2. American poetry—Collections
ISBN 0-618-06892-9
LC 00-31947

"Morrison's selections tell of real and imagined girls and women famous or nameless, but all true-to-life. . . . These poems are accessible, inspiring, and challenging. . . . Boyajian's black-and-white spot illustrations decorate every page without hampering the effect of the words." SLJ

My America; a poetry atlas of the United States; selected by Lee Bennett Hopkins; illustrated by Stephen Alcorn. Simon & Schuster Bks. for Young Readers 2000 83p il $21.95 (4 and up) **811.008**
1. United States—Poetry 2. American poetry—Collections
ISBN 0-689-81247-7
LC 98-47402

A collection of poems evocative of seven geographical regions of the United States, including the Northeast, Southeast, Great Lakes, Plains, Mountain, Southwest, and Pacific Coast States.

"Some poems are purposive, but the best . . . capture places and people in all their diversity. Stephen Alcorn's handsome, multi-textured pictures . . . avoid literal interpretation and capture the sweep of the land and the rhythm of the words." Booklist

My kingdom for a horse; an anthology of poems about horses; edited by Betty Ann Schwartz; illustrated by Alix Berenzy. Holt & Co. 2001 45p il $17.95 (2-4) **811.008**
1. Horses—Poetry 2. American poetry—Collections
ISBN 0-8050-6212-2
LC 00-40976

"The mostly brief, one-page poems cover everything from racing horses to police mounts. . . . The poets include Walt Whitman, Jack Prelutsky, Robert Frost, Christina Rossetti, Navajo Indians, and William Shakespeare. What really makes this anthology stand out are the impressionistic illustrations. Working in pastels and pencils, the artist has created soft-focus images with small dots and patches of color. . . . The pictures, both in color and black and white, are a perfect companion to the printed word and genuinely bring the selections to life." SLJ

Oh, no! Where are my pants? and other disasters; poems; edited by Lee Bennett Hopkins; pictures by Wolf Erlbruch. HarperCollins 2005 32p il $15.99; lib bdg $16.89 (2-4) **811.008**
1. American poetry—Collections
ISBN 0-688-17860-X; 0-688-17861-8 (lib bdg)
LC 2003-24272

"These 14 short poems all depict little moments of being human. . . . Embarrassment, shame, fear, chagrin: all of these feelings are so common in childhood that a collection of poems about them seems natural. Erlbruch . . . creates pictures that show this range of emotions beautifully. . . . A winner from a prolific poet/editor/compiler and a talented illustrator." SLJ

Opening days; sports poems; selected by Lee Bennett Hopkins; illustrated by Scott Medlock. Harcourt Brace & Co. 1996 37p il $16 (4 and up) **811.008**
1. Sports—Poetry 2. American poetry—Collections
ISBN 0-15-200270-7 LC 94-43364
"A collection of eighteen poems focusing on a variety of athletic endeavors includes Jane Yolen's 'Karate Kid,' Arnold Adoff's 'I Am the Running Girl,' and Gary Soto's 'Ode to Weight Lifting.' . . . Enhanced by oil paintings with lustrous color." Horn Book Guide

The **Oxford** book of children's verse in America; edited by Donald Hall. Oxford Univ. Press 1985 xxxviii, 319p $39.95; pa $19.95 **811.008**
1. American poetry—Collections
ISBN 0-19-503539-9; 0-19-506761-4 (pa)
LC 84-20755
"Hall's intention, expressed in the introduction, is to create an anthology of American poetry actually written for or adopted by children during a particular historical period. The emphasis is on authenticity rather than personal taste." SLJ
"A fine and carefully winnowed collection of American poetry is gathered in a book that will interest students of children's literature and young people who simply enjoy browsing." Horn Book

The **Oxford** illustrated book of American children's poems; edited by Donald Hall. Oxford Univ. Press 1998 96p il $19.95 **811.008**
1. American poetry—Collections
ISBN 0-19-512373-5 LC 99-34419
The poems in this anthology "date back to Native American cradle songs and an alphabet from a 1727 primer, and include contemporary works by Gary Soto, Sandra Cisneros and Janet S. Wong. The wide-ranging selections include both fresh and familiar poems, many of which are set off by period artwork, some from early children's magazines." Publ Wkly

The **Palm** of my heart; poetry by African American children; edited by Davida Adedjouma; illustrated by Gregory Christie; introduction by Lucille Clifton. Lee & Low Bks. 1996 unp il $15.95; pa $6.95 **811.008**
1. American poetry—African American authors—Collections 2. African Americans—Poetry 3. Children's writings
ISBN 1-880000-41-5; 1-880000-76-8 (pa)
LC 96-13426
A Coretta Scott King honor book for illustration, 1997
"Twenty short poems by African-American students are gathered in this picture-book-sized collection that celebrates being black. Stunning acrylic and colored-pencil illustrations enhance brief moodpieces. . . . Exaggerated and elongated human figures stand against blocks of color and suggested shapes, reflecting the energy and passion of the text." Bull Cent Child Books

Pass it on; African-American poetry for children; selected by Wade Hudson; illustrated by Floyd Cooper. Scholastic 1993 32p il $15.95 (k-3) **811.008**
1. American poetry—African American authors—Collections
ISBN 0-590-45770-5 LC 92-16034
An illustrated collection of poetry by such Afro-American poets as Langston Hughes, Nikki Giovanni, Eloise Greenfield, and Lucille Clifton
"Cooper's beautifully individualized oil-wash portraits express the energy, the yearning, and the heartfelt emotion of this fine anthology." Booklist

A **Pet** for me; poems; selected by Lee Bennett Hopkins; pictures by Jane Manning. HarperCollins Pubs. 2003 44p il $15.99; lib bdg $16.89 (k-3) **811.008**
1. Pets—Poetry 2. American poetry—Collections
ISBN 0-06-029111-7; 0-06-029112-5 (lib bdg)
LC 2002-8339
"An I can read book"
"A collection of 20 easy-to-read poems that celebrate pets of all shapes and sizes. Featuring such poets as J. Patrick Lewis, Tony Johnston, and Alice Schertle, among others, the selections sing the praises of turtles, ants, iguanas, and tarantulas along with more common animals like cats and dogs. Manning's cheerful watercolor illustrations suit both the format and the poetry perfectly." SLJ

The **Place** my words are looking for; what poets say about and through their work; selected by Paul B. Janeczko. Bradbury Press 1990 150p il $17.95 (4 and up) **811.008**
1. American poetry—Collections 2. Poetics
ISBN 0-02-747671-5 LC 89-39331
"More than forty contemporary poets are included: Eve Merriam, X. J. Kennedy, Felice Holman, Gary Soto, Mark Vinz, Karla Kuskin, and John Updike, among others. Their contributions vary widely in theme and mood and style, though the preponderance of the pieces are written in modern idiom and unrhymed meter. The accompanying comments frequently are as insightful and eloquent as the poems themselves." Horn Book

Pocket poems; selected by Bobbi Katz; illustrated by Marylin Hafner. Dutton Children's Books 2004 28p il $15.99 (k-3) **811.008**
1. American poetry—Collections
ISBN 0-525-47172-3 LC 2003-60667
A collection of short poems by such authors as Gwendolyn Brooks, Emily Dickinson, Emily George, Nikki Giovanni, Eve Merriam, and Charlotte Pomerantz.
This is a "child-friendly collection of short, bouncy poems. . . . The verses range from humorous . . . to introspective. . . . Hafner's whimsical watercolor-and-pen illustrations skillfully decorate the pages, visually enhancing the experience of each composition." SLJ

A **Poke** in the I; [selected by] Paul Janeczko; illustrated by Chris Raschka. Candlewick Press 2001 35p il $16.99; pa $7.99 (4 and up)

811.008

1. American poetry—Collections

ISBN 0-7636-0661-8; 0-7636-2376-8 (pa)

LC 00-33675

"Thirty concrete poems of all shapes and sizes are carefully laid on large white spreads, extended by Raschka's quirky watercolor and paper-collage illustrations. . . . Beautiful and playful, this title should find use in storytimes, in the classroom, and just for pleasure anywhere." SLJ

Read a rhyme, write a rhyme; poems selected by Jack Prelutsky; illustrated by Meilo So. Alfred A. Knopf 2005 23p il $16.95 (2-4)

811.008

1. American poetry—Collections 2. Poetics

ISBN 0-375-82286-0

LC 2004-26501

"Prelutsky designed this collection to jumpstart children's creative juices. Three short poems were chosen for each theme: dogs, food, birthdays, bugs, cows, friends, snow, turtles, rain, and self. He also includes a poemstart: an unfinished verse, along with advice and lists of rhyming words, so that readers can complete the poem on their own. The compiler displays a fine sense for lighthearted, kid-friendly poetry. . . . So's watercolor-and-ink illustrations add playfully jumbled perspectives." SLJ

Salting the ocean; 100 poems by young poets; selected by Naomi Shihab Nye; pictures by Ashley Bryan. Greenwillow Bks. 2000 111p il $16.99 (4 and up)

811.008

1. Children's writings 2. American poetry—Collections

ISBN 0-688-16193-6

LC 99-30590

"These poems are divided into four topics: The Self and the Inner World, Where We Live, Anybody's Family, and the Wide Imagination." Horn Book Guide

"Nye presents the exceptional work of students in grades 1 through 12. . . . Illustrated with Ashley Bryan's signature bright-hued, bold-lined paintings and multicultural imagery, the poems are varied in both sophistication and subject." Booklist

Includes bibliographical references

Soul looks back in wonder; [illustrated by] Tom Feelings. Dial Bks. 1993 unp il $16.99; pa $7.99 (4 and up)

811.008

1. American poetry—African American authors—Collections

ISBN 0-8037-1001-1; 0-14-056501-9 (pa)

LC 93-824

Coretta Scott King award for illustrations, 1994

Artwork and poems by such writers as Maya Angelou, Langston Hughes, and Askia Toure portray the creativity, strength, and beauty of their African American heritage

"This thoughtful collection of poetry is unique. . . . Feelings selected sketches done while he was in West Africa, South America, and at home in America. The original drawings were enhanced with colored pencils, colored papers, stencil cut-outs, and other techniques to give a collage effect. Marbled textures bring vibrancy to the work." Horn Book

Spectacular science; a book of poems; selected by Lee Bennett Hopkins; illustrated by Virginia Halstead. Simon & Schuster Bks. for Young Readers 1999 37p il $17 (2-4)

811.008

1. Science—Poetry 2. American poetry—Collections

ISBN 0-689-81283-3

LC 97-46695

A collection of poems about science by a variety of poets, including Carl Sandburg, Valerie Worth, and David McCord

"Enticing double-spread pictures, large, imaginative, and blooming with color, will work well with small groups; and Hopkins . . . has rounded up a satisfying variety of works." Booklist

Sports! sports! sports! a poetry collection; selected by Lee Bennett Hopkins; pictures by Brian Floca. HarperCollins Pubs. 1999 48p il lib bdg $14.89; pa $3.95 (k-2)

811.008

1. Sports—Poetry 2. American poetry—Collections

ISBN 0-06-027801-3 (lib bdg); 0-06-443713-2 (pa)

LC 98-8509

"An I can read book"

"Ice skating, baseball, and scuba diving are but three of the activities showcased in this collection of sports poetry, which includes work by editor Hopkins, Myra Cohn Livingston, Nikki Grimes, and others. The excitement, the sweet success, the thrill of competition are all here in the brief, lively poems, accompanied by equally lively cartoon-style artwork that bursts with action." Booklist

Stone bench in an empty park; selected by Paul Janeczko; with photographs by Henri Silberman. Orchard Bks. 2000 unp il $15.95 (4 and up)

811.008

1. City and town life—Poetry 2. Haiku 3. Poetry—Collections

ISBN 0-531-30259-8

LC 99-44282

"The poets, ranging from Buson to James Berry, capture urban sights and scenes in haiku that, while including city images of icicles, cats, and spring winds, also celebrate newsstands, car washes, traffic, and stickball." Horn Book

Silberman's black-and-white photographs "were taken in response to the selected haikus, and they offer visuals that are sometimes elucidation, sometimes illustration, and sometimes counterpoint." Bull Cent Child Books

The **Sun** in me; poems about the planet; compiled by Judith Nicholls; illustrated by Beth Krommes. Barefoot Bks. (NY) 2003 40p il $16.99 (2-4)

811.008

1. Nature poetry 2. Poetry—Collections

ISBN 1-84148-058-4

A collection of poems about nature

"Nicholls shows herself to be a master anthologist. . . . The selections range over time and cultures, but each one shines in its crisp vision of the natural world. . . . Krommes's extraordinary scratchboard-and-watercolor illustrations extend the mood of each poem." SLJ

The **sun,** the moon, and the stars; poems; collected, written, and illustrated by Nancy Elizabeth Wallace. Houghton Mifflin 2003 unp il $12 (k-2)   **811.008**

1. Stars—Poetry 2. Moon—Poetry 3. Sun—Poetry

ISBN 0-618-26353-5   LC 2002-151186

A collection of more than thirty poems, some by the compiler, others by Walter de la Mare, Russell Hoban, Frank Asch, Jane Taylor, and others

"Each colorful page is beautifully designed, and the well-executed cut-paper collages draw readers into the poems, enhancing the mood suggested by the words. . . . All of the selections are appealing, amusing, and gentle in tone." SLJ

This place I know; poems of comfort; poems selected by Georgia Heard; illustrations by eighteen renowned picture book artists. Candlewick Press 2006 c2002 46p il $12.99 (3-5)   **811.008**

1. American poetry—Collections

ISBN 0-7636-2875-1

A re-formatted edition of the title first published 2002

"Poems by Eloise Greenfield, Walt Whitman, Karla Kushkin, Wendell Berry, and others share space with full-page illustrations . . . to offer children consolation after the sorrow of September 11. Illustrators include Peter Sis, Elsa Kleven, and Yumi Heo." Booklist

"A multicultural dimension to the words and pictures gives this title universal application, as life throughout the world is celebrated." SLJ

Whisper and shout; poems to memorize; edited by Patrice Vecchione. Cricket Bks. 2002 120p $16.95 (4 and up)   **811.008**

1. American poetry—Collections

ISBN 0-8126-2656-7   LC 2002-591

A collection of poems on different subjects and in different styles, that lend themselves to memorization. Among the poets represented are Jack Prelutsky, Edward Lear, Ogden Nash, T. S. Eliot, Edna St. Vincent Millay, Christina Rossetti, and Lewis Carroll

"With a lengthy, enthusiastic introduction and a generous final section of resources and biographies, this anthology will get as much use in the classroom as with individual readers." Booklist

Includes bibliographical references

Wicked poems; edited by Roger McGough; illustrated by Neal Layton. Bloomsbury Children's Books 2004 208p il $15 (4 and up)   **811.008**

1. Good and evil—Poetry 2. Poetry—Collections

ISBN 1-58234-854-5   LC 2002-38551

"The 134 poems in this . . . collection focus on people exhibiting various degrees of wickedness. The book includes works from well-known poets . . . and children's authors such as Shel Silverstein, Eve Merriam, Myra Cohn Livingston, and Jack Prelutsky. . . . Childlike, black-and-white cartoons are laugh-out-loud funny. . . . A perfect choice for reading aloud as well as independent browsing." SLJ

Wings on the wind; bird poems; collected and illustrated by Kate Kiesler. Clarion Bks. 2002 40p il $14 (k-3)   **811.008**

1. Birds—Poetry 2. American poetry—Collections

ISBN 0-618-13333-X   LC 2001-37103

A collection of serious and humorous poems about birds by such authors as Eleanor Farjeon, Carl Sandburg, and Edward Lear

These poems "should delight young readers. . . . Kiesler's oil paintings offer vivid landscapes and bird closeups." Booklist

Words with wings; a treasury of African-American poetry and art; selected by Belinda Rochelle. HarperCollins Pubs. 2001 unp il lib bdg $16.99 (4 and up)   **811.008**

1. American poetry—African American authors—Collections 2. African Americans in art 3. African Americans—Poetry

ISBN 0-688-16415-3   LC 00-26864

"Amistad"

Pairs twenty works of art by African-American artists such as Horace Pippin and Jacob Lawrence with twenty poems by African-American poets such as Langston Hughes, Countee Cullen, and Lucille Clifton

"Most of the combinations are stunning. . . . Short biographical paragraphs on each poet and artist round out this moving presentation." SLJ

812   American drama

Bruchac, Joseph

Pushing up the sky: seven Native American plays for children; illustrated by Teresa Flavin. Dial Bks. for Young Readers 2000 94p il $18.99; pa $8.99 (3-5)   **812**

1. Native Americans—Drama

ISBN 0-8037-2168-4; 0-8037-2535-3 (pa)

LC 98-20483

Uses drama to tell seven different stories from Native American traditions including the Abenaki, Ojibway, Cherokee, Cheyenne, Snohomish, Tlingit, and Zuni

"The short, simple scripts are accessible to young, inexperienced actors. . . . Suggestions are given for easy-to-make costumes, props, and scenery. A variety of pen-and-ink drawings illustrate the plays, as well as one lively gouache illustration per selection." SLJ

Includes bibliographical references

Lohnes, Marilyn

Fractured fairy tales; puppet plays & patterns. UpstartBooks 2002 157p il pa $16.95   **812**

1. Puppets and puppet plays

ISBN 1-57950-073-0   LC 2002-12882

This "contains 10 puppet plays, all loosely based on well-known fairy tales, representing different themes, environments and holidays. . . . The book begins with an extensive discussion of the history of puppetry, types of puppets, manipulation of the puppets, voices and all that goes into staging a puppet show. Patterns for creating . . . puppetry and storytelling resources are also included." Publisher's note

Lohnes, Marilyn—*Continued*
"The style of the fractured tales is lively, irreverent, funny, and appealing. A solid addition to classroom and library collections for storytelling, puppetry, and creative dramatics." SLJ

Shepard, Aaron
Stories on stage; children's plays for reader's theater (or readers theatre), with 15 Play scripts from 15 authors. 2nd ed. Shepard 2005 160p pa $15   **812**
1. Readers' theater 2. Drama—Collections
ISBN 0-938497-22-7
First published 1993 in H. W. Wilson Co.
A collection of twenty-two plays adapted from folk tales, short stories, myths, and novels and intended for use in reader's theater programs
"With its mix of humor, fantasy, and multicultural tales . . . this book gives teachers both a fun and useful tool for bringing reading and literature to their students." SLJ

812.008   American drama--Collections

You're on!: seven plays in English and Spanish; selected by Lori Marie Carlson. Morrow Junior Bks. 1999 139p $17 (4 and up)
                                                          812.008
1. Hispanic Americans—Drama 2. American drama—Collections 3. Bilingual books—English-Spanish
ISBN 0-688-16237-1   LC 99-17222
This includes plays by Gary Soto, Pura Belpré, Denise Ruiz, Federico Garcia Lorca, Elena Castedo, Alfonsina Storni, and Oscar Hijuelos
"Each play is presented in both English and Spanish. Although the selections are short (anywhere from 3 to 10 pages), they vary greatly in complexity and style. . . . This unique resource will enrich any library's performing arts collection and be especially useful for those libraries serving Latino communities." Booklist

813.009   American fiction--History and criticism

The **wand** in the word; conversations with writers of fantasy; compiled and edited by Leonard S. Marcus. 1st ed. Candlewick Press 2006 202p il $19.99 (6 and up)   **813.009**
1. Fantasy fiction—History and criticism 2. Authors, American 3. Authors, English
ISBN 0-7636-2625-2   LC 2005046913
"Marcus presents interviews with 13 fantasy luminaries, including Lloyd Alexander, Susan Cooper, Nancy Farmer, Brian Jacques, Garth Nix, Tamora Pierce, and Philip Pullman. The writers' distinct personalities and career paths emerge, as do intriguing similarities. . . . . Each profile includes a black-and-white author's photo, a reading list, and a bit of ephemera, often a handwritten manuscript page. . . . . [This is] a rich resource that will be consulted as frequently by children's literature professionals as by genre fans themselves." Booklist

818   American miscellany

Brewer, Paul
You must be joking! lots of cool jokes; compiled and illustrated by Paul Brewer; foreword by Kathleen Krull. Cricket Books 2003 107p il $16.95 (3-6)   **818**
1. Jokes 2. Riddles 3. Wit and humor
ISBN 0-8126-2661-3   LC 2002-13926
A collection of over two hundred jokes and riddles, grouped by subject, plus tips on writing, learning, and telling jokes.
"The cartoon sketches scattered throughout the text add to the humor. A gem among joke books." SLJ

Sandburg, Carl
The Sandburg treasury; prose and poetry for young people; introduction by Paula Sandburg; illustrated by Paul Bacon. Harcourt Brace Jovanovich 1970 480p il pa $24 hardcover o.p. (5 and up)   **818**
ISBN 0-15-202678-9 (pa)
"Including, 'Rootabaga stories,' 'Early moon,' 'Wind song,' 'Abe Lincoln grows up,' 'Prairie-town boy.'" Title page
This volume brings together all of Sandburg's books for young people; his whimsical stories, two books of poetry, a version of his biography of Abraham Lincoln, and portions of his autobiography specially edited for children

820.8   English literature--Collections

Krull, Kathleen
A pot o' gold; a treasury of Irish stories, poetry, folklore, and (of course) blarney; selected and adapted by Kathleen Krull; illustrated by David McPhail. Hyperion Books For Children 2004 181p il map $19.99 (3-6)   **820.8**
1. Irish literature 2. Folklore—Ireland
ISBN 0-7868-0625-7   LC 2001-39058
A collection of stories, folklore, poetry, and songs from Ireland, including works by authors such as James Joyce and Oscar Wilde as well as classic myths, stories and poems about Finn McCool, fairies, leprechauns and saints Patrick and Bridget
"Children will love the limericks and the folk riddles. McPhail's signature full-color illustrations enliven the pages and add tremendous appeal for younger readers. The stunning cover and spine shimmer with the gold promised in the title and honor the intricate designs found in the Book of Kells. This is an eclectic grouping and an excellent introduction to the country's culture." SLJ
Includes bibliographical references

821 English poetry

Berry, James
A nest full of stars; poems; pictures by Ashley Bryan. Greenwillow Books 2004 95p il $15.99; lib bdg $16.89 (2-5)   **821**
1. Jamaican poetry 2. Caribbean region—Poetry
ISBN 0-06-052747-1; 0-06-052748-X (lib bdg)
                                        LC 2002-32176
A collection of poems reflecting Caribbean culture including "Old man called Arawak," "Woods whisperings," and "Not one weak day"
"All of the poems . . . will hold kids rapt with their sheer musicality—especially if read aloud. . . . Bryan provides bold, black-and-white illustrations that allow Berry's words plenty of room to resonate." Booklist

Browning, Robert
The Pied Piper of Hamelin; with illustrations by Kate Greenaway. Knopf 1993 104p il $12.95
                                        821
ISBN 0-679-42812-7   LC 93-11265
Also available in paperback from Dover Publs.
A reissue of the edition first published 1880 in the United Kingdom; first United States edition 1882 by Lyman & Curtis
The Pied Piper pipes the village free of rats, and when the villagers refuse to pay him for the service he exacts a terrible revenge
Includes bibliographical references

Carroll, Lewis
Jabberwocky; illustrated by Joel Stewart. Candlewick Press 2003 unp il $15.99 (k-3)
                                        821
1. Nonsense verses
ISBN 0-7636-2018-1   LC 2002-71425
An illustrated version of the classic nonsense poem from "Through the Looking Glass"
"Joel Stewart's version succeeds very well, indeed; his imagery suggests the time period in which 'Jabberwocky' was written and his illustrations have the manic fluidity of Carroll's own accomplished art. . . . The pictures depict a funny, childlike world that little ones can easily enter." Booklist

Cohen, Barbara
Canterbury tales; [by] Geoffrey Chaucer; selected, translated, and adapted by Barbara Cohen; illustrated by Trina Schart Hyman. Lothrop, Lee & Shepard Bks. 1988 87p il $24.99 (4 and up)   **821**
1. Chaucer, Geoffrey, d. 1400—Adaptations
ISBN 0-688-06201-6   LC 86-21045
Contents: The nun's priest's tale; The pardoner's tale; The wife of Bath's tale; The franklin's tale
"Cohen's evident love and respect for Chaucer's writing keep her close to the text. Her writing retains the flavor of the times and the spirit of Chaucer's words while her prose retelling, enriched by Hyman's lively full-color paintings, enhances the book's appeal to young people. . . . An excellent introduction to *The Canterbury Tales* for young readers." Booklist

Dahl, Roald
Vile verses. Viking 2005 191p il $25 (4-6)
                                        821
1. Humorous poetry
ISBN 0-670-06042-9
A collection of Roald Dahl's poems, many previously published in his novels, such as *Charlie and the Chocolate Factory* and *James and the, Giant Peach*, and illustrated by various artists such as Tony Ross, Lane Smith, Quentin Blake, and Chris Riddle
"This vivacious addition to poetry collections will amuse a broad audience." SLJ

Hirsch, Robin
F E G: ridiculous stupid poems for intelligent children; with the assistance of Benjamin Joshua Jaglom Hirsch and a critical introduction by Alexander Max Jaglom Hirsch; illustrated by Ha. Little, Brown 2002 48p il $15.95 (5 and up)
                                        821
1. Humorous poetry
ISBN 0-316-36344-8   LC 00-64965
"Megan Tingley books"
Title appears with "stupid" crossed out
This "collection celebrates wordplay, including acrostics, palindromes, and spoonerisms, within the confines of various poetic forms. Lengthy footnotes—usually meandering, sometimes goofy—help elucidate the clever poetry." Horn Book Guide
Includes glossary

Howitt, Mary Botham
The spider and the fly; based on the poem by Mary Howitt; with illustrations by Tony DiTerlizzi. Simon & Schuster Bks. for Young Readers 2002 unp il $16.95 (k-3)   **821**
1. Spiders—Poetry 2. Flies—Poetry
ISBN 0-689-85289-4   LC 2002-5760
An illustrated version of the well-known poem about a wily spider who preys on the vanity and innocence of a little fly
"Rendered in black-and-white gouache and pencil, then reproduced in silver-and-black duotone, the paintings have a spooky quality perfectly suited to retelling this melancholy tale. Ms. Fly, with her whimsical flower umbrella and Roaring '20s attire, captures the flavor of an old-time Hollywood heroine." SLJ

Hughes, Shirley
Rhymes for Annie Rose; [by] Shirley Hughes. 1st Candlewick Press ed. Candlewick Press 2006 c1995 unp il $16.99 (k-2)   **821**
ISBN 0-7636-2940-5   LC 2005054286
A reissue of the title first published 1995 by Lothrop Lee
A collection of more than twenty poems about young Annie Rose and the daily activities of a child
"Annie Rose and her brother, Alfie, play and dream and discover the world. With wonderful domestic detail, Hughes' line-and-watercolor pictures capture the toddler's joy and mischief, fear and affection. . . . The words have a physicalness and a beat that children will love." Booklist

Hughes, Ted

The cat and the cuckoo; illustrated by Flora McDonnell. Roaring Brook Press 2003 unp il $15.95; lib bdg $22.90 (3-6)   **821**
1. Animals—Poetry
ISBN 0-7613-1548-9; 0-7613-2572-7 (lib bdg)
LC 2001-48296
First published 1987 in the United Kingdom
Illustrated poems about an otter, a dragonfly, a cow, a robin, and many other creatures of the land, sea, and air
"With physical immediacy, the 28 poems in this children's collection . . . bring readers and listeners close to each animal's sounds and movements. . . . McDonnell's black-and-white wash illustrations . . . capture the silliness as well as realism and mystery." Booklist

Lear, Edward

The complete verse and other nonsense; compiled and edited with an introduction and notes by Vivien Noakes. Penguin Bks. 2002 566p il pa $18   **821**
ISBN 0-14-200227-5   LC 2002-28998
This volume "presents all of Lear's verse and other nonsense writings, including stories, letters, and illustrated alphabets, as well as previously unpublished material, line drawings, and . . . [an] introduction by scholar Vivien Noakes." Publisher's note
Includes bibliographical references

Edward Lear; edited by Edward Mendelson; illustrated by Laura Huliska-Beith. Sterling 2002 c2001 48p il (Poetry for young people) $14.95 (4 and up)   **821**
1. Nonsense verses 2. Limericks
ISBN 0-8069-3077-2   LC 2001-20112
"In an analytical introduction, Mendelson looks at Lear's serious and silly sides before selecting 15 limericks and 18 longer poems, all of which feature odd creatures adapting to, or reveling in, their differences. Huliska-Beit's smiling, rubber-limbed figures dance through vertiginously tilted, brightly colored minimalist settings. . . . Thought- and laugh-provoking." Booklist

The owl and the pussycat   **821**
1. Nonsense verses
LC 84-24897
Some editions are:
HarperCollins Pubs. $15.95 Illustrated by James Marshall (ISBN 0-06-205010-9)
Putnam $14.95; pa $6.95 Illustrated by Jan Brett (ISBN 0-399-21925-0; 0-698-11367-5)
First published 1871
After a courtship voyage of a year and a day, Owl and Pussy finally buy a ring from Piggy and are blissfully wed

The pelican chorus and other nonsense; illustrated by Fred Marcellino. HarperCollins Pubs. 1995 unp il $14.95   **821**
1. Nonsense verses
ISBN 0-06-205062-1   LC 94-78570
"Michael di Capua books"

"Three great nonsense rhymes by the inimitable Edward Lear—'The Pelican Chorus,' 'The Owl and the Pussycat,' and 'he New Vestments'—are presented with wildly comic illustrations, uniquely suited to their era and content. . . . Fred Marcellino's bouncy, humorous, and expressive illustrations enlarge and expand the narratives of all three verses. A great treat for lovers of Lear." Horn Book

Milne, A. A. (Alan Alexander)

Now we are six; with decorations by Ernest H. Shepard. Dutton 1961 c1927 104p il $22.99; pa $4.99 (k-3)   **821**
ISBN 0-525-44960-4; 0-14-0361234-3 (pa)
First published 1927. "Reprinted September 1961 in this completely new format designed by Warren Chappell." Verso of title page
"The boy or girl who has liked 'When were were very young' and 'Winnie-the-Pooh' will enjoy reading about Alexander Beetle who was mistaken for a match, the knight whose armor didn't squeak, and the old sailor who had so many things which he wanted to do. There are other entertaining poems, also, and many pictures as delightful as the verses." Pittsburgh

When we were very young; with decorations by Ernest H. Shepard. Dutton 1961 c1924 102p il $10.99; pa $4.99 (k-3)   **821**
ISBN 0-525-44445-9; 0-14-036123-5 (pa)
First published 1924. "Reprinted September 1961 in this completely new format designed by Warren Chappell." Verso of title page
Verse "written for Milne's small son Christopher Robin, which for its bubbling nonsense, its whimsy, and the unexpected surprises of its rhymes and rhythms, furnishes immeasurable joy to children." Right Book for the Right Child
"Mr. Milne's gay jingles have found a worthy accompaniment in the charming illustrations of Mr. Shepard." Saturday Rev

Simon, Francesca

Toddler time; illustrated by Susan Winter. Orchard Bks. 2000 36p il $15.95 (k-1)   **821**
ISBN 0-531-30251-2   LC 99-32942
"This collection of nursery-type rhymes and poems is about everyday activities and occurrences. . . . The verses . . . are action packed and colorfully illustrated. The watercolor paintings reflect the joy of discovery, natural curiosity, and energy that toddlers possess." SLJ

Stevenson, Robert Louis

A child's garden of verses il (k-4)   **821**
1. Scottish poetry
Some editions are:
Abrams $17.95 Illustrated by Joanna Isles (ISBN 0-8109-3196-6; LC 93-74829)
Knopf (Everyman's library children's classics) $14.95 Illustrated by Charles Robinson (ISBN 0-679-41799-0; LC 92-53175)
Simon & Schuster $18.95 Illustrated by Tasha Tudor (ISBN 0-689-823802-7)

Stevenson, Robert Louis—*Continued*
"Verses known and loved by one generation after another. Among the simpler ones for pre-school children are: Rain; At the Seaside; and Singing." Right Book for the Right Child

821.008   English poetry--Collections

Ghost poems; edited by Daisy Wallace; illustrated by Tomie de Paola. Holiday House 1979 30p il lib bdg $14.95; pa $4.95 (1-4)   **821.008**
1. Ghosts—Poetry 2. English poetry—Collections 3. American poetry—Collections
ISBN 0-8234-0344-0 (lib bdg); 0-8234-0849-3 (pa)
LC 78-11028
"Mostly inducing titters rather than terrors—is this collection by rhymsters with an active sense of the absurd. . . . Among the 17 entertainers are the old Scottish prayers ('Ghosties and Ghoulies'), two American Indian songs and contributions from conjurers of the past and present: Nancy Willard, Lilian Moore. X. J. Kennedy, Jack Prelutsky, et al., as well as anonymous selections from legends." Publ Wkly
"Illustrated with a quick and fearsome flourish by Tomie de Paola. . . . Here are wonderful poems to frighten young children with—but not really." N Y Times Book Rev

The **Kingfisher** book of family poems; selected by Belinda Hollyer; illustrated by Holly Swain. Kingfisher (NY) 2003 223p il $18.95 (3-6)
821.008
1. Family life—Poetry 2. Poetry—Collections
ISBN 0-7534-5557-9   LC 2002-34032
A collection of poetry that captures many aspects of family relationships and interactions by such poets as Arnold Adoff, Ogden Nash, Janet S. Wong, James Berry, Lucille Clifton, Jack Prelutsky, Lewis Carroll, Eloise Greenfield, Shel Silverstein, and Langston Hughes
"Loving, angry, raucous, tender: the 159 poems in this lively anthology are about all kinds of families and all kinds of feelings. . . . Hollyer has brought together many of the best children's poets." Booklist

The **Kingfisher** book of funny poems; selected by Roger McGough; illustrated by Caroline Holden. Kingfisher (NY) 2002 256p il $18.95 (4 and up)
821.008
1. Humorous poetry 2. English poetry—Collections 3. American poetry—Collections
ISBN 0-7534-5480-7   LC 2001-38942
A collection of over 200 poems, limericks, and verses from such authors as Emily Dickinson, Lewis Carroll, and Shel Silverstein
"This collection is chock-full of wacky, witty, and whimsical poems that will hook readers from the first stanza to the last. . . . What really brings out the humor are the equally zany black-and-white drawings that appear on almost every page." SLJ

The **Oxford** book of children's verse. Oxford Univ. Press 1973 xxxi, 407p pa $15.85 hardcover o.p.   **821.008**
1. English poetry—Collections 2. American poetry—Collections
ISBN 0-19-282349-3 (pa)
Arranged chronologically, these 332 selections from British and American children's poetry include works by such poets as Chaucer, Charles and Mary Lamb, Kipling, Farjeon, Milne, Eliot and Nash

Poems for the very young; selected by Michael Rosen; illustrated by Bob Graham. Kingfisher (NY) 1993 77p il $18.95; pa $9.95 (k-3)
821.008
1. Poetry—Collections
ISBN 1-85697-908-3; 0-7534-5816-0 (pa)
LC 92-45574
This "is a mix of traditional rhymes, verse by poets, and pieces written by children that ranges over time and cultures, united by a sure sense of the richness of well-chosen words. The obvious care behind each poem's selection is matched by Graham's humorous watercolor cartoons that extend, interpret, and celebrate their subjects." SLJ

Poetry by heart; a child's book of poems to remember; foreword by Andrew Motion; compiled by Liz Attenborough. Scholastic 2001 124p il $17.95 (3-5)   **821.008**
1. Poetry—Collections
ISBN 0-439-29657-9
"The Chicken House"
This anthology includes more than 100 poems by such poets as Beatrice Schenk de Regniers, William Blake, Emily Dickinson, Roald Dahl, Edward Lear, and Judith Viorst, each illustrated by a different artist
"The poems in this large-size anthology are great for chanting, reading aloud, and reciting silently." Booklist

The **Random** House book of poetry for children; selected and introduced by Jack Prelutsky; illustrated by Arnold Lobel. Random House 1983 248p il $19.95; lib bdg $21.99
821.008
1. American poetry—Collections 2. English poetry—Collections
ISBN 0-394-85010-6; 0-394-95010-0 (lib bdg)
LC 83-2990
Opening poems for each section especially written for this anthology by Jack Prelutsky
In this anthology emphasis "is placed on humor and light verse; but serious and thoughtful poems are also included. . . . Approximately two thirds of the selections were written within the past forty years—the splendid contributions of such writers as John Ciardi, Aileen Fisher, Dennis Lee, Myra Cohn Livingston, David McCord, Eve Merriam, and Lilian Moore. [There are] . . . samplings of earlier poets from Shakespeare and Blake to Emily Dickinson and Walter de la Mare." Horn Book

Read-aloud rhymes for the very young; selected by Jack Prelutsky; illustrated by Marc Brown; with an introduction by Jim Trelease. Knopf 1986 98p il $19.95; lib bdg $21.99 (k-2)

821.008

1. English poetry—Collections 2. American poetry—Collections 3. Nursery rhymes

ISBN 0-394-87218-5; 0-394-97218-X (lib bdg)

LC 86-7147

"Prelutsky has selected and combined joyous, sensitive poems . . . by such traditional poets as Dorothy Aldis and A. A. Milne, as well as by more contemporary poets such as Karla Kuskin, Dennis Lee, and Prelutsky himself. All are lively, rhythmic poems that young children will enjoy. . . . Brown's bright pastel illustrations effectively use framing, action, and cheerful creatures to echo the light tone of the book. The poems are arranged with others of the same topic and include popular concerns of small children such as animals, bath time, dragons, and play. Teachers and librarians will appreciate poems about seasons, months, holidays, and special events that can be easily incorporated into story hours and classroom life." SLJ

Talking like the rain; a first book of poems; selected by X. J. Kennedy and Dorothy Kennedy; illustrated by Jane Dyer. Little, Brown 1992 96p il $19.95 (k-3)

821.008

1. English poetry—Collections 2. American poetry—Collections

ISBN 0-316-48889-5

LC 89-13504

This is an "assortment of classic and contemporary verse for children. From Robert Louis Stevenson to Dennis Lee, with samples of most of the best children's poets ranging among the 123 selections, there's a sense of rolling rhyme that carries the reader from one singing page to another. And there are many pages, each designed to surround the poetry or set it into neat, discreet illustrations that project graphic images from verbal ones. . . . In selection, scope, and visual format, this is likely to be a volume many times revisited." Bull Cent Child Books

822.3 William Shakespeare

Aliki

William Shakespeare & the Globe; written & illustrated by Aliki. HarperCollins Pubs. 1999 48p il $15.95; lib bdg $15.89; pa $6.99 (4 and up)

822.3

1. Shakespeare, William, 1564-1616 2. Globe Theatre (London, England) 3. Shakespeare's Globe (London, England)

ISBN 0-06-027820-X; 0-06-027821-8 (lib bdg); 0-06-443722-1 (pa)

LC 98-7903

The "text describes Shakespeare's life, the Elizabethan world and entertainments, and the ups and downs of the theatrical industry . . . including tidbits such as the Burbage brothers' piece-by-piece theft of the original Globe Theatre. A fast-forward to the twentieth century then treats Sam Wanamaker's dream of making the Globe rise again." Bull Cent Child Books

"A logically organized and engaging text, plenty of detailed illustrations with informative captions, and a clean design provide a fine introduction to both bard and theater." Horn Book Guide

Chrisp, Peter

Welcome to the Globe; the story of Shakespeare's theater; written by Peter Chrisp. Dorling Kindersley 2000 48p il $12.95; pa $3.95 (1-3)

822.3

1. Shakespeare, William, 1564-1616 2. Globe Theatre (London, England)

ISBN 0-7894-6641-4; 0-7894-6640-6 (pa)

LC 00-21931

"Dorling Kindersley readers"

Various characters, including a waterman, an actor, a gallant, and an apple seller, from Shakespeare's London describe the Globe Theatre from their own perspective

"Illustrations and photographs are excellent, showing details of the building and the people." SLJ

Includes glossary

Coville, Bruce

William Shakespeare's A midsummer night's dream; retold by Bruce Coville; pictures by Dennis Nolan. Dial Bks. 1996 unp il $17.95; pa $7.99 (5 and up)

822.3

1. Shakespeare, William, 1564-1616—Adaptations

ISBN 0-8037-1784-9; 0-14-250168-9 (pa)

LC 94-12600

A simplified prose retelling of Shakespeare's play about the strange events that take place in a forest inhabited by fairies who magically transform the romantic fate of two young couples

"Coville introduces the story and also conveys something of the poetry and drama. Nolan's framed graphite and watercolor paintings express the dreaminess and absurdity of the play, and the pictures have a theatrical flair." Booklist

William Shakespeare's Hamlet; retold by Bruce Coville; illustrated by Leonid Gore. Dial Bks. 2004 unp il $16.99 (5 and up)

822.3

1. Shakespeare, William, 1564-1616—Adaptations

ISBN 0-8037-2708-9

LC 2002-13743

Retells, in simplified prose, William Shakespeare's play about a prince of Denmark who seeks revenge for his father's murder

"Not only is the text incredibly faithful to the original, but the language that surrounds the quoted dialogue is also amazingly rich. . . . Done predominantly in shades of blue and orange, Gore's acrylic-and-pastel artwork underscores the sharp contrast between the protagonist's periods of brooding and his angry outbursts." SLJ

William Shakespeare's Macbeth; retold by Bruce Coville; pictures by Gary Kelley. Dial Bks. 1997 unp il $18 hardcover o.p. (5 and up)

822.3

1. Shakespeare, William, 1564-1616—Adaptations

ISBN 0-8037-1899-3

LC 97-7582

A simplified prose retelling of Shakespeare's play about a man who kills his king after hearing the prophesies of three witches

Coville, Bruce—*Continued*

"Kelley's framed pastel illustrations of the hideous hags will hold kids from the start, and Coville's dramatic narrative will keep them reading. . . . Words and pictures are true to the dark, brooding spirit of the play." Booklist

William Shakespeare's Romeo and Juliet; retold by Bruce Coville; pictures by Dennis Nolan. Dial Bks. 1999 unp il $16.99 (5 and up)

822.3

1. Shakespeare, William, 1564-1616—Adaptations
ISBN 0-8037-2462-4   LC 98-36178
A simplified prose retelling of Shakespeare's play about two young people who defy their warring families' prejudices and dare to fall in love

"Coville's treatment is generally faithful to the original and is nicely enhanced by Dennis Nolan's lushly romantic illustrations. . . . This is an accessible and enticing introduction to one of Shakespeare's most popular works." Booklist

William Shakespeare's Twelfth night; retold by Bruce Coville; illustrated by Tim Raglin. Dial Bks. 2003 unp il $16.99 (5 and up)   **822.3**
1. Shakespeare, William, 1564-1616—Adaptations
ISBN 0-8037-2318-0   LC 2001-28252
This "provides a short, prose version of Shakespeare's *Twelfth Night*. . . . Though simplified, the story is intact and bits of the original language are preserved. Large-scale ink drawings, warmed with tints of color and shaded with cross-hatching, clearly depict the action." Booklist

Lamb, Charles

Tales from Shakespeare; by Charles & Mary Lamb (5 and up)   **822.3**
1. Shakespeare, William, 1564-1616—Adaptations
Hardcover and paperback editions available from various publishers
First published 1807
A now classic collection of twenty plays by Shakespeare adapted as prose stories—the comedies by Mary Lamb, the tragedies by Charles Lamb

"The *Tales* were the first version of 'Shakespeare' to be published specifically for children. They are written in a clear, vigorous style, not often encumbered by the attempt to make the language resemble that of the original. A lot is left out. . . . But the literary quality of the *Tales* makes them outshine almost every other English children's book of this period, and they proved an immediate and lasting success." Oxford Companion to Child Lit

Nettleton, Pamela Hill

William Shakespeare; playwright and poet; by Pamela Hill Nettleton. Compass Point Books 2005 112p il map (Signature lives) $30.60 (5 and up)
822.3
1. Shakespeare, William, 1564-1616
ISBN 0-7565-0816-9   LC 2004-23081
Contents: All the world's a stage; Shakespeare's time; Shakespeare as a boy; At school and beyond; Shakespeare in love; Shakespeare in London; Shakespeare's poems; Success as a playwrite; At the peak of his powers; The final years

Profiles the life and work of William Shakespeare

"This biography is one of the best available for younger students. Nettleton supplements what little is actually known about the bard's life with detailed and accurate information about everyday life in England during the period, the theater, and publishing practices of the time. The text is enhanced by full-color illustrations and black-and-white reproductions." SLJ
Includes bibliographical references

Packer, Tina

Tales from Shakespeare; retold by Tina Packer; illustrated by Gail de Marcken . . . [et al.] Scholastic Press 2004 192p il $24.95 (5 and up)
822.3
1. Shakespeare, William, 1564-1616—Adaptations
ISBN 0-439-32107-7   LC 2003-42710
Tina Packer retells ten of Shakespeare's plays. The stories are illustrated by various artists: Macbeth by Barry Moser, The Tempest by Mark Teague, Othello by Kadir Nelson, Twelfth Night by Chesley McLaren, Romeo and Juliet by David Shannon, Much Ado About Nothing by Mary GrandPre, King Lear by Leo and Diane Dillon, As You Like It by Barbara McClintock, A Midsummer Night's Dream by Gail De Marcken, and Hamlet by P.J. Lynch.

This is "a treasure trove of well-told tales. In these adaptations, Packer captures the essence of the playwright's words and ideas, placing them in concise and clearly told stories. . . . Each illustrator sets the appropriate tone for and conveys the mood of the tale, and the breadth of artistic interpretations gives the book appeal to a wide audience." SLJ

Rosen, Michael

Shakespeare; his work and his world; illustrated by Robert Ingpen. Candlewick Press 2001 96p il $19.99 (6 and up)   **822.3**
1. Shakespeare, William, 1564-1616
ISBN 0-7636-1568-4   LC 00-66689
"The volume begins with plot teasers from the plays and progresses through an explanation of Shakespeare's time and the locations important to his life and works. . . . There is a plethora of historical information, as well as an explanation of the types of theaters and plays common at the time." Book Rep

"In exceptionally fresh and vivid terms, the author plies readers with abundant, accurate information. . . . The copious and engaging pencil-and-watercolor illustrations have the burnished look of old pictures and are as glorious as the text." SLJ
Includes bibliographical references

Stanley, Diane

Bard of Avon: the story of William Shakespeare; by Diane Stanley and Peter Vennema; illustrated by Diane Stanley. Morrow Junior Bks. 1992 unp il $16.99; lib bdg $17.89; pa $6.99 (4 and up)   **822.3**
1. Shakespeare, William, 1564-1616
ISBN 0-688-09108-3; 0-688-09109-1 (lib bdg); 0-688-16294-0 (pa)
                    LC 90-46564

Stanley, Diane—*Continued*

A brief biography of the world's most famous playwright, using only historically correct information

"A remarkably rounded picture of Shakespeare's life and the period in which he lived is presented . . . together with a thoughtful attempt to relate circumstances in his personal life to the content of his plays. . . . The text is splendidly supported by the illustrations, which are stylized, yet recognizable, and present a clear view of life in the late sixteenth century. A discerning, knowledgeable biography, rising far above the ordinary." Horn Book

Includes bibliographical references

823.009 English fiction--History and criticism

Colbert, David

The magical worlds of Harry Potter; a treasury of myths, legends, and fascinating facts. Berkeley Hills Bks. 2002 c2001 209p il pa $14 (5 and up)
823.009

1. Rowling, J. K.—Characters 2. Fantasy fiction—History and criticism

ISBN 0-425-19891-X   LC 2002-20857

First published 2001 in the United Kingdom

"The 53 entries, most of them two to six pages in length, are arranged in alphabetical order by a highlighted keyword. For example, words such as 'Alchemy,' 'Animagus,' 'Grindylows,' 'Voldemort,' and 'wizards' are defined, traced to their usage in other tales, and given an expanded description. . . . Long after the enthusiasm for Harry and friends has abated, this small volume will serve as a resource to answer questions that may result from reading other stories in the genre." SLJ

Includes bibliographical references

Cooling, Wendy

D is for Dahl; a gloriumptious A-Z guide to the world of Roald Dahl; illustrations by Quentin Blake; compiled by Wendy Cooling. Viking 2005 149p il $15.99 (4 and up)   **823.009**

1. Dahl, Roald 2. Authors, English

ISBN 0-670-06023-2

This is an alphabetically arranged collection of facts about the life and work of the popular author of children's books.

"This dictionary-of-sorts is entertaining, insightful, and of particular interest to Dahl's fans. . . . The writing is clear, wicked, and fun. An occasional black-and-white photograph complements Blake's illustrations." SLJ

Kronzek, Allan Zola

The sorcerer's companion; a guide to the magical world of Harry Potter; [by] Allan Zola Kronzek and Elizabeth Kronzek. Broadway Bks. 2001 286p il pa $15.95 (4 and up)
823.009

1. Rowling, J. K.—Characters 2. Fantasy fiction—History and criticism

ISBN 0-7679-1944-0   LC 2001-35659

Explores the true history, folklore, and mythology behind the magical practices, creatures and personalities that appear in J. K. Rowling's Harry Potter books

"The material is interesting and informative, easy to read, and fairly wide-ranging." SLJ

Includes bibliographical references

828 English miscellany

Thomas, Dylan

A child's Christmas in Wales   **828**

1. Christmas—Wales

Some editions are:

Candlewick Press $17.99 illustrated by Chris Raschka (ISBN 0-7636-2161-7)

Godine $16.95 illustrated by Edward Ardizzone (ISBN 0-8792-3339-7)

Holiday House $16.95 illustrated by Trina Schart Hyman (ISBN 0-8234-0565-6)

First published 1954

A portrait of Christmas Day in a small Welsh town and of the author's childhood there

"The language is enchanting and the poetry shines with an unearthly radiance." NY Times Book Rev

841 French poetry

Cendrars, Blaise

Shadow; translated and illustrated by Marcia Brown from the French of Blaise Cendrars. Scribner 1982 unp il $17; pa $6.99 (1-3)
841

1. French poetry 2. Africa—Poetry 3. Shades and shadows—Poetry

ISBN 0-684-17226-7; 0-689-71875-6 (pa)

LC 81-9424

Awarded the Caldecott Medal, 1983

Original text first published in France

This is the French poet's "version of a West African folk tale about a spirit that is at once elusive and multiform." N Y Times Book Rev

"Inspired by the exotic atmosphere and the dramatic possibilities of the text, Brown has choreographed a sequence of almost theatrical illustrations, placing human and animal figures—and their shadows—against brilliant, contrasting, always changing settings. Resplendent—yet controlled—in color, texture, and form, the work is an impressive, sophisticated example of the art of the picture book." Horn Book

861 Spanish poetry

Argueta, Jorge

A movie in my pillow; story by Jorge Argueta; illustrations by Elizabeth Gómez. Children's Bk. Press 2001 31p il $15.95 (3-6)   **861**

1. Bilingual books—English-Spanish 2. Immigrants—Poetry 3. Hispanic Americans—Poetry

ISBN 0-89239-165-0   LC 00-55582

Text and title page in English and Spanish

Argueta, Jorge—*Continued*

These poems recount Argueta's "childhood experiences of being an immigrant and having dual homelands, with roots in El Salvador and a new life in San Francisco's Mission District." Booklist

"Gómez's rich and bright paintings fill every spread with . . . joy and literal humor. . . . An excellent addition to any poetry collection." SLJ

861.008   Spanish poetry--Collections

Messengers of rain and other poems from Latin America; edited by Claudia M. Lee; illustrated by Rafael Yockteng; translations by Andrew C. Leone . . . [et al.] Douglas & McIntyre 2002 80p il $18.95 (3-6)   **861.008**
1. Spanish poetry—Collections
ISBN 0-88899-470-2

"A Groundwood book"

"The 64 poems from 19 countries include 20th-century classics and more recent selections, and represent women, indigenous writers, and widely published names such as Octavio Paz and Rafael Pombo. . . . Yockteng's fanciful watercolors head each section with a full-page spread, and spots brighten the pages between, here and there, without distracting from the poems." SLJ

883   Classical Greek epic poetry and fiction

Osborne, Mary Pope

The gray-eyed goddess; with artwork by Troy Howell. Hyperion Bks. for Children 2003 120p il (Mary Pope Osborne's Tales from the Odyssey) $9.99; pa $4.99 (4 and up)   **883**
1. Homer—Adaptations 2. Odysseus (Greek mythology)
ISBN 0-7868-0773-3; 0-7868-0931-0 (pa)

Retells a part of the Odyssey in which Odysseus' wife, Penelope, and their son, Telemachus, are desperately warding off the men who want to marry her. Then a visit from a mysterious stranger gives Telemachus the courage to confront the suitors, and to search for his long-lost father

The land of the dead; illustrated by Troy Howell. Hyperion Bks. for Children 2002 105p il (Mary Pope Osborne's Tales from the Odyssey) $9.99; pa $4.99 (4 and up)   **883**
1. Homer—Adaptations 2. Odysseus (Greek mythology)
ISBN 0-7868-0771-7; 0-7868-0929-9 (pa)
                       LC 2002-69078

A retelling of part of the Odyssey in which Odysseus and his fleet continue their journey and encounter giant cannibals, a beautiful witch, and the Land of the Dead

"Osborne's simple, engaging narrative will surely capture interest as it presents a great hero in bold, yet human, dimensions." Booklist

The one-eyed giant; with artwork by Troy Howell. Hyperion Bks. for Children 2002 105p il (Mary Pope Osborne's Tales from the Odyssey) $9.99 (4 and up)   **883**
1. Homer—Adaptations 2. Odysseus (Greek mythology)
ISBN 0-7868-0770-9   LC 2002-68539

Retells a part of the Odyssey in which King Odysseus fights the cyclops

"In brief chapters and concise sentences, Osborne pares down . . . [this adventure] into easily absorbed, swiftly paced episodes." Publ Wkly

Return to Ithaca; with artwork by Troy Howell. Hyperion Books for Children 2004 105p (Mary Pope Osborne's Tales from the Odyssey) $9.99 (4 and up)   **883**
1. Homer—Adaptations 2. Odysseus (Greek mythology)
ISBN 0-7868-0774-1   LC 2003-60355

Retells part of Homer's Odyssey in which Odysseus, with the help of the goddess Athena, plans to get revenge on those who have plagued his wife and son during his absence

Sirens and sea monsters; with artwork by Troy Howell. Hyperion Bks. for Children 2003 105p il (Mary Pope Osborne's Tales from the Odyssey) $9.99 (4 and up)   **883**
1. Homer—Adaptations 2. Odysseus (Greek mythology)
ISBN 0-7868-0772-5   LC 2003-284359

Retells a part of the Odyssey in which Odysseus and his men, returning from the Land of the Dead determined to sail home to Ithaca, encounter Scylla, the six-headed monster, and Charybdis, the deadly whirlpool

"Osborne pares down the story to its essential elements. . . . The result is a respectful though short retelling in clear, simple language complemented by large type and generous spacing." Booklist

895.6   Japanese literature

Demi

In the eyes of the cat; Japanese poetry for all seasons; selected and illustrated by Demi; translated by Tze-si Huang. Holt & Co. 1992 unp il pa $8.95   **895.6**
1. Animals—Poetry 2. Japanese poetry—Collections
ISBN 0-8050-3383-1   LC 91-27728

"The poems were selected from the works of the Japanese masters and organized according to the seasons. Each depicts an animal, from the familiar kittens to the less familiar heron and egret. The poems evoke multisensory images because of the carefully selected words and the deceptively simplistic, brilliant illustrations. A book to read, re-read and treasure." Child Book Rev Serv

896 African literatures

Talking drums; a selection of poems from Africa south of the Sahara; edited and illustrated by Véronique Tadjo. . Bloomsbury Children's Books 2003 96p il map $15.95 (5 and up)

896

1. African poetry—Collections

ISBN 1-58234-813-8 LC 2003-52173

Contents: Our universe; The animal kingdom; Love and celebrations; People; Death; Pride and defiance; The changing times

A collection of traditional and twentieth-century poems from sub-Saharan Africa, written in or translated into English, that expresses the spirit and history of this region.

"The contemporary and the traditional are both well represented in this lively anthology. . . . Illustrated with small, black-and-white folk-art drawings, the collection ranges widely, including poems of love, sorrow, and pride. . . . This [is a] fine resource for social studies and literature classes, which will also be great for reading aloud." Booklist

Includes glossary

897 North American native literatures

Dancing teepees: poems of American Indian youth; selected by Virginia Driving Hawk Sneve, with art by Stephen Gammell. Holiday House 1989 32p il $17.95 paperback o.p. (3-5)

897

1. Native Americans—Poetry

ISBN 0-8234-0724-1 LC 88-11075

An illustrated collection of poems from the oral tradition of Native Americans

This is an "eclectic collection, drawn from a variety of tribal traditions. Printed on heavy paper, the book is illustrated with a catalogue of marvelously rendered designs and motifs, ranging from those of the Northwest Coast to the intricate beadwork patterns of the Great Lakes and the zigzag geometric borders of Southwestern pottery." N Y Times Book Rev

900 HISTORY & GEOGRAPHY

902 History--Miscellany. Chronologies

Tomaselli-Moschovitis, Valerie

Junior timelines on file. Updated ed. Facts on File 2002 various paging il $185

902

1. Historical chronology 2. World history

ISBN 0-8160-5122-4 LC 2002-27167

Also available CD-ROM version

First published 1997

This looseleaf binder provides more than 250 reproducible timelines covering "the history of the world on a country-by-country basis; different periods of time, such as the Reorganization of Empires (300 A.D. to 1500 A.D.) and Nationalism, Imperialism, and Revolution (1700 to 1914); human thought and achievement within various fields." Publisher's note

Includes bibliographical references

904 Collected accounts of events

Blackwood, Gary L.

Enigmatic events; [by] Gary L. Blackwood. Marshall Cavendish Benchmark 2005 72p il (Unsolved history) lib bdg $29.93 (4 and up)

904

1. History—Miscellanea 2. Disasters 3. Curiosities and wonders

ISBN 0-7614-1889-X LC 2004-23755

Contents: The death of the dinosaurs; The lost colony; The Salem witch trials; The *Mary Celeste*; The *Maine*; The Tunguska event; The *Hindenburg*

Explores several events that have baffled scientists and historians for years, such as the demise of the dinosaurs, the "lost colony" of Roanoke, the sinking of the Main, and the Hindenberg disaster

This collection of "tidbits about lingering mysteries of the past . . . [offers] more substance than most. . . . [This offers] a full-page illustration opening each chapter; reproductions, many in color; and a generously spaced format." SLJ

Includes glossary and bibliographical references

909 World history. Civilization

Brimson, Samuel

Nations of the world. World Almanac Library 2004 8v il map set $240 (5 and up) **909**

1. Geography—Encyclopedias 2. World history—Encyclopedias 3. Civilization—Encyclopedias

ISBN 0-8368-5484-5

This is a "reference guide to the geography, history, economy, government, peoples and languages, religions and culture of every sovereign nation. . . . Each entry includes a detailed fact box for a quick overview of key facts and statistics, plus full-color photos, locator map and national flag." Publisher's note

"This attractive set presents excellent overviews of national histories. . . . The entries are liberally illustrated with captioned, high-quality color photos that offer glimpses of scenery, events, buildings, and native peoples. The text is quite readable." SLJ

Haskins, James

Count your way through the Arab world; by Jim Haskins; illustrations by Dana Gustafson. Carolrhoda Bks. 1987 unp il lib bdg $19.95; pa $5.95 (2-4) **909**

1. Arab countries

ISBN 0-87614-304-4 (lib bdg); 0-87614-487-3 (pa)

LC 87-6391

Uses Arabic numerals from one to ten to introduce concepts about Arab countries and Arab culture

The **Kingfisher** history encyclopedia. rev ed.
Kingfisher 2004 491p il map $24.95 (5 and up)
909

1. World history
ISBN 0-7534-5784-9
First published 1999
A reference guide to world history, featuring a timeline, key date boxes, and biographies of historical figures
"Students will find this tool useful and engaging." Booklist

Knight, Margy Burns
Talking walls; illustrated by Anne Sibley O'Brien. Tilbury House 1992 unp il map $17.95; pa $8.95 (3-5) **909**
1. Walls 2. World history
ISBN 0-88448-102-6; 0-88448-154-9 (pa)
LC 91-67867
An illustrated description of walls around the world and their significance
"A praiseworthy celebration of similarities and differences among the world's peoples. . . . Young readers will recognize such landmarks as the Great Wall of China, the cave walls of Lascaux, the Wailing Wall and the Vietnam Memorial. More surprising selections feature the work of Australian aborigines, Indian Hindus, Islamic Egyptians, Native Americans and Africans. The narrative is respectful and egalitarian, with the clear intent of valuing no one people over another. O'Brien's . . . well-designed and affecting pastels cover each spread." Publ Wkly

Talking walls: the stories continue; illustrated by Anne Sibley O'Brien. Tilbury House 1996 unp il $17.95; pa $8.95 (3-5) **909**
1. Walls 2. World history
ISBN 0-88448-164-6; 0-88448-165-4 (pa)
LC 96-15123
Introduces different cultures around the world by telling the stories of walls, from the Maya murals in Bonampak, Mexico, to dikes in the Netherlands
"Warm watercolors create just the right mood for the text. Some of the stories are sad, some are inspiring, and some mysterious, but each one says something unique about the people who constructed these structures." SLJ

909.07   World history -- ca. 500-1450/1500

Stefoff, Rebecca
The medieval world. Benchmark Books 2004 c2005 48p il map (World historical atlases) lib bdg $18.95 (5 and up) **909.07**
1. Middle Ages 2. Medieval civilization
ISBN 0-7614-1642-0   LC 2003-22139
This history of the medieval world briefly describes the rise of European states, including the Byzantine Empire, The Franks, England, Germany, and the Papacy, the conquering powers, including Islam, the Vikings, the Crusades, the Mongols and the Turks, and the late Middle Ages, including the Black Death, peasant uprisings,

merchants and trade, and the growth of cities.
The book will "prove helpful to those who know little about the subject. Sidebars, maps, and well-reproduced color art appear throughout." Horn Book Guide
Includes glossary and bibliographical references

909.82   World history--20th century, 1900-1999

Feinstein, Stephen
Decades of the 20th Century [series] rev ed. Enslow Pubs. 2006 10v il ea $27.93 (5 and up)
909.82
1. World history—20th century
First published 2001
Contents: The 1900s, from Teddy Roosevelt to flying machines; The 1910s, from World War I to ragtime music; The 1920s, from Prohibition to Charles Lindbergh; The 1930s, from the Great Depression to the Wizard of Oz; The 1940s, from World War II to Jackie Robinson; The 1950s, from the Korean War to Elvis; The 1960s, from the Vietnam War to Flower Power; The 1970s, from Watergate to disco; The 1980s, from Ronald Reagan to MTV; The 1990s, from the Persian Gulf War to Y2K
"Taking a popular-culture approach, each book begins with a look at 'Lifestyles, Fashion, and Fads,' followed by arts and entertainment, sports, and then politics, with science, technology, and medicine coming last. . . . The books are visually exciting, and the texts are clear and vigorous." SLJ
Includes bibliographical references

Jennings, Peter
The century for young people; [by] Peter Jennings, Todd Brewster; adapted by Jennifer Armstrong; photographs edited by Katherine Bourbeau. Random House 1999 245p il $29.95 (4 and up) **909.82**
1. World history—20th century
ISBN 0-385-32708-0
An adaptation of the authors' The century published 1998 by Doubleday
The "authors use primary sources throughout the narrative to highlight the events and people of the 1900s. . . . Excellent-quality, archival photos capture the moments on almost every page. This is a unique and valuable book." SLJ

909.83 World history--21st century, 2000-2099

Torres, John Albert
Disaster in the Indian Ocean, Tsunami 2004; [by] John A. Torres. Mitchell Lane 2005 48p il map (Monumental milestones) lib bdg $19.95 (5 and up) **909.83**
1. Indian Ocean earthquake and tsunami, 2004
ISBN 1-58415-344-X
This "emerges from the author's personal trip to Indonesia after the December 26, 2004, catastrophe. . . . Primary-source accounts, many taken from Torres' own interviews, chillingly recreate the tsunami's initial strike, its chaotic aftermath, and the challenges of recovery." Booklist
Includes bibliographical references

910 Geography and travel

The **Blackbirch** kid's visual reference of the world; by the editors of Blackbirch Press; maps, charts, and graphs by Bob Italiano. Blackbirch Press 2001 360p il map $49.95 (5 and up) **910**
1. Geography
ISBN 1-56711-579-9   LC 2001-3056
"More than 2,500 graphs, charts, maps, and photos that cover the most important and interesting facts about every country on the planet!" Title page
"This visually appealing resource is packed with geographic information presented in a colorful and easy-to-follow fashion." SLJ

Jenkins, Steve
Hottest, coldest, highest, deepest. Houghton Mifflin 1998 unp il $16 (k-2)   **910**
1. Geography
ISBN 0-395-89999-0   LC 97-53080
Describes some of the remarkable places on earth, including the hottest, coldest, windiest, snowiest, highest, and deepest.
This book "uses striking colorful paper collage illustrations. . . . This eye-catching introduction to geography will find a lot of use in libraries and classrooms." SLJ
Includes bibliographical references

Rockwell, Anne F.
Our earth; written and illustrated by Anne Rockwell. Harcourt Brace & Co. 1998 unp il $13; pa $6 (k-2)   **910**
1. Geography
ISBN 0-15-201679-1; 0-15-202383-6 (pa)
          LC 97-1247
A simple introduction to geography which explains such things as how the earth was shaped, how islands are born from volcanoes, and how gushing springs affect rivers
"The watercolor-and-gouache illustrations are very accessible. The pictures should provoke questions; parents and teachers can use the answers to provide kids with more information." Booklist

910.3 Geography--Dictionaries, encyclopedias, gazetteers

Gifford, Clive
The Kingfisher geography encyclopedia. Kingfisher 2003 488p il map $39.95 (4 and up) **910.3**
1. Geography—Encyclopedias
ISBN 0-7534-5591-9   LC 2003-47420
Contents: The physical earth; The Arctic; North America; Central America; The Caribbean; South America; Europe; Russian Federation; Asia; Indian subcontinent; Eastern Asia; Southeast Asia; Africa; Australasia; Oceania; Antarctica
Statistics, text, and color maps reveal the physical geography, peoples, politics, governments, languages, religions, and currencies of each nation of the world
"The arrangement is logical and the format accessible. . . . Striking color photographs and informative captions highlight the uniqueness of each locale." SLJ

Junior worldmark encyclopedia of the nations; [Timothy L. Gall and Susan Bevan Gall, editors] 4th ed. UXL 2004 10v set $335 (5 and up)   **910.3**
1. Geography—Encyclopedias 2. World history—Encyclopedias
ISBN 0-7876-9215-8   LC 2004-6311
First published 1996
Contents: v1 Afghanistan to Bolivia; v2 Bosnia and Herzegovina to Congo, Democratic Republic of the; v3 Congo, Republic of the to Fiji; v4 Finland to Indonesia; v5 Iran to Lebanon; v6 Liberia to Mozambique; v7 Myanmar to Poland; v8 Portugal to Somalia; v9 South Africa to Tuvalu; v10 Uganda to Zimbabwe
"Articles on 193 countries are presented in alphabetical order. Each article begins with a black-and-white illustration of the nation's flag and seal and a summary list that includes capital city, title or beginning line of anthem, monetary unit, weights and measures, holidays, and time. This data is followed by 35 uniform sections of narrative covering topics such as topography, history, government, industry, and health. Each profile ends with names of famous people and a bibliography. . . . This is an exemplary set for all school and public libraries." Booklist

The **World** Book encyclopedia of people and places. World Bk. 6v il maps set $329 (5 and up)   **910.3**
1. Geography—Dictionaries
First published 1992. Revised annually
This set profiles close to 200 countries. Coverage of each country includes an overview of its history, geography, economy, people, culture and government; a physical/political map; a locator map; and fact box

910.4   Accounts of travel and facilities for travelers

Adams, Simon

Titanic; written by Simon Adams. rev ed. DK Pub. 2004 72p il (DK eyewitness books) $15.99; lib bdg $19.99 (4 and up)   **910.4**
1. Titanic (Steamship) 2. Shipwrecks
ISBN 0-7566-0733-7; 0-7566-0732-9 (lib bdg)
First published 1999
Detailed descriptions of the Titanic, including its accommodations, and a retelling of its sinking in the North Atlantic in April, 1912.

Ballard, Robert D.

Ghost liners; exploring the world's greatest lost ships; by Robert D. Ballard and Rick Archbold; illustrations by Ken Marschall. Little, Brown 1998 64p il $19.95 (4 and up)   **910.4**
1. Shipwrecks
ISBN 0-316-08020-9   LC 98-3412
"A Madison Press book"
Depicts five famous ships that have been lost at sea in modern times, the Empress of Ireland, the Lusitania, the Andrea Doria, the Brittanic, and the Titanic
"The large, attractive format and informative text combine to make this an appealing book on a subject that continues to fascinate young people." Booklist
Includes glossary and bibliographical references

Butterfield, Moira

Pirates & smugglers; foreword by Captain Stephen Bligh. Kingfisher 2005 63p il map (Kingfisher knowledge) $12.95 (5 and up)
      910.4
1. Pirates 2. Smuggling
ISBN 0-7534-5864-0
This is an "introduction to the highwaymen and women of the seas from the cruel Cilician pirates who terrorized the Mediterranean more than 2,000 years ago to the . . . modern-day buccaneers who target supertankers on the South China Sea and the loot they plunder and smuggle." Publisher's note
This offers "stunning illustrations and engaging text. . . . This book is fascinating. Photographs from the movies mix with drawings and reproductions to clarify the text." SLJ
Includes glossary

Explorers and exploration. Marshall Cavendish 2005 11v il map set $471.36 (5 and up)
      910.4
1. Explorers—Encyclopedias 2. Exploration—Encyclopedias
ISBN 0-7614-7535-4   LC 2004-48292
"This set includes more than 100 biographical entries and 50 topical articles, organized alphabetically. A thematic table of contents in the first volume conveniently groups the explorers geographically and divides the articles into broad categories. Most entries are between two and eight pages long, with plenty of illustrative material.

The clearly written text provides solid overviews, along with key dates and details." SLJ
Includes bibliographical references

Fritz, Jean

Around the world in a hundred years; from Henry the Navigator to Magellan; illustrated by Anthony Bacon Venti. Putnam 1994 128p il maps $18.99; pa $6.99 (4 and up)   **910.4**
1. Explorers
ISBN 0-399-22527-7; 0-698-11638-0 (pa)
       LC 92-27042
"Fritz examines the voyages of ten explorers, acknowledging that their contributions, though deserving of recognition, were dearly bought. Opening and closing chapters summarize the fourteenth-century world view and indicate later expansion of geographic understanding. As always, Fritz tempers scholarship with humor in this brief volume—illustrated with drawings in pencil—which reads like an adventure story." Horn Book Guide
Includes bibliographical references

Gibbons, Gail

Sunken treasure. Crowell 1988 32p il lib bdg $15.89; pa $6.95 (k-3)   **910.4**
1. Nuestra Señora de Atocha (Ship) 2. Buried treasure 3. Shipwrecks
ISBN 0-690-04736-3 (lib bdg); 0-06-446097-5 (pa)
       LC 87-30114
"Gibbons concentrates on the ancient Spanish galleon, the *Atocha*, which sank off the coast of Florida in 1662, describing under labeled headings the sinking, the search, the find, recording, salvage, restoration and preservation, cataloguing, and eventual distribution of the treasure. . . . A handsomely designed book, well organized, and easily accessible to younger readers." Horn Book

Kentley, Eric

Story of the Titanic; illustrated by Steve Noon; written by Eric Kentley. DK Pub. 2001 32p il $17.95 (4 and up)   **910.4**
1. Titanic (Steamship) 2. Shipwrecks
ISBN 0-7894-7943-5   LC 2001-28432
"Each spread features one paragraph of text superimposed on a large, colorful drawing of the ill-fated luxury liner. The pictures detail the building of the ship through the rescue of its survivors. Borders contain facts and trivia and duplications of small scenes and figures from within each picture that readers can search for in the spread." SLJ
"This book, with its oversize format, brief, informative text, and large illustrations, will be a first choice for many children." Booklist
Includes glossary

Marschall, Ken

Inside the Titanic; illustrated by Ken Marschall; text by Hugh Brewster. Little, Brown 1997 32p il $19.95 (4 and up)   **910.4**
1. Titanic (Steamship) 2. Shipwrecks
ISBN 0-316-55716-1   LC 97-382
"A Madison Press book"

Marschall, Ken—_Continued_
"Color cutaway paintings of the _Titanic_ in this over-size book allow readers to view every deck as they follow two 12-year-old boys exploring the vessel, and to see how the liner struck the iceberg and sank." Booklist
Includes glossary and bibliographical references

Matsen, Bradford
The incredible search for the treasure ship Atocha; [by] Brad Matsen. Enslow Pubs. 2003 48p il map (Incredible deep-sea adventures) lib bdg $18.95 (4 and up)   **910.4**
1. Fisher, Mel 2. Nuestra Señora de Atocha (Ship) 3. Buried treasure 4. Shipwrecks
ISBN 0-7660-2193-9   LC 2002-14311
Contents: Today's the day; The sinking of the Atocha, 1622; Mel Fisher's quest for the ghost galleons; The search goes on and on and on; Atocha's treasure is worth more than money
Presents background information about the sinking of the Spanish galleon, Atocha, in 1622 and describes efforts to locate the wreck and successfully salvage its treasure more than 300 years later
"A credible title about an amazing adventure. . . . The colorful illustrations include numerous underwater photos, period reproductions, and a map." SLJ
Includes glossary and bibliographical references

Matthews, Rupert
Explorer; written by Rupert Matthews. rev ed. DK Pub. 2005 72p il map (DK eyewitness books) $15.99; lib bdg $19.99 (4 and up)   **910.4**
1. Exploration 2. Explorers
ISBN 0-7566-1072-9; 0-7566-1071-0 (lib bdg)
First published 1991 by Knopf
Photographs and text examine the history of explorers and exploration, and highlight many of their discoveries.

Platt, Richard
Shipwreck; written by Richard Platt; photographed by Alex Wilson and Tina Chambers. rev ed. DK Pub. 2005 72p il (DK eyewitness books) $15.99; lib bdg $19.99 (4 and up)
910.4
1. Shipwrecks
ISBN 0-7566-1089-3; 0-7566-1090-7 (lib bdg)
First published 1997 by Knopf
Describes the history of shipwrecks, famous wrecks, causes, navigation and rescue techniques, and underwater archeology and the exploration of wrecks.

Stefoff, Rebecca
Exploration. Benchmark Books 2004 c2005 48p il map (World historical atlases) lib bdg $18.95 (5 and up)   **910.4**
1. Exploration
ISBN 0-7614-1640-4   LC 2003-12032
Contents: A widening world: Ancient explorers; Chinese travelers; Viking voyages; The journey of Marco Polo; Ibn Battuta explores the Islamic world; The Great Age of European exploration: The Portuguese navigators;

To the Indies; The unexpected Americas; Around the World; Into the Pacific; Filling in the blanks: American interiors; African riddles; Forbidden Asia; The frozen north; Antarctica
This "offers a brief overview of world exploration, beginning with ancient Mediterranean travelers and closing with the polar expeditions of Shackleton and Amundsen. . . . Numerous maps depicting travelers' routes across the globe are noteworthy, and the text provides a solid starting place for further research." Booklist
Includes glossary and bibliographical references

911 Historical geography

Leacock, Elspeth
Places in time; a new atlas of American history; [by] Elspeth Leacock and Susan Buckley; illustrations by Randy Jones. Houghton Mifflin 2001 48p il $15; pa $6.95 (4 and up)
911
1. United States—Historical geography
ISBN 0-395-97958-7; 0-618-3113-0 (pa)
LC 00-59741
This book presents "20 sites in American history at the moment of their historical significance, beginning in 1200 (Cahokia) and ending in 1953. Places and times include New Plymouth—1627, Charlestown—1739, Saratoga—1777, Philadelphia—1787, Abilene—1871, and Chicago—1893. The detailed cutaway views of homes, forts, and mills are impressive enough to keep readers looking again and again. These fascinating slices of life stir the imagination and lead to questions and further research." SLJ
Includes bibliographical references

912 Atlases. Maps

Atlas of North America; H.J. de Blij, editor; [cartography by Philip's] Oxford University Press 2004 320p il map $125 (5 and up)
912
1. Atlases
ISBN 0-19-516993-X   LC 2004-45005
This "atlas of the three largest countries of North America . . . [features a] thematic section covering physical, historic, economic, urban, social, and cultural topics ranging from environmental change to religious practice and from indigenous peoples to migration patterns." Publisher's note
"This exhaustive, authoritative resource presents a dynamic view of Canada, the U.S., and Mexico." SLJ

Atlas of the world; [prepared by National Geographic Maps for the Book Division] 8th ed. National Geographic Society 2005 various paging il map $165 (5 and up)   **912**
1. Atlases
ISBN 0-7922-7543-8   LC 2004-45002
First published 1963
At head of title: National Geographic
This edition features 60 political maps, 17 thematic maps, and 10 panoramic satellite views of the world.

Atlas of the world—*Continued*
Also includes views of all five ocean floors and both polar regions, the latest imagery from the Hubble Space Telescope, and new information from Mars. A world-thematic section addressing such global concerns as biodiversity, the world economy, and terrorism is also provided. The Web site that accompanies the atlas includes interactive maps
For a review see: Booklist, Feb. 15, 2005

Goode's world atlas. Rand McNally $49.95 (4 and up) 912
1. Atlases
First published 1922 with title: Goode's school atlas. (21st edition revised 2005) Periodically revised
"Contains thematic maps and tables showing distribution of population, minerals, manufacturing, and other subjects. Also included are metropolitan-area maps, physical-political maps of regions, geographic tables, and ocean-floor maps showing earth movement. Pronouncing index included." N Y Public Libr Book of How & Where to Look It Up

Johnson, Sylvia A.
Mapping the world. Atheneum Bks. for Young Readers 1999 32p il map $16.95 (4 and up) 912
1. Maps
ISBN 0-689-81813-0 LC 98-7858
"Johnson traces the history of cartography from an early Babylonian image scratched into a clay tablet to maps developed with satellite and computer technology. . . . The slender book contains a number of clear full-color reproductions that suitably illustrate Johnson's descriptions. The writing is smooth and lucid and the material is well organized." SLJ
Includes bibliographical references

National Geographic world atlas for young explorers. Rev & expanded ed. National Geographic Soc. 2003 192p il maps $29.95 (3-6) 912
1. Atlases
ISBN 0-7922-2879-0
First published 1998
This atlas includes photographs taken from space, political and physical maps, flags and statistics
"This new edition of an essential resource incorporates the latest global changes in place-names, boundaries, and statistics. . . . The oversized, attractive layout and engaging, easy-to-read text make this the clear choice for reference collections." SLJ

Rubel, David
Scholastic atlas of the United States. new and updated. Scholastic Reference 2003 144p il map lib bdg $24.95; pa $10.95 (4 and up) 912
1. United States—Maps
ISBN 0-439-55494-2 (lib bdg); 0-439-47436-1 (pa)
"An Agincourt Press book"
First published 2000
This atlas "offers students a detailed map of each of the 50 states plus the District of Columbia and Puerto

Rico. [It] also features an information page about each state that uses photos, graphics, . . . facts, and a brief essay to explain what makes each state unique." Publisher's note

Scholastic atlas of the world. Scholastic Ref. 2001 224p il map $19.95; lib bdg $24.95; pa $12.95 (4 and up) 912
1. Atlases
ISBN 0-439-08795-3; 0-439-55496-9 (lib bdg); 0-439-52797-X (pa)
In this atlas each topographical map "locates important cities, mountains, deserts, and bodies of water, indicating border countries and national capitals. The culture and geography of each country are explored through . . . essays and . . . full-color photographs." Publisher's note

Student atlas. 3rd ed. DK Pub. 2004 160p il map $20 (5 and up) 912
1. Atlases
ISBN 0-7566-0338-2
First published 1998
"The atlas opens with a chapter on map skills. . . . The next chapter focuses on the world as a whole, providing demographic, relief, and climatological maps. Subsequent chapters focus on regions and certain nations contained within a specific continent. . . . There are photographs scattered throughout the text and page layouts are colorful, with graphics appropriate to the target audience. Due to its size, multiple copies of this atlas might be a helpful alternative to the more traditional behemoths." Am Ref Books Annu, 2005

Wilkinson, Philip
The Kingfisher student atlas. Kingfisher 2003 128p il map $24.95 (5 and up) 912
1. Atlases
ISBN 0-7534-5589-7
This "volume presents maps of planet Earth, the poles, the oceans, North and South America, Europe, Africa, Asia, and Oceania. . . . Introductory material is provided on the solar system and on Earth's geological features, climate, and various habitats. Full-color photographs and maps give readers concrete examples of the facts given in the text. . . . A glossary, index, and a wall map of North America are appended, and a MAC or PC compatible CD that can be used to print more than 40 maps is housed in the front cover. This is an easy-to-use resource for home and classroom use." SLJ

Wright, David
The Facts on File children's atlas; [by] David and Jill Wright. Facts on File il maps (2-6) 912
1. Atlases
First published 1987. (2006 edition) Frequently revised
This "atlas for the elementary-through junior-high-age student goes from a global perspective to the various continents and then to specific countries or regions within the continent. . . . The level of detail in the maps provides more information that can be found in some other atlases for children. Additional material includes statistics; quiz or puzzle questions; representations of flags, postage stamps, and coinage; and sidebars highlighting aspects of history or culture." Booklist

920 Biography

Books of biography are arranged as follows: 1. Biographical collections (920) 2. Biographies of individuals alphabetically by name of biographee (92)

Aaseng, Nathan

Business builders in sweets and treats; [by] Nathan Aaseng. Oliver Press 2005 160p il (Business builders) $24.95 (5 and up)   **920**

1. Food industry 2. Businesspeople
ISBN 1-881508-84-6   LC 2003-64984

Contents: Milton Hershey: dreams made of chocolate; William Wrigley Jr.: Chicago's chewing-gum empire; Frand and Forrest Mars: first family of candy; Vernon Rudolph: Krispy Kreme Donuts: hottest brand going; Ellen Gordon: Tootsie Roll: making millions on penny candy; Wally Amos: the cookie manager; Ben Cohen and Jerry Greenfield: good will, good times, good ice cream

This is a "study of Hershey and chocolate, Wrigley and chewing gum, Ben and Jerry and ice cream, and others who make things we love to eat. . . . A few well-chosen sidebars document sweets that don't get a whole chapter. Excellent sources and citations, boxed facts, a lively style, and sometimes mouthwatering pictures finish the package." Booklist

Includes bibliographical references

Altman, Susan

Extraordinary African-Americans. Children's Press 2001 288p il (Extraordinary people) $39; pa $16.95 (5 and up)   **920**

1. African Americans—Biography
ISBN 0-516-22549-9; 0-516-25962-8 (pa)
LC 00-52373

First published 1988 with title: Extraordinary Black Americans: from colonial to contemporary times

This "profiles more than 100 African-American achievers, including writers, artists, musicians, athletes, activists, politicians, and others who have made headlines. It also includes descriptions of important periods in African-American history, including the Harlem Renaissance, Reconstruction, the Great Northern Migration, and the civil rights movement." SLJ

"Perfect for quick reference, in an attractive layout that will appeal to even the most reluctant researchers." Voice Youth Advocates

Includes bibliographical references

Atkins, Jeannine

How high can we climb? the story of women explorers; pictures by Dušan Petričic. . Farrar, Straus and Giroux 2005 209p il $17 (5 and up)   **920**

1. Explorers 2. Women—Biography
ISBN 0-374-33503-6   LC 2003-56378

Profiles twelve women explorers of the land, sea, and air: Jeanne Baret, Florence Baker, Annie Smith Peck, Josephine Peary, Arnarulunguaq, Elisabeth Casteret, Nicole Maxwell, Sylvia Earle, Junko Tabei, Kay Cottee, Sue Hendrickson, and Ann Bancroft.

"The stories, illustrated with Petričic's winsome pen-and-ink drawings, are greatly fictionalized. . . . The strongest justifications for purchase are the thrilling adventures and the introductions to daring, accomplished, and, in some cases, nearly forgotten women who changed history." Booklist

Bausum, Ann

Our country's presidents; with a foreword by George W. Bush. rev ed. National Geographic 2005 207p il $24.95; lib bdg $45.90 (5 and up)   **920**

1. Presidents—United States
ISBN 0-7922-9329-0; 0-7922-9330-4 (lib bdg)
First published 2001

This briefly discusses such topics as "the role of vice presidents, . . . the Electoral College, past presidents as elder statesmen, presidential security, and the expanding global role of the president. The short profiles provide essential information for report writers. The book includes an appended chart of election results . . . and information on America's changing role in the world, the White House, military conflicts throughout our history, political parties and campaigns, and important historical events of the time. The beautiful illustrations . . . current information, and user-friendly layout make this title a solid addition for most libraries." SLJ

Includes bibliographical references

Blackwood, Gary L.

Debatable deaths; [by] Gary L. Blackwood. 1st ed. Marshall Cavendish Benchmark 2005 72p il (Unsolved history) lib bdg $29.93 (4 and up)   **920**

1. Death
ISBN 0-7614-1888-1   LC 2004-22237

Explores the mystery surrounding the deaths of various historical figures: Tutkankhamen, the English Princes in the Tower, Christopher Marlowe, Mozart, Meriwether Lewis, and Amelia Earhart

This collection of "tidbits about lingering mysteries of the past . . . [offers] more substance than most. . . . [It offers] a full-page illustration opening each chapter; reproductions, many in color; and a generously spaced format." SLJ

Includes glossary and bibliographical references

Perplexing people; [by] Gary L. Blackwood. Marshall Cavendish Benchmark 2006 72p il (Unsolved history) lib bdg $29.93 (4 and up)   **920**

1. Impostures and imposture
ISBN 0-7614-1890-3   LC 2004-22238

Describes various famous pretenders in history, including those individuals who claimed to be Joan of Arc, Anastasia, the French Dauphin who would have been King Louis XVII, and the outlaw Billy the Kid

This collection "of tidbits about lingering mysteries of the past . . . [offers] more substance than most. . . . [It offers] a full-page illustration opening each chapter; reproductions, many in color; and a generously spaced format." SLJ

Includes glossary and bibliographical references

Bolden, Tonya

Portraits of African-American heroes; paintings by Ansel Pitcairn. Dutton Children's Books 2003 88p il $18.99 (4 and up)   **920**

1. African Americans—Biography

ISBN 0-525-47043-3   LC 2002-75911

Contents: Frederick Douglass; Matthew Henson; W.E.B. Du Bois; Mary McLeod Bethune; Bessie Coleman; Paul Robeson; Satchel Paige; Thurgood Marshal; Pauli Murray; Joe Louis; Gwendolyn Brooks; Jacob Lawrence; Dizzy Gillespie; Shirley Chisholm; Malcolm X; Martin Luther King, Jr.; Charlayne Hunter-Gault; Judith Jamison; Ruth Simmons; Ben Carson

"Bolden profiles 20 people, ranging from Matthew Henson, Thurgood Marshall, and Martin Luther King, Jr., to Paul Robeson, Ruth Simmons, Judith Jamison, and Charlayne Hunter-Gault." SLJ

"Each profile lists expected biographical information, but offers even more by way of keen insights into a subject's personality based on interviews and information drawn from personal memoirs. . . . Pitcairn's beautifully rendered sepia-toned portraits make each subject jump from the page, beckoning children to come ever closer and learn." Booklist

Bostrom, Kathleen Long

Winning authors; profiles of the Newbery medalists; [by] Kathleen Long Bostrom. Libraries Unlimited 2003 338p il (Popular authors series) $52   **920**

1. Authors, American 2. Newbery Medal

ISBN 1-56308-877-0   LC 2003-53878

This "resource opens with a brief history of the Newbery Medal. . . . Entries featuring each winner from 1922 to 2002 follow with basic information about the authors, including useful listings of all awards and honors they have won, a full listing of their books, and sources for further information. A two to three-page narrative linking life experiences to themes of their books is also included." SLJ

Includes bibliographical references

Chin-Lee, Cynthia

Amelia to Zora; twenty-six women who changed the world; illustrated by Megan Halsey and Sean Addy. Charlesbridge 2005 32p il $15.95 (4 and up)   **920**

1. Women—Biography

ISBN 1-57091-522-9

"An introduction to 26 diverse, 20th-century women who have made a difference in such varied fields as the arts, sports, journalism, science, and entertainment. The entries include Dolores Huerta, Frida Kahlo, Lena Horne, Maya Lin, and Patricia Schroeder." SLJ

"The illustrations are done in a remarkable mix of media. . . . The text portions are short . . . but they are enticing. By choosing her subjects from every culture, the author introduces children to the scope of the struggles and achievements of women from many times and many places." Booklist

Delano, Marfe Ferguson

American heroes. National Geographic 2005 191p il $24.95; lib bdg $45.90 (5 and up)   **920**

1. United States—Biography

ISBN 0-7922-7208-0; 0-7922-7215-3 (lib bdg)

This profiles 50 Americans each "chosen for his or her vision, strength, and commitment to exploration or change. . . . Organized chronologically from pre-Colonial times through today, the . . . entries range from Pocahontas to Senator Daniel K. Inouye. . . . The clearly written, beautifully laid out profiles include an information box with basic chronology, milestones, landmarks, honors, and a bulleted list of facts." SLJ

Includes bibliographical references

Fradin, Dennis B.

The founders; the 39 stories behind the U.S. Constitution; [by] Dennis Brindell Fradin; illustrated by Michael McCurdy. Walker & Co. 2005 162p il map $22.95; lib bdg $23.95 (4 and up)   **920**

1. United States. Constitution 2. Statesmen—United States 3. United States—Politics and government—1783-1809

ISBN 0-8027-8972-2; 0-8027-8973-0 (lib bdg)

"The makers of the U.S. Constitution are profiled in two or three pages each, in sections introduced by a brief note about their home states. McCurdy's black-and-white scratchboard illustrations are properly stately and engaging. Readers will find great nuggets of fact." Booklist

Includes bibliographical references

The signers; the fifty-six stories behind the Declaration of Independence; [by] Dennis Brindell Fradin; illustrations by Michael McCurdy. Walker & Co. 2002 164p il map $22.95; lib bdg $23.85 (4 and up)   **920**

1. United States. Declaration of Independence 2. Statesmen—United States 3. United States—Politics and government—1775-1783, Revolution

ISBN 0-8027-8849-1; 0-8027-8850-5 (lib bdg)

LC 2002-66364

Profiles each of the fifty-six men who signed the Declaration of Independence, giving historical information about the colonies they represented. Includes the text of the Declaration and its history

"Fradin gives brief, fascinating glimpses into the people who have been overlooked as well as those with whom readers might be familiar. . . . An excellent resource for report writing." SLJ

Includes bibliographical references

Freedman, Russell

Indian chiefs. Holiday House 1987 151p il lib bdg $22.95; pa $12.95 (6 and up)   **920**

1. Native Americans—Biography

ISBN 0-8234-0625-3 (lib bdg); 0-8234-0971-6 (pa)

LC 86-46198

This "book chronicles the lives of six renowned Indian chiefs, each of whom served as a leader during a critical period in his tribe's history. . . . The text relates information about the lives of each chief and aspects of Indi-

Freedman, Russell—*Continued*

an/white relationships that illuminate his actions. Interesting vignettes and quotations are well integrated into the narrative as are dramatic accounts of battles. While the tone of the text is nonjudgmental, an underlying sympathy for the Indians' situation is apparent." Horn Book

Includes bibliographical references

George-Warren, Holly

Honky-tonk heroes & hillbilly angels; the pioneers of country & western music; words by Holly George-Warren; pictures by Laura Levine. Houghton Mifflin 2006 32p il $16 (3-6)
920

1. Country music 2. Musicians
ISBN 0-618-19100-3   LC 2003-5364
Profiles important and influential performers of country and western music, including the Carter Family, Roy Acuff, Gene Autry, Bill Monroe, Patsy Cline, and Loretta Lynn.

"Concise but thorough. . . . Colorful, stylized, folk art of the performers and/or their instruments is included." SLJ

Shake, rattle, & roll; the founders of rock & roll; words by Holly George-Warren; pictures by Laura Levine. Houghton Mifflin 2001 unp il $15; pa $5.95 (4 and up)
920

1. Musicians 2. Rock music
ISBN 0-618-05540-1; 0-618-43229-9 (pa)
LC 00-33480
"Brief profiles of 15 men and women whose music 'created a sound that changed our culture forever,' including Bill Haley, Fats Domino, Little Richard, Elvis Presley, Carl Perkins, Wanda Jackson and Ritchie Valens." N Y Times Book Rev

"A wonderfully entertaining browsing book that will also fill a gap in most music collections." SLJ

Greenfield, Eloise

Childtimes: a three-generation memoir; by Eloise Greenfield and Lessie Jones Little; with material by Pattie Ridley Jones; drawings by Jerry Pinkney and photographs from the authors' family albums. Crowell 1979 175p il lib bdg $15.89; pa $8.95 (4 and up)
920

1. African American women
ISBN 0-690-03875-5 (lib bdg); 0-06-446134-3 (pa)
LC 77-26581
Childhood memoirs of three African American women—grandmother, mother, and daughter—who grew up between the 1880's and the 1950's

"A carefully considered and thoughtful book, moving deliberately, constructed with loving care. The authors respect their child-readers (or listeners) and honor them with candor and honesty, tragedy and tears, providing chuckles and smiles as well." Interracial Books Child Bull

Hansen, Joyce

African princess; the amazing lives of Africa's royal women; illustrated by Laurie McGaw. . Jump at the Sun/Hyperion/Madison Press 2004 48p il lib bdg $16.99 (5 and up)
920

1. Princesses 2. Africa—Biography
ISBN 0-7868-5116-3   LC 2004-40634
This profiles six African royal women from ancient times to the present, including Hatshepsut of Egypt, Njinja of Matumba, Amina of Zaria, Tata Ajach of Dahomey, Taytu Betul of Ethiopia, and Elizabeth of Toro

"Meticulously researched and jammed with historical tidbits and surprises. . . . Each minibiography is illustrated with a stunning, golden-toned watercolor portrait." N Y Times Book Rev

Jones, Charlotte Foltz

Westward ho! eleven explorers of the West; [by] Charlotte Foltz Jones. Holiday House 2005 233p il map $22.95 (5 and up)
920

1. West (U.S.)—History
ISBN 0-8234-1586-4   LC 2003-57004
Contents: Robert Gray (1755-1806); George Vancouver (1757-1798); Alexander Mackenzie (1764-1820); John Colter (1774 or 1775-1813); Zebulon Montgomery Pike (1779-1813); Stephen Harriman Long (1784-1864); James Bridger (1804-1881); Jedediah Smith (1799-1831); Joseph Reddeford Walker (1798-1876); John C. Fremont (1813-1890); John Wesley Powell (1834-1902)

A collective biography of eleven men who explored the American West in the 18th and 19th centuries, including ship's officers, fur traders, and Army officers

"Jones makes history a lively endeavor by writing vivid accounts of lives that were sometimes stranger, and nearly always more exciting, than fiction. . . . Black-and-white reproductions of period drawings, paintings, prints, and photos illustrate the text." Booklist

Includes bibliographical references

Just like me; stories and self-portraits by fourteen artists; edited by Harriet Rohmer. Children's Bk. Press 1997 31p il $15.95
920

1. Artists
ISBN 0-89239-149-9   LC 97-4467
Fourteen artists and picture book illustrators present self-portraits and brief descriptions that explore their varied ethnic origins, their work, and their feelings about themselves. Mira Reisberg, Stephen Von Mason, Carmen Lomas Garza, and George Littlechild are among the artists included

"This is a wonderful browsing item as well as an excellent teaching tool." SLJ

Kimmel, Elizabeth Cody

The look-it-up book of explorers. Random House 2004 128p il map $17.99; pa $10.99 (5 and up)
920

1. Explorers 2. Exploration
ISBN 0-375-92478-7; 0-375-82478-2 (pa)
"Beginning with Leif Ericksson and his trip to Greenland and the Americas to Robert Ballard's 1985 expedition to search for the *Titanic*, the chronlogically arranged spreads give readers a better understanding of how the

Kimmel, Elizabeth Cody—*Continued*
world was explored. . . . Informative black-and-white photos and reproductions appear throughout. . . . This is an excellent quick resource that will appeal to researchers and general readers alike." SLJ

Krull, Kathleen
The book of rock stars; 24 musical icons that shine through history; written by Kathleen Krull; art by Stephen Alcorn. Hyperion Bks. for Children 2003 44p il $16.99 (4 and up)　　　**920**
　　1. Rock musicians
　　ISBN 0-7868-1950-2　　　　　　LC 2002-191901
An illustrated collection of twenty mini-biographies of such rock music legends as Jimi Hendrix, Janis Joplin, Bruce Springsteen, and Carlos Santana
"Krull's hard to top for energy and passion. Alcorn's full-page polychrome relief prints hark back to the psychedelic posters of the '60s. . . . Readers will not only be caught up in the swirl of one of the past century's central cultural currents but also find this an irresistible gateway to the music." Booklist
Includes bibliographical references

Lives of extraordinary women; rulers, rebels (and what the neighbors thought); written by Kathleen Krull; illustrated by Kathryn Hewitt. Harcourt 2000 95p il $20 (4 and up)　　　**920**
　　1. Women in politics
　　ISBN 0-15-200807-1　　　　　　LC 99-6840
"The subjects range from Cleopatra in ancient Egypt to contemporary activists Wilma Mankiller, Aung San Suu Kyi, and Rigoberta Menchu." Voice Youth Advocates
"Each entry offers a tightly written biography, often filled with delicious anecdote. . . . Each biographical essay is accompanied by one of Hewitt's full-page, full-color caricatures. Both artful and witty, the illustrations provide perfect accompaniments to the often breezy and accessible text." N Y Times Book Rev
Includes bibliographical references

Lives of the artists; masterpieces, messes (and what the neighbors thought); written by Kathleen Krull; illustrated by Kathryn Hewitt. Harcourt Brace & Co. 1995 96p il $20 (4 and up)
　　　　　　　　　　　　　　　　　　920
　　1. Artists
　　ISBN 0-15-200103-4　　　　　　LC 94-35357
Also available from Raintree Steck-Vaughn Pubs.
"Krull's brief biographies provide basic facts as well as intriguing details. The subjects chosen range from the famous (Michelangelo Buonarroti) to the infamous (Andy Warhol) to the less well known. Hewitt's caricaturelike illustrations reflect and extend the lively text." Horn Book Guide
Includes glossary and bibliographical references

Lives of the athletes; thrills, spills (and what the neighbors thought); written by Kathleen Krull; illustrated by Kathryn Hewitt. Harcourt Brace & Co. 1997 96p il $20 (4 and up)　　　**920**
　　1. Athletes
　　ISBN 0-15-200806-3　　　　　　LC 95-50702
Also available from Raintree Steck-Vaughn Pubs.

"Krull profiles twenty legendary athletes of the twentieth century who broke new ground in their sports and often broke through racial or gender barriers as well. . . . The brief biographies are enhanced by unusual details of personality and Hewitt's lively caricatures of the subjects." Horn Book
Includes bibliographical references

Lives of the musicians; good times, bad times (and what the neighbors thought); written by Kathleen Krull; illustrated by Kathryn Hewitt. Harcourt Brace Jovanovich 1993 96p il $20 (4 and up)　　　　　　　　　　　　　　　　　　**920**
　　1. Composers
　　ISBN 0-15-248010-2　　　　　　LC 91-33497
Also available from Raintree Steck-Vaughn Pubs.
"Twenty (including both Gilbert and Sullivan) composers, from Vivaldi to Gershwin, are here profiled in a series of irreverent, anecdotal vignettes, each stylishly illustrated with an elegant caricature." Bull Cent Child Books
Includes glossary and bibliographical references

Lives of the presidents; fame, shame (and what the neighbors thought); illustrated by Kathryn Hewitt. Harcourt Brace & Co. 1998 96p il $20 (4 and up)　　　　　　　　　　　　　　　　　　**920**
　　1. Presidents—United States
　　ISBN 0-15-200808-X　　　　　　LC 97-33069
Also available from Raintree Steck-Vaughn Pubs.
Focuses on the lives of presidents as parents, husbands, pet-owners, and neighbors while also including humorous anecdotes about hairstyles, attitudes, diets, fears, and sleep patterns
"Packed with enough detail for brief reports, these articles are also just plain entertaining. . . . Hewitt's spirited watercolor cartoons add to the presentation immensely." SLJ
Includes bibliographical references

Lives of the writers; comedies, tragedies (and what the neighbors thought); written by Kathleen Krull; illustrated by Kathryn Hewitt. Harcourt Brace & Co. 1994 96p il (4 and up)　　　**920**
　　1. Authors
　　ISBN 0-15-248009-9　　　　　　LC 93-32436
Also available from Raintree Steck-Vaughn Pubs.
This offers "views of twenty writers . . . from various countries and historical periods. Included are William Shakespeare, Edgar Allan Poe, Mark Twain, Zora Neale Hurston, Isaac Bashevis Singer, and many others." Publisher's note
The "authors profiled are cleverly chosen. . . . Hewitt provides a full-page color portrait, part caricature, part realistic, for each, and Krull's text includes hard facts as well as enough lively anecdotes to make clear that the writers are human." Booklist
Includes glossary and bibliographical references

Lester, Julius

The blues singers; ten who rocked the world; illustrated by Lisa Cohen. Jump at the Sun 2001 47p il $15.99; lib bdg $16.49 (5 and up)

920

1. Blues music 2. African American singers

ISBN 0-7868-0463-7; 0-7868-2405-0 (lib bdg)

LC 00-59019

"Lester profiles 10 blues, or blues-inspired, legends including Bessie Smith, Muddy Waters, B. B. King and Billie Holiday as well as Mahalia Jackson . . . and Little Richard. . . . Lester's anecdotal approach, his leisurely pacing and abundance of colorful, down-home similes give the famous figures a tangible presence." Publ Wkly

Includes discography and bibliographical references

Major, John S.

Caravan to America; living arts of the Silk Road; [by] John S. Major and Betty J. Belanus. Cricket Bks. 2002 130p il map $24.95; pa $15.95 (4 and up)

920

1. Arts

ISBN 0-8126-2666-4; 0-8126-2677-X (pa)

LC 2002-5477

"A Marcato book"

Contents: Qi Shu Fang: Peking opera performer; Doug Kim: Korean American martial artist; Yeshi Dorjee: Tibetan artist-monk; Abdul Khaliq Muradi: Turkmen rug restorer; Tamara Katayev: Bukharan singer; Najmieh Batmanglij: Iranian American cook; La Verne J. Magarian: Armenian American calligrapher and paper artist; Peter Kyvelos, Greek American oud maker

Profiles eight artists and artisans now living in America who are originally from the "Silk Road," an ancient network of caravan trails through which trade goods, ideas, and arts pass between Asia and the Mediterranean

"Full of colorful and informative archival and contemporary photographs and drawings. . . . Each person's story is told in an interesting manner, and information about their specialty and its history is woven throughout the text. . . . Not only is the work informative, but it is handsome as well." SLJ

Includes glossary and bibliographical references

Meltzer, Milton

Ten kings; and the worlds they ruled; illustrated by Bethanne Andersen. Orchard Bks. 2002 132p il map $21.95 (5 and up)

920

1. Kings and rulers

ISBN 0-439-31293-0

LC 2001-33202

This "volume comprises biographies of ten legendary leaders, including Hammurabi, Alexander the Great, Attila, Kublai Khan, and Peter the Great. Meltzer's sources for discussing these lives and their cultural contexts are impeccable, and he writes knowledgeably and thoughtfully." Horn Book Guide

Includes bibliographical references

Ten queens; portraits of women of power; illustrated by Bethanne Andersen. Dutton Children's Bks. 1998 134p il maps pa $14.99 (5 and up)

920

1. Queens

ISBN 0-525-47158-8 (pa); 0-525-45643-0 (hc)

LC 97-36428

"The 10 women Meltzer showcases are Esther, Cleopatra, Boudicca, Zenobia, Eleanor of Aquitaine, Isabella of Spain, Elizabeth I, Christine of Sweden, Maria Theresa, and Catherine the Great." Booklist

Meltzer "has a storyteller's flair and an eye for the small details and anecdotes that bring these queens to life. . . . Colorful expressionistic paintings, boldly stroked onto unframed panels, enrich the pages." SLJ

Includes bibliographical references

Mulvihill, Margaret

The treasury of saints and martyrs. Viking 1999 80p il $19.99 (5 and up)

920

1. Christian saints

ISBN 0-670-88789-7

LC 99-70893

"Oversize and illustrated with museum art, the book introduces more than 40 saints, from the beginning of Christianity to the modern day. The life of each saint is discussed in a page or two of straightforward text that also features several illustrations. . . . A pleasure to look at and often inspiring. A calendar of saints and glossary are appended." Booklist

Orgill, Roxane

Shout, sister, shout! the girl singers who shaped a century. Margaret K. McElderry Bks. 2001 148p il $19.95 (6 and up)

920

1. Popular music 2. Singers

ISBN 0-689-81991-9

LC 99-54374

"The lives of ten 'girl singers,' representing different genres of popular music, from vaudeville to blues to jazz to country, are arranged by decade. Profiles of Sophie Tucker, Ma Rainey, Bessie Smith, Ethel Merman, Judy Garland, Anita O'Day, Joan Baez, Bette Midler, Madonna, and Lucinda Williams are included." Voice Youth Advocates

Includes discography and bibliographical references

Pinkney, Andrea Davis

Let it shine; stories of Black women freedom fighters; illustrated by Stephen Alcorn. Harcourt 2000 107p il $20 (4 and up)

920

1. African American women 2. African Americans—Civil rights 3. United States—Race relations

ISBN 0-15-201005-X

LC 99-42806

"Gulliver books"

This "collective biography tells of 10 extraordinary black women. From Sojourner Truth to Shirley Chisholm, this is also a view of African American history through individual lives. . . . Stephen Alcorn's allegorical oil portraits are dramatic and beautiful. . . . The immediacy of the text and the spacious design of the large volume make this a natural for reading aloud." Booklist

Includes bibliographical references

Piven, Hanoch

What presidents are made of. Atheneum Bks for Young Readers 2004 unp il $15.95 (2-4)

920

1. Presidents—United States
ISBN 0-689-86880-4

"Piven presents the characters and interests of 17 U.S. presidents in text and collage portraits that make use of small toys and objects." Booklist

"This book exhibits Piven's flair for creativity and whimsy. . . . Children will be fascinated by the imaginative, humorous artwork and will appreciate the anecdotes." SLJ

Rappaport, Doreen

We are the many; a picture book of American Indians; illustrated by Cornelius Van Wright and Ying-Hwa Hu. HarperCollins Pubs. 2002 28p il $15.99; lib bdg $17.89 (2-4) **920**

1. Native Americans—Biography
ISBN 0-688-16559-1; 0-06-001139-4 (lib bdg)

LC 2001-39820

"One incident from each person's life is re-created, giving a quick, snapshot-style view of the individual's contribution to the world. . . . The text is large, and sentences are accessible to emerging readers. . . . There is some fictionalizing . . . but it is limited and does not detract from the overall worth of the title." SLJ

Robinson Masters, Nancy

Extraordinary patriots of the United States of America; Colonial times to pre-Civil War; [by] Nancy Robinson Masters. Children's Press 2005 288p il (Extraordinary people) $40 (5 and up)

920

1. United States—Biography
ISBN 0-516-24404-3   LC 2004030940

"This book provides biographical sketches of dozens of individuals and groups of people. The three to five-page sketches are arranged chronologically by the patriot's birth year, beginning with Benjamin Franklin and ending with Sam Houston. . . . Although these sketches are very brief, they are interesting and readable." SLJ

Includes bibliographical references

Rubel, David

Scholastic encyclopedia of the presidents and their times; with a foreword by James M. McPherson. Scholastic Reference 2005 244p il $19.95 (5 and up) **920**

1. Presidents—United States
ISBN 0-439-28323-X   LC 2004-52564
First published 1994

This reference "documents the tenure of each of the American presidents. It also includes information about the headlines, people, and fads that were defining America during each presidency. . . . Each profile includes a fact box that lists the president's birthday, birthplace, vice president, wife, children, and nickname." Publisher's note

"This is an attractive, inexpensive resource . . . providing concise information in an easy-to-read format." Booklist [review of 1997 edition]

Sinnott, Susan

Extraordinary Asian Americans and Pacific Islanders. rev ed. Children's Press 2003 288p il (Extraordinary people) lib bdg $39; pa $16.95 (5 and up) **920**

1. Asian Americans—Biography
ISBN 0-516-22655-X (lib bdg); 0-516-29355-9 (pa)

LC 2002-11220

First published 1993 with title: Extraordinary Asian-Pacific Americans

Biographical sketches of notable Asian Americans and Pacific Islander Americans, from the nineteenth century up to the present

"This well-written resource is accompanied by black-and-white photographs, and will be useful for both browsers and report writers." SLJ

Includes bibliographical references

Sullivan, Otha Richard

African American inventors; Jim Haskins, general editor. Wiley 1998 164p il (Black stars) $24.95 (5 and up) **920**

1. African American inventors
ISBN 0-471-14804-0   LC 97-46932

Profiles the lives of twenty-five African American inventors who made significant scientific contributions from the eighteenth century to modern times

This is "a particularly engaging book to read; Sullivan highlights those aspects of the subjects' lives that will interest readers the most and writes about them with insight. The book is attractive, too, with lots of historical engravings and photographs." Booklist

Includes bibliographical references

African American millionaires. John Wiley & Sons 2004 c2005 158p il (Black stars) $24.95

920

1. African Americans—Biography
ISBN 0-471-46928-9   LC 2004-14694

Contents: William Alexander Leidesdorff, 1810-1848; Mary Ellen Pleasant, 1814-1904; Bridget "Biddy" Mason, 1818-1891; Anthony Overton, 1864-1946; Abraham Lincoln Lewis, 1865-1947; Madame C.J. Walker, 1867-1919; Annie Turnbo Malone, 1869-1957; Robert S. Abbott, 1870-1940; George Baker "Father Divine", 1879-1965; Arthur George Gaston, 1892-1906; S.B. Fuller, 1905-1988; John H. Johnson, 1918; Crispus Attucks Wright, 1913-2001; Matel "Mat" Dawson, 1922-2002; Ray Charles, 1930; Quincy Jones, 1933; Earl G. Graves, 1935; Joe L. Dudley, 1937; Bill and Camille Cosby, 1937, 1944; Eddie Brown, 1940; Reginald F. Lewis, 1942-1993; Don Barden, 1943; Robert L. Johnson, 1946; Willie Gary, 1947; Oprah Winfrey, 1954; Spike Lee, 1957; Russell Simmons, 1957; Earvin Magic Johnson, 1959; Kenneth "Babyface" Edmonds, 1959; Trish Millines, 1958; Sean "Puffy" Combs (P. Diddy), 1969; Tyra Banks, 1973; Tiger Woods, 1975

This profiles 25 African American millionaires

"Sullivan offers an exemplary compilation of a relatively unexplored subject area. . . . The book is well organized, highly readable, and inspiring." SLJ

Includes bibliographical references

Talking with adventurers; conversations with Christina M. Allen [et al.]; compiled and edited by Pat Cummings and Linda Cummings. National Geographic Soc. 1998 95p il maps $19.95 (4-6) **920**

1. Scientists

ISBN 0-7922-7068-1   LC 98-11457

Twelve men and women who work in the field of science discuss and explain their occupations, including what they might do in a day and the scariest thing that ever happened to them

"This well-organized book, with spectacular, well-placed, captioned photos, is sure to enhance classroom science studies and please the ever curious reader." Booklist

Includes glossary

Thimmesh, Catherine

Girls think of everything; illustrated by Melissa Sweet. Houghton Mifflin 2000 57p $16; pa $6.95 (5 and up) **920**

1. Women inventors 2. Inventions

ISBN 0-395-93744-2; 0-618-19563-7 (pa)

LC 99-36270

"Ten women and two girls are given a few pages each. Included are Mary Anderson, who invented the windshield wiper (after she was told it wouldn't work); Ruth Wakefield, who, by throwing chunks of chocolate in her cookie batter, gave Toll House cookies to the world; and young Becky Schroeder, who invented Glo-paper because she wanted to write in the dark. The text is written in a fresh, breezy manner, but it is the artwork that is really outstanding." Booklist

Madam president; the extraordinary, true (and evolving) story of women in politics; illustrated by Douglas B. Jones. Houghton Mifflin 2004 80p il $17 (4 and up) **920**

1. Women in politics

ISBN 0-618-39666-7   LC 2004-1053

"Thimmesh's collective biography profiles women who took up the fight for women's political rights. . . . Divided into groups such as suffragettes, First Ladies, and politicians in the U.S and around the world, the profiles include Edith Wilson, Jeanette Rankin, Margaret Chase Smith, Frances Perkins, Nancy Pelosi, and Sirimavo Bandaranaike of Ceylon (Sri Lanka). The one to two-page profiles are incisively written, highlighted by a quote, and illustrated with a wonderful, telling picture of each woman." Booklist

Includes bibliographical references

Winter, Jonah

Beisbol! Latino baseball pioneers and legends; introduction by Felipe Alou. Lee & Low Bks. 2001 unp il $16.95 (3-6) **920**

1. Baseball—Biography 2. Hispanic Americans—Biography

ISBN 1-58430-012-4   LC 00-35419

"Winter presents one-page biographical sketches of 14 players who played between 1900 and the 1960s, including Dolf Luque, Cristóbal Torriente, and Martin Dihigo. He includes a couple of fascinating facts after listing pertinent details such as years played, main teams, position, and similar stats found on the back of baseball cards. Each profile faces a colorful acrylic painting on a background that resembles an old card." SLJ

Zalben, Jane Breskin

Paths to peace; people who changed the world; [by] Jane Breskin Zalben. 1st ed. Dutton Children's Books 2006 46p il $18.99 (4 and up) **920**

ISBN 0-525-47470-6   LC 2005004793

This "volume highlights 16 individuals who have worked to improve conditions for others through their words and actions. Included are writers, philosophers, Civil Rights advocates, and politicians, many of whom are Nobel Peace Prize recipients. The book focuses on celebrated individuals such as John Fitzgerald Kennedy, Martin Luther King, Jr., Eleanor Roosevelt, Cesar Chavez, and Elie Wiesel. Also covered are those newer to recognition, such as Wangari Maathai, who works for conservation in Kenya, and Aung San Suu Kyi, who fights for democracy in Myanmar. . . . Made from fabric, etchings, watercolor, and found objects, the collages reflect Zalbens interpretation of these individuals. . . . The accomplished, vibrant artwork and the graceful narrative clearly express each persons character, approach to life, and accomplishments." SLJ

Includes glossary and bibliographical references

920.003 Biographical reference works

Biography for beginners: world explorers; Laurie Lanzen Harris, editor. Favorable Impressions 2003 xxi, 598p il maps $55 (3-5) **920.003**

1. Explorers—Dictionaries

ISBN 1-931360-20-0   LC 2003-1942

Profiles 107 world explorers, from 500 B.C. when Carthaginian explorer Hanno colonized West Africa, to such present-day adventurers as astronaut Neil Armstrong and ocean explorer Sylvia Earle

"This title would be a useful addition in elementary-school libraries as well as in public libraries." Booklist

Explorers; from ancient times to the space age; consulting editors, John Logan Allen, E. Julius Dasch, Barry M. Gough. Macmillan Ref. USA 1999 3v il maps set $370 (5 and up) **920.003**

1. Explorers—Dictionaries

ISBN 0-02-864893-5   LC 98-8809

"This set profiles 333 world explorers, including cartographers, merchants, navigators, botanists, archaeologists, treasure hunters, and astronauts. . . . Well-selected, high-quality black-and-white portraits and maps abound. . . . This is a solid resource with considerable browsing appeal." SLJ

Favorite children's authors and illustrators; E. Russell Primm, III, editor-in-chief. Tradition Bks. 2003 6v il set $357 **920.003**

1. Authors—Dictionaries 2. Illustrators—Dictionaries

ISBN 1-59187-026-7   LC 2002-7129

Favorite children's authors and illustrators—
Continued

Contents: v1 Verna Aardema to Brock Cole; v2 Joanna Cole to Jack Gantos; v3 Carmen Lomas Garza to Edward Lear; v4 Ursula K. Le Guin to Helen Oxenbury; v5 Barbara Park to Peter Sis; v6 David Small to Gene Zion

Provides biographical information about authors and illustrators of books for children and young adults, arranged in dictionary form

"Each essay is a brief but informative four pages in length and contains a wealth of information useful to student researchers. All entries include a photograph of the author or illustrator, dates of birth and death (if applicable), quotes from and about the subject, reproductions of book covers, and footnotes of interesting facts. . . . This set is well designed and easily accessible." Booklist

Murphy, Barbara Thrash

Black authors and illustrators of books for children and young adults; a biographical dictionary; foreword by E.J. Josey. 3rd ed. Garland 1999 xxiii, 513p il $95   **920.003**

1. Children's literature—Bio-bibliography 2. Illustrators

ISBN 0-8153-2004-3   LC 98-42690

First published 1988 under the authorship of Barbara Rollock with title: Black authors and illustrators of children's books

This volume offers 274 biographical sketches. "Each entry ranges in length from a paragraph to two pages and includes such information as year and place of birth, influences, approaches to writing and or illustrating, achievements, awards, and a selected bibliography of works. Photographs of the authors or illustrators are included when available. An appendix of sample book covers and jackets is included, followed by an appendix listing books that have received awards or honors." Booklist

Includes bibliographical references

Ninth book of junior authors and illustrators; edited by Connie C. Rockman. H.W. Wilson 2004 [i.e. 2005] 583p il $105   **920.003**

1. Authors—Dictionaries 2. Illustrators—Dictionaries 3. Children's literature—Bio-bibliography

ISBN 0-8242-1043-3   LC 2004-61627

Previous volumes in Junior authors and illustrators series available in print and electronic editions

This volume covers some 200 authors and illustrators of books for children and young adults including Kate DiCamillo, Pura Belpré, Julia Alvarez and Kadir Nelson. For 20 authors and artists whose careers include significant new works and honors since their profile in earlier editions of the series, newly written entries are featured

This "offers solid and appealing information for students, librarians, and educators. . . . School and public libraries would be well served by this informative and easy-to-read text." Booklist

Something about the author; facts and pictures about authors and illustrators of books for young people. Gale Res. il ea $140   **920.003**

1. Authors—Dictionaries 2. Illustrators—Dictionaries 3. Children's literature—Bio-bibliography

ISSN 0276-816X

Also available Major authors and illustrators for children and young adults: a selection of sketches from Something about the author, 8 volume set $605 (ISBN 0-7876-1234-0)

First published 1971. Frequency varies

Editors vary

"This important series gives comprehensive coverage of the individuals who write and illustrate books for children. Each new volume adds about 100 profiles. Entries include career and personal data, a bibliography of the author's works, information on works in progress and references to further information." Safford. Guide to Ref Materials for Sch Libr Media Cent. 5th edition

Something about the author: autobiography series. Gale Res. il ea $149   **920.003**

1. Authors—Dictionaries 2. Illustrators—Dictionaries 3. Children's literature—Bio-bibliography

ISSN 0885-6842

First published 1986

Editors vary

An "ongoing series in which juvenile authors discuss their lives, careers, and published works. Each volume contains essays by 20 established writers or illustrators (e.g., Evaline Ness, Nonny Hogrogian, Betsy Byars, Jean Fritz) who represent all types of literature, preschool to young adult. . . . Some articles focus on biographical information, while others emphasize the writing career. Most, however, address young readers and provide family background, discuss the writing experience, and cite some factors that influenced it. Illustrations include portraits of the authors as children and more recent action pictures and portraits. There are cumulative indexes by authors, important published works, and geographical locations mentioned in the essays." Safford. Guide to Ref Books for Sch Libr Media Cent. 5th edition

92   Individual biography

Lives of individuals are arranged alphabetically under the name of the person written about. A number of subject headings have been added to the entries in this section to aid in curriculum work. It is not necessarily recommended that these subjects be used in the library catalog.

Aaron, Hank, 1934-

Golenbock, Peter. Hank Aaron; brave in every way; illustrated by Paul Lee. Harcourt 2001 unp il $16 (1-3)   **92**

1. Baseball—Biography 2. African American athletes

ISBN 0-15-202093-4   LC 00-8855

A biography of the Hall of Fame baseball player who broke Babe Ruth's career home run record

"This richly illustrated biography . . . deftly tells the athlete's story. . . . Lee's strong, full-page acrylic illustrations in rich tones and textures work well and give the story depth and intensity." SLJ

Ada, Alma Flor, 1938-

Ada, Alma Flor. Under the royal palms; a childhood in Cuba. Atheneum Bks. for Young Readers 1998 85p il $15 (4 and up)   **92**

1. Authors, American 2. Women authors 3. Cuba—Social life and customs

ISBN 0-689-80631-0   LC 97-48887

Companion volume to Where the flame trees bloom (1994)

The author recalls her life and impressions growing up in Cuba

"The attention paid to small daily things as well as the occasional awareness of historical events will encourage readers to look for their own family stories." Booklist

Adams, Abigail, 1744-1818

St. George, Judith. John & Abigail Adams. See entry under Adams, John, 1735-1826

Wallner, Alexandra. Abigail Adams; written and illustrated by Alexandra Wallner. Holiday House 2001 unp il $16.95 (1-3)   **92**

1. Presidents' spouses—United States

ISBN 0-8234-1442-6   LC 00-23149

A biography of Abigail Adams, wife of second United States President John Adams, and a dedicated wife and mother who spoke up against slavery and for women's rights

"Full-page, colorful pictures in a folk-art style contribute greatly to the text, capturing the daily life, clothing, and household routines of the times." SLJ

Adams, John, 1735-1826

Harness, Cheryl. The revolutionary John Adams; written and illustrated by Cheryl Harness. National Geographic Soc. 2003 39p il map $17.95 (3-6)   **92**

1. Presidents—United States 2. United States—History—1775-1783, Revolution

ISBN 0-7922-6970-5   LC 2002-11271

A biography of John Adams with emphasis on his role in the American Revolution

"Harness' warm, friendly, mixed-media illustrations, which range from full-color, double-page spreads to labeled diagrams to black-line silhouettes, will delight children, and quotes from Adams' letters, including many letters to his wife, Abigail, are a bonus. A fascinating book for young history buffs." Booklist

Includes bibliographical references

St. George, Judith. John & Abigail Adams; an American love story. Holiday House 2001 147p il $22.95 (6 and up)   **92**

1. Adams, Abigail, 1744-1818 2. Presidents—United States 3. Presidents' spouses—United States

ISBN 0-8234-1571-6   LC 00-48226

"John and Abigail Adams's marriage lasted 54 years, surviving wars, tragedies, politics, and frequent separations. During these absences, the Adamses wrote the letters upon which this biography is based." SLJ

"There's a good deal of information here, and the dual approach is a fine way to introduce children to two remarkable people." Booklist

Includes bibliographical references

Adams, Samuel, 1722-1803

Adler, David A. A picture book of Samuel Adams; by David A. Adler and Michael S. Adler; illustrated by Ronald Himler. 1st ed. Holiday House 2005 unp il $16.95 (1-3)   **92**

1. United States—History—1775-1783, Revolution

ISBN 0-8234-1846-4   LC 2004-49346

"The Adlers recount Adams's life, particularly his contributions to the American Revolution." Horn Book Guide

"The story offers a good introduction to Adams and his times. Himler's pencil drawings with muted watercolor washes provide a series of handsome pictures illustrating moments of reflection as well as scenes of action." Booklist

Includes bibliographical references

Fradin, Dennis B. Samuel Adams; the father of American Independence; [by] Dennis Brindell Fradin. Clarion Bks. 1998 182p il $18 (6 and up)   **92**

1. United States—History—1775-1783, Revolution

ISBN 0-395-82510-5   LC 97-20027

"Archival reproductions effectively complement a descriptive and accurate narrative that imaginatively integrates details of Adams's life with the social and political milieu of the time." Horn Book Guide

Includes bibliographical references

Fritz, Jean. Why don't you get a horse, Sam Adams? illustrated by Trina Schart Hyman. Coward, McCann & Geoghegan; distributed by Putnam Pub. Group 1974 47p il $15.99; pa $5.99 (2-4)   **92**

1. United States—History—1775-1783, Revolution

ISBN 0-399-23401-2; 0-698-11416-7 (pa)

"A piece of history far more entertaining and readable than most fiction. . . . The author has humanized a figure of the Revolution: Adams emerges a marvelously funny and believable man. The illustrations play upon his foibles; they are, in fact, even more outrageously mocking than the text. A tour de force, for both author and illustrator." Horn Book

Ailey, Alvin

Pinkney, Andrea Davis. Alvin Ailey; illustrated by Brian Pinkney. Hyperion Bks. for Children 1993 unp il pa $4.95 hardcover o.p. (k-3)   **92**

1. African American dancers

ISBN 0-7868-1077-7 (pa); 1-56282-413-9 (hc)

          LC 92-54865

Describes the life, dancing, and choreography of Alvin Ailey, who created his own modern dance company to explore the black experience

"Brian Pinkney's marvelously detailed scratchboard drawings are tinted with pastels to show the sweep and flow of dancers caught in the act of leaping, twirling, and soaring through the air. . . . The book is both informative and inspiring." SLJ

Aldrin, Buzz

Aldrin, Buzz. Reaching for the moon; paintings by Wendell Minor. 1st ed. HarperCollins Children's Books 2005 unp il $15.99; lib bdg $16.89 (2-4) **92**

1. Astronauts

ISBN 0-06-055445-2; 0-06-055446-0 (lib bdg)

LC 2004-6247

"In this picture book, Aldrin, the second man to step foot on the moon, relates the life events that led him to the space program and his assignment on Apollo 11. . . . Minor's colorful and precisely rendered illustrations help this effort really take off, especially in the images of Aldrin's space journeys." Booklist

Alexander, the Great, 356-323 B.C.

Adams, Simon. Alexander; the boy soldier who conquered the world. National Geographic 2005 64p il map (World history biographies) $17.95; lib bdg $27.90 (4 and up) **92**

1. Ancient civilization

ISBN 0-7922-3660-2; 0-7922-3661-0 (lib bdg)

This describes the life and times of Alexander the Great.

This is a "handsomely designed [book]. . . . illustrated with maps and many color photographs of art and sculpture that give substance to [the era]. . . . Adams does not downplay Alexander's brutality or all-consuming ambition and includes examples of both." SLJ

Includes bibliographical references

Ali, Muhammad, 1942-

Bolden, Tonya. The champ! the story of Muhammad Ali; illustrated by R. Gregory Christie. 1st ed. Alfred A. Knopf 2004 unp il $17.95; lib bdg $19.99 (2-5) **92**

1. Boxing—Biography 2. African American athletes

ISBN 0-375-82401-4; 0-375-92401-9 (lib bdg)

LC 2004-10082

A biography of the African American boxer

"In simple, clear, and lively text, Bolden introduces both Ali the fighter and Ali the activist. . . . The words interact well with Christie's sturdy acrylic paintings." Booklist

Haskins, James. Champion: the story of Muhammad Ali; [by] Jim Haskins; illustrations by Eric Velasquez. Walker & Co. 2002 unp il $17.95; lib bdg $18.85 (3-5) **92**

1. Boxing—Biography 2. African American athletes

ISBN 0-8027-8784-3; 0-8027-8785-1 (lib bdg)

LC 2001-45374

A biography of Muhammad Ali, from his childhood in Louisville, Kentucky, his legendary boxing career, and his conversion to Islam and opposition to the war in Vietnam, to his appearance at the 1996 summer Olympics in Atlanta.

Written in "plainspoken, economical prose. . . . Haskins's text . . . ably portrays Ali's personal and spiritual joruneys, while Velasquez's page-dominating oil paintings offer pleasing stylistic variations." Horn Book Guide

Shange, Ntozake. Muhammad Ali: the man who could float like a butterfly and sting like a bee; story by Ntozake Shange; illustrated by Edel Rodriguez. Jump at the Sun 2002 unp il $15.99 (k-3) **92**

1. Boxing—Biography 2. African American athletes

ISBN 0-7868-0554-4   LC 2002-72920

Cover title: Float like a butterfly

An introduction to the legendary boxer, Muhammad Ali, including his accomplishments as a fighter and his contributions to society.

"The chronology at the end of the volume fills in the factual gaps, allowing Shange's spare, lyrical text and Rodriguez's theatrical, posterlike mixed-media illustrations—rendered in pastels, ink, gouache, and even spray paint—to simply honor and celebrate the perseverance, generosity, and humanity of this 'hero for all time.'" Horn Book

Allende, Isabel

Benatar, Raquel. Isabel Allende; illustrated by Fernando Molinari; English translation by Patricia Petersen. Piñata Books 2004 unp il $14.95 (3-5) **92**

1. Women authors 2. Bilingual books—English-Spanish

ISBN 1-55885-379-0

A simple description of the childhood and youth of the Chilean author Isabel Allende.

"The brief evocative text outlines the author's life and influences. . . . The colored-pencil illustrations, done in shades of green and gray, are detailed and intriguing, ably communicating a sense of the mysterious. The English translation moves as briskly as the Spanish original and is easy to read aloud. An excellent introduction to Allende and a look at the roots of the creative process." SLJ

Andersen, Hans Christian, 1805-1875

Hesse, Karen. The young Hans Christian Andersen; illustrated by Erik Blegvad. Scholastic Press 2005 48p il $16.99 (2-4) **92**

1. Authors, Danish

ISBN 0-439-67990-7   LC 2004-29100

The story of the early days of the Danish author.

"Hesse uses evocative images and metaphors that parallel Andersen's own writing style to convey some of the formative childhood experiences that appear so poignantly in his fairy tales. . . . Blegvad's bucolic illustrations of ponds, swans, and cottages are done in soft, warm, and sunny colors, and offer lovely images of Denmark in the early 1800s." SLJ

Varmer, Hjørdis. Hans Christian Andersen; his fairy tale life; illustrated by Lilian Brogger; translated by Tiina Nunnally. Groundwood Books 2005 111p il $19.95 (5 and up) **92**

1. Authors, Danish

ISBN 0-88899-690-X

"Most of this book describes Andersen's childhood and belated schooling, showing his poverty and the grief he experienced over the death of his beloved father, as well as several horrifying events such as being forced by

Andersen, Hans Christian, 1805-1875—*Continued*

a teacher to witness the beheading of three young people. . . . The biography is divided into 11 chapters, set up as if they were stories. . . . The writing flows smoothly, with many details provided to help students picture the places and events. Brøgger's haunting, mixed-media illustrations add to the somber and at times surreal feeling of the text." SLJ

Yolen, Jane. The perfect wizard; Hans Christian Andersen; illustrated by Dennis Nolan. Dutton Children's Books 2005 unp il $16.99 (2-4)
92

1. Authors, Danish
ISBN 0-525-46955-9   LC 2003-55717
A biography of the famous Danish writer of fairy tales, interspersed with excerpts from his stories.
"This volume, with its patrician wallpaper and sepia-tinged pastel pictures framed with gentle arches, is handsome. . . . This is a carefully crafted, lovely, and loving tribute to the father of the modern fairy tale." SLJ

Anderson, Marian, 1897-1993

Freedman, Russell. The voice that challenged a nation; Marian Anderson and the struggle for equal rights. Clarion Books 2004 114p il $18 (5 and up)
92

1. African American singers 2. African American women 3. African Americans—Civil rights
ISBN 0-618-15976-2   LC 2003-19558
Contents: Easter Sunday, April 9, 1939; Twenty-five cents a song; A voice in a thousand four: Marian fever; Banned by the DAR; Singing to the nation; Breaking barriers; "What I had was singing."
In the mid-1930s, Marian Anderson was a famed vocalist who had been applauded by European royalty and welcomed at the White House. But, because of her race, she was denied the right to sing at Constitution Hall in Washington, D.C. This is the story of her resulting involvement in the civil rights movement of the time.
"In his signature prose, plain yet eloquent, Freedman tells Anderson's triumphant story, with numerous black-and-white photos and prints that convey her personal struggle, professional artistry, and landmark civil rights role." Booklist
Includes bibliographical references

McKissack, Patricia C. Marian Anderson; a great singer; [by] Patricia and Fredrick McKissack. rev ed. Enslow Pubs. 2001 32p il (Great African Americans) lib bdg $14.95 (1-3)   **92**

1. African American singers 2. African American women
ISBN 0-7660-1676-5   LC 00-12149
Replaces the edition published 1991
Tells the story of the African-American singer who struggled against prejudice to become one of the great opera performers of the century
Includes glossary and bibliographical references

Ryan, Pam Muñoz. When Marian sang: the true recital of Marian Anderson, the voice of a century; libretto by Pam Muñoz Ryan; staging by Brian Selznick. Scholastic Press 2002 unp il $16.95 (2-4)
92

1. African American singers 2. African American women
ISBN 0-439-26967-9   LC 2001-49508
An introduction to the life of Marian Anderson, extraordinary singer and civil rights activist, who was the first African American to perform at the Metropolitan Opera, whose life and career encouraged social change
"This book masterfully distills the events in the life of an extraordinary musician. . . . Working with a sepia-toned palette, Selznick's paintings shimmer with emotion." Publ Wkly

Andrews, Roy Chapman, 1884-1960

Bausum, Ann. Dragon bones and dinosaur eggs: a photobiography of Roy Chapman Andrews. National Geographic Soc. 2000 64p il map $17.95 (5 and up)   **92**

1. Fossils 2. Dinosaurs 3. Naturalists
ISBN 0-7922-7123-8   LC 99-38363
A biography of the great explorer-adventurer, who discovered huge finds of dinosaur bones in Mongolia, pioneered modern paleontology field research, and became the director of the American Museum of Natural History
"Bausum's account reads smoothly, and a layout dense with captioned sepia photographs and quotes from Andrews provides plenty of oases for readers as they follow him through the desert." Bull Cent Child Books
Includes bibliographical references

Marrin, Albert. Secrets from the rocks: dinosaur hunting with Roy Chapman Andrews. Dutton Children's Bks. 2002 64p il map $18.99 (4 and up)
92

1. Fossils 2. Dinosaurs 3. Naturalists
ISBN 0-525-46743-2   LC 2001-47084
A biography of the scientist-adventurer, Roy Chapman Andrews, focusing on the expeditions he led for New York's American Museum of Natural History to the Gobi Desert in Mongolia in an effort to uncover dinosaur fossils
This "is a colorful portrait that offers thought-provoking insight into the constantly shifting nature of scientific discovery." Booklist
Includes bibliographical references

Anning, Mary, 1799-1847

Atkins, Jeannine. Mary Anning and the sea dragon; pictures by Michael Dooling. Farrar, Straus & Giroux 1999 unp il $16 (k-3)
92

1. Fossils
ISBN 0-374-34840-5   LC 97-47547
An account of the finding of the first entire skeleton of an ichthyosaur, an extinct sea reptile, by a twelve-year-old English girl who went on to become a paleontologist
Anning's "patience and persistence, are emphasized in a smoothly crafted narrative. . . . Dooling's watercolors on textured paper employ a predominantly blue, gray, and brown palette." SLJ

Anning, Mary, 1799-1847—*Continued*

Brown, Don. Rare treasure: Mary Anning and her remarkable discoveries; written and illustrated by Don Brown. Houghton Mifflin 1999 unp il $15 (k-3)   **92**
1. Fossils
ISBN 0-395-92286-0   LC 98-32372
Describes the life of the English girl whose discovery of an Ichthyosaurus fossil led to a lasting interest in other prehistoric animals
"Brown dwells on Mary's self-determination, focusing on her adventurous spirit . . . and lifelong quest for knowledge in her chosen field of study. . . . The understated watercolors suit the mood. Their subdued palette (ocean blues, sand browns) and simple compositions are undistracting." Bull Cent Child Books

Anthony, Susan B., 1820-1906

Hopkinson, Deborah. Susan B. Anthony; fighter for women's rights; by Deborah Hopkinson; illustrated by Amy Bates. 1st Aladdin Paperbacks ed. Aladdin 2005 30p il (Ready-to-read stories of famous Americans) lib bdg $11.89; pa $3.99 (2-4)   **92**
1. Women—Suffrage 2. Feminism
ISBN 0-689-86910-x (lib bdg); 0-689-86909-6 (pa)
LC 2004031074
"This biography presents Anthony as a lifelong advocate for women's equality. . . . Soft-edged illustrations complement the simple yet accurate text that informs emergent and reluctant readers of both the historical context and lasting importance of Anthony's contributions to the suffrage movement." SLJ

Antin, Mary, 1881-1949

Wells, Rosemary. Streets of gold; pictures by Dan Andreasen. Dial Bks. for Young Readers 1999 39p il $15.99 (3-6)   **92**
1. Jews—Biography 2. United States—Immigration and emigration
ISBN 0-8037-2149-8   LC 97-50377
Based on: The promised land, by Mary Antin
"This picture-book biography is based upon the life of Masha (Mary) Antin, who emigrated from Russia in 1894. This account has been adapted from her memoir, *The Promised Land*. . . . This beautiful story of hope and inspiration captures the spirit of those who gave up everything for a chance at a better life. The oil paintings provide an evocative accent to the narrative." SLJ

Appleseed, Johnny, 1774-1845

Kellogg, Steven. Johnny Appleseed; a tall tale retold and illustrated by Steven Kellogg. Morrow Junior Bks. 1988 unp il $16.95; lib bdg $16.89 (k-3)   **92**
1. Frontier and pioneer life
ISBN 0-688-06417-5; 0-688-06418-3 (lib bdg)
LC 87-27317
Also available Big book edition
"Oversize pages have given Kellogg a fine opportunity for pictures that are on a large scale, colorful and animated if often busy with details. His version of Chapman's life is more substantial than the subtitle (*A Tall Tale*) would indicate, since the text makes clear the difference between what Chapman really did and what myths grew up about his work, his life, his personality, and his achievements. There's some exaggeration, but on the whole the biography is factual and written with clarity." Bull Cent Child Books

Moses, Will. Johnny Appleseed; the story of a legend. Philomel Bks. 2001 unp il $16.99 (3-6)   **92**
1. Frontier and pioneer life
ISBN 0-399-23153-6   LC 00-44600
This is a "picture-book biography of John Chapman, aka Johnny Appleseed. . . . Starting in 1774, the year of Chapman's birth, Moses briefly covers Chapman's early childhood, and then quickly moves on to his young adult years, when he leaves home for the frontier. The bulk of the book documents Chapman's rich adult life and celebrates his odd ways. . . . The paintings . . . are filled with rich detail and are unforgettable." Booklist
Includes bibliographical references

Archimedes, ca. 287-212 B.C.

Gow, Mary. Archimedes; mathematical genius of the ancient world. Enslow Pub. 2005 128p il (Great minds of science) lib bdg $26.60 (5 and up)   **92**
1. Mathematicians
ISBN 0-7660-2502-0 (lib bdg)   LC 2004-28480
"Because more information has survived about Archimedes's contributions than about his life, most of this book wisely focuses on his mathematical observations 22 centuries ago. Descriptions of Syracuse and Alexandria . . . introduce readers to ancient Greek society and give them a fuller understanding of the importance of Archimedes's discoveries. The next chapters describe the significance of his work regarding levers, buoyancy, geometry, and pi; and of such inventions as the pulley and Archimedes's screw. . . . Good-quality, black-and-white illustrations add information to the clear text." SLJ
Includes glossary and bibliographical references

Aristotle, 384-322 B.C.

Anderson, Margaret Jean. Aristotle; philosopher and scientist; [by] Margaret J. Anderson and Karen F. Stephenson. Enslow Publishers 2004 112p il map (Great minds of science) $26.60 (5 and up)   **92**
1. Philosophers 2. Scientists
ISBN 0-7660-2096-7   LC 2003-2270
Contents: Living in interesting times; Aristotle's childhood; Athens, the City of Wonder; The Academy; A new direction; The Father of Zoology; Alexander; The Lyceum; "A Desire for Knowledge"; The end of the road; His writings live on; Aristotle's influence
"After opening with an overview of the time during which Aristotle lived, the authors discuss his childhood, his student days at the Academy in Athens, his tutoring of Alexander, and his founding of the Lyceum. The bulk of the text focuses on Aristotle's contributions to philosophy and science. . . . The text is clear and concise.

Aristotle, 384-322 B.C.—*Continued*
. . . This easy-to-understand offering will prove useful
for reports." SLJ
Includes bibliographical references

Armstrong, Lance
Armstrong, Kristin Richard. Lance Armstrong;
the race of his life; by Kristin Armstrong;
illustrated by Ken Call with photographs. Grosset
& Dunlap 2000 47p il $13.89; pa $3.90 (1-3)
92
1. Bicycle racing
ISBN 0-448-42415-0; 0-448-42407-X (pa)
LC 00-56199
"All aboard reading"
The wife of the cyclist describes his Tour de France
victory and his battle with cancer
A "captivating, well-paced biography. . . . Written in
language suitable for readers almost ready to make the
transition to chapter books, the text is spiced with personal details that will interest a wide range of children."
Booklist

Donovan, Sandra. Lance Armstrong; by Sandy
Donovan. Lerner Sports 2005 32p il (Amazing
athletes) lib bdg $22.60; pa $5.95 (2-4)
92
1. Bicycle racing
ISBN 0-8225-3691-9 (lib bdg); 0-8225-2039-7 (pa)
LC 2003-23306
Contents: Climbing the mountain; Young athlete; Be-
coming a cyclist; Finding fame; Setback; Tour de France
champion; Selected career highlights
This is a biography of the cycling champion who
overcame cancer and was the first person to win six
Tour de France races.
This offers "exciting color photographs and a lucid,
direct narrative." Booklist
Includes glossary and bibliographical references

Armstrong, Louis, 1900-1971
Collier, James Lincoln. The Louis Armstrong
you never knew. Children's Press 2004 80p il
$25.50 (4 and up)
92
1. Jazz musicians 2. African American musicians
ISBN 0-516-24429-9
LC 2003-28307
Contents: The waif; The music apprentice; Greatness;
The popular band leader; The international star
A biography of the African American jazz trumpeter
and singer
This is "inviting. . . . Excellent photographs bring
Armstrong . . . to life." SLJ
Includes bibliographical references

Kimmel, Eric A. A horn for Louis; by Eric A.
Kimmel; illustrated by James Bernardin. Random
House 2005 86p il $11.95; lib bdg $13.99 (2-4)
92
1. Jazz musicians 2. African American musicians
ISBN 0-375-83252-1; 0-375-93252-6 (lib bdg)
LC 2005004151
"A Stepping Stone book"

"Adapted from an unpublished memoir, this beginning
chapter book is an account of [Louis] Armstrong's
youthful acquisition of his first true horn. . . . Kimmel's
skilled narrative accentuates the diversity of the boys surroundings and the early influence of local music upon his
innate gift. Bernardins dynamic black-and-white artwork
captures the vivacious subject well and includes many
period and cultural details." SLJ

Armstrong, Neil, 1930-
Brown, Don. One giant leap: the story of Neil
Armstrong. Houghton Mifflin 1998 unp il $16
(k-3)
92
1. Astronauts
ISBN 0-395-88401-2
LC 97-42152
Discusses the life and accomplishments of astronaut
Neil Armstrong, from his childhood in Ohio to his fa-
mous moon landing
"The sense of Armstrong as a boy growing into his
childhood dream is strong in the well-constructed text,
and that feeling is extended through watercolors with an
airy sense of lightness that suits the emotional tone."
Bull Cent Child Books

Byers, Ann. Neil Armstrong; the first man on
the moon; [by] Ann Byers. Rosen Pub. Group
2004 112p il (Library of astronaut biographies) lib
bdg $29.95 (4 and up)
92
1. Astronauts
ISBN 0-8239-4461-1
LC 2003-14301
Discusses the life and training as an astronaut of Neil
Armstrong, the first man to set foot on the moon.
"The writing is fast paced and lively. Many color photographs and occasional full-page sidebars enhance the
[text]." SLJ
Includes bibliographical references

Ashe, Arthur, 1943-1993
Cunningham, Kevin. Arthur Ashe; athlete and
activist; by Kevin Cunningham. Child's World
2005 40p il (Journey to freedom) lib bdg $28.50
(5 and up)
92
1. Tennis—Biography 2. African American athletes
ISBN 1-59296-228-9
LC 2003-27076
"With an open design, clear text, and lots of action
photographs, this biography . . . tells the compelling story of the tennis champion and his politics. The facts of
prejudice are here as Ashe learns tennis on segregated
courts. But words and pictures show him in glorious action on the court, where he makes sports history."
Booklist
Includes glossary and bibliographical references

Audubon, John James, 1785-1851
Armstrong, Jennifer. Audubon; painter of birds
in the wild frontier; illustrated by Jos. A. Smith.
Abrams 2003 unp il $17.95 (2-4)
92
1. Artists—United States 2. Naturalists
ISBN 0-8109-4238-0
LC 2002-11921
Briefly tells the story of this nineteenth-century painter
and naturalist who is most famous for his detailed paintings of birds

Audubon, John James, 1785-1851—*Continued*

"This stunning picture book presents intriguing episodes from the life of the acclaimed American naturalist. . . . Smith's watercolor illustrations are so lifelike that one can virtually feel the beat of the swans' wings as the birds attack a pack of wolves. Several samples of Audubon's own artwork add to the artistic appeal of the book. The text is well documented." SLJ

Burleigh, Robert. Into the woods: John James Audubon lives his dream; paintings by Wendell Minor. Atheneum Bks. for Young Readers 2003 unp il $16.95 (3-5)   **92**
   1. Naturalists 2. Artists—United States
   ISBN 0-689-83040-8   LC 2001-22954

This is a "portrayal of artist-naturalist John James Audubon, revealed through an imagined conversation between Audubon and his father. Brief, rhymed lines of conversation followed by italicized quotes from Audubon's actual journals explain why Audubon chose to forego the ordinary life of a shopkeeper to explore nature and develop his art. Brightly toned watercolors that realistically recreate the scenery and the wildlife of the early 1800s are accentuated with spot-art cameos of birds from Audubon's paintings. Full-page pictures on the right-hand pages alternate with double-page spreads to create a visual rhythm that matches the spare, poetic text." Booklist

Davies, Jacqueline. The boy who drew birds: a story of John James Audubon; illustrated by Melissa Sweet. Houghton Mifflin Co 2004 unp il map $15 (2-4)   **92**
   1. Artists—United States 2. Naturalists 3. Birds
   ISBN 0-618-24343-7   LC 2004-971

This describes how John James Audubon studied and painted birds.

"Sweet's mixed-media collage artwork includes sensitive pencil sketches and ink drawings washed with watercolors and gouache, as well as elements such as photos of bird nests and bones. . . . This handsome book makes a beguiling introduction to the painter." Booklist

Includes bibliographical references

Bach, Johann Sebastian, 1685-1750

Winter, Jeanette. Sebastian: a book about Bach. Harcourt Brace & Co. 1999 unp il $16 (k-3)   **92**
   1. Composers
   ISBN 0-15-200629-X   LC 98-5543

Describes how Johann Sebastian Bach survived the sorrows of his childhood and composed the music the world has come to love.

"Winter's spare poetic text is beautiful. . . . In brilliant colors, with lots of blue and purple, the framed acrylic quiltlike paintings have depth and clear detail." Booklist

Balboa, Vasco Núñez de, 1475-1519

Otfinoski, Steven. Vasco Nuñez de Balboa; explorer of the Pacific; by Steven Otfinoski. Benchmark Books 2005 79p il map (Great explorations) lib bdg $29.93 (5 and up)   **92**
   1. Explorers 2. America—Exploration
   ISBN 0-7614-1609-9   LC 2003-14927

Contents: A daring youth; To the New World; From stowaway to governor; The first conquistador; To the South Sea; Discoverer of the Pacific; A new rival; Last adventure; The final treachery

Describes the life of Vasco Nuñez de Balboa, the Spanish explorer who was the first European to see the Pacific Ocean and who conceived the idea of a canal connecting the Atlantic and Pacific.

Includes bibliographical references

Ballard, Robert D., 1942-

Hill, Christine M. Robert Ballard; oceanographer who discovered the Titanic. Enslow Pubs. 1999 128p il (People to know) lib bdg $20.95 (5 and up)   **92**
   1. Oceanography—Biography
   ISBN 0-7660-1147-X   LC 98-54437

A biography which covers the life and professional work of the man whose numerous missions to study the ocean floor led to the discovery of the wreck of the Titanic

"A valuable source. . . . A chronology, glossary, and meticulous endnotes add to the strength of this fine work." Booklist

Banneker, Benjamin, 1731-1806

Ferris, Jeri. What are you figuring now? a story about Benjamin Banneker; illustrations by Amy Johnson. Carolrhoda Bks. 1988 64p il (Carolrhoda creative minds book) lib bdg $21.27; pa $5.95 (3-5)   **92**
   1. Astronomers 2. African Americans—Biography
   ISBN 0-87614-331-1 (lib bdg); 0-87614-521-7 (pa)
                 LC 88-7267

"A Carolrhoda creative minds book."

A biography of the African American farmer and self-taught mathematician, astronomer, and surveyor for the new capital city of the United States in 1791, who also calculated a successful almanac notable for its preciseness

"Ferris' judicious use of dialogue and Johnson's full-page gray washes enhance this smooth, engaging biographical story; the mature style and succinct text make this a good choice for reluctant readers." Booklist

Hinman, Bonnie. Benjamin Banneker; American mathematician and astronomer; Arthur M. Schlesinger, senior consulting editor. Chelsea House 2000 79p il (Colonial leaders) lib bdg $21.85; pa $8.95 (5 and up)   **92**
   1. Astronomers 2. African Americans—Biography
   ISBN 0-7910-5348-2 (lib bdg); 0-7910-5691-0 (pa)
                 LC 99-24118

A biography of the eighteenth-century African American who taught himself mathematics and astronomy and helped survey what would become Washington, D.C

Banneker's "life, efforts, and achievements are described in a most engaging manner." Sci Books Films

Includes bibliographical references

Banneker, Benjamin, 1731-1806—*Continued*

Pinkney, Andrea Davis. Dear Benjamin Banneker; illustrated by Brian Pinkney. Harcourt Brace & Co. 1994 unp il $16; pa $6 (2-4)

92

1. Astronomers 2. African Americans—Biography
ISBN 0-15-200417-3; 0-15-201892-1 (pa)

LC 93-31162

"Gulliver books"

"The Pinkneys chronicle Banneker's work on his almanac and, most particularly, his letter to Thomas Jefferson, then secretary of state, protesting the country's—and Jefferson's—involvement in slavery." Bull Cent Child Books

This offers "lucid text and striking illustrations, rendered on scratchboard and colored with oil paint." Publ Wkly

Wadsworth, Ginger. Benjamin Banneker; pioneering scientist; illustrations by Craig Orback. Carolrhoda Books 2003 47p il lib bdg $22.60; pa $5.95 (3-5)

92

1. Astronomers 2. African Americans—Biography
ISBN 0-87614-916-6 (lib bdg); 0-87614-104-1 (pa)

LC 2002-985

Introduces Benjamin Banneker, a free black man of the eighteenth century who loved to learn and used his knowledge and observations to build a wooden clock, write an almanac, and help survey the streets of Washington, D.C.

Barton, Clara, 1821-1912

Koestler-Grack, Rachel A. The story of Clara Barton. Chelsea Clubhouse 2004 32p il (Breakthrough biographies) lib bdg $14.95 (2-4)

92

1. American Red Cross 2. Nurses
ISBN 0-7910-7312-2

LC 2003-267

Describes the life of the nurse who served on the battlefields of the Civil War and later founded the American Red Cross

"The book is illustrated with historical documents, original art, and color photographs of places that still exist. The captions are clear and informative." SLJ

Includes glossary and bibliographical references

Bartram, John, 1699-1777

Ray, Deborah Kogan. Flower hunter. See entry under Bartram, William, 1739-1823

Bartram, William, 1739-1823

Ray, Deborah Kogan. Flower hunter; William Bartram, America's first naturalist. Frances Foster Books/Farrar, Straus and Giroux 2004 unp il $17 (3-5)

92

1. Bartram, John, 1699-1777 2. Botanists
3. Naturalists
ISBN 0-374-34589-9

LC 2002-23186

Young Billy Bartram keeps a journal of his experiences learning about the plants of the colonial United States from his father, John Bartram, as they travel together gathering specimens and planting seeds.

"Large watercolor, gouache, and colored-pencil illustrations interpret the story with great warmth and beauty. This unique book offers students a different perspective on life in eighteenth-century America." Booklist

Bates, Katharine Lee, 1859-1929

Younger, Barbara. Purple mountain majesties: the story of Katharine Lee Bates and "America the beautiful"; illustrated by Stacey Schuett. Dutton Children's Bks. 1998 unp il $16.99 (2-4)

92

1. America the beautiful (Song) 2. Women authors
3. Authors, American
ISBN 0-525-45653-8

LC 98-12884

A brief biography of the author and college professor whose travels across the United States inspired her to write the poem which became the song "America the Beautiful"

This book "has much to recommend it, from its concise but engagingly informative text to its single and double-page spreads illustrating the panorama of Bates' America." Bull Cent Child Books

Bates, Peg Leg, 1907-1998

Barasch, Lynne. Knockin' on wood; starring Peg Leg Bates; by Lynne Barasch. 1st ed. Lee & Low Books 2004 unp il $16.95 (2-4)

92

1. African American dancers 2. Tap dancing
3. Handicapped
ISBN 1-58430-170-8

LC 2003-22905

A picture book biography of Clayton "Peg Leg" Bates, an African American who lost his leg in a factory accident at the age of twelve and went on to become a world-famous tap dancer.

"Sprightly ink-and-watercolor art ably depicts both the poverty of Bates' early life and the colorful world of entertainment. . . . Barasch subtly sets the story against American racism." Booklist

Bearden, Romare, 1914-1988

Greenberg, Jan. Romare Bearden; collage of memories. Abrams 2003 52p il $17.95 (4 and up)

92

1. African American artists
ISBN 0-8109-4589-4

LC 2002-153715

Recounts the life of the twentieth-century African-American collage artist who used his southern childhood, New York City, jazz, and Paris to influence his art

"This beautiful, large-size volume with exquisite reproductions of [Bearden's] art is both a biography and an exciting accessible introduction to his amazing work." Booklist

Includes bibliographical references

Bell, Alexander Graham, 1847-1922

Durrett, Deanne. Alexander Graham Bell. KidHaven Press 2003 48p il map (Inventors and creators) $18.95 (4-6)

92

1. Inventors
ISBN 0-7377-0991-X

LC 2001-6610

Bell, Alexander Graham, 1847-1922—*Continued*
Discusses the early childhood, education, interests, and
inventions of Alexander Graham Bell
"This title is a solid resource. . . . The content is well
written and easy to understand. . . . Photographs and
drawings enhance the story and offer readers a glimpse
of this time in history." Libr Media Connect
Includes glossary and bibliographical references

Matthews, Tom L. Always inventing: a
photobiography of Alexander Graham Bell.
National Geographic Soc. 1999 64p il $17.95 (4
and up)   **92**
1. Inventors
ISBN 0-7922-7391-5   LC 98-27209
A biography, with photographs and quotes from Bell
himself, which follows this well known inventor from his
childhood in Scotland through his life-long efforts to
come up with ideas that would improve people's lives
"Succinct, lively, and readable, the text is illustrated
with many well-captioned period photographs of Bell, his
family, his associate, and his inventions as well as a host
of diagrams." Booklist
Includes bibliographical references

Bemelmans, Ludwig, 1898-1962
Marciano, John Bemelmans. Bemelmans; the
life & art of Madeline's creator; by John
Bemelmans Marciano. Viking 1999 151p il $40
                                                     92
1. Authors, American 2. Illustrators
ISBN 0-670-88460-X   LC 99-25646
"The grandson of Ludwig Bemelmans writes an entirely affectionate biography, 'one with obvious and un-
apologetic bias,' of the *bon vivant* grandfather whose
range of talent extended far beyond his signature Madeline books. . . . Marciano's attractive portrait of his
grandfather is done 'with loving care,' the very words inscribed on the Madeline sketch that ends this enchanting
tale of talent." Horn Book
Includes bibliographical references

Benedict, Saint, Abbot of Monte Cassino
Norris, Kathleen. The holy twins: Benedict and
Scholastica; written by Kathleen Norris; illustrated
by Tomie De Paola. Putnam 2001 unp il $16.99
(3-5)   **92**
1. Scholastica, Saint, 6th cent 2. Christian saints
ISBN 0-399-23424-1   LC 00-40294
"This fictionalized biography of Saints Benedict and
Scholastica, twins who lived in sixth-century Italy, is told
in a lively, authoritative manner. . . . dePaola's elegant,
stylized artwork seems particularly well suited to the
eternal quality of religious subjects. The framed spreads
are painted in soft, warm acrylics on tea-stained watercolor paper, which gives the semblance of an old manuscript." SLJ

Bentley, Wilson Alwyn, 1865-1931
Martin, Jacqueline Briggs. Snowflake Bentley;
illustrated by Mary Azarian. Houghton Mifflin
1998 unp il $16 (k-3)   **92**
1. Snow 2. Scientists
ISBN 0-395-86162-4   LC 97-12458

Awarded the Caldecott Medal, 1999
A biography of a self-taught scientist who photographed thousands of individual snowflakes in order to
study their unique formations
"Azarian's woodblock illustrations, hand tinted with
watercolors, blend perfectly with the text and recall the
rural Vermont of Bentley's time. . . . The story of this
man's life is written with graceful simplicity." SLJ

Berenstain, Jan, 1923-
Berenstain, Stan. Down a sunny dirt road. See
entry under Berenstain, Stan, 1923-2005

Berenstain, Stan, 1923-2005
Berenstain, Stan. Down a sunny dirt road; an
autobiography; [by] Stan & Jan Berenstain.
Random House 2002 202p il $20 (4 and up)
                                                     92
1. Berenstain, Jan, 1923- 2. Authors, American
ISBN 0-375-81403-5   LC 2001-48317
In alternating chapters Stan and Jan Berenstain, creators of the Berenstain Bears, tell their own stories from
early childhood until their marriage, then continue the
tale together to the present day
"Their illustrations of themselves jitterbugging or
playing field hockey (rendered in the Berenstain's familiar, contemporary style) demonstrate the impressive ver-
satility of the couple's talents. Though sometimes long
on detail, this breezy, humorous saga makes for an intriguing publishing tale." Publ Wkly
Includes bibliographical references

Blériot, Louis, 1872-1936
Provensen, Alice. The glorious flight: across the
Channel with Louis Blériot, July 25, 1909; [by]
Alice and Martin Provensen. Viking 1983 39p il
pa $6.99 hardcover o.p. (1-4)   **92**
1. Air pilots 2. Airplanes—Design and construction
ISBN 0-14-050729-9 (pa)   LC 82-7034
Awarded the Caldecott Medal, 1984
This book "recounts the persistence of a Frenchman,
Louis Blériot, to build a flying machine to cross the English Channel. For eight years (1901-1909) he tries and
tries again to create a kind of contraption light enough
to lift him off the ground and yet strong enough to keep
from falling apart." SLJ
"A pleasing text recounts Bleriot's adventures with
gentle humor and admiration for his earnest, if accident-
prone, determination. Best of all, the pictures shine with
the illustrator's delight in the wondrous flying machines
themselves." Horn Book

Bloomer, Amelia Jenks, 1818-1894
Corey, Shana. You forgot your skirt, Amelia
Bloomer; a very improper story; illustrated by
Chesley McLaren. Scholastic Press 2000 unp il lib
bdg $16.95 (k-2)   **92**
1. Feminism 2. Clothing and dress 3. Women's rights
ISBN 0-439-07819-9   LC 99-27181
This is a "biography of the woman who briefly rocked
the nineteenth-century American fashion world with her

Bloomer, Amelia Jenks, 1818-1894—*Continued*
liberating, eccentric pantaloon-styled garb." Bull Cent
Child Books

"With an irresistible blend of humor, history and panache, this tale demonstrates how one woman's fashion
statement reflected the changing role of women in society." Publ Wkly

Bly, Nellie, 1864-1922
Christensen, Bonnie. The daring Nellie Bly;
America's star reporter. Knopf 2003 unp il $16.95;
lib bdg $18.99 (3-5) **92**
1. Women journalists
ISBN 0-375-81568-6; 0-375-91568-0 (lib bdg)
LC 2002-152478
Introduces the life of Nellie Bly who, as a "stunt reporter" for the New York World newspaper in the late
1800s, championed women's rights and traveled around
the world faster than anyone ever had

"In an easy-to-read style, Christensen lets Bly's story
tell itself, and her art . . . is powerful and rich in color.
She uses strong black line to outline figures, add detail,
and emphasize vivid facial expression in over-size pictures that are full of movement and action." Booklist
Includes bibliographical references

Booth, Edwin, 1833-1893
Giblin, James. Good brother, bad brother. See
entry under Booth, John Wilkes, 1838-1865

Booth, John Wilkes, 1838-1865
Giblin, James. Good brother, bad brother; the
story of Edwin Booth and John Wilkes Booth.
Clarion Books 2005 244p il $22 (5 and up)
92
1. Booth, Edwin, 1833-1893 2. Lincoln, Abraham,
1809-1865—Assassination 3. Actors 4. United
States—History—1861-1865, Civil War 5. Brothers
ISBN 0-618-09642-6 LC 2004-21260
Giblin "frames the intertwined tale of two brothers
with accounts of their families, friends, the Civil War,
and nineteenth-century theater. . . . Alcoholism and depression afflicted the family, but Giblin is brilliant at
showing that darkness was only one part of a life. . . .
Giblin's book will engross readers until the very last
footnote." Booklist
Includes bibliographical references

Braille, Louis, 1809-1852
Adler, David A. A picture book of Louis
Braille; illustrated by John & Alexandra Wallner.
Holiday House 1997 unp il $16.95; pa $6.95 (1-3)
92
1. Blind
ISBN 0-8234-1291-1; 0-8234-1413-2 (pa)
LC 96-38453
Presents the life of the nineteenth-century Frenchman,
accidentally blinded as a child, who originated the raised
dot system of reading and writing used by the blind
throughout the world

"The text is simple yet informative. . . . Adler sprinkles in interesting facts about early 19th-century France
that help readers better grasp Braille's world. . . . Softly
colored illustrations in line and watercolor add visual
clues for younger children." SLJ

Freedman, Russell. Out of darkness: the story of
Louis Braille; illustrated by Kate Kiesler. Clarion
Bks. 1997 81p il $16.95; pa $7.95 (4 and up)
92
1. Blind
ISBN 0-395-77516-7; 0-395-96888-7 (pa)
LC 95-52353
This biography "tells about Braille's life and the de-
velopment of his alphabet system for the blind." SLJ

"Without melodrama, Freedman tells the momentous
story in quiet chapters in his best plain style, making the
facts immediate and personal. . . . A diagram explains
how the Braille alphabet works, and Kate Kessler's full-
page shaded pencil illustrations are part of the understated poignant drama." Booklist

Breckinridge, Mary, 1881-1965
Wells, Rosemary. Mary on horseback; three
mountain stories; pictures by Peter McCarty. Dial
Bks. for Young Readers 1998 53p il $16.99; pa
$4.99 (4 and up) **92**
1. Nurses
ISBN 0-670-88923-7; 0-14-130815-x (pa)
LC 97-43409
Tells the stories of three families who were helped by
the work of Mary Breckinridge, the first nurse to go into
the Appalachian Mountains and give medical care to the
isolated inhabitants. Includes an afterword with facts
about Breckinridge and the Frontier Nursing Service she
founded

"These beautifully written stories will remain with the
reader long after the book is closed." Booklist

Bridges, Ruby
Bridges, Ruby. Through my eyes: the
autobiography of Ruby Bridges; articles and
interviews compiled and edited by Margo Lundell.
Scholastic Press 1999 63p il $16.95 (4 and up)
92
1. African Americans—Civil rights 2. New Orleans
(La.)—Race relations
ISBN 0-590-18923-9 LC 98-49242
Ruby Bridges recounts the story of her involvement,
as a six-year-old, in the integration of her school in New
Orleans in 1960

"Profusely illustrated with sepia photos—including
many gritty journalistic reproductions—this memoir
brings some of the raw emotions of a tumultuous period
into sharp focus. . . . A powerful personal narrative that
every collection will want to own." SLJ

Brown, Clara, 1800-1885

Lowery, Linda. Aunt Clara Brown; official pioneer; illustrations by Janice Lee Porter. Carolrhoda Bks. 1999 48p il (On my own biography) lib bdg $19.93; pa $5.95 (2-4)

92

1. African American women 2. Frontier and pioneer life
ISBN 1-57505-045-5 (lib bdg); 1-57505-416-7 (pa)
LC 98-24259

A biography of the freed slave who made her fortune in Colorado and used her money to bring other former slaves there to begin new lives

"The well-defined primitivist shapes, canvas-y textures, and muted earth tones of the illustrations perfectly evoke the roughness of the terrain and the historical period, as well as the powerful basic emotions motivating the characters. The straightforward text allows the facts speak for themselves. . . . A good story and a solid resource." Bull Cent Child Books

Brown, Molly, 1867-1932

Landau, Elaine. Heroine of the Titanic: the real unsinkable Molly Brown. Clarion Bks. 2001 132p il $18 (5 and up)

92

ISBN 0-395-93912-7   LC 00-57015

This is a biography of the survivor of the Titanic who supported such causes as worker's rights and feminism

"A realistic biography of an independent and strong-willed woman. . . . Black-and-white archival illustrations and photos highlight her life as well as greater relevant aspects of the period in which she lived." SLJ

Includes bibliographical references

Bunting, Eve, 1928-

McGinty, Alice B. Meet Eve Bunting. PowerKids Press 2003 24p il map (About the author) lib bdg $18.95 (1-3)

92

1. Authors, American 2. Women authors
ISBN 0-8239-6411-6   LC 2002-153

A short biography of the Irish-born author who has written over 200 books, including "Smoky Night," which won the Caldecott Medal in 1995

This combines a "simply written . . . [account of Bunting's] youth, career, and particular interests with tempting sample passages of that author's work and a bright, generous array of baby pictures, family photos, portraits, and book covers." Booklist

Includes glossary

Bush, George W.

Kachurek, Sandra J. George W. Bush. Enslow Publishers 2004 128p il (United States presidents) lib bdg $26.60 (4 and up)

92

1. Presidents—United States
ISBN 0-7660-2040-1   LC 2003-19539

Discusses the life and political career of George W. Bush, up through the events of September 11, 2001, and the subsequent War on Terror.

"This biography is a solid introduction to the forty-third president. . . . The writing is involving, and Kachurek's coverage is evenhanded. . . . Studding the text are crisply reproduced, black-and-white photos." Booklist

Includes bibliographical references

Byars, Betsy Cromer, 1928-

Cammarano, Rita. Betsy Byars. Chelsea House 2002 106p il (Who wrote that?) $22.95 (4 and up)

92

1. Authors, American 2. Women authors
ISBN 0-7910-6720-3   LC 2001-8337

Contents: Planes, people and pets; Miss Harriet, Bubba, and the zoo; Books, a river, and a fox; Swan time; Wings and things; From swimming to soaring; Golly blossom bingo; Reaching for the moon; A well that never goes dry

Describes the personal life and successful writing career of the Newbery Award-winning author, whose memorable characters include Bingo Brown, Herculeah Jones, and the Golly sisters

"An excellent resource for author studies and creative writing classes." Book Rep

Includes bibliographical references

Carr, Emily, 1871-1945

Debon, Nicolas. Four pictures by Emily Carr. Douglas & McIntyre 2003 unp il $15.95 (4 and up)

92

1. Artists, Canadian 2. Women artists
ISBN 0-88899-532-6

"Debon has distilled four periods in the Canadian artist's life (1871-1945) into enticing vignettes that illuminate her passions, determination, health problems, relationships with fellow Group of Seven artists, and, most of all, her dramatic progression as a painter. . . . Engaging artwork and brisk storytelling make this a consideration for most libraries." SLJ

Carson, Rachel, 1907-1964

Ehrlich, Amy. Rachel: the story of Rachel Carson; illustrated by Wendell Minor. Silver Whistle/Harcourt 2003 unp il $16 (2-4)

92

1. Women scientists
ISBN 0-15-216227-5   LC 00-13115

This "anecdotal biography of nature writer and environmentalist Carson focuses on incidents that influenced Carson's thinking and career aspirations. . . . Minor's . . . impressively realistic watercolor and gouache paintings lend a pleasing cohesiveness to the volume." Publ Wkly

Gow, Mary. Rachel Carson; ecologist and activist. Enslow Pubs. 2005 128p il (Great minds of science) lib bdg $31.93 (5 and up)

92

1. Women scientists
ISBN 0-7660-2503-9

A biography of the environmentalist and author of "Silent Spring."

Includes glossary and bibliographical references

Carter, Jimmy, 1924-
Kent, Deborah. Jimmy Carter; [by] Deborah Kent. Children's Press 2005 110p il (Encyclopedia of presidents) $34 (4 and up) **92**
1. Presidents—United States
ISBN 0-516-22975-3   LC 2004-17772
Contents: The morning bell; To see the world; Peanuts and politics; From Atlanta to Washington; The greatest challenge of all; Citizen Jimmy Carter
This offers a "look at Carter's youth and presidency plus tributes to his humanitarian work for Habitat for Humanity and the Jimmy Carter Center. . . . This provides insight into both the man and his career and makes an excellent choice for middle-grade assignments." Booklist
Includes bibliographical references

Carver, George Washington, 1864?-1943
Adler, David A. A picture book of George Washington Carver; illustrated by Dan Brown. Holiday House 1999 unp il $16.95; pa $6.95 (1-3) **92**
1. Scientists 2. African Americans—Biography
ISBN 0-8234-1429-9; 0-8234-1633-X (pa)
     LC 98-20261
A brief biography of the African American scientist who overcame tremendous hardship to make unusual and important discoveries in the field of agriculture
"The colorful illustrations complement the simple, but informative text to give children a solid introduction to one of America's most important scientists." SLJ
Includes bibliographical references

Mitchell, Barbara. A pocketful of goobers: a story about George Washington Carver; illustrations by Peter E. Hanson. Carolrhoda Bks. 1986 64p il (Carolrhoda creative minds book) lib bdg $21.27; pa $5.95 (3-5) **92**
1. Scientists 2. African Americans—Biography
ISBN 0-87614-292-7 (lib bdg); 0-87614-474-1 (pa)
     LC 86-2690
Relates the scientific efforts of George Washington Carver, especially his production of more than 300 uses for the peanut
"This book tells his remarkable story accurately, sympathetically, and felicitously." Sci Books Films

Cassatt, Mary, 1844-1926
Casey, Carolyn. Mary Cassatt; the life of an artist. Enslow Publishers 2004 48p il (Artist biographies) $23.93 (2-4) **92**
1. Artists—United States 2. Women artists
ISBN 0-7660-2093-2   LC 2003-17616
Discusses the life and the work of the Impressionist painter Mary Cassatt
Includes glossary and bibliographical references

O'Connor, Jane. Mary Cassatt; family pictures; illustrated by Jennifer Kalis. Grosset & Dunlap 2003 unp il (Smart about art) lib bdg $14.89; pa $5.99 (2-4) **92**
1. Artists—United States 2. Women artists
ISBN 0-448-43153-X (lib bdg); 0-448-43152-1 (pa)
     LC 2002-151305

Discusses the life and the work of the Impressionist painter Mary Cassatt in the form of a child's school report
"The vivid illustrations are a combination of reproductions of Cassatt's work, Claire's cartoon drawings, and a few family photos. . . . [A] slim, exuberant introduction to Cassatt's life and art." SLJ

Cézanne, Paul, 1839-1906
Burleigh, Robert. Paul Cezanne; a painter's journey. H.N. Abrams 2006 31p il $17.95 (4 and up) **92**
1. Artists, French
ISBN 0-8109-5784-1   LC 2005011779
Published in association with the National Gallery of Art
"Burleigh offers brief insights into Cézanne's personal life, such as his relationship with his father, who did not support his sons interest in art. However, the emphasis is on interpreting some individual paintings and understanding the artist's various styles, including the impact of the Impressionists and his evolution to a freer and simpler manner of expression in his later years. . . . The high-quality reproductions demonstrate Burleigh's points. . . . A solid, lively introduction." SLJ

Chagall, Marc, 1887-1985
Markel, Michelle. Dreamer from the village; the story of Marc Chagall; illustrated by Emily Lisker. 1st ed. H. Holt 2005 unp il $16.95 (k-3) **92**
1. Artists, Russian
ISBN 0-8050-6373-0   LC 2003-22498
"Opening with the artist's dramatic birth during a fire in a small Russian village, Markel describes Chagall's childhood and early career. The village, his extended family, and deep Jewish roots are all emphasized, elements that are central to understanding his art. . . . The language is often poetic. . . . The vivid illustrations are inspired by Chagall, but Lisker doesn't attempt to copy his style directly. . . . [This is] an excellent portrait of an artist that will open and expand children's minds." SLJ

Chaka, Zulu Chief, 1787?-1828
Stanley, Diane. Shaka, king of the Zulus; [by] Diane Stanley and Peter Vennema; illustrated by Diane Stanley. Morrow Junior Bks. 1988 unp il pa $5.95 hardcover o.p. (4 and up) **92**
1. Zulu (African people)
ISBN 0-688-13114-X (pa)   LC 87-27376
A biography of the nineteenth-century military genius and Zulu chief
"Diane Stanley and Peter Vennema have culled the massive amount of historical material that exists about this strange and fascinating figure. Their text is lucid; the incidents are tactfully within the scope and decorum of a children's book but representative and true to the facts. . . . The rhythm of the illustrations . . . makes each page not only a realistic representation but also an artistic composition." N Y Times Book Rev
Includes bibliographical references

Champlain, Samuel de, 1567-1635

Faber, Harold. Samuel de Champlain; explorer of Canada; Harold Faber. Benchmark Books 2005 80p il map (Great explorations) lib bdg $29.93 (5 and up)   92

1. Explorers 2. America—Exploration

ISBN 0-7614-1608-0   LC 2003-974

Contents: Growing up; First voyage to Canada; The fur trade; Founding of Quebec; The battle of Lake Champlain; More voyages to Canada; Disappointments; Governor of New France

"Faber draws on Champlain's own accounts to trace his exploration of and dogged determination to colonize Canada. . . . Illustrated with beautiful reproductions of period illustrations, paintings, and maps. . . . Well-written." SLJ

Includes bibliographical references

Champollion, Jean François, 1790-1832

Rumford, James. Seeker of knowledge; the man who deciphered Egyptian hieroglyphs. Houghton Mifflin 2000 unp il $15 (3-5)   92

1. Hieroglyphics

ISBN 0-395-97934-X   LC 99-37254

A biography of the French scholar whose decipherment of the Egyptian hieroglyphic language made the study of ancient Egypt possible

"Despite the book's traditional picture-book appearance, with a short text and nicely rendered watercolor art, the topic requires and gets sturdy treatment. . . . Those intrigued by hieroglyphs . . . will find this a useful introduction." Booklist

Chavez, Cesar, 1927-1993

Krull, Kathleen. Harvesting hope: the story of Cesar Chavez; illustrated by Yuyi Morales. Harcourt 2003 unp il $17 (2-4)   92

1. Mexican Americans—Biography 2. Migrant labor

ISBN 0-15-201437-3   LC 2002-5096

A biography of Cesar Chavez, from age ten when he and his family lived happily on their Arizona ranch, to age thirty-eight when he led a peaceful protest against California migrant workers' miserable working conditions

"The brief text creates a remarkably complex view of Chavez—his experiences and feelings. Krull's empathetic words are well paired with artist Yuyi Morales's mixed-media acrylic paintings, which are suffused with a variety of emotions. . . . The pictures glow with intense shades of gold, green, pink, and orange." Horn Book

Wadsworth, Ginger. Cesar Chavez; by Ginger Wadsworth; illustrations by Mark Schroder. Carolrhoda Books 2005 48p il (On my own biography) lib bdg $23.93; pa $5.95 (2-4)   92

1. Mexican Americans—Biography 2. Migrant labor

ISBN 1-57505-652-6 (lib bdg); 1-57505-826-X (pa)   LC 2004-6571

Contents: Arizona; Hard times; Growing up; Action!; After the strike

This "picture book combines the history of the migrant farm workers' struggle with Chavez's personal story. The clear, direct text tells how Chavez . . . grew up to organize the first farm workers union with Dolores Huerta, and led a successful, five-year grape boycott in the 1960s. . . . Schroder's realistic color, often full-page illustrations show Chavez with his people, working in the fields and on the march. . . . A good way to introduce children to the hero and to the issues." Booklist

Churchill, Sir Winston, 1874-1965

Binns, T. B. Winston Churchill; soldier and politician; [by] Tristan Boyer Binns. Franklin Watts 2004 127p il (Great life stories) $30.50 (5 and up)   92

1. Prime ministers—Great Britain 2. Great Britain—Politics and government—20th century

ISBN 0-531-12361-8   LC 2004-2946

Contents: The early years; Enter the army; The young statesman; World War One; Roaring through the twenties; The wilderness years; Back in power; The tide turns; Victory in Europe; After the war; A great life ends

This is an introduction to the life of Winston Churchill, British Prime Minister during World War II

"Binns does an excellent job of looking at the statesman's major successes, struggles, downfalls, and rises to political prominence. . . . Archival photographs and reproductions and boxes of information are attractive." SLJ

Includes bibliographical references

Clark, Eugenie

Ross, Michael Elsohn. Fish watching with Eugenie Clark; illustrations by Wendy Smith. Carolrhoda Bks. 2000 48p il (Naturalist's apprentice) $19.93 (4 and up)   92

1. Women scientists 2. Fishes

ISBN 1-57505-384-5   LC 99-19963

Describes the life and career of ichthyologist Eugenie Clark, who began her research observing fresh-water aquarium fishes and moved on to the underwater study of sharks and other marine animals. Includes observation tips and and related activities

"Ross presents a bright, readable, up-to-the-minute biography. . . . The well-organized text is illustrated with a number of somewhat unpretentious black-and-white and full-color photos, but they are almost eclipsed by Smith's colorful drawings of a wide variety of fish mentioned in Clark's studies." SLJ

Includes bibliographical references

Clemente, Roberto, 1934-1972

Ford, Carin T. Roberto Clemente; baseball legend. Enslow Pubs. 2005 128p il (Latino biography library) lib bdg $31.93 (5 and up)   92

1. Baseball—Biography 2. Puerto Ricans—Biography

ISBN 0-7660-2485-7

This "account of the major leagues' first Puerto Rican superstar highlights the player's extraordinary talent and humanitarian drive as well as his less-admirable hot temper and often cocky demeanor. . . . The basic arc of Clemente's biography, particularly his tragic death, ensures an exciting read, with special appeal for sports fans." Booklist

Includes bibliographical references

Clemente, Roberto, 1934-1972—*Continued*

Márquez, Herón. Roberto Clemente; baseball's humanitarian hero; by Herón Márquez. Carolrhoda Books 2005 112p il (Trailblazer biography) lib bdg $27.93 (4 and up)   **92**

1. Baseball—Biography 2. Puerto Ricans—Biography
ISBN 1-57505-767-0   LC 2004-2319

Contents: Introduction; Field of dreams; Turning heads, turning pro; Don't cry for me, Puerto Rico; The man of steel; Good night, Clemente; An immortal moment; Death of a hero

This "biography of the baseball great begins with Clemente's early life in Puerto Rico and ends with his death delivering supplies to earthquake victims in Nicaragua in 1972." Booklist

"This excellent biography is well organized and enlivened with interesting details and anecdotes. . . . Balancing facts with insightful perspective, this is a readable, well-rounded portrait." SLJ

Includes bibliographical references

Winter, Jonah. Roberto Clemente; pride of the Pittsburgh Pirates; illustrated by Raul Colón. Atheneum Books for Young Readers 2005 unp il $16.95 (2-4)   **92**

1. Baseball—Biography 2. Puerto Ricans—Biography
ISBN 0-689-85643-1   LC 2003-25546

"An Anne Schwartz book"

"Winter tells the . . . story of how Clemente's passionate love of the game and unrivaled work ethic took him from poverty in Puerto Rico . . . to World Series triumph with the Pittsburgh Pirates and, later . . . to near-mythic status as a role model for young Latino ballplayers. Soaked in pastoral greens and browns, Colon's evocatively grainy, soft-focus illustrations, rendered with a mix of watercolors, colored pencils, and litho pencils, capture perfectly the worlds in which Clemente was most at home. . . . Baseball history brought vividly to life for a younger audience." Booklist

Cleopatra, Queen of Egypt, d. 30 B.C.

Stanley, Diane. Cleopatra; [by] Diane Stanley, Peter Vennema; illustrated by Diane Stanley. Morrow Junior Bks. 1994 unp il maps $16.95; lib bdg $17.89; pa $6.99 (4 and up)   **92**

1. Queens 2. Egypt—History
ISBN 0-688-10413-4; 0-688-10414-2 (lib bdg);
0-688-15480-8 (pa)   LC 93-27032

This is a biography of the ancient Egyptian queen

"Lucid writing combines with carefully selected anecdotes, often attributed to the Greek historian Plutarch to create an engaging narrative. . . . Stanley's stunning, full-color gouache artwork is arresting in its large, well-composed images executed in flat Greek style." SLJ

Includes bibliographical references

Cohen, Sasha, 1984-

Cohen, Sasha. Fire on ice; autobiography of a champion figure skater; [by] Sasha Cohen with Amanda Maciel; photographs by Kathy Goedeken. 1st Avon ed. Avon Books 2005 172p il $16.99; pa $9.99 (4 and up)   **92**

1. Ice skating
ISBN 0-06-072489-7; 0-06-072490-0 (pa)
                                      LC 2004-21618

"Cohen tells of her switch at age seven from gymnastics to ice skating, the sport in which she leapt to fame at the 1999 Nationals. Her subsequent struggles with injury, nerves, and finding the right costumes and coaches dominate the book's latter half." Booklist

"Cohen tells her story with frankness and humor. . . . Black-and-white and color family and competition photographs add to the narrative. A thoroughly enjoyable read." SLJ

Coleman, Bessie, 1896?-1926

Grimes, Nikki. Talkin' about Bessie: the story of aviator Elizabeth Coleman; illustrated by E. B. Lewis. Orchard Bks. 2002 unp il $16.95 (3-5)
                                              92

1. Women air pilots 2. African American pilots
ISBN 0-439-35243-6

Coretta Scott King award for illustration, 2003

"Following a brief introduction to Coleman's life, the story, couched in a fictional framework, opens in the parlor of a house in Chicago, where friends and relatives gather to mourn Bessie's death. Each spread features one person speaking about Bessie. . . . Lewis' paintings, subdued in tone and color, reflect the spirit of the verse through telling details and sensitive, impressionistic portrayals." Booklist

Includes bibliographical references

Collins, Michael, 1930-

Schyffert, Bea Uusma. The man who went to the far side of the moon: the story of Apollo 11 astronaut Michael Collins. Chronicle 2003 77p il $14.95 (5 and up)   **92**

1. Astronauts 2. Space flight
ISBN 0-8118-4007-7

A biography of the astronaut, Michael Collins, who circled the moon in the Apollo 12 space capsule while his colleagues Neil Armstrong and Buzz Aldrin landed the lunar module and walked on the moon.

"This excellent book—illustrated scrapbook-style with a cleverly presented mix of photographs, illustrations, and charts—communicates the excitement of space travel." Booklist

Columba, Saint, 521-597

Brown, Don. Across a dark and wild sea; written and illustrated by Don Brown; calligraphy by Deborah Nadel. Roaring Brook Press 2002 unp il $15.95; lib bdg $22.90 (2-5)   **92**

1. Christian saints
ISBN 0-7613-1534-9; 0-7613-2415-1 (lib bdg)
                                       LC 2001-19355

Columba, Saint, 521-597—*Continued*
The author "traces the life of Columcille. Better known as Saint Columba, Columcille was born a prince of a sixth-century Irish clan, and became a monk and a scribe. . . . This picture-book biography is gracefully written and illustrated with great delicacy and finesse, and the pictures are evidently ink drawings washed in watercolors of muted green, gray, and tan." Booklist
Includes bibliographical references

Columbus, Christopher
Fritz, Jean. Where do you think you're going, Christopher Columbus? pictures by Margot Tomes. Putnam 1980 80p il maps $15.99; pa $5.99 (2-4)   **92**
1. Explorers 2. America—Exploration
ISBN 0-399-20723-6; 0-698-11580-5 (pa)
                                        LC 80-11377
Discusses the voyages of Christopher Columbus who was determined to beat everyone in the race to the Indies
"Reducing a life as well-documented as Columbus's to 80 pages must result in some simplifications of fact or context, but in this case they are not readily apparent. Mrs. Fritz's breezy narrative gives us a highly individual Columbus. . . . Margot Tomes's three-color illustrations are attractive, amusing and informative." N Y Times Book Rev

Sís, Peter. Follow the dream. Knopf 1991 unp il map pa $6.99 hardcover o.p. (k-3)   **92**
1. Explorers 2. America—Exploration
ISBN 0-679-88088-7 (pa)   LC 90-45276
Cover title: Follow the dream: the story of Christopher Columbus
In a pictorial retelling, Christopher Columbus overcomes a number of obstacles to fulfill his dream of sailing west to find a new route to the Orient
"The text is smoothly written and informative. Yet it is Sis's illustrations that make *Follow the Dream* so distinctive; his pictures, executed in oil, ink and watercolor, and gouache, complement and extend the narrative, adding additional facts and capturing young readers' interest by humanizing Columbus and vividly rendering his vision of a new world." Horn Book

Confucius
Freedman, Russell. Confucius; the golden rule; illustrated by Frédéric Clément. Levine Bks. 2002 48p il $15.95 (4 and up)   **92**
1. Philosophers
ISBN 0-439-13957-0   LC 2001-29372
This is a "biography of the 5th-century B.C. philosopher Confucius, whose teachings have influenced the development of modern government and education in both China and the West." Publ Wkly
"The fascinating narrative seamlessly intersperses stories from the *Analects* with Chinese history and biographical information about Confucius. . . . Clement's muted, elegant paintings of towns, temples, and the bucktoothed Confucius himself have a suitably ancient feel with jagged borders and fading colors." Booklist

Copernicus, Nicolaus, 1473-1543
Fradin, Dennis B. Nicolaus Copernicus; the earth is a planet; by Dennis Brindell Fradin; illustrated by Cynthia von Buhler. Mondo 2003 32p il $15.95 (3-6)   **92**
1. Astronomers
ISBN 1-59336-006-1   LC 2003-56147
A biography of astronomer Nicolaus Copernicus, who challenged the belief of his age that Earth was the center of the universe and proved that it is, instead, a planet orbiting the Sun.
"The text is beautifully supported by dramatic oil-on-gesso artwork. . . . Von Buhler's style suggests the muted colors and two-dimensional quality of late-medieval illustration. . . . This is a useful and accessible introduction to Copernicus's life and works." SLJ

Ingram, Scott. Nicolaus Copernicus; father of modern astronomy; [by] Scott Ingram. Blackbirch Press 2004 64p il (Giants of science) $24.95 (5 and up)   **92**
1. Astronomers
ISBN 1-56711-489-X   LC 2003-16229
Contents: The importance of Copernicus; A new view of the world; The power of the Church; Sharing the theory
Discusses the youth, education, scientific observations, conflict with religious teachings and the Church, and legacy of Nicolaus Copernicus.
This is "clearly written. . . . Black-and-white and full-color photos and reproductions add interest." SLJ
Includes bibliographical references

Craft, Ellen, 1826-1891
Moore, Cathy. The daring escape of Ellen Craft; illustrations by Mary O'Keefe Young. Carolrhoda Bks. 2002 48p il (On my own history) lib bdg $22.60; pa $5.95 (1-3)   **92**
1. Craft, William, 19th cent. 2. Slavery—United States
ISBN 0-87614-462-8 (lib bdg); 0-87614-787-2 (pa)
                                        LC 2001-220
"Ellen and William Craft were slaves determined to escape to freedom. Their daring plan involved Ellen traveling as a white male slave master with William as her slave. Risking everything, they embarked on their journey from Georgia on December 21, 1848. . . . This account of a real event employs a suspenseful text that will keep readers engaged to the very end. . . . Soft watercolor paintings illustrate almost every page and there are reproductions of a period drawing and photograph of Ellen Craft. . . . A great nonfiction choice for newly independent readers." SLJ
Includes bibliographical references

Crandall, Prudence, 1803-1890
Jurmain, Suzanne. The forbidden schoolhouse; the true and dramatic story of Prudence Crandall and her students. Houghton Mifflin 2005 150p il $18 (5 and up)   **92**
1. African Americans—Education 2. Educators 3. Abolitionists
ISBN 0-618-47302-5
This is the story of Prudence Crandall, who, in 1831, opened a school for African American girls in Canter-

Crandall, Prudence, 1803-1890—*Continued*
bury, Connecticut.

"A compelling, highly readable book. . . . Writing with a sense of drama that propels readers forward . . . Jurmain makes painfully clear what Crandall and her students faced. . . . Including a number of sepia-toned and color photographs as well as historical engravings, the book's look will draw in readers." Booklist

Includes bibliographical references

Crazy Horse, Sioux Chief, ca. 1842-1877
Freedman, Russell. The life and death of Crazy Horse; drawings by Amos Bad Heart Bull. Holiday House 1996 166p il maps $22.95 (5 and up)
92
1. Oglala Indians
ISBN 0-8234-1219-9   LC 95-33303
A biography of the Oglala Indian leader who relentlessly resisted the white man's attempt to take over Indian lands
This is "a compelling biography that is based on primary source documents and illustrated with pictographs by a Sioux band historian." Voice Youth Advocates
Includes bibliographical references

Crews, Donald
Crews, Donald. Bigmama's. Greenwillow Bks. 1991 unp il $16; lib bdg $15.93; pa $5.95 (k-3)
92
1. Authors, American 2. African Americans—Biography 3. Country life
ISBN 0-688-09950-5; 0-688-09951-3 (lib bdg); 0-688-15842-0 (pa)   LC 90-33142
Visiting Bigmama's house in the country, young Donald Crews finds his relatives full of news and the old place and its surroundings just the same as the year before
"This is an evocative celebration of the joy and wonder of childhood; would that every child had such a summer. The last page is a hauntingly lovely remembrance. The illustrations are perfect and make this a truly beautiful book." Child Book Rev Serv

Crum, George, fl. 1853
Taylor, Gaylia. George Crum and the Saratoga chip; by Gaylia Taylor; illustrated by Frank Morrison. 1st ed. Lee & Low Books 2006 unp il $16.95 (2-4)
92
1. Cooking 2. Racially mixed people 3. United States—Race relations
ISBN 9781584302551; 1584302550
LC 2005015313
"Part Native American, part African American, George Crum coped with prejudice as a boy in New York State during the 1830s. As a young man, he became an excellent cook and was hired as a chef at a renowned restaurant in Saratoga Springs. . . . Once . . . Crum retrieved [a] dish of French fries, whittled them into very thin slices, and cooked them in hot oil, creating the forerunner of the potato chip. . . . This picture-book biography describes dramatic moments that reveal Crum's creativity, artistic temperament, and relentless

pursuit of perfection. Buoyant acrylic illustrations accentuate the absurdity of situations, depicting the jaunty chef, all angles and energy." Booklist

Includes bibliographical references

Cruz, Celia, 1929-2003
Chambers, Veronica. Celia Cruz, Queen of salsa; illustrated by Julie Maren. Dial Books for Young Readers 2005 unp il $15.99 (2-4)
92
1. Singers 2. Cuban Americans
ISBN 0-8037-2970-7   LC 2004-18960
"In this picture-book biography, Chambers offers a . . . tribute to salsa superstar Celia Cruz. Short paragraphs follow the vocalist from her Havana childhood . . . to her . . . emigration from Cuba and worldwide stardom. . . . Chambers' enthusiasm for her subject is contagious, and the bright, uncluttered paintings of rounded, stylized figures in saturated, tropical hues echo the energy in the words." Booklist

Curie, Marie, 1867-1934
MacLeod, Elizabeth. Marie Curie; a brilliant life; written by Elizabeth MacLeod. Kids Can Press 2004 32p il $14.95; pa $6.95 (5 and up)
92
1. Chemists 2. Women scientists
ISBN 1-55337-570-X; 1-55337-571-8 (pa)
"The drive and self-sacrifice that enabled Marie Curie to win two Nobel Prizes and become the most acclaimed female scientist to date are explored in this accessible biography, which covers Curie's personal and professional lives. Illustrated with well-chosen archival photos." Horn Book Guide

McClafferty, Carla Killough. Something out of nothing; Marie Curie and radium. Farrar, Straus & Giroux 2006 134p il $18 (5 and up)   **92**
1. Chemists 2. Women scientists
ISBN 0-374-38036-8   LC 2004-56414
This "biography examines Curie's life and work as a groundbreaking scientist and as an independent woman. . . . The groundbreaking science is as thrilling as the personal story. . . . The spacious design makes the text easy to read, and occasional photos . . . bring the story closer." Booklist

Poynter, Margaret. Marie Curie: discoverer of radium. Enslow Pubs. 1994 128p il maps (Great minds of science) lib bdg $26.60; pa $10.95 (4 and up)   **92**
1. Chemists 2. Women scientists
ISBN 0-89490-477-9 (lib bdg); 0-7660-1875-X (pa)
LC 93-21224
This "biography emphasizes Marie Curie's early life of poverty, desire to study, and contributions to the fields of chemistry, physics, and medicine." Horn Book Guide
"The writing style is straightforward, with a combination of personal detail and scientific explanation. . . . Sure to be in demand for those middle-grade biography and science assignments." Booklist

Includes glossary and bibliographical references

Custer, George Armstrong, 1839-1876

Anderson, Paul Christopher. George Armstrong Custer; the Indian Wars and the Battle of the Little Bighorn; Paul Christopher Anderson. 1st ed. PowerPlus Books 2004 112p il (Library of American lives and times) $31.95 (4 and up)

92

1. Little Bighorn, Battle of the, 1876 2. Native Americans—Wars 3. Generals

ISBN 0-8239-6631-3   LC 2002-153404

Contents: Remembering Custer; The boy from New Rumley; School and skins; Autie Custer's first war; Wolverine in blue; A warrior without a war; Frustrated frontiersman; A life on the Plains; To the Little Bighorn and beyond; Heroes and history

A biography of the Civil War general who died at the Battle of the Little Bighorn.

This "is not an apologia but a carefully measured analysis. . . . Stunning reproductions and photos provide a clear sense of the times and settings." SLJ

Includes bibliographical references

Dalai Lama XIV, 1935-

Demi. The Dalai Lama; a biography of the Tibetan spiritual and political leader. Holt & Co. 1998 unp il $18.95 (3-6)   92

1. Buddhism 2. Tibet (China)

ISBN 0-8050-5443-X   LC 97-30654

In this biography of the Buddhist spiritual leader, Demi "uses straightforward prose and fluid, eastern-influenced art—small pen-and-ink and watercolor images with fine, intricate detail. . . . Told with respect and devotion, this is an inspirational picture-book biography." Horn Book

Darwin, Charles, 1809-1882

Lawson, Kristan. Darwin and evolution for kids; his life and ideas, with 21 activities. Chicago Review Press 2003 146p il map $16.95 (4 and up)

92

1. Naturalists 2. Evolution

ISBN 1-55652-502-8   LC 2003-7473

A biography of the English naturalist who, after collecting plants and animals from around the world, postulated the theory of evolution by natural selection. Includes related activities.

"A thorough introduction to the life and work of this naturalist and thinker. . . . The writing is consistently clear and lively." SLJ

Includes bibliographical references

Sís, Peter. The tree of life: a book depicting the life of Charles Darwin, naturalist, geologist & thinker. Frances Foster Bks./Farrar, Straus & Giroux 2003 unp il map $18 (4 and up)

92

1. Naturalists

ISBN 0-374-45628-3   LC 2002-40706

Presents the life of the famous nineteenth-century naturalist using text from Darwin's writings and detailed drawings by Sís

"Muted tones of blue, green, and tan, and finely hatched drawings in the manner of old prints lend a peri-od look to the pages. Beautifully conceived and executed, the presentation is a humorous and informative tour de force that will absorb and challenge readers." SLJ

David-Neel, Alexandra, 1868-1969

Brown, Don. Far beyond the garden gate: Alexandra David-Neel's journey to Lhasa. Houghton Mifflin 2002 unp il $16 (3-5)

92

1. Tibet (China) 2. Travelers 3. Buddhism

ISBN 0-618-08364-2   LC 2002-222

Describes the life and travels of Alexandra David-Neel, who became a scholar of Buddhism and Tibet in the early twentieth century and trekked thousands of miles to reach Llasa, the Tibetan capital.

This "tells a fascinating tale. . . . David-Neel's vivid quotes are interspersed throughout the story. . . . The beiges, grays, and whites of Brown's palette capture the feeling of the unfamiliar world into which the woman and her companion ventured." SLJ

Includes bibliographical references

De Kooning, Willem, 1904-1997

Hawes, Louise. Willem de Kooning; the life of an artist. Enslow Pubs. 2002 48p il (Artist biographies) $23.93 (2-4)   92

1. Artists—United States

ISBN 0-7660-1884-9   LC 2002-11986

Contents: Cowboy dreams; New York! New York!; Painting in action; Bill's "girls"; Back to the sea; The last paintings

Discusses the private and professional life of the twentieth-century American painter who was part of the Abstract Expressionism movement of art

Includes glossary and bibliographical references

De Paola, Tomie, 1934-

De Paola, Tomie. 26 Fairmount Avenue; written and illustrated by Tomie dePaola. Putnam 1999 56p il $13.99 (2-4)   92

1. Authors, American 2. Illustrators

ISBN 0-399-23246-X   LC 98-12918

A Newbery Medal honor book, 2000

Children's author-illustrator Tomie De Paola describes his experiences at home and in school when he was a boy

"A disarmingly unselfconscious reminiscence. . . . The immediacy of detail resists nostalgia, and dePaola is wise to what recent graduates of his picture books will find interesting. Neat sketches and silhouettes will draw browsers in to this satisfying easy chapter book." Horn Book Guide

Followed by Here we all are

De Paola, Tomie. Here we all are; a 26 Fairmount Avenue book; written and illustrated by Tomie DePaola. Putnam 2000 26p il $13.99 (2-4)

92

1. Authors, American 2. Illustrators

ISBN 0-399-23496-9   LC 99-46747

"Continuing the memoir begun in dePaola's Newbery Honor Book 26 *Fairmount Avenue* (1999), this short

De Paola, Tomie, 1934-—*Continued*
chapter book shows young Tomie as he takes tap dancing lessons, finds his way in kindergarten, and waits a
seemingly interminable 10 days for his mother and new
baby sister to come home from the hospital. . . . Another satisfying book in a warm episodic family story that
makes writing autobiography look easy." Booklist

Followed by On my way

De Paola, Tomie. I'm still scared; a 26
Fairmount Avenue book, book 6; written and
illustrated by Tomie dePaola. G. P. Putnam's Sons
2006 83p il $13.99 (2-4) **92**
  1. Authors, American 2. Illustrators 3. World War,
1939-1945—United States
  ISBN 0-399-24502-2   LC 2005-13500
"DePaola picks up his autobiographical series right
where his last title, *Things Will Never Be the Same*
(2003), left off: December, 7, 1941. Now in second
grade, little Tomie describes the reactions to the Pearl
Harbor bombings, first at home, then at church, and finally at school. . . . Once again, the warm, childlike narration captures both the specifics of the time and universal experiences that will connect with most children. The
shaded, black-and-white sketches on each page extend
the story's small, revealing moments." Booklist

De Paola, Tomie. On my way; a 26 Fairmount
Avenue book; written and illustrated by Tomie
dePaola. Putnam 2001 73p il $13.99 (2-4) **92**
  1. Authors, American 2. Illustrators
  ISBN 0-399-23583-3   LC 00-38229
"The saga of dePaola's early life related in *26
Fairmount Avenue* . . . and *Here We All Are* . . . continues with this reminiscence of kindergarten and first
grade. de Paola describes his baby sister Maureen's recovery from pneumonia, a family trip to the 1939
World's Fair, and his theatrical debut as the blushing
bride in a 'Tiny Tot Bridal Party.' . . . The humor is
clear and the selection of incidents indicates the author
has a comfortable familiarity with the concerns of his audience." Bull Cent Child Books

Followed by What a year!

De Paola, Tomie. Things will never be the
same; a 26 Fairmount Avenue book; written and
illustrated by Tomie dePaola. Putnam 2003 69p il
$13.99 (2-4) **92**
  1. Authors, American 2. Illustrators
  ISBN 0-399-23982-0   LC 2002-5995
This fifth volume in DePaola's autobiographical 24
Fairmount Avenue series "takes the budding artist into
his seventh year. . . . [This] re-creates the joys of sledding, the dangers of polio, and the glories of the Ferris
wheel." Horn Book Guide
"Livening nearly every page with vignettes or larger
drawings, the author again draws children into a vanished, but somehow universal, world with his youthful
narration, convincingly childlike sensibility, and irrepressible spirit." Booklist

Followed by I'm still scared

De Paola, Tomie. What a year! a 26 Fairmount
Avenue book; written and illustrated by Tomie
dePaola. Putnam 2002 72p il $13.99 (2-4) **92**
  1. Authors, American 2. Illustrators
  ISBN 0-399-23797-6   LC 2001-19921
"The fourth volume in dePaola's autobiographical 24
Fairmont Avenue series opens with the beginning of first
grade in September 1940 and ends on New Year's Eve.
DePaola appears to remember his childhood in vivid detail. . . . Small silhouette drawings and paintings bright-
en nearly every page. Young readers will gain a sense of
period and feel empathy with young Tomie in this appealing episodic chapter book." Booklist

Followed by Things will never be the same

Elleman, Barbara. Tomie de Paola; his art & his
stories. Putnam 1999 218p il $35 **92**
  1. Authors, American 2. Illustrators 3. Children's literature—History and criticism
  ISBN 0-399-23129-3   LC 98-19821
"After summarizing dePaola's life, with particular reference to events most significant to his work in children's books, Elleman presents these books by category:
autobiographical, religious, Christmas, folktales, Strega
Nona, informational, etc." Horn Book
"Well-chosen examples of dePaola's art effectively illustrate Elleman's critical insights, photographs and illustrations on nearly every page create an appealing presentation. While children will enjoy poring over the collected illustrations, they are not the primary audience for this
scholarly text." SLJ

Includes bibliographical references

Degas, Edgar, 1834-1917
Cocca-Leffler, Maryann. Edgar Degas: paintings
that dance; written and illustrated by Maryann
Cocca-Leffler. Grosset & Dunlap 2001 unp il
(Smart about art) $14.89; pa $5.99 (2-4) **92**
  1. Artists, French
  ISBN 0-448-42520-3; 0-448-42520-3 (pa)
      LC 2001-23149
Written in the format of a school report by a fictitious
student named Kristin Cole, this recounts events in the
life of the French artist Degas and offers insight into his
work
Illustrated with "charming childlike drawings and reproductions of the artist's paintings in scrapbook-style
layouts. . . . [This] is a successful blend of fact and humor that makes sophisticated concepts completely accessible and even entertaining." Booklist

Rubin, Susan Goldman. Degas and the dance;
the painter and the petits rats, perfecting their art.
Abrams 2002 31p il $17.95 (3-6) **92**
  1. Artists, French 2. Ballet
  ISBN 0-8109-0567-1   LC 2001-6580
"Degas depicted the young girls of the Paris Opéra
corps over and over again in painting and sculpture from
1855 to 1905. This book traces that artistic involvement,
discussing the hard life of the 'little rats' of the ballet
and Degas' interest in various aspects of that life; it also
addresses Degas' technique . . . and changing approach

Degas, Edgar, 1834-1917—*Continued*
as his sight dimmed. . . . The art history is skillfully
blended with the ballet interest . . . and Rubin's fluid
text provides a measured and elegant entree to both."
Bull Cent Child Books

Includes bibliographical references

Dickens, Charles, 1812-1870
Rosen, Michael. Dickens; his work and his
world; illustrated by Robert Ingpen. Candlewick
Press 2005 95p il $19.99 (5 and up)   **92**
   1. Authors, English
   ISBN 0-7636-2752-6   LC 2004-61847
"Opening with Dickens's touring life and final London
performance, Rosen then turns to the writer's humble beginnings and nomadic childhood, paying particular attention to the people he met, the sights he saw, and the situations he endured—all of which were to find their way
into his writings. The author looks at 1800s London,
pointing out the societal changes that were to influence
Dickens's progressive thinking." SLJ
"The art adds to the richness of a volume designed
and written with care." Booklist

Stanley, Diane. Charles Dickens; the man who
had great expectations; [by] Diane Stanley & Peter
Vennema; illustrated by Diane Stanley. Morrow
Junior Bks. 1993 unp il $15; lib bdg $14.93 (4
and up)   **92**
   1. Authors, English
   ISBN 0-688-09110-5; 0-688-09111-3 (lib bdg)
                LC 91-41552
"This picture-book biography of the great English
novelist is attractive and appealing. Stanley's full-color,
full-page gouache paintings are expressive and inviting;
the abbreviated text covers all of the major events in
Dickens's life." SLJ

Includes bibliographical references

Douglass, Frederick, 1817?-1895
McKissack, Patricia C. Frederick Douglass;
leader against slavery; [by] Patricia and Fredrick
McKissack. rev ed. Enslow Pubs. 2002 32p il
(Great African Americans) lib bdg $18.60 (2-4)
     92
   1. Abolitionists 2. African Americans—Biography
   ISBN 0-7660-1696-X   LC 00-12415
   First published 1991
A biography of the African American abolitionist
Ths contains "many facts presented in a readable
style. . . . Attractive." SLJ

Includes bibliographical references

Earhart, Amelia, 1898-1937
Adler, David A. A picture book of Amelia
Earhart; illustrated by Jeff Fisher. Holiday House
1998 unp il $16.95; pa $6.95 (1-3)   **92**
   1. Women air pilots
   ISBN 0-8234-1315-2; 0-8234-1517-1 (pa)
                LC 96-54854

Discusses the life of the pilot who was the first woman to cross the Atlantic by herself in a plane
This offers "a straightforward, informative text full of
detail. The illustrations ably reflect both the humorous
and more serious moments in the narrative." Horn Book
Guide

Includes bibliographical references

Lauber, Patricia. Lost star: the story of Amelia
Earhart. Scholastic 1988 106p il maps pa $4.50
hardcover o.p. (5 and up)   **92**
   1. Women air pilots
   ISBN 0-590-41159-4 (pa)   LC 88-3043
"Earhart's early life is covered succinctly, including
the family problems that resulted from her father's alcoholism. Close to half of the book is concerned with the
details of the last flight around the world and the mysterious disappearance, sure to hold the attention of readers.
Small but very clear black-and-white photographs are included." SLJ

Includes bibliographical references

Ederle, Gertrude, 1905-2003
Adler, David A. America's champion swimmer:
Gertrude Ederle; written by David A. Adler;
illustrated by Terry Widener. Harcourt 2000 unp il
$16 (2-4)   **92**
   1. Swimming—Biography 2. Women athletes
   ISBN 0-15-201969-3   LC 98-54954
   "Gulliver books"
Describes the life and accomplishments of Gertrude
Ederle, the first woman to swim the English Channel and
a figure in the early women's rights movement
This book "illustrated with richly colored acrylic
paintings . . . captures the highlights of Ederle's life in
evocative images and telling details that will appeal to
children." N Y Times Book Rev

Edison, Thomas A. (Thomas Alva), 1847-1931
Delano, Marfe Ferguson. Inventing the future: a
photobiography of Thomas Alva Edison. National
Geographic Soc. 2002 64p il $18.95 (5 and up)
     92
   1. Inventors
   ISBN 0-7922-6721-4   LC 2001-7357
Presents a biography of the tireless Thomas Edison, illustrated with many photos of his life and inventions
"Well-written and -illustrated. . . . This biography
would inspire young people who are interested in experimenting with new ideas and methods." Libr Media Connect

Includes bibliographical references

Dooling, Michael. Young Thomas Edison; [by]
Michael Dooling. 1st ed. Holiday House 2005 unp
il $16.95 (1-3)   **92**
   1. Inventors
   ISBN 0-8234-1868-5   LC 2004-49345
"Dooling has brought Edison's boyhood into focus
through careful attention to visual detail and a readable
text. What emerges is a story of a determined, focused
young man who, despite significant hearing loss and other setbacks, continued to experiment and create inven-

Edison, Thomas A. (Thomas Alva), 1847-1931—
Continued
tions that we still benefit from today. . . . Dooling's somber oil-on-canvas illustrations use a dark palette and are extraordinarily beautiful." SLJ

Includes bibliographical references

Thomas Edison; a brilliant inventor; by the editors of Time for kids; with Lisa DeMauro. HarperCollins Pubs. 2005 44p (Time for kids biographies) $14.99 (2-4) **92**
1. Inventors
ISBN 0-06-057612-X
A brief illustrated biography of the inventor
This is "sure to be highly popular with students. . . . Pages feature eye-catching sidebars with . . . photographs and brightly colored drawings. . . . [It features] short lively [text]." Lib Media Connect

Einstein, Albert, 1879-1955
Brown, Don. Odd boy out: young Albert Einstein. Houghton Mifflin 2004 unp il $16 (2-4) **92**
1. Physicists
ISBN 0-618-49298-4   LC 2003-17701
An introduction to the work and early life of the twentieth-century physicist whose theory of relativity revolutionized scientific thinking.
"Brown's pen-and-ink and watercolor illustrations [are] rendered in a palette of dusky mauve and earthy brown. . . . Through eloquent narrative and illustration, Brown offers a thoughtful introduction to an enigmatic man." SLJ

Delano, Marfe Ferguson. Genius; a photobiography of Albert Einstein. National Geographic 2005 64p il $17.95; lib bdg $27.90 (5 and up) **92**
1. Physicists
ISBN 0-7922-9544-7; 0-7922-9545-5 (lib bdg)
          LC 2004-15001
A biography of the German American physicist.
This "combines a solid text with a particularly attractive format. . . . Delano offers just enough information about Einstein's theories to give a sense of his work. . . . Oversize and filled with well-selected photographs, the book is very handsome." Booklist

Lassieur, Allison. Albert Einstein; genius of the twentieth century. Franklin Watts 2005 128p il (Great life stories) lib bdg $30.50 (5 and up) **92**
1. Physicists
ISBN 0-531-12401-0   LC 2004-14313
"A clear, chronological look at Einstein's life and contributions with respect to gravity, energy, matter, light, and time. . . . Photo captions and sidebars provide further insights into this Noble Prize winner." SLJ
Includes bibliographical references

MacLeod, Elizabeth. Albert Einstein; a life of genius; written by Elizabeth MacLeod. Kids Can Press 2003 32p il $14.95; pa $6.95 (4 and up) **92**
1. Physicists
ISBN 1-55337-396-0; 1-55337-397-9 (pa)
A brief introduction to the life and work of the physicist
"It looks like a scrapbook, with information offered in small bites accompanied by lots of small photos and illustrations, but this introduction to the life of Einstein is as informative as it is appealing. . . . This is concise, but there's still plenty here for students and browsers alike." Booklist

Severance, John B. Einstein; visionary scientist. Clarion Bks. 1999 144p il $15 (5 and up) **92**
1. Physicists
ISBN 0-395-93100-2   LC 98-51396
"Severance opens with a chapter designed to establish Einstein's place in and contribution to history in which he outlines how Einstein's theories sparked advances in many scientific fields. The succeeding chapters deal with Einstein's life chronologically, from his childhood, when he was thought to be learning disabled, to his later years, when his genius became apparent." Bull Cent Child Books
The author "does a commendable job of conveying both the complicated ideas that revolutionized the study of physics and the life of the thinker behind them." Publ Wkly
Includes bibliographical references

Sullivan, Anne Marie. Albert Einstein. Mason Crest Publs. 2003 unp il $19.95 (4 and up) **92**
1. Physicists
ISBN 1-59084-140-9   LC 2003-6034
This is a brief introduction to the life and work of the physicist
"Einstein comes alive in this delightful, entertaining, well-written, and beautifully illustrated biography." Libr Media Connect

Elizabeth I, Queen of England, 1533-1603
Adams, Simon. Elizabeth I; the outcast who became England's queen; [by] Simon Adams. National Geographic 2005 64p il map (World history biographies) $17.95; lib bdg $27.90 (4 and up) **92**
1. Great Britain—History—1485-1603, Tudors
2. Queens
ISBN 0-7922-3649-1; 0-7922-3654-8 (lib bdg)
          LC 2005001359
An illustrated introduction to the life and times of the 16th century queen of England
"Accomplishments and hardships are clearly explained with supporting quotes and facts. . . . Beautifully illustrated and visually appealing." SLJ
Includes glossary and bibliographical references

Elizabeth I, Queen of England, 1533-1603—
Continued

Mannis, Celeste A. The Queen's progress; an Elizabethan alphabet; by Celeste Davidson Mannis; illustrations by Bagram Ibatoulline. Viking 2003 unp il $16.99 (3-5)   **92**
1. Queens 2. Great Britain—Kings and rulers 3. Great Britain—History—1485-1603, Tudors 4. Alphabet
ISBN 0-670-03612-9   LC 2002-10174

Uses the letters of the alphabet to provide an account of Queen Elizabeth's annual holiday, known as a "royal progress"

"Ibatoulline's acrylic paintings are superb in their elegance and fascinating in their detail. . . . A plus for any collection." SLJ

Stanley, Diane. Good Queen Bess: the story of Elizabeth I of England; by Diane Stanley and Peter Vennema; illustrated by Diane Stanley. HarperCollins Pubs. 2001 c1990 unp il $16.99 (4 and up)   **92**
1. Queens 2. Great Britain—Kings and rulers 3. Great Britain—History—1485-1603, Tudors
ISBN 0-688-17961-4   LC 00-47267

A reissue of the title first published 1990 by Four Winds Press

Follows the life of the strong-willed queen who ruled England in the time of Shakespeare and the defeat of the Spanish Armada

"The handsome illustrations . . . are worthy of their subject. Although the format suggests a picture-book audience, this biography needs to be introduced to older readers who have the background to appreciate and understand this woman who dominated and named an age." SLJ

Includes bibliographical references

Ellington, Duke, 1899-1974

Pinkney, Andrea Davis. Duke Ellington; the piano prince and his orchestra; illustrated by Brian Pinkney. Hyperion Bks. for Children 1998 unp il $15.95; lib bdg $16.49 (2-4)   **92**
1. Jazz musicians 2. African Americans—Biography
ISBN 0-7868-0178-6; 0-7868-2150-7 (lib bdg)
    LC 96-46031

A Caldecott Medal honor book, 1999; Coretta Scott King honor book for illustration, 1999

A brief recounting of the career of this jazz musician and composer who, along with his orchestra, created music that was beyond category

This is "written in a folksy, colloquial style. . . . The warmly colored, exquisitely designed scratchboard illustrations have a grand time evoking the sounds of Ellington's music." Horn Book Guide

Includes bibliographical references

Eratosthenes, 3rd cent. B.C.

Lasky, Kathryn. The librarian who measured the earth; illustrated by Kevin Hawkes. Little, Brown 1994 48p il $16.95 (2-5)   **92**
1. Astronomers
ISBN 0-316-51526-4   LC 92-42656

Describes the life and work of Eratosthenes, the Greek geographer and astronomer who accurately measured the circumference of the Earth

"Illustrating the text with warmth and humor, Hawkes' acrylic paintings capture the period details of the setting and clarify the geometric concepts used in the measurement. The often dramatic compositions vary from page to page, while the sunlit reds, oranges, and yellows glow brightly against the cooler blues and greens. . . . Entertaining as well as instructional." Booklist

Includes bibliographical references

Farragut, David Glasgow, 1801-1870

Roop, Peter. Take command, Captain Farragut! [by] Peter Roop and Connie Roop; illustrated by Michael McCurdy. Atheneum Bks. for Young Readers 2002 44p il $16 (4-6)   **92**
1. Admirals
ISBN 0-689-83022-X   LC 00-38612

"Thirteen-year-old American naval officer Farragut, imprisoned onboard ship by the British, writes his father a series of letters in which he reflects on his three years at sea. . . . Though the book seems to straddle fiction and nonfiction, the first-person voice gives the narrative an immediacy sometimes lacking in historical writing and biography. McCurdy's illustrations, apparently scratchboard, have a period look well suited to the book's setting and design." Booklist

Includes glossary and bibliographical references

Fitzgerald, Ella

Pinkney, Andrea Davis. Ella Fitzgerald; the tale of a vocal virtuosa; by Andrea Davis Pinkney with Scat Cat Monroe; illustrated by Brian Pinkney. Hyperion 2002 unp il $16.99; lib bdg $17.49 (2-4)   **92**
1. African American singers 2. African American women
ISBN 0-7868-0568-4; 0-7868-2493-X (lib bdg)

"Scat Cat Monroe, a jazzy feline in a zoot suit, tells Fitzgerald's life story. . . . The general details of an extraordinary life—when, what, where, and how—are related in rhythmic, vivid language that matches the verve of the hand-colored scratchboard illustrations." Bull Cent Child Books

Fleischman, Sid, 1920-

Fleischman, Sid. The abracadabra kid; a writer's life. Greenwillow Bks. 1996 198p il $16.99; pa $4.95 (5 and up)   **92**
1. Authors, American
ISBN 0-688-14859-X; 0-688-15855-2 (pa)
    LC 95-47382

This autobiography, "turns real life into a story complete with cliffhangers. And it's a classic *boy's* story, from card tricks and traveling magic shows to World War II naval experiences and screen-writing gigs for John Wayne movies. En route, we learn how Fleischman learned the craft of writing." Bull Cent Child Books

Includes bibliographical references

Fleischman, Sid, 1920——_Continued_

Freedman, Jeri. Sid Fleischman; Jeri Freedman. 1st ed. Rosen Pub. Group 2004 112p (Library of author biographies) $26.50 (5 and up)   **92**

1. Authors, American 2. Authorship

ISBN 0-8239-4019-5   LC 2003-5203

Discusses the life and work of this popular author, including his writing process and methods, inspirations, a critical discussion of his books, biographical timeline, and awards.

"Libraries looking to expand their biography section will be well served by [this] informative [title]." SLJ

Includes bibliographical references

Fleming, Alexander, 1881-1955

Tocci, Salvatore. Alexander Fleming; the man who discovered penicillin. Enslow Pubs. 2002 128p il (Great minds of science) lib bdg $26.60 (5 and up)   **92**

1. Penicillin 2. Bacteriologists

ISBN 0-7660-1998-5   LC 2001-3072

A biography of Alexander Fleming, the discoverer of penicillin

"Large type and lots of white space make this title accessible, and the black-and-white photographs enhance the well-written text. Activities for students reinforce the principles that are presented." SLJ

Includes glossary and bibliographical references

Fletcher, Ralph, 1953-

Fletcher, Ralph. Marshfield dreams; when I was a kid. Holt & Co. 2005 183p il $16.95 (4 and up)   **92**

1. Authors, American

ISBN 0-8050-7242-X   LC 2004-60746

"Fletcher reminisces about growing up in Marshfield, VT, recalling boyhood friendships, sibling attachments, and romps through the woods. . . . Written with sagacious eloquence and gentle humor, this work stands strong in the ranks of authors' memoirs and autobiographies." SLJ

Fortune, Amos, 1709 or 10-1801

Yates, Elizabeth. Amos Fortune, free man; illustrations by Nora S. Unwin. Dutton 1950 181p il $16.99; pa $5.99 (4 and up)   **92**

1. African Americans—Biography 2. Slavery—United States

ISBN 0-525-25570-2; 0-14-034158-7 (pa)

Awarded the Newbery Medal, 1951

"Born free in Africa, Amos Fortune was sold into slavery in America in 1725. After more than 40 years of servitude Amos was able to purchase his freedom and, in time, that of several others. He died a tanner of enviable reputation, a landowner, and a respected citizen of his community. Based on fact, this is a . . . story of a life dedicated to the fight for freedom and service to others." Booklist

Fossey, Dian

Matthews, Tom L. Light shining through the mist: a photobiography of Dian Fossey. National Geographic Soc. 1998 64p il $17.95 (4 and up)   **92**

1. Gorillas 2. Women scientists

ISBN 0-7922-7300-1   LC 97-34084

Traces the adventurous life of the American woman who worked as a zoologist among the mountain gorillas of the Virunga area of central Africa

"Gorgeous color photographs will be the main draw to this biography of the controversial primatologist, but Matthews's text also does a fine job." Horn Book

Includes bibliographical references

Frank, Anne, 1929-1945

Frank, Anne. The diary of a young girl; translated from the Dutch by B. M. Mooyaart-Doubleday (6 and up)   **92**

1. World War, 1939-1945—Jews 2. Netherlands—History—1940-1945, German occupation 3. Jews—Netherlands 4. Holocaust, 1933-1945

Various editions available

This is the diary of a "German-Jewish girl who hid from the Nazis with her parents, their friends, and some other fugitives in an Amsterdam warehouse from 1942 to 1944. Her diary, covering the years of hiding, was found by friends and published as _Het achterhu_ (1947); it was later published in English as _The Diary of a Young Girl_ (1952). . . . Written with humor as well as insight, it shows a growing girl with all the preoccupations of adolescence and first love. The diary ends three days before the Franks and their group were discovered by the Nazis." Reader's Ency. 4th edition

Frank, Anne. The diary of a young girl: the definitive edition; edited by Otto H. Frank and Mirjam Pressler; translated by Susan Massotty. Doubleday 1995 340p $27.50; pa $12.95 (6 and up)   **92**

1. World War, 1939-1945—Jews 2. Netherlands—History—1940-1945, German occupation 3. Jews—Netherlands 4. Holocaust, 1933-1945

ISBN 0-385-47378-8; 0-385-42360-8 (pa)

LC 94-41379

"This new translation of Frank's famous diary includes material about her emerging sexuality and her relationship with her mother that was originally excised by Frank's father, the only family member to survive the Holocaust." Libr J

Gold, Alison Leslie. Memories of Anne Frank; reflections of a childhood friend. Scholastic 1997 135p il pa $5.99 hardcover o.p. (5 and up)   **92**

1. Pick-Goslar, Hannah 2. Jews—Netherlands 3. Holocaust, 1933-1945

ISBN 0-590-90723-9   LC 96-41185

This "story of Anne Frank's neighbor and friend, Hannah Elizabeth Pick-Goslar, recounts the tragedy of World War II through a young girl's eyes. . . . The account traces the childhood friendship of the two girls from the time Anne disappeared to the removal of Hannah and her family to concentration camps. The narrative also tells of

Frank, Anne, 1929-1945—*Continued*

the brief meeting between Anne and Hannah at Bergen-Belsen shortly before Anne's death." SLJ

"Gold uses carefully chosen details and specific incidents to communicate the horrors of the Holocaust. . . . Readers drawn to Anne Frank's diary will be grateful for the fuller picture rendered here." Publ Wkly

Hurwitz, Johanna. Anne Frank: life in hiding; illustrated by Vera Rosenberry. Jewish Publ. Soc. 1988 62p il map $13.95 (3-5)   **92**

1. Jews—Netherlands 2. Holocaust, 1933-1945
ISBN 0-8276-0311-8   LC 87-35263
Also available in paperback from HarperCollins

The author "gives a concise explanation of the political and economic background to the Holocaust and provides a map of Europe and a chronology. She ably covers the events of Anne's life before, during, and after the period covered by the 'Diary of Anne Frank,' explaining the significance and importance of the 'Diary' throughout the world." SLJ

Koestler-Grack, Rachel A. The story of Anne Frank. Chelsea Clubhouse 2004 32p il (Breakthrough biographies) lib bdg $14.95 (2-4)   **92**

1. Jews—Netherlands 2. Holocaust, 1933-1945
ISBN 0-7910-7311-4   LC 2003-266
Discusses the life of Anne Frank and her family, who hid from soldiers in Nazi-occupied Holland for over two years by staying in a secret attic. Includes brief quotations from her diary.

"Chapters are written in a clear manner and accompanied by photographs, reproductions, and quotations. . . . [This volume is] carefully researched, presenting good and respectful coverage." SLJ

Includes glossary and bibliographical references

Poole, Josephine. Anne Frank; illustrations by Angela Barrett. Knopf 2005 unp il $17.95 (2-4)   **92**

1. Jews—Netherlands 2. Holocaust, 1933-1945
ISBN 0-375-83242-4   LC 2004-15099
This biography "tells of Anne Frank's childhood up through the moment her family's hideout is raided by the Nazis." Publ Wkly

"The familiar yet compelling story is told with simple poignancy and dignity. . . . Both the text and illustrations quickly create a sense of foreboding. Spreads are dominated by Barrett's realistically rendered paintings done in subdued tones." SLJ

Rol, Ruud van der. Anne Frank, beyond the diary; a photographic remembrance; by Ruud van der Rol and Rian Verhoeven; in association with the Anne Frank House; translated by Tony Langham and Plym Peters; with an introduction by Anna Quindlen. Viking 1993 113p il maps $17; pa $10.99 (5 and up)   **92**

1. Jews—Netherlands 2. Holocaust, 1933-1945
ISBN 0-670-84932-4; 0-14-036926-0 (pa)
LC 92-41528
Original Dutch edition, 1992

Photographs, illustrations, and maps accompany historical essays, diary excerpts, and interviews, providing an insight to Anne Frank and the massive upheaval which tore apart her world

"Readers will become absorbed in the richness of the detail and careful explanation which revisit and expand the familiar, well-loved story." Horn Book

Sawyer, Kem Knapp. Anne Frank. DK Pub 2004 127p il (DK biography) $14.99 (5 and up)   **92**

1. Jews—Netherlands 2. Holocaust, 1933-1945
ISBN 0-7566-0341-2   LC 2004-8450
For this biography "Sawyer drew extensively on several sources, including the diary in its various versions and accounts by Anne's father and their rescuer Miep Gies. Her clear history makes this a good place to start research." Booklist

Includes bibliographical references

Franklin, Benjamin, 1706-1790

Adler, David A. B. Franklin, printer. Holiday House 2001 126p il lib bdg $19.95 (4 and up)   **92**

ISBN 0-8234-1675-5   LC 2001-24535
This "surveys Benjamin Franklin's life as a printer, a scientist, an inventor, a writer, and a statesman. . . . Throughout the book, details, anecdotes, and quotations bring the man's portrait into clearer focus, while period illustrations . . . help readers envision the background of his times." Booklist

Includes bibliographical references

Ashby, Ruth. The amazing Mr. Franklin, or, The boy who read everything; [by] Ruth Ashby. 1st ed. Peachtree 2004 104p il $12.95 (3-5)   **92**

ISBN 1-56145-306-4   LC 2003-18740
Introduces the life of inventor, statesman, and founding father Benjamin Franklin, whose love of books led him to establish the first public library in the American colonies.

"Ashby's clearly written narrative . . . flows smoothly and will hold the interest of children." SLJ

Benjamin Franklin; a man of many talents; by the editors fo Time for kids; with Kathryn Hoffman Satterfield. HarperCollins Pubs. 2005 44p il (Time for kids biographies) $14.99 (2-4)   **92**

ISBN 0-06-057610-3
A brief illustrated biography of the statesman and inventor

This is "sure to be highly popular with students. . . . Pages feature eye-catching sidebars with . . . brightly colored original drawings. . . . [It features] short lively [text]." Lib Media Connect

Fleming, Candace. Ben Franklin's almanac; being a true account of the good gentleman's life. Atheneum Bks. for Young Readers 2003 120p il $19.95 (5 and up)   **92**

ISBN 0-689-83549-3   LC 2002-6136
"An Anne Schwartz book"

Brings together eighteenth century etchings, artifacts, and quotations to create the effect of a scrapbook of the

Franklin, Benjamin, 1706-1790—*Continued*

life of Benjamin Franklin

"An authoritative work of depth, humor, and interest, presenting Franklin in all his complexity, ranging from the heroic to the vulgar, the saintly to the callous." SLJ

Ford, Carin T. Benjamin Franklin; inventor and patriot. Enslow Pubs. 2003 32p il map (Famous inventors) $22.70 (1-3) **92**

ISBN 0-7660-1859-8   LC 2002-487

Contents: Boyhood in Boston; Printer for the Colonies; Experimenting with electricity; Preparing for revolution; Diplomat for America

"Organized chronologically, the book moves from Franklin's childhood to his early career as a printer, introduces some of his inventions, and then covers his roles as a leader in the American Revolution and a diplomat to France. The print is large, the layout is colorful and inviting, and many reproductions are included." SLJ

Includes bibliographical references

Fritz, Jean. What's the big idea, Ben Franklin? illustrated by Margot Tomes. Coward, McCann & Geoghegan; distributed by Putnam Pub. Group 1976 46p il $15.99; pa $5.99 (2-4) **92**

ISBN 0-399-23487-X; 0-698-11372-1 (pa)

The text "focuses on Franklin's multifaceted career but also gives personal details and quotes some of his pithy sayings. Enough background information about colonial affairs is given to enable readers to understand the importance of Franklin's contributions to the public good but not so much that it obtrudes on his life story. Although the text is not punctuated by references or footnotes, a page of notes (with numbers for pages referred to) is appended." Bull Cent Child Books

Harness, Cheryl. The remarkable Benjamin Franklin; written & illustrated by Cheryl Harness. National Geographic Society 2005 47p il $17.95 (2-4) **92**

ISBN 0-7922-7882-8   LC 2004-20504

"Beginning with Franklin's birth, Harness explores the activities that filled his days from his quest to open his own print shop to his role in the American Revolution to his personal intrigues and inventions. Her conversational writing style and vivid illustrations will appeal to readers just becoming acquainted with this important figure." SLJ

Includes bibliographical references

Franklin, Rosalind, 1920-1958

Senker, Cath. Rosalind Franklin. Raintree Steck-Vaughn Pubs. 2003 48p il (Scientists who made history) lib bdg $27.12 (5 and up) **92**

1. Women scientists 2. DNA

ISBN 0-7398-5226-4   LC 2001-48961

Describes the life and career of Rosalind Franklin, a British molecular biologist who played a vital role in the discovery of the structure of DNA

This book has "ample full-color and black-and-white photos, reproductions, and maps to supplement the accessible [text]." SLJ

Includes glossary and bibliographical references

Fritz, Jean

Fritz, Jean. Homesick: my own story; illustrated with drawings by Margot Tomes and photographs. Putnam 1982 163p il $16.99; pa $5.99 (5 and up) **92**

1. China 2. Women authors

ISBN 0-399-20933-6; 0-698-11782-4 (pa)

LC 82-7646

A Newbery Medal honor book, 1983

Companion volume to China homecoming

This is a somewhat fictionalized memoir of the author's childhood in China. "Born in Hankow, where her father was director of the YMCA, Jean loved the city. . . . But she knew she 'belonged on the other side of the world'—in Pennsylvania with her grandmother and her other relations." Horn Book

"The descriptions of places and the times are vivid in a book that brings to the reader, with sharp clarity and candor, the yearnings and fears and ambivalent loyalties of a young girl." Bull Cent Child Books

Fulton, Robert, 1765-1815

Pierce, Morris A. Robert Fulton and the development of the steamboat. PowerPlus Books 2003 112p il map (Library of American lives and times) lib bdg $31.95 (4 and up) **92**

1. Inventors 2. Steamboats

ISBN 0-8239-5737-3   LC 2001-5541

Contents: Childhood, 1765-1780; Apprentice, 1780-1787; Artist, 1787-1793; Canal engineer, 1793-1797; Submarines, 1797-1802; Steamboats, 1802-1804; Torpedoes, 1804-1806; Pioneer, 1806-1807; Entrepreneur, 1807-1815

"The life and times of this complex and creative man are captured in this attractive presentation replete with maps and full-color reproductions of building sketches and period paintings." SLJ

Includes glossary and bibliographical references

Galilei, Galileo, 1564-1642

Panchyk, Richard. Galileo for kids; his life and ideas: 25 activities; foreword by Buzz Aldrin. Chicago Review Press 2005 166p il map pa $16.95 (5 and up) **92**

1. Astronomers

ISBN 1-55652-566-4   LC 2004-22936

A biography of the Renaissance scientist and his times with related activities

"Clear . . . writing places Galileo squarely within the historical context of the turbulent Italian Renaissance. . . . Panchyk's title is a good choice for those interested in integrating history and science curriculums." SLJ

Includes bibliographical references

Sís, Peter. Starry messenger; a book depicting the life of a famous scientist, mathematician, astronomer, philosopher, physicist, Galileo Galilei; created and illustrated by Peter Sís. Farrar, Straus & Giroux 1996 unp il $17; pa $6.95 **92**

1. Astronomers

ISBN 0-374-37191-1; 0-374-47027-8 (pa)

LC 95-44986

A Caldecott Medal honor book, 1997

"Frances Foster books"

Galilei, Galileo, 1564-1642—*Continued*

Describes the life and work of the man who changed the way people saw the galaxy, by offering objective evidence that the earth was not the fixed center of the universe

"Large, beautiful drawings reflect the ideas, events, books, maps, world view, and symbolism of the times. These intricate ink drawings, idiosyncratic in concept and beautifully tinted with delicate watercolor washes, are complemented by smaller drawings and prints that illustrate a side-text of significant dates, time lines, quotations, comments, and explanations. . . . Those drawn to the book will find that it works on many levels, offering not just facts but intuitive visions of another world." Booklist

Steele, Philip. Galileo; the genius who faced the Inquisition. National Geographic 2005 64p il (World history biographies) $17.95; lib bdg $27.90 (4 and up)   **92**
  1. Astronomers
  ISBN 0-7922-3656-4; 0-7922-3657-2 (lib bdg)
                                              LC 2005-01357
An illustrated introduction to the 16th century astronomer and his times

"Accomplishments and hardships are clearly explained wiwth supporting quotes and facts. . . . Beautifully illustrated and visually appealing." SLJ

Gama, Vasco da, 1469-1524

Calvert, Patricia. Vasco da Gama; so strong a spirit; [by] Patricia Calvert. Benchmark Books 2005 96p il map (Great explorations) lib bdg $29.93 (5 and up)   **92**
  1. Explorers
  ISBN 0-7614-1611-0   LC 2003-22946
Recounts the voyages undertaken by fifteenth-century Portuguese explorer Vasco da Gama to strengthen his nation's power by establishing a sea trade route to India.
Includes bibliographical references

Goodman, Joan E. A long and uncertain journey: the 27,000 mile voyage of Vasco da Gama; by Joan Elizabeth Goodman; illustrated by Tom McNeely. Mikaya Press 2001 47p il map (Great explorers book) $19.95 (4 and up)
                                                     92
  1. Explorers
  ISBN 0-9650493-7-X   LC 00-63795
"Goodman reviews the accomplishments of 15th century Portuguese explorer Vasco da Gama and his role in the rise of the Portuguese Empire." Book Rep

"McNeely's full-page illustrations, which vibrate with life and action, lighten the format, and quotations from the diary of an anonymous sailor on the voyage add fascinating detail and vivid description. . . . A good resource for reports, but the book is also intelligently written and exciting." Booklist

Ganci, Peter J., d. 2001

Ganci, Chris. Chief: the life of Peter J. Ganci, a New York City firefighter. Orchard Bks. 2003 unp il $16.95 (3-6)   **92**
  1. Fire fighters
  ISBN 0-439-44386-5   LC 2002-72816

"The author describes his dad . . . [Peter J. Ganci, who] became a member of the FDNY in 1968 and, in 1999, became Chief of the New York City Fire Department. . . . He lost his life on September 11, 2001, saving countless others, inside the raging inferno at the World Trade Center. . . . The text is balanced with large and small photos, in color and black and white. . . . The narrative is compelling, and children are likely to add Chief Ganci to the top of their list of heroes." SLJ

Gandhi, Mahatma, 1869-1948

Demi. Gandhi. Margaret K. McElderry Bks. 2001 unp il $19.95 (3-6)   **92**
  1. India—Politics and government 2. Passive resistance
  ISBN 0-689-84149-3   LC 00-32911
Maps on lining papers
"Beginning with Gandhi's failure as a student in India, this . . . biography traces Gandhi's life, from his first rallies against prejudice in South Africa to his remarkable victory over colonialism in India. . . . With extraordinarily detailed illustrations, decorated with gold leaf . . . and accessible, flowing text, veteran artist-author Demi reveals how a simple man who spun his own cloth became one of history's most important political and spiritual leaders." Booklist

Severance, John B. Gandhi, great soul. Clarion Bks. 1997 143p il map $18 (5 and up)
                                                     92
  1. India—Politics and government 2. Passive resistance
  ISBN 0-395-77179-X   LC 95-20887
Severance "begins with an introduction to Gandhi's message and gives a brief overview of the mahatma's personal evolution as well as India's external and internal struggles. He then chronicles Gandhi's life. . . . Severance details Gandhi's philosophy of *satyagraha*, or peaceful resistance." Booklist
"It is not only Gandhi who comes alive in this considered, well-documented biography but the multifarious personalities and politics of his world." Horn Book Guide
Includes bibliographical references

Wilkinson, Philip. Gandhi; the young protester who founded a nation. National Geographic 2005 64p il (World history biographies) $17.95; lib bdg $27.90 (4 and up)   **92**
  1. India—Politics and government 2. Passive resistance
  ISBN 0-7922-3647-5; 0-7922-3648-3 (lib bdg)
"Double-page spreads describe phases in Gandhi's life, from childhood to his tragic death, detailed in Wilkinson's straightforward, succinct language and in anecdotes, which will capture young people's attention and also humanize the great leader." Booklist
Includes glossary and bibliographical references

Gates, Bill, 1955-

Woog, Adam. Bill Gates. KidHaven Press 2003 48p il (Famous people) $23.70 (4 and up)
92

1. Microsoft Corporation 2. Computer software industry 3. Businessmen
ISBN 0-7377-1400-X   LC 2002-8897
Contents: A need to win; Boy meets computer; Starting Microsoft; Playing to win; Businessman, family man, philanthropist

Examines the life of Bill Gates, his early interest in computers, the founding of Microsoft, his success as a businessman, his family life and philanthropic activities

"Concise and well illustrated. . . . Readers will enjoy the personal anecdotes. . . . Color photos include an aerial shot of Gates' lavish home, as well as excellent images of him as a smug, gangly adolescent." Booklist

Gehrig, Lou, 1903-1941

Adler, David A. Lou Gehrig; the luckiest man; illustrated by Terry Widener. Harcourt Brace & Co. 1997 unp il $16 (2-4)   92

1. Baseball—Biography
ISBN 0-15-200523-4   LC 95-7997
"Gulliver books"
Traces the life of the Yankees' star ballplayer, focusing on his character and his struggle with the terminal disease amyotrophic lateral sclerosis

"Adler's restrained tone makes his description of Gehrig's stoic and uncomplaining struggle all the more moving. The illustrations, meticulously detailed . . . also pack an emotional wallop." Horn Book Guide

Viola, Kevin. Lou Gehrig; by Kevin Viola. LernerSports 2005 106p il (Sports heroes and legends) lib bdg $26.60 (4 and up)   92

1. Baseball—Biography
ISBN 0-8225-1794-9   LC 2003-23649
Contents: Prologue: The luckiest man; Little Lou; Another Babe?; Lou Lewis; Earning his stripes; The greatest team of all time; Ups and downs; Love and marriage; Captain Lou; A new partner; The streak and the slump; Epilogue: The pride of the Yankees

This "begins with the shy player's farewell at Yankee Stadium after being diagnosed with ALS. It then goes back to describe his early life as the son of German immigrants and how his enormous talent lifted his family from poverty. There is plenty of detail about the games he played and the records he broke, but the book also lends insight into the man himself." Booklist

Includes bibliographical references

Gehry, Frank

Greenberg, Jan. Frank O. Gehry; outside in; by Jan Greenberg and Sandra Jordan. DK Ink 2000 47p il $19.95 (4 and up)   92

1. Architects
ISBN 0-7894-2677-3   LC 99-46871
This book follows "Gehry from his modest upbringing in Canada . . . to his current international acclaim as architect of the Guggenheim Bilbao." Booklist

"Filled with childhood memories, personal quotes, and gorgeous full-color photographs of his work, this volume is a wonderful introduction to a creative and intuitive artist." SLJ

Includes glossary and bibliographical references

George III, King of Great Britain, 1738-1820

Fritz, Jean. Can't you make them behave, King George? pictures by Tomie de Paola. Putnam 1977 45p il $15.99; pa $6.99 (2-4)   92

1. Great Britain—Kings and rulers
ISBN 0-399-23304-0; 0-698-11402-7 (pa)
LC 75-33722
"As a boy, George is seen to have had struggles in deportment; as King George III, he is mystified that the colonists refuse to be taught. Bits of history, a sense of George's personality, and the loneliness of being king are all conveyed with good humor. The artist's drawings evoke more chuckles." LC. Child Books, 1977

George, Jean Craighead, 1919-

George, Jean Craighead. A tarantula in my purse; and 172 other wild pets; written and illustrated by Jean Craighead George. HarperCollins Pubs. 1996 134p il $15.99; pa $4.99 (4-6)   92

1. Women authors 2. Authors, American 3. Naturalists 4. Pets
ISBN 0-06-023626-4; 0-06-446201-3 (pa)
LC 95-54151
"George tells of the many wild pets that lived with her family, particularly while her children were growing up. Each chapter describes a different animal or incident." Booklist

"Told in a casual and thoroughly engaging manner, the stories will enchant all animal lovers and even those who aren't." SLJ

Giff, Patricia Reilly

Giff, Patricia Reilly. Don't tell the girls; a family memoir; by Patricia Reilly Giff. 1st ed. Holiday House 2005 131p il $16.95 (4 and up)
92

1. Women authors 2. Authors, American
ISBN 0-8234-1813-8   LC 2004-47452
"Giff reflects on her childhood and her family, going back through several generations. Spotlighting her two grandmothers, she lovingly relates remembered conversations and incidents involving the one she knew well before turning to the other grandmother, whom she never met. . . . This little book has much to offer thoughtful children. . . . With . . . sharply reproduced family photos and documents, this handsome book's small format reflects its intimate, conversational style." Booklist

Glenn, John, 1921-

Ashby, Ruth. Rocket man; the Mercury adventure of John Glenn. Peachtree 2004 il $12.95 (4-6)   92

1. Project Mercury 2. Astronauts 3. Statesmen
ISBN 1-56145-323-4
A biography of astronaut and U.S. Senator John Glenn

"This book describes Glenn's life in a highly readable style. Ashby also skillfully includes historical events in the narrative." SLJ

Glover, Savion

Glover, Savion. Savion!: my life in tap; by Savion Glover and Bruce Weber. Morrow 2000 79p il $19.95 (5 and up)   **92**

1. African American dancers 2. Choreographers 3. Tap dancing

ISBN 0-688-15629-0   LC 98-31517

Examines the life and career of the young tap dancer who speaks with his feet and who choreographed the Tony Award-winning Broadway show "Bring in da Noise, Bring in da Funk"

"Glover comes across in this vibrant book as confident but not arrogant. The black, white, and red text dances around the pages in a style and format that complement the subject matter." Voice Youth Advocates

Gogh, Vincent van, 1853-1890

Bassil, Andrea. Vincent van Gogh; by Andrea Bassil. New ed. World Almanac Library 2004 48p il (Lives of the artists) lib bdg $30; pa $11 (4 and up)   **92**

1. Artists, Dutch

ISBN 0-8368-5602-3 (lib bdg); 0-8368-5607-4 (pa)
                LC 2003-67236

Original Italian edition 2003

This is a biography of the Dutch painter.

This is "concise and straightforward, and there's no sensationalizing: Van Gogh's famous ear injury is only mentioned in a brief, matter-of-fact note. The interesting mix of photos and art is the biggest attraction." Booklist

Goodall, Jane, 1934-

Goodall, Jane. My life with the chimpanzees. rev ed. Pocket Bks. 1996 156p il pa $4.99 hardcover o.p. (3-6)   **92**

1. Chimpanzees 2. Women scientists

ISBN 0-671-56271-1 (pa)   LC 97-122051

"A Byron Preiss book. A Minstrel book"

First published 1988

The well-known English zoologist describes her early interest in animals and how this led to her study of chimpanzees at the Gombe Stream Reserve in Tanzania

"Family snapshots add to the special feeling of being let into Goodall's circle of friends as the famous scientist recounts her adventures with the chimps and illustrates many of her subjects' distinctive personalities. . . . This outstanding autobiography will be a noteworthy choice for school and public libraries." Booklist

Greene, Charles Sumner, 1868-1957

Thorne-Thomsen, Kathleen. Greene & Greene for kids; art, architecture, activities. Gibbs Smith 2004 112p il $17.95 (5 and up)   **92**

1. Greene, Henry Mather, 1870-1954 2. Architecture 3. Handicraft

ISBN 1-58685-440-2

" "Charlie and Henry Greene were born in Cincinnati, OH, during the late 19th century, a time period the author elucidates through full-color photographs and illustrations to make it more accessible to her audience. . . . The book [introduces] readers to their architecture after detailing a history of their ideas, concepts, and life expe-

riences. . . . Thorne-Thomsen presents the history, culture, and art of Greene and Greene through clear descriptions, fun activities, and lots of pictures." SLJ

Greene, Henry Mather, 1870-1954

Thorne-Thomsen, Kathleen. Greene & Greene for kids. See entry under Greene, Charles Sumner, 1868-1957

Grimm, Jacob, 1785-1863

Hettinga, Donald R. The Brothers Grimm; two lives, one legacy. Clarion Bks. 2001 180p il $22 (5 and up)   **92**

1. Grimm, Wilhelm, 1786-1859 2. Folklore—Germany

ISBN 0-618-05599-1   LC 00-65598

A biography of the brothers famous for collecting German folk tales

"No book for young readers presents the Grimms' intertwined lives against the larger background of early 19th-century Europe in such fascinating detail as this absorbing new biography. . . . Students will find it an excellent resource for term papers, yet it is written so clearly that it makes for enjoyable pleasure reading." SLJ

Includes bibliographical references

Grimm, Wilhelm, 1786-1859

Hettinga, Donald R. The Brothers Grimm. See entry under Grimm, Jacob, 1785-1863

Guthrie, Woody, 1912-1967

Christensen, Bonnie. Woody Guthrie, poet of the people. Knopf 2001 unp il $16.95; lib bdg $18.99 (3-6)   **92**

1. Singers

ISBN 0-375-81113-3; 0-375-91113-8 (lib bdg)
                LC 00-65504

Christensen tells "the life story of American songwriter Woody Guthrie. . . . The book both describes Guthrie's personal involvement in historical events such as the Dust Bowl drought and the rise of unionism and demonstrates those connections with short excerpts from songs he wrote at the time." Bull Cent Child Books

"Christensen makes a fine union of a spirited, vibrant text and hand-colored woodcuts that are sinewy and emotionally compelling." Booklist

Neimark, Anne E. There ain't nobody that can sing like me: the life of Woody Guthrie. Atheneum Bks. for Young Readers 2002 122p il $17.95 (5 and up)   **92**

1. Singers

ISBN 0-689-83369-5   LC 00-56933

The author "chronicles the tragedy-and triumph-laced life of folksinger and activist Woody Guthrie." Publ Wkly

The author's "ideas are cohesive and well developed, yet she writes with an energy reflective of young Woody hurrying to get words on paper as his thoughts seemingly spilled off his pencil. She doesn't ignore Woody's imperfections. . . . And his political leanings and influence are given their due. But with quotes from *Bound for Glory*

Guthrie, Woody, 1912-1967—*Continued*

and plentiful reproduction of his song lyrics, it is Woody's own voice that takes center stage here." Horn Book

Includes bibliographical references

Hancock, John, 1737-1793

Fritz, Jean. Will you sign here, John Hancock? pictures by Trina Schart Hyman. Coward, McCann & Geoghegan; distributed by Putnam Pub. Group 1976 47p il $16.99; pa $5.99 (2-4)   **92**

1. United States—History—1775-1783, Revolution
ISBN 0-399-23306-7; 0-698-11440-X (pa)

"A straightforward biography of the rich Boston dandy with the gigantic signature. When he signed the Declaration of Independence he quipped, 'There! George the Third can read "that" without his spectacles. Now he can double his reward for my head.'" Saturday Rev

"An affectionate look at a flamboyant, egocentric, but kindly, patriot, the book is a most enjoyable view of history. . . . The delightful illustrations exactly suit the times and the extraordinary character of John Hancock." Horn Book

Handel, George Frideric, 1685-1759

Anderson, M. T. Handel, who knew what he liked; illustrated by Kevin Hawkes. Candlewick Press 2001 unp $16.99; pa $6.99 (4-6)   **92**

1. Composers
ISBN 0-7636-1046-1; 0-7636-2562-0 (pa)
LC 00-57210

In this biography Handel, who would later compose some of the world's most beautiful music, is shown as a stubborn little boy with a mind of his own

The author "infuses the composer's story with warmth and color, humor and humanity. . . . Relating pithy stories with plain words and short sentences, Anderson never forgets his audience in his enthusiasm for his subject." Booklist

Harrison, John, 1693-1776

Dash, Joan. The longitude prize; pictures by Dučsan Petrčci'c. Foster Bks. 1999 200p il $16 (5 and up)   **92**

1. Longitude
ISBN 0-374-34636-4
LC 97-44257

The story of John Harrison, inventor of watches and clocks, who spent forty years working on a time-machine which could be used to accurately determine longitude at sea

"Students looking for new subjects for reports will discover . . . an excellent resource on a topic seldom addressed in a book for youth. Charming ink drawings by Dusan Petricic illustrate. A glossary, an afterword, a time line, and a bibliography conclude." Booklist

Haskell, Katharine Wright, 1874-1929

Maurer, Richard. The Wright sister; Katharine Wright and her famous brothers. Millbrook Press 2003 127p il $18.95; lib bdg $25.90 (5 and up)   **92**

1. Wright, Wilbur, 1867-1912 2. Wright, Orville, 1871-1948 3. Air pilots
ISBN 0-7613-1546-2; 0-7613-2564-6 (lib bdg)
LC 2002-151080

"Maurer chronicles the events surrounding Wilbur and Orville, while all along filling in the details of their younger sister's life and the relationship among the three." SLJ

"Quotations from diaries and letters bring the close-knit Wright family to life. . . . The layout is spacious, and the many well chosen, black-and-white photos help visualize the Wrights and their times." Booklist

Hatshepsut, Queen of Egypt

Galford, Ellen. Hatshepsut; the princess who became king. National Geographic 2005 64p il map (World history biographies) $17.95; lib bdg $27.90 (4 and up)   **92**

1. Egypt—Civilization 2. Egypt—History
ISBN 0-7922-3645-9; 0-7922-3646-7 (lib bdg)

This "presents the life of Queen Hatshepsut, who ruled Egypt as pharaoh during the New Kingdom, around 3500 years ago. Illustrated with clear, color photos of artifacts and sites as well as colorful maps, the text discusses aspects of Egyptian life such as education and religion in Hatshepsut's life. . . . With a clearly written text and many handsome photos, this provides an accessible introduction to Hatshepsut and her times." Booklist

Hawkins, Benjamin Waterhouse

Kerley, Barbara. The dinosaurs of Waterhouse Hawkins; an illuminating history of Mr. Waterhouse Hawkins, artist and lecturer; with drawings by Brian Selznick, many of which are based on the original sketches of Mr. Hawkins. Scholastic 2001 unp il $16.95 (3-5)   **92**

1. Dinosaurs
ISBN 0-439-11494-2
LC 00-58376

A Caldecott Medal honor book, 2002

"A true dinosaur story—in three ages—from a childhood love of art, to the monumental dinosaur sculptures at the Crystal Palace in England, to the thwarted work in New York's Central Park . . . it's all here!" Title page

The true story of Victorian artist Benjamin Waterhouse Hawkins, who built life-sized models of dinosaurs in the hope of educating the world about these awe-inspiring ancient animals and what they were like

"Kerley suffuses her text with a sense of wonder and amazement, a tone well-matched by Selznick's lush, dramatic illustrations." Publ Wkly

Henry, Patrick, 1736-1799

Fritz, Jean. Where was Patrick Henry on the 29th of May? illustrated by Margot Tomes. Coward, McCann & Geoghegan; distributed by Putnam Pub. Group 1975 47p il $16.99; pa $6.99 (2-4)   **92**

1. United States—History—1600-1775, Colonial period

ISBN 0-399-23305-9; 0-698-11439-6 (pa)

A "portrait of a founding father. Patrick Henry was born on May 29, and the author uses this date to focus on significant periods in his life. Henry's skill at oratory is shown in development as well as his anger at English laws, until they peak in his famous speech." Child Book Rev Serv

"The color pictures are artful evocations of the [18th] century in America and the text presents Patrick Henry as a human being—not a sterilized historic 'figure.'" Publ Wkly

Henson, Matthew Alexander, 1866-1955

Ferris, Jeri. Arctic explorer: the story of Matthew Henson. Carolrhoda Bks. 1989 80p il maps lib bdg $24.50; pa $6.25 (3-6)   **92**

1. Explorers 2. North Pole 3. African Americans—Biography

ISBN 0-87614-370-2 (lib bdg); 0-87614-507-1 (pa)
                                    LC 88-34449

"A high adventure biography of Matthew Henson, the black explorer who accompanied Robert Peary on six expeditions to the North Pole. Henson's great courage, determination, and adaptability were crucial elements in the success of the expeditions. Black-and-white photographs supplement well-written text." Sci Child

Includes bibliographical references

Johnson, Dolores. Onward; a photobiography of African-American polar explorer Matthew Henson. National Geographic 2006 64p il $17.95 (5 and up)   **92**

1. Explorers 2. North Pole 3. African Americans—Biography

ISBN 0-7922-7914-X   LC 2005-05837

"The quest to be the first to reach the North Pole is an exciting adventure story, and Henson got there first, as part of the ninth expedition led by Robert Peary in 1909. But Henson was African American, labeled as Peary's 'Negro manservant,' and he did not get full recognition until 2001. This . . . focuses on the physical details of the dangerous Arctic journeys . . . the repeated failures and the teamwork, as well as Henson's skills, stamina, and essential role in forging relationships with the Inuit. . . . The book design is beautiful: thick paper, spacious type, and stirring photos that capture the icy storms as well as the people involved in the history." Booklist

Herrera, Juan Felipe, 1948-

Herrera, Juan Felipe. The upside down boy; story by Juan Felipe Herrera; illustrations by Elizabeth Gómez. Children's Bk. Press 2000 31p il $15.95 (k-3)   **92**

1. Poets 2. Mexican Americans—Biography 3. Bilingual books—English-Spanish

ISBN 0-89239-162-6   LC 99-49113

Title page and text in English and Spanish

The author recalls the year when his farm worker parents settled down in the city so that he could go to school for the first time

"Herrera's poetic prose sings with a unique voice in both languages, and Gómez's illustrations are colorful and ethereal." Horn book guide

Hillary, Sir Edmund

Brennan, Kristine. Sir Edmund Hillary, modern day explorer. Chelsea House 2001 63p il (Explorers of new worlds) lib bdg $21.85; pa $11.95 (4 and up)   **92**

1. Mount Everest (China and Nepal)
2. Mountaineering

ISBN 0-7910-5953-7 (lib bdg); 0-7910-6163-9 (pa)
                                    LC 00-43077

A biography of the New Zealander who, with his Sherpa climbing partner Tenzing Norgay, first reached the Summit of Mount Everest in 1953

"Accessible and well organized. . . . Fresh, appealing, and well written." SLJ

Includes glossary and bibliographical references

Coburn, Broughton. Triumph on Everest: a photobiography of Sir Edmund Hillary. National Geographic Soc. 2000 64p il map $17.95 (4 and up)   **92**

1. Mount Everest (China and Nepal)
2. Mountaineering

ISBN 0-7922-7114-9   LC 00-27009

A biography of Edmund Hillary, whose love of snow, mountains, and the outdoor life culminated in his conquering the highest peak in the world

"Threaded with quotes from Hillary's own writings, and full of fine, blue-toned photographs, the engrossing text presents the life of a reticent but world-renowned mountaineer, adventurer, and philanthropist." SLJ

Includes bibliographical references

Hokusai (Katsushika Hokusai), 1760-1849

Ray, Deborah Kogan. Hokusai; the man who painted a mountain. Foster Bks. 2001 unp il $18 (3-6)   **92**

1. Artists, Japanese

ISBN 0-374-33263-0   LC 00-50395

"The life of the iconoclastic Japanese artist who produced more than thirty thousand works of art." Booklist

"The text and evocative artwork provide details and scenes of everyday Japanese life in the 19th century. The illustrations include accomplished soft watercolor and colored-pencil paintings, labeled Chinese characters, drawings from the artist's sketchbooks, and a reproduction of Hokusai's 'The Great Wave off Kanagawa.'" SLJ

Includes bibliographical references

Hopper, Edward, 1882-1967

Spangenburg, Ray. Edward Hopper; the life of an artist; [by] Ray Spangenburg and Kit Moser. Enslow Pubs. 2002 48p il (Artist biographies) $23.93 (2-4)   **92**

1. Artists—United States

ISBN 0-7660-1881-4   LC 2002-11984

Hopper, Edward, 1882-1967—*Continued*
Examines the life and work of the American realist painter, describing and giving examples of his art
Includes glossary and bibliographical references

Houdini, Harry, 1874-1926
Fleischman, Sid. Escape! the story of the great Houdini; [by] Sid Fleischman. Greenwillow Books 2006 210p il $18.99; lib bdg $19.89 (5 and up)
92
1. Magicians
ISBN 978-0-06-085094-4; 0-06-085094-9; 978-0-06-085095-1 (lib bdg) LC 2005052631
"Fleischman looks at Houdini's life through his own eyes, as a fellow magician. . . . Fleischman's tone is lively and he develops a relationship with readers by revealing just enough truth behind Houdini's razzle-dazzle to keep the legend alive. . . . Engaging and fascinating." SLJ
Includes bibliographical references

Krull, Kathleen. Houdini; the world's greatest mystery man and escape king; in a production written by Kathleen Krull; and illustrated by Eric Velasquez. Walker & Co 2005 unp il $16.95; lib bdg $17.85 (2-4) **92**
1. Magicians
ISBN 0-8027-8953-6; 0-8027-8954-4 (lib bdg) LC 2004-49493
"Framed descriptions of some of Houdini's most famous stunts are interspersed within the overview of his life. The author's crisp narrative style and careful choice of detail are evident here. . . . Velasquez's impressive framed, posed oil paintings portray the magician's intensity and sense of showmanship." SLJ
Includes bibliographical references

MacLeod, Elizabeth. Harry Houdini; a magical life; written by Elizabeth MacLeod. Kids Can Press 2005 32p il $14.95 (4-6) **92**
1. Magicians
ISBN 1-55337-769-9
"The world's best-known magician began performing as an acrobat in his neighborhood at the age of nine to make money desperately needed by his family. MacLeod provides a straightforward history of her colorful subject. . . . Reproduced images of photos, handbills, and advertisements bring the text on each double-page spread to life." Booklist

Houston, Samuel, 1793-1863
Fritz, Jean. Make way for Sam Houston; illustrations by Elise Primavera. Putnam 1986 109p il map $16.99; pa $5.99 (4 and up)
92
ISBN 0-399-21303-1; 0-698-11646-1 (pa) LC 85-25601
This is a biography of the "lawyer, governor of Tennessee, general in the wars against Santa Anna, president of the Republic of Texas, and finally U.S. senator and governor of the state of Texas." Horn Book
"Artfully weaving the threads of fact, Fritz creates a biography that is both interesting and informative. Devel-

oping Houston as a human character that readers can identify with as well as admire, and drawing him against the scene of America's own political turmoil, Fritz gives us a book to be read and to be felt." Voice Youth Advocates
Includes bibliographical references

Hughes, Langston, 1902-1967
Cooper, Floyd. Coming home; from the life of Langston Hughes. Philomel Bks. 1994 unp il lib bdg $16.95; pa $6.99 (k-3) **92**
1. Poets, American 2. African American authors
ISBN 0-399-22682-6 (lib bdg); 0-698-11612-7 (pa) LC 93-36332
This "biography highlights pivotal events in Hughes's life, emphasizing his loneliness as a child and his development as a poet. . . . Cooper's hazy illustrations in gold, brown, and sepia tones reveal keen observations of people and neighborhood. The text and art combine to create a fine tribute and introduction to the writer's life." Horn Book
Includes bibliographical references

Walker, Alice. Langston Hughes, American poet; paintings by Catherine Deeter. HarperCollins Pubs. 2002 37p il $16.95; lib bdg $16.89; pa $7.99 (2-5) **92**
1. Poets, American 2. African American authors
ISBN 0-06-021518-6; 0-06-021519-4 (lib bdg); 0-06-079889-0 (pa) LC 92-28540
"Amistad"
A newly illustrated edition of the title first published 1974 by Crowell
An illustrated biography of the Harlem poet whose works gave voice to the joy and pain of the black experience in America.
This "is an excellent introduction to Hughes, focusing mainly on his adolescence and early adulthood. . . . The engaging, anecdotal style is perfect for read-alouds, and the brief sentences and simple vocabulary make the book a good choice for beginning and struggling readers. Deeter's realistic paintings capture the text's pivotal moments." Booklist

Hurston, Zora Neale, 1891-1960
Miller, William. Zora Hurston and the chinaberry tree; illustrated by Cornelius Van Wright and Ying-hwa Hu. Lee & Low Bks. 1994 unp il $15.95; pa $6.95 (k-3) **92**
1. African American authors 2. Women authors
ISBN 1-880000-14-8; 1-880000-33-4 (pa) LC 94-1291
"This biography, which covers a brief period in Zora Neale Hurston's childhood, ends with the young girl grieving over her mother's death but finding inner power and strength from her mother's life." Horn Book
"Conveying the changing expressions on the face of the young Hurston as easily as they show the grandeur of the sky at nightfall, the versatile artists neatly capture the emotions in this lucidly told story." Publ Wkly

Hurston, Zora Neale, 1891-1960—*Continued*

Porter, A. P. Jump at de sun: the story of Zora Neale Hurston; foreword by Lucy Ann Hurston. Carolrhoda Bks. 1992 95p il pa $6.95 hardcover o.p. (4 and up)   **92**

1. African American authors 2. Women authors

ISBN 0-87614-546-2 (pa)   LC 91-37241

Follows the life of the African American writer known for her novels, plays, articles, and collections of folklore

This is "written in engagingly fresh prose and attractively laid out in a large, clear type. . . . The well-chosen and appropriately placed black-and-white photographs serve not only to extend the text, but also to put faces on the many names that crop up in the story of Hurston's eventful life." SLJ

Includes bibliographical references

Huynh, Quang Nhuong

Huynh, Quang Nhuong. The land I lost: adventures of a boy in Vietnam; with pictures by Vo-Dinh Mai. Harper & Row 1982 115p il pa $4.99 hardcover o.p. (5 and up)   **92**

1. Vietnam—Social life and customs

ISBN 0-06-440183-9 (pa)   LC 80-8437

"Each chapter in this book of reminiscence about the author's boyhood in a hamlet in the Vietnamese highlands, is a separate episode, although the same characters appear in many of the episodes. . . . The writing has an ingenuous quality that adds to the appeal of the strong sense of familial and communal ties that pervades the story." Bull Cent Child Books

Huynh, Quang Nhuong. Water buffalo days; growing up in Vietnam; pictures by Jean and Mou-sien Tseng. HarperCollins Pubs. 1997 116p il $13.95; pa $4.95 (3-5)   **92**

1. Vietnam—Social life and customs 2. Water buffalo

ISBN 0-06-024957-9; 0-06-446211-0 (pa)

LC 96-35058

The author describes his close relationship to his water buffalo, Tank, when he was growing up in a village in the central highlands of Vietnam

"Most of the incidents described are entertaining and readers will learn fascinating information about the importance of these animals in this culture. . . . The Tsengs' soft sketches show Tank, his young master, and the various villagers mentioned in the text." SLJ

Hypatia, ca. 370-415

Love, D. Anne. Of numbers and stars; the story of Hypatia; by D. Anne Love; illustrated by Pam Paparone. 1st ed. Holiday House 2006 unp il $16.95 (2-4)   **92**

1. Women mathematicians 2. Philosophers

ISBN 0-8234-1621-6   LC 2003064725

"In fourth-century C.E. Egypt, women had few opportunities. How Hypatia, daughter of mathematician Theon, became one of the greatest philosophers of her day makes fascinating reading. . . . Attractive paintings add life to a clear and captivating text that offers a unique contribution to units about Egypt, philosophers, or women in history." SLJ

Includes bibliographical references

Ibn Battuta, 1304-1377

Rumford, James. Traveling man: the journey of Ibn Battuta, 1325-1354; written, illustrated, and illuminated by James Rumford. Houghton Mifflin 2001 unp il map $16 (3-6)   **92**

1. Voyages and travels 2. Asia—Description

ISBN 0-618-08366-9   LC 00-57257

This describes the "journey of Ibn Battuta, the celebrated 14th-century scholar and cultural geographer from Tangier who spent 29 years wandering through Africa, the Middle East and Asia." N Y Times Book Rev

"Rumford's presentation is lavish and undeniably impressive. Ibn Battuta's route snakes across the spreads to create an extended map, with text boxes serving as stopping points along the way. Lush watercolor scenes, awash in gold highlights, are frequently borded by equally lush calligraphy quotes, rendered in Arabic, Persian, or Chinese." Bull Cent Child Books

Includes glossary

Ives, Charles Edward, 1874-1954

Gerstein, Mordicai. What Charlie heard. Foster Bks. 2001 unp il $17 (k-3)   **92**

1. Composers

ISBN 0-374-38292-1   LC 00-25557

Describes the life of American composer Charles Ives, who wrote music which expressed all the sounds he heard in the world, but which was not well received during his lifetime

"Gerstein creates a rousing visual cacophony that echoes Ives's compositions in this inspired picture-book biography." Publ Wkly

Jackson, Mahalia, 1911-1972

Orgill, Roxane. Mahalia; a life in gospel music. Candlewick Press 2002 132p il $19.99 (5 and up)   **92**

1. Gospel music 2. African American singers 3. African American women

ISBN 0-7636-1011-9   LC 00-48669

This is a "portrait of a passionately religious woman devoted to bringing the gospel to audiences around the world through her music. . . . Rhythmic sentences, sometimes fragments, capture the beat of gospel music and incorporate vernacular African-American speech patterns from the 1920s to the early 1970s. Events in the singer's personal life and musical career are skillfully blended with material about the social climate of the times." SLJ

Jackson, Stonewall, 1824-1863

Fritz, Jean. Stonewall; with drawings by Stephen Gammell. Putnam 1979 152p il map $16.99; pa $5.99 (4 and up)   **92**

1. Generals 2. United States—History—1861-1865, Civil War

ISBN 0-399-20698-1; 0-698-11552-X (pa)

LC 79-12506

A biography of the brilliant southern general who gained the nickname Stonewall by his stand at Bull Run during the Civil War

"Fritz's trenchant, compassionate life of General

Jackson, Stonewall, 1824-1863—*Continued*
Thomas Jonathan Jackson grips the reader and makes one understand why Stonewall is an honored legend in American history. . . . The tragic irony of his death at age 39 is movingly described." Publ Wkly

Includes bibliographical references

Jefferson, Thomas, 1743-1826
Adler, David A. A picture book of Thomas Jefferson; illustrated by John & Alexandra Wallner. Holiday House 1990 unp il lib bdg $16.95; pa $6.95 (1-3)   **92**
1. Presidents—United States
ISBN 0-8234-0791-8 (lib bdg); 0-8234-0881-7 (pa)
LC 89-20076
Traces the life and achievements of the architect, bibliophile, president, and author of the Declaration of Independence
"The book includes an amazing amount of material. An appealing package with simple language and detailed drawings." Horn Book

Jemison, Mae C.
Alagna, Magdalena. Mae Jemison; the first African American woman in space; by Magdalena Alagna. 1st ed. Rosen Pub. Group 2004 112p il (Women hall of famers in mathematics and science) lib bdg $29.25 (4 and up)   **92**
1. Astronauts 2. African American women
ISBN 0-8239-3878-6   LC 2002-11132
Provides insights into the life of Mae Jemison, the first female African American astronaut, including some of the steps she took to reach her goals.
This "well-written [volume has an] interesting [story], well-documented facts, well-chosen photographs, and an easy and enjoyable writing style." SLJ

Includes bibliographical references

Jemison, Mae C. Find where the wind goes; moments from my life; [by] Mae Jemison. Scholastic Press 2001 196p il $16.95; pa $4.99 (5 and up)   **92**
1. Astronauts 2. African American women
ISBN 0-439-13195-2; 0-439-13196-0 (pa)
LC 00-41008
"Dr. Jemison, the first woman of color to travel in space, shares her life story in this autobiographical selection." Book Rep
"Jemison's vitality, intelligence, and humor shine through the book, and she has a fascinating and inspiring life story to tell." Booklist

Joan, of Arc, Saint, 1412-1431
Hodges, Margaret. Joan of Arc; the Lily Maid; illustrated by Robert Rayevsky. Holiday House 1999 unp il $16.95 (2-4)   **92**
1. Christian saints 2. France—History—1328-1589, House of Valois
ISBN 0-8234-1424-8   LC 98-24260
A biography of the fifteenth-century peasant girl who led a French army to victory against the English, witnessed the crowning of King Charles VII, and was later burned at the stake for witchcraft
"Hodges tells Joan's story with simplicity, distilling the myriad events of bravery and betrayal down to their essence. . . . The pictures are full of action and naive charm, and they have the same strong simplicity as the text. Rayevsky incorporates medieval styles and techniques into his artwork, using two printmaking techniques: dry point and etching." Booklist

Poole, Josephine. Joan of Arc; illustrated by Angela Barrett, research by Vincent Helyas. Knopf 1998 unp il $18; pa $6.99 (2-4)   **92**
1. Christian saints 2. France—History—1328-1589, House of Valois
ISBN 0-679-89041-6; 0-375-80355-6 (pa)
LC 97-46667
This is a "biography of Saint Joan, the 15th-century farmer's daughter who heard voices from heaven directing her to lead the French in battle during the Hundred Years' War." Publ Wkly
"The text mixes the high adventure of Joan's crusade with the maiden's most personal reactions to the dramatic events engulfing her life. . . . Barrett's lovely illustrations are alternately pastoral, celestial, and spirited. The spreads sweep along and will gather younger readers with their zeal." Booklist

Stanley, Diane. Joan of Arc. Morrow Junior Bks. 1998 unp il $16 (4 and up)   **92**
1. Christian saints 2. France—History—1328-1589, House of Valois
ISBN 0-688-14329-6   LC 97-45652
A biography of the fifteenth-century peasant girl who led a French army to victory against the English and was burned at the stake for witchcraft
Stanley "orchestrates the complexities of history into a gripping, unusually challenging story in this exemplary biography. . . . Judiciously chosen details build atmosphere in both the text and the artwork—painstakingly wrought, gilded paintings modeled after the illuminated manuscripts of Joan's day." Publ Wkly

Includes bibliographical references

Johnson, Mamie, 1935-
Green, Michelle Y. A strong right arm: the story of Mamie "Peanut" Johnson; introduction by Mamie Johnson. Dial Bks. for Young Readers 2002 111p il $15.99; pa $5.99 (4 and up)
92
1. Baseball—Biography 2. Women athletes 3. African American athletes
ISBN 0-8037-2661-9; 0-14-240072-6 (pa)
LC 2001-28616
"Johnson was a pitcher with the Negro Leagues' Indianapolis Clowns from 1953 to 1955. In the introduction, Johnson speaks directly and movingly to the reader about her meeting with author Green, who then lets the famous ballplayer tell her own story in a lively first-person narrative. Johnson's ebullient personality and determination fairly leap off the page." Booklist

Includes bibliographical references

Jones, Mother, 1830-1930

Koestler-Grack, Rachel A. The story of Mother Jones. Chelsea Clubhouse 2004 32p il (Breakthrough biographies) lib bdg $14.95 (2-4)

92

1. Reformers 2. Labor—United States
ISBN 0-7910-7316-5   LC 2003-367

A biography of the labor leader who grew up in Ireland, emigrated to the United States, lost her family to yellow fever, and helped the mistreated working class, from coal miners to child mill workers, achieve better working conditions in the late 1800s and early 1900s.

Includes bibliographical references

Jones, John Paul, 1747-1792

Haugen, Brenda. John Paul Jones; father of the American Navy; by Brenda Haugen. Compass Point Books 2005 112p il map (Signature lives) $30.60 (4 and up)

92

1. United States—History—1775-1783, Revolution
ISBN 0-7565-0829-0   LC 2004-23133

Contents: Not yet begun to fight; Dreams of the sea; Captain Jones; Sailing for the United States; Fighting in Great Britain; Sailing on the Bonhomme Richard; Battle with the Serapis; A hero on two continents; Adventures after the Revolutionary War; The final years

"Jones' life is traced from his childhood in London through his controversial career as a British merchant seaman. . . . Attractively designed and illustrated, this fast-paced, informative biography has many useful appendixes, including a chronology of Jones' life and times, source notes, and a selective bibliography." Booklist

Includes bibliographical references

Joseph, Nez Percé Chief, 1840-1904

Englar, Mary. Chief Joseph, 1840-1904; by Mary Englar. Blue Earth Books 2004 32p (American Indian biographies) $23.93 (3-5)

92

1. Nez Percé Indians
ISBN 0-7368-2444-8   LC 2003-11071

Contetnts: "I will fight no more forever"; Life in Wallowa Valley; The white men come; Joseph becomes chief; The Nez Perce war; Life after the war

A biography of the peace chief who ended the Nez Percé War by surrendering to United States soldiers in 1877, believing that he would be permitted lead his people back to their ancestral lands in Idaho. Includes a recipe for berry fritters and directions for "the stick game."

This "very accessible [title is] well illustrated with maps, photographs, and paintings, and [it offers] an introduction to American Indian history as well as specific information for reports." Booklist

Juana Inés de la Cruz, 1651-1695

Mora, Pat. A library for Juana: the world of Sor Juana Inés; illustrated by Beatriz Vidal. Knopf 2002 unp il $15.95 (2-4)

92

1. Women authors 2. Authors, Mexican 3. Nuns
ISBN 0-375-80643-1   LC 2001-50851

A biography of the seventeenth-century Mexican poet, learned in many subjects, who became a nun later in life

"Mora's beautifully crafted text does credit to its subject. . . . The text is perfectly complemented by Vidal's brilliant, detailed illustrations that have the look and exactitude of Renaissance miniatures." SLJ

Includes glossary

Kahlo, Frida, 1907-1954

Frith, Margaret. Frida Kahlo; the artist who painted herself; written by Margaret Frith; illustrated by Tomie DePaola. Grosset & Dunlap 2003 unp il (Smart about art) lib bdg $14.89; pa $5.99 (2-4)

92

1. Artists, Mexican 2. Women artists
ISBN 0-448-43239-0 (lib bdg); 0-448-42677-3 (pa)
                                LC 2003-5221

Biography of Mexican artist Frida Kahlo, written as a child's school report

"Kahlo's story is clear, concise, and accessible. All of the basic facts are here, along with many personal details that enliven the narrative. . . . The well-written prose is beautifully complemented both by photos of Kahlo and of some of her best-known paintings and by dePaola's splendid trademark illustrations, all set against vividly colored backgrounds." SLJ

Laidlaw, Jill A. Frida Kahlo. Watts 2003 46p il (Artists in their time) lib bdg $22.50; pa $6.95 (5 and up)

92

1. Women artists 2. Artists, Mexican
ISBN 0-531-12236-0 (lib bdg); 0-531-16642-2 (pa)
                                LC 2003-535333

A biography of the Mexican artist and Communist activist

"The text is clear, concise, and written with vigor. . . . The large, full-color reproductions of [Kahlo's] paintings are excellent, and numerous archival photographs and quotes add a personal and immediate connection to the artist's life." SLJ

Sabbeth, Carol. Frida Kahlo and Diego Rivera: their lives and ideas; 24 activities; [by] Carol Sabbeth. 1st ed. Chicago Review Press 2005 147p il map pa $17.95 (5 and up)

92

1. Rivera, Diego, 1886-1957 2. Artists, Mexican
ISBN 1-55652-569-9   LC 2004-24525

"An overview of two complicated and controversial figures whose personal affairs, political ideas and affiliations, and artworks were out of the mainstream, even radical. . . . The pages are colorfully designed with bright borders at the tops of the pages, colored sidebars, and appropriately placed photos and reproductions, including works by both artists. The 24 related activities range from artwork to cultural projects." SLJ

Includes bibliographical references

Winter, Jonah. Frida; illustrated by Ana Juan. Levine Bks. 2002 unp il $16.95; pa $5.99 (k-3)

92

1. Artists, Mexican 2. Women artists
ISBN 0-590-20320-7; 0-590-20321-5 (pa)
                                LC 00-51421

Also available Spanish language edition

Kahlo, Frida, 1907-1954—*Continued*

This "illustrated short biography argues that the seeds of iconic painter Frida Kahlo's genius were planted during her childhood. . . . Winter consistently manages to convey much with a few well-chosen words, and the illustrations are appropriately awash with traditional Mexican folk art motifs and characters. Especially pleasing are Juan's surreal, Kahlo like touches." Horn Book

Kaiulani, Princess of Hawaii, 1875-1899

Stanley, Fay. The last princess: the story of Princess Ka'iulani of Hawai'i; illustrated by Diane Stanley. HarperCollins Pubs. 2001 40p il map $15.95; lib bdg $15.89 (4 and up)   **92**

1. Princesses 2. Hawaii—History

ISBN 0-688-18020-5; 0-06-029215-6 (lib bdg)

LC 00-32048

A reissue of the title first published 1991 by Four Winds Press

Recounts the story of Hawaii's last heir to the throne, who was denied her right to rule when the monarchy was abolished

"The princesses's story sheds new light on long-forgotten history; the vibrant, handsome gouache illustrations establish the lush Hawaiian background and provide historic detail." Horn Book

Includes bibliographical references

Keats, Ezra Jack, 1916-1983

Engel, Dean. Ezra Jack Keats; a biography with illustrations; [by] Dean Engel and Florence B. Freedman. Silver Moon Press 1995 81p il $24.95 (3-5)   **92**

1. Authors, American 2. Illustrators

ISBN 1-881889-65-3   LC 94-34960

A "profile of a significant creator of twentieth-century children's books, this study of Ezra Jack Keats for young readers is based on reminiscences of conversations with and autobiographical essays by the subject. . . . The illustrations, most from published works, integrate Keats's persona with that of his characters." Horn Book

"This attractive, oversized volume is a must read for Keats's many fans and a marvelous way to introduce (or reintroduce) children to his work." SLJ

Kehret, Peg, 1936-

Kehret, Peg. Five pages a day; a writer's journey. Whitman, A. 2002 185p $14.95 (4 and up)   **92**

1. Authors, American 2. Women authors

ISBN 0-8075-8650-1   LC 2002-16768

A biography of the author of numerous books for young people, describing her childhood bout with polio, how she became a writer, family relationships, and the importance of writing in her life

"With the same eye for well-chosen details that characterizes her other writing, [Kehret] mines her experiences for anecdotes young readers will appreciate." Booklist

Kehret, Peg. Small steps: the year I got polio. Whitman, A. 1996 179p il $14.95; pa $5.95 (4-6)   **92**

1. Poliomyelitis 2. Authors, American 3. Women authors

ISBN 0-8075-7457-0; 0-8075-7458-9 (pa)

LC 95-52641

This "memoir takes readers back to 1949 when the author, at age 12, contracted polio. . . . She describes her seven-month ordeal—her diagnosis and quarantine, her terrifying paralysis, her slow and difficult recuperation—and the people she encountered along the way." Booklist

Kehret "writes in an approachable, familiar way, and readers will be hooked from the first page on." SLJ

Keita, Soundiata, d. 1255

Wisniewski, David. Sundiata; lion king of Mali; story and pictures by David Wisniewski. Clarion Bks. 1992 unp il $17; pa $5.95 (1-4)   **92**

1. Mali—History

ISBN 0-395-61302-7; 0-395-76481-5 (pa)

LC 91-27951

The story of Sundiata, who overcame physical handicaps, social disgrace, and strong opposition to rule Mali in the thirteenth century

"Passed down through oral tradition, this historical account has the drama and depth of a folktale. The illustrations—elaborate collages inspired by the artifacts and culture of the Malinke—create a series of dramatic images. The intricacy of the paper-cuts and the richness of the colors and patterns give the artwork visual as well as narrative strength." Booklist

Keller, Helen, 1880-1968

Adler, David A. A picture book of Helen Keller; illustrated by John & Alexandra Wallner. Holiday House 1990 unp il lib bdg $16.95; pa $6.95 (1-3)   **92**

1. Blind 2. Deaf

ISBN 0-8234-0818-3 (lib bdg); 0-8234-0950-3 (pa)

LC 89-77510

A brief biography of the woman who overcame her handicaps of being both blind and deaf

"The Wallners' line and watercolor cartoons match the simple text and are appropriate to the book's tone." SLJ

Dash, Joan. The world at her fingertips: the story of Helen Keller. Scholastic Press 2001 235p $15.95; pa $4.99 (5 and up)   **92**

1. Blind 2. Deaf

ISBN 0-590-90715-8; 0-590-90716-6 (pa)

LC 00-34502

In this "biography, Dash recaps the life of an extraordinary woman. The popularly known events of Helen Keller's early years—the arrival of teacher Annie Sullivan and her efforts to break through to Helen—are encapsulated in the first few chapters, after which the text turns to Keller's continuing education, her years at Radcliffe, and her growing autonomy." Bull Cent Child Books

"A smooth, readable narrative. . . . The use of primary-source material . . . brings the subject's vibrant personality, intelligence, and sensitivity to life." SLJ

Includes bibliographical references

Keller, Helen, 1880-1968—*Continued*

Garrett, Leslie. Helen Keller. DK Publishing 2004 127p il (DK biography) $14.99; pa $4.99 (5 and up)   **92**

1. Blind 2. Deaf
ISBN 0-7566-0488-5; 0-7566-0339-0 (pa)
                                          LC 2004-8451
This is a "first look at the . . . woman, blind and deaf since childhood, who . . . learned to read and speak and traveled the world as an inspiring public speaker and political activist. The . . . illustration-rich page design works well . . . and the smooth [narrative is] broken up on every page with boxed facts and quotes as well as well-chosen, small color photos." Booklist
Includes bibliographical references

Koestler-Grack, Rachel A. The story of Helen Keller. Chelsea Clubhouse 2004 32p il (Breakthrough biographies) lib bdg $14.95 (2-4)
                                                    92

1. Blind 2. Deaf
ISBN 0-7910-7315-7   LC 2003-366
Introduces Helen Keller and tells of her childhood struggles with deafness and blindness which led her to a successful career as a public speaker, writer, and champion of rights for the disabled
"Interesting and readable. . . . [This volume is] carefully researched, presenting good and respectful coverage." SLJ
Includes glossary and bibliographical references

Lawlor, Laurie. Helen Keller: rebellious spirit. Holiday House 2001 168p il $22.95 (5 and up)
                                                    92

1. Blind 2. Deaf
ISBN 0-8234-1588-0   LC 00-36950
A "biography of the most famous deaf and blind person in history. Drawing on social and scientific studies of deafness and blindness as well as on American history texts, Lawlor puts Keller's experiences in context. . . . At the same time, readers get a strong feel for Keller's personality and for the personalities of Annie Sullivan, Alexander Graham Bell, and other major figures in her life. Aided by numerous well-chosen photographs and excerpts from Keller's writings." Horn Book
Includes bibliographical references

MacLeod, Elizabeth. Helen Keller; a determined life; written by Elizabeth MacLeod. Kids Can Press 2004 32p il (Snapshots: Images of People and Places in History) $14.95; pa $6.95 (3-6)
                                                    92

1. Blind 2. Deaf
ISBN 1-55337-508-4; 1-55337-509-2 (pa)
An illustrated biography of the woman renowned for overcoming her handicaps of being blind and deaf
"This biography tells Keller's story in a readable, sometimes fictionalized narrative and busy, colorful page layouts. On each spread, the main text appears on the left, while the opposite page consists of a visually appealing collage of black-and-white, full-color, and tinted photos and interesting tidbits set against a pastel background." SLJ

Kennedy, John F. (John Fitzgerald), 1917-1963
Adler, David A. A picture book of John F. Kennedy; illustrated by Robert Casilla. Holiday House 1991 unp il lib bdg $16.95; pa $6.95 (1-3)
                                                    92

1. Presidents—United States
ISBN 0-8234-0884-1 (lib bdg); 0-8234-0976-7 (pa)
                                          LC 90-23589
Depicts the life and career of John F. Kennedy
"Adler presents a brief, clearly written text that provides basic information about his subject in an appealing format. . . . Casilla's watercolors are full-color copies of famous photographs." SLJ

Heiligman, Deborah. High hopes; a photobiography of John F. Kennedy; by Deborah Heiligman. National Geographic 2003 63p il map $17.95 (4 and up)   **92**

1. Presidents—United States
ISBN 0-7922-6141-0   LC 2003-7819
Photographs and text trace the life of President John F. Kennedy.
The text "successfully captures the spirit that makes Kennedy an enduring figure in our history. . . . This well-designed book features large, well-chosen, black-and-white photographs." SLJ
Includes bibliographical references

Sommer, Shelley. John F. Kennedy; his life and legacy; introduction by Caroline Kennedy. HarperCollins Publishers 2005 152p il $16.99; lib bdg $17.89 (5 and up)   **92**

1. Presidents—United States
ISBN 0-06-054135-0; 0-06-054136-9 (lib bdg)
A "portrait of our 35th president. In discussing his curious mind, his love of reading, and his sense of humor, Sommer creates an empathetic connection with readers early in the book. . . . In an easy-to-read style, Sommer does a fine job of painting an interesting and sympathetic picture of a leader who left his mark." SLJ
Includes bibliographical references

King, Martin Luther, Jr., 1929-1968
Adler, David A. Dr. Martin Luther King, Jr.; illustrated by Colin Bootman. Holiday House 2001 48p il $14.95 (1-3)   **92**

1. African Americans—Biography 2. African Americans—Civil rights
ISBN 0-8234-1572-4   LC 00-24314
"A Holiday House reader"
Tells the story of Dr. Martin Luther King, Jr., his life, accomplishments in the civil rights movement, and his impact on American history
"Adler presents short, moving vignettes about the people and events that influenced the child and man. . . . Bootman's full-and double-page realistic paintings help to fill in the details for the author's spare but well-chosen words." SLJ
Includes bibliographical references

King, Martin Luther, Jr., 1929-1968—*Continued*

Farris, Christine. My brother Martin; a sister remembers growing up with the Rev. Dr. Martin Luther King Jr.; by Christine King Farris; illustrated by Chris Soentpiet. Simon & Schuster Bks. for Young Readers 2003 35p il $17.95 (k-3)
92
1. African Americans—Biography 2. African Americans—Civil rights
ISBN 0-689-84387-9   LC 2001-44681
Looks at the early life of Martin Luther King, Jr., as seen through the eyes of his older sister.
"The warmth of the text is exquisitely echoed in Soentpiet's realistic, light-filled watercolor portraits. . . . This outstanding book belongs in every collection." SLJ

Marzollo, Jean. Happy birthday, Martin Luther King; illustrated by J. Brian Pinkney. Scholastic 1993 unp il $15.95 (k-3)
92
1. African Americans—Biography 2. African Americans—Civil rights
ISBN 0-590-44065-9   LC 91-42137
Also available Big book edition
"This very easy biography of Martin Luther King is distinguished by its succinct explanations of King's achievements. . . . The narrative of King's life is smooth and accessible. Pinkney's scratchboard paintings are fluidly drawn, warm, and dignified." Bull Cent Child Books

Myers, Walter Dean. I've seen the promised land; the life of Dr. Martin Luther King, Jr.; illustrated by Leonard Jenkins. HarperCollins Publishers 2004 unp il $15.99; lib bdg $16.89 (k-3)
92
1. African Americans—Biography 2. African Americans—Civil rights
ISBN 0-06-027703-3; 0-06-027704-1 (lib bdg)
LC 2003-4098
Pictures and easy-to-read text introduce the life of civil rights leader Dr. Martin Luther King, Jr.
"This eloquent picture book presents a brief overview of King's life and accomplishments. . . . Jenkins's stunning collage artwork dramatically reflects the events described in the narrative." SLJ

Rappaport, Doreen. Martin's big words: the life of Dr. Martin Luther King, Jr.; illustrated by Bryan Collier. Hyperion Bks. for Children 2001 unp il $15.99; lib bdg $16.49 (k-3)
92
1. African Americans—Biography 2. African Americans—Civil rights
ISBN 0-7868-0714-8; 0-7868-2591-X (lib bdg)
LC 00-40957
A Caldecott Medal honor book, 2002; A Coretta Scott King honor book for illustration, 2002
The author "has taken key phrases from King's early life and from his speeches, and used them as markers in telling a simplified story of his life." N Y Times Book Rev
"Rappaport's spare narrative captures the essentials of the man, the movement he led, and his policy of nonviolence. . . . Collier's collage art is glorious. Combining cut-paper, photographs, and watercolor he expresses his own Christian faith and King's power 'to make many different things one.' " Booklist

King-Smith, Dick, 1922-

King-Smith, Dick. Chewing the cud; illustrated by Harry Horse. Knopf 2002 c2001 196p il $16.95; lib bdg $18.99 (5 and up)   **92**
1. Authors, English
ISBN 0-375-81459-0; 0-375-91459-5 (lib bdg)
LC 2002-67128
First published 2001 in the United Kingdom
Dick King-Smith recounts his life from soldier to farmer to salesman to factory worker to teacher to, finally, author
This is a "warm and witty memoir. . . . These pages reveal a gifted writer with an affection for animals and a simple country life, a passion for his work, and sheer goodness of heart." Publ Wkly

Knight, Margaret, 1838-1914

McCully, Emily Arnold. Marvelous Mattie; how Margaret E. Knight became an inventor. Farrar, Straus & Giroux 2006 unp il $16 (k-3)
92
1. Women inventors
ISBN 0-374-34810-3   LC 2004-56415
Margaret (or Mattie) "Knight's design for a safer loom saved textile workers from injuries and death. . . . She fought in court and won the right to patent her most famous invention, a machine that would make paper bags. Mattie's story is told in a style that is not only easy to understand, but that is also a good read-aloud. The watercolor-and-ink illustrations capture the spirited inventor and support the text in style and design." SLJ

Kobayashi, Issa, 1763-1827

Gollub, Matthew. Cool melons—turn to frogs!: the life and poems of Issa; story and Haiku translations by Matthew Gollub; illustrations by Kazuko G. Stone; calligraphy by Keiko Smith. Lee & Low Bks. 1998 unp il $16.95 (3-6)   **92**
1. Poets
ISBN 1-880000-71-7   LC 98-13087
A biography and introduction to the work of the Japanese haiku poet whose love for nature finds expression in the more than thirty poems included in this book
This contains the life of the poet "told in simple language; lots of his exquisite and accessible haiku; limpid watercolor and colored pencil illustrations reminiscent of Japanese prints and drawings; and beautiful Japanese calligraphy." Booklist

Korczak, Janusz, 1878-1942

Adler, David A. A hero and the holocaust: the story of Janusz Korczak and his children; illustrated by Bill Farnsworth. Holiday House 2002 unp il $16.95 (3-5)   **92**
1. Holocaust, 1933-1945 2. Jews—Biography
ISBN 0-8234-1548-1   LC 2001-59409
A brief biography of the Polish doctor, author, founder of orphanages, and promoter of children's rights, who lost his life trying to protect his orphans from the Nazis
"Moving quotes from Korczak's diary are part of the text. . . . The illustrations, oil paintings on linen in sepia tones, are unforgettable." Booklist
Includes bibliographical references

La Salle, Robert Cavelier, sieur de, 1643-1687

Goodman, Joan E. Despite all obstacles: La Salle and the conquest of the Mississippi; by Joan Elizabeth Goodman; illustrated by Tom McNeely. Mikaya Press 2001 47p il map (Great explorers book) $19.95 (4 and up)   **92**

1. Explorers 2. Mississippi River valley
ISBN 1-931414-01-7   LC 2001-31732

A biography of the man who explored the St. Lawrence, Ohio, Illinois, and Mississippi rivers, and who claimed America's heartland for King Louis XIV and France

"Vivid color illustrations and Goodman's exciting writing style will attract both researchers and pleasure readers." Voice Youth Advocates

Lafayette, Marie Joseph Paul Yves Roch Gilbert du Motier, marquis de, 1757-1834

Fritz, Jean. Why not, Lafayette? illustrated by Ronald Himler. Putnam 1999 87p il $16.99; pa $5.99 (5 and up)   **92**

1. United States—History—1775-1783, Revolution
ISBN 0-399-23411-X; 0-698-11882-0 (pa)
LC 98-31417

Traces the life of the French nobleman who fought for democracy in revolutions in both the United States and France

This biography is "chock-full of quotes, anecdotes, and wry humor." Booklist

Includes bibliographical references

Lange, Dorothea, 1895-1965

Partridge, Elizabeth. Restless spirit: the life and work of Dorothea Lange. Viking 1998 122p il $19.99; pa $10.99 (6 and up)   **92**

1. Women photographers
ISBN 0-670-87888-X; 0-14-230024-1 (pa)
LC 98-9807

A biography of Dorothea Lange, whose photographs of migrant workers, Japanese American internees, and rural poverty helped bring about important social reforms

"Generously placed throughout this accessibly written biography are the photographic images that make Lange a pre-eminent artist of the century. The book is elegantly designed and the photographic reproductions are excellent." Bull Cent Child Books

Includes bibliographical references

Law, Westley Wallace, 1923-2002

Haskins, James. Delivering justice; W.W. Law and the fight for civil rights; [by] Jim Haskins; illustrated by Benny Andrews. Candlewick Press 2005 unp il $16.99 (2-4)   **92**

1. African Americans—Civil rights
ISBN 0-7636-2592-2   LC 2005-47114

A biography of Westley (W. W.) Law, a mail carrier who played a leading role in the cvil rights movement.

"With handsome, full-page illustrations in oil and collage, this picture-book biography tells the stirring story of a quiet hero." Booklist

Lawrence, Jacob, 1917-2000

Duggleby, John. Story painter: the life of Jacob Lawrence. Chronicle Bks. 1998 55p il $16.95 (4 and up)   **92**

1. African American artists
ISBN 0-8118-2082-3   LC 98-4513

A biography of the African American artist who grew up in the midst of the Harlem Renaissance and became one of the most renowned painters of the life of his people

"Lawrence's expressionistic, stark paintings, in excellent full-page color reproduction . . . nicely complement Duggleby's measured account of a materially poor but culturally rich childhood and Lawrence's subsequent struggles and successes." Publ Wkly

Includes bibliographical references

Lee, Sammy, 1920-

Yoo, Paula. Sixteen years in sixteen seconds; the Sammy Lee story; illustrations by Dom Lee. 1st ed. Lee & Low Books 2005 unp il $16.95 (2-4)   **92**

1. Diving 2. Korean Americans
ISBN 1-58430-247-X   LC 2004-20962

"Yoo introduces Sammy Lee, the son of Korean immigrants who overcame formidable odds to become an Olympic diving champion as well as a doctor. . . . Washed in nostalgic sepia tones, Dom Lee's acrylic-and-wax textured illustrations are reminiscent of his fine work in Ken Mochizuki's watershed *Baseball Saved Us* (1993) and like Yoo's understated words, the uncluttered images leave a deep impression." Booklist

Leeper, David Rohrer, 1832-1900

Leeper, David Rohrer. The diary of David R. Leeper; rushing for gold; edited by Connie and Peter Roop; illustrations and map by Laszlo Kubinyi. Benchmark Bks. 2001 78p il (In my own words) lib bdg $24.21 (4 and up)   **92**

1. Overland journeys to the Pacific 2. Frontier and pioneer life—West (U.S.) 3. California—Gold discoveries
ISBN 0-7614-1011-2   LC 00-23840

A young prospector describes his experiences traveling overland to the California gold fields and during the five years he spent digging for gold

"Leeper's story, taken from a book he published in 1894 . . . is a lively account of his life as forty-niner." Booklist

Includes glossary and bibliographical references

Lennon, John, 1940-1980

Rappaport, Doreen. John's secret dreams; the life of John Lennon; written by Doreen Rappaport; illustrated by Bryan Collier. Hyperion Books for Children 2004 unp il $16.99 (4 and up)
92

1. Rock musicians
ISBN 0-7868-0817-9   LC 2003-57116

"Using a combination of simple prose, song lyrics, and illustration, this heartfelt picture-book biography traces Lennon's life from his childhood to his death.

Lennon, John, 1940-1980—*Continued*

Striking in both its simplicity and complexity, it captures this enigmatic singer, artist, songwriter, and folk hero in a way that will move and fascinate those too young to remember the man but are surrounded by his music and myth." SLJ

Leonardo, da Vinci, 1452-1519

Anderson, Maxine. Amazing Leonardo da Vinci inventions you can build yourself. Nomad Press 2006 122p il map (Learn some hands-on history) pa $14.95 **92**

1. Inventions 2. Handicraft 3. Artists, Italian

ISBN 0-9749344-2-9

"Anderson has combined biography with doable activities that mirror ideas found in Leonardo's notebooks. Using common household objects (duct tape, foil, cereal boxes, paper-towel tubes, etc.), readers can make a parachute, hydrometer, invisible ink, walk-on-water shoes, etc. Anderson introduces each project with an explanation of why Leonardo came up with the idea and whether he created just the sketch or the sketch and the object. Detailed steps and illustrations provide clarity." SLJ

Byrd, Robert. Leonardo, beautiful dreamer. Dutton Children's Bks. 2003 unp il $17.99 (3-6) **92**

1. Artists, Italian

ISBN 0-525-47033-6   LC 2003-44860

Illustrations and text portray the life of Leonardo da Vinci, who gained fame as an artist through such works as the Mona Lisa, and as a scientist by studying various subjects including human anatomy and flight

"The brilliant, full-page ink-and-watercolor paintings characterize da Vinci's life in a cartoonlike manner. The animated artwork and lively text that brings together facts and anecdotes keep interest high." SLJ

Krull, Kathleen. Leonardo da Vinci; illustrated by Boris Kulikov. Viking 2005 128p il (Giants of science) $15.99 (5 and up) **92**

1. Scientists 2. Artists, Italian 3. Renaissance

ISBN 0-670-05920-X

This is a "biography of Leonardo da Vinci that highlights his scientific approach to understanding the physical world. The first half of the book describes Leonardo's apprenticeship and his work as an artist in Milan. The second half relates events in his later life, emphasizing his observation and investigation of the human body and nature. . . . Six excellent ink drawings illustrate this attractive volume. A very readable, vivid portrait set against the backdrop of remarkable times." Booklist

Includes bibliographical references

O'Connor, Barbara. Leonardo da Vinci; Renaissance genius. Carolrhoda Bks. 2003 112p il (Trailblazer biography) lib bdg $27.93 (5 and up) **92**

1. Artists, Italian

ISBN 0-87614-467-9   LC 2001-6470

A biography of the notable Italian Renaissance artist, scientist, and inventor

"Outstanding writing and design result in a compelling and accessible portrait of this master artist." SLJ

Includes bibliographical references

Reed, Jennifer. Leonardo da Vinci: genius of art and science; [by] Jennifer Reed. 1st ed. Enslow 2005 128p il (Great minds of science) lib bdg $26.60 (5 and up) **92**

1. Artists, Italian

ISBN 0-7660-2500-4   LC 2004-13401

Contents: Renaissance genius; Young Leonardo; Art, queen of science; Engineer and the architect; Prophet of automation; The earth and the universe; Leonardo's polyhedron; The human body; Other wonderful ideas; A great mind gone

"Da Vinci's inventions, observations, and artistic creations are described, and readers see that they are still influential in a variety of areas. . . . His grand achievements are illustrated throughout with black-and-white photos and reproductions. . . . Readers are introduced to a brilliant visionary whose passion for learning and creating might prove infectious." SLJ

Stanley, Diane. Leonardo da Vinci. Morrow Junior Bks. 1996 unp il $16.95; lib bdg $15.93; pa $6.95 (4 and up) **92**

1. Artists, Italian

ISBN 0-688-10437-1; 0-688-10438-X (lib bdg); 0-688-16155-3 (pa)   LC 95-35227

"Stanley begins with a brief introduction to the Italian Renaissance and then looks at the life of the artist. The text pages feature a series of sketches from Leonardo's notebooks. These vivid drawings, chosen to reflect ideas and events in the story, juxtapose well with the large illustrations created with colored pencil, gouache, and watercolors on the facing pages. . . . The craftsmanship that makes this biography so solid in concept, appealing in design, and accessible in presentation extends to the scholarship behind it, as glimpsed in the appended postscript and bibliographies." Booklist

Lester, Helen, 1936-

Lester, Helen. Author; a true story. Houghton Mifflin 1997 32p il $11 (k-3) **92**

1. Women authors

ISBN 0-395-82744-2   LC 96-9645

An "autobiographical look at the evolution of a writer describes Lester's experiences—including her earliest three-year-old scribbles and the acceptance of her first manuscript (on the seventh try). Illustrated with Lester's own rather childlike illustrations, this lighthearted but realistic (and helpful) guide for the writer has lots of fresh tips for young authors-in-the-making." Horn Book Guide

Lester, Julius

Lester, Julius. On writing for children & other people. Dial Books 2004 159p il $16.99 **92**

1. Children's literature 2. Authorship 3. African American authors

ISBN 0-8037-2867-0   LC 2003-27090

"This book is autobiographical, philosophical, and academic in nature, as Lester explores his evolution into the writer that he is today, describing the familial, social, racial, religious, and environmental influences that etched the jigsaw of his life. . . . This title will be well received by educators looking for books detailing the impact of spiritual, multicultural, and ethnic issues in children's literature." SLJ

Limón, José, 1908-1972

Reich, Susanna. José! born to dance: the story of José Limón; illustrated by Raúl Colón. Simon & Schuster Books for Young Readers 2005 unp il $16.95 (2-4) **92**

1. Dancers 2. Choreographers 3. Mexican Americans—Biography

ISBN 0-689-86576-7   LC 2004-4776

"A Paula Wiseman book"

"This picture-book biography tells the story of Jose Limon, who became a legendary figure in the history of American dance. . . . Sensitively written and beautifully illustrated, this picture book offers a soaring portrayal of achievement. Colon's distinctive watercolor-and-colored-pencil artwork includes many strong compositions that are fundamentally narrative yet emotionally resonate and often memorable." Booklist

Includes bibliographical references

Lincoln, Abraham, 1809-1865

Cohn, Amy L. Abraham Lincoln; [by] Amy L. Cohn and Suzy Schmidt; pictures by David A. Johnson. Scholastic Press 2002 unp il $16.95 (k-3) **92**

1. Presidents—United States

ISBN 0-590-93566-6   LC 96-48709

A simple biography of the Illinois lawyer who served the country as president through the difficulties of the Civil War

"The writing is lively and irresistible. . . . There's a tall-tale feel to the text and to the illustrations. . . . Pictures are done in pen and ink with watercolor washes. The palette is soft and muted." SLJ

Includes bibliographical references

Freedman, Russell. Lincoln: a photobiography. Clarion Bks. 1987 149p il $18; pa $7.95 (5 and up) **92**

1. Presidents—United States 2. United States—History—1861-1865, Civil War

ISBN 0-89919-380-3; 0-395-51848-2 (pa)

    LC 86-33379

Awarded the Newbery Medal, 1988

The author "begins by contrasting the Lincoln of legend to the Lincoln of fact. His childhood, self-education, early business ventures, and entry into politics comprise the first half of the book, with the rest of the text covering his presidency and assassination." SLJ

This is "a balanced work, elegantly designed and enhanced by dozens of period photographs and drawings, some familiar, some refreshingly unfamiliar." Publ Wkly

Includes bibliographical references

Harness, Cheryl. Abe Lincoln goes to Washington, 1837-1865; written and illustrated by Cheryl Harness. National Geographic Soc. 1997 unp il maps $18 (2-4) **92**

1. Presidents—United States

ISBN 0-7922-3736-6   LC 96-9587

Companion volume to Young Abe Lincoln: the frontier days, 1809-1837 (1996)

Portrays Lincoln's life as a lawyer in Springfield, a devoted husband and father, and president during the Civil War years

"The text gallops through years of history, with sudden stops for surprisingly vivid little scenes. . . . Filled with color and action, Harness' paintings and maps dominate the pages and provide a wealth of historical detail as well as a humanizing view of the Lincolns." Booklist

Includes bibliographical references

Sullivan, George. Abraham Lincoln. Scholastic Ref. 2000 128p il (In their own words) $12.95 (4 and up) **92**

1. Presidents—United States 2. United States—History—1861-1865, Civil War

ISBN 0-439-09554-9   LC 99-33387

Presents a biography, including excerpts from his speeches, letters, and other writings, of the man who was President during the Civil War

This book features "black-and-white photos and reproductions, a useful index, a short bibliography of primary and secondary sources, and a short list of further readings, along with places to contact for further information." SLJ

Includes bibliographical references

Turner, Ann Warren. Abe Lincoln remembers; [by] Ann Turner; pictures by Wendell Minor. HarperCollins Pubs. 2001 unp il $15.95; lib bdg $15.89 (k-3) **92**

1. Presidents—United States 2. United States—History—1861-1865, Civil War

ISBN 0-06-027577-4; 0-06-027578-2 (lib bdg)

    LC 98-50937

A simple description of the life of Abraham Lincoln, presented from his point of view

"Turner's free-verse reminiscence gracefully ties images and themes from Lincoln's youth to those of his adult years. . . . Minor's well-composed paintings, best seen from a little distance, effectively portray the man as he ages." Booklist

Winters, Kay. Abraham Lincoln: the boy who loved books; illustrated by Nancy Carpenter. Simon & Schuster Bks. for Young Readers 2003 unp il $16.95 (k-2) **92**

1. Presidents—United States

ISBN 0-689-82554-4   LC 00-52223

The author "recounts events from Lincoln's childhood in Kentucky and Indiana and his young adulthood in New Salem, Illinois. The engaging narrative emphasizes Lincoln's love of books and reading, which flourished despite his lack of formal education. Carpenter's oil-on-canvas illustrations include many details of pioneer life and focus on Lincoln's humble beginnings. . . . This will be a good choice for reading aloud." Booklist

Lindbergh, Charles, 1902-1974

Burleigh, Robert. Flight: the journey of Charles Lindbergh; illustrated by Mike Wimmer; introduction by Jean Fritz. Philomel Bks. 1991 unp il $16.99; pa $5.99 (2-4) **92**

1. Aeronautics—Flights 2. Air pilots

ISBN 0-399-22272-3; 0-698-11425-6 (pa)

    LC 90-35401

Describes how Charles Lindbergh achieved the remarkable feat of flying nonstop and solo from New York

Lindbergh, Charles, 1902-1974—_Continued_
to Paris in 1927

"Using Charles Lindbergh's autobiography, _The Spirit of St. Louis_, as the basis for his text, Burleigh vividly creates that first solo flight in words, while Wimmer fashions exhilarating pictures that are, above all else, emotional. . . . This artistic emotion . . . works terrifically with the terseness of the near-poetic text." Booklist

Louis, Joe, 1914-1981
Adler, David A. Joe Louis; America's fighter; written by David A. Adler; illustrated by Terry Widener. Harcourt 2005 unp il $16 (2-4)

92

1. Boxing—Biography 2. African American athletes
ISBN 0-15-216480-4   LC 2003-12817
"Gulliver books"

The life story of Joe Louis, heavyweight champion boxer, with the complete history of his career in the ring.

"This creative team's collaboration packs a powerful punch. . . . The action-packed acrylics capture the setting and emotions—Widener's signature muscular figures are particularly apt here." SLJ

Includes bibliographical references

Lowry, Lois
Lowry, Lois. Looking back; a book of memories. Houghton Mifflin 1998 181p il $17 (5 and up)

92

1. Authors, American 2. Women authors
ISBN 0-395-89543-X   LC 98-11376
Also available in paperback from Delacorte Press
"A Walter Lorraine book"

Using family photographs and quotes from her books, the author provides glimpses into her life

"A compelling and inspirational portrait of the author emerges from these vivid snapshots of life's joyful, sad and surprising moments." Publ Wkly

Lyons, Maritcha Rémond, 1848-1929
Bolden, Tonya. Maritcha; a nineteenth-century American girl. Abrams 2005 47p il $17.95 (4 and up)

92

1. African American women 2. New York (N.Y.)—Race relations 3. African Americans—New York (N.Y.)
ISBN 0-8109-5045-6   LC 2004-05849

This is a "life history of Maritcha Rémond Lyons, born a free black in 1848 in lower Manhattan. The author draws her biographical sketch primarily from Lyons's unpublished memoir, dated one year before her death in 1929. . . . One of the . . . sections of the book documents the Draft Riots . . . of July 1868, and the impact of them on Maritcha and other citizens." Publ Wkly

"The high quality of writing and the excellent documentation make this a first choice for all collections." SLJ

Madison, James, 1751-1836
Fritz, Jean. The great little Madison. Putnam 1989 159p il $16.99; pa $5.99 (5 and up)

92

1. Presidents—United States
ISBN 0-399-21768-1; 0-698-11621-6 (pa)
LC 88-31584

"Small, soft-spoken, and by nature diffident, James Madison found it difficult to speak in the midst of controversy, but his zeal and his convictions in the struggle between Republicans and Federalists gave him confidence, and his successes brought him to the presidency. Fritz has given a vivid picture of the man and an equally vivid picture of the problems—especially the internal dissension—that faced the leaders of the new nation. . . . Notes by the author and a bibliography are appended." Bull Cent Child Books

Magellan, Ferdinand, 1480?-1521
Levinson, Nancy Smiler. Magellan and the first voyage around the world. Clarion Bks. 2001 132p il map $19 (5 and up)

92

1. Explorers 2. Voyages around the world
ISBN 0-395-98773-3   LC 00-52350

This "biography of the great explorer, navigator, and adventurer presents him as a man of action who overcame political, social, and financial obstacles to sail around the globe." Horn Book Guide

"This clearly written book shows through involving narrative and vivid detail what a monumental achievement the journey was. . . . A well-designed volume, useful for research and interesting as biography." Booklist

Includes bibliographical references

Malcolm X, 1925-1965
Myers, Walter Dean. Malcolm X; a fire burning brightly; illustrated by Leonard Jenkins. HarperCollins Pubs. 2000 unp il $15.95 (3-6)

92

1. African Americans—Biography
ISBN 0-06-027707-6   LC 99-21527

This biography of the civil rights activist "combines quotes from interviews and speeches." Bull Cent Child Books

"Myers's spare and eloquent narrative makes the complexities of Malcolm X's story accessible without compromising its integrity. The book has appeal for reluctant teen readers as well as younger readers. The sophisticated paintings blend realism with abstraction to heighten the underlying emotional drama of scenes." Horn Book Guide

Mandela, Nelson
Cooper, Floyd. Mandela; from the life of the South African statesman; written and illustrated by Floyd Cooper. Philomel Bks. 1996 unp il $15.95; pa $6.99 (2-4)

92

1. South Africa—Race relations 2. South Africa—Politics and government
ISBN 0-399-22942-6; 0-698-11816-2 (pa)
LC 95-19639

Mandela, Nelson—*Continued*

In this biography "the author focuses more closely on Mandela's boyhood and schooling than on his adulthood as an anti-apartheid activist or his ascension to the presidency of South Africa." Publ Wkly

"Cooper's oil paintings are infused with golden light. Elegant composition and subtle shifts in perspective add emotional value to the carefully focused account." SLJ

Includes bibliographical references

Kramer, Ann. Mandela; the rebel who led his nation to freedom. National Geographic 2005 63p il (World history biographies) $17.95; lib bdg $27.90 (4 and up) **92**

1. South Africa—Race relations 2. South Africa—Politics and government

ISBN 0-7922-3658-0; 0-7922-3659-9 (lib bdg)

"This biography introduces readers not only to Mandela, but also to the political turmoil that affected South Africa for over a century. It begins with his birth, and covers his school years, his political ventures, imprisonment, release, presidency, Nobel Peace Prize, and retirement. Full-color photographs appear throughout and a time line runs along the bottom of each spread. . . . the book is well worth purchasing." SLJ

Includes glossary and bibliographical references

McDonough, Yona Zeldis. Peaceful protest: the life of Nelson Mandela; illustrations by Malcah Zeldis. Walker & Co. 2002 unp il $16.95; lib bdg $17.85 (2-5) **92**

1. South Africa—Race relations 2. South Africa—Politics and government

ISBN 0-8027-8821-1; 0-8027-8823-8 (lib bdg)

LC 2002-23462

Map of South Africa on endpapers

A biography of the black South African leader who became a civil rights activist, political prisoner, and president of South Africa

This is an "easy-to-read but engaging biography. . . . Zeldis's brightly colored folk-art illustrations reflect her subject's life and struggle with candid simplicity." SLJ

Includes bibliographical references

Mantle, Mickey, 1931-1995

Marlin, John. Mickey Mantle; by John Marlin. LernerSports 2005 106p il (Sports heroes and legends) lib bdg $26.60 (4 and up) **92**

1. Baseball—Biography

ISBN 0-8225-1796-5 LC 2003-22798

Contents: The "Washington Wallop;" Born for baseball; Close call; The windup; The waiting game; Too much, too soon; Turning point; Crown prince; Perfect game; The M&M boys; Hall of Famer

A biography of the Yankee baseball player known as the "Washington Wallop."

This is a "good, solid [biography]. . . . [The book is] engagingly written." Booklist

Includes bibliographical references

Marshall, Thurgood, 1908-1993

Adler, David A. A picture book of Thurgood Marshall; illustrated by Robert Casilla. Holiday House 1997 unp il $16.95; pa $6.95 (1-3) **92**

1. United States. Supreme Court 2. African Americans—Biography 3. Judges

ISBN 0-8234-1308-X; 0-823-41506-6 (pa)

LC 96-37248

Follows the life of the first African American to serve as a judge on the United States Supreme Court

"Adler presents the high points of Marshall's life with enough detail to humanize the man. . . . Sensitive line-and-watercolor illustrations on every page add warmth to the story as they define people and settings." Booklist

Martini, Helen, 1912-

Lyon, George Ella. Mother to tigers; illustrations by Peter Catalanotto. Atheneum Bks. for Young Readers 2003 unp il lib bdg $16.95 (k-3) **92**

1. Zoos

ISBN 0-689-84221-X LC 00-45375

"A Richard Jackson book"

"Helen Martini cared for both lion and tiger cubs in her New York City apartment before building the Bronx Zoo's first nursery back in 1944." SLJ

"Lyon's succinct, yet elegant, prose emphasizes Martini's dedication to the animals in her care. . . . Catalanotto's watercolor, charcoal, and torn-paper art is particularly effective here." Booklist

Matisse, Henri

Hollein, Nina. Matisse; cut-out fun with Matisse; make your own cut-outs like Matisse! [text and picture selection by Nina and Max Hollein] Prestel Verlag 2002 28p il (Adventures in art) $14.95 (3-5) **92**

1. Artists, French 2. Paper crafts

ISBN 3-7913-2858-1

Includes 4 pull-out sheets of coloured paper; Translated from the German

"Focusing on the artist's interest in paper cutouts, this book describes these works, portraying them as though they have a life of their own. . . . Throughout the book, readers will experience the course of Matisse's imagination and the excitement of his technique. . . . Full-color reproductions of the works as well as black-and-white photos of the man accompany the poetic, interpretive text. . . . Concluding pages outline Matisse's life, describe how and why he developed his techniques, and encourage readers to make these art forms themselves." SLJ

Welton, Jude. Henri Matisse. Watts 2002 46p il (Artists in their time) $22; pa $6.95 (5 and up) **92**

1. Artists, French

ISBN 0-531-12228-X; 0-531-16621-X (pa)

LC 2002-69106

Discusses the life and career of this French artist, describing and giving examples of his work

This offers a "clear and lively [text]. . . . Captioned, full-color and black-and-white photographs and art reproductions are liberally scattered throughout." SLJ

Matzeliger, Jan, 1852-1889

Mitchell, Barbara. Shoes for everyone: a story about Jan Matzeliger; illustrations by Hetty Mitchell. Carolrhoda Bks. 1986 63p il (Carolrhoda creative minds book) lib bdg $21.27; pa $5.95 (3-5)   **92**

1. Shoe industry 2. African American inventors
ISBN 0-87614-290-0 (lib bdg); 0-87614-473-3 (pa)
                                    LC 86-4157

A biography of the half-Dutch half-black Surinamese man who, despite the hardships and prejudice he found in his new Massachusetts home, invented a shoe-lasting machine that revolutionized the shoe industry in the late nineteenth century

This is "a compelling story of human endeavor. A clear text blessedly allows the extraordinary individual in focus, Jan Matzeliger, . . . to emerge without undue exclamatory adulation." Bull Cent Child Books

McCarty, Oseola

Coleman, Evelyn. The riches of Oseola McCarty; illustrated by Daniel Minter. Whitman, A. 1998 48p il $14.95 (3-5)   **92**

1. African American women
ISBN 0-8075-6961-5   LC 98-11570

A brief biography of Oseola McCarty, a hard-working washer woman who, without a formal education herself, donated a portion of her life savings to the University of Southern Mississippi to endow a scholarship fund for needy students

"Coleman conducted interviews with McCarty, her friends, and family, and this original research shows in the solid text. . . . Daniel Minter's wonderful woodcuts enliven the text and add depth to the story." Booklist
Includes bibliographical references

Menchú, Rigoberta

Menchú, Rigoberta. The girl from Chimel; [by] Rigoberta Menchú with Dante Liano; pictures by Domi; translated by David Unger. House of Anansi Press 2005 54p il $16.95 (4 and up)
                                    92

1. Guatemala 2. Mayas
ISBN 0-88899-666-7

This is "Menchú's account of her childhood in the small village of Chimel, Guatamala. . . . Short sketches provide glimpses of Menchú's early years; lyrical language and repeated phrases such as 'when I was a girl in Chimel' link the text to oral storytelling. . . . Each chapter sports a vivid oil painting by Domi, featuring thick strokes of bright oranges, purples, greens, and reds and a naive approach that lends a folk-art feel, effectively capturing the action and emotion of the stories." Bull Cent Child Books

Michelangelo Buonarroti, 1475-1564

Stanley, Diane. Michelangelo. HarperCollins Pubs. 2000 unp il $16.99; lib bdg $17.89; pa $7.99
                                    92

1. Artists, Italian
ISBN 0-688-15085-3; 0-688-15086-1 (lib bdg);
0-06-052113-9 (pa)

A biography of the Renaissance sculptor, painter, architect, and poet, well known for his work on the Sistine Chapel in Rome's St. Peter's Cathedral

This is "as readable as it is useful. . . . Integrating Michelangelo's art with Stanley's watercolor, gouache, and colored-pencil figures and settings has the desired effect: readers will be dazzled with the master's ability, while at the same time pulled into his daily life and struggles." SLJ
Includes bibliographical references

Miller, Norma, 1919-

Miller, Norma. Stompin' at the Savoy; the story of Norma Miller; collected and edited by Alan Govenar; illustrated by Martin French. Candlewick Press 2006 54p il $15.99 (3-6)   **92**

1. African American dancers 2. African American women
ISBN 0-7636-2244-3   LC 2004-57916

This is an autobiography of the African American jazz dancer of the Harlem Renaissance

This "sizzles with spirit and swings with vitality. . . . Miller tells her story with humor and candor. . . . Stylized black-and-white illustrations, produced digitally and in mixed media, nearly swing right off the pages." SLJ

Monet, Claude, 1840-1926

Kelley, True. Claude Monet: sunshine and waterlilies; written and illustrated by True Kelley. Grosset & Dunlap 2001 unp il (Smart about art) $14.89; pa $7.50 (2-4)   **92**

1. Artists, French
ISBN 0-448-42613-7; 0-448-42522-X (pa)
                                    LC 2001-23147

Written in the format of a school report by a fictitious student named Kristin Cole, this recounts the events in the life of the French artist and offers insight into his work

Illustrated with "charming childlike drawings and reproductions of the artist's paintings in scrapbook-style layouts. . . . [This] is a successful blend of fact and humor that makes sophisticated concepts completely accessible and even entertaining." Booklist

Morgan, Ann Haven, 1882-1966

Ross, Michael Elsohn. Pond watching with Ann Morgan; illustrations by Wendy Smith. Carolrhoda Bks. 2000 48p il $19.93 (4 and up)   **92**

1. Women scientists
ISBN 1-57505-385-3   LC 99-24953

Describes the life and work of Ann Haven Morgan, who studied, taught, and wrote about the animals of ponds and streams and the importance of an ecological approach to conservation. Includes related activities

"A unique combination of biography and natural histo-

Morgan, Ann Haven, 1882-1966—*Continued*
ry. . . . The photographs and full-color illustrations amplify the text." SLJ
Includes glossary and bibliographical references

Morrison, Toni, 1931-
Haskins, James. Toni Morrison; the magic of words; [by] Jim Haskins. Millbrook Press 2001 48p il (Gateway biography) lib bdg $23.90 (4 and up) **92**
1. Authors, American 2. African American authors 3. Women authors
ISBN 0-7613-1806-2   LC 00-32868
Haskins discusses Morrison's "childhood, her career as an editor . . . and he gives a very brief outline of each of her books and its critical reception, from *The Bluest Eye* to *Beloved*." Booklist
"This introductory biography is well organized, attractive, and inspiring." SLJ
Includes bibliographical references

Mozart, Wolfgang Amadeus, 1756-1791
Sís, Peter. Play, Mozart, play! Greenwillow Books 2006 unp il $16.99 (k-2)   **92**
1. Composers
ISBN 0-06-112181-9   LC 2005-30152
"Recognizing his son's talent at a very young age, Mozart's stern father resolutely turned him into a child sensation! . . . . Illustrations give a hint of a unique boy who, despite a childhood of narrow restrictions, was released by the freedom he found in his music and his imagination. The clear, brief, readable text is augmented by a biographical afterword." SLJ

Muir, John, 1838-1914
Lasky, Kathryn. John Muir; America's first environmentalist; illustrated by Stan Fellows. Candlewick Press 2006 41p il $16.99 (3-5)
92
1. Naturalists
ISBN 0-7636-1957-4
A biography of John Muir, naturalist and founder of the Sierra Club, whose travels, speeches and writings led directly to the creation of the Yosemite National Park in 1890 and other national parks that followed.
"Lasky's clear prose quotes liberally from diary entries Muir recorded. . . . True to Muir's vision, Fellows' spacious double-page watercolors show the beauty of the wide landscapes in storm and sunshine as well as the tiny details in a single meadow." Booklist
Includes bibliographical references

Locker, Thomas. John Muir, America's naturalist. Fulcrum 2003 30p il $17.95 (2-4)
92
1. Naturalists 2. Nature conservation
ISBN 1-55591-393-8   LC 2002-153593
Presents an overview of the life of the naturalist who founded the Sierra Club and was influential in establishing the national park system
"This handsome book provides a few lines of text and a quote from Muir's writing on each left-hand page; fac-ing is a full-page painting. . . . Locker's individual paintings, which clearly illustrate the text, are well-composed, delicately colored, and suitable-for-framing beautiful." Booklist

Nakahama, Manjirō, 1827-1898
Blumberg, Rhoda. Shipwrecked!: the true adventures of a Japanese boy. HarperCollins Pubs. 2000 80p il map $16.95; pa $7.99 (5 and up)
92
1. Japan—History
ISBN 0-688-17484-1; 0-688-17485-X (pa)
LC 99-86664
In 1841, rescued by an American whaler after a terrible shipwreck leaves him and his four companions castaways on a remote island, fourteen-year-old Manjiro learns new laws and customs as he becomes the first Japanese person to set foot in the United States
"Exemplary in both her research and writing, Blumberg hooks readers with anecdotes that astonish without sensationalizing, and she uses language that's elegant and challenging, yet always clear. Particularly notable is the well-chosen reproductions of original artwork." Booklist
Includes bibliographical references

Newton, Sir Isaac, 1642-1727
Krull, Kathleen. Isaac Newton; illustrated by Boris Kulikov. Viking 2006 126p il (Giants of science) $15.99 (5 and up)   **92**
1. Scientists
ISBN 0-670-05921-8   LC 2005017741
This "profiles Sir Isaac Newton, the secretive, obsessive, and brilliant English scientist who invented calculus, built the first reflecting telescope, developed the modern scientific method, and discerned many of our laws of physics and optics. . . . The lively, conversational style will appeal to readers. . . . Kulikov's humorous pen-and-ink drawings complement the lighthearted text of this fascinating introduction." Booklist

Nicholas, Saint, Bishop of Myra
Demi. The legend of Saint Nicholas. Margaret K. McElderry Bks. 2003 unp il $19.95 (3-6)
92
1. Christian saints 2. Santa Claus
ISBN 0-689-84681-9   LC 2002-8426
Recounts pivotal events in the history and life of Saint Nicholas, including how he came to be associated with Christmas and Santa Claus
"The gilded paintings are full of absorbing . . . details. . . . The greatest strength of this book is its straightforward, affectionate depiction of a person who, by his deep love for the young and the needy, embodies the spirit of Christmas." SLJ

Nightingale, Florence, 1820-1910

Gorrell, Gena K. (Gena Kinton). Heart and soul: the story of Florence Nightingale. Tundra Bks. 2000 146p il maps $18.95 (5 and up)   **92**
1. Nurses
ISBN 0-88776-494-0
A biography of the 19th century English woman known as the founder of modern nursing
"This highly readable and well-researched biography does an excellent job of integrating the social and medical conditions of Nightingale's time. . . . Enlivening the narrative are black-and-white reproductions of drawings . . . and period photographs." SLJ
Includes bibliographical references

Nixon, Joan Lowery, 1927-2003

Nixon, Joan Lowery. The making of a writer. Delacorte Press 2002 97p il $14.95; lib bdg $16.99; pa $4.99   **92**
1. Authors, American 2. Women authors
ISBN 0-385-73000-4; 0-385-90046-5 (lib bdg); 0-440-41905-0 (pa)   LC 2001-53909
The author recalls events from her childhood and adolescence before and during World War II that contributed to her development as a writer
"This will be of tremendous value to adults who teach writing to children, but it will also appeal to Nixon's legion of fans, including those who have no desire to write a word of their own; it's a delightful look back at a time and a life." Booklist

Oakley, Annie, 1860-1926

Macy, Sue. Bulls-eye: a photobiography of Annie Oakley. National Geographic Soc. 2001 64p il $17.95 (4 and up)   **92**
ISBN 0-7922-7008-8   LC 2001-125
A biography of the woman born Phoebe Ann Moses, who, under the name Annie Oakley, became a famous sharpshooter touring with Buffalo Bill's Wild West Show
"This book is exemplary nonfiction: well documented, lots of period photos with credits, a resource list, and a chronology. Equally important is its engaging and well crafted account of this famous woman of the West." SLJ
Includes bibliographical references

Obama, Barack, 1961-

Brill, Marlene Targ. Barack Obama; working to make a difference; [by] Marlene Targ Brill. Millbrook Press 2006 48p il (Gateway biography) $23.93 (5 and up)   **92**
1. Racially mixed people 2. African Americans—Biography 3. Politicians—United States
ISBN 0-822-53417-7; 9780822534174
      LC 2005016298
"Brill offers a warm, personal portrait of the politician, beginning with his parents' disparate backgrounds and his multinational upbringing and moving through his political awakenings, higher education, and public life. . . . Brill offers an intimate portrait that is bolstered by her own interviews with Obama's colleagues, schoolmates, and friends." Booklist
Includes bibliographical references

Obata, Chiura, 1888-1975

Ross, Michael Elsohn. Nature art with Chiura Obata; illustrations by Wendy Smith. Carolrhoda Bks. 2000 48p il (Naturalist's apprentice) $19.93 (4 and up)   **92**
1. Artists 2. Japanese Americans
ISBN 1-57505-378-0   LC 98-49073
Describes the life and work of nature artist and Japanese American Chiura Obata. Includes tips on how readers can make their own nature art
"This well-written, historically illuminating biography will inspire appreciation of the beauty and wonder in nature, and teachers will appreciate the art exercises that are included." Booklist
Includes glossary and bibliographical references

O'Keeffe, Georgia, 1887-1986

Bryant, Jennifer. Georgia's bones; [illustrated by] Bethanne Anderson. 1st ed. Eerdmans Books for Young Readers 2005 32p il $16 (k-3)
      92
1. Women artists 2. Artists—United States
ISBN 0-8028-5217-3   LC 2004-6800
Artist Georgia O'Keeffe was interested in the shapes she saw around her, from her childhood on a Wisconsin farm to her adult life in New York City and New Mexico.
"Bryant writes in spare, lyrical verse, honoring her subject's idiosyncratic impressions and precise observation of the natural world. . . . Cow skulls, southwestern landscapes, and oversize flowers are present and accounted for, but the swooping brushstrokes and earthy textures are unmistakably Andersen's own." Booklist

Rodriguez, Rachel. Through Georgia's eyes; illustrated by Julie Paschkis. 1st ed. H. Holt and Co. 2006 unp il $16.95 (k-3)   **92**
1. Women artists 2. Artists—United States
ISBN 9780805077407; 0-8050-7740-5
      LC 2005012479
"Rodríguez gently tells this inspirational artist's story . . . with quiet simplicity. . . . Using short, strong sentences and phrases, the author emphasizes the artist's creative force. Paschkis extends the words with the visual simplicity of colorful, cut-paper collages." SLJ

Spangenburg, Ray. Georgia O'Keeffe; the life of an artist; [by] Ray Spangenburg and Kit Moser. Enslow Pubs. 2002 48p il (Artist biographies) $23.93 (2-4)   **92**
1. Women artists 2. Artists—United States
ISBN 0-7660-1882-2   LC 2002-11985
Contents: I'm going to be an artist; Finding the artist inside; O'Keeffe and Stieglitz; Giant blossoms and city scenes; Bleached bones and desert dust; Lone artist at Abiquiu; Fading light
Presents the life of the twentieth-century American painter who drew much of her artistic inspiration from nature
"The use of full color, good paper, large type, and uncluttered design results in [a book] that [offers] several excellent reproductions of artworks, and the relatively simple [text respects] the capabilities of a young audience." Booklist

O'Keeffe, Georgia, 1887-1986—*Continued*

Winter, Jeanette. My name is Georgia; a portrait. Harcourt Brace & Co. 1998 unp il $16 (k-3)   **92**
1. Women artists 2. Artists—United States
ISBN 0-15-201649-X   LC 97-7087
Presents, in brief text and illustrations, the life of the painter who drew much of her inspiration from nature
"Winter mirrors the artist's stark imagery and strong personality in spare, poetic text and folk art—inspired illustrations." Publ Wkly
Includes bibliographical references

Oppenheimer, J. Robert, 1904-1967

Allman, Toney. J. Robert Oppenheimer; theoretical physicist, atomic pioneer; [by] Toney Allman. Blackbirch Press 2005 64p il map (Giants of science) $24.95 (5 and up)   **92**
1. Physicists 2. Atomic bomb
ISBN 1-56711-889-5   LC 2004-11199
Subtitle on cover: Father of the atomic bomb
This is a biography of the nuclear physicist who was instrumental in the development of the atomic bomb in the United States
This is a "readable, inviting overview. . . . Full-color and black-and-white photographs and diagrams energize the text and clarify the complex ideas discussed." SLJ
Includes bibliographical references

Owens, Jesse, 1913-1980

Adler, David A. A picture book of Jesse Owens; [by] David Adler; illustrated by Robert Casilla. Holiday House 1992 unp il lib bdg $16.95; pa $6.95 (1-3)   **92**
1. African American athletes 2. Track athletics
ISBN 0-8234-0966-X (lib bdg); 0-8234-1066-8 (pa)
     LC 91-44735
A simple biography of the noted black track star who competed in the 1936 Berlin Olympics
"The portrait presented, although brief, is accurate and touches on the major events of the track-and-field champion's life. . . . Casilla contributes full-page watercolor paintings that nicely complement and expand the writing." SLJ

Paige, Satchel, 1906-1982

Cline-Ransome, Lesa. Satchel Paige; paintings by James E. Ransome. Simon & Schuster Bks. for Young Readers 2000 unp il $16 (2-4)   **92**
1. Baseball—Biography 2. African American athletes
ISBN 0-689-81151-9   LC 97-13790
Examines the life of the legendary baseball player, who was the first African-American to pitch in a Major League World Series
"Cline-Ransome plays up the mythic elements of the Paige story in her rollicking narrative, while Ransome's paintings jump off the page with bright colors and startling contrasts." Booklist
Includes bibliographical references

Parker, John P., 1827-1900

Rappaport, Doreen. Freedom river; pictures by Bryan Collier. Jump at the Sun 2000 unp il map $14.99 (2-5)   **92**
1. Underground railroad 2. Slavery—United States 3. African Americans—Biography
ISBN 0-7868-0350-9   LC 99-33438
Coretta Scott King honor book for illustration, 2001
Map on lining papers
Describes an incident in the life of John Parker, an ex-slave who became a successful businessman in Ripley, Ohio, and who repeatedly risked his life to help other slaves escape to freedom
This book "combines an exciting, heartrending narrative with dramatic collage and watercolor pictures." Booklist
Includes bibliographical references

Parks, Rosa, 1913-2005

Giovanni, Nikki. Rosa; illustrated by Bryan Collier. Henry Holt 2005 32p il $16.95 (3-5)
    92
1. African American women 2. African Americans—Civil rights
ISBN 0-8050-7106-7
A Caldecott Medal honor book, 2006
A picture book biography of the Alabama black woman whose refusal to give up her seat on a bus helped establish the civil rights movement.
"Paired very effectively with Giovanni's passionate, direct words, Collier's large watercolor-and-collage illustrations depict Parks as an inspiring force that radiates golden light, and also as part of a dynamic activist community." Booklist

Parks, Rosa. I am Rosa Parks; by Rosa Parks with Jim Haskins; pictures by Wil Clay. Dial Bks. for Young Readers 1997 48p il $13.99; lib bdg $13.89 (1-3)   **92**
1. African American women 2. African Americans—Civil rights
ISBN 0-8037-1206-5; 0-8037-1207-3 (lib bdg)
     LC 96-896
"Dial easy-to-read"
"The famous civil rights activist has simplified her YA autobiography, *Rosa Parks: My Story*, and made it accessible to beginning readers. . . . The style is clear and direct. . . . The design is spacious, with big type, and Clay's paintings, some of them based on famous photographs, capture the segregation scene and the fight to end it." Booklist

Parks, Rosa. Rosa Parks: my story; by Rosa Parks with Jim Haskins. Dial Bks. 1992 192p il $17.99; pa $6.99 (5 and up)   **92**
1. African American women 2. African Americans—Civil rights
ISBN 0-8037-0673-1; 0-14-130120-7 (pa)
     LC 89-1124
Rosa Parks describes her early life and experiences with race discrimination, and her participation in the Montgomery bus boycott and the civil rights movement
"A remarkable story, a record of quiet bravery and modesty, a document of social significance, a taut drama told with candor." Bull Cent Child Books

Patrick, Saint, 373?-463?

De Paola, Tomie. Patrick: patron saint of Ireland. Holiday House 1992 unp il lib bdg $16.95; pa $6.95 (k-3)   **92**
   1. Christian saints
   ISBN 0-8234-0924-4; 0-8234-1077-3 (pa)
                     LC 91-19417
Relates the life and legends of Patrick, the patron saint of Ireland
"The combination of book design, text, and illustration is suitably reverent but never saccharine; the whole is a well-executed treatment of an appealing subject." Horn Book

Paulsen, Gary

Fine, Edith Hope. Gary Paulsen; author and wilderness adventurer. Enslow Pubs. 2000 128p il (People to know) lib bdg $26.50 (5 and up)
                              92
   1. Authors, American
   ISBN 0-7660-1146-1   LC 99-37950
A biography of the outdoor adventurer and author, whose writing includes adventure stories, historical novels, sports books, and nature stories
"Those who have read Paulsen's books are sure to enjoy this biography, and those who have not will definitely be inspired to look for them." SLJ
Includes bibliographical references

Paulsen, Gary. Caught by the sea; my life on boats. Delacorte Press 2001 103p maps $15.95; pa $5.50 (5 and up)   **92**
   1. Authors, American 2. Boats and boating 3. Ocean travel
   ISBN 0-385-32645-9; 0-440-40716-8 (pa)
                    LC 2001-17336
"Paulsen traces his life at sea, from buying his first sailboat to getting lost in the Pacific to encountering sharks. . . . His sometimes comic, sometimes near-fatal sea-going errors make for absorbing, captivating reading." Booklist

Paulsen, Gary. How Angel Peterson got his name; and other outrageous tales about extreme sports. Wendy Lamb Bks. 2003 111p $12.95; lib bdg $14.99 (5 and up)   **92**
   1. Authors, American
   ISBN 0-385-72949-9; 0-385-90090-2 (lib bdg)
                    LC 2002-7668
Author Gary Paulsen relates tales from his youth in a small town in northwestern Minnesota in the late 1940s and early 1950s, such as skiing behind a souped-up car and imitating daredevil Evel Knievel
"Writing with humor and sensitivity, Paulsen shows boys moving into adolescence believing they can do anything. . . . None of them dies (amazingly), and even if Paulsen exaggerates the teensiest bit, his tales are side-splittingly funny and more than a little frightening." Booklist

Paulsen, Gary. My life in dog years; with drawings by Ruth Wright Paulsen. Delacorte Press 1998 137p il $15.95; pa $5.99 (4 and up)
                              92
   1. Authors, American 2. Dogs
   ISBN 0-385-32570-3; 0-440-41471-7 (pa)
                    LC 97-40254
Also available Thorndike Press large print edition
The author describes some of the dogs that have had special places in his life, including his first dog, Snowball, in the Philippines; Dirk, who protected him from bullies; and Cookie, who saved his life
"Paulsen differentiates his canine friends beautifully, as only a keen observer and lover of dogs can. At the same time, he presents an intimate glimpse of himself, a lonely child of alcoholic parents, who drew strength and solace from his four-legged companions and a love of the great outdoors. Poignant but never saccharine, honest, and open." Booklist

Peet, Bill

Peet, Bill. Bill Peet: an autobiography. Houghton Mifflin 1989 190p il $22; pa $15 (4 and up)   **92**
   1. Walt Disney Productions 2. Authors, American 3. Illustrators
   ISBN 0-395-50932-7; 0-395-68982-1 (pa)
                    LC 88-37067
A Caldecott Medal honor book, 1990
This memoir "describes the life of the well-known children's book author who worked as an illustrator for Walt Disney from the making of 'Dumbo' until 'Mary Poppins.'" N Y Times Book Rev
"Every page of this oversized book is illustrated with Peet's unmistakable black-and-white drawings of himself and the people, places, and events described in the text. Familiar characters from his books and movies appear often." SLJ

Penn, William, 1644-1718

Kroll, Steven. William Penn; founder of Pennsylvania; illustrated by Ronald Himler. Holiday House 2000 unp il $16.95 (3-5)
                              92
   1. Society of Friends 2. Pennsylvania—History
   ISBN 0-8234-1439-6   LC 98-18932
A biography of William Penn, founder of the Quaker colony of Pennsylvania, who struggled throughout his life for the freedom to practice his religion
"The watercolor, pencil, and gouache paintings light up the book with their mix of dramatic scenes and sensitive portraits. . . . This biographical picture book will be a useful and certainly a handsome addition to library collections." Booklist

Peter I, the Great, Emperor of Russia, 1672-1725

Stanley, Diane. Peter the Great. Morrow Junior Bks. 1999 32p il $16 (4 and up)   **92**
   1. Russia—Kings and rulers
   ISBN 0-688-16708-X   LC 98-45250
A reissue of the title first published 1986 by Four Winds Press

Peter I, the Great, Emperor of Russia, 1672-1725—*Continued*

A biography of the tsar who began the transformation of Russia into a modern state in the late seventeenth-early eighteenth centuries

The author's "material is presented with a modicum of oversimplification and a plethora of details that are sure to fascinate children. But what really makes this biography shine are its breathtaking illustrations. The meticulously researched, vivid scenes of Russian life during Peter's reign—courts, countryside, architecture, costumes—are beautifully rendered." Publ Wkly

Picasso, Pablo, 1881-1973

Hodge, Susie. Pablo Picasso; by Susie Hodge. new ed. World Almanac Library 2004 48p il (Lives of the artists) lib bdg $30; pa $11 (4 and up)   **92**
1. Artists, French
ISBN 0-8368-5601-5 (lib bdg); 0-8368-5606-6 (pa)
LC 2003-67238
Original Italian edition 2003
This discusses the life and work of the twentieth century artist
This is "concise and straightforward. . . . [It] includes remarkably accomplished sketches and paintings from the artist's childhood and adolescence." Booklist
Includes bibliographical references

Jacobson, Rick. Picasso; soul on fire; [by] Rick Jacobson; illustrated by Laura Fernandez & Rick Jacobson. Tundra Books 2004 unp il $15.95 (3-5)
92
1. Artists, French
ISBN 0-88776-599-8
This is an introduction the life of the artist, exploring his influences, selected works, and his creative processes.
"Written in simple, clear language. . . . The softly radiant oil paintings are mostly full page and enhance the enjoyment of the book. . . . This eloquent tribute will serve as an introduction to Picasso and to an artist's inspirations." SLJ

Scarborough, Kate. Pablo Picasso. Watts 2002 46p il map (Artists in their time) lib bdg $22; pa $6.95 (5 and up)   **92**
1. Artists, French
ISBN 0-531-12229-8; 0-531-16622-8 (pa)
LC 2002-27017
Discusses the life, art, and legacy of the artist Pablo Picasso. Includes a timeline linking the events in his life with world events
This offers a "clear and lively [text]. . . . Captioned, full-color and black-and-white photographs and art reproductions are liberally scattered throughout." SLJ
Includes glossary

Pick-Goslar, Hannah

Gold, Alison Leslie. Memories of Anne Frank. See entry under Frank, Anne, 1929-1945

Pickett, Bill, ca. 1860-1932

Pinkney, Andrea Davis. Bill Pickett, rodeo ridin' cowboy; written by Andrea D. Pinkney; illustrated by Brian Pinkney. Harcourt Brace & Co. 1996 unp il $16; pa $6 (k-3)   **92**
1. Cowhands 2. African Americans—Biography 3. Rodeos
ISBN 0-15-200100-X; 0-15-202103-5 (pa)
LC 95-35920
"Gulliver books"
Describes the life and accomplishments of the son of a former slave whose unusual bulldogging style made him a rodeo star
"The story is told with verve, relish, and just enough of a cowboy twang, with Pinkney giving an excellent overview of the history of rodeos and black cowboys in a closing note. Husband Brian Pinkney's pictures, in his typical scratchboard technique, are well suited to the story, their lines and colors swirling with movement and excitement on the deep black surface." Booklist
Includes bibliographical references

Pike, Zebulon Montgomery, 1779-1813

Calvert, Patricia. Zebulon Pike; lost in the Rockies; by Patricia Calvert. Benchmark Books 2005 96p il map (Great explorations) lib bdg $29.93 (5 and up)   **92**
1. Explorers 2. West (U.S.)—Exploration
ISBN 0-7614-1612-9   LC 2003-17583
This "discusses the explorer's military service, relationship with the corrupt general James Wilkinson, the historical speculation about his motives for his meandering expedition to the Spanish west, and his failure to climb the mountain named for him. . . . Illustrated with beautiful reproductions of period illustrations, paintings, and maps. . . . Well-written." SLJ
Includes bibliographical references

Pinchot, Gifford, 1865-1946

Hines, Gary. Midnight forests; a story of Gifford Pinchot and our national forests; illustrated by Robert Casilla. 1st ed. Boyds Mills Press 2005 unp il $16.95 (3-5)   **92**
1. Conservationists 2. Forests and forestry
ISBN 1-56397-148-8   LC 2003-26876
"This picture-book biography introduces Gifford Pinchot, a wealthy young American who studied forestry in France and returned home to put his knowledge to good use in his own country. Appointed Secretary of Agriculture in 1898, he later joined forces with Theodore Roosevelt to turn 16 million acres into national forests. . . . Mirroring the quiet prose, the dignified pencil-and-watercolor illustrations depict Pinchot at work and in quiet contemplation." Booklist
Includes bibliographical references

Pinkwater, Daniel Manus, 1941-
McGinty, Alice B. Meet Daniel Pinkwater.
PowerKids Press 2003 24p il (About the author)
lib bdg $18.75 (1-3) **92**
1. Authors, American
ISBN 0-8239-6406-X LC 2002-136
A short biography of the author of more than seventy
books for children, Daniel Pinkwater
"Each spread has photographs and drawings on one
side and text and a sidebar with interesting or fun facts
on the other." SLJ
Includes glossary and bibliographical references

Pitcher, Molly, 1754-1832
Rockwell, Anne F. They called her Molly
Pitcher; by Anne Rockwell; illustrated by Cynthia
von Buhler. Knopf 2002 unp il $16.95; lib bdg
$17.99 (3-5) **92**
1. United States—History—1775-1783, Revolution
ISBN 0-679-89187-0; 0-679-99187-5 (lib bdg)
LC 2001-29422
A biography of the woman who was named a sergeant
in the Continental Army by George Washington for her
bravery in the Battle of Monmouth
"The language is inviting, the story, exciting. Von
Buhler's illustrations, which appear crackled, as if they
were painted during this period, make the book shine."
SLJ

Pizarro, Francisco, ca. 1475-1541
Meltzer, Milton. Francisco Pizarro; the conquest
of Peru; by Milton Meltzer. Benchmark Books
2005 80p il map (Great explorations) lib bdg
$29.93 (5 and up) **92**
1. Explorers 2. America—Exploration
ISBN 0-7614-1607-2 LC 2002-156000
Contents: Where Pizarro came from; The Spanish conquistadores; The business of conquest; A glimpse of
gold; The Inca empire; Epidemics and civil wars; The
decisive day; Turning an empire into a colony
Introduces the life of the explorer who was sent to
Peru in the sixteenth century by the king of Spain to
conquer the Incas and claim their land and wealth for the
Spanish crown.
Includes bibliographical references

Pollock, Jackson, 1912-1956
Greenberg, Jan. Action Jackson; [by] Jan
Greenberg and Sandra Jordan; illustrated by Robert
Andrew Parker. Roaring Brook Press 2002 32p il
$16.95; lib bdg $22.90 (3-6) **92**
1. Artists—United States
ISBN 0-7613-1682-5; 0-7613-2770-3 (lib bdg)
LC 2002-6211
Imagines Jackson Pollock at work during the creation
of one of his paint-swirled and splattered canvasses
"Using spare, lyrical words, the authors layer the ex-
citing story with deep observations about what art is and
how it is made. . . . Parker's scribbly pen-and-
watercolor illustrations get the mood just right; the loose
lines have an improvised, energetic quality that echoes
Pollock's painting." Booklist
Includes bibliographical references

Ponce de Leon, Juan, 1460?-1521
Otfinoski, Steven. Juan Ponce de Leon;
discoverer of Florida; by Steven Otfinoski.
Benchmark Books 2005 77p il map (Great
explorations) lib bdg $29.93 (5 and up)
92
1. Explorers 2. America—Exploration
ISBN 0-7614-1610-2 LC 2003-17582
Contents: The soldier's way; Westward with Colum-
bus; The Governor of Higuey; Father of Puerto Rico;
The Fountain of Youth; An island called Florida; The
King's favorite; At war with the Carib; To die in Florida
A biography of the Spanish explorer who was called
the Father of Puerto Rico and who discovered Florida in
his search for the Fountain of Youth.
Includes bibbliographical references

Potter, Beatrix, 1866-1943
Winter, Jeanette. Beatrix: various episodes from
the life of Beatrix Potter. Farrar, Straus & Giroux
2003 62p il $15 (k-3) **92**
1. Authors, English 2. Women authors 3. Women artists
ISBN 0-374-30655-9 LC 2002-69724
"Frances Foster books"
This simple biography of Beatrix Potter, best known
for writing *The Tale of Peter Rabbit*, includes excerpts
from her published letters and journals and reveals why
she drew and wrote about animals.
"The text is spare, just two to five sentences per page;
the paintings, in Winter's characteristic muted tones and
flat style, are delicately outlined in black ink. Brief as it
is, the book successfully conveys Potter's life and personality." Booklist
Includes bibliographical references

Powell, Colin L., 1937-
Waxman, Laura Hamilton. Colin Powell; [by]
Laura Hamilton Waxman. Lerner Publications Co
2005 47p il (History maker bios) lib bdg $25.26
(2-5) **92**
1. Generals 2. Statesmen 3. African Americans—Biography
ISBN 0-8225-2433-3 LC 2004-2595
Contents: Growing up in the Bronx; Army life; Life
in Washington, D.C; War with Iraq; Secretary of State
"This clearly written, interesting biography begins
with Powell's childhood in the Bronx and focuses on the
man's distinguished career in the military and in government, with additional information about how he was affected by discrimination and segregation. . . . Black-and-
white and color photos are included." SLJ
Includes bibliographical references

Quezada, Juan, 1939-
Andrews-Goebel, Nancy. The pot that Juan
built; pictures by David Diaz. Lee & Low Bks.
2002 unp il $16.95 (k-3) **92**
1. Pottery
ISBN 1-58430-038-8 LC 2001-38139
A cumulative rhyme summarizes the life's work of renowned Mexican potter, Juan Quezada. Additional infor-

Quezada, Juan, 1939-—*Continued*

mation describes the process he uses to create his pots after the style of the Casas Grandes people.

"This unusual book is set up to allow for differing levels of reading expertise. . . . One page contains a catchy cumulative rhyme modeled on 'This Is the House That Jack Built,' which outlines the process of making a pot. The facing page offers a clearly written prose presentation. . . . Diaz's arresting illustrations, rendered in Adobe Photoshop, use yellows, oranges, and reds in a layered effect that seems to glow with an inward light." SLJ

Quimby, Harriet, 1875-1912

Moss, Marissa. Brave Harriet; the first woman to fly the English Channel; illustrated by C.F. Payne. Silver Whistle Bks. 2001 unp il $16 (k-3)

92

1. Women air pilots

ISBN 0-15-202380-1   LC 99-50463

Harriet Quimby, the first American woman to have received a pilot's license, describes her April 1912 solo flight across the English Channel, the first such flight by any woman

"Moss writes effectively in first person, putting readers in touch with Quimby's dreams and determination through direct, vivid language. The mixed media artwork combines paints and pastels in a series of beautiful scenes." Booklist

Ramon, Ilan, 1954-2003

Stone, Tanya Lee. Ilan Ramon, Israel's first astronaut; Tanya Lee Stone. Millbrook Press 2003 48p il lib bdg $16.70 (3-5)   92

1. Astronauts 2. Space shuttles—Accidents

ISBN 0-7613-2888-2   LC 2003-9254

A biography of Israeli astronaut Ilan Ramon, who died in the explosion of the space shuttle Columbia on February 1, 2003.

"The excellent-quality color photos show Ramon at work and in his private life, and the author's research is impeccably documented. Overall, an appealing and informative book." SLJ

Includes bibliographical references

Ramsey, Alice Huyler, d. 1983

Brown, Don. Alice Ramsey's grand adventure; written and illustrated by Don Brown. Houghton Mifflin 1997 32p il $16; pa $5.95 (k-3)

92

1. Automobile travel 2. United States—Description and travel

ISBN 0-395-70127-9; 0-618-07316-7 (pa)

LC 96-31783

Describes the difficulties faced by the first woman to make a cross-country journey from New York to San Francisco in an automobile in 1909

"Brown tells the tale in dramatic fashion, choosing entertaining details with a sure hand. His ink-and-watercolor sketches depict an intrepid-looking figure in heavy duster and goggles, steering a ramshackle Maxwell through a succession of rough, lonely landscapes." SLJ

Reiss, Johanna

Reiss, Johanna. The upstairs room. Crowell 1972 273p $16.99; pa $5.99 (5 and up)

92

1. World War, 1939-1945—Jews 2. Netherlands—History—1940-1945, German occupation 3. Jews—Netherlands 4. Holocaust, 1933-1945—Personal narratives

ISBN 0-690-85127-8; 0-06-440370-X (pa)

Also available Spanish language edition

A Newbery Medal honor book, 1973

"In a vital, moving account the author recalls her experiences as a Jewish child hiding from the Germans occupying her native Holland during World War II. . . . Ten-year-old Annie and her twenty-year-old sister Sini, . . . are taken in by a Dutch farmer, his wife, and mother who hide the girls in an upstairs room of the farm house. Written from the perspective of a child the story affords a child's-eye-view of the war." Booklist

Followed by The journey back

Rembert, Winfred

Rembert, Winfred. Don't hold me back; my life and art; with Charles and Rosalie Baker. Cricket Books 2003 40p il $19.95 (4 and up)   92

1. African Americans—Biography 2. African American artists

ISBN 0-8126-2703-2   LC 2003-9980

"A Marcato book"

Through words and paintings, an artist tells about growing up on a cotton plantation in Cuthbert, Georgia, serving time in prison for his actions during a civil rights demonstration, and finding a purpose and direction in life.

"Rembert's unusual pictures are classified as 'outsider art.' . . . Each one is a piece of leather that has been carved, tooled, and dyed with rich colors. . . . This beautifully designed, very accessible book offers a vivid impression of an African American man's experiences in the mid-twentieth-century South." Booklist

Includes bibliographical references

Revere, Paul, 1735-1818

Fritz, Jean. And then what happened, Paul Revere? pictures by Margot Tomes. Coward, McCann & Geoghegan; distributed by Putnam Pub. Group 1973 45p il $16.99; pa $5.99 (2-4)

92

1. United States—History—1775-1783, Revolution

ISBN 0-399-23337-7; 0-698-11351-9 (pa)

This "description of Paul Revere's ride to Lexington is funny, fast-paced, and historically accurate; it is given added interest by the establishment of Revere's character: busy, bustling, versatile, and patriotic, a man who loved people and excitement. The account of his ride is preceded by a description of his life and the political situation in Boston, and it concludes with Revere's adventures after reaching Lexington." Bull Cent Child Books

Rey, H. A. (Hans Augusto), 1898-1977

Borden, Louise. The journey that saved Curious George. See entry under Rey, Margret

Rey, Margret

Borden, Louise. The journey that saved Curious George; the true wartime escape of Margret and H. A. Rey; illustrated by Allan Drummond. Houghton Mifflin 2005 72p il $17 (3-6)   **92**

1. Rey, H. A. (Hans Augusto), 1898-1977 2. Authors, American 3. Jewish refugees

ISBN 0-618-33924-8   LC 2004-01015

This "book tells the story of Margret and H. A. Rey. Part 1 concerns their childhoods in Germany, their lives together in Rio de Janeiro and Paris in the 1920s and 1930s, and the growing menace after war broke out in 1939. As German-born Jews, they were suspect in many quarters. Part 2 recalls the Reys' flight from Paris and the couple's escape to Lisbon, Rio, and finally New York. They were carrying several illustrated manuscripts, including *The Adventures of FiFi*, later retitled *Curious George*. Photos, reproductions of documents, and artwork appear throughout the book, as do Drummond's spirited ink-and-watercolor illustrations, brimming with action and details. The text . . . reads well." Booklist

Rice, Condoleezza, 1954-

Cunningham, Kevin. Condoleezza Rice; U. S. Secretary of State; by Kevin Cunningham. Child's World 2004 40p il (Journey to freedom) lib bdg $28.50 (5 and up)   **92**

1. Statesmen—United States 2. African American women

ISBN 1-59296-231-9   LC 2003-27077

Contents: Daughter of teachers; A change of plans; A booming career; Today and tomorrow; Timeline

This describes the life and career of the George W. Bush's Secretary of State.

This is a "quality [title] both in content and design. . . . Excellent historical and current photos enhance the easy-to-read [text] on every spread." SLJ

Includes bibliographical references

Ripken, Cal, Jr.

Herman, Gail. Cal Ripken, Jr.; play ball! by Cal Ripken, Jr. and Mike Bryan; adapted by Gail Herman; illustrated by Stan Silver. Dial Bks. for Young Readers 1999 48p il $13.99; pa $3.99 (1-3)   **92**

1. Baltimore Orioles (Baseball team) 2. Baseball—Biography

ISBN 0-8037-2415-2; 0-14-130184-8 (pa)

LC 98-26366

"Dial easy-to-read"

Adaptation of The only way I know, by Cal Ripken, Jr. and Mike Bryan (1997)

A simple biography of the highly honored player for the Baltimore Orioles, who in 1995 broke the record for playing the most games in a row

This "is sure to be a hit with young baseball fans, but its appeal will not be limited to them. . . . The text is nicely balanced with portrayals of both slumps and streaks, anecdotes and statistics. The combination of first-person narration with full-color photographs and realistic paintings . . . will pull kids into the life and thoughts of this hardworking player." SLJ

Rivera, Diego, 1886-1957

Sabbeth, Carol. Frida Kahlo and Diego Rivera: their lives and ideas. See entry under Kahlo, Frida, 1907-1954

Winter, Jonah. Diego; [illustrated] by Jeanette Winter; text by Jonah Winter; translated from the English by Amy Prince. Knopf 1991 unp il pa $6.99 hardcover o.p. (k-3)   **92**

1. Artists, Mexican 2. Bilingual books—English-Spanish

ISBN 0-679-85617-X (pa)   LC 90-25923

This book "in both Spanish and English, chronicles the life of Mexican muralist Diego Rivera. . . . Jonah Winter's crisp text and Jeanette Winter's elaborately bordered, dynamic illustrations successfully convey the spirit of the man and his work." Publ Wkly

Rivera, Tomás

Medina, Jane. Tomás Rivera; [by] Jane Medina; illustrated by Edward Martinez. [1st Green Light Readers ed.] Harcourt 2004 unp il $12.95; pa $3.95 (k-2)   **92**

1. Authors, American 2. Mexican American authors

ISBN 0-15-205145-7; 0-15-205146-5 (pa)

LC 2003-17482

"Green light readers"

"This simple story recounts an incident from the childhood of Mexican American writer and educator Tomás Rivera and suggests its far-reaching effects on his life. After a day of hard work picking farm crops with his family in the 1940s, young Tomas enjoys hearing his grandfather tell stories. When Tomas confides that he wants to tell stories, too, Grandpa takes him to the library, and soon the boy begins writing stories of his own. When he becomes an adult, his stories are published and a library is named after him. . . . Medina's straightforward writing is enhanced by the warm depictions of Rivera and his family in the painterly illustrations." Booklist

Robinson, Jackie, 1919-1972

Adler, David A. A picture book of Jackie Robinson; illustrated by Robert Casilla. Holiday House 1994 unp il $16.95; pa $6.95 (1-3)   **92**

1. Baseball—Biography 2. African American athletes

ISBN 0-8234-1122-2; 0-8234-1304-7 (pa)

LC 93-27224

"A brief look at the life of baseball great Jackie Robinson. The subject's childhood, sporting accomplishments, and later endeavors are touched upon, as are the bigotry and prejudice he faced as the first African American to play in the major leagues. . . . Casilla's full-and double-page watercolors provide attractive backgrounds for the text. A sound introduction to a significant figure." SLJ

Robinson, Jackie, 1919-1972—*Continued*

Ford, Carin T. Jackie Robinson; hero of baseball. Enslow Pubs. 2006 32p il (Heroes of American History) lib bdg $22.60 (2-4)

92

1. Baseball—Biography 2. African American athletes
ISBN 0-7660-2600-0

"Ford presents a straightforward account of memories and milestones from Robinson's life. . . . With large type and a photo on nearly every page, the book offers a very readable, short account of Robinson's life and achievements." Booklist

Includes glossary and bibliographical references

Golenbock, Peter. Teammates; written by Peter Golenbock; designed and illustrated by Paul Bacon. Harcourt Brace Jovanovich 1990 unp il $16; pa $7 (1-4)

92

1. Reese, Pee Wee, 1919-1999 2. Brooklyn Dodgers (Baseball team) 3. Baseball—Biography 4. African American athletes
ISBN 0-15-200603-6; 0-15-284286-1 (pa)

LC 89-38166

"Gulliver books"

Describes the racial prejudice experienced by Jackie Robinson when he joined the Brooklyn Dodgers and became the first black player in Major League baseball and depicts the acceptance and support he received from his white teammate Pee Wee Reese

"Golenbock's bold and lucid style distills this difficult issue, and brings a dramatic tale vividly to life. Bacon's spare, nostalgic watercolors, in addition to providing fond glimpses of baseball lore, present a haunting portrait of one man's isolation. Historic photographs of the major characters add interest and a touch of stark reality to an unusual story, beautifully rendered." Publ Wkly

Robinson, Sharon. Promises to keep: how Jackie Robinson changed America. Scholastic 2004 64p il $16.95 (4 and up)

92

1. Baseball—Biography 2. African American athletes
ISBN 0-439-42592-1   LC 2003-42709

"Robinson's daughter, Sharon, describes her father's youth, his rise to become major-league baseball's first African American player, and his involvement in the civil rights movement. . . . Her private view of her father's accomplishments, placed within the context of American sports and social history, makes for absorbing reading. An excellent selection of family and team photographs and other materials . . . illustrate this fine tribute." Booklist

Rockwell, Norman, 1894-1978

Gherman, Beverly. Norman Rockwell; storyteller with a brush. Atheneum Bks. for Young Readers 2000 57p il $19.95 (4 and up)

92

1. Artists—United States
ISBN 0-689-82001-1   LC 98-36546

Describes the life and work of the popular American artist who depicted both traditional and contemporary subjects, including children, family scenes, astronauts, and the poor

"The format of the biography is appealing and attrac-

tive. The pages are replete with color reproductions of Rockwell's paintings as well as photographs of the man and his family. The text is well researched and authentic; the writing style is free-flowing and the words capture the naturalness of Rockwell's paintings." SLJ

Includes bibliographical references

Roy, Jennifer Rozines. Norman Rockwell; the life of an artist; [by] Jennifer Rozines Roy and Gregory Roy. Enslow Pubs. 2002 48p il (Artist biographies) $23.93 (2-4)

92

1. Artists—United States
ISBN 0-7660-1883-0   LC 2002-11982

Examines the life and work of the twentieth-century artist, who for sixty-five years portrayed America for Americans as they liked to see themselves

Includes glossary and bibliographical references

Rogers, Will, 1879-1935

Keating, Frank. Will Rogers: an American legend; written by Frank Keating; illustrated by Mike Wimmer. Silver Whistle/Harcourt 2002 unp il $16 (k-3)

92

1. Entertainers 2. Humorists
ISBN 0-15-202405-0   LC 2001-5949

A biography of the man from Oklahoma, known for his wise and witty sayings

"The highly episodic text, presented in the form of typewritten pages to evoke Rogers' own typed newspaper columns, makes good use of quotations from its subject. . . . The adulatory, iconographic tone is reinforced by Wimmer's full-page oil paintings. Inarguably beautiful, accomplished, and occasionally witty." Booklist

Roosevelt, Eleanor, 1884-1962

Cooney, Barbara. Eleanor. Viking 1996 unp il $15.99; pa $6.99 (k-3)

92

1. Presidents' spouses—United States
ISBN 0-670-86159-6; 0-14-055583-8 (pa)

LC 96-7723

"Beginning the story with Eleanor Roosevelt's mother's disappointment at her birth, the author emphasizes the girl's lonely and often fearful childhood. . . . The book ends with Eleanor's public role still to come. A brief afterword provides information about her worldwide influence in her later life." SLJ

"There are many biographies of Eleanor Roosevelt but this one is special. Not only does it boast Cooney's artwork, but it also gets to the heart of a young girl, which in many ways is as interesting as Roosevelt's later, well-known accomplishments." Booklist

Fleming, Candace. Our Eleanor; a scrapbook look at Eleanor Roosevelt's remarkable life; [by] Candace Fleming. 1st ed. Atheneum Books for Young Readers 2005 176p il $19.95 (5 and up)

92

1. Presidents' spouses—United States
ISBN 0-689-86544-9   LC 2004-22825

"An Anne Schwartz book"

Told in scrapbook style, this biography looks behind the politics to present First Lady Eleanor Roosevelt in her many roles: wife and mother, United Nations dele-

Roosevelt, Eleanor, 1884-1962—*Continued*

gate, popular columnist, civil rights crusader, and champion of the underprivileged.

"Each of the seven chapters leads readers through the subject's busy life with short sections of text filled with well-documented first-person accounts and direct quotes. . . . Not a spread goes by without incredible archival photographs or reproductions, newspaper and magazine clippings, handwritten letters, and diary entries. . . . They all provide relevant and fascinating insight." SLJ

Freedman, Russell. Eleanor Roosevelt; a life of discovery. Clarion Bks. 1993 198p il $17.95; pa $10.95 (5 and up)   **92**

1. Presidents' spouses—United States
ISBN 0-89919-862-7; 0-395-84520-3 (pa)
                                                 LC 92-25024

"Readers are made privy to the telling details of a full life through numerous quotes from Roosevelt and her wide inner circle in this frank, well-documented portrait of the 'First Lady of the World.' A superlative biography." SLJ

Includes bibliographical references

Koestler-Grack, Rachel A. The story of Eleanor Roosevelt. Chelsea Clubhouse 2004 32p il (Breakthrough biographies) lib bdg $14.95 (2-4)
                                                          92

1. Presidents' spouses—United States
ISBN 0-7910-7313-0   LC 2003-269

Chronicles the life of Eleanor Roosevelt, from her privileged childhood, to her accomplishments as First Lady of the United States, to her work with the United Nations

"The style and design are just right for middlegraders. The type is spacious, illustrations appear on every page. . . . [This volume] will stimulate readers to find out more." Booklist

Includes glossary and bibliographical references

Roosevelt, Franklin D. (Franklin Delano), 1882-1945

Freedman, Russell. Franklin Delano Roosevelt. Clarion Bks. 1990 200p il $20; pa $9.95 (5 and up)   **92**

1. Presidents—United States 2. United States—Politics and government—1933-1945
ISBN 0-89919-379-X; 0-395-62978-0 (pa)
                                                 LC 89-34986

The author "traces the personal and public events in a life that led to the formation of one of the most influential and magnetic leaders of the twentieth century." Horn Book

"The carefully researched, highly readable text and extremely effective coordination of black-and-white photographs chronicle Roosevelt's priviledged youth, his early influences, and his maturation. . . . Even students with little or no background in American history will find this an intriguing and inspirational human portrait." SLJ

Includes bibliographical references

Roosevelt, Theodore, 1858-1919

Fritz, Jean. Bully for you, Teddy Roosevelt! illustrations by Mike Wimmer. Putnam 1991 127p il $16.99; pa $5.99 (5 and up)   **92**

1. Presidents—United States
ISBN 0-399-21769-X; 0-698-11609-7 (pa)
                                                 LC 90-8142

Follows the life of the twenty-sixth president, discussing his conservation work, hunting expeditions, family life, and political career

"Jean Fritz gives a rounded picture of her subject and deftly blends the story of a person and a picture of an era." Bull Cent Child Books

Includes bibliographical references

Kraft, Betsy Harvey. Theodore Roosevelt; champion of the American spirit. Clarion Bks. 2003 180p il $19 (5 and up)   **92**

1. Presidents—United States
ISBN 0-618-14264-9   LC 2002-152825

Contents: The strenuous life; The sweetness of home; Darling wifie; The wild west; My literary work; We stirred things up; Man's work; Immense fun; A great historical expedition; New York politics; A most honorable office; I felt at once that he had bad news; A household of children; No easy job; A coal famine; Roosevelt's corollary; In the interest of the United States; If elected...; A square deal; The bride at every wedding; Carry a big stick; Good-bye, Mr. President; My hat is in the ring; The rights of the people; My last chance to be a boy

A biography of the energetic New Yorker who became the twenty-sixth president of the United States and who once exclaimed "No one has ever enjoyed life more than I have"

"Interwoven with the well-told story of Roosevelt's public activities is Kraft's vivid portrayal of his personal life, laced with anecdotes and quotations (mainly from letters) that help bring the famous figure to life. The spacious layout and the many black-and-white reproductions of photos, drawings, and prints add to the book's appeal." Booklist

Includes bibliographical references

Rowling, J. K.

Boekhoff, P. M. J.K. Rowling; [by] P.M. Boekhoff and Stuart A. Kallen. KidHaven Press 2003 48p il (Inventors and creators) $23.70 (4-6)
                                                          92

1. Authors, English 2. Women authors
ISBN 0-7377-1368-2   LC 2002-3292

A biography of the author of the Harry Potter series

"There have been other books written about Rowling, but none as entertaining and easily read. . . . Color photographs add to the text." Libr Media Connect

Includes glossary and bibliographical references

Chippendale, Lisa A. Triumph of the imagination: the story of writer J.K. Rowling; introduction by James Scott Brady. Chelsea House 2002 112p il (Overcoming adversity) lib bdg $22.95 (5 and up)   **92**

1. Authors, English 2. Women authors
ISBN 0-7910-6312-7   LC 2001-47604

Rowling, J. K.—*Continued*

"This title blends biographical data, literary review, and the effects of the 'Harry Potter' books on the world, written at a reading level that is accessible to many of Rowling's fans." SLJ

Includes bibliographical references

Rudolph, Wilma, 1940-1994

Krull, Kathleen. Wilma unlimited: how Wilma Rudolph became the world's fastest woman; illustrated by David Diaz. Harcourt Brace & Co. 1996 unp il $16; pa $6 (2-4) **92**

1. African American athletes 2. Women athletes 3. Track athletics—Biography

ISBN 0-15-201267-2; 0-15-202098-5 (pa)

LC 95-32105

A biography of the African-American woman who overcame crippling polio as a child to become the first woman to win three gold medals in track in a single Olympics

"Brightly colored paintings contrast with sepia-toned photographic backgrounds, creating juxtapositions that extend both the text and the pictures in the foreground. Krull's understated conversational style is perfectly suited to Rudolph's remarkable and inspiring story." Horn Book Guide

Sacagawea, b. 1786

Adler, David A. A picture book of Sacagawea; illustrated by Dan Brown. Holiday House 2000 unp il $16.95; pa $6.95 (1-3) **92**

1. Lewis and Clark Expedition (1804-1806) 2. Shoshoni Indians

ISBN 0-8234-1485-X; 0-8234-1665-8 (pa)

LC 99-37135

A biography of the Shoshone woman who joined the Lewis and Clark Expedition

"The narrative is clear, direct, and never fictionalized. . . . The soft watercolor art is more successful in depicting landscapes than human figures." Booklist

Includes bibliographical references

St. George, Judith. Sacagawea. Putnam 1997 115p maps $16.99 (4-6) **92**

1. Lewis and Clark Expedition (1804-1806) 2. Shoshoni Indians

ISBN 0-399-23161-7 LC 96-49311

Tells the story of the Shoshoni Indian girl who served as interpreter, peacemaker, and guide for the Lewis and Clark Expedition to the Northwest in 1805-1806

"In a well-written and well-researched account, St. George humanizes her subject. . . . Adventure lovers will find much to like in the book." Booklist

Includes bibliographical references

Sachar, Louis, 1954-

Greene, Meg. Louis Sachar. Rosen Pub. Group 2004 112p il (Library of author biographies) lib bdg $26.50 (5 and up) **92**

1. Authors, American

ISBN 0-8239-4017-9 LC 2002-154252

Contents: Meet Louis Sachar; "Louis the yard teacher"; Success; From middle school to grade school; Holes; How does he do it?; Interview with Louis Sachar; Timeline

Discusses life and work of the popular children's author, including his writing process and methods, inspirations, a critical discussion of his books, biographical timeline, and awards

A "solid [introduction]. . . . Libraries looking to expand their biography section will be well served by [this] informative [title]." SLJ

Includes bibliographical references

Saladin, Sultan of Egypt and Syria, 1137-1193

Stanley, Diane. Saladin: noble prince of Islam. HarperCollins Pubs. 2002 unp il $16.99; lib bdg $18.89 (4 and up) **92**

1. Crusades 2. Kings and rulers

ISBN 0-688-17135-4; 0-688-17136-2 (lib bdg)

LC 2001-24636

A biography of the Islamic leader who defended his people during the Crusades

The author demonstrates "her trademark ability to research and then distill complex topics in terms accessible to middle-graders. . . . Stanley's precise, detailed artwork pays homage to period architecture. She evokes the colors of Persian miniatures (and medieval stained glass) as her paintings incorporate the complex patterning associated with Islamic art." Publ Wkly

Includes glossary and bibliographical references

Sandburg, Carl, 1878-1967

Niven, Penelope. Carl Sandburg: adventures of a poet; with poems and prose by Carl Sandburg; illustrated by Marc Nadel. Harcourt 2003 unp il $17 (3-6) **92**

1. Poets, American

ISBN 0-15-204686-0 LC 2002-14592

Traces the life of the American poet, journalist, and historian who won the Pulitzer Prize for Poetry and the Pulitzer Prize for History

"Pairing readable, carefully selected biographical details with a specific poem or prose excerpt on facing pages, this book makes Sandburg accessible to young readers. . . . Nadel's masterful watercolor-and-crosshatch illustrations give additional visual information." SLJ

Sargent, John Singer, 1856-1925

Kreiter, Eshel. John Singer Sargent; the life of an artist; [by] Eshel Kreiter, Marc Zabludoff. Enslow Pubs. 2002 48p il (Artist biographies) $23.93 (2-4) **92**

1. Artists—United States

ISBN 0-7660-1879-2 LC 2001-1813

A biography of the late 19th and early 20th century American painter known for his portraits

"The use of full color, good paper, large type, and uncluttered design results in [a book] that [offers] several excellent reproductions of artworks, and the relatively simple [text respects] the capabilities of a young audience." SLJ

Includes glossary and bibliographical references

Sasaki, Sadako, 1943-1955

Coerr, Eleanor. Sadako; illustrated by Ed Young. Putnam 1993 unp il $17.95; pa $6.99 (1-4)
92

1. Leukemia 2. Atomic bomb—Physiological effect
3. Hiroshima (Japan)—Bombardment, 1945
ISBN 0-399-21771-1; 0-698-11588-0 (pa)
LC 92-41483

"This is the same story as the author's *Sadako and the Thousand Paper Cranes*, told through an entirely new text. In this abbreviated version, the beautiful, limpid prose and crisp dialogue further telescope Sadako's fight with leukemia. . . . Young's pastels vividly capture all the moods of the narrative, place, and characters. . . . A masterful collaboration." SLJ

Coerr, Eleanor. Sadako and the thousand paper cranes; paintings by Ronald Himler. Putnam 1977 64p il $16.99; pa $4.99 (3-6)
92
1. Leukemia 2. Atomic bomb—Physiological effect
3. Hiroshima (Japan)—Bombardment, 1945
ISBN 0-399-20520-9; 0-698-11802-2 (pa)
LC 76-9872

Also available Spanish language edition

"A story about a young girl of Hiroshima who died from leukemia ten years after the dropping of the atom bomb. Her dreams of being an outstanding runner are dimmed when she learns she has the fatal disease. But her spunk and bravery, symbolized in her efforts to have faith in the story of the golden crane, are beautifully portrayed by the author." Babbling Bookworm

Satie, Erik, 1866-1925

Anderson, M. T. Strange Mr. Satie; illustrated by Petra Mathers. Viking 2003 unp il $16.99 (2-4)
92
1. Composers
ISBN 0-670-03637-4
LC 2003-949

Introduces the life of the French composer, Erik Satie, who spent his entire career challenging established conventions in music

"A splendid alliance of topic, text, and illustration produces a hauntingly compelling biography. . . . Mathers's illustrations are superb in their crisp, colorful clarity." SLJ

Scholastica, Saint, 6th cent

Norris, Kathleen. The holy twins: Benedict and Scholastica. See entry under Benedict, Saint, Abbot of Monte Cassino

Schumann, Clara, 1819-1896

Reich, Susanna. Clara Schumann; piano virtuoso. Clarion Bks. 1999 118p il $18; pa $9.95 (5 and up)
92
1. Pianists 2. Women composers
ISBN 0-395-89119-1; 0-618-55160-3 (pa)
LC 98-24510

Describes the life of the German pianist and composer who made her professional debut at age nine and who devoted her life to music and to her family

"This thoroughly researched book draws on primary sources, both Clara's own diaries and her voluminous correspondence with her husband. . . . Reich's lucid, quietly passionate biography is liberally illustrated with photographs and reproductions." Horn Book Guide

Scott, Blanche Stuart, 1886-1970

Cummins, Julie. Tomboy of the air: daredevil pilot Blanche Stuart Scott. HarperCollins Pubs. 2001 80p il $16.95; lib bdg $16.89 (3-6)
92
1. Women air pilots
ISBN 0-06-029138-9; 0-06-029243-1 (lib bdg)
LC 00-32009

Blanche Stuart "Scott had many firsts in the air: first public flight by a woman, first woman test pilot, first American woman to fly in a jet. This illustrated biography is full of details about early aviation." N Y Times Book Rev

"A spellbinding biography, adroitly told. . . . Archival photographs, many with chatty captions, further enhance the engaging text." SLJ

Includes bibliographical references

Selkirk, Alexander, 1676-1721

Kraske, Robert. Marooned; the strange but true adventures of Alexander Selkirk, the real Robinson Crusoe; illustrated by Robert Andrew Parker. Clarion Books 2005 120p il map $15 (5 and up)
92
1. Survival after airplane accidents, shipwrecks, etc.
ISBN 0-618-56843-3
LC 2004-28769

"In 1704, English sailing master Alexander Selkirk was marooned on Juan Fernandez, an isolated Pacific island. . . . In 1709, two English ships rescued him, hired him as a second mate, and later captured a Spanish treasure ship. . . . Kraske offers a well-focused look at life in several quite different settings during the early eighteenth century as well as an absorbing telling of Selkirk's story." Booklist

Includes glossary and bibliographical references

Sennett, Mack, 1880-1960

Brown, Don. Mack made movies. 1st ed. Roaring Brook Press 2003 unp il $16.95; lib bdg $23.90 (2-4)
92
1. Motion picture producers and directors 2. Actors
ISBN 0-7613-1538-1; 0-7613-2504-2 (lib bdg)
LC 2002-6357

A simple biography of the director whose silent films immortalized such slapstick clowns as the Keystone Kops, Charlie Chaplin, Fatty Arbuckle, Mabel Normand, and Ben Turpin

This offers a "concise, brilliantly understated text. . . . Especially fine in conveying facial expression, Brown's spare, fluid sketches, softly washed in sepia and butterscotch tones, cunningly capture the look of the times." Booklist

Sequoyah, 1770?-1843

Dennis, Yvonne Wakim. Sequoyah, 1770?-1843; by Yvonne Wakim Dennis. Blue Earth Books 2004 32p il map (American Indian biographies) $23.93 (3-6) **92**

1. Cherokee Indians
ISBN 0-7368-2447-2   LC 2003-17584

Contents: A gift for the Cherokee; Growing up Cherokee; Inventor and soldier; Sequoyah seeks an answer; The syllabary spreads; A quiet ending

The story of Sequoyah's life is "told in easy-to-read prose that is amplified by handsome works of art . . . colorful and dramatic maps, and games and recipes." SLJ

Includes bibliographical references

Rumford, James. Sequoyah; the Cherokee man who gave his people writing. Houghton Mifflin 2004 unp il $16 (1-4) **92**

1. Cherokee Indians
ISBN 0-618-36947-3   LC 2004-00980

"Rumford presents the seminal events in Sequoyah's life, culminating in his invention of the Cherokee syllabary. The author writes with a concise eloquence that echoes the oral tradition and makes this one of those rare gems of read-aloud nonfiction. . . . Done in ink, watercolor, pastel, and pencil, the illustrations were adhered to a rough piece of wood, and its textures were highlighted through the use of chalk and colored pencil. . . . The parallel text in Cherokee . . . makes this beautiful book readily accessible to Cherokee children in their own language." SLJ

Seuss, Dr.

Cohen, Charles D. The Seuss, the whole Seuss, and nothing but the Seuss; a visual biography of Theodor Seuss Geisel. Random House 2004 390p il $35; lib bdg $36.99 **92**

1. Authors, American 2. Illustrators
ISBN 0-375-82248-8; 0-375-92248-2 (lib bdg)
LC 2003-20526

This is a "profile of the creator of Horton, the Grinch, and the Cat in the Hat. . . . Crisp full-color illustrations on every page of the coffee-table volume will pull readers into Cohen's accessible recap of Theodore Geisel's career, which is enhanced with just enough personal information to bring everything together. . . . [The volume includes] clear reproductions of posters, book illustrations, newspaper cartoons, and book pages, with intriguing background information." Booklist

Dean, Tanya. Theodor Geisel. Chelsea House 2002 112p il (Who wrote that?) $22.95 (4 and up) **92**

1. Authors, American 2. Illustrators
ISBN 0-7910-6724-6   LC 2002-166

Describes the life and career of the author and illustrator known as Dr. Seuss who created such popular children's picture books as The cat in the hat, How the Grinch stole Christmas, and Horton hears a Who

"Well organized and clearly written." Booklist

Includes bibliographical references

Krull, Kathleen. The boy on Fairfield Street: how Ted Geisel grew up to become Dr. Seuss; paintings by Steve Johnson and Lou Fancher; with decorative illustrations by Dr. Seuss. Random House 2004 43p il $16.95; lib bdg $18.99 (k-3) **92**

1. Authors, American 2. Illustrators
ISBN 0-375-82298-4; 0-375-92298-9 (lib bdg)
LC 2003-1754

Introduces the life of renowned children's author and illustrator Ted Geisel, popularly known as Dr. Seuss, focusing on his childhood and youth in Springfield, Massachusetts

"Johnson and Fancher's lovely, full-page illustrations are supplemented by samples of Dr. Seuss's artwork. . . . Krull's work is a terrific look at the boyhood of one of the most beloved author/illustrators of the 20th century." SLJ

Shackleton, Sir Ernest Henry, 1874-1922

Kostyal, K. M. Trial by ice: a photobiography of Sir Ernest Shackleton. National Geographic Soc. 1999 64p il map $17.95 (4 and up) **92**

1. Explorers 2. Antarctica—Exploration
ISBN 0-7922-7393-1   LC 99-20980

Traces the adventurous life of the South Pole explorer whose ship, the Endurance, was frozen in ice and crushed, leaving the captain and crew to fight for survival

"The stunning, archival black-and-white photographs are this book's strength." SLJ

Includes bibliographical references

Shepard, Alan B., Jr.

Orr, Tamra. Alan Shepard; the first American in space; [by] Tamra B. Orr. 1st ed. Rosen Pub. Group 2004 112p il (Library of astronaut biographies) lib bdg $29.95 (4 and up)
92

1. Astronauts
ISBN 0-8239-4455-7   LC 2003-10703

Contents: A decade of contrasts; The launching of a future astronaut; The Mercury 7 astronauts; Freedom 7; The terror and triumph of Apollo; Into the business world; A quiet ending

This describes Alan Shepard's childhood, education, and training as an astronaut.

"The writing is fast paced and lively. Many color photographs and occasional full-page sidebars enhance the [text]." SLJ

Includes glossary and bibliographical references

Sholem Aleichem, 1859-1916

Silverman, Erica. Sholom's treasure; how Sholom Aleichem became a writer; pictures by Mordicai Gerstein. 1st ed. Farrar, Straus and Giroux 2005 unp il $16 (k-3) **92**

1. Authors, Yiddish 2. Jews—Biography
ISBN 0-374-38055-4   LC 2002-44672

Describes some events in the life of Sholem Aleichem, the Yiddish author who wrote stories about Jewish life in nineteenth-century Russia.

Sholem Aleichem, 1859-1916—*Continued*

"Silverman keeps her focus on the things about Aleichem's life that will appeal most to young readers. . . . Gerstein's ink-and-watercolor paintings appear as full-page art and strips of illustration, both of which are equally adept at capturing the pathos and absurdities of everyday life." Booklist

Simmons, Philip

Lyons, Mary E. Catching the fire: Philip Simmons, blacksmith; with photographs by Mannie Garcia. Houghton Mifflin 1997 47p il $17 (4 and up)   92

1. African American artists
ISBN 0-395-72033-8   LC 96-38643

Tells the story of this African American artist, the great-grandson of slaves, who has achieved fame and admiration for his ornamental wrought-iron creations

"The narrative, based on Simmons' memories and words, involves readers through its lively presentation of an intriguing subject. . . . Photographs appear on every spread, with black-and-white pictures of Simmons' early days and beautifully lit and composed color shots of the man today." Booklist

Includes bibliographical references

Sitting Bull, Dakota Chief, 1831-1890

Bruchac, Joseph. A boy called Slow: the true story of Sitting Bull; illustrated by Rocco Baviera. Philomel Bks. 1994 unp il $16.99; pa $6.99 (1-3)   92

1. Dakota Indians
ISBN 0-399-22692-3; 0-698-11616-X (pa)
                                      LC 93-21233

The author "recounts the early years of the young Lakota boy who grows from an unprepossessing child named 'Slow,' to a youth whose careful and deliberate actions bring honor to the name, to a young warrior whose courage in defeating the Crow earns him his father's vision name Tatan'ka Iyota'ke—Sitting Bull." Bull Cent Child Books

"Baviera's darkly atmospheric, dramatic paintings frequently feature startling bits of bright color, as in the setting sun or a piece of sky visible through the smoke hole of a family's tipi. The pictures evoke a sense of timelessness and distance, possessing an almost mythic quality that befits this glimpse into history." Horn Book

Slocum, Joshua, b. 1844

Lasky, Kathryn. Born in the breezes: the seafaring of Joshua Slocum; illustrated by Walter Lyon Krudop. Orchard Bks. 2001 unp il $16.95 (3-6)   92

1. Sailors 2. Voyages around the world
ISBN 0-439-29305-7   LC 00-66565

"Joshua Slocum, who grew up in Nova Scotia in the mid-1800s, went to sea in his teens and spent his life as a sailor and later a captain of sailing ships. He married an adventurous woman, who joined him on his travels and raised their children at sea. . . . He repaired an old sloop and, in 1898, became the first man to sail around the world alone. This smoothly written story is illustrated with handsome oil paintings. . . . An interesting introduction to an intriguing man." Booklist

Snicket, Lemony, 1970-

Haugen, Hayley Mitchell. Daniel Handler; the real Lemony Snicket. Kidhaven Press 2005 48p il (Inventors and Creators) $23.70 (4 and up)   92

1. Authors, American
ISBN 0-7377-3117-6

In this biography of the author of the A Series on Unfortunate Events series "Haugen explains Handler's reasons for writing under a pen name. . . . He also explains Snicket's many interruptions, for vocabulary lessons, throughout the titles. A brief section presents some of the criticism of the series and Snicket's creative allusions to other literature and authors within his work. The full-color photos of Handler are sure to please the fans who've been longing for a glimpse. . . . This book will be read for reports and by adoring fans." SLJ

Soyer, Alexis, 1809-1858

Arnold, Ann. The adventurous chef: Alexis Soyer. Foster Bks. 2002 unp il $17 (3-5)   92

1. Cooking
ISBN 0-374-31665-1   LC 2002-19224

A biography of a flamboyant, successful French chef and inventor of kitchen tools who opened soup kitchens during the Irish potato famine and taught the army how to feed itself during the Crimean War

"The writing is simple and straightforward, with touches of wry humor throughout, and the graceful watercolors add mood, detail, and a sense of time and place." SLJ

Spinelli, Jerry, 1941-

Spinelli, Jerry. Knots in my yo-yo string; the autobiography of a kid. Knopf 1998 148p il lib bdg $16.99; pa $10.95 (4 and up)   92

1. Authors, American
ISBN 0-679-98791-6 (lib bdg); 0-679-88791-1 (pa)
                                      LC 97-30827

Also available Thorndike Press large print edition

This Italian-American Newbery Medalist presents a humorous account of his childhood and youth in Norristown, Pennsylvania

"There is an 'everyboy' universality to Spinelli's experiences, but his keen powers of observation and recall turn the story into a richly rewarding personal history." Horn Book Guide

Stanton, Elizabeth Cady, 1815-1902

Fritz, Jean. You want women to vote, Lizzie Stanton? illustrated by DyAnne DiSalvo-Ryan. Putnam 1995 88p il $16.99; pa $5.99 (2-4)   92

1. Feminism 2. Women—Suffrage
ISBN 0-399-22786-5; 0-698-11764-6 (pa)
                                      LC 94-30018

This is a biography of the 19th century feminist and advocate of women's suffrage

"With remarkable clarity, sensitivity, and momentum, Fritz has captured—but never imprisoned [Stanton's] spirit in an accessible, fascinating portrait." Horn Book

Includes bibliographical references

Starr, Belle, 1848-1889

Naden, Corinne J. Belle Starr and the Wild West; by Corinne J. Naden and Rose Blue. Blackbirch Press 2000 112p il maps (Notorious Americans and their times) lib bdg $19.95 (5 and up) **92**

1. West (U.S.)

ISBN 1-56711-223-4   LC 00-8437

A biography of the legendary outlaw known as the Bandit Queen. Sidebars describe the history, daily life, and people of the Wild West

"Fascinating black-and-white illustrations and reproductions and informative sidebars are the highlights of this biography." SLJ

Includes bibliographical references (p. 108-109) and index

Stetson, John Batterson, 1830-1906

Carlson, Laurie M. Boss of the plains; the hat that won the West; by Laurie Carlson; pictures by Holly Meade. DK Pub. 1998 unp il $16.95; pa $5.95 (k-3) **92**

1. Hats

ISBN 0-7894-2479-7; 0-7894-2657-9 (pa)

LC 97-30995

"A Melanie Kroupa book"

The story of John Stetson and how he came to create the most popular hat west of the Mississippi

"Carlson's storytelling prose sets the scene and tells the tale concisely and enticingly, and Meade's mixed-media illustrations have an appropriately rough-and-ready feel." Horn Book Guide

Includes bibliographical references

Stevenson, Robert Louis, 1850-1894

Murphy, Jim. Across America on an emigrant train. Clarion Bks. 1993 150p il $18; pa $9.95 (5 and up) **92**

1. Authors, Scottish 2. Railroads—History 3. United States—Description and travel

ISBN 0-395-63390-7; 0-395-76483-1 (pa)

LC 92-38650

"Murphy presents a forthright and thoroughly engrossing history of the transcontinental railway, with entries from Robert Louis Stevenson's 1879 journal as he rode cross country. It's also an inviting introduction to Stevenson, with a romance in the bargain." SLJ

Includes bibliographical references

Stiles, Jackie, 1978-

Stewart, Mark. Jackie Stiles; gym dandy. Millbrook Press 2002 48p il (Basketball's new wave) lib bdg $22.90 (4 and up) **92**

1. Basketball 2. Women athletes

ISBN 0-7613-2614-6   LC 2002-2670

A biography of WNBA star Jackie Stiles, a guard for the Portland Fire who was named Rookie of the Year in 2001

This title is distinguished by "a breezy, narrative style and well-selected color photos. . . . [This is a] solid, well-presented [volume]." Booklist

Stowe, Harriet Beecher, 1811-1896

Adler, David A. A picture book of Harriet Beecher Stowe; illustrated by Colin Bootman. Holiday House 2003 unp il $17.95; pa $6.95 (k-3) **92**

1. Women authors 2. Authors, American 3. Abolitionists

ISBN 0-8234-1646-1; 0-8234-1878-2 (pa)

LC 2002-27626

Details the life and achievements of abolitionist Harriet Beecher Stowe whose book, Uncle Tom's Cabin, is said to have started the Civil War

"This biography offers easily accessible information supported by realistic, evocative oil paintings." SLJ

Includes bibliographical references

Fritz, Jean. Harriet Beecher Stowe and the Beecher preachers. Putnam 1994 144p il $15.99; pa $5.99 (5 and up) **92**

1. Beecher family 2. Women authors 3. Authors, American 4. Abolitionists

ISBN 0-399-22666-4; 0-698-11660-7 (pa)

LC 93-6408

This is a biography of the abolitionist author of "Uncle Tom's Cabin" with an emphasis on the influence of her preacher father and her family on her life and work.

"Written with vivacity and insight, this readable and engrossing biography is an important contribution to women's history as well as to the history of American letters." Horn Book

Includes bibliographical references

Tallchief, Maria

Tallchief, Maria. Tallchief; America's prima ballerina; by Maria Tallchief with Rosemary Wells; illustrations by Gary Kelley. Viking 1999 unp il $15.99 (3-5) **92**

1. Ballet dancers 2. Native American women

ISBN 0-670-88756-0   LC 98-35783

Ballerina Maria Tallchief describes her childhood on an Osage reservation, the development of her love of dance, and her rise to success in that field

"Through eloquent words, readers are immediately drawn into the first-person narrative. . . . As beautiful as the text is, so too are Kelley's pictures. The large illustrations, several covering double-page spreads, are rendered in soft pastels." SLJ

Taylor, Mildred D.

Houghton, Gillian. Mildred Taylor. Rosen Pub. Group 2005 112p il (Library of author biographies) lib bdg $26.50 (5 and up) **92**

1. Women authors 2. African American authors

ISBN 1-4042-0330-3

"Houghton presents readers with an understanding of Taylor's work as based on family stories and the history of African Americans in the United States. The result is a blend of history with the author's life and literature. . . . [This is] well-written." SLJ

Tecumseh, Shawnee Chief, 1768-1813

Collier, James Lincoln. The Tecumseh you never knew; [by] James Lincoln Collier; [illustrations by Greg Copeland] Children's Press 2004 80p il map lib bdg $25.95 (4 and up)
92

1. Shawnee Indians
ISBN 0-516-24426-4   LC 2003-28205
Contents: An Indian boy grows up; The war heats up; Rebuilding the confederacy; Tippecanoe; Triumph and tragedy

A biography of the Shawnee Indian chief who struggled to build a confederacy of Indians in order to thwart American expansionism after the Revolutionary war.

"A mix of realistic paintings and reproductions depict Tecumseh's life. Easy-to-read type on spacious white pages may tempt children into reading biographies." SLJ

Includes bibliographical references

Tillage, Leon, 1936-

Tillage, Leon. Leon's story; [by] Leon Walter Tillage; collage art by Susan L. Roth. Farrar, Straus & Giroux 1997 107p il $15; pa $4.95 (4 and up)
92

1. African Americans—Biography 2. North Carolina—Race relations
ISBN 0-374-34379-9; 0-374-44330-0 (pa)
     LC 96-43544
The son of a North Carolina sharecropper recalls the hard times faced by his family and other African Americans in the first half of the twentieth century and the changes that the civil rights movement helped bring about

The author's "voice is direct, the words are simple. There is no rhetoric, no commentary, no bitterness. . . . This quiet drama will move readers of all ages . . . and may encourage them to record their own family stories." Booklist

Toulouse-Lautrec, Henri de, 1864-1901

Burleigh, Robert. Toulouse-Lautrec; the Moulin Rouge and the City of Light. Abrams 2005 32p il $17.95 (3-5)
92

1. Artists, French
ISBN 0-8109-5867-8
This "volume introduces the life and art of Toulouse-Lautrec. . . . Burleigh relates the facts in a way that is comprehensible to children, without talking down to them. . . . The book's format allows for many illustrations, including period photos and paintings of Paris by artists such as Pissarro and Renoir, which are cleverly mingled with reproductions of Toulouse-Lautrec's arresting drawings, paintings, and lithographs, many in color. . . . A beautifully designed book that provides a lively, accessible introduction to the artist's life and work." Booklist

Truth, Sojourner, d. 1883

Adler, David A. A picture book of Sojourner Truth; illustrated by Gershom Griffith. Holiday House 1994 unp il $16.95; pa $6.95 (1-3)
92

1. African American women 2. Abolitionists 3. Feminism
ISBN 0-8234-1072-2; 0-8234-1262-8 (pa)
     LC 93-7478
An introduction to the life of the woman born into slavery who became a well-known abolitionist and crusader for the rights of African Americans in the United States

The author "portrays his subject in a realistic manner, discussing slavery and other issues in an easy-to-read style. The quotes, while undocumented, are simple enough for the target audience and help to place events in context. Excellent-quality watercolor illustrations capture the action and provide effective representations and details of the time period." SLJ

Butler, Mary G. Sojourner Truth; from slave to activist for freedom. PowerPlus Bks. 2003 112p il map (Library of American lives and times) lib bdg $31.95 (5 and up)
92

1. African American women 2. Abolitionists 3. Feminism
ISBN 0-8239-5736-5   LC 2001-6169
Contents: Slavery in America; The slave Isabella; Living free; The sojourn begins; The Northampton Association; On the lecture circuit; The Battle Creek years; The legend grows; The nation divided; The last crusade

A biography of the former slave who became an abolitionist and advocate for women's rights

"The text is well documented, and the numerous illustrations, photos, and reproductions, both in color and in black and white, are authoritative and informative." SLJ

Includes glossary and bibliographical references

McKissack, Patricia C. Sojourner Truth; a voice for freedom; [by] Patricia and Fredrick McKissack. rev ed. Enslow Pubs. 2001 32p il (Great African Americans) lib bdg $18.60 (1-3)
92

1. African American women 2. Abolitionists 3. Feminism
ISBN 0-7660-1693-5   LC 00-12420
First published 1992

Describes the life of the anti-slavery and women's rights activist, from her beginnings in slavery to her tireless campaign for the rights and welfare of the freedmen

"Short sentences, large, well-spaced text, and a blend of black-and-white photographs and sketches. . . . [This] will give an overview of that great woman's achievements." SLJ [review of 1992 edition]

Includes glossary and bibliographical references

Rockwell, Anne F. Only passing through: the story of Sojourner Truth; by Anne Rockwell; illustrated by Gregory Christie. Knopf 2000 unp il $16.95; lib bdg $18.99 (3-5)
92

1. African American women 2. Abolitionists 3. Feminism
ISBN 0-679-89186-2; 0-679-99186-7 (lib bdg)
     LC 00-35736

Truth, Sojourner, d. 1883—_Continued_

"Rockwell traces the life of 'Isabella,' who renamed herself Sojourner Truth when she began her journeys at the age of forty-six to speak out for the abolition of slavery." Horn Book

Rockwell's narrative "is both conversational and immediately riveting. . . . The semi-abstract paintings are inspirational rather than representational, their authority residing in the presence Christie imparts to this heroine." Bull Cent Child Books

Roop, Peter. Sojourner Truth; [by] Peter Roop and Connie Roop. Scholastic 2002 128p il (In their own words) pa $4.50 (3-6)   92
1. African American women 2. Abolitionists 3. Feminism
ISBN 0-439-26323-9   LC 2001-32025

"The Roops make use of recollections, historical photos, letters, and newspaper articles to reveal the personality behind Truth's famous rousing oratory, 'Ain't I a Woman?' The biography covers the subjects birth into enslavement through her tireless travels across the country speaking out against slavery and fighting for social reforms, and her death at age 86 in 1883. . . . This book gives a complete picture, providing facts and insight into the woman's character and convictions." SLJ

Includes bibliographical references

Tubman, Harriet, 1815?-1913

Adler, David A. A picture book of Harriet Tubman; illustrated by Samuel Byrd. Holiday House 1992 unp il $16.95; pa $6.95 (1-3)
92
1. African American women 2. Underground railroad
ISBN 0-8234-0926-0; 0-8234-1065-X (pa)
LC 91-19628

Biography of the black woman who escaped from slavery to become famous as a conductor on the Underground Railroad

This book features "brief, easy-to-read text. . . . Byrd's appealing, colorful illustrations convey the quiet dignity of a brave heroine." Booklist

Ferris, Jeri. Go free or die: a story about Harriet Tubman; illustrations by Karen Ritz. Carolrhoda Bks. 1988 63p il (Carolrhoda creative minds book) $21.27; pa $5.95 (3-5)   92
1. African American women 2. Underground railroad
ISBN 0-87614-317-6; 0-87614-504-7 (pa)
LC 87-18279

This is "the story of Harriet Tubman, born a slave in Maryland in 1820. Fiercely determined to 'go free or die,' Tubman, aided by the Quakers, mastered the intricate maneuvering of the Underground Railroad, and from 1850 to 1861 made 19 trips leading more than 300 slaves to freedom, never losing one. Using a clear direct style, Ferris does not dwell on the brutal injustices . . . but rather on [her] against-all-odds perseverance to fight for equal rights. Ritz' illustrations have a haunting antique-photo quality." Booklist

Koestler-Grack, Rachel A. The story of Harriet Tubman. Chelsea Clubhouse 2004 32p il (Breakthrough biographies) lib bdg $14.95 (2-4)
92
1. African American women 2. Underground railroad
ISBN 0-7910-7314-9   LC 2003-271

A biography of American abolitionist Harriet Tubman, who escaped slavery and led others to freedom as a conductor on the Underground Railroad

"Interesting and readable. . . . [This volume is] carefully researched, presenting good and respectful coverage." SLJ

Includes glossary and bibliographical references

Schraff, Anne E. Harriet Tubman; Moses of the Underground Railroad. Enslow Pub 2001 128p il map (African-American biographies) lib bdg $26.60 (5 and up)   92
1. African American women 2. Underground railroad
ISBN 0-7660-1548-3   LC 00-10953

This biography describes Tubman's "life from her birth into slavery on a Maryland plantation around 1820 . . . until her death in 1913. In discussing Tubman's life as a slave, Schraff does not gloss over the harsh treatment her subject received. The book also mentions Tubman's service to the Union during the Civil War, working as a nurse, scout, and spy." SLJ

Includes bibliographical references

Tutankhamen, King of Egypt

Sabuda, Robert. Tutankhamen's gift; written and illustrated by Robert Sabuda. Atheneum Pubs. 1994 unp il $17; pa $6.99 (k-3)   92
1. Egypt—Antiquities
ISBN 0-689-31818-9; 0-689-81730-4 (pa)
LC 93-5401

"His tutor foresees that little Tutankhamen's 'gift for the gods' will someday be revealed. That day comes sooner than expected, when the young boy becomes pharaoh after his brother's death and rebuilds the beautiful temples created by his father and destroyed by his brother. Bold pictures outlined in black against a background of painted, handmade Egyptian papyrus illustrate the book, and an afterword provides historical details." Horn Book Guide

Twain, Mark, 1835-1910

Brown, Don. American boy: the adventures of Mark Twain; written and illustrated by Don Brown. Houghton Mifflin 2003 unp il $16 (2-4)
92
1. Authors, American
ISBN 0-618-17997-6   LC 2002-151177

Provides a brief biography of the noted American writer who was born Samuel Clemens

"The boyhood of writer Samuel Clemens is irresistible, with much of his youth inspiring scenes in his works that have become folklore in their own right. Brown does a spirited job of telling some of those stories. . . . Brown's strengths as an artist, making evocative vistas and suggesting architecture and flora, are in evidence here." Booklist

Includes bibliographical references

Twain, Mark, 1835-1910—*Continued*

Collier, James Lincoln. The Mark Twain you never knew; [by] James Lincoln Collier; [illustrations by Greg Copeland] Children's Press 2004 80p il $25.50 (4 and up) **92**
1. Authors, American
ISBN 0-516-24430-2   LC 2003-28305
Contents: A writer's boyhood; Earning a living; Roughing it; Writing the classics; The masterpiece
A biography of the American author.
"Excellent photographs bring . . . Twain to life. . . . [This offers] easy-to-read type on spacious white pages." SLJ
Includes bibliographical references

Harness, Cheryl. Mark Twain and the queens of the Mississippi. Simon & Schuster Bks. for Young Readers 1998 unp il pa $6.99 hardcover o.p. (3-5) **92**
1. Authors, American 2. Mississippi River 3. Steamboats
ISBN 0-689-85549-4 (pa); 0-689-81542-5 (hc)
     LC 97-40799
Focuses on this American author's connection with steamboats on the Mississippi River while also presenting a history of the craft
"Full of action and color, the watercolor-and-colored-pencil illustrations give readers many vivid images of the river, the people who traveled it, the events that marked Twain's times, and the man himself. . . . An unusually lively picture-book biography and an accessible, informative introduction to the life of Mark Twain." Booklist
Includes bibliographical references

Lasky, Kathryn. A brilliant streak: the making of Mark Twain; illustrated by Barry Moser. Harcourt Brace & Co. 1998 41p il $18 (4 and up) **92**
1. Authors, American
ISBN 0-15-252110-0   LC 95-18479
An illustrated biography of young Samuel Clemens
"An obvious delight in her subject makes Lasky's biography an appealing choice, and a similar enthusiasm invests Moser's illustrations." Horn Book Guide
Includes bibliographical references

Valentine, Saint

Sabuda, Robert. Saint Valentine; retold and illustrated by Robert Sabuda. Atheneum Pubs. 1992 unp il $16.95; pa $5.99 (1-3) **92**
1. Christian saints
ISBN 0-689-31762-X; 0-689-82429-7 (pa)
     LC 91-25012
Recounts an incident in the life of St. Valentine, a physician who lived some 200 years after Christ, in which he treated a small child for blindness
"The fluid, straightforward retelling of the legend is accompanied by evocative, mosaiclike illustrations created from colored cut paper. Varying sizes of illustrations, careful page placement, and effective use of white space create the impression of the large-scale period mosaics. A fine melding of text and art." SLJ

Velázquez, Diego, 1599-1660

Venezia, Mike. Diego Velázquez; written and illustrated by Mike Venezia. Children's Press 2004 32p il (Getting to know the world's greatest artists) lib bdg $26; pa $6.95 (k-3) **92**
1. Artists, Spanish
ISBN 0-516-22580-4 (lib bdg); 0-516-26980-1 (pa)
     LC 2003-4590
Describes the life and career of the seventeenth-century Spanish artist famous for his portraits of royalty.
"The unusually abundant full-color reproductions more than justify this series' longevity, as do Venezia's light-hearted cartoons, which foster welcome associations between 'art appreciation' and 'fun.'" Booklist

Waldman, Neil, 1947-

Waldman, Neil. Out of the shadows; an artist's journey. Boyds Mills Press 2006 144p il $21.95 (5 and up) **92**
1. Illustrators 2. Artists—United States 3. Jews—Biography
ISBN 1-59078-411-1
Neil Waldman reveals how his passion for art emerged in the kitchen of his family's apartment, where he discovered the work of Vincent Van Gogh and the ability to use illustration as a means to escape the sadness that plagued his home.
"Young artists, as well as readers who wonder about the person behind the pictures they have seen, will appreciate every element of this book: well-constructed story, visual richness, and uncompromising honesty." Booklist

Walker, C. J., Madame, 1867-1919

Lasky, Kathryn. Vision of beauty: the story of Sarah Breedlove Walker; illustrated by Nneka Bennett. Candlewick Press 2000 unp il $16.99 (3-5) **92**
1. African American businesspeople 2. African American women
ISBN 0-7636-0253-1   LC 99-19594
A biography of Sarah Breedlove Walker who, though born in poverty, pioneered in hair and beauty care products for black women, and became a great financial success
"Lasky's engaging account moves smoothly through events in Walker's life. . . . The illustrations . . . are attractive and rich in historical detail." Booklist

McKissack, Patricia C. Madam C.J. Walker; self-made millionaire; [by] Patricia and Fredrick McKissack. rev ed. Enslow Pubs. 2001 32p $18.60 (1-3) **92**
1. African American businesspeople 2. African American women
ISBN 0-7660-1682-X   LC 00-10055
First published 1992
Describes the life of the black laundress who founded a cosmetics company and became the first female self-made millionaire in the United States

Washington, Booker T., 1856-1915

McKissack, Patricia C. Booker T. Washington; leader and educator; [by] Patricia and Fredrick McKissack. rev ed. Enslow Pubs. 2001 32p il $18.60 (1-3)　　**92**

1. Tuskegee Institute 2. African American educators
ISBN 0-7660-1679-X　　LC 00-10056
First published 1992
A biography of the former slave who founded Tuskegee University and later became the most powerful African American leader at the turn of the century
This is a "solid, straightforward [biography]." Booklist

Washington, George, 1732-1799

Adler, David A. George Washington; an illustrated biography; by David A. Adler. 1st ed. Holiday House 2004 274p il map $24.95 (5 and up)　　**92**

1. Presidents—United States
ISBN 0-8234-1838-3　　LC 2003-67606
This "look at America's premier founding father literally spans his lifetime and attempts to focus . . . on how Washington's early character formation impacted his decisions as a military officer and later as president. . . . The illustrations are largely engravings from the late 19th century. . . . The writing style is accessible without ever falling prey to oversimplification." SLJ

Bial, Raymond. Where Washington walked; [by] Raymond Bial. Walker & Co 2004 48p il $17.95; lib bdg $18.85 (3-6)　　**92**

1. Presidents—United States
ISBN 0-8027-8899-8; 0-8027-8900-5 (lib bdg)
　　LC 2004-41931
"Bial briefly recounts the life of his subject with reference to the places he lived and worked." SLJ
"This well-designed book introduces George Washington through a clearly written biographical account of his life and achievements, illustrated with many sharply focused, well-composed photographs and a few reproductions of period paintings and prints." Booklist
Includes bibliographical references

Harness, Cheryl. George Washington. National Geographic Soc. 2000 48p il $17.95 (3-5)
　　92

1. Presidents—United States
ISBN 0-7922-7096-7　　LC 99-29920
Presents the life of George Washington, focusing on the Revolutionary War years and his presidency
"Detailed paintings, full of action and rich with color, portray Washington as well as important moments in American history. . . . This heavily illustrated biography serves as a good introduction to Washington." Booklist
Includes bibliographical references

Jurmain, Suzanne. George did it; by Suzanne Tripp Jurmain; illustrated by Larry Day. Dutton Children's Books 2006 40p il $16.99 (2-4)
　　92

1. Presidents—United States
ISBN 0-525-47560-5　　LC 2004-25068

"This picture book focuses on George Washington as a reluctant first president. . . . The lively text follows Washington as friends such as Jefferson convince him to accept the challenge. . . . The text is studded with short quotes and memorable details. . . . Brightened with watercolor washes, Day's strong drawings illustrate the story with wit and finesse." Booklist
Includes bibliographical references

Washington, Mary Ball, 1708-1789

Fritz, Jean. George Washington's mother; illustrated by DyAnne DiSalvo-Ryan. Grosset & Dunlap 1992 48p il $7.99; pa $3.99 (1-3)
　　92

1. Washington, George, 1732-1799 2. Presidents—United States—Mothers
ISBN 0-448-40385-4; 0-448-40384-6 (pa)
　　LC 91-34247
"All aboard reading"
At head of title: All aboard reading
Describes the life of the mother of our first president and her relationship with her children
"Fritz brings the excitement of history to newly independent readers. . . . Using factual data and funny incidents, the author humorously depicts Mary Ball Washington as a manipulative and stubborn worrywart. The numerous, half- and full-page, pencil-and-watercolor illustrations . . . complement the text and extend the humor." SLJ

Weber, EdNah New Rider

Weber, EdNah New Rider. Rattlesnake Mesa; stories from a native American childhood; by EdNah New Rider Weber; photographs by Richela Renkun. 1st ed. Lee & Low Books 2004 132p il $18.95 (4 and up)　　**92**

1. Native Americans
ISBN 1-58430-231-3　　LC 2004-2385
"Weber grew up in the early twentieth century on the Crown Point Navajo Reservation . . . and she attended a government boarding school for Native American children. She recounts childhood experiences in both places." Booklist
"Weber describes her experiences with warmth and affection in this unusually compelling memoir. Striking black-and-white photos . . . add to the book's appeal." Horn Book Guide

Wells-Barnett, Ida B., 1862-1931

Fradin, Dennis B. Ida B. Wells; mother of the civil rights movement; [by] Dennis Brindell Fradin and Judith Bloom Fradin. Clarion Bks. 2000 178p il $19 (5 and up)　　**92**

1. African American women 2. African Americans—Civil rights
ISBN 0-395-89898-6　　LC 99-37038
This "biography chronicles the life of teacher, writer, publisher and civil rights champion, Ida B. Wells." ALAN
"This stellar biography of one of history's most inspiring women offers an excellent overview of Wells's life and contributions. . . . Black-and-white photographs and reproductions enhance the clear, well-written text." SLJ
Includes bibliographical references

West, Benjamin, 1738-1820
Brenner, Barbara. The boy who loved to draw: Benjamin West; illustrated by Olivier Dunrea. Houghton Mifflin 1999 unp il $15 (k-3)
                                                                         92
1. Artists—United States
ISBN 0-395-85080-0   LC 97-5183
Recounts the life story of the Pennsylvania artist who began drawing as a boy and eventually became well known on both sides of the Atlantic
"Naive in style and reminiscent of some colonial art, the illustrations present clear visual expressions of the activities and emotions related in the story. . . . A fascinating look at art in colonial times, and a likable portrait of the artist as a young boy." Booklist

Wheatley, Phillis, 1753-1784
Lasky, Kathryn. A voice of her own: the story of Phillis Wheatley, slave poet; illustrated by Paul Lee. Candlewick Press 2003 unp il $16.99 (3-5)
                                                                         92
1. Poets, American 2. African American authors 3. Women poets 4. Slavery—United States
ISBN 0-7636-0252-3   LC 2001-47139
A biography of an African girl brought to New England as a slave in 1761 who became famous on both sides of the Atlantic as the first Black poet in America
Written "in evocative language that's rich with historical detail. . . . This will serve as a good introduction to Wheatley's life and times for young children, who will appreciate Lee's full-page, historically accurate acrylics." Booklist

Whitman, Walt, 1819-1892
Kerley, Barbara. Walt Whitman; words for America; illustrated by Brian Selznick. Scholastic Press 2004 unp il $16.95 (4 and up)   92
1. Poets, American
ISBN 0-439-35791-8   LC 2003-20085
A biography of the American poet whose compassion led him to nurse soldiers during the Civil War, to give voice to the nation's grief at Lincoln's assassination, and to capture the true American spirit in verse
"Delightfully old-fashioned in design, [the book's] oversized pages are replete with graceful illustrations and snippets of poetry. The brilliantly inventive paintings add vibrant testimonial to the nuanced text." SLJ

Wickenheiser, Hayley, 1978-
Etue, Elizabeth. Hayley Wickenheiser; born to play. Kids Can Press 2005 40p il pa $6.95 (4 and up)   92
1. Hockey 2. Women athletes
ISBN 1-55337-791-5
"The first woman to play professional hockey, Hayley Wickenheiser took up the sport in her family's backyard rink in a small Saskatchewan town at the age of three. . . . In 2003, Wickenheiser played professional hockey in a men's league in Finland. Fully illustrated with clear, colorful photos of Wickenheiser in action as well as posed shots off the ice, this appealing, large-format paperback offers a look at one woman's career in a 'man's' sport and shows the drive that propelled her to the top." Booklist

Wild Boy of Aveyron, d. 1828
Gerstein, Mordicai. The wild boy; based on the true story of the Wild Boy of Aveyron. Foster Bks. 1998 39p il $16 (k-3)   92
1. Wild children
ISBN 0-374-38431-2   LC 97-37246
Relates the story of a boy who grew up wild in the forests of France and was captured in 1800, studied and cared for and named Victor, but who never learned to speak
"Gerstein's prose finds power in its simplicity and emotional resonance in its declarative understatement. . . . The narrative strength and energy of the illustrations expand the inherent drama of Victor's situation. Together, Gerstein's text and pictures work to create an unforgettable story." Booklist

Wilder, Laura Ingalls, 1867-1957
Anderson, William T. Pioneer girl: the story of Laura Ingalls Wilder; by William Anderson; illustrated by Dan Andreasen. HarperCollins Pubs. 1998 unp il $15.95; lib bdg $15.89; pa $5.35 (2-4)
                                                                         92
1. Authors, American 2. Women authors 3. Frontier and pioneer life
ISBN 0-06-027243-0; 0-06-027244-9 (lib bdg); 0-06-446234-X (pa)   LC 96-31203
Recounts the life story of the author of the "Little House" books, from her childhood in Wisconsin to her old age at Rocky Ridge Farm
"Laura Ingalls Wilder's many fans will delight in this inviting biographical overview in a picture-book format, graced by Andreasen's dreamy landscapes, glowing prairie skies and warm character portraits." Publ Wkly

Wilder, Laura Ingalls. A Little House traveler; writings from Laura Ingalls Wilder's journeys across America; by Laura Ingalls Wilder. HarperCollins 2006 344p il $16.99 (5 and up)
                                                                         92
1. Women authors 2. Authors, American 3. United States—Description and travel
ISBN 9780060724917   LC 2005014975
"This volume combines three Wilder travel diaries: On the Way Home, recounting the 1894 trip from South Dakota to Missouri, with husband Almanzo and daughter Rose; West from Home, featuring letters written by Laura to Almanzo during her 1915 solo visit to Rose in San Francisco; and The Road Back, highlighting Laura's previously unpublished record of a 1931 trip with Almanzo to De Smet, South Dakota, and the Black Hills. . . . This offers an amazing look at a beloved author, as well as a fascinating account of travel before interstate highways and air-conditioning." Booklist

Wilder, Laura Ingalls. West from home; letters of Laura Ingalls Wilder to Almanzo Wilder, San Francisco, 1915; edited by Roger Lea MacBride; historical setting by Margot Patterson Doss. Harper & Row 1974 124p il $16.95; pa $5.95 (6 and up)
                                                                         92
1. San Francisco (Calif.)—Description 2. Authors, American 3. Women authors
ISBN 0-06-024110-1; 0-06-440081-6 (pa)
                                            LC 73-14342

Wilder, Laura Ingalls, 1867-1957—*Continued*

This collection is "edited from letters sent to her beloved husband while Laura spent two months in late 1915 visiting their daughter and immersing herself in the sights of bustling San Francisco and the exciting Panama-Pacific Exposition. Wilder readers of all ages will lose themselves in this trip—the adults with nostalgia and wholesome pleasure, the youth with wonder and awe over the sights vividly described in her inimitable combination of homespun literary and journalistic styles." Child Book Rev Serv

Williams, Roger, 1604?-1683

Avi. Finding Providence: the story of Roger Williams; story by Avi; illustrations by James Watling. HarperCollins Pubs. 1997 46p il pa $3.99 hardcover o.p. (2-4)   92

1. United States—History—1600-1775, Colonial period 2. Rhode Island—History

ISBN 0-06-444216-0; .   LC 95-46360

"An I can read chapter book"

After being forced to leave the Massachusetts Bay Colony, Roger Williams travels south and, with the help of the Narragansett Indians, founds Providence, Rhode Island.

"Plentiful dialogue speeds the action along, and even the philosophical issues are cogently presented for young readers in the form of Williams' interrogation at the trial. Watling's watercolors have a roughhewn quality appropiate to the early colonies, and his grave figures are charged with tension." Bull Cent Child Books

Wonder, Stevie

Troupe, Quincy. Little Stevie Wonder; by Quincy Troupe; illustrated by Lisa Cohen. Houghton Mifflin 2005 unp il $18 (k-3)
92

1. African American musicians 2. Blind

ISBN 0-618-34060-2   LC 2003-17703

Includes an audio CD with two songs

"This tribute introduces young readers to the life and music of . . . Stevie Wonder. Echoes from his song lyrics . . . highlight his early life and reveal the evolution of his musical genius. . . . The acrylic paintings perfectly match the joyful nature of the narrative." SLJ

Wood, Grant, 1892-1942

Duggleby, John. Artist in overalls: the life of Grant Wood. Chronicle Bks. 1996 56p il map $15.95 (4 and up)   92

1. Artists—United States

ISBN 0-8118-1242-1   LC 95-34070

Follows the life of the Iowa farm boy who struggled to realize his talents and who painted in Paris but returned home to focus on the land and people he knew best

"The text provides a good, basic introduction to Wood's work and his life as an artist. Throughout the book, reproductions (most in full color) of the paintings and black-and-white photographs of the artist add greatly to the book's usefulness and visual appeal." Booklist

Wright, Orville, 1871-1948

Borden, Louise. Touching the sky: the flying adventures of Wilbur and Orville Wright; [by] Louise Borden & Trish Marx; illustrated by Peter Fiore. Margaret K. McElderry Bks. 2003 unp il maps $18.95 (3-5)   92

1. Wright, Wilbur, 1867-1912 2. Aeronautics—History

ISBN 0-689-84876-5   LC 2002-12041

A look at how the Wright Brothers became the first celebrities of the twentieth century through their 1909 public flying exhibitions in New York City and Germany

"Fiore's detailed watercolors dramatically and accurately record the two venues. The narrative, too, is laced with engaging facts that are successfully married to the pictures." SLJ

Busby, Peter. First to fly: how Wilbur & Orville Wright invented the airplane; paintings by David Craig; diagrams by Jack McMaster; historical consultation by Fred E. C. Culick. Crown 2002 32p il $19.95; lib bdg $21.99 (3-6)   92

1. Wright, Wilbur, 1867-1912 2. Aeronautics—History

ISBN 0-375-81287-3; 0-375-91287-8 (lib bdg)
LC 2002-849

"A Madison Press book"

A look at the lives of the Wright brothers, from their childhood interest in flight, through their study of successful gliders and other flying machines, to their triumphs at Kitty Hawk and beyond

"The pages are filled with large, sumptuous paintings that add a flavor of realism and an almost nostalgic feel. In addition, well-chosen images and reproductions help to inform the text. Archival photos from the Wright brothers' own collection and diagrams created by a mechanical engineer/aeronautics expert do much to help readers understand the concepts of flight. . . . This book engages readers quickly and maintains interest throughout." SLJ

Includes glossary and bibliographical references

Collins, Mary. Airborne: a photobiography of Wilbur and Orville Wright. National Geographic Soc. 2003 63p il maps $18.95 (4 and up)
92

1. Wright, Wilbur, 1867-1912 2. Aeronautics—History

ISBN 0-7922-6957-8   LC 2002-5279

Examines the lives of the Wright brothers and discusses their experiments and triumphs in the field of flight

"The well-chosen photos give readers a feel for Kitty Hawk—windy, sandy, solitary. This is an exceptionally well-informed picture of the Wright brothers and what their 100-year-old achievement really meant." SLJ

Freedman, Russell. The Wright brothers: how they invented the airplane; with original photographs by Wilbur and Orville Wright. Holiday House 1991 129p il $22.95 hardcover o.p.; pa $14.94   92

1. Wright, Wilbur, 1867-1912 2. Aeronautics—History

ISBN 0-8234-0875-2; 0-8234-1082-X (pa)
LC 90-48440

A Newbery Medal honor book, 1992

In this "combination of photography and text, Freedman reveals the frustrating, exciting, and ultimately suc-

Wright, Orville, 1871-1948—*Continued*
cessful journey of these two brothers from their bicycle shop in Dayton, Ohio, to their Kitty Hawk flights and beyond. . . . An essential purchase for younger YAs." Voice Youth Advocates

Includes bibliographical references

Old, Wendie. To fly: the story of the Wright brothers; illustrated by Robert Andrew Parker. Clarion Bks. 2002 48p il $16 (3-5) **92**
1. Wright, Wilbur, 1867-1912 2. Aeronautics—History
ISBN 0-618-13347-X   LC 2001-47219
Traces the work that the two Wright brothers did together to develop the first machine-powered aircraft.
"Old writes in a clear, straightforward manner, using intriguing details to enliven the account. . . . The innocence and optimism reflected in illustrations catch the tone of the story." Booklist

Includes bibliographical references

Wright, Wilbur, 1867-1912
Borden, Louise. Touching the sky: the flying adventures of Wilbur and Orville Wright. See entry under Wright, Orville, 1871-1948

Busby, Peter. First to fly: how Wilbur & Orville Wright invented the airplane. See entry under Wright, Orville, 1871-1948

Collins, Mary. Airborne: a photobiography of Wilbur and Orville Wright. See entry under Wright, Orville, 1871-1948

Freedman, Russell. The Wright brothers: how they invented the airplane. See entry under Wright, Orville, 1871-1948

Old, Wendie. To fly: the story of the Wright brothers. See entry under Wright, Orville, 1871-1948

Yep, Laurence
Yep, Laurence. The lost garden. Messner 1991 117p il (In my own words) (5 and up) **92**
1. Authors, American 2. Chinese Americans
LC 90-40647
Available in paperback from HarperCollins Pubs. pa $4.95 (0-688-13701-6)
The author describes how he grew up as a Chinese American in San Francisco and how he came to use his writing to celebrate his family and his ethnic heritage
"The writing is warm, wry, and humorous. . . . *The Lost Garden* will be welcomed as a literary autobiography for children and, more, a thoughtful probing into what it means to be an American." SLJ

Yolen, Jane
McGinty, Alice B. Meet Jane Yolen. PowerKids Press 2003 24p il (About the author) lib bdg $18.75 (1-3) **92**
1. Authors, American 2. Women authors
ISBN 0-8239-6407-8   LC 2002-116

A short biography of Jane Yolen, a prolific and well-known writer of juvenile literature
This "book is filled with vintage black-and-white and full-color photographs of . . . [Yolen] from early childhood to the present. Reprints of book covers, illustrations, and excerpts from the authors' works are also found throughout." SLJ

Includes glossary

Zaharias, Babe Didrikson, 1911-1956
Freedman, Russell. Babe Didrikson Zaharias; the making of a champion. Clarion Bks. 1999 192p il $18 (5 and up) **92**
1. Women athletes
ISBN 0-395-63367-2   LC 98-50208
A biography of Babe Didrikson, who broke records in golf, track and field, and other sports, at a time when there were few opportunities for female athletes
"Freedman's measured yet lively style captures the spirit of the great athlete. . . . Plenty of black-and-white photos capture Babe's spirit and dashing good looks; the documentation . . . is impeccable." Horn Book

Includes bibliographical references

929   Genealogy, names, insignia

Taylor, Maureen
Through the eyes of your ancestors. Houghton Mifflin 1999 86p il $17; pa $8.95 (4 and up) **929**
1. Genealogy
ISBN 0-395-86980-3; 0-395-86982-X (pa)
LC 98-8776
Discusses genealogy, the study of one's family, examining how such an interest develops, how to get started, how to use family stories and keepsakes, where to get help, and the positive effects of such study
"Motivated young researchers with adult help will find the book a good starting place." SLJ

Includes bibliographical references

929.9   Flags

Bateman, Teresa
Red, white, blue, and Uncle who? the stories behind some of America's patriotic symbols; illustrated by John O'Brien. Holiday House 2001 64p il $16.95; pa $6.95 (4 and up) **929.9**
1. National emblems 2. National monuments
ISBN 0-8234-1285-7; 0-8234-1784-0 (pa)
LC 00-57258
This "volume presents 17 'patriotic symbols,' an umbrella term that encompasses everything from the flag to Uncle Sam, from Mount Rushmore to the Korean War Memorial. Bateman finds plenty of interesting information to share about each symbol or site, and browsers will be entertained by the many stories of origination, construction, and history." Booklist

Includes bibliographical references

Haban, Rita D.

How proudly they wave; flags of the fifty states. Lerner Publs. 1989 111p il lib bdg $23.95 (4 and up) **929.9**

1. Flags—United States

ISBN 0-8225-1799-X   LC 89-2302

"Haban presents full-color pictures of the 50 state flags. . . . Two-page descriptions explain who designed the flag, what the design means, and when each flag was officially adopted. . . . A glossary lists flag-related terms, and an accompanying diagram shows the parts of a flag. An enormously useful reference source for both school and public librarians." Booklist

Smith, Whitney

Flag lore of all nations. Millbrook Press 2001 112p il map $29.90; pa $12.95 (4 and up) **929.9**

1. Flags

ISBN 0-7613-1753-8; 0-7613-1899-2 (pa)

LC 00-48973

"Arranged alphabetically, each country's flag is illustrated, with an accompanying text covering its history, symbolism, and lore, if appropriate. . . . With two countries per page, readers can easily locate the material. Flags and any images on them are crisply and cleanly displayed, with colors remaining true." SLJ

Includes glossary and bibliographical references

930   History of ancient world to ca.499

Merrill, Yvonne Young

Hands-on ancient people. Kits Pub. 2003-2004 2v il map pa ea $20 (5 and up) **930**

1. Ancient civilization 2. Handicraft

ISBN 0-9643177-8-8 (v1); 0-9643177-9-6 (v2)

Contents: v1 Art activities about Mesopotamia, Egypt, and Islam; v2 Art activities about Minoans, Trojans, Ancient Greeks, Etruscans and Romans

Each volume offers instructions for creating 60 objects based on ancient artifacts such as a cardboard model of the Parthenon, masks, Greek vases, war shields, mosaics, toys, banners, tomb paintings, a wheel, board games, and the ziggurat.

"These exciting art projects are illustrated with dramatic full-page, full-color photographs. Each activity occupies an inviting spread with a list of materials, clear instructions, and background information on the artifacts and the culture they represent." SLJ [review of v2]

Includes bibliographical references

930.1   Archaeology

Barnes, Trevor

Archaeology; foreword by Tony Robinson. Kingfisher 2004 63p il map (Kingfisher knowledge) $11.95 (5 and up) **930.1**

1. Archeology

ISBN 0-7534-5768-7

Explores the science of excavating and examining the debris of centuries of human life, from the Iron Age to recent history

Includes glossary and bibliographical references

Deem, James M.

Bodies from the bog. Houghton Mifflin 1998 42p il $16; pa $5.95 (4 and up) **930.1**

1. Mummies 2. Prehistoric peoples 3. Archeology

ISBN 0-395-85784-8; 0-618-35402-6 (pa)

LC 97-12010

Describes the discovery of bog bodies in northern Europe and the evidence which their remains reveal about themselves and the civilizations in which they lived

"The text is engaging and accessible, and the starkly dramatic photos are given dignity by the spacious and understated page design." Horn Book Guide

Getz, David

Frozen man; illustrated by Peter McCarty. Holt & Co. 1994 68p il maps $14.95; pa $8.95 (5 and up) **930.1**

1. Mummies 2. Prehistoric peoples 3. Archeology

ISBN 0-8050-3261-4; 0-8050-4645-3 (pa)

LC 94-9109

"A Redfeather book"

"This is an account of the mummified stone-age corpse who was found in Austria in 1991. . . . Getz's generally well-organized information and smooth exposition makes the effort to understand the Iceman, as this book calls him, into an intriguing detective story. This could well stimulate the interest of kids who didn't think they liked science or archeology. Black-and-white drawings include useful maps and diagrams." Bull Cent Child Books

Includes glossary and bibliographical references

McIntosh, Jane

Archeology; written by Jane McIntosh. Dorling Kindersley 2000 63p il (DK eyewitness books) $15.99; lib bdg $19.99 (4 and up) **930.1**

1. Archeology

ISBN 0-7894-5864-0; 0-7894-6605-8 (lib bdg)

First published 1994 by Knopf

This book contains "photographs, illustrations, and terms covering the specialized field of archeology. Inside are a contents page, an index, and 26 sections of two to three pages each, covering . . . the various techniques used by archeologists and historians to learn about past civilizations." Sci Books Films [review of 1994 edition]

Panchyk, Richard

Archaeology for kids; uncovering the mysteries of our past: 25 activities. Chicago Review Press 2001 146p il map pa $14.95 (5 and up)

930.1

1. Archeology 2. Ancient civilization 3. Antiquities

ISBN 1-55652-395-5   LC 2001-42134

Twenty five activities support an overview of the science of archaeology as well as some of the secrets it has revealed from ancient civilizations throughout the world

"Panchyk explains things clearly and vividly. . . . Illustrations are plentiful, and suggested activities are practical and illuminate the subject matter well." Booklist

Includes bibliographical references

Reinhard, Johan

Discovering the Inca Ice Maiden; my adventures on Ampato. National Geographic Soc. 1998 48p il $17.95 (5 and up)   **930.1**

1. Mummies 2. Peru—Antiquities 3. Incas 4. Archeology

ISBN 0-7922-7142-4   LC 97-31291

A first-person account of the 1995 discovery of the over 500-year-old Peruvian ice mummy on Mount Ampato and a description of the subsequent retrieval and scientific study.

"Vibrant color photographs of the mummy and Incan artifacts found on the expedition illustrate the engrossing text." Horn Book Guide

Includes glossary

931 China to 420 A.D.

Cole, Joanna

Ms. Frizzle's adventures: Imperial China; illustrated by Bruce Degen. Scholastic Press 2005 39p il $16.95 (2-4)   **931**

1. China—Civilization 2. China—History

ISBN 0-590-10822-0

Ms. Frizzle and her tour group are transported to China 1000 years in the past, where they learn how rice, tea and silk are grown and harvested, and visit the Emperor in the Forbidden City.

"Readers will savor sidebars touting Chinese contributions to society, pore over Degen's delightfully cluttered compositions and lovely chinoiserie embellishments." Booklist

Cotterell, Arthur

Ancient China; written by Arthur Cotterell. rev ed. Dorling Kindersley 2005 63p il map (DK eyewitness books) $15.99 (4 and up)   **931**

1. China—Civilization

ISBN 0-7566-1391-4

First published 1994 by Knopf

"This volume touches upon such topics as Chinese history, the first emperor, inventions, health and medicine, waterways, food and drink, clothing, the Silk Road, and arts and crafts. Material from as recent as the last dynasty, which ended in 1911, is included." SLJ [review of 1994 edition]

Dean, Arlan

Terra-cotta soldiers; army of stone; [by] Arlan Dean. Children's Press 2005 48p il map (Digging up the past) lib bdg $23; pa $6.95 (4 and up)

931

1. Ch'in Shih-huang, Emperor of China, 259-210 B.C.—Tomb 2. China—Antiquities

ISBN 0-516-25124-4 (lib bdg); 0-516-25093-0 (pa)
                LC 2005002699

"Hi-lo interest books"

This "discusses ancient Chinese history, including the first emperor and his tomb, which was found to contain 8000 clay soldiers, made to protect him in his afterlife. Beliefs about life after death are explained. The author also discusses Qin Shi Huangdis role in creating the Great Wall." SLJ

This consists of "short chapters, with text sharing space with mostly snapshot-size photos. . . . Reluctant readers at ease with the High Interest series format may want to start with this." Booklist

Includes glossary and bibliographical references

O'Connor, Jane

The emperor's silent army; terracotta warriors of Ancient China. Viking 2002 48p il $17.99 (4 and up)   **931**

1. Ch'in Shih-huang, Emperor of China, 259-210 B.C.—Tomb 2. China—Antiquities

ISBN 0-670-03512-2   LC 2001-46900

Describes the archaeological discovery of thousands of life-sized terracotta warrior statues in northern China in 1974, and discusses the emperor who had them created and placed near his tomb

"This intriguing book is enhanced by beautiful illustrations—pictures of stone engravings, colorful paintings, drawings, and maps—while numerous photographs show the clay soldiers from different perspectives. . . . The author's writing style is entertaining, yet informative." Book Rep

Includes bibliographical references

Schomp, Virginia

The ancient Chinese; written by Virginia Schomp. Franklin Watts 2004 112p il map (People of the ancient world) $29.50; pa $9.95 (5 and up)

931

1. China—Civilization

ISBN 0-531-11817-7; 0-531-16737-2 (pa)
                LC 2004-2174

Contents: At the center of the world; Kings and emperors; Civil servants and nobles; Philosophers and holy men; Peasant farmers and soldiers; Artisans and silk makers; Merchants and traders; Inventors, scientists, and healers; Writers and artists; The legacy of ancient China

"Focusing mainly on the Shang, Zhou, Qin, and Han dynasties, this book explores ancient China through its social structure. It takes a look at its people and details the duties of an emperor, the activities of a merchant, and . . . more. It also describes some of the discoveries and writings that have led to our present-day understanding of this . . . civilization." Publisher's note

"Crisp reproductions of visuals, along with impressive ancilliary content. . . . help make [this title] among the best available on ancient [China]." Booklist

Includes bibliographical references

Shuter, Jane

Ancient China; [by] Jane Shuter. Heinemann Library 2006 48p il map (Excavating the past) lib bdg $31.43 (4-6)   **931**

1. China—Civilization 2. China—Antiquities 3. Excavations (Archeology)—China

ISBN 1-4034-5995-9   LC 2005009178

"Ancient China covers the region's history from the first single kingdom dynasty, Xia (2205 B.C.E. to 1700 B.C.E), to the conquering of China by Mongols in C.E.1279. Shuter includes a history of archaeology conducted by Westerners and by the Chinese government. Artifacts and a few well-preserved burial sites reveal lifestyles of the powerful and wealthy. Short chapters describe living conditions of the poor and of skilled workers as well." SLJ

Includes bibliographical references

932   Egypt to 640 A.D.

Biesty, Stephen

Egypt in spectacular cross-section; text by Stewart Ross. Scholastic Nonfiction 2005 28p il $18.99 (4 and up)   **932**

1. Egypt—Antiquities 2. Egypt—Civilization

ISBN 0-439-74537-3   LC 2004-59185

"Employing his large, trademark cross-section or cutaway style illustrations that are full of detail and bustling small figures, Biesty, supported by Ross, uses the fictional construct of family members traveling to a wedding as a way of exploring various aspects of daily life in Egypt around the year 1230 B.C.E." SLJ

Includes glossary

Chrisp, Peter

Ancient Egypt revealed; written by Peter Chrisp. DK Pub. 2002 37p il map $12.99 (4 and up)   **932**

1. Egypt—Civilization

ISBN 0-7894-8883-3   LC 2003-268199

"Each spread covers a different topic about life on the Nile, such as rulers and gods, warriors, notions of beauty, craftsmanship, methods of writing, techniques for building tombs, and mummification." Booklist

"A dazzling look at Egyptian artifacts and architecture. Hundreds of excellent-quality, captioned, full-color photographs and reproductions demonstrate various aspects of culture and life. . . . This spectacular presentation is easy to read and a delight to browse through." SLJ

Frank, John

The tomb of the boy king; a true story in verse; pictures by Tom Pohrt. Foster Bks. 2001 unp il $16 (3-6)   **932**

1. Tutankhamen, King of Egypt—Tomb 2. Carter, Howard, 1874-1939

ISBN 0-374-37674-3   LC 99-27597

Tells, in rhyming text, the story of Howard Carter's efforts to find Tutankhamen's tomb and of what he did discover in the Valley of the Kings

"When read aloud the text is full and dynamic, packing in an amazing amount of information. . . . Pohrt's colored pencil and ink artwork . . . is expertly executed and has the feel of a book or magazine from Carter's time." Booklist

Giblin, James

Secrets of the Sphinx; by James Cross Giblin; illustrated by Bagram Ibatoulline. Scholastic Press 2004 47p il map $17.95 (4 and up)   **932**

1. Egypt—Antiquities 2. Egypt—Civilization

ISBN 0-590-09847-0   LC 2003-19666

Discusses some of Egypt's most famous artifacts and monuments, including the pyramids, the Rosetta Stone, and, especially, the Great Sphinx, presenting research and speculation about their origins and their future

"In his signature plain style the . . . author presents a wealth of scholarship. . . . He vividly conveys the drama of recent discoveries. . . . The photorealistic gouache and watercolor illustrations are beautiful." Booklist

Includes bibliographical references

Hawass, Zahi A.

Curse of the pharaohs; my adventures with mummies. National Geographic Society 2004 144p il $19.95; lib bdg $29.90 (5 and up)   **932**

1. Egypt—Antiquities 2. Archeology

ISBN 0-7922-6963-2; 0-7922-6665-X (lib bdg)

     LC 2003-18813

"Hawass delineates and attempts to debunk the alleged curses attached to the entering of the pharaohs' tombs." Publ Wkly

"Hawass' writing is passionate, informative, and kid friendly. . . . Even so, what will probably most attract aspiring archeologists are the National Geographic-quality photographs, which lend tantalizing immediacy to real-life tales from the crypt." Booklist

Includes glossary and bibliographical references

Tutankhamun; the mystery of the boy king; by Zahi Hawass. National Geographic 2005 64p il $17.95; lib bdg $27.90 (3-6)   **932**

1. Tutankhamen, King of Egypt 2. Egypt—Civilization 3. Egypt—History

ISBN 0-7922-8354-6; 0-7922-8355-4 (lib bdg)

     LC 2004-15002

Contents: The great discovery; Egypt before Tutankhamun; Tutankhamun, king of Egypt; The life of the boy king; Death and burial; After King Tut

"Hawass, director of excavations at the Giza pyramids and head of Egypt's archaeological council, . . . offers a solid summary . . . of the complex and controversial 18th dynasty in which Tut lived. . . . Black-and-white shots from the past join rich color photographs that almost glow. Especially marvelous is a stunning recreation, employing current reconstructive techniques, of what Tut might have looked like. . . . A first-rate investigation enriched by beautiful artwork." SLJ

Includes bibliographical references

Langley, Andrew

Ancient Egypt; [by] Andrew Langley. Raintree 2005 48p il map (History in art) $31.43 (4 and up)
932

1. Egyptian art 2. Egypt—Civilization
ISBN 1-4109-0518-7   LC 2004-7524

Contents: Art of ancient Egypt; Art as evidence; Beginnings; The old kingdom; The middle kingdom; The new kingdom; Land of the pharaohs; Building the pyramids; Trade and empire; The Valley of the Kings; Greeks and Romans; Homes and families; Eating and drinking; At work; Entertainment; Scribes and hieroglyphs; Gods and the afterlife; Mummification; Burial; Priests and rituals

This book has "a depth of content that is unusual in art-history books for this age group. . . . [It] is amply illustrated with full-color photographs and reproductions. . . . Well-written, informative." SLJ

Includes bibliographical references

Logan, Claudia

The 5,000-year-old puzzle; solving a mystery of Ancient Egypt; illustrated by Melissa Sweet. Farrar, Straus & Giroux 2001 41p il $17 (2-4)
932

1. Reisner, George Andrew, 1867-1942 2. Egypt—Civilization 3. Excavations (Archeology)
ISBN 0-374-32335-6   LC 00-60243
"Melanie Kroupa books"
With the cooperation of the Museum of Fine Arts, Boston

An account of Dr. George Reisner's 1925 discovery and excavation of a secret tomb in Giza, Egypt, based on archival documents and records, but told through the fictionalized experiences of a young boy named Will who accompanies his father on the dig.

"There's considerable value to the sidebar information . . . and the journal-style exposition of the excavation's painstaking pace. Snapshots and photographed artifacts from the expedition mingle with Sweet's golden acrylic and watercolor scenes, and readers who patiently sift through the fictional bits will be rewarded with an intriguing glimpse of an important excavation." Bull Cent Child Books

Malam, John

Ancient Egyptian jobs. Heinemann Lib. 2003 48p il map (People in the past) $29.93; pa $8.50 (5 and up)
932

1. Egypt—Civilization
ISBN 1-4034-0311-2; 1-4034-0515-8 (pa)
LC 2002-12595
Contents: Egypt: gift of the Nile; Who worked in ancient Egypt?; Organizing the workforce; Professions of ancient Egypt; Priest; Doctor; Merchant; Dancer; Farmer; Fisher; Hunter; Baker; Carpenter; Spinner and weaver; Jeweler; Who built the tombs of ancient Egypt?; Pyramid builder; Artist; Embalmer; How do we know?

This "volume begins with a brief introduction that offers geographical and historical background. [It] covers an assortment of workers including scribe, priest, dancer, baker, hunter, pyramid builder, and embalmer. Training, daily routines, and other pertinent information is includ-

ed. . . . Color photographs of sites and artifacts and maps enhance the [presentation]. Insets provide additional tidbits of information." SLJ

Includes bibliographical references

Nardo, Don

King Tut's tomb; by Don Nardo. KidHaven Press 2005 48p il map (Wonders of the world) lib bdg $23.70 (3-6)
932

1. Tutankhamen, King of Egypt 2. Egypt—Civilization
ISBN 0-7377-2352-1   LC 2004-17024
Contents: The brief life of a boy-king; The discovery of Tut's tomb; The tomb's fabulous contents; The curse : scary or silly?; How did King Tut die?

"Nardo covers the life of King Tut and devotes a chapter to speculation as to how he died, as well as the discovery of his tomb and its contents. Beautiful, colorful photographs and reproductions round out the nicely prepared text." SLJ

Includes bibliographical references

Perl, Lila

The ancient Egyptians; written by Lila Perl. Franklin Watts 2004 112p il map (People of the ancient world) $29.50; pa $9.95 (5 and up)
932

1. Egypt—Civilization
ISBN 0-531-12345-6; 0531-16738-0 (pa)
LC 2004-1940
Contents: How we know about ancient Egypt; Farmers, bakers, and brewers; Priests and scribes; Kings, queens, and pharaohs; Builders in stone; Quarrymen and craft workers; Warriors and captives; Mummy makers; The legacy of ancient Egypt

"Crisp reproductions of visuals, along with impressive ancillary content. . . . help make [this title] among the best available on ancient [Egypt]." Booklist

Includes bibliographical references

Smith, Stuart Tyson

Valley of the Kings; [by] Stuart Tyson Smith and Nancy Stone Bernard. Oxford Univ. Press 2002 47p il map (Digging for the past) $19.95 (4 and up)
932

1. Egypt—Antiquities
ISBN 0-19-514770-7   LC 2002-4288
Contents: Tourists and plunderers; Explorers, observers, and patrons; Sensation of the century; The last lost tomb?; Where did all the mummies go?; Interview with Stuart Tyson Smith

Explores Egypt's Valley of the Kings, a vast burial ground containing more than seventy tombs, and discusses archaeologists' findings and challenges during nearly two hundred years of excavation

"The easy-to-read text is enhanced by good-quality, color photographs of artifacts, period photographs, reproductions of artwork, and maps." SLJ

Includes glossary and bibliographical references

Taylor, John H.

Mummy; the inside story. Abrams 2004 48p il map pa $14.95 (5 and up)   **932**

1. Mummies 2. Egypt—Antiquities

ISBN 0-8109-9181-0

Using non-invasive cutting-edge technology, this exhibit by the British Museum reveals the secrets of one mummy, the priest Nesperennub, while leaving him undisturbed.

"There are many excellent mummy books available, but this one explores the impact and potential of cutting-edge technology especially well." SLJ

933   Palestine to 70 A.D.

Waldman, Neil

Masada; written and illustrated by Neil Waldman. Boyds Mills Press 2003 c1998 64p il map $18.95 (4 and up)   **933**

1. Jews—History 2. Excavations (Archeology) 3. Masada Site (Israel)

ISBN 1-59078-063-9

A reissue of the title first published 1998 by Morrow Junior Bks.

Discusses the history of Masada, from the building of Herod's Temple through its use by Zealots as a refuge from the Romans to its rediscovery in the mid-20th century

"Dramatic illustrations and two large maps, all in charcoal shades of acrylic and India ink, show realistic scenes, many of them painted from photos, relief sculptures, and artifacts found during the excavation of Masada." SLJ

Includes glossary and bibliographical references

934   India to 647 A.D.

Schomp, Virginia

Ancient India; written by Virginia Schomp. 1st ed. Franklin Watts 2005 112p il map (People of the ancient world) lib bdg $30.50; pa $9.95 (5 and up)   **934**

1. India—Civilization

ISBN 0-531-12379-0 (lib bdg); 0-531-16846-8 (pa)

LC 2004-25156

Contents: Brahman priests; Kings, queens, and princes; Government leaders and warriors; Farmers and merchants; Servants, laborers, and craftspeople; Outcastes and slaves; Poets and playwrights

This examines the society of ancient India through its "literature, artifacts, and documents. Religion, farming, levels of society, art, government, and fine arts are covered in [this] well-written and attractive [book]. . . . Quality full-color photos and reproductions on glossy pages will give readers insight into the daily lives, arts, and contributions of [this culture.]" SLJ

Includes bibliographical references

935   Mesopotamia and Iranian Plateau to 637 A.D.

Chrisp, Peter

Mesopotamia; Iraq in ancient times. Enchanted Lion 2004 32p il (Picturing the past) $15.95 (5 and up)   **935**

1. Iraq—Civilization

ISBN 1-59270-024-1

This introduction to Mesopotamia "covers such topics as farming, writing, craft, trade, domestic life, religion, warfare, burial, kingship and law. [It includes descriptions of] artifacts, . . . geographical sites, and archaeological evidence." Publisher's note

"Brief but substantive, [this] attractive [title] will spark students' curiosity about the specifics of ancient life and the importance of archaeology." Booklist

Includes glossary and bibliographical references

Schomp, Virginia

Ancient Mesopotamia; the Sumerians, Babylonians, and Assyrians; written by Virginia Schomp. Franklin Watts 2004 112p il map (People of the ancient world) $29.50; pa $9.95 (5 and up)   **935**

1. Iraq—Civilization

ISBN 0-531-11818-5; 0-531-16741-0 (pa)

LC 2004-1947

Contents: Cradle of civilization; The warrior-kings; Nobles, government officials, and priests; Merchants and traders; Artisans and artists; Peasant farmers; Soldiers and slaves; Doctors and scientists; Scribes and poets; The legacy of ancient Mesopotamia

"This book explores the cultures of ancient Mesopotamia through their social structure. It takes a look at the people and details the duties of a king, the activities of a peasant farmer, and . . . more. It also describes some of the discoveries and writings that have led to our present-day understanding of this . . . civilization." Publisher's note

"Crisp reproductions of visuals, along with impressive ancillary content . . . help make [this title] among the best available on ancient [Mesopotamia]." Booklist

Includes bibliographical references

Shuter, Jane

Mesopotamia; [by] Jane Shuter. Heinemann Library 2006 48p il map (Excavating the past) lib bdg $31.43 (4-6)   **935**

1. Iraq—Antiquities 2. Sumerians 3. Excavations (Archeology)—Iraq

ISBN 1-4034-5998-3   LC 2005009177

Contents: Archaeology and Mesopotamia; Rediscovering the Sumerians; The importance of writing; City-states; What was a city like?; Outside the city; Beliefs and burials; Temples; Burial and the afterlife; Royal tombs; Daily life; Skilled work; Travel and trade; Archaeology in modern Iraq

"Photos, maps, diagrams, and sidebars combine with an accessible text to demonstrate the roles of archaeological discoveries and scientific advancement in providing an accurate history of [this] ancient civilization." Horn Book Guide

936 Europe north and west of Italian peninsula to ca. 499 A.D.

Calvert, Patricia

The ancient Celts; written by Patricia Calvert. Watts 2005 112p il map (People of the ancient world) $29.50; pa $9.95 (5 and up) **936**

1. Celts

ISBN 0-531-12359-6; 0-531-16845-X (pa)

This book portrays the lives of the ancient Celts "by examining their arts, culture, economy, government, religious beliefs, and societal [structure]. . . . Attractively designed and illustrated, the [book features] excellent color representations of architecture, artwork, and other cultural and historical artifacts." SLJ

Includes bibliographical references

936.1 Scotland to 410 A.D.

Arnold, Caroline

Stone Age farmers beside the sea; Scotland's prehistoric village of Skara Brae; photographs by Arthur P. Arnold. Clarion Bks. 1997 48p il map $15.95 (4 and up) **936.1**

1. Scotland—Antiquities 2. Prehistoric peoples

ISBN 0-395-77601-5 LC 96-20021

Describes the Stone Age settlement preserved in the sand dunes on one of Scotland's Orkney Islands, telling how it was discovered and what it reveals about life in prehistoric times

Arnold "carefully distinguishes between what is known and what is surmised about the people who lived at Skara Brae. . . . The photos' clear images, subtle colors, and pleasing compositions give the book its pervasive sense of beauty." Booklist

Includes glossary

937 Roman Empire

Biesty, Stephen

Rome: in spectacular cross section; text by Andrew Solway. Scholastic Nonfiction 2003 29p il $18.95 (4 and up) **937**

1. Rome—Civilization 2. Rome—Social life and customs

ISBN 0-439-45546-4 LC 2002-70694

Detailed illustrations with explanatory captions and narrative text survey some sites in ancient Rome, including the house of a wealthy family, the Colosseum, the Baths of Trajan, and the Temple of Jupiter

This "is a visually intriguing, reader-friendly introduction to ancient Rome." Booklist

Includes glossary

Blacklock, Dyan

The Roman Army; the legendary soldiers who created an empire; illustrations by David Kennett. Walker & Company 2004 48p il map $17.95; lib bdg $18.85 (4 and up) **937**

1. Rome—Military history

ISBN 0-8027-8896-3; 0-8027-8897-1 (lib bdg)

LC 2003-57574

An illustrated history of the Roman Army, including information about its composition, organization, training, methods, weapons, and campaigns.

"Blacklock's writing is clear and lively and the book, packed with dramatic cartoon illustrations, will captivate readers." SLJ

Includes bibliographical references

Caselli, Giovanni

In search of Pompeii; uncovering a buried Roman city; written and illustrated by Giovanni Caselli. Bedrick Bks. 1999 44p il (In search of) $18.95 (3-5) **937**

1. Pompeii (Extinct city)

ISBN 0-87226-545-5 LC 99-21352

Describes the discovery and excavation of the ruins of the ancient city of Pompeii, buried by the eruption of Mount Vesuvius in 79 A.D., and what has been learned about life there

Corbishley, Mike

Ancient Rome. rev ed. Facts on File 2003 96p il map (Cultural atlas for young people) $35 (5 and up) **937**

1. Rome—History 2. Rome—Civilization

ISBN 0-8160-5147-X LC 2003-40258

Text, maps, illustrations, charts, tables, and chronologies depict the history, society, and political life of ancient Rome and its vast empire

This is "valuable for research and for a brief overview of the history of [this civilization.]" SLJ

Includes glossary and bibliographical references

Deem, James M.

Bodies from the ash. Houghton Mifflin 2005 50p il $16 (4 and up) **937**

1. Pompeii (Extinct city)

ISBN 0-618-47308-4 LC 2004-26553

"On August 24, 79 C.E., the long-silent Mt. Vesuvius erupted, and volcanic ash rained down on the 20,000 residents of Pompeii. This photo-essay explains what happened when the volcano exploded—and how the results of this disaster were discovered hundreds of years later. . . . [This offers an] enormous amount of information. . . . But the jewels here are the numerous . . . photographs, especially those featuring the plaster casts and skeletons of people in their death throes. . . . Excellent for browsers as well as researchers." Booklist

James, Simon

Ancient Rome; written by Simon James. rev ed. DK Pub. 2004 72p il (DK eyewitness books) $15.99; lib bdg $19.99 **937**

1. Rome—Civilization 2. Rome—Antiquities

ISBN 0-7566-0651-9; 0-7566-0650-0 (lib bdg)

First published 1990 by Knopf

A photo essay documenting ancient Rome and the people who lived there as revealed through the many artifacts they left behind, including shields, swords, tools, toys, cosmetics, and jewelry.

Lassieur, Allison

The ancient Romans; written by Allison Lassieur. Franklin Watts 2004 112p il map (People of the ancient world) lib bdg $29.50; pa $9.95 (5 and up) **937**

1. Rome—Civilization

ISBN 0-531-12338-3 (lib bdg); 0-531-16742-9 (pa)

LC 2004-1955

Contents: The rulers of Rome; Power and influence of the Roman senate; People of the Roman government; Scholars and writers; Soldiers and the Roman army; The lives of Roman women; Priests and the Roman religion; Architects and engineers; Working-class Romans; Slaves and slavery; Legacy of the Roman empire

"This attractive, thorough, and comprehensible book . . . offers a stellar introduction to life in ancient Rome." Booklist

Includes bibliographical references

Osborne, Mary Pope

Pompeii; lost & found; frescoes by Bonnie Christensen. Knopf 2006 unp il $16.95; lib ed $18.99 **937**

1. Pompeii (Extinct city)

ISBN 0-375-82889-3; 0-375-92889-8 (lib ed)

LC 2005-09331

"After brief accounts of the events of 79 A.D. and the first archaeological investigations of the city that lay beneath the fields surrounding Mt. Vesuvius, Osborne's straightforward text focuses on the life at Pompeii at the time of the volcano's eruption. . . . Christensen's distinctive, haunting frescoes are reminiscent of the art found throughout the site. . . . Osborne's text . . . will serve as an enticing introduction to this legendary city frozen in time." SLJ

Watkins, Richard Ross

Gladiator; by Richard Watkins. Houghton Mifflin 1997 80p il map $17; pa $7.95 (4 and up) **937**

1. Gladiators 2. Rome—Social life and customs

ISBN 0-395-82656-X; 0-618-07032-X (pa)

LC 96-21107

Describes the history of gladiators, including types of armor, use of animals, amphitheaters, and how the practice fit into Roman society for almost 700 years

"In a balanced treatment of a potentially sensational topic, Watkins provides colorfully written, detailed accounts of the fights as well as pithy discussions of what gladiators meant to the Romans and what they tell us

about Roman society. . . . The solid gray-and-white drawings illustrate the text effectively." Booklist

Includes glossary and bibliographical references

938 Greece to 323 A.D.

Hart, Avery

Ancient Greece! 40 hands-on activities to experience this wondrous age; [by] Avery Hart & Paul Mantell; illustrations by Michael Kline. Williamson 1999 104p il pa $12.95 (4 and up) **938**

1. Greece—Civilization 2. Handicraft

ISBN 1-885593-25-2 LC 98-35762

"A Kaleidoscope Kids book"

Introduces the places, people, historical events, myths, culture, and philosophy of ancient Greece. Includes forty hands-on activities, such as making an early Greek theater, building an Ionic temple, and pressing olives for oil

This is "a clever title that encourages learning and creativity." SLJ

Includes bibliographical references

Lassieur, Allison

The ancient Greeks; written by Allison Lassieur. Franklin Watts 2004 112p il map (People of the ancient world) $29.50 (5 and up) **938**

1. Greece—Civilization

ISBN 0-531-12339-1 LC 2004-1942

Contents: The people of the government; Scientists of Greece; Greek athletes and sport; Philosophers and thinkers; Priests, priestesses, and the Greek religion; Poets and playwrights; Artists and architects; Warriors; Slaves and workers; Legacy of the ancient Greeks

This title offers "useful information that would help report writers and would also engage interested readers." SLJ

Includes bibliographical references

Malam, John

Ancient Greece. Enchanted Lion 2004 32p il map (Picturing the past) $15.95 (5 and up) **938**

1. Greece—Civilization 2. Greece—Antiquities

ISBN 1-59270-022-5

This "touches on such topics as ancient Greek religion, sport, theater, and government, each one introduced with an accompanying image of painted pottery, a statue, or photos of the present-day ruins of ancient structures. . . . Brief but substantive, [this] attractive [title] will spark students' curiosity about the specifics of ancient life and the importance of archaeology." Booklist

Includes bibliographical references

Pearson, Anne

Ancient Greece. DK Pub. 2004 72p il map (DK eyewitness books) $15.99; lib bdg $19.99 (4 and up) **938**

1. Greece—Civilization

ISBN 0-7566-0649-7; 0-7566-0648-9 (lib bdg)

LC 2004304193

Pearson, Anne—_Continued_
First published 1992 by Knopf
Describes the land, history, and civilization of ancient Greece.

Powell, Anton
Ancient Greece; updated by Sean Sheehan. rev ed. Facts on File 2003 96p il map (Cultural atlas for young people) $35 (5 and up)   **938**
1. Greece—History—0-323 2. Greece—Civilization
ISBN 0-8160-5146-1   LC 2003-40864
First published 1989
Maps, charts, illustrations, and text explore the history and culture of Ancient Greece
This is "valuable for research and for a brief overview of the history of [this civilization.]" SLJ
Includes glossary and bibliographical references

Stefoff, Rebecca
The ancient Mediterranean. Benchmark Books 2004 c2005 48p il map (World historical atlases) lib bdg $18.95 (5 and up)   **938**
1. Mediterranean region—History 2. Greece—History—0-323 3. Rome—Civilization 4. Greece—Civilization
ISBN 0-7614-1641-2   LC 2003-12027
Contents: Greece: Bronze Age ancestors; The Dark Age; Greek civilization is born; The Persian wars; Athens against Sparta; Alexander's empire: Macedonian might; To rule the world; The Hellenistic age; Conquest by Rome; Rome: The Kingdom; The Republic; Conquest and war; The birth of an empire; East and West; An empire falls
Text plus historical and contemporary maps provide a look at the history of cultures that flourished along the Mediterranean Sea
The text is "clearly written and well organized. The [book includes] large, full-color photographs and illustrations reproduced from original pieces of art found in diverse national museums. Maps placed throughout clearly show the boundaries and areas of the empires. [This volume makes an] excellent [supplement] to history lessons and [a] good starting [point] for research." SLJ

939   Other parts of ancient world to ca. 640

Sonneborn, Liz
The ancient Kushites. Franklin Watts 2005 112p il map (People of the ancient world) lib bdg $30.50; pa $9.95 (5 and up)   **939**
1. Cushites
ISBN 0-531-12380-4 (lib bdg); 0-531-16847-6 (pa)
          LC 2004-13908
This book portrays the lives of the ancient Kushites "by examining their arts, culture, economy, government, religious beliefs, and societal [structure]. . . . Attractively designed and illustrated, the [book features] excellent color representations of architecture, artwork, and other cultural and historical artifacts." SLJ
Includes bibliographical references

Stefoff, Rebecca
The ancient Near East; [by] Rebecca Stefoff. Benchmark Books 2004 c2005 48p il map (World historical atlases) lib bdg $27.07 (5 and up)
          939
1. Middle East—History 2. Middle East—Civilization
ISBN 0-7614-1639-0   LC 2003-12030
Contents: Mesopotamia – Empires and invasions: Beginnings; The rise of city-states; Sumer and Akkad; Babylonia and Assyria; The Persian conquest; Anatolia – Cultures of the crossroads: Where three worlds meet; Early Anatolian states; Trade and war; The Hittite empire; Phrygia and Lydia; Egypt – Land of the river: Before the pharaohs; The old kingdom; The middle kingdom; The new kingdom; Foreign rulers
Text plus historical and contemporary maps provide a look at the history of the Ancient Near East
This is "clearly written and well organized. The [book includes] large, full-color photographs and illustrations reproduced from original pieces of art found in diverse national museums. . . . [This volume makes an] excellent [supplement] to history lessons and [a] good starting [point] for research." SLJ
Includes bibliographical references

940   History of Europe

Peoples of Europe. Benchmark Bks. 2002 c2003 11v il map set $329.95 (5 and up)   **940**
1. Europe—Encyclopedias
ISBN 0-7614-7378-5   LC 2002-19490
Contents: v1 Albania–Belgium; v2 Bosnia and Herzegovina–Czech Republic; v3 Denmark–France; v4 Germany–Hungary; v5 Iceland–Liechtenstein; v6 Lithuania–Netherlands; v7 Norway–Romania; v8 Russia–Slovakia; v9 Slovenia–Switzerland; v10 Ukraine–Yugoslavia; v11 Index volume
This "set 'uses geography and national identity to organize information' on 44 countries. Entries are arranged alphabetically by country. Each contains a short introduction to the country, including its landscape, climate, and history. . . . All of the following areas are treated: religion, housing, clothing, language, health and education, food and drink, family and social life, and art and music. Political upheavals, economic turmoil and hardship, war, and ethnic disputes are covered with commendable frankness and clarity. . . . Given the wealth of information, excellent indexing, and attractive format, this is a recommended purchase for middle-school, high-school, and public libraries." Booklist
Includes bibliographical references

940.1   Europe--Early history to 1453

Aliki
A medieval feast; written and illustrated by Aliki. Crowell 1983 unp il lib bdg $15.89; pa $6.95 (2-5)   **940.1**
1. Dining—History 2. Courts and courtiers 3. Medieval civilization 4. Festivals—History
ISBN 0-690-04246-9 (lib bdg); 0-06-446050-9 (pa)
          LC 82-45923

Aliki—*Continued*

"In pictures of minute, charming detail and vibrant, translucent colors, Aliki takes us through the ritual of preparation and the enthusiastic consumption of a medieval feast served to a king and his retinue when they stop for a few days at Camdenton Manor. Not to be outdone by the art, the text has its own various facets. There is the fictional story set in type outside the art and there is within the paintings a collection of delightful historical, gastronomical, agricultural, and zoological facts printed by hand. And throughout the spendid whole are border decorations worthy of the great illuminated manuscripts." Child Book Rev Serv

Chrisp, Peter

Town and country life; by Peter Chrisp. Lucent Books 2004 48p il (Medieval realms) $28.70 (5 and up)   **940.1**
1. Medieval civilization
ISBN 1-59018-536-6   LC 2003-24516
This briefly describes life in Europe in the Middle Ages for landholders, peasants, monks and nuns, on manors and in churches and villages.
Includes glossary and bibliographical references

Corbishley, Mike

The Middle Ages. rev ed. Facts on File 2003 96p il map (Cultural atlas for young people) $35 (5 and up)   **940.1**
1. Medieval civilization 2. Middle Ages
ISBN 0-8160-5150-X   LC 2003-40260
First published 1989
Maps, charts, illustrations, and text explore the history and culture of the Middle Ages
This "is replete with enough colorful maps, time lines, photographs, and illustrations to satisfy even the most finicky student." Voice Youth Advocates
Includes glossary and bibliographical references

Galloway, Priscilla

Archers, alchemists, and 98 other medieval jobs you might have loved or loathed; art by Martha Newbigging. Annick Press 2003 96p il lib bdg $24.95; pa $14.95 (3-6)   **940.1**
1. Medieval civilization
ISBN 1-55037-811-2 (lib bdg); 1-55037-810-4 (pa)
"Galloway introduces medieval Europe from 1000 to 1500 not by recounting dates, wars, and rulers but by discussing the occupations available in the society. . . . The jaunty, cartoonlike ink drawings, brightened with color washes, heighten the informal, upbeat tone of the informative text." Booklist
Includes bibliographical references

Gibbons, Gail

Knights in shining armor. Little, Brown 1995 unp il lib bdg $15.95; pa $4.95 (k-3)
      940.1
1. Knights and knighthood 2. Medieval civilization
ISBN 0-316-30948-6; 0-316-30038-1 (pa)
      LC 94-35525

The author "covers tournaments, chivalry, and what happened when a bad knight was caught. Legendary knights such as Sir Gawain and the knights of the Round Table are briefly described, as is St. George and the dragon, and Gibbons also discusses present-day knights. The watercolor-and-ink pictures are some of Gibbons' liveliest and most attractive." Booklist

Gravett, Christopher

Knight; written by Christopher Gravett; photographed by Geoff Dann. rev ed. DK Pub. 2004 72p il (DK eyewitness books) $15.99; lib bdg $19.99 (4 and up)   **940.1**
1. Knights and knighthood 2. Medieval civilization
ISBN 0-7566-0696-9; 0-7566-0695-0 (lib bdg)
First published 1993 by Knopf
Discusses the age of knighthood, covering such aspects as arms, armor, training, ceremonies, tournaments, the code of chivalry, and the Crusades

Hart, Avery

Knights & castles; 50 hands-on activities to experience the Middle Ages; [by] Avery Hart & Paul Mantell. Williamson 1998 96p il pa $10.95 (4 and up)   **940.1**
1. Medieval civilization 2. Middle Ages 3. Knights and knighthood 4. Handicraft
ISBN 1-885593-17-1   LC 97-32863
"A Kaleidoscope Kids book"
Introduces the Middle Ages, including activities and crafts that are representative of medieval life, for example creating an hour glass, a catapult, a coat of arms, and a code of honor
"The text is written in a breezy tone and illustrated with a combination of line drawings and blue-or-purple-ink reproductions of medieval art and woodcuts." SLJ
Includes bibliographical references

Langley, Andrew

Medieval life; written by Andrew Langley; photographed by Geoff Brightling. rev ed. DK Pub. 2004 72p il (DK eyewitness books) $15.99; lib bdg $19.99 (4 and up)   **940.1**
1. Medieval civilization
ISBN 0-7566-0705-1; 0-7566-0704-3 (lib bdg)
First published 1996 by Knopf
An illustrated look at various aspects of life in medieval Europe, covering everyday life, religion, royalty, and more.

Martin, Alex

Knights & castles; exploring history through art; [by] Alex Martin. Two-Can Pub 2005 64p il (Picture that!) $19.95 (5 and up)   **940.1**
1. Knights and knighthood 2. Castles 3. Medieval civilization 4. Medieval art
ISBN 1-58728-441-3   LC 2004-14902
This "introduces readers to the . . . world of the medieval knight and his entourage. Including works by Paolo Uccello, Lucas Cranach, Pietr Brueghel the Younger, and Hieronymous Bosch, the book [also examines]

Martin, Alex—_Continued_

. . . a section of the Bayeux tapestry and . . . [the] illuminated manuscript, _Les Tres Riches Heures du Duc de Berry_." Publisher's note

"Art and history meld with entertaining and successful results. . . . [This] unique, well-thought-out [title is] good for reports, and browsers would enjoy [it] too." SLJ

Includes glossary and bibliographical references

Ross, Stewart

Monarchs; [by] Stewart Ross. Lucent 2004 48p il map (Medieval realms) $28.70 (5 and up)

940.1

1. Kings and rulers 2. Medieval civilization

ISBN 1-59018-535-8   LC 2003-60387

This describes medieval kings and queens of Europe and their governments, courts, succession, relationships to the church, wars, the Crusades, and the beginnings of nations.

This is "attractive, informative. . . . Well reproduced and mostly colorful, the illustrations include a great many reproductions of period paintings and prints, along with maps and a few photos." Booklist

Includes glossary and bibliographical references

Woolf, Alex

Education; by Alex Woolf. Lucent Books 2004 48p il map (Medieval realms) $28.70 (5 and up)

940.1

1. Medieval civilization 2. Education—History

ISBN 1-59018-532-3   LC 2003-18309

Contents: Education in 1000 AD; Education during the Dark Ages; Charlemagne; The role of the Church; Beliefs and ideas in education; Who went to school?; What did children learn at school?; Song schools; Grammar schools; Monastic schools; School life; Teachers; Chivalric education; Apprenticeship; The education of girls; The rise of universities; The university curriculum; University life; The great universities of Europe; The rise of humanism; The spread of humanism

Discusses the development of formal education during the Middle Ages, describing various methods of education, types of schools, curricula, who went to school, the rise of higher education, and more.

"Clear, well-organized [text] along with full-color reproductions of art and artifacts and photos of period structures immerse readers in . . . medieval life and offer sufficient information for reports." SLJ

Includes glossary and bibliographical references

940.2   Europe--1453-

Wood, Tim

The Renaissance. Viking 1993 48p il maps (See through history) $19.99 (4 and up)   **940.2**

1. Renaissance

ISBN 0-670-85149-3   LC 93-60028

Drawings, photographs, and text describe 15th and 16th century European civilization. Four see-through acetate pages lift to reveal the inner structures of three buildings and Columbus' ship, the Santa Maria

Includes glossary

940.3   World War I, 1914-1918

Adams, Simon

World War I; written by Simon Adams; photographed by Andy Crawford. rev ed. DK Pub. 2004 72p il (DK eyewitness books) $15.99; lib bdg $19.99 (4 and up)   **940.3**

1. World War, 1914-1918

ISBN 0-7566-0740-X; 0-7566-0741-8 (lib bdg)

First published 2001

This study covers how and why the First World War started, equipment used, and what it was like in trenches and at home

Gay, Kathlyn

World War I; [by] Kathlyn Gay, Martin Gay. 21st Cent. Bks. (NY) 1995 64p il maps (Voices from the past) lib bdg $25.90 (5 and up)

940.3

1. World War, 1914-1918

ISBN 0-8050-2848-X   LC 95-12300

An illustrated look at America's role in World War I on the battlefield and on the home front. Includes excerpts from letters, diaries and newspaper accounts

Includes bibliographical references

940.4   World War I, 1914-1918 (Military conduct of the war)

Myers, Walter Dean

The Harlem Hellfighters; when pride met courage; [by] Walter Dean Myers and Bill Miles. HarperCollins 2006 150p il maps lib bdg $17.89; $16.99 (5 and up)   **940.4**

1. World War, 1914-1918 2. African American soldiers

ISBN 0-06-991137-8 (lib bdg); 0-06-001136-X

LC 2005-08951

This is a "tribute to the 369th Infantry Regiment, comprised entirely of African American soldiers (many from Harlem), who fought in World War I. . . . The clear prose; effective use of white space; and numerous, often full-page black-and-white photographs will attract reluctant readers while enticing more dedicated history buffs." Booklist

Includes bibliographical references

Preston, Diana

Remember the Lusitania. Walker & Co. 2003 102p il maps $22.95; lib bdg $23.85 (5 and up)

940.4

1. Lusitania (Steamship) 2. World War, 1914-1918—Naval operations

ISBN 0-8027-8846-7; 0-8027-8847-5 (lib bdg)

LC 2002-27444

An account of the World War I German torpedo attack on and sinking of the passenger liner, the Lusitania, describing the experiences of some of those involved

"Most material is derived from a broad spectrum of

Preston, Diana—*Continued*

primary sources . . . and this adherence to firsthand accounts pays off in the riveting immediacy of Preston's prose. Plentiful illustrations (including historical photographs, documents, and maps) help bring the presentation well within the grasp of able younger readers." Bull Cent Child Books

940.53   World War II, 1939-1945

Adams, Simon

World War II; written by Simon Adams; photographed by Andy Crawford. rev ed. DK Pub. 2004 il (DK eyewitness books) $15.99; lib bdg $19.99 (4 and up)   **940.53**
1. World War, 1939-1945
ISBN 0-7566-0742-6; 0-7566-0743-4 (lib bdg)
First published 2000

In photographs and text this introduces the events of World War II, briefly covering such topics as bombing raids, the role of women, the atomic bomb, the American home front, the Holocaust, the D-Day invasion and propaganda.

Adler, David A.

Hiding from the Nazis; illustrated by Karen Ritz. Holiday House 1997 unp il $15.95; pa $6.95 (2-4)   **940.53**
1. Baer, Lore, 1938- 2. Holocaust, 1933-1945 3. World War, 1939-1945—Jews 4. Jews—Netherlands
ISBN 0-8234-1288-1; 0-8234-1666-6 (pa)
       LC 96-38451

The true story of Lore Baer who as a four-year-old Jewish child was placed with a Christian family in the Dutch farm country to avoid persecution by the Nazis

"Adler includes a lot of factual information about the history of the time and about the people in the story, before and after the war. Ritz's realistic watercolors in warm shades of brown focus on the small girl whose childhood games of hide-and-seek become a terrifying reality." Booklist

Ambrose, Stephen E.

The good fight; how World War II was won. Atheneum Bks. for Young Readers 2001 96p il maps $19.95 (5 and up)   **940.53**
1. World War, 1939-1945
ISBN 0-689-84361-5   LC 00-49600
"A Byron Preiss Visual Publications Inc. book"

"Beginning with an explanation of the origin of the war in Europe and Asia, the text moves on to Pearl Harbor through the major battles to the war-crimes trials and the Marshall Program." SLJ

"An excellent balance between the big picture and the humanizing details, well supported by fact boxes, tinted photographs, and battlefield maps that are both simple and clear. . . . Ambrose's style is authoritative and warm." Booklist

Includes glossary and bibliographical references

Bachrach, Susan D.

Tell them we remember; the story of the Holocaust. Little, Brown 1994 109p il maps $21.95; pa $14.95 (5 and up)   **940.53**
1. United States Holocaust Memorial Museum 2. Holocaust, 1933-1945
ISBN 0-316-69264-6; 0-316-07484-5 (pa)
       LC 93-40090
"United States Holocaust Memorial Museum."

"Intended to extend the experience of the United States Holocaust Memorial Museum beyond its walls, this book reproduces some of its artifacts, photographs, maps, and taped oral and video histories. . . . Bachrach makes the victims of Hitler's cruelty immediate to readers, showing that, like readers, they were individuals with hobbies and desires, friends and families. . . . This is a very personal approach to Holocaust history and a very effective one." SLJ

Includes glossary and bibliographical references

Greenfeld, Howard

After the Holocaust. Greenwillow Bks. 2001 146p il maps $18.95; lib bdg $19.89 (6 and up)   **940.53**
1. Holocaust survivors 2. Holocaust, 1933-1945 3. Jewish refugees
ISBN 0-688-17752-2; 0-06-029420-5 (lib bdg)
       LC 00-52798
"Eight Jewish survivors (five women, three men) share their personal experiences of what happened after the defeat of Hitler." SLJ

"The readable, slightly oversize design features lots of black-and-white photographs, news photos, and family snapshots. . . . The truth of the individual voices gives the history immediacy." Booklist

Includes bibliographical references

The hidden children. Ticknor & Fields Bks. for Young Readers 1993 118p il $17; pa $7.95 (4 and up)   **940.53**
1. Holocaust, 1933-1945—Personal narratives 2. Jews—Europe
ISBN 0-395-66074-2; 0-395-86138-1 (pa)
       LC 93-20326
Describes the experiences of those Jewish children who were forced to go into hiding during the Holocaust and survived to tell about it

"Illustrated with black-and-white photographs, the moving stories and dramatic facts make inspiring, and often troubling, reading. A lovely, important book about heroism and survival." Horn Book Guide

Includes bibliographical references

Holocaust memories; speaking the truth in their own words; [compiled] by Elaine Landau. Watts 2001 95p il (In their own voices) lib bdg $24 (5 and up)   **940.53**
1. Holocaust, 1933-1945—Personal narratives
ISBN 0-531-11742-1   LC 00-32511
These personal narratives of the Holocaust include "accounts of *Kristallnacht*, the Warsaw Ghetto rebellion against the Nazi army, the Nazi medical mutilations of Jews, and the Allied liberation of the death camps. . . . The easy-to-read, very revealing, and unsparingly honest

Holocaust memories—*Continued*

text is accompanied by black-and-white maps and some remarkable photos depicting the horrors of the Nazi genocide." SLJ

Includes bibliographical references

King, David C.

World War II days; discover the past with exciting projects, games, activities, and recipes; illustrations by Cheryl Kirk Noll. Wiley 2000 100p il (American kids in history) pa $12.95 (3-6) **940.53**

1. World War, 1939-1945—United States

ISBN 0-471-37101-7 LC 00-20474

Discusses American life during World War II, depicts a year in the lives of two fictional families, and presents projects and activities, such as deciphering codes, making a mobile out of found objects, and baking a sweet potato pie

"This is a valuable historical resource with unusual crafts that both entertain and educate." SLJ

Includes bibliographical references

Krinitz, Esther Nisenthal

Memories of survival; [by] Esther Nisenthal Krinitz & Bernice Steinhardt. Hyperion Books for Children 2005 63p il $15.99 (6 and up) **940.53**

1. Holocaust, 1933-1945—Personal narratives 2. Jews—Poland

ISBN 0-7868-5126-0

"Krinitz set down the story of her Holocaust survival in a series of 36 exquisite, hand-embroidered fabric collages and hand-stitched narrative captions. For this picture-book presentation, Steinhardt, Krinitz's daughter, reproduced those panels, adding eloquent commentary to fill in the facts and the history. . . . The telling is quiet, and the hand-stitched pictures are incredibly detailed, with depth and color that will make readers look closely." Booklist

Leapman, Michael

Witnesses to war; eight true-life stories of Nazi persecution. Viking 1998 127p il maps pa $7.99 hardcover o.p. (5 and up) **940.53**

1. Holocaust, 1933-1945 2. World War, 1939-1945—Children

ISBN 0-14-130841-9 (pa); 0-670-87386-1 (hc)

LC 98-208868

Facsimiles on end-papers

The author "suggests the far reaches of Nazi terror by focusing on the experiences of eight children, each victimized during WWII." Publ Wkly

"Leapman presents an authoritative, informative, and attractive work. . . . The narrative is riveting." Voice Youth Advocates

Lee, Carol Ann

A friend called Anne; one girl's story of war, peace, and a unique friendship with Anne Frank; by Jacqueline van Maarsen; retold for children by Carol Ann Lee. Viking Children's Books 2005 163p il $15.99 (4 and up) **940.53**

1. Frank, Anne, 1929-1945 2. Jews—Netherlands 3. Holocaust, 1933-1945

ISBN 0-670-05958-7 LC 2004-21418

Contents: The Road to war; Anne; Getting to know each other; Separation; Removing the yellow star; Last goodbyes; The hunger winter; Liberation; The Diary of Anne Frank; Fame

"Jacqueline van Maarsen met Anne Frank in 1941, and the two girls quickly became best friends. A Friend Called Anne details their relationship. . . . The book also shares Jacqueline's own chilling experience of narrowly escaping Nazi deportation thanks to her Catholic mother." Publisher's note

"This is a clearly written, demonstrative memoir. . . . Black-and-white photos of family and school settings, letters, poems, and a time line of events in wartime Netherlands are included." SLJ

Levine, Karen

Hana's suitcase; a true story. Whitman, A. 2003 111p il lib bdg $15.95 (4 and up) **940.53**

1. Brady, Hana 2. Holocaust, 1933-1945

ISBN 0-8075-3148-0 LC 2002-27439

Also available in paperback with CD-ROM from Second Story Press

First published 2002 in Canada

A biography of a Czech girl who died in the Holocaust, told in alternating chapters with an account of how the curator of a Japanese Holocaust center learned about her life after Hana's suitcase was sent to her

"The account, based on a radio documentary Levine did in Canada . . . is part history, part suspenseful mystery, and always anguished family drama, with an incredible climactic revelation." Booklist

Meltzer, Milton

Never to forget: the Jews of the Holocaust. Harper & Row 1976 217p maps pa $8.99 hardcover o.p. (6 and up) **940.53**

1. Holocaust, 1933-1945

ISBN 0-06-446118-1 (pa)

"The mass murder of six million Jews by the Nazis during World War II is the subject of this compelling history. Interweaving background information, chilling statistics, individual accounts and newspaper reports, it provides an excellent introduction to its subject." Interracial Books Child Bull

Includes bibliographical references

Rescue: the story of how Gentiles saved Jews in the Holocaust. Harper & Row 1988 168p maps $16.89; pa $9.99 (6 and up) **940.53**

1. Holocaust, 1933-1945 2. World War, 1939-1945—Jews—Rescue

ISBN 0-06-024210-8; 0-06-446117-3 (pa)

LC 87-47816

Meltzer, Milton—*Continued*

A recounting drawn from historic source material of the many individual acts of heroism performed by righteous gentiles who sought to thwart the extermination of the Jews during the holocaust

"This is an excellent portrayal of a difficult topic. Meltzer manages to both explain without accusing, and to laud without glorifying. . . . The discussion of the complicated relations between countries are clear, but not simplistic. An impressive aspect of this book is its lack of didacticism." Voice Youth Advocates

Includes bibliographical references

Millman, Isaac

Hidden child. Farrar, Straus and Giroux 2005 73p il $18 (4 and up)   **940.53**
1. Holocaust, 1933-1945—Personal narratives 2. Jews—France
ISBN 0-374-33071-9   LC 2003-60688
"Frances Foster books"

The author details his difficult experiences as a young Jewish child living in Nazi-occupied France during the 1940s.

"Millman tells his story in a straightforward, yet compelling voice. . . . Dense text pages—with occasional black-and-white photos—alternate with double-page montage paintings in which Millman presents images that emphasize his fears, emotions, and reactions to the events he describes. . . . An inspiring and powerful view of this tragic period in human history." SLJ

Mochizuki, Ken

Passage to freedom; the Sugihara story; written by Ken Mochizuki; illustrated by Dom Lee; afterword by Hiroki Sugihara. Lee & Low Bks. 1997 unp il $15.95 (3-6)   **940.53**
1. Sugihara, Sempo, 1900-1986 2. Holocaust, 1933-1945 3. World War, 1939-1945—Jews—Rescue
ISBN 1-880000-49-0   LC 96-35359
"The story of a Japanese diplomat who saved thousands of Jewish refugees in defiance of official government orders." SLJ

"Lee's stirring mixed-media illustrations in sepia shades are humane and beautiful. . . . The immediacy of the narrative will grab kids' interest and make them think." Booklist

Nicholson, Dorinda Makanaõnalani

Remember World War II; kids who survived tell their stories. National Geographic 2005 61p il map $17.95; lib bdg $27.90 (5 and up)   **940.53**
1. World War, 1939-1945—Personal narratives
ISBN 0-7922-7179-3; 0-7922-7191-2 (lib bdg)

This book offers "views of the Second World War through the eyes of those who experienced it as children. . . . Providing enough background information to give a framework for the progression of the war as a whole and the particular conditions and events surrounding the interviewees' memories, Nicholson lets the first-person accounts bring the experiences to life. Photographs of these individuals as children, other period photos, excellent maps, and pictures of artifacts illustrate the text." Booklist

Includes bibliographical references

Perl, Lila

Four perfect pebbles; a Holocaust story; by Lila Perl and Marion Blumenthal Lazan. Greenwillow Bks. 1996 130p il $16.99; pa $5.99 (6 and up)   **940.53**
1. Holocaust, 1933-1945—Personal narratives 2. Jews—Germany
ISBN 0-688-14294-X; 0-380-73188-6 (pa)
     LC 95-9752

"Starting with a description of one of the days that Marion Blumenthal Lazan survived in Bergen-Belsen, this chronicle of her experiences during the Holocaust then goes further back for a look at her family's secure prewar life in Germany." Bull Cent Child Books

"This book warrants attention both for the uncommon experiences it records and for the fullness of that record. . . . Quotes from Lazan's 87-year-old mother are invaluable—her memories of the family's experiences afford Marion's story a precision and wholeness rarely available to child survivors." Publ Wkly

Includes bibliographical references

Rosenberg, Maxine B.

Hiding to survive; stories of Jewish children rescued from the Holocaust. Clarion Bks. 1994 166p il pa $8.95 (5 and up)   **940.53**
1. Holocaust, 1933-1945—Personal narratives 2. Jews—Europe
ISBN 0-395-90020-4 (pa); 0-395-65014-3 (hc)
     LC 93-28328

First person accounts of fourteen Holocaust survivors who as children were hidden from the Nazis by non-Jews

"Told in the plain, unvarnished language of childhood memories, these harrowing first-person accounts are particularly moving in their straightforward simplicity, and all are accompanied by photos of the survivors as children and as they are today." Voice Youth Advocates

Includes glossary and bibliographical references

Rubin, Susan Goldman

The cat with the yellow star; coming of age in Terezin; by Susan Goldman Rubin with Ela Weissberger. 1st ed. Holiday House 2006 40p il $16.95 (3-6)   **940.53**
1. Holocaust, 1933-1945 2. Jews—Czechoslovakia 3. Terezin (Czechoslovakia: Concentration camp)
ISBN 0-8234-1831-6   LC 2004057582

"In 1942, at age 11, Ela Weissberger was transported with her Czech family to the Nazi concentration camp Terezin. She survived, and now, based on extensive personal interviews, Rubin tells Weissberger's story of being a Jewish child in that camp, including how the young prisoners rehearsed and performed the opera *Brundibar*." Booklist

"This finely tuned collaboration weaves together narrative and memories into one cohesive story of trauma, friendship, and survival. . . . Extensive use of historical photographs, drawings, and primary visual sources brings even greater depth to readers' understanding." SLJ

Rubin, Susan Goldman—*Continued*

The flag with fifty-six stars; a gift from the survivors of Mauthausen; illustrated by Bill Farnsworth. 1st ed. Holiday House 2005 39p il $16.95 (3-5)   **940.53**
1. Holocaust, 1933-1945 2. World War, 1939-1945—Germany 3. Jews—Germany 4. Flags—United States
ISBN 0-8234-1653-4   LC 2004-47457
"In the spring of 1945, U.S. troops marched into the Mauthausen concentration camp in Austria to liberate surviving prisoners and were given an American flag that had been secretly made by a group of detainees there. This is an inspiring account of the camp, its survivors, and its liberators. . . . Nazi atrocities are muted here, but the sorrow, hunger, hopelessness, and, finally, optimism shine through in the pictures and in the text." SLJ
Includes bibliographical references

Russo, Marisabina

Always remember me; how one family survived World War II; [by] Marisabina Russo. 1st ed. Atheneum Books for Young Readers 2005 unp il $16.95 (3-5)   **940.53**
1. Jews—Germany 2. Holocaust, 1933-1945
ISBN 0-689-86920-7   LC 2004-4228
"Russo tells her Jewish family's story of Holocaust survival. She remembers herself as a small child visiting her grandmother, Oma, who tells Russo the family history with photos stretching back to Oma's youth and marriage before World War I. . . . Russo personalizes the history with photo-album entries printed on the endpapers, and her gouache illustrations, framed like photos, show the individuality and strength of family members." Booklist
Includes glossary

Schroeder, Peter W.

Six million paper clips; the making of a children's Holocaust memorial; [by] Peter W. Schroeder & Dagmar Schroeder-Hildebrand. Kar-Ben Publishing 2004 64p il lib bdg $17.95; pa $7.95 (5 and up)   **940.53**
1. Holocaust, 1933-1945—Study and teaching
ISBN 1-58013-169-7 (lib bdg); 1-58013-176-X (pa)
                                LC 2004-19598
"In rural Whitwell, Tennessee, all 1,600 residents are alike, 'white, Anglo-Saxon, and Protestant.' When the community middle school decided to teach diversity by focusing on the Holocaust, the students did not believe that the Nazis had killed six million Jews and five million others. To help them grasp the numbers, they collected 11 million paper clips, which they placed in a memorial made from a German World War II railcar." Booklist
"With clear and concise language, color photographs, and an attractive layout, this book tells [an] inspiring and touching story." SLJ

Talbott, Hudson

Forging freedom; a true story of heroism during the Holocaust. Putnam 2000 64p il $15.99 (4 and up)   **940.53**
1. Penraat, Jaap 2. World War, 1939-1945—Jews—Rescue 3. Holocaust, 1933-1945
ISBN 0-399-23434-9   LC 99-52551
"Talbott tells the story of his friend Jaap Penraat, who, as a young architectural student in Amsterdam under the Nazi occupation, saved hundreds of Jews from arrest, first by forging their ID cards, and then by devising an elaborate escape plan to smuggle them over the border to freedom." Booklist

Tunnell, Michael O.

The children of Topaz; the story of a Japanese-American internment camp; based on a classroom diary; by Michael O. Tunnell and George W. Chilcoat. Holiday House 1996 74p il $19.95 (5 and up)   **940.53**
1. Central Utah Relocation Center 2. Japanese Americans—Evacuation and relocation, 1942-1945 3. World War, 1939-1945—Children
ISBN 0-8234-1239-3   LC 95-49360
"Interned behind barbed wire in a desert relocation camp in Topaz, Utah, Japanese American teacher Lillian 'Anne' Yamauchi Hori kept a classroom diary with her third-grade class from May to August 1943. . . . Twenty of the small diary entries appear in this book, together with several black-and-white archival photos of the camps. Tunnell and Chilcoat provide a long historical introduction and then detailed commentary that puts each diary entry in the context of what was happening in the camp and in the country at war. . . . The primary sources have a stark authority; it's the very ordinariness of the children's concerns that grabs you." Booklist
Includes bibliographical references

Warren, Andrea

Surviving Hitler; a boy in the Nazi death camps. HarperCollins Pubs. 2001 146p il $16.99; lib bdg $17.89; pa $6.99 (5 and up)   **940.53**
1. Mandelbaum, Jack 2. Holocaust, 1933-1945
ISBN 0-688-17497-3; 0-06-029218-0 (lib bdg); 0-06-000767-2 (pa)   LC 00-38899
"Jack Mandelbaum, a Polish Jew, had a happy family life until 1939, when Germany invaded Poland, beginning World War II. Fifteen-year-old Jack is sent to Nazi concentration camps. Despite fear, starvation, and other horrors, he survives." Voice Youth Advocates
"Simply told, Warren's powerful story blends the personal testimony of Holocaust survivor Jack Mandelbaum with the history of his time, documented by stirring photos from the archives of the U.S. Holocaust Memorial Museum. . . . An excellent introduction for readers who don't know much about the history." Booklist
Includes bibliographical references

Whiteman, Dorit Bader

Lonek's journey; the true story of a boy's escape to freedom; by Dorit Bader Whiteman. Star Bright Books 2005 141p il map $15.95 (5 and up)
940.53

1. Holocaust, 1933-1945 2. Jews—Poland 3. Jewish refugees

ISBN 1-59572-021-9   LC 2005010898

"Lonek is 11 when the Nazis invade his Polish hometown in 1939. First he hides in a hole under the stable of friendly neighbors; then his family makes the dangerous escape to Russian-occupied Poland, from where the family members are deported in a horrific three-week crossing to the harsh Siberian slave-labor camps. But following a deal with the British, Stalin lets them go, and for two years Lonek travels on foot, by train, and by ship, until, with 1,000 other orphans, he reaches safety in Palestine. . . . The story . . . is told in short, stark chapters, each ending on a note of mounting suspense. . . . With occasional black-and-white photos, clear maps, and extensive historical notes, this is an important addition to history collections." Booklist

940.54 World War II, 1939-1945 (Military conduct of the war)

Allen, Thomas B.

Remember Pearl Harbor; American and Japanese survivors tell their stories; foreword by Robert D. Ballard. National Geographic Soc. 2001 57p il maps $17.95 (5 and up)   **940.54**

1. Pearl Harbor (Oahu, Hawaii), Attack on, 1941
2. World War, 1939-1945—Personal narratives

ISBN 0-7922-6690-0   LC 2001-796

Personal accounts of the Japanese attack on Pearl Harbor, with background information

"Eyewitness testimony of Japanese and American men and women from various backgrounds enriches this balanced treatment of World War II. . . . The first-person voices along with dozens of black-and-white photos and several full-color maps make this a draw for both browsers and World War II buffs." Booklist

Includes bibliographical references

Drez, Ronald J.

Remember D-day; the plan, the invasion, survivor stories. National Geographic Books 2004 61p il map $17.95 (5 and up)   **940.54**

1. World War, 1939-1945—Campaigns—France

ISBN 0-7922-6666-8   LC 2003-17733

Discusses the events and personalities involved in the momentous Allied invasion of France on June 6, 1944.

"This well-organized, clearly written account provides a solid overview for readers unfamiliar with the subject. A first-rate purchase." SLJ

Includes bibliographical references

Kuhn, Betsy

Angels of mercy; the Army nurses of World War II. Atheneum Bks. for Young Readers 1999 114p il map $18 (5 and up)   **940.54**

1. United States. Army Nurse Corps 2. World War, 1939-1945—Women 3. Women in the armed forces

ISBN 0-689-82044-5   LC 98-36610

Relates the experiences of World War II Army nurses, who brought medical skills, courage, and cheer to hospitals throughout Europe, North Africa, and the Pacific

"Excellent reproductions, maps and a time line accompany the clear, well-written text." SLJ

Includes bibliographical references

Lawton, Clive

Hiroshima; the story of the first atom bomb; [by] Clive A. Lawton. 1st U.S. ed. Candlewick Press 2004 48p il map $18.99 (5 and up)
940.54

1. Hiroshima (Japan)—Bombardment, 1945
2. Atomic bomb 3. World War, 1939-1945—Japan

ISBN 0-7636-2271-0   LC 2004-45166

The author "explores the politics and the science behind the military decision that began the nuclear arms race. . . . He investigates the events that led up to the disaster at Hiroshima in 1945 and discusses the consequences that we are still living with today." Publisher's note

"Engaging text and powerful photographs are intricately woven together to make a long-lasting impact on readers." Libr Media Connect

Maruki, Toshi

Hiroshima no pika; words and pictures by Toshi Maruki. Lothrop, Lee & Shepard Bks. 1982 c1980 unp il $17.99 (5 and up)   **940.54**

1. Hiroshima (Japan)—Bombardment, 1945
2. Atomic bomb 3. World War, 1939-1945—Japan

ISBN 0-688-01297-3   LC 82-15365

First published 1980 in Japan

Focusing on the experiences of a real family "the horrifying story of the atomic bombing or 'flash' of Hiroshima is told here with a remarkable eloquence, including many poignant details. The story is terribly disturbing and painful to read, but the narrative is at the same time so spare and compelling one must go on. . . . Young people twelve and over, as well as adults, should know this terrible story. This superb book can begin to tell it to them." Appraisal

McGowen, Tom

Germany's lightning war; Panzer divisions of World War II. 21st Cent. Bks. (Brookfield) 1999 64p il (Military might) lib bdg $26.90 (5 and up)
940.54

1. World War, 1939-1945—Germany 2. Military tanks

ISBN 0-7613-1511-X   LC 98-44009

Discusses the development and actions of German tank units in World War II, covering specific battles and the changes that tanks brought to warfare in general

This book "should inspire youngsters to pursue their interest in the subject." SLJ

McGowen, Tom—*Continued*

Sink the Bismarck; Germany's super-battleship of World War II. 21st Cent. Bks. (Brookfield) 1999 64p il (Military might) lib bdg $26.90 (5 and up) **940.54**

1. Bismarck (Battleship) 2. World War, 1939-1945—Naval operations

ISBN 0-7613-1510-1   LC 98-48500

Describes the actions of the German battleship "Bismarck" during World War II and the operations of the British navy to destroy this ship

The presentation is "straightforward, simple. . . . The writing is . . . easy to follow." SLJ

Tanaka, Shelley

Attack on Pearl Harbor; the true story of the day America entered World War II; text by Shelley Tanaka; paintings by David Craig; maps by Jack McMaster; historical consultation by John Lundstrom. Hyperion Bks. for Children 2001 64p il $19.99 (4 and up) **940.54**

1. Pearl Harbor (Oahu, Hawaii), Attack on, 1941 2. World War, 1939-1945

ISBN 0-7868-0736-9   LC 2001-16634

"An I was there book; A Hyperion/Madison Press book"

"Tanaka reconstructs key events of the attack on Pearl Harbor, based on the harrowing, real-life experiences of four young men. . . . The account is riveting. She includes plenty of sensory details and writes in a clipped, concise manner that clearly conveys the danger and frenzied pace of the events. . . . Dramatic, full-color paintings, black-and-white photos, maps, and diagrams contribute much to the readers' understanding of the events." Booklist

Includes glossary and bibliographical references

Williams, Barbara

World War II, Pacific; by Barbara Williams: . Lerner Publications 2005 96p il map (Chronicle of America's wars) lib bdg $27.93 (5 and up) **940.54**

1. World War, 1939-1945

ISBN 0-8225-0138-4   LC 2004-3371

This chronicles World War II in the Pacific focusing on the war's impact on America and its people.

"A precise, well-documented chronology of the major battles in the Pacific theater. Though the narration is brief, it is informative and avoids misconceptions." SLJ

Includes glossary and bibliographical references

941   British Isles

Fuller, Barbara

Britain. 2nd ed. Benchmark Books 2005 144p il map (Cultures of the world) lib bdg $37.07 (5 and up) **941**

1. Great Britain

ISBN 0-7614-1845-8

First published 1994

Cover title: Great Britain

"Explores the geography, history, government, people, and culture of Britain" Publisher's note

Includes glossary and bibliographical references

Gordon, Sharon

Great Britain. Benchmark Bks. 2003 c2004 48p il map (Discovering cultures) lib bdg $25.64 (2-4) **941**

1. Great Britain

ISBN 0-7614-1717-6   LC 2003-6956

Contents: Where in the world is Great Britain?; What makes Great Britain British?; Living in Great Britain; School days; Just for fun; Let's celebrate!

Highlights the geography, people, food, schools, recreation, celebrations, and language of Great Britain

Includes glossary and bibliographical references

941.1   Scotland

Levy, Patricia

Scotland. Benchmark Bks. 2001 128p il map (Cultures of the world) lib bdg $37.07 (5 and up) **941.1**

1. Scotland

ISBN 0-7614-1159-3   LC 00-39831

An illustrated look at the geography, history, government, politics, people, religion, language, food and culture of Scotland

Includes glossary and bibliographical references

Oxlade, Chris

A visit to Scotland; [by] Chris Oxlade and Anita Ganeri. Heinemann Lib. 2003 32p il map (Visit to) lib bdg $22.79 (1-4) **941.1**

1. Scotland

ISBN 1-4034-0966-8   LC 2002-7409

Contents: Scotland; Land; Landmarks; Homes; Food; Clothes; Work; Transportation; Language; School; Free time; Celebrations; The arts; Fact file

An introduction to the history, geography, and culture of Scotland

"Despite the simple language, the subject matter is not oversimplified and the [book is] jam-packed with interesting facts. Crisp, full-color photographs on every page add meaning to the ideas presented and provide visual treats." SLJ

Includes glossary and bibliographical references

941.5   Ireland

January, Brendan

Ireland. Children's Press 1999 47p il map lib bdg $22; pa $6.95 (2-4) **941.5**

1. Ireland

ISBN 0-516-21186-2; 0-516-26493-1 (pa)

LC 98-15762

"A True book"

Presents an overview of the history, geography, climate, and culture of Ireland

January, Brendan—*Continued*

"Almost all of the pages include a glossy, full-color photograph or a historical reproduction with highlighted, easy-to-read captions. . . . The information is sufficient for basic reports." SLJ

Includes bibliographical references

Levy, Patricia

Ireland. 2nd ed. Benchmark Books 2004 144p il map (Cultures of the world) lib bdg $29.95 (5 and up)   **941.5**

1. Ireland

ISBN 0-7614-1784-2   LC 2004-12902

First published 1994

This describes the geography, history, government, economy, environment, lifestyle, religion, and culture of Ireland.

Includes glossary and bibliographical references

Murphy, Patricia

Ireland; by Patricia J. Murphy. Benchmark Bks. 2003 48p il map (Discovering cultures) lib bdg $25.64 (2-4)   **941.5**

1. Ireland

ISBN 0-7614-1515-7   LC 2002-15303

Contents: Where in the world is Ireland?; What makes Ireland Irish?; Living in Ireland; School days; Just for fun; Let's celebrate!

Highlights the geography, people, food, schools, recreation, celebrations, and language of Ireland

"Illustrated with clear color photos [and] simply written." Horn Book Guide

Includes glossary and bibliographical references

942   England and Wales

Blashfield, Jean F.

England. Children's Press 1997 143p il map (Enchantment of the world, second series) $33 (5 and up)   **942**

1. England

ISBN 0-516-20471-8   LC 97-5662

Describes the geography, history, economy, language, religions, culture, people, plants, and animals of England

Includes bibliographical references

Oxlade, Chris

A visit to England; [by] Chris Oxlade and Anita Ganeri. Heinemann Lib. 2003 32p il map (Visit to) lib bdg $22.79 (1-4)   **942**

1. England

ISBN 1-4034-0965-X   LC 2002-7415

Contents: England; Land; Landmarks; Homes; Food; Clothes; Work; Transportation; Language; School; Free time; Celebrations; The arts; Fact file

An introduction to the land and culture of England

This is "clear, concise, . . . reader-friendly, [and] informative. . . . Accurate, up-to-date material is supported by large, full-color photographs on each spread." SLJ

Includes glossary and bibliographical references

942.01   England--Early history to 1066

Crossley-Holland, Kevin

The world of King Arthur and his court; people, places, legend, and lore; illustrated by Peter Malone. Dutton Children's Bks. 1999 c1998 125p il pa $14.99 hardcover o.p. (5 and up)

                        942.01

1. Arthur, King 2. Great Britain—History—0-1066 3. Middle Ages

ISBN 0-525-47321-1 (pa)   LC 98-37698

First published 1998 in the United Kingdom

Surveys the known history of King Arthur, the legends and lore surrounding him, his treatment in literature, and the possible historical background of his associates and stories

An "eminently browsable, stylishly written trove of Arthuriana. . . . Lavishly detailed, both the full-spread paintings and spot illustrations are ripe with mystery and romance." Publ Wkly

942.03   England--Period of House of Plantagenet, 1154-1399

Tanaka, Shelley

In the time of knights; the real-life history of history's greatest knight; illustrations by Greg Ruhl. Hyperion 2000 48p il $16.99 (4 and up)

                        942.03

1. Pembroke, William Marshal, Earl of, 1144?-1219 2. Knights and knighthood 3. Great Britain—History—1154-1399, Plantagenets

ISBN 0-7868-0651-6   LC 00-29552

"An I was there book"

This "tells the life story of William Marshal, one of the most successful knights of the twelfth century and regent to Henry, the son of Eleanor of Aquitaine." Horn Book Guide

"Tanaka weaves a fascinating tale filled with plenty of historical detail. . . . She draws on documents, maps, period reproductions, and other primary sources. Clear, colorful photos of sites and artifacts and original art complement the story line. Excellent organization is an added plus." SLJ

Includes glossary and bibliographical references

942.1   London

Stacey, Gill

London; by Gill Stacey. World Almanac Library 2004 48p il map (Great cities of the world) lib bdg $30; pa $11.95 (4 and up)   **942.1**

1. London (England)

ISBN 0-8368-5022-X (lib bdg); 0-8368-5182-X (pa)

                   LC 2003-49693

Contents: Introduction; History of London; People of London; Living in London; London at work; London at play; Looking forward

Stacey, Gill—*Continued*

This "up-to-date, attractively formatted [title contains an] interesting, informative [text] set in an easy-to-read font. Well-chosen, excellent-quality color photos, quotations, and sidebars appear throughout." SLJ

Includes bibliographical references

942.9 Wales

Oxlade, Chris

A visit to Wales; [by] Anita Ganeri and Chris Oxlade. Heinemann Lib. 2003 32p il map (Visit to) lib bdg $22.79 (1-4)   **942.9**

1. Wales

ISBN 1-4034-0967-6   LC 2002-7417

Contents: Wales; Land; Landmarks; Homes; Food; Clothes; Work; Transportation; Language; School; Free time; Celebrations; The arts; Fact file

An introduction to the history, geography, and culture of Wales

This is "clear, concise, . . . reader-friendly, [and] informative. . . . Accurate, up-to-date material is supported by large, full-color photographs on each spread." SLJ

Includes glossary and bibliographical references

943 Central Europe. Germany

Allan, Tony

The Rhine. World Almanac 2003 48p il maps (Great rivers of the world) lib bdg $26.60 (4 and up)   **943**

1. Rhine River

ISBN 0-8368-5446-2   LC 2002-34318

Contents: The course of the Rhine; The Rhine in history; Cities and settlements; Economic activity; Animals and plants; Environmental issues; Recreation and leisure; The future

The Rhine river's "flow, history, ecological concerns, tourism, flora and fauna, etc., are explained. . . . Clear and colorful photos appear on every page." SLJ

Includes glossary and bibliographical references

Fuller, Barbara

Germany; [by] Barbara Fuller, Gabriele Vossmeyer. 2nd ed. Benchmark Bks. 2003 c2004 144p il map (Cultures of the world) lib bdg $37.07 (5 and up)   **943**

1. Germany

ISBN 0-7614-1667-6   LC 2003-8186

First published 1993

Explores the geography, history, government, economy, people, and culture of Germany

Includes glossary and bibliographical references

Gordon, Sharon

Germany; by Sharon Gordon. Benchmark Books 2004 48p il map (Discovering cultures) lib bdg $25.64 (2-4)   **943**

1. Germany

ISBN 0-7614-1792-3   LC 2004-6132

Contents: Where in the world is Germany?; What makes Germany German?; Living in Germany; School days; Just for fun; Let's celebrate!

An introduction to the geography, history, people, and culture of Germany

Includes glossary and bibliographical references

Stein, R. Conrad

Berlin. Children's Press 1997 64p il maps (Cities of the world) lib bdg $26.50 (5 and up)   **943**

1. Berlin (Germany)

ISBN 0-516-20582-X   LC 96-50147

Describes the history, culture, people, daily life, and points of interest of Germany's major city

Includes bibliographical references

943.6 Austria and Liechtenstein

Sheehan, Sean

Austria. 2nd ed. Benchmark Bks. 2003 144p il map (Cultures of the world) lib bdg $25.95 (5 and up)   **943.6**

1. Austria

ISBN 0-7614-1497-5   LC 2002-11623

First published 1993

Presents the geography, history, economy, and social life and customs of Austria, the birthplace of such people as Kurt Waldheim, Wolfgang Amadeus Mozart, Sigmund Freud, and Arnold Schwarzenegger

Includes glossary and bibliographical references

943.7 Czech Republic and Slovakia

Sioras, Efstathia

Czech Republic. Benchmark Bks. 1999 128p il maps (Cultures of the world) lib bdg $37.07 (5 and up)   **943.7**

1. Czech Republic

ISBN 0-7614-0870-3   LC 98-30290

Describes the geography, history, government, economy, people, lifestyle, religion, language, arts, leisure, festivals, and food of the Czech Republic

Includes glossary and bibliographical references

943.8 Poland

Gordon, Sharon

Poland. Benchmark Bks. 2004 48p il map (Discovering cultures) lib bdg $25.64 (2-4)   **943.8**

1. Poland

ISBN 0-7614-1724-9   LC 2003-19101

Contents: Where in the world is Poland?; What makes Poland Polish?; Living in Poland; School days; Just for fun; Let's celebrate!

An introduction to the geography, history, people, and culture of Poland

Includes bibliographical references

Heale, Jay

Poland; [by] Jay Heale & Pawel Grajnert. 2nd ed. Benchmark Books 2005 144p il map (Cultures of the world) lib bdg $37.07 (5 and up)

943.8

1. Poland
ISBN 0-7614-1847-4
First published 1994

Describes the geography, history, government, economy, environment, people, and culture of Poland

"Richly detailed and illustrated with numerous striking, full-color photographs. . . . [This is] well-organized, carefully researched, readable." SLJ

Includes glossary and bibliographical references

Hintz, Martin

Poland. Children's Press 1998 144p il map (Enchantment of the world, second series) lib bdg $35 (5 and up) **943.8**

1. Poland
ISBN 0-516-20605-2   LC 97-25559

Describes the history, geography, economy, plants and animals, language, religion, sports, arts, and people of this central European country which has ties to both East and West

Includes bibliographical references

943.9 Hungary

Esbenshade, Richard S.

Hungary. 2nd ed. Benchmark Books 2005 144p il map (Cultures of the world) lib bdg $37.07 (5 and up) **943.9**

1. Hungary
ISBN 0-7614-1846-6
First published 1994

Describes the geography, history, government, economy, environment, and culture of Hungary

Includes glossary and bibliographical references

944 France and Monaco

Landau, Elaine

France. Children's Press 2000 47p il lib bdg $25 (2-4) **944**

1. France
ISBN 0-516-21173-0   LC 99-14956

"A True book"

Describes the geography, history, culture, and people of France, the largest country in Western Europe

Includes bibliographical references

Nardo, Don

France. Children's Press 2000 144p il (Enchantment of the world, Second series) lib bdg $36 (5 and up) **944**

1. France
ISBN 0-516-21052-1   LC 99-12685

Describes the geography, plants, animals, history, economy, language, sports, arts, religions, culture, and people of France

Includes bibliographical references

NgCheong-Lum, Roseline

France. Stevens, G. 1999 96p il (Countries of the world) lib bdg $30 (4 and up) **944**

1. France
ISBN 0-8368-2260-9   LC 98-33770

An overview of France, discussing its history, geography, government, economy, culture, and relations with North America

"The full-color photos on every page are outstanding and the style of writing is graceful." SLJ

Includes glossary and bibliographical references

945 Italian Peninsula and adjacent islands. Italy

Behnke, Alison

Italy in pictures. Lerner Publs. 2003 80p il maps (Visual geography series) lib bdg $27.93 (5 and up) **945**

1. Italy
ISBN 0-8225-0368-9   LC 2001-5483

A historical and current look at Italy, discussing the land, the government, the people, and the economy

Includes glossary and bibliographical references

Macaulay, David

Rome antics. Houghton Mifflin 1997 79p il $18 (4 and up) **945**

1. Rome (Italy)—Description and travel
ISBN 0-395-82279-3   LC 97-20941

"Modern Rome is seen through the skewed perspective of a homing pigeon's erratic flight through the city streets as she delivers a message to an artist in a garret. . . . Macaulay adds sly touches of humor to the pen-and-ink sketches. . . . The book includes a map of the city 'As the pigeon flies' with each structure numbered, and an addendum shows the 22 featured buildings with a paragraph or two of interesting facts about each one." SLJ

Malone, Margaret Gay

Italy. Benchmark Bks. 2002 c2003 48p il map (Discovering cultures) lib bdg $25.64 (2-4)

945

1. Italy
ISBN 0-7614-1176-3   LC 2001-7458

Contents: Where in the world is Italy?; What makes Italy Italian?; Living in Italy; School days; Just for fun; Let's celebrate!

Highlights the geography, people, food, schools, recreation, celebrations, and language of Italy

Includes glossary and bibliographical references

Sheehan, Sean
Malta. Benchmark Bks. 2000 128p il map
(Cultures of the world) lib bdg $37.07 (5 and up)
945

1. Malta
ISBN 0-7614-0993-9   LC 99-53436
The text covers Malta's "government, economy, people, lifestyles, religion, language, arts and leisure, festivals, and food. . . . Copious colorful photographs and reproductions complement and reinforce the facts presented." SLJ
Includes glossary and bibliographical references

Winter, Jane Kohen
Italy; [by] Jane Kohen Winter, Leslie Jermyn.
2nd ed. Benchmark Bks. 2003 144p il maps
(Cultures of the world) lib bdg $37.07 (5 and up)
945

1. Italy
ISBN 0-7614-1500-9   LC 2002-11628
First published 1995
Describes the geography, history, government, economy, and culture of Italy
"Colorful photographs with informative captions decorate almost every page of [this book]." SLJ
Includes glossary and bibliographical references

946   Iberian Peninsula and adjacent islands. Spain

Kohen, Elizabeth
Spain; [by] Elizabeth Kohen, Marie Louise
Elias. 2nd ed. Benchmark Bks. 2003 144p il maps
(Cultures of the world) lib bdg $37.07 (5 and up)
946

1. Spain
ISBN 0-7614-1501-7   LC 2002-11626
First published 1996
Introduces the geography, history, economy, culture, and people of Spain
"Colorful photographs with informative captions decorate almost every page of [this book]." SLJ
Includes glossary and bibliographical references

Parker, Lewis K.
Spain. Benchmark Bks. 2003 48p il maps
(Discovering cultures) lib bdg $25.64 (2-4)
946

1. Spain
ISBN 0-7614-1520-3   LC 2002-15301
Contents: Where in the world is Spain?; What makes Spain Spanish?; Living in Spain; School days; Just for fun; Let's celebrate!
An introduction to Spain, highlighting the country's geography, people, foods, schools, recreation, celebrations, and language
This title is "illustrated with clear color photos [and is] simply written." Horn Book Guide
Includes glossary and bibliographical references

946.9   Portugal

Heale, Jay
Portugal; [by] Jay Heale & Angeline Koh. 2nd
ed. Marshall Cavendish Benchmark 2006 144p il
map (Cultures of the world) lib bdg $37.07 (5 and up)
946.9

1. Portugal
ISBN 0-7614-2053-3   LC 2005022922
First published 1995
Describes the geography, history, government, economy, culture, peoples, and religion of Portugal
Includes glossary and bibliographical references

947   Eastern Europe. Russia

De Capua, Sarah
Russia. Benchmark Bks. 2003 c2004 48p il map
(Discovering cultures) lib bdg $25.64 (2-4)
947

1. Russia
ISBN 0-7614-1716-8   LC 2003-6957
Contents: Where in the world is Russia?; What makes Russia Russian?; Living in Russia; School days; Just for fun; Let's celebrate!
Highlights the geography, people, food, schools, recreation, celebrations, and language of Russia
Includes glossary and bibliographical references

Torchinskiĭ, Oleg
Russia; [by] Oleg Torchinsky, Angela Black.
2nd ed. Benchmark Books 2005 144p il map
(Cultures of the world) lib bdg $37.07 (5 and up)
947

1. Russia
ISBN 0-7614-1849-0
First published 1994
Describes the history, geography, government, economy, environment, and culture of Russia
"This title provides a well-written look at Russian history and culture up to the present day. . . . The high-quality, full-color photographs and reproductions are crisply printed, well composed, and perfectly placed." SLJ
Includes glossary and bibliographical references

947.5   Caucasus

Beliaev, Edward
Dagestan; [by] Edward Beliaev & Oksana
Buranbaeva. 1st ed. Marshall Cavendish
Benchmark 2006 144p il map (Cultures of the world) lib bdg $37.07 (5 and up)
947.5

1. Dagestan (Russia)
ISBN 0-7614-2015-0   LC 2005013698
An exploration of the geography, history, government, economy, people, and culture of the former Soviet republic of Dagestan
Includes glossary and bibliographical references

King, David C.

Azerbaijan; [by] David C. King. 1st ed. Marshall Cavendish Benchmark 2006 144p il map (Cultures of the world) lib bdg $37.07 (5 and up)

947.5

1. Azerbaijan

ISBN 0-7614-2011-8   LC 2004028443

An overview of the history, culture, peoples, religion, government, and geography of Azerbaijan

Includes glossary and bibliographical references

947.6 Moldova

Sheehan, Patricia

Moldova. Benchmark Bks. 2000 128p il map (Cultures of the world) lib bdg $37.07 (5 and up)

947.6

1. Moldova

ISBN 0-7614-0997-1   LC 99-53433

An illustrated look at the history and culture of the small landlocked country between Russia and the Ukraine that proclaimed its independence in August, 1991

Includes glossary and bibliographical references

947.7 Ukraine

Kummer, Patricia K.

Ukraine. Children's Press 2001 144p il (Enchantment of the world, Second series) lib bdg $35 (5 and up)

947.7

1. Ukraine

ISBN 0-516-21101-3   LC 00-57040

Describes the geography, history, culture, and people of Ukraine

The chapters "are clearly written and have the details needed for reports, but many of the sidebars set off within the chapters are more engaging. . . . Excellent-quality, full-color photos and reproductions enhance the presentation." SLJ

Includes bibliographical references

947.9 Lithuania, Latvia, Estonia

Barlas, Robert

Latvia. Benchmark Bks. 2000 128p il map (Cultures of the world) lib bdg $37.07 (5 and up)

947.9

1. Latvia

ISBN 0-7614-0977-7   LC 99-30168

Describes the geography, history, government, economy, people, religion, language, arts, leisure, festivals, and food of Latvia

Includes glossary and bibliographical references

Spilling, Michael

Estonia. Benchmark Bks. 1999 128p il maps (Cultures of the world) lib bdg $37.07 (5 and up)

947.9

1. Estonia

ISBN 0-7614-0951-3   LC 98-43682

Introduces the geography, history, government, economy, culture, and people of Estonia, the northernmost and least populated of the three Baltic states

Includes glossary and bibliographical references

948 Scandinavia

Berger, Melvin

The real Vikings; craftsmen, traders, and fearsome raiders; [by] Melvin and Gilda Berger. National Geographic Society 2003 55p il map $18.95 (4 and up)

948

1. Vikings

ISBN 0-7922-5132-6   LC 2002-154474

This book offers an "introduction to the Vikings, beginning with their attack on Lindisfarne in 793 and ending, in 1066, with William the Conqueror." SLJ

"The many illustrations include maps, drawings, prints, and paintings from many periods in addition to color photographs of Viking artifacts and sites. . . . Visually appealing and quite informative, the book will appeal to browsers as well as young researchers" Booklist

Margeson, Susan M.

Viking; written by Susan M. Margeson; photographed by Peter Anderson. rev ed. DK Pub. 2005 72p il map (DK eyewitness books) $15.99; lib bdg $19.99 (4 and up)

948

1. Vikings

ISBN 0-7566-1095-8; 0-7566-1096-6 (lib bdg)

First published 1994 by Knopf

Presents an illustrated look at the Vikings - their ships and weapons, heroes and myths, and great adventures in war and exploration.

Schomp, Virginia

The Vikings. Franklin Watts 2005 112p il map (People of the ancient world) lib bdg $30.50; pa $9.95 (5 and up)

948

1. Vikings

ISBN 0-531-12382-0 (lib bdg); 0-531-16849-2 (pa)

LC 2004-24311

Contents: Legends and history; Warrior kings; Upper-class men and women; Farmers and settlers; Artisans and artists; Merchants and traders; Warriors; Poets and rune masters; Slaves; The legacy of the Vikings

This examines the culture of the Vikings "through their literature, artifacts, and documents. Religion, farming, levels of society, art, government, and fine arts are covered in [this] well-written and attractive [book]." Booklist

Includes bibliographical references

948.5   Sweden

Gan, Delice
Sweden; [by] Delice Gan, Leslie Jermyn. 2nd ed. Benchmark Bks. 2003 144p il maps (Cultures of the world) lib bdg $37.07 (5 and up)
948.5
1. Sweden
ISBN 0-7614-1502-5   LC 2002-152559
First published 1993 under the authorship of Delice Gan
Introduces the geography, history, economy, culture, and people of the fourth largest country in Europe
Includes glossary and bibliographical references

948.9   Denmark and Finland

Pateman, Robert
Denmark; [by] Robert Pateman. 2nd ed. Marshall Cavendish Benchmark 2006 144p il map (Cultures of the world) lib bdg $37.07 (5 and up)
948.9
1. Denmark
ISBN 0-7614-2024-X   LC 2005021610
First published 1995
Introduces the geography, history, economics, culture, and people of Denmark
Includes glossary and bibliographical references

948.97   Finland

McNair, Sylvia
Finland. Children's Press 1997 143p il map (Enchantment of the world, second series) $33 (5 and up)
948.97
1. Finland
ISBN 0-516-20472-6   LC 97-4972
Describes the geography, plants, animals, history, economy, language, religions, culture, sports, arts, and people of Finland
Includes bibliographical references

949.12   Iceland

McMillan, Bruce
Going fishing; written and photo-illustrated by Bruce McMillan. Houghton Mifflin Co 2005 32p il $16 (2-4)
949.12
1. Iceland 2. Fishing
ISBN 0-618-47201-0   LC 2004-15506
"Walter Lorraine books"
"This narrative photo-essay follows a young boy from Reykjavik to the fishing village where his two grandfathers live. Each takes his grandson out on his own boat to catch a type of fish important to Iceland. . . . The clarity of the color photos brings the people, their surroundings, and the process of fishing sharply into focus. . . . A delightfully illustrated presentation of fishing, family, and, of course, Iceland." Booklist

949.2   Netherlands

Seward, Pat
Netherlands; [by] Pat Seward & Sunandini Arora Lal. 2nd ed. Marshall Cavendish Benchmark 2006 144p il map (Cultures of the world) lib bdg $37.07 (5 and up)
949.2
1. Netherlands
ISBN 0-7614-2052-5   LC 2005019823
First published 1995
Describes the geography, history, government, economy, culture, peoples, and religion of the Netherlands.
Includes glossary and bibliographical references

949.3   Southern Low Countries. Belgium

Burgan, Michael
Belgium. Children's Press 2000 144p il (Enchantment of the world, second series) $33 (5 and up)
949.3
1. Belgium
ISBN 0-516-21006-8   LC 99-21338
Describes the geography, plants and animals, history, economy, language, religions, culture, sports and arts, and people of Belgium
Includes bibliographical references

949.35   Luxembourg

Sheehan, Patricia
Luxembourg. Benchmark Bks. 1997 128p il maps (Cultures of the world) lib bdg $37.07 (5 and up)
949.35
1. Luxembourg
ISBN 0-7614-0685-9   LC 96-53367
Discusses the geography, history, government, economy, and customs of the smallest of the Benelux countries
This is "lucidly written. . . . Informative chapters include discussion about body language, religion, education, and women." Horn Book Guide
Includes glossary and bibliographical references

949.4   Switzerland

Levy, Patricia
Switzerland; [by] Patricia Levy & Richard Lord. 2nd ed. Benchmark Books 2005 144p il map (Cultures of the world) lib bdg $37.70 (5 and up)
949.4
1. Switzerland
ISBN 0-7614-1850-4
First published 1994
Describes the geography, history, government, economy, people, and culture of Switzerland.
Includes glossary and bibliographical references

949.5   Greece

DuBois, Jill
  Greece; [by] Jill Dubois, Xenia Skoura, Olga Gratsaniti. 2nd ed. Benchmark Bks. 2003 143p il maps (Cultures of the world) lib bdg $37.07 (5 and up)   **949.5**
  1. Greece
  ISBN 0-7614-1499-1   LC 2002-11625
  First published 1992 under the authorship of Jill DuBois
  Introduces the geography, history, economics, culture, and people of the Mediterranean country of Greece
  "An attractive, lively, and perceptive look at Greece." SLJ
  Includes glossary and bibliographical references

Gordon, Sharon
  Greece. Benchmark Bks. 2004 48p il maps (Discovering cultures) lib bdg $25.64 (2-4)   **949.5**
  1. Greece
  ISBN 0-7614-1718-4   LC 2003-8130
  Contents: Where in the world is Greece?; What makes Greece Greek?; Living in Greece; School days; Just for fun; Let's celebrate!
  An introduction to the history, geography, language, schools, and social life and customs of Greece
  Includes glossary and bibliographical references

949.6   Balkan Peninsula

Barber, Nicola
  Istanbul; [by] Nicola Barber. World Almanac Library 2006 48p il map (Great cities of the world) lib bdg $30 (3-6)   **949.6**
  1. Istanbul (Turkey)
  ISBN 0-8368-5050-5   LC 2005042112
  This describes the geography, culture, work, play, history, and religion of Istanbul, Turkey.
  This is "attractive, informative. . . . straightforward and objective." SLJ
  Includes bibliographical references

949.65   Albania

Knowlton, MaryLee
  Albania; by MaryLee Knowlton. Marshall Cavendish Benchmark 2005 144p il map (Cultures of the world) lib bdg $37.07 (5 and up)   **949.65**
  1. Albania
  ISBN 0-7614-1852-0   LC 2004-22236
  Contents: Geography; History; Government; Economy; Environment; Albanians; Lifestyle; Religion; Language; Arts; Leisure; Festivals; Food
  An overview of the history, culture, peoples, religion, government, and geography of Albania
  Includes glossary and bibliographical references

Wright, David K.
  Albania. Children's Press 1997 143p il map (Enchantment of the world, second series) $33 (5 and up)   **949.65**
  1. Albania
  ISBN 0-516-20468-8   LC 97-4973
  Describes the geography, plants, animals, history, economy, language, religions, culture, sports, arts, and people of Albania
  Includes bibliographical references

949.7   Serbia and Montenegro, Croatia, Slovenia, Bosnia and Hercegovina, Macedonia

Cooper, Robert
  Croatia. Benchmark Bks. 2001 128p il map (Cultures of the world) lib bdg $37.07 (5 and up)   **949.7**
  1. Croatia
  ISBN 0-7614-1156-9   LC 00-29510
  "The initial chapters go over basic geography, history, and government, while the bulk of the book examines Croatia's culture and contemporary life. The short chapters are divided into highlighted segments of a page or two. This format allows easy access to information." SLJ
  Includes glossary and bibliographical references

Halilbegovich, Nadja
  My childhood under fire; a Sarajevo diary. Kids Can Press 2006 120p il $14.95 (5 and up)   **949.7**
  1. Yugoslav War, 1991-1995 2. Sarajevo (Bosnia and Hercegovina)
  ISBN 1-55337-797-4
  "In 1992, when the bombing started in Sarajevo, Halilbegovich, 12, kept a diary of her terrifying daily life under siege. Her terse vignettes replay the horror of her comfortable home torn apart." Booklist

King, David C.
  Serbia and Montenegro; by David C. King. Benchmark Bks. 2005 144p il map (Cultures of the world) lib bdg $37.07 (5 and up)   **949.7**
  1. Serbia 2. Montenegro
  ISBN 0-7614-1855-5   LC 2004-22248
  Contents: Geography; History; Government; Economy; Environment; Serbs and Montenegrins; Lifestyle; Religion; Language; Arts; Leisure; Festivals; Food
  This offers "historical, geographical, and cultural information as well as observations about contemporary lifestyles and issues. In general the writing is clear; at times it is lively. . . . The photographs are excellent." SLJ
  Includes glossary and bibliographical references

Knowlton, MaryLee
Macedonia; by MaryLee Knowlton. Benchmark Books 2005 144p il map (Cultures of the world) lib bdg $25.95 (5 and up)   **949.7**
1. Macedonia (Republic)
ISBN 0-7614-1854-7   LC 2004-22735
Contents: Geography; History; Government; Economy; Environment; Macedonians; Lifestyle; Religion; Language; Arts; Leisure; Festivals; Food
Describes the geography, history, government, economy, people, and culture of Macedonia
Includes glossary and bibliographical references

Milivojevic, JoAnn
Bosnia and Herzegovina. Children's Press 2004 144p il map (Enchantment of the world, Second series) lib bdg $35 (5 and up)   **949.7**
1. Bosnia and Hercegovina
ISBN 0-516-24247-4   LC 2002-15581
Contents: Wrapped; Land of forests and mountains; What lives high and low; Bosnia through the centuries; Forming a new country; Economy past, present, future; One country, three ethnic groups; Three faiths; Artistic expressions; Enjoying life
Describes the history, geography, economy, and culture of Bosnia and Herzegovina
This offers "lucid commentary, digestible quantities of facts and statistics, eye-catching color photos, and eminently useful back matter." Booklist
Includes bibliographical references

Serbia. rev ed. Children's Press 2003 144p il map (Enchantment of the world, Second series) lib bdg $35 (5 and up)   **949.7**
1. Serbia
ISBN 0-516-22695-9   LC 2002-8262
First published 1999
Contents: Crossroads; From the mountains to the Valleys; Where the wild things grow; When Serbia began; Citizens revolt, a new president leads; Money, money, money; Who lives in Serbia?; Traditions, faith, and folklore; Pictures, words, and music; At home, school, and play
An introduction to the geography, history, economy, government, and culture of Serbia
Includes bibliographical references

Orr, Tamra
Slovenia; by Tamra Orr. Children's Press 2004 144p il map (Enchantment of the world, Second series) lib bdg $35 (5 and up)   **949.7**
1. Slovenia
ISBN 0-516-24249-0   LC 2003-15253
Contents: A small but mighty country; Frigid Alps to underground caverns; Animal and plant life; From instability to independence; A new independence; Economic stability and strength; Proud Slovenes; Faith and tradition; The arts and sports; Daily life
Discusses the geography and climate, history, wildlife, economy, government, people, religion, and culture of Slovenia.
This "basically well-written [book] should engage a wide range of readers with varied interests. . . . The ex-

cellent quality of the photos contributes to the attractiveness of [this volume.]" SLJ
Includes bibliographical references

950   Asia. Orient. Far East

Peoples of Eastern Asia. Marshall Cavendish 2004 11v il map set $329.95 (5 and up)   **950**
1. Asia
ISBN 0-7614-7547-8   LC 2003-69645
Contents: v1 Bangladesh-Brunei; v2 Cambodia-China; v3 China-East Timor; v4 India; v5 Indonesia; v6 Japan-Korea, North; v7 Korea, South-Malaysia; v8 Mongolia-Nepal; v 9 Philippines-Sri Lanka; v10 Taiwan-Vietnam; v11 Index
This "alphabetically arranged set covers the countries ranging from India in the West to the island nations of the western Pacific, and from Mongolia southward through Indonesia. . . . The entries open with a brief geographical introduction and map, a facts and figures box, and information on the nation's history with a time line running along the bottom of the page. The text then discusses the people, minority populations, lifestyles, religion, jobs, foods . . ., transportation, health, education, architecture, the performing and visual arts, literature, recreation, and festivals. . . . Numerous full-color and archival black-and-white photographs lend appeal. . . . This useful set is reliable." SLJ
Includes bibliographical references

Stefoff, Rebecca
The Asian empires; by Rebecca Stefoff. Benchmark Books 2004 c2005 48p il map (World historical atlases) lib bdg $27.07 (5 and up)
950
1. China—History 2. China—Civilization 3. India 4. Turkey
ISBN 0-7614-1643-9   LC 2004-8703
This introduces the empires of Imperial China, early India, and Ottoman Turkey
This is "clearly written and well organized. The [book includes] large, full-color photographs and illustrations reproduced from original pieces of art found in diverse national museums. . . . [This volume makes an] excellent [supplement] to history lessons and [a] good starting [point] for research." SLJ
Includes bibliographical references

951   China and adjacent areas

Asher, Sandy
China. Benchmark Bks. 2003 48p il map (Discovering cultures) lib bdg $16.95 (2-4)
951
1. China
ISBN 0-7614-1179-8   LC 2001-7293
Includes index
Highlights the geography, people, food, schools, recreation, celebrations, and language of China
Includes glossary and bibliographical references

Dramer, Kim

People's Republic of China. Children's Press 1999 144p il map (Enchantment of the world, second series) lib bdg $33 (5 and up)

951

1. China

ISBN 0-516-21077-7   LC 98-17643

Describes the geography, plants and animals, history, economy, language, religions, culture, and people of the People's Republic of China, home of one of the world's oldest continuous civilizations

"An attractive, insightful book with a broad scope." SLJ

Includes glossary and bibliographical references

Ferroa, Peggy Grace

China; [by] Peggy Ferroa, Elaine Chan. 2nd ed. Benchmark Bks. 2002 144p il map (Cultures of the world) lib bdg $37.07 (5 and up)   **951**

1. China

ISBN 0-7614-1474-6   LC 2002-19209

First published 1991

Describes the geography, history, government, economy, environment, people, and culture of China

Includes glossary and bibliographical references

Kummer, Patricia K.

Tibet; [by] Patricia K. Kummer. Children's Press 2003 144p il map (Enchantment of the world, second series) lib bdg $35 (5 and up)

951

1. Tibet (China)

ISBN 0-516-22693-2   LC 2002-156704

Introduces Tibet, including its geography and climate, history, government, economy, people, culture, religion, language, and activities of daily life

Includes bibliographical references

Sís, Peter

Tibet; through the red box. Farrar, Straus & Giroux 1998 unp il maps $25   **951**

1. Tibet (China)

ISBN 0-374-37552-6   LC 97-50175

A Caldecott Medal honor book, 1999

"Frances Foster books"

"When Sis opens the red lacquered box that has sat on his father's table for decades, he finds the diary his father kept when he was lost in Tibet in the mid-1950s. The text replicates the diary's spidery handwriting, while the illustrations depict elaborate mazes and mandalas, along with dreamlike spreads that are filled with fragmented details of the father's and son's lives. . . . Impeccably designed and beautifully made, the book has a dreamlike quality that will keep readers of many ages coming back to find more in its pages." Booklist

951.05   China--Period of People's Republic, 1949-

Fritz, Jean

China homecoming; with photographs by Michael Fritz. Putnam 1985 143p il $19.99 (6 and up)

951.05

1. China

ISBN 0-399-21182-9   LC 84-24775

Companion volume to Homesick: my own story

This account of the author's return to Hankow after four decades "is intended for a slightly older readership than 'Homesick' . . . as it is not only an autobiography, but also a glimpse of Chinese history and a social commentary. It is, however, a book to be read and reread." SLJ

Includes bibliographical references

Jiang, Ji-li

Red scarf girl; a memoir of the Cultural Revolution; foreword by David Henry Hwang. HarperCollins Pubs. 1997 285p $16.99; pa $6.99 (6 and up)

951.05

1. China—History—1949-1976—Personal narratives

ISBN 0-06-027585-5; 0-06-446208-0 (pa)

LC 97-5089

"This is an autobiographical account of growing up during Mao's Cultural Revolution in China in 1966. . . . Jiang describes in terrifying detail the ordeals of her family and those like them, including unauthorized search and seizure, persecution, arrest and torture, hunger, and public humiliation. . . . Her voice is that of an intelligent, confused adolescent, and her focus on the effects of the revolution on herself, her family, and her friends provides an emotional focal point for the book, and will allow even those with limited knowledge of Chinese history to access the text." Bull Cent Child Books

Ma Yan

The diary of Ma Yan; the struggles and hopes of a Chinese schoolgirl; edited and introduced by Pierre Haski; translated from the French by Lisa Appignanesi. 1st American ed. HarperCollins 2005 166p $15.99; lib bdg $16.89 (5 and up)

951.05

1. China

ISBN 0-06-076496-1; 0-06-076497-X (lib bdg)

LC 2004-16136

Original French edition, 2002

"The diaries were originally translated from the Mandarin by He Yanping."

"In 2001, while a French journalist was visiting remote Ningxia province in northwest China, a Muslim woman wearing the white headscarf of the Hui people thrust the diaries of her daughter into his hands. The three small notebooks described the girl's struggle to get an education despite extreme poverty. . . . The girl's feelings for her mother were powerful and complex, and she alternated between overwhelming love and rage at the injustices she suffered." SLJ

Zhang, Ange
Red land, yellow river; a story from the Cultural Revolution. Douglas & McIntyre 2004 55p il $16.95 (5 and up)   **951.05**
1. China—History—1949-1976—Personal narratives
ISBN 0-88899-489-3
"A Groundwood book"
"Zhang was a teen living in Beijing when Mao Zedong began the Cultural Revolution. In a youthful voice he records his experiences in the early years of that turbulent decade that began in 1966. . . . This moving account of a youngster swept up in the revolutionary fervor and then beginning to question its goals is accompanied by attractive, digitally rendered illustrations." SLJ

951.2   Taiwan, Hong Kong, Macau

Waterlow, Julia
The Yangtze. World Almanac Lib. 2003 48p il map (Great rivers of the world) lib bdg $26.60; pa $14.60 (4 and up)   **951.2**
1. Yangtze River valley (China)
ISBN 0-8368-5447-0 (lib bdg); 0-8368-5454-3 (pa)
LC 2002-33134
Contents: The course of the Yangtze; The Yangtze in history; Cities and settlements; Farming, transportation and industry; Animals and plants; Environmental issues; Recreation and leisure; The future
This covers the Yangtze River's "geography, wildlife, and history . . . and its impact on nearby peoples. The presentation is exceptionally clear and lively. . . . Exquisite, full-color photos and maps." SLJ
Includes glossary and bibliographical references

951.7   Mongolia

Pang, Guek-Cheng
Mongolia. Benchmark Bks. 1999 128p il maps (Cultures of the world) lib bdg $37.07 (5 and up)
951.7
1. Mongolia
ISBN 0-7614-0954-8   LC 98-31897
Describes the geography, history, government, economy, people, lifestyle, religion, language, arts, leisure, festivals, and food of Mongolia
"High-quality, full-color photography combines with clearly written text and meaningful sidebars." SLJ
Includes glossary and bibliographical references

951.9   Korea

Ashabranner, Brent K.
Remembering Korea; the Korean War Veterans Memorial; [by] Brent Ashabranner; photographs by Jennifer Ashabranner. 21st Cent. Bks. (Brookfield) 2001 64p il (Great American memorials) lib bdg $25.90 (4 and up)   **951.9**
1. Korean War Veterans Memorial (Washington, D.C.)
2. Korean War, 1950-1953
ISBN 0-7613-2156-X   LC 00-68282

This "book begins at the memorial's dedication ceremony and gives an account of the planning, funding, site choice and the controversy surrounding the design. There is also an account of the Korean War. . . . Throughout, the writing is crisp and informative; excellent photographs, including evocative, black-and-white photos from the war and color photos of the dedication ceremony, and the memorial expand the text." Booklist
Includes bibliographical references

De Capua, Sarah
Korea. Benchmark Books 2004 c2005 48p il map (Discovering cultures) lib bdg $25.64 (2-4)
951.9
1. Korea
ISBN 0-7614-1794-X   LC 2004-6140
Contents: Where in the world is Korea?; What makes Korea Korean?; Living in Korea; School days; Just for fun; Let's celebrate!
An introduction to the geography, history, people, and culture of Korea
Includes glossary and bibliographical references

DuBois, Jill
Korea. 2nd ed. Benchmark Books 2004 144p il map (Cultures of the world) lib bdg $25.95 (5 and up)   **951.9**
1. Korea
ISBN 0-7614-1786-9   LC 2004-7678
First published 1994
Describes the geography, history, government, economy, environment, people, and culture of Korea
Includes glossary and bibliographical references

Feldman, Ruth Tenzer
The Korean War; by Ruth Tenzer Feldman. Lerner Publications Co 2004 88p il map (Chronicle of America's wars) lib bdg $27.93 (5 and up)   **951.9**
1. Korean War, 1950-1953
ISBN 0-8225-4716-3   LC 2002-156557
Contents: Korea sometime in January 1951; Drawing the line; Storm!; Saving the South; North to the Yalu almost; "An entirely new war"; Setting limits; The talking war; Epilogue; Timeline
This "begins briefly with the events that led to Korea's division before focusing in greater detail on North Korea's invasion of South Korea. The author offers good overviews of the roles of the major players, and she outlines the significant battles and campaigns, and the lengthy negotiations that resulted in armistice. . . . [This is] abundantly illustrated with color and black-and-white photographs as well as maps." Booklist
Includes glossary and bibliographical references

952   Japan

Behnke, Alison
Japan in pictures. Lerner Publs. 2003 79p il map (Visual geography series) lib bdg $27.93 (5 and up)   **952**
1. Japan
ISBN 0-8225-1956-9   LC 2001-2955

Behnke, Alison—*Continued*
First published 1989, catalogued under title
This describes Japan's "land, history and government, people, cultural life, and economy. Other information includes a timeline, fast facts, currency, flag, national anthem, famous people, sights to see . . . and Web sites. The [book is] visually appealing with photos and sidebars that complement the text." Libr Media Connect
Includes glossary and bibliographical references

Blumberg, Rhoda
Commodore Perry in the land of the Shogun. Lothrop, Lee & Shepard Bks. 1985 144p il map $18.95; pa $7.95 (5 and up)   **952**
1. Perry, Matthew Calbraith, 1794-1858 2. United States Naval Expedition to Japan (1852-1854) 3. United States—Foreign relations—Japan 4. Japan—Foreign relations—United States 5. Japan—History
ISBN 0-688-03723-2; 0-06-008625-4 (pa)
LC 84-21800
A Newbery Medal honor book, 1986
"The diplomatic expeditions of Commodore Matthew C. Perry to secure a treaty to provide for U.S. trade with Japan are described. The black-and-white period illustrations and informative text provide an in-depth and intimate view of nineteenth century Japan, Japanese and U.S. values and attitudes, and treaty negotiations." Soc Educ
Includes bibliographical references

Haskins, James
Count your way through Japan; by Jim Haskins; illustrations by Martin Skoro. Carolrhoda Bks. 1987 unp il lib bdg $19.93; pa $5.95 (2-4)
952
1. Japan
ISBN 0-87614-301-X (lib bdg); 0-87614-485-7 (pa)
LC 87-6398
Presents the numbers one to ten in Japanese, using each number to introduce concepts about Japan and its culture

Heinrichs, Ann
Japan. Children's Press 1998 143p il map (Enchantment of the world, second series) lib bdg $35 (5 and up)   **952**
1. Japan
ISBN 0-516-20649-4   LC 97-38771
Describes the history, geography, plants and animals, economy, language, people and culture of the island nation of Japan
"The writing is clear . . . the topics covered are broad in scope and will be suitable for assignments. Good-quality, full-color photographs, reproductions, and maps are interspersed throughout." SLJ
Includes bibliographical references

Reiser, Robert
Japan. Benchmark Bks. 2003 48p il map (Discovering cultures) lib bdg $25.64 (2-4)
952
1. Japan
ISBN 0-7614-1177-1   LC 2001-7459

Contents: Where in the world is Japan?; What makes Japan Japanese?; Living in Japan; School days; Just for fun; Let's celebrate
An introduction to the geography, history, people, and culture of Japan
Includes glossary and bibliographical references

Takabayashi, Mari
I live in Tokyo; written & illustrated by Mari Takabayashi. Houghton Mifflin 2001 unp il map $16 (k-3)   **952**
1. Tokyo (Japan) 2. Japan—Social life and customs
ISBN 0-618-07702-2   LC 00-5964
"Seven-year-old narrator Mimiko takes readers on a month-by-month tour of contemporary Tokyo, briefly describing one or two festivals, customs, or facets of life each month. The narrative remains consistently childlike throughout. . . . This book is a model of efficiency and elegance, cramming numerous details into a small space in a compact and attractive manner." Horn Book

953   Arabian Peninsula and adjacent areas

Augustin, Byron
United Arab Emirates. Children's Press 2002 144p il map (Enchantment of the world, Second series) lib bdg $35 (5 and up)   **953**
1. United Arab Emirates
ISBN 0-516-20473-4   LC 00-65958
Describes the geography, history, culture, economy, and people of the United Arab Emirates
"This attractive title enhanced with full-color photographs provides everything that most students need for a basic understanding of the country." SLJ
Includes bibliographical references

Foster, Leila Merrell
Oman. Children's Press 1999 144p il map (Enchantment of the world, second series) lib bdg $33 (5 and up)   **953**
1. Oman
ISBN 0-516-20964-7   LC 98-19572
Describes the geography, plants and animals, history, economy, language, religions, culture, and people of Oman, a small nation strategically located on the eastern part of the Arabian peninsula
Includes bibliographical references

953.3   Yemen

Hestler, Anna
Yemen. Benchmark Bks. 1999 128p il maps (Cultures of the world) lib bdg $37.07 (5 and up)
953.3
1. Yemen
ISBN 0-7614-0956-4   LC 98-53993
Presents information about the geography, history, government, and economy of this country located on the

Hestler, Anna—*Continued*
southwestern tip of the Arabian Peninsula and describes
many aspects of the lifestyle of its people
Includes glossary and bibliographical references

953.67   Kuwait

Foster, Leila Merrell
Kuwait. Children's Press 1998 143p il map
(Enchantment of the world, second series) lib bdg
$35 (5 and up)   **953.67**
1. Kuwait
ISBN 0-516-20604-4   LC 97-23845
Describes the history, geography, economy, language,
religion, sports, arts, and people of this oil-rich country
located on the northwestern shore of the Persian Gulf
Includes bibliographical references

O'Shea, Maria
Kuwait. Benchmark Bks. 1999 128p il maps
(Cultures of the world) lib bdg $37.07 (5 and up)
                                                  953.67
1. Kuwait
ISBN 0-7614-0871-1   LC 98-25833
Introduces the geography, history, religious beliefs,
government, and people of Kuwait, a small country on
the Persian Gulf
Includes glossary and bibliographical references

953.8   Saudi Arabia

Fazio, Wende
Saudi Arabia. Children's Press 1999 47p il lib
bdg $22; pa $6.95 (2-4)   **953.8**
1. Saudi Arabia
ISBN 0-516-21190-0 (lib bdg); 0-516-26502-4 (pa)
                                                LC 98-12273
"A True book"
Provides an overview of the geography, history, and
culture of the Kingdom of Saudi Arabia
"An informative text is coupled with crisp photo-
graphs." Horn Book Guide
Includes glossary and bibliographical references

Janin, Hunt
Saudi Arabia; [by] Hunt Janin, Margaret
Besheer. 2nd ed. Benchmark Bks. 2003 144p il
map (Cultures of the world) lib bdg $37.07 (5 and
up)   **953.8**
1. Saudi Arabia
ISBN 0-7614-1666-8   LC 2003-6931
First published 1993
Contents: Geography; History; Government; Economy;
Environment; Saudi Arabians; Lifestyle; Religion; Lan-
guage; Arts; Leisure; Festivals; Food; Map of Saudi Ara-
bia; About the economy; About the culture; Time line
Includes glossary and bibliographical references

954   South Asia. India

Engfer, Lee
India in pictures. Lerner Publs. 2003 80p il map
(Visual geography series) lib bdg $27.93 (5 and
up)   **954**
1. India
ISBN 0-8225-0371-9   LC 2002-950
Contents: The land; History and government; The peo-
ple; Cultural life; The economy
Text and illustrations present detailed information on
the geography, history and government, economy, people,
cultural life and society of traditional and modern India
The book is "visually appealing with photos and
sidebars that complement the text." Libr Media Connect
Includes bibliographical references

Guile, Melanie
Culture in India; [by] Melanie Guile. 1st ed.
Raintree 2005 32p il map lib bdg $29.29 (4 and
up)   **954**
1. India
ISBN 1-4109-1134-9   LC 2004-16649
Contents: Culture in India; Traditions and customs;
Minority groups; Costume and clothing; Food; Performing arts; Literature; Film and television; Arts and crafts
This "title includes a map and picture of the nation's
flag as well as color photographs that bring to life the
wide range of topics addressed. Two to four-page chapters briefly cover languages, history, people, religions,
holidays and festivals, customs, minority groups, costumes and clothing, food, and arts and crafts, providing
students with lots of cultural information. Text is well
spaced in an overall neat and pleasing manner." SLJ
Includes bibliographical references

Murphy, Patricia
India; by Patricia J. Murphy. Benchmark Bks.
2003 48p il map (Discovering cultures) lib bdg
$25.64 (2-4)   **954**
1. India
ISBN 0-7614-1516-5   LC 2002-15306
Highlights the geography, people, food, schools, recre-
ation, celebrations, and languages of the largest country
in Southeast Asia
"Report writers will appreciate [this] simply written
[volume]. . . . Illustrated with clear color photos." Horn
Book Guide
Includes glossary and bibliographical references

Srinivasan, Radhika
India; [by] Radhika Srinivasan, Leslie Jermyn.
2nd ed. Benchmark Bks. 2002 144p il maps
(Cultures of the world) $37.07 (5 and up)
                                                  954
1. India
ISBN 0-7614-1354-5   LC 2001-28608
First published 1990
This describes the geography, history, government,
economy, environment, people, and culture of India
Includes glossary and bibliographical references

954.91   Pakistan

Sheehan, Sean
    Pakistan; by Sean Sheehan. 2nd ed. Benchmark Books 2004 144p il map (Cultures of the world) lib bdg $37.07 (5 and up)   **954.91**
    ISBN 0-7614-1787-7   LC 2004-7677
    First published 1994
    Contents: Geography; History; Government; Economy; Environment; Pakistanis; Lifestyle; Religion; Language; Arts; Leisure; Festivals; Food
    An introduction to the geography, history, government, and culture of Pakistan
    "Excellent-quality, full-color photographs and sidebars highlight special information and make this book accessible and appealing. . . . A gold mine of information for reports." SLJ
    Includes glossary and bibliographical references

954.93   Sri Lanka

Wanasundera, Nanda P.
    Sri Lanka; [by] Nanda Pethiyagoda Wanasundera. 2nd ed. Benchmark Bks. 2002 144p il maps (Cultures of the world) lib bdg $37.07 (5 and up)   **954.93**
    1. Sri Lanka
    ISBN 0-7614-1477-0   LC 2002-25980
    First published 1990
    Describes the geography, history, government, economy, social life and customs, religion, culture, and more of this island country in the Indian Ocean
    Includes glossary and bibliographical references

954.96   Nepal

Burbank, Jon
    Nepal. 2nd ed. Benchmark Bks. 2002 144p il map (Cultures of the world) lib bdg $37.07 (5 and up)   **954.96**
    1. Nepal
    ISBN 0-7614-1476-2   LC 2002-25994
    First published 1991
    Describes the geography, history, government, economy, people, religion, language, and culture of Nepal, a predominantly Hindu country located north of India. Includes several recipes
    Includes glossary and bibliographical references

Kalz, Jill
    Mount Everest; by Jill Kalz. 1st ed. Creative Education 2004 32p il map (Natural wonders of the world) lib bdg $27.10 (4-6)   **954.96**
    1. Mount Everest (China and Nepal)
    ISBN 1-58341-325-1   LC 2003-65232
    This describes Mount Everest's "geological formation and climate, ecology and wildlife, and human inhabitants and expeditions. A final chapter is devoted to tourism. . . . The [text], sufficient in informational quantity and

quality for short reports, [is] briskly and engagingly written. But the real selling point here is the gorgeous color photographs." SLJ

955   Iran

Rajendra, Vijeya
    Iran; [by] Vijeya Rajendra, Gisela Kaplan, Rudi Rajendra. 2nd ed. Benchmark Bks. 2003 c2004 144p il map (Cultures of the world) lib bdg $37.07 (5 and up)   **955**
    1. Iran
    ISBN 0-7614-1665-X   LC 2003-8257
    First published 1993
    Contents: Geography; History; Government; Economy; Environment; Iranians; Lifestyle; Religion; Language; Arts; Leisure; Festivals; Food
    Explores the geography, history, government, economy, people, and culture of Iran
    Includes glossary and bibliographical references

956.04   Middle East--1945-1980

Senker, Cath
    The Arab-Israeli conflict; [by] Cath Senker. Smart Apple Media 2005 64p il map (Questioning history) $29.95 (5 and up)   **956.04**
    1. Israel-Arab conflicts
    ISBN 1-58340-441-4   LC 2003-65917
    This describes current conditions in Israel and the occupied territories and includes a history of major events and political developments
    "A complex situation is clearly explained. . . . [This is] well-illustrated . . . Throughout, the tone is nonjudgmental." SLJ
    Includes bibliographical references

956.1   Turkey

Orr, Tamra
    Turkey. Children's Press 2003 144p il map (Enchantment of the world, second series) lib bdg $34 (5 and up)   **956.1**
    1. Turkey
    ISBN 0-516-22679-7   LC 2002-1590
    Contents: Traveling through time; A unique meeting point; The flora and the fauna; A 3,000 year history; The new face of the government; Shifting the economy; The richness of the people; The ways of a spiritual life; The expanding world of Turkish culture; Daily life in Turkey; Timeline; Fast facts
    This describes the history, culture, flora and fauna, government, and economy of Turkey
    "Good-quality graphics and lively . . . [text makes this title] readable and visually enticing." SLJ
    Includes bibliographical references

Sheehan, Sean

Turkey. 2nd ed. Benchmark Bks. 2004 144p il map (Cultures of the world) lib bdg $25.95 (5 and up) **956.1**

1. Turkey
ISBN 0-7614-1705-2   LC 2003-20885
First published 1993

Contents: Geography; History; Government; Economy; Environment; The Turks; Lifestyle; Religion; Language; Arts; Leisure; Festivals; Food

Examines the geography, history, government, economy, people, and culture of Turkey

Includes glossary and bibliographical references

956.7   Iraq

Augustin, Byron

Iraq; by Byron Augustin and Jake Kubena. Rev. ed. Children's Press 2006 144p il map (Enchantment of the world, second series) lib bdg $36 (5 and up) **956.7**

1. Iraq
ISBN 0516248529   LC 2005032181
First published 1998

This describes the geography, history, culture, people, and government of Iraq.

This edition "focuses far less on Saddam Hussein and includes more details about the nation's different ethnic groups, environmental issues and wildlife, and information about the current political situation. . . . [The book contains] more full-color photographs than the previous [edition]. . . . Libraries will definitely want [this volume]." SLJ

Includes bibliographical references

Gaag, Nikki van der

Baghdad. World Almanac Lib. 2005 48p il map (Great cities of the world) lib bdg $30 (3-6) **956.7**

1. Baghdad (Iraq)
ISBN 0-8368-5049-1

This describes the geography, culture, work, play, history, and religion of Bagdad, Iraq.

This is "attractive, informative . . . straightforward and objective." SLJ

Hassig, Susan M.

Iraq; [by] Susan M. Hassig, Laith Muhmood Al Adely. 2nd ed. Benchmark Bks. 2003 144p il maps (Cultures of the world) lib bdg $37.07 (5 and up) **956.7**

1. Iraq
ISBN 0-7614-1668-4   LC 2003-10082
First published 1993

Explores the geography, history, government, economy, people, and culture of Iraq

Rau, Dana Meachen

Iraq. Benchmark Bks. 2004 48p il map (Discovering cultures) lib bdg $25.64 (2-4) **956.7**

1. Iraq
ISBN 0-7614-1726-5   LC 2003-19100

Contents: Where in the world is Iraq?; What makes Iraq Iraqi?; Living in Iraq; School days; Just for fun; Let's celebrate!

An introduction to the geography, history, people, and culture of Iraq

This book is "informative and balanced." SLJ

Includes glossary and bibliographical references

956.91   Syria

South, Coleman

Syria; by Coleman South & Leslie Jermyn. 2nd ed. Marshall Cavendish Benchmark 2006 144p il map (Cultures of the world) lib bdg $37.07 (5 and up) **956.91**

1. Syria
ISBN 0-7614-2054-1   LC 2005023848
First published 1995

This describes the geography, history, government, economy, culture, peoples, and religion of Syria

"Straightforward, up-to-date. . . . well-written. . . . The attractive layout features a high-quality full-color photo on each page." SLJ

Includes glossary and bibliographical references

956.93   Cyprus

Spilling, Michael

Cyprus. Benchmark Bks. 2000 128p il map (Cultures of the world) lib bdg $37.07 (5 and up) **956.93**

1. Cyprus
ISBN 0-7614-0978-5   LC 99-31942

Discusses the geography, history, government, economy, people, and culture of Cyprus

Includes glossary and bibliographical references

956.94   Palestine. Israel

Bowden, Rob

Jerusalem; [by] Rob Bowden. World Almanac Library 2006 48p il map (Great cities of the world) lib bdg $30 (3-6) **956.94**

1. Jerusalem
ISBN 0-8368-5051-3   LC 2005043586

This describes the geography, cultures, work, play, history, and religions of Jerusalem.

This is "attractive, informative. . . . straightforward and objective." SLJ

Includes bibliographical references

DuBois, Jill

Israel; by Jill DuBois, Mair Rosh. 2nd ed. Benchmark Bks. 2003 c2004 144p il map (Cultures of the world) lib bdg $37.07 (5 and up)
    956.94

1. Israel
ISBN 0-7614-1669-2   LC 2003-10083
First published 1993
Explores the geography, history, government, economy, people, and culture of Israel
Includes glossary and bibliographical references

Ellis, Deborah

Three wishes; Palestinian and Israeli children speak. Groundwood Bks. 2004 110p il map $16.95 (5 and up)
    956.94

1. Israel-Arab conflicts 2. Palestinian Arabs
ISBN 0-88899-608-X
"Growing up separate and apart in a world of bombs, bullets, removals, checkpoints, and curfews, 20 Israeli and Palestinian young people talk about how the war has affected them." Booklist
"An excellent presentation of a confusing historic struggle, told within a palpable, perceptive and empathetic format." SLJ
Includes bibliographical references

Grossman, Laurie M.

Children of Israel; written and photographed by Laurie M. Grossman. Carolrhoda Bks. 2000 48p il (World's children) lib bdg $23.93 (2-4)
    956.94

1. Israel
ISBN 1-57505-448-5   LC 99-50907
Introduces the history, geography, and culture of Israel through the daily lives of children who live there
"At least one captivating, full-color photograph illustrates each page. [This book] also includes a helpful pronunciation guide and a map." SLJ

Haskins, James

Count your way through Israel; illustrations by Rick Hanson. Carolrhoda Bks. 1990 unp il lib bdg $19.93; pa $5.95 (2-4)
    956.94
1. Israel
ISBN 0-87614-415-6 (lib bdg); 0-87614-558-6 (pa)
      LC 90-1594
An introduction to the land and people of Israel accompanied by instructions on how to read and pronounce the numbers one through ten in Hebrew

Roy, Jennifer Rozines

Israel. Benchmark Bks. 2003 48p il maps (Discovering cultures) lib bdg $25.64 (2-4)
    956.94

1. Israel
ISBN 0-7614-1720-6   LC 2003-8127
Contents: Where in the world is Israel?; What makes Israel Israeli?; Living in Israel; School days; Just for fun; Let's celebrate!
Highlights the geography, people, food, schools, recreation, celebrations, and language of Israel
Includes glossary and bibliographical references

958.1   Afghanistan

Behnke, Alison

Afghanistan in pictures. rev and expanded. Lerner Publs. 2003 80p il map (Visual geography series) lib bdg $27.93 (5 and up)   **958.1**
1. Afghanistan
ISBN 0-8225-4683-3   LC 2002-13613
First published 1989
An introduction to the geography, history, government, people, and economy of this landlocked country with a long history of warfare and conquest
Includes glossary and bibliographical references

Greenblatt, Miriam

Afghanistan; [by] Miriam Greenblatt. Children's Press 2003 144p il map (Enchantment of the world, Second series) lib bdg $35 (5 and up)
    958.1

1. Afghanistan
ISBN 0-516-22696-7   LC 2002-156471
Contents: A troubled land; A difficult environment; Forests, flowers, animals, and plants; A turbulent history; A transitional government; Earning a living; A varied population; Religious beliefs; An active culture; Lifestyles; Timeline; Fast facts
An introduction to the geography, history, economy, government, and culture of Afghanistan

Kazem, Halima

Afghanistan. Stevens, G. 2003 96p il map (Countries of the world) lib bdg $29.26 (4 and up)
    958.1

1. Afghanistan
ISBN 0-8368-2357-5   LC 2002-75787
Discusses the geography, history, government, economy, people, politics, and culture of Afghanistan
"A well-organized title that fills the need for an up-to-date book on this country. Clearly written information . . . is illustrated with vibrant color photographs on almost every page." SLJ
Includes glossary and bibliographical references

958.4   Turkestan

King, David C.

Kyrgyzstan; [by] David C. King. 1st ed. Marshall Cavendish Benchmark 2005 144p il map (Cultures of the world) lib bdg $37.07 (5 and up)
    958.4

1. Kyrgyzstan
ISBN 0-7614-2013-4   LC 2005001314
Describes the geography, history, government, economy, people, and culture of Kyrgyzstan
Includes glossary and bibliographical references

958.5   Turkmenistan

Knowlton, MaryLee
  Turkmenistan; [by] MaryLee Knowlton. 1st ed.
Marshall Cavendish Benchmark 2006 144p il map
(Cultures of the world) lib bdg $37.07 (5 and up)
958.5
  1. Turkmenistan
  ISBN 0-7614-2014-2   LC 2005006455
  Describes the geography, history, government, econo-
my, people, and culture of Turkmenistan
  Includes glossary and bibliographical references

958.6   Tajikistan

Abazov, Rafis
  Tajikistan; [by] Rafis Abazov. 1st ed. Marshall
Cavendish Benchmark 2006 144p il map (Cultures
of the world) lib bdg $37.07 (5 and up)
958.6
  1. Tajikistan
  ISBN 0-7614-2012-6   LC 2005001166
  Describes the geography, history, government, econo-
my, people, and culture of the former Soviet republic of
Tajikistan
  Includes glossary and bibliographical references

958.7   Uzbekistan

Knowlton, MaryLee
  Uzbekistan; [by] MaryLee Knowlton. Marshall
Cavendish Benchmark 2005 144p il map (Cultures
of the world) lib bdg $37.07 (5 and up)
958.7
  1. Uzbekistan
  ISBN 0-7614-2016-9   LC 2005016875
  An examination of the geography, history, govern-
ment, economy, culture, and peoples of Uzbekistan
  Includes glossary and bibliographical references

959.1   Myanmar

Yin, Saw Myat
  Myanmar. 2nd ed. Benchmark Bks. 2002 144p
il map (Cultures of the world) lib bdg $37.07 (5
and up)   **959.1**
  1. Myanmar
  ISBN 0-7614-1353-7   LC 2001-25412
  First published 1990
  This describes the geography, history, government,
economy, environment, people, and culture of Myanmar
  Includes glossary and bibliographical references

959.3   Thailand

Goodman, Jim
  Thailand. 2nd ed. Benchmark Bks. 2003 144p il
map (Cultures of the world) lib bdg $37.07 (5 and
up)   **959.3**
  1. Thailand
  ISBN 0-7614-1478-9   LC 2002-25979
  First published 1990
  Describes the geography, history, government, econo-
my, people, religion, language, and culture of Thailand,
a predominantly Buddhist country located in Southeast
Asia. Includes several recipes
  Includes glossary and bibliographical references

Morris, Ann
  Tsunami; helping each other; by Ann Morris &
Heidi Larson. Millbrook Press 2005 32p il map
$15.95 (3-5)   **959.3**
  1. Tsunamis 2. Indian Ocean earthquake and tsunami,
2004 3. Thailand
  ISBN 0-7613-9501-6   LC 2005-13616
  The story of how one family in Thailand survived the
tsunami of December 26, 2004, and, with the help of
others, began to rebuild their lives.
  "The brisk and straightforward text is enhanced by
many excellent well-captioned color photos." Horn Book
Guide

959.5   Commonwealth of Nations territories. Malaysia

Guile, Melanie
  Culture in Malaysia; [by] Melanie Guile. 1st ed.
Raintree 2005 32p il map lib bdg $29.29 (4 and
up)   **959.5**
  1. Malaysia
  ISBN 1-4109-1133-0   LC 2004-16650
  Contents: Culture in Malaysia; Traditions and customs; Minority groups; Costume and clothing; Food; Performing arts; Folklore and literature; Film and television;
Arts and crafts
  This "title includes a map and picture of the nation's
flag as well as color photographs that bring to life the
wide range of topics addressed. Two to four-page chapters briefly cover languages, history, people, religions,
holidays and festivals, customs, minority groups, costumes and clothing, food, and arts and crafts, providing
students with lots of cultural information. Text is well
spaced in an overall neat and pleasing manner." SLJ
  Includes bibliographical references

959.57   Singapore

Layton, Lesley
  Singapore; [by] Lesley Layton, Pang Guek
Cheng. 2nd ed. Benchmark Bks. 2002 144p il map
(Cultures of the world) lib bdg $37.07 (5 and up)
959.57
  1. Singapore
  ISBN 0-7614-1352-9   LC 2001-25413

Layton, Lesley—*Continued*
First published 1990
This describes the geography, history, government, economy, environment, people, and culture of Singapore
Includes glossary and bibliographical references

Rau, Dana Meachen
Singapore. Benchmark Bks. 2004 48p il map (Discovering cultures) lib bdg $25.64 (2-4)
959.57
1. Singapore
ISBN 0-7614-1727-3   LC 2003-19102
Contents: Where in the world is Singapore?; What makes Singapore Singaporean?; Living in Singapore; School days; Just for fun; Let's celebrate!
An introduction to the geography, history, people, and culture of Singapore
This book is "informative and balanced." SLJ
Includes glossary and bibliographical references

959.7 Vietnam

Guile, Melanie
Culture in Vietnam; [by] Melanie Guile. 1st ed. Raintree 2005 32p il map lib bdg $29.29 (4 and up)
959.7
1. Vietnam
ISBN 1-4109-1135-7   LC 2004-16651
Contents: Culture in Vietnam; Traditions and customs; Minority groups; Costume and clothing; Food; Performing arts; Film and television; Literature; Arts and crafts
This "title includes a map and picture of the nation's flag as well as color photographs that bring to life the wide range of topics addressed. Two to four-page chapters briefly cover languages, history, people, religions, holidays and festivals, customs, minority groups, costumes and clothing, food, and arts and crafts, providing students with lots of cultural information. Text is well spaced in an overall neat and pleasing manner." SLJ
Includes bibliographical references

959.704 Vietnam--1949-

Canwell, Diane
African Americans in the Vietnam War; [by] Diane Canwell and Jon Sutherland. World Almanac Library 2005 48p il map (American experience in Vietnam) lib bdg $30; pa $11.95 (5 and up)
959.704
1. Vietnam War, 1961-1975 2. African American soldiers
ISBN 0-8368-5772-0 (lib bdg); 0-8368-5779-8 (pa)
LC 2004-58096
This is an illustrated history of the role of American Americans in the Vietnam War.
"Browsers will gravitate to this . . . given the personal stories as well as the quality . . . and subject matter of the full-color photos. . . . Readers will pick up some sense of the history here." Booklist
Includes bibliographical references

Levy, Debbie
The Vietnam War; by Debbie Levy. Lerner Publications 2004 88p il map (Chronicle of America's wars) lib bdg $27.93 (5 and up)
959.704
1. Vietnam War, 1961-1975
ISBN 0-8225-0421-9   LC 2002-156558
Contents: A history of struggle; Deadly dominoes; From Cold War to hot war; Americans at war; Turning point; The end begins; America lets go
This describes the events of the Vietnam War, focusing on the impact the war had on America and its people.
Includes glossary and bibliographical references

Seah, Audrey
Vietnam; [by] Audrey Seah, Charissa M. Nair. 2nd ed. Benchmark Books 2004 144p il map (Cultures of the world) lib bdg $37.07 (5 and up)
959.704
1. Vietnam
ISBN 0-7614-1789-3   LC 2004-12903
First published 1994
Contents: Geography; History; Government; Economy; Environment; Vietnamese; Lifestyle; Religion; Language; Arts; Leisure; Festivals; Food
This describes the geography, history, government, economy environment, and culture of Vietnam
Includes glossary and bibliographical references

959.9 Philippines

Gordon, Sharon
Philippines. Benchmark Bks. 2003 48p il map (Discovering cultures) lib bdg $25.64 (2-4)
959.9
1. Philippines
ISBN 0-7614-1518-1   LC 2002-15304
Highlights the geography, people, food, schools, recreation, celebrations, and languages of the Philippines
"Report writers will appreciate [this] simply written [volume]. . . . Illustrated with clear color photos." Horn Book Guide
Includes glossary and bibliographical references

Tope, Lily Rose R.
Philippines; [by] Lily R. Tope, Detch P. Nonan-Mercado. 2nd ed. Benchmark Bks. 2002 144p il maps (Cultures of the world) lib bdg $37.07 (5 and up)
959.9
1. Philippines
ISBN 0-7614-1475-4   LC 2002-19725
First published 1990
Discusses the geography, history, government, economy, people, and culture of the Philippines, an archipelago of many islands in the Western Pacific
Includes glossary and bibliographical references

960 Africa

961.2 Libya

Haskins, James

African beginnings; [by] James Haskins & Kathleen Benson; paintings by Floyd Cooper. Lothrop, Lee & Shepard Bks. 1998 48p il map $17.99; lib bdg $17.89 (4 and up)   **960**

1. Africa—History
ISBN 0-688-10256-5; 0-688-10257-3 (lib bdg)
                                    LC 94-9848
This is an "overview of the great African kingdoms between 3800 B.C. and A.D. 1800. Sections on the kingdoms of Nubia, Egypt, Jenne-Jeno, Ghana, Mao, Songhay, etc., briefly discuss trade, education, art, agriculture, and other practices." Bull Cent Child Books
Cooper "fills in the geographical and cultural details with soft-edged, luminous oil paintings." Publ Wkly
Includes bibliographical references

Malcolm, Peter

Libya; [by] Peter Malcolm, Elie Losleben. 2nd ed. Benchmark Bks. 2004 144p il map (Cultures of the world) lib bdg $37.07 (5 and up)
                                    961.2

1. Libya
ISBN 0-7614-1702-8   LC 2003-20887
First published 1993
Contents: Geography; History; Government; Economy; Environment; Libyans minority; Lifestyle; Religion; Language; Arts; Leisure; Festivals; Food
Examines the geography, history, government, economy, people, and culture of Libya
Includes glossary and bibliographical references

962 Egypt and Sudan

Bowden, Rob

The Nile; [by] Rob Bowden. Raintree Steck-Vaughn Publishers 2004 48p il map (River journey) lib bdg $29.93 (5 and up)   **962**
1. Nile River 2. Nile River valley
ISBN 0-7398-6072-0   LC 2002-155378
Contents: The source of the Nile; Calming the Nile; The rivers meet; The Nile cataracts; The Nile Valley; The Nile Delta
The author presents information about the Nile River "as though readers are taking a trip from the river's source to where it meets the sea. This approach works surprisingly well at drawing youngsters in. . . . The author presents an integrated view of the geological, economic, and cultural aspects of [The Nile], and does not shy away from realities, such as how thousands of people lose their homes when dams are built, or the pollution that threatens wildlife. Full-color photographs appear throughout." SLJ

Musgrove, Margaret

Ashanti to Zulu: African traditions; pictures by Leo and Diane Dillon. Dial Bks. for Young Readers 1976 unp il $15.99; pa $5.99 (3-6)
                                    960

1. Africa—Social life and customs 2. Ethnology—Africa
ISBN 0-8037-0357-0; 0-14-054604-9 (pa)
Awarded the Caldecott Medal, 1977
"In brief texts arranged in alphabetical order, each accompanied by a large framed illustration, the author introduces 'the reader to twenty-six African peoples by depicting a custom important to each.' . . . In most of the paintings the artists 'have included a man, a woman, a child, their living quarters, an artifact, and a local animal' and have, in this way, stressed the human and the natural ambience of the various peoples depicted." Horn Book
"The writing is dignified and the material informative, but it is the illustrations that make the book outstanding." Bull Cent Child Books

Cumming, David

The Nile. World Almanac Lib. 2003 48p il maps (Great rivers of the world) lib bdg $26.60 (4 and up)   **962**
1. Nile River 2. Nile River valley
ISBN 0-8368-5445-4   LC 2002-33139
Contents: The course of the river; The Nile in history; Cities and settlements; Farming, trade, and industry; Animals and plants; Environmental issues; Recreation and leisure; The future
This describes the geography, wildlife, and history of the Nile River and its impact on people of the Nile River valley
"The presentation is exceptionally clear and lively. . . . Exquisite, full-color photos and maps show the beauty and dangers of the [river]. . . . Useful for reports and enjoyable as recreational reading." SLJ
Includes glossary and bibliographical references

961.1 Tunisia

Brown, Roslind Varghese

Tunisia. Benchmark Bks. 1998 128p il maps (Cultures of the world) lib bdg $37.07 (5 and up)
                                    961.1

1. Tunisia
ISBN 0-7614-0690-5   LC 97-15883
Examines the history, economy, people, lifestyles, and culture of this Arab country in northern Africa
Includes glossary and bibliographical references

Parker, Lewis K.

Egypt. Benchmark Bks. 2003 48p il map (Discovering cultures) lib bdg $25.64 (2-4)

962

1. Egypt

ISBN 0-7614-1519-X　　　　LC 2002-15305

Highlights the geography, people, food, schools, recreation, celebrations, and language of Egypt

This "is written in simple prose and illustrated with appealing color photos. The emphasis is on child-friendly topics. . . . Helpful for school reports." Horn Book Guide

Includes glossary and bibliographical references

Pateman, Robert

Egypt; [by] Robert Pateman, Salwa El-Hamamsy. 2nd ed. Benchmark Bks. 2003 144p il map (Cultures of the world) lib bdg $37.07 (5 and up)

962

1. Egypt

ISBN 0-7614-1670-6　　　　LC 2003-9859

First published 1993

Contents: Geography; History; Government; Economy; Environment; Egyptians; Lifestyle; Religion; Language; Arts; Leisure; Festivals; Food; Map of Egypt; About the economy; About the culture

Explores the geography, history, government, economy, people, and culture of Egypt

Includes glossary and bibliographical references

Zuehlke, Jeffrey

Egypt in pictures. Lerner Publs. 2003 80p il map (Visual geography series) lib bdg $27.93 (5 and up)

962

1. Egypt

ISBN 0-8225-0367-0　　　　LC 2001-6613

Contents: The land, the Nile River and Delta, deserts, the Aswan High Dam, climate, Flora and Fauna, natural resources, Cairo, ports, secondary cities; History and government, the age of the pyramids, the middle kingdom, the new kingdom, Greek and Roman rule, early Arab rulers, the Fatimids, the Mamluks, the Ottoman Empire, Muhammad Ali Pasha, European intervention, independence, the revolution of 1952, the Suez war, union with Syria, the Six-Day war, Anwar el-Sadat, peace with Israel, Hosni Mubarak government; The People, ethnic groups, way of life, health, education, langauge; Cultural life, religion, architecture, literature, marriage, social life and customs, festivals and food, sports and recreation; The Economy, agriculture, industry, transportation, trade, tourism, the future

Discusses the physical features, history, government, people, culture, and economy of Egypt

Includes bibliographical references

964　Northwest African coast and offshore islands. Morocco

Seward, Pat

Morocco; [by] Pat Seward & Orin Hargraves. 2nd ed. Marshall Cavendish Benchmark 2006 144p il map (Cultures of the world) lib bdg $37.07 (5 and up)

964

1. Morocco

ISBN 0-7614-2051-7　　　　LC 2005020782

First published 1995

Describes the geography, history, government, economy, people, and culture of Morocco

Includes glossary and bibliographical references

965　Algeria

Hintz, Martin

Algeria; by Martin Hintz. rev ed. Children's Press 2006 144p il map (Enchantment of the world, second series) lib bdg $30 (5 and up)

965

1. Algeria

ISBN 0516248553　　　　LC 2005007825

First published 1993

Describes the history, geography, people, culture, and government of Algeria

This edition "has less discussion of the French colonial experience and includes more about the current government, a section on rai music, and a new chapter depicting a day in the life of a typical Algerian boy.[The book contains] more full-color photographs than the previous [edition], and the statistics, time lines, and Web sites have been . . . added. . . . Libraries will definitely want [this volume]." SLJ

Includes bibliographical references

966.2　Mali, Burkina Faso, Niger

McKissack, Patricia C.

The royal kingdoms of Ghana, Mali, and Songhay; life in medieval Africa; [by] Patricia and Fredrick McKissack. Holt & Co. 1993 142p il maps pa $9.95 hardcover o.p. (5 and up)

966.2

1. Ghana Empire 2. Songhai Empire 3. Mali—History

ISBN 0-8050-4259-8 (pa)　　　　LC 93-4838

Examines the civilizations of the Western Sudan which flourished from 700 to 1700 A.D., acquiring such vast wealth that they became centers of trade and culture for a continent

"The McKissacks are careful to distinguish what is known from what is surmised; they draw on the oral tradition, eyewitness accounts, and contemporary scholarship; and chapter source notes discuss various conflicting views of events." Booklist

Includes bibliographical references

966.23 Mali

Brook, Larry
Daily life in ancient and modern Timbuktu; illustrations by Ray Webb. Runestone Press 1999 64p il (Cities through time) lib bdg $25.26 (4 and up) **966.23**
1. Tombouctou (Mali)
ISBN 0-8225-3215-8   LC 98-18314
Examines the history of the city of Timbuktu, or Tombouctou, from its time as a camping site for nomadic Tuaregs through its prominence in the sixteenth century to the current decline it faces
"Brook presents the political and social history of the city known as the 'Pearl of Africa' in clean, engaging prose." Horn Book Guide
Includes bibliographical references

966.26 Niger

Seffal, Rabah
Niger. Benchmark Bks. 2001 128p il maps (Cultures of the world) lib bdg $35.64 (5 and up) **966.26**
1. Niger
ISBN 0-7614-0995-5   LC 99-55064
A history and geography as well as a description of the government, economy, people, lifestyle, religion, language, arts, leisure time activities, festivals, and food of this landlocked West African country
Includes glossary and bibliographical references

966.3 Senegal

Berg, Elizabeth
Senegal; [by] Elizabeth L. Berg. Benchmark Bks. 1999 128p il maps (Cultures of the world) lib bdg $37.07 (5 and up) **966.3**
1. Senegal
ISBN 0-7614-0872-X   LC 98-7790
Describes the geography, history, economy, lifestyle, and religion of Senegal, as well as its people, languages, and festivals
Includes glossary and bibliographical references

966.68 Ivory Coast

Sheehan, Patricia
Côte d'Ivoire. Benchmark Bks. 2000 128p il map (Cultures of the world) lib bdg $37.07 (5 and up) **966.68**
1. Ivory Coast
ISBN 0-7614-0980-7   LC 99-27250
Surveys the geography, history, government, economy, and culture of Côte d'Ivoire, formerly known as the Ivory Coast
Includes glossary and bibliographical references

966.7 Ghana

Levy, Patricia
Ghana. Benchmark Bks. 1999 128p il map (Cultures of the world) lib bdg $37.07 (5 and up) **966.7**
1. Ghana
ISBN 0-7614-0952-1   LC 98-49004
Describes the geography, history, government, economy, people, lifestyle, religion, language, arts, leisure, festivals, and food of Ghana
This offers "a readable text along with plenty of clear color photos." Horn Book Guide
Includes glossary and bibliographical references

966.9 Nigeria

Levy, Patricia
Nigeria. 2nd ed. Benchmark Bks. 2004 144p il map (Cultures of the world) lib bdg $25.95 (5 and up) **966.9**
1. Nigeria
ISBN 0-7614-1703-6   LC 2003-20886
First published 1993
Contents: Geography; History; Government; Economy; Environment; Nigerians; Lifestyle; Religion; Language; Arts; Leisure; Festivals; Food
Examines the geography, history, government, economy, people, and culture of Nigeria
Includes glossary and bibliographical references

Murphy, Patricia
Nigeria. Benchmark Books 2004 c2005 48p il map (Discovering cultures) lib bdg $25.64 (2-4) **966.9**
1. Nigeria
ISBN 0-7614-1795-8
An introduction to the geography, history, people, and culture of Nigeria
Includes glossary and bibliographical references

967.51 Democratic Republic of the Congo

Heale, Jay
Democratic Republic of the Congo. Benchmark Bks. 1999 128p il maps (Cultures of the world) lib bdg $37.07 (5 and up) **967.51**
1. Congo (Republic)
ISBN 0-7614-0874-6   LC 98-28538
Describes the geography, history, government, economy, people, lifestyle, religion, languages, arts, leisure, festivals, and food of the third largest country in Africa, a former colony of Belgium
Includes glossary and bibliographical references

Willis, Terri

Democratic Republic of the Congo. Children's
Press 2004 143p il map (Enchantment of the
world, Second series) lib bdg $34.50 (5 and up)
967.51

1. Congo (Republic)
ISBN 0-516-24250-4   LC 2003-504
Contents: Collapsing under its weight; The country
and the river; Congo's bountiful diversity; Kingdoms,
colonies, and corruption; Moving toward freedom; Poverty amidst plenty; People of the Congo; Overlapping
faiths; Expression through the arts; Life in Congo;
Timeline; Fast facts
Discusses the geography and climate, history, wildlife,
economy, government, people, religion, and culture of
the Congo.
This offers "lucid commentary, digestible quantities of
facts and statistics, eye-catching color photos, and eminently useful back matter." Booklist
Includes bibliographical references

967.6   Uganda and Kenya

Barlas, Robert

Uganda. Benchmark Bks. 2000 128p il map
(Cultures of the world) lib bdg $37.07 (5 and up)
967.6

1. Uganda
ISBN 0-7614-0981-5   LC 99-27577
Discusses the geography, history, government, econo-
my, people, and culture of the African nation of Uganda
Includes glossary and bibliographical references

967.62   Kenya

Broberg, Catherine

Kenya in pictures. rev and expanded. Lerner
Publs. 2003 80p il map (Visual geography series)
lib bdg $27.93 (5 and up)   **967.62**
1. Kenya
ISBN 0-8225-1957-7   LC 2001-3829
First published 1988 under the authorship of Joel Reu-
ben
A brief overview of Kenya's land, history, govern-
ment, people, and culture
The book is "visually appealing with photos and
sidebars that complement the text." Libr Media Connect
Includes bibliographical references

Pateman, Robert

Kenya; by Robert Pateman. 2nd ed. Benchmark
Bks. 2004 144p il map (Cultures of the world) lib
bdg $37.07 (5 and up)   **967.62**
1. Kenya
ISBN 0-7614-1701-X   LC 2003-20921
First published 1993
Contents: Geography; History; Government; Economy;
Environment; Kenyans; Lifestyle; Religion; Language;
Arts; Leisure; Festivals; Foods
Examines the geography, history, government, econo-
my, people, and culture of Kenya
Includes glossary and bibliographical references

967.8   Tanzania

Heale, Jay

Tanzania. Benchmark Bks. 1998 128p il maps
(Cultures of the world) lib bdg $37.07 (5 and up)
967.8

1. Tanzania
ISBN 0-7614-0809-6   LC 97-42180
Describes the geography, history, government, econo-
my, ethnic groups, lifestyle, religion, language, arts, lei-
sure, festivals, and food of this Eastern African nation
This offers "a clear and informative text [and] . . .
captioned color photographs." Horn Book Guide
Includes glossary and bibliographical references

968   Southern Africa. Republic of South Africa

Blauer, Ettagale

South Africa; [by] Ettagale Blauer and Jason
Lauré. rev ed. Children's Press 2006 144p il map
(Enchantment of the world, second series) lib bdg
$25.20 (5 and up)   **968**
1. South Africa
ISBN 0-516-24853-7
First published 1998
This survey of South Africa "covers geography, history, constitutional development, the economy, language,
religion, and current challenges. . . . Color photos are
clear and thoughtfully placed. . . . Not only is the text
accurate, but it also captures some of the cultural, economic, and social complexities and contradictions in a
succinct and even elegant way. " SLJ

Murphy, Patricia

South Africa. Benchmark Bks. 2004 48p il map
(Discovering cultures) lib bdg $25.64 (2-4)
968

1. South Africa
ISBN 0-7614-1719-2   LC 2003-8129
An introduction to the history, geography, language,
schools, and social life and customs of South Africa
Includes glossary and bibliographical references

Rosmarin, Ike

South Africa; [by] Ike Rosmarin, Dee Rissik.
2nd ed. Benchmark Bks. 2004 144p il map
(Cultures of the world) lib bdg $37.07 (5 and up)
968

1. South Africa
ISBN 0-7614-1704-4   LC 2003-20923
First published 1993
Contents: Geography; History; Government; Economy;
Environment; South Africans; Lifestyle; Religion; Lan-
guage; Arts; Leisure; Festivals; Food
Examines the geography, history, government, econo-
my, people, and culture of South Africa
Includes glossary and bibliographical references

968.8 Namibia, Botswana, Lesotho, Swaziland

Brandenburg, Jim
Sand and fog; adventures in Southern Africa; edited by JoAnn Bren Guernsey. Walker & Co. 1994 44p il map pa $6.95 hardcover o.p. (4 and up)   **968.8**
1. Namibia 2. Desert ecology 3. Photography of animals
ISBN 0-8027-7476-8 (pa)   LC 93-30425
This is a "collection of images of life—both human and animal—in the desert realms of Namibia." Publ Wkly
The author "combines exquisite color pictures with a first-person narrative to produce a book noteworthy for its craftsmanship, artistry, and perspective." Horn Book Guide

968.91 Zimbabwe

Sheehan, Sean
Zimbabwe. 2nd ed. Benchmark Bks. 2004 144p il map (Cultures of the world) lib bdg $37.07 (5 and up)   **968.91**
1. Zimbabwe
ISBN 0-7614-1706-0   LC 2003-20883
Contents: Geography; History; Government; Economy; Environment; Zimbabweans; Lifestyle; Religion; Language; Arts; Leisure; Festivals; Foods
Examines the geography, history, govenment, economy, people, and culture of Zimbabwe
Includes glossary and bibliographical references

970 North America

Peoples of the Americas. Marshall Cavendish 1999 11v set $471.36 (5 and up)   **970**
1. Ethnology—America
ISBN 0-7614-7050-6   LC 98-2801
Contents: v1 Anguilla-Belize; v2 Bermuda-Brazil; v3 Canada-Cayman Islands; v4 Chile-Costa Rica; v5 Cuba-French Guiana; v6 Greenland-Jamaica; v7 Martinique-Paraguay; v8 Peru-Turks and Caicos Islands; v9 United States of America; v10 United States of America-Virgin Islands
"The 50 entries, arranged alphabetically by country, vary in length from 2 to 74 pages and focus on native, ethnic, and immigrant groups in these nations. Discussions center on their way of life; on their contributions, both cultural and political; and often, on their struggle for survival." SLJ
"The amount of information, logical organization, multiple access points, and attractive layout combine to create a reference tool that most school and public libraries will want in their collections." Booklist
Includes bibliographical references

970.004 North American native peoples

Ancona, George
Powwow; photographs and text by George Ancona. Harcourt Brace Jovanovich 1993 unp il $17; pa $9 (3-6)   **970.004**
1. Crow Fair (Crow Agency, Mont.) 2. Native Americans—Rites and ceremonies
ISBN 0-15-263268-9; 0-15-263269-7 (pa)
LC 92-15912
A photo essay on the pan-Indian celebration called a powwow, this particular one being held on the Crow Reservation in Montana
The book is "illustrated with well-placed, full-color photos that clearly reflect the text. . . . An exquisite kaleidoscope of Native American music, customs, and crafts." SLJ

Andryszewski, Tricia
The Seminoles; people of the Southeast. Millbrook Press 1995 64p il map (Native Americans) lib bdg $22.90 (4-6)   **970.004**
1. Seminole Indians
ISBN 1-56294-530-0   LC 94-21819
This book describes the history and culture of the Seminoles of Florida. A traditional recipe, game and story are included
Includes glossary and bibliographical references

Arnold, Caroline
The ancient cliff dwellers of Mesa Verde; photographs by Richard Hewett. Clarion Bks. 1992 64p il $15.95; pa $6.95 (4 and up)
970.004
1. Pueblo Indians
ISBN 0-395-56241-4; 0-618-05149-X (pa)
LC 91-8145
Discusses the native Americans known as the Anasazi, who migrated to southwestern Colorado in the first century A.D. and mysteriously disappeared in 1300 A.D. after constructing extensive dwellings in the cliffs of the steep canyon walls
"A thorough and attractive introduction to the Anasazi people with outstanding photographs of the dramatic vistas and ceremonial chambers within this national park." SLJ
Includes glossary

Baylor, Byrd
When clay sings; illustrated by Tom Bahti. Scribner 1972 unp il $16 (1-4)   **970.004**
1. Native American art 2. Native Americans—Southwestern States 3. Pottery
ISBN 0-684-18829-5
Also available in paperback from Aladdin paperbacks
A Caldecott Medal honor book, 1973
"A lyrical tribute to an almost forgotten time of the prehistoric Indian of the desert West presents broken bits of pottery from this ancient time. The designs and drawings, done in rich earth tones, are derived from prehistoric pottery found in the American Southwest." Read Ladders for Hum Relat. 6th edition

Bealer, Alex W.

Only the names remain; the Cherokees and the Trail of Tears; illustrated by Kristina Rodanas. Little, Brown 1996 79p il pa $4.95 hardcover o.p. (4-6) **970.004**

1. Cherokee Indians

ISBN 0-316-08519-7 (pa)

A reissue with new illustrations of the title first published 1972

The author describes "the rise of the Cherokee Nation, with its written language, constitution, and republican form of government, and its tragic betrayal in the 1830s." Chicago Public Libr

A **Braid** of lives; Native American childhood; edited by Neil Philip. Clarion Bks. 2000 81p il $20 (4 and up) **970.004**

1. Native Americans

ISBN 0-395-64528-X   LC 00-21343

This "book presents the remembrances of 33 individuals from 22 different American Indian nations, ranging from anonymous men and women to such well-known figures as Black Elk and Sarah Winnemucca Hopkins." SLJ

"This is an excellent choice for curriculum support and brief read-aloud material." Booklist

Includes bibliographical references

Bruchac, Joseph

The Trail of Tears; illustrated by Diana Magnuson. Random House 1999 46p il lib bdg $11.99; pa $3.99 (2-4) **970.004**

1. Cherokee Indians

ISBN 0-679-99052-6 (lib bdg); 0-679-89052-1 (pa)
                                      LC 98-36199

"Step into reading"

Recounts how the Cherokees, after fighting to keep their land in the nineteenth century, were forced to leave and travel 1200 miles to a new settlement in Oklahoma, a terrible journey known as the Trail of Tears

"Magnuson's colorful pictures, packed with people and action, are a little bright for the subject, but strong new readers will find that nonfiction can tell a powerful story." Booklist

Corriveau, Danielle

The Inuit of Canada. Lerner Publs. 2002 48p il (First peoples) lib bdg $23.93 (4-6) **970.004**

1. Inuit

ISBN 0-8225-4850-X   LC 00-12183

This describes the culture of the Inuit, explaining the role of plants, animals, and the climate on such topics as housing, clothing, and transportation

"Color photographs and blocks of focused text organized into concise, double-page-spread chapters effectively introduce readers to [the Inuit]." Booklist

Includes bibliographical references

Dennis, Yvonne Wakim

Children of native America today; [by] Yvonne Wakim Dennis & Arlene Hirschfelder; with a foreword by Buffy Sainte-Marie. Charlesbridge Pub. 2003 64p il map lib bdg $19.95 (3-6) **970.004**

1. Native Americans

ISBN 1-57091-499-0   LC 2002-2272

"Shakti for children"

"This photo-essay features 25 of the more than 500 native cultures of the U.S. as well as a section on urban Indians. In this 'book of few words and many pictures,' the clear, captioned photographs speak eloquently of contemporary Native American young people. . . . An excellent resource for multicultural studies, this handsome album will also attract browsers." Booklist

Includes glossary and bibliographical references

Ehrlich, Amy

Wounded Knee: an Indian history of the American West; adapted for young readers by Amy Ehrlich from Dee Brown's Bury my heart at Wounded Knee. Holt & Co. 1974 202p il maps pa $13.95 hardcover o.p. (6 and up) **970.004**

1. Native Americans—West (U.S.) 2. Native Americans—Wars 3. West (U.S.)—History

ISBN 0-8050-2700-9 (pa)

This book traces the plight of the Navaho, Apache, Cheyenne and Sioux Indians in their struggles against the white man in the West between 1860 and 1890. It recounts battles and their causes, participants, and consequences during this era

"Some chapters [of the original] have been deleted, others condensed, and in some instances sentence structure and language have been simplified. The editing is good, and this version is interesting, readable, and smooth." SLJ

Includes bibliographical references

Flanagan, Alice K.

The Pueblos. Children's Press 1998 47p il maps lib bdg $25 (2-4) **970.004**

1. Pueblo Indians

ISBN 0-516-20626-5   LC 97-12683

"A True book"

Examines the culture, history, and society of the Pueblos

Includes bibliographical references

The Zunis. Children's Press 1998 47p il lib bdg $25 (2-4) **970.004**

1. Zuni Indians

ISBN 0-516-20630-3   LC 97-6712

"A True book"

Examines the history, culture, and society of the Zuni Indians, one of the groups of Pueblo Indians living in New Mexico

Includes bibliographical references

Freedman, Russell

Buffalo hunt. Holiday House 1988 52p il lib bdg $21.95; pa $8.95 (4 and up)   **970.004**

1. Native Americans—Great Plains 2. Bison
ISBN 0-8234-0702-0 (lib bdg); 0-8234-1159-1 (pa)
LC 87-35303

The author discusses the importance of the buffalo in the lore and day-to-day life of the Indian tribes of the Great Plains. He describes hunting methods, the uses found for each part of the animal, and the near disappearance of the buffalo as white hunters, traders and settlers moved west

"Freedman has hit his stride in terms of selection, style, and illustration: the color reproductions of historical art work form a stunning complement to the carefully researched, graceful presentation of information." Bull Cent Child Books

Goble, Paul

All our relatives; traditional Native American thoughts about nature; compiled and illustrated by Paul Goble. World Wisdom 2005 unp il $15.95 (5 and up)   **970.004**

1. Native Americans 2. Philosophy of nature
ISBN 0-941532-77-1   LC 2005004285

"The pages of this book are chock-full of quotations, songs, and brief stories that exemplify Native American attitudes toward nature. . . . Black Elk, Standing Bear, Brave Buffalo, and others observe the importance of various animals and the sacred qualities of all living things. . . . The spaces between text blocks are filled with Goble's familiar illustrations based on traditional Native American designs and colors." SLJ

Includes bibliographical references

Hoyt-Goldsmith, Diane

Pueblo storyteller; photographs by Lawrence Migdale. Holiday House 1991 26p il $16.95; pa $6.95 (3-5)   **970.004**

1. Pueblo Indians
ISBN 0-8234-0864-7; 0-8234-1080-3 (pa)
LC 90-46405

A young Cochiti Indian girl living with her grandparents in the Cochiti Pueblo near Santa Fe, New Mexico, describes her home and family and the day-to-day life and customs of her people

"The bright, crisp, almost shadowless photographs smoothly integrate additional details into the lively text." Publ Wkly

Includes glossary

King, Sandra

Shannon: an Ojibway dancer; photographs by Catherine Whipple; with a foreword by Michael Dorris. Lerner Publs. 1993 48p il map (We are still here: Native Americans today) pa $6.95 hardcover o.p. (3-6)   **970.004**

1. Ojibwa Indians
ISBN 0-8225-9643-1 (pa)   LC 92-27261

Shannon, a twelve-year-old Ojibwa Indian living in Minneapolis, Minnesota, learns about her tribe's traditional costumes from her grandmother and gets ready to dance at a powwow

"Numerous, colorful photographs show Shannon's daily activities as well as the costumes and dances at the powwow. The photos combine with a contemporary focus and straightforward text to make the book an excellent choice for middle readers." Booklist

Includes glossary and bibliographical references

Left Hand Bull, Jacqueline

Lakota hoop dancer; text by Jacqueline Left Hand Bull and Suzanne Haldane; with photographs by Suzanne Haldane. Dutton Children's Bks. 1999 unp il $15.99 (3-6)   **970.004**

1. Teton Indians 2. Native American dance
ISBN 0-525-45413-6   LC 98-21905

Follows the activities of Kevin Locke, a Hunkpapa Indian, as he prepares for and performs the traditional Lakota hoop dance

"The well-written narrative is nicely matched with large full-color photos showing Locke's costumes, various dance designs, homeland, and family." Booklist

Includes glossary and bibliographical references

McCurdy, Michael

An Algonquian year; the year according to the full moon; written and illustrated by Michael McCurdy. Houghton Mifflin 2000 unp il map $15 (3-5)   **970.004**

1. Algonquian Indians
ISBN 0-618-00705-9   LC 99-87157

"The clean, elegant lines of McCurdy's informative prose echo the bold cross-hatching and linear detail of his artwork; he frames resonant black-and-white vignettes, united by a recurring lunar motif, with a brick red border." Publ Wkly

Includes bibliographical references

Molin, Paulette Fairbanks

American Indian stereotypes in the world of children; a reader and bibliography. 2nd ed, by Arlene Hirschfelder, Paulette Fairbanks Molin, Yvonne Wakim. Scarecrow Press 1999 343p il $45; pa $32.50   **970.004**

1. Native Americans 2. Race awareness
ISBN 0-8108-3612-2; 0-8108-3613-0 (pa)
LC 98-49654

First published 1982

"This volume presents a collection of . . . articles detailing uses and abuses of Native American symbols, images, ideas, and stories that are directed at youth in the mass media. Toys, cartoons, textbooks, general reading, media portrayals, sports, logos, nicknames and more are discussed in stand-alone articles." Voice Youth Advocates

Includes bibliographical references

Murdoch, David Hamilton

North American Indian; written by David Murdoch; chief consultant, Stanley A. Freed; photographed by Lynton Gardiner. rev ed. DK Pubs. 2005 72p il (DK eyewitness books) $15.99; lib bdg $19.99 (4 and up)   970.004

1. Native Americans

ISBN 0-7566-1082-6; 0-7566-1082-6 (lib bdg)

First published 1995 by Knopf

Published in association with the American Museum of Natural History

This is a guide to the civilizations of North American Indians including full-color photographs of artifacts and descriptions ceremonies and customs.

Patterson, Lotsee

Indian terms of the Americas; [by] Lotsee Patterson, Mary Ellen Snodgrass; original illustrations by Dan Timmons. Libraries Unlimited 1994 275p il maps $35   970.004

1. Native Americans—Dictionaries

ISBN 1-56308-133-4   LC 93-47170

"Each of the approximate 850 entries provides a pronunciation guide for the term, an alternate form or spelling, a definition of Indian vocabulary, people, places, and events, boldface words that refer to other listings in the book, and other related terms for more information. . . . Drawings and photos greatly enhance the meaning of the terms." Book Rep

Peters, Russell M.

Clambake; a Wampanoag tradition; photographs by John Madama; with a foreword by Michael Dorris. Lerner Pubs. 1992 48p il (We are still here: Native Americans today) lib bdg $21.27; pa $6.95 (3-6)   970.004

1. Wampanoag Indians

ISBN 0-8225-2651-4 (lib bdg); 0-8225-9621-0 (pa)
LC 92-8423

"The traditional clambake, or Apponaug, of the Wampanoag Indians of the Northeastern American coast holds important spiritual and cultural meaning for the people of the tribe. This is the story of how young Steven, a Mashpee Wampanoag, celebrates his first Apponaug with friends and relatives on tribal lands of Cape Cod, Massachusetts." Publisher's note

"The full-color photographs illustrate the clearly written text and portray real people who are part of the contemporary world, passing on old traditions to their children." SLJ

Includes glossary and bibliographical references

Powell, Suzanne I.

The Pueblos; [by] Suzanne Powell. Watts 1993 64p il lib bdg $22.50; pa $6.95 (4 and up)
970.004

1. Pueblo Indians

ISBN 0-531-20068-X (lib bdg); 0-531-15703-2 (pa)
LC 93-18368

"A First book"

Discusses the traditional and modern way of life of the Pueblos, examining their history, culture, religion, and ability to survive and thrive in difficult conditions

Includes glossary and bibliographical references

Roessel, Monty

Songs from the loom; a Navajo girl learns to weave; text and photographs by Monty Roessel. Lerner Publs. 1995 48p il (We are still here: Native Americans today) lib bdg $21.27; pa $6.95 (3-6)   970.004

1. Navajo Indians 2. Weaving

ISBN 0-8225-2657-3 (lib bdg); 0-8225-9711-X (pa)
LC 94-48765

"Ten-year-old Jaclyn's grandmother teaches her the art of traditional Navajo rug-weaving. Jaclyn learns the songs and stories that invest the weaving with meaning, as well as the use of the proper tools and techniques. The color photographs of contemporary Navajo life are clear and engrossing, enhancing the solid text." Horn Book Guide

Includes glossary and bibliographical references

Sneve, Virginia Driving Hawk

The Apaches; illustrated by Ronald Himler. Holiday House 1997 32p il (First Americans book) $16.95 (3-5)   970.004

1. Apache Indians

ISBN 0-8234-1287-3   LC 96-41358

Describes the social structure, daily life, religion, government relations, and history of the Apache people

"Sneve's text is not exhaustive, but it does provide some detailed information. Himler's atmospheric oil paintings expand on the words to give readers a fuller appreciation of the subject." SLJ

The Cherokees; illustrated by Ronald Himler. Holiday House 1996 32p il maps (First Americans book) $16.95 (3-5)   970.004

1. Cherokee Indians

ISBN 0-8234-1214-8   LC 95-24099

"This brief description of the Cherokee nation begins with a creation myth and includes some traditions, history, and contemporary socio-cultural information." Bull Cent Child Books

This "is a sound treatment of the Cherokee people that will encourage youngsters to read further. . . . Himler's nicely executed paintings add detail, clarify the text, and contribute to the reader's understanding of history." Horn Book Guide

The Cheyennes; illustrated by Ronald Himler. Holiday House 1996 32p il maps (First Americans book) $16.95 (3-5)   970.004

1. Cheyenne Indians

ISBN 0-8234-1250-4   LC 95-50696

The author describes "Cheyenne creation stories, westward migration, culture, history, and conditions for the tribe today. . . . The tragic heritage of Cheyenne-white violence takes up the bulk of the text. Himler's watercolors take the form of clear maps and marvelously rendered characters. . . . A worthy addition that brings to life these people and their culture." SLJ

The Hopis; illustrated by Ronald Himler. Holiday House 1995 32p il maps (First Americans book) $16.95 (3-5)   970.004

1. Hopi Indians

ISBN 0-8234-1194-X   LC 95-1259

Sneve, Virginia Driving Hawk—*Continued*
"After opening with a retelling of the creation myth, Sneve goes on to provide a fair amount of detail about the religion, social structure, and general way of life of the Hopi. . . . Sneve's prose is simple and straightforward, with short, clear sentences. Himler's appealing oil paintings lend a rich atmosphere to the book." SLJ

The Navajos; illustrated by Ronald Himler. Holiday House 1993 32p il (First Americans book) pa $6.95 hardcover o.p. (3-5)   **970.004**
1. Navajo Indians
ISBN 0-8234-1168-0 (pa)   LC 92-40330
Provides an overview of the history, culture, and way of life of the Navajo Indians
"Himler's paintings enliven the matter-of-fact text." Booklist

The Nez Percé; illustrated by Ronald Himler. Holiday House 1994 32p il map (First Americans book) $16.95 (3-5)   **970.004**
1. Nez Percé Indians
ISBN 0-8234-1090-0   LC 93-38598
This discussion of the Nez Percé Indians "begins with a Chopunnish creation story, followed by descriptions of daily life and an abbreviated history. Himler's paintings beautifully enhance the text." Booklist

The Seminoles; illustrated by Ronald Himler. Holiday House 1994 32p il map (First Americans book) $16.95 (3-5)   **970.004**
1. Seminole Indians
ISBN 0-8234-1112-5   LC 93-14316
Discusses the history, lifestyle, customs, and current situation of the Seminoles
"The writing is smooth, if necessarily generalized, and Himler's watercolors are especially suited to the swampy backdrops and dramatic action that characterized the Seminoles' struggle to survive." Bull Cent Child Books

Terry, Michael Bad Hand
Daily life in a Plains Indian village, 1868. Clarion Bks. 1999 48p il map $20; pa $9.95 (4 and up)   **970.004**
1. Native Americans—Great Plains
ISBN 0-395-94542-9; 0-395-97499-2 (pa)
          LC 98-32382
Depicts the historical background, social organization, and daily life of a Plains Indian village in 1868, presenting interiors, landscapes, clothing, and everyday objects
"The author presents short paragraphs of fascinating information accompanied by visuals that explain even more than the text." SLJ
Includes glossary

970.01 North America--Early history to 1599

Lauber, Patricia
Who came first; new clues to prehistoric Americans. National Geographic Soc. 2003 64p il maps $18.95 (5 and up)   **970.01**
1. Native Americans—Origin 2. America—Antiquities
ISBN 0-7922-8228-0   LC 2002-5278

Contents: A surprising discovery; The mystery; Searching for South American settlers; A second look at North America; Skulls, languages, and genetics; The search goes on
Presents recent archaeological findings about the first people to settle the Americas, how they got here, and from what continent they came
"In a lively narrative that draws readers right into crucial research going on now, Lauber weaves together geology, archaeology, genetics, anthropology [and] language. . . . The inviting, spacious, magazine-style design, with lots of paintings, maps, photos, and screened insets, makes the complex information accessible." Booklist
Includes bibliographical references

Maestro, Betsy
The discovery of the Americas; by Betsy and Giulio Maestro. Lothrop, Lee & Shepard Bks. 1990 48p il maps $16.95; pa $6.95 (2-4)   **970.01**
1. America—Exploration
ISBN 0-688-06837-5; 0-688-11512-8 (pa)
          LC 89-32375
Discusses both hypothetical and historical voyages of discovery to America by the Phoenicians, Saint Brendan of Ireland, the Vikings, and such later European navigators as Columbus, Cabot, and Magellan
"The dazzlingly clean and accurate prose and the exhilarating beauty of the pictures combine for an extraordinary achievement in both history and art." SLJ

Exploration and conquest; the Americas after Columbus, 1500-1620; [by] Betsy & Giulio Maestro. Lothrop, Lee & Shepard Bks. 1994 48p il maps lib bdg $15.93; pa $6.95 (2-4)   **970.01**
1. America—Exploration
ISBN 0-688-09268-3 (lib bdg); 0-688-15474-3 (pa)
          LC 93-48618
This is a "discussion of the European exploration and conquest of the 'New World.' The author carefully explains that, 'The great gain of one people was the great loss of another' and traces the disastrous effects that the Portuguese, Spanish, English, French, and Dutch had on the native peoples of the Americas, while acknowledging the benefits the Europeans enjoyed." SLJ
"The book's most outstanding feature is its full-color artwork. Large, double-page spreads give scope to dramatic landscapes, while smaller pictures on every page show events, places, and maps pertinent to the text. . . . This book provides a useful overview of the period." Booklist

Sattler, Helen Roney
The earliest Americans; illustrated by Jean Day Zallinger. Clarion Bks. 1993 125p il maps $19 (5 and up)   **970.01**
1. Native Americans—Antiquities 2. Prehistoric peoples 3. America—Antiquities
ISBN 0-395-54996-5   LC 91-9463
Covers the history of early man in America from the earliest known sites to approximately 1492 A.D

Sattler, Helen Roney—*Continued*
"A readable archaeologically based account of pre-Columbian history, profusely illustrated in meticulous detail." SLJ
Includes bibliographical references

Steins, Richard
Exploration and settlement. Raintree Steck-Vaughn Pubs. 2000 96p il maps (Making of America) $28.55 (5 and up)   **970.01**
1. America—Exploration 2. Native Americans
ISBN 0-8172-5700-4   LC 99-46961
Recounts the stories of the French, English, and Dutch in the New World, their reasons for settlement, and their relations with the native Americans
"Back matter includes glossaries, bibliographies, time lines, and Web sites. Colorfully illustrated with maps as well as period prints, paintings, and drawings." Booklist

Wood, Marion
Ancient America; updated by Brian Williams. rev ed. Facts on File 2003 96p il map (Cultural atlas for young people) $35 (5 and up)
      970.01
1. Native Americans—Antiquities 2. America—Antiquities
ISBN 0-8160-5145-3   LC 2003-40863
First published 1990
Maps and text offer information on the cultures and histories of native groups in both North and South America
This offers "facts, figures, and plenty of visuals that young researchers will find useful. . . . Each spread contains several colorful photographs, drawings, diagrams, and/or maps that will help readers visualize the places and cultures discussed." SLJ
Includes glossary and bibliographical references

971   Canada

Bowers, Vivien
Crazy about Canada! amazing things kids want to know; illustrated by Dianne Eastman. Maple Tree Press 2006 96p il map (Canadian geographic for kids) $28.95; pa $18.95 (4-6)   **971**
1. Canada
ISBN 1-897066-47; 1-897066-48-1 (pa)
"Organized into topical chapters dealing with animals, landforms, and Canadians themselves, the book follows two bespectacled cartoon researchers, Vivien and Morton, as they encounter an assortment of creatures and experts who help them answer their questions. Frequent clear, full-color photographs, drawings, graphs, and sidebars break up the text and flesh out the commentary." Booklist

Wow Canada! exploring this land from coast to coast to coast; illustrated by Dan Hobbs and Dianne Eastman. Owl Bks. (Toronto) 2000 c1999 160p il maps $29.95; pa $19.95 (3-6)
      971
1. Canada
ISBN 1-895688-93-0; 1-895688-94-9 (pa)
In this "travel story a family tours the Canadian provinces from British Columbia to Newfoundland and back across the Northwest Territories, Nunavut, and the Yukon. . . . This brightly illustrated introduction to Canada is informal, often humorous, and always informative." Booklist

Braun, Eric
Canada in pictures. Lerner Publs. 2003 80p il map (Visual geography series) lib bdg $27.93 (5 and up)   **971**
1. Canada
ISBN 0-8225-4679-5   LC 2002-8107
First published 1989, catalogued under title
A historical and current look at Canada, discussing the land, the government, the culture, the people, and the economy
"An excellent introduction. . . . [This offers] easy-to-read and informative text, maps, charts, and full-color photographs." SLJ
Includes glossary and bibliographical references

Harris, Tim
The Mackenzie River; by Tim Harris. Gareth Stevens Pub 2003 32p il map (Rivers of North America) lib bdg $24.67 (5 and up)   **971**
1. Mackenzie River (N.W.T.)
ISBN 0-8368-3756-8   LC 2003-42741
Contents: River of the North; From source to mouth; The life of the river; Northern people; Land of black gold; Places to visit
This describes the longest river in Canada, which runs from its source east of the Rocky Mountains in the Northwest Territories to its mouth at the Arctic Ocean.
This "clearly describes [the Mackenzie River's], colorful history, and strong impact on the development of towns found along its banks. In well-organized fashion, the [author delves] into wild life, environmental issues facing [this region], and the people who live there. The color photographs enhance the [text] nicely to enrich readers' understanding." SLJ
Includes bibliographical references

Murphy, Patricia
Canada. Benchmark Bks. 2004 48p il map (Discovering cultures) lib bdg $25.64 (2-4)
      971
1. Canada
ISBN 0-7614-1725-7   LC 2003-19098
Contents: Where in the world is Canada?; What makes Canada Canadian?; School days; Just for fun; Let's celebrate!
An introduction to the geography, history, people, and culture of Canada
This book is "informative and balanced." SLJ
Includes glossary and bibliographical references

Pang, Guek-Cheng
Canada. 2nd ed. Benchmark Books 2004 144p il map (Cultures of the world) lib bdg $37.07 (5 and up) **971**
1. Canada
ISBN 0-7614-1788-5 LC 2004-8584
First published 1994
This describes the geography, history, government, economy, environment, and culture of Canada.
"There is excellent coverage of Canadian arts. . . . Full-color photos appear throughout, and the maps are current and easy to read." SLJ
Includes glossary and bibliographical references

Rowe, Percy
Toronto; by Percy Rowe. World Almanac Library 2004 48p il map (Great cities of the world) $30 (3-6) **971**
1. Toronto (Ont.)
ISBN 0-8368-5026-2 LC 2003-53477
Contents: History of Toronto; People of Toronto; Living in Toronto; Toronto at work; Toronto at play; The future of Toronto
This "provides a concise overview of the history, geography, economy, and population of [Toronto] as well as a good sense of the residents' lifestyles, including work, shopping, religion, and more. Useful maps and statistics are included, and clear, color photographs convey the city's flavor." SLJ

971.27   Manitoba

Kurelek, William
A prairie boy's summer; paintings and story by William Kurelek. Houghton Mifflin 1975 unp il (3-5) **971.27**
1. Children—Canada   2. Farm life—Canada   3. Summer
Available in paperback from Tundra Bks. $10.95 (088776-116-X)
This book shows "many details of the artist's life when he was a boy growing up on a farm in Western Canada." Horn Book
"It is, of course, the pictures by this distinguished Canadian artist that give the book its distinction; each full-color page glows with life and vigor, and the paintings have both a felicity of small details and a remarkable evocation of the breadth and sweep of the Manitoba prairie." Bull Cent Child Books

A prairie boy's winter; paintings and story by William Kurelek. Houghton Mifflin 1973 unp il pa $8.95 hardcover o.p. (3-5) **971.27**
1. Children—Canada   2. Farm life—Canada   3. Winter
ISBN 0-395-36609-7 (pa)
The author depicts the rigors and pleasures of boyhood winters on a Manitoba farm in the 1930's including hauling hay, playing hockey, and surviving a blizzard

971.3   Ontario

Greenwood, Barbara
A pioneer sampler; the daily life of a pioneer family in 1840; illustrated by Heather Collins. Ticknor & Fields Bks. for Young Readers 1995 240p il $18.95; pa $10.95 (4 and up) **971.3**
1. Frontier and pioneer life
ISBN 0-395-71540-7; 0-395-88393-8 (pa)
LC 94-12829
First published 1994 in Canada with title: A pioneer story
"Using a combination of fiction and fact-filled supplementary commentary, with illustrations inspired by Garth Williams, the author tells the story of the Robertsons, a large, hardworking farm family. Good projects for school or home." N Y Times Book Rev

971.9   Northern territories of Canada

Walsh Shepherd, Donna
The Klondike gold rush. Watts 1998 64p il maps pa $6.95 hardcover o.p. (4 and up) **971.9**
1. Klondike River valley (Yukon)—Gold discoveries
ISBN 0-531-15909-4 (pa); 0-531-20360-3 (hc)
LC 97-38340
"A First book"
Describes the adventures of those who flocked to the Klondike after gold was discovered there in 1896
"Short enough to appeal to reluctant researchers and long enough to provide a basic grasp of the events, the book succeeds admirably." SLJ
Includes bibliographical references

972   Middle America. Mexico

Ancona, George
Charro; the Mexican cowboy. Harcourt Brace & Co. 1999 unp il $18; pa $9 (3-6) **972**
1. Cowhands   2. Mexico—Social life and customs
ISBN 0-15-201047-5; 0-15-201046-7 (pa)
LC 98-13396
Text and photographs present the traditions and the annual celebration of the charro, the Mexican cowboy
"Ancona's pictures just keep getting better and better, moving readers forward with motion, color, and excitement. A 'don't miss' from a master." SLJ
Includes glossary

Hamilton, Janice
Mexico in pictures. Lerner Publs. 2003 80p il map (Visual geography series) lib bdg $27.93 (5 and up) **972**
1. Mexico
ISBN 0-8225-1960-7 LC 2001-4238
First published 1987, catalogued under title

Hamilton, Janice—*Continued*

A historical and current look at Mexico, discussing the land, the government, the people, and the economy

The book is "visually appealing with photos and sidebars that complement the text." Libr Media Connect

Includes glossary and bibliographical references

Kimmel, Eric A.

Montezuma and the fall of the Aztecs; illustrated by Daniel San Souci. Holiday House 2000 unp il $16.95 (3-5)   **972**

1. Montezuma II, Emperor of Mexico, ca. 1480-1520 2. Aztecs 3. Mexico—History

ISBN 0-8234-1452-3   LC 99-37134

"Hernán Cortés and his small force of Spanish soldiers arrived on the coast of Mexico in 1519. Within three years . . . the Aztec empire had collapsed. Kimmel prefaces his account of these events with a few pages of background information on the empire and Montezuma's rule. The story of Cortés's marches inland, his capture of the native leader, and the siege on Tenochtitlan is simply but dramatically told. San Souci's light-filled, detailed watercolors paint a vivid picture of these adversaries." SLJ

Includes bibliographical references

Milord, Susan

Mexico! 40 activities to experience Mexico past & present; illustrations by Michael Kline. Williamson 1998 96p il maps pa $10.95

972

1. Mexico 2. Handicraft

ISBN 1-88559-322-8   LC 98-34153

"A Kaleidoscope kids book"

"Milord provides an amazing amount of information about Mexico, ranging from ancient history through the Spanish conquest to contemporary life. Activities include such standards as making an *Ojo de Dios* and a *piñata*, but there are also directions for creating marzipan skulls for the Day of the Dead celebration, as well as recipes for salsa, tortillas, and hot chocolate. . . . This is an excellent starting point for students investigating this culture." SLJ

Includes bibliographical references

Perl, Lila

The ancient Maya. Franklin Watts 2005 112p il map (People of the ancient world) $29.50; pa $9.95 (5 and up)   **972**

1. Mayas

ISBN 0-531-12381-2; 0-531-16848-4 (pa)

This book portrays the lives of the ancient Maya "by examining their arts, culture, economy, government, religious beliefs, and societal structures. . . . Attractively designed and illustrated, the [book features] excellent color representations of architecture, artwork, and other cultural and historical artifacts." SLJ

Includes bibliographical references

Reilly, Mary-Jo

Mexico; by Mary-Jo Reilly, Leslie Jermyn. 2nd ed. Benchmark Bks. 2002 144p il map (Cultures of the world) lib bdg $37.07 (5 and up)

972

1. Mexico

ISBN 0-7614-1363-4   LC 2001-47760

First published 1991

Presents the history, geography, economy, people, and social life and customs of Mexico

Includes glossary and bibliographical references

Sonneborn, Liz

The ancient Aztecs; written by Liz Sonneborn. Franklin Watts 2005 112p il map (People of the ancient world) lib bdg $30.50; pa $9.95 (5 and up)

972

1. Aztecs

ISBN 0-531-12362-6 (lib bdg); 0-531-16844-1 (pa)

LC 2004-13909

Contents: Introduction; Commoners, nobles, and rulers; Warriors; Priests and scholars; Merchants and craftspeople; Farmers; Conquest and survival

This examines ancient Aztec society "through their literature, artifacts, and documents. Religion, farming, levels of society, art, government, and fine arts are covered in [this] well-written and attractive [book]." SLJ

Includes bibliographical references

Stein, R. Conrad

The Aztec empire. Benchmark Bks. 1996 80p il (Cultures of the past) $28.50 (4 and up)

972

1. Aztecs

ISBN 0-7614-0072-9   LC 95-7333

An illustrated look at Aztec art, architecture, religion, mythology, government and society

Includes glossary and bibliographical references

Tanaka, Shelley

Lost temple of the Aztecs; what it was like when the Spaniards invaded Mexico; illustrations by Greg Ruhl; diagrams and maps by Jack McMaster; historical consultation by Eduardo Matos Moctezuma. Hyperion Bks. for Children 1998 48p il maps (I was there books) $16.95; pa $7.99 (4 and up)   **972**

1. Aztecs 2. Mexico—History

ISBN 0-7868-0441-6; 0-7868-1542-6 (pa)

LC 98-10986

"A Hyperion/Madison Press book"

Uses the discovery of the temple in Mexico City, what was the Aztec city of Tenochtitlan, to introduce the story of the Spanish conquest of Moctezuma and his empire in the sixteenth century

"Lavishly illustrated with full-color photos, period artwork, and dramatic full-page paintings, the book is handsome and eye-catching." SLJ

Includes glossary and bibliographical references

972.8   Central America

Shields, Charles J.
Central America: facts and figures. Mason Crest Pubs. 2003 63p il maps (Discovering Central America) lib bdg $19.95 (4 and up)
972.8
1. Central America
ISBN 1-59084-099-2   LC 2002-9194
This title "looks at the region as a whole, briefly reviewing geography and history and providing a glimpse of the area's peoples and cultures. . . . Tailored for the quick research needs of students, the . . . [title presents its] information smoothly and in well-organized fashion." Booklist
Includes glossary and bibliographical references

972.81   Guatemala

Mann, Elizabeth
Tikal; the center of the Maya world; with illustrations by Tom McNeely. Mikaya Press 2002 47p il map (Wonders of the world) $19.95 (4 and up)
972.81
1. Mayas—Antiquities
ISBN 1-931414-05-X   LC 2002-29599
A history of the Maya Indians in the city of Tikal, founded in 800 B.C.
"Mann's narrative flows smoothly, and frequent, full-color illustrations . . . help to clarify the details mentioned in the text." Booklist
Includes glossary

Sheehan, Sean
Guatemala. Benchmark Bks. 1998 128p il maps (Cultures of the world) lib bdg $37.07 (5 and up)
972.81
1. Guatemala
ISBN 0-7614-0812-6   LC 97-44619
Introduces the geography, history, religion, government, economy, and culture of Guatemala
"A good-quality full-color photograph, reproduction, or map appears on most pages. This [is a] solid volume." SLJ
Includes glossary and bibliographical references

972.82   Belize

Jermyn, Leslie
Belize. Reference ed. Benchmark Bks. 2001 128p il map (Cultures of the world) lib bdg $37.07 (5 and up)
972.82
1. Belize
ISBN 0-7614-1190-9   LC 00-65699
This offers "information on the geography, history, government, lifestyles, religion, festivals, arts, and contemporary life in [Belize]. . . . The concise writing offers enough material for report writers without overwhelming them." SLJ
Includes glossary and bibliographical references

Shields, Charles J.
Belize. Mason Crest Pubs. 2003 63p il map (Discovering Central America) lib bdg $19.95 (4 and up)
972.82
1. Belize
ISBN 1-59084-092-5   LC 2002-8937
Contents: A warm, sultry land cooled by sea breezes; A history different from the rest of Central America; Careful land use strengthens the economy; A mosaic of backgrounds and languages; Communities and cultures clustered by districts; A calendar of Belizean festivals; Recipes
This describes the history, geography, and culture of Belize
"Tailored for the quick research needs of students, the . . . [title presents its] information smoothly and in well-organized fashion." Booklist
Includes glossary and bibliographical references

972.83   Honduras

McGaffey, Leta
Honduras. Benchmark Bks. 1999 128p il maps (Cultures of the world) lib bdg $37.07 (5 and up)
972.83
1. Honduras
ISBN 0-7614-0955-6   LC 98-54908
This is a look at the Central American nation. "Following introductory chapters on the geography, history, and government, the clearly written book focuses on contemporary life. The economy, population, religion, leisure activities, holidays, indigenous and ethnic groups, and rural and urban lifestyles are all covered. . . . A quality, full-color photograph appears on almost every page." SLJ
Includes glossary and bibliographical references

Shields, Charles J.
Honduras. Mason Crest Pubs. 2003 63p il map (Discovering Central America) lib bdg $19.95 (4 and up)
972.83
1. Honduras
ISBN 1-59084-096-8   LC 2002-9089
Contents: Honduras, the knee of Central America; Honduras becomes the "Banana Republic"; A fragile economy; The people of Honduras; Language, religion, and home life; A calendar of Honduran festivals; Recipes
This describes the history, geography, and culture of Honduras
This is "jam-packed with useful information. . . . [It contains] straightforward writing, clearly titled chapters, high quality color, and well-captioned photographs and graphics." Libr Media Connect
Includes glossary and bibliographical references

972.84   El Salvador

Foley, Erin
El Salvador; [by] Erin Foley, Rafiz Hapipi. 2nd ed. Benchmark Bks. 2005 144p il map (Cultures of the world) lib bdg $37.07 (5 and up)
          972.84

1. El Salvador
ISBN 0-7614-1967-5   LC 2005009360
First published 1994
This describes the geography, history, government, economy, environment, people, lifestyle, religion, language, arts, leisure, festivals, and food of El Salvador
Includes glossary and bibliographical references

972.85   Nicaragua

Kott, Jennifer
Nicaragua; [by] Jennifer Kott, Kristi Streiffert. 2nd ed. Benchmark Bks. 2005 144p il map (Cultures of the world) lib bdg $37.07 (5 and up)
          972.85

1. Nicaragua
ISBN 0-7614-1969-1   LC 2005009240
First published 1994
An illustrated overview of the geography, economy, history, government, politics, and culture of Nicaragua
Includes glossary and bibliographical references

972.86   Costa Rica

Morrison, Marion
Costa Rica. Children's Press 1998 144p il map (Enchantment of the world, second series) lib bdg $35 (5 and up)   **972.86**
1. Costa Rica
ISBN 0-516-20469-6   LC 97-40665
Describes the geography, history, culture, religion, and people of the small Central American nation of Costa Rica
Includes bibliographical references

972.9   West Indies and Bermuda

Karwoski, Gail
Miracle; the true story of the wreck of the Sea Venture; by Gail Langer Karwoski. Darby Creek Pub. 2004 64p il map $28.95 (4-6)   **972.9**
1. Sea Venture (Ship) 2. Bermuda 3. Jamestown (Va.)—History
ISBN 1-58196-015-8
This is an "account of the 17th-century British sailing ship *Sea Venture*, flagship of nine vessels bound for the colony of Jamestown. A powerful hurricane forced it to break from the fleet. . . . Eventually [it ran] aground on the shores of the Bermuda islands. . . . Karwoski offers a wealth of historical information through a well-researched narrative. . . . [An] attractive, well-designed title." SLJ
Includes bibliographical references

972.91   Cuba

Ancona, George
Cuban kids. Marshall Cavendish 2000 40p il $15.95 (3-5)   **972.91**
1. Cuba—Social life and customs
ISBN 0-7614-5077-7   LC 00-29522
"Photojournalist George Ancona takes his camera back to Cuba 40 years after his first visit, which was right in the middle of the revolution. What he finds four decades later is a country rich in history, culture, and traditions but short on things Americans take for granted like paper, gasoline, and medicine. Superb color photographs show children at work and play. . . . The well-written text also touches on the impact of communism, Castro, and other important names like Ché Guevara and José Marti. A very fine portrait of modern Cuba." Booklist

Gordon, Sharon
Cuba. Benchmark Bks. 2003 48p il map music (Discovering cultures) lib bdg $25.64 (2-4)
          972.91
1. Cuba
ISBN 0-7614-1517-3   LC 2002-15302
Contents: Where in the world is Cuba?; What makes Cuba Cuban?; Living in Cuba; School days; Just for fun; Let's celebrate!
Highlights the geography, people, food, schools, recreation, celebrations, and language of Cuba
"Gordon includes lots of interesting specifics that convey a strong sense of daily life." Booklist
Includes glossary and bibliographical references

Sheehan, Sean
Cuba; [by] Sean Sheehan, Leslie Jermyn. 2nd ed. Benchmark Bks. 2005 144p il map (Cultures of the world) lib bdg $37.07 (5 and up)
          972.91
1. Cuba
ISBN 0-7614-1965-9   LC 2005009362
First published 1994
This describes the geography, history, government, economy, population, lifestyle, religion, language, arts, leisure, festivals, and food of Cuba
Includes glossary and bibliographical references

972.92   Jamaica and Cayman Islands

Roy, Jennifer Rozines
Jamaica; [by] Jennifer Rozines Roy and Gregory Roy. Benchmark Books 2004 48p il map (Discovering cultures) lib bdg $25.64 (2-4)
          972.92
1. Jamaica
ISBN 0-7614-1793-1   LC 2004-6142
Contents: Where in the world is Jamaica?; What makes Jamaica Jamaican?; Living in Jamaica; School days; Just for fun; Let's celebrate!
An introduction to the geography, history, people, and culture of Jamaica
Includes bibliographical references

Sheehan, Sean

Jamaica; [by] Sean Sheehan & Angela Black. 2nd ed. Benchmark Books 2004 144p il map (Cultures of the world) lib bdg $37.07 (5 and up)
972.92

1. Jamaica

ISBN 0-7614-1785-0   LC 2004-7676

First published 1996

Introduces the geography, history, religion, government, economy, and culture of Jamaica

"An informative book with captivating pictures, a visually attractive layout, and flowing text. . . . A well-balanced and interesting look at one country's culture." SLJ

Includes glossary and bibliographical references

972.93   Dominican Republic

De Capua, Sarah

Dominican Republic. Benchmark Bks. 2004 48p il map (Discovering cultures) lib bdg $25.64 (2-4)
972.93

1. Dominican Republic

ISBN 0-7614-1722-2   LC 2003-19099

Contents: Where in the world is the Dominican Republic?; What makes the Dominican Republic Dominican?; Living in the Dominican Republic; School days; Just for fun; Let's celebrate!

An introduction to the geography, history, people, and culture of the Dominican Republic.

Includes glossary and bibliographical references

Foley, Erin

Dominican Republic; [by] Erin Foley & Leslie Jermyn. 2nd ed. Marshall Cavendish Benchmark 2005 144p (Cultures of the world) lib bdg $25.95 (5 and up)
972.93

1. Dominican Republic

ISBN 0-7614-1966-7

First published 1995

"Explores the geography, history, government, economy, people, and culture of the Dominican Republic." Publisher's note

"The material is well organized in easily readable sections, accurately illustrated with well-placed, full-color photographs on every page." SLJ

972.94   Haiti

Cheong-Lum, Roseline Ng

Haiti; [by] Roseline Ng Cheong-Lum & Leslie Jermyn. 2nd ed. Marshall Cavendish Benchmark 2005 144p il map (Cultures of the world) lib bdg $37.07 (5 and up)
972.94

1. Haiti

ISBN 0-7614-1968-3

First published 1995

Describes the geography, history, government, economy, culture, peoples, and religion of Haiti

Includes glossary and bibliographical references

Hintz, Martin

Haiti. Children's Press 1998 143p il map (Enchantment of the world, second series) lib bdg $33 (5 and up)
972.94

1. Haiti

ISBN 0-516-20603-6   LC 97-25518

Describes the geography, history, government, people, and culture of the second oldest republic in the Western Hemisphere

Includes bibliographical references

972.95   Puerto Rico

Levy, Patricia

Puerto Rico; [by] Patricia Levy & Nazry Bahrawi. 2nd ed. Marshall Cavendish Benchmark 2005 144p il map (Cultures of the world) lib bdg $37.07 (5 and up)
972.95

1. Puerto Rico

ISBN 0-7614-1970-5

First published 1995

This introduction to Puerto Rico "covers geography, history, government, economy, population, lifestyle, religion, language, arts, leisure, festivals, and food. . . . The material is well organized in easily readable sections, accurately illustrated with well-placed, full-color photographs on every page." SLJ

Includes glossary and bibliographical references

972.96   Bahama Islands

Barlas, Robert

Bahamas. Benchmark Bks. 2000 128p il map (Cultures of the world) lib bdg $37.07 (5 and up)
972.96

1. Bahamas

ISBN 0-7614-0992-0   LC 99-88028

Introduces the geography, history, government, economy, religion, language, arts, leisure activities, festivals, food, and people of this archipelago lying in the Atlantic Ocean off the coast of Florida

Includes bibliographical references

Hintz, Martin

The Bahamas; by Martin & Stephen Hintz. Children's Press 1997 143p il map (Enchantment of the world, second series) $33 (5 and up)
972.96

1. Bahamas

ISBN 0-516-20583-8   LC 97-596

Describes the geography, plants, animals, history, economy, language, religions, culture, sports, arts, and people of the Bahamas

Includes bibliographical references

972.983   Trinidad and Tobago

Hernandez, Romel
    Trinidad & Tobago. Mason Crest Pubs. 2003
63p il map (Discovering the Caribbean) lib bdg
$19.95 (4 and up)   **972.983**
  1. Trinidad and Tobago
  ISBN 1-59084-304-5   LC 2002-75112
  Presents the geography, history, economy, cities and
communities, and people and culture of Trinidad and Tobago. Includes recipes, related projects, and a calendar of
festivals
  The author's "readable [style] will capture children's
interest . . . [The book is] illustrated with full-color photographs and include[s] quick-facts inserts, easy-to-
prepare recipes . . . and useful project and report ideas."
SLJ
  Includes glossary and bibliographical references

973   United States

America the beautiful, second series. Children's
    Press 1998-2001 53v il map ea $32 lib bdg ea
    $35 (5 and up)   **973**
  1. United States
  Also available online version
  Replaces titles in the original series published 1987-
1992
  Contents: Alabama, by L. Davis; Alaska, by D. Walsh
Shepherd; Arizona by J. F. Blashfield; Arkansas by S.
McNair; California, by A. Heinrichs; Colorado, by J. F.
Blashfield; Connecticut, by S. McNair; Delaware by J. F.
Blashfield; Florida, by A. Heinrichs; Georgia, by N.
Robinson Masters; Hawaii, by M. Hintz; Idaho by L. &
C. George; Illinois, by A. Santella; Indiana, by A.
Heinrichs; Iowa, by M. Hintz; Kansas, by N. Robinson
Masters; Kentucky, by R. C. Stein; Louisiana, by M.
Hintz; Maine, by D. Kent; Maryland by M. Burgan;
Massachusetts, by S. McNair; Michigan, by M. Hintz;
Minnesota, by M. Hintz; Mississippi, by C. George; Mis-
souri, by M. Hintz; Nebraska, by S. McNair; Nevada, by
R. C. Stein; New Hampshire by R. Stein; New Jersey, by
R. C. Stein; New Mexico, by D. Kent; New York, by A.
Heinrichs; North Carolina, by M. Hintz; North Dakota by
M. Hintz; Ohio, by A. Heinrichs; Oklahoma, by J.
Reedy; Oregon, by S. Ingram; Pennsylvania by A.
Heinrichs; Puerto Rico, by L. Davis; Rhode Island, by S.
McNair; South Carolina, by R. C. Stein; Tennessee by D.
Kent; Texas, by A. Heinrichs; U. S. Territories by S.
McNair; Utah by D. Kent; Vermont by A. Heinrichs;
Virginia, by J. F. Blashfield; Washington by J. F.
Blashfield; Washington, D.C., by R. C. Stein; Wisconsin,
by J. F. Blashfield; Wyoming by D. Kent
  "Several chapters on the history of the state begin
each book; sections on geography, government and poli-
tics, the economy, diversity of the population, education,
arts and leisure, famous citizens, and museums and historical sites follow." SLJ
  These books "are solid purchases for many libraries.
They feature clear, lively writing with considerable
amounts of information. . . . Maps are a particularly
strong feature." Booklist

The **Blackbirch** kid's visual reference of the
    United States; by the editors of Blackbirch
    Press; maps, charts, and graphs by Bob Italiano.
    Blackbirch Press 2003 336p il maps $49.94 (4
    and up)   **973**
  1. United States
  ISBN 1-56711-659-0   LC 2002-4239
  An alphabetical presentation of brief statistics and pictorial information about each of the United States, as
well as U.S. territories and possessions
  "This colorful, fact-filled work will be an ideal addition to elementary and middle school libraries as well as
children's reference collections in public libraries." Am
Ref Books Annu, 2003

Bockenhauer, Mark H.
    Our fifty states; by Mark H. Bockenhauer and
Stephen F. Cunha; foreword by former president
Jimmy Carter. National Geographic Society 2004
239p il map $25.95; lib bdg $45.90 (4 and up)
                         973
  1. United States
  ISBN 0-7922-6402-9; 0-7922-6992-6 (lib bdg)
                        LC 2004-1190
  This "book is organized by regions: the Northeast,
Southeast, Midwest, Southwest, and West, with a map of
each region and a short history. Four pages are devoted
to each state and include basic facts and a map. The full-
color photographs are outstanding. Reproductions of archival illustrations depict four important events from
each state's history. The final sections offer a paragraph
about each of the territories and a page of facts and figures about the United States." SLJ
  Includes bibliographical references

Celebrate the states. 2nd ed. Benchmark Bks.
    2005-2006 c2006-2007 15v il map lib bdg Each
    group 5v set $185.36; lib bdg   **973**
  1. United States
  ISBN 0-7614-1733-8 (group 1); 0-7614-2017-7 (group
2)
  Also available separate volumes $37.07 each
  Replaces the set published 1996-2001
  Contents: Group 1: California by Linda Jacobs
Altman; Illinois by Marlene Targ Brill; New York by
Virginia Schomp; Texas by Carmen Bredeson and Mary
Dodson Wade; Virginia by Tracy Barrett; Group 2: Colo-
rado by Eleanor Ayer and Dan Elish; Indiana by Marlene
Targ Brill; Louisiana by Suzanne LeVert; Oregon by Re-
becca Stefoff; Vermont by Dan Elish; Group 3: Alaska
by Rebecca Stefoff; Connecticut by Victoria Sherrow;
South Dakota by Melissa McDaniel; Tennessee byTracy
Barrett; Wisconsin by Karen Zeinert and Joyce Hart
  These volumes describe each state's geography, histo-
ry, people, government, economy, and landmarks.

Cole, Sheila
    To be young in America; growing up with the
country, 1776-1940; [by] Sheila Cole. 1st ed.
Little, Brown 2005 146p il $19.99 (5 and up)
                         973
  1. Children—United States 2. United States—Social
life and customs
  ISBN 0-316-15196-3   LC 2004-15109

Cole, Sheila—*Continued*

"Using topics such as home, life in an orphanage, sickness and health, work, school, crime, and war, [the author] shows how each one affected young people over the course of American history. For each of these subject areas, she highlights the experiences of one real child, drawing on historical diaries and other documents that give readers an opportunity to learn about life through that individual's own voice. This is a fascinating book, and also a beautiful one." SLJ

Includes bibliographical references

Hakim, Joy

A history of US. 3rd ed. Oxford University Press 2003 11v il map set $219.45; pa $175.45 (5 and up)   **973**

1. United States—History

ISBN 0-19-515256-8; 0-19-515259-X (pa)

LC 2002-25169

First published 1993-1995

Contents: bk 1 The first Americans; bk 2 Making thirteen colonies; bk 3 From colonies to country; bk 4 The new nation; bk 5 Liberty for all?; bk 6 War, terrible war; bk 7 Reconstructing America; bk 8 An age of extremes; bk 9 War, peace, and all that jazz; bk 10 All the people; bk 11 Sourcebook and index

Presents the history of America from the earliest times of the Native Americans to the administration of George W. Bush

Includes bibliographical references

Hoose, Phillip M.

We were there, too! young people in U.S. history; [by] Phillip Hoose. Farrar, Straus & Giroux 2001 264p il $28 (5 and up)   **973**

1. United States—History 2. Children 3. Youth

ISBN 0-374-38252-2   LC 99-89052

"Melanie Kroupa books"

Biographies of dozens of young people who made a mark in American history, including explorers, planters, spies, cowpunchers, sweatshop workers, and civil rights workers

"A treasure chest of history come to life, this is an inspired collection. . . . Because the book is packed with historical documents, evocatively illustrated . . . and full of eyewitness quotations, it should prove valuable to young historians and researchers." SLJ

Includes bibliographical references

It's my state! [series] Benchmark Bks. 2003-2006 42v il map lib bdg ea $27.07 (4 and up)

973

1. United States

Contents: Alaska, by R. Bjorklund; Arizona, by K. Derzipilski; California, by M. Burgan; Colorado, by L. J. Altman; Connecticut by M. Burgan; Delaware, by D. C. King; Florida, by D. Hess; Georgia by K. Haywood; Idaho by D. Sanders; Illinois, by C. Price-Groff; Kansas by D. C. King; Kentucky, by A. G. Gaines; Louisiana by R. Bjorklund; Maine by T. A. Hicks; Maryland, by S. Otfinoski; Massachusetts, by R. Bjorklund; Michigan by J. Haney; Minnesota, by M. T. Brill; Missouri by S. Sanders; Montana by R. Bjorklund; Nebraska by D. Sanders; Nevada by T. Allan Hicks; New Hampshire by

T. A. Hicks; New Jersey, by D. C. King; New Mexico, by R. Bjorklund; New York, by D. Elish; North Carolina, by A. G. Gaines; North Dakota by D. Sanders; Ohio by J. Hart; Oklahoma by D. Sanders; Oregon by J. Hart; Pennsylvania by J. Hart; Rhode Island by R. Petreycik; South Carolina by D. Hess; South Dakota, by R. Bjorkland; Tennessee by R. Petreycik; Texas, by L. J. Altman; Utah, by D. Sanders; Vermont by M. Dornfeld; Virginia by D. C. King; Washington, by S. Otfinoski; Wisconsin, by M. Dornfeld

Each book in the series covers "the state's topography, climate, and wildlife; history; lifestyle and population; government; and major industries and resources. Several spreads offer quick reference for state facts, such as the state flower, flag, and seal; famous residents; etc. The texts are basic and informative, providing solid insight into local life and culture." Booklist

Johnston, Robert D. (Robert Dougall)

The making of America; the history of the United States from 1492 to the present; with a foreword by Laura Bush. National Geographic Soc. 2002 240p il maps $29.95 (5 and up)

973

1. United States—History

ISBN 0-7922-6944-6   LC 2002-4825

Contents: A new world from many old worlds: beginnings to 1763; A revolutionary age: 1763-1789; The new republic: 1789-1848; A new birth of freedom: Civil War and Reconstruction, 1848-1877; Industry and empire: 1876-1900; Progressivism and the New Deal, 1900-1941; War, prosperity, and social change: 1941-1968; The age of conservatism: 1969-present

This is a "narrative of American history from Columbus through the terrorist attacks on Sept. 11, 2001." Libr Media Connect

"Johnston takes on an enormous, complex topic and presents an excellent overview for young people. . . . This well-written book does a particularly good job of balancing political and social history." Booklist

Includes bibliographical references

Junior state maps on file. Facts on File 2002 unp il loose-leaf $185 (4 and up)   **973**

1. United States—Maps

ISBN 0-8160-4752-9

Also available CD-ROM version

"This title offers more than 400 reproducible state maps and fact sheets in a looseleaf, three-ring binder format. . . . After a general section on the United States and its regions, the maps are arranged by geographic region. . . . Five maps and a fact sheet are provided for each state: major cities, outline map, physical features, industry, agriculture and state facts and flag. . . . This is an excellent U.S. geography resource for school and public libraries that do not subscribe to the online version." Am Ref Books Annu, 2003

Leacock, Elspeth

Journeys in time; a new atlas of American history; [by] Elspeth Leacock and Susan Buckley; illustrations by Rodica Prato. Houghton Mifflin 2001 48p il maps $15; pa $6.95 (4 and up)

973

1. United States—History 2. United States—Historical geography

ISBN 0-395-97956-0; 0-618-31114-9 (pa)

LC 00-40803

Each double-page spread of this book "takes an individual who was part of a historic movement (such as the Underground Railroad or immigration) and gives a brief narrative outlining his or her circumstances. Added to the text are sequential numbers that indicate major events in each of the twenty journeys. A double-page location map traces the routes each took, using illustrative vignettes marked with corresponding numbers that reference the text." Horn Book

Leedy, Loreen

Celebrate the 50 states; written and illustrated by Loreen Leedy. Holiday House 1999 32p il maps $16.95; pa $6.95 (k-3)

973

1. United States

ISBN 0-8234-1431-0; 0-8234-1631-3 (pa)

LC 99-10986

Introduces statistics, emblems, notable cities, products, and other facts about the fifty states, United States territories, and Washington, D.C

"Brightly colored and amusingly designed, this is a simple yet winning introduction to the U.S." Booklist

Sís, Peter

The train of states; [by] Peter Sis. Greenwillow Books 2004 unp il $17.99; lib bdg $18.89 (2-4)

973

1. United States

ISBN 0-06-057838-6; 0-06-057839-4 (lib bdg)

LC 2003-56826

"Using the motif of a circus train, Sís has designed a different car for each state in the Union and a caboose for Washington, DC. . . . The cars are lined up chronologically according to their date of statehood and are decorated with the state flag, nickname, motto, bird, tree, and animal as well as important people or sites." SLJ

"The wagons—with their rococo embellishments and glorious gallimaufry of visual factoids, trivia, hoopla, and American hyperbole . . . command attention and invite endless, wondering reexamination." Booklist

St. George, Judith

So you want to be president? by Judith St. George; illustrated by David Small. Updated and rev ed. Philomel Books 2004 52p il $17.99 (3-6)

973

1. Presidents—United States

ISBN 0-399-24317-8   LC 2004-4464

2000 edition awarded the Caldecott Medal, 2001

First published 2000

This book presents an assortment of facts about the qualifications and characteristics of U.S. presidents, from George Washington to George W. Bush.

This book "is easy enough to read even for children in the lower grades, but like many such books it is ideally enjoyed by a child with an adult. That way, its rich anecdotes provoke questions, answers, definitions, recollections and more anecdotes." NY Times Book Rev [review of 2000 edition]

World Almanac Library of the States series. World Almanac 2002-2003 52v il map (4 and up)

973

1. United States

each $30, pa $11.95; set $1560, pa $569.40

Contents: Alabama by Michael A. Martin; Alaska by Isaac Seder; Arizona by Michael A. Martin; Arkansas by Darice Bailer; California by Scott Ingram; Colorado by Megan Elias; Connecticut by Darice Bailer; Delaware by Justine Fontes; Florida by Patricia Chui; Georgia by Eric Siegfried Holtz; Hawaii by Robin S. Doak; Idaho by Karen Edwards; Illinois by Kathleen Feeley; Indiana by Lynn Brunelle; Iowa by Michael E. Martin; Kansas by Scott Ingram; Kentucky by Miriam Heddy Pollack; Louisiana by Leslie S. Gildart; Maine by Deborah H. DeFord; Maryland by Michael A. Martin; Massachusetts by Rachel Barenblat; Michigan by Rachel Barenblat; Minnesota by Miriam Heddy Pollack; Mississippi by Acton Figueroa; Missouri by Scott Ingram; Montana by Kris Hirschmann; Nebraska by Michael Flocker; Nevada by Jon Hana; New Hampshire by Joanne Mattern; New Jersey by Eric Siegfried Holtz; New Mexico by Michael Burgan; New York by Jacqueline A. Ball; North Carolina by Sarah Rafle; North Dakota by Justine Fontes; Ohio by Michael A. Martin; Oklahoma by Michael A. Martin; Oregon by Scott Ingram; Pennsylvania by Scott Ingram; Puerto Rico and other outlying areas by Michael Burgan; Rhode Island by Joanne Mattern; South Carolina by Ann Volkwein; South Dakota by Kris Hirschmann; Tennessee by Barbara Peck; Texas by Rachel Barenblat; Utah by Kris Hirschmann; Vermont by Michael Flocker; Virginia by Pamela Pollack; Washington by Rachel Barenblat; Washington D.C. by Acton Figueroa; West Virginia by Justine Fontes; Wisconsin by Rachel Barenblat; Wyoming by Justine Fontes

Each of these "titles briefly outlines the state's history, politics, government, culture, etc., and includes numerous colorful sidebars, charts, graphs, maps, and photographs that illustrate or supplement the texts. An introductory 'Almanac' lists state emblems and provides an assortment of facts. A time line presents state events. . . . Brief biographical sketches of notable native sons and daughters are included. . . . Most libraries will want to consider adding these books." SLJ

Yorinks, Adrienne

Quilt of states; quilts by Adrienne Yorinks; written by Adrienne Yorinks and 50 librarians from across the nation; librarian contributions compiled and edited by Jeanette Larson. National Geographic 2005 122p il $19.95 (5 and up)

973

1. United States

ISBN 0-7922-7285-4   LC 2004-17796

Yorinks, Adrienne—*Continued*

"The United States is stitched together chronologically in this stunning book that features a quilted spread for each state. Yorinks enlisted a librarian from each state to contribute a short entry to point up a few significant facts that add to the tapestry of the emerging nation. . . . The quilted representations are not only artistically intricate and beautiful, but also informative. A handsome book to linger over and learn from." SLJ

973.03   United States--History-- Encyclopedias and dictionaries

Brownstone, David M.

Frontier America; [by] David M. Brownstone, Irene M. Franck. Grolier 2004 10v il map set $369 (5 and up)   **973.03**

1. United States—History—Encyclopedias

ISBN 0-7172-5990-0   LC 2004-42445

Contents: v1 A new world; v2 West to the Pacific; v3 Acadia-Butterfield Overland Stage; v4 Cabeza de Vaca-Custer; v5 Delaware-Homestead Act; v6 Horses-Louisiana Purchase; v7 Mail-Northwest Territory; v8 Oakley-Roanoke Island; v9 Rocky Mountains-Turnpike; v10 Utah-Young

"The first two volumes present the overall history of the American frontier, with volume 2 containing a chronology of key events and a map of the lower 48 states. Volumes 3 through 10 offer alphabetically organized articles on events, people, and places. . . . The writing style is brisk and engaging enough to hold the attention of younger researchers. Coverage is evenhanded." Booklist

Junior Worldmark encyclopedia of the states; [Timothy L. Gall and Susan Bevan Gall, editors] 4th ed. UXL 2004 4v il map set $195 (5 and up)   **973.03**

1. United States—Encyclopedias

ISBN 0-7876-9197-6   LC 2004-8306

First published 1996

Contents: v1 Alabama to Illinois; v2 Indiana to Nebraska; v3 Nevada to South Dakota; v4 Tennesse to Wyoming, Washington D.C., Puerto Rico, U.S. Pacific and Caribbean dependencies, and U.S. overview, cumulative index

"Each entry begins with an introductory section of about 20 quick facts such as origin of the name, nickname(s), capital, motto, description of the flag, and title of the state song. There are also small black-and-white line drawings of the seal and flag. . . . Following this introduction is the profile containing 40 numbered subsections with information on topics such as location, topography, population, ethnic groups, religion, arts, communications, and famous people. . . . The entries have been thoughtfully arranged to make them easy to use. The introductory section contains all those quick facts that students need for reports, and the arrangement of the meatier profile sections facilitates comparison between different states." Booklist

Includes bibliographical references

The **student** encyclopedia of the United States. Kingfisher 2005 776p il map $29.95 (5 and up)   **973.03**

1. United States—Encyclopedias

ISBN 0-7534-5925-6

"Designed to be a starting place for young researchers and browsers alike, this reference tool explains topics relating to the 'people, places, and events that have shaped the United States.' . . . More than 1,200 entries are arranged alphabetically and range in length from one paragraph to two pages. Entries are illustrated throughout with more than 2,000 full-color photographs, illustrations, diagrams, charts, time lines, and maps. . . . Students will find this tool useful, and school and public libraries will want to purchase both reference and circulating copies." Booklist

973.2   United States--Colonial period, 1607-1775

Burgan, Michael

Colonial and revolutionary times; a Watts guide; historical consultant, W. Guthrie Sayen. Watts 2003 144p il map lib bdg $40 (5 and up)   **973.2**

1. United States—History—1600-1775, Colonial period 2. United States—History—1775-1783, Revolution

ISBN 0-531-15453-X   LC 2002-27029

A guide to the major people, places, ideas, and events of colonial and revolutionary times

"Sidebars highlight interesting anecdotes and personalities, and offer other supplements to the readable text. Excellent-quality, color photos, diagrams, and reproductions of period prints and documents add to the presentation." SLJ

Includes glossary and bibliographical references

Doherty, Craig A.

The thirteen colonies [series]; by Craig A. Doherty and Katherine M. Doherty. Facts on File 2005 13v il map set $455 (4-6)   **973.2**

1. United States—History—1600-1775, Colonial period

ISBN 0-8160-5406-1

Also available as separate volumes $35 each

Contents: Connecticut; Delaware; Georgia; Maryland; Massachusetts; New Hampshire; New Jersey; New York; North Carolina; Pennsylvania; Rhode Island; South Carolina; Virginia

"Beginning with a brief introduction that discusses some of the broad reasons why Europeans came to the New World, both as explorers and settlers, each book's . . . narrative highlights the people, places, and events that were important to the development of each colony." Publisher's note

"The clear narrative style is interesting and accessible. . . . Clear explanations of events often explored in classrooms make this a valuable resource for school libraries." Voice Youth Advocates

Includes bibliographical references

King, David C.

Colonial days; discover the past with fun projects, games, activities, and recipes. Wiley 1998 118p il (American kids in history) pa $12.95 (3-6)

973.2

1. United States—Social life and customs—1600-1775, Colonial period

ISBN 0-471-16168-3   LC 97-16083

"A Roundtable Press book"

Illustrations by Bobbie Moore

Discusses colonial life in America, depicts a year in the life of a fictional colonial family, and presents projects and activities, such as butter churning, candle dipping, baking bread, and playing colonial games

"Explanatory text alternates with instructions and other sidebars that provide brief history lessons. The materials needed are readily accessible in grocery, hobby, or craft stores. The line drawings are clear and helpful." SLJ

Includes glossary and bibliographical references

Maestro, Betsy

The new Americans; colonial times, 1620-1689; illustrated by Giulio Maestro. Lothrop, Lee & Shepard Bks. 1998 48p il maps $16.95; lib bdg $16.89 (2-4)

973.2

1. United States—History—1600-1775, Colonial period 2. Canada—History—0-1763 (New France)

ISBN 0-688-13448-3; 0-688-13449-1 (lib bdg)

     LC 95-19636

Traces the competition among the American Indians, French, English, Spanish, and Dutch for land, furs, timber, and other resources of North America

This is "accessibly written and meticulously illustrated. . . . Giulio Maestro's carefully detailed watercolor and color-pencil art includes maps, closely focused spot illustrations and dramatic spreads, which together provide a vivid picture of the century's pivotal events." Publ Wkly

Struggle for a continent; the French and Indian Wars, 1689-1763; illustrated by Giulio Maestro. HarperCollins Pubs. 2000 48p il maps (American story series) $15.95; lib bdg $15.89 (3-6)

973.2

1. United States—History—1600-1775, Colonial period 2. United States—History—1755-1763, French and Indian War

ISBN 0-688-13450-5; 0-688-13451-3 (lib bdg)

     LC 99-11500

Discusses the relations between the European colonists and the Native Americans, the disputes between settlers from France, England, and Spain, and the role these conflicts played in the history of North America

"The text is a model of clarity, balance, and nuance. . . . A wide variety of beautifully delineated pictures—maps, townscapes, seascapes, battlefields, and portraits—add to the spirited sweep of the text. A fine resource." Booklist

Stanley, George Edward

The European settlement of North America (1492-1763); by George E. Stanley. World Almanac Library 2005 48p il (Primary source history of the United States) $30 (5 and up)

973.2

1. America—Exploration 2. Frontier and pioneer life 3. United States—History—1600-1775, Colonial period

ISBN 0-8368-5824-7

"Stanley includes the efforts of Columbus to gain the support of the Spanish royals, a lithograph of Columbus and Queen Isabella, and primary-source material containing the permission for exploration. The motivation of other early explorers and their financial supporters is treated in a similar manner. Coverage of Native Americans includes text from the Constitution of the Iroquois Confederation, c. 1500, used by Benjamin Franklin during the creation of the United States Constitution. . . . Well-organized, highly attractive." SLJ

Includes bibliographical references

The New Republic (1763-1815); by George E. Stanley. World Almanac Library 2005 48p il (Primary source history of the United States) lib bdg $30 (5 and up)

973.2

1. United States—History—1600-1775, Colonial period 2. United States—History—1775-1783, Revolution 3. United States—History—1783-1865

ISBN 0-8368-5825-5

"The series of events that lead to the American Revolution is explained, helping readers to understand the connections of events inherent in historical study. Stanley's analysis of the constitutional debates of the Federalists and Anti-Federalists is exceptionally clear. Well-organized, highly attractive." SLJ

Includes bibliographical references

Tunis, Edwin

Colonial living; written and illustrated by Edwin Tunis. Johns Hopkins paperbacks ed. Johns Hopkins Univ. Press 1999 155p il pa $18.95

973.2

1. United States—Social life and customs—1600-1775, Colonial period

ISBN 0-8018-6227-2   LC 99-22591

A reprint of the title first published 1957 by World Pub. Co.

"Common everyday aspects of colonial living from 1564-1770 are highlighted by the detailed descriptions and numerous black and white illustrations of items such as tools, home furnishings, clothing, etc." N Y Public Libr. Ref Books for Child Collect

Voices from colonial America [series] National Geographic 2005-2006 10v il map ea $21.95 (5 and up)

973.2

1. United States—History—1600-1775, Colonial period

Contents: California 1542-1850 by Robin Doak with Andrés Reséndez; Delaware 1638-1776 by Karen Hossel with Karin Wulf; Georgia 1521-1776 by Robin Doak; Louisiana 1682-1803 by Richard Worth; Massachusetts 1620-1776 by Michael Burgan; New Jersey 1609-1776

Voices from colonial America [series]—Continued

by Robin Doak with Brendan McConville; New York 1609-1776 by Michael Burgan; Pennsylvania 1643-1776 by Lisa Trumbauer; Texas 1527-1836 by Michael Teitelbaum; Virginia 1607-1776 by Sandy Pobst

Each volume in this series describes the colonial history of a state illustrated with historical maps and reprints of period artwork, and includes excerpts from first-person accounts.

"Presented in clear, succinct text. . . . this resource, containing a great deal of information, will be a welcome addition to history classes and a great source for report writers." Booklist [review of New Jersey volume]

Includes bibliographical references

973.3 United States--Periods of Revolution and Confederation, 1775-1789

The **American** revolutionaries: a history in their own words, 1750-1800; edited by Milton Meltzer. Crowell 1987 210p il pa $8.99 hardcover o.p. (6 and up) **973.3**
1. United States—History—1775-1783, Revolution 2. United States—History—1755-1763, French and Indian War
ISBN 0-06-446145-9 (pa) LC 86-47846
"Meltzer has assembled a collage of eyewitness accounts, speech and diary excerpts, letters, and other documents for a chronological account of the half century that included the American Revolution. . . . The voices of women who accompanied the troops and of blacks who fought with the army are both represented." Bull Cent Child Books

Bobrick, Benson
Fight for freedom; the American Revolutionary War. Atheneum Books for Young Readers 2004 96p il map $22.95 (5 and up) **973.3**
1. United States—History—1775-1783, Revolution
ISBN 0-689-86422-1 LC 2003-25548
"This large-format volume profiles significant individuals and discusses the progress of the Revolutionary War. . . . Printed in color, most of the illustrations are period paintings and prints. . . . Students will find the book a well-organized and clearly written introduction to the war." Booklist
Includes glossary and bibliographical references

Bohannon, Lisa Frederiksen
The American Revolution; [by] Lisa Frederiksen Bohannon. Lerner Publications Co 2004 88p il (Chronicle of America's wars) lib bdg $27.23 (5 and up) **973.3**
1. United States—History—1775-1783, Revolution
ISBN 0-8225-4717-1 LC 2002-10036
Chronicles the American Revolution, including the causes, strategies, and characters of the war, both famous and lesser-known.
"The clear, well-written text is enhanced with black-and-white and sepia reproductions and woodcuts, eyewitness quotes, and sidebars." SLJ
Includes bibliographical references

Brenner, Barbara
If you were there in 1776. Bradbury Press 1994 136p il $17.95 (4-6) **973.3**
1. United States. Declaration of Independence 2. United States—Social life and customs
ISBN 0-02-712322-7 LC 93-24060
Demonstrates how the concepts and principles expressed in the Declaration of Independence were drawn from the experiences of living in America in the late eighteenth century, with emphasis given to how children lived on a New England farm, a Southern plantation, and the frontier
"The author's inclusion of details of how peoples' lives began to change as a result of the Revolution and her accessible style are the selling points here. Both budding historians and report writers will find this title worth their time." SLJ
Includes bibliographical references

Cox, Clinton
Come all you brave soldiers; blacks in the Revolutionary War. Scholastic 1999 182p il $15.95; pa $4.99 (6 and up) **973.3**
1. African American soldiers 2. United States—History—1775-1783, Revolution
ISBN 0-590-47576-2; 0-590-47577-0 (pa)
LC 97-44198
Tells the story of the thousands of black men who served as soldiers fighting for independence from England during the American Revolutionary War.
"An interesting and informative survey. . . . Black-and-white reproductions of period prints, documents, and paintings are included." SLJ
Includes bibliographical references

The **Declaration** of Independence; inscribed and illustrated by Sam Fink. Scholastic Ref. 2002 160p il $19.95 **973.3**
1. United States. Declaration of Independence 2. United States—Politics and government—1775-1783, Revolution
ISBN 0-439-40700-1 LC 2001-58194
The text of the Declaration of Independence is accompanied by illustrations meant to help explain its meaning
"Infused with humor and a contagious patriotism. . . . Fink breaks up this fervent, articulate proclamation into brief, elegantly hand-lettered phrases, which he pairs with etching-like artwork. . . . [This is a] clever and inspiring volume." Publ Wkly
Includes glossary and bibliographical references

Ferrie, Richard
The world turned upside down; George Washington and the Battle of Yorktown. Holiday House 1999 168p il map $18.95 (5 and up) **973.3**
1. Washington, George, 1732-1799 2. Yorktown (Va.)—History—Siege, 1781
ISBN 0-8234-1402-7 LC 98-19574

Ferrie, Richard—*Continued*

This examination of the events surrounding the pivotal Revolutionary War battle that led to the defeat of the British forces at Yorktown, Virginia, focuses on the central role of General George Washington

An "exemplary and readable history. . . . The text is engrossing, the format inviting, the facts accurate, and the illustrative material—maps, photographs, and reproductions—informative." Horn Book

Includes bibliographical references

Fradin, Dennis B.

Let it begin here! Lexington & Concord: first battles of the American Revolution; [by] Dennis Brindell Fradin; illustrations by Larry Day. Walker & Co 2005 unp il maps $16.95; lib bdg $17.85 (2-4)   **973.3**

1. Lexington (Mass.), Battle of, 1775 2. Concord (Mass.), Battle of, 1775

ISBN 0-8027-8945-5; 0-8027-8946-3 (lib bdg)

LC 2004-49473

This is an "account of Paul Revere's actions on the night of April 18, 1775, and the battles in Lexington and Concord on the following day. . . . Well-composed double-page illustrations, ink drawings with watercolor and gouache, highlight the human drama implicit in the text." Booklist

Includes bibliographical references

Freedman, Russell

Give me liberty! the story of the Declaration of Independence. Holiday House 2000 90p il $24.95; pa $12.95 (5 and up)   **973.3**

1. United States. Declaration of Independence 2. United States—Politics and government—1775-1783, Revolution

ISBN 0-8234-1448-5; 0-8234-1753-0 (pa)

LC 99-57513

Describes the events leading up to the Declaration of Independence as well as the personalities and politics behind its framing

"Handsomely designed with a generous and thoughtful selection of period art, the book is dramatic and inspiring." Horn Book

Includes bibliographical references

Herbert, Janis

The American Revolution for kids; a history with 21 activities. Chicago Review Press 2002 139p il pa $14.95 (4-6)   **973.3**

1. United States—History—1775-1783, Revolution

ISBN 1-55652-456-0   LC 2002-7938

Discusses the events of the American Revolution, from the hated Stamp Act and the Boston Tea Party to the British surrender at Yorktown and the writing of the Constitution. Activities include making a tricorn hat and discovering local history

"Achieving a good balance between textual material, illustration, and projects, the book immerses children in the milieu of these years. . . . The directions are detailed enough and adequately illustrated with pencil drawings to make them exciting and easy to follow." SLJ

Includes glossary and bibliographical references

Krensky, Stephen

Paul Revere's midnight ride; illustrations by Greg Harlin. HarperCollins Pubs. 2002 unp il $15.99; lib bdg $17.89 (2-4)   **973.3**

1. Revere, Paul, 1735-1818 2. Lexington (Mass.), Battle of, 1775 3. Concord (Mass.), Battle of, 1775 4. United States—History—1775-1783, Revolution

ISBN 0-688-16409-9; 0-688-16410-2 (lib bdg)

LC 00-66220

This "narrative recounts the eventful night of April 18, 1775, when Paul Revere rode from Boston to Concord to warn that British troops were on their way to seize the rebels' military supplies." Publ Wkly

"As an alternative to galloping through a picture-book edition of Longfellow's 'Paul Revere's Ride,' teachers may want to read aloud this more accurate, prose version about the same subject. . . . Painted with a dusky palette well suited to the many night scenes, the nicely composed, often dramatic pictures bring the story to life." Booklist

Kroll, Steven

The Boston Tea Party; illustrated by Peter Fiore. Holiday House 1998 unp il $17.95; pa $5.95 (3-5)   **973.3**

1. Boston Tea Party, 1773 2. United States—History—1775-1783, Revolution

ISBN 0-8234-1316-0; 0-8234-1557-0 (pa)

LC 96-54855

Describes the events preceding, during, and following the event which helped precipitate the American Revolutionary War

This book offers a "brief text written in a matter-of-fact style. . . . Presented in the format of a long picture book and illustrated with full-page watercolor art, the story unfolds step by step." SLJ

Maestro, Betsy

Liberty or death; the American Revolution, 1763-1783; illustrated by Giulio Maestro. HarperCollins 2005 64p il map (American story series) $15.99; lib bdg $16.89 (3-6)   **973.3**

1. United States—History—1775-1783, Revolution

ISBN 0-688-08802-3; 0-688-08803-1 (lib bdg)

LC 00-54042

The author and illustrator describe "the 20 years leading up to, and fighting, the American Revolution. A simple narrative, largely from the Colonists' perspective, touches on the major events, players, and ideas of the times, beginning with the Stamp Act and ending with Yorktown and the subsequent peace treaty. . . . Full-color ink, colored-pencil, and watercolor illustrations . . . grace the page in a pleasing, uncluttered way. . . . This book serves as a good introductory overview." SLJ

Miller, Brandon Marie

Declaring independence; life during the American Revolution; by Brandon Marie Miller. Lerner Publications Co 2005 112p il map (People's history) lib bdg $26.60 (5 and up)   **973.3**

1. United States—History—1775-1783, Revolution 2. United States—Social conditions

ISBN 0-8225-1275-0   LC 2004-17917

Miller, Brandon Marie—*Continued*

Contents: The people are ripe for mischief; They feel their importance; You are now my enemy; Free and independent states; The ragged lousey naked regiment; Where God can we fly from danger; The revolution just accomplished

This describes the lives of American colonists in the late 1700s and the fight for independence from Great Britain with emphasis on "firsthand accounts, contemporary writings, and official documents. Miller does a good job of chronicling the history, presenting the information in a clear, concise, and well-organized manner." SLJ

Includes bibliographical references

Growing up in revolution and the new nation, 1775 to 1800. Lerner Publs. 2003 59p il map (Our America) $26.60 (5 and up)   **973.3**
1. United States—History—1775-1783, Revolution 2. United States—Social life and customs 3. Children—United States
ISBN 0-8225-0078-7   LC 2001-4654
Presents details of daily life of American children during the period from 1775 to 1800
The author "does a good job presenting this information by using quotes from primary sources, historical photographs, and artwork from this time period." Libr Media Connect
Includes bibliographical references

Minor, Wendell

Yankee Doodle America; the spirit of 1776 from A to Z; [by] Wendell Minor. G.P. Putnam's Sons 2006 unp il $16.99 (2-4)   **973.3**
1. United States—History—1775-1783, Revolution 2. Alphabet
ISBN 0-399-24003-9   LC 2005025174
"In colonial America, the public houses served as the news hubs of their surrounding areas. . . . Using hand-carved replicas of the signs for these inns and taverns to share facts about the American Revolution, Minor, in concert with master woodworker John Reichling, has created an unusual alphabet book. . . . The factual material is correct, clearly stated, and intriguing." SLJ
Includes bibliographical references

Murphy, Jim

A young patriot; the American Revolution as experienced by one boy. Clarion Bks. 1996 101p il maps $16; pa $7.95 (5 and up)   **973.3**
1. Martin, Joseph Plumb, 1760-1850 2. United States—History—1775-1783, Revolution
ISBN 0-395-60523-7; 0-395-90019-0 (pa)
                LC 93-38789
"Using Joseph Plumb Martin's first person account of his participation in the Revolutionary War as primary source material, Murphy intertwines this story of one teenager's life as a soldier with broader information about the Revolution, to put Martin's story in context. The handsome, informative, and fascinating look at American history is illustrated with many period reproductions." Horn Book Guide
Includes bibliographical references

Rappaport, Doreen

Victory or death! eight stories of the American Revolution; by Doreen Rappaport and Joan Verniero; illustrated by Greg Call. HarperCollins 2003 120p il map $16.99; lib bdg $17.89 (4-6)
                973.3
1. United States—History—1775-1783, Revolution
ISBN 0-06-029515-5; 0-06-029516-3 (lib bdg)
                LC 2002-12837
Contents: The soldier with the pen: Peter Brown; The oath: Francis Salvador; "Yours, Portia": Abigail Adams; The decision: George Washington; Tarnation Sybil!: Sybil Ludington; A question of justice: Grace Growden Galloway; The spy: James Armistead; The recruit: Robert Shurtliff
This tells the stories of eight people who displayed courage during the American Revolution
"A well-researched and thoroughly engaging approach to history." SLJ

Schanzer, Rosalyn

George vs. George; the American Revolution as seen from both sides. National Geographic 2004 60p il maps $16.95 (3-6)   **973.3**
1. Washington, George, 1732-1799 2. George III, King of Great Britain, 1738-1820 3. United States—History—1775-1783, Revolution
ISBN 0-7922-7349-4   LC 2003-20843
Explores how the characters and lives of King George III of England and George Washington affected the progress and outcome of the American Revolution
"A carefully researched, evenhanded narrative with well-crafted, vibrant, watercolor illustrations. . . . This is a lovely book, showing historical inquiry at its best." SLJ
Includes bibliographical references

Sheinkin, Steve

The American Revolution. Summer Street Press 2005 155p il map (Storyteller's history) pa $10.95 (4 and up)   **973.3**
1. United States—History—1775-1783, Revolution
ISBN 0-9766367-0-0
Contains true stories and real quotes about the American Revolution not often found in formal history texts, and includes notes on the later lives of key figures in the conflict
"The quotes, often displayed in cartoon word balloons, are woven neatly into a well-organized narrative. . . . Along with famous figures, readers hear from soldiers, farmers, and other lesser-known folk. . . . There's an irreverent tone to the text that makes all of these figures seem more human, though no less worthy of respect. . . . Wry chapter titles and cartoon figure sketches match the light tone of the text." SLJ

St. George, Judith

The journey of the one and only Declaration of Independence; illustrated by Will Hillenbrand. Philomel Books 2005 unp il $16.99 (2-4)
                973.3
1. United States. Declaration of Independence 2. United States—Politics and government—1775-1783, Revolution
ISBN 0-399-23738-0   LC 2004-13567

St. George, Judith—*Continued*

This describes how the Declaration of Independence was written and how the document was preserved and displayed throughout American history

"Readers will learn fascinating details. . . . Hillenbrand's lively mixed-media illustrations are a perfect match for the text, filling the pages with visual energy and humor. . . . This well-researched, readable, and well-illustrated book belongs on the shelves of all public and school libraries." SLJ

Includes bibliographical references

Stein, R. Conrad

Valley Forge. Children's Press 1994 28p il (Cornerstones of freedom) lib bdg $20.50; pa $5.95 (4-6)　　　　　　　**973.3**

1. Washington, George, 1732-1799 2. United States—History—1775-1783, Revolution

ISBN 0-516-06683-8 (lib bdg); 0-516-46683-6 (pa)

LC 94-9490

First published 1985 with title: The story of Valley Forge

The author "describes how, routed at the Battle of Brandywine, Washington's forces retreated to Valley Forge. Quotations personalize their suffering, their resolve, and their loyalty to Washington. The addition of full-color and black-and-white photos, period paintings, and reproductions adds enormously to the book's appeal." SLJ

973.4　United States--Constitutional period, 1789-1809

Schlaepfer, Gloria G.

The Louisiana Purchase; [by] Gloria G. Schlaepfer. Franklin Watts 2005 63p il map lib bdg $25.50 (5 and up)　　　　　　　**973.4**

1. Louisiana Purchase

ISBN 0-531-12300-6　　　　　　LC 2005001465

"Watts library"

"Schlaepfer tells the story of 'the greatest land deal in American history.'. . . Black-and-white and color illustrations, maps, sidebars, and time lines enhance the well-organized [text]." SLJ

Includes bibliographical references

973.5　United States--1809-1845

Childress, Diana

The War of 1812; [by] Diana Childress. Lerner Publications Co 2004 80p il map (Chronicle of America's wars) lib bdg $27.93 (5 and up)

973.5

1. War of 1812

ISBN 0-8225-0800-1　　　　　　LC 2003-18805

Contents: The road to war; Losses on land, victories at sea; The pattern changes; A new front and a victory in the Northwest; The Creek vanquished, the last invasion; The British counterattack; A dramatic end

This describes the events of the War of 1812 and focusing on the impact the war had on America and its people.

Includes glossary and bibliographical references

Edelman, Rob

The War of 1812; by Rob Edelman and Audrey Kupferberg. Blackbirch Press 2005 48p il map (People at the center of) $23.70 (5 and up)

973.5

1. War of 1812

ISBN 1-56711-926-3　　　　　　LC 2004-16944

This profiles 15 people connected with the War of 1812 such as Thomas Jefferson, Tecumseh, Jean Laffite, Francis Scott Key, William Henry Harrison, and Oliver Hazard Perry.

Includes bibliographical references

Marquette, Scott

War of 1812. Rourke Pub. 2002 48p il map (America at war) lib bdg $29.93; pa $6.95 (4 and up)　　　　　　　**973.5**

1. War of 1812

ISBN 1-58952-389-X (lib bdg); 1-58952-475-6 (pa)

LC 2002-1239

Contents: Introduction: The strangest war; Map of the U.S., 1812-1815; Timeline; Sea battles and Indian wars; Victory at sea, defeat on land; "We have met the enemy"; America in Flames; The mistaken victory; "Don't give up the ship"

Discusses the events connected with the conflict between the United States and England during the early years of the nineteenth century

This "works very well in terms of both design and information. Large print on glossy pages, plenty of color photographs, and clear, simple text invite readers into [the book]. Marquette writes simply but supplies children with facts set firmly into context." Booklist

Includes glossary and bibliographical references

Stefoff, Rebecca

First frontier. Benchmark Bks. 2001 48p il maps (North American historical atlases) lib bdg $16.95 (4 and up)　　　　　　　**973.5**

1. Frontier and pioneer life 2. United States—Territorial expansion

ISBN 0-7614-1059-7　　　　　　LC 99-47936

Chronicles the exploration and settlement of lands west of the Appalachian Mountains during the late 1700s and early 1800s

"Facts are presented in an easy-to-read manner and sidebars provide additional information. Numerous full-color historical maps and reproductions with lengthy captions illuminate the events described." SLJ

Includes glossary and bibliographical references

The War of 1812. Benchmark Bks. 2001 48p il maps (North American historical atlases) lib bdg $16.95 (4 and up)　　　　　　　**973.5**

1. War of 1812

ISBN 0-7614-1060-0　　　　　　LC 00-20086

Stefoff, Rebecca—*Continued*

This describes the causes of the War of 1812, "land and sea battles, and the end of the conflict. . . . Facts are presented in an easy-to-read manner and sidebars provide additional information. Numerous full-color historical maps and reproductions with lengthy captions illuminate the events described." SLJ

Includes glossary and bibliographical references

973.6   United States--1845-1861

Bardhan-Quallen, Sudipta

The Mexican-American War; by Sudipta Bardhan-Quallen. Blackbirch Press 2005 48p il map (People at the center of) $23.70 (5 and up)
973.6

1. Mexican War, 1846-1848

ISBN 1-56711-927-1   LC 2004-13973

This offers biographical profiles of 15 people prominent in the Mexican War of 1846-1848.

This is a "unique and easily accessible [presentation] of biographical and historical information. . . . Maps, photos, drawings, . . . add to the appeal. . . . Great for reports." SLJ

Includes bibliographical references

Feldman, Ruth Tenzer

The Mexican-American War; [by] Ruth Tenzer Feldman. Lerner Publications Co 2004 88p il map (Chronicle of America's wars) lib bdg $27.93 (5 and up)
973.6

1. Mexican War, 1846-1848

ISBN 0-8225-0831-1   LC 2003-23395

Contents: Bordering on war; Manifest destiny; Rough and ready; Continuing conflict; Conquering peace; March to Mexico City; The struggle for peace; Two nations, one border

This chronicles the events of the Mexican War of 1846-1848 focusing the impact the war had on America and its people.

Includes glossary and bibliographical references

973.7   United States--Administration of Abraham Lincoln, 1861-1865. Civil War

Anderson, Dale

World Almanac library of the Civil War [series] World Almanac Library 2004 8v il map set $180; pa $87.60 (4-6)
973.7

1. United States—History—1861-1865, Civil War

Also available as separate volumes ea $30; pa $11.95

Contents: The aftermath of the Civil War; The causes of the Civil War; The Civil War at sea; The Civil War in the East (1861-July 1863); The Civil War in the West (1861-July 1863); The home fronts in the Civil War; A soldier's life in the Civil War; The Union victory (July 1863-1865)

"While series on the Civil War are rather common, this one stands apart by presenting a wide breadth of topics in a concise way. These . . . titles offer accessible overviews for students just becoming acquainted with this period in American history. . . . Clear maps and extremely helpful photographs, illustrations, and reproductions are everywhere, many in full color." SLJ

Includes bibliographical references

Armentrout, David

The Emancipation Proclamation; [by] David & Patricia Armentrout. Rourke Pub 2005 48p il map (Documents that shaped the nation) $29.93 (4 and up)
973.7

1. Lincoln, Abraham, 1809-1865 2. Emancipation Proclamation (1863) 3. Slavery—United States 4. United States—Politics and government—1861-1865

ISBN 1-59515-233-4   LC 2004-14418

The book introduces "the cultural and political factors that lead to the creation of [The Emancipation Proclamation], admirably distilling pertinent events into simple language that still manages to explain the complex issues and connections. . . . A wide mix of archival etchings, portraits, maps, and other images illustrate the [text]. . . . Clearly written and organized." Booklist

Includes glossary and bibliographical references

Beller, Susan Provost

Billy Yank & Johnny Reb; soldiering in the Civil War. 21st Cent. Bks. (Brookfield) 2000 96p il lib bdg $26.90 (5 and up)
973.7

1. United States—History—1861-1865, Civil War 2. Soldiers—United States

ISBN 0-7613-1869-0   LC 99-462169

Describes military life for the average soldier in the Civil War, including camp life, diseases, and conditions for the wounded and prisoners of war. Includes excerpts from first-person accounts, letters, and diaries

The author "presents a good deal of solid information in an interesting manner. . . . Good black-and-white reproductions, mainly of photographs from the 1860s, appear throughout the book." Booklist

Includes bibliographical references

Bolotin, Norm

Civil War A to Z; a young readers' guide to over 100 people, places, and points of importance; [by] Norman Bolotin. Dutton Children's Bks. 2002 148p il map $19.99 (4 and up)
973.7

1. United States—History—1861-1865, Civil War

ISBN 0-525-46268-6   LC 2001-33370

Alphabetically arranged articles present over 100 people, places, and points of importance of the Civil War

"Bolotin has a good eye for what students need to understand about the war and provides a great deal of information, skillfully whittled down to its most salient points. . . . The format is attractive, with numerous photographs." Booklist

Includes glossary and bibliographical references

The **Civil** War. Grolier 2004 10v il map set $309
(5 and up)   **973.7**
1. United States—History—1861-1865, Civil War
ISBN 0-7172-5883-1   LC 2003-49315

Contents: v1 Abolition-Camp followers; v2 Camp life-
Custer, George A.; v3 Daily life-Flags; v4 Florida-Hill,
Ambrose P.; v5 Home Front, Confederacy-Legacy of the
Civil War; v6 Lincoln, Abraham-Mobile Bay, Battle of
; v7 Money and banking-Politics, Confederate; v8 Poli-
tics, Union-Shenandoah Valley; v9 Sheridan, Philip H.-
Trade; v10 Training-Zouaves

This set "features detailed multipage articles that address significant individuals, battles, events, and conditions of the American Civil War." Booklist

"The variety of topics addressed in this set will give
students a wide perspective on the conflict. . . . The
clearly written, objective entries, ranging in length from
one to six pages, all offer basic analysis." SLJ

Clinton, Catherine
Hold the flag high; illustrated by Shane W.
Evans. 1st ed. Katherine Tegen Books 2005 unp il
$15.99; lib bdg $16.89 (2-4)   **973.7**
1. Carney, William, 1840-1908 2. United States—History—1861-1865, Civil War 3. African American soldiers
ISBN 0-06-050428-5; 0-06-050429-3 (lib bdg)
                                       LC 2003-11956
"Amistad"

Describes the Civil War battle of Morris Island, South
Carolina, during which Sargeant William H. Carney be-
came the first African American to earn a Congressional
Medal of Honor

"The story captures the fear and horror of battle as
well as the bravery of the soldiers. . . . Evans' paintings
convey the emotions of the characters as well as their actions." Booklist

Includes bibliographical references

Ford, Carin T.
African-American soldiers in the Civil War;
fighting for freedom; [by] Carin T. Ford. Enslow
Publishers 2004 48p il (Civil War library) lib bdg
$23.93 (4-6)   **973.7**
1. United States—History—1861-1865, Civil War
2. African American soldiers
ISBN 0-7660-2254-4   LC 2003-13724

Contents: A new country; The way is barred; Recruitment; The first regiments; Separate but unequal

"Ford discusses the laws and practices that hindered
African Americans from becoming soldiers as well as the
inequalities they experienced once the need for more
Union men increased, leading Congress to pass legislation permitting black recruitment. . . . The text, illustrations, photographs, and time line all play an important
role in conveying the struggles and triumphs experienced
by these men." SLJ

Includes bibliographical references

The American Civil War; an overview; [by]
Carin T. Ford. Enslow Publishers 2004 48p il map
(Civil War library) lib bdg $23.93 (4-6)
                                          973.7
1. United States—History—1861-1865, Civil War
ISBN 0-7660-2255-2   LC 2003-23773

Contents: North vs. South; War; Battles; The tide
turns; Peace?

This is an overview of the events of the American
Civil War.

This is "brief, yet factual and informative. Pages that
look like parchment are covered with colorful maps, illustrations, historical paragraphs, and sidebars." SLJ

Includes bibliographical references

The Battle of Gettysburg and Lincoln's
Gettysburg Address; [by] Carin T. Ford. Enslow
Publishers 2004 48p il map (Civil War library) lib
bdg $23.93 (4-6)   **973.7**
1. Lincoln, Abraham, 1809-1865 2. Gettysburg (Pa.),
Battle of, 1863
ISBN 0-7660-2253-6   LC 2003-13723

Contents: Invading the North; Second day of the battle; Pickett's charge; After the battle; Remembrance

A detailed account of the three days of the Battle of
Gettysburg plus an examination of Abraham Lincoln's
Gettysburg address.

"Appropriately placed period reproductions and photos
extend the text, and the maps and battle plans are helpful
in clarifying troop movements. This attractively designed
book gives enough information for reports." SLJ

Includes bibliographical references

Daring women of the Civil War. Enslow
Publishers 2004 48p il (Civil War library) lib bdg
$18.95 (3-5)   **973.7**
1. United States—History—1861-1865, Civil War—
Women
ISBN 0-7660-2250-1   LC 2003-6479

Contents: Women's work; The home front; Serving as
nurses; Fighting as soldiers; Fighting as spies

This "book begins with a description of women's traditional roles in the United States in the 1800s and highlights several female abolitionists. The changes caused by
the Civil War are then enumerated, as women took on
the 'men's work' at home, held jobs in offices and factories, served as nurses, disguised themselves as soldiers,
and . . . functioned as spies. . . . [The text is] well organized, [contains] quotes from primary sources, and
[presents] enough information to cover the [topic]. . . .
Abundant photographs, reproductions, and sidebars complement the [narrative]." SLJ

Includes glossary and bibliographical references

Lincoln, slavery, and the Emancipation
Proclamation; [by] Carin T. Ford. Enslow
Publishers 2004 48p il map (Civil War library) lib
bdg $23.93 (4-6)   **973.7**
1. Lincoln, Abraham, 1809-1865 2. Slavery—United
States 3. United States—History—1861-1865, Civil
War
ISBN 0-7660-2252-8   LC 2003-13720

Contents: Slavery takes root; The battle over slavery;
A nation torn apart; Taking action; Let freedom ring;
Timeline

This discusses the establishment of slavery in the
United States, the growing Northern opposition to the institution of slavery, the ensuing war and the signing of
the Emancipation Proclamation.

This is "brief, yet factual and informative. . . . [The]
attractive and inviting layout will hook readers." SLJ

Includes glossary and bibliographical references

Fraser, Mary Ann

Vicksburg—the battle that won the Civil War. Holt & Co. 1999 104p il map $17.95 (4 and up)
973.7

1. Vicksburg (Miss.)—Siege, 1863
ISBN 0-8050-6106-1   LC 99-19701

Describes the events preceding and during the key Civil War battle of Vicksburg, its significance, and its aftermath

"Bringing the history to life, quotations from diaries, memoirs, and other sources give voices to the participants. Illustrations . . . include black-and-white photographs, maps, and engravings. Source notes, a glossary, and lists of books and Internet sites are appended." Booklist

Friedman, Robin

The silent witness; a true story of the Civil War; illustrated by Claire A. Nivola. Houghton Mifflin Co 2005 unp il $16 (k-3)   **973.7**

1. McLean family 2. United States—History—1861-1865, Civil War 3. Virginia—History
ISBN 0-618-44230-8   LC 2004-1013

"Young Lula McLean watched the Civil War begin and end: General Beauregard used her family's Virginia home as his headquarters, and Lee surrendered at their second home. The finely executed, primitive-like paintings accentuate the idea that this war was an intimate part of everyday life in the South, and the small telling details show a personal side of the war." Horn Book Guide

Hansen, Joyce

Freedom roads: searching for the Underground Railroad; [by] Joyce Hansen and Gary McGowan. Cricket Bks. 2003 164p il maps $18.95 (5 and up)
973.7

1. Underground railroad 2. Slavery—United States
ISBN 0-8126-2673-7   LC 2002-13711

Contents: Running South: artifacts from Fort Mose; Land of the free: History on a ship's log; A more perfect Union: learning from the law; Running: The WPA slave narratives; Steal away: the enslaved speak through spirituals; I will be heard: archaeology meets an oral tradition; Midnight seekers after liberty: anecdotes and memories uncover the past; The last stop: outrunning the fugitive slave laws; A mystery: when history keeps a secret; The search continues

The authors "explore the ways historians have traced the path of the enslaved as they traveled northward to freedom. . . . The authors demonstrate how the study of artifacts, laws, slave narratives and more contribute to an understanding of how this crucial chapter of American history evolved. Reproductions of period photographs and documents extend the value of this well-researched volume." Publ Wkly

Includes bibliographical references

Holzer, Harold

The president is shot! the assassination of Abraham Lincoln. Boyds Mills Press 2004 181p il $17.95 (5 and up)   **973.7**

1. Lincoln, Abraham, 1809-1865—Assassination
ISBN 1-56397-985-3

This is a "description of the violent end to Lincoln's life. Holzer provides the Civil War context of the event and then details April 14 and 15, 1865." SLJ

"A page-turner of a text, a fascinating array of photos and archival illustrations, and an event that changed the course of history: all these elements combine in this strong, highly readable book." Booklist

Includes bibliographical references

Landau, Elaine

Fleeing to freedom on the Underground Railroad; the courageous slaves, agents, and conductors; [by] Elaine Landau. Twenty-First Century Books 2006 88p il map (People's history) lib bdg $26.60 (5 and up)   **973.7**

1. Underground railroad 2. Slavery—United States 3. Abolitionists
ISBN 0-8225-3490-8   LC 2005020358

"Landau discusses the history of slavery in the United States, slave life, the Underground Railroad, and the leaders, both black and white, of antislavery organizations. Three chapters outline specifics of slaves' escapes. . . . An outstanding feature of this book is the use of primary sources and quotes from former slaves, contemporary newspaper accounts, and reminiscences of escaped slaves. . . . Excellent historical photographs and illustrations enhance the text." SLJ

Includes bibliographical references

McKissack, Patricia C.

Days of Jubilee; the end of slavery in the United States; [by] Patricia C. & Fredrick L. McKissack. Scholastic Press 2003 134p il $18.95 (5 and up)   **973.7**

1. Slavery—United States 2. African Americans—History 3. United States—History—1861-1865, Civil War
ISBN 0-590-10764-X   LC 2001-57568

Uses slave narratives, letters, diaries, military orders, and other documents to chronicle the various stages leading to the emancipation of slaves in the United States

"The balanced perspective, vivid telling, and well-chosen details give this book an immediacy that many history books lack." Booklist

McPherson, James M.

Fields of fury; the American Civil War. Atheneum Bks. for Young Readers 2002 96p il map $22.95 (5 and up)   **973.7**

1. United States—History—1861-1865, Civil War
ISBN 0-689-84833-1   LC 2001-46048

"A Byron Preiss Visual Publications, Inc. book"

Examines the events and effects of the American Civil War

"McPherson writes with authority, offering a broad overview as well as many details and anecdotes that give his account a human dimension. . . . The many fine il-

McPherson, James M.—*Continued*

lustrations include period photographs, paintings, prints, some excellent maps." Booklist

Includes glossary and bibliographical references

Murphy, Jim

The boys' war; Confederate and Union soldiers talk about the Civil War. Clarion Bks. 1990 110p il $18; pa $8.95 (5 and up)　　　　　**973.7**

1. United States—History—1861-1865, Civil War
ISBN 0-89919-893-7; 0-395-66412-8 (pa)

LC 89-23959

This book includes diary entries, personal letters, and archival photographs to describe the experiences of boys, sixteen years old or younger, who fought in the Civil War

"An excellent selection of more than 45 sepia-toned contemporary photographs augment the text of this informative, moving work." SLJ

Includes bibliographical references

The long road to Gettysburg. Clarion Bks. 1992 116p il maps $17; pa $7.95 (5 and up)

973.7

1. Gettysburg (Pa.), Battle of, 1863
ISBN 0-395-55965-0; 0-618-05157-0 (pa)

LC 90-21881

Describes the events of the Battle of Gettysburg in 1863 as seen through the eyes of two actual participants, nineteen-year-old Confederate lieutenant John Dooley and seventeen-year-old Union soldier Thomas Galway. Also discusses Lincoln's famous speech delivered at the dedication of the National Cemetery at Gettysburg

The author "uses all of his fine skills as an information writer—clarity of detail, conciseness, understanding of his age group, and ability to find the drama appealing to readers—to frame a well-crafted account of a single battle in the war." Horn Book

Includes bibliographical references

Rappaport, Doreen

United no more! stories of the Civil War; by Doreen Rappaport and Joan Verniero; illustrated by Rick Reeves. 1st ed. HarperCollinsPublishers 2006 132p il map $15.99; lib bdg $16.89 (4 and up)　　　　　**973.7**

1. United States—History—1861-1865, Civil War
ISBN 0-06-050599-0; 0-06-050600-8 (lib bdg)

LC 2005005724

"An interesting and readable introduction to the Civil War. Drawn from primary sources, the seven short narratives reflect the experiences of people on both sides of the conflict. . . . Maps and occasional black-and-white, pen-and-ink drawings add detail and drama to the narratives." SLJ

Includes bibliographical references

Rossi, Ann

Freedom struggle; the anti-slavery movement in America 1830-1865. National Geographic 2005 40p il (Crossroads America) $12.95; lib bdg $21.90 (4-6)　　　　　**973.7**

1. Slavery—United States 2. Abolitionists
ISBN 0-7922-7828-3; 0-7922-8061-X (lib bdg)

LC 2003-19824

Contents: America in 1860; Slavery, right or wrong?; The Underground Railroad; Slavery divides the nation; Should slavery be abolished?; The Path to War; Uncle Tom's Cabin; Fighting for freedom

This discusses the Abolitionist Movement in the United States, profiling some of its leaders and its role in the Civil War.

"Period photographs, drawings, and cartoons; primary-source material; and biographical content make [this] introductory [title] interesting and accessible." SLJ

Includes glossary

Stanchak, John E.

Civil War; written by John Stanchak. Dorling Kindersley 2000 64p il map (DK eyewitness books) $15.95 (4 and up)　　　　　**973.7**

1. United States—History—1861-1865, Civil War
ISBN 0-7894-6302-4　　　　　LC 00-20431

Examines many aspects of the Civil War, including the issue of slavery, secession, the raising of armies, individual battles, the commanders, Northern life, Confederate culture, the surrender of the South, and the aftermath

This "offers a stunning array of reproductions and photographs of the sites, people, and artifacts associated with the war. . . . A paragraph of text introduces each topic and informative, often lengthy, captions accompany the numerous black-and-white and full-color illustrations." SLJ

973.8　United States--Reconstruction period, 1865-1901

Custer, Elizabeth Bacon

The diary of Elizabeth Bacon Custer; on the plains with General Custer; edited by Nancy Plain; illustrations and map by Laszlo Kubinyi. Benchmark Bks. 2004 95p il map (In my own words) lib bdg $18.95 (5 and up)　　　　　**973.8**

1. Custer, George Armstrong, 1839-1876 2. Native Americans—Wars
ISBN 0-7614-1647-1　　　　　LC 2003-1432

Presents the diary of the wife of General George Armstrong Custer, focusing on their life on the Great Plains from 1873 to 1876, when Custer and his Seventh Cavalry were clearing the way for the Northern Pacific Railroad and battling Native Americans

This offers "an engaging history lesson." Horn Book Guide

Includes glossary and bibliographical references

January, Brendan
Little Bighorn, June 25, 1876; . Enchanted Lion
Books 2004 32p il map (American battlefields)
$14.95 (5 and up)   **973.8**
1. Little Bighorn, Battle of the, 1876 2. Native Americans—Great Plains
ISBN 1-59270-028-4   LC 2003-64300
This "describes the Native American and U.S. Cavalry
clashes at Little Bighorn: the history, the leaders and
their actions on that day, and the aftermath of the battle.
. . . The [text is] well written . . . The books' many illustrations . . . include excellent reproductions of period
photos, drawings, engravings, and paintings, along with
clearly drawn maps and a few photos of sites." Booklist
Includes glossary and bibliographical references

Kupferberg, Audrey E.
The Spanish-American War; by Audrey
Kupferberg. Blackbirch Press 2005 48p il (People
at the center of) $23.70 (5 and up)   **973.8**
1. Spanish-American War, 1898
ISBN 1-56711-924-7
This profiles 15 people connected with the Spanish-
American War, such as Grover Cleveland, Clara Barton,
Mark Twain, Theodore Roosevelt, and William McKin-
ley.

Uschan, Michael V.
The Battle of the Little Bighorn. World
Almanac 2002 48p il map (Landmark events in
American history) lib bdg $26.60 (5 and up)
                                          973.8
1. Custer, George Armstrong, 1839-1876 2. Little Bighorn, Battle of the, 1876
ISBN 0-8368-5338-5   LC 2002-24632
Describes the causes, events, and aftermath of the
fateful encounter at the Little Bighorn River on June 25,
1876, between the Seventh Cavalry troops commanded
by Lieutenant Colonel Custer and the Cheyenne and
Lakota Sioux led by Chiefs Sitting Bull and Crazy Horse
The "design is attractive, with drawings, maps, paintings, and photos; primary sources, such as excerpts from
diaries, letters, and newspapers, support and enhance the
[text]." Booklist
Includes glossary and bibliographical references

973.91   United States--1901-1953

Stanley, George Edward
An emerging world power (1900-1929); [by]
George E. Stanley. World Almanac Library 2005
48p il (Primary source history of the United
States) lib bdg $30 (5 and up)   **973.91**
1. United States—Politics and government—1919-
1933 2. United States—History—1919-1933
3. United States—Foreign relations
ISBN 0-8368-5828-X   LC 2004-61501
The author describes United States politics and foreign
relations in the 1920s.
"Stanley explains and connects events utilizing clear
language and a blending of text, images, and primary accounts. . . . Well-organized, highly attractive." SLJ
Includes bibliographical references

973.917   United States--
Administration of Franklin D.
Roosevelt, 1933-1945

Cooper, Michael L.
Dust to eat; drought and depression in the
1930's. Clarion Books 2004 81p il map $15 (4
and up)   **973.917**
1. Great Depression, 1929-1939 2. Migrant labor
3. Droughts
ISBN 0-618-15449-3   LC 2003-17807
Contents: The "Okie" problem; The dirty thirties;
"Dust to eat, dust to breathe, dust to drink"; California-
bound; Harvest gypsies; Crisis in the valley; World War
II ends the Depression
This is a history of the Great Depression and the Dust
Bowl drought of the 1930s that drove desperate families
to California in search of work.
This includes "lots of stunning black-and-white archi-
val photos and a clear, spacious text that draws on elo-
quent eyewitness reports—including comments from John
Steinbeck and Woody Guthrie. . . . This is an excellent
historical account." Booklist
Includes bibliographical references

973.92   United States--1953-2001

Anderson, Dale
The Cold War years. Raintree Steck-Vaughn
Pubs. 2001 96p il (Making of America) lib bdg
$35.64 (5 and up)   **973.92**
1. Cold war 2. United States—History—1945-
3. United States—Social conditions
ISBN 0-8172-5711-X   LC 00-62827
This discusses factors that led to the Cold War and
the formation of alliances in reaction to it, as well as domestic issues such as the demand for equality for women
and African Americans
"Written in a clear and concise fashion [this book pro-
vides] . . . enough details to give a taste for the era
without overwhelming students." SLJ
Includes bibliographical references

Stanley, George Edward
America in today's world (1969-2004); by
George E. Stanley. World Almanac Library 2005
48p il (Primary source history of the United
States) lib bdg $30 (5 and up)   **973.92**
1. United States—Politics and government—1945-
2. United States—History—1945- 3. Presidents—United States
ISBN 0-8368-5831-X
This "covers the end of the Vietnam War through the
2004 presidential election. The terms of Presidents Nixon
through George W. Bush are highlighted through brief
but evenhanded descriptions of the major events of each
administration. . . . Well-organized, highly attractive."
SLJ
Includes bibliographical references

973.922   United States-- Administration of John F. Kennedy, 1961-1963

Hampton, Wilborn

Kennedy assassinated! the world mourns: a reporter's story. Candlewick Press 1997 96p il $17.99; pa $8.99 (5 and up)   **973.922**

1. Kennedy, John F. (John Fitzgerald), 1917-1963—Assassination 2. Journalism

ISBN 1-56402-811-9; 0-7636-1564-1 (pa)

         LC 96-25801

This is the author's "account of November 22, 1963, when, as a cub reporter for UPI in Dallas, he was drafted to cover JFK's assassination. His personal response to the tragedy is fluidly juxtaposed with the nuts and bolts of scooping the story in this insider's view of one of the most pivotal events of our nation's recent history." Publ Wkly

Includes bibliographical references

973.931   United States-- Administration of George W. Bush, 2001-

Marquette, Scott

America under attack. Rourke Pub. 2003 48p il (America at war) lib bdg $29.93; pa $6.95 (4 and up)   **973.931**

1. September 11 terrorist attacks, 2001 2. Terrorism 3. United States—Foreign relations—Middle East

ISBN 1-58952-386-5 (lib bdg); 1-58952-471-3 (pa)

         LC 2002-1215

Contents: Introduction: "A War to Save Civilization"; Map of Middle East/Central Asia, 2001; Timeline; Roots of terror; "An Act of War"; A war of many fronts; "The New Normal"; America changed forever

The author "begins with 9/11 and then presents a chronology of prior events of terrorism against the U.S. He goes on to describe the war in Afghanistan and changes in American life. Even within the limits of 48 pages, he is able to point out some of the dissent in American policy concerning the Patriot Act." Booklist

Includes glossary and bibliographical references

A **Nation** challenged; a visual history of 9/11 and its aftermath; [by] The New York Times; introduction by Howell Raines; photographs edited by Nancy Lee and Lonnie Schlein; text edited by Mitchel Levitas. Young reader's ed. Scholastic 2002 96p il map $18.95 (4 and up)   **973.931**

1. September 11 terrorist attacks, 2001—Pictorial works 2. Terrorism

ISBN 0-439-48803-6   LC 2002-26879

Contents: September 11, 2001; The days after; Meeting the challenge abroad; Meeting the challenge at home

In this Young Reader's edition of the title published for adults by the New York Times and Calloway, text, photographs, and illustrations from the New York Times

section, "A Nation Challenged," record how the world was changed due to the September 11, 2001, terrorist attacks on the United States and their aftermath

This "is beautifully designed with unforgettable images on every page. . . . The book is an excellent resource for every library desiring a sweeping visual account of this momentous time in America's history." Libr Media Connect

Includes glossary and bibliographical references

974   Northeastern United States

Rylant, Cynthia

Appalachia; the voices of sleeping birds; illustrated by Barry Moser. Harcourt Brace Jovanovich 1991 21p il $17; pa $6   **974**

1. Appalachian region

ISBN 0-15-201605-8; 0-15-201893-X (pa)

         LC 90-36798

"This is a running narrative description of the dogs, people, houses, seasons, and lifestyles of Appalachia." Bull Cent Child Books

"Taking her subtitle from a passage by James Agee, the author conveys with a marvelous economy of words the essence of the very special part of America where she was raised. A poetic text projects emotion as well as information. . . . Moser's watercolors capture the scene perfectly. . . . The book is a treasure—simply a beautiful combination of text and art." Horn Book

974.4   Massachusetts

Armentrout, David

The Mayflower Compact; [by] David & Patricia Armentrout. Rourke Pub 2005 48p il map (Documents that shaped the nation) $29.93; pa $8.45 (4 and up)   **974.4**

1. Mayflower (Ship) 2. Pilgrims (New England colonists) 3. Massachusetts—History—1600-1775, Colonial period

ISBN 1-59515-229-6; 1-59515-334-9 (pa)

         LC 2004-14413

Contents: The Pilgrims; Before the Pilgrims; The Church of England; The Scrooby separatists; William Bradford; Escape; Life in Holland; Choosing America; Merchant adventurers; Saints and strangers; A leaky mess; The Mayflower; Life at sea; Land!; The Mayflower Compact; A new settlement

The book introduces "the cultural and political factors that lead to the creation of [The Mayflower Compact], admirably distilling pertinent events into simple language that still manages to explain the complex issues and connections. . . . A wide mix of archival etchings, portraits, maps, and other images illustrate the [text]." Booklist

Includes glossary and bibliographical references

Bowen, Gary

Stranded at Plimoth Plantation, 1626; words and woodcuts by Gary Bowen; introduction by David Freeman Hawke. HarperCollins Pubs. 1994 81p il map pa $12.95 hardcover o.p. (4 and up)

974.4

1. Pilgrims (New England colonists) 2. Massachusetts—History—1600-1775, Colonial period

ISBN 0-06-440719-5 (pa)   LC 93-31016

The author "gives an account of the year 1626 at the by-then-well-established Pilgrim colony, rendered in the form of a journal kept by an orphaned 13-year-old. Shipwrecked on the way to Jamestown, taken in by the settlers at Plimoth, Christopher Sears observes their customs, planting, harvesting, home tutoring, the eight-hour Sabbath meeting, court day, the use of the stocks, etc." Publ Wkly

"The youthful voice and observations, in language that is a remarkable blend of clarity and period flavor, provide a more intimate and involving picture of the period than more straightforward factual accounts." SLJ

Fritz, Jean

Who's that stepping on Plymouth Rock? illustrated by J. B. Handelsman. Coward, McCann & Geoghegan 1975 30p il $15.99; pa $6.99 (2-4)

974.4

1. Plymouth Rock

ISBN 0-698-20325-9; 0-698-11681-X (pa)

An "account of the Rock which is visited yearly by about one and a half million people. It stands now under a monument on the waterfront of Plymouth, Massachusetts, sacred to the memory of the First Comers (Pilgrims) but it has figured in many adventures since the Pilgrims did—or did not—step upon it in 1620." Publ Wkly

"Both a delightful story and a perceptive commentary on how the mythmaking process works in American history." N Y Times Book Rev

Sewall, Marcia

The pilgrims of Plimoth; written and illustrated by Marcia Sewall. Atheneum Pubs. 1986 48p il $16.95; pa $5.99 (3-6)   **974.4**

1. Pilgrims (New England colonists) 2. Massachusetts—History—1600-1775, Colonial period

ISBN 0-689-31250-4; 0-689-80861-5 (pa)

LC 86-3362

The author provides a "first-person narrative account of the Mayflower voyage of 1620 and the early years of the Plymouth colony. This is not the personal diary of an individual, but rather a journal of the community." Booklist

"Translating narrative and descriptive details into visual images, the illustrations accompany every page of text, occasionally overspreading double pages for panoramic effects. Combining subtle, modulating color with a spiritual as well as an actual luminosity, the paintings—done in gouache—are vibrant with the daily pulse of life among an energetic, enterprising people." Horn Book

Waters, Kate

On the Mayflower; voyage of the ship's apprentice & a passenger girl; photographs by Russ Kendall. Scholastic 1996 40p il $16.95; pa $5.99 (2-4)   **974.4**

1. Mayflower (Ship) 2. Pilgrims (New England colonists) 3. Massachusetts—History—1600-1775, Colonial period

ISBN 0-590-67308-4; 0-439-09941-2 (pa)

LC 95-43980

"Waters tells a story of the *Mayflower's* passage to America through the characters of William Small, the apprentice to the master of the ship, and Ellen Moore, an eight-year-old passenger. The text is based on historical documents. . . . Kendall's clear, full-color photographs, shot on the *Mayflower II*, complement the story. This book is well written, designed, and photographed." SLJ

Includes glossary

Samuel Eaton's day; a day in the life of a Pilgrim boy; photographs by Russ Kendall. Scholastic 1993 40p il $16.95; pa $5.99 (2-4)

974.4

1. Pilgrims (New England colonists) 2. Massachusetts—History—1600-1775, Colonial period

ISBN 0-590-46311-X; 0-590-48053-7 (pa)

LC 92-32325

Text and photographs follow a six-year-old Pilgrim boy through a busy day during the spring harvest in 1627

"The photographs, taken at Plimoth Plantation, an outdoor living history museum, entice the reader back into the seventeenth century with their authenticity and detail. A vivid description of the hardships endured as well as the pride felt by these English colonists in their new American community." Horn Book

Includes glossary

Sarah Morton's day; a day in the life of a pilgrim girl; photographs by Russ Kendall. Scholastic 1989 32p il $16.95; pa $5.99 (2-4)

974.4

1. Pilgrims (New England colonists) 2. Massachusetts—History—1600-1775, Colonial period

ISBN 0-590-42634-6; 0-590-44871-4 (pa)

LC 88-35581

Text and photographs of Plimouth Plantation follow a pilgrim girl through a typical day as she milks the goats, cooks and serves meals, learns her letters, and adjusts to her new stepfather

Includes glossary

974.7 New York

Bial, Raymond

Tenement; immigrant life on the Lower East Side. Houghton Mifflin 2002 48p il $16 (4 and up)   **974.7**

1. Poor 2. Immigrants—United States 3. Lower East Side (New York, N.Y.)

ISBN 0-618-13849-8   LC 2002-00407

Bial, Raymond—*Continued*

Presents a view of New York City's tenements during the peak years of foreign immigration, discussing living conditions, laws pertaining to tenements, and the occupations of their residents

"The writing is particularly clear and sharp. Calling upon and quoting the writing of reformer Jacob Riis (and featuring his compelling photographs), Bial explains simply, yet engagingly, what tenement life was like. . . . Along with Riis' photographs, Bial provides some of his own, taken at the Lower East Side Tenement Museum in New York City." Booklist

Includes bibliographical references

Curlee, Lynn

Liberty. Atheneum Bks. for Young Readers 2000 41p $18 (3-6)   **974.7**

1. Bartholdi, Frédéric Auguste, 1834-1904 2. Statue of Liberty (New York, N.Y.)

ISBN 0-689-82823-3   LC 98-44732

The author narrates the "story of Liberty's creation, from its conception by French professor Édouard de Laboulaye (who proposed the idea at a dinner party attended by young sculptor Frédéric-Auguste Bartholdi) to the fulfillment of Bartholdi's obsession to create a monument to liberty that would rival the Colossus of Rhodes." Horn Book

"Curlee's illustrations—bold, bright full-page acrylic paintings, most dramatically composed—are helpful in conveying technical details and in portraying the various stages in the creation of the statue. But they are also quite beautiful, for they communicate not just information but also excitement and sentiment." N Y Times Book Rev

Includes bibliographical references

Hess, Debra

The Statue of Liberty; by Debra Hess. Benchmark Books 2004 40p il (Symbols of America) $25.64 (3-5)   **974.7**

1. Statue of Liberty (New York, N.Y.)

ISBN 0-7614-1707-9   LC 2003-4272

Traces the origins of the Statue of Liberty, its creators, the different symbols and their meanings, and what it stands for today.

This is "engaging [and] well-written." SLJ

Includes bibliographical references

Hopkinson, Deborah

Shutting out the sky; life in the tenements of New York, 1880-1924. Orchard Bks. 2003 134p il $17.95 (5 and up)   **974.7**

1. Poor 2. Immigrants—United States 3. Lower East Side (New York, N.Y.)

ISBN 0-439-37590-8   LC 2002-44781

Contents: Coming to the golden land; Tenements: shutting out the sky; Settling in: greenhorns and boarders; Everyone worked on; On the streets: pushcarts, pickles and play; A new language, a new life; Looking to the future: will it ever be different?

Photographs and text document the experiences of five individuals who came to live in the Lower East Side of New York City as children or young adults from Belarus, Italy, Lithuania, and Romania at the turn of the twentieth century

"The text is supported by numerous tinted archival photos of living and working conditions. Although this book will appeal to students looking for material for projects, the writing lends immediacy and vivid images make it simply a fascinating read." SLJ

Includes bibliographical references

Kalman, Maira

Fireboat; the heroic adventures of the John J. Harvey. Putnam 2002 unp il $16.99 (k-3)   **974.7**

1. John J. Harvey (Fireboat) 2. September 11 terrorist attacks, 2001

ISBN 0-399-23953-7   LC 2002-2423

A fireboat, launched in 1931, is retired after many years of fighting fires along the Hudson River, but is saved from being scrapped and then called into service again on September 11, 2001

"Among the many literary tributes to 9-11 heroism, Kalman's is particularly exciting, uplifting, and child-sensitive." Bull Cent Child Books

Maestro, Betsy

The story of the Statue of Liberty; [by] Betsy & Giulio Maestro. Lothrop, Lee & Shepard Bks. 1986 39p il pa $5.95 hardcover o.p. (k-3)   **974.7**

1. Bartholdi, Frédéric Auguste, 1834-1904 2. Statue of Liberty (New York, N.Y.)

ISBN 0-688-08746-9 (pa)   LC 85-11324

"Although Maestro simplifies the story—including only the most important people's names, for example—she still presents an accurate account of what happened. The exceptional drawings are visually delightful—primarily in the blue-green range, although they are in full color—and cover most of every page. Human figures—workers, tourists—are included in many drawings, indicating the statue's tremendous scale. Further, the drawings involve viewers through the use of unusual perspectives and angles and by placing the statue in scenes of city life." SLJ

Includes bibliographical references

Marcus, Leonard S.

Storied city; a children's book, walking-tour guide to New York City. Dutton Children's Bks. 2003 154p il map pa $12.99   **974.7**

1. New York (N.Y.) 2. New York (N.Y.) in literature 3. Literary landmarks—United States

ISBN 0-525-46924-9   LC 2002-69283

"Including both fiction and nonfiction, some popular titles and some less well known, Marcus has created a fascinating array of walking tours of New York City. . . . Touring through each section, Marcus introduces history, characters, authors, anecdotes, quotes, and often parts of the specific stories from children's books. . . . Historical background on authors, illustrators, and publishing helps tie the books into the history of the city, and a bibliography of children's books set in New York City is included." SLJ

Matsen, Bradford

Go wild in New York City; [by] Brad Matsen; illustrations by Paul Corio; scientific illustration by Kate Lake. National Geographic 2005 79p il map $16.95 (4 and up)   **974.7**

1. Natural history 2. New York (N.Y.)
ISBN 0-7922-7982-4

This is a "picture-book tour through New York City's 'true wildness,' with chapters that cover the area's water, rocks, air, plants, and animals as well as a closing section about food production and waste removal. . . . Packed with color photographs, cartoons, diagrams, and numerous sidebars. . . . There's an impressive array of basic science here, described mostly in accessible, enthusiastic text. Students will find enough to support reports, and the open format will attract browsers. " Booklist

Melmed, Laura Krauss

New York, New York; the Big Apple from A to Z; illustrated by Frané Lessac. HarperCollins Pub. 2005 unp il $16.99; lib bdg $17.89 (k-3)   **974.7**

1. New York (N.Y.) 2. Alphabet
ISBN 0-06-054674-6; 0-06-054876-2 (lib bdg)

"From the American Museum of Natural History to the Bronx Zoo, each letter is accompanied by a peppy eight-line poem as well as multiple sidebars, factoids, and tidbits about the sights described. Melmed brilliantly touches on all the major sights of NYC." SLJ

Shea, Pegi Deitz

Liberty rising; the story of the Statue of Liberty; illustrated by Wade Zahares. 1st ed. Henry Holt 2005 unp il $17.95 (2-4)   **974.7**

1. Bartholdi, Frédéric Auguste, 1834-1904 2. Statue of Liberty (New York, N.Y.)
ISBN 0-8050-7220-9   LC 2004-24279

In this account of the building of the Statue of Liberty "Shea introduces the size and scale of creating such a large object. . . . Each step in the process . . . is told in simple text. . . . The book is easy to read, with three-quarter spreads of illustration and single columns of text. The stylized graphic art is fairly realistic with bold colors and unusual angles to create a sense of excitement." SLJ

Includes bibliographical references

974.8   Pennsylvania

Hess, Debra

The Liberty Bell; [by] Debra Hess. Benchmark Books 2004 40p il (Symbols of America) $25.64 (3-5)   **974.8**

1. Liberty Bell
ISBN 0-7614-1713-3   LC 2003-4463

Contents: Cracked bells; The American Revolution; A symbol of freedom

Traces the history of the Liberty Bell, including its role in the American Revolution, its famous crack, and how it became a symbol of the United States.

This is "engaging [and] well-written." SLJ

Includes bibliographical references

975   Southeastern United States. Southern States

Erickson, Paul

Daily life on a Southern plantation, 1853. Lodestar Bks. 1998 c1997 48p il pa $7.99 hardcover o.p. (4 and up)   **975**

1. Plantation life 2. Slavery—United States
ISBN 0-14-056668-6 (pa)   LC 97-22540
First published 1997 in the United Kingdom

Recreates a southern plantation of 1853 and describes the daily lives of its owners and of the slaves who worked there

"Erickson uses a family to make the information in the text accessible. This book follows two families . . . one living in the 'Big House'; and the other a slave family, through a typical day—a technique that provides a personal, well-informed view of slavery." Horn Book Guide

Includes glossary

975.3   District of Columbia (Washington)

Ashabranner, Brent K.

No better hope; what the Lincoln Memorial means to America; [by] Brent Ashabranner; photographs by Jennifer Ashabranner. 21st Cent. Bks. (Brookfield) 2001 64p il (Great American memorials) lib bdg $25.90 (4 and up)   **975.3**

1. Lincoln, Abraham, 1809-1865 2. Lincoln Memorial (Washington, D.C.)
ISBN 0-7613-1523-3   LC 00-61546

"Seven brief chapters review Lincoln's presidency, discuss preliminary plans for a permanent memorial, describe the processes by which architect Henry Bacon and sculptor Daniel French developed and executed their creation, and suggest how the site has 'become a symbol of the "patient confidence" that Lincoln had in the wisdom and courage of the common people.'" Bull Cent Child Books

A "well-designed volume. . . . Excellent color photographs by Jennifer Ashabranner appear throughout the book." Booklist

Includes bibliographical references

Curlee, Lynn

Capital. Atheneum Bks. for Young Readers 2003 40p il map $17.95 (3-6)   **975.3**

1. National monuments 2. Washington (D.C.)
ISBN 0-689-84947-8   LC 2001-56083

Provides a history of Washington, D.C., focusing on the National Mall, its monuments and surrounding buildings

"Curlee brings history to life with small details and historical incidents. . . . With clean lines, muted colors, dramatic lighting, and dignified compositions, Curlee's acrylic art faithfully represents these structures, while placing them within a human context." Booklist

Includes bibliographical references

Grace, Catherine O'Neill
The White House; an illustrated history.
Scholastic 2003 144p il $19.95 (3-6)
975.3

1. White House (Washington, D.C.)
ISBN 0-439-42971-4   LC 2002-30603
Explores the history, architecture, and symbolism of
the White House, which serves as a museum, office, ceremonial site, and a home to presidents and their families.
"Published in cooperation with the White House Historical Association, this is a fascinating and beautifully
produced gem. . . . This accessible volume is filled with
many interesting facts, and is a handsomely designed
tribute." SLJ
Includes bibliographical references

Hess, Debra
The White House; by Debra Hess. Benchmark
Books 2004 40p il $25.24 (3-5)   **975.3**
1. White House (Washington, D.C.)
ISBN 0-7614-1712-5   LC 2003-4462
Contents: A home for the president; Living in the
White House; The twentieth century and beyond
Traces the history of the White House, including its
construction, repairs and renovations through the years,
uses, and what it means to Americans today.
This "offers a fascinating look at the mansion, how it
has changed over the years, and why it is so important.
[The title has] full-color photographs and reproductions
of famous paintings." SLJ
Includes bibliographical references

975.5   Virginia

Chorao, Kay
D is for drums; a Colonial Williamsburg ABC;
[by] Kay Chorao. Harry N. Abrams 2004 unp il
$16.95 (k-3)   **975.5**
1. Colonial Williamsburg (Williamsburg, Va.)
2. Alphabet
ISBN 0-8109-4927-X   LC 2003-25793
"Chorao has created a large, visually charming, and
fact-rich look at Colonial Williamsburg. Endpaper maps
of the city's streets show everything from a shoemaker's
shop to the Governor's Palace. Each page in between
displays a huge capital letter decorated with drawings
that showcase an alliterative list of words. . . . Chorao
selected items to foster chuckles and amazement. Her
pen-and-ink and watercolor drawings of children and animals add energy to the stunning layouts." SLJ

Richards, Norman
Monticello. Children's Press 1995 30p il
(Cornerstones of freedom) lib bdg $20.50; pa
$5.95 (4-6)   **975.5**
1. Jefferson, Thomas, 1743-1826—Homes and haunts
ISBN 0-516-06695-1 (lib bdg); 0-516-46695-X (pa)
      LC 94-35654
A revised and newly illustrated edition of The story of
Monticello, published 1970

The construction and furnishing of the home of Thomas Jefferson "are described as they relate to the events of
Jefferson's life and to the founding of our country. The
well-written text is handsomely enhanced by full-color
and black-and-white photographs and illustrations of the
house, gardens, and Jefferson's inventions. His beliefs
and feelings about slavery are briefly discussed." SLJ

Rosen, Daniel
New beginnings; Jamestown and the Virginia
Colony, 1607-1699; [by] Daniel Rosen. National
Geographic 2005 40p il map (Crossroads America)
$12.95 (4-6)   **975.5**
1. Jamestown (Va.)—History 2. Virginia—History
3. United States—History—1600-1775, Colonial peri-
od
ISBN 0-7922-8277-9   LC 2004007101
First published 2004 with title: Jamestown and the
Virginia Colony

This describes colonial Virginia, from the founding of
Jamestown to the building of Williamsburg.
This "solid [title] for report writers may even pull in
a few curious browsers because of [its] plentiful, full-
color photos and reproductions. The [layout is] inviting,
and the [text is] clear, informative, and readable." SLJ
Includes glossary

Sewall, Marcia
James Towne: struggle for survival; written and
illustrated by Marcia Sewall. Atheneum Bks. for
Young Readers 2001 40p il $16 (3-5)
      975.5
1. Jamestown (Va.)
ISBN 0-689-81814-9   LC 99-32167
"The story of the first permanent English settlement in
North America is narrated here by an 18-year-old carpen-
ter who in 1607, along with 104 other Englishmen estab-
lished the colony of Jamestown, Virginia." Booklist
"Sewall's art . . . is subtle, thoughtful, and dignified.
It appeals to the intellect, not to raw emotion, yet is
moving and evocative—like the text." Horn Book
Includes glossary and bibliographical references

975.6   North Carolina

Fritz, Jean
The Lost Colony of Roanoke; illustrated by
Hudson Talbott. G.P. Putnam's Sons 2004 58p il
map $16.99 (3-6)   **975.6**
1. Roanoke Island (N.C.)—History
ISBN 0-399-24027-6   LC 2002-152000
Describes the English colony of Roanoke, which was
founded in 1585, and discusses the mystery of its disappearance.
"Talbott's softly colored watercolor illustrations . . .
are at once detailed and impressionistic. Clever touches
of humor abound. . . . Fritz has scored again, making
history breathe while showing both historians and archaeologists at their reconstructive best." SLJ

975.9 Florida

George, Jean Craighead
Everglades; paintings by Wendell Minor. HarperCollins Pubs. 1995 unp il $15.95; lib bdg $16.89; pa $6.95 (2-4)   **975.9**
1. Everglades (Fla.)
ISBN 0-06-021228-4; 0-06-021229-2 (lib bdg); 0-06-446194-7 (pa)   LC 92-9517
"Though structured as a tale told to five children whom a storyteller has poled into the Everglades, the narrative focuses on the history of that unusual ecosystem. The narrator tells how the Everglades became 'a living kaleidoscope of color and beauty,' filled with plants and animals, and how human involvement has changed the ecology, devastating the area. . . . When the children ask about what happened to the orchids, egrets, and alligators, the storyteller suggests that they can make a happy ending to the story when they grow up." Booklist
"The story and the art create a mystical tale that flows from a serene start to a powerful conclusion." SLJ

976.4 Texas

Lourie, Peter
Rio Grande; from the Rocky Mountains to the Gulf of Mexico. Boyds Mills Press 1999 46p il $17.95; pa $9.95 (4 and up)   **976.4**
1. Rio Grande valley
ISBN 1-56397-706-0; 1-56397-896-2 (pa)
LC 97-77907
The author "reports on his 1,900-mile journey down the Rio Grande, from its headwaters near a former silver town in Colorado to its inconspicuous outlet into the Gulf. In dramatic prose . . . he not only describes the passing scenery but also evokes some of its colorful history. . . . Unusually well-chosen photographs enhance the connections between the river's past and present with a mix of historical shots, new portraits, and landscapes in sharp color, and even a satellite picture." Booklist

Murphy, Jim
Inside the Alamo. Delacorte Press 2003 121p il map $16.95; lib bdg $18.99 (5 and up)
976.4
1. Alamo (San Antonio, Tex.) 2. Texas—History
ISBN 0-385-32574-6; 0-385-90092-9 (lib bdg)
LC 2002-24029
An overview of the struggle between the Texan settlers and Mexico's General Santa Anna for control of Texas, with a detailed description of the 1836 siege of the Alamo. Includes biographical sketches and quotations of some of those involved
This is "an absorbing, interpretive, highly readable account. . . . Murphy has done an admirable job of separating prejudicial speculation (by survivors on both sides) from documentation." SLJ
Includes bibliographical references

977 North Central United States. Lake states

Walsh, Kieran
The Mississippi. World Almanac 2003 48p il map (Great rivers of the world) lib bdg $26.60; pa $14.60 (4 and up)   **977**
1. Mississippi River 2. Mississippi River valley
ISBN 0-8368-5444-6 (lib bdg); 0-8368-5451-9 (pa)
LC 2002-34315
Contents: The course of the Mississippi; The Mississippi in history; Cities and settlements; Trade, transportation, and industry; Animals and plants; Environmental issues; Recreation and leisure; The future
This explains the Mississippi River's "flow, history, ecological concerns, tourism, flora and fauna, etc. . . . Clear and colorful photos appear on every page." SLJ
Includes glossary and bibliographical references

977.3 Illinois

Murphy, Jim
The great fire. Scholastic 1995 144p il maps $16.95 (5 and up)   **977.3**
1. Fires—Chicago (Ill.)
ISBN 0-590-47267-4   LC 94-9963
Newbery honor book, 1996
"Firsthand descriptions by persons who lived through the 1871 Chicago fire are woven into a gripping account of this famous disaster. Murphy also examines the origins of the fire, the errors of judgment that delayed the effective response, the organizational problems of the city's firefighters, and the postfire efforts to rebuild the city. Newspaper lithographs and a few historical photographs convey the magnitude of human suffering and confusion." Horn Book Guide
Includes bibliographical references

978 Western United States

Bial, Raymond
Ghost towns of the American West. Houghton Mifflin 2001 48p il $16 (3-6)   **978**
1. Ghost towns 2. West (U.S.)—History
ISBN 0-618-06557-1   LC 00-31895
"This photo-essay offers views of America's ghost towns and discusses their place in history. Several period photographs from the 1800s show these communities while they flourished, but the book's most effective illustrations are the evocative color photos of ghost towns today." Booklist
Includes bibliographical references

Blumberg, Rhoda
The incredible journey of Lewis and Clark. Lothrop, Lee & Shepard Bks. 1987 143p il maps pa $12.99 (5 and up)   **978**
1. Lewis, Meriwether, 1774-1809 2. Clark, William, 1770-1838 3. Lewis and Clark Expedition (1804-1806) 4. West (U.S.)—Exploration
ISBN 0-688-14421-7 (pa)   LC 87-4235

Blumberg, Rhoda—*Continued*

Also available in hardcover from Smith, P.

Describes the expedition led by Lewis and Clark to explore the unknown western regions of America at the beginning of the nineteenth century

"Blumberg's writing is dignified but never dry, and her sense of narrative makes familiar history an exciting story." Bull Cent Child Books

Includes bibliographical references

York's adventures with Lewis and Clark; an African-American's part in the great expedition. HarperCollins 2004 88p il map $17.99; lib bdg $18.89 (5 and up)   **978**

1. York, ca. 1775-ca. 1815 2. Lewis and Clark Expedition (1804-1806) 3. West (U.S.)—Exploration 4. African Americans—Biography
ISBN 0-06-009111-8; 0-06-009112-6 (lib bdg)
LC 2003-9425

Relates the adventures of York, a slave and "body servant" to William Clark, who journeyed west with the Lewis and Clark Expedition of 1804-1806

"This well-researched selection helps to round out the study of an amazing event in our country's history. . . . Meticulously documented and illustrated with black-and-white photos and reproductions, this is a solid purchase for all collections." SLJ

Includes bibliographical references

Calabro, Marian

The perilous journey of the Donner Party. Clarion Bks. 1999 192p il maps $20 (5 and up)
978

1. Donner party 2. Frontier and pioneer life—West (U.S.) 3. Overland journeys to the Pacific
ISBN 0-395-86610-3   LC 98-29610

Uses materials from letters and diaries written by survivors of the Donner Party to relate the experiences of that ill-fated group as they endured horrific circumstances on their way to California in 1846-47

"Calabro's offering is a fine addition to the Donner Party canon and particularly well suited to its young audience, for whom the story of hardship and survival will be nothing short of riveting. . . . From the haunting cover with its lonely campfire to the recounting of a survivors' reunion, this is a page-turner." Booklist

Includes bibliographical references

Freedman, Russell

Children of the wild West. Clarion Bks. 1983 104p il map $18; pa $6.95 (4 and up)
978

1. Children—West (U.S.) 2. Frontier and pioneer life—West (U.S.) 3. West (U.S.)—History
ISBN 0-89919-143-6; 0-395-54785-7 (pa)
LC 83-5133

"A smooth narrative and numerous historical photographs combine for an intriguing backward look at how children fared in pioneer times." Booklist

An Indian winter; paintings and drawings by Karl Bodmer. Holiday House 1992 88p il $21.95; pa $12.95 (6 and up)   **978**

1. Wied, Maximilian, Prinz von, 1782-1867 2. Native Americans—Missouri River valley 3. Missouri River valley
ISBN 0-8234-0930-9; 0-8234-1158-3 (pa)
LC 91-24205

Relates the experiences of a German prince, his servant, and a young Swiss artist as they traveled through the Missouri River Valley in 1833 learning about the territory and its inhabitants and recording their impressions in words and pictures

"The pictures are particularly effective in presenting rich details of village life, clothing, ceremonies, and customs. Both the book's specific information about native peoples and its use of primary-source material make it a valuable creation." Horn Book

Includes bibliographical references

Galford, Ellen

The trail West; exploring history through art; [by] Ellen Galford. Two-Can Pub 2005 64p il (Picture that!) $19.95 (5 and up)   **978**

1. West (U.S.)—History 2. West (U.S.) in art
ISBN 1-58728-442-1   LC 2004-8334

Contents: Heading West; The travellers' rest: Benjamin Franklin Reinhart; Fur-trapping trip: George Caleb Bingham; Hunting buffalo: George Catlin; Trouble on the trail: Charles Ferdinand Wimar; At home in the wilderness: Cornelius Krieghoff; Home by the fireside: Eastman Johnson; A Mandan village: George Catlin; A sacred festival: Silver Horn; The shooting match: George Caleb Bingham; Schooldays: Winslow Homer; At the trading post: Alfred Jacob Miller; Life in the saddle: Frederic Remington; Gold rush: Charles Christian Nahl; End of the line: O.E. Berninghaus

This examines pioneer life in the American West through the works of such artists as Wislow Homer, Eastman Johnson, George Catlin, and George Caleb Bingham

"Art and history meld with entertaining and successful results. . . . [This] unique, well-thought-out [title is] good for reports, and browsers would enjoy [it], too." SLJ

Grupper, Jonathan

Destination: Rocky Mountains. National Geographic Soc. 2001 31p il $16.95 (3-6)
978

1. Rocky Mountains
ISBN 0-7922-7722-8   LC 00-55926

"A hypothetical trek up the Rocky Mountains provides the framework for . . . information about its animals and the vegetation that sustains them at elevations beyond fourteen thousand feet. Each animal—from huge grizzly bear to tiny pika—has a double-page spread, lavishly illustrated with well-chosen color photographs. The text and graphics work well together." Horn Book Guide

Johmann, Carol

Going west! journey on a wagon train to settle a frontier town; [by] Carol A. Johmann, Elizabeth J. Rieth; illustrations by Michael Kline. Williamson 2000 96p il pa $10.95 (3-6) **978**

1. Frontier and pioneer life—West (U.S.) 2. Overland journeys to the Pacific 3. West (U.S.)—History

ISBN 1-88559-338-4   LC 99-89622

"A Kaleidoscope Kids book"

Describes the choices and decisions the pioneers faced as they traveled to the American West and built settlements there. Includes activities

"A good combination of history lesson, craft instruction, critical-thinking activities, and story." SLJ

Includes bibliographical references

Josephson, Judith Pinkerton

Growing up in pioneer America, 1800 to 1890. Lerner Publs. 2003 64p il map (Our America) lib bdg $26.60   **978**

1. Frontier and pioneer life—West (U.S.) 2. West (U.S.)—History

ISBN 0-8225-0659-9   LC 2001-6825

Describes what life was like for young people moving to and living on the western frontier

"Primary-source materials including selections from letters and diaries join numerous reproductions and archival photos to deliver a clear picture of the varied experiences of children living in the U.S. during the 1800s. Accessible, attractive, and useful." SLJ

Includes bibliographical references

Katz, William Loren

Black women of the Old West. Atheneum Bks. for Young Readers 1995 84p il $19.95 (5 and up) **978**

1. African American women 2. Frontier and pioneer life—West (U.S.) 3. West (U.S.)—History

ISBN 0-689-31944-4   LC 95-9969

This work contains "vignettes and photographs of dozens of women, some famous, others unknown outside their own family circles, who lived across the West in the 19th and early 20th centuries." N Y Times Book Rev

"Katz succeeds in establishing that women of color were an important, if unsung, presence on the westward-shifting frontier." Bull Cent Child Books

Kimmel, Elizabeth Cody

As far as the eye can reach; Lewis and Clark's westward quest. Random House 2003 119p il maps $14.95; lib bdg $16.99 (4 and up) **978**

1. Lewis, Meriwether, 1774-1809 2. Clark, William, 1770-1838 3. Lewis and Clark Expedition (1804-1806) 4. West (U.S.)—Exploration

ISBN 0-375-81348-9; 0-375-91348-3 (lib bdg)
          LC 2002-31621

"Landmark books"

An account of the journey across the unexplored territory west of the Mississippi River undertaken by Meriwether Lewis and William Clark in the early eighteen hundreds by order of President Jefferson

"Chock-full of historical detail, Kimmel's account of Lewis and Clark's expedition is an eye-opener. . . . A book such as this can excite young readers to delve further into U.S. history." SLJ

Includes bibliographical references

King, David C.

Pioneer days; discover the past with fun projects, games, activities, and recipes. Wiley 1997 118p il (American kids in history) pa $12.95 (3-6) **978**

1. Frontier and pioneer life—West (U.S.) 2. West (U.S.)—Social life and customs

ISBN 0-471-16169-1   LC 96-37495

This book is an "assortment of history, culture, crafts, and stories to teach about the daily life of the pioneers. . . . [Crafts and recipes include] air-dried flowers, toys and games, homemade soda pop, johnny-cakes, and various holiday ornaments. The author's research is evident, and the presentation of the activities and recipes is so engaging that the book will appeal to a wide audience." SLJ

Includes glossary and bibliographical references

Wild West days; discover the past with fun projects, games, activities, and recipes. Wiley 1998 118p il (American kids in history) pa $12.95 (3-6) **978**

1. Ranch life 2. West (U.S.)—Social life and customs

ISBN 0-471-23919-4   LC 97-48557

Discusses what life was like for the people who settled the West between 1870 and 1900, follows a year in the life of a fictional family of that time, and presents projects and activities, such as designing a brand stamp and making a yarn picture

Includes glossary and bibliographical references

Lavender, David Sievert

Snowbound; the tragic story of the Donner Party; by David Lavender. Holiday House 1996 87p il maps $22.95 (4 and up) **978**

1. Donner party 2. Frontier and pioneer life—West (U.S.) 3. Overland journeys to the Pacific

ISBN 0-8234-1231-8   LC 95-41266

Relates the ordeals faced by a group of pioneers on their journey from Illinois to California in 1846

The author "draws on authentic primary documents, combining a vivid narrative with his analysis of what happened and why. His handsomely designed, slightly oversize volume has lots of photos of the places and people." Booklist

Includes bibliographical references

Meltzer, Milton

Driven from the land; the story of the Dust Bowl. Benchmark Bks. 2000 111p il (Great journeys) lib bdg $32.79 (4 and up) **978**

1. Great Plains—History 2. Dust storms 3. Great Depression, 1929-1939

ISBN 0-7614-0968-8   LC 98-47501

Meltzer, Milton—*Continued*
Describes the economic and environmental conditions
that led to the Great Depression and the horrific dust
storms that drove people from their homes westward during the 1930s
"Well-reproduced photographs by Dorothea Lange and
others of the time greatly enhance the text." Booklist
Includes bibliographical references

Miller, Brandon Marie
Buffalo gals; women of the old West. Lerner
Publs. 1995 88p il (People's history series) lib bdg
$22.60; pa $8.95 (5 and up)   **978**
1. Women—West (U.S.) 2. Frontier and pioneer life—
West (U.S.) 3. West (U.S.)—History
ISBN 0-8225-1730-2 (lib bdg); 0-8225-9772-1 (pa)
           LC 94-5063
"Westward migration, housekeeping difficulties, professions, forms of entertainment, and intercultural relations are some of the topics discussed in this . . .
overview of women's experiences in getting to and surviving in the West." Bull Cent Child Books
The author "catches both the bone-wearying labor and
the excitement that sometimes made living in the West
worthwhile. She deftly augments her text with excerpts
from journals and memoirs as well as photographs from
regional archives, which are especially effective because
the images are not familiar ones." Booklist
Includes bibliographical references

Patent, Dorothy Hinshaw
Animals on the trail with Lewis and Clark;
photographs by William Muñoz. Clarion Bks. 2002
118p il map $18 (4 and up)   **978**
1. Lewis and Clark Expedition (1804-1806)
2. Animals—United States 3. West (U.S.)—Exploration
ISBN 0-395-91415-9   LC 2001-42200
Retraces the Lewis and Clark journey and blends their
observations of previously unknown animals with modern information about those same animals
"The spacious page layouts, beautiful illustrations, and
well-written text help ensure that this historically significant story will be read and enjoyed." Booklist
Includes bibliographical references

The Lewis and Clark trail; then and now;
photographs by William Muñoz. Dutton Children's
Bks. 2002 60p il maps $19.99 (4 and up)
      978
1. Lewis and Clark Expedition (1804-1806) 2. West
(U.S.)—Exploration
ISBN 0-525-46912-5   LC 2002-70857
Patent provides a "narrative account of the Lewis and
Clark Expedition, beginning with a realistically harsh,
you-are-there introduction to life with the Corps of Discovery. Among the many books on the subject appearing
in time for the bicentennial of that event . . . this one
distinguishes itself by incorporating information about
how the land, rivers, vegetation, wildlife and trails today
differ from what Lewis and Clark saw 200 years ago.
. . . A well-written presentation of the topic." Booklist
Includes bibliographical references

Plants on the trail with Lewis and Clark;
photographs by William Muñoz. Clarion Bks. 2003
104p il map $18 (4 and up)   **978**
1. Lewis and Clark Expedition (1804-1806)
2. Plants—United States 3. West (U.S.)—Exploration
ISBN 0-618-06776-0   LC 2002-10383
Contents: Jefferson, Lewis, and plants; The importance
of trees; Plants as food; Wildflowers and their uses; The
fate of Lewis's specimens
Describes the journey of Lewis and Clark through the
western United States, focusing on the plants they cata-
loged, their uses for food and medicine, and the plant
lore of Native American people
"Good-quality, full-color photos and reproductions
clearly extend the text. . . . The author's knowledge of
and keen interest in her subject matter is very evident in
this fascinating account." SLJ
Includes bibliographical references

Pringle, Laurence P.
Dog of discovery; a Newfoundland's adventures
with Lewis and Clark; by Laurence Pringle. Boyds
Mills Press 2002 149p $17.95 (4-6)   **978**
1. Lewis and Clark Expedition (1804-1806) 2. Dogs
3. West (U.S.)—Exploration
ISBN 1-59078-028-0   LC 2002-102046
This is "a lightly fictionalized account of the Lewis
and Clark expedition. . . . It focuses on Seaman,
Meriwether Lewis' Newfoundland dog, who proved himself a worthy member of the Corps of Discovery. . . .
The result is a very informative story, illustrated with
small drawings and photos, studded with sidebars that
carry related facts, and bolstered by an afterword, a dated
list of entries about Seaman from expedition members'
journals, lists of resources, and an index." Booklist

Sakurai, Gail
Asian-Americans in the old West. Children's
Press 2000 30p il (Cornerstones of freedom) $21;
pa $5.95 (4 and up)   **978**
1. West (U.S.)—History 2. Asian Americans
ISBN 0-516-21152-8; 0-516-27035-4 (pa)
          LC 99-24463
Describes the important role of the Chinese, Japanese,
and other Asians in the settlement of the American West

Savage, Candace
Born to be a cowgirl; a spirited ride through the
old West. Tricycle Press 2001 64p il $15.95; pa
$9.95 (4 and up)   **978**
1. Cowhands 2. Women—West (U.S.) 3. Frontier and
pioneer life—West (U.S.)
ISBN 1-58246-019-1; 1-58246-020-5 (pa)
          LC 00-61559
"This survey highlights the vigorous horse-women
who helped shape the West . . . focuses on the daring
girls and women who defied convention to ride horses,
lasso cattle and buck broncos." Publ Wkly
"Sepia tones and leather-textured framing for the illustrations add flavor to this nifty piece of bookmaking. An
exemplary work." SLJ
Includes glossary and bibliographical references

Schanzer, Rosalyn

How we crossed the West; the adventures of Lewis & Clark. National Geographic Soc. 1997 unp il $18 (3-5)   **978**

1. Lewis, Meriwether, 1774-1809 2. Clark, William, 1770-1838 3. Lewis and Clark Expedition (1804-1806)

ISBN 0-7922-3738-2   LC 96-6585

This "account of the 1804-1805 journey [has]. . . . a text composed of brief excerpts drawn from the actual journals and letters written by Lewis and Clark and members of the expedition." SLJ

"Pithy and sometimes humorous, the text tells of contacts with Native Americans, encounters with wildlife . . . and the hardships of the trail. Warm in color and accessible in style, the acrylic paintings have a folk-art inspiration." Booklist

Scott, Ann Herbert

Cowboy country; pictures by Ted Lewin. Clarion Bks. 1993 unp il $16; pa $6.95 (k-3)

978

1. Cowhands 2. West (U.S.)

ISBN 0-395-57561-3; 0-395-76482-3 (pa)

LC 92-24499

An "old buckaroo" tells how he became a cowboy, what the work was like in the past, and how this life has changed

The author "succinctly captures the laconic speaking rhythms and distinctive jargon of her subject. . . . Lewin's . . . well-lit watercolors suggest the affability of the weathered narrator and the awe of the boy with him." Publ Wkly

Sonneborn, Liz

The Mormon Trail; [by] Liz Sonneborn. Franklin Watts 2005 63p il $25.50 (5 and up)

978

1. Mormons 2. Frontier and pioneer life—West (U.S.)

ISBN 0-531-12317-0   LC 2005001466

"Watts library"

This "title tells how in the 19th century Mormons traveled west to establish a community where they could practice their religion without fear of persecution. Black-and-white and color illustrations, maps, sidebars, and time lines enhance the well-organized [text]." SLJ

Includes bibliographical references

Steele, Christy

Cattle ranching in the American West; by Christy Steele. World Almanac Library 2005 48p il map (America's westward expansion) lib bdg $30; pa $11.95 (5 and up)   **978**

1. Ranch life 2. Cattle 3. West (U.S.)—History

ISBN 0-8368-5787-9 (lib bdg); 0-8368-5794-1 (pa)

LC 2004-56769

This volume describing Western cattle ranching is "richly illustrated with historical photographs, illustrations, maps, and quotes from primary sources presented in sidebars." SLJ

Includes bibliographical references

Famous wagon trails; by Christy Steele. World Almanac Library 2005 48p il map (America's westward expansion) lib bdg $30; pa $11.95 (5 and up)   **978**

1. Frontier and pioneer life 2. West (U.S.)—History 3. Overland journeys to the Pacific

ISBN 0-8368-5788-7 (lib bdg); 0-8368-5795-X (pa)

LC 2004-57822

This description of famous wagon trails in the West is "richly illustrated with historical photographs, illustrations, maps, and quotes from primary sources presented in sidebars." SLJ

Includes bibliographical references

Pioneer life in the American West; by Christy Steele. World Almanac Library 2005 48p il map (America's westward expansion) lib bdg $30; pa $11.95 (5 and up)   **978**

1. Frontier and pioneer life 2. West (U.S.)—History

ISBN 0-8368-5790-9 (lib bdg); 0-8368-5797-6 (pa)

LC 2004-56772

This description of pioneer life in the American West is "richly illustrated with historical photographs, illustrations, maps, and quotes from primary sources presented in sidebars." SLJ

Includes bibliographical references

Waldman, Stuart

The last river; John Wesley Powell & the Colorado River Exploration Expedition; by Stuart Waldman; illustrated by Gregory Manchess. Mikaya Press 2005 47p il map (Great explorers book) $19.95 (3-6)   **978**

1. Powell, John Wesley, 1834-1902 2. Colorado River (Colo.-Mexico) 3. West (U.S.)—Exploration

ISBN 1-931414-09-2   LC 2005041580

"In 1869 the Colorado River Exploring Expedition set forth from Green River City led by John Wesley Powell, a one-armed explorer who was determined to reach the Colorado's canyons to study their geology. . . . Waldman relates their story clearly in the main text, while occasional sidebars carry short excerpts from the men's journals and letters. Illustrations include clear nineteenth-century photos as well as handsome full and double-page paintings. . . . Rich in color, strong in composition, and beautifully executed, these often-dramatic paintings bring the story to life." Booklist

Includes bibliographical references

978.8   Colorado

Quigley, Mary

Mesa Verde; [by] Mary Quigley. Heinemann Library 2006 48p il (Excavating the past) lib bdg $31.43 (4-6)   **978.8**

1. Native Americans—Antiquities 2. Excavations (Archeology)—United States 3. Mesa Verde National Park (Colo.)

ISBN 1403459975   LC 2005009179

"*Mesa Verde* explains how these ancient people reached North and South America using the land bridge and settled down to farm in the Four Corners area.

Quigley, Mary—*Continued*
Quigley uses the term Ancestral Puebloans rather than the sometimes derogatory Anasazi and explains why. She describes the daily lives of the people and includes current theories about why they may have abandoned this site. Activities and discoveries by the Wetherill brothers and other archaeologists as well as cultural information from modern-day people bring knowledge about the ancients up to date. This [is an] excellent title." SLJ
Includes bibliographical references

979.4 California

Jaskol, Julie
City of angels; in and around Los Angeles; by Julie Jaskol & Brian Lewis; illustrated by Elisa Kleven. Dutton Children's Bks. 1999 47p il $16.99 (2-4)   **979.4**
1. Los Angeles (Calif.)
ISBN 0-525-46214-7   LC 99-35233
Surveys the history, historic sites, ethnic neighborhoods, festivals, and culture of the Los Angeles area
This offers "bright, exuberant collages filled with fascinating, minute details and a few paragraphs of text equally jam-packed with tidbits of information." SLJ

O'Donnell, Kerri
The gold rush; a primary source history of the search for gold in California. Rosen Central Primary Source 2003 64p il maps (Primary sources in American history) lib bdg $29.25 (4 and up)
979.4
1. California—Gold discoveries 2. Frontier and pioneer life—California
ISBN 0-8239-3682-1   LC 2002-1367
Contents: El Dorado; Timeline; The great discovery; Gold fever; To California by sea; The Overlanders; Life in the mines; The lawless West
Uses primary source documents, narrative, and illustrations to recount how the mid-nineteenth century California gold rush affected Americans and immigrants and how it shaped history
This "will be extremely effective when introducing students to primary source material." Libr Media Connect
Includes glossary and bibliographical references

Tanaka, Shelley
Earthquake! on a peaceful spring morning disaster strikes San Francisco; text by Shelley Tanaka; paintings by David Craig; historical consultation by Gladys Hansen. 1st U.S. ed. Hyperion Books for Children 2004 48p il map (Day that changed America) $16.99 (4 and up)
979.4
1. San Francisco (Calif.)—History 2. Earthquakes
ISBN 0-7868-1882-4   LC 2004-44457
"A Hyperion/Madison Press book"
"Using dramatic material culled from the adult recollections of four survivors . . . Tanaka recreates a series of events during and following the great San Francisco earthquake of April 18, 1906." SLJ

"Attractively illustrated and designed, this book offers a good story as well as solid information." Booklist
Includes glossary and bibliographical references

979.5 Oregon. Pacific Northwest

Fisher, Leonard Everett
The Oregon Trail. Holiday House 1990 64p il maps $18.95 (4 and up)   **979.5**
1. Oregon Trail 2. Overland journeys to the Pacific 3. Frontier and pioneer life—West (U.S.)
ISBN 0-8234-0833-7   LC 90-55103
Charts the journey of those who followed the Oregon Trail in the first half of the nineteenth century
"Fisher brings this migration to life with a clear, readable text that makes generous use of the emigrants' own journal entries. . . . The illustrations are many and varied, including maps, photographs, drawings, documents, and paintings." Booklist

981 Brazil

Fitzpatrick, Anne
Amazon River; [by] Anne Fitzpatrick. Creative Education 2004 c2005 32p il map (Natural wonders of the world) $27.10 (4-6)   **981**
1. Amazon River 2. Amazon River valley
ISBN 1-58341-322-7   LC 2003-62574
The describes the Amazon River's "geological formation and climate, ecology and wildlife, and human inhabitants and expeditions. A final chapter is devoted to tourism. . . . The [text], sufficient in informational quantity and quality for short reports, [is] briskly and engagingly written. But the real selling point here is the gorgeous color photographs." SLJ

Galvin, Irene Flum
Brazil; many voices, many faces. Benchmark Bks. 1996 64p il maps (Exploring cultures of the world) lib bdg $27.07 (4 and up)   **981**
1. Brazil
ISBN 0-7614-0200-4   LC 95-44087
An illustrated look at the geography, history, people and culture of the largest country in South America
Includes bibliographical references

Heinrichs, Ann
Brazil. Children's Press 1997 144p il map (Enchantment of the world, second series) $33 (5 and up)   **981**
1. Brazil
ISBN 0-516-20602-8   LC 97-14376
Describes the geography, plants, animals, history, economy, culture, and people of Brazil
Includes bibliographical references

Reiser, Robert

Brazil. Benchmark Bks. 2003 48p il map (Discovering cultures) lib bdg $25.64 (2-4)

981

1. Brazil
ISBN 0-7614-1180-1   LC 2001-7292
Contents: Where in the world is Brazil?; What makes Brazil Brazilian?; Living in Brazil; School days; Just for fun; Let's celebrate
An introduction to the geography, history, people, and culture of Brazil
Includes glossary and bibliographical references

Richard, Christopher

Brazil; [by] Christopher Richard, Leslie Jermyn. 2nd ed. Benchmark Bks. 2002 144p il map (Cultures of the world) lib bdg $37.07 (5 and up)

981

1. Brazil
ISBN 0-7614-1359-6   LC 2001-47263
First published 1991
Presents the geography, history, government, economy, and social life and customs of the South American country of Brazil
Includes glossary and bibliographical references

Streissguth, Thomas

Brazil in pictures; by Tom Streissguth. rev and expanded. Lerner Publs. 2003 80p il map (Visual geography series) lib bdg $21.27 (5 and up)

981

1. Brazil
ISBN 0-8225-1959-3   LC 2001-3275
Replaces the edition published 1987 prepared by Nathan A. Haverstock
An introduction to Brazil, discussing its history, government, economy, people, and culture
Includes bibliographical references

982   Argentina

Gofen, Ethel

Argentina; by Ethel Caro Gofen, Leslie Jermyn. 2nd ed. Benchmark Bks. 2002 144p il map (Cultures of the world) lib bdg $37.07 (5 and up)

982

1. Argentina
ISBN 0-7614-1358-8   LC 2001-47759
First published 1991
Presents the history, geography, government, economy, people, and social life and customs of Argentina
Includes glossary and bibliographical references

Gordon, Sharon

Argentina. Benchmark Bks. 2004 48p il map (Discovering cultures) lib bdg $25.64 (2-4)

982

ISBN 0-7614-1723-0   LC 2003-19097
Contents: Where in the world is Argentina?; What makes Argentina Argentinean?; Living in Argentina; School days; Just for fun; Let's celebrate!

An introduction to the geography, history, people, and culture of Argentina
Includes glossary and bibliographical references

Lourie, Peter

Tierra del Fuego; a journey to the end of the earth. Boyds Mills Press 2002 47p il map $19.95 (4 and up)

982

1. Tierra del Fuego (Argentina and Chile)
ISBN 1-56397-973-X   LC 2001-96395
The author describes his travels in Tierra del Fuego and provides historical background on the area
"Lourie's smooth, first-person narrative mixes history, adventure, and personal insights, while glorious photographs of the remarkable land at the southernmost point of the world enhance his travelogue. . . . Highly informative for reports, this fascinating account will also appeal to young readers with wanderlust." SLJ

983   Chile

Winter, Jane Kohen

Chile; by Jane Kohen Winter, Susan Roraff. 2nd ed. Benchmark Bks. 2002 144p il map (Cultures of the world) lib bdg $37.07 (5 and up)

983

1. Chile
ISBN 0-7614-1360-X   LC 2001-47827
First published 1991
Introduces the history, geography, culture, and lifestyles of Chile
Includes glossary and bibliographical references

985   Peru

Calvert, Patricia

The ancient Inca; written by Patricia Calvert. Franklin Watts 2004 128p il (People of the ancient world) lib bdg $29.50; pa $9.95 (5 and up)

985

1. Incas
ISBN 0-531-12358-8 (lib bdg); 0-531-16740-2 (pa)
LC 2004-1956
Contents: The science of the past: why it matters; Before the Inca; Children of the sun; Life in a highland family; Growing up among the Inca; Medicine, magic, and death; The top of the Inca pyramid; Warriors, war, and keeping the peace; Buildings, bridges, and roads; The war of two brothers; Suncasapa, the bearded one; The aftermath of conquest
This "well-written, attractive [title has] extensive collections of quality color photographs of ruins and artifacts." SLJ
Includes bibliographical references

De Capua, Sarah

Peru; by Sarah De Capua. Benchmark Books 2004 48p il map (Discovering cultures) lib bdg $25.64 (2-4)

985

1. Peru
ISBN 0-7614-1796-6   LC 2004-6125

De Capua, Sarah—_Continued_

Contents: Where in the world is Peru?; What makes Peru Peruvian?; Living in Peru; School days; Just for fun; Let's celebrate!

An introduction to the geography, history, people, and culture of Peru

Includes glossary and bibliographical references

Lewin, Ted

Lost city; the discovery of Machu Picchu. Philomel Bks. 2003 unp il $16.99 (2-4)

985

1. Machu Picchu (Peru)

ISBN 0-399-23302-4   LC 2002-4461

In 1911, Yale professor Hiram Bingham discovers a lost Incan city with the help of a young Peruvian boy

"The language is graceful and uncomplicated, weaving in bits of background history along the way. . . . Full-page watercolors spreads of the stunning vistas and thick forests contrast with dark, intimate views of Bingham inside homes and walking along walled city streets. . . . An exciting, eye-catching story." Booklist

986.1   Colombia

De Capua, Sarah

Colombia. Benchmark Bks. 2004 48p il maps (Discovering cultures) $25.64 (2-4)   **986.1**

1. Colombia

ISBN 0-7614-1715-X   LC 2003-8128

Contents: Where in the world is Colombia?; What makes Colombia Colombian?; Living in Colombia; School days; Just for fun; Let's celebrate!

Highlights the geography, people, food, schools, recreation, celebrations, and language of Colombia

Includes glossary and bibliographical references

DuBois, Jill

Colombia; by Jill DuBois, Leslie Jermyn. 2nd ed. Benchmark Bks. 2002 144p il map (Cultures of the world) lib bdg $37.07 (5 and up)

986.1

1. Colombia

ISBN 0-7614-1361-8   LC 2001-47264

First published 1991

Presents the geography, history, government, economy, and social life and customs of the country of Colombia

Includes glossary and bibliographical references

Markham, Lois

Colombia; the gateway to South America. Benchmark Bks. 1997 64p il (Exploring cultures of the world) lib bdg $27.07 (4 and up)

986.1

1. Colombia

ISBN 0-7614-0140-7   LC 96-51580

Introduces the geography, history, people, and culture of the country known as the Gateway to South America

"Although Colombia's poverty, civil unrest, and drug trafficking are briefly mentioned, the volume concen-

trates on sunnier topics, such as family relationships, festivals, and the arts. . . . The clear text is accessible and readable." Horn Book Guide

Includes glossary and bibliographical references

Morrison, Marion

Colombia. Children's Press 1999 144p il map (Enchantment of the world, second series) lib bdg $33 (5 and up)   **986.1**

1. Colombia

ISBN 0-516-21106-4   LC 98-19307

Describes the geography, history, economy, natural resources, culture, religion, and people of the South American country of Colombia

Includes bibliographical references

986.6   Ecuador

Foley, Erin

Ecuador; [by] Erin L. Foley & Leslie Jermyn. 2nd ed. Marshall Cavendish Benchmark 2006 144p il map (Cultures of the world) lib bdg $37.07 (5 and up)   **986.6**

1. Ecuador

ISBN 0-7614-2050-9   LC 2005022671

First published 1995

This briefly describes Ecuador's "history, government, economy, and geography. . . . Particularly useful is the information on religion, the arts, food, leisure activities, and social roles. The [book has] great visual appeal with excellent full-color photographs on every page. [It] is especially successful in explaining social and economic hierarchies within the country." SLJ

Includes glossary and bibliographical references

Lourie, Peter

Lost treasure of the Inca. Boyds Mills Press 1999 48p il map $18.95 (4 and up)   **986.6**

1. Incas 2. Ecuador 3. Buried treasure

ISBN 1-56397-743-5

The author describes his search in the mountains of Ecuador for gold hidden by the Incas

Lourie "succumbed to altitude sickness and had to descend without discovering a glimmer of the gold. But he did return with a ripping good yarn to tell . . . and some breathtaking photographs of the mistshrouded volcanic peaks. This should be a hot pick for armchair travelers." Bull Cent Child Books

Includes glossary

987   Venezuela

Winter, Jane Kohen

Venezuela; [by] Jane Kohen Winter, Kitt Baguley. 2nd ed. Benchmark Bks. 2002 144p il map (Cultures of the world) lib bdg $37.07 (5 and up)   **987**

1. Venezuela

ISBN 0-7614-1362-6   LC 2001-53877

First published 1990

Winter, Jane Kohen—*Continued*
Presents the geography, history, economy, and social life and customs of Venezuela
Includes glossary and bibliographical references

988.1   Guyana

Jermyn, Leslie
Guyana. Benchmark Bks. 2000 128p il map (Cultures of the world) lib bdg $37.07 (5 and up) **988.1**
1. Guyana
ISBN 0-7614-0994-7   LC 99-55063
Examines the geography, history, government, economy, people, and culture of Guyana
Includes glossary and bibliographical references

Morrison, Marion
Guyana. Children's Press 2003 144p il map (Enchantment of the world, Second series) lib bdg $34.50 (5 and up)   **988.1**
1. Guyana
ISBN 0-516-22377-1   LC 2001-6915
Describes the geography, history, culture, religion, and people of Guyana
Includes bibliographical references

989.2   Paraguay

Jermyn, Leslie
Paraguay. Benchmark Bks. 2000 128p il map (Cultures of the world) lib bdg $37.07 (5 and up)   **989.2**
1. Paraguay
ISBN 0-7614-0979-3   LC 99-27257
Describes the geography, history, government, economy, people, lifestyle, religion, language, arts, leisure, festivals, and food of Paraguay
Includes glossary and bibliographical references

989.5   Uruguay

Jermyn, Leslie
Uruguay. Benchmark Bks. (Tarrytown) 1999 128p il maps (Cultures of the world) lib bdg $37.07 (5 and up)   **989.5**
1. Uruguay
ISBN 0-7614-0873-8   LC 98-27375
Describes the geography, history, government, economy, people, lifestyle, religion, language, arts, leisure, festivals, and food of the smallest country in South America
Includes glossary and bibliographical references

993   New Zealand

Smelt, Roselynn
New Zealand. Benchmark Bks. (Tarrytown) 1998 128p il maps (Cultures of the world) lib bdg $37.07 (5 and up)   **993**
1. New Zealand
ISBN 0-7614-0808-8   LC 97-42179
Introduces the geography, history, religion, government, economy, and culture of a Pacific-island country first populated by the Maori, to whom it was the "Land of the Long White Cloud"
Includes glossary and bibliographical references

994   Australia

Arnold, Caroline
Uluru, Australia's Aboriginal heart; photographs by Arthur Arnold. Clarion Books 2003 64p il $16 (5 and up)   **994**
1. Aboriginal Australians 2. Australia 3. Uluru-Kata Tjuta National Park (Australia)
ISBN 0-618-18181-4   LC 2002-15542
Describes Uluru, formerly known as Ayers Rock, in Australia's Uluru-Kata Tjuta National Park, its plant and animal life, and the country's Aboriginal people for whom the site is sacred
"The book's greatest accomplishment . . . is to give readers a sense of the ongoing spiritual importance of Uluru to the Anangu, who have lived around it for 10,000 years. Clear, colorful photos of Uluru and its surroundings appear on nearly every page, illustrating the text with beauty and finesse." Booklist

Gordon, Sharon
Australia. Benchmark Books 2004 c2005 48p il map (Discovering cultures) lib bdg $25.64 (2-4)   **994**
1. Australia
ISBN 0-7614-1791-5   LC 2004-6136
An introduction to the geography, history, people, and culture of Australia
Includes glossary and bibliographical references

Heinrichs, Ann
Australia. Children's Press 1998 144p il map (Enchantment of the world, second series) $35 (5 and up)   **994**
1. Australia
ISBN 0-516-20648-6   LC 98-15780
Explores the geography, history, arts, religions, and everyday life of the Land Down Under, also called the Lucky Country
Includes bibliographical references

Lewin, Ted

Top to bottom down under; [by] Ted and Betsy Lewin. 1st ed. HarperCollins Pub. 2005 40p il $15.99; lib bdg $16.89 (2-4) **994**

1. Australia 2. Animals—Australia 3. Natural history—Australia

ISBN 0-688-14113-7; 0-688-14114-5 (lib bdg)

LC 2003-26934

"The Lewins share their . . . journey to the land down under in a fresh, funny, fact-filled travelogue that meanders from Kakadu National Park to Kangaroo Island. Striking, realistic watercolor landscapes are juxtaposed with comical sketches and circa-1900 spot illustrations of Aboriginals killing snakes and riding on paperbark rafts. The pictures catch attention, and the text is intelligently written." Booklist

Petersen, David

Australia. Children's Press 1998 47p il maps $22 (2-4) **994**

1. Australia

ISBN 0-516-20765-2 LC 97-33041

"A True book"

An illustrated introduction to the geography, history, wildlife, and people of Australia

Includes bibliographical references

Rajendra, Vijeya

Australia; [by] Vijeya & Sundran Rajendra. 2nd ed. Benchmark Bks. 2002 143p il map (Cultures of the world) lib bdg $37.07 (5 and up) **994**

1. Australia

ISBN 0-7614-1473-8 LC 2002-19206

First published 1990

Presents the history, geography, government, economy, environment, religion, people, and social life and customs of the island continent of Australia

Includes glossary and bibliographical references

995.3 Papua New Guinea. New Guinea region

Gascoigne, Ingrid

Papua New Guinea. Benchmark Bks. (Tarrytown) 1998 128p il maps (Cultures of the world) lib bdg $37.07 (5 and up) **995.3**

1. Papua New Guinea

ISBN 0-7614-0813-4 LC 97-43611

Discusses the geography, history, economy, government, varied culture and peoples of the country made up of more than 600 islands and archipelagos

Includes glossary and bibliographical references

996 Polynesia and Micronesia

Arnold, Caroline

Easter Island; giant stone statues tell of a rich and tragic past; text and photographs by Caroline Arnold. Clarion Bks. 2000 48p il map $15; pa $5.95 (5 and up) **996**

1. Easter Island

ISBN 0-395-87609-5; 0-618-48605-4 (pa)

LC 99-27189

Describes the formation, geography, ecology, and inhabitants of the isolated Easter Island in the Pacific Ocean

This is a "straightforward account of what archaeologists have determined about the history of the Rapanui people and their monuments. The clearly written text is accompanied by breathtaking color photographs that show the beauty of the island and its rich collection of archaeological features." Horn Book

Includes bibliographical references

Underwood, Deborah

The Easter Island statues; by Deborah Underwood. KidHaven Press 2005 48p il map (Wonders of the world) lib bdg $23.70 (3-6) **996**

1. Easter Island

ISBN 0-7377-3065-X LC 2004-12062

Contents: Land of the stone giants; Who made the statues?; Carving and moving the Moai; The end of the statue carving

"Underwood discusses the geography, history, and people of Easter Island and of the statues, including who made them, how they were constructed, and what they represent. The last chapter includes information about their restoration and conservation. The illustrations include many full-page, full-color photographs and maps. . . . Attractive, readable." SLJ

Includes bibliographical references

Webster, Christine

Polynesians; [by] Christine Webster. Weigl Publishers 2004 32p il map (Indigenous peoples) lib bdg $26 (3-5) **996**

1. Polynesians

ISBN 1-59036-123-7 LC 2003-3963

Contents: Where in the world?; Stories and legends; Out of the past; Social structures; Communication; Law and order; Celebrating cultures; Art and design; Dressing up; Food and fun; Great ideas; At issue; Into the future; Fascinating facts

This discusses the history, social structure, language, culture, and current issues facing the Polynesian people.

This provides "a wealth of information. . . . The well-designed pages provide a mixture of vivid color photographs, historical drawings, and eye-catching graphics." SLJ

Includes bibliographical references

998 Arctic islands and Antarctica

Beattie, Owen

Buried in ice; by Owen Beattie and John Geiger with Shelley Tanaka. Scholastic 1992 64p il maps (Time quest book) pa $6.95 hardcover o.p. (4 and up) **998**

1. Franklin, Sir John, 1786-1847 2. Arctic regions

ISBN 0-590-43839-2 (pa)   LC 91-23897

"A Scholastic/Madison Press book"

Probes the tragic and mysterious fate of Sir John Franklin's failed expedition to the Arctic to find the Northwest Passage in 1845

"The narrative is interspersed with an imaginative section that relates the story of the expedition from the point of view of 19-year-old Luke, a member of the crew. While the text is exciting, the book's greatest strength is its superb illustrations: drawings, paintings, and historic and present day photographs are used to enrich each page." SLJ

Includes glossary and bibliographical references

Bledsoe, Lucy Jane

How to survive in Antarctica; written and photographed by Lucy Jane Bledsoe. Holiday House 2006 101p il map $16.95 (5 and up) **998**

1. Antarctica

ISBN 0-8234-1890-1

"Bledsoe, who made three trips to study Antarctica, bases her informal, chatty narrative on her thrilling adventure, bringing close the amazing science and geography as well as the gritty facts of human survival in the frigid environment. . . . Bledsoe's own black-and-white photos . . . will grab students across the curriculum." Booklist

Includes glossary

Burleigh, Robert

Black whiteness; Admiral Byrd alone in the Antarctic; illustrated by Walter Lyon Krudop. Atheneum Bks. for Young Readers 1998 36p il $16 (3-5) **998**

1. Byrd, Richard Evelyn, 1888-1957 2. Antarctica—Exploration

ISBN 0-689-81299-X   LC 96-21999

"Byrd's solitary sojourn at Little America during the unimaginably cold, dark Antarctic winter of 1934 is captured in a lyrical text strengthened by dramatic, impressive paintings." SLJ

Dewey, Jennifer

Antarctic journal; four months at the bottom of the world. HarperCollins Pubs. 2001 64p il $16.99; lib bdg $17.89 (4 and up) **998**

1. Antarctica

ISBN 0-06-028586-9; 0-06-028587-7 (lib bdg)

LC 99-89065

"Dewey relates the experience of her four-month trip to the Antarctic peninsula in diary entries, letters, sketch-

es, and photographs." Bull Cent Child Books

A "well-written, eye-opening book. . . . This is a remarkable read." Booklist

Includes bibliographical references

Kimmel, Elizabeth Cody

Ice story; Shackleton's lost expedition. Clarion Bks. 1999 120p il maps $18 (4 and up) **998**

1. Shackleton, Sir Ernest Henry, 1874-1922 2. Endurance (Ship) 3. Imperial Trans-Antarctic Expedition (1914-1917) 4. Antarctica—Exploration

ISBN 0-395-91524-4   LC 98-29956

Describes the events of the 1914 Shackleton Antarctic expedition, when the ship the Endurance was crushed in a frozen sea and the men made the perilous journey across ice and stormy seas to reach inhabited land

"The amazing story is well served in this account, which includes photos by expedition photographer Frank Hurley." Horn Book Guide

Includes bibliographical references

Levinson, Nancy Smiler

North Pole, South Pole; illustrated by Diane Dawson Hearn. Holiday House 2002 40p il $14.95 (k-3) **998**

1. North Pole 2. South Pole

ISBN 0-8234-1737-9   LC 2001-59419

An introduction to the geography, climate, and inhabitants of the polar regions at the top and the bottom of the earth where the North Pole and the South Pole are located

"Beginning readers can find a clear and concise discussion of the differences between the poles. . . . Hearn's colorful illustrations in white, blue, and teal green depict a number of the animal inhabitants, all identified." SLJ

Love, Ann

The kids book of the Far North; written by Ann Love & Jane Drake; illustrated by Jocelyne Bouchard. Kids Can Press 2000 48p il $15.95 (3-6) **998**

1. Arctic regions

ISBN 1-55074-563-8

"The book introduces the Arctic's landscape and rigorous climate, natural resources, early human settlement, European exploration, and the life ways of its peoples, both traditional and contemporary." Booklist

"The information will encourage meaningful discussions of topics often glossed over in other books about the Arctic. . . . An up-to-date, accessible overview." SLJ

Martin, Jacqueline Briggs

The lamp, the ice, and the boat called Fish; based on a true story; pictures by Beth Krommes. Houghton Mifflin 2001 unp il $15 (3-6) **998**

1. Karluk (Ship) 2. Canadian Arctic Expedition (1913-1918) 3. Inuit 4. Arctic regions

ISBN 0-618-00341-X   LC 99-35303

Martin, Jacqueline Briggs—*Continued*

"Trapped and drifting amid the ice floes, the 1913 Canadian Arctic Expedition aboard the *Karluk* may well have been doomed, save for the resilience of her crew and the particular resourcefulness of the Inupiat who were hired as provisioners and guides. . . . Martin recounts their frigid adventures." Bull Cent Child Books

"The quiet, intriguing language, with a poet's attention to sound, will lull young ones into the story's drama, as will Beth Krommes' captivating scratchboard illustrations." Booklist

Scott, Elaine

Poles apart; why penguins and polar bears will never be neighbors; by Elaine Scott. Viking 2004 63p il maps $17.99 (5 and up) **998**

1. Arctic regions 2. Antarctica

ISBN 0-670-05925-0 LC 2004-4270

Contents: Drifting apart: Gondwanaland and Eurasia; Poles apart: summer and winter; Mutual attraction: the magnetic poles; The people: Inuit and None; Never neighbors: penguins in the south; Never neighbors: polar bears in the north; Great races: first to see them; Great races: first to claim them; The poles today: lessons from the ice

This "book introduces the North and South Poles: their origins, seasons, composition, magnetism, people, animals, exploration, and recent changes. . . . The many excellent color illustrations include clear photographs of wildlife and mysterious, beautiful shots of the northern lights as well as maps and period photos. Scott writes well, never talking down to her audience but making scientific and historical information understandable." Booklist

Fic FICTION

A number of subject headings have been added to the books in this section to aid in curriculum work. It is not necessarily recommended that these subjects be used in the library catalog.

Abbott, Tony

Kringle; illustrated by Greg Call. Scholastic Press 2005 324p il $14.99 (5 and up) **Fic**

1. Santa Claus—Fiction 2. Fantasy fiction 3. Orphans—Fiction

ISBN 0-439-74942-5 LC 2005-12697

In the fifth century A.D., as order retreats from Britain with the departing Roman Army, orphaned, twelve-year-old Kringle determines to rescue his beloved guardian from the evil goblins who terrorize the countryside by kidnapping and enslaving humans and, in the process, with the help of elves and others along the way, discovers his true destiny.

"The enticing premise, appealing young hero, and nonstop action will appeal to many fantasy lovers." Booklist

Abraham, Susan Gonzales

Cecilia's year; by Susan Gonzales Abraham & Denise Gonzales Abraham. 1st ed. Cinco Puntos Press 2004 210p il $16.95 (4 and up) **Fic**

1. Poverty—Fiction 2. Sex role—Fiction 3. Hispanic Americans—Fiction 4. New Mexico—Fiction

ISBN 0-938317-87-3 LC 2004-13374

Nearly fourteen and poor, Ceclia Gonzales wants desperately to go to high school and become a teacher until her mother's old-fashioned ideas about a woman's place threaten her dreams.

"The cultural details are vivid and integrated into the story, providing a rich context and a snapshot of an entire community. . . . This fictionalized biography succeeds on several levels." SLJ

Another title about Cecilia is:

Surprising Cecilia (2005)

Ackerman, Karen

The night crossing; illustrated by Elizabeth Sayles. Knopf 1994 56p il pa $4.50 hardcover o.p. (3-5) **Fic**

1. Holocaust, 1933-1945—Fiction 2. Jews—Fiction

ISBN 0-679-87040-7 (pa) LC 94-10805

In 1938, having begun to feel the persecution that all Jews are experiencing in their Austrian city, Clara and her family escape over the mountains into Switzerland

"Ackerman's writing is clear and direct; despite its simplicity, it is never banal. This is an excellent fictional introduction to the Holocaust." SLJ

Adams, Richard

Watership Down. Scribner classics ed. Scribner 1996 c1972 429p $30 (6 and up) **Fic**

1. Rabbits—Fiction 2. Allegories

ISBN 0-684-83605-X

Also available in paperback from Simon & Schuster

First published 1972 in the United Kingdom; first United States edition 1974 by Macmillan

"Faced with the annihilation of its warren, a small group of male rabbits sets out across the English downs in search of a new home. Internal struggles for power surface in this intricately woven, realistically told adult adventure when the protagonists must coordinate tactics in order to defeat an enemy rabbit fortress. It is clear that the author has done research on rabbit behavior, for this tale is truly authentic." Shapiro Fic for Youth. 3d edition

Adler, David A.

Cam Jansen and the mystery of the stolen diamonds; illustrated by Susanna Natti. Viking 1980 58p il $13.99; pa $3.99 (2-4) **Fic**

1. Mystery fiction

ISBN 0-670-20039-5; 0-14-034670-8 (pa)

LC 79-20695

Easy-to-read titles about Cam Jansen are also available

Cam Jansen, a fifth-grader with a photographic memory, and her friend Eric help solve the mystery of the stolen diamonds

This is a "fast-action uncomplicated adventure . . . [with] a touch of humor, a breezy writing style, and some very enjoyable pen-and-ink drawings." Booklist

Other titles about Cam Jansen are:

Adler, David A.—*Continued*

Cam Jansen and the barking treasure mystery (1999)
Cam Jansen and the birthday mystery (2000)
Cam Jansen and the catnapping mystery (1998)
Cam Jansen and the chocolate fudge mystery (1993)
Cam Jansen and the first day of school mystery (2002)
Cam Jansen and the ghostly mystery (1996)
Cam Jansen and the mystery at the haunted house (1992)
Cam Jansen and the mystery at the monkey house (1985)
Cam Jansen and the mystery of Flight 54 (1989)
Cam Jansen and the mystery of the Babe Ruth baseball (1982)
Cam Jansen and the mystery of the carnival prize (1984)
Cam Jansen and the mystery of the circus clown (1983)
Cam Jansen and the mystery of the dinosaur bones (1981)
Cam Jansen and the mystery of the gold coins (1982)
Cam Jansen and the mystery of the monster movie (1984)
Cam Jansen and the mystery of the stolen corn popper (1986)
Cam Jansen and the mystery of the television dog (1981)
Cam Jansen and the mystery of the UFO (1980)
Cam Jansen and the scary snake mystery (1997)
Cam Jansen and the school play mystery (2001)
Cam Jansen and the snowy day mystery (2004)
Cam Jansen and the tennis trophy mystery (2003)
Cam Jansen and the Triceratops Pops mystery (1995)
Cam Jansen and the Valentine baby mystery (2005)

Ahlberg, Allan

The cat who got carried away; illustrated by Katharine McEwen. Candlewick Press 2003 79p il $15.99 (2-4)   **Fic**

1. Family life—Fiction
ISBN 0-7636-2073-4   LC 2002-73718

It is an exciting couple of days for the Gaskitt family and their community—with missing pets, an unusual substitute teacher, and a special addition to their household

"Ahlberg's characteristically droll narration provides for many laugh-out-loud moments. . . . McEwen's watercolor and crayon illustrations are themselves witty compositions." Bull Cent Child Books

Other titles about the Gaskitt family are:
The children who smelled a rat (2005)
The man who wore all his clothes (2001)
The woman who won things (2002)

Aiken, Joan

The wolves of Willoughby Chase; illustrated by Pat Marriott. Delacorte Press 2000 c1962 181p $16.95; pa $5.99 (5 and up)   **Fic**

1. Great Britain—Fiction
ISBN 0-385-32790-0; 0-440-49603-9 (pa)
First published 1962 in the United Kingdom; first United States edition 1963 by Doubleday

"In this burlesque of a Victorian melodrama, two London children are sent to a country estate while their parents are away. Here they outwit a wicked governess, escape from packs of hungry wolves, and restore the estate to its rightful owner." Hodges. Books for Elem Sch Libr

"Plot, characterization, and background blend perfectly into an amazing whole. . . . Highly recommended." SLJ
Other titles in this series are:

Black hearts in Battersea (1964)
Cold Shoulder Road (1996)
The cuckoo tree (1971)
Dangerous games (1999)
Is underground (1993)
Midwinter nightingale (2003)
The stolen lake (1981)
The witch of Clatteringshaws (2005)

Alcock, Vivien

The cuckoo sister. Delacorte Press 1986 c1985 160p (6 and up)   **Fic**

1. Sisters—Fiction 2. London (England)—Fiction
LC 85-20648
Available in paperback from Houghton Mifflin
First published 1985 in the United Kingdom

"Eleven year old Kate Seton becomes very upset when an underfed 13-year-old shows up at her parents' home with a letter stating that she is Kate's sister—stolen from a pram outside a store where Mrs. Seton had been shopping. Rosie doesn't believe the story that she is Emma Seton and frantically tries to find her mother who has left with no trace. Kate eventually comes to love Rosie and tries to provide a clue that will enable her to stay. Characterizations are very vivid and although it definitely has a British flavor, students will empathize with Kate and Rosie." Voice Youth Advocates

Alcott, Louisa May

Little women; or Meg, Jo, Beth and Amy (5 and up)   **Fic**

1. Family life—Fiction 2. New England—Fiction
Available from various publishers
First published 1868

The tale is "related with sympathy, humour, and sincerity. This lively natural narrative of family experience is as well-loved today as when it first appeared." Toronto Public Libr. Books for Boys & Girls

Other titles about members of the March family are:
Eight cousins (1875)
Jo's boys (1886)
Little men (1871)
Rose in bloom (1876)

An old-fashioned Thanksgiving (3-5)
Fic

1. Family life—Fiction 2. Thanksgiving Day—Fiction
3. New England—Fiction
Various editions available

"In this story, which first appeared in 'St. Nicholas' magazine in 1881, Alcott recounts the escapades of a New Hampshire farm family in the 1820s. When the parents are unexpectedly called away on Thanksgiving Day, the children pitch in to make their version of the traditional holiday feast and, with little knowledge and less caution, bumble along toward a culinary catastrophe reminiscent of Meg and Jo's dinner in 'Little Women.'" Booklist

Alexander, Lloyd

The Arkadians. Dutton Children's Bks. 1995 272p $17.99; pa $6.99 (5 and up)   **Fic**

1. Fantasy fiction
ISBN 0-525-45415-2; 0-14-038073-6 (pa)
LC 94-35025

Alexander, Lloyd—*Continued*

To escape the wrath of the king and his wicked sooth-sayers, Lucian joins with Fronto, a poet-turned-jackass, and Joy-in-the-Dance, a young girl with mystical powers, on a series of epic adventures

"On one level, this is a rousing adventure complete with cliffhangers and do-or-die situations. On another, readers familiar with Greek mythology will find clever hints at the myths' purpose and genesis." SLJ

The book of three. rev ed. Holt & Co. 1999 190p (Chronicles of Prydain) $19.95 (5 and up)
Fic
1. Fantasy fiction
ISBN 0-8050-6132-0   LC 98-40901
Also available in paperback from Yearling Bks
First published 1964

"The first of five books about the mythical land of Prydain finds Taran, an assistant pig keeper, fighting with Prince Gwydion against the evil which theatens the kingdom." Hodges. Books for Elem Sch Libr

"Related in a simple, direct style, this fast-paced tale of high adventure has a well-balanced blend of fantasy, realism, and humor." SLJ

Other titles about the mythical land of Prydain are:
The black cauldron (1965)
The castle of Llyr (1966)
The foundling and other tales of Prydain (1999)
The high king (1968)
Taran Wanderer (1967)

The cat who wished to be a man. Dutton 1973 107p pa $4.99 hardcover o.p. (4-6)   **Fic**
1. Cats—Fiction
ISBN 0-14-130704-8 (pa)   LC 73-77447
When he begins dealing with humanity, Lionel the cat begins to understand why his wizard master was reluctant to change him into a man

This is "a comic and ebullient fantasy; just right for reading aloud." Horn Book

The Gawgon and The Boy. Dutton Children's Bks. 2001 199p $17.99; pa $5.99 (5 and up)
Fic
1. Philadelphia (Pa.)—Fiction 2. Aunts—Fiction 3. Great Depression, 1929-1939—Fiction
ISBN 0-525-46677-0; 0-14-250000-3 (pa)
LC 00-47541
In Depression-era Philadelphia, when eleven-year-old David is too ill to attend school, he is tutored by the unique and adventurous Aunt Annie, whose teaching combines with his imagination to greatly enrich his life

"The unusual novel has a subtle charm and a cast of memorable eccentrics, and the relationship between David and the Gawgon is tender without being maudlin." Horn Book Guide

Gypsy Rizka. Dutton Children's Bks. 1999 195p $16.99; pa $5.99 (5 and up)   **Fic**
1. Gypsies—Fiction 2. Fantasy fiction
ISBN 0-525-46121-3; 0-14-130980-6 (pa)
LC 98-41399
Living alone in her wagon on the outskirts of a Greater Dunitsa while waiting for her father's return, Rizka, a Gypsy and a trickster, exposes the ridiculous foibles of some of the townspeople

"Scenes of broad slapstick effervesce with mind-tickling repartee in this book that is . . . lively, satirical, and with a core of pure gold." Horn Book Guide

The high king. rev ed. Holt & Co. 1999 c1968 253p (Chronicles of Prydain) $19.95 (5 and up)
Fic
1. Fantasy fiction
ISBN 0-8050-6135-5   LC 98-40900
Also available in paperback from Yearling Bks.
Awarded The Newbery Medal, 1969
Concluding title in the chronicles of Prydain which include: The book of three, The black cauldron, The castle of Llyr, and Taran Wanderer
First published 1968
This edition includes a pronunciation guide

In this final volume Taran, the assistant pig-keeper "becomes High King of Prydain, Princess Eilonwy becomes his queen, the predictions of Taran's wizard guardian Dallben are fulfilled, and the forces of black magic led by Arawn, Lord of Annuvin, Land of the Dead, are vanquished forever." SLJ

"The fantasy has the depth and richness of a medieval tapestry, infinitely detailed and imaginative." Saturday Rev

The Illyrian adventure. Dutton 1986 132p pa $5.99 hardcover o.p. (5 and up)   **Fic**
1. Adventure fiction
ISBN 0-14-130313-1 (pa)   LC 85-30762
"Sixteen-year-old Vesper Holly drags her long-suffering guardian, Brinnie, off to Illyria to vindicate her late father's reputation as a scholar. With humor, beguiling charm, and intelligence she manages to find a treasure, thwart a conspiracy to murder Illyria's King Osman, and guide two rival factions to the peace table." Wilson Libr Bull

"Alexander's archeological mystery has intricate plotting and witty wording." Bull Cent Child Books

Other adventure titles featuring Vesper Holly are:
The Drackenberg adventure (1988)
The El Dorado adventure (1987)
The Jedera adventure (1989)
The Philadelphia adventure (1990)
The Xanadu adventure (2005)

The iron ring. Dutton Children's Bks. 1997 283p pa $5.99 hardcover o.p. (5 and up)
Fic
1. Adventure fiction 2. India—Fiction
ISBN 0-14-130348-4 (pa)   LC 96-29730
"Young Tamar, ruler of a small Indian kingdom, wagers with a visiting king and loses his kingdom and his freedom. Traveling to the king's land to make good on his debt, he collects quite an entourage and eventually overcomes his enemies with his friends' help. This tale offers delightful characters, a philosophical interest in the meaning of life, a thoughtful look at the caste system, and a clever use of Indian animal folktales." Horn Book Guide

Alexander, Lloyd—*Continued*

The marvelous misadventures of Sebastian; grand extravaganza, including a performance by the entire cast of the Gallimaufry-Theatricus. Dutton 1970 204p pa $5.99 hardcover o.p. (4 and up) **Fic**

1. Adventure fiction 2. Musicians—Fiction
ISBN 0-14-130816-8 (pa)   LC 70-116879

"Sebastian, a teenage fiddler, gets involved in court intrigue and muddles his way to eventual success in ousting a cruel usurper from the throne." Natl Counc of Teach of Engl. Adventuring with Books

"The intricacy of plot, the humor and allusiveness of the writing, the exaggerated characterization, and the derring-do of romantic adventures are knit into a lively and elaborate tale that can be enjoyed for its action and appreciated for its subtler significance." Sutherland. The Best in Child Books

The remarkable journey of Prince Jen. Dutton Children's Bks. 1991 273p pa $6.99 hardcover o.p. (5 and up) **Fic**

1. Adventure fiction 2. China—Fiction
ISBN 0-14-240225-7 (pa)   LC 91-13720

Bearing six unusual gifts, young Prince Jen in Tang Dynasty China embarks on a perilous quest and emerges triumphantly into manhood

"Alexander satisfies the taste for excitement, but his vivid characters and the food for thought he offers will nourish long after the last page is turned." SLJ

The rope trick. Dutton Children's Bks. 2002 195p $16.99; pa $5.99 (4 and up) **Fic**

1. Magicians—Fiction 2. Adventure fiction 3. Italy—Fiction
ISBN 0-525-47020-4; 0-14-240119-6 (pa)
     LC 2002-67497

Motivated by her quest to learn a legendary rope trick, the magician Princess Lidi and her troupe embark on a journey through Renaissance Italy that intertwines adventure, love, and mystery

"Even as the outsize characterizations and rollicking adventure amuse, the compassionate vision of life's possibilities is likely to bring a lump to the throat." Publ Wkly

Westmark. Dutton 1981 184p pa $5.99 hardcover o.p. (5 and up) **Fic**

1. Adventure fiction
ISBN 0-14-131068-5 (pa)

A boy fleeing from criminal charges falls in with a charlatan, his dwarf attendant, and an urchin girl, travels with them about the kingdom of Westmark, and ultimately arrives at the palace where the king is grieving over the loss of his daughter

The author "peoples his tale with a marvelous cast of individuals, and weaves an intricate story of high adventure that climaxes in a superbly conceived conclusion, which, though predictable, is reached through carefully built tension and subtly added comic relief." Booklist

Other titles in this series are:
The Beggar Queen (1984)
The Kestrel (1982)

Allison, Jennifer

Gilda Joyce, psychic investigator; by Jennifer Allison. 1st ed. Sleuth/Dutton 2005 321p $10.99 (5 and up) **Fic**

1. Mystery fiction 2. Cousins—Fiction
ISBN 0-525-47375-0   LC 2004-10834

During the summer before ninth grade, intrepid Gilda Joyce invites herself to the San Francisco mansion of distant cousin Lester Splinter and his thirteen-year-old daughter, where she uses her purported psychic abilities and detective skills to solve the mystery of the mansion's boarded-up tower.

"Allison pulls off something special here. She not only offers a credible mystery . . . but also . . . provides particularly strong characterizations." Booklist

Almond, David

Heaven Eyes. Delacorte Press 2001 c2000 233p $15.95; pa $5.50 (5 and up) **Fic**

1. Orphans—Fiction 2. Adventure fiction
ISBN 0-385-32770-6; 0-440-22910-3 (pa)
     LC 00-31798

First published 2000 in the United Kingdom

Having escaped from their orphanage on a raft, Erin, January, and Mouse float down into another world of abandoned warehouses and factories, meeting a strange old man and an even stranger girl with webbed fingers and little memory of her past

"The ambiguous and surreal setting and the lyricism of the metaphor-laden prose make this a compelling and original novel." SLJ

Kit's wilderness. Delacorte Press 1999 229p $15.95; pa $5.99 (5 and up) **Fic**

1. Coal mines and mining—Fiction 2. Ghost stories 3. Great Britain—Fiction
ISBN 0-385-32665-3; 0-440-41605-1 (pa)
     LC 99-34332

Thirteen-year-old Kit goes to live with his grandfather in the decaying coal mining town of Stoneygate, England, and finds both the old man and the town haunted by ghosts of the past

The author "explores the power of friendship and family, the importance of memory, and the role of magic in our lives. This is a highly satisfying literary experience." SLJ

Skellig. Delacorte Press 1999 c1998 182p $16.95; pa $5.50 (5 and up) **Fic**

1. Fantasy fiction
ISBN 0-385-32653-X; 0-440-41602-7 (pa)
     LC 98-23121

First published 1998 in the United Kingdom

Unhappy about his baby sister's illness and the chaos of moving into a dilapidated old house, Michael retreats to the garage and finds a mysterious stranger who is something like a bird and something like an angel

"The plot is beautifully paced and the characters are drawn with a graceful, careful hand. . . . A lovingly done, thought-provoking novel." SLJ

Alvarez, Julia

How Tía Lola came to visit/stay. Knopf 2001
147p $15.95; lib bdg $17.99; pa $5.50 (4 and up)
Fic

1. Aunts—Fiction 2. Dominican Americans—Fiction
3. Divorce—Fiction 4. Vermont—Fiction

ISBN 0-375-80215-0; 0-375-90215-5 (lib bdg);
0-440-41870-4 (pa)   LC 00-62932

On title page "visit" is crossed out

Although ten-year-old Miguel is at first embarrassed
by his colorful aunt, Tia Lola, when she comes to Vermont from the Dominican Republic to stay with his
mother, his sister, and him after his parents' divorce, he
learns to love her

"Readers will enjoy the funny situations, identify with
the developing relationships and conflicting feelings of
the characters, and will get a spicy taste of Caribbean
culture in the bargain." SLJ

Andersen, Hans Christian

The little match girl; illustrated by Rachel
Isadora. Putnam 1987 30p il $16.99 (3-5)
Fic

ISBN 0-399-21336-8   LC 85-30082

The wares of the poor little match girl illuminate her
cold world, bringing some beauty to her brief, tragic life

"Isadora follows Andersen's lead, neither
sensationalizing nor apologizing for the tale's potentially
sentimental plot. . . . A moving, original picture-book
interpretation of the classic tale." Booklist

The princess and the pea; illustrated by
Dorothée Duntze. North-South Bks. 1985 unp il
$16.95; pa $7.95 (k-3)   **Fic**

1. Fairy tales

ISBN 1-55858-034-4; 1-55858-381-5 (pa)
                                      LC 85-7199

A young girl feels a pea through twenty mattresses
and twenty featherbeds and proves she is a real princess

"This classic Andersen fairy tale is presented in simple text and with elaborate illustrations. . . . Duntze appears to set the story during the Renaissance, and her illustrations are precise, intricate and detailed." SLJ

Anderson, Janet

The last treasure; [by] Janet S. Anderson.
Dutton 2003 257p il $17.99 (5 and up)
Fic

1. Family life—Fiction 2. Buried treasure—Fiction

ISBN 0-525-46919-2   LC 2002-74143

Thirteen-year-old Ellsworth leaves his father to visit
the relatives he has never met and eventually joins forces
with Jess, his distant cousin, to uncover family secrets
and search for their ancestor's hidden treasure

"Anderson has conjured up a fascinating read for puzzle lovers while sandwiching in an important message
about intergenerational relationships." SLJ

Anderson, Jodi Lynn

May Bird and The Ever After; book one;
illustrations by Leonid Gore. Atheneum Books for
Young Readers 2005 317p il $15.95 (5 and up)
Fic

1. Fantasy fiction

ISBN 0-689-86923-1   LC 2004-17829

Lonely and shy, ten-year-old May Ellen Bird has no
idea what awaits her when she falls into the lake and enters The Ever After, home of ghosts and the Bogeyman.

"Anderson sets the unsettling, nightmarish tone of her
offbeat fantasy in the first paragraph, then compounds
the horror chapter after scary chapter. . . . The first of
a trilogy, this book leaves loads of tantalizing, unanswered questions." Booklist

Anderson, Laurie Halse

Fever, 1793. Simon & Schuster Bks. for Young
Readers 2000 251p pa $5.99 hardcover o.p. (5 and
up)   **Fic**

1. Yellow fever—Fiction 2. Epidemics—Fiction
3. Philadelphia (Pa.)—Fiction

ISBN 0-689-84891-9 (pa)   LC 00-32238

In 1793 Philadelphia, sixteen-year-old Matilda Cook,
separated from her sick mother, learns about perseverance and self-reliance when she is forced to cope with
the horrors of a yellow fever epidemic

"A vivid work, rich with well-drawn and believable
characters. Unexpected events pepper the top-flight novel
that combines accurate historical detail with a spellbinding story line." Voice Youth Advocates

Anderson, M. T.

The Game of Sunken Places; [by] M. T.
Anderson. Scholastic Press 2004 260p $16.95; pa
$5.99 (5 and up)   **Fic**

1. Games—Fiction 2. Vermont—Fiction

ISBN 0-439-41660-4; 0-439-41661-2 (pa)
                                      LC 2003-20055

When two boys stay with an eccentric relative at his
mansion in rural Vermont, they discover an old-fashioned
board game that draws them into a mysterious adventure.

"Deliciously scary, often funny, and crowned by a pair
of deeply satisfying surprises, this tour de force leaves
one marveling at Anderson's ability to slip between
genres as fluidly as his middle-grade heroes straddle
worlds." Booklist

Whales on stilts; illustrations by Kurt Cyrus.
Harcourt 2005 188p il $15; pa $5.95 (4 and up)
Fic

1. Science fiction

ISBN 0-15-205340-9; 0-15-205394-8 (pa)
                                      LC 2004-17754

Racing against the clock, shy middle-school student
Lily and her best friends, Katie and Jasper, must foil the
plot of her father's conniving boss to conquer the world
using an army of whales.

"A story written with the author's tongue shoved firmly into his cheek. . . . It's full of witty pokes at other
series novels and Jasper's nutty inventions." SLJ

Another title about Lily, Kate, and Jasper is:
The clue of the linoleum lederhosen (2006)

Armstrong, Alan

Whittington; illustrated by S. D. Schindler. Random House 2005 191p il $14.95; lib bdg $16.99 (4-6)   **Fic**
1. Cats—Fiction 2. Domestic animals—Fiction
ISBN 0-375-82864-8; 0-375-92864-2 (lib bdg)
LC 2004-05789
A Newbery Medal honor book, 2006
Whittington, a feline descendant of Dick Whittington's famous cat of English folklore, appears at a rundown barnyard plagued by rats and restores harmony while telling his ancestor's story.
"The story works beautifully, both as historical fiction about medieval street life and commerce and as a witty, engaging tale of barnyard camaraderie and survival." Booklist

Armstrong, William Howard

Sounder; [by] William H. Armstrong; illustrations by James Barkley. Harper & Row 1969 116p il $15.99; pa $5.99 (5 and up)
Fic
1. Dogs—Fiction 2. African Americans—Fiction 3. Family life—Fiction
ISBN 0-06-020143-6; 0-06-440020-4 (pa)
Awarded the Newbery Medal, 1970
"Set in the South in the era of sharecropping and segregation, this succinctly told tale poignantly describes the courage of a father who steals a ham in order to feed his undernourished family; the determination of the eldest son, who searches for his father despite the apathy of prison authorities; and the devotion of a coon dog named Sounder." Shapiro. Fic for Youth. 3d edition

Arrington, Frances

Bluestem. Philomel Bks. 2000 140p $16.99 (4-6)   **Fic**
1. Sisters—Fiction 2. Frontier and pioneer life—Fiction
ISBN 0-399-23564-7   LC 99-53726
With their father away and their mother traumatized by some unknown event, eleven-year-old Polly and her younger sister are left to take care of themselves and their prairie homestead
"Arrington uses poetic language and deep description to provide her audience with a clear vision of the open prairie. Her characters are realistic and their struggle evident." ALAN

Prairie whispers. Philomel Bks. 2003 184p $17.99 (5 and up)   **Fic**
1. Frontier and pioneer life—Fiction 2. Family life—Fiction 3. South Dakota—Fiction
ISBN 0-399-23975-8   LC 2002-6698
Only twelve-year-old Colleen knows that her baby sister died just after she was born and that Colleen put another baby in her place, until the baby's father shows up and makes trouble for her and her family on the South Dakota prairie in the 1860s
"The story is rich in atmosphere, both literal and emotional. . . . This is a suspenseful and well-told tale." Horn Book

Atinsky, Steve

Tyler on prime time. Delacorte Press 2002 168p $14.95 (5 and up)   **Fic**
1. Television—Fiction
ISBN 0-385-72917-0   LC 2001-32468
While visiting his uncle, a writer on the most popular show on television, twelve-year-old Tyler auditions for a part on the show
"Written with a light touch, the novel features likable characters and a well-detailed setting. . . . The vagaries of show business . . . are convincingly portrayed." Horn Book Guide

Atwater, Richard Tupper

Mr. Popper's penguins; [by] Richard and Florence Atwater; illustrated by Robert Lawson. Little, Brown 1938 138p il $18.99; pa $6.99 (3-5)
Fic
1. Penguins—Fiction
ISBN 0-316-05842-4; 0-316-05843-2 (pa)
A Newbery Medal honor book, 1939
When Mr. Popper, a mild little painter and decorator with a taste for books and movies on polar explorations, was presented with a penguin, he named it Captain Cook. From that moment on life was changed for the Popper family
"To the depiction of the penguins in all conceivable moods Robert Lawson [the] artist has brought not only his skill but his individual humor, and his portrayal of the wistful Mr. Popper is memorable." N Y Times Book Rev

Auch, Mary Jane

I was a third grade science project; illustrated by Herm Auch. Holiday House 1998 96p il $15.95 (2-4)   **Fic**
1. School stories 2. Hypnotism—Fiction
ISBN 0-8234-1357-8   LC 97-41996
Also available in paperback from Bantam Bks.
While trying to hypnotize his dog for the third grade science fair, Brian accidentally makes his best friend Josh think he's a cat
"Auch's wisecracking third-graders and superb comic timing will have readers rolling on the floor." Booklist
Other titles about Brian are:
I was a third grade bodyguard (2003)
I was a third grade spy (2001)

Journey to nowhere. Holt & Co. 1997 202p pa $4.99 hardcover o.p. (4 and up)   **Fic**
1. Frontier and pioneer life—Fiction 2. New York (State)—Fiction
ISBN 0-440-41491-1 (pa)   LC 96-42249
This is the first title in the Genesee trilogy. In 1815, while traveling by covered wagon to settle in the wilderness of western New York, eleven-year-old Mem experiences a flood and separation from her family
"A well-written, realistic, and thoroughly researched novel." Booklist
Other titles in the Genesee trilogy are;
Frozen summer (1998)
The road to home (2000)

Auch, Mary Jane—*Continued*

Wing nut; [by] MJ Auch. 1st ed. Henry Holt 2005 231p $16.95 (5 and up)   **Fic**
1. Moving—Fiction 2. Birds—Fiction 3. Old age—Fiction
ISBN 0-8050-7531-3   LC 2004-54046
When twelve-year-old Grady and his mother relocate yet again, they find work taking care of an elderly man, who teaches Grady about cars, birds, and what it means to have a home
"Auch's story . . . is engaging. . . . What will attract readers . . . is the author's careful integration of bird lore and the unusual challenges of creating and maintaining a purple martin colony." Booklist

Augarde, Steve

The Various. David Fickling Books 2004 447p $16.95; lib bdg $18.99 (5 and up)   **Fic**
1. Fantasy fiction 2. Fairies—Fiction
ISBN 0-385-75029-3; 0-385-75037-4 (lib bdg)
     LC 2003-56548
First published 2003 in the United Kingdom
While staying on her uncle's rundown farm in the Somerset countryside, twelve-year-old Midge discovers that she has a special connection to the Various, a tribe of "strange, wild-and sometimes deadly" fairies struggling to maintain their existence in the nearby woods.
"Painstakingly crafted right down to dialects spoken by the tribes, this sweeping fantasy will engross fans of the 'little people' genre . . . as well as works . . . which open a window to a previously unimagined society in peril." Booklist

Avi

Abigail takes the wheel; story by Avi; pictures by Don Bolognese. HarperCollins Pubs. 1999 54p il lib bdg $17.89 (2-4)   **Fic**
1. Ships—Fiction 2. New York (N.Y.)—Fiction
ISBN 0-06-027663-0   LC 98-36887
"An I can read chapter book"
When the first mate of the freight boat Neptune falls ill, it is up to Abigail, the captain's daughter, to steer the ship up the Hudson River from New Jersey to New York City
"Avi's generous dose of adventure and suspense, combined with his straightforward yet compelling storytelling style, custom-fit this tale for new chapter-book readers. Bolognese's subdued watercolors create a turn-of-the-century nautical atmosphere." Horn Book Guide

The barn. Orchard Bks. 1994 106p $14.95; lib bdg $15.99 (4 and up)   **Fic**
1. Farm life—Fiction 2. Frontier and pioneer life—Fiction 3. Father-son relationship—Fiction
ISBN 0-531-06861-7; 0-531-08711-5 (lib bdg)
     LC 94-6920
Also available in paperback from Avon Bks.
"A Richard Jackson book"
In an effort to fulfill their dying father's last request, nine-year-old Ben and his brother and sister construct a barn on their land in the Oregon Territory in the 1850s
"While focusing mainly on his characters, Avi presents a vivid picture of the time and place, including fair-ly involved details about how the barn is constructed. This novel . . . is a thought-provoking and engaging piece of historical fiction." SLJ

Blue heron. Bradbury Press 1992 186p (5 and up)   **Fic**
1. Family life—Fiction 2. Herons—Fiction
ISBN 0-02-707751-9   LC 91-4308
Available in paperback from HarperTrophy
While spending the month of August on the Massachusetts shore with her father, stepmother, and their new baby, almost thirteen-year-old Maggie finds beauty in and draws strength from a great blue heron, even as the family around her unravels
"Maggie emerges as a sensitive heroine whose perceptions are genuine as well as compelling. Reflecting the complexity of people and their emotions, this novel explores rather than solves the conflicts introduced." Publ Wkly

The Book Without Words; a fable of medieval magic. Hyperion Books for Children 2005 203p $15.99 (5 and up)   **Fic**
1. Supernatural—Fiction 2. Magic—Fiction 3. Middle Ages—Fiction 4. Great Britain—History—0-1066—Fiction
ISBN 0-7868-0829-2
"At the dawning of the Middle Ages, Thorston, an old alchemist, works feverishly to create gold and to dose himself with a concoction that will enable him to live forever. The key to his success lies in a mysterious book with blank pages that can only be read by desperate, green-eyed people. . . . Avi's compelling language creates a dreary foreboding. . . . Clearly this is a story with a message, a true fable. Thoughtful readers will devour its absorbing plot and humorous elements, and learn a 'useful truth' along the way." SLJ

Crispin; the cross of lead. Hyperion Bks. for Children 2002 262p $15.99; lib bdg $16.49; pa $6.99 (5 and up)   **Fic**
1. Orphans—Fiction 2. Middle Ages—Fiction 3. Great Britain—History—1154-1399, Plantagenets—Fiction
ISBN 0-7868-0828-4; 0-7868-2647-9 (lib bdg); 0-7868-1658-9 (pa)   LC 2001-51829
Awarded the Newbery Medal, 2003
Falsely accused of theft and murder, an orphaned peasant boy in fourteenth-century England flees his village and meets a larger-than-life juggler who holds a dangerous secret
This "book is a page-turner from beginning to end. . . . A meticulously crafted story, full of adventure, mystery, and action." SLJ

Don't you know there's a war on? HarperCollins Pubs. 2001 200p $14.95; pa $5.99 (4 and up)   **Fic**
1. World War, 1939-1945—Fiction 2. Teachers—Fiction 3. Brooklyn (New York, N.Y.)—Fiction
ISBN 0-380-97863-6; 0-380-81544-3 (pa)
     LC 00-46102
In wartime Brooklyn in 1943, eleven-year-old Howie Crispers mounts a campaign to save his favorite teacher from being fired

Avi—*Continued*

"The 1943 Brooklyn setting is well evoked in Howie's lively, slang-spangled narration. The novel's uncomplicated, compact structure invites reading aloud." Horn Book Guide

The end of the beginning; being the adventures of a small snail (and an even smaller ant); with illustrations by Tricia Tusa. Harcourt 2004 143p il $14.95 (3-5) **Fic**

1. Snails—Fiction 2. Ants—Fiction
ISBN 0-15-204968-1   LC 2004-2696

Avon the snail and Edward, a take-charge ant, set off together on a journey to an undetermined destination in search of unspecified adventures.

"Whimsical pen-and-ink sketches add much to this wise little book. It's perfect for reading and discussing." SLJ

The good dog. Atheneum Bks. for Young Readers 2001 243p $16; pa $5.99 (4-6)

Fic

1. Dogs—Fiction 2. Wolves—Fiction
ISBN 0-689-83824-7; 0-689-83825-5 (pa)
                LC 00-53600

"A Richard Jackson book"

McKinley, a malamute, is torn between the domestic world of his human family and the wild world of Lupin, a wolf that is trying to recruit dogs to replenish the dwindling wolf pack

"Falling somewhere between a naturalistic account of animal life and a fantasy, the strongest parts of the book depict the communication gap between McKinley and the human family with whom he resides." Horn Book Guide

Midnight magic. Scholastic Press 1999 249p $15.95; pa $5.99 (5 and up) **Fic**

1. Magicians—Fiction 2. Renaissance—Fiction
3. Italy—Fiction
ISBN 0-590-36035-3; 0-439-24219-3 (pa)
                LC 98-50192

In Italy in 1491, Mangus the magician and his apprentice are summoned to the castle of Duke Claudio to determine if his daughter is indeed being haunted by a ghost.

An "entertaining tale of mystery and intrigue." SLJ

Never mind! a twin novel; [by] Avi and Rachel Vail. HarperCollins 2004 200p $15.99; lib bdg $16.89 (5 and up) **Fic**

1. Twins—Fiction 2. New York (N.Y.)—Fiction
ISBN 0-06-054314-0; 0-06-054315-9 (lib bdg)
                LC 2003-21439

Twelve-year-old New York City twins Meg and Edward have nothing in common, so they are just as shocked as everyone else when Meg's hopes for popularity and Edward's mischievous schemes coincidentally collide in a hilarious showdown.

"The dialogue is great, especially the conversations that reveal how hard it is to listen and to say what you mean. . . . The wit and slapstick carry the story, which has moments of sadness that raise serious issues everyone will recognize. Best of all is the message: laugh at yourself." Booklist

Poppy; illustrated by Brian Floca. Orchard Bks. 1995 147p il $16.95 (3-5) **Fic**

1. Animals—Fiction 2. Allegories
ISBN 0-531-09483-9   LC 95-6040

Also available in paperback from HarperCollins

"A Richard Jackson book"

"As ruler of Dimwood Forest, Ocax the hoot owl has promised to protect the mice occupying an abandoned farmhouse as long as they ask permission before 'moving about.' Poppy, a timid dormouse, is a loyal, obedient subject—until she sees Ocax devour her fiancé and hears the owl deny her father's request to seek new living quarters. To prove that the intimidating ruler is really a phony, Poppy embarks on a dangerous and eye-opening quest, which ends with her one-on-one battle with Ocax. . . . An engaging blend of romance, suspense and parody." Publ Wkly

Other titles about Dimwood Forest are:
Ereth's birthday (2000)
Poppy and Rye (1998)
Poppy's return (2005)
Ragweed (1999)

Prairie school; story by Avi; pictures by Bill Farnsworth. HarperCollins Pubs. 2001 47p il $14.95; lib bdg $14.89 (2-4) **Fic**

1. Books and reading—Fiction 2. Aunts—Fiction
3. Frontier and pioneer life—Fiction 4. Physically handicapped—Fiction
ISBN 0-06-027664-9; 0-06-027665-7 (lib bdg)
                LC 00-38834

"An I can read chapter book"

In 1880, Noah's aunt teaches the reluctant nine-year-old how to read as they explore the Colorado prairie together, Noah pushing Aunt Dora in her wheelchair

"Warm, soft-edged illustrations capture the intimacy of the loving family relationships and the vastness of the landscape. . . . This gentle story with a great message . . . would make a pleasant read-aloud as well as a good addition to easy chapter-book collections." SLJ

S.O.R. losers. Atheneum 2000 c1984 96p $15.95 (5 and up) **Fic**

1. Soccer—Fiction 2. School stories
ISBN 0-689-84157-4

Also available in paperback from HarperTrophy

A reissue of the title first published 1984 by Bradbury Press

Each member of the South Orange River eighth-grade soccer team has qualities of excellence, but not on the soccer field.

"Short, pithy chapters highlighting key events maintain the pace necessary for successful comedy. . . . The style is vivid, believably articulate." Horn Book

The secret school. Harcourt 2001 153p $16; pa $5.95 (4 and up) **Fic**

1. School stories 2. Colorado—Fiction
ISBN 0-15-216375-1; 0-15-204699-2 (pa)
                LC 2001-629

In 1925, fourteen-year-old Ida Bidson secretly takes over as the teacher when the one-room schoolhouse in her remote Colorado area closes unexpectedly

"This carefully plotted, enjoyable, old-fashioned tale of children taking control of a bad situation is a welcome addition to the literature of empowerment." SLJ

Avi—*Continued*

The true confessions of Charlotte Doyle. 1st Orchard Classics ed. Orchard Books 2003 c1990 215p il $9.95 (6 and up)   **Fic**
1. Sea stories
ISBN 0-439-32731-8
A Newbery Medal honor book, 1991
First published 1990
"Includes a new preface from Avi and a discussion guide."

As the only passenger, and the only female, on a transatlantic voyage in 1832, thirteen-year-old Charlotte finds herself caught between a murderous captain and a mutinous crew.

The author has "fashioned an intriguing, suspenseful, carefully crafted tale, with nonstop action on the high seas." Booklist

Ayres, Katherine
Macaroni boy. Delacorte Press 2003 182p $15.95; lib bdg $17.99 (5 and up)   **Fic**
1. School stories 2. Great Depression, 1929-1939—Fiction
ISBN 0-385-73016-0; 0-385-90085-6 (lib bdg)
LC 2002-6768
In Pittsburgh in 1933, sixth-grader Mike Costa notices a connection between several strange occurrences, but the only way he can find out the truth about what's happening is to be nice to the class bully. Includes historical facts
"Actual places and events are interwoven with a heartwarming story of a close-knit family facing difficult times." Voice Youth Advocates

Babbitt, Natalie
The eyes of the Amaryllis. Farrar, Straus & Giroux 1977 127p pa $4.95 hardcover o.p. (5 and up)   **Fic**
1. Sea stories 2. Grandmothers—Fiction
ISBN 0-374-42238-9 (pa)   LC 77-11862
"The sea holds countless mysteries and gives up very few secrets; when she does, it is truly a remarkable event, an event that eleven-year-old Geneva Reade experiences when she visits her grandmother who lives in a house by the water's edge. Sent for to tend her Gran through a broken leg, Jenny is put to work, at once, combing the beach for a sign from her grandfather, a captain lost at sea with his ship and crew thirty years ago." Child Book Rev Serv
"The book succeeds as a well-wrought narrative in which a complex philosophic theme is developed through the balanced, subtle use of symbol and imagery. It is a rare story." Horn Book

Kneeknock Rise; story and pictures by Natalie Babbitt. Farrar, Straus & Giroux 1970 117p il pa $5.95 hardcover o.p. (4-6)   **Fic**
1. Allegories 2. Superstition—Fiction
ISBN 0-374-44260-6 (pa)
A Newbery Medal honor book, 1971
"Did you ever meet a Megrimum? There is one in KneeKnock Rise, and on stormy nights the villagers of

Instep tremble in delicious delight as its howls echo over the Mammoth Mountains. Egan learns a lesson when he climbs to meet and conquer the Megrimum." Best Sellers
"An enchanting tale imbued with a folk flavor, enlivened with piquant imagery and satiric wit." Booklist

The search for delicious. Farrar, Straus & Giroux 1969 167p il $17; pa $5.95 (5 and up)   **Fic**
1. Fantasy fiction
ISBN 0-374-36534-2; 0-374-46536-3 (pa)
"An Ariel book"
The Prime Minister is compiling a dictionary and when no one at court can agree on the meaning of delicious, the King sends his twelve-year-old messenger to poll the country
"The theme, foolish arguments can lead to great conflict, may not be clear to all children who will enjoy this fantasy." Best Sellers

Tuck everlasting. Farrar, Straus & Giroux 1975 139p $16; pa $5.95 (5 and up)   **Fic**
1. Fantasy fiction
ISBN 0-374-37848-7; 0-374-48009-5 (pa)
The Tuck family is confronted with an agonizing situation when they discover that a ten-year-old girl and a malicious stranger now share their secret about a spring whose water prevents one from ever growing any older
"The story is macabre and moral, exciting and excellently written." N Y Times Book Rev

Baccalario, Pierdomenico
The door to time; [translated from Italian by Leah Janeczko; illustrated by Iacopo Bruno] Scholastic 2006 222p il (Ulysses Moore) $12.99 (4-6)   **Fic**
1. Twins—Fiction 2. Adventure fiction 3. Mystery fiction
ISBN 0-439-77438-1
Original Italian edition 2004
After moving from London to an old mansion on the English coast, eleven-year-old twins Jason and Julia discover that their new home has twisting tunnels, strange artifacts from around the world, and a mysterious, locked door.
"The book offers a well-paced adventure story, attractive line drawings, and the promise of many time-travel fantasies to come in the series." Booklist
Another title in this series is:
The long-lost map (2006)

Bagnold, Enid
National Velvet (5 and up)   **Fic**
1. Horses—Fiction 2. Great Britain—Fiction
Available from Buccaneer Bks. and in paperback from HarperTrophy
First published 1935
An English girl, Velvet Brown, wins a magnificent piebald horse in a lottery and determines to enter and win the Grand National Steeplechase even though girls are not allowed to ride in that race

Baker, Olaf

Where the buffaloes begin; illustrated by Stephen Gammell. Puffin Bks. 1985 c1981 unp il pa $6.99 (2-4)   **Fic**
   1. Native Americans—Fiction 2. Bison—Fiction
   ISBN 0-14-050560-1   LC 85-5682
   A Caldecott Medal honor book, 1982
   First published in book form 1981 by Warne
   "Originally published in 1915 in 'St. Nicholas Magazine,' the story tells in four short chapters of the adventure of Little Wolf, a ten-year-old Indian boy. He was fascinated by a tribal legend about a lake to the south, a sacred spot where the buffaloes were said to originate. . . . Narrated in cadenced prose rich in images, the story evokes the Plains Indians' feelings of reverence for the buffalo. Magnificent full- and double-page pencil drawings . . . capture the immensity of the prairie and the mighty strength of the awesome beasts." Horn Book

Balliett, Blue

Chasing Vermeer; illustrated by Brett Helquist. Scholastic Press 2004 254p il $16.95 (5 and up)   **Fic**
   1. Vermeer, Johannes, 1632-1675—Fiction
   2. Mystery fiction 3. Art—Fiction
   ISBN 0-439-37294-1   LC 2002-152106
   When seemingly unrelated and strange events start to happen and a precious Vermeer painting disappears, eleven-year-olds Petra and Calder combine their talents to solve an international art scandal.
   Balliett's purpose "seems to be to get children to think—about relationships, connections, coincidences, and the subtle language of artwork. . . . [This is] a book that offers children something new upon each reading. . . . Helquist . . . outdoes himself here, providing an interactive mystery in his pictures." Booklist
   Another title about Petra and Calder is:
The Wright 3 (2006)

Banks, Kate

Dillon Dillon. Foster Bks. 2002 150p $16 (4 and up)   **Fic**
   1. Family life—Fiction 2. Adoption—Fiction
   3. Loons—Fiction 4. New Hampshire—Fiction
   ISBN 0-374-31786-0   LC 2001-33207
   During the summer that he turns ten years old, Dillon Dillon learns the surprising story behind his name and develops a relationship with three loons, living on the lake near his family's New Hampshire cabin, that help him make sense of his life
   This "succeeds as an emotionally intricate, quietly well-observed, symbolically charged novel." Horn Book

Banks, Lynne Reid

The Indian in the cupboard. Doubleday 1980 181p il $16.95 (5 and up)   **Fic**
   1. Fantasy fiction
   ISBN 0-385-17051-3   LC 79-6533
   Also available in paperback from Avon Bks.
   Illustrated by Brock Cole
   A nine-year-old boy receives a plastic Indian, a cupboard, and a little key for his birthday and finds himself involved in adventure when the Indian comes to life in the cupboard and befriends him

Other titles in this series are:
The key to the Indian (1998)
The mystery of the cupboard (1993)
The return of the Indian (1986)
The secret of the Indian (1989)

Barrett, Tracy

Cold in summer. Holt & Co. 2003 203p $16.95 (5 and up)   **Fic**
   1. Ghost stories 2. Tennessee—Fiction
   ISBN 0-8050-7052-4   LC 2002-67888
   At the beginning of seventh grade, Ariadne moves to a Tennessee town near a former farming community submerged under a man-made lake and meets the ghost of a girl from the past
   "This is a straightforward ghost tale with a doughty main character, a strong sense of history, and solid secondary players." Bull Cent Child Books

On Etruscan time. Henry Holt 2005 172p $16.95 (5 and up)   **Fic**
   1. Archeology—Fiction 2. Etruscans—Fiction
   3. Italy—Fiction
   ISBN 0-8050-7569-0   LC 2004-52341
   While spending the summer on an archaeological dig near Florence, Italy, with his mother, eleven-year-old Hector meets an Etruscan boy who needs help to foil his treacherous uncle's plan to make him a human sacrifice-1,000 years in the past.
   "Barrett's accurate description of the archaeological dig and the details of Etruscan daily life are well researched and interesting. The plot holds excitement and suspense." SLJ

Barrie, J. M. (James Matthew)

Peter Pan (3-5)   **Fic**
   1. Fairy tales
   Some editions are:
Everyman's Lib. Children's Classics $15.95 Illustrated by F. D. Bedford (ISBN 0-679-41792-3)
Henry Holt & Co. $22.50 Illustrated by Michael Hague (ISBN 0-8050-7245-4)
Orchard Books $17.95 Illustrated by Robert R. Ingpen (ISBN 0-439-67257-0) Has title: Peter Pan and Wendy
Viking $22.99 Illustrated by Scott Gustafson (ISBN 0-670-84180-3)
   First published 1911 by Scribner with title: Peter and Wendy
   This is the story of "how Wendy, John, and Michael flew with Peter Pan, the boy who never grows up, to adventures in the Never-Never Land with pirates, redskins, and the fairy Tinker Bell. [It is] in Barrie's inimitable style, pleasing the child with delightful absurdities and the adult with good-humored satire." Right Book for the Right Child

Barron, T. A.

The lost years of Merlin. Philomel Bks. 1996 326p $19.99 (6 and up)   **Fic**
   1. Merlin (Legendary character)—Fiction 2. Fantasy fiction
   ISBN 0-399-23018-1   LC 96-33920
   Also available in paperback from Ace Bks.

Barron, T. A.—*Continued*

"A boy, hurled on the rocks by the sea, regains consciousness unable to remember anything—not his parents, not his own name. He is sure that the secretive Branwen is not his mother, despite her claims, and that Emrys is not his real name. The two soon find themselves feared because of Branwen's healing abilities and Emrys' growing powers. . . . Barron has created not only a magical land populated by remarkable beings but also a completely magical tale, filled with ancient Celtic and Druidic lore, that will enchant readers." Booklist

Other titles in this series are:

The fires of Merlin (1998)

The mirror of Merlin (1999)

The seven songs of Merlin (1997)

The wings of Merlin (2000)

Barrows, Annie

Ivy + Bean; written by Annie Barrows; illustrated by Sophie Blackall. Chronicle Books 2006 113p il $14.95 (1-3)   **Fic**

1. Friendship—Fiction

ISBN 978-0-8118-4903-6; 0-8118-4903-1

LC 2005023944

When seven-year-old Bean plays a mean trick on her sister, she finds unexpected support for her antics from Ivy, the new neighbor, who is less boring than Bean first suspected.

"The deliciousness here is in the details, with both girls drawn distinctly and with flair. . . . Even with all the text's strong points, what takes the book to a higher level is Blackall's artwork, which captures the girls' spirit." Booklist

Barry, Dave

Peter and the starcatchers; by Dave Barry and Ridley Pearson. Hyperion 2004 451p il $17.99 (5 and up)   **Fic**

1. Fairy tales 2. Pirates—Fiction

ISBN 0-7868-5445-6   LC 2004-55275

Soon after Peter, an orphan, sets sail from England on the ship Never Land, he befriends and assists Molly, a young Starcatcher, whose mission is to guard a trunk of magical stardust from a greedy pirate and the native inhabitants of a remote island.

"The authors plait multiple story lines together in short, fast-moving chapters. . . . Capitalizing on familiar material, this adventure is carefully crafted to set the stage for Peter's later exploits. This smoothly written page-turner just might send readers back to the original." SLJ

Another title about Peter is:

Peter and the shadow thieves (2006)

Bartek, Mary

Funerals & fly fishing; [by] Mary Bartek. 1st ed. H. Holt 2004 148p $16.95 (4 and up)   **Fic**

1. Grandfathers—Fiction 2. Funeral rites and ceremonies—Fiction 3. Pennsylvania—Fiction

ISBN 0-8050-7409-0   LC 2003-57046

The summer after sixth grade, Brad Stanislawski travels to Pennsylvania by himself to visit the grandfather he

has never met before, and overcomes some of the preconceived ideas he has gotten from his mother

"The characters are believable and well developed. . . . There is enough action to keep children's attention." SLJ

Bartoletti, Susan Campbell

A coal miner's bride; the diary of Anetka Kaminska. Scholastic 2000 219p il (Dear America) $10.95; lib bdg $12.95 (4 and up)   **Fic**

1. Polish Americans—Fiction 2. Immigrants—Fiction 3. Coal mines and mining—Fiction

ISBN 0-439-05386-2; 0-439-55510-8 (lib bdg)

LC 99-29864

A diary account of thirteen-year-old Anetka's life in Poland in 1896, immigration to America, marriage to a coal miner, widowhood, and happiness in finally finding her true love

"Bartoletti paints an accessible and evocative picture of life in a harsh era." SLJ

The journal of Finn Reardon; a newsie. Scholastic 2003 156p il (My name is America) $10.95 (4 and up)   **Fic**

1. Irish Americans—Fiction 2. New York (N.Y.)—Fiction 3. Newspaper carriers—Fiction

ISBN 0-439-18894-6   LC 2002-30874

Finn Reardon, a thirteen-year-old Irish-American newspaper carrier who hopes to be a journalist someday, keeps a journal of his experiences living in New York City in 1899. Includes historical notes

This "is a standout in the series. . . . It's entertaining and the characters leap off the pages." SLJ

Baskin, Nora Raleigh

What every girl (except me) knows; a novel. Little, Brown 2001 213p $16.95; pa $4.99 (4 and up)   **Fic**

1. Mothers—Fiction 2. Friendship—Fiction 3. Death—Fiction

ISBN 0-316-07021-1; 0-440-41852-6 (pa)

LC 00-40557

"Twelve-year-old Gabby feels like she's speeding into womanhood without a map, since her mother died when she was small. . . . She's convinced that girls with mothers have knowledge to which she's not privy, and one of the benefits of her friendship with new girl Taylor is a helpful dose of female camaraderie. . . . The book's depiction of Gabby's family dynamics . . . is perceptive and sympathetic." Bull Cent Child Books

Bateman, Colin

Running with the Reservoir Pups; [by] Colin Bateman. Delacorte Press 2005 c2003 263p (Eddie & the gang with no name) $15.95; lib bdg $17.99 (5 and up)   **Fic**

1. Gangs—Fiction 2. Divorce—Fiction 3. Northern Ireland—Fiction

ISBN 0-385-73244-9; 0-385-90268-9 (lib bdg)

LC 2004-43912

First published 2003 in the United Kingdom

Bateman, Colin—*Continued*

When his parents divorce and his mother moves with him to Belfast, Northern Ireland, twelve-year-old Eddie contends with the Reservoir Pups, a gang of children who rule his neighborhood.

This "author's hilarious, dark Northern Irish wit, penchant for action-packed mayhem, sense of irony, and snappy dialogue are all evident in this [book]." SLJ

Another title about Eddie is:

Bring me the head of Oliver Plunkett (2005)

Bateson, Catherine

Stranded in Boringsville. Holiday House 2005 138p $16.95 (5 and up)   **Fic**
1. Moving—Fiction 2. Divorce—Fiction
3. Friendship—Fiction 4. Australia—Fiction
ISBN 0-8234-1969-X

First published 2002 in Australia with title: Rain May and Captain Daniel

"Twelve year-old Rain's parents have separated. Her father has moved in with his trendy, younger girlfriend, and her mother has turned in her business suits for yoga and a simpler life in 'Boringsville,' tiny Clarkson, Central Victoria. . . . Her neighbor Daniel is almost 12, . . . and, as Rain learns, cruelly bullied at school. In alternating chapters, . . . Bateson deftly allows Rain and Daniel to chronicle their budding friendship. . . . Readers will ache for the kids, whose conflicted feelings seem all too real." Booklist

Bath, K. P.

The secret of Castle Cant; being an account of the remarkable adventures of Lucy Wickwright, maidservant and spy; with artistic embellishments by David Christiana. Little, Brown 2004 291p il $16.99 (5 and up)   **Fic**
1. Orphans—Fiction 2. Fantasy fiction
ISBN 0-316-10848-0   LC 2004-03643

When twelve-toed orphan Lucy Wickwright is brought to Castle Cant to be serving girl to the Baron's daughter, the Adorable & Honorable Pauline, she becomes involved with revolutionaries and uncovers surprising palace intrigues.

"Bath deals with a familiar fairy-tale theme: the discovery of noble lineage in a maidservant. His treatment, however, is quirky, funny, and rife with social satire; his style, full of puns, similes, alliteration, and just the right tone of tongue-in-cheek pomposity, is delightful." SLJ

Bauer, Marion Dane

A bear named Trouble. Clarion Books 2005 120p $15 (3-6)   **Fic**
1. Bears—Fiction 2. Zoos—Fiction 3. Alaska—Fiction
ISBN 0-618-51738-3   LC 2004-21259

In Anchorage, Alaska, two lonely boys make a connection—a brown bear injured just after his mother sends him out on his own, and a human whose father is a new keeper at the Alaska Zoo and whose mother and sister are still in Minnesota.

"With a strong plot, well-developed characters, and an engaging writing format, this book is a great choice for young readers." SLJ

The blue ghost; illustrated by Suling Wang. Random House 2005 85p il $11.95; lib bdg $13.99 (2-4)   **Fic**
1. Ghost stories
ISBN 0-375-83179-7; 0-375-93179-1 (lib bdg)

"A Stepping Stone book."

At her grandmother's log cabin, nine-year-old Liz is led to make contact with children she believes may be her ancestors.

"This gentle ghost story, written in simple prose, blends mild suspense with a look at how the past connects to and influences the present. Mystery fans will enjoy the spooky premise, and Wang's softly rendered black-and-white drawings increase the ghostly atmosphere." Booklist

The double-digit club. Holiday House 2004 118p $15.95 (3-5)   **Fic**
1. Friendship—Fiction
ISBN 0-8234-1805-7   LC 2003-047862

Nine-year-old Sarah is excited about summer vacation, but she faces unexpected crises when her best friend Paige becomes old enough to join a local girls' clique, and when she makes choices which affect her relationship with an elderly blind neighbor.

"While many of the story elements will be familiar to readers, they are presented here in a meaningful and thoughtful way." SLJ

On my honor. Clarion Bks. 1986 90p $15 (4 and up)   **Fic**
1. Accidents—Fiction
ISBN 0-89919-439-7   LC 86-2679

Also available in paperback from Dell

A Newbery Medal honor book, 1987

When his best friend drowns while they are both swimming in a treacherous river that they had promised never to go near, Joel is devastated and terrified at having to tell both sets of parents the terrible consequences of their disobedience

"Bauer's association of Joel's guilt with the smell of the polluted river on his skin is particularly noteworthy. Its miasma almost rises off the pages. Descriptions are vivid, characterization and dialogue natural, and the style taut but unforced. A powerful, moving book." SLJ

Runt. Clarion Bks. 2002 138p $14 (4 and up)   **Fic**
1. Wolves—Fiction
ISBN 0-618-21261-2   LC 2002-3965

Runt, the smallest wolf cub in the litter, seeks to prove himself to his father King and the rest of the pack and to earn a new name

The author's "passion for the animals is evident throughout this compelling, poignant story." Booklist

Baum, L. Frank

The Wizard of Oz (3-6)   **Fic**
1. Fantasy fiction

Also available Simon & Schuster Commemorative Pop-Up edition for younger readers illustrated by Robert Sabuda

Some editions are:

Baum, L. Frank—*Continued*

HarperCollins $24.99 Illustrated by William Wallace Denslow (ISBN 0-06-029323-3)

Holt & Co. $34.95 Illustrated by Michael Hague (ISBN 0-8050-6430-3)

North-South Bks. $19.95 Illustrated by Lisbeth Zwerger (ISBN 1-55858-638-5)

Pavilion Bks. $29.99 Illustrated by Michael Foreman (ISBN 1-86205-343-X)

First published 1900 with title: The wonderful Wizard of Oz

Here are the adventures of Dorothy who, in her dreams, escapes from her bed in Kansas to visit the Emerald City and to meet the wonderful Wizard of Oz, the Scarecrow, the Tin Woodman, and the Cowardly Lion

Other titles about the land of Oz are:

Dorothy and the Wizard in Oz (1908)

The land of Oz (1904)

Little Wizard stories of Oz (1985)

The magic of Oz (1919)

The marvelous land of Oz (1904)

Ozma of Oz (1907)

The patchwork girl of Oz (1913)

The tin woodsman of Oz (1918)

Bawden, Nina

Granny the Pag. Clarion Bks. 1996 184p $15 (4 and up) **Fic**

1. Grandmothers—Fiction 2. Parent-child relationship—Fiction

ISBN 0-395-77604-X   LC 95-38191

Also available in paperback from Puffin Bks.

First published 1995 in the United Kingdom

Originally abandoned by her actor parents who later attempt to gain custody, Cat wages a spirited campaign to decide her own fate and remain with her grandmother

"Bawden has created some enormously appealing characters in this funny and very touching novel." SLJ

Humbug. Clarion Bks. 1992 133p $15 (4 and up) **Fic**

1. Truthfulness and falsehood—Fiction

ISBN 0-395-62149-6   LC 91-33900

Also available in paperback from Puffin Bks.

When eight-year-old Cora is sent to stay next door with the seemingly pleasant woman called Aunt Sunday, she is tormented by Aunt Sunday's mean-spirited, deceitful daughter, but finds an ally in Aunt Sunday's elderly mother

"Characters are beautifully and intricately drawn. . . . Bawden deals forthrightly with harsh truths; she acknowledges that children can hate, and she shatters a host of childhood notions about grown-ups, honesty, and fairness. Along with that, she delivers a riveting plot and a totally credible Cora." Booklist

Beard, Darleen Bailey

Operation Clean Sweep; [by] Darleen Bailey Beard. 1st ed. Farrar Straus Giroux 2004 151p $16 (3-6) **Fic**

1. Women—Suffrage—Fiction 2. Elections—Fiction 3. Oregon—Fiction

ISBN 0-374-38034-1   LC 2003-49430

In 1916, just four years after getting the right to vote, the women of Umatilla, Oregon band together to throw the mayor and other city officials out of office, replacing them with women.

"Beard's story, based on real events, features believable characters, strong local color, and a plot that gently makes its point without offending anyone." Booklist

Beatty, Patricia

Turn homeward, Hannalee. Morrow 1984 193p $16.99; pa $5.99 (5 and up) **Fic**

1. United States—History—1861-1865, Civil War—Fiction 2. Georgia—Fiction 3. Child labor—Fiction

ISBN 0-688-03871-9; 0-688-16676-8 (pa)

LC 84-8960

This "historical fiction shows how the Civil War affected one segment of the population—the southern mill workers—and is based on fact. . . . The protagonists are Hannalee and Jem, twelve and ten, who are shipped from their Georgia town (and their recently widowed, pregnant mother) to Indiana, where they are offered as workers to anyone who wants them." Bull Cent Child Books

"The story is vintage Beatty, with a forthright, plain-spoken heroine who has gumption to spare. As a period piece, it is a vivid, seemingly authentic picture of what times might have been like for a hardworking, white, Southern family." Booklist

Bell, Hilari

The wizard test. Eos 2005 166p $15.99; lib bdg $16.89 (5 and up) **Fic**

1. Magicians—Fiction 2. Fantasy fiction

ISBN 0-06-059940-5; 0-06-059941-3 (lib bdg)

Fourteen year-old Dayven is devastated when he learns he has wizard powers, since wizards are considered to be disloyal deceivers who believe in nothing, until he undergoes wizard training and discovers a new way of looking at the world that will change his values, friendships, and future.

"Hard questions are asked and answered in a slim book that will find a wide audience and spark much discussion." SLJ

Bell, Joanne

Breaking trail. Groundwood books/House of Anansi Press 2005 135p $15.95 (5 and up) **Fic**

1. Yukon River valley (Yukon and Alaska)—Fiction 2. Sled dog racing—Fiction 3. Depression (Psychology)—Fiction

ISBN 0-88899-630-6

"Becky has always lived with her family in a log cabin in the Yukon, but when the fur market dwindled away, her father, a dog musher and trapper, had to quit trapping and she and her family moved into town. Now her father is depressed. . . . [Becky's plan is] to train her own dog team to race in the Junior Quest, a challenging five-day dog race across Alaska, in hopes of making her father happy." Publisher's note

"Although there are no easy solutions to the difficulties that confront this family, their love and support for one another are touching and believable." SLJ

Bellairs, John

The curse of the blue figurine. Dial Bks. for Young Readers 1983 200p pa $5.99 hardcover o.p. (5 and up) **Fic**

1. Mystery fiction

ISBN 0-14-038005-1 (pa); 0-8446-7138-4 (hc)

LC 82-73217

Also available Brad Strickland's titles based on John Bellairs characters; Hardcover available from P. Smith

"The terror for young Johnny Dixon begins when cranky eccentric Professor Childermass tells him that St. Michael's Church is haunted by Father Baart, an evil sorcerer who mysteriously disappeared years ago. When Johnny finds a blue Egyptian figurine hidden in the church basement, he takes it home in spite of the warning note from Father Baart threatening harm to anyone who removes it from the church." SLJ

The author "intertwines real concerns with sorcery in a seamless fashion, bringing dimension to his characters and events with expert timing and sharply honed atmosphere." Booklist

Other titles about Johnny Dixon and Professor Childermass are:

The chessmen of doom (1989)

The eyes of the killer robot (1986)

The mummy, the will and the crypt (1983)

The revenge of the wizard's ghost (1985)

The secret of the underground room (1990)

The spell of the sorcerer's skull (1984)

The trolley to yesterday (1989)

The house with a clock in its walls; pictures by Edward Gorey. Dial Bks. for Young Readers 1973 179p il pa $5.99 o.p. (5 and up) **Fic**

1. Witchcraft—Fiction

ISBN 0-14-240257-5 (pa)

Also available Brad Strickland's titles based on John Bellair's characters

In 1948, Lewis, a ten-year-old orphan, goes to New Zebedee, Michigan with his warlock Uncle Jonathan, who lives in a big mysterious house and practices white magic. Together with their neighbor, Mrs. Zimmerman, a witch, they search to find a clock that is programmed to end the world and has been hidden in the walls of the house by the evil Isaac Izard

"Bellairs's story and Edward Gorey's pictures are satisfyingly frightening." Publ Wkly

Other titles about Lewis are:

The doom of the haunted opera (1995)

The figure in the shadows (1975)

The ghost in the mirror (1993)

The letter, the witch, and the ring (1976)

The vengeance of the witch-finder (1993)

Bernstein, Nina

Magic by the book; pictures by Boris Kulikov. Farrar, Straus and Giroux 2005 227p il $17 (4-6) **Fic**

1. Magic—Fiction 2. Books and reading—Fiction

ISBN 0-374-34718-2   LC 2004-43329

"Frances Foster books"

After returning from a trip to the library, eleven-year-old Anne and her younger brother and sister discover a magic book which sends them on adventures in which they meet Robin Hood, giant bugs, and a dark, sinister man with a wolfish face.

"Between bouts of brisk action, Bernstein probes realistic childhood themes—sibling tensions, ambivalence about growing up, the thrill of mastering a challenge." Booklist

Betancourt, Jeanne

My name is brain Brian. Scholastic 1993 128p pa $4.50 hardcover o.p. (4-6) **Fic**

1. Dyslexia—Fiction 2. School stories 3. Friendship—Fiction

ISBN 0-590-44922-2 (pa)   LC 92-16513

On title page the word "brain" appears with an "X" through it

Although he is helped by his new sixth grade teacher after being diagnosed as dyslexic, Brian still has some problems with school and with people he thought were his friends

"Betancourt's depiction of Brian's emotional and psychological growth is believable and involving." Booklist

Bianco, Margery Williams

The velveteen rabbit; or, How toys become real; by Margery Williams (2-4) **Fic**

1. Toys—Fiction 2. Rabbits—Fiction 3. Fairy tales

Some editions are:

Doubleday $13.95 illustrated by William Nicholson (ISBN 0-385-07725-4)

Holt & Co. $16.95 Illustrated by Michael Hague (ISBN 0-8050-0209-X)

First published 1922 by Doran

"The story of a toy rabbit that becomes real through the love of a child and the intervention of a fairy." Bull Cent Child Books

Billingsley, Franny

The Folk Keeper. Atheneum Bks. for Young Readers 1999 162p $16.95; pa $4.99 (5 and up) **Fic**

1. Fantasy fiction

ISBN 0-689-82876-4; 0-689-84461-1 (pa)

LC 98-48778

"A Jean Karl book"

Orphan Corinna disguises herself as a boy to pose as a Folk Keeper, one who keeps the Evil Folk at bay, and discovers her heritage as a seal maiden when she is taken to live with a wealthy family in their manor by the sea

"The intricate plot, vibrant characters, dangerous intrigue, and fantastical elements combine into a truly remarkable novel steeped in atmosphere." Horn Book

Well wished. Atheneum Bks. for Young Readers 1997 170p $16.95; pa $4.99 (4-6) **Fic**

1. Wishes—Fiction 2. Magic—Fiction 3. Fantasy fiction

ISBN 0-689-81210-8; 0-689-83255-9 (pa)

LC 96-24511

"A Jean Karl book"

"In Nuria's town, a magical wishing well grants individuals one wish per lifetime, but if possible, twists the requests to produce a ruinous outcome. When Nuria

Billingsley, Franny—*Continued*

wishes that her crippled friend 'had a body just like mine,' the girls switch bodies. Fantasy elements play a pivotal role in the plot, but keen character development leaves the strongest impression in this well-constructed, thought-provoking first novel." Horn Book Guide

Birdsall, Jeanne

The Penderwicks; a summer tale of four sisters, two rabbits, and a very interesting boy. Knopf 2005 262p $15.95; lib bdg $17.77 (3-6)

Fic

1. Sisters—Fiction 2. Single parent family—Fiction
ISBN 0-375-83143-6; 0-375-93143-0 (lib bdg)
LC 2004-20364

While vacationing with their widowed father in the Berkshire Mountains, four lovable sisters, ages four through twelve, share adventures with a local boy, much to the dismay of his snobbish mother.

"This comforting family story . . . [offers] . . . four marvelously appealing sisters, true childhood behavior . . ., and a writing style that will draw readers close." Booklist

Birney, Betty G.

The seven wonders of Sassafras Springs; written by Betty Birney; illustrated by Matt Phelan. 1st ed. Atheneum Books for Young Readers 2005 210p il $16.95 (3-6) **Fic**

1. Country life—Fiction 2. Family life—Fiction
ISBN 0-689-87136-8   LC 2004-11399

Eben McAllister searches his small town to see if he can find anything comparable to the real Seven Wonders of the World.

"Black-and-white sketches enhance the text and its folksy character. Perfect for reading aloud." SLJ

Björk, Christina

Linnea in Monet's garden; text, Christina Björk; drawings, Lena Anderson. R & S Bks. 1987 52p il $14 (3-5) **Fic**

1. Monet, Claude, 1840-1926—Fiction 2. Paris (France)—Fiction
ISBN 91-29-58314-4   LC 87-45163

Also available Spanish language edition
Original Swedish edition, 1985

"Linnea and her elderly friend Mr. Bloom travel to Paris, visit Monet's home in Giverny, picnic in the artist's garden, and admire the waterlilies and the Japanese bridge which he often painted. In Paris, the two companions stop at a museum to see Impressionist paintings, view the sunlight over the Seine, and chatter about the life and times of the artist. The book ends with a page of information about things to do and see in Paris." SLJ

"In addition to the long but smooth text peppered with dialogue are photographs of Monet's paintings, house, and family as well as colorful drawings of the little girl's excursion. . . . A splendid way to introduce children to impressionism and to the man behind the masterpieces." Booklist

Vendela in Venice; pictures by Inga-Karin Eriksson; translated by Patricia Crampton. R & S Bks. 1999 93p il $18 (4 and up) **Fic**

1. Venice (Italy)—Fiction
ISBN 91-296-4559-X   LC 98-49243

Originally published in Sweden

On a visit to Venice with her father, Vendela experiences the richness and beauty of the city and its palaces, gondolas, and statues

"The illustrations comprise Inga-Karin Eriksson's beautifully composed paintings, photographs, maps, and sketches. Asides and appendixes add to the book's value as source and, since they are all written in the same winsome style, will increase the reader's delight." Booklist

Blackwood, Gary L.

Second sight; [by] Gary Blackwood. Dutton 2005 279p $16.99 (5 and up) **Fic**

1. Lincoln, Abraham, 1809-1865—Fiction 2. United States—History—1861-1865, Civil War—Fiction 3. Washington (D.C.)—Fiction 4. Clairvoyance—Fiction
ISBN 0-525-47481-1

In Washington, D.C., during the last days of the Civil War, a teenage boy who performs in a mind reading act befriends a clairvoyant girl whose frightening visions foreshadow an assassination plot.

"This is a well-researched, engrossing story grounded in historical detail." SLJ

The Shakespeare stealer; [by] Gary Blackwood. Dutton Children's Bks. 1998 216p $15.99; pa $5.99 (5 and up) **Fic**

1. Shakespeare, William, 1564-1616—Fiction 2. Theater—Fiction 3. Orphans—Fiction 4. Great Britain—History—1485-1603, Tudors—Fiction
ISBN 0-525-45863-8; 0-14-130595-9 (pa)
LC 97-42987

A young orphan boy is ordered by his master to infiltrate Shakespeare's acting troupe in order to steal the script of "Hamlet," but he discovers instead the meaning of friendship and loyalty

"Wry humor, cliffhanger chapter endings, and a plucky protagonist make this a fitting introduction to Shakespeare's world." Horn Book

Other titles in this series are:
Shakespeare's scribe (2000)
Shakespeare's spy (2003)

Bledsoe, Lucy Jane

Cougar canyon. Holiday House 2001 130p $16.95 (4 and up) **Fic**

1. Pumas—Fiction 2. Wildlife conservation—Fiction 3. Mexican Americans—Fiction
ISBN 0-8234-1599-6   LC 2001-16718

After hearing that people are planning to kill a mountain lion in the wilds near her neighborhood, twelve-year-old Izzie decides that it is her duty to protect the animal

"An entertaining adventure story with fast-paced action and a strong female protagonist." SLJ

Blegvad, Lenore

Kitty and Mr. Kipling; neighbors in Vermont; illustrated by Erik Blegvad. 1st ed. Margaret K. McElderry Books 2005 131p il $16.95 (3-5)

Fic

1. Kipling, Rudyard, 1865-1936—Fiction 2. Vermont—Fiction 3. Friendship—Fiction 4. Authorship—Fiction

ISBN 0-689-87363-8   LC 2004-4143

In 1892, eight-year-old Kitty learns about writing and the world beyond her Dummerston, Vermont, home when she befriends her new neighbors, author Rudyard Kipling and his family, who have recently arrived from England.

"Erik Blegvad's soft drawings give readers a good sense of time and place. . . . This is a fast read, and a good recommendation for those looking for historical fiction for younger readers." SLJ

Blos, Joan W.

A gathering of days: a New England girl's journal, 1830-32; a novel. Scribner 1979 144p $16.95; pa $4.99 (6 and up)   **Fic**

1. New Hampshire—Fiction

ISBN 0-684-16340-3; 0-689-71419-X (pa)

LC 79-16898

Awarded the Newbery Medal, 1980

The journal of a 14-year-old girl, kept the last year she lived on the family farm, records daily events in her small New Hampshire town, her father's remarriage, and the death of her best friend

"The 'simple' life on the farm is not facilely idealized, the larger issues of the day are felt . . . but it is the small moments between parent and child, friend and friend that are at the fore, and the core, of this low-key, intense, and reflective book." SLJ

Blume, Judy

Are you there God?, it's me, Margaret. rev format ed. Atheneum 2001 c1970 149p $17.95 (5 and up)   **Fic**

1. Religion—Fiction

ISBN 0-689-84158-2

Also available in paperback from Dell

A reissue of the first published 1970 by Bradbury Press

A "story about the emotional, physical, and spiritual ups and downs experienced by 12-year-old Margaret, child of a Jewish-Protestant union." Natl Counc of Teach of Engl. Adventuring with Books. 2d edition

"The writing style is lively, the concerns natural, and the problems are treated with both humor and sympathy, but the story is intense in its emphasis on the four girls' absorption in, and discussions of, menstruation and brassieres." Bull Cent Child Books

Freckle juice; illustrated by Sonia O. Lisker. Four Winds Press 1971 40p il lib bdg $17.95 (2-4)

Fic

ISBN 0-02-711690-5

Also available in paperback from Dell

"A gullible second-grader pays 50¢ for a recipe to grow freckles." Best Books for Child

"Spontaneous humor, sure to appeal to the youngest reader." Horn Book

Otherwise known as Sheila the Great. Dutton 1972 188p pa $5.99 hardcover o.p. (4-6)

Fic

1. Fear—Fiction

ISBN 0-525-36455-2 (pa)

Ten-year-old Sheila is secretly afraid of dogs, spiders, bees, ghosts and the dark. When she and her family leave New York for their summer home, she has to face up to her problems

"An unusual and merry treatment of the fears of a young girl. . . . This is a truly appealing book in which the author makes her points without a single preachy word." Publ Wkly

Tales of a fourth grade nothing. Dutton Children's Books 2002 c1972 120p $15.99 (3-6)

Fic

1. Brothers—Fiction 2. Family life—Fiction

ISBN 0-525-46931-1

Also available in paperback from Puffin Bks.

A reissue of the title first published 1972

"Jacket illustration c2002 by Peter Reynolds."

This story describes the trials and tribulations of nine-year-old Peter Hatcher who is saddled with a pesky two-year-old brother named Fudge who is constantly creating trouble, messing things up, and monopolizing their parents' attention. Things come to a climax when Fudge gets at Peter's pet turtle

"The episode structure makes the book a good choice for reading aloud." Saturday Rev

Other titles about Peter and Fudge are:

Double Fudge (2002)

Fudge-a-mania (1990)

Superfudge (1980)

Bode, N. E.

The Anybodies. HarperCollins 2004 276p il $15.99; lib bdg $16.89 (5 and up)   **Fic**

1. Magic—Fiction

ISBN 0-06-055735-4; 0-06-055736-2 (lib bdg)

After learning that she is not the biological daughter of boring Mr. and Mrs. Drudger, Fern embarks on magical adventures with her real father and finally finds "a place that feels like home."

"The writing is fluid, the characters are multifaceted, and the situations range from poignant to gloriously silly. Eye-catching, black-and-white sketches echo the story's nuances and add to the atmosphere. There's laugh-out-loud humor, fantasy, mystery, real-life family drama." SLJ

Another title about these characters is:

The nobodies (2005)

Boles, Philana Marie

Little divas. Amistad 2006 164p $16.89 (5 and up)   **Fic**

1. African Americans—Fiction 2. Father-daughter relationship—Fiction 3. Divorce—Fiction 4. Cousins—Fiction

ISBN 0-06-073300-4

"Amistad"

The summer before seventh grade, Cassidy Carter must come to terms with living with her father, practical-

Boles, Philana Marie—*Continued*

ly a stranger, as well as her relationships with her cousins, all amidst the overall confusion of adolescence.

"Boles portrays this variable age well, and readers will feel for Cassidy's trials." SLJ

Boling, Katharine

January 1905. Harcourt 2004 170p $16 (5 and up) **Fic**

1. Twins—Fiction 2. Sisters—Fiction 3. Child labor—Fiction

ISBN 0-15-205119-8   LC 2003-24470

In a 1905 mill town, eleven-year-old twin sisters, Pauline, who goes to work with the rest of the family, and Arlene, whose crippled foot keeps her home doing the cooking, cleaning, and washing, are convinced that the other sister has an easier life until a series of incidents helps them see each other in a new light.

"This vivid account will draw readers into the period." Horn Book Guide

Bond, Michael

A bear called Paddington; with drawings by Peggy Fortnum. Houghton Mifflin 1998 c1958 128p il $15; pa $4.95 (2-5) **Fic**

1. Bears—Fiction 2. Great Britain—Fiction

ISBN 0-395-92951-2; 0-618-15071-4 (pa)

Picture books about Paddington for younger readers are also available

First published 1958 in the United Kingdom; first United States edition 1960

"Mr. and Mrs. Brown first met Paddington on a railway platform in London. Noticing the sign on his neck reading 'Please look after this bear. Thank you,' they decided to do just that. From there on home was never the same though the Brown children were delighted." Publ Wkly

Other titles about Paddington Bear are:
More about Paddington
Paddington abroad
Paddington at large
Paddington at work
Paddington goes to town
Paddington helps out
Paddington marches on
Paddington on screen
Paddington on stage
Paddington on top
Paddington takes the air
Paddington takes the test
Paddington takes to TV
Paddington treasury

Bond, Nancy

A string in the harp. Atheneum Pubs. 1976 370p il $19.95; pa $5.99 (6 and up) **Fic**

1. Taliesin—Fiction 2. Fantasy fiction 3. Wales—Fiction

ISBN 0-689-50036-X; 0-689-80445-8 (pa)
      LC 75-28181

"A Margaret K. McElderry book"

"Present-day realism and the fantasy world of sixth-century Taliesin meet in an absorbing novel set in Wales.

The story centers around the Morgans—Jen, Peter, Becky, and their father—their adjustment to another country, their mother's death, and especially, Peter's bitter despair, which threatens them all." LC. Child Books, 1976

Bonk, John J.

Dustin Grubbs; one-man show; [by] John J. Bonk. 1st ed. Little, Brown and Co. 2005 243p $15.99 (5 and up) **Fic**

1. School stories 2. Theater—Fiction

ISBN 0-316-15636-1   LC 2004021268

A sixth-grader, who longs to see his name in lights, recounts life at Buttermilk Falls Elementary in preparation for the school drama production.

"There are plenty of hilarious scenes, occasionally interrupted by thoughtful, bittersweet moments; and everything is wrapped up with a very satisfying ending." Booklist

Another title about Dustin Grubbs is:
Dustin Grubbs: take two (2006)

Bonners, Susan

Edwina victorious; story and pictures by Susan Bonners. Farrar, Straus & Giroux 2000 131p il $16 (3-5) **Fic**

1. Letter writing—Fiction 2. Political activists—Fiction

ISBN 0-374-31968-5   LC 00-24229

Edwina follows in the footsteps of her namesake great-aunt when she begins to write letters to the mayor about community problems and poses as Edwina the elder

"Occasional soft cartoon drawings bring the characters and town to life. This charming tale is an easy fit for lessons on social activism, letter writing, and even plagiarism." SLJ

Borden, Louise

Across the blue Pacific; a World War II story; illustrated by Robert Andrew Parker. Houghton Mifflin 2006 unp il $17 (2-5) **Fic**

1. World War, 1939-1945—Fiction

ISBN 0-618-33922-1   LC 2004-9206

A woman reminisces about her neighbor's son who was the object of a letter writing campaign by some fourth-graders when he went away to war in 1943.

"Beautifully written in an understated tone, the story offers a believable picture of life during the war. . . . Restrained yet expressive, the artwork conveys moods and mindsets as well as a strong sense of the time and place." Booklist

The greatest skating race; a World War II story from the Netherlands; illustrated by Niki Daly. Margaret K. McElderry Books 2004 44p il $18.95 (2-5) **Fic**

1. World War, 1939-1945—Fiction 2. Netherlands—Fiction 3. Ice skating—Fiction

ISBN 0-689-84502-2   LC 2002-12040

During World War II in the Netherlands, a ten-year-old boy's dream of skating in a famous race allows him

Borden, Louise—*Continued*

to help two children escape to Belgium by ice skating past German soldiers and other enemies.

"Told with immediacy and suspense. . . . The gorgeously detailed watercolor illustrations capture a sense of the time. The subdued, winter hues of brown and smoky gray are those often found in the oil paintings of Dutch and Flemish masters and match the quiet tone of the text." SLJ

The last day of school; written by Louise Borden; illustrated by Adam Gustavson. 1st ed. Margaret K. McElderry Books 2005 unp il $15.95 (2-4)   **Fic**

1. School stories 2. Gifts—Fiction
ISBN 0-689-86869-3   LC 2003025124

Matthew Perez, the official timekeeper of Mrs. Mallory's third-grade class, has a special goodbye gift for her.

"Varied sizes of colorful oil illustrations accompany the tale of Matts patient delivery of the perfect gift. True to a childs remembrance of final school days, each page recalls memorable moments for students and teachers." SLJ

Bornstein, Ruth Lercher

Butterflies and lizards, Beryl and me. Marshall Cavendish 2002 144p $14.95 (4 and up)   **Fic**

1. Great Depression, 1929-1939—Fiction
2. Missouri—Fiction
ISBN 0-7614-5118-8   LC 2001-47473

In 1934, eleven-year-old Charlotte and her mother move to tiny Valley Junction, Missouri, where Charlotte befriends an eccentric old woman in spite of her mother's and others' warnings

"The characters are drawn with aching truth." Booklist

Boston, L. M. (Lucy Maria)

The children of Green Knowe; illustrated by Peter Boston. Harcourt 2002 c1954 183p il $17; pa $6 (4-6)   **Fic**

1. Fantasy fiction 2. Great Britain—Fiction
ISBN 0-15-202462-X; 0-15-202468-9 (pa)
LC 2001-51806

First published 1954 in the United Kingdom
"An Odyssey/Harcourt young classic"

Tolly comes to live with his great-grandmother at the ancient house of Green Knowe and becomes friends with three children who lived there in the seventeenth century.

"A special book for the imaginative child, in which mood predominates and fantasy and realism are skillfully blended." Booklist

Other titles about Green Knowe are:
An enemy of Green Knowe (c1976)
The river of Green Knowe (c1959)
A stranger of Green Knowe (c1961)
The treasure of Green Knowe (c1958)

Bowdish, Lynea

Brooklyn, Bugsy, and me; pictures by Nancy Carpenter. Farrar, Straus & Giroux 2000 83p il $15 (3-5)   **Fic**

1. Grandfathers—Fiction 2. Moving—Fiction
3. Brooklyn (New York, N.Y.)—Fiction
ISBN 0-374-30993-0   LC 99-36267

In 1953 nine-year-old Sam moves with his mother from West Virginia to Brooklyn and finds that his grandfather, a well-liked neighborhood character nicknamed Bugsy, does not seem to want him in his life

"Short, easy reading that is both well developed and satisfying." Horn Book Guide

Bower, Tamara

How the Amazon queen fought the prince of Egypt; written and illustrated by Tamara Bower. 1st ed. Atheneum Books for Young Readers 2005 40p il $16.95 (3-6)   **Fic**

1. Assyria—Fiction 2. Amazons—Fiction 3. Sex role—Fiction 4. Egypt—Fiction
ISBN 0-689-84434-4   LC 2004-1781

Serpot leads her Amazon warriors in battle against Prince Pedikhons of Egypt, who has come to see for himself if women can equal men, even in battle.

"Inspired by Egyptian and Assyrian art, the striking watercolor-and-gouache illustrations emulate ancient reliefs and feature rich, saturated earth colors. . . . Excellent appended notes provide historical background and information about the hieroglyphs and symbols. . . . This slender offering will enrich ancient-civilization collections and attract budding Egyptologists as well." Booklist

Includes bibliographical references

Bradley, Kimberly Brubaker

The President's daughter; [by] Kimberly Brubaker Bradley. Delacorte Press 2004 166p $15.95; lib bdg $17.99 (3-5)   **Fic**

1. Derby, Ethel Roosevelt, 1891-1977—Fiction
2. Roosevelt, Theodore, 1858-1919—Fiction
3. Presidents—Fiction
ISBN 0-385-73147-7; 0-385-90179-8 (lib bdg)
LC 2003-19018

A fictionalized account of ten-year-old Ethel Roosevelt's early experiences in the White House after her father, Theodore Roosevelt, becomes president in 1901.

"Loaded with historical details . . . the novel rings true and the people come to life." SLJ

Ruthie's gift; illustrated by Dave Kramer. Delacorte Press 1998 150p il $14.95; pa $4.50 (3-5)   **Fic**

1. Farm life—Fiction 2. Family life—Fiction
3. Siblings—Fiction 4. Indiana—Fiction
ISBN 0-385-32525-8; 0-440-41405-9 (pa)
LC 97-19396

Just before the beginning of World War I, eight-year-old Ruthie, who lives with her parents and six brothers on a farm in Indiana, wishes for a sister and tries to behave like the lady her mother wants her to be

"Brisk pacing, affectionate humor and an unforgettable heroine." Publ Wkly

Bradley, Kimberly Brubaker—*Continued*

Weaver's daughter. Delacorte Press 2000 166p $14.95 (4 and up) **Fic**

1. Asthma—Fiction 2. Frontier and pioneer life—Fiction 3. Tennessee—Fiction

ISBN 0-385-32769-2   LC 00-26193

In 1791 after her family's journey from Pennsylvania, ten-year-old Lizzie suffers from the disease of asthma in her new home in the Southwest Territory (present-day Tennessee)

"Lizzy's a sympathetic heroine who faces uncertainty with aplomb. This well-developed story also offers insight into early medical practices." Horn Book Guide

Branford, Henrietta

Fire, bed, & bone. Candlewick Press 1998 122p $16.99 (5 and up) **Fic**

1. Dogs—Fiction 2. Middle Ages—Fiction 3. Great Britain—History—1154-1399, Plantagenets—Fiction

ISBN 0-7636-0338-4   LC 97-17491

In 1381 in England, a hunting dog recounts what happens to his beloved master Rufus and his family when they are arrested on suspicion of being part of the peasants' rebellion led by Wat Tyler and the preacher John Ball

"The dog's observant eye, sympathetic personality, and courageous acts hook the reader into what is both irresistible adventure and educational historical fiction." Booklist

Bredsdorff, Bodil

The Crow-girl; the children of Crow Cove; translated from the Danish by Faith Ingwersen. Farrar Straus Giroux 2004 155p map $16 (4 and up) **Fic**

1. Orphans—Fiction 2. Grandmothers—Fiction 3. Denmark—Fiction

ISBN 0-374-31247-8   LC 2003-49310

Original Danish editon, 1993

After the death of her grandmother, a young orphaned girl leaves her house by the cove and begins a journey which leads her to people and experiences that exemplify the wisdom her grandmother had shared with her

"Touching on universal themes, this quiet adventure story has the depth and flavor of a tale from long ago and far away." SLJ

Brink, Carol Ryrie

Caddie Woodlawn; illustrated by Trina Schart Hyman. Macmillan 1973 275p il $17.95; pa $5.99 (4-6) **Fic**

1. Frontier and pioneer life—Fiction 2. Wisconsin—Fiction

ISBN 0-02-713670-1; 0-689-71370-3 (pa)

Awarded the Newbery Medal, 1936

First published 1935

Caddie Woodlawn was eleven in 1864. Because she was frail, she had been allowed to grow up a tomboy. Her capacity for adventure was practically limitless, and there was plenty of adventure on the Wisconsin frontier in those days. The story covers one year of life on the pioneer farm, closing with the news that Mr. Woodlawn

had inherited an estate in England, and the unanimous decision of the family to stay in Wisconsin. Based upon the reminiscences of the author's grandmother

The typeface "is eminently clear and readable, and the illustrations in black and white . . . are attractive and expressive." Wis Libr Bull

Broach, Elise

Shakespeare's secret; [by] Elise Broach. Henry Holt 2005 250p il $16.95 (5 and up) **Fic**

1. Mystery fiction

ISBN 0-8050-7387-6   LC 2004-54020

Named after a character in a Shakespeare play, misfit sixth-grader Hero becomes interested in exploring this unusual connection because of a valuable diamond supposedly hidden in her new house, an intriguing neighbor, and the unexpected attention of the most popular boy in school.

"The mystery alone will engage readers. . . . The main characters are all well developed, and the dialogue is both realistic and well planned." SLJ

Brockmeier, Kevin

Grooves; a kind of mystery; [by] Kevin Brockmeier. 1st ed. Katherine Tegen Books 2006 199p $15.99; lib bdg $16.89 (4 and up) **Fic**

1. Jeans (Clothing)—Fiction 2. Factories—Fiction 3. Mystery fiction

ISBN 0-06-073691-7; 0-06-073692-5 (lib bdg)

LC 2004-22683

After seventh-grader Dwayne Ruggles discovers that the grooves in his Thigpen-brand blue jeans are encoded with a cry for help, he sets out to save the factory workers from greedy entrepreneur Howard Thigpen.

"Brockmeier constructs a frothy, fanciful, and entertaining blend of science fiction and mystery." Booklist

Brooks, Bruce

Everywhere. Harper & Row 1990 70p lib bdg $16.89 (4 and up) **Fic**

1. Grandfathers—Fiction 2. Death—Fiction

ISBN 0-06-020729-9   LC 90-4073

Afraid that his beloved grandfather will die after suffering a heart attack, a nine-year-old boy agrees to join ten-year-old Dooley in performing a mysterious ritual called soul switching

"Echoes of the great Southern writers with their themes of loneliness and faith can be heard in this masterly novella. . . . Brooks's precise use of language is a tour de force." Horn Book

Brooks, Walter R.

Freddy the detective; illustrated by Kurt Wiese. Overlook Press 1997 256p il $23.95; pa $7.99 (3-5) **Fic**

1. Pigs—Fiction 2. Mystery fiction

ISBN 0-87951-809-X; 0-14-131234-3 (pa)

LC 97-10214

A reissue of the title first published 1932 by Knopf

Brooks, Walter R.—*Continued*

Freddy the pig does some detective work in order to solve the mystery of a missing toy train

"This book will be great fun for all who have not outgrown the gift of fitting becoming personalities to our animal friends." N Y Her Trib Books

Other titles about Freddy are:

Freddy and Mr. Camphor (1944)

Freddy and the baseball team from Mars (1955)

Freddy and the bean home news (1943)

Freddy and the dragon (1958)

Freddy and the ignormus (1941)

Freddy and the space ship (1953)

Freddy goes to Florida (1949) First published 1927 with title: To and again

Freddy goes to the North Pole (1951) First published 1930 with title: More to and again

Freddy the pilot (1952)

Freddy the politician (1948) First published 1939 with title: Wiggins for President

Brown, Jackie

Little Cricket. Hyperion Bks. for Children 2004 252p $15.99 (4-6)   **Fic**

1. Hmong (Asian people)—Fiction 2. Immigrants—Fiction 3. Minnesota—Fiction

ISBN 0-786-81852-2

After the upheaval of the Vietnam War reaches them, twelve-year-old Kia and her Hmong family flee from the mountains of Laos to a refugee camp in Thailand and eventually to the alien world of Saint Paul, Minnesota.

"Brown's debut is both a gripping survival story and a gentle, heart-wrenching portrait of an immigrant family." Booklist

Bruchac, Joseph

The arrow over the door; pictures by James Watling. Dial Bks. for Young Readers 1998 89p il $15.99; pa $4.99 (4-6)   **Fic**

1. Native Americans—Fiction 2. Society of Friends—Fiction 3. United States—History—1775-1783, Revolution—Fiction

ISBN 0-8037-2078-5; 0-14-130571-1 (pa)

LC 96-36701

"In this fictionalized account of a Quaker assembly's encounter with a band of Indian scouts in service to King George's Loyalists, Bruchac alternates the viewpoints of fourteen-year-old Samuel Russell and his Abenaki counterpart, Stands Straight." Bull Cent Child Books

"Bruchac's elegant and powerful writing fills in much of the fascinating detail of this serendipitous wartime friendship. . . . Watling's rugged, textured pen-and-ink drawings provide an atmospheric backdrop." Publ Wkly

Children of the longhouse. Dial Bks. for Young Readers 1996 150p $14.99; pa $5.99 (4 and up)
Fic

1. Mohawk Indians—Fiction 2. Siblings—Fiction 3. Twins—Fiction

ISBN 0-8037-1793-8; 0-14-038504-5 (pa)

LC 95-11344

Eleven-year-old Ohkwa'ri and his twin sister Otsi:stia must make peace with a hostile gang of older boys in their Mohawk village during the late 1400s

"This is a fascinating story that will leave the middle-grade reader with an appreciation for Mohawk culture." Book Rep

The dark pond; illustrations by Sally Wern Comport. 1st ed. HarperCollins 2004 142p il $15.99; lib bdg $16.89 (5 and up)   **Fic**

1. Ponds—Fiction 2. Monsters—Fiction 3. Shawnee Indians—Fiction

ISBN 0-06-052995-4; 0-06-052997-0 (lib bdg)

LC 2003-22212

After he feels a mysterious pull drawing him toward a dark, shadowy pond in the woods, Armie looks to old Native American tales for guidance about the dangerous monster lurking in the water

"Effectively illustrated by Comport, this eerie story skillfully entwines Native American lore, suspense, and the realization that people and things are not always what they seem to be on the surface. . . . A perfect choice for reluctant readers." SLJ

Skeleton man. HarperCollins Pubs. 2001 114p il $15.99; lib bdg $16.89; pa $4.99 (4 and up)
Fic

1. Kidnapping—Fiction 2. Mohawk Indians—Fiction

ISBN 0-06-029075-7; 0-06-029076-5 (lib bdg); 0-06-440888-4 (pa)   LC 00-54345

After her parents disappear and she is turned over to the care of a strange "great-uncle," Molly must rely on her dreams about an old Mohawk story for her safety and maybe even for her life

"The mix of traditional and contemporary cultural references adds to the story's haunting appeal, and the quick pace and suspense . . . will likely hold the interest of young readers." Publ Wkly

Another title about Skeleton man is:

The return of Skeleton man (2006)

Whisper in the dark; illustrations by Sally Wern Comport. 1st ed. HarperCollins Pub. 2005 174p il $15.99; lib bdg $16.89 (5 and up)   **Fic**

1. Narragansett Indians—Fiction 2. Traffic accidents—Fiction 3. Horror fiction 4. Rhode Island—Fiction

ISBN 0-06-058087-9; 0-06-058088-7 (lib bdg)

LC 2004-22561

An ancient and terrifying Narragansett native-American legend begins to come true for a teenage long-distance runner, whose recovery from the accident that killed her parents has stunned everyone, including her guardian aunt in Providence, Rhode Island.

"This fast-paced, macabre novel is perfect for reluctant readers." SLJ

The winter people. Dial Bks. 2002 168p $16.99; pa $5.99 (5 and up)   **Fic**

1. Abnaki Indians—Fiction 2. United States—History—1755-1763, French and Indian War—Fiction

ISBN 0-8037-2694-5; 0-14-240229-X (pa)

LC 2002-338

As the French and Indian War rages in October of 1759, Saxso, a fourteen-year-old Abenaki boy, pursues the English rangers who have attacked his village and taken his mother and sisters hostage

"The narrative itself is thrilling, its spiritual aspects enlightening." Booklist

Buchanan, Jane

Goodbye, Charley; [by] Jane Buchanan. 1st ed. Farrar Straus Giroux 2004 165p $16 (5 and up) **Fic**

1. World War, 1939-1945—Fiction 2. Monkeys—Fiction 3. Family life—Fiction 4. Massachusetts—Fiction

ISBN 0-374-35020-5   LC 2003-61054

In 1943, twelve-year-old Celie's father brings home a rhesus monkey that helps Celie deal with all the difficulties that the war has brought into her life in Gloucester, Massachusetts.

"An engaging, insightful novel that weaves timeless themes into a historical setting." Booklist

Buckley-Archer, Linda

Gideon the cutpurse; being the first part of the Gideon trilogy; [by] Linda Buckley-Archer. 1st U.S. ed. Simon & Schuster Books for Young Readers 2006 404p $17.95 (5 and up)   **Fic**

1. Science fiction 2. Thieves—Fiction 3. Great Britain—History—1714-1837—Fiction

ISBN 9781416915256   LC 2006042204

Ignored by his father and sent to Derbyshire for the weekend, twelve-year-old Peter and his new friend, Kate, are accidentally transported back in time to 1763 England where they are befriended by a reformed cutpurse

"This wonderfully rich and complex novel, written in lyrical and vivid language, is destined to be a classic." SLJ

Bulla, Clyde Robert

The Paint Brush Kid; illustrated by Ellen Beier. Random House 1999 64p il lib bdg $11.99; pa $3.99 (2-4)   **Fic**

1. Artists—Fiction 2. Mexican Americans—Fiction

ISBN 0-679-99282-0 (lib bdg); 0-679-89282-6 (pa)
LC 97-51153

"A Stepping Stone book"

Nine-year-old Gregory paints pictures representing the life of the Mexican American old man known as Uncle Pancho and attempts to save him from losing his house

"The conclusion is realistic—satisfying, yet containing some unresolved conflict." Horn Book Guide

The sword in the tree; illustrated by Paul Galdone. Crowell 1956 113p il lib bdg $15.89; pa $4.25 (3-5)   **Fic**

1. Arthur, King—Fiction 2. Knights and knighthood—Fiction

ISBN 0-690-79909-8 (lib bdg); 0-064-42132-5 (pa)

A story of England in King Arthur's days. Shan, the son of Lord Weldon, takes on the duties of a knight and seeks redress against his uncle, who had usurped his father's rights. A picture of the Knights of the Round Table and King Arthur develops

"A good story for beginning readers, this is also excellent for the older child who is a slow reader, because of the stimulating combination of exciting adventure, short sentences, and easy vocabulary." N Y Times Book Rev

Bunting, Eve

Blackwater. HarperCollins Pubs. 1999 146p lib bdg $15.89; pa $5.99 (5 and up)   **Fic**

1. Death—Fiction 2. Guilt—Fiction

ISBN 0-06-027843-9 (lib bdg); 0-06-440890-6 (pa)
LC 99-24895

"Joanna Cotler books"

When a boy and girl are drowned in the Blackwater River, thirteen-year-old Brodie must decide whether to confess that he may have caused the accident

"Bunting's thought-provoking theme, solid characterization and skillful juggling of suspense and pathos make this a top-notch choice." Publ Wkly

Nasty, stinky sneakers. HarperCollins Pubs. 1994 105p $15.95; lib bdg $15.89; pa $4.99 (4-6)   **Fic**

ISBN 0-06-024236-1; 0-06-024237-X (lib bdg); 0-06-440507-9 (pa)   LC 93-34641

Will ten-year-old Colin find his missing stinky sneakers in time to enter The Stinkiest Sneakers in the World contest?

"A fast-paced, funny book that should elicit some delighted groans." Horn Book Guide

Some frog! illustrated by Scott Medlock. Harcourt Brace & Co. 1998 unp il $15 (2-4)   **Fic**

1. Father-son relationship—Fiction 2. Divorce—Fiction

ISBN 0-15-277082-8   LC 96-24844

Billy is disappointed when his father doesn't show up to help him catch a frog for the frog-jumping competition at school, but the one he and his mother catch wins the championship and Billy begins to accept his father's absence

"The author does an excellent job of presenting a realistic situation and its resolution in straightforward yet eloquent prose. Medlock's bright oil illustrations appear on almost every page, adroitly mirroring the child's emotions and the contest events." SLJ

Spying on Miss Müller. Clarion Bks. 1995 179p $15 (5 and up)   **Fic**

1. World War, 1939-1945—Fiction 2. School stories 3. Ireland—Fiction

ISBN 0-395-69172-9   LC 94-15003

Also available in paperback from Fawcett Bks.

At Alveara boarding school in Belfast at the start of World War II, thirteen-year-old Jessie must deal with her suspicions about a teacher whose father was German and with her worries about her own father's drinking problem

"A thoughtful, moving coming-of-age novel. Jessie and her world . . . are portrayed with page-turning immediacy." Horn Book

Burch, Robert

Ida Early comes over the mountain. Viking 1980 145p pa $4.99 hardcover o.p. (4 and up)   **Fic**

1. Great Depression, 1929-1939—Fiction 2. Country life—Fiction 3. Georgia—Fiction

ISBN 0-14-034534-5 (pa)   LC 79-20532

Burch, Robert—*Continued*

"Set in the mountains of rural Georgia during the Depression. Ida Early arrives one day to the motherless Sutton family of four children. Mr. Sutton agrees to hire her as a temporary housekeeper." Interracial Books Child Bull

"The book works on two levels—the hilarious account of Ida Early's exotic housekeeping in which real cleverness and skill is as effective and amazing as any fantasy magic, and the gentle, touching story of an ungainly woman's longing for beauty and femininity. . . . [A] fine book." SLJ

Another title about Ida Early is:
Christmas with Ida Early (1983)

Queenie Peavy; illustrated by Jerry Lazare. Viking 1966 159p il pa $5.99 hardcover o.p. (5 and up) **Fic**
1. Georgia—Fiction
ISBN 0-14-032305-8 (pa)

"Defiant, independent and intelligent, 13-year-old Queenie idolized her father who was in jail and was neglected by her mother who had to work all the time. Growing up in the [Depression] 1930's in Georgia, Queenie eventually understands her father's real character, herself and her relationships to those about her." Wis Libr Bull

"Queenie is so real that the reader becomes deeply involved in everything that concerns her." Horn Book

Burgess, Melvin

Kite. Farrar, Straus & Giroux 2000 c1997 181p $16 (5 and up) **Fic**
1. Birds—Fiction 2. Endangered species—Fiction 3. Great Britain—Fiction
ISBN 0-374-34228-8 LC 99-46872
First published 1997 in the United Kingdom

Although the landowner for whom his father works as a gamekeeper hates all birds of prey, Taylor and his friend raise an endangered red kite in secret

"Burgess offers a compellingly detailed view of a way of life and ways of thinking that may attract young naturalists." Bull Cent Child Books

Burnett, Frances Hodgson

A little princess (4-6) **Fic**
1. School stories 2. Great Britain—Fiction
Available from various publishers, including a HarperCollins paperback edition illustrated by Tasha Tudor
First American edition published 1892 by Scribner in shorter form with title: Sara Crewe

The story of Sara Crewe, a girl who is sent from India to a boarding school in London, left in poverty by her father's death, and rescued by a mysterious benefactor

"The story is inevitably adorned with sentimental curlicues but the reader will hardly notice them since the story itself is such a satisfying one. Tasha Tudor's gentle, appropriate illustrations make this a lovely edition." Publ Wkly

The secret garden (4-6) **Fic**
1. Gardens—Fiction 2. Great Britain—Fiction
Some editions are:

Books of Wonder $21.95 Illustrated by Saelig Gallagher (ISBN 0-688-14582-5)
HarperCollins Pubs. lib bdg $14.89; pa $3.50 Illustrated by Tasha Tudor; 0-397-32162-7; 0-06-440-188-X)
Knopf (Everyman's library children's classics) $14.95 illustrated by Charles Robinson (ISBN 0-679-42309-5)
First published 1909 by Stokes

"Neglected by his father because of his mother's death at his birth, Colin lives the life of a spoilt and incurable invalid until, on the arrival of an orphaned cousin, the two children secretly combine to restore his mother's locked garden and Colin to health and his father's affection." Four to Fourteen

Burns, Khephra

Mansa Musa; the lion of Mali; illustrated by Leo & Diane Dillon. Harcourt 2001 unp il $18 (4 and up) **Fic**
1. Musa, d. 1337—Fiction 2. Mali—Fiction
ISBN 0-15-200375-4 LC 97-50559
"Gulliver books"

A fictional account of the nomadic wanderings of the boy who grew up to become Mali's great fourteenth-century leader, Mansa Musa

This is "part coming-of-age tale, part cautionary tale, and part fairy tale. . . . Burn's story moves in a languid magical atmosphere beautifully supported by the Dillons' jewel-like illustrations and stylized text ornaments, which, together with parchment-colored pages, give the impression of an illuminated manuscript." Horn Book

Butterworth, Oliver

The enormous egg; illustrated by Louis Darling. Little, Brown 1956 187p il pa $6.99 hardcover o.p. (4 and up) **Fic**
1. Dinosaurs—Fiction
ISBN 0-316-11920-2 (pa)

"Up in Freedom, New Hampshire, one of the Twitchell's hens laid a remarkable egg. . . . Six weeks later when a live dinosaur hatched from the egg, the hen was dazed and upset, the Twitchells dumbfounded, and the scientific world went crazy. Twelve-year-old Nate who had taken care of the egg and made a pet out of the triceratops tells of the hullabaloo." Booklist

This story is "great fun. . . . And if you have any trouble visualizing a Triceratops moving placidly through the twentieth-century world you need only turn to Louis Darling's illustrations to believe." NY Times Book Rev

Byars, Betsy Cromer

The burning questions of Bingo Brown; [by] Betsy Byars. Viking 1988 166p pa $5.99 hardcover o.p. (4 and up) **Fic**
1. School stories
ISBN 0-14-032479-8 (pa) LC 87-21022
Also available Spanish language edition

A boy is puzzled by the comic and confusing questions of youth and worried by disturbing insights into adult conflicts

"A fully worked out novel. . . . Readers will recognize the pitfalls, agonies, and joys of elementary school life in this book. . . . The short chapters and comic style are designed to appeal to young readers and to move them right into other books." Christ Sci Monit

Byars, Betsy Cromer—*Continued*

Other titles about Bingo Brown are:

Bingo Brown and the language of love (1989)

Bingo Brown, gypsy lover (1990)

Bingo Brown's guide to romance (1992)

Cracker Jackson; [by] Betsy Byars. Viking Kestrel 1985 147p pa $5.99 hardcover o.p. (5 and up)   **Fic**

1. Wife abuse—Fiction 2. Child abuse—Fiction

ISBN 0-670-80546-7 (pa)   LC 84-24684

"Young Jackson discovers that his ex-baby sitter has been beaten by her husband; and, spurred by affection for her, the boy enlists his friend Goat to help drive her to a home for battered women. The pathetic story of Alma, with her adored baby, tidy home, and treasured collection of Barbie dolls, is relieved by flashbacks to the two boys' antics at school and by their hilarious, if potentially lethal, attempt to drive her to safety." Horn Book

"Suspense, danger, near-tragedy, heartbreak and tension-relieving, unwittingly comic efforts at seriously heroic action mark this as the best of middle-grade fiction to highlight the problems of wife-battering and child abuse." SLJ

The Cybil war; [by] Betsy Byars; illustrated by Gail Owens. Viking 1981 126p il pa $5.99 hardcover o.p. (4-6)   **Fic**

1. Friendship—Fiction

ISBN 0-14-034356-3 (pa)   LC 80-26912

"Simon is deeply smitten by Cybil, a fourth-grade classmate, and just as deeply angered by his once-closest friend Tony who persists in telling fibs to and about Cybil to strengthen his cause: Tony is also smitten by Cybil." Bull Cent Child Books

"In her gently comic style, Byars presents Simon and the other people in her . . . story (even nasty Tony) as subteens who are people dealing with real problems. . . . Owens has illustrated sympathetically, making up a book that readers will take to their hearts." Publ Wkly

The dark stairs; a Herculeah Jones mystery; by Betsy Byars. Viking 1994 130p $14.99; pa $5.99 (4 and up)   **Fic**

1. Mystery fiction

ISBN 0-670-85487-5; 0-14-036996-1 (pa)

LC 94-14012

The intrepid Herculeah Jones helps her mother, a private investigator, solve a puzzling and frightening case

"There is plenty to laugh at in this book, including classic chapter headings guaranteed to cause shivers for the uninitiated; practiced mystery readers may feel that they are in on a bit of a joke and appreciate the hint of parody. This is a page-turner that is sure to entice the most reluctant readers." SLJ

Other titles about Herculeah Jones are:

Dead letter (1996)

Death's door (1997)

Disappearing acts (1998)

King of murder (2006)

Tarot says beware (1995)

The house of wings; [by] Betsy Byars; illustrated by Daniel Schwartz. Viking 1972 142p il pa $5.99 hardcover o.p. (4-6)   **Fic**

1. Cranes (Birds)—Fiction 2. Grandfathers—Fiction

ISBN 0-14-031523-3 (pa)

"A young boy reeling from the pain of temporary parental abandonment forges a relationship with an eccentric grandfather whom he despises. In attempting to rescue and mend a wounded crane, they come to respect each other for what they are, and as men." Book World

This story "has an unsentimental and potent message about wildlife and draws a telling portrait of a human relationship. . . . The book's spare construction makes it strong." Saturday Rev

The keeper of the doves; by Betsy Byars. Viking 2002 121p $14.99; pa $5.99 (4 and up)   **Fic**

1. Sisters—Fiction 2. Family life—Fiction 3. Kentucky—Fiction

ISBN 0-670-03576-9; 0-14-240063-7 (pa)

LC 2002-9283

In the late 1800s in Kentucky, Amie McBee and her four sisters both fear and torment the reclusive and seemingly sinister Mr. Tominski, but their father continues to provide for his needs

"This is Byars at her best—witty, appealing, thought-provoking." Horn Book

Little Horse; [by] Betsy Byars; illustrated by David McPhail. Holt & Co. 2001 45p il $15.95 (1-3)   **Fic**

1. Horses—Fiction

ISBN 0-8050-6413-3   LC 00-40983

"An Early chapter book"

Little Horse falls into the stream and is swept away into a dangerous adventure and a new life

"Byars deftly combines crisp action with a lyrically evoked setting. Language is simple, but not simplistic; uncommon terms are clearly defined in the text and the soft black-and-white art." Horn Book Guide

Another title about Little Horse is:

Little Horse on his own (2004)

Me Tarzan; by Betsy Byars; illustrations by Bill Cigliano. HarperCollins Pubs. 2000 86p il $14.99 (3-5)   **Fic**

1. School stories 2. Acting—Fiction 3. Animals—Fiction

ISBN 0-06-028706-3   LC 99-34512

When Dorothy gets the part of Tarzan in the class play, her tremendous yell attracts the attention of increasingly larger and wilder animals

"This very funny story, peppered with likable characters and on-target dialogue, will delight readers." SLJ

The not-just-anybody family; [by] Betsy Byars; illustrated by Jacqueline Rogers. Delacorte Press 1986 149p il pa $5.50 hardcover o.p. (5 and up)   **Fic**

1. Siblings—Fiction 2. Family life—Fiction

ISBN 0-440-45951-6 (pa)   LC 85-16184

"It's an ordinary day in the Blossom family: Junior, with Maggie and Vernon watching, is poised to fly off the barn in homemade wings; Mom's on the rodeo cir-

Byars, Betsy Cromer—*Continued*

cuit; and Pap and his dog, Mud, are in town. By evening, Pap's in jail; Junior's in the hospital; Mud is gone; and Maggie helps Vernon break into jail to be with their grandfather." Publisher's note

"The story of the pathetically self-reliant, eccentric, but deeply loving family makes a book that is funny and sad, warm and wonderful." Horn Book

Other titles about the Blossom family are:

A Blossom promise (1987)

The Blossoms and the Green Phantom (1987)

The Blossoms meet the Vulture Lady (1986)

Wanted—Mud Blossom (1991)

The pinballs; [by] Betsy Byars. Harper & Row 1977 136p lib bdg $16.89; pa $5.99 (5 and up)
Fic

1. Foster home care—Fiction 2. Friendship—Fiction

ISBN 0-06-020918-6 (lib bdg); 0-06-440198-7 (pa)

"Pinballs go where they're pushed—and life's 'tilts' have thrown together three misfits. Suddenly finding themselves in a warm, loving foster home are Thomas J., eight, who is homeless now that his octogenarian twin guardians are hospitalized; Harvey, 13, whose mother ran off to a commune and whose hard-drinking father ran over him in a car; and Carlie, 15, who cannot get along with a succession of stepfathers—or the rest of the world, for that matter." SLJ

"A deceptively simple, eloquent story, its pain and acrimony constantly mitigated by the author's light, offhand style and by Carlie's wryly comic view of life." Horn Book

The SOS file; [by] Betsy Byars, Betsy Duffey, Laurie Myers; illustrated by Arthur Howard. Henry Holt 2004 71p il $15.95 (3-5)   **Fic**

1. School stories

ISBN 0-8050-6888-0   LC 2003-18240

The students in Mr. Magro's class submit stories for the SOS file about their biggest emergencies, and then they read them aloud for extra credit

"Some tales are poignant, others are humorous; all are as credible as the characters sketched. . . . Lighthearted sketches enhance characterization. . . . [An] engaging, plausible, and highly readable collection of anecdotes." SLJ

The summer of the swans; [by] Betsy Byars; illustrated by Ted CoConis. Viking 1970 142p il $15.99; pa $5.99 (5 and up)   **Fic**

1. Mentally handicapped children—Fiction 2. Siblings—Fiction

ISBN 0-670-68190-3; 0-14-031420-2 (pa)

Awarded the Newbery Medal, 1971

"The thoughts and feelings of a young girl troubled by a sense of inner discontent which she cannot explain are tellingly portrayed in the story of two summer days in the life of fourteen-year-old Sara Godfrey. Sara is jolted out of her self-pitying absorption with her own inadequacies by the disappearance of her ten-year-old retarded brother who gets lost while trying to find the swans he had previously seen on a nearby lake. Her agonizing, albeit ultimately successful, search for Charlie and the reactions of others to this traumatic event help Sara gain a new perspective on herself and life." Booklist

Tornado; by Betsy Byars; illustrations by Doron Ben-Ami. HarperCollins Pubs. 1996 49p il lib bdg $15.89; pa $4.99 (2-4)   **Fic**

1. Dogs—Fiction 2. Tornadoes—Fiction

ISBN 0-06-026452-7 (lib bdg); 0-06-442063-9 (pa)

LC 95-41584

As they wait out a tornado in their storm cellar, a family listens to their farmhand tell stories about the dog that was blown into his life by another tornado when he was a boy

"The handsome illustrations by Doron Ben-Ami give the volume a more distinguished, less juvenile look than the typical chapter book and convey the story's drama, warmth, and occasional humor. Parents and teachers will find this an excellent book to read aloud, and dog lovers of any age will find it irresistible." Booklist

Calhoun, Dia

The Phoenix Dance; [by] Dia Calhoun. 1st ed. Farrar, Straus and Giroux 2005 273p $17 (5 and up)   **Fic**

1. Fairy tales 2. Manic-depressive illness—Fiction

ISBN 0-374-35910-5   LC 2004-56281

Phoenix Dance battles an illness of her mind and emotions, realizes her dream of becoming shoemaker to the Royal Household, and attempts to discover what magic compels the twelve princesses of Windward to wear out their shoes each night.

"The story is well crafted and offers excellent insight into the life of an individual suffering from bipolar disorder. . . . The prose is straightforward, yet maintains the fairy-tale essence of the setting." SLJ

Cameron, Ann

Colibri. Farrar, Straus & Giroux 2003 227p $17 (5 and up)   **Fic**

1. Kidnapping—Fiction 2. Mayas—Fiction

ISBN 0-374-31519-1   LC 2002-192542

"Frances Foster books"

Kidnapped when she was very young by an unscrupulous man who has forced her to lie and beg to get money, a twelve-year-old Mayan girl endures an abusive life, always wishing she could return to the parents she can hardly remember

"The taut, chilling suspense and search for riches will keep readers flying through the pages. But it's Cameron's beautiful language and Rosa's larger identity quest that make this novel extraordinary." Booklist

Gloria's way; pictures by Lis Toft. Farrar, Straus & Giroux 2000 96p il $15 (2-4)
Fic

1. Friendship—Fiction 2. Family life—Fiction 3. African Americans—Fiction

ISBN 0-374-32670-3   LC 99-12104

Also available in paperback from Puffin Bks.

"Frances Foster books"

This companion volume to the series featuring Julian and Huey centers on their friend Gloria. Gloria shares special times with her mother and father and with her friends

"Lis Toft's shaded pencil drawings portray these African American characters and their predicaments with warmth and humor." Booklist

Cameron, Ann—*Continued*

Another title about Gloria is:
Gloria rising (2002)

The stories Julian tells; illustrated by Ann Strugnell. Pantheon Bks. 1981 71p il pa $4.99 hardcover o.p. (2-4)   **Fic**

1. Family life—Fiction 2. African Americans—Fiction
ISBN 0-394-82892-5 (pa)   LC 80-18023

"When seven-year-old Julian tells his little brother, Huey, that cats come from catalogues, Huey believes him. But when he flips the pages of the catalogue and doesn't find any cats, he begins to cry and Julian has some fast explaining to do. . . . A loving family is the center for six happy stories about catalog cats, strange teeth, a garden, a birthday fig tree and a new friend." West Coast Rev Books

"Strugnell's delightful drawings depict Julian, his little brother Huey and their parents as black, but they could be members of any family with a stern but loving and understanding father." Publ Wkly

Other titles about Julian and his family are:
Julian, dream doctor (1990)
Julian, secret agent (1988)
Julian's glorious summer (1987)
More stories Huey tells (1997)
More stories Julian tells (1986)
The stories Huey tells (1995)

Cameron, Eleanor

The court of the stone children. Dutton 1973 191p pa $6.99 hardcover o.p. (5 and up)
Fic

1. Museums—Fiction 2. Mystery fiction
ISBN 0-14-034289-3 (pa)

Also available in hardcover from P. Smith

In a San Francisco museum of French art and furniture, Nina encounters the ghost of Dominique, a girl who lived in the nineteenth-century. Spurred on by the appearance of the ghost, Nina sets out to untangle a murder mystery which had remained unsolved since Napoleon's day

"A nice concoction of mystery, fantasy, and realism adroitly blended in a contemporary story. . . . The characters are interesting, the plot threads nicely integrated." Bull Cent Child Books

The wonderful flight to the Mushroom Planet; with illustrations by Robert Henneberger. Little, Brown 1954 214p il pa $7.99 hardcover o.p. (4-6)
Fic

1. Science fiction
ISBN 0-316-12540-7 (pa)

Also available in hardcover from P. Smith

"An Atlantic Monthly Press book"

Two boys help a neighbor build a space ship in answer to an ad and take off for the dying planet of Basidium. There they help the inhabitants to restore an essential food to their diets and thereby save the life of the planet

"Scientific facts are emphasized in this well-built story. Since they are necessary to the development of the story the reader absorbs them naturally as he soars with the boys on the mission." N Y Times Book Rev

Cannon, A. E. (Ann Edwards)

Charlotte's Rose. Wendy Lamb Bks. 2002 246p $15.95; pa $5.50 (5 and up)   **Fic**

1. Infants—Fiction 2. Frontier and pioneer life—Fiction 3. Immigrants—Fiction 4. Mormons—Fiction
ISBN 0-385-72966-9; 0-440-41840-2 (pa)
LC 2002-427

As Charlotte, twelve-year-old Welsh immigrant, carries a motherless baby along the Mormon Trail in 1856, she comes to love the baby as her own and fear the day the baby's father will reclaim her

"Based on historical fact, the book offers a genuine headstrong girl in hardscrabble circumstances with a lightness of heart and a strong will to do right." SLJ

Carbone, Elisa Lynn

Blood on the river; James Town 1607; [by] Elisa Carbone. Viking 2006 237p $16.99 (5 and up)   **Fic**

1. Jamestown (Va.)—History—Fiction 2. Powhatan Indians—Fiction 3. United States—History—1600-1775, Colonial period—Fiction
ISBN 0-670-06060-7   LC 2005023646

Traveling to the New World in 1606 as the page to Captain John Smith, twelve-year-old orphan Samuel Collier settles in the new colony of James Town, where he must quickly learn to distinguish between friend and foe.

"A strong, visceral story of the hardship and peril settlers faced, as well as the brutal realities of colonial conquest." Booklist

Storm warriors; [by] Elisa Carbone. Knopf 2001 168p $16.95; lib bdg $18.99 (4 and up)
Fic

1. United States. Life-Saving Service—Fiction 2. African Americans—Fiction 3. North Carolina—Fiction
ISBN 0-375-80664-4; 0-375-90664-9 (lib bdg)
LC 00-59924

In 1895, after his mother's death, twelve-year-old Nathan moves with his father and grandfather to Pea Island off the coast of North Carolina, where he hopes to join the all-black crew at the nearby lifesaving station, despite his father's objections

"This thoughtfully crafted first-person narrative combines historical figures with created characters in the best traditions of the historical novel." Horn Book Guide

Carlson, Natalie Savage

The family under the bridge; pictures by Garth Williams. Harper & Row 1958 99p il lib bdg $16.89; pa $5.99 (3-5)   **Fic**

1. Tramps—Fiction 2. Christmas—Fiction 3. Paris (France)—Fiction
ISBN 0-06-020991-7 (lib bdg); 0-06-440250-9 (pa)

A Newbery Medal honor book, 1959

"Old Armand, a Parisian hobo, enjoyed his solitary, carefree life. . . . Then came a day just before Christmas when Armand, who wanted nothing to do with children because they spelled homes, responsibility, and regular work, found that three homeless children and their working mother had claimed his shelter under the bridge. How the hobo's heart and life become more and more

Carlson, Natalie Savage—*Continued*

deeply entangled with the little family and their quest for a home is told." Booklist

"Garth Williams' illustrations are perfect for this thoroughly delightful story of humor and sentiment." Libr J

Carman, Patrick

The Dark Hills divide; the land of Elyon, book 1; [by] Patrick Carman. 1st Orchard Books ed. Orchard Books 2005 253p $11.95 (5 and up)
Fic

1. Fantasy fiction

ISBN 0-439-70093-0   LC 2004-16312

When she finds the key to a secret passageway leading out of the walled city of Bridewell, twelve-year-old Alexa realizes her lifelong wish to explore the mysterious forests and mountains that lie beyond the wall.

"Narrator Aasne Vigesaa clearly portrays Alexa's thoughtful, inquisitive nature and unsettled feelings. . . . Vigesaa's excellent use of pace, pitch, and tone help differentiate each character." SLJ

Other titles in this series are:
Beyond the Valley of Thorns (2005)
The tenth city (2006)

Carroll, Lewis

Alice through the looking glass; illustrated by Helen Oxenbury. Candlewick Press 2005 224p $24.99 (4 and up)   **Fic**

1. Fantasy fiction

ISBN 0-7636-2892-1

First published 1871 with title: Through the looking-glass and what Alice found there

In this edition of Lewis Carroll's classic which follows Alice in Wonderland, Alice "steps through the looking glass and into a world depicted in warm watercolors, sepia-toned illustrations, and line drawings. Not a word of the original tale has been altered. The artwork echoes the whimsy of the language." SLJ

Alice's adventures in Wonderland (4 and up)
Fic

1. Fantasy fiction

Some editions are:
Books of Wonder $16.95 Illustrated by John Tenniel
(ISBN 0-688-11087-8)
Candlewick Press $24.99 Illustrated by Helen Oxenbury
(ISBN 0-7636-0804-1)
North-South Bks. $19.95 Illustrated by Lisbeth Zwerger
(ISBN 0-7358-1166-0)

"First told in 1862 to the little Liddell girls. Written out for Alice Liddell, published, and first copy given to her in 1865." Arnold

Variant title: Alice in Wonderland

"A rabbit who took a watch out of his waistcoat pocket seemed well-worth following to Alice so she hurried after him across the field, down the rabbit hole, and into a series of adventures with a group of famous and most unusual characters." Let's Read Together

This fantasy "is one of the most quoted books in the English language. Every child should be introduced to Alice, though its appeal will not be universal." Natl Counc of Teach of Engl. Adventuring with Books

Followed by Through the looking glass, and what Alice found there

Alice's adventures in Wonderland, and Through the looking glass (4 and up)   **Fic**

1. Fantasy fiction

Available from various publishers including a Dell paperback edition illustrated by John Tenniel

A combined edition of the two titles first published 1865 and 1872 respectively. Through the looking glass, the sequel to Alice's adventures in Wonderland, "tells of Alice's experiences when, curious about the world behind the mirror, she climbs over the mantel through the glass. In looking-glass country, everything is reversed, just as reflections are reversed in a mirror. Brooks and hedges divide the land into a checkerboard, and Alice finds herself a white pawn in the whimsical and fantastic game of chess that constitutes the bulk of the story. . . . The ballad 'Jabberwocky' is found in the tale." Reader's Ency. 4th edition

Cassidy, Cathy

Dizzy; a novel; by Cathy Cassidy. Viking 2004 247p $15.99 (5 and up)   **Fic**

1. Mother-daughter relationship—Fiction 2. Great Britain—Fiction

ISBN 0-670-05936-6   LC 2004-1642

After an eight-year absence, Dizzy's "New Age traveler" mother suddenly shows up on her twelfth birthday and whisks her away to a series of festivals throughout Scotland in her rattletrap van.

"The eclectic characters and their lifestyle are presented as captivating yet questionable in the girl's first-person narrative, and the well-developed plot fosters concern for Dizzy from the beginning. A unique, satisfying story." SLJ

Indigo Blue. Viking 2005 215p $15.99 (5 and up)   **Fic**

1. Moving—Fiction 2. Abused women—Fiction 3. Great Britain—Fiction

ISBN 0-670-05927-7

Eleven-year-old Indigo, her mother, and her toddler sister have to move out of their apartment because of troubles with Mum's boyfriend, while Indie is also having best friend problems at school, leaving her stressed, confused, and lonely.

"This British story of domestic abuse is firmly child-centered, and Indigo's confusion and fear . . . are sensitively portrayed. . . . The hopeful ending rings true." Booklist

Chabon, Michael

Summerland. Hyperion Bks. for Children 2002 500p $22.95; pa $8.95 (5 and up)   **Fic**

1. Fantasy fiction 2. Baseball—Fiction 3. Magic—Fiction

ISBN 0-7868-0877-2; 0-7868-1615-5 (pa)
          LC 2002-27497

Ethan Feld, the worst baseball player in the history of the game, finds himself recruited by a 100-year-old scout to help a band of fairies triumph over an ancient enemy

"Much of the prose is beautifully descriptive as Chabon navigates vividly imagined other worlds and offers up some timeless themes." Horn Book

Cheaney, J. B.

My friend, the enemy. Knopf 2005 266p $15.95;
lib bdg $17.99 (5 and up) **Fic**

1. Japanese Americans—Fiction 2. Friendship—Fiction
3. World War, 1939-1945—Fiction

ISBN 0-375-81432-9; 0-375-91432-3 (lib bdg)

LC 2004-26927

During World War II, a twelve-year-old girl becomes
friends with a young Japanese-American boy she discovers being sheltered and hidden by her neighbor.

"Written in first person, this novel offers quiet but
finely tuned portrayal of the stresses that changed life on
the home front and one child's attempts to cope with it
all." Booklist

Cheng, Andrea

Honeysuckle house. Front Street 2004 136p
$16.95 (3-5) **Fic**

1. Friendship—Fiction 2. Chinese Americans—Fiction
3. Immigrants—Fiction

ISBN 1-886910-99-5

An all-American girl with Chinese ancestors and a
new immigrant from China find little in common when
they meet in their fourth grade classroom, but they are
both missing their best friends and soon discover other
connections.

"Told in first person in alternating chapters, the narratives balance well between large issues . . . and more
intimate ones. . . . With a smoothly drawn and interesting plot, strong characters, and graceful writing, the story
has more immediacy than much realistic contemporary
fiction." SLJ

The key collection; illustrated by Yangsook
Choi. Holt & Co. 2003 117p il $15.95 (3-5)
Fic

1. Chinese Americans—Fiction 2. Grandmothers—Fiction

ISBN 0-8050-7153-9 LC 2002-68921

A ten-year-old boy in the Midwest misses his Chinese
grandmother, who always lived next door until her health
caused her to move

"There's unusual warmth and depth in the details of
the story; and Choi's realistic drawings enhance the
open, inviting format." Horn Book

The lace dowry. Front Street 2005 113p $16.95
(4 and up) **Fic**

1. Friendship—Fiction 2. Sex role—Fiction
3. Hungary—Fiction

ISBN 1-932425-20-9 LC 2004-21186

In Hungary in 1933, a twelve-year-old from Budapest
befriends the Halas village family of lacemakers hired to
stitch her dowry.

"Cheng tells a familiar story of children discovering
empathy across class and cultural divides, enriching the
theme with a vivid historical setting and Juli's strong
narration, which is written in spare language and a believable voice." Booklist

Shanghai messenger; illustrated by Ed Young.
Lee & Low 2005 unp il $18.95 (3-6) **Fic**

1. Chinese Americans—Fiction 2. China—Fiction

ISBN 1-58430-238-0 LC 2004-4025934

A free-verse novel about eleven-year-old Xiao Mei's
visit with her extended family in China, where the Chinese-American girl finds many differences but also the
similarities that bind a family together.

"Cheng does an admirable job of capturing this experience from the perspective of a child, and each free-
verse chapter is brief but satisfying. . . . Young's illustrations delicately intertwine with the text, gently supporting each vignette. This is a superb book." SLJ

Child, Lauren

Clarice Bean spells trouble; [by] Lauren Child.
Candlewick Press 2005 189p il $15.99 (3-5)
Fic

1. Authorship—Fiction 2. Friendship—Fiction

ISBN 0-7636-2813-1

Picture book titles about Clarice Bean also available

Clarice Bean, aspiring actress and author, unsuccessfully tries to avoid getting into trouble as she attempts to
help a friend in need by following the rules of the fictional spy, Ruby Redfort.

This is written "with fresh, childlike turns of phrase
and a hyperawareness of words. . . . With a sprinkling
of small, childlike line drawings, a few other illustrations, and some creative typography, this entertaining
chapter book will please readers." Booklist

Another title about Clarice Bean is:

Utterly me, Clarice Bean (2003)

Choi, Sook Nyul

Year of impossible goodbyes. Houghton Mifflin
1991 171p $16 (5 and up) **Fic**

1. Korea—Fiction

ISBN 0-395-57419-6 LC 91-10502

Also available in paperback from Dell

Sookan, a young Korean girl survives the oppressive
Japanese and Russian occupation of North Korea during
the 1940s, to later escape to freedom in South Korea

"Tragedies are not masked here, but neither are they
overdramatized. . . . The observations are honest, the details authentic, the characterizations vividly developed."
Bull Cent Child Books

Other titles about Sookan are:

Echoes of the white giraffe (1993)

Gathering of pearls (1994)

Choldenko, Gennifer

Al Capone does my shirts. G.P. Putnam's Sons
2004 225p il $15.99 (5 and up) **Fic**

1. Alcatraz Island (Calif.)—Fiction 2. Autism—Fiction
3. Siblings—Fiction

ISBN 0-399-23861-1 LC 2002-31766

A Newbery Medal honor book, 2005

A twelve-year-old boy named Moose moves to Alcatraz Island in 1935 when guards' families were housed
there, and has to contend with his extraordinary new environment in addition to life with his autistic sister.

"With its unique setting and well-developed characters, this warm, engaging coming-of-age story has plenty
of appeal, and Choldenko offers some fascinating historical background on Alcatraz Island in an afterword."
Booklist

Choldenko, Gennifer—*Continued*

Notes from a liar and her dog. Putnam 2001
216p $16.99; pa $5.99 (5 and up)   **Fic**
1. Family life—Fiction 2. Truthfulness and falsehood—Fiction
ISBN 0-399-23591-4; 0-14-250068-2 (pa)
LC 00-55354

Eleven-year-old Ant, stuck in a family that she does
not like, copes by pretending that her "real" parents are
coming to rescue her, by loving her dog Pistachio, by
volunteering at the zoo, and by bending the truth and
telling lies

"Choldenko's writing is snappy and tender, depicting
both Ant's bravado and her isolation with sympathy."
Bull Cent Child Books

Christopher, John

The White Mountains. 35th anniversary ed.
Simon & Schuster Bks. for Young Readers 2003
c1967 164p $16.95   **Fic**
1. Science fiction
ISBN 0-689-85504-4   LC 2002-70808

A reissue of the title first published 1967 by Macmillan

Young Will Parker and his companions make a perilous journey toward an outpost of freedom where they
hope to escape from the ruling Tripods, who capture mature human beings and make them docile, obedient servants

This "remarkable story . . . belongs to the school of
science-fiction which puts philosophy before technology
and is not afraid of telling an exciting story." Times Lit
Suppl

Other available titles about the Tripods are:
The city of gold and lead (2003 c1967)
The pool of fire (2003 c1968)
When the Tripods came (2003 c1988)

Christopher, Matt

The dog that called the pitch; illustrated by
Daniel Vasconcellos. Little, Brown 1998 34p il
$14.95 (2-4)   **Fic**
1. Dogs—Fiction 2. Extrasensory perception—Fiction
3. Baseball—Fiction
ISBN 0-316-14207-7   LC 97-28224

Mike and his dog Harry, the Airedale with ESP, are
shocked to discover that the new umpire for Mike's
baseball games can hear their mental conversations

"With plenty of illustrations, the text tells a fast-paced
story, just right for newly independent readers." Horn
Book Guide

Tennis ace. Little, Brown 2000 116p $15.95; pa
$4.50 (3-6)   **Fic**
1. Tennis—Fiction 2. Parent-child relationship—Fiction 3. Siblings—Fiction
ISBN 0-316-13519-4; 0-316-13491-0 (pa)
LC 99-48067

Steve and Ginny are frustrated because their father ignores her talent as a tennis player while pushing him
harder and harder to win at the sport

"The plot is transparent but the lively action throughout will keep young players intrigued." SLJ

Clark, Clara Gillow

Hill Hawk Hattie. Candlewick Press 2003 159p
$15.99 (5 and up)   **Fic**
1. Father-daughter relationship—Fiction 2. Death—
Fiction 3. Sex role—Fiction
ISBN 0-7636-1963-9   LC 2002-73740

"With beautiful rhythmic sentences, the simple first-
person narrative captures [Hattie's] rustic innocence, the
thrilling rafting adventure, and the heartfelt struggle of a
tough girl who feels useful to her father only in the role
of a boy." Booklist

Another title about Hattie is:
Hattie on her way (2005)

Cleary, Beverly

Dear Mr. Henshaw; illustrated by Paul O.
Zelinsky. Morrow 1983 133p il $15.99; lib bdg
$16.89 (4 and up)   **Fic**
1. Divorce—Fiction 2. Parent-child relationship—Fic-
tion 3. School stories
ISBN 0-688-02405-X; 0-688-02406-8 (lib bdg)
LC 83-5372

Also available in paperback from Avon Bks.; Spanish
language edition also available

Awarded the Newbery Medal, 1984

"Leigh Botts started writing letters to his favorite author, Boyd Henshaw, in the second grade. Now, Leigh is
in the sixth grade, in a new school, and his parents are
recently divorced. This year he writes many letters to
Mr. Henshaw, and also keeps a journal. Through these
the reader learns how Leigh adjusts to new situations,
and of his triumphs." Child Book Rev Serv

"The story is by no means one of unrelieved gloom,
for there are deft touches of humor in the sentient, subtly
wrought account of the small triumphs and tragedies in
the life of an ordinary boy." Horn Book

Followed by Strider

Ellen Tebbits; illustrated by Louis Darling.
Morrow 1951 160p il $15.99; lib bdg (3-5)
Fic
1. School stories
ISBN 0-688-21264-6; 0-688-31264-0

Also available in paperback from Avon Bks.

"Ellen Tebbits is eight years old, takes ballet lessons,
wears bands on her teeth, and has a secret—she wears
woolen underwear. But she finds a friend in Austine, a
new girl in school, who also wears woolen underwear.
They have the usual troubles that beset 'best friends' in
grade school plus some that are unusual." Carnegie Libr
of Pittsburgh

"Their experiences in the third grade are comical and
very appealing to children in the middle grades."
Hodges. Books for Elem Sch Libr

Henry Huggins; illustrated by Louis Darling.
HarperCollins Pubs. 2000 155p il $15.99; lib bdg
$16.89; pa $5.99 (3-5)   **Fic**
1. Family life—Fiction 2. School stories
ISBN 0-688-21385-5; 0-688-31385-X (lib bdg);
0-380-70912-0 (pa)   LC 00-27567

Also available Spanish language edition

A reissue of the title first published 1950 by Morrow

Cleary, Beverly—*Continued*

"Henry Huggins is a typical small boy who, quite innocently, gets himself into all sorts of predicaments—often with the very apt thought, 'Won't Mom be surprised.' There is not a dull moment but some hilariously funny ones in the telling of Henry's adventures at home and at school." Booklist

Other titles about Henry Huggins are:

Henry and Beezus (1952)
Henry and Ribsy (1954)
Henry and the clubhouse (1962)
Henry and the paper route (1957)
Ribsy (1964)

Mitch and Amy; illustrated by Bob Marstall. Morrow Junior Bks. 1991 222p il $16.99 (3-5)

Fic

1. Twins—Fiction 2. School stories
ISBN 0-688-10806-7   LC 91-25657

Also available in paperback from Avon Bks.

A newly illustrated edition of the title first published 1967

"The twins Mitch and Amy are in the fourth grade. Mitch is plagued by a bully and by reading difficulties, Amy struggles with multiplication tables, and their patient mother mediates their squabbles." SLJ

"The writing style and dialogue, the familial and peer group relationships, the motivations and characterizations all have the ring of truth. Written with ease and vitality, lightened with humor, the story is perhaps most appealing because it is clear that the author respects children." Bull Cent Child Books

The mouse and the motorcycle; illustrated by Louis Darling. Morrow 1965 158p il $16 (3-5)

Fic

1. Mice—Fiction
ISBN 0-688-21698-6

Also available in paperback from Avon Bks.

"A fantasy about Ralph, a mouse, who learns to ride a toy motorcycle and goes on wild rides through the corridors of the hotel where he lives. Keith, the boy to whom the motorcycle belongs, becomes fast friends with Ralph and defends him when danger threatens." Hodges. Books for Elem Sch Libr

"The author shows much insight into the thoughts of children. She carries the reader into an imaginative world that contains many realistic emotions." Wis Libr Bull

Other titles about Ralph are:

Ralph S. Mouse (1982)
Runaway Ralph (1970)

Muggie Maggie; illustrated by Kay Life. Morrow Junior Bks. 1990 70p il $15.99; lib bdg (2-4)   **Fic**

1. Handwriting—Fiction 2. School stories
ISBN 0-688-08553-9; 0-688-08554-7

LC 89-38959

Also available in paperback from Avon Bks.; Spanish language edition also available

Maggie resists learning cursive writing in the third grade, until she discovers that knowing how to read and write cursive promises to open up an entirely new world of knowledge for her

"This deceptively simple story is accessible to prima-ry-grade readers able to read longhand, as some of the text is in script. . . . Everything in this book rings true, and Cleary has created a likable, funny heroine about whom readers will want to know more." SLJ

Otis Spofford; illustrated by Louis Darling. Morrow 1953 191p il $16.99; lib bdg (3-5)

Fic

1. School stories
ISBN 0-688-21720-6; 0-688-31720-0

Also available in paperback from Avon Bks.

"Otis, a mischievous, fun loving boy, is always getting in and out of trouble. His mother, a dancing teacher, is busy and often leaves Otis on his own. This book tells of several episodes in Otis's life—from his sneaking vitamins to a white rat to 'disprove' a diet experiment, to getting his final 'come-uppance' when a trick on Ellen Tebbits backfires." Read Ladders for Hum Relat. 6th edition

"This writer has her elementary school down pat, and manages to report her growing boys, teachers, and P.T.A. meetings so that parents chuckle and boys laugh out loud." N Y Her Trib Books

Ramona the pest; illustrated by Louis Darling. Morrow 1968 192p il $16; lib bdg $15.93 (3-5)

Fic

1. Kindergarten—Fiction 2. School stories
ISBN 0-688-21721-4; 0-688-31721-9 (lib bdg)

Also available in paperback from Avon Bks.; Spanish language edition also available

"Ramona Quimby comes into her own. Beezus keeps telling her to stop acting like a pest, but Ramona is five now, and she is convinced that she is 'not' a pest; she feels very mature, having entered kindergarten, and she immediately becomes enamoured of her teacher. Ramona's insistence on having just the right kind of boots, her matter-of-fact interest in how Mike Mulligan got to a bathroom, her determination to kiss one of the boys in her class, and her refusal to go back to kindergarten because Miss Binney didn't love her any more—all of these incidents or situations are completely believable and are told in a light, humorous, zesty style." Bull Cent Child Books

Other titles about Ramona are:

Beezus and Ramona (1955)
Ramona and her father (1977)
Ramona and her mother (1979)
Ramona, forever (1984)
Ramona Quimby, age 8 (1981)
Ramona the brave (1975)
Ramona's world (1999)

Socks; illustrated by Beatrice Darwin. Morrow 1973 156p il $16.99; lib bdg $17.89 (3-5)

Fic

1. Cats—Fiction 2. Infants—Fiction
ISBN 0-688-20067-2; 0-688-30067-7 (lib bdg)

Also available in paperback from Avon Bks.

"The Brickers' kitten, Socks, is jealous when they bring a baby home from the hospital. How he copes with this rivalry makes an amusing story true to cat nature." Cleveland Public Libr

"Not being child-centered, this may have a smaller audience than earlier Cleary books, but it is written with the same easy grace, the same felicitous humor and sharply observant eye." Bull Cent Child Books

Cleary, Beverly—*Continued*

Strider; illustrated by Paul O. Zelinsky. Morrow Junior Bks. 1991 179p il $15.95; lib bdg $16.89 (4 and up)   **Fic**
1. Dogs—Fiction 2. Divorce—Fiction
ISBN 0-688-09900-9; 0-688-09901-7 (lib bdg)
                                                      LC 90-6608
Also available in paperback from Avon Bks.; Spanish language edition also available

Sequel to Dear Mr. Henshaw

In a series of diary entries, Leigh tells how he comes to terms with his parents' divorce, acquires joint custody of an abandoned dog, and joins the track team at school.

"The development of the narrative is vintage Beverly Cleary, an inimitable blend of comic and poignant moments." Horn Book

Cleaver, Vera

Where the lillies bloom; [by] Vera & Bill Cleaver; illustrated by Jim Spanfeller. Lippincott 1969 174p il $15.95; pa $5.99 (5 and up)
                                                            Fic
1. Orphans—Fiction 2. Siblings—Fiction
3. Appalachian region—Fiction
ISBN 0-397-31111-7; 0-06-447005-9 (pa)
Mary Call Luther is "fourteen years old and made of granite. When her sharecropper father dies, Mary Call becomes head of the household, responsible for a boy of ten and a retarded, gentle older sister. Mary and her brother secretly bury their father so they can retain their home [in the Appalachian hills]; tenaciously she fights to keep the family afloat by selling medicinal plants and to keep them together by fending off [Kiser Pease, their landlord], who wants to marry her sister." Saturday Rev

"The setting is fascinating, the characterization good, and the style of the first-person story distinctive." Bull Cent Child Books

Followed by Trial Valley (1977)

Clements, Andrew

Frindle; pictures by Brian Selznick. Simon & Schuster Bks. for Young Readers 1996 105p il $15.95; pa $5.99 (4-6)   **Fic**
1. School stories
ISBN 0-689-80669-8; 0-689-81876-9 (pa)
                                                      LC 95-26671
When he decides to turn his fifth grade teacher's love of the dictionary around on her, clever Nick Allen invents a new word and begins a chain of events that quickly moves beyond his control

"Sure to be popular with a wide range of readers, this will make a great read-aloud as well." Booklist

The janitor's boy; a novel; by the best-selling author of Frindle. Simon & Schuster Bks. for Young Readers 2000 140p pa $5.99 hardcover o.p. (4-6)   **Fic**
1. Father-son relationship—Fiction 2. School stories
ISBN 0-689-83585-X (pa)   LC 99-47457
Fifth grader Jack finds himself the target of ridicule at school when it becomes known that his father is one of the janitors, and he turns his anger onto his father

"Clements' strength is his realistic depiction of public schools. . . . Jack's antics and those of his classmates ring true, as do the behaviors of the teachers and administrators." Booklist

The Landry News; illustrations by Salvatore Murdocca. Simon & Schuster Bks. for Young Readers 1999 123p il $15.95; pa $5.99 (4-6)
                                                            Fic
1. Newspapers—Fiction 2. Teachers—Fiction
3. School stories
ISBN 0-689-81817-3; 0-689-82868-3 (pa)
                                                      LC 98-34376
A fifth-grader starts a newspaper with an editorial that prompts her burnt-out classroom teacher to really begin teaching again, but he is later threatened with disciplinary action as a result

"The text flows effortlessly yet explores thought-provoking issues such as intellectual freedom that are likely to engender further exploration." Horn Book Guide

Lunch money; illustrations by Brian Selznick. Simon & Schuster Books for Young Readers 2005 222p il $15.95 (4-6)   **Fic**
1. Money-making projects for children—Fiction
2. Cartoons and comics—Fiction 3. School stories
ISBN 0-689-86683-6   LC 2005-00061
Twelve-year-old Greg, who has always been good at moneymaking projects, is surprised to find himself teaming up with his lifelong rival, Maura, to create a series of comic books to sell at school.

"The characters are rich with interesting quirks and motivations. . . . Along with providing a fast-paced and humorous story line, the author examines concepts of true wealth, teamwork, community mindedness, and the value of creative expression. Selznick's pencil sketches add comic touches throughout." SLJ

The report card. Simon & Schuster Books for Young Readers 2004 173p $15.95 (4-6)
                                                            Fic
1. School stories
ISBN 0-689-84515-4   LC 2003-7384
Fifth-grader Nora Rowley has always hidden the fact that she is a genius from everyone because all she wants is to be normal, but when she comes up with a plan to prove that grades are not important, things begin to get out of control.

"Clements has . . . built a solid story around a controversial issue for which there is no easy answer, and to his credit, he never tries to offer one. . . . A novel sure to generate strong feelings and discussion." Booklist

The school story; illustrated by Brian Selznick. Simon & Schuster Bks. for Young Readers 2001 196p il $16; pa $5.99 (4 and up)   **Fic**
1. Authorship—Fiction 2. Publishers and publishing—Fiction
ISBN 0-689-82594-3; 0-689-85186-3 (pa)
                                                      LC 00-49683
After twelve-year-old Natalie writes a wonderful novel, her friend Zoe helps her devise a scheme to get it accepted at the publishing house where Natalie's mother works as an editor

"The girls are believable characters. . . . Selznick's black-and-white illustrations add humorous details. A comic novel that's a sure winner." SLJ

Clifford, Eth

Help! I'm a prisoner in the library; illustrated by
George Hughes. Houghton Mifflin 1979 105p il
$16 (3-5) **Fic**

1. Libraries—Fiction 2. Blizzards—Fiction

ISBN 0-395-28478-3 LC 79-14447

Also available in paperback from Scholastic

"Caught in a blinding snowstorm with their car out of
gas, Mary Rose and Jo-Beth are told to stay put while
their father finds fuel for the stalled vehicle. Jo-Beth,
however, develops 'an emergency' and Mary Rose takes
her to a nearby library to find a restroom. . . . Without
warning the girls find themselves locked in when the
building closes early. As the storm worsens, the lights
and telephone go out and a series of flying objects,
creaking noises, and moaning sounds thoroughly frighten
the girls. . . . Clifford uses a light touch while evoking
a pleasingly scary atmosphere that children will enjoy.
Spirited dialogue and swift pace are an additional plus."
Booklist

The remembering box; illustrated by Donna
Diamond. Houghton Mifflin 1985 70p il $16 (3-5)
Fic

1. Grandmothers—Fiction 2. Jews—Fiction 3. Death—
Fiction

ISBN 0-395-38476-1 LC 85-10851

Also available in paperback from Beech Tree Bks.

Nine-year-old Joshua's weekly visits to his beloved
grandmother on the Jewish Sabbath give him an understanding of love, family, and tradition which helps him
accept her death

"This warm and loving relationship between a boy and
his grandmother is beautifully depicted. . . . Diamond's
silhouettes, used for the stories that Grandma tells Joshua, are dramatic, and her meticulously detailed black-
and-white illustrations of Joshua and his grandmother are
both expressive and moving." SLJ

Clifton, Lucille

The times they used to be; illustrated by Earl B.
Lewis. Delacorte Press 2000 41p il $12.95 (4 and
up) **Fic**

1. African Americans—Fiction

ISBN 0-385-32126-0 LC 99-42411

A newly illustrated edition of the title first published
1974 by Holt, Rinehart and Winston

A young black girl relates the adventures of the summer her Uncle Sunny died and her best friend broke out
in sin because she wasn't saved.

"Clifton's plainspoken narrative poem has been newly
illustrated with beautiful, realistic charcoal pictures. . . .
The words are easy, the rhythms conversational, the people never idealized. Lewis' pictures [have] extraordinary
detail and depth." Booklist

Coatsworth, Elizabeth Jane

The cat who went to heaven; [by] Elizabeth
Coatsworth; illustrated by Lynd Ward. Macmillan
1958 62p il $17.95; pa $4.99 (4 and up)
Fic

1. Cats—Fiction 2. Japan—Fiction

ISBN 0-02-719710-7; 0-689-71433-5 (pa)

LC 58-10917

First published 1930. The 1958 edition is a reprint
with new illustrations of the book which won the
Newbery Medal award in 1931

"Watched by his little cat, Good Fortune, a Japanese
artist paints a picture of the Buddha receiving homage
from the animals. By tradition the cat should not be
among them, but the artist risks his reputation by adding
Good Fortune and is vindicated by a miracle." Hodges.
Books for Elem Sch Libr

"Into this lovely and imaginative story the author has
put something of the serenity and beauty of the East and
of the gentleness of a religion that has a place even for
the humblest of living creatures." N Y Times Book Rev

Cohen, Barbara

Thank you, Jackie Robinson; drawings by
Richard Cuffari. Lothrop, Lee & Shepard Bks.
1974 125p il pa $4.99 hardcover o.p. (4-6)
Fic

1. Baseball—Fiction 2. Friendship—Fiction
3. African Americans—Fiction

ISBN 0-688-15293-7 (pa)

"When 60-year-old Davey (Black) comes to work at
the inn for Sam's mother, Sam (Jewish and fatherless)
gains a friend. Davey takes Sam to see the Brooklyn
Dodgers (circa 1945), and an avid, statistic-spouting
Dodger fan is born. When Davey becomes ill, Sam gets
Jackie Robinson and his teammates to autograph a ball
for Davey." Child Book Rev Serv

"Cohen's characters have unusual depth and her story
succeeds as a warm, understanding consideration of
friendship and, finally, death." Booklist

Cohen, Miriam

Mimmy and Sophie all around the town;
pictures by Thomas F. Yezerski. Farrar, Straus and
Giroux 2004 68p il $16 (2-4) **Fic**

1. Sisters—Fiction 2. Brooklyn (New York, N.Y.)—
Fiction

ISBN 0-374-34989-4 LC 2003-48059

Features the same characters as the picture book
Mimmy & Sophie (1999)

"Frances Foster books"

Describes the experiences of two sisters growing up in
Brooklyn in the time of Shirley Temple movies and trolleys

"With plenty of dialogue and straightforward action,
this charming story is just right for newly independent
readers. Yezerski's black-and-white drawings illustrate
the era, while conveying all of the energy of the characters." SLJ

Cohn, Rachel

The Steps. Simon & Schuster Bks. for Young
Readers 2003 137p $15.95 (5 and up) **Fic**

1. Stepfamilies—Fiction 2. Family life—Fiction
3. Australia—Fiction

ISBN 0-689-84549-9 LC 2001-57566

Over Christmas vacation, Annabel goes from her
home in Manhattan to visit her father, his new wife, and
her half- and step-siblings in Sydney, Australia

"Packed with humorous incident, life lessons learned,
Australian travel tidbits, and a litany of preteen-girl
touchstones." Horn Book

Cohn, Rachel—*Continued*
Another title about this family is:
Two steps forward (2006)

Colfer, Eoin
Artemis Fowl. Hyperion Bks. for Children 2001 277p $16.95; pa $7.99 (5 and up)   **Fic**
1. Fairies—Fiction 2. Fantasy fiction
ISBN 0-7868-0801-2; 0-7868-1707-0 (pa)
LC 2001-16632
When a twelve-year-old evil genius tries to restore his family fortune by capturing a fairy and demanding a ransom in gold, the fairies fight back with magic, technology, and a particularly nasty troll
"Colfer's antihero, techno fantasy is cleverly written and filled to the brim with action, suspense, and humor." SLJ
Other titles in this series are:
Artemis Fowl: the Arctic incident (2002)
Artemis Fowl: the Eternity code (2003)
Artemis Fowl: the Opal deception (2005)

Half-Moon investigations. Miramax Books/Hyperion Books for Children 2006 290p $16.95 (4 and up)   **Fic**
1. Mystery fiction
ISBN 0-7868-4957-6
"Diminutive Fletcher Moon may not be the most popular 12-year-old in his Irish town but he's proud . . . of the badge that he constantly flashes to let everyone know that he's an online graduate of a private detective academy in Washington, DC. . . . But when . . . April Devereux hires him to find a lock of a pop star's hair that she claims was stolen . . . everything starts going wrong for Fletcher." SLJ
"The private-eye lingo has a great, comical grade-school snap, and . . . the kid's goofy charm and stubborn dedication to crime solving will win him a hefty, enthusiastic following." Booklist

Collier, James Lincoln
The empty mirror. Bloomsbury 2004 192p $16.95 (5 and up)   **Fic**
1. Ghost stories 2. Influenza—Fiction 3. Orphans—Fiction
ISBN 1-58234-949-5
"Nick's an admitted troublemaker, but when his mysterious doppledanger starts committing increasingly sinister crimes, his small New England town is ready to string Nick up. The secret of this ghostly presence might lie in the recent influenza epidemic of 1918. . . . Collier's challenging novel effectively combines historical fiction with a genuinely spooky supernatural tale." Horn Book Guide

Jump ship to freedom; [by] James Lincoln Collier, Christopher Collier. Delacorte Press 1981 198p pa $5.99 hardcover o.p. (6 and up)   **Fic**
1. United States—History—1783-1809—Fiction 2. Slavery—Fiction 3. African Americans—Fiction
ISBN 0-440-44323-7 (pa)   LC 81-65492
Companion volume to War comes to Willie Freeman and Who is Carrie?

In 1787 Dan Arabus, a fourteen-year-old slave, anxious to buy freedom for himself and his mother, escapes from his dishonest master and tries to find help in cashing the soldier's notes received by his father, Jack Arabus, for fighting in the Revolution
"The period seems well researched, and the speech has an authentic ring without trying to imitate a dialect." SLJ

Me and Billy; [by] James Lincoln Collier. 1st ed. Marshall Cavendish 2004 185p $15.95 (5 and up)   **Fic**
1. Swindlers and swindling—Fiction 2. Orphans—Fiction 3. Friendship—Fiction
ISBN 0-7614-5174-9   LC 2003-26865
After escaping the orphanage where they have spent their lives together, two boys become assistants to a con artist, and while Possum objects to the lying, stealing, and cheating, Billy only cares about making money and taking life easy.
"A small gem. . . . The book's momentum is sustained by the author's wonderful use of vernacular and the friendship/tension between the boys." SLJ

My brother Sam is dead; by James Lincoln Collier and Christopher Collier. Four Winds Press 1985 c1974 216p $17.95 (6 and up)   **Fic**
1. United States—History—1775-1783, Revolution—Fiction
ISBN 0-02-722980-7   LC 84-28787
Also available in paperback from Scholastic
A reissue of the title first published 1974
"In 1775 the Meeker family lived in Redding, Connecticut, a Tory community. Sam, the eldest son, allied himself with the Patriots. The youngest son, Tim, watched a rift in the family grow because of his brother's decision. Before the war was over the Meeker family had suffered at the hands of both the British and the Patriots." Shapiro. Fic for Youth. 3d edition

War comes to Willy Freeman; [by] James Lincoln Collier, Christopher Collier. Delacorte Press 1983 178p pa $5.99 hardcover o.p. (6 and up)   **Fic**
1. United States—History—1775-1783, Revolution—Fiction 2. African Americans—Fiction 3. Slavery—Fiction
ISBN 0-440-49504-0 (pa)   LC 82-70317
This deals with events prior to those in Jump ship to freedom, and involves members of the same family.
"Willy is thirteen when she begins her story, which takes place during the last two years of the Revolutionary War; her father, a free man, has been killed fighting against the British, her mother has disappeared. Willy makes her danger-fraught way to Fraunces Tavern in New York, her uncle, Jack Arabus, having told her that Mr. Fraunces may be able to help her. She works at the tavern until the war is over, goes to the Arabus home to find her mother dying, and participates in the trial (historically accurate save for the fictional addition of Willy) in which her uncle sues for his freedom and wins." Bull Cent Child Books

Collins, Suzanne

Gregor the Overlander. Scholastic Press 2003
311p $16.95; pa $5.99 (4 and up) **Fic**
1. Fantasy fiction
ISBN 0-439-43536-6; 0-439-67813-7 (pa)
LC 2002-155865

When eleven-year-old Gregor and his two-year-old
sister are pulled into a strange underground world, they
trigger an epic battle involving men, bats, rats, cockroaches, and spiders while on a quest foretold by ancient
prophecy

"Collins creates a fascinating, vivid, highly original
world and a superb story to go along with it." Booklist
Other titles in this series are:
Gregor and the curse of the warmbloods (2005)
Gregor and the marks of secret (2006)
Gregor and the prophecy of Bane (2004)

Collodi, Carlo

The adventures of Pinocchio (3-6) **Fic**
1. Puppets and puppet plays—Fiction 2. Fairy tales
Some editions are:
Candlewick Press $18.99 illustrated by Sara Fanelli
(ISBN 0-7636-2261-3)
Creative Editions $19.95 illustrated by Roberto Innocenti
(ISBN 1-56846-190-9)
Purple Bear $19.95 illustrated by Robert Ingpen (ISBN
1-93327-00-6)
Simply Read Books $24.95 illustrated by Iassen
Ghiuselev (ISBN 0-968876-80-3)
An Italian classic for children, written late in the 19th
century. Variant title: Pinocchio

"When Geppetto discovered a piece of wood which
talked, he carved it into a marionette and named him
Pinocchio. Although he is a wooden boy, Pinocchio has
a lively and nimble mind and an ardent curiosity which
lead to unexpected and extraordinary results. A lighthearted and original fantasy in which children can identify themselves with Pinocchio and grasp the simple and
practical morality which underlies the story." Toronto
Public Libr. Books for Boys & Girls

Coman, Carolyn

The big house; drawings by Rob Shepperson.
Front Street 2004 220p il $16.95 (3-6)
Fic
1. Siblings—Fiction 2. Crime—Fiction
ISBN 1-932425-09-8 LC 2004-40425
When Ivy and Ray's parents are sent to jail, and left
in the custody of their parent's accusers, they decide to
look for evidence that will "spring" their parents.

This is "an enjoyable romp. . . . Shepperson's drawings make the story even more amusing. This farcical,
pseudo-Victorian drama of crime and punishment is sure
to be a crowd pleaser." SLJ

What Jamie saw. Front St. 1995 126p $13.95 (5
and up) **Fic**
1. Child abuse—Fiction
ISBN 1-886910-02-2 LC 95-23545
Available in paperback from Puffin Bks.
A Newbery Medal honor book, 1996
Having fled to a family friend's hillside trailer after
his mother's boyfriend tried to throw his baby sister

against a wall, nine-year-old Jamie finds himself living
an existence full of uncertainty and fear

"Shocking in its simple narration and child's-eye
view, *What Jamie Saw* is a bittersweet miracle in understated language and forthright hopelessness." SLJ

Conford, Ellen

Annabel the actress starring in "Gorilla my
dreams"; illustrated by Renée Williams-Andriani.
Simon & Schuster Bks. for Young Readers 1999
64p il $14; pa $3.99 (2-4) **Fic**
1. Actors—Fiction 2. Parties—Fiction
ISBN 0-689-81404-6; 0-689-83883-2 (pa)
LC 97-39449
Though a little disappointed that her first acting part
is to be a gorilla at a birthday party, Annabel determines
to really get into the role

"The vocabulary is appropriate for those graduating
from easy-readers, but the language is never stilted.
Amusing pen-and-ink illustrations appear on almost every
page." SLJ
Other titles about Annabel are:
Annabel the actress starring in "Hound of the
Barkervilles" (2002)
Annabel the actress, starring in "Camping it up" (2004)
Annabel the actress, starring in "Just a little extra"
(2000)

A case for Jenny Archer; illustrated by Diane
Palmisciano. Little, Brown 1988 61p il pa $4.99
hardcover o.p. (2-4) **Fic**
1. Mystery fiction
ISBN 0-316-15352-4 (pa) LC 88-14169
"A Springboard book"
After reading three mysteries in a row, Jenny becomes
convinced that the neighbors across the street are up to
no good and decides to investigate

"This lots-of-fun advanced easy reader contains eight
chapters, all about three pages long, with large, clear
print, and lots of white space. . . . The children here are
lively, the adults funny, wise, and supportive." SLJ
Other titles about Jenny Archer are:
Can do, Jenny Archer (1991)
Get the picture, Jenny Archer (1994)
Jenny Archer, author (1989)
Jenny Archer to the rescue (1990)
A job for Jenny Archer (1988)
Nibble, nibble, Jenny Archer (1993)
What's cooking, Jenny Archer (1989)

Conly, Jane Leslie

Crazy lady! HarperCollins Pubs. 1993 180p lib
bdg $16.89; pa $5.99 (5 and up) **Fic**
1. Prejudices—Fiction 2. Death—Fiction
3. Alcoholism—Fiction 4. Mentally handicapped—Fic-
tion
ISBN 0-06-021360-4 (lib bdg); 0-06-440571-0 (pa)
LC 92-18348
A Newbery Medal honor book, 1994
"A Laura Geringer book"
As he tries to come to terms with his mother's death,
Vernon finds solace in his growing relationship with the
neighborhood outcasts, an alcoholic and her retarded son

The narration "is fast and blunt, and the conversations
are lively and true." Bull Cent Child Books

Conly, Jane Leslie—*Continued*

Racso and the rats of NIMH; illustrations by Leonard Lubin. Harper & Row 1986 278p il lib bdg $17.89; pa $5.99 (4 and up)   **Fic**
1. Mice—Fiction 2. Rats—Fiction
ISBN 0-06-021362-0 (lib bdg); 0-06-440245-2 (pa)
LC 85-42634

Sequel to Mrs. Frisby and the rats of NIMH by Robert C. O'Brien

This book "continues the NIMH saga with a focus on the second rodent generation: Timothy, Mrs. Frisby's son, and Racso, son of the rebel rat Jenner. On his way to classes at Thorn Valley, Timothy saves Racso's life but is himself severely injured. Both reach the Utopian colony only to discover that the valley and surrounding farms are to be turned into a tourist lake and campgrounds." SLJ

"The book is cleverly and gracefully built upon both the philosophy of self-sufficiency and the details of the plot of its predecessor. Given the difficulty of writing good sequels, *Racso and the Rats of NIMH* is an outstanding success." Horn Book

Another title about the rats of NIMH by this author is:
RT, Margaret, and the rats of NIMH (1990)

While no one was watching. Holt & Co. 1998 233p $16.95 (5 and up)   **Fic**
1. Poverty—Fiction
ISBN 0-8050-3934-1   LC 97-48718
Also available in paperback from HarperCollins

This "story is told from the point of view of five characters: siblings Earl, Frankie, and Angela (on their own after their aunt disappears on a drinking binge) and, from a very different part of the city, Maynard and Addie (whose pet rabbit has been stolen by affection-starved, seven-year-old Frankie). Conly writes convincingly and unsentimentally about the working class poor in an urban setting." Horn Book Guide

Conrad, Pam

My Daniel. Harper & Row 1989 137p lib bdg $16.89; pa $5.99 (5 and up)   **Fic**
1. Nebraska—Fiction
ISBN 0-06-021314-0 (lib bdg); 0-06-440309-2 (pa)
LC 88-19850

"When she's 80 years old, Julia Summerwaithe decides to visit her grandchildren, Ellie and Stevie, in New York City, for the first time. She has something important to show them; in the Natural History Museum is the dinosaur she and her brother discovered on their farm in Nebraska when they were young. But even more important to Julia than seeing the dinosaur is sharing her memories of the discovery and excavation with her grandchildren." SLJ

"Rendering scenes from both the past and the present with equal skill, Conrad is at the peak of her storytelling powers." Publ Wkly

Prairie songs; illustrations by Darryl S. Zudeck. Harper & Row 1985 167p il pa $5.99 (5 and up)   **Fic**
1. Frontier and pioneer life—Fiction 2. Nebraska—Fiction
ISBN 0-06-440206-1 (pa); 0-06-021337-X (hc)
LC 85-42633

"The deterioration of the frail, young wife of a doctor who is unable to adapt to the harshness of prairie life is made more vivid because the reader views it through the eyes of an adolescent girl who lives nearby. Set in Nebraska at the turn of the century, this story is rich with detail about the beauty and hardships of pioneer life in the American West." Soc Educ

Stonewords; a ghost story. Harper & Row 1990 130p pa $5.99 hardcover o.p. (5 and up)
    Fic
1. Ghost stories 2. Space and time—Fiction
ISBN 0-06-440354-8 (pa)   LC 89-36382

Zoe discovers that her house is occupied by the ghost of an eleven-year-old girl, who carries her back to the day of her death in 1870 to try to alter that tragic event

"The supernatural and time-travel elements of the book are viscerally convincing, and the desperate neediness of both girls is fierce and real. The disquieting ending is in the richest gothic tradition, resolving one mystery only to reveal another even more frightening. This is a very scary book." Bull Cent Child Books

Cooper, Susan

The Boggart. Margaret K. McElderry Bks. 1993 196p $15.95; pa $5.99 (4 and up)   **Fic**
1. Supernatural—Fiction 2. Scotland—Fiction 3. Canada—Fiction
ISBN 0-689-50576-0; 0-689-86930-4 (pa)
LC 92-15527

After visiting the castle in Scotland which her family has inherited and returning home to Canada, twelve-year-old Emily finds that she has accidentally brought back with her a boggart, an invisible and mischievous spirit with a fondness for practical jokes

"Using both electronics and theater as metaphors for magic, Cooper has extended the world of high fantasy into contemporary children's lives through scenes superimposing the ordinary and the extraordinary." Bull Cent Child Books

Another title about the Boggart is:
The Boggart and the monster (1997)

The grey king; illustrated by Michael Heslop. Atheneum Pubs. 1975 208p il $18.95; pa $4.99 (5 and up)   **Fic**
1. Wales—Fiction 2. Good and evil—Fiction 3. Fantasy fiction
ISBN 0-689-50029-7; 0-689-82984-1 (pa)
Awarded the Newbery Medal, 1976
"A Margaret K. McElderry book"

"In the fourth of Cooper's Arthurian fantasies, Will Stanton, last and youngest of the Old Ones, the strange Welsh boy, Bran, and the sheep dogs and ghostly gray foxes of the mountains are drawn into the epic struggles of a world beyond time." SLJ

"So well-crafted that it stands as an entity in itself, the novel . . . is nevertheless strengthened by its relationship to the preceding volumes—as the individual legends within the Arthurian cycles take on deeper significance in the context of the whole. A spellbinding tour de force." Horn Book

Cooper, Susan—*Continued*

King of shadows. Margaret K. McElderry Bks. 1999 186p $16; pa $4.99 (5 and up) **Fic**
1. Shakespeare, William, 1564-1616—Fiction
2. Globe Theatre (London, England)—Fiction
3. Actors—Fiction
ISBN 0-689-82817-9; 0-689-84445-X (pa)
LC 98-51127

While in London as part of an all-boy acting company preparing to perform in a replica of the famous Globe Theatre, Nat Field suddenly finds himself transported back to 1599 and performing in the original theater under the tutelage of Shakespeare himself

"Cleverly explicating old and new acting and performance techniques, Susan Cooper entertains her contemporary readers while giving them a first-rate theatrical education." N Y Times Book Rev

The magician's boy; illustrated by Serena Riglietti. Margaret K. McElderry Bks. 2005 il $15.95 (2-4) **Fic**
1. Fairy tales 2. Magicians—Fiction
ISBN 0-689-87622-X

A boy who works for a magician meets familiar fairy tale characters when he is transported to the Land of Story in search of a missing puppet.

"Fanciful and mildly amusing, the dreamlike story flows along smoothly through a strange yet vaguely familiar wonderland. Riglietti contributes a series of expressive, stylized illustrations." Booklist

Over sea, under stone; illustrated by Margery Gill. Harcourt Brace Jovanovich 1966 c1965 252p il $18; pa $4.99 (5 and up) **Fic**
1. Fantasy fiction 2. Good and evil—Fiction 3. Great Britain—Fiction
ISBN 0-15-259034-X; 0-689-84035-7 (pa)
Also available in paperback from Simon & Schuster
First published 1965 in the United Kingdom

In this series about the "conflict between the good of the Servants of Light and the evil of the Powers of Dark, Cooper has created an intricate fantasy. Ancient lore and mythology are believably interwoven into a modern setting. Ostensibly, the three Drew children, on a holiday in Cornwall, find an old map and, aided by their uncle, they begin a search for an ancient treasure linked with King Arthur. With each book, more reliance is placed on folklore and legend. There is much action and excitement included in the carefully wrought stories." Roman. Sequences

Other titles in The dark is rising series are:
The dark is rising (1973)
Greenwitch (1974)
The grey king (1975)
Silver on the tree (1977)

Corbett, Sue

Free baseball; [by] Sue Corbett. 1st ed. Dutton Children's Books 2006 152p $15.99 (5 and up) **Fic**
1. Baseball—Fiction 2. Cuban Americans—Fiction 3. Florida—Fiction
ISBN 0-525-47120-0
LC 2005004792

Angry with his mother for having too little time for him, eleven-year-old Felix takes advantage of an opportunity to become bat boy for a minor league baseball team, hoping to someday be like his father, a famous Cuban outfielder. Includes glossaries of baseball terms and Spanish words and phrases.

"An engaging, well-written story with a satisfying ending." SLJ

Corder, Zizou

Lionboy. Dial Books 2004 275p il $15.99; pa $6.99 (4 and up) **Fic**
1. Kidnapping—Fiction 2. Lions—Fiction 3. Circus—Fiction 4. Voyages and travels—Fiction
ISBN 0-8037-2982-0; 0-14-240226-5 (pa)
Also available Spanish language edition

In the near future, Charlie Ashanti, a boy who can speak the language of cats, sets out from London to find his kidnapped parents and finds himself on a Paris-bound circus ship learning to train lions

This is a "fast-paced, original adventure." Voice Youth Advocates

Other titles in this series are:
Lionboy: the chase (2004)
Lionboy: the truth (2005)

Cottrell Boyce, Frank

Millions. HarperCollins 2004 247p $15.99; lib bdg $16.89 (5 and up) **Fic**
1. Money—Fiction 2. Great Britain—Fiction
ISBN 0-06-073330-6; 0-06-073331-4 (lib bdg)

After their mother dies, two brothers find a huge amount of money which they must spend quickly before England switches to the new European currency, but they disagree on what to do with it.

"The humor, the strong family story, and Damian's narrative voice make this satisfying novel succeed on several levels." SLJ

Couloumbis, Audrey

Getting near to baby. Putnam 1999 211p $17.99; pa $5.99 (5 and up) **Fic**
1. Sisters—Fiction 2. Death—Fiction 3. Aunts—Fiction
ISBN 0-399-23389-X; 0-698-11892-8 (pa)
LC 99-18191

A Newbery Medal honor book, 2000

Although thirteen-year-old Willa Jo and her Aunt Patty seem to be constantly at odds, staying with her and Uncle Hob helps Willa Jo and her younger sister come to terms with the death of their family's baby

"Couloumbis's writing is strong; she captures wonderfully the Southern voices of her characters and conveys with great depth powerful emotions. . . . A compelling novel." SLJ

The misadventures of Maude March; or, Trouble rides a fast horse; [by] Audrey Couloumbis. Random House 2005 295p $15.95; lib bdg $17.99 (5 and up) **Fic**
1. Frontier and pioneer life—Fiction 2. Orphans—Fiction 3. Adventure fiction
ISBN 0-375-83245-9; 0-375-93245-3 (lib bdg)
LC 2004-16464

Couloumbis, Audrey—*Continued*

After the death of the stern aunt who raised them since they were orphaned, eleven-year-old Sallie and her fifteen-year-old sister escape their self-serving guardians and begin an adventure resembling those in the dime novels Sallie loves to read.

"Sallie's narration is delightful, with understatements that are laugh-out-loud hilarious. . . . Hard to put down, and a fun read-aloud." SLJ

Coville, Bruce

Jennifer Murdley's toad; a magic shop book; illustrated by Gary A. Lippincott. Harcourt 2002 c1992 159p il $17 (4-6)   **Fic**
1. Toads—Fiction 2. Fantasy fiction
ISBN 0-15-204613-5   LC 2002-24107
A reissue of the title first published 1992
When an ordinary-looking fifth grader purchases a talking toad, she embarks on a series of extraordinary adventures
"This light, fast-paced fantasy has touches of humor (at times low comedy), an implicit moral, and a hint that Jennifer may be in for more adventures." Booklist

Jeremy Thatcher, dragon hatcher; a magic shop book; illustrated by Gary A. Lippincott. Harcourt 2002 c1991 151p il $17 (4-6)   **Fic**
1. Dragons—Fiction 2. Fantasy fiction
ISBN 0-15-204614-3   LC 2002-68714
A reissue of the title first published 1991
Small for his age but artistically talented, twelve-year-old Jeremy Thatcher unknowingly buys a dragon's egg
This is "right on target. Not only is the story involving but the reader can really get a feeling for Jeremy as a person. Coville's technique of combining the real world with a fantasy one works well in this story." Voice Youth Advocates

Juliet Dove, Queen of Love; a magic shop book. Harcourt 2003 190p $17 (4-6)   **Fic**
1. Magic—Fiction 2. Classical mythology—Fiction
ISBN 0-15-204561-9   LC 2003-11846
A shy twelve-year-old girl must solve a puzzle involving characters from Greek mythology to free herself from a spell which makes her irresistible to boys
"Although humorous, the story has surprising depth. . . . Coville capably interweaves mythological characters with realistic modern ones, keeping readers truly absorbed." SLJ

The skull of truth; a magic shop book; illustrated by Gary A. Lippincott. Harcourt 2002 c1997 194p il $17 (4-6)   **Fic**
1. Truthfulness and falsehood—Fiction 2. Fantasy fiction
ISBN 0-15-204612-7   LC 2002-24244
A reissue of the title first published 1997
Charlie, a sixth-grader with a compulsion to tell lies, acquires a mysterious skull that forces its owner to tell only the truth, causing some awkward moments before he understands its power
"Coville has structured the story very carefully, with a great deal of sensitivity to children's thought processes and emotions. The mood shifts from scary to funny to serious are fused with understandable language and sentence structures." SLJ

Thor's wedding day; by Thialfi, the goat boy; as told to and translated by Bruce Coville; illustrations by Matthew Cogswell. Harcourt 2005 137p il $15 (4 and up)   **Fic**
1. Norse mythology—Fiction 2. Giants—Fiction
ISBN 0-15-201455-1   LC 2004-29580
Thialfi, the Norse thunder god's goat boy, tells how he inadvertently helped the giant Thrym to steal Thor's magic hammer, the lengths to which Thor must go to retrieve it, and his own assistance along the way.
"Coville takes a Norse poem called the Thrymskvitha and turns it into a delightful prose romp. . . . Throughout, he injects a modern sensibility while keeping the feel of the original myth." Booklist

Cox, Judy

Butterfly buddies; illustrated by Blanche Sims. Holiday House 2001 86p il $15.95 (2-4)
                                          Fic
1. School stories 2. Friendship—Fiction 3. Butterflies—Fiction
ISBN 0-8234-1654-2   LC 2001-16720
Third grader Robin has a series of mishaps and learns the value of honesty as she tries to become best friends with Zoey, her partner for a class project on raising butterflies. Includes butterfly care tips
"Written in simple, highly descriptive language that brings settings and characters alive, and sprinkled with lively drawings, this warmhearted friendship story is a good choice for readers transitioning to chapter books." Booklist

That crazy Eddie and the science project of doom; illustrated by Blanche Sims. Holiday House 2005 88p il $15.95 (2-4)   **Fic**
1. Friendship—Fiction 2. School stories
ISBN 0-8234-1931-2   LC 2004-52316
Best friends Matt and Eddie have a falling out that threatens to ruin their science fair project. Includes instructions for making a model of an erupting volcano.
"Believable characters and situations as well as large print and short chapters make this story easily accessible to newly independent readers. Sims' black-line, cartoon-style drawings add to the appeal." Booklist

Weird stories from the Lonesome Café; illustrated by Diane Kidd. Harcourt 2000 72p il $15 (2-4)   **Fic**
1. Restaurants—Fiction 2. Uncles—Fiction 3. Nevada—Fiction
ISBN 0-15-202134-5   LC 98-56016
"Browndeer Press"
Sam moves to Nevada with his uncle to run a café in the middle of nowhere, and although Uncle Clem insists that nothing ever happens there, his clientele consists of a number of strange characters, including Dorothy and Toto, Elvis, and Bigfoot
This "will satiate kids with an appetite for shenanigans, and Kidd's black-and-white cartoon art dishes out an extra dollop of fun." Publ Wkly

Craig, Joe

Jimmy Coates: assassin? HarperCollins Pubs.
2005 218p $15.99; lib bdg $16.89 (5 and up)
Fic

1. Robots—Fiction 2. Adventure fiction
ISBN 0-06-077263-8; 0-06-077264-6 (lib bdg)

While escaping from the strange men that are after
him in London, Jimmy discovers he possesses many unusual talents for an eleven-year-old boy.

"Jimmy's convivial ensemble of helpful adults and
peers leavens the propulsive suspense." Booklist

Creech, Sharon

Absolutely normal chaos. HarperCollins Pubs.
1995 c1990 230p $16.99; lib bdg $16.89; pa $5.99
(5 and up) **Fic**

1. Family life—Fiction
ISBN 0-06-026989-8; 0-06-026992-8 (lib bdg);
0-06-440632-6 (pa) LC 95-22448

First published 1990 in the United Kingdom

"Mary Lou Finney's summer journal describes family
life in a high-spirited household in Ohio that includes
five children." N Y Times Book Rev

"Those in search of a light, humorous read will find
it; those in search of something a little deeper will also
be rewarded." SLJ

Bloomability. HarperCollins Pubs. 1998 273p
$16.99; pa $5.99 (5 and up) **Fic**

1. School stories 2. Switzerland—Fiction
ISBN 0-06-026993-6; 0-06-440823-X (pa)
LC 98-14601

"Joanna Cotler books"

When her aunt and uncle take her from New Mexico
to Lugano, Switzerland, to attend an international school,
thirteen-year-old Dinnie discovers her world expanding

"As if fresh, smart characters in a picturesque setting
weren't engaging enough, Creech also poses an array of
knotty questions, both personal and philosophical. . . . A
story to stimulate both head and heart." Booklist

Chasing Redbird. HarperCollins Pubs. 1997
261p $16.99; pa $5.99 (5 and up) **Fic**

1. Family life—Fiction 2. Kentucky—Fiction
ISBN 0-06-026987-1; 0-06-440696-2 (pa)
LC 96-44128

"Joanna Cotler books"

Thirteen-year-old Zinnia Taylor uncovers family secrets and self truths while clearing a mysterious settler
trail that begins on her family's farm in Kentucky

"With frequent flashbacks, the narrative makes clear
the complexities of the story, while the unsolved puzzles
lead the reader on to the end. The writing is laced with
figurative language and folksy comments that intensify
both atmosphere and emotion." Horn Book Guide

Granny Torrelli makes soup; drawings by Chris
Raschka. HarperCollins Pubs. 2003 141p il $15.99;
lib bdg $16.89 (4-6) **Fic**

1. Grandmothers—Fiction
ISBN 0-06-029290-3; 0-06-029291-1 (lib bdg)
LC 2002-152662

With the help of her wise old grandmother, twelve-
year-old Rosie manages to work out some problems in

her relationship with her best friend, Bailey, the boy next
door who is blind

"This gets high marks for its unique voice (make that
voices) and for the way the subtleties that are woven into
the story." Booklist

Heartbeat. HarperCollins 2004 180p $15.99; lib
bdg $16.89 (4 and up) **Fic**

1. Friendship—Fiction 2. Grandfathers—Fiction
3. Pregnancy—Fiction 4. Running—Fiction
ISBN 0-06-054022-2; 0-06-054023-0 (lib bdg)
LC 2003-7832

"Joanna Cotler books"

Twelve-year-old Annie ponders the many rhythms of
life the year that her mother becomes pregnant, her
grandfather begins faltering, and her best friend (and running partner) becomes distant

"A tenderhearted story told in spare, free-verse poems.
. . . This is vintage Creech, and its richness lies in its
sheer simplicity." SLJ

Love that dog. HarperCollins Pubs. 2001 86p
$15.99; lib bdg $14.89; pa $5.99 (4 and up)
Fic

1. Poetry—Fiction 2. School stories
ISBN 0-06-029287-3; 0-06-029289-X (lib bdg);
0-06-440959-7 (pa) LC 00-54233

"Joanna Cotler books"

"Jack's free-verse journal charts his evolution from
doubt to delight in poetry. His teacher, Miss
Stretchberry, introduces him to poetry, serves as an advocate for his writing, and flatters him into believing he's
a poet." Horn Book

"Creech has created a poignant, funny picture of a
child's encounter with the power of poetry. . . . This
book is a tiny treasure." SLJ

Replay; a new book. Joanna Cotler Books 2005
180; 31p $15.99; lib bdg $16.89 (5 and up)
Fic

1. Family life—Fiction 2. Theater—Fiction 3. Italian
Americans—Fiction
ISBN 0-06-054019-2; 0-06-054020-6 (lib bdg)

While preparing for a role in the school play, twelve-
year-old Leo finds an autobiography that his father wrote
as a teenager and ponders the ways people change as
they grow up. Includes the text for the play, "Rumpopo's
Porch."

"Both uproarious and tender, this story . . . captures
[Leo's] big, noisy, extended Italian family with pitch-
perfect dialogue that will sweep readers right to the end
of the story." Booklist

Ruby Holler. HarperCollins Pubs. 2002 310p
$16.99; lib bdg $16.89; pa $5.99 (4 and up)
Fic

1. Orphans—Fiction 2. Twins—Fiction 3. Country
life—Fiction
ISBN 0-06-027732-7; 0-06-027733-5 (lib bdg);
0-06-056015-0 (pa) LC 00-66371

"Joanna Cotler books"

Thirteen-year-old fraternal twins Dallas and Florida
have grown up in a terrible orphanage but their lives
change forever when an eccentric but sweet older couple
invites them each on an adventure, beginning in an al-

Creech, Sharon—*Continued*
most magical place called Ruby Holler
"This poignant story evokes a feeling as welcoming as
fresh-baked bread. . . . The novel celebrates the healing
effects of love and compassion." Publ Wkly

Walk two moons. HarperCollins Pubs. 1994
280p $16.99; lib bdg $17.89; pa $6.99 (6 and up)
Fic
1. Death—Fiction 2. Grandparents—Fiction 3. Family
life—Fiction 4. Friendship—Fiction
ISBN 0-06-023334-6; 0-06-023337-0 (lib bdg);
0-06-440517-6 (pa)   LC 93-31277
Awarded the Newbery Medal, 1995
After her mother leaves home suddenly, thirteen-year-
old Sal and her grandparents take a car trip retracing her
mother's route. Along the way, Sal recounts the story of
her friend Phoebe, whose mother also left
"An engaging story of love and loss, told with humor
and suspense. . . . A richly layered novel about real and
metaphorical journeys." SLJ

The Wanderer; drawings by David Diaz.
HarperCollins Pubs. 2000 305p $16.99; lib bdg
$17.89; pa $6.99 (5 and up)   **Fic**
1. Sailing—Fiction 2. Family life—Fiction 3. Sea stories
ISBN 0-06-027730-0; 0-06-027731-9 (lib bdg);
0-06-076673-5 (pa)   LC 99-42699
A Newbery Medal honor book, 2001
"Joanna Cotler books"
Thirteen-year-old Sophie and her cousin Cody record
their transatlantic crossing aboard the Wanderer, a forty-
five foot sailboat, which, along with uncles and another
cousin, is en route to visit their grandfather in England
"The story is exciting, funny, and brimming with life.
. . . This is a beautifully written and imaginatively constructed novel." SLJ

Crew, Gary
Troy Thompson's excellent peotry book; [by]
Gary Crew; [illustrated by] Craig Smith.
Kane/Miller 2003 unp il $14.95 (4 and up)
Fic
1. Poetry—Fiction 2. Authorship—Fiction
ISBN 1-929132-52-2
Troy Thompson, a grade six student at Daggaburra
State School, writes poems in order to win contest prize.
"This colorful book resembles a student's notebook.
. . . The poems are typewritten, handwritten, or printed
from a computer and 'pasted' into his book. This title is
complete with silliness and serious topics." SLJ

Crilley, Mark
Billy Clikk: creatch battler; . Delacorte Press
2004 246p $10.95; lib bdg $12.99 (3-5)
Fic
1. Monsters—Fiction 2. Adventure fiction
ISBN 0-385-73111-6; 0-385-90136-4 (lib bdg)
LC 2003-17906
Twelve-year-old Billy discovers that his parents' ex-
termination business is really a cover for something a
whole lot more sinister.

"The author of the Akiko graphic novels gives kids
with a budding taste for sf and an established delight in
the witty and the gross a new hero. . . . [The] story is
light but far from fluffy." Booklist
Another title about Billy Clikk is:
Billy Clikk: Rogmasher rampage (2005)

Crocker, Carter
The tale of the swamp rat; illustrated by the
author. Philomel Bks. 2003 232p il $16.99 (4 and
up)   **Fic**
1. Rats—Fiction 2. Florida—Fiction
ISBN 0-399-23964-2   LC 2003-429
Guided by an ancient alligator, a silent young rat
learns to find his own way in the drought-stricken
swamp, despite having been orphaned under circumstances that sometimes cause other animals to reject him
"All the characters are well drawn. . . . But the
swamp itself is the star of this story, and Crocker evokes
its complex ecology with clever phrasing and a laid-back
southern storytelling style. . . . The writing is uncommonly evocative, and this is the kind of folkloric fiction
that kids can treasure." Booklist

Cruise, Robin
Fiona's private pages. Harcourt 2000 195p $15
(5 and up)   **Fic**
1. Diaries—Fiction
ISBN 0-15-202210-4   LC 99-50559
Eleven-year-old Fiona "and her younger brother, Sam,
are adjusting to life in two households after their parents'
divorce. . . . Her favorite teacher moves away, her parents are both involved in new relationships, and her
grandmother develops Alzheimer's. . . . Her biggest
challenge, though, is deciding what to do when she discovers that a friend has anorexia." SLJ
"The writing style is energetic and highly believable,
with a voice that sounds just like a bright, reasonably
sensitive sixth-grade girl." Booklist
Another title about Fiona is:
The top-secret journal of Fiona Clare Jardin (1998)

Cummings, Priscilla
Saving Grace. Dutton Children's Bks. 2003
240p $16.99 (5 and up)   **Fic**
1. Family life—Fiction 2. Great Depression, 1929-
1939—Fiction 3. Washington (D.C.)—Fiction
4. Family life—Fiction
ISBN 0-525-47123-5   LC 2002-31539
When Grace's family is evicted from their Washington, D.C., apartment just before Christmas 1932, and she
and her younger brothers are sent to the Mission, Grace
wonders what will become of her sick older brother, her
pregnant mother, and her out-of-work father
"The realistic historical detail is an integral part of the
family drama, but the class differences and adoption conflicts are universal." Booklist

Currier, Katrina Saltonstall

Kai's journey to Gold Mountain; an Angel Island story; illustrated by Gabhor Utomo. Angel Island Association 2005 39p il $16.95 (4 and up)

Fic

1. Chinese Americans—Fiction 2. Immigrants—Fiction 3. Los Angeles (Calif.)—Fiction

ISBN 0-9667352-4-2   LC 2004-14821

In 1934, twelve-year-old Kai leaves China to join his father in America, but first he must take a long sea voyage, then endure weeks of crowded conditions and harsh examinations on Angel Island, fearing that he or his new friend will be sent home.

"The character Kai is based on a real person, whose photos, then and now, are part of the historical notes at the back of the book. Opposite each page of the intensely moving, detailed text are beautiful full-page watercolor-and-pencil illustrations that capture the crowded holding place, and, in unforgettable closeups, the characters' heartbreak and strength." Booklist

Curry, Jane Louise

The Black Canary. Margaret K. McElderry Books 2005 279p $16.95 (5 and up)   **Fic**

1. Essex, Robert Devereux, 2nd Earl of, 1566-1601—Fiction 2. Racially mixed people—Fiction 3. Singers—Fiction 4. London (England)—Fiction 5. Great Britain—History—1485-1603, Tudors—Fiction

ISBN 0-689-86478-7   LC 2003-26150

As the child of two musicians, twelve-year-old James has no interest in music until he discovers a portal to seventeenth-century London in his uncle's basement, and finds himself in a situation where his beautiful voice and the fact that he is biracial might serve him well.

"A genuinely good story that conveys a sense of darkness and mystery in the textured backdrop of a storied time and place." Booklist

Curtis, Christopher Paul

Bucking the Sarge. Wendy Lamb Books 2004 259p $15.95; lib bdg $17.99 (5 and up)

Fic

1. Mothers—Fiction 2. Fraud—Fiction 3. African Americans—Fiction

ISBN 0-385-32307-7; 0-385-90159-3 (lib bdg)

Deeply involved in his cold and manipulative mother's shady business dealings in Flint, Michigan, fourteen-year-old Luther keeps a sense of humor while running the Happy Neighbor Group Home For Men, all the while dreaming of going to college and becoming a philosopher.

This is a "hilarious, anguished novel. . . . There are some real surprises in plot and character. . . . The farce and the failure tell the truth in this gripping story." Booklist

Bud, not Buddy. Delacorte Press 1999 245p $16.95; pa $6.50 (4 and up)   **Fic**

1. Orphans—Fiction 2. African Americans—Fiction 3. Great Depression, 1929-1939—Fiction

ISBN 0-385-32306-9; 0-440-41328-1 (pa)

LC 99-10614

Awarded the Newbery Medal, 2000; Coretta Scott King Award for text, 2000

Ten-year-old Bud, a motherless boy living in Flint, Michigan, during the Great Depression, escapes a bad foster home and sets out in search of the man he believes to be his father—the renowned bandleader, H. E. Calloway of Grand Rapids

"Curtis says in a afterword that some of the characters are based on real people, including his own grandfathers, so it's not surprising that the rich blend of tall tale, slapstick, sorrow, and sweetness has the wry, teasing warmth of family folklore." Booklist

Mr. Chickee's funny money. Wendy Lamb Books 2005 151p il (Flint future detective series) $15.95; lib bdg $17.99 (3-6)   **Fic**

1. Mystery fiction 2. African Americans—Fiction

ISBN 0-385-32772-2; 0-385-90936-5 (lib bdg)

LC 2004-30863

Flint Future Detective Club members Steven Carter, his friend Russell, and Russell's huge dog Zoopy solve the mystery of a quadrillion-dollar bill with the image of James Brown on it.

"A humorous and exciting tall tale. . . . Curtis piles the laughs on in this fast-paced mystery." SLJ

The Watsons go to Birmingham—1963; a novel. Delacorte Press 1995 210p $16.95; pa $6.50 (4 and up)   **Fic**

1. African Americans—Fiction 2. Family life—Fiction 3. Prejudices—Fiction

ISBN 0-385-32175-9; 0-440-41412-1 (pa)

LC 95-7091

A Newbery Medal honor book, 1996

The ordinary interactions and everyday routines of the Watsons, an African American family living in Flint, Michigan, are drastically changed after they go to visit Grandma in Alabama in the summer of 1963

"Curtis's ability to switch from fun and funky to pinpoint-accurate psychological imagery works unusually well. . . . Ribald humor, sly sibling digs, and a totally believable child's view of the world will make this book an instant hit." SLJ

Cushman, Karen

The ballad of Lucy Whipple. Clarion Bks. 1996 195p $15 (5 and up)   **Fic**

1. Frontier and pioneer life—Fiction 2. Family life—Fiction 3. California—Gold discoveries—Fiction

ISBN 0-395-72806-1   LC 95-45257

Also available in paperback from HarperCollins

In 1849, twelve-year-old California Morning Whipple, who renames herself Lucy, is distraught when her mother moves the family from Massachusetts to a rough California mining town

"Cushman's heroine is a delightful character, and the historical setting is authentically portrayed." SLJ

Catherine, called Birdy. Clarion Bks. 1994 169p $16 (6 and up)   **Fic**

1. Middle Ages—Fiction 2. Great Britain—Fiction

ISBN 0-395-68186-3   LC 93-23333

Also available in paperback from HarperCollins

A Newbery Medal honor book, 1995

The fourteen-year-old daughter of an English country knight keeps a journal in which she records the events

Cushman, Karen—*Continued*

of her life, particularly her longing for adventures beyond the usual role of women and her efforts to avoid being married off

"In the process of telling the routines of her young life, Birdy lays before readers a feast of details about medieval England. . . . Superb historical fiction." SLJ

Matilda Bone. Clarion Bks. 2000 167p $15; pa $5.99 (5 and up) **Fic**

1. Physicians—Fiction 2. Middle Ages—Fiction 3. Great Britain—Fiction

ISBN 0-395-88156-0; 0-440-41822-4 (pa)

LC 00-24032

Fourteen-year-old Matilda, an apprentice bonesetter and practitioner of medicine in a village in medieval England, tries to reconcile the various aspects of her life, both spiritual and practical

"A fascinating glimpse into the colorful life and times of the 14th century. . . . Cushman's character descriptions are spare, with each word carefully chosen to paint wonderful pictures." SLJ

Includes bibliographical references

The midwife's apprentice. Clarion Bks. 1995 122p $12 (6 and up) **Fic**

1. Middle Ages—Fiction 2. Midwives—Fiction 3. Great Britain—Fiction

ISBN 0-395-69229-6 LC 94-13792

Also available in paperback from HarperCollins

Awarded the Newbery Medal, 1996

In medieval England, a nameless, homeless girl is taken in by a sharp-tempered midwife, and in spite of obstacles and hardship, eventually gains the three things she most wants: a full belly, a contented heart, and a place in this world

"Earthy humor, the foibles of humans both high and low, and a fascinating mix of superstition and genuinely helpful herbal remedies attached to childbirth make this a truly delightful introduction to a world seldom seen in children's literature." SLJ

Rodzina. Clarion Bks. 2003 215p $16 (5 and up) **Fic**

1. Polish Americans—Fiction 2. Orphans—Fiction

ISBN 0-618-13351-8 LC 2002-15976

A twelve-year-old Polish American girl is boarded onto an orphan train in Chicago with fears about traveling to the West and a life of unpaid slavery

"The story features engaging characters, a vivid setting, and a prickly but endearing heroine. . . . Rodzina's musings and observations provide poignancy, humor, and a keen sense of the human and topographical landscape." SLJ

Cutler, Jane

Common sense and fowls; [by] Jane Cutler; pictures by Lynne Barasch. 1st ed. Farrar, Straus and Giroux 2005 135p $16 (3-5) **Fic**

1. Pigeons—Fiction

ISBN 0-374-32262-7 LC 2004-47189

When a group of their neighbors plans to oust Mrs. Krnc because she feeds the pigeons that cause a mess, Rachel and her great uncle Benson work to encourage

better communication and search for an alternate solution.

"The cast of likable and interesting characters all take a hand in working things out. Barasch's soft, black-and-white illustrations have the same gentle tone as the text." SLJ

Another title about Rachel and Uncle Benson is:

Family dinner (1991)

Rats! pictures by Tracey Campbell Pearson. Farrar, Straus & Giroux 1996 114p il $14; pa $5.95 (3-5) **Fic**

1. Brothers—Fiction 2. Family life—Fiction

ISBN 0-374-36181-9; 0-374-46203-8 (pa)

LC 95-22953

Fourth-grader Jason and his younger brother Edward shop for school clothes, get ready for Halloween, acquire a couple of pet rats, and deal with not-birthday presents from Aunt Bea

"The brothers, alternately squabbling and supporting each other, are convincing in this lighthearted episodic novel." Horn Book Guide

Other titles about Jason and Edward are:

'Gator aid (1999)

Leap, frog (2002)

No dogs allowed (1992)

D'Adamo, Francesco

Iqbal; a novel; written by Francesco D'Adamo; translated by Ann Leonori. Atheneum Bks. for Young Readers 2003 120p $15.95 (5 and up) **Fic**

1. Masih, Iqbal, d. 1995—Fiction 2. Child labor—Fiction 3. Pakistan—Fiction

ISBN 0-689-85445-5 LC 2002-153498

Original Italian edition, 2001

A fictionalized account of the Pakistani child who escaped from bondage in a carpet factory and went on to help liberate other children like him before being gunned down at the age of thirteen

"The situation and setting are made clear in this novel. Readers cannot help but be moved by the plight of these youngsters. . . . This readable book will certainly add breadth to most collections." SLJ

Dahl, Roald

The BFG; pictures by Quentin Blake. Farrar, Straus & Giroux 1982 219p il $17 (4-6) **Fic**

1. Giants—Fiction 2. Orphans—Fiction

ISBN 0-374-30469-6 LC 82-15548

Also available in paperback from Penguin Bks.

Kidsnatched from her orphanage by a BFG (Big Friendly Giant), who spends his life blowing happy dreams to children, Sophie concocts with him a plan to save the world from nine other man-gobbling cannybull giants

This "is a book not all adults will like, but most kids will. . . . Highly unusual, often hilarious, and occasionally vulgar, even grisly." Booklist

Dahl, Roald—*Continued*

The enormous crocodile; illustrated by Quentin Blake. Knopf 2000 c1978 unp il pa $5.99 hardcover o.p. (2-4)   **Fic**

1. Crocodiles—Fiction 2. Animals—Fiction

ISBN 0-14-036556-7 (pa)

"A Borzoi Bk."

A reissue of the title first published 1978

"'For my lunch today,' says the crocodile, 'I would like a nice juicy little child.' To this end, he sets off from the muddy river to go to town. On his way he meets Humpy Rumpy the hippo, Trunky the elephant, Muggle-Wump the monkey, and the Roly-Poly bird, all of whom are horrified by his quest. Each in turn manages to foil one of his attempts on unsuspecting children." SLJ

"Mr. Dahl's gift for sonorous and inventive language carries the story along merrily . . . and Quentin Blake's squidgy jungle and scaly villain, colorful crowds and righteous elephant couldn't be improved upon." N Y Times Book Rev

James and the giant peach; a children's story; illustrated by Lane Smith. Knopf 1996 126p il $16; lib bdg $17.99 (4-6)   **Fic**

1. Fantasy fiction

ISBN 0-679-88090-9; 0-679-98090-3 (lib bdg)

                   LC 91-33489

Also available in paperback from Penguin Bks.; Spanish language edition also available

A newly illustrated edition of the title first published 1961

After the death of his parents, little James is forced to live with Aunt Sponge and Aunt Spike, two cruel old harpies. A magic potion causes the growing of a giant-sized peach on a puny peach tree. James sneaks inside the peach and finds a new world of insects. With his new family, James heads for many adventures

"A 'juicy' fantasy, 'dripping' with humor and imagination." Commonweal

The magic finger; illustrated by Quentin Blake. Viking 1995 62p il $16.99; pa $4.99 (2-4)   **Fic**

1. Hunting—Fiction 2. Magic—Fiction

ISBN 0-670-85252-X; 0-14-130229-1 (pa)

                   LC 92-31443

A newly illustrated edition of the title first published 1966 by Harper & Row

Angered by a neighboring family's sport hunting, an eight-year-old girl turns her magic finger on them

This is an "original and intriguing fantasy." Booklist

Matilda; illustrations by Quentin Blake. Viking Kestrel 1988 240p il $15.99; pa $6.99 (4-6)   **Fic**

1. School stories

ISBN 0-670-82439-9; 0-14-130106-6 (pa)

                   LC 88-40312

Also available Spanish language edition

"Matilda knows how to be extremely and creatively naughty—lining her father's hat with super glue, putting her mother's hair bleach in her father's hair tonic bottle, for example. This streak of imaginative wickedness not only allows her to make a loyal friend, Lavender, but

also to wreak revenge on her unloving parents, defeat the fiendish headmistress, Miss Turnbull, and return her victimized teacher, the enchanting Miss Honey, to her rightful place in the world." N Y Times Book Rev

"Dahl has written another fun and funny book with a child's perspective on an adult world. As usual, Blake's comical sketches are the perfect complement to the satirical humor." SLJ

Daley, Michael J.

Space station rat; by Michael J. Daley. 1st ed. Holiday House 2005 181p $15.95 (4-6)

                                   Fic

1. Rats—Fiction 2. Science fiction

ISBN 0-8234-1866-9   LC 2004-40534

A lavender rat that has escaped from a laboratory, and Jeff, a lonely boy whose parents are scientists, meet on an orbiting space station, communicate by email, and ultimately find themselves in need of each other's help and friendship.

"The point of view shifts between Jeff and Rat. . . . The developing interspecies communication raises interesting questions about the nature of intelligence and individuality. A thoughtful and satisfying adventure." SLJ

Dalgliesh, Alice

The bears on Hemlock Mountain; illustrated by Helen Sewell. Scribner c1952 unp il pa $4.99 hardcover o.p. (1-4)   **Fic**

1. Bears—Fiction

ISBN 0-689-71604-4 (pa)

A Newbery Medal honor book, 1953

"This is the story of a little boy sent by his mother to borrow an iron from an aunt who lived on the other side of Hemlock Mountain—really only a hill. Jonathan's mother did not believe that there were bears on Hemlock Mountain but Jonathan did. . . . The two-color, somewhat stylized illustrations seem right for the story." Booklist

"Jonathan's adventure is a tall tale passed down in Pennsylvania, which might have happened to a pioneer boy almost anywhere. Full of suspense and humor, it will make good reading aloud." N Y Her Trib Books

The courage of Sarah Noble; illustrations by Leonard Weisgard. Scribner 1986 c1954 52p il $16.99; pa $4.99 (2-4)   **Fic**

1. Frontier and pioneer life—Fiction 2. Native Americans—Fiction 3. Connecticut—Fiction

ISBN 0-684-18830-9; 0-689-71540-4 (pa)

                   LC 86-26191

Also available Spanish language edition

A Newbery Medal honor book, 1955

A reissue of the title first published 1954

"Sarah, though only eight, cooked for her father while he made a new home for the family in the Connecticut wilderness of 1707. When Mr. Noble returned to Massachusetts for the rest of the family, leaving Sarah with a friendly Indian, her courage was sorely tested." Hodges. Books for Elem Sch Libr

"Based on a true incident in Connecticut history—the founding of New Milford—this story is one to be long remembered for its beautiful simplicity and dignity. Leonard Weisgard's pictures add just the right sense of background." N Y Times Book Rev

Danziger, Paula

Amber Brown is not a crayon; illustrated by Tony Ross. Putnam 1994 80p il $15.99 (2-4) **Fic**
1. Friendship—Fiction 2. Moving—Fiction 3. School stories
ISBN 0-399-22509-9   LC 92-34678
Also available in paperback from Scholastic; Also available easy-to-read titles about Amber Brown in series: A is for Amber
The year she is in the third grade is a sad time for Amber because her best friend Justin is getting ready to move to a distant state
"Ross's black-and-white sketches throughout add humor and keep the pages turning swiftly. Danziger reaches out to a younger audience in this funny, touching slice of third-grade life, told in the voice of a feisty, lovable heroine." SLJ
Other titles about Amber Brown are:
Amber Brown goes fourth (1995)
Amber Brown is feeling blue (1998)
Amber Brown is green with envy (2003)
Amber Brown sees red (1997)
Amber Brown wants extra credit (1996)
Forever Amber Brown (1996)
I, Amber Brown (1999)
You can't eat your chicken pox, Amber Brown (1995)

P.S. Longer letter later; [by] Paula Danziger & Ann M. Martin. Scholastic 1998 234p $16.95; pa $4.99 (5 and up) **Fic**
1. Friendship—Fiction 2. Letters—Fiction
ISBN 0-590-21310-5; 0-590-21311-3 (pa)
LC 97-19120
Companion volume to Snail mail no more
Twelve-year-old best friends Elizabeth and Tara-Starr continue their friendship through letter-writing after Tara-Starr's family moves to another state
"The authenticity of the well-drawn characters gives life and vitality to the story. . . . Readers will thoroughly enjoy this fast-paced read." SLJ

Snail mail no more; [by] Paula Danziger & Ann M. Martin. Scholastic Press 2000 307p $16.95; pa $5.99 (5 and up) **Fic**
1. Friendship—Fiction 2. Letters—Fiction
ISBN 0-439-06335-3; 0-439-06336-1 (pa)
LC 99-33593
Companion volume to P.S. Longer letter later
Now that they live in different cities, thirteen-year-old Tara and Elizabeth use e-mail to "talk" about everything that is occurring in their lives and to try to maintain their closeness as they face big changes
"A funny, thought-provoking page-turner that will delight readers and leave them ready for more messages." Booklist

United Tates of America; a novel with scrapbook art. Scholastic Press 2002 123p il $17.95; pa $5.99 (4 and up) **Fic**
1. School stories 2. Friendship—Fiction 3. Death—Fiction
ISBN 0-590-69221-6; 0-590-69222-4 (pa)
LC 2001-42019

Eleven-year-old Skate Tate experiences many changes when she enters middle school, finds her best friend drifting away from her, and loses her beloved Great Uncle Mort, or GUM
"Young scrapbook artists, in particular, will take delight in this book's unique artwork. . . . The pictures (collages of photos, stickers, cut-outs and humorous captions) synchronize perfectly with Danziger's . . . sparkling narrative." Publ Wkly

Davis, Michele Ivy

Evangeline Brown and the Cadillac Motel; [by] Michele Ivy Davis. 1st ed. Dutton Children's Books 2004 181p $16.99 (4-6) **Fic**
1. Hotels and motels—Fiction 2. Alcoholism—Fiction 3. Father-daughter relationship—Fiction 4. Florida—Fiction
ISBN 0-525-47221-5   LC 2003-21562
"Sixth-grader Evangeline Dawn Brown is embarrassed about . . . her father's rundown motel . . . in Paradise, FL. Even more embarrassing is the fact that since her mother died, her father has become an alcoholic. Fortunately, a new friend, Farrell . . . lives nearby. . . . Likable characters are developed in a satisfying, linear plot that explores the challenges of living with dysfunctional adults." SLJ

De Angeli, Marguerite Lofft

The door in the wall; by Marguerite de Angeli. Doubleday 1989 c1949 120p il $16.95; pa $4.99 (4-6) **Fic**
1. Physically handicapped children—Fiction 2. Great Britain—Fiction 3. Middle Ages—Fiction
ISBN 0-385-07283-X; 0-440-22779-8 (pa)
Awarded the Newbery Medal, 1950
First published 1949
Robin, a crippled boy in fourteenth-century England, proves his courage and earns recognition from the King
"An enthralling and inspiring tale of triumph over handicap. Unusually beautiful illustrations, full of authentic detail, combine with the text to make life in England during the Middle Ages come alive." N Y Times Book Rev

Thee, Hannah! written and illustrated by Marguerite de Angeli. Herald Press 2000 99p il pa $15.99 (3-5) **Fic**
1. Society of Friends—Fiction 2. Philadelphia (Pa.)—Fiction
ISBN 0-8361-9106-4   LC 99-52422
A reissue of the title first published 1940 by Doubleday
Nine-year-old Hannah, a Quaker living in Philadelphia just before the Civil War, longs to have some fashionable dresses like other girls but comes to appreciate her heritage and its plain dressing when her family saves the life of a runaway slave
"Hannah and the other children are very real and, in addition to the [author's] lovely pictures that follow the story, the street cries of old Philadelphia are effectively introduced and illustrated at the beginning of each chapter." Libr J

De Guzman, Michael

The bamboozlers; [by] Michael de Guzman. 1st ed. Farrar, Straus & Giroux 2005 167p $16 (5 and up)   **Fic**

1. Grandfathers—Fiction 2. Swindlers and swindling—Fiction

ISBN 0-374-30512-9   LC 2004-57670

Nothing exciting ever happens to twelve-year-old Albert Rosegarden until he meets his grandfather for the first time, and the pair travel to Seattle, Washington, where Albert becomes a partner in his grandfather's elaborate scheme to "con a con man."

"Plot progression is steady, well paced, and broken up into short chapters of clear, concise detail. Language and writing style are visual and uncomplicated, with engaging characters that lend an authentic feel to the story." SLJ

Beekman's big deal; [by] Michael de Guzman. 1st ed. Farrar Straus Giroux 2004 213p $16 (5 and up)   **Fic**

1. New York (N.Y.)—Fiction 2. Moving—Fiction

ISBN 0-374-30672-9   LC 2003-60773

Tired of the frequent moves that he and his father must make, twelve-year-old Beekman begins to make connections with neighbors and classmates after settling in a small, unusual New York City neighborhood

"Featuring interesting, well-developed characters and sprinkled with gentle humor, this novel strikes a pleasing balance between heart-wrenching and heartwarming moments." SLJ

Deans, Sis Boulos

Every day and all the time; [by] Sis Deans. Holt & Co. 2003 234p $16.95 (5 and up)   **Fic**

1. Bereavement—Fiction 2. Ballet—Fiction

ISBN 0-8050-7337-X   LC 2002-38893

Eleven-year-old Emily, still reeling from the car accident that took her older brother's life and badly injured her, uses psychotherapy and ballet dancing to cope with her parents' decision to sell their house—the only place she can still feel and talk to her brother

"In the hands of a lesser author this could have been maudlin, but Deans wisely adds a humorous subplot involving the naive realtor that lightens the goings-on just enough. She also realistically shepherds her characters through their grief, before permitting the closure that allows them to move forward." Booklist

Deedy, Carmen Agra

The yellow star; the legend of King Christian X of Denmark; illustrated by Henri Sørensen. Peachtree Pubs. 2000 unp il $16.95 (3-5)
                                                    Fic

1. Christian X, King of Denmark, 1870-1947—Fiction 2. Denmark—Fiction 3. World War, 1939-1945—Fiction 4. Holocaust, 1933-1945—Fiction

ISBN 1-56145-208-4   LC 00-20602

Retells the story of King Christian X and the Danish resistance to the Nazis during World War II

"Deedy's language is simple and rhythmic. . . . This is an interesting and thought-provoking piece of work." SLJ

DeFelice, Cynthia C.

The apprenticeship of Lucas Whitaker; [by] Cynthia DeFelice. Farrar, Straus & Giroux 1996 151p $16 (5 and up)   **Fic**

1. Apprentices—Fiction 2. Orphans—Fiction 3. Physicians—Fiction

ISBN 0-374-34669-0   LC 95-26728

Also available in paperback from Avon Bks.

"Orphaned Lucas Whitaker has lost all his family to consumption, the scourge of the mid-nineteenth century. His grief leads him away from the family's marginal hill farm, and he stumbles into an apprenticeship with Doc Beecher, a rare college-trained physician. The pace of this fine piece of historical fiction is brisk in spite of a wealth of detail that not only establishes the setting but exposes beliefs and attitudes of the day regarding health, hygiene, and witchcraft." Horn Book

Death at Devil's Bridge; [by] Cynthia DeFelice. Farrar, Straus & Giroux 2000 181p $16 (5 and up)
                                                    Fic

1. Drug traffic—Fiction 2. Fishing—Fiction 3. Martha's Vineyard (Mass.)—Fiction

ISBN 0-374-31723-2   LC 99-56097

Also available in paperback from HarperCollins

Sequel to Devil's Bridge (1992)

Despite a great summer job as first mate on a fishing boat out of Martha's Vineyard, thirteen-year-old Ben gets caught up with illegal drugs and possible murder

"The lively prose style, a plot that keeps readers wondering, and generally fleshed-out characters create a selection that will hook its target audience to the end." SLJ

The ghost and Mrs. Hobbs; [by] Cynthia DeFelice. Farrar, Straus & Giroux 2001 180p $16; pa $5.99 (4-6)   **Fic**

1. Ghost stories

ISBN 0-374-38046-5; 0-06-001172-6 (pa)
                                  LC 00-52827

Also available Thorndike Press large print edition

Hindered by a fight with her friend Dub and a series of mysterious fires, eleven-year-old Allie investigates the fire seventeen years earlier which claimed the lives of the husband and infant son of a school cafeteria worker, as well as the handsome young man whose ghost asks Allie for help

"This is a diverting and suspenseful ghost story offering a likable protagonist and a thrilling romantic spark." Horn Book

The ghost of Fossil Glen; [by] Cynthia DeFelice. Farrar, Straus & Giroux 1998 167p $16 (4-6)   **Fic**

1. Ghost stories

ISBN 0-374-31787-9   LC 97-33230

Also available in paperback from Avon Bks.

"Sixth-grader Allie Nichols encounters the ghost of Lucy Stiles and becomes involved with Lucy's unsolved death, eventually finding proof that Lucy was murdered." Horn Book Guide

"A supernatural cliff-hanger with breathless chases and riveting suspense." SLJ

DeFelice, Cynthia C.—*Continued*

The missing manatee; [by] Cynthia DeFelice. 1st ed. Farrar, Straus and Giroux 2005 181p $16 (5 and up)   **Fic**
1. Fishing—Fiction 2. Mystery fiction 3. Florida—Fiction
ISBN 0-374-31257-5   LC 2004-50633

While coping with his parents' separation, eleven-year-old Skeet spends most of Spring Break in his skiff on a Florida river, where he finds a manatee shot to death and begins looking for the killer.

"DeFelice offers a realistic adventure story that is fast paced and full of drama. . . . The characters are multifaceted and well developed, and the story should prompt readers to think about cause and effect." SLJ

Weasel; [by] Cynthia DeFelice. Macmillan 1990 119p $15 (4 and up)   **Fic**
1. Frontier and pioneer life—Fiction 2. Ohio—Fiction
ISBN 0-02-726457-2   LC 89-37794
Also available in paperback from Avon Bks.

Alone in the Ohio frontier wilderness in the winter of 1839 while his father is recovering from an injury, eleven-year-old Nathan runs afoul of the renegade killer known as Weasel and makes a surprising discovery about the concept of revenge

"Despite its clear point of view, the book is ideal for discussion and debate—a fine choice as a novel to teach in a literature-based curriculum, where children can be stimulated to think about moral choices and about some of the unhappy truths of frontier settlement." Booklist

DeJong, Meindert

The house of sixty fathers; pictures by Maurice Sendak. Harper & Row 1956 189p il lib bdg $15.89; pa $5.39 (4-6)   **Fic**
1. Sino-Japanese Conflict, 1937-1945—Fiction 2. China—Fiction
ISBN 0-06-021481-3 (lib bdg); 0-06-440200-2 (pa)
A Newbery Medal honor book, 1957

This story is set in "China during the early days of the Japanese invasion. Tien Pao, a small Chinese boy, and his family fled inland on a sampan when the Japanese attacked their coastal village, but Tien Pao was separated from his parents during a storm and swept back down the river on the sampan. . . . [The author paints] starkly realistic word pictures that give the reader the full impact of the terror, pain, hunger and finally the joy that Tien Pao knew during his search for his family." Bull Cent Child Books

The wheel on the school; pictures by Maurice Sendak. Harper & Row 1954 298p il $16.99; lib bdg $17.89; pa $5.99 (4-6)   **Fic**
1. Netherlands—Fiction 2. Storks—Fiction 3. School stories
ISBN 0-06-021585-2; 0-06-021586-0 (lib bdg); 0-06-440021-2 (pa)
Also available Spanish language edition
Awarded the Newbery Medal, 1955

"Six Dutch children encouraged by a sensitive schoolmaster search for a wheel to place on the schoolhouse roof as a nesting place for storks. Their efforts and ultimate success lead to better understanding among the children and closer ties to older members of the community." Read Ladders for Hum Relat

"This author goes deeply into the heart of childhood and has written a moving story, filled with suspense and distinguished for the quality of its writing." Child Books Too Good To Miss

Delaney, Joseph

The last apprentice: Revenge of the witch; book one; illustrations by Patrick Arrasmith. Greenwillow Bks. 2005 344p il $14.99; lib bdg $15.89 (5 and up)   **Fic**
1. Supernatural—Fiction 2. Witches—Fiction
ISBN 0-06-076618-2; 0-06-076619-0 (lib bdg)
LC 2004-54003

Young Tom, the seventh son of a seventh son, starts work as an apprentice for the village spook, whose job is to protect ordinary folk from "ghouls, boggarts, and all manner of wicked beasties."

"Delaney grabs readers by the throat and gives them a good shake in a smartly crafted story. . . . This is a gristly thriller. . . . Yet the twisted horror is amply buffered by an exquisitely normal young hero, matter-of-fact prose, and a workaday normalcy." Booklist

Delaney, M. C. (Michael Clark)

Birdbrain Amos; written and illustrated by Michael Delaney. Philomel Bks. 2002 153p il $14.99 (3-5)   **Fic**
1. Hippopotamus—Fiction 2. Birds—Fiction
ISBN 0-399-23614-7   LC 00-66932

When Amos the hippopotamus advertises for a bird to help him with his bug problem, the tick bird who answers his ad creates a different set of problems for him by building a nest on Amos's head

"Droll, cartoon drawings embellish the very funny story, which has large type and short chapters made-to-order for a good early chapter book." Booklist
Another title about Amos is:
Birdbrain Amos, Mr. Fun (2006)

Delton, Judy

Angel's mother's wedding; illustrated by Margot Apple. Houghton Mifflin 1987 166p il $16 (3-5)
                                                      Fic
1. Weddings—Fiction 2. Family life—Fiction
ISBN 0-395-44470-5   LC 87-16937

"Angel's capacity for worry, added to her friend Edna's knowledge of how a wedding should be properly organized, leads to confusions and misunderstandings that reach almost epic proportions. . . . Humor, affection, and action narrowly skirting disaster mark each chapter in the progress from bridal shower to wedding march. Angel, her family, and friends are all pleasantly ordinary folk with a singular capacity to bring near-chaos into the normally quiet routines and celebrations of their daily life." Horn Book
Other titles about Angel are:
Angel bites the bullet (2000)
Angel in charge (1985)
Angel spreads her wings (1999)
Angel's mother's baby (1989)
Angel's mother's boyfriend (1986)
Back yard Angel (1983)

Denslow, Sharon Phillips

Georgie Lee; pictures by Lynne Rae Perkins.
Greenwillow Bks. 2002 91p il $15.95; lib bdg
$15.89 (2-4)   **Fic**
1. Farm life—Fiction 2. Grandmothers—Fiction
ISBN 0-688-17940-1; 0-688-17941-X (lib bdg)
LC 00-52797
Nine-year-old J.D. and his grandmother share all sorts
of adventures on her farm with her cat Boots and her
cow Georgie Lee
"J.D. and Grandmother enjoy plenty of engagingly
offbeat dialogue in Denslow's appealingly eventful story.
Perkins's illustrations suggest setting and characters with
understated ease." Horn Book Guide

DiCamillo, Kate

Because of Winn-Dixie. Candlewick Press 2000
182p $15.99; pa $5.99 (4 and up)   **Fic**
1. Dogs—Fiction 2. Florida—Fiction
ISBN 0-7636-0776-2; 0-7636-1605-2 (pa)
LC 99-34260
A Newbery honor book, 2001
Ten-year-old India Opal Buloni describes her first
summer in the town of Naomi, Florida, and all the good
things that happen to her because of her big ugly dog
Winn-Dixie
"This well-crafted, realistic, and heartwarming story
will be read and reread as a new favorite deserving a
long-term place on library shelves." SLJ

The miraculous journey of Edward Tulane;
illustrated by Bagram Ibatoulline. 1st ed.
Candlewick Press 2006 198p il $18.99 (3-6)
                                                Fic
1. Toys—Fiction 2. Rabbits—Fiction
ISBN 0-7636-2589-2   LC 2004-56129
Edward Tulane, a coldhearted and proud toy rabbit,
loves only himself until he is separated from the little
girl who adores him and travels across the country, acquiring new owners and listening to their hopes, dreams,
and histories.
"This achingly beautiful story shows a true master of
writing at her very best. . . . Ibatoulline's lovely sepia-
toned gouache illustrations and beautifully rendered color
plates are exquisite." SLJ

The tale of Despereaux; being the story of a
mouse, a princess, some soup, and a spool of
thread; illustrated by Timothy Basil Ering.
Candlewick Press 2003 267p il $17.99 (3-6)
                                                Fic
1. Fairy tales 2. Mice—Fiction
ISBN 0-7636-1722-9   LC 2002-34760
Awarded the Newbery Medal, 2004
The adventures of Despereaux Tilling, a small mouse
of unusual talents, the princess that he loves, the servant
girl who longs to be a princess, and a devious rat determined to bring them all to ruin
"Forgiveness, light, love, and soup. These essential ingredients combine into a tale that is as soul stirring as
it is delicious. . . . Ering's soft pencil illustrations reflect
the story's charm." Booklist

Dickinson, Peter

Inside Grandad. Wendy Lamb Books 2004 117p
$15.95; lib bdg $17.99 (4 and up)   **Fic**
1. Grandfathers—Fiction 2. Stroke—Fiction
3. Scotland—Fiction
ISBN 0-385-74641-5; 0-385-90873-3 (lib bdg)
LC 2003-7862
"Gavin tries to enlist the help of selkies—seal people—to communicate with his comatose grandfather."
Bull Cent Child Books
The "simple, beautiful words . . . root the fantasy in
real places and daily routine. . . . The love and grief in
the story will touch many readers." Booklist

DiSalvo-Ryan, DyAnne

The sloppy copy slipup; [by] Dyanne DiSalvo.
Holiday House 2006 103p il $16.95 (2-4)
                                                Fic
1. School stories 2. Authorship—Fiction
ISBN 0-8234-1947-9
Fourth-grader Brian Higman worries about how his
teacher Miss Fromme—nicknamed The General—will re-
act when he fails to hand in a writing assignment, but he
ends up being able to tell his story, after all.
"DiSalvo combines spot-on humor, vivid classroom
scenes, and tension that builds from the first page, and
Brian's story . . . will keep children eagerly engaged."
Booklist

Divakaruni, Chitra Banerjee

The conch bearer. Roaring Brook Press 2003
265p $16.95; pa $5.99 (5 and up)   **Fic**
1. Magic—Fiction 2. India—Fiction
ISBN 0-7613-1935-2; 0-6898-7242-9 (pa)
LC 2003-8578
"A Neal Porter book"
In India, a healer invites twelve-year-old Anand to
join him on a quest to return a magical conch to its safe
and rightful home, high in the Himalayan mountains
"Divakaruni keeps her tale fresh and riveting." Publ
Wkly
Another title about Anand is:
The mirror of fire and dreaming (2005)

Dodge, Mary Mapes

Hans Brinker; or, The silver skates (4 and up)
                                                Fic
1. Ice skating—Fiction
Various editions available
First published 1865
A new friend gives Hans and his sister Gretel enough
money for one pair of ice skates, so Hans insists that
Gretel enter the grand competition for silver skates,
while he seeks the great Doctor who consents to try to
restore their father's memory

Donaldson, Julia

The Giants and the Joneses; illustrated by Greg
Swearingen. Holt & Co. 2005 215p il $14.95 (3-5)
                                                Fic
1. Giants—Fiction 2. Fantasy fiction
ISBN 0-8050-7805-3   LC 2004-60727

Donaldson, Julia—*Continued*

When Jumbeelia, an eight-year-old giant, climbs down a beanstalk and collects some "iggly plops," the little people of children's stories, she treats them like toys, unaware that she is endangering their lives.

"An exciting story with a subtle message about respect and cooperation." SLJ

Dorris, Michael

Morning Girl. Hyperion Bks. for Children 1992 74p pa $4.99 hardcover o.p. (4 and up)

Fic

1. Taino Indians—Fiction 2. America—Exploration—Fiction

ISBN 0-78681-358-X   LC 92-52989

Also available Spanish language edition

Twelve year old Morning Girl, a Taino Indian who loves the day, and her younger brother Star Boy, who loves the night, take turns describing their life on a Bahamian island in 1492; in Morning Girl's last narrative, she witnesses the arrival of the first Europeans to her world

"The author uses a lyrical, yet easy-to-follow, style to place these compelling characters in historical context. . . . Dorris does a superb job of showing that family dynamics are complicated, regardless of time and place. . . . A touching glimpse into the humanity that connects us all." Horn Book

Sees Behind Trees. Hyperion Bks. for Children 1996 104p pa $4.99 hardcover o.p. (4 and up)

Fic

1. Native Americans—Fiction 2. Vision disorders—Fiction

ISBN 0-7868-1357-1 (pa)   LC 96-15859

"For the partially sighted Walnut, it is impossible to prove his right to a grown-up name by hitting a target with his bow and arrow. With his highly developed senses, however, he demonstrates that he can do something even better: he can see 'what cannot be seen' which earns him the name Sees Behind Trees. . . . Set in sixteenth-century America, this richly imagined and gorgeously written rite-of-passage story has the gravity of legend. Moreover, it has buoyant humor and the immediacy of a compelling story that is peopled with multidimensional characters." Booklist

Dowell, Frances O'Roark

Chicken boy. Atheneum Books for Young Readers 2005 201p $15.95 (4 and up)   Fic

1. Chickens—Fiction 2. Friendship—Fiction 3. Family life—Fiction

ISBN 0-689-85816-7   LC 2004-10928

Since the death of his mother, Tobin's family life and school life have been in disarray, but after he starts raising chickens with his seventh-grade classmate, Henry, everything starts to fall into place.

"There is no glib resolution, here. But the strong narration and the child's struggle with forgiveness make for poignant, aching drama." Booklist

Dovey Coe. Atheneum Bks. for Young Readers 2000 181p $16; pa $5.99 (5 and up)   Fic

1. Mountain life—Fiction 2. North Carolina—Fiction

ISBN 0-689-83174-9; 0-689-84667-3 (pa)

LC 99-46870

When accused of murder in her North Carolina mountain town in 1928, Dovey Coe, a stronged-willed twelve-year-old girl, comes to a new understanding of others, including her deaf brother

"Dowell has created a memorable character in Dovey, quick-witted and honest to a fault. . . . This is a delightful book, thoughtful and full of substance." Booklist

The secret language of girls. Atheneum Books for Young Readers 2004 247p $15.95 (5 and up)

Fic

1. Friendship—Fiction 2. School stories

ISBN 0-689-84421-2   LC 2003-12026

Marylin and Kate have been friends since nursery school, but when Marylin becomes a middle school cheerleader and Kate begins to develop other interests, their relationship is put to the test.

"Excellent characterization, an accurate portrayal of the painful and often cruel machinations of preteens, and evocative dialogue will make this tale resonate with most readers." SLJ

Where I'd like to be. Atheneum Bks. for Young Readers 2003 232p $15.95 (4 and up)   Fic

1. Foster home care—Fiction 2. Tennessee—Fiction 3. Friendship—Fiction

ISBN 0-689-84420-4   LC 2002-2183

"When a new girl moves into the East Tennessee Children's Home, her charisma has an immediate effect on Maddie, the story's narrator. Maddie's scrapbooks filled with pictures of the houses she dreams of living in serve as a catalyst for Murphy, as she gathers a fledgling group of unlikely friends around her. . . . The foster children's backgrounds are believable, diverse, and engaging, and readers familiar with eastern Tennessee will appreciate the references to real towns and cities that are sprinkled throughout the text." SLJ

Downer, Ann

Hatching magic. Atheneum Bks. for Young Readers 2003 242p $16.95 (4 and up)   Fic

1. Dragons—Fiction 2. Magic—Fiction

ISBN 0-689-83400-4   LC 00-56570

When a thirteenth-century wizard confronts twenty-first century Boston while seeking his pet dragon, he is followed by a rival wizard and a very unhappy demon, but eleven-year-old Theodora Oglethorpe may hold the secret to setting everything right

"With likable characters, and laced with plenty of humor and adventure, Downer's fantasy will have solid appeal for young genre fans." Booklist

Another title about Theodora is:

The dragon of never-was (2006)

Draanen, Wendelin van

Flipped. Knopf 2001 212p $14.95; lib bdg $16.99; pa $8.95 (6 and up)   Fic

ISBN 0-375-81174-5; 0-375-91174-X (lib bdg); 0-375-82544-4 (pa)   LC 2001-29238

In alternating chapters, eighth-graders Juli and Bryce, describe how their feelings about themselves, each other, and their families have changed over the years

"There's lots of laugh-out-loud egg puns and humor in this novel. There's also, however, a substantial amount

Draanen, Wendelin van—_Continued_

of serious social commentary woven in, as well as an exploration of the importance of perspective in relationships." SLJ

Sammy Keyes and the hotel thief. Knopf 1998 163p il $4.99 hardcover o.p. (4 and up) **Fic**

1. Mystery fiction
ISBN 0-679-89264-8 (pa)   LC 97-40776

Thirteen-year-old Sammy's penchant for speaking her mind gets her in trouble when she involves herself in the investigation of a robbery at the "seedy" hotel across the street from the seniors' building where she is living with her grandmother

"This is a breezy novel with vivid characters." Bull Cent Child Books

Other titles about Sammy Keyes are:
Sammy Keyes and the art of deception (2003)
Sammy Keyes and the curse of Moustache Mary (2000)
Sammy Keyes and the dead giveaway (2005)
Sammy Keyes and the Hollywood mummy (2001)
Sammy Keyes and the psycho Kitty Queen (2004)
Sammy Keyes and the runaway elf (1999)
Sammy Keyes and the search for snake eyes (2002)
Sammy Keyes and the Sisters of Mercy (1999)
Sammy Keyes and the skeleton man (1998)

Shredderman: Secret identity; illustrated by Brian Biggs. Knopf 2004 138p il $12.95; lib bdg $14.99 (3-5)   **Fic**

1. School stories
ISBN 0-375-82351-4; 0-375-92351-9 (lib bdg)
        LC 2003-17856

Fifth-grader Nolan Byrd, tired of being called names by the class bully, has a secret identity—Shredderman!

"This entertaining story . . . will keep even reluctant readers laughing and wanting more stories about this cyber superhero. Droll, black-and-white cartoons are a perfect accompaniment to the clever text." SLJ

Other titles about Shredderman are:
Shredderman: Attack of the tagger (2004)
Shredderman: Enemy spy (2005)
Shredderman: Meet the gecko (2005)

Du Bois, William Pène

The twenty-one balloons; written and illustrated by William Pène Du Bois. Viking 1947 179p il $16.99; pa $5.99 (5 and up)   **Fic**

1. Balloons—Fiction
ISBN 0-670-73441-1; 0-14-032097-0 (pa)

Awarded the Newbery Medal, 1948

"Professor Sherman set off on a flight across the Pacific in a giant balloon, but three weeks later the headlines read 'Professor Sherman in wrong ocean with too many balloons.' This book is concerned with the professor's explanation of this phenomenon. His account of his one stopover on the island of Krakatoa which blew up with barely a minute to spare to allow time for his escape, is the highlight of this hilarious narrative." Ont Libr Rev

Dudley, David L.

The bicycle man. Clarion Books 2005 249p $16 (4-6)   **Fic**

1. Country life—Fiction 2. African Americans—Fiction 3. Georgia—Fiction
ISBN 0-618-54233-7   LC 2005-06409

In poor, rural Georgia in 1927, twelve-year-old Carrisa and her suspicious mama take in an elderly drifter with a shiny bicycle, never expecting how profoundly his wise and patient ways will affect them.

Readers "will find complex characters and rich themes. . . . There is much here to digest and a wealth of material for book discussions." SLJ

Duey, Kathleen

Lara and the gray mare; Hoofbeats, book one; by Kathleen Duey. Dutton Children's Books 2005 140p $15.99; pa $4.99 (4-6)   **Fic**

1. Horses—Fiction 2. Ireland—Fiction
ISBN 0-525-47332-7; 0-14-240230-3 (pa)
        LC 2004-53521

While her father is away fighting the Normans and other Irish clans, nine-year-old Lara works hard to help harvest food and also cares for the pregnant gray mare that she loves

"Writing with a keen appreciation for everyday goings-on in thirteenth-century Ireland and an unusual ability to bring the past to life, Duey creates a convincing setting, a thoroughly likable heroine, and a strong narrative." Booklist

Other titles in the Hoofbeats series are:
Lara and the Moon-colored filly (book two) (2005)
Lara at Athnery Castle (book three) (2005)
Lara at the silent place (book four) (2005)

Duffey, Betsy

Spotlight on Cody; illustrated by Ellen Thompson. Viking 1998 74p il $14.99; pa $4.99 (2-4)   **Fic**

1. School stories
ISBN 0-670-88077-9; 0-14-130987-3 (pa)
        LC 98-17461

Nine-year-old Cody Michaels is bound for stardom in the third grade talent show just as soon as he figures out his talent

"Truly funny scenes juxtaposed with Cody's distress at his situation and lively pacing combine to make this a very appealing chapter book." Booklist

Other titles about Cody are:
Cody unplugged (1999)
Cody's secret admirer (1998)
Hey, new kid! (1996)
Virtual Cody (1997)

Dunrea, Olivier

Hanne's quest; [by] Olivier Dunrea. Philomel Books 2005 95p il $16.99 (3-5)   **Fic**

1. Fairy tales 2. Chickens—Fiction 3. Scotland—Fiction
ISBN 0-399-24216-3   LC 2004-9091

On an island off the coast of Scotland, a young hen must prove herself pure, wise, and brave in a quest to

Dunrea, Olivier—_Continued_
help her beloved owner, Mem Pocket, from losing her family's farm.

"Beautifully composed and often darkly atmospheric, the handsome full-page paintings rival . . . those in the best picture books. This handsome, well-written book will find a rapt audience among children who prefer sturdy, homespun fairy tales." Booklist

DuPrau, Jeanne
The city of Ember. Random House 2003 270p $15.95; lib bdg $17.99 (5 and up)   **Fic**
1. Science fiction
ISBN 0-375-82273-9; 0-375-92274-1 (lib bdg)
           LC 2002-10239

"More than 200 years after an unspecified holocaust, the residents of Ember have lost all knowledge of anything beyond the area illuminated by the floodlamps on their buildings. . . . Food and other supplies are running low, and the power failures that plunge the town into impenetrable darkness are becoming longer and more frequent. Then Lina, a young foot messenger, discovers a damaged document from the mysterious Builders that hints at a way out." SLJ

"The writing and storytelling are agreeably spare and remarkably suspenseful." Horn Book
Followed by The people of Sparks

The people of Sparks. Random House 2004 338p $15.95; lib bdg $17.99 (5 and up)
           Fic
1. Science fiction
ISBN 0-375-82824-9; 0-375-92824-3 (lib bdg)
           LC 2003-20760

Sequel to The City of Ember
"DuPrau continues the adventures of Lina and Doon, who have led the 400 residents from the underground city of Ember to the unfamiliar world above. The refugees are tentatively welcomed, housed, and fed by the people of Sparks, located near the wasteland left by the long-ago Disaster that destroyed most of civilization. Conflicts arise between the two groups. . . . DuPrau clearly explores themes of nonviolence and when to stand up for oneself. The text smoothly involves new readers and fans of the first story, creating a range of three-dimensional characters." Booklist

Durbin, William
Blackwater Ben. Wendy Lamb Bks. 2003 199p $15.95; lib bdg $17.99 (5 and up)   **Fic**
1. Lumber and lumbering—Fiction 2. Father-son relationship—Fiction 3. Frontier and pioneer life—Fiction 4. Minnesota—Fiction
ISBN 0-385-72928-6; 0-385-90149-6 (lib bdg)
           LC 2002-155586

In the winter of 1898, a seventh-grade boy drops out of school to work with his father, the cook at Blackwater Logging Camp in Minnesota
"Lively details about logging add depth to this warm, colorful historical novel." Booklist

The journal of Sean Sullivan; a Transcontinental Railroad worker. Scholastic 1999 188p il (My name is America) $10.95 (5 and up)   **Fic**
1. West (U.S.)—Fiction 2. Railroads—Fiction
ISBN 0-439-04994-6   LC 98-47705

In 1867, fifteen-year-old Sean experiences both hardships and rewards when he joins his father in working on the building of the Transcontinental Railroad

This "focuses on historic details to bring the Old West vibrantly alive. . . . Durbin expertly handles racial issues and also does a good job of being authentic to the time and place, yet sensitive to modern sensibilities." Booklist

Durrant, Lynda
The beaded moccasins; the story of Mary Campbell. Clarion Bks. 1998 183p $15; pa $5.50 (5 and up)   **Fic**
1. Campbell, Mary, fl. 1764—Fiction 2. Delaware Indians—Fiction
ISBN 0-395-85398-2; 0-440-41591-8 (pa)
           LC 97-16288

Also available in paperback from Dell
After being captured by a group of Delaware Indians and given to their leader as a replacement for his dead granddaughter, twelve-year-old Mary Campbell is forced to travel west with them to Ohio

"Based on a 1759 historical incident. . . . Thoughtful characterizations, a strong sense of place, and an involving present tense narration make this a solid historical novel." Horn Book Guide

Eager, Edward
Half magic; illustrated by N. M. Bodecker; introduction by Jack Gantos. 50th anniversary ed. Harcourt 2004 c1954 217p il $18.95 (4-6)
           Fic
1. Fantasy fiction
ISBN 0-15-205302-6

A reissue with a new introduction of the title first published 1954

Faced with a dull summer in the city, Jane, Mark, Katharine, and Martha suddenly find themselves involved in a series of extraordinary adventures after Jane discovers an ordinary-looking coin that seems to grant wishes

"Entertaining and suspenseful fare for readers of make-believe." Booklist
Other titles in this series are:
Knight's castle (1956)
Magic by the lake (1957)
The time garden (1958)

Magic or not? illustrated by N. M. Bodecker. Harcourt Brace & Co. 1999 c1959 197p il $17; pa $5.40 (4-6)   **Fic**
1. Fantasy fiction
ISBN 0-15-202081-0; 0-15-202080-2 (pa)
           LC 99-22566

A reissue of the title first published 1959
"An Odyssey/Harcourt Brace young classic."
When the family moves to Connecticut, twins James and Laura make new friends and begin a series of unusual adventures after discovering an old well that seems to be magic in their backyard

"The children are lifelike and likable, their doings are entertaining." Booklist

Eager, Edward—*Continued*
Another title in this series is:
The well-wishers (1960)

Seven-day magic; illustrated by N.M. Bodecker. Harcourt Brace & Co. 1999 190p il $17; pa $6 (4-6)   **Fic**
1. Fantasy fiction
ISBN 0-15-202079-9; 0-15-202078-0 (pa)
                                        LC 99-22563
A reissue of the title first published 1962
"Five children find a magic book that describes themselves, and realize that they can create their own magic by wishing with the book. . . . The children are lively and a bit precocious. . . . [The book has] humor, and some fresh and imaginative situations." Bull Cent Child Books

Easton, Richard
A real American. Clarion Bks. 2002 156p $15 (5 and up)   **Fic**
1. Farm life—Fiction 2. Immigrants—Fiction 3. Coal mines and mining—Fiction 4. Pennsylvania—Fiction
ISBN 0-618-13339-9   LC 2001-53876
With his older brother dead, his best friend moved away, and his father busy trying to save the family's farm in western Pennsylvania, eleven-year-old Nathan needs a friend, but can he find one among the immigrants who have come to work in the new coal mines?
"The setting is realistic, and the characters are drawn with complexity." Booklist
Includes bibliographical references

Eckert, Allan W.
Incident at Hawk's Hill; with illustrations by John Schoenherr. Little, Brown 1998 173p il $15.95; pa $5.95 (6 and up)   **Fic**
1. Badgers—Fiction 2. Wilderness survival—Fiction 3. Saskatchewan—Fiction
ISBN 0-316-21905-3; 0-316-20948-1 (pa)
A Newbery Medal honor book, 1972
First published 1971
This account of an actual incident in Saskatchewan at the turn of the century tells of six-year-old Ben Macdonald, more attuned to animals than to people, who gets lost on the prairie and is nurtured by a female badger for two months before being found. Although a strange bond continues between the boy and the badger, the parents' understanding of their son and his communication with them improve as a result of the bizarre experience
"A very deeply moving, well written book." Jr Bookshelf
Followed by Return to Hawk's Hill (1998)

Edwards, Michelle
The talent show. Harcourt 2002 56p il $14; pa $5.95 (1-3)   **Fic**
1. School stories
ISBN 0-15-216403-0; 0-15-205760-9 (pa)
                                        LC 2001-1227
"A Jackson friends book"

Second-grader Howardina Geraldina Paulina Maxina Gardenia Smith is sure she will be the star of the talent show, but when she gets up to sing at the dress rehearsal, she gets stage fright
"This combines strong characterizations with a heartfelt story that touches on real emotions. The pen-and-ink and watercolor-and-gouache artwork is very imaginative." Booklist
Other titles in the Jackson friends series are:
Pa Lia's first day (1999)
Stinky Stern forever (2005)
Zero grandparents (2001)

Ellis, Sarah
The several lives of Orphan Jack; pictures by Bruno St-Aubin. Douglas & McIntyre 2003 84p il $14.95 (3-6)   **Fic**
1. Orphans—Fiction 2. Adventure fiction
ISBN 0-88899-529-6
"A Groundwood book"
When, at the age of twelve, he is sent out from the Opportunities School for Orphans and Foundlings to be a bookkeeper's apprentice, Jack finds his heretofore predictable life full of unusual adventures.
"Ellis has created a small gem here, with messages about following your heart tucked into the sentences, phrases, thoughts, and ideas that she seamlessly weaves together." Booklist

English, Karen
Francie. Farrar, Straus & Giroux 1999 199p $17; pa $5.95 (5 and up)   **Fic**
1. African Americans—Fiction 2. Race relations—Fiction 3. Alabama—Fiction
ISBN 0-374-32456-5; 0-374-42459-4 (pa)
                                        LC 98-53047
Coretta Scott King honor book for text, 2000
"The best student in her small, all-black school in preintegration Alabama, 12-year-old Francie hopes for a better life. . . . When Jessie, an older school friend who is without family, is forced on the run by a racist employer, Francie leaves her mother's labeled canned food for him in the woods. Only when the sheriff begins searching their woods . . . does she realize the depth of the danger she may have brought to her family. Francie's smooth-flowing, well-paced narration is gently assisted by just the right touch of the vernacular. Characterization is evenhanded and believable, while place and time envelop readers." SLJ

Enright, Elizabeth
Gone-Away Lake; illustrated by Beth and Joe Krush. Harcourt 2000 c1957 256p il $17; pa $6 (4-6)   **Fic**
ISBN 0-15-202274-0; 0-15-202272-4 (pa)
                                        LC 99-55281
A Newbery Medal honor book, 1958
"An Odyssey/Harcourt young classic"
A reissue of the title first published 1957
Portia and her cousin Julian discover adventure in a hidden colony of forgotten summer houses on the shores of a swampy lake
"Excellent writing, clear in setting of scene and details of nature, and strong in appeal for children." Horn Book

Enright, Elizabeth—*Continued*
Another title about Gone-Away Lake is:
Return to Gone-Away Lake (1961)

Erdrich, Louise
The birchbark house. Hyperion Bks. for Children 1999 244p il $17.99; pa $6.99 (5 and up)
Fic

1. Ojibwa Indians—Fiction
ISBN 0-7868-0300-2; 0-7868-1454-3 (pa)
LC 98-46366
Omakayas, a seven-year-old Native American girl of the Ojibwa tribe, lives through the joys of summer and the perils of winter on an island in Lake Superior in 1847.
"Erdrich crafts images of tender beauty while weaving Ojibwa words seamlessly into the text. Her gentle spot art throughout complements this first of several projected stories that will 'attempt to retrace [her] own family's history.'" Horn Book Guide

The game of silence; [by] Louise Erdrich. 1st ed. HarperCollins 2004 256p $15.99; lib bdg $16.89 (5 and up)
Fic
1. Ojibwa Indians—Fiction
ISBN 0-06-029789-1; 0-06-029790-5 (lib bdg)
LC 2004-6018
Sequel to The birchbark house
Nine-year-old Omakayas, of the Ojibwa tribe, moves west with her family in 1849.
"Erdrich's captivating tale of four seasons portrays a deep appreciation of our environment, our history, and our Native American sisters and brothers." SLJ

Estes, Eleanor
The Alley; illustrated by Edward Ardizzone. Harcourt 2003 c1964 283p il $17; pa $5.95 (4-6)
Fic
1. Brooklyn (New York, N.Y.)—Fiction 2. Mystery fiction
ISBN 0-15-204917-7; 0-15-204918-5 (pa)
LC 2003-45290
"An Odyssey/Harcourt young classic"
A reissue of the title first published 1964
Ten-year-old Connie, who lives in the Brooklyn neigborhood called The Alley, investigates a burglary with her friend Billy Maloon
"Even the minor characters are deftly drawn. A book with substance and a great deal of humor." Horn Book
Followed by The tunnel of Hugsy Goode

Ginger Pye; with illustrations by the author. Harcourt 2000 c1951 306p il $17; pa $6 (4-6)
Fic
1. Dogs—Fiction
ISBN 0-15-202499-9; 0-15-202505-7 (pa)
LC 00-26700
Awarded the Newbery Medal, 1952
"An Odyssey/Harcourt young classic"
A reissue of the title first published 1951
The disappearance of a new puppy named Ginger and the appearance of a mysterious man in a mustard yellow hat bring excitement into the lives of the Pye children

Estes' drawings are "vivid, amusing sketches that point up and confirm the atmosphere of the story. It is a book to read and reread." Saturday Rev
Another title about the Pye family is:
Pinky Pye (1958)

The hundred dresses; illustrated by Louis Slobodkin. New ed. Harcourt 2004 c1944 80p il $16 (4-6)
Fic
ISBN 0-15-205170-8   LC 2003-57037
A reissue of the title first published 1944
"The 100 dresses are just dream dresses, pictures Wanda Petronski has drawn, but she describes them in self-defense as she appears daily in the same faded blue dress. Not until Wanda, snubbed and unhappy, moves away leaving her pictures at school for an art contest, do her classmates realize their cruelty." Books for Deaf Child
"Written with great simplicity it reveals, in a measure, the pathos of human relationships and the suffering of those who are different. Mr. Slobodkin's watercolors interpret the mood of the story and fulfill the quality of the text." N Y Public Libr

The Moffats; illustrated by Louis Slobodkin. Harcourt 2001 c1941 290p il $17; pa $6 (4-6)
Fic
1. Family life—Fiction
ISBN 0-15-202535-9; 0-15-202541-3 (pa)
LC 00-39726
"An Odyssey/Harcourt Young Classic"
A reissue of the title first published 1941
Relates the adventures and misadventures of the four Moffat children living with their widowed mother in a yellow house on New Dollar Street in the small town of Cranbury, Connecticut
"A captivating family story with highly individual characters. Each chapter is a separate episode, suitable for reading aloud." Hodges. Books for Elem Sch Libr
Other titles about the Moffats are:
The middle Moffat (1942)
The Moffat Museum (1983)
Rufus M. (1943)

The witch family; illustrated by Edward Ardizzone. Harcourt 2000 223p il $17; pa $6 (4-6)
Fic
1. Witches—Fiction
ISBN 0-15-202604-5; 0-15-202610-X (pa)
LC 99-89152
"An Odyssey/Harcourt young classic"
A reissue of the title first published 1960
"The Old Witch, the Little Witch Girl and Witch Baby are all the creations of crayons wielded by Amy and Clarissa. . . . As their imaginations run riot, the witches take on an independent life of their own, and the two groups mix and mingle." Libr J
"A very special book that is certain to give boundless pleasure." Horn Book

Etchemendy, Nancy

The power of Un. Front St./Cricket Bks. 2000
148p $15.95; pa $4.99 (4 and up) **Fic**
1. Fantasy fiction
ISBN 0-8126-2850-0; 0-4393-1331-7 (pa)
LC 99-58281

When he is given a device that will allow him to
"undo" what has happened in the past, Gib Finney is not
sure what event from the worst day in his life he should
change in order to keep his sister from being hit by a
truck

The author has a "knack for writing hilarious dialogue
that perfectly paints the funny, poignant, and altogether
unpredictable world of eleven and twelve year olds. . . .
A unique, thought-provoking book." Voice Youth Advocates

Evangelista, Beth

Gifted. Walker & Co. 2005 180p $16.95 (5 and
up) **Fic**
1. Gifted children—Fiction 2. Camping—Fiction
3. Bullies—Fiction
ISBN 0-8027-8994-3

Arrogant, mentally gifted George Clark has dreaded
the eighth-grade class camping trip and its inevitable bullying, but a hurricane and a friend's loyalty make him
realize what is important in life.

"It's hard to write a successful book with an unlikable
protagonist . . . but that's what first-time author
Evangelista has done. . . . Fresh and funny." Booklist

Fardell, John

The 7 professors of the Far North. G. P.
Putnam's Sons 2005 217p il $14.99 (4 and up)
Fic
1. Adventure fiction 2. Arctic regions—Fiction
3. Science fiction
ISBN 0-399-24381-X

Eleven-year-old Sam finds himself involved in a dangerous adventure when he and his new friends, brother
and sister Ben and Zara, set off for the Arctic to try and
rescue the siblings' great-uncle and five other professors
from the mad scientist holding them prisoner.

"Action is nonstop and very exciting. This inventive,
funny, suspenseful, and exciting book will appeal to most
readers." SLJ

Farley, Walter

The Black Stallion; illustrated by Domenick
D'Andrea; with a new foreword. Golden
anniversary ed. Random House 1991 196p il $17;
pa $5.50 (4 and up) **Fic**
1. Horses—Fiction
ISBN 0-679-81349-7; 0-679-81343-8 (pa)
LC 90-53670

A newly illustrated edition of the title first published
1941

Young Alec Ramsay is shipwrecked on a desert island
with a horse destined to play an important part in his
life. Following their rescue their adventure continues in
America

This story "continues to please. Each energetic black-
and-white pencil drawing done by D'Andrea . . . shows
the glossy Black in action." Horn Book Guide

Other titles about the Black Stallion are:
The Black Stallion and Flame (1960)
The Black Stallion returns (1945)
The Black Stallion's ghost (1969)
Son of the Black Stallion (1947)
The young Black Stallion (1989)

Farmer, Nancy

The Ear, the Eye, and the Arm; a novel.
Orchard Bks. 1994 311p $18.95; lib bdg $19.99 (6
and up) **Fic**
1. Science fiction 2. Zimbabwe—Fiction
ISBN 0-531-06829-3; 0-531-08679-8 (lib bdg)
LC 93-11814

Also available in paperback from Puffin Bks. and
Thorndike Press large print edition

A Newbery Medal honor book, 1995

"A Richard Jackson book"

In 2194 in Zimbabwe, General Matsika's three children Tendai, Rita, and Kuda, are kidnapped and put to
work in a plastic mine, while three mutant detectives
named The Ear, the Eye and the Arm use their special
powers to search for them

"Throughout the story, it's the thrilling adventure that
will grab readers, who will also like the comic, tender
characterizations." Booklist

A girl named Disaster. Orchard Bks. 1996 309p
$19.95 (6 and up) **Fic**
1. Supernatural—Fiction 2. Adventure fiction
3. Mozambique—Fiction 4. Zimbabwe—Fiction
ISBN 0-531-09539-8 LC 96-15141

Also available in paperback from Penguin Bks.

A Newbery Medal honor book, 1997

"A Richard Jackson book"

While journeying from Mozambique to Zimbabwe to
escape an arranged marriage, eleven-year-old Nhamo
struggles to escape drowning and starvation and in so doing comes close to the luminous world of the African
spirits

"This story is humorous and heartwrenching, complex
and multilayered." SLJ

The Sea of Trolls. Atheneum Books for Young
Readers 2004 459p $17.95 (5 and up) **Fic**
1. Norse mythology—Fiction 2. Druids and Druidism—Fiction 3. Vikings—Fiction 4. Fantasy fiction
ISBN 0-689-86744-1 LC 2003-19091

"A Richard Jackson book"

After Jack becomes apprenticed to a Druid bard, he
and his little sister Lucy are captured by Viking Berserk-
ers and taken to the home of King Ivar the Boneless and
his half-troll queen, leading Jack to undertake a vital
quest to Jotunheim, home of the trolls.

"This exciting and original fantasy will capture the
hearts and imaginations of readers." SLJ

Includes bibliographical references

Feiffer, Jules

A room with a zoo. Hyperion Books for
Children 2005 182p il $16.95 (3-5) **Fic**
1. Pets—Fiction 2. Family life—Fiction
ISBN 0-7868-3702-0 LC 2005-922875
"Michael di Capua books"

Feiffer, Jules—*Continued*

Nine-year-old Julie loves animals. So much it seems that she's assembling a zoo in her room. But, what she really wants is a dog.

"This is briskly written with lots of amusing moments. . . . Feiffer's distinctive drawings delectably capture the rousing events." Booklist

Fenner, Carol

The king of dragons. Margaret K. McElderry Bks. 1998 216p $17; pa $4.99 (5 and up)

Fic

1. Homeless persons—Fiction
ISBN 0-689-82217-0; 0-689-83540-X (pa)

LC 98-15434

Having lost access to the old railroad station where they had been staying, homeless Ian and his father move into an unused city courthouse and try to avoid being discovered by the authorities

"The characters are sharply etched, and the narrative moves swiftly, with moments of poignancy and suspense." Horn Book Guide

Snowed in with Grandmother Silk; illustrated by Amanda Harvey. Dial Books for Young Readers 2003 75p il $14.99 (2-4) Fic

1. Grandmothers—Fiction 2. Snow—Fiction
ISBN 0-8037-2857-3

LC 2002-152296

Ruddy is disappointed when his parents go on a cruise and he must stay with his fussy grandmother for a whole week, but an unexpected snowstorm reveals a surprising side of Grandmother Silk

"Harvey's pencil-and-watercolor artwork extends the warmth and gentle humor in this chapter book, which will be a good choice for beginning readers as well as for reading aloud." Booklist

Yolonda's genius. Margaret K. McElderry Bks. 1995 211p $17.95 hardcover o.p.; pa $5.99 (4-6)

Fic

1. Siblings—Fiction 2. Musicians—Fiction 3. African Americans—Fiction
ISBN 0-689-80001-0; 0-689-81327-9 (pa)

LC 94-46962

A Newbery Medal honor book, 1996

After moving from Chicago to Grand River, Michigan, fifth grader Yolonda, big and strong for her age, determines to prove that her younger brother is not a slow learner but a true musical genius

"In this brisk and appealing narrative, readers are introduced to a close-knit, middle-class African-American family. . . . [This novel] is suffused with humor and spirit." Horn Book

Ferris, Jean

Much ado about Grubstake. Harcourt, Inc. 2006 265p $17 (5 and up) Fic

1. Gold mines and mining—Fiction 2. Orphans—Fiction 3. City and town life—Fiction 4. Colorado—Fiction
ISBN 0-15-205706-6

When two city folks arrive in the depressed mining town of Grubstake, Colorado in 1888, sixteen-year-old

orphaned Arley tries to discover why they want to buy the supposedly worthless mines in the area.

"Ferris combines adventure, love, and off-the-wall characters in a page-turning story full of good laughs and common sense messages." Voice Youth Advocates

Field, Rachel

Hitty: her first hundred years; with illustrations by Dorothy P. Lathrop. Macmillan 1929 207p il $18.95; pa $5.95 (4 and up) Fic

1. Dolls—Fiction
ISBN 0-02-734840-7; 0-689-82284-7 (pa)

Awarded the Newbery Medal, 1930

"Hitty, a doll of real character carved from a block of mountain ash, writes a story of her eventful life from the security of an antique-shop window which she shares with Theobold, a rather over-bearing cat. . . . The illustrations by Dorothy P. Lathrop are the happiest extension of the text." Cleveland Public Libr

Fine, Anne

The diary of a killer cat; [by] Anne Fine; pictures by Steve Cox. 1st American ed. Farrar, Straus and Giroux 2006 c1994 58p il $15 (2-4)

Fic

1. Cats—Fiction
ISBN 0-374-31779-8

LC 2004-56212

First published 2001 in the United Kingdom

Tuffy the pet cat tries to defend himself against accusations of terrifying other animals and murdering the neighbor's rabbit

"The book is funny throughout. . . . The black-and-white sketches, some full page, bring movement and personality to the characters." SLJ

Notso hotso; [by] Anne Fine; pictures by Tony Ross. 1st American ed. Farrar, Straus and Giroux 2006 c2001 92p il $15 (2-4) Fic

1. Dogs—Fiction
ISBN 0-374-35550-9

LC 2004-56282

First published 2001 in the United Kingdom

Anthony, a neglected pet dog, develops an irritating skin condition and has most of his hair shaved off, which embarrasses him greatly until he realizes he now looks like a lion and can frighten other animals and people

"Ross' line drawings, full of action and expression, effectively capture the transformation. [This book] will be great for reading aloud and reading alone." Booklist

The true story of Christmas. Delacorte Press 2003 133p $15.95; lib bdg $17.99 (4 and up)

Fic

1. Christmas—Fiction 2. Family life—Fiction
ISBN 0-385-73130-2; 0-385-90156-9 (lib bdg)

LC 2003-5166

"Banished to his room on Christmas Day, Ralph recounts the disasters that occur when his highly eccentric relatives come together to celebrate the holiday. Funny dialogue . . . unique characters, from a demonic preschooler to a daft great-aunt; and hilarious but believable situations make this book a great read-aloud." SLJ

Fine, Anne—*Continued*

Up on cloud nine. Delacorte Press 2002 151p
$15.95; lib bdg $17.99; pa $4.99 (5 and up)

                                  Fic

1. Friendship—Fiction 2. Suicide—Fiction
ISBN 0-385-73009-8; 0-385-90058-9 (lib bdg);
0-440-41916-6 (pa)   LC 2001-53937

While Stolly struggles to regain consciousness in a
hospital bed after falling, or possibly jumping, from a
third story window, Ian recalls some of their best and
worst times together

"It's rare for such a serious subject to be accessibly
addressed for readers of this age group, and it's even
rarer for it to be addressed in an easygoing yet thoughtful story of friendship." Bull Cent Child Books

Finney, Patricia

I, Jack; by Jack the dog, as told to Patricia
Finney; illustrated by Peter Bailey. 1st U.S. ed.
HarperCollins 2004 c2000 178p il $15.99; lib bdg
$16.89 (3-6)   **Fic**

1. Dogs—Fiction
ISBN 0-06-052207-0; 0-06-052208-9 (lib bdg)
                             LC 2003-47856

First published 2000 in the United Kingdom

Jack, a Labrador Retriever, tells about his daily life of
food, walks, and the "apedogs" and "funny-looking
dogs" (cats) in his pack, as well as how everything
changes when a pretty girl dog moves into the neighborhood. Includes explanatory footnotes written by the cats

"Finney does a good job of weaving realistically believable canine behavior and slapstick humor throughout." SLJ

Fisher, Dorothy Canfield

Understood Betsy; with new illustrations by
Kimberly Bulcken Root. Holt & Co. 1999 229p il
$17.95 (4-6)   **Fic**

1. Farm life—Fiction 2. Vermont—Fiction
ISBN 0-8050-6073-1   LC 99-25265

Also available in paperback from Hardscrabble Bks.

A newly illustrated edition of the title first published
1917

Timid and small for her age, nine-year-old Elizabeth
Ann discovers her own abilities and gains a new perception of the world around her when she goes to live with
relatives on a farm in Vermont

"Kimberly Bulcken Root's inviting, unaffected pencil
drawings have a cozy feel to them. . . . 'Understood
Betsy' is sure to delight a new generation." N Y Times
Book Rev

Fitzgerald, John D.

The Great Brain; illustrated by Mercer Mayer.
Dial Bks. for Young Readers 1967 175p $9.99 (4
and up)   **Fic**

1. Utah—Fiction
ISBN 0-8037-2590-6

Also available in paperback from Dell

"The Great Brain was Tom Dennis ('T.D.') Fitzgerald,
age ten, of Adenville, Utah; the time, 1896. . . . This
autobiographical yarn is spun by his brother John Dennis

('J.D.'), age seven . . . who can tell stories about himself and his family with enough tall-tale exaggeration to
catch the imagination." Horn Book

Other titles about the Great Brain are:
The Great Brain at the academy (1972)
The Great Brain does it again (1975)
The Great Brain is back (1995)
The Great Brain reforms (1973)
Me and my little brain (1971)
More adventures of the Great Brain (1969)
The return of the Great Brain (1974)

Fitzhugh, Louise

Harriet, the spy; written and illustrated by
Louise Fitzhugh. Delacorte Press 2000 c1964 300p
il $15.95 (4 and up)   **Fic**

1. School stories
ISBN 0-385-32783-8   LC 00712298

A reissue of the title first published 1964 by Harper
& Row

Eleven-year-old Harriet keeps notes on her classmates
and neighbors in a secret notebook, but when some of
the students read the notebook, they seek revenge.

"A very, very funny and a very, very affective story;
the characterizations are marvelously shrewd, the pictures
of urban life and of the power structure of the sixth
grade class are realistic." Bull Cent Child Books

Another title about Harriet is:
The long secret (1965)

Flanagan, John

Ranger's apprentice; book one: the ruins of
Gorlan. Philomel Bks. 2005 249p $15.99 (5 and
up)   **Fic**

1. Fantasy fiction
ISBN 0-399-24454-9

When fifteen-year-old Will is rejected by battleschool,
he becomes the reluctant apprentice to the mysterious
Ranger Halt, and winds up protecting the kingdom from
danger.

"Flanagan concentrates on character, offering readers
a young protagonist they will care about and relationships that develop believably over time." Booklist

Another title in this series is:
The burning bridge (2006)

Fleischman, Paul

The borning room. HarperCollins Pubs. 1991
101p pa $4.99 hardcover o.p. (6 and up)

                                  Fic

1. Frontier and pioneer life—Fiction 2. Ohio—Fiction
ISBN 0-06-447099-7 (pa)   LC 91-4432

"A Charlotte Zolotow book"

Lying at the end of her life in the room where she
was born in 1851, Georgina remembers what it was like
to grow up on the Ohio frontier

"Fleischman successfully tackles many important
themes and once again gifts readers with writing lush
with similes, metaphors, and allusions, so subtly woven
into the mesh of the narrative that they enrich without
distracting. A memorable novel, rich and resonant in familial love and the strength of connection and tradition."
SLJ

Fleischman, Paul—*Continued*

Bull Run; woodcuts by David Frampton. HarperCollins Pubs. 1993 104p il lib bdg $16.89; pa $4.99 (6 and up) **Fic**

1. Bull Run, 1st Battle of, 1861—Fiction 2. United States—History—1861-1865, Civil War—Fiction

ISBN 0-06-021447-3 (lib bdg); 0-06-440588-5 (pa)

LC 92-14745

"A Laura Geringer book"

"In a sequence of sixty one- to two-page narratives, fifteen fictional characters (and one real general) recount their experiences during the Civil War. A few encounter each other, most meet unawares or not at all, but they have in common a battle, Bull Run, that affects—and sometimes ends—their lives." Bull Cent Child Books

"Abandoning the conventions of narrative fiction, Fleischman tells a vivid, many-sided story in this original and moving book. An excellent choice for readers' theater in the classroom or on stage." Booklist

The Half-a-Moon Inn; illustrated by Kathy Jacobi. Harper & Row 1980 88p il pa $4.99 hardcover o.p. (4-6) **Fic**

1. Kidnapping—Fiction 2. Physically handicapped children—Fiction 3. Hotels and motels—Fiction

ISBN 0-06-440364-5 (pa) LC 79-2010

"A mute boy, Aaron, leaves the cottage he shares with his mother to search for her when she is days late returning from market. Lost in a blizzard, he seeks shelter at the Half-A-Moon Inn. Here the evil crone Miss Grackle, who owns the place, forces Aaron to abet her thieving. The boy tries to warn guests against Miss Grackle but none of them can read his hastily written notes. . . . The ending is a terrific twist." Publ Wkly

"Despite the grimness of Aaron's predicament, accentuated by dark scratch drawings of figures in grotesque proportion, the story's tone is hopeful and its style concrete and brisk. Elements of folklore exist in the story's characterization, structure, and narration." SLJ

Lost! a story in string; illustrated by C.B. Mordan. Holt & Co. 2000 unp il $16.95

Fic

1. Wilderness survival—Fiction 2. Grandmothers—Fiction 3. String figures—Fiction

ISBN 0-8050-5583-5 LC 99-27997

A grandmother tells a story about a young girl who uses her wits and what is available to her to help her survive when she is lost in the snow. Includes instructions for creating a number of string figures mentioned in the story

"Mordan depicts the unfolding action in elegant ink drawings that have the look of woodcuts. . . . This story celebrates the power of the imagination while providing an interactive opportunity for children to participate." Booklist

Saturnalia. Harper & Row 1990 113p pa $5.95 hardcover o.p. (6 and up) **Fic**

1. Narragansett Indians—Fiction 2. Apprentices—Fiction 3. Prejudices—Fiction 4. Boston (Mass.)—Fiction

ISBN 0-06-447089-X (pa) LC 89-36380

"A Charlotte Zolotow book"

This novel is set in Boston in 1681. Fourteen-year-old William, a Narraganset Indian captured six years earlier in a raid, is apprenticed to Mr. Currie, a printer. "William's accomplishments enrage Mr. Baggot, the tithingman whose grandsons were killed by Indians. . . . William often wanders the streets after curfew playing an Indian melody on a small bone flute in the hope of finding his lost brother. One night, the melody does bring him to an uncle and young cousin, now servants of a cruel eyeglass maker. When the eyeglass maker is found murdered, . . . [Mr. Baggot] accuses William of the crime." Horn Book

"While William is the main focus of the story, there are several bubbling subplots that illuminate the texture of Puritan colonial life. . . . Especially welcome as a support for history units, this absorbing story exemplifies Fleischman's graceful, finely honed use of the English language." Booklist

Seedfolks; illustrations by Judy Pedersen. HarperCollins Pubs. 1997 69p $14.99; lib bdg $15.89; pa $4.99 (4 and up) **Fic**

1. Gardens—Fiction 2. City and town life—Fiction

ISBN 0-06-027471-9; 0-06-027472-7 (lib bdg); 0-06-447207-8 (pa) LC 96-26696

"Joanna Cotler books"

This "novel tells about an urban garden started by a child and nurtured by people of all ages and ethnic and economic backgrounds. Each of the thirteen chapters is narrated by a different character, allowing the reader to watch as a community develops out of disconnected lives and prior suspicions." Horn Book Guide

"The characters' vitality and the sharply delineated details of the neighborhood make this not merely an exercise in craftsmanship or morality but an engaging, entertaining novel as well." Booklist

Fleischman, Sid

The 13th floor; a ghost story; illustrations by Peter Sis. Greenwillow Bks. 1995 134p il $15.99 (4-6) **Fic**

1. Fantasy fiction 2. Pirates—Fiction

ISBN 0-688-14216-8 LC 94-42806

Also available in paperback from Dell

When his older sister disappears, twelve-year-old Buddy Stebbins follows her back in time and finds himself aboard a seventeenth-century pirate ship captained by a distant relative

"Liberally laced with dry wit and thoroughly satisfying. . . . Readers could hardly ask for more." Publ Wkly

Bandit's moon; illustrations by Jos. A. Smith. Greenwillow Bks. 1998 136p $16.99 (4-6)

Fic

1. Murieta, Joaquín, d. 1853—Fiction 2. Thieves—Fiction 3. California—Gold discoveries—Fiction 4. Adventure fiction

ISBN 0-688-15830-7 LC 97-36197

Also available in paperback from Dell

Twelve-year-old Annyrose relates her adventures with Joaquin Murieta and his band of outlaws in the California gold-mining region during the mid-1800s

"A quick read, with lots of twists, wonderful phrasing, historical integrity, and a bit of the tall tale thrown in." SLJ

Fleischman, Sid—*Continued*

Bo & Mzzz Mad. Greenwillow Bks. 2001 103p
$14.99; lib bdg $15.89; pa $4.99 (5 and up)

Fic

1. Family life—Fiction 2. Gold mines and mining—
Fiction 3. Orphans—Fiction 4. Mojave Desert
(Calif.)—Fiction
ISBN 0-06-029397-7; 0-06-029398-5 (lib bdg);
0-06-440972-4 (pa)   LC 00-56198

When his father dies, Bo Gamage warily moves to the
Mojave Desert home of his distant and estranged relatives, the Martinkas, and finds that "Mad" lives up to her
name, PawPaw despises him, and Aunt Juna hopes he'll
help search for the gold mine that started a family feud

"Fleischman does a first-rate job, using some clever
twists and snappy repartee. . . . Add to that a shot of
genuine suspense, and you have a quick, enjoyable read
that will fly off the shelves." Booklist

By the Great Horn Spoon! illustrated by Eric
von Schmidt. Little, Brown 1963 193p il $16.95;
pa $6.99 (4-6)   **Fic**

1. California—Gold discoveries—Fiction
ISBN 0-316-28577-3; 0-316-28612-5 (pa)

"An Atlantic Monthly Press book"

"Jack and his aunt's butler, Praiseworthy, stow away
on a ship bound for California. Here are their adventures
aboard ship and in the Gold Rush of '49." Publ Wkly

The ghost on Saturday night; illustrated by
Laura Cornell. Greenwillow Bks. 1997 53p il $15;
pa $4.99 (3-5)   **Fic**

1. Ghost stories 2. West (U.S.)—Fiction 3. Thieves—
Fiction
ISBN 0-688-14919-7; 0-688-14920-0 (pa)
                                                LC 96-43551

A newly illustrated edition of the title first published
1974 by Little, Brown

When Professor Pepper gives Opie tickets to a ghost-
raising instead of a nickel in payment for being guided
through the dense fog, Opie manages to make money
anyway by helping to thwart a bank robbery

"This story is filled with the hyperbole, piquant phrasing, and bravura that make Fleischman's books so much
fun to read." Horn Book Guide

The Giant Rat of Sumatra; [illustrations by]
John Hendrix. Greenwillow Books 2005 194p il
$15.99; lib bdg $16.89; pa $5.99 (4 and up)

Fic

1. Pirates—Fiction 2. Mexican War, 1846-1848—Fiction 3. California—Fiction 4. Adventure fiction
ISBN 0-06-074238-0; 0-06-074239-9 (lib bdg);
0-06-074240-2 (pa)   LC 2004-42457

"First shipwrecked and then captured by pirates,
young Edmund Amos Peters winds up in sunny San Diego. . . . The year is 1846, and the U.S. is at war with
Mexico, which puts Edmund, an American, once more in
jeopardy. . . . Fleischman has written another tale that
seamlessly blends rousing adventure and good humor."
Booklist

Here comes McBroom! three more tall tales;
illustrated by Quentin Blake. Greenwillow Bks.
1992 79p il pa $4.95 hardcover o.p. (3-5)

Fic

1. Farm life—Fiction 2. Tall tales
ISBN 0-688-16364-5 (pa)   LC 91-32689

Also available in hardcover from P. Smith

The stories were originally published separately by
Grosset and Dunlap

Contents: McBroom the rainmaker (c1973);
McBroom's ghost (c1971); McBroom's zoo (c1972)

The tall tale adventures of a farm family

Fleischman's "humor is still as fresh as ever, and
Quentin Blake's illustrations continue to delight."
Booklist

Other titles about McBroom are:
McBroom tells a lie (1976)
McBroom tells the truth (1981)
McBroom's wonderful one-acre farm: three tall tales
(1992)

The midnight horse; illustrations by Peter Sis.
Greenwillow Bks. 1990 84p il $16.99 (3-6)

Fic

1. Magicians—Fiction 2. Ghost stories 3. Orphans—
Fiction
ISBN 0-688-09441-4   LC 89-23441

Also available in paperback from Dell

Touch enlists the help of The Great Chaffalo, a ghost-
ly magician, to thwart his great-uncle's plans to put
Touch into the orphan house and swindle The Red Raven
Inn away from Miss Sally

"The prose is colorful and earthy. . . . Good and bad
are clearly defined, a happy ending is never in doubt,
and the reader must accept in good faith the capricious
appearances of a deceased but still-practicing magician."
Horn Book

Mr. Mysterious & Company; illustrated by Eric
von Schmidt. Greenwillow Bks. 1997 153p il pa
$5.99 hardcover o.p. (5 and up)   **Fic**

1. Magic—Fiction 2. Overland journeys to the Pacific—Fiction
ISBN 0-688-14922-7 (pa); 0-688-14921-9 (hc)
                                                LC 96-41225

A reissue of the title first published 1962 by Little,
Brown

Story of a covered wagon family who traveled across
the country to California in 1884, giving magic shows to
earn their living

"A lighthearted and delightful family story." Booklist

The whipping boy; illustrations by Peter Sis.
Greenwillow Bks. 1986 90p il $16.99 (5 and up)

Fic

1. Thieves—Fiction 2. Adventure fiction
ISBN 0-688-06216-4   LC 85-17555

Also available in paperback from HarperTrophy

Awarded the Newbery Medal, 1987

"A round tale of adventure and humor, this follows
the fortunes of Prince Roland (better known as Prince
Brat) and his whipping boy, Jemmy, who has received
all the hard knocks for the prince's mischief. . . .
There's not a moment's lag in pace, and the stock char-

Fleischman, Sid—*Continued*

acters, from Hold-Your-Nose Billy to Betsy's dancing bear Petunia, have enough inventive twists to project a lively air to it all." Bull Cent Child Books

Fleming, Candace

Lowji discovers America. Atheneum Books for Young Readers 2005 152p $15.95 (3-5)

Fic

1. Moving—Fiction 2. East Indians—United States—Fiction

ISBN 0-689-86299-7   LC 2004-6899

"An Anne Schwartz book"

A nine-year-old East Indian boy tries to adjust to his new life in suburban America.

"Fleming tells a gentle, effective story about the loneliness and bewilderment that come with moving, and her brisk, lively sentences make this a good choice for readers gaining confidence with chapter books." Booklist

Fleming, Ian

Chitty chitty bang bang. Random House 2003 c1964 149p il $15.95 (4-6)   **Fic**

1. Automobiles—Fiction

ISBN 0-375-82591-6

A newly illustrated edition of the title first published 1964

"An ingenious nonsense tale about an English family and their remarkable old car. Gifted with the ability to navigate land, sea, and air, Chitty-Chitty-Bang-Bang rescues the family from floods, traffic jams, and gangsters." Hodges. Books for Elem Sch Libr

Fletcher, Ralph

Fig pudding. Clarion Bks. 1995 136p $15 (4 and up)   **Fic**

1. Family life—Fiction 2. Death—Fiction

ISBN 0-395-71125-8   LC 94-3654

Also available in paperback from Dell

"Twelve-year-old Cliff, the oldest of six children . . . recalls the past year in episodes focusing on his brothers and his sister. . . . There were good times, but there were also ones he'd like to forget—among them, the death of one brother." Booklist

"Written with humor, perception, and clarity of language, the book resonates with laughter and sorrow." SLJ

Flying solo. Clarion Bks. 1998 138p $15 (5 and up)   **Fic**

1. School stories 2. Death—Fiction

ISBN 0-395-87323-1   LC 98-10775

Also available in paperback from Dell

Rachel, having chosen to be mute following the sudden death of a classmate, shares responsibility with the other sixth-graders who decide not to report that the substitute teacher failed to show up

"Fletcher expertly balances a wide variety of emotions, giving readers a story that is by turns sad, poignant, and funny." Booklist

Fletcher, Susan

Shadow spinner. Atheneum Bks. for Young Readers 1998 219p $17; pa $4.99 (6 and up)

Fic

1. Storytelling—Fiction 2. Physically handicapped—Fiction 3. Iran—Fiction

ISBN 0-689-81852-1; 0-689-83051-3 (pa)

LC 97-37346

"A Jean Karl book"

When Marjan, a thirteen-year-old crippled girl, joins the Sultan's harem in ancient Persia, she gathers for Shahrazad the stories which will save the queen's life

"An elegantly written novel that will delight and entertain even as it teaches." SLJ

Forbes, Esther

Johnny Tremain; illustrated by Michael McCurdy. Houghton Mifflin 1998 293p il $22 (5 and up)   **Fic**

1. Boston (Mass.)—Fiction 2. United States—History—1775-1783, Revolution—Fiction

ISBN 0-395-90011-5   LC 98-228478

Also available in paperback from Dell; and Thomson Gale large print edition

Awarded the Newbery Medal, 1944

A newly illustrated edition of the title first published 1943

After injuring his hand, a silversmith's apprentice in Boston becomes a messenger for the Sons of Liberty in the days before the American Revolution

"This sumptuous new gift edition is illustrated with vigorous woodcuts." Horn Book Guide

Ford, Christine

Scout; [by] Christine Ford. Delacorte Press 2006 213p $14.95; lib bdg $16.99 (5 and up)

Fic

1. Friendship—Fiction 2. Family life—Fiction 3. Texas—Fiction

ISBN 0-385-73234-1; 0-385-90260-3 (lib bdg)

LC 2005005696

After her mother dies, eleven-year-old Cecelia befriends a new boy at school, but soon realizes that the scruffy youth's home life is the reason for his introspective personality, which is so much like her own.

"With short lines and an immediate first-person narrative, the free verse in this first novel is that rare combination—an easy read and beautiful poetry." Booklist

Fox, Helen

Eager. Wendy Lamb Books 2004 280p $15.95; lib bdg $17.99 (5 and up)   **Fic**

1. Robots—Fiction 2. Science fiction

ISBN 0-385-74672-5; 0-385-90903-9 (lib bdg)

LC 2003-19489

Unlike Grumps, their old-fashioned robot, the Bell family's new robot, Eager, is programmed to not merely obey but to question, reason, and exercise free will.

"There is a lot of warmth and humor in this engaging . . . novel. . . . The characters are well developed and the action moves quickly. The author also raises thought-provoking questions about what it means to be human, the dangers of technology, and the concept of free will." SLJ

Fox, Helen—*Continued*

Another title about Eager is:

Eager's nephew (2006)

Fox, Paula

One-eyed cat; a novel. Bradbury Press 1984
216p pa $5.99 hardcover o.p. (5 and up)

                                            Fic

1. Firearms—Fiction 2. Cats—Fiction

ISBN 0-689-83970-7 (pa)   LC 84-10964

Also available in paperback from Dell; Spanish language edition also available

A Newbery Medal honor book, 1985

"Told by his father that he's too young for the air rifle an uncle gives him as a birthday present, Ned sneaks the gun out one night and takes a shot at a shadowy creature. He is subsequently smitten with guilt when he sees a one-eyed feral cat, and the knowledge that he may have been responsible as well as [having disobeyed] his father colors all his days." Bull Cent Child Books

The author's "writing is sure. Her characterization is outstanding, and she creates a strong sense of place and mood." SLJ

The slave dancer; a novel; with illustrations by
Eros Keith. Bradbury Press 1973 176p il $17.95 (5
and up)   **Fic**

1. Slave trade—Fiction 2. Sea stories

ISBN 0-02-735560-8   LC 73-80642

Also available in paperback from Dell; Spanish language edition also available

Awarded the Newbery Medal, 1974

"Thirteen-year-old Jessie Bollier is kidnapped from New Orleans and taken aboard a slave ship. Cruelly tyrannized by the ship's captain, Jessie is made to play his fife for the slaves during the exercise period into which they are forced in order to keep them fit for sale. When a hurricane destroys the ship, Jessie and Ras, a young slave, survive. They are helped by an old black man who finds them, spirits Ras north to freedom, and assists Jessie to return to his family." Shapiro. Fic for Youth. 3d edition

The stone-faced boy; illustrated by Donald A.
Mackay. Bradbury Press 1968 106p il (4-6)

                                            Fic

1. Siblings—Fiction 2. Family life—Fiction

Available in paperback from Front Street; Also available Spanish language edition

"The story is a perceptive character study of a lonely, timid middle child in a family of five self-possessed, individualistic children. To save himself from teasing by classmates and siblings, Gus Oliver has learned to mask his feelings so well that he has lost all ability to show emotion. Even the startling and unexpected arrival of an eccentric, outspoken great-aunt appears to leave Gus unmoved but the night his sister inveigles him into going out in the dark and the cold to rescue a stray dog, he gains a new-found confidence in himself." Booklist

Frank, Lucy K.

Lucky stars; [by] Lucy Frank. Atheneum Books
for Young Readers 2005 295p $16.95 (5 and up)

                                            Fic

1. Musicians—Fiction 2. School stories

ISBN 0-689-85933-3   LC 2004-10299

"A Richard Jackson book"

Music entwines Kira, a thirteen-year-old singer who hates that her father makes her perform for money on New York City subway platforms; Eugene, the class clown; and Jake, who longs to sing and to approach Kira, but feels held back by his stuttering.

"Deft characterization, an authentic sense of place, and a good mix of serious and funny scenes make this a better-than-average novel." SLJ

Franklin, Kristine L.

Grape thief. Candlewick Press 2003 290p il
$16.99 (5 and up)   **Fic**

1. Croatian Americans—Fiction

ISBN 0-7636-1325-8   LC 2002-23774

In 1925, in a small Washington State community made up of families from different ethnic backgrounds, twelve-year-old Cuss tries to stay in school as he watches those around him struggle with various financial difficulties

"Franklin has drawn on her Croatian father's stories to create a strong sense of the multiethnic community in that time and place. . . . . Cuss' fast, first-person narrative rings true." Booklist

Lone wolf. Candlewick Press 1997 220p pa
$4.99 hardcover o.p. (4 and up)   **Fic**

1. Friendship—Fiction 2. Family life—Fiction

ISBN 0-7636-0480-1 (pa)   LC 96-33287

When a large family moves into the house near where he and his father live in the woods, Perry's friendship with the oldest girl helps him come to terms with his sister's death and his parents' divorce

"Strong characters, a plot that works on many levels, and an engaging background make this . . . a standout." SLJ

Frederick, Heather Vogel

The voyage of Patience Goodspeed. Simon &
Schuster Bks. for Young Readers 2002 219p
$16.95; pa $4.99 (5 and up)   **Fic**

1. Seafaring life—Fiction 2. Whaling—Fiction
3. Navigation—Fiction

ISBN 0-689-84851-X; 0-689-84869-2 (pa)

                                          LC 2001-49039

Following their mother's death in Nantucket, Captain Goodspeed brings twelve-year-old Patience and six-year-old Tad aboard his whaling ship, where a new crew member incites a mutiny and Patience puts her mathematical ability to good use

"This is an exciting voyage of peril and self-discovery." N Y Times Book Rev

Another title about Patience is:

The education of Patience Goodspeed (2004)

Freeman, Martha

The trouble with cats; illustrated by Cat Bowman Smith. Holiday House 2000 77p il $15.95 (2-4) **Fic**

1. School stories 2. Stepfathers—Fiction 3. Cats—Fiction 4. San Francisco (Calif.)—Fiction

ISBN 0-8234-1479-5 LC 99-29291

After a difficult first week of third grade, Holly begins to adjust to her new school and living in her new stepfather's tiny apartment with his four cats

"Bowman contributes pen-and-ink drawings with lines that quiver with energy. . . . Freeman has a knack for wholesome, undemanding fiction . . . with enough action and humor to carry the plot." Bull Cent Child Books

Another title about Holly is
The trouble with babies (2002)

Who stole Halloween? Holiday House 2005 232p il $16.95 (4-6) **Fic**

1. Mystery fiction 2. Cats—Fiction 3. Halloween—Fiction

ISBN 0-8234-1962-2

When nine-year-old Alex and his friend Yasmeen investigate the disappearance of cats in their neighborhood, they stumble onto a larger mystery involving a haunted house and a ghostly cat.

"The story unfolds to a satisfying resolution . . . Characters are well drawn, and the book will entice even reluctant readers with its action and humor." SLJ

Another title about Alex and Yasmeen is:
Who is stealing the 12 days of Christmas (2003)

French, Simon

Where in the world. Peachtree Publishers 2003 174p $14.95 (5 and up) **Fic**

1. Musicians—Fiction 2. Australia—Fiction 3. Immigrants—Fiction 4. Grandfathers—Fiction

ISBN 1-56145-292-0 LC 2003-43867

First published 2002 in Australia

When Ari and his mother leave their home in Germany for a new life and family in Australia, he parts from the grandfather who taught him to play violin, but finds that his music and memories are intertwined.

"The lyrical writing style suits the theme of musical improvisation in a story that's poignant without being overly sentimental." Booklist

Fritz, Jean

The cabin faced west; illustrated by Feodor Rojankovsky; distributed by Putnam Pub. Group 1958 124p il $15.99; pa $5.99 (3-6) **Fic**

1. Scott, Ann Hamilton—Fiction 2. Frontier and pioneer life—Fiction 3. Pennsylvania—Fiction

ISBN 0-698-20016-0; 0-14-032256-6 (pa)

"Ann is unhappy when her family moves from Gettysburg to the Pennsylvania frontier, but she soon finds friends and begins to see that there is much to enjoy about her new home—including a visit from General Washington." Hodges. Books for Elem Sch Libr

Frost, Helen

Spinning through the universe; a novel in poems from room 214. Farrar Straus and Giroux 2004 93p $16 (4 and up) **Fic**

1. School stories 2. Poetry

ISBN 0-374-37159-8 LC 2003-48056

"Frances Foster books"

A collection of poems written in the voices of Mrs. Williams of room 214, her students, and a custodian about their interactions with each other, their families, and the world around them. Includes notes on the poetic forms represented.

"Interwoven dramatic stories and interesting poetic patterns give this book extra appeal. A boon for poetry classes." SLJ

Funke, Cornelia Caroline

Dragon rider; [by] Cornelia Funke; translated by Anthea Bell. Scholastic 2004 523p il $12.95 (5 and up) **Fic**

1. Dragons—Fiction 2. Fantasy fiction

ISBN 0-439-45695-9 LC 2004-45419

Original German edition 1997

After learning that humans are headed toward his hidden home, Firedrake, a silver dragon, is joined by a brownie and an orphan boy in a quest to find the legendary valley known as the Rim of Heaven, encountering friendly and unfriendly creatures along the way, and struggling to evade the relentless pursuit of an old enemy.

"Funke proves she knows how to tickle the imaginations of younger readers. . . . This is a good, old-fashioned ensemble-cast quest." Booklist

Fuqua, Jonathon Scott

Darby. Candlewick Press 2002 242p $16.99 (4 and up) **Fic**

1. Race relations—Fiction 2. African Americans—Fiction 3. South Carolina—Fiction

ISBN 0-7636-1417-3 LC 2001-35061

In 1926, nine-year-old Darby Carmichael stirs up trouble in Marlboro County, South Carolina, when she writes a story for the local newspaper promoting racial equality

"Darby's voice, rich with Southern idiom, rings true." Horn Book Guide

Gaiman, Neil

Coraline; [by] Neil Gaiman; with illustrations by Dave McKean. HarperCollins Pubs. 2002 162p il $15.99; lib bdg $17.89; pa $5.99 (5 and up) **Fic**

1. Supernatural—Fiction

ISBN 0-380-97778-8; 0-06-623744-0 (lib bdg); 0-380-80734-3 (pa) LC 2002-18937

Looking for excitement, Coraline ventures through a mysterious door into a world that is similar, yet disturbingly different from her own, where she must challenge a gruesome entity in order to save herself, her parents, and the souls of three others

"Gaiman twines his taut tale with a menacing tone and crisp prose fraught with memorable imagery . . . yet keeps the narrative just this side of terrifying." Publ Wkly

Gannett, Ruth Stiles

My father's dragon; illustrated by Ruth Chrisman Gannett. Random House 1948 86p il pa $6.95 hardcover o.p. (1-4)   **Fic**

1. Dragons—Fiction 2. Fantasy fiction 3. Animals—Fiction

ISBN 0-394-89048-5 (pa)

A Newbery Medal honor book, 1949

This is a combination of fantasy, sense, and nonsense. It describes the adventures of a small boy, Elmer Elevator, who befriended an old alley cat and in return heard the story of the captive baby dragon on Wild Island. Right away Elmer decided to free the dragon. The tale of Elmer's voyage to Tangerina and his arrival on Wild Island, his encounters with various wild animals, and his subsequent rescue of the dragon follows

Other available titles in this series are:

The dragons of Blueland (1951)

Elmer and the dragon (1950)

Gantos, Jack

Heads or tails; stories from the sixth grade. Farrar Straus Giroux 1994 151p il $16; pa $4.95 (5 and up)   **Fic**

1. Diaries—Fiction 2. Family life—Fiction 3. School stories

ISBN 0-374-32909-5; 0-374-42923-5 (pa)

LC 93-43117

"Jack is trying to survive his sixth-grade year, and he narrates, through a series of short-stories-cum-chapters, his difficulties in dodging the obstacles life throws in his path. . . . The writing is zingy and specific, with snappily authentic dialogue and a vivid sense of juvenile experience. . . . Jack and his family have a recognizably thorny relationship. This is a distinctive and lively sequence of everyday-life stories." Bull Cent Child Books

Other titles about Jack are:

Jack adrift (2003)

Jack on the tracks (1999)

Jack's black book (1997)

Jack's new power (1995)

Joey Pigza swallowed the key. Farrar, Straus & Giroux 1998 153p $16 (5 and up)   **Fic**

1. Attention deficit disorder—Fiction 2. School stories

ISBN 0-374-33664-4   LC 98-24264

Also available in paperback from HarperCollins

To the constant disappointment of his mother and his teachers, Joey has trouble paying attention or controlling his mood swings when his prescription meds wear off and he starts getting worked up and acting wired

This "frenetic narrative pulls at heartstrings and tickles funny bones." SLJ

Other titles about Joey Pigza are:

Joey Pigza loses control (2000)

What would Joey do? (2002)

Gardiner, John Reynolds

Stone Fox; illustrated by Marcia Sewall. Crowell 1980 81p il $15.99; lib bdg $16.89; pa $5.50 (2-5)   **Fic**

1. Sled dog racing—Fiction 2. Dogs—Fiction

ISBN 0-690-03983-2; 0-690-03984-0 (lib bdg); 0-06-440132-4 (pa)   LC 79-7895

Also available Spanish language edition

"When his usually spry grandfather won't get out of bed Willy searches for a remedy. Back taxes are the problem and the only way to get the money is to win the dogsled race. Stone Fox, a towering Indian who has never lost a race, is primary competition. Both want the prize money for the government—Willy for taxes and Stone Fox to buy his native land back." SLJ

This story "is rooted in a Rocky Mountain legend, a locale faithfully represented in Sewall's wonderful drawings. . . . In Gardiner's bardic chronicle, the tension is teeth rattling, with the tale flying to a conclusion that is almost unbearably moving, one readers won't soon forget." Publ Wkly

Garfield, Leon

Black Jack. Farrar, Straus & Giroux 2000 197p $18; pa $6.95 (6 and up)   **Fic**

1. Apprentices—Fiction 2. Adventure fiction 3. London (England)—Fiction

ISBN 0-374-30827-6; 0-374-40696-0 (pa)

LC 99-57836

A reissue of the title first published 1968 in the United Kingdom; first United States edition 1969 by Pantheon

A young apprentice in eighteenth-century London begins a strange adventure when he inadvertently becomes involved with a wanted criminal and a girl who is reputedly mad

"The cast of characters is intriguing and the atmosphere of the times zestfully portrayed." Booklist

Smith. Farrar, Straus & Giroux 2000 195p $18; pa $7.95 (6 and up)   **Fic**

1. Thieves—Fiction 2. Adventure fiction 3. London (England)—Fiction

ISBN 0-374-37082-6; 0-374-46762-5 (pa)

LC 99-57837

A reissue of the title first published 1967 by Pantheon

Moments after he steals a document from a man's pocket, an illiterate young pickpocket in eighteenth-century London witnesses the man's murder by two men who want the document

"A lusty, flavorsome tale of adventure." Booklist

Garza, Xavier

Lucha libre: the Man in the Silver Mask; a bilingual cuento; written & illustrated by Xavier Garza. Cinco Puntos Press 2005 unp il $17.95 (2-5)   **Fic**

1. Uncles—Fiction 2. Wrestling—Fiction 3. Mexico—Fiction 4. Bilingual books—English-Spanish

ISBN 0-938317-92-X   LC 2004-29756

When Carlitos attends a wrestling match in Mexico City with his father, his favorite masked-wrestler has eyes that are strangely familiar.

"Smoothly integrated information in fluid colloquial English and Spanish combines with grainy graphic-novel-style illustrations executed in acrylic to create an oddly compelling and sophisticated package. An informative endnote, in English only, presents a brief but engrossing history of lucha libre." SLJ

Gates, Doris

Blue willow; illustrated by Paul Lantz. Viking 1940 172p il pa $5.99 hardcover o.p. (4 and up)

Fic

1. Migrant labor—Fiction 2. California—Fiction
ISBN 0-14-030924-1 (pa)

Also available in hardcover from P. Smith

"Having to move from one migrant camp to another intensifies Janey Larkin's desire for a permanent home, friends, and school. The only beautiful possession the family has is a blue willow plate handed down from generation to generation. It is a reminder of happier days in Texas and represents dreams and promises for a better future. Reading about this itinerant family's ways of life, often filled with despair and yet always hopeful, leaves little room for the reader's indifference." Read Ladders for Hum Relat. 6th edition

Gauch, Patricia Lee

This time, Tempe Wick? illustrated by Margot Tomes. Boyds Mills Press 2003 c1974 43p il $16.95; pa $9.95 (3-5)

Fic

1. United States—History—1775-1783, Revolution—Fiction
ISBN 1-59078-179-1; 1-59078-185-6 (pa)

A reissue of the title first published 1974 by Coward, McCann & Geoghegan

Everyone knows Tempe Wick is a most surprising girl, but she exceeds even her own reputation when two mutinous Revolutionary soldiers try to steal her beloved horse.

"The writing is the perfect vehicle for the illustrations—in the artist's inimitable style—which capture the down-to-earth, unpretentious, and humorous quality of the storytelling." Horn Book

Thunder at Gettysburg; drawings by Stephen Gammell. Boyds Mills Press 2003 c1975 46p il $16.95; pa $9.95 (3-5)

Fic

1. Gettysburg (Pa.), Battle of, 1863—Fiction
ISBN 1-59078-180-5; 1-59078-186-4 (pa)

A reissue of the title first published 1975 by Coward, McCann & Geoghegan

Fourteen-year-old Tillie becomes involved in the tragic battle of July 13, 1863

"Gauch has drawn on the experiences of a real person, in this case Tillie Pierce Alleman, whose 1889 book 'At Gettysburg' provided the basis of the story. Gammell's thorough pencilled scenes are full of atmosphere and acute emotion, their escalating drama effectively congruent with that of the story." Booklist

Geisert, Bonnie

Prairie summer; illustrated by Arthur Geisert. Houghton Mifflin 2002 113p il $15 (4-6)

Fic

1. Farm life—Fiction 2. Family life—Fiction
ISBN 0-618-21293-0   LC 2001-4176

Ten-year-old Rachel demonstrates the maturity gained from her experiences growing up with three sisters on a farm in South Dakota

"Geisert skillfully uses the plot and the setting to reveal the relationships and develop the characters. . . . A poignant family story that's true to a child's point of view." SLJ

Another title about Rachel is:
Lessons (2005)

George, Jean Craighead

Charlie's raven; written and illustrated by Jean Craighead George. Dutton Children's Books 2004 190p il $15.99 (5 and up)

Fic

1. Ravens—Fiction 2. Grandfathers—Fiction
3. Naturalists—Fiction
ISBN 0-525-47219-3

Charlie's friend, Singing Bird, a Teton Sioux, tells him that ravens have curing powers, so Charlie steals a baby bird from its nest, hoping to heal his ailing Granddad, a retired naturalist.

"The story is technically accurate and offers a vivid sense of place and a window into Native American beliefs through storytelling." SLJ

Julie; illustrated by Wendell Minor. HarperCollins Pubs. 1994 226p il pa $5.99 hardcover o.p. (6 and up)

Fic

1. Inuit—Fiction 2. Arctic regions—Fiction
3. Wolves—Fiction
ISBN 0-06-440573-7 (pa); 0-06-023528-4 (hc)

LC 93-27738

This sequel to Julie of the wolves "details Julie's adjustment to family and modernization after returning home. Her father's musk oxen enterprise depicts the problems inherent to environment-versus-economics issues as Julie struggles to save her wolf friends." Sci Child

Followed by Julie's wolf pack

Julie of the wolves; pictures by John Schoenherr. Harper & Row 1972 170p il $15.99; lib bdg $16.89; pa $5.99 (6 and up)

Fic

1. Inuit—Fiction 2. Arctic regions—Fiction
3. Wilderness survival—Fiction 4. Wolves—Fiction
ISBN 0-06-021943-2; 0-06-021944-0 (lib bdg); 0-06-440058-1 (pa)

Awarded the Newbery Medal, 1973

"Lost in the Alaskan wilderness, thirteen-year old Miyax [Julie in English], an Eskimo girl, is gradually accepted by a pack of Arctic wolves that she comes to love." Booklist

"The superb narration includes authentic descriptions and details of the Eskimo way-of-life and of Eskimo rituals. . . . The whole book has a rare, intense reality which the artist enhances beautifully with animated drawings." Horn Book

Followed by Julie

My side of the mountain trilogy; written and illustrated by Jean Craighead George. Dutton Children's Books 2000 xii, 177, 170, 258p il $24.99 (5 and up)

Fic

1. Wilderness survival—Fiction 2. Falcons—Fiction
3. New York (State)—Fiction
ISBN 0-525-46269-4   LC 00-712305

Also available in paperback from Puffin as separate volumes

Originally published as three separate volumes, 1959, 1990, and 1999 respectively

Contents: My side of the mountain; On the far side of the mountain; Frightful's mountain

George, Jean Craighead—*Continued*

In *My Side of the Mountain* Sam Gribley tells of his year in the wilderness of the Catskill Mountains. In *On the Far Side of the Mountain* Sam's peaceful existence in his wilderness home is disrupted when his sister runs away and his pet falcon is confiscated by a conservation officer. In *Frightful's Mountain* Sam's pet falcon must learn to live as a wild bird.

There's an owl in the shower; illustrated by Christine Herman Merrill. HarperCollins Pubs. 1995 133p il pa $5.99 hardcover o.p. (3-5)

Fic

1. Owls—Fiction 2. Endangered species—Fiction
ISBN 0-06-440682-2 (pa); 0-06-024891-2 (hc)
LC 94-38893

Because protecting spotted owls has cost Borden's father his job as a logger in the old growth forest of northern California, Borden intends to kill any spotted owl he sees, until he and his father find themselves taking care of a young owlet

"George's writing skill and knowledge of animal behavior turn what could have been nothing but a message into an absorbing story that shows both sides of the controversy. . . . Merrill's drawings perfectly capture the engaging bird and the family's affection for it." SLJ

Giblin, James

The boy who saved Cleveland; based on a true story; [by] James Cross Giblin; illustrated by Michael Dooling. 1st ed. Henry Holt and Company 2006 64p il $15.95 (3-5)   **Fic**

1. Frontier and pioneer life—Fiction 2. Epidemics—Fiction 3. Malaria—Fiction 4. Ohio—Fiction
ISBN 0-8050-7355-8   LC 2005021695

During a malaria epidemic in late eighteenth-century Cleveland, Ohio, ten-year-old Seth Doan surprises his family, his neighbors, and himself by having the strength to carry and grind enough corn to feed everyone.

"Young readers will enjoy the clear writing and plot-driven pace. Dooling's full-page pencil-on-paper illustrations convey the time period as well as the emotional tone. A solid choice for those seeking pioneer fiction and strong characters." Booklist

Giff, Patricia Reilly

All the way home. Delacorte Press 2001 169p $15.95; pa $5.99 (4 and up)   **Fic**

1. Poliomyelitis—Fiction 2. Apples—Fiction 3. Friendship—Fiction 4. Brooklyn (New York, N.Y.)—Fiction
ISBN 0-385-32209-7; 0-440-41182-3 (pa)
LC 2001-28174

In 1941, circumstances bring together Brick, a boy from New York's apple country, and Mariel, a young girl made shy by her bout with polio, and the two make a journey from Brooklyn back to help Brick's elderly neighbors save their apple crop and to help Mariel learn about her past

"A compelling story of two unforgettable youngsters, their strength, and their friendship." SLJ

A house of tailors. Wendy Lamb Books 2004 148p $15.95; lib bdg $17.99 (5 and up)

Fic

1. Immigrants—Fiction 2. German Americans—Fiction 3. Brooklyn (New York, N.Y.)—Fiction
ISBN 0-385-73066-7; 0-385-90879-2 (lib bdg)
LC 2003-26103

When thirteen-year-old Dina emigrates from Germany to America in 1871, her only wish is to return home as soon as she can, but as the months pass and she survives a multitude of hardships living with her uncle and his young wife and baby, she finds herself thinking of Brooklyn as her home.

"This novel is rich with believable, endearing characters as well as excitement and emotion." SLJ

Kidnap at the Catfish Cafe; illustrated by Lynne Cravath. Viking 1998 73p il lib bdg $13.99; pa $4.99 (3-5)   **Fic**

1. Mystery fiction
ISBN 0-670-88180-5 (lib bdg); 0-14-130821-4 (pa)
LC 98-5711

Assisted by her cat Max, sixth grader Minnie starts up her new detective agency by investigating a kidnapping and a thief who will steal anything, even a hot stove

"Young mystery lovers will enjoy the witty story with its standout characters." Booklist

Another title about Minnie and Max is:
Mary Moon is missing (1998)

Lily's crossing. Delacorte Press 1997 180p $15.95; pa $6.50 (4 and up)   **Fic**

1. World War, 1939-1945—Fiction 2. Friendship—Fiction
ISBN 0-385-32142-2; 0-440-41453-9 (pa)
LC 96-23021

A Newbery honor book, 1998

During a summer spent at Rockaway Beach in 1944, Lily's friendship with a young Hungarian refugee causes her to see the war and her own world differently

"Gentle elements of danger and suspense . . . keep the plot moving forward, while the delicate balance of characters and setting gently coalesces into an emotional whole that is fully satisfying." Bull Cent Child Books

Nory Ryan's song. Delacorte Press 2000 148p $15.95; pa $5.99 (5 and up)   **Fic**

1. Ireland—Fiction 2. Famines—Fiction
ISBN 0-385-32141-4; 0-440-41829-1 (pa)
LC 00-27690

When a terrible blight attacks Ireland's potato crop in 1845, twelve-year-old Nory Ryan's courage and ingenuity help her family and neighbors survive

"Giff brings the landscape and the cultural particulars of the era vividly to life and creates in Nory a heroine to cheer for. A beautiful, heart-wrenching novel that makes a devastating event understandable." Booklist

Another title about Nory is:
Maggie's door (2003)

Giff, Patricia Reilly—*Continued*

Pictures of Hollis Woods. Wendy Lamb Bks. 2002 166p $15.95; lib bdg $17.99; pa $6.50 (5 and up) **Fic**
1. Artists—Fiction 2. Foster home care—Fiction 3. Old age—Fiction
ISBN 0-385-32655-6; 0-385-90070-8 (lib bdg); 0-440-41578-0 (pa) LC 2002-426
A Newbery Medal honor book, 2003
"She was named for the place where she was found as an abandoned baby. Twelve-year-old Hollis Woods has been through many foster homes—and she runs away, every time. In her latest placement, with an artist named Josie, the tightly wound Hollis begins to relax ever so slightly. . . . But Josie is slowly slipping into dementia, and Hollis knows that she'll be taken away from her if Josie is found out. . . . Giff has a sure hand with language, and the narrative is taut and absorbing." Booklist

Willow run. Wendy Lamb Bks. 2005 149p $15.95 (4 and up) **Fic**
1. World War, 1939-1945—Fiction
ISBN 0-385-73067-5 LC 2004-24541
During World War II, after moving with her parents to Willow Run, Michigan, when her father gets a job in the B24 bomber-building factory, eleven-year-old Meggie learns about different kinds of bravery from all of the people around her.
"Giff artfully carves the sentiments so prevalent in times of war—anxiety, inspiration, boredom—into sharp relief while creating a cast of finely drawn characters." Booklist

Gilliland, Judith Heide

Strange birds. Farrar, Straus and Giroux 2006 231p $17 (3-6) **Fic**
1. Horses—Fiction 2. Magic—Fiction 3. Trees—Fiction
ISBN 0-374-37275-6
"Melanie Kroupa Books"
With her parents lost at sea, eleven-year-old Anna finds comfort in a tree with magical properties which suddenly becomes home to some amazing creatures who may need her help.
"This fast-paced fantasy features an appealing heroine who must deal with grief and loneliness as well as the everyday insecurities of middle school." SLJ

Gilman, Laura Anne

Grail quest: the Camelot spell; book one. HarperCollins 2006 291p $10.99; lib bdg $14.89 (5 and up) **Fic**
1. Arthur, King—Fiction 2. Knights and knighthood—Fiction 3. Middle Ages—Fiction 4. Magic—Fiction
ISBN 0-06-077279-4; 0-06-077280-8 (lib bdg)
Three teenagers living in Camelot are forced to undertake a dangerous mission when King Arthur's court falls under a mysterious enchantment on the eve of the quest for the Holy Grail.
"The believable dialogue, succint plot, and uncomplicated references to court life will appeal to middle graders who are beginning to explore Aurthurian legend." Voice Youth Advocates

Another title in this series is:
Grail quest: Morgain's revenge (2006)

Gilson, Jamie

4B goes wild; illustrated by Linda Strauss Edwards. Lothrop, Lee & Shepard Bks. 1983 160p il lib bdg $16 (4-6) **Fic**
1. Camping—Fiction 2. School stories
ISBN 0-688-02236-7 LC 83-948
"Hobie Hanson, a sensitive fourth grader, tells of the time two fourth grade classes went on a three day camping trip." Child Book Rev Serv
"The writing style is breezy and comic . . . The dialogue is natural." Bull Cent Child Books
Other titles about Hobie Hanson are:
Double dog dare (1988)
Hobie Hanson, you're weird (1987)
Thirteen ways to sink a sub (1982)

Bug in a rug; illustrated by Diane deGroat. Clarion Bks. 1998 69p il $15; pa $4.95 (2-4) **Fic**
1. School stories 2. Clothing and dress—Fiction 3. Uncles—Fiction
ISBN 0-395-86616-2; 0-618-31670-1 (pa) LC 97-16437
Seven-year-old Richard is self-conscious when he receives a pair of purple pants from his aunt and uncle and has to wear them to school, but he is even more worried when his uncle shows up for a visit to his classroom
"Gilson captures the thoughts and fears of second graders through authentic dialogue and solid characterization." SLJ

Do bananas chew gum? Lothrop, Lee & Shepard Bks. 1980 158p pa $5.99 hardcover o.p. (4-6) **Fic**
1. Reading—Fiction 2. Learning disabilities—Fiction
ISBN 0-688-15294-5 (pa) LC 80-11414
Able to read and write at only a second grade level, sixth-grader Sam Mott considers himself dumb until he is prompted to cooperate with those who think something can be done about his problem
"This is a wonderfully written story, with real situations and a main character for whom the reader feels anguish at his fear of his learning disability being discovered, but also exultation when he correctly reads a long and difficult word. . . . This is a story that leaves you feeling good." Voice Youth Advocates

Hello, my name is Scrambled Eggs; illustrated by John Wallner. Lothrop, Lee & Shepard Bks. 1985 159p il (4 and up) **Fic**
1. Vietnamese—United States—Fiction
ISBN 0-688-04095-0 LC 84-10075
Available in paperback from Pocket Bks.
"A humorous account of what happens when a Vietnamese family, sponsored by the church, moves into Harvey's home temporarily. To make himself feel more important, Harvey decides to make educating and Americanizing the 12-year-old boy his project. By the end of the book, Tuan is not the only one who has received an education." SLJ
"Entertaining and also thought-provoking, this is a popular-reading item that has nice substance." Booklist

Gilson, Jamie—*Continued*

Stink Alley. HarperCollins Pubs. 2002 183p
$15.95; lib bdg $15.89 (4 and up)   **Fic**
1. Brewster, William, 1566 or 7-1644—Fiction 2.
Rembrandt Harmenszoon van Rijn, 1606-1669—Fiction 3. Puritans—Fiction 4. Artists—Fiction
5. Netherlands—Fiction
ISBN 0-688-17864-2; 0-06-029217-2 (lib bdg)
           LC 2001-39515

Living in Holland in 1614 with the harsh Puritan leader, William Brewster, and working for the family of a mischievous Dutch boy named Rembrandt, Lizzie, a spirited twelve-year-old orphan girl struggles to do what is right

"Gilson adds information about the real-life characters . . . in a historical note, but the story will first of all resound with young readers as a coming-of-age tale. It's a deftly woven mix of adventure, youthful ingenuity, and overcoming the odds." Horn Book

Gipson, Frederick Benjamin

Old Yeller; [by] Fred Gipson; drawings by Carl Burger. Harper & Row 1956 158p il $23; pa $5.99
(6 and up)   **Fic**
1. Dogs—Fiction 2. Texas—Fiction 3. Frontier and pioneer life—Fiction
ISBN 0-06-011545-9; 0-06-440382-3 (pa)
           LC 56-8780

A Newbery Medal honor book, 1957

"Travis at fourteen was the man of the family during the hard summer of 1860 when his father drove his herd of cattle from Texas to the Kansas market. It was the summer when an old yellow dog attached himself to the family and won Travis' reluctant friendship. Before the summer was over, Old Yeller proved more than a match for thieving raccoons, fighting bulls, grizzly bears, and mad wolves. This is a skillful tale of a boy's love for a dog as well as a description of a pioneer boyhood and it can't miss with any dog lover." Horn Book

Glaser, Linda

Bridge to America; based on a true story.
Houghton Mifflin Co. 2005 200p $16 (4-6)
          Fic
1. Immigrants—Fiction 2. Jews—Fiction
ISBN 0-618-56301-6

Eight-year-old Fivel narrates the story of his family's Atlantic Ocean crossing to reunite with their father in the United States, from its desperate beginning in a shtetl in Poland in 1920 to his stirrings of identity as an American boy.

"Even reluctant readers will enjoy this riveting account and sensitive portrayal of what it means to be an immigrant." SLJ

Gleitzman, Morris

Toad rage; [by] Morris Gleitzman. 1st American ed. Random House 2004 c1999 165p $14.95; lib bdg $16.99; pa $4.99 (3-6)   **Fic**
1. Toads—Fiction 2. Australia—Fiction
ISBN 0-375-82762-5; 0-375-92762-X (lib bdg);
0-375-82763-3 (pa)   LC 2003-8620

Determined to understand why humans hate cane toads and to improve relations between the species, Limpy embarks on a dangerous trek from his swamp to the Summer Olympics in Sydney, Australia

"This funny tale of one toad's bold quest to reach out to another species will give readers plenty of laughs." Booklist

Other titles in this series are:
Toad away (2006)
Toad heaven (2005)

Goble, Paul

Beyond the ridge; story and illustrations by Paul Goble. Bradbury Press 1989 unp il pa $6.99 hardcover o.p. (2-4)   **Fic**
1. Native Americans—Fiction
ISBN 0-689-71731-8 (pa)   LC 87-33113

At her death an elderly Plains Indian woman experiences the afterlife believed in by her people, while the surviving family members prepare her body according to their custom

"Goble's illustrations—in a double spread of gray rocks, smoothly surfaced in a skyscape of flying vultures—make a dignified context for a moving, direct discussion of death." Bull Cent Child Books

Godden, Rumer

The doll's house; illustrated by Tasha Tudor. Viking 1962 c1947 136p il pa $5.99 hardcover o.p. (2-4)   **Fic**
1. Dollhouses—Fiction 2. Dolls—Fiction
ISBN 0-14-030942-X (pa)

Available in hardcover from P. Smith

First published 1947 in the United Kingdom; first United States edition illustrated by Dana Saintsbury published 1948

Adventures of a brave little hundred-year-old Dutch farthing doll, her family, their Victorian dollhouse home and the two little English girls to whom they all belonged. Tottie's great adventure was when she went to the exhibition, Dolls through the ages, and was singled out for notice by the Queen who opened the exhibition

"Each doll has a firmly drawn, recognizably true character; the children think and behave convincingly. . . . The story is enthralling, and complete in every detail." Spectator

Gordon, Amy

The Gorillas of Gill Park. Holiday House 2003 247p il $16.95 (4 and up)   **Fic**
1. Parks—Fiction 2. Friendship—Fiction 3. Aunts—Fiction
ISBN 0-8234-1751-4   LC 2002-69092

While spending the summer before seventh grade with his aunt, Willy Wilson finds his first friends ever in the colorful characters who all love the neighborhood park owned by an eccentric old man

"The protagonist's first-person narration is both humorous and insightful. . . . An action-filled bildungsroman with quirky, unforgettable characters." SLJ

Another title about Gill Park is:
Return to Gill Park (2006)

Gorman, Carol

Dork in disguise. HarperCollins Pubs. 1999 164p $15.95; lib. bdg $15.89; pa $5.99 (4 and up)

Fic

1. School stories

ISBN 0-06-024866-1; 0-06-024867-X (lib bdg); 0-06-440891-4 (pa)   LC 99-27898

Starting middle school in a new town, brainy Jerry Flack changes his image from "dork" to "cool kid," only to discover that he'd rather be himself

"Humor keeps the plot jumping, and the novel's resolution is admirably restrained." Horn Book Guide

Other titles about Jerry are:

Dork on the run (2002)

A midsummer night's Dork (2004)

Goscinny

Nicholas; [by] Rene Goscinny & [illustrated by] Jean-Jacques Sempe; translated by Anthea Bell. Phaidon 2005 126p $19.95 (4-6)   **Fic**

1. School stories

ISBN 0-7148-4529-9

"This classic book about a mischievous schoolboy and his friends, originally published in French in 1959, is now available in English. The expertly translated text is enlivened by artwork by a New Yorker cartoonist to create the unforgettable milieu of Nicholas and his rowdy friends. A collection of 19 escapades, the stories introduce the protagonist and his cohorts as they wreak havoc out of simple, everyday situations at school, on the playground, and at home." SLJ

Another title about Nicholas is:

Nicholas again (2006)

Graff, Serena

Blackwell's Island; [by] Serena Graff. Delacorte Press 2005 185p $14.95; lib bdg $16.99 (5 and up)

Fic

1. New York (N.Y.)—Fiction 2. Supernatural—Fiction

ISBN 0-385-74670-9; 0-385-90901-2 (lib bdg)

LC 2004-8823

In 1914, eleven-year-old Alex and his nine-year-old sister, Anna, are taken from New York City's Lower East Side to Blackwell's Island, where there are lunatics, prisoners, evil caretakers, ghouls, and, perhaps, their missing mother.

"This fast-paced novel . . . combines history, mystery, and adventure." SLJ

Grahame, Kenneth

The reluctant dragon (3-5)   **Fic**

1. Dragons—Fiction 2. Fairy tales

Some editions are:

Holiday House $15.95; pa $6.95 Illustrated by Ernest H. Shepard (ISBN 0-8234-0093-X; 0-8234-0755-1)

Holt & Co. pa $7.95 Illustrated by Michael Hague (ISBN 0-8050-0802-0)

This chapter from Dream days was first published 1938 by Holiday House

This "is the droll tale of a peace-loving dragon who is forced to fight St. George. The dragon's friend, called simply the Boy, arranges a meeting between St. George

and the dragon, and a mock fight is planned. St. George is the hero of the day, the dragon is highly entertained at a banquet, and the Boy is pleased to have saved both the dragon and St. George." Huck. Child Lit in the Elem Sch. 3d edition

The wind in the willows (4-6)   **Fic**

1. Animals—Fiction

Some editions are:

Candlewick Press $19.99 Illustrated by Inga Moore (ISBN 0-7636-2242-7)

Harcourt $24 Illustrated by Michael Foreman (ISBN 0-15-216807-9)

St. Martin's Press $19.95 Illustrated by Patrick Benson (ISBN 0-312-13624-2)

First published 1908 by Scribner

In this fantasy "the characters are Mole, Water Rat, Mr. Toad, and other small animals, who live and talk like humans but have charming individual animal characters. The book is a tender portrait of the English countryside." Reader's Ency

Gray, Luli

Falcon's egg. Houghton Mifflin 1995 133p $16 (3-5)   **Fic**

1. Dragons—Fiction 2. New York (N.Y.)—Fiction

ISBN 0-395-71128-2   LC 94-16731

Also available in paperback from Bantam Bks.

"Falcon is an 11-year-old girl in New York City and the egg is red, hot, and discovered in Central Park. Falcon enlists the help of an older friend and neighbor to hide it until it hatches, fearing that her mother won't let her keep it. Soon elderly Aunt Emily; her ornithologist friend, Fernando Maldonado; and Falcon's younger brother join the cozy group that gathers to ponder the egg. When Egg hatches, she is a dragon. . . . Each of the characters is rich in wit, wisdom, and human foibles. . . . The real world blends well with the fantasy elements as tidbits of lore and locale are woven seamlessly." SLJ

Other titles about Falcon are:

Falcon and the carousel of time (2005)

Falcon and the Charles Street Witch (2002)

Greene, Bette

Philip Hall likes me, I reckon maybe; pictures by Charles Lilly. Dial Bks. for Young Readers 1974 135p il pa $5.99 hardcover o.p. (4-6)

Fic

1. Friendship—Fiction 2. African Americans—Fiction 3. Arkansas—Fiction

ISBN 0-14-130312-3 (pa)

A Newbery Medal honor book, 1975

Eleven-year-old Beth, an African American girl from Arkansas, thinks that Philip Hall likes her, but their on-again, off-again relationship sometimes makes her wonder

"The action is sustained; . . . the illustrations are excellent black-and-white pencil sketches." Read Teach

Other titles about Beth and Philip Hall are:

Get out of here, Philip Hall (1981)

I've already forgotten your name, Philip Hall (2004)

Greene, Bette—*Continued*

Summer of my German soldier. Dial Bks. for Young Readers 1973 230p pa $6.99 hardcover o.p. (6 and up)　　　　　　　　**Fic**

1. World War, 1939-1945—Fiction 2. German prisoners of war—Fiction 3. Arkansas—Fiction

ISBN 0-14-130636-X (pa)

"Patty knows the pain of loneliness, rejection, and beatings in a family where she is the ugly duckling, unable to gain her parents' love. This is in contrast to the affection shown to her beautiful and submissive sister. Anton Reiker is a German prisoner-of-war in a camp outside of Jenkinsville, Arkansas, and when he escapes, Patty helps him. Because her family is Jewish, she pays dearly for this intervention." Shapiro. Fic for Youth. 3d edition

Followed by Morning is a long time coming (1978)

Greene, Stephanie

Falling into place. Clarion Bks. 2002 124p $15 (3-5)　　　　　　　　**Fic**

1. Grandmothers—Fiction 2. Stepfamilies—Fiction 3. Family life—Fiction

ISBN 0-618-17744-2　　　　　LC 2002-2744

As eleven-year-old Margaret struggles to find a way of coping with the hassles of a new stepfamily, she learns that her Gran is facing similar concerns after moving to a retirement community and becoming a widow

"The reading is easy, and the plot moves along quickly, naturally, and with some humor." SLJ

Moose's big idea; illustrated by Joe Mathieu. Marshall Cavendish 2005 51p il (Moose and Hildy) $14.95 (1-3)　　　　　　　　**Fic**

1. Moose—Fiction 2. Pigs—Fiction

ISBN 0-7614-5212-5　　　　　LC 2004-22536

"Moose is sad upon losing his very large antlers, but cheers up a bit when his pig friend, Hildy, is now able to observe his pretty eyes and muscular legs. . . . In the next chapter, he stays inside during hunting season. . . . When cabin fever ensues, Moose gets the idea to sell doughnuts, coffee, and original artwork to hunters. . . . making a sale to a naive hunter. In another chapter, this same man finds Moose's old antlers but won't give them back. Finally, Moose's new antlers begin to grow. . . . Readers stepping up to chapter books will laughingly turn these pages and clamor for more. Mathieu's frequent black-and-white illustrations expand on the fun." SLJ

Other titles about Moose and Hildy are:

Moose crossing (2005)

Pig pickin' (2006)

Owen Foote, frontiersman; illustrated by Martha Weston. Clarion Bks. 1999 88p il $14; pa $4.95 (2-4)　　　　　　　　**Fic**

1. Outdoor life—Fiction

ISBN 0-395-61578-X; 0-618-24620-7 (pa)

LC 98-44843

Second grader Owen Foote is looking forward to spending time with his friend Joseph in their tree fort, until some bullies visiting his neighbor, Mrs. Gold, threaten to wreck the fort

"Real-boy characters with an appealingly loyal friendship, a good balance of narrative and dialogue, and an honestly childlike sense of the way the world works." Horn Book

Other titles about Owen Foote are:

Owen Foote, mighty scientist (2004)

Owen Foote, money man (2000)

Owen Foote, second grade strongman (1997)

Owen Foote, super spy (2001)

Owen Foote, soccer star (1998)

Queen Sophie Hartley; [by] Stephanie Greene. Clarion Books 2005 136p $15 (3-5)　　　　　　　　**Fic**

1. Family life—Fiction 2. Old age—Fiction

ISBN 0-618-49461-8　　　　　LC 2004-20106

A suggestion from her mother leads Sophie to befriend the new girl at school and an elderly, grouchy woman, and helps her overcome the feeling that she is not good at anything.

"The family dynamics are nicely developed and believable. . . . Sophie is likable and resilient, and readers will identify with her." SLJ

Greenfield, Eloise

Sister; drawings by Moneta Barnett. Crowell 1974 83p il pa $4.99 hardcover o.p. (4 and up)　　　　　　　　**Fic**

1. Sisters—Fiction 2. Single parent family—Fiction 3. African Americans—Fiction

ISBN 0-06-440199-5 (pa); 0-690-00497-4 (hc)

A 13-year-old black girl whose father is dead watches her 16-year-old sister drifting away from her and her mother and fears she may fall into the same self-destructive behavior herself. While waiting for her sister's return home, she leafs through her diary, reliving both happy and unhappy experiences while gradually recognizing her own individuality

"The book is strong . . . strong in perception, in its sensitivity, in its realism." Bull Cent Child Books

Greenwald, Sheila

Rosy Cole's worst ever, best yet tour of New York City. Farrar, Straus & Giroux 2003 121p il $16 (3-5)　　　　　　　　**Fic**

1. Cousins—Fiction 2. Family life—Fiction 3. New York (N.Y.)—Fiction

ISBN 0-374-36349-8　　　　　LC 2002-192526

"Melanie Kroupa books"

Rosy plans to show her small-town cousin all the amazing sights that make New York City such a great place to live, but things do not go as she had hoped

"Expressive ink drawings reflect the story's energy and humor." Booklist

Other titles about Rosy Cole are:

Give us a great big smile, Rosy Cole (1981)

Here's Hermione: a Rosy Cole production (1991)

Rosy Cole discovers America! (1992)

Rosy Cole: she grows and graduates (1997)

Rosy Cole: she walks in beauty (1994)

Rosy Cole's great American guilt club (1985)

Rosy Cole's memoir explosion (2006)

Rosy's romance (1989)

Write on, Rosy! (a young author in crisis (1988)

Valentine Rosy (1984)

Griffin, Adele

Hannah, divided. Hyperion Bks. for Children 2002 264p $15.99; pa $5.99 (4 and up)

Fic

1. Mathematics—Fiction 2. Great Depression, 1929-1939—Fiction 3. Pennsylvania—Fiction
ISBN 0-7868-0879-9; 0-7868-1727-5 (pa)

LC 2002-68929

In 1934, a thirteen-year-old with a gift for numbers is offered the chance to leave her family's dairy farm to spend one term at an exclusive Philadelphia girls' school preparing for a scholarship exam

"Griffin does a marvelous job of presenting a girl who is very different and letting readers peek inside her head. She also touches characters and situations with a freshness that sets her writing apart." Booklist

The other Shepards. Hyperion Bks. for Children 1998 218p pa $5.99 hardcover o.p. (6 and up)

Fic

1. Sisters—Fiction 2. New York (N.Y.)—Fiction
ISBN 0-7868-1333-4 (pa); 0-7868-043-8 (hc)

LC 98-12609

Teenage Holland and her younger sister Geneva, having always lived under the shadow of siblings who died before they were born, struggle to establish separate identities and escape from the oppressive weight of their parents' continuing grief

"This is a stunning, quietly moving novel." SLJ

Griffin, Peni R.

The ghost sitter. Dutton Children's Bks. 2001 131p $14.99; pa $5.99 (4 and up)

Fic

1. Ghost stories
ISBN 0-525-46676-2; 0-14-230216-3 (pa)

LC 00-65859

When she realizes that her new house is haunted by the ghost of a ten-year-old girl who used to live there, Charlotte tries to help her find peace

"Griffin's book has several strong appeals: new best friends solving a mystery together, a just-scary-enough ghost girl, and a deathless bond between sisters that provides the book with its resoundingly satisfying conclusion and bang-up last sentence." Horn Book

Switching well. Margaret K. McElderry Bks. 1993 218p $17 hardcover o.p. (5 and up)

Fic

1. Space and time—Fiction 2. Texas—Fiction
ISBN 0-689-50581-7

LC 92-38442

Also available in paperback from Puffin Bks.

Two twelve-year-old girls in San Antonio, Texas, Ada in 1891 and Amber in 1991, switch places through a magic well and try desperately to return to their own times

"A fine blend of time travel and friendship, laced with insight into social history and attitudes." SLJ

Grossman, David

Duel; a mystery; translated by Betsy Rosenberg. Bloomsbury 2004 112p $15.95 (5 and up)

Fic

1. Jews—Fiction 2. Jerusalem—Fiction 3. Mystery fiction
ISBN 1-58234-930-4

LC 2003-47198

In Jerusalem, when elderly Mr. Rosenthal receives a threatening letter accusing him of stealing a painting and challenging him to a duel, twelve-year-old David needs to find who really stole it before someone gets hurt.

"This mystery reads like a tall tale, with larger-than-life characters and dire circumstances. The translation is natural and seamless. The memorable characters and quirky situation make this a great read-aloud." SLJ

Gündisch, Karin

How I became an American; translated from German by James Skofield. Cricket Publs. 2001 120p $15.95 (4 and up)

Fic

1. German Americans—Fiction 2. Immigrants—Fiction
ISBN 0-8126-4875-7

LC 01-37223

Original German edition, 2000
Translation of: Das Paradies liegt in Amerika

In 1902, ten-year-old Johann and his family, Germans who had been living in Austria-Hungary, board a ship to immigrate to Youngstown, Ohio, where they make a new life as Americans

"This upbeat, often humorous, realistic narrative incorporates songs used to encourage or discourage potential emigrants and even neatly ties in the story of the Pied Piper of Hamlin." SLJ

Gutman, Dan

The homework machine; [by] Dan Gutman. 1st ed. Simon & Schuster Books for Young Readers 2006 146p $15.95 (4-6)

Fic

1. School stories
ISBN 0-689-87678-5

LC 2005-19785

Four fifth-grade students—a geek, a class clown, a teacher's pet, and a slacker—as well as their teacher and mothers, each relate events surrounding a computer programmed to complete homework assignments.

"This fast-paced, entertaining book has something for everyone: convincing characters deftly portrayed . . . ; points of discussion on ethics and student computer use; and every child's dream machine." Booklist

The million dollar strike; [by] Dan Gutman. 1st ed. Hyperion Books For Children 2004 176p $15.99 (4-6)

Fic

1. Bowling—Fiction 2. Horror fiction 3. Mystery fiction
ISBN 0-7868-1880-8

LC 2004-40614

Best friends Ouchie and Squishy, who love bowling and horror movies respectively, meet the eccentric owner of a local bowling alley and try to help him save Bowl-A-Rama from the wrecking ball and a destructive psychotic lunatic.

"Filled with humor and suspense, this fast-paced novel is a good choice for reluctant readers." SLJ

Shoeless Joe & me; a baseball card adventure. HarperCollins Pubs. 2002 163p $15.95 (4 and up)

Fic

1. Jackson, Joe, 1888-1951—Fiction 2. Baseball—Fiction
ISBN 0-06-029253-9

LC 2001-24638

Joe Stoshack travels back to 1919, where he meets Shoeless Joe Jackson and tries to prevent the fixing of

Gutman, Dan—*Continued*

the World Series in which Jackson was wrongly implicated

"A not-quite-believable, but still highly enjoyable time-travel adventure." Booklist

Other titles in the Baseball card adventures series are:

Abner & me (2005)
Babe & me (2000)
Honus & me (1997)
Jackie & me (1999)
Mickey & me (2003)
Satch & me (2006)

Gwaltney, Doris

Homefront. Simon & Schuster Books for Young Readers 2006 310p $16.99 (5 and up) **Fic**

1. Family life—Fiction 2. World War, 1939-1945—Fiction 3. Virginia—Fiction

ISBN 0-689-86842-1

"As Margaret Ann Motley looks forward to seventh grade, the only changes she sees on the horizon are her sister's leaving for college and, immediately afterwards, moving . . . into her sister's old room. With the U.S. on the brink of World War II, though, greater changes are in store. . . . Gwaltney provides vivid character portrayals. . . . Well grounded in the Tidewater area of Virginia, the novel's social context is made real." Booklist

Haas, Jessie

Birthday pony; pictures by Margot Apple. Greenwillow Books 2004 80p il $14.99; lib bdg $15.89 (2-4) **Fic**

1. Horses—Fiction 2. Horsemanship—Fiction 3. Grandmothers—Fiction

ISBN 0-06-057359-7; 0-06-057360-0 (lib bdg)

LC 2003-57286

Grandma Aggie tries to help her granddaughter Jane and the independent pony Popcorn, who were born on the same day, become riding partners

"Sentences are short and prose style and vocabulary are accessible to youngsters who are making the transition from beginning readers to chapter books. This delightful story is enhanced by Apple's black-and-white pencil drawings." SLJ

Jigsaw pony; pictures by Ying-hwa Hu. Greenwillow Books 2005 128p il lib bdg $15.89; $14.99 (2-4) **Fic**

1. Horses—Fiction 2. Twins—Fiction 3. Sisters—Fiction

ISBN 0-06-078250-1 (lib bdg); 0-06-078245-5

LC 2004-60724

Twins Kiera and Fran have never agreed on anything but when their dream comes true and their father surprises them with a pony, they must learn to work together to care for their new pet.

This is "a very pleasing tale . . . with large, easy-to-read type and a spacious layout that make it ideal for readers new to chapter books." Booklist

Runaway Radish; pictures by Margot Apple. Greenwillow Bks. 2001 56p il $15.95; lib bdg $15.89 (2-4) **Fic**

1. Horses—Fiction

ISBN 0-688-16688-1; 0-06-029159-1 (lib bdg)

LC 99-54088

When Radish the pony grows too big for the girls who own him, he goes to live at a horse camp where there are always new children for him to train

"With basic language, short sentences, and plenty of details about horse care and riding technique, this beginning chapter book is a sure bet for children with horse fever. Margot Apple's handsome, nostalgic illustrations of horses in action enliven nearly every page." Booklist

Haddix, Margaret Peterson

Say what? illustrated by James Bernardin. Simon & Schuster Books for Young Readers 2004 91p il $12.95 (2-4) **Fic**

1. Family life—Fiction

ISBN 0-689-86255-5 LC 2002-155512

When their parents begin saying the wrong thing every time six-year-old Sukey and her older brothers misbehave, the children discover that it is a plot and fight back with their own wrong phrases

"Lighthearted and humorous, this easy chapter book is made all the more appealing by Bernardin's comical black-and-white illustrations." Booklist

Hahn, Mary Downing

Anna all year round; illustrated by Diane deGroat. Clarion Bks. 1999 133p il $15 (3-5) **Fic**

1. Family life—Fiction 2. Baltimore (Md.)—Fiction

ISBN 0-395-86975-7 LC 98-19985

Eight-year-old Anna experiences a series of episodes, some that are funny, others sad, involving friends and family during a year in Baltimore just before World War I

"Based on the childhood of the author's mother. . . . Hahn's use of the present tense helps keep nostalgia at bay, as does the energetic, just-dashed-off quality of deGroat's rough pencil sketches." Horn Book Guide

Another title about Anna is:

Anna on the farm (2001)

Daphne's book. Clarion Bks. 1983 177p $15 (5 and up) **Fic**

1. School stories 2. Friendship—Fiction 3. Authorship—Fiction 4. Family life—Fiction

ISBN 0-89919-183-5 LC 83-7348

Also available in paperback from Avon Bks.

As author Jessica and artist Daphne collaborate on a picture book for a seventh-grade English class contest, Jessica becomes aware of conditions in Daphne's home life that seem to threaten her health and safety

"The story is compelling in its portrayal of peer group cruelty and the disturbing dilemma Daphne faces. Jessica's own conflict about how long to shield Daphne will provoke its share of thought too. Characterizations are strong and the situations pressing." Booklist

Hahn, Mary Downing—*Continued*

The doll in the garden; a ghost story. Clarion Bks. 1989 128p $15 (4-6)   **Fic**

1. Space and time—Fiction 2. Ghost stories

ISBN 0-89919-848-1   LC 88-20365

Also available in paperback from Avon Bks.

After Ashley and Kristi find an antique doll buried in old Miss Cooper's garden, they discover that they can enter a ghostly turn-of-the-century world by going through a hole in the hedge

"Hahn's elegant use of language, as well as her ability to probe complex emotions at a child's level, elevates this above-the-ordinary ghost tale into a story with universal themes." Booklist

The Gentleman Outlaw and me—Eli; a story of the Old West. Clarion Bks. 1996 212p $16 (5 and up)   **Fic**

1. Frontier and pioneer life—Fiction 2. West (U.S.)—Fiction

ISBN 0-395-73083-X   LC 95-18802

Also available in paperback from Avon Bks.

In 1887 twelve-year-old Eliza, disguised as a boy and traveling towards Colorado in search of her missing father, falls in with Calvin Featherbone, a "Gentleman Outlaw" and joins him in his illegal schemes

Hahn "succeeds in bringing the ambiance of the Old West to her novel. The result is a fast, funny, and entertaining adventure." SLJ

Hear the wind blow. Clarion Bks. 2003 212p $15 (5 and up)   **Fic**

1. United States—History—1861-1865, Civil War—Fiction 2. Siblings—Fiction

ISBN 0-618-18190-3   LC 2002-15977

With their mother dead and their home burned, a thirteen-year-old boy and his little sister set out across Virginia in search of relatives during the final days of the Civil War

The author "gives readers an entertaining and thought-provoking combination: a strong adventure inextricably bound to a specific time and place, but one that resonates with universal themes." Horn Book

The old Willis place; a ghost story. Clarion Books 2004 199p $15 (5 and up)   **Fic**

1. Ghost stories

ISBN 0-618-43018-0   LC 2004-2345

Tired of the rules that have bound them ever since "the bad thing happened," twelve-year-old Diana ignores her brother's warnings and befriends the daughter of the new caretaker, setting in motion events that lead to the release of the spirit of an evil, crazy woman who once ruled the old Willis place

"The story is taut, spooky, and fast-paced with amazingly credible, memorable characters." SLJ

Stepping on the cracks. Clarion Bks. 1991 216p $16 (5 and up)   **Fic**

1. World War, 1939-1945—Fiction

ISBN 0-395-58507-4   LC 91-7706

Also available in paperback from Avon Bks.

In 1944, while her brother is overseas fighting in World War II, eleven-year-old Margaret gets a new view of the school bully Gordy when she finds him hiding his

own brother, an army deserter, and decides to help him

"Well-drawn characters and a satisfying plot. . . . There is plenty of action and page-turning suspense to please those who want a quick read, but there is much to ponder and reflect on as well." SLJ

Time for Andrew; a ghost story. Clarion Bks. 1994 165p $15 (5 and up)   **Fic**

1. Ghost stories 2. Space and time—Fiction

ISBN 0-395-66556-6   LC 93-2877

Also available in paperback from Avon Bks.

When he goes to spend the summer with his great-aunt in the family's old house, eleven-year-old Drew is drawn eighty years into the past to trade places with his great-great-uncle who is dying of diphtheria

"There's plenty to enjoy in this delightful time-slip fantasy: a fascinating premise, a dastardly cousin, some good suspense, and a roundup of characters to care about." Booklist

Wait till Helen comes; a ghost story. Clarion Bks. 1986 184p $15 (4-6)   **Fic**

1. Ghost stories 2. Stepchildren—Fiction

ISBN 0-89919-453-2   LC 86-2648

Also available in paperback from Avon Bks.

Molly and Michael dislike their spooky new stepsister Heather but realize that they must try to save her when she seems ready to follow a ghost child to her doom

"Intertwined with the ghost story is the question of Molly's moral imperative to save a child she truly dislikes. Though the emotional turnaround may be a bit quick for some, this still scores as a first-rate thriller." Booklist

Hale, Marian

The truth about sparrows; [by] Marian Hale. 1st ed. H. Holt 2004 260p $16.95 (5 and up)
                    Fic

1. Friendship—Fiction 2. Moving—Fiction 3. Great Depression, 1929-1939—Fiction

ISBN 0-8050-7584-4   LC 2003-56981

Twelve-year-old Sadie promises that she will always be Wilma's best friend when their families leave drought-stricken Missouri in 1933, but once in Texas, Sadie learns that she must try to make a new home—and new friends, too

"Rich with social history, this first novel is informative, enjoyable, and evocative." SLJ

Halpern, Sue

Introducing . . . Sasha Abramowitz; [by] Sue Halpern. Farrar, Straus and Giroux 2005 281p $17 (5 and up)   **Fic**

1. Tourette syndrome—Fiction 2. Siblings—Fiction 3. Family life—Fiction

ISBN 0-374-38432-0   LC 2004-53269

"Frances Foster books"

When eleven-year-old Sasha tries to ignore the fact that her brother has Tourette's Syndrome, it takes a classmate to help her understand and accept the situation.

The author "turns her considerable talents to envisioning the impact a devastating illness can have on a family, at the same time creating a lively, engaging protagonist whose first-person narrative incorporates wry asides as well as painful truths." Booklist

Hamilton, Virginia

The bells of Christmas; illustrations by Lambert Davis. Harcourt Brace Jovanovich 1989 59p $19; pa $10 (4-6) **Fic**
1. Christmas—Fiction 2. Family life—Fiction 3. African Americans—Fiction 4. Ohio—Fiction
ISBN 0-15-206450-8; 0-15-201550-7 (pa)
LC 89-7468
"On Christmas Day, 1890, in Ohio, the Bell family comes along the National Road to spend the holiday with Jason and his family. The gentle story is stuffed like a proper plum pudding with specific details of rural life almost a century ago." N Y Times Book Rev

Cousins. Philomel Bks. 1990 125p $17.99 o.p. (5 and up) **Fic**
1. Death—Fiction 2. Cousins—Fiction 3. Grandmothers—Fiction 4. African Americans—Fiction
ISBN 0-399-22164-6 LC 90-31451
Also available in paperback from Scholastic
Concerned that her grandmother may die, Cammy is unprepared for the accidental death of her cousin Patty Ann
"The book deals essentially with emotions and sensations, and the writing reverberates with honesty and truth. Virginia Hamilton encases the story in family tradition, which offsets the instabilities of contemporary life, and she beautifully counterposes superstition and rationality, separation and reconciliation, love and death." Horn Book
Followed by Second Cousins (1998)

Drylongso; illustrated by Jerry Pinkney. Harcourt Brace Jovanovich 1992 54p il pa $10 hardcover o.p. (3-5) **Fic**
1. Droughts—Fiction 2. Farm life—Fiction 3. African Americans—Fiction
ISBN 0-15-201587-6 (pa) LC 91-25575
As a great wall of dust moves across their drought-stricken farm, a family's distress is relieved by a young man called Drylongso, who literally blows into their lives with the storm
"In an understand story of drought and hard times and longing for rain, a great writer and a great artists have pared down their rich, exuberant styles to something quieter but no less intense." Booklist

The house of Dies Drear; illustrated by Eros Keith. Macmillan 1968 246p il $18.95; pa $5.99 (5 and up) **Fic**
1. African Americans—Fiction 2. Mystery fiction 3. Ohio—Fiction
ISBN 0-02-742500-2; 0-02-043520-7 (pa)
"A hundred years ago, Dies Drear and two slaves he was hiding in his house, an Underground Railroad station in Ohio, had been murdered. The house, huge and isolated, was fascinating, Thomas thought, but he wasn't sure he was glad Papa had bought it—funny things kept happening, frightening things." Bull Cent Child Books
"The answer to the mystery comes in a startling dramatic dénouement that is pure theater. This is gifted writing; the characterization is unforgettable, the plot imbued with mounting tension." Saturday Rev
Followed by The mystery of Drear House (1987)

M.C. Higgins, the great; [by] Virginia Hamilton. Simon & Schuster 1999 c1974 232p $18; pa $5.99 (5 and up) **Fic**
1. African Americans—Fiction 2. Family life—Fiction 3. Appalachian region—Fiction
ISBN 0-689-83074-2; 0-689-71694-X (pa)
LC 99014288
Awarded the Newbery Medal, 1975
"A reissue of the title first published 1974 by Macmillan"
'25th anniversary edition'--T.p. verso.
As a slag heap, the result of strip mining, creeps closer to his house in the Ohio hills, fifteen-year-old M.C. is torn between trying to get his family away and fighting for the home they love.
"This is a deeply involving story possessing a folkorish quality." Child Book Rev Serv

Plain City. Blue Sky Press (NY) 1993 194p pa $5.99 hardcover o.p. (5 and up) **Fic**
1. Racially mixed people—Fiction 2. African Americans—Fiction
ISBN 0-590-47365-4 (pa); 0-590-47364-6 (hc)
LC 93-19910
Twelve-year-old Buhlaire, a "mixed" child who feels out of place in her community, struggles to unearth her past and her family history as she gradually discovers more and more about her long-missing father
"Richly textured with a cast of unforgettable characters, this extraordinary novel offers a rare glimpse of unconditional love, family loyalty and compassion." Publ Wkly

The planet of Junior Brown. Macmillan 1971 210p pa $5.99 hardcover o.p. (6 and up) **Fic**
1. Friendship—Fiction 2. African Americans—Fiction
ISBN 0-02-742510-X (pa); 0-689-71721-0 (hc)
"This is the story of a crucial week in the lives of two black, eighth-grade dropouts who have been spending their time with the school janitor. Each boy is presented as a distinct individual. Jr. is a three-hundred pound musical prodigy as neurotic as his overprotective mother. Buddy has learned to live by his wits in a world of homeless children. Buddy becomes Jr. Brown's protector and says to the other boys, 'We are together because we have to learn to live for each other.'" Read Ladders for Hum Relat. 6th edition

Time pieces; the book of times. Blue Sky Press (NY) 2002 199p $16.95; pa $5 (5 and up) **Fic**
1. Family life—Fiction 2. African Americans—Fiction 3. Ohio—Fiction
ISBN 0-590-28881-4; 0-439-51714-1 (pa)
LC 2001-43608
Valena, her family, and dog live in rural Ohio, where she and her cousin Melinda share experiences that include seeing the aurora borealis, surviving a tornado, and going to an amazing circus
"The simplicity and directness of the language serve the subject matter beautifully." SLJ

Hamilton, Virginia—_Continued_

Zeely; illustrated by Symeon Shimin. Macmillan 1967 122p il $17.95; pa $4.99 (4 and up)

Fic

1. African Americans—Fiction
ISBN 0-02-742470-7; 0-689-71695-8 (pa)

"Imaginative eleven-year-old Geeder is stirred when she sees Zeely Tayber, who is dignified, stately, and six-and-a-half feet tall. Geeder thinks Zeely looks like the magazine picture of the Watusi queen. Through meeting Zeely personally and getting to know her, Geeder finally returns to reality." Read Ladders for Hum Relat. 5th edition

Hannigan, Katherine

Ida B; —and her plans to maximize fun, avoid disaster, and (possibly) save the world. Greenwillow Books 2004 246p $15.99; lib bdg $16.89 (4-6)

Fic

1. Cancer—Fiction 2. Family life—Fiction 3. School stories 4. Wisconsin—Fiction
ISBN 0-06-073024-2; 0-06-073025-0 (lib bdg)

LC 2003-25625

In Wisconsin, fourth-grader Ida B spends happy hours being home-schooled and playing in her family's apple orchard, until her mother begins treatment for breast cancer and her parents must sell part of the orchard and send her to public school

"Through a masterful use of voice, Hannigan's first-person narration captures an unforgettable heroine with intelligence, spirit, and a unique imagination." SLJ

Hansen, Brooks

Caesar's antlers; with drawings by the author. Farrar, Straus & Giroux 1997 217p il $16; pa $6.95 (5 and up)

Fic

1. Reindeer—Fiction 2. Sparrows—Fiction
ISBN 0-374-31024-6; 0-374-41072-0 (pa)

LC 96-53148

Bette, a mother sparrow separated by accident from her mate, takes her chicks on a long search when a faithful reindeer permits her to make a nest in his antlers

"Simply written, yet full of wonder and magic, the story builds to a satisfying, if tragic conclusion. . . . Spare ink drawings add to the quiet mood." SLJ

Haptie, Charlotte

Otto and the flying twins; the first book of the Karmidee; [by] Charlotte Haptie. 1st ed. Holiday House 2004 304p il $17.95 (4 and up)

Fic

1. Fantasy fiction 2. Magic—Fiction
ISBN 0-8234-1826-X   LC 2003-57135
First published 2002 in the United Kingdom

Young Otto comes to the rescue when he discovers that his family and city are the last remnants of an ancient magical world now under threat from the Normal Police.

"The amazing oddities and quirks of this world and its residents are described with delicious nonchalance. . . . The characters are equally surprising and unpredictable. . . . The writing is as fresh and invigorating as the setting." SLJ

Hardinge, Frances

Fly by night; [by] Frances Hardinge. 1st U.S. ed. HarperCollinsPublishers 2006 487p $16.99; $16.99; lib bdg $17.89; lib bdg $17.89 (5 and up)

Fic

1. Fantasy fiction
ISBN 9780060876272; 0060876271; 9780060876296 (lib bdg); 0060876298 (lib bdg)   LC 2005020598
First published 2005 in the United Kingdom

Mosca Mye and her homicidal goose, Saracen, travel to the city of Mandelion on the heels of smooth-talking con-man, Eponymous Clent.

"Through rich, colorful language and a sure sense of plot and pacing, Hardinge has created a distinctly imaginative world full of engaging characters, robust humor, and true suspense." SLJ

Harlow, Joan Hiatt

Star in the storm. Margaret K. McElderry Bks. 2000 150p $16; pa $4.99

Fic

1. Dogs—Fiction 2. Newfoundland—Fiction
ISBN 0-689-82905-1; 0-689-84621-5 (pa)

LC 99-20416

In 1912, fearing for the safety of her beloved Newfoundland dog Sirius because of a new law outlawing non-sheepherding dogs in her Newfoundland village, twelve-year-old Maggie tries to save him by keeping him hidden

"Containing many authentic details of life in a remote region in days gone by, this story is educational as well as exciting." Booklist

Harrison, Barbara

Theo. Clarion Bks. 1999 166p $15 (5 and up)

Fic

1. World War, 1939-1945—Fiction 2. Greece—Fiction 3. Orphans—Fiction 4. Puppets and puppet plays—Fiction
ISBN 0-89919-959-3   LC 98-45823

Theo, an orphaned puppeteer performs bravely on and off the stage after joining the Greek resistance movement during World War II

"A story full of intensity that resonates with humor, hope, and—above all—goodness." Horn Book

Harvey, Brett

Cassie's journey; going West in the 1860s; illustrated by Deborah Kogan Ray. Holiday House 1988 unp il lib bdg $14.35; pa $6.95 (2-4)

Fic

1. Overland journeys to the Pacific—Fiction 2. Frontier and pioneer life—Fiction 3. West (U.S.)—Fiction
ISBN 0-8234-0684-9 (lib bdg); 0-8234-1172-9 (pa)

LC 87-23599

A young girl relates the hardships and dangers of traveling with her family in a covered wagon from Illinois to California during the 1860's

"Harvey has based this story of westward migration on the diaries of pioneer women. . . . [This is] a fascinating piece of historical fiction. . . . Ray's soft charcoal drawings carry a solemnity that gives the account a serious edge while evoking the loneliness and breadth of the landscape." Booklist

Harvey, Brett—*Continued*

My prairie Christmas; illustrations by Deborah Kogan Ray. Holiday House 1990 unp il $17.95; pa $5.95 (2-4) **Fic**
1. Christmas—Fiction 2. Frontier and pioneer life—Fiction 3. West (U.S.)—Fiction
ISBN 0-8234-0827-2; 0-8234-1064-1 (pa)
LC 90-55104
On the first Christmas after Eleanor's family moves to a house on the prairie, everyone becomes worried when Papa goes out to cut down a Christmas tree and does not come back
"Ray's soft-edged illustrations capture the prairie vistas and the warm family interactions well. The narrative is flowing and comfortable." Booklist

Haseley, Dennis

The amazing thinking machine. Dial Bks. 2002 117p $17.99 (4 and up) **Fic**
1. Great Depression, 1929-1939—Fiction 2. Inventions—Fiction 3. Poverty—Fiction
ISBN 0-8037-2609-0 LC 00-63860
During the Great Depression, while their father is away looking for work, eight-year-old Patrick and thirteen-year-old Roy create a machine to help their mother make ends meet, even as she is helping tramps
"Thoughtfully written, the novel is alternately poignant and humorous, with a satisfying resolution." Horn Book Guide

Heide, Florence Parry

The shrinking of Treehorn; drawings by Edward Gorey. Holiday House 1971 unp il lib bdg $16.95; pa $6.95 (2-5) **Fic**
ISBN 0-8234-0189-8 (lib bdg); 0-8234-0975-9 (pa)
Treehorn spends an unhappy day and night shrinking. Yet when he tells his mother, father, teacher and principal of his problem they're all too busy to do anything about it. To Treehorn's great relief he finally discovers a magical game that restores him to his natural size, but then he starts turning green!
This "is an imaginative little whimsy, whose sly humor and macabre touches are perfectly matched in Edward Gorey's illustrations." Book World

Henkes, Kevin

The birthday room. Greenwillow Bks. 1999 152p $15.99 (5 and up) **Fic**
1. Family life—Fiction 2. Uncles—Fiction
ISBN 0-688-16733-0 LC 98-39887
Also available in paperback from Puffin Bks.
"For his twelfth birthday, Ben Hunter receives a room that he can use as an art studio and a letter from his uncle—the one responsible for the loss of Ben's little finger when Ben was a toddler. . . . Mrs. Hunter, who has been angry at her brother since the accident, reluctantly agrees to go to Oregon with Ben." Booklist
"Told in spare, unobtrusive prose, a story that helps us see our own chances for benefiting from mutual tolerance, creative conflict resolution, and other forms of good will." Horn Book

Olive's ocean. Greenwillow Bks. 2003 217p $15.99; lib bdg $16.89 (5 and up) **Fic**
1. Grandmothers—Fiction 2. Family life—Fiction
ISBN 0-06-053543-1; 0-06-053544-X (lib bdg)
LC 2002-29782
A Newbery Medal honor book, 2004
On a summer visit to her grandmother's cottage by the ocean, twelve-year-old Martha gains perspective on the death of a classmate, on her relationship with her grandmother, on her feelings for an older boy, and on her plans to be a writer.
"Rich characterizations move this compelling novel to its satisfying and emotionally authentic conclusion." SLJ

Protecting Marie. Greenwillow Bks. 1995 195p $18.99 (5 and up) **Fic**
1. Father-daughter relationship—Fiction 2. Dogs—Fiction
ISBN 0-688-13958-2 LC 94-16387
Also available in paperback from Puffin Bks.
Relates twelve-year-old Fanny's love-hate relationship with her father, a temperamental artist, who has given Fanny a new dog
"The characters ring heartbreakingly true in this quiet, wise story; they are complex and difficult—like all of us—and worthy of our attention." Horn Book

Sun & Spoon. Greenwillow Bks. 1997 135p $15.99 (4 and up) **Fic**
1. Grandmothers—Fiction 2. Death—Fiction
ISBN 0-688-15232-5 LC 96-46259
Also available in paperback from Puffin Bks.
"Spoon, 10, spends his summer trying to reconfigure his world, which seems strangely out of kilter since his grandmother's death." SLJ
"Sensitively placed metaphors enrich the narrative, embuing its perceptive depictions of grief with a powerful message of affirmation." Publ Wkly

Words of stone. Greenwillow Bks. 1992 152p $18.99 (5 and up) **Fic**
1. Friendship—Fiction
ISBN 0-688-11356-7 LC 91-28543
Also available in paperback Puffin Bks.; Spanish language edition also available
Busy trying to deal with his many fears nd his troubled feelings for his dead mother, ten-year-old Blaze has his life changed when he meets the boisterous and irresistible Joselle
"A story rich in characterization, dramatic subplots, and some very creepy moments." SLJ

Henry, Marguerite

Brighty of the Grand Canyon; illustrated by Wesley Dennis. Rand McNally 1953 222p il (4 and up) **Fic**
1. Donkeys—Fiction 2. Grand Canyon (Ariz.)—Fiction
LC 53-7233
Available in hardcover from P. Smith and in paperback from Aladdin Bks.
Drawn from a real-life incident, this is the story of "Brighty, the shaggy little burro who roamed the canyons of the Colorado River [and] had a will of his own. He

Henry, Marguerite—*Continued*

liked the old prospector and Uncle Jim and he helped solve a mystery, but chiefly he was the freedom-loving burro." Chicago Public Libr

"Only those who are unfamiliar with the West would say it is too packed with drama to be true. . . . The author's . . . superb ability as a story teller [makes] this a vivid tale." Christ Sci Monit

Justin Morgan had a horse; illustrated by Wesley Dennis. Simon & Schuster Bks. for Young Readers 2002 c1954 169p il $17.95; pa $4.99 (4 and up)   **Fic**

1. Horses—Fiction 2. Vermont—Fiction

ISBN 0-689-85279-7; 0-689-71534-X (pa)

A Newbery Medal honor book, 1946

A reissue of the edition first published 1954 by Rand McNally; an expanded version of the book first published 1945 by Wilcox & Follett

An unusual work horse raised in Vermont and known originally as [Little Bub] becomes the sire of a famous American breed and takes the name of his owner, Justin Morgan

A horse story "in a book that is rich in human values—the sort of book that makes you proud and sometimes brings a lump to your throat." Book Week

King of the wind; illustrated by Wesley Dennis. Macmillan 1991 172p il $18.95; pa $5.99 (4 and up)   **Fic**

1. Horses—Fiction

ISBN 0-02-743629-2; 0-689-71486-6 (pa)

LC 91-13474

Awarded the Newbery Medal, 1949

A reissue of the title first published 1948 by Rand McNally

"A beautiful, sympathetic story of the famous [ancestor of a line of great thoroughbred horses] . . . and the little mute Arabian stable boy who accompanies him on his journey across the seas to France and England [in the eighteenth century]. The lad's fierce devotion to his horse and his great faith and loyalty are skillfully woven into an enthralling tale which children will long remember. The moving quality of the writing is reflected in the handsome illustrations." Wis Libr Bull

Misty of Chincoteague; illustrated by Wesley Dennis. Macmillan 1991 173p il $21.95; pa $5.99 (4 and up)   **Fic**

1. Horses—Fiction 2. Chincoteague Island (Va.)—Fiction

ISBN 0-02-743622-5; 0-689-71492-0 (pa)

LC 90-27237

A Newbery Medal honor book, 1948

First published 1947 by Rand McNally

"The islands of Chincoteague and Assateague, just off the coast of Virginia, are the setting. . . . Two children have their hearts set on owning a wild pony and her colt, descendants, so legend says, of the Moorish ponies who were survivors of a Spanish galleon wrecked there long ago." Booklist

"The beauty and pride of the wild horses is the highpoint in the story, and skillful drawings of them reveal their grace and swiftness." Ont Libr Rev

Other titles about the ponies of Chincoteague Island are:

Sea star, orphan of Chincoteague (1949)

Stormy, Misty's foal (1963)

Hermes, Patricia

Emma Dilemma and the new nanny; by Patricia Hermes. Marshall Cavendish 2006 106p $15.95 (2-4)   **Fic**

1. Family life—Fiction

ISBN 0-7614-5286-9   LC 2005024668

Emma tries to help her parents understand that, although their beloved new nanny has made a few mistakes, no one can behave perfectly responsibly all the time

"The tumult in a family with five preteen children, several pets, and two working parents provides a lively setting, and the author lightly but effectively conveys the ideas that adults aren't perfect and that admitting mistakes is often the first step toward solutions that leave everyone pleased." Booklist

Summer secrets. Marshall Cavendish 2004 141p $15.95 (5 and up)   **Fic**

1. Mental illness—Fiction 2. Race relations—Fiction 3. Mississippi—Fiction

ISBN 0-7614-5074-2   LC 2003-17669

Twelve-year-old Missy tries to learn more about her mother's odd behavior as she and her two friends share some secrets during a long, hot summer in Mississippi toward the end of World War II

"Hermes's child's-eye view of a small southern town is on target. . . . An evocative and satisfying coming-of-age story." SLJ

Hesse, Karen

Just Juice; pictures by Robert Andrew Parker. Scholastic 1998 138p il $15.95; pa $4.99 (3-5)   **Fic**

1. Literacy—Fiction 2. Family life—Fiction 3. Poverty—Fiction

ISBN 0-590-03382-4; 0-590-03383-2 (pa)

LC 98-13375

Realizing that her father's lack of work has endangered her family, nine-year-old Juice decides that she must return to school and learn to read in order to help their chances of surviving and keeping their house

"Hesse's plain, beautiful words tell of the harsh dailiness of poverty through the eyes of a child." Booklist

Letters from Rifka. Holt & Co. 1992 148p $16.95 (5 and up)   **Fic**

1. Immigrants—Fiction 2. Jews—Fiction 3. Letters—Fiction

ISBN 0-8050-1964-2   LC 91-48007

Also available in paperback from Puffin Bks.

In letters to her cousin, Rifka, a young Jewish girl, chronicles her family's flight from Russia in 1919 and her own experiences when she must be left in Belgium for a while when the others emigrate to America

"Based on the true story of the author's great-aunt, the moving account of a brave young girl's story brings to life the day-to-day trials and horrors experienced by many immigrants as well as the resourcefulness and strength they found within themselves." Horn Book

Hesse, Karen—*Continued*

A light in the storm; the Civil War diary of
Amelia Martin. Scholastic 1999 169p (Dear
America) $10.95 (5 and up)　　　　　**Fic**
1. United States—History—1861-1865, Civil War—
Fiction 2. Delaware—Fiction
ISBN 0-590-56733-0　　　　　　LC 98-49204
"Amelia Martin is a fictional character, created by the
author, and her diary and its epilogue are works of fic-
tion"

In 1860 and 1861, while working in her father's lighthouse on an island off the coast of Delaware, fifteen-
year-old Amelia records in her diary how the Civil War
is beginning to devastate her divided state
"This well-paced story features a seamless combination of history, sociology, drama, and romance." Horn
Book

Out of the dust. Scholastic 1997 227p $16.95;
pa $6.99 (5 and up)　　　　　　　**Fic**
1. Dust storms—Fiction 2. Farm life—Fiction
3. Great Depression, 1929-1939—Fiction
4. Oklahoma—Fiction
ISBN 0-590-36080-9; 0-590-37125-8 (pa)
　　　　　　　　　　LC 96-40344
Also available Thomson Gale large print edition; and
Spanish language edition
Awarded the Newbery Medal, 1998
"After facing loss after loss during the Oklahoma Dust
Bowl, Billie Jo begins to reconstruct her life." SLJ
"Hesse's writing transcends the gloom and transforms
it into a powerfully compelling tale of a girl with enor-
mous strength, courage, and love. The entire novel is
written in very readable blank verse." Booklist

Sable; illustrated by Marcia Sewall. Holt & Co.
1994 81p il $15.95; pa $7.95 (2-4)　　　**Fic**
1. Dogs—Fiction
ISBN 0-8050-2416-6; 0-8050-5772-2 (pa)
　　　　　　　　　　LC 93-33646
"A Redfeather book"
Tate Marshall is delighted when a stray dog turns up
in the yard one day, but Sable, named for her dark, silky
fur, causes trouble with the neighbors and has to go
"The early chapter book relates a dog tale sweet and
scary enough for any budding pet lover." Horn Book
Guide

Stowaway; with drawings by Robert Andrew
Parker. Margaret K. McElderry Bks. 2000 319p il
$17.95; pa $6.99 (5 and up)　　　　　**Fic**
1. Cook, James, 1728-1779—Fiction 2. Voyages
around the world—Fiction 3. Sea stories
ISBN 0-689-83987-1; 0-689-83989-8 (pa)
　　　　　　　　　　LC 00-56976
A fictional journal relates the experiences of Nicholas,
a young stowaway, from 1768 to 1771 aboard the Endeavor which sailed around the world under Captain
James Cook
"Hesse is a master storyteller who gives Nicholas an
authentic voice. . . . The author's subtle yet thorough attention to detail creates a memorable tale that is a virtual
encyclopedia of life in the days when England ruled the
seas." SLJ

Witness. Scholastic Press 2001 161p $16.95; pa
$5.99 (6 and up)　　　　　　　　**Fic**
1. Ku Klux Klan—Fiction 2. Prejudices—Fiction
3. Vermont—Fiction
ISBN 0-439-27199-1; 0-439-27200-9 (pa)
　　　　　　　　　　LC 00-54139
A series of poems express the views of eleven people
in a small Vermont town, including a young black girl
and a young Jewish girl, during the early 1920s when the
Ku Klux Klan is trying to infiltrate the town
"The story is divided into five acts, and would lend itself beautifully to performance. The plot unfolds smoothly, and the author creates multidimensional characters."
SLJ

Hiaasen, Carl

Flush. Knopf 2005 263p $16.95 (5 and up)
　　　　　　　　　　　　　　Fic
1. Environmental protection—Fiction 2. Florida—Fiction 3. Boats and boating—Fiction
ISBN 0-375-82182-1　　　　　LC 2005-05259
With their father jailed for sinking a river boat, Noah
Underwood and his younger sister, Abbey, must gather
evidence that the owner of this floating casino is empty-
ing his bilge tanks into the protected waters around their
Florida Keys home.
"This quick-reading, fun, family adventure harkens
back to the Hardy Boys in its simplicity and quirky characters." SLJ

Hoot. Knopf 2002 292p $15.95; lib bdg $17.99;
pa $8.95 (5 and up)　　　　　　　**Fic**
1. Owls—Fiction 2. Environmental protection—Fiction
3. Florida—Fiction
ISBN 0-375-82181-3; 0-375-92181-8 (lib bdg);
0-375-82916-4 (pa)　　　　　LC 2002-25478
Roy, who is new to his small Florida community, becomes involved in another boy's attempt to save a colony of burrowing owls from a proposed construction site
"The story is full of offbeat humor, buffoonish yet
charming supporting characters, and genuinely touching
scenes of children enjoying the wildness of nature."
Booklist

Hicks, Betty

Busted! [by] Betty Hicks. 1st ed. Roaring Brook
Press 2004 168p $15.95 (5 and up)　　　**Fic**
1. Mothers—Fiction 2. Single parent family—Fiction
ISBN 1-59643-004-4　　　　　LC 2003-17830
"A Deborah Brodie book"
"Twelve-year-old Stuart Ellis finds that his relation-
ship with his single-parent mom is becoming increasingly
prickly. When he is forced to quit the soccer team after
he breaks a household rule, he asks his best friend,
Mack, for help." Booklist
"A winning combination of sports and humor with a
subtle message about personal responsibility." SLJ

Out of order; [by] Betty Hicks. 1st ed. Roaring
Brook Press 2005 169p $15.95 (4-6)　　　**Fic**
1. Stepfamilies—Fiction
ISBN 1-59643-061-3　　　　　LC 2004-30107
"A Deborah Brodie book."

Hicks, Betty—*Continued*

Four youngsters, ages nine to fifteen, narrate one side of the story of their newly blended family's adjustment, interwoven with grief and loss.

"Hicks provides readers with a fresh look at blended families, offering much food for thought and several multilayered characters." SLJ

Hill, Elizabeth Starr

Bird Boy; pictures by Lesley Liu. Farrar, Straus & Giroux 1999 55p il pa $5.95 hardcover o.p. (2-4)   **Fic**
1. Birds—Fiction 2. Fishing—Fiction 3. Physically handicapped—Fiction 4. China—Fiction
ISBN 0-374-40659-6 (pa); 0-374-30723-7 (hc)
LC 98-51942

Chang, a mute Chinese boy whose father uses cormorants to fish, is pleased when he is finally old enough to help with the Big Catch and the raising of a new bird

"Youngsters, especially those with disabilities, will strongly identify with Chang, and Lesley Liu's detailed drawings capture the flavor of the Chinese landscape." Booklist

Chang and the bamboo flute; pictures by Lesley Liu. Farrar, Straus & Giroux 2002 57p il $15 (3-5)
Fic
1. Fishing—Fiction 2. Flutes—Fiction 3. China—Fiction
ISBN 0-374-31238-9   LC 2002-20722

Chang, a mute Chinese boy whose father uses cormorants to fish, becomes a hero when a heavy rain strands his father's fishing raft

"This simply told story with its unusual locale offers lessons in friendship, cooperation, and acceptance of disability. The many evocative illustrations and the good-size typeface makes this an enticing package that children will take to eagerly." Booklist

Hill, Kirkpatrick

The year of Miss Agnes. Margaret K. McElderry Bks. 2000 115p $16 (3-5)   **Fic**
1. School stories 2. Teachers—Fiction 3. Athapascan Indians—Fiction 4. Alaska—Fiction
ISBN 0-689-82933-7   LC 99-46912

Ten-year-old Fred (short for Frederika) narrates the story of school and village life among the Athapascans in Alaska during 1948 when Miss Agnes arrived as the new teacher

"Hill has created more than just an appealing cast of characters; she introduces readers to a whole community and makes a long-ago and faraway place seem real and very much alive. This is an inspirational story." SLJ

Himelblau, Linda

The trouble begins. Delacorte Press 2005 200p $14.95 (4 and up)   **Fic**
1. Vietnamese Americans—Fiction 2. Immigrants—Fiction
ISBN 0-385-73273-2   LC 2004-28253

"After years in a refugee camp in the Philippines, Du Nguyen and his grandmother are finally joining the rest of the family, who escaped Vietnam long ago. American life is nothing like he imagined. . . . Du's narration nimbly conveys not just his own cultural confusion but also how he is misunderstood by others. . . . The book is often funny and bitter-sweet simultaneously." Horn Book

Hirsch, Odo

Bartlett and the ice voyage; illustrated by Andrew McLean. Bloomsbury Pub. 2002 168p il $14.95 (3-6)   **Fic**
1. Queens—Fiction 2. Adventure fiction
ISBN 1-58234-797-2   LC 2002-18481

When an impatient queen longs to taste the delicious but fragile melidrop fruit, two explorers use "Inventiveness, Desperation, and Perseverance" to try to bring it to her

"Hirsch blends sparkling wit with engaging characters and great pacing that follows through till the suspensefully timed end. Drawings washed in pale colors add to the charm." Booklist
Other titles in this series are:
Bartlett and the City of Flames (2003)
Barlett and the Forest of Plenty (2004)

Hobbs, Valerie

Defiance. Farrar, Straus and Giroux 2005 116p $16 (5 and up)   **Fic**
1. Cancer—Fiction 2. Death—Fiction 3. Country life—Fiction
ISBN 0-374-30847-0   LC 2004-61524
"Frances Foster books."

While vacationing in the country, eleven-year-old Toby, a cancer patient, learns some important lessons about living and dying from an elderly poet and her cow.

"Spare, graceful writing, with just enough detail to bring the characters and setting to life, skillfully paces the action and keeps the focus on Toby's conflicted feelings. . . . A quiet, yet resonant story." SLJ

Sheep. Farrar, Straus and Giroux 2006 115p $16 (3-5)   **Fic**
1. Dogs—Fiction 2. Sheep—Fiction
ISBN 0-374-36777-9   LC 2005-46356
"Frances Foster books"

After a fire destroys the farm where he was born, a young border collie acquires a series of owners and learns about life as he seeks a home and longs to fulfill his life's purpose of shepherding sheep.

"The classic foundling story is beautifully told in the dog's simple, first-person voice." Booklist

Hobbs, Will

Jackie's Wild Seattle. HarperCollins Pubs. 2003 200p $15.99; lib bdg $16.89 (5 and up)
Fic
1. Uncles—Fiction
ISBN 0-688-17474-4; 0-06-051631-3 (lib bdg)
LC 2002-13386

Fourteen-year-old Shannon and her little brother, Cody, spend the summer with their uncle, helping at a wildlife rescue center named Jackie's Wild Seattle

"This story is packed with action. Each character has a storm to weather, which is ultimately confronted in a way that seems a natural part of the overall plot." Booklist

Hobbs, Will—*Continued*

Jason's gold. Morrow Junior Bks. 1999 221p
$16.99; pa $5.99 (5 and up)   **Fic**
1. Klondike River Valley (Yukon)—Gold discoveries—Fiction 2. Voyages and travels—Fiction
3. Orphans—Fiction
ISBN 0-688-15093-4; 0-380-72914-8 (pa)
LC 99-17973
When news of the discovery of gold in Canada's Yukon Territory in 1897 reaches fifteen-year-old Jason, he
embarks on a 10,000-mile journey to strike it rich
"The successful presentation of a fascinating era, coupled with plenty of action, makes this a good historical
fiction choice." SLJ
Followed by Down the Yukon (2001)

Kokopelli's flute. Atheneum Bks. for Young
Readers 1995 148p $16.95 (5 and up)   **Fic**
1. Flutes—Fiction 2. Magic—Fiction 3. Native Americans—Fiction 4. New Mexico—Fiction
ISBN 0-689-31974-6   LC 95-8422
Also available in paperback from Avon Bks.
Thirteen-year-old Tepary discovers an old flute in a
cliff dwelling in New Mexico, and through its power he
learns about ancient Native American magic
"Outstanding characters, plot, mood, and setting combine in this satisfying and memorable book." SLJ

Hodges, Margaret

Gulliver in Lilliput; retold by Margaret Hodges
from Gulliver's travels by Jonathan Swift;
illustrated by Kimberly Bulcken Root. Holiday
House 1995 unp il $17.95; pa $6.95 (3-6)
Fic
1. Fantasy fiction
ISBN 0-8234-1147-8; 0-8234-1303-9 (pa)
LC 94-15037
On a voyage in the South Seas, an Englishman finds
himself shipwrecked in Lilliput, a land of people only six
inches high
"Hodges's adaptation of Part I of *Gulliver's Travels* is
a masterful retelling of the 18th-century classic. While
condensing the story considerably, she has retained not
only the important details of the involved plot, but also
the flavor of Swift's rich, descriptive language. . . .
Root's stunning pen-and-watercolor illustrations do much
to bring the fanciful tale to life." SLJ

Hoeye, Michael

Time stops for no mouse; a Hermux Tantamoq
adventure. Putnam 2002 250p $14.99; pa $7.99 (5
and up)   **Fic**
1. Mice—Fiction 2. Animals—Fiction 3. Mystery fiction
ISBN 0-399-23878-6; 0-698-11991-6 (pa)
LC 2001-48486
Also available in paperback from Terfle Bks.
First published 2000 by Terfle Bks.
When Linka Perflinger, a jaunty mouse, brings a
watch into his shop to be repaired and then disappears,
Hermux Tantamoq is caught up in a world of dangerous
search for eternal youth as he tries to find out what hap-

pened to her
"The snappy, sophisticated writing makes this adventure a delight from start to finish. The city of Pinchester
comes alive brilliantly with its multispecies population of
rats, mice, gophers, and other small furry folk. . . . A
delightful romp for imaginative readers and fantasy
fans." Voice Youth Advocates
Other titles in this series are:
No time like show time (2004)
The sands of time (2002)

Hoffman, Mary

Starring Grace; illustrated by Caroline Binch.
Fogelman Pub. 2000 95p il $14.99; pa $4.99 (3-5)
Fic
1. African Americans—Fiction 2. Grandmothers—Fic-
tion
ISBN 0-8037-2559-0; 0-14-230022-5 (pa)
Picture book titles about Grace are also available
Grace and her friends have all sorts of adventures dur-
ing their summer vacation—going to the circus, taking
an imaginary safari, making friends with an elderly
neighbor, pretending to be astronauts, and calling the
paramedics when her grandmother has an accident.
"Hoffman's text reads easily and is filled with humor
and the wide-eyed innocence of young children at play."
SLJ
Other chapter-book titles about Grace are:
Bravo Grace! (2005)
Encore Grace! (2003)

Hoffmann, E. T. A. (Ernst Theodor Amadeus)

Nutcracker; pictures by Maurice Sendak;
translated by Ralph Manheim. Crown 1984 102p
il $40 (4 and up)   **Fic**
1. Fairy tales 2. Christmas—Fiction
ISBN 0-609-61049-X   LC 83-25266
This "book stems from Sendak's costume and set designs for the Pacific Northwest Ballet's 1981 production.
That production, and this volume, differ from the traditional ballet as they are based on Hoffmann's original
1816 long short story, rather than a French version of
Hoffmann's tale." SLJ
"The smooth, elegant, new translation re-creates the
flavor of the period and does justice to the story. . . .
The occasional quirkiness of the pictures . . . eerily reflect the mysterious story. Altogether a magnificent,
splendid combination of talents." Horn Book

Holling, Holling C.

Paddle-to-the-sea; written and illustrated by
Holling Clancy Holling. Houghton Mifflin 1941
unp il lib bdg $20; pa $11.95 (4-6)   **Fic**
1. Great Lakes region—Fiction
ISBN 0-395-15082-5 (lib bdg); 0-395-29203-4 (pa)
A Caldecott Medal honor book, 1942
A toy canoe with a seated Indian figure is launched
in Lake Nipigon by the Indian boy who carved it and in
four years travels through all the Great Lakes and the St.
Lawrence River to the Atlantic. An interesting picture of
the shore life of the lakes and the river with striking full
page pictures in bright colors and marginal pencil drawings

Holling, Holling C.—_Continued_

"The canoe's journey is used to show the flow of currents and of traffic, and each occurrence is made to seem plausible. . . . There are also diagrams of a sawmill, a freighter, the canal locks at the Soo, and Niagara Falls." Libr J

Holm, Anne

I am David; translated from the Danish by L.W. Kingsland. Harcourt 2004 239p $17; pa $5.95 (6 and up)   **Fic**
1. Refugees—Fiction
ISBN 0-15-205161-9; 0-15-205160-0 (pa)
LC 2003-57006
Original Danish edition 1963; first United States edition published 1965 with title: North to freedom

After escaping from an Eastern European concentration camp where he has spent most of his life, a twelve-year-old boy struggles to cope with an entirely strange world as he flees northward to freedom in Denmark

Holm, Jennifer L.

Our only May Amelia. HarperCollins Pubs. 1999 253p il $16.99; lib bdg $15.89; pa $5.99 (5 and up)   **Fic**
1. Frontier and pioneer life—Fiction 2. Family life—Fiction 3. Finnish Americans—Fiction 4. Washington (State)—Fiction
ISBN 0-06-027822-6; 0-06-028354-8 (lib bdg); 0-06-440856-6 (pa)   LC 98-47504
Also available Thorndike Press large print edition
A Newbery Medal honor book, 2000

As the only girl in a Finnish American family of seven brothers, May Amelia Jackson resents being expected to act like a lady while growing up in Washington State in 1899

"The voice of the colloquial first-person narrative rings true and provides a vivid picture of frontier and pioneer life. . . . An afterword discusses Holm's research into her own family's history and that of other Finnish immigrants." Horn Book Guide

Holt, Kimberly Willis

Dancing in Cadillac light. Putnam 2001 167p $16.99; pa $5.99 (5 and up)   **Fic**
1. Grandfathers—Fiction 2. Old age—Fiction 3. Texas—Fiction
ISBN 0-399-23402-0; 0-698-11970-3 (pa)
LC 00-40267
Also available Thorndike Press large print edition
In 1968, eleven-year-old Jaynell's life in the town of Moon, Texas, is enlivened when her eccentric Grandpap comes to live with her family

"This nostalgic parable about loss and redemption is at once gritty and poetic, stark and sentimental, howlingly funny and depressingly sad, but it is a solid page-turner." SLJ

Mister and me; with illustrations by Leonard Jenkins. Putnam 1998 74p $13.99; pa $4.99 (3-5)   **Fic**
1. Remarriage—Fiction 2. African Americans—Fiction 3. Louisiana—Fiction
ISBN 0-399-23215-X; 0-698-11869-3 (pa)
LC 97-40329

In a small Louisiana mill town in 1940, Jolene does not want her Momma to marry the logger who is courting her, but it seems that even her most defiantly bad behavior cannot make him go away

"This heartfelt story is filled with richly developed characters who deal with all-too-real problems." Booklist

When Zachary Beaver came to town. Holt & Co. 1999 227p $16.95 (5 and up)   **Fic**
1. Obesity—Fiction 2. Friendship—Fiction 3. Texas—Fiction
ISBN 0-8050-6116-9   LC 99-27998
Also available in paperback from Dell; and Thomson Gale large print edition

During the summer of 1971 in a small Texas town, thirteen-year-old Toby and his best friend Cal meet the star of a sideshow act, 600-pound Zachary, the fattest boy in the world

"Holt writes with a subtle sense of humor and sensitivity, and reading her work is a delightful experience." Voice Youth Advocates

Hopkinson, Deborah

Birdie's lighthouse; written by Deborah Hopkinson; illustrated by Kimberly Bulcken Root. Atheneum Bks. for Young Readers 1997 unp il pa $6.99 hardcover o.p. (1-3)   **Fic**
1. Lighthouses—Fiction 2. Maine—Fiction
ISBN 0-689-83529-9 (pa); 0-689-81052-0 (hc)
LC 94-24097

"An Anne Schwartz book"
Written in diary form, this "book tells the story of Birdie Holland, daughter of a lighthouse keeper on a tiny island off the Maine coast in 1855. Her brother helps their father in the lighthouse until he becomes a fisherman and leaves the island. Then Birdie must take his place. When her father becomes ill during a severe northeaster, she must carry out the duties alone." SLJ

"With an exemplary assemblage of genre paintings perfectly attuned to the flow of the text, the whole is restrained yet charged with emotion." Horn Book

Pioneer summer; illustrated by Patrick Faricy. Simon & Schuster 2002 74p il lib bdg $15; pa $3.99 (2-4)   **Fic**
1. Frontier and pioneer life—Fiction 2. Family life—Fiction 3. Kansas—Fiction
ISBN 0-689-84350-X (lib bdg); 0-689-84349-6 (pa)
LC 2002-107354

"Ready for chapters"
"When the first book in the Prairie Skies series opens, it's 1885, and Charlie Keller's family is leaving Massachusetts with other abolitionists bound for Kansas to prevent its becoming a slave-holding state. . . . The characters are engaging." Booklist

Other titles in the Prairie skies series are:
Cabin in the snow (2002)
Our Kansas home (2003)

Horowitz, Anthony

The Devil and his boy. Philomel Bks. 2000
c1998 182p $17.99; pa $5.99 (5 and up)

Fic

1. Theater—Fiction 2. Adventure fiction 3. London
(England)—Fiction

ISBN 0-399-23432-2; 0-698-11913-4 (pa)

LC 99-39791

First published 1998 in the United Kingdom

In 1593, thirteen-year-old Tom travels through the English countryside to London, where he falls in with a
troupe of actors and finds himself in great danger from
several sources

"In this delightful and inventive mixture of historical
fact and grand storytelling, Horowitz has conjured a fabulous, fast-paced tale of humor, intrigue, magic, and adventure." Voice Youth Advocates

Public enemy number two; a Diamond brothers
mystery. Philomel Books 2004 c1997 190p $16.99;
pa $5.99 (5 and up)   Fic

1. Mystery fiction

ISBN 0-399-24154-X; 0-14-240218-4 (pa)

LC 2004-10418

When thirteen-year-old Nick is framed for a jewel
robbery, he and his brother, the bumbling detective Tim
Diamond, attempt to clear his name by capturing the
master criminal known as the Fence.

"Horowitz has a knack for puns and humor, and he
successfully combines it with a nonstop action mystery
that has everything from hydraulically controlled buses to
secret caverns. A readable and exciting adventure." SLJ

Other titles in the Diamond Brothers Mystery series are:

The falcon's Maltester (2004)

South by southeast (2005)

Three of Diamonds (2005)

Stormbreaker. Philomel Bks. 2001 c2000 192p
$17.99; pa $5.99 (5 and up)   Fic

1. Spies—Fiction 2. Terrorism—Fiction 3. Orphans—
Fiction 4. Great Britain—Fiction

ISBN 0-399-23620-1; 0-14-240165-X (pa)

LC 00-63683

First published 2000 in the United Kingdom

After the death of the uncle who had been his guardian, fourteen-year-old Alex Rider is coerced to continue
his uncle's dangerous work for Britain's intelligence
agency, MI6

"Horowitz thoughtfully balances Alex's super-spy finesse with typical teen insecurities to create a likable
hero living a fantasy come true. An entertaining, nicely
layered novel." Booklist

Other titles about Alex Rider are:

Alex Rider, the gadgets (2006)

Ark angel (2006)

Eagle strike (2004)

Point blank (2002)

Scorpia (2005)

Skeleton key (2003)

Horvath, Polly

Everything on a waffle. Farrar, Straus & Giroux
2001 149p $16; pa $5.95 (4 and up)   Fic

1. Uncles—Fiction 2. British Columbia—Fiction

ISBN 0-374-32236-8; 0-374-42208-7 (pa)

LC 00-35399

A Newbery Award honor book, 2002

Eleven-year-old Primrose living in a small fishing village in British Columbia recounts her experiences and all
that she learns about human nature and the unpredictabil-
ity of life in the months after her parents are lost at sea

"The story is full of subtle humor and wisdom, presented through the eyes of a uniquely appealing young
protagonist." SLJ

The Pepins and their problems; pictures by
Marylin Hafner. Farrar Straus Giroux 2004 179p il
$16 (3-6)   Fic

1. Family life—Fiction

ISBN 0-374-35817-6   LC 2003-60196

"Portions of this work originally appeared in somewhat different form in Cricket magazine" T.p. verso.

The reader is invited to help solve the Pepin family's
unusual problems, which include having a cow who
creates lemonade rather than milk and having to cope
with a competitive neighbor

"Horvath spins a delightful yarn. . . . Absurd characters and situations and witty repartee are Horvath's
strengths, and . . . the wordplay is a great argument for
reading this aloud." Booklist

The trolls. Farrar, Straus & Giroux 1999 135p
$16; pa $5.95 (3-6)   Fic

1. Aunts—Fiction 2. Family life—Fiction
3. Siblings—Fiction

ISBN 0-374-37787-1; 0-374-47991-7 (pa)

LC 98-34375

Eccentric Aunt Sally comes from Canada to babysit
the Anderson children while their parents are on a trip
to Paris and every night the bedtime story adds another
piece to a very suspect family history

"A surprisingly poignant undercurrent adds even greater depth to this skillfully written comic novel." Horn
Book Guide

When the circus came to town. Farrar, Straus &
Giroux 1996 138p pa $5.95 hardcover o.p. (4-6)

Fic

1. Circus—Fiction 2. Prejudices—Fiction
3. Friendship—Fiction 4. Family life—Fiction

ISBN 0-374-48367-1 (pa); 0-374-38308-1 (hc)

LC 96-11591

Although Ivy and her family welcome the Halibuts,
and their son Alfred becomes her best friend, not all the
townspeople are pleased to have circus people as neighbors, especially as other circus families move in

"With snappy dialogue and a witty text, Horvath
makes a point about discrimination and tolerance, yet
keeps the tone animated and humorous." SLJ

Houston, James A.

Frozen fire; a tale of courage; by James
Houston; drawings by the author. Atheneum Pubs.
1977 149p il pa $4.95 hardcover o.p. (6 and up)

Fic

1. Wilderness survival—Fiction 2. Arctic regions—
Fiction 3. Inuit—Fiction

ISBN 0-689-71612-5 (pa); 0-689-50083-1 (hc)

LC 77-6366

"A Margaret K. McElderry book"

Houston, James A.—*Continued*

"Based on the true and dramatic ordeal of an Eskimo boy in the 1960's, this adventure story is set . . . in the far north. Kayak, a classmate of Matthew Morgan's in their Baffin Island school, suggests to his new friend Mattoosie (Matthew) that they take a snowmobile and go to the rescue of Mattoosie's father when the latter, a prospector, disappears. The spare can of gasoline leaks, and the two boys face a homeward trek through seventy-five miles of whirling snow and bitter cold." Bull Cent Child Books

"Convincing dialogue, good pace, and lean style mark this as first-class adventure with a partial basis in fact." SLJ

Followed by Black diamonds (1982)

Howard, Ellen

The gate in the wall. Atheneum Bks. for Young Readers 1999 148p il $16 (5 and up)   **Fic**

1. Canals—Fiction 2. Orphans—Fiction 3. Great Britain—Fiction 4. Child labor—Fiction

ISBN 0-689-82295-2   LC 98-22250

"A Jean Karl book"

In nineteenth-century England, ten-year-old Emma, accustomed to long working hours at the silk mill and the poverty and hunger of her sister's house, finds her life completely changed when she inadvertently gets a job on a canal boat carrying cargoes between several northern towns

"Howard has given her story a highly interesting venue and has created a cast of characters who are fully dimensional and engaging." Horn Book Guide

Howe, Deborah

Bunnicula; a rabbit-tale of mystery; by Deborah and James Howe; illustrated by Alan Daniel. 25th anniversary edition. Atheneum Books for Young Readers 2004 c1979 92p il $16.95 (4-6)   **Fic**

1. Animals—Fiction 2. Mystery fiction

ISBN 0-689-86775-1

A reissue of the title first published 1979

Other books about Bunnicula by James Howe

Though scoffed at by Harold the dog, Chester the cat tries to warn his human family that their foundling baby bunny must be a vampire

This book is "blithe, sophisticated, and distinguished for the wit and humor of the dialogue." Bull Cent Child Books

Howe, James

Dew drop dead; a Sebastian Barth mystery. Atheneum Pubs. 1990 156p $16.95; pa $4.99 (4-6)   **Fic**

1. Mystery fiction 2. Homeless persons—Fiction

ISBN 0-689-31425-6; 0-689-80760-0 (pa)

LC 89-34697

"A Jean Karl book"

"Sebastian Barth and his friends Corrie and David discover what appears to be a dead body in the long-abandoned Dew Drop Inn. But when they return with the police, the body has vanished. Police theory—that the 'body' was a homeless man passed-out drunk—is refuted when the kids find the body again in the woods, undeniably dead and possibly murdered." SLJ

"The story is well crafted and has substance beyond escapist fare as a result of Howe's inclusion of secondary storylines involving the homeless and Sebastian's own worries about his father's pending job loss." Booklist

Other titles about Sebastian Barth are:

Eat your poison, dear (1986)
Stage fright (1986)
What Eric knew (1985)

It came from beneath the bed! illustrated by Brett Helquist. Atheneum Bks. for Young Readers 2002 90p il (Tales from the House of Bunnicula) $9.95 (3-5)   **Fic**

1. Authorship—Fiction 2. Dogs—Fiction

ISBN 0-689-83947-2   LC 2001-22985

With help from his Uncle Harold, who wrote books about Bunnicula, Howie the wire-haired dachshund writes a story in which he saves the world from a science experiment gone awry

"The chapters alternate between Howie's journal, filled with droll observations and tongue-in-cheek humor that stem from Harold's writing instruction, and chapters in Howie's own tales. Real author Howe has provided elementary students with an ingenious lesson in how to write, seamlessly blended with . . . [a] first-rate [tale] starring a whimsical protagonist." Booklist

Other titles in the Tales from the House of Bunnicula series are:

Bud Barkin, private eye (2004)
Howie Monroe and the Doghouse of Doom (2002)
Invasion of the mind swappers from Asteroid 6! (2002)
The odorous adventures of Stinky Dog (2004)
Screaming mummies of the pharaoh's tomb II (2003)

Hughes, Pat

The breaker boys. Farrar, Straus and Giroux 2004 247p $18 (5 and up)   **Fic**

1. Coal mines and mining—Fiction 2. Immigrants—Fiction 3. Labor movement—Fiction 4. Pennsylvania—Fiction

ISBN 0-374-30956-6   LC 2003-49433

In 1897, Nate Tanner, the hot-tempered twelve-year-old son of wealthy Pennsylvania mine owners, goes against his father's wishes by befriending some of the boys who work in the mines and gets caught up in a disasterous clash between mine workers and the law.

"Hughes has created a complex protagonist who's likable even when acting 'ugly.' The author doesn't provide pat answers, but offers the hope that the questions Nate faces will be resolved." SLJ

Hughes, Ted

The iron giant; a story in five nights; illustrated by Andrew Davidson. Knopf 1999 79p il pa $4.99 hardcover o.p. (4-6)   **Fic**

1. Science fiction

ISBN 0-375-80153-7 (pa)   LC 98-41368

A newly illustrated edition of the title first published 1968 by Harper & Row; published in the United Kingdom with title: The iron man

Hughes, Ted—*Continued*

This is the story of an Iron Giant "who appears from nowhere and stalks the earth, devouring tractors and barbed wire for his supper. . . . But in the end he has to save the world from a creature from Outer Space." NY Times Book Rev

Hunter, Mollie

The mermaid summer. Harper & Row 1988 118p lib bdg $15.89; pa $5.99 (4 and up)

Fic

1. Mermaids and mermen—Fiction 2. Grandfathers—Fiction
ISBN 0-06-022628-5 (lib bdg); 0-06-440344-0 (pa)
LC 87-45984

"A Charlotte Zolotow book"

With the help of her brother, Jon, nine-year-old Anna daringly seeks to discover the secret means to undo a mermaid's curse upon their grandfather

"Hunter's atmospherically rich story, set about a century ago, unfolds against a tapestry of local color. The delicately intertwining plot skeins reveal both tightly controlled suspense and an intriguing puzzle. Characters are well realized and fit the time and setting as well as the folkloric mold that Hunter once again uses to thoroughly enchant her readers." Booklist

Hurst, Carol Otis

You come to Yokum; with illustrations by Kay Life. Houghton Mifflin Co. 2005 137p il $15 (3-5)

Fic

1. Women—Suffrage—Fiction 2. Family life—Fiction 3. Feminism—Fiction 4. Massachusetts—Fiction
ISBN 0-618-55122-0

"Walter Lorraine books"

Twelve-year-old Frank witnesses his mother's struggles to muster support for women's right to vote even as the family's life is transformed by a year running a lodge in western Massachusetts in the early 1920s.

"With mostly short chapters and charming black-and-white illustrations, this is a satisfying read." SLJ

Hurwitz, Johanna

The adventures of Ali Baba Bernstein; illustrated by Gail Owens. Morrow 1985 82p il $16.95 (2-4)

Fic

1. Personal names—Fiction
ISBN 0-688-04161-2
LC 84-27387

Also available in paperback from Avon Bks.

"Tired of his ordinary name, David Bernstein, age eight, decides he wants to be called Ali Baba, and he has a series of . . . adventures, culminating in a birthday party to which he invites every David Bernstein in the Manhattan telephone directory. That's when he realizes how different people with the same name can be, and he decides that some day he might go back to calling himself David." Bull Cent Child Books

"Hurwitz' characters, as always, are believable, the situations realistic and the plot well developed." SLJ

Another title about Ali Baba Bernstein is:
Hurray for Ali Baba Bernstein (1989)

Baseball fever; illustrated by Ray Cruz. Morrow 1981 128p il (3-5) **Fic**

1. Baseball—Fiction 2. Father-son relationship—Fiction
LC 81-5633

Available in paperback from Avon Bks.

"Ten-year-old Ezra suffers from 'Baseball Fever' and a father who has no interest in the sport. Mr. Feldman is constantly nagging Ezra to show an interest in chess. A weekend trip that takes the pair to Cooperstown and the Hall of Fame sets the stage for father-and-son rapprochement." SLJ

"A brisk, breezy story about a believable family is told with warmth and humor." Bull Cent Child Books

Class clown; illustrated by Sheila Hamanaka. Morrow 1987 98p il $15.99 (2-4) **Fic**

1. School stories
ISBN 0-688-06723-9
LC 86-23624

Also available in paperback from Scholastic

Lucas Cott "is the problem child in class; although extremely bright, he acts out involuntarily at the most inopportune moments. Even when he is trying his best to do assignments properly, things go wrong." Horn Book

"There are some very funny moments here, as well as some gentle and touching ones. . . . This [is] a fine choice for children just beginning chapter books." SLJ

Other titles in this series are:
Class president (1990)
Fourth-grade fuss (2004)
School spirit (1994)
School's out (1990)
Spring break (1997)
Teacher's pet (1988)

Faraway summer; illustrated by Mary Azarian. Morrow Junior Bks. 1998 155p pa $4.95 hardcover o.p. (4-6) **Fic**

1. Farm life—Fiction 2. Vermont—Fiction 3. Jews—Fiction
ISBN 0-380-73256-4 (pa)
LC 97-36363

"It's the summer of 1910, and Hadassah Rabinowitz, called Dossi, a Russian Jewish immigrant girl living in New York City, sets off for a Fresh Air Fund holiday on a farm in Vermont." N Y Times Book Rev

"Mary Azarian's occasional small woodcuts in black and white help create a sense of the period. . . . The warm characterization will keep readers interested in a story that shows how the hosts as well as the visitor benefit from the encounter with the stranger." Booklist

Other titles in this series are:
Dear Emma (2002)
The unsigned valentine (2006)

The hot & cold summer; illustrated by Gail Owens. Morrow 1984 160p il lib bdg $16 (3-5)

Fic

1. Friendship—Fiction
ISBN 0-688-02746-6
LC 83-19336

Also available in paperback from Scholastic

"Ten-year-olds Rory and Derek are best friends—a unit that does not need outsiders. So when their neighbor tells them that her niece is coming for the summer and that she expects they'll be great chums, Rory decides that the best attack is to ignore the girl from the start.

Hurwitz, Johanna—*Continued*

But Bolivia . . . is not to be shunted aside. With the help of her talking parrot, she knows how to get attention and, once gotten, how to keep it. . . . This episodic novel is cheerful and perceptive—right on target for both boys and girls." Booklist

Other titles about Rory, Derek, and Bolivia are:
The cold & hot winter (1988)
The down & up fall (1996)
The up & down spring (1993)

Oh no, Noah! illustrated by Mike Reed. SeaStar Bks. 2002 134p il $14.95 (2-4)　　　　**Fic**
1. Moving—Fiction 2. Friendship—Fiction 3. Family life—Fiction
ISBN 1-58717-133-3　　　　LC 2001-49888
Noah struggles to impress the kids he meets when he and his family move to a new house
"Reed's full-page, digitally prepared black-and-white illustrations add just the right touch. With realistic dialogue, short sentences, and large print, this warm, amusing transitional novel is ideal for reluctant readers." SLJ

PeeWee's tale; illustrated by Patience Brewster. SeaStar 2000 104p il $13.95 (2-4)　　　　**Fic**
1. Guinea pigs—Fiction 2. Squirrels—Fiction 3. New York (N.Y.)—Fiction
ISBN 1-58717-027-2　　　　LC 00-26177
When his owner's parents let him go in Central Park, PeeWee, a young guinea pig, learns to survive in the natural world with the help of a "park-wise" squirrel, named Lexi while trying to find his way back home
"Through PeeWee's perspective, Hurwitz delivers some humorous and insightful observations about the urban outdoors. . . . Brewster's engaging, black-and-white spot art will draw readers into this story." Publ Wkly
Other titles about PeeWee and Lexi are:
Lexi's tale (2001)
PeeWee & Plush (2002)

Rip-roaring Russell; illustrated by Lillian Hoban. Morrow 1983 80p il pa $4.95 hardcover o.p. (2-4)
Fic
1. Family life—Fiction 2. School stories
ISBN 0-688-16664-4 (pa)　　　　LC 83-1019
Russell "faces the challenges of growing up in his own inimitable way. . . . Being a big brother disturbs him because baby Elisa takes altogether too much of his mother's time, but by the book's end, he decides that it isn't so bad." SLJ
"The action is low-keyed. . . . This is both realistic and sunny, with good adult-child relationships, the appeal of everyday life experiences, and a light, humorous treatment." Bull Cent Child Books
Other titles about Russell and Elisa are:
E is for Elisa (1991)
Elisa in the middle (1995)
Elisa Michaels, bigger and better (2003)
Ever clever Elisa (1997)
Make room for Elisa (1993)
Russell and Elisa (1989)
Russell rides again (1985)
Russell sprouts (1987)
Russell's secret (2001)
Summer with Elisa (2000)

Ibbotson, Eva

Dial-a-ghost; illustrated by Kevin Hawkes. Dutton Children's Bks. 2001 195p $15.99 (4-6)
Fic
1. Orphans—Fiction 2. Ghost stories 3. Great Britain—Fiction
ISBN 0-525-46693-2　　　　LC 00-52287
A family of nice ghosts protects a British orphan from the diabolical plans of his evil guardians
"The book is filled with a large and delightful cast of characters. . . . The black-and-white illustrations have an eerie charm." SLJ
Another title about the nice ghosts is:
The great ghost rescue (2002)

The haunting of Granite Falls; illustrated by Kevin Hawkes. Dutton Children's Books 2004 216p il $15.99 (4-6)　　　　**Fic**
1. Ghost stories
ISBN 0-525-47192-8　　　　LC 2003-60669
When twelve-year-old Alex's Scottish castle of Carra is sold, dismantled, and moved to Texas, the ghosts that raised him from a child have difficulty relocating.
The author "excels in her depiction of quirky characters, and the idea of Scottish ghosts in rural Texas adds absurdity to the convoluted, comical plot." Booklist

Journey to the river sea; illustrated by Kevin Hawkes. Dutton Children's Bks. 2002 298p il $17.99; pa $5.99 (5 and up)　　　　**Fic**
1. Orphans—Fiction 2. Amazon River valley—Fiction 3. Brazil—Fiction
ISBN 0-525-46739-4; 0-14-250184-0 (pa)
　　　　LC 2001-28733
Sent with her governess to live with the dreadful Carter family in exotic Brazil in 1910, Maia endures many hardships before fulfilling her dream of exploring the Amazon River
"The unconventional cast of characters is highly appealing, and Ibbotson does a wonderful job of turning genre themes topsy-turvy in delightfully humorous style, at the same time adding fine details that expand and enrich the traditional orphan-adventure plot." Booklist

The secret of platform 13; illustrated by Sue Porter. Dutton Children's Bks. 1998 c1994 231p il $15.99; pa $5.99 (5 and up)　　　　**Fic**
1. Fantasy fiction
ISBN 0-525-45929-4; 0-14-130286-0 (pa)
　　　　LC 97-44601
First published 1994 in the United Kingdom
Odge Gribble, a young hag, accompanies an old wizard, a gentle fey, and a giant ogre on their mission through a magical tunnel from their Island to London to rescue their King and Queen's son who had been stolen as an infant
"Lively, funny fantasy with a case of mistaken identity and a cast of eccentric characters." SLJ

The star of Kazan; illustrated by Kevin Hawkes. Dutton 2004 405p il $16.99 (5 and up)
Fic
1. Vienna (Austria)—Fiction 2. Germany—Fiction 3. Mystery fiction
ISBN 0-525-47347-5　　　　LC 2004-45455

Ibbotson, Eva—*Continued*

After twelve-year-old Annika, a foundling living in late nineteenth-century Vienna, inherits a trunk of costume jewelry, a woman claiming to be her aristocratic mother arrives and takes her to live in a strangely decrepit mansion in Germany

"This is a rich saga . . . full of stalwart friends, sly villains, a brave heroine, and good triumphing over evil. . . . An intensely satisfying read." SLJ

Irving, Washington

Rip Van Winkle (5 and up)   **Fic**
1. New York (State)—Fiction
Some editions are:
Dover Pub. pa $12.95 Illustrated by Arthur Rackham (ISBN 0-486-44242-X)
Morrow (Books of Wonder) $22.95 Illustrated by N. C. Wyeth (ISBN 0-688-07459-6)
Originally appeared 1819 in Irving's The sketch book of Geoffrey Crayon, Gent.

Rip Van Winkle "is based on a folk tale. Henpecked Rip and his dog Wolf wander into the Catskill mountains before the Revolutionary War. There they meet a dwarf, whom Rip helps to carry a keg. They join a group of dwarfs playing ninepins. When Rip drinks from the keg, he falls asleep and wakes 20 years later, an old man. Returning to his town, he discovers his termagant wife dead, his daughter married, and the portrait of King George replaced by one of George Washington. Irving uses the folk tale to present the contrast between the new and old societies." Reader's Ency. 3d edition

Ives, David

Scrib; some characters, adventures, letters and conversations from the year 1863, including a deadly chase in the wilderness of the Fearsome Canyon, all as told by Billy Christmas, who was there; a novel; . . HarperCollins 2005 188p $15.99; lib bdg $16.89 (5 and up)   **Fic**
1. West (U.S.)—Fiction 2. United States—History—1861-1865, Civil War—Fiction 3. Adventure fiction
ISBN 0-06-059841-7; 0-06-059842-5 (lib bdg)
                                    LC 2004-12483

In 1863, a sixteen-year-old boy nicknamed Scrib travels around the West making his living writing and delivering letters, an occupation that leads to him nearly getting killed, being jailed as a criminal, joining up with the notorious Crazy James Kincaid, and delivering a letter from President Abraham Lincoln to a Paiute Indian.

"Ives's witty wordplay is lively and the plot is fast and funny in this great read-aloud." Horn Book Guide

Jackson, Alison

Rainmaker. Boyds Mills Press 2005 192p $16.95 (5 and up)   **Fic**
1. Droughts—Fiction 2. Great Depression, 1929-1939—Fiction 3. Florida—Fiction
ISBN 1-59078-309-3

"For 13-year-old Pidge Martin, the summer of 1939 brings changes and challenges. Her town, Frostfree, Florida, faces its longest drought in 40 years, and if it doesn't rain soon, area families . . . may lose their farms. A miracle is in order, and Pidge's father hopes a

rainmaker can provide one. . . . Pidge is a well-characterized, sympathetic protagonist that readers will connect with." Booklist

Jacobson, Jennifer

Winnie (dancing) on her own; by Jennifer Richard Jacobson; illustrated by Alissa Imre Geis. Houghton Mifflin 2001 105p il $15 (2-4)
                                            Fic
1. Friendship—Fiction 2. Ballet—Fiction
ISBN 0-618-13287-2   LC 00-53929

Winnie is worried when her best friends Zoe and Vanessa enroll her in ballet classes with them, since she would rather go to the library and read like they always do

"Geis's uncomplicated pencil drawings capture the girls' energy and personalities. . . . A good title for those who are just beginning to read chapter books." SLJ
Other titles about Winnie are:
Truly Winnie (2003)
Winnie at her best (2006)

Jacques, Brian

Redwall; illustrated by Gary Chalk. Philomel Bks. 1986 351p il $23.99; pa $7.99 (6 and up)
                                            Fic
1. Mice—Fiction 2. Animals—Fiction 3. Fantasy fiction
ISBN 0-399-21424-0; 0-14-230237-6 (pa)
                                    LC 86-25467

"Only the lost sword of Martin the Warrior can save Redwall Abbey from the evil rat Cluny and his greedy horde. The young mouse Matthias (formerly Redwall's most awkward novice) vows to recover the legendary weapon." Publ Wkly

"Thoroughly engrossing, this novel captivates despite its length. . . . The theme will linger long after the story is finished." Booklist
Other titles about Redwall Abbey are:
The Bellmaker (1995)
High Rhulain (2005)
The legend of Luke (2000)
Loamhedge (2003)
The long patrol (1998)
Lord Brocktree (2000)
Mariel of Redwall (1992)
Marlfox (1998)
Martin the Warrior (1994)
Mattimeo (1990)
Mossflower (1998)
The outcast of Redwall (1996)
Pearls of Lutra (1997)
Rakkety Tam (2004)
Salamandastron (1993)
Taggerung (2001)
Triss (2002)

James, Mary

Shoebag. Scholastic 1990 135p pa $4.50 hardcover o.p. (5 and up)   **Fic**
1. Cockroaches—Fiction 2. Fantasy fiction
ISBN 0-590-43030-0 (pa)   LC 89-10828

James, Mary—_Continued_

Shoebag, a happy young cockroach who finds himself suddenly changed into a little boy, changes the lives of those around him before returning to his former life as an insect

"Fans of the improbable will find this cockroach fantasy holds appeal, while the combination of humor and possible discussion topics offers opportunities for interchange." Booklist

Another title about Shoebag is:

Shoebag returns (1996)

Jansson, Tove

Moominsummer madness; translated by Thomas Warburton. Farrar, Straus & Giroux 1991 c1955 159p il $13.95; pa $5.95 (4-6)   **Fic**

1. Fantasy fiction

ISBN 0-374-35039-6; 0-374-45310-1 (pa)

LC 90-56150

Original Swedish edition 1954; this translation first published 1955 in the United Kingdom; first United States edition 1961 by Henry Z. Walck

A flood hits Moomin Valley and triggers a series of adventures for the Moomins

"Newcomers to the long-established Moominvalley series might first glance at the simple, playfully illustrated appendix—'Moomin Gallery'—to acquaint themselves with the host of Moomin-species that adorn the plot. Once initiated, it's difficult not to be drawn in by the inventive adventures of Moomintroll and his family." Publ Wkly

Other titles about the Moomintrolls are:

Comet in Moominland (1968)

Finn Family Moomintroll (1965)

Moominland midwinter(1967)

Moominpapa at sea (1967)

Moominpapa's memoirs (1994)

Moominvalley in November (1971)

Tales from Moominvalley (1964)

Jarrell, Randall

The animal family; decorations by Maurice Sendak. HarperCollins Pubs. 1996 179p il $16.99; pa $8.95 (4 and up)   **Fic**

1. Animals—Fiction 2. Fantasy fiction

ISBN 0-06-205088-5; 0-06-205904-1 (pa)

LC 94-76270

"Michael di Capua books"

A reissue of the title first published 1965 by Pantheon Bks.

A lonely hunter living in the wilderness beside the sea gains a family made up of a mermaid, a bear, a lynx, and a boy

This story is "sensitively related with touches of humor and wisdom. A delight for the imaginative reader." Booklist

The bat-poet; pictures by Maurice Sendak. HarperCollins Pubs. 1996 42p il $15.95; pa $7.95 (2-4)   **Fic**

1. Bats—Fiction 2. Poetry—Fiction

ISBN 0-06-205084-2; 0-06-205905-X (pa)

LC 94-76271

"Michael di Capua books"

A reissue of the title first published 1964 by MacMillan

A bat who can't sleep days makes up poems about the woodland creatures he now perceives for the first time

"A lovely book, perfectly illustrated—one well worth a child's attention and affection." Publ Wkly

Jarvis, Robin

The alchemist's cat; book one of the Deptford histories. Seastar Books 2004 304p $17.95 (5 and up)   **Fic**

1. Witchcraft—Fiction 2. Horror fiction 3. London (England)—Fiction

ISBN 1-58717-257-7

Prequel to the Deptford mice trilogy that includes The dark portal, The crystal prison, and The final reckoning

First published 1989 in the United Kingdom

When Will Godwin, assistant to a wicked alchemist in 1664 London, takes in a mother cat and her kittens, a story of villainy unfolds which reveals how Jupiter, Lord of Darkness, became so evil and powerful.

"Jarvis delivers a vivid tale of treachery, cruelty, and sorcery, leavened only by Will's innate goodness. It's also a real page-turner." Booklist

Followed by The oaken throne

The dark portal; book one of the Deptford mice trilogy. SeaStar Bks. 2000 243p il $17.95; pa $6.95 (5 and up)   **Fic**

1. Mice—Fiction 2. Rats—Fiction 3. Fantasy fiction

ISBN 1-58717-021-3; 1-58717-112-0 (pa)

LC 00-26517

"Books of wonder"

First published 1989 in the United Kingdom

While on a rescue mission, a few daring mice journey below to the sewers to an evil world populated by rats who peel mice before eating them and worship the Dark Lord

This "is a spooky and enthralling animal fantasy. . . . Jarvis provides counterpoint to the heart-racing adventure with scenes of haunting beauty." Publ Wkly

Other titles in the Deptford mice trilogy are:

The crystal prison (2001)

The final reckoning (2002)

The oaken throne; book two of the Deptford histories. SeaStar Books 2005 382p $17.95 (5 and up)   **Fic**

1. Bats—Fiction 2. Squirrels—Fiction 3. Supernatural—Fiction

ISBN 1-58717-277-1

Sequel to The alchemist's cat

"A Peter Glassman book"

First published 1993 in the United Kingdom

As a series of dark wars between the bats and the squirrels rage, Vesper, a young bat, and the squirrel maiden Ysabelle are unaware of the devastating events that are unfolding, but they will soon be drawn into a nightmarish journey and a desperate attempt to save their lands from destruction.

"This novel is even darker in tone than the previous book, with full of terrifying and gory scenes, but it is also filled with inspiring heroics, and its sentient characters are true to their animal natures." Booklist

Jennings, Patrick

Out standing in my field; by Patrick Jennings. 1st ed. Scholastic Press 2005 165p $16.95 (4-6)   **Fic**

1. Baseball—Fiction 2. Father-son relationship—Fiction

ISBN 0-439-46581-8   LC 2004-41619

Although fifth-grader Ty Cutter is named after baseball great Ty Cobb, he is the worst player on the Brewer's team—which happens to be coached by his overly-competitive father.

"The book is funny, poignant, and deeper than one might think at first glance." SLJ

The weeping willow; an Ike and Mem story; illustrated by Anna Alter. Holiday House 2002 56p il $15.95 (2-4)   **Fic**

1. Siblings—Fiction 2. Friendship—Fiction

ISBN 0-8234-1671-2   LC 2002-20544

While trying to build a tree house for guys, Ike and his best friend Buzzy argue so much that Ike builds his sister Mem a play house instead, but still misses his friend

"Sentences are short, and the vocabulary is simple and descriptive. There are also touches of humor throughout the story. . . . A well-written, perceptive story with likable characters." Booklist

Other titles about Ike and Mem are:

The bird shadow (2001)

The ears of corn (2003)

The lightning bugs (2003)

The tornado watches (2002)

Jennings, Richard W.

My life of crime. Houghton Mifflin 2002 145p $15 (5 and up)   **Fic**

1. Parrots—Fiction 2. Theft—Fiction 3. School stories

ISBN 0-618-21433-X   LC 2002-1183

"Walter Lorraine books"

A sixth grader's discovery of a bedraggled classroom pet parrot sets him on an adventure with real ethical and legal implications

This is a "buoyant, briskly paced novel." Publ Wkly

Orwell's luck; [by] Richard Jennings. Houghton Mifflin 2000 146p $15; pa $6.95 (5 and up)   **Fic**

1. Rabbits—Fiction 2. Magic—Fiction

ISBN 0-618-03628-8; 0-618-69335-1 (pa)

       LC 99-33501

"Walter Lorraine books"

While caring for an injured rabbit which becomes her confidant, horoscope writer, and source of good luck, a thoughtful seventh grade girl learns to see things in more than one way

"This absolutely captivating tale is about everyday magic . . . filled with quiet humor and seamless invention. The characters . . . are the sort that readers fall in love with." Booklist

Jiménez, Francisco

Breaking through. Houghton Mifflin 2001 195p il $15; pa $6.95 (5 and up)   **Fic**

1. Mexican Americans—Fiction 2. Migrant labor—Fiction

ISBN 0-618-01173-0; 0-618-34248-6 (pa)

       LC 2001-16941

Sequel to The circuit

Having come from Mexico to California ten years ago, fourteen-year-old Francisco is still working in the fields but fighting to improve his life and complete his education

"For all its recounting of deprivation, this is a hopeful book, told with rectitude and dignity." Horn Book

Jocelyn, Marthe

Mable Riley; a reliable record of humdrum, peril, and romance. Candlewick Press 2004 279p $15.99 (5 and up)   **Fic**

1. Teachers—Fiction 2. Women's rights—Fiction 3. Canada—Fiction

ISBN 0-7636-2120-X   LC 2003-55322

In 1901, fourteen-year-old Mable Riley dreams of being a writer and having adventures while stuck in Perth County, Ontario, assisting her sister in teaching school and secretly becoming friends with a neighbor who holds scandalous opinions on women's rights.

"This book is a funny and inspiring tale of a young girl finding her voice and the courage to make it heard." Voice Youth Advocates

Johnson, Angela

Bird. Dial Books 2004 133p $15.99 (5 and up)   **Fic**

1. Runaway teenagers—Fiction 2. Stepfathers—Fiction 3. African Americans—Fiction 4. Alabama—Fiction

ISBN 0-8037-2847-6   LC 2003-22793

Devastated by the loss of a second father, thirteen-year-old Bird follows her stepfather from Cleveland to Alabama in hopes of convincing him to come home, and along the way helps two boys cope with their difficulties

"Johnson writes with a poet's knowledge of rhythm and knows how to use the space between words. . . . Johnson also creates a visceral sense of each character's search for love and connection." Booklist

A cool moonlight. Dial Bks. 2003 133p $14.99 (5 and up)   **Fic**

1. Skin—Diseases—Fiction

ISBN 0-8037-2846-8   LC 2002-31521

Nine-year-old Lila, born with xeroderma pigmentosum, a skin disease that make her sensitive to sunlight, makes secret plans to feel the sun's rays on her tenth birthday

"The book's real magic resides in the spell cast by Johnson's spare, lucid, lyrical prose. Using simple words and vivid sensory images, she creates Lila's inner world as a place of quiet intensity." Booklist

Heaven. Simon & Schuster Bks. for Young Readers 1998 138p $16.95; pa $5.99 (6 and up)   **Fic**

1. Adoption—Fiction 2. African Americans—Fiction

ISBN 0-689-82229-4; 0-689-82290-1 (pa)

       LC 98-3291

Johnson, Angela—*Continued*

Coretta Scott King Award for text, 1999

Fourteen-year-old Marley's seemingly perfect life in the small town of Heaven is disrupted when she discovers that her father and mother are not her real parents

"In spare, often poetic prose . . . Johnson relates Marley's insightful quest into what makes a family." SLJ

Songs of faith. Orchard Bks. 1998 103p $15.95 (5 and up)   **Fic**

1. Divorce—Fiction 2. African Americans—Fiction

ISBN 0-531-30023-4   LC 97-40216

Also available in paperback from Knopf

Living in a small town in Ohio in 1975 and desperately missing her divorced father, thirteen-year-old Doreen comes to terms with disturbing changes in her family life

"Johnson has set attractive and realistic African-American characters in situations in which race is not the focus. This short, sensitive book will appeal most to reflective readers." SLJ

Johnson, Gillian

Thora; written and illustrated by Gillian Johnson. . Katherine Tegen Books 2005 c2003 229p il $12.99; lib bdg $15.89 (4-6)   **Fic**

1. Mermaids and mermen—Fiction 2. Magic—Fiction

ISBN 0-06-074378-6; 0-06-074379-4 (lib bdg)

LC 2004-14904

First published 2003 in Australia

Ten-year-old Thora, daughter of a mermaid mother and a human father, has many adventures at sea until she must return to the English seaside town of Grimli and save her mother who has been captured by the greedy real estate developer, Frooty de Mare.

"This entertaining fantasy will charm children who like their magic with its feet on the ground. . . . Lively, witty line drawings illustrate the action." Booklist

Johnston, Tony

Any small goodness; a novel of the barrio; illustrations by Raúl Colón. Blue Sky Press (NY) 2001 128p il $16.95; pa $4.99 (4 and up)   **Fic**

1. Mexican Americans—Fiction 2. Los Angeles (Calif.)—Fiction

ISBN 0-439-18936-5; 0-439-23384-4 (pa)

LC 99-59877

Arturo and his family and friends share all kinds of experiences living in the barrio of East Los Angeles—reclaiming their names, playing basketball, championing the school librarian, and even starting their own gang

"The characters are likable and warm. . . . The message is positive and the episodes, while occasionally serious, are more often humorous and gratifying." SLJ

The spoon in the bathroom wall; . Harcourt 2005 134p $16 (3-5)   **Fic**

1. Magic—Fiction 2. Fantasy fiction

ISBN 0-15-205292-5   LC 2004-17415

Living in the boiler room of the school where her father is janitor seems normal to fourth grader Martha Snapdragon, until she has experiences with an evil principal, the class bully, and a mysterious giant spoon, all

reminiscent of the Arthurian legends.

"This delightful story is filled with humor, wisdom, and wonderful sayings." Lib Media Connect

Jones, Diana Wynne

Castle in the air. Greenwillow Bks. 1991 199p pa $6.99 hardcover o.p. (6 and up)   **Fic**

1. Fantasy fiction

ISBN 0-06-447345-7 (pa); 0-688-09686-7 (hc)

LC 90-30266

In this "follow-up to *Howl's Moving Castle* . . . the protagonist is a young carpet merchant called Abdullah, who spends much of his time creating a richly developed daydream in which he is the long-lost son of a great prince, kidnapped as a child by a villainous bandit. . . . Feisty Sophie and the Wizard Howl (from *Howl's Moving Castle* do not become apparent till late in the story, but their fortunes do link up with those of Abdullah and his love. Jones maintains both suspense and wit throughout, demonstrating once again that frequently nothing is what it seems to be." Booklist

Howl's moving castle. Greenwillow Bks. 1986 212p pa $6.99 hardcover o.p. (6 and up)

Fic

1. Fantasy fiction

ISBN 0-06-441034-X (pa); 0-688-06233-4 (hc)

LC 85-21981

Available in paperback from HarperTrophy $6.99 (ISBN 0-06-441034-X)

"When the wicked Witch of the Waste turns Sophie Hatter into an ugly crone, the girl seeks refuge in Wizard Howl's moving castle. To her surprise and dismay, she finds herself embroiled in a contest between the witch and the wizard, in the tangled love affairs of the wizard, and in a perplexing mystery." Child Book Rev Serv

"Satisfyingly, Sophie meets a fate far exceeding her dreary expectations. This novel is an exciting, multi-faceted puzzle, peopled with vibrant, captivating characters. A generous sprinkling of humor adds potency to this skillful author's spell." Voice Youth Advocates

Jordan, Rosa

Lost Goat Lane; by Rosa Jordan. 1st ed. Peachtree Publisher 2004 197p $14.95 (5 and up)

Fic

1. Goats—Fiction 2. Race relations—Fiction 3. African Americans—Fiction 4. Florida—Fiction

ISBN 1-56145-325-0   LC 2004-5343

Two families—one white, one black—living near one another in rural Florida overcome their suspicions of each other and find ways to work together, with the help of their children and a few goats

"The fully realized characters and the warmth of the story make up for the small sermons. A tender, satisfying offering." SLJ

Joseph, Lynn

The color of my words. HarperCollins Pubs. 2000 138p $14.99; lib bdg $15.89 (5 and up)

Fic

1. Family life—Fiction 2. Siblings—Fiction 3. Dominican Republic—Fiction

ISBN 0-06-028232-0; 0-06-028233-9 (lib bdg)

LC 00-22440

"Joanna Cotler books"

When life gets difficult for Ana Rosa, a twelve-year-old would-be writer living in a small village in the Dominican Republic, she can depend on her older brother to make her feel better—until the life-changing events on her thirteenth birthday

"A finely crafted novel, lovely and lyrical." SLJ

Jung, Reinhardt

Dreaming in black and white; translated by Anthea Bell. Phyllis Fogelman Books 2003 112p $15.99 (5 and up)

Fic

1. Handicapped—Fiction 2. Germany—Fiction 3. Holocaust, 1933-1945—Fiction

ISBN 0-8037-2811-5

LC 2002-19918

Original German edition, 1996

A boy dreams that he is a student during the period of the Nazi Third Reich in Germany, where he is persecuted for being physically handicapped

"This spare, deeply felt novel adds a new dimension to Holocaust literature." Horn Book Guide

Juster, Norton

The phantom tollbooth; illustrated by Jules Feiffer. Random House 1961 255p il $19.95; pa $6.50 (5 and up)

Fic

1. Fantasy fiction

ISBN 0-394-81500-9; 0-394-82037-1 (pa)

"Milo, a boy who receives a surprise package which, when put together, is a toll-booth, goes off in a toy automobile on a tour of an imaginary country." Bull Cent Child Books

"It's all very clever. The author plays most ingeniously on words and phrases . . . and on concepts of averages and infinity and such . . . while the pictures are even more diverting than the text, for they add interesting details." N Y Her Trib Books

Kadohata, Cynthia

Kira-Kira. Atheneum Bks. for Young Readers 2004 244p $15.95 (5 and up)

Fic

1. Sisters—Fiction 2. Japanese Americans—Fiction 3. Death—Fiction 4. Georgia—Fiction

ISBN 0-689-85639-3

Awarded the Newbery Medal, 2005

"This beautifully written story tells of a girl struggling to find her own way in a family torn by illness and horrendous work conditions. . . . All of the characters are believable and well developed." SLJ

Weedflower. Atheneum Books for Young Readers 2006 260p $16.95

Fic

1. Japanese Americans—Evacuation and relocation, 1942-1945—Fiction 2. World War, 1939-1945—Fiction 3. Arizona—Fiction

ISBN 0-689-86574-0

LC 2004-24912

After twelve-year-old Sumiko and her Japanese-American family are relocated from their flower farm in southern California to an internment camp on a Mojave Indian reservation in Arizona, she helps her family and neighbors, becomes friends with a local Indian boy, and tries to hold on to her dream of owning a flower shop.

Sumiko "is a sympathetic heroine, surrounded by well-crafted, fascinating people. The concise yet lyrical prose conveys her story in a compelling narrative." SLJ

Karr, Kathleen

The great turkey walk. Farrar, Straus & Giroux 1998 197p $17; pa $5.95 (5 and up)

Fic

1. Turkeys—Fiction 2. West (U.S.)—Fiction

ISBN 0-374-32773-4; 0-374-42798-4 (pa)

LC 97-38859

In 1860, a somewhat simple-minded fifteen-year-old boy attempts to herd one thousand turkeys from Missouri to Denver, Colorado, in hopes of selling them at a profit

"Based on an actual event, this is a lively and entertaining story." Horn Book Guide

Man of the family. Farrar, Straus & Giroux 1999 178p $16 (4 and up)

Fic

1. Hungarian Americans—Fiction 2. Family life—Fiction

ISBN 0-374-34764-6

LC 99-26051

During the 1920s, life for Istvan, the eldest child of a Hungarian-American family, holds both joy and sadness

"The episodes are amusing and sometimes fascinating, but the warm relationship between father and son lies at the heart of this excellent novel." SLJ

Worlds apart; by Kathleen Karr. Marshall Cavendish 2005 196p $15.95 (4 and up)

Fic

1. United States—History—1600-1775, Colonial period—Fiction 2. Native Americans—Fiction 3. Friendship—Fiction 4. South Carolina—Fiction

ISBN 0-7614-5195-1

LC 2004-19455

In 1670, soon after arriving in the Carolinas with a group of colonists from England, fifteen-year-old Christopher West befriends a young Sewee Indian, Asha-po, and learns some hard lessons about survival, slavery, and friendship.

"This thoughtful novel offers extensive information as well as a gripping story of friendship and adventure." SLJ

Keehn, Sally M.

Gnat Stokes and the Foggy Bottom Swamp Queen; [by] Sally M. Keehn. Philomel Books 2005 152p il $16.99 (5 and up)

Fic

1. Magic—Fiction 2. Tennessee—Fiction

ISBN 0-399-24287-2

LC 2003-26635

In Mary's Cove, Tennessee, in 1869, twelve-year-old Gnat Stokes decides to prove she's not just a trouble maker by rescuing a boy who was spirited away seven years earlier by the evil Swamp Queen of Foggy Bottom.

"Keehn's tale is by turns, creepy, laugh-aloud funny, touching, and utterly satisfying. Her voice is sassy and straight out of the Tennessee hills." Booklist

Kehret, Peg

Abduction! [by] Peg Kehret. 1st ed. Dutton Children's Books 2004 215p $16.99 (5 and up) **Fic**

1. Kidnapping—Fiction
ISBN 0-525-47294-0 LC 2003-63531

Thirteen-year-old Bonnie has a feeling of foreboding on the very day that her six-year-old brother Matt and their dog Pookie are abducted, and she becomes involved in a major search effort as well as a frightening adventure

"This novel has enough suspense to keep children interested, and it will also appeal to reluctant readers." SLJ

Don't tell anyone. Dutton Children's Bks. 2000 137p $15.99; pa $5.99 (5 and up) **Fic**

1. Cats—Fiction 2. Criminals—Fiction
ISBN 0-525-46388-7; 0-14-230031-4 (pa)
LC 99-89605

Twelve-year-old Megan does not realize that feeding a group of feral cats living in a field near her house will involve her as a witness to a traffic accident and in the dangerous plan of an unstable criminal

"There are subplots galore in this quick read . . . but they all hang together, and thanks to Kehret's even tone, the scary aspects won't frighten younger readers." Booklist

Earthquake terror. Cobblehill Bks. 1996 132p pa $4.99 (4-6) **Fic**

1. Earthquakes—Fiction 2. Siblings—Fiction
3. Physically handicapped—Fiction
ISBN 0-14-038343-3 (pa) LC 95-20462

When an earthquake hits the isolated island in northern California where his family had been camping, twelve-year-old Jonathan Palmer must find a way to keep himself, his partially paralyzed younger sister, and their dog alive until help arrives

"The accessible, dramatic survival story explores themes of responsibility and bravery, and the fast pace will keep readers turning the pages." Horn Book Guide

The ghost's grave. Dutton Children's Books 2005 210p $16.99 (5 and up) **Fic**

1. Ghost stories 2. Coal miners—Fiction
3. Washington (State)—Fiction
ISBN 0-525-46162-0 LC 2004-22064

Apprehensive about spending the summer in Washington State with his Aunt Ethel when his parents get an overseas job, twelve-year-old Josh soon finds adventure when he meets the ghost of a coal miner.

"This fast-paced and engaging book should be a hit with fans of ghost stories. Josh is a rich character to whom readers can relate." SLJ

Keith, Harold

Rifles for Watie. Crowell 1957 332p lib bdg $16.89; pa $5.99 (6 and up) **Fic**

1. Watie, Stand, 1806-1871—Fiction 2. United States—History—1861-1865, Civil War—Fiction
ISBN 0-690-04907-2 (lib bdg); 0-06-447030-X (pa)
Awarded the Newbery Medal, 1958

"Young Jeff Bussey longs for the life of a Union soldier during the Civil War, but before long he realizes the cruelty and savagery of some men in the army situation. The war loses its glamor as he sees his very young friends die. When he is made a scout, his duties take him into the ranks of Stand Watie, leader of the rebel troops of the Cherokee Indian Nation, as a spy." Stensland. Lit By & About the Am Indian

Kelly, Katy

Lucy Rose, here's the thing about me. Delacorte Press 2004 137p il $12.95; lib bdg $14.99 (2-4) **Fic**

1. Moving—Fiction 2. Family life—Fiction 3. School stories 4. Washington (D.C.)—Fiction
ISBN 0-385-73203-1; 0-385-90234-4 (lib bdg)
LC 2003-20754

Eight-year-old Lucy Rose keeps a diary of her first year in Washington, D.C., her home since her parents separation, where she spends time with her grandparents, makes new friends, and longs to convince her teacher to let her take care of the class pet during a holiday.

"There's something especially endearing about Lucy Rose, and her interactions with her parents, grandparents, teacher, and friends seem believable and comfortable." Booklist

Another title about Lucy Rose is:
Lucy Rose, big on plans (2005)

Kendall, Carol

The Gammage Cup; a novel of the Minnipins; illustrated by Erik Blegvad. Harcourt 2000 c1959 283p il $17; pa $6 (5 and up) **Fic**

1. Fantasy fiction
ISBN 0-15-202487-5; 0-15-202493-X (pa)
LC 99-55279

A Newbery Medal honor book, 1960
"An Odyssey/Harcourt young classic"
A reissue of the title first published 1959

A handful of Minnipins, a sober and sedate people, rise up against the Periods, the leading family of an isolated mountain valley, and are exiled to a mountain where they discover that the ancient enemies of their people are preparing to attack

"An original and wholly delightful tale." Booklist

Another title about the Minnipins is:
The whisper of Glocken (1965)

Kerrin, Jessica Scott

Martin Bridge: ready for takeoff! written by Jessica Scott Kerrin; illustrated by Joseph Kelly. Kids Can Press 2005 120p il $14.95; pa $4.95 (2-4) **Fic**

ISBN 1-55337-688-9; 1-55337-772-9 (pa)

"Martin Bridge usually has a scheme or project under way. In the three school and home stories presented in this beginning chapter book, he sees how a happy surprise intended for one person makes a positive difference for another, figures out what to say to a little girl whose hamster has died, and suffers the consequences of jealousy. . . . [Martin's] responses are on target for a third grader. Kerrin relates the episodes in a straightforward way that incorporates rich language. Kelly's full-page illustrations and spot art follow the narrative closely enough to support the newly independent readers for whom this book is written." SLJ

Kerrin, Jessica Scott—*Continued*
Other titles about Martin Bridge are:
Martin Bridge blazing ahead (2006)
Martin Bridge on the lookout! (2005)

Ketchum, Liza

Orphan journey home; by Liza Ketchum; illustrated by C.B. Mordan. Avon Bks. 2000 162p $15 (4-6) **Fic**
1. Frontier and pioneer life—Fiction 2. Voyages and travels—Fiction 3. Orphans—Fiction
ISBN 0-380-97811-3 LC 99-42649
In 1828, while traveling from Illinois to Kentucky, twelve-year-old Jesse and her two brothers and sister lose their parents to the milk sickness and must try to finish the dangerous journey by themselves
"Originally published as a newspaper serial, the fast-paced, present-tense narrative is written in short, cliffhanger chapters, each accompanied by an effective illustration." Horn Book Guide

Where the great hawk flies. Clarion Books 2005 264p $16 (5 and up) **Fic**
1. Prejudices—Fiction 2. Pequot Indians—Fiction 3. Vermont—Fiction
ISBN 0-618-40085-0 LC 2004-29832
Years after a violent New England raid by the Redcoats and their Revolutionary War Indian allies, two families, one that suffered during that raid and one with an Indian mother and Patriot father, become neighbors and must deal with past trauma and prejudices before they can help each other in the present. Based on the author's family history. Includes historical notes and notes on the Pequot Indians.
The author writes "in prose as sturdy and well crafted as a cedar-frame wigwam or hand-pegged pine barn." Booklist

Kimmel, Elizabeth Cody

In the stone circle. Scholastic 1998 225p pa $4.50 hardcover o.p. (5 and up) **Fic**
1. Ghost stories 2. Wales—Fiction
ISBN 0-439-06259-4 (pa); 0-590-21308-3 (hc)
LC 97-14737
While spending the summer in an old stone house in Wales, fourteen-year-old Cristyn comes to terms with the death of her mother while satisfying the request of a thirteenth-century princess
"Kimmel handles the history and the ghost of the girl Carwen with a deft naturalness that keeps both vivid, and the resolution of all the plots strands is satisfying without being overly pat." Booklist

To the frontier; [by] E. Cody Kimmel; illustrated by Scott Snow. HarperCollins Pubs. 2002 182p il $15.95; lib bdg $15.89 (4 and up) **Fic**
1. Buffalo Bill, 1846-1917—Fiction 2. Frontier and pioneer life—Fiction 3. Kansas—Fiction
ISBN 0-06-029117-6; 0-06-029118-4 (lib bdg)
LC 00-63170
After the death of his brother, eight-year-old Bill Cody and his family set out from Iowa to make a new home for themselves in the volatile Kansas Territory
This "is more than a solid read. Its characters are well defined, its protagonist is engaging, and it is a good introduction to frontier life." Booklist
Other titles in this series are:
In the eye of the storm (2003)
One sky above us (2002)
West on the wagon train (2003)

Visiting Miss Caples. Dial Bks. 2000 168p $17.99 (6 and up) **Fic**
1. Old age—Fiction 2. Friendship—Fiction
ISBN 0-8037-2502-7 LC 99-27899
The elderly shut-in she visits once a week becomes an unexpected source of friendship and strength for thirteen-year-old Jenna, and they help each other face and overcome painful aspects of their lives
"Young readers coping with difficult changes at school and at home will respond to this thoughtful story." Booklist

King-Smith, Dick

Babe; the gallant pig; illustrated by Maggie Kneen. Twentieth anniversary edition. Knopf 2005 130p il $16.95; lib bdg $18.99 (3-5) **Fic**
1. Pigs—Fiction
ISBN 0-375-82970-9; 0-375-92970-3 (lib bdg)
LC 2004-5832
First published 1983 in the United Kingdom with title: The sheep-pig; first United States edition 1985 by Crown
A piglet destined for eventual butchering arrives at the farmyard, is adopted by an old sheep dog, and discovers a special secret to success
"Mary Rayner's engaging black-and-white drawings capture the essence of Babe and the skittishness of sheep and enhance this splendid book-which should once and for all establish the intelligence and nobility of pigs." Horn Book

The Catlady; [by] Dick King-Smith; illustrated by John Eastwood. Knopf 2006 c2004 71p il $15.95; lib bdg $17.99 (2-4) **Fic**
1. Cats—Fiction 2. Great Britain—Fiction
ISBN 0-375-82985-7; 0-375-92985-1 (lib bdg)
LC 2005009507
First published 2004 in the United Kingdom
Muriel Ponsonby, the Catlady, lives with dozens of cats, many of whom she believes are reincarnated friends, relatives, and even royalty.
"Creating setting and characters in a few sure strokes, King-Smith sets the story in motion and carries his readers along in a quietly engaging way. . . . Illustrated with many appealing ink drawings." Booklist

Funny Frank; illustrated by John Eastwood. Knopf 2002 c2001 108p il $14.95; lib bdg $16.99 (3-5) **Fic**
1. Chickens—Fiction 2. Ducks—Fiction
ISBN 0-375-81460-4; 0-375-91460-9 (lib bdg)
LC 2001-29539
First published 2001 in the United Kingdom
Gertie the hen is appalled when her son Frank wants to swim with the ducks, but Jemima and her mother, the farmer's wife, make him a special outfit so that his

King-Smith, Dick—*Continued*

dream can come true

"Illustrated with comic line drawings, the short chapter book is entertaining and easy to read." Horn Book Guide

The golden goose; illustrated by Ann Kronheimer. Knopf 2005 c2003 113p il $15.95; lib bdg $17.99 (2-4) **Fic**

1. Geese—Fiction 2. Farm life—Fiction

ISBN 0-375-82984-9; 0-375-92984-3 (lib bdg)

LC 2004-40842

First published 2003 in the United Kingdom

Farmer Skint and his family on Woebegone Farm have fallen on hard times, but their luck changes with the arrival of a special golden goose.

"The novel's breezy premise, Kronheimer's simple and appealing halftone illustrations, the text's relatively large typeface and brief chapters make this perhaps best suited to those just embarking on chapter books, but reluctant readers will also take a fancy to it. And all will be tickled by the uplifting conclusion that caps this engaging story." Publ Wkly

Lady Lollipop; illustrated by Jill Barton. Candlewick Press 2001 120p il $14.99 (3-5)
Fic

1. Princesses—Fiction 2. Pigs—Fiction

ISBN 0-7636-1269-3 LC 00-58498

A quick-witted swineherd and a pig named Lollipop are royally rewarded after they reform a spoiled princess

"The short chapters and the book's open, lively design and engaging pencil illustrations add to this amusing book's appeal." Horn Book Guide

Another title about Lollipop is:

Clever Lollipop (2003)

The nine lives of Aristotle; illustrated by Bob Graham. Candlewick Press 2003 75p il $14.99 (2-4) **Fic**

1. Cats—Fiction 2. Witches—Fiction

ISBN 0-7636-2260-5 LC 2003-40942

Aristotle, a little white kitten, goes to live with a witch in an old cottage, where he finds so many opportunities for risky adventures that he soon has only one life left

"With winsome watercolor-and-ink illustrations, this short, lighthearted fantasy will appeal to beginning chapter-book readers." SLJ

Kinsey-Warnock, Natalie

Lumber camp library; illustrated by James Bernardin. HarperCollins Pubs. 2002 87p il $14.95; lib bdg $14.89 (3-5) **Fic**

1. Books and reading—Fiction 2. Lumber and lumbering—Fiction 3. Blind—Fiction

ISBN 0-06-029321-7; 0-06-029322-5 (lib bdg)

LC 2001-39684

Ruby wants to be a teacher, but after her father's death in a logging accident she must quit school to care for her ten brothers and sisters, until a chance meeting with a lonely old blind woman transforms her life

"Kinsey-Warnock's likable characters work hard to overcome the obstacles life has dealt them. The simple, direct language and short, accessible chapters will appeal to beginning chapter-book readers." Booklist

Kipling, Rudyard

The elephant's child **Fic**

1. Elephants—Fiction

Some editions are:

Harcourt pa $6.95 Illustrated by Lorinda Bryan Cauley (ISBN 0-15-225386-6)

Crocodile Bks. USA pa $6 Illustrated by Jan Mogensen (ISBN 0-940793-77-6)

Originally published 1902 as part of Kipling's Just so stories

"This well-known whimsical fantasy that explains how the insatiably curious elephant child got his trunk is a fine example of one of Kipling's greatest classics." Adventuring with Books

Kirkpatrick, Katherine A.

Escape across the wide sea; by Katherine Kirkpatrick. 1st ed. Holiday House 2004 210p $17.95 (5 and up) **Fic**

1. Huguenots—Fiction 2. Voyages and travels—Fiction 3. Slavery—Fiction

ISBN 0-8234-1854-5 LC 2003-68563

After escaping religious persecution in France in 1686, a young Huguenot boy and his parents travel on a slave ship to West Africa, then to the Caribbean, and finally to New York, where they help found the town of New Rochelle.

"This strong historical novel presents a realistic account of slavery, religious intolerance, and French immigration in Colonial times." SLJ

Kladstrup, Kristin

The book of story beginnings. Candlewick Press 2006 360p $15.99 (4 and up) **Fic**

1. Authorship—Fiction 2. Storytelling—Fiction 3. Magic—Fiction 4. Space and time—Fiction

ISBN 0-7636-2609-0 LC 2005054262

After moving with her parents to Iowa, twelve-year-old Lucy discovers a mysterious notebook that can bring stories to life and which has a link to the 1914 disappearance of her great uncle.

"Kladstrup's first novel offers mystery, adventure, and fantasy, as well as reflections on family dynamics, time travel, and the structure of stories." Booklist

Kline, Suzy

Herbie Jones; illustrated by Richard Williams. Putnam 1985 95p il $15.99; pa $4.99 (3-5)
Fic

1. School stories

ISBN 0-399-21183-7; 0-14-032071-7 (pa)

LC 84-24915

Herbie's experiences in the third grade include finding bones in the boy's bathroom, wandering away from his class on their field trip, and being promoted to a higher reading group

This is "filled with light humor in its accounts of classroom incidents." Bull Cent Child Books

Other titles about Herbie Jones are:

Herbie Jones and Hamburger Head (1989)

Herbie Jones and the birthday showdown (1993)

Herbie Jones the the class gift (1987)

Herbie Jones and the dark attic (1992)

Kline, Suzy—Continued
Herbie Jones and the monster ball (1988)
Herbie Jones and the second grade slippers (2006)
Herbie Jones moves on (2003)
Herbie Jones sails into second grade (2006)
What's the matter with Herbie Jones? (1986)

Horrible Harry in room 2B; pictures by Frank
Remkiewicz. Viking Kestrel 1988 56p il pa $3.99
hardcover o.p. (2-4)   **Fic**
1. School stories
ISBN 0-14-038552-5 (pa)   LC 88-14204
Harry "is the devilish second grader who plays pranks
and gets into mischief but can still end up a good friend.
In a series of brief scenes, children meet Harry as he
shows a garter snake to Song Lee and later ends up being a snake himself for Halloween. His trick to make
scary people out of pencil stubs backfires when no one
is scared, and his budding romance with Song Lee goes
nowhere on the trip to the aquarium. . . . This story
should prove to be popular with those just starting chap-
ter books." SLJ
Other titles about Horrible Harry and Song Lee are:
Horrible Harry and the ant invasion (1989)
Horrible Harry and the Christmas surprise (1991)
Horrible Harry and the dragon war (2002)
Horrible Harry and the Drop of Doom (1998)
Horrible Harry and the dungeon (1996)
Horrible Harry and the goog (2005)
Horrible Harry and the green slime (1989)
Horrible Harry and the holidaze (2003)
Horrible Harry and the kickball wedding (1992)
Horrible Harry and the locked closet (2004)
Horrible Harry and the mud gremlins (2003)
Horrible Harry and the purple people (1997)
Horrible Harry at Halloween (2000)
Horrible Harry goes to the moon (2000)
Horrible Harry moves up to third grade (1998)
Horrible Harry takes the cake (2006)
Horrible Harry's secret (1990)
Song Lee and Leech Man (1995)
Song Lee and the hamster hunt (1994)
Song Lee and the "I hate you" notes (1999)
Song Lee in room 2B (1993)

Klise, Kate
Regarding the sink; where, oh where, did
Waters go? illustrated by M. Sarah Klise. Harcourt
2004 127p il $15 (4 and up)   **Fic**
1. School stories
ISBN 0-15-205019-1   LC 2003-26560
A series of letters reveals the selection of the famous
fountain designer, Florence Waters, to design a new sink
for the Geyser Creek Middle School cafeteria, her subse-
quent disappearance, and the efforts of a class of sixth-
graders to find her
"Piecing the story and clues together is satisfying. In-
troduce this book to savvy readers who are ready for the
jump to a clever, unconventional reading experience."
SLJ
Other titles in this series are:
Regarding the bathrooms (2006)
Regarding the fountain (1998)
Regarding the trees (2005)

Knight, Joan
Charlotte in Giverny; by Joan MacPhail Knight;
watercolor illustrations by Melissa Sweet.
Chronicle Bks. 2000 unp il $16.95 (3-6)
     Fic
1. Artists—Fiction 2. France—Fiction
ISBN 0-8118-2383-0   LC 99-6878
While living in France in 1892, Charlotte, a young
American girl, writes a journal of her experiences including those among the Impressionist painters at the artist
colony of Giverny. Includes profiles of artists who appear in the journal and a glossary of French words
"The profuse illustrations, a mix of 1890s postcards
and other memorabilia, reproductions of (mostly) impressionistic paintings by the mentioned artists, and Melissa
Sweet's delicately drawn vignettes of vegetables and other items, lay an air of sunny, well-bred tranquility over
the scene." Booklist

Kochenderfer, Lee
The victory garden. Delacorte Press 2001 167p
$14.95 (5 and up)   **Fic**
1. World War, 1939-1945—Fiction 2. Gardens—Fic-
tion 3. Kansas—Fiction
ISBN 0-385-32788-9   LC 2001-28614
Hoping to contribute to the war effort during World
War II, eleven-year-old Teresa organizes her friends to
care for an ill neighbor's victory garden
"There are no heavy messages, only surprising revela-
tions, rooted in character and place." Booklist

Konigsburg, E. L.
From the mixed-up files of Mrs. Basil E.
Frankweiler; written and illustrated by E. L.
Konigsburg. Atheneum Pubs. 1967 162p il $16; pa
$5.50 (4-6)   **Fic**
1. Metropolitan Museum of Art (New York, N.Y.)—
Fiction
ISBN 0-689-20586-4; 0-689-71181-6 (pa)
Also available in paperback from Dell
Awarded the Newbery Medal, 1968
"Claudia, feeling misunderstood at home, takes her
younger brother and runs away to New York where she
sets up housekeeping in the Metropolitan Museum of
Art, making ingenious arrangements for sleeping, bath-
ing, and laundering. She and James also look for clues
to the authenticity of an alleged Michelangelo statue, the
true story of which is locked in the files of Mrs.
Frankweiler, its former owner. Claudia's progress toward
maturity is also a unique introduction to the Metropolitan
Museum." Moorachian. What is a City?

Jennifer, Hecate, Macbeth, William McKinley,
and me, Elizabeth; written and illustrated by E. L.
Konigsburg. Atheneum Pubs. 1967 117p il $16
(4-6)   **Fic**
1. Friendship—Fiction 2. Witchcraft—Fiction
3. African Americans—Fiction
ISBN 0-689-30007-7
Also available in paperback from Dell
A Newbery Medal honor book, 1968
"Two fifth grade girls, one of whom is the first black
child in a middle-income suburb, play at being apprentice witches in this amusing and perceptive story." NY
Public Libr. Black Exper in Child Books

Konigsburg, E. L.—*Continued*

A proud taste for scarlet and miniver; written and illustrated by E. L. Konigsburg. Atheneum Pubs. 1973 201p il $18.95 (5 and up)　　**Fic**
　　1. Eleanor, of Aquitaine, Queen, consort of Henry II, King of England, 1122?-1204—Fiction
　　ISBN 0-689-30111-1

Also available in paperback from Aladdin Bks.

This is an historical novel about the 12th century queen, Eleanor of Aquitaine, wife of kings of France and England and mother of King Richard the Lion Hearted and King John. Impatiently awaiting the arrival of her second husband, King Henry II, in heaven, she recalls her life with the aid of some contemporaries

The author "has succeeded in making history amusing as well as interesting. . . . The characterization is superb. . . . The black-and-white drawings are skillfully as well as appropriately modeled upon medieval manuscript illuminations and add their share of joy to the book." Horn Book

Up from Jericho Tel. Atheneum Pubs. 1986 178p $17; pa $4.99 (5 and up)　　**Fic**
　　1. Actors—Fiction 2. Mystery fiction
　　ISBN 0-689-31194-X; 0-689-82332-0 (pa)
　　　　　　　　　　　　　　LC 85-20061

"Jeanmarie and Malcolm are both unpopular, both bossy, both latchkey children; both live in a trailer park, and both want to be famous. Jeanmarie knows that she will be a famous actress and that Malcolm will one day be a famous scientist. These two friends embark on a series of adventures encouraged by the spirit of the long dead actress, Tallulah. Yes, presumably 'the' Tallulah! Tallulah, as a ghost, has the ability to make them invisible, and in that state the kids are sent to find the missing Regina Stone." Voice Youth Advocates

"Konigsburg always provides fresh ideas, tart wit and humor, and memorable characters. As for style, she is a natural and gifted storyteller. . . . This is a lively, clever, and very funny book." Bull Cent Child Books

The view from Saturday. Atheneum Bks. for Young Readers 1996 163p $16.95; pa $5.99 (4 and up)　　**Fic**
　　1. School stories 2. Friendship—Fiction 3. Physically handicapped—Fiction
　　ISBN 0-689-80993-X; 0-689-81721-5 (pa)
　　　　　　　　　　　　　　LC 95-52624

Awarded the Newbery Medal, 1997

"A Jean Karl book"

Four students, with their own individual stories, develop a special bond and attract the attention of their teacher, a paraplegic, who choses them to represent their sixth-grade class in the Academic Bowl competition

"Glowing with humor and dusted with magic. . . . Wrought with deep compassion and a keen sense of balance." Publ Wkly

Koppe, Susanne

The Nutcracker; [by] E. T. A. Hoffmann; illustrated by Lisbeth Zwerger; retold by Susanne Koppe; translated from the German by Anthea Bell; North-South Books 2004 $15.95; lib bdg $16.50 (3-5)　　**Fic**
　　1. Fairy tales 2. Christmas—Fiction
　　ISBN 0-7358-1733-2; 0-7358-1734-0 (lib bdg)

In this retelling of the original 1816 German story, Godfather Drosselmeier gives young Marie a nutcracker for Christmas, and she finds herself in a magical realm where she saves a boy from an evil curse.

"This version features somewhat surreal, almost theatrically presented tableaux, delicately and darkly rendered in pen and ink and watercolor. . . . Koppe's retelling is . . . accessible and detailed." SLJ

Korman, Gordon

The sixth grade nickname game. Hyperion Bks. for Children 1998 154p pa $5.99 hardcover o.p. (4 and up)　　**Fic**
　　1. Nicknames—Fiction 2. School stories
　　ISBN 0-7868-5190-2 (pa); 0-7868-0432-7 (hc)
　　　　　　　　　　　　　　LC 98-12343

Eleven-year-old best friends Jeff and Wiley, who like to give nicknames to their classmates, try to find the right one for the new girl Cassandra, while adjusting to the football coach who has become their new teacher

"This is a funny, fast-paced grade-school romp." Bull Cent Child Books

Kornblatt, Marc

Izzy's place. Margaret K. McElderry Bks. 2003 118p $16.95 (4-6)　　**Fic**
　　1. Death—Fiction
　　ISBN 0-689-84639-8　　　　　LC 2002-6185

While spending the summer at his grandmother's Indiana home, ten-year-old Henry Stone gets help from a new friend in coping with the recent death of his grandfather and the possibility of his parents getting divorced

"In straightforward language, Kornblatt writes a realistic, affecting account of the challenges of coming to terms with grief and family difficulties and the process of acceptance and healing." Booklist

Koss, Amy Goldman

The girls. Dial Bks. for Young Readers 2000 121p $16.99; pa $5.99 (5 and up)　　**Fic**
　　1. Friendship—Fiction
　　ISBN 0-8037-2494-2; 0-14-230033-0 (pa)
　　　　　　　　　　　　　　LC 99-19318

Also available Thorndike Press large print edition

"One Saturday morning a girl finds out that her group of friends, for reasons unknown, has decided to exclude her. As the short novel moves over the course of the weekend, five girls narrate in turns, each moving the story forward as well as providing sometimes unwitting commentary on her friends' versions of events." Horn Book Guide

"This provocative page-turner will be passed from one girl to the next." SLJ

Koss, Amy Goldman—*Continued*

How I saved Hanukkah; pictures by Diane deGroat. Dial Bks. for Young Readers 1998 88p il $15.99; pa $4.99 (3-5) **Fic**

1. Hanukkah—Fiction 2. Jews—Fiction

ISBN 0-8037-2241-9; 0-14-130982-2 (pa)

LC 96-52715

Marla, the only Jewish student in her fourth-grade class, wishes she celebrated Christmas like her best friend Lucy, until one year when she decides to learn all about Hanukkah and to teach her family about it too

"Koss keeps this hoary-sounding plot fresh and believable by talking up, not down, to readers and by virtue of a witty, warmly realized cast." Publ Wkly

Stolen words. Pleasant 2001 145p il $14.95; pa $5.95 (4 and up) **Fic**

1. Death—Fiction 2. Aunts—Fiction 3. Austria—Fiction

ISBN 1-58485-377-8; 1-58485-376-X (pa)

LC 2001-22149

"AG fiction"

In her diary, eleven-year-old Robyn describes her family's visit to Austria, from the disastrous theft of their luggage to adventures in the countryside, while she tries to recover from the death of her Aunt Beth

"Detailed, often humorous descriptions and commentary on the Austrian people and places alternate with poignant reflections on Aunt Beth and family experiences. Heavier issues are presented well and fairly." Booklist

Stranger in Dadland. Dial Bks. 2001 119p $16.99 (5 and up) **Fic**

1. Father-son relationship—Fiction 2. Divorce—Fiction 3. California—Fiction

ISBN 0-8037-2563-9

LC 99-462100

Twelve-year-old John develops a new understanding of his divorced father during an eventful summer visit to California

"What readers will appreciate is John's honest vacillation between anger and longing for his dad's attention. The first-person dialogue crisply captures John's angst." Booklist

Strike two. Dial Bks. for Young Readers 2001 134p $16.99; pa $5.99 (4 and up) **Fic**

1. Strikes—Fiction 2. Softball—Fiction 3. Cousins—Fiction

ISBN 0-8037-2607-4; 0-14-250024-0 (pa)

LC 00-38365

Haley's hope of spending the summer playing softball and hanging out with her cousin Gwen is ruined when her father and her uncle land on opposite sides of the local newspaper strike

"Gwen is a wonderfully spunky kid who has real problems, creative solutions, and the guts to admit that she has a lot to learn about others' needs." Booklist

Krensky, Stephen

Dangerous crossing; the revolutionary voyage of John Quincy Adams; by Stephen Krensky; illustrated by Greg Harlin. 1st ed. Dutton Children's Books 2005 unp il $16.99 (2-4) **Fic**

1. Adams, John Quincy, 1767-1848—Fiction 2. Adams, John, 1735-1826—Fiction 3. Voyages and travels—Fiction 4. United States—History—1775-1783, Revolution—Fiction

ISBN 0-525-46966-4 LC 2003-40852

In 1778, ten-year-old Johnny Adams and his father make a dangerous midwinter voyage from Massachusetts to Paris in hopes of gaining support for the colonies during the American Revolution.

"Harlin's richly atmospheric paintings dramatize scene after scene with subtle hues and lighting effects. . . . The story offers a stirring account of life aboard ship, spiced with details from the voyage. An appended author's note comments on the story's source and the illustrious careers of the two Adamses." Booklist

Krumgold, Joseph

Onion John; illustrated by Symeon Shimin. Crowell 1959 248p il lib bdg $15.89; pa $5.95 (5 and up) **Fic**

1. Friendship—Fiction

ISBN 0-690-04698-7 (lib bdg); 0-06-440144-8 (pa)

Awarded the Newbery Medal, 1960

The story "of Andy Rusch, twelve, and European-born Onion John, the town's odd-jobs man and vegetable peddler who lives in a stone hut and frequents the dump. Andy . . . tells of their . . . friendship and of how he and his father, as well as Onion John, are affected when the Rotary Club, at his father's instigation, attempts to transform Onion John's way of life." Booklist

"The writing has dignity and strength. There is conflict, drama, and excellent character portrayal." SLJ

Kurtz, Jane

The storyteller's beads. Harcourt Brace & Co. 1998 154p $15 (5 and up) **Fic**

1. Friendship—Fiction 2. Prejudices—Fiction 3. Blind—Fiction 4. Ethiopia—Fiction

ISBN 0-15-201074-2 LC 97-42312

"Gulliver books"

During the political strife and famine of the 1980's, two Ethiopian girls, one Christian and the other Jewish and blind, struggle to overcome many difficulties, including their prejudices about each other, as they make the dangerous journey out of Ethiopia

"The novel presents an involving portrait of Ethiopian culture through the eyes of two well-defined characters." Horn Book Guide

LaFaye, A.

Worth. Simon & Schuster Books for Young Readers 2004 144p $15.95 (5 and up) **Fic**

1. Frontier and pioneer life—Fiction 2. Orphans—Fiction 3. Nebraska—Fiction

ISBN 0-689-85730-6 LC 2003-8101

LaFaye, A.—*Continued*

After breaking his leg, eleven-year-old Nate feels useless because he cannot work on the family farm in nineteenth-century Nebraska, so when his father brings home an orphan boy to help with the chores, Nate feels even worse.

"This short tale has a quietly epic sweep." Horn Book Guide

Langrish, Katherine

Troll Fell. HarperCollins 2004 264p $15.99; lib bdg $16.89 (5 and up)   **Fic**

1. Orphans—Fiction 2. Fantasy fiction

ISBN 0-06-058304-5; 0-06-058305-3 (lib bdg)

LC 2003-17480

Forced to live with his evil identical-twin uncles after his father's death, twelve-year-old Peer tries to find a way to stop their plan to sell the neighbor's children to the trolls.

"Langrish's tense, quick-paced story will keep readers glued to the page." Booklist

Another title about Peer is:

Troll Mill (2006)

Langton, Jane

The fledgling. Harper & Row 1980 182p il lib bdg $15.89; pa $5.95 (5 and up)   **Fic**

1. Geese—Fiction 2. Fantasy fiction

ISBN 0-06-023679-5 (lib bdg); 0-06-440121-9 (pa)

LC 79-2008

A Newbery Medal honor book, 1981

"An Ursula Nordstrom book"

"Quiet, introspective Georgie . . . yearns to fly. An encounter with a large, old Canadian goose, which stops at Walden Pond on its migratory journey south, brings her that chance. . . . Then neighboring Mr. Preek, who tries to save Georgie from what he thinks is an attacking predator, and Miss Prawn, who sees the girl's feat as a saintly sign, interfere." Booklist

"The writing is alternately solemn and funny, elevated and colloquial. It is mythic, almost sacred, in passages involving Georgie and the goose; it is satiric, almost irreverent, when it relates to Mr. Preek and Miss Prawn." Horn Book

Lasky, Kathryn

Broken song; by Kathryn Lasky. Viking 2005 154p $15.99 (5 and up)   **Fic**

1. Jews—Fiction 2. Russia—Fiction 3. Violinists—Fiction

ISBN 0-670-05931-5   LC 2004-17741

In 1897, fifteen-year-old Reuven Bloom, a Russian Jew, must set aside his dreams of playing the violin in order to save himself and his baby sister after the rest of their family is murdered

"Through rich prose filled with imagery, distinct characterization, and historical research, Lasky breathes life into the horrific history of anti-Semitism in Russia in the late-19th and early-20th centuries." SLJ

Dancing through fire. Scholastic Inc. 2005 172p (Portraits) $9.99 (4-6)   **Fic**

1. Ballet—Fiction 2. Paris (France)—Fiction

ISBN 0-439-71009-X

Sylvie dreams of being a prima ballerina. When the Franco-Prussian war begins in 1870, Sylvie is thrown into turmoil and tragedy. Sylvie must rely on the strength that ballet gives her in order to survive and acheive her goal.

"Though readers may be unfamiliar with this historical period, they will be swept along by the strong story line. Young dancers will particularly enjoy the evocative passages when Sylvie is on stage or in class." Booklist

Dreams in the golden country; the diary of Zipporah Feldman, a Jewish immigrant girl. Scholastic 1998 188p il (Dear America) $10.95; lib bdg $12.95 (4 and up)   **Fic**

1. Jews—Fiction 2. Immigrants—Fiction 3. New York (N.Y.)—Fiction

ISBN 0-590-02973-8; 0-439-55502-7 (lib bdg)

LC 97-26213

Twelve-year-old Zippy, a Jewish immigrant from Russia, keeps a diary account of the first eighteen months of her family's life on the Lower East Side of New York City in 1903-1904

"The hopes and dreams of a young girl are beautifully portrayed through Lasky's eloquent and engaging narrative." SLJ

Elizabeth I; red rose of the House of Tudor. Scholastic 1999 237p il (Royal diaries) $10.95 (4 and up)   **Fic**

1. Elizabeth I, Queen of England, 1533-1603—Fiction 2. Great Britain—History—1485-1603, Tudors—Fiction

ISBN 0-590-68484-1   LC 99-11178

In a series of diary entries, Princess Elizabeth, the eleven-year-old daughter of King Henry VIII, celebrates holidays and birthdays, relives her mother's execution, revels in her studies, and agonizes over her father's health

"Well written and captivating." Voice Youth Advocates

Marie Antoinette; princess of Versailles. Scholastic 2000 236p il (Royal diaries) $10.95 (4 and up)   **Fic**

1. Marie Antoinette, Queen, consort of Louis XVI, King of France, 1755-1793—Fiction

ISBN 0-439-07666-8   LC 99-16804

In 1769, thirteen-year-old Maria Antonia Josepha Johanna, daughter of Empress Maria Theresa, begins a journal chronicling her life at the Austrian court and her preparations for her future role as queen of France

"Quality writing, lively characterizations, and abundant historical detail." Booklist

The night journey; with drawings by Trina Schart Hyman. Warne 1981 149p il pa $4.99 o.p. (4 and up)   **Fic**

1. Jews—Fiction 2. Russia—Fiction

ISBN 0-14-032048-2 (pa)   LC 81-2225

This novel "describes the escape of a Jewish family from the persecutions and pogroms of Tsarist Russia.

Lasky, Kathryn—*Continued*

. . . It is told as a story-within-a-story, as thirteen-year-old Rachel learns, bit by bit, what her great-grandmother went through as a child." Bull Cent Child Books

"The novel shifts back and forth from the dangerous journey out of Russia to Rachel's own casual, secure life at home and school. These transitions are handled with a smoothness that doesn't break the intrinsic tension of the story, and the contrast between the two lives demonstrates with poignant clarity the real meaning of freedom. The portrayal of warm, supportive families in both stories becomes a link between past and present." SLJ

Lawlor, Laurie

He will go fearless; [by] Laurie Lawlor. Simon & Schuster Books for Young Readers 2006 210p $15.95 (5 and up)   **Fic**

1. Father-son relationship—Fiction 2. United States—History—1865-1898—Fiction 3. Overland journeys to the Pacific—Fiction

ISBN 0-689-86579-1   LC 2005-06129

With the Civil War ended and Reconstruction begun, fifteen-year-old Billy resolves to make the dangerous and challenging journey West in search of real fortune – his true father.

"Danger, adventure, and survival combine to make this a richly detailed story." SLJ

The school at Crooked Creek; illustrated by Ronald Himler. Holiday House 2004 83p il map $15.95 (3-5)   **Fic**

1. Frontier and pioneer life—Fiction 2. School stories 3. Indiana—Fiction

ISBN 0-8234-1812-X   LC 2003-56759

Living on the nineteenth-century Indiana frontier with his parents and irritable older sister Louise, six-year-old Beansie dreads his first day of school, but his resilience surprises even his sister.

"The book is rich with colloquial language, superstitions, and information about the lifestyle of this pioneer family. Nicely done shaded, pencil drawings help set the tone." SLJ

Lawrence, Iain

The convicts; [by] Iain Lawrence. Delacorte Press 2005 198p $15.95; lib bdg $17.99 (5 and up)   **Fic**

1. Prisoners—Fiction 2. Adventure fiction

ISBN 0-385-73087-X; 0-385-90109-7 (lib bdg)
    LC 2004-14968

His efforts to avenge his father's unjust imprisonment force thirteen-year-old Tom Tin into the streets of nineteenth-century London, but after he is convicted of murder, Tom is eventually sent to Australia where he has a surprise reunion.

"The story abounds in terrifying villains, grime, misery, and cruelty. Yet it also serves up a fair share of optimism. . . . This book is . . . action packed and . . . thoroughly researched. . . . Give it to reluctant readers who are looking for an exciting adventure." SLJ

Another title about Tom Tin is:
The cannibals (2005)

Lord of the nutcracker men. Delacorte Press 2001 212p map $15.95; lib bdg $17.99; pa $5.99 (5 and up)   **Fic**

1. World War, 1914-1918—Fiction

ISBN 0-385-72924-3; 0-385-90024-4 (lib bdg); 0-440-41812-7 (pa)   LC 2001-17254

Johnny, a ten year old English boy, comes to believe that the battles he enacts with his toy soldiers control the war his father is fighting on the front in World War I

"There's realism in the grief of the village people and also in Dad's poignant letters. . . . This will be a fine introduction to World War I, both for personal interest and for curriculum use." Booklist

The wreckers. Delacorte Press 1998 196p $15.95; pa $5.99 (5 and up)   **Fic**

1. Shipwrecks—Fiction 2. Adventure fiction 3. Great Britain—History—1714-1837—Fiction

ISBN 0-385-32535-5; 0-440-41545-4 (pa)
    LC 97-31625

"In 1799 fourteen-year-old John Spencer survives a shipwreck on the coast of Cornwall. To his horror, he soon learns that the villagers are not rescuers, but pirates who lure ships ashore in order to plunder their cargoes. . . . Lawrence creates an edge-of-the-chair survival/mystery story. Fast-moving, mesmerizing." Horn Book Guide

Other titles in this series are:
The buccaneers (2001)
Ghost boy (2000)
The smugglers (1999)

Lawson, Robert

Ben and me; a new and astonishing life of Benjamin Franklin, as written by his good mouse Amos; lately discovered, edited and illustrated by Robert Lawson. Little, Brown 1939 113p il $16.95; pa $5.95 (5 and up)   **Fic**

1. Franklin, Benjamin, 1706-1790—Fiction 2. Mice—Fiction

ISBN 0-316-51732-1; 0-316-51730-5 (pa)

"How Amos, a poor church mouse, oldest son of a large family, went forth into the world to make his living, and established himself in Benjamin Franklin's old fur cap, 'a rough frontier-cabin type of residence,' and made himself indispensable to Ben with his advice and information, and incidentally let himself in for some very strange experiences is related here in a merry compound of fact and fancy." Bookmark

"The sophisticated and clever story is illustrated by even more sophisticated and clever line drawings." Roundabout of Books

Mr. Revere and I; set down and embellished with numerous drawings by Robert Lawson. Little, Brown 1953 152p il pa $5.95 hardcover o.p. (5 and up)   **Fic**

1. Revere, Paul, 1735-1818—Fiction 2. Horses—Fiction 3. United States—History—1775-1783, Revolution—Fiction

ISBN 0-316-51729-1 (pa)

"Being an account of certain episodes in the career of Paul Revere, Esq., as recently revealed by his horse, Scheherazade, late pride of His Royal Majesty's 14th Regiment of Foot." Subtitle

Lawson, Robert—*Continued*

"A delightful tale which is perfect for reading aloud to the whole family. The make-up is excellent, illustrations are wonderful, and the reader will get a very interesting picture of the American Revolution." Libr J

Rabbit Hill. Viking 1944 127p il lib bdg $16.99; pa $4.99 (3-6) **Fic**
1. Rabbits—Fiction 2. Animals—Fiction
ISBN 0-670-58675-7 (lib bdg); 0-14-031010-X (pa)
Awarded the Newbery Medal, 1945

"Story of the great rejoicing among the wild creatures when the news goes round that new people are coming to live in the big house. For people in the big house will mean a garden and a garden means food. Their hopes are rewarded. The new people are 'planting folks' and the garden is big enough to provide for all." Wis Libr Bull

"Robert Lawson, because he loves the Connecticut country and the little 'animals of field and wood and looks at them with the eye of an artist, a poet and a child, has created for the boy and girl, indeed for the sensitive reader of any age, a whole, fresh, lively, amusing world." N Y Times Book Rev

Followed by The tough winter (1954)

Le Guin, Ursula K.

Catwings; illustrations by S. D. Schindler. Orchard Bks. 1988 39p il pa $3.99 hardcover o.p. (2-4) **Fic**
1. Cats—Fiction 2. Fantasy fiction
ISBN 0-439-55189-7 (pa)   LC 87-33104
"A Richard Jackson book"

"When four kittens with wings are born in a rough city neighborhood, their mother nurtures and protects them as they grow and learn to fly. At her urging they soon escape the dangerous streets and alleys, flying to a forest where they find more enemies but, finally, new friends." Booklist

"Le Guin's adroit writing style, the well-observed feline detail, the thematic concern for natural victims of human environment, and the gentle humor make this a prime choice for reading aloud, although one would not want children to miss the fine-line hatch drawings that further project the satisfying sense of reality." Bull Cent Child Books

Other titles about Catwings are:
Catwings return (1989)
Jane on her own (1999)
Wonderful Alexander and the Catwings (1994)

A wizard of Earthsea; drawings by Ruth Robbins. Parnassus Press 1968 205p il pa $7.99 o.p. (6 and up) **Fic**
1. Fantasy fiction
ISBN 0-553-26250-5 (pa)   LC 68-21992
"An imaginary archipelago is the setting for . . . [this] fantasy about a talented but proud, overzealous student of wizardry. In a willful misuse of his limited powers, the novice wizard unleashes a shadowy, malevolent creature that endangers his life and the world of Earthsea. To atone for his misdeed, Ged goes on a perilous journey through the island kingdom to find the baleful beast and destroy its evil influence." Booklist

A "powerful fantasy-allegory. Though set as prose, the rhythms of the language are truly and consistently poetical." Read Ladders for Hum Relat. 6th edition

Other titles in this series are:
The farthest shore (1972)
Tehanu (1990)
The Tombs of Atuan (1971)

Lee, Milly

Landed; [by] Milly Lee; pictures by Yangsook Choi. Farrar, Straus & Giroux 2006 unp il $16 **Fic**
1. Immigrants—Fiction 2. Chinese Americans—Fiction 3. San Francisco (Calif.)—Fiction
ISBN 0-374-34314-4   LC 2004-47216
"Frances Foster books."

After leaving his village in southeastern China, twelve-year-old Sun is held at Angel Island, San Francisco, before being released to join his father, a merchant living in the area. Includes historical notes

"The story is told with quiet restraint. . . . Choi's beautiful, full-page oil paintings, in sepia tones and shades of green, are quiet and packed with feeling." Booklist

L'Engle, Madeleine

Meet the Austins. Farrar, Straus & Giroux 1997 216p $17 (5 and up) **Fic**
1. Family life—Fiction 2. Orphans—Fiction
ISBN 0-374-34929-0   LC 96-27655
Also available in paperback from Dell

A revised edition of the title first published 1960 by Vanguard Press

This edition includes a "chapter titled 'The Anti-Muffins,' which deals with being concerned for others and true to oneself." Book Rep

A "story of the family of a country doctor, told by the twelve-year-old daughter, during a year in which a spoiled young orphan, Maggy, comes to live with them. . . . [This is an] account of the family's adjustment to Maggy and hers to them." Horn Book

Other titles about the Austins are:
The moon by night (1963)
A ring of endless light (1980)
Troubling a star (1994)

A wrinkle in time. Farrar, Straus & Giroux 1962 211p $17 (5 and up) **Fic**
1. Fantasy fiction
ISBN 0-374-38613-7
Awarded the Newbery Medal, 1963

"A brother and sister, together with a friend, go in search of their scientist father who was lost while engaged in secret work for the government on the tesseract problem. A tesseract is a wrinkle in time. The father is a prisoner on a forbidding planet, and after awesome and terrifying experiences, he is rescued, and the little group returns safely to Earth and home." Child Books Too Good to Miss

"It makes unusual demands on the imagination and consequently gives great rewards." Horn Book

Followed by A wind in the door (1973)

Leonard, Elmore

A coyote's in the house. HarperEntertainment 2004 149p il $15.95 (5 and up)   **Fic**

1. Dogs—Fiction 2. Coyotes—Fiction 3. Hollywood (Calif.)—Fiction

ISBN 0-06-054404-X   LC 2003-71050

"Hip coyote Antwan. . . . is foraging for garbage when he makes the acquaintance of German shepherd Buddy, a retired film star. Buddy is bored and has decided he'd like the freedom of the coyote's life in the wild, while Antwan. . . . is interested in getting to know Miss Betty, a prizewinning poodle who lives with Buddy's family. . . . The story is good fun, but the real pleasure here . . . lies in listening to the characters banter with one another. . . . A poignant ending gives the tale just the right edge." Booklist

Lester, Julius

The old African; illustrated by Jerry Pinkney. Dial Bks. 2005 79p il $19.99 (3-6)   **Fic**

1. Slavery—Fiction 2. African Americans—Fiction 3. Extrasensory perception—Fiction

ISBN 0-8037-2564-7   LC 2003-15671

An elderly slave uses the power of his mind to ease the suffering of his fellow slaves and eventually lead them back to Africa.

"The stirring illustrations, glowing with color and swirling with action, beautifully depict the dramatic escape fantasy (which is based on legend), but they never deny the horror." Booklist

Levin, Betty

Shadow-catcher. Greenwillow Bks. 2000 152p $15.95 (5 and up)   **Fic**

1. Grandfathers—Fiction 2. Photography—Fiction 3. Mystery fiction

ISBN 0-688-17862-6   LC 99-45087

Although he often fancied himself a detective, Jonathan must become a real sleuth when he attempts to solve a mystery while accompanying his grandfather, a Civil War veteran and traveling photographer in Maine

"The well-crafted, engaging mystery . . . neatly frames a story of character growth and development." Booklist

Levine, Gail Carson

Dave at night. HarperCollins Pubs. 1999 281p lib bdg $16.99; pa $5.99 (5 and up)   **Fic**

1. Orphans—Fiction 2. Jews—Fiction 3. African Americans—Fiction 4. New York (N.Y.)—Fiction

ISBN 0-06-028154-5 (lib bdg); 0-06-440747-0 (pa)
      LC 98-50069

When orphaned Dave is sent to the Hebrew Home for Boys where he is treated cruelly, he sneaks out at night and is welcomed into the music- and culture-filled world of the Harlem Renaissance

"The magic comes from Levine's language and characterization. This novel will provide inspiration for all children while offering a unique view of a culturally diverse New York City." SLJ

Ella enchanted. HarperCollins Pubs. 1997 232p $16.99; lib bdg $17.89; pa $6.50 (5 and up)
    Fic

1. Fantasy fiction

ISBN 0-06-027510-3; 0-06-027511-1 (lib bdg); 0-06-440705-5 (pa)   LC 96-30734

A Newbery Medal honor book, 1998

In this novel based on the story of Cinderella, Ella struggles against the childhood curse that forces her to obey any order given to her

"As finely designed as a tapestry, Ella's story both neatly incorporates elements of the original tale and mightily expands them." Booklist

Fairy dust and the quest for the egg; [by] Gail Carson Levine; illustrated by David Christiana. Disney Press 2005 188p il $16.99 (3-5)
    Fic

1. Fairies—Fiction

ISBN 0-7868-3491-9

After a hurricane injures the fairies' godlike Mother Dove, whose magical feathers and precious egg are of powerful importance to both fairies and Neverland itself, it falls to newcomer Prilla and two companions to set things right.

This is "an engaging tale. The story is exciting, the characters accessible . . . and Christiana's lush, full-color illustrations breathtaking." SLJ

The princess test; illustrated by Mark Elliott. HarperCollins Pubs. 1999 91p il (Princess tales) $9.99 (4 and up)   **Fic**

1. Andersen, Hans Christian, 1805-1875—Adaptations 2. Fairy tales

ISBN 0-06-028062-X   LC 98-27960

In this humorous retelling of Hans Christian Andersen's "The Princess and the Pea," Lorelei must pass many difficult tests in order to prove that she is a true princess and win the hand of Prince Nicholas

"Breezily told, with a wealth of comic detail, slyly contemporary dialogue, and genuine affection for the genre that inspired [it]." Bull Cent Child Books

Other titles in the Princess tales series are:

Cinderellis and the glass hill (2000)
The fairy's mistake (1999)
The fairy's return (2002)
For Biddle's sake (2002)
Princess Sonora and the long sleep (1999)

The two princesses of Bamarre. HarperCollins Pubs. 2001 241p $15.99; lib bdg $16.89; pa $5.99 (5 and up)   **Fic**

1. Fantasy fiction 2. Sisters—Fiction 3. Princesses—Fiction

ISBN 0-06-029315-2; 0-06-029316-0 (lib bdg); 0-06-440966-X (pa)   LC 00-47953

With her adventurous sister, Meryl, suffering from the Gray Death, meek and timid Princess Addie sets out to find a cure

"A lively tale with vivid characters and an exciting plot." Book Rep

Levitin, Sonia

Journey to America; illustrated by Charles Robinson. Atheneum Pubs. 1993 c1970 150p il pa $4.99 hardcover o.p. (4 and up) **Fic**

1. World War, 1939-1945—Fiction 2. Jewish refugees—Fiction 3. Family life—Fiction

ISBN 0-689-71130-1 (pa) LC 93-163980

A reissue of the title first published 1970

"In a strong immigration story, Lisa Platt, the middle daughter, tells how her family is forced to leave Nazi Germany and make a new life in the United States. First their father leaves, then the others escape to Switzerland, where they endure harsh conditions. After months of separation, the family is reunited in New York." Rochman. Against borders

Followed by Silver days (1989) and Annie's promise (1993)

The return. Atheneum Pubs. 1987 213p map pa $5.99 o.p. (6 and up) **Fic**

1. Jews—Fiction 2. Antisemitism—Fiction 3. Ethiopia—Fiction

ISBN 0-449-70280-4 (pa) LC 86-25891

"In a docunovel of a Jewish Ethiopian family's flight to Israel, Levitin focuses on an orphan, Desta, whose older brother, Joas, persuades her to leave the village where hunger and political recriminations constantly threaten their lives." Bull Cent Child Books

"A vivid and compelling book. . . . Levitin's tour de force is sensitively written; her command of the language is impressive and she uses Ethiopian terms effectively, interspersing them in ways readers will understand." Booklist

Levy, Elizabeth

My life as a fifth-grade comedian. HarperCollins Pubs. 1997 184p $15.95; pa $4.95 (4-6) **Fic**

1. School stories

ISBN 0-06-026602-3; 0-06-440723-3 (pa) LC 97-3842

"Bobby loves to joke around, but his constant misbehavior in class is about to land him in the School for Intervention. That's where his older brother went before he got kicked out of school and out of the house. Bobby's last chance to prove himself to his teacher, the principal, and his sarcastic father is to organize a school-wide stand-up comedy contest." Publisher's note

"Levy incorporates a cornucopia of jokes and a wealth of subtle advice on becoming a comic. There is great pleasure in seeing Bobby and his father's earlier sarcasm and angry dialogue transformed by a turn of attitude into universal, and really funny comedy." SLJ

Seventh grade tango. Hyperion Bks. for Children 2000 153p $15.99 (5 and up) **Fic**

1. Dancers—Fiction 2. Friendship—Fiction 3. School stories

ISBN 0-7868-0498-X LC 99-53124

When Rebecca, a seventh-grader, is paired up with her friend Scott for a dance class at school, she learns a lot about who her real friends are

"Descriptive prose, snappy dialogue, and diverse characters enhance the story, which notably portrays ballroom dance as a hip, fun activity." Booklist

Lewis, C. S. (Clive Staples)

The lion, the witch, and the wardrobe; illustrated by Pauline Baynes. HarperCollins Pubs. 1994 189p il $16.99; lib bdg $17.89; pa $7.99 (4 and up) **Fic**

1. Fantasy fiction

ISBN 0-06-023481-4; 0-06-023482-2 (lib bdg); 0-06-440499-4 (pa) LC 93-8889

A reissue of the title first published 1950 by Macmillan

Four English schoolchildren find their way through the back of a wardrobe into the magic land of Narnia and assist Aslan, the golden lion, to triumph over the White Witch, who has cursed the land with eternal winter

This begins "the 'Narnia' stories, outstanding modern fairy tales with an underlying theme of good overcoming evil." Child Books Too Good to Miss

Other titles about Narnia are:
The horse and his boy (1954)
The last battle (1956)
The magician's nephew (1956)
Prince Caspian (1951)
The silver chair (1953)
The voyage of the Dawn Treader (1952)

Lewis, J. Patrick

The Last Resort; [illustrated by] Roberto Innocenti; [written by] J. Patrick Lewis. Creative Eds. 2002 48p il $17.95 (3-6) **Fic**

1. Artists—Fiction

ISBN 1-56846-172-0 LC 2001-47536

A writer who can't find anything to write about goes for a drive and meets literary figures of the past who inspire him

"The book is gloriously illustrated, and the text is charming enough to make you forgive its obscurities." NY Times Book Rev

Lewis, Maggie

Morgy makes his move; illustrated by Michael Chesworth. Houghton Mifflin 1999 74p il $15 (2-4) **Fic**

1. Moving—Fiction 2. School stories 3. Massachusetts—Fiction

ISBN 0-395-92284-4 LC 98-43245

When third-grader Morgy MacDougal-MacDuff moves from California to Massachusetts with his parents, he has a lot of new things to get used to before he feels comfortable

"Heavy issues are handled lightly; language is simple and straightforward; Michael Chesworth's illustrations are funny and exaggerated." Booklist

Another title about Morgy is:
Morgy coast to coast (2005)

Lin, Grace

The year of the dog; a novel. Little, Brown 2006 134p il $14.99 (3-5) **Fic**

1. Taiwanese Americans—Fiction 2. Chinese New Year—Fiction

ISBN 0-316-06000-3 LC 2005-02586

Lin, Grace—*Continued*

Frustrated at her seeming lack of talent for anything, Pacy, a young Taiwanese American girl, sets out to apply the lessons of the Chinese Year of the Dog, those of making best friends and finding oneself, to her own life.

"The story . . . is entertaining and often illuminating. Appealing, childlike decorative drawings add a delightful flavor to a gentle tale full of humor." Horn Book

Lindgren, Astrid

Pippi Longstocking; translated from the Swedish by Florence Lamborn; illustrated by Louis S. Glanzman. Viking 1950 158p il lib bdg $15.99; pa $5.99 (3-6)   **Fic**

1. Sweden—Fiction

ISBN 0-670-55745-5 (lib bdg); 0-14-032772-4 (pa)

The adventures of Pippi Longstocking, omnibus volume of the three titles about Pippi, is also available

Original Swedish edition, 1945

"There were no more dull days for Tommy and Annika after they made the acquaintance of Pippi Longstocking. Pippi was nine years old, her strength—and her imagination—was prodigious, and except for her monkey and horse, she lived alone unrestrained by adults." Booklist

Other titles about Pippi Longstocking are:

Pippi goes on board (1957)
Pippi in the South Seas (1959)

Ronia, the robber's daughter; translated by Patricia Crampton. Viking 1983 176p $12.50 (4-6)   **Fic**

1. Thieves—Fiction 2. Middle Ages—Fiction

ISBN 0-670-60640-5   LC 82-60081

Original Swedish edition, 1981

Ronia, who lives with her father and his band of robbers in a castle in the woods, causes trouble when she befriends the son of a rival robber chieftain

"The book is full of high adventure, hairsbreadth escapes, droll earthy humor, and passionate emotional energy; and cast over the whole narrative is a primitive, ecstastic respones to the changing seasons and the wonders of nature." Horn Book

Lisle, Janet Taylor

Afternoon of the elves. Orchard Bks. 1989 122p $15.95; lib bdg $16.99 (4-6)   **Fic**

1. Friendship—Fiction 2. Mentally ill—Fiction

ISBN 0-531-05837-9; 0-531-08437-X (lib bdg)

LC 88-35099

A Newbery Medal honor book, 1990

"Nine-year-old Hillary has a happy home, all the material possessions she wants, and plenty of friends at school. Eleven-year-old Sara-Kate is an outcast, thin, poorly dressed, with failing grades, a decrepit house, and a weedy yard adjoining Hillary's neat garden. But Sara-Kate has an elf village, and with it she hooks Hillary into a friendship that thrives on elf stories but suffers from Sara-Kate's stormy moods and prickly pride. It is for Hillary to discover that Sara-Kate alone is caring for a mother who is mentally ill, penniless, and unable to provide the most basic physical or emotional necessities." Bull Cent Child Books

"'Afternoon of the elves' is a distinctive portrayal of

the way children figure out ways to inhabit the world when there aren't any adults around." N Y Times Book Rev

The art of keeping cool. Atheneum Bks. for Young Readers 2000 207p $17; pa $4.99 (5 and up)   **Fic**

1. World War, 1939-1945—Fiction 2. Rhode Island—Fiction

ISBN 0-689-83787-9; 0-689-83788-7 (pa)

LC 00-32778

"A Richard Jackson book"

In 1942, Robert and his cousin Elliot uncover long-hidden family secrets while staying in their grandparents' Rhode Island town, where they also become involved with a German artist who is suspected of being a spy

"Lisle develops an unforgettable cast of characters placed against a fully realized setting. Engrossing, challenging, and well paced." Horn Book

How I became a writer and Oggie learned to drive. Philomel Bks. 2002 155p $16.99; pa $5.99 (4 and up)   **Fic**

1. Brothers—Fiction 2. Authorship—Fiction 3. Gangs—Fiction 4. Divorce—Fiction

ISBN 0-399-23394-6; 0-14-250167-0 (pa)

LC 2001-36205

"After their parents break up, aspiring writer Archie, eleven, and his six-year-old brother Oggie move to a dangerous neighborhood with their mother. When Oggie's wallet is stolen by a gang, Archie promises to get it back but must join the gang to do so." Horn Book Guide

"It's a tribute to Lisle's powers as a writer that this frightening scenario never overpowers the real essence of the book, which is about how fiction and life are different and equally useful to one another. Such great truths are stated simply and shown in the action at the same time. . . . [A] fast-paced, adventure-filled title." SLJ

The lost flower children; illustrated by Satomi Ichikawa. Philomel Bks. 1999 122p il $16.99; pa $4.99 (4-6)   **Fic**

1. Sisters—Fiction 2. Aunts—Fiction 3. Gardens—Fiction

ISBN 0-399-23393-8; 0-698-11880-4 (pa)

LC 98-34912

After their mother's death, Olivia and Nellie go to live with their Great Aunt Minty where they discover a tiny tea cup in the garden and a storybook about children turned into flowers by a fairy spell

"Humorous, poignant, and magical, this story has a fantastical, creative story-within-a-story, characters of depth and appeal, and an irresistible mystery resulting in personal transformation." Booklist

Lisle, Rebecca

Copper. G. P. Putnam's Sons 2004 c2002 186p $16.99 (3-6)   **Fic**

1. Magic—Fiction

ISBN 0-399-24211-2   LC 2003-5973

First published 2002 in United Kingdom

Pursued by enemies of the family she never knew she had, ten-year-old Copper Beach flees to Spindle House,

Lisle, Rebecca—*Continued*

her paternal home, and decides to uncover the truth about a feud between the Stone and Wood clans that sent her into exile six years earlier.

"The writing is lively, with humor, tension, and fast-paced dialogue. . . . With enough excitement to be an excellent read-aloud, this well-crafted fantasy provides children with a solid entry into the genre." SLJ

Little, Jean

From Anna; pictures by Joan Sandin. Harper & Row 1972 201p il pa $4.95 hardcover o.p. (4-6)
                                    Fic

1. Vision disorders—Fiction 2. Family life—Fiction 3. Germans—Canada—Fiction

ISBN 0-06-440044-1 (pa)

"Often ridiculed by her older brothers and sisters and chided by her mother for her awkwardness and lack of ability, nine-year-old Anna is prickly and uncommunicative, but when her family moves to Canada in 1933 to get away from the growing oppression in their native Germany a doctor discovers that Anna has an acute vision problem. Fitted with glasses and sent to a special school for visually handicapped children Anna is slowly drawn out of her shell by an understanding teacher and new friends. . . . This is an engaging story of Anna's adjustment to life and her family's to a new homeland." Booklist

Followed by Listen for the singing (1977)

Littman, Sarah

Confessions of a closet Catholic; [by] Sarah Darer Littman. 1st ed. Dutton Children's Books 2005 193p $15.99 (5 and up)   **Fic**

1. Jews—Fiction 2. Catholics—Fiction

ISBN 0-525-47365-3   LC 2004-10829

To be more like her best friend, eleven-year-old Justine decides to give up Judaism to become Catholic, but after her beloved, religious grandmother dies, she realizes that she needs to seek her own way of being Jewish.

"The novel is injected with humor throughout and written with the voice of a contemporary adolescent. Readers can't help but laugh and cry with this winning protagonist." SLJ

Lobel, Arnold

Fables; written and illustrated by Arnold Lobel. Harper & Row 1980 40p il $15.95; lib bdg $15.89; pa $6.95 (3-5)   **Fic**

1. Animals—Fiction

ISBN 0-06-023973-5; 0-06-023974-3 (lib bdg); 0-06-443046-4 (pa)   LC 79-2004

Awarded the Caldecott Medal, 1981

"Short, original fables, complete with moral, poke subtle fun at human foibles through the antics of 20 memorable animal characters. . . . Despite the large picture-book format, the best audience will be older readers who can understand the innuendos and underlying messages. Children of all ages, however, will appreciate and be intrigued by the artist's fine, full-color illustrations. Tones are deftly blended to luminescent shadings, and the pictorial simplicity of ideas, droll expressions, and caricature of behavior work in many instances as complete and humorous stories in themselves." Booklist

Lofting, Hugh

The voyages of Doctor Dolittle; told by Hugh Lofting; illustrated by Michael Hague; edited with a foreword by Patricia C. McKissack and Fredrick L. McKissack; afterword by Peter Glassman. HarperCollins Pubs. 2001 355p il $22.95 (4 and up)   **Fic**

1. Animals—Fiction 2. Fantasy fiction

ISBN 0-688-14002-5

Awarded the Newbery Medal, 1923

"Books of wonder"

A newly illustrated and revised edition of the title first published 1922 by Stokes

When his colleague Long Arrow disappears, Dr. Dolittle sets off with his assistant, Tommy Stubbins, his dog, Jip, and Polynesia the parrot on an adventurous voyage over tropical seas to floating Spidermonkey Island

London, Jack

The call of the wild; pictures by Wendell Minor. Atheneum Books for Young Readers 1999 112p il $24 (5 and up)   **Fic**

1. Dogs—Fiction 2. Alaska—Fiction

ISBN 0-689-81836-X   LC 97-45019

Also available from other publishers

First published 1903 by Macmillan

"Buck, half-St. Bernard, half-Scottish sheepdog, is stolen from his comfortable home in California and pressed into service as a sledge dog in the Klondike. At first he is abused by both man and dog, but he learns to fight ruthlessly. He becomes lead dog on a sledge team, after bettering Spitz, the vicious old leader, in a brutal fight to the death. In John Thornton, he finally finds a master whom he can respect and love. When Thornton is killed by Indians, Buck breaks away to the wilds and becomes the leader of a wolf pack, returning each year to the site of Thornton's death." Reader's Ency. 4th edition

White Fang; pictures by Ed Young. Atheneum Books for Young Readers 2000 260p il $25 (5 and up)   **Fic**

1. Dogs—Fiction 2. Alaska—Fiction

ISBN 0-689-82431-9   LC 98-19241

Also available from other publishers

First published 1906

White Fang "is about a dog, a cross-breed, sold to Beauty Smith. This owner tortures the dog to increase his ferocity and value as a fighter. A new owner Weedom Scott, brings the dog to California, and, by kind treatment, domesticates him. White Fang later sacrifices his life to save Scott." Haydn. Thesaurus of Book Dig

Look, Lenore

Ruby Lu, brave and true; illustrated by Anne Wilsdorf. Atheneum Books for Young Readers 2004 105p il $15.95 (1-3)   **Fic**

1. Chinese Americans—Fiction

ISBN 0-689-84907-9   LC 2003-3605

"An Anne Schwartz book"

"Almost-eight-year-old" Ruby Lu spends time with her baby brother, goes to Chinese school, performs mag-

Look, Lenore—*Continued*

ic tricks and learns to drive, and has adventures with
both old and new friends.

This is a "funny and charming chapter book. . . . [It
offers] generous font, ample white space, and animated
and active illustrations rendered in India ink." SLJ

Another title about Ruby Lu is:

Ruby Lu, empress of everything (2006)

Lord, Bette Bao

In the Year of the Boar and Jackie Robinson;
illustrations by Marc Simont. Harper & Row 1984
169p il lib bdg $15.89; pa $4.95 (4-6)
                                                    Fic
1. Chinese Americans—Fiction 2. School stories
ISBN 0-06-024004-0 (lib bdg); 0-06-440175-8 (pa)
                                        LC 83-48440

"In a story based in part on the author's experience as
an immigrant, Shirley Temple Wong . . . arrives in
Brooklyn and spends her first year in public school."
Bull Cent Child Books

"Warm-hearted, fresh, and dappled with humor, the
episodic book, which successfully encompasses both Chinese dragons and the Brooklyn Dodgers, stands out in
the bevy of contemporary problem novels. And the unusual flavor of the text infiltrates the striking illustrations
picturing the pert, pigtailed heroine making her way in
'Mei Guo'—her new 'Beautiful Country.'" Horn Book

Lottridge, Celia Barker

Berta: a remarkable dog; with pictures by Elsa
Myotte. Groundwood Bks. 2002 99p il $14.95; pa
$4.95 (3-5)   **Fic**
1. Dogs—Fiction 2. Farm life—Fiction
ISBN 0-88899-461-3; 0-88899-469-9 (pa)

"Berta the dachshund lives with nine-year-old Marjory
and her parents on their hobby farm. Told from Marjory's . . . viewpoint . . . the chapter book follows Berta
as she helps the family care for a newborn lamb rejected
by its mother." Horn Book Guide

"Illustrated with softly shaded drawings, this short
chapter book will intrigue readers with its appealing story and its details of farm life." Booklist

Love, D. Anne

A year without rain. Holiday House 2000 118p
$15.95 (5 and up)   **Fic**
1. Family life—Fiction 2. Frontier and pioneer life—
Fiction 3. Remarriage—Fiction 4. South Dakota—Fiction
ISBN 0-8234-1488-4   LC 99-35825

Her mother's death and a year-long drought has made
life difficult for twelve-year-old Rachel and her family
on their farm in the Dakotas, but when she learns that
her father plans to get married again, it is almost more
than Rachel can bear

This "is simply yet artfully told with characters both
realistic and endearing." SLJ

Lovelace, Maud Hart

Betsy-Tacy; illustrated by Lois Lenski.
HarperCollins Pubs. 1994 c1940 112p il $15.99;
pa $5.99 (2-4)   **Fic**
1. Friendship—Fiction 2. Minnesota—Fiction
ISBN 0-06-024415-1; 0-06-440096-4 (pa)

A reissue of the title first published 1940 by Crowell

Betsy and Tacy (short for Anastacia) were two little
five-year-olds, such inseparable friends that they were regarded almost as one person. This is the story of their
friendship in a little Minnesota town in the early 1900's

The author "has written a story of real literary merit
as well as one with good story interest." Libr J

Other titles about Betsy through adolescence and young
    womanhood with reading levels to grade 5 and up are:

Betsy and Joe (1948)
Betsy and Tacy go downtown (1943)
Betsy and Tacy go over the big hill (1942)
Betsy and the great world (1952)
Betsy in spite of herself (1946)
Betsy, Tacy and Tib (1941)
Betsy was a junior (1947)
Betsy's wedding (1955)
Heavens to Betsy (1945)

Lowry, Lois

Anastasia Krupnik. Houghton Mifflin 1979 113p
$16 (4-6)   **Fic**
1. Family life—Fiction
ISBN 0-395-28629-8

Also available in paperback from Dell

Anastasia's 10th year has some good things like falling in love and really getting to know her grandmother
and some bad things like finding out about an impending
baby brother.

"Anastasia's father and mother—an English professor
and an artist—are among the most humorous, sensible,
and understanding parents to be found in . . . children's
fiction, and Anastasia herself is an amusing and engaging
heroine." Horn Book

Other titles about Anastasia Krupnik and her family are:
All about Sam (1988)
Anastasia, absolutely (1995)
Anastasia again! (1981)
Anastasia, ask your analyst (1984)
Anastasia at this address (1991)
Anastasia at your service (1982)
Anastasia has the answers (1986)
Anastasia on her own (1985)
Anastasia's chosen career (1987)
Attaboy Sam! (1992)
See you around Sam! (1996)
Zooman Sam (1999)

Autumn Street. Houghton Mifflin 1980 188p
$16 (4 and up)   **Fic**
1. World War, 1939-1945—Fiction 2. Friendship—
Fiction
ISBN 0-395-27812-0   LC 80-376

Also available in paperback from Dell

"Elizabeth, the teller of the story, feels danger around
her when her father goes to fight in World War II. She,
her older sister, and her pregnant mother go to live with
her grandparents on Autumn Street. Tatie, the black
cook-housekeeper, and her street-wise grandson Charley

Lowry, Lois—*Continued*

love Elizabeth and reassure her during this difficult time." Child Book Rev Serv

"Characters, dialogue, believable plot combine in this well written story to capture the mind and heart of all who read this memorable and touching book." Voice Youth Advocates

Gathering blue. Houghton Mifflin 2000 215p $16 (5 and up) **Fic**
1. Science fiction
ISBN 0-618-05581-9   LC 00-24359
Also available in paperback from Laurel Leaf
"Walter Lorraine books"

Lame and suddenly orphaned, Kira is mysteriously removed from her squalid village to live in the palatial Council Edifice, where she is expected to use her gifts as a weaver to do the bidding of the all-powerful Guardians

"Lowry has once again created a fully realized world full of drama, suspense, and even humor." SLJ

The giver. Houghton Mifflin 1993 180p $16 (6 and up) **Fic**
1. Science fiction
ISBN 0-395-64566-2   LC 92-15034
Also available Thorndike Press large print edition and in paperback from Dell
Awarded the Newbery Medal, 1994

Given his lifetime assignment at the Ceremony of Twelve, Jonas becomes the receiver of memories shared by only one other in his community and discovers the terrible truth about the society in which he lives

"A riveting, chilling story that inspires a new appreciation for diversity, love, and even pain. Truly memorable." SLJ

Gooney Bird Greene; illustrated by Middy Thomas. Houghton Mifflin 2002 88p il $15 (2-4) **Fic**
1. Storytelling—Fiction 2. School stories
ISBN 0-618-23848-4   LC 2002-1478
"Walter Lorraine books"

A most unusual new student who loves to be the center of attention entertains her teacher and fellow second graders by telling absolutely true stories about herself, including how she got her name

"Lowry's masterful writing style reaches directly into her audience, managing both to appeal to young listeners and to engage older readers." Bull Cent Child Books
Another title about Gooney Bird is:
Gooney Bird and the room mother (2005)

Gossamer; [by] Lois Lowry. Houghton Mifflin 2006 140p $16 (5 and up) **Fic**
1. Dreams—Fiction 2. Foster home care—Fiction 3. Child abuse—Fiction
ISBN 0-618-68550-2   LC 2005030849
"Walter Lorraine books"

While learning to bestow dreams, a young dream giver tries to save an eight-year-old boy from the effects of both his abusive past and the nightmares inflicted on him by the frightening Sinisteeds.

"Lowry's prose is simple and clear. This carefully plotted fantasy has inner logic and conviction. . . . This is a beautiful novel with an intriguing premise." SLJ

Messenger. Houghton Mifflin 2004 169p $16 (6 and up) **Fic**
1. Science fiction
ISBN 0-618-40441-4   LC 2003-14789
"Walter Lorraine books"

In this novel that unites characters from "The Giver" and "Gathering Blue," Matty, a young member of a utopian community that values honesty, conceals an emerging healing power that he cannot explain or understand.

"Lowry's skillful writing imbues the story with a strong sense of foreboding. . . . The shocking conclusion without benefit of denouement is bound to spark much discussion and debate." SLJ

Number the stars. Houghton Mifflin 1989 137p $16 (4 and up) **Fic**
1. World War, 1939-1945—Fiction 2. Jews—Fiction 3. Friendship—Fiction 4. Denmark—Fiction
ISBN 0-395-51060-0   LC 88-37134
Also available in paperback from Dell
Awarded the Newbery Medal, 1990

In 1943, during the German occupation of Denmark, ten-year-old Annemarie learns how to be brave and courageous when she helps shelter her Jewish friend from the Nazis.

"The appended details the historical incidents upon which Lowry bases her plot. . . . The whole work is seamless, compelling, and memorable." Horn Book

The one hundredth thing about Caroline. Houghton Mifflin 1983 150p $16 (5 and up) **Fic**
1. Single parent family—Fiction
ISBN 0-395-34829-3   LC 83-12629

"Caroline, fascinated by dinosaurs, spends much of her free time prowling New York's Museum of Natural History; her best friend, Stacy, practices being an investigative reporter. The combination proves disastrous when Caroline's mother becomes interested in Frederick Fiske, the mysterious man in the fifth-floor apartment who looks, Caroline is convinced, like the evil 'Tyrannosaurus rex' and who seemingly wants to eliminate Caroline and her brother, J.P." Booklist

"Lowry's style is bright, fast-paced and funny, with skillfully-drawn, believable characters." SLJ
Followed by Switcharound (1985)

Rabble Starkey. Houghton Mifflin 1987 192p $16 (5 and up) **Fic**
1. Friendship—Fiction
ISBN 0-395-43607-9   LC 86-27542
Also available in paperback from Dell

"Parable Starkey and her mother, Sweet Hosanna, move into the Bigelows' house to take charge of the children after Mrs. Bigelow's hospitalization for mental illness. . . . [This is] a smooth first-person narrative that quietly takes on class as well as individual differences. In the end, Lowry has managed to portray a large, diverse cast by carefully and consistently focusing the point of view as one of a maturing observer." Bull Cent Child Books

Stay! Keeper's story. Houghton Mifflin 1997 127p il $15 (5 and up) **Fic**
1. Dogs—Fiction
ISBN 0-395-87048-8   LC 97-1569

Lowry, Lois—*Continued*

Also available in paperback from Dell

"The canine narrator is a mongrel with class, a poetically inclined, refined animal of good upbringing if not bloodlines. He leaves the relative safety of his first home (an alley outside a French restaurant) for the perils of the wide world in search of a human friend." Bull Cent Child Books

"The author proves she is as well versed in animal behavior as in human sensibilities. Her warm sense of humor and vivid imagination . . . accentuate Keeper's unorthodox perceptions of the world." Publ Wkly

A summer to die; illustrated by Jenni Oliver. Houghton Mifflin 1977 154p il $16 (5 and up)
Fic

1. Sisters—Fiction 2. Death—Fiction
ISBN 0-395-25338-1 LC 77-83
Also available in paperback from Bantam Bks.

"Meg, 13, envies her older sister's popularity and prettiness and finds it difficult to cope with Molly's degenerating illness and eventual death." Booklist

"As told by Meg, the chronicle of this experience is a sensitive exploration of the complex emotions underlying the adolescent's first confrontation with human mortality; the author suggests nuances of contemporary conversation and situations without sacrificing the finesse with which she limns her characters." Horn Book

Your move, J.P.! Houghton Mifflin 1990 122p $16 (5 and up) **Fic**
1. School stories
ISBN 0-395-53639-1 LC 89-24707
Also available in paperback from Dell

Caroline's older brother, twelve-year-old J.P. Tate, who appeared in The one hundredth thing about Caroline and Switcharound, has a "crush on Angela Galsworthy, newly arrived at his private school from London, England. . . . Anxious to sustain Angela's interest, J.P. tells her that he is suffering from triple framosis, a rare but fatal disease. Angela believes him and J.P. is stuck with his lie." Bull Cent Child Books

"The author makes the most of the humor in J.P.'s antics but maintains a rueful sympathy throughout for his plight and for his eventual admission of truth." Horn Book

Lunn, Janet Louise Swoboda

Laura Secord: a story of courage; [by] Janet Lunn; illustrated by Maxwell Newhouse. Tundra Bks. 2001 unp il maps $16.95 (3-5) **Fic**
1. Secord, Laura, d. 1868—Fiction 2. War of 1812—Fiction
ISBN 0-88776-538-6

This is the fictionalized story of Laura "Secord's 19-mile journey to inform British Lieutenant FitzGibbon of the American plan for a surprise attack during the War of 1812." SLJ

"The folkloric rhythm of the tale is underscored in the dramatically colored, naively rendered illustrations." Horn Book Guide

Lupica, Mike

Heat. Philomel Books 2006 220p $16.99 (5 and up) **Fic**
1. Baseball—Fiction 2. Orphans—Fiction 3. Illegal aliens—Fiction 4. Cubans—Fiction
ISBN 0-399-24301-1 LC 2005-13521

Pitching prodigy Michael Arroyo is on the run from social services after being banned from playing Little League baseball because rival coaches doubt he is only twelve years old and he has no parents to offer them proof.

"The dialogue crackles, and the rich cast of supporting characters' . . . nearly steals the show. Topnotch entertainment." Booklist

Ly, Many

Home is east; [by] Many Ly. Delacorte Press 2005 294p $15.95; lib bdg $17.99 (5 and up)
Fic
1. Cambodian Americans—Fiction 2. Divorce—Fiction 3. Moving—Fiction 4. California—Fiction
ISBN 0-385-73222-8; 0-385-73223-6 (lib bdg)
LC 2004-14969

After her mother moves out, Amy, a Cambodian American girl, and her old-fashioned father leave their home in Florida to begin a new life in San Diego, experiencing turmoil and change as they slowly adjust to their new circumstances.

"Amy's narration is convincingly plainspoken, believable in its limitations but subtle in its understandings, and she's joined by a cast of compelling supporting characters." Bull Cent Child Books

Lyons, Mary E.

Letters from a slave girl; the story of Harriet Jacobs. Scribner 1992 146p il pa $4.99 hardcover o.p. (6 and up) **Fic**
1. Jacobs, Harriet A. (Harriet Ann), 1813-1896 or 7—Fiction 2. Slavery—Fiction 3. African Americans—Fiction 4. Letters—Fiction
ISBN 0-689-80015-0 (pa) LC 91-45778

A fictionalized version of the life of Harriet Jacobs, told in the form of letters that she might have written during her slavery in North Carolina and as she prepared for escape to the North in 1842

This "is historical fiction at its best. . . . Mary Lyons has remained faithful to Jacobs's actual autobiography throughout her readable, compelling novel. . . . Her observations of the horrors of slavery are concise and lucid. The letters are written in dialect, based on Jacobs's own writing and on other slave narrations of the period." Horn Book

MacDonald, Betty

Mrs. Piggle-Wiggle; illustrated by Hilary Knight. Lippincott 1957 c1947 118p il $15.99; pa $4.99 (2-4) **Fic**
ISBN 0-397-31712-3; 0-06-440148-0 (pa)
First published 1947

From her upside-down house, the eccentric Mrs. Piggle-Wiggle issues to parents her marvelous cures for such common children's diseases as Won't-Put-

MacDonald, Betty—*Continued*

AwayToys-itis, Answer-backism, and Fighter-Quarrelitis.

The author "mixes a little psychology with a lot of common sense, and seasons with nonsense, to produce the most palatable type of lecture on good behavior. Hilary Knight's illustrations catch the mood of the whole delightful business." Chicago Sunday Trib

Other titles about Mrs. Piggle-Wiggle are:

Hello, Mrs. Piggle-Wiggle (1957)

Mrs. Piggle-Wiggle's farm (1954)

Mrs. Piggle-Wiggle's magic (1949)

MacDonald, George

At the back of the North Wind (4-6)

Fic

1. Fairy tales

Available from various publishers, including a Knopf hardcover edition illustrated by Arthur Hughes

First published 1871

"There is a rare quality in Macdonald's lovely fairy tales which relates spiritual ideals with the everyday things of life. This one tells of Diamond, the little son of a coachman, and his friendship with the North Wind who appears to him in various guises." Toronto Public Libr. Books for Boys & Girls

The light princess; with pictures by Maurice Sendak. Farrar, Straus & Giroux 1969 110p il pa $5.95 hardcover o.p. (3-6) **Fic**

1. Fairy tales

ISBN 0-374-44458-7 (pa)

This fairy story originally appeared 1864 in the author's novel Adela Cathcart and was reprinted in his 1867 story collection Dealings with the fairies

"The problems of the princess who had been deprived, as an infant, of her gravity and whose life hung in the balance when she grew up are amusing as ever and the sweet capitulation to love that brings her (literally) to her feet, just as touching. All of the best of Macdonald is reflected in the Sendak illustrations: the humor and wit, the sweetness and tenderness, and the sophistication—and they are beautiful." Sutherland. The Best in Child Books

The princess and the goblin (3-6) **Fic**

1. Fairy tales

Some editions are:

Knopf (Everyman's library children's classics) $12.95 Illustrated by Arthur Hughes (ISBN 0-679-42810-0)

Morrow (Books of Wonder) $22.95 Illustrated by Jessie Willcox Smith (ISBN 0-688-06604-6)

First published 1872

"Living in a great house on the side of a mountain in a country where hideous spiteful goblins inhabit the dark caverns below the mines, little Princess Irene and Curdie the miner's son have many strange adventures. . . . To adults Macdonald's stories have an allegorical significance, to each succeeding generation of children they are wonderful fairytale adventures." Four to Fourteen

Followed by The princess and Curdie

Mackel, Kathy

MadCat; [by] Kathy Mackel. 1st ed. HarperCollins 2005 185p $15.99; lib bdg $16.89 (5 and up) **Fic**

1. Softball—Fiction 2. Friendship—Fiction 3. Women athletes—Fiction

ISBN 0-06-054869-X; 0-06-054870-3 (lib bdg)

LC 2004-6618

Fast-pitch softball catcher MadCat Campione's love for the sport—and her relationship with her best friends—is strained when her team competes on a national level.

"With a credible plot, a distinct narrative voice, and sparky dialogue, this is a winner in any league." Booklist

MacLachlan, Patricia

Arthur, for the very first time; illustrated by Lloyd Bloom. Harper & Row 1980 117p il lib bdg $15.89; pa $4.95 (4-6) **Fic**

ISBN 0-06-024047-4 (lib bdg); 0-06-440288-6 (pa)

LC 79-2007

A "recounting of ten-year-old Arthur's activities and introspections during a summer spent with a great-uncle and a great-aunt. The offbeat relatives cultivate equally offbeat friends, climb trees, and speak French to their pet chicken. Arthur also enjoys the companionship of a veterinarian's granddaughter." Horn Book

"Good-hearted good humor. . . . The colorfulness of the characters is unrelenting; each is more exaggeratedly unique and zany than the other." SLJ

Baby. Delacorte Press 1993 132p $15.95 (5 and up) **Fic**

1. Infants—Fiction 2. Death—Fiction 3. Islands—Fiction

ISBN 0-385-31133-8 LC 93-22117

Also available in paperback from Dell

Taking care of a baby left with them at the end of the tourist season helps a family come to terms with the death of their own infant son

"Short, spare, powerful, this is a story which touches deep emotions and lingers in the heart." Horn Book

The facts and fictions of Minna Pratt. Harper & Row 1988 136p lib bdg $14.89; pa $4.95 (4 and up) **Fic**

1. Musicians—Fiction

ISBN 0-06-024117-9 (lib bdg); 0-06-440265-7 (pa)

LC 85-45388

"A Charlotte Zolotow book"

"Minna Pratt plays the cello and wishes she would get her vibrato. She wishes someone would answer her questions about herself and life and love. . . . Then she meets Lucas Ellerby. His life seems so perfect and he has a vibrato. As their friendship develops Minna finds that life is not always as it seems and even when you think you know someone or something there may be a hidden side that will surprise you." Voice Youth Advocates

"Ms. MacLachlan's skillful handling of her subject, and above all her vivid characterization . . . place her story in the ranks of outstanding middle-grade fiction." N Y Times Book Rev

MacLachlan, Patricia—*Continued*

Journey. Delacorte Press 1991 83p pa $5.50 hardcover o.p. (4 and up)   **Fic**

1. Family life—Fiction

ISBN 0-440-40809-1 (pa)   LC 90-21052

When their mother goes off, leaving her two children with their grandparents, they feel as if their past has been erased until Grandfather finds a way to restore it to them

"This is a spellbinding tale, lean only in its length. The author's clipped dialogue and meticulously pared-down descriptions convey a deceptive simplicity—there are deep, intricate rumblings beneath the surface calm of MacLachlan's words." Publ Wkly

Sarah, plain and tall. Harper & Row 1985 58p $14.99; lib bdg $15.89; pa $4.99 (3-5)   **Fic**

1. Stepmothers—Fiction 2. Frontier and pioneer life—Fiction

ISBN 0-06-024101-2; 0-06-024102-0 (lib bdg); 0-06-440205-3 (pa)   LC 83-49481

Awarded the Newbery Medal, 1986

"A Charlotte Zolotow book"

When their father invites a mail-order bride to come live with them in their prairie home, Caleb and Anna are captivated by their new mother and hope that she will stay

"It is the simplest of love stories expressed in the simplest of prose. Embedded in these unadorned declarative sentences about ordinary people, actions, animals, facts, objects and colors are evocations of the deepest feelings of loss and fear, love and hope." N Y Times Book Rev

Other titles in this series are:

Caleb's story (2001)

Grandfather's dance (2006)

More perfect than the moon (2004)

Skylark (1994)

Seven kisses in a row; pictures by Maria Pia Marrella. Harper & Row 1983 56p il lib bdg $15.89; pa $4.95 (2-4)   **Fic**

1. Aunts—Fiction 2. Uncles—Fiction 3. Family life—Fiction

ISBN 0-06-024084-9 (lib bdg); 0-06-440231-2 (pa)   LC 82-47718

"A Charlotte Zolotow book"

"How different life is for Emma and Zachary when Aunt Evelyn and Uncle Elliott babysit for them while their parents attend an 'eyeball meeting'! No seven kisses before breakfast or divided grapefruit with cherry. Nevertheless both learn from the others—Emma learns to eat broccoli and her aunt and uncle learn about babies and what they do." Child Book Rev Serv

"The brief understated story makes few demands on the reader, but it is full of humor and the warmth of family caring and mutual affection. Informal, offhand pen-and-ink drawings reflect the tone of both story and style." Horn Book

MacLean, Christine Kole

Mary Margaret and the perfect pet plan. Dutton Children's Books 2004 168p $15.99 (3-5)   **Fic**

1. Pets—Fiction 2. Family life—Fiction

ISBN 0-525-47183-9   LC 2003-55430

During the summer that she turns nine, Mary Margaret tries very hard to persuade her parents to let her have a pet, makes a new neighbor friend and helps her brother keep an old one, and looks forward to the new baby's arrival because then her mother will be less "crabby."

"MacLean's heroine is lively, spirited, and full of energy. All of the characters are well drawn and the narrative sparkles with humor." SLJ

Another title about Mary Margaret is:

Mary Margaret, center stage (2006)

Madden, Kerry

Gentle's Holler; by Kerry Madden. Viking 2005 237p $16.99 (5 and up)   **Fic**

1. Family life—Fiction 2. Poverty—Fiction 3. North Carolina—Fiction

ISBN 0-670-05998-6   LC 2004-18424

In the early 1960s, twelve-year-old songwriter Livy Two Weems dreams of seeing the world beyond the Maggie Valley, North Carolina, holler where she lives in poverty with her parents and eight brothers and sisters, but understands that she must put family first.

"Livy's narration rings true and is wonderfully voiced, and Madden's message about the importance of forgiveness will be well received." SLJ

Maguire, Gregory

The good liar. Clarion Bks. 1999 129p $15 (4 and up)   **Fic**

1. World War, 1939-1945—Fiction 2. France—Fiction

ISBN 0-395-90697-0   LC 98-19981

Also available in paperback from HarperTrophy

First published 1995 in Ireland

Now an old man living in the United States, Marcel recalls his childhood in German-occupied France, especially the summer that he and his older brother Rene befriended a young German soldier

"At once poignant, thoughtful, and laced with humor, the book offers readers an unusual perspective on history." Horn Book Guide

Seven spiders spinning; illustrated by Dirk Zimmer. Clarion Bks. 1994 132p il $16 (4-6)   **Fic**

1. Spiders—Fiction 2. School stories

ISBN 0-395-68965-1   LC 93-30478

Also available in paperback from HarperCollins

Seven prehistoric spiders that had been trapped in ice for thousands of years bring excitement to rural Vermont and briefly unite two rival clubs at a local elementary school.

"There is quite a bit of tongue-in-cheek humor here. . . . Characters are almost caricatures. . . . Yet, somehow it all comes together to create a funny, shivery story." SLJ

Other titles in this series are:

A couple of April fools (2004)

Five alien elves (1998)

Four stupid Cupids (2000)

One final firecracker (2005)

Six haunted hairdos (1997)

Three rotten eggs (2002)

Mankell, Henning

Secrets in the fire; translated by Anne Connie Stuksrud. Annick Press 2003 166p $17.95; pa $7.95 (5 and up)   **Fic**

1. Mozambique—Fiction 2. War stories
ISBN 1-55037-801-5; 1-55037-800-7 (pa)
Originally published in Sweden

Sofia, who lost her legs from landmines in Mozambique, attempts to make a new life for herself.

"A hard-hitting, eye-opening novel that brings readers face-to-face with the horrors of war. . . . Mankell's language and style are spare, but elicit a deeply emotional response. " SLJ

Marsden, Carolyn

The gold-threaded dress. Candlewick Press 2002 73p $13.99 (3-5)   **Fic**

1. Thai Americans—Fiction 2. Prejudices—Fiction 3. School stories
ISBN 0-7636-1569-2   LC 2001-25132

When Oy and her Thai American family move to a new neighborhood, her third-grade classmates tease and exclude her because she is different

"Marsden writes with keen observation and finesse about the social dynamics of the classroom and with simplicity reveals the layers of emotion experienced by Oy." Booklist

Another title about Oy is:
The Quail Club (2006)

Mama had to work on Christmas; illustrations by Robert Casilla. Viking 2003 73p il $14.99 (2-4)   **Fic**

1. Christmas—Fiction 2. Work—Fiction
ISBN 0-670-03635-8   LC 2003-943

Gloria's Christmas begins with frustration when she is forced to go to work with Mama, but by the end of the day, she appreciates her family and enjoys the holiday

"The tone is matter-of-fact and engaging, and Gloria is an appealing character." SLJ

Moon runner; [by] Carolyn Marsden. 1st ed. Candlewick Press 2005 97p $15.99 (3-5)   **Fic**

1. Friendship—Fiction 2. Running—Fiction
ISBN 0-7636-2117-X   LC 2004-58143

When Mina discovers that she can run faster than her athlete friend, Ruth, she thinks she must choose between running and friendship.

"A quiet, lyrical story that sensitively explores issues of friendship and being true to oneself. . . . The lucid prose is full of haunting metaphors. " SLJ

Silk umbrellas; [by] Carolyn Marsden. Candlewick Press 2004 134p $15.99 (3-6)   **Fic**

1. Thailand—Fiction 2. Family life—Fiction 3. Artists—Fiction
ISBN 0-7636-2257-5   LC 2003-55323

Eleven-year-old Noi worries that she will have to stop painting the silk umbrellas her family sells at the market near their Thai village and be forced to join her older sister in difficult work at a local factory instead.

"In simple, lucid prose, Marsden tells a story that is foreign in detail and texture but universal in appeal. . . . This gracefully told story will resonate with many young readers." Booklist

Martin, Ann M.

Belle Teal. Scholastic Press 2001 214p $15.95 (4 and up)   **Fic**

1. School stories 2. Race relations—Fiction
ISBN 0-439-09823-8   LC 00-136292

Belle Teal Harper is from a poor family in the country, and beginning fifth-grade is a challenge as her grandmother's memory is slipping away, her brother and father are fighting again, and she becomes involved with the two new African American children in her class.

"This is a solid piece of work with an absorbing plot." SLJ

A corner of the universe. Scholastic Press 2002 189p $15.95; pa $5.99 (5 and up)   **Fic**

1. Uncles—Fiction 2. Mentally handicapped—Fiction 3. Friendship—Fiction
ISBN 0-439-38880-5; 0-439-38881-3 (pa)
   LC 2001-57611

The summer that Hattie turns twelve, she meets the childlike uncle she never knew and becomes friends with a girl who works at the carnival that comes to Hattie's small town

"Martin delivers wonderfully real characters and an engrossing plot through the viewpoint of a girl who tries so earnestly to connect with those around her." SLJ

The doll people; by Ann M. Martin and Laura Godwin; with pictures by Brian Selznick. Hyperion Bks. for Children 2000 256p il $15.99; lib bdg $16.49 (3-5)   **Fic**

1. Dolls—Fiction
ISBN 0-7868-0361-4; 0-7868-2372-0 (lib bdg)
   LC 98-12344

A family of porcelain dolls that has lived in the same house for one hundred years is taken aback when a new family of plastic dolls arrives and doesn't follow The Doll Code of Honor

"A lighthearted touch and a dash of drama make this a satisfying read." SLJ

Another title about the doll family is:
The meanest doll in the world (2003)

Here today. Scholastic 2004 308p $16.95 (5 and up)   **Fic**

1. Mothers—Fiction 2. Family life—Fiction
ISBN 0-439-57944-9   LC 2004-41620

In 1963, Ellie's mother was crowned a grocery store beauty queen, her classmates treated her cruelly, and President Kennedy was killed. It was also when Ellie realized that in trying to keep her life together she had to let pieces of it go

"Martin paints a well-articulated picture of the times, but it is her memorable child and adult characters that shine here." SLJ

Martin, Nora

Flight of the Fisherbird. Bloomsbury Children's Bks. 2003 150p il $16.95 (5 and up)   **Fic**
1. Uncles—Fiction 2. Chinese Americans—Fiction 3. Washington (State)—Fiction
ISBN 1-58234-814-6   LC 2002-35628

In 1889 in the islands off the coast of Washington State, thirteen-year-old Clementine pulls a nearly drowned Chinese man out of the sea and begins to suspect that her beloved uncle may have been involved in his attempted murder as well as other treacherous deeds.

"A fast-paced, high-stakes historical mystery." SLJ

Martino, Carmela A.

Rosa, sola. Candlewick Press 2005 236p $15.99 (4-6)   **Fic**
1. Bereavement—Fiction 2. Italian Americans—Fiction 3. Chicago (Ill.)—Fiction
ISBN 0-7636-2395-4   LC 2004-62875

Longing for a sibling in 1966 Chicago, fourth-grader Rosa is delighted with her mother's pregnancy, until tragedy strikes and her family struggles to deal with its grief.

"Offering a great deal of nuance within an approachable narrative, this tender novel glows with affection and hope for its grieving family." Booklist

Masefield, John

Jim Davis; a high-sea adventure. Scholastic 2002 c1911 224p $15.95 (5 and up)   **Fic**
1. Pirates—Fiction 2. Adventure fiction
ISBN 0-439-40436-3   LC 2002-21175
"The Chicken House"
First published 1911 in the United Kingdom

Jim Davis is a twelve-year-old boy whose life takes a terrifying turn when he stumbles upon a ring of bloodthirsty pirates

"Masefield was England's poet laureate, and his prose has a poet's grace and attention to detail. The language, however, doesn't get in the way of the rip-roaring plot, which taps into the rich vein of classic sea stories." Booklist

Mason, Simon

The Quigleys at large; illustrated by Helen Stephens. David Fickling Bks. 2003 148p il $14.95; lib bdg $16.99 (2-4)   **Fic**
1. Family life—Fiction
ISBN 0-385-75022-6; 0-385-75031-5 (lib bdg)
LC 2003-47036

The adventures and misadventures of the four members of the Quigley family. "Dad's elaborate trap to catch the family's pet budgie entangles him instead of the bird. Will gets locked inside the school when he goes back on the weekend to find his lost coat. Mum resists everyone's attempt to keep her inactive at a fete because of recent dental surgery. . . . Lucy breaks the language barrier in order to make a friend when the family goes camping in France." SLJ

"The humor is all human foible-based, and so very warm and not at all brittle." Horn Book
Other titles about the Quigley family are:
The Quigleys (2002)
The Quigleys in a spin (2006)
The Quigleys not for sale (2004)

Matas, Carol

Sparks fly upward. Clarion Bks. 2002 180p $15 (4 and up)   **Fic**
1. Jews—Fiction 2. Prejudices—Fiction 3. Canada—Fiction
ISBN 0-618-15964-9   LC 2001-47188

In 1910, when a family of Russian Jews moves from Saskatchewan to Winnipeg, Canada, twelve-year-old Rebecca must live with Christians temporarily and struggles with anti-Semitism, confusion about God, and changing relationships with family and friends

"There's no sentimentality in the characterization . . . and the history is well researched. Most compelling, though, is Rebecca's personal struggle with faith, friendship, and loyalty." Booklist

The war within; a novel of the Civil War. Simon & Schuster Bks. for Young Readers 2001 151p $16; pa $4.99 (5 and up)   **Fic**
1. United States—History—1861-1865, Civil War—Fiction 2. Jews—Fiction 3. Prejudices—Fiction
ISBN 0-689-82935-3; 0-689-84358-5 (pa)
LC 00-45068
Also available Thorndike Press large print edition

In 1862, after Union forces expel Hannah's family from Holly Springs, Mississippi, because they are Jews, Hannah re-examines her views regarding slavery and the war

"Readers will find themselves swept along by the riptide of action and the appealing cast of strong, vivid characters." Booklist

Mazer, Norma Fox

Good night, Maman. Harcourt Brace & Co. 1999 185p $16 (5 and up)   **Fic**
1. Holocaust, 1933-1945—Fiction 2. World War, 1939-1945—Fiction 3. Jewish refugees—Fiction
ISBN 0-15-201468-3   LC 98-49220
Also available in paperback from HarperCollins

After spending years fleeing from the Nazis in war-torn Europe, twelve-year-old Karin Levi and her older brother Marc find a new home in a refugee camp in Oswego, New York

"Mazer convincingly constructs a fictional yet moving memoir of one girl's forever-altered life, and in Karin she gives readers a memorable heroine." Bull Cent Child Books

McAllister, Margaret

Ghost at the window. Dutton Children's Bks. 2002 160p $15.99 (5 and up)   **Fic**
1. Space and time—Fiction 2. Ghost stories 3. Scotland—Fiction
ISBN 0-525-46852-8   LC 2001-40395

Life at Ninian House, Ewan's Scottish home that slips back and forth in time, becomes even more unpredictable when a ghostly girl from 1937 shares a frightening secret with him.

"McAllister's prose moves quickly, and her characters, setting, and events are easy to visualize. . . . Part mystery, part ghost story, part morality tale, the novel has a good deal to offer." Booklist

McCaughrean, Geraldine

The kite rider; a novel. HarperCollins Pubs. 2002 272p maps $15.95; lib bdg $16.89; pa $6.99 (5 and up) **Fic**

1. Kublai Khan, 1216-1294—Fiction 2. China—Fiction 3. Kites—Fiction

ISBN 0-06-623874-9; 0-06-623875-7 (lib bdg); 0-06-441091-9 (pa) LC 2001-39522

In thirteenth-century China, after trying to save his widowed mother from a horrendous second marriage, twelve-year-old Haoyou has life-changing adventures when he takes to the sky as a circus kite rider and ends up meeting the great Mongol ruler Kublai Khan

"The story is a genuine page-turner. . . . McCaughrean fully immerses her memorable characters in the culture and lore of the ancient Chinese and Mongols, which make this not only a solid adventure story but also a window to a fascinating time and place." Booklist

Stop the train! a novel. HarperCollins Pubs. 2003 289p $16.99; lib bdg $17.89 (5 and up) **Fic**

1. Frontier and pioneer life—Fiction 2. Oklahoma—Fiction

ISBN 0-06-050749-7; 0-06-050750-0 (lib bdg) LC 2002-27340

Despite the opposition of the owner of the Red Rock Runner railroad in 1893, the new settlers of Florence, Oklahoma, are determined to build a real town

"There is much tongue-in-cheek humor in this rollicking tale, and wonderful figurative language abounds." SLJ

McCloskey, Robert

Homer Price. Viking 1943 149p il $15.99; pa $4.99 (4-6) **Fic**

ISBN 0-670-37729-5; 0-14-030927-6 (pa)

Six "stories about the exploits of young Homer Price, who divides his time between school and doing odd jobs at his father's filling station and in his mother's tourist lunchroom two miles outside of Centerburg." Bookmark

"Text and pictures are pure Americana, hilarious and convincing in their portrayal of midwestern small-town life." Child Books Too Good to Miss

Another title about Homer Price is:
Centerburg tales (1951)

McCully, Emily Arnold

The bobbin girl. Dial Bks. for Young Readers 1996 unp il $15.99 (3-5) **Fic**

1. Strikes—Fiction 2. United States—History—1815-1861—Fiction 3. Massachusetts—Fiction 4. Factories—Fiction

ISBN 0-8037-1827-6 LC 95-6997

Rebecca, a ten-year-old bobbin girl working in a textile mill in Lowell, Massachusetts, in the 1830s, must make a difficult decision—will she participate in the first workers' strike in Lowell?

"McCully weaves historical facts and fictional characters into an intriguing story. The author's note details the background, incidents, and people who inspired the book. Beautifully composed watercolor paintings give a vivid impression of America in the 1830s and bring the period to life." Booklist

Hurry! illustrated by Emily Arnold McCully, adapted from Farewell to the Farivox by Harry Hartwick. Harcourt 2000 unp il $16 (2-4) **Fic**

1. Wildlife conservation—Fiction

ISBN 0-15-201579-5 LC 97-45564

"Browndeer Press"

In 1916, a young boy named Tom Elson living in Iowa meets a stranger who has an unusual animal called a Farivox, maybe the last of its kind, and Tom becomes determined to buy it

"The tale gently but firmly makes its point and provides an excellent springboard for discussion. . . . The illustrations are vintage McCully, perfectly capturing the time period and its ambience with brightly colored but soft-edged watercolors." SLJ

McDonald, Megan

All the stars in the sky; the Santa Fe trail diary of Florrie Mack Ryder. Scholastic 2003 187p il (Dear America) $10.95 (4 and up) **Fic**

1. Santa Fe Trail—Fiction 2. Frontier and pioneer life—Fiction 3. Overland journeys to the Pacific—Fiction

ISBN 0-439-16963-1 LC 2002-44579

A girl's diary records the year 1848 during which she, her brother, mother, and stepfather traveled the Santa Fe trail from Independence, Missouri, to Santa Fe.

"The writing is excellent, developing a compelling narrative." SLJ

Judy Moody; illustrated by Peter Reynolds. Candlewick Press 2000 160p il $15.99; pa $5.99 (2-4) **Fic**

1. School stories

ISBN 0-7636-0685-5; 0-7636-1231-6 (pa) LC 99-13464

Third grader Judy Moody is in a first day of school bad mood until she gets an assignment to create a collage all about herself and begins creating her masterpiece, the Me collage.

"This beginning chapter book features large type; simple, expressive prose and dialogue; and plenty of child-appealing humor." Booklist

Other titles about Judy Moody are:
Judy Moody: around the world in 8 1/2 days (2006)
Judy Moody declares independence (2005)
Judy Moody gets famous (2001)
Judy Moody M.D., the doctor is in (2004)
Judy Moody predicts the future (2003)
Judy Moody saves the world (2002)

Stink; the incredible shrinking kid; illustrated by Peter H. Reynolds. 1st ed. Candlewick Press 2005 102p il $12.99 (2-4) **Fic**

1. School stories

ISBN 0-7636-2025-4 LC 2003-65246

The shortest kid in the second grade, James Moody, also known as Stink, learns all about the shortest president of the United States, James Madison, when they celebrate Presidents' Day at school.

"Delightful full-page and spot-art cartoons and playful language in large type bring the child's adventures to life." SLJ

Another title about Stink is:

McDonald, Megan—*Continued*

Stink and the incredible super-galactic jawbreaker (2006)

McDonough, Yona Zeldis

The doll with the yellow star; illustrated by Kimberly Bulcken Root. 1st ed. H. Holt 2005 90p il $16.95 (3-5)   **Fic**

1. Holocaust, 1933-1945—Fiction 2. Dolls—Fiction 3. Jews—Fiction

ISBN 0-8050-6337-4   LC 2002-27554

When France falls to Germany at the start of World War II, nine-year-old Claudine must leave her beloved parents and friends to stay with relatives in America, accompanied by her doll, Violette.

"This fiction book is informative, enjoyable, and passionately written." Libr Media Connect

McGhee, Alison

Snap; a novel. Candlewick Press 2004 129p $15.99 (5 and up)   **Fic**

1. Friendship—Fiction 2. Grandmothers—Fiction 3. Death—Fiction

ISBN 0-7636-2002-5   LC 2002-34998

Eleven-year-old Edwina confronts old and new challenges when her longtime best friend Sally faces the inevitable death of the grandmother who raised her.

This "features memorable characters and a tolerance for eccentricity, emotional subtlety and complexity, themes of acceptance of death and love, and a spare and poetic text that begs to be reread and savored." SLJ

McGraw, Eloise Jarvis

The moorchild; [by] Eloise McGraw. Margaret K. McElderry Bks. 1996 241p $17; pa $4.99 (4 and up)   **Fic**

1. Fantasy fiction 2. Fairies—Fiction

ISBN 0-689-80654-X; 0-689-82033-X (pa)

LC 95-34107

Also available Thorndike Press large print edition

Newbery Medal honor book, 1997

"Saaski, a half-human, half-Moorfolk child, is banished from the Mound and placed as a changeling in a human village, where she is regarded with suspicion and treated with scorn." Horn Book Guide

"Incorporating some classic fantasy motifs and icons, McGraw . . . conjures up an appreciably familiar world that, as evidence of her storytelling power, still strikes an original chord." Publ Wkly

McKay, Hilary

Dog Friday. Margaret K. McElderry Bks. 1995 135p $16.95; pa $4.99 (4-6)   **Fic**

1. Dogs—Fiction 2. Great Britain—Fiction

ISBN 0-689-80383-4; 0-689-81765-7 (pa)

LC 95-4446

First published 1994 in the United Kingdom

Ten-year-old Robin Brogan is determined to keep the dog he finds abandoned on the beach from being impounded by the police

"The sharply realized characters, fast-paced story, and witty dialogue make this English novel both distinctive and refreshing." Booklist

Other titles about the Brogan family and their friends are:

The amber cat (1997)

Dolphin luck (1999)

Saffy's angel. Margaret K. McElderry Bks. 2002 152p $16; pa $4.99 (5 and up)   **Fic**

1. Family life—Fiction 2. Adoption—Fiction

ISBN 0-689-84933-8; 0-689-84934-6 (pa)

LC 2001-44110

First published 2001 in the United Kingdom

After learning that she was adopted, thirteen-year-old Saffron's relationship with her eccentric, artistic family changes, until they help her go back to Italy where she was born to find a special momento of her past

"Like the Casson household itself, the plot is a chaotic whirl that careens off in several directions simultaneously. But McKay always skillfully draws each clearly defined character back into the story with witty, well-edited details; rapid dialogue; and fine pacing." Booklist

Other titles in this series are:

Caddy ever after (2006)

Indigo's star (2004)

Permanent Rose (2005)

McKissack, Patricia C.

Abby takes a stand; illustrated [by] Gordon C. James. Viking 2005 104p il (Scraps of time) $14.99 (2-4)   **Fic**

1. Civil rights demonstrations—Fiction 2. African Americans—Fiction 3. Tennessee—Fiction

ISBN 0-670-06011-9   LC 2004-21641

Gee recalls for her grandchildren what happened in 1960 in Nashville, Tennessee, when she, aged ten, passed out flyers while her cousin and other adults held sit-ins at restaurants and lunch counters to protest segregation.

"Although short and simply told, the book gives readers a kid's-eye view of important happenings and reminds them that history is something that is always in the making. Fine black-and-white art adds to the ambience of the time." Booklist

Color me dark; the diary of Nellie Lee Love, the great migration North. Scholastic 2000 218p (Dear America) $10.95 (4 and up)   **Fic**

1. African Americans—Fiction 2. Chicago (Ill.)—Fiction

ISBN 0-590-51159-9   LC 99-16459

Eleven-year-old Nellie Lee Love records in her diary the events of 1919, when her family moves from Tennessee to Chicago, hoping to leave the racism and hatred of the South behind

"The strong narrative will keep children involved and give them a great deal of social history to absorb along the way." Booklist

Nzinga, warrior queen of Matamba; by Patricia McKissack. Scholastic 2000 136p (Royal diaries) $10.95 (5 and up)   **Fic**

1. Nzinga, Queen of Matamba, 1582-1663—Fiction 2. Angola—Fiction 3. Princesses—Fiction 4. Slave trade—Fiction

ISBN 0-439-11210-9   LC 00-24216

McKissack, Patricia C.—*Continued*

Presents the diary of thirteen-year-old Nzingha, a sixteenth-century West African princess who loves to hunt and hopes to lead her kingdom one day against the invasion of the Portuguese slave traders

"The diary format will appeal to readers and the author's use of time lines, seasons, and actual place names makes the story believable and interesting." SLJ

A picture of Freedom; the diary of Clotee, a slave girl. Scholastic 1997 192p il maps (Dear America) $10.95 (4 and up)   **Fic**
1. Slavery—Fiction 2. Underground railroad—Fiction 3. Books and reading—Fiction 4. African Americans—Fiction
ISBN 0-590-25988-1   LC 96-25673
In 1859 twelve-year-old Clotee, a house slave who must conceal the fact that she can read and write, records in her diary her experiences and her struggle to decide whether to escape to freedom
"McKissack brings Clotee alive through touching and sobering details of slave life." SLJ

Tippy Lemmey; illustrated by Susan Keeter. Simon & Schuster 2003 59p il lib bdg $11.89; pa $3.99 (2-4)   **Fic**
1. Dogs—Fiction 2. African Americans—Fiction 3. Tennessee—Fiction
ISBN 0-689-85594-X (lib bdg); 0-689-85019-0 (pa)
"Ready-for-chapters"
"In 1951, in Templeton, TN, Leanne Martin and her friends Paul and Jeannie are at war with Tippy Lemmey, a dog that frightens them. . . . The kids learn that Tippy is simply a puppy who wants to play, and that his owner is fighting in Korea. Leanne remains unconvinced about the dog's good intentions, but when the friends see thieves stealing him and other neighborhood dogs to sell across state, they rescue the animals and are rewarded when Tippy gets them out of a dangerous situation. . . . This charming and humorous story moves along at a fast pace, making it perfect for readers just venturing into chapter-book territory." SLJ

McMullan, Margaret

How I found the Strong; a Civil War story. Houghton Mifflin 2004 136p $15 (5 and up)   **Fic**
1. United States—History—1861-1865, Civil War—Fiction 2. Mississippi—Fiction 3. Slavery—Fiction
ISBN 0-618-35008-X   LC 2003-12294
Frank Russell, known as Shanks, wishes he could have gone with his father and brother to fight for Mississippi and the Confederacy, but his experiences with the war and his changing relationship with the family slave, Buck, change his thinking.
"The crisply written narrative is full of regional speech and detail, creating a vivid portrait." Voice Youth Advocates

McNamee, Graham

Sparks. Wendy Lamb Bks. 2002 119p $15.95; lib bdg $17.99 (4-6)   **Fic**
1. Benga, Ota, d. 1916—Fiction 2. Learning disabilities—Fiction 3. Prejudices—Fiction 4. Friendship—Fiction 5. School stories
ISBN 0-385-72977-4; 0-385-90054-6 (lib bdg)
LC 2001-50693
When Todd is both happy and anxious about trying to fit in with the regular fifth grade class but feels confused about how to relate to his former friends in the Special Needs class, a school assignment on the exploited pygmy, Ota Benga, helps give him confidence and clarity
"McNamee crafts a warm and humorous story about a boy's struggle to overcome his learning difficulties and his own self-doubt. A solid choice for any reader, but especially reluctant ones." SLJ

McPhail, David M.

Piggy's pancake parlor; [by] David McPhail. Dutton Children's Bks. 2002 48p il $15.99 (1-3)
Fic
1. Pigs—Fiction 2. Foxes—Fiction 3. Restaurants—Fiction
ISBN 0-525-45930-8   LC 2001-47143
Piggy and Fox open a restaurant where they serve the delicious pancakes that Piggy makes by adding a secret ingredient
"McPhail's understated narrative and winsome watercolor-and-ink pictures serve up generous portions of humor, making this delectable fare that goes down easily." Publ Wkly

McSwigan, Marie

Snow treasure; [by] Marie McSwigan; illustrated by Mary Reardon. 1st ed. Dutton's Children's Books 2005 c1942 196p il $10.99 (3-6)
Fic
1. World War, 1939-1945—Fiction 2. Norway—Fiction
ISBN 0-525-47626-1   LC 2005042108
A reissue of the title first published 1942
In 1940, when the Nazi invasion of Norway reaches their village in the far north, twelve-year-old Peter and his friends use their sleds to transport nine million dollars worth of gold bullion past the German soldiers to the secret harbor where Peter's uncle keeps his ship ready to take the gold for safekeeping in the United States.
"A dramatic reconstruction of an actual happening. . . . Well written." Booklist

Mead, Alice

Crossing the Starlight Bridge. Bradbury Press 1994 122p il $15; pa $4.50 (3-5)   **Fic**
1. Penobscot Indians—Fiction
ISBN 0-02-765950-X; 0-689-80105-X (pa)
LC 93-40978
Nine-year-old Rayanne's life turns upside down when her father leaves and she has to move off the Penobscot reservation and go to live with her grandmother
"Mead deftly establishes a child's point of view with

Mead, Alice—_Continued_

simple and unpretentious language. . . . This is a gentle
and understanding story of a young girl's adjustment to
change." Bull Cent Child Books

Girl of Kosovo. Farrar, Straus & Giroux 2001
113p $16 (5 and up)   **Fic**
1. Kosovo (Serbia)—Fiction
ISBN 0-374-32620-7   LC 00-44239
Also available in paperback from Yearling

Although Zana, an eleven-year-old Albanian girl, experiences the turmoil and violence of the 1999 conflict
in her native Kosovo, she remembers her father's admonition to not let her heart become filled with hate

"Mead writes lucidly and honestly about a child of
war." Horn Book Guide

Junebug. Farrar, Straus & Giroux 1995 101p
$16 (3-5)   **Fic**
1. African Americans—Fiction 2. Sailing—Fiction
ISBN 0-374-33964-3   LC 95-5421
Also available in paperback from Dell

"Junebug approaches his tenth birthday with fear because he knows he'll be forced by the older boys in his
housing project to join a gang. On his birthday, with
luck and persistence, Junebug realizes his secret dream
of one day sailing a boat. The novel contains vivid descriptions of the grim realities of inner-city life but also
demonstrates that strong convictions and warm hearts can
bring about change." Horn Book Guide

Other titles about Junebug are:
Junebug and the Reverend (1998)
Junebug in trouble (2003)

Madame Squidley and Beanie. Farrar Straus
Giroux 2004 137p $16 (3-5)   **Fic**
1. School stories 2. Chronic fatigue syndrome—Fiction 3. Friendship—Fiction 4. Mothers—Fiction
ISBN 0-374-34688-7   LC 2003-48057

Ten-year-old Beanie struggles with the start of a new
school year, being excluded from the fifth grade in-
crowd, and the extra burdens her mother's Chronic Fatigue Syndrome places on her.

"Beanie's friendship with classmate Charles adds texture to this ultimately insightful portrait of a girl and her
family adjusting to a worrisome illness." Booklist

Meddaugh, Susan

Lulu's hat. Houghton Mifflin 2002 74p il $15
(3-5)   **Fic**
1. Magicians—Fiction
ISBN 0-618-15277-6   LC 2001-16787
"Walter Lorraine books"

"Lulu is adopted and thought to be unable to inherit
her family's magic abilities. But when she finds a hat at
the bottom of her magician uncle's truck, it allows her
to do magic after all—even if it's somewhat unpredictable." Horn Book Guide

"With plot twists, cliff-hanger chapter endings, a large
dose of originality, sparkling humor, and even an epilogue, this witty chapter book will hold readers' attention." SLJ

Menotti, Gian Carlo

Amahl and the night visitors; illustrated by
Michèle Lemieux. Morrow 1986 64p il $21 (2-4)
                                             Fic
1. Jesus Christ—Fiction 2. Magi—Fiction
ISBN 0-688-05426-9   LC 84-27196

Relates how a crippled young shepherd comes to accompany the three Kings on their way to pay hommage
to the newborn Jesus

"Some of the pictures, which are dominated by reddish brown, have rich tension and composition, as in the
one of Amahl's mother contemplating theft, or in the
portrait of Melchior describing the Christ child. . . .
There is a great deal to look at, and the story, popular
since the opera's 1951 debut, has sentimental appeal, humor, and some commanding moments." Bull Cent Child
Books

Meyer, Carolyn

Isabel; jewel of Castilla. Scholastic 2000 204p
(Royal diaries) $10.95 (4 and up)   **Fic**
1. Isabella I, Queen of Spain, 1451-1504—Fiction
2. Spain—Fiction
ISBN 0-439-07805-9   LC 99-16805

While waiting anxiously for others to choose a husband for her, Isabella, the future Queen of Spain, keeps
a diary account of her life as a member of the royal family

"The writing flows well and is age appropriate, and
Meyer makes a distinction between history and fiction in
the appended historical notes. A family tree and glossary
of characters are included." Horn Book Guide

Mikaelsen, Ben

Petey. Hyperion Bks. for Children 1998 280p
$15.95; pa $5.99 (5 and up)   **Fic**
1. Cerebral palsy—Fiction 2. Physically handicapped—Fiction 3. Old age—Fiction
ISBN 0-7868-0426-2; 0-7868-1336-9 (pa)
                                      LC 98-10183

In 1922 Petey, who has cerebral palsy, is
misdiagnosed as an idiot and institutionalized; sixty years
later, still in the institution, he befriends a boy and
shares with him the joy of life

"Mikaelsen successfully conveys Petey's strangled attempts to communicate. He captures the slow passage of
time, the historical landscape encompassed. He brings
emotions to the surface and tears to readers' eyes." SLJ

Miles, Miska

Annie and the Old One; illustrated by Peter
Parnall. Little, Brown 1971 44p il lib bdg $16.95;
pa $7.95 (1-4)   **Fic**
1. Navajo Indians—Fiction 2. Death—Fiction
ISBN 0-316-57117-2 (lib bdg); 0-316-57120-2 (pa)
A Newbery Medal honor book, 1972
"An Atlantic Monthy Press book"

"Annie, a young Navajo girl, struggles with the realization that her grandmother, the Old One, must die.
Slowly and painfully, she accepts the fact that she cannot
change the cyclic rhythms of the earth to which the Old
One has been so sensitively attuned." Wis Libr Bull

Miles, Miska—*Continued*

This is "a poignant, understated, rather brave story of a very real child, set against a background of Navajo traditions and contemporary Indian life. Fine expressive drawings match the simplicity of the story." Horn Book

Miller, Kirsten

Kiki Strike; inside the shadow city; [by] Kirsten Miller. 1st U.S. ed. Bloomsbury Children's Books 2006 387p $16.95; $16.95 (5 and up)   **Fic**
1. Mystery fiction 2. New York (N.Y.)—Fiction
ISBN 9781582349602; 1-58234-960-6
LC 2005030945
Life becomes more interesting for Ananka Fishbein when, at the age of twelve, she discovers an underground room in the park across from her New York City apartment and meets a mysterious girl called Kiki Strike who claims that she, too, wants to explore the subterranean world.
"If a 12-year-old can be a hardboiled detective, Ananka Fishbein is one. Her narration is fresh and funny, and the author's unadorned, economical, yet descriptive style carries her character through with verve." SLJ

Mills, Claudia

7 x 9 = trouble! pictures by G. Brian Karas. Farrar, Straus & Giroux 2002 103p il $15 (2-4)
Fic
1. School stories 2. Mathematics—Fiction
ISBN 0-374-36746-9   LC 2001-16028
Third-grader Wilson struggles with his times-tables in order to beat the class deadline
"Mills' sympathetic and detailed treatment of Wilson's travails makes this both a suspenseful and satisfying beginning chapter book." Bull Cent Child Books

Alex Ryan, stop that! Farrar, Straus & Giroux 2003 151p $16 (5 and up)   **Fic**
1. School stories 2. Fathers—Fiction
ISBN 0-374-34655-0   LC 2002-25009
Sequel to Lizzie at last
Seventh-grader Alex Ryan enjoys attracting attention, though he never seems to impress his father, but when his antics cause problems with his would-be girlfriend on a school outing, he has second thoughts about his actions
"Mills has a great ear for middle-school dialogue, and her characters ring true." Booklist

Lizzie at last. Farrar, Straus & Giroux 2000 151p $16 (5 and up)   **Fic**
1. School stories
ISBN 0-374-34659-3   LC 99-47621
Also available in paperback from Hyperion
"Sequel to *Losers, Inc.* and *You're a Brave Man, Julius Zimmerman* gives the title character of the latter novel a minor role, while placing the refreshingly candid Lizzie Archer center stage. Determined to shake off her reputation as a nerd, Lizzie puts on a new face at the start of seventh grade." Publ Wkly
"Mills has all the elements of middle school in place and deftly weaves a story that is both sensitive and humorous." SLJ

Makeovers by Marcia. Farrar, Straus and Giroux 2005 149p $16 (5 and up)   **Fic**
1. Old age—Fiction 2. School stories
ISBN 0-374-34654-2   LC 2004-53248
At the beginning of eighth grade, all Marcia can think about is what nail polish to use, how to lose weight, and whether Alex will ask her to the dance, but after giving makeovers in a nursing home for a school project, she begins to appreciate the value of inner beauty.
"This humorous, appealing tale is realistic, touching, and evenly paced." SLJ

Trading places; [by] Claudia Mills. 1st ed. Farrar, Straus and Giroux 2006 137p $16 (3-5)
Fic
1. Twins—Fiction 2. School stories 3. Family life—Fiction
ISBN 0-374-31798-4   LC 2005-46371
When fifth-grade twins, Amy and Todd, tackle a school project, they also have to cope with issues of friendship at school and problems at home, including their father's unemployment.
"Turnarounds at home and in the classroom, told in the third person from the twins' alternating viewpoints, grow naturally from beautifully drawn characters." Booklist

Milne, A. A. (Alan Alexander)

The complete tales of Winnie-the-Pooh; with decorations by Ernest H. Shepard. Dutton Children's Bks. 1996 344p il $35 (1-4)
Fic
1. Bears—Fiction 2. Animals—Fiction 3. Toys—Fiction
ISBN 0-525-45723-2
A combined edition of Winnie-the-Pooh and The House at Pooh Corner

The House at Pooh Corner; with decorations by Ernest H. Shepard. Dutton c1928 180p il $9.95; pa $4.99 (1-4)   **Fic**
1. Bears—Fiction 2. Animals—Fiction 3. Toys—Fiction
ISBN 0-525-32302-3; 0-14-036122-7 (pa)
First published 1928
"Pooh and Piglet built a house for Eeyore at Pooh Corner. They called it that because it was shorter and sounded better than did Poohanpiglet Corner. Christopher Robin, Rabbit, and other old acquaintances of 'Winnie-the-Pooh' appear, and a new friend, Tigger, is introduced." Carnegie Libr of Pittsburgh
"It is hard to tell what Pooh Bear and his friends would have been without the able assistance of Ernest H. Shepard to see them and picture them so cleverly. . . . They are, and should be, classics." N Y Times Book Rev

Winnie-the-Pooh; illustrated by Ernest H. Shepard, colored by Hilda Scott. Dutton 1974 c1926 161p il $10.99; pa $4.99 (1-4)   **Fic**
1. Bears—Fiction 2. Animals—Fiction 3. Toys—Fiction
ISBN 0-525-44443-2; 0-14-036121-9 (pa)
First published 1926

Milne, A. A. (Alan Alexander)—*Continued*
"The kindly, lovable Pooh is one of an imaginative cast of animal characters which includes Eeyore, the wistfully gloomy donkey, Tigger, Piglet, Kanga, and Roo, all living in a fantasy world presided over by Milne's young son, Christopher Robin. Many of the animals are drawn from figures in Milne's life, though each emerges as a universally recognizable type." Reader's Ency

The world of Pooh; the complete Winnie-the-Pooh and The House at Pooh Corner; with decorations and new illustrations in full color by E. H. Shepard. Dutton 1957 314p il $21.99 (1-4) **Fic**
1. Bears—Fiction 2. Animals—Fiction 3. Toys—Fiction
ISBN 0-525-44447-5
This combined edition of Winnie-the-Pooh and The House at Pooh Corner contains the original black and white "illustrations and eight delightful new full-page pictures printed in lovely soft colors." Publ Wkly

Mitchell, Stephen
The nightingale; by Hans Christian Andersen; retold by Stephen Mitchell; illustrated by Bagram Ibatoulline. Candlewick Press 2002 unp il $17.99 (2-4) **Fic**
1. Andersen, Hans Christian, 1805-1875—Adaptations 2. Fairy tales 3. Nightingales—Fiction
ISBN 0-7636-1521-8 LC 2001-25144
Though the emperor banishes the nightingale in preference of a jeweled mechanical imitation, the little bird remains faithful and returns years later when the emperor is near death and no one else can help him
"This is an elegant piece of bookmaking. Mixed-media illustrations (ink, gouache, watercolor) based on Chinese art and costume are rendered in a ceremonial, fairy-tale style." Bull Cent Child Books

Mohr, Nicholasa
Going home. Dial Bks. for Young Readers 1986 192p pa $4.95 hardcover o.p. (4-6) **Fic**
1. Puerto Ricans—New York (N.Y.)—Fiction 2. Puerto Rico—Fiction
ISBN 0-14-130644-0 (pa) LC 85-20621
Feeling like an outsider when she visits her relatives in Puerto Rico for the first time, eleven-year-old Felita tries to come to terms with the heritage she always took for granted
"This is a convincing story that captures the universality of preteen relationships." Rochman. Against borders
Another title about Felita is:
Felita (1979)

Montgomery, L. M. (Lucy Maud)
Anne of Green Gables (5 and up) **Fic**
1. Adoption—Fiction 2. Prince Edward Island—Fiction
Available from various publishers
First published 1908 by Page

"Daily doings and dreams from her 10th to 17th year of a lively, imaginative child, adopted by an elderly brother and sister on a Prince Edward Island farm." N Y State Libr
Other titles about Anne are:
Anne of Avonlea (1909)
Anne of Ingleside (1939)
Anne of the island (1915)
Anne of Windy Poplars (1936)
Anne's house of dreams (1917)

Moranville, Sharelle Byars
Over the river. Holt & Co. 2002 228p $16.95 (5 and up) **Fic**
1. Family life—Fiction 2. Illinois—Fiction
ISBN 0-8050-7049-4 LC 2002-24308
Also available in paperback from Dell
In 1947, after the war, Willa Mae's father returns to the Illinois town where she has lived with her maternal grandparents for the last five of her eleven years, and Willa Mae finds herself struggling to understand old family tensions and secrets
"Suspense builds and the troubling secrets are revealed, but there's no tidy resolution. . . . This is the best kind of historical fiction, where details of time and place are not a picturesque backdrop but an integral part of the story." Booklist

Morey, Walt
Gentle Ben; illustrated by John Schoenherr. Dutton 1965 191p il pa $4.99 hardcover o.p. (5 and up) **Fic**
1. Bears—Fiction 2. Alaska—Fiction
ISBN 0-14-036035-2 (pa)
Set in Alaska before statehood, this is the story of 13-year-old Mark Anderson who befriends a huge brown bear which has been chained in a shed since it was a cub. Finally Mark's father buys the bear, but Orca City's inhabitants eventually insist that the animal, named Ben, be shipped to an uninhabited island. However, the friendship of Mark and Ben endures
The author "has written a vivid chronicle of Alaska, its people and places, challenges and beauties. Told with a simplicity and dignity which befits its characters, human and animal, {it} is a memorable reading experience." SLJ

Morgan, Clay
The boy who spoke dog. Dutton Children's Bks. 2003 166p $15.99 (5 and up) **Fic**
1. Survival after airplane accidents, shipwrecks, etc.—Fiction 2. Dogs—Fiction 3. Orphans—Fiction 4. New Zealand—Fiction
ISBN 0-525-47159-6 LC 2003-45223
After being marooned on an island near New Zealand, Jack, an orphaned cabin boy from San Francisco, becomes allied with a group of dogs who protect the local sheep from wild dogs
"Morgan delivers an unusual, engrossing novel, using vivid language to project the reader into the sounds and smells of the animal world as he examines the ancient bonds between humans and dogs." Booklist

Morgan, Nicola

Chicken friend; [by] Nicola Morgan. 1st U.S. ed. Candlewick Press 2005 148p $15.99 (5 and up)   **Fic**
1. Diabetes—Fiction 2. Country life—Fiction 3. Friendship—Fiction 4. Great Britain—Fiction
ISBN 0-7636-2735-6   LC 2004-54608

When her parents decide to move their family to the English countryside, homeschool their children, and raise chickens, Becca tries to make friends with her new neighbors by hiding her diabetes and throwing a twelfth birthday party for herself.

"The girl is believable and likable as both character and narrator, which turns an apparently simple story into one that is funny, insightful, and moving." SLJ

Morgenstern, Susie Hoch

A book of coupons; by Susie Morgenstern; illustrated by Serge Bloch; translated by Gill Rosner. Viking 2001 62p il $12.99 (3-5)   **Fic**
1. Teachers—Fiction 2. School stories
ISBN 0-670-89970-4   LC 00-11940
Original French edition, 1999

Elderly Monsieur Noel, the very unconventional new teacher, gives coupon books for such things as dancing in class and sleeping late, which are bound to get him in trouble with the military discipline of Principal Incarnation Perez

"Morgenstern's witty and poignant tribute to great teachers everywhere proclaims what education should be about. Her message may be pointed, but no reader will be unmoved." Horn Book Guide

Morpurgo, Michael

Arthur, high king of Britain; illustrated by Michael Foreman. Harcourt Brace & Co. 1995 137p il $22 (4 and up)   **Fic**
1. Arthur, King—Fiction 2. Arthurian romances
ISBN 0-15-200080-1   LC 93-33620
First published 1994 in the United Kingdom

A twelve-year-old boy comes across Arthur Pendragon, who has just awakened from his long sleep beneath the earth, and hears from him some of the exciting stories of his past

The author "follows in a time-honored tradition of adaptation and abridgment, but he never neglects the integrity and authenticity of the stories he tells. . . . [Foreman's] soft watercolor scenes are pricked with a cool freshness; blues, greens, golds, and purples shimmer together." Bull Cent Child Books

Kensuke's kingdom. Scholastic Press 2003 c1999 164p $16.95 (4 and up)   **Fic**
1. Survival after airplane accidents, shipwrecks, etc.—Fiction
ISBN 0-439-38202-5   LC 2002-9078
First published 1999 in the United Kingdom

When Michael is swept off his family's yacht, he washes up on a desert island, where he struggles to survive—until he finds he is not alone

This is "highly readable. . . . The end is bittersweet but believable, and the epilogue is a sad commentary on the long-lasting effects of war." Booklist

Waiting for Anya. Viking 1991 c1990 172p $14.99; pa $4.99 (5 and up)   **Fic**
1. World War, 1939-1945—Fiction 2. Jews—Fiction 3. France—Fiction
ISBN 0-670-83735-0; 0-14-038431-6 (pa)
LC 90-50560
First published 1990 in the United Kingdom

"A World War II adventure story set in Vichy, France, this centers on a young shepherd, Jo, who becomes involved in smuggling Jewish children across the border from his mountain village to Spain. Morpurgo has injected the basic conventions of heroism and villainy with some complexities of character. . . . Independent readers will appreciate the simple, clear style and fast-paced plot of the book, which will also hold up well in group read-alouds, commanding attention to ethics as well as action." Bull Cent Child Books

Moss, Marissa

Amelia's 6th-grade notebook; [by] Marissa Moss. 1st ed. Simon & Schuster Books for Young Readers 2005 unp il $9.95 (4-6)   **Fic**
1. School stories
ISBN 0-689-87040-X   LC 2004-45309
"A Paula Wiseman book"

Problems arise for Amelia when she starts sixth grade at the same middle school where her older sister Cleo is an eighth-grader, and she gets the school's meanest teacher for three of her classes.

"Both insightful and entertaining, Amelia's first-person narrative rings true. . . . [This] features a handwritten format; colorful, cartoonlike illustrations; and charming doodles with descriptive asides." Booklist

Other titles about Amelia are:
The all-new Amelia (1999)
Amelia hits the road (1997)
Amelia lends a hand (2002)
Amelia takes command (1998)
Amelia works it out (2000)
Amelia writes again (1996)
Amelia's book of notes & note passing (2006)
Amelia's boredom survival guide (1999)
Amelia's bully survival guide (1998)
Amelia's family ties (2000)
Amelia's longest, biggest, most-fights-ever family reunion (2006)
Amelia's most unforgettable embarrassing moments (2005)
Amelia's notebook (1995)
Luv, Amelia luv, Nadia (1999)
Oh boy, Amelia! (2001)

Murray, Martine

The slightly true story of Cedar B. Hartley; (who planned to live an unusual life). Levine Bks. 2003 233p $15.95 (5 and up)   **Fic**
1. Acrobats and acrobatics—Fiction 2. Friendship—Fiction 3. Australia—Fiction
ISBN 0-439-48622-X   LC 2002-12113

When twelve-year-old Cedar loses her dog, it sets off a chain of events leading her to find a new friend, become an acrobat, and learn some bitter-sweet truths about family, community, and herself

"With unique and fully realized supporting characters

Murray, Martine—*Continued*

and a multiethnic, urban environment, this story vibrates with authenticity. . . . Small, wonderfully quirky line drawings accompany this breezy yet serious novel." SLJ

Mwangi, Meja

The Mzungu boy. House of Anansi Press 2005 150p $15.95 (5 and up)　　　　　　　　**Fic**

1. Kenya—Fiction 2. Friendship—Fiction 3. Race relations—Fiction

ISBN 0-88899-653-5; 0-88899-664-0 (pa)

"A Groundwood book"

First published 1990 in Canada with title: Little white man

"A story set in Kenya during the early 1950s. . . . Much of the land at this time was held by European settlers, and native Kenyans were relegated to working as tenant farmers under exploitative and demeaning conditions. Against this backdrop, the author created this story of a friendship between two boys, Nigel, white and British, grandson of a brutal landowner." Booklist

"The pace is quick, and the story is exciting, action-packed, and full of detail. . . . This is a riveting tale." SLJ

Myers, Laurie

Lewis and Clark and me; a dog's tale; illustrations by Michael Dooling. Holt & Co. 2002 64p il $16.95 (3-6)　　　　　　　　**Fic**

1. Lewis, Meriwether, 1774-1809—Fiction 2. Clark, William, 1770-1838—Fiction 3. Lewis and Clark Expedition (1804-1806)—Fiction 4. Dogs—Fiction

ISBN 0-8050-6368-4　　　　　　LC 00-47298

Seaman, Meriwether Lewis's Newfoundland dog, describes Lewis and Clark's expedition, which he accompanied from St. Louis to the Pacific Ocean

"Myers is a dog lover, and that respect comes through in the dignified portrayal of Seaman. Attractive, realistic paintings illustrate the book, giving a feel for the period and, most importantly, a visual personality to Seaman." SLJ

Includes bibliographical references

Myers, Walter Dean

The journal of Joshua Loper; a black cowboy. Scholastic 1999 158p il (My name is America) $10.95 (5 and up)　　　　　　　　**Fic**

1. Cowhands—Fiction 2. African Americans—Fiction 3. West (U.S.)—Fiction

ISBN 0-590-02691-7　　　　　　LC 98-18661

In 1871 Joshua Loper, a sixteen-year-old black cowboy, records in his journal his experiences while making his first cattle drive under an unsympathetic trail boss

"With characteristic research, sensitivity, and insight, Myers offers a lively, youthful portrait of the life and times of this black cowboy." SLJ

The journal of Scott Pendleton Collins; a World War II soldier. Scholastic 1999 140p il (My name is America) $10.95 (5 and up)　　　　　　**Fic**

1. World War, 1939-1945—Fiction

ISBN 0-439-05013-8　　　　　　LC 99-13615

A seventeen-year-old soldier from central Virginia records his experiences in a journal as his regiment takes part in the D-Day invasion of Normandy and subsequent battles to liberate France

"This brief novel presents an accurate depiction of the horror of battle. The narrative voice is engaging and believable." SLJ

Three swords for Granada; illustrated by John Speirs. Holiday House 2002 154p il $15.95 (3-6)
　　　　　　　　Fic

1. Cats—Fiction 2. Dogs—Fiction 3. Fantasy fiction 4. Spain—Fiction

ISBN 0-8234-1676-3　　　　　　LC 2001-59357

In 1420 Spain, three young cat friends join the warrior cats as they struggle to save their beloved Granada from the vicious dogs of the Fidorean Guard

"The snappy dialogue, flashing swords, and daring action, as well as the charming ink-and-wash drawings, will appeal to readers who enjoy high adventure laced with a touch of whimsy." SLJ

Myracle, Lauren

Eleven. Dutton Children's Books 2004 201p $16.99 (4 and up)　　　　　　　　**Fic**

1. Friendship—Fiction 2. Family life—Fiction

ISBN 0-525-47165-0　　　　　　LC 2003-49076

The year between turning eleven and turning twelve bring many changes for Winnie and her friends.

"The inclusion of details about the everyday lives of these girls . . . will make this novel enjoyable, even for reluctant readers. However, it's the book's occasional revelation of harder truths that lifts it out of the ordinary." SLJ

Nagda, Ann Whitehead

Dear Whiskers; illustrated by Stephanie Roth. Holiday House 2000 75p il $15.95 (2-4)
　　　　　　　　Fic

1. School stories 2. Immigrants—Fiction 3. Friendship—Fiction

ISBN 0-8234-1495-7　　　　　　LC 00-35013

Fourth-grader Jenny is discouraged when her second grade penpal turns out to be a new student from Saudi Arabia who does not speak English very well, but as she works with her they slowly become friends

"Vividly re-creating classroom culture, Nagda portrays the seesawing emotions of schoolchildren with empathy and finesse. Stephanie Roth's expressive illustrations capture the tone and characterization as well as the incidents of the story." Booklist

Meow means mischief; illustrated by Stephanie Roth. Holiday House 2003 92p il $15.95 (2-4)
　　　　　　　　Fic

1. Cats—Fiction 2. Grandparents—Fiction 3. East Indians—United States—Fiction

ISBN 0-8234-1786-7　　　　　　LC 2002-192208

Companion volume to Dear Whiskers

A stray kitten turns out to be the perfect way to help Rana make friends in her new school and to feel more comfortable with her grandparents, who are visiting from India while her parents are away

Nagda, Ann Whitehead—*Continued*

"Nagda clearly understands the problems and concerns of middle-grade children, and her situations and upbeat solutions ring true. Young readers will enjoy the humor." Booklist

Naidoo, Beverley

Journey to Jo'burg; a South African story; illustrations by Eric Velasquez. Lippincott 1986 80p il lib bdg $16.89; pa $4.99 (5 and up)

Fic

1. South Africa—Race relations—Fiction
ISBN 0-397-32169-4 (lib bdg); 0-06-440237-1 (pa)

LC 85-45508

"This touching novel graphically depicts the plight of Africans living in the horror of South Africa. Thirteen-year-old Maledi and her 9-year-old brother leave their small village, take the perilous journey to the city, and encounter, firsthand, the painful struggle for justice, freedom, and dignity in the 'City of Gold.' A provocative story with a message readers will long remember." Soc Educ

Followed by Chain of fire (1990)

No turning back; a novel of South Africa. HarperCollins Pubs. 1997 c1995 189p lib bdg $15.89 hardcover o.p.; pa $5.99 (5 and up)

Fic

1. Runaway children—Fiction 2. South Africa—Fiction
ISBN 0-06-027506-5 (lib bdg); 0-06-440749-7 (pa)

LC 96-28980

First published 1995 in the United Kingdom

When the abuse at home becomes too much for twelve-year-old Sipho, he runs away to the streets of Johannesburg and learns to survive in the post-apartheid world

"Charged with a rhythm that begins beating on the first page and carries through until the last, Naidoo's novel is a can't-put-it-down account." Horn Book

The other side of truth. HarperCollins Pubs. 2001 c2000 252p $16.99; lib bdg $17.89; pa $5.99 (5 and up)

Fic

1. Africans—Fiction 2. London (England)—Fiction
3. Refugees—Fiction 4. Nigeria—Fiction
ISBN 0-06-029628-3; 0-06-029629-1 (lib bdg); 0-06-441002-1 (pa)

LC 00-54112

First published 2000 in the United Kingdom

Smuggled out of Nigeria after their mother's murder, Sade and her younger brother are abandoned in London when their uncle fails to meet them at the airport and they are fearful of their new surroundings and of what may have happened to their journalist father back in Nigeria

"Part survival adventure, part docudrama, the narrative stays true to Sade's viewpoint. . . . This powerful novel brings the news images very close." Booklist

Followed by Web of lies (2006)

Namioka, Lensey

Yang the youngest and his terrible ear; illustrated by Kees de Kiefte. Little, Brown 1992 134p il pa $4.50 o.p. (4-6)

Fic

1. Chinese—United States—Fiction 2. Family life—Fiction
ISBN 0-440-40917-9 (pa)

LC 91-30345

"Joy Street books"

Recently arrived in Seattle from China, musically untalented Yingtao is faced with giving a violin performance to attract new students for his father when he would rather be working on friendships and playing baseball

"Namioka explores issues of diversity, self-realization, friendship, and duty with sensitivity and a great deal of humor." Horn Book

Other titles about the Yang family are:
Yang the eldest and his odd jobs (2000)
Yang the second and her secret admirers (1998)
Yang the third and her impossible family (1995)

Napoli, Donna Jo

The king of Mulberry Street; [by] Donna Jo Napoli. Wendy Lamb Books 2005 245p $15.95; lib bdg $17.99 (5 and up)

Fic

1. Immigrants—Fiction 2. Italian Americans—Fiction
3. Jews—Fiction
ISBN 0-385-74653-9; 0-385-90890-3 (lib bdg)

LC 2004-30860

In 1892, Dom, a nine-year old Jewish stowaway from Naples, Italy, arrives in New York and must learn to survive the perils of street life in the big city.

"The characters are drawn with depth . . . and the unsentimental story is honest about the grinding poverty and the prejudice among various immigrant groups." Booklist

The prince of the pond; otherwise known as De Fawg Pin; illustrated by Judy Schachner. Dutton Children's Bks. 1992 151p il $15.99; pa $4.99 (4-6)

Fic

1. Frogs—Fiction
ISBN 0-525-44976-0; 0-14-037151-6 (pa)

LC 91-40340

This story based on the frog prince motif is "told from the point of view of Jade, a female frog. . . . Pin (as the Prince calls himself, hampered in his speech by a long, fat tongue attached at the front of his mouth) is handsome, but strangely ignorant of everything . . . so Jade must teach him the ropes. . . . Eventually, when the opportunity of kissing a princess represents itself, Pin leaps at it and disappears from Jade's life forever." Booklist

"An animal fantasy that fairy tale readers will relish. . . . Schachner's numerous ink-and-wash drawings go far in supporting the characterization." Bull Cent Child Books

Sly the Sleuth and the pet mysteries; by Donna Jo Napoli and Robert Furrow; illustrated by Heather Maione. Dial Books for Young Readers 2005 96p il $15.99 (2-4)

Fic

1. Mystery fiction 2. Pets—Fiction
ISBN 0-8037-2993-6

LC 2003-24090

Contents: Case #1: Sly and the fat cat; Case #2: Sly and the Wish Fish; Case #3: Sly and the third case

Napoli, Donna Jo—*Continued*

Sly the Sleuth, also known as Sylvia, solves three mysteries for her friends and neighbors, all involving pets, through her detective agency, Sleuth for Hire.

"The stories are easy to read and engaging, the pen-and-ink illustrations convey the light tone of the adventures, and Sly's first-person narration is convincing." Horn Book Guide

Another title about Sly the Sleuth is:
Sly the Sleuth and the sports mysteries (2006)

Stones in water. Dutton Children's Bks. 1997 209p pa $5.99 hardcover o.p. (5 and up)   **Fic**
1. World War, 1939-1945—Fiction
ISBN 0-14-130600-9 (pa); 0-525-45842-5 (hc)
LC 97-14253

After being taken by German soldiers from a local movie theater along with other Italian boys including his Jewish friend, Roberto is forced to work in Germany, escapes into the Ukrainian winter, before desperately trying to make his way back home to Venice

This is a "gripping, meticulously researched story (loosely based on the life of an actual survivor)." Publ Wkly

Naylor, Phyllis Reynolds

The agony of Alice. Atheneum Pubs. 1985 131p $16; pa $4.99 (5 and up)   **Fic**
1. Teachers—Fiction 2. School stories
ISBN 0-689-31143-5; 0-689-81672-3 (pa)
LC 85-7957

Also available titles about Alice in adolescence for older readers, and prequels about Alice for younger readers

Eleven-year-old, motherless Alice decides she needs a gorgeous role model who does everything right; and when placed in homely Mrs. Plotkin's class she is greatly disappointed until she discovers it's what people are inside that counts

"The lively style exhibits a deft touch at capturing the essence of an endearing heroine growing up without a mother." SLJ

Other titles about Alice are:
Achingly Alice (1998)
Alice in April (1993)
Alice in lace (1996)
Alice in rapture, sort of (1989)
Alice in-between (1994)
Alice on the outside (1999)
Alice the brave (1995)
All but Alice (1992)
The grooming of Alice (2000)
Outrageously Alice (1997)
Patiently Alice (2003)
Reluctantly Alice (1991)
Simply Alice (2002)

The fear place. Atheneum Pubs. 1994 118p pa $4.99 hardcover o.p. (5 and up)   **Fic**
1. Brothers—Fiction 2. Pumas—Fiction 3. Camping—Fiction
ISBN 0-689-80442-3 (pa)   LC 93-38891

When he and his older brother Gordon are left camping alone in the Rocky Mountains, twelve-year-old Doug faces his fear of heights and his feelings about Gordon—with the help of a cougar

This is "a solid action story, tense and involving. . . . A satisfying wilderness adventure." Publ Wkly

The grand escape; illustrated by Alan Daniel. Atheneum Pubs. 1993 148p il $16.95 o.p.; pa $5.50 (4-6)   **Fic**
1. Cats—Fiction 2. Adventure fiction
ISBN 0-689-31722-0; 0-689-87407-3 (pa)
LC 91-40816

After years of being strictly house cats, Marco and Polo escape into the wonderful, but dangerous outside world and are sent on three challenging adventures by a group of cats known as the Club of Mysteries

"While Naylor's feline explorers are amusing and lovable, their behavior is always catlike, and their interpretation of human foibles is often hilarious." Booklist

Other titles Marco and Polo are:
Carlotta's kittens and the Club of Mysteries (2000)
The healing of Texas Jake (1997)
Polo's mother (2005)

Peril in the Bessledorf Parachute Factory. Atheneum Bks. for Young Readers 2000 c1999 148p $16 (4-6)   **Fic**
ISBN 0-689-82539-0   LC 98-36606
"A Jean Karl book"

Bernie's attempt to marry off his sister Delores results in mystery and near-disaster at the Bessledorf Parachute Factory

"The humor is right on target for middle-graders." Booklist

Other titles in the Bessledorf series are:
Bernie Magruder & the bats in the belfry (2003)
The bomb in the Bessledorf bus depot (1996)
The face in the Bessledorf funeral parlor (1993)
The treasure of Bessledorf Hill (1997)

Roxie and the Hooligans; with illustrations by Alexandra Boiger. Atheneum Books for Young Readers 2006 115p il $15.95 (3-5)   **Fic**
1. Adventure fiction
ISBN 1-4169-0243-0   LC 2004-24645
"Ginee Seo books."

Roxie Warbler, the niece of a famous explorer, follows Uncle Dangerfoot's advice on how to survive any crisis when she becomes stranded on an island with a gang of school bullies and a pair of murderous bank robbers.

This "mixes fantasy, absurdity, and reality in a way that never diminishes or overwhelms the story's heart. Boiger's black-and-white illustrations catch the energy of Naylor's over-the-top yet sympathetically portrayed characters." Booklist

Shiloh. Atheneum Pubs. 1991 144p $15; pa $5.50 (4-6)   **Fic**
1. Dogs—Fiction 2. West Virginia—Fiction
ISBN 0-689-31614-3; 0-689-83583-3 (pa)
LC 90-603

Also available Shiloh trilogy as a boxed set $35; pa $14.99 (ISBN 0-689-82327-4; 0-689-01525-9 pa

Awarded the Newbery Medal, 1992

Naylor, Phyllis Reynolds—*Continued*
When he finds a lost beagle in the hills behind his West Virginia home, Marty tries to hide it from his family and the dog's real owner, a mean-spirited man known to shoot deer out of season and to mistreat his dogs

"A credible plot and characters, a well-drawn setting, and nicely paced narration combine in a story that leaves the reader feeling good." Horn Book

Other titles about Shiloh are:
Saving Shiloh (1997)
Shiloh season (1996)

Starting with Alice. Atheneum Bks. for Young Readers 2002 181p $15.95 (3-6)   **Fic**
1. Family life—Fiction 2. Friendship—Fiction 3. School stories
ISBN 0-689-84395-X   LC 2001-53610
This, the first of three prequels to the series about Alice, is written for younger readers. After she, her older brother, and their father move from Chicago to Maryland, Alice has trouble fitting into her new third grade class, but with the help of some new friends and her own unique outlook, she survives

"New characters and realistic third-grade situations are explored, but young Alice's humor and earnestness are refreshingly the same." Horn Book

Other prequels to the Alice series are:
Alice in Blunderland (2003)
Lovingly Alice (2004)

Neale, Jonathan
Himalaya. Houghton Mifflin 2004 153p $16 (5 and up)   **Fic**
1. Mountaineering—Fiction 2. Wilderness survival—Fiction 3. Siblings—Fiction 4. Himalaya Mountains—Fiction
ISBN 0-618-41200-X   LC 2004-973
In alternating chapters, twelve-year-old Orrie and her older brother Jack tell the story of a doomed mountain-climbing expedition in which they, their younger brother, their divorced father, and his girlfriend attempt to climb Island Peak in Nepal.

"The adventure is true enough to make readers sweat, and the cultural details are convincingly integrated. The description of the trek . . . is accurate in many details." SLJ

Another title about Orrie and Jack is:
Lost at sea (2002)

Nelson, Theresa
And one for all. Orchard Bks. 1989 182p $16.95 (5 and up)   **Fic**
1. Vietnam War, 1961-1975—Fiction 2. Siblings—Fiction
ISBN 0-531-05804-2   LC 88-22490
Also available in paperback from Dell
"A Richard Jackson book"
Geraldine's close relationship with her older brother Wing and his friend Sam changes when Wing joins the Marines and Sam leaves for Washington to join a peace march

"Plot, dialogue, and setting are effortlessly authentic and never overwhelmed by the theme. . . . Smoothly written and easily read, this also manages to challenge

assumptions in a thought-provoking probe of the past." Bull Cent Child Books

Ruby electric; a novel. Atheneum Bks. for Young Readers 2003 264p $16.95 (5 and up)
   Fic
1. Fathers—Fiction 2. Siblings—Fiction 3. Authorship—Fiction 4. California—Fiction
ISBN 0-689-83852-2   LC 2002-8034
"A Richard Jackson book"
Twelve-year-old Ruby Miller, movie buff and aspiring screen writer, tries to resolve the mysteries surrounding her little brother's stuffed woolly mammoth and their father's five year absence

"Ruby's voice is electric, and she is an unforgettable character with courage, a cause, and imagination." Booklist

Nesbit, E. (Edith)
The enchanted castle; illustrated by Paul O. Zelinsky; afterword by Peter Glassman. Morrow Junior Bks. 1992 292p il lib bdg $22.95 (4-6)
   Fic
1. Fantasy fiction 2. Great Britain—Fiction
ISBN 0-688-05435-8   LC 91-46267
First published 1907 in the United Kingdom; first United States edition 1908 by Harper & Brothers

Four English children find a wonderful world of magic through an enchanted wishing ring

"With fine, cross-hatched lines tinted in luminous colors, Zelinsky's artwork is as lively as the story and very much of the period." Booklist

Five children and it; illustrated by Paul O. Zelinsky. Morrow 1999 242p il $22 (4-6)
   Fic
1. Fantasy fiction 2. Great Britain—Fiction
ISBN 0-688-13545-5   LC 98-50391
Also available in paperback from Puffin Bks.
"Books of Wonder"
First published 1902 in the United Kingdom; first United States edition 1905 by Dodd, Mead & Co.

When four brothers and sisters discover a Psammead, or sand-fairy, in the gravel pit near the country house where they are staying, they have no way of knowing all the adventures its wish-granting will bring them

This "features twelve appropriately Edwardian watercolor paintings by Zelinsky." Horn Book

Other titles in this series are:
The Phoenix and the carpet (1904)
The story of the amulet (1907)

The railway children; with illustrations by C.E. Brock; afterword by Peter Glassman. SeaStar Books 2005 225p il $14.95 (4-6)   **Fic**
1. Family life—Fiction 2. Railroads—Fiction 3. Great Britain—Fiction
ISBN 1-58717-279-8
"A Peter Glassman book"
A reissue of the title first published 1906 by MacMillan

When their father is sent away to prison, three London children move to the country where they keep busy pre-

Nesbit, E. (Edith)—*Continued*

venting accidents on the nearby railway, making many new friends, and generally learning a good deal about themselves

Neufeld, John

Almost a hero. Atheneum Bks. for Young Readers 1995 147p $15; pa $3.99 (5 and up)

Fic

1. Child abuse—Fiction 2. Homeless persons—Fiction 3. Death—Fiction

ISBN 0-689-31971-1; 0-689-80740-6 (pa)

LC 94-12785

"Ben Derby is a 12-year-old whose teacher has assigned to him a week of charitable work during spring break. Ben works at a day care center for homeless children, one of whom Ben thinks he sees being abused in the grocery store. When 'the system' is too cautious in its response, Ben and his friends plan a bold rescue of the child." Booklist

"Ben ponders some difficult questions in ways that young readers, who may face similar moral challenges themselves, will relate to." Bull Cent Child Books

Neville, Emily Cheney

It's like this, Cat; [by] Emily Neville; pictures by Emil Weiss. Harper & Row 1963 180p il lib bdg $15.89; pa $3.95 (5 and up)   **Fic**

1. Cats—Fiction 2. New York (N.Y.)—Fiction

ISBN 0-06-024391-0 (lib bdg); 0-06-440073-5 (pa)

Awarded the Newbery Medal, 1964

This is the "story of a fourteen-year-old growing up in the neighborhood of Gramercy Park in New York City. He tells of life in the city and his relationships with his parents, neighbors, and friends. It is his pet, a stray tom cat whom he adopts, that brings him two new friends, one a troubled boy and the other his first girl." Wis Libr Bull

"A story told with a great amount of insight into human relationships. . . . This all provides a wonderfully real picture of a city boy's outlets and of one likable adolescent's inner feelings. An exceedingly fresh, honest, and well-rounded piece of writing." Horn Book

Newman, Lesléa

Hachiko waits; illustrated by Machiyo Kodaira. 1st ed. H. Holt 2004 96p il $15.95 (3-5)

Fic

1. Dogs—Fiction 2. Japan—Fiction

ISBN 0-8050-7336-1   LC 2003-68589

Professor Ueno's loyal Akita, Hachiko, waits for him at the train station every afternoon, and even after the professor has a fatal heart attack while at work, Hachiko faithfully continues to await his return until the day the dog dies. Based on a true story.

"Yasuo brings a childhood focus to the poignant story . . . and Kodaira's soft, black-and-white sketches help to break up the chapters for younger readers and add interest to the story." Booklist

Newman, Robert

The case of the Baker Street Irregular; a Sherlock Holmes story. Atheneum Pubs. 1978 216p pa $4.95 hardcover o.p. (5 and up)

Fic

1. Mystery fiction 2. London (England)—Fiction

ISBN 0-689-70766-5   LC 77-15463

Also available in hardcover from P. Smith

Brought to London under mysterious circumstances by his tutor, young Andrew Tillett seeks the help of Sherlock Holmes when his tutor is kidnapped and he himself is threatened with the same fate

"The author is as urbane and fluent as the legendary Mr. Holmes; he seems thoroughly comfortable with the characters, the atmosphere, and the turn-of-the century London setting; and the story moves along with unflagging energy." Horn Book

Nichol, Barbara

Beethoven lives upstairs; illustrated by Scott Cameron. Orchard Bks. 1994 c1993 unp il $15.95; pa $5.95 (3-5)   **Fic**

1. Beethoven, Ludwig van, 1770-1827—Fiction 2. Uncles—Fiction

ISBN 0-531-06828-5; 0-531-7118-9 (pa)

LC 93-5774

First published 1993 in Canada

The letters that ten-year-old Christoph and his uncle exchange show how Christoph's feelings for Mr. Beethoven, the eccentric boarder that shares his house, change for anger and embarrassment to compassion and admiration

"The oil pictures are rich and dark, with glowing, candlelit interiors, they define the period while giving a strong sense of character. But it's the story that holds you, as tension builds until the triumphant first performance of the Ninth." Booklist

Nixon, Joan Lowery

Aggie's home. Delacorte Press 1998 116p il (Orphan train children) $9.95 (3-5)   **Fic**

1. Orphans—Fiction 2. Women—Suffrage—Fiction

ISBN 0-385-32295-X   LC 97-47760

A clumsy and unattractive twelve-year-old, Aggie is sure no one will want to adopt her when she rides the orphan train out west, but when she meets the eccentric Bradon family she begins to have some hope. Includes historical information about orphan trains and the woman's suffrage movement

"Readers will enjoy watching this spirited child stick up for herself despite the consequences." SLJ

Other titles in the Orphan train children series are:
David's search (1998)
Lucy's wish (1998)
Will's choice (1998)

A family apart. Stevens, G. 2000 162p il $21.27 (5 and up)   **Fic**

1. Foster home care—Fiction

ISBN 0-8368-2638-8   LC 99-55932

Also available in paperback from Bantam Bks.

A reissue of the title first published 1987 by Bantam Bks.

Nixon, Joan Lowery—*Continued*

The first volume in the "Orphan train" series is set in 1860. When their widowed mother can no longer support them, Frances Kelley and her five brothers and sisters are sent on the orphan train by the Children's Aid Society of New York City to live with farm families in Missouri

"The plot is rational and well paced; the characters are real and believable; the time setting important to U.S. history, and the values all that anyone could ask for." Voice Youth Advocates

Other titles in the Orphan train series are:

Caught in the act (1988)

Circle of love (1997)

A dangerous promise (1994)

In the face of danger (1988)

Keeping secrets (1995)

A place to belong (1989)

Laugh till you cry; . Delacorte Press 2004 99p $15.95; lib bdg $17.99 (5 and up) **Fic**

1. Moving—Fiction 2. Family life—Fiction 3. School stories

ISBN 0-385-73027-6; 0-385-90186-0 (lib bdg)

LC 2004-9557

Thirteen years old and a budding comedian, Cody has little to laugh about after he and his mother move from California to Texas to help his sick grandmother and he finds himself framed by his jealous cousin for calling in bomb threats to their school.

"The pacing of the story, Cody's humorous side, and the book's length make this mystery ideal for reluctant readers." SLJ

Nordin, Sofia

In the wild; translated by Maria Lundin. House of Anansi Press 2005 115p $15.95; pa $6.95 (4 and up) **Fic**

1. Bullies—Fiction 2. Wilderness survival—Fiction

ISBN 0-88899-648-9; 0-88899-663-2 (pa)

Originally published in Swedish

"Amanda, the target of harassment by her classmates, is on an adventure trip with her sixth-grade class. When she and one of the bullies, Philip, are separated from the group and become lost in the wilderness, they are forced to work together to survive. . . . Nordin realistically depicts the psychological effects of relentless hounding. . . . The translation is smooth and the text flows naturally. . . . Well written, and a lightning-fast read." SLJ

Norton, Mary

Bed-knob and broomstick; illustrated by Erik Blegvad. Harcourt 2000 227p il $17; pa $6 (3-6) **Fic**

1. Fantasy fiction 2. Witchcraft—Fiction

ISBN 0-15-202450-6; 0-15-202456-5 (pa)

LC 99-89153

"An Odyssey/Harcourt young classic"

A combined edition of The magic bed-knob (1943) and Bonfires and broomsticks (1947); present title is a reissue of the 1957 edition

With the powers they acquire from a spinster who is studying to be a witch, three English children have a series of exciting and perilous adventures traveling on a flying bed that takes them to a London police station, a tropical island, and back in time to the seventeenth century

The borrowers; foreword by Leonard S. Marcus; interior illustrations by Diana Stanley. Fiftieth Anniversary ed. Harcourt 2003 148p il $19.95 (3-6) **Fic**

1. Fantasy fiction

ISBN 0-15-204928-2 LC 2003-4406

A newly illustrated edition of the title first published 1952 in the United Kingdom; first United States edition 1953

Miniature people who live in an old country house by borrowing things from the humans are forced to emigrate from their home under the clock. Includes a letter and a sketch of Homily and Arrietty by the author

"A remarkably consistent and sensitively written fantasy." Bookmark

Other titles about the Borrowers are:

The Borrowers afield (1955)

The Borrowers afloat (1959)

The Borrowers aloft (1961)

The Borrowers avenged (1982)

O'Brien, Robert C.

Mrs. Frisby and the rats of NIMH; illustrated by Zena Bernstein. Atheneum Pubs. 1971 223p il lib bdg $18; pa $5.99 (4 and up) **Fic**

1. Mice—Fiction 2. Rats—Fiction

ISBN 0-689-20651-8 (lib bdg); 0-689-71068-2 (pa)

Awarded the Newbery Medal, 1972

"Mrs. Frisby, a widowed mouse, is directed by an owl to consult with the rats that live under the rosebush about her problem of moving her sick son from the family's endangered home. Upon entering the rats' quarters, Mrs. Frisby discovers to her astonishment that the rats are not ordinary rodents, but highly intelligent creatures that escaped from an NIMH laboratory after being taught to read." Booklist

"The story is fresh and ingenious, the style witty, and the plot both hilarious and convincing." Saturday Rev

Followed by Racso and the rats of NIMH by Jane Leslie Conly

O'Connor, Barbara

Fame and glory in Freedom, Georgia. Frances Foster Bks./Farrar, Straus & Giroux 2003 104p $16 (4 and up) **Fic**

1. School stories 2. Contests—Fiction

ISBN 0-374-32258-9 LC 2002-190212

"An idiosyncratic group of characters play out this touching and well-paced story about friendship, family, and connection." Horn Book

Me and Rupert Goody. Foster Bks. 1999 105p $15 (4-6) **Fic**

1. Mentally handicapped—Fiction 2. Racially mixed people—Fiction 3. Mountain life—Fiction

ISBN 0-374-34904-5 LC 98-30235

Also available Thorndike Press large print edition

Eleven-year-old Jennalee is jealous when Rupert Goody, a slow-thinking black man, arrives in her Smoky

O'Connor, Barbara—*Continued*

Mountains community and claims to be the son of Uncle Beau, the owner of the general store and Jennalee's only friend

"An absorbing story peopled with carefully drawn and memorable characters." SLJ

Taking care of Moses; [by] Barbara O'Connor. 1st ed. Frances Foster Books/Farrar, Straus and Giroux 2004 134p $16 (4-6)   **Fic**

1. Abandoned children—Fiction 2. South Carolina—Fiction

ISBN 0-374-38038-4   LC 2003-49466

When dissension erupts in the town of Foley, South Carolina, after a baby is left on the steps of the Rock of Ages Baptist Church, eleven-year-old Randall must decide whether or not to keep secret his knowledge of who the foundling's mother is.

The author "creates a strong sense of this small South Carolina community. . . . Against this realistic backdrop, she places characters whose idiosyncrasies make them believable. . . . A rewarding read." Booklist

O'Dell, Kathleen

Agnes Parker . . . girl in progress. Dial Bks. 2003 156p $16.99 (4 and up)   **Fic**

1. Friendship—Fiction 2. School stories

ISBN 0-8037-2648-1   LC 2001-58256

As she starts in the sixth grade, Agnes faces challenges with her old best friend, a longtime bully, a wonderful new classmate and neighbor, and herself

"This is a thoughtful, gently humorous, and resonant cusp-of-coming-of-age novel." Horn Book Guide

Another available title about Agnes Parker is:

Agnes Parker . . . Happy camper? (2005)

O'Dell, Scott

The black pearl; illustrated by Milton Johnson. Houghton Mifflin 1967 140p il $17 (6 and up)   **Fic**

1. Pearl fisheries—Fiction 2. Baja California (Mexico: Peninsula)—Fiction

ISBN 0-395-06961-0

Also available in paperback from Dell

A Newbery Medal honor book, 1968

In claiming as his own the magnificent black pearl he finds, sixteen-year-old Ramón Salazar enrages El Manta Diablo, the sea devil, who legend says is its owner.

"The stark simplicity of the story and the deeper significance it holds in the triumph of good over evil add importance to the book, but even without that the book would be enjoyable as a rousing adventure tale with supernatural overtones." Bull Cent Child Books

The captive. Houghton Mifflin 1979 210p $16 (6 and up)   **Fic**

1. Mayas—Fiction 2. Mexico—Fiction

ISBN 0-395-27811-2   LC 79-15809

This story set in the 16th century "centers on the adventures of a young Jesuit seminarian who goes to the New World as part of a Spanish expedition. Full of Christian idealism, Julián Escobar believes his role is to convert the savages. Instead, he succumbs to the tempta-

tion to pose as the reincarnated Mayan deity [Kukulcán]." Child Book Rev Serv

"Characterizations are all finely drawn, and Julián's transformation from insecure, humane seminarian to pretend god is remarkable in its honest development." SLJ

Island of the Blue Dolphins; illustrated by Ted Lewin. Houghton Mifflin 1990 181p il $22 (5 and up)   **Fic**

1. Native Americans—Fiction 2. Wilderness survival—Fiction 3. San Nicolas Island (Calif.)—Fiction

ISBN 0-395-53680-4   LC 90-35331

Also available in paperback from Dell; Spanish language edition also available

Awarded the Newbery Medal, 1961

A reissue with new illustrations of the title first published 1960

"Unintentionally left behind by members of her California Native American tribe who fled a tragedy-ridden island, young Karana must construct a life for herself. Without bitterness or self-pity, she is able to extract joy and challenge from her eighteen years of solitude." Shapiro. Fic for Youth. 2d edition

Followed by Zia

The King's fifth; decorations and maps by Samuel Bryant. Houghton Mifflin 1966 264p $17 (5 and up)   **Fic**

1. Estevan, d. 1539—Fiction 2. Mexico—Fiction

ISBN 0-395-06963-7

A Newbery Medal honor book, 1967

"Fifteen-year-old Esteban sailed with Admiral Alarcon as a cartographer; carrying supplies for Coronado, the expedition went astray and a small group was put ashore to find Coronado's camp. Thus begins a harrowing story of the exciting and dangerous journey in search of the fabled gold of Cibola." Sutherland. The Best in Child Books

Sarah Bishop. Houghton Mifflin 1980 184p $16 (6 and up)   **Fic**

1. United States—History—1775-1783, Revolution—Fiction 2. American Loyalists—Fiction 3. New York (State)—Fiction

ISBN 0-395-29185-2   LC 79-28394

Also available in paperback from Scholastic

"Surrounded by war, prejudice, and fear, fifteen-year-old Sarah Bishop quietly determines to live her own kind of life in the wilderness that was Westchester County, New York, during the Revolution." Child Book Rev Serv

"O'Dell's messages about the bitterness and folly of war, the dangers of superstition, and the courage of the human spirit are smoothly woven into the story, as are the telling details of period and place." Bull Cent Child Books

Sing down the moon. Houghton Mifflin 1970 137p $18 (5 and up)   **Fic**

1. Navajo Indians—Fiction

ISBN 0-395-10919-1

Also available in paperback from Laurel Leaf

A Newbery Medal honor book, 1971

This story is told "through the eyes of a young Navaho girl as she sees the rich harvest in the Canyon de Chelly in 1864 destroyed by Spanish slavers and the sub-

O'Dell, Scott—*Continued*

sequent destruction by white soldiers which forces the Navahos on a march to Fort Sumner." Publ Wkly

"There is a poetic sonority of style, a sense of identification, and a note of indomitable courage and stoicism that is touching and impressive." Saturday Rev

Streams to the river, river to the sea; a novel of Sacagawea. Houghton Mifflin 1986 191p $16 (5 and up)   **Fic**
1. Sacagawea, b. 1786—Fiction 2. Lewis and Clark Expedition (1804-1806)—Fiction 3. Native Americans—Fiction
ISBN 0-395-40430-4   LC 86-936
Also available in paperback from Fawcett Bks.

This novel "tells the story of the Lewis and Clark expedition through the eyes of the young Shoshone woman who served as interpreter and, often, guide." Soc Educ

"An informative and involving choice for American history students and pioneer-adventure readers." Bull Cent Child Books

Oppel, Kenneth

Silverwing. Simon & Schuster Bks. for Young Readers 1997 217p pa $4.99 hardcover o.p. (5 and up)   **Fic**
1. Bats—Fiction
ISBN 0-689-82558-7 (pa)   LC 97-10977
When a newborn bat named Shade but sometimes called "Runt" becomes separated from his colony during migration, he grows in ways that prepare him for even greater journeys

"Oppel's bats are fully developed characters who, if not quite cuddly, will certainly earn readers' sympathy and respect. In *Silverwing* the author has created an intriguing microcosm of rival species, factions, and religions." Horn Book
Other titles in this series are:
Firewing (2003)
Sunwing (2000)

Orgel, Doris

The devil in Vienna. Dial Bks. for Young Readers 1978 246p pa $5.99 hardcover o.p. (6 and up)   **Fic**
1. Austria—Fiction 2. Holocaust, 1933-1945—Fiction 3. Friendship—Fiction 4. Jews—Fiction
ISBN 0-14-032500-X (pa)   LC 78-51319
"Although fictional, the events in this story about the Nazi occupation of Austria are based on the author's experiences as a child in Vienna. Inge is Jewish, her best friend Lieselotte is the daughter of a Nazi officer so devoted to Hitler that he had moved his family to Germany, returning only after the Anschluss. Although the girls have been forbidden to meet by both sets of parents, Inge knows her friend is loyal; when her parents are having difficulty in leaving the country, Inge turns to Lieselotte's uncle, a Catholic priest, for help. The story ends with the refugees' safe arrival in Yugoslavia." Bull Cent Child Books

"The book arouses in its readers anguish, fury, admiration, scorn—it couldn't be a more effective story or a more powerful illustration of the reason 'never to forget.'" Publ Wkly

Orlev, Uri

The island on Bird Street; translated by Hillel Halkin. Houghton Mifflin 1984 162p $16; pa $5.95 (5 and up)   **Fic**
1. Holocaust, 1933-1945—Fiction 2. Jews—Fiction 3. World War, 1939-1945—Fiction 4. Poland—Fiction
ISBN 0-395-33887-5; 0-395-61623-9 (pa)
                                     LC 83-26524
Original Hebrew edition, copyright 1981

This is the "story of an 11-year-old boy's life during the Holocaust. Alex, entirely on his own in an empty Polish ghetto, is sustained by his father's admonition to wait for him. Over rooftops, through attics and basements he traverses the deserted sector in his struggle for life." SLJ

"The author has written a book that offers on one level a first-rate survival story and on another a haunting glimpse of the war's effects on individual people." Horn Book

The man from the other side; translated from the Hebrew by Hillel Halkin. Houghton Mifflin 1991 186p $16 (6 and up)   **Fic**
1. World War, 1939-1945—Fiction 2. Holocaust, 1933-1945—Fiction
ISBN 0-395-53808-4   LC 90-47898
Also available in paperback from Puffin Bks.

Living on the outskirts of the Warsaw Ghetto during World War II, fourteen-year-old Marek and his grandparents shelter a Jewish man in the days before the Jewish uprising

"Strong emotions and swift actions bombard the reader in this fact-based book. The well-done translation projects the book's intensity." Child Book Rev Serv

Osborne, Mary Pope

Adaline Falling Star. Scholastic Press 2000 170p $16.95; pa $5.99 (5 and up)   **Fic**
1. Carson, Kit, 1809-1868—Fiction 2. Arapaho Indians—Fiction 3. Racially mixed people—Fiction
ISBN 0-439-05947-X; 0-439-05948-8 (pa)
                                     LC 99-30689
Feeling abandoned by her deceased Arapaho mother and Kit Carson, her explorer father, Adaline Falling Star runs away from the prejudiced cousins with whom she is staying and comes close to death in the wilderness, with only a mongrel dog for company

"Told in the girl's colorful frontier voice, this is an engaging tale of true grit and self-discovery." Booklist

My brother's keeper; Virginia's diary. Scholastic 2000 109p (My America) $8.95 (3-5)   **Fic**
1. Gettysburg (Pa.), Battle of, 1863—Fiction 2. United States—History—1861-1865, Civil War—Fiction
ISBN 0-439-15307-7   LC 00-20200
In 1863, as the Civil War approaches her quiet town of Gettysburg, Pennsylvania, nine-year-old Virginia records in a journal the horrible things she witnesses before, during, and after the Battle of Gettysburg

"Osborne successfully creates individual characters, and she poses difficult questions about war and the waste of human life." SLJ

Oswald, Nancy

Nothing here but stones; a Jewish pioneer story; [by] Nancy Oswald. 1st ed. H. Holt 2004 215p $16.95 (5 and up) **Fic**

1. Jews—Fiction 2. Frontier and pioneer life—Fiction 3. Colorado—Fiction 4. Immigrants—Fiction

ISBN 0-8050-7465-1 LC 2003-56969

In 1882, ten-year-old Emma and her family, along with other Russian Jewish immigrants, arrive in Cotopaxi, Colorado, where they face inhospitable conditions as they attempt to start an agricultural colony, and lonely Emma is comforted by the horse whose life she saved.

"This well-paced, vivid account should capture readers' attention." SLJ

Paratore, Coleen

The wedding planner's daughter; [by] Coleen Murtagh Paratore. Simon & Schuster Books for Young Readers 2005 200p $15.95 (4-6) **Fic**

1. Mother-daughter relationship—Fiction 2. Weddings—Fiction

ISBN 0-689-87340-9 LC 2004-14502

Willa, a romantic girl who wants a father, tries to find a husband for her mother, Cape Cod's most popular wedding planner.

"This book is as sweet a confection as the cherry cordials its 12-year-old protagonist is so fond of eating. . . . The girl's letter to her mother . . . provides emotional heft to what has up to that point been just a pleasant story." SLJ

Park, Barbara

Junie B. Jones and her big fat mouth; illustrated by Denise Brunkus. Random House 1993 69p il lib bdg $11.99; pa $3.99 (2-4) **Fic**

1. School stories

ISBN 0-679-94407-9 (lib bdg); 0-679-84407-4 (pa) LC 92-50957

"A First stepping stone book"

When her kindergarten class has Job Day, Junie B. goes through much confusion and excitement before deciding on the "bestest" job of all

"Brunkus' energetic drawings pick up the slapstick action and the spunky comic hero." Booklist

Other titles about Junie B. Jones are:

Junie B. Jones and a little monkey business (1993)
Junie B. Jones and some sneaky peeky spying (1994)
Junie B. Jones and that meanie Jim's birthday (1996)
Junie B. Jones and the mushy gushy valentine (1999)
Junie B. Jones and the stupid smelly bus (1992)
Junie B. Jones and the yucky blucky fruitcake (1995)
Junie B. Jones, first grader: Aloha-ha-ha (2006)
Junie B. Jones, first grader (at last!) (2001)
Junie B. Jones, first grader: boo . . . and I mean it! (2003)
Junie B. Jones, first grader: boss of lunch (2002)
Junie B. Jones, first grader: cheater pants (2003)
Junie B. Jones, first grader: jingle bells, Batman smells! (p.s. so does May) (2005)
Junie B. Jones, first grader: one-man band (2003)
Junie B. Jones, first grader: shipwrecked (2003)
Junie B. Jones, first grader: toothless wonder (2002)
Junie B. Jones has a monster under her bed (1997)

Junie B. Jones has a peep in her pocket (2000)
Junie B. Jones is a beauty shop guy (1998)
Junie B. Jones is a graduation girl (2001)
Junie B. Jones is a party animal (1997)
Junie B. Jones is (almost) a flower girl (1999)
Junie B. Jones is Captain Field Day (2000)
Junie B. Jones is not a crook (1997)
Junie B. Jones loves handsome Warren (1996)
Junie B. Jones smells something fishy (1998)

Mick Harte was here. Apple Soup Bks. 1995 89p $15; pa $4.99 (4-6) **Fic**

1. Siblings—Fiction 2. Death—Fiction

ISBN 0-679-87088-1; 0-679-88203-0 (pa) LC 94-27272

Thirteen-year-old Phoebe recalls her younger brother Mick and his death in a bicycle accident

"The author is adept at portraying the stages of grief and the effects of this sudden tragedy on the family. The book's tone of sadness is mitigated by humor, reassurance, and hope." SLJ

My mother got married (and other disasters). Knopf 1989 138p pa $4.99 hardcover o.p. (4-6) **Fic**

1. Stepfamilies—Fiction

ISBN 0-394-85059-9 (pa) LC 88-27257

Twelve-year-old Charles experiences many difficulties in adjusting to a new stepfather, stepsister, and stepbrother

"Stories about divorce are nothing new, but Parks does a superb job of giving this one a fresh feel. Charlie's first-person dialogue is humorous but also realistically bitter. . . . A story of surprising depth." Booklist

Park, Linda Sue

Archer's quest. Clarion Books 2006 167p $16 (4 and up) **Fic**

1. Science fiction 2. Korea—Fiction 3. Korean Americans—Fiction

ISBN 9780618596317 LC 2005-29789

Twelve-year-old Kevin Kim helps Chu-mong, a legendary king of ancient Korea, return to his own time. This "is a breezy, fun read." Voice Youth Advocates

The kite fighters; decorations by Eung Won Park. Clarion Bks. 2000 136p $15 (4-6) **Fic**

1. Kites—Fiction 2. Brothers—Fiction 3. Korea—Fiction

ISBN 0-395-94041-9 LC 99-36936

In Korea in 1473, eleven-year-old Young-sup overcomes his rivalry with his older brother Kee-sup, who as the first-born son receives special treatment from their father, and combines his kite-flying skill with Kee-sup's kite-making skill in an attempt to win the New Year kite-fighting competition

"Besides catching the excitement of the ancient sport, the novel deals with intense sibling rivalry. . . . [The story feels] consistently well-grounded in its time and place." Booklist

Park, Linda Sue—Continued

Project Mulberry; a novel. Clarion 2005 225p
$16 (5 and up)   **Fic**
1. Korean Americans—Fiction
ISBN 0-618-47786-1   LC 2004-18159
While working on a project for an afterschool club,
Julia, a Korean American girl, and her friend Patrick
learn not just about silkworms, but also about tolerance,
prejudice, friendship, patience, and more. Between the
chapters are short dialogues between the author and main
character about the writing of the book.
"The unforgettable family and friendship story, the
quiet, almost unspoken racism, and the excitement of the
science make this a great cross-curriculum title." Booklist

A single shard. Clarion Bks. 2001 152p $15 (5
and up)   **Fic**
1. Pottery—Fiction 2. Korea—Fiction
ISBN 0-395-97827-0   LC 00-43102
Also available Thorndike Press large print edition and
in paperback from Yearling
Awarded the Newbery Medal, 2002
Tree-ear, a thirteen-year-old orphan in medieval Korea, lives under a bridge in a potters' village, and longs
to learn how to throw the delicate celadon ceramics himself
"This quiet, but involving, story draws readers into a
very different time and place. . . . A well-crafted novel
with an unusual setting." Booklist

When my name was Keoko. Clarion Bks. 2002
199p $16 (5 and up)   **Fic**
1. Korea—Fiction 2. World War, 1939-1945—Fiction
ISBN 0-618-13335-6   LC 2001-32487
With national pride and occasional fear, a brother and
sister face the increasingly oppressive occupation of Korea by Japan during World War II, which threatens to
suppress Korean culture entirely
"Park is a masterful prose stylist, and her characters
are developed beautifully. She excels at making traditional Korean culture accessible to Western readers." Voice
Youth Advocates
Includes bibliographical references

Parker, Toni Trent

Sienna's scrapbook; our African American
heritage trip; with illustrations by Janell Genovese.
Chronicle Books 2005 61p il $15.95 (3-5)
                                                  Fic
1. African Americans—Fiction 2. Historic sites—Fiction 3. Scrapbooks—Fiction 4. Diaries—Fiction
ISBN 0-8118-4300-9
A young girl's parents take her and her brother on a
summer trip to visit the sites of African American history.
"A combination of scrapbook and journal, this refreshing retrospective of African-American history is engaging
and entertaining. . . . The chosen sites are both significant and fascinating. . . . Engaging illustrations include
childlike drawings and doodles, photos, paintings, and
replicas of ticket stubs and other ephemera." SLJ

Paterson, Katherine

Bridge to Terabithia; illustrated by Donna
Diamond. Crowell 1977 128p il $15.99; lib bdg
$16.89; pa $5.99 (4 and up)   **Fic**
1. Friendship—Fiction 2. Death—Fiction 3. Virginia—
Fiction
ISBN 0-690-01359-0; 0-690-04635-9 (lib bdg);
0-06-440184-7 (pa)   LC 77-2221
Awarded the Newbery Medal, 1978
The life of Jess, a ten-year-old boy in rural Virginia
expands when he becomes friends with a newcomer who
subsequently meets an untimely death trying to reach
their hideaway, Terabithia, during a storm
"Jess and his family are magnificently characterized;
the book abounds in descriptive vignettes, humorous
sidelights on the clash of cultures, and realistic depictions of rural school life." Horn Book

Come sing, Jimmy Jo. Lodestar Bks. 1985 193p
$15.99; pa $5.99 (5 and up)   **Fic**
1. Country music—Fiction 2. Family life—Fiction
ISBN 0-525-67167-6; 0-14-037397-7 (pa)
                                      LC 84-21123
Also available Spanish language edition

When his family becomes a successful country music
group and makes him a featured singer, eleven-year-old
James has to deal with big changes in all aspects of his
life, even his name
"What Katherine Paterson does so well is catch the
cadence of the locale without sounding fake. There isn't
a false note in her diction. She has created a West Vir-
ginian world that is entirely believable: homely, honest,
goodhearted. . . . This book is James's personal inward
journey, and it is deeply felt." Christ Sci Monit

The great Gilly Hopkins. Crowell 1978 148p
$15.99; lib bdg $16.89; pa $5.99 (5 and up)
                                                  Fic
1. Foster home care—Fiction
ISBN 0-690-03837-2; 0-690-03838-0 (lib bdg);
0-06-440201-0 (pa)   LC 77-27075
"Cool, scheming, and deliberately obstreperous, 11-
year-old Gilly is ready to be her usual obnoxious self
when she arrives at her new foster home. . . . But Gilly's old tricks don't work against the all-encompassing
love of the huge, half-illiterate Mrs. Trotter. . . . Determined not to care she writes a letter full of wild exaggerations to her real mother that brings, in return, a surprising visit from an unknown grandmother." Booklist
"A well-structured story, [this] has vitality of writing
style, natural dialogue, deep insight in characterization,
and a keen sense of the fluid dynamics in human relationships." Bull Cent Child Books

Jip; his story. Lodestar Bks. 1996 181p pa $5.99
hardcover o.p. (5 and up)   **Fic**
1. Slavery—Fiction 2. African Americans—Fiction
3. Vermont—Fiction 4. Racially mixed people—Fiction
ISBN 0-14-038674-2 (pa); 0-525-67543-4 (hc)
                                      LC 96-2680
While living on a Vermont poor farm during 1855 and
1856, Jip learns that his mother was a runaway slave,
and that his father, the plantation owner, plans to reclaim
him as property

Paterson, Katherine—*Continued*

"This historically accurate story is full of revelations and surprises, one of which is the return appearance of the heroine of *Lyddie*. . . . The taut, extremely readable narrative and its tender depictions of friendship and loyalty provide first-rate entertainment." Publ Wkly

Lyddie. Lodestar Bks. 1991 182p $17.99; pa $6.99 (5 and up)   **Fic**
1. United States—History—1815-1861—Fiction
2. Massachusetts—Fiction 3. Factories—Fiction
ISBN 0-525-67338-5; 0-14-034981-2 (pa)
          LC 90-42944
Impoverished Vermont farm girl Lyddie Worthen is determined to gain her independence by becoming a factory worker in Lowell, Massachusetts, in the 1840s

"Not only does the book contain a riveting plot, engaging characters, and a splendid setting, but the language—graceful, evocative, and rhythmic—incorporates the rural speech patterns of Lyddie's folk, the simple Quaker expressions of the farm neighbors, and the lilt of fellow mill girl Bridget's Irish brogue. . . . A superb story of grit, determination, and personal growth." Horn Book

Park's quest. Lodestar Bks. 1988 148p pa $5.99 hardcover o.p. (5 and up)   **Fic**
1. Farm life—Fiction 2. Vietnamese Americans—Fiction
ISBN 0-14-034262-1   LC 87-32422
Also available Spanish language edition
Eleven-year-old Park makes some startling discoveries when he travels to his grandfather's farm in Virginia to learn about his father who died in the Vietnam War and meets a Vietnamese-American girl named Thanh

The author "confronts the complexity, the ambiguity, of the war and the emotions of those it involved with an honesty that young readers are sure to recognize and appreciate." N Y Times Book Rev

Preacher's boy. Clarion Bks. 1999 168p $15; pa $4.95 (5 and up)   **Fic**
1. Family life—Fiction 2. Christian life—Fiction
3. Vermont—Fiction
ISBN 0-395-83897-5; 0-06-447233-7 (pa)
          LC 98-50083
Also available Thorndike Press large print edition
In 1899, ten-year-old Robbie, son of a preacher in a small Vermont town, gets himself into all kinds of trouble when he decides to give up being Christian in order to make the most of his life before the end of the world

"With warmth, humor, and her powerful yet plain style, Paterson draws empathetic and memorable characters." SLJ

The same stuff as stars. Clarion Bks. 2002 242p $15 (5 and up)   **Fic**
ISBN 0-618-24744-0   LC 2002-3967
When Angel's self-absorbed mother leaves her and her younger brother with their poor great-grandmother, the eleven-year-old girl worries not only about her mother and brother, her imprisoned father, the frail old woman, but also about a mysterious man who begins sharing with her the wonder of the stars

"Paterson's deft hand at characterization, her insight into the human soul, and her glorious prose make this book one to rejoice over." Voice Youth Advocates

Patron, Susan

Maybe yes, maybe no, maybe maybe; pictures by Dorothy Donahue. Orchard Bks. 1993 87p il $15.95 (3-5)   **Fic**
1. Moving—Fiction 2. Sisters—Fiction
ISBN 0-531-05482-9   LC 92-34067
"A Richard Jackson book"
When her hardworking mother decides to move, eight-year-old PK uses her imagination and storytelling to help her older and younger sisters adjust

"The author's distinctive voice and characters drive this engaging novel, with its easy vocabulary, large type, and scattered, full-page wash paintings." Horn Book Guide

Paulsen, Gary

Alida's song. Delacorte Press 1999 88p pa $5.50 hardcover o.p. (5 and up)   **Fic**
1. Grandmothers—Fiction 2. Farm life—Fiction
ISBN 0-440-41474-1 (pa); 0-385-32586-X (hc)
          LC 98-37015
In this sequel to The cookcamp, "Grandma Alida once again steps in at a troubled time in her grandson's life. Now the boy is 14; living with violent, drunken parents. . . . [A] letter arrives from his grandmother offering him a summer job as a hired hand on a farm. . . . He accepts the offer and experiences a season of hard work, music, dancing, and hearty meals served up with warmth, love, and understanding. . . . This beautifully written novella is a quiet tribute to a loving relative." SLJ

The cookcamp. Orchard Bks. 1991 115p $15.95 (5 and up)   **Fic**
1. Grandmothers—Fiction 2. World War, 1939-1945—Fiction
ISBN 0-531-05927-8   LC 90-7734
Also available in paperback from Dell
"A Richard Jackson book"
During World War II, a little boy is sent to live with his grandma, a cook in a camp for workers building a road through the wilderness

"Paulsen's simply told story strikes extraordinary emotional chords. . . . Those hungry for adventure stories, as well as more introspective readers, will be spellbound by this stirring novel." Publ Wkly

Followed by Alida's song

Dogsong. Bradbury Press 1985 177p (6 and up)   **Fic**
1. Inuit—Fiction 2. Arctic regions—Fiction
          LC 84-20443
Available in hardcover $16 (ISBN 0-698-83960-X) and paperback $5.99 (ISBN 0-689-82700-8) from Atheneum
A Newbery Medal honor book, 1986
A fourteen-year-old Eskimo boy who feels assailed by the modernity of his life takes a 1400-mile journey by dog sled across ice, tunda, and mountains seeking his own "song" of himself

The author's "mystical tone and blunt prose style are well suited to the spare landscape of his story, and his depictions of Russell's icebound existence add both authenticity and color to a slick rendition of the vision-quest plot, which incorporates human tragedy as well as promise." Booklist

Paulsen, Gary—*Continued*

Mr. Tucket. Delacorte Press 1994 166p $15.95;
pa $4.50 (5 and up)   **Fic**
  1. Frontier and pioneer life—Fiction 2. West (U.S.)—
Fiction
  ISBN 0-385-31169-9; 0-440-41133-5 (pa)
                        LC 93-31180
In 1848, while on a wagon train headed for Oregon,
fourteen-year-old Francis Tucket is kidnapped by Pawnee
Indians and then falls in with a one-armed trapper who
teaches him how to live in the wild
  "Superb characterizations, splendidly evoked setting
and thrill-a-minute plot make this book a joy to gallop
through." Publ Wkly
  Other titles about Francis Tucket are:
Call me Francis Tucket (1995)
Tucket's gold (1999)
Tucket's home (2000)
Tucket's ride (1997)

The quilt. Wendy Lamb Books 2004 83p
$15.95; lib bdg $17.99 (5 and up)   **Fic**
  1. Grandmothers—Fiction 2. World War, 1939-1945—
Fiction
  ISBN 0-385-72950-2; 0-385-90886-5 (lib bdg)
                       LC 2003-11912

This is a "World War II novel, about a six-year-old
boy living with his grandmother, Alida, in a Norwegian
immigrant community. . . . As Alida and other women
gather to help a farmer's wife give birth, they hold a
quilting bee and tell stories of their family and neighbors
who have died, each one remembered in a patch of cloth.
The simple, poignant prose speaks gently about the elemental domestic dramas of birth and death." Booklist

The winter room. Orchard Bks. 1989 103p
$16.95 (5 and up)   **Fic**
  1. Farm life—Fiction 2. Minnesota—Fiction
  ISBN 0-531-05839-5   LC 89-42541
  Also available in paperback from Dell
  A Newbery Medal honor book, 1990
  "A Richard Jackson book"
A young boy growing up on a northern Minnesota
farm describes the scenes around him and recounts his
old Norwegian uncle's tales of an almost mythological
logging past
  "While this seems at first to be a collection of anecdotes organized around the progression of the farm calendar, Paulsen subtly builds a conflict that becomes apparent in the last brief chapters, forceful and well-
prepared. . . . Lyrical and only occasionally sentimental,
the prose is clean, clear, and deceptively simple." Bull
Cent Child Books

Paver, Michelle

Wolf brother; Chronicles of ancient darkness,
book one; by Michelle Paver. 1st American ed.
HarperCollins 2005 c2004 295p $16.99; lib bdg
$17.89 (5 and up)   **Fic**
  1. Prehistoric peoples—Fiction 2. Wolves—Fiction
3. Demoniac possession—Fiction 4. Bears—Fiction
  ISBN 0-06-072825-6; 0-06-072826-4 (lib bdg)
                      LC 2004-8857

First published 2004 in the United Kingdom
6,000 years in the past, twelve-year-old Tarak and his
guide, a wolf cub, set out on a dangerous journey to fulfill an oath the boy made to his dying father—to travel
to the Mountain of the World Spirit seeking a way to destroy a demon-possessed bear that threatens all the clans.
  "Paver's depth of research into the spiritual world of
primitive peoples makes this impressive British import,
slated to be the first in a six-book series, intriguing and
believable." SLJ
  Another title in this series is:
Spirit walker (2006)

Pearce, Philippa

The little gentleman; drawings by Tom Pohrt.
Greenwillow Books 2004 200p il $15.99; lib bdg
$16.89 (3-5)   **Fic**
  1. Moles (Animals)—Fiction 2. Magic—Fiction
  ISBN 0-06-073160-5; 0-06-073161-3 (lib bdg)
                      LC 2003-67530
A young girl's dull life is transformed when she meets
and befriends an extraordinary talking mole that likes to
be read to and tell of his own past exploits throughout
the centuries.
  "There are plenty of exciting and dangerous events in
this humorous and moving novel." SLJ

Tom's midnight garden; illustrated by Susan
Einzig. Lippincott 1959 c1958 229p il lib bdg
$15.89; pa $5.95 (4 and up)   **Fic**
  1. Fantasy fiction 2. Space and time—Fiction
  ISBN 0-397-30477-3 (lib bdg); 0-06-440445-5 (pa)
  First published 1958 in the United Kingdom
  "Daytime life for Tom at his aunt's home in England
is dull, but each night he participates through fantasy in
the lives of the former inhabitants of the interesting old
house in which he is spending an enforced vacation. The
book is British in setting and atmosphere. The element
of mystery is well sustained, and the reader is left to
make his own interpretation of the reality of the story."
Adventuring with Books

Pearsall, Shelley

Crooked river; [by] Shelley Pearsall. 1st ed.
Knopf 2005 249p $15.95; lib bdg $17.99 (5 and
up)   **Fic**
  1. Ojibwa Indians—Fiction 2. Frontier and pioneer
life—Fiction 3. Ohio—Fiction
  ISBN 0-375-82389-1; 0-375-92389-6 (lib bdg)
                      LC 2004-10310
When twelve-year old Rebecca Carter's father brings
a Native American accused of murder into their 1812
Ohio settlement town, Rebecca, witnessing the town's reaction to the Indian, struggles with the idea that an innocent man may be convicted and sentenced to death.
  "Pearsall quickly engages readers with her captivating
tale of fear, ignorance, and bravery. . . . Packed with believable characters wrapped in a thoroughly researched
plot." SLJ

Pearsall, Shelley—*Continued*

Trouble don't last. Knopf 2002 237p $14.95; lib bdg $16.99 (5 and up)   **Fic**
1. Slavery—Fiction 2. African Americans—Fiction 3. Underground railroad—Fiction
ISBN 0-375-81490-6; 0-375-91490-0 (lib bdg)
            LC 2001-38109

Samuel, an eleven-year-old Kentucky slave, and Harrison, the elderly slave who helped raise him, attempt to escape to Canada via the Underground Railroad

This offers "strong characters and an inventive, suspenseful plot. . . . This is a compelling story that will expand young readers' understanding of the Underground Railroad." SLJ

Includes bibliographical references

Peck, Richard

Fair weather; a novel. Dial Bks. 2001 130p il $16.99; pa $5.99 (5 and up)   **Fic**
1. Buffalo Bill, 1846-1917—Fiction 2. Russell, Lillian, 1861-1922—Fiction 3. Family life—Fiction 4. Chicago (Ill.)—Fiction
ISBN 0-8037-2516-7; 0-14-250034-8 (pa)
            LC 00-55561

Also available Thorndike Press large print edition

In 1893, thirteen-year-old Rosie and members of her family travel from their Illinois farm to Chicago to visit Aunt Euterpe and attend the World's Columbian Exposition which, along with an encounter with Buffalo Bill and Lillian Russell, turns out to be a life-changing experience for everyone

"Peck's unforgettable characters, cunning dialogue and fast-paced action will keep readers in stitches." Publ Wkly

Here lies the librarian. Dial Books 2006 145p $16.99   **Fic**
1. Automobiles—Fiction 2. Librarians—Fiction 3. Country life—Fiction 4. Indiana—Fiction
ISBN 0-8037-3080-2   LC 2005-20279

Fourteen-year-old Eleanor "Peewee" McGrath, a tomboy and automobile enthusiast, discovers new possibilities for her future after the 1914 arrival in her small Indiana town of four young librarians.

"Another gem from Peck, with his signature combination of quirky characters, poignancy, and outrageous farce." SLJ

A long way from Chicago; a novel in stories. Dial Bks. for Young Readers 1998 148p $15.99; pa $5.99 (5 and up)   **Fic**
1. Grandmothers—Fiction 2. Great Depression, 1929-1939—Fiction
ISBN 0-8037-2290-7; 0-14-240110-2 (pa)
            LC 98-10953

A Newbery Medal honor book, 1999

Joe recounts his annual summer trips to rural Illinois with his sister during the Great Depression to visit their larger-than-life grandmother

"The novel reveals a strong sense of place, a depth of characterization, and a rich sense of humor." Horn Book

Followed by A year down yonder

Lost in cyberspace. Dial Bks. for Young Readers 1995 151p $16.99; pa $5.99 (5 and up)   **Fic**
1. Space and time—Fiction 2. School stories
ISBN 0-8037-1931-0; 0-14-037856-1 (pa)
            LC 94-48330

While dealing with changes at home, sixth-grader Josh and his friend Aaron use the computer at their New York prep school to travel through time, learning some secrets from the school's past and improving Josh's home situation

This "will appeal to today's computer-literate generation while allowing their imaginations to soar. A time-traveling journey that will keep the reader on the edge of his seat—or computer." Child Book Rev Serv

The teacher's funeral; a comedy in three parts; [by] Richard Peck. Dial Books 2004 190p $16.99 (5 and up)   **Fic**
1. Teachers—Fiction 2. Indiana—Fiction 3. Country life—Fiction
ISBN 0-8037-2736-4   LC 2004-4361

In rural Indiana in 1904, fifteen-year-old Russell's dream of quitting school and joining a wheat threshing crew is disrupted when his older sister takes over the teaching at his one-room schoolhouse after mean, old Myrt Arbuckle "hauls off and dies."

"The dry wit and unpretentious tone make the story's events comical, its characters memorable, and its conclusion unexpectedly moving." Booklist

A year down yonder. Dial Bks. for Young Readers 2000 130p $16.99; pa $5.99 (5 and up)   **Fic**
1. Grandmothers—Fiction 2. Great Depression, 1929-1939—Fiction
ISBN 0-8037-2518-3; 0-14-230070-5 (pa)
            LC 99-43159

Awarded the Newbery Medal, 2001

This sequel to A long way from Chicago "tells the story of Joey's younger sister, Mary Alice, 15, who spends the year of 1937 back with Grandma Dowdel in a small town in Illinois." Booklist

"Peck has created a delightful, insightful tale that resounds with a storyteller's wit, humor, and vivid description." SLJ

Peck, Robert Newton

Soup; illustrated by Charles C. Gehm. Knopf 1974 96p il pa $5.50 hardcover o.p. (5 and up)   **Fic**
1. Friendship—Fiction 2. Vermont—Fiction
ISBN 0-679-89261-3 (pa)

"Soup was Robert Peck's best friend during his boyhood, and this is an episodic account of some of the ploys and scrapes the two shared when they were in elementary school." Bull Cent Child Books

"Rural Vermont during the 1920's is the setting for this nostalgic account. . . . In a laconic and wryly humorous style, the author relates the activities of the mischievous twosome. . . . The black-and-white pencil drawings, artistically executed in the manner of Norman Rockwell, reflect the understated story." SLJ

Other titles about the author and his friend Soup are:

Peck, Robert Newton—*Continued*

Soup 1776 (1995)

Soup ahoy (1994)

Soup for president (1978)

Soup in love (1992)

Soup on wheels (1981)

Soup's hoop (1990)

Pennac, Daniel

Dog; translated by Sarah Adams. Candlewick Press 2004 c2002 181p $15.99 (3-5) **Fic**

1. Dogs—Fiction

ISBN 0-7636-2421-7

Original French edition 1982

Rescued from certain death by a kindly dog at the city dump, an abandoned puppy grows up fending for himself until he finds a home with a willful little girl. Could she be the mistress of his dreams?

"The omniscient narrator fills the reader in on the behavior of both dogs and humans, and the tone is melancholy but, in the end, triumphant and loving." Horn Book Guide

Pennypacker, Sara

Stuart's cape; illustrated by Martin Matje. Orchard Bks. 2002 55p il $15.95 (2-4)

Fic

ISBN 0-439-30180-7 LC 2001-37480

Bored because there is nothing to do in the house to which his family has just moved and worried about starting third grade in a new school, Stuart makes a magical cape out of his uncle's ties and has a series of adventures

"The story is hilariously descriptive and will appeal to both slower and more proficient readers, and its engaging flow makes for a great read-aloud. Matje's quirky cartoon pencil drawings add to the weird flavor of the book." SLJ

Another title about Stuart is:

Stuart goes to school (2003)

Pérez, Amada Irma

My diary from here to there; story, Amada Irma Pérez; illustrations, Maya Christina Gonzalez. Children's Bk. Press 2002 unp il $16.95 (2-4)

Fic

1. Mexican Americans—Fiction 2. Immigrants—Fiction 3. Bilingual books—English-Spanish

ISBN 0-89239-175-8 LC 2001-58251

Text and title page in English and Spanish

A young girl describes her feelings when her father decides to leave their home in Mexico to look for work in the United States

"The diary entries, written in conversational English and Spanish, resonate with the tensions of the experience. . . . The full-page, bright acrylic paintings complement the text, with the blocky primitive forms adding a reassuring note to the whole." SLJ

Perkins, Lynne Rae

All alone in the universe. Greenwillow Bks. 1999 140p il $15.95; pa $5.99 (5 and up)

Fic

1. Friendship—Fiction

ISBN 0-688-16881-7; 0-380-73302-1 (pa)

LC 98-50093

Debbie is dismayed when her best friend Maureen starts spending time with ordinary, boring Glenna

"A poignant story written with sensitivity and tenderness." SLJ

Criss cross; by Lynne Rae Perkins. Greenwillow Books 2005 337p $16.99; lib bdg $17.89 (6 and up) **Fic**

ISBN 0-06-009272-6; 0-06-009273-4 (lib bdg)

LC 2004-54023

Awarded the Newbery Medal, 2006

Teenagers in a small town in the 1960s experience new thoughts and feelings, question their identities, connect, and disconnect as they search for the meaning of life and love

"Debbie . . . and Hector . . . narrate most of the novel. Both are 14 years old. Hector is a fabulous character with a wry humor and an appealing sense of self-awareness. . . . The descriptive, measured writing includes poems, prose, haiku, and question-and-answer formats. There is a great deal of humor in this gentle story." SLJ

Petry, Ann Lane

Tituba of Salem Village; [by] Ann Petry. Crowell 1964 254p pa $4.95 hardcover o.p. (6 and up) **Fic**

1. Tituba—Fiction 2. Salem (Mass.)—Fiction 3. African Americans—Fiction 4. Witchcraft—Fiction

ISBN 0-694-40403-X (pa)

"From the beauty of the island of Barbados, Tituba is uprooted to the dreary, gray cold of Boston. As the slave in the household of the minister, Samuel Parris, Tituba cooks, nurses, and attends to his sickly wife, daughter, and niece. When the minister moves to a new post in Salem Village, Tituba becomes the central figure in a witchcraft trial." Shapiro. Fic for Youth. 3d edition

Philbrick, W. R. (W. Rodman)

REM world; [by] Rodman Philbrick. Blue Sky Press (NY) 2000 192p $16.95; pa $5.99 (4 and up)

Fic

1. Fantasy fiction

ISBN 0-439-08362-1; 0-439-08363-4 (pa)

LC 99-54843

Eleven-year-old Arthur Woodbury's attempt to lose weight fast and escape his nickname of Biscuit Butt takes him to an endangered dream world where he faces fantastic adventures and learns the true meaning of courage

"Imaginative characters and a string of cliffhangers make [this] . . . novel a fun and fast-paced read." Publ Wkly

Philbrick, W. R. (W. Rodman)—*Continued*

The young man and the sea; [by] Rodman Philbrick. Blue Sky Press 2004 192p $16.95 (5 and up)   **Fic**
1. Fishing—Fiction
ISBN 0-439-36829-4   LC 2003-050233
After his mother's death, twelve-year-old Skiff Beaman decides that it is up to him to earn money to take care of himself and his father, so he undertakes a dangerous trip alone out on the ocean off the coast of Maine to try to catch a hugh bluefin tuna.

"This excellent maritime bildungsroman has all of the makings of a juvenile classic: wide-open adventure, heart-pounding suspense, and just the right amount of tear-jerking pathos, all neatly wrapped up in an ending that . . . is purely triumphant." SLJ

Pierce, Tamora

Magic steps; book one of the Circle opens quartet. Scholastic Press 2000 264p pa $5.99 hardcover o.p. (5 and up)   **Fic**
1. Fantasy fiction
ISBN 0-590-39605-6 (pa)   LC 99-31943
Based on characters in the author's Circle of Magic quartet

Sandry "is a 'stitch witch' who can weave magic as well as cloth. She reluctantly takes on twelve-year-old Pasco as a student, and the plot revolves around her struggles as a first-time teacher and her involvement in investigating a series of vicious murders." Horn Book Guide

"Using descriptive, personable prose, Pierce combines dimensional characters, intricate details, plot twists, and alternating story lines for a gripping read. . . . There is some vivid violence." Booklist
Other titles in this series are:
Cold fire (2002)
Shatterglass (2003)
Street magic (2001)

Pinkney, Jerry

The nightingale; [by] Hans Christian Andersen; adapted and illustrated by Jerry Pinkney. Phyllis Fogelman Bks. 2002 unp il $16.99 (2-4)
                                           Fic
1. Andersen, Hans Christian, 1805-1875—Adaptations
2. Fairy tales 3. Nightingales—Fiction
ISBN 0-8037-2464-0   LC 2001-47601
Despite being neglected by the emperor for a jewel-studded bird, the little nightingale revives the dying ruler with its beautiful song. A retelling set in Morocco

This "is a pleasing version of the classic, fresh in its interpretation but true to the spirit of the original. . . . Each double-page spread is illuminated by artwork that glows with rich colors and teems with lively details. Done in graphic, gouache, and watercolor, the large, gracefully composed illustrations feature a profusion of patterns." Booklist

Pinkwater, Daniel Manus

Fat men from space; written and illustrated by Daniel Manus Pinkwater. Dodd, Mead 1977 57p il (3-6)   **Fic**
1. Food—Fiction 2. Science fiction
                              LC 77-6091
Available in paperback from Dell
"Young William goes to the dentist and comes out with a filling that receives radio programs. Exploring the infinite possibilities of a tooth radio, he attaches a wire to a chainlink fence, touches it to his molar, and tunes in on an invading 'spaceburger' from the planet Spiegel. Before he can warn anyone of earth's peril, he is captured and 'floated' up to the spaceburger where he meets the invaders—fat men with glasses, wearing plaid sport jackets. Their raid is successful—Earth is stripped of all its junk food." SLJ

"Message books aren't usually this much fun, but Pinkwater makes his a polished romp." Bull Cent Child Books

The Hoboken chicken emergency; illustrated by Jill Pinkwater. Atheneum Pubs. 1999 108p il lib bdg $15; pa $4.99 (3-6)   **Fic**
1. Chickens—Fiction
ISBN 0-689-83060-2 (lib bdg); 0-689-82889-6 (pa)
                              LC 00-268579
A newly illustrated edition of the title first published 1977 by Prentice-Hall

Arthur Bobowicz goes to pick up the turkey for Thanksgiving dinner but comes back with a 260-pound chicken and names her Henrietta.

"A contemporary tall tale that will stretch middle graders' imagination, sense of humor, and enthusiasm for reading." Booklist
Other titles about Henrietta the chicken are:
The Artsy Smartsy Club (2005)
Looking for Bobowicz (2004)

Lizard music; written and illustrated by D. Manus Pinkwater. Dodd, Mead 1976 157p il (4 and up)   **Fic**
1. Science fiction
Available in paperback from Bantam Bks
"Left alone when his parents go on a vaction, Victor discovers, through late-night TV, a community of intelligent lizards and the Chicken Man. The succeeding adventures take Victor through some strange but thought-provoking escapades. Children associate with the ending—a return to normal but dull life when the rest of the family returns. A good read-aloud book." Read Teach

Place, François

The old man mad about drawing; a tale of Hokusai; translated from the French by William Rodarmor. David R. Godine 2004 105p il $19.95 (3-6)   **Fic**
1. Hokusai (Katsushika Hokusai), 1760-1849—Fiction
2. Japan—Fiction 3. Artists—Fiction
ISBN 1-56792-260-0   LC 2003-13521
Tojiro, a young seller of rice cakes in the Japanese capital of Edo, later known as Tokyo, is amazed to discover that the grumpy and shabby old man who buys his cakes is a famous artist renowned for his sketches, prints,

Place, François—*Continued*

and paintings of flowers, animals, and landscapes.

This book "features fine reproductions of Hokusai's work, as well as Rodarmore's elegant detailed sketches of the quiet studio and crowded streets." Booklist

Platt, Richard

Castle diary; the journal of Tobias Burgess, page; transcribed by Richard Platt; illuminated by Chris Riddell. Candlewick Press 1999 64p il $21.99 (4 and up)   **Fic**
1. Castles—Fiction 2. Middle Ages—Fiction
ISBN 0-7636-0489-5   LC 98-42779

As a page in his uncle's castle in thirteenth-century England, eleven-year-old Tobias records in his journal his experiences learning how to hunt, play games of skill, and behave in noble society. Includes notes on noblemen, castles, and feudalism

"Rewarding observant viewers with dramatic or humorous details of gesture and expression, Chris Riddell's deftly drawn ink-and-watercolor illustrations brighten the pages and complement the lively tone of the text." Booklist
Other titles in this series are:
Egyptian diary (2005)
Pirate diary (2001)
Includes bibliographical references

Polacco, Patricia

The butterfly. Philomel Bks. 2000 unp il $16.99 (2-4)   **Fic**
1. Jews—Fiction 2. World War, 1939-1945—Fiction 3. France—Fiction
ISBN 0-399-23170-6   LC 99-30038

During the Nazi occupation of France, Monique's mother hides a Jewish family in her basement and tries to help them escape to freedom

"Polacco's use of color has never been more effective. . . . The bold pattern and heightened color of the insect provides a counterpoint to the equally dynamic black-on-red swastikas. Convincing in its portrayal of both the disturbing and humanitarian forces of the time." SLJ

Christmas tapestry. Philomel Bks. 2002 unp il $16.95 (2-4)   **Fic**
1. Christmas—Fiction 2. Jews—Fiction 3. Tapestry—Fiction
ISBN 0-399-23955-3   LC 2001-7392

A tapestry that is being used to cover a hole in a church wall at Christmas brings together an elderly Jewish couple who were separated during World War II

"The tender colors and gestures in the illustrations echo the text to make a satisfying whole." Booklist

When lightning comes in a jar. Philomel Bks. 2002 unp il $16.99 (2-4)   **Fic**
1. Family reunions—Fiction 2. Grandmothers—Fiction 3. Family life—Fiction
ISBN 0-399-23164-1   LC 2001-45925

A young girl describes the family reunion at her grandmother's house, from the food and baseball and photos to the flickering fireflies on the lawn

"The watercolor-and-pencil illustrations, skillfully

composed on the pages, expressively sketch the characters. . . . This autobiographical story will convey the joys of family." Booklist

Polikoff, Barbara Garland

Life's a funny proposition, Horatio. Holt & Co. 1992 103p $14.95 (5 and up)   **Fic**
1. Death—Fiction 2. Grandfathers—Fiction
ISBN 0-8050-1972-3   LC 91-46724

Also available in paperback from Puffin Bks.

As Horatio tries to adjust to the death of his father from lung cancer, O.P., Horatio's grandfather, mourns the loss of his dog Mollie

"While capable of great tenderness, the understated writing style is both bracing and poignantly funny." Bull Cent Child Books

Why does the coqui sing? y. Holiday House 2004 213p $16.95 (5 and up)   **Fic**
1. Puerto Ricans—Fiction 2. Puerto Rico—Fiction 3. Moving—Fiction
ISBN 0-8234-1817-0   LC 2003-56776

When thirteen-year-old Luz and her family move from Chicago to her stepfather's native home of Puerto Rico, she and her brother Rome struggle to adjust and to decide where it is they really belong

"Luz, an aspiring poet, beautifully describes the pain of leaving and resettling in a sensitive, sometimes lyrical voice that's always true to her age." Booklist

Porte, Barbara Ann

If you ever get lost; the adventures of Julia and Evan; pictures by Nancy Carpenter. Greenwillow Bks. 2000 80p il $15.95 (2-4)   **Fic**
1. Siblings—Fiction
ISBN 0-688-16947-3   LC 98-32133

Julia and her younger brother Eric share several adventures, including getting lost at a marathon race, going grocery shopping, helping to catch two thieves at a pet store, and learning to speak Spanish

"The book has a sweet, old-fashioned air. Nancy Carpenter's lively line drawings with gray washes balance that feeling with an appealing, modern look." Booklist

Porter, Pamela Paige

The crazy man; [by] Pamela Porter. Groundwood Books 2005 214p $15.95 (5 and up)
                                                  Fic
1. Mentally ill—Fiction 2. Prejudices—Fiction 3. Farm life—Fiction 4. Saskatchewan—Fiction
ISBN 0-88899-694-2

"After Emaline, 11, is crippled by an accident with her father's tractor in 1965, Daddy kills her beloved dog, Prince, and walks away from the farm on the Saskatchewan prairie. Mom takes in Angus from the local mental hospital to help with the farm work, but the neighbors jeer and complain about the 'subhuman' crazy man on the loose. . . . Narrated by Emaline in short lines of free verse, the story is a very easy read, its plain, lyrical words capturing the beauty of the flat prairie under the huge sky and the sounds of wind, trains, and coyotes in the night, as well as the harsh community prejudice." Booklist

Porter, Pamela Paige—*Continued*

Sky; [by] Pamela Porter; with pictures by Mary Jane Gerber. Groundwood Books 2004 83p il $15.95; pa $5.95 (3-5)   **Fic**
1. Floods—Fiction 2. Horses—Fiction 3. Montana—Fiction
ISBN 0-88899-563-6; 0-88899-607-1 (pa)
"Georgia Salois, 11, lives with her grandparents in 1964 Montana. . . . A flood completely destroys the family's house and barn. . . . Georgia discovers a foal that survived the flood, adopts her, and names her Sky. . . . Georgia tells her story in a straightforward manner. . . . Lovely black-and-white illustrations bring the characters and events to life and add to the book's charm." SLJ

Potter, Ellen

Olivia Kidney; illustrated by Peter Reynolds. Philomel Bks. 2003 155p il $15.99 (3-6)
     Fic
1. Apartment houses—Fiction 2. New York (N.Y.)—Fiction
ISBN 0-399-23850-6   LC 2002-3660
Twelve-year-old Olivia explores her new apartment building and finds a psychic, talking lizards, a shrunken ex-pirate, an exiled princess, ghosts, and other unusual characters
"Potter has written a first-rate novel to be enjoyed on many levels. Its plot is so tightly woven that it's difficult to separate the mystical from the fantastical. Occasional full-page illustrations add another dimension to this narrative, which is wonderful medicine for the lonely." SLJ
Another title about Olivia Kidney is:
Olivia Kidney and the Exit Academy (2005)

Pratchett, Terry

Only you can save mankind. HarperCollins 2005 c1992 207p $15.99; lib bdg $16.89 (5 and up)
     Fic
1. Computer games—Fiction 2. War stories
ISBN 0-06-054185-7; 0-06-054186-5 (lib bdg)
First published 1992 in the United Kingdom
Twelve-year-old Johnny endures tensions between his parents, watches television coverage of the Gulf War, and plays a computer game called Only You Can Save Mankind, in which he is increasingly drawn into the reality of the alien ScreeWee.
This is "a wild ride, full of Pratchett's trademark humor; digs at primitive, low-resolution games . . . ; and some not-so-subtle philosophy about war and peace." Booklist
Another title about Johnny is:
Johnny and the dead (2006)

Propp, Vera W.

When the soldiers were gone. Putnam 1999 101p $14.99 (3-5)   **Fic**
1. Jews—Fiction 2. Netherlands—Fiction
ISBN 0-399-23325-3   LC 97-50169
After the German occupation of the Netherlands, Benjamin leaves the Christian family with whom he had

been living and reunites with his real parents who returned from hiding
"The miracle of this tale, based on an actual wartime story, is the constancy of Henk's voice; we see his world entirely through his eyes." Horn Book Guide

Prue, Sally

Cold Tom; a novel. Scholastic Press 2003 c2001 187p $15.95; pa $5.99 (5 and up)   **Fic**
1. Fantasy fiction
ISBN 0-439-48268-2; 0-439-48269-0 (pa)
     LC 2002-75802
First published 2001 in the United Kingdom
Struggling to find a place for himself, Tom flees the elven parents who hunt to kill him and becomes involved with human "demons" in the nearby city
"A thoughtful and engaging fantasy that explores multiple real-life themes while telling a compelling story." SLJ

Pullman, Philip

Clockwork; or, All wound up; with illustrations by Leonid Gore. Levine Bks. 1998 c1996 112p il pa $4.99 (4 and up)   **Fic**
1. Supernatural—Fiction
ISBN 0-590-12998-8 (pa); 0-590-12999-6 (hc)
     LC 97-27458
First published 1996 in the United Kingdom
Long ago in Germany, a storyteller's story and an apprentice clockwork-maker's nightmare meet in a menacing, lifelike figure created by the strange Dr. Kalmenius
"Pullman laces his tale with subtle humor while maintaining the suspense until the end. Misty, moody, and atmospheric black-and-white drawings by Leonid Gore make a perfect fit for this gothic gem." Voice Youth Advocates

The firework-maker's daughter; illustrations by S. Saelig Gallagher. Levine Bks. 1999 97p il $15.95; pa $4.99 (4 and up)   **Fic**
1. Fireworks—Fiction 2. Magic—Fiction 3. Adventure fiction 4. Elephants—Fiction
ISBN 0-590-18719-8; 0-439-22420-9 (pa)
     LC 98-41048
In a country far to the east, Chulak and his talking white elephant Hamlet help Lila seek the Royal Sulphur from the sacred volcano so that she can become a master maker of fireworks like her father
"This story is abundantly good natured and rich with humorous scenes and philosophical underpinings." Booklist

I was a rat! illustrated by Kevin Hawkes. Knopf 2000 164p $15.95; lib bdg $17.99; pa $4.99 (4 and up)   **Fic**
1. Fantasy fiction
ISBN 0-375-80176-6; 0-375-90176-0 (lib bdg); 0-440-41661-2 (pa)   LC 99-31806
First published 1999 in the United Kingdom with illustrations by Peter Bailey
"Pullman tells what happens to Cinderella's rat-turned-pageboy, who, busily sliding down banisters at the palace, misses the pumpkin-coach ride home and gets

Pullman, Philip—*Continued*
trapped in boy form. Young readers will find the story
completely entertaining, whether or not they appreciate
the playful spoofing of sensational news stories, mob
mentality, and the royal family." Horn Book Guide

The scarecrow and his servant; illustrated by
Peter Bailey. Knopf 2005 229p il $15.95; lib bdg
$17.99 (4-6)   **Fic**
  1. Scarecrows—Fiction 2. Fairy tales
  ISBN 0-375-81531-7; 0-375-91531-1 (lib bdg)
A scarecrow and his boy servant, Jack, set off on a
dangerous adventure as they try to outwit the crooked
Buffaloni family and stake their claim to valuable Spring
Valley.
"Pullman's clever employment of fairy-tale conventions, his superb use of language, and his engaging dialogue make it a wholly satisfying yarn of ridiculous proportions, and Bailey's line drawings provide just the
right feeling of long ago." SLJ

Quattlebaum, Mary
Grover G. Graham and me. Delacorte Press
2001 179p $14.95 (4 and up)   **Fic**
  1. Foster home care—Fiction 2. Infants—Fiction
  ISBN 0-385-32277-1   LC 2001-23510
In his eighth foster home since the death of his great-
grandmother, eleven-year-old Ben becomes very attached
to a baby living with the same family and worries when
the baby's biological mother takes him away
"Ben is a likable, multilayered character, and his lively, descriptive narrative, peppered with dry wit and intimate detail, is both an engaging read and an exploration
of foster care." Booklist

Jackson Jones and Mission Greentop. Delacorte
Press 2004 101p $15.95; lib bdg $17.99 (3-5)
                                    Fic
  1. Gardens—Fiction 2. African Americans—Fiction
  ISBN 0-385-73114-0; 0-385-90139-9 (lib bdg)
                           LC 2003-11823
His plot in a community garden brings 10-year-old
Jackson Jones more zucchini than he cares to see and the
unwanted attention of a bully, but when a company plans
to destroy the garden, Jackson turns his attention to trying to save it.
"Quattlebaum's talent for depicting a lively, diverse
neighborhood and funny interchanges between kids remains strong, as does her gift for simple conversational
writing." Horn Book Guide
 Another title about Jackson Jones is:
Jackson Jones and the puddle of thorns (1995)

Radin, Ruth Yaffe
Escape to the forest; based on a true story of the
Holocaust; illustrated by Janet Hamlin.
HarperCollins Pubs. 2000 90p il $13.95; lib bdg
$13.89 (3-6)   **Fic**
  1. Holocaust, 1933-1945—Fiction 2. Jews—Fiction
  ISBN 0-06-028520-6; 0-06-028521-4 (lib bdg)
                           LC 99-26426
Sarah, a young Jewish girl living with her family in
Poland at the beginning of World War II, recalls the hor-

rors of life under first the Russians then the Nazis, before fleeing to join Tuvia Bielski, a partisan who tried to
save as many Jews as possible. Based on a true story
"Stylistically simple but strongly plotted, the narrative
makes good use of suspense and contrast." Bull Cent
Child Books

Rand, Gloria
Sailing home; a story of a childhood at sea; told
by Gloria Rand; illustrated by Ted Rand.
North-South Bks. 2001 unp il $15.95; lib bdg
$15.88 (2-4)   **Fic**
  1. Madsen, Mads Albert—Fiction 2. Seafaring life—
  Fiction 3. Family life—Fiction
  ISBN 0-7358-1539-9; 0-7358-1540-2 (lib bdg)
                          LC 2001-34429
"A Cheshire Studio book"
Captain Madsen's four children fondly recall their exciting experiences sailing with their father and mother on
the bark John Ena at the turn of the twentieth century
"This story has an authentic ring and provides a fascinating glimpse into an era and way of life probably unfamiliar to most young readers. Ted Rand's characteristically vibrant and expressive color illustrations bring this
family saga to life." SLJ

Raskin, Ellen
The mysterious disappearance of Leon (I mean
Noel). Dutton 1971 149p il pa $5.99 hardcover
o.p. (4 and up)   **Fic**
  1. New York (N.Y.)—Fiction 2. Mystery fiction
  ISBN 0-14-032945-5 (pa)
"Wed at the age of five to a seven-year-old husband
(it solved a business difficulty for their two families), the
very young Mrs. Leon Carillon immediately loses her
spouse, who is sent off to boarding school. This is the
hilarious account of her search for Leon, aided by adopted twins, when she is older. With clever clues to stimulate the reader's participation, the story is a bouquet of
wordplay garnished with jokes, sly pokes at our society,
daft characters, and soupcon of slapstick. Fresh and funny, it's the kind of book that passes from child to child."
Saturday Rev

The Westing game. Dutton Children's Books
2003 182p $16.99; pa $5.99 (5 and up)
                                      Fic
  1. Mystery fiction
  ISBN 0-525-47137-5; 0-14-240120-X (pa)
                           LC 2004-268658
Awarded the Newbery medal, 1979
First published 1978
"This mystery puzzle . . . centers on the challenge set
forth in the will of eccentric multimillionaire Samuel
Westing. Sixteen heirs of diverse backgrounds and ages
are assembled in the old 'Westing house,' paired off, and
given clues to a puzzle they must solve—apparently in
order to inherit." SLJ
"The rules of the game make eight pairs of the players; each oddly matched couple is given a ten thousand
dollar check and a set of clues. The result is a fascinating medley of word games, disguises, multiple aliases
and subterfuges—in a demanding but rewarding book."
Horn Book

Rawlings, Marjorie Kinnan

The yearling; with pictures by N. C. Wyeth. Scribner 1985 c1938 400p il $28; pa $5.95 (6 and up)   **Fic**

1. Deer—Fiction 2. Florida—Fiction

ISBN 0-684-18461-3; 0-02-044931-3 (pa)

                 LC 85-40301

First published 1938; this is a reissue of the 1939 edition

"Young Jody Baxter lives a lonely life in the scrub forest of Florida until his parents unwillingly consent to his adopting an orphan fawn. The two become inseparable until the fawn destroys the meager crops. Then Jody realizes that this situation offers no compromise. In the sacrifice of what he loves best, he leaves his own yearling days behind." Read Ladders for Hum Relat. 5th edition

Rawls, Wilson

Where the red fern grows; the story of two dogs and a boy. Bantam Bks. 212p $16.95; pa $5.99 (4 and up)   **Fic**

1. Dogs—Fiction 2. Ozark Mountains—Fiction

ISBN 0-385-32330-1; 0-440-41267-6 (pa)

First published 1961 by Doubleday

"Looking back more than 50 years to his boyhood in the Ozarks, the narrator, recalls how he achieved his heart's desire in the ownership of two redbone hounds, how he taught them all the tricks of hunting, and how they won the championship coon hunt before Old Dan was killed by a mountain lion and Little Ann died of grief. Although some readers may find this novel hackneyed and entirely too sentimental, others will enjoy the fine coonhunting episodes and appreciate the author's feelings for nature." Booklist

Ray, Delia

Ghost girl; a Blue Ridge Mountain story. Clarion Bks. 2003 216p il $15 (5 and up)   **Fic**

1. Hoover, Herbert, 1874-1964—Fiction 2. Hoover, Lou Henry, 1874-1944—Fiction 3. School stories 4. Teachers—Fiction 5. Virginia—Fiction

ISBN 0-618-33377-0   LC 2003-4115

Eleven-year-old April is delighted when President and Mrs. Hoover build a school near her Madison County, Virginia, home but her family's poverty, grief over the accidental death of her brother, and other problems may mean that April can never learn to read from the wonderful teacher, Miss Vest

"This excellent portrayal of four important years in a girl's life rises to the top. Based on a real school and teacher, this novel seamlessly incorporates historical facts into the narrative." SLJ

Reaver, Chap

Bill. Delacorte Press 1994 216p pa $3.99 hardcover o.p. (5 and up)   **Fic**

1. Dogs—Fiction 2. Father-daughter relationship—Fiction 3. Prohibition—Fiction

ISBN 0-440-41153-X (pa)   LC 93-35491

With the help of her faithful dog Bill and the officer responsible for putting her father in jail, thirteen-year-old Jessica faces changes in her life when she realizes that her father will not stop drinking and making moonshine

"The story contains everything a reader could want—spunky, intriguing characters; a smart, loyal dog; hidden treasure; a raft trip; and a happy ending. Never lapsing into melodrama, the gripping novel depicts a girl and her dog who never give up and never let go of each other." Horn Book Guide

Recorvits, Helen

Goodbye, Walter Malinski; pictures by Lloyd Bloom. Foster Bks. 1999 85p il $15 (3-6)   **Fic**

1. Great Depression, 1929-1939—Fiction 2. Family life—Fiction 3. Death—Fiction 4. Polish Americans—Fiction

ISBN 0-374-32747-5   LC 97-35451

"Fifth-grader Wanda narrates a quiet portrait of Polish immigrants struggling to make ends meet in 1934. Out-of-work Pa takes out his frustrations on Wanda's older brother Walter. When Walter dies in an accident, the shock is great, but the family . . . is brought together with new affection. Beautifully composed illustrations add to the period atmosphere conveyed in the accessible, simply phrased narrative." Horn Book Guide

Reeder, Carolyn

Across the lines. Atheneum Bks. for Young Readers 1997 220p (5 and up)   **Fic**

1. United States—History—1861-1865, Civil War—Fiction 2. African Americans—Fiction 3. Race relations—Fiction

ISBN 0-689-81133-0   LC 96-31068

Available in paperback from HarperCollins

Edward, the son of a white plantation owner, and his black house servant and friend Simon witness the siege of Petersburg during the Civil War

"Told in the alternating voices of Edward and Simon, this thoughtful Civil War story resonates with authenticity." Horn Book Guide

Reiche, Dietlof

I, Freddy; book one in the golden hamster saga; translated from the German by John Brownjohn; illustrated by Joe Cepeda. Scholastic Press 2003 201p il $15.95; pa $4.99 (3-5)   **Fic**

1. Hamsters—Fiction

ISBN 0-439-28356-6; 0-439-28357-4 (pa)

                 LC 2002-6981

Freddy, a remarkably intelligent golden hamster, learns how to read and how to write on a computer and escapes captivity to become an independent and civilized creature

"Illustrated with amusing black-ink sketches, this engaging story will appeal to fans of animal fantasies." SLJ

Other titles about Freddy are:

Freddy in peril (2004)

Freddy to the rescue (2005)

The haunting of Freddy (2006)

Richards, Justin

Double life; [by] Justin Richards. G.P. Putnam's Sons 2005 c2003 204p (Invisible detective) $10.99 (5 and up) **Fic**

1. Mystery fiction

ISBN 0-399-24313-5   LC 2004-9536

First published 2003 in the United Kingdom

After finding a mysterious stone and an old casebook, fourteen-year-old Arthur finds himself remembering the 1936 adventures of a boy named Art who, under the identity of the Invisible Detective, works with three friends in London to solve the mystery of sinister puppets who are replacing real people.

This is a "fast-paced, action-packed [story] for mystery fans." SLJ

Other titles in the Invisible detective series are:

Ghost soldiers (2006)

Shadow beast (2005)

Richardson, Charisse K.

The real slam dunk; illustrated by Kadir Nelson. Dial Books for Young Readers 2005 64p il $15.99; pa $4.99 (2-4) **Fic**

1. Basketball—Fiction 2. African Americans—Fiction

ISBN 0-8037-3050-0; 0-14-240212-5 (pa)

     LC 2004-54880

Ten-year-old Marcus plans to become a professional basketball player, but when he, his twin sister Mia, and their classmates meet a real star on a school field trip, they learn the importance of dreaming more than one career dream.

"Marcus is an appealing character, and the easy format makes it a slam dunk for reluctant readers." Horn Book Guide

Another title about Marcus and Mia is:

The real lucky charm (2005)

Rinaldi, Ann

The journal of Jasper Jonathan Pierce, a pilgrim boy. Scholastic Press 2000 155p il (My name is America) $10.95 (4 and up) **Fic**

1. Pilgrims (New England colonists)—Fiction
2. Massachusetts—Fiction

ISBN 0-590-51078-9   LC 99-26028

A fourteen-year-old indentured servant keeps a journal of his experiences on the Mayflower and during the building of Plimoth Plantation in 1620 and 1621

"Written in a believable voice, the novel offers an interesting perspective on life aboard the ship and among the first colonists." Horn Book Guide

Riskind, Mary

Apple is my sign. Houghton Mifflin 1981 146p $14.95; pa $5.95 (5 and up) **Fic**

1. Deaf—Fiction

ISBN 0-395-30852-6; 0-395-65747-4 (pa)

"The story is set in Pennsylvania at the time of the first horseless carriages . . . in a school for the deaf. Ten-year-old Harry is at first homesick, but he soon makes friends, becomes excited about learning to draw and learning to talk. Aware that his father is ashamed of his own deafness (both parents are deaf) and that his

mother is not, Harry learns to accept his situation." Bull Cent Child Books

"In a lengthy note the author explains that she had deaf parents and learned sign language before she learned to speak. She also explores some characteristics of sign language, which has been translated into print via sentence syntax and spelling. A warm, unpretentious story." Booklist

Ritter, John H.

The boy who saved baseball. Philomel Bks. 2003 216p $17.99 (5 and up) **Fic**

1. Baseball—Fiction

ISBN 0-399-23622-8   LC 2002-15792

The fate of a small California town rests on the outcome of one baseball game, and Tom Gallagher hopes to lead his team to victory with the secrets of the now disgraced player, Dante Del Gato

"This tale is peppered with both optimism and dilemmas; it has plenty of play-by-play action, lots of humor, and a triumphant ending." SLJ

Over the wall. Philomel Bks. 2000 312p $17.99 (6 and up) **Fic**

1. Baseball—Fiction 2. New York (N.Y.)—Fiction

ISBN 0-399-23489-6   LC 99-49911

Thirteen-year-old Tyler, who has trouble controlling his anger, spends an important summer with his cousins in New York City, playing baseball and sorting out how he feels about violence, war, and in particular the Vietnamese conflict that took his grandfather's life

"Sports are just a part of this ambitious work that presents a compelling, multilayered story." SLJ

Roberts, Kristi

My 13th season; [by] Kristi Roberts. Henry Holt 2005 154p $15.95 (5 and up) **Fic**

1. Baseball—Fiction 2. Sex role—Fiction
3. Bereavement—Fiction

ISBN 0-8050-7495-3   LC 2004-52368

Already downhearted due to the loss of her mother and her father's overwhelming grief, thirteen-year-old Fran decides to give up her dream of becoming the first female in professional baseball after a coach attacks her just for being a girl.

"Funny, harsh, and poignant by turns, this strong first-person narrative establishes Fran's character through the most colorful, accessible side of her story before gradually letting readers in on her rich inner life of imagination, memory, and dreams." Booklist

Roberts, Willo Davis

The girl with the silver eyes. Atheneum Pubs. 1980 181p pa $4.50 o.p. (4-6) **Fic**

1. Psychokinesis—Fiction

ISBN 0-590-44248-1 (pa)   LC 80-12391

"Silver eyes are not all that set ten-year-old Katie apart from her peers—she's able to move things by thinking about them and talk to animals. Living with her mother for the first time since she was three, Katie tries to adjust to the other adults in the building, to her mom's male friend, and to her own strange situation." SLJ

Roberts, Willo Davis—*Continued*

"Much of the book's first half relies on diverting readers with examples of Katie's powers . . . while the second section builds more suspensefully around her efforts to track down the source of her problem, other children who might share it, and someone who will help her deal with it. . . . Roberts' smooth writing will lure them right to the end." Booklist

The kidnappers. Atheneum Bks. for Young Readers 1998 137p $15; pa $4.99 (4 and up)

                    Fic

1. Kidnapping—Fiction 2. Wealth—Fiction 3. New York (N.Y.)—Fiction

ISBN 0-689-81394-5; 0-689-81393-7 (pa)

                LC 96-53677

"A Jean Karl book"

No one believes eleven-year-old Joey, who has a reputation for telling tall tales, when he claims to have witnessed the kidnapping of the class bully outside their expensive New York City private school

"The combination of a witty narrative and a suspenseful plot makes this a good page-turner that will leave even the most reluctant readers glued to their seats." Booklist

The one left behind; [by] Willo Davis Roberts. 1st ed. Atheneum Books for Young Readers 2006 139p $16.95 (5 and up) **Fic**

1.   Sisters—Fiction   2.   Twins—Fiction 3. Bereavement—Fiction 4. Kidnapping—Fiction

ISBN 9-780-689-85075-2   LC 2005018196

"Since losing her vivacious twin sister, Angel, nearly a year ago, . . . 11-year-old [Mandy] drifts through the days, aching for her dead sister's company. But when someone breaks into the house and steals food, Mandy snaps into action and investigates what might be going on. . . . The suspense mounts to a desperate climax before all is resolved safely. An introspective page-turner." Booklist

Scared stiff. Atheneum Pubs. 1991 188p $16 (5 and up) **Fic**

1. Mystery fiction 2. Amusement parks—Fiction 3. Brothers—Fiction

ISBN 0-689-31692-5   LC 90-37732

"A Jean Karl book"

When their mother disappears, two brothers go to stay with a great uncle in a mobile home park next to an abandoned amusement park and begin a search which puts themselves in danger

"The brisk pace, fluid style, and excitement of the novel are sure to entertain readers, while the sensitive handling of such issues as separation and alcoholism, and the not-perfect ending make the book a cut above the general fare." SLJ

The view from the cherry tree. Atheneum Pubs. 1975 181p $16; pa $4.99 (5 and up) **Fic**

1. Mystery fiction

ISBN 0-689-30483-8; 0-689-71131-X (pa)

"Thoroughly disgruntled by the furor which accompanies his sister's wedding, eleven-year-old Rob Mallory retires to his favorite perch in the cherry tree. There, he is a horrified witness to the murder of an unpleasant

neighborhood recluse. Because of the wedding preparations and the arrival of hordes of relatives, no adult will believe Rob's story. Soon, he finds that someone knows—and is trying to kill him, too." Child Book Rev Serv

"Although written in a direct and unpretentious style, this is essentially a sophisticated story, solidly constructed, imbued with suspense, evenly paced, and effective in conveying the atmosphere of a household coping with the last-minute problems and pressures of a family wedding." Bull Cent Child Books

Robertson, Keith

Henry Reed, Inc.; illustrated by Robert McCloskey. Viking 1958 239p il pa $4.99 hardcover o.p. (4-6) **Fic**

ISBN 0-14-034144-7 (pa)

"Henry Reed, on vacation from the American School in Naples, keeps a record of his research into the American free-enterprise system, to be used as a school report on his return. With a neighbor, Midge Glass, he starts a business in pure and applied research, which results in some very free and widely enterprising experiences, all recorded deadpan in his journal. Very funny and original escapades." Hodges. Books for Elem Sch Libr

Another title about Henry Reed is:

Henry Reed's babysitting service (1966)

Robinet, Harriette Gillem

Forty acres and maybe a mule. Atheneum Bks. for Young Readers 1998 132p $16; pa $4.99 (4 and up) **Fic**

1. African Americans—Fiction 2. Reconstruction (1865-1876)—Fiction 3. United States—History—1865-1898—Fiction

ISBN 0-689-82078-X; 0-689-83317-2 (pa)

                LC 97-39169

Also available Thorndike Press large print edition

"A Jean Karl book"

Born with a withered leg and hand, Pascal, who is about twelve years old, joins other former slaves in a search for a farm and the freedom which it promises

"Robinet skillfully balances her in-depth historical knowledge with the feelings of her characters, creating a story that moves along rapidly and comes to a bittersweet conclusion." Booklist

Walking to the bus-rider blues. Atheneum Bks. for Young Readers 2000 146p $16; pa $4.99 (5 and up) **Fic**

1. African Americans—Fiction 2. Race relations—Fiction

ISBN 0-689-83191-9; 0-689-83886-7 (pa)

                LC 99-29054

"A Jean Karl book"

Twelve-year-old Alfa Merryfield, his older sister, and their grandmother struggle for rent money, food, and their dignity as they participate in the Montgomery, Alabama bus boycott in the summer of 1956

"Ingredients of mystery, suspense, and humor enhance and personalize this well-constructed story that offers insight into a troubled era." SLJ

Robinson, Barbara

The best Christmas pageant ever; pictures by Judith Gwyn Brown. Harper & Row 1972 80p il $15.99; lib bdg $16.89; pa $5.99 (4-6)

Fic

1. Christmas—Fiction 2. Pageants—Fiction
ISBN 0-06-025043-7; 0-06-025044-5 (lib bdg); 0-06-447044-X (pa)

In this story the six Herdmans, "absolutely the worst kids in the history of the world," discover the meaning of Christmas when they bully their way into the leading roles of the local church nativity play

The story "romps through the festive preparations with comic relish, and if the Herdmans are so gauche as to seem exaggerated, they are still enjoyable, as are the not-so-subtle pokes at pageant-planning in general." Bull Cent Child Books

Other titles about the Herdmans are:
The best Halloween ever (2004)
The best school year ever (1994)

Rocklin, Joanne

Strudel stories. Delacorte Press 1999 131p $14.95; pa $4.50 (4 and up)   Fic

1. Storytelling—Fiction 2. Jews—Fiction 3. Family life—Fiction
ISBN 0-385-32602-5; 0-440-41509-8 (pa)

LC 98-23141

Also available Thorndike Press large print edition

"Members of a Jewish family tell their stories across generations while baking strudel in kitchens from Odessa to New York's lower east side to Los Angeles. . . . Rocklin based her fiction on 'the memoirs of ordinary people,' and each of her narrators has an individual, personal voice that rings true." Bull Cent Child Books

Rockwell, Thomas

How to eat fried worms; pictures by Emily McCully. Watts 1973 115p il lib bdg $25 (3-6)

Fic

1. Worms—Fiction
ISBN 0-531-02631-0

Also available in paperback from Dell

"The stakes are high when Alan bets $50 that his friend Billy can't eat 15 worms (one per day). . . . Billy's mother, instead of upchucking, comes to her son's aid by devising gourmet recipes like Alsatian Smothered Worm. Alan wants to win as desperately as Billy, who is itching to buy a used minibike, and few holds are barred in the contest." SLJ

"A hilarious story that will revolt and delight bumptious, unreachable, intermediate-grade boys and any other less particular mortals that read or listen to it. . . . The characters and their families and activities are natural to a T, and this juxtaposed against the uncommon plot, makes for some colorful, original writing in a much-needed comic vein." Booklist

Rodda, Emily

Rowan of Rin. Greenwillow Bks. 2001 c1993 151p il $15.99; pa $5.99 (4-6)   Fic

1. Fantasy fiction
ISBN 0-06-029707-7; 0-06-056071-1 (pa)

LC 00-63619

First published 1993 in Australia

Because only he can read the magical map, young, weak and timid Rowan joins six other villagers to climb a mountain and try to restore their water supply, as fears of a dragon and other horrors threaten to drive them back

The author has created "a fully conceived fantasy world complete with its own flora and fauna, a well-developed back story, and fascinating characters." Booklist

Other titles about Rowan are:
Rowan and the Ice creepers (2003)
Rowan and the Keeper of the Crystal (2002)
Rowan and the travelers (2001)
Rowan and the Zebak (2002)

Rodgers, Mary

Freaky Friday. Harper & Row 1972 145p $15.95; lib bdg $16.89; pa $5.99 (4 and up)

Fic

1. Mother-daughter relationship—Fiction
ISBN 0-06-025048-8; 0-06-025049-6 (lib bdg); 0-06-057010-5 (pa)

"'When I woke up this morning, I found I'd turned into my mother.' So begins the most bizarre day in the life of 13-year-old Annabel Andrews, who discovers one Friday morning she has taken on her mother's physical characteristics while retaining her own personality. Readers will giggle in anticipation as Annabel plunges madly from one disaster to another trying to cope with various adult situations." Publ Wkly

"A fresh, imaginative, and entertaining story." Bull Cent Child Books

Rodman, Mary Ann

Yankee girl. Farrar, Straus and Giroux 2004 219p $17 (4 and up)   Fic

1. Race relations—Fiction 2. School stories 3. Mississippi—Fiction
ISBN 0-374-38661-7   LC 2003-49048

When her FBI-agent father is transferred to Jackson, Mississippi, in 1964, eleven-year-old Alice wants to be popular but also wants to reach out to the one black girl in her class in a newly-integrated school.

"Rodman shows characters grappling with hard choices, sometimes courageously, sometimes willfully, sometimes inconsistently, but invariably believably." Publ Wkly

Rodowsky, Colby F.

The next-door dogs; [by] Colby Rodowsky; pictures by Amy June Bates. . Farrar Straus & Giroux 2005 103p il $15 (2-4)   Fic

1. Dogs—Fiction 2. Fear—Fiction
ISBN 0-374-36410-9   LC 2004-43333

Although terrified of dogs, nine-year-old Sara forces herself to face a labrador retriever and a dalmatian when she must help her next-door neighbor, who has fallen and broken her leg.

"Rodowsky makes Sara's fear palpable and her eventual recovery believable. Plentiful pencil illustrations add to the book's accessibility." Horn Book Guide

Rodowsky, Colby F.—_Continued_

Not my dog; pictures by Thomas F. Yezerski. Farrar, Straus & Giroux 1999 69p il $15 (2-4) **Fic**

1. Dogs—Fiction
ISBN 0-374-35531-2   LC 98-26126

Eight-year-old Ellie has to give up her life-long dream of getting a puppy after her parents agree to take in the dog that Great-aunt Margaret can no longer keep

"The author writes a genuine, gently humorous and uncomplicated story about compromise and love." Publ Wkly

Spindrift; [by] Colby Rodowsky. Farrar, Straus & Giroux 2000 136p $16 (5 and up) **Fic**

1. Sisters—Fiction 2. Divorce—Fiction
ISBN 0-374-37155-5   LC 99-36263

During the summer after seventh grade, Cassie sees her close-knit family life in Bethany Beach, Delaware, changing drastically as her older sister has a baby, reveals the true nature of her husband, and announces the breakup of her marriage

"Readers drawn more to emotional drama than to action plots will find much to satisfy them in this realistic family story." Booklist

Rosen, Michael J.

Elijah's angel; a story for Chanukah and Christmas; illustrated by Aminah Brenda Lynn Robinson. Harcourt Brace Jovanovich 1992 unp il pa $6 hardcover o.p. (2-4) **Fic**

1. Pierce, Elijah, 1892-1984—Fiction 2. Artists—Fiction 3. Jews—Fiction 4. Christmas—Fiction 5. Hanukkah—Fiction
ISBN 0-15-201556-2 (pa)   LC 91-37552

At Christmas-Hanukkah time, Elijah Pierce, a black Christian woodcarver gives a carved angel to Michael, a young Jewish friend, who struggles with accepting the Christmas gift until he realizes that friendship means the same thing in any religion

"Perhaps because it's based on reality, Michael and Elijah's relationship rings sweetly true. The naive-style paintings, done in house paint on scrap rags, boldly simulate woodcuts, and though the artwork is not pretty, it, too, has the feel of reality." Booklist

A school for Pompey Walker; illustrated by Aminah Brenda Lynn Robinson. Harcourt Brace & Co. 1995 unp il $16 (2-4) **Fic**

1. Slavery—Fiction 2. African Americans—Fiction
ISBN 0-15-200114-X   LC 94-6240

This "story is based on the life of Gussie West, a slave who sold himself into slavery again and again, escaped each time with the help of his white friend, and used the money to build a school for freed black children. . . . Drawing on slave memoirs, Rosen imagines Pompey Walker telling his story, an elderly man remembering and talking to the children in his school." Booklist

"The narrator's voice is startlingly clear and natural. . . . Using dyes and bold, sinuous lines to suggest the rich, transparent coloring and stylized figures of stained glass, Robinson's full- and half-page illustrations convey strong feelings through facial expressions and gnarled, slightly oversized hands." SLJ

Ross, Adrienne

In the quiet. Delacorte Press 2000 148p $14.95 (5 and up) **Fic**

1. Aunts—Fiction 2. Death—Fiction
ISBN 0-385-32678-5   LC 99-35219

Eleven-year-old Sammy must deal with the death of her mother and the arrival of her mother's long-lost sister, who has a special gift

"The introspective first-person narrative effectively conveys Sammy's struggle and the story's hopeful resolution." Horn Book Guide

Rowling, J. K.

Harry Potter and the sorcerer's stone; illustrations by Mary Grandpré. Levine Bks. 1998 c1997 309p il $19.95; pa $6.99 (4 and up) **Fic**

1. Fantasy fiction 2. Witches—Fiction
ISBN 0-590-35340-3; 0-590-35342-X (pa)
   LC 97-39059

First published 1997 in the United Kingdom with title: Harry Potter and the philosopher's stone

Rescued from the outrageous neglect of his aunt and uncle, a young boy with a great destiny proves his worth while attending Hogwarts School for Witchcraft and Wizardry.

This "is a brilliantly imagined and beautifully written fantasy." Booklist

Other titles about Harry Potter are:
Harry Potter and the Chamber of Secrets (1999)
Harry Potter and the goblet of fire (2000)
Harry Potter and the half-blood prince (2005)
Harry Potter and the Order of the Phoenix (2003)
Harry Potter and the prisoner of Azkaban (1999)

Roy, Jennifer Rozines

Yellow star; by Jennifer Roy. Marshall Cavendish 2006 227p $16.95; $16.95 (5 and up) **Fic**

1. Holocaust, 1933-1945—Fiction 2. Jews—Fiction 3. Poland—Fiction
ISBN 978-0-7614-52; 0-7614-5277-X
   LC 2005-50788

From 1939, when Syvia is four and a half years old, to 1945 when she has just turned ten, a Jewish girl and her family struggle to survive in Poland's Lodz ghetto during the Nazi occupation.

"In a thoughtful, vividly descriptive, almost poetic prose, Roy retells the true story of her Aunt Syvia's experiences. . . . This book is a standout in the genre of Holocaust literature." SLJ

Ruby, Laura

Lily's ghosts. HarperCollins Pubs. 2003 258p $16.99; lib bdg $17.89 (5 and up) **Fic**

1. Ghost stories
ISBN 0-06-051829-4; 0-06-051830-8 (lib bdg)
   LC 2002-154315

Strange goings-on at her great-uncle's summer home in Cape May, New Jersey, draw Lily and a new friend into a mystery involving lost treasure, a fake medium, and ghosts of all sizes, shapes, and dispositions

Ruby, Laura—*Continued*
"Ruby doesn't horrify so much as she insinuates, in gracefully nuanced language that provides chilling support for the action." Bull Cent Child Books

The Wall and the Wing; [by] Laura Ruby. 1st ed. Eos 2006 327p $16.99; lib bdg $17.89 (5 and up) **Fic**
1. Orphans—Fiction 2. Fantasy fiction 3. New York (N.Y.)—Fiction
ISBN 978-0-06-075255-2; 0-06-075255-6; 978-0-06-075256-9 (lib bdg); 0-06-075256-4 (lib bdg)
LC 2005-23170
In a future New York where most people can fly and cats are a rarity, a nondescript resident of Hope House for the Homeless and Hopeless discovers that although she is shunned as a "leadfoot," she has the surprising ability to become invisible.
"This poor-little-rich-girl story is packed with wildly eccentric characters. . . . All of this fast-paced wackiness is told with humor, often black, that will have young readers giggling." SLJ

Ruckman, Ivy
Night of the twisters. Crowell 1984 153p lib bdg $15.89; pa $5.99 (4 and up) **Fic**
1. Tornadoes—Fiction 2. Nebraska—Fiction
ISBN 0-690-04409-7 (lib bdg); 0-06-440176-6 (pa)
LC 83-46168
"Twelve-year-old Dan describes the events leading up to the hour that his town was struck seven times by tornadoes. Alone at home, [in Grand Island, Nebraska] Dan, his baby brother, and his best friend Arthur ride out the storm huddled in the shower stall in Dan's basement and then begin the search for their parents." Sci Child
"Ruckman does a good job of creating and maintaining suspense, produces dialogue that sounds appropriate for a stress situation, and gives her characters some depth and differentiation." Bull Cent Child Books

Ruskin, John
The king of the Golden River **Fic**
1. Fairy tales
Available Simply Read edition illustrated by Iassen Ghiuselev
Written 1841
After Gluck's cruel and greedy older brothers refuse hospitality to a mysterious visitor, their prosperous farm fails and one by one each brother makes the perilous journey to find treasure in the nearby Golden River
"As a piece of literature it is excellent, with its charming descriptions full of color and sound." Johnson. Anthology of Children's Literature

Ryan, Pam Muñoz
Becoming Naomi León; [by] Pam Muñoz Ryan. 1st ed. Scholastic Press 2004 246p $16.95 (5 and up) **Fic**
1. Mexican Americans—Fiction 2. Mexico—Fiction 3. Family life—Fiction
ISBN 0-439-26969-5 LC 2004-346

When Naomi's absent mother resurfaces to claim her, Naomi runs away to Mexico with her great-grandmother and younger brother in search of her father
"Ryan has written a moving book about family dynamics. . . . All of the characters are well drawn." SLJ

Esperanza rising. Scholastic Press 2000 262p $15.95; pa $4.99 (5 and up) **Fic**
1. Mexican Americans—Fiction 2. Agricultural laborers—Fiction 3. California—Fiction
ISBN 0-439-12041-1; 0-439-12042-X (pa)
LC 00-24186
Esperanza and her mother are forced to leave their life of wealth and privilege in Mexico to go work in the labor camps of Southern California, where they must adapt to the harsh circumstances facing Mexican farm workers on the eve of the Great Depression
"Ryan writes movingly in clear, poetic language that children will sink into, and the [book] offers excellent opportunities for discussion and curriculum support." Booklist

Rylant, Cynthia
A blue-eyed daisy. Bradbury Press 1985 99p $15 (5 and up) **Fic**
1. Family life—Fiction 2. West Virginia—Fiction
ISBN 0-02-777960-2 LC 84-21554
This story "describes a year in a child's life. . . . Ellie is eleven, youngest of five girls. She wishes her father didn't drink but understands his frustration. . . . It is a bond between them when they acquire a hunting dog. . . . She also acquires a best friend during the year, gets her first kiss (and is surprised to see that she enjoys it) and adjusts to the fact that some of the events in her life will be sad ones." Bull Cent Child Books
"Episodic in nature, the story captures, as if in a frozen frame, the brief moments between childhood and adolescence." Horn Book

A fine white dust. Bradbury Press 1986 106p $16; pa $4.99 (5 and up) **Fic**
1. Religion—Fiction 2. Friendship—Fiction 3. Family life—Fiction
ISBN 0-02-777240-3; 0-689-80462-8 (pa)
LC 86-1003
Also available Thorndike Press large print edition
A Newbery Medal honor book, 1987
The visit of the traveling Preacher Man to his small North Carolina town gives new impetus to thirteen-year-old Peter's struggle to reconcile his own deeply felt religious belief with the beliefs and non-beliefs of his family and friends
"Blending humor and intense emotion with a poetic use of language, Cynthia Rylant has created a taut, finely drawn portrait of a boy's growth from seeking for belief, through seduction and betrayal, to a spiritual acceptance and a readiness 'for something whole.'" Horn Book

Missing May. Orchard Bks. 1992 89p $14.95; pa $5.99 (5 and up) **Fic**
1. Death—Fiction 2. West Virginia—Fiction
ISBN 0-531-05996-0; 0-439-61383-3 (pa)
LC 91-23303
Awarded the Newbery Medal, 1993
"A Richard Jackson book"

Rylant, Cynthia—*Continued*

After the death of the beloved aunt who has raised her, twelve-year-old Summer and her uncle Ob leave their West Virginia trailer in search of the strength to go on living

"There is much to ponder here, from the meaning of life and death to the power of love. That it all succeeds is a tribute to a fine writer who brings to the task a natural grace of language, an earthly sense of humor, and a well-grounded sense of the spiritual." SLJ

Sachar, Louis

Holes. Farrar, Straus & Giroux 1998 233p $17 (5 and up)   **Fic**
1. Juvenile delinquency—Fiction 2. Friendship—Fiction 3. Buried treasure—Fiction
ISBN 0-374-33265-7   LC 97-45011
Also available Thorndike Press large print edition and in paperback from Yearling
Awarded the Newbery Medal, 1999
"Frances Foster books"
As further evidence of his family's bad fortune which they attribute to a curse on a distant relative, Stanley Yelnats is sent to a hellish correctional camp in the Texas desert where he finds his first real friend, a treasure, and a new sense of himself

"This delightfully clever story is well-crafted and thought-provoking, with a bit of a folklore thrown in for good measure." Voice Youth Advocates
Another title about these characters is:
Small steps (2006)

Marvin Redpost, kidnapped at birth? illustrated by Neal Hughes. Random House 1992 68p il pa $3.99 hardcover o.p. (2-4)   **Fic**
ISBN 0-679-91946-5 (pa)   LC 91-51105
"A First Stepping Stone book"
Red-haired Marvin is convinced that the reason he looks different from the rest of his family is that he is really the lost prince of Shampoon

"Written almost completely in dialogue, the story is fast paced, easy to read, and full of humor." SLJ
Other titles about Marvin Redpost are:
Marvin Redpost, a flying birthday cake (1999)
Marvin Redpost, a magic crystal (2000)
Marvin Redpost, alone in his teacher's house (1994)
Marvin Redpost, class president (1999)
Marvin Redpost, is he a girl? (1993)
Marvin Redpost, superfast, out of control (2000)
Marvin Redpost, why pick on me? (1993)

Wayside School gets a little stranger; illustrated by Joel Schick. Morrow Junior Bks. 1995 168p il pa $4.95 hardcover o.p. (3-6)   **Fic**
1. School stories
ISBN 0-380-72381-6 (pa); 0-688-13694-X (hc)
      LC 94-25448
This is "about the zany goings-on in [an] unorthodox 30-story-tall school. . . . The narrative revolves around the wacky substitute teachers who take Mrs. Jewls's place when she is on maternity leave." Publ Wkly

"Sachar's offering contains hilarity, malevolence, romance, relentless punning, goofiness, inspiration, revenge, and poignancy." SLJ
Other titles about Wayside School are:

Sideways stories from Wayside School (1978)
Wayside School is falling down (1989)

Sachs, Marilyn

The four ugly cats in apartment 3D; illustrations by Rosanne Litzinger. Atheneum Bks. for Young Readers 2002 67p il $15 (3-5)   **Fic**
1. Cats—Fiction 2. Apartment houses—Fiction
ISBN 0-689-84581-2   LC 00-140225
"A Richard Jackson book"
After a neighbor in her apartment building dies, ten-year-old Lily tries to find homes for his four ugly, noisy cats

"Young readers . . . will appreciate the realism and suspense in this simple, warm story, nicely illustrated by stylized spot drawings." Booklist

Lost in America. Roaring Brook Press 2005 150p $16.95 (5 and up)   **Fic**
1. Jews—Fiction 2. Immigrants—Fiction 3. Holocaust, 1933-1945—Fiction
ISBN 1-59643-040-0   LC 2004-17551
Sequel to A pocket full of seeds (1973)
"A Deborah Brodie book"
Follows the experiences of Nicole, a teenaged French Jew, from 1943 to 1948, as she loses her parents and sister to the concentration camps and then leaves her native France to make a new life for herself in New York City.

"This is a moving coming-of-age story of a courageous girl." SLJ

Sage, Angie

Magyk; Septimus Heap, book one; illustrations by Mark Zug. Katherine Tegen Books 2005 576p il $16.99; lib bdg $17.89 (5 and up)   **Fic**
1. Fantasy fiction 2. Magic—Fiction
ISBN 0-06-057731-2; 0-06-057732-0 (lib bdg)
      LC 2003-28185
After learning that she is the Princess, Jenna is whisked from her home and carried toward safety by the Extraordinary Wizard, those she always believed were her father and brother, and a young guard known only as Boy 412, pursued by agents of those who killed her mother ten years earlier.

"Youngsters will lose themselves happily in Sage's fluent, charismatic storytelling, which enfolds supportive allies and horrific enemies, abundant quirky details, and poignant moments of self-discovery." Booklist
Another title in this series is:
Flyte (2006)

Saint-Exupéry, Antoine de

The little prince; written and illustrated by Antoine de Saint-Exupery; translated from the French by Richard Howard. Harcourt 2000 83p il $18; pa $12   **Fic**
1. Air pilots—Fiction 2. Extraterrestrial beings—Fiction
ISBN 0-15-202398-4; 0-15-601219-7 (pa)
      LC 99-50439
A new translation of the title first published 1943 by Reynal & Hitchcock

Saint-Exupéry, Antoine de—*Continued*

"This many-dimensional fable of an airplane pilot who has crashed in the desert is for readers of all ages. The pilot comes upon the little prince soon after the crash. The prince tells of his adventures on different planets and on Earth as he attempts to learn about the universe in order to live peacefully on his own small planet. A spiritual quality enhances the seemingly simple observations of the little prince." Shapiro. Fic for Youth. 3d edition

Salisbury, Graham

Lord of the deep. Delacorte Press 2001 182p $15.95; lib bdg $17.99; pa $7.99 (5 and up)
Fic

1. Fishing—Fiction 2. Stepfathers—Fiction 3. Hawaii—Fiction

ISBN 0-385-72918-9; 0-385-90013-9 (lib bdg); 0-440-22911-1 (pa) LC 00-60280

Working for Bill, his stepfather, on a charter fishing boat in Hawaii teaches thirteen-year-old Mikey about fishing, and about taking risks, making sacrifices, and facing some of life's difficult choices

"With its vivid Hawaiian setting, this fine novel is a natural for book-discussion groups that enjoy pondering moral ambiguity. Its action-packed scenes will also lure in reluctant readers." SLJ

Salten, Felix

Bambi; a life in the woods il (4-6) **Fic**

1. Deer—Fiction

Various editions available

Original German edition, 1923; first United States edition published 1928 by Simon & Schuster

"Bambi is a young deer, growing up in a forest, at first a curious child playing about his mother in glade and meadow, conversing with grasshoppers, squirrels and his own little cousins, Faline and Gobo." N Y Libr

"Felix Stalten's story of deer life in the woods that fringe the Danube is neither sentimental nor used to point a moral. It derives its dramatic value, legitimately, from the animals' fear and terror of their historic enemy—man. . . . In his absorption with details that author has brought his whole forest to life, yet these details are selected with a poet's intuition for delicacy of effect." NY Her Trib Books

San Souci, Robert

Kenneth Grahame's The reluctant dragon; retold by Robert D. San Souci; illustrated by John Segal. Orchard Books 2004 39p $16.95 (2-4)
Fic

1. Grahame, Kenneth, 1859-1932—Adaptations 2. Dragons—Fiction 3. Fairy tales

ISBN 0-439-45581-2 LC 2003-16678

"Jack meets the dragon and learns that he is a poet who would rather write than fight knights and breathe fire. . . . One day, Saint George rides into town to slay the beast, but the dragon refuses to take part in something so uncivilized. So with the help of Jack, they agree to stage a mock battle." Publisher's note

"For this elegantly designed volume, San Souci . . . breathes new life into the sword-and-scales genre with a snappy adaptation of Kenneth Grahame's 1898 short story. . . . Matching the text's dynamism, Segal's . . . illustrations seem a happy cross between medieval manuscripts and comic book panels." Publ Wkly

Sawyer, Ruth

Roller skates; written by Ruth Sawyer and illustrated by Valenti Angelo. Viking 1995 c1936 186p il $15.99; pa $5.99 (4-6) **Fic**

1. New York (N.Y.)—Fiction

ISBN 0-670-60310-4; 0-14-030358-8 (pa)
LC 85-43418

Also available in hardcover from P. Smith

Awarded the Newbery Medal, 1937

A reissue of the title first published 1936

"For one never-to-be forgotten year Lucinda Wyman (ten years old) was free to explore New York on roller skates. She made friends with Patrick Gilligan and his hansom cab, with Policeman M'Gonegal, with the fruit vendor, Vittore Coppicco and his son Tony, and with many others. All Lucinda's adventures are true and happened to the author herself as is borne out by the occasional pages of Lucinda's diary which are a part of the story." Horn Book

Schirripa, Steven R.

Nicky Deuce; welcome to the family; [by] Steven R. Schirripa & Charles Fleming. Delacorte Press 2005 167p $15.95 (4-6) **Fic**

1. Italian Americans—Fiction 2. Grandmothers—Fiction 3. Uncles—Fiction 4. Brooklyn (New York, N.Y.)—Fiction

ISBN 0-385-73257-0 LC 2004-28810

While his parents are on a cruise, twelve-year-old Nicholas spends his summer in Brooklyn with his grandmother and uncle and learns, with unintended results, about his Italian-American heritage.

The authors "have created a warm, funny story with memorable characters and enough shady intrigue to keep readers turning the pages." Booklist

Schmidt, Gary D.

Anson's way. Clarion Bks. 1999 213p $15 (5 and up) **Fic**

1. Ireland—Fiction

ISBN 0-395-91529-5 LC 98-29220

While serving as a British Fencible to maintain the peace in Ireland, Anson finds that his sympathy for a hedge master places him in conflict with the law of King George II

"Wonderfully descriptive, captivating prose and well-defined characters draw readers into eighteenth-century Ireland." Booklist

Schnur, Steven

The shadow children; illustrated by Herbert Tauss. Morrow Junior Bks. 1994 86p il $16; lib bdg $15.95 (5 and up) **Fic**

1. Holocaust, 1933-1945—Fiction 2. Ghost stories 3. France—Fiction

ISBN 0-688-13281-2; 0-688-13831-4 (lib bdg)
LC 94-5098

Schnur, Steven—*Continued*

While spending the summer on his grandfather's farm in the French countryside, eleven-year-old Etienne discovers a secret dating back to World War II and encounters the ghosts of Jewish children who suffered a dreadful fate under the Nazis

"The prose is spare and beautiful, and the expressive charcoal illustrations move from the warm affection of the present to the shadowy horror that won't go away." Booklist

Schulman, Janet

The nutcracker; [by] E.T.A. Hoffmann; adapted by Janet Schulman; illustrated by Renée Graef; audio CD narrated by Claire Bloom with music by Peter Ilyich Tchaikovsky. HarperCollins Pubs. 1999 34p il $19.95 (4 and up)   **Fic**

1. Fairy tales 2. Christmas—Fiction

ISBN 0-06-027814-5   LC 97-22346

This adaptation of the Nutcracker with illustrations by Kay Chorao was published 1979 by Dutton

One Christmas after hearing how the toy nutcracker made by her godfather got his ugly face, a little girl helps break the spell and watches him change into a handsome prince

"Graef's illustrations are floridly old-fashioned, with careful attention to period detail." Booklist

Schumacher, Julie

The chain letter. Delacorte Press 2005 195p $15.95; lib bdg $17.99 (5 and up)   **Fic**

1. Superstition—Fiction 2. Letters—Fiction

ISBN 0-385-73169-8; 0-385-90205-0 (lib bdg)

                           LC 2004-73

When sixth-grader Livvie decides to throw a chain letter in the trash, bad luck ensues.

"Readers . . . will appreciate the story's suspense, humor, and many examples of fine prose." SLJ

Schur, Maxine

The circlemaker; by Maxine Rose Schur. Dial Bks. for Young Readers 1994 179p pa $4.99 hardcover o.p. (5 and up)   **Fic**

1. Jews—Fiction 2. Russia—Fiction

ISBN 0-14-037997-5 (pa)   LC 93-17983

In mid-nineteenth century Russia, Mendel Cholinsky, a twelve-year-old Jewish boy tries to escape to America to avoid being taken into the Czar's army for twenty-five years of military service

"The action and suspense will draw readers to a book that could also be used by teachers and librarians for units on Russia, Judaism, multiculturalism, and prejudice." Book Rep

Scieszka, Jon

Knights of the kitchen table; illustrated by Lane Smith. Viking 1991 55p il (Time Warp Trio) $14.99; pa $4.99 (3-5)   **Fic**

1. Fantasy fiction

ISBN 0-670-83622-2; 0-14-034603-1 (pa)

                         LC 90-51009

"Transported to the Middle Ages, three friends save themselves from a dragon and a giant through quick thinking. The tongue-in-cheek narrative makes for laugh-out-loud enjoyment, and the easy-to-read sentences and zany dialogue perfectly suit the breathless pace." SLJ

Other titles about The Time Warp Trio are:

2095 (1995)

Da wild, da crazy, da Vinci (2004)

The good, the bad, and the goofy (1992)

Hey kid, want to buy a bridge? (2002)

It's all Greek to me (1999)

The not-so-jolly Roger (1991)

Oh say I can't see (2005)

Sam Samurai (2001)

See you later, gladiator (2000)

Summer reading is killing me! (1998)

Tut, tut (1996)

Viking it & liking it (2002)

Your mother was a Neanderthal (1993)

Seen Art? [by] Jon Scieszka and Lane Smith. Viking 2005 unp il $16.99   **Fic**

1. Museum of Modern Art (New York, N.Y.)—Fiction 2. Art appreciation—Fiction

ISBN 0-670-05986-2

While looking for his friend Art, a boy wanders through the Museum of Modern Art and is amazed by what he discovers there.

"The unusually long and narrow shape of the book and the stylized characters echo the modern-art theme while the muted background tones are an effective foil for the well-reproduced if sometimes diminutive artwork. . . . For anyone planning a trip to MoMA with a youngster, this is a provocative read." SLJ

Sebestyen, Ouida

Out of nowhere; a novel. Orchard Bks. 1994 183p lib bdg $17.99 (5 and up)   **Fic**

1. Dogs—Fiction 2. Foster home care—Fiction

ISBN 0-531-08689-5   LC 93-37759

Also available in paperback from Puffin Bks.

"A Melanie Kroupa book"

When he no longer fits into his vagabond mother's life, thirteen-year-old Harley adopts an abandoned dog and falls in with an outspoken old woman, a cantankerous junk collector, and an energetic and loving teenage girl

"This poignant story is beautifully written, and readers will delight in it." SLJ

Words by heart. Little, Brown 1979 162p pa $4.99 o.p. (5 and up)   **Fic**

1. African Americans—Fiction 2. Race relations—Fiction 3. Family life—Fiction

ISBN 0-440-22688-0 (pa)   LC 78-27847

"An Atlantic Monthly Press book"

"It is 1910, and Lena's family is the only black family in her small Southwestern town. When Lena wins a scripture reciting contest that a white boy is supposed to win, her family is threatened. Lena's father tries to make her understand that by hating the people who did this, the problems that cause their behavior are not solved. Only more hatred and violence cause Lena and the village to understand the words of her father." ALAN

Followed by On fire (1985)

Seidler, Tor

Brainboy and the Deathmaster. Laura Geringer Bks. 2003 311p $16.99; lib bdg $17.89 (5 and up) **Fic**

1. Orphans—Fiction 2. Video games—Fiction 3. Science fiction

ISBN 0-06-029181-8; 0-06-029182-6 (lib bdg)

LC 2002-33918

When Darryl, a twelve-year-old orphan, is adopted by a technology genius, he finds himself the star of his very own life-threatening video game

"A fast-paced, science-fiction adventure. . . . Seidler has created empathetic characters and writes at a level that is accessible even to readers not usually drawn to this genre." SLJ

The dulcimer boy; illustrations by Brian Selznick. Laura Geringer Bks. 2003 153p il $15.99; lib bdg $16.89 (4 and up) **Fic**

1. Dulcimers—Fiction 2. Twins—Fiction 3. Brothers—Fiction 4. New England—Fiction

ISBN 0-06-623609-6; 0-06-623610-X (lib bdg)

LC 2001-23875

A newly illustrated edition of the title first published 1979 by Viking Press

"Tracing the footsteps of musically gifted William Carbuncle from his arrival on his uncaring uncle's doorstep in a box containing him, his brother, and a silver-stringed dulcimer, the story follows William's escape and journey south. . . . Seidler's simple yet eloquent prose likens William's plight to a caged songbird. . . . Selznick's detailed sense of light and shadow shines as his soft-textured acrylic paintings not only echo the novel's overall poetic melancholy, but also serve as integral pieces of the plot itself." SLJ

The steadfast tin soldier; [by] Hans Christian Andersen; illustrated by Fred Marcellino; retold by Tor Seidler. HarperCollins Pubs. 1992 28p il $14.95; pa $6.95 (1-4) **Fic**

1. Andersen, Hans Christian, 1805-1875—Adaptations 2. Toys—Fiction 3. Fairy tales

ISBN 0-06-205000-1; 0-06-205900-9 (pa)

LC 92-52690

"Michael di Capua books"

This is a retelling of Andersen's fairy tale in which the one-legged tin soldier falls in love with a paper ballerina

The text is "lively and readable. . . . Marcellino . . . creates an exceptionally handsome version of the tale. Set in the nineteenth century, presumably in Denmark, the book includes impressive outdoor scenes under a pewter gray winter sky and domestic indoor scenes golden with the diffuse light of candles. Softly delineated forms and figures appear in a series of formally composed scenes sometimes reminiscent of dramatic tableaux. Designed with a sense of quiet elegance." Booklist

The Wainscott weasel; illustrated by Fred Marcellino. HarperCollins Pubs. 1993 193p il lib bdg $19.89; pa $11.95 (4-6) **Fic**

1. Weasels—Fiction 2. Animals—Fiction

ISBN 0-06-205033-8 (lib bdg); 0-06-205911-4 (pa)

LC 92-54526

"The weasels' summer begins with the visiting Wendy being charmed by both Zeke and Bagley Jr. . . . But Bagley pines for Bridget, a beautiful fish who lives in the nearby brook. . . . When Bridget's life is in danger, Bagley learns he can be a hero." Child Book Rev Serv

"Seidler's pacing is superb; he builds a solid structure within each chapter. A dry wit inspires his characterizations. . . . Marcellino enhances and even extends the beguiling ambiance with his exceptionally expressive art." Publ Wkly

Selden, George

The cricket in Times Square; illustrated by Garth Williams. Farrar, Straus & Giroux 1960 151p il $16 (3-6) **Fic**

1. Cats—Fiction 2. Crickets—Fiction 3. Mice—Fiction 4. New York (N.Y.)—Fiction

ISBN 0-374-31650-3

Also available in paperback from Dell

A Newbery Medal honor book, 1961

"An Ariel book"

"A touch of magic comes to Times Square subway station with Chester, a cricket from rural Connecticut. He is introduced to the distinctive character of city life by three friends: Mario Bellini, whose parents operate a newsstand; Tucker, a glib Broadway mouse; and Harry, a sagacious cat. Chester saves the Bellinis' business by giving concerts from the newsstand, bringing to rushing commuters moments of beauty and repose. This modern fantasy shows that, in New York, anything can happen." Moorachian. What is a City?

Other titles about Chester and his friends are:

Chester Cricket's new home (1983)

Chester Cricket's pigeon ride (1981)

Harry Cat's pet puppy (1974)

Harry Kitten and Tucker Mouse (1986)

The old meadow (1987)

Tucker's countryside (1969)

The genie of Sutton Place. Farrar, Straus & Giroux 1973 175p pa $4.95 hardcover o.p. (4 and up) **Fic**

ISBN 0-374-42530-2 (pa)

Also available in hardcover from P. Smith

Adapted from the television play written by the author and Kenneth Heuer

"Tim turns to his dead father's diaries for some occult wisdom to help him keep Sam, a beloved mongrel his aunt has banished from their apartment. What he finds is a spell that summons the genie Abdullah from a thousand years' captivity in a woven carpet." Booklist

"The speedy action and clever dialogue in this witty book are sure to entice readers." SLJ

Sendak, Maurice

Higglety pigglety pop! or, There must be more to life; story and pictures by Maurice Sendak. HarperCollins Pubs. c1967 69p il $14.95; pa $8.95 (2-4) **Fic**

1. Dogs—Fiction

ISBN 0-06-028479-X; 0-06-443021-9 (pa)

Copyright renewed 1995

Sendak, Maurice—*Continued*

In this modern fairy tale "Jennie, the Sealyham terrier, leaves home because 'there must be more to life than having everything.' When she applies for a job as the leading lady of the World Mother Goose Theater, she discovers that what she lacks is experience. What follows are her adventures and her gaining of experience; finally Jennie becomes the leading lady of the play." Wis Libr Bull

"The story has elements of tenderness and humor; it also has . . . typically macabre Sendak touches. . . . The illustrations are beautiful, amusing, and distinctive." Sutherland. The Best in Child Books

Seredy, Kate

The Good Master; written and illustrated by Kate Seredy. Viking 1935 210p il pa $4.99 hardcover o.p. (4-6)   **Fic**

1. Farm life—Fiction 2. Hungary—Fiction
ISBN 0-14-030133-X (pa)

A Newbery Medal honor book, 1936

Into this story of Jancsi, a ten-year-old Hungarian farm boy and his little hoyden of a cousin Kate from Budapest, is woven a description of Hungarian farm life, fairs, festivals, and folk tales. Under the tutelage of Jancsi's kind father, called by the neighbors The Good Master, Kate calms down and becomes a more docile young person

"The steady warm understanding of the wise father, the Good Master, is a shining quality throughout." Horn Book

Followed by The singing tree (1939)

The white stag; written and illustrated by Kate Seredy. Viking 1937 94p il pa $4.99 hardcover o.p. (4-6)   **Fic**

1. Hungary—Fiction
ISBN 0-14-031258-7 (pa)

Awarded the Newbery Medal, 1938

"Striking illustrations interpret this hero tale of the legendary founding of Hungary, when a white stag and a red eagle led the people to their promised land." Hodges. Books for Elem Sch Libr

Serraillier, Ian

The silver sword; illustrated by C. Walter Hodges. Phillips 1959 c1956 187p il $31.95 (5 and up)   **Fic**

1. World War, 1939-1945—Fiction 2. Polish refugees—Fiction
ISBN 0-87599-104-1

First published 1956 in the United Kingdom; first United States edition published 1959 by Criterion Books

"As a result of World War II, the Balicki family of Warsaw are separated from one another. Living in bombed-out cellars or the countryside the children are helped by Edek until his arrest for smuggling and from then on by Jan, a sullen orphan. The privations of each member of the family, especially the children, are graphically described as each works toward their rendezvous, Switzerland, and freedom. A suspense-filled, exciting story." Read Ladders for Hum Relat. 5th edition

Service, Pamela F.

Stinker from space. Scribner 1988 83p pa $5.99 o.p. (4-6)   **Fic**

1. Science fiction
ISBN 0-449-70330-4 (pa)   LC 87-25266

An agent of the Sylon Confederacy, fleeing from enemy ships, crash lands on Earth, transfers his mind to the body of a skunk, and enlists the aid of two children in getting back to his home planet

"A first-class, funny science fantasy that will hook middle-grade readers right from the first scene. . . . The situation is gratifyingly absurd, the development satisfyingly natural." Bull Cent Child Books

Setterington, Ken

The wild swans; an adventure in six parts. Tundra Books 2003 35p il $17.95 (4-6)

                                  Fic

1. Fairy tales
ISBN 0-88776-615-3

"Borrowing from European folklore . . . and illustrated with traditional cut-paper art, this . . . fairy tale tells of brave Elise, who weaves stinging nettles into shirts that save her 11 brothers from a curse that has transformed them into swans. The clear storytelling style blends the contemporary . . . with the traditional. . . . The small, intricate, black-and-white illustrations, delicate and formal in design, fit well with the story. . . . A long, fascinating chapter at the back fills in facts about the history and tradition of cut-paper art." Booklist

Seuling, Barbara

Robert and the back-to-school special; illustrated by Paul Brewer. Cricket Bks. 2002 104p il $15.95 (2-4)   **Fic**

1. School stories 2. Halloween—Fiction
ISBN 0-8126-2662-1   LC 2002-9325

The new school year gets off to a not-so-good start when Robert gets a bad haircut, but things improve when his father helps him plan a party for Halloween

"This book offers a lot of chuckles. The resolutions to Robert's problems are all within a child's realm, and the dynamics of his family ring true. The soft, black-and-white illustrations are upbeat." SLJ

Other titles about Robert are:

Oh no, its Robert (1999)
Robert and the great escape (2003)
Robert and the great pepperoni (2001)
Robert and the lemming problem (2003)
Robert and the practical jokes (2006)
Robert and the weird & wacky facts (2002)
Robert finds a way (2005)
Robert takes a stand (2004)

Sewell, Anna

Black Beauty (4-6)   **Fic**

1. Horses—Fiction 2. Great Britain—Fiction

Some editions are:

Grosset & Dunlap (Illustrated junior library) $14.95 Illustrated by Fritz Eichenberg (ISBN 0-448-40942-9)

Knopf (Everyman's library children's classics) $13.95 Illustrated by Lucy Kemp-Welch (ISBN 0-679-42811-9)

First published 1877 in the United Kingdom; first United States edition, 1891

Sewell, Anna—*Continued*

This is "the most celebrated 'Animal Story' of the 19th cent., an account of a horse's experiences at the hands of many owners, ranging from the worthy Squire Gordon to a cruel cab-owner." Oxford Companion to Child Lit

Shafer, Anders C.

The fantastic journey of Pieter Bruegel. Dutton Children's Bks. 2002 unp il $18.99 (4 and up) **Fic**

1. Brueghel, Pieter, the Elder, 1522?-1569—Fiction 2. Voyages and travels—Fiction 3. Artists—Fiction

ISBN 0-525-46986-9   LC 2002-25024

For over two years in the mid-1500s, Pieter Bruegel keeps a journal of his trip from his home in Antwerp, The Netherlands, to Rome, where he studies art before returning home again

"The illustrations are well imagined, beautifully rendered drawings washed with watercolors and acrylics. . . . The book ends with two solid, instructive additions . . . a four-page section with 16 very small, color reproductions of Bruegel's paintings, each accompanied by identifying notes and a well-written paragraph of comments, as well as a page about the artist's life and works." Booklist

Shalant, Phyllis

Bartleby of the mighty Mississippi; with illustrations by Anna Vojtech. Dutton Children's Bks. 2000 164p il $15.99 (3-6) **Fic**

1. Turtles—Fiction

ISBN 0-525-46033-0   LC 99-89893

After being abandoned in a pond, Bartleby, a pet turtle, meets many other creatures, learns to survive in the wild, and decides to go in search of his birthplace

"Shalant's novel is a sweet, warm allegory about the pains of growing up." SLJ

Another title about Bartleby is:
Bartleby of the big bad bayou (2005)

Beware of kissing Lizard Lips. Dutton Children's Bks. 1995 183p $14.99 (4-6) **Fic**

1. School stories 2. Martial arts—Fiction 3. Korean Americans—Fiction

ISBN 0-525-45199-4   LC 94-44389

"Zach wants to stop being Mouseboy, the smallest in the sixth grade, and at the mercy of Lizard Lips, the tallest girl. He finds some hope, physically and spiritually, from learning tae kwon do and becomes interested in a girl in his class." SLJ

"This is a laugh-out-loud story about growing up male, written without a trace of condescension." Booklist

When pirates came to Brooklyn. Dutton Children's Bks. 2002 212p $16.99 (4 and up) **Fic**

1. Jews—Fiction 2. Brooklyn (New York, N.Y.)—Fiction 3. Friendship—Fiction

ISBN 0-525-46920-6

"Lee Bloom, 10, is an imaginative, intelligent, but lonely girl living in Brooklyn, NY, in 1960. . . . When Lee meets vibrant Polly Burke . . . the two girls know that they have found a kindred spirit in one another. However, Lee is Jewish, Polly is Catholic, and their bigoted mothers are fiercely prejudiced against the girls' friendship. . . . Elements of magical realism enhance the story, as do scenes filled with humor, and the themes of prejudice and injustice may prompt readers toward further thought and discussion." SLJ

Shearer, Alex

The Great Blue Yonder. Clarion Bks. 2002 c2001 184p $15 (5 and up) **Fic**

1. Future life—Fiction

ISBN 0-618-21257-4   LC 2001-47741

First published 2001 in the United Kingdom

This "novel tells the story of Harry, killed in a bicycle accident. Initially confused by his new existence in the Other Side, the flippant 12-year-old realizes he cannot move toward the peace of the Great Blue Yonder until he has addressed the unfinished business in his life. . . . Amusing, poignant, and deeply moving. A great main character and unusual topical matter combine to make a unique winner of a book that will leave readers laughing through their tears." SLJ

Sherlock, Patti

Letters from Wolfie. Viking 2004 232p $16.99 (5 and up) **Fic**

1. Dogs—Fiction 2. Vietnam War, 1961-1975—Fiction

ISBN 0-670-03694-3   LC 2003-24316

Certain that he is doing the right thing by donating his dog, Wolfie, to the Army's scout program in Vietnam, thirteen-year-old Mark begins to have second thoughts when the Army refuses to say when and if Wolfie will ever return.

"In this topnotch novel, Sherlock weaves together numerous threads of emotion, information, and plot so seamlessly that readers will be surprised by how much they've learned by the time they finish this deceptively simple story." SLJ

Sheth, Kashmira

Blue jasmine; [by] Kashmira Sheth. 1st ed. Hyperion Books for Children 2004 186p $15.99; pa $5.99 (5 and up) **Fic**

1. Immigrants—Fiction 2. East Indians—Fiction 3. India—Fiction

ISBN 0-7868-1855-7; 0-7868-5565-7 (pa)

LC 2003-50818

When twelve-year-old Seema moves to Iowa City with her parents and younger sister, she leaves friends and family behind in her native India but gradually begins to feel at home in her new country.

"Seema's story, which articulates the ache for distant home and family, will resonate with fellow immigrants and enlighten their classmates." Booklist

Shipton, Paul

The pig scrolls; by Gryllus the pig; [by] Paul Shipton. Candlewick Press 2005 c2004 274p $15.99 (5 and up) **Fic**

1. Pigs—Fiction 2. Classical mythology—Fiction

ISBN 0-7636-2702-X   LC 2005-50177

Shipton, Paul—*Continued*

A translation of an ancient Greek manuscript written by Gryllus, a talking pig who was once a man, which describes the many adventures that he and his companions—a junior prophetess named Sybil and a bumbling goatherd—experience while traveling to Delphi to try to prevent the universe from coming to an end.

"Shipton combines humor and action with bits of abstract thought about death and life. . . . More farce than epic, this story does manage to provide a little bit to chew on after the laughter stops." SLJ

Shreve, Susan Richards

Blister; by Susan Shreve. Levine Bks. 2001 153p $15.95 (4 and up) **Fic**

1. Family life—Fiction 2. Moving—Fiction

ISBN 0-439-19313-3 LC 00-61887

When a family tragedy occurs, ten-year-old Alyssa "Blister" Reed changes schools, moves to an apartment with her depressed mother while her father gets his own place, and tries to believe her grandmother, who tells her she is "elastic" and can handle it all

"With a tightly woven plot, entirely convincing characters and flashes of humor. . . . Shreve again proves herself an inspired and inspiring storyteller." Publ Wkly

The flunking of Joshua T. Bates; [by] Susan Shreve; illustrated by Diane de Groat. Knopf 1984 82p il pa $4.99 hardcover o.p. (3-5) **Fic**

1. School stories 2. Teachers—Fiction 3. Family life—Fiction

ISBN 0-679-84187-3 (pa) LC 83-19636

"Sometimes children, especially boys, are held back in school even if they are smart. To his dismay, Joshua T. Bates was supposed to repeat the whole third grade, but he was lucky enough to have a very sympathetic teacher." N Y Times Book Rev

"In addition to the warm depiction of a teacher-pupil relationship, the story has other relationships, astutely drawn: Joshua's parents, the former classmate who teases Joshua, the best friend who stoutly defends him. The dialogue is particularly good, often contributing to characterization, just as often crisply humorous." Bull Cent Child Books

Other titles about Joshua are:

Joshua T. Bates in trouble again (1997)

Joshua T. Bates takes charge (1993)

Trout and me. Knopf 2002 136p $15.95; lib bdg $17.99; pa $4.99 (5 and up) **Fic**

1. Friendship—Fiction 2. Attention deficit disorder—Fiction 3. School stories

ISBN 0-375-81219-9; 0-375-91219-3 (lib bdg); 0-0440-41902-6 (pa) LC 2002-22858

Ben's troubles at school get progressively worse when he starts hanging around Trout, a new boy in his fifth grade class, who is also labeled as learning disabled

"Fusing humor and pathos, Shreve introduces characters of uncommon dimension and complexity—and leaves readers with subtle issues to ponder." Publ Wkly

Under the Watson's porch; [by] Susan Shreve. 1st ed. Alfred A. Knopf 2004 199p $15.95; lib bdg $17.99 (5 and up) **Fic**

1. Friendship—Fiction

ISBN 0-375-82630-0; 0-375-92630-5 (lib bdg)

LC 2003-61383

Twelve-year-old Ellie's boring summer becomes exciting when she develops a crush on her new next-door neighbor, an older boy with a troubled past, whom her parents have forbidden her to see.

"Ellie's first-person narration is utterly and immediately believable. . . . Shreve imagines a troubled kid with unusual sensitivity and depth, and this novel will be treasured by readers." Booklist

Shulevitz, Uri

The travels of Benjamin of Tudela; through three continents in the twelfth century; [by] Uri Shulevitz. Farrar, Straus & Giroux 2005 unp il maps $17 (4 and up) **Fic**

1. Benjamin, of Tudela, 12th cent.—Fiction 2. Jews—Fiction 3. Middle Ages—Fiction 4. Voyages and travels—Fiction

ISBN 0-374-37754-5 LC 2004-40434

A fictionalized account of the travels of Benjamin, a Jewish man from Tudela, Spain, who, in 1159, set out on a fourteen-yearlong journey that took him to Italy, Greece, Palestine, Persia, China, Egypt, and Sicily.

"The richly painted scenes, which vary in style and color according to their location, are highlighted by collage accents. Together with the evocative text, they capture the sweep of mysterious and faraway places." Booklist

Includes bibliographical references

Shyer, Marlene Fanta

Fleabiscuit sings! Marshall Cavendish 2005 150p $15.95 (3-5) **Fic**

1. Dogs—Fiction 2. New York (N.Y.)—Fiction

ISBN 0-7614-5213-3 LC 2004-19454

A down-on-their luck New York City family thinks they can make some money when they discover that their neighbor's dog can sing harmony in the family's subway singing act.

"Interesting details flesh out the quirky characters. A lively read." SLJ

Siebold, Jan

My nights at the Improv; by Jan Siebold. Albert Whitman & Co. 2005 98p $14.95 (4 and up) **Fic**

1. Moving—Fiction 2. Acting—Fiction 3. School stories

ISBN 0-8075-5630-0 LC 2005004590

"Lizzie, an eighth-grader struggling with a move to a new town, feels as though her voice is on 30-second delay. . . . She learns to confront her fear of speaking out by secretly observing a community-education class on improvisational-drama techniques. . . . Improvisational theater is a fascinating topic that is not often represented in fiction for this age group; the concept is well covered in this high-interest novel." SLJ

Singer, Isaac Bashevis

The fools of Chelm and their history; pictures by Uri Shulevitz; translated by the author and Elizabeth Shub. Farrar, Straus & Giroux 1973 57p il $14; pa $4.95 (4 and up)   **Fic**

1. Jews—Fiction

ISBN 0-374-32444-1; 0-374-42429-2 (pa)

The "town of Chelm is just like every place else, only worse, as numerous shortages, foolish citizens, and inept leaders combine to make life thoroughly miserable. . . . Singer mocks the 'advantages'—such as war, crime, and revolution—that civilization brings to Chelm, as the leadership changes but never improves." Booklist

"An amusing story, well-told. The pen-and-ink illustrations embellish the text, adding droll touches of their own." Horn Book

Skurzynski, Gloria

The virtual war. Simon & Schuster Bks. for Young Readers 1997 152p $16; pa $4.99 (6 and up)   **Fic**

1. Science fiction 2. Virtual reality—Fiction

ISBN 0-689-81374-0; 0-689-82425-4 (pa)

LC 96-35346

In a future world where global contamination has necessitated limited human contact, three young people with unique genetically engineered abilities are teamed up to wage a war in virtual reality

"Skurzynski's anti-war message is clear yet never didactic; her characters are complex and fully realized, the pacing brisk, and the story compelling." Bull Cent Child Books

Other titles in this series are:

The clones (2002)

The revolt (2005)

Sleator, William

The beasties. Dutton Children's Bks. 1997 198p $15.99; pa $5.99 (6 and up)   **Fic**

1. Ecology—Fiction 2. Horror fiction

ISBN 0-525-45598-1; 0-14-130639-4 (pa)

LC 97-6147

"In this horror tale, Doug and his sister are captured by the beasties who live in tunnels underneath the forest. Threatened and genetically mutated by the destruction of the wilderness, the beasties have taken to kidnapping people and amputating body parts they need. Sleator handles the ickier aspects of the story with aplomb, and the menacing atmosphere and suspense-serving pace are all they should be." Horn Book Guide

The boxes. Dutton Children's Bks. 1998 196p $15.99; pa $4.99 (6 and up)   **Fic**

1. Science fiction

ISBN 0-525-46012-8; 0-14-130810-9 (pa)

LC 98-9285

When she opens two strange boxes left in her care by her mysterious uncle, fifteen-year-old Annie discovers a swarm of telepathic creatures and unleashes a power capable of slowing down time

"Sleator has written a page-turner. . . . His writing is crisp and clean, letting the story speak for itself." Voice Youth Advocates

Interstellar pig. Dutton 1984 197p pa $6.99 hardcover o.p. (5 and up)   **Fic**

1. Science fiction

ISBN 0-14-037595-3 (pa)   LC 84-4132

"Solitary and bored, Barney is quickly attracted by the exotic appearance and protean personalities of Zena, Manny, and Joe, who have rented the summer house next door. The interest of the sophisticated adults in sixteen-year-old Barney at first flatters, then intrigues, and finally terrifies him as he becomes absorbed in their compulsion to possess 'The Piggy.' When he realizes that the talisman has power, the game expands in significance." Horn Book

The author "draws the reader in with intimations of danger and horror, but the climactic battle is more slapstick than horrific, and the victor's prize could scarcely be more ironic. Problematic as straight science fiction but great fun as a spoof on human-alien contact." Booklist

Another title about Barney is:

Parasite Pig (2002)

Into the dream; illustrated by Ruth Sanderson. Dutton 1979 137p il pa $4.99 hardcover o.p. (5 and up)   **Fic**

1.   Extrasensory   perception—Fiction 2. Psychokinesis—Fiction 3. Unidentified flying objects—Fiction

ISBN 0-14-130814-1 (pa)   LC 78-11825

When two youngsters realize they are having the same frightening dream, they begin searching for an explanation for this mysterious coincidence

"Tightly woven suspense and an ingenious, totally involving plot line . . . make this a thriller of top-notch quality." Booklist

Slepian, Jan

The Broccoli tapes. Philomel Bks. 1989 157p $15.99 (5 and up)   **Fic**

1. Cats—Fiction 2. Death—Fiction 3. Hawaii—Fiction

ISBN 0-399-21712-6   LC 88-25490

"Both 12-year-old Sara and her 13-year-old brother, Sam, have trouble adjusting to Hawaii during the five months that their family is living there. . . . When Sara and Sam rescue a wild cat (who is later named Broccoli), they meet Eddie Nutt. At first Eddie is as suspicious and untrusting as Broccoli until the bonds of friendship gradually develop. The story unfolds through Sara's cassette tapes sent to her teacher and classmates back home." SLJ

"Slepian is a fine writer, and the elements of her story are smoothly meshed, the action and characterization mutually affective. The message that love is worth the chance of pain is given by the people in her story, not didactically imposed by the author." Bull Cent Child Books

Slote, Alfred

Finding Buck McHenry. HarperCollins Pubs. 1991 250p lib bdg $15.89; pa $4.95 (4-6)   **Fic**

1. Baseball—Fiction 2. African Americans—Fiction

ISBN 0-06-021653-0 (lib bdg); 0-06-440469-2 (pa)

LC 90-39190

Slote, Alfred—*Continued*

Eleven-year-old Jason, believing the school custodian Mack Henry to be Buck McHenry, a famous pitcher from the old Negro League, tries to enlist him as a coach for his Little League team by revealing his identity to the world

"Slote skillfully blends comedy, suspense and baseball in a highly entertaining tale." Publ Wkly

Hang tough, Paul Mather. Lippincott 1973 156p pa $4.95 hardcover o.p. (4-6)   **Fic**
1. Leukemia—Fiction 2. Baseball—Fiction
ISBN 0-06-440153-7 (pa)

"Paul Mather, a Little League star pitcher before he contracted leukemia, is unable to resist the temptation to demonstrate his skill when his family moves to Michigan and he ends up in the hospital." Booklist

"The story of Paul's candor and courage is convincing, sad but never morbid, in a book that has depth and integrity." Bull Cent Child Books

The trading game. Lippincott 1990 200p pa $4.95 hardcover o.p. (4-6)   **Fic**
1. Baseball cards—Fiction 2. Grandfathers—Fiction
ISBN 0-06-440438-2 (pa)   LC 89-12851

"Andy Harris' baseball-card collection, inherited from his recently deceased father, contains some valuable items, including a 1952 Mickey Mantle card worth $2500. He's willing, however, to trade Mantle for a 25-cent card that pictures his grandfather, Jim 'Ace 459' Harris, whom Andy idolizes. . . . It's not until Grampa coaches Andy that he learns why the relationship between his father and grandfather was strained." SLJ

"Slote does a masterful job grounding the moral dilemmas of growing up within the rigorously measured world of the baseball diamond. Friendship, father-son intimacy, and the rough edges of adult life are all examined and filtered through the eyes of a boy who instinctively understands more than he knows." Booklist

Smith, Cynthia Leitich

Indian shoes; illustrated by Jim Madsen. HarperCollins Pubs. 2002 66p il $15.95; lib bdg $15.89 (3-5)   **Fic**
1. Grandfathers—Fiction 2. Native Americans—Fiction
ISBN 0-06-029531-7; 0-06-029532-5 (lib bdg)
LC 2001-39510

Together with Grampa, Ray Halfmoon, a Seminole-Cherokee boy, finds creative and amusing solutions to life's challenges

"The writing is warm and lively; the situations are sometimes humorous, sometimes poignant; and Ray and Grampa's loving relationship is depicted believably and without sentimentality." Horn Book Guide

Smith, D. James

The boys of San Joaquin; a novel. Atheneum Books for Young Readers 2005 231p $15.95 (5 and up)   **Fic**
1. Family life—Fiction 2. Italian Americans—Fiction 3. Deaf—Fiction 4. California—Fiction
ISBN 0-689-87606-8   LC 2004-3075
"A Richard Jackson book"

In a small California town in 1951, twelve-year-old Paolo and his deaf cousin Billy get caught up in a search for money missing from the church collection, leading them to complicated discoveries about themselves, other family members, and townspeople they thought they knew.

"Narrator Paolo has an appealingly distinctive voice and a keen eye for observing people, and the supporting characters are equally memorable." Booklist

Smith, Doris Buchanan

A taste of blackberries; illustrated by Charles Robinson. Crowell 1973 58p il lib bdg $14.89; pa $4.95 (4-6)   **Fic**
1. Death—Fiction 2. Friendship—Fiction
ISBN 0-690-80512-8 (lib bdg); 0-06-440238-4 (pa)

A "portrayal of the death of a close friend. While gathering Japanese beetles to help a neighbor, Jamie is stung by a bee and falls screaming and writhing to the ground. His best friend (never named) disgustedly stalks off, only to find later that Jamie is dead of the bee sting. The boy feels guilty because he thought Jamie was clowning and didn't try to help. The boy is very withdrawn the week of the funeral, but comes to grips with the tragedy and learns to manage his grief." SLJ

"A difficult and sensitive subject, treated with taste and honesty, is woven into a moving story about a believable little boy. The black-and-white illustrations are honest, affective, and sensitive." Horn Book

Smith, Janice Lee

The kid next door and other headaches; stories about Adam Joshua; drawings by Dick Gackenbach. Harper & Row 1984 143p il lib bdg $14.89 (2-4)   **Fic**
1. Friendship—Fiction
ISBN 0-06-025793-8   LC 83-47689
"Adam Joshua and Nelson, who are best friends as well as next-door neighbors, play and battle as best friends do. Their finest hour is coping with a visit from Nelson's truly horrid cousin Cynthia." N Y Times Book Rev

"This book has all the ingredients necessary for the often reluctant transition from easy readers to chapter books: large print and an ample supply of dialogue, humor and wonderfully funny black-and-white illustrations." SLJ

Other titles about Adam Joshua are:
The monster in the third dresser drawer and other stories about Adam Joshua (1981)
The show-and-tell war and other stories about Adam Joshua (1988)

Smith, Robert Kimmel

Bobby Baseball; illustrated by Alan Tiegreen. Delacorte Press 1989 165p il pa $4.50 hardcover o.p. (4-6)   **Fic**
1. Father-son relationship—Fiction 2. Baseball—Fiction
ISBN 0-440-40417-7 (pa)   LC 89-1175
Ten-year-old Bobby is passionate about baseball and convinced that he is a great player. The only problem is to get a chance to prove his skill, especially to his father

Smith, Robert Kimmel—*Continued*

"Baseball fans who share Bobby's fantasies will admire his determination and empathize with his stinging realization. Smith's crisp dialogue vivifies the book's appealing characters, and Tiegreen's illustrations lend an antic touch to Bobby's predicaments. This is an upbeat, refreshing celebration of the spirit of our national pastime." Publ Wkly

Chocolate fever; illustrated by Gioia Fiammenghi. Putnam 1989 c1972 93p il $13.89 (4-6) **Fic**

ISBN 0-399-61224-6   LC 88-23508

Also available in paperback from Dell

A reissue of the title first published l972 by Coward-McCann

"You've heard of too much of a good thing? You've never heard of it the way it happens to Henry Green. Henry's a chocolate maven, first class. No, that's too mild. Henry's absolutely freaky over chocolate, loco over cocoa. He can't get enough, until—aaarrrfh! Brown spots, brown bumps all over Henry. It's (gulp) 'Chocolate Fever.'" N Y Times Book Rev

"It's all quite preposterous and lots of laughs, and so are the cartoon illustrations." Publ Wkly

The war with Grandpa; illustrated by Richard Lauter. Delacorte Press 1984 141p il pa $4.99 hardcover o.p. (4-6) **Fic**

1. Grandfathers—Fiction 2. Family life—Fiction

ISBN 0-440-49276-9 (pa)   LC 83-14366

"Pete's Grandpa comes to live with the family and bumps Pete out of the room he's had 'forever.' Egged on by his buddies, Pete starts a war of notes and practical jokes. To his surprise, Grandpa enjoys the skirmishes and the two carry on a quiet campaign for a while. In the final episode, Pete realizes just how wrong he has been and Grandpa comes up with a happy solution. This should be a winner with the middle grade set." Child Book Rev Serv

Smith, Roland

Cryptid hunters. Hyperion Books for Children 2005 348p $15.99 (5 and up) **Fic**

1. Twins—Fiction 2. Congo (Republic)—Fiction 3. Adventure fiction

ISBN 0-7868-5161-9

Twins, Grace and Marty, along with a mysterious uncle, are dropped into the middle of the Congolese jungle in search of their missing photojournalist parents.

"The action is nonstop in this well-paced jungle adventure, and Smith adds a deeper layer in scenes of Marty and Grace discovering truths about their complicated family relationships." Booklist

Sneve, Virginia Driving Hawk

High Elk's treasure; illustrated by Oren Lyons. Holiday House 1995 c1972 96p il $15.95

Fic

1. Dakota Indians—Fiction

ISBN 0-8234-0212-6

A reissue of the title first published 1972

"When Joe High Elk and his sister take refuge from a storm in a cave used by their revered ancestor Steps High Like an Elk, Joe finds a mysterious package that may shed light on the true story of the Battle of the Little Big Horn. . . . [This] paints an authentic portrait of modern Sioux life and culture." Horn Book Guide

Snicket, Lemony

The bad beginning; illustrations by Brett Helquist. HarperCollins Pubs. 1999 162p il (Series of unfortunate events) $11.99; lib bdg $15.89 (4 and up) **Fic**

1. Orphans—Fiction

ISBN 0-06-440766-7; 0-06-028312-2 (lib bdg)

LC 99-14750

After the sudden death of their parents, the three Baudelaire children must depend on each other and their wits when it turns out that the distant relative who is appointed their guardian is determined to use any means necessary to get their fortune

"While the misfortunes hover on the edge of being ridiculous, Snicket's energetic blend of humor, dramatic irony, and literary flair makes it all perfectly believable. . . . Excellent for reading aloud." SLJ

Other titles about the Baudelaire children are:

The austere academy (2000)
The carnivorous carnival (2003)
The ersatz elevator (2000)
The grim grotto (2004)
The hostile hospital (2001)
The miserable mill (2000)
The penultimate peril (2005)
The reptile room (1999)
The slippery slope (2003)
The vile village (2001)
The wide window (2000)

Lemony Snicket: the unauthorized autobiography. HarperCollins Pubs. 2002 212p il $11.99; lib bdg $14.89 (4 and up) **Fic**

ISBN 0-06-000719-2; 0-06-000720-6 (lib bdg)

LC 2001-51745

"The story of the fictitious Lemony Snicket and how he has dedicated his life to the case of the orphaned Baudelaire children. . . . Snicket tells you what he cannot tell you and then tells you, but what he tells you makes no sense. . . . [A] hilarious and clever book. . . . Lemony Snicket fans will love it, and new readers will laugh so much that they will want to read the series." Voice Youth Advocates

Snyder, Zilpha Keatley

Cat running. Delacorte Press 1994 168p $15.95; pa $4.99 (4 and up) **Fic**

1. Great Depression, 1929-1939—Fiction 2. Running—Fiction

ISBN 0-385-31056-0; 0-440-41152-1 (pa)

LC 94-447

"Sixth grader Cat Kinsey is sure she is the fastest runner in Brownwood School until Zane Perkins arrives barefoot and clothed in ragged overalls. He's an 'Okie,' and to most Californians during the Great Depression, that automatically translates to 'lazy, dirty, and shiftless.' When Cat's father forbids her to wear slacks because he

Snyder, Zilpha Keatley—*Continued*
feels they are unseemly, she ignores Zane's challenge and refuses to race during the school's annual Play Day. . . . This story is both appealing and informative. The characters are well drawn and beautifully motivated." SLJ

The Egypt game; drawings by Alton Raible. Atheneum Pubs. 1967 215p il $17 (5 and up) **Fic**

ISBN 0-689-30006-9

Also available in paperback from Dell

A Newbery Medal honor book, 1968

"Six children of different ethnic backgrounds secretly play a game invented by a white girl and a [black] girl who are fascinated by their own imaginations and by ancient Egypt. The Egypt game helps solve one girl's personal problems and it leads to the capture of a mentally ill murderer who attacks one of the girls." Wis Libr Bull

This book "is strong in characterization, the dialogue is superb, the plot is original, and the sequences in which the children are engaged in sustained imaginative play are fascinating, and often very funny." Saturday Rev

The ghosts of Rathburn Park. Delacorte Press 2002 182p $15.95; lib bdg $17.99; pa $5.50 (5 and up) **Fic**

1. Ghost stories

ISBN 0-385-32767-6; 0-385-90064-3 (lib bdg); 0-440-41711-2 (pa) LC 2002-848

Lost in the woods of Rathburn Park, eleven-year-old Matthew weighs the odds of dying from thirst, embarrassment, or at the hands of the forest's reputed ghostly inhabitants

"This skillfully told story is full of both history and middle-grade concerns about peer pressure and acceptance." SLJ

The headless cupid; illustrated by Alton Raible. Atheneum Pubs. 1971 203p il $17 (5 and up) **Fic**

1. Occultism—Fiction

ISBN 0-689-20687-9

Also available in paperback from Dell

A Newbery Medal honor book, 1972

"Story of an unhappy adolescent's preoccupation with the occult, her relationships with her step-siblings, and her eventual acceptance of the tangible world. Set in present-day California." Publisher's note

"The author portrays children with acute understanding, evident both in her delineation of Amanda and David and of the distinctively different younger children. Good style, good characterization, good dialogue, good story." Sutherland. The Best in Child Books

Libby on Wednesdays. Delacorte Press 1990 196p pa $4.99 hardcover o.p. (5 and up) **Fic**

1. Authorship—Fiction 2. Friendship—Fiction 3. School stories

ISBN 0-440-40498-3 (pa) LC 89-34959

"Libby, age eleven, very bright and the only child in an unconventional but strong household, has heretofore been home-educated. She is enrolled in public school for 'socialization' but soon finds that her peers tease her and

mock her enormous wealth of knowledge. Only when she is selected for a writer's group does she forge ties to some equally gifted students." Child Book Rev Serv

"Vivid descriptions and clear portraits of the characters give an honest, forthright picture of these classmate-turned-friends who come to accept their difficulties and to care about each other. It's an absorbing story, filled with real young people and genuine concerns." SLJ

The magic nation thing; [by] Zilpha Keatley Snyder. Delacorte Press 2005 164p $15.95; lib bdg $17.99 (4 and up) **Fic**

1. Extrasensory perception—Fiction 2. San Francisco (Calif.)—Fiction

ISBN 0-385-73085-3; 0-385-90107-0 (lib bdg) LC 2004-10105

Although twelve-year-old Abby has always tried to deny that she has some kind of weird psychic power, she takes advantage of it to help her mother, a struggling private investigator, and, more importantly, to find her best friend's little brother when he goes missing at a ski resort.

"Readers will delight in Snyder's vivid descriptions of Abby's special powers, but what will draw them most is the warm, believable story." Booklist

The runaways. Delacorte Press 1999 245p $15.95; pa $4.99 (4 and up) **Fic**

1. Runaway children—Fiction 2. Nevada—Fiction

ISBN 0-385-32599-1; 0-440-41512-8 (pa) LC 98-22258

Twelve-year-old Dani hates living in the small desert town of Rattler Springs, Nevada, but her plans to run away get complicated when nine-year-old Stormy and an imaginative new girl named Pixie decide they want to go along

"The book is set in the 1950s, and the dying town and desperate people are very real and touching. The plight of these creative and neglected children will keep readers turning the pages." SLJ

Spyhole secrets. Delacorte Press 2001 186p $15.95; lib bdg $17.99 (4 and up) **Fic**

1. Death—Fiction 2. Moving—Fiction

ISBN 0-385-32764-1; 0-385-32764-1 (lib bdg) LC 00-48508

When Hallie and her mother move to a new town after her father's sudden death, Hallie begins to spy on a troubled family living in a nearby building and her involvement helps her begin to handle her feelings of anger and grief

"This complex, appealing novel combines edgy Hitchcockian suspense with an insightful exploration of a young person's coping with loss." Booklist

The Unseen. Delacorte Press 2004 199p $15.95; lib bdg $17.99 (5 and up) **Fic**

1. Supernatural—Fiction

ISBN 0-385-73084-5; 0-385-90106-2 (lib bdg) LC 2003-46299

Feeling angry and out-of-place in her large family, twelve-year-old Xandra finds a magical key to a world of ghostly, sometimes frightening, phantoms that help her see herself and her siblings more clearly.

"This book is a wonderful ride into fantasy, with a lot of realistic touches to think about and relationships to

Snyder, Zilpha Keatley—*Continued*

ponder. . . . This perceptive story is not to be missed."
SLJ

The witches of Worm; illustrated by Alton
Raible. Atheneum Pubs. 1972 183p il $17 (5 and
up)   **Fic**
1. Witchcraft—Fiction 2. Cats—Fiction
ISBN 0-689-30066-2

Also available in paperback from Dell
A Newbery Medal honor book, 1973

Jessica, the neglected child of a divorcee, "finds a deserted, new-born kitten which she calls 'Worm' since it
is virtually hairless and blind. When this Worm turns—
daily becoming more dominant over its mistress—Jessica
is convinced she is in the grip of a hellish force that
makes her play harmful tricks on her mother and on her
few friends." Publ Wkly

"This is a haunting story of the power of mind and
ritual, as well as of misunderstanding, anger, loneliness
and friendship. It is written with humor, pace, a sure
feeling for conversation and a warm understanding of human nature." Commonweal

Sobol, Donald J.

Encyclopedia Brown, boy detective; illustrated
by Leonard Shortall. Dutton Children's Bks. 1963
88p il pa $4.50 o.p. (3-5)   **Fic**
1. Mystery fiction
ISBN 0-553-15724-8 (pa)

First published by Thomas Nelson

"Leroy Brown earns his nickname by applying his encyclopedic learning to community mysteries. The reader
is asked to anticipate solutions before checking them in
the back of the book." Natl Counc of Teach of Engl. Adventuring with Books. 2d edition

"The answers are logical; some are tricky, but there
are no trick questions, and readers who like puzzles
should enjoy the . . . challenge. The episodes are lightly
humorous, brief, and simply written." Bull Cent Child
Books

Other titles about Encyclopedia Brown are:
Encyclopedia Brown and the case of the dead eagles
   (1975)
Encyclopedia Brown and the case of the disgusting
   sneakers (1990)
Encyclopedia Brown and the case of the jumping frogs
   (2003)
Encyclopedia Brown and the case of the midnight visitor
   (1977)
Encyclopedia Brown and the case of the mysterious
   handprints (1985)
Encyclopedia Brown and the case of Pablo's nose (1996)
Encyclopedia Brown and the case of the secret pitch
   (1965)
Encyclopedia Brown and the case of the sleeping dog
   (1998)
Encyclopedia Brown and the case of the slippery sala-
   mander (1999)
Encyclopedia Brown and the case of the treasure hunt
   (1988)
Encyclopedia Brown and the case of the two spies
   (1994)
Encyclopedia Brown finds the clues (1966)
Encyclopedia Brown gets his man (1967)

Encyclopedia Brown keeps the peace (1969)
Encyclopedia Brown lends a hand (1974)
Encyclopedia Brown saves the day (1970)
Encyclopedia Brown sets the pace (1982)
Encyclopedia Brown shows the way (1972)
Encyclopedia Brown solves them all (1968)
Encyclopedia Brown takes the cake! (1983)
Encyclopedia Brown takes the case (1973)
Encyclopedia Brown tracks them down (1971)

Sorensen, Virginia Eggertsen

Miracles on Maple Hill; [by] Virginia Sorensen;
illustrated by Beth and Joe Krush. Harcourt 2003
232p il $17; pa $5.95 (4 and up)   **Fic**
1. Family life—Fiction 2. Country life—Fiction
3. Pennsylvania—Fiction
ISBN 0-15-204719-0; 0-15-204718-2 (pa)
                                      LC 2003-49939

Awarded the Newbery Medal, 1957
"An Odyssey/Harcourt Young Classic"
A reissue of the title first published 1956

After her father returns from the war moody and tired,
Marly's family decides to move from the city to Maple
Hill Farm in the Pennsylvania countryside where they
share many adventures which help restore their spirits
and their bond with each other

"Vivid descriptions of the countryside and excellent
characterization mark each page of the book." Booklist

Soto, Gary

Taking sides. Harcourt Brace Jovanovich 1991
138p $17; pa $5.95 (5 and up)   **Fic**
1. Hispanic Americans—Fiction 2. Basketball—Fiction
ISBN 0-15-284076-1; 0-15-204694-1 (pa)
                                      LC 91-11082

Fourteen-year-old Lincoln Mendoza, an aspiring basketball player, must come to terms with his divided loyalties when he moves from the Hispanic inner city to a
white suburban neighborhood

This is a "light but appealing story. . . . Because of
its subject matter and its clear, straightforward prose, it
will be especially good for reluctant readers." SLJ

Includes glossary

Speare, Elizabeth George

The bronze bow. Houghton Mifflin 1961 255p
$16; pa $6.95 (6 and up)   **Fic**
1. Jesus Christ—Fiction 2. Christianity—Fiction
3. Palestine—Fiction
ISBN 0-395-07113-5; 0-395-13719-5 (pa)

Awarded the Newbery Medal, 1962

"Daniel had sworn vengence against the Romans who
had killed his parents, and he had become one of a band
of outlaws. . . . Each time he saw the Rabbi Jesus, the
youth was drawn to his cause; at last he resolved his
own conflict by giving up his hatred and, as a follower
of the Master, accepting his enemies. The story has drama and pace, fine characterization, and colorful background detail." Bull Cent Child Books

The sign of the beaver. Houghton Mifflin 1983
135p $16 (5 and up)   **Fic**
1. Frontier and pioneer life—Fiction 2. Native Americans—Fiction 3. Friendship—Fiction
ISBN 0-395-33890-5   LC 83-118

Speare, Elizabeth George—*Continued*

Also available in paperback from Dell

A Newbery Medal honor book, 1984

Left alone to guard the family's wilderness home in eighteenth-century Maine, Matt is hard-pressed to survive until local Indians teach him their skills

Matt "begins to understand the Indians' ingenuity and respect for nature and the devastating impact of the encroachment of the white man. In a quiet but not unsuspenseful story . . . the author articulates historical facts along with the adventures and the thoughts, emotions, and developing insights of a young adolescent." Horn Book

The witch of Blackbird Pond. Houghton Mifflin 1958 249p $16 (6 and up)   **Fic**

1. Connecticut—History—1600-1775, Colonial period—Fiction 2. Witchcraft—Fiction 3. Puritans—Fiction

ISBN 0-395-07114-3   LC 58-11063

Also available in paperback from Dell

Awarded the Newbery Medal, 1959

"Headstrong and undisciplined, Barbados-bred Kit Tyler is an embarrassment to her Puritan relatives, and her sincere attempts to aid a reputed witch soon bring her to trial as a suspect." Child Books Too Good to Miss

Sperry, Armstrong

Call it courage; illustrations by the author. Macmillan 1940 95p il $16; pa $4.99 (5 and up)   **Fic**

1. Courage—Fiction 2. Polynesia—Fiction

ISBN 0-02-786030-2; 0-689-71391-6 (pa)

Also available Spanish language edition

Awarded the Newbery Medal, 1941

"Because he fears the ocean, a Polynesian boy is scorned by his people and must redeem himself by an act of courage. His lone journey to a sacred island and the dangers he faces there earn him the name Mafatu, 'Stout Heart.' Dramatic illustrations add atmosphere and mystery." Hodges. Books for Elem Sch Libr

Spinelli, Jerry

Crash. Knopf 1996 162p $16; pa $4.99 (5 and up)   **Fic**

1. Football—Fiction 2. Grandfathers—Fiction 3. Friendship—Fiction

ISBN 0-679-87957-9; 0-679-88550-1 (pa)

                LC 95-30942

"Crash is a star football player. He torments Penn, a classmate who is everything Crash is not—friendly, small, and a pacifist. When his beloved grandfather comes to live with his family and suffers a debilitating stroke, Crash begins to see value in many of the things he has scorned." Horn Book Guide

"Readers will devour this humorous glimpse at what jocks are made of while learning that life does not require crashing helmet-headed through it." SLJ

Loser. HarperCollins Pubs. 2002 218p $15.99; lib bdg $16.89; pa $5.99 (4 and up)   **Fic**

1. School stories 2. Family life—Fiction

ISBN 0-06-000193-3; 0-06-000483-5 (lib bdg); 0-06-054074-5 (pa)   LC 2001-47484

"Joanna Cotler books"

Even though his classmates from first grade on have considered him strange and a loser, Daniel Zinkoff's optimism and exuberance and the support of his loving family do not allow him to feel that way about himself

"This novel is an offbeat, affectionate, colorful, and melancholy work." Voice Youth Advocates

Maniac Magee; a novel. Little, Brown 1990 184p $16.99 (5 and up)   **Fic**

1. Orphans—Fiction 2. Homeless persons—Fiction 3. Race relations—Fiction

ISBN 0-316-80722-2   LC 89-27144

Also available Thorndike Press large print edition and in paperback from HarperCollins Pubs.

Awarded the Newbery Medal, 1991

"Orphaned at three, Jeffery Lionel Magee, after eight unhappy years with relatives, one day takes off running. A year later, he ends up 200 miles away in Two Mills, a highly segregated community. Part tall tale and part contemporary realistic fiction, this unusual novel magically weaves timely issues of homelessness, racial prejudice, and illiteracy into an energetic story that bursts with creativity, enthusiasm, and hope for the future. In short, it's a celebration of life." Booklist

There's a girl in my hammerlock. Simon & Schuster Bks. for Young Readers 1991 199p pa $4.99 hardcover o.p. (5 and up)   **Fic**

1. Wrestling—Fiction 2. Sex role—Fiction 3. School stories

ISBN 0-671-86695-8 (pa)   LC 91-8765

Thirteen-year-old Maisie joins her school's formerly all-male wrestling team and tries to last through the season, despite opposition from other students, her best friend, and her own teammates

The author "tackles a meaty subject—traditional gender roles—with his usual humor and finesse. The result, written in a breezy, first-person style, is a rattling good sports story that is clever, witty and tightly written." Publ Wkly

Wringer. HarperCollins Pubs. 1997 228p $16.99; lib bdg $16.89; pa $6.50 (4 and up)   **Fic**

1. Courage—Fiction 2. Violence—Fiction 3. Pigeons—Fiction

ISBN 0-06-024913-7; 0-06-024914-5 (lib bdg); 0-06-440578-8 (pa)   LC 96-37897

A Newbery Medal honor book, 1998

"Joanna Cotler books"

"During the annual pigeon shoot, it is a town tradition for 10-year-old boys to break the necks of wounded birds. In this riveting story told with verve and suspense, Palmer rebels." SLJ

Spinner, Stephanie

Be first in the universe; [by] Stephanie Spinner and Terry Bisson. Delacorte Press 2000 133p $14.95; pa $4.99 (4-6)   **Fic**

1. Twins—Fiction 2. Science fiction 3. Extraterrestrial beings—Fiction

ISBN 0-385-32687-4; 0-440-41639-6 (pa)

                LC 99-39933

Spinner, Stephanie—*Continued*

While staying with their hippie grandparents, ten-year-old twins, Tod and Tessa, discover an unusual shop at the nearby mall, where they find a lie-detecting electronic pet, a Do-Right machine, and other alien gadgets which help them foil their nemeses, the evil Gneiss twins

"Spinner and Bisson . . . write with verve and wit, and a good time will be had by all." Booklist

Springer, Nancy

The case of the missing marquess; an Enola Holmes mystery. Philomel Books 2006 216p $10.99 (5 and up) **Fic**

1. Mystery fiction
ISBN 0-399-24304-6

Enola Holmes, much younger sister of detective Sherlock Holmes, must travel to London in disguise to unravel the disappearance of her missing mother.

"Enola's loneliness, intelligence, sense of humor, and sheer pluck make her an extremely appealing heroine." SLJ

Rowan Hood, outlaw girl of Sherwood Forest. Philomel Bks. 2001 170p $16.99 (4 and up) **Fic**

1. Robin Hood (Legendary character)—Fiction
2. Middle Ages—Fiction 3. Adventure fiction
ISBN 0-399-23368-7   LC 00-63694

In her quest to connect with Robin Hood, the father she has never met, thirteen-year-old Rosemary disguises herself as a boy, befriends a half-wolf, half-dog, a runaway princess, and an overgrown boy whose singing is hypnotic, and makes peace with her elfin heritage

"This tale is a charmer, filled with exciting action, plenty of humor, engaging characters, and a nice fantasy twist." Booklist

Other titles about Rowan Hood are:
Lionclaw (2002)
Outlaw princess of Sherwood (2003)
Rowan Hood returns (2005)
Wild boy (2004)

Spyri, Johanna

Heidi (4 and up) **Fic**

1. Switzerland—Fiction 2. Alps—Fiction
Some editions are:
Grosset & Dunlap (Illustrated junior library) $17.99 Illustrated by William Sharp (ISBN 0-448-40563-6)
Morrow Junior Bks. (Books of Wonder) $24.99 Illustrated by Jessie W. Smith (ISBN 0-688-14519-1)
First published 1880

"The story of Heidi is the story of the greatness of her affection for her pet goats, for Peter and her grandfather, and for her mountain home. Permeating the whole tale is the play of sunshine and shadow on the slopes of the jagged peaks of the great, glittering, snow-capped mountains of Heidi's [Swiss] Alpine home. A book which finds a responsive chord in every young heart." Toronto Public Libr

St. Anthony, Jane

The summer Sherman loved me; [by] Jane St. Anthony. 1st ed. Farrar Straus Giroux 2006 136p $16 **Fic**

1. Family life—Fiction 2. Mother-daughter relationship—Fiction 3. Friendship—Fiction
ISBN 0-374-3728-6   LC 2005046361

In addition to coping with her changing relationship with her mother, twelve-year-old Margaret spends her summer trying to sort out her feelings for the boy next door who claims to love her.

"This fluidly told, well-paced novel is set in a more innocent time. . . . The emotions experienced by the well-drawn characters, however, remain universal. A fresh and refreshing coming-of-age story." SLJ

Stanek, Muriel

I speak English for my mom; illustrations by Judith Friedman. Whitman, A. 1989 unp il lib bdg $13.95 (2-4) **Fic**

1. Mexican Americans—Fiction 2. Mother-daughter relationship—Fiction
ISBN 0-8075-3659-8   LC 88-20546

Lupe, a young Mexican American, must translate for her mother who speaks only Spanish until Mrs. Gomez decides to learn English in order to get a better job

"Stanek provides a nicely rounded look at a situation common to immigrant families." Booklist

Stanley, Diane

Bella at midnight; illustrated by Bagram Ibatoulline. 1st ed. HarperCollins Pub. 2006 278p il $15.99; lib bdg $16.89 (5 and up) **Fic**

1. Knights and knighthood—Fiction 2. Fairy tales
ISBN 0-06-077573-4; 0-06-077574-2 (lib bdg); 9780060775742 (lib bdg)   LC 2005-05906

Raised by peasants, Bella discovers that she is actually the daughter of a knight and finds herself caught up in a terrible plot that will change her life and the kingdom forever.

"What raises this above other recreated fairy tales is the quality of the writing, dotted with jeweled description and anchored by the strong values—loyalty, truth, honor." Booklist

Roughing it on the Oregon Trail; illustrated by Holly Berry. HarperCollins Pubs. 2000 unp il (Time-traveling twins) $15.95; lib bdg $15.89 (2-4) **Fic**

1. Oregon Trail—Fiction 2. Overland journeys to the Pacific—Fiction 3. Frontier and pioneer life—Fiction
ISBN 0-06-027065-9; 0-06-027066-7 (lib bdg)
LC 98-41711

"Joanna Cotler Books"

Twins Liz and Lenny, along with their time-traveling grandmother, join a group of pioneers journeying west on the Oregon Trail in 1843

"An engaging trip and a painless history lesson." SLJ
Other titles in this series are:
Joining the Boston Tea Party (2001)
Thanksgiving on Plymouth Plantation (2004)

Staples, Suzanne Fisher

The green dog; a mostly true story. Farrar, Straus & Giroux 2003 119p $16 (4-6)   **Fic**

1. Dogs—Fiction 2. Summer—Fiction
ISBN 0-374-32779-3   LC 2002-26575
"Frances Foster books"

During the summer before fifth grade, Suzanne, a day-dreaming loner who likes to fish and walk through the woods, acquires a canine companion. Based on the author's childhood in northeastern Pennsylvania

The author's "writing is rich and descriptive, yet clear and simple." SLJ

Stauffacher, Sue

Donuthead. Knopf 2003 144p $15.95; lib bdg $17.99 (4-6)   **Fic**

1. Fear—Fiction 2. Friendship—Fiction
ISBN 0-375-82468-5; 0-375-92468-X (lib bdg)
         LC 2003-40073

Franklin Delano Donuthead, a fifth-grader obsessed with hygiene and safety, finds an unlikely friend and protector in Sarah Kervick, the tough new student who lives in a dirty trailer, bonds with his mother, and is as "irregular" as he is

"It's refreshing for a novel with problem situations to be so light and funny. An appealing story with some memorable characters and a lot of heart." SLJ

Harry Sue; [by] Sue Stauffacher. 1st ed. Knopf 2005 288p $15.95; lib bdg $17.99 (5 and up)   **Fic**

1. Prisoners—Fiction 2. Handicapped—Fiction
3. Mother-daughter relationship—Fiction
ISBN 0-375-83274-2; 0-375-93274-7 (lib bdg)
         LC 2004-16945

Although tough-talking Harry Sue would like to start a life of crime in order to be "sent up" and find her incarcerated mother, she must first protect the children at her neglectful grandmother's home day care center and befriend a paralyzed boy.

"This is a riveting story, dramatically and well told, with characters whom readers won't soon forget." SLJ

Steele, William Owen

The perilous road; [by] William O. Steele; with an introduction by Jean Fritz. Harcourt 2004 c1958 156p $17; pa $5.95 (5 and up)   **Fic**

1. United States—History—1861-1865, Civil War—Fiction 2. Tennessee—Fiction
ISBN 0-15-205203-8; 0-15-205204-8 (pa)
A Newbery Medal honor book, 1959
"An Odyssey/Harcourt young classic"
A reissue of the title first published 1958

Fourteen-year-old Chris, bitterly hating the Yankees for invading his Tennessee mountain home, learns a difficult lesson about the waste of war and the meaning of tolerance and courage when he reports the approach of a Yankee supply troop to the Confederates, only to learn that his brother is probably part of that troop.

"Mr. Steele makes the tensions and excitements of the Brother's War very real, and customs of the mountain people, the speech and setting are well integrated into the narrative." NY Times Book Rev

Steig, William

Abel's island. Farrar, Straus & Giroux 1976 117p il $15; pa $4.95 (3-5)   **Fic**

1. Mice—Fiction 2. Survival after airplane accidents, shipwrecks, etc.—Fiction
ISBN 0-374-30010-0; 0-374-40016-4 (pa)

Castaway on an uninhabited island, Abel, a very civilized mouse, finds his resourcefulness and endurance tested to the limit as he struggles to survive and return to his home.

"The line drawings washed with gray faithfully and delightfully record not only the rigors of Abel's experiences but the refinement of his domestic existence." Horn Book

Dominic; story and pictures by William Steig. Farrar, Straus & Giroux 1972 145p il pa $4.95 hardcover o.p. (3-5)   **Fic**

1. Dogs—Fiction
ISBN 0-374-41826-8 (pa)

Dominic, a gregarious dog, sets out on the high road one day, going no place in particular, but moving along to find whatever he can. And that turns out to be plenty, including an invalid pig who leaves Dominic his fortune; a variety of friends and adventures; and even—in the end—his life's companion

"A singular blend of naiveté and sophistication, comic commentary and philosophizing, the narrative handles situation clichés with humor and flair—perhaps because of the author's felicitous turn of phrase, his verbal cartooning, and his integration of text and illustrations. A chivalrous and optimistic tribute to gallantry and romance." Horn Book

The real thief; story and pictures by William Steig. Farrar, Straus & Giroux 1973 58p il pa $3.95 hardcover o.p. (3-5)   **Fic**

1. Animals—Fiction 2. Thieves—Fiction
ISBN 0-374-46208-9 (pa)

"Proud of his job as guard to the Royal Treasury, loyal to his king (Basil the bear) Gawain the goose is baffled by the repeated theft of gold and jewels from the massive building to which only Gawain and Basil have keys. He is heartsick when the king dismisses him publicly and calls him a disgrace to the kingdom. Sentenced to prison, the goose flies off to isolation. The true thief, a mouse, is penitent and decides that he will go on stealing so that the king will know Gawain is innocent." Bull Cent Child Books

"Steig's gray line-and-wash drawings provide a charming accompaniment to a wholly winning story." SLJ

Stevenson, Robert Louis

The strange case of Dr. Jekyll and Mr. Hyde; illustrations by François Place. Viking 2000 105p il (Whole story) $25.99 (5 and up)   **Fic**

ISBN 0-670-88865-6   LC 99-75659
First published 1886; this illustrated edition published 1999 in France

"The story follows Dr. Jekyll, by day a respectable doctor, who by night roams the back alleys of London as a monstrous criminal." Publisher's note

"This edition of Stevenson's classic tale gives the flavor of late Victorian England through its lively ink-and-

Stevenson, Robert Louis—*Continued*

watercolor illustrations and plentiful reproductions of period photos, sketches, engravings, and paintings. Marginal notes comment on Stevenson and on aspects of the story and of Victorian culture that might be obscure to modern readers." Booklist

Treasure Island (6 and up)   **Fic**
1. Buried treasure—Fiction 2. Pirates—Fiction
Hardcover and paperback editions available from various publishers

First published 1882

Young Jim Hawkins discovers a treasure map in the chest of an old sailor who dies under mysterious circumstances at his mother's inn. He shows it to Dr. Livesey and Squire Trelawney who agree to outfit a ship and sail to Treasure Island. Among the crew is the pirate Long John Silver and his followers who are in pursuit of the treasure

"A masterpiece among romances. . . . Pew, Black Dog, and Long John Silver are a villainous trio, strongly individualized, shedding an atmosphere of malignancy and terror. The scenery of isle and ocean contrasts vividly with the savagery of the action." Baker. Guide to the Best Fic

Stewart, Paul

Beyond the Deepwoods; [by] Paul Stewart, Chris Riddell. David Fickling Bks. 2004 c1998 276p il (Edge chronicles) $12.95; lib bdg $14.99 (4-6)   **Fic**
1. Fantasy fiction
ISBN 0-385-75068-4; 0-385-75069-2 (lib dg)

First published 1998 in the United Kingdom

Thirteen-year-old Twig, having always looked and felt different from his woodtroll family, learns that he is adopted and travels out of his Deepwoods home to find the place where he belongs.

"Those with hearty appetites for adventure (and strong stomachs) will find this a tremendously exciting fantasy. Riddell's wonderfully detailed ink drawings, on nearly every page, create a strong sense of the believable, well-imagined otherworld and bring its strange creatures to life." Booklist

Other titles in The Edge Chronicles series are:
The curse of the Gloamglozer (2005)
Freeglader (2006)
The last of the sky pirates (2005)
Midnight over Sanctaphrax (2004)
Stormchaser (2004)
VOX (2005)

Stockton, Frank

The bee-man of Orn; [by] Frank R. Stockton; illustrated by P.J. Lynch. Candlewick Press 2003 unp il $17.99 (2-4)   **Fic**
1. Fairy tales
ISBN 0-7636-2239-7   LC 2003-48454

Story first published in St. Nicholas magazine 1883

When a Sorcerer tells him that he has been transformed from another sort of being, the Beeman sets out to discover what he was in his earlier incarnation. Story is accompanied by a DVD which provides a behind-the-scenes look at the illustrator at work.

"Lynch's spirited artwork, richly detailed and darkly atmospheric, provides a series of imaginative settings and creates a romantic and broadly appealing vision of this original fairy tale. . . . This edition is a read-aloud treasure for good listeners." Booklist

Stolz, Mary

A dog on Barkham Street; pictures by Leonard Shortall. Harper & Row 1960 184p il lib bdg $15.89; pa $4.95 (4-6)   **Fic**
1. Dogs—Fiction
ISBN 0-06-025841-1 (lib bdg); 0-06-440160-X (pa)

"Fifth-grader Edward Frost has two seemingly insurmountable problems—to rid himself of the constant tormenting by the bully who lives next door and to convince his parents that he is responsible enough to have a dog. It is the coming of his irresponsible vagabond uncle with a beautiful young collie that precipitates the solution of Edward's problems." Booklist

"Simple, everyday events and very familiar people make up this story. . . . This author has a remarkable ability to get inside her characters." Horn Book

Another title about Edward Frost and Martin Hastings is:
The bully of Barkham Street (1963)

Go fish; illustrated by Pat Cummings. HarperCollins Pubs. 1991 69p il pa $4.99 hardcover o.p. (2-4)   **Fic**
1. Grandfathers—Fiction 2. Fishing—Fiction 3. African Americans—Fiction
ISBN 0-06-440466-8 (pa); 0-06-025822-4 (lib bdg)
     LC 90-4860

After spending the day fishing in the Gulf of Mexico with Grandfather, eight-year-old Thomas has a quiet evening on the porch hearing more about his African heritage

"The text is easy to read, laced with gentle humor, and designed with rounded, black-and-white pictures in a pop-art style. . . . A book that's all the more effective for its low-key, companionable tone." Bull Cent Child Books

Other titles about Thomas and his grandfather are:
Stealing home (1992)
Storm in the night (1988)

Strickland, Brad

The hand of the necromancer; frontispiece by Edward Gorey. Dial Bks. for Young Readers 1996 168p lib bdg $14.89; pa $4.99 (5 and up)
     Fic
1. Mystery fiction
ISBN 0-8037-1830-6 (lib bdg); 0-14-038695-5 (pa)
     LC 95-47222

Continues John Bellairs' series about Johnny Dixon and Professor Childermass

Thirteen-year-old Johnny Dixon and his friend Professor Childermass battle an evil wizard for possession of a bewitched hand which can be used to rule the world

Other titles about Johnny Dixon and Professor Childermass by Brad Strickland are:
The bell, the book and the spellbinder (1997)
The wrath of the grinning ghost (1999)

Strickland, Brad—_Continued_

John Bellairs's Lewis Barnavelt in The specter
from the magician's museum; frontispiece by
Edward Gorey. Dial Bks. for Young Readers 1998
149p $15.99; pa $5.99 (5 and up)   **Fic**
1. Witchcraft—Fiction
ISBN 0-8037-2202-8; 0-14-038652-1 (pa)
LC 97-47167

Continues John Bellairs' series about Lewis Barnavelt
Based on the characters of John Bellairs

When the evil sorceress Belle Frisson ensnares Rose
Rita Pottinger in a magic web in order to steal her life
force, Lewis Barnavelt must risk his own life to save his
friend

Other titles about Lewis Barnavelt by Brad Strickland
are:

The beast under the wizard's bridge (2000)
The tower at the end of the world (2001)
The whistle, the grave, and the ghost (2003)

Sturtevant, Katherine

At the sign of the star. Farrar, Straus & Giroux
2000 140p $16; pa $5.95 (5 and up)   **Fic**
1. London (England)—Fiction 2. Sex role—Fiction
3. Booksellers and bookselling—Fiction
ISBN 0-374-30449-1; 0-374-40458-5 (pa)
LC 00-20448

In seventeenth-century London, Meg, who has little
interest in cooking, needlework, or other homemaking
skills, dreams of becoming a bookseller and someday in-
heriting her widowed father's book store

"The author's thorough research of Restoration England makes for an enjoyable and an informative read."
ALAN

Swope, Sam

Jack and the seven deadly giants; pictures by
Carll Cneut. Farrar, Straus and Giroux 2004 99p il
$16 (3-5)   **Fic**
1. Fairy tales 2. Giants—Fiction
ISBN 0-374-33670-9   LC 2003-54199

While hoping to find his mother, Jack encounters sev-
en deadly giants: the Giant Poet, the Terrible Glutton,
Mrs. Roth, the Wild Tickler, Avaritch, Orgulla the Great,
and the Green Queen.

"The plot details and use of language are often clever
as the story comes full circle to its satisfying conclusion.
Semi-abstract, black-and-white sketches punctuate the absurdity of the tale." SLJ

Tacang, Brian

Bully-be-gone; [by] Brian Tacang. 1st ed.
HarperCollins 2006 216p (Misadventures of
Millicent Madding) $15.99; lib bdg $16.89 (3-6)
Fic
1. Bullies—Fiction   2. Inventions—Fiction
3. Friendship—Fiction
ISBN 0-06-073911-8; 0-06-073912-6 (lib bdg)
LC 2005-07777

Budding-inventor Millicent Madding launches her latest invention to disastrous results, and she has only days
to create an antidote before the local bullies wreak havoc

and her dearest friendships are destroyed forever.

"The book has zippy dialogue and brilliant use of alliteration. . . . The eccentric characters are fun, and the
silly but substantive plot will surely appeal to children."
SLJ

Taylor, Mildred D.

The friendship; pictures by Max Ginsburg. Dial
Bks. for Young Readers 1987 53p il $15.99; pa
$4.99 (4 and up)   **Fic**
1. African Americans—Fiction 2. Race relations—Fic-
tion 3. Mississippi—Fiction
ISBN 0-8037-0417-8; 0-14-038964-4 (pa)
LC 86-29309

Coretta Scott King Award for text, 1988

This "story about race relations in rural Mississippi
during the Depression focuses on an incident between an
old Black man, Mr. Tom Bee, and a white storekeeper,
Mr. John Wallace. Indebted to Tom for saving his life as
a young man, John had promised they would always be
friends. But now, years later, John insists that Tom call
him 'Mister' and shoots the old man for defiantly—and
publicly—calling him by his first name. Narrator Cassie
Logan and her brothers . . . are verbally abused by Wallace's villainous sons before witnessing the encounter."
Bull Cent Child Books

The gold Cadillac; pictures by Michael Hays.
Dial Bks. for Young Readers 1987 43p il $16.99;
pa $4.99 (4 and up)   **Fic**
1. African Americans—Fiction 2. Prejudices—Fiction
3. Race relations—Fiction
ISBN 0-8037-0342-2; 0-14-038963-6 (pa)
LC 86-11526

"The shiny gold Cadillac that Daddy brings home one
summer evening marks a stepping stone in the lives of
Wilma and 'lois, two black sisters growing up in Ohio
during the fifties. At first neighbors and relatives shower
them with attention. But when the family begins the long
journey to the South to show off the car to their Mississippi relatives, the girls, for the first time, encounter the
undisguised ugliness of racial prejudice." Horn Book

"Full-page sepia paintings effectively portray the characters, setting, and mood of the story events as Hays
ably demonstrates his understanding of the social and
emotional environments which existed for blacks during
this period." SLJ

Let the circle be unbroken. Dial Bks. for Young
Readers 1981 394p $17.99; pa $7.99 (4 and up)
Fic
1. African Americans—Fiction 2. Mississippi—Fiction
3. Great Depression, 1929-1939—Fiction
ISBN 0-8037-4748-9; 0-14-034892-1 (pa)
LC 81-65854

Sequel to Roll of thunder, hear my cry

This novel featuring the Logans covers "a series of
tangential events so that it is a family record, a picture
of the depression years in rural Mississippi, and an in-
dictment of black-white relations in the Deep South. A
young friend is convicted of a murder of which he is innocent, a pretty cousin is insulted by some white boys
and her father taunted because he married a white woman, an elderly neighbor tries to vote, the government
pays farmers to plow their crops under, etc." Bull Cent

Taylor, Mildred D.—*Continued*
Child Books
The author "provides her readers with a literal sense of witnessing important American history. . . . Moreover, [she] never neglects the details of her volatile 9-year-old heroine's interior life. The daydreams, the jealousy, the incredible ardor of that age come alive." N Y Times Book Rev

Mississippi bridge; by Mildred Taylor; pictures by Max Ginsburg. Dial Bks. for Young Readers 1990 62p il pa $4.99 hardcover o.p. (4 and up)
Fic
1. Race relations—Fiction 2. African Americans—Fiction 3. Prejudices—Fiction 4. Mississippi—Fiction
ISBN 0-14-130817-6 (pa)   LC 89-27898
Available in hardcover from P. Smith
In this story featuring the children of Mississippi's Logan family, "Jeremy Simms, a 10-year-old white neighbor, describes a harrowing incident after the Logans and other blacks are ordered off the weekly bus in a foggy rainstorm." N Y Times Book Rev
"Taylor has shaped this episode into a haunting meditation that will leave readers vividly informed about segregation practices and the unequal rights that prevailed in that era. . . . The incident and its context constitute a telling piece of social history." Booklist

The road to Memphis; by Mildred Taylor. Dial Bks. 1989 290p $16.99; pa $6.99 (4 and up)
Fic
1. Race relations—Fiction 2. African Americans—Fiction 3. Mississippi—Fiction
ISBN 0-8037-0340-6; 0-14-036077-8 (pa)
LC 88-33654
Coretta Scott King award for text, 1989
Sadistically teased by two white boys in 1940's rural Mississippi, Cassie Logan's friend, Moe, severely injures one of the boys with a tire iron and enlists Cassie's help in trying to flee the state
"Taylor's continued smooth, easy language provides readability for all ages, with a focus on universal human pride, worthy values, and individual responsibility. This action-packed drama is highly recommended." Voice Youth Advocates

Roll of thunder, hear my cry. 25th anniversary ed. Phyllis Fogelman Books 2001 276p $17.99 (4 and up)
Fic
1. African Americans—Fiction 2. Mississippi—Fiction
ISBN 0-8037-2647-3   LC 00-39378
Also available in paperback from Puffin Bks.
Awarded the Newbery medal, 1977
First published 1976 by Dial Press
"The time is 1933. The place is Spokane, Mississippi where the Logans, the only black family who own their own land, wage a courageous struggle to remain independent, displeasing a white plantation owner bent on taking their land. But this suspenseful tale is also about the story's young narrator, Cassie, and her three brothers who decide to wage their own personal battles to maintain the self-dignity and pride with which they were raised. . . . Ms. Taylor's richly textured novel shows a strong, proud black family . . . resisting rather than succumbing to oppression." Child Book Rev Serv
Followed by Let the circle be unbroken

Song of the trees; pictures by Jerry Pinkney. Dial Bks. for Young Readers 1975 48p il $16.99; pa $5.99 (4 and up)
Fic
1. African Americans—Fiction 2. Great Depression, 1929-1939—Fiction 3. Mississippi—Fiction
ISBN 0-8037-5452-3; 0-14-250075-5 (pa)
Eight-year-old Cassie Logan tells how her family "leaving Mississippi during the Depression was cheated into selling for practically nothing valuable and beautiful giant old pines and hickories, beeches and walnuts in the forest surrounding their house." Adventuring with Books

The well; David's story. Dial Bks. for Young Readers 1995 92p $16.99; pa $5.99 (4 and up)
Fic
1. African Americans—Fiction 2. Race relations—Fiction 3. Mississippi—Fiction
ISBN 0-8037-1802-0; 0-14-038642-4 (pa)
LC 94-25360
"David Logan (Cassie's father) tells this story from his childhood. . . . There's a drought, and the Logans possess the only well in the area that has not gone dry. Black and white alike come for water freely given by the family, but the Simms boys can't seem to stand the necessary charity, and their resentment explodes when David's big brother Hammer beats Charlie Simms after Charlie hits David." Bull Cent Child Books
This story "delivers an emotional wallop in a concentrated span of time and action. . . . This story reverberates in the heart long after the final paragraph is read." Horn Book

Taylor, Sydney
All-of-a-kind family; illustrations by Helen John. Delacorte Press 2005 c1951 188p il $15.95; lib bdg $17.99; pa $5.99 (4-6)
Fic
1. Jews—Fiction 2. New York (N.Y.)—Fiction
ISBN 0-385-73295-3; 0-0385-90316-2 (lib bdg); 0-440-40059-7 (pa)
First published 1951 by Follett
"Five little Jewish girls grow up in New York's lower east side in a happy home atmosphere before the first World War." Carnegie Libr of Pittsburgh
"A genuine and delightful picture of a Jewish family . . . with an understanding mother and father, rich in kindness and fun though poor in money. The important part the public library played in the lives of these children is happily evident; and the Jewish holiday celebrations are particularly well described." Horn Book
Other titles about this family are:
All-of-a-kind family downtown (1957)
All-of-a-kind family uptown (1957)
Ella of all-of-a-kind family (1978)
More all-of-a-kind family (1954)

Taylor, Theodore
The cay. Delacorte Press c1969 137p $16.95; pa $5.50 (5 and up)
Fic
1. Race relations—Fiction 2. Caribbean region—Fiction 3. Survival after airplane accidents, shipwrecks, etc.—Fiction 4. Blind—Fiction
ISBN 0-385-07906-0; 0-440-22912-X (pa)
Also available in paperback from HarperCollins

Taylor, Theodore—*Continued*
When the freighter on which they are traveling is torpedoed by a German submarine during World War II, Phillip, an adolescent white boy blinded by a blow on the head, and Timothy, an old black man, are stranded on a tiny Caribbean island where the boy acquires a new kind of vision, courage, and love from his old companion.
"Starkly dramatic, believable and compelling." Saturday Rev
Followed by Timothy of the cay

Ice drift; [by] Theodore Taylor. Harcourt 2005 224p $16 (4 and up)   **Fic**
1. Inuit—Fiction 2. Brothers—Fiction 3. Arctic regions—Fiction
ISBN 0-15-205081-7   LC 2003-27783
Two Inuit brothers must fend for themselves while stranded on an ice floe that is adrift in the Greenland Strait.
This is "a masterful and detailed look into a culture unfamiliar to most Americans, a gripping adventure, and a moving depiction of brotherly love." SLJ

Teetoncey. Harcourt 2004 c1974 208p $17; pa $5.95 (5 and up)   **Fic**
1. Amnesia—Fiction 2. North Carolina—Fiction
ISBN 0-15-205298-4; 0-15-205294-1 (pa)
       LC 2003-67745
"An Odyssey/Harcourt young classic"
A reissue of the title first published 1974 by Doubleday
In this first novel of the Cape Hatteras trilogy, eleven-year-old Ben rescues an English girl from a shipwreck off the Outer Banks of North Carolina; and, though she becomes part of his family, she never speaks.
"The novel is rich with details of of local geography, history, and folklore." Horn Book
Other titles in the Cape Hatteras trilogy are:
The odyssey of Ben O'Neal (2004 c1977)
Teetoncey and Ben O'Neal (2004 c1975)

Timothy of the cay. Harcourt Brace & Co. 1993 161p $16 (5 and up)   **Fic**
1. Race relations—Fiction 2. Caribbean region—Fiction 3. Survival after airplane accidents, shipwrecks, etc.—Fiction 4. Blind—Fiction
ISBN 0-15-288358-4   LC 93-7898
Also available in paperback from HarperCollins
Sequel to The cay
Having survived being blinded and shipwrecked on a tiny Caribbean island with the old black man Timothy, twelve-year-old white Phillip is rescued and hopes to regain his sight with an operation. Alternate chapters follow the life of Timothy from his days as a young cabin boy
"Somewhat more thoughtful than its well-loved antecedent, this boldly drawn novel is no less commanding." Publ Wkly

The trouble with Tuck. Doubleday 1981 110p $15.95; pa $4.50 (5 and up)   **Fic**
1. Dogs—Fiction 2. Blind—Fiction
ISBN 0-385-17774-7; 0-440-41696-5 (pa)
       LC 81-43139

Helen trains her blind dog Tuck to follow and trust a seeing-eye companion dog
This is "a touching dog story, written with good flow, pace, and structure." Bull Cent Child Books
Another title about Helen and Tuck is:
Tuck triumphant (1991)

Temple, Frances
The Ramsay scallop; a novel. Orchard Bks. 1994 310p (6 and up)   **Fic**
1. Middle Ages—Fiction 2. Pilgrims and pilgrimages—Fiction
ISBN 0-531-06836-6   LC 93-29697
Available in paperback from HarperCollins
"A Richard Jackson book"
At the turn of the fourteenth century in England, fourteen-year-old Elenor finds her betrothal to an ambitious lord's son launching her on a memorable pilgrimage to far-off Spain
"With a nod to *The Canterbury Tales*, the book highlights the stories that their fellow pilgrims share with Elenor and Thomas; the stories are sad, romantic, and instructive, and all help shape the journey into the special thing it becomes for the duo. . . . The leisurely pace of the pilgrimage allows the author to introduce a large cast of characters and to decorate her story with historical details that enlighten and intrigue." Booklist

Tonight, by sea; a novel. Orchard Bks. 1995 152p (6 and up)   **Fic**
1. Haiti—Fiction 2. Refugees—Fiction
ISBN 0-531-06899-4   LC 94-32167
Available in paperback from HarperCollins
"A Richard Jackson book"
As governmental brutality and poverty become unbearable, Paulie joins with others in her small Haitian village to help her uncle secretly build a boat they will use to try to escape to the United States
"In an elegant prose style [the author] captures the lyrical cadence of Creole speech and paints an affecting portrait of a proud, resourceful people trying to survive in the face of lawlessness and tyranny." SLJ

Testa, Maria
Almost forever. Candlewick Press 2003 69p $14.99 (3-5)   **Fic**
1. Vietnam War, 1961-1975—Fiction
ISBN 0-7636-1996-5   LC 2002-34757
In free verse, a young girl describes what she, her brother, and their mother do during the year that her doctor father is serving in the Army in Vietnam
This is "sensitive and moving. . . . Testa's poems give her young speaker a believable, sympathetic voice." Publ Wkly

Thomas, Jane Resh
The comeback dog; drawings by Troy Howell. Clarion Bks. 1981 62p il $16 (3-5)   **Fic**
1. Dogs—Fiction 2. Farm life—Fiction
ISBN 0-395-29432-0   LC 80-12886
Also available in paperback from Bantam Bks.

Thomas, Jane Resh—*Continued*

"Grieving over the loss of his dog, Daniel claims he doesn't want another dog, but when he finds one that is near death, he takes her home and gives her loving care. The dog, Lady, gets well but seems fearful and hostile; irritated, Daniel lets her off the leash to run away. When she comes back, some weeks later, her face bristling with porcupine quills, he's again irritated but quickly decides to help Lady and is then gratified when she shows trust and affection." Bull Cent Child Books

"The matter-of-fact, life-must-go-on attitude of Daniel's concerned parents is particularly well communicated. . . . Numerous soft pencil drawings greatly enhance the exceptionally gentle, poignant story." Horn Book

Thurber, James

Many moons; illustrated by Louis Slobodkin. Harcourt Brace 1943 unp il $16; pa $7 (1-4)

Fic

1. Fairy tales
ISBN 0-15-251873-8; 0-15-251877-9 (pa)
Also available with illustrations by Marc Simont for $14.95 (ISBN 0-15-251872-X); pa $7 (ISBN 0-15-201895-6)

Awarded the Caldecott Medal, 1944

This is "the story of a little princess who fell ill of a surfeit of raspberry tarts and would get well only if she could have the moon. The solving of this baffling court problem, how to get the moon, results in an original and entertaining picture-storybook." Booklist

"Louis Slobodkin's pictures float on the pages in four colors: black and white cannot represent them. They are the substance of dreams . . . the long thoughts little children, and some adults wise as they, have about life." N Y Her Trib Books

Tolan, Stephanie S.

Listen! HarperCollins Publishers 2006 197p $15.99; lib bdg $16.89 (4 and up)

Fic

1. Dogs—Fiction 2. Bereavement—Fiction 3. Wounds and injuries—Fiction
ISBN   9780060579357;   0-06-057935-8; 9780060579364 (lib bdg); 0-06-057936-6 (lib bdg)

LC 2005-17792

During her solitary convalescence from a crippling accident, twelve-year-old Charley finds a wild dog, and the arduous process of training him leads her to explore her feelings about her mother's death two years earlier.

"This is a sweet, gentle story of healing and the strong bond that can develop between humans and animals. The lovely imagery and involving plot should appeal to more than just animal lovers." SLJ

Save Halloween! Morrow Junior Bks. 1993 168p $16; pa $4.95 (5 and up)

Fic

1. Halloween—Fiction 2. Christian life—Fiction 3. School stories
ISBN 0-688-12168-3; 0-688-15497-2 (pa)

LC 93-10635

Eleven-year-old Johnna, who is deeply involved in the sixth grade Halloween pageant although her family views it as a celebration of an un-Christian holiday, decides that she must follow her own beliefs

"Thoughtful, pithy, and entertaining, this will intrigue readers from cover to cover." Booklist

Tolkien, J. R. R. (John Ronald Reuel)

The hobbit, or, There and back again; by J.R.R. Tolkien. Houghton Mifflin 2001 330p il $18 (4 and up)

Fic

1. Fantasy fiction
ISBN 0-618-16221-6   LC 2001276594

A reissue of the title first published 1938

"Text of this edition is based on that first published in Great Britain by Collins Modern Classics in 1998 . . . corrections have been made to that setting"--T.p. verso

"This fantasy features the adventures of hobbit Bilbo Baggins, who joins a band of dwarves led by Gandalf the Wizard. Together they seek to recover the stolen treasure that is hidden in Lonely Mountain and guarded by Smaug the Dragon. This book precedes the Lord of the Rings trilogy." Shapiro. Fic for Youth. 3d edition

Followed by The lord of the rings, a trilogy intended for older readers

Travers, P. L. (Pamela L.)

Mary Poppins; illustrated by Mary Shepard. rev ed. Harcourt Brace & Co. 1997 c1981 202p il $18; pa $6 (4-6)

Fic

1. Fantasy fiction
ISBN 0-15-252595-5; 0-15-201717-8 (pa)

LC 97-223987

First published 1934; this is a reissue of the 1981 revised edition

An extraordinary English nanny blows in on the East Wind with her parrot-headed umbrella and magic carpetbag and introduces her charges, Jane and Michael Banks, to some delightful people and experiences

"The chapter 'Bad Tuesday,' in which Mary and the Banks children travel to the four corners of the earth and meet the inhabitants, has been criticized for portraying minorities in an unfavorable light. . . . [In] the revised edition . . . the entourage meet up with a polar bear, macaw, panda, and dolphin instead of Eskimos, Africans, Chinese, and American Indians." Booklist

Other titles about Mary Poppins are:
Mary Poppins comes back (1935)
Mary Poppins in the kitchen (1975)
Mary Poppins in the park (1952)
Mary Poppins opens the door (1943)

Treviño, Elizabeth Borton de

I, Juan de Pareja. Farrar, Straus & Giroux 1965 180p $17 o.p.; pa $6.95 (6 and up)

Fic

1. Juan, de Pareja—Fiction 2. Velázquez, Diego, 1599-1660—Fiction 3. Artists—Fiction 4. Spain—Fiction 5. Slavery—Fiction
ISBN 0-374-33531-1; 0-374-43525-1 (pa)

LC 65-19330

Awarded the Newbery Medal, 1966

"Bell books"

The black slave boy, Juan de Pareja, "began a new life when he was taken into the household of the Spanish painter, Velázquez. As he worked beside the great artist learning how to grind and mix colors and prepare canvases, there grew between them a warm friendship based on mutual respect and love of art. Created from meager but authentic facts, the story, told by Juan, depicts the life and character of Velázquez and the loyalty of the talented seventeenth-century slave who eventually won his freedom and the right to be an artist." Booklist

Tunis, John R.

The Kid from Tomkinsville; illustrated by Jay Hyde Barnum. Harcourt 1940 355p il pa $6 hardcover o.p. (5 and up)   **Fic**

1. Baseball—Fiction
ISBN 0-15-242567-5 (pa)

As the newest addition to the Brooklyn Dodgers, young Roy Tucker's pitching helps pull the team out of a slump; but, when a freak accident ends his career as a pitcher, he must try to find another place for himself on the team

Other titles about Roy Tucker and the Brooklyn Dodgers are:
Keystone kids (1943)
The kid comes back (1946)
Rookie of the year (1944)
World Series (1941)

Turner, Ann Warren

Grasshopper summer. Macmillan 1989 166p pa $4.99 hardcover o.p. (4-6)   **Fic**

1. Frontier and pioneer life—Fiction 2. South Dakota—Fiction
ISBN 0-689-83522-1 (pa)   LC 88-13847

In 1874 eleven-year-old Sam and his family move from Kentucky to the southern Dakota Territory, where harsh conditions and a plague of hungry grasshoppers threaten their chances for survival

"Carefully selected details, skillfully woven into the story line, evoke a sense of place and time. . . . Both a family story and an account of pioneer living, the book is accessible as well as informative." Horn Book

Love thy neighbor; the Tory diary of Prudence Emerson. Scholastic 2003 188p il (Dear America) $10.95 (4 and up)   **Fic**

1. United States—History—1775-1783, Revolution—Fiction
ISBN 0-439-15308-5   LC 2002-73345

In Greenmarsh, Massachusetts, in 1774, thirteen-year-old Prudence keeps a diary of the troubles she and her family face as Tories surrounded by American patriots at the start of the American Revolution

"Details of Colonial life are intricately interwoven. . . . The action and suspense build steadily and will keep readers hooked." SLJ

Nettie's trip South; [by] Ann Turner; illustrated by Ronald Himler. Macmillan 1987 unp il $16; pa $5.99 (3-5)   **Fic**

1. Slavery—Fiction
ISBN 0-02-789240-9; 0-689-80117-3 (pa)
     LC 86-18135

"In 1859 Nettie is allowed to accompany her brother, who has been assigned his first newspaper story, and an older sister on the trip from Albany, New York, to Richmond. The text appears in the form of a letter Nettie writes to a friend, and . . . the story recounts her poignantly felt reactions to the viewing of slave quarters and an auction of black men and women." Horn Book

"Himler's charcoal drawings fashion scenes rich with character and emotion. . . . A vivid piece of history for early elementary students or older picture-book audiences." Booklist

Twain, Mark

The adventures of Huckleberry Finn; illustrated by Steven Kellogg; afterword by Peter Glassman. Books of Wonder 1994 348p il $24.99 (5 and up)   **Fic**

1. Mississippi River—Fiction 2. Missouri—Fiction
ISBN 0-688-10656-0
Other editions also available
First published 1885

The adventures of a boy and a runaway slave as they travel down the Mississippi River on a raft.

The adventures of Tom Sawyer; illustrated by Barry Moser; afterword by Peter Glassman. Books of Wonder 1989 261p il $24.99 (5 and up)   **Fic**

1. Mississippi River—Fiction 2. Missouri—Fiction
ISBN 0-688-07510-X
Other editions also available
First published 1876

The adventures and pranks of a mischievous boy growing up in a Mississippi River town on the early nineteenth century.

Uchida, Yoshiko

A jar of dreams. Atheneum Pubs. 1981 131p $16.95; pa $4.99 (5 and up)   **Fic**

1. Japanese Americans—Fiction 2. Family life—Fiction 3. Prejudices—Fiction 4. California—Fiction
ISBN 0-689-50210-9; 0-689-71672-9 (pa)
     LC 81-3480

"A Margaret K. McElderry book"

"A story of the Depression Era is told by eleven-year-old Rinko, the only girl in a Japanese-American family living in Oakland and suffering under the double burden of financial pressure and the prejudice that had increased with the tension of economic competition. Into the household comes a visitor who is a catalyst for change." Bull Cent Child Books

"Rinko in her guilelessness is genuine and refreshing, and her worries and concerns seem wholly natural, honest, and convincing." Horn Book

Other titles about Rinko Tsujimura and her family are:
The best bad thing (1983)
The happiest ending (1985)

Journey home; illustrated by Charles Robinson. Atheneum Pubs. 1978 131p il $16; pa $4.99 (5 and up)   **Fic**

1. Japanese Americans—Fiction 2. Prejudices—Fiction 3. Family life—Fiction
ISBN 0-689-50126-9; 0-689-70755-X (pa)
     LC 78-8792

Sequel to Journey to Topaz
"A Margaret K. McElderry book"

After their release from an American concentration camp, Yuki and her family try to reconstruct their lives amidst strong anti-Japanese feelings which breed fear, distrust, and violence

Uchida, Yoshiko—*Continued*

Journey to Topaz; a story of the Japanese-American evacuation; illustrated by Donald Carrick. Scribner 1971 149p il (5 and up)

Fic

1. Japanese Americans—Evacuation and relocation, 1942-1945—Fiction

Available Heyday Bks. paperback edition $9.95 (ISBN 1-890771-91-0)

This is the story of eleven-year-old Yuki, her eighteen-year-old brother and her mother, who were uprooted, evacuated and interned in Topaz, the War Relocation Center in Utah during World War II

"This tragic herding of innocent people is described with dignity and a sorrowful sense of injustice that never becomes bitter." Saturday Rev

Followed by Journey home

Umansky, Kaye

The silver spoon of Solomon Snow. Candlewick Press 2005 289p $14.99 (5 and up)   **Fic**

1. Orphans—Fiction

ISBN 0-7636-2792-5

Ten-year-old Solomon Snow, a foundling who was discovered with a distinctive silver spoon in his mouth, sets out to find his parents and receives help along the way from an aspiring writer, a precocious young circus performer, and several orphans.

This is "an entertaining farce. . . . After adventures aplenty, all is satisfactorily resolved, but not without a clever authorial twist to ensure a sequel." Horn Book

Vail, Rachel

Daring to be Abigail; a novel. Orchard Bks. 1996 128p $15.95; lib bdg $16.99 (4-6)

Fic

1. Camps—Fiction

ISBN 0-531-09517-7; 0-531-08867-7 (lib bdg)

LC 95-33531

Also available in paperback from Puffin Bks.

"A Richard Jackson book"

"Eleven-year-old Abigail plans to 'reinvent herself' at summer camp. Instead, torn between her newfound popularity and her empathy for the camp outcast, she learns more about who she really is." Horn Book Guide

"The dialogue is fresh and genuine. Readers will be drawn to the novel's authenticity and will find themselves empathizing with Abby, yet laughing at her escapades." SLJ

Van Leeuwen, Jean

Bound for Oregon; pictures by James Watling. Dial Bks. for Young Readers 1994 167p il map pa $5.99 hardcover o.p. (4-6)   **Fic**

1. Todd, Mary Ellen, 1843-1924—Fiction
2. Overland journeys to the Pacific—Fiction
3. Oregon Trail—Fiction

ISBN 0-14-038319-0 (pa)   LC 93-26709

A fictionalized account of the journey made by nine-year-old Mary Ellen Todd and her family from their home in Arkansas westward over the Oregon Trail in 1852

"The appealing narrator, the forthright telling, and the concrete details of life along the Oregon Trail will draw readers into the story." Booklist

Cabin on Trouble Creek. Dial Books for Young Readers 2004 119p $16.99 (4 and up)   **Fic**

1. Frontier and pioneer life—Fiction 2. Brothers—Fiction 3. Ohio—Fiction

ISBN 0-8037-2548-5   LC 2003-14151

In 1803 in Ohio, two young brothers are left to finish the log cabin and guard the land while their father goes back to Pennsylvania to fetch their mother and younger siblings.

"Excellent pacing is what makes this novel work so well. . . . The suspense builds consistently. The boys' struggle is portrayed realistically, without sugarcoating nature's harshness." SLJ

The Great Googlestein museum mystery; pictures by R.W. Alley. Phyllis Fogelman Bks. 2003 197p il $16.99 (3-5)   **Fic**

1. Solomon R. Guggenheim Museum—Fiction
2. Mice—Fiction 3. New York (N.Y.)—Fiction

ISBN 0-8037-2765-8   LC 2001-51273

Other titles about Marvin, Raymond, and Fats are: The great cheese conspiracy (1969), The great Christmas kidnapping caper (1975), The great rescue operation (1982), The great summer camp catastrophe (1992)

Marvin, Raymond, and Fats, three adventurous mice, escape from their home at Macy's department store and spend an exciting week in the Guggenheim Museum, creating a sensation in the art world

"Van Leeuwen's characters are appealing, both for their mouselike behaviors and their childlike personalities. Alley's black-and-white sketches add to the fun." Booklist

Vande Velde, Vivian

Smart dog. Harcourt Brace & Co. 1998 145p $16 (4-6)   **Fic**

1. Dogs—Fiction

ISBN 0-15-201847-6   LC 98-4771

Also available in paperback from Dell

Fifth grader Amy finds her life growing complicated when she meets and tries to hide an intelligent, talking dog who has escaped from a university lab

"The accessible vocabulary, quick-moving plot, and humor make the novel appealing for reluctant readers as well as a good choice for reading aloud." Horn Book

There's a dead person following my sister around. Harcourt Brace & Co. 1999 143p $16 (4 and up)   **Fic**

1. Ghost stories 2. Slavery—Fiction 3. Underground railroad—Fiction

ISBN 0-15-202100-0   LC 99-11462

Also available in paperback from Puffin Bks.

Ted becomes concerned and intrigued when his five-year-old sister Vicki begins receiving visits from the ghosts of two runaway slaves

"There is sufficient humor, action, and scariness to keep readers engaged." SLJ

Vande Velde, Vivian—*Continued*

Three good deeds. Harcourt 2005 147p $16
(3-5)   **Fic**

1. Geese—Fiction 2. Witches—Fiction
ISBN 0-15-205382-4   LC 2004-29578

Caught stealing some goose eggs from a witch, Howard is cursed for his heartlessness and turned into a
goose himself, and he can only become human again by
performing three good deeds.

"With well-spaced print, plenty of dialogue, a strong
dose of humor, and more invention than many books
written at this level, this goose tale is a nicely accomplished, entertaining read." Booklist

Wizard at work; a novel in stories. Harcourt
2003 134p $16 (3-6)   **Fic**

1. Magic—Fiction 2. Princesses—Fiction
ISBN 0-15-204559-7   LC 2002-68665

A young wizard, who runs a school to teach wizards,
looks forward to a quiet summer off but is drawn into
adventures with princesses, unicorns, and ghosts instead

"A lot of fairy-tale conventions are turned on their
heads. . . . The language sparkles with sunny good humor. . . . Lighthearted and sly." Booklist

Vega, Denise

Click here; (to find out how I survived seventh
grade). Little, Brown 2005 211p $15.99 (5 and up)
       Fic

1. Friendship—Fiction 2. School stories
ISBN 0-316-98560-0

Seventh-grader Erin Swift writes about her friends and
classmates in her private blog, but when it accidentally
gets posted on the school Intranet site, she learns some
important lessons about friendship.

"The characters and situations are believable, and
readers will relate to and sympathize with Erin's dilemmas." SLJ

Velmans, Hester

Isabel of the whales; [by] Hester Velmans.
Delacorte Press 2005 192p $15.95; lib bdg $17.99
(5 and up)   **Fic**

1. Whales—Fiction 2. Massachusetts—Fiction
ISBN 0-385-73202-3; 0-385-90233-6 (lib bdg)
       LC 2004-546

On a whale watch trip with her class off the coast of
Cape Cod, Isabel, who has always had an affinity for
whales, falls overboard and discovers as she finds herself
swimming underwater with whales all around her that
she is one of the Chosen who can change shape from human to whale and back again.

"An excellent choice for readers who enjoy animal
stories, domestic fantasy, or even nonfiction." SLJ

Verne, Jules

20,000 leagues under the sea; illustrated by the
Dillons; translated by Anthony Bonner.
HarperCollins Pubs. 2000 394p il $21.95 (5 and
up)   **Fic**

1. Science fiction 2. Submarines—Fiction
ISBN 0-688-10535-1   LC 00-24336

Also available other translations from various publishers

"Books of Wonder"
Original French edition, 1870
Translation of: Vingt milles lieues sous les mers

Retells the adventures of a French professor and his
two companions as they sail above and below the
world's oceans as prisoners on the fabulous electric submarine of the deranged Captain Nemo

Vining, Elizabeth Gray

Adam of the road; illustrated by Robert Lawson.
Viking 1942 317p il $19.99 hardcover o.p.; pa
$7.99 (5 and up)   **Fic**

1. Minstrels—Fiction 2. Middle Ages—Fiction
3. Great Britain—Fiction
ISBN 0-670-10435-3; 0-14-032464-X (pa)
Awarded the Newbery Medal, 1943

Tale of a minstrel and his son Adam, who wandered
through southeastern England in the thirteenth century.
Adam's adventures in search of his lost dog and his beloved father led him from St. Alban's Abbey to London,
and thence to Winchester, back to London, and then to
Oxford where the three were at last reunited

Voigt, Cynthia

Dicey's song. Atheneum Pubs. 1982 196p
$17.95 (6 and up)   **Fic**

1. Grandmothers—Fiction 2. Siblings—Fiction
ISBN 0-689-30944-9   LC 82-3882
Also available in paperback from Fawcett Bks.
Awarded the Newbery Medal, 1983
Sequel to Homecoming

Dicey "had brought her siblings to the grandmother
they'd never seen when their mother (now in a mental
institution) had been unable to cope. This is the story of
the children's adjustment to Gram (and hers to them) and
to a new school and a new life—but with some of the
old problems." Bull Cent Child Books

"The vividness of Dicey is striking; Voigt has
plumbed and probed her character inside out to fashion
a memorable protagonist." Booklist

Homecoming. Atheneum Pubs. 1981 312p
$18.95 (6 and up)   **Fic**

1. Siblings—Fiction 2. Abandoned children—Fiction
ISBN 0-689-30833-7   LC 80-36723
Also available in paperback from Fawcett Bks.

"When their momma abandons them in a shopping
center, Dicey Tillerman and her three younger brothers
and sisters set out on foot for where momma was ostensibly taking them—to Great-Aunt Cilla's in Bridgeport,
Connecticut." Booklist

"The characterizations of the children are original and
intriguing, and there are a number of interesting minor
characters encountered in their travels." SLJ

Followed by Dicey's song

Vos, Ida

Anna is still here; translated by Terese Edelstein
and Inez Smidt. Houghton Mifflin 1993 139p $15
(4 and up)   **Fic**

1. Holocaust, 1933-1945—Fiction 2. Jews—Fiction
3. Netherlands—Fiction
ISBN 0-395-65368-1   LC 92-1618

Vos, Ida—*Continued*

Also available in paperback from Puffin Bks.

Original Dutch edition, 1986

In this sequel to Hide and seek, Anna now thirteen "has been reunited with her parents, who are loving but still unable to speak of their own time in hiding or of the loss of family and friends. . . . The story mainly concerns the rebuilding of her relationship with her parents and a tenuous friendship with Mrs. Neumann, a woman who is searching for her little daughter, lost in the tides of war. . . . A striking, and ultimately hopeful, account of how the human spirit survives and recovers." Horn Book

Hide and seek; translated by Terese Edelstein and Inez Smidt. Houghton Mifflin 1991 132p $15 (4 and up) **Fic**

1. Holocaust, 1933-1945—Fiction 2. Jews—Fiction 3. Netherlands—Fiction

ISBN 0-395-56470-0   LC 90-4980

Also available in paperback from Puffin Bks.

Original Dutch edition, 1981

Anna, a young Jewish girl living in Holland, tells of her experiences during the Nazi occupation, her years in hiding, and the after shock when the war finally ends

"Drawing on her own experiences during WW II, Vos fills the narrative with understated but painfully realistic moments. . . . Vos's novel deserves special attention for its sensitive and deeply affecting consideration of life after liberation." Publ Wkly

Followed by Anna is still here

Wait, Lea

Wintering well; [by] Lea Wait. 1st ed. Margaret K. McElderry Books 2004 186p $16.95 (5 and up) **Fic**

1. Siblings—Fiction 2. Handicapped—Fiction 3. Maine—Fiction

ISBN 0-689-85646-6   LC 2003-19322

Fifteen-year-old Will Ames and his sister Cassie go to stay with their sister in nearby Wiscasset, Maine, after a disabling accident ruins Will's plans for a career in farming.

"Limned with just the right amount of detail about the realities of life in the early nineteenth century, this is a quiet story of seeking." Booklist

Wallace, Barbara Brooks

Cousins in the castle. Atheneum Bks. for Young Readers 1996 152p $16; pa $3.99 (4-6) **Fic**

1. Orphans—Fiction 2. Mystery fiction

ISBN 0-689-80637-X; 0-689-80778-3 (pa)

LC 95-23484

"A Jean Karl book"

"When the recently orphaned Amelia sails from Victorian England to her guardian in America, she finds herself the target of a plan to steal her fortune. It's a close call for Amelia, but the scheme fails, and all ends well. Wallace weaves long-lost relatives, goodhearted helpers, and despicable kidnappers—not to mention improbable plot twists—into an enjoyable story fraught with Gothic atmosphere." Horn Book Guide

Ghosts in the gallery. Atheneum Bks. for Young Readers 2000 136p $16; pa $4.99 (5 and up)

Fic

1. Orphans—Fiction 2. Grandfathers—Fiction

ISBN 0-689-83175-7; 0-689-83915-4 (pa)

LC 99-29055

"A Jean Karl book"

When eleven-year-old Jenny arrives at her grandfather's house but is not recognized as one of the family because of a servant's intrigue, the young orphan endures a difficult fate

"Guaranteed thrills and chills." Horn Book Guide

The twin in the tavern. Atheneum Pubs. 1993 179p $15; pa $4.99 (4-6) **Fic**

1. Orphans—Fiction 2. Twins—Fiction 3. Mystery fiction

ISBN 0-689-31846-4; 0-689-80167-X (pa)

LC 92-36429

"A Jean Karl book"

Taddy, a young orphan, afraid of being sent to the workhouse, finds himself at the mercy of the unsavory owner of a tavern in Alexandria, Virginia, while he tries to solve the mystery surrounding his past and a missing twin

"With a fine hand for Gothic embroidery and a nifty surprise conclusion that ties up all the loose ends, Wallace has delivered [a] . . . very satisfying read." SLJ

Wallace, Bill

Beauty. Holiday House 1988 177p $16.95 (4-6)

Fic

1. Horses—Fiction 2. Farm life—Fiction

ISBN 0-8234-0715-2   LC 88-6422

Also available in paperback from Pocket Bks.

Unhappy about his parents splitting up and moving with his mother to Grandpa's farm, eleven-year-old Luke finds comfort in riding and caring for a horse named Beauty

"Wallace's horse story is strong on sentiment, and its tear-jerker finale packs a wallop. . . . The story will stir up genuine emotion." Booklist

A dog called Kitty. Holiday House 1980 153p $15.95 (4-6) **Fic**

1. Dogs—Fiction 2. Farm life—Fiction

ISBN 0-8234-0376-9   LC 80-16293

Also available in paperback from Minstrel Bks.

Afraid of dogs since he was attacked by a mad one as a baby, Ricky resists taking in a homeless pup that shows up at the farm

"Some minor plot elements are contrived enough to strain credibility, but Ricky is real, as are his family and friends, and there is no lack of action. Recommended also for older reluctant readers for its fast pace, popular appeal, and second-to-third-grade reading level." Booklist

Skinny-dipping at Monster Lake. Simon & Schuster Bks. for Young Readers 2003 212p $16.95 (4 and up) **Fic**

ISBN 0-689-85150-2   LC 2002-152820

When twelve-year-old Kent helps his father in a daring underwater rescue, he wins the respect he has always craved.

Wallace, Bill—*Continued*

"This old-fashioned adventure has wide appeal, and the youngsters' games and camaraderie will hook even reluctant readers." SLJ

Wallace-Brodeur, Ruth

Blue eyes better. Dutton Children's Bks. 2002 106p il $15.99; pa $5.99 (4-6)   **Fic**
1. Death—Fiction
ISBN 0-525-46836-6; 0-14-250086-0 (pa)
         LC 2001-45205

When her older brother is killed in an accident, ten-year-old Tessa and her parents find it difficult to overcome their grief and return to living normally

"From the first words, this small, beautiful novel is rooted in hard fact. . . . The images are simple poetry. . . . This is gripping family drama." Booklist

Walter, Mildred Pitts

Justin and the best biscuits in the world; with illustrations by Catherine Stock. Lothrop, Lee & Shepard Bks. 1986 122p il $16 (3-6)   **Fic**
1. Sex role—Fiction 2. Grandfathers—Fiction 3. Family life—Fiction 4. African Americans—Fiction
ISBN 0-688-06645-3   LC 86-7148
Also available in paperback from Knopf
Coretta Scott King Award for text, 1987

"Justin can't seem to do anything right at home. His sisters berate his dishwashing and his mother despairs of his ever properly tidying his room. As for Justin, he angrily rejects the tasks as 'women's work.' Enter now Justin's widowed grandfather, who sizes up the situation, invites Justin for a visit to his ranch, and through daily routines quietly shows Justin that 'it doesn't matter who does the work, man or woman, when it needs to be done.'" Booklist

"The strong, well-developed characters and humorous situations in this warm family story will appeal to intermediate readers; the large print will draw slow or reluctant readers." SLJ

Suitcase; illustrated by Teresa Flavin. Lothrop, Lee & Shepard Bks. 1999 107p il $13.50 (3-6)
         Fic
1. Artists—Fiction 2. African Americans—Fiction
ISBN 0-688-16547-8   LC 99-11488

Despite his love of drawing and his feelings of inadequacy as an athlete, sixth-grader Xander "Suitcase" Bingham works to become a baseball player to win the approval of his father

"The book is reassuring in its honest portrayal of his insecurities and his willingness to persevere." Horn Book Guide

Ward, Lynd Kendall

The silver pony; a story in pictures; by Lynd Ward. Houghton Mifflin 1973 174p il $18; pa $6.95 (2-4)   **Fic**
1. Horses—Fiction 2. Stories without words
ISBN 0-395-14753-0; 0-395-64377-5 (pa)

"Eighty pictures in shades of gray, black, and white tell the story of a lonely farm boy whose dreams of his

adventures on a winged horse become confused with reality. One night the boy leans out his window fantasizing that the horse is carrying him to the moon; but the dream turns into a nightmare as rockets and missiles fill the air around them, then explode, killing the horse and sending the boy hurtling through space—really out the window to his own yard below. The boy recovers physically and, with the help of his parents, doctor, and a real colt, emotionally. This is a complex story subtly conveyed without words—a unique experience for readers and nonreaders alike." Booklist

Warner, Sally

Only Emma; illustrated by Jamie Harper. Viking 2004 115p il $14.99 (2-4)   **Fic**
ISBN 0-670-05979-X   LC 2004-12478

Third-grader Emma's peaceful life as an only child is disrupted when she has to temporarily share her tidy bedroom with four-year-old Anthony Scarpetto.

"The black-and-white illustrations are charming, and thumbnail sidebars present fun scientific facts about animals mentioned in the story. . . . Emma is a likable character whose feelings and behaviors are common to many children." SLJ

Another title about Emma is:
Not-so-weird Emma (2005)

This isn't about the money. Viking 2002 209p $15.99; pa $5.99 (5 and up)   **Fic**
1. Death—Fiction 2. Orphans—Fiction 3. California—Fiction
ISBN 0-670-03574-2; 0-14-240221-4 (pa)
         LC 2001-56797

Twelve-year-old Janey tries to adjust in the aftermath of an automobile accident that kills her parents, severely injures her face, and forces her and her younger sister to move from Arizona to California to live with their grandfather and great-aunt

"Warner's dialog and characterization are rich and real." Booklist

Waters, Fiona

Oscar Wilde's The selfish giant; retold by Fiona Waters; illustrated by Fabian Negrin. Knopf 2000 c1999 il $16.95; lib bdg $18.99 (2-5)   **Fic**
1. Fairy tales 2. Giants—Fiction
ISBN 0-375-80319-X; 0-375-90319-4 (lib bdg)
         LC 99-32495

This retelling first published 1999 in the United Kingdom

A once selfish giant welcomes the children to his previously forbidden garden and is eventually rewarded by an unusual little child

"Water's retelling of Wilde's allegorical fairy tale stays close to the original, and Negrin's lavish, theatrical illustrations express the dramatic contrasts at the heart of the story." Booklist

Watkins, Yoko Kawashima

My brother, my sister, and I. Bradbury Press 1994 275p pa $5.99 hardcover o.p. (6 and up)
         Fic
1. World War, 1939-1945—Fiction 2. Japan—Fiction 3. Korea—Fiction
ISBN 0-689-80656-6 (pa)   LC 93-23535

Watkins, Yoko Kawashima—*Continued*

"The author continues her autobiographical account begun in *So Far from the Bamboo Grove* with the story of how the two sisters, Ko and Yoko, now reunited with their brother Hideyo, try to survive in postwar Japan." Horn Book

"Watkins's first-person narrative is beautifully direct and emotionally honest." Publ Wkly

So far from the bamboo grove. Lothrop, Lee & Shepard Bks. 1986 183p map pa $5.99 hardcover o.p. (6 and up) **Fic**
1. World War, 1939-1945—Fiction 2. Korea—Fiction 3. Japan—Fiction
ISBN 0-688-13115-8 (pa) LC 85-15939
A fictionalized autobiography in which eight-year-old Yoko escapes from Korea to Japan with her mother and sister at the end of World War II

"An admirably told and absorbing novel." Horn Book
Followed by My brother, my sister and I

Waugh, Sylvia

The Mennyms. Greenwillow Bks. 1994 c1993 212p $16 (5 and up) **Fic**
1. Dolls—Fiction 2. Family life—Fiction 3. Great Britain—Fiction
ISBN 0-688-13070-4 LC 93-15901
Also available in paperback from Avon Bks.
First published 1993 in the United Kingdom
The Mennyms, a family of life-size rag dolls living in a house in England and pretending to be human, see their peaceful existence threatened when the house's owner announces he is coming from Australia for a visit

"The suspenseful, seamless fantasy is rich in detail and imagination." Horn Book Guide
Other titles about the Mennyms are:
Mennyms alive (1997)
Mennyms alone (1996)
Mennyms in the wilderness (1995)
Mennyms under siege (1996)

Space race. Delacorte Press 2000 241p $15.95 (4-6) **Fic**
1. Extraterrestrial beings—Fiction 2. Science fiction
ISBN 0-385-37266-8 LC 99-55399
When he learns that he and his father must soon leave Earth to return to the planet Ormingat, eleven-year-old Thomas Derwent is upset, but a terrible accident that separates the two of them makes Thomas's situation much worse

This "is a thoughtful examination of friendship, loyalty, and love. Readers will enjoy the exciting plot and fast-moving action, and the sympathetic characters will stay with them long after the book is closed." SLJ
Other titles in this series are:
Earthborn (2002)
Who goes home (2004)

Weeks, Sarah

Jumping the scratch; [by] Sarah Weeks. 1st ed. Laura Geringer Books 2006 167p il $15.99; lib bdg $16.89 (5 and up) **Fic**
1. Child sexual abuse—Fiction 2. Memory—Fiction 3. Aunts—Fiction
ISBN 978-0-06-054109-5; 978-0-06-054110-1 (lib bdg); 0-06-054110-5 (lib bdg) LC 2005017776
After moving with his mother to a trailer park to care for an injured aunt, eleven-year-old Jamie Reardon struggles to cope with a deeply buried secret.

"Weeks alludes to sexual abuse, but with a broad brush and no graphic details. . . . Weeks perfectly captures not only the guilt, shame, and pain of the abused boy but also the tenor of a fifth-grade classroom from the point of view of a new student who is friendless, targeted, and belittled by an insensitive teacher. Touches of humor ameliorate the pain and poignancy." SLJ

Regular Guy. HarperCollins Pubs. 1999 120p $14.95; lib bdg $14.89; pa $4.99 (4-6) **Fic**
1. Parent-child relationship—Fiction
ISBN 0-06-028367-X; 0-06-028368-8 (lib bdg); 0-06-440782-9 (pa) LC 99-12118
"A Laura Geringer book"
Because he is so different from his eccentric parents, twelve-year-old Guy is convinced he has been switched at birth with a classmate whose parents seem more normal

"Weeks treats the situation with wild exaggeration, a farcical plot, and just a touch of tenderness. . . . Many middle-graders will enjoy the gross humor (lots of snot and clatter and fishy smells) as much as the view of embarrassing adults who love you even though they drive you nuts." Booklist
Other titles about Guy are:
Guy time (2000)
Guy wire (2002)
My Guy (2001)

So B. it; a novel. Laura Geringer Books 2004 245p $15.99 (5 and up) **Fic**
1. Mentally handicapped—Fiction 2. Mental illness—Fiction
ISBN 0-06-623622-3 LC 2003-15643
After spending her life with her mentally retarded mother and agoraphobic neighbor, twelve-year-old Heidi sets out from Reno, Nevada, to New York to find out who she is.

"This is lovely writing—real, touching, and pared cleanly down to the essentials." Booklist

Wells, Rosemary

Wingwalker; illustrated by Brian Selznick. Hyperion Bks. for Children 2002 63p il $15.99; lib bdg $16.49 (3-6) **Fic**
1. Great Depression, 1929-1939—Fiction 2. Fairs—Fiction 3. Stunt flying—Fiction
ISBN 0-7868-0397-5; 0-7868-2347-X (lib bdg) LC 2001-39087
During the Depression, Reuben and his out-of-work parents move from Oklahoma to Minnesota, where his father gets a job as a carnival wingwalker and Reuben

Wells, Rosemary—*Continued*

has a chance to overcome his terror of flying

"This is a beautifully crafted book. Wells has chosen her words with precision. . . . As fine as the text are Selznick's insightful Norman Rockwell-like pictures, brushed with Oklahoma dust." Booklist

Weston, Carol

The diary of Melanie Martin; or, How I survived Matt the Brat, Michelangelo, and the Leaning Tower of Pizza. Knopf 2000 144p $15.95; lib bdg $17.99 (3-6)   **Fic**

1. Voyages and travels—Fiction 2. Family life—Fiction 3. Italy—Fiction

ISBN 0-375-80509-5; 0-375-90509-X (lib bdg)

LC 99-53384

Fourth-grader Melanie Martin writes in her diary, describing her family's trip to Italy and all that she learned

"Sections of the book are laugh-out-loud funny and Weston's descriptions will have readers wanting to see the country for themselves. An enjoyable read." SLJ

Other titles about Melanie Martin are:

Melanie in Manhattan (2005)

Melanie Martin goes Dutch (2002)

With love from Spain, Melanie Martin (2005)

Weston, Martha

Act I, act II, act normal. Roaring Brook Press 2003 148p $15.95; lib bdg $22.90 (5 and up)   **Fic**

1. Theater—Fiction 2. School stories 3. Family life—Fiction

ISBN 0-7613-1779-1; 0-7613-2859-9 (lib bdg)

LC 2002-14222

Topher Blakely gets the lead in the eighth-grade play, but unfortunately the play is "Rumpelstiltskin," the class bully picks on him relentlessly, and his beloved cat dies, all of which teach him a lot about compassion, friendship, and life

"Lighthearted and humorous, this novel presents a realistic and insightful look at artistic young people." SLJ

Whelan, Gloria

Goodbye, Vietnam. Knopf 1992 135p pa $5.50 hardcover o.p. (4 and up)   **Fic**

1. Refugees—Fiction 2. Vietnamese—Fiction

ISBN 0-679-82376-X (pa)   LC 91-3660

Thirteen-year-old Mai and her family embark on a dangerous sea voyage from Vietnam to Hong Kong to escape the unpredictable and often brutal Vietnamese government

"While the book has the suspense and appeal of any good escape story, Whelan is neither melodramatic nor sentimental, and the sometimes horrific details of the scary voyage are plain but understated." Bull Cent Child Books

Homeless bird. HarperCollins Pubs. 2000 216p $15.95; lib bdg $16.89; pa $5.99 (6 and up)

     Fic

1. Women—India—Fiction 2. India—Fiction

ISBN 0-06-028454-4; 0-06-028452-8 (lib bdg); 0-06-440819-1 (pa)   LC 99-33241

When thirteen-year-old Koly enters into an ill-fated arranged marriage, she must either suffer a destiny dictated by India's tradition or find the courage to oppose it

"This beautifully told, inspiring story takes readers on a fascinating journey through modern India and the universal intricacies of a young woman's heart." Booklist

Listening for lions. HarperCollins 2005 194p $15.99; lib bdg $16.89 (5 and up)   **Fic**

1. Orphans—Fiction 2. East Africa—Fiction 3. Physicians—Fiction 4. Great Britain—Fiction

ISBN 0-06-058174-3; 0-06-058175-1 (lib bdg)

Left an orphan after the influenza epidemic in British East Africa in 1918, thirteen-year-old Rachel is tricked into assuming a deceased neighbor's identity to travel to England, where her only dream is to return to Africa and rebuild her parents' mission hospital.

"In a straightforward, sympathetic voice, Rachel tells an involving, episodic story." Booklist

The turning; [by] Gloria Whelan. 1st ed. HarperCollins 2006 213p $15.99; lib bdg $16.89 (5 and up)   **Fic**

1. Soviet Union—Fiction 2. Ballet—Fiction

ISBN 0-06-075593-8; 0-06-075594-6 (lib bdg)

LC 2005-08777

In the months leading up to the August 1991 coup attempt that resulted in the collapse of communism in the Soviet Union, a young dancer with the Kirov Ballet struggles to decide whether to defect while on an upcoming trip to Paris.

"The author has successfully woven Russian history and culture into this story. . . . Tanya is an appealing, thoughtful heroine whose political awareness and integrity will encourage readers to think about the importance of decisions and events in peoples lives." SLJ

White, E. B. (Elwyn Brooks)

Charlotte's web; pictures by Garth Williams. Harper & Row 1952 184p il $16.95; lib bdg $16.89; pa $5.95   **Fic**

1. Pigs—Fiction 2. Spiders—Fiction

ISBN 0-06-026385-7; 0-06-026386-5 (lib bdg); 0-06-440055-7 (pa)

Also available Spanish language edition

A Newbery Medal honor book, 1953

The story of a little girl who could talk to animals, but especially the story of the pig, Wilbur, and his friendship with Charlotte, the spider, who could not only talk but write as well

"Illustrated with amusing sketches . . . [this] story is a fable for adults as well as children and can be recommended to older children and parents as an amusing story and a gentle essay on friendship." Libr J

Stuart Little; pictures by Garth Williams. Harper & Row 1945 131p il $16.95; lib bdg $16.89; pa $5.95 (3-6)   **Fic**

1. Mice—Fiction

ISBN 0-06-026395-4; 0-06-026396-2 (lib bdg); 0-06-440056-5 (pa)

Also available Spanish language edition

This is "the story of a 'Tom Thumb'-like child born to a New York couple who is to all intents and purposes

White, E. B. (Elwyn Brooks)—*Continued*

a mouse. . . . The first part of the book explores, with dead-pan humour, the advantages and disadvantages of having a mouse in one's family circle. Then Stuart sets out on a quest in search of his inamorata, a bird named Margalo, and the story ends in mid-air. The book is outstandingly funny and sometimes touching." Oxford Companion to Child Lit

The trumpet of the swan; illustrated by Fred Marcellino. HarperCollins Pubs. 2000 251p il $16.95; lib bdg $16.89; pa $5.95 (3-6)

Fic

1. Swans—Fiction
ISBN 0-06-028935-X; 0-06-028936-8 (lib bdg); 0-06-440867-1 (pa)   LC 99-44250
Also available Spanish language edition
A newly illustrated edition of the title first published 1970

Louis, a voiceless Trumpeter swan, finds himself far from his wilderness home when he determines to communicate by learning to play a stolen trumpet
The author "deftly blends true birdlore with fanciful adventures in a witty, captivating fantasy." Booklist

White, Ruth

Belle Prater's boy. Farrar, Straus & Giroux 1996 196p $17 (5 and up)   **Fic**
1.   Cousins—Fiction   2.   Virginia—Fiction
3. Appalachian region—Fiction
ISBN 0-374-30668-0   LC 94-43625
Also available in paperback from Random House
A Newbery Medal honor book, 1997
"Gypsy and her cousin Woodrow become close friends after Woodrow's mother disappears. Both sixth-graders feel deserted by their parents—Gypsy discovers that her father committed suicide—and need to define themselves apart from these tragedies. White's prose evokes the coal mining region of Virginia and the emotional quality of her characters' transformations." Horn Book Guide
Another title about Belle Prater is:
The search for Belle Prater (2005)

Tadpole. Farrar, Straus & Giroux 2003 198p $16 (4 and up)   **Fic**
1. Child abuse—Fiction 2. Orphans—Fiction
3. Family life—Fiction
ISBN 0-374-31002-5   LC 2002-20707
In rural Kentucky in 1955, Serilda Collins, single mother of four lively girls, discovers that her orphaned nephew is being subjected to brutality
"White skillfully re-creates the time and place, and her superbly drawn characters possess the resiliency of spirit necessary to transform themselves." SLJ

White, T. H. (Terence Hanbury)

The sword in the stone; with illustrations by Dennis Nolan. Putnam 1993 256p il $22.99 (4 and up)   **Fic**
1. Arthur, King—Fiction 2. Merlin (Legendary character)—Fiction
ISBN 0-399-22502-1   LC 92-24808
Also available in paperback from Dell

A newly illustrated edition of the title first published 1938 in the United Kingdom; first United States edition 1939 by G.P Putnam's Sons
"In White's classic story about the boyhood of King Arthur, Wart—unaware of his true identity—is tutored by Merlyn, who occasionally transform the young boy into various animals as part of his schooling. Contemporary children will still enjoy the text, which is both fantastical and down-to-earth." Horn Book Guide

Whittenberg, Allison

Sweet Thang. Delacorte Press 2006 149p $15.95; lib bdg $17.99 (5 and up)   **Fic**
1. African Americans—Fiction 2. Family life—Fiction
3. School stories
ISBN 0-385-73292-9; 0-385-90313-8 (lib bdg)
                                        LC 2005-03809
In 1975, life is not fair for fourteen-year-old Charmaine Upshaw, who shares a room with her brother, tries to impress a handsome classmate, and acts as caretaker for a rambunctious six-year-old cousin who has taken over the family.
"Whittenberg has created a refreshing cast and a good read." SLJ

Wiggin, Kate Douglas Smith

The Bird's Christmas Carol; by Kate Douglas Wiggin; illustrated by Jessie Gillespie. Memorial ed. Houghton Mifflin 1941 84p il $9.95; pa $4.95 (3-5)   **Fic**
1. Christmas—Fiction
ISBN 0-395-07205-0; 0-395-89110-8 (pa)
First published 1888
"The story of Carol Bird, an invalid girl so named because she was born at Christmas." Oxford Companion to Child Lit

Rebecca of Sunnybrook Farm; with illustrations by Helen Mason Grose; afterword by Peter Glassman. Morrow 1994 291p il $12.95 (4 and up)   **Fic**
1. Aunts—Fiction 2. New England—Fiction
ISBN 0-688-13481-5   LC 94-9899
Also available various hardcover reprint and paperback editions
A reissue of the title first published 1903 by Houghton, Mifflin
Talkative, ten-year-old Rebecca goes to live with her spinster aunts, one harsh and demanding, the other soft and sentimental, with whom she spends seven difficult but rewarding years growing up
"Six full-color illustrations and numerous pen-and-ink drawings attractively depict the familiar characters and old-time setting of the classic novel. Wiggin's story . . . continues to hold appeal." Horn Book Guide

Wilde, Oscar

The selfish giant (2-5)   **Fic**
1. Fairy tales 2. Giants—Fiction
Available Putnam & Grosset Group edition illustrated by Saelig Gallagher
This is the "story of a giant whose garden is wrapped in winter until he shares it with the children who live nearby." Booklist

Wilder, Laura Ingalls

Little house in the big woods; illustrated by
Garth Williams. newly illustrated, uniform ed.
Harper & Row 1953 237p il $16.95; lib bdg
$16.89; pa $3.50 (4-6)   **Fic**
1. Frontier and pioneer life—Fiction 2. Wisconsin—
Fiction
ISBN 0-06-026430-6; 0-06-026431-4 (lib bdg);
0-06-107005-X (pa)
First published 1932
This book "tells the story of the author's earliest days
'in the Big Woods of Wisconsin, in a little grey house
made of logs.' The style of narrative is simple, almost
naive, but the pioneer life is described unsqueamishly,
with attention to such details as the butchering of the
family hog. As in later books, the author refers to herself
in the third person as 'Laura.' The record of daily life far
from any town is punctuated with stories told in the eve-
nings by Pa, who is also a great singer of folk-songs."
Oxford Companion to Child Lit
 Other titles in the Little House series are:
By the shores of Silver Lake (1939)
Farmer boy (1933)
The first four years (1971)
Little house on the prairie (1935)
Little town on the prairie (1941)
The long winter (1940)
On the banks of Plum Creek (1937)
These happy golden years (1943)

Wiles, Deborah

Each little bird that sings; [by] Deborah Wiles.
Harcourt, Inc 2005 247p $16 (4-6)   **Fic**
1.   Death—Fiction   2.   Bereavement—Fiction
3. Undertakers and undertaking—Fiction 4. Family
life—Fiction
ISBN 0-15-205113-9   LC 2004-13631
Comfort Snowberger is well acquainted with death
since her family runs the funeral parlor in their small
southern town, but even so the ten-year-old is unprepared
for the series of heart-wrenching events that begins on
the first day of Easter vacation with the sudden death of
her beloved great-uncle Edisto
"Sensitive, funny, and occasionally impatient, Comfort
is a wholly sympathetic protagonist. . . . This is a deeply felt novel." SLJ

Love, Ruby Lavender. Harcourt 2001 188p il
$16 (4-6)   **Fic**
1. Grandparents—Fiction 2. Mississippi—Fiction
ISBN 0-15-202314-3   LC 00-11159
"Gulliver books"
When her quirky grandmother goes to Hawaii for the
summer, nine-year-old Ruby learns to survive on her
own in Mississippi by writing letters, befriending chickens as well as the new girl in town, and finally coping
with her grandfather's death
"The engaging narrative . . . is witty and fast paced
and the quirky, diverse cast of human and poultry characters is colorful and spirited, if not totally realistic." SLJ

Wilkinson, Carole

Dragon keeper. Hyperion Books for Children
2005 c2003 352p $16.99 (5 and up)   **Fic**
1. Dragons—Fiction 2. China—Fiction
ISBN 0-7868-5581-9
First published 2003 in Australia
An orphan slave girl becomes a Dragon Keeper when
she heroically comes to the aid of an aging dragon and
both go on a dangerous journey across China to protect
a mysterious stone vital to the dragon's legacy.
"The relationship between the child and the beast
stands at the heart of this compelling adventure, which
is infused with humor as well as peril." Booklist

Williams, Laura E.

The executioner's daughter. Holt & Co. 2000
134p $15.95 (6 and up)   **Fic**
1. Middle Ages—Fiction
ISBN 0-8050-6234-3   LC 99-49259
Thirteen-year-old Lily, daughter of the town's executioner living in fifteenth-century Europe, decides whether
to fight against her destiny or to rise above her fate
" This well-written story is an excellent vehicle for
demonstrating the harsh realities of life in the Middle
Ages." SLJ

Williams, Mary

Brothers in hope; the story of the Lost Boys of
Sudan; illustrated by R. Gregory Christie. Lee &
Low Books 2005 unp il $17.95 (3-5)   **Fic**
1. Refugees—Fiction 2. Sudan—Fiction 3. War stories
ISBN 1-58430-232-1   LC 2004-20965
Eight-year-old Garang, orphaned by a civil war in Sudan, finds the inner strength to help lead other boys as
they trek hundreds of miles seeking safety in Ethiopia,
then Kenya, and finally in the United States.
"Christie's distinctive acrylic illustrations, done in
broad strokes of predominantly green, yellow, and burnt
orange, are arresting in their combination of realism and
the abstract. . . . This important profile in courage is one
that belongs in most collections." SLJ

Williams, Vera B.

Scooter. Greenwillow Bks. 1993 147p il $15; lib
bdg $14.93 (3-5)   **Fic**
1.   Moving—Fiction   2.   Friendship—Fiction
3. Divorce—Fiction
ISBN 0-688-09376-0; 0-688-09377-9 (lib bdg)
                                      LC 90-38489
After her parent's divorce "Elana Rose Rosen and her
mother relocate to an apartment in a big city housing
project where 'Lanny' spends the summer making friends
and practicing her favorite scooter tricks." Publ Wkly
"The voice is totally authentic, and Williams peppers
the pages with ink drawings that have an equally authentic childlike zest." Bull Cent Child Books

Willis, Patricia

The barn burner. Clarion Bks. 2000 196p $15 (5
and up)   **Fic**
1. Great Depression, 1929-1939—Fiction 2. Runaway
children—Fiction 3. Family life—Fiction
ISBN 0-395-98409-2   LC 99-42223

Willis, Patricia—*Continued*

Also available in paperback from Scholastic

In 1933 while running from a bad situation at home and suspected of having set fire to a barn, fourteen-year-old Ross finds a haven with a loving family which helps him make an important decision

"By tying an unsentimental look at the era together with a mystery, the author has created a story that is both appealing and of literary merit." SLJ

Willner-Pardo, Gina

Daphne Eloise Slater, who's tall for her age; illustrated by Glo Coalson. Clarion Bks. 1997 39p il $15 (2-4) **Fic**

1. School stories

ISBN 0-395-73080-5 LC 95-44050

Daphne didn't mind being the tallest girl in her class until third grade, when a classmate begins teasing her about her height and she must decide whether to retaliate

"The situations are realistic, and Willner-Pardo captures the importance of the small events that make up life in the elementary school. Coalson's light watercolors . . . are warm and lively." Horn Book Guide

Figuring out Frances. Clarion Bks. 1999 134p $14 (4-6) **Fic**

1. Friendship—Fiction 2. Grandmothers—Fiction 3. Alzheimer's disease—Fiction

ISBN 0-395-91510-4 LC 98-50082

Ten-year-old Abigail's neighbor Travis, her best friend although he is at a different school, upsets her when he transfers to her school, ignores her, and laughs at her grandmother's Alzheimer's along with his new friends

"The writing is witty, sincere, and insightful. This is a gem of a book." SLJ

Wilson, Diane L.

I rode a horse of milk white jade; [by] Diane Lee Wilson. Orchard Bks. 1998 232p $18.95 (6 and up) **Fic**

1. Horses—Fiction

ISBN 0-531-30024-2 LC 97-23838

Also available in paperback from HarperCollins

Oyuna tells her granddaughter the story of how love for her horse enabled her to win a race and bring good luck to her family living in Mongolia in 1339

This "story is an exciting one that will reward diligent, proficient readers." SLJ

Wilson, Jacqueline

The illustrated Mum; [by] Jacqueline Wilson. Delacorte Press 2005 282p $15.95; lib bdg $17.99 (5 and up) **Fic**

1. Manic-depressive illness—Fiction 2. Mother-daughter relationship—Fiction 3. Sisters—Fiction 4. Tattooing—Fiction

ISBN 0-385-73237-6; 0-385-90263-8 (lib bdg)
LC 2003-70123

First published 1999 in the United Kingdom

Ten-year-old Dolphin is determined to stay with her family, no matter what, but when her sister goes to live with her newly-discovered father, sending their mother

further into manic-depression, Dolphin's life takes a turn for the better.

"Dolphin is a sympathetic character and the relationship between the sisters is realistically portrayed, as is Marigold's mental illness." SLJ

Wilson, Nancy Hope

Mountain pose. Farrar, Straus & Giroux 2001 233p $17 (5 and up) **Fic**

1. Grandmothers—Fiction 2. Diaries—Fiction 3. Vermont—Fiction

ISBN 0-374-35078-7 LC 00-57269

Also available in paperback from Scholastic

When twelve-year-old Ellie inherits an old Vermont farm from her cruel and heartless grandmother Aurelia, she reads a set of diaries written by an ancestor and discovers secrets from the past

"Beautifully written and suspenseful, this novel explores the many emotions associated with the tragedy of spousal and child abuse." Voice Youth Advocates

Winerip, Michael

Adam Canfield of the Slash. Candlewick Press 2005 326p $15.99 (5 and up) **Fic**

1. Journalism—Fiction 2. School stories

ISBN 0-7636-2340-7

While serving as co-editors of their school newspaper, middle-schoolers Adam and Jennifer uncover fraud and corruption in their school and in the city's government.

"This is a deceptively fun read that somehow manages to present kids with some of the most subtle social and ethical questions currently shaping their futures." SLJ

Winthrop, Elizabeth

The castle in the attic; frontispiece and chapter title decorations by Trina Schart Hyman. Holiday House 1985 179p il $15.95 (4-6) **Fic**

1. Fantasy fiction

ISBN 0-8234-0579-6 LC 85-5607

Also available in paperback from Dell

A gift of a toy castle, complete with silver knight, introduces William to an adventure involving magic and a personal quest.

"Well-crafted, easy to follow, this excursion into knightly times and affairs is further enhanced by the cover art, chapter decorations and, most important of all, a thoughtful floor plan of the castle." Horn Book

Another available title about William and Sir Simon is:
The battle for the castle (1993)

Wise, William

Christopher Mouse; the tale of a small traveler; illustrations by Patrick Benson. Bloomsbury Children's Books 2004 152p il $15.95 (3-5) **Fic**

1. Mice—Fiction

ISBN 1-58234-878-2 LC 2003-56393

After being sold to an unscrupulous pet store owner, a young mouse lives with several owners and has many adventures, before ending up with an appreciative family.

"The writing is nicely mannered but very accessible,

Wise, William—*Continued*

making the book not only a winner for reading aloud but also a delightful offering for children moving past beginning readers. The ink illustrations and the enticing cover will help them along." Booklist

Wiseman, David

Jeremy Visick. Houghton Mifflin 1981 170p pa $5.95 hardcover o.p. (5 and up)   **Fic**

1. Space and time—Fiction 2. Supernatural—Fiction 3. Great Britain—Fiction 4. Miners—Fiction
ISBN 0-618-34514-0 (pa)   LC 80-28116

Twelve-year-old Matthew is drawn almost against his will to help a boy his own age who was lost in a mining disaster a century before.

"This story blends the mystery and awe of the supernatural with the real terror and peril of descending the shaft of an 1850 Cornish copper mine." SLJ

Wisler, G. Clifton

Mr. Lincoln's drummer. Lodestar Bks. 1995 131p $15.99; pa $4.99 (4 and up)   **Fic**

1. Johnston, William J., b. 1850—Fiction 2. United States—History—1861-1865, Civil War—Fiction
ISBN 0-525-67463-2; 0-14-038542-8 (pa)
LC 94-20328

Recounts the courageous exploits of Willie Johnston, an eleven-year-old Civil War drummer, who became the youngest recipient of the Congressional Medal of Honor

"Lively dialogue, vivid battle scenes, unsentimentalized heroism, and a fair amount of wry humor make this an especially good choice for history-shy readers." Bull Cent Child Books

Red Cap. Lodestar Bks. 1991 160p pa $5.99 hardcover o.p. (4 and up)   **Fic**

1. Powell, Ransom J., 1849-1899—Fiction 2. Andersonville Prison—Fiction 3. United States—History—1861-1865, Civil War—Fiction
ISBN 0-14-036936-8 (pa)   LC 90-21944

A young Yankee drummer boy displays great courage when he's captured and sent to Andersonville Prison

The author "presents a well-researched view of the war. He effectively interweaves the known facts of Powell's life with first-person accounts of other soldiers and prisoners to create an exciting story." SLJ

Wojciechowska, Maia

Shadow of a bull; drawings by Alvin Smith. Atheneum Pubs. 1964 165p il $16; pa $4.99 (6 and up)   **Fic**

1. Spain—Fiction 2. Bullfights—Fiction
ISBN 0-689-30042-5; 0-689-71567-6 (pa)

Awarded the Newbery Medal, 1965

"Manolo was the son of the great bullfighter Juan Olivar. Ever since his father's death the town of Arcangel [Spain] has waited for [the time] when Manolo would be twelve and face his first bull." Publ Wkly

"In spare, economical prose [the author] makes one feel, see, smell the heat, endure the hot Andalusian sun and shows one the sand and glare of the bullring. Above all, she lifts the veil and gives glimpses of the terrible loneliness in the soul of a boy. . . . Superbly illustrated." N Y Times Book Rev

Wolfson, Jill

What I call life. Holt & Co. 2005 270p $16.95 (5 and up)   **Fic**

1. Foster home care—Fiction
ISBN 0-8050-7669-7

Placed in a group foster home, eleven-year-old Cal Lavender learns how to cope with life from the four other girls who live there and from their storytelling guardian, the Knitting Lady.

"Wolfson paints her characters with delightful authenticity. Her debut novel is a treasure of quiet good humor and skillful storytelling that conveys subtle messages about kindness, compassion, and the gift of family regardless of its configuration." Booklist

Woodruff, Elvira

The Ravenmaster's secret. Scholastic Press 2003 225p $15.95 (5 and up)   **Fic**

1. Tower of London (England)—Fiction 2. Great Britain—History—1714-1837—Fiction 3. Ravens—Fiction 4. London (England)—Fiction
ISBN 0-439-28133-4   LC 2002-15963

The eleven-year-old son of the Ravenmaster at the Tower of London befriends a Jacobite rebel being held prisoner there.

"An absorbing historical adventure with a unique and colorful setting. . . . The novel can be read for its exciting plot and sympathetic characters, but readers will also sense its underlying theme of courage." Booklist

Woods, Brenda

The red rose box. Putnam 2002 136p $16.99; pa $5.99 (5 and up)   **Fic**

1. African Americans—Fiction 2. Louisiana—Fiction 3. Los Angeles (Calif.)—Fiction
ISBN 0-399-23702-X; 0-14-250151-4 (pa)
LC 2001-18354

In 1953, Leah Hopper dreams of leaving the poverty and segregation of her home in Sulphur, Louisiana, and when Aunt Olivia sends train tickets to Los Angeles as part of her tenth birthday present, Leah gets a first taste of freedom

"In language made musical with southern phrases, this . . . novel shapes the era and characters with both well-chosen particulars and universal emotions." Booklist

Wrede, Patricia C.

Dealing with dragons. Harcourt Brace Jovanovich 1990 212p $17; pa $5.95 (6 and up)
Fic

1. Fairy tales 2. Dragons—Fiction
ISBN 0-15-222900-0; 0-15-204566-X (pa)
LC 89-24599

Also available in paperback from Scholastic

"Jane Yolen books"

Bored with traditional palace life, a princess goes off to live with a group of dragons and soon becomes involved with fighting against some disreputable wizards who want to steal away the dragons' kingdom

"A decidedly diverting novel with plenty of action and many slightly skewed fairy-tale conventions that add to the laugh-out-loud reading pleasure and give the story a wide appeal. The good news is that this is book one in the Enchanted Forest Chronicles." Booklist

Wrede, Patricia C.—*Continued*
Other titles in the Enchanted Forest Chronicles are:
Calling on dragons (1993)
Searching for dragons (1991)
Talking to dragons (1993)

Wright, Betty Ren
Crandall's castle. Holiday House 2003 177p
$16.95 (4 and up) **Fic**
1. Ghost stories 2. Orphans—Fiction
3. Clairvoyance—Fiction 4. Cousins—Fiction
ISBN 0-8234-1726-3 LC 2002-38783
Charli's impulsive uncle, Will Crandall, decides to
buy the town's abandoned, possibly haunted castle and
fix it up as a bed-and-breakfast, but Charli and Sophia,
a clairvoyant orphan who has come to stay with the
Crandall family, know his plan is somehow dangerous
"Wright characteristically combines a well-written,
shivery ghost story with distinctively drawn, appealing
protagonists whose issues and dilemmas are sympathetically portrayed." Booklist

The dollhouse murders. Holiday House 1983
149p $15.95 (4 and up) **Fic**
1. Mystery fiction
ISBN 0-8234-0497-8 LC 83-6147
Also available in paperback from Scholastic
A dollhouse filled with a ghostly light in the middle
of the night and dolls that have moved from where she
last left them lead Amy and her retarded sister to unravel
the mystery surrounding grisly murders that took place
years ago
"More than just a mystery, this offers keen insight
into the relationship between handicapped and
nonhandicapped siblings and glimpses into the darker
adult emotions of guilt and anger. A successful, full-
bodied work." Booklist

The ghost in Room 11; illustrated by Jacqueline
Rogers. Holiday House 1998 112p il $15.95 (3-5)
Fic
1. Ghost stories 2. School stories
ISBN 0-8234-1318-7 LC 96-53696
When his family moves to a small town near Milwau-
kee, Matt's efforts to fit into his new fourth-grade class
are complicated by his poor spelling and his encounter
with the ghost of one of the school's former teachers
"Wright offers another intriguing variation on the classic ghost narrative, one that focuses on emotions and maturity instead of fear." Booklist

The ghosts of Mercy Manor. Scholastic 1993
172p pa $3.99 hardcover o.p. (4 and up)
Fic
1. Ghost stories 2. Orphans—Fiction 3. Mystery fiction
ISBN 0-590-43602-3 (pa) LC 92-21557
Twelve-year-old Gwen, an orphan who comes to live
with the Mercy family, discovers that the house is haunted by the ghost of a sad-looking young girl and is determined to solve the mystery behind her appearances
"Superbly written and suspenseful throughout." Voice
Youth Advocates

Nothing but trouble; drawings by Jacqueline
Rogers. Holiday House 1995 119p il $15.95 (4
and up) **Fic**
1. Aunts—Fiction 2. Dogs—Fiction 3. Mystery fiction
ISBN 0-8234-1175-3 LC 94-34285
Also available in paperback from Scholastic
"When Vannie Kirkland is dropped off with an aged
aunt she's never met while her parents search for work
in California, things don't look great. For one, aunt Bert
thinks Vannie's diminutive dog, Muffy, is a noisy, destructive little bundle. But Aunt Bert's less prickly side
is revealed when mysterious prowlers start vandalizing
her farm." Booklist
"The plot is cleanly structured and should hold readers' interest. . . . Overall, a satisfying story for a wide
range of mystery fans." SLJ

Princess for a week; illustrated by Jacqueline
Rogers. Holiday House 2006 105p il $16.95 (2-4)
Fic
1. Ghost stories 2. Mystery fiction
ISBN 0-8234-1945-2 LC 2005-50288
When a confident girl named Princess arrives to spend
a week at Roddy's house, she encourages him to help
her investigate the suspicious activities happening at a
supposedly haunted house.
"The story moves quickly and is excellently paced.
. . . The full-page illustrations add realism and depth to
the story." SLJ

Wyatt, Leslie J.
Poor is just a starting place; by Leslie J. Wyatt.
1st ed. Holiday House 2005 196p $16.95 (5 and
up) **Fic**
1. Great Depression, 1929-1939—Fiction 2. Poverty—
Fiction 3. Kentucky—Fiction
ISBN 0-8234-1884-7 LC 2004-47451
During the Great Depression, twelve-year-old Artie
Wilson, determined to escape plowing and planting the
fields and milking the cow on her family's farm, longs
to leave Buck Creek, Kentucky, and her life of poverty.
"Written with spare beauty, this first novel tells a
moving story." Booklist

Wyss, Johann David
The Swiss family Robinson (5 and up)
Fic
1. Survival after airplane accidents, shipwrecks, etc.—
Fiction
Some editions are:
Grosset & Dunlap (Illustrated junior library) $16.99 Illus-
trated by Lynd Kendall Ward (ISBN 0-448-06022-1)
Knopf (Everyman's library children's classics) $14.95 Il-
lustrated by Louis Rhead (ISBN 0-679-43640-5)
Originally published 1812-1813 in Switzerland
"A Swiss family—a pastor, his wife, and four boys—
are shipwrecked on an uninhabited island. They gradually
establish an attractive way of life for themselves, and
their many adventures are used by their father to form
the basis of lessons in natural history and the physical
sciences." Oxford Companion to Child Lit

Wyss, Thelma Hatch

Bear dancer; the story of a Ute girl. Margaret K. McElderry Books 2005 181p il $15.95 (5 and up) **Fic**

1. Ute Indians—Fiction

ISBN 1-4169-0285-0 LC 2005-40620

In late ninetenth-century Colorado, Elk Girl, sister of Ute chief Ouray, is captured by Cheyenne and Arapaho warriors, rescued by the white "enemy," and finally returned to her home. Includes historical notes.

"This fascinating story is based on a real person. . . . An excellent addition to historical-fiction collections." SLJ

Yee, Lisa

Millicent Min, girl genius. Arthur A. Levine Books 2003 248p $16.95; pa $4.99 (5 and up) **Fic**

1. Gifted children—Fiction 2. School stories 3. Chinese Americans—Fiction

ISBN 0-439-42519-0; 0-439-42520-4 (pa)

LC 2003-3747

"At the tender age of eleven, Millicent Min has completed her junior year of high school. Summer school is Millie's idea of fun, so she is excited that her parents are allowing her to take a college poetry course. . . . The tension between Millie's formal, overly intellectual way of expressing herself and her emotional immaturity makes her a very funny narrator. . . . Readers considerably older than Millicent's eleven years will enjoy this strong debut novel." Voice Youth Advocates

Another title about Millicent Min and her friends is: Stanford Wong flunks big-time (2005)

Yep, Laurence

The amah. Putnam 1999 181p $15.99; pa $5.99 (5 and up) **Fic**

1. Family life—Fiction 2. Chinese Americans—Fiction

ISBN 0-399-23040-8; 0-698-11878-2 (pa)

LC 98-49046

"When her mother becomes the amah (Chinese governess) for a wealthy white girl, twelve-year-old Amy must skip her ballet classes—in which she is preparing for the role of Cinderella's mean stepsister—to baby-sit her siblings." Horn Book Guide

"An enjoyable book about friendship, family, and traditions." Voice Youth Advocates

Angelfish. Putnam 2001 216p $16.99 (5 and up) **Fic**

1. Chinese Americans—Fiction 2. Racially mixed people—Fiction 3. Ballet—Fiction

ISBN 0-399-23041-6 LC 00-62676

Robin, a young ballet dancer who is half Chinese and half white, works in a fish store for Mr. Tsow, a brusque Chinese who accuses her of being a half-person and who harbors a bitter secret

"An entertaining read with an engaging and resourceful protagonist." SLJ

Child of the owl. Harper & Row 1977 217p pa $6.99 hardcover o.p. (5 and up) **Fic**

1. Chinese Americans—Fiction 2. Grandmothers—Fiction 3. San Francisco (Calif.)—Fiction

ISBN 0-06-440336-X (pa); 0-06-026743-7 (hc)

LC 76-24314

"Casey, a 12-year-old Chinese American girl, is more American than Chinese. When her father, a compulsive gambler, is hospitalized after a severe beating, Casey moves in with her grandmother in San Francisco's Chinatown. Although she is a street-smart child, Casey finds that she is an outsider in this community. Her grandmother teaches her something of her heritage and what it means to be 'a child of the owl.'" Shapiro. Fic for Youth. 3d edition

Dragon's gate. HarperCollins Pubs. 1993 273p $16.99; pa $6.99 (6 and up) **Fic**

1. Chinese—United States—Fiction 2. Railroads—Fiction

ISBN 0-06-022971-3; 0-06-440489-7 (pa)

LC 92-43649

A Newbery Medal honor book, 1994

Sequel to The serpent's children (1984) and Mountain light (1985)

When he accidentally kills a Manchu, a fifteen-year-old Chinese boy is sent to America to join his father, an uncle, and other Chinese working to build a tunnel for the transcontinental railroad through the Sierra Nevada mountains in 1867

"Yep has succeeded in realizing the primary characters and the irrepressibly dramatic story. . . . The carefully researched details will move students to thought and discussion." Bull Cent Child Books

Dragonwings. Harper & Row 1975 248p lib bdg $16.89; pa $6.99 (5 and up) **Fic**

1. Chinese Americans—Fiction 2. San Francisco (Calif.)—Fiction

ISBN 0-06-026738-0 (lib bdg); 0-06-440085-9 (pa)

"In 1903 Moon Shadow, eight years old, leaves China for the 'Land of the Golden Mountains,' San Francisco, to be with his father, Windrider, a father he has never seen. There, beset by the trials experienced by most foreigners in America, Moonrider shares his father's dream—to fly. This dream enables Windrider to endure the mockery of the other Chinese, the poverty he suffers in this hostile place—the land of the white demons—and his loneliness for his wife and his own country." Shapiro. Fic for Youth. 3d edition

Hiroshima; a novella. Scholastic 1995 56p pa $4.99 (4 and up) **Fic**

1. Hiroshima (Japan)—Bombardment, 1945—Fiction

ISBN 0-590-20833-0 (pa); 0-590-20832-2 (hc)

LC 94-18195

"This moving and detailed narrative chronicles the dropping of the atomic bomb on Hiroshima and its effects on its citizens, especially on twelve-year-old Sachi. Based on true accounts, this book describes the horrors and sadness as well as the courage and hope that result from war." Soc Educ

Yep, Laurence—*Continued*

The journal of Wong Ming-Chung; a Chinese miner. Scholastic 2000 219p il (My name is America) $10.95 (4 and up)   **Fic**

1. California—Gold discoveries—Fiction 2. Chinese—United States—Fiction

ISBN 0-590-38607-7   LC 99-28405

A young Chinese boy nicknamed Runt records his experiences in a journal as he travels from southern China to California in 1852 to join his uncle during the Gold Rush

"The engrossing story involves readers from start to finish. . . . An engaging book with strong characters that successfully weaves fact with fiction." SLJ

The magic paintbrush; drawings by Suling Wang. HarperCollins Pubs. 2000 89p il $13.95; lib bdg $13.89 (3-5)   **Fic**

1. Chinese Americans—Fiction 2. Magic—Fiction

ISBN 0-06-028199-5; 0-06-028200-2 (lib bdg)

LC 99-34959

A magic paintbrush transports Steve and his elderly caretakers from their drab apartment in Chinatown to a world of adventures

"Yep's crisp style keeps the pages turning, and he leavens his story with snappy dialogue, realistic characters and plenty of wise humor." Publ Wkly

Skunk scout. Hyperion Bks. for Children 2003 177p $15.99 (4-6)   **Fic**

1. Camping—Fiction 2. Brothers—Fiction 3. Uncles—Fiction 4. Chinese Americans—Fiction

ISBN 0-7868-0670-2   LC 2002-68909

Companion volume to Later, gator (1995) and Cockroach cooties (2000)

Teddy is not thrilled with the present his uncle gives him for his tenth birthday—a camping trip for him and his younger brother—but on his first outing away from San Francisco's Chinatown, Teddy learns some interesting facts about nature, about his uncle, and about himself

"Teddy is a lively, funny narrator. In between the laughs, he gains personal insight into himself and his family." Booklist

Thief of hearts. HarperCollins Pubs. 1995 197p pa $6.99 hardcover o.p. (5 and up)   **Fic**

1. Chinese Americans—Fiction 2. Friendship—Fiction 3. San Francisco (Calif.)—Fiction 4. Racially mixed people—Fiction

ISBN 0-06-440591-5 (pa)   LC 94-18703

"Stacy is not pleased that she's been elected by her parents to show a new girl from China around school, particularly when it turns out that Hong Ch'un is snotty and difficult, even calling Stacy *t'ung chung*, 'mixed seed.' Stacy's mother (whose story was told in *Child of the Owl* . . . is of Chinese descent, and her father Caucasian, and when Hong Ch'un is accused by the other kids of stealing, Stacy feels torn between parental instruction, ethnic loyalty, and peer acceptance." Bull Cent Child Books

"Told with candor and controlled emotion, this first-person narrative presents a difficult topic in a manner accessible to a wide audience." Horn Book

The traitor; Golden Mountain chronicles, 1885. HarperCollins Pubs. 2003 310p $16.99; lib bdg $17.89 (5 and up)   **Fic**

1. Prejudices—Fiction 2. Friendship—Fiction 3. Chinese Americans—Fiction

ISBN 0-06-027522-7; 0-06-027523-5 (lib bdg)

LC 2002-22534

Sequel to Dragon's gate

In 1885, a lonely illegitimate American boy and a lonely Chinese American boy develop an unlikely friendship in the midst of prejudices and racial tension in their coal mining town of Rock Springs, Wyoming

"The short chapters read quickly, and readers will become involved through the first-person voices that capture each boy's feelings of being an outsider and a traitor." Booklist

When the circus came to town; drawings by Suling Wang. HarperCollins Pubs. 2002 113p il $14.95; lib bdg $14.89 (3-5)   **Fic**

1. Frontier and pioneer life—Fiction 2. Chinese New Year—Fiction 3. Circus—Fiction 4. Chinese Americans—Fiction

ISBN 0-06-029325-X; 0-06-029326-8 (lib bdg)

LC 2001-39290

An Asian cook and a Chinese New Year celebration help ten-year-old Ursula at a Montana stage coach station to regain her confidence after smallpox scars her face

"Yep has based his novel on a true story, and his writing is, by turns, direct, humorous, and poignant." Booklist

Ylvisaker, Anne

Dear Papa. Candlewick Press 2002 184p $15.99 (4 and up)   **Fic**

1. Fathers—Fiction 2. Death—Fiction 3. Family life—Fiction 4. Minnesota—Fiction

ISBN 0-7636-1618-4   LC 2001-37608

In September of 1943, one year after her father's death, nine-year-old Isabelle begins writing him letters, which are interspersed with letters to other members of her family, relating important events in her life and how she feels about them

"The letters are personal and immediate, and the story is full of daily details that evoke the historical period." Booklist

Yolen, Jane

The dragon's boy. Harper & Row 1990 120p $14.95 (5 and up)   **Fic**

1. Arthur, King—Fiction 2. Merlin (Legendary character)—Fiction

ISBN 0-06-026789-5   LC 89-24642

"This is a retelling of the education and coming of age of 13-year-old Artos (Arthur). Old Linn (Merlin) is to be his teacher, but, doubting he can command the boy's attention, he constructs a fire-breathing dragon as a façade." SLJ

"Scattered throughout the book are broad hints of Artos's identity, but even children unfamiliar with the legendary King Arthur should find the crisply told story accessible and entertaining." Horn Book

Yolen, Jane—*Continued*

Odysseus in the serpent maze; by Jane Yolen &
Robert J. Harris. HarperCollins Pubs. 2001 248p
(Young heroes) $14.95; lib bdg $14.89 (4 and up)
Fic

1. Odysseus (Greek mythology)—Fiction
2. Adventure fiction 3. Classical mythology—Fiction
ISBN 0-06-028734-9; 0-06-028735-7 (lib bdg)
LC 00-33584

Thirteen-year-old Odysseus, who longs to be a hero,
has many opportunities to prove himself during an adventure which involves pirates and satyrs, a trip to
Crete's Labyrinth, and the two young girls, Penelope and
Helen, who play a major role in his future life

This offers "cliffhanger chapter endings, snappy humor, and breakneck adventure. . . . The characters are
richly drawn. . . . Well-integrated historical detail and
an authors' note enhance this page-turner." Booklist

Other titles in the Young heroes series are:
Atalanta and the Arcadian beast (2003)
Hippolyta and the curse of the Amazons (2002)
Jason and the Gorgan's blood (2004)

Young, Ed

Pinocchio; adaptation from C. Collodi's [by] Ed
Young. Philomel Bks. 1995 44p il $18.95 (3-6)
Fic

1. Puppets and puppet plays—Fiction 2. Fairy tales
ISBN 0-399-22941-8 LC 95-10127

"Adapted from the original version of The adventures
of Pinocchio, translated by M. A. Murray and published
in the United Kingdom in 1892." Verso of title page

"Ed Young presents an illustrated edition of this famous Italian fantasy. Although his version of the story is
considerably shorter than Collodi's text, it retains a sense
of the adventure, humor, and pathos that made the original *Pinocchio* a classic. In the full-color, collage
artwork, Young builds scenes from deftly cut and composed materials that include cloth as well as textured,
painted, and printed papers highlighted with pastels."
Booklist

Zalben, Jane Breskin

Unfinished dreams; a novel. Simon & Schuster
Bks. for Young Readers 1996 160p $16 (5 and up)
Fic

1. Jews—Fiction 2. AIDS (Disease)—Fiction
3. School stories 4. Violinists—Fiction
ISBN 0-689-80033-9 LC 95-44424

In this "story about Jason, a twelve-year-old Jewish
fledgling violinist who must suffer the slings of the class
bully, AIDS becomes the background thread as a beloved
principal enters the final stages of the disease. The naturalness of the dialogue, the richness of emotion, and the
views expressed about valuing individual strengths, talents, and differences make this book a recommended
read." Horn Book Guide

Zemser, Amy Bronwen

Beyond the mango tree. Greenwillow Bks. 1998
166p $15; pa $4.95 (5 and up) **Fic**

1. Diabetes—Fiction 2. Liberia—Fiction
ISBN 0-688-16005-0; 0-06-440786-1 (pa)
LC 97-32268

While living in Liberia with her possessive, diabetic
mother and often-absent father, twelve-year-old Sarina
longs for a friend with whom to experience the world
beyond her yard

"Zemser's poetic, wrenching narrative transports readers to a foreign land, but the truths they uncover will
surely hit home." Publ Wkly

Zimmer, Tracie Vaughn

Sketches from a spy tree; poems by Tracie
Vaughn Zimmer; illustrated by Andrew Glass.
Clarion Books 2005 63p il $16 (3-6) **Fic**

1. Twins—Fiction 2. Sisters—Fiction 3. Divorce—Fiction 4. Stepfamilies—Fiction
ISBN 0-618-23479-9 LC 2003-27768

In a series of poems, narrator Anne Marie paints pictures of family life from grief to hope after her father
abandons his "four girls" Anne Marie and her mother
and twin and baby sister.

"The writing is lyrical yet fresh. . . . Glass's remarkable watercolors, sketches, photographs, and collages
bring Anne Marie's experiences to life." SLJ

Zinnen, Linda

The dragons of Spratt, Ohio; by Linda Zinnen.
1st ed. HarperCollins Publishers 2004 233p
$15.99; lib bdg $16.89 (5 and up) **Fic**

1. Dragons—Fiction 2. Ohio—Fiction
ISBN 0-06-000021-X; 0-06-000022-8 (lib bdg)
LC 2003-19610

Seventh-grader John Salt, a budding animal behavior-
ist, and his best friend's sister become unlikely allies in
an attempt to protect a pack of dragons from an unscrupulous cosmetics researcher.

"This is an exciting fantasy with a subtle message
about self-acceptance and individuality." SLJ

S C STORY COLLECTIONS

Books in this class include collections of short stories by one
author and collections by more than one author. Folk tales are
entered in class 398.2. Collections of general literature, American
literature, English literature, etc.--which may include but are not
limited to short stories--are entered in classes 808.8, 810.8, 820.8,
etc.

Aiken, Joan

Shadows and moonshine; stories; illustrations by
Pamela Johnson. Godine 2001 171p il $18.95 (4
and up) **S C**

1. Fantasy fiction 2. Short stories
ISBN 1-56792-167-1 LC 2001-23830

This is a collection 13 stories about such things as
witches, enchanted pigs, mermaids, and dragons, selected
from the author's earlier anthologies

"Whether scary, satiric, or poetic, Aiken's tales have
strong settings, memorable characters, insight, and humor." SLJ

Alexander, Lloyd

The foundling and other tales of Prydain. rev & expanded ed. Holt & Co. 1999 98p $19.95 (5 and up) **S C**

1. Fantasy fiction 2. Short stories
ISBN 0-8050-6130-4   LC 98-42807
Also available in paperback from Penguin

First published 1973; this revised and expanded edition includes two additional stories Coll and his white pig and The truthful harp, first published separately 1965 and 1967 respectively

Eight short stories dealing with events that preceded the birth of Taran, the Assistant Pig-Keeper and key figure in the author's five works on the Kingdom of Prydain which began with The book of three

"The stories are written with vivid grace and humor." Chicago. Children's Book Center [review of 1973 edition]

Andersen, Hans Christian

Fairy tales of Hans Christian Andersen; [translated by Neil Philip; illustrated by Isabelle Brent] Reader's Digest 2005 352p il $27.95 (3-6) **S C**

1. Fairy tales
ISBN 0-276-42830-7

"By ably retranslating 40 of Andersen's best-known tales, [Neil] Philip succeeds in restoring the original conversational intimacy between the storyteller and listeners. . . . [Philip offers] a substantive and informative introduction. Brent's elegant watercolors make frequent use of gold leaf as emphasis and borders for both the illustrations and each page of text. Families will find much to cherish in this beautifully designed presentation." SLJ

Hans Christian Andersen's Fairy Tales; selected and illustrated by Lisbeth Zwerger; translated by Anthea Bell. Minedition 2006 c1991 104p il $19.99 (4 and up) **S C**

1. Fairy tales 2. Short stories
ISBN 0-698-40035-6

A reissue of the edition first published 1991

"This collection of . . . tales includes relatively unknown stories, such as 'The Rose Tree Regiment,' along with such familiar favorites as 'The Princess & the Pea.' Bell's finesse in writing is well matched by Zwerger's delicate, understated approach in the illustrations, which are introspective rather than dramatic. Sophisticated in design, the book features fluid watercolors and wide-bordered text on tall, white pages." Booklist

The swan's stories; selected and translated by Brian Alderson; illustrated by Chris Riddell. Candlewick Press 1997 143p il $22.99 **S C**

1. Fairy tales 2. Short stories
ISBN 1-56402-894-1   LC 96-47197
A collection of Andersen's stories, including "The Steadfast Tin Soldier," "The Fir Tree," and "The Money Pig"

These are "excellent translations that flow smoothly with a casual and comfortable feel. The illustrations are superb." Horn Book Guide

Tales of Hans Christian Andersen; translated and introduced by Naomi Lewis; illustrated by Joel Stewart. 1st U.S. ed. Candlewick Press 2004 207p il $22.99 (4 and up) **S C**

1. Fairy tales
ISBN 0-7636-2515-9   LC 2004-45171
Contents: The princess and the pea; The tinderbox; Thumbelina; The emperor's new clothes; The little mermaid; The steadfast tin soldier; Wild swans; The flying trunk; The ugly duckling; The nightingale; The snow queen; The little match girl; The goblin at the grocer's

A collection of 13 of Andersen's fairy tales

This is a "lavishly illustrated volume. In new introductions to each story, Lewis provides background and context, connecting the tale to Andersen's life and offering her own interpretation of its theme. Stewart's digitally created drawings shed fresh light on the stories as well." SLJ

Avi

Strange happenings; five tales of transformation. Harcourt 2006 147p $15 (5 and up) **S C**

1. Supernatural—Fiction 2. Short stories
ISBN 0-15-205790-0   LC 2004-29579
"In this short story collection, Avi offers five fantastical tales, set in both contemporary and fairy-tale lands, that explore the notion of transformation. . . . The pieces are vividly imagined and shot through with a captivating, edgy spookiness, which, along with their brevity and some droll, crackling dialogue, makes them great choices for sharing aloud in class or as inspiration in creative-writing units." Booklist

What do fish have to do with anything? and other stories; illustrated by Tracy Mitchell. Candlewick Press 1997 202p il pa $5.99 hardcover o.p. (4 and up) **S C**

1. Short stories
ISBN 0-7636-0412-7 (pa)   LC 97-1354
"Willie believes a homeless man possesses a cure for unhappiness. A minister dares his devilish son to be good. Pet-obsessed Eve receives visitations from two deceased cats. . . . These are among seven . . . stories dealing with communication in troubled relationships." Publisher's note

"While Avi's endings are not tidy, they are effective: each story brings its protagonist beyond childhood self-absorption to the realization that one is an integral part of a bigger picture." Horn Book

Babbitt, Natalie

The Devil's other storybook; stories and pictures by Natalie Babbitt. Farrar, Straus & Giroux 1987 81p il pa $4.95 hardcover o.p. (4-6) **S C**

1. Devil—Fiction 2. Short stories
ISBN 0-374-41704-0 (pa)   LC 86-32760
"Michael di Capua books"

Featuring the same creature as in The Devil's storybook, this companion volume contains 10 additional tales

Babbitt, Natalie—*Continued*

The Devil's storybook; stories and pictures by Natalie Babbitt. Farrar, Straus & Giroux 1974 101p il pa $3.95 hardcover o.p. (4-6)

S C

1. Devil—Fiction 2. Short stories
ISBN 0-374-41708-3 (pa)

Ten "stories about the machinations of the Devil to increase the population of his realm. He is not always successful and, despite his clever ruses, meets frustration as often as his intended victims do." Horn Book

"Twists of plot within traditional themes and a briskly witty style distinguish this book, illustrated amusingly with black-and-white line drawings." Booklist

Byars, Betsy Cromer

My dog, my hero; [by] Betsy Byars, Betsy Duffey, Laurie Myers; illustrated by Loren Long. Holt & Co. 2000 47p il $16 (3-6)   S C

1. Dogs—Fiction 2. Short stories
ISBN 0-8050-6327-7   LC 99-44496

In this collection of eight short stories, a panel of three judges has to decide which dog out of eight finalists deserves to win the title of My Hero

"Drama, humor, excitement, and love fuel these short, well-written stories." Booklist

Conrad, Pam

Our house; by Pam Conrad; pictures by Brian Selznick. 10th anniversary ed. Scholastic Press 2005 c1995 130p il $16.99 (4 and up)

S C

1. Short stories 2. Levittown (N.Y.)—Fiction
ISBN 0-439-74508-X   LC 2004065082

A reissue of the title first published 1995. Includes a new artist's note by Brian Selznick

Six stories, one from each decade from the 1940s to the 1990s, about children growing up in Levittown, New York

"Vivid descriptions and poignant observations leave indelible impressions. . . . Conrad's fresh, imaginative approach to the concept of 'home' makes this an ideal starting point for discussion, creative writing, and other class activities." Booklist

Delacre, Lulu

Salsa stories; stories and linocuts by Lulu Delacre. Scholastic Press 2000 105p il $15.95; pa $4.50 (4-6)   S C

1. Latin America—Fiction 2. Family life—Fiction 3. Short stories
ISBN 0-590-63118-7; 0-590-63121-7 (pa)

LC 99-25534

A collection of stories within the story of a family celebration where the guests relate their memories of growing up in various Latin American countries. Also contains recipes

"Kids will respond to both the warmth and the anxiety of the family life described in the vivid writing, and in Delacre's nicely composed linocuts." Booklist

Fire and wings: dragon tales from East and West; edited by Marianne Carus; illustrated by Nilesh Mistry; with an introduction by Jane Yolen. Cricket Bks. 2002 146p il $17.95 (4 and up)

S C

1. Dragons—Fiction 2. Short stories
ISBN 0-8126-2664-8   LC 2002-5792

A collection of stories about all kinds of dragons, by such authors as Jane Yolen, Patricia MacLachlan, Eric A. Kimmel, Vida Chu, and E. Nesbit

"The writing is smooth and the black-and-white illustrations are skillfully done, with especially graceful line work." SLJ

Fleischman, Paul

Graven images; three stories; by Paul Fleischman; illustrations by Bagram Ibatoulline. Candlewick Press 2006 116p il $16.99; pa $5.99 (5 and up)   S C

1. Supernatural—Fiction 2. Short stories
ISBN 0763627755; 0763629847 (pa)

LC 2005054283

A Newbery Medal honor book, 1983

A newly illustrated edition with a new afterword of the title first published 1982 by Harper & Row

A collection of three stories about a child who reads the lips of those who whisper secrets into a statue's ear; a daydreaming shoemaker's apprentice who must find ways to make the girl he loves notice him; and a stone carver who creates a statue of a ghost.

"Readers will be delighted with the return to print of [this title] with haunting new acrylic gouache illustrations . . . evoking the spinetingling aspects of this trio of tales. . . . Via a new afterword, the author explains the stories' inspiration and describes this book's significance early in his career." Publ Wkly

Friends; stories about new friends, old friends, and unexpectedly true friends; edited by Ann M. Martin and David Levithan. Scholastic Press 2005 185p $16.95 (5 and up)   S C

1. Friendship—Fiction 2. Short stories
ISBN 0-439-72991-2   LC 2004-27758

Contents: The friend who changed my life by Pam Muñoz Ryan; My best friend by Jennifer L. Holm; Connie Hunter Williams, psychic teacher by Meg Cabot; Squirrel by Ann M. Martin; Smoking lessons by Patricia McCormick; Shashikala: a brief history of love and khadi by Tanuja Desai Hidier; The Wild Prince by Brian Selznick; Flit by Patrick Jennings; The Justice League by David Levithan; Minka and Meanie by Rachel Cohn; Doll by Virginia Euwer Wolff

"This collection of stories by well-known authors spans a broad definition of the term 'friend,' and also approaches the topic from a wide variety of viewpoints. . . . The selections by Ann M. Martin, Pam Muñoz Ryan, Rachel Cohn, David Levithan, and Patricia McCormick are among the more outstanding entries. . . . It is also likely that every reader will find at least one that hits home." SLJ

A **Glory** of unicorns; compiled by Bruce Coville; illustrated by Alix Berenzy. Scholastic 1998 198p il pa $4.99 (5 and up)   S C

1. Unicorns—Fiction 2. Short stories
ISBN 0-439-06628-X (pa)   LC 97-13689

A Glory of unicorns—*Continued*

Eleven stories and one poem, by such authors as Nancy Varian Berberick, Gregory Maguire, and Margaret Bechard, about unicorns in both mythical and contemporary settings

"Exciting and thought-provoking. Even readers who shy away from the science fiction/fantasy genres will enjoy these short tales and their special messages." Voice Youth Advocates

Horse tales; collected by June Crebbin; illustrated by Inga Moore. 1st U.S. ed. Candlewick Press 2005 il $18.99 (4 and up) **S C**
1. Horses—Fiction 2. Short stories
ISBN 0-7636-2657-0   LC 2004-51897

Contents: Orange pony by Wendy Douthwaite; Snow pony by Alison Lester; Bucephalus: a king's horse by Alice Gall & Fleming Crew; Mud pony retold by Caron Lee Cohen; Gift horse by June Crebbin; Christmas pony by Lincoln Steffens; War horse by Michael Morpurgo; Black Beauty by Anna Sewell; I rode a horse of milk white jade by Diane Lee Wilson; Misty of Chincoteague by Marguerite Henry; Pony in the dark by K.M. Peyton; Unicorn by Peter Dickinson; Chestnut gray retold by Helen Cooper; The gray palfrey retold by Barbara Leonie Pickard

In these "short stories, the remarkable nature of the horse is revealed. . . . The offerings excerpted from novels work well as short stories here and may inspire readers to look for the full-length books. . . . This is an excellently conceived and executed collection with wonderful art." SLJ

Hughes, Ted

How the Whale became and other stories; illustrated by Jackie Morris. Orchard Bks. 2000 94p il $25 (4-6) **S C**
1. Creation—Fiction 2. Animals—Fiction 3. Short stories
ISBN 0-531-30303-9   LC 99-85992

A newly illustrated edition of the title first published 1963 in the United Kingdom; first United States edition 1964 by Atheneum

A collection of creation stories explaining why owls hunt at night, why the dog was chosen to guard farm animals, why polar bears live at the North Pole, and how the elephant came to accept its unique and wonderful qualities

"Hughes' prose, both comical and elegantly spare, finds a worthy match in Morris' lavish, detailed watercolors." Booklist

Jiménez, Francisco

The circuit: stories from the life of a migrant child. University of N.M. Press 1997 134p pa $10.95 (5 and up) **S C**
1. Mexican Americans—Fiction 2. Migrant labor—Fiction 3. Short stories
ISBN 0-8263-1797-9   LC 97-4844

Also available in hardcover from Houghton Mifflin

A collection of twelve short stories about Mexican American migrant farmworkers

"Each of these short stories builds quietly to a surprise that reveals the truth, and together the stories lead to the tearing climax." Booklist

Jones, Diana Wynne

Mixed magics. Greenwillow Bks. 2001 138p $15.95; lib bdg $15.89 (5 and up) **S C**
1. Fantasy fiction 2. Short stories
ISBN 0-06-029705-0; 0-06-029706-9 (lib bdg)
LC 00-62277

Four separate incidents test the power of the Chrestomanci, a powerful enchanter with nine lives, to control misuses of magic on various worlds

"Three of the stories have already appeared in U.S. editions. . . . 'Stealer of Souls' is a good, strong story, notable for its creepiness as well as a bit of humor." Booklist

Kimmel, Eric A.

The jar of fools: eight Hanukkah stories from Chelm; illustrated by Mordicai Gerstein. Holiday House 2000 56p il $18.95 (4 and up)
S C
1. Hanukkah—Fiction 2. Short stories 3. Jews—Fiction
ISBN 0-8234-1463-9   LC 99-57823

Drawing on traditional Jewish folklore, these Hanukkah stories relate the antics of the people of Chelm, thought—perhaps incorrectly—to be a town of fools

"Kimmel gets the shtetl setting, the humanity, and the farce. . . . Gerstein's detailed ink-on-oil paint artwork, one full-page picture per story, captures the intricate silliness and slapstick." Booklist

Sword of the samurai; adventure stories from Japan. Harcourt Brace & Co. 1999 114p (4 and up) **S C**
1. Japan—Fiction 2. Adventure fiction 3. Short stories
ISBN 0-15-201985-5   LC 98-16633

Available in paperback from HarperCollins $4.99 (0-06-442131-7)

"Browndeer Press"

Eleven short stories about samurai warriors, their way of life, courage, wit, and foolishness

"These selections offer something for everyone: humor, wisdom and adventure along with a gentle and graceful introduction to the code of ethics that continues to shape Japan today." Publ Wkly

Kipling, Rudyard

A collection of Rudyard Kipling's Just so stories. 1st ed. Candlewick Press 2004 127p il $22.99 (3-6) **S C**
1. Animals—Fiction 2. India—Fiction 3. Short stories
ISBN 0-7636-2629-5   LC 2004-45858

Contents: How the whale got his throat illustrated by Peter Sis; How the camel got his hump illustrated by Clare Melinsky; How the rhinoceros got his skin illustrated by Christopher Corr; How the leopard got his spots illustrated by Cathie Felstead; The elephant's child illustrated by Louise Voce; The sing-song of Old Man Kangaroo illustrated by Jeff Fisher; The beginning of the armadillos illustrated by Jane Ray; The cat that walked by himself illustrated by Satoshi Kitamura

"This colorful collection of eight tales distinguishes itself with its range of artwork. Well-known children's book artists, including Peter Sis, Jane Ray, and Satoshi

Kipling, Rudyard—*Continued*

Kitamura, contributed the art, each one illustrating a different story. The vibrant mix of styles and materials adds new dimension to favorite stories. . . . A lively, accessible edition." Booklist

The jungle book: Mowgli's story; [illustrated by] Nicola Bayley. Candlewick Press 2005 151p il $19.99 (3-6)   **S C**

1. Animals—Fiction 2. India—Fiction 3. Short stories
ISBN 0-7636-2317-2

"Three stories–'Mowgli's Brothers,' 'Kaa's Hunting,' and 'Tiger! Tiger!'–and six of the poetic songs from Kipling's classic work are accompanied by painterly illustrations. . . . A combination of detailed miniature drawings and small framed paintings is strategically placed throughout the text. . . . The masterful use of light, detail, rich color, and texture creates striking and evocative visual effects." SLJ

The jungle book: the Mowgli stories; illustrated by Jerry Pinkney; afterword by Peter Glassman. Morrow 1995 258p il $22.95 (4 and up)
     S C

1. Animals—Fiction 2. India—Fiction 3. Short stories
ISBN 0-688-09979-3   LC 92-1415

Selected stories from Kipling's two "Jungle Books" chronicle the adventures of Mowgli, the boy reared by a pack of wolves in an Indian jungle. Also includes "Rikki-Tikki-Tavi"

The handsome illustrations in dappled watercolors show to admiration the lush jungle growth, the watchful animals, and Mowgli himself. A glorious pairing of text and illustration." Horn Book

Just so stories; illustrated by Barry Moser; afterword by Peter Glassman. Morrow 1996 148p il $24.99 (3-6)   **S C**

1. Animals—Fiction 2. India—Fiction 3. Short stories
ISBN 0-688-13957-4 (Morrow)   LC 95-13714
First published 1902

A set of tales that "give far-fetched humorous explanations of the chief physical characteristics of certain animals." Oxford Companion to Child Lit

Konigsburg, E. L.

Altogether, one at a time; illustrated by Gail E. Haley [et al.] Atheneum Pubs. 1971 79p il pa $4.99 hardcover o.p. (4-6)   **S C**

1. Short stories
ISBN 0-689-71290-1 (pa)

"Compelled to invite a child he doesn't want to his birthday party in 'Inviting Jason,' Stanley likes the boy even less afterwards, but for a different reason. A 10-year-old boy learns something about old age in 'The Night of the Leonids' when he realizes his grandmother has lost her chance to see a shower of stars that occurs only once every 33⅓ years. The spirit of a long dead camp counselor helps an obese girl make up her mind that she will never have to attend Camp Fat again. In 'Momma at the Pearly Gates,' Momma tells the story of how, as a girl, she was called a 'dirty nigger' by a white classmate." Libr J

Marcantonio, Patricia Santos

Red ridin' in the hood; and other cuentos; pictures by Renato Alarcão. Farrar, Straus & Giroux 2005 181p il $16 (3-5)   **S C**

1. Fairy tales 2. Hispanic Americans—Fiction 3. Short stories
ISBN 0-374-36241-6

"The fractured fairy tale gets cool Latino flavor in this lively collection of 11 fresh retellings, with witty reversals of class and gender roles and powerful, full-page pictures that set the drama in venues ranging from the desert and the barrio to a skyscraper." Booklist

Marshall, James

Rats on the range and other stories. Dial Bks. for Young Readers 1993 80p $13.99; pa $3.99 (2-4)   **S C**

1. Animals—Fiction 2. Short stories
ISBN 0-8037-1384-3; 0-14-038645-9 (pa)
     LC 92-28918

In eight animal stories the reader meets a rat family that vacations at a dude ranch, a pig who takes lessons in table manners, a mouse who keeps house for a tomcat, and a buzzard who leaves his money to the Society for Stray Cats—or does he?

"In this collection, which brilliantly demonstrates Marshall's gift for humor, there are eight gems." Horn Book Guide

Rats on the roof, and other stories. Dial Bks. for Young Readers 1991 79p il lib bdg $12.89; pa $4.99 (2-4)   **S C**

1. Animals—Fiction 2. Short stories
ISBN 0-8037-0835-1 (lib bdg); 0-14-038646-7 (pa)
     LC 90-44084

An illustrated collection of seven stories about various animals, including a frog with magnificent legs, a hungry brontosaurus, and a mouse who gets married

"Marshall's fertile imagination gets lots of exercise here as does his sardonic wit, and he's included plenty of expressive illustrations, all done in his signature style." Booklist

McKissack, Patricia C.

The dark-thirty; Southern tales of the supernatural; illustrated by Brian Pinkney. Knopf 1992 122p il $18.95; lib bdg $20.99; pa $6.50 (4 and up)   **S C**

1. Ghost stories 2. African Americans—Fiction 3. Short stories
ISBN 0-679-81863-4; 0-679-91853-9 (lib bdg); 0-679-89006-8 (pa)   LC 92-3021
Also available in paperback from Dell

A Newbery Medal honor book, 1993; Coretta Scott King Award for text, 1993

A collection of ghost stories with African American themes, designed to be told during the Dark Thirty—the half hour before sunset—when ghosts seem all too believable

"Strong characterizations are superbly drawn in a few words. The atmosphere of each selection is skillfully developed and sustained to the very end. Pinkney's stark scratchboard illustrations evoke an eerie mood, which heightens the suspense of each tale." SLJ

Medearis, Angela Shelf

Haunts; five hair-raising tales; drawings by Trina Schart Hyman. Holiday House 1996 37p il $15.95 (4 and up)   S C

1. Ghost stories 2. Short stories

ISBN 0-8234-1280-6   LC 96-17336

This includes "five short stories about creepy, crawly horrors, spooky ghosts, and things that go bump in the night." Publisher's note

These stories are "accessibly short, gleefully scary, and blessed with terrifically horrific cover and interior art by Trina Schart Hyman." Bull Cent Child Books

Naidoo, Beverley

Out of bounds: seven stories of conflict and hope. HarperCollins Pubs. 2003 c2001 175p $16.99; lib bdg $17.89 (5 and up)   S C

1. South Africa—Race relations—Fiction 2. Short stories

ISBN 0-06-050799-3; 0-06-050800-0 (lib bdg)
LC 2002-68901

First published 2001 in the United Kingdom

Seven stories, spanning the time period from 1948 to 2000, chronicle the experiences of young people from different races and ethnic groups as they try to cope with the restrictions placed on their lives by South Africa's apartheid laws

"Naidoo's book reveals our humanity and inhumanity with starkness and precision. . . . She honors her country's past, present, and future with these brave tales." Horn Book

Nixon, Joan Lowery

Ghost town; seven ghostly stories. Delacorte Press 2000 147p $14.95; pa $4.99   S C

1. Ghost stories 2. West (U.S.)—Fiction 3. Short stories

ISBN 0-385-32681-5; 0-440-41603-5 (pa)
LC 99-36340

A collection of stories about eerie encounters in various Western ghost towns. Each story is accompanied by an afterword about the actual town on which the story is based

"Readers will get shivers and laughs from this collection. . . . This well-researched and enjoyable book will be useful in cross-curricular units." Book Rep

San Souci, Robert

Dare to be scared; thirteen stories to chill and thrill; illustrations by David Ouimet. Cricket Bks. 2003 159p il $15.95 (4 and up)   S C

1. Horror fiction 2. Short stories

ISBN 0-8126-2688-5   LC 2002-152827

"From a horrible dream a boy can't wake up to from to an alien-driven bus to an eerie house with an alarming inhabitant, these stories cover the gamut of scary themes." SLJ

"With crisp, straightforward delivery and some intriguing endings, these 13 tales are great fun for young readers who like to be spooked." Booklist

Double-dare to be scared: another thirteen chilling tales; [by] Robert D. San Souci; illustrated by David Ouimet. Cricket Books 2004 170p il $15.95 (4 and up)   S C

1. Horror fiction 2. Short stories

ISBN 0-8126-2716-4   LC 2003-26610

Companion volume to Dare to be scared (2003)

This is a "collection of 13 tales. . . . Most of the main characters are menaced by a variety of scary, unexpected threats: a madman in the woods, a giant spider, unforgiving leprechauns, and exceptionally hungry Appalachian children." Booklist

"San Souci uses elements of urban legend and folklore to weave powerful and suspenseful yet age-appropriate stories that youngsters will revisit, finding new meaning with each reading." SLJ

Sandburg, Carl

More Rootabaga stories; illustrated by Maud and Miska Petersham. Harcourt 2003 c1923 158p il $17; pa $5.95   S C

1. Fairy tales 2. Short stories

ISBN 0-15-204713-1; 0-15-204706-9 (pa)
LC 2002-191948

"An Odyssey/Harcourt young classic"

First published 1923; previously published as Rootabaga stories, part two

A selection of tales from Rootabaga Country peopled with such characters as the Huckabuck Family, Big Buff Banty Hen, Dippy the Wisp, and many others

Rootabaga stories; illustrated by Maud and Miska Petersham. Harcourt 2003 c1922 176p il $17; pa $5.95   S C

1. Fairy tales 2. Short stories

ISBN 0-15-204709-3; 0-15-204714-X (pa)
LC 2002-191949

Newly illustrated edition of Rootabaga stories. Two volume edition by Michael Hague published 1988-1989 available

"An Odyssey/Harcourt young classic"

First published 1922; previously published as: Rootabaga stories, part one

A selection of tales from Rootabaga Country peopled with such characters as the Potato Face Blind Man, the Blue Wind Boy, and many others

Shelf life: stories by the book; edited by Gary Paulsen. Simon & Schuster Bks. for Young Readers 2003 173p $16.95 (5 and up)   S C

1. Books and reading—Fiction 2. Short stories

ISBN 0-689-84180-9   LC 2002-66901

Contents: In your hat, by E. Conford; Escape, by M. P. Haddix; Follow the water, by J. L. Holm; Testing, testing 1 . . . 2 . . . 3, by A. La Faye; Tea party ends in bloody massacre, film at 11, by G. Maguire; What's a fellow to do, by K. Karr; Wet hens, by E. Wittlinger; The good deed, by M. D. Bauer; Bacarole for paper and bones, by M. T. Anderson; Clean sweep, by J. Bauer

Ten short stories in which the lives of young people in different circumstances are changed by their encounters with books

"Covering almost every genre of fiction, including

Shelf life: stories by the book—*Continued*

mystery, SF, fantasy and realism, these well-crafted stories by familiar authors offer sharply drawn characterizations and intriguing premises." Publ Wkly

Singer, Isaac Bashevis

The power of light; eight stories for Hanukkah; with illustrations by Irene Lieblich. Farrar, Straus & Giroux 1980 86p il pa $10.95 hardcover o.p. (4 and up)   **S C**

1. Hanukkah—Fiction 2. Short stories 3. Jews—Fiction

ISBN 0-374-36099-5 (pa); 0-374-45984-3 (hc)

LC 80-20263

"The stories, bound together by recurring Hanukkah motifs—the lamp, the dreidel, and the pancakes, tell chiefly of events affecting the lives of Eastern European Jews. Ranging from such somber happenings as the drafting of small Jewish boys to serve in the Russian army during the nineteenth century through the bombing and burning of the Warsaw ghetto, the harrowing events are seen in the context of the celebration of Hanukkah." Horn Book

"The stories vary from realism to incorporation of the miraculous . . . but are united in their strong piety as they are in the polished craftsmanship and warmth with which they are written." Bull Cent Child Books

Stories for children. Farrar, Straus & Giroux 1984 337p $22.95; pa $14 (4 and up)
S C

1. Jews—Fiction 2. Short stories

ISBN 0-374-37266-7; 0-374-46489-8 (pa)

LC 84-13612

This collection of thirty-six stories includes "parables, beast fables, allegories and reminiscences. Some stories are silly and charming, while others are wildly fantastic, dealing with savagery and miracles in mythical, medieval Poland. Frequently they are about scary situations, but all tend to end happily, with an edifying idea. Most appealing is the Nobel Prize winner's sheer story-telling power. In this respect, he has no equal among contemporaries." N Y Times Book Rev

Soto, Gary

Baseball in April, and other stories. 10th anniversary ed. Harcourt Brace Jovanovich 2000 c1990 111p $16; pa $6 (5 and up)   **S C**

1. Mexican Americans—Fiction 2. California—Fiction 3. Short stories

ISBN 0-15-202573-1; 0-15-202567-7 (pa)

Also available Spanish language edition

A reissue of the title first published 1990

A collection of eleven short stories focusing on the everyday adventures of Hispanic young people growing up in Fresno, California

Each story "gets at the heart of some aspect of growing up. The insecurities, the embarrassments, the triumphs, the inequities of it all are chronicled with wit and charm. Soto's characters ring true and his knowledge of, and affection for, their shared Mexican-American heritage is obvious and infectious." Voice Youth Advocates

Petty crimes. Harcourt Brace & Co. 1998 157p $16 (5 and up)   **S C**

1. Mexican Americans—Fiction 2. Short stories

ISBN 0-15-201658-9   LC 97-37114

A collection of short stories about Mexican American youth growing up in California's Central Valley

"A sense of family strength relieves the under-current of sadness in these raw stories." Horn Book Guide

Spinelli, Jerry

The library card. Scholastic 1997 148p pa $4.99 (4 and up)   **S C**

1. Books and reading—Fiction 2. Short stories

ISBN 0-590-38633-6 (pa)   LC 96-18412

"A library card is the magical object common to each of these four stories in which a budding street thug, a television addict, a homeless orphan, and a lonely girl are all transformed by the power and the possibilities that await them within the walls of the public library. Spinelli's characters . . . are unusual and memorable; his writing both humorous and convincing." Horn Book Guide

Sports shorts. Darby Creek Pub. 2005 127p il $15.99 (5 and up)   **S C**

1. Sports—Fiction 2. Short stories

ISBN 1-58196-040-9

Contents: Bombardment by Joseph Bruchac; Two left feet, two left hands, and too left on the bench by David Lubar; First position by Marilyn Singer; Finishing blocks and deadly hook shots by Terry Trueman; Finding high-jump fame by Dorian Cirrone; Line drive by Tanya West; Riding the century by Alexandra Siy; On being written in by Jamie McEwan.

A collection of eight semi-autobiographical stories about the authors' experiences with sports while growing up.

"Some of the vignettes are laugh-out-loud funny. . . . The book's smaller-than-standard trim size and inviting page design will help attract readers to this rewarding collection." Booklist

Stine, R. L.

The haunting hour. HarperCollins Pubs. 2001 153p il $11.95; lib bdg $14.89 (4 and up)
S C

1. Horror fiction 2. Short stories

ISBN 0-06-623604-5; 0-06-623605-3 (lib bdg)

LC 2001-39142

"A Parachute Press book"

A collection of ten short horror stories featuring a ghoulish Halloween party, a long, mysterious car trip, and a very dangerous imaginary friend. Each story includes drawings by a different illustrator

"The predictability of the stories and the unsophisticated storytelling won't keep Stine fans old and new from swallowing this down in one big gulp." Bull Cent Child Books

Swan sister; fairy tales retold; edited by Ellen Datlow and Terri Windling. Simon & Schuster Bks. for Young Readers 2003 165p $16.95 (5 and up)   **S C**

1. Fairy tales 2. Short stories

ISBN 0-689-84613-4   LC 2002-30409

Swan sister—*Continued*

Contents: Greenkid by Jane Yolen; Golden fur by Midori Snyder; Chambers of the heart by Nina Kiriki Hoffman; Little Red and the Big Bad by Will Shetterly; The Fish's story by Pat York; The Children of Tilford Fortune by Christopher Rowe; The Girl in the attic by Lois Metzger; The Harp that sang by Gregory Frost; A life in miniature by Bruce Coville; Lupe by Kathe Koja; Awake by Tanith Lee; Inventing Aladdin by Neil Gaiman; My swan sister by Katherine Vaz

"In this anthology, noted children's and adult fantasy writers play with the bones of traditional stories, songs, and characters to create 13 vibrant, imaginative short stories. . . . There's something for everyone in this anthology." SLJ

Tripping over the lunch lady and other school stories; edited by Nancy E. Mercado. Dial Books 2004 177p $16.99 (4 and up)

S C

1. School stories 2. Short stories

ISBN 0-8037-2873-5   LC 2003-15905

Contents: Tripping over the lunch lady by Angela Johnson; How I got my English A by Avi; Experts, incorporated by Sarah Weeks; Apple blossoms by Terry Trueman; Science friction by David Lubar; The grade school zone by James Proimos, illustrated by David Fremont; The desk by Lee Wardlaw; The crush by Rachel Vail; The girls room by Susan Shreve; Tied to Zelda by David Rice

An "anthology of 10 short stories, by authors such as Avi, Angela Johnson, David Lubar, and Rachel Vail." SLJ

"In these first-person narratives, sharply defined details and keenly observed nuances of school life often set the stage for moments of wit, surprise, realization, and tenderness." Booklist

Wynne-Jones, Tim

Some of the kinder planets: stories. Orchard Bks. 1995 c1993 130p $15.95; lib bdg $16.99 (4 and up)   **S C**

1. Short stories

ISBN 0-531-09451-0; 0-531-08751-4 (lib bdg)

     LC 94-33009

Also available in paperback from Puffin Bks.

First published 1993 in Canada

"This collection of nine short stories offers offbeat vignettes of contemporary life as well as tales of ghosts, aliens, and historical figures. Clear writing combines with clever concepts and varied subject matter to make the book accessible and enjoyable to a wide audience." SLJ

E EASY BOOKS

This section consists chiefly of fiction books that would interest children from pre-school through third grade. Easy books that have a definite nonfiction subject content are usually classified with other nonfiction books. Easy books listed here include:

1. Picture books, whether fiction or nonfiction, that the young child can use independently

2. Fiction books with very little or scattered text, with large print and with vocabulary suitable for children with reading levels of grades 1-3

3. Picture storybooks with a larger amount of text to be used primarily by or with children in pre-school through grade 3

Ackerman, Karen

Song and dance man; illustrated by Stephen Gammell. Knopf 1988 unp il lib bdg $17.99; pa $6.99   **E**

1. Entertainers—Fiction 2. Grandfathers—Fiction

ISBN 0-394-99330-6 (lib bdg); 0-679-81995-9 (pa)

     LC 87-3200

Awarded the Caldecott Medal, 1989

"Grandpa takes three grandchildren up to the attic, where he arranges lights and gives a performance that enchants his audience. They tell him they wish they could have seen him dance in 'the good old days' but he says he wouldn't trade a million good old days for the time he spends with the narrators." Bull Cent Child Books

The illustrator "captures all the story's inherent joie de vivre with color pencil renderings that fairly leap off the pages." Booklist

Adler, David A.

The Babe & I; written by David A. Adler; illustrated by Terry Widener. Harcourt Brace & Co. 1999 unp il $16   **E**

1. Ruth, Babe, 1895-1948—Fiction 2. Great Depression, 1929-1939—Fiction

ISBN 0-15-201378-4   LC 97-37580

"Gulliver books"

While helping his family make ends meet during the Depression by selling newspapers, a boy meets Babe Ruth

"Widener's illustrations evoke the ambiance of the period in this book that is carefully paced and remarkable for its unified focus." Horn Book Guide

Young Cam Jansen and the dinosaur game; illustrated by Susanna Natti. Viking 1996 32p il $13.99; pa $3.99   **E**

1. Mystery fiction

ISBN 0-670-86399-8; 0-14-037779-4 (pa)

     LC 95-46463

Titles about Cam Jansen for older readers are also available

"A Viking easy-to-read"

"At Jane's birthday party, everyone guesses the number of toy dinosaurs in a big jar. Jennifer 'the Camera' Jansen's photographic memory helps her nab Robert, who has cheated in order to win all the dinosaurs. Observant readers can follow Cam's reasoning and solve the mystery, too." Horn Book Guide

Other easy-to-read titles about Cam Jansen are:

Adler, David A.—*Continued*

Young Cam Jansen and the baseball mystery (1999)

Young Cam Jansen and the double beach mystery (2002)

Young Cam Jansen and the ice skate mystery (1998)

Young Cam Jansen and the library mystery (2001)

Young Cam Jansen and the lost tooth (1997)

Young Cam Jansen and the missing cookie (1996)

Young Cam Jansen and the new girl mystery (2004)

Young Cam Jansen and the pizza shop mystery (2000)

Young Cam Jansen and the substitute mystery (2005)

Young Cam Jansen and the zoo note mystery (2003)

Adoff, Arnold

Black is brown is tan; pictures by Emily Arnold McCully. HarperCollins Pubs. 2002 unp il $15.99; lib bdg $15.89   E

1. Racially mixed people—Fiction 2. Family life—Fiction

ISBN 0-06-028776-4; 0-06-028777-2 (lib bdg)

LC 00-44864

A newly illustrated edition of the title first published 1973

Describes in verse a family with a brown-skinned mother, white-skinned father, two children, and their various relatives

"Children everywhere will love the simple, joyful rhythmic words in Adoff's signature 'shaped speech' style, with McCully's beautiful dancing watercolors." Booklist

Agee, Jon

Milo's hat trick; story and pictures by Jon Agee. Hyperion Bks. for Children 2001 unp il $15.95

E

1. Magicians—Fiction 2. Bears—Fiction

ISBN 0-7868-0902-7

"Michael di Capua books"

In the busy city, there are lots of people with hats. But there is only one guy with a bear in his hat. That's Milo The Magician

"Agee's bold, angular pencil-and-paint illustrations drive this warm story about perseverance, luck, and courage." Booklist

Terrific; story and pictures by Jon Agee. Hyperion Books for Children 2005 unp il $15.95

E

1. Shipwrecks—Fiction 2. Parrots—Fiction

ISBN 0-7868-5184-8   LC 2004-117133

"Michael di Capua books"

"Terrific," says Eugene when he wins an all-expenses-paid cruise to Bermuda. "I'll probably get a really nasty sunburn." But Eugene's luck is much worse than that. His ship sinks, and he ends up stranded on a tiny island with a talking parrot.

"With pithy humor and a knack for comic timing, Agee has created a character who will endear himself to readers despite his curmudgeonly exterior and posturing. . . . The cartoon illustrations feature strong lines and soft colors that contrast wonderfully with the story line." SLJ

Z goes home. Hyperion Bks. for Children 2003 unp il $16.95   E

1. Alphabet

ISBN 0-786-81987-1   LC 2002-114205

"Michael di Capua books"

"The letter Z abandons its allotted spot in the City Zoo sign and heads off in Agee's innovative alphabet book. Children can track the red Z's journey past an Alien, over a Bridge, into some Cake, and over Hurdles until the red-letter moment when it finally finds its way to its similarly colored friends. . . . Each letter is exemplified by a noun . . . but to make matters more interesting, the object is also shaped like the letter. . . . Bold shapes and lines create a clean, comical look." Booklist

Ahlberg, Allan

A bit more Bert; [by] Allan Ahlberg & Raymond Briggs. Farrar, Straus & Giroux 2002 unp il $16   E

ISBN 0-374-32489-1   LC 2001-59777

Companion volume to The adventures of Bert (2001)

Bert receives a disastrous haircut, loses his dog, and discovers that there are many other Berts in the world

"Briggs's illustrations are sublime . . . with Bert evoked in all his cherry-nosed, red-haired . . . affability." Horn Book

The shopping expedition; illustrated by André Amstutz. 1st U.S. ed. Candlewick Press 2005 unp il $16.99   E

1. Imagination—Fiction 2. Shopping—Fiction

ISBN 0-7636-2586-8   LC 2003-69674

A routine shopping trip becomes a grand adventure in the eyes of a little girl.

"Amstutz's richly colored illustrations have a painterly look, often with visible brush strokes, that really suits the imaginative subject matter. The repetitive phrase keeps the pace of the story going and works well for reading aloud." SLJ

Ahlberg, Janet

Each peach pear plum; [by] Janet and Allan Ahlberg. 25th anniversary ed. Viking 2004 c1978 unp il $18.92; pa $4.99   E

1. Stories in rhyme

ISBN 0-670-05897-1; 0-14-050639-X (pa)

Also available board book edition

First published 1978 in the United Kingdom; a reissue of the edition published 1979 in the United States

Rhymed text and illustrations invite the reader to play "I Spy" with a variety of Mother Goose and other folklore characters.

"This is a lovely small book, well-conceived and very well drawn, gentle, humorous, unsentimental." NY Times Book Rev

Alborough, Jez

Duck in the truck. HarperCollins Pubs. 2000 unp il $14.95   E

1. Ducks—Fiction 2. Animals—Fiction 3. Stories in rhyme

ISBN 0-06-028685-7   LC 99-60934

Alborough, Jez—Continued

"A rhyming text relates the troubles of a duck whose truck gets stuck in the muck. . . . The art makes the most of the story's physical comedy, with exaggerated humor and an engaging animal cast, including a frog, a sheep, and a goat who all come to help out." Horn Book Guide

Other titles about Duck are:
Captain Duck (2003)
Duck's key, where can it be (2005)
Fix-it Duck (2002)
Hit the ball Duck (2006)

Some dogs do. Candlewick Press 2003 unp il $15.99 **E**
1. Dogs—Fiction 2. Stories in rhyme
ISBN 0-7636-2201-X LC 2002-41760
When Sid tries to convince his doggy classmates that he flew to school, they do not believe him.
"Done in gouache, the illustrations glow with bright colors. . . . A wonderful addition to any library and a great choice for storytime." SLJ

Tall. Candlewick Press 2005 unp il $15.99 **E**
1. Chimpanzees—Fiction 2. Size—Fiction
ISBN 0-7634-2784-4 LC 2004-062941
Illustrations and just a few words depict how various jungle animals help Bobo the chimp to feel that he is tall.
"Bobo embodies an impressive range of identifiable emotions. Alborough's adept pen-and-gouache illustrations make each feeling and point of view crystal clear. . . . A must-have title for any children who have ever felt less than enchanted with their diminutive status." SLJ

Another title about Bobo the chimp is:
Hug (2000)

Alda, Arlene

Arlene Alda's 1 2 3. Tricycle Press 1998 unp il $12.95; pa $6.96 **E**
1. Counting
ISBN 1-883672-71-6; 1-58246-119-8 (pa)
LC 98-5966
Also available, Arlene Alda's a b c
"The numerals 1 through 10 and back again are portrayed with great imagination in fine, full-color photographs. The examples reflect the shapes of the numbers themselves: four is formed by the crossed legs of a flamingo, eight is two bagels frosted with cream cheese lying on a plate. . . . A unique, challenging concept book." SLJ

Did you say pears? Tundra Books 2006 31p il $16.95 **E**
1. English language—Homonyms
ISBN 0-88776-739-7
"A marvelously imaginative pairing (sorry) of homonyms (words that sound alike but have different meanings and the same spelling) and homophones (words that sound alike but have different meanings and different spellings), wrapped up in a rhyme of amazingly few words and terrific offbeat photographs." Booklist

Alexander, Lloyd

The fortune-tellers; illustrated by Trina Schart Hyman. Dutton Children's Bks. 1992 unp il pa $6.99 hardcover o.p. **E**
1. Fortune telling—Fiction 2. Cameroon—Fiction
ISBN 0-14-056233-8 (pa) LC 91-30684
A carpenter goes to a fortune teller and finds the predictions about his future coming true in an unusual way
"Alexander's rags-to-riches story combines universal elements of the trickster character and the cumulative disaster tale. Hyman's pictures set it all in a vibrant community in Cameroon, West Africa. . . . The energetic, brilliantly colored paintings are packed with people and objects that swirl around the main characters. . . . With its ups and downs, this is a funny, playful story that evokes the irony of the human condition." Booklist

How the cat swallowed thunder; illustrated by Judith Byron Schachner. Dutton Children's Bks. 2000 unp il $16.99 **E**
1. Cats—Fiction
ISBN 0-525-46449-2 LC 00-24530
Warned not to get into his usual mischief, Mother Holly's cat tries to tidy up all the mess he has made while she is away
"Alexander's original tale progresses with the easy feel of folklore, and children will delight in this mischievous *pourquoi* tale about how Cat got his purr." Bull Cent Child Books

Alexander, Martha G.

I'll never share you, Blackboard Bear; [by] Martha Alexander. 1st ed. Candlewick Press 2003 unp il $12.99 **E**
1. Bears—Fiction
ISBN 0-7636-1590-0 LC 2001-58120
After the bear he has drawn on the blackboard comes to life, Anthony does not want to share him with Gloria and Stewart.
"Alexander combines uncomplicated language with engaging watercolor illustrations to reveal positive solutions to typical emotional dilemmas." SLJ
Other titles about Blackboard Bear are:
And my mean old mother will be sorry, Blackboard Bear (1972)
Blackboard Bear (1969)
I sure am glad to see you, Blackboard Bear (1976)
We're in big trouble, Blackboard Bear (2001)
You're a genius, Blackboard Bear (1995)

Aliki

All by myself! written and illustrated by Aliki. HarperCollins Pubs. 2000 unp il $14.95; lib bdg $14.89 **E**
ISBN 0-06-028929-5; 0-06-028930-9 (lib bdg)
LC 99-51672
A child shows all the things he has learned to do all on his own
"Aliki's colorful illustrations closely match the moods and energy levels of a five- or six-year-old. . . . The text has a hand-printed appearance, large and easy to read. . . . A good choice for story-hours and beginning readers." SLJ

Aliki—*Continued*

Painted words: Marianthe's story one. Greenwillow Bks. 1998 unp il $16.99; lib bdg $17.89 **E**

1. School stories 2. Immigrants—Fiction
ISBN 0-688-15661-4; 0-688-15662-2 (lib bdg)
LC 97-34653

Bound back to back with: Spoken memories: Marianthe's story two

Two separate stories, the first telling of Mari's starting school in a new land, and the second describing village life in her country before she and her family left in search of a better life

"In simple, understated language, Aliki has captured the emotions and experiences of many of today's children. Colored-pencil and crayon illustrations in soft primary and secondary colors reinforce the mood of the text." SLJ

A play's the thing; written and illustrated by Aliki. 1st ed. HarperCollins 2005 32p il $16.99; lib bdg $17.89 **E**

1. School stories 2. Theater—Fiction
ISBN 0-06-074355-7; 0-06-074356-5 (lib bdg)
LC 2004-22101

"When Miss Brilliant's class decides to put on a fractured version of [Mary Had a Little Lamb], José must learn to work with his classmates and overcome his antisocial tendencies. . . . This is . . . the type of work that children will be drawn to again and again because they recognize their world so aptly captured in both word and art. Each time they revisit, they will find something new in the colorful cartoon illustrations." SLJ

The two of them; written and illustrated by Aliki. Greenwillow Bks. 1979 unp il pa $6.99 hardcover o.p. **E**

1. Grandfathers—Fiction 2. Death—Fiction
ISBN 0-688-07337-9 (pa)
LC 79-10161

Describes the relationship of a grandfather and his granddaughter from her birth to his death

"The eloquent illustrations in muted full color and the smaller soft-pencil drawings show the life the two shared as well as the tenderness and pure pleasure implicit in their relationship." Horn Book

We are best friends. Greenwillow Bks. 1982 unp il $16.99; pa $5.99 **E**

1. Friendship—Fiction
ISBN 0-688-00822-4; 0-688-07037-X (pa)
LC 81-6549

When Robert's best friend Peter moves away, both are unhappy, but they learn that they can make new friends and still remain best friends

"Brightly lit pictures in cheerful primary colors portray with just a stroke of the pen the misery of losing a friend who must move away and the tentative beginnings of a new companionship. . . . Details of school and home abound in the lively pictures." Horn Book

Another title about Robert and Peter is:
Best friends together again (1995)

Welcome, little baby. Greenwillow Bks. 1987 unp il $15.99 **E**

1. Infants—Fiction 2. Mothers—Fiction
ISBN 0-688-06810-3
LC 86-7648

A mother welcomes her newborn infant, and tells what life will be like as the child grows older

"Tender pictures in pastel colors are appropriate for a minimal text, not substantial but effective in its message of love." Bull Cent Child Books

Allard, Harry

Miss Nelson is missing! [by] Harry Allard, James Marshall. Houghton Mifflin 1977 32p il $16; pa $5.95 **E**

1. School stories 2. Teachers—Fiction
ISBN 0-395-25296-2; 0-395-40146-1 (pa)
LC 76-55918

Also available Spanish language edition

"The kids in room 207 were so fresh and naughty that they lost their sweet-natured teacher, the blonde Miss Nelson, and got in her place the sour-souled Miss Swamp." N Y Times Book Rev

"Humor and suspense fill the pages of [this book]." Christ Sci Monit

Other titles about Miss Nelson are:
Miss Nelson has a field day (1985)
Miss Nelson is back (1982)

Allen, Debbie

Dancing in the wings; pictures by Kadir Nelson. Dial Bks. for Young Readers 2000 unp il $16.99 **E**

1. Ballet—Fiction 2. African Americans—Fiction
ISBN 0-8037-2501-9
LC 99-462181

Sassy tries out for a summer dance festival in Washington, D.C., despite the other girls' taunts that she is much too tall

"Allen's dialogue is realistic, and Nelson's illustrations of the predominantly African-American cast ably capture Sassy's love of dance and her lively personality." Horn Book Guide

Allen, Jonathan

I'm not cute! Hyperion Books for Children 2006 unp il $14.99 **E**

1. Owls—Fiction
ISBN 0-7868-3720-9

Little Owl wants to be strong, brave, and fearsome—not cute! But he is cute and no one can resist telling him so.

The "minimalist, black-outlined watercolors capture plenty of facial expressions. A fresh story line and . . . cartoons make this a crowd-pleaser." SLJ

Alvarez, Julia

A gift of gracias; the legend of Altagracia; written by Julia Alvarez; illustrated by Beatriz Vidal. Knopf 2005 unp $15.95 **E**

1. Oranges—Fiction 2. Dominican Republic—Fiction 3. Saints—Fiction
ISBN 0-375-82425-1

Also available Spanish language edition

Maria's family is almost forced to leave their farm on the new island colony, until a mysterious lady appears in Maria's dream.

Alvarez, Julia—*Continued*

"Rich in cultural authenticity and brimming with the magical realism that is characteristic of Hispanic literature, this elegantly woven tale introduces the legend of Our Lady of Altagracia, the patron saint of the Dominican Republic. . . . With an exquisite use of watercolor and gouache, Vidal has painted colorful, yet warm illustrations that add depth to the story." SLJ

Anaya, Rudolfo A.

The farolitos of Christmas; [by] Rudolfo Anaya; illustrated by Edward Gonzales. Hyperion Bks. for Children 1995 unp il $16.95   E

1. Christmas—Fiction 2. Mexican Americans—Fiction
ISBN 0-7868-0060-7   LC 94-48073

With her father away fighting in World War II and her grandfather too sick to create the traditional luminaria, Luz helps create farolitos, little lanterns, for their Christmas celebration instead

"The narrative provides a satisfying explanation for the Mexican tradition of *farolitos*. Paintings complement the text of this warm family story, which naturally incorporates Spanish words." Horn Book Guide

Another title about Luz is:
Farolitos for Abuelo (1998)

Andersen, Hans Christian

The emperor's new clothes; translated and introduced by Naomi Lewis; illustrated by Angela Barrett. Candlewick Press 1997 unp il $15.99; pa $5.99   E

1. Fairy tales
ISBN 0-7636-0119-5; 0-7636-1281-2 (pa)
LC 96-45004

Two rascally weavers convince the emperor they are making him beautiful new clothes, visible only to those fit for their posts, but when he wears them during a royal procession, a child recognizes that the emperor has nothing on

This book "introduces the Emperor and his problems in a sophisticated setting that looks much like pre-World War I Monaco. Lewis's . . . translation is smooth and contemporary and easily transmits the wry humor that distinguishes the story. The illustrations, incorporated into a design of exceptional cleverness and wit, are spectacular." Horn Book

The emperor's new clothes; designed and illustrated by Virginia Lee Burton. Houghton Mifflin 2004 c1949 44p il $16   E

1. Fairy tales
ISBN 0-618-34421-7

A reissue of the edition first published 1949

Weavers convince the vain emperor that the clothing they make for him can only be seen by those who are not fools, but only the child recognizes the truth

"Burton's sense of pageantry sets forth in beautiful colors the magnificence of the Empereror's doman and entourage; her sense of humor brings out rightly the ridiculous situation with all its implications." Horn Book Guide

Thumbeline; illustrated by Lisbeth Zwerger; translated by Anthea Bell. North-South Bks. 2000 unp il $15.95; pa $7.99   E

1. Fairy tales
ISBN 0-7358-1213-6; 0-7358-1210-1 (pa)
LC 99-57073

"A Michael Neugebauer book"

A reissue of 1985 edition published by Picture Book Studio

The adventures of a tiny girl no bigger than a thumb and her many animal friends

"The book's squarish design . . . draws the reader's attention to the exceptional art. Lovely, lean, lithe lines combine with a palette of tawny earth tones to create a minimalist world redolent with grace and rich with imagination." Horn Book Guide

Anderson, Christine

Bedtime! [by] Christine Anderson; illustrated by Steven Salerno. Philomel Books 2005 unp il $14.99   E

1. Bedtime—Fiction
ISBN 0-399-24004-7   LC 2004-9460

When Melanie is too busy playing to get ready for bed, her mother gives the special bedtime treatment to the dog, and Melanie misses some of the best parts of the routine.

"Salerno's watercolor, gouache, and ink artwork has a stylized, modern retro look and a dynamic use of line. The illustrations maximize the action and provide plenty of humorous touches. This is an irresistible approach to the ups and downs of bedtime rituals." SLJ

Anderson, Lena

Tea for ten; translated by Elisabeth Kallick Dyssegaard. R & S Bks. 2000 unp il $14   E

1. Counting
ISBN 91-29-64557-3   LC 99-52906

Original Swedish edition, 1998
Translated from the Swedish

Hedgehog is lonely until nine of her friends arrive, introducing the numbers from one to ten

"The text is simply written and complemented by gentle, childlike watercolor illustrations." SLJ

Anno, Mitsumasa

Anno's counting book. Crowell 1977 c1975 unp il $16.95; lib bdg $16.89; pa $6.99   E

1. Counting 2. Seasons—Fiction 3. Stories without words
ISBN 0-690-01287-X; 0-690-01288-8 (lib bdg); 0-06-443123-1 (pa)   LC 76-28977

Original Japanese edition, 1975

"A distinctive, beautifully conceived counting book in which twelve full-color doublespreads show the same village and surrounding countryside during different hours (by the church clock) and months. Both the seasons and community changes are studied, as such components of the scene as flowers, trees, animals, people, and buildings increase from one to twelve." LC. Child Books, 1977

Anno, Mitsumasa—*Continued*

Anno's Spain. Philomel Books 2004 unp il $17.99 **E**

1. Spain—Pictorial works 2. Stories without words
ISBN 0-399-24238-4

Original Japanese edition 2003

"Anno takes us through Spain . . . featuring twenty-one colorful, wordless spreads, depicting the . . . cities and eras of this . . . country. [The illustrations include] historic moments, hidden literary and artistic details, and . . . Anno himself, as he wanders the unfolding countrysides." Publisher's note

"Detailed pen and ink and watercolors illustrate this wordless travelogue. Anno's aerial tour of Spanish landscapes and townscapes is timeless." SLJ

Antle, Nancy

Sam's Wild West Christmas; pictures by S.D. Schindler. Dial Bks. for Young Readers 2001 40p il $13.99 **E**

1. Christmas—Fiction 2. Santa Claus—Fiction
ISBN 0-8037-2199-4   LC 99-47057

"Dial easy-to-read"

On Christmas Eve, Sam and the members of his Wild West Show help a trainful of people robbed by outlaws who have just captured a very special holiday traveler in red

"The fine-lined ink and watercolor illustrations are as deadpan as the humorous text." Horn Book Guide

Appelbaum, Diana Karter

Cocoa ice; by Diana Appelbaum; pictures by Holly Meade. Orchard Bks. 1997 unp il $16.95; lib bdg $17.99 **E**

1. Ice—Fiction
ISBN 0-531-30040-4; 0-531-33040-0 (lib bdg)
          LC 96-40365

A girl in Santo Domingo tells how cocoa is harvested during the late 1800s while at the same time her counterpart in Maine tells about the harvesting of ice

"Meade's vibrant cut-paper and gouache illustrations capture the action, industry, and natural beauty of each locale. Filled with fascinating, child-centered details and engaging artwork." SLJ

Appelt, Kathi

Bats around the clock; illustrated by Melissa Sweet. HarperCollins Pubs. 2000 unp il $15.99; lib bdg $16.89 **E**

1. Bats—Fiction 2. Rock music—Fiction 3. Stories in rhyme
ISBN 0-688-16469-2; 0-688-16470-6 (lib bdg)
          LC 99-15502

Click Dark hosts a special twelve-hour program of American Bat Stand where the bats rock and roll until the midnight hour ends.

"The rhymes are delightful and the narrative jives right along." SLJ

Other titles about the bats are:
The bat jamboree (1996)
Bats on parade (1999)

Bubba and Beau, best friends; [illustrated by] Arthur Howard. Harcourt 2002 unp il $16; pa $6 **E**

1. Infants—Fiction 2. Dogs—Fiction
ISBN 0-15-202060-8; 0-15-205580-0 (pa)
          LC 2001-1987

When Mamma Pearl washes their favorite blanket it's a sad day for best friends Bubba and Beau, but it gets worse when she decides the baby boy and his puppy need baths, too.

"Appelt's snappy text is a readaloud romp, and Howard's equally snappy watercolors provide an offbeat, slyly funny subtext. Uncluttered compositions, a clean pastel palette, solid drafting, and terrifically expressive faces combine with the conversational, cheeky text." Bull Cent Child Books

Other titles about Bubba and Beau are:
Bubba and Beau go night-night (2003)
Bubba and Beau meet the relatives (2004)

Cowboy dreams; illustrated by Barry Root. HarperCollins Pubs. 1999 unp il $14.95; lib bdg $14.89 **E**

1. Cowhands—Fiction 2. West (U.S.)—Fiction 3. Stories in rhyme
ISBN 0-06-027763-7; 0-06-027764-5 (lib bdg)
          LC 98-18316

A little cowpoke is lulled to sleep by dreams of the sights and sounds of the Western landscape at night.

"Rhythmic rhymes and imaginative artwork combine in a cozy bedtime tale." SLJ

Oh my baby, little one; pictures by Jane Dyer. Harcourt Brace & Co. 2000 unp il $16 **E**

1. Mother-child relationship—Fiction 2. Stories in rhyme
ISBN 0-15-200041-0   LC 99-6363

"An exploration of the love that exists between mother and child, even when Mama Bird must leave her baby at nursery school. Told in rhyming verse, each four-line stanza is a reassurance that mama's love will permeate all areas of Baby Bird's day." SLJ

"The light, bright pictures will charm young listeners, who will find this book best enjoyed while cuddled up next to Mama." Booklist

Where, where is Swamp Bear? pictures by Megan Halsey. HarperCollins Pubs. 2002 unp il $15.95; lib bdg $15.89 **E**

1. Bears—Fiction 2. Wetlands—Fiction 3. Grandfathers—Fiction
ISBN 0-688-17102-8; 0-688-17103-6 (lib bdg)
          LC 00-33582

"On a fishing trip with his Granpere through the swamp, a young Cajun named Pierre ponders the life of the elusive (and now endangered) Louisiana black bear. . . . Appelt . . . infuses the text with a gentle rhyme and rhythm that never intrudes into the subtle science lesson. Although Pierre gets a look at many other swamp creatures, the bear remains unseen, to him and Granpere, at least—attentive readers will spot it on every one of Halsey's . . . dusky, subtly textured cut-paper spreads." Publ Wkly

Argueta, Jorge

Moony Luna; story, Jorge Argueta; illustrations, Elizabeth Gómez. Children's Book Press 2005 31p il $16.95   E

1. School stories 2. Bilingual books—English-Spanish

ISBN 0-89239-205-3   LC 2004-56047

"This bilingual picture book presents . . . the fears five-year-old Luna experiences as she faces her first day of school. The little girl gives shape to her anxiety by visualizing it as the monster from a book her mother read to her the night before. The Spanish text . . . has a pleasing poetic structure and a comforting rhythm that will reassure young listeners. . . . The illustrations, well matched to the story, have the flat perspective and the vibrant colors of contemporary Latin American art." Booklist

Armstrong, Jennifer

Magnus at the fire; illustrated by Owen Smith. Simon & Schuster Books for Young Readers 2005 unp il $15.95   E

1. Horses—Fiction 2. Fire fighting—Fiction

ISBN 0-689-83922-7   LC 2004-11487

When the Broadway Fire House acquires a motorized fire engine, Magnus the fire horse is not ready to retire.

A "stirring historical story. . . . Impressive oil paintings in vibrant colors capture the drama of firefighting in the 1800s." SLJ

Arnold, Caroline

The terrible Hodag and the animal catchers; [by] Caroline Arnold; illustrated by John Sandford. 1st ed. Boyds Mills Press 2006 unp il $15.95
E

1. Monsters—Fiction 2. Lumber and lumbering—Fiction

ISBN 1-59078-166-X   LC 2005021141

When animal catchers come to the forest looking for the scary-looking, but very kindly, Hodag to take him to a zoo, a group of lumberjacks must find a way to protect their friend.

"The black-and-white prints . . . enhance the woodsy tale with a style that places the adventure at the turn of the 20th century." SLJ

Arnold, Katya

Me too! two small stories about small animals; retold and illustrated by Katya Arnold; based on stories by V. Suteev. Holiday House 2000 unp il $15.95

1. Animals—Fiction

ISBN 0-8234-1483-3   LC 99-16696

"In 'Me Too,' Chick copies all of Duckling's actions, until his friend goes swimming, whereupon Chick learns that following suit is not always a good idea. In 'Three Kittens,' a black, a gray, and a white kitten all turn white when they jump into a canister of flour while chasing a mouse." SLJ

"The simple, light-hearted tellings . . . are well matched by Arnold's distinctive illustrations, drawn with playful, energetic black line and colored with bright acrylics." Horn Book

Arnold, Marsha Diane

Heart of a tiger; pictures by Jamichael Henterly. Dial Bks. for Young Readers 1995 unp il $16.99
E

1. Cats—Fiction 2. Tigers—Fiction 3. India—Fiction

ISBN 0-8037-1695-8   LC 94-17126

"Small kitten Number Four must find a name for himself for his naming day. Not wanting to be called Smallest of All, he searches out Bengal, the beautiful tiger whose ways he greatly admires. He learns much from the big cat, and when he saves the tiger's life, he earns the name Heart of a Tiger. Arnold's original story has the feel of an oft-told tale, and Henterly's watercolors reward a lingering look." Horn Book Guide

Prancing, dancing Lily; pictures by John Manders. Dial Books for Young Readers 2004 unp il $16.99   E

1. Cattle—Fiction 2. Dance—Fiction

ISBN 0-8037-2823-9   LC 2002-5852

Lily will someday be the "bell cow," leading her herd, but because her prancing and dancing only disrupts their order, she travels the world looking for the right place and dance for her

"Arnold's amusing characters and clever text come to life through Manders's comical cartoon illustrations." SLJ

The pumpkin runner; pictures by Brad Sneed. Dial Bks. for Young Readers 1998 unp il $16.99
E

1. Running—Fiction 2. Pumpkin—Fiction 3. Australia—Fiction

ISBN 0-8037-2124-2   LC 97-26666

An Australian sheep rancher who eats pumpkins for energy enters a race from Melbourne to Sydney, despite people laughing at his eccentricities

"Sneed's cleverly skewed perspectives and Arnold's engaging style make this book, like its star, an easy winner." Publ Wkly

Arnosky, Jim

Beaver pond, moose pond. National Geographic Soc. 2000 unp il $15.95   E

1. Beavers—Fiction 2. Moose—Fiction

ISBN 0-7922-7692-2   LC 00-28377

A beaver and a moose share a pond, each thinking that the body of water belongs to him

"A touch of tension and some gentle humor enliven this brief nature lesson in story form. . . . Striking acrylic paintings show the changing light as the day passes and employ interesting perspectives." SLJ

Grandfather Buffalo; [by] Jim Arnosky. G.P. Putnam's Sons 2006 unp il $16.99   E

1. Bison—Fiction 2. Old age—Fiction

ISBN 0-399-24169-8   LC 2005003535

When Grandfather Buffalo, the oldest bull of the herd, trails behind the group, he finds that he is joined by a newborn calf.

"Arnosky's signature artwork, which beautifully evokes the western landscape, is especially effective showing the buffalo closeup, and the writer-artist's respect for nature is clearly reflected in the simple, poignant story." Booklist

Arnosky, Jim—*Continued*

Turtle in the sea. Putnam 2002 unp il $16.99
    E

1. Sea turtles—Fiction
ISBN 0-399-22757-1   LC 2001-48123

A sea turtle "escapes from a shark, a boat, a water-spout, and a fisherman's net to drag her scarred body onto a beach to lay her eggs. Arnosky has chosen clear, candy colors for his illustrations—pink, lavender, turquoise—all surrounded by a sunny lemon yellow. . . . The text is often lyrical." SLJ

Aroner, Miriam

Clink, clank, clunk! story by Miriam Aroner; pictures by Dominic Catalano. 1st ed. Boyds Mills Press 2005 unp il $15.95   E

1. Automobiles—Fiction 2. Animals—Fiction
ISBN 1-59078-270-4   LC 2005020113

"Rabbit, driving his purple convertible to town, picks up Mole, Squirrel, Porcupine, Possum, Beaver, Crow, Skunk, Fox, and Cow. As each animal climbs into the old junker, something else goes amiss with it. . . . Simple, rhythmic text with plenty of action words and lively pastel illustrations make this a good choice for sharing aloud with preschoolers." SLJ

Aruego, Jose

The last laugh; [by] Jose Aruego & Ariane Dewey. Dial Books for Young Readers 2006 unp il $12.99   E

1. Snakes—Fiction 2. Ducks—Fiction 3. Stories without words
ISBN 0-8037-3093-4   LC 2005-48461

A wordless tale in which a clever duck outwits a bullying snake.

"In comic-strip panels, Aruego and Deweys signature pen-and-ink and gouache art is droll and accessible. . . . Young readers will find the format and the karmic justice of this story appealing." SLJ

Asch, Frank

Baby Bird's first nest. Harcourt Brace & Co. 1999 unp il $15   E

1. Birds—Fiction 2. Frogs—Fiction
ISBN 0-15-201726-7   LC 97-32653
"Gulliver books"

When Baby Bird takes a tumble from her mama's nest in the middle of the night, she finds a friend in Little Frog.

"A satisfying read-aloud with just enough adventure, wit, and common sense to engage listeners and vocabulary easy enough for beginning readers. . . . Asch's trademark pen-and-ink drawings have been 'colorized' in Adobe Photoshop. The technique is very effective with deep, rich color fading to lighter shades." SLJ

Baby Duck's new friend; [by] Frank Asch and Devin Asch. Harcourt 2001 unp il $15   E

1. Ducks—Fiction
ISBN 0-15-202257-0   LC 00-8189
"Gulliver books"

Baby Duck follows a rubber ducky down waterfalls, through the woods, and far away from home, not realizing that he will have to find his own way back

"Baby Duck's adventures are told with delightful, subtle humor in both the text and illustrations." Horn Book guide

Barnyard lullaby. Simon & Schuster Bks. for Young Readers 1998 unp il music $15   E

1. Domestic animals—Fiction 2. Lullabies 3. Bedtime—Fiction
ISBN 0-689-81363-5   LC 96-44987

Although the farmer only hears animal noises, when the different barnyard animals sing lullabies to their respective children, the babies understand the words. Includes music.

"Soothing lullabies combine with the deep evening palette of Asch's trademark illustrations to make this a comforting bedtime read." Horn Book Guide

Like a windy day; [by] Frank Asch & Devin Asch. Harcourt 2002 unp il $15   E

1. Winds—Fiction
ISBN 0-15-216376-X   LC 2001-5260
"Gulliver books"

A young girl discovers all the things the wind can do, by playing and dancing along with it

Written "in a poetic text. . . . The brief story is filled with action verbs. . . . The exciting pen-and-ink illustrations were colorized in Adobe Photoshop. Broad and sweeping spreads are filled with movement." SLJ

Moonbear's dream. Simon & Schuster Bks. for Young Readers 1999 unp il $15   E

1. Bears—Fiction 2. Birds—Fiction 3. Dreams—Fiction
ISBN 0-689-82244-8   LC 98-24133

When Moonbear and his friend Little Bird see a kangaroo in the backyard, they think they must be dreaming, so they do things they would not do if they were awake.

"Asch's familiar restrained illustrations . . . neatly reflect the story's understated humor and the beloved silliness of Moonbear's world." Booklist

Other titles in this series are:
Good night Baby Bear (1998)
Goodbye house (1985)
Happy birthday, Moon (1982)
Just like Daddy (1981)
Moonbear's pet (1997)
Mooncake (1983)
Moondance (1993)
Moongame (1984)

Mr. Maxwell's mouse; written by Frank Asch; illustrated by Devin Asch. Kids Can Press 2004 unp il $15.95   E

1. Cats—Fiction 2. Mice—Fiction 3. Restaurants—Fiction
ISBN 1-55337-486-X

"An urbane, executive-level cat on his lunch break orders a live mouse . . . and finds himself in conversation with his entrée." Horn Book Guide

"Readers will relish the formal language as a tongue-in-cheek counterpoint to a very funny, if macabre, story. In keeping with the black humor, dark but lush illustrations, rendered in Adobe Photoshop and Corel Painter, depict an Edwardian setting." SLJ

Asch, Frank—*Continued*

The sun is my favorite star. Harcourt 2001 unp il $15   E
    1. Sun—Fiction
    ISBN 0-15-202127-2   LC 98-46383
    "Guilliver books"
    Celebrates a child's love of the sun and the wondrous ways in which it helps the earth and the life upon it
    "Asch strikes just the right tone for his audience. . . . With colors as warm as a summer day, he creates a series of large-scale illustrations that reflect the direct unaffected tone of the writing." Booklist

Ashman, Linda

Babies on the go; illustrated by Jane Dyer. Harcourt 2003 unp il $16   E
    1. Animal babies 2. Animal locomotion
    ISBN 0-15-201894-8   LC 2002-6310
    Illustrations and rhyming text show how different animals carry their babies when they are on the move
    "The large, soft watercolor illustrations and rhyming text make this celebration of parent/child love a natural for toddler storytime, and it's also perfect for one-on-one sharing." SLJ

Castles, caves, and honeycombs; illustrated by Lauren Stringer. Harcourt 2001 unp il $16   E
    1. Home 2. Animals—Habitations 3. Stories in rhyme
    ISBN 0-15-202211-2   LC 99-50801
    Describes some of the unique places where animals build their homes such as in a heap of twigs, on a castle tower, in a cave, or in the hollow space inside a tree
    "The concise text and womb-like illustrations convey the feelings of love, safety, and security that a home should have." Horn Book Guide

Mama's day; [by] Linda Ashman; [illustrated by] Jan Ormerod. 1st ed. Simon & Schuster Books for Young Readers 2006 unp il $15.95   E
    1. Mother-child relationship—Fiction 2. Stories in rhyme
    ISBN 0-689-83475-6   LC 00-45063
    In rhyming text, mothers and their babies are described sharing in a variety of activities, from playing at the ocean to reading books and taking a bath.
    "Ashman's skillful verse and Ormerod's cozy ink-and-gouache artwork improve upon many other picture-book fulminations on mother love. A lilting line of verse appears on each spread, illustrated by a neatly framed scene of a different mother-child pair (including a demure image of breastfeeding) as well as a crew of charming, multicultural babies." Booklist

To the beach! illustrated by Nadine Bernard Westcott. Harcourt 2005 unp il $16   E
    1. Family life—Fiction 2. Beaches—Fiction
    ISBN 0-15-216490-1   LC 2003-19444
    A family keeps forgetting the things they need to take to the beach
    "Rhyming text and bouncy and boldly colored illustrations in acrylic on watercolor paper capture the frenzy surrounding this hilarious . . . family. A rip-roaring fun read-aloud." SLJ

Atwell, Debby

Barn; written and illustrated by Debby Atwell. Houghton Mifflin 1996 unp il $15.95   E
    ISBN 0-395-78568-5   LC 96-11044
    Follows the life of a country barn from the late eighteenth-century to the present day
    "The charming folk-art-style paintings complement the text perfectly and give added meaning to this unusual and warm story about the rhythms of time and our own haunting continuity with the past." Booklist

The Thanksgiving door. Houghton Mifflin 2003 31p il $15   E
    1. Thanksgiving Day—Fiction 2. Immigrants—Fiction
    ISBN 0-618-24036-5   LC 2002-414
    "Walter Lorraine books"
    After burning their Thanksgiving dinner, Ann and Ed head for the local cafe, where they are welcomed by an immigrant family into an unusual celebration that gives everyone cause to be thankful
    "Atwell's luminous folk-art illustrations expand the story through details such as Russian onion domes in a picture on the wall, fur hats on the men, scarves on the women. . . . A fine addition to holiday collections and for those looking for immigrant stories." SLJ

Auch, Mary Jane

Bantam of the opera; written and illustrated by Mary Jane Auch. Holiday House 1997 unp il $17.95   E
    1. Singers—Fiction 2. Opera—Fiction 3. Roosters—Fiction
    ISBN 0-8234-1312-8   LC 96-40169
    Luigi the rooster wins fame and fortune when the star of the Cosmopolitan Opera Company and his understudy both come down with chicken pox on the same night
    "The brightly colored illustrations capture the exaggerated humor of the text." Booklist

Peeping Beauty; written and illustrated by Mary Jane Auch. Holiday House 1993 unp il $16.95; pa $6.95   E
    1. Chickens—Fiction 2. Ballet—Fiction
    ISBN 0-8234-1001-3; 0-8234-1170-2 (pa)
                                  LC 92-16374
    Poulette the dancing hen falls into the clutches of a hungry fox, who exploits her desire to become a great ballerina
    "The language is lively, and filled with witty phrases and ballet references. Using bright colors and just enough detail, Auch sets her cast of characters against a simple backdrop." SLJ
    Another title about Poulette is:
    Hen Lake (1995)

Avi

Silent movie; Avi, the author; C.B. Mordan, the illustrator. Atheneum Bks. for Young Readers 2002 unp il $16.95   E
    1. Immigrants—Fiction 2. Silent films—Fiction
    ISBN 0-689-84145-0   LC 2001-33025
    "An Anne Schwartz book"

Avi—*Continued*

In the early years of the twentieth century, a Swedish family encounters separation and other hardships upon immigrating to New York City until the son is cast in a silent movie, in a picture book that evokes an actual silent movie

"Clear, beautiful ink-on-clayboard illustrations; white type on thick, glossy black paper; and cinematic lighting effects combine to evoke the historical period." Booklist

Aylesworth, Jim

The full belly bowl; illustrated by Wendy Halperin. Atheneum Bks. for Young Readers 1998 unp il $16.95   E

1. Fairy tales

ISBN 0-689-81033-4   LC 98-14052

In return for the kindness he showed a wee small man, a very old man is given a magical bowl that causes problems when it is not used properly

"From the dainty pictures on the endpapers to the stunning artwork inside, this book is a feast for the eyes. The story . . . is just as good, smoothly blending folktale conventions with touches of magic and a dusting of comedy." Booklist

Old black fly; illustrations by Stephen Gammell. Holt & Co. 1992 unp il $16.95; pa $6.95   E

1. Flies—Fiction 2. Alphabet 3. Stories in rhyme

ISBN 0-8050-1401-2; 0-8050-3924-4 (pa)

LC 91-26825

Rhyming text and illustrations follow a mischievous old black fly through the alphabet as he has a very busy bad day landing where he should not be

Aylesworth's "snappy couplets constitute a waggish presentation of a basic concept. . . . Gammell's paintings are exuberant splashes of mayhem—rainbows of splattered hues from which truly memorable characters emerge. His appropriately bug-eyed (and cross-eyed) fly and gap-toothed humans sporting crazy hairdos provide a level of dementia that children will relish." Publ Wkly

Azarian, Mary

A farmer's alphabet. Godine 1981 61p il $19.95; pa $14.95   E

1. Alphabet 2. Farm life

ISBN 0-87923-394-X; 0-87923-397-4 (pa)

LC 80-84938

"Large, bold woodcuts make up an album of farming scenes obviously from New England—for example, 'M' is for maple sugar. A few scenes look cold and stern—showing winter and icicles—but there are children jumping in hay and flying a kite as well as . . . 'N' for neighbor and 'G' for a garden bursting with vegetables." Horn Book

A gardener's alphabet. Houghton Mifflin 2000 unp il $16; pa $5.95   E

1. Alphabet 2. Gardening

ISBN 0-618-03380-7; 0-618-54881-5 (pa)

LC 99-44242

An alphabet book featuring words associated with gardening, including bulbs, compost, digging, insects, and weeds

"The stunning black wood-cuts, hand tinted with strong watercolors, are full of action and detail." SLJ

Bahrampour, Ali

Otto, the story of a mirror. Farrar, Straus & Giroux 2003 unp il $16   E

1. Mirrors—Fiction 2. Voyages and travels—Fiction

ISBN 0-374-27078-3   LC 00-64628

Tired of reflecting the customers at Mr. Topper's Hat Store, Otto manages to escape and have the adventures he had always dreamed of having

"The unique protagonist and appealing cartoon illustrations will pique the interest of young readers. Numerous details reward the observant." SLJ

Baicker, Karen

You can do it too! illustrations by Ken Wilson-Max. Handprint 2005 24p $13.95

E

1. Siblings—Fiction

ISBN 1-59354-080-9

"An affectionate older sister encourages her brother to follow her lead in games from morning 'til night in this bright, appealing offering. . . . The short, direct rhymes, printed in a large, energetic black font, scan smoothly, and Wilson-Max's textured paintings, colored in rich, bright hues and accented with thick black lines, keep the focus on the palpable warmth between the siblings and the everyday images from a child's multicultural world." Booklist

Another title about these characters is:

I can do it too (2003)

Baker, Barbara

Anna shares; pictures by Catharine O'Neill. Dutton Children's Books 2004 unp il $8.99

E

ISBN 0-525-47111-1   LC 2003-55718

When Justin comes to play with Anna, her mother tries to teach her how to share.

"O'Neill's breezy ink drawings, brightened with washes in cheerful hues, contribute to the [story's] simple narrative appeal and visual charm." Booklist

Another title about Anna published in 2004 is:

Anna's book

Digby and Kate and the beautiful day; pictures by Marsha Winborn. Dutton Children's Bks. 1998 48p il $13.99   E

1. Dogs—Fiction 2. Cats—Fiction

ISBN 0-525-45855-7

Digby the dog and Kate the cat disagree about many things but they remain best friends

"The artwork . . . together with the cheerful stories make up good, light fare for beginning readers." Horn Book Guide

Other titles about Digby and Kate are:

Digby and Kate (1988)

Digby and Kate 1 2 3 (2004)

Digby and Kate again (1989)

Baker, Jeannie

Home. Greenwillow Books 2004 unp il $15.99; lib bdg $16.09   E
1. Stories without words 2. City and town life
ISBN 0-06-623935-4; 0-06-623934-6 (lib bdg)
LC 2003-49287
A wordless picture book that observes the changes in a neighborhood from before a girl is born until she is an adult, as it first decays and then is renewed by the efforts of the residents
"Baker uses natural materials to create detailed, arresting collages that tell a story in which words are superfluous. Children can pore over these pages again and again and make fresh discoveries with each perusal." SLJ

Where the forest meets the sea; story and pictures by Jeannie Baker. Greenwillow Bks. 1988 c1987 unp il $16   E
1. Australia—Fiction 2. Rain forests—Fiction
ISBN 0-688-06363-2   LC 87-7551
First published 1987 in the United Kingdom
On a camping trip in an Australian rain forest with his father, a young boy thinks about the history of the plant and animal life around him and wonders about their future
The illustrations "are relief collages 'constructed from a multitude of materials, including modeling clay, papers, textured materials, preserved natural materials, and paints.' Integrated by the artist's vision, the collages create three-dimensional effects on two-dimensional pages drawing the reader into each scene as willing observer and explorer." Horn Book

Window. Greenwillow Bks. 1991 unp il lib bdg $16.89   E
1. Stories without words 2. Human ecology—Fiction 3. Australia—Fiction
ISBN 0-688-08918-6   LC 90-3922
"The story in this wordless book is told through the outdoor scene viewed over time from one child's bedroom window. Initially, a mother holding her infant son gazes out at the lush Australian bush; as the boy gets older, civilization swallows up the wilderness." Horn Book Guide
"Filled with marvelous detail, the textured collages make an affecting statement about the erosion of the planet Earth." SLJ

Baker, Keith

Little Green. Harcourt 2001 unp il $16
     E
1. Hummingbirds—Fiction 2. Stories in rhyme
ISBN 0-15-292859-6   LC 99-50831
A young boy paints the flight of a hummingbird as it zips, loops, and zigzags around his garden
"Filled with simple, active words and printed in large type suitable for beginning readers, the rhyming text captures the bird's exciting energy, which is extended in Baker's bright collage pictures." Booklist

The magic fan; written and illustrated by Keith Baker. Harcourt Brace Jovanovich 1989 unp il $16; pa $8   E
1. Japan—Fiction
ISBN 0-15-250750-7; 0-15-200983-3 (pa)
LC 88-18727

Despite the laughter of his fellow villagers, Yoshi uses his building skills to make a boat to catch the moon, a kite to reach the clouds, and a bridge that mimics the rainbow
"The artwork, acrylics on illustration board, is framed within the outline of an open fan. The text appears outside this frame, and fan-shaped die-cuts allow the reader to turn the inner page and see a second picture on each double-page spread. . . . An entertaining tale as well as an elegant addition to the picture-book shelf." Booklist

Meet Mr. and Mrs. Green. Harcourt 2004 71p il $16; pa $5.95   E
1. Alligators—Fiction
ISBN 0-15-204954-1; 0-15-204955-X (pa)
LC 2001-1955
First published 2002
A loving alligator couple enjoy going camping, eating pancakes, and visiting the county fair
"The acrylic illustrations have a loud, oversized presence that is complemented by the strong text." SLJ
Other titles about Mr. and Mrs. Green are:
Lucky days with Mr. and Mrs. Green (2005)
More Mr. and Mrs. Green (2004)
On the go with Mr. and Mrs. Green (2006)

Quack and count. Harcourt Brace & Co. 1999 unp il $15; pa $6   E
1. Addition 2. Ducks 3. Counting
ISBN 0-15-292858-8; 0-15-205025-6 (pa)
LC 98-7924
"Seven uniquely marked ducklings slide, chase bees, and play peekaboo as they group on double-spread pages to illustrate ways to add up to their sum. . . . Jaunty scenes in cut-paper collage with a gracious array of colors offer plenty of extras." SLJ

Baker, Leslie

You bad dog! Dutton Children's Bks. 2003 unp il $15.99   E
1. Dogs—Fiction
ISBN 0-5254-7127-8
"All Bridget the Rottweiler wants is to be left alone so she can 'practice her snoozing.' But along comes trouble in the form of Lulu, a sparkplug of a pup." Publ Wkly
"The simple, child-friendly text consists of no more than three short sentences per page. Baker's winsome representations of rottweiler Bridget and terrier Lulu are rendered in smudgy, floodlit watercolors." SLJ

Balian, Lorna

Humbug witch; [by] Lorna Balian. Star Bright Books 2003 c1965 unp il $12.95   E
1. Witches—Fiction
ISBN 1-932065-32-6   LC 2003-16979
A reissue of the title first published 1965 by Abingdon Press
Despite looking the part, a little witch cannot seem to do the things that witches are supposed to do.
This is a "warm-hearted, conversational story. . . . [Illustrated with] friendly ink drawings in black, red, and yellow." Horn Book Guide

Ballard, Robin

My day, your day. Greenwillow Bks. 2001 unp
il $14.95   **E**

1. Day care centers—Fiction 2. Work—Fiction
ISBN 0-688-17796-4   LC 99-86462

Children have a busy day at day care while their parents have a busy day at work

"A happy calm pervades both the succinct text and warmly hued watercolor and ink drawings." Publ Wkly

Bang, Molly

Goose; written and illustrated by Molly Bang.
Blue Sky Press (NY) 1996 unp il $10.95
                                             E

1. Geese—Fiction
ISBN 0-590-89005-0   LC 95-47616

Adopted by woodchucks at birth, a baby goose never feels she truly belongs—until the day she discovers she can fly

"The telling is simple and lovely, not one word too many. . . . Bang's animals are exquisitely drawn, both fragile and sturdy." Booklist

The Grey Lady and the Strawberry Snatcher.
Four Winds Press 1980 unp il $16; pa $6.99
                                             E

1. Strawberries—Fiction 2. Stories without words
ISBN 0-02-708140-0; 0-689-80381-8 (pa)
                                  LC 79-21243

A Caldecott Medal honor book, 1981

The strawberry snatcher tries to wrest the strawberries from the grey lady but as he follows her through shops and woods he discovers some delicious blackberries instead

"Bang's illustrations are unparalleled in effects, full-color paintings and collages in which the surrealistic and the representational combine to tell a story without words." Publ Wkly

The paper crane. Greenwillow Bks. 1985 unp il
$16.99; pa $5.95   **E**

ISBN 0-688-04108-6; 0-688-07333-6 (pa)
                                  LC 84-13546

"Bang gives a modern setting and details to the consoling story of a good man, deprived by unlucky fate of his livelihood, whose act of kindness and generosity is repaid by the restoration of his fortunes, through the bringing to life of a magical animal—the paper crane." SLJ

"Every detail of the restaurant interior, from the strawberries on the cake to the floral centerpieces, is a delight to the eye and imagination. . . . The book successfully blends Asian folklore themes with contemporary Western characterization." Horn Book

Ten, nine, eight. Greenwillow Bks. 1983 unp il
$15.99; lib bdg $16.89; pa $5.99   **E**

1. Bedtime—Fiction 2. Counting
ISBN 0-688-00906-9; 0-688-00907-7 (lib bdg);
0-688-10480-0 (pa)   LC 81-20106

Also available Board book edition and Spanish language edition

A Caldecott Medal honor book, 1984

"In countdown style, the text of this counting book begins with '10 small toes all washed and warm,' and ends with '1 big girl all ready for bed.' The captions rhyme . . . and the pictures—warm, bright paintings—show a black father and child snuggling in a chair, the child yawning, and the child hugging her toy bear after some loving good night kisses." Bull Cent Child Books

When Sophie gets angry—really, really angry.
Blue Sky Press (NY) 1999 unp il $15.95
                                             E

1. Anger—Fiction
ISBN 0-590-18979-4   LC 97-42209

A Caldecott Medal honor book, 2000

"Sophie loses a tug-of-war altercation with her sister over a stuffed monkey, and her anger propels her out of the house and into an anger-reducing run. After running, crying, climbing a tree, and being soothed by the breeze, Sophie feels better and goes home, where everyone is happy to see her." Bull Cent Child Books

"The text is appropriately brief, for it is Bang's double-page illustrations, vibrating with saturated colors, that reveal the drama of the child's emotions." SLJ

Bang-Campbell, Monika

Little Rat sets sail; illustrated by Molly Bang.
Harcourt 2002 unp il $14; pa $5.95   **E**

1. Rats—Fiction 2. Sailing—Fiction
ISBN 0-15-216297-6; 0-15-204769-7 (pa)
                                  LC 2001-1959

With a little courage and a lot of practice, Little Rat overcomes her fear of sailing

The text shows "a remarkable understanding of childhood feelings. . . . Molly Bang's illustrations are both gorgeous and functional, saturated not only with color . . . but also with character and mood and narrative." Horn Book

Another title about Little Rat is:
Little Rat rides (2004)

Bania, Michael

Kumak's fish; a tall tale from the far north; by
Michael Bania. Alaska Northwest Books 2004 unp
il $15.95; pa $8.95   **E**

1. Inuit—Fiction 2. Fishing—Fiction 3. Arctic regions—Fiction
ISBN 0-88240-583-7; 0-88240-584-5 (pa)
                                  LC 2003-70852

On a beautiful Arctic morning when Kumak and his family go ice fishing, Kumak hooks what seems like an enormous fish, and the entire village gets involved.

"Joyful watercolor and pen-and-ink illustrations capture the . . . landscape and . . . the expressive faces of the . . . villagers. . . . This delightful blend of art and text brings the rich traditions and culture of the peoples of the Far North to life." SLJ

Another title about Kumak is:
Kumak's house (2002)

Banks, Kate

And if the moon could talk; pictures by Georg Hallensleben. Foster Bks. 1998 unp il $15
E

1. Bedtime—Fiction 2. Night—Fiction 3. Moon—Fiction

ISBN 0-374-30299-5   LC 97-29770

"Originally published in France"--page facing t.p

As evening progresses into nighttime, the moon looks down on a variety of nocturnal scenes, including a child getting ready for bed

"The deeply saturated tones of the lovely, impressionistic oil paintings perfectly match the somnolent feeling of the text." SLJ

Baboon; pictures by Georg Hallensleben. Farrar, Straus & Giroux 1997 unp il $14   E

1. Baboons—Fiction

ISBN 0-374-30474-2   LC 96-20888

"Frances Foster books"

Original French edition, 1994

"A baby baboon sees a forest and concludes that the world is green, but then his mother takes him farther afield. . . . Everything he encounters expands his understanding, and when night falls, he has seen with his own eyes that the world is a big and varied place." Publisher's note

"Visible brush-strokes give texture to the impressionistic paintings, and adept lighting evokes sunlight and shadow. The simple, eloquent text is as subtly understated." Horn Book Guide

The cat who walked across France; pictures by Georg Hallensleben. Farrar, Straus and Giroux 2004 unp il $16   E

1. Cats—Fiction 2. France—Fiction

ISBN 0-374-39968-9   LC 2002-25091

"Frances Foster Books"

After his owner dies, a cat wanders across the countryside of France, unable to forget the home he had in the stone house by the edge of the sea

"Banks uses simple, lovely words to tell the elemental story of an outcast's journey home. . . . The paintings are exquisite . . . but what kids will like best is the cat's adventure and the loving welcome he receives." Booklist

Close your eyes; pictures by Georg Hallensleben. Foster Bks. 2002 unp il $16
E

1. Tigers—Fiction 2. Dreams—Fiction 3. Sleep—Fiction

ISBN 0-374-31382-2   LC 99-46430

A mother tiger entices her child to sleep by telling of all that can been seen with one's eyes closed

"Banks' language will delight young children with its delicious rhythms, patterned sounds, and the mystery in the poetic imagery. . . . Hallensleben's thick, expressive brush strokes occasionally blur shapes and details, but the vividly colored dreamscapes . . . will capture young imaginations and reassure children who . . . harbor secret fears of falling asleep." Booklist

A gift from the sea; pictures by Georg Hallensleben. Foster Bks. 2001 unp il $16
E

1. Rocks—Fiction

ISBN 0-374-32566-9   LC 00-26503

Unaware of its eons-old history, a boy finds a rock and takes it home to a shelf beside his sea glass and starfish

"Banks uses graceful and rhythmic language that hums with the sense and sound of the words." Booklist

The great blue house; pictures by Georg Hallensleben. 1st ed. Farrar Straus Giroux 2005 unp il $16   E

1. Houses—Fiction 2. Seasons—Fiction

ISBN 0-374-32769-6   LC 2003-54886

"Frances Foster books"

When its owners leave, a summer house comes alive with the sounds of a mouse nibbling crumbs in the fall, a cat taking shelter in the winter, and rain falling on the roof in the spring.

"In spare, poetic sentences, Banks' precise sounds and cyclical rhythms amplify the hypnotic sensory impressions. . . . Hallensleben's beautiful, thickly brushed, impressionistic paintings evoke a sense of noise and life in rooms painted shocking blue and rich, bright red." Booklist

The night worker; pictures by Georg Hallensleben. Farrar, Straus & Giroux 2000 unp il $16   E

1. Night—Fiction 2. Work—Fiction 3. Building—Fiction

ISBN 0-374-35520-7   LC 99-27595

"Frances Foster books"

Alex wants to be a "night worker" like his father who goes to work at a construction site after Alex goes to bed

"Banks' elegant, simple words and poetic images and rhythms evoke the book's exciting activity and the secure comfort Alex feels with his father. With thick brush strokes and deep, satisfying primary and earth colors, Hallensleben's paintings extend the story's balance of exhilarating intensity and reassuring calm." Booklist

Bannerman, Helen

The story of Little Babaji; illustrated by Fred Marcellino. HarperCollins Pubs. 1996 unp il $16.99; pa $7.95   E

1. India—Fiction 2. Tigers—Fiction

ISBN 0-06-205064-8; 0-06-008093-0 (pa)

"Michael di Capua books"

In this edition of the Story of Little Black Sambo, originally published 1899, the characters have been given Indian names

Babaji gives his new clothing to tigers who threaten to eat him, but they chase one another around a tree until they turn to butter

"Marcellino has set the story of Little Black Sambo in India. . . . Except for a change of names . . . Bannerman's text is essentially unaltered, retaining the narrative rhythm that has always paced a tightly patterned plot. Marcellino's watercolor paintings project a toy-like quality that emphasizes humor over suspense." Bull Cent Child Books

Bányai, István

The other side. Chronicle Books 2005 unp il $15.95   E

1. Stories without words

ISBN 0-8118-4608-3   LC 2004-63448

Bányai, István—*Continued*

"Banyai explores the concept of 'the other side' through visual vignettes offering contrasting perspectives on dreamlike scenarios, often revealing previously hidden information that significantly alters how a scene is perceived." Booklist

"This is a challenging book, one that allows for creative speculation. The graphite-rendered artwork is quirky as well as infinitely interesting." SLJ

Zoom. Viking 1995 unp il $16.99; pa $6.99
         E
1. Stories without words
ISBN 0-670-85804-8; 0-14-055774-1 (pa)
         LC 94-33181
Also available Re-zoom (1995)
A wordless picture book presents a series of scenes, each one from farther away, showing, for example, a girl playing with toys which is actually a picture on a magazine cover, which is part of a sign on a bus, and so on

"If the concept is not wholly new, the execution is superior. Readers are in for a perpetually surprising—and even philosophical—adventure." Publ Wkly

Barasch, Lynne

A country schoolhouse; [by] Lynne Barasch. 1st ed. Farrar, Straus and Giroux 2004 unp il $16
         E
1. School stories 2. Grandfathers—Fiction
ISBN 0-374-31577-9   LC 2002-40759
"Frances Foster books"
A grandfather relates to his grandson tales of the small country school he attended in the 1940s.

"The watercolor-and-ink illustrations create a solid sense of time and place. This gentle story unfolds nicely, captivating children and raising intriguing questions about the effectiveness of a 'country school' education." SLJ

Radio rescue. Farrar, Straus & Giroux 2000 unp il $16
         E
1. Amateur radio stations—Fiction 2. Cipher and telegraph codes—Fiction
ISBN 0-374-36166-5   LC 99-22384
"Frances Foster books"
In 1923, after learning Morse code and setting up his own amateur radio station, a twelve-year-old boy sends a message that leads to the rescue of a family stranded by a hurricane in Florida. Based on experiences of the author's father

"In a well-designed mix of insets, brief sketches, and full-page drawings, the author's uncluttered color cartoons do an excellent job of illustrating the technology and the code, at the same time creating likeable, expressive characters." Booklist

The reluctant flower girl; story and pictures by Lynne Barasch. HarperCollins Pubs. 2001 unp il $14.95; lib bdg $14.89
         E
1. Sisters—Fiction 2. Weddings—Fiction
ISBN 0-06-028809-4; 0-06-028810-8 (lib bdg)
         LC 00-61352
"Saddened at the prospect of seeing her older sister (and best friend) Annabel get married and leave home,

April does everything she can to sabotage the big day." Publ Wkly

"Appealing cartoon illustrations wedded with the light-hearted text make for a satisfying story." SLJ

Barbour, Karen

Mr. Williams. 1st ed. Henry Holt and Co 2005 29p il $16.95   E
1. African Americans 2. Louisiana 3. Country life
ISBN 0-8050-6773-6   LC 2004-22182
"Recounting stories told by J. W. Williams, a friend of her mother's, Barbour captures the essence of a black Louisiana farmer's life in the early 20th century. . . . The words are succinct but evocative of a larger picture. . . . The ink-and-gouache illustrations, punctuated with well-placed bits of fabric collage, are perfect." SLJ

Barner, Bob

Bug safari; [by] Bob Barner. 1st ed. Holiday House 2004 unp il $16.95   E
1. Insects—Fiction 2. Ants—Fiction
ISBN 0-8234-1707-7   LC 2003-56619
"A young explorer describes his experiences as he tracks an army of ants through 'a bug-infested jungle,' observing their progress through a magnifying glass." SLJ

"The bright, cut-paper collages will appeal to the youngest bug lovers, but the funny, dramatically told story is tailored to a more sophisticated young entomologist." Booklist

Fish wish. Holiday House 2000 unp il $16.95; pa $6.95   E
1. Coral reefs and islands—Fiction
ISBN 0-8234-1482-5; 0-82341-663-1 (pa)
         LC 99-44491
A young boy's dream sends him on an underwater journey through a coral reef. Includes factual information on coral reefs and the animals that live in them

"The impressive collage illustrations combine pieces of torn, cut, and sometimes painted papers with found objects and bits of fabric. Bold forms and striking color combinations give the double-page spreads a vibrant sense of place and motion." Booklist

Barracca, Debra

The adventures of Taxi Dog; by Debra and Sal Barracca; pictures by Mark Buehner. Dial Bks. for Young Readers 1990 30p il $16.99; pa $5.99
         E
1. Dogs—Fiction 2. Stories in rhyme
ISBN 0-8037-0671-5; 0-14-056665-1 (pa)
         LC 89-1056
"In snappy, rhymed lines, Maxi recalls his days as a stray and his adoption by taxi-driving Jim. Applying oil paint over acrylics, Buehner creates color with lush character. The hues' intense depth, coupled with the artist's finesse with perspective, will draw readers into the action." Booklist

Other titles about Maxi, the Taxi Dog are:
Maxi, the hero (1991)
Maxi, the star (1993)
A Taxi Dog Christmas (1994)

Barron, T. A.

High as a hawk; a brave girl's historic climb; illustrated by Ted Lewin. Philomel Books 2004 unp il $16.99   E
    1. Mills, Enos, 1870-1922—Fiction
2. Mountaineering—Fiction 3. Colorado—Fiction
    ISBN 0-399-23704-6   LC 2003-12405
In 1905, eight-year-old Harriet Peters fulfills her dead mother's dream by climbing Long's Peak in Colorado with the help of an old mountain guide, Enos Mills.
"This poignant tale, based on a true story, is retold in lyrical language and accompanied by dazzling watercolors." SLJ

Where is Grandpa? illustrated by Chris K. Soentpiet. Philomel Bks. 2000 unp il $15.99; pa $6.99   E
    1. Grandfathers—Fiction 2. Death—Fiction
    ISBN 0-399-23037-8; 0-698-11904-5 (pa)
    LC 97-29549
As his family reminisces after his beloved grandfather's death, a boy realizes that his grandfather is still with him in all the special places they shared
"The reassuring message is fitting, and the realistic watercolors are suitably expressive and luminous." Horn Book Guide

Barroux, Stephane

Where's Mary's hat? [by] Barroux. Viking 2003 unp il $15.99   E
    1. Animals—Fiction 2. Hats—Fiction
    ISBN 0-670-03601-3   LC 2002-152341
When Mary the cow cannot find her favorite hat, she asks one animal after another, but no one has seen it
"The brightly colored acrylic artwork complements this delightfully understated story to a tee. Many of the stylized illustrations have clever details and are quite humorous." SLJ

Barry, Frances

Duckie's ducklings; a one-to-ten counting book. Candlewick 2005 unp il $7.99   E
    1. Counting 2. Ducks—Fiction
    ISBN 0-7636-2514-0
Duckie is ready to take the family for a swim. But where are her ducklings? Turn the shaped pages to find out!
"Barry's uncluttered paper collages are excellent. The elemental shapes and vivid, saturated colors nicely fit the book's handsome design." Booklist

Bartoletti, Susan Campbell

Nobody's diggier than a dog; illustrated by Beppe Giacobbe. Hyperion 2005 unp il $15.99
    E
    1. Dogs—Fiction
    ISBN 0-7868-1824-7
"Bouncy, alliterative phrases describe the characteristics of all kinds of canines in this humorous ode to man's best friend. . . . The short verses are just right for sharing aloud with young children and easy enough for beginning readers to handle on their own. . . . Done in flat colors, the cartoon artwork features many different breeds engaged in a variety of activities." SLJ

Barton, Byron

Bones, bones, dinosaur bones. Crowell 1990 unp il $16.99   E
    1. Dinosaurs 2. Fossils
    ISBN 0-690-04825-4   LC 89-71306
"From the field search for dinosaur bones to reconstructed skeletons for museum display, paleontology as process is revealed in simple text, bold print, and flat illustrations with heavy, black outlines. Includes labeled illustrations of eight dinosaurs." Sci Child

Dinosaurs, dinosaurs. Crowell 1989 unp il $15.95; lib bdg $15.89; pa $5.95   E
    1. Dinosaurs
    ISBN 0-694-00269-0; 0-690-04768-1 (lib bdg); 0-06-443298-X (pa)   LC 88-22938
Also available Big book edition and Board book edition
This book examines the many different kinds of dinosaurs, big and small, those with spikes and those with long, sharp teeth
"Barton conveys the primordial sense of excitement that draws children to these beasts. . . . The endpapers identify the creatures by scientific name and pronunciation. Barton wisely keeps his text simple, describing dinosaurs only by size and physical features." SLJ

My car. Greenwillow Bks. 2001 unp il $14.95; lib bdg $14.89   E
    1. Automobiles—Fiction
    ISBN 0-06-029624-0; 0-06-029625-9 (lib bdg)
    LC 00-50334
Sam describes in loving detail his car and how he drives it
"The chunky blocks of color and minimalist text will withstand countless readings." Publ Wkly

Bartone, Elisa

Peppe the lamplighter; illustrations by Ted Lewin. Lothrop, Lee & Shepard Bks. 1993 unp il $16.99; lib bdg $16.89; pa $5.99   E
    1. Italian Americans—Fiction 2. New York (N.Y.)—Fiction
    ISBN 0-688-10268-9; 0-688-10269-7 (lib bdg); 0-688-15469-7 (pa)   LC 92-1397
A Caldecott Medal honor book, 1994
Peppe's father is upset when he learns that Peppe has taken a job lighting the gas street lamps in his New York City neighborhood
"Peppe's quiet quest for familial respect and pleasure in his work is touching and rhythmically written. The early-American city scenes are dark but have a nice period luminescence in the myriad street and table lamps, and the earth-toned watercolors lend the bustling streets and interiors of Little Italy an air both somber and lively." Bull Cent Child Books

Bass, L. G.

A three hat day; [by] Laura Geringer; pictures by Arnold Lobel. Harper & Row 1985 30p il lib bdg $15.89; pa $5.99   E
    1. Hats—Fiction
    ISBN 0-06-021989-0 (lib bdg); 0-06-443157-6 (pa)
    LC 85-42640

Bass, L. G.—*Continued*

This "is about R.R. Pottle the Third, an inveterate collector of hats. Wearing one at a time usually suits him, but on days when he is depressed, he wears three all at once. It is on such a day that he meets Ida, the shop clerk, and not long after, R.R. Pottle the Fourth is born—an inveterate collector of shoes." Wilson Libr Bull

"Lobel's energetic line drawings with warm, full-color washes contribute their own dignity and humor to the characters. . . . With its light touch, good pacing, and satisfying symmetry, this is a pleasing choice to read aloud." Booklist

Bateman, Teresa

April foolishness; illustrated by Nadine Bernard Westcott. Albert Whitman & Co 2004 unp il $15.95　　　　E

1. April Fools' Day—Fiction 2. Farm life—Fiction 3. Stories in rhyme
ISBN 0-8075-0404-1　　　　LC 2004-825

"Grandpa thinks he's wise to his grandchildren's April Fools' Day tricks and ignores their warnings of animals run amok." SLJ

"Bateman's verse prances along in a pleasing way, never sounding a false note or tripping over its metric feet. Bright with colorful washes, Westcott's ink drawings illustrate the action with equal lightness and grace. . . . Zany and inventive, the artwork amplifies the story's humor." Booklist

The Bully Blockers Club; illustrated by Jackie Urbanovic. Albert Whitman & Co 2004 unp il $15.95　　　　E

1. School stories
ISBN 0-8075-0918-3　　　　LC 2004-524

When Lottie is bothered by a bully at school, she helps start a club where everyone is welcome.

"Although this story is purposeful, it is told with humor and drama. The illustrations are colorful and engaging." SLJ

Farm flu; illustrated by Nadine Bernard Westcott. Whitman, A. 2001 unp il lib bdg $15.95　　　　E

1. Influenza—Fiction 2. Domestic animals—Fiction 3. Stories in rhyme
ISBN 0-8075-2274-0　　　　LC 00-8158

When the farm animals seem to catch the flu one after another, a young boy does his best to take care of them

"A humorous rhyming story that's as much fun to look at as it is to read. . . . Westcott's lively illustrations add comedic touches throughout." SLJ

Harp o' gold; illustrated by Jill Weber. Holiday House 2001 unp il $16.95　　　　E

1. Fairy tales
ISBN 0-8234-1523-6　　　　LC 99-18821

A poor musician who dreams of riches and fame trades his beloved but worn harp for one made of gold, but when he becomes famous he finds that something is missing

"Acrylic paintings rendered in a blue-green palette with flat tilty perspectives complement this bittersweet cautionary tale set in an Irish-looking countryside." Horn Book Guide

Bates, Katharine Lee

America the beautiful; illustrated by Chris Gall. Little, Brown 2004 unp il $16.95　　　　E

1. United States—Poetry 2. Songs—United States
ISBN 0-316-73743-7　　　　LC 2003-54552

"Megan Tingley books"

Four verses of the nineteenth-century poem later set to music, illustrated by the author's great-great-grandnephew

"Children will be stirred by Gall's pictures. Using hand engraving on clay-covered board and enhancing elements such as color with a computer, he offers a series of pictures resembling woodcuts in form and WPA paintings in style." Booklist

Bauer, Marion Dane

Jason's bears; illustrated by Kevin Hawkes. Hyperion Bks. for Children 2000 unp il $14.99
　　　　E

1. Bears—Fiction
ISBN 0-7868-0356-8　　　　LC 98-52968

Jason's enthusiasm for bears is dampened when his big brother tells him that they are going to eat him up

"Richly colored, humorous acrylic paintings show Jason overcoming his fears with his own bravery in this good read-aloud choice." Horn Book Guide

Bayer, Jane

A my name is Alice; pictures by Steven Kellogg. Dial Bks. for Young Readers 1984 unp il $16.99; pa $6.99　　　　E

1. Stories in rhyme 2. Alphabet
ISBN 0-8037-0123-3; 0-14-054668-5 (pa)
　　　　LC 84-7059

"Each page contains (in the border above the illustration) the name of an animal ('A my name is Alice') and its spouse ('and my husband's name is Alex.'), their locale ('We come from Alaska') and occupation ('and we sell ants.'). Two sentences appear beneath the illustrations on each page identifying the kind of animals in the verse (Alice is an 'Ape.' Alex is an 'Anteater.')." SLJ

"It is a superlative blend of visual and textual nonsense because the visual surprises keep the repetitive pattern in the text from becoming tedious. The verbal parts gradually expand in their ludicrousness, in their cataloging of zany characters and occupations." Wilson Libr Bull

Baylor, Byrd

Hawk, I'm your brother; illustrated by Peter Parnall. Scribner 1976 unp il lib bdg $17.95; pa $6.99　　　　E

1. Hawks—Fiction
ISBN 0-684-14571-5 (lib bdg); 0-689-71102-6 (pa)

A Caldecott Medal honor book, 1977

"Driven by the desire to fly, Rudy Soto steals a baby hawk from its nest in the hope that having a hawk as his 'brother' will somehow enable him to take flight. Seeing the hawk's frustration in confinement, the boy finally releases it." Interracial Books Child Bull

"In the poetic simplicity of the writing, Baylor echoes the quietness of the desert and she captures the essence

Baylor, Byrd—*Continued*

of the desert people's affinity for natural things. Both are reflected in Parnall's spacious illustrations, as clean and poetic as is the writing." Bull Cent Child Books

Beames, Margaret

Night cat; illustrated by Sue Hitchcock. Scholastic 2003 c2000 unp il $15.95   E

1. Cats—Fiction 2. Night—Fiction 3. Gardens—Fiction

ISBN 0-439-38576-8   LC 2002-75790

First published 2000 in New Zealand with title: Oliver in the garden

New Zealand ed. has title: Oliver in the garden

At first, Oliver the cat is excited about staying out all night in the fascinating garden, but then unexpected adventures leave him ready for his indoor cushion.

"Scenes of Oliver's nighttime playground coupled with his cat's-eye-view narration result in a hauntingly ambient picture book. Exquisite art design and painstaking attention to detail are evident." SLJ

Beard, Darleen Bailey

Twister; pictures by Nancy Carpenter. Farrar, Straus & Giroux 1999 unp il $16; pa $5.95

    E

1. Tornadoes—Fiction 2. Siblings—Fiction

ISBN 0-374-37977-7; 0-374-48014-1 (pa)

    LC 95-13862

"Lucille and her little brother, Natt, are partaking in the idle pleasures of summer when a storm blows up; when the storm throws a funnel cloud, Mama commands her brood out of their mobile home to safety in the storm cellar . . . while she goes in search of an elderly neighbor. . . . Lucille's present-tense first-person narration is unforcedly full of telling details that make the account immediate. . . . Carpenter's thick, smudgy pastels deftly convey the viscousness of summer air before a storm and the weight of the threatening skies and the inky cellar dark." Bull Cent Child Books

Bearden, Romare

Li'l Dan, the drummer boy; a Civil War story; foreword by Henry Louis Gates Jr. Simon & Schuster Bks. for Young Readers 2003 unp il $18.95   E

1. African Americans—Fiction 2. Drums—Fiction 3. United States—History—1861-1865, Civil War—Fiction

ISBN 0-689-86237-7   LC 2003-3548

When a company of black Union soldiers tells Li'l Dan that he is no longer a slave, he follows them, and uses his beloved drum to save them from attack

This "work by the renowned African-American artist is not to be missed. . . . Although the story is worthy in its own right, the 21 mixed-media paintings are the outstanding element here. With rich colors and bold black outlines, the dramatic art shows the influence of abstract expressionism. . . . On the accompanying CD, Maya Angelou's mellow voice and easy pace complement this beautiful, creative work." SLJ

Beaumont, Karen

Baby danced the polka; pictures by Jennifer Plecas. Dial Books for Young Readers 2004 unp il $12.99   E

1. Infants—Fiction

ISBN 0-8037-2587-6

"Mama and Papa put their baby down for a nap, but the youngster feels like dancing. Each time the adults set out to do a chore, Baby escapes the crib and boogie-woogies, cha-chas, or shooby-doobies with a different stuffed-animal companion." SLJ

"What a happy, rollicking baby. And what a rolling, rhythmic text. . . . The sprightly pen-and-watercolor artwork bears a very strong resemblance to the work of Helen Oxenbury." Booklist

Duck, duck, goose! a coyote's on the loose! illustrated by Jose Aruego and Ariane Dewey. HarperCollins Pub. 2004 unp il $15.95; lib bdg $16.89   E

1. Animals—Fiction 2. Stories in rhyme

ISBN 0-06-050802-7; 0-06-050804-3 (lib bdg)

    LC 2003-8734

Several farm animals try to evade a coyote that they think is dangerous.

"Aruego and Dewey use bold paints as varied as a child's imagination to color their comically rendered farmyard animals. A suspenseful romp that will strike a chord with children." SLJ

I ain't gonna paint no more! illustrated by David Catrow. Harcourt 2005 unp il $16

    E

1. Painting—Fiction 2. Stories in rhyme

ISBN 0-15-202488-3   LC 2003-27739

"To the tune of 'It Ain't Gonna Rain No More,' one creative kid floods his world with color, painting first the walls, then the ceiling, then HIMSELF!" Publisher's note

"Catrow splashes color all over, uses white space cleverly, and includes playful flourishes. . . . Elongated figures and exaggerated expressions match the silly tone of the story. . . . With rhymes that invite audience participation and scenes that draw the eye, this is a strong storytime choice." SLJ

Bechtold, Lisze

Edna's tale; written & illustrated by Lisze Bechtold. Houghton Mifflin 2001 unp il $15

    E

1. Cats—Fiction

ISBN 0-618-09164-5   LC 00-36945

Edna, a cat known for her beautiful tail, is in for a couple of surprises when she goes into the woods to meet the new cat in the neighborhood

"With bold, deep navy strokes outlining Edna and most objects, the bright gouache art will show up exceedingly well at story hours. Everything shimmers with movement and shines with fun in this witty, well-conceived offering." Booklist

Beck, Scott

Pepito the brave. Dutton Children's Bks. 2001
unp il $12.99   E
1. Birds—Fiction
ISBN 0-525-46524-3
A "red bird that is afraid of heights is faced with a
challenge when it comes time to leave his nest. Rather
than risk flying, Pepito sets off on a trek during which
he meets animals that inspire him to run, hop, swim, burrow, and climb." SLJ
"The book's flat, candy-colored illustrations are like
its plot: simple and sweet." Horn Book Guide

Bedford, David

The way I love you. Simon & Schuster Books
for Young Readers 2005 unp il $12.95   E
1. Dogs—Fiction
ISBN 0-689-87625-4   LC 2004-3964
First published 2004 in Australia with title: I love
A little girl celebrates all of the ways she loves her
puppy.
"Loose charcoal lines provide texture and motion,
while splashes of pastel-hued watercolors keep the pictures warm and cozy. . . . The simple language and
clean, colorful artwork make this book just right for the
youngest pet lovers." SLJ

Bell, Anthea

The Snow Queen; a fairy tale; by Hans
Christian Andersen; translated and adapted by
Anthea Bell; illustrated by Bernadette Watts.
North-South Bks. 1987 unp il $15.95; pa $7.95
       E
1. Andersen, Hans Christian, 1805-1875—Adaptations
2. Fairy tales
ISBN 1-55858-053-0; 1-55858-779-9 (pa)
       LC 87-1518
After the Snow Queen abducts her friend Kai, Gerda
sets out on a perilous and magical journey to find him
"The story is written with clarity and simplicity.
Watts' paintings are full of atmosphere, thoughtfully
composed, and likely to appeal to children." Booklist

Belle, Jennifer

Animal stackers; pictures by David McPhail.
Hyperion Books for Children 2005 unp il $15.99
       E
1. Alphabet 2. Animals
ISBN 0-7868-1834-4
"An acrostic, alphabet, and poetry book all rolled into
one. From Ant to Zebra, animals are presented in colorful single and double-page entries. The letters of the
creatures' names are arranged vertically
on the pages, and each one begins a line of poetry. The
verses are delightful, funny, and sweet. . . . The pictures
are filled with vibrant colors and amusing details and
have an old-fashioned quality that works well with the
tone of the text." SLJ

Belton, Sandra

Beauty, her basket; illustrated by Cozbi A.
Cabrera. Greenwillow Books 2004 unp il $15.99;
lib bdg $16.89   E
1. Gullahs—Fiction 2. African Americans—Fiction
3. Baskets—Fiction
ISBN 0-688-17821-9; 0-688-17822-7 (lib bdg)
       LC 2003-40599
While visiting her grandmother in the Sea Islands, a
young girl hears about her African heritage and learns to
weave a sea grass basket.
"Fullbleed illustrations in darkly brilliant acrylics float
and swirl across the page, complementing the lush, evocative tone of the text." SLJ

Pictures for Miss Josie; pictures by Benny
Andrews. Greenwillow Bks. 2003 40p il $16.99;
lib bdg $17.89   E
1. African Americans—Fiction
ISBN 0-688-17480-9; 0-688-17481-7 (lib bdg)
       LC 2002-6797
"Amistad"
When his father first takes him to meet Miss Josie, a
young boy is somewhat intimidated by her, but through
the coming years he comes to treasure her friendship and
support and passes on his love of her to his own son.
Based on the life of Josephine Carroll Smith
"The large, brightly colored folk paintings, done in oil
and collage, are in harmony with the quiet, lyrical narrative." SLJ

Bemelmans, Ludwig

Madeline; story and pictures by Ludwig
Bemelmans. Viking 1985 c1939 unp il $16.99; pa
$6.99   E
1. Paris (France)—Fiction 2. Stories in rhyme
ISBN 0-670-44580-0; 0-14-056439-X (pa)
Also available Big book edition
A Caldecott Medal honor book, 1940
A reissue of the title first published 1939 by Simon &
Schuster
"Madeline is a nonconformist in a regimented world—
a Paris convent school. This rhymed story tells how she
made an adventure out of having appendicitis." Hodges.
Books for Elem Sch Libr
Other titles about Madeline are:
Madeline and the bad hat (1957)
Madeline and the gypsies (1959)
Madeline in London (1961)
Madeline's Christmas (1985)
Madeline's rescue (1985)

Madeline's rescue; story and pictures by Ludwig
Bemelmans. Viking 1985 c1953 unp il $16.99; pa
$7.99   E
1. Dogs—Fiction 2. Paris (France)—Fiction 3. Stories
in rhyme
ISBN 0-670-44716-1; 0-14-056651-1 (pa)
Awarded the Caldecott Medal, 1954
First published 1953
A picture-story book with rhymed text about little
Madeline in Paris. This time she falls into the Seine and
is rescued by 'a dog that kept its head.' The dog, named
Genevieve, was promptly adopted by Madeline's board-

Bemelmans, Ludwig—_Continued_

ing school mistress and her twelve pupils. When Genevieve was turned out by snobbish trustees the little girls
were inconsolable, until Genevieve solved their problem

Benchley, Nathaniel

A ghost named Fred; pictures by Ben Shecter.
Harper & Row 1968 unp il lib bdg $16.89

E

1. Ghost stories
ISBN 0-06-020474-5
"An I can read mystery"
"George, an imaginative child used to playing alone,
went into an empty house to get out of the rain; there he
met an absent-minded ghost named Fred, who knew
there was a treasure but had forgotten where. Only when
Fred opened an umbrella for George's homeward journey
did the treasure materialize." Bull Cent Child Books
"More humorous than scary . . . this is a pleasing and
acceptable ghost story for beginning readers." Booklist

Bercaw, Edna Coe

Halmoni's day; pictures by Robert Hunt. Dial
Bks. for Young Readers 2000 unp il $15.99

E

1. Grandmothers—Fiction 2. Korean Americans—Fiction 3. School stories
ISBN 0-8037-2444-6   LC 98-47169
Jennifer, a Korean American, is worried that her
grandmother, visiting from Korea, will embarrass her on
her school's Grandparents' Day, but the event brings her
understanding and acceptance
"The heartwarming resolution is credible and satisfying. . . . The oil facial portraits radiate the mix of emotions in both grandchild and grandparent." Booklist

Berenzy, Alix

Sammy the classroom guinea pig; [by] Alix
Berenzy. 1st ed. Henry Holt 2005 unp il $16.95

E

1. Guinea pigs—Fiction 2. School stories
ISBN 0-8050-4024-2   LC 2004-10136
Ms. B. and her students try to understand what is
bothering Sammy, the classroom guinea pig
"The pastel-and-colored-pencil illustrations are very
successful in depicting the characters, particularly the endearing little animal with a variety of facial expressions.
. . . Through simple text and engaging artwork, Berenzy
shows the proper setup of a guinea-pig cage, what foods
are best for these creatures, and how responsive they are
to humans." SLJ

Bergman, Mara

Snip snap! what's that? illustrated by Nick
Maland. 1st American ed. Greenwillow Books
2005 unp il $15.99   E
1. Alligators—Fiction
ISBN 0-06-077754-0   LC 2004-13420
Three siblings are frightened by the wide mouth, long
teeth, and strong jaws of the alligator that has crept up
the stairs—until they decide they have had enough.

"Using elements of rhythm and rhyme as well as an
enjoyably predictable question-and-answer refrain, the
text maintains a playful tone beneath the scary details.
. . . Expressive line drawings, brightened with watercol-
or washes, illustrate the story with wit and style."
Booklist

Berry, Lynne

Duck skates; [by] Lynne Berry; illustrated by
Hiroe Nakata. 1st ed. Henry Holt and Co 2005
unp il $15.95   E
1. Ducks—Fiction 2. Snow—Fiction 3. Stories in
rhyme
ISBN 0-8050-7219-5   LC 2004-22176
Five little ducks skate, romp, and play in the snow.
"The illustrations follow the text exactly, allowing
children to count the ducks engaged in each activity. The
watercolor-and-ink pictures convey the playfulness in
warm, cozy tones, and a surprising amount of expression
is conveyed in simple lines." SLJ

Bertrand, Lynne

Granite baby; pictures by Kevin Hawkes. 1st ed.
Farrar, Straus and Giroux 2005 unp il $16

E

1. Infants—Fiction 2. New Hampshire—Fiction
3. Tall tales
ISBN 0-374-32761-0   LC 2002-192882
"Melanie Kroupa books"
Five talented New Hampshire sisters try to care for a
baby that one of them has carved out of granite.
"Together with Bertrand's rollicking text, Hawkes'
broad double-page paintings make this ideal for sharing
with groups." Booklist

Best, Cari

Are you going to be good? pictures by G. Brian
Karas. 1st ed. Farrar, Straus and Giroux 2005 unp
il $16   E
1. Parties—Fiction 2. Etiquette—Fiction 3. Old age—
Fiction
ISBN 0-374-30394-0   LC 2004-46945
"Melanie Kroupa books"
While attending his first "night party" to celebrate
Great-Gran Sadie's 100th birthday, Robert's manners dis-
appoint family members and relatives but please the
guest of honor who loves his dance steps.
"Karas's spirited color illustrations portray the family
gathering from a child's view. . . . Attempts to meet
adults' expectations will resonate with most readers."
SLJ

Goose's story; pictures by Holly Meade. Farrar,
Straus & Giroux 2002 unp il $16   E
1. Geese—Fiction
ISBN 0-374-32750-5   LC 2001-27285
"Melanie Kroupa books"
A young girl finds a Canada goose with a badly in-
jured foot and looks for her each day to see how she is
doing
"Holly Meade's animated paper collage enhances
Best's poignant story. . . . Best tells the story from the
girl's point of view, and her language is appropriately
childlike and empathetic." Horn Book

Best, Cari—*Continued*

Sally Jean, the Bicycle Queen; Cari Best; pictures by Christine Davenier. 1st ed. Farrar, Straus and Giroux 2005 unp il $16   **E**

1. Bicycles—Fiction 2. Cycling—Fiction
ISBN 0-374-36386-2   LC 2004-40461
When Sally Jean outgrows her beloved bicycle, Flash, she experiments with various ideas for acquiring a new, bigger one.
"Davenier's ink-and-watercolor illustrations are light and airy and convey a variety of emotions and delightful details. Sally Jean is a real charmer, and children will appreciate her resourcefulness and tenacity." SLJ

Shrinking Violet; illustrated by Giselle Potter. Farrar, Straus & Giroux 2001 unp il $16   **E**

1. School stories 2. Theater—Fiction
ISBN 0-374-36882-1   LC 99-88966
"Melanie Kroupa books"
Violet, who is very shy and hates for anyone to look at her in school, finally comes out of her shell when she is cast as Lady Space in a play about the solar system and saves the production from disaster
"In wry, well-paced prose, Best . . . tells a good-natured story. . . . Potter's charming, signature-style illustrations, filled with wacky angles and proportions, rich colors, and slightly nostalgic details, extend the story's drama and warmth." Booklist

Three cheers for Catherine the Great; illustrated by Giselle Potter. DK Pub. 1999 unp il $16.95   **E**

1. Grandmothers—Fiction 2. Birthdays—Fiction 3. Gifts—Fiction 4. Russian Americans—Fiction
ISBN 0-7894-2622-6   LC 98-41153
Also available in paperback from Farrar, Straus & Giroux
"A Melanie Kroupa book"
Sara's Russian grandmother has requested that there be no presents at her seventy-eighth birthday party so Sara must think of a gift from her heart
"In lively, lyrical prose, Best celebrates a special family relationship, and conveys the unique challenges and joys of an immigrant's new life. . . . Potter's festive, whimsical artwork is an irresistible play of vibrant colors and patterns, filled with rich detail and diverse, expressive characters." Booklist
Another title about Sara and her grandmother is:
When Catherine the Great and I were eight! (2003)

Bildner, Phil

Shoeless Joe & Black Betsy; illustrated by C.F. Payne. Simon & Schuster Bks. for Young Readers 2002 unp il $17   **E**

1. Jackson, Joe, 1888-1951—Fiction 2. Baseball—Fiction
ISBN 0-689-82913-2   LC 99-40563
Shoeless Joe Jackson, said by some to be the greatest baseball player ever, goes into a hitting slump just before he is to start his minor league career, so he asks his friend to make him a special bat to help him hit
This is "told in a folksy, Southern voice, with many

of the stylistic elements of a tall tale. . . . The mixed-media illustrations are layered and rich in texture, qualities that add depth and drama." SLJ

Birtha, Becky

Grandmama's pride; illustrated by Colin Bootman. Albert Whitman 2005 unp il $16.95   **E**

1. Grandmothers—Fiction 2. African Americans—Fiction 3. Segregation—Fiction
ISBN 0-8075-3028-X   LC 2005003991
While on a trip in 1956 to visit her grandmother in the South, six-year-old Sarah Marie experiences segregation for the first time, but discovers that things have changed by the time she returns the following year.
"The strong, sensitive writing is enhanced by beautiful watercolor paintings filled with chips of light." SLJ

Blackstone, Stella

My granny went to market; a round-the-world counting rhyme; written by Stella Blackstone; illustrated by Christopher Corr. Barefoot Books 2005 unp il $16.99   **E**

1. Voyages and travels—Fiction 2. Grandmothers—Fiction 3. Counting 4. Stories in rhyme
ISBN 1-84148-792-9   LC 2004-17394
A child's grandmother travels around the world, buying things in quantities that illustrate counting from one to ten.
"The brightly colored gouache illustrations have the feel of Mexican folk art, and endpaper maps route Granny's travels, with a one-page legend showing her purchases—from one carpet to 10 llamas. A cheery, global shopping trip, fun to read alone and also useful in the classroom." Booklist

Secret seahorse; written by Stella Blackstone; illustrated by Clare Beaton. Barefoot Books 2004 unp il $15.99; pa $6.99   **E**

1. Sea horses—Fiction 2. Coral reefs and islands—Fiction 3. Stories in rhyme
ISBN 1-8414-8704-X; 1-8414-8937-9 (pa)
       LC 2003-19085
Also available board book edition
A sea horse leads the reader past coral reefs and underwater creatures to a sea horse family hidden in a cave. Includes notes on coral reefs and various marine animals.
"The involving quest and appealing fabric collages make this rhyming hide-and-seek tale great for reading together or enjoying alone." Booklist

Who are you, baby kangaroo? written by Stella Blackstone; illustrated by Clare Beaton. Barefoot Books 2004 unp il $14.99   **E**

1. Animals—Fiction 2. Stories in rhyme
ISBN 1-84148-217-X   LC 2004-4652
A curious puppy leads the reader to a number of animal babies in search of the name for a baby kangaroo. Includes notes on animal mothers and various infant animals.
"The rhyming, repetitive text makes this book perfect for reading aloud. . . . Made of felt, antique fabrics, buttons, beads, and sequins, Beaton's illustrations are filled with bright colors and interesting details." SLJ

Blake, Robert J.

Akiak; a tale from the Iditarod. Philomel Bks. 1997 unp il lib bdg $16.99   **E**

1. Dogs—Fiction 2. Iditarod Trail Sled Dog Race, Alaska—Fiction 3. Alaska—Fiction

ISBN 0-399-22798-9   LC 97-2251

Akiak the sled dog refuses to give up after being injured during the Iditarod sled dog race

"The story is stirring and involving. . . . Blake's oils are snow-blown and vivid, with varying perpectives but an emphasis on dog-level views. . . . An endpaper map depicts Iditarod routes and makes it easy to follow Akiak's journey; an author's note gives a little more background about the race and the relevant details." Bull Cent Child Books

Togo. Philomel Bks. 2002 unp il $16.99   **E**

1. Dogs 2. Alaska

ISBN 0-399-23381-4   LC 2001-45926

In 1925, Togo, a Siberian husky who loves being a sled dog, leads a team that rushes to bring diphtheria antitoxin from Anchorage to Nome, Alaska

The author "paints a vivid word-picture of bitter, deadly conditions and the grueling effort required to surmount them, reinforcing it with dramatic art." Booklist

Blomgren, Jennifer

Where do I sleep? a Pacific Northwest lullabye; illustrated by Andrea Gabriel. Sasquatch Bks. 2001 unp il $15.95   **E**

1. Animals—Fiction 2. Sleep—Fiction 3. Pacific Northwest—Fiction 4. Stories in rhyme

ISBN 1-57061-258-7   LC 2001-20940

Rhyming text describes some of the young animals—from a gray wolf pup and a horned puffin to a cougar kit and a small brown bat—as they settle down to sleep

"Kids get an opportunity to practice map skills, learn about new animals, find out why Alaska's summer days are so long, and add such unfamiliar words as *tundra* to their vocabulary. . . . Gabriel's gorgeous artwork reflects the beauty and diversity of the wildlife and landscape." Booklist

Blood, Charles L.

The goat in the rug; as told to Charles L. Blood & Martin Link by Geraldine; illustrated by Nancy Winslow Parker 1976 unp il   **E**

1. Goats—Fiction 2. Navajo Indians—Fiction 3. Rugs and carpets—Fiction

Available in paperback from Aladdin Books

"A goat's-eye view of how a Navajo rug is made, from the shearing of our supposed narrator ('Geraldine') to the dyeing and weaving. By the time the rug is finished, Geraldine has grown enough wool to start another one." Saturday Rev

"Parker's vivid primary colored illustrations are as enjoyable and humorous as the instructive text." SLJ

Bloom, Suzanne

The bus for us. Boyds Mills Press 2001 unp il $10.95   **E**

1. School stories 2. Vehicles—Fiction

ISBN 1-56397-932-2   LC 00-102348

"At the bus stop, young Tess asks, 'Is this the bus for us, Gus?' every time an unusual vehicle goes by. . . . Gus patiently identifies each vehicle, from taxi to backhoe, until their school bus arrives. In the attractive illustrations, readers can enjoy not only the parade of vehicles but also the antics of the waiting children." Horn Book Guide

A splendid friend, indeed; written and illustrated by Suzanne Bloom. Boyds Mills Press 2005 unp il $15.95   **E**

1. Polar bear—Fiction 2. Geese—Fiction 3. Friendship—Fiction

ISBN 1-59078-286-0   LC 2004-10780

When a studious polar bear meets an inquisitive goose, they learn to be friends.

"The cool palette of the pastel illustrations, consisting of shades of blue and white and touches of violet, sets a quiet, friendly tone, and the animals' priceless expressions tell all. The gentle humor will elicit giggles." SLJ

Blume, Judy

The Pain and the Great One; illustrations by Irene Trivas. rev format ed. Atheneum Books for Young Readers 2002 c1984 unp il $17.95   **E**

1. Siblings—Fiction

ISBN 0-689-85507-9

First published 1984 by Bradbury Press

A six-year-old (The Pain) and his eight-year-old sister (The Great One) see each other as troublemakers and the best-loved in the family

"Young readers, depending on their position within the family, will readily identify with either character and may learn empathy for the other. Used in a group, this will provide much healthy discussion. . . . Trivas' vibrant colors add depth and humor to a valuable book on sibling relationships." SLJ

Blumenthal, Deborah

Ice palace; illustrated by Ted Rand. Clarion Bks. 2003 32p il $16   **E**

1. Winter—Fiction 2. Festivals—Fiction 3. New York (State)—Fiction

ISBN 0-618-15960-6   LC 2002-155648

A girl and her father help plan the annual winter carnival in Saranac Lake Village, New York, as the girl's uncle and other prisoners work together to build its centerpiece, the ice palace

"The text is poetic yet approachable. The description of the prison is straightforward without being alarming. . . . Rand's watercolor-and-acrylic illustrations capture the icy-blue feel of a small town in winter, with the brush strokes providing texture and layer to the story." SLJ

Bogan, Paulette

Goodnight Lulu. Bloomsbury Children's Bk. 2003 unp il $15.95   **E**

1. Chickens—Fiction 2. Bedtime—Fiction

ISBN 1-58234-803-0   LC 2002-27825

Bogan, Paulette—*Continued*

When her mother tucks her in for the night, Lulu the chicken worries what would happen if a bear or a tiger or an alligator should come in during the night

This is a "funny, original, and reassuring tale. . . . The saturated watercolor and ink spreads deftly capture the night's ominous as well as cozy qualities." Horn Book Guide

Bolliger, Max

The happy troll; [by] Max Bolliger; illustrated by Peter Sis; translated from the German by Nina Ignatowicz. 1st American ed. Henry Holt and Co 2005 unp il $16.95   E

1. Singing—Fiction 2. Happiness—Fiction

ISBN 0-8050-6982-8   LC 2004-8984

Originally published in Switzerland in 1998 by Bohem Press

Gus, a troll who loves to sing, makes everyone happy with his songs until his desire for gold becomes so strong that he no longer has time to use his beautiful voice.

"Using oil pastels on gesso, Sís creates a miniature world of childlike trolls in colorful suits. . . . Bolliger's simple, eloquent language perfectly taps into a child's sensibilities." SLJ

Bond, Rebecca

This place in the snow. Dutton Children's Books 2004 unp il $16.99   E

1. Snow—Fiction

ISBN 0-525-47308-4

"Bond explores the magic of waking up to a world blanketed with snow. . . . The freeflowing, poetic text uses strong imagery. . . . The full-color illustrations dance across the pages, suffused with shades of blue in the snow and surrounded by white inside the houses." SLJ

Bonsall, Crosby Newell

The case of the hungry stranger; by Crosby Bonsall. HarperCollins Pubs. 1992 64p il lib bdg $16.89; pa $3.99   E

1. Mystery fiction

ISBN 0-06-020571-7 (lib bdg); 0-06-444026-5 (pa)
LC 91-13345

Also available Spanish language edition

"An I can read book"

A reissue of the title first published 1963. This edition has full color illustrations

Wizard and his friends are clueless when they are sent on the trail of a blueberry pie thief, until Wizard hits on a plan that is sure to nab the sweet-toothed pilferer

This offers "suspense and humor." Horn Book

Other titles in this series are:

The case of the cat's meow (1965)
The case of the double cross (1980)
The case of the dumb bells (1966)
The case of the scaredy cats (1971)

The day I had to play with my sister; story and pictures by Crosby Bonsall. newly il ed. HarperCollins Pubs. 1999 32p il lib bdg $14.89; pa $3.99   E

1. Siblings—Fiction

ISBN 0-06-028181-2 (lib bdg); 0-06-444253-5 (pa)
LC 98-20342

"My first I can read book"

A newly illustrated edition of the title first published 1972

A young boy becomes very frustrated when he tries to teach his little sister to play hide-and-seek

"The extremely simple text . . . is one with which children can readily identify. . . . The realistic atmosphere makes Bonsall's book an excellent addition to the very early reading shelves." SLJ

Mine's the best. newly il ed. HarperCollins Pubs. 1996 32p il lib bdg $16.89; pa $3.99
E

ISBN 0-06-027091-8 (lib bdg); 0-06-444213-6 (pa)
LC 95-12405

"My first I can read book"

A newly illustrated edition of the title first published 1973

Two little boys meet at the beach, each sure that his balloon is better

"The playful illustrations tell their own story; the extremely brief text (not to mention the head start provided by the two initial wordless spreads) will give new readers a sense of accomplishment." Horn Book Guide

Who's a pest? Harper & Row 1962 64p il lib bdg $15.89; pa $3.99   E

ISBN 0-06-020621-7 (lib bdg); 0-06-444099-0 (pa)

"An I can read book"

"In this truly funny . . . book a small boy named Homer proves that he is not a pest as his four sisters, a rabbit, chipmunk, and lizard claim. The drawings are as laughable as the text and the tongue-twisting dialog begs to be read aloud." Booklist

Another title about Homer is:

Piggle (1973)

Who's afraid of the dark? by Crosby Bonsall. Harper & Row 1980 32p il lib bdg $16.89; pa $3.99   E

1. Night—Fiction 2. Fear—Fiction

ISBN 0-06-020599-7 (lib bdg); 0-06-444071-0 (pa)
LC 79-2700

"An Early I can read book"

"A little boy describes to a friend the nighttime fears of his dog Stella. Stella shivers in the dark, he claims; she sees shapes and hears scary sounds. The doubting but sympathetic friend offers a suggestion—hug Stella in the night and comfort her until her fears go away. . . . The illustrations in shades of light blue and brown are filled with as much life and warmth as ever." Horn Book

Borden, Louise

The A+ custodian; illustrated by Adam Gustavson. Margaret K. McElderry Books 2004 unp il $15.95   E

1. School stories 2. Janitors—Fiction

ISBN 0-689-84995-8   LC 2002-12029

Borden, Louise—*Continued*

The students and teachers at Dublin Elementary School make banners, posters, and signs for their school custodian to show how much they appreciate him and all the work he does

"The simple, unrhymed poetic words and the realistic oil paintings create a strong sense of a diverse school community and a man in flannel shirt and worn leather shoes." Booklist

A. Lincoln and me; illustrated by Ted Lewin. Scholastic 1999 unp il pa $5.99 hardcover o.p.

E

1. Lincoln, Abraham, 1809-1865—Fiction
ISBN 0-590-45715-2 (pa); 0-590-45714-4 (hc)
LC 98-51921

With the help of his teacher, a young boy realizes that he not only shares his birthday and similar physical appearance with Abraham Lincoln, but that he is like him in other ways as well

"Borden's text flows nicely, creating imagery of the physical presence of the man. Lewin's distinctive watercolors lend style and substance to the book, producing a treat for the eyes." SLJ

Good luck, Mrs. K! written by Louise Borden; illustrated by Adam Gustavson. Margaret K. McElderry Bks. 1999 unp il pa $6.99 hardcover o.p.

E

1. Teachers—Fiction 2. Cancer—Fiction 3. School stories
ISBN 0-689-85119-7 (pa)
LC 97-50553

"Ann loves her third-grade teacher, who makes every child feel special and who introduces subjects with great zest. When Mrs. K. has cancer surgery the students are sad, but they (and their teacher) survive the year to return in the fall." Horn Book Guide

"A truly endearing story. Gustavson's watercolor illustrations exude all of the warmth and vibrancy of Borden's words." SLJ

The little ships; the heroic rescue at Dunkirk in World War II; illustrated by Michael Foreman. Margaret K. McElderry Bks. 1997 unp il pa $6.99 hardcover o.p.

E

1. Dunkerque (France), Battle of, 1940—Fiction
2. World War, 1939-1945—Fiction
ISBN 0-689-85396-3 (pa)
LC 95-52557

A young English girl and her father take their sturdy fishing boat and join the scores of other civilian vessels crossing the English Channel in a daring attempt to rescue Allied and British troops trapped by Nazi soldiers at Dunkirk

"Borden's descriptive style is potent, and Foreman's watercolors perfectly express the dulled and watery scenes of devastation, the exhausted and hopeful soldiers awaiting rescue." Horn Book Guide

Sleds on Boston Common; a story of the American Revolution; written by Louise Borden; illustrated by Robert Andrew Parker. Margaret K. McElderry Bks. 2000 unp il $17

E

1. Gage, Thomas, 1721-1787—Fiction 2. Boston (Mass.)—Fiction 3. United States—History—1600-1775, Colonial period—Fiction
ISBN 0-689-82812-8
LC 99-18080

Henry complains to the royal governor, General Gage, after his plan to sled down the steep hill at Boston Common is thwarted by the masses of British troops camped there

"Based on local folklore, Borden's story paints an authentic picture of life in colonial Boston. . . . Robert Parker's watercolor illustrations include many setting details and complement Borden's lyrical text nicely." Booklist

Bottner, Barbara

Rosa's room; written by Barbara Bottner; illustrated by Beth Spiegel. Peachtree 2004 unp il $15.95

E

1. Moving—Fiction
ISBN 1-56145-302-1
LC 2003-16837

Rosa searches for things that will fill her room in her new home, but it feels empty until she discovers exactly what is missing

"Through simple language and age-appropriate details, Bottner does a good job of capturing a child's point of view. Done in watercolor, gouache, and India ink, the illustrations enhance the mood of the text." SLJ

The Scaredy Cats; pictures by Victoria Chess. Simon & Schuster Bks. for Young Readers 2003 unp il $14.95

E

1. Cats—Fiction 2. Fear—Fiction
ISBN 0-689-83786-0
LC 00-45059

When the Scaredy Cat family's fears keep them from doing things, Baby Scaredy Cat suggests they might be missing good things as well

"Bottner's serious tone is a perfect counterpoint to the increasing ridiculousness of the Scaredy Cats' fear, and Chess pushes the story from funny to hilarious with her watercolor depictions of the wide-eyed, terrified felines." SLJ

Wallace's lists; y; [by] Barbara Bottner and Gerald Kruglik; illustrated by Olof Landström. 1st ed. Katherine Tegen Books 2004 unp il $15.99; lib bdg $16.89

E

1. Mice—Fiction 2. Friendship—Fiction
ISBN 0-06-000224-7; 0-06-000225-5 (lib bdg)
LC 2003-8431

Devoted to making lists about everything in his life, Wallace the mouse discovers the joys of spontaneity and adventure when he becomes friends with his neighbor Albert.

"The writing is memorable, and the authors provide just the right details. . . . Landstrom's pictures are expressive and witty, with soft colors, strong lines, and lots of personality." SLJ

Bradby, Marie

Momma, where are you from? illustrated by Chris K. Soentpiet. Orchard Bks. 2000 unp il $16.95

E

1. African Americans—Fiction 2. Mother-daughter relationship—Fiction
ISBN 0-531-30105-2
LC 99-23068

Momma describes the special people and surroundings of her childhood, in a place where the edge of town met

Bradby, Marie—*Continued*
the countryside, in a time when all the children at school
were brown.

"Soentpiet's detailed, beautifully lit paintings freeze
the mother's vivid memories, culminating in a dreamy,
gray-toned montage of all the previous scenes. Children
will be inspired by the mother's eloquent, proud answer
to her daughter's essential question." Booklist

More than anything else; story by Marie
Bradby; pictures by Chris K. Soentpiet. Orchard
Bks. 1995 unp il $15.95   E
  1. Washington, Booker T., 1856-1915—Fiction
2. African Americans—Fiction 3. Books and reading—Fiction
  ISBN 0-531-09464-2   LC 94-48804
"A Richard Jackson book"
Nine-year-old Booker works with his father and brother at the saltworks, but dreams of the day when he'll be
able to read.
"An evocative text combines with well-crafted, dramatic watercolors to provide a stirring, fictionalized account of the early life of Booker T. Washington." Horn
Book

Bradford, Karleen
You can't rush a cat; [by] Karleen Bradford &
Leslie Elizabeth Watts. Orca Book Pub. 2004 unp
il $16.95   E
  1. Cats—Fiction 2. Grandfathers—Fiction
  ISBN 1-55143-247-1
"Jessica helps her grandfather slowly lure a small orange stray inside. . . . When the man is disappointed
that she remains hidden, Jessica reminds him, 'You can't
rush a cat.' . . . Portraying an adorable and irresistible
kitten, the soft watercolor illustrations effectively capture
the emotions of each moment." SLJ

Bradley, Kimberly Brubaker
Ballerino Nate; illustrated by R.W. Alley. Dial
Books for Young Readers 2006 unp il $16.99
                                                    E
  1. Ballet—Fiction 2. Sex role—Fiction
  ISBN 0-8037-2954-5   LC 2004-17822
After seeing a ballet performance, Nate decides he
wants to learn ballet but he has doubts when his brother
Ben tells him that only girls can be ballerinas.
"Bradley writes smoothly and insightfully about
Nate's experiences. . . . Alley's watercolor-and-pencil
contributions, portraying an entirely canine universe, capture both the warm family dynamics and Nate's zooming, irrepressible energy. " Booklist

Bradman, Tony
Daddy's lullaby; illustrated by Jason Cockcroft.
Margaret K. McElderry Bks. 2002 c2001 unp il
$16.95   E
  1. Fathers—Fiction 2. Infants—Fiction
  ISBN 0-689-84295-3   LC 2001-31280
First published 2001 in the United Kingdom
A father takes his baby on a midnight stroll through
the house, trying to get the baby to sleep

"This slice of life is simply told and depicted in softly
rendered, realistic paintings across spreads that capture
the quiet of a sleeping household and a father's tenderness." SLJ

Brandenberg, Alexa
Ballerina flying. HarperCollins Pubs. 2002 unp
il $15.95; lib bdg $15.89   E
  1. Ballet—Fiction
  ISBN 0-06-029549-X; 0-06-029550-3 (lib bdg)
                                     LC 00-56721
Mina, who loves dance and especially ballet, is off to
her Tuesday afternoon class with Miss Viola
"Children who like dancing will enjoy this delightful
encounter. . . . From arabesques to pirouettes, examples
of each position are clearly and colorfully illustrated."
Booklist

Branford, Henrietta
Little Pig Figwort can't get to sleep; illustrated
by Claudio Muñoz. Clarion Bks. 2002 c2000 unp
il $14   E
  1. Sleep—Fiction 2. Bedtime—Fiction 3. Pigs—Fic-
tion
  ISBN 0-618-15968-1   LC 2001-42093
First published 2000 in the United Kingdom with title:
Little Pig Figwort
Little Pig Figwort cannot sleep, so he goes off to the
North Pole, the moon, and the bottom of the sea
"Rich language makes this a good read-aloud, and the
spirited illustrations . . . bring Pig Figwort and his adventures to life." Horn Book Guide

Braun, Trudi
My goose Betsy; illustrated by John
Bendall-Brunello. Candlewick Press 1999 unp il
$16.99; pa $6.99   E
  1. Geese—Fiction
  ISBN 0-7636-0449-6; 0-7636-1714-8 (pa)
                                     LC 98-3456
Betsy the goose makes a cozy nest, lays her eggs, and
tends to them until her little goslings are hatched. Includes a section with facts about geese
"Down-to-earth language, a minimum of detail, and an
abundance of large yet cozy illustrations make this just
right for the intended audience." Horn Book Guide

Brenner, Barbara
Good morning, garden; illustrated by Denise
Ortakales. Northword Press 2004 unp il $15.95
                                                    E
  1. Gardens—Fiction 2. Stories in rhyme
  ISBN 1-55971-888-9
Upon entering a garden one morning, a child greets
the flowers, plants, insects, and animals there.
"The alliterative tone and subtle rhyme scheme continue throughout this joyful celebration. . . . Ortakales
works with sculpted paper to convey the depth and detail
of a garden replete with luscious plants and friendly
creatures." SLJ

Brenner, Barbara—*Continued*

Wagon wheels; story by Barbara Brenner; pictures by Don Bolognese. newly il ed. HarperCollins Pubs. 1993 il pa $3.99 hardcover o.p. E

1. Frontier and pioneer life—Fiction 2. African Americans—Fiction

ISBN 0-06-444052-4 (pa)   LC 92-18780

"An I can read book"

A newly illustrated edition of the title first published 1978

Shortly after the Civil War a black family travels to Kansas to take advantage of the free land offered through the Homestead Act

"The based-on-fact story . . . is as fascinating as ever. Beautifully narrated with sensitivity, compassion, and just the right amount of suspense, and featuring new full-color illustrations." Horn Book Guide

Brett, Jan

Annie and the wild animals; written and illustrated by Jan Brett. Houghton Mifflin 1985 unp il lib bdg $16; pa $5.95 E

1. Animals—Fiction 2. Cats—Fiction

ISBN 0-395-37800-1 (lib bdg); 0-395-51006-6 (pa)
LC 84-19818

When Annie's cat disappears, she attempts friendship with a variety of unsuitable woodland animals, but with the emergence of Spring, everything comes right

"Miss Brett uses colorful borders filled with detail to provide miniature previews of the narrative action and a story around a story, so that the reader instantly becomes an insider. The small glimpses of the world outside Annie's cottage move the tale forward and embellish the pages with grace and skill." N Y Times Book Rev

Daisy comes home. Putnam 2002 unp il $16.99
E

1. Chickens—Fiction 2. China—Fiction

ISBN 0-399-23618-X   LC 00-40295

Daisy, an unhappy hen in China, floats down the river in a basket and has an adventure

"Brett's attention to detail is matched by her skill in representing the story's viewpoint and movement. . . . Particularly eye-catching are the richly hued pictures, bursting with Chinese life." Booklist

The hat. Putnam 1997 unp il $16.95   E
1. Hedgehogs—Fiction 2. Animals—Fiction
3. Clothing and dress—Fiction

ISBN 0-399-23101-3   LC 96-54015

When Lisa hangs her woolen clothes in the sun to air them out for winter, the hedgehog, to the amusement of the other animals, ends up wearing a stocking on his head

This story "has charm and humor. . . . The setting is the Danish countryside (detailed down to the moss on a tree) on a day when the first snow begins to fall, and Brett conveys the season with such loving spirit that children will almost wish for winter." Booklist

Honey . . . honey . . . lion! a story from Africa. G.P. Putnam's Sons 2005 unp il $16.99
E

1. Badgers—Fiction 2. Honeyguides (Birds)—Fiction
3. Africa—Fiction

ISBN 0-399-24463-8   LC 2005-00449

After working together to obtain honey, the African honey badger always shares it with his partner, the honeyguide bird, until one day when the honey badger becomes greedy and his feathered friend decides to teach him a lesson.

"Brett has created another lush winner with beautifully detailed illustrations of the animals and a clear, fast-paced story." SLJ

On Noah's ark. Putnam 2003 unp il $16.99
E

1. Noah's ark—Fiction

ISBN 0-399-24028-4   LC 2003-1281

Noah's granddaughter helps him bring the animals onto the ark, calm them down, and get them to sleep

"The words are basic and effective; it's the detailed watercolors of the animals that are the real attraction here. In precise brushstrokes and vivid colors, Brett creates incredibly textured feathers and fur." Booklist

Trouble with trolls. Putnam 1992 unp il $16.99; pa $6.99   E

1. Fairy tales

ISBN 0-399-22336-3; 0-698-11791-3 (pa)
LC 91-41061

While climbing Mt. Baldy, Treva outwits some trolls who want to steal her dog

"Bursting with energy and fine detail, the double-page spreads, which escape their cross-stitch borders, depict a beautiful mountain landscape, dotted with trees and rocks that make excellent hiding places for the pesky trolls. Cutaway scenes beneath the spreads tell a concurrent story, picturing the trolls readying their home for Tuffi while an uninvited guest works its way down the chimney, then inside. Playful and funny, with a valiant female protagonist, this is a first-rate read." Booklist

The wild Christmas reindeer; written and illustrated by Jan Brett. Putnam 1990 unp il $17.99   E

1. Reindeer—Fiction 2. Christmas—Fiction

ISBN 0-399-22192-1   LC 89-36095

"The story's heroine is Teeka, who is asked by Santa to get the reindeer ready to fly. . . . Only when she realizes that hugging works better than bossing, do the reindeer unite into the working team that Santa needs to bring Christmas to the world. . . . Brett provides ornamental pictures, heavily detailed and decoratively bordered. . . . Beautifully conceived and finely wrought." Booklist

Briant, Ed

Seven stories; [written and illustrated by] Ed Briant. Roaring Brook Press 2005 unp il $16.95
E

1. Apartment houses—Fiction

ISBN 1-59643-056-7   LC 2004-24351

Briant, Ed—*Continued*

A girl in a seven-story apartment building has trouble sleeping because of her disruptive neighbors, who all seem to be characters from fairy tales.

"This comical take on familiar events features freely limned art, offbeat characterizations, a retro urban setting, and perky snatches of dialogue." Horn Book Guide

Bridges, Margaret Park

I love the rain! illustrated by Christine Davenier. Chronicle Books 2005 unp $15.95   **E**

1. Rain—Fiction

ISBN 1-58717-208-9   LC 2004-10823

Molly hates the rain, but Sophie enjoys how it makes shiny black streets, forms fun puddles, and sounds like tap dancers on the roof of the bus.

"The loose, scratchy pen-and-ink drawings, augmented with vibrant watercolors, lend an evocative atmosphere to the text. . . . The author and artist have created both a concrete and an interpretive vision that captures the delight of childhood and an appreciation for nature." SLJ

Bridges, Shirin Yim

Ruby's wish; illustrated by Sophie Blackall. Chronicle Bks. 2002 unp il $15.95   **E**

1. Sex role—Fiction 2. Education—Fiction 3. China—Fiction

ISBN 0-8118-3490-5   LC 2001-7406

In China, at a time when few girls are taught to read or write, Ruby dreams of going to the university with her brothers and male cousins

"This true story about Bridges' own grandmother has a gentle momentum. . . . Blackall's gouache illustrations have a quietly historical air, their palette subtly shaded with smoky inks and highlighted with touches of brilliant red." Bull Cent Child Books

Briggs, Raymond

The snowman. Random House 1978 unp il $17; pa $7.99   **E**

1. Stories without words 2. Dreams—Fiction 3. Snow—Fiction

ISBN 0-394-83973-0; 0-394-88466-3 (pa)

LC 78-55904

Also available Board book edition

A "wordless picture book about a small boy who expertly fashions a snowman and then dreams that his splendid creation comes alive. Affably greeting the child, the snowman enters the house and is introduced to the delights and dangers of gadgetry. . . . Finally, no longer earthbound, the two friends go soaring over city and countryside, magical in their snowy beauty." Horn Book

"The pastel-toned pencil-and-crayon pictures in their neat rectangular frames will hold the attention of primary 'readers.'" SLJ

Brimner, Larry Dane

The littlest wolf; illustrated by Jose Aruego and Ariane Dewey. HarperCollins Pubs. 2002 unp il $15.95   **E**

1. Wolves—Fiction

ISBN 0-06-029039-0   LC 00-33581

"Being the smallest wolf in the pack is not easy, especially when the other pups can roll in straighter lines, pounce higher, and run faster. Big Gray comforts Little Wolf each time he compares himself to his siblings. . . . Brimner's gentle and encouraging story will speak to those children who feel less capable or talented than their siblings. Aruego and Dewey's charming pictures perfectly portray Little Wolf's attempts to run, pounce, and jump, and imbue the characters with lots of personality." SLJ

Brisson, Pat

I remember Miss Perry; illustrated by Stéphane Jorisch. Dial Books for Young Readers 2006 unp il $16.99   **E**

1. School stories 2. Teachers—Fiction 3. Death—Fiction 4. Bereavement—Fiction

ISBN 0-8037-2981-2   LC 2004-24070

When his teacher, Miss Perry, is killed in a car accident, Stevie and his elementary school classmates take turns sharing memories of her, especially her fondest wish for each day.

"The delicate pen-and-ink, watercolor, and gouache illustrations reflect the varied emotions evoked by this treasured individual." SLJ

Mama loves me from away; illustrated by Laurie Caple. Boyds Mills 2004 unp il $15.95

E

1. Prisoners—Fiction 2. Mother-daughter relationship—Fiction

ISBN 1-56397-966-7

When a mother and daughter are separated by the mother's incarceration, they find a special way to keep their loving relationship alive

"The warm, first-person narrative and realistic double-page art show the loving bond between Sugar and her single-parent mom." Booklist

The summer my father was ten; illustrated by Andrea Shine. Boyds Mills Press 1998 unp il $15.95; pa $8.95   **E**

ISBN 1-56397-435-5; 1-56397-829-6 (pa)

LC 97-72769

A father tells his daughter the story of how he damaged a neighbor's garden when he was a boy and what he did to make amends

"The personal narrative voice, the heartfelt characters, and the daily gardening work . . . are celebrated in the gorgeously detailed pictures that show how a garden transforms a vacant lot." Booklist

Tap-dance fever; illustrated by Nancy Cote. 1st ed. Boyds Mills Press 2004 unp il $15.95

E

1. Tap dancing—Fiction

ISBN 1-59078-290-9   LC 2004-14575

Annabelle Applegate will not stop tap-dancing no matter what the frustrated citizens of Fiddlers Creek do to make her quit

"A deliciously tall tale with an appealing young heroine, the story of Annabelle's troubles and triumph reads aloud well. Just as amusing are Cote's fanciful watercolor-and-gouache paintings of a multicultural, rural community." Booklist

Brown, Craig McFarland

Barn raising; [by] Craig Brown. Greenwillow
Bks. 2002 unp il $15.99; lib bdg $17.89
E

1. Barns—Fiction 2. Farm life—Fiction 3. Amish—
Fiction
ISBN 0-06-029399-3; 0-06-029400-0 (lib bdg)
LC 00-63644

An Amish community gathers to erect a barn in one
day, and finishes in time for the owner's cows to be
milked there that very evening

"In this attractive picture book, Brown does a good,
solid job of depicting an Amish barn raising. . . . Brown
offers a series of large outdoor scenes drawn in ink and
warmed with muted colors." Booklist

Brown, Jeff

Flat Stanley; pictures by Tomi Ungerer. Harper
& Row 1964 unp il lib bdg $16.89; pa $4.99
E

ISBN 0-06-020681-0 (lib bdg); 0-06-009791-4 (pa)

"When an enormous bulletin board fell on him as he
lay in bed Stanley Lambchop emerged as flat as a pancake. Once he got used to his half-inch thickness Stanley
came to enjoy it and so did his parents—he could be
lowered through sidewalk gratings, mailed to California,
rolled up like wallpaper and tied with a string for carrying, and disguised as a framed picture to help catch art
thieves in the museum. Comical colored pictures accentuate the humor of this rib-tickling story." Booklist

Brown, Ken

The scarecrow's hat; written and illustrated by
Ken Brown. Peachtree Pubs. 2001 unp il $15.95
E

1. Chickens—Fiction 2. Scarecrows—Fiction
ISBN 1-56145-240-8
LC 00-46957

First published 2000 in the United Kingdom

Chicken thinks Scarecrow's hat will make a nice nest,
but first she must swap with Badger, Crow, Sheep, Owl,
and Donkey

"Realistic watercolors greatly enhance this plucky, humorous tale." Booklist

Brown, Marc Tolon

Arthur's nose; by Marc Brown. Little, Brown
1976 32p il $15.95; pa $5.95
E

1. Nose—Fiction 2. Aardvark—Fiction
ISBN 0-316-11193-7; 0-316-11070-1 (pa)

Books about Arthur are also available in other formats
including board books, easy-to-read books, and chapter
books

"An Atlantic Monthly Press book"

"Arthur the aardvark is unhappy with his long nose.
When he finally decides to visit a rhinologist to have it
changed, he discovers that he can't come up with a different kind of nose that suits him. No alterations are
done, for Arthur comes to realize that 'I'm just not me
without my nose.' The . . . lesson is pleasantly conveyed with surprisingly little text and large and colorful
illustrations." SLJ

Other titles about Arthur are:

Arthur babysits (1992)
Arthur goes to camp (1982)
Arthur, it's only rock 'n roll (2002)
Arthur lost and found (1998)
Arthur meets the president (1991)
Arthur writes a story (1996)
Arthur's April Fool (1983)
Arthur's baby (1987)
Arthur's birthday (1989)
Arthur's chicken pox (1994)
Arthur's Christmas (1985)
Arthur's computer disaster (1997)
Arthur's eyes (1979)
Arthur's family vacation (1993)
Arthur's first sleepover (1994)
Arthur's Halloween (1982)
Arthur's new puppy (1993)
Arthur's perfect Christmas (2000)
Arthur's pet business (1990)
Arthur's teacher trouble (1986)
Arthur's Thanksgiving (1983)
Arthur's tooth (1985)
Arthur's TV trouble (1995)
Arthur's underwear (1999)
Arthur's valentine (1980)

D.W. all wet; [by] Marc Brown. Little, Brown
1988 unp il pa $5.95 hardcover o.p.
E

1. Beaches—Fiction 2. Siblings—Fiction
3. Aardvark—Fiction
ISBN 0-316-11077-9 (pa); 0-316-11268-2 (hc)
LC 87-15752

Also available Board book edition

"Joy Street books"

Arthur the Aardvark's little sister D.W. "announces 'I
don't like the beach, and I don't like to get wet.' She
asks to leave the minute she arrives, she won't play and
she's afraid of getting sunburned. It's Arthur who helps
change D.W.'s mind about the beach by unexpectedly
tossing her into very shallow water." Publ Wkly

"A simple, even predictable vignette, but entertaining
nonetheless because of Brown's warm pictures." Booklist

Other titles about D.W. are:

D.W. flips (1987)
D.W. go to your room! (1999)
D.W. rides again (1993)
D.W. the picky eater (1995)
D.W. thinks big (1993)
D.W.'s guide to perfect manners (2006)
D.W.'s guide to preschool (2003)
D.W.'s library card (2001)
D.W.'s lost blankie (1998)

Brown, Margaret Wise

Another important book; pictures by Chris
Raschka. HarperCollins Pubs. 1999 unp il $15.99;
lib bdg $16.89
E

1. Growth—Fiction 2. Counting 3. Stories in rhyme
ISBN 0-06-026282-6; 0-06-026283-4 (lib bdg)
LC 98-7212

Also available The important book $16.99; lib bdg
$16.89 (ISBN 0-06-020720-5; 0-06-020721-3)

"Joanna Cotler books"

Illustrations and simple rhyming text describe how a
child grows from ages one through six

Brown, Margaret Wise—*Continued*

"Raschka assigns each age group a geometric shape: a simple circle represents age one, pairs of stacked squares indicate two, a five-pointed star signifies five and so on. . . . It's a pleasure to hear the organic rhythms of Brown's prose . . . and Raschka paints in boisterous surprises." Publ Wkly

Big red barn; pictures by Felicia Bond. newly il ed. Harper & Row 1989 unp il $16.99; lib bdg $17.89 **E**
1. Animals—Fiction 2. Farm life—Fiction 3. Stories in rhyme
ISBN 0-06-020748-5; 0-06-020749-3 (lib bdg)
LC 85-45814

Also available Board book edition

A newly illustrated edition of the title first published 1956

Rhymed text and illustrations introduce the many different animals that live in the big red barn

"The large illustrations are somewhat stylized, but still have a strong sense of detail and reality. The bright colors will attract young readers. The short text on each page is superimposed on the picture, but always in a way that is easy to read. Children will enjoy studying each of the pages as the day progresses from early morning to night." SLJ

Bunny's noisy book; pictures by Lisa McCue. Hyperion 2000 unp il $14.99 **E**
1. Rabbits—Fiction 2. Sound—Fiction
ISBN 0-7868-0472-6 LC 99-19024

A little bunny listens to noises all around him and then makes some of his own

"McCue's brightly colored, detailed illustrations depicting a warm spring day from sunup to sundown are eye-catching and engaging. . . . This joyful adventure will work well as a lap-sit or storytime selection." SLJ

A child's good night book; pictures by Jean Charlot. HarperCollins Pubs. 1992 unp il $14.99
E
1. Night—Fiction 2. Bedtime—Fiction
ISBN 0-06-021028-1 LC 91-45340

Also available Board book edition

A Caldecott Medal honor book, 1944

A reissue of the title first published 1943 by W. R. Scott

As an invitation to sleepiness the author writes of birds and animals, sailboats, automobiles and little children as they settle down for the night

"Soft, colored-crayon drawings show night coming on. . . . A quiet, tender, bedtime book, gently, but not prosaically, illustrated." Horn Book

The fierce yellow pumpkin; story by Margaret Wise Brown; pictures by Richard Egielski. HarperCollins Pubs. 2003 unp il $15.99; lib bdg $16.89 **E**
1. Pumpkin—Fiction
ISBN 0-06-024479-8; 0-06-024481-X (lib bdg)
LC 2002-8338

A little pumpkin dreams of the day when he will be a big, fierce, yellow pumpkin who frightens away the field mice as the scarecrow does

"Egielski's artwork features subtle shadings and interesting juxtapositions of colors. . . . The story rolls along smoothly with a clear plot line and some nice phrasing." Booklist

The good little bad little pig; illustrated by Dan Yaccarino. Hyperion Bks. for Children 2002 unp il $15.99; lib bdg $16.49 **E**
1. Pigs—Fiction
ISBN 0-7868-0600-1; 0-7868-2514-6 (lib bdg)
LC 2001-39083

First published 1939 in the author's collection The fish with the deep sea smile

Peter's wish comes true when he gets a little pet pig who is sometimes good and sometimes bad

"The narrative flows naturally, it has sound effects . . . and even depth. . . . The retro style of the illustrations is just right for this old-fashioned, simple tale." SLJ

Goodnight moon; pictures by Clement Hurd. Harper & Row 1947 unp il $15.99; lib bdg $16.89; pa $5.99 **E**
1. Rabbits—Fiction 2. Night—Fiction 3. Stories in rhyme
ISBN 0-06-020705-1; 0-06-020706-X (lib bdg); 0-06-443017-0 (pa)

Also available Board book edition

"The coming of night is shown in pictures which change from bright to dark as a small rabbit says good night to the familiar things in his nest." Hodges. Books for Elem Sch Libr

"A clever goodnight book in which pages are progressively darker as the leaves are turned. There are many objects to identify and children enjoy picking out familiar words." Books for Deaf Child

Little Fur family; illustrated by Garth Williams. HarperCollins Pubs. 1991 unp il $15.95 **E**
1. Bedtime—Fiction
ISBN 0-06-020745-0

First published 1946; this is a reissue of the 1951 edition

"This story of a little fur child's day in the woods ends when his parents sing him to sleep with a lovely bedtime song." Publisher's note

This "book will still charm readers. . . . Williams's softly lit illustrations are enchanting." Horn Book

The little island; with illustrations by Leonard Weisgard. Doubleday Bks. for Young Readers 2003 c1946 unp il $14.95 **E**
1. Islands—Fiction
ISBN 0-385-74640-7

Awarded the Caldecott Medal, 1947

A reissue of the title first published 1946 under the pseudonym Golden MacDonald

There was a little island in the ocean and his book is about how the seasons and the storm and the day and night changed it, how the lobsters and seals and gulls and everything else lived on it, and what the kitten who came to visit found out about it

Brown, Margaret Wise—_Continued_

The little scarecrow boy; pictures by David Diaz. newly il ed. HarperCollins Pubs. 1998 unp il $15.99; lib bdg $16.89; pa $6.99   E
1. Scarecrows—Fiction
ISBN 0-06-026284-2; 0-06-026290-7 (lib bdg); 0-06-77891-1 (pa)   LC 97-32558
"Joanna Cotler books"
Early one morning, a little scarecrow whose father warns him that he is not fierce enough to frighten a crow goes out into the cornfield alone
"Diaz provides wonderful illustrations for a story Brown wrote in the 1940s. . . . Brown's masterful use of repetition and rhythm creates a fine read-aloud story. The warm watercolor illustrations incorporate straw and patchwork." SLJ

The runaway bunny; pictures by Clement Hurd. HarperCollins Publishers 2005 c1942 unp il $16.99; lib bdg $17.89   E
1. Rabbits—Fiction
ISBN 0-06-077582-3; 0-06-077583-1 (lib bdg)
Also available Spanish language edition
A reissue, with some illustrations redrawn, of the title first published 1942
"Within a framework of mutual love, a bunny tells his mother how he will run away and she answers his challenge by indicating how she will catch him." SLJ
"The text has the simplicity of a folk tale and the illustrations are black and white or double page drawings in startling colour." Ont Libr Rev

Two little trains; pictures by Leo and Diane Dillon. HarperCollins Pubs. 2001 unp il $15.95; lib bdg $15.89   E
1. Railroads—Fiction
ISBN 0-06-028376-9; 0-06-028377-7 (lib bdg)   LC 00-40798
A newly illustrated edition of the title first published 1949 by Scott
Two little trains, one streamlined, the other old-fashioned, puff, puff, puff, and chug, chug, chug, on their way West
"The rhythms, the word sounds and the resonant echo of folk song set up a veritable hypnotic chant. . . . [The] soft-grained paintings . . . are beautifully composed in both form and color. A handsome reinterpretation." Booklist

Where have you been? pictures by Leo and Diane Dillon. HarperCollins 2004 unp il $15.99; lib bdg $16.89   E
1. Animals—Fiction 2. Stories in rhyme
ISBN 0-06-028378-5; 0-06-028379-3 (lib bdg)   LC 2003-49981
A newly illustrated edition of the title first published 1952 by Crowell
In rhyming verse, various animals tell where they have been.
"Children fond of call-and-response will enjoy this humorous nursery rhyme. . . . The illustrations are as lively as they are charming, and have enough detail to keep children interested." SLJ

Brown, Ruth

A dark, dark tale; story and pictures by Ruth Brown. Dial Bks. for Young Readers 1981 unp il pa $6.99 hardcover o.p.   E
1. Cats—Fiction
ISBN 0-14-054621-9 (pa)
In a "style used by storytellers of ghostly tales, Brown begins 'Once upon a time there was a dark, dark moor' and goes on to describe the 'dark, dark wood' on the moor, the 'dark, dark house' in the wood and the stygian rooms in the huge place. A nimble black cat accompanies explorers of the mansion and leaps with them in gleeful terror when the final 'dark, dark thing' is discovered." Publ Wkly
"The book's mysterious power is engendered by the illustrations of weed-choked gardens and abandoned, echoing halls, of mullioned windows and blowing curtains." Time

Ten seeds. Knopf 2001 unp il $9.95   E
1. Counting 2. Plants
ISBN 0-375-80697-0   LC 00-46960
This "counting book with a gardening theme takes young children through the life cycle of a sunflower from seed to plant and back again." Horn Book
"With accuracy and charm, the handsome, realistic, double-page watercolor illustrations bring the cycle to life." SLJ

Browne, Anthony

Into the forest. Candlewick Press 2004 unp il $16.99   E
1. Fathers—Fiction 2. Grandmothers—Fiction
ISBN 0-7636-2511-6   LC 2003-69576
After his father seems to disappear, a boy takes a cake to his ill grandmother, traveling through the forest in a journey reminiscent of the story of Little Red Riding Hood.
Browne's "hyperrealistic, pencil-and-watercolor illustrations are full of rich details. Each child may take something different from this psychological picture book, but the reassuring ending is especially comforting." SLJ

My dad. Farrar, Straus & Giroux 2001 c2000 unp il $16   E
1. Fathers—Fiction
ISBN 0-374-35101-5   LC 00-37951
First published 2000 in the United Kingdom
A child describes the many wonderful things about "my dad," who can jump over the moon, swim like a fish, and be as warm as toast
"The offhand affection is genuinely moving as well as funny." Booklist

My mom; [by] Anthony Browne. 1st American ed. Farrar Straus Giroux 2005 unp il $16   E
1. Mothers—Fiction
ISBN 0-374-35098-1   LC 2004-47173
A child describes the many wonderful things about "my mom," who can make anything grow, roar like a lion, and be as comfy as an armchair.
"Browne's paintings hold attention, whether depicting images true to life or flights of fancy, and the honesty of the narrator's emotions and Mom's devotion shine through." Booklist

Browne, Anthony—*Continued*

Piggybook. Knopf 1986 unp il pa $7.99
hardcover o.p.   **E**
1. Mothers—Fiction 2. Family life—Fiction
ISBN 0-679-80837-X (pa)   LC 86-3008
When Mrs. Piggott unexpectedly leaves one day, her
demanding family begins to realize just how much she
did for them
"As in most of Browne's art, there is more than a
touch of irony and visual humor here, bringing off the
didactic with a light touch and turning the lesson into
satire." Bull Cent Child Books

The shape game. Farrar, Straus & Giroux 2003
unp il $16   **E**
1. Illustrators 2. Art museums 3. Art appreciation
ISBN 0-374-36764-7   LC 2002-192894
The author/illustrator describes how his mother's wish
to spend her birthday visiting an art museum with her
family changed the course of his life forever.
"This personal, playful introduction to art and drawing
may well give readers a fresh take on both." Publ Wkly

Voices in the park. DK Ink 1998 unp il $15.95
E
1. Gorillas—Fiction
ISBN 0-7894-2522-X   LC 97-48730
"A simple outing is described by two parents and two
children, each with a different point of view and emotional outlook. Intriguing illustrations of the gorilla characters and surreal touches add layers of visual humor."
SLJ

Willy the dreamer. Candlewick Press 1998 unp
il $16.99   **E**
1. Chimpanzees—Fiction
ISBN 0-7636-0378-3   LC 97-2135
Also available Spanish language edition
Willy the chimp dreams of being a movie star, a sing-
er, a sumo wrestler, an artist, a giant, and other exciting
figures.
"Whether readers are wholly untutored or art history
experts, the closer they look, the more jokes they will
find. Fresh, funny and full of surprises." Publ Wkly
Other titles about Willy are:
Willy and Hugh (1991)
Willy the champ (1986)
Willy the wizard (1995)
Willy's pictures (2000)

Bruchac, Joseph

Crazy Horse's vision; illustrated by S.D. Nelson.
Lee & Low Bks. 2000 unp il $16.95   **E**
1. Crazy Horse, Sioux Chief, ca. 1842-1877—Fiction
2. Oglala Indians—Fiction
ISBN 1-880000-94-6   LC 99-47451
A story based on the life of the dedicated young
Lakota boy who grew up to be one of the bravest de-
fenders of his people.
"Bruchac has created a memorable tale about Crazy
Horse's childhood. . . . In beautiful illustrations inspired
by the ledger book style of the Plains Indians, Sioux artist Nelson fills the pages with both action and quiet drama." Booklist

Bruel, Nick

Boing! [by] Nick Bruel. 1st ed. Roaring Brook
Press 2004 unp il $15.95; lib bdg $22.90
E
1. Kangaroos—Fiction
ISBN 0-7613-2428-3; 0-7613-3412-2 (lib bdg)
LC 2003-18135
A mother kangaroo and various woodland animals
coach her joey as she attempts her first jump.
"Told mainly through bright, cheerful pictures that are
enhanced by bits of dialogue and pertinent sound effects,
this simple story will make children smile." SLJ

Brun-Cosme, Nadine

No, I want daddy! illustrated by Michel Backès.
1st American ed. Clarion Books 2004 unp il $14
E
1. Mother-daughter relationship—Fiction 2. Foxes—
Fiction
ISBN 0-618-38157-0   LC 2003-1165
Anna the fox is unhappy when her tired mother says
no to all of her after-school plans but after an evening
of letting only Daddy do things for her, Anna cannot go
to sleep until she and Mama make up.
"Simple sentences tell this universal story and make it
ring true. The illustrations feature thick black lines and
an earthy palette of tans, greens, and a foxlike reddish
brown." SLJ

Brunhoff, Jean de

The story of Babar, the little elephant; translated
from the French by Merle S. Haas. Random House
1937 c1933 47p il $15.95; lib bdg $17.99
E
1. Elephants—Fiction
ISBN 0-394-80575-5; 0-394-90575-X (lib bdg)
Additional titles about Babar by Laurent de Brunhoff
are available
Original French edition, 1931; this is a reduced format
version of the 1933 United States edition
"Babar runs away from the jungle and goes to live
with an old lady in Paris, where he adapts quickly to
French amenities. Later he returns to the jungle and be-
comes king. Much of the charm of the story is contribut-
ed by the author's gay pictures." Hodges. Books for
Elem Sch Libr
Other titles about Babar are:
Babar and Father Christmas (1940)
Babar and his children (1938)
Babar the king (1935)
Bonjour, Babar (2000)
Travels of Babar (1934)

Brusca, María Cristina

Three friends. Tres amigos; a counting book;
[by] María Cristina Brusca and Toña Wilson;
illustrated by María Cristina Brusca. Holt & Co.
1995 unp il $16.95   **E**
1. Counting 2. Bilingual books—English-Spanish
ISBN 0-8050-3707-1   LC 94-44648
This "bilingual text teaches the numbers one to ten by
incorporating a Southwestern flavor. Brief sentences

Brusca, María Cristina—*Continued*

count objects, while the illustrations show the adventures of two cowboys. The artwork is amusing, and a picture glossary contains terms for objects that are in the illustrations but not mentioned in the text." Horn Book Guide

Bruss, Deborah

Book! book! book! illustrated by Tiphanie Beeke. Levine Bks. 2001 unp il $15.95 **E**

1. Domestic animals—Fiction 2. Libraries—Fiction 3. Books and reading—Fiction

ISBN 0-439-13525-7 LC 99-59758

When the children go back to school, the animals on the farm are bored, so they go into the library in town trying to find something to do

"Soft, naive watercolor paintings illustrate the satisfying story, which, with its witty conclusion, will be a sure winner at story time." Horn Book Guide

Brust, Beth Wagner

The great tulip trade; by Beth Wagner Brust; illustrated by Jenny Mattheson. 1st ed. Random House 2005 47p lib bdg $11.99; pa $3.99

E

1. Netherlands—Fiction 2. Tulips—Fiction 3. Birthdays—Fiction 4. Father-daughter relationship—Fiction

ISBN 0-375-92573-2 (libdg); 0-375-82573-8 (pa)

LC 2004008067

"Step into reading"

In Holland in the 1600s, a birthday gift of eight precious tulip bulbs is traded into livestock, furniture, and a valuable painting.

The author "takes a complicated topic . . . and makes it into a credible story-for beginning readers! . . . Delightful illustrations that have the dimension of collage and the soft edges of digital art add to the accessibility." Booklist

Brutschy, Jennifer

Just one more story; illustrated by Cat Bowman Smith. Orchard Bks. 2002 unp il $16.95

E

1. Storytelling—Fiction 2. Musicians—Fiction

ISBN 0-439-31767-3 LC 99-58610

Austin and his parents travel around the country in their trailer performing with their band, and every night Austin's father tells him one bedtime story, until the night they stay in a two-story house instead of their trailer

"Pitch-perfect southwestern idioms set the tone and enhance the sense of place. Loose, carefree watercolors include fanciful touches." Horn Book Guide

Buck, Pearl S. (Pearl Sydenstricker)

Christmas day in the morning; illustrated by Mark Buehner. HarperCollins Pubs. 2002 unp il $16.99; lib bdg $18.89 **E**

1. Christmas—Fiction 2. Farm life—Fiction

ISBN 0-688-16267-3; 0-688-16268-1 (lib bdg)

LC 2001-39497

Story originally published 1955

A boy surprises his father on Christmas morning by getting up early and milking the cows on their farm.

"Buck invests a simple story with poetic dignity and teaches a bone-deep lesson about love. . . . Buehner's paintings enhance the story, capturing the deep blue-white of a snowy farmland." Booklist

Buckley, Helen E. (Helen Elizabeth)

Grandfather and I; [illustrated by] Jan Ormerod. Lothrop, Lee & Shepard Bks. 1994 unp il $15.95; lib bdg $15.89; pa $5.99 **E**

1. Grandfathers—Fiction

ISBN 0-688-12533-6; 0-688-12534-4 (lib bdg); 0-688-17526-0 (pa) LC 93-22936

A newly illustrated edition of the title first published 1959

A child considers how Grandfather is the perfect person to spend time with because he is never in a hurry

"Ormerod's full-color paintings teem with the warmth of a loving intergenerational family and fairly burst from the pages." SLJ

Grandmother and I; [illustrated by] Jan Ormerod. Lothrop, Lee & Shepard Bks. 1994 unp il $16.99; pa $5.99 **E**

1. Grandmothers—Fiction

ISBN 0-688-12531-X; 0-688-17525-2 (pa)

LC 93-22937

A newly illustrated edition of the title first published 1961

A child considers how Grandmother's lap is just right for those times when lightning is coming in the window or the cat is missing

"The watercolor art, done mostly in earth tones, varies from soft to sassy, but most of all, it is honest. Any child who has shared the unconditional love of a grandparent will see that love reflected here." Booklist

Buehner, Caralyn

Fanny's dream; pictures by Mark Buehner. Dial Bks. for Young Readers 1996 unp il $15.99; pa $6.99 **E**

1. Marriage—Fiction 2. Farm life—Fiction

ISBN 0-8037-1496-3; 0-14-250060-7 (pa)

LC 94-31910

Fanny Agnes is a sturdy farm girl who dreams of marrying a prince, but when her fairy godmother doesn't show up, she decides on a local farmer instead

"Fanny Agnes is a delight: a feminist with a wry sense of humor, she balances her dreams with common sense and a loving heart. What's more, there's plenty for youngsters to enjoy in the robust, bucolic pictures, which seem almost to jump off the page." Booklist

I did it, I'm sorry; pictures by Mark Buehner. Dial Bks. for Young Readers 1998 unp il $16.99; pa $6.99 **E**

1. Animals—Fiction

ISBN 0-8037-2010-6; 0-14-056722-4 (pa)

LC 97-10216

Ollie Octopus, Bucky Beaver, Howie Hogg, and other animal characters encounter moral dilemmas involving such virtues as honesty, thoughtfulness, and trustworthi-

Buehner, Caralyn—*Continued*

ness. The reader is invited to select the appropriate behavior from a series of choices, and the letter for the correct answer is hidden in the pictures

The artist has "concealed bumblebees, cats, rabbits and dinosaurs, among other things, in each of his lush and expressive oil-and-acrylic paintings. . . . Caralyn Buehner's snappy, alliterative text makes for an exuberant read-aloud." Publ Wkly

Snowmen at night; pictures by Mark Buehner. Phyllis Fogelman Bks. 2002 unp il $15.99

E

1. Snow—Fiction 2. Stories in rhyme
ISBN 0-8037-2550-7   LC 2001-33517
Snowmen play games at night when no one is watching

The "text has bouncy rhymes, but it's the artwork that is spectacular. Acrylic-over-oil paintings feature fat, happy snowpeople who practically jump—or sled—off the pages." Booklist

Another title about the snowmen is:
Snowmen at Christmas (2005)

Superdog; the heart of a hero; illustrated by Mark Buehner. HarperCollins 2004 unp il $15.99; lib bdg $16.89

E

1. Dogs—Fiction
ISBN 0-06-623620-7; 0-06-623621-5 (lib bdg)
                    LC 2002-3540
Tired of being overlooked because he is so small, a big-hearted dog named Dexter transforms himself into a superhero

"Solid shapings, surprising perspectives, and thick paints in dynamic colors combine for artwork that practically jumps off the page. There's plenty of wit, too." Booklist

Bulla, Clyde Robert

The chalk box kid; illustrated by Thomas B. Allen. Random House 1987 unp il $11.99; pa $3.99

E

ISBN 0-394-99102-8; 0-394-89102-3 (pa)
                    LC 87-4683
"Gregory's family moves to a smaller house in a poorer part of town; the father has lost his factory job. There is no yard at the new house in which to play, but Gregory explores a nearly burnt-out building that formerly was a chalk factory. Gregory finds plenty of chalk in the debris as he cleans up, and the artist in him soars." Publ Wkly

"Bulla manages a poignant depth within the confines of simple style and narrative. Understated and easy to read, this nevertheless tackles problems that are not easy to solve without exercising the imagination." Bull Cent Child Books

Daniel's duck; pictures by Joan Sandin. Harper & Row 1979 60p il lib bdg $16.89; pa $3.99

E

1. Wood carving—Fiction
ISBN 0-06-020909-7 (lib bdg); 0-06-444031-1 (pa)
                    LC 77-25647

"An I can read book"

Daniel "carved a duck with its head looking backward. At the fair, people laughed when they saw the carving, and Daniel thought his work was being ridiculed; but he was more than consoled by a famous local wood-carver, who not only praised Daniel's duck but offered to buy it. The easy-to-read story and the simple format are excellently served by the subdued three-color illustrations, which round out the account of a traditional Appalachian family." Horn Book

Bunting, Eve

The bones of Fred Mcfee; illustrated by Kurt Cyrus. Harcourt 2002 unp il $16   E

1. Halloween—Fiction 2. Stories in rhyme
ISBN 0-15-202004-7   LC 2001-2414
A toy skeleton at Halloween provides menace and mystery

"The story, told in rhyme keeps readers on the edge of their seats. . . . Cyrus's detailed, realistic illustrations, done in scratchboard and watercolor, are appropriately dark and are a perfect complement to the subtly scary mood of the text." SLJ

Butterfly house; illustrated by Greg Shed. Scholastic Press 1999 unp il $16.95   E

1. Butterflies—Fiction 2. Grandfathers—Fiction
3. Stories in rhyme
ISBN 0-590-84884-4   LC 98-16349
With the help of her grandfather, a little girl makes a house for a larva and watches it develop before setting it free, and every summer after that butterflies come to visit her

"Shed's gouache-on-canvas paintings evoke feelings of warmth and nostalgia suited to the quiet story. Earth tones predominate, especially the browns and oranges found in this species. Appended with directions for raising a butterfly." Booklist

Can you do this, Old Badger? illustrated by LeUyen Pham. Harcourt Brace & Co. 2000 unp $15   E

1. Badgers—Fiction 2. Old age—Fiction
ISBN 0-15-201654-6   LC 98-39809
Although Old Badger cannot do some things as easily as he used to, he can still teach Little Badger the many things he knows about finding good things to eat and staying safe and happy

"Cozy woodland scenes, rendered in dusky forest greens, royal blue, and earth tones, illustrate a satisfying yarn that hints at the natural life cycle." Horn Book Guide

Other titles about the Badgers are:

Little Badger, terror of the seven seas (2001)
Little Badger's just-about birthday (2002)

Cheyenne again; illustrated by Irving Toddy. Clarion Bks. 1995 unp il $16; pa $5.95

E

1. Cheyenne Indians—Fiction 2. School stories
ISBN 0-395-70364-6; 0-618-19465-7 (pa)
                    LC 94-43287

Young Bull, "a young Cheyenne boy tells how he's taken from his parents on the reservation in the late 1880s and sent to a boarding school, where he's forced

Bunting, Eve—*Continued*

to learn white ways. . . . This is a picture book for older readers, a grim story of painful separation and forced assimilation. . . . The short, spare lines of free verse are illustrated by double-page-spread oil and acrylic paintings that contrast the open landscape with the stiffness of figures forced into uniform and regimentation." Booklist

Christmas cricket; illustrated by Timothy Bush. Clarion Bks. 2002 32p il $15   E
1. Crickets—Fiction 2. Christmas—Fiction
ISBN 0-618-06554-7   LC 2001-55266
On Christmas Eve, a little cricket finds its way into a house where its singing is thought to be the voice of an angel
"Bush's watercolor pictures celebrate the story's cheerful warmth while their varying sizes and shapes create a cinematic effect that cleverly captures both the rhythm of the text and a cricket's kinetic spirit." Booklist

Dandelions; illustrated by Greg Shed. Harcourt Brace & Co. 1995 unp $16   E
1. Frontier and pioneer life—Fiction 2. Family life—Fiction 3. Nebraska—Fiction
ISBN 0-15-200050-X   LC 94-27104
"Like the dandelions she plants on the roof of their Nebraska soddie, Zoe believes that the transplanting of her family will 'take,' despite the difficult transition. Young Zoe's narration conveys both youthful confidence and fear as the family work to adjust to their new life. Gouache illustrations effectively portray the vast, sun-drenched prairie and complement the text." Horn Book Guide

December; illustrated by David Diaz. Harcourt Brace & Co. 1997 unp il $16; pa $7   E
1. Christmas—Fiction 2. Homeless persons—Fiction
ISBN 0-15-201434-9; 0-15-202422-0 (pa)
LC 96-21148
A homeless family's luck changes after they help an old woman who has even less than they do at Christmas
"Using elements of traditional folktales, Bunting provides a simply told story that is infused with the miraculous. . . . The artwork . . . is top-notch, intricate collages created from scraps of newspaper and images from the story make an arresting backdrop for the bold acrylic-and-watercolor pictures." Booklist

Flower garden; written by Eve Bunting; illustrated by Kathryn Hewitt. Harcourt Brace & Co. 1994 unp il $16; pa $6   E
1. Flowers—Fiction 2. Birthdays—Fiction 3. Stories in rhyme
ISBN 0-15-228776-0; 0-15-202372-0 (pa)
LC 92-25766
Also available Big book edition
"The young narrator has, with the help of her father, assembled a 'garden in a shopping cart' to take home and plant in a window box high above the city as a birthday gift for her mother." Horn Book Guide
"The simple rhymed verse, which skips along in pace with the child's anticipation, is smoothly integrated with the vibrant, lifelike paintings." Booklist

Fly away home; illustrated by Ronald Himler. Clarion Bks. 1991 32p il $16; pa $5.95
E
1. Homeless persons—Fiction 2. Airports—Fiction
ISBN 0-395-55962-6; 0-395-66415-2 (pa)
LC 90-42353
A homeless boy who lives in an airport with his father, moving from terminal to terminal and trying not to be noticed, is given hope when he sees a trapped bird find its freedom
"Himler's quiet paintings echo the economy and the touching quality of the story, which is all the more effective in depicting the plight of the homeless because it is so low-keyed." Bull Cent Child Books

Girls A to Z; illustrated by Suzanne Bloom. Boyds Mills Press 2002 unp il $15.95   E
1. Occupations 2. Alphabet
ISBN 1-56397-147-X
Girls with names ranging from Aliki to Zoe imagine themselves in various fun and creative professions
"Bunting has created a winning alphabet book that is playful, inventive, and (coincidentally) politically correct. Accompanied by Bloom's exuberant watercolor portraits." SLJ

How many days to America? a Thanksgiving story; illustrated by Beth Peck. Clarion Bks. 1988 unp il lib bdg $16; pa $5.95   E
1. Refugees—Fiction 2. Thanksgiving Day—Fiction
ISBN 0-89919-521-0 (lib bdg); 0-395-54777-6 (pa)
LC 88-2590
Refugees from an unnamed Caribbean island embark on a dangerous boat trip to America where they have a special reason to celebrate Thanksgiving
"Bunting's simple tale focuses on the hardships of the journey and on the American ideals of freedom and safety. She wisely leaves aside the issues of politics in the homeland or in this country. Her prose is poetically spare. . . . Peck's richly colored crayon drawings yield added enjoyment. . . . A poignant story and a thought-provoking discussion starter." SLJ

Jin Woo; illustrated by Chris K. Soentpiet. Clarion Bks. 2001 30p il $16   E
1. Adoption—Fiction 2. Brothers—Fiction 3. Korean Americans—Fiction
ISBN 0-395-93872-4   LC 00-38408
Davey is dubious about having a new adopted brother from Korea, but when he finds out that his parents still love him, he decides that having a baby brother will be fine
"Soentpiet's watercolors are suffused with light and perfectly capture the characters' expressions. . . . The story's emotional veracity will speak to any new sibling." SLJ

Little Bear's little boat; illustrated by Nancy Carpenter. Clarion Bks. 2003 32p il $12
E
1. Growth—Fiction 2. Bears—Fiction
ISBN 0-395-97462-3   LC 2001-37233
When Little Bear can no longer fit into his boat he finds someone else who can use it
"This is a sensitive, affecting story about growing up

Bunting, Eve—*Continued*

and leaving favorite things behind, with charming ink-and-paint illustrations that echo the spare clarity of the words." Booklist

The memory string; pictures by Ted Rand. Clarion Bks. 2000 32p il $15　　　　　　**E**

1. Memory—Fiction 2. Stepmothers—Fiction

ISBN 0-395-86146-2　　　　　　LC 99-42771

While still grieving for her mother and unable to accept her stepmother, Laura clings to the memories represented by forty-three buttons on a string

"Rand's realistic artwork concentrates on the faces of the family and the emotions that cross them. Some children will find this touches them very deeply." Booklist

My special day at Third Street School; illustrated by Suzanne Bloom. Boyds Mills Press 2004 unp il $15.95　　　　　　**E**

1. Authors—Fiction 2. School stories

ISBN 1-59078-075-2

A school visit from children's book author Amanda Drake brings a day full of fun.

"Just as Bunting's writing captures the action and the children's emotions in a convincing way, Bloom's gouache, colored pencil, and crayon artwork illustrates the contemporary classroom setting and the children's body language to perfection." Booklist

Night tree; illustrated by Ted Rand. Harcourt Brace Jovanovich 1991 unp il $16; pa $6　　　　　　**E**

1. Trees—Fiction 2. Christmas—Fiction

ISBN 0-15-257425-5; 0-15-200121-2 (pa)

　　　　　　LC 90-36178

A family makes its annual pilgrimage to decorate an evergreen tree with food for the forest animals at Christmastime

"Bunting's quiet text and Rand's watercolors have just the right nighttime mood, capturing the mystery of the woods where there are 'secrets all around us.'" Bull Cent Child Books

One candle; illustrated by K. Wendy Popp. HarperCollins Pubs. 2002 unp il $15.99; lib bdg $17.89　　　　　　**E**

1. Hanukkah—Fiction 2. Holocaust, 1933-1945—Fiction 3. Jews—Fiction

ISBN 0-06-028115-4; 0-06-028116-2 (lib bdg)

　　　　　　LC 2001-47205

"Joanna Cotler books"

Every year a family celebrates Hanukkah by retelling the story of how Grandma and her sister managed to mark the day while in a German concentration camp

"Popp invests her art with all the emotion of Bunting's heartfelt text. . . . A gentle but forthright opening for discussion about the Holocaust." Booklist

One green apple; by Eve Bunting; illustrated by Ted Lewin. Clarion Books 2006 unp il $16

　　　　　　E

1. Immigrants—Fiction 2. Apples—Fiction 3. Muslims—Fiction 4. School stories

ISBN 0-618-43477-1　　　　　　LC 2005011378

While on a school field trip to an orchard to make cider, a young immigrant named Farah gains self-confidence when the green apple she picks perfectly complements the other students' red apples.

"Young readers will respond as much to Bunting's fine first-person narrative as to Lewin's double-page, photorealistic watercolors." Booklist

A picnic in October; illustrated by Nancy Carpenter. Harcourt Brace & Co. 1999 unp il $16; pa $6　　　　　　**E**

1. Statue of Liberty (New York, N.Y.)—Fiction 2. Immigrants—Fiction 3. Italian Americans—Fiction

ISBN 0-15-201656-2; 0-15-205065-5 (pa)

　　　　　　LC 98-20044

A boy finally comes to understand why his grandmother insists that the family come to Ellis Island each year to celebrate Lady Liberty's birthday

"The talented Bunting makes this into a real story with characters that ring true. Carpenter's art, vibrant with sea and sky blues, has the same realistic feel." Booklist

Secret place; illustrated by Ted Rand. Clarion Bks. 1996 26p il $16　　　　　　**E**

1. City and town life—Fiction 2. Nature—Fiction

ISBN 0-395-64367-8　　　　　　LC 95-20466

"A little boy learns that the city, with all its grime and smoke and noise, can also be home for wildlife, when he discovers a 'secret place' in a river flowing between concrete walls. . . . Bunting's prose is evocative . . . and Rand's paintings vividly convey both the grayness of the city and the colors of the graceful wild creatures." Booklist

Smoky night; written by Eve Bunting; illustrated by David Diaz. Harcourt Brace & Co. 1994 unp il $16; pa $6　　　　　　**E**

1. Riots—Fiction 2. Los Angeles (Calif.)—Fiction 3. African Americans—Fiction 4. Korean Americans—Fiction

ISBN 0-15-269954-6; 0-15-201884-0 (pa)

　　　　　　LC 93-14885

Awarded the Caldecott Medal, 1995

When the Los Angeles riots break out in the streets of their neighborhood, Daniel and his mother, African Americans, make friends with Mrs. Kim, a Korean grocer from across the street

"Thick black lines border vibrant acrylic paintings. . . . Diaz places these dynamic paintings on collages of real objects that, for the most part, reinforce the narrative action. . . . Both author and illustrator insist on a headlong confrontation with the issue of rapport between different races, and the result is a memorable, thought-provoking book." Horn Book

So far from the sea; illustrated by Chris K. Soentpiet. Clarion Bks. 1998 30p il $16

　　　　　　E

1. Japanese Americans—Evacuation and relocation, 1942-1945—Fiction

ISBN 0-395-72095-8　　　　　　LC 97-28176

When seven-year-old Laura and her family visit Grandfather's grave at the Manzanar War Relocation Center, the Japanese American child leaves behind a special symbol

Bunting, Eve—*Continued*

"Soentpiet's impressionistic watercolors perfectly complement Bunting's evocative text." SLJ

Someday a tree; illustrated by Ronald Himler. Clarion Bks. 1993 unp il $16; pa $5.95

E

1. Trees—Fiction 2. Pollution—Fiction
ISBN 0-395-61309-4; 0-395-76478-5 (pa)

LC 92-24074

Alice, her parents, and their neighbors try to save an old oak tree that has been poisoned by pollution

"Himler's soft, realistic watercolors spread over double pages and complement the sensitive, poetic mood of the story." SLJ

That's what leprechauns do; illustrated by Emily Arnold McCully. Clarion Books 2005 32p il $16

E

1. Leprechauns—Fiction 2. Ireland—Fiction
ISBN 0-618-35410-7

When leprechauns Ari, Boo, and Col need to place the pot of gold at the end of the rainbow, they cannot help getting into mischief along the way.

"McCully graces this lighthearted story with her characteristically expressive and charming watercolors that eloquently capture the verdant beauty of the Irish countryside and the irrepressible personalities." SLJ

Train to Somewhere; illustrated by Ronald Himler. Clarion Bks. 1996 32p il $16; pa $5.95

E

1. Orphans—Fiction 2. Adoption—Fiction
3. Abandoned children—Fiction
ISBN 0-395-71325-0; 0-618-04031-5 (pa)

LC 95-6787

"Traveling on an Orphan Train in the late 1800s, Marianne tells herself that her mother, who went west some time ago, will surely come to meet her. At the last stop in Somewhere, Iowa, she finds not her mother, but an unlikely-looking older couple who just may be the family she needs. The illustrations convey the poignancy and historical setting of Marianne's journey." Horn Book Guide

The Wall; illustrated by Ronald Himler. Clarion Bks. 1990 unp il $16; pa $5.95   E

1. Vietnam Veterans Memorial (Washington, D.C.)—Fiction
ISBN 0-395-51588-2; 0-395-62977-2 (pa)

LC 89-17429

"A father and his young son come to the Vietnam Veterans Memorial to find the name of the grandfather the boy never knew. This moving account is beautifully told from a young child's point of view; the watercolors capture the impressive mass of the wall of names as well as the poignant reactions of the people who visit there." Horn Book Guide

The Wednesday surprise; illustrated by Donald Carrick. Clarion Bks. 1989 unp il lib bdg $16; pa $5.95   E

1. Grandmothers—Fiction 2. Reading—Fiction
ISBN 0-89919-721-3 (lib bdg); 0-395-54776-8 (pa)

LC 88-12117

This "first-person account tells of the special gift that seven-year-old Anna and her grandmother have planned for her dad's birthday: secretly, the two read books together until finally, the grandmother has learned to read." SLJ

"Bunting's writing is simple and warm and direct. . . . Carrick's pictures echo the warmth, especially in the faces of the family, painted in realistically detailed watercolors with a careful attention to familial resemblance. A gentle charmer." Bull Cent Child Books

Burleigh, Robert

Home run; the story of Babe Ruth; illustrated by Mike Wimmer. Harcourt Brace & Co. 1998 unp il $16   E

1. Ruth, Babe, 1895-1948—Fiction 2. Baseball—Fiction
ISBN 0-15-200970-1

LC 95-10038

"A Silver Whistle book"

A poetic account of the legendary Babe Ruth as he prepares to make a home run

"With a flowing minimal text, Burleigh brings the Babe to life through the moment of one at bat. . . . Wimmer's sprawling, photorealistic oil paintings depict the larger-than-life figure and his surroundings with folksy Norman Rockwell-like charm." SLJ

Messenger, messenger; illustrated by Barry Root. Atheneum Bks. for Young Readers 2000 unp il $16   E

1. City and town life—Fiction 2. Cycling—Fiction
3. Stories in rhyme
ISBN 0-689-82103-4

LC 98-20566

Calvin Curbhopper, a bicycle messenger, makes his way through the city in all kinds of conditions to make sure that his messages get delivered on time

"The brightly colored gouache spreads extend the kinetic rhythms in the rhyming text. In realistic detail, they convey the city's buzzing workday activity." Booklist

The secret of the great Houdini; [illustrated by] Leonid Gore. Atheneum Bks. for Young Readers 2002 unp il $16.95   E

1. Houdini, Harry, 1874-1926—Fiction 2. Magicians—Fiction
ISBN 0-689-83267-2

LC 00-38057

As Sam and Uncle Ezra watch, the Great Houdini escapes from a trunk at the bottom of the river. Includes factual information about Houdini and his career as a magician and escape artist.

"The suspense is palpable, and Gore's subtly tinted, atmospheric artwork reinforces the deep mystery of what really went on underwater." Booklist

Burningham, John

Mr. Gumpy's outing. Holt & Co. 1971 c1970 unp il $16.95; pa $6.95   E

1. Animals—Fiction
ISBN 0-8050-0708-3; 0-8050-1315-6 (pa)
Also available Big book edition
First published 1970 in the United Kingdom

"Mr. Gumpy is about to go off for a boat ride and is asked by two children, a rabbit, a cat, a dog, and other

Burningham, John—*Continued*

animals if they may come. To each Mr. Gumpy says yes, if—if the children don't squabble, if the rabbit won't hop, if the cat won't chase the rabbit or the dog tease the cat, and so on. Of course each does exactly what Mr. Gumpy forbade, the boat tips over, and they all slog home for tea in friendly fashion." Sutherland. The Best in Child Books

Another title about Mr. Gumpy is:

Mr. Gumpy's motor car (1976)

Burton, Virginia Lee

Katy and the big snow; story and pictures by Virginia Lee Burton. Houghton Mifflin 1943 32p il $16; pa $6.95   E

1. Tractors—Fiction 2. Snow—Fiction

ISBN 0-395-18155-0; 0-395-18562-9 (pa)

"Katy was a beautiful red crawler tractor. In summer she wore a bulldozer to push dirt with. In winter she wore a snowplow. She was big and strong and the harder the job the better she liked it. When the Big Snow covered the city of Geoppolis like a thick blanket, Katy cleared the city from North to South and East to West." Ont Libr Rev

The little house; story and pictures by Virginia Lee Burton. Houghton Mifflin 1942 40p il $14.95; pa $5.95   E

1. Houses—Fiction 2. City and town life—Fiction

ISBN 0-395-18156-9; 0-395-25938-X (pa)

Awarded the Caldecott Medal, 1943

"The little house was very happy as she sat on the quiet hillside watching the changing seasons. As the years passed, however, tall buildings grew up around her, and the noise of city traffic disturbed her. She became sad and lonely until one day someone who understood her need for twinkling stars overhead and dancing apple blossoms moved her back to just the right little hill." Child Books Too Good to Miss

Maybelle, the cable car; written and illustrated by Virginia Lee Burton. Houghton Mifflin 1996 42p il $16; pa $5.95   E

1. Cable railroads—Fiction 2. San Francisco (Calif.)—Fiction

ISBN 0-395-82847-3; 0-395-84003-1 (pa)

LC 96-9845

A reissue of the title first published 1952

Maybelle loves to carry people up and down the hilly streets of San Francisco, until the City Fathers decide that she should be taken out of service in the name of progress

"The brightly colored line drawings are baroque in flavor, in keeping with the whimsey of the story, which is done in a loose-jointed blank verse, fine for reading aloud." N Y Times Book Rev

Mike Mulligan and his steam shovel; story and pictures by Virginia Lee Burton. Houghton Mifflin 1939 unp il $16; pa $6.95   E

1. Steam-shovels—Fiction

ISBN 0-395-16961-5; 0-395-25939-8 (pa)

Also available Spanish language edition

"Mike Mulligan remains faithful to his steam shovel, Mary Anne, against the threat of the new gas and Diesel-engine contraptions and digs his way to a surprising and happy ending." New Yorker

"One of the most convincing personifications of a machine ever written. Lively pictures, dramatic action, and a satisfying conclusion." Adventuring with Books. 2d edition

Butler, John

Can you cuddle like a koala? Peachtree 2003 unp il $15.95   E

1. Animals—Fiction 2. Stories in rhyme

ISBN 1-56145-298-X   LC 2003-4334

Rhyming text describes how various animals move.

"The art, with its delicate colors and detailed rendering of the layered textures of fur, gives the animals a soft, huggable look, making this a perfect title for curling up together during one-on-one reading." SLJ

Whose baby am I? Viking 2001 unp il $10.99   E

1. Animal babies

ISBN 0-670-89683-7   LC 00-11200

Under each "illustration of a young animal is the question, 'whose baby am I?' Turn the page, and the baby is identified and shown with a parent. Nine animals, including a koala, panda, and penguin, are introduced. The final page shows the words for the baby animals such as *foal*, *joey*, and *cub*." Horn Book Guide

"Each creature is handsomely presented in acrylic-and-colored pencil art, its 'babyness' distinct and appealing. . . . An effective, attractive presentation that should also work well at toddler story hours." Booklist

Buzzeo, Toni

Dawdle Duckling; illustrated by Margaret Spengler. Dial Bks. for Young Readers 2003 unp il $15.99   E

1. Ducks—Fiction

ISBN 0-8037-2731-3   LC 2001-49913

Mama Duck tries to keep Dawdle Duckling together with his siblings, but he wants to dawdle and dream, preen and play, splash and spin

"The smile-provoking pastel illustrations put the characters front and center. . . . The repetitive text will hold children's attention, and the bit of tension at the book's conclusion adds sparkle." Booklist

Another title about Dawdle Duckling is:

Ready or not, Dawdle Ducking (2005)

The sea chest; illustrated by Mary GrandPré. Dial Bks. for Young Readers 2002 unp il $16.99   E

1. Lighthouses—Fiction 2. Islands—Fiction 3. Sisters—Fiction 4. Maine—Fiction

ISBN 0-8037-2703-8   LC 2001-28255

A young girl listens as her great-aunt, a lighthouse keeper's daughter, tells of her childhood living on a Maine island, and of the infant that washed ashore after a storm

"GrandPré's oil paintings create the dramatic effects of the story. . . . This lovely book has an intimacy that is enhanced by reading it aloud." SLJ

Byars, Betsy Cromer

The Golly sisters go West; by Betsy Byars; pictures by Sue Truesdell. Harper & Row 1986 c1985 64p il lib bdg $16.89; pa $3.99   E
1. Entertainers—Fiction 2. Frontier and pioneer life—Fiction 3. West (U.S.)—Fiction
ISBN 0-06-020884-8 (lib bdg); 0-06-444132-6 (pa)
LC 84-48474
"An I can read book"
May-May and Rose, the singing, dancing Golly sisters, travel west by covered wagon, entertaining people along the way
"The dialogue and antics are convincingly like those of rivalrous young siblings anywhere on the block. The story lines are cleverer than much easy-to-read fare, and the old-West setting adds flair. The accompanying watercolors, too, add a generous dollop of humor." Bull Cent Child Books
Other titles about the Golly sisters are:
The Golly sisters ride again (1994)
Hooray for the Golly sisters! (1990)

My brother, Ant; by Betsy Byars; illustrated by Marc Simont. Viking 1996 31p il $13.99; pa $3.99   E
1. Brothers—Fiction
ISBN 0-670-86664-4; 0-14-038345-X (pa)
LC 95-23725
In four separate stories, Ant's older brother gets rid of the monster under Ant's bed, forgives Ant for drawing on his homework, tries to read a story, and helps Ant writes a letter to Santa
"The affectionate relationship between the boys underscores all the stories. Simont's lively, realistic watercolors enhance the understated humor." SLJ
Another title about Ant is:
Ant plays Bear (1997)

Bynum, Eboni

Jamari's drum; [by] Eboni Bynum and Roland Jackson; pictures on glazed tiles by Baba Wagué Diakité. Groundwood Books 2004 unp il $16.95   E
1. Drums—Fiction 2. Africa—Fiction 3. Volcanoes—Fiction
ISBN 0-88899-531-8
When Jamari forgets to heed Baba Mdogo's warning to play the drum in the village every day, he narrowly averts disaster from a volcano.
"The beautifully executed, folk-style artwork swirls with bold lines and bright patterns, incorporating backgrounds that blend earth tones with the blues and purples of the sky. . . . This book makes an excellent read-aloud." SLJ

Byrd, Robert

Saint Francis and the Christmas donkey. Dutton Children's Bks. 2000 unp il $15.99   E
1. Francis, of Assisi, Saint, 1182-1226—Fiction 2. Jesus Christ—Nativity 3. Donkeys—Fiction
ISBN 0-525-46480-8   LC 00-25415
Saint Francis, who loves all animals, explains to a sullen donkey why his kind have always had to work hard, but also tells him of a donkey's role in the first Christmas
"Byrd's evocative language . . . will attract readers and listeners of many ages. The pace of his story is measured and calm, and the paintings are large and spacious, some glittering with details, others open and peaceful." Booklist

Cabrera, Jane

If you're happy and you know it; [by] Jane Cabrera. 1st ed. Holiday House 2005 unp il $16.95   E
1. Songs 2. Animals—Fiction
ISBN 0-8234-1881-2   LC 2004-47264
An elephant, a monkey, and a giraffe join other animals to sing different verses of this popular song that encourages everyone to express their happiness through voice and movement.
"Cheerful painterly pictures in a kaleidoscope of colors enhance the jovial mood of the song." SLJ

Mommy, carry me please! [by] Jane Cabrera. 1st ed. Holiday House 2006 unp il $16.95   E
1. Mother-child relationship—Fiction 2. Animals—Fiction
ISBN 0-8234-1935-5   LC 2004048862
"On each spread of this warm lapsit book, a baby animal asks its mother to carry me please. Each mother accommodates by transporting the youngster in that animals special way: lemur under its belly, kangaroo in a pouch, tiger in its mouth, crocodile in teeth, penguin on its feet, and so on until the cozy ending when a human child is carried in the mothers arms. The art features Cabrera's trademark breezy, blocky, and bold animals in bright and energetic colors that focus childrens eye and attention." SLJ

Calhoun, Mary

Cross-country cat; illustrated by Erick Ingraham. Morrow 1979 unp il pa $5.99 hardcover o.p.   E
1. Cats—Fiction
ISBN 0-698-06519-8 (pa)   LC 78-31718
When he becomes lost in the mountains, Henry, a cat with the unusual ability of walking on two legs finds his way home on cross-country skis
"Only the careful blending of skills by a talented author and illustrator could turn such a farfetched plot into a warm, rich, and rewarding story. The realistic illustrations seem to be enveloped in a glowing light and invite the reader to step right into the story." Child Book Rev Serv
Other titles about Henry the cat are:
Blue-ribbon Henry (1999)
Henry the Christmas cat (2004)
Henry the sailor cat (1994)
High-wire Henry (1991)
Hot-air Henry (1981)

Flood; illustrated by Erick Ingraham. Morrow Junior Bks. 1997 unp il $15.95   E
1. Floods—Fiction
ISBN 0-688-13919-1   LC 96-14836

Calhoun, Mary—*Continued*

One fictional Midwestern family is forced to leave their home during the flooding of the Mississippi River in 1993

"Powerful in its understatement. . . . The storytelling is quiet, but it is tightly paced as it moves inexorably to the climax. . . . Ingraham's pastel pencil and watercolor illustrations are extraordinary, both the sweeping views of the stormy midwestern landscape and the interior close-up scenes of the family facing their loss together." Booklist

Campbell, Bebe Moore

Sometimes my mommy gets angry; illustrated by E. B. Lewis. Putnam 2003 unp il $16.99
E

1. Mother-child relationship—Fiction 2. Mentally ill—Fiction 3. African Americans—Fiction
ISBN 0-399-23972-3   LC 2003-1279

Annie copes with her mother's mental illness, with the help of her grandmother and friends

"Lewis makes excellent use of light and shadow in his watercolors. . . . The multicultural cast is depicted with realistic sensitivity. . . . A skillful treatment of a troubling subject." SLJ

Campbell, Nicola I.

Shi-shi-etko; pictures by Kim La Fave. Groundwood Books 2005 unp il $16.95   E

1. Native Americans—Fiction 2. Canada—Fiction
ISBN 0-88899-659-4

"This is a moving story set in Canada about the practice of removing Native children from their villages and sending them to residential schools to learn the English language and culture. . . . Shi-shi-etko counts down her last four days before going away. . . . The vivid, digital illustrations rely on a red palette, evoking not only the land but also the sorrow of the situation and the hope upon which the story ultimately ends." SLJ

Campbell, Rod

Dear zoo; a pop-up book. Little Simon 2005 c1982 unp il $12.95   E

1. Animals—Fiction
ISBN 0-689-87751-X

First published as a board book in the United Kingdom 1982; first published as a pop-up book 2004 in the United Kingdom

Each animal arriving from the zoo as a possible pet fails to suit its prospective owner, until just the right one is found.

Campos, Tito

Muffler man; illustrations by Lamberto Alvarez; Spanish translation by Evangelina Vigil-Piñón. Piñata Bks. 2001 unp il $14.95   E

1. Fathers—Fiction 2. Sculpture—Fiction 3. Mexican Americans—Fiction 4. Bilingual books—English-Spanish
ISBN 1-55883-318-9   LC 00-53735

Text and title page in English and Spanish

Chuy works hard at the muffler shop to earn enough money to join his father in America, where together they create an army of "muffler men," statues made from old muffler parts, that they scatter around the city

"The folksy prose with its gently delivered message is extended by eye-catching artwork. Somber hues and forms surrounded by heavy black lines coupled with odd perspectives give this book the look of revisionist woodblock prints." SLJ

Campoy, F. Isabel

Rosa Raposa; illustrated by Jose Aruego and Ariane Dewey. Harcourt 2002 unp il $16
E

1. Foxes—Fiction 2. Jaguars—Fiction
ISBN 0-15-202161-2   LC 2001-5322

"Gulliver books"

A wily fox outwits Jaguar in three trickster tales set in the jungles of South America

"Aruego and Dewey's signature pen-and-ink, gouache, and watercolor illustrations play up the trickery's humor and cheerfulness with expressive characters and bright, tropical colors." Booklist

Cannon, Janell

Crickwing; written and illustrated by Janell Cannon. Harcourt 2000 unp il $16   E

1. Cockroaches—Fiction 2. Ants—Fiction
ISBN 0-15-201790-9   LC 99-50456

A lonely cockroach named Crickwing has a creative idea that saves the day for the leaf-cutter ants when their fierce forest enemies attack them

"An amusing tale lightly rooted in natural history. . . . Cannon's illustrations skillfully blur the line between fact and fancy." Publ Wkly

Stellaluna. Harcourt Brace Jovanovich 1993 unp il $16   E

1. Bats—Fiction
ISBN 0-15-280217-7   LC 92-16439

After she falls headfirst into a bird's nest, a baby bat is raised like a bird until she is reunited with her mother

"Cannon's delightful story is full of gentle humor. . . . [She] provides good information about bats in the story, amplifying it in two pages of notes at the end of the book. Her full-page colored-pencil-and-acrylic paintings fairly glow." Booklist

Verdi. Harcourt Brace & Co. 1997 unp il $16
E

1. Snakes—Fiction 2. Old age—Fiction
ISBN 0-15-201028-9   LC 96-18442

A young python does not want to grow slow and boring like the older snakes he sees in the tropical jungle where he lives

"Cannon's acrylic-and pencil illustrations look almost three-dimensional with the blend of plain gray pencil and brightly colored paints. . . . Cannon blends natural science with story, providing a double-page spread of added information on snakes." Booklist

Caple, Kathy

The friendship tree. Holiday House 2000 48p il lib bdg $15.95 **E**

1. Sheep—Fiction 2. Trees—Fiction 3. Friendship—Fiction

ISBN 0-8234-1376-4　　　　　　LC 98-39043

"A Holiday House reader"

This book "includes four little stories about trees. Best friends Blanche and Otis are sheep who live next door to each other and share their sorrows and joys. . . . The line-and-watercolor illustrations reflect the sweet, gentle tone of the text with the soft, pastel shades." Booklist

Capucilli, Alyssa

Biscuit's new trick; story by Alyssa Capucilli; pictures by Pat Schories. HarperCollins Pubs. 2000 unp il $12.95; lib bdg $15.89; pa $3.99

E

1. Dogs—Fiction

ISBN 0-06-028067-0; 0-06-028068-9 (lib bdg); 0-06-444308-6 (pa)　　　　LC 99-23004

Also available board books about Biscuit

"My first I can read book"

"While his owner tries to teach him to fetch a ball, Biscuit the dog chews his bone or chases the cat—that is, until the ball lands in a mud puddle. . . . The simple language . . . and playful watercolor illustrations make this an appealing choice for beginning readers." Horn Book Guide

Other titles about Biscuit are:

Bathtime for Biscuit (1998)
Biscuit (1996)
Biscuit and the baby (2005)
Biscuit finds a friend (1997)
Biscuit goes to school (2002)
Biscuit visits the big city (2006)
Biscuit wants to play (2001)
Biscuit wins a prize (2004)
Biscuit's big friend (2003)
Biscuit's new trick (2000)
Biscuit's picnic (1998)
Happy birthday, Biscuit! (1999)
Hello, Biscuit! (1998)

Carle, Eric

10 little rubber ducks; by Eric Carle. 1st ed. HarperCollins 2005 unp il $19.99; lib bdg $20.89

E

1. Toys—Fiction 2. Counting

ISBN 0-06-074075-2; 0-06-074076-0 (lib bdg)

LC 2004-1420

When a storm strikes a cargo ship, ten rubber ducks are tossed overboard and swept off in ten different directions. Based on a factual incident.

"Carle's signature cut-paper collages burst with color, texture, light, and motion, delighting the eye and bringing out the text's nuances." SLJ

Do you want to be my friend? Crowell 1971 unp il $15.99; lib bdg $16.99; pa $6.99

E

1. Mice—Fiction 2. Stories without words

ISBN 0-690-24276-X; 0-690-01137-7 (lib bdg); 0-06-443127-4 (pa)

Also available Board book edition

"The only text is the title question at the start and a shy 'Yes' at the close. The pictures do the rest, as the hopeful mouse overtakes one large creature after another. With each encounter, the mouse sees (on the right-hand page) an interesting tail. Turn the page, and there is a huge lion, or a malevolent fox, or a peacock, and then, at last another wee mouse." Saturday Rev

"Good material for discussion and guessing games. . . . The pictures tell an amusing story and they are good to look at as well." Times Lit Suppl

Does a kangaroo have a mother, too? HarperCollins Pubs. 2000 unp il $16.99; lib bdg $17.89; pa $6.99 **E**

1. Animals

ISBN 0-06-028768-3; 0-06-028767-5 (lib bdg); 0-06-443642-X (pa)　　　　LC 99-36147

"The repetitive text is perfect for the toddler set. 'Does a lion have a mother, too? Yes! A lion has a mother. Just like me and you.' The text is repeated on every spread as the author showcases a dozen different animal mothers and their babies. . . . The vibrant artwork is classic Carle and should delight its audience." SLJ

From head to toe. HarperCollins Pubs. 1997 unp il $16.99; lib bdg $17.89; pa $6.95 **E**

1. Exercise 2. Animals

ISBN 0-06-023515-2; 0-06-023516-0 (lib bdg); 0-06-443596-2 (pa)　　　　LC 95-53141

Also available Board book edition

"A giraffe bends its neck, a monkey waves its arms, etc. The repetitive text has the animal stating the movement and asking, 'Can you do it?' Each child responds, 'I can do it!' Carle's vivid cut-paper collages are striking and invite sharing individually or with a group." SLJ

The grouchy ladybug. HarperCollins Pubs. 1996 unp il $16.99; lib bdg $17.89; pa $7.99

E

1. Ladybugs—Fiction

ISBN 0-06-027087-X; 0-06-027088-8 (lib bdg); 0-06-443450-8 (pa)　　　　LC 95-26581

Also available Board book edition

A reissue of the title first published 1977 by Crowell

A grouchy ladybug, looking for a fight, challenges everyone she meets regardless of their size or strength

"The finger paint and collage illustrations—as bold as the feisty hero—are satisfyingly placed on pages sized to suit the successive animals that appear. . . . Tiny clocks show the time of each enjoyable encounter, with the sun rising and setting as the action proceeds." SLJ

A house for Hermit Crab. Picture Bk. Studio 1988 c1987 unp il $17.95 **E**

1. Crabs—Fiction

ISBN 0-88708-056-1　　　　　　LC 87-29261

Also available Miniature editon

"Hermit Crab, having outgrown his old shell, sets out to find a new one. He's a bit frightened at first, but over the course of the next year acquires not only a shell, but also an array of sea creatures to decorate, clean, and protect his new home. The story ends with him once again outgrowing his shell." SLJ

"The bright illustrations in Carle's familiar style, which seems particularly suited to undersea scenes, and the cumulative story are splendid." Horn Book

Carle, Eric—*Continued*

Mister Seahorse. Philomel Books 2004 unp il
$16.99 **E**
1. Sea horses—Fiction 2. Fishes—Fiction 3. Fathers—
Fiction
ISBN 0-399-24269-4 LC 2003-17125

After Mrs. Seahorse lays her eggs on Mr. Seahorse's
belly, he drifts through the water, greeting other fish fathers who are taking care of their eggs

"With each encounter comes a delightful surprise: an
acetate overlay camouflages the sea creatures as Mister
Seahorse passes by. . . . Awash with the wonders of undersea life, this is a stunning, ingeniously conceived lesson in nature as well as a celebration of fatherly affection." Booklist

The mixed-up chameleon; by Eric Carle.
Crowell 1984 unp il $16.99; lib bdg $17.89; pa
$6.99 **E**
1. Chameleons—Fiction
ISBN 0-690-04396-1; 0-690-04397-X (lib bdg);
0-06-443162-2 (pa) LC 83-45950
Also available Board book edition

A revised and newly illustrated edition of the title first
published 1975

"A chameleon goes to a zoo where it wishes it could
become like the different animals it sees. It does, but
then isn't happy until it wishes it could be itself again."
Child Book Rev Serv

The author "has replaced the heavy-lined, childlike,
scrawled colors with crisp, appealing collages and has
streamlined the text. The cutaway pages have been retained, and none of the humor has been lost. The simpler
text results in a smoother flow, and children will enjoy
the resulting repetition." Booklist

"Slowly, slowly, slowly," said the sloth.
Philomel Bks. 2002 unp il $16.99 **E**
1. Sloths—Fiction 2. Animals—Fiction
ISBN 0-399-23954-5 LC 2002-16057

Challenged by the other jungle animals for its seemingly lazy ways, a sloth living in a tree explains the
many advantages of his slow and peaceful existence

"Carle's art is at its best with a brightly colored selection of painted tissue-paper collage that captures 25 rainforest denizens." SLJ

The very busy spider. Philomel Bks. 1984 unp
il $20.99; pa $7.95 **E**
1. Spiders—Fiction
ISBN 0-399-21166-7; 0-399-21592-1 (pa)
LC 84-5907
Also available Board book edition

The farm animals try to divert a busy little spider
from spinning her web, but she persists and produces a
thing of both beauty and usefulness.

This book "has a disarming ingenuousness and a repetitive structure that will capture the response of preschool audiences. Of special note is the book's use of
raised lines for the spider, its web, and an unsuspecting
fly. Both sighted and blind children will be able to follow the action with ease." Booklist

The very clumsy click beetle. Philomel Bks.
1999 unp il $21.99 **E**
1. Beetles—Fiction 2. Animals—Fiction
ISBN 0-399-23201-X LC 97-33417

A clumsy young click beetle learns to land on its feet
with encouragement from various animals and a wise old
beetle. An electronic chip with a built-in battery creates
clicking sounds to accompany the story

"Done in colored tissue-paper collage, the illustrations
burst from the pages and are charmingly rendered. . . .
A well-crafted story, joyfully illustrated." SLJ

The very hungry caterpillar. Philomel Bks. 1981
c1970 unp il $21.99 **E**
1. Caterpillars—Fiction
ISBN 0-399-20853-4
Also available Board book edition and Miniature edition

First published 1970 by World Publishing Company

"This caterpillar is so hungry he eats right through the
pictures on the pages of the book—and after leaving
many holes emerges as a beautiful butterfly on the last
page." Best Books for Child, 1972

The very lonely firefly. Philomel Bks. 1995 unp
il $22.99 **E**
1. Fireflies—Fiction
ISBN 0-399-22774-1 LC 94-27827
Also available Board book edition

A lonely firefly goes out into the night searching for
other fireflies

"The illustrations are painted cut-paper collages, designed to draw the eye to the page. This is a compelling
accomplishment." SLJ

The very quiet cricket. Philomel Bks. 1990 unp
il $21.99 **E**
1. Crickets—Fiction
ISBN 0-399-21885-8 LC 89-78317
Also available Board book edition

A very quiet cricket who wants to rub his wings together and make a sound as do so many other animals
finally achieves his wish

"The text is skillfully shaped; the illustrations convey
energy and immediacy; and, in a surprise ending, a
microchip inserted in the last page replicates the cricket's
chirp." Horn Book Guide

Where are you going? To see my friend! [by]
Eric Carle & Kazuo Iwamura. Orchard Bks. 2003
c2001 unp il $19.95 **E**
1. Animals—Fiction 2. Friendship—Fiction
3. Bilingual books—English-Japanese
ISBN 0-439-41659-0 LC 2002-70396
Original Japanese edition, 2001

This "bilingual picture book is told in dialogue, with
rebuslike symbols used to identify speakers. It details an
energetic romp with a dog, cat, rooster, goat, rabbit, and
a child, all of whom become friends. Carle's familiar
collage technique is employed in the book's first half,
while Iwamura's gentle watercolor illustrations, combined with the Japanese text, make up the second half.
. . . An irresistible, spirited ode to friendship." SLJ

Carling, Amelia Lau

Mama & Papa have a store; story and pictures by Amelia Lau Carling. Dial Bks. for Young Readers 1998 unp il $16.99　　　　E
　1. Retail trade—Fiction　2. Chinese—Fiction　3. Guatemala—Fiction
　ISBN 0-8037-2044-0　　　　LC 97-10217
Also available Spanish language edition
A little girl describes what a day is like in her parents' Chinese store in Guatemala City
"Carling's lovingly detailed watercolors in candy-box colors illustrate [the author's] memories. . . . A pleasant family story that should enrich library collections, especially those looking for multicultural themes." SLJ

Sawdust carpets; story and pictures by Amelia Lau Carling. Douglas & McIntyre 2005 unp il $16.95　　　　E
　1. Chinese—Fiction　2. Guatemala—Fiction　3. Easter—Fiction
　ISBN 0-88899-625-X
Also available Spanish language edition
"A Groundwood book"
"A Chinese family living in Guatemala visits relatives in Antigua during Holy Week. . . . [This is an] intriguing, unusual multicultural offering. . . . In watercolors, pastels, and colored pencils, the lively illustrations offer colorful impressions of the characters and places of the story." Booklist

Carlson, Nancy L.

Get up and go! by Nancy Carlson. Viking 2006 unp il $15.99　　　　E
　1. Exercise
　ISBN 0-670-05981-1　　　　LC 2005003864
Text and illustrations encourage readers, regardless of shape or size, to turn off the television and play games, walk, dance, and engage in sports and other forms of exercise.
"Bright and sassy, the clearly delineated drawings with vivid washes provide a light, sometimes-comical tone that makes the lessons easier to take. With a short, simple text and a cheerful look, this will suit preschool and kindergarten teachers looking for an accessible book on exercise." Booklist

Harriet and the roller coaster. 20th Anniversary ed. Carolrhoda Books 2003 unp il $15.95; pa $6.95　　　　E
　1. Dogs—Fiction　2. Rabbits—Fiction　3. Roller coasters—Fiction
　ISBN 1-57505-053-6; 1-57505-202-4 (pa)
　　　　LC 2002-13922
A reissue of the title first published 1982
Harriet accepts her friend George's challenge to ride the frightening roller coaster, and finds out that she is the brave one
"This emotionally satisfying story is illustrated with simple colorful art. This edition is slightly larger than the original but otherwise unchanged." Horn Book Guide

Henry's show and tell. Viking 2004 unp il $15.99　　　　E
　1. School stories　2. Mice—Fiction
　ISBN 0-670-03695-1　　　　LC 2003-19481

Henry the mouse likes everything about kindergarten except show-and-tell, but with the help of his teacher and his pet lizard he is able to overcome his fear.
"The story tackles public-speaking fears in an ideal way for very young children. . . . Carlson's bright, humorous gouache illustrations add an extra dose of fun." SLJ
Other titles about Henry are:
First grade, here I come! (2006)
Henry's 100 days of kindergarten (2005)

Hooray for Grandparent's Day; [by] Nancy Carlson. Viking 2000 unp il $15.99　　　　E
　1. Grandparents—Fiction　2. School stories
　ISBN 0-670-88876-1　　　　LC 99-46237
Arnie doesn't have grandparents to come to school on Grandparent's Day, but it turns out he has a lot of people who can substitute
"Bright, cheery, cartoonlike illustrations of the animal characters carry out the upbeat tone of the story." SLJ

I like me! [by] Nancy Carlson. Viking Kestrel 1988 unp il lib bdg $15.99; pa $5.99　　　　E
　1. Pigs—Fiction
　ISBN 0-670-82062-8 (lib bdg); 0-14-050819-8 (pa)
　　　　LC 87-32616
Also available Big book edition
By admiring her finer points and showing that she can take care of herself and have fun even when there's no one else around, a charming pig proves the best friend you can have is yourself
This book is "visually interesting, with sturdy animals drawn in a deliberately artless style. Simple shapes, strong lines, and clear colors, with lots of pattern mixing, show what is not described in the minimal text. The text is hand-lettered." SLJ
Another title about this pig is:
ABC I like me! (1997)

Carlstrom, Nancy White

Giggle-wiggle wake-up! illustrated by Melissa Sweet. Knopf 2003 unp il $15.95　　　　E
　1. Stories in rhyme
　ISBN 0-375-81350-0　　　　LC 2002-43320
Sammy wakes up to Monday morning sunshine, has breakfast, and heads to preschool
"There is lots of wordplay and rhyme, with rich, playful, and splashy colors." SLJ

Jesse Bear, what will you wear? illustrations by Bruce Degen. Macmillan 1986 unp il $16.95; pa $6.99　　　　E
　1. Bears—Fiction　2. Stories in rhyme
　ISBN 0-02-717350-X; 0-689-80623-X (pa)
　　　　LC 85-10610
Also available Board book edition
"The happy, singsong verse of the title follows Jesse Bear through the changes of clothes and activities of his day, even to bath and bed." N Y Times Book Rev
"The big, cheerful watercolor paintings show the baby bear in loving relation to his family and world. Without crossing the line into sentimentality, this offers a happy, humorous soundfest that will associate reading aloud with a sense of play." Bull Cent Child Books
Other titles about Jesse Bear are:

Carlstrom, Nancy White—*Continued*

Better not get wet, Jesse Bear (1988)
Climb the family tree, Jesse Bear (2004)
Guess who's coming, Jesse Bear (1998)
Happy birthday, Jesse Bear (1994)
How do you say it today, Jesse Bear? (1992)
It's about time, Jesse Bear, and other rhymes (1990)
Let's count it out, Jesse Bear (1996)
What a scare, Jesse Bear! (1999)
Where is Christmas, Jesse Bear? (2000)

Carrick, Carol

Mothers are like that; illustrated by Paul
Carrick. Clarion Bks. 2000 unp il $15   **E**
    1. Mothers 2. Animals
    ISBN 0-395-88351-2   LC 99-16587
A simple description of animal and human mothers
caring for their young
"The text in this gentle, lulling bedtime story of maternal love is brief but complete. The acrylic paintings
. . . brim with child-appealing, close-up portraits of
mother animals and their babies." Horn Book Guide

Patrick's dinosaurs; pictures by Donald Carrick.
Clarion Bks. 1983 unp il lib bdg $16; pa $5.95
                                       E
    1. Dinosaurs—Fiction 2. Brothers—Fiction
    ISBN 0-89919-189-4 (lib bdg); 0-89919-402-8 (pa)
                                        LC 83-2049
When his older brother talks about dinosaurs during a
visit to the zoo, Patrick is afraid, until he discovers they
all died millions of years ago.
"The Carricks do a particularly good job of creating
an impressive array of creatures both in text and illustrations—realistic pencil drawings washed in muted greens,
browns and oranges." SLJ
   Other titles about Patrick's dinosaurs are:
Patrick's dinosaurs on the Internet (1999)
What happened to Patrick's dinosaurs? (1986)

Carryl, Charles E.

The camel's lament; a poem by Charles Edward
Carryl; illustrated by Charles Santore. Random
House 2004 unp il $16.95; lib bdg $18.99
                                         E
    1. Camels—Poetry 2. Animals—Poetry
    ISBN 0-375-81426-4; 0-375-91426-9 (lib bdg)
                                   LC 2003-22271
A poem in which a camel compares his life with that
of other animals of the world
This poem "has all the hallmarks of child-friendly
verse: a clever idea, humor, and a sprightly rhyme. . . .
But it's really Santore's fabulous artwork that will catapult this into kids' eager hands. . . . Richly colored and
intensely detailed . . . the closeup art, set against crisp
white backgrounds, will be fun to look at by individuals
or in groups." Booklist

Carson, Jo

You hold me and I'll hold you; story by Jo
Carson; pictures by Annie Cannon. Orchard Bks.
1992 unp il $15.95; pa $6.95   **E**
    1. Death—Fiction 2. Bereavement—Fiction
    ISBN 0-531-05895-6; 0-531-07088-3 (pa)
                                   LC 91-16370
"A Richard Jackson book"
When a great-aunt dies, a young girl finds comfort in
being held by her father and in holding, too
"Lightly tinted watercolors with collaged-in materials
provide an unthreatening setting, and Cannon . . . paints
a family of reassuringly lovable people. . . . A moving
and sensitive exploration of a difficult topic." Publ Wkly

Carter, David A.

One red dot; a pop-up book for children of all
ages. Little Simon 2005 unp il $19.95   **E**
    1. Counting 2. Puzzles
    ISBN 0-689-87769-2
    Original Italian edition 2004
"A graphically bold pop-up book that entices readers
to find the one red dot that is hidden on each paper
sculpture. Going from 1 to 10, Carter creates a visual
hide-and-seek game, ranging from flip-flop flaps to flut-
tering flicker clickers that really click to orbs that tower
above the page. Bold primary colors and a silver-black
text give the book a very slick, modern feel." SLJ

Carville, James

Lu and the swamp ghost; [by] James Carville
with Patricia C. McKissack; illustrated by David
Catrow. 1st ed. Atheneum Books for Young
Readers 2004 unp il $17.95   **E**
    1. Great Depression, 1929-1939—Fiction
    2. Friendship—Fiction 3. Louisiana—Fiction
    ISBN 0-689-86560-0   LC 2003-14679
"An Anne Schwartz book"
During the Depression in the Louisiana bayou, a curious young girl helps the "Swamp Ghost" that her cousins
warned her about and finds herself with one good friend.
"Carville tells this humorous . . . story . . . with gusto. Catrow's wildly bright watercolor-and-pencil illustrations fill the pages with wonderful swamp critters and an
indomitable red-haired heroine." SLJ

Casanova, Mary

One-dog canoe; pictures by Ard Hoyt. Farrar,
Straus & Giroux 2003 unp il $16.50   **E**
    1. Canoes and canoeing—Fiction 2. Animals—Fiction
    3. Stories in rhyme
    ISBN 0-374-35638-6   LC 2002-25096
"Melanie Kroupa books"
A girl and her dog set out in their canoe one morning,
only to be insistently joined by a series of animals, large
and small
"The hilariously exaggerated facial expressions on the
animals are the highlight of Hoyt's softly colored illustrations." Booklist

Caseley, Judith

On the town; a community adventure. Greenwillow Bks. 2002 unp il $15.95; lib bdg $15.89   E

1. Community life—Fiction

ISBN 0-06-029584-8; 0-06-029585-6 (lib bdg)

LC 2001-23896

Charlie and his mother walk around the neighborhood doing errands so that Charlie can write in his notebook about the people and places that make up his community

"Written from a child's perspective, the story has a cheerful tone and enough variety to keep the expedition interesting. The lively ink, watercolor, and colored-pencil illustrations are full of intriguing details." Booklist

Casey, Patricia

One day at Wood Green Animal Shelter. Candlewick Press 2001 29p il $16.99   E

1. Animal shelters

ISBN 0-7636-1210-3   LC 00-47404

It is a very busy day at Wood Green Animal Shelter, where the workers take care of a variety of animals that need their help

"The story and intriguing photo-collage and watercolor illustrations are based on Casey's own observations at the shelter." Horn Book Guide

Castañeda, Omar S.

Abuela's weave; illustrated by Enrique O. Sanchez. Lee & Low Bks. 1993 unp il $16.95; pa $6.95   E

1. Grandmothers—Fiction 2. Guatemala—Fiction 3. Weaving—Fiction

ISBN 1-880000-00-8; 1-880000-20-2 (pa)

LC 92-71927

Also available Spanish language edition

A young Guatemalan girl and her grandmother grow closer as they weave some special creations and then make a trip to the market in hopes of selling them

"Castañeda affectingly portrays the loving rapport between a child and her grandmother, as well as the beauty of his homeland's cultural traditions. Sanchez's bright, richly grained acrylic-on-canvas paintings bring dimension to the characters and authenticity to the setting." Publ Wkly

Catalanotto, Peter

Emily's art. Atheneum Bks. for Young Readers 2001 unp il $16   E

1. Artists—Fiction 2. Contests—Fiction

ISBN 0-689-83831-X   LC 00-29293

"A Richard Jackson book"

Emily paints four pictures and enters one in the first-grade art contest, but the judge interprets Emily's entry as a rabbit instead of a dog

"Filled with touches of humor and authentically child-like emotions, this book explores the subjectivity of opinion and the importance of personal conviction." Horn Book Guide

Kitten red, yellow, blue. Atheneum Books for Young Readers 2005 unp il $15.95   E

1. Color—Fiction 2. Cats—Fiction 3. Occupations—Fiction

ISBN 0-689-86562-7   LC 2003-19584

"A Richard Jackson book"

After placing the red kitten with Dave the firefighter and the blue kitten with Francine the police officer, Mrs. Tuttle finds homes for fourteen other colorful kittens.

"The art has a lot of child appeal, as do the popular concepts, and the text is bold and easy to read." SLJ

Cates, Karin

A far-fetched story; pictures by Nancy Carpenter. HarperCollins Pubs. 2002 unp il $15.89   E

1. Grandmothers—Fiction 2. Quilts—Fiction

ISBN 0-688-15938-9   LC 2001-16152

With a hard winter on the way, Grandmother uses her family's rags and stories to create a cozy quilt

"The conclusion is one that anyone can enjoy. Pen-and-ink with watercolor illustrations enhance the text." Horn Book Guide

The Secret Remedy Book; a story of comfort and love; illustrated by Wendy Anderson Halperin. Orchard Bks. 2003 unp il $16.95   E

1. Aunts—Fiction

ISBN 0-439-35226-6   LC 2002-35475

Although Lolly loves to visit her Auntie Zep's house, she feels homesick when she actually gets there, and so Auntie Zep retrieves the Secret Remedy Book from an old trunk

"This wonderfully warm and satisfying story is paired with Halperin's lovely illustrations. Her trademark details and patterns abound, with softened edges, muted colors, and quiet landscapes." SLJ

Cauley, Lorinda Bryan

Clap your hands. Putnam 1992 unp il $16.99; pa $6.99   E

1. Animals—Fiction 2. Stories in rhyme

ISBN 0-399-22118-2; 0-698-11428-0 (pa)

LC 91-12863

Rhyming text instructs the listener to find something yellow, roar like a lion, give a kiss, tell a secret, spin in a circle, and perform other playful activities along with the human and animal characters pictured

"The illustrations feature glowing colors and make good use of Cauley's gift for characterization. . . . Some parts of the book would be fun as action rhymes for preschool story time." Booklist

Cave, Kathryn

One child, one seed; a South African counting book; photographs by Gisèle Wulfsohn. Holt & Co. 2003 unp il $16.95   E

1. Counting 2. Pumpkin 3. South Africa—Social life and customs

ISBN 0-8050-7204-7   LC 2002-24098

"Children count from 1 to 10 with Nothando as she plants a pumpkin seed that grows to bear fruit for a deli-

Cave, Kathryn—*Continued*

cious stew. . . . In a harmonious partnership of narrative and crisp, beautifully composed photographs that show the individuality of each person, readers get a glimpse into the life of an extended family living in a rural South African community. . . . The recipe for *isijingi*, the pumpkin stew, is included as are some basic geographical facts and a simple map. The writing has good rhythm, and reads aloud well." SLJ

Cazet, Denys

Elvis the rooster almost goes to heaven. HarperCollins Pubs. 2003 48p il $15.99; lib bdg $16.89   **E**

1. Roosters—Fiction
ISBN 0-06-000500-9; 0-06-000501-7 (lib bdg)
                                   LC 2002-14416

"An I can read book"

Elvis the rooster thinks he has died when he fails to crow at the rising of the sun but the chickens find a way to restore his cluck

"Cazet's writing is filled with quirky characters, simple wordplay, and gentle humor. The cartoon artwork perfectly reflects the tone of the text." SLJ

The octopus; Grandpa Spanielson's Chicken pox stories, story #1; [by] Denys Cazet. 1st ed. HarperCollins 2005 46p il (Grandpa Spanielson's chicken pox stories, story #1) $15.99; lib bdg $16.89   **E**

1. Octopuses—Fiction   2.   Dogs—Fiction
3. Chickenpox—Fiction
ISBN 0-06-051088-9; 0-06-051089-7 (lib bdg)
                                   LC 2003-26557

"An I Can Read book, level 2."

Grandpa Spanielson helps his favorite grandpup to avoid scratching his chicken pox by telling how he once had to fight off an octopus during a terrible storm.

"Beginning readers will love the humor, action, and compassion in this story, brought to life in the fun-filled text and superb cartoon illustrations." SLJ

Another title about Grandpa Spanielson is:
A snout for Christmas (2006)

The perfect pumpkin pie. Atheneum Books for Young Readers 2005 unp il $15.95   **E**

1. Ghost stories 2. Halloween—Fiction 3. Cooking—Fiction 4. Pies—Fiction
ISBN 0-689-86467-1

"A Richard Jackson book"

Mr. Wilkerson, lover of pie, returns as a ghost on Halloween to demand some good pie from Jack and his grandmother.

"This tale makes a great read-aloud, complete with [a] catchy refrain. . . . The watercolor cartoons are dynamic and funny, bursting with details that kids will love." SLJ

Chaconas, Dori

Christmas mouseling; written by Dori Chaconas; illustrated by Susan Kathleen Hartung. Viking 2005 unp il $15.99   **E**

1. Jesus Christ—Nativity 2. Mice—Fiction
3. Christmas—Fiction
ISBN 0-670-05984-6   LC 2005-04458

When her shivering baby is born on a cold winter night, a mouse follows some animals to a special manger where she receives help from another mother.

"Chaconas' text will easily draw in young listeners with its lyrical language, gentle humor . . . and an infectious, rhyming refrain. . . . Hartung's delicate, soft-toned illustrations, decorated with plate-sized, filigreed snowflakes, amplify the contrast between the blustery winter forest and the safety and warmth of the manger." Booklist

Cork & Fuzz; illustrated by Lisa McCue. Viking 2005 32p il $13.99   **E**

1.   Opossums—Fiction   2.   Muskrats—Fiction
3. Friendship—Fiction
ISBN 0-670-03602-1   LC 2004-13613

"A Viking easy-to-read"

A possum and a muskrat become friends despite their many differences.

"The story's repeated words and entire sentences will help beginning readers feel successful. McCue's endearing drawings add personality and humor to the animals' faces. An excellent addition to easy-reader collections." SLJ

Another title about Cork & Fuzz is:
Cork & Fuzz: short and tall (2006)

One little mouse; illustrated by LeUyen Pham. Viking 2002 unp il $15.99   **E**

1. Mice—Fiction 2. Animals—Fiction 3. Stories in rhyme 4. Counting
ISBN 0-670-88947-4   LC 2001-6109

Woodland animals, from two moles to ten opossums, offer to share their homes with a little mouse who is dissatisfied with his own

"A charming counting book that will appeal especially to the read-aloud set. . . . Pham's watercolor-and-gouache illustrations . . . do an excellent job of expressing the adorable mouse's emotions at each home he visits." SLJ

Chall, Marsha Wilson

Bonaparte; illustrations by Wendy Anderson Halperin. DK Ink 2000 unp il $16.95   **E**

1. Dogs—Fiction 2. School stories 3. France—Fiction
ISBN 0-7894-2617-X   LC 00-21282

When a young French boy goes away to school, he and his dog are sad to be separated until they find a way to change the school's rules about dogs

"Halperin's highly detailed, realistic watercolor-and-pencil illustrations are wonderfully expressive and humorous. . . . This humorous and heartwarming tale will engage youngsters." Booklist

Chamberlin, Mary

Mama Panya's pancakes; written by Mary and Rich Chamberlin; illustrated by Julia Cairns. Barefoot Books 2005 unp il map $16.99

                                             E

1. Kenya—Fiction 2. Cooking—Fiction
ISBN 1-8414-8139-4   LC 2004-17781

Mama Panya has just enough money to buy ingredients for a few pancakes, so when her son Adika invites

Chamberlin, Mary—*Continued*

all their friends to join them, she is sure there will not be enough to go around.

"A recipe, map, details about daily life, and facts about Kiswahili and Kenya are included. With their bold colors, vivid patterns, and lush scenery, the illustrations will transport readers into this country." SLJ

Chambers, Roland

Rooftop rocket party. Roaring Brook Press 2003 unp il $16.95   E
    1. Moon—Fiction 2. New York (N.Y.)—Fiction
    ISBN 0-7613-1888-7   LC 2002-11809
"A Neal Porter book"

"This whimsical, challenging story leaves plenty of things unexplained . . . but children will easily connect with Finn's triumph. . . . Chambers' lively, boldly outlined paintings, filled with sly humor, will transport kids to a joyous nighttime rumpus." Booklist

Chandra, Deborah

George Washington's teeth; written by Deborah Chandra & Madeleine Comora; pictures by Brock Cole. Farrar, Straus & Giroux 2003 unp il $16
           E
    1. Washington, George, 1732-1799 2. Teeth
    ISBN 0-374-32534-0   LC 2002-25086

A rollicking rhyme portrays George Washington's life-long struggle with bad teeth. A timeline taken from diary entries and other nonfiction sources follows

This is written "with wit, verve, and a generous amount of sympathy for poor Washington and his dental woes. . . . Illustrator Cole is at his absolute best here, totally at ease with human gesture and expression." Booklist

Charlip, Remy

Hooray for me! by Remy Charlip & Lilian Moore; paintings by Vera B. Williams. Tricycle Press 1996 unp il $14.95   E
    ISBN 1-88367-243-0   LC 96-2449
A reissue of the title first published 1975 by Parents' Magazine Press

"Two kids realize they are both 'me' and then continue the discussion with a whole crowd, discovering that 'me' can be an aunt, a nephew, a second cousin, a great-grandfather. Bright, dreamlike watercolors enhance this joyful look at self-discovery." Horn Book Guide

Little Old Big Beard and Big Young Little Beard; a short and tall tale; pictures by Remy Charlip & Tamara Rettenmund. Marshall Cavendish 2003 unp il $16.95   E
    1. Cowhands—Fiction 2. Lost and found possessions—Fiction
    ISBN 0-7614-5142-0   LC 2002-155930

Two cowboys in search of their lost cow, Grace, are delighted when she finally finds them

"Told with a storyteller's ear for repetition and alliteration, the story begs for listeners to provide punch lines and chant along with the narration. The almost childlike watercolor illustrations feature simple lines and curves and warm, rich tones." SLJ

Sleepytime rhyme. Greenwillow Bks. 1999 unp il $15.95; lib bdg $15.89   E
    1. Mothers—Fiction 2. Stories in rhyme
    ISBN 0-688-16271-1; 0-688-16272-X (lib bdg)
           LC 98-41040

Illustrations and rhyming text convey a mother's love for her child

"The artwork is crisp, simple, and bright. The equally simple rhyming text chronicles all the parts of the baby its mother loves." Booklist

Why I will never ever ever ever have enough time to read this book; pictures by Jon J. Muth. Tricycle Press 2000 unp il $14.95   E
    1. Time—Fiction 2. Books and reading—Fiction
    ISBN 1-58246-018-3   LC 99-52825

A busy girl recounts all of the things she has to do in a day as she tries to find time to read

"The true charm of the book lies in its tongue-in-cheek presentation and lively watercolor illustrations." SLJ

Chen, Chih-Yuan

Guji Guji. Kane/Miller 2004 unp il $15.95
           E
    1. Ducks—Fiction 2. Crocodiles—Fiction
    ISBN 1-929132-67-0
Crocodile Guji Guji, who was raised by a family of ducks, meets three crocodiles who tell him that he was not a duck. When the crocodiles ask Guji Guji to help them trap the ducks he saves the duck family.

"This beautifully written story has much to say about appreciating families and differences. . . . Chen's unique illustrations are compelling. . . . The rich blues and earth tones and dramatic page layouts create moving scenes, but the quirky details and characters' expressions are hilarious." SLJ

On my way to buy eggs; written and illustrated by Chih-Yuan Chen. Kane/Miller 2003 unp il $15.95   E
    ISBN 1-929132-49-2   LC 2002-117381
First published 2001 in Taiwan

"A young girl's errand to the store turns into a sensory adventure. . . . After a make-believe game with the shopkeeper and more adventures along the way, Shau-yu returns home to her loving dad. The story is basic, but the simple words and phrases easily show Shau-yu's delight in transforming small things. The earth-tone colors in the crisp paper-and-pencil collages are as quiet as the story." Booklist

Cheng, Andrea

Anna the bookbinder; illustrations by Ted Rand. Walker & Co. 2003 unp il $16.95; lib bdg $17.85
           E
    1. Bookbinding—Fiction
    ISBN 0-8027-8831-9; 0-8027-8832-7 (lib bdg)
           LC 2003-544865

When her bookbinder father cannot complete an order for an important customer in time, Anna decides to take the fate of the family business into her own hands

"Warm watercolors limn an early-twentieth-century home and shop of beautifully rendered accoutrements and equipment." Booklist

Cheng, Andrea—*Continued*

The lemon sisters; [by] Andrea Cheng; illustrated by Tatjana Mai-Wyss. G.P. Putnam's Sons 2006 unp il $16.99   **E**

1. Sisters—Fiction 2. Snow—Fiction 3. Old age—Fiction 4. Birthdays—Fiction

ISBN 0-399-24023-3   LC 2005002208

On her 80th birthday, a woman watches three young sisters play outside in the snow, remembers good times with her own sisters, and receives several birthday surprises.

"Mai-Wyss's attractive illustrations, done in watercolor, gouache, and collage, are filled with colorful patterns. . . . Despite the snowy backdrop, this book leaves readers with a warm glow inside." SLJ

Cherry, Lynne

The great kapok tree; a tale of the Amazon rainforest. Harcourt Brace Jovanovich 1990 unp il $16; pa $7   **E**

1. Rain forests—Fiction

ISBN 0-15-200520-X; 0-15-202614-2 (pa)

LC 89-2208

Also available Big book edition

"Gulliver books"

The many different animals that live in a great kapok tree in the Brazilian rainforest try to convince a man with an ax of the importance of not cutting down their home

"A carefully researched picture book. . . . Cherry captures the Amazonian proportions of the plants and animals that live there by using vibrant colors, intricate details, and dramatic perspectives. . . . The writing is simple and clear." Booklist

How Groundhog's garden grew. Blue Sky Press (NY) 2003 unp il $15.95   **E**

1. Marmots—Fiction

ISBN 0-439-32371-1   LC 2002-3428

Squirrel teaches Little Groundhog how to plant and tend a vegetable garden

The author "tells a charming and also informative story about plants, gardening, and environmental respect. Her beautiful, full-color illustrations—realistic and wonderfully detailed—often incorporate spot-art borders of labeled seedlings and plants, highlighting a diverse array of wildlife." Booklist

The sea, the storm, and the mangrove tangle. Farrar, Straus and Giroux 2004 unp il $16

     E

1. Wetlands—Fiction 2. Ecology—Fiction 3. Marine animals—Fiction 4. Caribbean region—Fiction

ISBN 0-374-36482-6   LC 2002-29705

A seed from a mangrove tree floats on the sea until it comes to rest on the shore of a faraway lagoon where, over time, it becomes a mangrove island that shelters many birds and animals, even during a hurricane.

"Cherry paints lustrous, detailed scenes that, together with her accessible narrative, will spark children's interest in a magnificent, endangered ecosystem." Booklist

Chesworth, Michael

Alphaboat. Farrar, Straus & Giroux 2002 unp il $16   **E**

1. Alphabet 2. Stories in rhyme

ISBN 0-374-30244-8   LC 2001-40287

Rhyming text full of puns tells the story of the letters of the alphabet sailing off to look for a buried treasure

"Each full-color watercolor-and-ink illustration is framed within neat black borders and extends the text with a wealth of visual jokes, hints, and goofy asides." SLJ

Child, Lauren

I am too absolutely small for school. Candlewick 2004 unp il $16.99   **E**

1. School stories 2. Siblings—Fiction

ISBN 0-7636-2403-9   LC 2003-65576

When Lola is worried about starting school, her older brother Charlie reassures her

"The children's relationship is refreshingly noncombative. . . . Incorporating photos, fabric, and appealingly childlike cartoon renderings of the siblings, the mixed-media illustrations are a visual treat of color and texture." SLJ

Other titles about Lola and Charlie are:

But excuse me that is my book (2006)

I am not sleepy and I will not go to bed (2001)

I will never not eat a tomato (2000)

The princess and the pea in miniature; after the fairy tale by Hans Christian Andersen. Hyperion Books for Children 2006 unp il $16.99   **E**

1. Andersen, Hans Christian, 1805-1875—Adaptations 2. Fairy tales

ISBN 0-7868-3886-8

Presents a retelling of the well-known fairy tale of a young girl feels a pea through twenty mattresses and twenty featherbeds and proves she is a real princess.

"Child has expanded Andersen's tale from a one-page gem into a humorous picture book that will delight the whole family. Color photographs of a cleverly designed, three-dimensional, miniature world of dolls reveal wonderful details." SLJ

Chinn, Karen

Sam and the lucky money; illustrated by Cornelius Van Wright, and Ying-Hwa Hu. Lee & Low Bks. 1995 unp $16.95; pa $6.95   **E**

1. Chinese New Year—Fiction 2. Chinese Americans—Fiction

ISBN 1-880000-13-X; 1-880000-53-9 (pa)

LC 94-11766

This is a "tale of a young boy eager to spend his 'lucky money' on Chinese New Year day. As Sam searches the streets of Chinatown for ways to spend his four dollars, he stumbles upon a stranger in need. After he decides to give, rather than spend, his money, Sam realizes that he's 'the lucky one.'" Horn Book Guide

"The illustrators masterfully combine Chinatown's exotic setting with the universal emotions of childhood through expressive portraits of the characters." SLJ

Chodos-Irvine, Margaret

Best best friends; [by] Margaret Chodos-Irvine.
Harcourt 2006 unp il $16   E
  1. Friendship—Fiction 2. Birthdays—Fiction
  3. School stories
  ISBN 0-15-205694-7   LC 2005002251
Mary and Clare do everything together at preschool,
but Mary's birthday celebration puts a strain on the girls'
friendship.
"In spot-on words and crisp, gaily patterned prints, the
[author-illustrator] captures the unselfconscious affection
and quicksilver shifts in mood that characterize preschool
friendships." Booklist

Ella Sarah gets dressed. Harcourt 2003 unp il
$16   E
  1. Clothing and dress—Fiction
  ISBN 0-15-216413-8   LC 2002-5097
A Caldecott Medal honor book, 2004
Despite the advice of others in her family, Ellah Sarah
persists in wearing the striking and unusual outfit of her
own choosing
"With minimal words and her signature art marked by
bright, bold prints, Chodos-Irvine perfectly captures a
universal childhood struggle." Booklist

Choi, Sook Nyul

Halmoni and the picnic; illustrated by Karen
Milone. Houghton Mifflin 1993 31p il $16
                                                 E
  1. Korean Americans—Fiction 2. Grandmothers—Fiction
  ISBN 0-395-61626-3   LC 91-34121
A third grade class helps Halmoni, Yunmi's newly arrived Korean grandmother, feel more comfortable with
her life in the United States
This book is "is pleasing . . . thanks to the lovely
bordered watercolor art and the subtle text, both of
which display a fine sensitivity." Booklist
  Another title about Yunmi and Halmoni is:
Yunmi and Halmoni's trip (1997)

Chorao, Kay

Here comes Kate. Dutton Children's Bks. 2000
48p il $13.99   E
  1. Elephants—Fiction 2. Family life—Fiction
  ISBN 0-525-46443-3   LC 00-20936
"Dutton easy reader"
In four stories, Kate, a young elephant, plays in the
snow, learns to appreciate her new quilt, fusses over a
lost toy, and quiets the crying of her baby cousin
"Both the issues and the resolutions are appropriate
for the target age. . . . Full-page color illustrations portray a cozy suburban world and a warm, loving family.
A first-choice addition to easy-reader collections." SLJ

Pig and Crow. Holt & Co. 2000 unp il $16.95
                                                 E
  1. Pigs—Fiction 2. Crows—Fiction
  ISBN 0-8050-5863-X   LC 99-31776
"Crow trades a series of three 'magic' items for lonely
Pig's baked goods. Magic seeds grow into nonmagic
pumpkins. A magic worm changes into a butterfly and,

heartbreakingly for Pig, flies away. Finally, Crow brings
a magic egg, which hatches into a companionable
goose." Horn Book Guide
"Chorao's gouache-and-ink illustrations are so wonderfully expressive that the joy on Pig's face when the butterfly hatches and the horror as it flies away tell the story as effectively as the words." Booklist

Christelow, Eileen

Five little monkeys jumping on the bed; retold
and illustrated by Eileen Christelow. Clarion Bks.
1989 unp il $15; pa $5.95   E
  1. Monkeys—Fiction 2. Counting
  ISBN 0-89919-769-8; 0-395-55701-1 (pa)
                                  LC 88-22839
Also available Board book edition
A counting book in which one by one the five little
monkeys jump on the bed only to fall off and bump their
heads
"Squiggling, swirling lines of color capture the sense
of unbridled motion as the monkeys bounce and, one by
one, topple from the bed. After all five bandaged young-
sters finally fall asleep, a relaxed mama gratefully retires
to her room . . . to bounce on 'her' bed. An amusingly
presented counting exercise." Booklist
  Other titles about the five little monkeys are:
Don't wake up Mama! (1992)
Five little monkeys play hide and seek (2004)
Five little monkeys sitting in a tree (1991)
Five little monkeys wash the car (2000)
Five little monkeys with nothing to do (1996)

Church, Caroline

One smart goose; [by] Caroline Jayne Church.
Orchard Books 2005 c2003 unp il $16.95
                                                 E
  1. Geese—Fiction 2. Foxes—Fiction
  ISBN 0-439-68765-9
First published 2003 in the United Kingdom
A goose who likes to wash in a muddy pond is teased
by the other geese, until they realize that he is the only
one not chased by the fox
"The clever story will hold the attention of young
children, but the illustrations are the book's most striking
feature. Bold black lines define the forms of the geese,
the fox, and the setting, while textured papers, buts of
smudgy print, and collage elements enrich the simple
compositions." Booklist

Cleary, Beverly

The hullabaloo ABC; illustrated by Ted Rand.
rev ed. Morrow Junior Bks. 1998 unp il $16.99;
lib bdg $15.89   E
  1. Noise—Fiction 2. Farm life—Fiction 3. Stories in
  rhyme 4. Alphabet
  ISBN 0-688-15182-5; 0-688-15183-3 (lib bdg)
                                  LC 97-6457
A revised and newly illustrated edition of the title first
published 1960 by Parnassus Press
An alphabet book in which two children demonstrate
all the fun that is to be had by making and hearing every
kind of noise as they dash about on the farm
"Rand's expert watercolor illustrations on crisp white
backgrounds bring the action to life with just the
slightest touch of nostalgia." SLJ

Clements, Andrew

Circus family dog; illustrated by Sue Truesdell. Clarion Bks. 2000 32p il $16 **E**

1. Dogs—Fiction 2. Circus—Fiction

ISBN 0-395-78648-7 LC 99-52657

Grumps is content to do his one trick in the center ring at the circus, until a new dog shows up and steals the show—temporarily

"The combination of Clements's impeccable storyteller pacing and Truesdell's creative and whimsical cartoons create a reading and visual experience second only to actually being at the circus. The illustrator uses a mixture of watercolors with pen and ink to bring the action to life in vibrant colors." SLJ

Clifton, Lucille

Everett Anderson's 1-2-3; illustrations by Ann Grifalconi. Holt & Co. 1992 unp il $14.95 **E**

1. Remarriage—Fiction 2. African Americans—Fiction 3. Stories in rhyme

ISBN 0-8050-2310-0 LC 92-8031

A reissue of the title first published 1977 by Holt, Rinehart & Winston

As a small boy's mother considers remarriage, he considers the numbers one, two, and three—sometimes they're lonely, sometimes crowded, but sometimes just right.

"The illustrations, strongly drawn with bold, broken lines, are large in scale, almost all pictures of the three characters with only minimal background details. The text is tender, artful in the simplicity and brevity with which it gets to the gist of the matter." Bull Cent Child Books

Other titles about Everett Anderson are:

Everett Anderson's Christmas coming (c1971)
Everett Anderson's friend (c1976)
Everett Anderson's goodbye (c1983)
Everett Anderson's nine month long (c1978)
Everett Anderson's year (c1974)
One of the problems of Everett Anderson (2001)
Some of the days of Everett Anderson (c1970)

Climo, Shirley

Cobweb Christmas; story by Shirley Climo; illustrations by Jane Manning. 1st ed. HarperCollins 2001 unp il $16.99 **E**

1. Christmas—Fiction 2. Spiders—Fiction

ISBN 0-06-029033-1 LC 00-47955

A revised and newly illustrated edition of the title first published 1982 by Crowell

Long ago in Germany, an old woman cleans her house and decorates her Christmas tree, hoping that this year she will witness some special Christmas Eve magic.

"The modest text revisions result in a trimmer, more succinct story, while the new illustrations (still retaining a folkloric, old-fashioned quality) and larger format enhance the book's use in group storytime." SLJ

Coerr, Eleanor

The big balloon race; pictures by Carolyn Croll. Harper & Row 1981 62p il pa $3.99 hardcover o.p.; lib bdg **E**

1. Balloons—Fiction

ISBN 0-06-444053-2 (pa); 0-06-021353-1
LC 80-8368

"An I can read book"

The author "recounts the winning of a hydrogen balloon race by Carlotta Myers, a famous aeronaut, and her stowaway daughter Ariel. Balloon facts are slipped naturally and painlessly into the story, which moves cogently along. The novel subject matter, straightforward mother-daughter relationship, and clear composition of the orange, blue and gray illustrations . . . make for a high-flying new look at a piece of the past." SLJ

Chang's paper pony; pictures by Deborah Kogan Ray. Harper & Row 1988 64p il lib bdg $15.89; pa $3.99 **E**

1. Chinese Americans—Fiction 2. Horses—Fiction 3. Gold mines and mining—Fiction

ISBN 0-06-021329-9 (lib bdg); 0-06-444163-6 (pa)
LC 87-45679

"An I can read book"

In San Francisco during the 1850's gold rush, Chang, the son of Chinese immigrants, wants a pony but cannot afford one until his friend Big Pete finds a solution.

"Ray's forceful drawings support the text well and firmly establish the dusty mining-town environment. She is particularly adept at showing the vulnerability of children, as well as the ways in which large and small joys affect them." Publ Wkly

The Josefina story quilt; pictures by Bruce Degen. Harper & Row 1986 64p il $15.99; lib bdg $16.89; pa $3.99 **E**

1. Quilts—Fiction 2. Overland journeys to the Pacific—Fiction

ISBN 0-06-021348-5; 0-06-021349-3 (lib bdg); 0-06-444129-6 (pa) LC 85-45260

"An I can read book"

While traveling west with her family in 1850, a young girl makes a patchwork quilt chronicling the experiences of the journey and reserves a special patch for her pet hen Josefina

"The story makes the history go down easily, and an author's note at the end fills in facts about the western trip and the place of quilts as pioneer diaries. The charcoal and blue/yellow wash illustrations are clear and natural . . . A good introduction to historical fiction that children can read for themselves." SLJ

Cohen, Barbara

Molly's pilgrim; illustrated by Daniel Mark Duffy. Lothrop, Lee & Shepard Bks. 1998 unp il $15; pa $3.95 **E**

1. Jews—Fiction 2. School stories 3. Thanksgiving Day—Fiction 4. Immigrants—Fiction

ISBN 0-688-16279-7; 0-688-16280-0 (pa)
LC 98-9227

A newly illustrated edition of the title first published 1983

Cohen, Barbara—*Continued*

Told to make a Pilgrim doll for the Thanksgiving display at school, Molly is embarassed when her mother tries to help her out by creating a doll dressed as she herself was dressed before leaving Russia to seek religious freedom

Cohen, Miriam

My big brother; art by Ronald Himler. Star Bright 2005 unp il $15.95   E

1. Brothers—Fiction 2. Family life—Fiction 3. Soldiers—Fiction

ISBN 1-59572-007-3   LC 2004-16056

When his big brother leaves to become a soldier, a boy does what he can to take his place in the family.

"This quiet picture book packs a strong emotional wallop. Himler's artwork, pencil with watercolor washes, sensitively depicts each character's emotions through body language and facial expressions." Booklist

Colato Laínez, René

Playing loteria; illustrated by Jill Arena. Luna Rising 2005 unp il $15.95   E

1. Grandmothers—Fiction 2. Mexican Americans— Fiction 3. Mexico—Fiction 4. Games—Fiction 5. Bilingual books—English-Spanish

ISBN 0-87358-881-9

A boy has a good time attending a fair with his grandmother in San Luis de La Paz, Mexico, as she teaches him Spanish words and phrases and he teaches her English.

"This is a warm and reassuring story of a boy's involvement not only with his family but also his culture. The prose flows easily in both English and Spanish. [This is illustrated with] spirited primitive acrylics." SLJ

Cole, Brock

Buttons. Farrar, Straus & Giroux 2000 unp il $16.99; pa $6.95   E

ISBN 0-374-31001-7; 0-374-41013-5 (pa)

      LC 99-27162

When their father eats so much that he pops the buttons off his britches, each of his three daughters tries a different plan to find replacements

"A delectable tall tale. . . . Cole's narrative has a humorous lilt that's as much fun as his rollicking illustrations." Horn Book Guide

Fair Monaco. Front Street 2004 c2003 unp il $16.95   E

1. Grandmothers—Fiction 2. Dreams—Fiction

ISBN 1-932425-07-1   LC 2004-43273

Maggie, Katie, and Nora try to help their always-worried and fearful grandmother by entering her dreams and replacing her fears of burglars, trains, and bills with images of sails, sun, and the sea.

"The illustrations are reminiscent of Margot Zemach, in bulbous-nosed kind-eyed characters who manage to be both earthy and airy. The rhythm and interaction of text and pictures is faultless. . . . The implicit message . . . is powerful in its understated and joyful conviction." Horn Book

Larky Mavis. Farrar, Straus & Giroux 2001 unp il $16   E

ISBN 0-374-34365-9   LC 00-51419

Having found a tiny baby in a peanut shell, Larky Mavis calls him Heart's Delight and carries him around as he grows bigger, to the confusion and anger of the adults around her

"The prose is lyrical, peppered with quaint speech patterns and lively dialogue that is a delight to read aloud. . . . The rumpled, animated line-and-watercolor illustrations extend the charming story beyond his tightly constructed prose." SLJ

Cole, Henry

I took a walk. Greenwillow Bks. 1998 unp il lib bdg $16.99   E

1. Animals—Fiction 2. Nature—Fiction

ISBN 0-688-15115-9   LC 97-6692

A visit to woods, pasture, and pond brings encounters with various birds, insects, and other creatures of nature. Flaps fold out to reveal the animals hidden on each two-page spread

"Executed in acrylic paint, the realistic nature scenes invite close and careful inspection." Horn Book Guide

On the way to the beach. Greenwillow Bks. 2003 unp il $15.99   E

1. Nature

ISBN 0-688-17515-5   LC 2002-23537

On a walk through the woods and a marsh to the seashore, the reader is encouraged to notice all sorts of plants, animals, insects, and shells

"Each locale . . . is gloriously depicted in a three-page foldout that is entered through a die-cut. . . . The outstanding realistic acrylic illustrations depict the scenes in an almost three-dimensional perspective. . . . This beautiful, interactive book encourages discussion, develops observation skills, and provides a learning experience that will bring children closer to nature." SLJ

Cole, Joanna

When Mommy and Daddy go to work; illustrated by Maxie Chambliss. HarperCollins Pubs. 2001 unp il $5.95   E

1. Day care centers—Fiction

ISBN 0-688-17044-7   LC 00-57254

Carly is sad when her parents leave her at daycare to go to work, but when reminded that they'll be back later, she soon begins having fun with her friends

"The simplicity and sensitivity of the writing is well matched by Chambliss' line and watercolor wash illustrations." Booklist

Collard, Sneed B., III

Butterfly count; illustrated by Paul Kratter. Holiday House 2002 unp il $16.95   E

1. Butterflies—Fiction 2. Wildlife conservation—Fiction 3. Prairies—Fiction

ISBN 0-8234-1607-0   LC 2001-24114

Amy and her mother look for a very special butterfly while attending the annual Fourth of July Butterfly Count at a prairie restoration site. Includes factual information

Collard, Sneed B., III—_Continued_

about butterflies and how to attract and watch them

"A gentle family story with an environmental message. . . . Soft watercolor illustrations of prairie grasses, plants, and butterflies quietly illuminate this tranquil tale." SLJ

Collicutt, Paul

This truck. Farrar, Straus and Giroux 2004 unp il $15   E

1. Trucks

ISBN 0-374-37496-1   LC 2002-192896

Simple text and illustrations present different types of trucks and the work they do.

"Colorful, large, and realistic paintings of trucks will entice readers who love big rigs. . . . The youngest transportation fans will enjoy having the book read to them, while the large print on white space and repetition aid beginning readers." SLJ

Collier, Bryan

Uptown. Holt & Co. 2000 unp il $16.95   E

1. African Americans—Fiction 2. Harlem (New York, N.Y.)—Fiction

ISBN 0-8050-5721-8   LC 99-31774

Coretta Scott King award for illustration, 2001

A tour of the sights of Harlem, including the Metro-North Train, brownstones, shopping on 125th Street, a barber shop, summer basketball, the Boy's Choir, and sunset over the Harlem River

"Collier's evocative watercolor-and-collage illustrations create a unique sense of mood and place. Bold color choices for text as well as background pages complement engagingly detailed pictures of city life." SLJ

Colón, Raúl

Orson blasts off! Atheneum Books for Young Readers 2004 unp il $15.95   E

1. Imagination—Fiction 2. Play—Fiction

ISBN 0-689-84278-3   LC 2003-45362

"An Anne Schwartz book"

When his computer breaks down, Orson discovers that imagination is way more fun than a computer game.

"The clever story is enhanced by glowing, textured artwork, rendered in watercolors, colored pencils, and litho pencils, which will draw children right into Orson's daydream world." Booklist

Compestine, Ying Chang

The runaway rice cake; pictures by Tungwai Chau. Simon & Schuster Bks. for Young Readers 2001 unp il $16.95   E

1. Chinese New Year—Fiction 2. China—Fiction

ISBN 0-689-82972-8   LC 99-462168

After chasing the special rice cake, Nian Gao, that their mother has made to celebrate the Chinese New Year, three poor brothers share it with an elderly woman and have their generosity richly rewarded

"Compestine's engaging tale brims with intriguing details of the traditions that surround the holiday. . . . Chau makes a splash with vibrant acrylics whose textured surface and controlled, sophisticated blending of shades mimic the look of pastels." Publ Wkly

Connor, Leslie

Miss Bridie chose a shovel; illustrated by Mary Azarian. Houghton Mifflin 2004 unp il $16

                                                          E

1. Immigrants—Fiction

ISBN 0-618-30564-5   LC 2003-12290

Miss Bridie emigrates to America in 1856 and chooses to bring a shovel, which proves to be a useful tool throughout her life.

" Azarian's sturdy woodcuts are an excellent choice to illustrate daily life in mid-nineteenth-century America, and her pictures catch some of the emotions that the text shies away from. . . . This is a simple pleasure that will be truly appreciated by those old enough to understand the message." Booklist

Conover, Chris

Over the hills & far away; retold and with pictures by Chris Conover. 1st ed. Farrar Straus Giroux 2004 unp il $16   E

1. Musicians—Fiction 2. Stories in rhyme 3. Animals—Fiction

ISBN 0-374-38043-0   LC 2003-54878

"This version of the nursery rhyme 'Tom, the Piper's Son' features a bright-eyed otter pup. . . . He and his bagpipes encourage the woodland animals to drop their cares and dance. . . . The text remains true in spirit to the original. The detailed illustrations are a joy to behold. . . . Done in muted earth tones, the . . . paintings are festive, yet serene." SLJ

Conway, David

The most important gift of all; illustrated by Karin Littlewood. Gingham Dog Press 2006 unp il $15.95   E

1. Love—Fiction 2. Infants—Fiction 3. Siblings—Fiction 4. Kenya—Fiction

ISBN 0-7696-4618-2

"Ama is excited when her baby brother is born, and like all the people of her Kenyan village, she wants to bring him a gift. Because Grandma tells her that love is the most important gift of all, the small girl goes in search of it. . . . The beautiful blend of the traditional storytelling pattern and contemporary realism is expressed in Littlewood's double-page spreads." Booklist

Cook, Bernadine

The little fish that got away; story by Bernadine Cook; pictures by Crockett Johnson. HarperCollins Publishers 2005 c1956 unp il $15.89   E

1. Fishing—Fiction

ISBN 0-06-055714-1

A reissue of the title first published 1956 by Addison Wesley

"A determined little boy goes fishing every day and never catches anything, until one amazing day when his luck finally turns. The minimal text and simple pictures (in a new color palette) make this story just right for three-year-old to memorize and 'read' to themselves over and over." Horn Book Guide

Cook, Sally

Good night pillow fight; illustrated by Laura Cornell. Joanna Cotler Books 2004 unp il $15.99; lib bdg $16.89   E

1. Bedtime—Fiction 2. Stories in rhyme

ISBN 0-06-205189-X; 0-06-205190-3 (lib bdg)

LC 2003-8933

Rhyming bedtime conversation between a city full of parents and their children, who are much more interested in playing than sleeping.

"This charming story will delight youngsters. . . . Cornell's ink-and-watercolor cartoons work beautifully in scenes that range from closeups to vignettes to detailed two-page paintings." SLJ

Cooke, Trish

Full, full, full of love; illustrated by Paul Howard. Candlewick Press 2003 unp il $15.99
                                                          E

1. Grandmothers—Fiction 2. African Americans—Fiction

ISBN 0-7636-1851-9   LC 2001-43761

For young Jay Jay, Sunday dinner at Gran's house is full of hugs and kisses, tasty dishes, all kinds of fishes, happy faces, and love

"Howard's generous, full-bleed illustrations capture the loving, bountiful spirit of a big family meal with a colorful palette and expressive eyes and smiles." Booklist

Cooney, Barbara

Chanticleer and the fox; adapted and illustrated by Barbara Cooney. Crowell 1958 unp il $16.99; lib bdg $17.89; pa $6.99   E

1. Chaucer, Geoffrey, d. 1400—Adaptations 2. Fables 3. Foxes—Fiction

ISBN 0-690-18561-8; 0-690-18562-6 (lib bdg); 0-06-443087-1 (pa)

Awarded the Caldecott Medal, 1959

"Adaptation of the 'Nun's Priest's Tale' from the Canterbury Tales." Verso of title page

"Chanticleer, the rooster, learns the pitfalls of vanity, while the fox who captures, then loses him, learns the value of self-control." Books for Deaf Child

This adaptation "retains the spirit of the original in its telling and in the beautiful, strongly colored illustrations softened by detailed lines. . . . [It] will be excellent for reading aloud to children." Libr J

Miss Rumphius; story and pictures by Barbara Cooney. Viking 1982 unp il $16.99   E

1. Aunts—Fiction

ISBN 0-670-47958-6   LC 82-2837

As a child Great-aunt Alice Rumphius resolved that when she grew up she would go to faraway places, live by the sea in her old age, and do something to make the world more beautiful—and she does all those things, the last being the most difficult of all

"The idea of offering beauty as one's heritage is appealing, the story is nicely told, and the illustrations are quite lovely, especially the closing scenes of a hill covered with flowers being gathered by children." Bull Cent Child Books

Cooper, Elisha

A good night walk. Orchard Books 2005 unp il $16.99   E

1. Bedtime—Fiction 2. Walking—Fiction

ISBN 0-439-68783-7   LC 2004-23571

The reader is taken on a journey through a neighborhood and shown the sights, sounds, and smells as evening approaches.

"The clear, unfussy compositions echo the poetic words' soothing, elemental sounds . . . which beautifully capture the soft, slowdown rhythms of dusk. Children will find much that's cozy, reassuring, and familiar in the scenes, . . . depicted in luminous watercolors and firmly penciled shapes" Booklist

Magic thinks big. Greenwillow Books 2004 unp il $14.99; lib bdg $15.89   E

1. Cats—Fiction

ISBN 0-06-058164-6; 0-06-058165-4 (lib bdg)

LC 2003-12566

A cat sits in the doorway and tries to decide whether to go inside where he might get fed again, go outside where he might have an adventure, or stay where he is.

"The simple text is full of dry humor and whimsy. The dreamy pencil-and-watercolor illustrations are a pleasing mixture of soft colors and thick lines." SLJ

Cooper, Helen

Pumpkin soup. Farrar, Straus & Giroux 1999 c1998 unp il $16   E

1. Cats—Fiction 2. Squirrels—Fiction 3. Ducks—Fiction

ISBN 0-374-36164-9   LC 98-18677

First published 1998 in the United Kingdom

The Cat and the Squirrel come to blows with the Duck in arguing about who will perform what duty in preparing their pumpkin soup, and they almost lose the Duck's friendship when he decides to leave them

"Cooper serves up a well-rounded tale told with storyteller's cadences. . . . Rich autumn colors and enchanting details on large spreads and spot illustrations embellish characterizations and setting." SLJ

Another title about Cat, Squirrel and Duck is:

A pipkin of pepper (2005)

Cooper, Susan

Frog; illustrated by Jane Browne. Margaret K. McElderry Bks. 2002 unp il $17   E

1. Swimming—Fiction 2. Frogs—Fiction

ISBN 0-689-84302-X   LC 2001-30825

A young boy learns how to swim by watching a small frog that makes its way into the family swimming pool

"Both text and art are stripped down to the essentials, with short, simple sentences and uncomplicated, expressive paintings telling the story." Horn Book Guide

Coppinger, Tom

Curse in reverse; [illustrated by] Dirk Zimmer. Atheneum Bks. for Young Readers 2003 unp il $16.95   E

1. Fairy tales 2. Witches—Fiction

ISBN 0-689-83096-3   LC 2001-22952

Coppinger, Tom—*Continued*

After a witch places a curse on them, a childless couple lives in fear for many years before coming to understand that the curse is really a blessing in disguise

The author "writes with lively dramatic language that is just right for read-alouds, while Zimmer's textured ink-and-watercolor illustrations capture the humor and farce." Booklist

Cordsen, Carol Foskett

The milkman; illustrated by Douglas Jones. Dutton Children's Books 2005 unp il $15.99

E

1. Stories in rhyme
ISBN 0-525-47208-8   LC 2004-21459

In the early, early morning, the milkman makes his rounds, helping his neighbors in a variety of ways.

"Cordsen tells the story in laconic phrases that read aloud well, but this picture book's most distinctive feature is its appealing, retro artwork." Booklist

Corey, Shana

Players in pigtails; illustrated by Rebecca Gibbon. Scholastic Press 2003 unp il $16.95

E

1. All-American Girls Professional Baseball League—Fiction 2. Baseball—Fiction 3. Sex role—Fiction
ISBN 0-439-18305-7   LC 2002-3445

Katie Casey, a fictional character, helps start the All-American Girls Professional Baseball League, which gave women the opportunity to play professional baseball while America was involved in World War II

"Kids, both girls and boys, will revel in the energy and joy Corey packs into her story. Gibbon's pictures look straight out of the 1940s, with vintage details and an evocative color palette. They also possess a winsome charm that plays nicely with the text." Booklist

Cousins, Lucy

Hooray for fish! Candlewick 2005 unp il $14.99

E

1. Fishes—Fiction
ISBN 0-763602741-0

Little Fish has all sorts of fishy friends in his underwater home, but loves one of them most of all.

"This winning title . . . features . . . bright hues and cheerful, childlike creatures. The stars here are fish, and Cousins matches a gloriously decorated assortment of them with rhyming text that encourages children to look carefully and think about similarities and differences." Booklist

Cowley, Joy

Red-eyed tree frog; story by Joy Cowley; illustrated with photographs by Nic Bishop. Scholastic Press 1999 unp il $16.95   E

1. Frogs—Fiction 2. Rain forests—Fiction
ISBN 0-590-87175-7   LC 98-15674

This frog found in the rain forest of Central America spends the night searching for food while also being careful not to become dinner for some other animal

"Stunning color photographs and a gripping interactive text." Booklist

Where horses run free; a dream for the American mustang; paintings by Layne Johnson. Boyds Mills Press 2003 unp il $15.95   E

1. Horses—Fiction
ISBN 1-59078-062-0

When a cowboy comes across a penned-up herd of wild horses, he vows to find a home where horses can run free.

"Readers come away with a feeling of overwhelming optimism shown by one man's ability to correct an injustice. The illustrations superbly convey the magnificence of the wilderness and the adaptation of rejuvenated, galloping residents to it." SLJ

Cox, Judy

Go to sleep, Groundhog! illustrated by Paul Meisel. Holiday House 2004 unp il $16.95

E

1. Marmots—Fiction 2. Groundhog Day—Fiction
ISBN 0-8234-1645-3   LC 2002-24124

When Groundhog is unable to sleep, he experiences autumn and winter holidays he never knew about, and then he finally falls asleep before Groundhog Day

"An endnote discussing the tradition of using critters as meteorologists makes this a useful as well as a charming answer to the scarcity of engaging material on Groundhog Day." Booklist

My family plays music; illustrated by Elbrite Brown. Holiday House 2003 unp il $16.95

E

1. Musicians—Fiction 2. Musical instruments—Fiction 3. Family life—Fiction
ISBN 0-8234-1591-0   LC 00-44903

A musical family with talents for playing a variety of instruments enjoys getting together to celebrate

"The paper-cut illustrations vibrate with color and—almost—with sound. The multiracial family with its rainbow of skin tones is not only a lovely multicultural statement but also a vivid reflection of contemporary families and musical tastes." Booklist

Coy, John

Strong to the hoop; illustrations by Leslie Jean-Bart. Lee & Low Bks. 1999 unp il $16.95

E

1. Basketball—Fiction
ISBN 1-880000-80-6   LC 98-33264

Ten-year-old James tries to hold his own and prove himself on the basketball court when the older boys finally ask him to join them in a game

"Coy's text moves with all the free-wheeling speed of playground ball. . . . Best of all, though, are Jean-Bart's collage-style illustrations, produced by combining Polaroid photographs and scratchboard drawings." Booklist

Vroomaloom zoom; illustrated by Joe Cepeda. Crown 2000 unp il $15.95; lib bdg $17.99

E

1. Sound—Fiction 2. Automobile travel—Fiction 3. Bedtime—Fiction
ISBN 0-517-80009-8; 0-517-80010-1 (lib bdg)
LC 99-462103

Coy, John—*Continued*

Daddy takes Carmela on a car ride, lulling her to sleep with various sounds, from the wurgle lurgle of swamps to the hoopty doopty swoopty loopty of driving in circles

"The rhythmic, repetitive text and the vibrant pictures against colorful pages make this story a perfect read-aloud." SLJ

Crews, Donald

Carousel. Greenwillow Bks. 1982 unp il lib bdg $16.89   **E**

ISBN 0-688-00909-3   LC 82-3062

"Crews uses both color photography of words and paintings in Art Deco style of the carousel; a brief text describes the ride, from the horses waiting, silent and still, to the end of a whirling ride. The speeded, blurred pictures of the carousel in motion and of the words (boom, too) that signify the calliope sounds are very effective. Despite the lack of story line, this should appeal to children because of the brilliant color, the impression of speed, and the carousel itself." Bull Cent Child Books

Freight train. Greenwillow Bks. 1978 unp il $16.99; lib bdg $17.89; pa $6.99   **E**

1. Railroads 2. Color
ISBN 0-688-80165-X; 0-688-84165-1 (lib bdg); 0-688-11701-5 (pa)   LC 78-2303

Also available Board book edition and Big book edition

A Caldecott Medal honor book, 1979

"Crews, with a minimum of descriptive words, has drawn a stylized freight train passing by, slowly at first, then in a blur of black and bright color." Babbling Bookworm

"The young child can learn to identify the engine, the caboose and the different cars. . . . A delightful introduction to railroad transportation and to the colors in the spectrum." America

Harbor. Greenwillow Bks. 1982 unp il lib bdg $15.89; pa $5.99   **E**

1. Harbors 2. Ships
ISBN 0-688-00862-3 (lib bdg); 0-688-07332-8 (pa)   LC 81-6607

"Liners, tankers, barges, and freighters move in and out. Ferryboats shuttle from shore to shore. Busiest of all are the tugboats as they push and tow the big ships to their docks. The New York harbor is full of action." Publisher's note

This book "is an exciting, educational and beautiful show-and-tell. . . . The full-page, full-color paintings will delight children." Publ Wkly

Night at the fair; pictures and words by Donald Crews. Greenwillow Bks. 1998 unp il $16.99   **E**

1. Fairs—Fiction
ISBN 0-688-11483-0   LC 96-48780

Nighttime is a wonderful time to enjoy the lights, the games, and the rides at a fair

"Each borderless double-page spread bursts with color and light and action and noise. . . . A minimal text acts for the most part as captioning or clues us in to what's coming next in this truly spectacular visual experience." Horn Book Guide

Parade. Greenwillow Bks. 1983 unp il lib bdg $15.93; pa $5.99   **E**

1. Parades
ISBN 0-688-01996-X (lib bdg); 0-688-06520-1 (pa)   LC 82-20927

Illustrations and brief text present the various elements of a parade-the spectators, street vendors, marchers, bands, floats, and the cleanup afterwards.

The author/illustrator's "refined poster-art approach to evoking an event works again here. . . . A polished assembly of crisp shapes, effective compositions, and pure, bright color." Booklist

Sail away. Greenwillow Bks. 1995 unp il $16.99; pa $6.99   **E**

1. Sailing—Fiction
ISBN 0-688-11053-3; 0-688-17517-1 (pa)   LC 94-6004

A family takes an enjoyable trip in their sailboat and watches the weather change throughout the day.

"To read any Crews book is to be immersed in sights and sounds vividly rendered and perfectly phrased, and this book proves no exception. The paintings move and swell; the words are haiku-like in their efficiency and implication." Horn Book

School bus. Greenwillow Bks. 1984 unp il $15.99; lib bdg $16.89; pa $5.99   **E**

1. School stories 2. Buses—Fiction
ISBN 0-688-02807-1; 0-688-02808-X (lib bdg); 0-688-12267-1 (pa)   LC 83-18681

Follows the progress of school buses as they take children to school and bring them home again

"The author-artist cleverly avoids monotony in his subject matter by using different size buses and a pleasing variety of background, perspectives, and the directions in which they travel. . . . The . . . yellow of the buses provides both a unifying element and a contrast for the cheerful colors of the children's clothing and for the bustle of city streets." Horn Book

Shortcut. Greenwillow Bks. 1992 unp il $16.99; lib bdg $17.89; pa $6.99   **E**

1. Railroads—Fiction 2. African Americans—Fiction
ISBN 0-688-06436-1; 0-688-06437-X (lib bdg); 0-688-813576-5 (pa)   LC 91-36312

Children taking a shortcut by walking along a railroad track find excitement and danger when a train approaches

"The story . . . is a perfect foil for the artist's masterful renderings of trains. . . . Scenes portraying the frightened children are equally effective in this out of the ordinary drama set forth with uncommon artistry." Publ Wkly

Truck. Greenwillow Bks. 1980 unp il $17.89; lib bdg $15.89; pa $5.99   **E**

1. Trucks
ISBN 0-688-80244-3; 0-688-84244-5 (lib bdg); 0-688-10481-9 (pa)   LC 79-19031

Also available Board book edition

A Caldecott Medal honor book, 1981

A bright red tractor-trailer truck "pushes its way across the United States to deliver its prized cargo of tricycles." Christ Sci Monit

Crews, Donald—*Continued*

"Although there is no text, the story is far from wordless; trucks, buses, and vans are emblazoned with letters and emblems, the streets are lined with familiar traffic signs, and a truck stop is festooned with advertisements in neon lights. . . . [This is] an imaginative, almost pop-art view of mobile America." Horn Book

Cronin, Doreen

Click, clack, moo; cows that type; pictures by Betsy Lewin. Simon & Schuster Bks. for Young Readers 2000 unp il $15   **E**

1. Cattle—Fiction

ISBN 0-689-83213-3   LC 97-29718

A Caldecott Medal honor book, 2001

When Farmer Brown's cows find a typewriter in the barn they start making demands, and go on strike when the farmer refuses to give them what they want

"A laugh-out-loud look at life on a very funny farm. . . . Lewin's hilarious cartoons deftly capture the farmer's exasperation and the animals' sheer determination." SLJ

Click, clack, quackity-quack; an alphabetical adventure; by Doreen Cronin and [illustrated by] Betsy Lewin. . Atheneum Books for Young Readers 2005 unp il $12.95   **E**

1. Animals—Fiction 2. Alphabet

ISBN 0-689-87715-3   LC 2004-20212

The cows invite "all of their animal friends . . . to a picnic. The alphabetical adventure begins as the Animals awake and ends 25 letters later with them peacefully snoring Zzzzzzzz. . . . This author-illustrator team works in perfect harmony to create a colorful and funny story with highly expressive animals." SLJ

Diary of a spider; pictures by Harry Bliss. 1st ed. Joanna Cotler Books 2005 unp il $15.99; lib bdg $16.89   **E**

1. Spiders—Fiction

ISBN 0-06-000153-4; 0-06-000154-2 (lib bdg)
     LC 2004-11549

A young spider discovers, day by day, that there is a lot to learn about being a spider, including how to spin webs and avoid vacuum cleaners.

"The amusing pen-and-ink and watercolor cartoons, complete with funny asides in dialogue balloons, expand the sublime silliness of some of the scenarios." SLJ

Diary of a worm; pictures by Harry Bliss. HarperCollins Pubs. 2003 unp il $15.99; lib bdg $16.89   **E**

1. Worms—Fiction

ISBN 0-06-000150-X; 0-06-000151-8 (lib bdg)
     LC 2002-7949

A young worm discovers, day by day, that there are some very good and some not so good things about being a worm in this great big world

"Bliss's droll watercolor illustrations are a marvel. He gives each worm an individual character with a few deft lines. . . . Inventive and laugh-out-loud funny, this worm's-eye view of the world will be a sure-fire hit." Publ Wkly

Duck for President; illustrated by Betsy Lewin. Simon & Schuster Books for Young Readers 2004 unp il $15.95   **E**

1. Ducks—Fiction 2. Elections—Fiction

ISBN 0-689-86377-2   LC 2003-21923

When Duck gets tired of working for Farmer Brown, his political ambition eventually leads to his being elected President.

"Lewin's characteristic humorous watercolors with bold black outlines fill the pages with color and jokes. Cronin's text is hilarious for kids and adults and includes a little math and quite a bit about the electoral process." SLJ

Giggle, giggle, quack; pictures by Betsy Lewin. Simon & Schuster Bks. for Young Readers 2002 unp il $15.95   **E**

1. Ducks—Fiction 2. Domestic animals—Fiction

ISBN 0-689-84506-5   LC 2001-32201

When Farmer Brown goes on vacation, leaving his brother Bob in charge, Duck makes trouble by changing all his instructions to notes the animals like much better

"Cronin again balances wit and jovial warmth in scenarios that will have readers laughing out loud." Publ Wkly

Wiggle; art by Scott Menchin. Atheneum Books for Young Readers 2005 unp il $12.95   **E**

1. Dogs—Fiction 2. Stories in rhyme

ISBN 0-689-86375-6   LC 2004-3326

"A spotted dog on the cover, vigorously working a hula hoop, leads children through a wiggling world. . . . The delightful cartoon-style, ink-and-watercolor artwork is highlighted by tidbits of collage. . . . Every candy-colored page features the funny, frenetic dog involved in some furious activity, and the sense of motion and movement is palpable each time." Booklist

Crowther, Robert

Opposites. Candlewick Press 2005 unp il $12.99
     E

1. Opposites

ISBN 0-7636-2783-6

"Each page features a word and readers must take some action—pulling a tab or turning a wheel—to discover its opposite. The pictures incorporate easy-to-understand examples in creative ways. . . . Warmly colored backgrounds and simply rendered images keep kids' attention focused on the task at hand, and the volume's sturdy pages and reinforced tabs will survive lots of use." SLJ

Cruise, Robin

Little Mamá forgets; [by] Robin Cruise; pictures by Stacey Dressen-McQueen. 1st ed. Farrar, Straus and Giroux 2006 unp il $16   **E**

1. Grandmothers—Fiction 2. Memory—Fiction 3. Mexican Americans—Fiction 4. Family life—Fiction

ISBN 0-374-34613-5   LC 2004-40462

"Melanie Kroupa books"

Although her Mexican-American grandmother now forgets many things, Luciana finds that she still remem-

Cruise, Robin—*Continued*

bers the things that are important to the two of them. Includes glossary of Spanish words used

"The story is bittersweet, but Lucy's ability to look on the bright side, and the obvious love that she and Little Mama share, wrap the events in affection and warmth. Dressen-McQueen's artwork is outstanding. . . . The Mexican family . . . comes alive in pictures that show the vibrancy of the happy household." Booklist

Crumpacker, Bunny

Alexander's pretending day; illustrated by Dan Andreasen. 1st ed. Dutton Children's Books 2005 unp il $15.99   E
1. Mother-child relationship—Fiction 2. Imagination—Fiction
ISBN 0-525-46936-2   LC 2004-12094
When Alexander asks his mother questions, they use their imaginations to play together.

"Andreasen's feathery, soft-tone paintings of a shape-shifting Alexander extend the humor and affection in the rhythmic words." Booklist

Cullen, Catherine Ann

Thirsty baby; illustrated by David McPhail. Little, Brown 2003 unp il $14.95   E
1. Infants—Fiction 2. Stories in rhyme
ISBN 0-316-16357-0   LC 2002-22493
"A baby's nigh-unquenchable thirst leads him to drain a bottle, a bathtub, a pond, a river, and finally the sea before he's replete—at least until bedtime. The tight rhymes are full of snappy repetitive elements . . . and the watercolor and ink illustrations reinforce the humor by contrasting the plot's absurdities with naturalistic details." Horn Book Guide

Cummings, Pat

Angel baby. Lothrop, Lee & Shepard Bks. 2000 unp il $16.99   E
1. Infants—Fiction 2. Siblings—Fiction 3. African Americans—Fiction 4. Stories in rhyme
ISBN 0-688-14821-2   LC 99-11502
In her mother's eyes, Amanda Lynne's baby brother is a perfect angel, but to Amanda the baby doesn't always seem so angelic

"Cummings captures the lot of the older sister in a readable rhyme, while her artwork shows the mischievousness of the little 'angel'. . . . The two-page spreads are brightly colored and full of nuance." Booklist

Cumpiano, Ina

Quinito's neighborhood; story Ina Cumpiano; illustrations José Ramirez. Children's Book Press 2005 22p il $16.95   E
1. Occupations—Fiction 2. Bilingual books—English-Spanish
ISBN 0-89239-209-6
Quinito not only knows everyone in his neighborhood, he also knows that each person in his community has a different, important occupation.

"Ramírez's vibrant acrylic-on-canvas paintings bring

this community to life, the primitive forms fairly bursting from the book's pages with their deep hues and sense of emotional warmth. The simple text, equally good in both English and Spanish, is in a font that resembles a child's printing." SLJ

Cunnane, Kelly

For you are a Kenyan child; [by] Kelly Cunnane; art by Ana Juan. 1st ed. Atheneum Books for Young Readers 2005 unp il $16.95
                                                                E
1. Kenya—Fiction
ISBN 0-689-86194-X   LC 2004-17060
"An Anne Schwartz book"
From rooster crow to bedtime, a Kenyan boy plays and visits neighbors all through his village, even though he is supposed to be watching his grandfather's cows.

This story is told "through vivid, descriptive text. . . . The brilliant, colorful, and humorous illustrations stand out against the white backgrounds and are large enough for group viewing. A gentle story about family, responsibility, and a curious little boy." SLJ

Curtis, Carolyn

I took the moon for a walk; written by Carolyn Curtis; illustrated by Alison Jay. Barefoot Books 2004 unp il $16.99   E
1. Moon—Fiction 2. Stories in rhyme
ISBN 1-84148-611-6   LC 2003-19087
"A young boy takes the moon on a stroll around his neighborhood. Curtis' rhyming text is rich with descriptive language and images. . . . Jay's surreal . . . illustrations not only greatly enhance the dreamlike quality of the text but also provide visual images for some of the unfamiliar words and unusual phrasings." Booklist

Curtis, Gavin

The bat boy & his violin; illustrated by E.B. Lewis. Simon & Schuster Bks. for Young Readers 1998 il $16.95; pa $6.99   E
1. Violinists—Fiction 2. Baseball—Fiction 3. Father-son relationship—Fiction 4. African Americans—Fiction
ISBN 0-689-80099-1; 0-689-84115-9 (pa)
                                        LC 97-25417
Reginald is more interested in practicing his violin than in his father's job managing the worst team in the Negro Leagues, but when Papa makes him the bat boy and his music begins to lead the team to victory, Papa realizes the value of his son's passion

"Lewis's soft watercolor illustrations portray the characters with depth and beauty, resulting in a very special book." SLJ

Curtis, Jamie Lee

I'm gonna like me; letting off a little self-esteem; illustrated by Laura Cornell. HarperCollins Pubs. 2002 unp il $16.99; lib bdg $17.89   E
1. Stories in rhyme
ISBN 0-06-028761-6; 0-06-028762-4 (lib bdg)
                                        LC 2002-1300

Curtis, Jamie Lee—_Continued_

"Joanna Cotler books"

"In rhyming text, a boy and a girl describe how they will like themselves whether things are going right or wrong." SLJ

"Though the message is both catchy and effective in its delivery, it's Cornell's humorous, detailed, ink-and-watercolor illustrations that give this volume true pizzazz." Publ Wkly

Tell me again about the night I was born; illustrated by Laura Cornell. HarperCollins Pubs. 1996 unp il $16.99; lib bdg $17.89; pa $5.99

E

1. Adoption—Fiction 2. Infants—Fiction

ISBN 0-06-024528-X; 0-06-024529-8 (lib bdg); 0-06-443581-4 (pa)   LC 95-5412

Also available Board book edition

"Joanna Cotler books"

"The young female narrator asks her adoptive parents to 'tell me again' the story of her birth and introduction into the family she is now a part of. . . . The humorous, cartoon-style pictures by Laura Cornell . . . are a perfect visual counterpart to the text." Horn Book

Cushman, Doug

Inspector Hopper; story and pictures by Doug Cushman. HarperCollins Pubs. 2000 64p il $14.95; lib bdg $14.89; pa $3.99   E

1. Insects—Fiction 2. Mystery fiction

ISBN 0-06-028382-3; 0-06-028383-1 (lib bdg); 0-06-444260-8 (pa)   LC 99-30878

"An I can read book"

Inspector Hopper and his perpetually hungry assistant McBugg solve three mysteries for their insect friends

"Beginning readers will find a familiar structure, natural language, compelling plot, supporting illustrations, and engaging characters. . . . The light watercolors define the characters as soft-boiled while slyly playing on stereotypes out of film noir." Horn Book Guide

Another title about Inspector Hopper is:

Inspector Hopper's mystery year (2003)

Mystery at the Club Sandwich; written and illustrated by Doug Cushman. Clarion Books 2004 unp $15   E

1. Mystery fiction 2. Elephants—Fiction 3. Animals—Fiction

ISBN 0-618-41969-1   LC 2004-537

When Lola, famous singer at the Club Sandwich, loses her lucky marbles, elephant detective Nick Trunk, lover of peanut butter, takes the case.

"Readers will guess the villain early on but that won't interfere with their enjoyment of the droll story, which is greatly enhanced by delightful illustrations. Cushman uses black watercolor washes, colored pencil, and pastel against a stark white background, suggesting the silver nitrate photographs and popular black-and-white movies of the gumshoe era." SLJ

Cutler, Jane

The cello of Mr. O; illustrated by Greg Couch. Dutton Children's Bks. 1999 unp il $15.99

E

1. Violoncellos—Fiction 2. Musicians—Fiction

ISBN 0-525-46119-1   LC 98-42692

When a concert cellist plays in the square for his neighbors in a war-besieged city, his priceless instrument is destroyed by a mortar shell, but he finds the courage to return the next day to perform with a harmonica

Couch's "soft-focus watercolors in burnished shades of gold, copper and fiery red have a dreamlike quality that effectively contrast with the unsentimental narration." Publ Wkly

Rose and Riley; pictures by Thomas F. Yezerski. 1st ed. Farrar Straus Giroux 2005 48p il $15   E

1. Friendship—Fiction

ISBN 0-374-36340-4   LC 2003-54887

Together, Rose, a vole, and Riley, a groundhog, figure out how to prepare for the possibility of rain, how to celebrate un-birthdays, and what to do with worries.

"Soft pastel illustrations add to the warmth of the text while repetition eases the decoding. A sweet, thoughtful offering with two memorable characters." SLJ

Another title about Rose and Riley is:

Rose and Riley come and go (2005)

Cuyler, Margery

100th day worries; illustrated by Arthur Howard. Simon & Schuster Bks. for Young Readers 2000 unp il $16   E

1. School stories 2. Counting

ISBN 0-689-82979-5   LC 98-52887

Jessica worries about collecting 100 objects to take to class for the 100th day of school

"Energetic pen-and-ink squiggles and bright watercolors fill the pages with round-eyed figures and striped, dotted, and floral patterns as the groups of objects are described and counted." Booklist

The bumpy little pumpkin; illustrated by Will Hillenbrand. 1st ed. Scholastic Press 2005 unp il $15.95   E

1. Pumpkin—Fiction

ISBN 0-439-52835-6   LC 2004-12179

Little Nell chooses an unusual pumpkin for her Halloween jacko-lantern, despite her big sisters' criticisms.

"Cuyler's infectious, repetitive text, with its recurrent use of BIG, is perfectly paced for participatory read-alouds, and Hillenbrand's cheery, whimsical mixed-media illustrations show Little Nell's perspective." Booklist

Another title about Little Nell is:

The biggest, best snowman (1998)

Daly, Niki

My dad; story and pictures by Niki Daly. Margaret K. McElderry Bks. 1995 unp il $16

E

1. Alcoholism—Fiction 2. Fathers—Fiction

ISBN 0-689-50620-1   LC 94-14455

Daly, Niki—*Continued*

"Though the brother and sister featured here dearly love their father, they are embarrassed and increasingly anxious about his drinking. . . . A Friday-night school concert becomes the turning point; Dad shows up drunk and humiliates his children. . . . The tale ends on a hopeful note, however, with Dad persuaded to join Alcoholics Anonymous. Daly's gentle touch extends to both words and pictures: her sensitive, graceful prose is coupled with soft-focus watercolors that underscore the poignancy of her characters' struggles." Publ Wkly

Once upon a time; story & pictures by Niki Daly. Farrar, Straus & Giroux 2003 unp il $16

E

1. Reading—Fiction 2. Friendship—Fiction
ISBN 0-374-35633-5   LC 2002-24516

Sarie struggles when she reads aloud in class in her South African school, but then she and her friend Auntie Anna find a book about Cinderella in Auntie Anna's old car and begin to read together

"The beautiful watercolor illustrations, in Daly's typical style, ably capture the expanse of the South African setting and the depth of Sarie's emotion. The gentle, encouraging tone prevents the message from being heavy-handed or maudlin." Booklist

Ruby sings the blues; story and pictures by Niki Daly. Bloomsbury Children's Books 2005 unp il $16.95

E

1. Jazz music—Fiction 2. Singers—Fiction
ISBN 1-58234-995-9   LC 2004-54457

Ruby's loud voice annoys everyone around her, until she learns to control her volume with the help of her new jazz musician friends.

"The nicely paced, rhythmic text will read well to a crowd, and the lyrical descriptions of what Ruby learns to do . . . will introduce children to the musicianship and emotion singers bring to their work. Daly's mixed-media illustrations showcase a cast of urban hipsters wearing patterned outfits that extend the rhythms in the story." Booklist

Where's Jamela? story & pictures by Niki Daly. Farrar, Straus and Giroux 2004 unp il $16

E

1. Moving—Fiction 2. Blacks—Fiction 3. South Africa—Fiction
ISBN 0-374-38324-3   LC 2003-49485

When Mama gets a new job and a new house, everyone is excited about moving except Jamela who likes her old house just fine

"Daly's warm, easy watercolors are full of motion, and convey both the unique sun-seared heat of the South African setting and the universality of common human experience." SLJ

Other titles about Jamela are:
Happy birthday, Jamela! (2006)
Jamela's dress (1999)
What's cooking Jamela (2001)

D'Amico, Carmela

Ella the Elegant Elephant; by Carmela & Steven D'Amico. Arthur A. Levine Books 2004 unp il $16.95

E

1. Hats—Fiction 2. School stories 3. Elephants—Fiction
ISBN 0-439-62792-3   LC 2003-28081

Ella is nervous about the first day of school in her new town, but wearing her grandmother's good luck hat makes her feel better—until the other students tease her and call her names.

"Combining a fairy-tale quality with elements in story and setting that will be familiar to children, this has a charming protagonist, as well as lovely, whimsical art, in a soft rich palette. . . . The text is simple, descriptive, and often lively, making a good read-aloud." Booklist
Another title about Ella is:
Ella takes the cake (2005)

Danziger, Paula

It's Justin Time, Amber Brown; illustrated by Tony Ross. Putnam 2001 48p il (A is for Amber) $12.99; pa $3.99

E

1. Clocks and watches—Fiction 2. Time—Fiction 3. Birthdays—Fiction
ISBN 0-399-23470-5; 0-698-11907-X (pa)
                              LC 99-89396

This Amber Brown easy reader features the protagonist at a younger age than Amber Brown is not a crayon and others in that series

Unlike her best friend Justin, Amber Brown loves to measure time and hopes to receive a watch on her seventh birthday

"The illustrations capture the mood of the story, which is playful and spirited. Beginning readers will enjoy sharing Amber's pre-birthday anticipation and older readers may want to go back and see the early years of the characters they know and love." SLJ
Other easy-to-read titles about Amber Brown are:
Get ready for second grade, Amber Brown (2002)
It's a fair day, Amber Brown (2002)
Orange you glad it's Halloween, Amber Brown (2005)
Second grade rules, Amber Brown (2004)
What a trip, Amber Brown (2001)

Darrow, Sharon

Old Thunder and Miss Raney; illustrated by Kathryn Brown. Dorling Kindersley 2000 unp il $15.95

E

1. Tall tales
ISBN 0-7894-2619-6   LC 99-462361
"A DK Ink book"

Miss Raney is determined to win a ribbon for her biscuits at the county fair until a tornado changes her plans

"The entertaining pace and folksy dialogue make this a natural choice for reading aloud. Energetic illustrations extend the tongue-in-cheek humor and are as clever as the homespun tale." Horn Book Guide

Daugherty, James Henry

Andy and the lion; by James Daugherty. Viking 1938 unp il pa $5.99 hardcover o.p.   **E**

1. Lions—Fiction

ISBN 0-14-050277-7 (pa)

A Caldecott Medal honor book, 1939

A modern picture story of Androcles and the lion in which Andy, who read a book about lions, was almost immediately plunged into action. The next day he met a circus lion with a thorn in his paw. Andy removed the thorn and earned the lion's undying gratitude

"This is a tall tale for little children. It is typically American in its setting and its fun. The large full page illustrations are in yellow, black and white and the brief, hand-lettered text on the opposite page is clear and readable." Libr J

Davidson, Rebecca Piatt

All the world's a stage; pictures by Anita Lobel. Greenwillow Bks. 2003 unp il $15.99; lib bdg $16.89   **E**

1. Shakespeare, William, 1564-1616 2. Stories in rhyme

ISBN 0-06-029626-7; 0-06-029627-5 (lib bdg)

LC 2001-33274

An introduction to some of the characters and plays of William Shakespeare, written in the style of "The House That Jack Built"

"This is a clever introduction to Shakespeare's varied characters, and Lobel's beautifully detailed watercolor and white-gouache paintings breathe life into both the invented personages and the world of the Elizabethan theatre itself." SLJ

Davies, Nicola

Bat loves the night; illustrated by Sarah Fox-Davies. Candlewick Press 2001 28p il $15.99   **E**

1. Bats—Fiction

ISBN 0-7636-1202-2   LC 00-66681

Bat wakes up, flies into the night, uses the echoes of her voice to navigate, hunts for her supper, and returns to her roost to feed her baby

"An enticing picture book . . . that blends story with fact. . . . Lovely, atmospheric watercolor-and-pencil illustrations show surprising detail and succeed in making an oft-maligned animal appear realistically fuzzy and appealing." Booklist

Day, Alexandra

Carl's sleepy afternoon. Farrar Straus Giroux 2005 unp il $12.95   **E**

1. Dogs—Fiction

ISBN 0-374-31088-2

Carl's owners have many errands to do and expect Carl to sleep the entire afternoon. Instead, Carl the rottweiler roams the town assisting many people in their daily chores

"The entertaining story is told through the gently detailed, warmly realistic paintings." SLJ

Other titles about Carl are:

Carl goes shopping (1990)

Carl goes to daycare (1993)

Carl makes a scrapbook (1994)

Carl's afternoon in the park (1991)

Carl's birthday (1995)

Carl's Christmas (1990)

Carl's masquerade (1992)

Good dog, Carl (1985)

Follow Carl (1998)

De Groat, Diane

Trick or treat, smell my feet. Morrow Junior Bks. 1998 unp il $14.95; lib bdg $14.89; pa $4.95   **E**

1. Halloween—Fiction 2. Siblings—Fiction

ISBN 0-688-15766-1; 0-688-15767-X (lib bdg); 0-688-17061-7 (pa)   LC 97-32916

"When Gilbert and his sister accidentally bring each other's costumes to school for the annual Halloween parade, Gilbert ends up donning a ballerina outfit." Publ Wkly

"De Groat's funny watercolor pictures capture the various animal creatures' very human expressions and body language." Booklist

Other titles about Gilbert are:

Brand-new pencils, brand-new books (2005)

Good night, sleep tight, don't let the bedbugs bite! (2002)

Happy birthday to you, you belong in the zoo (1999)

Jingle, bells, homework smells (2000)

Liar, liar, pants on fire (2003)

No more pencils, no more books, no more teacher's dirty looks! (2006)

Roses are pink, your feet really stink (1996)

We gather together—now please get lost! (2001)

De Paola, Tomie

The baby sister; written and illustrated by Tomie dePaola. Putnam 1996 unp il $16.99; pa $5.99   **E**

1. Infants—Fiction 2. Siblings—Fiction 3. Grandmothers—Fiction

ISBN 0-399-22908-6; 0-698-11773-5 (pa)

LC 94-37218

"Tommy's mother is expecting a baby. Tommy helps get the baby's room ready and longs for a sister with a red ribbon in her hair. He's thrilled when the baby is a girl, but while his mother is away in the hospital, his Italian grandmother comes to stay, and he finds it hard to get along with her. . . . Simple lines and warm colors convey the affection in the extended family and the special closeness between Tommy and his parents." Booklist

Bill and Pete; story and pictures by Tomie de Paola. Putnam 1978 unp il pa $6.99 hardcover o.p.   **E**

1. Crocodiles—Fiction 2. Birds—Fiction

ISBN 0-698-11400-0 (pa)

"William Everett Crocodile chooses Pete the plover for his toothbrush, and they become friends as well. When the reptile scholar despairs of writing all the letters in his name, Pete has an idea and William passes the test by penning 'Bill.' Then, the Bad Guy (a human trapper) captures Bill and plans to make a suitcase of him." Publ

De Paola, Tomie—*Continued*

Wkly

"De Paola has . . . created an imaginative, humorous tale which he illustrates in happy pinks, greens, yellows, and blues." SLJ

Other titles about Bill and Pete are:
Bill and Pete go down the Nile (1987)
Bill and Pete to the rescue (1998)

An early American Christmas; written and illustrated by Tomie dePaola. Holiday House 1987 unp il lib bdg $16.95   E
1. Christmas—Fiction 2. German Americans—Fiction
ISBN 0-8234-0617-2   LC 86-3102

"A German family moves from the old country to a small New England town in the 1800's. The town doesn't celebrate Christmas, but the family forges ahead with bayberry candles, evergreen decorations, a Christmas tree in the parlor, and carols on the night air. Gradually, all the households become 'Christmas families.'" Child Book Rev Serv

"This provides a fascinating look at Christmas as it once was: a holiday whose customs were entwined with the season's natural bounty. . . . This is a warm and beautifully realized tribute to the spirit and traditions of the season." Publ Wkly

Guess who's coming to Santa's for dinner? written and illustrated by Tomie dePaola. Putnam's 2004 unp il $16.99   E
1. Christmas—Fiction 2. Santa Claus—Fiction 3. Family life—Fiction
ISBN 0-399-24271-6   LC 2003-26638

A houseful of relatives turns "Mrs. C." and Santa's Christmas into a string of surprises, from the arrival of a pet polar bear to Cousin James B.'s flaming plum pudding.

"The part comic strip-style format cleverly reflects the busy, everyone-talk-at-once hum of a big family gathering and serves up plenty of funny asides. Warm and wonderful as Christmas cake fresh out of the oven, dePaola's softly hued, rounded illustrations shine with holiday spirit." Booklist

Jamie O'Rourke and the pooka. Putnam 2000 unp il $16.99; pa $6.99   E
1. Ireland—Fiction
ISBN 0-399-23467-5; 0-698-11974-X (pa)
          LC 99-22469

While his wife is away, lazy Jamie O'Rourke relies on a pooka to clean up the messes that he and his friends make

"DePaola's cozy, colorful illustrations are a good match for the lighthearted, rhythmic text." Horn Book Guide

The knight and the dragon; story and pictures by Tomie de Paola. Putnam 1980 unp il $17.99; pa $5.99   E
1. Knights and knighthood—Fiction 2. Dragons—Fiction
ISBN 0-399-20707-4; 0-698-11623-2 (pa)
          LC 79-18131

"A boy knight feels he really ought to fight a dragon and, in a cave far away, a dragon begins to feel he ought

to defend his species' honor by a duel with a knight. . . . When the foes finally meet, the encounter becomes something else." Publ Wkly

"Very few words and typical de Paola illustrations make this lighthearted jest. . . . There's a chuckle on every page." Child Book Rev Serv

Marco's colors; red, yellow, blue. Putnam 2003 unp il $5.99   E
1. Color 2. Dogs—Fiction 3. Bilingual books—English-Spanish
ISBN 0-399-24010-1

In this board book Marcos, the younger adopted brother of the Barker twins, learns the names of colors in English from Morgie as he thinks of their Spanish equivalents

"DePaola's signature watercolors, featuring bright clear hues on a clean white background, have tremendous charm and child appeal." SLJ

Another title about Marcos is:
Marcos counts: one, two, three (2003)

Meet the Barkers; Morgan and Moffat go to school; written and illustrated by Tomie dePaola. Putnam 2001 unp il $13.99   E
1. School stories 2. Twins—Fiction 3. Dogs—Fiction
ISBN 0-399-23708-9   LC 00-55355

Bossy Moffie (a dog) and her quiet twin brother Morgie both enjoy starting school, especially getting gold stars and making new friends

"Genuinely expressive, lovable characters, depicted in warm tones on handmade watercolor paper, make this a great read-aloud." SLJ

Other titles about the Barkers are:
Boss for a day (2001)
Hide-and-seek all week (2001)
A new Barker in the house (2002)
Trouble in the Barkers' class (2003)

Nana Upstairs & Nana Downstairs; written and illustrated by Tomie dePaola. Putnam 1998 unp il $16.99; pa $6.99   E
1. Grandmothers—Fiction 2. Death—Fiction
ISBN 0-399-23108-0; 0-698-11836-7 (pa)
          LC 96-31908

A newly illustrated edition of the title first published 1973

"Every Sunday four-year-old Tommy's family goes to visit his grandparents. His grandmother is always busy downstairs, but his great-grandmother is always to be found in bed upstairs, because she is 94 years old. . . . [Tommy] is desolate when his upstairs nana dies, but his mother comforts him by explaining that 'she will come back in your memory whenever you think about her.'" Booklist

"The illustrations are vintage dePaola, and the warm palette conveys the boy's love for his elderly relatives." Horn Book Guide

The night of Las Posadas; written and illustrated by Tomie dePaola. Putnam 1999 unp il $15.99; pa $6.99   E
1. Mary, Blessed Virgin, Saint—Fiction 2. Joseph, Saint—Fiction 3. Christmas—Fiction 4. Santa Fe (N.M.)—Fiction
ISBN 0-399-23400-4; 0-698-11901-0 (pa)
          LC 98-36405

De Paola, Tomie—*Continued*

At the annual celebration of Las Posadas in old Santa Fe, the husband and wife slated to play Mary and Joseph are delayed by car trouble, but a mysterious couple appear who seem perfect for the part

"DePaola's talent for crafting folktales is honed to near-perfection, and his pages glow with the soft sunwashed hues of the Southwest." Publ Wkly

Now one foot, now the other; story and pictures by Tomie de Paola. Putnam 1981 unp il $15.99; pa $7.99 **E**

1. Grandfathers—Fiction 2. Old age—Fiction
ISBN 0-399-20774-0; 0-399-20775-9 (pa)

LC 80-22239

"Bobby's much loved grandfather has had a stroke. After a long hospitalization, the man returns home unable to speak, walk or care for himself. . . . Their roles reversed, the youngster helps his grandfather learn to walk again 'now one foot, now the other.'" SLJ

"De Paola sensitively provides an understanding portrayal about grandparents' illness. . . . Soft blues and tans, textured with pencil shadings, provide a tranquil backdrop for the emotion-filled faces that expressively suggest the changing relationship of the old man and the boy." Booklist

Pascual and the kitchen angels; written and illustrated by Tomie de Paola. G.P. Putnam 2004 unp il $16.99 **E**

1. Angels—Fiction 2. Cooking—Fiction 3. Christian life—Fiction
ISBN 0-399-24214-7 LC 2003-8521

Pascual, a boy blessed by angels at his birth, receives divine help when the Franciscan monks make him their cook.

"Acrylic illustrations with soft pastel backgrounds show Pascual as a little boy. . . . The winsome paintings capture his serene spirituality as he and the creatures lift their voices toward heaven. Simple, well-chosen words reflect the youngster's sincere love for God and all of His creatures." SLJ

Stagestruck; written and illustrated by Tomie dePaola. G.P. Putnam's Sons 2005 unp il $16.99
E

1. Theater—Fiction 2. School stories
ISBN 0-399-24338-0 LC 2004-9261

Although Tommy fails to get the part of Peter Rabbit in the kindergarten play, he still finds a way to be the center of attention on stage

"The gently delivered lesson at the end does not dampen the fun of watching this aspiring thespian get carried away. . . . With its warm palette, rounded shapes, and clarity of expression, dePaola's signature style makes Tommy's world an inviting place to visit." Booklist

Strega Nona: an old tale; retold and illustrated by Tomie de Paola. Simon & Schuster 1988 c1975 unp il $16.95; pa $7.99 **E**

1. Witches—Fiction 2. Italy—Fiction
ISBN 0-671-66283-X; 0-671-66606-1 (pa)

LC 88-11438

Also available Board book edition; Spanish language edition also available

A Caldecott Medal honor book, 1976

A reissue of the title first published 1975 by Prentice-Hall

In this Italian folk-tale set in Calabria, "Strega Nona, 'Grandma Witch,' leaves Big Anthony alone with her magic pasta pot. He decides to give the townspeople a treat. . . . Big Anthony doesn't know how to make the pot stop. The town is practically buried in spaghetti before Strega Nona returns to save the day." SLJ

"Tomie de Paola has used simple colors, simple line, and medieval costume and architecture in his spaciously composed humorous pictures." Bull Cent Child Books

Other titles about Strega Nona and Big Anthony are:
Big Anthony and the magic ring (1979)
Big Anthony: his story (1998)
Merry Christmas, Strega Nona (1986)
Strega Nona: her story (1996)
Strega Nona meets her match (1993)
Strega Nona takes a vacation (2000)
Strega Nona's magic lessons (1982)

Tom; written and illustrated by Tomie dePaola. Putnam 1993 unp il $16.99; pa $6.99 **E**

1. Grandfathers—Fiction
ISBN 0-399-22417-3; 0-698-11448-5 (pa)

LC 92-1022

"In a story based on his own childhood, Tomie dePaola tells about little Tommy's regular Sunday visits with his grandfather, Tom. . . . With gentle humor and his usual mastery of line and composition, dePaola conveys the strong bond of affection between Tom and little Tommy." Horn Book Guide

De Regniers, Beatrice Schenk

May I bring a friend? illustrated by Beni Montresor. Atheneum Pubs. 1964 unp il pa $5.99 hardcover o.p. **E**

1. Animals—Fiction
ISBN 0-689-71353-3 (pa); 0-689-20615-1 (hc)

Awarded the Caldecott Medal, 1965

"Each time the little boy in this picture book is invited to take tea or dine with the King and Queen, he brings along a somewhat difficult animal friend. Their Highnesses always cope and are wonderfully rewarded in the end." Publ Wkly

"Rich color and profuse embellishment adorn an opulent setting. Absurdities and contrasts are so imaginatively combined in a hilarious comedy of manners that the merriment can be enjoyed on several levels." Horn Book

Deacon, Alexis

Beegu. Farrar, Straus & Giroux 2003 unp il $16
E

1. Extraterrestrial beings—Fiction
ISBN 0-374-30667-2 LC 2002-192738

A small creature from space finds no welcome on Earth, until she meets a group of children on a playground

"Beegu's black outline and solid yellow center evoke a celestial simplicity. . . . The accomplished artwork underscores the children's easy acceptance of Beegu and highlights the book's uplifting message that acts of kindness have lasting effects." Publ Wkly

DeFelice, Cynthia C.

Old Granny and the bean thief; pictures by Cat Bowman Smith. Farrar, Straus and Giroux 2003 unp il $16   E

1. Grandmothers—Fiction 2. Thieves—Fiction

ISBN 0-374-35614-9   LC 2002-20770

After a thief steals Old Granny's beans while she is asleep at night, she gets some surprising help with catching him.

"The down-home narrative is folksy and fun to read aloud. . . . Smith uses a Southwestern palette in her cartoon-style paintings." SLJ

The real, true Dulcie Campbell; [by] Cynthia DeFelice; pictures by R.W. Alley. Farrar, Straus & Giroux 2002 unp il $16   E

1. Family life—Fiction 2. Princesses—Fiction 3. Books and reading—Fiction

ISBN 0-374-36220-3   LC 00-58736

Believing that she is a princess, Dulcie Campbell leaves home to seek her true family, but she finds by reading a book of fairy tales that being a princess is not what she thought

"The story radiates good humor as well as sympathy for the imaginative Dulcie. In Alley's lively, appealing watercolor paintings, Dulcie's royal fantasies appear in picture frames alongside homelier scenes of life on the farm." Booklist

Degen, Bruce

Jamberry; story and pictures by Bruce Degen. Harper & Row 1983 unp il $16.99; lib bdg $17.89; pa $6.99   E

1. Stories in rhyme 2. Berries—Fiction

ISBN 0-06-021416-3; 0-06-021417-1 (lib bdg); 0-06-443068-5 (pa)   LC 82-47708

Also available Board book edition

"Boy meets bear, and together they go berry-picking by canoe, through fields and by pony and 'Boys-in-Berries' train, all the way to Berryland." Child Book Rev Serv

"Berries and jam are roundly celebrated in a lilting rhyme that, coupled with the jaunty colored pictures, makes it . . . a good pick for sharing one on one, or fun to read aloud as a poetry introduction." Booklist

Del Negro, Janice

Willa and the wind; retold by Janice M. Del Negro; illustrated by Heather Solomon. Marshall Cavendish Children 2005 unp il $16.95   E

1. Winds—Fiction 2. Magic—Fiction

ISBN 0-7614-5232-X

A mischievous north wind and a dishonest innkeeper try to outsmart young Willa Rose Mariah McVale, who must use trickery to claim what is rightfully hers.

"Lively prose, eye-catching art, and a strong female protagonist characterize Del Negro's delightful story based on a Norwegian folktale. . . . Solomon's luminous artwork has a magical airiness about it." Booklist

Delacre, Lulu

Rafi and Rosi; by Lulu Delacre. 1st ed. HarperCollins Publishers 2004 63p il $15.99; lib bdg $16.89   E

1. Frogs—Fiction 2. Siblings—Fiction 3. Puerto Rico—Fiction

ISBN 0-06-009895-3; 0-06-009896-1 (lib bdg)
LC 2003-1204

Two tree frogs, mischievous Rafi and his younger sister Rosi, learn about the plants and animals of Puerto Rico together.

"The teasing banter and tender rapport between the siblings are the most appealing features of these stories. Delacre's brightly colored cartoon illustrations add detail and a light touch. There is also a helpful glossary of Spanish words/phrases, and an appended 'Did You Know About—' section adds some interesting facts about Puerto Rico." SLJ

Another title about Rafi and Rosi is:

Rafi and Rosi carnival! (2006)

Demas, Corinne

Saying goodbye to Lulu; illustrated by Ard Hoyt. Little, Brown 2004 unp il $15.95   E

1. Death—Fiction 2. Bereavement—Fiction 3. Dogs—Fiction

ISBN 0-316-70278-1   LC 2003-44690

When her dog Lulu dies, a girl grieves but then continues with her life.

"Hoyt's expressive illustrations, ink-and-colored-pencil drawings washed with watercolors, reflect the tone of the text and show the child's sadness without sentimentality. . . . A sensitive, hopeful portrayal." Booklist

Demi

The emperor's new clothes; a tale set in China. Margaret K. McElderry Bks. 2000 unp il $19.95
E

1. Andersen, Hans Christian, 1805-1875—Adaptations 2. Fairy tales 3. China—Fiction

ISBN 0-689-83068-8   LC 99-24883

In this retelling of Hans Christian Andersen's tale, two rascals sell a vain Chinese emperor an invisible suit of clothes

"Demi's retelling is lucid, graceful, and true to the original. . . . Figures are delicately outlined; they are painted with flat, jewel-like colors and metallic gold and set against subtly patterned grounds that resemble silk damask. . . . A lovely and meticulously wrought rendition." Horn Book Guide

The greatest power. Margaret K. McElderry Bks. 2004 unp $19.95   E

1. Power (Social sciences)—Fiction 2. China—Fiction

ISBN 0-689-84503-0   LC 2002-10869

Companion volume to The empty pot

Long ago, a Chinese emperor challenges the children of his kingdom to show him the greatest power in the world, and all are surprised at what is discovered

"The text and the handsomely designed, richly colored artwork, which is touched with gold leaf, are set within a circular motif that reinforces the idea of eternity. As usual, Demi ably combines striking artwork and a meaningful story, with quiet dignity and wisdom." Booklist

Demi—*Continued*

Kites; magic wishes that fly up to the sky. Crown 1999 unp il pa $6.99 hardcover o.p.; lib bdg   **E**
1. Kites—Fiction 2. China—Fiction
ISBN 0-375-81008-0 (pa); 0-517-80050-0 (lib bdg)
       LC 98-41372

"In long-ago China, a woman commissioned an artist to paint a special dragon kite for her son. . . . Word of the artist's talent traveled, and he was soon asked to create a wide variety of flyers for other villagers. The small, intricate, colorful kites illustrated in Demi's signature style and set against blues and greens are lovely to look at and will encourage readers to appreciate their beauty. Captions offer brief explanations of the different emblematic figures, creatures, and symbols. . . . There is also mention of a Chinese festival devoted to kites, as well as detailed instructions for making a kite." SLJ

Denslow, Sharon Phillips
In the snow; by Sharon Phillips Denslow; pictures by Nancy Tafuri. 1st ed. Greenwillow Books 2005 unp il $15.99; lib bdg $16.89
       E
1. Animals—Fiction 2. Snow—Fiction 3. Stories in rhyme
ISBN 0-06-059683-X; 0-06-059684-8 (lib bdg)
       LC 2003-56861
Forest animals come out after a fresh snow to eat the seeds a thoughtful child has scattered on the ground.

"The very short verses of the rhyming text, sometimes limited to one word per page, provide young children with a guide to what is happening in the illustrations. . . . Tafuri works her visual magic, so finely attuned to the sensibilities of young children while challenging them to observe the natural world." Booklist

DePalma, Mary Newell
A grand old tree. Arthur A. Levine Books 2005 unp il $16.99   **E**
1. Trees—Fiction
ISBN 0-439-62334-0

"For many years a tree flourishes. . . . After the old tree dies, it still provides a home to animals and insects as it slowly decomposes. . . . Neither sentimental nor unfeeling, this appealing picture book offers an appreciation of the cycle of life through a story that is accessible to young children." Booklist

Desimini, Lisa
My beautiful child; illustrated by Matt Mahurin. Blue Sky Press 2004 unp il $16.95   **E**
1. Parent-child relationship—Fiction
ISBN 0-439-45893-5   LC 2003-5566
Parents express their affection and hopes for their beautiful baby.

"Mahurin uses amazing colors in his eye-catching illustrations, the brightest of yellows and the most vivid greens. . . . This volume lends itself to imaginative contemplation in its sense of joy and wonder." SLJ

Dewan, Ted
Bing: paint day. David Fickling Books 2004 unp il $5.95   **E**
1. Rabbits—Fiction 2. Color—Fiction
ISBN 0-385-75021-8
Bing the bunny and Flop decide to paint, but Bing spills the water and that changes the colors.

"Illustrated with bold, computer-generated art, [this] small [book] will appeal to toddlers who will relate to a world in which everything can go wrong but come out right at the end." SLJ
Other titles about Bing are:
Bing: bed time (2004)
Bing: get dressed (2004)
Bing: go picnic (2005)
Bing: make music (2005)
Bing: something for Daddy (2004)
Bing: swing (2005)
Bing: Yuk! (2005)

Dewdney, Anna
Llama, llama red pajama; by Anna Dewdney. Viking 2005 unp il $15.99   **E**
1. Llamas—Fiction 2. Bedtime—Fiction 3. Mother-child relationship—Fiction 4. Stories in rhyme
ISBN 0-670-05983-8   LC 2004-25149
At bedtime, a little llama worries after his mother puts him to bed and goes downstairs.

"Dewdney gives a wonderfully fresh twist to a familiar nighttime ritual with an adorable bugeyed baby llama, staccato four-line rhymes, and page compositions that play up the drama. The simple rhymes call out for repeating." Booklist

Dewey, Ariane
Splash! [by] Ariane Dewey and Jose Aruego. Harcourt 2001 c2000 unp il $10.95; pa $3.95
       E
1. Bears—Fiction 2. Fishing—Fiction
ISBN 0-15-216256-9; 0-15-216262-3 (pa)
       LC 00-9723
"Green Light reader"
Two clumsy bears join in fishing fun at the river
"This combines big, silly ink-and-watercolor pictures with two or three lines of text on each page. New readers will enjoy the slapstick . . . and the sounds of such words as *splash* and *slip* add to the fun of the story." Booklist

Dewey, Jennifer
Once I knew a spider; [by] Jennifer Owens Dewey; illustrated by Jean Cassels. Walker & Co. 2002 unp il $16.95; lib bdg $17.85   **E**
1. Spiders—Fiction
ISBN 0-8027-8700-2; 0-8027-8701-0 (lib bdg)
       LC 2001-26345
An expectant mother watches as an orb weaver spider spins a web, lays her eggs, and stays with them over the winter
An "eloquent meditation on the cycle of life. The muted tones of Cassels's . . . austere interiors and the detailed paintings of the spider's behavior complement the calm, contemplative tone of the journal-like text." Publ Wkly

Diakité, Penda

I lost my tooth in Africa; by Penda Diakité and Baba Wagué Diakité; illustrated by Baba Wagué Diakité. Scholastic Press 2006 unp il $16.99

E

1. Mali—Fiction 2. Teeth—Fiction 3. Chickens—Fiction 4. Family life—Fiction

ISBN 0-439-66226-5   LC 2004-01933

While visiting her father's family in Mali, a young girl loses a tooth, places it under a calabash, and receives a hen and a rooster from the African Tooth Fairy.

"The vivid ceramic-tile illustrations expand the text, revealing a range of animals, houses, and greenery. At the end are the words to Grandma's Good Night Song, the recipe for African Onion Sauce, and a glossary of Bambara words, all of which add to the authentic feel of the story." SLJ

DiCamillo, Kate

Mercy Watson to the rescue; illustrated by Chris Van Dusen. Candlewick Press 2005 68p il $12.99

E

1. Pigs—Fiction

ISBN 0-7636-2270-2   LC 2004-51896

After Mercy the pig snuggles to sleep with the Watsons, all three awaken with the bed teetering on the edge of a big hole in the floor.

"Appropriate as both a picture book and a beginning reader, this joyful story combines familiar elements . . . with a raucous telling that lets readers in on the joke. . . . The gouache illustrations are polished to a sheen and have plenty of heft." Booklist

Another title about Mercy Watson is:

Mercy Watson goes for a ride (2006)

Dillon, Leo

Rap a tap tap; here's Bojangles—think of that! [by] Leo & Diane Dillon. Blue Sky Press (NY) 2002 unp il $15.95

E

1. Robinson, Bill, 1878-1949 2. Tap dancing 3. African Americans 4. Stories in rhyme

ISBN 0-590-47883-4   LC 2001-43896

In illustrations and rhyme describes the dancing of Bill "Bojangles" Robinson, one of the most famous tap dancers of all time

"The spreads feature a bouncy text and eye-catching art. . . . The paintings have the effect of collage and employ strong city shapes, with bridges, buildings, and park benches pressed against feather-white backgrounds." Booklist

DiSalvo-Ryan, DyAnne

A castle on Viola Street. HarperCollins Pubs. 2001 unp il $16.95; lib bdg $16.89

E

1. Houses—Fiction

ISBN 0-688-17690-9; 0-688-17691-7 (lib bdg)

LC 00-40889

A hardworking family gets their own house at last by joining a community program that restores old houses

"DiSalvo-Ryan shares an uplifting story of the importance and impact of community pride and support. . . . The colorful gouache, pen, and pencil pictures are folksy and warm." Booklist

A dog like Jack. Holiday House 1999 unp il $16.95; pa $6.95

E

1. Dogs—Fiction 2. Death—Fiction

ISBN 0-8234-1369-1; 0-8234-1680-1 (pa)

LC 97-41949

After a long life of chasing squirrels, licking ice cream cones, and loving his adoptive family, an old dog comes to the end of his days

"Thoughtful words and tender pictures beautifully convey the special relationship between a young boy and his dog." Booklist

Grandpa's corner store. HarperCollins Pubs. 2000 unp il $15.99

E

1. Grocery trade—Fiction 2. Grandfathers—Fiction

ISBN 0-688-16716-0   LC 99-15504

Grandfather's corner grocery business is threatened by a new supermarket, but his granddaughter, Lucy, organizes the neighbors to convince him to stay

"The characterizations are strong, the illustrations deft and affecting, the story complex and uplifting." Horn Book Guide

Uncle Willie and the soup kitchen. Morrow Junior Bks. 1991 unp il pa $5.99 hardcover o.p.

E

1. Uncles—Fiction 2. Poverty—Fiction

ISBN 0-688-15285-6 (pa)   LC 90-6375

A boy spends the day with Uncle Willie in the soup kitchen where he works preparing and serving food for the hungry

"The color-pencil and wash illustrations observe . . . [a] balance between attracting the viewer with softly blended colors and avoiding the sentimentality of glamorizing an essentially sad situation. Without sacrifice of story, the total effect leaves young listeners with new considerations of society and social service, a theme too often neglected in picture books." Bull Cent Child Books

DiTerlizzi, Tony

Jimmy Zangwow's out-of-this-world, moon pie adventure. Simon & Schuster Bks. for Young Readers 2000 unp il $16; pa $4.99

E

1. Space flight to the moon—Fiction

ISBN 0-689-80076-2; 0-689-87830-3 (pa)

LC 98-16602

When Jimmy's mother won't let him have any moon pies for a snack, he takes a trip to the moon to get some

"The dialogue includes quirky sayings like 'Holy macaroni!' and 'Jumping june bugs!,' which young readers will relish. Large double-page watercolor, gouache, and colored-pencil illustrations enhance the story." SLJ

Dodd, Emma

Dog's noisy day; a story to read aloud. Dutton Children's Bks. 2003 c2002 unp il $14.99

E

1. Dogs—Fiction 2. Noise—Fiction

ISBN 0-525-47015-8

First published 2002 in the United Kingdom

Dog's "adventure takes him around a barnyard to meet the noisy animals that live there. . . . Children will need little encouragement to make each sound as they enjoy

Dodd, Emma—*Continued*

this lively, well-paced story. The simple, digitally enhanced cartoons are done in vivid colors and the animals are all wonderfully expressive." SLJ

Other titles about Dog are:

Dog's ABC (2002)

Dog's colorful day (2001)

Dodds, Dayle Ann

Minnie's Diner; a multiplying menu; illustrated by John Manders. Candlewick Press 2004 unp il $16.99   **E**

1. Multiplication—Fiction 2. Stories in rhyme 3. Restaurants—Fiction

ISBN 0-7636-1736-9   LC 2002-34756

Rhyming tale of five boys and their father who forget about their chores on the farm to enjoy Minnie's good cooking, each requesting double what the previous one ordered

"Told in jaunty rhymes with varied type sizes for emphasis, this funny story is illustrated with colorful cartoons done in gouache. Children will appreciate the humor and groan with delight when they recognize the math pattern." SLJ

Where's Pup? pictures by Pierre Pratt. Dial Bks. for Young Readers 2003 unp il $12.99   **E**

1. Circus—Fiction 2. Clowns—Fiction 3. Dogs—Fiction 4. Stories in rhyme

ISBN 0-8037-2744-5   LC 2002-588

A circus clown's search for his partner leads him to the top of an acrobatic pyramid, found by unfolding the book's final page

"Relying on a jeweled palette of acrylic reds and oranges, the images are simple yet arresting and show the action from varying perspectives. A visually exciting charmer." SLJ

Donaldson, Julia

The snail and the whale; pictures by Axel Scheffler. Dial Books for Young Readers 2004 c2003 unp il $16.99   **E**

1. Snails—Fiction 2. Whales—Fiction 3. Stories in rhyme

ISBN 0-8037-2922-7   LC 2003-4133

First published 2003 in the United Kingdom

Wanting to sail beyond its rock, a tiny snail hitches a ride on a big humpback whale and then is able to help the whale when it gets stuck in the sand.

"The message that even the smallest among us can help others will not be lost on children, and neither will the poetic language. . . . Donaldson's smooth, sprightly rhyming scheme buoys the story and never falters. The flat, cartoonish look of Scheffler's multimedia illustrations perfectly complements the tone of the text." SLJ

Dorros, Arthur

Abuela; illustrated by Elisa Kleven. Dutton Children's Bks. 1991 unp il $16.99; pa $5.99   **E**

1. Imagination—Fiction   2. Flight—Fiction 3. Grandmothers—Fiction 4. New York (N.Y.)—Fiction 5. Hispanic Americans—Fiction

ISBN 0-525-44750-4; 0-14-056225-7 (pa)

LC 90-21459

While riding on a bus with her grandmother, a little girl named Rosalba imagines that they are carried up into the sky and fly over the sights of New York City

"Each illustration is a masterpiece of color, line, and form that will mesmerize youngsters. . . . The smooth text, interpersed with Spanish words and phrases, provides ample context clues, so the glossary, while helpful, is not absolutely necessary." Booklist

Another title about Rosalba and her grandmother is:

Isla (1995)

City chicken; illustrated by Henry Cole. HarperCollins Pubs. 2003 unp il $15.99; lib bdg $16.89   **E**

1. Chickens—Fiction 2. Country life—Fiction

ISBN 0-06-028482-X; 0-06-028483-8 (lib bdg)

LC 00-66363

Egged on by the cat next door, a chicken from the city visits the country to see what she's been missing, and finds that it's not "all it's cracked up to be"

"The lively language will entertain the picture-book crowd with age-appropriate jokes and wordplay. Cole's cartoonlike watercolors extend the humor and show Henry's hilariously misinformed view of the world." Booklist

Julio's magic; collages by Ann Grifalconi. 1st ed. HarperCollins 2005 32p il $15.99; lib bdg $16.89   **E**

1. Wood carving—Fiction 2. Mexico—Fiction

ISBN 0-06-029004-8; 0-06-029005-6 (lib bdg)

LC 2004-6616

A young artist in a Mexican village discovers the power of friendship when he helps his mentor win a prestigious wood-carving contest

"Grifalconi's photorealistic collages capture the texture, color, and feel of village life. This book will be excellent for art and social studies classrooms. . . . It is also a compassionate intergenerational story." SLJ

Radio Man. Don Radio; a story in English and Spanish; Spanish translation by Sandra Marulanda Dorros. HarperCollins Pubs. 1993 unp il pa $6.99 hardcover o.p.   **E**

1. Migrant labor—Fiction 2. Mexican Americans—Fiction 3. Bilingual books—English-Spanish

ISBN 0-06-443482-6 (pa)   LC 92-28369

As he travels with his family of migrant farmworkers, Diego relies on his radio to provide him with companionship and help connect him to all the different places in which he lives

"Spot art separates English and Spanish on text pages that alternate with affecting, primitive-like acrylic paintings." Publ Wkly

Dotlich, Rebecca Kai

Grandpa loves; illustrated by Kathryn Brown. 1st ed. HarperCollins 2005 unp il $15.99; lib bdg $16.89 **E**

1. Grandfathers—Fiction 2. Pigs—Fiction

ISBN 0-06-029405-1; 0-06-029406-X (lib bdg)

LC 2002-276320

A "young pig describes what he or she enjoys doing with Grandpa. . . . The illustrations alternate between scenes that chronicle everyday activities, from camping to building a tree house, and snapshots of these special times arranged as if in a photo album. . . . Painted in soft, warm colors, the artwork adds greatly to the feeling of love that pervades this book." SLJ

Dowson, Nick

Tigress; illustrated by Jane Chapman. Candlewick Press 2004 27p il $15.99 **E**

1. Tigers—Fiction

ISBN 0-7636-2325-3
LC 2003-55342

A mother tigress raises two cubs and teaches them all they need to know until they are ready to rely on themselves.

"The zoology is as exciting as the story in this action-packed picture book. . . . Chapman's bright, clear, double-page acrylic pictures show the camouflage drama. . . . On each spread, the simple poetic words are in bold type, and small notes in italics add fascinating facts." Booklist

Doyle, Malachy

One, two, three O'Leary; written by Malachy Doyle; with illustrations by Will Hillenbrand. 1st ed. Margaret K. McElderry Books 2004 unp il $15.95 **E**

1. Bedtime—Fiction 2. Counting 3. Stories in rhyme

ISBN 0-689-85513-3
LC 2003-7915

Rhythmic text based on traditional rhymes tells how their father and mother try to put the ten bouncy O'Leary children to bed.

"Featuring crisp, bold colors, the collage and mixed-media illustrations show this family enjoying a rip-roaring good time. The tongue-twisting text will have kids laughing out loud." SLJ

Dragonwagon, Crescent

And then it rained . . .; illustrated by Diane Greenseid. Atheneum Bks. for Young Readers 2003 unp il $17.95 **E**

1. Rain—Fiction

ISBN 0-689-81884-X
LC 2002-2169

Bound back-to-back with And then the sun came out . . .

Describes how different people in the city react to days of rain and days of hot sun

"Brilliantly colored acrylic illustrations, cleverly rendered from a variety of perspectives, are well matched to the lively onomatopoeic language." SLJ

Drummond, Allan

Liberty! Farrar, Straus & Giroux 2002 unp il $17 **E**

1. Statue of Liberty (New York, N.Y.)—Fiction

ISBN 0-374-34385-3
LC 2001-18777

"Frances Foster books"

"Drummond tells the story of October 28, 1886, the day the Statue of Liberty was first unveiled in New York harbor. A boy, whose name is now lost, is on the ground, ready to signal Bartholdi, the statue's sculptor, to release the tricolor veil that covers the Lady of Liberty's face. . . . This is an unusual offering. Drummond takes a kernel of history . . . and turns it into both a thoughtful lesson and a visual pageant. Scenes of the construction of France's gift to the U.S. are shown in finely wrought, energetic, pen-and-wash images that swirl through the text." Booklist

Dugan, Joanne

ABC NYC; a book about seeing New York City; by Joanne Dugan; design by Pamela Hovland; (inspiration from Hugo and Henry). Abrams 2005 unp il $14.95 **E**

1. Alphabet 2. New York (N.Y.)

ISBN 0-8109-5854-6

"Every letter of this New York City alphabet follows the same pattern while redefining the ABCs with surprising words and pictures. A photo or photos of the letter faces an example or two of something beginning with that letter. . . . The photographs . . . are captivating." SLJ

Dumont, Jean-François

A blue so blue; translated from the French by Michel Bourque. Sterling 2005 unp il $14.95 **E**

1. Color—Fiction

ISBN 1-4027-2139-0

"A boy who loves to draw starts dreaming about a certain blue. . . . One morning, the memory of it is so strong that he sets off in search of it." SLJ

"Complex both in its language and in the richly painted illustrations, this makes for an evocative yet gentle book. The endpapers give 18 samples of kinds of blue." Booklist

Dunbar, Polly

Dog Blue. Candlewick Press 2004 unp il $14.99 **E**

1. Dogs—Fiction

ISBN 0-7636-2476-4
LC 2003-65223

Bertie, who loves the color blue and really wants a dog, finally gets his wish even though the dog he meets is white with black spots

"Dunbar makes clever use of page turns, unfolding the story in pithy, alliterative prose. . . . In the end, the wish fulfillment is gratifying, but it's Bertie's ingenious self-sufficiency that truly resonates." Booklist

Flyaway Katie. Candlewick Press 2004 unp il $14.99 **E**

1. Color—Fiction 2. Imagination—Fiction

ISBN 0-7636-2366-0
LC 2003-51599

Dunbar, Polly—*Continued*

On a gray, gray day, a young girl named Katie finds that adding colors to her life brightens up her day

"The mixed-media illustrations perfectly capture Katie's transformation from a totally gray-outlined figure to a brightly hued creature with patterned feathers. . . . Told at just the right pace, this whimsical story presents a gentle reminder of the power of a child's imagination." SLJ

Duncan, Lois

I walk at night; paintings by Steve Johnson and Lou Fancher. Viking 2000 unp il $15.99; pa $6.99   E

1. Cats—Fiction

ISBN 0-670-87513-9; 0-14-230090-X (pa)

LC 99-32057

This is a "description of a cat's multifaceted personality—docile pet by day, untamed beast in dreams, adventurer by night." SLJ

"The paintings rely on the contrast between cobalt shadows and subtle light sources for emphasis, and the night-blue palette gives an air of mystery to the wanderings of the midnight cat." Bull Cent Child Books

Dunrea, Olivier

Bear Noel. Farrar, Straus & Giroux 2000 unp il $16   E

1. Bears—Fiction 2. Animals—Fiction 3. Christmas—Fiction

ISBN 0-374-39990-5   LC 99-27600

The animals of the North Woods react with excitement as they hear Bear Noel coming to bring them Christmas

"Dunrea beautifully creates the effect of falling snow throughout the pictures and uses a limited palette of browns, grays, and greens with flashes of fox red to lend a celebratory feel." Booklist

Gossie. Houghton Mifflin 2002 unp il $9.95   E

1. Geese—Fiction

ISBN 0-618-17674-8   LC 2002-214

Gossie is a gosling who likes to wear bright red boots every day, no matter what she is doing, and so she is heartbroken the day the boots are missing and she can't find them anywhere

The succinct text uses "repetition and predictability with great skill and will therefore work equally well with early independent readers and preschoolers. . . . The illustrations, focused against restful white space, are spare and expressive, models of composition and clarity." Horn Book

Other titles about Gossie and her friends are:

BooBoo (2004)

Gossie & Gertie (2002)

Ollie (2003)

Ollie the stomper (2003)

Peedie (2004)

It's snowing! Farrar, Straus & Giroux 2002 unp il $16   E

1. Snow—Fiction 2. Mothers—Fiction 3. Infants—Fiction

ISBN 0-374-39992-1   LC 00-42172

A mother shares the magic of a snowy night with her baby

"The gentle, rhythmical rocking of the text conveys a reassuring message that's beautifully supported by Dunrea's spare, snow-dappled gouache illustrations." Horn Book

Durango, Julia

Cha-cha chimps; illustrated by Eleanor Taylor. Simon & Schuster Books for Young Readers 2006 unp il $15.95   E

1. Chimpanzees—Fiction 2. Dance—Fiction 3. Stories in rhyme

ISBN 0-689-86456-6

In this counting book, "10 little chimps sneak out of their tree house to go dancing at Mambo Jambas, where a pig band plays music all night long. . . . The rhymes roll easily off the tongue, making the text fun to read aloud. . . . Done in watercolor and pencil, the illustrations are bright and lively." SLJ

Duval, Kathy

The Three Bears' Christmas; illustrated by Paul Meisel. 1st ed. Holiday House 2005 unp il $16.95   E

1. Bears—Fiction 2. Santa Claus—Fiction 3. Christmas—Fiction

ISBN 0-8234-1871-5   LC 2003-67646

After taking a walk on Christmas Eve while their freshly baked gingerbread cools, Papa, Mama, and Baby Bear arrive home to encounter another "trespasser," who does not have golden hair but wears a red suit and leaves presents.

"The old favorite gets wrapped in a Christmas bow, with excellent results. . . . The artwork is utterly childlike." Booklist

Duvoisin, Roger

Petunia. fiftieth anniversary edition. Knopf 2000 c1950 unp il $15.95; lib bdg $17.99   E

1. Geese—Fiction 2. Books and reading—Fiction

ISBN 0-394-90865-7; 0-394-90865-1 (lib bdg)

A reissue of the title first published 1950

Petunia, the goose, learns that possessing knowledge involves more than just carrying a book around under her wing

"Duvoisin's energetic drawings perfectly capture Petunia's growing arrogance." Horn Book Guide

Eastman, P. D. (Philip D.)

Are you my mother? written and illustrated by P. D. Eastman. Beginner Bks. 1960 63p il $8.99; lib bdg $11.99   E

1. Birds—Fiction 2. Bilingual books—English-Spanish

ISBN 0-394-80018-4; 0-394-90018-9 (lib bdg)

Also available Board book edition; Spanish-English edition also available

"A small bird falls from his nest and searches for his mother. He asks a kitten, a hen, a dog, a cow, a boat, [and] a plane . . . 'Are you my mother?' Repetition of words and phrases and funny pictures are just right for beginning readers." Chicago. Public Libr

Edwards, Michelle

Papa's latkes; illustrated by Stacey Schuett. Candlewick Press 2004 unp il $15.99   **E**
1. Hanukkah—Fiction   2. Jews—Fiction 3. Bereavement—Fiction
ISBN 0-7636-0779-7   LC 00-69801
On the first Hanukkah after Mama died, Papa and his two daughters try to make latkes and celebrate without her.
"The poignant text with touches of humor is nicely matched with warm and richly colored oil paintings. . . . A touching and uplifting story." SLJ

Edwards, Pamela Duncan

The leprechaun's gold; illustrated by Henry Cole. 1st ed. Katherine Tegen Books 2004 unp il $15.99; lib bdg $16.89   **E**
1. Leprechauns—Fiction   2. Musicians—Fiction 3. Ireland—Fiction
ISBN 0-06-623974-5; 0-06-623975-3 (lib bdg)
LC 2002-3150
A leprechaun intervenes with gold and magic when a greedy, boastful young harpist gains an unfair advantage for a royal harping contest.
"Cole's imaginative illustrations are a good match for the story, displaying both realism and fantasy. . . . An appealing tale that need not be limited to St. Patrick's Day storytime." Booklist

The neat line; illustrated by Diana Cain Bluthenthal. 1st ed. Katherine Tegen Books 2004 unp il $15.99; lib bdg $16.89   **E**
1. Nursery rhymes—Fiction
ISBN 0-06-623970-2; 0-06-623971-0 (lib bdg)
LC 2002-153424
A young scribble matures into a neat line, then wriggles into a book of nursery rhymes where he transforms himself into different objects to assist the characters he meets there.
This is a "brilliantly creative romp. . . . The large cartoon paintings . . . are appropriately outlined with thick, bold lines and are framed by book pages on either side." SLJ

Some smug slug; illustrated by Henry Cole. HarperCollins Pubs. 1996 32p il $15.99; lib bdg $16.89; pa $6.99   **E**
1. Slugs (Mollusks)—Fiction   2. Animals—Fiction
ISBN 0-06-024789-4; 0-06-024792-4 (lib bdg); 0-06-443502-4 (pa)   LC 94-18682
"A slug senses a slope and saunters on up, against the advice of a sparrow, a spider, and a skink, among others, and meets with a sudden, spontaneous demise. Such is the life of a slug told with a multitude of common and not so common 'S' words. . . . Realistically detailed, earth-toned illustrations focus attention on each scene. . . . This slug is so appealing and full of personality that it will certainly garner sympathy." SLJ

Egielski, Richard

Slim and Jim. HarperCollins Pubs. 2002 unp il $15.95; lib bdg $15.89   **E**
1. Rats—Fiction   2. Mice—Fiction   3. Cats—Fiction 4. Yo-yos—Fiction
ISBN 0-06-028352-1; 0-06-028353-X (lib bdg)
LC 00-67281
"Laura Geringer books"
Slim the rat and his new friend Jim the mouse find that their yo-yo tricks come in handy when they are threatened by a tough, old one-eyed cat
"The story is old-fashioned in the best sense of the term, but Egielski's sly wit is evident in both the text and the art. . . . This has a real story, with adventure, friendship, dastardly deeds—and yo-yos!" Booklist

Ehlert, Lois

Circus. HarperCollins Pubs. 1992 unp il $16.99
E
1. Circus—Fiction   2. Animals—Fiction
ISBN 0-06-020252-1   LC 91-12067
Leaping lizards, marching snakes, a bear on the high wire, and others perform in a somewhat unusual circus
"The book approximates a light show in visual intensity, with neon-bright illustrations set against black or bold backgrounds. . . . The sprightly rhythm of Ms. Ehlert's text complements her Day-Glo palette. Echoing a ringmaster's speech, she's afraid of neither alliteration . . . nor hyperbole." N Y Times Book Rev

Color farm. Lippincott 1990 unp il $16.99
E
1. Color   2. Shape
ISBN 0-397-32440-5   LC 89-13561
"A delightful die-cut exploration of how shapes and colors can be layered and overlapped to create the faces of farm animals. Includes geometric pictures of a rooster, a chicken, a goose, a duck, a cat, a dog, a sheep, a pig, and a cow." Sci Child

Color zoo. Lippincott 1989 unp il $16.99
E
1. Color   2. Shape
ISBN 0-397-32259-3   LC 87-17065
Also available Board book edition
A Caldecott Medal honor book, 1990
This "book features a series of cutouts stacked so that with each page turn, a layer is removed to reveal yet another picture. Each configuration is an animal: a tiger's face (a circle shape) and two ears disappear with a page turn to leave viewers with a square within which is a mouse. . . . There are three such series, and each ends with a small round-up of the shapes used so far. . . . On the reverse of the turned page is the shape cutout previously removed with the shape's printed name." SLJ
"Not only an effective method for teaching basic concepts, the book is also a means for sharpening visual perception, which encourages children to see these shapes in other contexts." Horn Book

Eating the alphabet; fruits and vegetables from A to Z. Harcourt Brace Jovanovich 1989 unp il $16; pa $7   **E**
1. Alphabet   2. Fruit   3. Vegetables
ISBN 0-15-224435-2; 0-15-224436-0 (pa)
LC 88-10906

Ehlert, Lois—*Continued*

Also available Board book edition

An alphabetical tour of the world of fruits and vegetables, from apricot and artichoke to yam and zucchini

"The objects depicted, shown against a white ground, are easily identifiable for the most part, and represent the more common sounds of the letter shown. . . . Both upper- and lower-case letters are printed in large, black type. A nice added touch is the glossary which includes the pronunciation and interesting facts about the origin of each fruit and vegetable, how it grows, and its uses. An exuberant, eye-catching alphabet book." SLJ

Feathers for lunch. Harcourt Brace Jovanovich 1990 unp il $16; pa $7   **E**

1. Cats—Fiction 2. Birds—Fiction 3. Stories in rhyme

ISBN 0-15-230550-5; 0-15-200986-8 (pa)

LC 89-29459

Also available Big book edition

This "book is both a story and a beginning nature guide. A pet cat wants to vary his diet with wild birds, but each attempt gains him only feathers. Twelve different bird species are . . . illustrated. . . . On each page, the bird's typical call is printed and plants pictured are named." SLJ

"Ehlert has attempted many things in these pages—for instance, the birds are all drawn life-size—and has succeeded in all of them; her lavish use of bold color against generous amounts of white space is graphically appealing, and the large type, nearly one-half-inch tall, invites attempts by those just beginning to read. An engaging, entertaining, and recognizably realistic story." Horn Book

Growing vegetable soup; written and illustrated by Lois Ehlert. Harcourt Brace Jovanovich 1987 unp il $16; pa $6   **E**

1. Vegetable gardening—Fiction

ISBN 0-15-232575-1; 0-15-232580-8 (pa)

LC 86-22812

Also available Big book edition and Spanish language edition

"Brightly-colored large illustrations and a boldly-worded text show how to plant and grow vegetables for Dad's soup. Shocking pinks, reds and greens give the illustrations an almost three-dimensional quality and will be good for large audiences of preschoolers." Child Book Rev Serv

Hands; growing up to be an artist. Harcourt 2004 unp il $14.95   **E**

ISBN 0-15-205107-4   LC 2004-1237

A reformatted edition of the title first published 1997

When a child works alongside her parents doing carpentry, sewing, and gardening, she thinks of being an artist as well when she grows up

This edition offers "slightly reworked trimmings, but keeps the same die-cut pages—in the shapes of scissors, seed packets and more—as well as a 'paint box' that opens." Publ Wkly

Leaf Man. Harcourt 2005 unp il $16   **E**

1. Leaves—Fiction 2. Winds—Fiction

ISBN 0-15-205304-2   LC 2004-9981

A man made of leaves blows away, traveling wherever the wind may take him.

This is an "eye-popping book. . . . Scalloped edgings on the tops of the pages, cut at varying heights, artfully give the effect of setting the action against a three-dimensional landscape." Booklist

Market day; a story told with folk art; written and designed by Lois Ehlert. Harcourt 2000 unp il $16   **E**

1. Markets—Fiction 2. Farm life—Fiction 3. Stories in rhyme

ISBN 0-15-202158-2   LC 99-6252

On market day, a farm family experiences all the fun and excitement of going to and from the farmers' market

"The very young will enjoy the spare, simple rhymes. . . . All ages will appreciate the illustrations, comprising images of folk art, primitive art, and textiles from around the world. An annotated inventory of the featured items is included." Horn Book Guide

Mole's hill; a woodland tale. Harcourt Brace & Co. 1994 unp il $17; pa $7   **E**

1. Moles (Animals)—Fiction

ISBN 0-15-255116-6; 0-15-201890-5 (pa)

LC 93-31151

When Fox tells Mole she must move out of her tunnel to make way for a new path, Mole finds an ingenious way to save her home

"Ehlert's language is compact and telling. . . . The art . . . is dark-hued, appropriately nocturnal without losing spirit or contrast, and the beads stippled across the cutout cloth shapes lend interesting texture to the planes of color. . . . The story (which Ehlert says she based on a fragment of a Seneca tale, with source completely cited in the book) has charm and vigor." Bull Cent Child Books

Nuts to you! Harcourt Brace Jovanovich 1993 unp il $16; pa $7   **E**

1. Squirrels—Fiction 2. Stories in rhyme

ISBN 0-15-257647-9; 0-15-205064-7 (pa)

LC 92-19441

"A frisky squirrel digs up bulbs and steals birdseed from a nearby feeder; in his boldest act, he enters the young narrator's apartment through a tear in the window screen. The quick-thinking child entices the mischievous squirrel back outside with some peanuts. . . . The story, told in brisk rhyme, is a fast-paced romp, and the large, dramatically styled collages will dazzle even the largest audiences. . . . The four concluding pages offer basic information about squirrels." Horn Book

Pie in the sky. Harcourt 2004 unp il $16   **E**

1. Cherries—Fiction 2. Pies—Fiction

ISBN 0-15-216584-3   LC 2003-4986

A father and child watch the cherry tree in their back yard, waiting until there are ripe cherries to bake in a pie. Includes a recipe for cherry pie

"The vibrant collage illustrations, made with an eclectic combination of materials—from paint and handmade papers to sheet metal, wires, and tree branches—celebrate the colors and simplified shapes of birds, insects, the cherry tree, and, yes, kitchen implements." Booklist

Ehlert, Lois—*Continued*

Planting a rainbow; written and illustrated by Lois Ehlert. Harcourt Brace Jovanovich 1988 unp il lib bdg $16; pa $7   **E**
1. Gardening—Fiction 2. Flowers—Fiction
ISBN 0-15-262609-3 (lib bdg); 0-15-262610-7 (pa)
LC 87-8528
Also available Big book edition and Spanish language edition
A mother and daughter plant a rainbow of flowers in the family garden
"The stylized forms of the plants are clearly and beautifully designed, and the primary, blazing colors of the blossoms dazzle in their resplendence. The minimal text, in very large print, is exactly right to set off the glorious illustrations, making a splendid beginning book of colors and flowers cleverly arranged for young readers." Horn Book

Snowballs. Harcourt Brace & Co. 1995 unp il $16; pa $7   **E**
1. Snow—Fiction
ISBN 0-15-200074-7; 0-15-202095-0 (pa)
LC 94-47183
"Using 'good stuff' like seeds, nuts, corn kernels, and colorful yarn kids create a wonderful snow family. Placed on vertical page spreads, the snow characters extend the full length of the book, a perspective that enhances the drama of their inevitable demise when the sun comes out. Large, well-designed illustrations effectively blend open space, colorful paper cutouts, and real objects." Horn Book Guide

Top cat. Harcourt Brace & Co. 1998 unp il $16
E
1. Cats—Fiction 2. Stories in rhyme
ISBN 0-15-201739-9   LC 97-8818
The top cat in a household is reluctant to accept the arrival of a new kitten but decides to share various survival secrets with it
"Ehlert creates a memorable cat duo in her trademark cut-paper collage style. . . . Children and other feline fans will quickly warm to this spunky story of rivalry and acceptance." Publ Wkly

Waiting for wings. Harcourt 2001 unp il $17
E
1. Butterflies 2. Stories in rhyme
ISBN 0-15-202608-8   LC 00-9765
Eggs clinging to leaves become caterpillars which become butterflies which lay their eggs
"A brief rhyming text and cheery tone invite readers to explore the full and half pages that form this brilliantly designed book-within-a book." Publ Wkly

Ehrlich, Amy

Leo, Zack, and Emmie together again; pictures by Steven Kellogg. Dial Bks. for Young Readers 1987 56p il pa $3.99 hardcover o.p.   **E**
1. Friendship—Fiction
ISBN 0-14-037946-0 (pa)   LC 86-16810
"An Easy-to-read book"
In this title "three second graders are involved . . . in four loosely connected episodes that take place in the

winter: they play in the snow, meet Santa Claus, suffer through chicken pox . . . and make Valentine cards. . . . Ehrlich's writing is direct and uncluttered. There is just enough conflict in the plot to create interest. Kellogg's full-color illustrations consistently add humor to the text and make this book hard to put down." SLJ
Another title about Leo, Zack, and Emmie is:
Leo, Zack, and Emmie (1981)

Thumbelina; by Hans Christian Andersen; retold by Amy Ehrlich; [illustrated by Susan Jeffers] Dutton Children's Books 2005 32p il $16.99
E
1. Andersen, Hans Christian, 1805-1875—Adaptations 2. Fairy tales
ISBN 0-525-47508-7   LC 2004028979
A reissue of the edition published 1979 by Dial Books for Young Readers
A retelling of Hans Christian Andersen's classic fairy tale about a girl who is only one inch tall.
"This sumptuous picture book version the classic Andersen story has been an adapted text that shows some softening of the tale's harsher edges. . . . [Readers will] be caught up in the action as depicted in Jeffers' striking, pastel-dominated pictures." Booklist

Ehrlich, Fred

Does an elephant take a bath? pictures by Emily Bolan. Blue Apple Books 2005 unp il (Early experiences) lib bdg $13.50; pa $5.95   **E**
1. Cleanliness 2. Baths 3. Animals
ISBN 1-59354-111-2 (lib bdg); 1-59354-123-5 (pa)
"Does a giraffe take a bath? The question is accompanied by a silly picture showing a giraffe standing in a foaming bathtub. Turn the page and the animal is in its natural habitat, grooming itself with its long tongue. . . . Following similar scenarios for an elephant, a zebra, a black rhino (a mud bath), and more, come several spreads showing how people keep clean and tidy." Booklist
"The humor is just right for the audience . . . and, like the text, the uncluttered illustrations . . . are both informative and amusing." Horn Book Guide
Other titles in the Early experiences series are:
Does a baboon sleep in a bed? (2005)
Does a chimp wear clothes? (2005)
Does a hippo say ahh? (2006)
Does a lion brush? (2005)
Does a panda go to school? (2006)
Does a pig flush? (2005)
Does a seal smile? (2006)
Does a tiger open wide? (2006)
Does a yak get a haircut? (2006)

Ehrlich, H. M.

Louie's goose; illustrated by Emily Bolam. Houghton Mifflin 2000 unp il $15   **E**
1. Toys—Fiction 2. Beaches—Fiction
ISBN 0-618-03023-9   LC 99-28566
"Walter Lorraine books"
While spending the summer at the beach with his parents, Louie has a wonderful time playing with his toy goose and even rescues her from a big wave
"This true-to-life look at a preschooler growing more

Ehrlich, H. M.—*Continued*

independent is low-key and natural. . . . Bolam's sunny paintings capture the seashore experience of a charming, lovable family." Booklist

Another title about Louie is:

Gotcha, Louie! (2002)

Eichenberg, Fritz

Ape in a cape; an alphabet of odd animals. Harcourt Brace & Co. 1952 unp il pa $8 hardcover o.p.   E

1. Animals 2. Alphabet

ISBN 0-15-607830-9 (pa)

A Caldecott Medal honor book, 1953

"Each letter of the alphabet from A for ape to Z for zoo is represented by a full-page picture of an animal with a brief nonsense rhyme caption explaining it. For example: mouse in a blouse, pig in a wig, toad on the road, whale in a gale." Publ Wkly

"The skill of a craftsman distinguishes this picture book illustrated with bold and lively drawings printed in three colors." N Y Public Libr

Eilenberg, Max

Cowboy Kid; illustrated by Sue Heap. Candlewick Press 2000 unp il $15.99   E

1. Bedtime—Fiction 2. Toys—Fiction

ISBN 0-7636-1058-5   LC 99-54076

Also available companion volume Cowboy Baby by Sue Heap

A young boy has difficulty getting to sleep because his toys seem to need so many hugs and kisses at bedtime

"Heap's bright acrylic and watercolor paintings feature striking yet simple figures in uncluttered compositions that are just right for the book's intended audience." Booklist

Ellis, Sarah

Ben over night; illustrated by Kim LaFave. Fitzhenry & Whiteside 2005 unp il $16.95

E

1. Fear—Fiction

ISBN 1-55041-807-6

"Little Ben loves to play at his friend Peter's house across the street, but every time he tries to sleep over, he wakens in the night and chickens out. His supportive parents suggest that he take his flashlight and security blanket, but nothing works until his big sister comes up with more imaginative ideas. Ellis tells Ben's story with economy and understanding. . . . With fresh colors and energetic line work, the apparently digital illustrations do a good job of expressing the characters' emotions as well as defining their actions." Booklist

Elvgren, Jennifer Riesmeyer

Josias, hold the book; [by] Jennifer Riesmeyer Elvgren; illustrated by Nicole Tadgell. 1st ed. Boyds Mills Press 2006 unp il $15.95   E

1. Haiti—Fiction 2. Gardening—Fiction 3. Education—Fiction

ISBN 1-59078-318-2   LC 2005024989

Each day Chrislove, who lives in Haiti, asks his friend Josias when he will "hold the book," or join them at school, but Josias can only think of tending the bean garden so that his family will have enough food.

"Elvgren has crafted a matter-of-fact snapshot of rural Haitian life. Tadgells muted watercolor spreads set the tone and enhance the text. Emotions are clearly depicted, giving the characters added dimension and believability." SLJ

Elya, Susan Middleton

Bebe goes shopping; illustrated by Steven Salerno. Harcourt 2006 unp il $16   E

1. Infants—Fiction 2. Shopping—Fiction 3. Spanish language—Vocabulary 4. Stories in rhyme

ISBN 0-15-205426-X

Rhyming text describes a trip to the grocery store for a mamá and her baby boy. Includes Spanish words.

"Almost all the words can be understood from the context or from the pictures. . . . Using gouache, watercolors, colored inks, and pencils, Salerno evokes the hip, retro style of 1950s cartoon-style advertisements. . . . Salerno is also a master at getting motion into his pictures, and his spreads rumble and tumble." Booklist

Cowboy José; illustrated by Tim Raglin. Putnam's 2005 unp il $15.99   E

1. Cowhands—Fiction 2. Mexico—Fiction 3. Stories in rhyme 4. Spanish language—Vocabulary

ISBN 0-399-23570-1   LC 2003-26636

A poor cowboy enters a rodeo to win a date from a pretty señorita, but afterwards wonders if he should spend his winnings on the girl, who is only interested in the money, or on his trusty horse, whose encouragement helped him win.

"Elya's engaging text features snappy rhymes and plenty of contextual clues for the Spanish words that appear in bold type. . . . Raglin's watercolor-and-colored-pencil artwork features bright south-of-the-border colors and characters in traditional dress to accentuate the story's Mexican setting." SLJ

Eight animals on the town; illustrated by Lee Chapman. Putnam 2000 unp il $15.99   E

1. Animals—Fiction 2. Counting 3. Bilingual books—English-Spanish 4. Stories in rhyme

ISBN 0-399-23437-3   LC 99-55269

Eight animals go to market, to supper, and to dance, introducing the numbers from one to eight and vocabulary in English and Spanish

"While the text has wit and whimsy, the illustrations are absolutely delectable. Bright oils on canvas capture qualities of Mexican folk art as tidy borders augment the text." SLJ

Other titles about the Eight animals are:

Eight animals bake a cake (2002)

Eight animals play ball (2003)

F is for fiesta; illustrated by G. Brian Karas. G.P. Putnam's Sons 2006 unp il $11.99

E

1. Spanish language—Vocabulary 2. Alphabet 3. Birthdays 4. Stories in rhyme

ISBN 0-399-24225-2   LC 2004-20478

Elya, Susan Middleton—*Continued*

A rhyming book that outlines the preparations for and celebration of a young boy's birthday, with Spanish words for each letter of the alphabet translated in a glossary.

"At their best, Elya's verses bounce as easily between languages as they did in *Oh, No, Gotta Go!* (2003), which was also buoyantly illustrated by Karas." Booklist

Fairy trails; a story told in English and Spanish; illustrated by Mercedes McDonald. Bloomsbury Children's Books 2005 unp il $16.95   E
1. Fairy tales 2. Stories in rhyme 3. Spanish language—Vocabulary
ISBN 1-58234-027-4

Miguel and Maria meet various fairy tale characters as they walk to their aunt's house. Includes some Spanish words

"Done in pastels, the warm and colorful illustrations have an appealing folk-art quality. . . . A glossary of the Spanish words is included, but the rhyming text provides ample context clues so that the story is accessible to non-Spanish speakers. Overall, Fairy Trails would be a great storytime choice for both bilingual and English-only audiences." SLJ

Oh no, gotta go! illustrated by G. Brian Karas. Putnam 2003 unp il $14.99   E
1. Bathrooms—Fiction 2. Spanish language—Vocabulary 3. Stories in rhyme
ISBN 0-399-23493-4   LC 2002-17703

As soon as she goes out for a drive with her parents, a young girl needs to find a bathroom quickly. Text includes some Spanish words and phrases

"The unexpected rhyming of the English and boldface Spanish words give the rhythmic text an ebullient humor enhanced by Karas' understated gouache, acrylic, pencil, and collage illustrations." Bull Cent Child Books

Emberley, Ed

Go away, big green monster! Little, Brown 1992 unp il $10.99   E
1. Monsters—Fiction 2. Fear—Fiction 3. Bedtime—Fiction
ISBN 0-316-23653-5   LC 92-6231

"In the first half of this fear-dispelling book, graphically distinctive die-cut pages reveal, bit by bit, a monster with 'sharp white teeth' and 'scraggly purple hair.' The process is then reversed as the text commands each scary feature to 'go away,' until there is nothing at all left of the monster but a black page instructing 'Don't Come Back! Until I say so.' Entertaining and empowering for young children." Horn Book Guide

Thanks, Mom! Little, Brown 2003 unp il $11.95   E
1. Mice—Fiction 2. Animals—Fiction
ISBN 0-316-24022-2   LC 2001-50715

Kiko the mouse finds some delicious cheese and gets help from his mother when a group of various animals tries to take it

"Using sunny yellow highlights and creatures constructed from bold, geometric shapes, Emberley creates an exciting, chaotic chase with sparse text and an impressive sense of graphic design." SLJ

The wing on a flea; a book about shapes; written and illustrated by Ed Emberley. Little, Brown 2001 unp il $15.95   E
1. Shape
ISBN 0-316-23487-7   LC 00-49725

A new version of the title first published 1961

Simple rhyming text and illustrations guide the reader to see triangles, rectangles, and circles in everyday things

Emberley's "breezy, rhyming text and cheerful visuals invite kids to explore the concept of shapes. More subtly, aspiring artists can follow Emberley's example of using basic shapes to create more complex pictures. Black pages effectively show off the bold, primary colors and shiny, gold leaf accents of the deceptively simple pictures." Publ Wkly

English, Karen

The baby on the way; pictures by Sean Qualls. Farrar, Straus and Giroux 2005 unp il $16   E
1. Grandmothers—Fiction 2. Childbirth—Fiction 3. Infants—Fiction 4. African Americans—Fiction
ISBN 0-374-37361-2   LC 2003-49047

Jamal, a young African American boy, asks his grandmother if she was ever a baby, she tells him the story of how she was born.

"The intimate artwork, in earth colors with pencil-thin line details, shows the loving bond between family members stretching back in time and into the future." Booklist

Hot day on Abbott Avenue; illustrated by Javaka Steptoe. Clarion Books 2004 32p il $15   E
1. Friendship—Fiction 2. Summer—Fiction 3. African Americans—Fiction 4. Rope skipping—Fiction
ISBN 0-395-98527-7   LC 2002-09043

After having a fight, two friends spend the day ignoring each other, until the lure of a game of jump rope helps them to forget about being mad.

"Steptoe's found-object and cut-paper collages highlight facial features and depict oppressive summertime weather to perfection. . . . English's simple narrative consists mostly of two to three sentences per page and ends on a gratifying note." SLJ

Speak to me; (and I will listen between the lines); pictures by Amy June Bates. Farrar Straus Giroux 2004 unp il $16   E
1. School stories 2. San Francisco (Calif.)—Fiction 3. African Americans—Fiction
ISBN 0-374-37156-3   LC 2002-192895

Describes events of one day at a San Francisco Bay Area school as perceived by different second-graders, from the observations of first to arrive on the playground to the walk home.

"English's rich descriptions and insights bring readers into the world of six inner-city . . . students. . . . Bates's watercolor-and-ink illustrations capture the characters' expressions and moods vividly." SLJ

Eriksson, Eva

Molly goes shopping; translated by Elisabeth Kallick Dyssegaard. R & S Bks.; distributed by Farrar, Straus & Giroux 2003 unp il $15

                            E

1. Shopping—Fiction 2. Pigs—Fiction
ISBN 91-29-65819-5
Translated from the Swedish
"Molly the pig walks to the store by herself, but once there, she gets a bit flustered and misremembers the order. Within this charming middle-class animal neighborhood, rendered in grainy colored pencils, Eriksson imbues her precocious piglet with a range of recognizable emotions and behaviors." Horn Book Guide
Another title about Molly is:
A crash course for Molly (2005)

Ernst, Lisa Campbell

Goldilocks returns. Simon & Schuster Bks. for Young Readers 2000 unp il $16.95   E
1. Bears—Fiction 2. Fairy tales
ISBN 0-689-82537-4   LC 98-30099
Fifty years after Goldilocks first met the three bears, she returns to fix up their cottage and soothe her guilty conscience.
"The spirited illustrations, featuring a stout, bespectacled Goldi, enchance the humor of this clever sequel to the familiar tale." Horn Book Guide

Sam Johnson and the blue ribbon quilt. Lothrop, Lee & Shepard Bks. 1983 32p il lib bdg $16.89; pa $5.99   E
1. Quilts—Fiction 2. Sex role—Fiction
ISBN 0-688-01517-4 (lib bdg); 0-688-11505-5 (pa)
                            LC 82-9980
While mending the awning over the pig pen, Sam discovers that he enjoys sewing the various patches together but meets with scorn and ridicule when he asks his wife if he could join her quilting club.
The illustrations "bring an old-timey, bucolic scene to life and show steps in an equal-rights issue." Publ Wkly

The turn-around upside-down alphabet book. Simon & Schuster Books for Young Readers 2004 unp il $15.95   E
1. Alphabet
ISBN 0-689-85685-7   LC 2003-16318
"With touches of humor and a great deal of creativity, Ernst fashioned this book out of cut paper and surrounded each block with a thick black border that sets off white words. Children will enjoy tilting the pages to see the transformations and will be motivated to come up with ideas of their own." SLJ

Zinnia and Dot. Viking 1992 unp il $16.99; pa $5.99   E
1. Chickens—Fiction
ISBN 0-670-83091-7; 0-14-054199-3 (pa)
                            LC 91-36178
Zinnia and Dot, self-satisfied hens who bicker constantly about who lays better eggs, put aside their differences to protect a prime specimen from a marauding weasel.
"Ernst has an easy storytelling style and a flair for

grouchy dialogue that clucks to be read aloud, and her line-and-wash paintings, lighted with gentle yellow tones, warm the comedy." Bull Cent Child Books

Esbaum, Jill

Ste-e-e-e-eamboat a-comin'! written by Jill Esbaum, poet; pictures by Adam Rex, craftsman. 1st ed. Farrar, Straus and Giroux 2005 unp il $16
                                 E
1. Steamboats—Fiction 2. Mississippi River—Fiction
3. Stories in rhyme
ISBN 0-374-37236-5   LC 2002-192541
A village comes to life when a Mississippi River steamboat arrives and unloads its goods.
"The terse, highly descriptive text features an ABB rhyme scheme with a catchy rhythm and introduces readers to interesting vocabulary. . . . Well-drawn details abound, making this an excellent resource for historical study. . . . This salute to a bygone transportation era is sure to engage children." SLJ

Ets, Marie Hall

Gilberto and the Wind. Viking 1963 32p il pa $5.99 hardcover o.p.   E
1. Winds—Fiction
ISBN 0-14-050276-9 (pa); 0-670-34025-1 (hc)
Also available Spanish language edition
"A little Mexican boy thinks aloud about all the things his playmate the wind does with him, for him, and against him. The wind calls him to play, floats his balloon, refuses to fly his kite, blows his soap bubble into the air, races with him, and rests with him under a tree." SLJ
"In brown, black, and white against soft gray pages, this author-artist has caught in a very appealing book . . . the emotions and attitudes of childhood." Horn Book

Play with me; story and pictures by Marie Hall Ets. Viking 1955 31p il pa $5.99 hardcover o.p.
                                 E
1. Animals—Fiction
ISBN 0-14-050178-9 (pa)
A Caldecott Medal honor book, 1956
On a sunny morning in the meadow an excited little girl tries to catch the meadow creatures and play with them. But, one by one, they all run away. Finally, when she learns to sit quietly and wait, there is a happy ending
The "pictures done in muted tones of brown, gray and yellow . . . accurately reflect the little girl's rapidly changing moods of eagerness, bafflement, disappointment and final happiness." N Y Times Book Rev

Everitt, Betsy

Mean soup. Harcourt Brace Jovanovich 1992 unp il $16; pa $7   E
ISBN 0-15-253146-7; 0-15-200227-8 (pa)
                            LC 91-15244
Horace feels really mean at the end of a bad day, until he helps his mother make Mean Soup
"The text features short sentences and easy but effective vocabulary, so the story bubbles with a building ex-

Everitt, Betsy—*Continued*

citement. Everitt's . . . stylized paintings and bold pal-ette—hot pinks, purples and black predominate—convey all of the feisty emotion of a frustrated youngster." Publ Wkly

Ewart, Claire

Fossil; [by] Claire Ewart. Walker 2004 unp il $16.89; lib bdg $17.85   E

1. Pterosaurs—Fiction 2. Fossils—Fiction 3. Stories in rhyme

ISBN 0-8027-8890-4; 0-8027-8891-2 (lib bdg)
                                              LC 2003-53469

Upon finding a special stone, a child imagines the life of a pterosaur, the ancient flying reptile that lived, died, and was fossilized into that stone. Includes facts about fossils and how they are formed.

"Ewart's inviting text and dramatic artwork work nice-ly together to describe the fossilization process in an en-grossing way." SLJ

Includes bibliographical references

Falconer, Ian

Olivia; written and illustrated by Ian Falconer. Atheneum Bks. for Young Readers 2000 unp il $16.95   E

1. Pigs—Fiction

ISBN 0-689-82953-1   LC 99-24003

Board books about Olivia also available

A Caldecott Medal honor book, 2001

"An Anne Schwartz book"

Whether at home getting ready for the day, enjoying the beach, or at bedtime, Olivia is a feisty pig who has too much energy for her own good

"The spacious design of the book; the appeal of the strong, clever art; and the humor that permeates every page make this a standout. . . . Falconer . . . renders Olivia's world in charcoal with dollops of red brighten-ing the pages." Booklist

Other titles about Olivia are:

Olivia . . . and the missing toy (2003)

Olivia forms a band (2006)

Olivia saves the circus (2001)

Faller, Régis

The adventures of Polo; [by] Roger Faller. 1st American ed. Roaring Brook 2006 75p il $16.95
                                                          E

1. Dogs—Fiction 2. Stories without words

ISBN 9781596431607; 1-59643-160-1
                                            LC 2005055261

Polo the dog sets out from his home and enjoys many adventures, including sailing his boat on top of a whale, roasting hot dogs over a volcano, and taking a ride in a spaceship built from a mushroom.

"Young readers will be charmed by this hound, and be awed by his ingenuity. Somewhat similar to a graphic-novel format, this wordless picture book contains bold, colorful, cartoon panels that are sure to captivate even the most finicky youngster." SLJ

Falwell, Cathryn

David's drawings; story and pictures by Cathryn Falwell. Lee & Low Bks. 2001 unp il $16
                                                          E

1. School stories 2. Drawing—Fiction 3. Friendship—Fiction 4. African Americans—Fiction

ISBN 1-58430-031-0   LC 2001-16450

A shy African American boy arriving at a new school makes friends with his classmates by drawing a picture of a tree

"The cut-paper-and-fabric collages are a good choice for the story. . . . Both theme and execution make this a fine choice for classroom read-alouds." Booklist

Turtle splash! countdown at the pond. Greenwillow Bks. 2001 unp il $15.95; lib bdg $15.89   E

1. Turtles—Fiction 2. Counting 3. Stories in rhyme

ISBN 0-06-029462-0; 0-06-029463-9 (lib bdg)
                                              LC 00-30918

As they are startled by the activities of other nearby creatures, the number of turtles on a log in a pond de-creases from ten to one

"The rhyming, alliterative text is energized with a roll-ing rhythm, suspense, and vivid, descriptive words. . . . Evocative woodland scenes spring to life with well-defined animals that are described in a final appended section." Booklist

Farish, Terry

The cat who liked potato soup; illustrated by Barry Root. Candlewick Press 2003 unp il $15.99
                                                          E

1. Cats—Fiction 2. Friendship—Fiction 3. Fishing—Fiction

ISBN 0-7636-0834-3   LC 2001-43533

The friendship between an old man and his cat, both of whom like potato soup, is strained after he goes fish-ing without her

"The carefully chosen words and charming simplicity of the illustrations lead to an unsentimental, but very sat-isfying tale of companionship." SLJ

Fearnley, Jan

Mr. Wolf's pancakes; [by] Jan Fearnley. Tiger Tales 2001 c1999 unp il $15.95; pa $6.95
                                                          E

1. Wolves—Fiction 2. Fairy tales

ISBN 1-58925-004-4; 1-58925-354-X (pa)
                                            LC 2001-834

First published 1999 in the United Kingdom

"Mr. Wolf seeks assistance from his neighbors, but Chicken Little, Wee Willy Winkle, the Gingerbread Man, Little Red Riding Hood and the Three Little Pigs all nas-tily refuse. Of course, when Mr. Wolf eventually whips up the pancakes all by himself, they demand a share of his culinary creation. Mr. Wolf . . . lets the marauders into the kitchen-and then gobbles them all up. . . . Chip-per watercolors depict a sunny storybook town. . . . A gleeful twist on a nursery staple." Publ Wkly

Another title about Mr. Wolf is:

Mr. Wolf and the three bears (2002)

Fearnley, Jan—*Continued*

Watch out! Candlewick Press 2004 unp il $15.99   **E**

1. Mice—Fiction 2. Mother-child relationship—Fiction
ISBN 0-7636-2318-0   LC 2003-48505

Wilf, a very energetic mouse who gets in a bit of trouble when he does not listen to his mother, makes her a special surprise.

"The large format and soft watercolor-and-ink illustrations perfectly demonstrate Wilf's exuberance and animatedly depict his numerous falls. . . . This is a tender, amusing offering, accomplished with unbridled enthusiasm." Booklist

Feelings, Muriel

Jambo means hello; Swahili alphabet book; pictures by Tom Feelings. Dial Bks. for Young Readers 1981 unp il pa $6.99 hardcover o.p.
    E

1. Alphabet 2. Swahili language 3. East Africa
ISBN 0-14-054652-1 (pa)

A Caldecott Medal honor book, 1975

This book "gives a word for each letter of the alphabet (the Swahili alphabet has 24 letters) save for 'q' and 'x', and a sentence or two provides additional information. A double-page spread of soft black and white drawings illustrates each word." Bull Cent Child Books

"Integrated totally in feeling and mood, the book has been engendered by an intense personal vision of Africa—one that is warm, all-enveloping, quietly strong and filled with love." Horn Book

Moja means one; Swahili counting book; pictures by Tom Feelings. Dial Bks. for Young Readers 1971 unp il pa $6.99 hardcover o.p.
    E

1. Counting 2. Swahili language 3. East Africa
ISBN 0-14-054662-6 (pa)

A Caldecott Medal honor book, 1972

The book "uses double-page spreads for each number, one to ten, with beautiful illustrations that depict aspects of East African culture as well as numbers of objects in relation to the various numbers." Publ Wkly

"A short introduction explaining the importance of Swahili and providing a map of the areas in which it is spoken expands the book's use beyond the preschool level of the text into the first three school grades." SLJ

Feiffer, Jules

Bark, George. HarperCollins Pubs. 1999 unp il $15.99   **E**

1. Dogs—Fiction
ISBN 0-06-205185-7

"Michael di Capua books"

"George the puppy has a problem—he just can't bark. He can meow, quack, oink, moo; but not bark." NY Times Book Rev

"Feiffer's characters are unforgettable, the text is brief and easy to follow, and the pictures burst with the sort of broad physical comedy that a lot of children just love." Booklist

Feiffer, Kate

Double pink; illustrated by Bruce Ingman. Simon & Schuster Books for Young Readers 2005 unp il $15.95   **E**

1. Color—Fiction
ISBN 0-689-87190-0   LC 2004--06582

"A Paula Wiseman Book"

Madison covers and surrounds herself with her favorite color, pink, until the day her mother has trouble finding her.

"Feiffer's simple text reads easily, and Ingman's playful acrylic-and-ink paintings take a light approach to this look at childhood obsession." SLJ

Fisher, Aileen Lucia

The story goes on; illustrated by Mique Moriuchi. 1st ed. Roaring Brook Press 2004 unp il $16.95   **E**

1. Food chains (Ecology) 2. Stories in rhyme
ISBN 1-59643-037-0   LC 2003-18143

An illustrated poem about the cycle of life—bug eats plant, frog eats bug, snake eats frog, hawk eats snake, and so on.

"With bright colors, rhyming text, and collage illustrations, this circular tale points out the interdependence of life. . . . This offering is a visual treat and an engaging opportunity to introduce the cycle of life to young readers." SLJ

Fisher, Leonard Everett

The ABC exhibit. Macmillan 1991 unp il $15.95   **E**

1. Alphabet
ISBN 0-02-735251-X   LC 90-6639

Introduces the letters of the alphabet in paintings of subjects from Acrobat to Zinnia

"The intensity of color and precision of detail invite readers to linger, to identify, and to observe. The alphabet is merely the framework; the lesson is in the appreciation of art." SLJ

Fisher, Valorie

My big brother. Atheneum Bks. for Young Readers 2002 unp il $15.95   **E**

1. Brothers—Fiction
ISBN 0-689-84327-5   LC 2001-22947

"An Anne Schwartz book"

Photographs and simple text depict a big brother from the point of view of his baby sibling

"The design is clean and strong, and the colors, textures, and lines all lead the eye to the important parts of the story. Together the text and the pictures tell a funny, very tender story of sibling relationships." Booklist

Flack, Marjorie

Ask Mr. Bear. Macmillan 1958 c1932 unp il $15; pa $5.99   **E**

1. Animals—Fiction 2. Birthdays—Fiction
ISBN 0-02-735390-7; 0-02-043090-6 (pa)

First published 1932

Flack, Marjorie—*Continued*

Danny did not know what to give his mother for a birthday present, so he set out to ask various animals—the hen, the duck, the goose, the lamb, the cow and others, but he met with very little success until he met Mr. Bear

This "will have a strong appeal to very young children because of its repetition, its use of the most familiar animals, its gay pictures and the cumulative effect of the story." N Y Times Book Rev

Fleischman, Paul

The animal hedge; illustrated by Bagram Ibatoulline. Candlewick Press 2003 unp il $16.99

E

1. Farmers—Fiction 2. Animals—Fiction
ISBN 0-7636-1606-0   LC 2002-23751
A newly illustrated edition of the title first published 1983 by Dutton

After being forced to sell the animals he loves, a farmer cuts his hedge to look like them and teaches his sons about following their hearts

"Ibatoulline's watercolor-and-gouache illustrations, inspired by 19th-century American folk-art paintings, are the perfect complement to this simple allegory." SLJ

Sidewalk circus; presented by Paul Fleischman and Kevin Hawkes. Candlewick Press 2004 unp il $15.99

E

1. City and town life—Fiction 2. Circus—Fiction
3. Stories without words
ISBN 0-7636-1107-7   LC 2002-74168
"As posters advertising the world-renowned Garibaldi circus are put up along a busy city block, a girl waiting for a bus watches the circus of everyday life unfold. There is no actual text to the book, just the words of store signs, a scrolling theater marquee, and the show bills. What the girl imagines is revealed through the playful shadows of the people on the street and the corresponding circus flyers. . . . Hawkes's richly colored acrylic paintings sustain interest and pacing throughout the book. . . . This delightful book will fascinate children and help them to see their world with new eyes." SLJ

Weslandia; illustrated by Kevin Hawkes. Candlewick Press 1999 unp il $15.99; pa $5.99

E

1. Plants—Fiction 2. Gardening—Fiction
ISBN 0-7636-0006-7; 0-7636-1052-6 (pa)
LC 98-30240
Wesley's garden produces a crop of huge, strange plants which provide him with clothing, shelter, food, and drink, thus helping him create his own civilization and changing his life

"This story about a nonconformist creating his own reality resonates with imagination and humor. . . . His natural creativity is reflected in Hawkes' vivid recreations of Wesley's altered environment, lush illustrations that have a realistic whimsy." Bull Cent Child Books

Fleming, Candace

Boxes for Katje; pictures by Stacey Dressen-McQueen. Farrar, Straus & Giroux 2003 unp il $16

E

1. World War, 1939-1945—Fiction 2. Netherlands—Fiction
ISBN 0-374-30922-1   LC 2002-20027
"Melanie Kroupa books"

After a young Dutch girl writes to her new American friend in thanks for the care package sent after World War II, she begins to receive increasingly larger boxes

The story is "moving, and Dressen-McQueen's lively illustrations, in colored pencil, oil pastel, and acrylic, pack lots of color, pattern, and historical details onto every expansive page." Booklist

The hatmaker's sign; a story; by Benjamin Franklin; retold by Candace Fleming; illustrated by Robert Andrew Parker. Orchard Bks. 1998 unp il $16.95; lib bdg $17.99

E

1. Jefferson, Thomas, 1743-1826—Fiction
2. Franklin, Benjamin, 1706-1790—Fiction
ISBN 0-531-30075-7; 0-531-33075-3 (lib bdg)
LC 97-27596
To heal the hurt pride of Thomas Jefferson as Congress makes changes to his Declaration of Independence, Benjamin Franklin tells his friend the story of a hatmaker and his sign

"Based on an anecdote in *The Papers of Thomas Jefferson*, the story has a folktale-like quality that lends itself to being read aloud. The illustrations give dimension to the characters and a sense of times past." Horn Book Guide

Muncha! Muncha! Muncha! illustrated by G. Brian Karas. Atheneum Bks. for Young Readers 2002 unp il $16; lib bdg $18.63

E

1. Rabbits—Fiction 2. Gardening—Fiction
ISBN 0-689-83152-8; 0-689-93652-X (lib bdg)
LC 99-24882
"An Anne Schwartz book"

After planting the garden he has dreamed of for years, Mr. McGreely tries to find a way to keep some persistent bunnies from eating all his vegetables

"Fleming's text is lilting and deftly paced, with sound effects . . . strategically and enjoyably employed. . . . Karas' mixed-media (gouache, acrylic, and pencil) illustrations offer a cornucopia of plot-enriching details." Bull Cent Child Books

Sunny Boy! the life and times of a tortoise; pictures by Anne Wilsdorf. 1st ed. Farrar, Straus and Giroux 2005 unp il $16

E

1. Turtles—Fiction
ISBN 0-374-37297-7   LC 2004-40451
"Melanie Kroupa books"

In this fictionalized account, Sunny Boy, a 100-year-old tortoise, describes various events in his long life including the dangerous barrel ride over Niagara Falls that he takes with his daredevil owner on July 5, 1930.

"This saga makes for wildly entertaining reading. . . . The comical cartoon narrative . . . enhances the textual flow of the story. Not to be missed is the author's fascinating historical note." SLJ

Fleming, Candace—*Continued*

This is the baby; pictures by Maggie Smith. 1st ed. Farrar, Straus and Giroux 2004 unp il $16.50
E

1. Infants—Fiction 2. Clothing and dress—Fiction 3. Stories in rhyme

ISBN 0-374-37486-4   LC 2002-70941

"Melanie Kroupa books"

A cumulative rhyme enumerating all the items of clothing that go on the baby who hates to be dressed, from the diaper often a mess to the jacket woolen and plaid.

"Smith's naive and rosy-cheeked characters, cozy textures, and crayon-box colors are a perfect accompaniment to Fleming's well-constructed, cumulative, 'House That Jack-Built' patterned story that positively insists on reader interaction." SLJ

When Agnes caws; written by Candace Fleming; illustrated by Giselle Potter. Atheneum Bks. for Young Readers 1999 unp il $16; pa $6.99
E

1. Birds—Fiction

ISBN 0-689-81471-2; 0-689-85118-9 (pa)
LC 97-32921

"An Anne Schwartz book"

When eight-year-old Agnes Peregrine, an accomplished birdcaller, travels with her parents to the Himalayas in search of the elusive pink-headed duck, she encounters a dastardly foe

"Gently distorted perspectives in the expressive illustrations add to the melodramatic spoofiness of this flibbertigibbet tale." Horn Book Guide

Fleming, Denise

Alphabet under construction. Holt & Co. 2002 unp il $16.95
E

1. Mice—Fiction 2. Alphabet

ISBN 0-8050-6848-1   LC 2001-5210

Companion volume to Lunch

A mouse works his way through the alphabet as he folds the "F," measures the "M," and rolls the "R"

"Fleming has poured colored cotton fiber through hand-cut stencils to make her illustrations, which are thus bold in outline and shape and vivid with an almost incandescent coloring. Although this has the simplicity of many alphabet books, it also has momentum . . . and ingenuity in its execution." Booklist

Barnyard banter. Holt & Co. 1994 unp il $16.95; pa $6.95
E

1. Animals—Fiction 2. Stories in rhyme

ISBN 0-8050-1957-X; 0-8050-5581-9 (pa)
LC 93-11032

Also available board book edition

All the farm animals are where they should be, clucking and mucking, mewing and cooing, except for the missing goose

"Strong rhythm and rhyme, plus fun onomatopoetic animal sounds, demand reading aloud. But even more delightful than the engaging text are Fleming's spectacular illustrations. . . . They create realistically textured, bold, bright settings for the whimsical critters to romp through." SLJ

Buster. Holt & Co. 2003 unp il $15.95
E

1. Dogs—Fiction 2. Cats—Fiction

ISBN 0-8050-6279-3   LC 2002-10857

Buster the dog thinks his perfect life is spoiled when Betty the cat comes to live with him, until he learns not to be afraid of cats

"Fleming's trademark handmade-paper artwork is awash with vibrant colors and dazzling details." SLJ

Count! Holt & Co. 1992 unp il $16.95; pa $6.95
E

1. Counting 2. Animals

ISBN 0-8050-1595-7; 0-8050-4252-0 (pa)
LC 91-25686

Also available Board book edition

The antics of lively and colorful animals present the numbers one to ten, twenty, thirty, forty, and fifty

"A fresh, upbeat concept book. Lizards, giraffes, toucans, butterflies are available for counting—if only they'll hold still long enough! Fuchsias and oranges, teals and purples, roll over the pages blending into each other in Fleming's beautiful couched paper with hand cut-stencil illustrations. Her explosions of color and motion are captivating and energizing." SLJ

The everything book. Holt & Co. 2000 64p il $18.95
E

ISBN 0-8050-6292-0   LC 99-53626

A collection of simple works which introduce colors, shapes, numbers, animals, food, and nursery rhymes

"The book includes everything needed to make it an anthology of preschool interests and concerns. . . . The very attractive illustrations, done in Fleming's characteristic bold and energetic style, were produced by pouring cotton pulp through hand-cut stencils, the result being simple forms that are attractively textured, with edges that are just fuzzy enough to look soft and friendly." SLJ

The first day of winter. Henry Holt and Co 2005 unp il $15.95
E

1. Snow—Fiction 2. Winter—Fiction

ISBN 0-8050-7384-1   LC 2004-22181

A snowman is built and is given special gifts to put on by his best friend each day for ten days with cumulative items of gifts.

"Fleming captures the tranquility and light of snowy days with her unique artistic style. Her paper-pulp and stencil illustrations depict a winter wonderland in which vibrant striped scarves, blue mittens, and red hats provide the color in a white, uncluttered landscape. . . . Quietly told and thoughtfully illustrated." SLJ

In the small, small pond. Holt & Co. 1993 unp il $16.95; pa $6.95
E

1. Pond ecology—Fiction 2. Stories in rhyme

ISBN 0-8050-2264-3; 0-8050-5983-0 (pa)
LC 92-25770

A Caldecott Medal honor book, 1994

Illustrations and rhyming text describe the activities of animals living in and near a small pond as spring progresses to autumn

"The brilliant, primitive illustrations were made by pouring colored cotton pulp through hand-cut stencils. Against the eye-catching colors, the four-word rhymes in

Fleming, Denise—*Continued*
bold black print dance, each double-page spread picturing and describing a different creature. Text, pictures, layout, and design are all beautifully done." SLJ

In the tall, tall grass. Holt & Co. 1991 unp il $16.95; pa $6.95   E
1. Animals—Fiction 2. Stories in rhyme
ISBN 0-8050-1635-X; 0-8050-3941-4 (pa)
LC 90-26444
Also available Big book edition
Rhymed text (crunch, munch, caterpillars lunch) presents a toddler's view of creatures found in the grass from lunchtime till nightfall, such as bees, ants, and moles
"Boldly colored in grassy greens, sunny yellows, and evening blues, the impressionistic illustrations make this a real treat for eyes as well as ears." Booklist

Lunch. Holt & Co. 1993 unp il $16.95; pa $6.95
E
1. Mice—Fiction 2. Color
ISBN 0-8050-1636-8; 0-8050-4646-1 (pa)
LC 92-178
Also available Board book edition
"A very hungry mouse nibbles and crunches his way through the various components of a vegetarian repast, while the text introduces readers to the individual foods and their respective colors." Publ Wkly
"Fleming continues to work in the medium of handmade paper built from layers of colored pulp that has been forced through a stencil. A huge typeface and the judicious use of large blocks of bold, solid color give this book a fresh look. Delectable fun, and, with its simple yet engaging plot, sure to be requested over and over by the youngest readers." Horn Book

Mama cat has three kittens. Holt & Co. 1998 unp il $16.95; pa $6.95   E
1. Cats—Fiction
ISBN 0-8050-5745-5; 0-8050-7162-8 (pa)
LC 98-12249
While two kittens copy everything their mother does, their brother naps
"Fleming's kittens, created by pouring colored cotton pulp through hand-cut stencils, are large and bold and set against colorful backdrops. An excellent choice for reading aloud to groups." SLJ

Pumpkin eye. Holt & Co. 2001 unp il $15.95
E
1. Halloween—Fiction 2. Stories in rhyme
ISBN 0-8050-6681-0   LC 00-44850
Simple rhymes describe the sights, sounds, and smells of Halloween
"Fleming's homemade paper landscapes set off their midnight-blue—well, probably eight-o'clock blue—backdrops with glowing orange and white accents as well as with the rainbow of colors represented in the trick-or-treaters' costumes. . . . This will be just the shivery ticket for kids looking to move from Halloween giggles to genuine spookiness." Bull Cent Child Books

Time to sleep. Holt & Co. 1997 unp il $16.95; pa $6.95   E
1. Winter—Fiction 2. Animals—Fiction
3. Hibernation—Fiction
ISBN 0-8050-3762-4; 0-8050-6767-1 (pa)
LC 96-37553
When Bear notices that winter is nearly here he hurries to tell Snail, after which each animal tells another until finally the already sleeping Bear is awakened in his den with the news
"Fleming's simple text is ripe with astute observations of the natural world and animal behavior. . . . Fleming's 'pulp painting' style results in lushly textured handmade paper compositions saturated with earthy browns, reds and golds." Publ Wkly

Floca, Brian
The racecar alphabet. Atheneum Bks. for Young Readers 2003 unp il $15.95   E
1. Automobile racing—Fiction 2. Alphabet
ISBN 0-689-85091-3   LC 2002-2198
"A Richard Jackson book"
Automobile races highlight the letters of the alphabet
"The alphabetical text often uses alliterative phrases. . . . Although a single race appears to proceed throughout the book, the cars, drivers, tracks, and spectators change considerably from the book's opening in 1901 . . . to the conclusion in 2001. . . . Large in scale, the ink-and-watercolor artwork is bold enough to share with a story hour or classroom group, yet young racing fans will find the details absorbing. Floca's introductory note on the history of racing may interest them as well." Booklist

Flournoy, Valerie
The patchwork quilt; pictures by Jerry Pinkney. Dial Bks. for Young Readers 1985 unp il $16.99
E
1. Quilts—Fiction 2. Family life—Fiction 3. African Americans—Fiction
ISBN 0-8037-0097-0   LC 84-1711
Coretta Scott King Award for illustrations, 1986
Using scraps cut from the family's old clothing, Tanya helps her grandmother and mother make a beautiful quilt that tells the story of her Afro-American family's life
"Plentiful full-page and double-page paintings in pencil, graphite and watercolor are vivid yet delicately detailed. . . . Giving a sense of dramatization to the text, . . . the illustrations provide just the right style and mood for the story." SLJ

Ford, Bernette
First snow; illustrated by Sebastien Braun. 1st ed. Holiday House 2005 unp il $16.95   E
1. Rabbits—Fiction 2. Snow—Fiction 3. Night—Fiction
ISBN 0-8234-1937-1   LC 2004-55257
A family of young rabbits goes into a meadow at night to explore and play in winter's first snow.
"Ford's text has a poetic rhythm that emphasizes the senses as the rabbits explore their wintry world. . . . Braun's illustrations . . . are particularly engaging and complement the story wonderfully." SLJ

Forward, Toby

What did you do today? the first day of school; illustrated by Carol Thompson. Clarion Books 2004 29p il $15 **E**

1. School stories 2. Mother-child relationship—Fiction

ISBN 0-618-49586-X   LC 2004-2467

A child describes the events of the first day of school, from making sandwiches for lunch to holding a parent's hand on the walk home

"The parallels between a child's day at school and his mother's day at work are shown with insight and love in this cleverly designed book. . . . Thompson varies her pen-and-watercolor illustrations in surprising and eye-catching ways." Booklist

Fox, F. G. (Frank G.)

Jean Laffite and the big ol' whale; pictures by Scott Cook. Farrar, Straus & Giroux 2003 unp il $16 **E**

1. Whales—Fiction 2. Mississippi River—Fiction 3. Tall tales

ISBN 0-374-33669-5   LC 99-43733

When a huge white whale gets stuck between the banks of the Mississippi River causing the water to stop flowing, Jean Laffite finds a way to get the river moving again

"This rollicking good yarn is brought to life with Cook's warm, glowing oil paintings full of action and humor." SLJ

Fox, Mem

Hattie and the fox; illustrated by Patricia Mullins. Bradbury Press 1987 c1986 unp il $16.95; pa $6.99 **E**

1. Chickens—Fiction 2. Foxes—Fiction

ISBN 0-02-735470-9; 0-689-71611-7 (pa)

LC 86-18849

First published 1986 in Australia

"Hattie is a fine, portly, and observant hen, and she knows there is something wrong when she spies a sharp foxy nose in the bushes. Her alarmist and ever escalating announcements, however, bring nothing but bored and languid replies." Horn Book

"Bright, whimsical tissue collage and crayon illustrations add zest to this simple cumulative tale, and reveal more action than is expressed by the text alone." SLJ

Hunwick's egg; illustrated by Pamela Lofts. Harcourt 2005 unp il $16 **E**

1. Bandicoots—Fiction 2. Australia—Fiction

ISBN 0-15-216318-2   LC 2003-16385

When a wild storm sends a beautiful egg to Hunwick the bandicoot's burrow, he decides to give it a home and become its friend.

"This slightly offbeat story . . . is accompanied by glowing watercolor pencil illustrations in orange, pink, and violet tones that showcase the flora and fauna of the Australian landscape, adding an interesting element to this charming title." SLJ

Koala Lou; illustrated by Pamela Lofts. Harcourt Brace Jovanovich 1989 c1988 unp il $16.95; pa $6.99 **E**

1. Koalas—Fiction

ISBN 0-15-200502-1; 0-15-200076-3 (pa)

LC 88-26810

"Gulliver books"

First published 1988 in Australia

This story is "set in the Australian bush. Koala Lou feels bereft when her mother becomes preoccupied with a growing brood of younger koala children. In her desire to recapture her mother's attention and affection, the enterprising Koala Lou decides to become a contestant in the Bush Olympics." Horn Book

"A reassuring story for the child who feels neglected when siblings arrive." Child Book Rev Serv

Night noises; written by Mem Fox; illustrated by Terry Denton. Harcourt Brace Jovanovich 1989 unp il $16; pa $6 **E**

1. Night—Fiction 2. Sleep—Fiction

ISBN 0-15-200543-9; 0-15-257421-2 (pa)

LC 89-2162

"Gulliver books"

Old Lily Laceby dozes by the fire with her faithful dog Butch Aggie at her feet as strange night noises herald a surprising awakening

"With an almost joltingly bright palette . . . Denton has divided up many of the double-page spreads into three scenes: the main one depicting Lily Laceby and Butch Aggie in various stages of alertness, another showing the chronology of Lily's life, and the third cleverly revealing clues to the mysterious activity outdoors. The text, in Mem Fox's Houdini-like hands, reads beautifully—the language, pacing, tension, and sparks of excitement absolutely at one with the artwork." Horn Book

Sleepy bears; illustrated by Kerry Argent. Harcourt Brace & Co. 1999 unp il $16; pa $6 **E**

1. Bears—Fiction 2. Bedtime—Fiction 3. Stories in rhyme

ISBN 0-15-202016-0; 0-15-216542-8 (pa)

LC 98-42640

"Mother Bear tucks in her six cubs, sending them off on dreamy adventures. Baxter dreams of pirates, Bella of the circus, Winifred of the jungle, Tosca of kingdoms, Ali of divine foods, and Baby Bear of moonbeams. . . . The rhymes are well written, and the charming pictures, done in gouache, watercolor, and colored pencil, are full of funny details." SLJ

Sophie; illustrated by Aminah Brenda Lynn Robinson. Harcourt Brace & Co. 1994 c1989 unp il $15; pa $6 **E**

1. Grandfathers—Fiction 2. African Americans—Fiction

ISBN 0-15-277160-3; 0-15-201598-1 (pa)

LC 94-1976

First published 1989 in Australia

"In this cyclical tale, Grandpa welcomes infant Sophie into the world; much later, Sophie is saddened when 'there was no Grandpa.' The birth of Sophie's own child completes the circle." Publ Wkly

"The artwork is rich, expressionist, heavily lined oil.

Fox, Mem—*Continued*

. . . The oversized hands depicted in many drawings exemplify the handholding theme, and the sunny hues of
earth and garden convey with warmth a loving and extended African-American family." Bull Cent Child Books

Tough Boris; illustrated by Kathryn Brown.
Harcourt Brace & Co. 1994 unp il $16; pa $6
E
1. Pirates—Fiction 2. Parrots—Fiction
ISBN 0-15-289612-0; 0-15-201891-3 (pa)
LC 92-8015
Boris von der Borch is a tough pirate but he weeps
when his parrot dies
"The text is deceptively simple, but the observant
child will quickly fill in the details, aptly provided in the
illustrations. The reassuring message, although under-
stated, is clear and effective." Horn Book Guide

Where is the green sheep? [by] Mem Fox and
[illustrated by] Judy Horacek. Harcourt 2004 unp
il $15
E
1. Sheep—Fiction 2. Stories in rhyme
ISBN 0-15-204907-X   LC 2003-4990
A story about many different sheep, and one that
seems to be missing.
"Until the lost sheep turns up, children will have fun
with the other sheep that make an appearance and perhaps, unbeknownst to them, also get lessons in colors
and comparisons. . . . In this neat and satisfying wedding of text and art, the squat, square format uses wool-
white backgrounds to display much of the amusing pen-
and-watercolor pictures." Booklist

Wombat divine; illustrated by Kerry Argent.
Harcourt Brace & Co. 1996 unp il $16; pa $6
E
1. Christmas—Fiction   2.   Wombats—Fiction
3. Animals—Fiction
ISBN 0-15-201416-0; 0-15-202096-9 (pa)
LC 96-5480
Wombat auditions for the Nativity play, but has trou-
ble finding the right part
"Fox spiffily combines a witty text with her wonderful
art. Here the fun comes with seeing all sorts of Austra-
lian animals (emu, bilby, kangaroo) decked out in their
Christmas-play garb." Booklist

Frame, Jeron Ashford

Yesterday I had the blues; illustrations by R.
Gregory Christie. Tricycle Press 2003 unp il
$14.95
E
1. Emotions—Fiction 2. African Americans—Fiction
3. Family life—Fiction
ISBN 1-58246-084-1   LC 2002-155295
A young African American boy ponders a variety of
emotions and how different members of his family experience them, from his own blues to his father's grays and
his grandmother's yellows
"Vibrant acrylic-and-gouache spreads give rhythm and
meaning to this child's interpretation of everyday life, his
neighborhood, and his family. The illustrations effectively express each individual's mood and beautifully capture
the cultural and artistic aspects of the family's life, while
the expressive text is engaging." SLJ

Francis, Panama

David gets his drum; [by] David "Panama"
Francis and Bob Reiser; illustrated by Eric
Velasquez. Marshall Cavendish 2002 unp il $16.95
E
1. Musicians—Fiction 2. Drums—Fiction
ISBN 0-7614-5088-2   LC 00-47425
In this story based on the life of drummer David
"Panama" Francis, a little boy named David dreams of
getting his own drum and marching in the Sunday parade
"The realistic oil paintings are framed in red and offer
varying perspectives and a sense of historical place that
invite readers into the story and lend an immediacy, yet
timelessness, to the text." SLJ

Frank, John

The toughest cowboy; or how the Wild West
was tamed; illustrated by Zachary Pullen. Simon &
Schuster Bks for Young Readers 2004 unp il
$16.95
E
1. Cowhands—Fiction 2. Dogs—Fiction 3. West
(U.S.)—Fiction
ISBN 0-689-83461-6
"Grizz Brickbottom, toughest cowboy in the West,
yearns for a companion and convinces his cattle-rustling
cohorts that they need a dog. . . . When the local saloon
goes out of business, the proprietor puts up a sign offering a free dog to a good home. Unexpectedly, it's a miniature poodle named Foofy. . . . Readers will return to
this one again and again to catch all of the humor and
nuances of both the text and illustrations." SLJ

Frasier, Debra

On the day you were born. Harcourt Brace
Jovanovich 1991 unp il $16
E
1. Earth 2. Childbirth
ISBN 0-15-257995-8   LC 90-36816
Also available with audio CD $17.95 (ISBN 0-15-
205567-3)
This combination of text and paper-collage graphics
depicts the earth's preparation for, and celebration of, the
birth of a newborn baby
"The text reads like unrhymed poetry, and both parents and educators will find themselves wanting to share
this book over and over with individuals and with
groups. A three-page appendix that includes miniature
versions of each spread elaborates on natural phenomena
for older readers—migrating animals, spinning Earth, rising tide, falling rain, growing trees, and more." SLJ

Frazee, Marla

Roller coaster. Harcourt 2003 unp il lib bdg $16
E
1. Roller coasters
ISBN 0-15-204554-6   LC 2002-7805
"Frazee does an extraordinary job of conveying motion by the placement of her images, her use of white
space, bright colors, and swooshing speed lines. . . .
What will keep children coming back for extra looks,
however, is Frazee's clever, dramatic depiction of the 12
riders and their wildly and amusingly different reactions
to the stomach-churning experience." Booklist

Frazee, Marla—*Continued*

Santa Claus, the world's number one toy expert.
Harcourt 2005 unp il $16   **E**
  1. Santa Claus—Fiction 2. Christmas—Fiction
  ISBN 0-15-204970-3   LC 2004-5228
Santa Claus has his own ways of knowing more about
children and toys than anyone else in the world.
  "Frazee, a master at creating scenes and moods in her
energetic drawings and spare text, fills these pages with
details and vignettes that readers will want to explore repeatedly." SLJ

Walk on! a guide for babies of all ages.
Harcourt, Inc. 2006 unp il $16   **E**
  1. Infants—Fiction 2. Walking—Fiction
  ISBN 0-15-205573-8 (lib bdg)   LC 2004-29895
  "In this how-to for little ones, a baby learns to walk
for the first time. . . . The pencil-and-gouache art has
the delightful feel of self-help pamphlets from an earlier
era. . . . This is one of those rare books that speaks to
crawling and walking babies who like to look at pictures
of creatures like themselves, preschoolers who enjoy stories about what they were like when they were little, and
older children and adults who will appreciate the wry humor." SLJ

Freedman, Claire

Gooseberry Goose; illustrated by Vanessa
Cabban. Tiger Tales 2003 unp il $15.95
                       E
  1. Geese—Fiction 2. Winter—Fiction 3. Animals—
Fiction
  ISBN 1-58925-030-3   LC 2003-12960
  As Gooseberry Goose practices flying on a beautiful
fall morning, his friends are preparing for winter, causing
Gooseberry to wonder if there is something else he
should be doing
  "The text is brought to life through the illustrations,
which are loose and lovely. Vibrant red and gold leaves
enliven the pages. Gooseberry is a bundle of expression.
. . . Readers will be captivated by this irrepressible gos-
ling's infectious charm." SLJ

Freeman, Don

Corduroy; story and pictures by Don Freeman.
Viking 1968 32p il lib bdg $15.99; pa $5.99
                       E
  1. Teddy bears—Fiction
  ISBN 0-670-24133-4 (lib bdg); 0-14-050173-8 (pa)
  Also available Big book edition and Spanish language
edition
  "One day Corduroy, a toy bear who lives in a big department store, discovers he has lost a button. That night
he goes to look for it and in his search he sees many
strange and wonderful things. He does not find his button, but the following morning he finds what he has always wanted—a friend, Lisa." Read Ladders for Hum
Relat. 6th edition
  "The art and story are direct and just right for the
very young who like bears and escalators." Book World
  Another title about Corduroy is:
A pocket for Corduroy (1978)

Earl the squirrel. Viking 2005 unp il $15.99
                       E
  1. Squirrels—Fiction
  ISBN 0-670-06019-4   LC 2005-03929
Earl the squirrel learns to gather acorns on his own.
  "The pictures are full of energy and detail, and Earl
is both cheeky and endearing. . . . The story is gentle,
innocent, and funny." SLJ

French, Jackie

Diary of a wombat; illustrated by Bruce
Whatley. Clarion Bks. 2003 c2002 unp il $14
                       E
  1. Wombats—Fiction
  ISBN 0-618-38136-8   LC 2003-829
  First published 2002 in Australia
  In his diary, a wombat describes his life of eating,
sleeping, and getting to know some new human neighbors
  The story is presented in "simple sentences and hilarious yet realistic acrylic illustrations. . . . Whatley gives
a sublime balance of the adorable charm of the creature,
along with its drawbacks as an acquaintance." SLJ

Pete the sheep-sheep; by Jackie French;
illustrated by Bruce Whatley. Clarion Books 2005
c2004 32p il $14   **E**
  1. Sheep—Fiction 2. Dogs—Fiction
  ISBN 0-618-56862-X   LC 2004030935
  First published 2004 in Australia with title: Pete the
sheep
  The sheep-shearers in Shaggy Gully all have a sheep
dog, but the new guy Shaun uses an extremely polite
sheep named Pete.
  "Cleanly designed illustrations work well with
French's understated text. Strong lines focus attention on
the expressive characters." Horn Book Guide

Freymann, Saxton

Dog food; written and illustrated by Saxton
Freymann. Levine Bks. 2002 unp il $12.95
                       E
  ISBN 0-439-11016-5   LC 2002-19572
  Dog figures carved out of different fruits and vegeta-
bles "act out" such phrases as "Bad dog," "Sick as a
dog," and "Doggy bag"
  The vegetable and fruit figures show "wit and a keen
design sensibility. . . . Whimsy prevails." Publ Wkly

Fast food; written and illustrated by Saxton
Freymann. Arthur A. Levine Books 2006 32p il
$12.99   **E**
  1. Transportation
  ISBN 0-439-11019-X
  "This picture book takes a theme (here, transportation)
and illustrates it with exceptionally clear color photos of
ephemeral, sometimes whimsical sculptures created from
fruits and vegetables. As quietly witty as its title, the
book is narrated by a little mushroom man who suggests
different ways of getting about. . . . The playful text
gallops along smoothly in rhymed couplets, while the illustrations work their inimitable charm." Booklist

Freymann, Saxton—*Continued*

Food for thought; the complete book of concepts for growing minds; written and illustrated by Saxton Freymann. Arthur A. Levine Books 2005 61p il $14.95　　　**E**

1. Concepts 2. Counting 3. Alphabet

ISBN 0-439-11018-1

This "covers basic shapes, colors, numbers, letters, and opposites—all introduced through images of artfully manipulated fruits and vegetables. . . . The simple, clean design is ideal for demonstrating the concepts. . . . But it's the playful, wonderfully clever transformation of familiar foods that will win an audience." Booklist

How are you peeling? foods with moods; [by] Saxton Freymann and Joost Elffers. Scholastic 1999 unp il $15.95; pa $5.99　　　**E**

1. Emotions

ISBN 0-439-10431-9; 0-439-59841-9 (pa)

LC 99-18162

"Arthur A. Levine books"

Brief text and photographs of carvings made from vegetables introduce the world of emotions by presenting leading questions such as "Are you feeling angry?"

"Kids will find the inherent silliness irresistible and be drawn in by the book's visual appeal: the colors are strong, the photography is excellent, and the expressions . . . are surprisingly masterful." Booklist

One lonely sea horse; [by Saxton Freymann and Joost Elffers] Scholastic 2000 unp il $15.95

E

1. Counting 2. Friendship—Fiction 3. Marine animals—Fiction 4. Stories in rhyme

ISBN 0-439-11014-9　　　LC 99-33396

"Arthur A. Levine books"

One lonely sea horse learns that she has a lot of friends—friends she can really "count" on

"In beautifully photographed dioramas, fruits and vegetables are transformed into sea flora and fauna. . . . The edible characters are wonderfully expressive, with a wide range of emotions captured through the use of a few simple slits and seeds." Booklist

Friedman, Ina R.

How my parents learned to eat; illustrated by Allen Say. Houghton Mifflin 1984 30p il $15; pa $5.95　　　**E**

1. Dining—Fiction 2. Japan—Fiction

ISBN 0-395-35379-3; 0-395-44235-4 (pa)

LC 83-18553

An American sailor courts a Japanese girl and each tries, in secret, to learn the other's way of eating

"The illustrations have precise use of line and soft colors, and the composition is economical. A warm and gentle story of an interracial family." Bull Cent Child Books

Friedrich, Elizabeth

Leah's pony; illustrated by Michael Garland. Boyds Mills Press 1996 unp il $16.95; pa $8.95

E

1. Farm life—Fiction 2. Great Depression, 1929-1939—Fiction

ISBN 1-56397-189-5; 1-56397-828-8 (pa)

LC 95-79657

"When drought in the 1930s turns their farm land into dust, Leah's papa has to put everything they own up for auction. Knowing how much he needs his tractor, Leah makes the decision to sell her beloved pony and bids all her money for the tractor—one dollar. Neighbors follow her example, placing penny bids and returning things to Leah's parents." Horn Book Guide

Friend, Catherine

Eddie the raccoon; illustrated by Wong Herbert Yee. Candlewick Press 2004 $12.99; pa $5.99

E

1. Raccoons—Fiction

ISBN 0-7636-2331-8; 0-7636-2334-2 (pa)

LC 2003-69717

"Brand new readers"

Eddie the "raccoon steals Big Chicken's eggs, gets his nose stuck in a jam jar, digs deep holes, and stumbles upon a grumpy bear's cave." SLJ

"Pleasant watercolors . . . provide ample visual clues to the accompanying sentence—usually comprising four or five basic vocabulary words. . . . Each setup packs a gently humorous punch that's easy enough for children to grasp and sweet enough to make their adult helpers chuckle." Booklist

Funke, Cornelia Caroline

The princess knight; by Cornelia Funke; illustrations by Kerstin Meyer; translated by Anthea Bell. Chicken House 2004 unp il $15.95

E

1. Princesses—Fiction 2. Knights and knighthood—Fiction

ISBN 0-439-53630-8

Original German edition 2001

"Raised by a widowed king, Princess Violetta is put through the same paces (swordplay, riding, jousting) as her older, brawnier brothers. Her practice pays off when her father holds a tournament—with Violetta as the grand prize—and she handily scuttles his plans. Bell translates Funke's story from the German with aplomb . . . and Meyer's effervescent line-and-watercolor artwork, as funny as it is lovely, stretches across each spread in horizontal strips." Booklist

Fusco Castaldo, Nancy

Pizza for the queen; by Nancy Castaldo; illustrated by Mélisande Potter. 1st ed. Holiday House 2005 unp il $16.95　　　**E**

1. Pizza—Fiction 2. Italy—Fiction 3. Cooking—Fiction

ISBN 0-8234-1865-0　　　LC 2004-58134

In 1889 Napoli, Italy, Raffaele Esposito prepares a special pizza for Queen Margherita. Based on a true sto-

Fusco Castaldo, Nancy—*Continued*
ry. Includes a recipe.

"The richly toned, detailed illustrations . . . extend the action and the sense of history in busy scenes in the kitchen and on the picturesque streets." Booklist

Gág, Wanda

Millions of cats. Putnam 2004 c1928 unp il $13.99   **E**

1. Cats—Fiction

ISBN 0-399-23315-6

A Newbery Medal honor book, 1929

A reissue of the title first published 1928 by Coward-McCann

A "story-picture book about a very old man and a very old woman who wanted one little cat and who found themselves with 'millions and billions and trillions of cats.'" St Louis Public Libr

It is "a perennial favorite among children and takes a place of its own, both for the originality and strength of its pictures and the living folktale quality of its text." NY Her Trib Books

Gaiman, Neil

The wolves in the walls; written by Neil Gaiman; illustrated by Dave McKean. HarperCollins Pubs. 2003 unp il $16.99   **E**

1. Wolves—Fiction

ISBN 0-380-97827-X   LC 2002-192194

Lucy is sure there are wolves living in the walls of her house, although others in her family disagree, and when the wolves come out, the adventure begins

"Gaiman's text rings with energetic confidence and an inviting tone. . . . McKean . . . expertly matches the tale's funny-scary mood . . . against shadow-filled backdrops that blend paint, digital manipulation and photography, his stylized human figures look right at home. His pen-and-inks of the wolves . . . suggest that they inhabit a world apart—or perhaps unreal?" Publ Wkly

Gammell, Stephen

Once upon MacDonald's farm. rev format ed. Simon & Schuster Bks. for Young Readers 2000 c1981 unp il $15   **E**

1. Farm life—Fiction 2. Animals—Fiction

ISBN 0-689-82885-3   LC 99-30691

First published 1981 by Four Winds Press

MacDonald tries farming with exotic circus animals, but has better luck with his neighbor's cow, horse, and chicken—or does he?

"The accomplished, shaded pencil drawings are well suited to this slyly humorous tale with an unexpected twist." Horn Book Guide

Gantos, Jack

Rotten Ralph; written by Jack B. Gantos; illustrated by Nicole Rubel. Houghton Mifflin 1976 unp il lib bdg $16; pa $7.95   **E**

1. Cats—Fiction

ISBN 0-395-24276-2 (lib bdg); 0-395-29202-6 (pa)

"The protagonist of this story is a mean and nasty cat, Ralph. As his young owner, Sarah, and her family say,

he is very difficult to love. Finally on a trip to the circus his behavior becomes unforgivable and they leave him. There he is treated as miserably as he has treated everyone else and he comes home a week later a wiser, more benevolent cat—well, almost." Child Book Rev Serv

The "bright watercolor scenes . . . capturing Ralph's demonic meanness and his family's chagrin are a perfect complement to the text." SLJ

Other titles about Rotten Ralph are:

Back to school for Rotten Ralph (1998)

Best in show for Rotten Ralph (2005)

Happy birthday Rotten Ralph (1990)

Not so Rotten Ralph (1994)

Practice makes perfect for Rotten Ralph (2002)

Rotten Ralph helps out (2001)

Rotten Ralph's rotten Christmas (1984)

Rotten Ralph's rotten romance (1997)

Rotten Ralph's show and tell (1989)

Rotten Ralph's trick or treat! (1986)

Wedding bells for Rotten Ralph (1999)

Worse than rotten, Ralph (1978)

Garden, Nancy

Molly's family; pictures by Sharon Wooding. Farrar Straus Giroux 2004 unp il $16   **E**

1. Family life—Fiction 2. School stories 3. Lesbians—Fiction

ISBN 0-374-35002-7   LC 2002-29784

When Molly draws a picture of her family for Open School Night, one of her classmates makes her feel bad because he says she cannot have a mommy and a momma

"By tying this specific household to the general diversity within all families, Garden manages to celebrate them all. The soft colored-pencil drawings with their many realistic details depict a room full of active kindergartners." SLJ

Garza, Carmen Lomas

Family pictures; paintings and stories [by] Carmen Lomas Garza. 15th anniversary edition. Children's Book Press 2005 30p il $16.95; pa $7.95   **E**

1. Hispanic Americans—Fiction 2. Bilingual books—English-Spanish

ISBN 0-89239-206-1; 0-89239-207-X (pa)

A re-designed edition with a new introduction of the title first published 1990

Text and title page in English and Spanish

The "Mexican-American artist shares memories of her childhood in Kingsville, Texas, through . . . paintings depicting the traditions of her family and community life. A fair in Mexico, the author's sixth birthday party, and a visit from a curandera (healer) represent a few of the scenes presented." Booklist

"An inspired celebration of American cultural diversity. . . . The English text is simple and reads smoothly, but it is Zubizarreta's Spanish rendition that has real verve and style. From the exquisite cut-paper images on the text pages, to the brilliant paintings, to the strong family bonds expressed in the text, Family Pictures/Cuadros de familia is a visual feast, and an aural delight." SLJ

Gauch, Patricia Lee

Aaron and the Green Mountain Boys; pictures by Margot Tomes. Boyds Mills Press 2005 c1972 64p il $16.95; pa $9.95   E

1. United States—History—1775-1783, Revolution—Fiction

ISBN 1-59078-335-2; 1-59078-354-9 (pa)

A reissue of the title first published 1972 by Coward, McCann & Geohegan

In 1777 nine-year-old Aaron would rather help the Green Mountain Boys fight the British than stay home and bake bread for them.

Tanya and the red shoes; illustrated by Satomi Ichikawa. Philomel Bks. 2002 unp il $16.99

E

1. Ballet—Fiction

ISBN 0-399-23314-8   LC 2001-33916

"Tanya confides her dreams of dancing *en pointe* like the dancer in the movie *The Red Shoes*. She finally gets her wish but discovers that the seemingly effortless beauty of the dance requires much work (and produces many blisters). The use of the present tense underscores the conversational tone, adding verisimilitude matched by Ichikawa's marvelously agile, expressive illustrations." Horn Book

Other titles about Tanya are:

Bravo Tanya (1992)
Dance Tanya (1989)
Presenting Tanya the Ugly Duckling (1999)
Tanya and the magic wardrobe (1997)

Geeslin, Campbell

Elena's serenade; written by Campbell Geeslin; illustrated by Ana Juan. Atheneum Books for Young Readers 2004 unp il $16.95   E

1. Mexico—Fiction 2. Glassblowing—Fiction 3. Sex role—Fiction

ISBN 0-689-84908-7   LC 2002-3233

"An Anne Schwartz book"

In Mexico a little girl disguised as a boy sets out for Monterrey determined to master the art of glassblowing, and in the process, experiences self-discovery along the way.

"The story flows well and Spanish words are smoothly incorporated into the text. The alluring acrylic-and-crayon illustrations have a stylized folk-art quality that helps to set the stage for the tale." SLJ

Geisert, Arthur

Lights out. Houghton Mifflin Co. 2005 32p il $16   E

1. Pigs—Fiction 2. Bedtime—Fiction 3. Inventions—Fiction

ISBN 0-618-47892-2   LC 2005-00555

"Walter Lorraine books"

Told by his parents that his light must be out at eight o'clock, a young piglet who is afraid of the dark devises an ingenious solution to the problem.

"Fans of roller-coaster construction, marble runs, and contraption-like machines will be immediately engaged, and the problem-solving humor is for everyone. The fine lines and small scale of Geisert's color art work perfectly to give an effect that is intimate, energetic, and delightful." SLJ

Pigs from 1 to 10. Houghton Mifflin 1992 32p il $16; pa $6.95   E

1. Counting 2. Pigs—Fiction

ISBN 0-395-58519-8; 0-618-21611-1 (pa)

LC 92-5097

Ten pigs go on an adventurous quest. The reader is asked to find all ten of them, and the numerals from zero to nine, in each picture

"Geisert's inventiveness knows no bounds, and his illustrations both inspire the imagination and convey a homey charm. The final page, a triumphant aggregation of pigs and numbers, is especially endearing." Publ Wkly

Pigs from A to Z. Houghton Mifflin 1986 unp il $18; pa $8.95   E

1. Alphabet 2. Pigs—Fiction

ISBN 0-395-38509-1; 0-395-77874-3 (pa)

LC 86-18542

Seven piglets cavort through a landscape of hidden letters as they build a tree house

"At the back of the book is a key that shows where the artist has secreted all the letters in each illustration; some are plain, some are subtle and every picture has, in addition to its principal letter, one or two from the alphabetical surroundings. . . . So 'Pigs From A to Z' succeeds as narrative, alphabet book, counting book (are all seven piglets in each etching?), puzzle book and as art." N Y Times Book Rev

Geisert, Bonnie

Mountain town; [by] Bonnie and Arthur Geisert. Houghton Mifflin 2000 32p il $16   E

1. Mountain life 2. Cities and towns 3. West (U.S.) 4. Seasons

ISBN 0-395-95390-1   LC 99-29856

"Walter Lorraine books"

Describes a year in the present-day life of a mountain town that was founded when prospectors searching for gold arrived in the Rocky Mountains in the mid-nineteenth century

"Etchings enhanced with watercolors provide sweeping panoramas. . . . Perspectives include bird's-eye views as well as above and belowground cross sections. The present-tense text occasionally provides helpful explanations for the already-informative pictures." SLJ

Other titles in this series are:

Prairie town (1998)
River town (1999)

Gelman, Rita Golden

Doodler doodling; pictures by Paul O. Zelinsky. Greenwillow Books 2003 unp il $15.99; lib bdg $16.89   E

1. Imagination—Fiction

ISBN 0-688-16645-8; 0-688-16646-6 (lib. bdg)

LC 2002-35326

"A young girl . . . scribbles doodles at her school desk, while behind her, a large sheet of notebook paper shows the multicolored line drawings of her imaginings, accompanied by a few explanatory words. 'Teachers teaching' . . . 'Fliers flying,' 'Fliers teaching,' 'Teachers flying'. . . . The minimal words make an appealing, rhythmic poem, but Zelinsky's whimsical illustrations give this title its gleeful, inventive humor." Booklist

George, Jean Craighead

Look to the North; a wolf pup diary; illustrated by Lucia Washburn. HarperCollins Pubs. 1997 unp il lib bdg $15.89; pa $5.99   E
1. Wolves—Fiction
ISBN 0-06-023640-X (lib bdg); 0-06-443510-5 (pa)
LC 95-39162
Brief diary entries that mark the passage of the seasons introduce the events in the lives of three wolves as they grow from helpless pups to participants in their small pack's hunt
"The delicately textured acrylic paintings offer lively yet loving views of the wolves, perfectly complementing George's appealing text." Booklist

Morning, noon, and night; paintings by Wendell Minor. HarperCollins Pubs. 1999 unp il $15.95; lib bdg $16.89   E
1. Day—Fiction 2. Animals—Fiction
ISBN 0-06-023628-0; 0-06-023629-9 (lib bdg)
LC 97-28796
Each day as the sun makes its dawn-to-dusk journey from the Eastern seaboard to the Pacific coast, the animals perform their daily activities
This offers "rhythmic, lyrical text. . . . Minor's lushly detailed paintings capture the beauty of both animals and landscape, elucidating the subtle journey the book makes from east coast to west." Horn Book Guide

Nutik, the wolf pup; illustrated by Ted Rand. HarperCollins Pubs. 2001 unp il $15.95; lib bdg $15.89   E
1. Inuit—Fiction 2. Wolves—Fiction 3. Arctic regions—Fiction
ISBN 0-06-028164-2; 0-06-028165-0 (lib bdg)
LC 99-10501
When his older sister Julie brings home two small wolf pups, Amaroq takes care of the one called Nutik and grows to love it, even though Julie tells him it cannot stay
"Rand's realistic paintings establish the Alaska setting and capture the affection between boy and pup. . . . First told in *Julie's Wolf Pack* (1997), the story is skillfully telescoped into a picture book with heart-tugging appeal." Booklist
Another title about Nutik and Amaroq is:
Nutik & Amaroq play ball (2001)

George, Kristine O'Connell

Book! illustrated by Maggie Smith. Clarion Bks. 2001 31p il $9.95   E
1. Books and reading—Fiction 2. Stories in rhyme
ISBN 0-395-98287-1   LC 00-65600
"When the toddler narrator opens a present and discovers a volume entitled Bunnies, he and the book immediately become inseparable." Publ Wkly
"Smith's deeply colored, playful acrylics depict the youngster through the day as he puts the book onto the shelf upside down, reads it to his cat, and uses it as a ticket to mom's lap for cozy storytime. Rounded, stiff paper pages ensure that this title will withstand repeated readings." SLJ

Hummingbird nest; a journal of poems; illustrated by Barry Moser. Harcourt 2004 unp il $16   E
1. Hummingbirds—Fiction 2. Stories in rhyme
ISBN 0-15-202325-9   LC 99-50909
When a mother hummingbird builds a nest on a family's porch, they watch and record her actions and the birth and development of her fledglings.
"Moser's quiet, exquisitely detailed pictures show the people watching and the small, delicate creatures. . . . The long, beautifully written notes with astonishing facts about hummingbirds make this a fine choice for both language arts and science classes." Booklist

Up! illustrated by Hiroe Nakata. Clarion Books 2005 32p il $15   E
1. Father-daughter relationship—Fiction 2. Stories in rhyme
ISBN 0-618-06489-3   LC 2004-10729
Rhyming text and illustrations animate the feeling of "up" as experienced by a little girl with her father.
"Nakata's airy, spirited watercolors beautifully expand on the words' carefree, physical elation with skewed angles, glorious fruit-juice colors, and leaping, tumbling toys and figures." Booklist

George, Lindsay Barrett

In the woods: who's been here? Greenwillow Bks. 1995 unp il $16.95; pa $6.99   E
1. Forest animals
ISBN 0-688-12318-X; 0-688-16163-4 (pa)
LC 93-16244
A boy and girl in the autumn woods find an empty nest, a cocoon, gnawed bark, and other signs of unseen animals and their activities
"Children will be drawn to George's vivid gouache paintings, especially those depicting the animals in their natural surroundings. . . . For most childen this will be an excellent introduction to classroom nature units and the perfect prelude to a walk in the woods." Booklist
Other titles in this series are:
Around the pond: who's been here? (1996)
Around the world: who's been here? (1999)
In the garden: who's been here? (2006)
In the snow: who's been here? (1995)

Inside mouse, outside mouse. Greenwillow Books 2004 unp il $15.99; lib bdg $16.89   E
1. Mice—Fiction
ISBN 0-06-000466-5; 0-06-000467-3 (lib bdg)
LC 2003-48497
Two mice, one who sleeps inside the house in a clock and one who sleeps outside the house in a stump, follow complicated but strangely parallel paths and meet each other at a window.
"The pictures are packed with interesting details just waiting to be explored. The simple text . . . compares and contrasts the animals' environments and lifestyles. The overall effect is mesmerizing" SLJ

George, William T.

Box Turtle at Long Pond; pictures by Lindsay Barrett George. Greenwillow Bks. 1989 unp il $15.99; lib bdg $15.89   E

1. Turtles—Fiction

ISBN 0-688-08184-3; 0-688-08185-1 (lib bdg)
LC 88-18787

On a busy day at Long Pond, Box Turtle searches for food, basks in the sun, and escapes a raccoon

"A beautifully illustrated book that introduces a pond environment. . . . The reader learns of other plants, animals, and insects that inhabit the pond." Sci Child

Other titles about Long Pond are:

Beaver at Long Pond (1988)

Christmas at Long Pond (1992)

Fishing at Long Pond (1991)

Geras, Adèle

Time for ballet; illustrated by Shelagh McNicholas. Dial Books for Young Readers 2004 unp il $16.99   E

1. Ballet—Fiction

ISBN 0-8037-2978-2   LC 2003-5751

Tilly, who loves ballet, plays the part of a cat in her class's dance recital.

"Tilly narrates in a fresh, childlike voice as the pictures offer an appealing look at her world. Well-observed details of everyday life create a sense of realism, and the artist's affection for her subject shines through in the warm colors and appealing drawings." Booklist

Gerber, Carole

Leaf jumpers; [illustrated by] Leslie Evans. Charlesbridge 2004 32p il $15.95   E

1. Leaves 2. Autumn

ISBN 1-57091-497-4   LC 2003-15846

Illustrations and rhyming text describe different leaves and the trees from which they fall

"Gerber's poetic text describes colors, shapes, and characteristics with an abundance of similes and metaphors. . . . Evans' vibrant hand-colored linoleum prints feature scenes of a brother and sister with the family dog enjoying traditional fall activities." Booklist

Gershator, David

Kallaloo! a Caribbean tale; by David and Phillis Gershator; illustrated by Diane Greenseid. 1st ed. Marshall Cavendish 2005 unp il $16.95   E

1. Caribbean region—Fiction

ISBN 0-7614-5110-2   LC 2004-14467

In this West Indian version of "Stone Soup," an old woman claims to have found a magic shell that can make kallaloo, a popular Caribbean gumbo.

"This humorous tale . . . is well suited to reading aloud. Greenseid's bright and vibrant acrylic illustrations are a perfect interpretation of the text and bring the setting to life. A well-written, engaging, and gentle story." SLJ

Gerstein, Mordicai

Carolinda clatter! Roaring Brook Press 2005 unp il $16.95   E

1. Fairy tales 2. Giants—Fiction

ISBN 1-59643-063-X   LC 2004-24258

The excessively quiet town of Pupickton and the sleeping lovesick giant upon which it was built, are both awakened by the joyful noise of a little girl's songs.

"Gerstein tells his whimsical tale with direct humor, and his lovely paint-and-ink illustrations extend the comedy." Booklist

The man who walked between the towers. Roaring Brook Press 2003 unp il $17.95; lib bdg $24.90   E

1. Petit, Philippe, 1949- 2. Tightrope walking

ISBN 0-7613-1791-0; 0-7613-2868-8 (lib bdg)
LC 2003-9040

Awarded the Caldecott Medal, 2004

A lyrical evocation of Philippe Petit's 1974 tightrope walk between the World Trade Center towers

"The pacing of the narrative is as masterful as the placement and quality of the oil-and-ink paintings. . . . Gerstein captures his subject's incredible determination, profound skill, and sheer joy." SLJ

Sparrow Jack. Frances Foster Bks. 2003 unp il $16   E

1. Bardsley, John, d. 1999—Fiction 2. Sparrows—Fiction 3. Immigrants—Fiction

ISBN 0-374-37139-3   LC 2001-23829

In 1868, John Bardsley, an immigrant from England, brought one thousand sparrows from his home country back to Philadelphia, where he hoped they would help save the trees from the inch-worms that were destroying them

"Though a few imaginative liberties are taken with the facts, Gerstein's cheerful tale is based on a true story. The humor of his whimsically witty text is beautifully captured and expanded by drawings that are filled with comic action and droll details." Booklist

Gibbons, Faye

Mama and me and the Model-T; illustrations by Ted Rand. Morrow Junior Bks. 1999 unp il lib bdg $15.89   E

1. Automobiles—Fiction 2. Sex role—Fiction 3. Mountain life—Fiction 4. Family life—Fiction

ISBN 0-688-15299-6 (lib bdg)   LC 98-31518

When Mama gets behind the wheel of the new Model-T which her husband just drove into the yard of their Georgia mountain home, she proves that she can drive a car as well as the men of the family

"Rand's delightful watercolors display the heartfelt warmth and humor of the noisy blended family." Booklist

Mountain wedding; illustrated by Ted Rand. Morrow Junior Bks. 1996 unp il $16; lib bdg $16.89   E

1. Weddings—Fiction 2. Mountain life—Fiction 3. Family life—Fiction

ISBN 0-688-11348-6; 0-688-11349-4 (lib bdg)
LC 95-18197

Gibbons, Faye—*Continued*

"Ma Searcy and Mr. Long stand before the preacher as the children, seven Longs and five Searcys, who clearly take exception to the marriage and to each other, stand in two opposing lines, prepared for battle. The children join forces, however, when a swarm of honeybees brings on a crisis. Gibbon's unassuming story of family solidarity unexpectedly achieved is splendidly augmented by Rand's funny and appealing watercolors." Horn Book Guide

Gibbons, Gail

The seasons of Arnold's apple tree. Harcourt Brace Jovanovich 1984 unp il $16; pa $6
E
1. Seasons—Fiction 2. Trees—Fiction
ISBN 0-15-271246-1; 0-15-271245-3 (pa)
LC 84-4484

Arnold enjoys his apple tree through the changing year: its springtime blossoms, the swing and tree-house it supports, its summer shade, its autumn harvest; in the winter, the tree's branches hold strings of popcorn and berries for the birds

"Two major concepts emerge here, the first being the passage of the seasons, the second the valuable resource Arnold has in his apple tree. . . . Gibbons' crisp pictures ensure that the multifaceted lesson is explicit, bright and cheery." Booklist

Giff, Patricia Reilly

Watch out, Ronald Morgan! illustrated by Susanna Natti. Viking Kestrel 1985 24p il pa $5.99 hardcover o.p.
E
1. Eyeglasses—Fiction 2. School stories
ISBN 0-14-050638-1 (pa)
LC 84-19623

Ronald has many humorous mishaps until he gets a pair of eyeglasses. Includes a note for adults about children's eye problems

"Told in a forthright manner but with appreciation for children's candor, the book's dialogue rings true with catchy humor. . . . Natti's illustrations show the characters to be bright, colorful informal figures who move with the text." SLJ

Other titles about Ronald Morgan are:
Good luck, Ronald Morgan (1996)
Happy birthday, Ronald Morgan! (1986)
Ronald Morgan goes to bat (1988)
Ronald Morgan goes to camp (1995)
Today was a terrible day (1980)

Giganti, Paul, Jr.

Each orange had 8 slices; a counting book; by Paul Giganti, Jr,; pictures by Donald Crews. Greenwillow Bks. 1992 unp il $15.99; pa $6.99
E
1. Counting 2. Mathematics
ISBN 0-688-10428-2; 0-688-13985-X (pa)
LC 90-24167

This volume presents a series of statements about the illustrations: "'On my way to Grandma's I saw 2 fat cows. Each cow had 2 calves. Each calf had 4 skinny legs,' and the questions follow: 'How many fat cows

. . . calves . . . legs were there in all?'" SLJ

"This bright, well-designed book challenges young children to think analytically about what's on its pages. . . . Since the objects are organized into sets and subsets, this could be used to introduce the concept of multiplication as well as counting and addition." Booklist

How many snails? a counting book; by Paul Giganti, Jr.; pictures by Donald Crews. Greenwillow Bks. 1988 unp il $15.99; lib bdg $15.89; pa $5.99
E
1. Counting
ISBN 0-688-06369-1; 0-688-06370-5 (lib bdg); 0-688-13639-7 (pa)
LC 87-26281

"Instead of inviting children to count static objects, Mr. Giganti poses a series of simple, direct questions designed to encourage youngsters to determine the often subtle differences between those objects. Donald Crews . . . concentrates here on decorating each page with objects that supply the necessary links to the text. Some of the pages—depicting a collection of motley dogs at the park or beautiful toy boats and trucks, cars and airplanes at a toy store—are a joy to look at." N Y Times Book Rev

Ginsburg, Mirra

The chick and the duckling; translated [and adapted] from the Russian of V. Suteyev; pictures by Jose & Ariane Aruego. Macmillan 1972 unp il pa $5.99 hardcover o.p.
E
1. Ducks—Fiction 2. Chickens—Fiction
ISBN 0-689-71226-X (pa)

"The adventures of a duckling who is a leader and a chick who follows suit. When the chick decides that an aquatic life is not for him, this brief selection for reading aloud comes to a humorous conclusion." Wis Libr Bull

"The sunny simplicity of the illustrations is just right for a slight but engaging text, and they add a note of humor that is a nice foil for the bland directness of the story." Bull Cent Child Books

Good morning, chick; by Mirra Ginsburg, adapted from a story by Korney Chukovsky; pictures by Byron Barton. Greenwillow Bks. 1980 unp il lib bdg $16.89; pa $5.99
E
1. Chickens—Fiction
ISBN 0-688-84284-4 (lib bdg); 0-688-08741-8 (pa)
LC 80-11352

"In this simple preschool tale . . . a chick hatches out of an egg ('like this'), learns to eat worms ('like this'), is scared by a cat ('like this'), falls in a pond ('like this'), and is coddled back to fluffiness by Mom ('like this')." SLJ

"Based upon a tale by the great Russian poet and storyteller, the totally childlike picture book for the very young employs an engaging device: The text, illustrated with a bright vignette, appears on each of the left-hand pages; then, after pausing briefly and leading the eye to the right, a sentence runs to completion on the opposite page with two words contained in a large storytelling picture done in bold, brilliant color." Horn Book

Glaser, Linda

Our big home; an Earth poem; illustrated by Elisa Kleven. Millbrook Press 2000 unp il $23.90; pa $7.95   **E**

  1. Nature—Fiction 2. Earth—Fiction
  ISBN 0-7613-1650-7; 0-7613-1776-7 (pa)
                                LC 99-45775

Describes the water, air, soil, sky, sun, and more shared by all living creatures on Earth

"A joyful celebration of the Earth. . . . Kleven's colorful artwork is full of subtle detail. . . . The artist uses an effective mix of media, from collage to chalk, to portray depth of scenes and vibrancy of detail." SLJ

Gliori, Debi

Flora's surprise! Orchard Bks. 2003 c2002 unp il $15.95   **E**

  1. Rabbits—Fiction 2. Gardens—Fiction
  ISBN 0-439-45590-1   LC 2002-30801
  First published 2002 in the United Kingdom

Flora, a young rabbit, tries to grow a house by planting a brick

"Gliori's bright, cheerful, full-color watercolor-and-ink art fills the spreads with the lush abundance of spring, summer, and fall gardens. Each illustration is full of homey details that children will want to pore over." SLJ

Mr. Bear's new baby. Orchard Bks. 1999 unp il $15.95   **E**

  1. Bears—Fiction 2. Infants—Fiction
  ISBN 0-531-30152-4   LC 98-30530

Mr. and Mrs. Bear and the other forest animals despair of ever getting Baby Bear to stop crying and go to sleep, but Small Bear knows just how to solve the problem

"Watercolor illustrations with pen-and-ink details depict interesting characters with expressive faces and a house agreeably cluttered with baby paraphernalia." Horn Book Guide

Other titles about the Bear family are:
Mr. Bear says "Are you there, Baby Bear?" (1999)
Mr. Bear to the rescue (2000)
Mr. Bear's vacation (2000)

No matter what. Harcourt Brace & Co. 1999 unp il $16   **E**

  1. Parent-child relationship—Fiction 2. Foxes—Fiction
  3. Stories in rhyme
  ISBN 0-15-202061-6   LC 98-47277

Small, a little fox, seeks reassurance that Large will always provide love, no matter what

"Gliori's whimsical illustrations use warm, inviting color to invoke the same sense of emotional security as the rhyming text." Booklist

Goble, Paul

Death of the iron horse; story and illustrations by Paul Goble. Bradbury Press 1987 unp il pa $6.99 hardcover o.p.   **E**

  1. Cheyenne Indians—Fiction 2. Railroads—Fiction
  ISBN 0-689-71686-9 (pa)   LC 85-28011

The author "has taken several accounts of the 1867 Cheyenne attack of a Union Pacific freight train . . . and combined them into a story from the Indians' viewpoint. As the Cheyenne Prophet Sweet Medicine had foretold, strange hairy people were invading the land, killing women and children and driving off the horses. Descriptions of the iron horse inspired curiosity and fear in the young braves who decided to go out and protect their village from this new menace. Keeping fairly close to actual Indian accounts, Goble presents the braves' bold attack on the train, glossing over the deaths of the train crew." SLJ

Godwin, Laura

Central Park serenade; pictures by Barry Root. HarperCollins Pubs. 2002 unp il $15.99; lib bdg $15.89   **E**

  1. Stories in rhyme 2. Central Park (New York, N.Y.)—Fiction
  ISBN 0-06-025891-8; 0-06-025892-6 (lib bdg)
                                  LC 99-30279
  "Joanna Cotler books"

Illustrations and rhyming text celebrate the sights and sounds of New York's Central Park in summer

"Godwin's lively, rhyming text uses onomatopeia and terrific descriptive language. . . . Root does an equally fine job providing visual stimulation in sun-drenched, double-page spreads depicting sidewalk artists sketching, sailboat races, seals splashing around at the park's zoo, and more." Booklist

Happy and Honey; written by Laura Godwin; pictures by Jane Chapman. Margaret K. McElderry Bks. 2000 unp il (Happy Honey) $12.95   **E**

  1. Dogs—Fiction 2. Cats—Fiction
  ISBN 0-689-83406-3   LC 99-46923

Honey the cat is determined to play with Happy the dog, even though he is trying to sleep

"The text is short and effective, and the delightful acrylic paintings, which are set against an expanse of white space, center on Happy and Honey, keeping children as focused on the goings-on as does the just-right text." Booklist

Other titles about Happy and Honey are:
The best fall of all (2002)
Happy Christmas, Honey (2002)
Honey helps (2000)

Golding, Kim

Counting kids. Dorling Kindersley 2000 unp il $9.95   **E**

  1. Counting
  ISBN 0-7894-2678-1   LC 99-47084

"A rhyming text and computer-enhanced photographs of children reinforce counting from 1 to 10. . . . An enjoyable counting book for both beginning counters and the more confident." Booklist

González, Rigoberto

Antonio's card; story, Rigoberto González; illustrations, Cecilia Concepción Alvarez. Children's Book Press 2005 30p $16.95

    E

1. Mother-son relationship—Fiction 2. Lesbians—Fiction 3. School stories 4. Bilingual books—English-Spanish

ISBN 0-89239-204-5   LC 2004-56046

With Mother's Day coming, Antonio finds he has to decide about what is important to him when his classmates make fun of the unusual appearance of his mother's partner, Leslie.

"Sensitively written in English, with an excellent translation by Jorge Argueta, the narrative captures the social worries and concerns that children in nontraditional families may experience. The acrylic illustrations are bright and colorful." SLJ

Goode, Diane

The most perfect spot; by Diane Goode. 1st ed. HarperCollins 2006 unp il $16.99; lib bdg $17.89

    E

1. Mother-son relationship—Fiction 2. Parks—Fiction 3. Brooklyn (New York, N.Y.)—Fiction

ISBN 0-06-072697-0; 0-06-072698-9 (lib bdg)

    LC 2004030058

"Young Jack wants to go on a picnic with his mother and thinks that he knows the perfect spot in Prospect Park. Maybe it is, but getting there is fraught with problems. . . . When the rain begins to pour down, Mama and Jack decide there's only one perfect spot for a picnic—back home. . . . Goode's art was inspired by the early years of the last century. . . . Full of amusing details and nice touches . . . this book will sustain more readings than one might expect." Booklist

Thanksgiving is here! HarperCollins Pubs. 2003 unp il $15.99; lib bdg $16.89   E

1. Thanksgiving Day—Fiction 2. Family life—Fiction

ISBN 0-06-051588-0; 0-06-051589-9 (lib bdg)

    LC f002-151781

A family gathers to celebrate Thanksgiving at Grandma's house

"The humorously detailed, pen-and-ink and watercolor, cartoon artwork is exuberant, mischievous, and full of surprises. This Thanksgiving book has something for everyone." SLJ

Gorbachev, Valeri

Ms. Turtle the babysitter. HarperCollins Pub. 2005 64p il $15.99; lib bdg $16.89   E

1. Babysitters—Fiction 2. Turtles—Fiction 3. Frogs—Fiction

ISBN 0-06-058073-9; 0-06-058074-7 (lib bdg)

    LC 2004-6234

"An I can read book"

Ms. Turtle babysits for three little frogs when their parents go out for the evening.

"Beginning readers will enjoy this chapter-style book. . . . The pen-and-ink and watercolor cartoons seamlessly complement the text. The expressions on the faces of these endearing frogs are priceless." SLJ

That's what friends are for. Philomel Books 2005 unp il $15.99   E

1. Friendship—Fiction 2. Goats—Fiction 3. Pigs—Fiction

ISBN 0-399-23966-9   LC 2004-18118

When Goat finds his friend Pig crying, he imagines all the terrible things that might have happened to cause his distress

"The book is a warm display of friendship and a caution against unnecessary worry. Soft-colored drawings supply details for the simple text." Horn Book Guide

Gower, Catherine

Long-Long's New Year; a story about the Chinese spring festival; illustrated by He Zhihong. Tuttle 2005 unp il $16.95   E

1. Chinese New Year—Fiction 2. China—Fiction 3. Grandfathers—Fiction

ISBN 0-8048-3666-3   LC 2004-111580

"To earn money for the upcoming Spring Festival (also known as Chinese New Year), Long-Long and his grandfather take a bicycle cart loaded with cabbages into town on market day." Booklist

"Gower's simple, appealing story aptly captures the details of the festival as well as specifics of Chinese life. Zhihong's softly colored, detailed drawings on tan rice paper evoke both the bustle of a preholiday marketplace as well as the gentle warmth shared by grandfather and grandchild." SLJ

Graham, Bob

Let's get a pup, said Kate. Candlewick Press 2001 unp il $14.99   E

1. Dogs—Fiction 2. Animal shelters—Fiction

ISBN 0-7636-1452-1   LC 00-57208

When Kate and her parents visit the animal shelter, an adorable puppy charms them, but it is very hard to leave an older dog behind

"Bob Graham's cozy watercolors, lightly held in place by loose, sketchy outlines, contribute to this story's feelings of warmth, family, and belonging." Horn Book

Max. Candlewick Press 2000 unp il $15.99

    E

1. Flight—Fiction

ISBN 0-7636-1138-7   LC 99-43704

Max, the young son of superheroes, is a late bloomer when it comes to flying, until he is inspired by the plight of a falling baby bird

"Here's a funny, comforting read for any child cowed by overachievers, or perhaps a sly gift for an overanxious parent." Bull Cent Child Books

Oscar's half birthday; [by] Bob Graham. 1st U.S. ed. Candlewick Press 2005 unp il $16.99

    E

1. Racially mixed people—Fiction 2. Birthdays—Fiction 3. Family life—Fiction

ISBN 0-7636-2699-6   LC 2004-57041

"A mixed-race family sets out for a picnic in the park to celebrate baby Oscar's half birthday. . . . The warm, expressive illustrations show a family apartment in which a mop, shoes, and toys all share floor space. . . . This is an effortlessly multicultural story, full of the joy of childhood, family, and community." SLJ

Gralley, Jean

The moon came down on Milk Street; written and illustrated by Jean Gralley. Holt 2004 unp il $16.95　　　　E

　　1. Moon—Fiction 2. Rescue work—Fiction 3. Stories in rhyme

　　ISBN 0-8050-7266-7

When the moon comes down in pieces, different helpers work to set things right again, including the Fire Chief, rescue workers, and helper dogs.

"Gralley presents a perceptive look at how individuals react to an unexpected crisis. . . . Done in gouache and mixed media, the large, uncluttered illustrations on white backgrounds contribute to the gentle nature of the story." SLJ

Gramatky, Hardie

Little Toot; pictures and story by Hardie Gramatky. Putnam c1939 unp il $16.99; pa $6.99
　　　　E

　　1. Tugboats—Fiction

　　ISBN 0-399-22419-X; 0-698-11576-7 (pa)

Also available Board book edition

Story and pictures describe the early career of a saucy little tug-boat too pleased with himself to do any real work until one day when he found himself out on the ocean in a storm. Then Little Toot earned the right to be called a hero

"Mr. Gramatky tells his story with humor and enjoyment, giving, too, a genuine sense of the water front in both pictures and story." Horn Book

Grant, Karima

Sofie and the city; [by] Karima Grant; illustrated by Janet Montecalvo. 1st ed. Boyds Mills Press 2006 unp il $15.95　　　　E

　　1. Immigrants—Fiction 2. African Americans—Fiction 3. City and town life—Fiction 4. Friendship—Fiction

　　ISBN 1-59078-273-9　　LC 2005020116

When Sofie calls her grandmother in Senegal on Sundays, she complains about the ugliness of the city she now lives in, but her life changes when she makes a new friend.

"Told in simple language, with dialogue matching that of a child learning English, the text and art show how upsetting any move can be and how it feels to be small in a large and unfamiliar place." SLJ

Gray, Libba Moore

My mama had a dancing heart; illustrated by Raúl Colón. Orchard Bks. 1995 unp il $15.95; lib bdg $16.99; pa $5.99　　　　E

　　1. Dance—Fiction 2. Mother-daughter relationship—Fiction 3. Seasons—Fiction

　　ISBN 0-531-09470-7; 0-531-08770-0 (lib bdg); 0-531-07142-1 (pa)　　LC 94-48802

"A Melanie Kroupa book"

"In spring, summer, fall and winter, a mother leads her young daughter in dancing a celebratory ballet, a hymn to the season. When the girl is older, she is a ballerina and remembers that her mother gave her a dancing heart. . . . Colón's etched watercolors in earth and mut-

ed jewel tones give the book an old-fashioned ambiance. . . . Gray's writing lends itself to reading aloud, but independent readers will also enjoy it." SLJ

Greenberg, David

Bugs! by David T. Greenberg; illustrated by Lynn Munsinger. Little, Brown 1997 unp il $14.95; pa $5.95　　　　E

　　1. Insects—Fiction 2. Stories in rhyme

　　ISBN 0-316-32574-0; 0-316-35576-3 (pa)

　　　　　　　　　　　　LC 96-23023

Celebrates the disgusting and horrible things you can do with a bunch of bugs

"These rhymes are ardently subversive. . . . Munsinger's pictures are sweetly colored, conferring a winsome giddiness on the proceedings." Horn Book Guide

Greene, Rhonda Gowler

Barnyard song; illustrated by Robert Bender. Atheneum Bks. for Young Readers 1997 unp il $16.95; pa $5.99　　　　E

　　1. Domestic animals—Fiction 2. Sick—Fiction 3. Stories in rhyme

　　ISBN 0-689-80758-9; 0-689-84054-3 (pa)

　　　　　　　　　　　　LC 96-1923

When the barnyard animals catch the flu, the farmer takes care of them until their usual voices return

"A playful read-aloud with a square-dance cadence and deeply saturated, warm-and-fuzzy colors." SLJ

Greenfield, Eloise

Africa dream; illustrated by Carole Byard. Crowell 1977 unp il lib bdg $15.89; pa $5.99
　　　　E

　　1. Africa—Fiction

　　ISBN 0-690-04776-2 (lib bdg); 0-06-443277-7 (pa)

　　　　　　　　　　　　LC 77-5080

Coretta Scott King Award, 1978

"As ethereal as the title implies, this sparsely worded prose-poem relates the benign dream experience of a young child who transports her mind to 'Long-ago Africa.'" Booklist

Grandpa's face; illustrated by Floyd Cooper. Philomel Bks. 1988 unp il lib bdg $16.99; pa $6.99　　　　E

　　1. Grandfathers—Fiction 2. Actors—Fiction

　　ISBN 0-399-21525-5 (lib bdg); 0-399-22106-9 (pa)

　　　　　　　　　　　　LC 87-16729

"Tamika fears that her grandfather, an actor, is incapable of loving her when she sees him practicing a cruel expression. The young girl's turmoil and its resolution are keenly felt through evocative text and striking pictures." SLJ

Me & Neesie; illustrated by Jan Spivey Gilchrist. HarperCollins 2005 unp il $15.99; lib bdg $16.89　　　　E

　　1. Imaginary playmates—Fiction 2. African Americans—Fiction 3. School stories

　　ISBN 0-06-000701-X; 0-06-000702-8 (lib bdg)

　　　　　　　　　　　　LC 2002-24241

Greenfield, Eloise—*Continued*

A newly illustrated edition of the title first published 1975

Janell's best friend is her invisible playmate Neesie, but things begin to change when Janell starts school.

This "features fresh, full-color watercolor-and-ink paintings. . . . All children will relate to the universal quest for friendship and security and will find comfort in this loving family's support during a time of transition." SLJ

Greenstein, Elaine

One little lamb. Viking 2004 unp il $10.99
E

1. Wool—Fiction 2. Sheep—Fiction
ISBN 0-670-03683-8

Describes how a lamb's coat is made into yarn, which is made into mittens worn by a little girl when she visits the lamb on the farm.

This is "illustrated by spot-on artwork that fills up the small pages. Kids will immediately be drawn by the cover art; the framed jacket painting of a sleeping lamb covered with curlicues of white wool is especially fetching." Booklist

One little seed. Viking 2004 unp il $10.99
E

1. Flowers—Fiction 2. Growth—Fiction
ISBN 0-670-03633-1

Follows a seed from the time it is planted until it grows into a beautiful flower.

"Folk-influenced, full-bleed watercolors balance facing pages where brief lyrical phrases and small circular insets float on white space." Publ Wkly

Gretz, Susanna

Riley and Rose in the picture; [by] Susanna Gretz. 1st U.S. ed. Candlewick Press 2005 unp il $16.99
E

1. Dogs—Fiction 2. Cats—Fiction 3. Friendship—Fiction
ISBN 0-7636-2681-3   LC 2004-54569

On a rainy day Reilly the dog and Rosa the cat decide to stay indoors and draw a picture together but have trouble agreeing on how to do it.

"The lively text is read-aloud friendly, incorporating child-familiar dialogue, interactions, and humor. The colorful gouache art is charming, too, filling the pages with expressive characters and distinctive childlike artwork that perfectly matches the story." Booklist

Grey, Mini

Traction Man is here! [by] Mini Grey. 1st American ed. Knopf; distributed by Random House 2005 unp il $15.95; lib bdg $17.99
E

1. Toys—Fiction 2. Imagination—Fiction
ISBN 0-375-83191-6; 0-375-93191-0 (lib bdg)
LC 2004-4452

Traction Man, a boy's courageous action figure, has a variety of adventures with Scrubbing Brush and other objects in the house.

And "imaginative and very funny romp. . . . The angular, full-color art sweeps across the pages and perfectly animates the antics of Traction Man and his enemies." SLJ

Griessman, Annette

The fire; [by] Annette Griessman; illustrated by Leonid Gore. G.P. Putnam's Sons 2005 unp il $16.99
E

1. Fires—Fiction 2. Family life—Fiction 3. Hispanic Americans—Fiction
ISBN 0-399-24019-5   LC 2003-24449

When their house is destroyed by fire and everything is lost except a stuffed bear and a family photograph, Mama reminds Maria and her little brother, Pepito, that they still have their most important possessions.

"The story contains descriptive images. . . . Beautiful, glowing illustrations done in acrylics and pastels illuminate it. . . . This fine book has a message that could help children experiencing any kind of life-changing disaster." SLJ

Grifalconi, Ann

The village that vanished; illustrated by Kadir Nelson. Dial Bks. for Young Readers 2002 unp il $16.99
E

1. Yao (African people)—Fiction 2. Escapes—Fiction 3. Slave trade—Fiction 4. Southern Africa—Fiction
ISBN 0-8037-2623-6   LC 00-38416

In southeastern Africa, a young Yao girl and her mother find a way for their fellow villagers to escape approaching slave traders

"This story celebrating resourcefulness, quick thinking, and community solidarity may inspire and empower readers. Nelson's pencil drawings enhanced with oil paints are wonderfully evocative of place, mood, posture, and expression." SLJ

Griffith, Helen V.

Grandaddy's place; pictures by James Stevenson. Greenwillow Bks. 1987 unp il pa $5.95 hardcover o.p.
E

1. Farm life—Fiction 2. Grandfathers—Fiction
ISBN 0-688-10491-6 (pa)   LC 86-19573

"Janetta accompanies her mother to the country to meet her grandfather for the first time. . . . This vacation in the country seems doomed until her grandfather tells of some absolutely incredible incidents that happened to him on this very farm. . . . Imaginative, tall-tale humor abounds throughout the smooth, well-paced text. . . . Watercolor illustrations, executed in warm pastels, lend visual clarity, exuding warmth and satisfaction." SLJ

Other titles about Janetta and her grandfather are:
Georgia music (1986)
Grandaddy and Janetta (1993)
Grandaddy's stars (1995)

Grindley, Sally

It's my school; [by] Sally Grindley; illustrations by Margaret Chamberlain. Walker & Company 2006 unp il $15.95; lib bdg $16.85   **E**

1. School stories 2. Siblings—Fiction

ISBN   978-0-8027-8086-7;   0-8027-8086-5;
978-0-8027-8087-4 (lib bdg)   LC 2005037181

Tom is not happy that his younger sister, Alice, is starting kindergarten at his school.

"The large illustrations . . . are depicted in soft pastel hues, capturing the siblings' facial expressions and the varying degress of emotion. . . . This is a new take on first-day-of-school stories, and a realistic choice to help children share their lives with a younger sibling." SLJ

Mucky Duck; illustrations by Neal Layton. Bloomsbury Pub. 2003 unp il $13.95   **E**

1. Ducks—Fiction 2. Cleanliness—Fiction

ISBN 1-58234-821-9   LC 2002-27824

Oliver and Mucky Duck, a duck who lives in the garden pond, have trouble staying clean because they love to do things like playing football and painting

"Layton's illustrations . . . are frenetic and fun. . . . Done in what appears to be a mix of watercolor, pencil, and collage, the mixed-media art carries the simple story." SLJ

Grobler, Piet

Hey, frog! Front St. 2002 unp il $15.95

          E

1. Frogs—Fiction 2. Animals—Fiction 3. Water—Fiction

ISBN 1-88691-084-7   LC 2002-70607

Originally published in Dutch

On a very hot day, the animals are roaring mad when a frog drinks up all of the water on the savannah, but each animal has an idea of how to get the water back

"The short text is nicely paced and tells a silly story that will capture young ones. But it's the uncluttered watercolor-and-ink illustrations . . . that really extend the laughs with quirky, slightly stylized depictions of animals and plants." Booklist

Little bird's ABC. Front Street 2005 unp il $8.95   **E**

1. Birds—Fiction 2. Alphabet

ISBN 1-932425-52-7

Originally published in Netherlands

As birds interact with what is going on around them, they make sounds that correspond to the letters of the alphabet.

"Elegantly impish watercolors and a soupSon of naughty humor make this one of the freshest primers in quite some time." Publ Wkly

Guarino, Deborah

Is your mama a llama? illustrated by Steven Kellogg. Scholastic 1989 unp il pa $5.99 hardcover o.p.   **E**

1. Llamas—Fiction 2. Animals—Fiction 3. Stories in rhyme

ISBN 0-590-44725-4 (pa)   LC 87-32315

Also available Board book edition and Big book edition; Spanish language edition also available

A young llama asks his friends if their mamas are llamas and finds out, in rhyme, that their mothers are other types of animals

"The lines are clean as well as exuberant, the colors well-blended as well as bright, and the compositions uncluttered as well as appealing. An ingenious page design invites choral participation, and the ending will encourage a cozy hiatus for bed/nap time." Bull Cent Child Books

Guback, Georgia

Luka's quilt. Greenwillow Bks. 1994 unp il $16.99   **E**

1. Quilts—Fiction 2. Grandmothers—Fiction 3. Hawaii—Fiction

ISBN 0-688-12154-3   LC 93-12241

When Luka's grandmother makes a traditional Hawaiian quilt for her, she and Luka disagree over the colors it should include

"Eye-catching collages of brightly painted papers, the illustrations express the characters' emotions and show a delight in the Hawaiian landscape and traditions. . . . An involving story that's all the more satisfying because the ending offers no mere emotional patch up but a real solution." Booklist

Guest, Elissa Haden

Iris and Walter; written by Elissa Haden Guest; illustrated by Christine Davenier. Harcourt 2000 43p il $14; pa $5.95   **E**

1. Country life—Fiction 2. City and town life—Fiction 3. Friendship—Fiction

ISBN 0-15-202122-1; 0-15-216442-1 (pa)

          LC 99-6242

"Gulliver books"

When Iris moves to the country, she misses the city where she formerly lived; but with the help of a new friend named Walter, she learns to adjust to her new home

"Christine Davenier's exuberant pen-and-ink drawings reveal all the delightful things Iris discovers with Walter. . . . An easy-to-read chapter book . . . just right for children ready to step up their skills." Booklist

Other titles about Iris and Walter are:

Iris and Walter and Baby Rose (2002)
Iris and Walter and Cousin Howie (2003)
Iris and Walter and the birthday party (2006)
Iris and Walter and the field trip (2005)
Iris and Walter and the substitute teacher (2004)
Iris and Walter, lost and found (2004)
Iris and Walter, the school play (2003)
Iris and Walter, the sleepover (2002)
Iris and Walter, true friends (2001)

Guilloppé, Antoine

One scary night. Milk & Cookies 2005 unp il $15.95   **E**

1. Stories without words 2. Fear—Fiction

ISBN 0-689-04636-7

"A suspenseful, wordless picture book. On a cold, dark night, a boy trudges through the snowy woods alone. A wolflike animal that appears to be stalking him sets readers' nerves on edge. When the animal finally

Guilloppé, Antoine—*Continued*

pounces, it looks as though the boy is in serious trouble. But . . . by the end, it is clear that the creature has saved the boy from a falling tree and the two are friends. The black-and-white images are stark, simple shapes with no shades of gray. Yet these sharp contrasts come together to create intricate visuals and a sense of optical illusion that keeps the story full of movement and tension. Many of the spreads are breathtaking and will have readers on the edge of their seats until the surprise happy ending." SLJ

Guy, Ginger Foglesong

Fiesta! pictures by Rene King Moreno. Greenwillow Bks. 1996 unp il $15.99　　　E
1. Parties—Fiction 2. Counting 3. Bilingual books—English-Spanish
ISBN 0-688-14331-8　　　　LC 95-35848
"Three children begin with *una canasta* (one basket) and proceed to fill it with scrumptious candies, trinkets, and toys in preparation for a Mexican fiesta. . . . A simple bilingual text provides numbers in English and Spanish. The soft-edged full-color illustrations done in pencils, pastels, and watercolors have a subtle folkloric quality." SLJ

Siesta; pictures by René King Moreno. Greenwillow Books 2005 unp il $15.99; lib bdg $16.89　　　　　　　　　　　　E
1. Color—Fiction 2. Bilingual books—English-Spanish
ISBN 0-06-056061-4; 0-06-056063-0 (lib bdg)
LC 2004-42464
A brother and sister and their teddy bear go through the house gathering items they will need for their siesta in the back yard.
This "uses a bilingual approach to reinforce an understanding of colors. . . . Highlighted text in the appropriate hue reinforces the color concept, as do Moreno's soft, appealing illustrations." Booklist

Haas, Irene

Bess and Bella; by Irene Haas. 1st ed. Margaret K. McElderry Books 2006 unp il $14.95
E
1. Birds—Fiction 2. Friendship—Fiction
ISBN 1-4169-0013-6　　　　LC 2004-12732
Bess is feeling terribly lonely when out of the sky tumbles a bird named Bella, her tiny suitcases packed with all manner of wonderful things.
"The venerable author-artist constructs another dreamlike tale from signature ingredients—chiffonlike watercolors, whimsically clothed animals, and themes of fantastical transformation." Booklist

Haas, Jessie

Hurry! pictures by Jos. A. Smith. Greenwillow Bks. 2000 unp il $15.95　　　　E
1. Grandparents—Fiction 2. Farm life—Fiction
ISBN 0-688-16889-2　　　　LC 99-30706
Nora helps her grandparents get the hay in before a rainstorm ruins the crop
"The text is filled with rich, sensory descriptions and brief, lyrical sentences that convey the smells, sounds, and rhythms of the task." Booklist

Scamper and the horse show; pictures by Margot Apple. Greenwillow Books 2004 unp il $14.99; lib bdg $15.89　　　　E
1. Horses—Fiction 2. Horsemanship—Fiction
ISBN 0-06-001338-9; 0-06-001339-7 (lib bdg)
LC 2003-49068
Molly and her sister hope that their horse Scamper's costume will win a blue ribbon in the horse show, but some unexpected rainfall changes the situation. Includes information on horse shows.
"This charming story presents an accurate and appealing look at the ambience of a local horse show. . . . The eye-pleasing, colored-pencil drawings show appealing young equestrians and their mounts in various shapes and sizes. . . . An excellent choice for young horse lovers." SLJ

Sugaring; pictures by Jos. A. Smith. Greenwillow Bks. 1996 unp il $15.99　　　　E
1. Maple sugar—Fiction 2. Grandfathers—Fiction
3. Horses—Fiction
ISBN 0-688-14200-1　　　　LC 95-38139
Nora wants to find a way to give the horses a special treat for helping her grandfather and her gather sap to make maple syrup
"The realistic watercolor illustrations effectively capture the scenes; color and texture are skillfully used to depict the cold, hard job of gathering the sap and the hot steamy atmosphere of the sugar house." SLJ

Hader, Berta

The big snow; by Berta and Elmer Hader. Macmillan 1948 unp il $17.95; pa $6.95
E
1. Animals—Fiction 2. Winter—Fiction
ISBN 0-02-737910-8; 0-02-043300-X (pa)
Awarded the Caldecott Medal, 1949
This book shows "the birds and animals which come for the food put out by an old couple after a big snow." Hodges. Books for Elem Sch Libr

Hall, Bruce Edward

Henry and the kite dragon; illustrated by William Low. Philomel Books 2004 unp il $15.99
E
1. Kites—Fiction 2. Chinese Americans—Fiction
3. Italian Americans—Fiction 4. New York (N.Y.)—Fiction
ISBN 0-399-23727-5　　　　LC 2003-16381
In New York City in the 1920s, the children from Chinatown go after the children from Little Italy for throwing rocks at the beautiful kites Grandfather Chin makes, not realizing that they have a reason for doing so.
The author "tells an engaging story about a vibrant community, which is beautifully captured in Low's detailed, dramatic paintings." Booklist

Hall, Donald

Ox-cart man; pictures by Barbara Cooney. Viking 1979 unp il $16.99; pa $6.99　　　E
1. New England—Fiction
ISBN 0-670-53328-9; 0-14-050441-9 (pa)
LC 79-14466

Hall, Donald—*Continued*

Awarded the Caldecott Medal, 1980

"It is fall and a farmer loads a cart with the year's produce, journeys to market, sells, buys, and returns to his family to begin the year's work anew. The journey, and the ensuing year, unfold at a stately pace against the rich 19th-century New England backdrop alive with the subtly changing colors and activities of the succeeding seasons." SLJ

"The stunning combination of text and illustrations, suggesting early American paintings on wood, depict the countryside through which [the farmer] travels, the jostle of the marketplace, and the homely warmth of family life." Horn Book

Hall, Zoe

Fall leaves fall! illustrated by Shari Halpern. Scholastic Press 2000 unp il $15.95　　E
1. Leaves—Fiction 2. Autumn—Fiction
ISBN 0-590-10079-3　　LC 98-26536
When fall comes, two brothers enjoy catching the falling leaves, stomping on them, kicking them, jumping in piles of them, and using them to make pictures. Includes a description of how leaves change through the year

"Exceptionally well-crafted paper-collage illustrations capture the children's easy exuberance while the simply written text is nicely paced for reading aloud." SLJ

Hamanaka, Sheila

All the colors of the earth. Morrow Junior Bks. 1994 unp il $16.99; lib bdg $17.89; pa $5.99
　　E
ISBN 0-688-11131-9; 0-688-11132-7 (lib bdg); 0-688-17062-5 (pa)　　LC 93-27118
Reveals in verse that despite outward differences children everywhere are essentially the same and all are lovable

"A poetic picture book and an exemplary work of art. . . . Hamanaka's oil paintings are all double-page spreads filled with the colors of earth, sky, and water, and the texture of the artist's canvas shines through. The text is arranged in undulant waves across each painting." SLJ

Grandparents song. HarperCollins Pubs. 2003 unp il $15.99; lib bdg $16.89　　E
1. Grandparents—Fiction 2. Racially mixed people—Fiction 3. Stories in rhyme
ISBN 0-688-17852-9; 0-688-17853-7 (lib bdg)
　　LC 00-47952
In verse "a young girl recounts the roots of her family tree. Fondly and respectfully, she describes her grandparents—one American Indian, one Irish, one Mexican, and one a descendent of African slaves. Beautifully rendered in calligraphy, the text is clean, simple, and lilting. . . . Filled with magnificent texture, Hamanaka's oil paintings are substantial and striking." SLJ

Hamilton, Virginia

Wee Winnie Witch's Skinny; an original African American scare tale; engravings by Barry Moser. Blue Sky Press 2004 unp il $16.95
　　E
1. Witches—Fiction 2. African Americans—Fiction
ISBN 0-590-28880-6　　LC 00-67999
James Lee and Uncle Big Anthony become victims of Wee Winnie Witch, who takes them on a ride up into the sky, but Mama Granny saves them.

This "is a wonderful horror story that draws on traditional beliefs about witches. . . . Moser's framed, colored wood engravings do a great job of bringing the wild, shivery adventure close to home, their black backgrounds and strong lines lit with garish Halloween images in green and red." Booklist

Hamm, Mia

Winners never quit! HarperCollins 2004 unp il $15.99; lib bdg $16.89　　E
1. Soccer
ISBN 0-06-074050-7; 0-06-074051-5 (lib bdg)
"Mia's favorite sport is soccer but she hates losing. In fact, she dislikes it so much that she quits in the middle of a game. . . . Mia learns quickly that there will be times when she will score a goal and those when she will not, but playing the game is the most fun of all. Bright, energetic cartoons depict the child's ups and downs." SLJ

Hanson, Mary Elizabeth

The difference between babies & cookies; [by] Mary Hanson; illustrated by Debbie Tilley. Silver Whistle/Harcourt 2002 unp il $16　　E
1. Infants—Fiction
ISBN 0-15-202406-9　　LC 00-8447
"A new big sister tries to make sense of her mother's teachings about babies. For example, babies are indeed as sweet as cookies, but they can't be dipped in milk; and despite their rosy cheeks, you can't give babies to teachers." Horn Book Guide

"The watercolor illustrations help set a light and breezy tone. A loose black line defines open-faced, cheerful characters. . . . Everything feels sunny and friendly, with plenty of innocent humor." SLJ

Harper, Dan

Sit, Truman! illustrated by Cara Moser & Barry Moser. Harcourt 2001 unp il $16　　E
1. Dogs—Fiction
ISBN 0-15-202616-9　　LC 00-9298
A busy day in the life of Truman the big dog includes walks, play time, and a little dog named Oscar

"Harper's minimal text and the Mosers' watercolor paintings are perfectly paired. Slobbery canine Truman is both exasperating and lovable." SLJ

Telling time with Big Mama Cat; illustrated by Barry Moser and Cara Moser. Harcourt Brace & Co. 1998 unp il $15　　E
1. Time—Fiction 2. Clocks and watches—Fiction 3. Cats—Fiction
ISBN 0-15-201738-0　　LC 97-18952

Harper, Dan—*Continued*

A cat describes her activities at various times throughout the day from morning to night. Features a clock with movable hands

"The simple, consistent arrangement of text and pictures on each page gently frames the humor and perfectly captures the everyday dramas of naptime and tea parties." SLJ

Harrington, Janice N.

Going north; pictures by Jerome Lagarrigue. Farrar, Straus and Giroux 2004 unp il $16

E

1. African Americans—Fiction 2. Moving—Fiction
ISBN 0-374-32681-9

A young African American girl and her family leave their home in Alabama and head for Lincoln, Nebraska, where they hope to escape segregation and find a better life.

"Lagarrigue's paintings are subdued but powerful and well-suited to Harrington's somber, poetic narrative voice." SLJ

Harris, Robie H.

Don't forget to come back! illustrated by Harry Bliss. Candlewick Press 2004 unp il $15.99

E

1. Babysitters—Fiction
ISBN 0-7636-1782-2   LC 2002-74169

A newly illustrated edition of the title first published 1978 by Knopf

When her parents go out for the evening, a little girl threatens to run off to Alaska but has a good time with the babysitter instead.

"Harris' playful, rhythmic text . . . skillfully conveys a child's attempt to mask fear and discomfort with blustering protests, and Bliss' winning ink-and-watercolor drawings add clever humor and spot-on details from a child's viewpoint." Booklist

Goodbye, Mousie; illustrated by Jan Ormerod. Margaret K. McElderry Bks. 2001 unp il $16

E

1. Death—Fiction 2. Mice—Fiction
ISBN 0-689-83217-6   LC 99-89167

A boy grieves for his dead pet Mousie, helps to bury him, and begins to come to terms with his loss

"Ormerod's honest pictures, black-pencil line drawings with watercolor washes on buff-colored paper, capture the emotions of the situation and chronicle the boy's move from disbelief to acceptance. . . . This covers all the bases of a frequently asked-for subject." Booklist

Happy birth day! illustrated by Michael Emberley. Candlewick Press 1996 unp il $17.99; pa $6.99

E

1. Childbirth—Fiction 2. Infants—Fiction
ISBN 1-56402-424-5; 0-763609-4-9 (pa)
LC 95-34547

A mother tells her child about its first day of life from the moment of birth through the end of the birth day

"The description of the infant's first sounds and actions is gentle and poetic. Emberley's illustrations in pencil and pastels fill the oversized pages with soft-focused, cozy colors and true-to-life detail." SLJ

I am not going to school today; illustrated by Jan Ormerod. Margaret K. McElderry Bks. 2003 unp il $16.95

E

1. School stories
ISBN 0-689-83913-8   LC 00-48053

A little boy decides to skip his very first day of school, because on the first day one doesn't know anything, but on the second, one knows everything

"Children with first-day jitters will take comfort in this story. . . . Ormerod's colorful, expressive illustrations capture a child's anxiety and the warmth of family with equal success." Booklist

Hartfield, Claire

Me and Uncle Romie; a story inspired by the life and art of Romare Bearden; paintings by Jerome Lagarrigue. Dial Bks. for Young Readers 2002 unp il $16.99

E

1. Bearden, Romare, 1914-1988—Fiction 2. Artists—Fiction 3. Uncles—Fiction 4. African Americans—Fiction
ISBN 0-8037-2520-5   LC 99-41390

A boy from North Carolina spends the summer in New York City visiting the neighborhood of Harlem, where his uncle, collage artist Romare Bearden, grew up. Includes a biographical sketch of Bearden and instructions on making a story collage

This is a "vibrant, evocative picture book. . . . Lagarrigue's lush, acrylic illustrations with collage elements recall the tones, brush strokes, and mixture of media that saturate Bearden's groundbreaking work." SLJ

Hartman, Bob

The wolf who cried boy. Putnam 2001 unp il $16.99

E

1. Wolves—Fiction
ISBN 0-399-23578-7   LC 2001-19604

Little Wolf is tired of eating lamburgers and sloppy does, but when he tricks his parents into thinking there is a boy in the woods, they could all miss a chance for a real feast

"Hartman's spare storytelling style is enhanced by Raglin's textured pen and colored-ink illustrations that are packed with nifty details." SLJ

Hartman, Gail

As the crow flies; a first book of maps; illustrated by Harvey Stevenson. Bradbury Press 1991 32p il map pa $6.99 hardcover o.p.

E

1. Animals—Fiction 2. Maps—Fiction
ISBN 0-689-71762-8 (pa)   LC 90-33982

"Simple words and pictures describe the travels of an eagle, a rabbit, a crow, a police horse, a seagull, and the moon. A pictorial map for each animal is given; all maps are joined in 'The Big Map' at the end." SLJ

"Stevenson's bright pen-and-ink with watercolor illustrations contain many interesting details, yet never seem overcluttered. . . . This is an attractive picture book that should find a niche in story hours and classrooms." Booklist

Harvey, Amanda

Dog eared. Doubleday Bks. for Young Readers 2002 unp il $17.99   **E**

1. Dogs—Fiction

ISBN 0-385-72911-1   LC 00-59033

Self-conscious about its ears, a dog named Otis tries doing a number of things to make them look better

"Harvey tells her story simply, and her illustrations are filled with humor and poignancy." Booklist

Other titles about Otis the dog are:

Dog days (2003)

Dog gone (2004)

Haseley, Dennis

The invisible moose; [by] Dennis Haseley; illustrated by Steven Kellogg. Dial Books for Young Readers 2005 unp il $16.99   **E**

1. Moose—Fiction 2. New York (N.Y.)—Fiction

ISBN 0-8037-2892-1   LC 2004-23102

When his beloved is captured by Steel McSteal, a shy moose summons his courage and, with the help of an invisibility potion, sets off to rescue her in New York City.

"The text and the watercolor illustrations are loaded with humorous touches and quirky details that will keep readers entertained for long periods." SLJ

Hassett, John

A mouse in the house; [by] John and Ann Hassett. Houghton Mifflin 2004 32p il $15

                    E

1. Animals—Fiction

ISBN 0-618-35317-8   LC 2003-14784

"Walter Lorraine books"

When Nana Quimby is upset by the mouse in the house, Father gets an owl, which also upsets Nana, so Mother gets a dog . . . until the family ends up with an elephant in the house

"The lighthearted illustrations increase the silliness and enjoyment of the story. Packed with amusing details." SLJ

Hautzig, Deborah

The Nutcracker ballet; retold by Deborah Hautzig; illustrated by Carolyn Ewing. Random House 2003 48p il lib bdg $11.99; pa $3.99

                    E

1. Fairy tales

ISBN 0-679-92385-3 (lib bdg); 0-679-82385-9 (pa)

                    LC 2002-13568

"Step into reading"

A reissue of the title first published 1992

A little girl helps break the spell on her toy nutcracker and watches him change into a handsome prince.

"Hautzig retells the story of 'The Nutcracker', concentrating on the narrative content of the first act. . . . The simple vocabulary makes this edition accessible to beginning readers; bright watercolor artwork adds an immediate appeal." Booklist

Havill, Juanita

Jamaica's find; illustrations by Anne Sibley O'Brien. Houghton Mifflin 1986 32p il $16; pa $5.95   **E**

1. African Americans—Fiction 2. Toys—Fiction

ISBN 0-395-39376-0; 0-395-45357-7 (pa)

                    LC 85-14542

Also available Spanish language edition

"When Jamaica discovers a raggedy stuffed dog at the park, she decides to take it home. Her family's reaction is lukewarm at best . . . and she broods over her mother's suggestion that she return it to the park desk. Reluctantly, she does. Just after that, Jamaica encounters a little girl named Kristin, who has come to search for her missing toy dog." Booklist

"This is a pleasant picture book with warm, expressive pictures and an appealing story line that encourages values clarification." Interracial Books Child Bull

Other titles about Jamaica are:

Brianna, Jamaica, and the Dance of Spring (2002)

Jamaica and Brianna (1993)

Jamaica and the substitute teacher (1999)

Jamaica tag-along (1989)

Jamaica's blue marker (1995)

Hayes, Joe

A spoon for every bite; illustrated by Rebecca Leer. Orchard Bks. 1996 unp il lib bdg $17.99

                    E

1. Wealth—Fiction 2. Hispanic Americans—Fiction

ISBN 0-531-08799-9   LC 95-22019

"Hayes combines two themes from Southwestern Hispanic tradition—rich and poor *compadres*, and the tortilla as an eating utensil—into a humorous tale in which a poor couple teaches their boastful neighbor a lesson. . . . Leer complements the lively text with pastel illustrations in rich and lustrous tones reminiscent of oil paintings." Bull Cent Child Books

Hays, Anna Jane

Ready, set, preschool! illustrated by True Kelley. Knopf 2005 30p il $16.95   **E**

1. School stories

ISBN 0-375-82519-3

A collection of simple stories, poems, and picture games designed to prepare children for preschool.

"With lots of cheerfully illustrated rhymes, stories, and interactive games, this big picture book is an excellent title to prepare kids for preschool." Booklist

Hazen, Barbara Shook

Digby; story by Barbara Shook Hazen; pictures by Barbara J. Phillips-Duke. HarperCollins Pubs. 1996 32p il $14.95; lib bdg $15.89; pa $4.99

                    E

1. Dogs—Fiction 2. Old age—Fiction

ISBN 0-06-026253-2; 0-06-026254-0 (lib bdg); 0-06-444239-X (pa)   LC 95-1689

"An I can read book"

"A boy wants the family dog to play ball, but his big sister explains that Digby is too old now to run and catch. . . . The story of aging and of time passing is told

Hazen, Barbara Shook—*Continued*

in very simple conversation . . . and the bright contemporary pictures show the bond between the African American brother and sister and their beloved pet." Booklist

Katie's wish; illustrated by Emily Arnold McCully. Dial Bks. for Young Readers 2003 unp il $15.99   E
  1.   Ireland—Fiction   2.   Famines—Fiction
  3. Immigrants—Fiction
  ISBN 0-8037-2478-0   LC 2001-28254

Soon after Katie wishes for her potatoes to disappear during dinner, a potato famine ravages her native Ireland, forcing her to leave for America

"The beautiful impressionistic watercolor paintings set the sturdy child against the background of the times. . . . In words and pictures, the narrative shows the hardship and the hope." Booklist

Heap, Sue

What shall we play? Candlewick Press 2002 unp il $13.99   E
  1. Play—Fiction
  ISBN 0-7636-1685-0   LC 2001-29511

Lily May and her friends have fun pretending to be trees, cars, cats, Jell-O, and fairies

"Heap's simple text effectively captures the rhythm of young children's imaginative play. Mixed-media illustrations mimic child-created art, combining paper collage (including shiny paper for fairy wings) with crayon scribbles." Bull Cent Child Books

Hearne, Betsy Gould

Seven brave women; illustrated by Bethanne Andersen. Greenwillow Bks. 1997 unp il $15.99; lib bdg $16.89; pa $6.99   E
  1.   Genealogy—Fiction   2.   Courage—Fiction
  3. Women—Fiction
  ISBN 0-688-14502-7; 0-688-14503-5 (lib bdg);
  0-060-79921-8 (pa)   LC 96-10414

"In this picture book divided into eight brief chapters, a young girl narrates the history of seven generations of brave women in her family, ending with her resolve to make history in her own way." Bull Cent Child Books

"Hearne's smooth writing style is suited to the succinct narrative; her carefully selected details help bring the past to life. . . . Andersen . . . has created oil paintings full of color, light, and movement." SLJ

Who's in the hall? a mystery in four chapters; by Betsy Hearne; illustrated by Christy Hale. Greenwillow Bks. 2000 29p il $15.95; lib bdg $15.89   E
  1. Apartment houses—Fiction
  ISBN 0-688-16262-2; 0-688-16262-2 (lib bdg)
                                  LC 99-42412

"Neighbors in an urban apartment building, Lizzy, Rowan, and Ryan (and their assorted sitters) cope with boredom, missing pets, and the strange disappearance of the building janitor." Bull Cent Child Books

"Betsy Hearne's dialogue is apt and funny, sparkling with rhyming repartee. . . . Christy Hale's dynamic car-

toon-style illustrations pick up the story's humor and help keep characters straight with a creative assortment of full-page art, vignettes, and frame sequences." Horn Book

Hegi, Ursula

Trudi & Pia; pictures by Giselle Potter. Atheneum Bks. for Young Readers 2003 unp il $16.95   E
  1. Dwarfs—Fiction
  ISBN 0-689-84683-5   LC 2001-55995
  "An Anne Schwartz book"

Adapted from the author's adult novel Stones from the river published 1994 by Poseidon Press

A dwarf girl goes to the circus where she meets another dwarf and realizes that she is not alone

"The story is well written and contains some dramatically effective imagery. . . . This sensitive story deals with a subject not frequently found in books for this audience. Potter's signature gouache illustrations have their usual quirky appeal and blend well with the tale." SLJ

Heide, Florence Parry

The day of Ahmed's secret; [by] Florence Parry Heide & Judith Heide Gilliland; illustrated by Ted Lewin. Lothrop, Lee & Shepard Bks. 1990 unp il pa $6.99 hardcover o.p.   E
  1. Cairo (Egypt)—Fiction
  ISBN 0-688-14023-8 (pa)   LC 90-52694

"Ahmed has monumental news to share with his family, but first he must complete the age-old duties of a butagaz boy, delivering cooking gas to customers all over Cairo. . . . Enhanced by Lewin's distinguished photorealistic watercolors, the sights, sounds, and smells of the exotic setting come to life. . . . At home at last, surrounded by his loving family, Ahmed demonstrates his newly acquired facility, proudly writing his name in Arabic." SLJ

Sami and the time of the troubles; [by] Florence Parry Heide & Judith Heide Gilliland; illustrated by Ted Lewin. Clarion Bks. 1992 unp il $16; pa $6.95   E
  1. Family life—Fiction 2. Lebanon—Fiction
  ISBN 0-395-55964-2; 0-395-72085-0 (pa)
                                  LC 91-14343

A ten-year-old Lebanese boy in Beirut goes to school, helps his mother with chores, plays with his friends, and lives with his family in a basement shelter when bombings occur and fighting begins on his street

This is "a powerful, poignant book. Heide and Gilliland's lyrically written, haunting story makes clear that war threatens not only physical existence but affects the human spirit as well. Lewin's watercolor illustrations capture contemporary Beirut with stunning clarity and drama." SLJ

Some things are scary; illustrated by Jules Feiffer. Candlewick Press 2000 unp il $15.99   E
  1. Fear
  ISBN 0-7636-1222-7   LC 00-25921

Heide, Florence Parry—*Continued*

A list of scary things includes "roller skating down hill when you haven't learned how to stop, getting hugged by somebody you don't like, and finding out your best friend has a best friend who isn't you"

"All the entries reflect the truth of childhood emotion. . . . Overall the tone is more light than dark, thanks in part to Jules Feiffer's energetic, spectacularly expressive illustrations." Horn Book

Helldorfer, Mary Claire

Hog music; by M. C. Helldorfer; illustrated by S. D. Schindler. Viking 2000 unp il $15.99
E

1. Frontier and pioneer life—Fiction 2. Voyages and travels—Fiction 3. Gifts—Fiction
ISBN 0-670-87182-6   LC 99-42059

Travelers along the National Road help make sure that the birthday gift that Lucy's great aunt has sent makes it all the way from Maryland to her family's farm in Illinois

"The period story gives a sense of nineteenth-century life—from its curious conveyances to the sense of adventure. While simplistic at times, the folk-art-like illustrations provide a homey, comfortable atmosphere." Horn Book Guide

Henderson, Kathy

Baby knows best; illustrated by Brita Granström. Little, Brown 2002 c2001 unp il $15.95
E

1. Infants—Fiction 2. Stories in rhyme
ISBN 0-316-60580-8   LC 00-107325

First published 2001 in the United Kingdom

"For this bubbling baby girl, keys are more fun than toys; newspapers more satisfying than books; a bath plug more engaging than tub toys; a birthday suit more comfortable than any clothes; and cuddles superior to stroller, bouncer, or playpen." SLJ

"The rhyming text is short and fun, and Granström's colorful watercolor illustrations get the point across." Booklist

Henkes, Kevin

Chester's way. Greenwillow Bks. 1988 unp il $15.99; lib bdg $16.89; pa $5.99   E

1. Mice—Fiction
ISBN 0-688-07607-6; 0-688-07608-4 (lib bdg); 0-688-15472-7 (pa)   LC 87-14882

The mice Chester and Wilson share the same exact way of doing things, until Lilly moves into the neighborhood and shows them that new ways can be just as good.

"Henkes' charming cartoons are drawn with pen-and-ink, washed over with cheerful watercolors. They give witty expressions to his characters." SLJ

Chrysanthemum. Greenwillow Bks. 1991 unp il $15.95; lib bdg $16.89; pa $6.99   E

1. Personal names—Fiction 2. School stories 3. Mice—Fiction
ISBN 0-688-09699-9; 0-688-09700-6 (lib bdg); 0-688-814732-1 (pa)   LC 90-39803

Also available Spanish language edition

Chrysanthemum, a mouse, loves her name, until she starts going to school and the other children make fun of it.

"The text, precise and evocative, uses contrast and repetition to achieve rhythm and balance; the illustrations are forthright yet delicately colored, remarkable for the agility of the fine line which creates setting and characters." Horn Book

Circle dogs; illustrated by Dan Yaccarino. Greenwillow Bks. 1998 unp il $16.99; lib bdg $14.89; pa $6.99   E

1. Dogs—Fiction 2. Shape—Fiction
ISBN 0-688-15446-8; 0-688-15447-6 (lib bdg); 0-06-443757-4 (pa)   LC 97-33037

Circle dogs live in a square house with a square yard and spend a busy day eating circle snacks, digging circle holes, and sleeping.

"The text is simple, almost primer-like, with lots of onomatopoeic words. . . . The lively gouache paintings in large flat areas of color have a retro look." SLJ

Jessica. Greenwillow Bks. 1989 unp il $15.99; lib bdg $15.89; pa $5.99   E

1. Imaginary playmates—Fiction
ISBN 0-688-07829-X; 0-688-07830-3 (lib bdg); 0-688-15847-1 (pa)   LC 87-38087

"A shy preschooler insists that her friend Jessica is not imaginary—and, in the end, she's absolutely correct. Henkes' depiction of play-alone and play-together time brims with buoyant camaraderie in this upbeat story of friendship fulfilled." SLJ

Julius, the baby of the world. Greenwillow Bks. 1990 unp il $16.99; lib bdg $16.89; pa $5.99
E

1. Mice—Fiction
ISBN 0-688-08943-7; 0-688-08944-5 (lib bdg); 0-688-14388-1 (pa)   LC 88-34904

Also available Spanish language edition

Lilly, the girl mouse who debuted in Chester's way "may still be the queen of the world, but her new brother 'Julius is the baby of the world.' Suffering from a severe case of sibling-itis, she warns pregnant strangers: 'You will live to regret that bump under your dress.' While her understanding parents shower her with 'compliments and praise and niceties of all shapes and sizes,' nothing works until snooty Cousin Garland comes for a visit." Booklist

"Magically, Henkes conveys a world of expressions and a wide range of complex emotions with a mere line or two upon the engaging mousey faces of Lilly and her family. A reassuring, funny book for all young children who suffer from new-sibling syndrome." SLJ

Kitten's first full moon. Greenwillow Books 2004 unp il $15.99; lib bdg $16.89   E

1. Cats—Fiction 2. Moon—Fiction
ISBN 0-06-058828-4; 0-06-058829-2 (lib bdg)   LC 2003-12564

Also available Spanish language edition

Awarded the Caldecott Medal, 2005

When Kitten mistakes the full moon for a bowl of milk, she ends up tired, wet, and hungry trying to reach it.

Henkes, Kevin—*Continued*

"Done in a charcoal and cream-colored palette, the understated illustrations feature thick black outlines, pleasing curves, and swiftly changing expressions that are full of nuance. The rhythmic text and delightful artwork ensure storytime success." SLJ

Lilly's purple plastic purse. Greenwillow Bks. 1996 unp il $16.99; lib bdg $16.89   **E**

1. Mice—Fiction 2. School stories

ISBN 0-688-12897-1; 0-688-12898-X (lib bdg)

        LC 95-25085

"Lilly loves everything about school. . . . But most of all, she loves her teacher, Mr. Slinger. . . . The little mouse will do anything for him—until he refuses to allow her to interrupt lessons to show the class her new movie-star sunglasses, three shiny quarters, and purple plastic purse. Seething with anger, she writes a mean story about him and places it in his book bag at the end of the day. . . . Rich vocabulary and just the right amount of repetition fuse perfectly with the watercolor and black-pen illustrations. . . . Clever dialogue and other funny details will keep readers looking and laughing." SLJ

Another title about Lilly is:

Lilly's big day (2006)

Oh! words by Kevin Henkes; pictures by Laura Dronzek. Greenwillow Bks. 1999 unp il $15.99; lib bdg $14.89   **E**

1. Snow—Fiction 2. Animals—Fiction

ISBN 0-688-17053-6; 0-688-17054-4 (lib bdg)

        LC 98-51890

The morning after a snowfall finds animals and children playing.

"Imbued with a soft, fuzzy quality, the full-color acrylic illustrations evoke the haziness of falling snow, and the illustrator's choice of blue and white as dominant colors is gently soothing. A winter book that's sure to please." SLJ

Owen. Greenwillow Bks. 1993 unp il $16.99; lib bdg $16.89   **E**

1. Blankets—Fiction

ISBN 0-688-11449-0; 0-688-11450-4 (lib bdg)

        LC 92-30084

Also available Spanish language edition

A Caldecott Medal honor book, 1994

Owen's parents try to get him to give up his favorite blanket before he starts school, but when their efforts fail, they come up with a solution that makes everyone happy.

This is "imbued with Henkes's characteristically understated humor, spry text and brightly hued watercolor-and-ink pictures." Publ Wkly

Sheila Rae, the brave. Greenwillow Bks. 1987 unp il $16.99; lib bdg $16.89; pa $5.99   **E**

1. Mice—Fiction

ISBN 0-688-07155-4; 0-688-07156-2 (lib bdg); 0-688-14738-0 (pa)   LC 86-25761

"A mouse both boastful and fearless, Sheila Rae decides to go home from school by taking a new route. She walks backwards with her eyes closed, growls at dogs

and cats, climbs trees, turns new corners and crosses different streets—and ends up in the middle of unfamiliar territory." Publ Wkly

"Bouncy watercolors in spring-like colors with some pen-and-ink detailing highlight Sheila Rae's bravado in an engaging and amusing way, and Henkes provides Sheila Rae, Louise, and their school friends with highly expressive faces." SLJ

So happy! pictures by Anita Lobel. Greenwillow Books 2005 unp il $15.99; lib bdg $16.89   **E**

1. Seeds—Fiction 2. Flowers—Fiction 3. Rabbits—Fiction

ISBN 0-06-056483-0; 0-06-056484-9 (lib bdg)

"A thirsty magic seed, a curious little rabbit, and a bored young boy all experience a great change when rain finally falls." Horn Book

"Lobel's vigorous artwork, a riot of color that pays homage to Van Gogh, locates events in a sun-toasted, south-of-the-border landscape, and captures the rhythm of Henkes' splitting, braided narratives in triptychs alternating with cohesive scenes." Booklist

Wemberly worried. Greenwillow Bks. 2000 unp il lib bdg $16.89   **E**

1. School stories 2. Mice—Fiction

ISBN 0-688-17028-5   LC 99-34341

A mouse named Wemberly, who worries about everything, finds that she has a whole list of things to worry about when she faces the first day of nursery school.

The author combines "good storytelling, careful characterization, and wonderfully expressive artwork to create an entertaining and reassuring picture book that addresses a common concern." SLJ

Hennessy, B. G. (Barbara G.)

Because of you; [by] B.G. Hennessy; illustrated by Hiroe Nakata. 1st ed. Candlewick Press 2005 unp il $15.99   **E**

ISBN 0-7636-1926-4   LC 2004-45168

"'Because of you,' Hennessy writes, 'there is one more person who will grow and learn,' but also 'one more person who can teach others.' . . . In an empowering conclusion, Hennessy widens the child's sphere of influence, seeing the 'small and precious' acts at home as the first step toward world peace—an ambitious goal made less daunting by Nakata's billowy, cotton candy-hued watercolors of smiling characters exchanging gestures of help and affection." Booklist

Henson, Heather

Angel coming; written by Heather Henson; illustrated by Susan Gaber. 1st ed. Atheneum Books for Young Readers 2005 unp il $15.95   **E**

1. Appalachian region—Fiction 2. Infants—Fiction

ISBN 0-689-85531-1   LC 2003-27981

A family makes preparations, eagerly awaiting the arrival of the angel who will come up the mountain bringing a new baby.

"Both story and art evoke the beauty of the Appalachian setting. Gaber's acrylic paintings portray the char-

Henson, Heather—*Continued*
acters and their surroundings with finesse. . . . The text is unrhymed, but its cadence has the grace of speech and the meter of song. A quiet, memorable picture book." Booklist

Herman, R. A. (Ronnie Ann)
Gomer & Little Gomer; illustrated by Steve Haskamp. Dutton Children's Books 2005 unp il $14.99   E
1. Dogs—Fiction 2. Toys—Fiction
ISBN 0-525-47359-9   LC 2004-17446
When Gomer the dog takes his toy with him everywhere he goes, his friend Chi Chi makes fun of him—but only at first.
"This satisfying story is accompanied by simple cartoon illustrations in bright primary colors." SLJ

Herold, Maggie Rugg
A very important day; illustrated by Catherine Stock. Morrow Junior Bks. 1995 unp il $16.99; lib bdg $15.89   E
1. Naturalization—Fiction 2. Immigrants—Fiction
3. New York (N.Y.)—Fiction
ISBN 0-688-13065-8; 0-688-13066-6 (lib bdg)
LC 94-16647
Two-hundred nineteen people from thirty-two different countries make their way to downtown New York in a snowstorm to be sworn in as citizens of the United States
"After the first quiet, gray-tone painting . . . this book bursts forth in a riot of color and activity. . . . A glossary supplies guidance for pronouncing names, and a clear, nicely detailed overview of the process of naturalization rounds things out. Pictures and story combine to make the joy of the day contagious." Booklist

Hesse, Karen
The cats in Krasinski Square; illustrated by Wendy Watson. Scholastic Press 2004 unp il $16.95   E
1. Poland—Fiction 2. Holocaust, 1933-1945—Fiction
3. Jews—Fiction 4. Cats—Fiction
ISBN 0-439-43540-4   LC 2003-27775
Two Jewish sisters, escapees of the infamous Warsaw ghetto, devise a plan to thwart an attempt by the Gestapo to intercept food bound for starving people behind the dark Wall.
"In luminous free verse [this] book tells a powerful story. . . . In bold black lines and washes of smoky gray and ochre, Watson's arresting images echo the pared-down language as well as the hope that shines like glints of sunlight on Kraskinski Square." Booklist

Come on, rain! pictures by Jon J. Muth. Scholastic Press 1999 unp il $15.95   E
1. Rain—Fiction 2. Summer—Fiction
ISBN 0-590-33125-6   LC 98-11575
A young girl eagerly awaits a coming rainstorm to bring relief from the oppressive summer heat
"Beautifully drafted watercolor paintings illustrate the lyrical text, creating a wonderful sense of atmosphere." Horn Book Guide

Hest, Amy
The Friday nights of Nana; illustrated by Claire A. Nivola. Candlewick Press 2001 unp il $15.99   E
1. Sabbath—Fiction 2. Grandmothers—Fiction
3. Jews—Fiction
ISBN 0-7636-0658-8   LC 00-39784
Jennie helps her grandmother prepare for a family Sabbath celebration
"The softly shaded watercolor and pen-and-ink pictures are lit with touches of jewel-bright color. . . . The words and pictures are quiet, yet precise and sustaining." Booklist

Guess who, Baby Duck! illustrated by Jill Barton. Candlewick 2004 unp il $15.99   E
1. Ducks—Fiction 2. Grandfathers—Fiction
ISBN 0-7636-1981-7
"Baby Duck has a cold and Grampa comes to visit, bringing a 'cheering-up present,' an album of her baby photos. Together they look at pictures of her on the day she was born, after her first bath, taking her first steps, and on her first birthday. She feels better and draws a picture of Grampa kissing her cheek, which is just what he does. . . . Barton's watercolor-and-pencil art is as warm and playful as Baby Duck herself." SLJ
Other titles about Baby Duck are:
Baby Duck and the bad eyeglasses (1996)
In the rain with Baby Duck (1995)
Make the team, Baby Duck (2003)
Off to school, Baby Duck (1999)
You're the boss, Baby Duck (1997)

Kiss good night; illustrated by Anita Jeram. Candlewick Press 2001 unp il $15.99   E
1. Bears—Fiction 2. Bedtime—Fiction
ISBN 0-7636-0780-0   LC 00-41372
Even after a story, being tucked in, and warm milk, Sam the bear is not ready to go to sleep until his mother kisses him good-night
"This is an enchanting little story, with homey illustrations that add to its appeal." SLJ
Other titles about Sam the bear are:
Don't you feel well, Sam? (2002)
You can do it, Sam (2003)

Mr. George Baker; illustrated by Jon J. Muth. Candlewick Press 2004 unp il $16.99   E
1. Reading—Fiction 2. Old age—Fiction 3. African Americans—Fiction 4. Friendship—Fiction
ISBN 0-7636-1233-2
Harry sits on the porch with Mr. George Baker, an African American who is one hundred years old but can still dance and play the drums, waiting for the school bus that will take them both to the class where they are learning to read.
This is "beautifully illustrated in subtle watercolors. Hest's understated, unhurried poetry echoes the syncopated rhythms of music. . . . Her book is a simple, sweet, moving portrait of a natural friendship between seniors and children." Booklist

The purple coat; pictures by Amy Schwartz. Four Winds Press 1986 unp il pa $5.99 hardcover o.p.   E
1. Coats—Fiction 2. Grandfathers—Fiction
ISBN 0-689-71634-6 (pa)   LC 85-29186

Hest, Amy—*Continued*

"Gabrielle has always gotten a navy coat in the fall, but, this year, to Mama's dismay, she yearns for a purple one. Grandpa, their favorite tailor, discovers a solution to please all." Child Book Rev Serv

"The artwork is full color, and the deep shades and vibrant colors (especially that purple) are arresting. The numerous details and patternings catch the eye and make for pictures that can be looked at over and over; each time the story's satisfying conclusion rings sweetly true." Booklist

When Jessie came across the sea; illustrated by P.J. Lynch. Candlewick Press 1997 unp il $16.99
                                                        E
1.   Immigrants—Fiction   2.   Jews—Fiction
3. Grandmothers—Fiction
ISBN 0-7636-0094-6   LC 97-6250

A thirteen-year-old Jewish orphan reluctantly leaves her grandmother and immigrates to New York City, where she works for three years sewing lace and earning money to bring Grandmother to the United States, too

"The elements of the plot fall neatly into place, and Hest communicates the heroine's courage and maturity convincingly and without fanfare. The subtle, emotional exposition is enriched by Lynch's . . . dramatically charged watercolor and gouache illustrations." Publ Wkly

Hester, Denia

Grandma Lena's big ol' turnip; written by Denia Hester; illustrated by Jackie Urbanovic. Albert Whitman & Co 2005 unp il $16.95   E
1. Turnips—Fiction 2. Cooking—Fiction 3. African Americans—Fiction 4. Tall tales
ISBN 0-8075-3027-1   LC 2004-18580

Grandma Lena grows a turnip so big that it takes her entire family pull it up and half of the town to eat it. Includes a note about cooking "soul food."

"Adapted from Aleksey Tolstoy's 'The Turnip,' this tale about teamwork and sharing in an extended African-American family is bubbling with warmth and Southern-style cooking. . . . Urbanovic's humorous watercolors are highlighted with charcoal detailing." SLJ

Heyward, DuBose

The country bunny and the little gold shoes; as told to Jenifer; pictures by Marjorie Flack. Houghton Mifflin 1939 unp il lib bdg $15; pa $5.95   E
1. Rabbits—Fiction 2. Easter—Fiction
ISBN 0-395-15990-3 (lib bdg); 0-395-18557-2 (pa)

This is an Easter story for young readers which grew out of a story the author has told and retold to his young daughter. It is of the little country rabbit who wanted to become one of the five Easter bunnies, and how she managed to realize her ambition

"It is really imaginative and well written. . . . The colored pictures are just right too." New Yorker

Hicks, Barbara Jean

Jitterbug jam; pictures by Alexis Deacon. 1st American ed. Farrar, Straus and Giroux 2005 c2004 unp il $16   E
1. Monsters—Fiction
ISBN 0-374-33685-7   LC 2004-46981
First published 2004 in the United Kingdom

Grandpa Boo-Dad not only believes that Bobo has seen a pink-skinned boy with orange fur on his head hiding under the bed, he knows exactly how a little monster can scare off such a horrible creature.

"Printed on luxurious, buff-colored paper, Deacon's line-and-watercolor artwork unites cleverly altered Victorian decorative elements . . . with the striking, varied design of contemporary graphic novels. . . . Hicks' folksy, slightly off-kilter language . . . keeps the sense of an exotic, alternate reality watertight." Booklist

High, Linda Oatman

Barn savers; illustrated by Ted Lewin. Boyds Mills Press 1999 unp il $15.95   E
1. Barns—Fiction
ISBN 1-56397-403-7

"Waking before dawn, a boy accompanies his father to an old barn. Their job is to save the barn from the bulldozers, taking it apart board by board so that the parts can be sold. . . . The illustrations, whether moonlit or washed by brilliant sunshine, reflect the dignity of the plain-spoken, first-person text." Booklist

The girl on the high-diving horse; illustrated by Ted Lewin. Philomel Bks. 2003 unp il $16.99
                                                        E
1. Stunt performers—Fiction
ISBN 0-399-23649-X   LC 2001-36441

Eight-year-old Ivy Cordelia spends the summer of 1936 in Atlantic City with her photographer father, and dreams of being the girl who perches on a horse as it dives into a tank of water

"High tells her warm, nostalgic story in musical, well-paced language filled with dialogue. . . . Lewin captures the sunny chaos of the boardwalk in busy, taffy-colored watercolor paintings." Booklist

Hill, Susan

Ruby bakes a cake; pictures by Margie Moore. HarperCollins 2004 28p il $15.99; lib bdg $16.89
                                                        E
1. Animals—Fiction 2. Raccoons—Fiction
ISBN 0-06-008975-X; 0-06-008976-8 (lib bdg)
                                      LC 2002-12740

"An I can read book"

Ruby the "raccoon asks her friends, 'What does it take to bake a cake?' She throws everything they suggest into the mix, including carrots, worms, flies, snails, and nuts. She bakes the terrible-smelling concoction, and when the friends sit down, they try their best to come up with nice things to say. Easy vocabulary and repetition make this a good choice for beginning readers, and the softly rendered pastel illustrations provide good picture clues." SLJ

Another title about Ruby is:
Ruby paints a picture (2005)

Hill, Susanna Leonard

Punxsutawney Phyllis; by Susanna Leonard Hill ; illustrated by Jeffrey Ebbeler. 1st ed. Holiday House 2005 unp il $16.95   E

1. Groundhog Day—Fiction 2. Marmots—Fiction 3. Sex role—Fiction

ISBN 0-8234-1872-3   LC 2003-67641

Although she can predict the weather much better than the boys in her family, no one thinks that Phyllis the groundhog has a chance of replacing the aging Punxsutawney Phil when Groundhog Day's official groundhog retires.

"Details about the origins of Groundhog Day and Punxsutawney Phil are appended. Ebbeler's full-bleed acrylic illustrations show an exuberant Phyllis skipping through a brook, sunbathing, and munching on berries." SLJ

Hills, Tad

Duck & Goose; written and illustrated by Tad Hills. 1st ed. Schwartz & Wade Books 2006 unp il $14.95   E

1. Ducks—Fiction 2. Geese—Fiction

ISBN 0-375-83611-X   LC 2005010849

Duck and Goose learn to work together to take care of a ball, which they think is an egg.

"While the narrative is fairly straightforward and has touches of childlike humor throughout, it's the bright and colorful artwork that will attract youngsters' attention. The cartoon-style oil paintings set against soft-focus, almost impressionistic backgrounds keep Duck and Goose center stage, and their expressions are priceless." SLJ

Himmelman, John

Frog in a bog. Charlesbridge 2004 unp il $15.95; pa $6.95   E

1. Marshes—Fiction

ISBN 1-57091-517-2; 1-57091-518-0 (pa)
LC 2003-3737

"Himmelman leads children through natural events that occur on a typical day in a bog, beginning with a frog hopping into some moss. . . . Throughout, readers are introduced to plant, insect, and animal names that may not be commonly known and the idea that some events trigger others. Some classification lessons are included at the end of the book. The watercolor illustrations are definitely a draw: the effect is soft and delicate. Detail is beautifully rendered. . . . This book will have broad appeal." SLJ

Includes bibliographical references

Hindley, Judy

Baby talk; a book of first words and phrases; illustrated by Brita Granström. Candlewick Press 2006 unp il $15.99   E

1. Infants—Fiction 2. Stories in rhyme

ISBN 0-7636-2971-5

Rhyming text describes the the activities in a baby's day and the words he says while going to the playground, eating dinner, and taking a bath.

"Hindley's unfussy rhyme offers on-target opportunities for concept development: low, high, bye, out. Granström's festive gouache-and-pencil cartoons shine." SLJ

Do like a duck does! illustrated by Ivan Bates. Candlewick Press 2002 unp il $14.99   E

1. Ducks—Fiction 2. Foxes—Fiction 3. Stories in rhyme

ISBN 0-7636-1668-0   LC 2001-25681

By challenging a hairy stranger to imitate the behavior of herself and her ducklings, a mother duck proves that he is a fox and not a duck

Hindley's "tight, percussive rhymes give the story a drumbeat momentum as the climax nears. Bates's . . . watercolors possess a sunlit, translucent grace, yet he still reaps plenty of comedy from his characterizations." Publ Wkly

Eyes, nose, fingers and toes; a first book about you; illustrated by Brita Granström. Candlewick Press 1999 unp il $15.99   E

1. Stories in rhyme

ISBN 0-7636-0440-2   LC 98-23597

A group of toddlers demonstrate all the fun things that they can do with their eyes, ears, mouths, hands, legs, feet—and everything in between

"With an exuberant rhyme and cheerful art . . . this should be an immediate hit both at story hours and on the home front." Booklist

Hines, Anna Grossnickle

Daddy makes the best spaghetti. Clarion Bks. 1986 unp il pa $5.95 hardcover o.p.   E

1. Father-son relationship—Fiction

ISBN 0-89919-794-9 (pa)   LC 85-13993

Also available Board book edition

"Corey and his father enjoy a close relationship that is aptly demonstrated in picture and story. He teases Corey and they spend time together doing things such as shopping for groceries and making a pot of spaghetti or being silly at bath time and getting ready for bed. Hines' simple but warm pencil drawings play out the scenes by capitalizing on the incidents described in the text; the strong sense of family (Mother is here too) is evident." Booklist

My grandma is coming to town; illustrated by Melissa Sweet. Candlewick Press 2003 unp il $13.99   E

1. Grandmothers—Fiction

ISBN 0-7636-1237-5   LC 00-49374

Albert and his grandma have a special long-distance relationship, but when she comes to visit, it takes him a little while to overcome his shyness

"Sweet's gentle, childlike illustrations, rendered in acrylic and colored pencil, do a great job of conveying the story from Albert's egocentric point of view, and Albert's first-person telling, as well as the actions of grown-ups, will really strike a chord with kids." Booklist

Ho, Minfong

Hush! a Thai lullaby; pictures by Holly Meade. Orchard Bks. 1996 unp il pa $6.99 hardcover o.p.   E

1. Thailand—Fiction 2. Lullabies

ISBN 0-531-07166-9 (pa)   LC 95-23251

A Caldecott Medal honor book, 1997

Ho, Minfong—*Continued*

"A mother goes to each animal, from lizard to water buffalo to elephant, trying to quiet noises that might wake her child. When the animals are silenced and the mother finally falls asleep, the baby lies awake, with wide eyes and a smile. Ho's rhythmic text is fine for reading aloud. . . . The setting, apparently a remote Thai village, is gently evoked in cut paper and ink pictures that are bold enough to be used with groups. . . . The comforting earth tones suit the quiet nature of the story." Booklist

Peek! a Thai hide-and-seek; illustrated by Holly Meade. Candlewick Press 2004 unp il $16.99
E
1. Play—Fiction 2. Thailand—Fiction 3. Stories in rhyme
ISBN 0-7636-2041-6 LC 2003-55835
A father and daughter play hide-and-seek in the midst of the animals near their house in Thailand
"From the rhymed verses and onomatopoeia to the nearly hidden toddler in each spread, this story is brimming with child appeal. Done in watercolor and cut-paper collage, the exuberant illustrations convey the energy of the high jinks." SLJ

Hoban, Lillian

Arthur's Christmas cookies; words and pictures by Lillian Hoban. Harper & Row 1972 63p il lib bdg $16.89; pa $3.99
E
1. Chimpanzees—Fiction 2. Christmas—Fiction
ISBN 0-06-022368-5 (lib bdg); 0-06-444055-9 (pa)
"An I can read book"
When Arthur decides to make Christmas cookies for his parents, a "disastrous mistake in the ingredients makes the cookies inedible but the story ends happily when Arthur turns them into holiday decorations." Publ Wkly
The characters are chimpanzees but "are endearingly like human children. . . . The Christmas setting is appealing, the plot has problem, conflict, and solution yet is not too complex for the beginning independent reader, and the simplicity and humor make the book an appropriate one for reading aloud to preschool children also." Bull Cent Child Books
Other titles about Arthur are:
Arthur's back to school day (1996)
Arthur's birthday party (1999)
Arthur's camp-out (1993)
Arthur's funny money (1981)
Arthur's great big valentine (1989)
Arthur's Halloween costume (1984)
Arthur's Honey Bear (1974)
Arthur's loose tooth (1985)
Arthur's pen pal (1976)
Arthur's prize reader (1978)

Silly Tilly's Thanksgiving dinner; story and pictures by Lillian Hoban. Harper & Row 1990 63p il lib bdg $15.89; pa $3.99
E
1. Thanksgiving Day—Fiction 2. Animals—Fiction
ISBN 0-06-022423-1 (lib bdg); 0-06-444154-7 (pa)
LC 89-29287
"An I can read book"

Forgetful Silly Tilly Mole nearly succeeds in ruining her Thanksgiving dinner, but her animal friends come to the rescue with tasty treats
"Watercolors in vibrant autumn hues accentuate this comedy of errors with quirky characterizations and fine brushwork." Booklist
Other titles about Silly Tilly are:
Silly Tilly and the Easter Bunny (1987)
Silly Tilly's valentine (1998)

Hoban, Russell

Bedtime for Frances; pictures by Garth Williams. HarperCollins Pubs. 1995 c1960 31p il $16.99; lib bdg $15.89; pa $5.99
E
1. Badgers—Fiction 2. Bedtime—Fiction
ISBN 0-06-027106-X; 0-06-027107-8 (lib bdg); 0-06-443451-6 (pa) LC 94-43809
Also available Spanish language edition
A reissue of the title first published 1960
"A little badger with a lively imagination comes up with one scheme after another to put off going to sleep but father badger proves himself as smart as his daughter." Bookmark
"The soft humorous pictures of these lovable animals in human predicaments are delightful." Horn Book
Other titles about Frances are:
A baby sister for Frances (1964)
A bargain for Frances (1970)
Best friends for Frances (1969)
A birthday for Frances (1968)
Bread and jam for Frances (1964)

Hoban, Tana

26 letters and 99 cents. Greenwillow Bks. 1987 unp il $15.99; lib bdg $16.89; pa $5.99
E
1. Alphabet 2. Counting 3. Coins
ISBN 0-688-06361-6; 0-688-06362-4 (lib bdg); 0-688-14389-X (pa) LC 86-11993
This concept book "is really two books in one. *26 Letters* is a delightful ABC handbook. Each page shows two letters (in both upper- and lowercase) paired with objects from airplane to zipper. Turning the book around reveals the even more creative *99 Cents*. Here Hoban clearly shows youngsters how to count by pairing photos of numbers with pennies, nickels, dimes and quarters in a variety of combinations. The book counts ones from 1¢ to 30¢, by fives from 30¢ to 50¢, by tens from 50¢ to 90¢, culminating in 99¢. . . . An extremely inventive approach that will be hailed by parents, teachers and librarians." Publ Wkly

Black on white. Greenwillow Bks. 1993 unp il $5.99
E
ISBN 0-688-11918-2 LC 92-18897
Black illustrations against a white background depict such objects as an elephant, butterfly, and leaf
This board book features "the stunning, sophisticated photography of Tana Hoban. . . . Simply the best for babies." Horn Book Guide

A children's zoo. Greenwillow Bks. 1985 unp il $16.99
E
1. Animals
ISBN 0-688-05202-9 LC 84-25318

Hoban, Tana—*Continued*

This is a photographic "portfolio of zoo denizens. . . . Each species is matted with a narrow white line, framed in black, and placed opposite a black page against which . . . white sans serif letters list three of that species' characteristics as well as its name." Horn Book

"For the most part, the photographs are standard zoo fare, but a few are truly different and amusing." SLJ

Includes glossary

Colors everywhere. Greenwillow Bks. 1995 unp il $16.99; lib bdg $17.89   **E**
1. Color
ISBN 0-688-12762-2; 0-688-12763-0 (lib bdg)
    LC 93-24847

"On each page of this wordless picture book is a color photograph accompanied by a bar graph that displays the spectrum of colors found in the photo." Booklist

"Very young children will enjoy naming the pictured objects, while older readers will be drawn into exploring the colors' varying tones. A book children will come back to over and over." Horn Book

Dots, spots, speckles, and stripes. Greenwillow Bks. 1987 unp il $16   **E**
ISBN 0-688-06862-6   LC 86-22919

Photographs show dots, spots, speckles, and stripes as found on clothing, flowers, faces, animals, and other places

"Not only are the photos in this title technically superb, but the composition and the subjects are imaginative yet clearly identifiable. . . . Going beyond a concept book on patterns, *Dots, Spots, Speckles, and Stripes* becomes a thought-provoking photo essay that can be appreciated by older children." Horn Book

Exactly the opposite. Greenwillow Bks. 1990 unp il $16.99; lib bdg $15.89; pa $5.99
    E
1. English language—Synonyms and antonyms
ISBN 0-688-08861-9; 0-688-08862-7 (lib bdg); 0-688-15473-5 (pa)   LC 89-27227

"Using a variety of people, animals, and objects found in outdoor settings of both the city and the country, [the author] introduces and expands on the concept of opposites in this wordless photographic book. The photographs are clear, bright, and enticing. Pairs of opposites are presented on facing pages." SLJ

Is it larger? Is it smaller? Greenwillow Bks. 1985 unp il pa $6.99 hardcover o.p.   **E**
1. Size
ISBN 0-688-15287-2 (pa)   LC 84-13719

"In each full-color photograph of the wordless picture book Hoban juxtaposes similar objects of differing size. In the simplest pictures only one kind of object is shown, such as three bright plastic sand cups in graduated sizes or three maple leaves. More complex compositions group several related items: measuring cups, bowls, and utensils; fish, shells, and pebbles in an aquarium. Still others contrast dissimilar objects that have common features. . . . In the photographs, Hoban demonstrates once again her mastery of the elements of composition, such as color, texture, and balance." Horn Book

Is it red? Is it yellow? Is it blue? an adventure in color. Greenwillow Bks. 1978 unp il lib bdg $15.99; pa $5.99   **E**
1. Color 2. Size 3. Shape
ISBN 0-688-84171-6 (lib bdg); 0-688-07034-5 (pa)
    LC 78-2549

Illustrations and brief text introduce colors and the concepts of shape and size

"The wordless book is simply designed and opens the eye to the marvelous world of color; each stark-white page contains one photograph which nearly fills it. In the bottom margin the predominant colors in the photograph are indicated by a row of corresponding circles." Horn Book

Is it rough? Is it smooth? Is it shiny? Greenwillow Bks. 1984 unp il $17.99   **E**
ISBN 0-688-03823-9   LC 83-25460

Color photographs without text introduce objects of many different textures, such as pretzels, foil, hay, mud, kitten, and bubbles

"Extraordinarily crisp, clean color photographs allow Hoban to call attention to textures." Booklist

Let's count. Greenwillow Bks. 1999 unp il $16.99; lib bdg $16.89   **E**
1. Counting
ISBN 0-688-16008-5; 0-688-16009-3 (lib bdg)
    LC 98-44739

Photographs and dots introduce the numbers one to one hundred

"Hoban brings us another dazzling picture book. . . . Her photos range from the simple—1 hen, 8 Dalmatian puppies—to the more sophisticated—6 twirling rings on the arms of a circus performer; 12 rolls of toilet paper unpacked and stored on a pantry shelf." Booklist

Look book. Greenwillow Bks. 1997 unp il $16.99   **E**
ISBN 0-688-14971-5   LC 96-46268

"Viewers first encounter a piece of an image, viewed through a small, die-cut circle on a black page. The full-color object—be it a flower, a pigeon, or a hot pretzel—is revealed with the turn of a page. Another turn of the page provides a larger view." SLJ

"Hoban presents a dazzling assortment of color photographs that celebrate the rich detail of everyday things." Booklist

Of colors and things. Greenwillow Bks. 1989 unp il pa $6.99 hardcover o.p.   **E**
1. Color
ISBN 0-688-04585-5 (pa)   LC 88-11101

Photographs of toys, food, and other common objects are grouped on each page according to color

"Hoban hits on a simple device to heighten a child's awareness, but what lifts this above the average concept book is the quality of its design and illustration." Booklist

Over, under & through, and other spatial concepts. Macmillan 1973 unp il $17   **E**
1. Vocabulary
ISBN 0-02-744820-7

In brief text and photographs, the author depicts several spatial concepts—over, under, through, on, in, around,

Hoban, Tana—*Continued*

across, between, beside, below, against, and behind

"Children who are confused by these concepts may need help understanding that many of the pictures illustrate more than one concept. However, both the photographs and the format, with the words printed large on broad yellow bands at the beginning of each section, are uncluttered and appealing." Booklist

Shadows and reflections. Greenwillow Bks. 1990 unp il $16.99   E

1. Shades and shadows
ISBN 0-688-07089-2   LC 89-30461

Photographs without text feature shadows and reflections of various objects, animals, and people

"This imaginative, wordless book of color photographs is a visual treat, offering witty and subtle sets of images for enriching the eyes of children and adults." SLJ

Shapes, shapes, shapes. Greenwillow Bks. 1986 unp il $16.99; lib bdg $16.89; pa $5.99

E

1. Shape
ISBN 0-688-05832-9; 0-688-05833-7 (lib bdg); 0-688-14740-2 (pa)   LC 85-17569

Photographs of familiar objects such as chair, barrettes, and manhole cover present a study of rounded and angular shapes

"Tana Hoban has created an excellent concept book that will encourage children to look for specific shapes in everyday urban scenes. . . . The photographs not only serve to teach shapes and colors but are works of art themselves." Appraisal

So many circles, so many squares. Greenwillow Bks. 1998 unp il $15; lib bdg $15.89   E

1. Shape
ISBN 0-688-15165-5; 0-688-15166-3 (lib bdg)
LC 97-10110

The geometric concepts of circles and squares are shown in photographs of wheels, signs, pots, and other familiar objects

"Teachers and young children will find plenty to talk about as they look at the colorful, well-composed, and clearly defined images." Booklist

White on black. Greenwillow Bks. 1993 unp il $5.99   E

ISBN 0-688-11919-0   LC 92-20092

In this board book, white illustrations against a black background depict such objects as a horse, baby bottle, and sailboat

"Hoban's compositions are so supple and her layouts so well balanced that she casts a kind of spell." Publ Wkly

Hoberman, Mary Ann

The two sillies; illustrated by Lynne Cravath. Harcourt 2000 unp il $16   E

1. Cats—Fiction 2. Mice—Fiction 3. Stories in rhyme
ISBN 0-15-202221-X   LC 98-51844

"Gulliver books"

"When Silly Lilly admires Sammy's cat and asks how to get one, he gives her step-by-step instructions that

seem to make no sense at all. . . . Short sentences use mono-syllabic words and rhyme to great effect. The brightly colored cartoon-style art adds just the right touch of exaggerated humor." Horn Book Guide

You read to me, I'll read to you; very short fairy tales to read together (in which wolves are tamed, trolls are transformed, and peas are triumphant); illustrated by Michael Emberley. Little, Brown 2004 32p il $16.95   E

1. Fairy tales
ISBN 0-316-14611-0   LC 2003-47445

"Megan Tingley books"

Contents: The three bears; The princess and the pea; Jack and the beanstalk; Little Red Riding Hood; Cinderella; The three little pigs; The little red hen and the grain of wheat; The three billy goats gruff

This is a "picture-book read-aloud with short, rhymed, illustrated scenarios for two voices. . . . The eight stories are . . . fractured fairy tales. . . . Each story ends with former enemies reading together." Booklist

"The two voices join seamlessly together to create a truly delightful reading ensemble. Emberley's humorous illustrations feature expressive characters drawn in pen, watercolor, and pastel." SLJ

Hoestlandt, Jo

Star of fear, star of hope; illustrations by Johanna Kang; translated from the French by Mark Polizzotti. Walker & Co. 1995 unp il pa $5.95 hardcover o.p.   E

1. Holocaust, 1933-1945—Fiction 2. Jews—Fiction 3. Paris (France)—Fiction
ISBN 0-8027-7588-8 (pa); 0-8027-8373-2 (hc)
LC 94-32378

Nine-year-old Helen is confused by the disappearance of her Jewish friend during the German occupation of Paris

"The pastel pictures in sepia tones are understated, with an old-fashioned, almost childlike simplicity. . . . Without being maudlin or sensational, the story brings the genocide home." Booklist

Hoff, Syd

Danny and the dinosaur; story and pictures by Syd Hoff. HarperFestival 1999 unp il $14.95

E

1. Dinosaurs—Fiction
ISBN 0-694-01297-1   LC 98-47691

Also available original edition in hardcover and paperback

"An I can read picture book"

A reissue of the title first published 1958 as An I can read book

A little boy is surprised and pleased when one of the dinosaurs from the museum agrees to play with him

"The bold, humorous, colored pictures convey the imaginative story. . . . Because of the simple vocabulary and sentence structure, first-graders can actually read this story." Libr J

Other titles about Danny and the dinosaur are:
Danny and the dinosaur go to camp (1996)
Happy birthday, Danny and the dinosaur (1995)

Hoff, Syd—*Continued*

Oliver; story and pictures by Syd Hoff. HarperCollins Pubs. 2000 64p il lib bdg $16.89; pa $3.99   E

1. Elephants—Fiction 2. Circus—Fiction
ISBN 0-06-028709-8 (lib bdg); 0-06-444272-1 (pa)
LC 99-25591

"An I can read book"
A newly illustrated edition of the title first published 1960
Oliver the elephant looks elsewhere for employment after learning that the circus already has enough elephants
"One of the most warm-hearted and appealing easy-to-read books available." SLJ

Sammy the seal; story and pictures by Syd Hoff. newly il ed. HarperCollins Pubs. 2000 64p il $15.99; lib bdg $15.89; pa $3.99   E

1. Seals (Animals)—Fiction 2. Zoos—Fiction
ISBN 0-06-028545-1; 0-06-028546-X (lib bdg); 0-06-444270-5 (pa)   LC 99-13805

"An I can read book"
A newly illustrated edition of the title first published 1959
Anxious to see what life is like outside the zoo, Sammy the seal explores the city, goes to school, and plays with the children but decides that there really is no place like home
"Happy adventures told in entertaining colored cartoonlike drawings and in simple vocabulary and short sentences which first graders can read with a minimum of help." Booklist

Hoffman, Mary

Amazing Grace; pictures by Caroline Binch. Dial Bks. for Young Readers 1991 unp il $16.99
E

1. African Americans—Fiction 2. Theater—Fiction
ISBN 0-8037-1040-2   LC 90-25108

Titles about Grace for older readers are also available
Although her classmates say that she cannot play Peter Pan in the school play because she is black and a girl, Grace discovers that she can do anything she sets her mind to do
"Gorgeous watercolor illustrations portraying a determined, talented child and her warm family enhance an excellent text and positive message of self-affirmation. Grace is an amazing girl and this is an amazing book." SLJ
Another picture book title about Grace is:
Boundless Grace (1995)

The color of home; pictures by Karin Littlewood. Phyllis Fogelman Bks. 2002 unp il $15.99   E

1. Refugees—Fiction 2. Immigrants—Fiction 3. Somalia—Fiction
ISBN 0-8037-2841-7   LC 2001-7393

Hassan, newly-arrived in the United States and feeling homesick, paints a picture at school that shows his old home in Somalia as well as the reason his family had to leave
"Readers gain a realistic child's perspective on what it is like to be forced to emigrate from a war-torn country. . . . Littlewood's impressionistic watercolor illustrations . . . beautifully convey Hassan's sadness, fear, and ultimate happiness." SLJ

Holabird, Katharine

Angelina Ballerina; story by Katharine Holabird; illustrations by Helen Craig. Viking 2006 c1983 unp il $12.99   E

1. Mice—Fiction 2. Ballet—Fiction
ISBN 0-670-06026-7

A reissue of the title first published 1983 by Potter
Angelina the mouse loves to dance and wants to become a ballerina more than anything else in the world
"Touches of humor, attention to detail, a feel for dance and truly anthropomorphic mice make the illustrations a major part of the book." Child Book Rev Serv
Other titles about Angelina are:
Angelina and Alice (1987)
Angelina and Henry (2002)
Angelina and the princess (1984)
Angelina at the fair (1985)
Angelina on stage (1986)
Angelina's baby sister (1991)
Angelina's Christmas (1985)
Angelina's Halloween (2000)

Holub, Joan

The garden that we grew; pictures by Hiroe Nakata. Viking 2001 unp il $13.99   E

1. Pumpkin—Fiction 2. Gardening—Fiction 3. Stories in rhyme
ISBN 0-670-89799-X   LC 00-10966

"A Viking easy-to-read"
"Level 2"--cover
Children plant pumpkin seeds, water and weed the garden patch, watch the pumpkins grow, pick them, and enjoy them in various ways
"The text blossoms with the ample warmth, light, and gentle sense of humor in the pictures." Horn Book

Hooks, Bell

Be boy buzz; illustrated by Chris Raschka. Hyperion Bks. for Children 2002 unp il $16.99
E

1. African Americans—Fiction
ISBN 0-7868-0814-4   LC 2001-42275

"Jump at the Sun"
Celebrates being Bold, All Bliss Boy, All Bad Boy Beast, Boy running, Boy Jumping, Boy Sitting Down, and being in Love With Being a Boy
"This spare, poetic riff on young manhood plumbs the delights and contradictions of what it means to be a boy—particulary an African-American boy—in a brief handful of sentences and with a few well-placed pastel lines that imply motion and emotion." Publ Wkly

Homemade love; with pictures by Shane W. Evans. Hyperion Bks. for Children 2002 unp il $16.99   E

1. Family life—Fiction 2. African Americans—Fiction
ISBN 0-7868-0643-5   LC 99-59839

Hooks, Bell—*Continued*

A girl who is Girlpie to her mama and Honey Bun Chocolate Dewdrop to her daddy savors the warmth and love of her family

"The rhythm of the words, the smoothness of the text, and the positive message all combine to make a lovely read-aloud. . . . Evans's folksy paintings, done in bright primary colors, are wonderful, with an appealing, dark-skinned, large-eyed little girl wearing dresses decorated with patterns that reflect the story." SLJ

Hopkinson, Deborah

Apples to Oregon; being the (slightly) true narrative of how a brave pioneer father brought apples, peaches, pears, plums, grapes, and cherries (and children) across the plains; illustrated by Nancy Carpenter. Atheneum Books for Young Readers 2004 unp il map $15.95　　　　**E**

1. Frontier and pioneer life—Fiction 2. Overland journeys to the Pacific—Fiction 3. Fruit culture—Fiction 4. Tall tales

ISBN 0-689-84769-6　　　　LC 2001-22949

"An Anne Schwartz book"

A pioneer father transports his beloved fruit trees and his family to Oregon in the mid-nineteenth century. Based loosely on the life of Henderson Luelling

"Carpenter's oil paintings are filled with vivid shades that reflect the changing scenery. Amusing details abound, and the slightly exaggerated humor of the pictures is in perfect balance with the tone of the text." SLJ

A band of angels; a story inspired by the Jubilee Singers; illustrated by Raúl Colón. Atheneum Bks. for Young Readers 1999 unp il $16.95; pa $6.99

E

1. Moore, Ella Sheppard, 1851-1914—Fiction 2. Jubilee Singers (Musical group)—Fiction 3. African Americans—Fiction 4. Gospel music—Fiction

ISBN 0-689-81062-8; 0-689-84887-0 (pa)

LC 96-20011

"An Anne Schwartz book"

Based on the life of Ella Sheppard Moore. The daughter of a slave forms a gospel singing group and goes on tour to raise money to save Fisk University

"Lilting prose, poignant historical details and arresting portraits of trailblazing singers lost in song contribute to this triumphant tale." Publ Wkly

Billy and the rebel; based on a true Civil War story; illustrated by Brian Floca. Atheneum Books for Young Readers 2002 44p il map $14.95

E

1. Gettysburg (Pa.), Battle of, 1863—Fiction 2. United States—History—1861-1865, Civil War—Fiction

ISBN 0-689-83964-2　　　　LC 2001-22982

"Ready-to-read"

During the Battle of Gettysburg in 1863, a mother and son shelter a young Confederate deserter. Includes a historical note on the incident.

"Based on the real William Bayly and his mother, Harriet Hamilton Bayly, [this book] . . . allows beginning readers and researchers some insight into life during

the Civil War. Full-page, full-spread, and spot art, executed mainly in shades of yellow and tan, add detail and expression to this story of courage and an unlikely friendship." SLJ

From slave to soldier; based on a true Civil War story; illustrated by Brian Floca. Atheneum Books for Young Readers 2005 44p $14.95　　　　**E**

1. Slavery—Fiction 2. African American soldiers—Fiction 3. United States—History—1861-1865, Civil War—Fiction

ISBN 0-689-83965-8

A boy who hates being a slave joins the Union Army to fight for freedom, and proves himself brave and capable of handling a mule team when the need arises.

This is written "in simple sentences for those who have just begun to read proficiently. . . . Short chapters and detailed watercolors aid the transition to more difficult text, while an exciting plot . . . keeps readers interested." SLJ

Girl wonder; a baseball story in nine innings; with pictures by Terry Widener. Atheneum Bks. for Young Readers 2003 unp il $16.95　　　　**E**

1. Weiss, Alta, 1890-1964—Fiction 2. Baseball—Fiction

ISBN 0-689-83300-8　　　　LC 99-47052

"An Anne Schwartz book"

In the early 1900s, Alta Weiss, a young woman who knows from an early age that she loves baseball, finds a way to show that she can play, even though she is a girl

"Hopkinson tells her story with practiced skill—vivid details, lively language, varied pacing. . . . The illustrations are . . . broad, somewhat exaggerated, but conveying much emotion and narrative content." Horn Book

Maria's comet; written by Deborah Hopkinson; illustrated by Deborah Lanino. Atheneum Bks. for Young Readers 1999 unp il $16; pa $6.99

E

1. Mitchell, Maria, 1818-1889—Fiction 2. Astronomers—Fiction

ISBN 0-689-81501-8; 0-689-85678-4 (pa)

LC 97-46676

"An Anne Schwartz book"

As a young girl, budding astronomer Maria Mitchell dreams of searching the night sky and some day finding a new comet

"Warm, deep tones of brown and midnight blue suffuse the soft-edged, full-page acrylic views of the house, sky, and seaside town. . . . The well-structured story is fanciful and rich in poetic imagery that will work for reading aloud." SLJ

A packet of seeds; pictures by Bethanne Andersen. Greenwillow 2004 unp il $15.99; lib bdg $16.89　　　　**E**

1. Frontier and pioneer life—Fiction 2. Gardens—Fiction 3. Infants—Fiction

ISBN 0-06-009089-8; 0-06-009090-1 (lib bdg)

LC 2003-5489

When a pioneer family moves west the mother misses home so much that she will not even name the new baby until her daughter thinks of just the right thing to cheer her up.

Hopkinson, Deborah—*Continued*

"Using clear language with a homespun flair, Hopkinson captures a child's perception of events. The illustrations, breathtakingly executed in gouache and oil paints, effectively depict the windswept prairie." SLJ

Saving Strawberry Farm; pictures by Rachel Isadora. 1st ed. Greenwillow Books 2004 unp il $16.99; lib bdg $17.89 **E**

1. Great Depression, 1929-1939—Fiction 2. Country life—Fiction
ISBN 0-688-17400-0; 0-688-17401-9 (lib bdg)

LC 2003-12565

During the Great Depression, Davey learns that a neighbor's property is about to be auctioned, and he rallies his friends, neighbors, and family to help save Strawberry Farm.

"Hopkinson's graceful text, filled with colloquial dialogue, doesn't mention the Great Depression until an appended author's note. But the details in her text and in Isadora's bright colored-pencil artwork bring a sharp focus to the day-today hardships, as well as simple pleasures such as making homemade lemonade." Booklist

Sky boys; how they built the Empire State Building; [by] Deborah Hopkinson & James E. Ransome. 1st ed. Schwartz & Wade Books 2006 unp il $16.95 **E**

1. Empire State Building (New York, N.Y.)—Fiction 2. Building—Fiction 3. New York (N.Y.)—Fiction
ISBN 0-375-83610-1   LC 2005010852

In 1931, a boy and his father watch as the world's tallest building, the Empire State Building, is constructed, step-by-step, near their Manhattan home.

"Crisp, lyrical free verse and bold paintings celebrate the skill and daring of those who constructed the Empire State Building. . . . Ransome's powerful acrylic paintings show the building in all stages of construction, and includes the workers' perilous views. A unique, memorable title." Booklist

Sweet Clara and the freedom quilt; paintings by James Ransome. Knopf 1993 unp il $15.95; lib bdg $17.99; pa $6.99 **E**

1. Slavery—Fiction 2. Quilts—Fiction
ISBN 0-679-82311-5; 0-679-92311-X (lib bdg); 0-679-87472-0 (pa)   LC 91-11601

Clara, a young slave, stitches a quilt with a map pattern which guides her to freedom in the North

"The smooth, optimistic, first-person vernacular of the story is ably accompanied by Ransome's brightly colored, full-page paintings." Horn Book Guide

Another title about Clara is:
Under the quilt of night (2001)

Horacek, Petr

Silly Suzy Goose. Candlewick Press 2006 unp il $14.99 **E**

1. Geese—Fiction 2. Lions—Fiction
ISBN 0-7636-3040-3

Suzy longs to be different from all the other geese, but learns that imitating a lion may not be the best way to express her individuality.

"Created in mixed media, the art jumps off the pages, a fitting verb for a clever, clever book, alive in every way." Booklist

Horenstein, Henry

A is for—? a photographer's alphabet of animals. Harcourt Brace & Co. 1999 unp il $16 **E**

1. Animals 2. Alphabet
ISBN 0-15-201582-5   LC 98-31424
"Gulliver books"

"More visual puzzle than early concept book, the title presents each letter alongside a photograph of the relevant creature—if you can figure out what the relevant creature is. Some letters are easy . . . but some are more challenging. . . . Even when the answer is fairly guessable, the view is original. . . . Artistic and creative." Bull Cent Child Books

Horning, Sandra

The giant hug; illustrated by Valeri Gorbachev. 1st ed. Knopf 2005 unp il $15.95; lib bdg $17.99 **E**

1. Grandmothers—Fiction 2. Postal service—Fiction 3. Pigs—Fiction
ISBN 0-375-82477-4; 0-375-92477-9 (lib bdg)

LC 2003-25883

When Owen the pig sends a real hug to his grandmother for her birthday he inadvertently brings cheer to the postal workers as they pass the hug along.

"Gorbachev's cast of animal characters, drawn with a . . . sense of whimsy, are well chosen to emphasize the relevant personality traits." Booklist

Horowitz, Ruth

Breakout at the bug lab; pictures by Joan Holub. Dial Bks. for Young Readers 2001 48p il $13.99 **E**

1. Cockroaches—Fiction 2. Brothers—Fiction
ISBN 0-8037-2510-8   LC 99-14274
Also available in paperback from Puffin Books
"Dial easy-to-read"

When a giant cockroach named Max escapes from their mother's bug laboratory, Leo and his brother receive help from a mysterious stranger who advises them to think like a bug in order to recapture the runaway roach

"Holub's appealing, bright illustrations capture this . . . book's humor and suspense, and readers will enjoy the fun facts woven into the lively, well-paced text." Booklist

Another title about Leo and his brother is:
Big surprise in the bug tank (2005)

Horse, Harry

Little Rabbit lost. Peachtree Pubs. 2002 unp il $15.95 **E**

1. Rabbits—Fiction 2. Birthdays—Fiction
ISBN 1-56145-273-4   LC 2002-2697
Also available board book edition

On his birthday Little Rabbit thinks that he is now a big rabbit, until he gets lost at the Rabbit World amusement park

"The lovely ink-and-watercolor illustrations are filled with clever details kids will enjoy—carrot-shaped paddleboats and bunny roller-coaster cars. Children will welcome this charming story." Booklist

Horse, Harry—*Continued*

Other titles about Little Rabbit are:

Little Rabbit goes to school (2004)

Little Rabbit runaway (2005)

Hort, Lenny

How many stars in the sky? paintings by James E. Ransome 1991 unp il pa $5.99 o.p.   **E**

1. Stars—Fiction 2. Father-son relationship—Fiction

ISBN 0-688-15218-X (pa); 0-688-0103-8 (hc)

LC 90-36044

Also availabel in paperback from HarperCollins Pubs.

One night when Mama is away, Daddy and child seek a good place to count the stars in the night sky

"Ransome uses thick, visible strokes in his dense oil paintings that completely fill each large-format page. In general they present a nice variety of scenes to match the flow of the text, and the closeness between the black father and son is warmly portrayed. A fresh look at an age-old concept." SLJ

Houston, Gloria

My great-aunt Arizona; illustrated by Susan Condie Lamb. HarperCollins Pubs. 1992 unp il $15.99; lib bdg $17.89; pa $6.99   **E**

1. Hughes, Arizona Houston, 1876-1969 2. Teachers 3. Appalachian region

ISBN 0-06-022606-4; 0-06-022607-2 (lib bdg); 0-06-443374-9 (pa)   LC 90-44112

The author tells the life story of "her great aunt Arizona who never traveled farther than the next town where she trained as a teacher before returning to her small Appalachian community's one-room schoolhouse. Though not well-traveled, Arizona encouraged her students to dream of faraway places and was always there to give them hugs and kisses." Child Book Rev Serv

"The pleasant, conversational rhythm of the prose, the unobtrusive use of repetition, and the ability to sum up the unique quality of a life in a few telling phrases give the writing its substance. . . . Sunny and lively, the watercolor paintings have a naive quality that suits the story well." Booklist

The year of the perfect Christmas tree; an Appalachian story; pictures by Barbara Cooney. Dial Bks. for Young Readers 1988 unp il $15.99; pa $6.99   **E**

1. Christmas—Fiction 2. Appalachian region—Fiction

ISBN 0-8037-0299-X; 0-14-055827-2 (pa)

LC 87-24551

"It's 1918 in the mountains of North Carolina, and the custom in the village is for one family to select and donate the Christmas tree each year. In the spring Ruthie and her father select a perfect balsam high on a rocky crag. Then Father goes to war. Still, on Christmas Eve the tree is in the church and Ruthie plays the angel. The winning illustrations perfectly match the tone of this affecting story, which comes from the author's family." NY Times Book Rev

Howard, Arthur

Hoodwinked. Harcourt 2001 unp il $16   **E**

1. Pets—Fiction 2. Witches—Fiction

ISBN 0-15-202656-8   LC 00-8318

Mitzi, a young witch, searches for a creepy pet, but finds that a cute kitten is perfect for her

"The pictures are perfect for this lively story—lots of fangs and slimy, scaly, weird, and wiggly outlines fill the pages." SLJ

Howard, Elizabeth Fitzgerald

Aunt Flossie's hats (and crab cakes later); by Elizabeth Fitzgerald Howard; paintings by James Ransome. 10th anniversary ed. Clarion Books 2001 31p il $16; pa $6.95   **E**

1. Hats—Fiction 2. Aunts—Fiction 3. African Americans—Fiction

ISBN 0-618-12038-6; 0-395-72077-X (pa)

LC 00-65757

A reissue of the title first published 1991

Includes an afterword with biographical information and photographs of the real Aunt Flossie

Sara and Susan share tea, cookies, crab cakes, and stories about hats when they visit their favorite relative, Aunt Flossie.

"This is an affecting portrait of a black American family. . . . Howard's quiet, sure telling is well matched by Ransome's art-elegant, expressive oil paintings that convey warmth, joy, tenderness and love." Publ Wkly

Virgie goes to school with us boys; illustrated by E.B. Lewis. Simon & Schuster Bks. for Young Readers 1999 unp il $16; pa $6.99   **E**

1. African Americans—Fiction

ISBN 0-689-80076-2; 0-689-87793-5 (pa)

LC 97-49406

In the post-Civil War South, a young African American girl is determined to prove that she can go to school just like her older brothers.

"The story is a superb tribute to the author's great aunt, the inspiration for this book. . . . Lewis's watercolor illustrations capture the characters with warmth and dignity." SLJ

Howe, James

Horace and Morris but mostly Dolores; written by James Howe; illustrated by Amy Walrod. Atheneum Bks. for Young Readers 1999 unp il $16; pa $6.99   **E**

1. Mice—Fiction 2. Friendship—Fiction 3. Sex role—Fiction

ISBN 0-689-31874-X; 0-689-85675-X (pa)

LC 96-17645

"An Anne Schwartz book"

"Three adventure-loving mice are best friends until gender stereotypes separate them, driving Horace and Morris into a rowdy boys-only clubhouse while Dolores reluctantly goes off to join the ultra-ladylike Cheese Puffs. The bold artwork suits the book's lively protest against conformity." Horn Book Guide

Another title about Horace, Morris, and Dolores is:

Horace and Morris join the chorus (but what about Dolores?) (2002)

Howe, James—*Continued*

Houndsley and Catina; [by] James Howe; illustrated by Marie-Louise Gay. 1st ed. Candlewick Press 2006 36p il $14.99   **E**
1. Cats—Fiction 2. Dogs—Fiction 3. Friendship—Fiction
ISBN 0-7636-2404-7   LC 2005050187
Houndsley, a dog, and Catina, a cat, run into trouble when they decide to prove that they are the best at cooking and writing, respectively.
"The lively, brisk writing is wonderfully extended in Gay's airy watercolor-and-pencil illustrations." Booklist

Kaddish for Grandpa in Jesus' name, amen; [illustrated by] Catherine Stock. Atheneum Books for Young Readers 2004 unp il $16.95   **E**
1. Funeral rites and ceremonies—Fiction 2. Death—Fiction 3. Grandfathers—Fiction 4. Judaism—Fiction 5. Christianity—Fiction
ISBN 0-689-80185-8   LC 2002-11569
Five-year-old Emily tries to understand her grandfather's death by exploring the Christian and Jewish rituals that her family practices during and after his funeral.
"The soft watercolor illustrations, done in pastel colors, are a perfect accompaniment to the story. This book is a good vehicle to explain the rituals of death to children." SLJ

Pinky and Rex; illustrated by Melissa Sweet. Atheneum Pubs. 1990 38p il $15; pa $3.99   **E**
1. Museums—Fiction 2. Friendship—Fiction 3. Toys—Fiction
ISBN 0-689-31454-X; 0-689-82348-7 (pa)
    LC 89-30786
"Pinky, a boy named for his favorite color, and Rex, a girl whose name reflects her interest in dinosaurs, live next door to each other; they each have twenty-seven stuffed animals and are best friends. . . . They go to the museum and discover that even best friends can vie with each other for the last remaining pink dinosaur in the museum store." Horn Book
"Sweet's gently washed, jovial illustrations reflect the unpretentious sincerity of Rex and Pinky's relationship, while Howe's readable text blending natural dialogue with narrative, is divided into individual chapters." Booklist
Other titles about Pinky and Rex are:
Pinky and Rex and the bully (1996)
Pinky and Rex and the double-dad weekend (1995)
Pinky and Rex and the just-right pet (2001)
Pinky and Rex and the mean old witch (1991)
Pinky and Rex and the new baby (1993)
Pinky and Rex and the new neighbors (1997)
Pinky and Rex and the perfect pumpkin (1998)
Pinky and Rex and the school play (1998)
Pinky and Rex and the spelling bee (1991)
Pinky and Rex get married (1990)
Pinky and Rex go to camp (1992)

Howland, Naomi
Latkes, latkes, good to eat; a Chanukah story. Clarion Bks. 1999 31p il $16; pa $5.95
    E
1. Magic—Fiction 2. Hanukkah—Fiction 3. Jews—Fiction
ISBN 0-395-89903-6; 0-618-49295-X (pa)
    LC 97-50616
In an old Russian village, Sadie and her brothers are poor and hungry until an old woman gives Sadie a frying pan that will make potato pancakes until it hears the magic words that make it stop
"Howland effectively sets her story in a Russian shtetl, using words, intonation, and especially pictures. Working in gouache and colored pencil, she offers a snowy landscape peopled with Jewish villagers who work hard and celebrate harder." Booklist

Hubbell, Will
Pumpkin Jack; written and illustrated by Will Hubbell. Whitman, A. 2000 unp il $15.95
    E
1. Pumpkin—Fiction 2. Halloween—Fiction
ISBN 0-8075-6665-9   LC 00-8282
After Halloween, Tim discards Jack, his jack-o'lantern, in the garden and during the following year it sprouts, blooms, and grows new pumpkins
"Satisfying and surprisingly varied in approach and perspective, Hubbell's colored pencil drawings illustrate the simple story in a series of well-imagined scenes." Booklist

Huck, Charlotte S.
A creepy countdown; by Charlotte Huck; pictures by Jos. A. Smith. Greenwillow Bks. 1998 unp il $15; lib bdg $14.93; pa $5.95   **E**
1. Halloween—Fiction 2. Counting 3. Stories in rhyme
ISBN 0-688-15460-3; 0-688-15461-1 (lib bdg); 0-688-17717-4 (pa)   LC 97-36283
Ten scary Halloween things, such as jack-o-lanterns, bats, and witches, count from one to ten and then back down again
"Huck's spirited counting rhyme . . . trips easily off the tongue, and Smith's black ink on scratchboard with watercolor overlays provide appropriate ghoulish harmony." SLJ

Hughes, Shirley
Annie Rose is my little sister. Candlewick Press 2003 unp il $15.99   **E**
1. Siblings—Fiction
ISBN 0-7636-1959-0   LC 2002-67695
Alfie describes all the things that he and his younger sister Annie Rose do together
"Few artists have recreated the young child's body language and surroundings as faithfully as Hughes. The gouache-and-oil pastel illustrations teem with well-observed details." Booklist

Hughes, Shirley—*Continued*

Ella's big chance; a Jazz-Age Cinderella; [by] Shirley Hughes. 1st U.S. ed. Simon & Schuster Books for Young Readers 2004 c2003 unp il $16.95   E

1. Fairy tales

ISBN 0-689-87399-9   LC 2003-27274

In this version of the Cinderella tale set in the 1920s, Ella has two men courting her—the handsome Duke of Arc and Buttons the delivery boy

"Hughes's gouache-and-pen-line illustrations exhibit her usual meticulous attention to detail. . . . This insightful retelling also offers a fascinating visual peek at a glamorous time." SLJ

Olly and me. Candlewick Press 2004 unp il $15.99   E

1. Siblings—Fiction 2. Family life—Fiction

ISBN 0-7636-2374-1   LC 2003-55088

Olly and his big sister Katie have a good time together, whether dancing, walking in the park with their parents, or playing with friends.

"Expressive gouache and oil pastels, full of realistic and child-centered detail, portray this loving, busy family as they go about their daily lives." SLJ

Out and about. Lothrop, Lee & Shepard Bks. 1988 unp il $16   E

1. Seasons—Fiction 2. Stories in rhyme

ISBN 0-688-07690-4   LC 87-17000

Rhyming text depicts the pleasures of the outdoors in all kinds of weather, through the four seasons

"The children who romp through these non-stop family scenes are rosy, cared-for, active, and enthusiastically messy. Hughes' drawing is always good, but the composition and coloration here mark some of her most cohesive book design and art work." Bull Cent Child Books

Stories by firelight. Lothrop, Lee & Shepard Bks. 1993 unp il $16   E

1. Winter—Fiction 2. Short stories

ISBN 0-688-04568-5   LC 92-38207

In a series of brief winter episodes, a child learns about a mythical sea creature, a boy and his grandfather build a bonfire, and Mrs. Toomly Stones pays a scary visit

"No one captures the real innocence and emotions of childhood with less sentimentality than Hughes. Designed with an appealing jacket and full-color illustrations on every page, this book will be in demand for reading aloud or reading alone." Booklist

The **human** alphabet; [by] Pilobolus; photographs by John Kane. Roaring Brook Press 2005 unp il $16.95   E

1. Alphabet

ISBN 1-59643-066-4   LC 2004-65052

The dancers of the Pilobolus Dance Theatre "join limbs, twist, and grip to form 26 letters—an alphabet made of the human body, captured in . . . color photographs. Alongside each letter, they've also composed a picture: Ants for A; Butterfly for B; Circus for C and so on through Z, a human Zipper." Publisher's note

This alphabet book "is one of the most striking ones around. . . . [This] is an extraordinarily inventive interpretation." SLJ

Huneck, Stephen

Sally goes to the beach; written and illustrated by Stephen Huneck. Abrams 2000 unp il $17.95   E

1. Dogs—Fiction 2. Beaches—Fiction

ISBN 0-8109-4186-4   LC 99-28421

Sally, a black Labrador retriever, goes to the beach, where she enjoys various activities with other visiting dogs

"The playful pup's enjoyment is conveyed through a simple but engaging text and beautiful, full-page woodblock prints." SLJ

Other titles about Sally are:

Sally goes to the farm (2002)

Sally goes to the mountains (2001)

Sally goes to the vet (2004)

Hurd, Edith Thacher

Johnny Lion's book; pictures by Clement Hurd. new ed. HarperCollins Pubs. 2001 63p il lib bdg $15.89; pa $3.99   E

1. Lions—Fiction

ISBN 0-06-029334-9 (lib bdg); 0-06-444297-7 (pa)

"An I can read book"

A reissue of the title first published 1965

When his parents go out hunting, Johnny Lion stays home and experiences exciting adventures reading a book about a baby lion who goes out into the world and gets lost

"A subtle boost for the joys of reading in a story with engaging illustrations." Booklist

Other titles about Johnny Lion are:

Johnny Lion's bad day (1970)

Johny Lion's rubber boots (1972)

Hurd, Thacher

Art dog. HarperCollins Pubs. 1996 unp il $15.99; lib bdg $15.89; pa $6.99   E

1. Dogs—Fiction 2. Artists—Fiction

ISBN 0-06-024424-0; 0-06-024425-9 (lib bdg); 0-06-443489-3 (pa)   LC 95-31092

When the Mona Woofa is stolen from the Dogopolis Museum of Art, a mysterious character who calls himself Art Dog tracks down and captures the thieves

"This is exuberantly drawn by Hurd, who has imbued Art Dog with the flash and dash every artist feels at times; but Hurd also captures the shyness that comes with displaying your art. Kids will respond not just to the pictures but also to a story that does as well with characters as with plot." Booklist

Mama don't allow; starring Miles and the Swamp Band. Harper & Row 1984 unp il lib bdg $16.89; pa $5.99   E

1. Bands (Music)—Fiction 2. Alligators—Fiction

ISBN 0-06-022690-0 (lib bdg); 0-06-443078-2 (pa)   LC 83-47703

Miles and the Swamp Band have the time of their lives playing at the Alligator Ball, until they discover the menu includes Swamp Band soup

"The multi-colored full-spread watercolor illustrations are stunningly bright and full of movement, far outpacing the story line in energy and imagination." SLJ

Hurd, Thacher—*Continued*

Sleepy Cadillac; a bedtime drive; by Thacher Hurd. HarperCollins 2005 unp il $15.99; lib bdg $16.89   E
1. Bedtime—Fiction 2. Automobiles—Fiction
ISBN 0-06-073020-X; 0-06-073021-8 (lib bdg)
LC 2004-7826
A nighttime ride in the Sleepy Cadillac ensures every passenger a night of happy dreams and cozy sleep.
"The text's present-tense, second-person voice . . . involves listeners directly in the nighttime enchantment, and repeated rhythms and alliterative sounds mimic an engine's hypnotic hum. Hurd's smudged, glowing pastels are equally lulling." Booklist

Zoom City. HarperCollins Pubs. 1998 unp il $6.99   E
1. Automobiles—Fiction
ISBN 0-694-01057-X   LC 96-49437
On board pages
Cars honk, beep, stop, go, zoom, crash, and get repaired
"A fast-paced, zip-zapping board book that begs to be read with as much gusto as possible. . . . The bright and busy illustrations are packed with energy." SLJ

Hurst, Carol Otis

Rocks in his head; pictures by James Stevenson. Greenwillow Bks. 2001 unp il $15.99; lib bdg $15.89   E
1. Rocks—Collectors and collecting
ISBN 0-06-029403-5; 0-06-029404-3 (lib bdg)
LC 00-56197
Hurst "recounts the story of her father, an avid rock collector from the time he was a boy. . . . Dominated by earth tones, Stevenson's artwork convincingly evokes both the personality of this endearing protagonist and the period in which he lived." Publ Wkly

Hurwitz, Johanna

New shoes for Silvia; illustrated by Jerry Pinkney. Morrow Junior Bks. 1993 unp il $16.99
E
1. Shoes—Fiction 2. Latin America—Fiction
ISBN 0-688-05286-X   LC 92-40868
Silvia receives a pair of beautiful red shoes from her Tia Rosita and finds different uses for them until she grows enough for them to fit
"This simple story, told in spare prose, speaks universally to the imagination and emotions. Pinkney's spirited watercolors animate the narrative and are large enough for group sharing." SLJ

Hutchins, Pat

1 hunter. Greenwillow Bks. 1982 unp il $16.99
E
1. Counting 2. Animals—Fiction
ISBN 0-688-00614-0   LC 81-6352
This is "a 1 to 10 and back again counting book. . . . Here, a Mr. Magoo-type hunter blunders through the jungle entirely missing the camouflaged elephants (2), giraffes (3), ostriches (4), etc." SLJ
"Humorous illustrations done in a flat, clear style make an outstanding counting book." Horn Book

The doorbell rang. Greenwillow Bks. 1986 unp il $15.99; lib bdg $16.89; pa $5.99   E
1. Division—Fiction 2. Cookies—Fiction
ISBN 0-688-05251-7; 0-688-05252-5 (lib bdg); 0-688-09234-9 (pa)   LC 85-12615
Also available Big book edition and Spanish language edition
"Victoria and Sam are delighted when Ma bakes a tray of a dozen cookies, even though Ma insists that her cookies aren't as good as Grandma's. They count them and find that each can have six. But the doorbell rings, friends arrive and the cookies must be re-divided. This happens again and again, and the number of cookies on each plate decreases as the visitors' pile of gear in the corner of the kitchen grows larger." SLJ
"Bright, joyous, dynamic, this wonderfully humorous piece of realism for the young is presented simply but with style and imagination." Horn Book

Rosie's walk. Macmillan 1968 unp il $16.95; pa $6.99   E
1. Chickens—Fiction 2. Foxes—Fiction
ISBN 0-02-745850-4; 0-02-043750-1 (pa)
Also available Spanish language edition
"Rosie the hen goes for a walk around the farm and gets home in time for dinner, completely unaware that a fox has been hot on her heels every step of the way. The viewer knows, however, and is not only held in suspense but tickled by the ways in which the fox is foiled at every turn by the unwitting hen. A perfect choice for the youngest." Booklist

Ten red apples. Greenwillow Bks. 2000 $15.99; lib bdg $16.89   E
1. Domestic animals—Fiction 2. Apples—Fiction
3. Counting 4. Stories in rhyme
ISBN 0-688-16797-7; 0-688-16798-5 (lib bdg)
LC 99-25065
In rhyming verses, one animal after another neighs, moos, oinks, quacks and makes other appropriate sounds as each eats an apple from the farmer's tree
"A concept book that blends rhyming, counting, repetition, and animal sounds into a charming, folksy story. . . . The gouache paintings are bright and clear." SLJ

There's only one of me! Greenwillow Bks. 2003 unp il $15.99; lib bdg $16.89   E
1. Family life—Fiction 2. Birthdays—Fiction
ISBN 0-06-029819-7; 0-06-029820-0 (lib bdg)
LC 2002-23546
A young girl describes her relationship to the various members of her family, including her stepfamily, as they all gather to celebrate her birthday
"Done in pen and ink and felt-tipped markers, the illustrations radiate color and merriment. . . . Popular subject matter, a repetitive text, and vibrant artwork result in a package that is sure to please." SLJ

We're going on a picnic! Greenwillow Bks. 2002 unp il $15.95; lib bdg $15.89   E
1. Chickens—Fiction 2. Ducks—Fiction
ISBN 0-688-16799-3; 0-688-16800-0 (lib bdg)
LC 00-62225
"Hen, Duck, and Goose intend to enjoy a picnic but are so busy searching for the perfect spot that they don't

Hutchins, Pat—_Continued_

notice the hungry animals taking up residence in their fruit-filled picnic basket." Horn Book Guide

"With an understated humor infusing both narrative and pictures, Hutchins successfully pulls off the child-pleasing contrivance of letting readers in on the secret." Publ Wkly

Ichikawa, Satomi

La La Rose. Philomel Books 2004 unp il $15.99
E

1. Lost and found possessions—Fiction 2. Paris (France)—Fiction 3. Gardens—Fiction
ISBN 0-399-24029-2   LC 2002-15366

La La Rose, a young girl's stuffed rabbit, gets lost in Luxembourg Gardens in Paris.

"Ichikawa's ink-and-watercolor paintings are a wonderful mix of action and thoughtfulness, sweetness and subtlety that extend the story and give it life past a first reading. . . . A very satisfying story that also captures the magic and excitement of a special place." Booklist

My pig Amarillo. Philomel Bks. 2003 c2002 unp il $15.99   **E**

1. Pigs—Fiction 2. Guatemala—Fiction
ISBN 0-399-23768-2   LC 2002-7318

Original French edition, 2002

Pablito, a Guatemalan boy whose pet pig Amarillo has disappeared, uses a kite to send him a message that he still loves him

"Ichikawa uses her Guatemalan setting very effectively, but she also wraps the story in universal emotions: love, longing, grief, hope. The pen-and-watercolor artwork brings children close to all facets of Pablito's story." Booklist

Isaacs, Anne

Swamp Angel; illustrated by Paul O. Zelinsky. Dutton Children's Bks. 1994 unp il $16.99; pa $6.99   **E**

1. Tall tales 2. Frontier and pioneer life—Fiction 3. Tennessee—Fiction
ISBN 0-525-45271-0; 0-14-055908-6 (pa)
          LC 93-43956

A Caldecott Medal honor book, 1995

Along with other amazing feats, Angelica Longrider, also known as Swamp Angel, wrestles a huge bear, known as Thundering Tarnation, to save the winter supplies of the settlers in Tennessee

"Isaacs tells her original story with the glorious exaggeration and uproarious farce of the traditional tall tale and with its typical laconic idiom—you just can't help reading it aloud. . . . Zelinsky's detailed oil paintings in folk-art style are exquisite, framed in cherry, maple, and birch wood grains." Booklist

Isadora, Rachel

At the crossroads. Greenwillow Bks. 1991 unp il pa $6.99 hardcover o.p.   **E**

1. Fathers—Fiction 2. South Africa—Fiction
ISBN 0-688-05271-1 (pa); 0-688-13103-4 (hc)
          LC 90-30751

South African children gather to welcome home their fathers who have been away for ten months working in the mines

"The characters' anticipation, patience, and joy speak loudest here, both in text and in brilliantly lit watercolor paintings." Bull Cent Child Books

Ben's trumpet. Greenwillow Bks. 1979 unp il $17.99; pa $6.99   **E**

1. Musicians—Fiction 2. African Americans—Fiction
ISBN 0-688-80194-3; 0-688-10988-8 (pa)
          LC 78-12885

A Caldecott Medal honor book, 1980

This is the story of Ben, a boy whose dream is to be a jazz trumpeter but who is too poor to own an instrument until a real musician, remembering his own dreams, puts one into the boy's hands

"The art is astonishingly varied in its brilliant recreation—in the margins, in the urban backgrounds—of the commercial art of the 20's and 30's." N Y Times Book Rev

Lili at ballet. Putnam 1993 unp il $17.99; pa $6.99   **E**

1. Ballet—Fiction
ISBN 0-399-22423-8; 0-698-11408-6 (pa)
          LC 92-8429

Lili dreams of becoming a ballerina and goes to her ballet lessons four afternoons a week

"Isadora uses pastel shades of purple, pink, green, and blue with bold splashes of black. This is a prettily illustrated book that captures the magic and hard work involved in ballet." SLJ

Other titles about Lili are:
Lili backstage (1997)
Lili on stage (1995)

Max; story & pictures by Rachel Isadora. Macmillan 1976 unp il pa $5.99 hardcover o.p.
          E

1. Baseball—Fiction 2. Ballet—Fiction
ISBN 0-02-043800-1 (pa)   LC 76-9088

Max "is the star of his baseball team. On a Saturday morning, he has time to spare before his game and accepts (with some hidden disdain) the invitation of his sister, Lisa, to watch her ballet class in action. Max is surprised to find himself interested and happy to join the students at their teacher's suggestion. . . . The experience pays off at the ball park where Max hits a home run. Now he warms up for the game each week at Lisa's dancing class. The pictures are an ebullient combination of grace and comedy, with the leggy students dipping and soaring, in contrast to Max in his uniform." Publ Wkly

On your toes; a ballet ABC. Greenwillow Bks. 2003 unp il $16.99; lib bdg $17.89   **E**

1. Ballet 2. Alphabet
ISBN 0-06-050238-X; 0-06-050241-X (lib bdg)
          LC 2002-23549

Each letter of the alphabet is represented by an illustration of a ballet-related word

"Ballet fans may pick up some information here, but they will return to the book mainly to look again at the richly colored, dynamic illustrations of the dancers." Booklist

Isadora, Rachel—*Continued*

What a family! a fresh look at family trees.
Putnam 2006 unp il $16.99   **E**
1. Family—Fiction
ISBN 0-399-24254-6   LC 2004-27543
"Charming illustrations highlight the similar traits
within an extended family, including those shared by
first cousins once removed, second or third cousins, or
even half-siblings. The endpapers consist of a genealogical diagram of the whole family, and include pictures of
everyone mentioned in the text." SLJ

Iwamatsu, Atushi Jun

Crow Boy; [by] Taro Yashima. Viking 1955
37p il lib bdg $17.99; pa $5.99   **E**
1. School stories 2. Japan—Fiction
ISBN 0-670-24931-9 (lib bdg); 0-14-050172-X (pa)
Also available Spanish language edition
A Caldecott Medal honor book, 1956
"A young boy from the mountain area of Japan goes
to school in a nearby village, where he is taunted by his
classmates and feels rejected and isolated. Finally an understanding teacher helps the boy gain acceptance. The
other students recognize how wrong they have been and
nickname him 'Crow Boy' because he can imitate the
crow's calls with such perfection." Adventuring with
Books. 2d edition
"A moving story interpreted by the author's distinctive
illustrations, valuable for human relations and for its picture of Japanese school life." Hodges. Books for Elem
Sch Libr

Umbrella; [by] Taro Yashima. Viking 1958 30p
il pa $6.99 hardcover o.p.   **E**
1. Umbrellas and parasols—Fiction
ISBN 0-14-050240-8 (pa); 0-670-73858-1 (hc)
A Caldecott Medal honor book, 1959
"Momo, given an umbrella and a pair of red boots on
her third birthday, is overjoyed when at last it rains and
she can wear her new rain togs." Hodges. Books for
Elem Sch Libr
In this simple tale, young children "will be carried
along by their identification with the actions of this very
real little girl. . . . The beauty of the book makes this
worthwhile." Horn Book

Jackson, Alison

The ballad of Valentine; illustrated by Tricia
Tusa. Dutton Children's Bks. 2001 unp il $16.99
    E
1. Valentines—Fiction 2. Stories in rhyme
ISBN 0-525-46720-3   LC 2001-42737
An ardent suitor tries various means of communication, from smoke signals to Morse code to skywriting, in
order to get his message to his Valentine
"Tusa uses sketchy, wispy lines to create loads of
droll details that are both funny and subtle. . . . Jackson
and Tusa make perfect harmony here—the cadence and
rhythm of text and the watercolor artwork are right on
pitch." Booklist

Jackson, Ellen B.

Cinder Edna; by Ellen Jackson; illustrated by
Kevin O'Malley. Lothrop, Lee & Shepard Bks.
1994 unp il $16.99; pa $5.99   **E**
1. Fairy tales
ISBN 0-688-12322-8; 0-688-16295-9 (pa)
     LC 92-44160
Cinderella and Cinder Edna, who live with cruel stepmothers and stepsisters, have different approaches to life;
and, although each ends up with the prince of her
dreams, one is a great deal happier than the other
"O'Malley's full-page, full-color illustrations are exuberant and funny. Ella is suitably bubble-headed and
self-absorbed while Edna is plain, practical, and bound to
enjoy life." SLJ

Jacobson, Jennifer

Andy Shane and the very bossy Dolores
Starbuckle; [by] Jennifer Richard Jacobson;
illustrated by Abby Carter. 1st ed. Candlewick
Press 2005 56p il $13.99   **E**
1. School stories 2. Grandmothers—Fiction
ISBN 0-7636-1940-X   LC 2004-57040
Andy Shane hates school, mainly because of a tattle-
tale know-it-all named Dolores Starbuckle, but Granny
Webb, who has taken care of him all his life, joins him
in class one day and helps him solve the problem.
"The characters are complex and realistic. . . . The
narrative voice is fresh and whimsical. . . . The pen-and-
ink illustrations effectively depict Andy's frustration, Dolores's temper, and Granny's zany self-assuredness." SLJ

James, Simon

Baby Brains. Candlewick Press 2004 unp il
$15.99   **E**
1. Infants—Fiction
ISBN 0-7636-2507-8   LC 2003-65528
Even though the new baby of Mr. and Mrs. Brains is
very intelligent, they realize that he is still just a baby
"This tongue-in-cheek tale will tickle the funny bones
of young listeners. The loose and playful lines of the watercolor-and-ink illustrations are used judiciously and to
great effect." SLJ
Another title about Baby Brains is:
Baby Brains superstar (2005)

Little One Step. Candlewick Press 2003 unp il
$15.99   **E**
1. Ducks—Fiction 2. Brothers—Fiction
ISBN 0-7636-2070-X   LC 2002-71407
As three duckling brothers cross forest and field to return to their mother, the older ones encourage the youngest by teaching him a game that earns him the name of
Little One Step
"Abundant white space surrounds the line drawings
suffused with buttery yellow and peach watercolor tones.
. . . This satisfying tale about perseverance will find an
eager audience at storytimes, on a parent's lap, and with
independent readers." SLJ

Jarrett, Clare

The best picnic ever. Candlewick Press 2004
unp il $16.99   **E**
1. Play—Fiction 2. Animals—Fiction
ISBN 0-7636-2370-9   LC 2003-55341
While his mother prepares a picnic, Jack invites a giraffe, an elephant, and other animals to lunch and each
eagerly agrees, as long as they can play first.
"The simple and repetitive text is perfectly suited to
this straightforward and sweetly innocent adventure. . . .
This paean to the joy of a robust imagination has great
child appeal." SLJ

Jay, Alison

ABC: a child's first alphabet book. Dutton
Children's Bks. 2003 unp il $15.99   **E**
1. Alphabet
ISBN 0-525-46951-6   LC 2003-45218
Also available board book edition
In this alphabet book, a is for apple and z is for zoo
"This imaginative alphabet book offers visual clues to
track and a story to tease out in its beautiful paintings.
. . . Older children will flip from page to page, finding
the simple story, drawing connections, and naming the
letter-related objects. Younger ones can simply enjoy the
delightful paintings with their crackle-glazed folk art
look and touches of humor." Booklist

Jenkins, Emily

Five creatures; pictures by Tomek Bogacki.
Foster Bks. 2001 unp il $16   **E**
1. Family life—Fiction 2. Cats—Fiction
ISBN 0-374-32341-0   LC 00-28771
In words and pictures, a girl describes the three humans and two cats that live in her house, and details
some of the traits that they share
"This clever, multilayered book is as much for sharing
and getting little ones on the path to deductive reasoning
as it is for reading. . . . The text encourages readers to
be observant. . . . Bogacki's colored chalk art . . . is
childlike in the best possible way—immediate, identifiable, and executed with soft colors and simple shapes."
Booklist

That new animal; pictures by Pierre Pratt.
Farrar, Straus and Giroux 2005 unp il $16
                                                E
1. Dogs—Fiction 2. Infants—Fiction
ISBN 0-374-37443-0   LC 2003-44058
"Frances Foster Books"
The lives of two dogs change after a new animal, a
baby, comes to their house.
"Both the author and illustrator demonstrate wonderful
insight into pet psychology and family dynamics, and the
elongated style of the vibrantly colored artwork strikes
just the right note of humor and whimsy." SLJ

Jenkins, Steve

Move! [written by Steve Jenkins and Robin
Page; illustrated by Steve Jenkins] Houghton
Mifflin 2006 unp il $16   **E**
1. Animal locomotion
ISBN 0-618-64637-X   LC 2005-19082

In this "book illustrated with cut and torn-paper collages, animals leap, swim, slide, swing, and waddle.
Each spread contains one action word and two animals
for whom that behavior is typical. . . . Jenkins uses brief
phrases as captions and provides a well-written, concise
appendix. . . . This book is gorgeous and educational."
SLJ

Jiménez, Francisco

The Christmas gift: El regalo de Navidad;
illustrated by Claire B. Cotts. Houghton Mifflin
2000 unp il $15   **E**
1. Migrant labor—Fiction 2. Mexican Americans—
Fiction 3. Christmas—Fiction 4. Bilingual books—English-Spanish
ISBN 0-395-92869-9   LC 99-26224
When his family has to move again a few days before
Christmas in order to find work, Panchito worries that he
will not get the ball he has been wanting
"This story, a version of which appeared in Jiménez's
. . .The Circuit, is presented here in a bilingual picture
book format with an excellent Spanish text. . . . Mural-
like illustrations soulfully depict the hard life and strong
people of the migrant labor camps." Horn Book Guide

Jocelyn, Marthe

ABC x 3; English, Español, Français; [illustrated
by] Tom Slaughter. Tundra Books 2005 unp il
$12.95   **E**
1. Alphabet 2. Spanish language—Vocabulary
3. French language—Vocabulary
ISBN 0-88776-707-9
"This alphabet book has an interesting twist: each letter is presented with text in three languages. What a terrific way to show the similarities among English, Spanish, and French, especially when the words are exactly
the same in each case for jaguar, kiwi, quetzal, radio,
and zigzag. . . . The illustrations are simple, painted paper cuts done in vibrant primary and secondary colors,
accented with black." SLJ

Hannah's collections. Dutton Children's Bks.
2000 unp il $14.99   **E**
1. Collectors and collecting—Fiction
ISBN 0-525-46442-5   LC 99-462104
Unable to decide which of her many collections to
take to school, Hannah surveys her collections of buttons, shells, feathers, and other wonderful objects and
comes up with a unique solution
"Spreads and individual scenes in this bright, boldly
graphic picture book possess startling clarity. . . . The
story framework presents ingenious opportunities for
preschoolers to practice some important thinking skills:
counting, mathematical grouping, naming objects, and
creative problem solving are all seamlessly wrapped up
in this fresh, visually vibrant display." Booklist
Another title about Hannah is:
Hannah and the seven dresses (1999)

Jocelyn, Marthe—*Continued*

Over under; [illustrated by] Tom Slaughter.
Tundra Books 2005 unp il $15.95   E
  1. Opposites
  ISBN 0-88776-708-7

"Minimal rhyming text and cut-paper illustrations of
animals in six basic colors introduce opposites: e.g. 'big'
and 'small' are represented by a black elephant and
mouse on a vibrant red background." Horn Book Guide

Johansen, Hanna

Henrietta and the golden eggs; Käthi Bhend,
pictures. Godine 2002 unp il $16.95   E
  1. Chickens—Fiction
  ISBN 1-56792-210-4   LC 2002-13477

The persistence of Henrietta, one of 3,333 chickens on
a chicken farm, leads to a better life for them all

"The pictures are quite extraordinary: hilarious depictions of chickens set free as well as somber drawings of
chickens stuffed in a modern-day chicken house that
goes on as far as the eye can see. This effective tale,
translated from the German, has layers of subtext in both
story and art." Booklist

Johnson, Angela

I dream of trains; illustrated by Loren Long.
Simon & Schuster Bks. for Young Readers 2003
unp il $16.95   E
  1. Jones, Casey, 1863-1900—Fiction 2. Railroads—
  Fiction 3. African Americans—Fiction
  ISBN 0-689-82609-5   LC 98-52886

The son of a sharecropper dreams of leaving Mississippi on a train with the legendary engineer Casey Jones

"Long's moody acrylic paintings, mainly in subdued
tones, are a sterling accompaniment to the book's provocative prose." SLJ

Just like Josh Gibson; written by Angela
Johnson; illustrated by Beth Peck. Simon &
Schuster Books for Young Readers 2004 unp il
$15.95   E
  1. Baseball—Fiction 2. Grandmothers—Fiction
  3. African Americans—Fiction
  ISBN 0-689-82628-1   LC 2001-49531

A young girl's grandmother tells her of her love for
baseball and the day they let her play in the game even
though she was a girl.

"Johnson tempers what could have been a sentimental
tale with Grandmama's contagious enthusiasm and sense
of empowerment, and her text has a baseball announcer's
suspenseful rhythm. . . . Peck's angular pastels . . .
skillfully capture the nostalgic sports action and celebration." Booklist

Tell me a story, Mama; pictures by David
Soman. Orchard Bks. 1989 unp il $16.95; lib bdg
$14.99; pa $6.95   E
  1. Mother-daughter relationship—Fiction 2. African
  Americans—Fiction
  ISBN 0-531-05794-1; 0-531-08394-2 (lib bdg);
  0-531-07032-8 (pa)   LC 88-17917

A young girl and her mother remember together all
the girl's favorite stories about her mother's childhood

"Soman's vivid, lively watercolors capture the essence
of the mood and message as they deftly portray the quo-
tidian portraits of two generations of a black family.
Both language and art are full of subtle wit and rich
emotion." SLJ

Violet's music; illustrated by Laura
Huliska-Beith. Dial Books for Young Readers
2004 unp il $16.99   E
  1. Music—Fiction 2. African Americans—Fiction
  ISBN 0-8037-2740-2   LC 2003-2037

From the days she banged her rattle in the crib, Violet
has been looking for friends to share her love of music.

"With an upbeat text that uses lots of sound words,
this tale celebrates music as much as it applauds being
true to what you love. . . . Done in acrylics and collage,
the lively illustrations seem to move on the page." SLJ

Johnson, Crockett

Harold and the purple crayon. Harper & Row
1955 unp il $15.99; lib bdg $15.89; pa $6.99
          E
  1. Drawing—Fiction
  ISBN 0-06-022935-7; 0-06-022936-5 (lib bdg);
  0-06-443022-7 (pa)
  Also available Spanish language edition

"As Harold goes for a moonlight walk, he uses his
purple crayon to draw a path and the things he sees
along the way, then draws himself back home." Hodges.
Books for Elem Sch Libr
  Other titles about Harold are:
Harold's ABC (1963)
Harold's circus (1959)
Harold's fairy tale (1986)
Harold's trip to the sky (1957)
A picture for Harold's room (1960)

Johnson, Dinah

Quinnie Blue; paintings by James Ransome.
Holt & Co. 2000 unp il $16.95   E
  1. Grandmothers—Fiction 2. African Americans—Fiction
  ISBN 0-8050-4378-0   LC 98-47830

Hattie wonders about the activities of her grandmother
Quinnie Blue when she was little

"In the rich oil illustrations for this poetic, celebratory
text, blue-bordered scenes of Grandma's childhood alternate with white-bordered scenes from the narrator's life."
Horn Book Guide

Johnson, Donald B. (Donald Barton)

Henry hikes to Fitchburg; [by] D. B. Johnson.
Houghton Mifflin 2000 unp il $15   E
  1. Thoreau, Henry David, 1817-1862—Fiction
  2. Nature—Fiction 3. Walking—Fiction 4. Bears—Fiction
  ISBN 0-395-96867-4   LC 99-35302

While his friend works hard to earn the train fare to
Fitchburg, Henry the bear walks the thirty miles through
woods and fields, enjoying nature and the time to think
great thoughts. Includes biographical information about
Henry David Thoreau

Johnson, Donald B. (Donald Barton)—*Continued*

"This splendid book works on several levels. Johnson's adaption of a paragraph taken from Thoreau's *Walden* (set down in an author's note) illuminates the contrast between materialistic and naturalistic views of life without ranting or preaching. His illustrations are breathtakingly rich and filled with lovingly rendered details." Booklist

Other titles about Henry the bear are:

Henry builds a cabin (2002)
Henry climbs a mountain (2003)
Henry works (2004)

Johnson, Paul Brett

On top of spaghetti; written and illustrated by Paul Brett Johnson; with lyrics by Tom Glazer. 1st ed. Scholastic Press 2006 unp il $15.99   **E**

1. Dogs—Fiction 2. Animals—Fiction 3. Songs 4. Meatballs—Fiction

ISBN 0-439-74944-1   LC 2005014311

"Expanding on the popular song, Johnson spins the tale of Yodeler Jones, a hound dog who serves nothing but meatballs and spaghetti at his dining establishment. When business begins to slow, Yodeler concocts a brand-new meatball, but before he can taste it, someone sneezes. . . . With original text printed in black and the lyrics sprinkled throughout in color, this story successfully marries the two. The loony illustrations, full of color and movement, effectively capture the zaniness." SLJ

Johnson, Stephen

Alphabet city; [by] Stephen T. Johnson. Viking 1995 unp il $16.99; pa $6.99   **E**

1. Alphabet

ISBN 0-670-85631-2; 0-14-055904-3 (pa)
                        LC 95-12335

A Caldecott Medal honor book, 1995

"Beginning with the *A* formed by a construction site's sawhorse and ending with the *Z* found in the angle of a fire escape, Johnson draws viewers' eyes to tiny details within everyday objects to find letters." SLJ

"Only after careful scrutiny will viewers realize that these arresting images aren't photographs but compositions of pastels, watercolors, gouache and charcoal. A visual tour de force, Johnson's ingenious alphabet book transcends the genre by demanding close inspection of not just letters, but the world." Publ Wkly

City by numbers. Viking 1998 unp il pa $6.99 hardcover o.p.   **E**

1. Counting

ISBN 0-14-056636-8 (pa)   LC 98-20391

Paintings of various sites around New York City—from a shadow on a building to a wrought iron-gate to the Brooklyn Bridge—depict the numbers from one to twenty-one

"The numbers are more difficult to read than the letters of 'Alphabet City,' but perhaps the stretching of vision for this companion book makes it a grander and more complex achievement." N Y Times Book Rev

Johnston, Tony

Alice Nizzy Nazzy, the Witch of Santa Fe; illustrated by Tomie dePaola. Putnam 1995 unp il pa $6.99 hardcover o.p.   **E**

1. Witches—Fiction 2. New Mexico—Fiction

ISBN 0-689-11650-X (pa)   LC 93-44375

Johnson and dePaola "transport Baba Yaga, one of Russia's great folklore figures, to the American Southwest. Incarnated here as Alice Nizzy Nazzy, the child-eating witch lives in an adobe hut perched on 'skinny roadrunner feet' and surrounded by a fence of prickly pear cactus. When Manuela wanders by in search of her lost sheep, she ends up in Alice's soup caldron." Publ Wkly

"Johnson's writing snaps with life. . . . dePaola has filled the book with the bright colors of the Southwest, using brick red borders and lots of teal, purple, and orange. Alice is a satisfying blend of spookiness and silliness." Bull Cent Child Books

Alien & Possum: hanging out; pictures by Tony DiTerlizzi. Simon & Schuster Bks. for Young Readers 2002 48p il $15   **E**

1. Opossums—Fiction 2. Extraterrestrial beings—Fiction 3. Friendship—Fiction

ISBN 0-689-83836-0   LC 00-52233

Two good friends, Possum and Alien, spend time together celebrating their birthdays, discovering their uniqueness, and hanging out together in a tree

Readers "will love the amusing illustrations of these two pals and their antics." SLJ

Another title about Alien & Possum is:

Alien & Possum: friends no matter what (2001)

The barn owls; illustrated by Deborah Kogan Ray. Charlesbridge Pub. 2000 unp il $16.95; pa $6.95   **E**

1. Owls—Fiction

ISBN 0-88106-981-7; 0-88106-982-5 (pa)
                        LC 99-18763

"A Talewinds book"

For at least one hundred years, generations of barn owls have slept, hunted, called, raised their young, and glided silently above the wheat fields around an old barn

"A few words of simple, poetic text accompany each picture, stressing the ebb and flow of life in and around the barn. . . . The pictures match the text's simplicity and understated tone, making this a quietly eloquent nature book." Booklist

Day of the Dead; illustrated by Jeanette Winter. Harcourt Brace & Co. 1997 unp il $14; pa $6   **E**

1. All Souls' Day—Fiction 2. Mexico—Fiction

ISBN 0-15-222863-2; 0-15-202446-8 (pa)
                        LC 96-2276

Describes a Mexican family preparing for and celebrating the Day of the Dead

"Spanish phrases are a natural part of the storytelling as the children ask questions about the cooking and preparations. . . . Winter's brilliantly colored, acrylic illustratons in folk-art style express the magic realism that is part of the ceremony under the stars." Booklist

Johnston, Tony—*Continued*

Desert song; illustrations by Ed Young. Sierra Club Bks. for Children 2000 unp il $15.95

E

1. Desert animals—Fiction
ISBN 0-87156-491-2   LC 99-36886
As the heat of the desert day fades into night, various nocturnal animals, including bats, coyotes, and snakes, venture out to find food
"Spare, lyrical words and luminous, richly textured pictures reveal the mysterious, hidden world of the desert night in this beautiful volume." Booklist

The quilt story; pictures by Tomie dePaola. Putnam 1985 unp il $16.99; pa $5.99   E
1. Quilts—Fiction 2. Mother-daughter relationship—Fiction
ISBN 0-399-21009-1; 0-399-21008-3 (pa)
                              LC 84-18212
A pioneer mother lovingly stitches a beautiful quilt which warms and comforts her daughter Abigail; many years later another mother mends and patches it for her little girl
"DePaola's full-color tempera illustrations add much to the story—the folk-art style matches the text perfectly and will grab the attention of young 'book browsers.'" SLJ

That summer; illustrated by Barry Moser. Harcourt 2002 unp il $16   E
1. Quilts—Fiction 2. Brothers—Fiction 3. Death—Fiction
ISBN 0-15-201585-X   LC 2001-1314
A boy "recalls a summer that started as always . . . but ended with the death of his younger brother, Joey. . . . To pass the time when he can't sleep, Joey learns quilting from his grandmother, and he pieces together patches with images that are meaningful to him. . . . When Joey dies, his older brother stitches the final piece and then whispers, 'Goodbye.' Never mawkish, Johnston's spare, understated text is emotionally eloquent and beautifully poetic in its use of simile and metaphor. . . . Moser's images are, alternately, vivid watercolors, full of summer's intensity, and haunting, gray-and-white 'snapshot' images executed in graphite and heightened with white chalk. They give the book the look of a treasured, old-fashioned family album." Booklist

Uncle Rain Cloud; illustrated by Fabricio Vanden Broeck. Charlesbridge Pub. 2001 unp il $15.95   E
1. Uncles—Fiction 2. Mexican Americans—Fiction 3. English language—Fiction
ISBN 0-88106-371-1   LC 99-54195
"A Talewinds book"
Carlos tries to help his uncle, who is frustrated and angry at his inability to speak English, adjust to their new home in Los Angeles
"Brisk pacing, sympathetic characters, and clear prose that uses embedded Spanish words effectively make a winner. VandenBroeck's acrylic and colored-pencil illustrations flesh out the narrative in soft, bright colors enhanced by dramatic shading." SLJ

The whole green world; pictures by Elisa Kleven. 1st ed. Farrar Straus Giroux 2001 unp il $15   E
1. Nature—Fiction 2. Stories in rhyme
ISBN 0-374-38400-2   LC 00-63625
"A spirited young girl, accompanied by her shaggy dog, describes how she plants some seeds, cares for them, and then enjoys the flowers and trees that make the 'whole round world' beautiful. . . . Johnston's repetitive language is playful and reads aloud smoothly. Done in a variety of mediums, the full-page folk-art paintings are filled to the brim with people, animals, bugs, and blooms." SLJ

Jonas, Ann

The quilt. Greenwillow Bks. 1984 unp il $16.99

E

1. Quilts—Fiction
ISBN 0-688-03825-5   LC 83-25385
Also available in paperback from Puffin Bks.
"A little girl is given a new patchwork quilt, and at bedtime she amuses herself by identifying the materials used in its making. Later, she has a colorful dream in which she almost loses her stuffed dog, Sally (a piece of Sally is in the quilt, too)." Child Book Rev Serv
"The intricate illustrations in Jonas's book can be described only in superlatives. Backed by a length of golden-yellow calico imprinted with small red flowers, a quilt fashioned from squares in a variety of colors is the prize shown to readers by a dear little girl." Publ Wkly

Reflections. Greenwillow Bks. 1987 unp il $16.99   E
1. Seashore—Fiction
ISBN 0-688-06140-0   LC 86-33545
"Imaginative book about a day at the seashore. At what is the end in most books, this book is reversed and read from back to front with re-interpreted artwork and new captions. Clever idea executed with skill, flare, and appealing, full-color illustrations. Excellent for encouraging observation and making predictions." Sci Child

Round trip. Greenwillow Bks. 1983 unp il $15.99; pa $5.99   E
1. City and town life—Fiction
ISBN 0-688-01772-X; 0-688-09986-6 (pa)
                              LC 82-12026
Black and white illustrations and text record the sights on a day trip to the city and back home again to the country. The trip to the city is read from front to back and the return trip, from back to front, upside down
"Although one or two pictures too easily suggest their upside-down images and the device is occasionally strained, the author-artist displays a fine sense of graphic design and balance, and pictorial beauty is never sacrificed for mere cleverness." Horn Book

Splash! Greenwillow Bks. 1995 unp il $16.99; pa $6.99   E
1. Counting 2. Animals—Fiction
ISBN 0-688-11051-7; 0-688-15284-8 (pa)
                              LC 94-4110
A little girl's turtle, fish, frogs, dog, and cat jump in and out of a backyard pond, constantly changing the an-

Jonas, Ann—*Continued*

swer to the question "How many are in my pond?"

"A clever concept book with physical humor and exciting acrylic paintings that capture the heat and drama of a sunny summer day." Booklist

Jonell, Lynne

Let's play rough; pictures by Ted Rand. Putnam 2000 unp il $13.99　　　　　　　　E

1. Father-son relationship—Fiction

ISBN 0-399-23039-4　　　　　LC 99-10624

A father and son have fun playing rough on the couch, grabbing, tossing, and tickling

"Wavy lines of type reflect the rambunctious mood, which is further enhanced by uncluttered illustrations." Horn Book Guide

When Mommy was mad; written by Lynne Jonell; illustrated by Petra Mathers. Putnam 2002 unp il $13.99　　　　　　　　E

1. Anger—Fiction 2. Mothers—Fiction

ISBN 0-399-23433-0　　　　　LC 00-68405

Robbie helps his mother realize how her bad mood is affecting everyone in the family

"Jonell's sentences are as crisp as the mother's trimmed bangs. . . . Mathers's artwork is fresh and alive, too. Her illustrations . . . look as if they've been done by a talented 8-year-old with a box full of crayons." N Y Times Book Rev

Other titles about Robbie and his brother Christopher are:

I need a snake (1998)

It's my birthday, too! (1998)

Mom pie (2001)

Mommy go away! (1997)

Jones, Sally Lloyd

Time to say goodnight; illustrated by Jane Chapman. HarperCollins Pubs. 2006 unp il $15.99; lib bdg $16.89　　　　　　　　E

1. Bedtime—Fiction 2. Animals—Fiction 3. Stories in rhyme

ISBN 0-06-054328-0; 0-06-054329-9 (lib bdg)

In the same way that baby animals stop whatever they are doing and close their eyes for the night, so a child must finally go to sleep when bedtime comes.

"Chapman's winsome creatures painted in rich jewel tones add to the charm of this gentle bedtime book. . . . A sweet rhyming story." SLJ

Jones, Ursula

The witch's children; written by Ursula Jones; illustrated by Russell Ayto. Holt & Co. 2003 unp il $16.95　　　　　　　　E

1. Witches—Fiction 2. Magic—Fiction 3. Parks—Fiction

ISBN 0-8050-7205-5　　　　　LC 2002-5943

When the two older witch's children use their magic to create trouble in the park, the Little One knows how to fix the problem

"Ayto's line-and-watercolor illustrations reflect the breezy nature of the sly, clever tale." Bull Cent Child Books

Joosse, Barbara M.

Hot city; by Barbara Joosse; illustrated by R. Gregory Christie. Philomel Books 2004 unp il $16.99　　　　　　　　E

1. City and town life—Fiction 2. Summer—Fiction 3. Libraries—Fiction 4. African Americans—Fiction

ISBN 0-399-23640-6　　　　　LC 2002-1254

Mimi and her little brother Joe escape from home and the city's summer heat to read and dream about princesses and dinosaurs in the cool, quiet library.

"This eloquently told story is boldly illustrated with evocative acrylic paintings in shades of orange, red, and yellow." SLJ

A houseful of Christmas; [by] Barbara Joosse; illustrated by Betsy Lewin. Holt & Co. 2001 unp il $14.95　　　　　　　　E

1. Family life—Fiction 2. Grandmothers—Fiction

ISBN 0-8050-6391-9　　　　　LC 00-47303

Snowed in after sharing Christmas with Grandma, a houseful of relatives settles in for the night

"Hectic, yet warm—that's the Christmastime of the text—but it's Lewin's artwork, watercolor washes outlined in thick black ink, that really captures all the frenetic fun." Booklist

Mama, do you love me? illustrated by Barbara Lavallee. Chronicle Bks. 1991 unp il $15.95　　　　　　　　E

1. Mother-daughter relationship—Fiction 2. Inuit—Fiction

ISBN 0-87701-759-X　　　　　LC 90-1863

Also available Board book edition

"A young girl asks how much her mother loves her, even when she is naughty, and receives warm, reassuring answers. The twist on this familiar theme is that the two are Inuits, and the text and pictures draw on their unique culture. . . . Two pages of back matter define and explain the functions of various terms in Inuit life past and present. Charming, vibrant watercolor illustrations expand the simple rhythmic text, adding to the characters' personalities and to the cultural information." SLJ

Papa, do you love me? illustrated by Barbara Lavallee. Chronicle Books 2005 unp il $15.95　　　　　　　　E

1. Father-son relationship—Fiction 2. Masai (African people)—Fiction 3. Africa—Fiction

ISBN 0-8118-4265-7　　　　　LC 2003-17344

When a Masai father in Africa answers his son's questions, the boy learns that his father's love for him is unconditional.

"Echoing the soothing rhythm of the poetic narrative, Lavallee's graceful watercolors feature a harmoniously balanced palette." Publ Wkly

Jordan, Deloris

Salt in his shoes; Michael Jordan in pursuit of a dream; by Deloris Jordan with Roslyn M. Jordan; illustrated by Kadir Nelson. Simon & Schuster Bks. for Young Readers 2000 unp il $16.95　　　　　　　　E

1. Jordan, Michael, 1963- 2. Basketball

ISBN 0-689-83371-7　　　　　LC 00-20539

Jordan, Deloris—*Continued*

Young Michael Jordan is smaller than the other basketball players, so his mother "recommends salt in his shoes and prayer, and even though the boy can't figure out how the salt's going to help, he takes his mother's advice. Michael doesn't just depend on salt and prayers, though; he constantly practices playing basketball." Bull Cent Child Books

"This readable and entertaining story will delight the superstar's fans. Nelson's illustrations bring the right blend of vivid color, realism, and personality." SLJ

Joyce, William

Dinosaur Bob and his adventures with the family Lazardo. new ed. HarperCollins Pubs. 1995 unp il $16.99; lib bdg $16.89   E

1. Dinosaurs—Fiction

ISBN 0-06-021074-5; 0-06-021075-3 (lib bdg)

LC 94-19100

"A Laura Geringer book"

A revised and enlarged edition of the title first published 1988

"The Lazardo family goes on safari to Africa where they find a dinosaur. They name him Bob and take him back to Pimlico Hills. . . . Bob soon becomes famous because he can play the trumpet, dance, and most importantly play baseball." Child Book Rev Serv [review of 1988 edition]

George shrinks; story and pictures by William Joyce. Harper & Row 1985 unp il $16.99; pa $6.99   E

1. Size—Fiction 2. Fantasy fiction

ISBN 0-06-023070-3; 0-06-443129-0 (pa)

LC 83-47697

Also available Miniature edition

"A young boy named George awakes from his nap to discover he has become as small as a mouse. . . . Resting against the alarm clock is a piece of poster-size paper on which parental instructions are written telling George all that he should do after getting up. . . . Most of the book's text consists of this note's contents." N Y Times Book Rev

"The colorful illustrations, executed with painstaking attention to detail, create a surreal landscape from an ordinary breakfast-cereal world, as familiar objects become monumental structures through which the diminutive George moves with panache." Horn Book

Juan, Ana

The Night Eater; by Ana Juan. 1st ed. Arthur A. Levine Books 2004 unp il $16.95   E

1. Night—Fiction

ISBN 0-439-48891-5   LC 2003-20197

The Night Eater, who brings each new day by gobbling up the darkness, decides he is too fat and stops eating, with dire consequences

"The sense of magic realism in this story is matched by in Juan's richly colored acrylic-and-wax paintings. . . . This delightful tale will definitely appeal to children's imaginations." SLJ

Juster, Norton

The hello, goodbye window; story by Norton Juster; pictures by Chris Raschka. Hyperion Books for Children 2005 unp il $15.95   E

1. Grandparents—Fiction

ISBN 0-7868-0914-0

Awarded the Caldecott Medal, 2006

"Michael di Capua Books"

"The window in Nanna and Poppy's kitchen is no ordinary window—it is the place where love and magic happens. . . . The first-person text is both simple and sophisticated, conjuring a perfectly child-centered world. . . . Using a bright rainbow palette of saturated color, Raschka's impressionistic, mixed-media illustrations portray a loving, mixed-race family." SLJ

Kain, Karen

The Nutcracker; paintings by Rajka Kupesic. Tundra Books 2005 unp il $18.95   E

1. Fairy tales 2. Christmas—Fiction

ISBN 0-88776-696-X

Based on The National Ballet of Canada's production

"Misha and Marie are thrilled that Christmas is coming. . . . But there's a disappointment in store. Instead of the beautiful doll she'd hoped for, the only thing strange old Uncle Nikolai has for Marie is a wooden nutcracker. . . . Little does she know that it will lead her and her brother on the adventure of a lifetime." Publisher's note

This is a "striking staging of the classic ballet. . . . The narrative reads smoothly, but it's the art that steals the show. Peopled with doll-like folk-art figures, Kupesic's full-page illustrations . . . are intense with luminous colors." Booklist

Kalan, Robert

Jump, frog, jump! pictures by Byron Baron. Greenwillow Books 1995 c1981 unp il $16.99; pa $6.99   E

1. Frogs—Fiction 2. Stories in rhyme

ISBN 0-688-13954-X; 0-688-09241-1 (pa)

Also available board book edition

A reissue of the title first published 1981

"When a frog catches a fly, he sets off a chain of predators. . . . The title answers the repeated refrain 'How did the frog get away?' and children will soon be chanting along with this cumulative tale enhanced by Barton's folk-art-style illustrations." Publ Wkly

Kalman, Maira

Next stop, Grand Central. Putnam 1999 unp il $16.99   E

1. Grand Central Terminal (New York, N.Y.)

ISBN 0-399-22926-4   LC 98-25135

A simple introduction to the thousands of activities going on everyday in Grand Central, a train station in New York City

"Capturing all the hustle, bustle, and throbbing life of Grand Central Station, Kalman maintains an appropriately frenetic pace, parading the nonstop activity across the pages in a conglomeration of colorful vignettes. Kalman's odd-ball humor is in full evidence here." Horn Book Guide

Kalman, Maira—*Continued*

Smartypants (Pete in school). Putnam 2003 unp il $15.99   **E**

1. Dogs—Fiction 2. School stories

ISBN 0-399-23478-0   LC 2003-6837

When Pete the dog, who has an insatiable appetite, arrives at school he and his owner are sent to the principal's office, where he devours a set of encyclopedias and is suddenly able to speak and answer any question

"The design and the artwork are signature Kalman: inventive, eye-catching, bold yet subtle. . . . With so many witty asides and quirky artistic tangents, saying that this will be read more than once is an understatement." Booklist

Another title about Pete the dog is:
What Pete ate from A to Z (2001)

Kanevsky, Polly

Sleepy boy; illustrated by Stephanie Anderson. Atheneum Books for Young Readers 2006 unp il $15.95   **E**

1. Bedtime—Fiction 2. Father-son relationship—Fiction

ISBN 0-689-86735-2

"A Richard Jackson Book"

Unable to fall asleep, a little boy lying next to his father experiences the various sensations of his body and remembers a lion cub he saw that day at the zoo

"Simple, physical words and full-page, unframed, sepia-toned watercolor-and-charcoal images combine to create a portrait of blissful intimacy between a toddler and his father." Booklist

Karas, G. Brian

Atlantic. Putnam 2002 unp il $15.99   **E**

1. Atlantic Ocean—Fiction

ISBN 0-399-23632-5   LC 2001-19602

"Written from the ocean's point of view, the . . . text comments on what it is, where it is, how the sun and moon affect it, and how it is known by scientists, explorers, artists, and poets. . . . The artwork, done in gouache, acrylic, and pencil, is both playful and inventive." Booklist

The class artist. Greenwillow Bks. 2001 unp il $15.95; lib bdg $15.89   **E**

1. Artists—Fiction 2. School stories

ISBN 0-688-17814-6; 0-688-17815-4 (lib bdg)

LC 00-48439

Despite the trouble he has at first working on art projects at school, Fred develops into the class artist

"Stylized, cartoon-like art and some creative arrangment of type keep the mood light. With understatement and subtle humor, Karas neatly delivers a lesson on perseverance and the importance of beliving in one's abilities." Publ Wkly

Karim, Roberta

Kindle me a riddle; a pioneer story; pictures by Bethanne Andersen. Greenwillow Bks. 1999 34p il $16; lib bdg $16.89   **E**

1. Frontier and pioneer life—Fiction 2. Family life—Fiction 3. Riddles—Fiction

ISBN 0-688-16203-7; 0-688-16204-5 (lib bdg)

LC 98-18955

The riddles that a pioneer family share explain the origin of such things in their lives as their log cabin, johnnycakes, the broom, a cloak, candles, and more

"Andersen matches Karim's homespun, image-rich language with vibrant, airy scenes of a cozy, well-appointed log cabin and rolling countryside amply dotted with trees." Publ Wkly

Kasza, Keiko

The dog who cried wolf; .; [by] Keiko Kasza. G.P. Putnam's Sons 2005 unp il $15.99   **E**

1. Dogs—Fiction 2. Wolves—Fiction

ISBN 0-399-24247-3   LC 2004-24737

Tired of being a house pet, Moka the dog moves to the mountains to become a wolf but soon misses the comforts of home.

"With an effective variety of page layouts, the expressive pen-and-watercolor pictures show [Moka] dashing off on his adventures. . . . Thanks to excellent pacing, children will get caught up in the childlike Moka's emotions." SLJ

My lucky day. Putnam 2003 unp il $15.99   **E**

1. Pigs—Fiction 2. Foxes—Fiction

ISBN 0-399-23874-3   LC 2001-57874

When a young pig knocks on a fox's door, the fox thinks dinner has arrived, but the pig has other plans

"Kasza's gouache art is as buoyant and comical as her narrative." Publ Wkly

The wolf's chicken stew. Putnam 1987 unp il $16.99; pa $6.99   **E**

1. Wolves—Fiction 2. Chickens—Fiction

ISBN 0-399-21400-3; 0-399-22000-9 (pa)

LC 86-12303

"An old plot takes a new turn after the wolf, determined to fatten a chicken for his stew, bakes goodies for her every day only to find them consumed by a horde of baby chicks who shame 'Uncle Wolf' with their adoring gratitude." Bull Cent Child Books

"Kasza combines quivery line and shaded color to turn Wolf and Chicken into scuptural forms. Landscape images are treated similarly. . . . Wolf is comically and suspensefully visualized, making the flimflamming refrains sound just right." Wilson Libr Bull

Katz, Karen

Mommy hugs; by Karen Katz. 1st ed. Margaret K. McElderry Books 2006 unp il $12.95   **E**

1. Mother-child relationship—Fiction 2. Counting

ISBN 0-689-87772-2   LC 2004025618

Katz, Karen—*Continued*

A loving mother counts the hugs she gives her baby throughout the day.

"Katz's trademark round-headed characters are cheerful and exude warmth. The sunny pictures capture familiar activities. . . . The collage, gouache, and colored-pencil illustrations have polka-dot and floral patterns that add visual interest." SLJ

My first Chinese New Year; [by] Karen Katz. 1st ed. H. Holt 2004 unp il $14.95 **E**
1. Chinese New Year—Fiction 2. Chinese Americans—Fiction
ISBN 0-8050-7076-1   LC 2003-23488

In this "picture book, a young girl prepares for and celebrates the Chinese New Year with her extended family. . . . The tale radiates warmth. . . . The collage illustrations, cut from paper with colorful Asian designs, also include paint and other media to capture the joyful celebrants." SLJ

Ten tiny tickles; by Karen Katz. 1st ed. Margaret K. McElderry Books 2004 unp il $14.95 **E**
1. Infants—Fiction 2. Counting
ISBN 0-689-85976-7   LC 2003-11821

Family members awaken a baby with tickles, from one little tickle on a lovely sleepy head to ten tiny tickles on chubby, tubby toes.

"Katz uses a bright, cheerful mix of collage, gouache, and colored pencils to produce artwork that has great visual appeal for the intended audience." Booklist

Kay, Verla

Covered wagons, bumpy trails; illustrated by S.D. Schindler. Putnam 2000 unp il $15.99 **E**
1. Overland journeys to the Pacific—Fiction 2. Frontier and pioneer life—Fiction 3. Stories in rhyme
ISBN 0-399-22928-0   LC 96-37478

Illustrations and simple rhyming text follow a family as they make the difficult journey by wagon to a new home across the Rocky Mountains

"Schindler handsomely augments the clip-clop rhyme with sweeping vistas and close-up views of the wagons, animals, and people through various stages of the journey." Horn Book Guide

Gold fever; illustrations by S.D. Schindler. Putnam 1999 unp il $15.99 **E**
1. California—Gold discoveries—Fiction 2. West (U.S.)—Fiction
ISBN 0-399-23027-0   LC 97-49634

In this brief rhyming story set during the gold rush, Jasper leaves his family and farm to pursue his dream of finding gold

"Schindler's colored pencil drawings convey the rugged scenery and the gritty enterprise of digging and sluicing for gold. Kay's tongue-in-cheek economy beautifully encapsulates this brief, colorful moment in history." Horn Book Guide

Keats, Ezra Jack

Apt. 3. Viking 1999 unp il $15.99; pa $6.99 **E**
1. City and town life—Fiction 2. Brothers—Fiction 3. Blind—Fiction
ISBN 0-670-88342-5; 0-14-056507-8 (pa)
                    LC 98-41043

A reissue of the title first published 1971 by Macmillan

On a rainy day two brothers try to discover who is playing the harmonica they hear in their apartment building

"The well-paced text is illustrated with shadowy paintings that capably convey both the dingy surroundings and the brothers' affection." Horn Book Guide

Clementina's cactus. Viking 1999 c1982 unp il $15.99 **E**
1. Cactus—Fiction 2. Deserts—Fiction 3. Stories without words
ISBN 0-670-88545-2   LC 98-47506

A reissue of the title first published 1982

"Little Clementina, a pioneer girl, examines an ugly cactus near her small shack. The next day after a storm, the cactus is abloom with brilliant yellow flowers. Showing both the sun-bleached vastness of a desert country as well as its brilliance, the wordless double-page spreads tell the story without a text." Horn Book Guide

Hi, cat! Viking 1999 unp il $15.99 **E**
1. Cats—Fiction 2. African Americans—Fiction
ISBN 0-670-88546-0   LC 98-37764

A reissue of the title first published 1970 by Macmillan

This book "tells the story of Peter's friend Archie and the inquisitive, nondescript, half-grown alley cat that tags after him and manages to make a shambles out of the boys' street carnival. The text provides an adequate framework for Keats's bold bright paintings of a lively city neighborhood." Horn Book Guide

Another title about Archie is:
Pet show! (1972)

Jennie's hat. Viking 2003 unp il $15.99; pa $6.99 **E**
1. Hats—Fiction
ISBN 0-670-03625-0; 0-14-250035-6 (pa)
                    LC 2002-11316

A reissue of the title published 1985 by Harper & Row

When the hat Jennie receives from her aunt is not as fancy as she had hoped, her bird friends decorate it for her

This fantasy "has a sense of freshness, of spring, about it. Attractive, colorful pictures make most telling use of collage." Christ Sci Monit

Louie. Greenwillow Bks. 1983 c1975 unp il lib bdg $16.89; pa $6.99 **E**
1. Puppets and puppet plays—Fiction
ISBN 0-688-02383-5 (lib bdg); 0-14-240080-7 (pa)
First published 1975

A shy, withdrawn boy loses his heart to a puppet

"This story is illustrated with the same glowing colors . . . and with some of the postercollage that is the art-

Keats, Ezra Jack—*Continued*

ist's trademark. The aura is touching without being maudlin, the writing simple and informal." Sutherland. The Best in Child Books

Other titles about Louie are:

Louie's search (1980)

Regards to the man in the moon (1981)

The trip (1978)

Over in the meadow; [written and] illustrated by Ezra Jack Keats. Viking 1999 unp il $16.99

E

1. Nursery rhymes 2. Animals—Poetry 3. Counting

ISBN 0-670-88344-1   LC 98-47037

A reissue of the title first published 1971 by Four Winds Press

Based on Southern Appalachian counting rhyme from late 1800's attributed to Olive A. Wadsworth

An old nursery poem introduces animals and their young and the numbers one through ten

"The book features Keats's illustrations that show animals in lively characteristic activity." Horn Book Guide

The snowy day. Viking 1962 31p il lib bdg $16.99; pa $5.99   E

1. Snow—Fiction

ISBN 0-670-65400-0 (lib bdg); 0-14-050182-7 (pa)

Also available Board book edition; Spanish language edition also available

Awarded the Caldecott Medal, 1963

A small "boy's ecstatic enjoyment of snow in the city is shown in vibrant pictures. Peter listens to the snow crunch under his feet, makes the first tracks in a clean patch of snow, makes angels and a snowman. At night in his warm bed he thinks over his adventures, and in the morning wakens to the promise of another lovely snowy day." Moorachian. What is a City?

Other titles about Peter are:

Goggles (1969)

A letter to Amy (1968)

Peter's chair (1967)

Whistle for Willie (1964)

Keller, Holly

Farfallina & Marcel. Greenwillow Bks. 2002 unp il $15.99; lib bdg $17.89; pa $5.99

E

1. Friendship—Fiction   2. Growth—Fiction
3. Caterpillars—Fiction 4. Geese—Fiction

ISBN 0-06-623932-X; 0-06-623933-8 (lib bdg); 0-06-443872-4 (pa)   LC 2001-51297

A caterpillar and a young goose become great friends, but as they grow up they undergo changes which separate them for awhile

"With bright, clear watercolors, Keller tells an appealing animal story. . . . The fantasy is rooted in the amazing true nature story of change and metamorphosis." Booklist

Geraldine's blanket. Greenwillow Bks. 1984 unp il pa $5.99 hardcover o.p.   E

1. Blankets—Fiction

ISBN 0-688-07810-9 (pa)   LC 83-14062

"Geraldine's pink blanket was a baby present from Aunt Bessie. It's worn now and patched, and when Aunt Bessie sends her a doll, Geraldine preserves and transfers her affections simultaneously by using the scraps for a doll dress." N Y Times Book Rev

"Simply but wonderfully expressive line drawings washed with pastel colors capture the gentleness and humor of the story." SLJ

Other titles about Geraldine are:

Geraldine and Mrs. Duffy (2000)

Geraldine first (1996)

Geraldine's baby brother (1994)

Geraldine's big snow (1988)

Merry Christmas, Geraldine (1997)

Grandfather's dream. Greenwillow Bks. 1994 unp il $16.99   E

1. Cranes (Birds)—Fiction 2. Grandfathers—Fiction
3. Vietnam—Fiction

ISBN 0-688-12339-2   LC 93-18186

After the end of the war in Vietnam, a young boy's grandfather dreams of restoring the wetlands of the Mekong delta, hoping that the large cranes that once lived there will return

"Keller uses simple, direct storytelling and vivid watercolor and ink illustrations to present a complex theme in a story of hope and rebirth." Horn Book Guide

Horace. Greenwillow Bks. 1991 unp il $16.99

E

1. Adoption—Fiction

ISBN 0-688-09831-2   LC 90-30750

"Horace is adopted. He is also spotted, and he is loved and cared for by his new mother and father—who are striped. But . . . Horace feels the need to search out his roots. And although he does find a brood that resembles him physically, it is not a family that truly loves him. . . . Keller . . . deals with a sensitive subject in a way that is perceptive but not sentimental. . . . The bright, boldly colored illustrations feature a lively animal cast and numerous amusing details." Publ Wkly

Other titles about Horace are:

Brave Horace (1998)

That's mine, Horace (2000)

Pearl's new skates; by Holly Keller. 1st ed. Greenwillow Books 2005 24p il $15.99; lib bdg $16.89   E

1. Ice skating—Fiction

ISBN 0-06-056280-3; 0-06-056281-1 (lib bdg)
          LC 2004-576

Pearl's birthday skates have a single blade and learning to use them is harder than she expects

"With her pitch-perfect text and uncluttered watercolor-and-ink pictures . . . Keller tells a tender story about accepting the failures and frustrations that come with learning something new." Booklist

Sophie's window; by Holly Keller. 1st ed. Greenwillow Books 2005 unp il $15.99; $16.89

E

1. Pigeons—Fiction 2. Dogs—Fiction

ISBN 0-06-056282-X; 0-06-056283-8 (lib bdg)
          LC 2004-42355

Keller, Holly—*Continued*

When Caruso, a little pigeon who is afraid to fly, is blown out of his home one windy night, he must rely on a new friend, Sophie the dog, to take him back to his parents

"Keller uses cheerful, airy yellows and blues that echo the story's gentle, empowering tone. . . . Written in appealing, short, rhythmic sentences, this is a fine choice for group sharing." Booklist

What a hat! Greenwillow Bks. 2003 unp il $15.99; lib bdg $16.89   E

1. Hats—Fiction 2. Cousins—Fiction 3. Rabbits—Fiction

ISBN 0-06-051479-5; 0-06-051480-9 (lib bdg)

LC 2002-29781

Henry makes fun of his cousin Newton for always wearing his hat, but the hat comes in handy for Henry's sister Wizzie

"Colorful illustrations featuring animals with expressive eyes and postures, all placed against uncluttered backgrounds, clearly depict the action in this amusing yet reassuring tale." SLJ

Kellogg, Steven

Best friends; story and pictures by Steven Kellogg. Dial Bks. for Young Readers 1986 unp il $16.99; pa $6.99   E

1. Friendship—Fiction

ISBN 0-8037-0099-7; 0-14-054607-3 (pa)

LC 85-15971

Kathy feels lonely and betrayed when her best friend Louise goes away for the summer and has a wonderful time

"The watercolor and ink illustrations are appealingly bright and magical. Kathy and Louise's daydreams are vividly and flamboyantly portrayed, with 'reality' just as attractively pictured." SLJ

The missing mitten mystery; story and pictures by Steven Kellogg. Dial Bks. for Young Readers 2000 unp il $15.99; pa $6.99   E

ISBN 0-8037-2566-3; 0-14-230192-2 (pa)

LC 99-54777

First published 1974 with title: The mystery of the missing red mitten

Annie searches the neighborhood for her red mitten, the fifth she's lost this winter

"Kellogg really outdoes himself with pictures that are filled with good cheer, warm spirits, and happy daydreams. . . . A book that's upbeat and touching by turns." Booklist

The mysterious tadpole; new illustrations and text by Steven Kellogg. 25th anniversary ed. Dial Bks. for Young Readers 2002 unp il $16.99

E

1. Pets—Fiction

ISBN 0-8037-2788-7   LC 2001-53776

First published 1977

"Louis receives a birthday present from his uncle in Scotland: Alphonse, an amiable tadpole that outgrows his bowl, the bathtub, and even the apartment. . . . The new illustrations are bigger, bolder, brighter, and brimming with lively details." Booklist

Pinkerton, behave! story and pictures by Steven Kellogg. Dial Books for Young Readers 2002 c1979 unp il $17.99; pa $6.99   E

1. Dogs—Fiction

ISBN 0-8037-2722-4; 0-14-230007-1 (pa)

A reissue of the title first published 1979

Pinkerton the Great Dane "doesn't understand his owner's commands. . . . Pinkerton's desperate owner sends him to obedience school, but he flunks out. . . . Then one night a burglar breaks into their house, and Pinkerton is able to put his bad habits to good use." Publisher's note

"Kellogg wittily captures expressions and movements of animal and human, wisely allowing the focal humor to emanate through the faces and action." Booklist

Other titles about Pinkerton are:

A penguin pup for Pinkerton (2001)

Prehistoric Pinkerton (1987)

A Rose for Pinkerton (1981)

Tallyho, Pinkerton (1982)

Kelly, John

The mystery of Eatum Hall; [by] John Kelly and Cathy Tincknell. 1st U.S. ed. Candlewick Press 2004 unp il $15.99   E

1. Pigs—Fiction 2. Geese—Fiction 3. Wolves—Fiction

ISBN 0-7636-2594-9   LC 2004-48507

Mr. and Mrs. Pork-Fowler (a pig and a goose respectively) are invited to spend a weekend of gourmet dining at a spooky castle where their host, Mr. Hunter (a wolf), is anxious to "meat" them.

"The digitally created pictures have an impressionistic quality that lends a look of unpolished spontaneity. There's beautiful use of color and exaggeration of all sorts to add atmosphere. A wealth of visual and verbal details will engage children on many levels." SLJ

Kenah, Katharine

The best seat in second grade; story by Katharine Kenah; pictures by Abby Carter. HarperCollins Pub. 2005 48p il $15.99; lib bdg $16.89   E

1. Hamsters—Fiction 2. School stories

ISBN 0-06-000734-6; 0-06-000735-4 (lib bdg)

LC 2004-178

"An I can read book"

Sam's favorite thing about second grade is the class pet, a hamster named George Washington, so when the class goes on a field trip to a science museum, Sam cannot resist bringing George along.

"Kenah has created an appealing cast of characters whose actions ring true. . . . Carter's watercolor illustrations add to the story's appeal." Booklist

Another title about this second grade is:

The best teacher in second grade (2006)

Kent, Jack

There's no such thing as a dragon. 1st Random House ed. Golden Book 2005 c1975 unp il $12.95; lib bdg $14.99   E

1. Dragons—Fiction

ISBN 0-375-83208-4; 0-375-93208-9 (lib bdg)

LC 2004-6123

Kent, Jack—*Continued*

First published 1975 by Western Pub.

"When Billy Bixbee wakes up and finds a dragon in his room, his mother tells him there is no such thing. The neglected dragon grows larger and larger, eventually walking off with the house, and the Bixbee family is forced to admit his existance. Practically a classic. . . for its neat story line and humorous cartoons of expressively suprised characters." Horn Book Guide

Kerley, Barbara

You and me together; moms, dads, and kids around the world; with a note by Marian Wright Edelman. National Geographic 2005 32p il $16.95; lib bdg $25.90 **E**

1. Parent-child relationship

ISBN 0-7922-8297-3; 0-7922-8298-1 (lib bdg)

"Using a simple rhyming text, Kerley captures the essence of childhood's special moments, accompanied by superb full-color photos. . . . Diverse cultures in various locations around the world are represented. . . . Children and parents engage in activities such as playing an instrument, taking a walk, making a meal, fishing, and dancing. . . . This book is an excellent tool for raising awareness of cultural differences and similarities." SLJ

Kerr, Judith

The other goose; story and pictures by Judith Kerr. HarperCollins Pubs. 2002 c2001 unp il $15.95; lib bdg $15.89 **E**

1. Geese—Fiction

ISBN 0-06-008254-2; 0-06-008583-5 (lib bdg)

LC 2001-39735

First published 2001 in the United Kingdom

Katerina the goose sees another goose in the side of Mr. Buswell's shiny car and wishes it would come join her in the town pond

"Lightly sketched in colored pencil, the illustrations complement the text perfectly, conveying humor and information." Horn Book Guide

Another title about Katrina is:

Goose in a hole (2006)

Kessler, Cristina

The best beekeeper of Lalibela; a tale from Africa; by Cristina Kessler; illustrated by Leonard Jenkins. 1st ed. Holiday House 2006 unp il $16.95 **E**

1. Beekeeping—Fiction 2. Sex role—Fiction 3. Ethiopia—Fiction

ISBN 0-8234-1858-8 LC 2005046217

In the Ethiopian mountain village of Lalibela a young girl named Almaz determines to find a way to be a beekeeper despite being told that is something only men can do.

"Jenkins follows the ups and downs of Almaz's labor in deep-hued, mixed-media scenes spread richly across double pages. . . . Kessler includes well-chosen details about the beekeeping project and a few words from the local Amharic and Tigringna languages." SLJ

Kessler, Leonard P.

Here comes the strikeout. newly il ed. HarperCollins Pubs. 1992 64p il lib bdg $16.89; pa $3.99 **E**

1. Baseball—Fiction

ISBN 0-06-023156-4 (lib bdg); 0-06-444011-7 (pa)

LC 91-14717

"An I can read book"

A revised and newly illustrated edition of the title first published 1965

This "concerns a boy who can't hit a baseball until he follows the advice of a friend. 'Lucky helmets won't do it. Lucky bats won't do it. Only hard work will do it.' . . . A winner." Booklist

Kick, pass, and run; story and pictures by Leonard Kessler. newly il ed. HarperCollins Pubs. 1996 64p il lib bdg $16.89; pa $3.99 **E**

1. Football—Fiction

ISBN 0-06-027105-1 (lib bdg); 0-06-444210-1 (pa)

LC 95-6185

"An I can read book"

A newly illustrated edition of the title first published 1966

"After a group of animal friends watches a boys' football team play, they are eager to have their own game. An apple serves as a ball until Frog eats it; a paper-bag football works until Duck kicks and pops it. The game is kept alive when a real football from the boys' game sails into the animals' midst. [A] simply told story with plenty of sports action." Horn Book Guide

Last one in is a rotten egg. newly il ed. HarperCollins Pubs. 1999 64p il lib bdg $14.89; pa $3.99 **E**

1. Swimming—Fiction

ISBN 0-06-028485-4 (lib bdg); 0-06-444262-4 (pa)

LC 98-50882

"An I can read book"

A newly illustrated edition of the title first published 1969

After Freddy is pushed into deep water by a couple of toughs, he decides to learn to swim

"This lively . . . sports story has been newly illustrated with a multicultural cast in a New York City neighborhood." Booklist

Ketteman, Helen

Armadilly chili; illustrated by Will Terry. Albert Whitman & Company 2004 unp il $16.95 **E**

1. Desert animals—Fiction

ISBN 0-8075-0457-2 LC 2003-14855

In this Texas-style adaptation of a traditional folktale, a tarantula, mockingbird, and horned toad refuse to help an armadillo prepare a batch of chili but nevertheless expect to eat it when it's ready.

"Done in jewel tones, the scenes depict the warmth of the desert landscape as well as that of the creatures' friendship. The rhythmic text reads aloud well and the dialogue has a western flavor." SLJ

Khan, Rukhsana

Ruler of the courtyard; illustrated by R. Gregory Christie. Viking 2003 unp il $15.99   **E**

1. Fear—Fiction

ISBN 0-670-03583-1   LC 2002-10167

After confronting what she believes to be a snake in the bath house, Saba finds the courage to overcome her fear of the chickens in the courtyard

"This spare tale . . . has wonderful energy and use of language. . . . Illustrator Christie gives us vibrant Picasso-esque chickens done as if in fingerpaints. He matches their vitality with an equally powerful landscape of oranges and yellows that frames Saba's pink house." Horn Book

Silly chicken; illustrated by Yunmee Kyong. Viking 2005 unp il $15.99   **E**

1. Chickens—Fiction 2. Pakistan—Fiction

ISBN 0-670-05912-9   LC 2004-15830

In Pakistan, Rani believes that her mother loves their pet chicken Bibi more than she cares for her, until the day that a fluffy chick appears and steals Rani's own affections.

"This picture book clearly depicts a child's jealousy. . . . Kyong . . . paints in a naive style, using fresh, warm colors. A pleasing book with an unusual setting." Booklist

Kimmel, Elizabeth Cody

My penguin Osbert; illustrated by H.B. Lewis. 1st ed. Candlewick Press 2004 unp il $16.99   **E**

1. Penguins—Fiction 2. Christmas—Fiction

ISBN 0-7636-1699-0   LC 2003-40981

When a boy finally gets exactly what he wants from Santa, he learns that owning a real penguin may not have been a good idea after all.

"Kimmel sneaks some sly humor into the well-told, nicely paced story, and Lewis' artwork, executed in watercolor and pastels and enhanced with digital renderings, has a soft look, colored in marshmallow tints." Booklist

Kimmel, Eric A.

Blackbeard's last fight; pictures by Leonard Everett Fisher. Farrar, Straus and Giroux 2006 32p il $17   **E**

1. Blackbeard, 1680?-1718—Fiction 2. Pirates—Fiction

ISBN 0-374-30780-6   LC 2003-69365

In 1718, off the coast of North Carolina, a young cabin boy assists in the final capture and execution of Blackbeard the pirate.

"The battle scenes are sea-sprayed and wonderfully choreographed, full of colorful corsairs and straight-faced sailors. Although not for the fainthearted, this tale is an exciting and satisfying read." SLJ

The Chanukkah guest; illustrated by Giora Carmi. Holiday House 1990 unp il $15.95; pa $6.95   **E**

1. Hanukkah—Fiction 2. Bears—Fiction 3. Jews—Fiction

ISBN 0-8234-0788-8; 0-8234-0978-3 (pa)

LC 89-20073

On the first night of Chanukkah, Old Bear wanders into Bubba Brayna's house and receives a delicious helping of potato latkes when she mistakes him for the rabbi

"In this comical story, Kimmel captures the kindness of an old woman and the innocence of a hungry bear in an unusual visit. Carmi's airy pastel illustrations shade the tale with a golden glow appropriate for the Festival of Lights." Publ Wkly

Don Quixote and the windmills; retold and adapted by Eric A. Kimmel from The ingenious hidalgo Don Quixote de la Mancha by Miguel de Cervantes Saavedra; pictures by Leonard Everett Fisher. Farrar, Straus and Giroux 2004 unp il $16   **E**

1. Spain—Fiction 2. Knights and knighthood—Fiction

ISBN 0-374-31825-5   LC 2002-67172

Immersed in tales of knights and dragons and sorcerers and damsels in distress, Senor Quexada proclaims himself a knight and sets out on his first adventure against some nearby windmills that he thinks are giants.

"Fisher's signature illustrations are the ideal accompaniment to the sprightly text. Making dramatic use of white highlights, the bold acrylic paintings have a kinetic momentum and power." SLJ

Four dollars and fifty cents; illustrated by Glen Rounds. Holiday House 1990 unp il lib bdg $16.95   **E**

1. Cowhands—Fiction 2. West (U.S.)—Fiction

ISBN 0-8234-0817-5   LC 89-77515

Originally published in Cricket Magazine

To avoid paying the Widow Macrae the four dollars and fifty cents he owes her, deadbeat cowboy Shorty Long plays dead and almost gets buried alive

"Rounds's outrageous, bold, line-and-crayon drawings perfectly suit the tale's Western flavor. A fast-paced, funny story." Horn Book

Grizz! illustrated by Andrew Glass. Holiday House 2000 unp il $16.95   **E**

1. Devil—Fiction 2. Cowhands—Fiction

ISBN 0-8234-1469-8   LC 98-43332

Cowboy Lucky Doolin makes a deal with the Devil, agreeing not to wash, shave, or change his clothes for seven years, thus earning a fortune and the hand of his true love

"This outwit-the-devil tale gets a wild west twist, enhanced by folksy prose and lively oil-and-watercolor illustrations." Booklist

Hershel and the Hanukkah goblins; written by Eric A. Kimmel; illustrated by Trina Schart Hyman. Holiday House 1989 unp il $16.95; pa $6.95   **E**

1. Hanukkah—Fiction 2. Fairies—Fiction 3. Jews—Fiction

ISBN 0-8234-0769-1; 0-8234-1131-1 (pa)

LC 89-1954

A Caldecott Medal honor book, 1990

"The setting is an Eastern European village, and the plot is a little like Halloween Hanukkah—it seems that goblins are occupying the synagogue on the hill. Along comes plucky Hershel of Ostropol, and he cleverly outwits the demons." N Y Times Book Rev

Kimmel, Eric A.—*Continued*

This "will fit companionably with haunted castle variants. Hyman is at her best with windswept landscapes, dark interiors, close portraiture, and imaginatively wicked creatures. Both art and history are charged with energy." Bull Cent Child Books

Zigazak! a magical Hanukkah night; illustrated by Jon Goodell. Doubleday Bks. for Young Readers 2001 unp il $15.95   **E**

1. Hanukkah—Fiction 2. Jews—Fiction
ISBN 0-385-32652-1   LC 98-46269

Two evil spirits wreak havoc on the town of Brisk's Hanukkah celebration, until the town's wise rabbi puts a stop to their mischief

"The text is safely boxed away from the devilry in double-page spreads in which intricately detailed art realistically depicts the furnishings, clothing, facial features, and even the townspeople's pets. Storytellers will have fun with the surprise ending." Booklist

Kinerk, Robert

Clorinda; illustrated by Steven Kellogg. Simon & Schuster Bks. for Young Readers 2003 unp il $15.95   **E**

1. Cattle—Fiction 2. Ballet—Fiction 3. Stories in rhyme
ISBN 0-689-86449-3   LC 2003-4559

"A Paula Wiseman book"

Defying the odds, Clorinda the cow follows her dream of becoming a ballet dancer

"As fine a mix of story and message as this is, it's the irrepressible art that makes this book shine. Kellogg is at the top of his game, finding the humor in every line." Booklist

King, Stephen Michael

Mutt dog! words and pictures by Stephen Michael King. Harcourt 2005 c2004 unp il $16   **E**

1. Dogs—Fiction 2. Homeless persons—Fiction
ISBN 0-15-205561-4

First published 2004 in Australia

A lonely dog finally finds a home after he makes friends with a woman who works at a homeless shelter.

"The presentation is well done, and the gentle pen-and-ink and watercolor cartoons tell the story beautifully. . . . The book's oversize format and clear wash illustrations on white backgrounds make this a good choice for storytimes." SLJ

Kinsey-Warnock, Natalie

Nora's ark; illustrated by Emily Arnold McCully. HarperCollins 2005 unp il $15.99; lib bdg $16.89   **E**

1. Floods—Fiction 2. Farm life—Fiction 3. Grandparents—Fiction 4. Vermont—Fiction
ISBN 0-688-17244-X; 0-06-029517-1 (lib bdg)
LC 2004-3444

During the Vermont flood of 1927, a girl and her grandparents share their new hilltop house with neighbors and animals.

This is a "well-told tale, based on an incident from the author's life. . . . [A] stunning picture is the wild, rainy scene showing houses bobbing along as the water pours down." Booklist

Kirk, Connie Ann

Sky dancers; illustrations by Christy Hale. 1st ed. Lee & Low Books 2004 unp il $16.95   **E**

1. Empire State Building (New York, N.Y.)—Fiction 2. Mohawk Indians—Fiction 3. Steel construction—Fiction 4. Father-son relationship—Fiction
ISBN 1-58430-162-7   LC 2004-1885

John Cloud, a Mohawk boy, lives in upstate New York, but he goes to visit his father who is working on the Empire State Building.

"Rich, sunlit gouache illustrations establish the 1930s setting for this well-told story." Horn Book Guide

Kitamura, Satoshi

Comic adventures of Boots. Farrar, Straus & Giroux 2002 unp il $16   **E**

1. Cats—Fiction
ISBN 0-374-31455-1

This consists of "three comic-strip adventures. There is 'Operation Fish Biscuit,' . . . in which clever Boots regains his prized sleeping spot from the local squatter cats. He tries to learn how to swim and fly from a duck in 'Pleased to Meet You, Madam Quark,' and plays in a wacky game of charades organized to ward off kitty boredom in 'Let's Play a Guessing Game.' . . . The pen-and-brush illustrations are zany and welcoming. . . . The humor is simultaneously sly and outrageous." SLJ

Other titles about Boots are:
Bath-time Boots (1997)
A friend for Boots (1998)

Me and my cat? Farrar, Straus & Giroux 2000 unp il $16; pa $6.95   **E**

1. Cats—Fiction 2. Magic—Fiction
ISBN 0-374-34906-1; 0-374-44796-9 (pa)
LC 99-16598

A young boy spends an unusual day after awakening to find that he and his cat have switched bodies

"Kitamura's oddball sense of humor finds a perfect outlet here, and readers will find a fresh and lively diversion in this uncommon adventure." Horn Book Guide

Kleven, Elisa

The paper princess. Dutton Children's Bks. 1994 unp il $15.99; pa $6.99   **E**

1. Drawing—Fiction
ISBN 0-525-45231-1; 0-14-056424-1 (pa)
LC 93-32612

A little girl makes a picture of a princess that comes to life and is carried off by the wind

"The jubilant, communicative collage art captivates the reader, as the winning text beguiles. A delightful reading experience." Horn Book Guide

Other titles about the paper princess are:
The paper princess finds her way (2003)
The paper princess flies again: (with her dog!) (2005)

Kleven, Elisa—*Continued*

Sun bread. Dutton Children's Bks. 2001 unp il $16.99   E

1. Bread—Fiction 2. Sun—Fiction 3. Stories in rhyme

ISBN 0-525-46674-6

Includes recipe on back cover

"In a rain-, snow-, and sleet-bound village of animals, everyone is miserable until the baker makes a loaf of bread shaped like the sun. The loaf brings such joy to the villagers that the actual sun makes an appearance. Gentle rhyming text joins delightful high-energy mixed-media illustrations with plenty of amusing details on each page." Horn Book Guide

Klinting, Lars

What do you want? Groundwood Books/House of Anansi Press 2006 unp il $15.95   E

ISBN 0-88899-636-5

Original Swedish edition 2003

"Each right-hand page of this little picture book begins with a phrase such as, 'The bumblebee wants . . . ' Turn the page, and the rest is revealed: 'its flower.' . . . This simple pattern repeats throughout the book, forming a guessing game." Booklist

"This diminutive book is mesmerizing in its calm simplicity. Cream-colored pages provide the backdrop to clear, precise color illustrations that are executed with artistic aplomb." SLJ

Klise, Kate

Shall I knit you a hat? a Christmas yarn; illustrated by M. Sarah Klise. 1st ed. H. Holt 2004 unp il $16.95   E

1. Rabbits—Fiction 2. Animals—Fiction 3. Christmas—Fiction 4. Hats—Fiction

ISBN 0-8050-7318-3   LC 2003-22497

When Mother Rabbit knits a warm winter hat for Little Rabbit, he likes it so much that he suggests they make hats for all of their friends as Christmas gifts

"The acrylic artwork glows with humor and radiates warmth." Booklist

Another title about Little Rabbit is:

Why do you cry?: not a sob story (2006)

Kloske, Geoffrey

Once upon a time, the end; (asleep in 60 seconds); by Geoffrey Kloske and Barry Blitt. Atheneum Books for Young Readers 2005 25p $15.95   E

1. Bedtime—Fiction 2. Fairy tales

ISBN 0-689-86619-4

"An Anne Schwartz Book"

A tired father takes only a few sentences to tell a number of classic tales in order to get the persistent listener to fall asleep.

"Blitt's ink-and-watercolor illustrations are amusing, with fine lines and soothing colors underscoring the comedy in the characters and situations." SLJ

Knowlton, Laurie Lazzaro

A young man's dance; [by] Laurie Knowlton; paintings by Layne Johnson. 1st ed. Boyds Mills Press 2006 unp il $15.95   E

1. Grandmothers—Fiction 2. Old age—Fiction 3. Alzheimer's disease—Fiction

ISBN 1-59078-259-3   LC 2005021138

Grandma Ronnie's grandson has a hard time adjusting to her needing a wheelchair, living in a nursing home, and not recognizing him when he comes to visit her.

"Swirling, dancing colors, both muted and sunny, accompany this lyrical story. . . . Oil paintings reveal clear, expressive faces on soft, fluid backgrounds that breathe action." SLJ

Koller, Jackie French

One monkey too many; illustrated by Lynn Munsinger. Harcourt Brace & Co. 1999 unp il $16; pa $6   E

1. Monkeys—Fiction 2. Stories in rhyme

ISBN 0-15-200006-2; 0-15-204764-6 (pa)

LC 96-50350

"Seven mischievous monkeys wreak havoc as 'one monkey too many' climbs first onto a bike made for one, then into a golf cart for two, then into a canoe for three, and so on." Horn Book Guide

"The joke is delightful, and Munsinger's boisterous illustrations, with animal characters galore . . . are full of expression, movement, and wacky comedy." Booklist

Another title about the seven monkeys is:

Seven spunky monkeys (2005)

Kono, Erin Eitter

Hula lullaby; [by] Erin Eitter Kono. 1st ed. Little, Brown 2005 unp il $15.99   E

1. Mother-child relationship—Fiction 2. Bedtime—Fiction 3. Hawaii—Fiction

ISBN 0-316-73591-4   LC 2004-10270

Against the backdrop of a beautiful Hawaiian landscape, a young girl cuddles and sleeps in her mother's lap.

"The rhyming text becomes almost hypnotic as night deepens around the two and, finally, the girl falls asleep. Glowing with warm colors, which seem all the more brilliant in the night scenes, the gouache-and-pencil illustrations create an idyllic vision of Hawaiian culture." Booklist

Koralek, Jenny

Night ride to Nanna's; illustrated by Mandy Sutcliffe. Candlewick Press 2000 unp il $15.99   E

1. Automobile travel—Fiction 2. Grandmothers—Fiction

ISBN 0-7636-1192-1   LC 99-58229

"When Amy and her family want to visit Nanna and Grandpa, they travel in the evening. . . . In both the glowing nighttime scenes that Amy views outside the car window and the images of the happy family gathering, the serene, cozily lit artwork complements the gentle tone of the text." Horn Book Guide

Koster, Gloria

The Peanut-Free Café; illustrated by Maryann Cocca-Leffler. Whitman, A. 2006 unp il $16.95

E

1. Allergy—Fiction 2. Peanuts—Fiction 3. School stories
ISBN 0-8075-6386-2

When a new classmate has a peanut allergy and has to sit in a special area of the lunchroom, Simon reconsiders his love for peanut butter.

"The cartoon-style art is fun, with some moments of exaggerated drama, as when Grant demonstrates what would happen to him if he ate just one peanut." Booklist

Kovalski, Maryann

Take me out to the ball game. Fitzhenry & Whiteside 2004 unp il $15.95   **E**

1. Baseball—Fiction 2. Grandmothers—Fiction
ISBN 1-55041-897-1

A new version of the title first published 1992 by Scholastic

"Grandma insists that Jenny and Joanna come on a surprise trip— even though it's a school day 'just this once.' Delighted when they arrive at Yankee Stadium, the girls break out into the title song." Publ Wkly

"Kovalski's watercolor illustrations project the vivacious personality of grandma and the joy of the experience beautifully. . . . This title is sure to be a hit with baseball fans young and old." SLJ

Kraus, Robert

Whose mouse are you? pictures by José Aruego. 30th anniversary ed. Simon & Schuster Books for Young Readers 2000 c1970 unp il $17.95

E

1. Mice—Fiction 2. Stories in rhyme
ISBN 0-689-84052-7

A reissue of the title first published 1970 by Macmillan

A lonely little mouse has to be resourceful in order to bring his family back together

"This is an absolute charmer of a picture book, original, tender, and childlike. The rhyming text is so brief, so catchy, and so right that a child will remember the words after one or two readings, and the large, uncluttered illustrations are gay and appealing." Booklist

Other titles about the mouse and his family are:
Come out and play, little mouse (1987)
Mouse in love (2000)
Where are you going, little mouse? (1986)

Krauss, Ruth

Bears; story by Ruth Krauss; pictures by Maurice Sendak. HarperCollins Pubs. 2005 unp il $14.95; lib bdg $15.89   **E**

1. Bears—Fiction
ISBN 0-06-027994-X; 0-06-075716-7 (lib bdg)

"Michael di Capua Books"

A newly illustrated edition of the title first published 1948

"The 27-word text is full of possibility: 'Bears—Under chairs—Washing hairs—Giving stares—Collecting

fares—.' . . . Sendak sets a full-color story in motion on the cover. In a scene both familiar and fresh, a boy in a wolf suit snuggles his stuffed bear in a themed room where the object of his affection is replicated on every conceivable surface. . . . Sure to spark laughter and original wordplay, this is the marriage of two masters." SLJ

The carrot seed; pictures by Crockett Johnson. Harper & Row 1945 unp il $14.99; pa $5.99

E

1. Gardening—Fiction
ISBN 0-06-023350-8; 0-06-443210-6 (pa)

Also available Board book edition; Spanish language edition also available

Simple text and picture show how the faith of a small boy, who planted a carrot seed, was rewarded

"Crockett Johnson's pictures are perfect and the brief text is just right." Book Week

Goodnight goodnight sleepyhead; illustrated by Jane Dyer. HarperCollins 2004 unp il $15.99

E

1. Bedtime—Fiction 2. Stories in rhyme
ISBN 0-06-028894-9

A newly illustrated edition of Eyes, nose, fingers, toes, published 1964 by Harper & Row

In simple rhyming text, a child says goodnight to the things around her.

"Dyer gives the old favorite a new title and creates new, clear, beautiful watercolor pictures." Booklist

The happy egg; story by Ruth Krauss; pictures by Crockett Johnson. HarperCollins Publishers 2005 unp il $15.89   **E**

1. Birds—Fiction 2. Eggs—Fiction
ISBN 0-06-076006-0

A reissue of the title first published 1967 by Scholastic

"A blue egg . . . is eventually hatched by a patient bird, and the baby bird walks, sings, and flies away. The circular ending is completely satisfying. The minimal text and simple pictures make this story just right for three-year-olds to memorize and 'read' to themselves over and over." Horn Book Guide

A very special house; by Ruth Krauss; pictures by Maurice Sendak. Harper Collins 1981 c1953 unp il $16.95   **E**

1. Imagination—Fiction
ISBN 0-06-028638-5   LC 2002511422

A Caldecott Medal honor book, 1954

A reissue of the title first published 1953

"The very special house is a house which exists in the imagination of a small boy—a house where the chairs are for climbing, the walls for writing on, and the beds for jumping on; a house where a lion, a giant, or a dead mouse is welcome, and where nobody ever says stop. Told in a chanting rhythm that demands participation by the reader; the imaginary characters, objects, and doings are pictured in line drawings almost as a child would scribble them while the real little boy stands out boldly in bright blue overalls." Booklist

Krensky, Stephen

How Santa got his job; illustrated by S.D. Schindler. Simon & Schuster Bks. for Young Readers 1998 unp il $15 **E**

1. Santa Claus—Fiction

ISBN 0-689-80697-3   LC 97-23474

This "peek at Santa's resumé reveals how various odd jobs, like chimney sweep and mail carrier, helped prepare him for his world-famous career. . . . [Schindler's] intricate pen-and-watercolor illustrations make Santa's evolution from boyish redhead to the familiar heavy-set, snowy-bearded character a joy to watch." Publ Wkly

Another title about Santa by this author and illustrator is:

How Santa lost his job (2001)

Lionel's birthday; pictures by Susanna Natti. Dial Bks. for Young Readers 2003 48p il $13.99 **E**

1. Birthdays—Fiction

ISBN 0-8037-2752-6   LC 2001-8501

"Dial easy-to-read"

Lionel counts down the days to his birthday party by making a time capsule and by letting his sister know what he wants for a present

This "is a warm, funny collection of three chapters. . . . Told mostly in dialogue in short sentences, and illustrated with clear, lovely pictures in pencil and bright colors." Booklist

Other titles about Lionel are:

Lionel and his friends (1996)
Lionel and Louise (1992)
Lionel at large (1986)
Lionel at school (2000)
Lionel in the fall (1987)
Lionel in the spring (1990)
Lionel in the summer (1998)
Lionel in the winter (1994)

Krishnaswami, Uma

Monsoon; pictures by Jamel Akib. Farrar, Straus & Giroux 2003 unp il $16 **E**

1. Monsoons—Fiction 2. India—Fiction

ISBN 0-374-35015-9   LC 2001-54753

A child in India describes waiting for the monsoon rains to arrive and the worry that they will not come

"Krishnaswami's poetic text rides faithfully on the child's sensibilities. . . . Akib's impressionistic, pastel illustrations make stunning use of extreme perspectives." SLJ

Kroeger, Mary Kay

Paperboy; by Mary Kay Kroeger and Louise Borden; illustrated by Ted Lewin. Clarion Bks. 1996 31p il $17 **E**

1. Newspaper carriers—Fiction 2. Boxing—Fiction

ISBN 0-395-64482-8   LC 94-34246

In Cincinnati in 1927, paperboy Willie Brinkman tries to sell extras on the Dempsey-Tunney boxing match in his workingman's neighborhood

"Lewin's watercolors bring Willie's Cincinnati to life. . . . Black-and-white 'stills' of Dempsey and Tunney share some pages with vivid, animated full-color scenes

of the Brinkman family. An engaging work that will bring home, through well-chosen details and a well-told story, the intimate connections one can make with 'famous facts' when the personal perspective is added." SLJ

Kroll, Steven

The biggest pumpkin ever; illustrated by Jeni Bassett. Holiday House 1984 unp il lib bdg $17.95 **E**

1. Pumpkin—Fiction 2. Halloween—Fiction 3. Mice—Fiction

ISBN 0-8234-0505-2   LC 83-18492

"A village mouse and a field mouse fall in love with the same pumpkin. Clayton feeds and waters it by day, while Desmond tends it at night. What a surprise when the two finally bump into eachother! Whose pumpkin is it—Clayton's for the pumpkin contest, or Desmond's for the jack-o'-lantern?" Publisher's note

"The cheerful, bright watercolor illustrations are as captivating as the text." Child Book Rev Serv

Patches: lost and found; illustrated by Barry Gott. Winslow Press (Delray Beach) 2001 unp il $16.95 **E**

1. Guinea pigs—Fiction 2. Drawing—Fiction 3. Authorship—Fiction

ISBN 1-89081-753-8   LC 00-31990

"When her guinea pig goes missing, Jenny draws imaginative pictures about what might have happened to him. Meanwhile, she is supposed to write a story for school but doesn't know where to start, until her drawings serve as inspiration." Horn Book Guide

"Written with a sure sense of narrative and an understanding of the concerns and the learning styles of children, the story finds apt expression in Gott's digital artwork, which has the appearance of cut-paper collage." Booklist

Krudop, Walter

The man who caught fish; [by] Walter Lyon Krudop. Farrar, Straus & Giroux 2000 unp il $16 **E**

1. Thailand—Fiction 2. Fairy tales

ISBN 0-374-34786-7   LC 98-49493

A stranger with a bamboo pole magically catches fish and hands them out to villagers, saying "One person, one fish," but the king will not be content until he receives a whole basket of fish

"Impressionistic pastel colors re-create a Thailand of long ago. . . . The tale speaks pointedly to the folly of pride; its lessons of generosity, peaceful resistance, and the temptations of privilege are universal." Horn Book Guide

Krull, Kathleen

M is for music; illustrated by Stacy Innerst. Harcourt 2003 unp il $16 **E**

1. Music 2. Alphabet

ISBN 0-15-201438-1   LC 2002-13037

An alphabet book introducing musical terms, from allegro to zarzuela

"The jazzy oil-and-acrylic collage assemblages include humorous touches to reinforce the concepts. The range of words explored is almost as vast as the world of music itself." SLJ

Kurtz, Jane

Faraway home; illustrated by E.B. Lewis. Harcourt Brace & Co. 2000 unp il $16　　　E

1. Father-daughter relationship—Fiction 2. African Americans—Fiction 3. Ethiopia—Fiction

ISBN 0-15-200036-4　　　LC 96-47664

"Gulliver books"

Desta's father, who needs to return briefly to his Ethiopian homeland, describes what it was like for him to grow up there

"Lewis captures the lyricism and rich imagery of the text with his evocative, realistic watercolors." SLJ

Water hole waiting; by Jane and Christopher Kurtz; illustrated by Lee Christiansen. Greenwillow Bks. 2002 unp il $15.95; lib bdg $15.89　　　E

1. Monkeys—Fiction 2. Animals—Fiction

ISBN 0-06-029850-2; 0-06-029851-0 (lib bdg)

LC 2001-23040

A thirsty monkey waits as the larger animals drink from the water hole on the African savanna

"Richly colored pastel drawings and precise, surprising word choices make this story a natural for sharing with a group." SLJ

Kushner, Lawrence

In God's hands; [by] Lawrence Kushner and Gary Schmidt; illustrated by Matthew J. Baek. Jewish Lights Pub. 2005 unp il $16.99　　　E

1. Jews—Fiction 2. Miracles—Fiction 3. Prayer—Fiction

ISBN 1-58023-224-8　　　LC 2005001669

While contemplating their problems in a synagogue, Jacob and David, one man rich, the other poor, come to realize their role in making miracles happen. Inspired by an ancient legend.

"This lovely piece of bookmaking combines a good tale with a strong, easily understood message. Baek's artwork, set against buff-colored pages and highlighted in shades of blue, uses a variety of angles, placements, and design elements to invite interest." Booklist

Kushner, Tony

Brundibar; retold by Tony Kushner; pictures by Maurice Sendak; after the opera by Hans Krása and Adolf Hoffmeister. Hyperion Bks. for Children 2003 unp il $19.95　　　E

1. Jews—Fiction 2. Holocaust, 1933-1945—Fiction

ISBN 0-7868-0904-3　　　LC 2001-99819

"Michael di Capua books"

"A picture book based on a 1938 Czech opera, originally performed by the children of Terezin. A brother and sister try to get milk for their sick mother. . . . Pepicek and Aninku then join voices with 300 other children and earn enough coins to fill their 'soon-to-be-milkbucket.' The playful language, with occasional rhyme and alliteration, is a perfect match for Sendak's spirited young heroes. The illustrations reflect varied undertones of a powerful story that works on different levels, including many references to the Holocaust." SLJ

Kuskin, Karla

I am me; illustrated by Dyanna Wolcott. Simon & Schuster Bks. for Young Readers 2000 unp il $14.95　　　E

1. Family life—Fiction

ISBN 0-689-81473-9　　　LC 98-7911

After being told how she resembles other members of her family, a young girl states positively and absolutely that she is "NO ONE ELSE BUT ME"

"The illustrations set the story during a family trip to the beach, and in Wolcott's brightly colored double-page spreads, all the rhythmic curves . . . show the natural connections around us, the loving family embrace across generations, and the child's exuberant energy as her own individual self." Booklist

So what's it like to be a cat? illustrated by Betsy Lewin. Atheneum Books for Young Readers 2005 unp il $15.95　　　E

1. Cats—Fiction

ISBN 0-689-84733-5　　　LC 2003-27338

A cat answers a young child's questions about such things as how much and where it sleeps, and whether or not it likes living with people.

"Lewin's charming, uncluttered watercolors extend the spare poetry's precise wit with swooping bold lines that beautifully capture both characters' movements and moods." Booklist

Under my hood I have a hat; illustrated by Fumi Kosaka. Laura Geringer Books 2004 unp il $14.99; lib bdg $15.89　　　E

1. Clothing and dress—Fiction 2. Winter—Fiction 3. Stories in rhyme

ISBN 0-06-057242-6; 0-06-057243-4 (lib bdg)

A child describes the many layers of clothing needed to brave the winter weather.

"Kosaka emulates the poem's unaffected charm in the large illustrations. . . . Featuring curving lines and warm, textured colors, the artwork will please young children as much as the satisfying verse." Booklist

Labatt, Mary

Pizza for Sam; written by Mary Labatt; illustrated by Marisol Sarrazin. Kids Can Press 2003 32p il $14.95; pa $3.95　　　E

1. Dogs—Fiction

ISBN 1-55337-329-4; 1-55337-331-6 (pa)

"Kids can read"

"Sam the dog watches eagerly as his owners set out cakes, cookies, and pies for a party. . . . Sam's presented with traditional dog food, but he turns up his snout, preferring to go hungry . . . until a pizza arrives and he finds his perfect puppy chow. Winsome pastel illustrations combine with a few large-type sentences per page in an attractive, uncluttered layout. The basic, repetitive text is filled with action, noise, and enough suspense and silliness to engage new readers." Booklist

Other titles about Sam are:

A friend for Sam (2003)

A parade for Sam (2005)

Sam at the seaside (2006)

Sam finds a monster (2004)

Sam gets lost (2004)

Labatt, Mary—*Continued*
Sam goes next door (2006)
Sam goes to school (2004)
Sam's first Halloween (2003)
Sam's snowy day (2005)

Lairla, Sergio
Abel and the wolf; written by Sergio Lairla; illustrated by Alessandra Roberti; translated by Marianne Martens. North-South Books 2004 unp il $15.95; lib bdg $16.50   E
1. Wolves—Fiction 2. Friendship—Fiction
ISBN 0-7358-1902-5; 0-7358-1903-3 (lib bdg)
Translated from the Italian
Abel leaves his loving home to make his way in the world, builds a house near a woodland brook, and tries to make friends with the powerful, jealous, and angry wolf who owns the woods
"Roberti's softly focused illustrations have the shimmering look of pointillism and complement the gentleness of the story, which ends on an upbeat note with a crystal-clear resolution." SLJ

Lakin, Pat
Fat chance Thanksgiving; illustrated by Stacey Schuett. Whitman, A. 2001 unp il $14.95
                E
1. Thanksgiving Day—Fiction 2. Apartment houses—Fiction 3. New York (N.Y.)—Fiction
ISBN 0-8075-2288-0   LC 2001-803
When their apartment burns down and they move to a much smaller place, Mama tells Carla they can't have Thanksgiving, but Carla thinks about all the hardships the Pilgrims faced and figures out a way
"A loving story of determination and sharing brought to life in richly colored, expressive artwork." Booklist

LaMarche, Jim
The raft. Lothrop, Lee & Shepard Bks. 2000 unp il $15.99; lib bdg $16.89   E
1. Grandmothers—Fiction 2. Rafting (Sports)—Fiction 3. Animals—Fiction
ISBN 0-688-13977-9; 0-688-13978-7 (lib bdg)
                LC 99-35546
Reluctuant Nicky spends a wonderful summer with Grandma who introduces him to the joy of rafting down the river near her home and watching the animals along the banks
"LaMarche introduces young readers to a visually resplendent, magical world. . . . Nicky's descriptive first-person narration supports the radiant, expressive illustrations." SLJ

Lamorisse, Albert
The red balloon. Doubleday 1957 c1956 unp il $16.95; pa $12.95   E
1. Balloons—Fiction 2. Paris (France)—Fiction
ISBN 0-385-00343-9; 0-385-14297-8 (pa)
Original French edition, 1956
"The chief feature of this book is the stunning photographs, many in color, which were taken during the filming of the French movie of the same name. A little French schoolboy Pascal catches a red balloon which turns out to be magic. The streets of Paris form a backdrop for a charming story and superb photographs." Libr J

Langston, Laura
Remember, Grandma? illustrated by Lindsey Gardiner. Viking 2004 unp il $15.99   E
1. Grandmothers—Fiction 2. Old age—Fiction 3. Memory—Fiction
ISBN 0-670-05898-X   LC 2003-19478
Lately Grandma has trouble remembering, and it makes Margaret sad until she learns about family love that endures even when memory does not. Includes recipe for Mile-high apple pie.

Lasky, Kathryn
Before I was your mother; written by Kathryn Lasky; illustrated by LeUyen Pham. Harcourt 2003 unp il $16   E
1. Mothers—Fiction
ISBN 0-15-201464-0   LC 2001-7544
A mother tells her own daughter what she was like and what she used to do when she was a little girl
"The watercolor and pen-and-ink illustrations, bursting with real life and remembrance, celebrate the story. Conversations galore will spring from this." Booklist

Lucille camps in; illustrated by Marylin Hafner. Knopf 2003 unp il $14.95   E
1. Camping—Fiction 2. Family life—Fiction 3. Pigs—Fiction
ISBN 0-517-80041-4   LC 2002-27493
When Lucille the pig is upset that she cannot go camping with her father and older siblings, she and her mother decide to go camping inside the house
"Lasky tells an endearing, realistic story in short sentences and simple language a new reader can handle, and Hafner perfectly captures Lucille's fury, brooding, excitement, and finally, the tenderness she shares with her mother." Booklist
Other titles about Lucille are:
Lucille's snowsuit (2000)
Starring Lucille (2001)

Marven of the Great North Woods; written by Kathryn Lasky; illustrated by Kevin Hawkes. Harcourt Brace & Co. 1997 unp il $16   E
1. Lumber and lumbering—Fiction 2. Minnesota—Fiction 3. Jews—Fiction
ISBN 0-15-200104-2   LC 96-2334
When his Jewish parents send him to a Minnesota logging camp to escape the influenza epidemic of 1918, ten-year-old Marven finds a special friend
"Inspired by her father's childhood, Lasky's handsomely crafted picture book is also a captivating survival story. . . . Contributing to the book's vivid sense of time and place are Hawkes' graphically accomplished paintings." Booklist

Lawrence, John

This little chick. Candlewick Press 2002 unp il
$15.99   **E**
1. Chickens—Fiction 2. Domestic animals—Fiction
3. Stories in rhyme
ISBN 0-7636-1716-4   LC 2001-35633
A little chick shows that he can make the sounds of
the animals in his neighborhood
"The silly farce and raucous noises will . . . delight
toddlers, and Lawrence coaxes plenty of character from
his boisterous, woodcut animal characters." Booklist

Lawson, Janet

Audrey and Barbara; written and illustrated by
Janet Lawson. Atheneum Bks. for Young Readers
2002 unp il $13.95   **E**
1. Cats—Fiction
ISBN 0-689-83896-4   LC 2001-22953
Audrey and her cat Barbara plan an adventure that
will take them across the ocean to India
"Lawson extends the humor with watercolor illustrations, in which sunny pastels serve as backdrops for entertaining cartoon-like images." Publ Wkly

Lawson, Julie

The Klondike cat; written by Julie Lawson;
illustrated by Paul Mombourquette. Kids Can Press
2002 unp il $15.95   **E**
1. Cats—Fiction 2. Klondike River Valley (Yukon)—
Gold discoveries—Fiction
ISBN 1-55337-013-9
Noah smuggles his cat aboard a steamship bound for
the 1896 gold rush in the Yukon
"This well-laid out picture book features a well-
written and engaging text, enlivened by Mombourquette's
atmospheric oil-paint illustrations." Booklist

Le Guin, Ursula K.

Tom Mouse; pictures by Julie Downing.
Roaring Brook Press 2002 unp il $15.95; lib bdg
$22.90   **E**
1. Mice—Fiction
ISBN 0-7613-1599-3; 0-7613-2663-4 (lib bdg)
      LC 2001-41893
"A Neal Porter book"
Tom Mouse hides on the train he has boarded for
travel and adventure, but an old woman finds and befriends him
"The quiet dignity of the telling shows respect for its
young audience. The warm colors and softly shaded
forms in Downing's artwork create a series of appealing
illustrations reflecting the story's essential charm."
Booklist

Leaf, Munro

The story of Ferdinand; illustrated by Robert
Lawson. Viking 1936 unp il $17.99; pa $6.99
      E
1. Bulls—Fiction 2. Bullfights—Fiction 3. Spain—Fic-
tion
ISBN 0-670-67424-9; 0-14-050234-3 (pa)
Also available Spanish language edition

"Ferdinand was a peace-loving little bull who pre-
ferred smelling flowers to making a reputation for himself in the bull ring. His story is told irresistbly in pictures and few words." Wis Libr Bull
"The drawings picture not only Ferdinand but Spanish
scenes and characters as well." N Y Public Libr

Leary, Mary

Karate girl. Farrar, Straus & Giroux 2003 unp il
$16   **E**
1. Karate—Fiction
ISBN 0-374-33977-5   LC 2002-35420
Hoping to protect her younger brother from school
bullies, a girl begins taking karate classes
"Leary uses clear, simple words to describe both karate's thoughtful, meditative purpose . . . and its high-
kicking, empowering action. The brightly colored illustrations, rendered in the fine lines and textures of colored
pencils, capture the girl's excitement." Booklist

Lee, Chinlun

Good dog, Paw! Candlewick Press 2004 unp il
$15.99   **E**
1. Dogs—Fiction 2. Veterinarians—Fiction
ISBN 0-7636-2178-1   LC 2003-48502
When April the veterinarian treats animals in her office, her well-loved dog Paw helps her and lets her patients know the secret of good health.
"Lee echoes a child's sensibilities in naive-style illustrations and repetitive words that reflect a young kid's
sweet, improvised nonsense." Booklist

Lee, Ho Baek

While we were out. Kane/Miller 2003 unp il
$15.95   **E**
1. Rabbits—Fiction
ISBN 1-929132-44-1   LC 2002-112325
"A white rabbit who lives on the patio notices that his
family has gone to Grandma's, leaving the house empty.
Now the house is hers. Simple line-and-wash pictures alternating with radiant full-page paintings follow the rabbit as she indulges in a multitude of obviously long-held
wishes. . . . This Korean import is amusing, yes, but
there is also a delicacy and intelligence that pervades the
tale. A definite cut above." Booklist

Lee, Jeanne M.

Bitter dumplings. Farrar, Straus & Giroux 2002
unp il $16   **E**
1. China—Fiction
ISBN 0-374-39966-2   LC 2001-41821
"In a story set in fifteenth-century China, dumplings
serve to bring together three people—a homeless girl, an
old hunchbacked woman, and an enslaved ship's carpenter—whose experiences have been painfully bitter. Lee's
delicately detailed art balances landscapes and domestic
scenes; the story's action is dramatically paced across
successive panels resembling Chinese screen paintings."
Horn Book Guide

Lee, Milly

Nim and the war effort; pictures by Yangsook Choi. Farrar, Straus & Giroux 1997 unp il $16

E

1. World War, 1939-1945—Fiction 2. Chinese Americans—Fiction

ISBN 0-374-35523-1   LC 96-11595

"Frances Foster books"

"It's the last day of the newspaper drive and Nim, a Chinese-American girl in San Francisco during World War II, is determined to win. . . . Nim's sweet seriousness and ingenuity are captured in the text and in the luminous, grave illustrations." N Y Times Book Rev

Lee, Spike

Please, baby, please; by Spike Lee and Tonya Lewis Lee; illustrated by Kadir Nelson. Simon & Schuster Bks. for Young Readers 2002 unp il $16.95; pa $6.99   E

1. African Americans—Fiction

ISBN 0-689-83233-8; 0-689-83457-8 (pa)

LC 99-462286

Also available: Please, puppy, please (2005)

A toddler's antics keep her mother busy as she tries to feed her, watch her on the playground, give her a bath, and put her to bed

"The litany of pleas will strike a chord with parents and caregivers, and will amuse children with its repetition and rhyme. Bright, full-bleed illustrations evoke the child-centered mayhem of this frazzled yet loving family." SLJ

Leedy, Loreen

The great graph contest; written and illustrated by Loreen Leedy. 1st ed. Holiday House 2005 32p il $16.95   E

1. Graphic methods 2. Frogs—Fiction 3. Lizards—Fiction 4. Snails—Fiction

ISBN 0-8234-1710-7   LC 2003-62549

Gonk the toad, Chester the snail, and Beezy the lizard hold a contest to see who can make better graphs.

"A splashy and colorful offering designed to inform and entertain. . . . The lively text, delivered in large type and contained in dialogue and thought balloons, is engaging and well supported by the vivid, cartoon illustrations." SLJ

Mapping Penny's world. Holt & Co. 2000 unp il maps $17   E

1. Maps—Fiction 2. Dogs—Fiction

ISBN 0-8050-6178-9   LC 99-48327

Companion volume to Measuring Penny

After learning about maps in school, Lisa maps all the favorite places of her dog Penny

"The concepts are clear, and the digital-painting and photo-collage illustrations are uncluttered and ably clarify the text." SLJ

Lehman, Barbara

Museum trip. Houghton Mifflin 2006 unp il $15

E

1. Art museums—Fiction 2. School stories 3. Stories without words

ISBN 0-618-58125-1   LC 2005052840

In this wordless picture book, a boy imagines himself inside some of the exhibits when he goes on a field trip to an art museum.

"The sturdiness and clarity of the ink-lined, watercolor-and-gouache art juxtaposes wonderfully with the story's airy world of imagination." Booklist

The red book. Houghton Mifflin 2004 unp il $12.95   E

1. Books and reading—Fiction 2. Stories without words

ISBN 0-618-42858-5

A Caldecott Medal honor book, 2005

This "wordless book tells the complex story of a reader who gets lost, literally, in a little book that has the magic to move her to another place. . . . Done in watercolor, gouache, and ink, the simple, streamlined pictures are rife with invitations to peek inside, to investigate further, and—like a hall of mirrors—reflect, refract, repeat, and reveal. Lehman's story captures the magical possibility that exists every time readers open a book." SLJ

Leopold, Nikia Speliakos Clark

K is for kitten; by Niki Clark Leopold; illustrated by Susan Jeffers. Putnam 2002 unp il $15.99   E

1. Cats—Fiction 2. Stories in rhyme 3. Alphabet

ISBN 0-399-23563-9   LC 2001-48252

A rhyming alphabet book which follows a kitten named Rosie from the alley in which she is found to the "ZZzzs" she enjoys with the family that gives her a home

"Jeffers's gouache and colored-ink illustrations are enchanting. This feline is a soft, yellow tabby with big green eyes that just about jumps off the page into readers' arms so that they can feel its fur. . . . The beauty of the book is in its simplicity and veracity." SLJ

Lessac, Frané

Island counting 1 2 3; by Frané Lessac. 1st U.S. ed. Candlewick Press 2005 unp il $12.99

E

1. Caribbean region—Fiction 2. Counting 3. Stories in rhyme

ISBN 0-7636-1960-4   LC 2003-69672

Counts from one to ten, featuring pictures and brief rhyming text with a Caribbean island theme.

"The text bounces along playfully. . . . Brightly colored and naive in approach. . . . A fresh, clear counting book for young children." Booklist

Lester, Alison

Are we there yet? a journey around Australia. Kane/Miller 2005 unp il $15.95   E

1. Australia—Fiction 2. Travel—Fiction

ISBN 1-929132-73-5

For six months, Grace and her family travel around Australia, seeing sights and meeting people.

"The text has a colloquial lilt and a consistently childlike point of view. . . . Lively and detailed, the colorful ink-and-watercolor artwork creates visual impressions through dozens of individual pictures." Booklist

Lester, Helen

Hooway for Wodney Wat; illustrated by Lynn Munsinger. Houghton Mifflin 1999 32p il $16

E

1. Speech disorders—Fiction 2. School stories
ISBN 0-395-92392-1   LC 98-46149
"Walter Lorraine books"

All his classmates make fun of Rodney because he can't pronounce his name, but it is Rodney's speech impediment that drives away the class bully

"Munsinger's watercolor with pen-and-ink illustrations positively bristle with humor and each rat, mouse, hamster, and capybara is fully realized as both rodent and child." SLJ

Something might happen; illustrated by Lynn Munsinger. Houghton Mifflin 2003 32p il $15

E

1. Fear—Fiction 2. Aunts—Fiction
ISBN 0-618-25406-4   LC 2002-156428
"Walter Lorraine books"

Twitchly Fidget the lemur worries about almost everything until his Aunt Bridget Fidget pays him a visit and shows him another way to live

"Lester elevates the story's simple messsage with upbeat words and appealing rhythms, while Munsinger's ink-and-watercolor pictures create an irresistible character in fretful Twitchly." Booklist

Three cheers for Tacky; illustrated by Lynn Munsinger. Houghton Mifflin 1994 32p il $16; pa $5.95   E

1. Penguins—Fiction   2. Contests—Fiction
3. Cheerleading—Fiction
ISBN 0-395-66841-7; 0-395-82-740-X (pa)
LC 93-14342

"Practicing with his classmates for a cheerleading contest, Tacky the penguin falls over his own feet, can't remember the right words, and looks simply slovenly. He finally gets it right, but, on the big day, he reverts to his usual form." Horn Book Guide

This "is a smooth, fun read. Munsinger's full-color illustrations are charming and subtle." SLJ

Other titles about Tacky are:
Tacky and the emperor (2000)
Tacky and the winter games (2005)
Tacky in trouble (1998)
Tacky the penguin (1988)
Tackylocks and the three bears (2002)

Lester, Julius

Black cowboy, wild horses; a true story; [by] Julius Lester, Jerry Pinkney. Dial Bks. 1998 unp il $18.99   E

1. Lemmons, Bob—Fiction 2. Horses—Fiction
3. Cowhands—Fiction 4. African Americans—Fiction
ISBN 0-8037-1787-3   LC 97-25210

A black cowboy is so in tune with wild mustangs that they accept him into the herd, thus enabling him singlehandedly to take them to the corral

This story is told in "vivid, poetic prose. . . . Pinkney's magnificent earth-toned paintings bring to life the wild beauty of the horses and the western plains." Horn Book Guide

Sam and the tigers; a new telling of Little Black Sambo; pictures by Jerry Pinkney. Dial Bks. for Young Readers 1996 unp il $16.99; pa $6.99

E

1. Tigers—Fiction
ISBN 0-8037-2028-9; 0-14-056288-5 (pa)
LC 95-43080

A boy named Sam, who lives in the land of Sam-sam-sa-mara, gives his new school clothes to tigers who threaten to eat him, but he re-claims them when the tigers chase one another until they turn into butter

"The rolling, lilting narrative is a model of harmony, clarity, and meticulously chosen detail. . . . Pinkney's lively pencil-and-watercolor illustrations sprawl extravagantly across double spreads and are smoothly integrated with the narrative." SLJ

What a truly cool world! illustrated by Joe Cepeda. Scholastic 1999 unp il $15.95   E
1. Creation—Fiction 2. God—Fiction 3. Angels—Fiction
ISBN 0-590-86468-8   LC 96-31438

Discovering that making a world takes a lot of work, God calls on his secretary Bruce and the angel Shaniqua to help him create bushes, grass, flowers, and butterflies

"The language is contemporary, colloquial, and humorous, and Cepeda's colorful, stylized illustrations capture the spirit of what Lester calls a 'black storytelling voice.'" Horn Book Guide

Another title about Bruce and Shaniqua is:
Why heaven is far away (2002)

Lester, Mike

A is for salad. Putnam & Grosset 2000 unp il $9.99   E
1. Alphabet
ISBN 0-399-23388-1   LC 99-20900

Each letter of the alphabet is presented in an unusual way, such as: "A is for salad" showing an alligator eating a bowl of greens

The author "makes parody into a hilarious farce that both mocks the original and creates its own wonderful silliness. Each wicked picture, in bright acrylics with thick, black lines, is an animal scenario that tells an outlandish story. . . . This isn't for very young children just learning their letters . . . it's for grade-schoolers who will get the jokes and love the irreverent nonsense." Booklist

Leuck, Laura

One witch; illustrations by S.D. Schindler. Walker & Co. 2003 unp il $15.95; lib bdg $16.85

E

1. Witches—Fiction   2.   Halloween—Fiction
3. Counting 4. Stories in rhyme
ISBN 0-8027-8860-2; 0-8027-8861-0 (lib bdg)
LC 2002-191049

A witch goes around to her fiendish friends—from two cats to ten werewolves—to gather the ingredients to make gruesome stew for her party

"Eerie yet amusing illustrations and a romping, rhyming text add up to fun in this Halloween counting book. Schindler's ink-and-watercolor artwork is a fine fit for Leuck's action-packed, easy-to-read text." SLJ

Lewin, Ted

Big Jimmy's Kum Kau Chinese take-out; written and illustrated by Ted Lewin. HarperCollins Pubs. 2002 unp il $16.95; lib bdg $16.89   **E**

1. Restaurants—Fiction 2. Chinese Americans—Fiction

ISBN 0-688-16026-3; 0-688-16027-1 (lib bdg)

LC 00-47954

The sights, sounds, and smells of a busy Chinese take-out restaurant are seen through the eyes of the owner's young son

"The realistic watercolor paintings bring the action up close; kids can almost smell what's cooking in the kitchen." Booklist

Lewis, J. Patrick

Isabella Abnormella and the very, very finicky Queen of Trouble; illustrations by Kyrsten Brooker. DK Ink 2000 unp il $15.95   **E**

1. Queens—Fiction 2. Sleep—Fiction 3. Stories in rhyme

ISBN 0-7894-2605-6   LC 99-14755

"A Richard Jackson book"

When the Queen of Trouble cannot sleep because all the beds she tries are uncomfortable, Isabella Abnormella saves the day by inventing the waterbed

"Brooker's comic scenes of the kingdom in turmoil smoothly blend paper, fabric, and paint. . . . Humorous details abound, punctuating and expanding the goofy verse." SLJ

The snowflake sisters; illustrated by Lisa Desimini. Atheneum Bks. for Young Readers 2003 unp il $16.95   **E**

1. Snow—Fiction 2. New York (N.Y.)—Fiction

ISBN 0-689-85029-8   LC 2002-6138

"An Anne Schwartz book"

Two snowflakes named Crystal and Ivory travel on Santa's sleigh and make their way through the wintry sky until they become part of a snowboy in Central Park

"The setting is New York City, captured through witty collage illustrations that make use of such materials as rice paper, maps, newsprint, and Scrabble letters. Lewis's elegant and fluid rhymed text offers surprises on every page." SLJ

Lewis, Kim

Good night, Harry. Candlewick Press 2004 c2003 unp il $15.99   **E**

1. Bedtime—Fiction 2. Sleep—Fiction 3. Elephants—Fiction

ISBN 0-7636-2206-0   LC 2002-41468

First published 2003 in the United Kingdom

When Harry, a toy elephant, has trouble sleeping, his friends help him.

"Lewis's meticulous illustrations were rendered in colored pencil and pastel, and the vivid, warm textures of the toys are sure to be appreciated by children. . . . This is a gentle book with illustrations that hum, and a bedtime story that's as warm as it is irresistible." SLJ

Other titles about Harry are:

Here we go Harry (2005)

Hooray for Harry (2006)

My friend Harry (1997)

Little Baa. Candlewick Press 2001 unp il $15.99   **E**

1. Sheep—Fiction

ISBN 0-7636-1447-5   LC 00-56423

Little Baa becomes separated from the rest of the sheep, but he is soon reunited with his Ma

"The spare text uses 'Ma' and 'Baa' repeatedly to recall sheep vocalizations, nicely capturing the mother's growing concern. Lewis's ethereal colored pencil drawings evoke the pastoral lushness of spring." Horn Book Guide

Lewis, Paeony

No more cookies! [illustrated by] Brita Granstrom. 1st American ed. Chicken HouseScholastic 2005 32p il $16.95   **E**

1. Cookies—Fiction 2. Toys—Fiction

ISBN 0-439-68332-7   LC 2004-52542

Florence and her toy monkey Arnold try to persuade her mother to let them eat more cookies. Includes a recipe for chocolate-covered bananas

"The humor will appeal to children, and Florence's first-person narrative reads quickly and smoothly. The cheery, cartoon illustrations match the light tone of the text." SLJ

Lewis, Rose A.

I love you like crazy cakes; written by Rose Lewis; illustrated by Jane Dyer. Little, Brown 2000 unp il $14.95   **E**

1. Adoption—Fiction 2. Infants—Fiction

ISBN 0-316-52538-3   LC 99-34175

A woman describes how she went to China to adopt a special baby girl. Based on the author's own experiences

"Dyer's simple watercolor layouts with expressive characters make this a calming read, befitting the gentle affection in the text." SLJ

Lexau, Joan M.

Who took the farmer's [hat]? [by] Joan L. Nodset; pictures by Fritz Siebel. Harper & Row 1963 unp il lib bdg $17.89; pa $6.99   **E**

1. Animals—Fiction

ISBN 0-06-024566-2 (lib bdg); 0-06-443174-6 (pa)

"Away flew the farmer's hat. In his search for it he found that his hat could be many things to many animals including, most permanently, a bird's nest." Publ Wkly

Lillegard, Dee

Tiger, tiger; illustrated by Susan Guevara. Putnam 2002 unp il $16.99   **E**

1. Tigers—Fiction 2. Magic—Fiction

ISBN 0-399-22633-8   LC 2002-272

A bored young boy uses a magic feather to form a tiger, and then must use the feather to save his village when the tiger gets hungry

"The suspenseful story reaches a dramatic climax, made all the more vivid by Guevara's highly charged artwork." Booklist

Lin, Grace

Dim sum for everyone! written and illustrated by Grace Lin. Knopf 2001 unp il $14.95; lib bdg $16.99　　　　　　　　　　　　　　　　E

1. Chinese Americans—Fiction 2. Restaurants—Fiction

ISBN 0-375-81082-X; 0-375-91082-4 (lib bdg)
　　　　　　　　　　　　　　　　LC 00-34813

A child describes the various little dishes of dim sum that she and her family enjoy on a visit to a restaurant in Chinatown

"Lin's paintings are graphically striking. They combine a simplicity of form and design with a delight of patterning that appears in clothing and in backgrounds. . . . Like the pleasures of dim sum, this is a compact treat." Booklist

Kite flying. Knopf 2002 unp il $14.95
　　　　　　　　　　　　　　　　E

1. Kites—Fiction

ISBN 0-375-81520-1　　　　　LC 2001-33456

"A Chinese girl describes how the members of her family come together to make and fly a dragon kite. . . . The overall simplicity is effective and appealing, and the spare text is accentuated by bright gouache illustrations, in colorful shapes and painted fabric patterns." Booklist

Olvina flies; written and illustrated by Grace Lin. Holt & Co. 2003 unp il $15.95　　　E

1. Fear—Fiction 2. Voyages and travels—Fiction 3. Pigs—Fiction

ISBN 0-8050-6711-6　　　　　LC 2002-8090

When Olvina, a chicken, receives an invitation to the annual Bird Convention in Hawaii, Will the pig and a fellow passenger help her to overcome her fear of flying

"The reassuring story gets a madcap twist from the artwork. Lin's jelly-bean-colored artwork, executed in gouache, finds humor in the small details." Booklist

Robert's snow; by Grace Lin. Viking 2004 unp il $15.99　　　　　　　　　　　E

1. Mice—Fiction 2. Snow—Fiction

ISBN 0-670-05911-0　　　　　LC 2003-25417

"Robert, a little mouse anxious to experience snow, falls out of his bedroom window in his family's boot home and has a snow adventure."

"Lin's bright watercolors combine sweetness and humor. . . . Young ones will identify with Robert's ebullience and his fear when he gets in (literally) over his head, as well as his satisfaction at being safely back home." Booklist

Lindbergh, Reeve

My hippie grandmother; illustrated by Abby Carter. Candlewick Press 2003 unp il $15.99
　　　　　　　　　　　　　　　　E

1. Grandmothers—Fiction 2. Hippies—Fiction 3. Stories in rhyme

ISBN 0-7636-0671-5　　　　　LC 00-37964

A young girl describes all the things she likes about her grandmother, including the purple bus she drives, growing vegetables, picketing City Hall, and playing the banjo

"A wonderful, poetic portrait. . . . Carter's colorful watercolor-and-gouache illustrations capture the happy mood of the verse." SLJ

Our nest; illustrated by Jill McElmurry. Candlewick Press 2004 unp il $15.99　　　E

1. Stories in rhyme

ISBN 0-7636-1286-3　　　　　LC 2001-58197

A rhymed view of the interrelatedness and belonging of all things and creatures in the universe, from the stars, to the sea, to a mouse, to a child.

"A honey of a poem, artwork at once timeless and innovative, and a sweetly optimistic message distinguish this soothing bedtime book. . . . McElmurry invests each of the ever-widening frames of reference with vibrancy and charm." Booklist

The visit; pictures by Wendy Halperin. Dial Books for Young Readers 2005 40p il $16.99
　　　　　　　　　　　　　　　　E

1. Country life—Fiction 2. Sisters—Fiction 3. Stories in rhyme

ISBN 0-8037-1189-1　　　　　LC 2002-13245

Sisters Beth and Jill share an experience of country life when they visit their aunt and uncle.

"Halperin's signature pencil-and-watercolor art, with arched frames for the main image and tiny story extenders in boxes at the bottom, complements the tone of Lindbergh's gently rhyming poem." SLJ

Lindgren, Barbro

Benny and the binky; [by] Barbro Lindgren, Olof Landstrom; translated by Elisabeth Kallick Dyssegaard. R & S Bks. 2002 unp il $15
　　　　　　　　　　　　　　　　E

1. Infants—Fiction 2. Brothers—Fiction 3. Pigs—Fiction

ISBN 91-29-65497-1

Companion volume to Benny's had enough (2000)

Original Swedish edition, 2001

"Benny the pig wanted a brother and now he has one. When the crying baby gets a binky, Benny wants one, too. His mother tells him he's too big for a pacifier so Benny takes things into his own hands." SLJ

"Lindgren sketches character, story, and mood with a few succinct phrases. The illustrations expand the slightly absurd narrative with great expression, movement, and detail." Horn Book Guide

Julia wants a pet; [by] Barbro Lindgren & [illustrated by] Eva Eriksson; translated by Elisabeth Kallick Dyssegaard. R & S Bks.; distributed by Farrar, Straus & Giroux 2003 unp il $15　　　　　　　　　　　　　　　E

1. Pets—Fiction

ISBN 91-29-65940-X

Original Swedish edition 2002

"On the lookout for a much-wished-for pet—preferably one that will fit in her baby carriage—Julia darts through town. . . . Lindgren's bracingly straightforward prose makes Julia's yearning and perversity feel immediate and authentic. . . . While Eriksson's brown-and-yellow-toned pictures may seem subdued at first glance, the earthtone colors and subtle pencil textures ground the heroine in the real world, while her yellow tutu and red baby carriage add playful tones." Publ Wkly

Lindsey, Kat

Sweet potato pie; by Kathleen D. Lindsey; illustrated by Charlotte Riley-Webb. 1st ed. Lee & Low Books 2003 unp il $16.95   **E**
  1. Farm life—Fiction 2. Family life—Fiction 3. African Americans—Fiction 4. Pies—Fiction
  ISBN 1-58430-061-2   LC 2002-30164
During a drought in the early 1900s, a large loving African American family finds a delicious way to earn the money they need to save their family farm
"Lindsey's down-home storytelling quality is charming. . . . The artwork's broad, energetic strokes and strong color palette sweep children into this tasty tale, and the included pie recipe makes the experience complete." Booklist

Lionni, Leo

Fish is fish. Alfred A. Knopf 2005 c1970 unp il $15.95   **E**
  1. Frogs—Fiction 2. Fishes—Fiction
  ISBN 0-394-80440-6
A reissue of the title first published 1970 by Pantheon Bks.
The frog tells the fish all about the world above the sea. The fish, however, can only visualize it in terms of fish-people, fish-birds and fish-cows.
"The story is slight but pleasantly and simply told, the illustrations are page-filling, deft, colorful, and amusing." Bull Cent Child Books

Frederick. Pantheon Bks. 1967 unp il $16.95; lib bdg $18.99; pa $5.99   **E**
  1. Mice—Fiction
  ISBN 0-394-81040-6; 0-394-91040-0 (lib bdg); 0-394-82614-0 (pa)
Also available Spanish language edition
A Caldecott Medal honor book, 1968
"While other mice are gathering food for the winter, Frederick seems to daydream the summer away. When dreary winter comes, it is Frederick the poet-mouse who warms his friends and cheers them with his words." Wis Libr Bull
"This captivating book . . . sings a hymn of praise to poets in a gentle story that is illustrated with gaiety and charm." Saturday Rev

Inch by inch. Astor-Honor 1960 unp il
   E
  1. Worms—Fiction 2. Birds—Fiction
  Available in paperback from HarperCollins
A Caldecott Medal honor book, 1961
This is a "small tale about an inchworm who liked to measure the robin's tail, the flamingo's neck, the whole of a hummingbird but not a nightingale's song." Christ Sci Monit
"This is a book to look at again and again. The semi-abstract forms are sharply defined, clean and strong, the colors subtle and glowing, and the grassy world of the inchworm is a special place of enchantment." N Y Times Book Rev

Little blue and little yellow; a story for Pippo and Ann and other children. Astor-Honor 1959 unp il   **E**
  1. Color—Fiction
  Available in paperback from HarperCollins

The author uses "splashes of color and abstract forms to tell the story of little blue and his friend little yellow who hugged and hugged each other until they were green—and unrecognizable to their parents." Booklist
"So well are the dots handled on the pages that little blue and little yellow and their parents seem to have real personalities. It should inspire interesting color play and is a very original picture book by an artist." N Y Her Trib Books

Swimmy. Pantheon Bks. c1963 unp il $16; pa $5.99   **E**
  1. Fishes—Fiction
  ISBN 0-394-81713-3; 0-394-82620-5 (pa)
A Caldecott Medal honor book, 1964
"Swimmy, an insignificant fish, escapes when a whole school of small fish are swallowed by a larger one. As he swims away from danger he meets many wonderful, colorful creatures and later saves another school of fish from the jaws of the enemy." Ont Libr Rev
"To illustrate his clever, but very brief story, Leo Lionni has made a book of astonishingly beautiful pictures, full of undulating, watery nuances of shape, pattern, and color." Horn Book

Lithgow, John

Micawber; illustrated by C.F. Payne. Simon & Schuster Bks. for Young Readers 2002 unp il $17.95   **E**
  1. Artists—Fiction 2. Squirrels—Fiction 3. Stories in rhyme 4. New York (N.Y.)—Fiction
  ISBN 0-689-83341-5   LC 2001-20919
Accompanied by CD recording of Lithgow reading his text
Micawber, a squirrel fascinated by art, leaves the Metropolitan Museum of Art with an art student, secretly uses her supplies to make his own paintings, and starts his own art museum atop Central Park's carousel
"The rhymed text sparkles with pleasing sounds. . . . Lithgow's reading on the CD is brimming with texture and playful pomposity. The mixed-media illustrations depict an utterly fetching protagonist displaying a range of moods and poses." SLJ

Little, Jean

Emma's yucky brother; story by Jean Little; pictures by Jennifer Plecas. HarperCollins Pubs. 2001 63p il $14.95; lib bdg $14.89   **E**
  1. Siblings—Fiction 2. Adoption—Fiction
  ISBN 0-06-028348-3; 0-06-028349-1 (lib bdg)
                         LC 99-34515
"An I can read book"
Emma finds out how hard it is to be a big sister when her family adopts a four-year-old boy named Max
"Heartfelt and honest. . . . Little's simple words and Plecas' clear, expressive line-and-watercolor illustrations tell an intense story." Booklist
Other titles about Emma are:
Emma's magic winter (1998)
Emma's strange pet (2003)

Liu, Jae Soo

Yellow umbrella; written and illustrated by Jae Soo Liu. Kane/Miller 2002 unp il $19.95　　E

1. Umbrellas and parasols—Fiction 2. Stories without words

ISBN 1-929132-36-0

Includes audio CD

A story, in pictures and music, of children on their way to school on a rainy day

"Originally published in South Korea, the volume is both delicate and handsome. . . . The joyful hues multiply with each successive spread. Composer Dong II Sheen gracefully glides between rhythms throughout the 15 tracks here [on the CD] . . . maintaining an overall happy tone." Publ Wkly

Livingstone, Star

Harley; illustrated by Molly Bang. SeaStar Bks. 2001 unp il $14.95; lib bdg $14.88　　E

1. Llamas—Fiction 2. Sheep—Fiction

ISBN 1-58717-048-5; 1-58717-049-3 (lib bdg)

LC 00-10434

Because Harley the llama does not get along with other llamas, he becomes a guard llama, protecting sheep from hungry coyotes and befriending a cantankerous ram

"The rustically textured illustrations warm the tone and highlight the action. This is a high adventure well told and respectful of both animal and audience." Horn Book Guide

Lobel, Anita

Alison's zinnia. Greenwillow Bks. 1990 unp il $16.99; pa $6.99　　E

1. Flowers—Fiction 2. Alphabet

ISBN 0-688-08865-1; 0-688-14737-2 (pa)

LC 89-23700

"More than two dozen little girls, a full alphabet of them, pick flowers for their friends: 'Alison acquired an Amaryllis for Beryl' and 'Nancy noticed a Narcissus for Olga' and so on till 'Zena zeroed in on a Zinnia for Alison.' Underneath each large handsome floral illustration is a smaller picture of the named child and her flower. Charming." N Y Times Book Rev

One lighthouse, one moon. Greenwillow Bks. 2000 40p il $15.95; lib bdg $15.89　　E

1. Days—Fiction 2. Months—Fiction 3. Counting

ISBN 0-688-15539-1; 0-688-15540-5 (lib bdg)

LC 98-50790

This is a "three-part introduction to days, seasons, colors, counting, and other basics. The first section pictures a little girl's feet as they journey through a week, with a different colored shoe marking each day's activity. . . . The second section shows Nini the cat in postcard-size images that reflect those from the 12 months of the year. The title section presents the numbers 1 through 10 in serene images of shoreline activity. . . . The simple phrases are lyrical in places, and Lobel's beautiful paintings, with their rich patterns and textures, luxurious detail, and sophisticated palette, will inspire children to linger over the pages and connect new words with images." Booklist

Lobel, Arnold

Frog and Toad are friends. Harper & Row 1970 64p il $15.99; lib bdg $16.89; pa $3.90　　E

1. Frogs—Fiction 2. Toads—Fiction

ISBN 0-06-023957-3; 0-06-023958-1 (lib bdg); 0-06-444020-6 (pa)

Also available Spanish language edition

A Caldecott Medal honor book, 1971

"An I can read book"

Here are five stories . . . which recount the adventures of two best friends—Toad and Frog. The stories are: Spring; The story; A lost button; A swim; The letter

The stories are told "with humor and perception. Illustrations in soft green and brown enhance the smooth flowing and sensitive story." SLJ

Other titles about Frog and Toad are:

Days with Frog and Toad (1979)

Frog and Toad all year (1976)

Frog and Toad together (1972)

Grasshopper on the road. Harper & Row 1978 62p il lib bdg $17.89; pa $3.99　　E

1. Grasshoppers—Fiction 2. Animals—Fiction

ISBN 0-06-023962-X (lib bdg); 0-06-444094-X (pa)

LC 77-25653

"An I can read book"

"Grasshopper's journey is divided into six chapters. In each chapter he meets a different animal or animals attending to a spectrum of tasks. The chapters weave a tale of habit—doing without questioning. Grasshopper gives his need-for-change reaction to each one, but only a worm in his apple home is open to change." Child Book Rev Serv

"The contemporary version of the fable of the ant and the grasshopper is told in a repetitive I-Can-Read text and extended in three-color illustrations which delicately capture the grasshopper's microcosmic world view." Horn Book

Ming Lo moves the mountain; written and illustrated by Arnold Lobel. Greenwillow Bks. 1982 unp il pa $5.99 hardcover o.p.　　E

1. Mountains—Fiction 2. Houses—Fiction

ISBN 0-688-10995-0 (pa)　　　　　　LC 81-13327

"Ming Lo and his wife love their house, but not the mountain that overshadows it. So, at his wife's bidding, Ming Lo undertakes to move the mountain by following the advice of a wise man." Child Book Rev Serv

"An original tale utilizing folkloric motifs, the book is Chinese-like rather than Chinese, for the artist has created an imagined landscape. The setting, shown in flowing lines and tones of delicate watercolors, provides a source of inspiration drawn from an ancient artistic tradition; particularly effective in conveying a sense of distance are the panoramic double-page spreads." Horn Book

Mouse soup. Harper & Row 1977 63p il $15.99; lib bdg $16.89; pa $3.99　　E

1. Mice—Fiction

ISBN 0-06-023967-0; 0-06-023968-9 (lib bdg); 0-06-444041-9 (pa)　　　　　　LC 76-41517

"An I can read book"

"In an effort to save himself from a weasel's stew pot, a little mouse tells the weasel four separate stories." West Coast Rev Books

Lobel, Arnold—*Continued*

"An artistic triumph with enough suspense, humor and wisdom to hold any reader who has a trace of curiosity and compassion. . . . The little one triumphs over the big one, and every child will rejoice. The exquisite wash drawings in mousey shades of grays, blues, greens and golds, have enough humor and pathos to exact repeated scrutiny. Like the stories, they improve with each reading." N Y Times Book Rev

Mouse tales. Harper & Row 1972 61p il $15.99; lib bdg $16.89; pa $3.99   E

1. Mice—Fiction

ISBN 0-06-023941-7; 0-06-023942-5 (lib bdg); 0-06-444013-3 (pa)

"An I can read book"

Contents: The wishing well; Clouds; Very tall mouse and very short mouse; The mouse and the winds; The journey; The odd mouse; The bath

Papa Mouse tells seven bedtime stories, one for each of his sons

"The illustrations have soft colors and precise, lively little drawings of the imaginative and humorous events in the stories. The themes are familiar to children: cloud shapes, wishing, a tall and a short friend who observe-and greet-natural phenomena on a walk, taking a bath, et cetera." Bull Cent Child Books

On Market Street; pictures by Anita Lobel; words by Arnold Lobel. Greenwillow Bks. 1981 c1980 unp il $16.99; lib bdg $17.89; pa $6.99   E

1. Shopping—Fiction 2. Alphabet 3. Stories in rhyme

ISBN 0-688-80309-1; 0-688-84309-3 (lib bdg); 0-688-08745-0 (pa)   LC 80-21418

A Caldecott Medal honor book, 1982

In this "alphabet book, a boy trots down Market Street buying presents for a friend, each one starting with a letter of the alphabet. Every letter is illustrated by a figure . . . composed of, for instance, apples or wigs or quilts or Xmas trees." Horn Book

"The artist has adapted the style of old French trade engravings, infusing it with a wonderful sense of color and detail. . . . Arnold Lobel's words ring of old rhymes, but it is these intricate, lovely drawings that take the day, and truly make it brighter." N Y Times Book Rev

Owl at home. Harper & Row 1982 64p il lib bdg $16.89; pa $3.99   E

1. Owls—Fiction

ISBN 0-06-023949-2 (lib bdg); 0-06-444034-6 (pa)

"An I can read book"

Five stories describe the adventures of a lovably foolish owl

"A child reader or listener in a kind of one-upmanship over wide-eyed tufted Owl will bristle with anxiety to have him perceive what causes two bewildering bumps under the blanket at the foot of his bed. The best scope for Lobel's inventiveness in drawing is, however, the opening episode where 'poor old' Winter makes a pushy entry into Owl's home. Muted browns and greys are countered by an animation that fully reveals Owl's distresses and contentments." Wash Post Child Book World

Small pig; story and pictures by Arnold Lobel. Harper & Row 1969 63p il lib bdg $16.89; pa $3.99   E

1. Pigs—Fiction

ISBN 0-06-023932-8 (lib bdg); 0-06-444120-2 (pa)

"An I can read book"

This "is the story of a pig who, finding the clean farm unbearable, runs away to look for mud—and ends up stuck in cement. His facial expressions alone are worth the price of the book; the illustrations, in blue, green, and gold, are a perfect complement to the story. Humor, adventure, and short, simple sentences provide a real treat for beginning readers." SLJ

A treeful of pigs; pictures by Anita Lobel. Greenwillow Bks. 1979 unp il lib bdg $17.89   E

1. Pigs—Fiction 2. Farm life—Fiction

ISBN 0-688-84177-5   LC 78-1810

A "story about a farmer's wife who tries everything to pry her lazy husband out of bed. He says he'll come to help her when the pigs grow on trees, fall from the sky, or 'bloom in the garden like flowers.' His wife knows how to work magic, and she makes each one of them happen with the help of a cooperative brood of piglets." Child Book Rev Serv

"The framed, full-color illustrations, characterized by intricately detailed designs in costumes and setting, are as elaborate as the diction is simple. The total effect, however, is one of unity." Horn Book

Uncle Elephant. Harper & Row 1981 62p il lib bdg $16.89; pa $3.99   E

1. Elephants—Fiction 2. Uncles—Fiction

ISBN 0-06-023980-8 (lib bdg); 0-06-444104-0 (pa)

LC 80-8944

"An I can read book"

Uncle Elephant takes care of his nephew whose parents are lost at sea. This book describes the way they lived together until the parents are rescued and little elephant rejoins them

"Nine gentle stories for the beginning independent reader; the soft grey, peach, and green tones of the deft pictures are an appropriate echo of the mood." Bull Cent Child Books

Locker, Thomas

Cloud dance. Silver Whistle/Harcourt 2000 unp il $16; pa $6   E

1. Clouds—Fiction

ISBN 0-15-202231-7; 0-15-204596-1 (pa)

LC 99-42642

Clouds of many shapes and sizes drift and dance across the sky. Includes factual information on the formation and different kinds of clouds

This "blends Locker's spare, poetic, informative text with his well-known Hudson River school-style landscapes. . . . The paintings speak eloquently of the complete, seamless quality of the elemental natural world." Booklist

Locker, Thomas—*Continued*

Walking with Henry; based on the life and works of Henry David Thoreau. Fulcrum 2002 unp il $17.95   **E**

1. Thoreau, Henry David, 1817-1862—Fiction 2. Wilderness areas—Fiction

ISBN 1-55591-355-5   LC 2002-3881

Introduces philosopher, writer, and environmentalist Henry David Thoreau, using selections from his own writings and an imaginary journey into the wilderness

This book "has simple, easy-to-understand text with beautiful art work which supports the theme of the book. The book is printed on a variety of colored paper that matches, tones to, or blends with the painting on the opposite page." Libr Media Connect

London, Jonathan

Baby whale's journey; illustrated by Jon Van Zyle. Chronicle Bks. 1999 unp il $15.95
E

1. Whales—Fiction

ISBN 0-8118-2496-9   LC 99-13020

Off the Pacific coast of Mexico, a baby sperm whale is born, feeds, speaks to her mother in clicks, and spends her days diving, spy-hopping, lob-tailing, and rolling as she grows and learns the ways of the sea

This book offers "London's lyrical text and Van Zyle's dramatic paintings dominated by blues and purples. . . . An informative afterword supplies additional facts about sperm whales, and a reader's guide offers thoughtful ideas for discussion of both the scientific and poetic aspects of the text." Horn Book Guide

Do your ABC's Little Brown Bear; illustrated by Margie Moore. Dutton Children's Books 2005 unp il $15.99   **E**

1. Father-son relationship—Fiction 2. Bears—Fiction 3. Alphabet

ISBN 0-525-47360-2

As they spend a day playing together near their home, Little Brown Bear goes through his ABCs for Papa Brown Bear.

"This sweet tale is accompanied by heartwarming illustrations that aptly depict the loving relationship." SLJ

Another title about Little Brown Bear is:

Count the ways, Little Brown Bear (2002)

Froggy learns to swim; illustrated by Frank Remkiewicz. Viking 1995 unp il $15.99; pa $5.99
E

1. Swimming—Fiction 2. Frogs—Fiction

ISBN 0-670-85551-0; 0-14-055312-6 (pa)

LC 94-43077

Froggy is afraid of the water until his mother, along with his flippers, snorkle, and mask, help him learn to swim

"Vivid watercolor cartoons add the humor, showing the comical facial expressions and hilarious beachwear. Froggy's childlike dialogue and the sound words—'zook! zik!'; 'flop flop . . . splash!'—make this story a wonderful read-aloud." SLJ

Other titles about Froggy are:

Froggy bakes a cake (2000)

Froggy eats out (2001)

Froggy gets dressed (1992)

Froggy goes to bed (2000)

Froggy goes to school (1996)

Froggy goes to the doctor (2002)

Froggy plays in the band (2002)

Froggy plays soccer (1999)

Froggy's baby sister (2003)

Froggy's best Christmas (2000)

Froggy's day with Dad (2004)

Froggy's first kiss (1998)

Froggy's Halloween (1999)

Froggy's sleepover (2005)

Let's go, Froggy! (1994)

Giving thanks; paintings by Gregory Manchess. 1st ed. Candlewick Press 2003 unp il $16.99
E

1. Prayer—Fiction 2. Nature—Fiction 3. Father-son relationship—Fiction

ISBN 0-7636-1680-X   LC 2002-23750

A boy's father celebrates the interconnectedness of the natural world through his daily words of thanks and assures his son . . . that it becomes a habit and makes one feel good.

"Manchess' illustrations are quite handsome. . . . A book that fosters respect for the natural world through a relatively simple text and illustrations that express the beauty and dignity of nature." Booklist

Mustang canyon; illustrated by Daniel San Souci. Candlewick Press 2002 unp il $15.99
E

1. Horses—Fiction

ISBN 0-7636-1554-4   LC 2001-25680

A young mustang is separated from its mother when a plane sweeps over the canyon and the horses run from the noise

"The words are spare, immediate, and informative, and San Souci's lavish, sharp watercolor artwork brings children close to the wild herd and the blistering desert heat." Booklist

Sled dogs run; illustrations by Jon Van Zyle. Walker 2005 unp il $16.95; lib bdg $17.85
E

1. Sledding—Fiction 2. Dogs—Fiction 3. Alaska—Fiction

ISBN 0-8027-8957-9; 0-8027-8958-7 (lib bdg)

LC 2004-52009

"A girl explains how she raises three Siberian husky pups from their birth in the spring through their summer and autumn training. Finally, in winter, they make their first sled run, which is also her first solo run as musher." Booklist

"The lyrical writing smoothly conveys information as well as the narrator's emotions. Illustrations done in acrylic on Masonite panels portray the snow-covered Alaskan countryside and the action." SLJ

A truck goes rattley-bumpa; illustrated by Denis Roche. 1st ed. Henry Holt and Co 2005 unp il $14.95   **E**

1. Trucks—Fiction 2. Stories in rhyme

ISBN 0-8050-7233-0   LC 2004-22174

"Short, rhyming couplets tell about a variety of trucks: what they look like, what sounds they make, where they

London, Jonathan—*Continued*
go, and what they do. Meanwhile, childlike gouache
paintings clearly illustrate the brief sentences or phrases
on each page." Booklist

Long, Melinda
How I became a pirate; written by Melinda
Long; illustrated by David Shannon. Harcourt
2003 unp il $16   **E**
1. Pirates—Fiction
ISBN 0-15-201848-4   LC 2002-6308
"Jeremy spies a pirate ship. When he's asked to join
its crew, he can't resist. On board, he does all sorts of
fun pirate stuff. . . . But, alas, Jeremy soon discovers,
there's no goodnight kiss or bedtime story, so there's
something to be said for home. . . . The rollicking tale
is a charmer, with a lively, witty, first-person narrative,
highly expressive characters, and farcical elements. . . .
Shannon's acrylic art is marvelously animated, with
bright, bold colors and extraordinary details." Booklist

Look, Lenore
Henry's first-moon birthday; illustrated by Yumi
Heo. Atheneum Bks. for Young Readers 2001 unp
il $16   **E**
1. Infants—Fiction 2. Grandmothers—Fiction
3. Chinese Americans—Fiction
ISBN 0-689-82294-4   LC 98-21626
"An Anne Schwartz book"
Jen helps her grandmother with preparations for the
traditional Chinese celebration to welcome her new baby
brother
"The words are clear and basic as well as creative
. . . and Jen's chatty narration infuses the book with the
cozy immediacy that's beautifully picked up in Heo's
swirling paint-and-paper collages." Booklist

Love as strong as ginger; illustrated by Stephen
T. Johnson. Atheneum Pubs. 1999 unp il $15
                                                  E
1. Chinese Americans—Fiction 2. Grandmothers—Fiction 3. Work—Fiction
ISBN 0-689-81248-5   LC 96-43459
"An Anne Schwartz book"
A Chinese American girl comes to realize how hard
her grandmother works to fulfill her dreams when they
spend a day together at the grandmother's job cracking
crabs
"Inspired by the author's memories of her grandmother, this gentle story is carefully and precisely told. . . .
Johnson's expressive pastel-and-watercolor illustrations
are rendered in muted colors and set within wide, softly
colored margins." SLJ

Uncle Peter's amazing Chinese wedding;
illustrated by Yumi Heo. Atheneum Books for
Young Readers 2006 unp il $16.95   **E**
1. Chinese Americans—Fiction 2. Weddings—Fiction
3. Uncles—Fiction
ISBN 0-689-84458-1   LC 2002-10740
Companion volume to Henry's first-moon birthday
"An Anne Schwartz book"

Jenny, a Chinese American girl, describes the festivities of her uncle's Chinese wedding and the customs behind them.
"Heo's child-inspired illustrations contribute to the
story's strong appeal with lively colors, perspectives, and
details that accentuate both Jenny's feelings and the wedding traditions. A delightful invitation to learn more
about Chinese traditions." SLJ

Lorbiecki, Marybeth
Sister Anne's hands; illustrated by K. Wendy
Popp. Dial Bks. for Young Readers 1998 unp il
$15.99; lib bdg $15.89   **E**
1. Race relations—Fiction 2. School stories
3. African Americans—Fiction 4. Nuns—Fiction
ISBN 0-8037-2038-6; 0-8037-2039-4 (lib bdg)
                                      LC 97-26671
Seven-year-old Anna has her first encounter with racism in the 1960s when an African American nun comes
to teach at her parochial school
"The story has honesty and integrity and the two main
characters are well crafted. The velvety pastel illustrations have the soft focus and pale palette of a distant
memory coupled with exquisite detail." SLJ

Lord, Janet
Here comes Grandma! [by] Janet Lord;
illustrated by Julie Paschkis. 1st ed. Henry Holt
and Co 2005 unp il $12.95   **E**
1. Grandmothers—Fiction 2. Transportation—Fiction
ISBN 0-8050-7666-2   LC 2004-22179
Grandma is coming to visit and she will use any possible method of transport, including a horse and a hot air
balloon, to get there.
"The simple, rhythmic text suits the mood of the story, and the vivid gouache illustrations have a warm, folk-
like quality." SLJ

Lord, John Vernon
The giant jam sandwich; story and pictures by
John Vernon Lord, with verses by Janet Burroway.
Houghton Mifflin 1973 c1972 32p il lib bdg $17;
pa $6.95   **E**
1. Wasps—Fiction 2. Stories in rhyme
ISBN 0-395-16033-2 (lib bdg); 0-395-44237-0 (pa)
First published 1972 in the United Kingdom
This is a story in rhymed verse "about the citizens of
Itching Down, who, attacked by four million wasps,
make a giant jam sandwich to attract and trap the insects.
With dump truck, spades, and hoes the people spread
butter and strawberry jam across an enormous slice of
bread; then, when the wasps settle, they drop the other
slice from five helicopters and a flying tractor." Booklist
"Highly amusing in the details of John Vernon Lord's
illustrations. . . . The figures are deliciously grotesque,
their expressions wickedly accurate and the colours
cheerfully vivid." Jr Bookshelf

Lotu, Denize

Running the road to ABC; by Denizé Lauture; illustrated by Reynold Ruffins. Simon & Schuster Bks. for Young Readers 1996 unp il $16.95; pa $6.99   **E**

1. Haiti—Fiction 2. School stories
ISBN 0-689-80507-1; 0-689-83165-X (pa)

                LC 95-38290

A Coretta Scott King honor book for illustration, 1997
Long before the sun even thinks of rising the Haitian children run to school where they learn the letters, sounds, and words of their beautiful books

"The rich lyrical language used by the author, a Haitian poet, creates a strong sense of place. . . . The lush, green country and sense of hope are reflected and enhanced by stylized, warmly detailed gouache paintings." Horn Book

Louie, Therese On

Raymond's perfect present; illustrated by Suling Wang. Lee & Low Bks. 2002 unp il $16.95   **E**

1. Gifts—Fiction 2. Mothers—Fiction 3. Chinese Americans—Fiction
ISBN 1-58430-055-8   LC 2002-16128

When Raymond's mother becomes sick, he remembers that she misses the living things of the country and, with the help of their neighbor, he tries to prepare the perfect present for her

"The pencil-and-computer-generated pictures accentuate Raymond's loneliness, worry, and love for his mother. The character's Asian features are subtly drawn." Booklist

Loupy, Christophe

Hugs and kisses; [by] Christophe Loupy, Eve Tharlet; translated by J. Alison James. North-South Bks. 2001 unp il $15.95; lib bdg $15.88   **E**

1. Dogs—Fiction 2. Animals—Fiction
ISBN 0-7358-1484-8; 0-7358-1485-6 (lib bdg)

                LC 2001-42595

"A Michael Neugebauer book"
Original German edition published 2001 in Switzerland

Hugs the puppy sets out to collect lots of wonderful kisses from his animal friends, but in the end he discovers that the best kiss of all is the one he gets from his loving mother

"With fur that seems real enough to touch, a sunny disposition, and sweet manners, Hugs is a real charmer." Booklist

Luciani, Brigitte

How will we get to the beach? illustrated by Eve Tharlet; translated by Rosemary Lanning. North-South Bks. 2000 unp il $14.95; lib bdg $14.88   **E**

1. Beaches—Fiction 2. Transportation—Fiction
ISBN 0-7358-1268-3; 0-7358-1269-1 (lib bdg)

                LC 99-57086

"A Michael Neugebauer book"

The reader is asked to guess what Roxanne must leave behind (ball, umbrella, book, turtle, or baby) as she tries various means of transportation to get to the beach

"The writing is spare, yet the story flows seamlessly. . . . Though on the surface the colorful pictures appear simple, details abound. . . . This book also introduces the concepts of color . . . and counting." SLJ

Lum, Kate

What! cried Granny; an almost bedtime story; pictures by Adrian Johnson. Dial Bks. for Young Readers 1999 unp il $16.99   **E**

1. Bedtime—Fiction 2. Grandmothers—Fiction
ISBN 0-8037-2382-2   LC 98-19642

First published 1998 in the United Kingdom with title: What!

"Sleeping over at Granny's for the first time, Patrick delays the inevitable, saying he can't go to bed because he doesn't even have a bed; or a blanket; or a teddy bear. In response to each legitimate complaint, Granny springs into action, chopping down a tree to build a bed, and so on." Horn Book Guide

This "combines the deadpan and the surreal in wild words and neon-colored acrylic illustrations." Booklist

Lund, Deb

Tell me my story, Mama; pictures by Hiroe Nakata. HarperCollins 2004 unp il $15.99   **E**

1. Pregnancy—Fiction 2. Childbirth—Fiction
ISBN 0-06-028876-0   LC 2002-68492

As they look forward to the arrival of a new baby, a mother tells her young daughter of the time when they waited for her to be born

"In simple, musical words, Lund tells a tender story. . . . Nakata's airy illustrations, in dabs and washes of sheer, pastel color, capture the story's freeflowing movement between then and now." Booklist

Luthardt, Kevin

Peep! Peachtree Pubs. 2003 unp il $15.95   **E**

1. Ducks—Fiction 2. Pets—Fiction
ISBN 1-56145-046-4   LC 2002-35910

"With just a dozen-plus words, Luthardt tells the story of a young boy's attachment to a duckling ('peep!') who grows up into a duck ('quack!') and grows away from the boy ('it's time'; 'bye bye'). . . . The book's strength is the directness and speed with which art and minimal text tell the story. Pastel and mixed-media illustrations are on colored paper, which imparts warmth and a pleasing texture." Horn Book

Lyon, George Ella

Weaving the rainbow; written by George Ella Lyon; illustrated by Stephanie Anderson. Atheneum Books for Young Readers 2004 unp il $15.95   **E**

1. Weaving—Fiction 2. Wool—Fiction 3. Sheep—Fiction
ISBN 0-689-85169-3
"A Richard Jackson book"

Lyon, George Ella—*Continued*

An artist raises sheep, shears them, cards and spins the wool, dyes it, and then weaves a colorful picture of the Kentucky pasture where her lambs were born.

"Lyon's writing is lyrical, and the gentle pacing is calming. . . . In her skillfully composed watercolor artwork, Anderson directs readers' eyes and shows them what to focus on." SLJ

Macaulay, David

Angelo. Houghton Mifflin 2002 48p il $16

E

1. Pigeons—Fiction 2. Rome (Italy)—Fiction
ISBN 0-618-16826-5   LC 2001-39536
"Walter Lorraine Books"

While restoring the front of a church in Rome, an old master plasterer rescues an injured pigeon and nurses her back to health

"The offbeat friendship is charming, there are entertaining details to discover throughout the book, and the grand old city is evoked in all her bustle and luminosity." Horn Book

Black and white. Houghton Mifflin 1990 unp il $17

E

1. Railroads—Fiction 2. Cattle—Fiction
ISBN 0-395-52151-3   LC 89-28888
Awarded the Caldecott Medal, 1990

Four brief "stories" about parents, trains, and cows, or is it really all one story? The author recommends careful inspection of words and pictures to both minimize and enhance confusion

"The magic of *Black and White* comes not from each story, . . . but from the mysterious interactions between them that creates a fifth story. . . . Eventually, the stories begin to merge into a surrealistic tale spanning several levels of reality. . . . *Black and White* challenges the reader to use text and pictures in unexpected ways." Publ Wkly

Shortcut. Houghton Mifflin 1995 unp il $15.95; pa $7.95

E

ISBN 0-395-52436-9; 0-618-00607-9 (pa)
LC 95-2542

"This picture book concerns six humans whose paths cross and recross in the eight chapters of brief text and distinctive artwork. Albert and his horse, June, take their wagon of melons to market, sell them, and go home. . . . Patty's pet pig, Pearl, wanders onto an abandoned railroad line. . . . Professor Tweet is studying birds when suddenly his hot air balloon breaks free and heads toward a nearby cathedral spire. . . . Seemingly inconsequential details in one story become the moving forces in another." Booklist

"Because *Shortcut* is not linear in its progression but rather an exploration of simultaneity and concepts of time and space, it is a picture book for sophisticated readers who enjoy puzzles and unraveling clues. . . . David Macaulay deserves applause for challenging his readers as well as entertaining them through boldly conceived illustrations with a cast of wonderfully caricatured characters." Horn Book

Why the chicken crossed the road. Houghton Mifflin 1987 31p il lib bdg $16; pa $6.95

E

ISBN 0-395-44241-9 (lib bdg); 0-395-58411-6 (pa)
LC 87-2908

"A ridiculous chicken sets off a circular story involving a herd of cows, a bridge, a train, a robber, the fire department and some hydrangeas. Chaos. The illustrations are suitably wild—painted with brilliant color and almost palpable energy." N Y Times Book Rev

Maccarone, Grace

A child's good night prayer; illustrated by Sam Williams. Scholastic 2001 unp il $10.95

E

1. Prayers 2. Bedtime
ISBN 0-439-23505-7   LC 00-41929

A "rhymed, very simple litany of blessings is asked upon things dear to little ones: the moon and stars; toy cars, trucks, and animals . . . and children everywhere. . . . The appealing pictures and gentle rhythm of the words should soothe any preschooler to sleep." SLJ

MacDonald, Ross

Achoo! Bang! Crash! the noisy alphabet. Roaring Brook Press 2003 unp il $16.95; lib bdg $23.90

E

1. Sound 2. Noise 3. Alphabet
ISBN 0-7613-1796-1; 0-7613-2900-5 (lib bdg)
LC 2003-9039

"A Neal Porter book"

Words about sound and noise illustrate the letters of the alphabet

"MacDonald treats readers and listeners to a bounty of sounds and an abundance of visual humor. . . . The illustrations, done in an old-fashioned cartoon style, were added after in a warm rainbow palette that totally supports the text." SLJ

Another perfect day. Millbrook Press 2002 unp il $15.95; lib bdg $22.90

E

ISBN 0-7613-1595-0; 0-7613-2659-6 (lib bdg)
LC 2002-18798

"A Neal Porter book"

What started out as another perfect day for Jack the superhero performing heroic feats suddenly goes awry

"With a beefy hero and graphics inspired by 1930-40s comic books, this impeccably designed volume features a forthright text that comically counterpoints a livelier tale told through the pictures." Publ Wkly

Another title about Jack is:
Bad baby (2005)

Macdonald, Suse

A was once an apple pie; adapted by Suse MacDonald from the poem by Edward Lear. Orchard Bks. 2005 unp il $12.99

E

1. Lear, Edward, 1812-1888—Adaptations
2. Alphabet 3. Nonsense verses
ISBN 0-439-66056-4   LC 2004-25683

A collection of twenty-six nonsense rhymes, one for each letter of the alphabet.

Macdonald, Suse—*Continued*

"MacDonald uses her acute sense of design and whimsy to introduce another generation to Lear's work. Children will delight in the zany lyrics that, for full effect, should be read aloud and repeated by a young audience. The illustrations are folksy paper collages . . . with large, bright shapes." SLJ

Alphabatics. Bradbury Press 1986 unp il $19.95; pa $7.99 **E**

1. Alphabet
ISBN 0-02-761520-0; 0-689-71625-7 (pa)

LC 85-31429

A Caldecott Medal honor book, 1987

MacDonald "maneuvers each letter to create a visual image as well as an object that begins with that letter." Child Book Rev Serv

The "*A* tilts, flops over, and literally becomes an ark as it turns itself around. An *N* turns over, glides up a tree trunk, and becomes a nest for three young birds. Crisp, fresh, and totally effective, it's a unique way of looking at the alphabet. This is a book for creative thinking and sheer enjoyment of MacDonald's precise graphics, rather than for object identification among the very young." SLJ

Look whooo's counting. Scholastic 2000 unp il $14.95 **E**

1. Counting 2. Animals—Fiction 3. Owls—Fiction
ISBN 0-590-68320-9 LC 99-87552

"As a young owl flies from dusk to dawn, she learns to count from one to ten. She spies one prairie dog on a hill, two mice in a field, three ducks flying over a pond, and so on. The feathers on Owl's wings change into the shape of each new number in clever cut-paper illustrations that also contain the numbers within the features of the animals themselves." Horn Book Guide

Sea shapes. Harcourt Brace & Co. 1994 unp il $15; pa $6 **E**

1. Shape 2. Marine animals
ISBN 0-15-200027-5; 0-15-201700-3 (pa)

LC 93-27957

"Gulliver books"

"Each double-page spread is devoted to a different shape. On each left-hand page, a sequence of simple pictures shows a basic shape evolving into the shape of a marine animal. The opposite page pictures the animal in the sea. The brightly colored paper collages make it easy to follow along as the sea animal develops. The shapes chosen go beyond the ordinary to include, for example, a fan shape, a diamond, a crescent, and a hexagon. MacDonald uses the three final pages to present some information about each animal." Booklist

Mackall, Dandi Daley

First day; illustrated by Tiphanie Beeke. Harcourt 2003 unp il $16 **E**

1. School stories 2. Stories in rhyme
ISBN 0-15-216577-0 LC 2002-933

"Silver Whistle"

The first day of school starts out filled with doubt, but after facing fear of the big kids, reciting the alphabet with ease, and learning about recess, a child can't help but look forward to day two.

"The rhyming text gives the story a sweet, singsong quality. . . . The softly colored, reassuring art works well with the simple text that is set on pastel backgrounds." SLJ

Macken, JoAnn Early

Sing-along song; written by JoAnn Early Macken; illustrated by LeUyen Pham. Viking 2004 unp il $15.99 **E**

ISBN 0-670-05890-4

A child sings along with the songs made by everyday sounds, from the chirping of a robin in the morning to the cooing of baby sister as she falls asleep in the evening.

"The rhythm, repetition, and tongue-twisting silliness of the text and the large, inviting pictures will entice even the youngest listeners to join this chorus." SLJ

MacLachlan, Patricia

All the places to love; paintings by Mike Wimmer. HarperCollins Pubs. 1994 unp il $16.99; lib bdg $17.89 **E**

1. Farm life—Fiction 2. Family life—Fiction
ISBN 0-06-021098-2; 0-06-021099-0 (lib bdg)

LC 92-794

A young boy describes the favorite places that he shares with his family on his grandparents' farm and in the nearby countryside

Wimmer's "paintings beautifully convey the splendor of nature, as well as the deep affection binding three generations. This inspired pairing of words and art is a timeless, uplifting portrait of rural family life." Publ Wkly

Bittle; by Patricia MacLachlan & Emily MacLachlan; illustrations by Dan Yaccarino. Joanna Cotler Books 2004 unp il $15.99; lib bdg $16.89 **E**

1. Infants—Fiction 2. Dogs—Fiction 3. Cats—Fiction
ISBN 0-06-000961-6; 0-06-000962-4 (lib bdg)

LC 2003-2357

Nigel the cat and Julia the dog think they will have no use for the new baby in their house, but after awhile they realize that they have come to love her

"The colors are bright, the lines simple. . . . The authors cleverly highlight the changes a new baby brings to a home, and the animals' growing affection for Bittle is humorous and heartwarming." SLJ

Painting the wind; by Patricia MacLachlan & Emily MacLachlan; illustrated by Katy Schneider. J. Cotler Bks. 2003 unp il $15.99; lib bdg $16.89 **E**

1. Artists—Fiction 2. Painting—Fiction
ISBN 0-06-029798-0; 0-06-029799-9 (lib bdg)

LC 2001-47549

Several artists who paint different things, with different kinds of paint, and at different times of the day, all paint the same island that they visit each summer

"The gentle prose pairs well with handsome artwork that evokes warm, strong sensory impressions through a combination of thick brushwork, texture, and a vibrant color palette." Booklist

MacLachlan, Patricia—*Continued*

Who loves me? illustrations by Amanda Shepherd. Joanna Cotler Books 2005 unp il $14.99; lib bdg $15.89   E

1. Bedtime—Fiction 2. Cats—Fiction

ISBN 0-06-027976-1; 0-06-027977-X (lib bdg)

LC 2004-697

At bedtime, a cat in the window reassures a little girl that family members, friends, her dog, and even her brother love her.

"Shepherd's stylized illustrations are bathed in rich, warm shades of goldenrod and ochre, through which MacLachlan's cozy, comforting dialogue meanders like a song. A warm and lyrical selection." SLJ

MacLean, Kerry Lee

Peaceful piggy meditation; written and illustrated by Kerry Lee MacLean. Albert Whitman & Co 2004 unp il $15.95   E

1. Meditation—Fiction 2. Pigs—Fiction

ISBN 0-8075-6380-3   LC 2004-526

Peaceful pigs demonstrate the many benefits of meditation.

"Even families that normally regard meditation as so much New Age folderol may find this chipper offering both endearing and persuasive." Booklist

Madrigal, Antonio Hernandez

Erandi's braids; written by Antonio Hernandez Madrigal; illustrated by Tomie dePaola. Putnam 1999 unp il $15.99   E

1. Hair—Fiction 2. Mother-daughter relationship—Fiction 3. Mexico—Fiction

ISBN 0-399-23212-5   LC 97-49631

In a poor Mexican village, Erandi surprises her mother by offering to sell her long, beautiful hair in order to raise enough money to buy a new fishing net

"This tale of love and sacrifice is based on an actual Mexican practice in the 1940s and 50s. The facial expressions in dePaola's warm illustrations add to the poignancy of the story." Horn Book Guide

Mahy, Margaret

17 kings and 42 elephants; pictures by Patricia MacCarthy. Dial Bks. for Young Readers 1987 26p il $16.99   E

1. Animals—Fiction 2. Stories in rhyme

ISBN 0-8037-0458-5   LC 87-5311

A newly illustrated edition of the title first published 1972 in the United Kingdom

Seventeen kings and forty-two elephants romp with a variety of jungle animals during their mysterious journey through a wild, wet night

"This book takes you on a jungle journey you will never forget. . . . The text is lyrical, humorous, and full of nonsense and fantasy. Children and adults will be charmed by the melodic use of language and the beautiful batik illustrations." Child Book Rev Serv

Maitland, Barbara

Moo in the morning; pictures by Andrew Kulman. Farrar, Straus & Giroux 2000 unp il $16   E

1. City and town life—Fiction 2. Farm life—Fiction 3. Sounds—Fiction

ISBN 0-374-35038-8   LC 97-17354

Tired of all the loud city noises early in the morning, a mother and child visit a farm, where very different noises greet them when the sun comes up

"Buoyant text captures the din of city traffic and farmyard animal sounds. Bold, vigorous images are rendered in varied perspectives and are well suited to the lively narrative." Horn Book Guide

Major, Kevin

Aunt Olga's Christmas postcards; illustrations by Bruce Roberts. House of Anansi Press 2005 unp il $16.95   E

1. Aunts—Fiction 2. Christmas—Fiction

ISBN 0-88899-593-8

"A Groundwood book"

Aunt Olga shares her collection of Christmas postcards and memories with her favorite niece, Anna.

The "story is expanded by Roberts' energetic drawings and the inclusion of dozens of postcards from the author's personal collection, which demonstrate that while the look of the season may have changed, its spirit remains the same." Booklist

Mak, Kam

My Chinatown; one year in poems. HarperCollins Pubs. 2002 unp il $16.95; lib bdg $16.89   E

1. Immigrants—Fiction 2. Chinese Americans—Fiction 3. Chinatown (New York, N.Y.)—Fiction

ISBN 0-06-029190-7; 0-06-029191-5 (lib bdg)

LC 2001-16686

A boy adjusts to life away from his home in Hong Kong, in the Chinatown of his new American city

"Extraordinary photo-realistic paintings and spare, free-verse poems bring New York's Chinatown to life in this picture book with appeal to a wide age group." Booklist

Mallat, Kathy

Mama love. Walker & Co 2004 unp il $15.95; lib bdg $16.85   E

1. Chimpanzees—Fiction 2. Mothers—Fiction 3. Stories in rhyme

ISBN 0-8027-8902-1; 0-8027-8904-8 (lib bdg)

LC 2003-57550

A young chimpanzee describes the different ways his mother shows her love for him; and how he loves her in return.

This offers "a gentle rhyming text and exquisite artwork. . . . The lush illustrations, done in oil pastels and colored pencils, show the two animals as they cuddle together, share food, and enjoy one another's company." SLJ

Manders, John

Señor Don Gato; a traditional song; illustrated by John Manders. Candlewick Press 2003 unp il music $15.99   **E**

1. Cats—Fiction 2. Songs

ISBN 0-7636-1724-5   LC 2001-52941

When he climbs on a roof to read a love letter, a cat has an unfortunate fall with unexpected consequences. Music and Spanish translation at back of book

"The bright, exuberant gouache illustrations, featuring a cast of bug-eyed cats . . . add the right amount of exaggeration and operatic flair to the entertaining story." Booklist

Mannis, Celeste A.

One leaf rides the wind; counting in a Japanese garden; by Celeste Davidson Mannis, pictures by Susan Kathleen Hartung. Viking 2002 unp il $15.99   **E**

1. Gardens—Poetry 2. Haiku 3. Counting

ISBN 0-670-03525-4   LC 2002-1024

In this collection of haiku poems, a young girl walks through a Japanese garden and discovers many delights, from one leaf to ten stone lanterns. Includes notes about Japanese religion and philosophy

"The book as a whole is elegantly and respectfully presented and the counting aspect is especially well crafted, capturing the meandering focus of a small child. Mannis's simple verses are complemented by Hartung's pleasing and evocative pen-and-ink and watercolor art." SLJ

Marcellino, Fred

I, crocodile. HarperCollins Pubs. 1999 unp il $18.99; lib bdg $15.89; pa $6.99   **E**

1. Napoleon I, Emperor of the French, 1769-1821— Fiction 2. Crocodiles—Fiction

ISBN 0-06-205168-7; 0-06-205199-7 (lib bdg); 0-06-008859-1 (pa)

"Michael di Capua books"

"The tale, inspired by a 19th-century French satire by an unknown author, centers on a crocodile captured in Egypt and transported to Paris by Napoleon, who decides to cook and eat the animal. But the crocodile . . . escapes into the sewers and makes his own dinner out of a lady of Napoleon's court." N Y Times Book Rev

"The text is reportorial in tone, a perfect complement to the extravagant, expressive illustrations. . . . A sophisticated picture book, this is one publication with appeal to many different audiences." Horn Book

Marino, Gianna

Zoopa; an animal alphabet. Chronicle Books 2005 unp il $14.95   **E**

1. Alphabet 2. Animals

ISBN 0-8118-4789-6   LC 2004-63449

"A bowl of tomato soup is the vehicle for introducing the letters of the alphabet and their corresponding animals. Beginning with a playful ant and an orange-and-purple butterfly, two to three animals and their first letters are introduced on each spread. As the menagerie multiplies, the creatures move around the pages, some-

times interacting with humorous results. . . . The playful gouache illustrations depict the colorful crew having as much fun as readers will surely have identifying them." SLJ

Markes, Julie

Good thing you're not an octopus! story by Julie Markes; pictures by Maggie Smith. HarperCollins Pubs. 2001 unp il $14.95; lib bdg $14.89   **E**

1. Animals—Fiction

ISBN 0-06-028465-X; 0-06-028466-8 (lib bdg)
LC 99-37139

"A boy who complains about getting dressed, riding in his car seat, and more is answered with funny worst-case scenarios: 'You don't like to take a nap? Its a good thing you're not a bear. If you were a bear, you would have to nap all winter long!' The tone is silly, and the cheerful illustrations convey the absurdity in the text." Horn Book Guide

I can't talk yet, but when I do...; illustrated by Laura Rader. HarperCollins Pubs. 2003 unp il $15.99   **E**

1. Infants—Fiction 2. Siblings—Fiction 3. Mice—Fiction

ISBN 0-06-009921-6

The author "gives voice to a mouse toddler that plans to thank its older sibling for sharing playthings and ice cream, being good company, tolerating a pull on the ear, etc. . . . Rader's whimsical illustrations are uncluttered and surrounded by lots of white space. They depict lively children, attuned parents, and typical childhood scenarios. . . . [This is a] simple, endearing read-aloud that has broad appeal." SLJ

Shhhhh! Everybody's sleeping; illustrated by David Parkins. 1st ed. HarperCollins 2005 unp il $14.99; lib bdg $15.89   **E**

1. Bedtime—Fiction 2. Sleep—Fiction 3. Stories in rhyme

ISBN 0-06-053790-6; 0-06-053791-4 (lib bdg)
LC 2003-27854

A young child is encouraged to go to sleep by the thought of everyone else sleeping, from teacher to baker to postman

"The text satisfyingly moves along while the artwork soars. . . . Glowing with warm colors in subdued hues, the sturdy pictures stretch wide across double-page spreads, offering surprisingly energetic, varied compositions." Booklist

Marshall, Edward

Fox and his friends; pictures by James Marshall. Dial Bks. for Young Readers 1982 56p il pa $3.99 hardcover o.p.   **E**

1. Foxes—Fiction

ISBN 0-14-037007-2 (pa)   LC 81-68769

"Dial easy-to-read"

"Fox has one objective—having fun with his motley group of friends. Unfortunately, his desires regularly conflict with his mother's insistence that he care for his younger sister Louise or with his responsibilities when

Marshall, Edward—*Continued*

assigned to traffic patrol." Horn Book

"The sibling exchanges and situations are comically true to life, as is Fox's duty/pleasure conflict. The red, green and black illustrations, showing a defiant Louise, a beleaguered Fox, a wonderful assortment of creature friends and a hilariously feeble group of old hounds pick the story up and add character embellishment and humor." SLJ

Other titles about Fox are:

Fox all week (1984)

Fox at school (1983)

Fox in love (1982)

Fox on wheels (1983)

Space case; pictures by James Marshall. Dial Bks. for Young Readers 1980 unp il $16.99; pa $6.99   E

1. Science fiction 2. Halloween—Fiction

ISBN 0-8037-8005-2; 0-14-054704-5 (pa)

LC 80-13369

"The 'thing'—a neon yellow robot-like creature from space—arrives on Halloween for a look around and is promptly mistaken for a costumed trick-or-treater. It spends the night with a friendly child . . . visits at school (the teacher takes it for a science project) and leaves promising to return for the next fun holiday, Christmas." SLJ

"The open ending of the brief story is as satisfying as it is original, for the small space traveler is thoroughly childlike in its insouciance, curiosity, and concern for self-gratification. The text is an economical, tongue-in-cheek accompaniment to the various levels of humor depicted in the illustrations." Horn Book

Three by the sea; pictures by James Marshall. Dial Bks. for Young Readers 1981 48p il pa $3.99 hardcover o.p.   E

1. Storytelling—Fiction

ISBN 0-14-037004-8 (pa)

"Dial easy-to-read"

"When Lolly, on a beach picnic with friends Sam and Spider, reads a story ('The rat saw the cat and the dog.') aloud, it is rated dull. So Sam uses the same rat and cat characters to tell one of his own, and Spider tops Sam's managing to scare the other two with his tale of a monster that passes by the rat and cat to find some tasty kids." SLJ

"The mild lunacy of the illustrations (an almost vertical hill, a neatly striped cat) with their ungainly, comical figures is nicely matched with the bland directness of the writing. This is good-humored and amusing." Bull Cent Child Books

Other titles about Spider, Sam, and Lolly are:

Four on the shore (1985)

Three up a tree (1986)

Marshall, James

George and Martha; written and illustrated by James Marshall. Houghton Mifflin 1972 46p il lib bdg $16; pa $6.95   E

1. Hippopotamus—Fiction 2. Friendship—Fiction

ISBN 0-395-16619-5 (lib bdg); 0-395-19972-7 (pa)

Also available Spanish language edition

In these five short episodes which include a misunderstanding about split pea soup, invasion of privacy and a crisis over a missing tooth, two not very delicate hippopotamuses reveal various aspects of friendship

"The pale pictures of these creatures and their adventures—in yellows, pinks, greens, and grays—capture the directness and humor of the stories." Horn Book

Other titles about George and Martha are:

George and Martha back in town (1984)

George and Martha encore (1973)

George and Martha, one fine day (1978)

George and Martha rise and shine (1976)

George and Martha round and round (1988)

George and Martha, tons of fun (1980)

Swine Lake; [pictures by] Maurice Sendak. HarperCollins Pubs. 1999 unp il $16.95   E

1. Ballet—Fiction 2. Wolves—Fiction 3. Pigs—Fiction

ISBN 0-06-205171-7   LC 98-73253

"Michael di Capua books"

A hungry wolf attends a performance of Swine Lake, performed by the Boarshoi Ballet, intending to eat the performers, but he is so entranced by the story unfolding that he forgets about his meal

"Both Marshall and Sendak are cleverly comic here . . . the text shines. Sendak's art captures the nuance as well as all the humor of the story." Booklist

Martin, Bill

Barn dance! by Bill Martin, Jr. and John Archambault; illustrated by Ted Rand. Holt & Co. 1986 unp il $16.95; pa $6.95   E

1. Stories in rhyme 2. Dance—Fiction 3. Country life—Fiction

ISBN 0-8050-0089-5; 0-8050-0799-7 (pa)

LC 86-14225

Unable to sleep on the night of a full moon, a young boy follows the sound of music across the fields and finds an unusual barn dance in progress

"The bouncy rhyme will be a pleasure for listeners and tellers as they pick up the twang and the barn-dance beat. Rand's raucous two-page watercolor spreads are as spirited as the story poem." Booklist

A beasty story; [written by] Bill Martin, Jr. & [illustrated by] Steven Kellogg. Harcourt Brace & Co. 1999 unp il $16   E

1. Mice—Fiction 2. Color—Fiction 3. Stories in rhyme

ISBN 0-15-201683-X   LC 97-49519

A group of mice venture into a dark, dark woods where they find a dark brown house with a dark red stair leading past other dark colors to a spooky surprise

"A rhymed narrative tells the story along the top of the pages, with the mice commenting in rhymed conversation as they move through the adventure. The silly resolution will appeal to young children. . . . Kellogg's lively ink-and-watercolor art strikes just the right note for the gently suspenseful story." Booklist

Brown bear, brown bear what do you see? pictures by Eric Carle. Holt & Co. 1992 unp il $16.95   E

1. Color—Fiction 2. Animals—Fiction 3. Stories in rhyme

ISBN 0-8050-1744-5   LC 91-29115

Martin, Bill—*Continued*

Also available Board book edition

A newly illustrated edition of the title first published 1967 by Holt, Rinehart & Winston

A chant in which a variety of animals, each one a different color, answers the question, "What do you see?"

"Carle's large, brilliantly colored animals set against a white background make the book perfect for sharing with a group of preschoolers, while Martin's repetitious text is eminently chantable—a boon for beginning readers." Horn Book

Chicka chicka 1, 2, 3; [by] Bill Martin, Jr. & Michael Sampson; illustrated by Lois Ehlert. Simon & Schuster Books for Young Readers 2004 unp il $15.95   **E**

1. Counting 2. Stories in rhyme

ISBN 0-689-85881-7   LC 2003-19106

Numbers from one to one hundred climb to the top of an apple tree in this rhyming chant.

"The chanting rhyme and eye-popping images have a contagious energy youngsters will find irresistible." Booklist

Chicka chicka boom boom; by Bill Martin, Jr. and John Archambault; illustrated by Lois Ehlert. Simon & Schuster Bks. for Young Readers 1989 unp il $15; pa $6.99   **E**

1. Alphabet 2. Stories in rhyme

ISBN 0-671-67949-X; 0-689-83568-X (pa)

LC 89-4315

An alphabet rhyme/chant that relates what happens when the whole alphabet tries to climb a coconut tree

"Ehlert's illustrations—bold, colorful shapes—are contained by broad polka-dotted borders, like a proscenium arch through which the action explodes. Tongue-tingling, visually stimulating, with an insistent repetitive chorus of 'chicka chicka boom boom,' the book demands to be read again and again and again." Horn Book

The ghost-eye tree; by Bill Martin, Jr. and John Archambault; illustrated by Ted Rand. Holt & Co. 1985 unp il $16.95; pa $6.95   **E**

1. Ghost stories 2. Fear—Fiction

ISBN 0-8050-0208-1; 0-8050-0947-7 (pa)

LC 85-8422

"On a dark and ghostly night a brother and sister are sent to fetch a pail of milk from the other end of town. They must pass the fearful ghost-eye tree, old and horribly twisted, looking like a monster, with a gap in the branches where the moon shines through like an eye. . . . The story is rhythmically told, sometimes rhyming, always moving ahead, sharp with the affectionate teasing of the brother and sister. The realistic watercolor illustrations are superb—strong, striking, very dark, with highlights of moonlight and lantern light that cast a spooky, scary spell. A splendidly theatrical book for storytelling and reading aloud." Horn Book

Knots on a counting rope; by Bill Martin, Jr. and John Archambault; illustrated by Ted Rand. Holt & Co. 1987 unp il $16.95; pa $6.95

      E

1. Native Americans—Fiction 2. Grandfathers—Fiction 3. Blind—Fiction

ISBN 0-8050-0571-4; 0-8050-5479-0 (pa)

LC 87-14858

Also available paperback Big edition

A different version of the title illustrated by Joe Smith was published in 1966

"Boy-Strength-of-Blue-Horses begs his grandfather to tell him again the story of the night he was born. In a question-and-answer litany, the boy and his grandfather share the telling of the events on that special night." SLJ

"The powerful spare poetic text is done full justice by Rand's fine full-color illustrations, which capture both the drama and brilliance of vast southwestern space and the intimacy of starlit camp-fire scenes." Booklist

The maestro plays; by Bill Martin, Jr.; pictures by Vladimir Radunsky. Holt & Co. 1994 unp il $15.95   **E**

1. Musicians—Fiction

ISBN 0-8050-1746-1   LC 94-1916

"At center stage is a clown-like creature, 'The Maestro,' who plays a progression of instruments. And how does he play? In an intriguing variety of ways, including some that are easy enough to understand ('flowingly, glowingly, knowingly, showingly, goingly') and some that will require youngsters to use their imaginations ('nippingly, drippingly, zippingly, clippingly, pippingly.'" Publ Wkly

"Radunsky's wonderfully bizarre illustrations, created from hand-colored cut paper, are a visual delight. . . . An infectious rhythm builds, at times lapsing into nonsense, but resulting in an almost perfect coupling of text and illustration." SLJ

Panda bear, panda bear, what do you see? by Bill Martin Jr.; pictures by Eric Carle. Holt & Co. 2003 unp il $15.95   **E**

1. Endangered species—Fiction 2. Animals—Fiction 3. Stories in rhyme

ISBN 0-8050-1758-5   LC 2002-10855

Illustrations and rhyming text present ten different endangered animals

"The pictures, featuring animals strolling, splashing, and soaring, are brilliant lessons in the application of color, shape, form, and texture. . . . A fine read-aloud with a subtle, yet clear, message." Booklist

Polar bear, polar bear, what do you hear? by Bill Martin, Jr.; pictures by Eric Carle. Holt & Co. 1991 unp il $16.95   **E**

1. Animals—Fiction 2. Stories in rhyme

ISBN 0-8050-1759-3   LC 91-13322

Also available Board book edition and paperback Big edition; Spanish language edition also available

Zoo animals from polar bear to walrus make their distinctive sounds for each other, while children imitate the sounds for the zookeeper

"Carle's characteristically inventive, jewel-toned artwork forms a seamless succession of images that fairly leap off the pages." Publ Wkly

Martin, Bill—*Continued*

Trick or treat? [by] Bill Martin, Jr. and Michael Sampson; illustrated by Paul Meisel. Simon & Schuster Bks. for Young Readers 2002 unp il $14.95   E

1. Halloween—Fiction 2. Magic—Fiction
ISBN 0-689-84968-0   LC 2002-70646

A child has a wonderful time collecting treats from the wacky neighbors until Magic Merlin decides that a trick would be more fun

"Meisel's cartoon illustrations take full advantage of the topsy-turvy story, adding lots of comic holiday detail to keep little ones alert. The fun is in the pictures, and the challenge is in figuring out the visual joke and the backward names." Booklist

Martin, David

Piggy and Dad go fishing; illustrated by Frank Remkiewicz. Candlewick Press 2005 unp il $14.99
                                                                E

1. Fishing—Fiction 2. Pigs—Fiction 3. Father-son relationship—Fiction
ISBN 0-7636-2506-X   LC 2004-51941

When his dad takes Piggy fishing for the first time and Piggy ends up feeling sorry for the worms and the fish, they decide to make some changes.

"The summery watercolor-and-pencil cartoon illustrations clue listeners into Piggy's emotions and create a bit of tension in the nicely paced story." Horn Book Guide
Other titles about Piggy and Dad are:
Piggy and Dad (2001)
Piggy and Dad play (2002)

Martin, Jacqueline Briggs

Grandmother Bryant's pocket; pictures by Petra Mathers. Houghton Mifflin 1996 48p il $14.95
                                                                E

1. Fear—Fiction 2. Grandmothers—Fiction 3. Maine—Fiction
ISBN 0-395-68984-8   LC 94-31309

"In 1787, Sarah Bryant is eight years old and lives on a farm in Maine. She and her spotted dog Patches are inseparable companions until that spring, when the barn burns down and Patches is killed in the fire. Sarah begins to have bad dreams . . . and so she is sent to her grandparents, an herbalist and a woodworker, for solace and healing." Horn Book

"Appealingly structured in one-and two-page chapters, the book is illustrated with watercolor paintings. Executed in naive style, the artwork has an unassuming sweetness." Booklist

On Sand Island; illustrated by David Johnson. Houghton Mifflin 2003 unp il $16   E

1. Islands—Fiction
ISBN 0-618-23151-X   LC 2002-5090

In 1916 on an island in Lake Superior, Carl builds himself a boat by bartering with the other islanders for parts and labor

"Martin's simple, poetic text deftly balances small, revealing details about the island's characters and Carl's life with the particulars of boat building. . . . The illustrations . . . capture the lake's translucent light and the

story's nostalgic mood in expert, geometric line drawings washed with watery blue-green and sunset-orange colors." Booklist

Martin, Rafe

The storytelling princess; illustrated by Kimberly Bulcken Root. Putnam 2001 unp il lib bdg $15.99   E

1. Fairy tales 2. Storytelling—Fiction
ISBN 0-399-22924-8   LC 98-4335

Having survived a shipwreck, a princess tries to tell a prince a story whose ending he does not know and thus qualify for his hand in marriage

"This original tale has a strong folkloric base, but there are no fragile folktale females here. Root's pencil and watercolor illustrations eschew gauzy images in favor of robust ones. . . . This is a dandy tale for telling or reading aloud." Bull Cent Child Books

Will's mammoth; illustrated by Stephen Gammell. Putnam 1989 unp il $16.99   E

1. Mammoths—Fiction
ISBN 0-399-21627-8   LC 88-11651

"Will loves mammoths—huge, hairy, woolly mammoths. His parents explain that there are no mammoths left in the world, but Will knows better. Off he goes into an iridescent, snowbound world of his own creation, where he quickly finds all manner of woolly prehistoric beasts." SLJ

"Gammell's depiction of a child's rich imagination is illustrated in vivid colors. The fantasy spreads use winter whites and blues as background for subtly individualized animals who move energetically across the pages." Booklist

Massie, Diane Redfield

The baby beebee bird; pictures by Steven Kellogg. Newly il ed. HarperCollins Pubs. 2000 unp il $16.99; lib bdg $16.89   E

1. Animals—Fiction 2. Sleep—Fiction
ISBN 0-06-028083-2; 0-06-028084-0 (lib bdg)
                                      LC 99-33421

A newly illustrated edition of the title first published 1963

The zoo animals find a way to keep the baby beebee bird awake during the day so that they can get some sleep at night

"The facial expressions on Kellogg's animals loom large, extending . . . the simple story and giving visual voice to a story big on child appeal." Booklist

Masurel, Claire

Two homes; illustrated by Kady MacDonald Denton. Candlewick Press 2001 unp il $14.99
                                                                E

1. Divorce—Fiction
ISBN 0-7636-0511-5   LC 00-41398

A young boy named Alex enjoys the homes of both of his parents who live apart but love Alex very much

"Parents looking for a book about separation or divorce will find few offerings as positive, matter-of-fact, or child-centered as this one. . . . Enhanced by Denton's sensitively drawn portrayals of the characters within well-imagined scenes of domestic life." Booklist

Mathers, Petra

Lottie's new beach towel. Atheneum Bks. for Young Readers 1998 unp il $15   **E**

1. Chickens—Fiction 2. Beaches—Fiction

ISBN 0-689-81606-5   LC 97-6689

"An Anne Schwartz book"

Lottie the chicken has a number of adventures at the beach, during which her new towel, a gift from her friend Herbie the duck, comes in handy.

"Pure fun, with a resourceful, big-hearted main character; humor in both text and pictures; and a good story, elegantly shaped." Horn Book

Other titles about Lottie and Herbie are:

A cake for Herbie (2000)

Herbie's secret Santa (2002)

Lottie's new friend (1999)

Maybarduk, Linda

James the dancing dog; illustrated by Gillian Johnson. Tundra 2004 unp il $15.95   **E**

1. Dogs—Fiction 2. Ballet—Fiction

ISBN 0-88776-619-6

James the beagle comes to the ballet studio every day, hoping some day to have his moment on stage.

"Johnson's cartoon ink-and-watercolor illustrations are light-filled and add detail and humor to Maybarduk's charming story." SLJ

Mayer, Mercer

A boy, a dog, and a frog. Dial Bks. for Young Readers 1967 unp il pa $4.99 hardcover o.p.

E

1. Frogs—Fiction 2. Stories without words

ISBN 0-14-054611-1 (pa)

"Without the need for a single word, humorous, very engaging pictures tell the story of a little boy who sets forth with his dog and a net on a summer day to catch an enterprising and personable frog. Even very young preschoolers will 'read' the tiny book with the greatest satisfaction and pleasure." Horn Book

Other titles in this series are:

A boy, a dog, a frog, and a friend (1971)

Frog goes to dinner (1974)

Frog on his own (1973)

Frog, where are you? (1969)

One frog too many (1975)

There's a nightmare in my closet. Dial Bks. for Young Readers 1968 unp il $16.99; pa $6.99

E

1. Fear—Fiction

ISBN 0-8037-8682-4; 0-14-054712-6 (pa)

"Childhood fear of the dark and the resulting exercise in imaginative exaggeration are given that special Mercer Mayer treatment in this dryly humorous fantasy. Young children will easily empathize with the boy and can be comforted by his experience." SLJ

Another title about this boy is:

There's an alligator under my bed (1987)

Mayhew, James

Katie's Sunday afternoon; by James Mayhew. 1st Scholastic ed. Orchard Books 2005 c2004 unp il $16.95   **E**

1. Art appreciation—Fiction 2. Impressionism (Art)—Fiction

ISBN 0-439-60678-0   LC 2004-2678

First published 2004 in the United Kingdom

On a hot day, Katie and her grandmother visit the art museum, where Katie climbs into the paintings of pointillist artists Seurat, Pisarro, and Signac.

"The watercolor artwork is in a simple impressionistic style. A note about the pointillists Georges Seurat, Paul Signac, and Camille Pissarro closes another of Mayhew's playful, imaginative celebrations of the happy fusion of life and art." Booklist

Other titles in this series are:

Katie and the Mona Lisa (1999)

Katie and the sunflowers (2001)

The knight who took all day. Scholastic Inc. 2005 unp il $15.99   **E**

1. Knights and knighthood—Fiction 2. Dragons—Fiction

ISBN 0-439-74829-1

"The Chicken House"

"Hoping to woo the princess, a knight readies to slay the dragon destroying her kingdom. However, this vain knight takes all day selecting his armor and when he is finally ready the princess has already tamed the dragon. Readers will enjoy observing the progress, buried in the quirky illustrations, of the princess quickly preparing to tame the dragon in this satisfying story." Horn Book Guide

Mayo, Margaret

Choo choo clickety-clack! written by Margaret Mayo; illustrated by Alex Ayliffe. 1st American ed. Carolrhoda Books 2005 unp il lib bdg $14.95

E

1. Noise—Fiction 2. Transportation—Fiction

ISBN 1-57505-819-7   LC 2004-11976

First published 2004 in the United Kingdom

Rhythmic sounds imitate trains, planes, and other busy transports that come and go.

"Short and snappy, four lines of text encapsulate the excitement that comes with getting in a car, sailing on a lake, or floating in a hot-air balloon. The graphic-style artwork is executed in a melange of pure colors." Booklist

McAllister, Angela

Barkus, Sly and the golden egg; illustrated by Sally Anne Lambert. Bloomsbury Children's Bks. 2002 unp il $15.95   **E**

1. Chickens—Fiction 2. Foxes—Fiction

ISBN 1-58234-764-6   LC 2001-43981

Published in the United Kingdom with title: The Baddies' goodies

Three inventive chickens find an ingenious way to escape from the two foxes that intend to eat them

"Having the universal appeal of the weak outwitting the strong, the story is told with delicious humor and good pacing, and the pleasing watercolor illustrations add much detail to the clever text." SLJ

McAllister, Angela—*Continued*

Take a kiss to school; by Angela McAllister; illustrated by Sue Hellard. 1st U.S. ed. Bloomsbury Children's Books 2006 unp il $15.95
E

1. School stories 2. Moles (Animals)—Fiction
ISBN 9781582347028   LC 2005053689

Digby's mother helps him make it through the second day of school by sending him off with a pocket full of kisses.

"Hellard's warm, humorous, ink-and-watercolor art keeps to the perspective of the shy, bespectacled mole—in the classroom, at the lunch table, and in the schoolyard, where he makes a friend." Booklist

McBratney, Sam

Guess how much I love you; illustrated by Anita Jeram. Candlewick Press 1995 unp il $15.99
E

1. Rabbits—Fiction 2. Father-son relationship—Fiction
ISBN 1-56402-473-3   LC 94-1599

Also available Board book edition; Spanish language edition also available

During a bedtime game, every time Little Nutbrown Hare demonstrates how much he loves his father, Big Nutbrown Hare gently shows him that the love is returned even more

"Neither sugary nor too cartoonlike, the watercolors, in soft shades of brown and greens with delicate ink-line details, warmly capture the loving relationship between parent and child as well as the comedy that stems from little hare's awe of his wonderful dad." Booklist

McCarty, Peter

Hondo and Fabian. Holt & Co. 2002 unp il $16.95
E

1. Dogs—Fiction 2. Cats—Fiction
ISBN 0-8050-6352-8   LC 2001-1884

A Caldecott Medal honor book, 2003

Hondo the dog gets to go to the beach and play with his friend Fred, while Fabian the cat spends the day at home

"McCarty's staccato text, one line to a page, captures a lot of action in a few words, but it is the pencil-on-watercolor-paper art that makes this so arresting. Each carefully shaded picture, in muted tones, has a smooth, solid look." Booklist

T is for terrible; written and illustrated by Peter McCarty. 1st ed. Henry Holt 2004 unp il $15.95
E

1. Dinosaurs—Fiction
ISBN 0-8050-7404-X   LC 2003-18246

A tyrannosaurus rex explains that he cannot help it that he is enormous and hungry and is not a vegetarian.

"Filled with textured lines and soft shading, the artwork glows with warmth and vitality. This beautifully formatted and well-conceived offering has creamy ivory pages that frame the subtle illustrations and spare text." SLJ

McClintock, Barbara

Dahlia. Farrar, Straus & Giroux 2002 unp il $16
E

1. Dolls—Fiction
ISBN 0-374-31678-3   LC 2001-18778

"Frances Foster books"

"Charlotte doesn't want a doll for a playmate. . . . She prefers to climb trees, make mud pies, and dig in the dirt. When her Aunt Edme sends her a doll that's dressed in lace, ribbons, and gloves, Charlotte wrinkles her nose and informs the doll that there will be no tea parties or riding in 'frilly prams!' . . . McClintock tells an engaging story about an unusual character. . . . In her trademark delicate pen-and-ink outline art—filled with soft watercolors—McClintock delightfully juxtaposes spirited Charlotte within the old-fashioned setting." Booklist

Molly and the magic wishbone. Foster Bks. 2001 unp il $16
E

1. Wishes—Fiction 2. Fairy tales
ISBN 0-374-34999-1   LC 98-31789

"Frances Foster books."

Molly's fairy godmother gives her a magic fishbone that will grant one wish, which the resourceful girl saves until she really needs it

"A Victorian setting and a family of kittens . . . are only part of the charm of this fairy tale, loosely based on a story by Charles Dickens. . . . McClintock's telling is well paced and nuanced." Booklist

McCloskey, Robert

Blueberries for Sal. Viking 1948 54p il $16.99; pa $7.99
E

1. Bears—Fiction 2. Maine—Fiction
ISBN 0-670-17591-9; 0-14-050169-X (pa)

A Caldecott Medal honor book, 1949

"The author-artist tells what happens on a summer day in Maine when a little girl and a bear cub, wandering away from their blueberry-picking mothers, each mistakes the other's mother for its own. The Maine hillside and meadows are real and lovely, the quiet humor is entirely childlike, and there is just exactly the right amount of suspense for small children." Wis Libr Bull

Another title about Sal is: One morning in Maine

Lentil. Viking 1940 unp il $18.99; pa $5.99
E

1. Harmonicas—Fiction 2. Ohio—Fiction
ISBN 0-670-42357-2; 0-14-050287-4 (pa)

Picture-story book about a small boy who could not sing, but who could work wonders on a simple harmonica, especially on the day when the great Colonel Carter returned to his home town

"Big, vigorous, amusing pictures in black-and-white, with an Ohio small-town background." New Yorker

Make way for ducklings. Viking 1941 unp $17.99; pa $7.99
E

1. Ducks—Fiction 2. Boston (Mass.)—Fiction
ISBN 0-670-45149-5; 0-14-056434-9 (pa)

Also available Spanish language edition

Awarded the Caldecott Medal, 1942

"A family of baby ducks was born on the Charles River near Boston. When they were old enough to fol-

McCloskey, Robert—*Continued*

low, Mother Duck, with some help from a friendly policeman, trailed them through Boston traffic to the pond
in the Public Garden." Bookmark

"There are some very beautiful drawings in this
book." Horn Book

One morning in Maine. Viking 1952 64p il
$17.99; pa $6.99 **E**
1. Maine—Fiction
ISBN 0-670-52627-4; 0-14-050174-6 (pa)

A Caldecott Medal honor book, 1953

The events of this "story—Sal's discovery of her first
loose tooth, the loss of the tooth while digging clams,
the consequent wish on a gull's feather, and the wish
come true—occur in the course of one morning in
Maine. The lovely Maine seacoast scenes and the doings
of Sal with her family and friends are drawn with enticing detail in beautiful, big double-spread lithographs
printed in dark blue." Booklist

Time of wonder. Viking 1957 63p il $18.99; pa
$6.99 **E**
1. Maine—Fiction
ISBN 0-670-71512-3; 0-14-050201-7 (pa)

Awarded the Caldecott Medal, 1958

"A summer on an island in Maine is described
through the simple everyday experiences of children, but
also reveals the author's deep awareness of an attachment to all the shifting moods of season and weather,
and the salty, downright character of the New England
people." Top News

McCully, Emily Arnold

The battle for St. Michaels. HarperCollins Pubs.
2002 64p il $15.99; lib bdg $17.89 **E**
1. War of 1812—Fiction
ISBN 0-06-028728-4; 0-06-028729-2 (lib bdg)
LC 2001-39814

"An I can read chapter book"

In 1813, nine-year-old Caroline, a fast runner, helps
the residents of Saint Michaels, Maryland, as they defend
their town against the British

"McCully's resourceful heroine, action-packed plot,
and dramatic watercolor paintings make for an exciting
slice of history for competent independent readers." SLJ

Beautiful warrior; the legend of the nun's kung
fu. Levine Bks. 1998 unp il $18.95 **E**
1. Martial arts—Fiction 2. China—Fiction
ISBN 0-590-37487-7 LC 97-3823

"Born near the end of the Ming Dynasty, a girl grows
up to become a fighting nun, renowned for her martial
arts. Later, when a timid village girl asks for help in de-
terring her loutish husband-to-be, the nun teaches her
kung fu so she can save herself. The story is intriguing,
and the watercolors . . . are filled with dramatic motion." Horn Book Guide

First snow. HarperCollins Publishers 2004 unp
il $15.99; lib bdg $16.89 **E**
1. Snow—Fiction 2. Sledding—Fiction 3. Mice—Fiction
ISBN 0-06-623852-8; 0-06-623853-6 (lib bdg)
LC 2003-44971

A timid little mouse discovers the thrill of sledding in
the first snow of the winter.

"First published as a wordless picture book in 1985,
First Snow is back with a brief text, enhanced illustrations, and a larger trim size. . . . This new edition has
brighter, deeper colors. . . . Full of exuberance and excitement." SLJ

Other titles about this young mouse are:
Picnic (2003)
School (2005)

The grandma mix-up; story and pictures by
Emily Arnold McCully. Harper & Row 1988 63p
il pa $5.99 hardcover o.p. **E**
1. Grandmothers—Fiction
ISBN 0-06-444150-4 (pa) LC 87-29378

"An I can read book"

Young Pip doesn't know what to do when two very
different grandmothers come to baby sit, each with her
own way of doing things

"McCully's two-color, line-and-wash drawings emphasize the personality differences by consciously flouting
stereotypes: Pip's laid-back Grandma Sal has white hair
and glasses, while his strict Grandma Nan dresses like a
teenager. Choice of words and sentence length will make
the sly humor easy for beginning readers to grasp."
Booklist

Other titles about Pip and his grandmothers are:
Grandmas at bat (1993)
Grandmas at the lake (1990)

Mirette on the high wire. Putnam 1992 unp il
$16.99; pa $6.99 **E**
1. Tightrope walking—Fiction 2. Paris (France)—Fiction
ISBN 0-399-22130-1; 0-698-11443-4 (pa)
LC 91-36324

Awarded the Caldecott Medal, 1993

Mirette learns tightrope walking from Monsieur Bellini, a guest in her mother's boarding house, not knowing
that he is a celebrated tightrope artist who has withdrawn
from performing because of fear

"With a rich palette of deep colors, the artist immerses
the reader in 19th-century Paris. Colorful theatrical personalities . . . fill the glowing interiors with robust life.
And the exterior scenes . . . are filled with the magic of
a Paris night when anything can happen. . . . An exuberant and uplifting picture book." N Y Times Book Rev

Other titles about Mirette and Bellini are:
Mirette & Bellini cross Niagra Falls (2000)
Starring Mirette and Bellini (1997)

Squirrel and John Muir. Farrar Straus Giroux
2004 unp il $16 **E**
1. Muir, John, 1838-1914—Fiction 2. California—Fiction
ISBN 0-374-33697-0 LC 2003-45511

In the early 1900s, a wild little girl nicknamed Squirrel meets John Muir, later to become a famous naturalist,
when he arrives at her parents' hotel in Yosemite Valley
seeking work and knowledge about the natural world.

"The afterword explains how this fictionalized retelling of an actual relationship reveals much about the compelling founder of the Sierra Club. . . . McCully's sure
watercolors capture the stunning natural beauty of the

McCully, Emily Arnold—*Continued*

area and provide a majestic backdrop for the small figure of Squirrel." SLJ

Includes bibliographical references

McDermott, Gerald

Creation. Dutton Children's Bks. 2003 unp il $16.99 **E**

1. Creation—Fiction

ISBN 0-525-46905-2

The author's meditation on the creation story based on Genesis I of Hebrew Bible. In it man and woman are created last to be the keepers of all this beauty

"McDermott casts the story of creation in strong poetic text and sweeping vibrant views. . . . Sumptuous, rhythmic, and mystical, this book is arresting and evocative." SLJ

Papagayo; the mischief maker; written and illustrated by Gerald McDermott. Harcourt Brace Jovanovich 1992 unp il $18; pa $8 **E**

1. Parrots—Fiction

ISBN 0-15-259465-5; 0-15-259464-7 (pa)

LC 91-40364

A reissue of the title first published 1980 by Windmill Bks.

Papagayo, the noisy parrot, helps the night animals save the moon from being eaten up by the moon dog

"McDermott's original story assumes folktale proportions. . . . Art for the story is striking; deep tropical colors seem intensified by glossy page surfaces, and they nearly vibrate against the intermittent deep-blue backdrop of a night sky." Booklist

McDonald, Megan

Ant and Honey Bee, what a pair! illustrated by G. Brian Karas. 1st ed. Candlewick Press 2005 unp il $13.99 **E**

1. Ants—Fiction 2. Bees—Fiction 3. Costume—Fiction

ISBN 0-7636-1265-0

LC 00-37888

Ant and Honey Bee try to come up with original outfits for a costume party and almost experience disaster.

"The clever writing is filled with puns and lighthearted jokes. Karas's artwork, done in gouache, acrylic, and pencil, is simple and engaging, adding warmth and humor to the story." SLJ

Baya, baya, lulla-by-a; pictures by Vera Rosenberry. Atheneum Bks. for Young Readers 2004 unp il $16.95 **E**

1. Mother-child relationship—Fiction 2. Birds—Fiction 3. India—Fiction 4. Lullabies—Fiction

ISBN 0-689-84932-X

LC 2001-53611

"A Richard Jackson book"

As a mother in rural India sings to her baby, a weaverbird builds a nest for its young.

"Weaving in Hindi words, the poetry is rhythmic and beautiful, and the richly detailed watercolors are filled with the movement, warmth, and patterns of cloth and quilt." Booklist

Insects are my life; story by Megan McDonald; pictures by Paul Brett Johnson. Orchard Bks. 1995 unp il $16.95 **E**

1. Insects—Fiction

ISBN 0-531-06874-9

LC 94-21960

"A Richard Jackson book"

No one at home or school understands Amanda Frankenstein's devotion to insects until she meets Maggie.

"Factual tidbits slipped surreptitiously into the appealing text add information to this spirited tale. . . . Full-page and vignette illustrations rendered in soft-hued watercolors, colored pencils, and pastels complement and add humor to the story." SLJ

Another title about Amanda and Maggie is:

Reptiles are my life (2001)

McElligott, Matthew

Absolutely not. Walker & Co 2004 unp il $16.95 **E**

1. Ants—Fiction

ISBN 0-8027-8888-2

LC 2003-47959

Gloria, an ant, takes her friend Frieda for a walk and tries to convince her not to always view the world as a frightening place

"McElligott's simple and attractive layout; the clean, orderly pencil-and-watercolor illustrations; and the straightforward text with its predictable aspects all work together to keep readers inside the joke." SLJ

McElmurry, Jill

I'm not a baby! [by] Jill McElmurry. 1st ed. Schwartz & Wade Books 2006 unp il $16.95

E

1. Growth—Fiction 2. Family life—Fiction

ISBN 0-375-83614-4

LC 2005012998

"An Anne Schwartz book"

I am not a baby!

As the years go by, the members of Leo Leotardi's family continue to think he is just a baby.

"The gouache illustrations on cream-colored paper present Leo's feckless family in a kind of Victorian tableau. The universality of Leo's lament and its wonderfully silly treatment will elicit giggles of recognition." SLJ

McGhee, Alison

Mrs. Watson wants your teeth; story by Alison McGhee; pictures by Harry Bliss. Harcourt 2004 unp il $16 **E**

1. School stories 2. Teachers—Fiction 3. Teeth—Fiction

ISBN 0-15-204931-2

LC 2003-21267

A first grader is frightened on her first day of school after hearing a rumor that her teacher is a 300-year-old alien with a purple tongue who steals baby teeth from her students.

"McGhee has the pulse of this blue-ribbon worrier. . . . Bliss's watercolor and black-ink illustrations feature distinctive, large-eyed classmates and a number of humorous toothy references on the walls in the hall and in the classroom." SLJ

McGill, Alice

Molly Bannaky; written by Alice McGill; pictures by Chris K. Soentpiet. Houghton Mifflin 1999 unp il $17   **E**

1. Banneker, Benjamin, 1731-1806—Fiction 2. Farm life—Fiction 3. United States—History—1600-1775, Colonial period—Fiction

ISBN 0-395-72287-X   LC 96-3000

Relates how Benjamin Banneker's grandmother journeyed from England to Maryland in the late seventeenth century, worked as an indentured servant, began a farm of her own, and married a freed slave

"The writing is descriptive but spare, the implied emotions more resonant echoes than obvious pronouncements. Soentpiet's watercolors use the contrasting play of light and dark to cast the figures in this family drama in bold relief. The compositions . . . have a weighty, monumental feel to them." Bull Cent Child Books

McGrory, Anik

Kidogo; [by] Anik McGrory. 1st U.S. ed. Bloomsbury Children's Books 2005 unp $15.95
          E

1. Elephants—Fiction 2. Size—Fiction

ISBN 1-58234-974-6   LC 2004-54729

Sure that he is the smallest creature on earth, a young elephant leaves home and journeys over woodlands, rivers, and plains searching for someone even smaller than he is.

"The poetic text is perfectly matched with pencil-and-watercolor illustrations that depict a warm and lovely home." SLJ

McKissack, Patricia C.

Flossie & the fox; pictures by Rachel Isadora. Dial Bks. for Young Readers 1986 unp il $15.99
          E

1. Foxes—Fiction 2. African Americans—Fiction

ISBN 0-8037-0250-7   LC 86-2024

A wily fox notorious for stealing eggs meets his match when he encounters a bold little girl in the woods who insists upon proof that he is a fox before she will be frightened

"The watercolor and ink illustrations, with realistic figures set on impressionistic backgrounds, enliven this humorous and well-structured story which is told in the black language of the rural south." SLJ

Goin' someplace special; [illustrated by] Jerry Pinkney. Atheneum Bks. for Young Readers 2001 unp il $16   **E**

1. Segregation—Fiction 2. African Americans—Fiction 3. Tennessee—Fiction

ISBN 0-689-81885-8   LC 99-88258

Coretta Scott King award for illustration, 2002

"An Anne Schwartz book"

In segregated 1950s Nashville, a young African American girl braves a series of indignities and obstacles to get to one of the few integrated places in town: the public library

"Pinkney's watercolor paintings are lush and sprawling as they evoke southern city streets and sidewalks as well as Tricia Ann's inner glow. . . . This book carries a strong message of pride and self-confidence as well as a pointed history lesson." Booklist

The honest-to-goodness truth; illustrated by Giselle Potter. Atheneum Pubs. 2000 unp il $16
          E

1. Honesty—Fiction

ISBN 0-689-82668-0   LC 98-47070

"An Anne Schwartz book"

After promising never to lie, Libby learns that it's not always necessary to blurt out the whole truth either

"The pastel watercolor and ink illustrations capture the story's Southern milieu, warmth, and humor." Horn Book Guide

Ma Dear's aprons; illustrations by Floyd Cooper. Atheneum Bks. for Young Readers 1997 unp il $16; pa $6.99   **E**

1. Mother-son relationship—Fiction 2. African Americans—Fiction

ISBN 0-689-81051-2; 0-689-83262-1 (pa)
          LC 94-48450

"An Anne Schwartz book"

"In this tribute to her great-grandmother, McKissack tells the story of Ma Dear, African-American single mother and domestic worker in the turn of the century South. Her son David Earl always knows what day it is by the 'clean, snappy-fresh apron Ma Dear is wearing—a different one for every day of the week.'" Bull Cent Child Books

"The homely reminiscence is aptly illustrated with Cooper's soft oil wash paintings. . . . Text and illustrations together create a portrait of a family working hard to survive but also finding much to be joyful about." Horn Book

Mirandy and Brother Wind; illustrated by Jerry Pinkney. Knopf 1988 unp il pa $6.99 hardcover o.p.   **E**

1. Dance—Fiction 2. Winds—Fiction 3. African Americans—Fiction

ISBN 0-679-88333-9 (pa)   LC 87-349

A Caldecott Medal honor book, 1989; Coretta Scott King award for illustrations, 1989

"Mirandy is sure that she'll win the cake walk if she can catch Brother Wind for her partner, but he eludes all the tricks her friends advise." Bull Cent Child Books

"Ms. McKissack and Mr. Pinkney's ebullient collaboration captures the texture of rural life and culture 40 years after the end of slavery." N Y Times Book Rev

Precious and the Boo Hag; [by] Patricia C. McKissack and Onawumi Jean Moss; illustrated by Kyrsten Brooker. Atheneum Books for Young Readers 2004 unp il $16.95   **E**

1. Monsters—Fiction 2. African Americans—Fiction

ISBN 0-689-85194-4   LC 2002-1571

"An Anne Schwartz book"

Home alone with a stomachache while the family works in the fields, a young girl faces up to the horrifying Boo Hag that her brother warned her about.

"With the grand feel of a folktale, this lively story speaks to choosing right in a world full of temptation and peril. . . . Expressive and fluid, Brooker's mixed-media art, comical yet scary, too, pops from the pages." Booklist

McLeod, Bob

SuperHero ABC; by Bob McLeod. 1st ed. HarperCollins Pubs. 2006 33p il $15.99; lib bdg $16.89　　　　　　　　　　　　　　　　E

　1. Heroes and heroines—Fiction 2. Alphabet

　ISBN 0-06-074514-2; 0-06-074515-0 (lib bdg)

　　　　　　　　　　　　　　LC 2004-22180

Humorous SuperHeroes such as Goo Girl and The Volcano represent the letters of the alphabet from A to Z.

　"There's strong appeal here for the youngest comic-book fans, with many doses of humor along the way. Each figure has special powers, of course, which readers learn about through alliterative captions and action-packed illustrations." SLJ

McLerran, Alice

Roxaboxen; illustrated by Barbara Cooney. Lothrop, Lee & Shepard Bks. 1991 unp il $16.99; lib bdg $17.89　　　　　　　　　　　　E

　1. Imagination—Fiction

　ISBN 0-688-07592-4; 0-688-07593-2 (lib bdg)

　　　　　　　　　　　　　　LC 89-8057

Also available in paperback from Puffin Bks.

A hill covered with rocks and wooden boxes in the desert becomes an imaginary town named Roxaboxen for Marian, her sisters, and their friends

　"A celebration of the transforming magic of the imagination, the story was inspired by McLerran's mother's reminiscences of her childhood in Yuma, Arizona. . . . The story, told as though from the memory of a Roxaboxenite, brings their play to life through concrete details and a spare, understated style. Equally vivid, Cooney's full-color artwork evokes the striking variety of colors and moods found in the desert landscape." Booklist

McMahon, Patricia

Just add one Chinese sister; by Patricia McMahon and Conor Clarke McCarthy; illustrated by Karen A. Jerome. Boyds Mills Press 2005 unp il $16.95　　　　　　　　　　　　　　E

　1. Adoption 2. Siblings

　ISBN 1-56397-989-6

This "picture book, based on a true story, is about an American family's adoption of a little Chinese girl. The story is told partly from the perspective of the girl's older American brother, Conor. . . . Enlivening the family's stories are Conor's journal entries, beginning with his anxiety and jealousy, and then gradually revealing the siblings' bond. . . . Expressive watercolor artwork, in bright hues, depicts the warm and intense feelings." Booklist

McMillan, Bruce

Growing colors. Lothrop, Lee & Shepard Bks. 1988 32p il $16.99; pa $5.99　　　　　　E

　1. Color 2. Vegetables 3. Fruit

　ISBN 0-688-07844-3; 0-688-13112-3 (pa)

　　　　　　　　　　　　　　LC 88-2767

　"A colors book using fruits and vegetables of every hue. Each double-page spread has a small photograph of the whole plant and a large close-up of the fruit or vegetable. The colors are announced in bold type tinted in the appropriate shade. . . . At the end of the book, there is a picture glossary of all the colors and plants used." Publ Wkly

　"A luscious-looking book that will help children identify colors. . . . This is notably a treat for kids and an example of photography as an art form in picture books." Bull Cent Child Books

Mouse views; what the class pet saw; written and photo-illustrated by Bruce McMillan. Holiday House 1993 32p il $17.95; pa $6.95　　　E

　1. Mice—Fiction

　ISBN 0-8234-1008-0; 0-8234-1132-X (pa)

　　　　　　　　　　　　　　LC 92-25921

Photographic puzzles follow an escaped pet mouse through a school while depicting such common school items as scissors, paper, books, and chalk. Readers are challenged to identify the objects as seen from the mouse's point of view

　"Children will see this brightly illustrated puzzle book, with its combination of story and game, as pure fun. Teachers will appreciate the chance to hone their students' observational skills and also to introduce mapping through the map at the book's conclusion." Booklist

The problem with chickens; illustrated with paintings by Gunnella. Houghton Mifflin 2005 32p il $16　　　　　　　　　　　　　　E

　1. Chickens—Fiction 2. Iceland—Fiction

　ISBN 0-618-58581-8　　　LC 2005-01225

　"Walter Lorraine books."

When women in an Icelandic village buy chickens to lay eggs for them to use, the chickens follow them, adopting human ways and forgetting their barnyard roots, until the ladies hatch a clever plan.

　"The playful text is both silly and joyous, without a wasted word. Gunnella's enchanting oil paintings are full of childlike humor and saturated with appealing primary colors." SLJ

McMullan, Kate

I stink! [by] Kate & Jim McMullan. HarperCollins Pubs. 2002 unp il $15.95; lib bdg $15.89　　　　　　　　　　　　　　E

　1. Refuse and refuse disposal—Fiction

　ISBN 0-06-029848-0; 0-06-029849-9 (lib bdg)

　　　　　　　　　　　　　　LC 00-54229

　"Joanna Cotler books"

A big city garbage truck makes its rounds, consuming everything from apple cores and banana peels to leftover ziti with zucchini

　"Kate McMullan creates an automotive beast whose narrative style reeks of personality, and Jim McMullan's renderings are a perfect match, coaxing steely features into flexible, expressive shapes." Bull Cent Child Books

I'm mighty! [by] Kate & Jim McMullan. Joanna Cotler Bks. 2003 unp il $15.99; lib bdg $16.89　　　　　　　　　　　　　　　　E

　1. Tugboats—Fiction

　ISBN 0-06-009290-4; 0-06-009291-2 (lib bdg)

　　　　　　　　　　　　　　LC 2002-7948

McMullan, Kate—*Continued*

A little tugboat shows how he can bring big ships into the harbor even though he is small

"The tugboat that narrates this picture book tells his story with more than a splash of moxie. Strong ink drawings define the harbor setting from a variety of perspectives and show the emotions of the anthropomorphic figures of boats and trucks, while color brightens the scenes and heightens the drama." Booklist

Papa's song; pictures by Jim McMullan. Farrar, Straus & Giroux 2000 unp il $15   E

1. Bears—Fiction 2. Sleep—Fiction

ISBN 0-374-35732-3   LC 99-34556

"Granny Bear, Grandpa Bear, and Mama Bear each take a turn at singing Baby to sleep, but only Papa Bear knows the 'right song'; he takes Baby out on the river where the soothing river sounds quickly put Baby Bear to sleep. The watercolors are likewise soothing, depicting a cradle-like boat on the blue moonlit river and a cozy bear home, aglow with candlelight and love." Horn Book Guide

Pearl and Wagner: two good friends; pictures by R. W. Alley. Dial Bks. for Young Readers 2003 48p il $13.99   E

1. Mice—Fiction 2. Rabbits—Fiction 3. Friendship—Fiction

ISBN 0-8037-2573-6   LC 2002-339

"Dial easy-to-read"

Pearl, a rabbit, and Wagner, a mouse, work together to build a robot for their science project and argue about a pair of new green boots

"McMullan's realistic portrayal of classroom friendship and activities will appeal to beginning readers as well as to older children polishing their skills. . . . The pen-and-ink, watercolor, and colored-pencil pictures feature bright colors that capture the trials and joys of school life." SLJ

Another title about Pearl and Wagner is:
Pearl and Wagner: three secrets (2004)

McNaughton, Colin

Once upon an ordinary school day; story by Colin McNaughton; pictures by Satoshi Kitamura. Farrar Straus & Giroux 2005 c2004 unp il $16
          E

1. School stories 2. Teachers—Fiction 3. Imagination—Fiction

ISBN 0-374-35634-3   LC 2004-105656

First published 2004 in the United Kingdom

"An ordinary boy awakens to an ordinary school day. The story opens with drab scenes depicted in shades of gray that turn to Technicolor several pages in, with the arrival of a new teacher in a yellow suit. . . . Deftly rendered cartoon drawings convey the expressive gestures and transformation of the characters and scenes. . . . An excellent selection to start the creative juices flowing or to enliven an ordinary day." SLJ

McPhail, David M.

Big Brown Bear's up and down day; [written and illustrated by] David McPhail. Harcourt 2003 unp il $16   E

1. Bears—Fiction 2. Rats—Fiction

ISBN 0-15-216407-3   LC 2002-15854

Big Brown Bear is visited by a rat who wants to use one of his slippers for a bed

"A warm and gentle story. . . . Beautiful watercolor and pen-and-ink paintings make the most of the size difference between the characters and help to create real personalities by capturing the emotions they experience." SLJ

Another title about Big Brown Bear is:
Big Brown Bear goes to town (2006)

Big Pig and Little Pig; by David McPhail. Harcourt 2001 c2000 unp il $10.95; pa $3.95
          E

1. Pigs—Fiction

ISBN 0-15-216516-9; 0-15-216510-X (pa)
          LC 00-9725

"Green light reader"

"Big Pig and Little Pig are hot. They each decide to make a pool—but in a different way. When Big Pig grabs for a shovel, Little Pig goes for an earthmover." Booklist

"McPhail's signature illustrations fill each page as he once again successfully manages to transfer human emotions to his lovable cartoon pigs. Well-chosen vocabulary and repetition of words make this story a suitable choice for those just learning to read." SLJ

Drawing lessons from a bear; [by] David McPhail. Little, Brown 2000 unp il $14.95
          E

1. Bears—Fiction 2. Artists—Fiction

ISBN 0-316-56345-5   LC 98-54966

A bear explains how he became an artist, first experimenting with simple drawings, then continuing to draw both things around him and things in his imagination. Includes tips for drawing

"This gentle story combines a humorous tone with warm, cozy watercolors to create inspiration for budding artists." SLJ

Edward and the pirates; [by] David McPhail. Little, Brown 1997 unp il $15.95   E

1. Books and reading—Fiction 2. Pirates—Fiction

ISBN 0-316-56344-7   LC 95-38451

Once Edward has learned to read, books and his vivid imagination provide him with great adventures

"McPhail's rich acrylic paintings exude a dark and mysterious aura and feature many sinister-looking characters from Edward's books lurking around every corner." Booklist

Other titles about Edward are:
Edward in the jungle (2001)
Santa's book of names (1993)

Emma in charge; by David McPhail. 1st ed. Dutton Children's Books 2005 unp il $12.99
          E

1. Bears—Fiction 2. Play—Fiction

ISBN 0-525-47411-0   LC 2004-21580

McPhail, David M.—*Continued*

Emma the bear pretends that she and her dolls spend a day at school.

"McPhail's watercolors are . . . expressive and winsome . . . and the short sentences, printed in bold type, are just right for read-alouds or for emerging readers to follow along." Booklist

Other titles about Emma are:

Emma's pet (1985)

Emma's vacation (1987)

Fix-it (1984)

Mole music; written and illustrated by David McPhail. Holt & Co. 1999 unp il $15.95

E

1. Moles (Animals)—Fiction 2. Violins—Fiction 3. Music—Fiction

ISBN 0-8050-2819-6   LC 98-21318

Feeling that something is missing in his simple life, Mole acquires a violin and learns to make beautiful, joyful music

"McPhail's delicate watercolor-and-ink illustrations work with the simple text to create a lyrical celebration of music and musicians." Booklist

My little brother; [by] David McPhail. Harcourt 2004 unp il $16   E

1. Brothers—Fiction

ISBN 0-15-204900-2   LC 2003-7716

A boy describes all the things that he does not like about having a younger brother—and the things he does like

"Each one of McPhail's clear, beautiful, soft-toned, line-and-watercolor pictures creates a world and leaves space for a story, a whole picture book on every page. The words are simple. . . . Kids will fill in their own scenarios of siblings they love." Booklist

Pigs aplenty, pigs galore! [by] David McPhail. Dutton Children's Bks. 1993 unp il $15.99; pa $6.99   E

1. Pigs—Fiction 2. Stories in rhyme

ISBN 0-525-45079-3; 0-14-055313-4 (pa)

LC 92-27986

"As pigs of every size, shape, and dress (including Elvis) arrive at his house in every possible vehicle, a riotous party begins and lasts through the night as the perplexed narrator looks on." SLJ

"The rhyme is bouncy enough, but it's the pictures that will have parents and kids howling. Using deep watercolors set against a black background, McPhail presents a magnificent group of porkers, whose capacity for costumes and capers is truly wondrous." Booklist

Other titles about the pigs are:

Pigs ahoy! (1995)

Those can-do pigs (1996)

Sisters; written and illustrated by David McPhail. Harcourt 2003 unp il $9.95   E

1. Sisters—Fiction

ISBN 0-15-204659-3   LC 2002-3755

A reissue with full color illustrations of the title first published 1984

Although two sisters are different in many ways, they are alike too—most importantly, in their love for each other

"Soft-toned watercolors . . . add gentle warmth without in any way detracting from the simple words and lively, detailed images of the two sisters together." Booklist

The teddy bear; written and illustrated by David McPhail. Holt & Co. 2002 unp il $15.95

E

1. Teddy bears—Fiction 2. Homeless persons—Fiction

ISBN 0-8050-6414-1   LC 2001-1500

"By accident a boy leaves his beloved bear in a diner. A homeless man finds it in the garbage and loves the bear as much as the boy did. Then one day the boy sees the bear on a park bench and joyfully grabs it. But when he recognizes the lonely man's sorrow at losing his friend, the child returns the toy. . . . It works because McPhail's beautiful soft-toned watercolor pictures with detailed ink cross-hatching tell the elemental story of shelter and love through the child's eyes." Booklist

Meade, Holly

Inside, inside, inside; written and illustrated by Holly Meade. 1st ed. Marshall Cavendish 2005 unp $16.95   E

1. Games—Fiction 2. Siblings—Fiction

ISBN 0-7614-5125-0   LC 2004-19321

Noah and Jenny play a game in which they place one item inside another, over and over, until they place it all in the shower, then imagine and draw the shower inside the house, inside the neighborhood, and all the way to the solar system.

"Meade cheerfully mixes cut-paper collage and watercolor, and sprinkles many homey details into the large and small scenes. . . . The messy game is fun, and the concept draws a useful lesson from creative play." SLJ

John Willy and Freddy McGee. Marshall Cavendish 1998 unp il $15.95   E

1. Guinea pigs—Fiction

ISBN 0-7614-5033-5   LC 97-50362

Two guinea pigs escape from their safe but boring cage and have an adventure in the tunnels of the family's pool table

"Zesty cut-paper collages track all of the details of this funny outing." SLJ

Meddaugh, Susan

The best place. Houghton Mifflin 1999 unp il $15   E

1. Wolves—Fiction 2. Animals—Fiction

ISBN 0-395-97994-3   LC 98-50184

After traveling around the world to make sure that the view from his screen porch is the best, an old wolf tries drastic measures to get his house back from the rabbit family that had bought it

"Meddaugh combines understated humor with her expressive watercolor illustratons to produce a delightful book." SLJ

Cinderella's rat. Houghton Mifflin 1997 32p il $15; pa $5.95   E

1. Rats—Fiction 2. Fairy tales

ISBN 0-395-86833-5; 0-618-12540-X (pa)

LC 97-2156

Meddaugh, Susan—*Continued*

One of the rats that was turned into a coachman by Cinderella's fairy godmother saves his rat sister's life, but an inept magician turns her into a girl who says "woof."

"The telling is a perfect example of a successful fractured fairy tale, with switched point of view. . . . The buoyant line drawings capture the whimsy." SLJ

Harry on the rocks. Houghton Mifflin 2003 32p il $15   **E**
1. Shipwrecks—Fiction
ISBN 0-618-27603-3   LC 2002-9740

"Walter Lorraine books"

Harry and his boat become stranded on an island, where he discovers an egg which hatches into a strange lizard with wings

This is "a well-paced, cleanly wrought piece of storytelling. The cheerful watercolor and colored-pencil art has a sturdy matter-of-factness that makes the fantasy endearingly domestic." Bull Cent Child Books

Hog-eye. Houghton Mifflin 1995 32p il $14.95; pa $5.95   **E**
1. Pigs—Fiction 2. Wolves—Fiction
ISBN 0-395-74276-5; 0-395-93746-9 (pa)
      LC 95-3951

Meddaugh presents a "story within a story as a piglet tells her family how she was caught by a wolf and nearly made into soup. Seeing that her captor is illiterate . . . she reads him a recipe that sends him on a wild wolf chase." SLJ

"The little pig's tale is fast-paced, funny, and creatively told. Clear typeface and conversation balloons combine with brightly animated, expressive illustrations that propel readers to the satisfying conclusion of this fresh cautionary tale." Horn Book Guide

Martha speaks. Houghton Mifflin 1992 unp il $16; pa $5.95   **E**
1. Dogs—Fiction
ISBN 0-395-63313-3; 0-395-72024-9 (pa)
      LC 91-48455

Also available Spanish language edition

Problems arise when Martha, the family dog, learns to speak after eating alphabet soup

"Good-natured and amusing, with cheerful illustrations of the delightfully stocky Martha and her amazed family." Horn Book

Other titles about Martha are:
Martha and Skits (2000)
Martha blah blah (1996)
Martha calling (1994)
Martha walks the dog (1998)
Perfectly Martha (2004)

The witch's walking stick. Houghton Mifflin 2005 32p il $16   **E**
1. Witches—Fiction 2. Magic—Fiction
ISBN 0-618-52948-9   LC 2004-17509

"Walter Lorraine books"

When a witch loses her magic walking stick, which has been used over the years to grant hundreds of miserable wishes, she tricks a young girl into finding and returning it, with unexpected results.

"Illustrated with watercolor and ink in a style that will put readers in mind of William Steig, Meddaugh's dry, quirky tale of the little guy triumphing over adversity will have children smiling and cheering." SLJ

Medearis, Angela Shelf

Seven spools of thread; a Kwanzaa story; illustrated by Daniel Minter. Whitman, A. 2001 unp il $15.95   **E**
1. Kwanzaa—Fiction 2. Brothers—Fiction 3. Blacks—Fiction 4. Ghana—Fiction
ISBN 0-8075-7315-9   LC 00-8101

When they are given the seemingly impossible task of turning thread into gold, the seven Ashanti brothers put aside their differences, learn to get along, and embody the principles of Kwanzaa. Includes information on Kwanzaa, West African cloth weaving, and instructions for making a belt

"Well-paced, the story incorporates the Kwanzaa values without spelling them out too much. Minter's attractively composed, dramatic painted linocuts, with strong community images and lively, silhouetted figures, root the story in a sun-drenched, magical landscape." Booklist

Snug in Mama's arms; illustrated by John Sandford. Gingham Dog Press 2004 unp il $14.95   **E**
1. Bedtime—Fiction 2. Mother-child relationship—Fiction 3. African Americans—Fiction 4. Stories in rhyme
ISBN 1-57768-430-3   LC 2004-40612

As she snuggles her daughter in her arms at bedtime, a mother describes how animals and children around the world go to sleep.

"The author's soothing rhymes are enhanced by the rich, earth-tone paintings that evoke the quiet mood." SLJ

Meggs, Libby Phillips

Go home! the true story of James the cat. Whitman, A. 2000 unp il $15.95   **E**
1. Cats—Fiction
ISBN 0-8075-2975-3   LC 99-41372

A homeless cat spends several seasons trying to survive the elements until at last a suburban family adopts him

"Meggs' lovely picture book, based on a true story, teaches children about kindness. . . . [She] captures the cat's lonely plight in watercolors that juxtapose the glow of firelight inside with the harsh winter landscape outside." Booklist

Meister, Cari

My pony Jack; illustrated by Amy Young. Viking 2005 32p il $13.99   **E**
1. Horses—Fiction 2. Stories in rhyme
ISBN 0-670-05917-X   LC 2004-21417

"Viking easy-to-read"

Easy-to-read, rhyming text follows Lacy as she spends a day with her pony, giving him exercise, grooming him, and feeding him oats and hay.

"The book has an attractive format, with colorful cartoon artwork and a small amount of text on each page. . . . A solid addition to easy-reader collections." SLJ

Meister, Cari—_Continued_
Other titles about Jack the pony are:
My pony Jack at riding lessons (2005)
My pony Jack at the horse show (2006)

Tiny's bath; illustrated by Rich Davis. Viking
1998 unp il $13.89; pa $3.99   E
1. Dogs—Fiction 2. Baths—Fiction
ISBN 0-670-87962-2; 0-14-130267-4 (pa)
                                 LC 98-3844
"A Viking easy-to-read"
Tiny is a very big dog who loves to dig, and when it
is time for his bath, his owner has trouble finding a place
to bathe him
"In this book for the least sophisticated beginning
readers, each sentence appears on a single line, and only
one sentence appears on a page. Illustrations mirror text,
providing clues that support readers as they decipher
both words and events. Add Tiny to the roll call of great
dogs in children's literature." Horn Book Guide
Other titles about Tiny are:
Tiny goes camping (2006)
Tiny goes to the library (2000)
Tiny the snow dog (2001)
When Tiny was tiny (1999)

Melmed, Laura Krauss
Little Oh; illustrated by Jim LaMarche. Lothrop,
Lee & Shepard Bks. 1996 unp il $16.99; lib bdg
$17.89   E
1. Origami—Fiction 2. Japan—Fiction
ISBN 0-688-14208-7; 0-688-14209-5 (lib bdg)
                                 LC 95-25427
This is an "original folk tale (set in Japan) . . . about
a little origami paper girl in a pink kimono who springs
to life one morning and adopts her astonished maker as
her mother." Bull Cent Child Books
"While the narrative echoes folktales told around the
world, the realistic colored paintings establish setting and
character with loving specificity." SLJ

Moishe's miracle; a Hanukkah story; illustrated
by David Slonim. HarperCollins Pubs. 2000 unp il
$15.95; lib bdg $15.98   E
1. Hanukkah—Fiction 2. Magic—Fiction 3. Jews—
Fiction
ISBN 0-688-14682-1; 0-688-14683-X (lib bdg)
                                 LC 99-27640
Moishe, a milkman who is kind to everyone in his
poor village of Wishniak, receives a magic frying pan
that produces an unlimited supply of delicious Hanukkah
latkes, but his wife, Baila, tries to use it selfishly
"It's the pictures more than the quirky story . . . that
will grab attention. Their rich golds and browns evoke
the bubbling goodness of the holiday's fried pancakes."
Booklist

Merrill, Jean
The Girl Who Loved Caterpillars; a twelfth
century tale from Japan; adapted by Jean Merrill;
illustrated by Floyd Cooper. Philomel Bks. 1992
unp il $16.99; pa $6.99   E
 1. Fairy tales 2. Japan—Fiction
ISBN 0-399-21871-8; 0-698-11393-4 (pa)
                                 LC 91-29054

In this retelling of an anonymous twelfth-century Japanese story, the young woman Izumi resists social and
family pressures as she befriends caterpillars and other
socially unacceptable creatures
"This story of an independent girl has a surprisingly
contemporary tone. . . . Merrill's adaptation is cleanly
yet elegantly styled, as are Cooper's pastel double
spreads, which elaborate on the many vivid images in the
story." Bull Cent Child Books

Meyers, Susan
Everywhere babies; illustrated by Marla Frazee.
Harcourt 2001 unp il $16   E
1. Infants 2. Stories in rhyme
ISBN 0-15-202226-0   LC 99-6288
Describes babies and the things they do from the time
they are born until their first birthday
"The rhythmic rhyming text hums along pleasantly.
. . . The many moods, expressions, and body movements
of babies are faithfully, gracefully rendered in the pencil
drawings, and brightened with watercolors in rather mut-
ed hues." Booklist

Puppies! Puppies! Puppies! illustrated by David
Walker. Harry N. Abrams 2005 unp il $15.95
                                             E
1. Dogs—Fiction
ISBN 0-8109-5856-2   LC 2004-12650
Rhyming text follows the life of all sorts of puppies
from when they are born through moving in with a new
family to learning how to do things grownup dogs do.
"The delightful acrylic illustrations are warm and child
friendly, yet specific enough to distinguish some of the
breeds represented. The dynamic language and large format make this engaging picture book a wonderful selection to read aloud at storytimes as well as to share one-
on-one." SLJ

This is the way a baby rides; illustrated by
Hiroe Nakata. Harry N. Abrams 2005 unp il
$15.95   E
1. Infants—Fiction 2. Animals—Fiction 3. Stories in
rhyme
ISBN 0-8109-5763-9   LC 2004023834
While on a picnic, an active baby plays, splashes, and
stretches, while imitating various animals.
"Splotchy watercolor-and-gouache art with comical,
elongated figures give a lightness and freshness to the
text, which is both a story about a family's day out and
an opportunity for little ones to relish the rhythmic
sounds of made-up words." Booklist

Michelson, Richard
Happy feet; the Savoy Ballroom Lindy Hoppers
and me; illustrated by E. B. Lewis. Harcourt 2005
unp il $16   E
1. Dance—Fiction 2. African Americans—Fiction
3. Harlem (New York, N.Y.)—Fiction 4. Father-son
relationship—Fiction
ISBN 0-15-205057-4   LC 2004-24399
"Gulliver books"
A young boy who loves to dance listens as his father
retells the story of the night he was born, which coincid-

Michelson, Richard—*Continued*

ed with the opening of the Savoy Ballroom in Harlem

"The story captures the mood and language of Harlem in the '20s and '30s. . . . Lewis's rich-toned watercolors bleed in and out of focus for the dancing scenes, transmitting excitement and joy." SLJ

Micklethwait, Lucy

I spy: an alphabet in art; devised & selected by Lucy Micklethwait. Greenwillow Bks. 1992 unp il $19.99; pa $10.99   E

1. Art appreciation 2. Alphabet

ISBN 0-688-11679-5; 0-688-14730-5 (pa)

        LC 91-42212

Presents objects for the letters of the alphabet through paintings by such artists as Magritte, Picasso, Botticelli, and Vermeer

"The author's stated intention of introducing young children to fine art, her choice of paintings, the handsome book design, and the quality of paper and reproduction take this beyond the usual alphabet book." Booklist

Other titles in this series are:

I spy a freight train: transportation in art (1996)

I spy a lion: animals in art (1994)

I spy shapes in art (2004)

I spy two eyes: numbers in art (1993)

Middleton, Charlotte

Do you still love me? Candlewick Press 2003 unp il $15.99   E

1. Dogs—Fiction 2. Chameleons—Fiction

ISBN 0-7636-2254-0   LC 2003-43835

Upset when the arrival of a new pet, a baby chameleon, seems to displace his role in the family, Dudley the dog finds a way to prove himself indispensable

"The large, mixed-media collage illustrations are rich in texture, color, and wit. This . . . is perfect for any small folk facing change, trying to understand their pets, or dealing with an addition to the family." SLJ

Milich, Zoran

City 1 2 3. Kids Can Press 2005 unp il $15.95   E

1. Counting

ISBN 1-55337-540-8

Photographs of objects such as skyscrapers, bags of leaves, fire trucks, and taxis illustrate numbers from 1 to 10

"An excellent, well-constructed concept book. . . . The superb pictures feature not only the required number of items, but the corresponding numeral as well." SLJ

The city ABC book. Kids Can Press 2001 unp il $15.95   E

1. Alphabet

ISBN 1-55074-942-0

"Milich searched Toronto for hidden geometrics—letters buried in everyday places. From window frames in the shape of As to steel-welded Zs that support a bridge, he finds and documents them—in black and white, highlighting each letter in stop-sign red. . . . Each picture is a wonder and every letter a clear, playful image to consider and behold." Booklist

City colors. Kids Can Press 2004 unp il $14.95   E

1. Color

ISBN 1-55337-542-4

This is a collection of color photographs of objects found in cities such as a red bus, a blue warehouse wall, and a yellow highway cone, a green swing, an orange cylindrical curb block, and a purple playground stool.

This is "a dazzling . . . concept book. . . . Precise partial photos inspire speculation on each verso with the recto revealing the complete image." SLJ

City signs. Kids Can Press 2002 unp il $15.95   E

1. Signs and signboards

ISBN 1-55337-003-1

"Milich took to the streets with his camera, looking for printed words found in various outdoor environments. The 30 photographs here demonstrate that even children who can't yet read a book understand many of the words they see around them. The quality of the pictures is very good. They are nicely composed, clear, and often colorful." Booklist

Miller, Margaret

Big and little. Greenwillow Bks. 1998 unp il $15.99   E

1. Size

ISBN 0-688-14748-8   LC 97-17242

Photographs and easy text introduce the concepts of size and opposites

"This book uses cheerful, clear color photos of active toddlers to teach basic concepts." Booklist

Guess who? Greenwillow Bks. 1994 unp il $16.99   E

1. Occupations

ISBN 0-688-12783-5   LC 93-26704

A child is asked who delivers the mail, gives haircuts, flies an airplane, and performs other important tasks. Each question has several different answers from which to choose

"Gender and ethnic representation are deftly handled. The author's sharp, clear full-color photographs are well composed, and her use of cropped photos and white space alternating with bled photos is an effective tool for involving youngsters." SLJ

Whose shoe? Greenwillow Bks. 1991 unp il $16.99   E

1. Shoes

ISBN 0-688-10008-2   LC 90-38491

Illustrates a variety of footwear and matches each wearer with the appropriate shoe

"Miller has consciously avoided stereotypes, picturing a male ballet dancer and children from many racial groups. She understands children's fascination with make-believe and dress-up, and this . . . book should spark much imaginative play." Horn Book

Miller, Sara Swan

Three more stories you can read to your dog; illustrated by True Kelley. Houghton Mifflin 2000 unp il $14 **E**

1. Dogs—Fiction

ISBN 0-395-92293-3   LC 99-39880

Stories addressed to dogs and written from a dog's point of view, featuring such topics as going to the vet, making friends with a rocklike creature, and getting a bath

"The witty, believable portrayal of canine thoughts and behavior will amuse readers. . . . True Kelley's lively ink-and-watercolor illustrations brighten every page." Booklist

Other titles in this series are:

Three more stories you can read to your cat (2002)

Three stories you can read to your cat (1997)

Three stories you can read to your dog (1995)

Three stories you can read to your teddy bear (2004)

Miller, William

Night golf; illustrated by Cedric Lucas. Lee & Low Bks. 1999 unp il $15.95 **E**

1. African Americans—Fiction 2. Golf—Fiction 3. Prejudices—Fiction

ISBN 1-880000-79-2   LC 98-47168

Despite being told that only whites can play golf, James becomes a caddy and is befriended by an older African American man who teaches him to play on the course at night

"Gentle paste and pencil illustrations support this quietly powerful story." Horn Book Guide

The piano; illustrated by Susan Keeter. Lee & Low Bks. 2000 unp il $16.95 **E**

1. Pianos—Fiction 2. Old age—Fiction 3. African Americans—Fiction

ISBN 1-880000-98-9   LC 99-38004

Tia's love of music leads her to a job in the home of an older white woman who not only teaches her to play the piano but also about caring for others

"The characters are brought to life and Tia's warm, open innocence is evident in the expressive artwork. This is a gentle story depicting a friendship that crosses age and racial barriers." SLJ

Rent party jazz; illustrated by Charlotte Riley-Webb. Lee & Low Bks. 2001 unp il $16.95 **E**

1. Jazz music—Fiction 2. New Orleans (La.)—Fiction

ISBN 1-58430-025-6   LC 2001-16449

When Sonny's mother loses her job in New Orleans during the Depression, Smilin' Jack, a jazz musician, tells him how to organize a rent party to raise the money they need

"Miller uses folksy dialogue to tell the story that celebrates both community and the uplifting power of music. Evocative artwork, done in broad, swirling strokes, fills pages with color and motion." Booklist

Richard Wright and the library card; illustrated by Gregory Christie. Lee & Low Bks. 1997 unp il $15.95; pa $6.95 **E**

1. Wright, Richard, 1908-1960—Fiction 2. African Americans—Fiction 3. Books and reading—Fiction

ISBN 1-880000-57-1; 1-880000-88-1 (pa)

LC 97-6847

Based on a scene from Wright's autobiography, Black boy, in which the seventeen-year-old African-American borrows a white man's library card and devours every book as a ticket to freedom

"Christie's powerful impressionistic paintings in acrylic and colored pencil show the harsh racism in the Jim Crow South. . . . Words and pictures express the young man's loneliness and confinement and, then, the power he found in books." Booklist

Millman, Isaac

Moses goes to school. Farrar, Straus & Giroux 2000 unp $16 **E**

1. Deaf—Fiction 2. Sign language—Fiction 3. School stories

ISBN 0-374-35069-8   LC 99-40582

"Frances Foster books"

Moses and his friends enjoy the first day of school at their special school for the deaf and hard of hearing, where they use sign language to talk to each other

"Child-friendly cartoon illustrations do a marvelous job of emphasizing the normalcy and charm of these youngsters. . . . The double-page layouts nicely accommodate the primary pictorial action along with written text and ASL inserts. . . . [This is a] great contribution to children's education about disabilities that also succeeds as effective storytelling in its own right." SLJ

Other titles about Moses are:

Moses goes to a concert (1998)

Moses goes to the circus (2003)

Moses sees a play (2004)

Mills, Claudia

Gus and Grandpa and the two-wheeled bike; pictures by Catherine Stock. Farrar, Straus & Giroux 1999 47p il $15 **E**

1. Cycling—Fiction 2. Grandfathers—Fiction

ISBN 0-374-32821-8   LC 97-44203

Gus doesn't want to give up the training wheels on his bike, even for a new five-speed bicycle, until Grandpa helps him learn how to get along without them

"Mills conveys strong sentiment without a trace of mawkishness, and Stock's illustrations in loose line and watercolor augment the story of this childhood rite of passage expressively." Horn Book Guide

Other titles about Gus and Grandpa are:

Gus and Grandpa (1997)

Gus and Grandpa and show-and-tell (2000)

Gus and Grandpa and the Christmas cookies (1997)

Gus and Grandpa and the Halloween costume (2002)

Gus and Grandpa and the piano lesson (2004)

Gus and Grandpa at basketball (2001)

Gus and Grandpa at the hospital (1998)

Gus and Grandpa go fishing (2003)

Gus and Grandpa ride the train (1998)

Mills, Claudia—*Continued*

Ziggy's blue-ribbon day; pictures by R. W. Alley. Farrar, Straus and Giroux 2005 unp il $16

E

1. Track athletics—Fiction 2. Drawing—Fiction 3. School stories

ISBN 0-374-32352-6   LC 2003-44057

Ziggy does not do well on the school track and field day events, but he feels much better after his classmates recognize his drawing talent.

"Mills offers a simple but heartening story for kids who don't excel on the playing field but have other talents. . . . Alley's paintings capture the school milieu with keenly observed details and a wry humor." Booklist

Mills, Lauren A.

Thumbelina; retold and illustrated by Lauren Mills. 1st ed. Little, Brown 2005 unp il $16.99

E

1. Andersen, Hans Christian, 1805-1875—Adaptations 2. Fairy tales

ISBN 0-316-57359-0   LC 2002-22491

After being kidnapped by a toad, a beautiful girl no bigger than a thumb has a series of dreadful experiences and makes many animal friends before meeting a fairy prince just her size.

"This is a charmingly illustrated Thumbelina, retold with just a few changes in detail and some omissions of lengthy description that make the story more readable. . . . In Mills's soft, detailed watercolor illustrations, the tiny red-haired girl appears fairylike in her filmy nightgown, then wears homespun jumpers and braids in the mouse's cozy burrow." SLJ

Milord, Susan

The ghost on the hearth; retold by Susan Milord; paintings by Lydia Dabcovich. Vermont Folklife Center; distributed by University Press of New England 2003 unp (Family heritage series) $15.95

E

1. Ghost stories 2. Québec (Province)—Fiction

ISBN 0-916718-18-2   LC 2002-24004

As was the custom in 1800s rural Quebec, Emily, the eldest of a poor family, is sent to live and work at a nearby farm, where her unexpected death is followed by a mysterious nocturnal event

"Milord's retelling keeps the action moving quickly and Dabcovich's folk-art illustrations build suspense and convey an eerie atmosphere. An afterword includes details about the tale's origins. A good addition to storytelling collections." SLJ

Love that baby! written and illustrated by Susan Milord. Houghton Mifflin 2005 unp il $7.95

E

1. Infants—Fiction

ISBN 0-618-56323-7   LC 2004-25119

"Each folded-over page poses a situation to ponder, while the unfolded spread beneath it suggests what to do next. A drawing of a . . . child . . . is accompanied by the words: 'Baby is hungry,' while the picture of father . . . gives the advice, 'Feed that baby!' Other pages offer suggested actions to take if the baby is napping, hiding, scared, sad, or sleepy. Simple drawings, soft colors in offbeat combinations, and a variety of patterns give this simple picture book visual appeal, while the lift-the-flap game will make it enjoyable for toddlers to revisit again and again." Booklist

Minarik, Else Holmelund

Little Bear; pictures by Maurice Sendak. Harper & Row 1957 63p il $15.99; lib bdg $16.89; pa $3.99

E

1. Bears—Fiction

ISBN 0-06-024240-X; 0-06-024241-8 (lib bdg); 0-06-444004-4 (pa)

"An I can read book"

Four episodes "about Little Bear . . . as he persuades his mother to make him a winter outfit—only to discover his fur coat is all he needs; makes himself some birthday soup—and then is surprised with a birthday cake; takes an imaginary trip to the moon, and finally goes happily off to sleep as his mother tells him a story about 'Little Bear.'" Bull Cent Child Books

The pictures "depict all the warmth of feeling and the special companionship that exists between a small child and his mother." Publ Wkly

Other titles about Little Bear are:

Father Bear comes home (1959)
A kiss for Little Bear (1968)
Little Bear's friend (1960)
Little Bear's visit (1961)

No fighting, no biting! pictures by Maurice Sendak. Harper & Row 1958 62p il lib bdg $16.89; pa $3.99

E

1. Alligators—Fiction

ISBN 0-06-024291-4 (lib bdg); 0-06-444015-X (pa)

"An I can read book"

"A young lady who is unable to read in peace because of two children squabbling beside her tells them a story about two little alligators whose fighting and biting almost lead to disastrous consequences with a big hungry alligator. Children are sure to accept and enjoy the lesson in this little adventure tale and be amused by the expressive old-fashioned drawings." Booklist

Miranda, Anne

To market, to market; written by Anne Miranda; illustrated by Janet Stevens. Harcourt Brace & Co. 1997 unp il $16

E

1. Stories in rhyme 2. Animals—Fiction

ISBN 0-15-200035-6   LC 95-26326

In this "riff on the old nursery rhyme, 'To market, to market, to buy a fat pig,' a plump matron makes a series of increasingly calamitous purchases of animals at the supermarket. Hungry and cranky after the raucous menagerie turns her house topsy-turvy, the lady . . . wisely decides to make vegetable soup instead." Publ Wkly

"Patterned, staccato verses tell the zany tale, but it is Stevens's wonderfully wild illustrations that bring it to life." SLJ

Mitchard, Jacquelyn

Baby bat's lullaby; illustrated by Julia Noonan. HarperCollins 2004 unp il $15.99; lib bdg $16.89

    E

1. Bats—Fiction 2. Bedtime—Fiction 3. Stories in rhyme

ISBN 0-06-050760-8; 0-06-050761-6 (lib bdg)

    LC 2002-10978

With loving words, a mother bat lulls her baby to sleep.

"With its spare, exquisite language and its evocative artwork, this lullaby is as soothing as it is entrancing." SLJ

Mitchell, Margaree King

Uncle Jed's barbershop; illustrated by James Ransome. Simon & Schuster Bks. for Young Readers 1993 unp il $17.95; pa $6.99   E

1. Uncles—Fiction 2. Barbers and barbershops—Fiction 3. African Americans—Fiction

ISBN 0-671-76969-3; 0-689-81913-7 (pa)

    LC 91-44148

Despite serious obstacles and setbacks Sarah Jean's Uncle Jed, the only black barber in the county, pursues his dream of saving enough money to open his own barbershop

"The author's convivial depictions of family life are enhanced by Ransome's . . . spirited oil paintings, which set the affectionate intergenerational cast against brightly patterned walls and crisp, leaf-strewn landscapes." Publ Wkly

Mitton, Tony

Goodnight me, goodnight you; illustrated by Mandy Sutcliffe. Little, Brown 2003 c2002 unp il $14.95   E

1. Bedtime—Fiction 2. Stories in rhyme

ISBN 0-316-73880-8   LC 2002-36850

When it is time for bed, a brother and sister say goodnight to things both inside and outside their house.

"Quiet rhyming couplets and richly colored paintings will help ease young children to sleep. . . . The oil paint on paper illustrations are soft and appealing." SLJ

Mochizuki, Ken

Baseball saved us; written by Ken Mochizuki; illustrated by Dom Lee. Lee & Low Bks. 1993 unp il $16.95; pa $6.95   E

1. Japanese Americans—Evacuation and relocation, 1942-1945—Fiction 2. World War, 1939-1945—Fiction 3. Baseball—Fiction 4. Prejudices—Fiction

ISBN 1-880000-01-6; 1-880000-19-9 (pa)

    LC 92-73215

Also available Spanish language edition

A Japanese American boy learns to play baseball when he and his family are forced to live in an internment camp during World War II, and his ability to play helps him after the war is over

"Fences and watchtowers are in the background of many of Lee's moving illustrations, some of which were inspired by Ansel Adams' 1943 photographs of Manzanar. . . . The baseball action will grab kids—and so will the personal experience of bigotry." Booklist

Heroes; written by Ken Mochizuki; illustrated by Dom Lee. Lee & Low Bks. 1995 unp il $15.95; pa $6.95   E

1. Japanese Americans—Fiction 2. Prejudices—Fiction

ISBN 1-880000-16-4; 1-880000-50-4 (pa)

    LC 94-26541

"In the 1960's Donnie Okada took a lot of razzing from the other boys in the neighborhood; they insisted that he had to be the enemy in their war games because he looked like the enemy, and they did not believe his father and uncle had served in the American military. Dad and Uncle Yosh give those boys a dignified and effective lesson." N Y Times Book Rev

"The book is a powerful exploration of the cruelty children can inflict upon one another and of the confusion and pain borne by the target of such unthinking racism." Horn Book

Modarressi, Mitra

Yard sale! DK Pub. 2000 unp il $15.95

    E

1. Garage sales—Fiction

ISBN 0-7894-2651-X   LC 99-27592

"A DK ink book"

"After Mr. Flotsam's yard sale, Spudville's residents are irritated to find that their unexpectedly magical purchases, such as a flying rug and a nonstop pasta maker, are threatening to disrupt their orderly lives. . . . The watercolor illustrations for this light, amusing tale show a multicultural cast of round-faced townspeople." Horn Book Guide

Mollel, Tololwa M. (Tololwa Marti)

My rows and piles of coins; illustrated by E. B. Lewis. Clarion Bks. 1999 32p il $15   E

1. Money—Fiction 2. Bicycles—Fiction 3. Tanzania—Fiction

ISBN 0-395-75186-1   LC 98-21586

A Coretta Scott King honor book for illustration, 2000

A Tanzanian boy saves his coins to buy a bicycle so that he can help his parents carry goods to market, but then he discovers that in spite of all he has saved, he still does not have enough money

"The story is natural and never excessively moralistic. The fluid, light-splashed watercolor illustrations lend a sense of place and authenticity." SLJ

Monjo, F. N.

The drinking gourd; a story of the Underground Railroad; pictures by Fred Brenner. newly il ed. HarperCollins Pubs. 1993 62p il lib bdg $16.89; pa $3.99   E

1. Underground railroad—Fiction

ISBN 0-06-024330-9 (lib bdg); 0-06-444042-7 (pa)

    LC 92-10823

"An I can read book"

First published 1970

Set in New England in the decade before the Civil War. For mischievous behavior in church, Tommy is sent home to his room, but wanders instead into the barn. There he discovers that his father is helping runaway slaves escape to Canada

Monjo, F. N.—*Continued*

"The simplicity of dialogue and exposition, the level of concepts, and the length of the story [makes] it most suitable for the primary grades reader. The illustrations are deftly representational, the whole a fine addition to the needed body of historical books for the very young." Bull Cent Child Books

Montenegro, Laura Nyman

A bird about to sing; written and illustrated by Laura Nyman Montenegro. Houghton Mifflin 2003 unp il $15   E

1. Poetry—Fiction

ISBN 0-618-18865-7   LC 2002-5091

Natalie, who likes to write poems, goes to a poetry reading and discovers that a poem needs to be read out loud at just the right time

"The surreal, stylized paintings of a fascinating cast of multicultural characters are awash in lovely, warm color." Booklist

Moodie, Fiona

Noko and the night monster. Marshall Cavendish 2001 unp il $15.95   E

1. Monsters—Fiction 2. Aardvark—Fiction 3. Porcupines—Fiction 4. Fear—Fiction

ISBN 0-7614-5093-9   LC 00-60376

Takadu the aardvark comes up with an ingenious plan to help his friend Noko the porcupine overcome his fear of the night monster

"Moodie's line-and-watercolor pictures capture the silliness and the warm friendship, with a nice edge of scariness." Booklist

Moon, Nicola

Tick-tock, drip-drop! a bedtime story; illustrated by Eleanor Taylor. Bloomsbury Children's Books 2004 unp il $16.95   E

1. Rabbits—Fiction 2. Moles (Animals)—Fiction 3. Bedtime—Fiction

ISBN 1-58234-944-4   LC 2003-55719

When Rabbit has trouble falling asleep because of various noises, Mole tries to help.

"Moon's simple text, with its building cacophony of noisy words, will delight children, who may want to join in the rhythmic chants. Taylor's warm watercolor images reinforce the humor and farce between the odd-couple roommates as well as the cozy allure of their snug, lamplit house." Booklist

Mora, Pat

Doña Flor; a tall tale about a giant woman with a great big heart; illustrated by Raul Colón. Knopf 2005 unp il $15.99; lib bdg $17.99   E

1. Giants—Fiction 2. Pumas—Fiction 3. Tall tales

ISBN 0-375-82337-9; 0-375-92337-3 (lib bdg)

Also available Spanish language edition

Doña Flor, a giant woman with a big heart, sets off to protect her neighbors from what they think is a dangerous animal, but soon discovers the tiny secret behind the huge noise.

"A charming tall tale. . . Colón uses his signature mix of watercolor washes, etching, and litho pencils for the art. There is great texture and movement on each page in the sunbaked tones of the landscape." SLJ

Tomás and the library lady; illustrated by Raúl Colón. Knopf 1997 unp il $17; lib bdg $18.99; pa $6.99   E

1. Rivera, Tomás—Fiction 2. Books and reading—Fiction 3. Libraries—Fiction 4. Migrant labor—Fiction 5. Mexican Americans—Fiction

ISBN 0-679-80401-3; 0-679-90401-8 (lib bdg); 0-375-80349-1 (pa)   LC 89-37490

While helping his family in their work as migrant laborers far from their home, Tomás finds an entire world to explore in the books at the local public library

"Mora's story is based on a true incident in the life of the famous writer Tomás Rivera, the son of migrant workers who became an education leader and university president. . . . Colón's beautiful scratchboard illustrations, in his textured, glowingly colored, rhythmic style, capture the warmth and the dreams that the boy finds in the world of books." Booklist

Uno, dos, tres: one, two, three; illustrated by Barbara Lavallee. Clarion Bks. 1996 43p il $15; pa $6.95   E

1. Mexico—Fiction 2. Counting 3. Stories in rhyme 4. Bilingual books—English-Spanish

ISBN 0-395-67294-5; 0-618-05468-5 (pa)

LC 94-15337

"Two girls search a Mexican market for gifts for their mother's birthday in this counting book in both English and Spanish. . . . Cheerful stylized paintings in muted reds, blues, and yellows depict designs from Mexican art and use pattern to highlight the number sequence." Horn Book Guide

Morgan, Michaela

Brave, brave mouse; illustrated by Michelle Cartlidge. Albert Whitman & Co 2004 unp il $15.95   E

1. Mice—Fiction 2. Courage—Fiction

ISBN 0-8075-0869-1   LC 2003-23874

After showing courage by trying many new things, Little Mouse becomes Brave Mouse when he realizes that it is sometimes good to say no to things he is not ready to try.

"Encouraging children while giving them permission not to be cajoled into exceeding their personal comfort zone is a powerful message. The ink-and watercolor illustrations are a counterpoint, simply executed in a childlike manner that makes use of a pastel palette." Booklist

Morrow, Barbara Olenyik

A good night for freedom; illustrated by Leonard Jenkins. Holiday House 2004 unp il $16.95   E

1. Coffin, Levi, 1789-1877—Fiction 2. Underground railroad—Fiction 3. Slavery—Fiction

ISBN 0-8234-1709-3   LC 2002-192207

Hallie discovers two runaway slaves hiding in Levi Coffin's home and must decide whether to turn them in

Morrow, Barbara Olenyik—*Continued*
or help them escape to freedom. Includes historical notes
on the Underground Railroad and abolitionists Levi and
Catharine Coffin.

"The well-written text smoothly blends fact and fiction. . . . Jenkins's mixed-media illustrations capture the
emotions of the characters as well as the details of pre-
Civil War life." SLJ

Includes bibliographical references

Morrow, Tara Jaye
Mommy loves her baby; pictures by Tiphanie
Beeke. HarperCollins Pubs. 2003 unp il $15.99; lib
bdg $16.89   E
1. Mothers—Fiction 2. Fathers—Fiction 3. Animals—
Fiction 4. Stories in rhyme
ISBN 0-06-029077-3; 0-06-029078-1 (lib bdg)
                                                     LC 2002-68560
Bound back-to-back with Daddy loves his baby
Compares the love Mommy and Daddy have for their
baby to the things that various animals love to do
"This is a striking book, making full use of Beeke's
warm palette and creatively fresh perspectives." SLJ

Mortensen, Denise Dowling
Good night engines; illustrated by Melissa Iwai.
Clarion Bks. 2003 32p il $15   E
1. Vehicles—Fiction 2. Stories in rhyme 3. Bedtime—
Fiction
ISBN 0-618-13537-5   LC 2002-155215
Rhyming verses describe how a variety of vehicles,
from locomotives to eighteen-wheelers to automobiles,
wind down for a night of rest
"The story is as smooth and easy as a familiar lullaby.
. . . Iwai's acrylic, full-page spreads match the quiet
text." SLJ

Moss, Lloyd
Zin! zin! zin! a violin; illustrated by Marjorie
Priceman. Simon & Schuster Bks. for Young
Readers 1995 unp il $17.95; pa $6.99   E
1. Musical instruments 2. Counting 3. Stories in
rhyme
ISBN 0-671-88239-2; 0-689-83524-8 (pa)
                                                     LC 93-37902
A Caldecott Medal honor book, 1996
"Rhyming couplets present 10 instruments and their
characteristics. . . . In the process of adding instruments,
the book teaches the names of musical groups up to a
chamber group of 10 as well as the categories into which
the instruments fall: strings, reeds, and brasses. Amazingly, Moss conveys this encyclopedic information while
keeping the poem streamlined and peppy. Priceman's
sprightly, sunny hued gouache paintings should take a
bow, too." Booklist

Moss, Marissa
Mighty Jackie: the strike out queen; illustrated
by C.F. Payne. Simon & Schuster Bks. for Young
Readers 2004 unp il $16.95   E
1. Mitchell, Jackie, 1914-1987 2. Baseball 3. Women
athletes
ISBN 0-689-86329-2   LC 2003-7382

"A Paula Wiseman book"
"In cadenced prose, Moss tells the story of the girl
who was taught to play—and to win—by her father and
Dazzy Vance, the Brooklyn Dodger. . . . Payne has well
and truly captured the tone with his wonderful pictures."
Booklist

Moss, Miriam
Don't forget I love you; illustrated by Anna
Currey. Dial Books for Young Readers 2004 unp
il lib bdg $15.99   E
1. Mother-son relationship—Fiction 2. Bears—Fiction
ISBN 0-8037-2920-0   LC 2002-152119
"Although Mama bear tries to hurry her son along, he
spends so much time getting his stuffed rabbit ready for
nursery school that they leave the house behind schedule.
. . . As the young bear unpacks his lunchbox in his
classroom, he laments, 'Mama didn't say I love you.'"
SLJ
"Currey's soft, rounded pastels underscore the warm,
cozy tone of this happily-after-all tale." Booklist

Most, Bernard
ABC T-Rex. Harcourt Brace & Co. 2000 unp il
$14; pa $6   E
1. Dinosaurs—Fiction 2. Alphabet
ISBN 0-15-202007-1; 0-15-205028-0 (pa)
                                                     LC 98-51128
A young T-Rex loves his ABCs so much that he eats
them up, experiencing on each letter a word that begins
with that letter
"Heavy black lines define the cartoonlike drawings,
brightened with a colorful palette emphasizing shades of
green, purple, and orange. Fun for alphabetically inclined
preschoolers." Booklist

How big were the dinosaurs. Harcourt Brace &
Co. 1994 unp il $16; pa $7   E
1. Dinosaurs
ISBN 0-15-236800-0; 0-15-200852-7 (pa)
                                                     LC 93-19152
Describes the size of different dinosaurs by comparing
them to more familiar objects, such as a school bus, a
trombone, or a bowling alley
"The colorful drawings, of children interacting with
dinosaurs, will be attractive to children. The text is easy
to read. This book will delight young dinosaur lovers."
Sci Books Films

Whatever happened to the dinosaurs? written
and illustrated by Bernard Most. Harcourt Brace
Jovanovich 1984 unp il lib bdg $16; pa $4.95
                                                        E
1. Dinosaurs—Fiction
ISBN 0-15-295295-0 (lib bdg); 0-15-295296-9 (pa)
                                                     LC 84-3779
Also available miniature edition
The author "offers various fantastic explanations to
answer his title question. 'Did the dinosaurs go to anoth-
er planet? . . . did a magician make them disappear?
. . . Are the dinosaurs in the hospital?'" SLJ
"A hilarious book, sure to be popular for individual
reading or with groups." Child Book Rev Serv

Munari, Bruno

Bruno Munari's zoo; [by] Bruno Munari. Chronicle Books 2005 c1963 unp il $17.95
E

1. Zoos 2. Animals
ISBN 0-8118-4830-2   LC 2004-21214

A reissue of the title first published 1963 by World Publishing

Illustrations and brief text introduce more than twenty zoo animals, including a rhinoceros that is always ready to fight and a peacock that struts proudly because he is the peacock.

"A stunning picture book of birds and beasts original in design, brilliant with color, and touched with humor." Booklist

Munro, Roxie

Doors. Chronicle 2004 unp il $15.95   E
ISBN 1-58717-247-X

Door-shaped flaps open to reveal such spaces as a fire station, a refrigerator, and a garage, and rhyming text lists objects hidden within each place

"The clever design is well integrated into the story. . . . The flaps' sturdy construction . . . will stand up to a great deal of wear and tear from eager young hands. This is a book that's sure to have kids lining up at your door." SLJ

Murphy, Mary

I kissed the baby. Candlewick Press 2003 unp il $12.99   E

1. Ducks—Fiction 2. Animals—Fiction
ISBN 0-7636-2122-6   LC 2002-31419

Various animals tell how they saw, fed, sang to, tickled, and kissed the new duckling

"Murphy makes creative use of color on the edges of the black-and-white pages, until the duckling appears in a splash of vibrant yellow, and the text changes to hot pink. This is an ideal book for little eyes and ears, for text, illustrations, and design meld perfectly." SLJ

Murphy, Stuart J.

Leaping lizards; illustrated by JoAnn Adinolfi. HarperCollins Pub. 2005 33p il (MathStart) $15.99; pa $4.99   E

1. Counting 2. Addition 3. Lizards—Fiction 4. Stories in rhyme
ISBN 0-06-000130-5; 0-06-000132-1 (pa)
LC 2004-22470

"This book introduces the multiples of five, as lizards of different colors travel through the pages on unicycles, a hot-air balloon, an airplane, and other modes of transport, while a green snake looks on. Finally, the number 50 is reached, and lizards explode in all directions. . . . An intelligent blending of white space and colors make each double-page spread visually stand out. A box on one side of each page helps children keep track of the multiplying lizards, and a closing section offers adults a few more ideas for easy math education." Booklist

Same old horse; illustrated by Steve Björkman. HarperCollins Pubs. 2005 31p (Mathstart) $15.99; pa $4.99   E

1. Horses—Fiction
ISBN 0-06-055770-2; 0-06-055771-0 (pa)

Hankie wants to be unpredictable, but the other horses are sure he'll always be the same old Hankie. Someone's in for a surprise in this story about making predictions.

This "is a lively story that encourages kids to work with numbers to find out what happens next. Bjorkman's clear, funny ink-and-watercolor pictures show horses in a barnyard acting just like children on a school playground." Booklist

Murray, Marjorie Dennis

Little Wolf and the moon; illustrated by Stacey Schuett. Marshall Cavendish 2002 unp il $16.95
E

1. Wolves—Fiction 2. Moon—Fiction
ISBN 0-7614-5100-5   LC 00-52317

Every night, Little Wolf looks up at the moon and wonders why it is the way it is

"This gentle, poetic narrative speaks to the sense of wonder that children have about the natural world. The overall tone of reverence, of awe of the grandness of nature . . . is carried through in the rich watercolor illustrations." SLJ

Museum ABC. Little, Brown 2002 unp il $16.95
E

1. Alphabet 2. Art appreciation
ISBN 0-316-07170-6

"Produced by the Department of Special publications, The Metropolitan Museum of Art"

This illustrates letters of the alphabet with reproductions of art works from the collections of the Metropolitan Museum of Art

"Imagination and creativity abound in this brilliantly simple alphabet book. . . . There are objects children see every day, an egg, a tree, an umbrella, and parts of themselves, such as feet, hair, and nose. . . . Pictures are taken from a timeless array of countries, media, and artists. Very pleasing to look upon, this illuminates lessons in color, form, shape, diversity, and artistic vision as well as the alphabet." Booklist

Museum shapes. Little, Brown 2005 unp il $16.99
E

1. Shape 2. Art appreciation
ISBN 0-316-05698-7

"Produced by the Department of Special Publications, The Metropolitan Museum of Art"

"An exercise in both art appreciation and recognizing shapes, this book invites children to find one of 10 geometric forms in tiled details taken from several dozen artworks owned by New York's Metropolitan Museum of Art." Booklist

"The concept is simple; what makes this book so wonderful is the art, which is varied in content, style, medium, culture, and period, and is beautifully reproduced." SLJ

Muth, Jon J.

The three questions; based on a story by Leo Tolstoy; written and illustrated by Jon J. Muth. Scholastic 2002 unp il $16.95 **E**
1. Conduct of life—Fiction 2. Animals—Fiction
ISBN 0-439-19996-4   LC 00-49673
Nikolai asks his animal friends to help him answer three important questions: "When is the best time to do things?" "Who is the most important?" and "What is the right thing to do?"

"Moral without being moralistic, the tale sends a simple and direct message unfreighted by pomp or pedantry. Muth's art is as carefully distilled as his prose. A series of misty, evocative watercolors in muted tones suggests the figures and their changing relationships to the landscape." Publ Wkly

Zen shorts; illustrated by Jon Muth. 1st ed. Scholastic Press 2005 unp il $16.95 **E**
1. Bears—Fiction 2. Storytelling—Fiction
ISBN 0-439-33911-1   LC 2003-20471
A Caldecott Medal honor book, 2006
When Stillwater the bear moves into the neighborhood, the stories he tells to three siblings teach them to look at the world in new ways.

This "is both an accessible, strikingly illustrated story and a thought-provoking mediation." Booklist

Myers, Christopher

Black cat. Scholastic Press 1999 unp il $16.95
E
1. Cats—Fiction 2. City and town life—Fiction
ISBN 0-590-03375-1   LC 98-28609
A Coretta Scott King honor book for illustration, 2000
A black cat wanders through the streets of a city
"With striking photo-collages enhanced with gouache and ink, this book captures the gritty beauty of the city." Horn Book Guide

Fly! by Christopher Myers. Jump at the Sun/Hyperion Bks. for Children 2001 unp il $15.99 **E**
1. Birds—Fiction 2. City and town life—Fiction 3. African Americans—Fiction
ISBN 0-7868-0652-4   LC 00-59726
On the roof of his building, lonely Jawanza meets a man who teaches him how to make friends with the sparrows and pigeons up there

"The dazzling illustrations are rife with contrasts, which reinforce the message that joy can be found amid harsh urban realities." Horn Book Guide

Wings. Scholastic Press 2000 unp il $16.95
E
1. Flight—Fiction 2. Classical mythology—Fiction
ISBN 0-590-03377-8   LC 99-87389
"Myers retells the myth of Icarus through the story of Ikarus Jackson, the new boy on the block, who can fly above the rooftops and over the crowd. In this contemporary version, the winged kid nearly falls from the sky . . . because jeering kids in the schoolyard and repressive adults don't like his being different and try to break his soaring spirit. . . . Myers' beautiful cut-paper collages are eloquent and open." Booklist

Myers, Tim

Basho and the river stones; illustrations by Oki S. Han. 1st ed. Marshall Cavendish 2004 unp il $16.95 **E**
1. Matsuo, Bashō, 1644-1694—Fiction 2. Foxes—Fiction 3. Poetry—Fiction 4. Japan—Fiction
ISBN 0-7614-5165-X   LC 2003-26245
Tricked by a fox into giving up his share of cherries, a famous Japanese poet is inspired to write a haiku and the fox, ashamed of his actions, must devise another trick to set things right.

"Han's expressive watercolors, with an unusual variety of perspectives, keep the story lively. A clever original fable." Booklist
Another title about Basho by this author and illustrator is:
Basho and the fox (2000)

Good babies; a tale of trolls, humans, a witch, and a switch; [by] Tim Myers; illustrated by Kelly Murphy. Candlewick Press 2005 unp $15.99
E
1. Infants—Fiction 2. Witches—Fiction 3. Norway—Fiction
ISBN 0-7636-2227-3
A wicked witch's plan to wreak havoc by switching a human baby and a troll baby backfires in a surprising way.

"Murphy's acrylic, watercolor, and gel illustrations are based in blue. The figures are simply drawn but the rich color and shading bring them to life. An enjoyable story." SLJ

Myers, Walter Dean

The blues of Flats Brown; illustrated by Nina Laden. Holiday House 2000 unp il $16.95
E
1. Dogs—Fiction 2. Blues music—Fiction
ISBN 0-8234-1480-9   LC 99-16695
To escape an abusive master, a junkyard dog named Flats runs away and makes a name for himself from Mississippi to New York City playing blues on his guitar
"The narrator's vernacular, rhythmic and easy-rolling, has the feel of a timeless legend, and the vibrant, jewel-toned illustrations, dominated by moody, bittersweet, tonal variations of blue, are filled with rich detail, expressive characters, and fantastic landscapes." Booklist

Patrol; an American soldier in Vietnam; collages by Ann Grifalconi. HarperCollins Pubs. 2002 unp il $16.95; lib bdg $16.89 **E**
1. Vietnam War, 1961-1975—Fiction 2. African American soldiers—Fiction
ISBN 0-06-028363-7; 0-06-028364-5 (lib bdg)
                LC 00-35009
A frightened American soldier faces combat in the lush forests of Vietnam and sees a young enemy soldier who is as frightened as he is
The story is told "in free verse that is at once ethereal and white-knuckle tense. . . . Grifalconi's intricate paper and photo collages juxtapose snips of explosion smoke, snapshot images of fleeing villagers, and paper constructions of burning huts against a landscape that approaches fantasy in its lush beauty." Bull Cent Child Books

Namioka, Lensey
The hungriest boy in the world; illustrated by Aki Sogabe. Holiday House 2001 unp il $16.95

E

1. Hunger—Fiction 2. Japan—Fiction
ISBN 0-8234-1542-2 LC 00-25142
After swallowing the Hunger Monster, Jiro begins eating everything in sight, until his family finds a way to lure the monster out of Jiro's stomach
"The story is told economically but with wit and humor. Sogabe's illustrations, created using cut paper over rice paper that has been colored by airbrush or watercolor, complement the text with their elegant simplicity." SLJ

Napoli, Donna Jo
Albert; illustrated by Jim LaMarche. Silver Whistle Bks. 2001 unp il $16

E

1. Birds—Fiction
ISBN 0-15-201572-8 LC 97-7089
One day when Albert is at his window, two cardinals come to build a nest in his hand, an event that changes his life
"Napoli has written a pleasing modern fairy tale, transformed into a picture book by LaMarche's appealing, shaded pencil drawings." Booklist

Flamingo dream; illustrated by Cathie Felstead. Greenwillow Bks. 2002 unp il $15.95; lib bdg $15.89

E

1. Death—Fiction 2. Fathers—Fiction
ISBN 0-688-16796-9; 0-688-17863-4 (lib bdg)
LC 2001-23072
Grieving over her father's death from cancer, a young girl celebrates their last year together by making a book that includes mementos and a story
"Napoli's simple and straightforward language describes what dying looks like to a young person and depicts the stages of grief in an accessible and age-appropriate manner. . . . This book succeeds beautifully." SLJ

Neitzel, Shirley
The jacket I wear in the snow; pictures by Nancy Winslow Parker. Greenwillow Bks. 1989 unp il $15.99; pa $5.99

E

1. Clothing and dress—Fiction 2. Snow—Fiction 3. Stories in rhyme
ISBN 0-688-08028-6; 0-688-04587-1 (pa)
LC 88-18767
Also available Big book edition
A young girl names all the clothes that she must wear to play in the snow
"Written in cheerful, cumulative verse that recalls the well-known favorite nursery rhyme 'The House That Jack Built,' the text, with its easy-going rhythm, will be simple for children to recite from memory. . . . The artist's drawings are executed in . . . watercolor, pencil, and pen; they combine with the large typeface and a generous amount of white space to create a tremendously appealing book." Horn Book

Our class took a trip to the zoo; pictures by Nancy Winslow Parker. Greenwillow Bks. 2002 unp il $15.95; lib bdg $15.89

E

1. Zoos—Fiction 2. Stories in rhyme
ISBN 0-688-15543-X; 0-688-15544-8 (lib bdg)
LC 2001-23670
A cumulative verse with rebuses in which a young boy has a wonderful day at the zoo, despite a series of mishaps with the animals
"Parker's charming watercolor, pencil, and ink illustrations are cheery and full of fun. Children will enjoy the format and chiming in on the repetitive verses." SLJ

Nelson, S. D.
The Star People; a Lakota story. Abrams 2003 unp il $14.95

E

1. Grandmothers—Fiction 2. Stars—Fiction
ISBN 0-8109-4584-3 LC 2002-156367
When Young Wolf and his older sister wander from their village and face the danger of a prairie fire, their deceased grandmother, now one of the Star People, appears to guide them
"In clear, captivating language, Nelson . . . tells a stirring, original story based on Lakota legend. An extensive author's note introduces Ledger Book Art, the nineteenth-century Plains Indian style of art that influenced Nelson's acrylic paintings." Booklist

Ness, Evaline
Sam, Bangs & Moonshine; written and illustrated by Evaline Ness. Holt & Co. 1966 unp il $17.95; pa $6.95

E

1. Imagination—Fiction
ISBN 0-8050-0314-2; 0-8050-0315-0 (pa)
Awarded the Caldecott Medal, 1967
Young Samantha, or Sam, "the fisherman's daughter, finally learns to draw the line between reality and the 'moonshine' [her fantasies] in which her mother is a mermaid, she owns a baby kangaroo, and can talk to her cat." Publisher's note
"In this unusually creative story the fantasy in which many, many children indulge is presented in a realistic and sympathetic context. The illustrations in ink and pale color wash (mustard, grayish-aqua) have a touching realism, too. This is an outstanding book." SLJ

Neubecker, Robert
Wow! city! Hyperion 2004 unp il $16.99

E

1. City and town life—Fiction
ISBN 0-7868-0951-5
Two-year-old toddler Izzy goes on a trip with her father and experiences in what she sees in the hustling-and-bustling, gigantic, crowded, loud, and colorful city.
"Drawn in India ink and vividly colored on a Macintosh computer using Adobe Photoshop, the illustrations are full of life, action, and detail." SLJ

Nevius, Carol
Karate hour; illustrated by Bill Thomson. 1st ed. Marshall Cavendish 2004 unp il $14.95

E

1. Karate—Fiction 2. Stories in rhyme
ISBN 0-7614-5169-2 LC 2003-27122

Nevius, Carol—*Continued*

Rhyming text portrays the exuberance of an hour of karate class. Includes nonfiction information at end

Nevius "deftly captures the excitement and energy of the experience as well as the discipline and commitment required to rise in rank. Thomson's realistic mixed-media artwork is a standout, using light, shadow, and perspective in a variety of interesting ways." SLJ

Newberry, Clare Turlay

April's kittens. HarperCollins Pubs. 1993 c1940 32p il $16.99   E

1. Cats—Fiction

ISBN 0-06-024400-3

A Caldecott Medal honor book, 1941

A reissue of the title first published 1940

"Though old-fashioned, the story of a small girl's yearning to keep both a mother cat and one of her kittens still speaks to pet owners young and old. Newberry's simple, charcoal drawings of the felines are as elegant and endearing as ever." Horn Book

Newcome, Zita

Head, shoulders, knees, and toes; and other action counting rhymes. Candlewick Press 2002 60p il $15.99   E

1. Nursery rhymes 2. Counting 3. Finger play

ISBN 0-7636-1899-3   LC 2002-17508

A collection of approximately fifty nursery and counting rhymes, most accompanied by fingerplays or other activities

"Each page includes the words of one rhyme and energetic watercolor-and-colored pencil illustrations of kids in action. . . . This is exercise and play as well as a lively celebration of the sound and beat of words in the nonsense rhymes that live on." Booklist

Newman, Lesléa

The best cat in the world; written by Lesléa Newman; illustrated by Ronald Himler. Eerdmans Books for Young Readers 2004 unp il $16

       E

1. Cats—Fiction 2. Death—Fiction

ISBN 0-8028-5252-1   LC 2003-13028

A young boy deals with the loss of his beloved cat Charlie, eventually accepting the arrival of another, very different cat.

"Himler's warm pencil-and-watercolor illustrations generously fill the pages. They portray the casually clad characters with tenderness and contrast the shape of the old and sick animal with that of the young and playful one. . . . For comfort and catharsis, Newman's fine story is the cat's pajamas." SLJ

A fire engine for Ruthie; illustrated by Cyd Moore. Clarion Books 2004 32p il $16   E

1. Play—Fiction 2. Grandmothers—Fiction 3. Sex role—Fiction

ISBN 0-618-15989-4   LC 2003-22791

Ruthie's Nana suggests playing tea party and fashion show during their visit, but Ruthie is much more interested in the vehicles that a neighbor boy is playing with as

they pass his house each day.

"This book hits the mark on three solid counts—a real story, good pacing, and deliciously full artwork that has its own momentum." Booklist

Runaway dreidel! illustrated by Kyrsten Brooker. Holt & Co. 2002 unp il $17.95

       E

1. Hanukkah—Fiction 2. Stories in rhyme

ISBN 0-8050-6237-8   LC 2001-5801

In this rhyming tale in the style of "The Night before Christmas," a family's preparations for Chanukah are disrupted by a wildly spinning dreidel

"The tale holds storytelling appeal in both text and humorous illustrations. Chagall-like oil paintings and cut-paper art lend an Old World feel to the story." SLJ

Where is bear? written by Lesléa Newman; illustrated by Valeri Gorbachev. Harcourt 2004 unp $16   E

1. Animals—Fiction 2. Stories in rhyme

ISBN 0-15-204936-3

"Gulliver books"

The animals in the forest are playing hide-and-seek, but none of them can find Bear anywhere.

"With charming pen-and-ink and watercolor spreads that depict the animals' bewilderment, this fun-loving, simply told story will appeal to the preschool set." SLJ

Another title about these animals is:

Skunk's spring surprise (2006)

Newman, Marjorie

Mole and the baby bird; illustrated by Patrick Benson. Bloomsbury Children's Bks. 2002 unp il $16.95   E

1. Moles (Animals)—Fiction 2. Birds—Fiction

ISBN 1-58234-784-0   LC 2001-52988

Mole rescues a baby bird, cares for it, and loves it, until the day he realizes it is because he loves it that he must set it free

"The message of making others happy through a selfless act and the true meaning of love comes across gently, and responsibility in dealing with wild animals is clearly presented. The endearing characters have both authenticity and appeal, and the countryside is vast yet delicately and precisely drawn." SLJ

Newsome, Jill

Dream dancer; story by Jill Newsome; illustrations by Claudio Muñoz. HarperCollins Pubs. 2002 unp il $15.95; lib bdg $15.89

       E

1. Ballet—Fiction 2. Dolls—Fiction

ISBN 0-06-000932-2; 0-06-001322-2 (lib bdg)

     LC 2001-39288

Lily loves to dance, but after she hurts her leg in an accident, she wonders if she will be able to dance again—until she finds encouragement in a gift from her grandmother

"The simple, straightforward language is nicely paced and great for read-alouds, and the appealing, loose-lined watercolors show the beauty and exhilaration of dance." Booklist

Newsome, Jill—*Continued*

Night walk; illustrations by Claudio Muñoz. Clarion Bks. 2003 unp il $15　　　　　**E**

1. Dogs—Fiction 2. Cats—Fiction

ISBN 0-618-32458-5　　　　LC 2002-10266

When Daisy, an adventurous dog, persuades Flute, a stay-at-home cat, to go for a walk one night, Flute gets more than she bargained for

"This suspenseful tale will keep children as wide-eyed as Flute. . . . The gracefully executed watercolors add charming details to the story and illustrate the bond of friendship . . . in an expressive manner." SLJ

Nicholls, Judith

Billywise; illustrated by Jason Cockcroft. Bloomsbury Children's Bks. 2002 unp il $16.95
　　　　　　　　　　　　　　　　　　E

1. Owls—Fiction 2. Stories in rhyme

ISBN 1-58234-778-6　　　　LC 2002-18339

The night finally arrives when Billywise the owlet, guided by his mother, jumps from the nest and flies

"Luminescent blues, greens, and rusts illuminate the dazzling illustrations, which elicit a sense of magical realism in the twilight setting." SLJ

Nikola-Lisa, W.

Setting the turkeys free; written by W. Nikola-Lisa; illustrated by Ken Wilson-Max. . Jump at the Sun/Hyperion Books for Children 2004 unp il $15.99　　　　　**E**

1. Turkeys—Fiction 2. Foxes—Fiction 3. Artists—Fiction

ISBN 0-7868-1952-9　　　　LC 2003-50928

When a sly, hungry fox threatens a flock of turkeys, the young artist who drew the birds must find a way to save them.

"Right at a preschooler's level, the artwork . . . has humor as well as momentum. . . . This clever mixing of art and a spot-on text provides a fun story as well as a surefire craft idea that kids will want to try." Booklist

Noble, Trinka Hakes

The day Jimmy's boa ate the wash; pictures by Steven Kellogg. Dial Bks. for Young Readers 1980 unp il $16.99; pa $6.99　　　　　**E**

1. Farm life—Fiction 2. Snakes—Fiction 3. School stories

ISBN 0-8037-1723-7; 0-8037-0094-6 (pa)

　　　　　　　　　　　　　　LC 80-15098

"One small girl, reporting to her mother after a class visit to a farm . . . describes . . . how Jimmy's boa escaped, set the hens in a flurry, precipitated an egg-throwing match, and so on." Bull Cent Child Books

"The illustrations, which depict disgruntled chickens, expressive pigs, and smiling cats as well as other individualized animal and human characters, show the artist's flair for humorous detail." Horn Book

Other titles about Jimmy's boa are:

Jimmy's boa and the big splash birthday bash (1989)
Jimmy's boa and the bungee jump slam dunk (2003)
Jimmy's boa bounces back (1984)

Nolan, Janet

The St. Patrick's Day shillelagh; illustrated by Ben F. Stahl. Whitman, A. 2002 unp il $15.95
　　　　　　　　　　　　　　　　　　E

1. Irish Americans—Fiction 2. Storytelling—Fiction 3. Immigrants—Fiction

ISBN 0-8075-7344-2　　　　LC 2002-1953

On his way from Ireland to America to escape the potato famine, young Fergus carves a shillelagh from his favorite blackthorn tree, and each St. Patrick's Day for generations, his story is retold by one of his descendants

"This account provides just enough historical context for each generation to be interesting. Stahl's realistic, acrylic illustrations adeptly convey the passage of time for this engaging family." SLJ

Nolen, Jerdine

Big Jabe; illustrations by Kadir Nelson. Lothrop, Lee & Shepard Bks. 2000 unp il $15.99; lib bdg $16.89　　　　　**E**

1. Slavery—Fiction 2. African Americans—Fiction

ISBN 0-688-13662-1; 0-688-13663-X (lib bdg)

　　　　　　　　　　　　　　LC 99-38001

Momma Mary tells stories about a special young man who does wondrous things, especially for the slaves on the Plenty Plantation

"Nolen recounts her original tale with a light touch and lyrical voices that add depth and resonance to its imagery and serious overtones. The gouache and watercolor illustrations convey both the lush summer and the rigorous life of the slaves. This powerful story will be particularly effective shared aloud." Horn Book Guide

Harvey Potter's balloon farm; [illustrated by] Mark Buehner. Lothrop, Lee & Shepard Bks. 1994 unp il $16.99; lib bdg $15.93; pa $5.99
　　　　　　　　　　　　　　　　　　E

1. Tall tales 2. Balloons—Fiction 3. Farm life—Fiction

ISBN 0-688-07887-7; 0-688-07888-5 (lib bdg); 0-688-15845-5 (pa)　　　　LC 91-38129

"Harvey Potter's unusual crop is balloons—which grow just like corn on long, sturdy stalks. Harvey Potter himself is not at all unusual, and his friend, a young African-American girl, is determined to uncover the secret of his curious harvest. The story is lively, but of even greater attraction are the vivid, air-brushed illustrations of balloons with expressive faces in every size, color, and shape." Horn Book Guide

Hewitt Anderson's great big life; illustrated by Kadir Nelson. Simon & Schuster Books for Young Readers 2005 unp il $16.95　　　　　**E**

1. Size—Fiction 2. Giants—Fiction

ISBN 0-689-86866-9　　　　LC 98-14039

"A Paula Wiseman book"

When tiny Hewitt is born into a family of giants, everyone learns that sometimes small is best of all.

"Nelson's funny, larger-than-life oil paintings warmly depict this African-American family and give readers a real sense of gigantic proportions. . . . Told in colorful language that begs to be read aloud, this humorous, oversize book offers a gentle look at accepting others as they are." SLJ

Nolen, Jerdine—*Continued*

Max and Jax in second grade; illustrated by Karen Lee Schmidt. Silver Whistle/Harcourt 2002 38p il $14   **E**
1. Alligators—Fiction
ISBN 0-15-201668-6   LC 98-5544
"Alligator twins Max and Jax both have plans for the summer: Max to catch fish with Dad, Jax to hold a sleepover. Both are happy when school is finally out— and Max catches a big fish with Jax's secret bait." Horn Book Guide
"Schmidt's vivid watercolors are perfectly matched to Nolen's bright writing, which will challenge new readers while delivering a story well told." Booklist

Raising dragons; illustrated by Elise Primavera. Silver Whistle Bks. 1998 unp il $16   **E**
1. Dragons—Fiction 2. Farm life—Fiction
ISBN 0-15-201288-5   LC 95-43307
A farmer's young daughter shares numerous adventures with the dragon that she raises from infancy
"Nolen's chimercial text meets its match in Primavera's imaginative and bold illustrations." Horn Book Guide

Thunder Rose; illustrated by Kadir Nelson. Harcourt 2003 unp il $16   **E**
1. Tall tales 2. African Americans—Fiction 3. West (U.S.)—Fiction
ISBN 0-15-216472-3   LC 2002-12287
Unusual from the day she is born, Thunder Rose performs all sorts of amazing feats, including building fences, taming a stampeding herd of steers, capturing a gang of rustlers, and turning aside a tornado
"Nolen and Nelson offer up a wonderful tale of joy and love, as robust and vivid as the wide West. The oil, watercolor, and pencil artwork is outstanding." SLJ

Norac, Carl

My daddy is a giant; illustrated by Ingrid Godon. 1st American ed. Clarion Books 2005 29p il $16   **E**
1. Father-son relationship—Fiction
ISBN 0-618-44399-1   LC 2004-12093
A little boy's father seems so large to him that he needs a ladder to cuddle him and birds nest in his father's hair.
"The simple premise captures the little boy's idolization of his dad well. . . . With the man so large that he often has to bend his head or crouch down to fit onto the page, and the full-bleed spreads overflowing the book, these pictures will engage even the children in the last row of storytime." SLJ

Noyes, Deborah

Hana in the time of the tulips; illustrated by Bagram Ibatoulline. Candlewick Press 2004 unp il $16.99   **E**
1. Rembrandt Harmenszoon van Rijn, 1606-1669— Fiction 2. Tulips—Fiction 3. Father-daughter relationship—Fiction 4. Netherlands—Fiction
ISBN 0-7636-1875-6   LC 2002-73900

A little girl who studies drawing with Rembrandt seeks to regain her father's attention during the tulipomania craze in seventeenth-century Holland.
"Noyes tells an unusual story with appealing rhythm and rich, fanciful language, while Ibatoulline's exquisite paintings and ink drawings evoke the historical setting and lively characters with an old master's precise attention to light, form, shadow, and texture." Booklist

Numeroff, Laura Joffe

Beatrice doesn't want to; illustrated by Lynn Munsinger. Candlewick Press 2004 unp il $15.99   **E**
1. Libraries—Fiction 2. Books and reading—Fiction
ISBN 0-7636-1160-3   LC 2002-73908
A newly illustrated edition of the title first published 1981 by Watts
On the third afternoon of going to the library with her brother Henry, Beatrice finally finds something she enjoys doing.
"Done in watercolor, ink, and pencil and featuring floppy-eared canine characters, the expressive illustrations perfectly capture the humor of the text." SLJ

The Chicken sisters; by Laura Numeroff; pictures by Sharleen Collicott. HarperCollins Pubs. 1997 unp il $15.99; pa $6.95   **E**
1. Chickens—Fiction 2. Sisters—Fiction 3. Wolves— Fiction
ISBN 0-06-026679-1; 0-06-443520-2 (pa)
     LC 96-30297
"A Laura Geringer book"
"Violet, Poppy, and Babs, the chicken sisters, possess talents that annoy the neighbors until a threatening wolf moves into the neighborhood. The illustrations achieve a captivating sense of texture that adds immediacy to the humorous story." Horn Book Guide

If you give a mouse a cookie; by Laura Numeroff; illustrated by Felicia Bond. Harper & Row 1985 unp il $15.99; lib bdg $16.89
    E
1. Mice—Fiction
ISBN 0-06-024586-7; 0-06-024587-5 (lib bdg)
     LC 84-48343
Also available Big book edition
Relating the cycle of requests a mouse is likely to make after you give him a cookie takes the reader through a young child's day
"Children love to indulge in supposition or to ask 'what will happen if . . .?' and here there is a long, satisfying chain of linked and enjoyably nonsensical causes and effects. . . . The illustrations, neatly drawn, spaciously composed, and humorously detailed, extend the story just the way picture book illustrations should." Bull Cent Child Books
Other titles in this series are:
If you give a moose a muffin (1991)
If you give a pig a pancake (1998)
If you give a pig a party (2005)
If you take a mouse to school (2002)
If you take a mouse to the movies (2000)

Numeroff, Laura Joffe—*Continued*

What mommies do best; by Laura Numeroff; illustrated by Lynn Munsinger. Simon & Schuster Bks. for Young Readers 1998 unp il $13.95   E

1. Mothers—Fiction 2. Fathers—Fiction 3. Sex role—Fiction

ISBN 0-689-80577-2   LC 96-44375

Bound back to back and inverted with: What daddies do best

"The first half shows a mother bear, pig, mouse, elephant, and porcupine engaging in everyday activities with her children. . . . Flip the book and read that Daddies can do the same thing. Munsinger's winsome water-color depictions of the animals are warm and humorous. A perfect cuddly bedtime or storytime read-aloud choice." SLJ

Other titles in this series are:

What aunts do best / What uncles do best (2004)
What grandmas do best / What grandpas do best (2000)

Nye, Naomi Shihab

Baby radar; pictures by Nancy Carpenter. Greenwillow Bks. 2003 unp il $15.99; lib bdg $16.89   E

ISBN 0-688-15948-6; 0-688-15949-4 (lib bdg)
LC 2002-23165

When her mother takes her out in her stroller, a toddler encounters a variety of things, people, and animals

"The brief, lyrical phrases, perfectly paired with realistic pen-and-watercolor illustrations set on a white expanse, give a toddler's view of the world—the humor, delight, and exuberance of life." SLJ

Ó Flatharta, Antoine

Hurry and the monarch; illustrated by Meilo So. 1st ed. Knopf 2005 unp il $14.95; lib bdg $16.99   E

1. Butterflies—Fiction 2. Turtles—Fiction

ISBN 0-375-83003-0; 0-375-93003-5 (lib bdg)
LC 2004-15984

Hurry the tortoise befriends a monarch butterfly when she stops in his garden in Wichita Falls, Texas, during her migration from Canada to Mexico. Includes facts about monarch butterflies

"Veined with a tracery of inked details, So's subtle watercolors reference both Asian nature-painting traditions and the limited palette of artwork in the early days of color printing. Together with its informative afterword, this is a particularly attractive, affecting introduction to the wonder of species diversity and the elegant continuum of life." Booklist

Oberman, Sheldon

The always prayer shawl; illustrated by Ted Lewin. Boyds Mills Press 1994 unp il $15.95   E

1. Jews—Fiction 2. Immigrants—Fiction

ISBN 1-878093-22-3

Also available in paperback from Puffin Bks.

This story "tells of the Jewish boy Adam, growing up in a shtetl, whose life drastically changes when famine and chaos in old Russia force his parents to immigrate to America. At parting, Adam's beloved grandfather gives the boy a gift, a prayer shawl . . . which was presented to the grandfather by *his* grandfather. . . . The watercolors are abundantly detailed and wonderfully expressive. . . . The pictures enrich the tranquil telling . . . as it movingly depicts how memory and tradition add texture and richness to our lives." Booklist

Ochiltree, Dianne

Sixteen runaway pumpkins; written by Dianne Ochiltree; illustrated by Anne-Sophie Lanquetin. 1st ed. Margaret K. McElderry Books 2004 unp il $16.95   E

1. Pumpkin—Fiction 2. Stories in rhyme

ISBN 0-689-85090-5   LC 2003-4655

"Sam, a raccoon, tours the pumpkin patch at harvest time, hoping to fill her wagon for Gramps. Peeking under vines for the fruit, she quickly counts her way from one to two to four, and then adds four more to her load. Now, 'Eight pumpkins thunk-clunk together.' . . . The rhyming text and action-packed illustrations express Sam's predicament as this spirited, energetic tale comes to a happy, surprise ending." SLJ

O'Connell, Rebecca

The baby goes beep; pictures by Ken Wilson-Max. Roaring Brook Press 2003 unp il $14.95; lib bdg $22.90   E

1. Infants—Fiction

ISBN 0-7613-1789-9; 0-7613-2867-X (lib bdg)
LC 2003-8579

A baby makes various sounds as he explores the world around him.

"The simple, repetitive text . . . will appeal to the very youngest listeners. Featuring bright colors and bold, clunky shapes outlined in black, the uncluttered illustrations perfectly complement the text." SLJ

O'Connor, Jane

The perfect puppy for me; by Jane O'Connor and Jessie Hartland; illustrated by Jessie Hartland. Viking 2003 unp il $15.99   E

1. Dogs—Fiction

ISBN 0-670-03614-5   LC 2002-15568

While waiting to get his very own puppy, a young boy spends time with various dogs and describes what the different breeds are like

"Each page is jam-packed with good advice, useful information, and bright and cleverly detailed paintings that successfully reflect the pertinent traits of the different canines." SLJ

Ogburn, Jacqueline K.

The bake shop ghost; illustrated by Marjorie Priceman. Houghton Mifflin 2005 unp il $16   E

1. Ghost stories 2. Cake—Fiction 3. Bakers and bakeries—Fiction

ISBN 0-618-44557-9

Miss Cora Lee Meriweather haunts her bake shop after her death, until Annie Washington, the new shop

Ogburn, Jacqueline K.—*Continued*

owner, makes a deal with her.

"Priceman's illustrations are charming, with dashes of color and humor and a sense of action in each one. . . . This is a delightful story with a satisfying conclusion." SLJ

The magic nesting doll; illustrated by Laurel Long. Dial Bks. 2000 unp il $16.99 **E**

1. Fairy tales 2. Russia—Fiction

ISBN 0-8037-2414-4   LC 98-34397

After her grandmother dies, Katya finds herself in a kingdom where the Tsarvitch has been turned into living ice and she uses the magic nesting dolls her babushka had given her to try to break the curse

"The writings is filled with description and poetic images. . . . Created using oil paints on paper primed with gesso, the illustrations are alive with detail and reminiscent of the miniaturist style used in Russian decorative items." SLJ

Okimoto, Jean Davies

The White Swan express; a story about adoption; by Jean Davies Okimoto and Elaine M. Aoki; illustrated by Meilo So. Clarion Bks. 2002 32p il $16 **E**

1. Adoption—Fiction 2. China—Fiction

ISBN 0-618-16453-7   LC 2002-5983

Across North America, people in four different homes prepare for a special trip to China, while four baby girls in China await their new adoptive parents

"The adoptive parents are a diverse group—two married couples, one white, the other Asian; a single woman; and a pair of women. . . . So's lovely watercolors are a whirl of activity. . . . A complement to the study of China as well a good book to explain adoption." Booklist

Olaleye, Isaac

Bitter bananas; illustrated by Ed Young. Boyds Mills Press 1994 unp il $15.95 **E**

1. Baboons—Fiction 2. Rain forests—Fiction 3. Africa—Fiction

ISBN 1-56397-039-2   LC 93-73306

Also available in paperback from Puffin Bks.

"Baboons are stealing the sweet palm sap that the young African boy Yusuf sells at market, and it takes patience, ingenuity, and several trials before Yusuf outwits his forest rivals with a lure of tempting sap and bananas—laced with wormwood." Bull Cent Child Books

"Olaleye's eminently readable text naturally calls for audience participation. Young renders the story beautifully in cut-paper collages of vibrant pink and lush green." Booklist

O'Malley, Kevin

Captain Raptor and the moon mystery; illustrations by Patrick O'Brien. Walker & Co 2005 unp il $16.95; lib bdg $17.85 **E**

1. Dinosaurs—Fiction 2. Science fiction

ISBN 0-8027-8935-8; 0-8027-8936-6 (lib bdg)

LC 2004-53624

When something lands on one of the moons of the planet Jurassica, Captain Raptor and his spaceship crew go to investigate.

"An action-packed science-fiction romp starring a cast of dinosaur characters. . . . Presented in comic-book style, this story blends an eye-catching layout with a quick-moving plot, tongue-in-cheek humor, and an imaginative setting." SLJ

Lucky leaf. Walker & Co 2004 unp il $15.95; lib bdg $16.85 **E**

1. Leaves—Fiction

ISBN 0-8027-8924-2; 0-8027-8925-0 (lib bdg)

LC 2003-68868

After his mother tells him to stop playing video games and go outside, a young boy tries to catch the last leaf on a tree, thinking it will bring him luck.

"Done in pen and ink and colored in PhotoShop, the illustrations feature crisp, vibrant colors that create a vivid setting. . . . The story is told through spare, but effective, dialogue presented in speech bubbles." SLJ

Once upon a cool motorcycle dude; written and illustrated by Kevin O'Malley; illustrated by Carol Heyer; illustrated by Scott Goto. Walker & Co 2005 unp il $16.95; lib bdg $17.85 **E**

1. Authorship—Fiction 2. Fairy tales

ISBN 0-8027-8947-1; 0-8027-8949-8 (lib bdg)

LC 2004-53613

Cooperatively writing a fairy tale for school, a girl imagines a beautiful princess whose beloved ponies are being stolen by a giant, and a boy conjures up the muscular biker who will guard the last pony in exchange for gold.

"The fun in this picture book comes in the contrasting styles of the illustrations. . . . The girl's story features bright colors, flowers, and long golden locks, while the boy's story is done in the dark, taut-muscled style of comic books." Booklist

O'Neill, Alexis

Estela's swap; illustrated by Enrique O. Sanchez. Lee & Low Bks. 2002 unp il $16.95

E

1. Mexican Americans—Fiction

ISBN 1-58430-044-2   LC 2001-38785

A young Mexican American girl accompanies her father to a swap meet, where she hopes to sell her music box for money for dancing lessons

"This is a warm, nicely paced story about sharing and bartering that's filled with sensory descriptions of the vibrant open market. The textured acrylics capture the hum and bustle of the stalls." Booklist

Orloff, Karen Kaufman

I wanna iguana; illustrated by David Catrow. Putnam 2004 unp il $15.99 **E**

1. Iguanas—Fiction 2. Pets—Fiction

ISBN 0-399-23717-8   LC 2002-10895

Alex and his mother write notes back and forth in which Alex tries to persuade her to let him have a baby iguana for a pet.

"This funny story is told through an amusing ex-

Orloff, Karen Kaufman—*Continued*

change of notes. . . . Featuring his signature cartoon characters, Catrow's illustrations provide a hilarious extension of the text." SLJ

Ormerod, Jan

If you're happy and you know it! [by] Jan Ormerod, Lindsey Gardiner. Star Bright Books 2003 unp il $15.95; pa $5.95   E
   1. Animals—Fiction 2. Stories in rhyme
ISBN 1-932065-07-5; 1-932065-10-5 (pa)
                 LC 2002-13692
A little girl and various animals sing their own versions of this popular rhyme
"Delightful, colorful animal figures cavort through the pages of this book that puts a twist on the familiar song. . . . The action on each spread gives the story a great deal of energy and the backgrounds are washes of color, from dark pink to yellow to blue." SLJ

Lizzie nonsense; a story of pioneer days. Clarion Books 2005 c2004 32p il lib bdg $15
                                     E
   1. Imagination—Fiction 2. Family life—Fiction
3. Australia—Fiction
ISBN 0-618-57493-X (lib bdg)   LC 2004-26642
First published 2004 in Australia
"Lizzie lives with her mother, father, and baby brother in a small, isolated house in the Australian bush. Her father has taken his sandalwood into town to sell and will be gone for weeks. Lizzie passes the lonely days by indulging in flights of fancy. . . . The text is simple yet evocative . . . while the skillfully rendered watercolors bring the unique setting to life." SLJ

Miss Mouse's day. HarperCollins Pubs. 2001 unp il $14.95; lib bdg $14.89   E
   1. Day—Fiction 2. Mice—Fiction
ISBN 0-688-16333-5; 0-688-16334-3 (lib bdg)
                 LC 99-27641
"Miss Mouse recounts her day as the stuffed-animal companion of an energetic little girl." Horn Book Guide
"The illustrations, in panels of varying sizes, brim with pattern, detail, and bright splashes of color. . . . Ormerod delightfully and realistically illustrates the challenges of energetic toddlerhood." Booklist
   Another title about Miss Mouse is:
Miss Mouse takes off (2001)

Osborne, Mary Pope

New York's bravest; paintings by Steve Johnson & Lou Fancher. Knopf 2002 unp il $15.95; lib bdg $17.99   E
   1. Fire fighters—Fiction 2. New York (N.Y.)—Fiction
ISBN 0-375-82196-1; 0-375-92196-6 (lib bdg)
                 LC 2002-455
Tells of the heroic deeds of the legendary New York firefighter, Mose Humphreys
"Boldly executed art supports the tall-tale flavor of a story that is both powerful and humane." Booklist

Pak, Soyung

Dear Juno; illustrated by Susan Kathleen Hartung. Viking 1999 unp il $15.99   E
   1. Grandmothers—Fiction 2. Letters—Fiction
3. Korean Americans—Fiction
ISBN 0-670-88252-6   LC 98-43408
Although Juno, a Korean American boy, cannot read the letter he receives from his grandmother in Seoul, he understands what it means from the photograph and dried flower that are enclosed and decides to send a similar letter back to her
"The handsome layout, featuring ample white space and illustrations that cover anywhere from one page to an entire spread, perfectly suit the gentle, understated tone of the text." SLJ

Palatini, Margie

Earthquack! illustrated by Barry Moser. Simon & Schuster Bks. for Young Readers 2002 unp il $15.95   E
   1. Domestic animals—Fiction
ISBN 0-689-84280-5   LC 2001-31302
When Chucky Ducky feels the earth beneath him grumble and rumble, he runs to alert the other barnyard animals to the coming earthquake, but just as a wily weasel is about to take advantage of their fears, the true source of the rumbling is revealed
"Moser captures the essence of Weasel's dark determination as well as the bug-eyed hysteria of the farm animals in his expressive graphite and transparent watercolor illustrations. . . . Palatini's text is funny, with contemporary dialogue, puns, and a fast-paced narrative rich in rhythm and alliteration." SLJ

Piggie pie! illustrated by Howard Fine. Clarion Bks. 1995 unp il $15; pa $5.95   E
   1. Witches—Fiction 2. Pigs—Fiction 3. Wolves—Fiction
ISBN 0-395-71691-8; 0-395-86618-9 (pa)
                 LC 94-19726
"Gritch the Witch sets out for Old MacDonald's Farm to get herself a meal of plump piggies. Alerted, however, . . . the swine hastily don sheep, cow, and other barnyard disguises and fool her. . . . The still-hungry Gritch is persuaded to give up by a Big Bad Wolf . . . and the two go off for lunch, each picturing the other made into a sandwich. . . . The exuberant illustrations are colorful and action-filled. Greedy (but not too bright) witch and wolf both get what they deserve in this thoroughly enjoyable romp." SLJ

Three French hens; a holiday tale; illustrations by Richard Egielski. Hyperion Books for Children 2005 unp il $15.99   E
   1. Chickens—Fiction 2. Foxes—Fiction
3. Christmas—Fiction 4. New York (N.Y.)—Fiction
ISBN 0-7868-5167-8
"The three French hens from the familiar Christmas song are sent by a Parisian lady to her boyfriend, Philippe Renard, in New York, and when they can't find Philippe in lost mail, they think perhaps they should translate his name: Phil Fox. They find Phil Fox, but he's a downtrodden fox living in the Bronx. . . . [This] is so much fun, it's hard to imagine an artist milking more laughs from it

Palatini, Margie—*Continued*

than Egielski. . . . Something really fresh for the holiday season." Booklist

The three silly billies; illustrated by Barry Moser. Simon & Schuster Books for Young Readers 2005 unp il $15.95   E

1. Goats—Fiction

ISBN 0-689-85862-0   LC 2002-155835

Three billy goats, unable to cross a bridge because they cannot pay the toll, form a car pool with The Three Bears, Little Red Riding Hood, and Jack of beanstalk fame to get past the rude Troll.

"Painted in cheery watercolors, Moser's figures are in contemporary dress and pop out from the white backgrounds. There is plenty of visual humor. . . . Palatini's hip and punny text is fun to read aloud." SLJ

Pallotta, Jerry

Ocean counting; odd numbers; illustrated by Shennen Bersani. Charlesbridge 2004 unp il $16.95; pa $6.95   E

1. Counting 2. Marine animals

ISBN 0-88106-151-4; 0-88106-150-6 (pa)

LC 98-46035

This "offering counts by twos to 50 and includes only odd numbers (except for the deliberate inclusion of 50 and 0). . . . Readers will find creatures from 9 little green crabs to 15 limpets to 33 sand dollars." Booklist

"Bersani's bright, realistic colored-pencil illustrations will lure readers into perusing the factoid-loaded, simple, conversational text. . . . This book offers a colorful, engaging, and intriguing slant on the technique of counting." SLJ

Panahi, H. L.

Bebop Express; illustrated by Steve Johnson and Lou Fancher. Laura Geringer Books 2005 unp il $15.99; lib bdg $16.89   E

1. Railroads—Fiction 2. Jazz music—Fiction 3. Stories in rhyme

ISBN 0-06-057190-X; 0-06-057191-8 (lib bdg)

LC 2003-24244

A rollicking rhythmic express train takes passengers on a jazzy journey that celebrates the United States and its unique musical culture.

"The intricate collages use old photographs and vintage fabrics to obtain a unique look. Teeming with life, the art visually complements the noisy text." Booklist

Parish, Peggy

Amelia Bedelia; pictures by Fritz Siebel. HarperFestival 1999 unp il $16.99   E

1. Household employees—Fiction

ISBN 0-694-01296-3   LC 98-31782

Also available in paperback with Audiobook

"An I can read picture book"

First published 1963; reissued 1992 as an I can read book (still available in hardcover and paperback)

"Amelia Bedelia is a maid whose talent for interpreting instructions literally results in comical situations, such as dressing the chicken in fine clothes." Hodges. Books for Elem Sch Libr

Other titles about Amelia Bedelia are:

Amelia Bedelia and the baby (1981)

Amelia Bedelia and the surprise shower (1996)

Amelia Bedelia, bookworm (2003) by Herman Parish

Amelia Bedelia goes camping (1985)

Amelia Bedelia 4 mayor (1999) by Herman Parish

Amelia Bedelia helps out (1979)

Amelia Bedelia, rocket scientist? (2005) by Herman Parish

Amelia Bedelia under construction (2006) by Herman Parish

Amelia Bedelia's family album (1988) by Herman Parish

Bravo Amelia Bedelia (1997) by Herman Parish

Calling Doctor Amelia Bedelia (2003) by Herman Parish

Come back, Amelia Bedelia (1971)

Good driving, Amelia Bedelia (1995) by Herman Parish

Good work, Amelia Bedelia (1976)

Happy haunting, Amelia Bedelia (2004) by Herman Parish

Merry Christmas, Amelia Bedelia (1986)

Play ball, Amelia Bedelia (1972)

Teach us, Amelia Bedelia (1977)

Thank you, Amelia Bedelia (1964)

Park, Frances

Good-bye, 382 Shin Dang Dong; [by] Frances and Ginger Park; illustrated by Yangsook Choi. National Geographic Soc. 2002 unp il $16.95

E

1. Immigrants—Fiction 2. Korea—Fiction

ISBN 0-7922-7985-9   LC 2001-2976

Jangmi finds it hard to say goodbye to relatives and friends, plus the food, customs, and beautiful things of her home in Korea, when her family moves to America

"The oil paintings done in a simple, childlike style are formally framed with white space. . . . Children will find the details of cultural differences and the immigrant experience well evoked." SLJ

The royal bee; by Frances Park and Ginger Park; illustrations by Christopher Zhong-Yuan Zhang. Boyds Mills Press 2000 unp il $16.95; pa $9.95   E

1. Korea—Fiction 2. Reading—Fiction

ISBN 1-56397-614-5; 1-56397-867-9 (pa)

LC 98-88234

"Song-ho is a poor peasant boy in Korea who eavesdrops outside a classroom that only admits privileged boys. The kindly teacher, however, allows him to attend, and so stellar is his academic performance that he represents the school in the Royal Bee—a yearly contest of knowledge." Horn Book Guide

"This simply and eloquently told tale is well paired with large, bold oil-paint-on-board illustrations." SLJ

Park, Linda Sue

Bee-bim bop! illustrated by Ho Baek Lee. Clarion Books 2005 31p $15   E

1. Cooking—Fiction 2. Korean Americans—Fiction 3. Stories in rhyme

ISBN 0-618-26511-2   LC 2003027697

"Bee-bim bop . . . is a traditional Korean dish of rice topped, and then mixed, with meat and vegetables. In . . . rhyming text, a hungry child tells about helping her

Park, Linda Sue—*Continued*
mother make bee-bim bop." Publisher's note
"Playful, cartoonlike drawings portray a round-faced girl helping her mother. . . . The illustrations . . . are very appealing. . . . The rhyme works well. A recipe follows the story." SLJ

The firekeeper's son; illustrated by Julie Downing. Clarion Books 2004 37p il $16
E
1. Korea—Fiction
ISBN 0-618-13337-2   LC 2002-13917
In eighteenth-century Korea, after Sang-hee's father injures his ankle, Sang-hee attempts to take over the task of lighting the evening fire which signals to the palace that all is well. Includes historical notes.
"Park's command of place, characterization, and language is as capable and compelling in this picture book as it is in her novels. . . . [This offers] lyrical prose and deftly realized watercolors and pastels." SLJ

Parr, Todd
The family book; [by] Todd Parr. 1st ed. Little, Brown 2003 unp il $9.99; lib bdg $15.95
E
1. Family life—Fiction
ISBN 0-316-15563-2; 0-316-73896-4 (lib bdg)
LC 2002-36843
"Megan Tingley books"
Represents a variety of families, some big and some small, some with only one parent and some with two moms or dads, some quiet and some noisy, but all alike in some ways and special no matter what.
This features "whimsical illustrations featuring neon colors and figures outlined in black. . . . This concept book celebrating the diversity of family groups is distinguished by its sense of fun." SLJ

Partridge, Elizabeth
Moon glowing; illustrated by Joan Paley. Dutton Children's Bks. 2002 unp il $16.99   E
1. Animals—Fiction 2. Autumn—Fiction
ISBN 0-525-46873-0   LC 2002-514965
"As autumn leaves fall, a squirrel, bat, beaver, and bear prepare for colder weather. . . . This deceptively straightforward tale subtly conveys the concept of hibernation to a young audience—its urgency, its inevitability, and its cozy and somnolent warmth. Each animal is composed of basic cut-paper shapes given furry texture with mixed-media decoration." SLJ

Oranges on Golden Mountain; illustrated by Aki Sogabe. Dutton Children's Bks. 2001 unp il $16.99   E
1. Immigrants—Fiction 2. Chinese Americans—Fiction 3. San Francisco (Calif.)—Fiction 4. China—Fiction
ISBN 0-525-46453-0   LC 99-462287
When hard times fall on his family, Jo Lee is sent from China to San Francisco, where he helps his uncle fish and dreams of being reunited with his mother and sister
"The spirited story is beautifully written. . . . The striking, skillful paper-cut illustrations . . . create a vivid sense of place and do much to explain and extend the story's action." Booklist

Whistling; story by Elizabeth Partridge; quilts by Anna Grossnickle Hines. Greenwillow Bks. 2003 unp il $15.99; lib bdg $16.89   E
1. Father-son relationship—Fiction 2. Camping—Fiction
ISBN 0-06-050235-5; 0-06-050236-3 (lib bdg)
LC 2002-23539
While on a camping trip with his father, a boy draws on the whistling practice they have shared and finally whistles up the sun
"A subdued palette of forest greens and a sky washed with shades of indigo evoke the stillness of the woods just before sunrise. . . . The fabric of the story is as carefully crafted as the quilts that serve as illustrations. . . . The final pages detail the quilter's technique so readers can create a story quilt of their own. " SLJ

Paterson, Katherine
Blueberries for the queen; [by] Katherine & John Paterson; illustrated by Susan Jeffers. HarperCollins 2004 unp il $17.99; lib bdg $18.89   E
1. Wilhelmina, Queen of the Netherlands, 1880-1962—Fiction 2. World War, 1939-1945—Fiction 3. Massachusetts—Fiction
ISBN 0-06-623942-7; 0-06-623943-5 (lib bdg)
LC 2003-13838
In the summer of 1942, when Queen Wilhelmina of the Netherlands lives down the road from his family's house in Massachusetts, young William decides to take her some of the blueberries he has picked.
"The innocence and naïveté of the place and time shine through. Jeffers's watercolor-and-ink illustrations perfectly juxtapose scenes of domestic reality with the boy's wistful daydreams of knights and heroic quests." SLJ

Marvin one too many; story by Katherine Paterson; pictures by Jane Clark Brown. HarperCollins Pubs. 2001 48p il $14.95; lib bdg $14.89   E
1. Reading—Fiction 2. School stories
ISBN 0-06-028769-1; 0-06-028770-5 (lib bdg)
LC 00-46128
"An I can read book"
When Marvin refuses to go back to his new school because he is the only one in his class who cannot read, his father decides to help him learn by reading with him
"There's no condescension in Paterson's gentle story about Marvin's trouble. . . . Brown's soft colored-pencil pictures capture Marvin's loneliness and shame and then the family warmth." Booklist

Pattison, Darcy S.
The journey of Oliver K. Woodman; written by Darcy Pattison; illustrated by Joe Cepeda. Harcourt 2003 unp il $16   E
1. Travel—Fiction
ISBN 0-15-202329-1   LC 2001-5320
Oliver K. Woodman, a man made of wood, takes a remarkable journey across America, as told through the postcards and letters of those he meets along the way
"The boldly colored, textured illustrations were made with oils over an acrylic under-painting on boards. . . . A fresh, unusual tale." SLJ

Pattison, Darcy S.—*Continued*

Another title about Oliver K. Woodman is:
Searching for Oliver K. Woodman (2005)

Payne, Emmy

Katy No-Pocket; pictures by H. A. Rey. Houghton Mifflin 1944 unp il lib bdg $17; pa $5.95   E

  1. Kangaroos—Fiction 2. Animals—Fiction

  ISBN 0-395-17104-0 (lib bdg); 0-395-13717-9 (pa)

Katy Kangaroo was most unfortunately unprovided with a pocket in which to carry her son Freddy. She asked other animals with no pockets how they carried their children but none of their answers seemed satisfactory. Finally a wise old owl advised her to try to find a pocket in the City, and so off she went and in the City she found just what she and Freddy needed

Peacock, Carol Antoinette

Mommy far, Mommy near; an adoption story; written by Carol Antoinette Peacock; illustrated by Shawn Brownell. Whitman, A. 2000 unp il $15.95   E

  1. Adoption—Fiction 2. Mother-child relationship—Fiction 3. Chinese Americans—Fiction

  ISBN 0-80755-234-8   LC 99-36108

Elizabeth, who was born in China, describes the family who has adopted her and tries to sort out her feelings for her mother back in China

"The situation is handled sensitively by the author, who writes from personal experience. . . . The faces deftly show the strong emotional bond between adoptive mother and daughter." Horn Book Guide

Pearson, Debora

Alphabeep; a zipping, zooming ABC; illustrated by Edward Miller. Holiday House 2003 unp il $16.95   E

  1. Vehicles 2. Alphabet

  ISBN 0-8234-1722-0   LC 2002-69053

Describes a vehicle or street sign for every letter of the alphabet from Ambulance to Zamboni

"This colorful picture book is a vehicle lover's dream. . . . The lively text frequently includes onomatopoeic words. . . . The book is stunningly illustrated in a deceptively simple stylized manner." SLJ

Pearson, Tracey Campbell

Bob. Farrar, Straus & Giroux 2002 unp il $16   E

  1. Roosters—Fiction 2. Animals—Fiction

  ISBN 0-374-39957-3   LC 2001-40439

While looking for someone to teach him how to crow, a rooster learns to sound like many different animals and finds that his new skills come in handy

"The droll, repetitious text, perfect for reading aloud, is delightfully complemented by bright, lively watercolor illustrations." SLJ

Myrtle. Farrar, Straus and Giroux 2004 unp il $15   E

  1. Mice—Fiction 2. Aunts—Fiction

  ISBN 0-374-35157-0   LC 2003-44059

With the help of her favorite Aunt Tizzy, Myrtle learns to overcome her fear of the mean next-door neighbor.

"Pearson uses a fruit-colored palette with lots of design work to showcase her delightful mouse characters, brimming with personality." Booklist

Pedersen, Janet

Millie wants to play! [by] Janet Pedersen. 1st ed. Candlewick Press 2004 unp il $15.99   E

  1. Cattle—Fiction 2. Domestic animals—Fiction

  ISBN 0-7636-1993-0   LC 2002-67665

Millie the cow is awake early in the morning but waits until she hears the other animals making noise before she joins them in play.

"Done in gouache, watercolor, crayon, and pen, the colorful cartoon illustrations are filled with movement and reflect the excitement of the text." SLJ

Another title about Millie is:
Millie in the meadow (2003)

Peet, Bill

Big bad Bruce. Houghton Mifflin 1977 38p il $17; pa $8.95   E

  1. Bears—Fiction 2. Witches—Fiction

  ISBN 0-395-25150-8; 0-395-32922-1 (pa)

           LC 76-62502

Bruce, a bear bully, never picks on anyone his own size until he is diminished in more ways than one by a small but very independent witch

"The language of the text is almost musical, with lots of words used for the sheer pleasure or appropriateness of their sounds. The illustrations are colorful and amusing." Child Book Rev Serv

Huge Harold; written and illustrated by Bill Peet. Houghton Mifflin 1961 unp il lib bdg $17; pa $8.95   E

  1. Rabbits—Fiction 2. Stories in rhyme

  ISBN 0-395-18449-5 (lib bdg); 0-395-32923-X (pa)

"Harold the rabbit grows and grows—to dimensions which deprive him of normal hiding places but help him, after a bizarre chase, to an astonishing and wonderful achievement." Horn Book

This story, "told in rhyming couplets and colored drawings, is action filled and laughable." Booklist

The whingdingdilly; written and illustrated by Bill Peet. Houghton Mifflin 1970 60p il $17; pa $9.95   E

  1. Dogs—Fiction 2. Witches—Fiction

  ISBN 0-395-24729-2; 0-395-31381-3 (pa)

"Scamps, the dog, wants to be a horse, but a well-meaning witch turns him into a Whingdingdilly with the hump of a camel, zebra's tail, giraffe's neck, elephant's front legs and ears, rhinoceros' nose, and reindeer's horns." Adventuring With Books. 2d edition

Pelletier, David

The graphic alphabet. Orchard Bks. 1996 unp il $17.95   E

  1. Alphabet

  ISBN 0-531-36001-6   LC 96-4001

Pelletier, David—*Continued*

A Caldecott Medal honor book, 1997

In this alphabet book "a stylized letter Y, pink against a black background, is turned on its side and looks like a mouth open in a yawn. . . . The letter Q is repeated in squares, becoming a handsome quilt, and a three-dimensional golden H hovers over a darkened sky. Even for those who know their letters very well, some of the pictures demand a second look before the artist's view is clear. But that's the point; things can be more than or different from what they seem. An engaging book that will certainly have art-class relevance." Booklist

Pérez, Amada Irma

My very own room; story by Amada Irma Pérez; illustrations by Maya Christina Gonzalez. Children's Bk. Press 2000 30p il $16.95

E

1. Mexican Americans—Fiction 2. Family life—Fiction 3. Bilingual books—English-Spanish
ISBN 0-89239-164-2   LC 00-20769
Title page and text in English and Spanish

With the help of her family, a resourceful Mexican American girl realizes her dream of having a space of her own to read and to think

"Gonzalez' palette is replete with joyfully exuberant colors; rich magentas, purples, and blues contrast with the warm golds of faces and arms, and the dark eyes and hair offer further contrast with the backgrounds and skin colors. Pérez based this story on her own life . . . and the text . . . exudes a comfortably familiar, accessible voice." Bull Cent Child Books

Pérez, L. King

First day in grapes; illustrated by Robert Casilla. Lee & Low Bks. 2002 unp il $16.95   E

1. Migrant labor—Fiction 2. Mexican Americans—Fiction 3. School stories 4. California—Fiction
ISBN 1-58430-045-0   LC 2001-38787

When Chico starts the third grade after his migrant worker family moves to begin harvesting California grapes, he finds that self confidence and math skills help him cope with the first day of school

This story "sheds light on the life of migrant children in a poignant, balanced manner. . . . The watercolor, colored-pencil, and pastel illustrations bring warmth and color to this portrait of life in rural California." SLJ

Perkins, Lynne Rae

Snow music. Greenwillow Bks. 2003 unp il $15.99; lib bdg $16.89   E

1. Snow—Fiction 2. Sound—Fiction
ISBN 0-06-623956-7; 0-06-623958-3 (lib bdg)
LC 2002-192758

When a dog gets loose from the house on a snowy day, his owner searches for him and experiences the sounds of various animals and things in the snow

"With whispery, musical words and detailed, soft-focus images that depict typical winter scenes, this gentle book gives children a sense of what snow is." SLJ

Peters, Lisa Westberg

Cold little duck, duck, duck; pictures by Sam Williams. Greenwillow Bks. 2000 unp il $15.99; lib bdg $16.89   E

1. Ducks—Fiction 2. Spring—Fiction 3. Stories in rhyme
ISBN 0-688-16178-2; 0-688-16179-0 (lib bdg)
LC 99-29880

Early one spring a little duck arrives at her pond and finds it still frozen, but not for long

"The poetic text, well served by expressive watercolors, is set in a large black typeface (inviting letter and word recognition); colorful and playful typefaces are used for the rhythmic three-word refrains." Horn Book Guide

Peterson, Jeanne Whitehouse

Don't forget Winona; illustrated by Kimberly Bulcken Root. Joanna Cotler Books 2004 unp il $14.99; lib bdg $15.89   E

1. Droughts—Fiction 2. Sisters—Fiction 3. Oklahoma—Fiction
ISBN 0-06-027197-3; 0-06-027198-1 (lib bdg)

A young girl describes her family's experiences—and her younger sister's antics—when a drought forces them to make their way on Route 66 from Oklahoma to California.

The text is "effective in setting the personal story against the larger one. Root's paintings are masterful pieces of storytelling on their own." Booklist

Pilkey, Dav

The Hallo-wiener. Blue Sky Press (NY) 1995 unp il $16.95; pa $5.99   E

1. Dogs—Fiction 2. Halloween—Fiction
ISBN 0-590-41703-7; 0-439-07946-2 (pa)
LC 94-40949

All the other dogs make fun of Oscar the dachshund until one Halloween when, dressed as a hot dog, Oscar bravely rescues the others

"Pilkey's bold, colorful illustrations add life to his simple tale of courage and friendship." Horn Book Guide

The paperboy; story and paintings by Dav Pilkey. Orchard Bks. 1996 unp il $16.95; lib bdg $16.99; pa $6.99   E

1. Newspaper carriers—Fiction
ISBN 0-531-09506-1; 0-531-08856-1 (lib bdg); 0-531-07139-1 (pa)   LC 95-30641

A Caldecott Medal honor book, 1997

"A Richard Jackson book"

"In the quiet hour before dawn, a boy and his dog get out of their warm bed, eat their breakfasts, and deliver the newspapers. . . . Happy together before the rest of the world awakes, they finish the job and head back home to bed, where they dream of flying across the night sky." Booklist

"The palette of the artwork is rich and inviting, and an emphasis is put on balance and geometric form, giving solidity to this celebration of routine. A meditative evocation of the extraordinary aspects of ordinary living." Horn Book Guide

Pinczes, Elinor J.

One hundred hungry ants; illustrated by Bonnie MacKain. Houghton Mifflin 1993 unp il $16; pa $5.95   **E**

1. Ants—Fiction 2. Mathematics—Fiction 3. Stories in rhyme

ISBN 0-395-63116-5; 0-395-97123-3 (pa)

LC 91-45415

One hundred hungry ants head towards a picnic to get yummies for their tummies, but stop to change their line formation, illustrating the various ways one hundred may be divided

"Kids will enjoy the bouncy rhyme and the comical portrayal of the ants, while teachers will appreciate the entertaining demonstration of a math concept. The illustrations, which look like linocuts tinted with flat colors, have a distinctive style and a definite sense of humor." Booklist

Pinkney, Andrea Davis

Fishing day; illustrated by Shane W. Evans. Jump at the Sun/ Hyperion Books for Children 2003 unp il $15.99; lib bdg $16.49   **E**

1. Fishing—Fiction 2. Race relations—Fiction 3. African Americans—Fiction

ISBN 0-7868-0766-0; 0-7868-2614-2 (lib bdg)

LC 2002-29421

When Reenie and her mother, who are African Americans, go fishing, Reenie decides to share the secret of their success with their needy white neighbors.

"Evans takes Pinkney's words and transforms them into powerfully expressive images. Readers will easily identify with the emotions of the characters, and gain a sense of time and place." SLJ

Mim's Christmas jam; illustrated by Brian Pinkney. Harcourt 2001 unp il $16   **E**

1. African Americans—Fiction 2. Christmas—Fiction 3. Family life—Fiction 4. Subways—Fiction

ISBN 0-15-201918-9   LC 99-6346

"Gulliver books"

When Pap goes away to build the New York City subway in 1915, his family sends him Mother's special jam which works magic in returning him home to celebrate Christmas

"This heartwarming tale not only reveals some history about one of the country's greatest engineering marvels but also portrays the essence of Christmas spirit. Brian Pinkney's trademark scratchboard illustrations are a fitting nostalgic accompaniment." Booklist

Peggony-Po; a whale of a tale; by Andrea Davis Pinkney; illustrated by Brian Pinkney. 1st ed. Jump at the Sun/Hyperion Books for Children 2006 unp il $16.99   **E**

1. Whales—Fiction 2. Whaling—Fiction 3. African Americans—Fiction 4. Tall tales

ISBN 0-7868-1958-8   LC 2005047537

Peggony-Po, carved out of wood by his father, a one-legged whaler, determines to catch the huge whale that ate his father's leg.

"Told with humor and verve, this [is a] rollicking tall tale. . . . The illustrations brim with activity and energy." SLJ

Pinkney, Brian

Cosmo and the robot. Greenwillow Bks. 2000 unp il $15.95; lib bdg $15.89   **E**

1. Robots—Fiction 2. Mars (Planet)—Fiction 3. Science fiction

ISBN 0-688-15940-0; 0-688-15941-9 (lib bdg)

LC 98-32209

Cosmo, a boy living on Mars, must come up with a quick solution when his malfunctioning robot Rex threatens his sister Jewel

Pinkney's "art, created on scratchboard with dyes and acrylic paints, presents a barren planet in the slightly kitschy tradition of '50s science fiction. Even with the outlandish plot and extraterrestrial setting, the author/artist lets ordinary family dynamics shine brightly." Publ Wkly

Pinkney, Gloria Jean

Back home; pictures by Jerry Pinkney. Dial Bks. for Young Readers 1992 unp il $16.99; pa $6.99   **E**

1. Farm life—Fiction 2. North Carolina—Fiction 3. African Americans—Fiction

ISBN 0-8037-1168-9; 0-14-056547-7 (pa)

LC 91-22610

Eight-year-old Ernestine returns to visit relatives on the North Carolina farm where she was born

"Gloria Pinkney's text has a relaxed pace that is perfectly suited to the summer setting. Her characterizations are particularly well drawn, and her dialogue thoroughly convincing. In some of Jerry Pinkney's finest work, sunlight filters through his pencil and watercolor illustrations, imbuing them with a feathery soft glow." Publ Wkly

Pinkney, Jerry

The little match girl; [by] Hans Christian Andersen; adapted and illustrated by Jerry Pinkney. Phyllis Fogelman Bks. 1999 unp il $16.99   **E**

1. Andersen, Hans Christian, 1805-1875—Adaptations 2. Fairy tales

ISBN 0-8037-2314-8   LC 99-13814

The wares of the poor little match girl illuminate her cold world, bringing some beauty to her brief, tragic life

"A faithful retelling of a classic tale. . . . The story's haunting death imagery . . . may disturb the very young, but ultimately Pinkney's vision proves as transcendent as Andersen's." Publ Wkly

Rikki-tikki-tavi; by Rudyard Kipling; adapted and illustrated by Jerry Pinkney. Morrow Junior Bks. 1997 unp il $16.99; lib bdg $15.93   **E**

1. Kipling, Rudyard, 1865-1936—Adaptations 2. Mongooses—Fiction 3. Cobras—Fiction 4. India—Fiction

ISBN 0-688-14320-2; 0-688-14321-0 (lib bdg)

LC 96-51194

This is a retelling of the story from Rudyard Kipling's The jungle book in which a mongoose saves an English boy and his family from cobras in their garden in India

"Dramatic in content, sensitive in line, and rich with

Pinkney, Jerry—*Continued*

color, the illustrations in this picture book make full use of the broad, double-page spreads. Children who are not familiar with the story will be captivated; those who have had the story read to them before will find new things to shiver over." Booklist

The ugly duckling; [by] Hans Christian Andersen; adapted and illustrated by Jerry Pinkney. Morrow Junior Bks. 1999 unp il $16.99; lib bdg $17.89　　　　　　　　　　　E

1. Andersen, Hans Christian, 1805-1875—Adaptations 2. Swans—Fiction 3. Fairy tales

ISBN 0-688-15932-X; 0-688-15933-8 (lib bdg)

LC 98-23604

A Caldecott Medal honor book, 2000

An ugly duckling spends an unhappy year ostracized by the other animals before he grows into a beautiful swan

"This is an elegantly accessible retelling, with illustrations full of lively, emotive animals and the kind of vigorous movement that young children are bound to find appealing." Bull Cent Child Books

Pinkney, Sandra L.

A rainbow all around me; photographs by Myles C. Pinkney. Scholastic 2002 unp il $14.95

E

1. Color

ISBN 0-439-30928-X　　　　　　LC 2001-40017

"Cartwheel books"

"Each spread is devoted to a hue and features a child from a different ethnic group wearing, eating, or holding objects of a particular color. Myles Pinkney's amazingly crisp, clear photographs are pleasingly arranged across the pages. Sandra Pinkney's carefully chosen words are given extra punch through a thoughtful use of changing colored fonts." SLJ

Read and rise; photographs by Myles C. Pinkney; foreword by Maya Angelou. Scholastic 2006 unp il $15.99　　　　　　　　　　　E

1. Reading 2. African American children

ISBN 0-439-30929-8

"Cartwheel books"

Photographs and poetic text celebrate reading as a means of encouraging African American children to pursue their dreams

"Powerful verbs match the vivid portrayal of children succeeding." SLJ

Shades of black; a celebration of our children; photographs by Myles C. Pinkney. Scholastic 2000 unp il $14.95　　　　　　　　　　　E

1. African Americans

ISBN 0-439-14892-8　　　　　　LC 99-86593

"Cartwheel books"

Photographs and text celebrate the beauty and diversity of African American children

"Wonderful, clear, full-color photographs of youngsters illustrate a poetic, vivid text that describes a range of skin and eye colors and hair textures." SLJ

Piper, Watty

The little engine that could; retold by Watty Piper; illustrated by George & Doris Hauman. 60th anniversary edition. Platt & Munk Pubs. 1990 c1930 unp il $16.99; pa $7.99　　　　　　E

1. Railroads—Fiction

ISBN 0-448-40041-3; 0-448-40520-2 (pa)

LC 89-81287

Also available 2005 Philomel edition illustrated by Loren Long

First published 1930

"When a train carrying good things to children breaks down, the little blue engine proves his courage and determination. The rhythmic, repetitive text encourages children to help tell the story." Hodges. Books for Elem Sch Libr

Pitzer, Susanna

Not afraid of dogs; [by] Susanna Pitzer; illustrations by Larry Day. Walker 2006 unp il $16.95; lib bdg $17.85; lib bdg　　　　　　E

1. Fear—Fiction 2. Dogs—Fiction

ISBN 9780802780676; 9780802780683 (lib bdg); 0-8027-8068-7　　　　　　LC 2005027500

Young Daniel must confront his fear of dogs when his mom dog-sits his aunt's pet.

"Day's sensitive ink drawings, brightened with watercolor and gouache washes, create a series of large-scale, double-page scenes that clearly illustrate the emotions as well as the actions and attitudes of the characters." Booklist

Polacco, Patricia

Babushka's doll. Simon & Schuster Bks. for Young Readers 1990 unp il $16.95; pa $6.95

E

1. Dolls—Fiction

ISBN 0-671-68343-8; 0-689-80255-2 (pa)

LC 89-6122

"When Natasha wants something, she wants it now—not after her grandmother, Babushka, has finished her chores. Babushka gets tired of this attitude, and finally goes off to the market, leaving Natasha to play with a special doll that she keeps on a high shelf. The doll comes to life and subjects Natasha to the same sort of insistent whining that Natasha used on Babushka." SLJ

"Polacco's distinctive artwork interprets the story with style and verve. Using pencil, marker, and paint, she creates a series of varied compositions, highlighting muted shades with an occasional flare of bright colors and strong patterns. . . . A good, original story, illustrated with panache." Booklist

The bee tree. Philomel Bks. 1993 unp il $16.99; pa $6.99　　　　　　　　　　　E

1. Books and reading—Fiction 2. Bees—Fiction

ISBN 0-399-21965-X; 0-698-11696-8 (pa)

LC 92-8660

To teach his daughter the value of books, a father leads a growing crowd in search of the tree where the bees keep all their honey

"With a lively plot and a beautifully depicted backdrop of a rural Michigan community early in the twentieth century, this book delivers its lovely sentiment with originality and verve." Booklist

Polacco, Patricia—*Continued*

Chicken Sunday. Philomel Bks. 1992 unp il
$16.99; pa $6.99   E
1. Easter—Fiction 2. Friendship—Fiction 3. Jews—
Fiction 4. African Americans—Fiction
ISBN 0-399-22133-6; 0-698-11615-1 (pa)
LC 91-16030
Also available Spanish language edition
To thank old Eula for her wonderful Sunday chicken
dinners, her two grandsons and their friend, a girl who
has "adopted" her since her own "babushka" died, sell
decorated eggs and buy her a beautiful Easter hat
"Without being heavy-handed, Polacco's text conveys
a tremendous pride of heritage as it brims with rich images from her characters' African American and Russian
Jewish cultures. Her vibrant pencil-and-wash illustrations
glow—actual family photographs have been worked into
several spreads." Publ Wkly

G is for goat. Philomel Bks. 2003 unp il $16.99
E
1. Goats 2. Alphabet 3. Stories in rhyme
ISBN 0-399-24018-7   LC 2002-11551
A rhyming celebration of goats and their antics, from
A to Z
"The charming animals will energize any storytime.
. . . The pencil-and-watercolor illustrations against white
backgrounds steal the spotlight, with charming details."
SLJ

John Philip Duck. Philomel Books 2004 unp il
$16.99   E
1. Ducks—Fiction 2. Hotels and motels—Fiction
3. Memphis (Tenn.)—Fiction
ISBN 0-399-24262-7
During the Depression, a young Memphis boy trains
his pet duck to do tricks in the fountain of a grand hotel
and ends up becoming the Duck Master of the Peabody
Hotel
"This is Polacco at the height of her form in terms of
both text and illustration. The story moves smoothly
from start to finish and has a refreshing air of innocence.
The artwork is simply beautiful as the artist orchestrates
a harmonious symphony of color." SLJ

The keeping quilt. rev format ed. Simon &
Schuster Bks. for Young Readers 1998 unp il
$17.95   E
1. Quilts—Fiction 2. Jews—Fiction
ISBN 0-689-82090-9   LC 97-47690
A reissue of the title first published 1988
A homemade quilt ties together the lives of four generations of an immigrant Jewish family, remaining a
symbol of their enduring love and faith
"Jewish customs and the way they've shifted through
the years are portrayed unobtrusively in the story, which
is illustrated in sepia pencil, except for the quilt, which
sparks every page with its strong colors." Booklist

Mommies say shhh! . Philomel Books 2005 unp
il $16.99   E
1. Domestic animals—Fiction 2. Sound—Fiction
ISBN 0-399-24341-0   LC 2004-9459

Animals make many different noises, but when they
make too much noise their mommies quiet them down
"The text is standard animal-noise fare, but the inclusion of the silent bunnies is a clever twist. . . .
Polacco's highly recognizable pencil-and-watercolor illustrations are full of life, with much to discover in repeated
readings." SLJ

Mr. Lincoln's way. Philomel Bks. 2001 unp il
$16.99   E
1. Prejudices—Fiction 2. School stories
ISBN 0-399-23754-2   LC 00-66939
When Mr. Lincoln, "the coolest principal in the whole
world," discovers that Eugene, the school bully, knows
a lot about birds, he uses this interest to help Eugene
overcome his intolerance
"The book may be useful to schools in need of a
springboard for discussion of the topic and is graced with
impressive watercolors." SLJ

Mrs. Katz and Tush. Bantam Bks. 1992 unp il
pa $6.99 hardcover o.p.   E
1. Friendship—Fiction 2. Jews—Fiction 3. African
Americans—Fiction
ISBN 0-440-40936-5 (pa)   LC 91-18710
"A Bantam little rooster book"
A long-lasting friendship develops between Larnel, a
young African-American, and Mrs. Katz, a lonely, Jewish widow, when Larnel presents Mrs. Katz with a
scrawny kitten without a tail
"Polacco has used loving details in both words and art
work to craft a moving and heartfelt story of a friendship
that reaches across racial and generational differences."
Horn Book

Mrs. Mack. Philomel Bks. 1998 38p il $16.99
E
1. Horses—Fiction 2. Michigan—Fiction
ISBN 0-399-23167-6   LC 97-52946
The author remembers the summer when she was ten
years old and staying with her father in Michigan where
she took riding lessons and became best friends with a
perfect horse
"Polacco uses her characteristic pencil sketches filled
in with warm colors to depict her characters, who come
across with down-to-earth realism suffused with tenderness." Booklist

My rotten redheaded older brother. Simon &
Schuster Bks. for Young Readers 1994 unp il
$17.95; pa $6.99   E
1. Polacco, Patricia 2. Siblings—Fiction
ISBN 0-671-72751-6; 0-689-82036-4 (pa)
LC 93-13980
"Featuring an obnoxious, freckle-faced, bespectacled
boy and a comforting, tale-telling grandmother, this autobiographical story is as satisfying as a warm slice of apple pie. Patricia can't quite understand how anyone could
possibly like her older brother Richard. Whether picking
blackberries or eating raw rhubarb, he always manages to
outdo her, rubbing it in with one of his 'extra-rotten,
weasel-eyed, greeny-toothed grins.' When their Bubbie
teaches Patricia to wish on a falling star, she knows just
what to ask for." SLJ

Polacco, Patricia—*Continued*

Oh, look! Philomel Books 2004 unp il $16.99
E

1. Goats—Fiction
ISBN 0-399-24223-6
Three goats visit a fair but run home after they seem
to encounter a troll.
"In this colorful picture book, the . . . author transfers
the rhythms and movement of the traditional bear-hunt
chant to safer ground. . . . Polacco's signature pencil-
and-watercolor paintings cascade across the pages, creating festive scenes and bright hues." SLJ

Pink and Say. Philomel Bks. 1994 unp il $16.99
E

1. Friendship—Fiction 2. African American soldiers—
Fiction 3. United States—History—1861-1865, Civil
War—Fiction
ISBN 0-399-22671-0   LC 93-36340
Also available Spanish language edition
Say Curtis describes his meeting with Pinkus Aylee,
a black soldier, during the Civil War, and their capture
by Southern troops
"Polacco pulls out all the stops in this heart-wrenching
tale . . . which has been passed through several generations of the author's family. . . . Polacco's signature
line-and-watercolor paintings epitomize heroism, tenderness, and terror. . . . Unglamorized details of the conventions and atrocities of the Civil War target readers
well beyond customary picture book age." Horn Book

Rechenka's eggs; written and illustrated by
Patricia Polacco. Philomel Bks. 1988 unp il lib
bdg $16.99; pa $6.99   E
1. Geese—Fiction 2. Easter—Fiction 3. Eggs—Fiction
ISBN 0-399-21501-8 (lib bdg); 0-698-11385-3 (pa)
LC 87-16588
An injured goose rescued by Babushka, having broken
the painted eggs intended for the Easter Festival in
Moscva, lays thirteen marvelously colored eggs to replace them, then leaves behind one final miracle in egg
form before returning to her own kind
"Polacco achieves optimal dramatic contrast by using
bold shapes against uncluttered white space and by contrasting rich colors and design details with faces in black
and white." Bull Cent Child Books

Thank you, Mr. Falker. Philomel Bks. 1998 unp
il $16.99   E
1. Reading—Fiction 2. Teachers—Fiction 3. Learning
disabilities—Fiction
ISBN 0-399-23166-8   LC 97-18685
At first, Trisha loves school, but her difficulty learning
to read makes her feel dumb, until, in the fifth grade, a
new teacher helps her understand and overcome her
problem
"Young readers struggling with learning difficulties
will identify with Trisha's situation and find reassurance
in her success. Polacco's gouache-and-pencil compositions deftly capture the emotional stages—frustration,
pain, elation—of Trisha's journey." Publ Wkly

The trees of the dancing goats. Simon &
Schuster Bks. for Young Readers 1996 unp il $16;
pa $6.99   E
1. Hanukkah—Fiction 2. Christmas—Fiction
3. Jews—Fiction
ISBN 0-689-80862-3; 0-689-83857-3 (pa)
LC 95-26670
"On the family farm in Michigan, Trisha and Richard
watch as Babushka and Grampa prepare for Hanukkah in
their native Russian way. . . . When scarlet fever debili-
tates their neighbors, Trisha's whole family pitches in to
make and deliver holiday dinners and Christmas trees."
Publ Wkly

Welcome Comfort. Philomel Bks. 1999 unp il
$16.99   E
1. Santa Claus—Fiction 2. Christmas—Fiction
3. Foster home care—Fiction
ISBN 0-399-23169-2   LC 98-29558
Welcome Comfort, a lonely foster child, is assured by
his friend the school custodian that there is a Santa
Claus, but he does not discover the truth until one wondrous and surprising Christmas Eve
"This warm blend of fantasy and reality delivers a satisfying surprise ending. . . . Polacco's artwork is even
more vibrant than usual, and her Santa scenes are sure-
fire crowd-pleasers." Publ Wkly

Politi, Leo
Song of the swallows. Scribner 1987 c1949 unp
il music $17.95; pa $6.99   E
1. Swallows—Fiction 2. California—Fiction
3. Missions—Fiction
ISBN 0-684-18831-7; 0-689-71140-9 (pa)
Awarded the Caldecott Medal, 1950
A reissue of title first published 1949
"The swallows always appeared at the old Mission of
Capistrano on St. Joseph's Day and Juan who lived nearby wondered how they could tell that from all others.
This tender poetic story of the coming of springtime is
touched by the kindliness of the good Fathers of the
Mission as a little boy knew it. Lovely pictures in soft
colors bring out the charm of the southern California
landscape and the melody of the swallow song adds to
the feeling of Spring." Horn Book

Pomerantz, Charlotte
The chalk doll; pictures by Frané Lessac.
Lippincott 1989 30p il pa $6.99 hardcover o.p.
E
1. Dolls—Fiction 2. Mother-daughter relationship—
Fiction 3. Jamaica—Fiction
ISBN 0-06-443333-1 (pa)   LC 88-872
"Rose has a cold and must stay in bed. Before she
settles in for a nap, she coaxes her mother to tell stories
of her Jamaican childhood. The scene shifts from Rose's
colorful room filled with toys to a simple little house in
the village where her mother grew up. The stories are
touching for the contrast between the poverty and yearning of these childhood memories and the obvious comfort of their present lives." Horn Book
"The stylized illustrations by the West Indian artists
Frané Lessac are primitive in bright, oscillating colors,
evoking poverty in a tropical paradise as well as mother-

Pomerantz, Charlotte—*Continued*
daughter affection in a well-appointed home." N Y
Times Book Rev

Pomeroy, Diana
One potato; a counting book of potato prints.
Harcourt Brace & Co. 1996 unp il pa $6
hardcover o.p.   E

1. Counting 2. Prints
ISBN 0-15-200330-5 (pa)   LC 95-10986
A counting book which uses images of fruits and vegetables to illustrate numbers from one to one hundred
and which also includes an explanation of how to do potato printing
"The counting is clear and progressively more challenging, and the botanical prints, made with potatoes, are
luscious and lovely." Booklist

Wildflower ABC; an alphabet of potato prints.
Harcourt Brace & Co. 1997 unp il $16; pa $6
                                                       E

1. Wild flowers 2. Alphabet
ISBN 0-15-201041-6; 0-15-202455-7 (pa)
                                    LC 96-19748
This is a "picture book illustrating wildflowers from
A to Z. Each bordered page features one plant; intricate
potato cuts are printed on cloth. . . . Two pages of appended notes in small type offer a few lines of information about each plant, including its scientific name, common names, plant family, myths, legends, and lore."
Booklist
The fine detail that Pomeroy "includes, her exceptional blends and shadings of color, and the rainbow palette
of the borders result in a stunning presentation." SLJ

Poole, Amy Lowry
The pea blossom; retold and illustrated by Amy
Poole. Holiday House 2005 unp il $16.95
                                                       E

1. Andersen, Hans Christian, 1805-1875—Adaptations
2. Fairy tales 3. China—Fiction
ISBN 0-8234-1864-2   LC 2003-67544
Based on the Hans Christian Andersen story: Five
peas in a pod
In a garden near Beijing, five peas in a shell grow and
wait to discover what fate has in store for them.
"Choosing to set her version in Beijing, China, Poole
illustrates her simple, elegant prose with watercolors on
rice paper that are clearly reminiscent of Chinese paintings." Booklist

Porte, Barbara Ann
Harry's birthday; story by Barbara Ann Porte;
pictures by Yossi Abolafia. HarperCollins Pubs.
2003 c1994 47p il $15.99; lib bdg $16.89; pa
$3.99   E

1. Birthdays—Fiction
ISBN 0-06-050355-6; 0-06-050356-4 (lib bdg);
0-06-050357-2 (pa)
"An I can read book"
A reissue of the title first published 1994 by
Greenwillow Bks.

Harry, who is hoping to get a cowboy hat for his
birthday, is quite surprised when he opens all the pres-
ents at his party
"Abolafia's pen-and-watercolor illustrations enhance
and extend to easy-to-read text." SLJ
Other titles about Harry are:
Harry gets an uncle (1991)
Harry in trouble (1989)
Harry's dog (1984)
Harry's mom (1985)
Harry's pony (1997)
Harry's visit (1983)

Potter, Beatrix
The story of Miss Moppet. Warne il $6.99
                                                       E

1. Cats—Fiction 2. Mice—Fiction
ISBN 0-7232-4790-0
First published 1906
Miss Moppet is a kitten who uses her wiles to capture
a curious mouse. But her trickery amounts to naught
when she herself is outwitted
Other titles about Moppet's brother Tom and sister Mit-
tens are:
The complete adventures of Tom Kitten and his friends
(1984)
The roly-poly pudding (1908)
The tale of Tom Kitten (1935)

The tailor of Gloucester. Warne il $6.99
                                                       E

1. Tailoring—Fiction 2. Mice—Fiction 3. Christmas—
Fiction
ISBN 0-7232-4772-2
First published in 1903
"The cat Simpkin looked after his master when he
was ill, but it was the nimble-fingered mice who used
snippets of cherry-coloured twist and so finished the embroidered waist coat for the worried tailor. A Christmastime story set in old Gloucester." Four to Fourteen
"A read-aloud classic in polished style, perfectly complemented by the author's exquisite watercolor illustrations." Hodges. Books for Elem Sch Libr

The tale of Jemima Puddle-duck. Warne il $6.99
                                                       E

1. Ducks—Fiction
ISBN 0-7232-4778-1
Also available French language and Spanish language
editions
First published 1908
"Jemima Puddle-duck's obstinate determination to
hatch her own eggs, makes a story of suspense and sly
humor." Toronto Public Libr. Books for Boys & Girls

The tale of Mr. Jeremy Fisher. Warne il $6.99
                                                       E

1. Frogs—Fiction
ISBN 0-7232-4776-5
First published 1906
A frog fishing from his lilly pad boat doesn't catch
any fish, but one catches him

Potter, Beatrix—*Continued*

The tale of Mrs. Tiggy-Winkle. Warne il $6.99

E

1. Hedgehogs—Fiction
ISBN 0-7232-4775-7
First published 1905

Lucie visits the laundry of Mrs. Tiggy-Winkle, a hedgehog, and finds her lost handerchiefs

The tale of Mrs. Tittlemouse. Warne il $6.99; pa $2.25

E

1. Mice—Fiction
ISBN 0-7232-3470-1; 0-7232-3495-7 (pa)
First published 1910

The story of a little mouse's funny house, the visitors she has there, and how she finally rids herself of the untidy, messy ones

The tale of Peter Rabbit. Warne il $6.99

E

1. Rabbits—Fiction
ISBN 0-7232-4770-6

Also available French language and Spanish language editions

First published 1903

All about the famous rabbit family consisting of Flopsy, Mopsy, Cotton-tail and especially Peter Rabbit who disobeys Mother Rabbit's admonishment not to go into Mr. McGregor's garden

"Distinctive writing and a strong appeal to a small child's sense of justice and his sympathies make this an outstanding story. The water color illustrations add charm to the narrative by their simplicity of detail and delicacy of color." Child Books Too Good to Miss

Other titles about Peter Rabbit and his family are:
The tale of Benjamin Bunny (1904)
The tale of Mr. Tod (1912)
The tale of the flopsy bunnies (1909)

The tale of Pigling Bland. Warne il $6.99

E

1. Pigs—Fiction
ISBN 0-7232-4784-6
First published 1913

"Pigling's story ends happily with a perfectly lovely little black Berkshire pig called Pigwig." Toronto Public Libr. Books for Boys & Girls

The tale of Squirrel Nutkin. Warne il $6.99

E

1. Squirrels—Fiction
ISBN 0-7232-4771-4
First published 1903

Each day the squirrels gather nuts, Nutkin propounds a riddle to Mr. Brown, the owl, until impertinent Nutkin, over-estimating Mr. Brown's patience, gets his due

The tale of Timmy Tiptoes. Warne il $6.99

E

1. Squirrels—Fiction
ISBN 0-7232-4781-1
First published 1911

An innocent squirrel accused of stealing nuts is forced down a hole in a tree, where he meets a friendly chipmunk

The tale of two bad mice. Warne il $6.99

E

1. Mice—Fiction
ISBN 0-7232-4774-9
First published 1904

"Two mischievous little mice pilfer a doll's house to equip their own. They are caught and finally make amends for what they have done. Perfectly charming illustrations and a most enticing tale." Adventuring With Books. 2d edition

Potter, Giselle

Chloe's birthday . . . and me. Atheneum Books for Young Readers 2004 unp il $15.95

E

1. Sisters—Fiction 2. Birthdays—Fiction 3. France—Fiction
ISBN 0-689-86230-X   LC 2002-38524
"An Anne Schwartz book"

When attention must be paid to her little sister Chloe's birthday, Giselle, who lives with her family in France, makes inappropriate gift suggestions and almost spoils the big day.

"The naive artwork, executed in pencil, ink, gouache, gesso, and watercolor, is colorful and interesting. . . . This [is a] refreshingly candid picture of a sibling relationship." SLJ

The year I didn't go to school. Atheneum Bks. for Young Readers 2002 unp il $16.95

E

1. Puppets and puppet plays 2. Italy—Social life and customs
ISBN 0-689-84730-0   LC 2001-46125
"An Anne Schwartz book"

Relates the experiences of children's author Giselle Potter who, at the age of seven, she toured Italy with her family's tiny theater company, The Mystic Paper Beasts

"The title is certain to pique children's curiosity, and the quirky autobiographical story will quickly pull them in. . . . Potter's pencil, ink gouache, and watercolor scenes capture classic details of Italian culture. . . . A madcap journey from a gifted storyteller." SLJ

Pow, Tom

Tell me one thing, Dad; illustrated by Ian Andrew. 1st U.S. ed. Candlewick Press 2004 unp il $15.99

E

1. Father-daughter relationship—Fiction 2. Bedtime—Fiction
ISBN 0-7636-2474-8   LC 2003-65272

Molly and her father play a bedtime game that shows how much they love each other

"The sharp yet simple text avoids the obvious, going for interesting images. . . . The watercolor-and-ink artwork . . . brims with whimsy in both design and execution." Booklist

Poydar, Nancy

The biggest test in the universe. Holiday House 2005 unp il $16.95 **E**

1. School stories 2. Examinations—Fiction

ISBN 0-8234-1944-4

Sam and his classmates dread Friday, the day they are to take the infamous Big Test.

"Enlivened by colorful and humorous illustrations depicting the students' worries, this book is fun and cheerful, as well as unique in its subject." SLJ

Priceman, Marjorie

Emeline at the circus. Knopf 1999 unp il $15; lib bdg $16.99 **E**

1. Circus—Fiction 2. Teachers—Fiction

ISBN 0-679-87685-5; 0-679-97685-X (lib bdg)

LC 98-28873

While her teacher Miss Splinter is lecturing her second-grade class about the exotic animals, clowns, and other performers they are watching at the circus, Emeline accidentally becomes part of the show

"Priceman captures the show's frenzied grace in freely painted forms that dance and swirl in a richly saturated palette." Horn Book Guide

Hot air; the (mostly) true story of the first hot-air balloon ride; [by] Marjorie Priceman. 1st ed. Atheneum Books for Young Readers 2005 unp il $16.95 **E**

1. Balloons

ISBN 0-689-82642-7

LC 2004-14743

A Caldecott Medal honor book, 2006

"An Anne Schwartz book"

"Combining fact and fancy, Priceman tells the story of the successful 1783 liftoff of a hot-air balloon, invented by the Montgolfier brothers, a flight made even more special because of its passengers: a duck, a sheep, and a rooster." Booklist

"With vibrant colors and varied use of panels, full-page illustrations, and spreads, Priceman paces the tale perfectly." SLJ

How to make an apple pie and see the world. Knopf 1994 unp il $16; pa $6.99 **E**

1. Baking—Fiction 2. Voyages and travels—Fiction

ISBN 0-679-83705-1; 0-679-88083-6 (pa)

LC 93-12341

Since the market is closed, the reader is led around the world to gather the ingredients for making an apple pie

"The perfect blend of whimsical illustrations and tongue-in-cheek humor makes this an irresistable offering. The recipe is included." Child Book Rev Serv

Prigger, Mary Skillings

Aunt Minnie McGranahan; illustrated by Betsy Lewin. Clarion Bks. 1999 31p il $15 **E**

1. Aunts—Fiction 2. Orphans—Fiction

ISBN 0-395-82270-X

LC 98-33501

The townspeople in St. Clere, Kansas, are sure it will never work out when the neat and orderly spinster, Minnie McGranahan, takes her nine orphaned nieces and nephews into her home in 1920

"In a dexterous style, Prigger employs repetitive elements to establish and maintain a spry tempo in clipped, spruce sentences. . . . The black outlines of Lewin's . . . witty, loose watercolors punctuate the pages in a flurry of scribbles, suggesting the kind of bursting-at-the-seams activity." Publ Wkly

Another title about Aunt Minnie is:

Aunt Minnie and the twister (2002)

Prince, April Jones

Twenty-one elephants and still standing; written by April Jones Prince; illustrated by Francois Roca. Houghton Mifflin 2005 unp il $16

E

1. Barnum, P. T. (Phineas Taylor), 1810-1891—Fiction 2. Brooklyn Bridge (New York, N.Y.)—Fiction 3. Elephants—Fiction

ISBN 0-618-44887-X

LC 2004-05229

Upon completion of the Brooklyn Bridge, P.T. Barnum and his twenty-one elephants parade across to prove to everyone that the bridge is safe.

A "well-researched, handsomely illustrated picture book. . . . The sparse, yet powerful text contains both alliteration and occasional rhyme, making it a pleasure for readers and listeners alike. Roca's masterful paintings capture both the spirit of the times and of the expansive bridge." SLJ

Prokofiev, Sergey

Peter and the wolf; translated by Maria Carlson; illustrated by Charles Mikolaycak. Viking 1982 unp il pa $5.99 hardcover o.p. **E**

1. Wolves—Fiction 2. Fairy tales

ISBN 0-14-050633-0 (pa)

LC 81-70402

This book retells the orchestral fairy tale of the boy who, ignoring his grandfather's warnings, proceeds to capture a wolf

"Prokofiev's classic, designed to teach children the instruments of an orchestra, has been published in picture book form before, but never better illustrated. The translation is smooth. . . . The paintings are rich in color, dramatic in details of costume or architecture, strong in composition, with distinctive individuality in the faces of people and of the wolf." Bull Cent Child Books

Prosek, James

A good day's fishing. Simon & Schuster Bks. for Young Readers 2004 unp il $15.95 **E**

1. Fishing—Fiction

ISBN 0-689-85327-0

LC 2003-7383

A child searches through the hooks, lures, bobbers, and other paraphernalia in his tacklebox for the one thing he needs to ensure a good day's fishing. Includes a detailed glossary

"A beautifully illustrated, simple story. . . . Young fishing enthusiasts will certainly learn more about which tackle works best to catch particular kinds of fish, while the wonderfully detailed, gentle watercolor illustrations of fish and gear offer a lovely introduction." Booklist

Provensen, Alice

A day in the life of Murphy. Simon & Schuster Bks. for Young Readers 2003 unp il $16.95

E

1. Dogs—Fiction 2. Farm life—Fiction
ISBN 0-689-84884-6   LC 2002-4309

Murphy, a farm terrier, describes a day in his life as he gets fed in the kitchen, hunts mice, goes to the vet, returns to the house for dinner, investigates a noise outside, and retires to the barn for sleep

"With charming, lively illustrations and peppy, descriptive prose, Provensen portrays the smells, sounds, and activities of a delightful, active pup." Booklist

Klondike gold. Simon & Schuster Books for Young Readers 2005 unp il $17.95   E
1. Howell, Bill—Fiction 2. Klondike River Valley (Yukon)—Gold discoveries—Fiction
ISBN 0-689-84885-8   LC 2004-28405

A fictionalized account of Bill Howell, a young prospector who braved the arduous journey from Boston to the Yukon Territory in search of gold in the Klondike River valley.

"In this rich historical nugget, art and text convey the danger, thrill, exhilaration and heartbreak experienced by these persevering prospectors." Publ Wkly

Pulver, Robin

Punctuation takes a vacation; illustrated by Lynn Rowe Reed. Holiday House 2003 unp il $16.95

E

1. Punctuation—Fiction 2. School stories
ISBN 0-8234-1687-9   LC 2002-68915

When all the punctuation marks in Mr. Wright's class decide to take a vacation, the students discover just how difficult life can be without them

"Pulver's clever story moves along at a nice clip and makes its point without belaboring the matter. Reed's acrylics-on-canvas illustrations are rich in color and texture, and add to the amusement of the story." SLJ

Purmell, Ann

Apple cider making days; illustrated by Joanne Friar. Millbrook Press 2002 unp il lib bdg $21.90

E

1. Apples—Fiction
ISBN 0-7613-2364-3   LC 2001-44920

Alex and Abigail join the whole family in processing and selling apples and apple cider at their grandfather's farm

"The comfortable, colorful art brings little ones up close to the process and gives them a good look at the conveyor belts and presses and other machinery involved. . . . A double-page spread, 'Cider Lore,' following the story, provides wonderful tidbits about the cider-making process. An excellent resource for autumn units or to use in preparation for a trip to the orchard." Booklist

Radunsky, Vladimir

The mighty asparagus. Silver Whistle/Harcourt 2004 unp il $16   E
1. Asparagus—Fiction 2. Italy—Fiction
ISBN 0-15-216743-9   LC 2003-12241

In Renaissance Italy, a large asparagus appears suddenly in the king's back yard, and he enlists the help of several people and animals, including a songbird, in order to get rid of it

"The lowbrow humor, the blind silliness, and the quirky exaggerations are childishness itself. For older children there is the appeal of random sarcasm and funky, distorted illustrations." SLJ

One; a nice story about an awful braggart. Viking 2003 unp il $16.99   E
1. Armadillos—Fiction
ISBN 0-670-03564-5   LC 2003-5790
Companion volume to Ten (2002)

When Six, a pink armadillo with nine green siblings, brags that he is "#1" in everything, his family expresses a different opinion

"The humor of Radunsky's text is enhanced by his whimsical, slightly surreal illustrations that turn these nocturnal mammals into amusing, endearing friends." Booklist

What does peace feel like? by V. Radunsky and children just like you from around the world. Atheneum Books for Young Readers 2004 unp il $14.95   E
1. Peace
ISBN 0-689-86676-3   LC 2003-11506
"An Anne Schwartz book"

Simple text and illustrations portray what peace looks, sounds, tastes, feels, and smells like to children around the world.

"As much a celebration of the five senses as an antiwar message, this bright picture book combines Radunsky's playful gouache double-page scenarios with quotes from grade-schoolers at an international school in Rome." Booklist

Rael, Elsa Okon

Rivka's first Thanksgiving; written by Elsa Okon Rael; illustrated by Maryann Kovalski. Margaret K. McElderry Bks. 2001 unp il $16

E

1. Thanksgiving Day—Fiction 2. Jews—Fiction
3. Immigrants—Fiction
ISBN 0-689-83901-4   LC 00-58738

Having heard about Thanksgiving in school, nine-year-old Rivka tries to convince her immigrant family and her rabbi that it is a holiday for all Americans, Jews and non-Jews alike

This offers "attractive milky sepia-tone acrylic and colored pencil illustrations. . . . The bustling backdrops and subdued interior tones add depth. Kids will be heartened by the reconciliation of the different traditions." Bull Cent Child Books

Ramirez, Antonio

Napi; story by Antonio Ramirez; pictures by Domi. Groundwood Books 2004 unp il $15.95

E

1. Native Americans—Mexico—Fiction 2. Herons—Fiction 3. Dreams—Fiction
ISBN 0-88899-610-1
Also available Spanish language edition

Ramirez, Antonio—*Continued*

Napi is a Mazatec Indian girl who loves to dream. One day, she dreams of becoming a heron and flying over the river.

"The clear, lyrical prose has a childlike charm that brilliantly recreates the joys of this child's experience. . . . Domi's primitive acrylic artwork enhances the sense of the story." SLJ

Rand, Gloria

Mary was a little lamb; illustrated by Ted Rand. 1st ed. H. Holt 2004 unp il $16.95   E

1. Sheep—Fiction

ISBN 0-8050-6816-3   LC 2003-7066

"Mary is a newborn lamb abandoned by her mother on a deserted farm on Cranberry Island. Mrs. Paradise adopts her, and the islanders quickly become fond of the animal—until she becomes a nuisance. . . . Mrs. Paradise finds the perfect solution: Mary is given to the mainland petting zoo. . . . Based on a true story, the text provides just enough detail to capture readers' interest, and the richly colored illustrations are expressive." SLJ

Rappaport, Doreen

Dirt on their skirts; the story of the young women who won the world championship; [by] Doreen Rappaport, Lyndall Callan; pictures by E.B. Lewis. Dial Bks. for Young Readers 1999 unp il $16.99   E

1. All-American Girls Professional Baseball League—Fiction 2. Baseball—Fiction

ISBN 0-8037-2042-4   LC 98-47080

Margaret experiences the excitement of watching the 1946 championship game of the All-American Girls Professional Baseball League as it goes into extra innings.

"With its economy of language and telling period details, this book provides an exciting slice of sports history and an appealing bit of Americana. . . . Lewis's finely wrought watercolor paintings deftly capture the crowd and the action on the field." SLJ

The secret seder; illustrated by Emily Arnold McCully. 1st ed. Hyperion Books For Children 2005 unp il $16.99 (2-4)   E

1. Holocaust, 1933-1945—Fiction 2. Jews—Fiction 3. France—Fiction 4. Passover—Fiction

ISBN 0-7868-077-6   LC 2003-57115

During the Nazi occupation of France, a boy and his father slip out of their village and into the mountains, where they join a group of fellow Jews at a humble seder table

"Rappaport interweaves themes and descriptive text to create a meaningful story in a distinctive setting. An excellent discussion starter." SLJ

Raschka, Christopher

Five for a little one; [by] Chris Raschka. 1st ed. Atheneum Books for Young Readers 2006 unp il $16.95   E

1. Senses and sensation—Fiction 2. Rabbits—Fiction 3. Counting 4. Stories in rhyme

ISBN 0-689-84599-5; 9780689845994

LC 2005-08963

"A Richard Jackson book"

"A buoyant bunny, drawn in thick ink outline with a fuzzy body and delightfully mismatched ears (one downy and one plain), introduces readers to the senses, numbering them one through five. The rhyming verses and ebullient artwork convey a child's curiosity and enthusiasm for investigating the world in various ways." SLJ

John Coltrane's Giant steps; remixed by Chris Raschka. Atheneum Bks. for Young Readers 2002 33p il $17   E

1. Jazz music

ISBN 0-689-84598-7   LC 2001-33755

"A Richard Jackson book"

John Coltrane's musical composition is performed by a box, a snowflake, some raindrops, and a kitten

"Like Coltrane, Raschka is creating something deeply personal here that we don't need to understand fully to appreciate. Instead, he asks us to trust our own understanding of raindrops, snowflakes, kittens, and music to experience the book. Anyone who's still intimidated by jazz after giving this book a chance is probably just trying too hard." Horn Book

Like likes like; [by] Chris Raschka. DK Pub. 1998 unp il $15.95   E

1. Cats—Fiction

ISBN 0-7894-2564-5   LC 98-3659

"A Richard Jackson book"

Two cats fall in love in a rose garden

"Raschka's text has a distinct rhythm that will carry readers along, and the energy of his pastel and watercolor illustrations is nearly palpable." Bull Cent Child Books

Mysterious Thelonious; [by] Chris Raschka. Orchard Bks. 1997 unp il $13.95; lib bdg $14.99   E

1. Monk, Thelonious, 1917-1982 2. Jazz musicians

ISBN 0-531-30057-9; 0-531-33057-5 (lib bdg)

LC 97-6994

Raschka "has created an unusual portrait of Thelonious Monk and 'Misterioso.' By matching the tones of the color wheel to the chromatic musical scale and then translating the notes of the piece into colors, Raschka captures its whimsical, lyrical and startling contours. . . . Raschka's truly remarkable watercolors capture with intense poignancy Monk's idiosyncratic postures." N Y Times Book Rev

New York is English, Chattanooga is Creek; by Chris Raschka. 1st ed. Atheneum Books for Young Readers 2005 unp il $16.95   E

1. Cities and towns—Fiction 2. Geographic names—Fiction

ISBN 0-689-84600-2   LC 2004-23188

"A Richard Jackson book"

New York City, though a bit boastful, decides to throw a party to make new friends of other unique cities like Chattanooga and Minneapolis

"This is both a fascinating exploration of the etymology and derivation of American city names and a characteristic Raschka farcical flight-of-fancy. . . . Raschka's illustrations rendered in ink and watercolor employ his loose, impressionistic, brushy style to perfect effect, giving the book its humor while artfully delivering his message and entertaining information." SLJ

Raschka, Christopher—*Continued*

Yo! Yes? by Chris Raschka. Orchard Bks. 1993
unp il $15.95; lib bdg $16.99; pa $6.95
                                                    E
1. Friendship—Fiction 2. Race relations—Fiction
3. African Americans—Fiction
ISBN 0-531-05469-1; 0-531-08619-4 (lib bdg);
0-531-07108-1 (pa)   LC 92-25644
A Caldecott Medal honor book, 1994
"A Richard Jackson book"
Two lonely characters, one black and one white, meet
on the street and become friends
"The design and drawing are bold, spare and expressive; the language has the strength and rhythm of a play-
ground chant." Bull Cent Child Books
Another title about these characters is:
Ring! Yo? (2000)

Rathmann, Peggy

10 minutes till bedtime. Putnam 1998 unp il
$16.99   E
1. Hamsters—Fiction 2. Bedtime—Fiction
ISBN 0-399-23103-X   LC 97-51295
A boy's hamster leads an increasingly large group of
hamsters on a tour of the boy's house, while his father
counts down the minutes to bedtime
"Children will pore over the comical details and follow closely the antics of the numbered hamsters, each
one with a personality of its own." SLJ

The day the babies crawled away. Putnam 2003
unp il $16.99   E
1. Infants—Fiction 2. Stories in rhyme
ISBN 0-399-23196-X   LC 2002-152002
A boy follows fives babies who crawl away from a
picnic and saves the day by bringing them back
This is a "rollicking rhyming tale, illustrated in nee-
dle-sharp, atmospheric silhouettes against twilight skies."
Publ Wkly

Good night, Gorilla. Putnam 1994 unp il $14.99;
pa $5.99   E
1. Zoos—Fiction 2. Animals—Fiction
ISBN 0-399-22445-9; 0-698-11649-6 (pa)
                                     LC 92-29020
Also available Board book edition
An unobservant zookeeper is followed home by all the
animals he thinks he has left behind in the zoo
"In a book economical in text and simple in illustration, the many amusing, small details, as well as the
tranquil tone of the story, make this an outstanding picture book." Horn Book Guide

Officer Buckle and Gloria. Putnam 1995 unp il
$16.99   E
1. School stories 2. Dogs—Fiction 3. Safety education—Fiction
ISBN 0-399-22616-8   LC 93-43887
Awarded the Caldecott Medal, 1996
"When rotund, good-natured officer Buckle visits
school assemblies to read off his sensible safety tips, the
children listen, bored and polite, dozing off one by one.
But when the new police dog, Gloria, stands behind him,

secretly miming the dire consequences of acting impru-
dently, the children suddenly become attentive, laughing
uproariously and applauding loudly. . . . The deadpan
humor of the text and slapstick wit of the illustrations
make a terrific combination. Large, expressive line drawings illustrate the characters with finesse, and the Kool-
Aid-bright washes add energy and pizzazz." Booklist

Rattigan, Jama Kim

Dumpling soup; illustrated by Lillian
Hsu-Flanders. Little, Brown 1993 unp il pa $6.99
hardcover o.p.   E
1. Family life—Fiction 2. New Year—Fiction
3. Hawaii—Fiction
ISBN 0-316-73047-5 (pa); 0-316-73445-4 (hc)
                                     LC 91-42949
"Marisa, a seven-year-old Asian-American girl who
lives in Hawaii, explains the traditions that exist in her
family to celebrate the New Year. Her family . . . consists of people who are Japanese, Chinese, Korean, Hawaiian, and *haole* (Hawaiian for white person). . . . A
glossary of English, Hawaiian, Japanese, and Korean
words provides pronunciations and definitions for many
of the possibly unfamiliar terms that weave in and out of
the text. A thoroughly enjoyable celebration of family
warmth and diverse traditions, illustrated with cheery watercolors." Horn Book

Rau, Dana Meachen

A star in my orange. Millbrook Press 2002 unp
il lib bdg $22.90   E
1. Shape
ISBN 0-7613-2414-3   LC 2001-32696
Photographs and simple text explain how various
shapes and patterns can be found all around in nature
"The concepts are a little less obvious than the commonly discussed shapes, but they are perfectly clear
within the colorful, well-focused photos of scenes in nature. . . . A very simple yet well-designed and effective
book." Booklist

Raven, Margot

Circle unbroken; the story of a basket and its
people; [by] Margot Theis Raven; pictures by E.B.
Lewis. Farrar, Straus and Giroux 2004 unp il lib
bdg $16   E
1. Baskets—Fiction 2. African Americans—Fiction
3. Gullahs—Fiction
ISBN 0-374-31289-3   LC 2002-24009
"Melanie Kroupa books"
A grandmother tells the tale of Gullahs and their
beautiful sweetgrass baskets that keep their African heritage alive.
"Raven's text masterfully frames several hundred
years of African-American history within the picture-
book format. Lewis's double-page, watercolor images are
poignant and perfectly matched to the text and mood."
SLJ

Ravishankar, Anushka

Tiger on a tree; [by] Anushka Ravishankar, Pulak Biswas. 1st American ed. Farrar, Straus and Giroux 2004 unp il $15   E

1. Tigers—Fiction 2. Stories in rhyme

ISBN 0-374-37555-0   LC 2003-49050

First published 1997 in India

After trapping a tiger in a tree, a group of men must decide what to do with it.

"This very simple chanting story is perfect for reading aloud with young preschoolers. . . . The thickly stroked illustrations, mostly black and white, have occasional splashes of orange." Booklist

Ray, Mary Lyn

All aboard! illustrated by Amiko Hirao. Little, Brown 2002 unp il $14.95   E

1. Railroads—Fiction

ISBN 0-316-73507-8   LC 00-51464

"Riding by herself on an overnight train to meet her grandparents, the girl finds comfort in imagining that her stuffed rabbit, Mr. Barnes, is a human-sized, confident rider of the rails, and that all the other passengers are animals." Publ Wkly

"This clever melding of real and imagined perfectly mimics the sensibilities and perceptions of young children. The sound words, repeated often throughout the text, as well as the swirling, curving lines of the cut-paper and colored-pencil illustrations, blend together well." SLJ

Basket moon; illustrated by Barbara Cooney. Little, Brown 1999 unp il $15.95   E

1. Basket making—Fiction 2. Father-son relationship—Fiction 3. Mountain life—Fiction 4. New York (State)—Fiction

ISBN 0-316-73521-3   LC 96-49013

After hearing some men call his father and him hillbillies on his first trip into the nearby town of Hudson, a young boy is not so sure he still wants to become a basket maker.

"The story is told by the boy in lyrical prose, and is graced by Cooney's soft-hued oil-and-acrylic paintings." SLJ

Red rubber boot day; illustrated by Lauren Stringer. Harcourt 2000 unp il $16   E

1. Rain—Fiction

ISBN 0-15-213756-4   LC 97-25676

A child describes all the things there are to do on a rainy day.

"The short text and appealing subject make this picture book accessible to young children. Stringer's acrylic paintings are as vivid as the text." Booklist

Recorvits, Helen

My name is Yoon; pictures by Gabi Swiatkowska. Frances Foster Bks. 2002 unp il $16   E

1. Korean Americans—Fiction 2. Immigrants—Fiction

ISBN 0-374-35114-7   LC 00-51395

Disliking her name as written in English, Korean-born Yoon, or "shining wisdom," refers to herself as "cat,"

"bird," and "cupcake," as a way to feel more comfortable in her new school and new country

"Swiatkowska's stunningly spare, almost surrealistic paintings enhance the story's message. . . . A powerful and inspiring picture book." SLJ

Another title about Yoon is:

Yoon and the Christmas mitten (2006)

Reid, Barbara

The Subway mouse. Scholastic Press 2005 c2003 unp il $15.95   E

1. Mice—Fiction 2. Subways—Fiction

ISBN 0-439-72827-4

First published 2003 in Canada

Remembering childhood stories of a beautiful but dangerous place called Tunnel's End, a mouse named Nib leaves his dirty, crowded home under a busy subway station and sets out on a long journey, joined by Lola, a mouse he meets along the way.

"Reid creates a charming, lively adventure in short, smoothly paced sentences, but it's her marvelous collage illustrations that really bring the characters and richly imagined world to life. Working in found materials and expertly molded, brightly colored plasticine, she sculpts remarkably expressive characters and a vivid, subterranean world." Booklist

Reiser, Lynn

Cherry pies and lullabies. Greenwillow Bks. 1998 39p il music $17.99   E

1. Mother-daughter relationship—Fiction 2. Grandmothers—Fiction

ISBN 0-688-13391-6   LC 95-2259

Companion volume to Tortillas and lullabies

This book "describes how traditions of baking, flower-wreathing, quilting, and lullaby singing are passed down from mother to daughter in one family." Horn Book Guide

"The well-executed watercolor-and-ink illustrations convey how the traditions alter through the years. . . . An ingenious family tree at the back of the book helps make the concept of generations enjoyable and clear." Booklist

Hardworking puppies. Harcourt 2006 unp il $16   E

1. Dogs—Fiction 2. Subtraction

ISBN 0-15-205404-9   LC 2004-21505

One by one, ten energetic puppies find important jobs as dogs who help people in different ways, including by pulling sleds and saving swimmers.

"Reiser's crisp, uncluttered, artful illustrations are the result of Sharpie markers, Wite-Out, watercolors, scissors, and other materials. A worthwhile purchase for storytime and as an introduction to subtraction." SLJ

The lost ball: la pelota perdida; translated by M.J. Infante. Greenwillow Bks. 2002 unp il $15.99; lib bdg $17.89   E

1. Lost and found possessions—Fiction 2. Bilingual books—English-Spanish

ISBN 0-06-029763-8; 0-06-029764-6 (lib bdg)

LC 2001-33272

Reiser, Lynn—*Continued*

English-speaking Richard and Spanish-speaking Ricardo and their dogs walk through the park, each looking for his lost ball

"The entire cleverly constructed concept hinges on charming, detailed pen-and-ink illustrations. English text is in orange on the verso of each spread. The Spanish text, in a sound translation, is on the recto in green. . . . Clever and eye-catching, the brief, repetitious text and slight tension of the hunt help readers assimilate the linguistic instruction painlessly." SLJ

Ten puppies. Greenwillow Bks. 2003 unp il $15.99; lib bdg $16.89   E
1. Dogs—Fiction 2. Addition 3. Counting
ISBN 0-06-008644-0; 0-06-008645-9 (lib bdg)
    LC 2002-23544

Puppies from one to ten are counted and sorted according to their different features

"In Reiser's skillfully informal watercolor art, the rambunctious pups occasionally breach the boxed frames that cage them. The pups' clearly differentiated characteristics offer all kinds of opportunities for observation and the exercise of logic." Horn Book

Tortillas and lullabies. Tortillas y cancioncitas; pictures by "Corazones Valientes;" coordinated and translated by Rebecca Hart. Greenwillow Bks. 1998 40p il $16.99; lib bdg $17.89   E
1. Mother-daughter relationship—Fiction
2. Grandmothers—Fiction 3. Bilingual books—English-Spanish
ISBN 0-688-14628-7; 0-688-14629-5 (lib bdg)
    LC 97-7096

Companion volume to Cherry pies and lullabies

In this "picture book, four everyday activities are depicted—making tortillas, gathering flowers, washing clothes, and singing a lullaby—as they are repeated by the women of a family over the last four generations. . . . Six Costa Rican women worked together to produce the striking acrylic folk-art paintings. With deeply saturated, glowing tones and a decidedly Central American style, the pictures enhance and extend the lyrical narrative, which is printed in English and in Spanish." SLJ

Rex, Michael

Truck Duck; [by] Michael Rex. G.P. Putnam 2004 unp il $9.99   E
1. Animals—Fiction 2. Vehicles—Fiction 3. Stories in rhyme
ISBN 0-399-24009-8   LC 2003-707

A variety of animals drive vehicles whose names rhyme with their own.

"This is the stuff of toddlers' play, with vrooming action and small characters in charge. The sounds of the words add to the fun, and to little ones' vocabularies. The vehicles are big, bright, and clear." Booklist

A companion to this title is:
Dunk skunk (2005)

Rey, H. A. (Hans Augusto)

Curious George. Houghton Mifflin 1941 unp il $16; pa $6.95   E
1. Monkeys—Fiction
ISBN 0-395-15993-8; 0-395-15023-X (pa)
Also available Spanish language edition

Curious George goes to the hospital was written by Margret Rey and H. A. Rey in collaboration with the Children's Hospital Medical Center; and Curious George flies a kite was written by Margret Rey with pictures by H. A. Rey

Colored picture book, with simple text, describing the adventures of a curious small monkey, and the difficulties he had in getting used to city life, before he went to live in the zoo

"The bright lithographs in red, yellow, and blue, are gay and lighthearted, following the story closely with the same speed and animated humour." Ont Libr Rev

Other titles about Curious George are:
Curious George flies a kite (1958)
Curious George gets a medal (1957)
Curious George goes to the hospital (1966)
Curious George learns the alphabet (1963)
Curious George rides a bike (1952)
Curious George takes a job (1947)

Rey, Margret

Whiteblack the penguin sees the world; [by] Margret & H. A. Rey. Houghton Mifflin 2000 unp il $15   E
1. Penguins—Fiction
ISBN 0-618-07389-2   LC 00-23196

In search of new stories for his radio program, Whiteblack the penguin sets out on a journey and has some interesting adventures

"The plot is very well crafted, and Whiteblack's adventures are appealingly silly, almost slapstick. H. A. Rey's watercolors make great use of the white paper, contrasting it with deep hues of yellow, red, and ultramarine blue and thick black outlines." Booklist

Reynolds, Aaron

Chicks and salsa; by Aaron Reynolds; illustrated by Paulette Bogan. 1st U.S. ed. Bloomsbury Children's Books 2005 unp il $15.95   E
1. Chickens—Fiction 2. Cooking—Fiction 3. Farm life—Fiction
ISBN 1-58234-972-X   LC 2005042137

Soon after the chickens tire of their feed and decide to make tortilla chips and salsa, all the other animals on Nuthatcher Farm start to crave southwestern cuisine.

"This story is a fun read, with a refrain and a smooth pattern. Bogan's humorous illustrations keep the action moving, and the pages are filled with saturated color and energy." SLJ

Reynolds, Peter

The dot; [by] Peter H. Reynolds. Candlewick Press 2003 unp il $14   E
1. Drawing—Fiction 2. School stories
ISBN 0-7636-1961-2   LC 2002-041113

Reynolds, Peter—*Continued*

Vashti believes that she cannot draw, but her art teacher's encouragement leads her to change her mind

"In this engaging, inspiring tale, Reynolds . . . demonstrates the power of a little encouragement. . . . Rendered in watercolor, ink and tea, Reynolds's spare, wispy illustrations exude a fresh, childlike quality pleasingly in sync with his hand-lettered text." Publ Wkly

Ish; [by] Peter H. Reynolds. Candlewick Press 2004 unp il $14   E
  1. Drawing—Fiction 2. Siblings—Fiction
  ISBN 0-7636-2344-X   LC 2003-66196
Ramon loses confidence in his ability to draw, but his sister gives him a new perspective on things

"The overriding theme about creativity versus exactitude will resonate with many. The line-and-color artwork is simple, but it has great emotion and warmth." Booklist

Rice, Eve

Sam who never forgets. Greenwillow Bks. 1977 unp il pa $5.99 hardcover o.p.   E
  1. Zoos—Fiction 2. Animals—Fiction
  ISBN 0-688-07335-2 (pa)   LC 76-30370
Sam is "a zoo keeper who 'never, never forgets' to feed the animals promptly at three o'clock. The beasts have their doubts when it looks like Sam has neglected to feed poor Elephant who is both hungry and crestfallen. Happily, Sam returns with a whole wagon of hay." SLJ

"A simple, unpretentious story with child appeal that lies in the naive, straightforward telling and elemental emotional interactions of the characters. . . . Rice has forsaken her pen drawings for bright, unlined colored shapes. The figures are pleasantly stylized, the scenes evenly composed." Booklist

Richards, Beah

Keep climbing, girls; by Beah E. Richards; illustrated by R. Gregory Christie; introduction by LisaGay Hamilton. Simon & Schuster Books for Young Readers 2006 unp il $15.95   E
  1. Girls—Poetry
  ISBN 1-4169-0264-3   LC 2004-29153
"In this picture-book rendition of Richards's 1951 poem of the same name, girls are urged to 'keep climbing' no matter what obstacles get in the way. Bold gouache illustrations create a beguiling green-and-gold landscape with an irresistible tree and a determined little girl who climbs it higher and higher with every page turn." SLJ

Richardson, Justin

And Tango makes three; by Justin Richardson and Peter Parnell; illustrated by Henry Cole. Simon & Schuster Bks. for Young Readers 2005 il $14.95   E
  1. Penguins—Fiction 2. Homosexuality—Fiction
  ISBN 0-689-87845-1
At New York City's Central Park Zoo, two male penguins fall in love and start a family by taking turns sitting on an abandoned egg until it hatches.

"Done in soft watercolors, the illustrations set the tone for this uplifting story, and readers will find it hard to resist the penguins' comical expressions. . . . This joyful story about the meaning of family is a must for any library." SLJ

Riddell, Chris

Platypus. Harcourt 2002 c2001 unp il $15   E
  1. Platypus—Fiction
  ISBN 0-15-216493-6   LC 2001-1228
First published 2001 in the United Kingdom
Platypus thinks he has found the perfect curly shell for his collection, but it keeps disappearing.

"The watercolor and black-ink illustrations have a soft, bright palette and simple, uncluttered style that extend the humor and charm of the tale." SLJ
  Other titles about Platypus are:
Platypus and the birthday party (2003)
Platypus and the lucky day (2002)

Riggio, Anita

Smack dab in the middle; written & illustrated by Anita Riggio. Putnam 2002 unp il $15.99   E
  1. Family life—Fiction
  ISBN 0-399-23700-3   LC 00-66472
Rosie is happy to be smack dab in the middle of her large family, but sometimes she feels neglected or ignored

"Digitally combining picture elements made with India ink, gouache, cut paper, and stamps, the artwork creates a 1950s' setting with a retro look, though the layout is fresh and the vitality of the line work is timeless. . . . A sympathetic tale that is expressively illustrated and nicely cadenced for reading aloud." Booklist

Riley, Linnea Asplind

Mouse mess; [by] Linnea Riley. Blue Sky Press (NY) 1997 unp il $16.95   E
  1. Mice—Fiction 2. Food—Fiction 3. Stories in rhyme
  ISBN 0-590-10048-3   LC 96-49499
A hungry mouse leaves a huge mess when it goes in search of a snack

"Cut-paper collages, set against black backgrounds, depict a chubby-cheeked mouse spilling, cutting, and eating a variety of colorful foods. . . . The rhyming text, filled with crunching and munching sounds, is rhythmic and fun to read aloud." SLJ

Ringgold, Faith

Tar Beach. Crown 1991 unp il $18; pa $6.99   E
  1. African Americans—Fiction 2. Dreams—Fiction
  3. Harlem (New York, N.Y.)—Fiction
  ISBN 0-517-58030-6; 0-517-58984-2 (pa)
                                        LC 90-40410
A Caldecott Medal honor book, 1992; Coretta Scott King Award for illustration, 1992
Eight-year-old Cassie dreams of flying above her Harlem home, claiming all she sees for herself and her fami-

Ringgold, Faith—*Continued*

ly. Based on the author's quilt painting of the same name

"Part autobiographical, part fictional, this allegorical tale sparkles with symbolic and historical references central to African-American culture. The spectacular artwork, a combination of primitive naive figures in a flattened perspective against a boldly patterned cityscape, resonates with color and texture." Horn Book

Another title about Cassie is:

Cassie's word quilt (2002)

Robert, François

Find a face; by François and Jean Robert, with Jane Gittings. Chronicle Books 2004 unp il $15.95
E

1. Face in art

ISBN 0-8118-4338-6   LC 2003-17593

Presents, with accompanying rhyming text, photographs of everyday objects depicting faces.

This is "a fun book that demonstrates that faces can be found anywhere if you look hard enough. . . . The photographs are clear and bright, and set against boldly colored backgrounds. Youngsters will never again look at a light switch in the same way." SLJ

Roberts, Bethany

May Belle and the Ogre; pictures by Marsha Winborn. Dutton 2003 48p il $14.99   E

1. Monsters—Fiction

ISBN 0-525-46855-2   LC 2003-273520

"Dutton easy reader"

May Belle "entertains herself with dress-up clothes, baking, and books until she meets the ogre, who seems scary at first . . . but eventually becomes a good friend. Well-crafted repetition helps make the text accessible to beginning readers. . . . Cheerful pictures . . . add color and personality." Booklist

Another title about May Belle and the Ogre is:

Ogre eats everything (2005)

Roberts, Lynn

Little Red; a fizzingly good yarn; retold by Lynn Roberts; illustrated by David Roberts. Harry N. Abrams 2005 32p il $16.95   E

1. Wolves—Fiction 2. Grandmothers—Fiction 3. Fairy tales

ISBN 0-8109-5783-3   LC 2004-29534

In this version of the Grimm fairy tale, Thomas—who is called Little Red—discovers a wolf in disguise at his grandmother's house and ingeniously uses ginger ale to save the day.

"The real strength of the book is David Roberts' stylish pen-and-ink and watercolor art, which creates a shadowy, detailed work that is deliciously creepy yet packed with humor." Bull Cent Child Books

Robins, Joan

Addie meets Max; pictures by Sue Truesdell. Harper & Row 1985 31p il pa $3.99 hardcover o.p.   E

1. Friendship—Fiction

ISBN 0-06-444116-4 (pa)   LC 84-48329

"An Early I can read book"

Addie discovers that the new boy next door, Max, and his dog are not so terrible when she helps him bury his newly lost tooth

"A realistic, mildly funny story is pleasant for reading aloud as well as for the beginning independent reader. The illustrations, line and wash, have vigor and humor." Bull Cent Child Books

Other titles about Addie and Max are:

Addie runs away (1989)

Addie's bad day (1993)

Roche, Denis

Little Pig is capable. Houghton Mifflin 2002 c2001 unp il $15   E

1. Pigs—Fiction 2. Wolves—Fiction 3. Scouts and scouting—Fiction

ISBN 0-395-91368-3   LC 2001-16583

Little Pig's parents worry about him so much that it's embarrassing, but all their warnings come in handy when he goes on a hike with his Snout Scout troop and their strange substitute troop leader

"Roche's playfully childlike artwork includes plenty of droll details . . . and extends the text's deadpan delivery. . . . Poking fun at overanxious parents, this picture book offers the kind of silly, subversive humor that kids eat up." Horn Book

Rockwell, Anne F.

100 school days; story by Anne Rockwell; pictures by Lizzy Rockwell. HarperCollins Pubs. 2002 unp il $12.99; lib bdg $14.89   E

1. Counting 2. School stories

ISBN 0-06-029144-3; 0-06-029145-1 (lib bdg)

LC 00-40704

The students in Mrs. Madoff's class keep track of the days they have been in school, marking each interval of ten, until they reach 100 days

"The simple text and the colorful paintings of familiar classroom and family activities will keep little ones involved." Booklist

Big wheels; by Anne Rockwell. Walker & Co. 2003 c1986 unp il $14.95   E

1. Vehicles 2. Machinery

ISBN 0-8027-8857-2   LC 2002-34348

A reissue of the title first published 1986 by Dutton Children's Bks.

Introduces a number of big-wheeled trucks, such as bulldozers, power shovels, and dump trucks, and explains what they do

"Although the author-artist has supplied a very brief text, she uses active, vivid verbs, such as *dig, dump,* and *chop up,* effectively conveying a sense of the machinery in the fewest words necessary. Likewise, her illustrations contain exactly the right amount of detail to satisfy but not confuse." Horn Book

Career day; story by Anne Rockwell; pictures by Lizzy Rockwell. HarperCollins Pubs. 2000 unp il $15.99; lib bdg $16.89   E

1. School stories 2. Occupations—Fiction

ISBN 0-06-027565-0; 0-06-027566-9 (lib bdg)

LC 97-20999

Rockwell, Anne F.—*Continued*

Each child in Mrs. Madoff's class brings a visitor who tells the group about his or her job

"Clearly laid out and cheerfully presented, this picture book strikes just the right tone for its intended audience." Booklist

Father's Day; by Anne Rockwell; pictures by Lizzy Rockwell. 1st ed. HarperCollins 2005 unp il $14.99; lib bdg $15.89   E
  1. Father's Day—Fiction 2. Fathers—Fiction
  ISBN 0-06-051377-2; 0-06-051378-0 (lib bdg)
                                          LC 2004-6243

For Fathers' Day, the students in Mrs. Madoff's class write and illustrate books about their dads.

"The best part of the book is the way it reflects the differences in dads. . . . The artwork, with rounded shapes and smooth colors, has a simple, friendly look that puts the focus on the characters." Booklist

Four seasons make a year; pictures by Megan Halsey. Walker & Co 2004 unp il $15.95; lib bdg $16.85   E
  1. Seasons
  ISBN 0-8027-8883-1; 0-8027-8885-8 (lib bdg)
                                          LC 2003-57171

Describes the passing of the seasons through the changes in plants and animals that occur on a farm.

"The first-person text is simple and childlike, a tone reflected in the clearly delineated collages. Combining ink drawings with acrylic paintings on torn paper, these illustrations create eye-catching compositions." Booklist

Good morning, Digger; by Anne Rockwell; illustrated by Melanie Hope Greenberg. Viking 2005 unp il $15.99   E
  1. Construction equipment—Fiction 2. Building—Fiction
  ISBN 0-670-05959-5   LC 2004-17398

Digger, Dump Truck, Cement Mixer, and their friends each do their part to build a community center.

"There can never be enough truck books for some preschoolers, and those who feel that way are sure to love this one—for the sound and rhythm of the words as well as clear, brightly colored pictures of machines in action." Booklist

Growing like me; [by] Anne Rockwell; illustrated by Holly Keller. Silver Whistle Bks. 2001 unp il $14   E
  1. Growth
  ISBN 0-15-202202-3   LC 99-50548

Explains how plants and animals of the meadow, woods, and pond grow and evolve, such as caterpillars changing into butterflies, eggs hatching into robins, and acorns becoming oaks

"Rockwell's very simple, rhythmic words and Keller's clear, bright watercolor-and-ink pictures work beautifully to show the surprising developments and connections." Booklist

Mother's Day; pictures by Lizzy Rockwell. HarperCollinsPub. 2004 unp il $14.99; lib bdg $15.89   E
  1. Mother's Day—Fiction 2. School stories
  ISBN 0-06-051374-8; 0-06-051375-6 (lib bdg)
                                          LC 2003-444

The students in Mrs. Madoff's class share how they will celebrate Mother's Day with their families.

"The simple text and vibrant illustrations work well together. . . . As a bonus, step-by-step directions for making flowers with construction paper, pipe cleaners, and buttons are included." SLJ

Thanksgiving Day; story by Anne Rockwell; pictures by Lizzy Rockwell. HarperCollins Pubs. 1999 unp il $14.95; lib bdg $16.89   E
  1. Thanksgiving Day—Fiction 2. School stories
  ISBN 0-06-027795-5; 0-06-028388-2 (lib bdg)
                                          LC 97-39290

Mrs. Madoff's preschool class learns about Thanksgiving and puts on a play about the origins of the holiday

"Rockwell's cartoon illustrations of dewy-eyed preschoolers in their various roles combine with the simple text to create an excellent example of a holiday concept book for inquisitive young readers." SLJ

The toolbox; by Anne & Harlow Rockwell. Walker & Company 2004 unp il $14.05
                                                                          E
  1. Tools
  ISBN 0-8027-8930-7   LC 2003-66562

A reissue of the title first published 1971 by Macmillan

An easy-to-read description of the basic tools found in a toolbox.

"The brief text is printed in clear, handsome type. . . . [The illustrations] make ingenious use of watercolor to show textures and surfaces of wood and metal." Horn Book

Two blue jays; [by] Anne Rockwell; pictures by Megan Halsey. Walker & Co. 2003 unp il $15.95; lib bdg $16.85   E
  1. Blue jays
  ISBN 0-8027-8840-8; 0-8027-8841-6 (lib bdg)
                                          LC 2002-31111

Miss Dana's class observes two blue jays as they make their nest, have babies, and teach them to fly. Includes information on the physical characteristics and behavior of blue jays

"Halsey's three-dimensional acrylic paintings . . . have been cut out and glued in layers. . . . An enjoyable informational story." SLJ

Valentine's Day; story by Anne Rockwell; pictures by Lizzy Rockwell. HarperCollins Pubs. 2001 unp il $14.95; lib bdg $14.89   E
  1. Valentine's Day—Fiction 2. School stories
  ISBN 0-06-027794-7; 0-06-028515-X (lib bdg)
                                          LC 97-17492

The children in Mrs. Madoff's class make special Valentine's cards to send to a friend in Japan and to share at their classroom celebration

"The friendly text matches the well-executed pictures of friends." Booklist

Rodman, Mary Ann

My best friend; illustrated by E.B. Lewis. Viking 2005 unp il $14.99   E
  1. Friendship—Fiction
  ISBN 0-670-05989-7   LC 2004-22778

Rodman, Mary Ann—*Continued*

Six-year-old Lily has a best friend all picked out for play group day, but unfortunately the differences between first-graders and second-graders are sometimes very large

"Rodman's honest text captures the girl's heartbroken disappointment and makes it real for young readers, and Lewis's shining, sun-drenched illustrations convey both the harshness and warmth of the bright days at the pool." SLJ

Rogers, Gregory

The boy, the bear, the baron, the bard. Roaring Brook 2004 unp il $15.95   E
1. Shakespeare, William, 1564-1616—Fiction 2. Stories without words
ISBN 1-59643-009-5

"A Neal Porter book"

A boy playing among the warehouses of London kicks a soccer ball into an abandoned theater. There he finds an enchanted cape that transports him back in time right onto the stage of one of William Shakespeare's plays

"The plot in this wordless picture book unfolds straightforwardly. . . . The full watercolor-and-ink panels give kids . . . the chance to peek into another era while sympathizing with a contemporary young protagonist." Booklist

Rohmann, Eric

Clara and Asha. Roaring Brook 2005 unp il $16.95   E
1. Imaginary playmates—Fiction 2. Fishes—Fiction 3. Bedtime—Fiction
ISBN 1-59643-031-1   LC 2005-04677

Young Clara would rather play with her imaginary giant fish, Asha, than settle down to sleep.

"The oil paintings portray a natural world in all its glorious seasons, brimming with mystery and delight. . . . Children will revel in the opportunity to see their dreams and longings realized so enchantingly." SLJ

My friend Rabbit. Roaring Brook Press 2002 unp il $15; lib bdg $22.90   E
1. Friendship—Fiction 2. Rabbits—Fiction 3. Mice—Fiction
ISBN 0-7613-1535-7; 0-7613-2420-8 (lib bdg)
   LC 2002-17764

Awarded the Caldecott Medal, 2003

Something always seems to go wrong when Rabbit is around, but Mouse lets him play with his toy plane anyway because he is his good friend

"The double-page, hand-colored relief prints with heavy black outlines are magnificent, and children will enjoy the comically expressive pictures of the animals." SLJ

Time flies. Crown 1994 unp il $17; lib bdg $17.99; pa $6.99   E
1. Stories without words 2. Birds—Fiction 3. Dinosaurs—Fiction
ISBN 0-517-59598-2; 0-517-59599-0 (lib bdg); 0-517-88555-7 (pa)   LC 93-28200

A Caldecott Medal honor book, 1995

A wordless tale in which a bird flying around the dinosaur exhibit in a natural history museum has an unsettling experience when the dinosaur seems to come alive and view the bird as a potential meal

"The handsome, atmospheric paintings heighten the drama as they tell their simple, somewhat mysterious, and quite short story." Booklist

Roome, Diana Reynolds

The elephant's pillow; pictures by Jude Daly. Farrar, Straus & Giroux 2003 unp il $16
   E
1. Elephants—Fiction 2. China—Fiction
ISBN 0-374-32015-2   LC 2002-192544

Sing Lo, a wealthy boy living in Peking, goes to visit the late emperor's Imperial Elephant and tries to cheer him up

"This picture book combines an original story with precise, delicate illustrations in which elements of clear, bright red glow against the more muted shades of brown, green, and blue." Booklist

Roosa, Karen

Beach day; illustrated by Maggie Smith. Clarion Bks. 2001 32p il $15   E
1. Beaches—Fiction 2. Stories in rhyme
ISBN 0-618-02923-0   LC 00-43010

Rhyming text describes a perfect day at the beach, complete with sandy knees, deviled eggs, and a castle with a moat

"The excitement and enthusiasm of the day are perfectly captured by the artist's bright, lively watercolors and the author's active, playful text." SLJ

Root, Barry

Gumbrella. Putnam 2002 unp il $15.99
   E
1. Elephants—Fiction 2. Animals—Fiction
ISBN 0-399-23347-4   LC 00-68406

Gumbrella the elephant loves nursing sick animals back to health, but she hates letting them go

"There's an appealing wackiness to this droll story of 'kindness to animals' carried too far. . . . Root's humorous paint and pastel illustrations are as solid and cheery as the elephant herself yet pleasantly soft around the edges." Bull Cent Child Books

Root, Phyllis

Big Momma makes the world; written by Phyllis Root; illustrated by Helen Oxenbury. Candlewick Press 2003 unp il $16.99   E
1. Creation—Fiction
ISBN 0-7636-1132-8   LC 2002-17498

Big Momma, with a baby on her hip and laundry piling up, makes the world and everything in it and, at the end of the sixth day, tells the people she has made that they must take care of her creation

"Root's text is strong and sassy, with a down-home cadence that has immediate appeal, and Oxenbury's Big Momma is the perfect embodiment of the story's earth mother." Booklist

Root, Phyllis—*Continued*
Grandmother Winter; pictures by Beth Krommes. Houghton Mifflin 1999 unp il $15

E

1. Winter—Fiction 2. Snow—Fiction 3. Animals—Fiction
ISBN 0-395-88399-7   LC 98-50515
When Grandmother Winter shakes out her feather quilt birds, bats, bears, and other creatures prepare themselves for the cold
"Root's cadenced text, lyrical and sweet, is nicely matched by Krommes's handsome stylized art rendered in scratchboard and watercolor." Horn Book Guide

If you want to see a caribou; illustrated by Jim Meyer. Houghton Mifflin 2004 unp il $16

E

1. Caribou—Fiction 2. Great Lakes region—Fiction
ISBN 0-618-39314-5   LC 2003-12291
Describes all the wonders of nature that the reader might see when setting out to find a caribou on an island in Lake Superior
"The restrained tone and natural rhythms of the language add depth to the telling. Meyer's woodblock prints . . . are ideally paired with the gentle narrative. The muted hues match the quiet mood of the text." SLJ

Kiss the cow; illustrated by Will Hillenbrand. Candlewick Press 2000 unp il $15.99   E
1. Cattle—Fiction
ISBN 0-7636-0298-1   LC 00-20926
Annalisa, the most curious and stubborn of Mama May's children, disobeys her mother and upsets the family's magic cow by refusing to kiss her in return for the milk she gives
"Elements of folklore echo through the story that reads aloud rhythmically with a satisfying, folksy sound. . . . The well-conceived illustrations, warm in color and graceful in line, depict a variety of scenes with style and panache." Booklist

The name quilt; pictures by Margot Apple. Farrar, Straus & Giroux 2003 unp il $16

E

1. Quilts—Fiction 2. Grandmothers—Fiction
ISBN 0-374-35484-7   LC 2002-69328
One of Sadie's favorite things to do when she visits her grandmother is to hear stories about the family members whose names are on a special quilt that Grandma had made, so Sadie is very sad when the quilt is blown away in a storm
"Root makes the most of the simple, intimate anecdotes that flow between generations, and the crayon-looking drawings bespeak a rustic informality." Publ Wkly

Rattletrap car; illustrated by Jill Barton. Candlewick Press 2001 unp il $15.99   E
1. Automobiles—Fiction
ISBN 0-7636-0819-6   LC 99-57833
Various disasters threaten to stop Poppa and the children from getting to the lake in their rattletrap car, but they manage to come up with an ingenious solution to each problem
"The internal rhymes, alliteration, and creative car sounds make a perfect read-aloud. The watercolor illustrations are full of action." SLJ

Rose, Deborah Lee
Birthday zoo; written by Lee Rose; illustrated by Lynn Munsinger. Whitman, A. 2002 unp il $15.95   E
1. Zoos—Fiction 2. Birthdays—Fiction 3. Animals—Fiction 4. Stories in rhyme
ISBN 0-8075-0776-8   LC 2002-1726
Rhyming text describes the preparations made for a boy's birthday party by his hosts, the animals at the zoo
"While Rose's strong rhythm and rhymes will charm youngsters in a storytime, Munsinger's lively pen-and-ink and watercolor illustrations beg for closer inspection." SLJ

One nighttime sea; an ocean counting rhyme; pictures by Steve Jenkins. Scholastic 2003 unp il $16.95   E
1. Counting 2. Marine animals 3. Night
ISBN 0-439-33906-5   LC 2002-8127
A counting book featuring nocturnal sea creatures, from one blue whale calf to ten turtle hatchlings, and back down to one seal pup. Includes facts about each of the twenty featured animals
"In a lapping, sealike rhythm, this enchanting counting book lulls its audience into the world beneath the waves. . . . Vivid cut-paper collages beautifully interplay with the rhymes." SLJ

Rosen, Michael
Michael Rosen's sad book; words by Michael Rosen; pictures by Quentin Blake. 1st U.S. ed. Candlewick Press 2005 unp il $16.99   E
1. Bereavement—Fiction
ISBN 0-7636-2597-3   LC 2004-45787
A man tells about all the emotions that accompany his sadness over the death of his son, and how he tries to cope.
"Blake's evocative watercolor-and-ink illustrations use shades of gray for the pictures where sadness has taken hold but brighten with color at the memory of happy times. This story is practical and universal and will be of comfort to those who are working through their bereavement. A brilliant and distinguished collaboration." SLJ

We're going on a bear hunt; retold by Michael Rosen; illustrated by Helen Oxenbury. Margaret K. McElderry Bks. 1989 unp il $17; pa $7.99

E

1. Bears—Fiction 2. Hunting—Fiction
ISBN 0-689-50476-4; 0-689-85349-1 (pa)
                          LC 88-13338
Also available Board book edition
"Glorious puddles of watercolor alternate with impish charcoal sketches in this refreshing interpretation of an old hand rhyme in which a man, four children, and a dog stalk the furry beast through mud and muck, high and low. A book with a genuine atmosphere of togetherness and boundless enthusiasm for the hunt." SLJ

Rosenberry, Vera
Vera's first day of school. Holt & Co. 1999 unp il $16.95; pa $6.95   E
1. School stories
ISBN 0-8050-5936-9; 0-8050-7269-1 (pa)
                          LC 98-43347

Rosenberry, Vera—_Continued_

Vera cannot wait for the day when she starts school, but the first day does not go exactly as she has anticipated

"Rosenberry's playful, brightly colored gouache illustrations capture Vera's jubilation-turned-dismay." Horn Book Guide

Other titles about Vera are:

Vera goes to the dentist (2002)

Vera rides a bike (2004)

Vera runs away (2000)

Vera's baby sister (2005)

When Vera was sick (1998)

Rosenthal, Amy Krouse

Cookies; bite-size life lessons; written by Amy Krouse Rosenthal; illustrated by Jane Dyer. 1st ed. HarperCollins Publishers 2006 unp il $12.99; lib bdg $13.89   **E**

1. Conduct of life 2. Cookies

ISBN 9780060580810 (trade bdg.); 0-06-058081-X; 9780060580827 (lib. bdg.); 0060580828 (lib bdg)
       LC 2005015134

"Using the activity of making and eating cookies, the author defines some important concepts for young children, such as respect, trustworthiness, patience, politeness, loyalty, etc. . . . Lovely pastel watercolor illustrations show appealing children and anthropomorphic animals interacting with one another and the treats. . . . The utilization of the cookies to explain the concepts is a brilliant idea and works well on a child's level. The text is short and clear, and the book is delightful to look at and browse through." SLJ

Rosoff, Meg

Meet wild boars; [written by] Meg Rosoff and [illustrated by] Sophie Blackall. 1st ed. Henry Holt and Co 2005 unp il $15.95   **E**

1. Boars—Fiction

ISBN 0-8050-7488-0   LC 2004-8985

It is very hard to be friends with wild boars because they are dirty and smelly, bad-tempered, and rude

This is "bitingly funny and deeply satisfying. . . . Blackall's roll-on-the-ground-in-laughter illustrations are incisively rendered in ink and gouache." Booklist

Ross, Pat

Meet M and M; pictures by Marylin Hafner. Pantheon Bks. 1980 41p il pa $4.99 hardcover o.p.
     E

1. Friendship—Fiction

ISBN 0-14-038731-5 (pa)   LC 79-190

"An I am reading book"

"Because they look so much alike, Mandy and Mimi like to pretend they're twins. . . . Then, 'one crabby day,' they have a squabble, it takes several miserable days more before they make up." Bull Cent Child Books

"Beginning readers will have no difficulty with the humorously told, very real incidents. . . . The many black-and-white pencil drawings capture the girls' facial expressions especially well." Horn Book

Other titles about M and M (Mandy and Mimi) are:

M and M and the bad news babies (1983)

M and M and the Halloween monster (1991)

M and M and the haunted house game (1980)

M and M and the mummy mess (1986)

Rostoker-Gruber, Karen

Rooster can't cock-a-doodle-doo. Dial Books for Young Readers 2004 unp il $15.99   **E**

1. Roosters—Fiction 2. Farm life—Fiction

ISBN 0-8037-2877-8

When Rooster's throat is too sore for him to crow, the other farm animals help both him and Farmer Ted.

"The story moves quickly and the text is packed with amusing puns. Cleanly executed in pencil, ink, marker, and colored pencil, the brightly colored, realistic cartoons add humor to the story." SLJ

Roth, Carol

The little school bus; illustrated by Pamela Paparone. North-South Bks. 2002 unp il $14.95; lib bdg $15.50   **E**

1. Animals—Fiction 2. Buses—Fiction 3. Stories in rhyme

ISBN 0-7358-1646-8; 0-7358-1647-6 (lib bdg)
       LC 2002-71417

An assortment of animals, including a goat in a coat, a quick chick, and a hairy bear, ride the bus to and from school

"Paparone's bright, sprightly illustrations feature plenty of cheery mugging out the windows and other amusing side business. . . . This will take children on a verbal and visual ride that they'll want to repeat as often as possible." Booklist

Roth, Susan L.

Hard hat area; [by] Susan Roth. 1st U.S. ed. Bloomsbury Children's Books 2004 unp il $17.95
     E

1. Construction workers—Fiction 2. Building—Fiction

ISBN 1-58234-946-0   LC 2003-65343

Construction workers ask Kristen, a young apprentice, to bring them snacks and supplies.

"Stunning collages showcase the workers, their jobs, and their equipment _in situ_; clear explanatory notes describe the work and responsibilities for each person involved in the construction." Horn Book Guide

Rounds, Glen

Once we had a horse. [new ed] Holiday House 1996 unp il $16.95   **E**

1. Horses—Fiction

ISBN 0-8234-1241-5   LC 95-25939

A revised and newly illustrated edition of the title first published 1971

Several children who live on a ranch in Montana spend the summer playing with a gentle old horse which had been left in their yard

This "is a delightful blend of Rounds's dry, witty storytelling with illustrations that capture the humor of the horse/child antics." SLJ

Rubin, Alan

How many fish? Yellow Umbrella Bks. 2003
17p il $14.60   E
1. Counting 2. Fishes
ISBN 0-7368-2013-2   LC 2003-924
"Yellow umbrella books for early readers"
Introduces counting by showing different numbers of
fish and other creatures swimming in the sea
"Not only can beginning readers feel successful at
mastering the short, repetitive sentences, but they can
also excel at counting the human feet and fish under the
water. Colorful illustrations enhance the text." SLJ

Ruelle, Karen Gray

The Thanksgiving beast feast. Holiday House
1999 32p il $15.95; pa $4.95   E
1. Thanksgiving Day—Fiction 2. Cats—Fiction
3. Animals—Fiction
ISBN 0-8234-1511-2; 0-8234-1802-2 (pa)
                                     LC 98-51339
"A Holiday House reader"
Harry the cat and his sister Emily celebrate Thanks-
giving by making a holiday feast for the animals in their
yard
"Simple and child-centered, the story reads well and
uses repetition in ways that sound natural, while reinforc-
ing word recognition. Pleasantly childlike, the naive ink
drawings are tinted with gentle washes." Booklist
Other titles about Harry and Emily are:
April fool (2002)
The crunchy, munchy Christmas tree (2003)
Dear Tooth Fairy (2006)
Easter egg disaster (2004)
Easy as apple pie (2002)
Great groundhogs! (2005)
Just in time for New Year's (2004)
The monster in Harry's backyard (1999)
Mother's Day mess (2003)
Snow valentines (2000)
Spookier than a ghost (2001)

Russell, Barbara T.

Maggie's Amerikay; by Barbara Timberlake
Russell; pictures by Jim Burke. Farrar, Straus and
Giroux 2006 unp il $17   E
1. Irish Americans—Fiction 2. Immigrants—Fiction
3. African Americans—Fiction 4. New Orleans
(La.)—Fiction
ISBN 0-374-34722-0   LC 2005040068
"Melanie Kroupa books"
This picture book, set in 1898 in New Orleans, "focuses on Maggie, an Irish immigrant child, who makes
friends with Nathan, an African American child . . . .
Maggie's Da gives Nathan a battered cornet, and Nathan
finds Maggie a job writing down the experiences of elderly Daddy Clements." Booklist
"Burke's realistic paintings are dark with a muted palette, capturing the period as well as the characters' sentiments. This handsome picture book reveals the plight of
immigrants at the turn of the century while paying tribute
to the city where jazz was born." SLJ

Russo, Marisabina

The big brown box. Greenwillow Bks. 2000 unp
il $16.99   E
1. Boxes—Fiction 2. Brothers—Fiction
ISBN 0-688-17096-X   LC 99-14871
As he plays in a very large box in his room and turns
it into a house, then a cave, then a boat, Sam is reluctant
to let his little brother Ben join him, but then he finds
the perfect way for them to share.
"The well-paced, child-centered text is complemented
by Russo's trademark two-dimensional gouache illustrations that realistically capture the creative play of children." SLJ

Come back, Hannah! Greenwillow Bks. 2001
unp il $15.95; lib bdg $15.89   E
1. Infants—Fiction 2. Mother-child relationship—Fiction
ISBN 0-688-17383-7; 0-688-17384-5 (lib bdg)
                                     LC 00-34133
Fast-crawling Hannah keeps Mama busy by getting
into all kinds of mischief around the house
"Russo's signature art, with appealing use of white
space and blocks of dense, solid color, catches all the action." Booklist

The trouble with Baby. Greenwillow Bks. 2003
unp il $15.99; lib bdg $16.89   E
1. Siblings—Fiction 2. Dolls—Fiction
ISBN 0-06-008924-5; 0-06-008925-3 (lib bdg)
                                     LC 2002-67857
Companion volume to Come back Hannah!
Sam and his big sister Hannah have fun playing together, until Hannah gets a new doll for her birthday and
begins paying so much attention to the doll that Sam
gets jealous
"The conflict and resolution is dealt with calmly and
without judgment. . . . The artist's signature-style illustrations—gouache paintings with a smooth application of
color—are flat yet detailed scenes of everyday life." SLJ

Ryan, Pam Muñoz

Amelia and Eleanor go for a ride; based on a
true story; story by Pam Muñoz Ryan; pictures by
Brian Selznick. Scholastic Press 1999 unp il
$16.95   E
1. Earhart, Amelia, 1898-1937—Fiction 2. Roosevelt,
Eleanor, 1884-1962—Fiction
ISBN 0-590-96075-X   LC 98-31788
A fictionalized account of the night Amelia Earhart
flew Eleanor Roosevelt over Washington, D.C. in an airplane
"Hewing closely to documented accounts, Ryan's inviting text adds drama and draws parallels between the
two protagonists with fictional touches. . . . Selznick's
illustrations, black-and-white graphite accented with
touches of purple pencil, both capture the vibrancy of his
subjects and evoke the feel of a more glamorous era."
Publ Wkly

Ryan, Pam Muñoz—*Continued*

There was no snow on Christmas Eve; illustrated by Dennis Ryan. Hyperion Books for Children 2005 unp il $15.99   **E**

1. Jesus Christ—Nativity 2. Christmas—Fiction 3. Stories in rhyme

ISBN 0-7868-5492-8

"On a wintry night two children and an adult walk outdoors and reflect on the contrast between the snowy scene that greets them and the balmy serenity in Jerusalem when Jesus was born. . . . The text is spare and lyrical, with hushed tones that underscore the significance of the momentous event. It's the evocative watercolor artwork, however, that really stands out, effectively and beautifully suggesting the different worlds of then and now." Booklist

Ryder, Joanne

Big Bear Ball; illustrations by Steven Kellogg. HarperCollins Pubs. 2002 unp il $15.95; lib bdg $15.89   **E**

1. Dance—Fiction 2. Bears—Fiction 3. Stories in rhyme

ISBN 0-06-027955-9; 0-06-027956-7 (lib bdg)

LC 00-56723

The moon is full and all the bears are gathered together for a ball under the stars

"The pages burst with vibrant reds and oranges for sunsets and every color in the rainbow appears. . . . The rhythmic rhyme, in large type, is strategically placed so as to keep children's attention on the exuberant and fun-loving action." SLJ

Come along, kitten; illustrated by Susan Winter. Simon & Schuster Bks. for Young Readers 2003 unp il $15.95   **E**

1. Cats—Fiction 2. Dogs—Fiction 3. Stories in rhyme

ISBN 0-689-83164-1   LC 2001-20953

"A wise old dog encourages a kitten to explore its world under his watchful eye. . . . Large watercolor and colored-pencil illustrations depict shining eyes and soft fur. Art and natural rhymes combine to make this book suitable for both storyhours and one-on-one sharing." SLJ

Each living thing; illustrations by Ashley Wolff. Harcourt 2000 unp il $16   **E**

1. Animals—Fiction 2. Stories in rhyme

ISBN 0-15-201898-0   LC 98-51832

"Gulliver Books"

Celebrates the creatures of the earth, from spiders dangling in their webs to owls hooting and hunting out of sight, and asks that we respect and care for them

"Wolff's intense gouache paintings, outlined in black, are as lyrical as the text, with just the right balance of simplicity and subtle detail." Booklist

A fawn in the grass; illustrated by Keiko Narahashi. Holt & Co. 2001 unp il $16.95   **E**

1. Animals—Fiction 2. Stories in rhyme

ISBN 0-8050-6236-X   LC 00-24284

"While walking in the woods, a child discovers many wonders of nature, from a fawn lying in the grass to a mole in a hole and a hawk circling in the sky." Horn Book Guide

"Simple rhyming words express the child's sense of wonder, and soft-toned gouache-and-watercolor pictures show more than the words say." Booklist

My father's hands; illustrated by Mark Graham. Morrow Junior Bks. 1994 unp il $16.99   **E**

1. Father-daughter relationship—Fiction 2. Gardening—Fiction

ISBN 0-688-09189-X   LC 93-27116

"A little girl and her father share the wonders of nature as they examine several small creatures in the garden—a pink worm, a golden beetle, a sliding snail, and a praying mantis. Graham's lovely double-page, impressionistic oil paintings clearly focus on the man and his daughter, with closeups of faces and hands in nearly every illustration. The garden in the background, lush with flowers and vegetable plants, provides a picturesque setting for this simple, straightforward description of a special parent/child outing." SLJ

Rylant, Cynthia

The case of the missing monkey; story by Cynthia Rylant; pictures by G. Brian Karas. Greenwillow Bks. 2000 48p il (High-rise private eyes) lib bdg $11.80; pa $3.99   **E**

1. Mystery fiction

ISBN 0-688-16305-X (lib bdg); 0-06-444306-X (pa)

LC 99-16878

While having breakfast at their favorite diner, two detectives, Bunny and Jack, find a missing glass monkey

"The full-color illustrations, rendered in acrylic gouache, and pencil, capture the cartoonlike animals' animated expressions and poses. . . . Children will enjoy searching the pages for the reported clues." SLJ

Other titles in the High-rise private eyes series are:

The case of the baffled bear (2004)

The case of the climbing cate (2000)

The case of the desperate duck (2005)

The case of the fidgety fox (2003)

The case of the puzzling possum (2001)

The case of the sleepy sloth (2002)

The case of the troublesome turtle (2001)

Christmas in the country; illustrated by Diane Goode. Blue Sky Press (NY) 2002 unp il $15.95   **E**

1. Christmas—Fiction 2. Country life—Fiction 3. Grandparents—Fiction

ISBN 0-439-07334-0   LC 2001-43213

A girl reflects on Christmas at her grandparents home in the country, with its fresh-cut tree, handmade ornaments, gifts from Santa, and special church services

"This gentle, first-person narrative shimmers with affection. The text is well matched with Goode's humorous pen-and-ink and watercolor pictures." SLJ

Henry and Mudge; the first book of their adventures; story by Cynthia Rylant; pictures by Suçie Stevenson. Bradbury Press 1987 39p il $15; pa $3.99   **E**

1. Dogs—Fiction

ISBN 0-689-81004-0; 0-689-71399-1 (pa)

LC 86-13615

Rylant, Cynthia—_Continued_

Also available Spanish language edition

This book tells "about a boy named Henry and his dog, Mudge. . . . Henry yearns for a dog and convinces his parents to get one. Mudge is small at first, but soon grows 'out of seven collars in a row' to become enormous, and Henry's best friend. Then comes a day when Mudge is lost, and boy and dog realize what they mean to each other." N Y Times Book Rev

"The stories are lighthearted and affectionate. Backed by line-and-wash cartoon drawings, they celebrate the familiar in a down-to-earth way that will please young readers." Booklist

Other titles about Henry and Mudge are:

Henry and Mudge and a very Merry Christmas (2004)
Henry and Mudge and Annie's good move (1998)
Henry and Mudge and Annie's perfect pet (2000)
Henry and Mudge and Mrs. Hopper's house (2003)
Henry and Mudge and the bedtime thumps (1991)
Henry and Mudge and the best day of all (1995)
Henry and Mudge and the big sleepover (2006)
Henry and Mudge and the careful cousin (1994)
Henry and Mudge and the forever sea (1989)
Henry and Mudge and the funny lunch (2004)
Henry and Mudge and the great grandpas (2005)
Henry and Mudge and the happy cat (1990)
Henry and Mudge and the long weekend (1992)
Henry and Mudge and the sneaky crackers (1998)
Henry and Mudge and the Snowman plan (1999)
Henry and Mudge and the starry night (1998)
Henry and Mudge and the tall tree house (1999)
Henry and Mudge and the tumbling trip (2005)
Henry and Mudge and the wild goose chase (2003)
Henry and Mudge and the wild wind (1993)
Henry and Mudge get the cold shivers (1989)
Henry and Mudge in puddle trouble (1987)
Henry and Mudge in the family trees (1997)
Henry and Mudge in the green time (1987)
Henry and Mudge in the sparkle days (1988)
Henry and Mudge take the big test (1991)
Henry and Mudge under the yellow moon (1987)

Moonlight: the Halloween cat; illustrated by Melissa Sweet. HarperCollins Pubs. 2003 unp il $14.99; lib bdg $15.89 **E**

1. Halloween—Fiction 2. Cats—Fiction

ISBN 0-06-029711-5; 0-06-029712-3 (lib bdg)

LC 2001-39511

Moonlight the cat loves everything about Halloween, from pumpkins to children to candy

"In simple, poetic prose, Rylant tracks the meandering cat's night journey. . . . Sweet's endearingly childlike, color-rich paintings convey an appreciation for the ever-deepening night. . . . A soothing, ghoul-free, utterly noncreepy Halloween picture book for the preschool set." Booklist

Mr. Putter and Tabby pour the tea; illustrated by Arthur Howard. Harcourt Brace & Co. 1994 unp il $14; pa $5.95 **E**

1. Cats—Fiction 2. Old age—Fiction

ISBN 0-15-256255-9; 0-15-200901-9 (pa)

LC 93-21470

"Mr. Putter, a lonely old man, finds a friend in Tabby, an elderly cat he gets from the pound." Booklist

"Rylant's charming story of two elderly characters is complemented and enhanced by Howard's delightful illustrations, done in pencil, watercolor, and gouache." SLJ

Other titles about Mr. Putter and Tabby are:

Mr. Putter and Tabby bake the cake (1994)
Mr. Putter and Tabby catch the cold (2002)
Mr. Putter and Tabby feed the fish (2001)
Mr. Putter and Tabby fly the plane (1997)
Mr. Putter and Tabby make a wish (2005)
Mr. Putter and Tabby paint the porch (2000)
Mr. Putter and Tabby pick the pears (1995)
Mr. Putter and Tabby row the boat (1997)
Mr. Putter and Tabby spin the yarn (2006)
Mr. Putter and Tabby stir the soup (2003)
Mr. Putter and Tabby take the train (1998)
Mr. Putter and Tabby toot the horn (1998)
Mr. Putter and Tabby walk the dog (1994)
Mr. Putter and Tabby write the book (2004)

Poppleton; book one; illustrated by Mark Teague. Blue Sky Press (NY) 1997 48p il pa $3.99 hardcover o.p. **E**

1. Pigs—Fiction 2. Friendship—Fiction

ISBN 0-590-84783-X (pa) LC 96-3365

"City pig Poppleton adjusts to small-town life in this . . . chapter book. In 'Neighbors,' the polite Poppleton tries to think up a polite way to say 'no thanks' to Cherry Sue, a friendly llama who invites him to breakfast, lunch and dinner every single day. . . . The second vignette, 'The Library,' details Poppleton's reading ritual, which demands solitude. Finally, 'The Pill' introduces Fillmore, a sick goat who refuses to take his pill unless Poppleton hides it in a cake. . . . [Rylant's] concise sentences mimic the characters' good manners and wryly point up the failures of etiquette. Teague contributes fetching watercolor-and-pencil images of the pudgy pig, slender llama and dignified goat." Publ Wkly

Other titles about Poppleton are:

Poppleton and friends (1997)
Poppleton everyday (1998)
Poppleton forever (1998)
Poppleton has fun (2000)
Poppleton in Fall (1999)
Poppleton in Spring (1999)
Poppleton in Winter (2001)
Poppleton through and through (2000)

The relatives came; story by Cynthia Rylant; illustrated by Stephen Gammell. rev format ed. Atheneum Books for Young Readers 2001 c1985 unp il $16.95; pa $6.99 **E**

1. Family life—Fiction

ISBN 0-689-84508-1; 0-689-71738-5 (pa)

A Caldecott Medal honor book, 1986

A reformatted edition of the title first published 1985 by Bradbury Press

"The relatives have come . . . bringing with them hugs and laughs, quiet talk, and, at night when all are asleep hither and yon." Booklist

"If there's anything more charming than the tone of voice in this story, it's the drawings that go with it. Stephen Gammell . . . fills the pages with bright, crayony pictures teeming with details that children should enjoy poring over for hours." NY Times Book Rev

Rylant, Cynthia—*Continued*

The stars will still shine; illustrated by Tiphanie Beeke. 1st ed. HarperCollins 2005 unp il $15.99; lib bdg $16.89   **E**
1. Stories in rhyme
ISBN 0-06-054639-5; 0-06-054640-9 (lib bdg)
                           LC 2004-14796

In pictures and rhyming text, this verse reassures the reader that life's familiar things, such as stars that shine and sleeping kittens, will continue as they always have.

"Beeke's artwork glows with color and light, creating a series of very different scenes, united by the style of illustration and the spirit of the work. A reassuring picture book for young children." Booklist

The ticky-tacky doll; illustrated by Harvey Stevenson. Harcourt 2002 unp il $16   **E**
1. Dolls—Fiction 2. School stories 3. Grandmothers—Fiction
ISBN 0-15-201078-5   LC 97-20281

When she has to go to school without her special doll, a little girl cannot focus on learning her letters and numbers, until her grandmother realizes what the problem is

"Rylant's dear, heartfelt text will remind children of their own treasured possessions and the feelings they evoke. . . . The cozy pictures, executed in crayon and acrylic oil, reflect the story's warmth." Booklist

When I was young in the mountains; illustrated by Diane Goode. Dutton 1982 unp il $15.99; pa $6.99   **E**
1. Appalachian region—Fiction
ISBN 0-525-42525-X; 0-525-44198-0 (pa)
                            LC 81-5359

A Caldecott Medal honor book, 1983

"Based on the author's memories of an Appalachian childhood. . . . The author reminisces about the busy, peaceful life of an extended family and their community." Bull Cent Child Books

"The people in the story are poor in material things, but rich in family pleasures. The title becomes a pleasing refrain. . . . Illustrations and text are placed on a bed of white space, without borders, which makes them look uncrowded and imparts a great feeling of freedom." SLJ

Sabuda, Robert

Alice's adventures in Wonderland; a pop-up adaptation of Lewis Carroll's original tale; illustrated by Robert Sabuda. Little Simon 2003 unp il $25.95   **E**
1. Fantasy fiction
ISBN 0-689-84743-2

A pop-up version of Lewis Carroll's classic tale of Alice who falls down the rabbit hole to find a new world.

"Sabuda brings Alice's world to life with breathtaking, three-dimensional images that are incredibly imaginative, intricately detailed, and perfectly executed. Carroll's text has been significantly abridged, and . . . the quickly paced narrative retains the flavor of the original." SLJ

The Christmas alphabet. deluxe anniversary edition. Orchard Books 2004 unp il $22.95
                                    E
1. Alphabet 2. Christmas
ISBN 0-439-67256-2
First published 1994

"Four large flaps per spread—each representing a letter of the alphabet— open to reveal sophisticated 3D images, some with parts that move in uncommonly inventive ways. Many of the pop-ups are obvious Christmas symbols. . . . Others have ambiguous—but resourceful—ties to the holiday. . . . A yuletide gem." Publ Wkly

Sakai, Komako

Emily's balloon. Chronicle Books 2006 unp il $14.95   **E**
1. Balloons—Fiction
ISBN 0-8118-5219-9   LC 2005-11283

A little girl's new friend is round, lighter than air, and looks like the moon at night.

"The yellow balloon and its blue string stand out in a simple color palette of white, gray, and tan with a few accents of red. The illustrations, rendered in watercolor and charcoal, are placed on tan pages and surrounded by unadorned thin, round-edged black frames. A tale of a common childhood experience, tenderly and sweetly told." SLJ

Saltzberg, Barney

Cornelius P. Mud, are you ready for bed? [by] Barney Saltzberg. 1st ed. Candlewick Press 2005 unp il $15.99   **E**
1. Pigs—Fiction 2. Bedtime—Fiction
ISBN 0-7636-2399-7   LC 2003-65273

Cornelius the pig has his own style when preparing for bed, but he does not really feel ready until he gets a hug.

"The oversize pictures offer plenty of space for humor, and Saltzberg employs comedy to full advantage. Using acrylics and pencils, he has created a little pig with a sweet smile and a devilish gleam in his eye." Booklist

Samuels, Barbara

Dolores on her toes. Farrar, Straus & Giroux 2003 unp il $16.50   **E**
1. Ballet—Fiction 2. Cats—Fiction 3. Sisters—Fiction
ISBN 0-374-31818-2   LC 2001-29384

"Melanie Kroupa books"

When her cat Duncan disappears just before Tutu Day, Dolores, with the help of her sister, realizes that Duncan does not want to be a ballerina

"There is a lot to look and laugh at in the illustrations. . . . This has all the elements of a terrific picture book: a fresh concept, a story and text that work together, and so much going on that children will want a second or third reading just to catch each hidden giggle." Booklist

Other titles about Dolores are:
Aloha Dolores (2000)
Duncan & Dolores (1986)
Happy birthday, Dolores (1989)
Happy Valentine's Day, Dolores (2005)

San Souci, Robert

The well at the end of the world; illustrated by Rebecca Walsh. Chronicle Books 2004 unp il $16.95

E

1. Fairy tales

ISBN 1-58717-212-7   LC 2004-41442

In this fairy tale, loosely based on English and Scottish lore, feisty Princess Rosamond, who prefers good books to good looks, risks her throne and all her wealth to save her father's life

"Done in a mixture of acrylic and watercolor, the richly hued illustrations vary in size from smaller vignettes to two-page paintings. They expand the narrative by imparting a fairy-tale setting and show lots of action and expression. Young viewers will enjoy the numerous small details." SLJ

Sandburg, Carl

The Huckabuck family and how they raised popcorn in Nebraska and quit and came back; pictures by David Small. Farrar, Straus & Giroux 1999 unp il $16

E

1. Farm life—Fiction

ISBN 0-374-33511-7   LC 98-6676

The text was originally published in 1923 by Harcourt, Brace & Company in the book Rootabaga stories

After the popcorn the Huckabucks had raised explodes in a fire and Pony Pony Huckabuck finds a silver buckle inside a squash, the family decides it is time for a change

"Small's watercolors have a translucent, airy quality that suits the fantastical elements of Sandburg's story. . . . Sandburg's language is as bracing as a tonic, and the inherent humor and rhythms of his tale are as invigorating today as when it was first written." Bull Cent Child Books

Santiago, Esmeralda

A doll for Navidades; illustrated by Enrique O. Sánchez. Scholastic Press 2005 unp $16.99

E

1. Christmas—Fiction 2. Puerto Rico—Fiction 3. Gifts—Fiction

ISBN 0-439-55398-9

While preparing for Christmas in Puerto Rico, seven-year-old Esmeralda asks the Three Magi for a baby doll like her cousin's, but when they bring something else instead she gains a deeper understanding of the meaning of the holiday.

"Santiago's autobiographical tale is both a universal story of holiday disappointment and a rich sensory portrait. . . . Sánchez's acrylic-on-canvas paintings add to the exotic flavor and the familiarity of the large family." SLJ

Saul, Carol P.

Barn cat; a counting book; illustrated by Mary Azarian. Little, Brown 1998 unp il lib bdg $15.95; pa $5.95

E

1. Cats—Fiction 2. Counting 3. Stories in rhyme

ISBN 0-316-76113-3; 0-316-71140-3 (pa)

LC 97-7052

Because she's looking for something special, the great barn cat notices but shows no interest in the activities of the animals which can be counted around her

"Azarian's exceedingly handsome woodcuts tether Saul's lyrical counting book to a pastoral setting." Publ Wkly

Say, Allen

Allison. Houghton Mifflin 1997 32p il $17

E

1. Adoption—Fiction 2. Japanese Americans—Fiction

ISBN 0-395-85895-X   LC 97-7528

When Allison realizes that she looks more like her Japanese doll than like her parents, she comes to terms with this unwelcomed discovery through the help of a stray cat

"A subtle, sensitive probing of interracial adoption, this exquisitely illustrated story will encourage thoughtful adult-child dialogue on a potentially difficult issue." Publ Wkly

The bicycle man. Parnassus Press 1982 unp il lib bdg $16; pa $5.95

E

1. Cycling—Fiction 2. Japan—Fiction

ISBN 0-395-32254-5 (lib bdg); 0-395-50652-2 (pa)

LC 82-2980

The amazing tricks two American soldiers do on a borrowed bicycle are a fitting finale for the school sports day festivities in a small village in occupied Japan

"The kindly, openhearted story is beautifully pictured in a profusion of delicate pen-and-ink drawings washed in gentle colors." Horn Book

Emma's rug. Houghton Mifflin 1996 32p il $16.95

E

1. Artists—Fiction 2. Rugs and carpets—Fiction

ISBN 0-395-74294-3   LC 96-14189

"Walter Lorraine books"

"From infancy, Emma has loved her rug. . . . When Emma begins to draw and paint, she amazes everyone. . . . Then disaster strikes: Mother dumps the 'dirty' rug in the washing-machine. All of Emma's quiet explodes in a picture of violent anguish." Booklist

Say's "deftly understated tale leaves ample room for readers' own interpretations. Yet it is his superb visual images, which have the semblance of faultlessly composed photographs, that make the most indelible mark here." Publ Wkly

Grandfather's journey; written and illustrated by Allen Say. Houghton Mifflin 1993 32p il $16.95

E

1. Japanese Americans—Fiction 2. Grandfathers—Fiction 3. Voyages and travels—Fiction 4. Japan—Fiction

ISBN 0-395-57035-2   LC 93-18836

Awarded the Caldecott Medal, 1994

A Japanese American man recounts his grandfather's journey to America which he later also undertakes, and the feelings of being torn by a love for two different countries

"The brief text is simple and unaffected, but the emotions expressed are deeply complex. The paintings are astonishingly still, like the captured moments found in a family photo album. Each translucent watercolor is suffused with light." SLJ

Say, Allen—*Continued*

Kamishibai man; written and illustrated by Allen Say. Houghton Mifflin Co. 2005 32p il $17

E

1. Entertainers—Fiction 2. Japan—Fiction
ISBN 0-618-47954-6

"Walter Lorraine books."

After many years of retirement, an old Kamishibai man—a Japanese street performer who tells stories and sells candies—decides to make his rounds once more even though such entertainment declined after the advent of television.

"The quietly dramatic, beautifully evocative tale contains a cliffhanger of its own, and its exquisite art, in the style of Kamishibai picture cards, will attract even the most jaded kid away from the TV to enjoy a good, good book." Booklist

The lost lake. Houghton Mifflin 1989 32p il $16; pa $6.95

E

1. Father-son relationship—Fiction 2. Camping—Fiction
ISBN 0-395-50933-5; 0-395-63036-3 (pa)

LC 89-11026

"Luke is disappointed in his relationship with his taciturn, work-absorbed father, with whom he is spending the summer. Early one morning his father awakens him with exciting news of a camping trip: they are going to find the Lost Lake, a very special and secret place Luke's father used to visit with his own father." Horn Book

"Using colors as crisp and clean as the outdoors, Say effectively alternates between scenes where father and son are the focus and those where the landscape predominates. Both in story and art, a substantial piece." Booklist

Music for Alice. Houghton Mifflin 2004 32p il $17

E

1. Japanese Americans—Fiction 2. Farms—Fiction 3. Dance—Fiction
ISBN 0-618-31118-1

LC 2003-14799

"Walter Lorraine Books"

A Japanese American farmer recounts her agricultural successes and setbacks and her enduring love of dance. Based on the true life story of Alice Sumida, who with her husband Mark, established the largest gladiola bulb farm in the country during the last half of the twentieth century.

"Say relates the true story . . . in an understated and eloquent style. . . . The masterful illustrations provide an emotional depth not always evident in the narration. . . . With proper introduction, this offering will be appreciated by sensitive and sophisticated youngsters." SLJ

Tea with milk. Houghton Mifflin 1999 32p il $17

E

1. Japanese Americans—Fiction 2. Japan—Fiction
ISBN 0-395-90495-1

LC 98-11667

"Walter Lorraine books"

After growing up near San Francisco, Masako (or May) returns with her parents to their native Japan, but she feels foreign and out of place until she finds a job in Osaka and marries a man with a similarly mixed background

"Say's masterfully executed watercolors tell as much of this story . . . as his eloquent prose." Publ Wkly

Tree of cranes; written and illustrated by Allen Say. Houghton Mifflin 1991 32p il $17.95

E

1. Christmas—Fiction 2. Mother-son relationship—Fiction 3. Japan—Fiction
ISBN 0-395-52024-X

LC 91-14107

A Japanese boy learns of Christmas when his mother decorates a pine tree with paper cranes

"The quiet, graciously told picture book is a perfect blend of text and art. Fine-lined and handsome, Say's watercolors not only capture fascinating details of the boy's far away home . . . but also depict, with simple grace, the rich and complex bond between mother and child that underlies the story." Booklist

Sayre, April Pulley

Dig, wait, listen; a desert toad's tale; pictures by Barbara Bash. Greenwillow Bks. 2001 unp il $15.95; lib bdg $15.89

E

1. Toads—Fiction 2. Desert animals—Fiction
ISBN 0-688-16614-8; 0-688-16615-6 (lib bdg)

LC 00-32111

A spadefoot toad waits under the sand for the rain, hears the sounds of other desert animals, and eventually mates and spawns other toads

"Created with pencil, pen and ink, and watercolor, Bash's pictures illustrate the desert scenes with pleasingly varied colors, perspectives, and layouts. Preschool and primary-grade children will find this well-crafted book a wholly satisfying introduction to the spadefoot toad in particular and desert animals and the idea of life cycles in general." Booklist

One is a snail, ten is a crab; a counting by feet book; [by] April Pulley Sayre and Jeff Sayre; illustrated by Randy Cecil. Candlewick Press 2003 unp il $15.99

E

1. Counting 2. Animals 3. Foot
ISBN 0-7636-1406-8

LC 2001-52494

A counting book featuring animals with different numbers of feet

"Very simple text in large type is appropriate for group use as well as beginning readers. Uncluttered, black-outlined, oil-on-paper pictures clearly illustrate the concepts, and Cecil's googly-eyed snails, sports-minded crabs, and other animals add a touch of humor." SLJ

Shadows; illustrated by Harvey Stevenson. Holt & Co. 2002 unp il $16.95

E

1. Shades and shadows—Fiction 2. Stories in rhyme
ISBN 0-8050-6059-6

LC 2001-196

Rhyming text describes the search of two young friends for shadows in the everyday world

"Anderson shows that everything has a shadow, and the tactile quality of his acrylic paintings will make children want to gaze longer and find more. . . . An engaging get-up-and-explore romp." Booklist

Schachner, Judith Byron

The Grannyman. Dutton Children's Bks. 1999 unp il $15.99

E

1. Cats—Fiction 2. Old age—Fiction
ISBN 0-525-46122-1

LC 98-52964

Schachner, Judith Byron—*Continued*

Simon the cat is so old that most of his parts have stopped working, but just when he is ready to breathe his last breath, his family brings home a new kitten for him to raise

"Schachner's expressive watercolor-and-mixed-media artwork mirrors the affection, humor, and warmth of her finely crafted text." Booklist

Schaefer, Carole Lexa

The biggest soap; pictures by Stacey Dressen-McQueen. Farrar, Straus and Giroux 2004 unp il $16   E

1. Oceania—Fiction 2. Storytelling—Fiction 3. Soap—Fiction

ISBN 0-374-30690-7   LC 2003-48512

When Kessy, who lives in the Truk Islands, is sent by his mother to buy laundry soap, he hurries back to listen to her storytelling, discovering that his own experience is a good story too

"Both the text and the pencil, oil pastel, and acrylic artwork, alive with the sun-drenched colors and patterns of the South Pacific, bubble with happiness. Refreshing, engaging, and thoroughly delightful." Booklist

Someone says; illustrated by Pierr Morgan. Viking 2003 unp il $15.99   E

1. Nursery schools—Fiction

ISBN 0-670-03664-1   LC 2003-952

A day at preschool has leaping frogs, dancing ponies, flapping wings, eating like tigers, and all the things that children can dream

"The simplicity of the story is enriched with rhythmic, playful language and the repetition of 'we do' as the children transform everyday activities into creative ideas and action. The exuberant art, combining Prismacolor markers and gouache, shows colorfully dressed youngsters bursting with energy." SLJ

Schaefer, Lola M.

An island grows; [by] Lola M. Schaefer; illustrated by Cathie Felstead. Greenwillow 2006 unp il $16.99   E

1. Islands—Fiction

ISBN 0-06-623930-3

An island is born and as it grows, lava flows, waves pound, sands mound, and life thrives.

"The colorful, bold collage illustrations are a perfect complement to the text. Like the narration, the seemingly elementary art is carefully composed, tells a complete story, and exudes energy." SLJ

Loose tooth; story by Lola M. Schaefer; pictures by Sylvie Wickstrom. 1st ed. HarperCollinsPublishers 2004 31p il $14.99; lib bdg $15.89; pa $3.99   E

1. Teeth—Fiction 2. Stories in rhyme

ISBN 0-06-052776-5; 0-06-052777-3 (lib bdg); 0-06-052778-1 (pa)   LC 2003-6322

"My first I can read book"

A young child experiences a loose tooth for the first time and eagerly waits for it to come out.

"With a few words, lots of repetition, some rhyme,

and good rhythm, this story is perfect for beginning readers. The cartoon illustrations add details to the plot and create interest." SLJ

This is the sunflower; pictures by Donald Crews. Greenwillow Bks. 2000 unp il $15.99; lib bdg $15.89   E

1. Sunflowers—Fiction 2. Stories in rhyme

ISBN 0-688-16413-7; 0-688-16414-5 (lib bdg)

LC 98-46682

A cumulative verse describing how a sunflower in a garden blossoms and, with the help of the birds, spreads its seeds to create an entire patch of sunflowers

"A beautiful, noteworthy title. The velvety watercolors are clearly defined and saturated with color. . . . This is perfect for story hours; also recommend it to budding ornithologists, who will appreciate the illustrated key identifying the birds pictured in the text." Booklist

What's up, what's down? pictures by Barbara Bash. Greenwillow Bks. 2002 unp il $15.99

E

1. Nature

ISBN 0-06-029757-3

"On each page is the question 'What's up if you're ...?' from the viewpoint of various flora and fauna: a mole, a root, grass, a toad. . . . The highest thing 'up' is the moon, and then it's time to turn the book upside down and move down through sky and water to see 'what's down.' Children will have a chance to stretch their imaginations as they get a rudimentary idea of how the natural world works. The artwork, executed in chalks, has a muscular look that brings nature home." Booklist

Schanzer, Rosalyn

Davy Crockett saves the world. HarperCollins Pubs. 2001 unp il $16.95; lib bdg $16.89

E

1. Crockett, Davy, 1786-1836—Fiction 2. Tall tales

ISBN 0-688-16991-0; 0-688-16992-9 (lib bdg)

LC 00-32021

Davy Crockett stops the evil Halley's Comet from destroying the world and wins the heart of Sally Sugartree in the process

"Full- and double-page frolicsome illustrations feature bold colors and cartoon characters that underline the humor of the story." SLJ

Scheer, Julian

Rain makes applesauce; by Julian Scheer & Marvin Bileck. Holiday House 1964 unp il $16.95

E

ISBN 0-8234-0091-3

A Caldecott Medal honor book, 1965

"A book of original nonsense, illustrated with intricate drawings. Small children live the refrains, 'Rain makes applesauce' and 'You're just talking silly talk,' and enjoy the fantastic details in the pictures." Hodges. Books for Elem Sch Libr

Scheer, Julian—*Continued*

A Thanksgiving turkey; illustrated by Ronald Himler. Holiday House 2001 unp il $16.95

        E

1. Grandfathers—Fiction 2. Turkeys—Fiction
3. Thanksgiving Day—Fiction 4. Virginia—Fiction
ISBN 0-8234-1674-7   LC 2001-16644

A thirteen-year-old boy and his mother move to a farm in rural Virginia, where he and his grandfather try to hunt a wild turkey

"Soft, watercolor illustrations and a story gently and respectfully told in the first person evoke memories of a time past." SLJ

Schertle, Alice

1, 2, I love you; illustrated by Emily Arnold McCully. Chronicle Books 2004 unp il $16.95

        E

1. Counting 2. Stories in rhyme 3. Elephants—Fiction
ISBN 0-8118-3518-9   LC 2003-21245

"A mother elephant addresses her little one as they engage in a variety of child-centered activities. . . . The numbers climb from 1 to 10 in the first half of the book, then descend until the end, when the little elephant goes to bed and to sleep. The rhythmic, rhyming verses are . . . engaging. . . . The colorful artwork features playful, large-scale paintings." Booklist

All you need for a beach; illustrated by Barbara Lavallee. Silver Whistle/Harcourt 2004 unp $16

        E

1. Beaches—Fiction 2. Stories in rhyme
ISBN 0-15-216755-2   LC 2002-151775

Rhyming text describes items essential for fun at the beach, from the first grain of sand, to a beach umbrella, to a bucket and shovel, to the waves rolling in to tickle your toes.

"Children will delight in the exuberance of the text and the vibrant illustrations that bring all of the sights, smells, and textures to life." SLJ

All you need for a snowman; illustrated by Barbara Lavallee. Silver Whistle/Harcourt 2002 unp il $16.95   **E**

1. Snow—Fiction
ISBN 0-15-200789-X   LC 2001-4787

Lists everything that one needs to build the perfect snowman, from the very first snowflake that falls

"The text is bouncy and light, and rolls like hand-packed snow. . . . The skill of both the author and the artist gives this book energy." SLJ

Down the road; illustrated by E.B. Lewis. Browndeer Press 1995 unp il $16; pa $6

        E

1. Eggs—Fiction 2. Country life—Fiction
ISBN 0-15-276622-7; 0-15-202471-9 (pa)
      LC 94-9901

"Browndeer press."

Hetty "makes her first solo jaunt to Mr. Birdie's store for fresh eggs, determined to prove how responsible she is. On the way home, temptation beckons in the guise of an apple tree; Hetty breaks the eggs while picking fruit, then hides among the branches in shame. Papa and

Mama take her failure better than she expects and, instead of scolding, join her in the tree and share apple pie for breakfast." Bull Cent Child Books

"The story is remarkable for its evocative imagery, and the loving interchange between the characters set a charming tone. The words are perfectly complemented by Lewis' dazzling, impressionistic watercolors." Booklist

Schick, Eleanor

Mama. Marshall Cavendish 2000 unp il $15.95

        E

1. Mothers—Fiction 2. Bereavement—Fiction
ISBN 0-7614-5060-2   LC 99-16373

A girl remembers special moments with Mama and starts to feel better after grieving over her death

"In keeping with the book's rich tone, Schick's watercolors have a softness broken only by occasional bare branches of the trees. The author . . . paints an honest portrait of one girl's grief that should resonate with children who have themselves experienced the death of a parent." Booklist

Schlein, Miriam

Hello, hello! illustrated by Daniel Kirk. Simon & Schuster Bks. for Young Readers 2002 unp il $16.95   **E**

1. Animal communication
ISBN 0-689-83435-7   LC 00-45061

"Schlein and Kirk depict animals across continents greeting one another: polar bears, chimps, wolves, beavers, zebras, penguins, elephants. The final spread brings all the animals together in a circle with a boy and his presumed mother giving one another a hug and a kiss." Booklist

"This introduction to animal communication radiates warmth and affection." Horn Book Guide

The story about me; illustrated by Kristina Stephenson. Albert Whitman & Co 2004 unp il $15.95   **E**

1. Infants—Fiction 2. Grandmothers—Fiction
3. Family life—Fiction
ISBN 0-8075-7631-X   LC 2003-17820

A little girl's grandmother describes how the different people in her extended family waited for her to be born

"The text is gentle and simply worded, and the illustrations are attractive and colorful, with scrapbooklike pictures showing various family members." SLJ

Schnur, Steven

Spring; an alphabet acrostic; illustrated by Leslie Evans. Clarion Bks. 1999 unp il $15   **E**

1. Spring 2. Alphabet
ISBN 0-395-82269-6   LC 98-22704

Describes spring, with its animals, green smells, and renewed outside activities. When read vertically, the first letters of the lines of text spell related words arranged alphabetically, from "April" to "zenith"

"The evocative free verse captures the season's promise, as do the colorful block-print illustrations." Horn Book Guide

Schnur, Steven—*Continued*

Spring thaw; illustrated by Stacey Schuett. Viking 2000 unp il $15.99 **E**

1. Spring—Fiction 2. Farm life—Fiction

ISBN 0-670-87961-4   LC 99-22543

"Schnur describes a rural landscape emerging from winter. From sun up till sun down on the small farm, the first signs of spring appear: a warm wind in the trees, the creaking of the old house, dripping icicles, and overflowing sap buckets. The soft edges and thick brush strokes of Schuett's paintings aptly capture the turning of the season." Horn Book Guide

Winter; an alphabet acrostic; illustrated by Leslie Evans. Clarion Bks. 2002 unp il $15

E

1. Winter 2. Alphabet

ISBN 0-618-02374-7   LC 2001-17358

Companion volume to Autumn (1997), Spring (1999), and Summer (2001)

"On each page, a winter-related word provides the basis for an acrostic that reads like a short poem. . . . A striking, hand-colored linoleum print illustrates each small, boxed acrostic." Booklist

Schories, Pat

Breakfast for Jack; [by] Pat Schories. Front Street 2004 unp il $13.95 **E**

1. Dogs—Fiction 2. Stories without words

ISBN 1-932425-16-0   LC 2004-46916

On a busy morning before school, the whole family leaves the house without giving Jack the dog his breakfast. A wordless picture book.

"Schories's likeness of a bouncing barker is right on target and her pastel palette and line drawings are pleasingly retro." SLJ

Other titles about Jack are:

Jack and the missing piece (2004)

Jack and the night visitors (2006)

Schotter, Roni

The boy who loved words; pictures by Giselle Potter. 1st ed. Schwartz & Wade Books 2006 unp il $16.95 **E**

1. English language—Fiction

ISBN 0-375-83601-2   LC 2005-10850

Selig, who loves words and copies them on pieces of paper that he carries with him, goes on a trip to discover his purpose.

"Potter's signature naive-style art is light and comical, while Schotter's words are a lovely celebration of the power and the music of language." Booklist

Missing Rabbit; illustrated by Cyd Moore. Clarion Bks. 2002 32p il $15 **E**

1. Divorce—Fiction 2. Toys—Fiction

ISBN 0-618-03432-3   LC 2001-32569

As Kara divides her time between Papa's house and Mama's house, she is comforted by the presence of her toy Rabbit

"Filled with comfortable routines, silly rhymes, and special games, the text reveals the loving bond Kara shares with each parent, which is echoed in charming cartoon drawings." Booklist

Another title about Kara and her family is:

Room for Rabbit (2003)

Schroeder, Alan

Minty: a story of young Harriet Tubman; pictures by Jerry Pinkney. Dial Bks. for Young Readers 1996 unp il $16.99; lib bdg $16.89; pa $6.99 **E**

1. Tubman, Harriet, 1815?-1913—Fiction 2. Slavery—Fiction

ISBN 0-8037-1888-8; 0-8037-1889-6 (lib bdg); 0-14-056196-X (pa)   LC 95-23499

Coretta Scott King Award for illustration, 1997

"Young Araminta, or 'Minty,' who will later in life be known as Harriet Tubman, proves too clumsy and defiant to be a house slave and is sent by Mistress Brodas to work in the fields. . . . The child purposely frees the muskrats from the traps she has been ordered to empty and is cruelly whipped and threatened to be sold 'downriver.' Certain that his headstrong daughter will one day attempt to run away, Minty's father begins to instruct her in outdoor survival and navigation." Bull Cent Child Books

Pinkney's "paintings, done in pencil, colored-pencils, and watercolor, use light and shadow to great effect. . . . This is a dramatic story that will hold listeners' interest and may lead them to biographical material." SLJ

Ragtime Tumpie; paintings by Bernie Fuchs. Little, Brown 1989 unp il pa $6.99 hardcover o.p.

E

1. Baker, Josephine, 1906-1975—Fiction 2. African Americans—Fiction 3. Dance—Fiction

ISBN 0-316-77504-6 (pa)   LC 87-37221

"Joy Street books"

A fictionalized account of "the childhood of Josephine Baker, the St. Louis girl who became the toast of Paris and, for many, epitomized the Jazz Age." Bull Cent Child Books

"This book evokes the magic of ragtime St. Louis, its down-and-out places and its joys. Both the prose and paintings are bursts of color." N Y Times Book Rev

Satchmo's blues; illustrated by Floyd Cooper. Doubleday Bks. for Young Readers 1996 unp il $15.95; pa $6.99 **E**

1. Armstrong, Louis, 1900-1971—Fiction 2. African American musicians—Fiction 3. New Orleans (La.)—Fiction

ISBN 0-385-32046-9; 0-440-41472-5 (pa)

LC 93-41082

A fictional recreation of the youth of trumpeter Louis Armstrong in New Orleans

"This book is full of gorgeous writing, accompanied by Cooper's atmospheric paintings." SLJ

Smoky Mountain Rose; an Appalachian Cinderella; pictures by Brad Sneed. Dial Bks. for Young Readers 1997 unp il pa $6.99 hardcover o.p. **E**

1. Fairy tales 2. Appalachian region—Fiction

ISBN 0-14-056673-2 (pa)   LC 92-1250

"Schroeder offers his own variant of the Cinderella story, using enough dialect to make an enjoyable read-

Schroeder, Alan—*Continued*

aloud. In his version, a hog plays the role of the fairy godmother, and Rose falls in love not with a prince, but with a wealthy man who 'made his fortune in sowbellies and grits.' The dynamic artwork features elongated figures in pleasing compositions." Horn Book Guide

Schuch, Steve

A symphony of whales; illustrated by Peter Sylvada. Harcourt Brace & Co. 1999 unp il $16

E

1. Whales—Fiction 2. Music—Fiction

ISBN 0-15-201670-8   LC 98-17248

Young Glashka's dream of the singing of whales, accompanied by a special kind of music, leads to the rescue of thousands of whales stranded in a freezing Siberian bay

"This is a quiet, powerful story, beautifully extended by Sylvada's paintings of ghostly whale shapes and glowing, fin-shaped skies." Booklist

Schumaker, Ward

In my garden; a counting book. Chronicle Bks. 2000 unp il $13.95   E

1. Gardens—Fiction 2. Counting

ISBN 0-8118-2689-9   LC 99-6880

In this garden the reader learns to count from one watering can to ten snails, from twenty weepy onions to fifty cherry pies and even to 233 peas

"The whimsical cartoons with soft, flat colors and outlined in black were rendered in Adobe Photoshop. The objects to be counted all have faces . . . and the 7 birds are singing from sheet music by Bach. This is a clever, enjoyable addition to the rich variety of counting books available." SLJ

Schwartz, Amy

Begin at the beginning; a little artist learns about life; [by] Amy Schwartz. newly il ed. Katherine Tegen Books 2005 unp il $15.99; lib bdg $16.89   E

1. Artists—Fiction

ISBN 0-06-000111-9; 0-06-000112-7 (lib bdg)

LC 2004-8081

A newly illustrated edition of the title first published 1983

Sara gets stuck when she must paint a picture for the second grade art show, until she discovers the best place to begin.

"Schwartz's watercolor-and-pencil drawings . . . extend the spot-on emotions in the smooth, well-paced text." Booklist

A glorious day. Atheneum Books for Young Readers 2004 unp il $16.95   E

1. Apartment houses—Fiction 2. Day—Fiction

ISBN 0-689-84802-1   LC 2003-3626

"A Richard Jackson book"

Describes a day in the life of the children, animals, parents, and babysitters in a small red brick apartment building.

"The minimalist pen-and-ink cartoons, with their loose and simple lines, are accented with soft analogous colors in gouache. . . . Youngsters will enjoy this peek into other children's daily routines and meals . . . as well as the constant action provided by the characters." SLJ

Some babies. Orchard Bks. 2000 unp il $15.95; lib bdg $16.99   E

1. Bedtime—Fiction 2. Infants—Fiction

ISBN 0-531-30287-3; 0-531-33287-X (lib bdg)

LC 99-56556

Companion volume to Teeny tiny baby (1994)

A talkative toddler delays going to sleep by asking about the activities of some babies in the park

"The soothing tone of the repetitive text balances nicely with the high-energy illustrations." SLJ

Things I learned in second grade. Katherine Tegen Books 2004 unp il $15.99; lib bdg $16.89

E

1. School stories

ISBN 0-06-050936-8; 0-06-050937-6 (lib bdg)

LC 2002-155507

A young boy shares all of the things he learned and how he changed in second grade, what he still wonders about, and what he hopes to accomplish when he is in third grade.

"This sweet story is accompanied by precisely drawn, softly colored illustrations of the boy engaged in a variety of activities at home and in the classroom, and the optimistic and cheerful ending pulls it together to a satisfactory conclusion." SLJ

What James likes best. Atheneum Bks. for Young Readers 2003 unp il $16.95   E

1. Transportation—Fiction

ISBN 0-689-84059-4   LC 2001-22988

"A Richard Jackson book"

James goes with his parents on an express bus to visit twins, in a taxi to visit Grandma, and in a car to see the county fair, then walks next door with his mother for a play date

"Schwartz's pristine illustrations are streamlined and clean; the lucid, transparent colors make her gouache and pen-and-ink illustrations . . . seem almost weightless. This is a terrifically simple, successful way to get readers and listeners to interact with printed text." Bull Cent Child Books

Schwartz, David M.

How much is a million? pictures by Steven Kellogg. Lothrop, Lee & Shepard Bks. 1985 unp il $16.99; lib bdg $17.89; pa $6.99   E

1. Million (The number) 2. Billion (The number) 3. Trillion (The number)

ISBN 0-688-04049-7; 0-688-04050-0 (lib bdg); 0-688-09933-5 (pa)   LC 84-5736

Also available paperback Big edition

"Marvelosissimo the Mathematical Magician leads the reader through Steven Kellogg's scenes of fantasy to express the concepts of a million, a billion and a trillion. The text is all printed in capital letters to point out the expanding scenes portrayed in the fabulous illustrations. The idea is to make possible to children the awesome concept of large numbers. It is a delightful fantasy as a picture book, but it is even more compelling as a first reader." Okla State Dept of Educ

Schwartz, David M.—*Continued*

If you made a million; pictures by Steven Kellogg. Lothrop, Lee & Shepard Bks. 1989 unp il $16.99; lib bdg $17.89; pa $6.99 E
1. Personal finance
ISBN 0-688-07017-5; 0-688-07018-3 (lib bdg); 0-688-13634-6 (pa) LC 88-12819
The author examines "how one earns money, how checks are used instead of cash, why banks pay interest on money deposited, [and] why interest is charged on loans." Booklist
"The concepts of banks and banking . . . are all explained with absurd and humorous examples involving Ferris wheels, ogres, and rhinoceroses. . . . The best advice of all is 'Enjoying your work is more important than money.' Steven Kellogg's splendidly funny illustrations contain a troupe of two cats, one dog, numerous kids, a unicorn, and the wonderful magician Marvelosissimo." Horn Book

Scieszka, Jon

Baloney (Henry P.); received and decoded by Jon Scieszka; visual recreation by Lane Smith. Viking 2001 unp il $15.99 E
1. Life on other planets—Fiction
ISBN 0-670-89248-3 LC 00-12041
A transmission received from outer space in a combination of different Earth languages tells of an alien schoolboy's fantastic excuse for being late to school again
"Every Earth kid will immediately recognize a soul mate in this extraterrestrial truth-stretcher and tall-tale teller. . . . Illustrator Smith has been having equal fun stretching the visual truth to create a vision of space that is not only artfully outer but also utterly outre. The result is wacky fun for everyone." Booklist

The Frog Prince continued; story by Jon Scieszka; paintings by Steve Johnson. Viking 1991 unp il $15.99; pa $6.99 E
1. Fairy tales 2. Frogs—Fiction
ISBN 0-670-83421-1; 0-14-054285-X (pa) LC 90-26537
After the frog turns into a prince, he and the Princess do not live happily ever after and the Prince decides to look for a witch to help him turn back into a frog
"The dialogue is witty, the plot, as logical as it is offbeat. Steve Johnson's paintings, executed in a rich and somber palette, are like stage settings; his depiction of the various characters is inspired." Horn Book

Math curse; illustrated by Lane Smith. Viking 1995 unp il $16.99 E
1. Mathematics—Fiction
ISBN 0-670-86194-4 LC 95-12341
When the teacher tells her class that they can think of almost everything as a math problem, one student acquires a math anxiety which becomes a real curse
"Bold in design and often bizarre in expression, Smith's paintings clearly express the child's feelings of bemusement, frustration, and panic as well as her eventual joy when she overcomes the math curse. . . . A child-centered, witty picture book." Booklist

Science verse; illustrated by Lane Smith. Viking 2004 unp il $16.99 E
1. Poetry—Fiction 2. Science—Fiction
ISBN 0-670-91057-0 LC 2004-1641
Companion volume to Math curse
When the teacher tells his class that they can hear the poetry of science in everything, a student is struck with a curse and begins hearing nothing but science verses that sound very much like some well known poems.
"Children need not be familiar with the works upon which the spoofs are based to enjoy the humor, but this is a perfect opportunity to introduce the originals and to discuss parody as a poetic form. The dynamic cartoons are an absolute delight." SLJ

Squids will be squids; fresh morals, beastly fables; by Jon Scieszka & Lane Smith; designed by Molly Leach. Viking 1998 unp il $17.99 E
1. Fables
ISBN 0-670-88135-X LC 98-5710
Contemporary fables with tongue-in-cheek morals address such topics as homework, curfews, and television commercials
"Smith ardently keeps pace with Scieszka's leaps of fancy, lending credence to a talking piece of toast, a walrus with a phone and a spiny, spiteful blowfish. . . . Beneath this duo's playful eccentricity readers will discover some powerful insights into human nature." Publ Wkly

The Stinky Cheese Man and other fairly stupid tales; [by Jon Scieszka & Lane Smith] Viking 1992 unp il $17.99 E
ISBN 0-670-84487-X LC 91-48194
A Caldecott Medal honor book, 1993
"Cinderumpelstiltskin and The Really Ugly Duckling are among the tales that Jack the narrator tries to present. But the Dedication is upside down; the Table of Contents is late; and Little Red Running Shorts and the wolf quit." Publisher's note
"The picture-book set will probably recognize the stories enough to know that what's going on isn't what's 'supposed' to happen. But *The Stinky Cheese Man* isn't a book for little ones. It will take older children (that's teens along with 10s) to follow the disordered story lines and appreciate the narrative's dry wit, wordplay, and wacky, sophomoric jokes. . . . Smith's New Wave art is an intricate part of the whole, extending as well as reinforcing the narrative; the pictures are every bit as comically insolent and deliberately clever as the words." Booklist

The true story of the 3 little pigs; pictures by Lane Smith. Viking Kestrel 1989 unp il $13.95; pa $7.99 E
1. Wolves—Fiction 2. Pigs—Fiction
ISBN 0-670-82759-2; 0-14-054451-8 (pa) LC 89-8953
The wolf gives his own outlandish version of what really happened when he tangled with the three little pigs
"The 'excited and funky' illustrations match the hilarious revisionist text to a standard story." N Y Times Book Rev

Scott, Ann Herbert

Brave as a mountain lion; illustrated by Glo Coalson. Clarion Bks. 1996 31p il $16 **E**

1. School stories 2. Shoshoni Indians—Fiction
ISBN 0-395-66760-7   LC 94-42906

Spider is afraid to get up on stage in front of everybody in the school spelling bee, but after listening to his father's advice, decides that he too will try to be as brave as his Shoshoni ancestors

"This story is well shaped and rhythmically told. Coalson's subdued watercolor and pastel illustrations depict the wintry landscapes and interiors with sensitivity and detail." SLJ

On Mother's lap; illustrated by Glo Coalson. Clarion Bks. 1992 32p il $16; pa $6.95   **E**

1. Inuit—Fiction 2. Mother-child relationship—Fiction
ISBN 0-395-58920-7; 0-395-62976-4 (pa)
     LC 91-17765

Also available Board book edition

A newly illustrated edition of the title first published 1972 by McGraw-Hill

"Sitting on his mother's lap, a young Eskimo boy gathers his belongings until he, some toys, his puppy, and a blanket are all crowded together in the rocking chair. When his baby sister cries, the boy claims there is no room for her, but Mother proves him wrong, and the threesome settle comfortably in the chair. Soft illustrations depict a cozy scene and a loving family." Horn Book

Scotton, Rob

Russell the sheep; by Rob Scotton. 1st ed. HarperCollins 2005 unp il $15.99; lib bdg $16.89   **E**

1. Sheep—Fiction 2. Bedtime—Fiction
ISBN 0-06-059848-4; 0-06-059849-2 (lib bdg)
     LC 2003-24274

Russell the sheep tries all different ways to get to sleep

"Scotton makes a captivating debut with this comical tale. He illustrates it with a witty, engaging, and fluffy character bathed in calming blue hues." SLJ

Another title about Russell is:
Russell and the lost treasure (2006)

Sedgwick, Marcus

The emperor's new clothes; retold by Marcus Sedgwick; illustrated by Alison Jay. Chronicle Books 2004 unp il $16.95   **E**

1. Andersen, Hans Christian, 1805-1875—Adaptations
2. Animals—Fiction 3. Fairy tales 4. Stories in rhyme
ISBN 0-8118-4569-9   LC 2004-2855

In this retelling of the Hans Christian Andersen story in which two rascals sell a vain emperor an invisible suit of clothes, all the characters are animals

"Sedgwick's . . . jaunty rhymed couplets and Jay's . . . signature stylized artwork ably accentuate the wry humor of this . . . tale." Publ Wkly

Includes bibliographical references

Seeger, Laura Vaccaro

The hidden alphabet. Roaring Brook Press 2003 unp il $17.95   **E**

1. Alphabet
ISBN 0-7613-1941-7   LC 2002-152838

"A Neal Porter book"

An alphabet book in which windows open to reveal the letters hidden within each picture

"From the black book jacket with cutout openings for each letter of the title to the vibrant, painterly strokes of yellow on the endpapers, Hidden Alphabet is a visual delight." SLJ

Lemons are not red. Roaring Brook Press 2004 unp il $14.95   **E**

1. Color
ISBN 1-59643-008-7

"A Neal Porter book"

"The first spread reads, 'Lemons are not/ RED.' The word 'RED' appears on a bright yellow page beneath the die-cut shape of a lemon with a red background showing through. When the page is turned, the die-cut shape falls on the correct yellow background, with the words 'Lemons are YELLOW' underneath. . . . This framework continues throughout the book. . . . Illustrated with richly colored yet simple oil paintings, this offering will delight preschoolers." SLJ

Walter was worried. Roaring Book Press 2005 unp il $15.95   **E**

1. Storms—Fiction 2. Emotions—Fiction
ISBN 1-59643-066-8   LC 2004-024558

"A Neal Porter book."

Children's faces, depicted with letters of the alphabet, react to the onset of a storm and its aftermath in this picture book, accompanied by simple alliterative text.

"The artwork uses bold colors with wide brush marks as backdrops and primary colors with almost graphic shapes to represent rain, snow flakes, leaves, and branches. With only one sentence per page, there is surprising depth in this wonderful collaboration of art and story." SLJ

Segal, John

Carrot soup; written and illustrated by John Segal. 1st ed. Margaret K. McElderry Books 2006 unp il $12.95   **E**

1. Carrots—Fiction   2. Rabbits—Fiction
3. Gardening—Fiction
ISBN 0-689-87702-1   LC 2004-16963

After working hard on his garden all spring and summer, Rabbit looks forward to harvest time when he can make soup, but every carrot disappears and Rabbit must find out who has taken them. Includes a recipe for carrot soup.

"The clues are in Segal's stylized pencil and watercolor pictures, and observant children won't have any trouble determining where the carrots went. The delicate springtime greens and browns used in the background contrast nicely with Rabbit's comically expressive face." Booklist

Segal, Lore Groszmann

Morris the artist; [by] Lore Segal; pictures by Boris Kulikov. Farrar, Straus & Giroux 2003 unp il $16   **E**

1. Birthdays—Fiction
ISBN 0-374-35063-9   LC 2002-66295
"Frances Foster books"

Morris buys a set of paints as a birthday present for Benjamin, but he wants to keep them for himself

"This simple and realistic tale is made fantastical by Kulikov's bizarrely sophisticated paintings. . . . Youngsters will enjoy the story, take the odd perspectives in stride, and maybe even learn a thing or two about friendship and generosity." SLJ

Seibold, J. Otto

Olive the other reindeer; by J. Otto Seibold and Vivian Walsh. Chronicle Bks. 1997 unp il $14.95   **E**

1. Reindeer—Fiction 2. Dogs—Fiction 3. Christmas—Fiction 4. Santa Claus—Fiction
ISBN 0-8118-1807-1   LC 97-9876

Thinking that "all of the other reindeer" she hears people singing about include her, Olive the dog reports to the North Pole to help Santa Claus on Christmas Eve

"Seibold has developed a signature style with computer digitized art, and his playful skewed lines and warm shades of ochre, pimento and olive green are user-friendly." Publ Wkly

Sendak, Maurice

Alligators all around; an alphabet. Harper & Row 1962 unp il lib bdg $15.89; pa $4.95   **E**

1. Alphabet
ISBN 0-06-025530-7 (lib bdg); 0-06-443254-8 (pa)

Originally published in smaller format as volume one of the "Nutshell library"

An alphabet book of alligators doing dishes, juggling jelly beans, throwing tantrums and wearing wigs, all from A to Z

Chicken soup with rice; a book of months. Harper & Row 1962 30p il lib bdg $16.89; pa $5.99   **E**

1. Seasons—Fiction 2. Stories in rhyme
ISBN 0-06-025535-8 (lib bdg); 0-06-443253-X (pa)

Also available Big book edition

Originally published in smaller format as volume two of the "Nutshell library"

Pictures and verse illustrate the delight of eating chicken soup with rice in every season of the year

In the night kitchen. 25th anniversary ed. HarperCollins Pubs. 1996 c1970 unp il $17.95; lib bdg $18.89; pa $6.95   **E**

1. Fantasy fiction
ISBN 0-06-026668-6; 0-06-026669-4 (lib bdg); 0-06-443436-2 (pa)

A Caldecott Medal honor book, 1971

First published 1970

"A small boy falls through the dark, out of his clothes, and into the bright, night kitchen where he is stirred into the cake batter and almost baked, jumps into the bread dough, kneads and shapes it into an airplane, and flies up over the top of the Milky Way to get milk for the bakers." Booklist

"A perfect midnight fantasy. The feelings, smells, sights, and comforting emotions which young children experience are here in lovely dream colors." Brooklyn. Art Books for Child

One was Johnny; a counting book. Harper & Row 1962 unp il lib bdg $15.89; pa $4.95   **E**

1. Counting
ISBN 0-06-025540-4 (lib bdg); 0-06-443251-3 (pa)

Originally published in smaller format as volume three of the "Nutshell library"

Counting from one to ten and back again to one, Johnny, who starts off alone, acquires too many numbered visitors for his own comfort, until they disappear one by one

Outside over there. Harper & Row 1981 unp il $21.95; pa $9.95   **E**

1. Fairy tales 2. Sisters—Fiction
ISBN 0-06-025523-4; 0-06-443185-1 (pa)
     LC 79-2682

A Caldecott Medal honor book, 1982

"An Ursula Nordstrom book"

With Papa off to sea and Mama despondent, Ida must go outside over there to rescue her baby sister from goblins who steal her to be a goblin's bride

"A gentle yet powerful story in the romantic tradition. . . . Soft in tones, rich in the use of light and color . . . the pictures are particularly distinctive for the tenderness with which the children's faces are drawn, the classic handling of texture, the imaginative juxtaposition of infant faces and the baroque landscape details that might have come from Renaissance paintings." Bull Cent Child Books

Pierre; a cautionary tale in five chapters and a prologue. Harper & Row 1962 48p il lib bdg $16.89; pa $5.99   **E**

1. Stories in rhyme
ISBN 0-06-025965-5 (lib bdg); 0-06-443252-1 (pa)

Originally published in smaller format as volume four of the "Nutshell library"

A story in verse about a little boy called Pierre who insisted upon saying 'I don't care' until he said it once too often and learned a well needed lesson

Where the wild things are; story and pictures by Maurice Sendak. Harper & Row 1963 unp il $16.95; lib bdg $17.89; pa $7.99   **E**

1. Fantasy fiction
ISBN 0-06-025492-0; 0-06-025493-9 (lib bdg); 0-06-443178-9 (pa)

Also available Spanish language edition

Awarded the Caldecott Medal, 1964

"A tale of very few words about Max, sent to his room for cavorting around in his wolf suit, who dreamed of going where the wild things are, to rule them and share their rumpus. Then a longing to be 'where some-

Sendak, Maurice—*Continued*

one loved him best of all' swept over him." Book Week

"This vibrant picture book in luminous, understated full color has proved utterly engrossing to children with whom it has been shared. . . . A sincere, preceptive contribution which bears repeated examination." Horn Book

Senisi, Ellen B.

Hurray for pre-K! text and photographs by Ellen Senisi. HarperCollins Pubs. 2000 unp il $12.95; lib bdg $12.89   **E**

1. Nursery schools

ISBN 0-06-028896-5; 0-06-028897-3 (lib bdg)

LC 99-45405

A child describes a day in pre-K, playing, snacking, resting, singing, and painting

"Each two-page spread highlights a word that describes things children do in school. The word is also used in a sentence, and is then repeated three times across the bottom right-hand page. Some children will be able to read these words. . . . New pre-schoolers will feel both comforted and enticed by these school scenes." Booklist

Serfozo, Mary

Plumply, dumply pumpkin; written by Mary Serfozo; illustrated by Valeria Petrone. Margaret K. McElderry Bks. 2001 unp il $12.95   **E**

1. Pumpkin—Fiction 2. Halloween—Fiction 3. Stories in rhyme

ISBN 0-689-83834-4   LC 00-32421

Peter finds the perfect pumpkin so that he and his Dad can make a jack-o-lantern

"Toddlers will relish the bouncy, rhyming stanzas and silly wordplay, which help make this a great, nonspooky Halloween storytime choice. The subtly textured computer-generated art has solid child appeal." Booklist

What's what? a guessing game; illustrated by Keiko Narahashi. Margaret K. McElderry Bks. 1996 unp il $15; pa $6.99   **E**

1. English language—Synonyms and antonyms

ISBN 0-689-80653-1; 0-689-83322-9 (pa)

LC 95-40098

Illustrations and rhyming text provide examples of what is soft and hard, warm and cold, wet and dry, long and short, and light and dark and describe how a puppy is all these things at once

"Narahashi's splendid watercolors . . . capture all of the joy and sense of wonder of the childhood investigations Serfozo names and celebrates." SLJ

Seuss, Dr.

The 500 hats of Bartholomew Cubbins. Random House 1990 c1938 unp il $14.95   **E**

1. Hats—Fiction

ISBN 0-394-84484-X   LC 88-38412

Also available Spanish language edition

"A Vanguard Press book"

A reissue of the title first published 1938 by Vanguard Press

"A read-aloud story telling what happened to Bartholomew Cubbins when he couldn't take his hat off before the King." Hodges. Books for Elem Sch Libr

"It is a lovely bit of tomfoolery which keeps up the suspense and surprise until the last page, and of the same ingenious and humorous imagination are the author's black and white illustrations in which a red cap and then an infinite number of red caps titillate the eye." N Y Times Book Rev

And to think that I saw it on Mulberry Street. Random House 1989 c1937 unp il $14.95; lib bdg $15.99   **E**

1. Stories in rhyme

ISBN 0-394-84494-7; 0-394-94494-1 (lib bdg)

LC 88-38411

"A Vanguard Press book"

A reissue of the title first published 1937 by Vanguard Press

This book tells in rhyme accompanied by pictures how little Marco saw a horse and wagon on Mulberry Street. Then "how that horse became a zebra, then a reindeer, then an elephant, and how the cart turned into a band wagon with a retinue of police to guide it through the traffic on Mulberry Street, only the book can properly explain." Christ Sci Monit

"A fresh, inspiring picture-story book in bright colors. . . . As convincing to a child as to the psychologist in quest of a book with an appeal to the child's imaginations." Horn Book

Bartholomew and the oobleck; written and illustrated by Dr. Seuss. Random House 1949 unp il $14.95   **E**

ISBN 0-394-80075-3

A Caldecott Medal honor book, 1950

"Bored with the same old kinds of weather, the King of Didd commanded his magicians to stir up something new and different. What they produced was a gooey, gummy green stuff which might have wrecked the kingdom had it not been for Bartholomew Cubbins, the page boy." Booklist

The cat in the hat. Random House 1957 61p il $8.99; lib bdg $11.99   **E**

1. Cats—Fiction 2. Stories in rhyme 3. Bilingual books—English-Spanish

ISBN 0-394-80001-X; 0-394-90001-4 (lib bdg)

Also available in a bilingual Spanish-English edition

A nonsense story in verse illustrated by the author about an unusual cat and his tricks which he displayed for the children one rainy day

Another title about The cat in the hat is:

The cat in the hat comes back! (1958)

Green eggs and ham. Beginner Bks. 1960 62p il $8.99; lib bdg $11.99; pa $9.95   **E**

1. Food—Fiction 2. Stories in rhyme

ISBN 0-394-80016-8; 0-394-90016-2 (lib bdg); 0-394-89220-8 (pa)

Also available Spanish language edition

This book is about "Sam-I-Am who wins a determined campaign to make another Seuss character eat a plate of green eggs and ham." Libr J

"The happy theme of refusal-to-eat changing to relish

Seuss, Dr.—*Continued*

will be doubly enjoyable to the child who finds many common edibles as nauseating as the title repast. The pacing throughout is magnificent, and the opening five pages, on which the focal character introduces himself with a placard: 'I am Sam,' are unsurpassed in the controlled-vocabulary literature." Saturday Rev

Hooray for Diffendoofer Day! [by] Dr. Seuss with some help from Jack Prelutsky & Lane Smith. Knopf 1998 unp il $17; lib bdg $18.99
E

1. School stories 2. Stories in rhyme
ISBN 0-679-89008-4; 0-679-99008-9 (lib bdg)
LC 97-39725

The students of Diffendoofer School celebrate their unusual teachers and curriculum, including Miss Fribble who teaches laughing, Miss Bonkers who teaches frogs to dance, and Mr. Katz who builds robotic rats

"Given an unfinished manuscript (some sketches, snippets of verse, and jottings of names—but no plot) retrieved after Seuss's death, Prelutsky and Smith have brought this fragment to fruition in a style that does credit to all three artists." Horn Book Guide

Horton hatches the egg. Random House 1940 unp il $14.95; lib bdg $15.99
E

1. Elephants—Fiction 2. Stories in rhyme
ISBN 0-394-80077-X; 0-394-90077-4 (lib bdg)

"Horton, the elephant, is faithful one hundred percent as he carries out his promise to watch a bird's egg while she takes a rest. Hilarious illustrations and a surprise ending." Adventuring with Books. 2d edition

Horton hears a Who! Random House 1954 unp il $14.95; lib bdg $16.99
E

1. Elephants—Fiction 2. Stories in rhyme
ISBN 0-394-80078-8; 0-394-90078-2 (lib bdg)

"Although considered the biggest blame fool in the Jungle of Nool, the faithful and kindhearted elephant of 'Horton hatches the egg' believing that a person's a person no matter how small, stanchly defends the Whos, too-small-to-be-seen inhabitants of Whoville, a town which exists on a dust speck." Booklist

"The verses are full of the usual lively, informal language and amazing rhymes that have delighted such a world-wide audience in the good 'doctor's' other books." N Y Her Trib Books

How the Grinch stole Christmas. Random House 1957 unp il $14
E

1. Christmas—Fiction 2. Stories in rhyme
ISBN 0-394-80079-6

Also available Spanish language edition

"The Grinch lived on a mountain where it was able to ignore the people of the valley except at Christmas time when it had to endure the sound of their singing. One year it decided to steal all the presents so there would be no Christmas, but much to its amazement discovered that people did not need presents to enjoy Christmas. It thereupon reformed, returned the presents and joined in the festivities." Bull Cent Child Books

"The verse is as lively and the pages are as bright and colorful as anyone could wish." Saturday Rev

If I ran the circus. Random House 1956 unp il $14.95
E

1. Circus—Fiction 2. Stories in rhyme
ISBN 0-394-80080-X

The author-illustrator "presents the fabulous Circus McGurkus with its highly imaginative young owner, Morris McGurk and its intrepid performer, Sneelock, behind whose store the circus is to be housed. There are the expected number of strange creatures with nonsensical names, but the real humor lies in the situations, and especially those involving Mr. Sneelock. There is fun for the entire family here." Bull Cent Child Books

If I ran the zoo. Random House 1950 unp il $14.95; lib bdg $16.99
E

1. Zoos—Fiction 2. Stories in rhyme
ISBN 0-394-80081-8; 0-394-90081-2 (lib bdg)

A Caldecott Medal honor book, 1951

"Assembled here are the rare and wonderful creatures which young Gerald McGrew collects from far and unusual places for the 'gol-darndest zoo on the face of the earth.'" Booklist

"As you turn the pages, the imaginings get wilder and funnier, the rhymes more hilarious. There will be no age limits for this book, because families will be forced to share rereading and quotation, for a long long time." NY Her Trib Books

McElligot's pool; written and illustrated by Dr. Seuss. Random House 1947 unp il $14.95
E

1. Fishing—Fiction 2. Stories in rhyme
ISBN 0-394-80083-4

A Caldecott Medal honor book, 1948

"In spite of warnings that there are no fish in McElligot's Pool, a boy continues to fish and to imagine the rare and wonderful denizens of the deep which he just 'might' catch." Hodges. Books for Elem Sch Libr

"Fine color surrounding a host of strange creatures enlivens this amazing fish story for all ages." Horn Book

Oh, the places you'll go! Random House 1990 unp il $17
E

1. Stories in rhyme
ISBN 0-679-80527-3
LC 89-36892

Also available Spanish language edition

Advice in rhyme for proceeding in life; weathering fear, loneliness, and confusion; and being in charge of your actions

"The combination of the lively text and wacky, offbeat pictures will delight both children and their parents." Child Book Rev Serv

Seymour, Tres

Auction! illustrated by Cat Bowman Smith. 1st ed. Candlewick Press 2005 unp il $16.99
E

1. Auctions—Fiction
ISBN 0-7636-1242-1
LC 2004-57072

No one ever outbids Aunt Lou or Miss Logsdon at local auctions, until a young girl sets her sights on a straw hat.

"Smith's detailed, muted watercolor illustrations add to the humor and movement of this satirical story." SLJ

Seymour, Tres—*Continued*

Hunting the white cow; story by Tres Seymour; pictures by Wendy Anderson Halperin. Orchard Bks. 1993 unp il $16.95 **E**

1. Cattle—Fiction 2. Farm life—Fiction

ISBN 0-531-05496-9 LC 92-43757

"A Richard Jackson book"

A child watches as more and more people join in the attempts to catch the family cow that has gotten loose, each remarking on how special the cow is

"Wendy Halperin's soft colored-pencil drawings of fields and woods that drift far back into the distant hills add to the mythic aura. A unique and imaginative book." Horn Book

Shahan, Sherry

Spicy hot colors: colores picantes; illustrated by Paula Barragan. August House 2004 unp il $16.95 **E**

1. Color 2. Bilingual books—English-Spanish

ISBN 0-87483-741-3

This is an "introduction to the names of nine colors in Spanish. Snappy, image-filled verses bring to life some of the hues and traditions of Latino culture. . . . Vibrant paintings that have both ethnic and fine-art references are appealing and attention grabbing." SLJ

Shange, Ntozake

Ellington was not a street; written by Ntozake Shange; illustrations by Kadir Nelson. Simon & Schuster Bks. for Young Readers 2004 unp il $15.95 **E**

1. African Americans—Poetry

ISBN 0-689-82884-5 LC 00-45060

"Nelson illustrates the noted poet's 'Mood Indigo,' from her collection entitled *A Daughter's Geography*. . . . In the poem, Shange recalls her childhood when her family entertained many of the . . . 'men/who changed the world,' including Paul Robeson, W.E.B. DuBois, Ray Barretto, Dizzy Gillespie, 'Sonny Til' Tilghman, Kwame Nkrumah, and Duke Ellington. Both the words and the rich, nostalgic illustrations are a tribute to these visionaries. . . . A biographical sketch of each man appears at the end, along with the poem reprinted on a single page." SLJ

Shannon, David

Alice the fairy. Blue Sky Press 2004 unp il $15.95 **E**

1. Imagination—Fiction 2. Fairies—Fiction

ISBN 0-439-49025-1 LC 2003-23478

Alice, who claims to be a Temporary Fairy, still has a lot to learn, such as how to make her clothes put themselves away in the closet.

"Kids will find most of the humor right at their level, in terms of both wit and imagination. The pictures are richly colored, some almost effervescent in their playfulness." Booklist

A bad case of stripes. Blue Sky Press (NY) 1998 unp il $16.95 **E**

ISBN 0-590-92997-6 LC 96-54643

In order to ensure her popularity, Camilla Cream always does what is expected, until the day arrives when she no longer recognizes herself

"Shannon's exaggerated, surreal, full-color illustrations take advantage of shadow, light, and shifting perspective to show the girl's plight. . . . This very funny tale speaks to the challenge many kids face in choosing to act independently." SLJ

Duck on a bike. Blue Sky Press (NY) 2002 unp il $15.95 **E**

1. Ducks—Fiction 2. Domestic animals—Fiction 3. Cycling—Fiction

ISBN 0-439-05023-5 LC 2001-35992

A duck decides to ride a bike and soon influences all the other animals on the farm to ride bikes too

"This delightful story will have youngsters chiming in on the repeated phrases and predicting, in no time, what will happen next, and the many animal sounds provide ample opportunities for role-playing. Shannon's brightly colored spreads are filled with humor." SLJ

Good boy, Fergus! [by] David Shannon. Blue Sky Press 2006 unp il $15.99 **E**

1. Dogs—Fiction

ISBN 0-439-49027-8 LC 2005-08541

Except for his bath, Fergus experiences the perfect doggy day, from chasing cats and motorcycles to being scratched on his favorite tickle spot.

"This book is all about the impressive, oversize visuals—pictures that show the adorable doggie in full canine-caper mode." Booklist

No, David! Blue Sky Press (NY) 1998 unp il $15.95 **E**

1. Mother-son relationship—Fiction

ISBN 0-590-93002-8 LC 97-35125

Also available Spanish language edition

A Caldecott Medal honor book, 1999

"All little David hears from his mother as he writes on the wall, runs naked down the road, lets water pour over the side of the tub, sticks his finger far, far up his nose, and the like is 'No, David!.'" Booklist

"The vigorous and wacky full-color acrylic paintings portray a lively and imaginative boy whose stick-figure body conveys every nuance of anger, exuberance, defiance, and best of all, the reassurance of his mother's love." SLJ

Other titles about David are:

David gets in trouble (2002))

David goes to school (1999)

The rain came down. Blue Sky Press (NY) 2000 unp il lib bdg $15.95 **E**

1. Rain—Fiction

ISBN 0-439-05021-9 LC 99-86363

"When the rain starts falling, a whole neighborhood is soon honking, bickering, and snapping at one another. . . . Calm and goodwill are finally restored when the rain stops and the sun comes out." Horn Book Guide

"This deceptively simple story showcases Shannon's quirky humor and offbeat illustrations." SLJ

Shannon, George

Lizard's guest; pictures by Jose Aruego and Ariane Dewey. Greenwillow Bks. 2003 unp il $15.99; lib bdg $16.89   **E**

1. Lizards—Fiction

ISBN 0-06-009083-9; 0-06-009084-7 (lib bdg)

LC 2002-23548

While dancing around, Lizard accidentally steps on Skunk's toes and then promises to take care of lazy Skunk until his foot is healed

"The color cartoon illustrations show the black-and-white striped skunk prancing about while his bright-green benefactor is away, and are a bouncy match for the humorous text and Lizard's energetic song." SLJ

Tippy-toe chick, go! pictures by Laura Dronzek. Greenwillow Bks. 2003 unp il $15.99; lib bdg $16.89   **E**

1. Chickens—Fiction 2. Dogs—Fiction

ISBN 0-06-029823-5; 0-06-029824-3 (lib bdg)

LC 2002-17509

When a mean dog blocks the path to the garden where a delicious breakfast awaits, Little Chick shows her family how brave and clever she is

"The narrative has a fresh, buoyant vitality that begs to be read aloud. . . . The bright, uncluttered acrylic illustrations neatly match the spare text." Booklist

Tomorrow's alphabet; pictures by Donald Crews. Greenwillow Bks. 1996 unp il $17; pa $6.99   **E**

1. Alphabet

ISBN 0-688-13504-8; 0-688-16424-2 (pa)

LC 94-19484

"In 26 double-page spreads, the letters of the alphabet are used to demonstrate where things come from. 'A is for seed' is followed on the next page with 'tomorrow's APPLE.' 'D is for puppy—tomorrow's DOG.'. . . All of the combinations are clever, well chosen, and well within youngsters' experience. . . . Each two-page spread offers brightly colored, large and realistic depictions of the objects named." SLJ

White is for blueberry; pictures by Laura Dronzek. 1st ed. Greenwillow Books 2005 unp il $15.99; lib bdg $16.89   **E**

1. Color

ISBN 0-06-029275-X; 0-06-029276-8 (lib bdg)

LC 2004-10147

"Shannon challenges color associations that become ingrained in early life by using unusual combinations of words and images. . . . Red poppies, for example, are black 'when we take the time to look inside.'" Booklist

"The bold, uncluttered scenes, rendered in acrylics, have a sweetness and strength that is quite pleasing to the eye. Easy to read and fun to share, this paean to the wonder of cycles and the rewards of close observation is the perfect prelude to a thoughtful excursion." SLJ

Shannon, Margaret

The red wolf; written and illustrated by Margaret Shannon. Houghton Mifflin 2002 unp il $15   **E**

1. Fairy tales 2. Princesses—Fiction

ISBN 0-618-05544-4   LC 00-56742

Roselupin, a princess locked in a tower by her over-protective father, uses yarn to knit a red wolf suit to free herself

"Shannon's brightly colored illustrations and the creative design and layout enrich this original, delightful tale. A thoroughly enjoyable story of empowerment." SLJ

Sharmat, Marjorie Weinman

Gila monsters meet you at the airport; pictures by Byron Barton. Macmillan 1980 unp il $16.95; pa $5.99   **E**

1. Moving—Fiction 2. West (U.S.)—Fiction

ISBN 0-02-782450-0; 0-689-71383-5 (pa)

LC 80-12264

A New York City boy's preconceived ideas of life in the West make him very apprehensive about the family's move there

"The exaggeration is amusing, the style yeasty, with a nice final touch; the illustrations are comic and awkward, but add little that's not inherent in the story." Bull Cent Child Books

Nate the Great; illustrated by Marc Simont. Coward, McCann & Geoghegan 1972 60p il pa $4.50 hardcover o.p.   **E**

1. Mystery fiction

ISBN 0-440-46126-X

Available in paperback from Dell

"A Break-of-day book"

Nate the Great, a junior detective who has found missing balloons, books, slippers, chickens and even a goldfish, is now in search of a painting of a dog by Annie, the girl down the street

"The illustrations capture the exaggerated, tongue-in-cheek humor of the story." Booklist

Other titles about Nate the Great are:

Nate the Great and me: the case of the fleeing fang (1998)

Nate the Great and the big sniff (2001)

Nate the Great and the boring beach bag (1987)

Nate the Great and the crunchy Christmas (1996)

Nate the Great and the fishy prize (1985)

Nate the Great and the Halloween hunt (1989)

Nate the Great and the lost list (1975)

Nate the Great and the missing key (1981)

Nate the Great and the monster mess (1999)

Nate the Great and the mushy valentine (1994)

Nate the Great and the musical note (1990)

Nate the Great and the phony clue (1977)

Nate the Great and the pillowcase (1993)

Nate the Great and the snowy trail (1982)

Nate the Great and the sticky case (1978)

Nate the Great and the stolen base (1992)

Nate the Great and the tardy tortoise (1995)

Nate the Great goes down in the dumps (1989)

Nate the Great goes undercover (1974)

Nate the Great on the Owl Express (2003)

Nate the Great, San Francisco detective (2000)

Nate the Great saves the King of Sweden (1997)

Nate the Great stalks stupidweed (1986)

Sharmat, Mitchell

Gregory, the terrible eater; illustrated by Jose Aruego and Ariane Dewey. Four Winds Press 1985 c1980 unp il $16.95   E

1. Goats—Fiction 2. Diet—Fiction
ISBN 0-02-782250-8   LC 85-29290
Also available in paperback from Scholastic
A reissue of the title first published 1980

"Gregory is not your average goat. In fact, he's the original goat gourmet, abandoning bottle caps in favor of bananas and trading last year's boots for bread and butter." SLJ

"Aruego and Dewey's illustrations are highly amusing, thanks to their goats' dot-eyed facial expressions. . . . There is energy in the pictures; they are beguiling and help to carry the humor." Booklist

Shaw, Charles

It looked like spilt milk. Harper & Row 1947 unp il $15.99; lib bdg $15.89; pa $5.95

                                        E

ISBN 0-06-025566-8; 0-06-025565-X (lib bdg); 0-06-443159-2 (pa)
Also available Board book edition and Big book edition

White silhouettes on a blue background with simple captions: "sometimes it looked like a tree," "Sometimes it looked like a bird," etc. lead to a surprise ending "sometimes it looked like spilt milk, but what it was was—"

"What one thing could look like all of these? On the last page you are told, and I could no more tell you now than I could spoil an adult mystery by a review that gives away its solution." N Y Her Trib Books

Shaw, Nancy

Raccoon tune; illustrated by Howard Fine. Holt & Co. 2003 unp il $15.95   E

1. Raccoons—Fiction 2. Stories in rhyme
ISBN 0-8050-6544-X   LC 2002-5945
A family of raccoons prowls around a neighborhood making a ruckus until they find supper

"Playful illustrations expand the lighthearted mood of the story. Fine's use of blues, greens, and light makes nighttime scenes almost as bright as the white of the raccoons' markings, and such objects as the metal trash cans shine with reflected moonlight." SLJ

Sheep in a jeep; illustrated by Margot Apple. Houghton Mifflin 1986 32p il lib bdg $15; pa $5.95   E

1. Sheep—Fiction 2. Stories in rhyme
ISBN 0-395-41105-X (lib bdg); 0-395-47030-7 (pa)
                                        LC 86-3101
Also available Board book edition

"When five sheep pile into one little jeep, there is trouble . . . [as] the poor woolly travelers push, shove, and attempt to drive their way from one calamity to another." Horn Book

"Shaw demonstrates a promising capacity for creating nonsense rhymes. . . . Veteran illustrator Apple's whimsical portraits of the sheep bring the story to life. Pleasing and lighthearted, this has much appeal for young readers." Publ Wkly

Other titles about the sheep are:
Sheep in a shop (1991)
Sheep on a ship (1989)
Sheep out to eat (1992)
Sheep take a hike (1994)
Sheep trick or treat (1997)

Shields, Carol Diggory

Lucky pennies and hot chocolate; illustrated by Hiroe Nakata. Dutton Children's Bks. 2000 unp il $13.99   E

1. Grandfathers—Fiction
ISBN 0-525-46450-6   LC 00-20967
A grandfather and his grandson enjoy sharing knock-knock jokes, playing games, hot chocolate, watching movies, reading books, playing baseball and just spending time together

"The illustrations are as warm, colorful, and winning as the story." Booklist

Shulevitz, Uri

Snow. Farrar, Straus & Giroux 1998 unp il $16
                                        E

1. Snow—Fiction
ISBN 0-374-37092-3   LC 97-37257
A Caldecott Medal honor book, 1999

As snowflakes slowly come down, one by one, people in the city ignore them, and only a boy and his dog think that the snowfall will amount to anything

"Passersby are caricatured into humorous figures bent into impossible postures, their tall hats, parasols, and funny shoes giving them an almost circus-clown appearance. . . . The elegantly stark text suits the elegant architectural lines of the cityscape." Bull Cent Child Books

So sleepy story. Farrar Straus Giroux 2006 unp il $16   E

1. Night—Fiction 2. Sleep—Fiction
ISBN 0-374-37031-1

"A sleepy sleepy boy is fast asleep in his sleepy sleepy bed along with everything else in his sleepy sleepy house until music comes drifting in, in ever louder tones. Then the child and his surroundings gradually come alive, dance, and shake to the beat, and drift back to sleep as the notes and instruments depart. The brief repetitive text takes a backseat to the whimsical watercolor-and-ink cartoon illustrations." SLJ

Shulman, Mark

Mom and Dad are palindromes; a dilemma for words . . . and backwards; by Mark Shulman; illustrated by Adam McCauley. Chronicle Books 2006 unp il $15.95   E

1. Palindromes—Fiction
ISBN 9780811843287   LC 2005023614
When Bob realizes that he is surrounded by palindromes, from his mom, dad, and sis Anna to his dog Otto, he discovers a way to deal with the palindrome puzzle.

"In all, Shulman cleverly weaves over 101 palindromes into the text. . . . The mixed-media cartoon art amplifies the zany situation." SLJ

Siddals, Mary McKenna

I'll play with you; illustrated by David Wisniewski. Clarion Bks. 2000 28p il $14

E

1. Play—Fiction
ISBN 0-395-90373-4   LC 99-57849

Children speak to the sun, wind, clouds, rain, stars, and moon, asking to play with them

"Despite the simplicity of the text, which is well suited for beginning readers, the words are poetic, mixing humor and glee into the reverence for nature. In his familiar cut-paper artwork, Wisniewski shows the children's profound satisfaction at play." Booklist

Siegelson, Kim L.

In the time of the drums; illustrated by Brian Pinkney. Hyperion Bks. for Children 1999 unp il $15.99; lib bdg $16.49

E

1. Slavery—Fiction 2. Gullahs—Fiction 3. Igbo (African people)—Fiction 4. Grandmothers—Fiction
ISBN 0-7868-0436-X; 0-7868-2386-0 (lib bdg)
LC 98-30347

"Jump at the sun"

Mentu, an American-born slave boy, watches his beloved grandmother, Twi, lead the insurrection at Teakettle Creek of Ibo people arriving from Africa on a slave ship

The "finely etched art dramatically captures the story's simultaneous sadness and hope. . . . At once magical yet chillingly real, this is a thought-provoking and memorable work." Publ Wkly

Sierra, Judy

Preschool to the rescue; illustrated by Will Hillenbrand. Harcourt 2001 unp il $15   E

1. Vehicles—Fiction 2. Stories in rhyme
ISBN 0-15-202035-7   LC 99-6475

"Gulliver books"

When a mud puddle traps a pizza van, police car, tow truck, and other vehicles, a group of preschoolers comes along and saves the day

"The repetition and rhyme carry the story along and the fun doesn't stop until the book is closed. The artwork is perfect." SLJ

Thelonius Monster's sky-high fly pie; illustrations by Edward Koren. 1st ed. Knopf 2006 unp il $16.95; lib bdg $18.99   E

1. Monsters—Fiction 2. Pies—Fiction 3. Flies—Fiction 4. Stories in rhyme
ISBN 0-375-83218-1; 0-375-93218-6 (lib bdg)
LC 2005-16773

A good-natured monster thinks a pie made out of flies would be a good dessert, and invites all his friends and relatives over to try it.

"An incomparable rhymester has teamed up with a master cartoonist to conjure up some haute cuisine on the fly. . . . The words are carefully chosen. . . . A lovable and entertaining work of art." SLJ

Wild about books; by Judy Sierra; pictures by Marc Brown. Knopf 2004 unp il $16.95

E

1. Animals—Fiction 2. Books and reading—Fiction 3. Libraries—Fiction 4. Stories in rhyme
ISBN 0-375-82538-X

A librarian named Mavis McGrew introduces the animals in the zoo to the joy of reading when she drives her bookmobile to the zoo by mistake.

"Sierra's text has a wacky verve and enough clever asides and allusions to familiar characters to satisfy bibliophiles of all ages. . . . Brown's cheerful, full-color illustrations stretch his trademark art with ever-so-slightly stylized spreads that are rich in pattern, texture, and nuance." SLJ

Silverman, Erica

Cowgirl Kate and Cocoa; written by Erica Silverman; painted by Betsy Lewin. Harcourt 2005 unp il $15   E

1. Horses—Fiction 2. Cowhands—Fiction
ISBN 0-15-202124-8   LC 2004-5739

Cowgirl Kate and her cowhorse Cocoa, who is always hungry, count cows, share a story, and help each other fall asleep.

"Children will . . . recognize the friends' good-natured banter and lively dialogue. . . . Lewin's bold-lined illustrations extend the comedy and the affectionate friendship." Booklist

Another title about Kate and Cocoa is:
Partners (2006)

When the chickens went on strike; a Rosh Hashanah tale; adapted from a story by Sholom Aleichem; illustrations by Matthew Trueman. Dutton Children's Bks. 2003 unp il $15.99

E

1. Sholem Aleichem, 1859-1916—Adaptations 2. Jews—Fiction 3. Rosh ha-Shanah—Fiction 4. Chickens—Fiction
ISBN 0-525-46862-5   LC 2001-40397

"In this Jewish New Year story . . . a young boy sneaks away from religious services to spy on a meeting of local chickens. The birds are upset about the tradition of Kapores, a custom involving twirling chickens overhead to symbolically rid a person of bad deeds. Declaring freedom for fowl, the birds go on strike. . . . Trueman's stylistically inventive mixed-media illustrations, rich in earth tones, are visually striking. They juxtapose well with Silverman's understated yet humorous text." Booklist

Simmons, Jane

Come along, Daisy! Little, Brown 1998 c1997 unp il $13.95   E

1. Ducks—Fiction
ISBN 0-316-79790-1   LC 97-26682

Also available Board book editions featuring Daisy the duck

First published 1997 in the United Kingdom

Daisy the duckling becomes so engrossed in playing with dragonflies and lily pads that she temporarily loses her mother

Simmons, Jane—*Continued*

"The inquisitive duckling is an expressive splash of yellow in Simmons's blue-green pondscapes; the story unfolds in a series of watery panoramas amid bold forms and broad strokes of color. . . . This is a gem of a story and a masterful piece of picture-book artistry." SLJ

Other titles about Daisy are:
Daisy and the Beastie (2000)
Daisy and the egg (1998)
Quack, Daisy, quack! (2002)

Simms, Laura

Rotten teeth; illustrated by David Catrow. Houghton Mifflin 1998 unp il $16   E

1. School stories 2. Teeth—Fiction
ISBN 0-395-82850-3   LC 97-2528

When Melissa takes a big glass bottle of authentic pulled teeth from her father's dental office for a show-and-tell presentation, she becomes a first-grade celebrity

"Catrow's watercolors are a suitably twisted complement to Simms' somewhat warped sense of humor (actually, it's perfect for this audience)." Bull Cent Child Books

Simont, Marc

The stray dog; retold and illustrated by Marc Simont from a true story by Reiko Sassa. HarperCollins Pubs. 2001 unp il $15.95; lib bdg $15.89   E

1. Dogs—Fiction
ISBN 0-06-028933-3; 0-06-028934-1 (lib bdg)

A Caldecott Medal honor book, 2002

"Two children play with a stray dog in the country one Saturday. The whole family thinks about him all week, and the next Saturday they return to the same picnic spot, where the children save the dog from the dog-catcher and adopt him." Horn Book Guide

"Simont's art and narrative play off each other strategically, together imparting the tale's humor and tenderness." Publ Wkly

Sís, Peter

Ballerina! Greenwillow Bks. 2001 unp il $14.95   E

1. Ballet—Fiction 2. Color
ISBN 0-688-17944-4   LC 00-35401

A little girl puts on costumes of different colors and imagines herself dancing on stage

Sis "creates a beautifully realized spot-on view of creative kids at play." Booklist

Dinosaur! Greenwillow Bks. 2000 unp il $15.99   E

1. Dinosaurs 2. Stories without words
ISBN 0-688-17049-8   LC 99-32923

While taking a bath, a young boy is joined by all sorts of dinosaurs

"A wordless picture book that takes readers on a wild adventure of the imagination. . . . This imaginative story with wonderful end-papers naming the creatures should appeal to all young dinosaur lovers. Sis's barely fleshed-out, cookie-cutter cartoons tell the story." SLJ

Fire truck. Greenwillow Bks. 1998 unp il $15.99   E

1. Fire engines—Fiction
ISBN 0-688-15878-1   LC 97-29320

Matt, who loves fire trucks, wakes up one morning to find that he has become a fire truck, with one driver, two ladders, three hoses, and ten boots. Features a gate-fold illustration that opens into a three-page spread

"Sis blends simple text with bold pictures to give insight into one boy's vivid imagination." SLJ

Komodo! Greenwillow Bks. 1993 il $16.99; lib bdg $17.89   E

1. Komodo dragon—Fiction 2. Indonesia—Fiction
ISBN 0-688-11583-7; 0-688-11584-5 (lib bdg)
          LC 92-25811

A young boy who loves dragons goes with his parents to the Indonesian island of Komodo in hopes of seeing a real dragon. Includes factual information about the Komodo dragon

"The story, assisted by the art in its moodily surreal tone, is simply written buy implies worlds." Bull Cent Child Books

Madlenka. Farrar, Straus & Giroux 2000 unp il $17   E

1. New York (N.Y.)—Fiction 2. Teeth—Fiction
ISBN 0-374-39969-7   LC 99-57730

"Frances Foster books"

Madlenka, whose New York City neighbors include the French baker, the Indian news vendor, the Italian ice-cream man, the South American grocer, and the Chinese shopkeeper, goes around the block to show her friends her loose tooth and finds that it is like taking a trip around the world

"The real magic comes in the cleverly cut-away windows in each storefront through which children glimpse complex, global dreamscapes. Madlenka journeys through these mystical places, too, and it is these surreal, wordless stories-within-the-story that will excite a wide range of children, launching them in their own imagined departures." Booklist

Another title about Madlenka is:
Madlenka's dog (2002)

Ship ahoy! Greenwillow Bks. 1999 unp il $14.95   E

1. Ships 2. Stories without words
ISBN 0-688-16644-X   LC 98-46673

A child on a sofa imagines it turning into a succession of ships, culminating in an encounter with a sea monster

This is a "wordless picture book. . . . The drawings are limned in shades of blue and green encircled by lots of clean, white space. The result is a charmingly simple, entrancing book." SLJ

A small tall tale from the far Far North. Foster Bks. 2001 unp il $17; pa $6.95   E

1. Welzl, Jan—Fiction 2. Inuit—Fiction 3. Arctic regions—Fiction
ISBN 0-374-37075-3; 0-374-46725-0 (pa)
          LC 00-34112

A reissue of the title first published 1993 by Knopf

With the help of Eskimos, Jan Welzl survives a perilous journey from central Europe to the Arctic regions in

Sís, Peter—*Continued*
the late 1800s

Sis "blends scraps of fact and fiction in writing about a little-known explorer and provides a short prologue and epilogue. Superb imaginative illustrations embellish the text of this most unusual picture story-book." Child Book Rev Serv

Trucks, trucks, trucks. Greenwillow Bks. 1999 il $15.99 E
1. Trucks—Fiction
ISBN 0-688-16276-2 LC 98-4482
A little boy cleans up his room using a variety of trucks and gives a one word description of their work such as hauling, plowing, and loading. Features a gatefold illustration that opens into a three-page spread

"Sis creates a simple, bold look. . . . Gouache paints in yellow, black, and gray are set off by plenty of white space. The single verbs on each page are rendered in shades of blue, purple, green, and orange. This cheery romp is perfect for toddlers." SLJ

Slate, Joseph
Miss Bindergarten celebrates the 100th day of kindergarten; illustrated by Ashley Wolff. Dutton Children's Bks. 1998 unp il $16.99 E
1. Kindergarten—Fiction 2. Animals—Fiction 3. Stories in rhyme
ISBN 0-525-46000-4 LC 98-10486
To celebrate one hundred days in Miss Bindergarten's kindergarten class, all her students bring one hundred of something to school, including a one hundred-year-old relative, one hundred candy hearts, and one hundred polka dots

"Wolff's sturdy, genially observed illustrations prove a perfect match for Slate's rhyming text." Publ Wkly
Other titles about Miss Bindergarten are:
Miss Bindergarten celebrates the last day of kindergarten (2006)
Miss Bindergarten gets ready for kindergarten (1996)
Miss Bindergarten has a wild day in kindergarten (2005)
Miss Bindergarten stays home from kindergarten (2000)
Miss Bindergarten takes a field trip with kindergarten (2001)
Miss Bindergarten's craft center (1999)

Sloat, Teri
Berry magic; written by Teri Sloat and Betty Huffmon; illustrated by Teri Sloat. Alaska Northwest Books 2004 unp il $15.95; pa $8.95 E
1. Berries—Fiction 2. Alaska—Fiction 3. Inuit—Fiction
ISBN 0-88240-575-6; 0-88240-576-4 (pa)
LC 2003-70851
Long ago, the only berries on the tundra were hard, tasteless, little crowberries. When Anana sings, she turns four dolls into little girls who run and tumble over the tundra creating patches of fat, juicy berries: blueberries, cranberries, salmonberries, and raspberries.

"Done in a palette of deep, earthy hues, ethereal blues, and bright highlights, Sloat's pictures are vibrant and engaging. . . . The rich language enlightens readers to different elements of the Eskimo culture." SLJ

I'm a duck! story and pictures by Teri Sloat. G.P. Putnam's Sons 2006 unp il $15.99 E
1. Ducks—Fiction 2. Stories in rhyme
ISBN 0-399-24274-0 LC 2004-20479
"From the moment he hatches, a duckling celebrates his duck-ness – his webbed feet, his perfect waddle, his strong quack, and his flapping wings. As he grows, he meets a mate, becomes a father, and continues his zestful take on life. Sloat's rhymed text captures the exuberance of this eternal optimist and gives a glimpse into the life cycle of a mallard. The full-color art is rendered in pastels and has bold lines and a variety of perspectives and page layouts." SLJ

There was an old lady who swallowed a trout; illustrated by Reynold Ruffins. Holt & Co. 1998 unp il $16.95 E
1. Stories in rhyme 2. Pacific Northwest—Fiction
ISBN 0-8050-4294-6 LC 98-11607
Set on the coast of the Pacific Northwest, this variation on the traditional cumulative rhyme describes the silly consequences of an old woman's fishy diet

"Ruffins's colorful illustrations reflect both the zaniness of the rhyme and the coastal locale." SLJ

Slobodkina, Esphyr
Caps for sale; a tale of a peddler, some monkeys & their monkey business; told and illustrated by Esphyr Slobodkina. Addison Wesley Longman 1947 unp il $16.99; pa $6.99 E
1. Monkeys—Fiction 2. Peddlers and peddling—Fiction
ISBN 0-201-09147-X; 0-06-443143-6 (pa)
Also available Big book edition and with Audiobook; Spanish language edition also available
A picture book story which "provides hilarious confusion. A cap peddler takes a nap under a tree. When he wakes up, his caps have disappeared. He looks up in the tree and sees countless monkeys, each wearing a cap and grinning." Parent's Guide To Child Read

Small, David
George Washington's cows. Farrar Straus Giroux 1994 unp il $16; pa $6.99 E
1. Washington, George, 1732-1799—Fiction 2. Animals—Fiction 3. Stories in rhyme
ISBN 0-374-32535-9; 0-374-42534-5 (pa)
LC 93-39989
Humorous rhymes about George Washington's farm where the cows wear dresses, the pigs wear wigs, and the sheep are scholars.

"Small's watercolors immeasurably extend his zany poem and make maximum use of the double-page spreads. Cleverly designed and well-executed scenes are filled with silly details that children will love." Booklist

Imogene's antlers; written and illustrated by David Small. Crown 2000 c1985 unp il $15.95; lib bdg $17.99; pa $6.99 E
ISBN 0-375-81048-X; 0-375-91048-4 (lib bdg); 0-517-56242-1 (pa)
First published 1985

Small, David—*Continued*

One Thursday Imogene wakes up with a pair of antlers growing out of her head and causes a sensation wherever she goes

The author "maximizes the inherent humor of the absurd situation by allowing the imaginative possibilities of Imogene's predicament to run rampant. The brief text is supported by Small's expansive watercolors. They brim with humorous details." SLJ

Smalls, Irene

My Pop Pop and me; by Irene Smalls; illustrated by Cathy Ann Johnson. 1st ed. Little, Brown 2006 unp il $15.99   **E**
    1. Grandfathers—Fiction 2. Baking—Fiction
3. Stories in rhyme
    ISBN 0-316-73422-5   LC 2005022559
"An African American grandfather, Pop Pop, and his grandson transform baking a lemon cake into a magical mystery tour of sound and rhythm. . . . Warm, soft, stylized watercolors add a surreal element to the lively story." Booklist

Smith, Cynthia Leitich

Jingle dancer; illustrated by Cornelius Van Wright and Ying-Hwa Hu. Morrow Junior Bks. 2000 unp il $15.99; lib bdg $16.89   **E**
    1. Creek Indians—Fiction 2. Native American dance—Fiction
    ISBN 0-688-16241-X; 0-688-16242-8 (lib bdg)
                                                          LC 99-15503
Jenna, a member of the Muscogee, or Creek, Nation, borrows jingles from the dresses of several friends and relatives so that she can perform the jingle dance at the powwow. Includes a note about the jingle dance tradition and its regalia
"The colorful, well-executed watercolor illustrations lend warmth to the story." Booklist

Smith, Lane

Glasses: who needs 'em? Viking 1991 unp il $16.99; pa $6.99   **E**
    1. Eyeglasses—Fiction
    ISBN 0-670-84160-9; 0-14-054484-4 (pa)
                                                          LC 91-9827
Also available Spanish language edition
"When a young patient states, 'I'm worried about looking like a dork,' the optometrist lists others who wear spectacles—'monster-movie' stuntpeople, famous inventors, entire planets. Just when he decides the doctor is crazy, the boy looks through the glasses and sees what he's been missing (almost everyone and everything in the world wearing glasses)." SLJ

The author's "outlandish, surreal illustrations combine with a loopy layout and fanciful type design to provide an abundance of laughter." Publ Wkly

Pinocchio, the boy; or, Incognito in Collodi. Viking 2002 various paging $16.99   **E**
    1. Fairy tales
    ISBN 0-670-03585-8   LC 2002-1020

Pinocchio has been turned into a boy but no one, not even he, realizes it as he walks through Collodi-town trying to get some hot chicken soup for Geppetto

"Smith's concept is clever and his telling buoyant. . . . The art is abundant in every way. . . . A clever, kooky offering that still allows children to feel the heart of a puppet-turned-boy." Booklist

Smith, Linda

Mrs. Biddlebox; illustrated by Marla Frazee. HarperCollins Pubs. 2002 unp il $15.99   **E**
    1. Stories in rhyme
    ISBN 0-06-028690-3   LC 00-63199
With baking magic, Mrs. Biddlebox uses fog, dirt, sky, and other ingredients of a rotten day to transform it into a sweet cake

"The jaunty rhythm of Smith's words captures the energy of her protagonist's out-of-the-box thinking and sheer determination. . . . Frazee . . . uses pencil lines and cross-hatching to dramatic effect." Publ Wkly

When Moon fell down; illustrated by Kathryn Brown. HarperCollins Pubs. 2001 unp il $15.95; lib bdg $15.89   **E**
    1. Moon—Fiction 2. Cattle—Fiction 3. Stories in rhyme
    ISBN 0-06-028301-7; 0-06-029497-3 (lib bdg)
                                                          LC 00-33580
The moon falls down to earth one night and roams about with a friendly cow before returning to the sky

"Soft, blue-toned watercolors capture the mood of the magical evening and depict the moon as a huge glowing orb atop a spindly human body." Horn Book Guide

Smothers, Ethel Footman

The hard-times jar; pictures by John Holyfield. Farrar, Straus and Giroux 2003 unp il $16
                                                          E
    1. Migrant labor—Fiction 2. Books and reading—Fiction 3. African Americans—Fiction
    ISBN 0-374-32852-8   LC 2002-26596
"Frances Foster books"
Emma, the daughter of poor migrant workers, longs to own a real book, and when she turns eight and must attend school for the first time, she is amazed to discover a whole library in her classroom

"Filled with descriptive language, the text flows smoothly and it clearly describes Emma's enthusiasm and fears. The richly textured browns, yellows, and greens of the paintings evoke a warm, orderly, and nonthreatening environment." SLJ

Soto, Gary

Chato's kitchen; illustrated by Susan Guevara. Putnam 1995 unp il $16.99; pa $6.99   **E**
    1. Cats—Fiction 2. Mice—Fiction
    ISBN 0-399-22658-3; 0-698-11600-3 (pa)
                                                          LC 93-43503
Also available Spanish language edition
To get the "ratoncitos," little mice, who have moved into the barrio to come to his house, Chato the cat prepares all kinds of good food: fajitas, frijoles, salsa, enchi-

Soto, Gary—*Continued*

ladas, and more

"Soto adeptly captures the flavor of life in *el barrio* in this amusing tale. The animal characters have distinct personalities, and their language, sprinkled with Spanish phrases and expressions, credibly brings them to life. Best of all, though, are Guevara's striking illustrations that enrich the text with delightful, witty details." SLJ

Other titles about Chato are:

Chato and the party animals (2000)

Chato goes cruisin' (2005)

If the shoe fits; illustrated by Terry Widener. Putnam 2002 unp il $15.99   E

1. Shoes—Fiction 2. Mexican Americans—Fiction

ISBN 0-399-23420-9   LC 00-68413

After being teased about his brand new loafers, Rigo puts them away for so long he grows out of them

"This subtle story is infused with an upbeat mood and nimble humor. The artwork is as inviting and unpretentious as Soto's prose." Horn Book Guide

Too many tamales; illustrated by Ed Martinez. Putnam 1992 unp il $16.99; pa $7.99   E

1. Christmas—Fiction 2. Mexican Americans—Fiction

ISBN 0-399-22146-8; 0-698-11412-4 (pa)

LC 91-19229

Maria tries on her mother's wedding ring while helping make tamales for a Christmas family get together, but panic ensues when hours later, she realizes the ring is missing

This is "a very funny story, full of delicious surprise. The handsome, realistic oil paintings, in rich shades of brown, red, and purple, are filled with light, evoking the togetherness of an extended family." Booklist

Sperring, Mark

The fairytale cake; made by Mark Sperring; decorated by Jonathan Langley. Scholastic 2005 unp il $15.95   E

1. Cake—Fiction 2. Fairy tales

ISBN 0-439-68329-7

"The Chicken House"

"An array of characters from Western fairy tales and nursery rhymes comes together to produce and deliver an enormous cake." SLJ

"The artwork adds to the brief text in a playful manner that invites participation. . . . Preschoolers who know their nursery tales and Mother Goose rhymes will want to linger on each page and identify every member of the crowd." Booklist

Spinelli, Eileen

The best time of day; written by Eileen Spinelli; illustrated by Bryan Langdo. Gulliver Books/Harcourt 2005 unp il $16   E

1. Farm life—Fiction 2. Stories in rhyme 3. Day—Fiction

ISBN 0-15-205051-5

Farmer Fred, various members of his family, his animals, and his neighbors each have a favorite time of day.

"Each spread's bouncing, rhyming text introduces diverse folks and everyday activities that kids will recognize as bright, detailed watercolor illustrations portray characters and an idyllic rural setting with cartoonlike simplicity and playful perspectives." Booklist

I know it's autumn; illustrated by Nancy Hayashi. 1st ed. HarperCollins Publishers 2004 unp il $15.99; lib bdg $16.89   E

1. Autumn—Fiction 2. Stories in rhyme

ISBN 0-06-029422-1; 0-06-029423-X (lib bdg)

LC 2003-4099

A rhyming celebration of the sights, smells, and sounds of autumn, such as pumpkin muffins, turkey stickers on spelling papers, and piles of raked leaves

"Large enough for group sharing and as quiet and comfortable as the text, Hayashi's illustrations feature rounded lines, soft shading, and gentle colors." Booklist

Night shift daddy; illustrated by Melissa Iwai. Hyperion Bks. for Children 2000 unp il $14.99; lib bdg $15.49   E

1. Father-daughter relationship—Fiction 2. Bedtime—Fiction 3. Stories in rhyme

ISBN 0-7868-0495-5; 0-7868-2424-7 (lib bdg)

LC 98-52499

A father shares dinner and bedtime rituals with his daughter before going out to work the night shift

"The rhyming text manages to convey many feelings—love, loneliness, anticipation—in few words; the mood is reinforced beautifully by the rich, detailed illustrations, especially those depicting a child's room at night." Horn Book Guide

Rise the moon; pictures by Raúl Colón. Dial Bks. for Young Readers 2003 unp il $16.99

E

1. Stories in rhyme 2. Moon—Fiction

ISBN 0-8037-2601-5   LC 00-34623

The moon lights the night for farmers, mothers and babies, wolves, and more

"Colón's distinctive illustrations full of cobalt and golden hues match the rich, glowing cadences of this delightful lullaby." SLJ

Sophie's masterpiece; a spider's tale; illustrations by Jane Dyer. Simon & Schuster Bks. for Young Readers 2001 unp il $16   E

1. Spiders—Fiction

ISBN 0-689-80112-2   LC 95-44063

Sophie the spider makes wondrous webs, but the residents of Beekman's Boarding House do not appreciate her until at last, old and tired, she weaves her final masterpiece

"The graceful telling glimmers with feeling and occasional humor, while the full-page watercolors and lacy spot art capture the delicate magic of Sophie's webs and enhance the tale's quiet mood." Horn Book Guide

Three pebbles and a song; pictures by S.D. Schindler. Dial Bks. for Young Readers 2003 unp il $16.99   E

1. Mice—Fiction 2. Winter—Fiction

ISBN 0-8037-2528-0   LC 2002-6822

As his mouse family endures a long, cold winter, Moses's contributions of a dance, a juggling act, and a little song prove more useful than he had supposed

Spinelli, Eileen—*Continued*

"The plot is well developed, the text contains many descriptive words, and emergent readers will appreciate the repetitive and predictable language. Done in gouache, watercolors, inks, pastels, and chalk, Schindler's painterly artwork captures perfectly the chill of the coming winter and the warmth of a happy home." SLJ

Wanda's monster; written by Eileen Spinelli; illustrated by Nancy Hayashi. Whitman, A. 2002 unp il $15.95   **E**
1. Monsters—Fiction 2. Grandmothers—Fiction
ISBN 0-8075-8656-0   LC 2002-1955

When Wanda fears that she has a monster in her closet, she takes her grandmother's advice and begins to look at things from the monster's point of view

"Hayashi's watercolor and colored-pencil illustrations do a great job of melding the real and the imaginary in Spinelli's story, staying true to the child's fearful fantasies and transforming them with warmth and affection." Booklist

When you are happy; illustrated by Geraldo Valério. Simon & Schuster Books for Young Readers 2006 unp il $16.95   **E**
1. Emotions—Fiction 2. Family life—Fiction
ISBN 0-689-86251-2

"Using a comforting refrain (When you are . . .), each member of the young girl's family reassures her when she is cold, sick, lonely, tired, grumpy, lost, and happy. . . . Appealingly offbeat, whimsical illustrations characterize the girl's emotions." Booklist

Spinner, Stephanie

It's a miracle! a Hanukkah storybook; written by Stephanie Spinner; illustrated by Jill McElmurry. Atheneum Bks. for Young Readers 2003 unp il $16.95   **E**
1. Hanukkah—Fiction 2. Grandmothers—Fiction
ISBN 0-689-84493-X   LC 2002-6137

"An Anne Schwartz book"

"Owen Block, aged six and a half, has just been named O.C.L.-Official Candle Lighter. Each night, as he performs his duty, he listens to Grandma Karen's cozy stories of family life. . . . A brief retelling of the Hanukkah legend and blessings in Hebrew, English, and transliteration appear at the end of the book. McElmurry's gouache illusrations add a light, humorous touch. Adults will appreciate the lessons gracefully imparted, and children will enjoy the silliness of Grandma's fanciful, zany family stories." SLJ

Spirin, Gennadiĭ

A apple pie; art by Gennady Spirin. Philomel Books 2005 unp il $16.99   **E**
1. Alphabet 2. Nursery rhymes
ISBN 0-399-23981-2   LC 2004030497

Introduces the letters A to Z while following the fortunes of an apple pie.

"Whimsically detailed watercolors revitalize an alphabet verse dating from the 1600s. . . . Delicately rendered vines and flowers are reminiscent of Victorian botanical prints. Busy details offer new discoveries with each reading. The letters, text, and paintings are unified in style and become a single work of art." SLJ

Martha. Philomel Books 2005 unp il $14.99   **E**
1. Crows 2. Russia
ISBN 0-399-23980-4   LC 2004-6735

The author relates how he and his Moscow family rescued Martha, a crow with a broken wing, and how she joined their household.

"The story will appeal to the picture book audience. . . . The lush art set in plentiful white space beautifully portrays a Moscow of a few decades ago." Horn Book Guide

Spirn, Michele

I am the turkey; story by Michele Sobel Spirn; pictures by Joy Allen. HarperCollins 2004 47p il $15.99; lib bdg $16.89   **E**
1. School stories 2. Theater—Fiction 3. Thanksgiving Day—Fiction
ISBN 0-06-053230-0; 0-06-053231-9 (lib bdg)

"An I can read book"

Mark does not want to play the turkey in the second grade Thanksgiving play, but then he ends up saving the day.

"Spirn's text is a graceful mix of quotes and narration in short sentences and basic, lively word choices that are just right for emerging readers, and Allen's ink-and-paint illustrations capture the action and comedy in scenes many kids will recognize." Booklist

Spohn, Kate

Turtle and Snake's day at the beach. Viking 2003 32p il $13.99   **E**
1. Beaches—Fiction 2. Turtles—Fiction 3. Snakes—Fiction
ISBN 0-670-03628-5   LC 2002-153376

"A Viking easy-to-read"

Turtle and Snake go to the beach, where they and some other animals participate in a sandcastle-making contest.

"Brightly colored, simple drawings capture the pleasure of this fun-in-the-sun day at the beach. . . . It's difficult to find easy-to-read books that have charm and a real story, and this one does." SLJ

Other titles about Turtle and Snake are:
Turtle and Snake and the Christmas tree (2000)
Turtle and Snake at work (1999)
Turtle and Snake fix it (2002)
Turtle and Snake go camping (2000)
Turtle and Snake's spooky Halloween (2002)
Turtle and Snake's Valentine's Day (2003)

Stamper, Judith Bauer

Breakfast at Danny's Diner; illustrated by Chris Demarest. Grosset & Dunlap 2003 46p il (All aboard math reader) lib bdg $13.89; pa $3.99   **E**
1. Restaurants—Fiction 2. Multiplication—Fiction
ISBN 0-448-43266-8 (lib bdg); 0-448-43210-2 (pa)
LC 2003-16833

Danny's twin niece and nephew help him prepare to open his diner one morning but are soon overwhelmed by the work, until they put their multiplication skills to

Stamper, Judith Bauer—*Continued*

work

"The simple text and watercolor cartoons capture the excitement and pressure of actually surviving the morning rush at a restaurant. . . . Real-life uses for math calculations and a fun story add up to a tasty treat." SLJ

Stanley, Diane

The Giant and the beanstalk; written and illustrated by Diane Stanley. HarperCollins Publishers 2004 unp il $15.99; lib bdg $16.89

E

1. Fairy tales

ISBN 0-06-000010-4; 0-06-000011-2 (lib bdg)

LC 2003-1818

In this version of the traditional tale, a young giant chases Jack down the beanstalk to rescue his beloved hen and meets other Jacks from various nursery rhymes along the way.

"Stanley injects her characteristic, understated humor into both text and art, and young ones will take pleasure in identifying the individual elements of the thoroughly mixed-up story." Booklist

Goldie and the three bears. HarperCollins Pubs. 2003 unp il $15.99; lib bdg $16.89 E
1. Friendship—Fiction 2. Bears—Fiction

ISBN 0-06-000008-2; 0-06-000009-0 (lib bdg)

LC 2002-23843

In this story, loosely based on that of Goldilocks, Goldie, who has yet to find a friend to "love with all her heart," makes an unplanned visit to the house of some bears

"The writing is smooth, concise, and rhythmic. . . . The pictures are marvelous, with fine lines; soft, glowing colors; and winsome, telling details." SLJ

Rumpelstiltskin's daughter. Morrow Junior Bks. 1997 unp il $16; lib bdg $15.93 E
1. Fairy tales

ISBN 0-688-14327-X; 0-688-14328-8 (lib bdg)

LC 96-14834

"Rumpelstiltskin's daughter relies on her cleverness instead of magic. When the king orders her to spin straw into gold, she tricks him out of his greedy ways and becomes prime minister of his kingdom. The illustrations provide splendid, detailed palace interiors and endow the characters, especially the king and his minions, with comically exaggerated features." Horn Book Guide

Saving Sweetness; illustrated by G. Brian Karas. Putnam 1996 unp il $16.99 E
1. Orphans—Fiction 2. West (U.S.)—Fiction

ISBN 0-399-22645-1 LC 95-10621

The sheriff of a dusty western town rescues Sweetness, an unusually resourceful orphan, from nasty old Mrs. Sump and her terrible orphanage

"Telling the tale from the sheriff's point of view, Stanley packs this fast-paced adventure full of language that begs to be read aloud. . . . Combining gouache, acrylic, and pencil drawings with cyanotype photographs, Karas's illustrations evoke the arid landscape of the West yet remain wonderfully original." SLJ

Another title about Sweetness is:

Raising Sweetness (1999)

Stauffacher, Sue

Bessie Smith and the night riders; [by] Sue Stauffacher; illustrated by John Holyfield. G. P. Putnam's Sons 2006 unp il $16.99 E
1. Smith, Bessie, 1894-1937—Fiction 2. Ku Klux Klan—Fiction 3. Blues music—Fiction 4. African Americans—Fiction 5. North Carolina—Fiction

ISBN 0-399-24237-6 LC 2005010399

Black blues singer Bessie Smith singlehandedly scares off Ku Klux Klan members who are trying to disrupt her show one hot July night in Concord, North Carolina. Includes historical note.

"Holyfield's brilliantly colored acrylic spreads aptly depict a larger-than-life individual. . . . The book is based on a true event. . . . This tale of courage would make a fine addition to units on the Civil Rights movement." SLJ

Includes bibliographical references

Steen, Sandra

Car wash; [by] Sandra Steen and Susan Steen; illustrated by G. Brian Karas. Putnam 2001 unp il $15.99 E
1. Automobiles—Fiction

ISBN 0-399-23369-5 LC 00-21402

"When their father takes a trip through the car wash, two children imagine a deep-sea adventure, rife with octopus arms and tidal waves." Horn Book Guide

"These offbeat pictures provide a perfect counterpart to a story that is firmly rooted in a familiar experience. Creative, clever, and original." SLJ

Steig, William

The amazing bone. Farrar, Straus & Giroux 1976 unp il $17; pa $6.95 E
1. Pigs—Fiction 2. Bones—Fiction

ISBN 0-374-30248-0; 0-374-40358-9 (pa)

A Caldecott Medal honor book, 1977

On her way home from school, Pearl finds an unusual bone that has unexpected powers

"Steig's marvelously straightfaced telling comes with a panoply of ultra-spring landscapes for pink-dressed Pearl to tiptoe through. And there's no holding back the chortles at the wonderfully expressive faces the artist delights in. This is a tight mesh of witty storytelling and art bound to please any audience." Booklist

Brave Irene. Farrar, Straus & Giroux 1986 unp il $17; pa $7.95 E
1. Blizzards—Fiction 2. Courage—Fiction

ISBN 0-374-30947-7; 0-374-40927-7 (pa)

LC 86-80957

Also available Spanish language edition

"Mrs. Bobbin has just finished a beautiful ballgown for the duchess, but she has a headache and can't deliver it. Brave and devoted daughter Irene takes charge . . . determinedly marching out into a raging snowstorm with the dress." Publ Wkly

"With sure writing and well-composed, riveting art, Steig keeps readers with Irene every step of the long way. The pictures . . . are done in winter blues, purples, and grays that gradually get darker as Irene trudges on." Booklist

Steig, William—*Continued*

Caleb & Kate. Farrar, Straus & Giroux 1977
unp il pa $6.95 hardcover o.p.   E
  1. Dogs—Fiction 2. Witches—Fiction
ISBN 0-374-41038-0 (pa)   LC 77-4947

"Though Caleb the carpenter loves Kate the weaver
very much, he leaves her one day because of a quarrel.
In the deep woods where he is resting Yedida the witch
turns him into a dog. The tale of his faithfulness and
love for his wife, even though he is a dog, is . . . told.
Their love is shared to the end, when a remarkable turn
of events enables him to return to his former self." Child
Book Rev Serv

"The well-cadenced storytelling has a certain old-
fashioned elegance of language, and the humor is emphasized by an atmosphere of mock-pathos." Horn Book

Doctor De Soto. Farrar, Straus & Giroux 1982
unp il $17; pa $6.95   E
  1. Dentists—Fiction 2. Mice—Fiction 3. Animals—
Fiction
ISBN 0-374-31803-4; 0-374-41810-1 (pa)
               LC 82-15701

Also available Spanish language edition

A Newbery Medal honor book, 1983

"Dr. De Soto is a mouse dentist who . . . treats all
creatures large and small but none that are injurious to
mice. When Fox begs for help, the couple face a dilemma. He is in pain and professional ethics demand that
they pull his aching tooth and replace it with a sound
one." Publ Wkly

"The story achieves comic heights partly through the
delightful irony of the situation. . . . Watercolor paintings, with the artist's firm line and luscious color, depict
with aplomb the eminently dentistlike mouse as he goes
about his business." Horn Book

Another title about Doctor De Soto is:
Doctor De Soto goes to Africa (1992)

Pete's a pizza. HarperCollins Pubs. 1998 unp il
$15.99; lib bdg $16.89   E
  1. Father-son relationship—Fiction
ISBN 0-06-205157-1; 0-06-205158-X (lib bdg)
               LC 97-78384

"Michael di Capua books"

Pete "moodily contemplates a rain-drenched landscape
when his understanding father decides to cheer him up
by transforming him into a pizza. The recipe: plenty of
kneading, stretching, twirling, and decorating with delica-
cies such as cheese (in reality pieces of paper) and tomatoes (checkers), plus tickling and obviously lots of love."
Horn Book

"The watercolor illustrations are executed in a clean
palette with precise lines in tightly controlled compositions, the semi-formality of which only add to the hilarity. . . . This is a jolly, affectionate story." Bull Cent
Child Books

Potch & Polly; with pictures by Jon Agee.
Farrar, Straus & Giroux 2002 unp il $16
                      E
  1. Love—Fiction
ISBN 0-374-36090-1   LC 00-29544

Lively Potch pursues the girl of his dreams, the darling Polly Pumpernickel

"This irresistible picture book has it all: a tongue-in-
cheek text brimming with deliciously alliterative phrases,
wry cartoons that mix visual gags with a comic-book
punch, and a plot featuring two lovers who are taunted
by twists of fate and turns of slapstick humor." SLJ

Sylvester and the magic pebble. Simon and
Schuster Books for Young Readers 2005 c1969
unp il $16.95   E
  1. Donkeys—Fiction
ISBN 1-4169-0206-6   LC 2004-15445

Awarded the Caldecott Medal, 1970

A reissue of the title first published 1969

This edition includes William Steig's Caldecott Award
acceptance speech

In a moment of fright, Sylvester the donkey asks his
magic pebble to turn him into a rock but then can not
hold the pebble to wish himself back to normal again.

"A remarkable atmosphere of childlike innocence pervades the book; beautiful pictures in full, natural color
show daily and seasonal changes in the lush countryside
and greatly extend the kindly humor and the warm, unselfconscious tenderness." Horn Book

When everybody wore a hat. Joanna Cotler Bks.
2003 unp il $17.99; lib bdg $18.89   E
ISBN 0-06-009700-0; 0-06-009701-9 (lib bdg)
               LC 2002-6512

"In 1916, Steig was eight years old. This autobiography describes that year of his life. . . . The childlike,
watercolor artwork that accompanies the memories features flattened tables, nostrils on the sides of noses, and
a sidewalk extending up into the air. Yet the illustrations' naiveté belies their underlying sophistication. With
a few spare lines, the artist manages to convey body language, facial expression, and gesture." SLJ

Stenmark, Victoria

The singing chick; illustrated by Randy Cecil.
Holt & Co. 1999 unp il $15.95   E
  1. Animals—Fiction 2. Singing—Fiction
ISBN 0-8050-5255-0   LC 98-6609

A newly hatched, happily singing chick is eaten by a
fox, who then starts singing before being eaten by a
wolf, and so begins a chain of eating and singing for a
series of animals

"Jaunty, lushy colored paintings wring every possible
bit of humor out of the goofy situation in this hugely
amusing read-aloud." Horn Book Guide

Steptoe, John

Baby says. Lothrop, Lee & Shepard Bks. 1988
unp il $15; lib bdg $16.89   E
  1. Brothers—Fiction 2. Infants—Fiction
ISBN 0-688-07423-5; 0-688-07424-3 (lib bdg)
               LC 87-17296

"Little brother keeps throwing his Teddy bear until he
finally topples the block city Big Brother is building. All
ends well when understanding Big Brother realizes that
Little Brother only wants to help. After hugs and kisses,
the project is started over again—together." Child Book
Rev Serv

"With simplicity of style and soft, pastel colored pen-

Steptoe, John—*Continued*

cil drawings the author-artist depicts the tender, caring relationship of an older brother for his baby brother." Horn Book

Stevens, Janet

Cook-a-doodle-doo! [by] Janet Stevens and Susan Stevens Crummel; illustrated by Janet Stevens. Harcourt Brace & Co. 1999 unp il $17

E

1. Cooking—Fiction 2. Animals—Fiction
ISBN 0-15-201924-3   LC 98-8853

With the questionable help of his friends, Big Brown Rooster manages to bake a strawberry shortcake which would have pleased his great-grandmother, Little Red Hen

"With the main story and each hilarious, mouthwatering double-page picture of pandemonium, there is a quiet sidebar in small type that explains what recipes are, what ingredients are, what measuring and baking means, and how to make a strawberry shortcake, step by step. The luscious illustrations on hand-made paper are beautifully drawn and deliciously textured. . . . The full recipe is printed on the last page." Booklist

The great fuzz frenzy; written by Janet Stevens and Susan Stevens Crummel; illustrated by Janet Stevens. Harcourt 2005 unp il $17   E

1. Prairie dogs—Fiction
ISBN 0-15-204626-7

When a fuzzy tennis ball lands in a prairie-dog town, the prairie dogs discover that their newfound frenzy for fuzz creates no end of trouble.

"The marvelously rendered mixed-media illustrations, with vivid blues, earthy browns, and that luminescent green, capture the true fuzzy nature and greenish glow of the ball." SLJ

Stevenson, James

Flying feet; a Mud Flat story. Greenwillow Books 2004 47p il $15.99; lib bdg $16.89

E

1. Tap dancing—Fiction 2. Animals—Fiction
ISBN 0-06-051975-4; 0-06-051976-2 (lib bdg)
LC 2002-29785

Stanley and the the other animals of Mud Flat take dance lessons from some touring tap dancers and prepare for a big show

"Stevenson's trademark pen-and-watercolor illustrations lovingly depict exuberant characters and provide lots of special details. . . . Children will enjoy this zany story." SLJ

Other titles about Mud Flat are:
Christmas at Mud Flat (2000)
Heat wave at Mud Flat (1997)
Mud Flat April Fool (1998)
The Mud Flat mystery (1997)
Mud Flat Olympics (1994)
Mud Flat spring (1999)
Yard sale (1996)

The most amazing dinosaur. Greenwillow Bks. 2000 unp il $15.95; lib bdg $15.89   E

1. Museums—Fiction 2. Rats—Fiction 3. Animals—Fiction
ISBN 0-688-16432-3; 0-688-16433-1 (lib bdg)
LC 99-25347

Wilfred the rat takes shelter in a natural history museum, where he befriends the animals living there and accidentally collapses a dinosaur skeleton, reassembling it in a creative way

"The humor and pacing of this story is absolutely perfect, with the matter-of-fact tone of the text heightened and expanded by Stevenson's quirky watercolor-and-pen illustrations." SLJ

No laughing, no smiling, no giggling. Farrar, Straus and Giroux 2004 unp il $16   E

1. Animals—Fiction
ISBN 0-374-31829-8   LC 2003-45508

Companion volume to Don't make me laugh (1999)

"Frances Foster books"

The reader joins Freddy Fafnaffer the pig as he deals with Mr. Frimdimpny, a crocodile who never laughs and who decides on the rules for reading this book.

"Children will enjoy the humorous cartoons and delight in helping Freddy out of his predicament. The act of inviting readers to actively participate in the plot has great appeal." SLJ

Stevenson, Robert Louis

Block city; illustrated by Daniel Kirk. Simon & Schuster Books for Young Readers 2005 unp il $14.95   E

1. Play—Fiction
ISBN 0-689-86964-9

A child creates a world of his own which has mountains and sea, a city and ships, all from toy blocks.

"This colorfully illustrated version of Stevenson's poem is as relevant today as when it was written for *A Child's Garden of Verses* in 1883. . . . Done in colored pencils and gouache in rich, deep colors, the large, clear pictures have a retro feel." SLJ

Stewart, Sarah

The friend; pictures by David Small. Farrar Straus Giroux 2004 unp il $16   E

1. Household employees—Fiction
ISBN 0-374-32463-8   LC 2003-64352

With Mom too busy and Dad away much of the time, Belle finds companionship with a household employee who after each day's work takes Belle "hand in hand" to the beach.

"David Small's elegant, moving illustrations . . . show the twosome touchingly small on the vast beach. . . . In both illustrations and text, Bea is not merely a playmate but her own person." NY Times Book Rev

The gardener; pictures by David Small. Farrar, Straus & Giroux 1997 unp il $16; pa $6.95

E

1. Gardening—Fiction 2. Letters—Fiction 3. Great Depression, 1929-1939—Fiction
ISBN 0-374-32517-0; 0-374-42518-3 (pa)
LC 96-30894

Stewart, Sarah—*Continued*

A Caldecott Medal honor book, 1998

"In the depth of the Depression, Lydia Grace Finch is sent to the big city to live with her dour Uncle Jim and cultivates an urban garden." N Y Times Book Rev

"Stewart's quiet story, relayed in the form of letters written by a little girl, focuses on a child who literally makes joy blossom. Small's illustrations . . . [offer] wonderfully expressive characters, ink-line details, and patches of pastel." Booklist

The journey; pictures by David Small. Farrar, Straus & Giroux 2001 unp il $16   E

1. Amish—Fiction 2. City and town life—Fiction

ISBN 0-374-33905-8   LC 99-31001

A young Amish girl tells her "silent friend," her diary, about all the wonderous experiences she has on her first trip to the city

"This title offers so much: a glimpse into Amish culture and Chicago treasures; a winsome main character and many sensitively depicted supporting personalities; a fresh, authentic voice; and a design perfectly melded to its subtle message." SLJ

The library; pictures by David Small. Farrar, Straus & Giroux 1995 unp il $16.50; pa $6.95
        E

1. Books and reading—Fiction 2. Stories in rhyme

ISBN 0-374-34388-8; 0-374-44394-7 (pa)
        LC 94-30320

Elizabeth Brown loves to read more than anything else, but when her collection of books grows and grows, she must make a change in her life

"Framed watercolors give the book an old-fashioned, scrapbooklike appearance. . . . Small black-ink line drawings decorate the verses below and often add an additional touch of humor. This is a funny, heartwarming story about a quirky woman with a not-so-peculiar obsession." SLJ

Stock, Catherine

Gugu's house. Clarion Bks. 2001 31p il $14
        E

1. Grandmothers—Fiction 2. Zimbabwe—Fiction

ISBN 0-618-00389-4   LC 00-43009

Kukamba loves helping her grandmother decorate her mud home in a dusty Zimbabwe village, but when the annual rains partially destroy all her art work, Kukamba learns to see the goodness of the rains

"Stock's watercolors capture not only the bright hues of landscape and traditional dress but also a clear sense of Gugu's deep serenity and the shared purpose that sends her and Kukamba striding back from their walk to restore the house to its former glory." Booklist

Stoeke, Janet Morgan

A hat for Minerva Louise. Dutton Children's Bks. 1994 unp il $13.99; pa $5.99   E

1. Chickens—Fiction 2. Hats—Fiction

ISBN 0-525-45328-8; 0-14-055666-4 (pa)
        LC 94-2139

Also available Minerva Louise Board books

Minerva Louise, a snow-loving chicken, mistakes a pair of mittens for two hats to keep both ends warm

This "is a rare find: a picture book exactly on target for preschoolers that sacrifices none of the essential elements of plot, character, and humor. . . . The pictures, in large rectangles of bright primary colors, are easy for preschoolers to 'read' and contain most of the book's considerable humor." Horn Book

Other titles about Minerva Louise are:

A friend for Minerva Louise (1997)

Minerva Louise (1988)

Minerva Louise and the colorful eggs (2006)

Minerva Louise at school (1996)

Minerva Louise at the fair (2000)

Waiting for May. Dutton Children's Bks. 2005 unp il $16.99   E

1. Adoption—Fiction 2. Siblings—Fiction

ISBN 0-525-47098-0

A young boy looks forward to the day when a new sister, who will be adopted from China, joins his family.

"The smoothly flowing text . . . imparts a surprising amount of information about requirements unique to international adoptions. . . . The colorful paintings enhance the narrative and capture the various emotions of the characters. . . . An excellent addition to all collections." SLJ

Stohner, Anu

Brave Charlotte; [illustrated by Henrike Wilson; translated from the German by Alyson Cole] Bloomsbury Children's Bks. 2005 unp il $16.95
        E

1. Sheep—Fiction

ISBN 1-58234-690-9

Charlotte, a headstrong sheep, rescues the flock when their shepherd is injured.

"There is a lot to like in 'Brave Charlotte': the gentle way the story unfolds, and the lovely way the illustrator . . . expresses an inviting, dingy fluffiness. . . . Each dreamlike image is suffused with colors that are rich yet subdued." NY Times Book Rev

Stojic, Manya

Rain; written and illustrated by Manya Stojic. Crown 2000 unp il $15.95; lib bdg $17.99
        E

1. Rain—Fiction 2. Animals—Fiction 3. Africa—Fiction

ISBN 0-517-80085-3; 0-517-80086-1 (lib bdg)
        LC 99-35298

The animals of the African savanna use their senses to predict and then enjoy the rain

"The brilliant double-page spreads, the play on the five senses, and a text that invites participation make this one trip to Africa you can't afford to miss!" SLJ

Stolz, Mary

Emmett's pig; illustrated by Garth Williams; watercolors by Rosemary Wells. HarperCollins Pubs. 2003 unp il $15.99; lib bdg $16.89

E

1. Pigs—Fiction
ISBN 0-06-028746-2; 0-06-028747-0 (lib bdg)
LC 2001-24750

A full-color edition of the title first published 1959 as an I can read book

"Although Emmett lives in a city apartment and is surrounded by toy pigs, pictures and books about pigs, his great desire for a real live pig is finally granted as a birthday present—a pig to be his own, but to be boarded on a farm outside the city." Wis Libr Bull

This book is "far above the average in both interest and illustration." Bookmark

Stowell, Penelope

The greatest potatoes; pictures by Sharon Watts. 1st ed. Jump at the Sun/Hyperion Books for Children 2004 unp il $15.99

E

1. Vanderbilt, Cornelius, 1794-1877—Fiction 2. Potatoes—Fiction 3. Restaurants—Fiction
ISBN 0-7868-5113-9
LC 2003-56954

In an effort to serve the perfect fried potato dish to the famous but fussy Cornelius Vanderbilt at the Moon's Lake Lodge House Restaurant in 1853, fry cook George Crum invents the potato chip. Based on true events.

"Lively ink-and-watercolor illustrations capture Crum's culinary attempts . . . with creativity. . . . The story is fun and animated, the subject appealing." Booklist

Stroud, Bettye

The patchwork path; a quilt map to freedom; illustrated by Erin Susanne Bennett. Candlewick Press 2005 32p il $15.99

E

1. Slavery—Fiction 2. Underground railroad—Fiction 3. Quilts—Fiction 4. African Americans—Fiction
ISBN 0-7636-2423-3
LC 2004-45786

While her father leads her toward Canada and away from the plantation where they have been slaves, a young girl thinks of the quilt her mother used to teach her a code that will help guide them to freedom.

"The exciting escape story makes the history immediate, and the fascinating quilt-code messages will have children revisiting the page that shows each symbol and its secret directions. Bennett's bright oil paintings make dramatic use of collage." Booklist

Sturges, Philemon

I love planes! illustrated by Shari Halpern. HarperCollins Pubs. 2003 unp il $12.99; lib bdg $14.89

E

1. Airplanes—Fiction
ISBN 0-06-028898-1; 0-06-028899-X (lib bdg)
LC 2001-26483

A child celebrates his love of planes by naming his favorite kinds and their notable characteristics

"The simplicity of the child's words is well matched by the colorful, uncluttered images, outlined in black." Booklist

I love school! illustrated by Shari Halpern. HarperCollins Pub. 2004 unp il $12.99; lib bdg $14.89

E

1. School stories 2. Stories in rhyme
ISBN 0-06-009284-X; 0-06-009285-8 (lib bdg)
LC 2002-68554

A brother and sister describe the things they love to do during their day at kindergarten.

This book "is a good way to prepare nervous new preschoolers and kindergartners. . . . [It features] simple, rhymed text and big, clear color pictures outlined in thick black line." Booklist

I love trains! illustrated by Shari Halpern. HarperCollins Pubs. 2001 unp il $12.95; lib bdg $13.89

E

1. Railroads—Fiction 2. Stories in rhyme
ISBN 0-06-028900-7; 0-06-028901-5 (lib bdg)
LC 99-86367

A boy expresses his love of trains, describing many kinds of train cars and their special jobs

This offers "clear, bright, double-page pictures with thick black lines and neon colors. . . . Toddlers will enjoy making the hoot, roar, and rumble sounds and identifying the various cars." Booklist

Stuve-Bodeen, Stephanie

Elizabeti's doll; illustrated by Christy Hale. Lee & Low Bks. 1998 unp il $15.95

E

1. Siblings—Fiction 2. Tanzania—Fiction
ISBN 1-880000-70-9
LC 98-13086

When a young Tanzanian girl gets a new baby brother, she finds a rock, which she names Eva, and makes it her baby doll

"Vibrant patterns and soft watercolor backgrounds evoke a sense of place and familial love." SLJ

Other titles about Elizabeti are:
Elizabeti's school (2002)
Mama Elizabeti (2000)

Suen, Anastasia

Red light, green light; written by Anastasia Suen; illustrated by Ken Wilson-Max. Harcourt 2005 unp il $16

E

1. Transportation—Fiction 2. Stories in rhyme
ISBN 0-15-202582-0

"Gulliver Books."

A young boy creates an imaginary world filled with zooming cars, flashing traffic lights, and racing fire engines.

"The flowing text rhymes and has a good pace and rhythm, which makes it an ideal read-aloud for transportation fans. The illustrations are bright and full of detail." SLJ

Subway; written by Anastasia Suen; illustrated by Karen Katz. Viking 2004 unp il $15.99

E

1. Subways—Fiction 2. Stories in rhyme
ISBN 0-670-03622-6
LC 2003-14020

"In brief, rhyming verses, an African-American child describes her ride on the subway. . . . The rhythmic language captures the feel of her journey and a repeated re-

Suen, Anastasia—*Continued*

frain invites readers to participate in the telling of the story. The bright, bold artwork depicts each scene in a realistic manner from the child's point of view." SLJ

Swallow, Pamela Curtis

Groundhog gets a say; as told to Pamela Curtis Swallow; illustrated by Denise Brunkus. G. P. Putnam's Sons 2005 unp il $15.99   E
1. Marmots—Fiction 2. Squirrels—Fiction 3. Crows—Fiction
ISBN 0-399-23876-X
A groundhog describes his various characteristics to a skeptical squirrel and crow. Text includes various facts about groundhogs.
"The humorous text is completed by Brunkus's finely executed, animated, watercolor-and-colored-pencil drawings." SLJ

Swanson, Susan Marie

The first thing my mama told me; illustrated by Christine Davenier. Harcourt 2002 unp il $16
                                                             E
1. Personal names—Fiction 2. Growth—Fiction
ISBN 0-15-201075-0   LC 2001-986
"Seven-year-old Lucy recounts childhood memories that all center on the importance of her name: her uncle building her a stool and painting her name on it, eating alphabet pancakes that spell her name, stomping her name in the snow." Horn Book Guide
"Davenier's delightful pictures are a great match for the text. Using a combination of pencil, ink, and pastel, she achieves a spunky, free-spirited look." Booklist

Sweet, Melissa

Carmine; a little more red; by Melissa Sweet. Houghton Mifflin 2005 unp il $16   E
1. Wolves—Fiction 2. Dogs—Fiction 3. Fairy tales 4. Alphabet
ISBN 0-618-38794-3   LC 2004-9212
While a little girl who loves red—and loves to dilly-dally—stops to paint a picture on the way to visit her grandmother, her dog Rufus meets a wolf and leads him directly to Granny's house.
"A fetching retelling of 'Little Red Riding Hood' that also works as an effective alphabet book. . . . The fresh and imaginative mixed-media art imitates the sketchbook of a child artist." SLJ

Swift, Fran

Old blue buggy; illustrated by Carol Thompson. Dutton Children's Bks. 2003 unp il $15.99
                                                             E
1. Carriages and carts—Fiction 2. Infants—Fiction
ISBN 0-525-45766-6   LC 2003-273255
"When baby Henry's mom finds an old blue buggy at a yard sale, she's delighted. . . . For Henry, the carriage means cozy naps, bouncy rides, and imaginary adventures. . . . After Henry outgrows the carriage, he is sad to let it go, but seeing it happily used by someone else makes Henry and his mom happy, too. Short, simple sen-

tences celebrate the everyday buggy as practical and fun. . . . Delightful illustrations, vibrant and animated, depict expressive characters, activities, and places in rich color and wonderfully appealing detail." Booklist

Swift, Hildegarde Hoyt

The little red lighthouse and the great gray bridge; by Hildegarde H. Swift and [illustrated by] Lynd Ward. Harcourt 2002 c1942 unp il $16
                                                             E
1. George Washington Bridge (N.Y. and N.J.)—Fiction 2. Lighthouses—Fiction
ISBN 0-15-204571-6   LC 2001-7106
A reissue of the title first published 1942
"After the great beacon atop the . . . George Washington Bridge was installed, the little red lighthouse feared he would no longer be useful, but when an emergency arose, the little lighthouse proved that he was still important." Hodges. Books for Elem Sch Libr
"The story is written with imagination and a gift for bringing alive this little lighthouse and its troubles. . . . [Lynd Ward's] illustrations have some distinction and one in particular, the fog creeping over the river clutching at the river boats, has atmosphere, rhythm and good colour." Ont Libr Rev

Swope, Sam

Gotta go! Gotta go! pictures by Sue Riddle. Farrar, Straus & Giroux 2000 unp il $13
                                                             E
1. Butterflies—Fiction 2. Caterpillars—Fiction
ISBN 0-374-32757-2   LC 99-28503
Although she does not know why or how, a caterpillar who becomes a monarch butterfly is certain that she must make her way to Mexico
"The rhythm and repetition are infectious; and the pen-and-ink and watercolor illustrations, set against expanses of white space, enlarge the book remarkably." Horn Book Guide

Taback, Simms

Joseph had a little overcoat. Viking 1999 unp il music $15.99   E
1. Clothing and dress—Fiction 2. Jews—Fiction
ISBN 0-670-87855-3   LC 98-47721
Awarded the Caldecott Medal, 2000
A newly illustrated edition of the title first published 1977 by Random House
Based on "... a Yiddish folk song..."
A very old overcoat is recycled numerous times into a variety of garments. Based on a Yiddish folk song, which is included
"Taback's inventive use of die-cut pages shows off his signature artwork. . . . This diverting, sequential story unravels as swiftly as the threads of Joseph's well-loved, patch-covered plaid coat." Publ Wkly

Simms Taback's big book of words. Blue Apple Books 2004 unp il $12.95   E
1. Vocabulary 2. Picture dictionaries
ISBN 1-59354-035-3
Illustrations and text present common toys, articles of clothing, foods and animals.

Taback, Simms—*Continued*

"A superb choice for emergent readers. The book's simple elegance is eye-catching. . . . The vibrant colors . . . draw children's attention to each picture." SLJ

Tafuri, Nancy

Five little chicks. Simon & Schuster Books for Young Readers 2006 unp il $14.95　　　**E**

1. Chickens—Fiction

ISBN 0-689-87342-5

Five chicks and their mother peck in the corn patch in search of breakfast.

"Created with brush pen, watercolor pencils, and ink, the gorgeous double-page spreads, in warm shades of red, yellow, and brown, manage to be both clear and fuzzy, simple and rich." Booklist

Goodnight, my duckling; by Nancy Tafuri. 1st ed. Scholastic Press 2005 unp il $16.95　　**E**

1. Ducks—Fiction 2. Bedtime—Fiction

ISBN 0-439-39881-9　　　　　LC 2003-25736

As a mother duck leads her ducklings home, one dawdles and is left behind but, luckily, a friend is there to help the little duckling back to his nest in time for bed

"Tafuri's 46-word text and feathery-textured, full-bleed watercolor spreads create a wonderfully reassuring and cozy whole."

Have you seen my duckling? Greenwillow Bks. 1984 unp il $16.99; lib bdg $17.89; pa $6.99

　　　　　　　　　　　　　　　　　　E

1. Ducks—Fiction

ISBN 0-688-02797-0; 0-688-02798-9 (lib bdg); 0-688-10994-2 (pa)　　　　　LC 83-17196

Also available Board book edition

A Caldecott Medal honor book, 1985

"In a picture book virtually wordless except for the repeated question of the title, seven ducklings obediently cluster in their nest, while the eighth—more daring and more curious—scrambles after an errant butterfly." Horn Book

"Tafuri's artwork . . . features clean lines, generous figures, and clear, cool colors. She also adds nice detail—feathers, for instance, that you can almost feel under your hands." Booklist

Mama's Little Bears. Scholastic 2002 unp il $15.95　　　　　　　　　　　　　　　**E**

1. Bears—Fiction

ISBN 0-439-27311-0　　　　　LC 2001-20935

The Little Bears explore their forest home but never stray too far from their Mama

"In her characteristic, child-friendly style, Tafuri matches large-print, simply phrased text to expressive, uncluttered paintings worked in watercolor enriched with pastel. Children will love this animal adventure." Booklist

Silly little goose! story and pictures by Nancy Tafuri. Scholastic Press 2001 unp il $15.95

　　　　　　　　　　　　　　　　　　E

1. Geese—Fiction

ISBN 0-439-06304-3　　　　　LC 00-25047

A goose tries out a few odd places to make her nest before finally settling on an old straw hat

"The large, uncluttered illustrations are full of interest, humor, and detail. The text is simple, with one sentence per spread alternating with a spread that contains the refrain, 'Silly little goose!' and the sounds of the animal babies. Perfect for lap-sits and toddler storytimes." SLJ

Spots, feathers, and curly tails. Greenwillow Bks. 1988 unp il $16.95; lib bdg $16.89

　　　　　　　　　　　　　　　　　　E

1. Domestic animals

ISBN 0-688-07536-3; 0-688-07537-1 (lib bdg)

　　　　　　　　　　　　　　LC 87-15638

Questions and answers highlight some outstanding characteristics of farm animals, such as a chicken's feathers and a horse's mane

"In the watercolor illustrations with black pen outline, Nancy Tafuri manages in the simplest style to give energy and personality to the animals through the angle of a head or the set of a snout. The story will provide a successful experience for both child and adult reader and is an ideal book for the beginning reader to entertain a younger sibling in a game they'll both enjoy." Horn Book

This is the farmer. Greenwillow Bks. 1994 unp il $16.99　　　　　　　　　　　　　　**E**

1. Farm life—Fiction

ISBN 0-688-09468-6　　　　　LC 92-30082

A farmer's kiss causes an amusing chain of events on the farm

"The well-defined, watercolor-and-ink double-spread illustrations are . . . of the highest quality. The brief story is rhythmic, predictable, and printed in extra-large type." SLJ

What the sun sees. Greenwillow Bks. 1997 unp il $16　　　　　　　　　　　　　　　**E**

1. Day—Fiction 2. Night—Fiction 3. Sun—Fiction 4. Moon—Fiction

ISBN 0-688-14493-4　　　　　LC 96-20976

Bound back to back and inverted with What the moon sees

"Tafuri uses a 'flip-book' technique to show readers similar settings first from the point of view of the sun, and then from that of the moon (or vice versa). . . . A spare and repetitious text reinforces the continuity and contrast of daytime and nightime experiences. A detached perspective and a panoramic distancing of colored-pencil and watercolor illustrations allow viewers to feel as though they are indeed looking down on the cycles on time." SLJ

You are special, Little one. Scholastic Press 2003 unp il $16.95　　　　　　　　　**E**

1. Animals—Fiction

ISBN 0-439-39879-7　　　　　LC 2002-151459

A variety of baby animals ask the question, "How am I special?" and receive loving answers from their mothers and fathers

"Tafuri's colored-pencil-and-watercolor art fills the oversize pages, depicting tranquil panoramas of various animal habitats as well as plenty of cozy close-ups of parents and children snuggling. Young children will be comforted by the text's rhythmic reassurances." Booklist

Tarpley, Natasha

Bippity Bop barbershop; by Natasha Anastasia Tarpley; illustrated by E.B. Lewis. Little, Brown 2002 unp il $15.95   **E**
  1. Barbers and barbershops—Fiction 2. African Americans—Fiction
ISBN 0-316-52284-8   LC 00-30188
"Megan Tingley books"
A story celebrating a young African-American boy's first trip to the barbershop
"Expressive watercolors showcase [the child's] curiosity, fear, and satisfaction, as well as a close father-son relationship." Horn Book Guide

Taulbert, Clifton L.

Little Cliff and the porch people; paintings by E.B. Lewis. Dial Bks. for Young Readers 1999 unp il $16.99; lib bdg $15.89   **E**
  1. African Americans—Fiction 2. Mississippi—Fiction
ISBN 0-8037-2174-9; 0-8037-2175-7 (lib bdg)
      LC 98-5503
Sent to buy special butter for Mama Pearl's candied sweet potatoes and told to get back lickety-split, Little Cliff is delayed by all his neighbors when they want to contribute their own ingredients
"The old Mississippi setting is authentic, the intergenerational relationships are realistic, and Lewis's illustrations add warmth to the simply told story." Horn Book Guide
  Other titles about Little Cliff are:
Little Cliff and the cold place (2002)
Little Cliff's first day of school (2001)

Tavares, Matt

Mudball; [by] Matt Tavares. 1st ed. Candlewick Press 2005 unp il $15.99   **E**
  1. Baseball—Fiction
ISBN 0-7636-2387-3   LC 2004-40671
During a rainy Minneapolis Millers baseball game in 1903, Little Andy Oyler has the chance to become a hero by hitting the shortest and muddiest home run in history.
"The large-scale, softly shaded pencil drawings have plenty of motion, just right for a sports story. . . . An attractive book for baseball fans who enjoy watching small heroes triumph and don't mind a bit of nostalgia." Booklist

Taylor, Debbie A.

Sweet music in Harlem; illustrated by Frank Morrison. Lee & Low Books 2004 unp il $16.95
     E
  1. Jazz musicians—Fiction 2. Harlem (New York, N.Y.)—Fiction 3. African Americans—Fiction
ISBN 1-58430-165-1   LC 2003-8994
C.J., who aspires to be as great a jazz musician as his uncle, searches for Uncle Click's hat in preparation for an important photograph and inadvertently gathers some of the greatest musicians of 1950s Harlem to join in on the picture.
"This dazzling tale is filled with energy, rhythm, and style from its attention-grabbing cover to its satisfying ending. . . . The acrylic illustrations make the text come alive." SLJ

Teague, Mark

Dear Mrs. LaRue; letters from obedience school; written and illustrated by Mark Teague. Scholastic Press 2002 unp il $15.95   **E**
  1. Dogs—Fiction
ISBN 0-439-20663-4   LC 2001-43479
Gertrude LaRue receives typewritten and paw-written letters from her dog Ike, entreating her to let him leave the Igor Brotweiler Canine Academy and come back home
"The humorous acrylic illustrations are, at times, a howl and the over-sized format is well-suited to storytelling." SLJ
  Another title about Mrs. LaRue and her dog Ike is:
Detective LaRue (2004)

Pigsty. Scholastic 1994 unp il $15.95; pa $5.99
     E
  1. Pigs—Fiction 2. Cleanliness—Fiction
ISBN 0-590-45915-5; 0-439-59843-5 (pa)
      LC 93-21179
When Wendell doesn't clean up his room, a whole herd of pigs comes to live with him
"Much of the tale's fun resides in Teague's quirky acrylic art. . . . Whether Wendell and his friends are jumping on the bed or playing Monopoly on the rug, their antics are rendered in the bold palette of a gleefully inventive imagination. Highly recommended for neat-freaks and mess-makers alike." Publ Wkly

Tekavec, Heather

Storm is coming! pictures by Margaret Spengler. Dial Bks. for Young Readers 2002 unp il $14.99
     E
  1. Storms—Fiction 2. Domestic animals—Fiction
ISBN 0-8037-2626-0   LC 00-34622
The animals misunderstand the farmer's "Storm" warning and expect someone scary and mean
"Children will giggle over the animals' confusion and enjoy the well-paced buildup of suspense. Inviting pastel illustrations feature round, cartoonlike animals and dramatic use of perspective." Horn Book Guide

Tenzing Norbu

Secret of the snow leopard; [by] Tenzing Norbu Lama; with Stéphane Frattini. Douglas & McIntyre 2004 unp il $16.95   **E**
  1. Nepal—Fiction 2. Himalaya Mountains—Fiction
ISBN 0-88899-544-X
Tsering, a boy from a small Nepali village, and "his stepfather accompany the village healer, who is gravely ill, on a journey to the monastery where he will seek a cure. . . . On the way home, Tsering . . . asserts his independence by climbing the dangerous pass where his father . . . lost his life. . . . Handsome earth-tone paintings, stylized and carefully composed, portray the people and animals that belong to this stark landscape. . . . The quiet authority of the artwork and the drama of the story will engage children emotionally." SLJ
  Another title about Tsering is:
Himalaya (2002)

Thayer, Jane

The popcorn dragon; written by Jane Thayer; illustrated by Lisa McCue. Morrow Junior Bks. 1989 unp il $16.99 **E**

1. Dragons—Fiction

ISBN 0-688-08340-4 LC 88-39855

A newly illustrated edition of the title first published 1953

Though his hot breath is the envy of all the other animals, a young dragon learns that showing off does not make friends

"McCue's new full-color illustrations capture the whimsical mood of the fable. The animals, although too coy, have appealing humanlike expressions which convey their envy and contempt." SLJ

The puppy who wanted a boy; illustrated by Lisa McCue. HarperCollins Pubs. 2003 unp il $14.99; lib bdg $15.89 **E**

1. Dogs—Fiction 2. Christmas—Fiction

ISBN 0-06-052696-3; 0-06-052697-1 (lib bdg)

A reissue of the edition published 1986 by Morrow; story first published 1958 with different illustrations

When Petey the puppy decides that he wants a boy for Christmas, he discovers that he must go out and find one on his own

"It is the same, somewhat sentimental but certainly appealing tale that Thayer fashioned in 1958, when this was originally published; however, McCue's affectionately drawn, warmly colored illustrations go a long way toward perking up the story." Booklist

Thiesing, Lisa

The Aliens are coming! Dutton Children's Books 2004 32p il $13.99 **E**

1. Pigs—Fiction 2. Rock musicians—Fiction

ISBN 0-525-47277-0 LC 2003-19303

Peggy the pig becomes very worried when she hears that the Aliens are coming, but then she learns that they are a rock band.

"This clever tale will appeal to newly independent readers." SLJ

Other titles about Peggy are:

A dark and noisy night (2005)

The Viper (2002)

Thomas, Eliza

The red blanket; illustrated by Joe Cepeda. Scholastic Press 2004 unp il $15.95 **E**

1. Adoption—Fiction 2. Single parent family—Fiction

ISBN 0-439-32253-7 LC 2003-5082

Tells the story of a single woman who goes to China to adopt a baby.

"Vibrantly colored oil illustrations dominate the pages. . . . The pictures convey the anxiety, the waiting, and the love that are a part of expanding a family. . . . This story, based on the author's experiences, is a welcome addition." SLJ

Thomas, Joyce Carol

I have heard of a land; illustrated by Floyd Cooper. HarperCollins Pubs. 1998 unp il $14.95; lib bdg $14.89; pa $6.99 **E**

1. Oklahoma—Fiction 2. Frontier and pioneer life—Fiction 3. African Americans—Fiction

ISBN 0-06-023477-6; 0-06-023478-4 (lib bdg); 0-06-443617-9 (pa) LC 95-48791

A Coretta Scott King honor book for illustration, 1999

"Joanna Cotler books"

Describes the joys and hardships experienced by an African-American pioneer woman who staked a claim for free land in the Oklahoma territory

"The strength and tenderness of Thomas' text are matched by Cooper's always evocative artwork." Booklist

Thomas, Shelley Moore

Good night, Good Knight; pictures by Jennifer Plecas. Dutton Children's Bks. 2000 47p il $13.99 **E**

1. Knights and knighthood—Fiction 2. Dragons—Fiction 3. Bedtime—Fiction

ISBN 0-525-46326-7 LC 99-28415

"Dutton easy reader"

A Good Knight helps three little dragons who are having trouble getting to sleep

"The short, simple, repetitive phrases are sure to capture the imaginations of young children. . . . With a palette dominated by the blues, grays, and purples of the nightime setting, Plecas's illustrations are a wonderful complement to this endearing tale." SLJ

Other titles about the Good Knight are:

Get well, Good Knight (2002)

Happy Birthday, Good Knight (2006)

Thomassie, Tynia

Feliciana Feyra LeRoux; a Cajun tall tale; illustrated by Cat Bowman Smith. Pelican 2005 c1995 unp il $15.95 **E**

1. Alligators—Fiction 2. Cajuns—Fiction 3. Louisiana—Fiction

ISBN 1-58980-286-1

A reissue of the title first published 1995 by Little, Brown

"Feliciana's grandpa won't let her go alligator hunting in the Louisiana Cajun bajou. When she sneaks out, Feliciana causes fun and excitement, and even becomes a heroine." Soc Educ

This "combines breezy watercolors and a swinging text that's perfect for reading aloud. A note on Cajun culture, a glossary, and a pronunciation guide are included." Booklist

Another title about Feliciana is:

Feliciana meets d'Loup Garou (1998)

Thompson, Kay

Kay Thompson's Eloise; including Eloise and the full-color Eloise scrapbook with rare photos & drawings from the files of Hilary Knight. Simon & Schuster Books for Young Readers 2005 c1955 65p $19.95   **E**

1. Hotels and motels—Fiction 2. New York (N.Y.)—Fiction

ISBN 1-4169-0823-4

Also available Ultimate edition which includes the original Eloise story, Eloise in Moscow, Eloise in Paris, Eloise at Christmastime, and a scrapbook of photographs, memorabilia, and drawings

A reissue of the title first published 1955

This is the "tale of the little girl who makes merry mayhem from her digs on the top floor of New York's Plaza Hotel." Horn Book

Other titles about Eloise are:

Eloise at Christmastime (1958)

Eloise in Paris (1957)

Eloise in Moscow (1959)

Eloise takes a bawth (2002)

Eloise's guide to life (2000)

Eloise's what I absolutely love, love, love (2005)

Thompson, Lauren

Little Quack; pictures by Derek Anderson. Simon & Schuster Bks. for Young Readers 2003 unp il $14.95   **E**

1. Ducks—Fiction 2. Counting

ISBN 0-689-84723-8   LC 2002-5567

One by one, four ducklings find the courage to jump into the pond and paddle with Mama Duck, until only Little Quack is left in the nest, trying to be brave

"Here's a familiar story kicked up a notch by a counting element and irresistible art. The story is reassuring and utterly straightforward. . . . The charm is in Anderson's comical, eye-commanding acrylics." Booklist

Other titles about Little Quack are:

Little Quack's bedtime (2005)

Little Quack's hide and seek (2004)

Little Quack's new friend (2006)

One riddle, one answer; illustrated by Linda Wingerter. Scholastic Press 2001 unp il $15.95   **E**

1. Riddles—Fiction 2. Mathematics—Fiction 3. Iran—Fiction

ISBN 0-590-31335-5   LC 99-89308

A sultan's daughter who loves numbers and riddles devises a plan to find the man who is best suited to be her husband

"Thompson's storytelling is simple and elegant; her language is graceful and understated. . . . Wingerter's paintings feature the delicate details of Persian miniatures." Bull Cent Child Books

Polar bear night; illustrated by Stephen Savage. Scholastic Press 2004 unp il $15.95   **E**

1. Polar bear—Fiction 2. Night—Fiction

ISBN 0-439-49524-5   LC 2003-27538

After wandering out at night to watch a magical star shower, a polar bear cub returns home to snuggle with her mother in their warm den.

"With comforting, carefully chosen words and soft pastels shading linocut prints, this book has all the elements to make it a bedtime favorite." SLJ

Thomson, Pat

Drat that fat cat! illustrated by Ailie Busby. Arthur A. Levine Books 2003 unp il $15.95   **E**

1. Cats—Fiction

ISBN 0-439-47195-8   LC 2002-8888

A fat cat in search of food eats up everything he meets until he swallows a bee.

"Busby's . . . droll watercolor cartoons make use of quirky shapes and perspectives. . . . Sheer enjoyable nonsense." Publ Wkly

Thomson, Sarah L.

Imagine a day; written by Sarah L. Thomson; paintings by Rob Gonsalves. Atheneum Books for Young Readers 2005 unp il $16.95   **E**

1. Imagination—Fiction

ISBN 0-689-85219-3   LC 2004-1033

"A Bryon Preiss visual publications, inc. book."

This presents a series of paintings, accompanied by brief text, which are intended to fool the eye and stretch the imagination.

"The text, though often lyrical, adds less to the book than the detailed pictures, which will stimulate wonder and imagination. An intriguing introduction to the surreal in art, this large-format book will fascinate children and adults with its realistic depiction of logical impossibilities." Booklist

A companion to this volume is:

Imagine a night (2003)

The sound of colors; a journey of imagination; [by] Jimmy Liao; English text adapted by Sarah L. Thornson. Little, Brown 2006 unp il $16.99   **E**

1. Blind—Fiction

ISBN 0-316-93992-7   LC 2004-025100

"A young girl's eyesight began slipping away a year ago. With her white cane in hand, she ventures on a subway trip using her imagination to take herself and readers on a journey. . . . Poetic, lyrical language is used in this translation from Chinese. The girl is strong and admirable. . . . Liao's watercolor illustrations invite readers to take time, slow down, and pore over the details." SLJ

Thong, Roseanne

One is a drummer; written by Roseanne Thong; illustrated by Grace Lin. Chronicle Books 2004 unp il $14.95   **E**

1. Counting 2. Chinese Americans—Fiction 3. Stories in rhyme

ISBN 0-8118-3772-6   LC 2003-10810

A young girl numbers her discoveries in the world around her, from one dragon boat to four mahjong players to ten bamboo stalks.

"The rhymes provide a pleasing framework for the book, and Lin's striking artwork gives it great visual appeal. . . . An appealing counting book, particularly for Chinese American children who want to learn a little about their heritage." Booklist

Thong, Roseanne—*Continued*

Red is a dragon; a book of colors; written by Roseanne Thong; illustrated by Grace Lin. Chronicle Bks. 2001 unp il $13.95 **E**

1. Color 2. Chinese Americans—Fiction 3. Stories in rhyme

ISBN 0-8118-3177-9　　　　　　LC 2001-93

Companion volume to Round is a mooncake: a book of shapes (2000)

A Chinese American girl provides rhyming descriptions of the great variety of colors she sees around her, from the red of a dragon, firecrackers, and lychees to the brown of her teddy bear

"Lin's simply drawn gouache illustrations, outlined in black, fairly explode with color. . . . This is a must-have for libraries serving Chinese American populations, and it will be a welcome addition to preschool story hours for children of all backgrounds." Booklist

Timberlake, Amy

The dirty cowboy; pictures by Adam Rex. Farrar, Straus & Giroux 2003 unp il $16

E

1. Cowhands—Fiction 2. Dogs—Fiction

ISBN 0-374-31791-7　　　　　LC 2001-53224

Telling his faithful dog to make sure nobody touches his clothes but him, a cowboy jumps into a New Mexico river for a bath, not realizing just how much the scrubbing will change his scent

"Told in descriptive language that rolls off the tongue, this story makes the most of a humorous situation. . . . The paintings have a gritty, sinewy look that matches the earthy tone of the tale." SLJ

Titherington, Jeanne

Pumpkin, pumpkin. Greenwillow Bks. 1986 23p il $16.99; lib bdg $17.89; pa $6.99 **E**

1. Gardening—Fiction 2. Pumpkin—Fiction

ISBN 0-688-05695-4; 0-688-05696-2 (lib bdg); 0-688-09930-0 (pa)　　　　　LC 84-25334

Jamie "plants a seed, then grows and harvests a pumpkin from which he saves seeds for next year. The large, detailed drawings capture Jamie's anticipation and pleasure just right. . . . Nonreaders can easily follow the story in pictures alone. Very large, clear print on facing pages makes the simple narrative inviting for beginning readers, too." SLJ

Todd, Mark

Monster trucks! Houghton Mifflin 2003 unp il $15 **E**

1. Trucks—Fiction 2. Stories in rhyme

ISBN 0-618-18208-X　　　　　LC 2002-155544

Illustrations and easy-to-read text depict a wide variety of trucks, including bulldozers, eighteen-wheelers, garbage trucks, and fire trucks

"Bright, solid-colored backgrounds allow the vehicles to take center stage. Large eyes glare from headlights and windshields, while grills and bumpers grin and grimace as the machines dig and lift, haul and move. . . . A good choice for storytime and one-on-one sharing." SLJ

Tompert, Ann

Grandfather Tang's story; illustrated by Robert Andrew Parker. Crown 1990 unp il $16; lib bdg $17.99; pa $6.99 **E**

1. Foxes—Fiction

ISBN 0-517-57487-X; 0-517-57272-9 (lib bdg); 0-517-88558-1 (pa)　　　　　LC 89-22205

"An old Chinese man sits beneath a tree with his granddaughter, telling her the tale of two foxes who change themselves into ever-fiercer animals as they compete for dominance. As he speaks, he rearranges two tangram puzzles to form the shapes of the animals. . . . Directions for making tangrams, described as ancient Chinese puzzles, appear on the book's last page." Booklist

"Parker's watercolor washes complement the text, adding energy and tension, as well as evoking oriental brushwork technique. . . . The text . . . will be valued by storytellers and listeners alike." SLJ

Torres, Leyla

The kite festival. Farrar Straus Giroux 2004 unp il $16 **E**

1. Kites—Fiction 2. Family life—Fiction 3. Hispanic Americans—Fiction

ISBN 0-374-38054-6

Also available Spanish language edition

While on a Sunday outing, Fernando and his family encounter a kite festival and decide to create a kite from scrap materials so that they can join in.

"The text is concise yet lyrical, and the soft watercolor illustrations enhance the gentle tone of the narrative." SLJ

Tresselt, Alvin R.

Hide and seek fog; by Alvin Tresselt; illustrated by Roger Duvoisin. Lothrop, Lee & Shepard Bks. 1965 unp il lib bdg $17.89; pa $6.99 **E**

1. Fog

ISBN 0-688-51169-4 (lib bdg); 0-688-07813-3 (pa)

A Caldecott Medal honor book, 1966

"This is . . . a mood picture book . . . describing a fog which rolls in from the sea to veil an Atlantic seacoast village for three days. The beautiful paintings . . . and the brief, poetic text sensitively and effectively evoke the atmosphere of the 'worst fog in twenty years' and depict the reactions of children and grown-ups to it." Booklist

White snow, bright snow; by Alvin Tresselt; illustrated by Roger Duvoisin. Lothrop, Lee & Shepard Bks. 1988 c1947 unp il $16.99; lib bdg $16.89; pa $5.99 **E**

1. Snow—Fiction

ISBN 0-688-41161-4; 0-688-51161-9 (lib bdg); 0-688-08294-7 (pa)　　　　　LC 88-10018

Awarded the Caldecott Medal, 1948

A reissue of the title first published 1947

When it begins to look, feel, and smell like snow, everyone prepares for a winter blizzard

Trivizas, Eugene

The three little wolves and the big bad pig;
illustrated by Helen Oxenbury. Margaret K.
McElderry Bks. 1993 unp il $17.95; pa $6.99

                                           E

1. Pigs—Fiction 2. Wolves—Fiction

ISBN 0-689-50569-8; 0-689-81528-X (pa)

                                    LC 92-24829

Also available Spanish language edition

"In this reverse of 'The Three Little Pigs' the wolves
build with cement, barbed wire and reinforced chains. In
response, the 'big bad pig' uses a sledgehammer, pneu-
matic drill and dynamite." Child Book Rev Serv

"Trivizas laces the text with funny, clever touches.
. . . Oxenbury's watercolors capture the story's broad
humor and add a wealth of supplementary details, with
exquisite renderings of the wolves' comic temerity and
the pig's bellicose stances." Publ Wkly

Trottier, Maxine

The paint box; [illustrations by] Stella East.
Fitzhenry & Whiteside 2003 32p il $16.95

                                           E

1. Tintoretto, Marietta, d. 1590—Fiction 2. Artists—
Fiction 3. Venice (Italy)—Fiction

ISBN 1-55041-801-7   LC 2003-464840

"'Long ago in Venice there was a girl named Marietta
who loved to paint. She was the daughter of the great
artist Tintoretto.' With her father's help, she disguises
herself as a boy in order to explore the art world of Venice. . . . Marietta befriends an enslaved cabin boy and
they spend their days sketching and exploring the city,
and telling one another about their lives. When it is time
for Piero's owner to leave the city, Marietta helps him
escape and return to his family. This poignant tale has its
roots in historical fact. . . . Trottier's fictional story
about Marietta and her friend seems plausible, due in
part to her descriptive and expressive writing style.
East's painterly illustrations are magnificent. Each spread
captures the feeling of Renaissance Venice and supports
the accompanying text." SLJ

Tryon, Leslie

Albert's birthday; written and illustrated by
Leslie Tryon. Atheneum Bks. for Young Readers
1999 unp il $16

                                           E

1. Birthdays—Fiction 2. Animals—Fiction

ISBN 0-689-82296-0   LC 98-36621

Patsy Pig plans a surprise birthday party for her friend
Albert, giving careful instructions to all their friends, but
she forgets to invite the guest of honor

"The prose is personable and engaging, and colorful,
exquisitely detailed illustrations portray the animal cast
in such familiar human settings as a classroom and a
town." Booklist

Other titles about Albert are:

Albert's alphabet (1991)

Albert's ballgame (1996)

Albert's Christmas (1997)

Albert's field trip (1993)

Albert's Halloween (1998)

Albert's play (1992)

Albert's Thanksgiving (1994)

Tsubakiyama, Margaret

Mei-Mei loves the morning; written by Margaret
Holloway Tsubakiyama; paintings by Cornelius
Van Wright & Ying-Hwa Hu. Whitman, A. 1999
unp il $15.95

                                           E

1. Grandfathers—Fiction 2. China—Fiction

ISBN 0-8075-5039-6   LC 97-26675

A young Chinese girl and her grandfather enjoy a typical morning riding on grandpa's bicycle to do errands
and meet friends in the park

"The gentle prose is accompanied by expressive, luminous watercolor paintings, detailing the people, places,
and activities that are characteristic of China." Booklist

Tucker, Kathy

The seven Chinese sisters; written by Kathy
Tucker; illustrated by Grace Lin. Whitman, A.
2003 unp il $15.95

                                           E

1. Sisters—Fiction 2. Dragons—Fiction 3. China—Fiction

ISBN 0-8075-7309-4   LC 2002-11330

When a dragon snatches the youngest of seven talented Chinese sisters, the other six come to her rescue

Lin "expertly captures the drama and humor of the
story with delightful paintings that reveal lovely Chinese
landscapes and a quirky, not-too-scary dragon. A wonderful read-aloud." Booklist

Tudor, Tasha

1 is one. Simon & Schuster Bks. for Young
Readers 2000 unp il $16

                                           E

1. Counting

ISBN 0-689-82843-8   LC 99-31290

A Caldecott Medal honor book, 1957

A reissue of the title first published 1956 by Oxford
University Press

"The author-artist has with characteristic charming
quaintness written and illustrated a counting book. Delicately tinted, decoratively bordered pictures and rhyming
lines of text count from one to twenty." Booklist

Turner, Ann Warren

Dust for dinner; story by Ann Turner; pictures
by Robert Barrett. HarperCollins Pubs. 1995 64p
il lib bdg $16.89; pa $3.99

                                           E

1. Great Depression, 1929-1939—Fiction 2. Family
life—Fiction 3. Farm life—Fiction

ISBN 0-06-023377-X (lib bdg); 0-06-444225-X (pa)

                                    LC 93-34634

"An I can read book"

Jake narrates the story of his family's life in the Oklahoma dust bowl and the journey from their ravaged farm
to California during the Great Depression

"Turner takes a sad episode in history and fashions it
into a story that has some depth as well as some drama.
. . . Realistic, nicely executed illustrations decorate every page." Booklist

Turner, Pamela S.

Hachiko; written by Pamela S. Turner; illustrated by Yan Nascimbene. Houghton Mifflin 2004 unp il $15   **E**

1. Dogs—Fiction 2. Japan—Fiction

ISBN 0-618-14094-8   LC 2002-155546

This "picture book pays tribute to one of the world's lesser-known animal heroes: Hachiko, a dog who kept vigil for nearly 10 years at a Tokyo train station, waiting for his deceased master to return from work. Turner unfolds this poignant true story in the natural, unaffected voice of Kentaro, a fictional little boy, who wonders at the dog's unswerving devotion. Unobtrusive details evoke a sense of place . . . as does Nascimbene's spare line-and-watercolor artwork, reminiscent of Japanese woodblock prints. . . . This will resonate with any child who has loved a dog and been loved in return." Booklist

Uchida, Yoshiko

The bracelet; story by Yoshiko Uchida; illustrated by Joanna Yardley. Philomel Bks. 1993 unp il $16.99; pa $6.99   **E**

1. Japanese Americans—Evacuation and relocation, 1942-1945—Fiction 2. World War, 1939-1945—Fiction 3. Friendship—Fiction

ISBN 0-399-22503-X; 0-698-11390-X (pa)

     LC 92-26196

Emi, a Japanese American in the second grade, is sent with her family to an internment camp during World War II, but the loss of the bracelet her best friend has given her proves that she does not need a physical reminder of that friendship

This "is a gentle, honest introduction to the treatment of the Japanese-Americans during the war, and Yardley's delicate pencil-and-watercolor paintings are cleanly drawn and richly colored." Bull Cent Child Books

Udry, Janice May

A tree is nice; pictures by Marc Simont. Harper & Row 1956 unp il $16.99; lib bdg $17.89; pa $6.99   **E**

1. Trees—Fiction

ISBN 0-06-026155-2; 0-06-026156-0 (lib bdg); 0-06-443147-9 (pa)

Also available Spanish language edition

Awarded the Caldecott Medal, 1957

"In childlike terms and in enticing pictures, colored and black and white, author and artist set forth reasons why trees are nice to have around—trees fill up the sky, they make everything beautiful, cats get away from dogs in them, leaves come down and can be played in, and trees are nice to climb in, to hang a swing in, or to plant. A picture book sure to please young children." Booklist

Uegaki, Chieri

Suki's kimono; written by Chieri Uegaki; illustrated by Stephane Jorisch. Kids Can Press 2003 unp il $15.95   **E**

1. Japanese—Fiction

ISBN 1-55337-084-8   LC 2003-495264

"On her first day of first grade [Suki] chooses to wear her beloved Japanese kimono to school, despite the ob-jections of her older sisters and the initial laughter of other children on the playground. . . . Her day ends in triumph, with her teacher and classmates won over by her impromptu dance performance. . . . This is an appealing story of courage and independence. Delicate, playful watercolor-and-ink illustrations perfectly capture the child's neighborhood and the characters' facial expressions." SLJ

Uff, Caroline

Lulu's busy day. Walker & Co. 2000 unp il $14.95   **E**

ISBN 0-8027-8716-9   LC 99-36100

Also available board book edition

Lulu enjoys many activities during the day, including drawing a picture, visiting the park, and reading a bedtime story

"The simple illustrations in a muted primary palette contain soft, round figures, and the spare text encourages children to point out favorite objects from their own busy days." Horn Book Guide

Other titles about Lulu are:

Happy birthday, Lulu! (2000)

Happy Christmas, Lulu (2002)

Hello, Lulu (1999)

Lulu's holiday (2004)

Uhlberg, Myron

Dad, Jackie, and me; illustrated by Colin Bootman. Peachtree Publishers 2005 unp il $16.95

    E

1. Robinson, Jackie, 1919-1972—Fiction 2. Deaf—Fiction 3. Father-son relationship—Fiction 4. Baseball—Fiction 5. Brooklyn (New York, N.Y.)—Fiction

ISBN 1-56145-329-3   LC 2004-16711

In Brooklyn, New York, in 1947, a boy learns about discrimination and tolerance as he and his deaf father share their enthusiasm over baseball and the Dodgers' first baseman, Jackie Robinson.

"Bootman's lovely watercolor paintings add detail and wistful nostalgia. . . . [Readers] will appreciate the story's insightful treatment of deafness as viewed through the eyes of a child." SLJ

Ungerer, Tomi

Crictor. Harper & Row 1958 32p il $16.99; pa $6.99   **E**

1. Snakes—Fiction

ISBN 0-06-026180-3; 0-06-443044-8 (pa)

A story "about the boa constrictor that was sent to Madame Bodot, who lived and taught school in a little French town. . . . The boys used him for a slide and the girls for a jump-rope. When Crictor captured a burglar by coiling around him until the police came, he was awarded impressive tokens of esteem and affection of the townspeople. Engaging line drawings echo the restrained and elegant absurdities of the text." Bull Cent Child Books

U'Ren, Andrea

Mary Smith. Farrar, Straus & Giroux 2003 unp il $16   **E**

1. City and town life—Fiction

ISBN 0-374-34842-1   LC 2002-69775

Early in the morning Mary Smith walks through the town, waking people up by shooting at their windows with her peashooter

"Outlined in black, U'Ren's art has a clean, graphic appearance that perfectly complements the simplicity of the story. . . . A historical note gives supplemental information about the real Mrs. Mary Smith and the role of the knocker-ups. A rollicking read." SLJ

Vail, Rachel

Sometimes I'm Bombaloo; illustrated by Yumi Heo. Scholastic Press 2001 unp il $15.95
E

1. Anger—Fiction

ISBN 0-439-08755-4   LC 99-58709

When Katie Honors feels angry and out of control, her mother helps her to be herself again

"Vail captures the intensity of emotion that children (and many adults) feel when they are angry, and then distills it with laughter. Heo uses lots of stripes and splotches of color to match Katie's emotions. . . . Kudos to Vail and Heo for making a scary subject manageable." Booklist

Valckx, Catharina

Lizette's green sock. Clarion Books 2005 unp il $15   **E**

1. Clothing and dress—Fiction 2. Birds—Fiction

ISBN 0-618-45298-2   LC 2004-12042

Original French edition, 2002

Lizette, a young bird, tries to figure out what to do with the one green sock that she finds while out walking one day.

"Utterly simple and springtime fresh. . . . Valckx conveys an impressive range of mood and action through spare, swooping brushstrokes, and pale tones of lemon, mint, and sky blue allow the kelly green of the sock to draw the eye instantly." Booklist

Van Allsburg, Chris

Bad day at Riverbend. Houghton Mifflin 1995 unp il $19.95   **E**

ISBN 0-395-67347-X   LC 95-4154

When Sheriff Hardy investigates the source of a brilliant light and shiny slime afflicting Riverbend, he finds that the village is becoming part of a child's coloring book streaked with greasy crayons

"Van Allsburg cuts loose with this inventive spoof that will keep readers guessing right up to the end. . . . Van Allsburg clearly had fun with his one, and readers likely will too." Publ Wkly

Ben's dream; story and pictures by Chris Van Allsburg. Houghton Mifflin 1982 31p il lib bdg $16.95   **E**

1. Dreams—Fiction

ISBN 0-395-32084-4   LC 81-20029

"When rain spoils Ben's ball game with Margaret, he returns to an empty house, falls asleep in his father's chair, and embarks on a dream. In a marvelous series of double-page black-and-white pictures meticulously textured with hatching, one shares Ben's voyage past such sights as the Statue of Liberty, the Sphinx, and the Mount Rushmore presidents, all with flood waters lapping about their respective chins and waists. . . . A visual tour de force." Horn Book

The garden of Abdul Gasazi; written and illustrated by Chris Van Allsburg. Houghton Mifflin 1979 unp il lib bdg $17.95   **E**

1. Magic—Fiction 2. Dogs—Fiction

ISBN 0-395-27804-X

A Caldecott Medal honor book, 1980

When the dog he is caring for runs away from Alan into the forbidden garden of a retired dog-hating magician, a spell seems to be cast over the contrary dog.

The full page "lithographlike drawings are astonishing—eerie, monumental, surreal and witty all at once—and the effect of the whole is original and unforgettable." Books of the Times

Jumanji; written and illustrated by Chris Van Allsburg. Houghton Mifflin 1981 unp il $18.95
E

1. Games—Fiction

ISBN 0-395-30448-2   LC 80-29632

Awarded the Caldecott Medal, 1982

Left on their own for an afternoon, two bored and restless children find more excitement than they bargained for in a mysterious and mystical jungle adventure board game.

"Through the masterly use of light and shadow, the interplay of design elements, and audacious changes in perspective and composition, the artist conveys an impression of color without losing the dramatic contrast of black and white." Horn Book

Just a dream. Houghton Mifflin 1990 unp il $18.95   **E**

1. Environmental protection—Fiction 2. Pollution—Fiction 3. Dreams—Fiction

ISBN 0-395-53308-2   LC 90-41343

When he has a dream about a future Earth devastated by pollution, Walter begins to understand the importance of taking care of the environment.

"Van Allsburg demonstrates his unique artistic magic in combining foresight, wisdom and striking artwork to deliver an ecological message concerning conservation and renewal." Child Book Rev Serv

The mysteries of Harris Burdick. Houghton Mifflin 1984 unp il lib bdg $18.95   **E**

1. Storytelling—Fiction 2. Imagination—Fiction

ISBN 0-395-35393-9   LC 84-9006

Also available Spanish language edition

Presents a series of loosely related drawings each accompanied by a title and a caption which the reader may use to make up his or her own story

Rendered in the author's "signature velvet black and white . . . the pictures are nothing short of spectacular. . . . While some may find this just an excuse for handsome artwork, others will see its great potential for

Van Allsburg, Chris—*Continued*
stretching a child's imagination. Although the book could
be used in countless ways, primarily it will make storytellers of children." Booklist

The Polar Express; written and illustrated by
Chris Van Allsburg. Houghton Mifflin 1985 unp il
$18.95   E
1. North Pole—Fiction 2. Santa Claus—Fiction
3. Christmas—Fiction
ISBN 0-395-38949-6   LC 85-10907
Also available Spanish language edition
Awarded the Caldecott Medal, 1986
A magical train ride on Christmas Eve takes a boy to
the North Pole to receive a special gift from Santa Claus
This offers "stunning paintings in which Van Allsburg
uses dark, rich colors and misty shapes in contrast with
touches of bright white-gold light to create scenes, interi-
or and exterior, that have a quality of mystery that imbues the strong composition to achieve a soft, evocative
mood." Bull Cent Child Books

The stranger. Houghton Mifflin 1986 unp il lib
bdg $18.95   E
1. Seasons—Fiction
ISBN 0-395-42331-7   LC 86-15235
The enigmatic origins of the stranger Farmer Bailey
hits with his truck and brings home to recuperate seem
to have a mysterious relation to the weather.
"The full-color illustrations, framed in white, evoke an
old-fashioned New England landscape at the end of summer; some are remarkably peaceful in tone, others slightly spooky by virtue of brooding colors, unexpected perspectives, or the stranger's peculiar expressions." Bull
Cent Child Books

The sweetest fig. Houghton Mifflin 1993 unp il
$18.95   E
1. Dreams—Fiction 2. Magic—Fiction 3. Dogs—Fiction
ISBN 0-395-67346-1   LC 93-12692
Also available Spanish language edition
After being given two magical figs that make his
dreams come true, Monsieur Bibot sees his plans for future wealth upset by his long-suffering dog
"The full-color, expressive illustrations are filled with
nuance, detail and mystery. Once again, Van Allsburg
weaves a spell with ultimate skill and creativity." Child
Book Rev Serv

The widow's broom. Houghton Mifflin 1992
unp il $18.95   E
1. Magic—Fiction 2. Witchcraft—Fiction
ISBN 0-395-64051-2   LC 92-7110
Also available Spanish language edition
A witch's worn-out broom serves a widow well, until
her neighbors decide the thing is wicked and dangerous
"In addition to being a neatly understated piece of storytelling, this fuels Van Allsburg's best kind of illustration—darkly rounded, speckle-textured art with eerie effects." Bull Cent Child Books

The wreck of the Zephyr; written and illustrated
by Chris Van Allsburg. Houghton Mifflin 1983
unp il lib bdg $18.95   E
ISBN 0-395-33075-0   LC 82-23371

A boy's ambition to be the greatest sailor in the world
brings him to ruin when he misuses his new ability to
sail his boat in the air.
This "displays recognizable hallmarks of the artist's
work: beauty of composition, striking contrasts of light
and shadow, and especially the fascinating ambiguity of
illusion and reality." Horn Book

The wretched stone. Houghton Mifflin 1991 unp
il $18.95   E
1. Sea stories
ISBN 0-395-53307-4   LC 91-11525
A strange glowing stone picked up on a sea voyage
captivates a ship's crew and has a terrible transforming
effect on them
"Although Van Allsburg clearly has a message to convey, he has added to the book an enjoyable and necessary dollop of humor. The story has a quiet, understated,
yet suspenseful tone; most of the plot's considerable drama is conveyed in the impressive illustrations." Horn
Book

The Z was zapped; a play in twenty-six acts;
performed by the Caslon Players; written and
directed by Chris Van Allsburg. Houghton Mifflin
1987 unp il $18.95   E
1. Alphabet
ISBN 0-395-44612-0   LC 87-14988
At head of title: The Alphabet Theatre proudly presents
Depicts how A was in an avalanche, B was badly bit-
ten, C was cut to ribbons, and the other letters of the alphabet suffered similar mishaps.
"Children can try to guess what action has occured,
thereby increasing their vocabulary and the fun, or they
can turn the page and read the text, or better yet—do
both. This clever romp resembles old vaudeville theater,
with one curious act following the next." SLJ

Zathura; a space adventure; written and
illustrated by Chris Van Allsburg. Houghton
Mifflin 2002 unp il $18   E
1. Games—Fiction
ISBN 0-618-25396-3   LC 2002-1751
Companion volume to Jumanji
"Danny and Walter Budwing, last seen on the final
page of *Jumanji*, find the magical game box in the park.
They discover a second game board inside, decorated
with space images. Once home, they begin to play, and
. . . they are instantly catapulted into the game's parallel
universe, which . . . involves meteor showers, pirate
aliens, violent robots, wild shifts in gravity, and a black
hole." Booklist
"Van Allsburg illustrates the surreal events in a grainy
charcoal-black that seems to shimmer on a rough, cream-
colored ground. His deathly quiet images . . . have a
frozen stillness that leaves all color and activity to the
imagination; with each new threat, the book seems to
hold its breath. . . . Zathura, like Jumanji, is a satisfying
enigma." Publ Wkly

Van Laan, Nancy

Moose tales; illustrated by Amy Rusch. Houghton Mifflin 1999 unp il $15; pa $5.95   **E**

1. Moose—Fiction 2. Animals—Fiction
ISBN 0-395-90863-9; 0-618-11128-X (pa)
LC 97-41273

Moose takes a walk, takes a nap under a tree that Beaver is gnawing, and finally joins all his friends in making an almost perfect snow creature with antlers

"The text is well paced, and the stories work either as read-alouds or independent reads. Rusch's illustrations feature the toothy, winsome forest dwellers. . . . Most children will enjoy their cheerful camaraderie and appreciate the gentle humor." SLJ

Another title about Moose is:
Busy, busy moose (2001)

Teeny tiny tingly tales; illustrated by Victoria Chess. Atheneum Bks. for Young Readers 2001 unp il $16   **E**

1. Horror fiction 2. Short stories 3. Stories in rhyme
ISBN 0-689-81875-0   LC 97-37452

"An Anne Schwartz book"

Three rhyming scary stories, including 'Old Doctor Wango Tango,' 'It,' and 'The Hairy Toe'

"Victoria Chess's squat figures, all teeth and beady eyes and unkempt hair, complement the zany, but a teeny-tiny bit scary, nature of these tales." Horn Book

When winter comes; illustrated by Susan Gaber. Atheneum Bks. for Young Readers 2000 unp il $16   **E**

1. Winter—Fiction 2. Animals—Fiction 3. Stories in rhyme
ISBN 0-689-81778-9   LC 97-32914

"An Anne Schwartz book"

Rhyming text asks what happens to different animals and plants "when winter comes and the cold wind blows"

"The rhyming answers use simple and accessible language. Gaber's exuberant acrylic paintings show a child, mother, father, and dog taking a walk through the woods during a snowfall." SLJ

Van Leeuwen, Jean

Benny & beautiful baby Delilah; pictures by LeUyen Pham. Dial Books for Young Readers 2006 32p il $16.99   **E**

1. Infants—Fiction 2. Siblings—Fiction
ISBN 0-8037-2891-3   LC 2004-19412

"Benny gets his very own little sister, but realizes pretty quickly that shes not much fun. . . . In the end, after a long session of crying, Benny takes charge and is able to get Delilah to smile. . . . While this well-paced story doesn't break any new ground thematically, it is realistic and heartwarming. What makes it truly shine is the art. . . . The characterizations, created with a heavy ink line, are expressive, jaunty, and lively." SLJ

Going West; pictures by Thomas B. Allen. Dial Bks. for Young Readers 1991 unp il $17.99; pa $5.99   **E**

1. Frontier and pioneer life—Fiction 2. Family life—Fiction
ISBN 0-8037-1027-5; 0-14-056096-3 (pa)
LC 90-20694

Follows a family's emigration by prairie schooner from the East, across the plains to Kansas

"Into a gentle text brimming with family warmth and love, Van Leeuwen . . . packs a wealth of emotional moments. . . . Allen's . . . scumbled, subdued pastel drawings, on sepia stock, masterfully conjure up the expanse of land and feelings." Publ Wkly

Nothing here but trees; pictures by Phil Boatwright. Dial Bks. for Young Readers 1998 unp il $15.99   **E**

1. Frontier and pioneer life—Fiction 2. Ohio—Fiction
ISBN 0-8037-2178-1   LC 97-34318

A close-knit pioneer family carves out a new home amidst the densely forested land of Ohio in the early nineteenth century

"Boatwright's handsome oil-and-acrylic paintings show the close-knit family in a wilderness that is lonely, scary, and exciting." Booklist

Tales of Oliver Pig; pictures by Arnold Lobel. Dial Bks. for Young Readers 1979 64p il pa $3.99 hardcover o.p.   **E**

1. Pigs—Fiction 2. Family life—Fiction
ISBN 0-14-036549-4 (pa)   LC 79-4276

"Dial easy-to-read"

"Oliver encounters many true-to-life situations and decides how to cope with them: what to do on a rainy day, how to make a bad day into a good one, what to do when Grandma comes, how to dress for the snow, and most confusing, what to do when Mother cries." Child Book Rev Serv

The book is "filled with the warmth of the commonplace, the jostling joys and sorrows of siblings and the love of a pig family. . . . Arnold Lobel's illustrations, often in miniature, carry on the tender, yet never sentimental tone." SLJ

Other titles about the Pig family are:
Amanda Pig and her best friend Lollipop (1998)
Amanda Pig and her big brother Oliver (1982)
Amanda Pig and the awful, scary monster (2003)
Amanda Pig and the really hot day (2005)
Amanda Pig on her own (1991)
Amanda Pig, school girl (1997)
More tales of Amanda Pig (1985)
More tales of Oliver Pig (1981)
Oliver, Amanda, and Grandmother Pig (1987)
Oliver and Albert, friends forever (2000)
Oliver and Amanda and the big snow (1995)
Oliver and Amanda's Christmas (1989)
Oliver and Amanda's Halloween (1992)
Oliver Pig and the best fort ever (2006)
Oliver Pig at school (1990)
Oliver the Mighty Pig (2004)
Tales of Amanda Pig (1983)

Vander Zee, Ruth

Mississippi morning; written by Ruth Vander Zee; illustrated by Floyd Cooper. Eerdmans Books for Young Readers 2004 unp il $16   **E**
1. Ku Klux Klan—Fiction 2. Race relations—Fiction 3. Father-son relationship—Fiction 4. Mississippi—Fiction
ISBN 0-8028-5211-4   LC 2002-151212
Amidst the economic depression and the racial tension of the 1930s, a boy discovers a horrible secret of his father's involvement in the Ku Klux Klan
"Cooper's large, warm oil paintings create the perfect sense of time, place, and atmosphere. . . . A sad and poignant story." SLJ

Varon, Sara

Chicken and Cat; by Sara Varon. 1st ed. Scholastic Press 2006 unp il $16.99   **E**
1. Cats—Fiction 2. Chickens—Fiction 3. City and town life—Fiction 4. Stories without words
ISBN 0-439-63406-7   LC 2003025297
When Cat feels sad about living in the hustle and bustle of the city, Chicken finds colorful ways to make Cat feel better.
"In this wordless story, bold, full-bleed cartoon illustrations are amiably cluttered. . . . This book has a funny, big-eyed sweetness, and is packed with details that kids will relish discovering in successive readings." SLJ

Vestergaard, Hope

Hello, snow! pictures by Nadine Bernard Westcott. 1st ed. Farrar, Straus and Giroux 2004 unp il $16   **E**
1. Snow—Fiction 2. Stories in rhyme
ISBN 0-374-32949-4   LC 2003-45509
"Melanie Kroupa books"
Children bundle up to spend a day in the snow with their father.
"Always upbeat and often comical, the artwork captures and extends the joyful tone of the text. . . . The illustrations, ink drawings with watercolor washes, are notable for their expressiveness, economy of line, and warmth of color." Booklist

Vidal, Beatriz

Federico and the Magi's gift; a Latin American Christmas story; by Beatriz Vidal. 1st ed. Knopf 2004 unp il $15.95; lib bdg $17.99   **E**
1. Epiphany—Fiction 2. Magi—Fiction 3. Latin America—Fiction
ISBN 0-375-82518-5; 0-375-92518-X (lib bdg)
          LC 2003-25880
Because he has misbehaved, four-year-old Federico is afraid the three kings will not bring him the toy horse he asked them for and, unable to sleep, he goes outside to await their arrival.
"Decoratively patterned, the gouache-and-watercolor paintings employ naive forms and glowing colors. . . . With its quiet narrative and beautiful illustrations, this celebrates the end of the Christmas season in a distinctly Latin American way." Booklist

Vigil-Piñón, Evangelina

Marina's muumuu; illustrations by Pablo Torrecilla. Arte Público Press 2001 unp il $14.95   **E**
1. Clothing and dress—Fiction 2. Bilingual books—English-Spanish
ISBN 1-55885-350-2   LC 2001-21487
Title page and text in English and Spanish
Marina has always dreamed of having a colorful muumuu, the traditional dress of the Hawaiian people, and finally goes to the bustling downtown with her grandmother to buy the fabric
"Gloriously bright tropical colors and patterns fill these gaily decorated pages." Booklist

Viorst, Judith

Alexander and the terrible, horrible, no good, very bad day; illustrated by Ray Cruz. Atheneum Pubs. 1972 unp il $15.95; pa $6.99   **E**
1. Day—Fiction
ISBN 0-689-30072-7; 0-689-71173-5 (pa)
Also available Spanish language edition
Recounts the events of a day when everything goes wrong for Alexander.
"Small listeners can enjoy the litany of disaster, and perhaps be stimulated to discuss the possibility that one contributes by expectation. The illustrations capture the grumpy dolor of the story, ruefully funny." Sutherland. The Best In Child Books
Other titles about Alexander are:
Alexander, who is not (do you hear me?) going (I mean it) to move (1995)
Alexander, who used to be rich last Sunday (1978)

Just in case; written by Judith Viorst; illustrated by Diana Cain Bluthenthal. 1st ed. Atheneum Books for Young Readers 2006 unp il $15.95
          E
ISBN 0-689-87164-3   LC 2003-26068
"Ginee Seo books."
Charlie likes to be ready for anything, imagining that his house could be flooded or a mermaid might kidnap him, but he learns that it is sometimes good to be unprepared.
"Blumenthal's colorful, mixed-media illustrations add some good cheer, sly wit, . . . and a companionable canine to the catalog of Charlie's hypothetical 'just in case' concerns." Booklist

The tenth good thing about Barney; illustrated by Erik Blegvad. Atheneum Pubs. 1971 25p il $15.95; pa $5.99   **E**
1. Death—Fiction 2. Cats—Fiction
ISBN 0-689-20688-7; 0-689-71203-0 (pa)
"A little boy saddened by the death of his cat thinks of nine good things about Barney to say at his funeral. Later his father helps him discover a tenth good thing: Barney is in the ground helping grow flowers and trees and grass.'" Booklist
"The author succinctly and honestly handles both the emotions stemming from the loss of a beloved pet and the questions about the finality of death . . . An unusually good book that handles a difficult subject straightforwardly." Horn Book

Voake, Charlotte

Ginger. Candlewick Press 1997 unp il $16.99;
pa $6.99   E
  1. Cats—Fiction
ISBN 0-7636-0108-X; 0-7636-0788-6 (pa)
                         LC 96-20890
When Ginger the cat gets fed up with dealing with her
owner's new kitten, it takes drastic measures to make the
two of them friends
  "The warm, expressive watercolor illustrations are a
perfect compliment to the winsome, enchanting text."
Child Book Rev Serv
 Another title about Ginger is:
Ginger finds a home (2003)

Vogel, Amos

How little Lori visited Times Square; pictures
by Maurice Sendak. HarperCollins Pubs. 2001 unp
il $14.95   E
  1. New York (N.Y.)—Fiction
ISBN 0-06-028462-5
A reissue of the title first published 1963
This "tells the story of Lori's many misadventures trying to get to Times Square on various modes of transportation, with a slow-moving turtle finally bearing him
off." Horn Book Guide

Waber, Bernard

Evie & Margie. Houghton Mifflin 2003 32p il
$15   E
  1. Friendship—Fiction 2. Theater—Fiction
3. Hippopotamus—Fiction
ISBN 0-618-34124-2   LC 2003-533
"Walter Lorraine books"
Best friends hippopotamuses, Evie and Margie, are
surprised to experience jealousy when they try out for
the same part in the school play
  "The book gets to the heart of what is important to
children, and the color illustrations are vintage Waber
with great facial expressions and humorous, child-
friendly images." SLJ

Ira sleeps over. Houghton Mifflin 1972 48p il
lib bdg $16; pa $5.95   E
  1. Teddy bears—Fiction 2. Friendship—Fiction
ISBN 0-395-13893-0 (lib bdg); 0-395-20503-4 (pa)
Ira is excited at the prospect of spending the night at
his friend's house but worries how he'll get along without his teddy bear.
  "An appealing picture book which depicts common
childhood qualms with empathy and humor in brief text
and colorful illustrations." Booklist
 Another title about Ira is:
Ira says goodbye (1988)

A lion named Shirley Williamson. Houghton
Mifflin 1996 40p il $15.95; pa $6.95   E
  1. Lions—Fiction 2. Zoos—Fiction
ISBN 0-395-80979-7; 0-618-05580-0 (pa)
                         LC 96-11187
Although a lion's unusual name causes confusion and
misunderstanding at the zoo, she becomes a favorite with
the public and with Seymour the zookeeper.

This is "a story that is both hysterical and poignant.
It succeeds at every level, offering a plot that prances
along, characters that show the inevitable tangle of emotions life elicits, and artwork that is so funny yet sly that
adults and children can both relish it." Booklist

Lyle, Lyle, crocodile. Houghton Mifflin 1965
48p il $16; pa $6.95   E
  1. Crocodiles—Fiction 2. New York (N.Y.)—Fiction
ISBN 0-395-16995-X; 0-395-13720-9 (pa)
Lyle the crocodile who lives in New York City
"wants desperately to win the friendship of the cat Loret-
ta two doors away but every time Loretta catches a
glimpse of him she flings herself into a nervous fit."
Booklist
  "The illustrations are cartoon-like, lively, and colorful.
. . . The situation is nicely exploited with a bland
daffiness." Bull Cent Child Books
 Other titles about Lyle are:
Funny, funny Lyle (1987)
The house on East 88th Street (1962)
Lovable Lyle (1969)
Lyle and the birthday party (1966)
Lyle at Christmas (1998)
Lyle at the office (1994)
Lyle finds his mother (1974)

The mouse that snored. Houghton Mifflin 2000
unp il $15   E
  1. Noise—Fiction 2. Mice—Fiction 3. Stories in
rhyme
ISBN 0-395-97518-2   LC 98-47276
"Walter Lorraine books"
A loudly snoring mouse disturbs the residents of a
quiet country house
  "Using characteristically humorous pictures and a delightful, rhyming text, Waber creates a world-weary
mouse with a snore that moves furniture." Booklist

Waddell, Martin

Can't you sleep, Little Bear? illustrated by
Barbara Firth. 2nd U.S. ed. Candlewick Press 1992
unp il $15.99; pa $5.99   E
  1. Bears—Fiction 2. Bedtime—Fiction
ISBN 1-56402-007-X; 1-56402-262-5 (pa)
                         LC 91-71858
First published 1988 in the United Kingdom
When bedtime comes Little Bear is afraid of the dark,
until Big Bear brings him lights and love
  "Firth's brightly lit watercolor and soft pencil illustra-
tions, framed in the dark blue of the night, capture the
cozy, physical affection of the story, the playfulness of
Little Bear, . . . the shadowy mystery of the moonlit
landscape, and the huge comforting presence of a parent
who is always there when you call." Booklist
 Other titles about Little Bear are:
Good job, Little Bear! (1999)
Let's go home, Little Bear (1993)
Little Bear's baby book (2000)
Sleep tight Little Bear (2005)
Well done, Little Bear (1999)
You and me, Little Bear (1996)

Waddell, Martin—_Continued_

Farmer duck; illustrated by Helen Oxenbury. Candlewick Press 1992 c1991 unp il $15.99; pa $5.99   E

1. Ducks—Fiction 2. Farm life—Fiction

ISBN 1-56402-009-6; 1-56402-596-9 (pa)

LC 91-71855

Also available Big book edition

First published 1991 in the United Kingdom

When a kind and hardworking duck nearly collapses from overwork, while taking care of a farm because the owner is too lazy to do so, the rest of the animals get together and chase the farmer out of town

"Hilarious art masterfully captures the expressions of the put-upon duck, the supportive cast, and the slovenly ergophobic who reads the newspaper and chomps on bonbons in bed. . . . With its lilting, large-print text and satisfying resolution, it's as perfect for beginning readers as it is for story hours." SLJ

Hi, Harry! illustrated by Barbara Firth. Candlewick Press 2003 unp il $14.99   E

1. Turtles—Fiction 2. Snails—Fiction 3. Friendship—Fiction

ISBN 0-7636-1802-0   LC 2001-47140

A tortoise tries to find someone who will play with him at his own speed

"Firth's pen-and-ink and watercolor illustrations aptly depict all of the characters. . . . The use of repetition within this simple text will engage listeners who will be touched by this tender story of friendship." SLJ

It's quacking time! illustrated by Jill Barton. 1st U.S. ed. Candlewick Press 2005 unp il $15.99

E

1. Ducks—Fiction 2. Eggs—Fiction

ISBN 0-7636-2738-0   LC 2004-57039

A duckling and all his family happily await the hatching of his parents' new egg.

"A warm tale. . . . Barton's expressive watercolor and pencil illustrations are appropriately full of life." Horn Book Guide

Owl babies; illustrated by Patrick Benson. Candlewick Press 1992 unp il $15.99   E

1. Owls—Fiction

ISBN 1-56402-101-7   LC 91-58750

Also available Board book edition and Spanish language edition

Three owl babies whose mother has gone out in the night try to stay calm while she is gone

"The illustrations, executed in black ink and watercolor, capture in every feather and expression the little owls' worry and watchfulness as well as their complete joy when Owl Mother returns." Horn Book

Snow bears; illustrated by Sarah Fox-Davies. Candlewick Press 2002 unp il $14.99   E

1. Bears—Fiction 2. Snow—Fiction

ISBN 0-7636-1906-X   LC 2001-58258

When three little bears play in the snow, they pretend to be "snow bears" and their mother goes along with the game

"Waddell's affectionate text offers an idyllic frosty gambol, and youngsters will appreciate the lulling repeti-

tion, the gentle trickery, and the smallest baby bear's struggles to keep up with her elder siblings." Bull Cent Child Books

Tiny's big adventure; illustrated by John Lawrence. Candlewick Press 2004 unp il $15.99

E

1. Mice—Fiction 2. Country life—Fiction 3. Siblings—Fiction

ISBN 0-7636-2170-6   LC 2002-35004

Katy Mouse teaches her younger brother, Tiny, the names of some of the things they see, including a boot, a snail, and a pheasant, when they go to the cornfield to play games.

"The rich mixture of vinyl engravings, watercolor washes, and printed wood textures gives a timeless flavor to the adventure, as do Waddell's sweet story line and clear sentences." Booklist

Wadsworth, Olive A.

Over in the meadow; a counting rhyme; illustrated by Anna Vojtech. North-South Bks. 2002 unp il $15.95; lib bdg $16.50   E

1. Counting 2. Nursery rhymes

ISBN 0-7358-1596-8; 0-7358-1597-6 (lib bdg)

LC 2001-51434

"A Cheshire Studio book"

An old nursery poem introduces animals and their young and the number one through ten

"Although many versions of the verse, both traditional and nontraditional, are available, this is an accessible rendition that children will enjoy in storytime and on their own." SLJ

Wahl, Jan

Candy shop; illustrated by Nicole Wong. Charlesbridge 2004 unp il lib bdg $15.95

E

1. Toleration—Fiction 2. Taiwanese Americans—Fiction 3. African Americans—Fiction

ISBN 1-57091-508-3   LC 2003-3695

When a boy and his aunt find that a bigot has written hurtful words on the sidewalk just outside the candy shop owned by "Miz Chu", a new immigrant from Taiwan, they set out to comfort her.

"The clean hues and supple lines of the pictures support Wahl's gentle message of comfort and tolerance." Booklist

Wallace, Carol

One nosy pup; illustrated by Steve Björkman. Holiday House 2005 40p $15.95   E

1. Dogs—Fiction 2. Hamsters—Fiction

ISBN 0-8234-1917-7

"A Holiday House reader"

After moving to a new house, Poky the beagle befriends Charlie the hamster, who was accidentally left behind by the previous owners.

"Wallace writes in short, simply constructed sentences and uses a brisk, basic vocabulary just right for new readers, and the expressive, color-washed art hums with activity and emotion." Booklist

Wallace, Carol—*Continued*

Turkeys together; illustrated by Jacqueline Rogers. . Holiday House 2005 38p il $15.95

E

1. Dogs—Fiction 2. Turkeys—Fiction 3. Eggs—Fiction

ISBN 0-8234-1895-2   LC 2004-52392

"A Holiday House reader"

A pointer dog puppy helps a mother turkey figure out how to protect her eggs from being stolen.

"A sweet tale about cooperation and friendship, with a satisfying conclusion. . . . Soft watercolor illustrations add meaning to the text and provide clues for some of the more difficult words. . . . The expressive animal faces are charming and realistic." SLJ

Wallace, Nancy Elizabeth

Pumpkin day! written and illustrated by Nancy Elizabeth Wallace. Marshall Cavendish 2002 unp il $16.95

E

1. Pumpkin—Fiction 2. Rabbits—Fiction

ISBN 0-7614-5128-5   LC 2002-834

Companion volume to Apples, apples, apples (2000)

A bunny family picks pumpkins at a local farm and learns pumpkin facts in the process

"Although there are many other books on the topic, this one stands apart because of its simple, yet dynamic collage artwork and the quality and quantity of information that is tucked into the text in all sorts of interesting ways." Booklist

Recycle every day! written and illustrated by Nancy Elizabeth Wallace. Marshall Cavendish 2003 unp il $16.95

E

1. Recycling—Fiction 2. Rabbits—Fiction

ISBN 0-7614-5149-8   LC 2001-26050

When Minna has a school assignment to make a poster about recycling, her entire rabbit family spends the week practicing various kinds of recycling and suggesting ideas for her poster

"Using found materials to create the lovely art, the author/illustrator practices what she preaches and invites readers to search for the recycled materials. An activity and a game are appended. While the book's message is obvious, there is enough of a story to keep youngsters interested." SLJ

Seeds! Seeds! Seeds! written and illustrated by Nancy Elizabeth Wallace. Marshall Cavendish 2004 unp il $16.95

E

1. Seeds—Fiction 2. Bears—Fiction

ISBN 0-7614-5159-5   LC 2003-9318

Buddy Bear learns about different kinds of seeds and their uses when he opens a package sent by his grandfather.

"The artwork consists of cut-paper collages with shadowing and life-sized photos of real seeds that look as though they can be picked right off the pages. The story is entertaining and educational." SLJ

Wallner, Alexandra

Sergio and the hurricane. Holt & Co. 2000 unp il $16

E

1. Hurricanes—Fiction 2. Puerto Rico—Fiction

ISBN 0-8050-6203-3   LC 99-40724

A young boy is excited when he hears that a hurricane is coming to his oceanfront home in San Juan, Puerto Rico, but when it comes, he learns how dangerous hurricanes can be

"Wallner's neatly drawn scenes, in muted colors, convey a sense of calm urgency before the hurricane, and her figures show restraint afterward." Booklist

Walsh, Ellen Stoll

Dot & Jabber and the big bug mystery. Harcourt 2003 unp il $15

E

1. Mice—Fiction 2. Insects—Fiction 3. Mystery fiction

ISBN 0-15-216518-5   LC 2002-11386

Dot and Jabber, mouse detectives, try to solve the mystery of the disappearing insects

"The distinctive cut-paper collages step nicely off the page for a 3-D look, and the earthy greens and browns are gentle and calming. A note on insects and camouflage is included." SLJ

Other titles about Dot & Jabber are:

Dot & Jabber and the great acorn mystery (2001)

Dot & Jabber and the mystery of the missing stream (2002)

For Pete's sake. Harcourt Brace & Co. 1998 unp il $15

E

1. Alligators—Fiction 2. Flamingos—Fiction

ISBN 0-15-200324-X   LC 97-25677

Pete, an alligator who thinks that he is a flamingo, worries when he begins to notice the differences between him and his flamingo friends

"Walsh's precise paper-cut collages are just right. Subtly textured and with spacious, stark white backgrounds, they are pleasingly simple, giving the comedy and the message plenty of unencumbered opportunity to sink in." Booklist

Mouse count. Harcourt Brace Jovanovich 1991 unp il lib bdg $14; pa $5.50

E

1. Mice—Fiction 2. Snakes—Fiction 3. Counting

ISBN 0-15-256023-8 (lib bdg); 0-15-200223-5 (pa)

LC 90-35915

Also available Board book edition

Ten mice outsmart a hungry snake

"Children will delight in this counting game that is couched in an exciting, original story. . . . The torn paper collage and tempra illustrations are lively and depict the story's unerring drama through an uncluttered form and line." SLJ

Another title about the mice is:

Mouse paint (1989)

Walter, Mildred Pitts

Alec's primer; illustrated by Larry Johnson. 1st ed. Vermont Folklife Center; distributed by University Press of New England 2004 unp il (Vermont Folklife Center children's book series) $15.95

E

1. Slavery—Fiction 2. African Americans—Fiction 3. Reading—Fiction

ISBN 0-916718-20-4   LC 2003-27716

Walter, Mildred Pitts—*Continued*

A young slave's journey to freedom begins when a plantation owner's granddaughter teaches him how to read. Based on the childhood of Alec Turner (1845-1923) who escaped from slavery by joining the Union Army during the Civil War and later became a landowner in Vermont

"Walter's spare, dramatic words and Johnson's stirring double-page paintings present a glimpse of the history in a brutal world." Booklist

Walters, Catherine

Time to sleep, Alfie Bear. Dutton Children's Bks. 2003 unp il $15.99   **E**
1. Bedtime—Fiction 2. Bears—Fiction
ISBN 0-525-47204-5   LC 2003-40962
On a night when Alfie Bear is not sleepy, he tries to join various nocturnal animals so that he can stay up later

"The sweet story is set off nicely by the lush, realistic single and double-page artwork. Young observers will appreciate the detailed illustrations." SLJ
Other titles about Alfie Bear are:
Are you there, Baby Bear? (1999)
Play gently, Alfie Bear (2002)
When will it be spring? (1998)
Where are you, Alfie Bear? (2002)

Walters, Virginia

Are we there yet, Daddy? illustrated by S. D. Schindler. Viking 1999 unp il $15.99   **E**
1. Automobile travel—Fiction 2. Maps—Fiction 3. Stories in rhyme
ISBN 0-670-87402-7   LC 97-18220
Colored map on folded page preceding t.p
A young boy describes the trip he and his father make to Grandma's house, measuring how many miles are left at various points on the trip

"This unique picture book combines maps and counting skills with a bouncy refrain that invites kids to join in. . . . The flat, pastel pictures add enlivening details to the repetitive text." SLJ

Walvoord, Linda

Razzamadaddy; illustrations by Sachiko Yoshikawa. 1st ed. Marshall Cavendish Children's Books 2004 unp il $14.95   **E**
1. Father-son relationship—Fiction 2. Beaches—Fiction 3. Stories in rhyme
ISBN 0-7614-5158-7   LC 2003-9319
A father and son spend a wonderful day together at the beach.

This offers a "lyrical, rhyming text. . . . The acrylic-and-pastel illustrations are done in bright, bold colors and reflect the enjoyment father and son experience during their day together." SLJ

Ward, Helen

The rooster and the fox; retold & illustrated by Helen Ward. Millbrook Press 2003 unp il $16.95; lib bdg $24.90   **E**
1. Chaucer, Geoffrey, d. 1400—Adaptations 2. Roosters—Fiction 3. Fables
ISBN 0-7613-1846-1; 0-7613-2920-X (lib bdg)
"A Templar book"
First published 2002 in the United Kingdom
An adaptation of the "Nun's priest's tale" from Geoffrey Chaucer's Canterbury tales

"After being outsmarted by a cunning fox, a cocky rooster gathers his wits and turns the tables on his captor. Chaucer's Chanticleer is brought to life through a riveting retelling and magnificent, edge-of-your-seat artwork." SLJ

Ward, Lynd Kendall

The biggest bear; by Lynd Ward. Houghton Mifflin 1988 84p il lib bdg $16; pa $6.95
E
1. Bears—Fiction
ISBN 0-395-14806-5 (lib bdg); 0-395-15024-8 (pa)
LC 88-176366
Awarded the Caldecott Medal, 1953
A reissue of the title first published 1952
"Johnny Orchard never did acquire the bearskin for which he boldly went hunting. Instead, he brought home a cuddly bear cub, which grew in size and appetite to mammoth proportions and worried his family and neighbors half to death." Child Books Too Good to Miss

Warhola, James

Uncle Andy's. Putnam 2003 unp il $16.99
E
1. Warhol, Andy, 1928?-1987 2. Artists—United States
ISBN 0-399-23869-7   LC 2002-7766
The author describes a trip to see his uncle, the soon-to-be-famous artist Andy Warhol, and the fun that he and his family had on the visit

"This catches the excitement that the creative process can engender, both for the established artist and for the dreamer." Booklist

Waring, Richard

Hungry hen; illustrated by Caroline Jayne Church. HarperCollins Pubs. 2001 unp il $14.95
E
1. Chickens—Fiction 2. Foxes—Fiction
ISBN 0-06-623880-3   LC 2001-24044
A greedy fox watches a hungry hen growing bigger every day, knowing that the longer he waits to eat her, the bigger she will be

"The story is simple and dramatic, with a perfect blend of words and pictures. . . . This is elemental storytelling, with tension rising until it's almost unbearable, and then the great surprise. The art is beautiful, with big, bright, clear shapes of the rosy hen and the sneaky fox on backgrounds of handmade paper." Booklist

Warnes, Tim

Mommy mine; by Tim Warnes; illustrated by Jane Chapman. 1st ed. HarperCollins 2005 unp il $15.99; lib bdg $16.89   **E**

1. Animals—Fiction 2. Mother-child relationship—Fiction 3. Stories in rhyme

ISBN 0-06-058947-7; 0-06-058948-5 (lib bdg)

LC 2003-24275

Whether it is by croak, flutter, or fur, all children claim their mothers as their own.

"The simple, chantable rhyme is filled with contrasts. . . . Human children safe in their own mother's embrace will point at the pictures, feel the excitement and connections, and act out the wildness and the hugs." Booklist

Watts, Bernadette

The ugly duckling; by Hans Christian Andersen; adapted and illustrated by Bernadette Watts. North-South Bks. 2000 unp il $15.95; lib bdg $16.95   **E**

1. Andersen, Hans Christian, 1805-1875—Adaptations 2. Swans—Fiction 3. Fairy tales

ISBN 0-7358-1388-4; 0-7358-1389-2 (lib bdg)

LC 00-35125

An ugly duckling spends an unhappy year ostracized by the other animals before he grows into a beautiful swan

The "detailed double-paged spreads are beautiful. . . . Watts' active pastoral landscapes, filled with light and movement, capture the changing seasons and the sturdy, unwanted outsider's search for home." Booklist

Weatherby, Brenda

The trucker; written by Brenda Weatherby; illustrated by Mark Weatherby. Scholastic 2004 unp il $15.95   **E**

1. Trucks—Fiction

ISBN 0-439-39877-0   LC 2002-70787

Wesley dreams his toy semi-flatbed rig grows big enough for him to have a trucking adventure but wakes to find he is in the back of his father's truck.

"The brief, simple text is filled with the lively sounds of the big machine on the road. . . . Using acrylic, sand, and, appropriately, road dirt, the pictures convey something of the story's blurry, dreamlike quality, while supplying plenty of realistic details of the trucker's life." Booklist

Weatherford, Carole Boston

Freedom on the menu; the Greensboro sit-ins; paintings by Jerome Lagarrigue. Dial Books for Young Readers 2005 unp il $16.99   **E**

1. African Americans—Fiction 2. Civil rights demonstrations—Fiction 3. Race relations—Fiction 4. North Carolina—Fiction

ISBN 0-8037-2860-3   LC 2002-13226

The 1960 civil rights sit-ins at the Woolworth's lunch counter in Greensboro, North Carolina, are seen through the eyes of a young Southern black girl.

"Simple and straightforward, the first-person narrative relates events within the context of one close-knit family. . . . The well-composed, painterly illustrations show up well from a distance. A handsome book." Booklist

Weeks, Sarah

Drip, drop; story by Sarah Weeks; pictures by Jane Manning. HarperCollins Pubs. 2000 32p il $14.95; lib bdg $14.89   **E**

1. Mice—Fiction 2. Rain—Fiction 3. Stories in rhyme

ISBN 0-06-028523-0; 0-06-028524-9 (lib bdg)

LC 00-21652

"An I can read book"

Pip Squeak the mouse is kept awake all night by the drips from his leaky roof

"Short, simple sentences keep the action moving along while a single problem focuses readers' attention. The snappy narrative is coupled with expressive, silly illustrations." SLJ

Two eggs, please; written by Sarah Weeks; illustrated by Betsy Lewin. Atheneum Bks. for Young Readers 2003 unp il $15.95   **E**

1. Eggs—Fiction 2. Restaurants—Fiction 3. Animals—Fiction

ISBN 0-689-83196-X   LC 2002-5291

"An all-night diner attracts a wide variety of customers in the middle of the night, including a rhino cab driver, two wolf police officers, and a crocodile street performer and his snake. One by one, they take stools at the counter and order the same thing, 'Two eggs, please,' but each order is different: soft-boiled, hard-boiled, poached, raw (for the snake). The premise is as basic as fried eggs, and handled with a light touch, but Lewin's inviting watercolor and ink illustrations add flavor and expand the story to involve young listeners and readers." Horn Book

Weigel, Jeff

Atomic Ace; (he's just my dad); written and illustrated by Jeff Weigel. Albert Whitman & Co 2004 unp il $15.95   **E**

1. Fathers—Fiction

ISBN 0-8075-3216-9   LC 2003-17523

In this rhyming story told in comic book format, a boy considers his family normal, though his superhero dad, Atomic Ace, does amazing feats, even battling the evil Insect King

"The juxtapositions between superheroics and regular-guy domesticity are clever, and Weigl's confident artwork . . . is guaranteed to satisfy children obsessed with caped crusaders." Booklist

Weiss, Nicki

Where does the brown bear go? Greenwillow Bks. 1989 unp il $16.99   **E**

1. Animals—Fiction 2. Night—Fiction

ISBN 0-688-07862-1   LC 87-36980

Also available Board book edition

When the lights go down on the city street and the sun sinks far behind the seas, the animals of the world are on their way home for the night

"The rich, dark colors of a velvet night sky, polka dotted with stars, form the background for this enchanting lullaby." Horn Book

Weitzman, Jacqueline Preiss

You can't take a balloon into the Metropolitan Museum; story by Jacqueline Preiss Weitzman; pictures by Robin Preiss Glasser. Dial Bks. for Young Readers 1998 37p il $18.99   **E**

1. Metropolitan Museum of Art (New York, N.Y.)—Fiction 2. New York (N.Y.)—Fiction 3. Stories without words

ISBN 0-8037-2301-6   LC 97-31629

In this wordless story, a young girl and her grandmother view works inside the Metropolitan Museum of Art, while the balloon she has been forced to leave outside floats around New York City causing a series of mishaps that mirror scenes in the museum's artworks

"Lively, squiggly ink sketches with characters picked out in watercolor and gouache for accent, along with reproductions of art from the Met . . . tell a vivid, happy tale." Booklist

Other titles in this series are:

You can't take a balloon into the Museum of Fine Arts (2002)

You can't take a balloon into the National Gallery (2000)

Weller, Frances Ward

The day the animals came; a story of Saint Francis Day; illustrated by Loren Long. Philomel Bks. 2003 unp il $16.99   **E**

1. Animals—Fiction 2. Hispanic Americans—Fiction 3. New York (N.Y.)—Fiction

ISBN 0-399-23630-9   LC 2002-6297

A young girl who misses her former home and her animal friends left behind in the West Indies makes new friends at the blessing of the animals at a cathedral in New York City on the Feast of St. Francis

"The acrylic paintings soar as Long looks at goings-on from many different perspectives. . . . Children will like seeing so many animals in such an unexpected place, and Ria's feeling of acceptance makes for a satisfying conclusion." Booklist

Wellington, Monica

Apple farmer Annie. Dutton Children's Bks. 2001 unp il $14.99   **E**

1. Apples—Fiction

ISBN 0-525-46727-0   LC 00-46203

Annie the apple farmer saves her most beautiful apples to sell fresh at the farmers' market

"Charming and cheery, [this] story makes a great read-aloud. The illustrations seem to step right out of a coloring book with simple shapes, objects, and bright, crayon-box colors." SLJ

Wells, Rosemary

Carry me! Hyperion Books for Children 2006 unp il $15.99   **E**

1. Parent-child relationship—Fiction 2. Rabbits—Fiction 3. Stories in rhyme

ISBN 0-7868-0396-7

"Sweet, signature watercolors highlight three poems told from a small bunny's point of view. Carry Me! Talk to Me! and Sing to Me! express the animal's desires: to be held close by a loving parent, read to, sung to, and told stories. Each picture, mainly in soft pastel hues, exemplifies a moment of shared happiness between child and parents." SLJ

Emily's first 100 days of school. Hyperion Bks. for Children 2000 unp il $16.99   **E**

1. School stories 2. Rabbits—Fiction 3. Counting

ISBN 0-7868-0507-2   LC 99-27021

Starting with number one for the first day of school, Emily the rabbit learns the numbers to one hundred in many different ways

"Wells manages to find fresh, engaging presentations for that many numbers. Alive with color and thematically relevant decoration, the oversized pages are sometimes divided into several panels, but never feel too busy." Horn Book Guide

Another title about Emily and her school is:

My kindergarten (2004)

Felix feels better. Candlewick Press 2001 unp il $12.99   **E**

1. Sick—Fiction 2. Medical care—Fiction 3. Guinea pigs—Fiction

ISBN 0-7636-0639-1   LC 00-41395

Felix feels bad and does not want to eat or play, so his mother takes him to Doctor Duck, who makes everything better

"This charming story reads beautifully, and subtly deals with children's fears. Felix is an adorable fellow and Wells expertly portrays his every mood through her art. Her delightful watercolor-and-ink illustrations add warmth and character to the tale." SLJ

Another title about Felix is:

Felix and the Worrier (2003)

McDuff moves in; pictures by Susan Jeffers. Hyperion Books for Children 2005 c1997 unp il $9.99   **E**

1. Dogs—Fiction

ISBN 0-7868-5677-7

A reissue of the title first published 1997

A white terrier "is rejected at several doors before finding a loving home, complete with an herbal bath and vanilla rice pudding." SLJ

"This collaboration by Wells and Jeffers is as sweet, substantial, and comforting as that bowl of rice pudding and will suit the many children who like stories with simple words, clear story lines, and happily-ever-after endings." Booklist

Other titles about McDuff are:

McDuff and the baby (1997)

McDuff comes home (1997)

McDuff goes to school (2001)

McDuff's Christmas (2005)

McDuff's favorite things (2004)

McDuff's new friend (1998)

McDuff saves the day (2001)

McDuff's wild romp (2005)

The miraculous tale of the two Maries; by Rosemary Wells; illustrated by Petra Mathers. Viking 2006 unp il $16.99   **E**

1. Miracles—Fiction 2. France—Fiction

ISBN 0-670-05960-9   LC 2005017743

Wells, Rosemary—*Continued*

After perishing in a boating accident, two sixteen-year-old girls, both named Marie, ask God to allow them to return to the earth and intervene in the lives of villagers.

"Anchoring the story's ethereal themes are palpable south-of-France details, from the narrative's occasional French phrases to Mathers' alluring artwork, which captures the region's azure skies and sunbaked, salt-cured colors." Booklist

Morris's disappearing bag. Viking 1999 unp il $15.99   **E**
1. Christmas—Fiction 2. Rabbits—Fiction
ISBN 0-670-88721-8   LC 00-267633
First published 1975 by Dial Bks. for Young Readers
New illustrations by the author

Morris is so disappointed with his Christmas present that he invents a disappearing bag, which gives him a chance to share his brother's and sister's gifts

In this version "Morris re-appears in a full-color, full-size edition of the Christmas day story." Horn Book Guide

Noisy Nora; with all new illustrations. Dial Bks. for Young Readers 1997 unp il $15.99; pa $5.99   **E**

1. Mice—Fiction 2. Stories in rhyme
ISBN 0-670-88722-6; 0-14-056728-3 (pa)

A newly illustrated edition of the title first published 1973

Little Nora, tired of being ignored, tries to gain her family's attention by being noisy. When this doesn't work Nora disappears but returns when she is sure she has been missed

"All new illustrations infuse this much-loved picture book . . . with energy. Vibrant colors and a larger format make the characters seem to jump out at readers." SLJ

Only you. Viking 2003 il $14.99   **E**
1. Mother-child relationship—Fiction 2. Bears—Fiction
ISBN 0-670-03634-X   LC 2002-15570
Also available bilingual English-Spanish edition $14.99 (0-670-03692-7)

A little bear describes how much his mother means to him

"Wells's illustrations are right on target. Most of them feature parent and child as the central characters, cozily enclosed in a square and surrounded by a soft, pastel border. . . . Perfect for one-on-one sharing." SLJ

Read to your bunny. Scholastic 1998 c1997 unp il $7.95; pa $3.99   **E**
1. Rabbits—Fiction 2. Books and reading—Fiction 3. Stories in rhyme
ISBN 0-590-30284-1; 0-439-08717-1 (pa)
      LC 97-17704

Brief rhyming text and colorful illustrations tell what happens when parents and children share twenty minutes a day reading

"Each line of text gets one of Wells' delightful bordered pictures of parents and children at all sorts of activities, from bathing to skating, but always with a book in hand." Booklist

Ruby's beauty shop. Viking 2002 unp il $15.99   **E**
1. Beauty shops—Fiction 2. Siblings—Fiction 3. Rabbits—Fiction
ISBN 0-670-03553-X   LC 2001-7730

Louise and Ruby use Louise's "Deluxe Beauty Kit" to give Max a make-over, but when Grandma calls to schedule her own make-over, she makes an appointment with Max

"Wells is in top form. . . . The author's affinity for kid-based glee is playfully evident." Bull Cent Child Books

Other titles about Max and Ruby are:
Bunny cakes (1997)
Bunny mail (2004)
Bunny money (1997)
Bunny party (2001)
Max and Ruby's first Greek myth: Pandora's box (1993)
Max and Ruby's Midas: another Greek myth (1995)
Max's ABC (2006)
Max cleans up (2000)
Max's bath (1985)
Max's bedtime (1985)
Max's birthday (1985)
Max's breakfast (1985)
Max's chocolate chicken (1989)
Max's Christmas (1986)
Max's dragon shirt (1991)
Max's first word (1979)
Max's new suit (1979)
Max's ride (1979)
Max's toys (1979)

Shy Charles; [by] Rosemary Wells. Viking 2001 c1988 unp il $15.99; pa $5.99   **E**
1. Mice—Fiction 2. Stories in rhyme
ISBN 0-670-88729-3; 0-14-056843-3 (pa)
      LC 2001-271649

A reissue of the title first published 1988 by Dial Books for Young Readers

"Charles, a young mouse, is perfectly happy playing by himself, and social contacts are an endless ordeal. . . . But when the baby sitter falls down the stairs, Charles is able to comfort her and call for help, before resuming his shy silence." NY Times Book Rev

"Wells' illustrations . . . show the plump, large-eared cast to be full of charm and cleverness. Facial expressions, posture, and background details substantially extend the humor of the story. The simple rhythm of the rhyming text is subtle and playful." SLJ

Timothy's tales from Hilltop School. Viking 2002 64p il $16.99   **E**
1. School stories 2. Animals—Fiction
ISBN 0-670-03554-8   LC 2001-7360

Companion volume to Timothy goes to school (1992)

A collection of six stories featuring the teachers and students of Hilltop School as they learn about taking turns, working together, and never giving up

"The language is evocative, the dilemmas are real, and the solutions are satisfying. Watercolor personality portraits and spot art throughout feature Wells' familiar and beloved animal characters." Bull Cent Child Books

Wells, Rosemary—*Continued*

Yoko. Hyperion Bks. for Children 1998 unp il
$14.95; lib bdg $15.49　　　　　　　　E
1. Food—Fiction 2. Japanese Americans—Fiction
3. Cats—Fiction 4. School stories
ISBN 0-7868-0395-9; 0-7868-2345-3 (lib bdg)
　　　　　　　　　　　　　　LC 98-12342
When Yoko the cat brings sushi to school for lunch,
her classmates make fun of what she eats—until one of
them tries it for himself
"Wells sets the story in an active preschool classroom,
and her clear ink-and-watercolor pictures have never
been more expressive and tender, with a range of animal
characters that are endearingly human in body language
and expression." Booklist
Other titles about Yoko are:
Yoko's paper cranes (2001)
Yoko's world of kindness (2005)

We're going on a lion hunt; [illustrated by] David
Axtell. Holt & Co. 2000 c1999 unp il $15.95
　　　　　　　　　　　　　　　　　E
1. Lions—Fiction 2. Africa—Fiction
ISBN 0-8050-6159-2　　　　　　LC 98-47507
First published 1999 in the United Kingdom
Two girls set out bravely in search of a lion, going
through long grass, a swamp, and a cave before they find
what they're looking for
"Axtell takes a storytime classic to the African savan-
na. . . . [His] sun-soaked, impressionistic oil paintings
offer beautiful landscapes and engaging details. . . .
Large figures on the page make this a good choice for
storytimes as well as lap times." SLJ

Weston, Tamson

Hey, pancakes! words by Tamson Weston;
pictures by Stephen Gammell. Harcourt 2003 unp
il $16　　　　　　　　　　　　　　E
1. Breakfasts—Fiction 2. Family life—Fiction
3. Stories in rhyme
ISBN 0-15-216502-9　　　　　　LC 2001-6867
The day gets off to a rough start, but soon the smell
of pancakes fills the air and a family gathers for a breakfast feast
"Weston's paean to pancakes has a bouncy breakfast
beat that lends itself to reading aloud. . . . Gammell's
pastel, pencil, and watercolor illustrations swirl around
like food coloring in an enthusiastic blend." Bull Cent
Child Books

Whatley, Bruce

Wait! No paint! written and illustrated by Bruce
Whatley. HarperCollins Pubs. 2001 31p il $15.95;
lib bdg $15.89　　　　　　　　　　E
1. Pigs—Fiction 2. Wolves—Fiction 3. Illustrators—
Fiction
ISBN 0-06-028270-3; 0-06-028271-1 (lib bdg)
　　　　　　　　　　　　　　LC 00-61351
The three little pigs are in their usual trouble with the
big bad wolf, until a mysterious Voice gets involved and
mixes things up
"The 'Voice' is the careless illustrator of the story,
and . . . he's run out of red paint! . . . A quirky retell-

ing of a perennial favorite, this may appeal most to ear-
ly-elementary-age children, who will delight in the picture's conceptual surprises." Booklist

Wheeler, Lisa

Bubble gum, bubble gum; illustrated by Laura
Huliska-Beith. Little, Brown and Co. 2004 unp il
$15.99　　　　　　　　　　　　　　E
1. Animals—Fiction 2. Stories in rhyme
ISBN 0-316-98894-4　　　　　　LC 2002-16268
After a variety of animals get stuck one by one in
bubble gum melting in the road, they must survive encounters with a big blue truck and a burly black bear.
"A fast-paced, rhyming story with vibrant, bouncing
illustrations." SLJ

Castaway cats; story by Lisa Wheeler; art by
Ponder Goembel. 1st ed. Atheneum Books for
Young Readers 2006 unp il $16.95　　　　E
1. Cats—Fiction 2. Survival after airplane accidents,
shipwrecks, etc.—Fiction 3. Stories in rhyme
ISBN 0-689-86232-6　　　　　　LC 2004-541
"A Richard Jackson book"
Fifteen felines find themselves marooned on an island
and are not sure what to do.
"This delightful book is told in verses that become
smoother as the cats cooperate and find their groove.
. . . Goembel's illustrations, done in acrylic and ink, are
fantastic and provide wonderful insight into the side stories developing as the book progresses." SLJ

Old Cricket; illustrations by Ponder Goembel.
Atheneum Bks. for Young Readers 2003 unp il
$16.95　　　　　　　　　　　　　　E
1. Crickets—Fiction
ISBN 0-689-84510-3　　　　　　LC 2002-2199
"A Richard Jackson book"
Old Cricket doesn't feel like helping his wife and
neighbors to prepare for winter and so he pretends to
have all sorts of ailments that require the doctor's care,
but hungry Old Crow has other ideas
"Wheeler invests her delightful tale with all the characteristics of a good fable, and Goembel's sharp, highly
detailed acrylic artwork gives a clever, humorous bug's-
eye view of the world." Booklist

Te amo, Bebé, little one; illustrated by Maribel
Suárez. Little, Brown 2004 unp il $15.95
　　　　　　　　　　　　　　　　　E
1. Mother-child relationship—Fiction 2. Infants—Fiction 3. Stories in rhyme
ISBN 0-316-61410-6
In this picture book "verses describe a baby's first
year of life. As the seasons change, the infant and mother are shown engaging in a variety of activities including
a trip to the beach, dancing to fiesta music at the country
fair, and enjoying a winter's night. . . . Spanish words
are smoothly incorporated into the text. The illustrations
are done in bright, bold colors. . . . This is a good
choice for intimate sharing with little ones. " SLJ

Whitman, Walt

When I heard the learn'd astronomer; words by Walt Whitman; pictures by Loren Long. Simon & Schuster Books for Young Readers 2004 unp il $16.95   E

1. Astronomy—Poetry
ISBN 0-689-86397-7   LC 2004-7538

"A little boy obsessed with outer space has been dragged to an astronomy lecture. . . . The fidgety youngster takes his toy rocket ship outside, where he marvels at the 'perfect silence of the stars, casting a decisive vote for creative speculation over chilly analysis.' The painterly artwork . . . gets its own injection of childlike wonder through playful doodles contributed by Long's two children." Booklist

Whybrow, Ian

Harry and the bucketful of dinosaurs; written by Ian Whybrow; illustrated by Adrian Reynolds. Random House 2003 c1999 unp il $14.95   E

1. Dinosaurs—Fiction 2. Toys—Fiction
ISBN 0-375-82541-X   LC 2003-270848
First published 1999 by Orchard Bks. with title: Sammy and the dinosaurs

Harry finds toy dinosaurs in the attic that come to life when he names each one

"Humorous illustrations show the dinosaurs coming to life for Harry in this charming story." Publ Wkly

Other titles in this series are:
Harry and the dinosaurs at the museum (2005)
Harry and the dinosaurs make a Christmas wish (2004)
Harry and the dinosaurs say "Raah!" (2004)

The noisy way to bed; illustrated by Tiphanie Beeke. Arthur A. Levine Books 2004 unp il $15.95   E

1. Bedtime—Fiction 2. Animals—Fiction 3. Stories in rhyme
ISBN 0-439-55689-9   LC 2003-2785

As a sleepy boy decides it is bedtime and sets out across the farm toward home, he meets several animals who, in their noisy way, express the same idea.

"This engaging bedtime story begs for participation from children. . . . [Beeke's] full-page, mixed-media pictures are captivating, providing an eye-pleasing blend of colors, textures, and facial expressions." SLJ

Wickstrom, Sylvie

I love you, Mister Bear. HarperCollins Publishers 2003 unp il $14.99; lib bdg $15.89   E

1. Teddy bears—Fiction
ISBN 0-06-029331-4; 0-06-029332-2 (lib bdg)
    LC 2003-1103

Young Sosha buys a shaggy old teddy bear at a yard sale and brings him home for some special care and love.

"Large white pages form the backdrop for the bold black outlines and painterly application of color that give Wickstrom's illustrations their distinctive look. . . . Well suited to reading aloud, this endearing story is simply told from the child's point of view and illustrated with affection and panache." Booklist

Wiesner, David

Free fall. Lothrop, Lee & Shepard Bks. 1988 unp il lib bdg $17.89; pa $6.99   E

1. Dreams—Fiction 2. Stories without words
ISBN 0-688-05584-2 (lib bdg); 0-688-10990-X (pa)
    LC 87-22834

A Caldecott Medal honor book, 1989

A young boy dreams of daring adventures in the company of imaginary creatures inspired by the things surrounding his bed

"Technical virtuosity is the trademark of the double-page watercolor spreads. Especially notable is the solidity of forms and architectural details." SLJ

Hurricane. Clarion Bks. 1990 unp il $16; pa $6.95   E

1. Hurricanes—Fiction 2. Brothers—Fiction
ISBN 0-395-54382-7; 0-395-62974-8 (pa)
    LC 90-30070

"A family weathers a hurricane; the next day, in the post-hurricane yard, the two boys in the family play on a great fallen elm, imagining it to be a jungle, a pirate ship, and a space ship. A handsome book, affording opportunities for sharing fears and dreams of adventure." Horn Book Guide

June 29, 1999. Clarion Bks. 1992 unp il $16; pa $5.95   E

1. Vegetables—Fiction
ISBN 0-395-59762-5; 0-395-72767-7 (pa)
    LC 91-34854

"Either Holly Evans's science project that sent vegetable seedlings into the ionosphere is enormously successful—or else something unearthly is going on." SLJ

"Here an understated, fairly straightforward text is a perfect foil for the outrageous scenes of vegetables run amok. Realistic watercolors reveal red peppers that need to be roped down, beans with bemused Arizona sheep clambering over them, and gargantuan peas floating down the Mississippi like logs to the sawmill. Fans of Wiesner's offbeat sense of humor will be delighted." Horn Book

Sector 7. Clarion Bks. 1999 unp il $16   E

1. Empire State Building (New York, N.Y.)—Fiction 2. Clouds—Fiction 3. Stories without words
ISBN 0-395-74656-6   LC 96-40343
A Caldecott Medal honor book, 2000

While on a school trip to the Empire State Building, a boy is taken by a friendly cloud to visit Sector 7, where he discovers how clouds are shaped and channeled throughout the country

"Wiesner's lofty watercolors render words superfluous as he transforms the sky into magical scenes of marine life, reminding children of the innate power of their own imagination." Publ Wkly

The three pigs. Clarion Bks. 2001 unp il $16   E

1. Pigs—Fiction
ISBN 0-618-00701-6   LC 00-57016
Awarded the Caldecott Medal, 2002

The three pigs escape the wolf by going into another world where they meet the cat and the fiddle, the cow

Wiesner, David—*Continued*

that jumped over the moon, and a dragon

"Wiesner's brilliant use of white space and perspective evokes a feeling that the characters can navigate endless possibilities—and that the range of story itself is limitless." Publ Wkly

Tuesday. Clarion Bks. 1991 unp il $17; pa $6.95   E

1. Frogs—Fiction

ISBN 0-395-55113-7; 0-395-87082-8 (pa)

LC 90-39358

Awarded the Caldecott Medal, 1992

Frogs rise on their lily pads, float through the air, and explore the nearby houses while their inhabitants sleep

"Wiesner offers a fantasy watercolor journey accomplished with soft-edged realism. Studded with bits of humor, the narrative artwork tells a simple, pleasant story with a consistency and authenticity that makes the fantasy convincing." Booklist

Wilcoxen, Chuck

Niccolini's song; illustrated by Mark Buehner. Dutton Children's Books 2004 unp il $16.99

E

1. Railroads—Fiction   2. Lullabies—Fiction 3. Bedtime—Fiction

ISBN 0-525-46805-6

A gentle night watchman at the railroad yard lulls anxious train engines to sleep by singing just the right song.

"The rhythmic pace of the text, short sentences, and alliterative phrases make this creative bedtime story ideal for reading aloud. Buehner's soft paintings are imbued with dusky, nighttime hues." SLJ

Wild, Margaret

Kiss kiss! [by] Margaret Wild & Bridget Strevens-Marzo. Simon & Schuster Books for Young Readers 2004 c2003 unp il $12.95

E

1. Hippopotamus—Fiction 2. Mother-child relationship—Fiction

ISBN 0-689-86279-2   LC 2002-154516

First published 2003 in Australia

Baby Hippo is in such a rush to play one morning he forgets to kiss his mama, but strangely all the jungle noises seem to remind him.

"This is a story filled with movement and physical affection. The lap-sit audience will love the squishy, lumpy sounds and the repetition of the text as they point to the animals in the clear, bright pictures." Booklist

Midnight babies; illustrated by Ann James. Clarion Bks. 2001 c1999 unp il $15   E

1. Infants—Fiction

ISBN 0-618-10412-7   LC 00-58978

First published 1999 in Australia

Baby Brenda and her friends have fun at the Midnight Cafe, enjoying a "wibble wobble" dance, a "jiggly-joggly" treat, and a dip in the sprinklers before going home to bed

"The art is bold and delicious; the text captures the pure exuberance of the sweet, silly action." Booklist

Our granny; story by Margaret Wild; pictures by Julie Vivas. Ticknor & Fields 1994 c1993 unp il $17; pa $5.95   E

1. Grandmothers—Fiction

ISBN 0-395-67023-3; 0-395-88395-4 (pa)

LC 93-11950

First published 1993 in Australia

"Two young children present a catalog of all the varying sizes, shapes, and types of grandmothers, interspersed with loving comments about their own granny, who has 'a wobbly bottom' and wears a funny bathing suit. . . . Vivas's lively illustrations capture the grandmothers in their most comic moments." Horn Book Guide

Tom goes to kindergarten; [illustrated by] David Legge. Whitman, A. 2000 unp il $15.95

E

1. Giant panda—Fiction 2. School stories

ISBN 0-8075-8012-0   LC 99-50420

When Tom, a young panda, goes to his very first day of kindergarten, his whole family stays and plays and wishes they could be in kindergarten too

"Large, bright, whimsical watercolors make this a perfect book both for group storytelling and for one-on-one sharing." SLJ

Wildsmith, Brian

ABC. Watts 1963 c1962 unp il   E

1. Alphabet

Available Board book edition; Spanish language Board book also available

First published 1962 in the United Kingdom

"An alphabet book which illustrates animals and objects, identifying each on a facing page in capital and lower case letters, setting off the first letter with special emphasis." N Y Times Book Rev

"Bold, original pictures drawn in the individual style of an artist provide an excellent beginning for a child's education." N Y Her Trib Books

A Christmas story. Eerdmans Bks. for Young Readers 1998 unp il $17   E

1. Jesus Christ—Fiction 2. Donkeys—Fiction

ISBN 0-8028-5173-8   LC 98-18067

A reissue of the title first published 1989 by Knopf

Rebecca, a young girl living in Nazareth, accompanies a small donkey searching for his mother to a stable in Bethlehem where they both witness a special event

"The story is very simple but incorporates details from the biblical account. Both homey and glorious, Wildsmith's paintings use muted browns and greens for the shepherds and their surroundings and bright gold for the star pointing them toward Bethlehem." Horn Book Guide

Wiles, Deborah

Freedom Summer; illustrated by Jerome Lagarrigue. Atheneum Bks. for Young Readers 2001 unp il $16   E

1. African Americans—Fiction 2. Race relations—Fiction 3. Friendship—Fiction

ISBN 0-689-82380-0   LC 98-52805

"An Anne Schwartz book"

Wiles, Deborah—*Continued*

In 1964, Joe is pleased that a new law will allow his best friend John Henry, who is colored, to share the town pool and other public places with him, but he is dismayed to find that prejudice still exists

"The text, though concise, is full of nuance, and the oil paintings shimmer with the heat of the South in summer." Horn Book Guide

Wilkes, Angela

My first word book. DK Pub. 1999 64p il $16.95   **E**

1. Vocabulary

ISBN 0-7894-3977-8   LC 99-206690

Also available Board book edition

A slightly revised edition of the title first published 1991

"Common, familiar objects, animals, and activities—featured in clear, bright photos set against a white background or in small drawings—are grouped together on double-page spreads with such headings as 'On the farm' and 'Colors, shapes, and numbers.' Children will be drawn to the bright, cheerful pages of this first vocabulary lesson." Horn Book Guide

Willans, Tom

Wait! I want to tell you a story; written and illustrated by Tom Willans. Simon & Schuster Books for Young Readers 2005 c2004 unp il $15.95   **E**

1. Storytelling—Fiction 2. Animals—Fiction

ISBN 0-689-87166-X

First published 2004 in the United Kingdom

"To avoid being eaten by a tiger, a fast-talking muskrat spins a tale about a frog who's about to be eaten by a shark who tells a story about a lizard who's about to be eaten by a snake, and so on. This bouncy repetitive tale with a twist is made all the funnier by the zany ink and watercolor illustrations." Horn Book Guide

Willard, Nancy

Sweep dreams; illustrated by Mary GrandPré. 1st ed. Little, Brown and Company 2005 unp il $16.99   **E**

1. Brooms—Fiction 2. Magic—Fiction

ISBN 0-316-94008-9   LC 2002-41635

A man who loves a magical, dancing broom learns how to make her happy, finds her after she is stolen, and finally sets her free and hopes that she will someday return home.

"GrandPré's oil-wash and colored-pencil artwork is as tender and expressive as the story." SLJ

Willems, Mo

Don't let the pigeon drive the bus! words and pictures by Mo Willems. Hyperion Bks. for Children 2003 unp il $12.99   **E**

1. Pigeons—Fiction 2. Buses—Fiction

ISBN 0-7868-1988-X

A Caldecott Medal honor book, 2004

"When a bus driver goes on break, he asks the audience to keep an eye on his vehicle and the daft, bug-eyed pigeon who desperately wants to drive it. The pigeon then relentlessly begs readers for some time behind the wheel." Publ Wkly

"An unflinching and hilarious look at a child's potential for mischief. In a plain palette, with childishly elemental line drawings, Willems has captured the essence of unreasonableness in the very young." SLJ

Other titles about the pigeon are:

Don't let the pigeon stay up late! (2006)

The pigeon finds a hot dog! (2004)

Knuffle bunny; a cautionary tale. Hyperion Books for Children 2004 unp il $15.99   **E**

1. Lost and found possessions—Fiction

ISBN 0-7868-1870-0

A Caldecott Medal honor book, 2005

After Trixie and daddy leave the laundromat, something very important turns up missing.

A "concise, deftly told narrative. . . . Printed on olive-green backdrops, the illustrations are a combination of muted, sepia-toned photographs upon which bright cartoon drawings of people have been superimposed. . . . A seamless and supremely satisfying presentation of art and text." SLJ

Leonardo, the terrible monster. Hyperion 2005 unp il $16.99   **E**

1. Monsters—Fiction

ISBN 0-7868-5294-1

Leonardo is a terrible monster he can't seem to frighten anyone. When he discovers the perfect nervous little boy, will he scare the lunch out of him? Or will he think of something better?

"Willems's familiar cartoon drawings work hand in glove with the brief text to tell this perfectly paced story." SLJ

Williams, Arlene

Tiny tortilla. Dutton Children's Bks. 2005 unp il $15.99   **E**

1. Tortillas—Fiction

ISBN 0-525-47382-3

Juan Carlos discovers that, with the right touch, he can transform some special tortilla dough into unexpected shapes.

"Karas' warm colored-pencil pictures in a lively folk-art style evoke a southwestern desert setting where magic can really happen, and the repeated action and tension make for a fun read-aloud." Booklist

Williams, Barbara

Albert's impossible toothache; illustrated by Doug Cushman. Candlewick Press 2003 unp il $15.99   **E**

1. Turtles—Fiction

ISBN 0-7636-1723-7   LC 2002-67059

A newly illustrated edition of Albert's toothache, published 1974 by Dutton

When Albert the turtle complains of a toothache, no one in his family believes him, until his grandmother takes the time to really listen to him

"This title is a worthwhile addition to any picture-book collection." SLJ

Williams, Karen Lynn

Galimoto; illustrated by Catherine Stock. Lothrop, Lee & Shepard Bks. 1990 unp il $16.95; pa $6.99   E

1. Toys—Fiction 2. Malawi—Fiction

ISBN 0-688-08789-2; 0-688-10991-8 (pa)

LC 89-2258

"In Malawi, Africa, according to the author's note, *galimoto* are intricate and popular push toys crafted by children. Williams tells the story of seven-year-old Kondi's quest to find ample scrap material to fashion his own toy pickup truck. . . . Kondi's perseverance and the pleasure he takes in his accomplishment are just two of the delights of this appealing story. Stock's graceful watercolors portray life in a bustling village and include enough detail . . . to give readers the flavor of a day in this southern African nation." Horn Book

Painted dreams; pictures by Catherine Stock. Lothrop, Lee & Shepard Bks. 1998 unp il $16; lib bdg $15.93   E

1. Haiti—Fiction 2. Artists—Fiction

ISBN 0-688-13901-9; 0-688-13902-7 (lib bdg)

LC 97-32920

Because her Haitian family is too poor to be able to buy paints for her, eight-year-old Ti Marie finds her own way to create pictures that make the heart sing

"Beautifully composed and full of life, Stock's watercolors suggest the personalities of the characters through their expressions and gestures." Booklist

Williams, Linda

The little old lady who was not afraid of anything; illustrated by Megan Lloyd. Crowell 1986 unp il $15.99; lib bdg $16.89; pa $5.99

E

1. Fear—Fiction

ISBN 0-690-04584-0; 0-690-04586-7 (lib bdg); 0-06-443183-5 (pa)   LC 85-48250

Also available Spanish language edition

A little old lady who is not afraid of anything must deal with a pumpkin head, a tall black hat, and other spooky objects that follow her through the dark woods trying to scare her

"A delightful picture book, perfect for both independent reading pleasure and for telling aloud." SLJ

Williams, Sherley Anne

Working cotton; written by Sherley Anne Williams; illustrated by Carole Byard. Harcourt Brace Jovanovich 1992 unp il $17; pa $7

E

1. Migrant labor—Fiction 2. Cotton—Fiction 3. African Americans—Fiction

ISBN 0-15-299624-9; 0-15-201482-9 (pa)

LC 91-21586

A Caldecott Medal honor book, 1993

A young black girl relates the daily events of her family's migrant life in the cotton fields of central California

"Byard's acrylic paintings contribute weight and emotion to Williams's spare text. The fields and family members fill each full-page spread, drawing the reader very close to the action of the story. The mural-like

paintings glow with blue and brown tones, recreating the textures and hues of the cotton fields. Williams's text, based on her poems, has a lyrical, rhythmic quality." Horn Book

Williams, Sheron

Imani's music; illustrated by Jude Daly. Atheneum Bks. for Young Readers 2000 unp il $17   E

1. Grasshoppers—Fiction 2. Slavery—Fiction 3. Music—Fiction

ISBN 0-689-82254-5   LC 98-19119

Imani, an African grasshopper, brings music to the new world when he travels aboard a slave ship

"The language is immediate and musical, and the strong blend of fantasy and history is beautifully extended in Daly's bright narrative watercolors in folk-art style." Booklist

Williams, Sue

Let's go visiting; written by Sue Williams; illustrated by Julie Vivas. Harcourt Brace & Co. 1998 unp il $16; pa $7   E

1. Domestic animals—Fiction 2. Counting 3. Stories in rhyme

ISBN 0-15-201823-9; 0-15-202410-7 (pa)

LC 97-34398

"Gulliver books"

A counting story in which a boy visits his farmyard friends, from one brown foal to six yellow puppies

"The bold illustrations, simple yet full of motion, combine with a lively text to make this perfect for toddler story hours." Booklist

Williams, Suzanne

Library Lil; illustrated by Steven Kellogg. Dial Bks. for Young Readers 1997 unp il $16.99; pa $6.99   E

1. Librarians—Fiction 2. Books and reading—Fiction 3. Tall tales

ISBN 0-8037-1698-2; 0-14-056837-9 (pa)

LC 95-23490

A formidable librarian makes readers not only out of the once resistant residents of her small town, but out of a tough-talking, television-watching motorcycle gang as well

"The silliness of both story and pictures are perfectly matched. Kellogg's distinctive toothy kids and laughing cats crowd the pages, fitting right in with the baby-faced biker banditos." SLJ

Williams, Vera B.

A chair for my mother. Greenwillow Bks. 1982 unp il $15.99; lib bdg $16.89; pa $6.99

E

1. Family life—Fiction 2. Saving and investment—Fiction 3. Chairs—Fiction

ISBN 0-688-00914-X; 0-688-00915-8 (lib bdg); 0-688-04074-8 (pa)   LC 81-7010

Also available Big book edition and Spanish language edition

A Caldecott Medal honor book, 1983

Williams, Vera B.—*Continued*

Rosa, her waitress mother, and her grandmother save dimes to buy a comfortable armchair after all their furniture is lost in a fire

"The cheerful paintings take up the full left-hand page and face, in most cases, a small chunk of the text set against a modulated wash of a complementing color; a border containing a pertinent motif surrounds the two pages, further unifying the design. The result is a superbly conceived picture book expressing the joyful spirit of a loving family." Horn Book

Other titles about Rosa and her family are:
Music, music for everyone (1984)
Something special for me (1983)

Cherries and cherry pits. Greenwillow Bks. 1986 unp il lib bdg $17.89; pa $6.99　　　　　E
1. African Americans—Fiction 2. Drawing—Fiction
ISBN 0-688-05146-4 (lib bdg); 0-688-10478-9 (pa)
LC 85-17156

"Bidemmi, a young black child, draws splendid pictures. 'As she draws, she tells the story of what she is drawing,' always starting with the word 'this.' . . . Finally, Bidemmi tells her story, revealing her wish for her neighborhood and her world. Each story involves cherries—buying, sharing, and enjoying them." SLJ

"Williams' portraits of Bidemmi drawing are done in watercolor; the drawings Bidemmi makes are done with bright markers, some being simple sketches, others filling the page with color, looking like naive, but glorious icons. The interior stories are well integrated with each other, and the whole adds up to a study of child as artist that is fresh, vibrant, and exciting." Bull Cent Child Books

Lucky song. Greenwillow Bks. 1997 unp il $15.99　　　　　E
1. Day—Fiction 2. Kites—Fiction 3. Songs—Fiction
ISBN 0-688-14459-4　　　　　LC 96-7151

"Evie flies the kite made by her grandfather until it's time to go home for supper all tired and ready for bed. This patterned story, showing a little girl surrounded by a loving family, ends by circling back to the beginning. It is illustrated using brilliantly colored watercolors." Child Book Rev Serv

"More more more" said the baby; 3 love stories. Greenwillow Bks. 1990 unp il $15.99; lib bdg $16.89; pa $5.99　　　　　E
1. Infants—Fiction 2. Family life—Fiction
ISBN 0-688-09173-3; 0-688-09174-1 (lib bdg); 0-688-814736-4 (pa)　　　　　LC 89-2023
Also available Board book edition
A Caldecott Medal honor book, 1991

Three babies are caught up in the air and given loving attention by a father, grandmother, and mother

"The pages reverberate with bright colors and vigorous forms, and the rhythmic language begs to be read aloud." Horn Book Guide

Stringbean's trip to the shining sea; greetings from Vera B. Williams, story and pictures; and Jennifer Williams, more pictures. Greenwillow Bks. 1987 unp il $16.99; lib bdg $17.89; pa $6.99　　　　　E
1. West (U.S.)—Fiction 2. Automobile travel—Fiction
ISBN 0-688-07161-9; 0-688-07162-7 (lib bdg); 0-688-16701-2 (pa)　　　　　LC 86-29502

"Stringbean and big brother Fred (joined en route by Potato, Stringbean's dog) take a car trip from their home in Kansas to the Pacific Ocean, and their pilgrimage is recorded herein in the form of a mock photo and postcard album." Bull Cent Child Books

"The use of mixed media—watercolors, Magic Markers, and colored pencils—is as aesthetically pleasing as it is skillful. Nothing has been forgotten; nothing more needs to be added. Not for the usual picture-book set, this travelogue storybook will appeal to slightly older audiences." Horn Book

Three days on a river in a red canoe. Greenwillow Bks. 1984 unp il lib bdg $16.89; pa $5.95　　　　　E
1. Canoes and canoeing—Fiction 2. Camping—Fiction
ISBN 0-688-84307-7 (lib bdg); 0-688-04072-1 (pa)
LC 80-23893

In this book, a "canoe trip for two children and two adults is recorded with all its interesting detail in a spontaneous first-person account and engaging full-color drawings on carefully designed pages. Driving to a river site, making camp, paddling the craft, negotiating a waterfall, swimming, fishing, dealing with a sudden storm, and even rescuing one overboard child are all described as important incidents in a summertime adventure." Horn Book

Willis, Jeanne

Susan laughs; illustrated by Tony Ross. Holt & Co. 2000 unp il $15　　　　　E
1. Play—Fiction 2. Physically handicapped—Fiction 3. Stories in rhyme
ISBN 0-8050-6501-6　　　　　LC 99-59560
Rhyming couplets describe a wide range of common emotions and activities experienced by a little girl who uses a wheelchair

"Without being condescending or preachy, the words, pictures, and design of this very simple picture book show that a physically disabled child is 'just like me, just like you.' Only on the very last page do we discover that Susan uses a wheelchair." Booklist

Wilson, Anna

Over in the grasslands; [by] Anna Wilson and Alison Bartlett. Little, Brown 2000 c1999 unp il $14.95　　　　　E
1. Grasslands—Fiction 2. Animals—Fiction 3. Stories in rhyme 4. Counting
ISBN 0-316-93910-2　　　　　LC 99-76633
First published 1999 in the United Kingdom

"This rhyming counting book, an adaptation of 'Over in the Meadow', takes readers on a safari through the African plains where mothers encourage their young ones—from one baby rhino to ten young monkeys—to

Wilson, Anna—*Continued*
eat, play, swim, or sleep" Horn Book Guide
"The bright colors and childlike quality of Bartlett's pictures will definitely attract the book's target audience." Booklist

Wilson, Karma
Bear snores on; illustrations by Jane Chapman. Margaret K. McElderry Bks. 2002 unp il $16

E
1. Bears—Fiction 2. Animals—Fiction 3. Parties—Fiction 4. Stories in rhyme
ISBN 0-689-83187-0   LC 00-28371
Also available board book edition
On a cold winter night many animals gather to party in the cave of a sleeping bear, who then awakes and protests that he has missed the food and the fun
"The characters are infused with warmth and humor. . . . The warm, soft tones of these acrylic illustrations perfectly capture the coziness of Bear's lair and capture the action." SLJ
Other titles in this series are:
Bear stays up for Christmas (2004)
Bear wants more (2003)
Bear's new friend (2006)

A frog in the bog; [illustrated by] Joan Rankin. Margaret K. McElderry Bks. 2003 unp il $16.95

E
1. Frogs—Fiction 2. Insects—Fiction 3. Stories in rhyme 4. Counting
ISBN 0-689-84081-0   LC 2002-5903
A frog in the bog grows larger and larger as he eats more and more bugs, until he attracts the attention of an alligator who puts an end to his eating
"This gastronomic adventure is told in catchy rhyming verse, complemented by soft, dreamy watercolors that perfectly recreate the bog. The illustrations are enhanced by humorous details." SLJ

Hilda must be dancing; illustrated by Suzanne Watts. Margaret K. McElderry Books 2004 unp il $15.95

E
1. Hippopotamus—Fiction 2. Dance—Fiction 3. Stories in rhyme
ISBN 0-689-84788-2   LC 2002-151109
None of her jungle friends can find Hilda Hippo a quieter, less disruptive replacement for dancing until Water Buffalo suggests an activity that allows Hilda to express her dance creativity in a new way.
"Watts illustrates this cartoon jungle with a palette of vibrant tropical colors and creates bold and humorous images that further energize an already active text. Told in rhyme with plenty of onomatopoeia, this delightfully noisy story is nonstop fun." SLJ

Mama always comes home; illustrated by Brooke Dyer. 1st ed. HarperCollins 2005 unp il $15.99; lib bdg $16.89

E
1. Mother-child relationship—Fiction 2. Animals—Fiction 3. Stories in rhyme
ISBN 0-06-057505-0; 0-06-057506-9 (lib bdg)
          LC 2003-26979

From Mama Bird to Mama Cat, mothers of all kinds come home to their children.
"The consistently tender illustrations follow the text's well-crafted rhymes. . . . Presented with a delicate and loving touch, this book embodies the power of thoughtful text supported by insightful pictures." SLJ

Wilson, Sarah
Big day on the river; illustrated by Randy Cecil. Holt & Co. 2003 unp il $16.95   E
1. Rafting (Sports)—Fiction 2. Family life—Fiction
ISBN 0-8050-6787-6   LC 2002-4358
Willie's relatives bring her so many provisions for her rafting trip that she almost does not get to go
"Wilson's folksy, well-paced words are perfect for story hours, as are Cecil's stylized, richly colored gouache paintings." Booklist

Winter, Jeanette
Calavera abecedario; a Day of the Dead alphabet. Harcourt 2004 unp il $16   E
1. All Souls' Day—Fiction 2. Alphabet 3. Spanish language—Vocabulary 4. Mexico—Social life and customs
ISBN 0-15-205110-4   LC 2004-1554
Every year Don Pedro makes papier-mache skeletons, or calaveras, for Mexico's Day of the Dead fiesta. From Angel to Unicornio, each letter of the alphabet has its own special calavera. Spanish words illustrate each letter of the alphabet.
This "features jaunty illustrations inspired by Mexican folk art. . . . This is a lovely book that approaches the Day of the Dead from an unusual angle." SLJ

Elsina's clouds. Frances Foster Books/Farrar, Straus and Giroux 2004 unp il $16   E
1. South Africa—Fiction 2. Rain—Fiction 3. Artists—Fiction
ISBN 0-374-32118-3   LC 2002-29704
In South Africa, a Basotho girl paints designs on her house as a prayer to the ancestors for rain.
"The story is elegant in its simplicity, and Winter frames the square pages with geometric folk artlike borders, echoing the designs Elsina paints." Horn Book Guide

Follow the drinking gourd; story and pictures by Jeanette Winter. Knopf 1988 unp il music pa $7.99 hardcover o.p.   E
1. Slavery—Fiction 2. Underground railroad—Fiction 3. African Americans—Fiction
ISBN 0-679-81997-5 (pa)   LC 88-9661
By following directions in a song, taught them by an old sailor, runaway slaves journey north along the Underground Railroad to freedom in Canada
"Complementing the few lines of text per page are dark-hued illustrations horizontally framed with a fine black line and plenty of white space. . . . The art carries the weight of introducing children to a riveting piece of U.S. history, and the music included at the end of the book will fix it in their minds." Bull Cent Child Books

Winter, Jeanette—*Continued*

Josefina. Harcourt Brace & Co. 1996 unp il $16

        E

1. Women artists—Fiction 2. Mexico—Fiction
3. Counting

ISBN 0-15-201091-2   LC 95-34110

"In a sunny patio in Mexico, there is one rising sun
in a sky where two angels keep watch over three houses.
. . . Throughout her life—from her childhood through
the deaths of her parents, her marriage to José, and the
birth of their nine children, Josefina works the soft clay
into figures to create this world. . . . Inspired by the
painted clay figures decorating Josefina Aguilar's patio
in Ocotlán, Mexico, Winter has crafted a picture-book vision of the folk artist's life that cleverly turns into a bilingual counting story. . . . Paired with a simple prose
narrative, the artwork creates an effect that is both elegant and soothing." Booklist

The librarian of Basra; a true story from Iraq.
Harcourt, Inc 2004 c2005 32p il $16   E

1. Baker, Alia Muhammad 2. Librarians 3. Iraq War,
2003 4. Books 5. Libraries

ISBN 0-15-205445-6   LC 2004-12969

The story of Alia Muhammad Baker, a librarian in
Basra, Iraq, who managed to rescue seventy percent of
the library's collection before the library burned in the
Iraq War in 2003.

"Winter's bright, folk-art style does much to mute the
horrific realties of war. . . . The librarian's quiet bravery
serves as a point of entry into a freighted topic."
Booklist

Mama; a true story in which a baby hippo loses
his mama during a tsunami, but finds a new home,
and a new mama. Harcourt 2006 unp il $16

        E

1. Hippopotamus 2. Turtles 3. Indian Ocean earthquake and tsunami, 2004

ISBN 0-15-205495-2   LC 2005-20905

Set against the backdrop of the devastating 2004 tsunami, this book reveals the true story of a rescued baby
hippo who adopts a new "mother" —a 130-year-old male
tortoise.

"This visually poetic book's subtitle is longer than its
entire text. . . . Winter reassuringly portrays how friendship can ease a devastating loss." Publ Wkly

Niño's mask. Dial Bks. for Young Readers 2003
unp il $15.99   E

1. Masks (Facial)—Fiction 2. Mexico—Fiction

ISBN 0-8037-2807-7   LC 2001-49912

Told that he is too young to wear a mask at the Fiesta, Niño makes his own mask and surprises his family
and the whole village. Includes a glossary of Spanish
words and an author's note

"Winter neatly slots her crisp prose into speech bubbles, lending the outing an inviting look and rapid pace.
She laces the pages not only with Spanish words but
with Mexican motifs (including) vibrant designs on the
townspeople's clothing." Publ Wkly

September roses. Farrar Straus Giroux 2004 unp
il $14   E

1. September 11 terrorist attacks, 2001 2. Roses
3. New York (N.Y.)

ISBN 0-374-36736-1   LC 2003-54877

"Frances Foster books"

"Two sisters fly to New York from South Africa with
thousands of roses meant for a flower show. The day
they fly is September 11, 2001, and after the attack they
are stranded at the airport with their flowers. They are
offered shelter and offer their roses in return: at Union
Square, they design two fallen towers made of roses.
Winter . . . makes beautiful patterns with her figures
and her roses using her signature thick black outlines.
. . . This is understated and full of tenderness." Booklist

Winters, Kay

My teacher for President; illustrated by Denise
Brunkus. 1st ed. Dutton Children's Books 2004
unp il $14.99   E

1. Teachers—Fiction 2. Presidents—Fiction

ISBN 0-525-47186-3   LC 2003-19222

A second-grader writes a television station with reasons why his teacher would make a good president, but
only if she can continue teaching till the end of the year.

"Brunkus' cheerful illustrations show a gray-haired
woman in large, round glasses. . . . The humorous tone
brings lofty ideals about desirable presidential qualities
down to an everyday, accessible level." Booklist

Winthrop, Elizabeth

Dumpy La Rue; illustrated by Betsy Lewin.
Holt & Co. 2001 unp il $15.95   E

1. Dance—Fiction 2. Pigs—Fiction 3. Domestic animals—Fiction 4. Stories in rhyme

ISBN 0-8050-6385-4   LC 99-53627

A rhyming story about Dumpy La Rue, a pig whose
passion for dancing becomes contagious

There's "plenty of bounce here . . . in the lively text
and the exuberant line-and-watercolor pictures, some of
which fairly leap off the pages." Booklist

Promises; illustrated by Betsy Lewin. Clarion
Bks. 2000 32p il $16   E

1. Cancer—Fiction 2. Mother-daughter relationship—
Fiction

ISBN 0-395-82272-6   LC 99-27186

"Sarah's mother is very sick, presumably with cancer,
and has lost all her energy and her hair. Sarah is alternately scared, angry, and sad until her mother begins her
gradual recovery. The characters are well developed, and
the sensitive, calm story offers realistic reassurances and
hope for children with a sick parent. Lewin's cartoon-
style pen-and-ink and watercolor illustrations help lighten
an otherwise serious book." Horn Book Guide

Shoes; illustrated by William Joyce. Harper &
Row 1986 19p il lib bdg $16.89; pa $5.99

        E

1. Shoes—Fiction 2. Stories in rhyme

ISBN 0-06-026592-2 (lib bdg); 0-06-443171-1 (pa)
        LC 85-45841

Also available Board book edition

"A jaunty rhyme about shoes of all kinds—'shoes for
fishing, shoes for wishing, shoes for muddy squishing.'
The roly-poly figures are drawn from a child's perspective." N Y Times Book Rev

"This lilting rhyme about shoes and feet easily

Winthrop, Elizabeth—*Continued*

pleases. . . . Backing the verses are full-color drawings of children busily involved with one kind of shoe or another. Joyce's pictures are animated, energetic, and warmly colored." Booklist

Squashed in the middle; illustrated by Pat Cummings. Holt 2005 unp il $16.95   E

1. Family life—Fiction 2. African Americans—Fiction

ISBN 0-8050-6497-4

When Daisy, a middle child, is invited to spend the night at her friend's house, her family finally pays attention to her.

"Cummings' recognizable robust style and intense palette are evident in the engaging design here, a bright amalgamation of bold full-page closeups that clearly reflect Daisy's feelings. . . . Homey and whimsical details . . . give Daisy and her African American family a thoroughly modern, familiar look." Booklist

Wise, William

Ten sly piranhas; a counting story in reverse (a tale of wickedness—and worse!); pictures by Victoria Chess. Dial Bks. for Young Readers 1993 unp il $16.99   E

1. Fishes—Fiction 2. Counting 3. Stories in rhyme

ISBN 0-8037-1200-6   LC 91-33704

A school of ten sly piranhas gradually dwindles as they waylay and eat each other, and the last is eaten by a crocodile

"The combination of a jaunty, rhymed text and gleefully fiendish illustrations demonstrates with delicious derring-do that the wicked frequently receive their just deserts." Horn Book

Wiseman, Bernard

Morris and Boris at the circus; by B. Wiseman. Harper & Row 1988 64p il lib bdg $16.89; pa $3.99   E

1. Moose—Fiction 2. Bears—Fiction 3. Circus—Fiction

ISBN 0-06-026478-0 (lib bdg); 0-06-444143-1 (pa)

LC 87-45682

"An I can read book"

"Morris the Moose and his friend Boris the Bear . . . take a trip to the circus. Morris has never gone before, so he doesn't quite have the big picture. He thinks the clown's nose is red because he has a cold, and when they join the performers in the ring, Morris rides 'bearback' on Boris, instead of on a horse." Booklist

"The cartoon illustrations with bold colors provide ample context clues for beginning readers. This delightful combination of text and illustrations will entice children to read and re-read this book." SLJ

Wisniewski, David

Rain player; story and pictures by David Wisniewski. Clarion Bks. 1991 unp il $17; pa $6.95   E

1. Mayas—Fiction 2. Games—Fiction

ISBN 0-395-55112-9; 0-395-72083-4 (pa)

LC 90-44101

To bring rain to his thirsty village, Pik challenges the rain god to a game of pok-a-tok

"This original tale combines research on Mayan history and legend with a suspenseful sports story. . . . Intricate and dramatic cut-paper illustrations powerfully recreate the foliage, landscape, architecture, and clothing of the Mayan classical period. . . . An author's note provides fascinating background information on Mayan civilization and gives in-depth explanations of some of the words and phrases used in the text." Horn Book

The wave of the Sea-Wolf; story and pictures by David Wisniewski. Clarion Bks. 1994 unp il $17; pa $5.95   E

1. Tlingit Indians—Fiction

ISBN 0-395-66478-0; 0-395-96892-5 (pa)

LC 93-18265

Kchokeen, a Tlingit princess, is rescued from drowning by a guardian spirit that later enables Kchokeen to summon a great wave and save her people from hostile strangers

"Vivid storytelling is complemented by textured cut-paper illustrations that paint the forest landscape in lacy layers. . . . Wisniewski's ability to convey both high drama and simple emotion lends a sense of authenticity to this original tale." Publ Wkly

Witte, Anna

The parrot Tico Tango; written and illustrated by Anna Witte. Barefoot Books 2004 unp il $15.99; pa $6.99   E

1. Parrots—Fiction 2. Rain forest animals—Fiction 3. Stories in rhyme

ISBN 1-84148-243-9; 1-84148-890-9 (pa)

LC 2004-17922

A cumulative rhyme in which a greedy parrot keeps taking fruit from the other creatures of the rainforest until he can hold no more.

"The rhymes are unusually taut and rhythmic, and the mixed-media art, which features fabric swatches, amounts to a feast of tropical colors." Horn Book Guide

Wojciechowski, Susan

The Christmas miracle of Jonathan Toomey; illustrated by P. J. Lynch. Candlewick Press 2004 c1995 unp il $12.99   E

1. Wood carving—Fiction 2. Christmas—Fiction 3. Friendship—Fiction

ISBN 0-7636-2621-X

A reissue of the title first published 1995

Includes audio CD, with story read aloud by James Earl Jones

The widow McDowell and her seven-year-old son Thomas ask the gruff Jonathan Toomey, the best woodcarver in the valley, to carve the figures for a Christmas creche

"The story verges on the sentimental, but it's told with feeling and lyricism. . . . Lynch's sweeping illustrations, in shades of wood grain, are both realistic and gloriously romantic, focusing on faces and hands at work before the fire and in the lamplight." Booklist

Wojciechowski, Susan—*Continued*

A fine St. Patrick's day; illustrated by Tom Curry. 1st ed. Random House 2004 unp il $15.95
E

1. Saint Patrick's Day—Fiction 2. Ireland—Fiction

ISBN 0-375-82386-7   LC 2002-11684

Two towns, Tralee and Tralah, compete in an annual St. Patrick's Day decorating contest which Tralah boastfully always wins, but when their hearts are put to the test by a little man with pointed ears, Tralee wins with no effort at all.

"Wojciechowski's charming tale is beautifully complemented by Curry's stylized depictions of green rolling hills and thatched-roof houses. Both text and art convey a sturdy feeling about community and charity, brushed with touch of whimsy." Booklist

Wolff, Ashley

Me baby, you baby. Dutton Children's Books 2004 unp il $14.99   E

1. Infants—Fiction 2. Zoos—Fiction 3. Stories in rhyme

ISBN 0-525-46952-4   LC 2003-45219

Simple rhyming text describes a day in the life of two babies as they greet the day, go to the zoo with their mothers, and return home at night.

"With its rhythmic text and delicate gouache artwork, this is a delightful book to share with two and three-year-olds." SLJ

Wolff, Ferida

It is the wind; illustrated by James Ransome. HarperCollins 2005 unp il $14.99; lib bdg $15.89
E

1. Bedtime—Fiction 2. Sound—Fiction

ISBN 0-06-028191-X; 0-06-028192-8 (lib bdg)
LC 00-63197

"In his room at night, a boy looks outside and tries to imagine what is making the noise he hears. . . . The mesmerizing effect of the verse makes this a good bedtime story. . . . Ransome makes the most of the simple story with graceful scenes of the African American boy and the rural night scenes he sees and imagines." Booklist

Wong, Janet S.

Apple pie 4th of July; pictures by Margaret Chodos-Irvine. Harcourt 2002 unp il $16
E

1. Fourth of July—Fiction 2. Chinese Americans—Fiction

ISBN 0-15-202543-X   LC 2001-1313

A Chinese American girl fears that the food her parents are preparing to sell on the Fourth of July will not be eaten

"An appealing story with believable characters and emotions, written in the girl's spare, lyrical voice. Chodos-Irvine . . . captures the story's uncluttered, elemental qualities in opaque prints that resemble paper cutouts." Booklist

Buzz; illustrated by Margaret Chodos-Irvine. Harcourt 2000 unp il $15   E

ISBN 0-15-201923-5   LC 99-6148

"A young child relates the simple morning events that happen in his house, all of which seem to make a buzz." Booklist

"Chodos-Irvine's use of various print-making techniques results in illustrations that are strongly geometric and graphically clean, in springtime colors that suit the cheerful tone of the text. The humor in both text and pictures contributes to the light-hearted atmosphere." Bull Cent Child Books

Hide & seek; pictures by Margaret Chodos-Irvine. Harcourt 2005 unp il $16
E

1. Counting

ISBN 0-15-204934-7   LC 2003-27737

In this counting book, a child and parent play hide-and-seek while they bake cookies.

"The rhythmic words capture the breathless excitement of searching and hiding, and Chodos-Irvine's prints, in her signature style of simple, dynamic shapes and bright, saturated hues, match the vibrant energy and elemental sounds in the simple words." Booklist

This next New Year; pictures by Yangsook Choi. Foster Bks. 2000 unp il $16   E

1. Chinese New Year—Fiction

ISBN 0-374-35503-7   LC 99-22377

"A Chinese-Korean boy reflects on what Chinese New Year means to him. By sweeping last year's mistakes and bad luck out of the house, he hopes to make room for 'a fresh start, my second chance.'" Horn Book Guide

"Choi's smooth, brightly colored paintings . . . ably illustrate the optimistic activity and the yearning in the accessible, rhythmic text." Booklist

Wood, Audrey

The Bunyans; illustrated by David Shannon. Blue Sky Press (NY) 1996 unp il $16.95
E

1. Bunyan, Paul (Legendary character) 2. Tall tales

ISBN 0-590-48089-8   LC 95-26170

Paul Bunyan "meets a gigantic woman, and he and Carrie are soon married. Two oversize children arrive and play a important role in the formation of many of America's natural wonders: Niagara Falls, Bryce Canyon, and Big Sur, among others. . . . Wood captures the tongue-in-cheek tone and the exaggeration bordering on the ridiculous that characterize American tall tales. . . . Shannon's realistic, full-color paintings provide a counterpoint to the text, serving to make it seem almost believable. The artist's figures are large and solid." SLJ

The deep blue sea; a book of colors; story by Audrey Wood; pictures of Bruce Wood. Blue Sky Press 2005 unp il $15.99   E

1. Color

ISBN 0-439-75382-1

Introduces various colors by presenting a colorful scene on a rock in the deep blue sea.

"Sharply focused, vividly hued artwork makes this concept book a standout. . . . The rhythmic text is enticing and reads aloud smoothly." SLJ

Wood, Audrey—*Continued*

Elbert's bad word; illustrated by Audrey and Don Wood. Harcourt Brace Jovanovich 1988 unp il $16; pa $6   **E**
    1. Parties—Fiction
    ISBN 0-15-225320-3; 0-15-201367-9 (pa)
                      LC 86-7557

"A bad word, spoken by a small boy at a fashionable garden party, creates havoc, and the child, Elbert, gets his mouth scrubbed out with soap. The bad word, in the shape of a long-tailed furry monster, will not go away until a wizard-gardener cooks up some really delicious, super-long words that everyone at the party applauds. This single-idea cautionary tale has lively, absurdist pictures of tiara-crowned, formally dressed adults recoiling in horror or cavorting with glee when Elbert, the only child at the party, speaks a word." SLJ

Heckedy Peg; illustrated by Don Wood. Harcourt Brace Jovanovich 1987 unp il lib bdg $16; pa $7   **E**
    1. Fairy tales 2. Witches—Fiction
    ISBN 0-15-233678-8 (lib bdg); 0-15-233679-6 (pa)
                      LC 86-33639

"The poor mother of seven children, each named for a day of the week, goes off to market promising to return with individual gifts that each child has requested and admonishing them to lock the door to strangers and not to touch the fire. The gullible children are tricked into disobeying their mother by the witch, Heckedy Peg, who turns them all into various kinds of food. The mother can rescue her children only by guessing which child is the fish, the roast rib, the bread. . . . This story, deep and rich with folk wisdom, is stunningly illustrated with Don Wood's luminous paintings. . . . With variety of color and line he enhances every nuance of the text." SLJ

King Bidgood's in the bathtub; written by Audrey Wood; illustrated by Don Wood. Harcourt Brace Jovanovich 1985 unp il lib bdg $16
                                E
    1. Kings and rulers—Fiction 2. Baths—Fiction
    ISBN 0-15-242730-9   LC 85-5472
    Also available with audio CD $17.95 (ISBN 0-15-205578-9); Big book edition also available
    A Caldecott Medal honor book, 1986
    Despite pleas from his court, a fun-loving king refuses to get out of his bathtub to rule his kingdom
    "The few simple words of text per large, well-designed page invite story-telling—but keep the group very small, so the children can be close enough to pore over the brilliant, robust illustrations." SLJ

The napping house; illustrated by Don Wood. Harcourt Brace Jovanovich 1984 unp il lib bdg $16   **E**
    1. Sleep—Fiction
    ISBN 0-15-256708-9   LC 83-13035
    Also available board book edition
    "In this sleepytime cumulative tale, all are pleasantly napping until a pesky flea starts the clamor that wakes up the whole family—mouse, cat, dog, child, and granny." Child Book Rev Serv
    "The cool blues and greens are superseded by warm colors and bursts of action as each sleeper wakes, ending in an eruption of color and energy as naptime ends. A deft matching of text and pictures adds to the appeal of cumulation, and to the silliness of the mound of sleepers—just the right kind of humor for the lap audience." Bull Cent Child Books

Wood, Don

Piggies; written by Don and Audrey Wood; illustrated by Don Wood. Harcourt Brace Jovanovich 1991 unp il $16; pa $7   **E**
    1. Bedtime—Fiction 2. Pigs—Fiction
    ISBN 0-15-256341-5; 0-15-200217-0 (pa)
                      LC 89-24598
    Also available Board book edition
    Ten little piggies dance on a young child's fingers and toes before finally going to sleep
    "A happy text and luxuriant, witty pictures make this a book to pore over again and again." Booklist

Wood, Douglas

What dads can't do; pictures by Doug Cushman. Simon & Schuster Bks. for Young Readers 2000 unp il $14   **E**
    1. Fathers—Fiction
    ISBN 0-689-82620-6   LC 98-41773
    "The young, green, reptilian narrator enumerates all the things dads—and especially the green reptilian one pictured—can never do. Dads 'can't cross the street without holding hands,' they 'lose at checkers and cards,' and 'Dads can push, but they can't swing.'" Horn Book Guide
    "This amusing picture book will tickle youngsters' funny bones and make every parent and child smile with recognition. . . . Cushman's large, delightful, pen-and-ink and watercolor cartoons . . . capture perfectly the father-and-son interactions." SLJ
    Other titles in this series are:
    What grandmas can't do (2005)
    What moms can't do (2000)
    What Santa can't do (2003)
    What teachers can't do (2000)

Woodruff, Elvira

The memory coat; story by Elvira Woodruff; illustrations by Michael Dooling. Scholastic Press 1999 unp il $16.95   **E**
    1. Ellis Island Immigration Station—Fiction 2. Immigrants—Fiction 3. Jews—Fiction
    ISBN 0-590-67717-9   LC 95-30048
    In the early 1900s, cousins Rachel and Grisha leave their Russian shtetl with the rest of their family to come to America, hopeful that they will all pass the dreaded inspection at Ellis Island
    This offers "warm, realistic period paintings, some in color, some in sepia shades. . . . In a long, interesting author's note, Woodruff discusses the shtetl and immigrant history." Booklist

Woodson, Jacqueline

Coming on home soon; illustrated by E.B. Lewis. Putnam's 2004 unp il $16.99   **E**
1. Mother-child relationship—Fiction 2. Grandmothers—Fiction 3. World War, 1939-1945—Fiction 4. African Americans—Fiction
ISBN 0-399-23748-8   LC 2003-21949
A Caldecott Medal honor book, 2005
After Mama takes a job in Chicago during World War II, Ada Ruth stays with Grandma but misses her mother who loves her more than rain and snow.
"Woodson and Lewis tell a moving historical story of longing and separation. . . . Lewis' beautiful watercolors establish the setting. . . . Period and place are wonderfully specific." Booklist

The other side; illustrations by E. B. Lewis. Putnam 2001 unp il $16.99   **E**
1. Race relations—Fiction 2. Friendship—Fiction 3. African Americans—Fiction
ISBN 0-399-23116-1   LC 99-42055
Two girls, one white and one black, gradually get to know each other as they sit on the fence that divides their town
"Lewis' watercolors provide a telling backdrop to the action. . . . This is an emotionally intricate tale presented simply and intimately." Bull Cent Child Books

Show way; illustrated by Hudson Talbott. G. P. Putnam's Sons 2005 unp il $16.99   **E**
1. Quilts—Fiction 2. Slavery—Fiction 3. African Americans—Fiction
ISBN 0-399-23749-6   LC 2004-28093
A Newbery Medal honor book, 2006
The making of "Show ways," or quilts which once served as secret maps for freedom-seeking slaves, is a tradition passed from mother to daughter in the author's family.
"The gorgeous, multimedia art includes chalk, watercolors, and muslin. An outstanding tribute, perfectly executed in terms of text, design, and illustration." SLJ

Visiting day; illustrated by James E. Ransome. Scholastic Press 2002 unp il $15.95   **E**
1. Prisoners—Fiction 2. Fathers—Fiction 3. African Americans—Fiction
ISBN 0-590-40005-3   LC 00-35772
A young girl and her grandmother visit the girl's father in prison
"The text is spare, gentle, and reassuring. . . . Ransome's vibrant acrylic paintings fill each page at home with intense pinks, yellows, greens, and blues in contrast to the monotone hue of the prison walls. Both author and illustrator provide notes that relate this story to their own personal experiences." SLJ

We had a picnic this Sunday past; illustrated by Diane Greenseid. Hyperion Bks. for Children 1998 c1997 unp il $14.95   **E**
1. Family life—Fiction 2. African Americans—Fiction
ISBN 0-7868-0242-1   LC 96-16312
Teeka describes her various relatives and the foods they bring to the annual family picnic
"If this is more character sketch than actual story, the solid acrylic paintings help bring all the people in this African American family to life." Booklist

Wormell, Christopher

Teeth, tails, & tentacles; an animal counting book. Running Press 2004 64p il $18.95   **E**
1. Animals 2. Counting
ISBN 0-7624-2100-2
The first portion of the work is a counting book covering the numbers one to twenty with block prints of animals. The second portion of the work has factual information concerning the animals.
"Within the art, limpid colors melt into single-hue light-to-dark continuums or flash in arresting contrast, while surprising shifts in perspective and shadow create an almost tangible visual texture and depth which invite repeated viewing." Bull Cent Child Books

Wright, Betty Ren

The blizzard; illustrated by Ronald Himler. Holiday House 2003 unp il $16.95   **E**
1. Birthdays—Fiction
ISBN 0-8234-1656-9   LC 2002-190764
Although a blizzard prevents his cousins from visiting for his birthday, a disappointed Billy ends up having a very special day when his teacher and classmates must stay overnight at his family's house to wait out the snowstorm
"This evocative story harkens back to an earlier, simpler time. . . . The feelings the events engender are tender and strong. Himler's artwork alternates between the white-gray of the blowing snow and the golden glow that comes from both inside the house and the hearts of those who live there." Booklist

Wright, Catherine

Steamboat Annie and the thousand-pound catfish; illustrated by Howard Fine. Philomel Bks. 2001 unp il $15.99   **E**
1. Fishes—Fiction 2. Tall tales
ISBN 0-399-23331-8   LC 00-32656
An ornery giant catfish that does not like singing causes trouble for the residents of a little town called Pleasant, until Steamboat Annie teaches him a lesson
"True to the genre, the highly humored telling is larger-than-life. . . . Fine's exaggerated perspectives in bold acrylic paintings contribute to the good fun." SLJ

Yacowitz, Caryn

Pumpkin fiesta; illustrated by Joe Cepeda. HarperCollins Pubs. 1998 unp il $16.99   **E**
1. Pumpkin—Fiction 2. Mexico—Fiction
ISBN 0-06-027658-4   LC 96-48580
Hoping to win a prize for the best pumpkin at the fiesta, Foolish Fernando tries to copy Old Juana's successful gardening techniques, but without really watching to see how much effort and love she puts into her work. Includes a recipe for pumpkin soup
"The warm-toned oil paintings contain flat but expressive figures. The book is both amusing and satisfying, competently executed, and good for read-aloud sharing." Horn Book Guide

Yang, Belle

Hannah is my name. Candlewick Press 2004 unp il $16.99   E

1. Chinese Americans—Fiction 2. Immigrants—Fiction 3. San Francisco (Calif.)—Fiction

ISBN 0-7636-2223-0   LC 2003-69675

A young Chinese girl and her parents emigrate to the United States and try their best to assimilate into their San Francisco neighborhood while anxiously awaiting the arrival of their green cards.

"The bright gouache pictures of San Francisco draw strongly on Chinese and American traditions. . . . The struggle with documentation and the celebration when the green cards finally arrive in the mail is a drama many immigrant families will recognize." Booklist

Yang, James

Joey and Jet; [by] James Yang. 1st ed. Atheneum Books for Young Readers 2004 unp il $15.95   E

1. Dogs—Fiction 2. English language—Terms and phrases

ISBN 0-689-86926-6   LC 2003-16758

"A Richard Jackson book"

A boy named Joey and his dog, Jet, play a game of fetch in a field of prepositions—among, between, past, and all around.

"This book will win fans with its simple text and retro-style illustrations rendered in a non-retro digital pen and ink." SLJ

Another title about Joey and Jet is:
Joey and Jet in Space (2006)

Yee, Wong Herbert

Tracks in the snow. H. Holt 2003 unp il $15.95   E

1. Animal tracks—Fiction 2. Snow—Fiction 3. Stories in rhyme

ISBN 0-8050-6771-X   LC 2002-10854

A little girl investigates tracks in the snow, trying to determine what could have made them.

"The gentle, rhyming text makes an ideal read-aloud, and young listeners will chime in on the repeated phrases. The soft-focus, colored-pencil illustrations portray a small Asian girl exploring her safe world, but a world transformed by the fresh snowfall." SLJ

Upstairs Mouse, downstairs Mole; . Houghton Mifflin Co 2005 unp il $15   E

1. Mice—Fiction 2. Moles (Animals)—Fiction 3. Friendship—Fiction

ISBN 0-618-47313-0   LC 2004-5238

Mouse and her downstairs neighbor, Mole, discover that when they help each other, housecleaning and other daily tasks are much easier.

"The expressive bamboo-pen and watercolor with colored-pencil illustrations capture the humor of the situations as well as the emotions of the characters. . . . A real winner." SLJ

Yezerski, Thomas

A full hand; [by] Thomas F. Yezerski. Farrar, Straus & Giroux 2002 unp il $16   E

1. Canals—Fiction

ISBN 0-374-42502-7   LC 00-140219

This "picture book describes the mule-drawn Morris Canal boats that transported coal through the American northeast over 100 years ago. . . . In this story, nine-year-old Asa is enlisted to help his father by taking the place of his hired mule handler. . . . The book relies primarily on its rustic watercolor-and-pen illustrations to communicate feeling and expression. . . . The book does a good job of explaining this obsolete and little-known method of transport." SLJ

Yin

Coolies; illustrated by Chris K. Soentpiet. Philomel Bks. 2001 unp il $16.99   E

1. Central Pacific Railroad—Fiction 2. Chinese Americans—Fiction 3. Brothers—Fiction

ISBN 0-399-23227-3   LC 98-40403

A young boy hears the story of his great-great-great-grandfather and his brother who came to the United States to make a better life for themselves helping to build the transcontinental railroad

"Soentpiet's strong, realistic watercolor paintings, in shades of blue and gold, show the bond between the brothers. . . . The American history is powerful. Yin provides notes and a bibliography for readers who want to know more." Booklist

Yolen, Jane

Baby Bear's chairs; written by Jane Yolen; illustrated by Melissa Sweet. Harcourt 2005 unp il $16   E

1. Bears—Fiction 2. Chairs—Fiction 3. Stories in rhyme

ISBN 0-15-205114-7   LC 2004-12227

"Gulliver books"

Baby Bear's favorite "chair" is his father's chest or lap, just before his father puts him to bed.

"Not only is the sound of the verse satisfying, the tone is also pleasing. . . . Fresh and bright, the large-scale pictures combine pencil, paint, and collage elements to illustrate the everyday activities of a likable little bear family at home while including a few fun-to-notice details." Booklist

Commander Toad and the voyage home; pictures by Bruce Degen. Putnam 1998 64p il $15.99; pa $5.99 (.)   E

1. Toads—Fiction 2. Science fiction

ISBN 0-399-23122-6; 0-698-11602-X (pa)

LC 96-21739

Commander Toad leads the lean green space machine "Star Warts" to find new worlds but runs into trouble when he sets course for home

"Yolen captures the high drama of space fiction in a delightful story that never loses sight of developing readers, who will be old enough to get the jokes but still young enough to relish the goofiness." Booklist

Other titles about Commander Toad are:

Yolen, Jane—*Continued*

Commander Toad and the big black hole (1996)
Commander Toad and the dis-asteroid (1996)
Commander Toad and the intergalactic spy (1997)
Commander Toad and the Planet of the Grapes (1996)
Commander Toad and the space pirates (1997)
Commander Toad in space (1996)

How do dinosaurs say goodnight? illustrated by Mark Teague. Blue Sky Press (NY) 2000 unp il $15.95   E
1. Bedtime—Fiction 2. Dinosaurs—Fiction 3. Stories in rhyme
ISBN 0-590-31681-8   LC 98-56134
Mother and child ponder the different ways a dinosaur can say goodnight, from slamming his tail and pouting to giving a big hug and kiss
"The text is sweet and simple—just right for the wonderful pictures that really make this picture book special. . . . Endpapers introduce the critter cast in all their gorgeous glory: tyrannosaurus rex, dimetrodon, and more, in vivid, yet still earthbound colors." Booklist
Other titles in this series are:
How do dinosaurs eat their food? (2005)
How do dinosaurs get well soon? (2003)

Off we go! illustrated by Laurel Molk. Little, Brown 2000 unp il lib bdg $12.95   E
1. Animals—Fiction 2. Grandmothers—Fiction 3. Stories in rhyme
ISBN 0-316-90228-4   LC 98-6893
One by one, baby woodland creatures leave home and sing their way to visit grandma
"Rhyme, repetition, and the playful, onomatopoeic language make this especially appealing for read-alouds. Large watercolors in earthy tones of gray, green, and brown are soft and fluid." Horn Book Guide

Owl moon; illustrated by John Schoenherr. Philomel Bks. 1987 unp il lib bdg $16.99
                    E
1. Owls—Fiction 2. Father-daughter relationship—Fiction
ISBN 0-399-21457-7   LC 87-2300
Awarded the Caldecott Medal, 1988
"The poetic narrative is told from the point of view of a child who 'has been waiting to go owling with Pa for a long, long time.' The father and child venture forth on a cold winter night not to capture, but to commune with, the great horned owl." SLJ
This book "conveys the scary majesty of winter woods at night in language that seldom overreaches either character or subject. . . . This book has a magic that is extremely rare in books for any age." N Y Times Book Rev

Yorinks, Arthur

Happy bees; by Arthur Yorinks; illustrated by Carey Armstrong-Ellis. Harry N. Abrams 2005 unp il $15.95   E
1. Bees—Fiction
ISBN 0-8109-5866-X   LC 2004-15454
Rhythmic text describes the carefree life of bees as they sting knees, munch on Swiss cheese, and laugh in

the breeze.
"The nonsensical text doubles as the lyrics of the first tune on the accompanying CD. . . . The happy-go-lucky insects have loads of personality. . . . Listeners will enjoy the romp, whether spoken or sung, and can discover more bee-guiling silliness in the other selections on the CD." SLJ

Hey, Al; story by Arthur Yorinks; pictures by Richard Egielski. Farrar, Straus & Giroux 1986 unp il $17; pa $6.95   E
1. Fantasy fiction 2. Birds—Fiction
ISBN 0-374-33060-3; 0-374-42985-5 (pa)
                    LC 86-80955
Awarded the Caldecott Medal, 1987
"Al, a janitor, and his faithful dog, Eddie, live in a single room on the West Side. . . . Their tiny home is crowded and cramped; their life is an endless struggle. Al and Eddie are totally miserable until a large and mysterious bird offers them a change of fortune." Publisher's note
"Egielski's solid naturalism provides just the visual foil needed to establish the surreal character of this fantasy. . . . Text and pictures work together to challenge readers' concept of reality." SLJ

You read to me & I'll read to you; 20th-century stories to share; selected by Janet Schulman. Knopf 2001 250p il $34.95   E
1. Short stories
ISBN 0-375-81083-8   LC 2001-29211
Companion volume to The 20th century children's book treasury (1998)
This is a collection of 26 picture books and selections from early chapter books by such authors as Maurice Sendak, William Steig, Dr. Seuss, and Florence Parry Heide
"A great choice for family or classroom sharing." SLJ

Young, Amy

Belinda, the ballerina. Viking 2002 unp il $15.99   E
1. Ballet—Fiction
ISBN 0-670-03549-1   LC 2001-8395
When Belinda auditions for the Spring Ballet Recital and the judges tell her she can not be a ballerina because her feet are too big, she tries to forget about dancing
This offers "spirited gouache paintings that capture the sadness, the humor and the triumph of Belinda's story. . . . The story puts physical defects into perspective and offers something to laugh about at the same time." Booklist
Another title about Belinda is:
Belinda in Paris (2005)

Young, Ed

Monkey King. HarperCollins Pubs. 2001 unp il $16.95; lib bdg $16.89   E
1. Monkeys—Fiction 2. China—Fiction
ISBN 0-06-027919-2; 0-06-027950-8 (lib bdg)
                    LC 00-38835
In this journey to a more enlightened state, a monkey must end his trickery and understand that thhere is

Young, Ed—*Continued*

strenggth in admittinf weakness. Based on a section of Chinese epic "Journey to the West"

"The language is lively and rich, and the lushly textured cut-paper collages, while abstract, beautifully illustrate the action-hero excitement." Booklist

My Mei Mei. Philomel Books 2006 unp il $16.99
E

1. Adoption—Fiction 2. Sisters—Fiction 3. Chinese Americans—Fiction 4. China—Fiction

ISBN 0-399-24339-9

Antonia gets her wish when her parents return to China to bring home a Mei Mei, or younger sister, for her.

"Young's vibrant collage illustrations joyously extend the spare, direct words." Booklist

Zemach, Harve

The judge; an untrue tale; with pictures by Margot Zemach. Farrar, Straus & Giroux 1969 unp il pa $6.95 hardcover o.p.
E

1. Judges—Fiction 2. Stories in rhyme

ISBN 0-374-43962-1 (pa)

A Caldecott Medal honor book, 1970

"Enthroned on his bench, a curmudgeon of a judge hears a prisoner plead that he didn't know that what he did was against the law, but that he had seen a horrible beast. 'This man has told an untrue tale. Throw him in jail!' Each additional prisoner adds to the story; each infuriates the judge." Sutherland. The Best in Child Books

Zemach, Kaethe

Just enough and not too much. Levine Bks. 2003 unp il $16.95
E

ISBN 0-439-37724-2   LC 2003-399

Simon the fiddler decides he needs more—more chairs, more hats, more stuffed animals—until he discovers that his house is too full and must think of a way to get back to having just enough

"The rich watercolor-and-gouache illustrations, many emphasizing rounded forms, are full of movement and joy. . . . Perfect for storyhours or individual readings." SLJ

Zemach, Margot

Eating up Gladys; illustrated by Kaethe Zemach. Arthur A. Levine Books 2005 unp $16.99
E

1. Sisters—Fiction

ISBN 0-439-66490-X

When Hilda and Rose get fed up with their older sister's bossiness, they get revenge by threatening to have her for dinner.

"The dialogue captures the essence of sibling interaction, and children will easily recognize themselves in these characters. The charming watercolor illustrations ensure the story remains lighthearted while clearly depicting the characters' many emotions." SLJ

Another title about Hilda and her sisters is:

To Hilda for helping (1977)

Ziefert, Harriet

A dozen ducklings lost and found; illustrated by Donald Dreifuss. Houghton Mifflin 2003 unp il $15
E

1. Ducks—Fiction 2. Counting

ISBN 0-618-14175-8   LC 2002-9403

Between the pond and the farm house some of Mother Duck's new babies get lost

"Dreifuss' naive, impressionistic paintings have a simplicity of composition that makes them easy to for group viewing, with the fluffy yellow ducklings standing out against the verdant background." Bull Cent Child Books

Home for Navidad; paintings by Santiago Cohen. Houghton Mifflin 2003 unp il $15
E

1. Mothers—Fiction 2. Christmas—Fiction 3. Mexico—Fiction

ISBN 0-618-34976-6   LC 2002-156430

Ten-year-old Rosa hopes that her mother, whom she has not seen for three years, will leave her job in New York and come home to Santa Catarina, Mexico, for Christmas and maybe even longer. Includes a glossary of Spanish words used

"The combination of simple words and bold, vibrant art relays the wrenching family separation from the child's viewpoint." Booklist

Lunchtime for a purple snake; written by Harriet Ziefert; paintings by Todd McKie. Houghton Mifflin 2003 unp il $15
E

1. Grandfathers—Fiction 2. Artists—Fiction 3. Color—Fiction

ISBN 0-618-31133-5   LC 2002-10295

Walter Lorraine Books

When Jessica visits her artist grandpa they make a painting together

Jessica's "artwork is as basic in form as a young child's would be—and it is full of a child's exuberance and imagination. Budding artists, at home or in class, will learn from this and receive inspiration." Booklist

One smart skunk; [by] Harriet Ziefert; illustrated by Santiago Cohen. 1st ed. Blue Apple Books 2004 unp il $15.95
E

1. Skunks—Fiction

ISBN 1-59354-064-7   LC 2004-10533

Rebecca the skunk lives under a suburban family's deck, eluding the traps set to ensnare her, but the smell of moth balls and the noise of rap music finally convince her that the suburbs are no place to raise her family.

"Cohen's illustrations are luminous, and the layout effectively varies text location and illustration size to create an appealing and modern background for this charming, informative text." SLJ

Zimmerman, Andrea Griffing

Dig! [by] Andrea Zimmerman and David Clemesha; illustrated by Marc Rosenthal. Silver Whistle/Harcourt 2004 unp il $16
E

1. Excavating machinery—Fiction 2. Construction workers—Fiction 3. Dogs—Fiction

ISBN 0-15-216785-4   LC 2003-4373

"Silver Whistle"

Zimmerman, Andrea Griffing—*Continued*

Follows Mr. Rally and his dog, Lightning, as they travel the town on a big yellow digging machine, taking care of five important jobs.

"Earth-tone illustrations are created with watercolor and Prismacolor pencil. . . . The pace, repetition, and word choices make the book appropriate for beginning readers. The uncluttered art, catchy refrain, and focus on heavy machinery make it a natural for storytimes." SLJ

Digger man; [by] Andrea Zimmerman & David Clemesha. Holt & Co. 2003 unp il $15.95
                                                        E
1. Steam-shovels—Fiction 2. Brothers—Fiction
ISBN 0-8050-6628-4   LC 2002-10856

A young boy imagines how he will use his digger to make a park where he and his little brother can play

"The joyful acrylic illustrations and the sparse, confident text will delight other digger-wannabes." Booklist

My dog Toby; [by] Andrea Zimmerman and David Clemesha; illustrated by True Kelley. Harcourt 2000 unp il $15   **E**
1. Dogs—Fiction
ISBN 0-15-202014-4   LC 98-35246
"Silver Whistle"

Toby the dog is a beloved pet, but he doesn't seem to be able to do any tricks

"The understated humor of the text is amplified by the buoyant spirits of Kelley's amusing illustrations. Black-ink drawings, vividly tinted with watercolors and acrylics, bring humor even to the most deadpan lines in the narration." Booklist

Trashy town; [by] Andrea Zimmerman and David Clemesha; illustrated by Dan Yaccarino. HarperCollins Pubs. 1999 unp il $15.99   **E**
1. Refuse and refuse disposal—Fiction
ISBN 0-06-027139-6   LC 98-27495

Little by little, can by can, Mr. Gillie, the trash man, cleans up his town

"Short energetic sentences propel the tale. . . . Employing primary colors dominated by bold blues, Yaccarino's vibrant art has a retro look." Booklist

Zion, Gene

Harry the dirty dog; pictures by Margaret Bloy Graham. Harper & Row 1956 unp il $15.99; lib bdg $17.89; pa $6.99   **E**
1. Dogs—Fiction
ISBN 0-06-026865-4; 0-06-026866-2 (lib bdg); 0-06-443009-X (pa)
Also available Spanish language edition

"A runaway dog becomes so dirty his family almost doesn't recognize him. Harry's flight from scrubbing brush and bath water takes him on a tour of the city." Moorachian. What is a City?

"Harry's fun and troubles are told simply, and the drawings are full of action and humor. The combination will have great appeal for the very young." Horn Book

Other titles about Harry are:
Harry and the lady next door (1960)
Harry by the sea (1965)
No roses for Harry! (1958)

Zolotow, Charlotte

The beautiful Christmas tree; illustrated by Yan Nacimbene. Houghton Mifflin 1999 32p il $15
                                                        E
1. City and town life—Fiction 2. Trees—Fiction 3. Christmas—Fiction
ISBN 0-395-91365-9   LC 98-50006

A newly illustrated edition of the title first published 1972 by Parnassus Press

Although his elegant neighbors do not appreciate his efforts, a kind old man transforms his rundown house and a small neglected pine tree into the best on the street

"In handsome depictions of the urban setting, Nacimbene's delicate watercolors convey the emotional warmth of Zolotow's testament to a simple man's faith and love." Horn Book Guide

The bunny who found Easter; illustrated by Helen Craig. Houghton Mifflin 1998 unp il $16
                                                        E
1. Rabbits—Fiction 2. Easter—Fiction
ISBN 0-395-86265-5   LC 97-36827

A newly illustrated edition of the title first published 1959 by Parnassus Press

A lonely rabbit searches for others of his kind from summer through winter until spring arrives and he finds one special bunny

"Zolotow's stylistic trademarks—tender lyricism, poetic prose, and a compassionate tone—continue to satisfy children. Craig's charming pastel paintings in ink, watercolor, and colored pencil bring the bunny to life." SLJ

Mr. Rabbit and the lovely present; pictures by Maurice Sendak. Harper & Row 1962 unp il $16.99; pa $5.99   **E**
1. Birthdays—Fiction 2. Color—Fiction 3. Rabbits—Fiction
ISBN 0-06-026945-6; 0-06-443020-0 (pa)
Also available Spanish language edition
A Caldecott Medal honor book, 1963

"A serious little girl and a tall, other-worldly white rabbit converse about a present for her mother. 'But what?' said the little girl. 'Yes, what?' said Mr. Rabbit. It requires a day of searching—for red, yellow, green, and blue, all things the mother likes, to make a basket of fruit for the present." Horn Book

"The quiet story, told in dialogue, is illustrated in richly colored pictures which exactly fit the fanciful mood." Hodges. Books for Elem Sch Libr

The old dog; paintings by James Ransome. rev and newly illustrated ed. HarperCollins Pubs. 1995 unp il $16.99   **E**
1. Dogs—Fiction 2. Death—Fiction
ISBN 0-06-024409-7   LC 93-41081

A revised and newly illustrated edition of the title first published 1972 by Coward, McCann & Geoghegan under the author's pseudonym Sarah Abbott

When Ben finds his old dog dead one morning, he spends the rest of the day thinking about all the good times they had together

"Zolotow's elemental story . . . is newly illustrated here with rich oil paintings. . . . An unsentimental story about connection and loss and renewal." Booklist

Zolotow, Charlotte—*Continued*

The seashore book; paintings by Wendell Minor. HarperCollins Pubs. 1992 unp il $16.99; pa $6.99

E

1. Seashore—Fiction 2. Mother-son relationship—Fiction

ISBN 0-06-020213-0; 0-06-443364-1 (pa)

LC 91-22783

A mother's words help a little boy imagine the sights and sounds of the seashore, even though he's never seen the ocean

"Minor's crisply detailed watercolors evoke place with imaginative accuracy and visual grace, and Zolotow's . . . spare, poetic text provides a lyrical and nostalgic paean to the wonders of seaside life." Publ Wkly

Sleepy book; pictures by Stefano Vitale. HarperCollins Pubs. 2001 unp $15.95; lib bdg $15.89

E

1. Sleep 2. Animals

ISBN 0-06-027873-0; 0-06-027874-9 (lib bdg)

LC 00-57252

A newly illustrated edition of the title first published 1958 by Lothrop

Describes how each animal sleeps in its own special place in its own special way

"The distinctive double-page spreads in deep autumn shades assure another round of applause for this celebrated nighttime piece." SLJ

A tiger called Thomas; story by Charlotte Zolotow; pictures by Diana Cain Bluthenthal. Hyperion Bks. for Children 2003 unp il $15.99

E

1. Halloween—Fiction

ISBN 0-7868-0517-X

LC 2001-51851

A newly illustrated edition of the title first published 1963 by Lothrop, Lee & Shepard

"Thomas is reluctant to meet his new neighbors, though he often watches them from his front stoop. When he dons a tiger costume for Halloween, Thomas feels bold enough to walk house to house and speak to people. . . . Bluthenthal's stylized illustrations use geometrical shapes and watercolors, chalks, ink, and collage to create a new and varied setting." Booklist

When the wind stops; illustrated by Stefano Vitale. rev and newly illustrated ed. HarperCollins Pubs. 1995 unp il $16.95; pa $6.99

E

1. Nature—Fiction

ISBN 0-06-025425-4; 0-06-443472-9 (pa)

LC 94-14477

A revised and newly illustrated edition of the title first published 1962 by Abelard-Schuman

A mother explains to her son that in nature an end is also a beginning as day gives way to night, winter ends and spring begins, and, after it stops falling, rain makes clouds for other storms

"The full-color scenes, painted on wood, gloriously depict heaven and earth and give concrete meaning to abstract concepts. Not only wonderful for lap sharing, this beautiful book will also be a rich supplement for a science unit on the elements or the seasons." Booklist

William's doll; pictures by William Pène Du Bois. Harper & Row 1972 30p il $15.99; lib bdg $16.89; pa $5.99

E

1. Dolls—Fiction 2. Sex role—Fiction

ISBN 0-06-027047-0; 0-06-027048-9 (lib bdg); 0-06-443067-7 (pa)

When little William asks for a doll, the other boys scorn him and his father tries to interest him in conventional boys' playthings such as a basketball and a train. His sympathetic grandmother buys him the doll, explaining his need to have it to love and care for so that he can practice being a father

"Very, very special. The strong, yet delicate pictures . . . convey a gentleness of spirit and longing most effectively, as William pantomimes his craving." N Y Times Book Rev

LIST OF RECOMMENDED PERIODICALS

The following list of recommended periodicals for a Children's Library is divided into two parts: Part I, Professional, which lists titles for librarians and teachers, and Part II, Children's, which lists titles for students. It is widely felt that a school library should introduce students to weekly news magazines and other popular general magazines as appropriate, but these types of materials are not listed below. Neither are popular magazines that are strictly for entertainment and have no educational content, which can be collected at the individual library's discretion.

PART I

PROFESSIONAL

Art Education. National Art Education Association $50 per year
ISSN 0004-3125

http://www.naea-reston.org
Bimonthly.

"Articles on current directions, problems, and exemplary approaches in visual art education at all instructional levels. Articles may focus on the art curriculum, teaching strategies, innovative programs, or a special area of the curriculum such as studio, art criticism, or art history. Each issue of Art Education includes four full-color reproductions of works of art, with commentary and lesson plan suggestions for use at both elementary and secondary levels." NAEA website

Arts and Activities; the nation's leading arts education magazine. Publishers Development Corp. $30 per year
ISSN 0004-3931

http://www.artsandactivities.com/
Monthly September through June.

"A magazine dedicated to providing an exchange of professional experiences, opinions, and new ideas for art educators. Contributors share strategies for art instruction, approaches to art history, techniques for engaging students in evaluating art, and programs and lessons to expand students' appreciation of art. Articles have covered a broad range of topics such as art appreciation, ceramics, computer art, drawing and painting, mixed media, papier-mache, collage, and three-dimensional design for grades K-12. A regular feature is a pullout clip-and-save art print. For the practitioner, the magazine publishes an annual buyers' guide and a listing of summer art programs." Katz. Mag for Libr. 13th edition

AudioFile; the magazine for people who love audiobooks. AudioFile Publs. $19.95 per year (individuals), $29.95 per year (institutions)
ISSN 1063-0244

http://www.audiofilemagazine.com/
6 times a year.

Price of subscription includes *AudioFile* issues and the *Audiobook Reference Guide*.

"AudioFile reviews unabridged and abridged audiobooks, original audio programs, commentary and dramatizations in the spoken-word format. Our focus is the audio presentation, not the critique of the written material." Publisher's note

Book Links; connecting books, libraries, and classrooms. American Library Association $39.95 per year
ISSN 1055-4742

http://www.ala.org/BookLinks/index.html
6 times a year.

This periodical "offers feature articles on children's books (e.g., best books of the year . . .) and regular columns that suggest ways to incorporate fine children's literature into the curriculum and day-care and nursery school programming. Background information on special topics . . . is accompanied by an annotated bibliography, complete with appropriate grade level. Columns devoted to specific children's books and interviews with authors and illustrators are a plus for the adult who wants to read or select books for children." Katz. Mag for Libr. 10th edition

Bookbird; a journal of international children's literature. University of Toronto Press, Journals Division $40 per year (individuals), $75 per year (institutions)
ISSN 0006-7377

http://www.utpjournals.com/jour.ihtml?lp=bookbird/bookbird.html
Quarterly.

Articles, criticism, and occasional brief book reviews survey the best of children's literature from an international perspective.

Booklist. American Library Association $89.95 per year
ISSN 0006-7385

http://www.booklistonline.com/
Bimonthly (22/yr.).

"Intended chiefly as a guide for librarians in public and school libraries, each issue covers titles in five major areas: forthcoming titles, adult books, books for youth, audiovisual media, and reference books. . . . Because of its selectivity, its early reviews, and its broad coverage of popular non-print media, Booklist is essential reading for public, school, and many academic libraries." Katz. Mag for Libr. 10th edition

Bulletin of the Center for Children's Books. University of Illinois Press $50 per year (individuals), $75 per year (institutions)
ISSN 0008-9036

http://bccb.lis.uiuc.edu/
Monthly (except combined issue July/Aug).

1057

Bulletin of the Center for Children's Books—
Continued

"This highly regarded reviewing source covers selected titles from the thousands of children's books published each year. In addition to complete bibliographic information, the critical annotations are supplemented by an indication of suitable age and/or grade level and a shorthand code noting a range of quality, from 'books of special distinction' to 'NR' for not recommended. . . . Librarians in schools, public libraries, and academic libraries with children's literature collections will find this an indispensable guide." Katz. Mag for Libr. 10th edition

Childhood Education. Association for Childhood Education International $65 per year
ISSN 0009-4056

http://www.acei.org/

Bi-monthly.

"The articles are well written and would provide valuable information to educators, education students, and childcare workers. The book review section includes a section for children's books, professional reading, and special publications pertaining to this area." Katz. Mag for Libr. 10th edition

Children's Magazine Guide; subject index to children's magazines and web sites. Greenwood Publishing Group $69.95 per year
ISSN 0743-9873

http://www.childrensmag.com/

9 times a year.

This publication indexes 65 "magazines for children ages 8 to 12. Entries are arranged under subject headings in alphabetical order by the title of the article. Bibliographic information includes article and journal titles, author's name (when available), issue month and year, and page numbers." Katz. Mag for Libr. 10th edition

Children's Technology Review. Active Learning Associates $26 per year
ISSN 1555-242X

http://www.childrenssoftware.com/

4 times a year.

This magazine reviews children's software, smart toys, video games, internet sites, and other interactive media for children. Reviews are based on both expert and child testing.

The **Education** Digest; essential readings condensed for quick review. Prakken Publications, Inc. $48 per year
ISSN 0013-127X

http://www.eddigest.com/

Monthly (nine issues a year, September through May).

"This publication provides a condensation of current articles on the themes chosen for the individual ED issues, allowing educators, students, and other interested readers an opportunity to quickly update their knowledge of particular education topics. In addition, there are regular columns such as the free-ranging discussions in 'The Teachers' Lounge,' capsules of education news in Washington and elsewhere, book reviews and lists, and web resources. This is a handy, pocket-sized resource that is useful for school and public libraries." Katz. Mag for Libr. 13th edition

Educational Leadership. Association for Supervision and Curriculum Development $36 per year
ISSN 0013-1784

http://www.ascd.org

Bimonthly September through May.

This magazine discusses "teaching and learning, new ideas and practices relevant to practicing educators, and the latest trends and issues affecting prekindergarten through higher education." ASCD website

Edutopia: The World of Learning. The George Lucas Educational Foundation Free to qualified personnel, otherwise $29.95 per year
ISSN 1552-9029

http://www.edutopia.org

Bimonthly.

Published by the George Lucas Foundation and evolved from their website that features multimedia streaming video to support many of the journal articles, Edutopia focuses on the newest research, theories, and practices in K-12 education and relates it to schools around the world that are already implementing them. Best New Publication 2005 Maggie Awards

Five Owls; a publication for readers, personally and professionally involved in children's literature. The Jara Society dba The Five Owls $35 per year
ISSN 0892-6735

http://www.fiveowls.com/

Quarterly.

"Each issue is approximately 22 pages and contains black-and-white photographs and illustrations. In addition to book reviews, there are articles about books and reading, and interviews with authors and illustrators. The reviews are comprehensive and include age recommendations. This would be a useful selection tool for a school or public library." Katz. Mag for Libr. 10th edition

Horn Book Guide to Children's and Young Adult Books. Horn Book, Inc. $35 for the first year, $49.50 per year afterward
ISSN 1044-405X

http://www.hbook.com/publications/guide/default.asp

Semi-annually.

"This offshoot of The Horn Book Magazine provides critical annotations on all hardcover trade children's and young adult books published in the United States during the previous six months. Fiction is arranged by grade level and genre (e.g., picture books, readers), nonfiction by the ten broad Dewey classes and then narrower topics. . . . Numerous indexes (author, illustrator, title, series, subject, and reissues) help the librarian track down particular titles." Katz. Mag for Libr. 10th edition

The **Horn** Book Magazine; recommending books for children and young adults. Horn Book, Inc. $34.95 for the first year, $49 per year afterward
ISSN 0018-5078

http://www.hbook.com/publications/magazine/default.asp

Bi-monthly.

The Horn Book Magazine—*Continued*

"One of the first magazines to treat children's literature as serious material for discussion and review. . . . The book reviews, most of which are for recommended titles, are grouped by age level and/or format (picture books, folklore, etc.). Other sections of the magazine include lists of new paperbacks and reissues, books in Spanish, and audiobooks." Katz. Mag for Libr. 10th edition

Instructor. Scholastic, Inc. $9.99 per year
ISSN 1532-0200

http://www.scholastic.com

Monthly August, September, October, March, and April. Bimonthly November/December, January/February, May/June.

This magazine is focused on elementary and middle school teachers with lots of classroom activities as well as feature articles, monthly columns and education news.

JOPERD. American Alliance for Health, Physical Education, Recreation and Dance $145 per year
ISSN 0730-3084

http://www.aahperd.org/aahperd/
template.cfm?template=johperd%5Fmain.html

Monthly (except June).

The Journal of Physical Education, Recreation & Dance is the professional magazine for the American Alliance of Health, Physical, Recreation, and Dance. It addresses a variety of HPERD issues including articles on teaching strategies, fitness, legal issues, assessment, dancing, teacher education, adapted physical education, leisure for older adults, the use of technology, and ethics and gender equity in sports and physical education.

Knowledge Quest. American Library Association $40 per year
ISSN 1094-9046

http://www.ala.org/aasl

Bimonthly September through May.

This publication, along with its companion website KQonline, "is devoted to offering substantive information to assist building-level library media specialists, supervisors, library educators, and other decision makers concerned with the development of school library media programs and services. Articles address the integration of theory and practice in school librarianship and new developments in education, learning theory, and relevant disciplines." ALA website

Language Arts. National Council of Teachers of English $25 per year (members)
ISSN 0360-9170

http://www.ncte.org

Bimonthly September-July.

"A professional journal for elementary and middle school teachers and teacher educators. It provides a forum for discussions on all aspects of language arts learning and teaching, primarily as they relate to children in prekindergarten through the eighth grade. Issues discuss both theory and classroom practice, highlight current research, and review children's and young adolescent literature, as well as classroom and professional materials of interest to language arts educators." NCTE website

Learning and Leading with Technology. International Society for Technology in Education Subscription included with membership
ISSN 1082-5754

http://www.iste.org

Monthly (except June, July, August), bimonthly December/January.

Member subscription of the International Society for Technology in Education, introduces classroom applications of newer technology, integration strategies, and leadership strategies for implementing instructional technology into schools.

Library Media Connection; magazine for secondary school library media and technology specialists. Linworth Publishing, Inc. $69 per year
ISSN 1542-4715

http://www.linworth.com/lmc.html

7 times a year.

The magazine provides articles and advice for managing school libraries, along with reviews of books, multimedia, and videos written by school librarians. Each review contains grade level recommendations.

Mailbox Bookbag; literacy ideas for teachers. Education Center, Inc. $39.95 per year
ISSN 1088-6397

http://www.theeducationcenter.com/cgi-bin/tec/
cdsSubscribe.jsp?Country=USA&Mag=BB

Bi-monthly.

"An excellent resource for elementary and middle school teachers and librarians, The Mailbox Bookbag provides brief descriptions of books and suggests activities for each title. Teaching units for chapter books and novels lay out chapter-by-chapter questions and follow-up activities to integrate literature with skills instruction. Reproducible worksheets reinforce reading vocabulary and comprehension skills and make connections to writing and math skills where applicable. The 'Bulletin Boards for Books' section illustrates classroom displays designed to attract students' attention while encouraging them to read." Katz. Mag for Libr. 13th edition

MultiMedia & Internet@Schools; the media and technology specialist's guide to electronic tools and resources for K-12. Information Today, Inc. $39.95 per year
ISSN 1546-4636

http://www.mmischools.com/

6 times a year.

This magazine for library media specialists and technology coordinators reviews and evaluates new software and hardware, offers purchasing recommendations and technical advice, and profiles high-tech products.

Nick Jr. Family. Nickelodeon Magazine, Inc. $14.85 per year
ISSN 1540-9333

http://www.nickjr.com

9 times a year.

This magazine for preschoolers and their parents features news articles, stories, and activities for parents and their children to do together. Features parenting tips and a pull-out section for preschoolers.

Phi Delta Kappan. Phi Delta Kappa International, Inc. $58 per year (members), $65 per year (institutions)
ISSN 0031-7217

http://www.pdkintl.org/kappan/kappan.htm

Monthly (except July and August).

"The professional print journal for education, addresses policy issues for educators at all levels. Advocating research-based school reform, the Kappan provides a forum for debate on controversial subjects." PDKINTL website

Preventing School Failure. Heldref Publications $54 per year (individuals), $123 per year (institutions)
ISSN 1045-988X

http://www.heldref.org

Quarterly.

"Helps educators and other professionals seeking to promote the success of students who have learning and behavioral problems. It offers examples of programs and practices that help children and youth in schools, clinics, correctional institutions, and other settings." Heldref website

The **Reading** Teacher. International Reading Association $61 per year (members), $122 per year (institutions)
ISSN 0034-0561

http://www.reading.org

Eight times per year.

Topics range from research-based suggestions about teaching phonics to the latest thinking about technology integration, and from reviews of children's books to ideas that promote learning from nonfiction text.

School Library Journal; the magazine of children, young adults & school librarians. Reed Business Information $129 per year
ISSN 0362-8930

http://www.slj.com

Monthly.

In addition to the feature articles this journal includes "a calendar of events, news from the field, notes on people, columns . . . as well as many reviews of professional reading, books for children and young adults, audiovisuals, and computer software. . . . This is an essential professional journal for school and public librarians." Katz. Mag for Libr. 10th edition

School Library Media Research. American Library Association Free
ISSN 1523-4320

http://www.ala.org/aasl/SLMR

5 times a year.

This is a web-based only publication

"An official journal of the American Association of School Librarians. It is the successor to School Library Media Quarterly Online. The purpose of School Library Media Research is to promote and publish high quality original research concerning the management, implementation, and evaluation of school library media programs. The journal will also emphasize research on instructional theory, teaching methods, and critical issues relevant to school library media." Publisher's note

Science and Children; the journal for elementary school science teachers. National Science Teachers Association $72 per year (members), $77 per year (institutions)
ISSN 0036-8148

http://www.nsta.org/elementaryschool#journal

8 times a year.

"A magazine for preschool through middle-level science teachers. The emphasis is on practical classroom activities, interdisciplinary learning, and current issues in elementary science education. . . . News excerpts of science discoveries or teaching and book and software reviews are also included." Katz. Mag for Libr. 10th edition

Science Books and Films. American Association for the Advancement of Science $45 per year
ISSN 1533-5046

http://SBFonline.com

Bimonthly.

"Published by the American Association for the Advancement of Science (AAAS), SB&F is the only critical review journal devoted exclusively to print and nonprint materials in all of the sciences and for all age groups. Every year, SB&F evaluates nearly 1,000 books, videos and DVDs, and software packages for general audiences, professionals, teachers, and students from kindergarten through college." AAAS website

Social Education. National Council for the Social Studies $55 per year (members), $75 per year (institutions)
ISSN 0037-7724

http://www.socialstudies.org

Monthly in September, October, March, April. Bimonthly November/December, January/February, May/June.

This journal, which includes the supplement *Middle Level Learning* featuring lesson ideas focused on the middle grades (3 times yearly) "contains a balance of theoretical content and practical ideas for classroom use. Our award-winning resources include techniques for using teaching materials in the classroom, information on the latest instructional technology, reviews of educational media, research on significant topics related to social studies, and lesson plans that can be applied to various disciplines." NCSS website

Teacher Librarian; the journal for school library professionals. Scarecrow Press, Inc. $54 per year
ISSN 1481-1782

http://www.teacherlibrarian.com/

5 times a year.

"This monthly publication provides useful information and resources for library staff who serve children and young adults. Feature articles cover a broad spectrum of topics, including management, advocacy, technology, leadership, information literacy, and collaboration. Reviews evaluate new books, e-zines, computer software, Internet resources, and electronic databases. Past issues have discussed gender discrimination in the school library, data use, strategic planning, and metacognition. Especially recommended for school librarians and library media specialists." Katz. Mag for Libr. 13th edition

Teacher Magazine. Editorial Projects in Education $17.94 per year
ISSN 1046-6193

http://www.teachermagazine.org

Teacher Magazine—*Continued*

Bimonthly (except for July and single-month October issue).

A sister publication of Education Week, Teacher Magazine is focused upon current news and stories of interest to classroom teachers.

Teaching Children Mathematics. National Council of Teachers of Mathematics Free to membership
ISSN 1073-5836

http://my.nctm.org/eresources/
journal%5Fhome.asp?journal%5Fid=4

Monthly September through May.

"This journal for teachers of math in grades K-6 presents articles on curriculum, learning, and instruction, reviews research and suggests practical ways to integrate the findings into the classroom. Regular columns review books for children and teachers, computer software, and other teaching materials." Katz. Mag for Libr. 10th edition

Teaching Exceptional Children. Council for Exceptional Children $135 per year (individuals), $170 per year (institutions)
ISSN 0040-0599

http://www.cec.sped.org

Bimonthly September-July.

"TEC, an official publication of the Council for Exceptional Children, is published specifically for teachers and administrators of children with disabilities and children who are gifted. TEC features . . . articles that present methods and materials for classroom use as well as current issues in special education teaching and learning. TEC also brings its readers the latest data on technology, assistive technology, and procedures and techniques with applications to students with exceptionalities." CEC website

Teaching PreK-8: Teacher Resources for Professional Development. Highlights for Children, Inc. $12 per year
ISSN 0891-4508

http://www.Teachingk-8.com

Monthly (except June, July, August, December).

This publication was Highlights Winner of the 2003 Association of Education Publishers Distinguished Achievement Award and includes reviews of classroom products, "Green Pages" listing ideas for classroom activities, and articles and columns written by teachers about their experiences.

Teaching Tolerance Magazine. Teaching Tolerance No charge to educators
ISSN 1066-2847

http://www.teachingtolerance.org

Twice a year.

"Founded in 1991 by the Southern Poverty Law Center, Teaching Tolerance provides educators with free educational materials that promote respect for differences and appreciation of diversity in the classroom and beyond. Published twice a year, our magazine profiles educators, schools and programs promoting diversity and equity in inspirational and replicable ways." Teaching Tolerance website

Technology and Learning. C M P Media Free to qualified personnel
ISSN 1053-6728

http://www.techlearning.com/

Monthly.

"The Resource for Education Technology Leaders" targets teachers as well as technology coordinators and administrators with ideas for and the theory behind the educational use of technology resources in the classroom.

PART II

CHILDREN'S

American Girl. Pleasant Company Publications $22.95 per year (3-6)
ISSN 1062-7812

http://www.americangirl.com/agmg/index.html

Bi-monthly.

This periodical features articles on American girls, games, arts and crafts, and short stories by children's authors.

AppleSeeds. Carus $29.95 per year (2-4)
ISSN 1099-7725

http://www.cobblestonepub.com/magazine/APP

9 times a year.

This social studies magazine features "articles, photographs, and activities that explore the history and culture of people and places both faraway and near. Each issue features puzzles, games, recipes, and the opportunity to join the 'Apple Corp' and submit their own stories." Publisher's note

Ask; arts and sciences for kids. Carus $32.97 per year (2-5)
ISSN 1535-4105

http://www.cobblestonepub.com/magazine/ASK

9 times a year.

This magazine "encourages young readers to explore the world with the greatest inventors, artists, thinkers, and scientists of the past and present, discovering how the ideas that shaped our lives were formed. . . . [It features] puzzles, word plays, riddles, activities, cartoons, photos, and . . . art." Publisher's note

Babybug. Carus $35.97 per year (PreK)
ISSN 1077-1131

http://www.cobblestonepub.com/magazine/BBB

10 times a year.

This magazine for children aged 6 months to 2 years features rhymes, word introductions, and simple stories.

Boys' Life. Boy Scouts of America $21.60 per year (5 and up)
ISSN 0006-8608

http://www.boyslife.org

Monthly.

This magazine covers scouting projects and profiles of scouts, as well as sports, science, hobbies, and other topics. It also features comics (including a Bible Heroes graphic strip), craft projects, and fiction. Some commercial content is included.

Boys' Quest. Bluffton News Printing & Publishing Co. $22.95 per year (K-7)
ISSN 1078-9006

http://www.funforkidzmagazines.com/
frameset.html?target=bq

Bi-monthly.

Boys' Quest—*Continued*

This magazine for boys contains stories, riddles and jokes, science experiments, projects, math puzzles, columns on topics such as cooking and computers, and contests.

Calliope. Carus $29.95 per year (4-6)
ISSN 1050-7086

http://www.cobblestonepub.com/magazine/CAL

9 times a year.

Each issue focuses on a single theme in world history, such as Mozart or the Mexican Revolution, and includes theme-related illustrations, maps, time lines, images of art from museums, activities and experiments, puzzles, and bibliographies.

Chickadee. Bayard Canada, The Owl Group $22 per year (K-3)
ISSN 0707-4611

http://www.owlkids.com/chickaDEE/index.html

10 times a year.

This "is a nature-oriented magazine for early elementary age children. It is bright, colorful, and filled with interesting content. Each issue follows a single theme through several avenues of interest. . . . The web site has a sampling of word games, activities, games, and some links to other web sites." Katz. Mag for Libr. 10th edition

ChildArt. International Child Art Foundation $30 per year (3-7)
ISSN 1096-9020

http://www.icaf.org

6 times a year.

This magazine focuses on famous art and artists and encourages young readers to express themselves in a variety of art forms. It explores themes, such as refugee art, peace through art, and art and culture, and includes games, wordplay, and profiles.

Chirp. Bayard Canada, The Owl Group $22 per year (PreK-1)
ISSN 1206-4580

http://www.owlkids.com/chirp/index.html

10 times a year.

This discovery magazine designed to teach children about animals, nature, and numbers and letters features fiction and artwork, puzzles, crafts, and comics.

Cicada. Carus $35.97 per year (4-9)
ISSN 1097-4008

http://www.cobblestonepub.com/magazine/CIC

Bimonthly.

This teen literary magazine features fiction and poetry often focused on themes of growing up. Submissions from young people are encouraged.

Click; opening windows for young minds. Carus $32.97 per year (2-4)
ISSN 1094-4273

http://www.cobblestonepub.com/magazine/CLK

9 times a year.

This science, nature and art magazine features articles, stories, poems, cartoons, activities, and games.

Cobblestone: discover American history. Carus $29.95 per year (4-8)
ISSN 0199-5197

http://www.cobblestonepub.com/magazine/COB

9 times a year.

Each issue of this historical magazine features a theme topic such as cowboys, Russians in America, or libraries, and contains articles, stories, and activities related to the issue's theme.

Creative Kids: the national voice for kids. Prufrock $19.95 per year (3-8)
ISSN 0892-9599

http://www.prufrock.com

4 times a year.

This magazine features "games, stories, and opinions all by and for kids ages 8-14." Publisher's note

Cricket: the magazine for children. Carus $35.97 per year (4-8)
ISSN 0090-6034

http://www.cricketmag.com/
ProductDetail.asp?pid=2

Monthly.

This magazine features fiction (including science fiction), biographies, fantasy, poetry, and folktales. It also "offers its readers cartoons, crossword puzzles, crafts, and recipes. In addition, CRICKET features story, poetry, art, and photography contests." Publisher's note

Dig Magazine. Carus $32.97 per year (4-8)
ISSN 1539-7130

http://www.cobblestonepub.com/magazine/DIG/

9 times a year.

This magazine features articles on archaeological discoveries, with topics ranging from mummies to dinosaurs. Each issue includes photo-illustrations, projects, puzzles and games.

Discovery Girls; a magazine created by girls, for girls. Discovery Girls $19.95 per year (3-6)
ISSN 1535-3230

http://www.discoverygirls.com/index.html

Bi-monthly.

This magazine "created for girls, by girls" includes articles on topics ranging from technology to fashion. The editors travel to a different part of the country every month to recruit a panel of twelve "Discovery Girls" that aid in the creation of the magazine.

Dolphin Log. Cousteau Society, Inc. $15 per year (3-7)
ISSN 8756-6362

http://www.cousteaukids.org/
frm%5FdolphinLog.html

Bi-monthly.

Also known as "Cousteau Kids," this magazine "is a publication (and record) of the Cousteau Society's famous adventures. . . . For environmental educators, teachers, and children ages 7 to 13 who are interested in marine life and the sea." Katz. Mag for Libr. 10th edition

Faces: people, places, & cultures. Carus $29.95 per year (4-6)
ISSN 0749-1387

http://www.cobblestonepub.com/magazine/FAC/

9 times a year.

Each issue of this 52-page magazine focuses on a different culture and includes maps, photographs, time lines, activities, contests, a crossword puzzle, bibliography, and Webography all related to that theme.

Girls' Life. Monarch Avalon $14.95 per year (4 and up)
ISSN 1078-3326

http://www.girlslife.com
Bimonthly.

In addition to articles on boys, school, fashion, celebrities, and family relationships, this magazine also features an advice column, craft projects, reviews, contests, quizzes, and profiles of notable teenage girls.

Highlights for Children; fun with a purpose. Highlights for Children, Inc. $29.64 per year (K and up)
ISSN 0018-165X

http://www.highlights.com/
Monthly.

This magazine "is intended for children of all ages . . . and carries stories, articles, and regular items appropriate to various reading and interest levels. The diversity of subject matter places this magazine among the few general-interest ones available for children. . . . [Included in each issue are] crafts and projects; puzzles, hidden pictures, and word games; and contributions from children." Richardson. Mag for Child. 2d edition

Hopscotch; for girls. Bluffton News Printing & Publishing Co. $22.95 per year (K-7)
ISSN 1044-0488

http://www.funforkidzmagazines.com/frameset.html?target=hs
Bi-monthly.

This magazine aimed at promoting reading and self-esteem among girls features stories, poetry, puzzles, crafts, science experiments, and contests.

Jack and Jill. Children's Better Health Institute $15.95 per year (2-4)
ISSN 0021-3829

http://cbhi.org/magazines/jackandjill/
Bi-monthly.

This health and safety magazine features articles on current events and other topics, stories, recipes, and puzzles.

Kids Discover. Kids Discover $19.95 per year (4-6)
ISSN 1054-2868

http://www.kidsdiscover.com
10 times a year.

Each theme-based issue features articles, bibliographies, experiments, and activities. Themes include topics as diverse as space exploration, weather, the pyramids, and the brain.

Ladybug; the magazine for young children. Carus Publishing Company $35.97 per year (PreK-1)
ISSN 1051-4961

http://www.cricketmag.com/ProductDetail.asp?pid=5&type=
Monthly.

A "beginning literary magazine for young children ages 2-6. The stories, poetry, and illustrations are engaging and new information is presented in stories and articles that are delightful. A parent section offers parent-child art activities. A 'Meet The Author' page and a list of book titles by the featured author are also included." Katz. Mag for Libr. 10th edition

Muse. Carus $32.97 per year (5 and up)
ISSN 1090-0381

http://www.cobblestonepub.com/magazine/MUS/
10 times a year.

This magazine aims to encourage kids to be more curious about the world around them and features articles on science, history, and art. "Each issue is filled with engaging photographs and illustrations, cartoons, a contest, activities, Web site recommendations, and reader letters." Publisher's note

National Geographic Kids. National Geographic Society $19.95 per year (4-6)
ISSN 1542-3042

http://www.nationalgeographic.com/ngkids
10 times a year.

Including games, posters, collectable cards, and stories, this is a "multitopic magazine covering animals, entertainment, science, technology, current events, and cultures from around the world." Publisher's note

New Moon: the magazine for girls and their dreams. New Moon $29.95 per year (5-9)
ISSN 1069-238X

http://www.newmoon.org
Bimonthly.

This periodical is edited by girls eight to 14 years old and features fiction, poems, articles, artwork, and letters from girls around the world.

Nickelodeon Magazine. Nickelodeon Magazine, Inc. $19.99 per year (3-9)
ISSN 1073-7510

http://www.nick.com/all%5Fnick/nick%5fmag/
10 times a year.

This magazine features stories, activities, cartoons, and articles on popular culture. Each issue of this magazine focuses on a special topic and features characters from programs aired on the Nickelodeon network.

Odyssey: adventures in science. Carus $29.95 per year (5-9)
ISSN 0163-0946

http://www.cobblestonepub.com/magazine/ODY/
9 times a year.

Each issue features articles on recent scientific discoveries, puzzles, hands-on activities, an animal column, a cartoon featuring astronomer Jack Horkheimer, and a monthly "Star Chart" for young astronomers. The magazine also publishes stories, poems, and artwork by kids.

Owl. Bayard Canada $33.99 per year (4-7)
ISSN 0382-6627

http://www.owlkids.com
10 times a year.

This magazine presents a variety of articles on science, art, and the environment. It also features an advice column, puzzles and activities.

Pack-O-Fun. Clapper $21.97 (4-7)
ISSN 0030-901X

http://www.pack-o-fun.com
6 times a year.

This magazine offers color photographs of finished themed arts and crafts projects. It includes step-by-step directions and lists of necessary materials for projects.

Plays; the drama magazine for young people. Plays Magazine $33 per year
ISSN 0032-1540

http://www.playsmag.com

Monthly October through May, except January/February combined.

Each issue of this magazine "offers approximately three plays for junior and senior high school students and three or more for the middle and lower grades. In addition, there is a dramatized classic and either a skit, a puppet play, or a choral reading. Production notes and stage directions accompany each play." Katz. Mag for Libr. 10th edition

Ranger Rick. National Wildlife Federation $17 per year (3 and up)
ISSN 0738-6656

http://www.nwf.org/gowild/

Monthly.

This magazine about animals and the environment for elementary school children "is filled with short stories and articles that are accompanied by colorful pictures and illustrations, often full-page." Katz. Mag for Libr. 10th edition

Sesame Street. Sesame Workshop $14.97 per year (PreK-1)
ISSN 0049-0253

http://www.sesameworkshop.org/sesamestreet/

10 times a year.

This magazine for young children teaches early learning concepts through stories and activities featuring the Sesame Street Muppets. Includes a separate Parents' Guide.

Skipping Stones: a multicultural magazine. Skipping Stones $35 per year (5-7)
ISSN 0899-529X

http://www.skippingstones.org

5 times a year.

This magazine features the writings and artwork of adults and young people from countries around the world, with an emphasis on international and multicultural education and communication.

Spider; the magazine for children. Carus Publishing Company $35.97 per year (1-3)
ISSN 1070-2911

http://www.cricketmag.com/ ProductDetail.asp?pid=9&type=

Monthly.

"A general-interest magazine with fiction, fairy and folk tales, poetry, crafts, and puzzles to interest early elementary age boys and girls. The large, lovely illustrations enhance the printed material. Opportunities are available for reader input and participation." Katz. Mag for Libr. 10th edition

Sports Illustrated for Kids. Time $24.95 per year (5 and up)
ISSN 1042-394X

http://www.sikids.com

Monthly.

Each issue features stories, trivia, color action photos, and posters for young sports fans.

Stone Soup: the magazine by young writers and artists. Children's Art Foundation $34 per year (4-7)
ISSN 0094-579X

http://www.stonesoup.com

6 times a year.

This magazine publishes works of fiction, poetry, and artwork by young people from around the world. It also pays a nominal fee for admissions that are accepted.

SuperScience. Scholastic Inc. $4.55 subscription per year per student for 10 or more copies (3-6)

http://teacher.scholastic.com/products/classmags/ superscience.htm

8 times a year (during school year).

"A science news magazine for grades 3-6. Each issue is theme-based and includes many color photos. Hands-on activities, experiments, and quizzes on the news stories actively engage students in the content. The teacher's guide provides background information, teaching strategies, discussion prompts, additional activities, reproducible worksheets, and answer keys. Feature articles are tied to curriculum areas through process skills addressed in each activity (e.g., observe, compare, use numbers, hypothesize, etc.). SuperScience features help teachers meet local, state, and national science education standards." Katz. Mag for Libr. 13th edition

Time for Kids Big Picture. Time, Inc $24.95 per year
ISSN 1528-6584

http://www.timeforkids.com/TFK/class/bp/

30 times a year.

This news magazine for grades K-1 "is for beginning readers with photos and easy-access text in two levels appropriate for emergent readers and readers moving into fluency. Connections to science, social studies, math, and the arts build vocabulary and prepare kids to read in the content areas." Katz. Mag for Libr. 13th edition

Time for Kids News Scoop. Time, Inc $24.95 per year

http://www.timeforkids.com/TFK/class/ns/

Weekly.

This news magazine "is for grades 2-3 and features a cover story with glossy photos, two shorter articles, and a game page called 'Time for Fun.'" Katz. Mag for Libr. 13th edition

Time for Kids World Report. Time, Inc $24.95 per year (4 and up)

http://www.timeforkids.com/TFK/class/wr/

Weekly.

This news magazine "introduces current events across the curriculum, and improves nonfiction reading skills. Writing assignments develop critical thinking skills, and passages similar to those found on benchmark tests help to prepare students for taking standardized tests." Katz. Mag for Libr. 13th edition

U S Kids. Children's Better Health Institute $22.95 per year (K-5)
ISSN 0895-9471

http://www.cbhi.org/magazines/uskids/

8 times a year.

This health and safety magazine publishes true-life stories about children around the same age as the readership, as well as games, puzzles, activities, and opportunities for readers to contribute to the magazine.

Wild Animal Baby. National Wildlife Federation $19.95 per year (PreK)
ISSN 1526-047X

http://www.nwf.org/wildanimalbaby/

10 times a year.

This magazine for very young children features stories, artwork, games, articles, and activities all featuring wild baby animals.

Your Big Backyard. National Wildlife Federation $15 per year (PreK-1)
ISSN 0886-5299

http://www.nwf.org/kids/kzPage.cfm?siteid=2

Monthly.

This magazine introduces children to science and nature through stories, riddles, poems, activities, and games.

Zoobooks. Wildlife Education Ltd. $20.95 per year (4-6)
ISSN 0737-9005

http://www.zoobooks.com

12 times a year.

Each issue features articles, color photographs, illustrations, and interactive games focused on a specific animal.

Zoonooz. Zoological Society of San Diego Free to membership
ISSN 0044-5282

http://www.sandiegozoo.org/membership/zoonooz.html

Monthly.

This magazine describes the activities and exhibits of the San Diego Zoo. It includes illustrated articles written by members of the Zoo's staff.

Zootles. Wildlife Education Ltd. $20.90 per year (PreK-1)

http://www.zoobooks.com/store/Zootles-Subscription-P224C0.aspx

6 times a year.

Each issue of this magazine for children ages 2 through 6 focuses on a different animal, describing its habitat, basic anatomy, and behavior. It also features activities, stories and cartoons.

LIST OF RECOMMENDED ELECTRONIC RESOURCES

A. Pintura: Art Detective. Educational Web Adventures Free (4 and up)

http://www.eduweb.com/pintura

An online game about art history and art composition, in which players attempt to identify a painting's artist by examining paintings by famous artists from Gauguin to Van Gogh for composition, style and subject. Three other art history games are linked.

Absurd Math. Learningwave Free (5 and up)

http://www.learningwave.com/abmath/

In this online interactive game, players work to overthrow a tyranny which punishes all thought, and mathematical thought in particular. They are presented with a series of pre-algebra problems of increasing difficulty as they approach success. The mathematics requires knowledge of arithmetic up to decimal fractions, and email help is available.

Academy of reading. TE21 Contact producer for pricing (K-12)

http://www.te21.com/academyofreading.asp

By subscription only. Tel. 843-579-2520

Designed to teach reading skills in a developmental continuum, Academy of Reading targets children at all levels, helping them sequentially improve phonemic awareness, reading subskills, word recognition, and oral/silent reading comprehension. Features a "Teacher Time" function that will not allow a child who is having difficulty with a concept to proceed until a teacher intervenes. Includes a management system, a metronome tool for nudging children forward, and student prizes for mastery of concepts (i.e., clues to complete a puzzle, etc.). Educators should note that consistent use of the program in short segments of fifteen to twenty minutes three to five days a week is recommended for optimal results.

Alien Empire. Public Broadcasting Service Free (3-6)

http://www.pbs.org/wnet/nature/alienempire/index.html

Provides pictures, sounds, animation, and videos on insects. Articles discuss insect reproduction, societies, migration, and survival strategies. Includes animated presentations on monarch butterflies, mayflies, and bees and a list of insect information resources.

All About Birds. Cornell Lab of Ornithology Free (4 and up)

http://www.birds.cornell.edu/AllAboutBirds/

Organized into six different sections (Birding 1-2-3, Bird Guide, Gear Guide, Attracting Birds, Learn about Birds, and Conservation), this beautiful site introduces hundreds of birds by taxonomy or alphabetically, followed by its description, sound, conservation status, cool facts, and other species accounts. Features such as Bird of the Week, Bird News, and an editor's blog keep this site fresh, while continuing to offer solid information for anyone interested in birds and their survival.

Amazon Interactive. Educational Web Adventures Free (3-6)

http://www.eduweb.com/amazon.html

Explains the geography of the Ecuadorian Amazon and the culture of the Quichua people through online games and activities. In one interactive game, players try to set up and manage a sustainable, community-based ecotourism project along the Río Napo.

America The Beautiful Online. Grolier Educational Contact producer for pricing; minimum of two databases (4 and up)

http://www.go.grolier.com

By subscription only. Tel. 888-326-6546

A national and state reference (including territories) with over 1000 articles covering: history, economy, government, cities and capitals, rivers and lakes, geography and landforms. Articles are enhanced with photos, maps, narrated slide shows, and pre-selected Web links on the Grolier Internet Index. Profiles of famous Americans include every president. Information on national parks, natural wonders, monuments, museums, zoos, and historical places is also included. Key word searches can be limited to article titles or full text with the use of Boolean operators. The site also includes an almanac and a dictionary. Lesson plans and activities are provided for teachers.

American Government. ABC-CLIO $499/yr. (6 and up)

http://www.abc-clio.com/products/overview.aspx?productid=109714

By subscription only. Tel. 800-368-6868

Comprehensive resource on all aspects of American Government that includes topic overviews, essays, court cases, biographies, speeches, and historical documents. Students can explore pre-designed topics such as Congressional Powers, the Presidency, Civil Rights, and Political Parties or search by key word. Advanced searches can be limited by topic and categories (movements, organizations, statistics, quotes, etc.). The Home page provides changing news articles and feature stories linked to related articles in the database. Instructors can customize the site by adding announcements, syllabi, calendar of assignments, tests, etc. Teachers also have access to professional articles and links to additional resources. Includes the *Merriam Webster Dictionary*.

"Well designed, with good content and strategically placed links. Students will enjoy digging deep into this source." Libr J

American History. ABC-CLIO $599/yr. (6 and up)

http://www.abc-clio.com/products/overview.aspx?productid=109716

By subscription only. Tel. 800-368-6868

Provides coverage and resources on American history from 1350 to the present. The Home page includes feature stories and current events with links to related articles. Information can be searched by key word or phrase

American History—*Continued*

as well as through advanced searches by category, including documents, quotes, timelines, and type of multimedia. Instructors can customize the site by adding announcements, syllabi, calendar of assignments, tests, etc. Teachers also have access to professional articles and links to additional resources. Includes the *Merriam Webster Dictionary.*

"An easily navigable, appealing and comprehensive resource that would be extremely useful for the study of United States history." Evalutech

America's Story. Library of Congress Free (5 and up)

http://www.americaslibrary.gov/cgi-bin/page.cgi

This site sets out to "put the story back in history" for children, using letters, diaries, records and tapes, films, sheet music, maps, prints, and photographs from the Library of Congress collections. Includes sections on famous Americans, on each historical period, and on popular culture.

Animals A to Z. Oakland Zoo Free (3-6)

http://www.oaklandzoo.org/atoz/atoz.html

A database of text, pictures, sounds, and video on approximately one hundred zoo animals.

Ask Dr. Math. Drexel University Free (1 and up)

http://mathforum.org/dr.math

This website, run by math majors at Drexel University, answers submitted mathematics questions and offers math advice for elementary, middle, high school, and college students.

Backyard biology. National Zoo Free (4 and up)

http://nationalzoo.si.edu/Animals/BackyardBiology/default.cfm

This site from the National Zoo in Washington, D.C. uses "its own grounds as a lens for learning about the 'backyard biology' that is present right within this major metropolitan area. The right-hand side of the site is well worth starting with, as it contains three thematic areas: 'Celebrate', 'Study', and 'Protect'. In each area, visitors may browse through a set of resources dedicated to science articles, identification guides, and other such materials." Internet Scout

Become A Historical Detective. Library of Congress Free (6 and up)

http://memory.loc.gov/learn/features/detect/detectiv.html

Teaches research by posing a question about a historical mystery and giving hints on finding the answer. Includes links to the American Memory collection of primary historical source materials.

Between the Lions: Get Wild About Reading. WGBH Boston and Sirius Thinking, Ltd., in association with Mississippi Public Broadcasting Free (K-3)

http://pbskids.org/lions/

Supporting the PBS television series by the same name, this site provides a Story of the Week, activities that build interest and strength pre-reading and reading and vocabulary skills, a list of recommended books, and usage tips for parents and teachers.

Biology of Plants. Missouri Botanical Garden Free (4 and up)

http://www.mbgnet.net/

Focusing on the growth and reproductive cycles of plants at a reading and interest level appropriate for children, this site offers videos and/or animations of processes such as germination, pollination, and seed dispersal.

BLS Career Information. U.S. Bureau of Labor Statistics Free (5 and up)

http://www.bls.gov/k12/

Provides ideas for what to do when one grows up, and how to set about doing so, for children interested in the arts, mathematics, science, physical activities, the outdoors, social science, or reading.

Born in Slavery. Library of Congress Free (5 and up)

http://memory.loc.gov/ammem/snhtml/snhome.html

Contains more than 2,300 first-person oral histories of slavery and 500 black-and-white photographs of former slaves collected in the 1930s as part of the Federal Writers' Project. Some narratives contain descriptions of shocking cruelty while others convey an almost nostalgic view of plantation life. Many narratives contain a word commonly used by African Americans in the 1930s South when speaking of themselves that some children may find horrifying.

British Library: Listen to Nature. British Library Free (4 and up)

http://www.bl.uk/listentonature

"The British Library's new Listen to Nature web site features 400 recordings selected from the more than 150,000 animal sounds held by the Library. Listen to Nature can be browsed by location, animal type, or habitat. Maps are provided with red dots plotting the locations of recordings; clicking any dot launches a player and the sound file. Alphabetical lists of animal sounds also accompany maps from the region." Internet Scout

Build a Prairie. Bell Museum of Natural History Free (3-6)

http://www.bellmuseum.org/distancelearning/prairie/

In this interactive game, players restore a prairie to its native state. They reintroduce native grasses, wildflowers, birds, animals, and insects, taking care not to introduce exotic, invasive species. Upon successfully completing each stage, they are shown an animation of their prairie's progress.

C.E.R.F. (Curriculum and Education Resource Finder). Media Flex $500/yr. (K and up)

http://www.cerfinfo.com/

By subscription only. Tel. 877-331-1022

A directory of weekly updated Web sites that have been pre-screened and selected for use in the instructional setting. Users can search for sites by key word (with Boolean operators), by topic lists, or by grade level range (including professional). Information about each site includes the title, hyperlinked URL, relevant subject areas, correlations to McREL standards, and cross references to related topics. Sites can also be saved to a bibliography with an option to e-mail results.

"A big plus for C.E.R.F. is the extensive use of links from outside the United States, giving a more global perspective to inquiry." Book Report

Cats: Plans for Perfection. National Geographic Society Free (3-6)

http://www.nationalgeographic.com/features/97/cats

This site is organized around the conceit that all feline species were designed by a team of engineers, who faced engineers' usual difficulties with budgets and schedules. As it tells the story of the design project's progress, the site teaches the relationship between feline structure and function.

Celebrate Hispanic heritage! Scholastic, Inc. Free (2 and up)

http://teacher.scholastic.com/activities/hispanic/

"This innovative site provides students with an opportunity to 'discover the contributions and rich cultures of Hispanics in the United States' through biographies, timelines links, and more. Students can access 'Hispanic History in the Americas' which opens an interactive map linked to information about Hispanic/Latino nations and people, 'Meet Famous Latinos,' a set of profiles of several noted celebrities, and 'Latinos in History,' a database of 25 biographies." SLJ

Children's Butterfly Site. Montana State University Free (4-6)

http://bsi.montana.edu/web/kidsbutterfly/

An expert on butterflies answers questions frequently asked by children and a gallery exhibits photographs of common butterflies from around the world, indexed by continent. Children may submit their own questions to the expert if they are not already answered on the site.

Children's Literature Comprehensive Database. CLCD Company, LLC. From $275/yr.

http://www.childrenslit.com/home.htm

By subscription only. Tel. 800-469-2070

The database contains more than 1,200,000 MARC records and 200,000 reviews from baby board books to young adult novels drawn from sources such as *Children's Literature Newsletter, Kirkus, Science Books and Films,* and *VOYA.* Reviews can be searched by key word with options to limit by category (fiction or nonfiction), genre, age, language, author/illustrator, publisher, publication date, and search term qualifiers such as exact phrase and singular or plural forms. Search results are ranked in relevancy order and each record provides a one-sentence annotation, text of reviews, as well as hyperlinks to related subject terms and other works by the author and reviewers.

"This is a great resource for librarians, media specialists, teachers, and parents." SLJ

Connected University. Classroom Connect Contact producer for pricing

http://www.cu.classroom.com

By subscription only. Tel. 800-638-1639

Connected University offers educators 24-hour a day access to instructor-led courses, self-paced courses, technology "how to" tips, and software tutorials. Courses are available on a broad range of topics from teaching reading standards to how to build a Web page. Graduate credits and continuing education units can be obtained from partner universities. Thousands of pre-screened, educator-friendly web sites are provided in the CU Library.

Cosmic Quest. Children's Museum of Indianapolis Free (4 and up)

http://www.childrensmuseum.org/cosmicquest/index.html

Site divided into three separate sections: Living in Space: Design a Space Station (a game); Field Guide to the Universe with detailed information about the planets, spacecraft, and astronomers; and Expedition to the Magnetic North Pole.

Curriculum Resource Center, Junior Edition. Facts on File Contact producer for pricing (3-6)

http://www.factsonfile.com/

By subscription only. Tel. 800-322-8755

Database of copyright-free, reproducible, black-and-white and color maps, historical maps, graphs, charts, timelines, illustrations, and other handout materials with visual content and text. Subjects dealt with are people and events in history, countries and states, science, and careers. The materials in this database display in Adobe Acrobat (link to free download provided).

Digital Learning Center for Microbial Ecology— The Microbe Zoo. Michigan State University Free (3-6)

http://commtechlab.msu.edu/sites/dlc-me/zoo/

Includes pictures and descriptions of microbes and explanations of how they interact with their environment and each other. Exhibits are arranged in pavilions representing the habitats in which they naturally dwell, such as the compost heap, the toxic waste dump, the human body, the termite gut, and several others.

DigitalCurriculum.com. AIMS Multimedia Contact producer for pricing

http://www.digitalcurriculum.com/

By subscription only. Tel. 800-367-2467

DigitalCurriculum.com provides access to over a thousand curriculum-based educational videos, or indexed key concept clips of the videos. The program sends these videos to the school via the Internet using video streaming/downloading technology. Schools and districts can also place the videos on their local or wide area network. The general program covers a variety of subjects including Science, Social Science, Language Arts, Reading, Health, Guidance, Mathematics, and Drivers Education.

Dino directory. The Natural History Museum Free (3-10)

http://internt.nhm.ac.uk/jdsml/nature-online/dino-directory/

"This database of dinosaur information and illustrations from the Natural History Museum in London, England, has an interface that provides multiple paths for accessing dinosaur data. The user may browse entries alphabetically, by geologic timeline (Upper Triassic to Upper Cretaceous periods), by geographic location, or by body shape. Each entry contains a black-and-white drawing and an enhanced action drawing (based on speculative estimates of coloring and habitats). . . . The text for each entry indicates such fundamental information as pronunciation, taxonomy, size, diet, and range. . . . Dino Directory serves admirably in its role as a well-organized source of basic information on these fascinating ancient reptiles." Evalutech

Discover the History of Life. University of California Museum of Paleontology Free (5 and up)

http://www.ucmp.berkeley.edu/historyoflife/histoflife.html

Discover the History of Life—*Continued*

Online exhibits explain how the theories of phylogeny, geology, and evolution fit together in paleontology. Also includes pages on special exhibits and a mystery fossil identification game.

Discovering Lewis and Clark. VIAs, Inc. Free (4-12)

http://www.lewis-clark.org/

"Discovering Lewis and Clark provides three paths to explore the most extraordinary journey in American history. Professor Harry Fritz's account of the adventure is divided into 19 segments, accessible from the 'Expedition' menu. Excerpts from the journal may be accessed directly from a menu of the entry dates. Finally, a 'Discovery Paths' menu leads to a fascinating series of special features that offer high interest information about various aspects of the expedition and the historical milieu. Multimedia materials include sound files, photographs, maps, and motion pictures. The value of this site in the American history classroom extends far beyond the scope of the expedition itself, due to its coverage of the societal context of the Jeffersonian era." Evalutech

Discovery School. Discovery Channel Free

http://school.discovery.com/

This site provides "teaching materials for teachers, . . . resources for students, and . . . advice for parents about how to help their kids enjoy learning and excel in school. The site is . . . reviewed for educational relevance by practicing classroom teachers in elementary school, middle school, and high school." Publisher's note

Dragonfly. University of Miami Free (3-5)

http://www.units.muohio.edu/dragonfly/

Clicking on a picture or on a list of topics moves one to sections containing articles, pictures, and interactive educational games on such subjects as animal flight, ecosystems, trees, skeletons, animal communication, navigation, and genetics.

Earth Science Explorer. Wheeling Jesuit University/NASA Free (4 and up)

http://www.cotf.edu/ete/modules/msese/explorer.html

This site is organized around the floor plan of a museum, one floor of which is devoted to earth sciences and the other of which is devoted to dinosaurs. The earth sciences section contains tutorials on geologic time, plate tectonics, geological cycles, and biomes. The dinosaur section presents various contending theories of dinosaur extinction and invites one to decide which is most plausible. Teacher section password protected.

Education world: math center. George Washington University Free

http://www.education-world.com/a%5Flesson/archives/math.shtml

"Education World offers a wealth of instructional resources for teachers. This section of the website is devoted to mathematics resources, primarily articles and lesson ideas. Each lesson idea lists the appropriate grade levels for the activity, the Standards and instructional goals addressed through the activity, supplies needed, key words to learn, and assessment strategies. The articles address various topics in teacher professional development and school administration." Internet Scout

eLibrary Elementary. ProQuest Contact producer for pricing (K-6)

http://www.proquestk12.com/productinfo/elibrary%5Felementary.shtml

By subscription only. Tel. 800-521-0600 x3344

Age appropriate online research of 130 full-text magazine, newspaper, book, and transcript resources, plus thousands of maps and pictures. Searches can be entered by key word with Boolean operators or in natural language format. There are options to limit searches by format: newspapers, magazine articles, reference books (*World Book*, *World Almanac for Kids*, *Webster's New World Dictionary*), pictures, maps, radio and television transcripts. Search results are listed with the reading level by grade and icons to designate the type of resource. Results can be sorted in relevancy order or by date, reading level, or media type. Includes a dictionary and a thesaurus.

eNature.com. Audubon Society Free (4 and up)

http://www.enature.com

Audubon field guides online and searchable, with descriptions and color photographs of over 4,800 North American plants and animals. If given a zip code, the site will provide descriptions and pictures of birds native to that region.

Encarta. Microsoft Corporation Free

http://encarta.msn.com/

Online access to the Encarta encyclopedia by entering a question or a keyword. Sections include: reference, homework, college prep, grad school, e-learning, parents, genealogy, and products. Quick reference tools include encyclopedia, dictionary and atlas. Content includes text, graphic, audio and video files. Quicktime three is needed for playing video files.

Encyclopedia of educational technology. San Diego State University Department of Educational Technology Free

http://coe.sdsu.edu/eet/admin/index.htm

"Offers a collection of short multimedia articles from various authors discussing topics related to the fields of instructional design, and education and training. . . . The Table of Contents is divided into the following main topics: Cognition and Learning, Analysis, Design, Development, Implementation, and Evaluation. For each subtopic the site provides a short explanation and related video demonstrations, images, or examples to help explain the topic, and links to related topics. Visitors will find overviews of topics such as Vygotsky's Zone of Proximal Development (ZPD), eLearning, Web accessibility, and authentic assessment." Internet Scout

Encyclopedia Smithsonian. Smithsonian Institution Free

http://www.si.edu/resource/faq/start.htm

This site provides an alphabetical list of links to Smithsonian resources, the subjects ranging from advertising to zoology.

eTAP. eTAP, Inc. $89/yr.

http://www.etap.org

By subscription only. Tel. 949-497-2200

Short for "electronic teaching assistance program," this resource provides a K-12 curriculum in the subjects of mathematics, English, history and science. It provides educators with lesson plans, instructions for assignments,

eTAP—*Continued*

links to web sites on key topics, practice exercises that can be used as worksheet assignments for students, tests modeled after standardized exams, and a problem section that can be printed out and used for student assessment.

Exploratorium. The museum of science, art and human perception at the Palace of Fine Arts, San Francisco Free (K and up)

http://www.exploratorium.edu

From frogs to Saturn, sports to optical illusions, this digital science museum takes kids and their teachers through a variety of high-interest topics. True to its name, the Exploratorium allows children to learn at their own speed, introducing them to solar flares through realtime tracking, gravity and momentum by examining skateboard physics, and the difference between cold-blooded and warm-blooded animals via an earlier frog exhibit. Teachers will appreciate the many science activities and experiments as well as an impressive digital library.

Exploring Leonardo. Boston Museum of Science Free (5 and up)

http://www.mos.org/sln/Leonardo/
LeoHomePage.html

Interactive site describes some of Leonardo's inventions, and gives a chance to analyze them and design others. Explains his system of perspective, provides a brief biography, and discusses his habit of writing in reverse.

Exploring the Planets. National Air and Space Museum Free (4 and up)

http://www.nasm.si.edu/research/ceps/etp/etp.htm

Explains how the planets of the solar system have been explored from Earth and by spacecraft. Includes information on and photographs of each planet, of asteroids, and of comets. In an activity, one describes satellite photographs and compares one's descriptions to those of an astronomer.

Fake Out. Houghton Mifflin Free (3-6)

http://www.eduplace.com/fakeout

In this variation of a classic word game, players are given an improbable, but actual, word and a set of plausible definitions among which to select. Players are invited to invent plausible definitions for upcoming words.

Federal Resources for Educational Excellence. U.S. Department of Education Free

http://www.ed.gov/free/index.html

Lists hundreds of educational Web sites supported by U.S. government agencies. Subjects include arts, educational technology, foreign languages, health and safety, language arts, mathematics, physical education, science, social studies, and vocational education.

FirstGov for Kids. Federal Citizen Information Center, U.S. General Services Administration Free (4 and up)

http://www.kids.gov/

The U.S. government gateway for children, which provides links to Federal kids' sites as well as those from other organizations. Websites are organized by subject, and subjects include arts, computers, health, and science and math.

Geography Software: Beginners Geography, USA Geography, World Geography, and Your State Geography. Click and Learn Software $995/yr.; available as a package with other Click and Learn products for $2995/yr., or $1495/yr. for schools with up to 300 users

http://www.clickandlearn.com

By subscription only. Tel. 888-254-2550

Geography Software: Beginners Geography, USA Geography, World Geography, and Your State Geography is an online product that features a Learning Machine with geographical instructional games for students and lesson plans for the teacher. It is also available as a package including other Click and Learn products (State Standards, Early Learning, Mathematics, Anatomy, Music, and Plate Tectonics).

Get Ready to Read! National Center for Learning Disabilities Free

http://www.getreadytoread.org/

Focused on early literacy, with an additional area for K-8 learning disabilities, this site provides an easy-to-administer, research-based screening tool and a variety of reading and pre-reading activities to early childhood educators, child care providers, and parents in order to help them prepare all children to learn to read and write. Includes a Spanish language section.

Ghosts in the Castle. National Geographic Society Free (3-6)

http://www.nationalgeographic.com/castles/
enter.html

As one tours a virtual castle, ghosts reminisce about their lives there.

Girl Power: Bodywise. U.S. Department of Health and Human Services Free (4 and up)

http://www.girlpower.gov/girlarea/bodywise/
Index.htm

Targets girls 9-13 to sustain positive body image by highlighting nutrition, fitness, body image, and facts about eating disorders.

Great Plant Escape. University of Illinois Extension in Urbana Free (4 and up)

http://www.urbanext.uiuc.edu/gpe/

This is "an elementary program for 4th and 5th grade students. Each of the lessons in this program is interdisciplinary, designed to introduce students to plant science and increase their understanding of how foods grow. Activities enhance student's math, science, language arts, social studies, music and art." Publisher's note

Great web sites for kids. American Library Association Free

http://www.ala.org/greatsites

Lists children's sites selected for clear statement of authorship and sponsorship, clearly defined purpose, good design, stability, and use of sound information to inform, educate, or entertain. Subjects include arts and entertainment, literature and language, people, geography, and science and technology.

Grolier Multimedia Encyclopedia Online. Grolier Educational Contact producer for pricing; minimum of two databases (5 and up)

http://www.go.grolier.com

Grolier Multimedia Encyclopedia Online—*Continued*

By subscription only. Tel. 888-326-6546

General encyclopedia covering all subjects with multimedia and current events. Information can be located by browsing categories such U.S. history, language and literature, life sciences, and technology or by key word searches. Advanced searches can be limited to article titles or full text with the use of Boolean operators. Articles include hyperlinked cross references, related Web links, and bibliographies. There are also links to related magazine articles provided by EBSCO. The Brain Jam feature changes frequently and explores a topic in more depth, enhanced with Web links, activities, and teacher resources.

"A wonderfully easy-to-use title that provides good overviews to large topics, good definitions and brief biographies, and highly useful cross-referencing. . . . Highly recommended for public and school libraries." Libr J

A Guided Tour of the Visible Human. MadSci Network Free (5 and up)

http://www.madsci.org/%7Elynn/VH/tour.html

The Visible Human Project has taken over 18,000 sections of a human body, scanned them, and made the images available over the Internet. This site uses some of the scanned images in an anatomy tutorial. Animations are used to explain how to visualize transverse, coronal, and sagittal sections in three dimensions.

Healthfinder Kids. Office of Disease Prevention and Health Promotion, U.S. Department of Health and Human Services Free (4 and up)

http://www.healthfinder.gov/kids/

This government site is divided into four categories: Cool and Uncool Stuff, Safe Surfing, Games, and Art Contests. The Cool and Uncool Stuff section provides links to both Federal sites and sites from other organizations related to health and medicine, and organized by subject. Subjects include alcohol, environmental health, and nutrition.

The Hero's Journey. Maricopa Center for Learning and Instruction Free (5 and up)

http://www.mcli.dist.maricopa.edu/smc/journey

In The Hero with a Thousand Faces, Joseph Campbell writes that hero myths follow a general formula. This site provides an interactive form based on this formula, with which writers can construct mythic, heroic stories.

History explorer. National Museum of American History Free (4 and up)

http://americanhistory.si.edu/explorer/index.cfm

"Allows those surfing the Web to browse through an interactive timeline of American history. The interface is composed of items from the Museum's various online collections, exhibitions and programs, such as Plymouth Rock and a world map from 1511. Visitors can zoom in and out through the timeline and its objects and also elect to toggle on or off various themes, such as 'Arts and Culture', 'Peopling America', and 'Politics and Reform'. Overall, this is a very well-thought-out tool for learning about American history and one that will engage a wide range of persons." Internet Scout

Homeroom.com. The Princeton Review Contact producer for pricing

http://k12.princetonreview.com/
homeroom%5Findex.asp

By subscription only. Tel. 800-REVIEW-2

Homeroom.com is a web based assessment and diagnostic tool containing over 130,000 math, reading, and language arts questions and over 10,000 instructional resources aligned to all state standards, major classroom textbooks, and specific state and national tests. There are an average of 10 instructional resources per tested skill. The program can be used to assess, analyze, and remediate strengths and weaknesses of student skills. It allows teachers to generate practice assessments that are correlated to state or city standards and the textbook used in the classroom. It directs teachers and students to targeted educational resources, customized to each tested skill, based on individual and group performance.

Homework Center. Multnomah Public Library Free

http://www.multcolib.org/homework/index.html

This browsable selection of internet resources is organized by topics most commonly requested for homework assignments. Sites are selected and annotated by librarians and an online question feature allows immediate access to a librarian of the Mulnomah Public Library.

How stuff works. BYG Publishing, Inc. Free (3-10)

http://www.howstuffworks.com/

This site "tackles typical childhood questions such as 'Why is the sky blue?' as well as more esoteric issues, such as 'What does WD-40 mean?' . . . A 'Question-of-the-Day' feature provides responses to reader questions and includes an archive that may be accessed in chronological order or by category. Additional useful features include a section on how to cite the articles, and lists of related Web sites. The expanded scope of How Stuff Works will make it an invaluable tool for the science class, as well as a potentially useful resource for other disciplines." Evalutech

How Things Work. University of Virginia Free (6 and up)

http://rabi.phys.virginia.edu/HTW/

A professor of physics answers email questions about how things—machines, everyday processes, toys, and games, among others—work. The explanations are as complete as they can be without mathematics, but the language is not needlessly technical. Includes an archive of answered questions.

Hunkin's Experiments. Pelham Projects Ltd. Free (4 and up)

http://www.HunkinsExperiments.com

A cartoonist with an engineering degree provides sketches of how to do hundreds of demonstrations, illusions, and tricks. Examples include how to move a mug of water by balloon, to peel bananas automatically, to photograph the path of a pendulum, to prove 1 = 2, to prove there is no black in a television picture, to pull a string through your neck, and to push a cube through the middle of a cube the same size.

InfoTrac Junior Edition. Gale Group Contact producer for pricing (5-8)

http://www.galegroup.com

By subscription only. Tel. 800-877-4253

InfoTrac Junior Edition features full-text articles from periodical titles relevant to the interests and curriculum needs of upper elementary, junior high, and middle school students. Broad search term results offer suggest-

InfoTrac Junior Edition—*Continued*
ed narrower terms with related subdivisions and types of source documents. An optional child-friendly interface is available that includes a Toolbox with tips for doing research and writing reports. Newspapers and magazines are updated daily. Includes a dictionary feature and maps.

Inside Art. Educational Web Adventures Free (4 and up)

http://www.eduweb.com/insideart/index.html

An online game which explores a painting from the inside out. During an art museum tour, players are sucked into a vortex and find themselves inside Van Gogh's Bank of the Oise at Auvers. Their only hope of escape is, with the help of a fish named Trish, to place the painting in its artistic and historical context.

Interactive Online Exhibits. London Natural History Museum Free (3 and up)

http://www.nhm.ac.uk/interactive/index.html

Among these exhibits are a video feed from a leafcutter ant colony, a database of dinosaur pictures, a multimedia presentation on eclipses, and an online game in which players use various instruments to identify objects from the museum's collection.

International Children's Digital Library. University of Maryland's Human-Computer Interaction Lab, and The Internet Archive Free (All ages)

http://www.icdlbooks.org/

The mission of the ICDL is to select, collect, digitize, and organize children's materials in their original languages and to create appropriate technologies for access and use by children 3-13 years old. To that end, over 1500 books are available in 10 different languages.

It's international. Topics Online Magazine Free (4-12)

http://www.topics-mag.com/internatl/center.htm

Published by an online magazine aimed at students and teachers of English as a second language, this site aims to create a forum for ESL students to share their experiences. Sections include "World of Tastes—Food, markets . . . and more!", "Holidays, Festivals, Celebrations" and "Traditional Clothing."

"Vivid details, illustrations, and photos of dress, food, and family traditions enhance instruction and student research." SLJ

Junior Reference Collection. Gale Group Contact producer for pricing (K-12)

http://www.gale.com/jrc/

By subscription only. Tel. 800-877-4253

This is an online version of the Gale Group's U·X·L electronic resources for students and librarians that combines the information from U·X·L Biographies 2.0, U·X·L Science, U·X·L Junior DISCovering Authors 2.0, U·X·L Junior Worldmark, U·X·L Multicultural, and U·X·L Encyclopedia of Science 2nd ed., with entries written at an appropriate reading level. The combined database provides an interface that permits searching by person, places, author, book, and multimedia, and it includes three Merriam-Webster dictionaries and a timeline with over 4000 entries.

"This database combines the wonderful UXL reference tools . . . in a user-friendly interface that is appropriate for upper elementary and middle school students." SLJ

Kid Territory. San Diego Zoo Free (3-6)

http://www.sandiegozoo.org/kids/index.html

Includes biographical profiles of zoo animals, job descriptions of zoo workers, articles on zookeeping, and games.

Kids InfoBits. Gale Group Contact producer for pricing (K-5)

http://www.gale.com/InfoBits/

By subscription only. Tel. 800-877-4253

This database offers a "user-friendly interface to children's and general interest periodicals, reference materials, and newspaper articles. . . . A sampling of the periodical titles includes Cobblestone, Current Science, Jack & Jill, National Geographic for Kids, and Ranger Rick. On the home page, cartoonlike icons represent 12 content areas, among them Animals, Geography, Stories and Literature, History and Social Studies, Transportation, Health, and Sports. . . . Kids InfoBits does an excellent job of preparing elementary-grade students to research other Gale databases and, by extension, databases in general." Booklist

Kids Space Connection. Kids Space Free (3-6)

http://www.ks-connection.org/home.cfm

Children may post messages or stories on bulletin boards, search for pen pals, and post links to their Web pages. Postings are screened to protect children's privacy and safety.

Kids Web Japan. Web Japan Free (4 and up)

http://web-japan.org/kidsweb/index.html

"Sponsored by the Japanese Ministry of Foreign Affairs, Kids Web Japan aims to introduce Japanese culture to students worldwide. Launched in 1996, the site is continuously updated and offers many links regarding the region, government, language, [folk legends,] and education." SLJ

Kids web: the digital library for K-12 students. Northeast Parallel Architectures Center at Syracuse University Free (K-12)

http://www.npac.syr.edu/textbook/kidsweb/

"Kids Web is a digital library for K-12 students that aims to 'present students with a subset of the Web that is very simple to navigate, and contains information targeted at the K-12 level.' . . . The collection of websites is organized into the following subject areas: Arts, Sciences, Social Studies, and Miscellaneous. The Miscellaneous section currently includes some games and reference resources, such as dictionaries and economic data. The Science section includes websites on topics such as mathematics, computers, technology, and meteorology." Internet Scout

KidsClick!. Ramapo Catskill Library System Free

http://www.kidsclick.org/

Lists sites selected to inform or entertain children from kindergarten to seventh grade in Dewey Decimal System order. Includes a child's search engine and a child's tutorial on Internet searching.

Landmarks for schools. The Landmark Project Free

http://www.landmark-project.com/index.php

Maintained and created by educator and consultant David Warlick, the site's features include the

Landmarks for schools—*Continued*
Blogmeister, a special blog for educators and their students; PiNet, a section that allows an educator to create and house a personal library of links; the New Century Schoolhouse where visitors can adopt a classroom and design it for 21st Century learning; the Education Podcast Network, a compilation of educational podcasting for teacher use; and a Web Tools site that includes a rubric builder and citation machine.

Lands and Peoples Online. Grolier Educational Contact producer for pricing; minimum of two databases (4 and up)

http://www.go.grolier.com

By subscription only. Tel. 888-326-6546

An international geography reference based on the print version. Articles have hyperlinked outlines and cross references and include photos, maps, flags, facts and figures, and Internet links. A Culture Cross feature enables users to compare two countries, continents, or states/provinces from the perspective of land, people, economy, history, or facts and figures. Also included are highlights of current events around the world, an atlas, an almanac, and games and quizzes for students.

"The ease of navigation and the multiple access points make it easy for beginning researchers to find what they need. The ability to create specific searches and locate precise elements of information make Lands and Peoples online attractive for more sophisticated assignments as well." Booklist

A **Lifetime** of Color. Sanford Free

http://www.sanford-artedventures.com/index.html

This site features four major sections: Create Art, Hands-on activities, technique demos and more; Study Art, Art history, glossary terms, and artist biographies; Play Art Games, ArtEdventures and online activities about art history and art concepts; and Teach Art, Lesson plans for classroom and art teachers.

Math Forum Problems. Drexel University Contact producer for pricing (4 and up)

http://mathforum.org/library/problems/

By membership only. Tel. 800-756-7823

An archive of elementary, middle school, geometry, algebra, discrete mathematics, trigonometry, and calculus word problems, each with a variety of solutions.

Mind Over Matter. National Institute on Drug Abuse Free (5 and up)

http://www.nida.nih.gov/mom/momindex.html

Describes the effects of specific drugs or drug types on the anatomy and physiology of the brain and the body and on the way in which these drug-induced changes affect both behavior and emotion. Care is taken to provide necessary background information on brain functioning.

Museum of Ancient Inventions. Smith College Free (4 and up)

http://www.smith.edu/hsc/museum/
ancient%5Finventions/hsclist.htm

Pictures and descriptions of replicas of forty-six ancient devices, with explanations of how they work and why they were important. Devices range from the distaff and the hoe, to toys and cosmetics, to a lighthouse and a ship breaker.

The **Mystery** Spot: Access Excellence Mysteries. National Health Museum Free (6 and up)

http://www.accessexcellence.org/AE/mspot

Interactive, online scientific mysteries teach problem-solving and inquiry. In one, players must decide whether an outbreak of sickness on a racing yacht is dangerous enough to require breaking off the race.

NASA Explores. NASA Free (4 and up)

http://www.nasaexplores.com/

This site contains articles discussing recent scientific research at NASA. Each article is available at reading levels appropriate for elementary school students, middle school students, and high school students and comes replete with teacher lesson plans and student worksheets.

National Geographic news. National Geographic Society Free (4 and up)

http://news.nationalgeographic.com/news/

"Provides access to many of the day's most compelling news, including updates on the Space Shuttle launches and new archaeological discoveries. The news stories are thematically organized around such familiar topics as animals and nature, health, and the environment. The feature section titled 'Pulse of the Planet' is a nice find, along with the 'Offbeat' area, which offers a bit of lighter news coverage." Internet Scout

Native languages of the Americas: facts for kids. Native Languages of the Americas Free (5 and up)

http://www.native-languages.org/kids.htm

"Over 30 tribal languages are described with alphabets, dictionaries, and pronunciation guides, and many come with sound files. Unfamiliar words, or Indian terms in general are highlighted and are linked to either a glossary, or another site with detailed explanations. Most of the individual language pages come with links to the homepages of the tribes themselves." SLJ

Natural History Notebooks. Canadian Museum of Nature Free (3-6)

http://www.nature.ca/NOTEBOOKS/english/
mon2.htm

Provides short descriptions and sketches of 246 animal species. The text is from the museum's book series of the same title and the sketches are by a former chief illustrator.

Nettrekker. Thinkronize $1,195/yr. (K-12)

http://www.nettrekker.com

By subscription only. Tel. 1-877-517-1125

An Internet search engine created specifically for the K-12 education community. Aligned with individual state standards and divided into Elementary and Secondary sites, Nettrekker highlights over 180,000 websites organized by basic subjects such as Math, Science, Technology, and Language Arts that in turn are broken down into smaller subsets that are ranked according to usefulness. Teacher Tools feature lesson plan and exercises, games, pictures, and videos. Nettrekker also features a Timeline feature showing the cross-curricular connection between important eras, famous people, events, arts and innovations during a specific period. Also available is Netrekker d.i., a version that supports differentiated instruction, for $1595/yr.

The **New** Book of Knowledge Online. Grolier Educational Contact producer for pricing; minimum of two databases (3 and up)

http://www.go.grolier.com

By subscription only. Tel. 888-326-6546

This elementary encyclopedia features not only traditional encyclopedia articles, but wonder questions, a science experiments and projects section, NBK News, an Encyclopedia Spotlight where kid-interest topics are explored, Web Feat highlighting educational games, puzzles, and activities, and extensive teacher resources.

The **New** Book of Popular Science Online. Grolier Educational Contact producer for pricing; minimum of two databases (5 and up)

http://www.go.grolier.com

By subscription only. Tel. 888-326-6546

A science and technology reference site with articles found in the print version along with science in the news. Articles are organized by broad topics and feature hyperlinked outlines and links to related topics. Key word searches can be limited to the full text of articles or article titles with the use of Boolean operators. Sidebars have options for selected readings, Web links, careers, etc. The resource includes news stories and a Skywatch section featuring a map of the heavens. There are puzzles and games for students and an option to communicate with a science expert via e-mail.

"The quantity and quality of graphics and features such as NewsBytes and SciZone are appealing to students, teachers, parents, and librarians." Libr J

North American mammals. The Smithsonian National Museum of Natural History Free (3-12)

http://web4.si.edu/mna/

"The content of two major reference books, The Smithsonian Book of North American Mammals (Don E. Wilson and Sue Ruff) and Mammals of North America (Roland W. Kays and Don E. Wilson), are incorporated into this interactive Web site. . . . Each of the over 400 profiles on the site includes scientific information such as average weight and length, a drawing of the animal, a map with its distribution range, and an explanation of the animal's habits, alternative names, and other characteristics. Some profiles include Quicktime panoramas that can be manipulated by the viewer, and several have sound clips such as a coyote's howl. . . . An interactive map search allows users to select an area of North America and identify the mammals in that range. . . . Students will find North American Mammals to be a delight for browsing as well as a valuable tool for research." Evalutech

NoveList K-8. EBSCO Publishing Contact producer for pricing (K-8)

http://www.epnet.com

By subscription only. Tel. 800-653-2726

"An annotated database of 38,000 picture book and fiction titles enhanced by teacher resources. . . . Searches produce lists of titles with Lexile ratings and descriptions, that usually include a book cover graphic, subject headings, plot summary, links to related Web resources, and reviews from standard sources. . . . Teacher resources include more than ten multidisciplinary thematic units, articles on using books with children, several hundred book talks for grades four and higher, and Boolean search options. . . . NoveList K-8 is a versatile and powerful resource for connecting readers with books, whether the need is to guide eager readers, support the

curriculum, suggest titles for summer reading, or develop customized reading plans based on Lexile level and personal interest." Evalutech

Nueva enciclopedia Cumbre en linea. Grolier Educational Contact producer for pricing; minimum of two databases (6 and up)

http://www.go.grolier.com

By subscription only. Tel. 888-326-6546

A Spanish-language encyclopedia covering all subjects. Articles can be located by keyword with the option of Boolean operators or by browsing broad categories. Web links, photos, maps, and audio recordings are included.

"Articles in NECEL are well written in clear, easy-to-read Spanish and generally reflect a Latin American perspective." Libr J

OLogy. American Museum of Natural History Free (3-6)

http://ology.amnh.org

Children are rewarded for going through science tutorials with electronic picture cards, which they can then arrange on their own page. Tutorials on astronomy, genetics, and paleontology, as well as an opportunity to submit questions to museum scientists by email are available.

Online Exhibits. Field Museum Free (3-6)

http://www.fmnh.org/exhibits/online%5Fexhib.htm

Collection of exhibits shows such things as photographs of a 19th-century hunt for two lions who had eaten 128 workers building a Ugandan railway bridge, an animated, insect's-eye view of life underground, and paintings of stages in the evolution of life.

Online Reader. EBSCO Publishing Contact producer for pricing (4-12)

http://www.epnet.com/
thisTopic.php?marketID=9&topicID=202

By subscription only. Tel. 800-653-2726

This database "is an interdisciplinary database of expository reading content designed to build students' reading comprehension skills across content areas. Its direct-assign format allows teachers to choose from high interest, nonfiction magazine articles and assign them to students according to individual reading needs. Lexile™ readability indicators are available for each article to facilitate selection. Each Online Reader article has a reading comprehension test that is automatically graded and question types are similar to those found on standardized tests. Online grade book and progress report features track student performance and achievement. Thematic teacher guides provide activities correlated to standards and explore expository writing and expression." Publisher's note

"An outstanding, valuable resource. Teachers can use it to improve student comprehension of informational material, provide background information, improve student test-taking skills, and much more. The program can be an important tool to help students prepare for state-administered tests nationwide." MultiMedia Schools

PBS Parents: Early Math. Public Broadcasting Service and WNET New York Free (K-2)

http://www.pbs.org/parents/earlymath/

Focused on developing young children's early math skills, this web site is divided into three age levels: In-

PBS Parents: Early Math—*Continued*
fants and Toddler, PK-K, and Grades 1-2. Each level features math games and activities that can be integrated into a young child's daily experiences. Links to PBS parenting sites and information expand the program's value for children, parents, and teachers.

Playmusic. American Symphony Orchestra League Free (K-3)

http://www.playmusic.org/

Designed to introduce younger children to the instruments in the orchestra, this website features each section and its instruments, plays selections that feature these instruments, and introduces young people who play in the Chicago Youth Orchestra to talk about their love of music and their enjoyment of playing together.

Primary Search. EBSCO Publishing Contact producer for pricing (3 and up)

http://www.epnet.com/
thisTopic.php?marketID=9&topicID=122

By subscription only. Tel. 800-653-2726

Children's periodical reference database for elementary schools and children's reading rooms. Provides full-text coverage for 67 elementary school magazines. The database also features student reference books (including the *American Heritage Children's Dictionary*); full-text student pamphlets; *the Encyclopedia of Animals*; *Funk & Wagnalls New World Encyclopedia*; images and maps, and Lexile reading level indicators. Uses a child-friendly "Searchosaurus" interface for locating information by key word or by subject.

Pupil pages. Online Solutions for Educators Contact producer for pricing (1-12)

http://www.pupilpages.com

By subscription only. Tel. 888-203-4704

An online portfolio system that enables students to create and manage electronic collections of their work for a single class, for several subjects, over many years, and among grade levels and/or schools. Each portfolio contains a Resume, a Journal, and a Biography that functions as the student's homepage. A Comment feature, which can be password protected, and a language filter allow visitors to provide low-risk feedback. The Portfolio-to-Go feature enables students to take their work with them when they graduate or transfer to another district.

Resources for K-12 Earth Science. Educators Geological Society of America (GSA) Free

http://www.geosociety.org/educate/resources.htm

"Offers lessons plans and additional resources covering virtually all topics in geology for K-12 students. The materials are divided into 12 topics, such as Environmental Science, Weather and Climate, and Plate Tectonics. Each of the topics has elementary, intermediate, and secondary lesson plans that offer details on the content, time required, materials needed, and directions for the project. The stimulating activities are a great way for students to understand otherwise difficult subjects and excite them about geology." Internet Scout

RIF Reading Planet. Reading is Fundamental, Inc. Free (All ages)

http://www.rif.org/readingplanet/

The kids' section of the Reading is Fundamental Web site focuses on making reading fun for children. The site is organized into four zones: Activity Lab, Game Station,

Express Yourself, and Book Zone; games and activities are book-based. Many of the resources are in Spanish as well as English.

Riverdeep.net. Riverdeep, Inc. Contact producer for pricing (4 and up)

http://www.riverdeep.net

By subscription only. Tel. 888-242-6747

A curriculum resource with a variety of programs, activities, and reference tools. The Destination Math program for grades four and up uses animation and natural language narration to provide self-paced tutorials and activities related to concepts such as numbers, fractions, decimals, and percents. For grades six and up the site offers the Logal Middle School Science Gateways and Explorer simulations and an EarthPulse Center for the middle school earth science curriculum. A Living Library section offers searchable reference materials such as the *World Book International*, Time.com for Kids, *Bartlett's Quotations*, almanacs, dictionaries, etc.

Robotics—Sensing-Thinking-Acting. Tech Museum of Innovation Free (4 and up)

http://www.thetech.org/robotics

This online exhibition explains what robots are, what they do, how they work, and who builds them. Includes video clips of researchers explaining how they design robots, ethicists discussing the moral problems of a successful artificial intelligence program, and artists discussing robots as art. Also includes an activity in which one tries to control an exploratory device over a great distance, so that there is a lag between command and response.

Scholastic READ 180. Scholastic, Inc. Contact producer for pricing (4-12)

http://teacher.scholastic.com/read180/

By subscription only. Tel. 877-234-READ

This research-based program "delivers individualized reading instruction to help students improve fluency, create mental models, and understand more complex written information through word analysis and vocabulary development. This is accomplished through a variety of reading experiences that integrate with History and Geography, People and Cultures, and Science and Math topics. The READ 180 model consists of a 90-minute rotation of activities. The four major components of READ 180 are Instructional Reading, Modeled Reading, Independent Reading, and Teacher-Directed Instruction. The program is available in three stages: Stage A (elementary), Stage B (middle school), and Stage C (high school). . . . Other program components include a management and assessment system that monitors student progress, and a reading diagnostic tool, the Scholastic Reading Inventory, that evaluates reading levels for student placement." Evalutech

Science buzz. Science Museum of Minnesota Free (4 and up)

http://ltc2.smm.org/buzz/

This site provides "information about a variety of science news stories that often do not receive adequate coverage elsewhere in the media. Some of the current stories on the site include West Nile virus, cloning, and even invasive flying carp. Visitors will want to start by perusing the 'What's Abuzz' section on the homepage. Here they can find about current science news stories and peruse previous stories as well. For persons who know what they are looking for there is a section titled 'I want to learn about', where they can go directly to stories about

Science buzz—*Continued*

such topical areas as physical science, math, or the history and nature of science." Internet Scout

Sharks: myth and mystery. Monterey Bay Aquarium Free (5 and up)

http://www.mbayaq.org/efc/sharks.asp

An online exhibit on the world of sharks that features of a gallery tour, which is organized by geographic region, such as Australia and Central America. In each area, visitors can learn about the individual species of shark in each region and how various human communities interact with these magnificent creatures. Visitors can also take a look through the live "Shark Cam" from the Aquarium's Australia Gallery. While sharks will be the draw here, visitors can also learn about and view penguins, jellyfish, sea otters, and octopi in other sections of the site.

Simple machines. Franklin Institute Online Free (4-8)

http://sln.fi.edu/qa97/spotlight3/spotlight3.html

"Learn about six simple machines and how they work at this Website that is almost as simple as the simple machines themselves. Basic definitions and samples of each simple machine are provided. There are examples of how simple machines are used to change the amount of force needed to move objects. Also given are links to other pages that go into more detail and provide activities and lesson plans." Florida's Instructional Technology Resource Center

SimScience. National Science Foundation Free (5 and up)

http://simscience.org

Provides tutorials on four areas of scientific research that depend on simulations done on supercomputers: membranes, fluid flow, dam cracking, and crackling noise. The tutorials are offered at three reading levels: elementary, secondary, and college-level.

SIRS Discoverer. ProQuest Contact producer for pricing (3-8)

http://www.proquestk12.com/productinfo/sirs%5Fdiscoverer.shtml

By subscription only. Tel. 800-521-0600 x3344

Reference database of full-text articles searchable by key words (options for Boolean operators, truncation, phrases, and natural language); subject tree (15 broad categories with sub-topics); and subject headings (primarily Library of Congress). Articles are drawn from newspapers, magazines, and U.S. government documents, as well as contributions by the SIRS staff. Articles are color-coded by reading level: easy (grades 1-4), moderate (grades 5-7), and challenging (grade 8 and beyond). The site includes Current Events articles updated daily, *The World Almanac for Kids, Funk and Wagnalls New Encyclopedia*, maps, a dictionary, and a thesaurus.

"SIRS Discoverer on the Web offers well-organized information and simplified search capabilities for student research." Evalutech

Smithsonian Expeditions. Smithsonian Institution Free (5 and up)

http://www.mnh.si.edu/anthro/laexped

Tells the story of the North and Latin American naturalists who collaborated on anthropological, botanical, and zoological expeditions to South America in the 19th and early 20th centuries.

SOS Math. Math Medics, L.L.C. Free (4 and up)

http://www.sosmath.com/index.html

Provides tutorials and practice exams on elementary to college-level mathematics.

Star Journey. National Geographic Free (4 and up)

http://www.nationalgeographic.com/features/97/stars

This site provides a star chart with embedded links to thirty-nine Hubble space telescope photographs of the corresponding heavenly bodies. Also includes articles on the Hubble space telescope and on constellations.

StarChild. NASA Free (4 and up)

http://starchild.gsfc.nasa.gov/docs/StarChild

Contains information on and photographs of the solar system, more distant heavenly bodies, and space exploration. All writing is available at both elementary and secondary reading levels.

Starfall.com. Stephen Schutz and Susan Polis Schutz Free (K-3)

http://www.starfall.com/

Starfall.com uses sound, animation, and video techniques to provide a learning environment that nurtures the beginning reader. The reading development program is based on the phonics model recommended by the California Department of Education. It "combines explicit instruction in letter-sound relationships, word recognition skills, and reading comprehension strategies with opportunities to apply and practice these skills in literature." Evalutech

State Geography. ABC-CLIO $499/yr. (4 and up)

http://www.abc-clio.com/products/overview.aspx?productid=109715

By subscription only. Tel. 800-368-6868

Covers the people, places, events, trends, statistics, news, attractions, politics, culture, environment, government, and history of all 50 states in the U.S. The site also includes biographies and primary source documents. Searchable by key word and advanced search options that allow filtering by categories. Teachers can customize the site by setting up classes and posting information such as announcements, syllabi, discussion questions, handouts, and tests. The Home page has frequently updated news articles and feature stories that are linked to related articles in the database. Includes the *Merriam Webster Dictionary*.

"The site's entries are authoritative and well linked. This online reference would be a boon to busy teachers who want to use the Internet in the instruction of geography. Highly recommended." Book Report

Storyline Online. Screen Actors Guild Foundation Free (K-3)

http://www.storylineonline.net/

Part of the BookPALS website, Storyline Online is a collection of high-quality online videos of actors reading picture books aloud. Each online video is accompanied by suggested activities and profiles of the book's author and the celebrity reader in Acrobat or text format.

testGEAR. Bridges Contact producer for pricing

http://www.testu.com/frameset.asp

By subscription only. Tel. 800-281-1168

testGEAR—*Continued*

This is a test preparation program that provides interactive instruction in English-Language Arts, mathmatics, social studies and science topics tested on the exit-level examination. It supplies lessons on test-taking strategies, and offers practice tests in a variety of formats.

Treehouses on the Tree of Life. Tree of Life Project Free

http://tolweb.org/tree/home.pages/treehouses.html

The Tree of Life is a web project developed by biologists around the world that is composed of more than 2,000 web pages and provides information about phylogeny and biodiversity. Treehouses is the section of the Tree of Life aimed at K-16 learners and teachers. The site features "treehouses" or sections including investigations (science reports and experiments with photos, diagrams, and videos), stories, games, and teacher resources.

unitedstreaming. Discovery Education Starting at $1,495/yr. for K-8 schools and $1,995/yr. for high schools

http://www.unitedstreaming.com

By subscription only. Tel. 800-323-9084

Unitedstreaming.com is an online library of over 50,000 video clips aligned to state standards for grades K-12. The library is searchable by keyword, subject area, grade level, and curriculum strand. Video clips are supported by materials for teachers and students, and can be steamed or downloaded as PDF files, printed, and distributed.

Unraveling the mysteries of King Tutankhamun. National Geographic Society Free (4 and up)

http://magma.nationalgeographic.com/ngm/tut/mysteries/index.html

This site "allows visitors to examine . . . [Tutankhamun's] body through the use of CT scan imagery and see how he might have looked. Clicking on the entrance to this multimedia feature, visitors are greeted by audio narration that complements a 360-degree view of the four walls of King Tut's tomb. Visitors can then look closer at each wall in detail by using a built-in interface to navigate the various decorative and symbolic markings on each side. After this first section, visitors can move to the 'Royal Wrappings' feature, which includes a detailed look at the many layers in which King Tut was entombed. The site is rounded out by a selection of additional links to such resources as articles from National Geographic dealing with Egyptian archaeology." Internet Scout

Virtual Renaissance. Twin Groves Junior High School Free (6 and up)

http://www.twingroves.district96.k12.il.us/Renaissance/VirtualRen.html

This tutorial on Renaissance history is presented as a trip back through time to various sites in Europe and England. Local people explain their lives and Renaissance art, science, exploration, trade, politics, war, religion, and society.

Visual thesaurus. Thinkmap, Inc. Contact producer for pricing (3-12)

http://www.visualthesaurus.com

By subscription only. Tel. 212-285-8600

Provides the meaning of 140,000 words meanings and explores their relationships to other words (ex. Antonym). Pdf Teachers Guide and Student Workbook included.

"The engaging, dynamic, and efficient interface is the great strength of this resource. Its responsive, animated interactivity draws students into a study of words. It also offers an excellent way for ESL students to develop a fuller understanding of English vocabulary." Evalutech

Weather Wiz Kids. Crystal Wicker Free (4 and up)

http://www.weatherwizkids.com/

This relatively simple, child-friendly website features the basics of clouds, wind, temperature, climate, and rain accompanied by drawings, diagrams, and photographs primarily presented in question and answer format. Severe weather events such as hurricanes, tornadoes, earthquakes, and winter storms are also highlighted. Weather experiments, simple games, quizzes, weather jokes, and weather folklore, as well as student-submitted art work and photographs, round out this fascinating website.

Web feet. Gale Group Contact producer for pricing (K-12)

http://www.gale.com/webfeet/

By subscription only. Tel. 800-877-4253

A collection of preselected, annotated, free websites that have been selected and evaluated by librarian and educators based on the criteria of source, information, timeliness, and appropriate links. Searchable by keyword [subject], grade level, and curriculum area or browsed by LC subject, title of Web site, author or sponsor of the site, or LC or Dewey call number. Sites, both curriculum specific and general interest, added on a bimonthly basis.

"The folks behind WEB FEET have done an outstanding job of selection. Every URL, with rare exception, took me straight to a page containing the exact information I was expecting to find. . . . WEB FEET ONLINE is a functional Internet subject guide, a truly useful resource for finding solid, trustworthy Web sites." Libr J

What works clearinghouse: middle school math curricula. U.S. Department of Education's Institute of Education Sciences Free

http://www.whatworks.ed.gov

"The What Works Clearinghouse was established 'to provide educators, policy-makers, researchers, and the public with a central and trusted source of scientific evidence of what works in education.' It has posted the results from its review of 'interventions based on a curriculum, which contain learning goals that spell out the mathematics that students should know and be able to do, instructional programs and materials that organize the mathematical content, and assessments.' The reviews are organized into three WWC Topic Reports that cover interventions for middle school mathematics, elementary school mathematics, and high school mathematics. For each intervention with at least one study that 'Meets Evidence Standards' or 'Meets Evidence Standards with Reservations,' the site provides a short review of the study and the findings." Internet Scout

The why files. The University of Wisconsin at Madison, The National Institute for Science Education Free (6-12)

http://whyfiles.org/

"The Why Files delves into the science behind the news headlines and draws a connection between science in the everyday world and science in the classroom. A major science-related story is posted every week in the 'In Depth' section. In addition to the mainstream science

The why files—*Continued*

disciplines (biology, environmental science, and physical science), these stories also cover the areas of sports, health, social science, and technology. The stories feature excellent navigational aids, and often have online videos and other multimedia enhancements. An archive of articles is maintained, and a site search engine provides flexible access. The 'In Brief' section offers pithy articles dealing with popular science mysteries, while 'In the News' selects stories from the Why Files database and relates them to current events. The site is nicely designed, well-written, and efficiently organized." Evalutech

World Atlas. Facts on File Contact producer for pricing (6 and up)

http://www.factsonfile.com/

By subscription only. Tel. 800-322-8755

An interactive database of maps and information related to geographic regions and countries of the world, as well as states and Canadian provinces. The site provides full-color political, elevation, and outline maps of each geographic area as well as multiple maps depicting information ranging from political and economic data to energy and natural resources. "Fact Files" have information on countries such as vital statistics, government, history, and chronologies. Links to related Web sites are included.

"Allows for easy access to current information in lieu of hard copy versions that become outdated quickly. This is a worthwhile purchase for classroom and media center use for research." Evalutech

World Book Online. World Book Publishing Contact producer for pricing (4 and up)

http://www.worldbookonline.com

By subscription only. Tel. 800-975-3250

General reference encyclopedia with all articles from the print version of World Book Encyclopedia along with multimedia elements and updated articles and information (750 new articles, 550 new Back in Time articles, 60 special reports, and 4500 revised articles were added in a single year). This online reference also has links to full text articles in over 250 magazines and newspapers as well as links to more than 10,000 editor approved Web sites. Back in Time articles, taken from World Book Yearbooks dating to 1922, provide coverage of people and events from the perspective of the times. A Surf the Millennium feature introduces the major political, cultural, and scientific events of the last 10 centuries. Includes a fully integrated dictionary.

"This flexible, easy-to-use, online resource is an excellent tool for student research. By integrating historical background and current information, it makes history more relevant to events of the day. Highly recommended." Book Report

World Geography. ABC-CLIO Contact producer for pricing (6 and up)

http://www.abc-clio.com/products/
overview.aspx?productid=109713

By subscription only. Tel. 800-368-6868

Provides information for a catalog of countries and regions. Each country page provides an overview of the nation, historical and governmental information, facts and figures, important events, biographies, primary source documents, lists of organizations, and maps. Articles are cross-referenced through hyperlinks. In addition to key word searches, there are advanced search options to limit by categories of information. Teachers can customize the site by adding discussion questions, handouts, tests, etc. The site also features daily news articles and feature stories with links to related articles. Includes the *Merriam-Webster Collegiate Dictionary* and *Merriam-Webster's Collegiate Thesaurus*.

"An excellent reference tool . . . that also can be used as a daily organizational resource for students logging on to find their assignments for the day." Evalutech

The Yuckiest Site on the Internet. Discovery Channel Free (3-5)

http://yucky.kids.discovery.com

Covers the coarser aspects of biology. Includes scientifically sound discussions of such topics as regurgitation, flatulence, cockroaches, and worms. Includes recordings of vulgar noises and a whack-a-roach game.

AUTHOR, TITLE, SUBJECT, AND ANALYTICAL INDEX

This index to the books in the Classified Catalog includes author, title, subject, and analytical entries; added entries for publishers' series, illustrators, joint authors, and editors of works entered under title; and name and subject cross-references; all arranged in one alphabet.

The number or symbol in bold face type at the end of each entry refers to the Dewey Decimal Classification or to the Fiction (Fic) or Story Collection (SC), or Easy Books (E) section where the main entry for the book will be found. Works classed in 92 are entered under the name of the person written about. The parenthetical notation following the the the title of a work indicates the grade level at which the item is most likely to be of interest.

For further directions for the use of this index and for examples of entries, see Directions for Use of the Catalog.

1, 2, 3 go!. Lee, H. V.	**495.1**
#1. See Radunsky, V. One	**E**
1, 2, I love you. Schertle, A.	**E**
1 hunter. Hutchins, P.	**E**
1 is one. Tudor, T.	**E**
2 x 2 = boo!. Leedy, L.	**513**
4B goes wild. Gilson, J.	**Fic**
4th of July See Fourth of July	
The **7** professors of the Far North. Fardell, J.	**Fic**
7 steps to an award-winning school library program. Martin, A. M.	**027.8**
7 x 9 = trouble!. Mills, C.	**Fic**
10 little rubber ducks. Carle, E.	**E**
10 minutes till bedtime. Rathmann, P.	**E**
The **11:59.** McKissack, P. C.	
In McKissack, P. C. The dark-thirty; Southern tales of the supernatural p35-42	**S C**
12 ways to get to 11. Merriam, E.	**510**
The **13th** floor. Fleischman, S.	**Fic**
17 kings and 42 elephants. Mahy, M.	**E**
The **20th** century children's poetry treasury	**811.008**
25 Latino craft projects. Pavon, A.-E.	**027.62**
26 Fairmount Avenue. De Paola, T.	**92**
26 letters and 99 cents. Hoban, T.	**E**
33 things every girl should know about women's history (5 and up)	**305.4**
50 words about plants. Armentrout, D.	**580**
100 best books for children. Silvey, A.	**011.6**
100 most popular children's authors. McElmeel, S. L.	**810.3**
100 most popular picture book authors and illustrators. McElmeel, S. L.	**810.3**
100 school days. Rockwell, A. F.	**E**
100th day worries. Cuyler, M.	**E**
201 awesome, magical, bizarre & incredible experiments, Janice VanCleave's. VanCleave, J. P.	**507.8**
202 oozing, bubbling, dripping & bouncing experiments, Janice VanCleave's. VanCleave, J. P.	**507.8**

The **500** hats of Bartholomew Cubbins. Seuss, Dr.	**E**
1,000 inventions & discoveries. Bridgman, R. F.	**609**
1621. Grace, C. O.	**394.26**
The **1900s,** from Teddy Roosevelt to flying machines. Feinstein, S.	
In Feinstein, S. Decades of the 20th Century [series]	**909.82**
The **1910s,** from World War I to ragtime music. Feinstein, S.	
In Feinstein, S. Decades of the 20th Century [series]	**909.82**
The **1920s,** from prohibition to Charles Lindbergh. Feinstein, S.	
In Feinstein, S. Decades of the 20th Century [series]	**909.82**
The **1930s,** from The Great Depression to The Wizard of Oz. Feinstein, S.	
In Feinstein, S. Decades of the 20th Century [series]	**909.82**
The **1940s,** from World War II to Jackie Robinson. Feinstein, S.	
In Feinstein, S. Decades of the 20th Century [series]	**909.82**
The **1950s,** from the Korean War to Elvis. Feinstein, S.	
In Feinstein, S. Decades of the 20th Century [series]	**909.82**
The **1960s,** from the Vietnam War to flower power. Feinstein, S.	
In Feinstein, S. Decades of the 20th Century [series]	**909.82**
The **1970s,** from Watergate fo disco. Feinstein, S.	
In Feinstein, S. Decades of the 20th Century [series]	**909.82**
The **1980s,** from Ronald Reagan to MTV. Feinstein, S.	
In Feinstein, S. Decades of the 20th Century [series]	**909.82**
The **1990s,** from the Persian Gulf War to Y2K. Feinstein, S.	
In Feinstein, S. Decades of the 20th Century [series]	**909.82**
The **2000** presidential election. Landau, E.	**324**

Adolescence—*Continued*
Jukes, M. It's a girl thing (5 and up)
           305.23
Madaras, L. The "what's happening to my body?" book for boys (4 and up)   **613.9**
Madaras, L. The "what's happening to my body" book for girls (4 and up)   **613.9**

Adolescents *See* Teenagers

Adoption
Krementz, J. How it feels to be adopted (4 and up)   **362.7**
McMahon, P. Just add one Chinese sister   **E**
See/See also pages in the following book(s):
Warren, A. Orphan train rider (4 and up)
           362.7

Fiction
Banks, K. Dillon Dillon (4 and up)   **Fic**
Bunting, E. Jin Woo   **E**
Bunting, E. Train to Somewhere   **E**
Curtis, J. L. Tell me again about the night I was born   **E**
Johnson, A. Heaven (6 and up)   **Fic**
Keller, H. Horace   **E**
Lewis, R. A. I love you like crazy cakes   **E**
Little, J. Emma's yucky brother   **E**
McKay, H. Saffy's angel (5 and up)   **Fic**
Montgomery, L. M. Anne of Green Gables (5 and up)   **Fic**
Okimoto, J. D. The White Swan express   **E**
Peacock, C. A. Mommy far, Mommy near   **E**
Say, A. Allison   **E**
Stoeke, J. M. Waiting for May   **E**
Thomas, E. The red blanket   **E**
Young, E. My Mei Mei   **E**

Adventure and adventurers
Fiction
See Adventure fiction

Adventure fiction
See also Science fiction; Sea stories
Alexander, L. The Illyrian adventure (5 and up)   **Fic**
Alexander, L. The iron ring (5 and up)   **Fic**
Alexander, L. The marvelous misadventures of Sebastian (4 and up)   **Fic**
Alexander, L. The remarkable journey of Prince Jen (5 and up)   **Fic**
Alexander, L. The rope trick (4 and up)   **Fic**
Alexander, L. Westmark (5 and up)   **Fic**
Almond, D. Heaven Eyes (5 and up)   **Fic**
Baccalario, P. The door to time (4-6)   **Fic**
Couloumbis, A. The misadventures of Maude March (5 and up)   **Fic**
Craig, J. Jimmy Coates: assassin? (5 and up)   **Fic**
Crilley, M. Billy Clikk: creach battler (3-5)   **Fic**
Ellis, S. The several lives of Orphan Jack (3-6)   **Fic**
Fardell, J. The 7 professors of the Far North (4 and up)   **Fic**
Farmer, N. A girl named Disaster (6 and up)   **Fic**
Fleischman, S. Bandit's moon (4-6)   **Fic**
Fleischman, S. The Giant Rat of Sumatra (4 and up)   **Fic**

Fleischman, S. The whipping boy (5 and up)   **Fic**
Garfield, L. Black Jack (6 and up)   **Fic**
Garfield, L. Smith (6 and up)   **Fic**
Hirsch, O. Bartlett and the ice voyage (3-6)   **Fic**
Horowitz, A. The Devil and his boy (5 and up)   **Fic**
Ives, D. Scrib (5 and up)   **Fic**
Kimmel, E. A. Sword of the samurai (4 and up)   **S C**
Lawrence, I. The convicts (5 and up)   **Fic**
Lawrence, I. The wreckers (5 and up)   **Fic**
Masefield, J. Jim Davis (5 and up)   **Fic**
Naylor, P. R. The grand escape (4-6)   **Fic**
Naylor, P. R. Roxie and the Hooligans (3-5)   **Fic**
Pullman, P. The firework-maker's daughter (4 and up)   **Fic**
Smith, R. Cryptid hunters (5 and up)   **Fic**
Springer, N. Rowan Hood, outlaw girl of Sherwood Forest (4 and up)   **Fic**
Yolen, J. Odysseus in the serpent maze (4 and up)   **Fic**

The **adventure** of the German student. San Souci, R.
    In San Souci, R. Short & shivery; thirty chilling tales p96-102   **398.2**

Adventures in art [series]
Hollein, N. Matisse   **92**

The **adventures** of Ali Baba Bernstein. Hurwitz, J.   **Fic**

The **Adventures** of Haroun-al-Raschid, Caliph of Bagdad
    In The Arabian nights entertainments p316-19   **398.2**

The **adventures** of Hershel of Ostropol. Kimmel, E. A.   **398.2**

The **adventures** of High John the Conqueror. Sanfield, S.   **398.2**

The **adventures** of Huckleberry Finn. Twain, M.   **Fic**

The **adventures** of Pinocchio. Collodi, C.   **Fic**

The **adventures** of Pinocchio. See Young, E. Pinocchio   **Fic**

The **adventures** of Polo. Faller, R.   **E**

The **Adventures** of Prince Camaralzaman and the Princess Badoura
    In The Arabian nights entertainments p216-66   **398.2**

The **adventures** of Simon and Susanna. Lester, J.
    In Lester, J. The last tales of Uncle Remus p151-56   **398.2**

The **adventures** of Taxi Dog. Barracca, D.   **E**

The **adventures** of Tintin, vol. 1. Hergé   **741.5**

The **adventures** of Tom Sawyer. Twain, M.   **Fic**

The **adventures** of Tom Thumb. Mayer, M.   **398.2**

Adventures of young Buffalo Bill [series]
Kimmel, E. C. To the frontier   **Fic**

African-American soldiers in the Civil War. Ford, C. T. **973.7**

African American women

Adler, D. A. A picture book of Harriet Tubman (1-3) **92**

Adler, D. A. A picture book of Sojourner Truth (1-3) **92**

Alagna, M. Mae Jemison (4 and up) **92**

Bolden, T. Maritcha [biography of Maritcha Rémond Lyons] (4 and up) **92**

Butler, M. G. Sojourner Truth (5 and up) **92**

Coleman, E. The riches of Oseola McCarty (3-5) **92**

Cunningham, K. Condoleezza Rice (5 and up) **92**

Ferris, J. Go free or die: a story about Harriet Tubman (3-5) **92**

Fradin, D. B. Ida B. Wells (5 and up) **92**

Freedman, R. The voice that challenged a nation [biography of Marian Anderson] (5 and up) **92**

Giovanni, N. Rosa [biography of Rosa Parks] (3-5) **92**

Jemison, M. C. Find where the wind goes (5 and up) **92**

Katz, W. L. Black women of the Old West (5 and up) **978**

Koestler-Grack, R. A. The story of Harriet Tubman (2-4) **92**

Lasky, K. Vision of beauty: the story of Sarah Breedlove Walker (3-5) **92**

Lowery, L. Aunt Clara Brown (2-4) **92**

McKissack, P. C. Madam C.J. Walker (1-3) **92**

McKissack, P. C. Marian Anderson (1-3) **92**

McKissack, P. C. Sojourner Truth (1-3) **92**

Miller, N. Stompin' at the Savoy [biography of Norma Miller] (3-6) **92**

Orgill, R. Mahalia [Jackson] (5 and up) **92**

Parks, R. I am Rosa Parks (1-3) **92**

Parks, R. Rosa Parks: my story (5 and up) **92**

Pinkney, A. D. Ella Fitzgerald (2-4) **92**

Pinkney, A. D. Let it shine (4 and up) **920**

Rockwell, A. F. Only passing through: the story of Sojourner Truth (3-5) **92**

Roop, P. Sojourner Truth (3-6) **92**

Ryan, P. M. When Marian sang: the true recital of Marian Anderson, the voice of a century (2-4) **92**

Schraff, A. E. Harriet Tubman (5 and up) **92**

Folklore

Hamilton, V. Her stories (4 and up) **398.2**

African American women writers. Wilkinson, B. S. **810.9**

African Americans

See also Gullahs

Barbour, K. Mr. Williams **E**

Dillon, L. Rap a tap tap **E**

Hoobler, D. The African American family album (5 and up) **305.8**

Kuklin, S. How my family lives in America (k-3) **305.8**

McKissack, P. C. Black hands, white sails (5 and up) **639.2**

Pinkney, S. L. Shades of black **E**

Bibliography

The Black experience in children's books **016.3058**

Rand, D. Black Books Galore!—guide to great African American children's books about boys **016.3058**

Biography

Adler, D. A. Dr. Martin Luther King, Jr. (1-3) **92**

Adler, D. A. A picture book of George Washington Carver (1-3) **92**

Adler, D. A. A picture book of Thurgood Marshall (1-3) **92**

Altman, S. Extraordinary African-Americans (5 and up) **920**

Blumberg, R. York's adventures with Lewis and Clark (5 and up) **978**

Bolden, T. Portraits of African-American heroes (4 and up) **920**

Brill, M. T. Barack Obama (5 and up) **92**

Crews, D. Bigmama's (k-3) **92**

Farris, C. My brother Martin [biography of Martin Luther King] (k-3) **92**

Ferris, J. Arctic explorer: the story of Matthew Henson (3-6) **92**

Ferris, J. What are you figuring now? a story about Benjamin Banneker (3-5) **92**

Hinman, B. Benjamin Banneker (5 and up) **92**

Hudson, W. Powerful words (5 and up) **808.8**

Johnson, D. Onward [biography of Matthew Henson] (5 and up) **92**

Marzollo, J. Happy birthday, Martin Luther King (k-3) **92**

McKissack, P. C. Frederick Douglass (2-4) **92**

Mitchell, B. A pocketful of goobers: a story about George Washington Carver (3-5) **92**

Myers, W. D. I've seen the promised land [biography of Martin Luther King] (k-3) **92**

Myers, W. D. Malcolm X (3-6) **92**

Pinkney, A. D. Bill Pickett, rodeo ridin' cowboy (k-3) **92**

Pinkney, A. D. Dear Benjamin Banneker (2-4) **92**

Pinkney, A. D. Duke Ellington (2-4) **92**

Rappaport, D. Freedom river [biography of John P. Parker] (2-5) **92**

Rappaport, D. Martin's big words: the life of Dr. Martin Luther King, Jr. (k-3) **92**

Rembert, W. Don't hold me back (4 and up) **92**

Sullivan, O. R. African American millionaires **920**

Tillage, L. Leon's story (4 and up) **92**

Wadsworth, G. Benjamin Banneker (3-5) **92**

Waxman, L. H. Colin Powell (2-5) **92**

Yates, E. Amos Fortune, free man (4 and up) **92**

Civil rights

Adler, D. A. Dr. Martin Luther King, Jr. (1-3) **92**

African Americans—Fiction—*Continued*

Johnson, A. Bird (5 and up)   **Fic**
Johnson, A. Heaven (6 and up)   **Fic**
Johnson, A. I dream of trains   **E**
Johnson, A. Just like Josh Gibson   **E**
Johnson, A. Songs of faith (5 and up)   **Fic**
Johnson, A. Tell me a story, Mama   **E**
Johnson, A. Violet's music   **E**
Johnson, D. Quinnie Blue   **E**
Joosse, B. M. Hot city   **E**
Jordan, R. Lost Goat Lane (5 and up)   **Fic**
Keats, E. J. Hi, cat!   **E**
Konigsburg, E. L. Jennifer, Hecate, Macbeth, William McKinley, and me, Elizabeth (4-6)   **Fic**
Kurtz, J. Faraway home   **E**
Lee, S. Please, baby, please   **E**
Lester, J. Black cowboy, wild horses   **E**
Lester, J. The old African (3-6)   **Fic**
Levine, G. C. Dave at night (5 and up)   **Fic**
Lindsey, K. Sweet potato pie   **E**
Lorbiecki, M. Sister Anne's hands   **E**
Lyons, M. E. Letters from a slave girl (6 and up)   **Fic**
McKissack, P. C. Abby takes a stand (2-4)   **Fic**
McKissack, P. C. Color me dark (4 and up)   **Fic**
McKissack, P. C. The dark-thirty (4 and up)   **S C**
McKissack, P. C. Flossie & the fox   **E**
McKissack, P. C. Goin' someplace special   **E**
McKissack, P. C. Let my people go (4 and up)   **221.9**
McKissack, P. C. Ma Dear's aprons   **E**
McKissack, P. C. Mirandy and Brother Wind   **E**
McKissack, P. C. A picture of Freedom (4 and up)   **Fic**
McKissack, P. C. Precious and the Boo Hag   **E**
McKissack, P. C. Tippy Lemmey (2-4)   **Fic**
Mead, A. Junebug (3-5)   **Fic**
Medearis, A. S. Snug in Mama's arms   **E**
Michelson, R. Happy feet   **E**
Miller, W. Night golf   **E**
Miller, W. The piano   **E**
Miller, W. Richard Wright and the library card   **E**
Mitchell, M. K. Uncle Jed's barbershop   **E**
Myers, C. Fly!   **E**
Myers, W. D. The journal of Joshua Loper (5 and up)   **Fic**
Nolen, J. Big Jabe   **E**
Nolen, J. Thunder Rose   **E**
Parker, T. T. Sienna's scrapbook (3-5)   **Fic**
Paterson, K. Jip (5 and up)   **Fic**
Pearsall, S. Trouble don't last (5 and up)   **Fic**
Petry, A. L. Tituba of Salem Village (6 and up)   **Fic**
Pinkney, A. D. Fishing day   **E**
Pinkney, A. D. Mim's Christmas jam   **E**
Pinkney, A. D. Peggony-Po   **E**
Pinkney, G. J. Back home   **E**
Polacco, P. Chicken Sunday   **E**
Polacco, P. Mrs. Katz and Tush   **E**

Quattlebaum, M. Jackson Jones and Mission Greentop (3-5)   **Fic**
Raschka, C. Yo! Yes?   **E**
Raven, M. Circle unbroken   **E**
Reeder, C. Across the lines (5 and up)   **Fic**
Richardson, C. K. The real slam dunk (2-4)   **Fic**
Ringgold, F. Tar Beach   **E**
Robinet, H. G. Forty acres and maybe a mule (4 and up)   **Fic**
Robinet, H. G. Walking to the bus-rider blues (5 and up)   **Fic**
Rosen, M. J. A school for Pompey Walker (2-4)   **Fic**
Russell, B. T. Maggie's Amerikay   **E**
Schroeder, A. Ragtime Tumpie   **E**
Sebestyen, O. Words by heart (5 and up)   **Fic**
Slote, A. Finding Buck McHenry (4-6)   **Fic**
Smothers, E. F. The hard-times jar   **E**
Stauffacher, S. Bessie Smith and the night riders   **E**
Stolz, M. Go fish (2-4)   **Fic**
Stroud, B. The patchwork path   **E**
Tarpley, N. Bippity Bop barbershop   **E**
Taulbert, C. L. Little Cliff and the porch people   **E**
Taylor, D. A. Sweet music in Harlem   **E**
Taylor, M. D. The friendship (4 and up)   **Fic**
Taylor, M. D. The gold Cadillac (4 and up)   **Fic**
Taylor, M. D. Let the circle be unbroken (4 and up)   **Fic**
Taylor, M. D. Mississippi bridge (4 and up)   **Fic**
Taylor, M. D. The road to Memphis (4 and up)   **Fic**
Taylor, M. D. Roll of thunder, hear my cry (4 and up)   **Fic**
Taylor, M. D. Song of the trees (4 and up)   **Fic**
Taylor, M. D. The well (4 and up)   **Fic**
Thomas, J. C. I have heard of a land   **E**
Wahl, J. Candy shop   **E**
Walter, M. P. Alec's primer   **E**
Walter, M. P. Justin and the best biscuits in the world (3-6)   **Fic**
Walter, M. P. Suitcase (3-6)   **Fic**
Weatherford, C. B. Freedom on the menu   **E**
Whittenberg, A. Sweet Thang (5 and up)   **Fic**
Wiles, D. Freedom Summer   **E**
Williams, S. A. Working cotton   **E**
Williams, V. B. Cherries and cherry pits   **E**
Winter, J. Follow the drinking gourd   **E**
Winthrop, E. Squashed in the middle   **E**
Woods, B. The red rose box (5 and up)   **Fic**
Woodson, J. Coming on home soon   **E**
Woodson, J. The other side   **E**
Woodson, J. Show way   **E**
Woodson, J. Visiting day   **E**
Woodson, J. We had a picnic this Sunday past   **E**

Folklore

Hamilton, V. Bruh Rabbit and the tar baby girl (k-3)   **398.2**

Afternoon of the elves. Lisle, J. T.   **Fic**

Age *See* Old age

The **age** of chivalry. Bulfinch, T.
    In Bulfinch, T. Bulfinch's mythology   **201**

The **age** of fable. Bulfinch, T.
    In Bulfinch, T. Bulfinch's mythology   **201**

Agee, Jon
    Elvis lives! and other anagrams   **793.73**
    Jon Agee's palindromania!   **793.73**
    Milo's hat trick   **E**
    Sit on a potato pan, Otis!   **793.73**
    So many dynamos! and other palindromes
        793.73
    Terrific   **E**
    Z goes home   **E**
    (il) Steig, W. Potch & Polly   **E**

Aggie's home. Nixon, J. L.   **Fic**

Aglebemu. Bruchac, J.
    In Bruchac, J. and Bruchac, J. When the
        Chenoo howls; native American tales of
        terror   **398.2**

Agnes, Michael
    (ed) Webster's New World children's dictionary.
    See Webster's New World children's dictio-
    nary   **423**

Agnes Parker . . . girl in progress. O'Dell, K.
    Fic

The **agony** of Alice. Naylor, P. R.   **Fic**

Agricultural laborers
    Ancona, G. Harvest (4 and up)   **331.5**
        Fiction
    Ryan, P. M. Esperanza rising (5 and up)
        Fic

Agricultural machinery
    Peterson, C. Fantastic farm machines (k-3)
        631.3

Agriculture
    Bial, R. Portrait of a farm family (4 and up)
        630.1
    Bowden, R. Food and farming (5 and up)
        363.8
    Halley, N. Farm (4 and up)   **630.1**

Aguinaldo. Delacre, L.
    In Delacre, L. Salsa stories p62-70   **S C**

Ah, music!. Aliki   **780**

Aher, Jackie
    (il) Madaras, L. The "what's happening to my
    body?" book for boys   **613.9**

Ahlberg, Allan
    A bit more Bert   **E**
    The cat who got carried away (2-4)   **Fic**
    The shopping expedition   **E**
    (jt. auth) Ahlberg, J. Each peach pear plum
        E

Ahlberg, Janet
    Each peach pear plum   **E**

AI (Artificial intelligence) *See* Artificial intelligence

Aïda. Verdi, G.   **792.5**

AIDS (Disease)
    Bardhan-Quallen, S. AIDS (4-6)   **616.97**
    McPhee, A. T. AIDS (5 and up)   **616.97**

    Fiction
    Zalben, J. B. Unfinished dreams (5 and up)
        Fic

Aiello, Laurel
    (il) Sabbeth, A. Rubber-band banjos and a java
    jive bass   **781**

Aiken, Joan
    Shadows and moonshine (4 and up)   **S C**
    Contents: Gift pig; Rocking donkey; Cooks and prophecies; Li-
    lac in the lake; Harp of fishbones; Small pinch of weather; King
    who stood all night; Cat's cradle; Moonshine in the mustard pot;
    Wolves and the mermaids; John Sculpin and the witches; Night
    the stars were gone; Boy with a wolf's foot
    The wolves of Willoughby Chase (5 and up)
        Fic

Ailey, Alvin
    About
    Pinkney, A. D. Alvin Ailey (k-3)   **92**

Aillaud, Cindy Lou
    Recess at 20 below (k-3)   **371.2**

Air
    Branley, F. M. Air is all around you (k-1)
        551.5
    Meiani, A. Air (4 and up)   **533**
    Parker, S. The science of air (4 and up)
        533
    Simon, S. Let's try it out in the air (k-2)
        533

Air is all around you. Branley, F. M.   **551.5**

Air pilots
    See also African American pilots; Women
    air pilots
    Burleigh, R. Flight: the journey of Charles Lind-
    bergh (2-4)   **92**
    Maurer, R. The Wright sister [biography of
    Katharine Wright Haskell] (5 and up)   **92**
    Provensen, A. The glorious flight: across the
    Channel with Louis Blériot, July 25, 1909
    (1-4)   **92**
    Fiction
    Saint-Exupéry, A. d. The little prince   **Fic**

Air pollution
    Dalgleish, S. Cleaning the air (3-6)   **363.7**

Airborne: a photobiography of Wilbur and Orville
    Wright. Collins, M.   **92**

Airplanes
    Barton, B. Airplanes (k-1)   **387.7**
    Barton, B. Airport (k-1)   **387.7**
    Bingham, C. Airplane (k-3)   **629.133**
    Hunter, R. A. Take off! (k-3)   **629.13**
    Design and construction
    Provensen, A. The glorious flight: across the
    Channel with Louis Blériot, July 25, 1909
    (1-4)   **92**
    Fiction
    Sturges, P. I love planes!   **E**
    Models
    Kelly, E. J. Paper airplanes (4 and up)
        745.592
    Simon, S. The paper airplane book (3-5)
        745.592

Airports—*Continued*
Piloting
See also Stunt flying
Airplanes, Jet propelled *See* Jet planes
Airports
  Barton, B. Airport (k-1)   **387.7**
Fiction
  Bunting, E. Fly away home   **E**
Airships
  O'Brien, P. The Hindenburg (4 and up)
       629.133

Ajmera, Maya
  Be my neighbor (k-2)   **307**
  Let the games begin! (3-5)   **796**
  To be an artist (k-3)   **700**
Akiak. Blake, R. J.   **E**
Akib, Jamel
  (il) Krishnaswami, U. Monsoon   **E**
Akiko pocket-size, vol. 1. Crilley, M.   **741.5**
Akkadians (Sumerians) *See* Sumerians
Al Adely, Laith Muhmood
  (jt. auth) Hassig, S. M. Iraq   **956.7**
Al Capone does my shirts. Choldenko, G.   **Fic**
ALA filing rules   **025.3**
ALA fundamentals series
  Sullivan, M. Fundamentals of children's services
       027.62

Alabama
  Davis, L. Alabama
    In America the beautiful, second series
       973
  Martin, M. A. Alabama
    In World Almanac Library of the States series
       973
Fiction
  English, K. Francie (5 and up)   **Fic**
  Johnson, A. Bird (5 and up)   **Fic**
Aladdin and the enchanted lamp. Doherty, B.
  In Doherty, B. Fairy tales   **398.2**
Aladdin and the enchanted lamp. Pullman, P.
       398.2
Aladdin and the wonderful lamp
  In The Arabian nights entertainments p295-
    315   **398.2**
  also in The Blue fairy book p72-85   **398.2**
Alagna, Magdalena
  Mae Jemison (4 and up)   **92**
Alamo (San Antonio, Tex.)
  Murphy, J. Inside the Alamo (5 and up)
       976.4
Alarcón, Francisco X.
  From the bellybutton of the moon and other
    summer poems (2-4)   **811**
  Iguanas in the snow and other winter poems
    (2-4)   **811**
  Laughing tomatoes and other spring poems (2-4)
       811
  Poems to dream together (3-5)   **811**
  (jt. auth) Garza, C. L. In my family   **305.8**
  (tr) Garza, C. L. Magic windows   **305.8**
Alaska
  Aillaud, C. L. Recess at 20 below (k-3)
       371.2

  Bjorklund, R. Alaska
    In It's my state! [series]   **973**
  Blake, R. J. Togo   **E**
  McMillan, B. Salmon summer (2-4)   **639.2**
  Miller, D. S. The great serum race (3-5)
       798.8
  Seder, I. Alaska
    In World Almanac Library of the States series
       973
  Stefoff, R. Alaska
    In Celebrate the states   **973**
  Walsh Shepherd, D. Alaska
    In America the beautiful, second series
       973
  Webb, S. Looking for seabirds (4 and up)
       598
Fiction
  Bauer, M. D. A bear named Trouble (3-6)
       Fic
  Blake, R. J. Akiak   **E**
  Hill, K. The year of Miss Agnes (3-5)   **Fic**
  London, J. Sled dogs run   **E**
  Morey, W. Gentle Ben (5 and up)   **Fic**
  Sloat, T. Berry magic   **E**
Natural history
  See Natural history—Alaska
Nome
  See Nome (Alaska)
Albania
  Knowlton, M. Albania (5 and up)   **949.65**
  Wright, D. K. Albania (5 and up)   **949.65**
Albert. Napoli, D. J.   **E**
Albert's birthday. Tryon, L.   **E**
Albert's impossible toothache. Williams, B.   **E**
Albert's toothache. See Williams, B. Albert's im-
  possible toothache   **E**
Alborough, Jez
  Duck in the truck   **E**
  Some dogs do   **E**
  Tall   **E**
Alcatraz Island (Calif.)
Fiction
  Choldenko, G. Al Capone does my shirts (5 and
    up)   **Fic**
The alchemist's cat. Jarvis, R.   **Fic**
Alcock, Vivien
  The cuckoo sister (6 and up)   **Fic**
Alcoholism
  Pringle, L. P. Drinking (5 and up)   **362.292**
Fiction
  Conly, J. L. Crazy lady! (5 and up)   **Fic**
  Daly, N. My dad   **E**
  Davis, M. I. Evangeline Brown and the Cadillac
    Motel (4-6)   **Fic**
Alcorn, Stephen
  (il) Home to me. See Home to me   **811.008**
  (il) Hoofbeats, claws, & rippled fins. See Hoof-
    beats, claws, & rippled fins   **811.008**
  (il) I, too, sing America. See I, too, sing Ameri-
    ca   **811.008**
  (il) Krull, K. The book of rock stars   **920**
  (il) My America. See My America   **811.008**
  (il) Pinkney, A. D. Let it shine   **920**

Alley, R. W. (Robert W.)—*Continued*

(il) DeFelice, C. C. The real, true Dulcie Campbell — **E**

(il) Katz, S. A revolutionary field trip — **811**

(il) McMullan, K. Pearl and Wagner: two good friends — **E**

(il) Mills, C. Ziggy's blue-ribbon day — **E**

(il) Singer, M. Family reunion — **811**

(il) Van Leeuwen, J. The Great Googlestein museum mystery — **Fic**

The **Alley**. Estes, E. — **Fic**

Alligators

Markle, S. Outside and inside alligators (2-4) — **597.98**

Simon, S. Crocodiles & alligators (4 and up) — **597.98**

Fiction

Baker, K. Meet Mr. and Mrs. Green — **E**

Bergman, M. Snip snap! — **E**

Hurd, T. Mama don't allow — **E**

Minarik, E. H. No fighting, no biting! — **E**

Nolen, J. Max and Jax in second grade — **E**

Thomassie, T. Feliciana Feyra LeRoux — **E**

Walsh, E. S. For Pete's sake — **E**

Alligators all around. Sendak, M. — **E**

Allison, Jennifer

Gilda Joyce, psychic investigator (5 and up) — **Fic**

Allison. Say, A. — **E**

Allman, Toney

From spider webs to man-made silk (4 and up) — **595.4**

J. Robert Oppenheimer (5 and up) — **92**

Allusions

Brewer's dictionary of phrase and fable — **803**

Almanacs

Chase's calendar of events — **394.26**

Information please almanac, atlas & yearbook — **031.02**

The World almanac and book of facts — **031.02**

The World almanac for kids — **031.02**

Almond, David

Heaven Eyes (5 and up) — **Fic**

Kit's wilderness (5 and up) — **Fic**

Skellig (5 and up) — **Fic**

Almost a hero. Neufeld, J. — **Fic**

Almost forever. Testa, M. — **Fic**

Almost late to school and more school poems. Shields, C. D. — **811**

Alphabatics. Macdonald, S. — **E**

Alphabeep. Pearson, D. — **E**

Alphabet

Ada, A. F. Gathering the sun (2-4) — **811**

Agee, J. Z goes home — **E**

Ashley Bryan's ABC of African-American poetry (k-3) — **811.008**

Aylesworth, J. Old black fly — **E**

Azarian, M. A farmer's alphabet — **E**

Azarian, M. A gardener's alphabet — **E**

Bayer, J. A my name is Alice — **E**

Belle, J. Animal stackers — **E**

Bunting, E. Girls A to Z — **E**

Chesworth, M. Alphaboat — **E**

Chorao, K. D is for drums (k-3) — **975.5**

Cleary, B. The hullabaloo ABC — **E**

Cronin, D. Click, clack, quackity-quack — **E**

Demarest, C. L. Firefighters A to Z (k-1) — **628.9**

Dugan, J. ABC NYC — **E**

Ehlert, L. Eating the alphabet — **E**

Eichenberg, F. Ape in a cape — **E**

Elya, S. M. F is for fiesta — **E**

Feelings, M. Jambo means hello — **E**

Fisher, L. E. The ABC exhibit — **E**

Fleming, D. Alphabet under construction — **E**

Floca, B. The racecar alphabet — **E**

Freymann, S. Food for thought — **E**

Geisert, A. Pigs from A to Z — **E**

Grobler, P. Little bird's ABC — **E**

Hoban, T. 26 letters and 99 cents — **E**

Horenstein, H. A is for—? — **E**

The human alphabet — **E**

Isadora, R. On your toes — **E**

Jay, A. ABC: a child's first alphabet book — **E**

Jocelyn, M. ABC x 3 — **E**

Johnson, S. Alphabet city — **E**

Kratter, P. The living rain forest (k-3) — **591.7**

Krull, K. M is for music — **E**

Leopold, N. S. C. K is for kitten — **E**

Lester, M. A is for salad — **E**

Lobel, A. Alison's zinnia — **E**

Lobel, A. On Market Street — **E**

London, J. Do your ABC's Little Brown Bear — **E**

MacDonald, R. Achoo! Bang! Crash! — **E**

Macdonald, S. A was once an apple pie — **E**

Macdonald, S. Alphabatics — **E**

Mannis, C. A. The Queen's progress [biography of Elizabeth I] (3-5) — **92**

Marino, G. Zoopa — **E**

Martin, B. Chicka chicka boom boom — **E**

McLeod, B. SuperHero ABC — **E**

Melmed, L. K. New York, New York (k-3) — **974.7**

Merriam, E. Spooky A B C (3-6) — **811**

Micklethwait, L. I spy: an alphabet in art — **E**

Mignon, P. Labyrinths (3-5) — **793.73**

Milich, Z. The city ABC book — **E**

Minor, W. Yankee Doodle America (2-4) — **973.3**

Most, B. ABC T-Rex — **E**

Museum ABC — **E**

Pearson, D. Alphabeep — **E**

Pelletier, D. The graphic alphabet — **E**

Polacco, P. G is for goat — **E**

Pomeroy, D. Wildflower ABC — **E**

Rankin, L. The handmade alphabet (k-3) — **419**

Rose, D. L. Into the A, B, sea (k-3) — **591.7**

Sabuda, R. The Christmas alphabet — **E**

Schnur, S. Spring — **E**

Schnur, S. Winter — **E**

Schwartz, D. M. G is for googol (4 and up) — **510**

Schwartz, D. M. Q is for quark (4 and up) — **500**

Seeger, L. V. The hidden alphabet — **E**

Sendak, M. Alligators all around — **E**

Shannon, G. Tomorrow's alphabet — **E**

Amendola, Dana
A day at the New Amsterdam Theatre (4 and up) **792.6**

America

See also Latin America

Antiquities
Lauber, P. Who came first (5 and up) **970.01**

Sattler, H. R. The earliest Americans (5 and up) **970.01**

Wood, M. Ancient America (5 and up) **970.01**

Exploration
Faber, H. Samuel de Champlain (5 and up) **92**

Fritz, J. Brendan the Navigator (3-5) **398.2**

Fritz, J. Where do you think you're going, Christopher Columbus? (2-4) **92**

Maestro, B. The discovery of the Americas (2-4) **970.01**

Maestro, B. Exploration and conquest (2-4) **970.01**

Meltzer, M. Francisco Pizarro (5 and up) **92**

Otfinoski, S. Juan Ponce de Leon (5 and up) **92**

Otfinoski, S. Vasco Nuñez de Balboa (5 and up) **92**

Sís, P. Follow the dream [biography of Christopher Columbus] (k-3) **92**

Stanley, G. E. The European settlement of North America (1492-1763) (5 and up) **973.2**

Steins, R. Exploration and settlement (5 and up) **970.01**

Exploration—Fiction
Dorris, M. Morning Girl (4 and up) **Fic**

America at war [series]
Marquette, S. America under attack **973.931**
Marquette, S. War of 1812 **973.5**

America in today's world (1969-2004). Stanley, G. E. **973.92**

America the beautiful (Song)
Younger, B. Purple mountain majesties: the story of Katharine Lee Bates and "America the beautiful" (2-4) **92**

America the beautiful. Bates, K. L. **E**

America the beautiful, second series (5 and up) **973**

America under attack. Marquette, S. **973.931**

America votes. Granfield, L. **324**

American art
Fisher, L. E. The limners (4 and up) **759.13**
Heart to heart (5 and up) **811.008**

American artists *See* Artists—United States

American Association of School Librarians
The Information-powered school. See The Information-powered school **027.8**
Information power **027.8**

American battlefields [series]
January, B. Little Bighorn, June 25, 1876 **973.8**

American bison *See* Bison

American bison. Berman, R. **599.64**

American boy: the adventures of Mark Twain. Brown, D. **92**

The **American** Civil War. Ford, C. T. **973.7**

American colonies *See* United States—History—1600-1775, Colonial period

American cooking *See* Cooking

American documents [series]
Finkelman, P. The Constitution **342**

American drama
Collections
You're on!: seven plays in English and Spanish (4 and up) **812.008**

American experience in Vietnam [series]
Canwell, D. African Americans in the Vietnam War **959.704**

American family albums [series]
Hoobler, D. The African American family album **305.8**
Hoobler, D. The Chinese American family album **305.8**
Hoobler, D. The Cuban American family album **305.8**
Hoobler, D. The German American family album **305.8**
Hoobler, D. The Irish American family album **305.8**
Hoobler, D. The Italian American family album **305.8**
Hoobler, D. The Japanese American family album **305.8**
Hoobler, D. The Jewish American family album **305.8**
Hoobler, D. The Mexican American family album **305.8**
Hoobler, D. The Scandinavian American family album **305.8**

American furniture
Fisher, L. E. The cabinetmakers (4 and up) **684.1**

The **American** Heritage Children's Dictionary (3-6) **423**

The **American** Heritage children's science dictionary (5 and up) **503**

The **American** Heritage children's thesaurus. Hellweg, P. **423**

The **American** Heritage picture dictionary (k-1) **423**

American heroes. Delano, M. F. **920**

American humane pet care library [series]
Jeffrey, L. S. Birds **636.6**
Jeffrey, L. S. Cats **636.8**
Jeffrey, L. S. Dogs **636.7**
Jeffrey, L. S. Fish **639.34**
Jeffrey, L. S. Hamsters, gerbils, guinea pigs, rabbits, ferrets, mice, and rats **636.9**
Jeffrey, L. S. Horses **636.1**

American Indian biographies [series]
Dennis, Y. W. Sequoyah, 1770?-1843 **92**
Englar, M. Chief Joseph, 1840-1904 **92**

American Indians *See* Native Americans

American kids in history [series]
King, D. C. Colonial days **973.2**
King, D. C. Pioneer days **978**
King, D. C. Wild West days **978**
King, D. C. World War II days **940.53**

American Library Association. Coretta Scott King Award Task Force

The Coretta Scott King Awards book, 1970-1999. See The Coretta Scott King Awards book, 1970-1999 **028.5**

American literature

See also various forms of American literature, e.g. American poetry

African American authors

The Coretta Scott King Awards book, 1970-1999 **028.5**

Hudson, W. Powerful words (5 and up)
808.8

Stephens, C. G. Coretta Scott King Award books **028.5**

Black authors

See American literature—African American authors

Collections

Girls got game (5 and up) **810.8**
Scared silly! (k-3) **810.8**
Yolen, J. Here there be dragons (5 and up)
810.8

Hispanic American authors—Bibliography

Day, F. A. Latina and Latino voices in literature
810.9
York, S. Children's and young adult literature by Latino writers **028.5**

Hispanic American authors—Bio-bibliography

York, S. Picture books by Latino writers
028.5

Hispanic American authors—Collections

Wáchale! poetry and prose on growing up Latino in America (5 and up) **810.8**

Native American authors—Collections

Rising voices (5 and up) **810.8**

American Loyalists

Fiction

O'Dell, S. Sarah Bishop (6 and up) **Fic**

American Museum of Natural History

Murdoch, D. H. North American Indian
970.004

American National Red Cross *See* American Red Cross

An **American** plague. Murphy, J. **614.5**

American poetry

African American authors—Collections

Ashley Bryan's ABC of African-American poetry (k-3) **811.008**
The entrance place of wonders (3-5)
811.008
I am the darker brother **811.008**
I, too, sing America (6 and up) **811.008**
The Palm of my heart **811.008**
Pass it on (k-3) **811.008**
Soul looks back in wonder (4 and up)
811.008
Words with wings (4 and up) **811.008**

Collections

The 20th century children's poetry treasury
811.008
The baby's playtime book (k-1) **811.008**
Big, bad, and a little bit scary (k-3)
811.008

The Blackbirch treasury of American poetry (5 and up) **811.008**
Carnival of the animals **811.008**
Christmas presents (k-3) **811.008**
Dinosaurs: poems (3-5) **811.008**
Extra innings (4 and up) **811.008**
The Fish is me (k-2) **811.008**
For laughing out loud **811.008**
Ghost poems (1-4) **821.008**
Good books, good times! (1-3) **811.008**
Grandad's tree (k-3) **811.008**
Halloween howls (k-3) **811.008**
Hanukkah lights (k-3) **811.008**
Heart to heart (5 and up) **811.008**
Home to me (3-5) **811.008**
Hoofbeats, claws, & rippled fins (3-6)
811.008
If you ever meet a whale (3-5) **811.008**
In daddy's arms I am tall **811.008**
It rained all day that night (3-6) **811.008**
The Kingfisher book of funny poems (4 and up)
821.008
Knock at a star **811.008**
Lives: poems about famous Americans (4 and up) **811.008**
Love to mamá (3-6) **811.008**
Marvelous math (4 and up) **811.008**
More spice than sugar (4 and up) **811.008**
My America (4 and up) **811.008**
My kingdom for a horse (2-4) **811.008**
Oh, no! Where are my pants? and other disasters (2-4) **811.008**
Opening days (4 and up) **811.008**
The Oxford book of children's verse
821.008
The Oxford book of children's verse in America
811.008
The Oxford illustrated book of American children's poems **811.008**
A Pet for me (k-3) **811.008**
The Place my words are looking for (4 and up)
811.008
Pocket poems (k-3) **811.008**
Poetry from A to Z (5 and up) **808.1**
A Poke in the I (4 and up) **811.008**
The Random House book of poetry for children
821.008
Read a rhyme, write a rhyme (2-4) **811.008**
Read-aloud rhymes for the very young (k-2)
821.008
Salting the ocean (4 and up) **811.008**
Spectacular science (2-4) **811.008**
Sports! sports! sports! (k-2) **811.008**
Talking like the rain (k-3) **821.008**
This place I know (3-5) **811.008**
Whisper and shout (4 and up) **811.008**
Wings on the wind (k-3) **811.008**

Hispanic American authors—Collections

Cool salsa (5 and up) **811.008**

American Red Cross

Koestler-Grack, R. A. The story of Clara Barton (2-4) **92**

The **American** Revolution. Bohannon, L. F.
973.3

The **American** Revolution. Sheinkin, S. **973.3**

The **American** Revolution for kids. Herbert, J.
973.3

The **American** revolutionaries: a history in their own words, 1750-1800 (6 and up) **973.3**

American science *See* Science—United States

American songs

See also Folk songs—United States; National songs—United States; Spirituals (Songs)

American story series

Maestro, B. Liberty or death **973.3**

Maestro, B. Struggle for a continent **973.2**

American tall tales. Osborne, M. P. **398.2**

Americanization

See also Naturalization

America's champion swimmer: Gertrude Ederle. Adler, D. A. **92**

America's leaders [series]

Ingram, S. The FBI director **363.2**

America's westward expansion [series]

Steele, C. Cattle ranching in the American West
978

Steele, C. Famous wagon trails **978**

Steele, C. Pioneer life in the American West
978

Ames, Gerald

(jt. auth) Wyler, R. Magic secrets **793.8**

Ames, Lee J.

[Draw 50 series] (4 and up) **743**

Amina, Queen of Zaria

See/See also pages in the following book(s):

Hansen, J. African princess (5 and up) **920**

Amiri, Fahimeh

(il) Rockwell, A. F. The Prince who ran away
294.3

Amish

Bial, R. Amish home (3-5) **289.7**

Fiction

Brown, C. M. Barn raising **E**

Stewart, S. The journey **E**

Amish home. Bial, R. **289.7**

Amistad (Schooner)

Myers, W. D. Amistad: a long road to freedom (5 and up) **326**

Ammon, Bette D.

Worth a thousand words **011.6**

Ammon, Richard

Conestoga wagons (2-5) **388.3**

Amnesia

Fiction

Taylor, T. Teetoncey (5 and up) **Fic**

Amos & Boris. Steig, W.

In You read to me & I'll read to you; 20th-century stories to share p2-9 **E**

Amos Fortune, free man. Yates, E. **92**

Amphibians

See also Frogs

Clarke, B. Amphibian (4 and up) **597.8**

Poetry

Florian, D. Lizards, frogs, and pollywogs
811

Amsha the giant. Schwartz, H.

In Schwartz, H. and Rush, B. A coat for the moon and other Jewish tales p42-45
398.2

Amusement parks

Fiction

Roberts, W. D. Scared stiff (5 and up) **Fic**

Amusements

See also Roller coasters

Becker, H. Boredom blasters (4-6) **793**

Blakey, N. Go outside! (3-6) **790.1**

Love, A. Kids and grandparents: an activity book (3-6) **790.1**

Williamson, S. Summer fun! **790.1**

Ananse and the birds. Badoe, A.

In Badoe, A. The pot of wisdom: Ananse stories
398.2

Ananse and the feeding pot. Badoe, A.

In Badoe, A. The pot of wisdom: Ananse stories
398.2

Ananse and the lizard. Cummings, P. **398.2**

Ananse and the pot of wisdom. Badoe, A.

In Badoe, A. The pot of wisdom: Ananse stories
398.2

Ananse and the singing cloak. Badoe, A.

In Badoe, A. The pot of wisdom: Ananse stories
398.2

Ananse becomes the owner of stories. Badoe, A.

In Badoe, A. The pot of wisdom: Ananse stories
398.2

Ananse the even-handed judge. Badoe, A.

In Badoe, A. The pot of wisdom: Ananse stories
398.2

Ananse the forgetful guest. Badoe, A.

In Badoe, A. The pot of wisdom: Ananse stories
398.2

Ananse the Spider in search of a fool. Bryan, A.

In Bryan, A. Ashley Bryan's African tales, uh-huh p1-8 **398.2**

Ananse's feast. Mollel, T. M. **398.2**

Anansi (Legendary character)

Aardema, V. Anansi does the impossible! (k-3)
398.2

Badoe, A. The pot of wisdom: Ananse stories
398.2

Cummings, P. Ananse and the lizard (k-3)
398.2

Haley, G. E. A story, a story (k-3) **398.2**

Kimmel, E. A. Anansi and the magic stick (k-3)
398.2

Kimmel, E. A. Anansi and the talking melon (k-3) **398.2**

Kimmel, E. A. Anansi goes fishing (k-3)
398.2

McDermott, G. Anansi the spider (k-3)
398.2

Mollel, T. M. Ananse's feast (k-3) **398.2**

Anansi and Nothing go hunting for wives. Courlander, H.

In Courlander, H. and Herzog, G. Cow-tail switch, and other West African stories p95-102 **398.2**

Anansi and the magic stick. Kimmel, E. A.
398.2

Anansi and the pig. Sierra, J.
   In Sierra, J. Nursery tales around the world
     p65-67   **398.2**
Anansi and the talking melon. Kimmel, E. A.
                           398.2
Anansi does the impossible!. Aardema, V.
                           398.2
Anansi goes fishing. Kimmel, E. A.   **398.2**
Anansi the spider. McDermott, G.   **398.2**
Anansi's fishing expedition. Courlander, H.
   In Courlander, H. and Herzog, G. Cow-tail
    switch, and other West African stories
    p47-58   **398.2**
Anansi's fishing expedition. Washington, D. L.
   In Washington, D. L. A pride of African tales
Anasazi culture *See* Pueblo Indians
Anastasia Krupnik. Lowry, L.   **Fic**
Anatomy
     See also Musculoskeletal system; Physiology
Anatomy, Human *See* Human anatomy
Anaya, Rudolfo A.
   The farolitos of Christmas   **E**
Ancient America. Wood, M.   **970.01**
Ancient art
     See also Greek art; Roman art
The **ancient** Aztecs. Sonneborn, L.   **972**
The **ancient** Celts. Calvert, P.   **936**
Ancient China. Anderson, D.   **709.51**
Ancient China. Cotterell, A.   **931**
Ancient China. Shuter, J.   **931**
The **ancient** Chinese. Schomp, V.   **931**
Ancient civilization
     See also Classical civilization
   Adams, S. Alexander (4 and up)   **92**
   Curlee, L. Seven wonders of the ancient world
    (3-6)   **709.01**
   Merrill, Y. Y. Hands-on ancient people (5 and
    up)   **930**
   Panchyk, R. Archaeology for kids (5 and up)
                       930.1
   Trumble, K. The Library of Alexandria (5 and
    up)   **027**
The **ancient** cliff dwellers of Mesa Verde. Arnold,
   C.   **970.004**
Ancient Egypt. Langley, A.   **932**
Ancient Egypt revealed. Chrisp, P.   **932**
Ancient Egyptian jobs. Malam, J.   **932**
The **ancient** Egyptians. Perl, L.   **932**
Ancient Greece!. Hart, A.   **938**
Ancient Greece. Langley, A.   **709.38**
Ancient Greece. Malam, J.   **938**
Ancient Greece. Pearson, A.   **938**
Ancient Greece. Powell, A.   **938**
The **ancient** Greek Olympics. Woff, R. **796.48**
The **ancient** Greeks. Lassieur, A.   **938**
The **ancient** Inca. Calvert, P.   **985**
Ancient India. Schomp, V.   **934**
The **ancient** Kushites. Sonneborn, L.   **939**

The **ancient** Maya. Perl, L.   **972**
The **ancient** Mediterranean. Stefoff, R.   **938**
Ancient Mesopotamia. Schomp, V.   **935**
The **ancient** Near East. Stefoff, R.   **939**
Ancient ones. Bash, B.   **585**
The **ancient** Romans. Lassieur, A.   **937**
Ancient Rome. Chrisp, P.   **709.37**
Ancient Rome. Corbishley, M.   **937**
Ancient Rome. James, S.   **937**
Ancona, George
   Carnaval (3-6)   **394.25**
   Charro (3-6)   **972**
   Cuban kids (3-5)   **972.91**
   Fiesta U.S.A. (k-3)   **394.26**
   The fiestas (2-4)   **394.26**
   Harvest (4 and up)   **331.5**
   Murals (3-6)   **751**
   Pablo remembers (k-3)   **394.26**
   The piñata maker: El piñatero (k-3) **745.594**
   Powwow (3-6)   **970.004**
And if the moon could talk. Banks, K.   **E**
And one for all. Nelson, T.   **Fic**
And Tango makes three. Richardson, J.   **E**
And then it rained . . . Dragonwagon, C.   **E**
And then the sun came out . . . *See*
   Dragonwagon, C. And then it rained . . .
                          E
And then what happened, Paul Revere? Fritz, J.
                           92
And to think that I saw it on Mulberry Street.
   Seuss, Dr.   **E**
And who cured the princess? Yolen, J.
   In Yolen, J. Mightier than the sword; world
    folktales for strong boys p69-73
                       398.2
Andersen, Bethanne
   (il) Hopkinson, D. A packet of seeds   **E**
   (il) Meltzer, M. Ten kings   **920**
   (il) Meltzer, M. Ten queens   **920**
   (il) Sasso, S. E. But God remembered **221.9**
Andersen, Hans Christian
   The emperor's new clothes [illustrated by Angela Barrett]   **E**
   The emperor's new clothes [illustrated by Virginia Lee Burton]   **E**
   The emperor's new clothes
    also in De Paola, T. Tomie dePaola's Favorite nursery tales p87-95   **398.2**
   Fairy tales of Hans Christian Andersen (3-6)
                       S C
   Hans Christian Andersen's Fairy Tales (4 and up)   **S C**
   Contents: The sandman; The jumpers Thumbeline; The tinderbox; The rose tree regiment; The naughty boy; The swineherd; The emperor's new clothes; The princess and the pea; The nightingale; The little match girl
   The little match girl (3-5)   **Fic**
   The little mermaid
    In Princess stories; a classic illustrated edition
                       398.2
   The nightingale
    also in Shedlock, M. L. The art of the storyteller p243-58   **372.6**

Andersen, Hans Christian—*Continued*

The princess and the pea [illustrated by Dorothee Duntze] (k-3)   **Fic**

The princess and the pea

also in Princess stories; a classic illustrated edition   **398.2**

also in De Paola, T. Tomie dePaola's Favorite nursery tales p64-67   **398.2**

The princess on the pea

In Shedlock, M. L. The art of the story-teller p259-60   **372.6**

The swan's stories   **S C**

Contents: The flying trunk; The steadfast tin soldier; The money pig; Jumpers; Lovers; The collar; The darning needle; Grief; The shepherdess and the chimney sweep; The browney at the grocer's; The snowman; The fir tree

The swineherd

In Shedlock, M. L. The art of the story-teller p235-42   **372.6**

Tales of Hans Christian Andersen (4 and up)   **S C**

Contents: The princess and the pea; The tinderbox; Thumbelina; The emperor's new clothes; The little mermaid; The steadfast tin soldier; The flying trunk; The ugly duckling; The nightingale; The snow queen; The little match girl; The goblin at the grocer's

Thumbeline   **E**

Andersen, Hans Christian, 1805-1875
About
Hesse, K. The young Hans Christian Andersen (2-4)   **92**

Varmer, H. Hans Christian Andersen (5 and up)   **92**

Yolen, J. The perfect wizard [biography of Hans Christian Andersen] (2-4)   **92**

See/See also pages in the following book(s):

Krull, K. Lives of the writers (4 and up)   **920**

Adaptations
Bell, A. The Snow Queen   **E**

Child, L. The princess and the pea in miniature   **E**

Demi. The emperor's new clothes   **E**

Ehrlich, A. Thumbelina   **E**

Levine, G. C. The princess test (4 and up)   **Fic**

Mills, L. A. Thumbelina   **E**

Mitchell, S. The nightingale (2-4)   **Fic**

Pinkney, J. The little match girl   **E**

Pinkney, J. The nightingale (2-4)   **Fic**

Pinkney, J. The ugly duckling   **E**

Poole, A. L. The pea blossom   **E**

Sedgwick, M. The emperor's new clothes **E**

Seidler, T. The steadfast tin soldier (1-4)   **Fic**

Watts, B. The ugly duckling   **E**

Anderson, Bethanne

(il) Bryant, J. Georgia's bones [biography of Georgia O'Keefe]   **92**

(il) Hearne, B. G. Seven brave women   **E**

(il) Karim, R. Kindle me a riddle   **E**

Anderson, Christine

Bedtime!   **E**

Anderson, Cynthia

Write grants, get money   **025.1**

Anderson, Dale

Ancient China (4 and up)   **709.51**

Arriving at Ellis Island (5 and up)   **325.73**

The Cold War years (5 and up)   **973.92**

World Almanac library of the Civil War [series] (4-6)   **973.7**

Anderson, Derek

(il) Thompson, L. Little Quack   **E**

Anderson, Janet

The last treasure (5 and up)   **Fic**

Anderson, Jill

Giraffes (k-2)   **599.63**

Anderson, Jodi Lynn

May Bird and The Ever After (5 and up) **Fic**

Anderson, Laurie Halse

Fever, 1793 (5 and up)   **Fic**

Anderson, Lena

Tea for ten   **E**

(il) Björk, C. Linnea in Monet's garden **Fic**

(il) Björk, C. Linnea's almanac   **508**

Anderson, M. T.

Bacarole for paper and bones

In Shelf life: stories by the book p127-49   **S C**

The Game of Sunken Places (5 and up)   **Fic**

Handel, who knew what he liked (4-6)   **92**

Strange Mr. Satie (2-4)   **92**

Whales on stilts (4 and up)   **Fic**

Anderson, Margaret Jean

Aristotle (5 and up)   **92**

Anderson, Marian, 1897-1993
About
Freedman, R. The voice that challenged a nation [biography of Marian Anderson] (5 and up)   **92**

McKissack, P. C. Marian Anderson (1-3) **92**

Ryan, P. M. When Marian sang: the true recital of Marian Anderson, the voice of a century (2-4)   **92**

Poetry
Livingston, M. C. Keep on singing (k-3) **811**

Anderson, Mary

See/See also pages in the following book(s):

Thimmesh, C. Girls think of everything (5 and up)   **920**

Anderson, Maxine

Amazing Leonardo da Vinci inventions you can build yourself   **92**

Anderson, Paul Christopher

George Armstrong Custer (4 and up)   **92**

Anderson, Peter

(il) Margeson, S. M. Viking   **948**

(il) Redmond, I. Gorilla, monkey & ape **599.8**

Anderson, Stephanie

(il) Kanevsky, P. Sleepy boy   **E**

(il) Lyon, G. E. Weaving the rainbow   **E**

Anderson, William T.

Pioneer girl: the story of Laura Ingalls Wilder (2-4)   **92**

Andersonville Prison
Fiction
Wisler, G. C. Red Cap (4 and up)   **Fic**

Andreasen, Dan
(il) Anderson, W. T. Pioneer girl: the story of Laura Ingalls Wilder **92**
(il) Crumpacker, B. Alexander's pretending day **E**
(il) Kroll, S. By the dawn's early light **782.42**
(il) Wells, R. Streets of gold [biography of Mary Antin] **92**

Andrew, Ian P.
(il) Pow, T. Tell me one thing, Dad **E**

Andrews, Benny
(il) Belton, S. Pictures for Miss Josie **E**
(jt. auth) Haskins, J. Delivering justice [biography of Westley Wallace Law] **92**
(il) Hughes, L. Langston Hughes **811**

Andrews, Linda Wasmer
Meditation (5 and up) **158**

Andrews, Roy Chapman, 1884-1960
About
Bausum, A. Dragon bones and dinosaur eggs: a photobiography of Roy Chapman Andrews (5 and up) **92**
Floca, B. Dinosaurs at the ends of the earth (3-5) **567.9**
Marrin, A. Secrets from the rocks: dinosaur hunting with Roy Chapman Andrews (4 and up) **92**

Andrews-Goebel, Nancy
The pot that Juan built [biography of Juan Quezada] (k-3) **92**

Andryszewski, Tricia
The Seminoles (4-6) **970.004**

Andy and the lion. Daugherty, J. H. **E**

Andy Shane and the very bossy Dolores Starbuckle. Jacobson, J. **E**

Anecdotes
See also Wit and humor
The **angel** and other stories. Stauffacher, S. **398.2**
The **angel** and the donkey. Paterson, K. **222**
Angel baby. Cummings, P. **E**
Angel coming. Henson, H. **E**
El **angel** de oro. Jiménez, F.
In Jiménez, F. The circuit: stories from the life of a migrant child p45-50 **S C**
The **Angel** of Death. Lester, J.
In Lester, J. When the beginning began; stories about God, the creatures, and us p25-30 **296.1**
Angel secrets. Chaikin, M. **296.1**
Angelfish. Yep, L. **Fic**
Angelina Ballerina. Holabird, K. **E**
Angelo, Master
(il) Grimes, N. A dime a dozen **811**
Angelo, Valenti
(il) Sawyer, R. Roller skates **Fic**
Angelo. Macaulay, D. **E**
Angels
Chaikin, M. Angel secrets (4 and up) **296.1**

Fiction
Chaikin, M. Angels sweep the desert floor (4 and up) **296.1**
De Paola, T. Pascual and the kitchen angels **E**
Lester, J. What a truly cool world! **E**
The **angel's** daughter. Schwartz, H.
In Schwartz, H. Invisible kingdoms; Jewish tales of angels, spirits, and demons p14-24 **398.2**
The **angel's** gift. Schwartz, H.
In Schwartz, H. Invisible kingdoms; Jewish tales of angels, spirits, and demons p3-8 **398.2**
Angel's mother's wedding. Delton, J. **Fic**
Angels of mercy. Kuhn, B. **940.54**
Angels sweep the desert floor. Chaikin, M. **296.1**
The **angel's** sword. Schwartz, H.
In Schwartz, H. Invisible kingdoms; Jewish tales of angels, spirits, and demons p9-13 **398.2**
Anger
Fiction
Bang, M. When Sophie gets angry—really, really angry **E**
Jonell, L. When Mommy was mad **E**
Vail, R. Sometimes I'm Bombaloo **E**
Angina pectoris *See* Heart diseases
Angles
Murphy, S. J. Hamster champs (1-3) **516**
Anglo-American cataloguing rules
Fritz, D. A. Cataloging with AACR2 and MARC21 **025.3**
Gorman, M. The concise AACR2 **025.3**
Anglo-American invasion of Iraq, 2003 *See* Iraq War, 2003
Angola
Fiction
McKissack, P. C. Nzinga, warrior queen of Matamba (5 and up) **Fic**
The **angry** woman. Lester, J.
In Lester, J. The last tales of Uncle Remus p56-61 **398.2**
Animal babies
Ashman, L. Babies on the go **E**
Bauer, M. D. If you were born a kitten (k-1) **591.3**
Butler, J. Whose baby am I? **E**
Fraser, M. A. How animal babies stay safe (k-1) **591.56**
Heller, R. Chickens aren't the only ones (k-1) **591.4**
Hickman, P. M. Animals and their young (3-5) **591.56**
Rose, D. L. Ocean babies (k-2) **591.3**
Ruurs, M. Wild babies (k-3) **591.3**
Swinburne, S. R. Safe, warm, and snug (k-3) **591.56**
Animal behavior
See also Animal defenses
Bancroft, H. Animals in winter (k-1) **591.56**
Bishop, N. The secrets of animal flight (3-6) **591.47**

Animal behavior—*Continued*

Collard, S. B., III. Animal dads (k-3)
591.56

Collard, S. B., III. Animals asleep (k-3)
591.56

Davies, N. Poop (2-5)   573.4

Fraser, M. A. Where are the night animals?
(k-1)   591.5

Goodman, S. The truth about poop (2-5)
573.4

Hickman, P. M. Animals and their mates (3-5)
591.56

Settel, J. Exploding ants (4 and up)   591.5

Stockdale, S. Carry me! (k-2)   591.56

Swinburne, S. R. Safe, warm, and snug (k-3)
591.56

Animal communication

Dudzinski, K. Meeting dolphins (4 and up)
599.5

Pfeffer, W. Dolphin talk (k-2)   599.5

Sayre, A. P. Secrets of sound (4 and up)
591.59

Schlein, M. Hello, hello!   E

Winer, Y. Frogs sing songs (k-3)   597.8

Animal courtship

Collard, S. B., III. Making animal babies (k-3)
571.8

Animal dads. Collard, S. B., III   591.56

Animal defenses

Jenkins, S. What do you do when something
wants to eat you? (k-3)   591.47

Zoehfeld, K. W. What lives in a shell? (k-1)
591.4

Animal fables from Aesop. McClintock, B.
398.2

The **animal** family. Jarrell, R.   Fic

The **animal** hedge. Fleischman, P.   E

Animal helpers for the disabled. Kent, D.
636.088

Animal introduction

Batten, M. Aliens from Earth (3-6)   577

Animal lives [series]

Tagholm, S. The rabbit   599.3

Animal locomotion

Ashman, L. Babies on the go   E

Hickman, P. M. Animals in motion (3-5)
591.47

Jenkins, S. Move!   E

Animal lore *See* Animals—Folklore

Animal migration *See* Animals—Migration

Animal mischief. Jackson, R. B.   811

Animal painting and illustration

See also Animals in art

Animal pounds *See* Animal shelters

Animal predators [series]

Markle, S. Crocodiles   597.98
Markle, S. Great white sharks   597
Markle, S. Killer whales   599.5
Markle, S. Lions   599.75
Markle, S. Owls   598
Markle, S. Polar bears   599.78
Markle, S. Wolves   599.77

Animal scavengers [series]

Markle, S. Vultures   598

Animal shelters

Casey, P. One day at Wood Green Animal Shelter   E

Fiction

Graham, B. Let's get a pup, said Kate   E

Animal snackers. Lewin, B.   811

Animal stories *See* Animals—Fiction

Animal tracks

Selsam, M. E. Big tracks, little tracks (k-3)
591.5

See/See also pages in the following book(s):

Arnosky, J. Field trips (3-6)   508

Fiction

Yee, W. H. Tracks in the snow   E

Animal welfare

See also Animal shelters

Animals

See also Dangerous animals; Pets; Prehistoric animals; Rare animals; Wildlife and names of orders and classes of the animal kingdom; kinds of animals characterized by their environments; and names of individual species

Aliki. My visit to the zoo (k-3)   590.73

Arnosky, J. Crinkleroot's guide to knowing animal habitats (k-3)   591.7

Arnosky, J. Crinkleroot's nature almanac (k-3)
508

Belle, J. Animal stackers   E

Bible. Selections. Animals of the Bible (1-4)
220.8

Carle, E. Does a kangaroo have a mother, too?
E

Carle, E. From head to toe   E

Carrick, C. Mothers are like that   E

DuQuette, K. They call me Woolly (k-3)
590

Ehrlich, F. Does an elephant take a bath?   E

Eichenberg, F. Ape in a cape   E

Fleming, D. Count!   E

Goodman, S. Claws, coats, and camouflage
(2-4)   591.4

Hoban, T. A children's zoo   E

Horenstein, H. A is for—?   E

Jenkins, S. Actual size (k-3)   591.4

Jenkins, S. Big & little (k-2)   591.4

Jenkins, S. Biggest, strongest, fastest (k-2)
590

Jenkins, S. I see a kookaburra! (k-3)   591.7

Krautwurst, T. Night science for kids (4-6)
591.5

Marino, G. Zoopa   E

Munari, B. Bruno Munari's zoo   E

Sayre, A. P. One is a snail, ten is a crab   E

Wormell, C. Teeth, tails, & tentacles   E

Zoehfeld, K. W. Wild lives (5 and up)
590.73

Zolotow, C. Sleepy book   E

Courtship

See Animal courtship

Encyclopedias

Dorling Kindersley animal encyclopedia (4 and up)   590.3

Animals—Encyclopedias—*Continued*

National Geographic animal encyclopedia (3-6)
590.3

Fiction

Alborough, J. Duck in the truck	**E**
Arnold, K. Me too!	**E**
Aroner, M. Clink, clank, clunk!	**E**
Avi. Poppy (3-5)	**Fic**
Barroux, S. Where's Mary's hat?	**E**
Beaumont, K. Duck, duck, goose!	**E**
Blackstone, S. Who are you, baby kangaroo?	**E**
Blomgren, J. Where do I sleep?	**E**
Brett, J. Annie and the wild animals	**E**
Brett, J. The hat	**E**
Brown, M. W. Big red barn	**E**
Brown, M. W. Where have you been?	**E**
Buehner, C. I did it, I'm sorry	**E**
Burningham, J. Mr. Gumpy's outing	**E**
Butler, J. Can you cuddle like a koala?	**E**
Byars, B. C. Me Tarzan (3-5)	**Fic**
Cabrera, J. If you're happy and you know it	**E**
Cabrera, J. Mommy, carry me please!	**E**
Campbell, R. Dear zoo	**E**
Carle, E. "Slowly, slowly, slowly," said the sloth	**E**
Carle, E. The very clumsy click beetle	**E**
Carle, E. Where are you going? To see my friend!	**E**
Casanova, M. One-dog canoe	**E**
Cauley, L. B. Clap your hands	**E**
Chaconas, D. One little mouse	**E**
Cole, H. I took a walk	**E**
Conover, C. Over the hills & far away	**E**
Cronin, D. Click, clack, quackity-quack	**E**
Cushman, D. Mystery at the Club Sandwich	**E**
Dahl, R. The enormous crocodile (2-4)	**Fic**
De Regniers, B. S. May I bring a friend?	**E**
Denslow, S. P. In the snow	**E**
Dunrea, O. Bear Noel	**E**
Edwards, P. D. Some smug slug	**E**
Ehlert, L. Circus	**E**
Elya, S. M. Eight animals on the town	**E**
Emberley, E. Thanks, Mom!	**E**
Ets, M. H. Play with me	**E**
Flack, M. Ask Mr. Bear	**E**
Fleischman, P. The animal hedge	**E**
Fleming, D. Barnyard banter	**E**
Fleming, D. In the tall, tall grass	**E**
Fleming, D. Time to sleep	**E**
Fox, M. Wombat divine	**E**
Freedman, C. Gooseberry Goose	**E**
Gammell, S. Once upon MacDonald's farm	**E**
Gannett, R. S. My father's dragon (1-4)	**Fic**
George, J. C. Morning, noon, and night	**E**
Grahame, K. The wind in the willows (4-6)	**Fic**
Grobler, P. Hey, frog!	**E**
Guarino, D. Is your mama a llama?	**E**
Hader, B. The big snow	**E**
Hartman, G. As the crow flies	**E**
Hassett, J. A mouse in the house	**E**
Henkes, K. Oh!	**E**
Hill, S. Ruby bakes a cake	**E**

Hoban, L. Silly Tilly's Thanksgiving dinner	**E**
Hoeye, M. Time stops for no mouse (5 and up)	**Fic**
Hoffman, M. Animals of the Bible (2-4)	**220.9**
Howe, D. Bunnicula (4-6)	**Fic**
Hughes, T. How the Whale became and other stories (4-6)	**S C**
Hutchins, P. 1 hunter	**E**
Jacques, B. Redwall (6 and up)	**Fic**
Jarrell, R. The animal family (4 and up)	**Fic**
Jarrett, C. The best picnic ever	**E**
Johnson, P. B. On top of spaghetti	**E**
Jonas, A. Splash!	**E**
Jones, S. L. Time to say goodnight	**E**
Kipling, R. A collection of Rudyard Kipling's Just so stories (3-6)	**S C**
Kipling, R. The jungle book: Mowgli's story (3-6)	**S C**
Kipling, R. The jungle book: the Mowgli stories (4 and up)	**S C**
Kipling, R. Just so stories (3-6)	**S C**
Klise, K. Shall I knit you a hat?	**E**
Kurtz, J. Water hole waiting	**E**
LaMarche, J. The raft	**E**
Lawson, R. Rabbit Hill (3-6)	**Fic**
Lexau, J. M. Who took the farmer's [hat]?	**E**
Lobel, A. Fables (3-5)	**Fic**
Lobel, A. Grasshopper on the road	**E**
Lofting, H. The voyages of Doctor Dolittle (4 and up)	**Fic**
Loupy, C. Hugs and kisses	**E**
Macdonald, S. Look whooo's counting	**E**
Mahy, M. 17 kings and 42 elephants	**E**
Markes, J. Good thing you're not an octopus!	**E**
Marshall, J. Rats on the range and other stories (2-4)	**S C**
Marshall, J. Rats on the roof, and other stories (2-4)	**S C**
Martin, B. Brown bear, brown bear what do you see?	**E**
Martin, B. Panda bear, panda bear, what do you see?	**E**
Martin, B. Polar bear, polar bear, what do you hear?	**E**
Massie, D. R. The baby beebee bird	**E**
Meddaugh, S. The best place	**E**
Meyers, S. This is the way a baby rides	**E**
Milne, A. A. The complete tales of Winnie-the-Pooh (1-4)	**Fic**
Milne, A. A. The House at Pooh Corner (1-4)	**Fic**
Milne, A. A. Winnie-the-Pooh (1-4)	**Fic**
Milne, A. A. The world of Pooh (1-4)	**Fic**
Miranda, A. To market, to market	**E**
Morrow, T. J. Mommy loves her baby	**E**
Murphy, M. I kissed the baby	**E**
Muth, J. J. The three questions	**E**
Newman, L. Where is bear?	**E**
Ormerod, J. If you're happy and you know it!	**E**
Partridge, E. Moon glowing	**E**
Payne, E. Katy No-Pocket	**E**
Pearson, T. C. Bob	**E**

Animals—Fiction—*Continued*

Rathmann, P. Good night, Gorilla	E
Rex, M. Truck Duck	E
Rice, E. Sam who never forgets	E
Root, B. Gumbrella	E
Root, P. Grandmother Winter	E
Rose, D. L. Birthday zoo	E
Roth, C. The little school bus	E
Ruelle, K. G. The Thanksgiving beast feast	E
Ryder, J. Each living thing	E
Ryder, J. A fawn in the grass	E
Sedgwick, M. The emperor's new clothes	E
Seidler, T. The Wainscott weasel (4-6)	**Fic**
Sierra, J. Wild about books	E
Slate, J. Miss Bindergarten celebrates the 100th day of kindergarten	E
Small, D. George Washington's cows	E
Steig, W. Doctor De Soto	E
Steig, W. The real thief (3-5)	**Fic**
Stenmark, V. The singing chick	E
Stevens, J. Cook-a-doodle-doo!	E
Stevenson, J. Flying feet	E
Stevenson, J. The most amazing dinosaur	E
Stevenson, J. No laughing, no smiling, no giggling	E
Stojic, M. Rain	E
Tafuri, N. You are special, Little one	E
Tryon, L. Albert's birthday	E
Van Laan, N. Moose tales	E
Van Laan, N. When winter comes	E
Varon, S. Sweaterweather (3-5)	**741.5**
Warnes, T. Mommy mine	E
Weeks, S. Two eggs, please	E
Weiss, N. Where does the brown bear go?	E
Weller, F. W. The day the animals came	E
Wells, R. Timothy's tales from Hilltop School	E
Wheeler, L. Bubble gum, bubble gum	E
Whybrow, I. The noisy way to bed	E
Willans, T. Wait! I want to tell you a story	E
Wilson, A. Over in the grasslands	E
Wilson, K. Bear snores on	E
Wilson, K. Mama always comes home	E
Yolen, J. Off we go!	E

Folklore

See also Dragons; Monsters; Mythical animals

Aardema, V. Rabbit makes a monkey of lion (k-3)	**398.2**
Aardema, V. Who's in Rabbit's house? (k-3)	**398.2**
Aardema, V. Why mosquitoes buzz in people's ears (k-3)	**398.2**
Blackstone, S. Storytime (k-1)	**398.2**
Brett, J. The mitten (k-2)	**398.2**
Bruchac, J. The great ball game (k-3)	**398.2**
Galdone, P. Henny Penny (k-2)	**398.2**
Grimm, J. The Bremen town musicians (k-3)	**398.2**
Hamilton, V. A ring of tricksters (3-6)	**398.2**
Kellogg, S. Chicken Little (k-3)	**398.2**

Leedy, L. There's a frog in my throat (2-5)	**428**
Lester, J. The last tales of Uncle Remus (4 and up)	**398.2**
MacDonald, M. R. A hen, a chick, and a string guitar (k-2)	**398.2**
Martin, F. Clever Tortoise (k-3)	**398.2**
McClintock, B. Animal fables from Aesop (1-4)	**398.2**
Orgel, D. The Bremen town musicians and other animal tales from Grimm (k-3)	**398.2**
Price, K. The Bourbon Street musicians (3-5)	**398.2**
Puttapipat, N. The musicians of Bremen (k-3)	**398.2**
Ross, G. How Turtle's back was cracked (k-3)	**398.2**
Thomas, J. C. What's the hurry, Fox? (k-3)	**398.2**
Tresselt, A. R. The mitten (k-2)	**398.2**
Wattenberg, J. Henny-Penny (k-3)	**398.2**

Habitations

Ashman, L. Castles, caves, and honeycombs	E

Hibernation

See Hibernation

Infancy

See Animal babies

Migration

Kaner, E. Animals migrating (2-4)	**591.5**
Rylant, C. The journey (2-4)	**591.56**
Simon, S. Ride the wind (4-6)	**591.56**

Photography

See Photography of animals

Pictorial works

See also Animals in art

Poetry

The baby's book of baby animals	**808.81**
The Beauty of the beast (4-6)	**811.008**
Big, bad, and a little bit scary (k-3)	**811.008**
Carnival of the animals	**811.008**
Carryl, C. E. The camel's lament	E
Cox, K. Mixed beasts (3-5)	**811**
Demi. In the eyes of the cat	**895.6**
Eric Carle's animals, animals	**808.81**
Florian, D. Beast feast	**811**
Florian, D. Omnibeasts	**811**
Florian, D. Zoo's who (k-3)	**811**
Galdone, P. The cat goes fiddle-i-fee (k-1)	**398.8**
Hoofbeats, claws, & rippled fins (3-6)	**811.008**
Hughes, T. The cat and the cuckoo (3-6)	**821**
Jackson, R. B. Animal mischief (2-4)	**811**
Keats, E. J. Over in the meadow	E
Larios, J. H. Yellow elephant	**811**
Lewin, B. Animal snackers (k-3)	**811**
My first Oxford book of animal poems (1-4)	**808.81**
Prelutsky, J. If not for the cat (1-4)	**811**
Ross, M. Wake up sleepy head! (k-1)	**811**
Singer, M. Fireflies at midnight (2-4)	**811**
Wise, W. Zany zoo (k-3)	**811**

Apartment houses
Fiction
Briant, E. Seven stories	E
Hearne, B. G. Who's in the hall?	E
Lakin, P. Fat chance Thanksgiving	E
Potter, E. Olivia Kidney (3-6)	Fic
Sachs, M. The four ugly cats in apartment 3D (3-5)	Fic
Schwartz, A. A glorious day	E

Apatosaurus and other giant long-necked plant-eaters. Schomp, V.
In Schomp, V. Prehistoric world [series] **567.9**

Ape in a cape. Eichenberg, F. **E**

Apes
See also Chimpanzees; Gorillas

Apiculture *See* Beekeeping; Bees

Apollo 11 (Spacecraft)
Hehner, B. First on the moon (4 and up) **629.45**
Thimmesh, C. Team moon (5 and up) **629.45**

Apollo moonwalks. Vogt, G. **629.45**

Apollo Project *See* Project Apollo

Apollo project
Bredeson, C. The moon (4 and up) **523.3**

Apoplexy *See* Stroke

Appalachia. Rylant, C. **974**

Appalachian Mountain region *See* Appalachian region

Appalachian Mountains
Folklore
See Folklore—Appalachian Mountains

Appalachian region
Houston, G. My great-aunt Arizona	E
Rylant, C. Appalachia	974

Fiction
Cleaver, V. Where the lillies bloom (5 and up)	Fic
Hamilton, V. M.C. Higgins, the great (5 and up)	Fic
Henson, H. Angel coming	E
Houston, G. The year of the perfect Christmas tree	E
Rylant, C. When I was young in the mountains	E
Schroeder, A. Smoky Mountain Rose	E
White, R. Belle Prater's boy (5 and up)	Fic

Apparitions. San Souci, R.
In San Souci, R. A terrifying taste of short & shivery; thirty creepy tales p30-34 **398.2**

Appelbaum, Diana Karter
Cocoa ice	E
Giants in the land (2-4)	634.9

Appelt, Kathi
Bats around the clock	E
Bubba and Beau, best friends	E
Cowboy dreams	E
Down Cut Shin Creek (4 and up)	027
Oh my baby, little one	E
Where, where is Swamp Bear?	E

Apple, Margot
(il) Delton, J. Angel's mother's wedding	Fic
(il) Haas, J. Birthday pony	Fic
(il) Haas, J. Runaway Radish	Fic
(il) Haas, J. Scamper and the horse show	E
(il) Root, P. The name quilt	E
(il) Shaw, N. Sheep in a jeep	E

Apple blossoms. Trueman, T.
In Tripping over the lunch lady and other school stories p43-57 **S C**

Apple cider making days. Purmell, A. **E**

Apple farmer Annie. Wellington, M. **E**

Apple for the teacher. Yolen, J. **782.42**

An **apple** from The Tree of Life. Schwartz, H.
In Schwartz, H. A journey to paradise and other Jewish tales p6-11 **398.2**

Apple is my sign. Riskind, M. **Fic**

Apple pie 4th of July. Wong, J. S. **E**

The **apple** pie tree. Hall, Z. **634**

Apples
Bulla, C. R. A tree is a plant (k-2)	582.16
Gibbons, G. Apples (k-3)	634
Hall, Z. The apple pie tree (k-1)	634
Landau, E. Apples (2-4)	634
Maestro, B. How do apples grow? (k-3)	634
Robbins, K. Apples (k-3)	634

Fiction
Bunting, E. One green apple	E
Giff, P. R. All the way home (4 and up)	Fic
Hutchins, P. Ten red apples	E
Purmell, A. Apple cider making days	E
Wellington, M. Apple farmer Annie	E

Apples to Oregon. Hopkinson, D. **E**

Appleseed, Johnny, 1774-1845
About
Kellogg, S. Johnny Appleseed (k-3)	92
Moses, W. Johnny Appleseed (3-6)	92

Poetry
Lindbergh, R. Johnny Appleseed (k-3) **811**

Appliances, Electric *See* Electric apparatus and appliances

Applied arts *See* Decorative arts

The **appointment**. Schwartz, A.
In Schwartz, A. Scary stories 3; more tales to chill your bones p7 **398.2**

Appointment in Samarra. San Souci, R.
In San Souci, R. Even more short & shivery; thirty spine-tingling stories p1-4 **398.2**

Apprentices
Fiction
DeFelice, C. C. The apprenticeship of Lucas Whitaker (5 and up)	Fic
Fleischman, P. Saturnalia (6 and up)	Fic
Garfield, L. Black Jack (6 and up)	Fic

The **apprenticeship** of Lucas Whitaker. DeFelice, C. C. **Fic**

Approximate computation
Murphy, S. J. Betcha! (1-3)	519.5
Murphy, S. J. Coyotes all around (1-3)	519

April foolishness. Bateman, T. **E**

April Fools' Day
Fiction
Bateman, T. April foolishness   **E**
April Mendez. Spinelli, J.
    In Spinelli, J. The library card   **S C**
April's kittens. Newberry, C. T.   **E**
Apt. 3. Keats, E. J.   **E**
Aquanauts *See* Underwater exploration
Aquariums
    See also Marine aquariums
Jeffrey, L. S. Fish (3-5)   **639.34**
Murphy, S. J. Room for Ripley (1-3)   **530.8**
Aquatic animals *See* Marine animals
Aquatic birds *See* Water birds
Aquatic life of the world (4 and up)   **578.7**
Aquatic plants *See* Marine plants
Arab Americans
Wolf, B. Coming to America (3-5)   **305.8**
The **Arab-Israeli** conflict. Senker, C.   **956.04**
Arab-Israeli conflicts *See* Israel-Arab conflicts
The **Arabian** nights entertainments (5 and up)
    398.2
Arabian Peninsula
    See also Oman
The **Araboolies** of Liberty Street. Swope, S.
    In You read to me & I'll read to you; 20th-
    century stories to share p78-83   **E**
Arabs
    See also Palestinian Arabs
Folklore
The Arabian nights entertainments (5 and up)
    398.2
Ben-´Ezer, E. Hosni the dreamer (2-4)   **398.2**
Pullman, P. Aladdin and the enchanted lamp
    (3-5)   **398.2**
Yeoman, J. The Seven voyages of Sinbad the
    Sailor (5 and up)   **398.2**
Arachne (Greek mythology)
Poetry
Hovey, K. Arachne speaks (4 and up)   **811**
Arachne speaks. Hovey, K.   **811**
Arachnida *See* Mites; Spiders
Arai, Tomie, 1949-
See/See also pages in the following book(s):
Just like me p2-3   **920**
Arapaho Indians
See/See also pages in the following book(s):
Ehrlich, A. Wounded Knee: an Indian history of
    the American West (6 and up)   **970.004**
Fiction
Osborne, M. P. Adaline Falling Star (5 and up)
    Fic
Arawak Indians *See* Taino Indians
Arbogast, Joan Marie
Buildings in disguise (4 and up)   **720**
Arbuthnot, Felicity
(jt. auth) Gaag, N. v. d. Baghdad   **956.7**
Arcella, Steve
(il) Sandburg, C. Carl Sandburg   **811**
Archaeology *See* Archeology
Archaeology. Barnes, T.   **930.1**

Archaeology for kids. Panchyk, R.   **930.1**
Archaeopteryx
Arnold, C. Dinosaurs with feathers (3-6)
    568
Zoehfeld, K. W. Did dinosaurs have feathers?
    (k-3)   **568**
Archaeopteryx and other flying dinosaurs.
    Schomp, V.
    In Schomp, V. Prehistoric world [series]
    567.9
Archambault, John
(jt. auth) Martin, B. Barn dance!   **E**
(jt. auth) Martin, B. Chicka chicka boom boom
    E
(jt. auth) Martin, B. The ghost-eye tree   **E**
(jt. auth) Martin, B. Knots on a counting rope
    E
Archbold, Rick
(jt. auth) Ballard, R. D. Ghost liners   **910.4**
Archeological specimens *See* Antiquities
Archeology
    See also Antiquities; Excavations (Archeol-
    ogy); Prehistoric peoples; Rock drawings,
    paintings, and engravings names of extinct
    cities; and names of groups of people and of
    cities (except extinct cities), countries, re-
    gions, etc., with the subdivision Antiquities
Barnes, T. Archaeology (5 and up)   **930.1**
Deem, J. M. Bodies from the bog (4 and up)
    930.1
Getz, D. Frozen man (5 and up)   **930.1**
Hawass, Z. A. Curse of the pharaohs (5 and up)
    932
McIntosh, J. Archeology (4 and up)   **930.1**
Panchyk, R. Archaeology for kids (5 and up)
    930.1
Reinhard, J. Discovering the Inca Ice Maiden (5
    and up)   **930.1**
See/See also pages in the following book(s):
Arnold, C. Stone Age farmers beside the sea (4
    and up)   **936.1**
Fiction
Barrett, T. On Etruscan time (5 and up)   **Fic**
Archers, alchemists, and 98 other medieval jobs
    you might have loved or loathed. Galloway,
    P.   **940.1**
Archer's quest. Park, L. S.   **Fic**
Archimedes, ca. 287-212 B.C.
About
Gow, M. Archimedes (5 and up)   **92**
Architects
Greenberg, J. Frank O. Gehry (4 and up)
    92
Zaunders, B. Gargoyles, girders, & glass houses
    (3-6)   **720.9**
The **architects.** Fisher, L. E.   **720.9**
Architectural engineering *See* Building
Architecture
Arbogast, J. M. Buildings in disguise (4 and up)
    720
Fisher, L. E. The architects (4 and up)
    720.9
Kent, P. Great building stories of the past (4
    and up)   **624**

Artists' materials—*Continued*

Sattler, H. R. Recipes for art and craft materials (4 and up) **745.5**

Arts

See also Surrealism

Ajmera, M. To be an artist (k-3) **700**

Major, J. S. Caravan to America (4 and up) **920**

Arts, Applied *See* Decorative arts

Arts, Decorative *See* Decorative arts

Arts and crafts *See* Handicraft

ArtStarts for little hands!. Press, J. **745.5**

Aruego, Jose

The last laugh **E**

Weird friends (k-3) **577.8**

(il) Beaumont, K. Duck, duck, goose! **E**

(il) Brimner, L. D. The littlest wolf **E**

(il) Bruchac, J. How Chipmunk got his stripes **398.2**

(il) Bruchac, J. Raccoon's last race **398.2**

(il) Bruchac, J. Turtle's race with Beaver **398.2**

(il) Campoy, F. I. Rosa Raposa **E**

(jt. auth) Dewey, A. Splash! **E**

(il) Ginsburg, M. The chick and the duckling **E**

(il) Kraus, R. Whose mouse are you? **E**

(il) Raffi. Five little ducks **782.42**

(il) Shannon, G. Lizard's guest **E**

(il) Sharmat, M. Gregory, the terrible eater **E**

(il) Sierra, J. Antarctic antics **811**

(il) Swinburne, S. R. Safe, warm, and snug **591.56**

Arzoumanian, Alik

(il) MacDonald, M. R. Tunjur! Tunjur! Tunjur! **398.2**

As far as the eye can reach. Kimmel, E. C. **978**

As the crow flies. Hartman, G. **E**

As you like it. Packer, T.

In Packer, T. Tales from Shakespeare p121-137 **822.3**

Asbjornsen, Peter Christen

Chicken Licken

In De Paola, T. Tomie dePaola's Favorite nursery tales p105-11 **398.2**

East of the sun and west of the moon [story]

In The Blue fairy book p19-29 **398.2**

also in Womenfolk and fairy tales p111-26 **398.2**

The house on the hill

In De Paola, T. Tomie dePaola's Favorite nursery tales p122-26 **398.2**

The husband who was to mind the house

In Womenfolk and fairy tales p106-110 **398.2**

The master-maid

In The Blue fairy book p120-35 **398.2**

The princess on the glass hill

In The Blue fairy book p332-41 **398.2**

The three billy goats gruff

In De Paola, T. Tomie dePaola's Favorite nursery tales p42-45 **398.2**

The three sisters who were entrapped into a mountain

In Womenfolk and fairy tales p156-63 **398.2**

Why the sea is salt

In The Blue fairy book p136-40 **398.2**

Asch, Devin

(jt. auth) Asch, F. Baby Duck's new friend **E**

(jt. auth) Asch, F. Like a windy day **E**

(il) Asch, F. Mr. Maxwell's mouse **E**

Asch, Frank

Baby Bird's first nest **E**

Baby Duck's new friend **E**

Barnyard lullaby **E**

Like a windy day **E**

Moonbear's dream **E**

Mr. Maxwell's mouse **E**

The sun is my favorite star **E**

Ashabranner, Brent K.

No better hope (4 and up) **975.3**

Remembering Korea (4 and up) **951.9**

Ashabranner, Jennifer

(il) Ashabranner, B. K. No better hope **975.3**

(il) Ashabranner, B. K. Remembering Korea **951.9**

Ashanti (African people)

Folklore

Courlander, H. Cow-tail switch, and other West African stories (4-6) **398.2**

McDermott, G. Anansi the spider (k-3) **398.2**

Mollel, T. M. Ananse's feast (k-3) **398.2**

Ashanti to Zulu: African traditions. Musgrove, M. **960**

Ashby, Ruth

The amazing Mr. Franklin, or, The boy who read everything [biography of Benjamin Franklin] (3-5) **92**

Pteranodon (1-3) **567.9**

Rocket man [biography of John Glenn] (4-6) **92**

Ashe, Arthur, 1943-1993

About

Cunningham, K. Arthur Ashe (5 and up) **92**

See/See also pages in the following book(s):

Krull, K. Lives of the athletes (4 and up) **920**

Asher, Sandy

China (2-4) **951**

Ashes. Babbitt, N.

In Babbitt, N. The Devil's storybook p63-71 **S C**

Ashley Bryan's ABC of African-American poetry (k-3) **811.008**

Ashley Bryan's African tales, uh-huh. Bryan, A. **398.2**

Ashman, Linda

Babies on the go **E**

Castles, caves, and honeycombs **E**

Mama's day **E**

To the beach! **E**

Atonement, Day of *See* Yom Kippur

Attack of the killer video book. Shulman, M.
778.59

Attack on Pearl Harbor. Tanaka, S. **940.54**

Attenborough, Liz
(comp) Poetry by heart. See Poetry by heart
821.008

Attention deficit disorder
Gold, S. D. Attention deficit disorder (4 and up)
616.85
Pigache, P. ADHD (5 and up) **616.85**
Trueit, T. S. ADHD (5 and up) **616.85**
Fiction
Gantos, J. Joey Pigza swallowed the key (5 and up) **Fic**
Shreve, S. R. Trout and me (5 and up) **Fic**

Attila, King of the Huns, d. 453
See/See also pages in the following book(s):
Meltzer, M. Ten kings (5 and up) 920

Attoe, Steve
(il) Thomas, K. Blades, boards & scooters
796.2

Atwater, Florence Carroll
(jt. auth) Atwater, R. T. Mr. Popper's penguins
Fic

Atwater, Richard Tupper
Mr. Popper's penguins (3-5) **Fic**

Atwell, Debby
Barn **E**
The Thanksgiving door **E**

Auch, Herm
(il) Auch, M. J. I was a third grade science project **Fic**

Auch, Mary Jane
Bantam of the opera **E**
I was a third grade science project (2-4) **Fic**
Journey to nowhere (4 and up) **Fic**
Peeping Beauty **E**
Wing nut (5 and up) **Fic**

Auction!. Seymour, T. **E**

Auctions
Fiction
Seymour, T. Auction! **E**

Audio video market place. See AV market place
371.3025

Audiovisual materials
Catalogs
Adamson, L. G. Literature connections to American history, K-6 **016.973**
Adamson, L. G. Literature connections to world history, K-6 **016.9**
Directories
AV market place 371.3025

Audrey and Barbara. Lawson, J. **E**

Audubon, John James, 1785-1851
About
Armstrong, J. Audubon (2-4) **92**
Burleigh, R. Into the woods: John James Audubon lives his dream (3-5) **92**
Davies, J. The boy who drew birds: a story of John James Audubon (2-4) **92**

Augarde, Steve
The Various (5 and up) **Fic**

August, Louise
(il) Jaffe, N. The way meat loves salt **398.2**
(il) Musleah, R. Why on this night? **296.4**

Augustin, Byron
Iraq (5 and up) **956.7**
United Arab Emirates (5 and up) **953**

Augustyn, Frank
Footnotes (5 and up) **792.8**

Aulnoy, Madame d'
Felicia and the pot of pinks
In The Blue fairy book p148-56 **398.2**
The story of Pretty Goldilocks
In The Blue fairy book p193-205 **398.2**
The White Cat
In The Blue fairy book p157-73 **398.2**
The wonderful sheep
In The Blue fairy book p214-30 **398.2**
The yellow dwarf
In The Blue fairy book p30-50 **398.2**

Aulnoy, Marie-Catherine Le Jumel de Barneville, comtesse d' *See* Aulnoy, Madame d', 1650 or 51-1705

Ault, Kelly
Let's sign! (k-1) **419**

Aung San Suu Kyi
See/See also pages in the following book(s):
Krull, K. Lives of extraordinary women (4 and up) **920**

Aunt Clara Brown. Lowery, L. **92**

Aunt Flossie's hats (and crab cakes later). Howard, E. F. **E**

Aunt Minnie McGranahan. Prigger, M. S. **E**

Aunt Olga's Christmas postcards. Major, K. **E**

Aunts
Fiction
Alexander, L. The Gawgon and The Boy (5 and up) **Fic**
Alvarez, J. How Tía Lola came to visit/stay (4 and up) **Fic**
Avi. Prairie school (2-4) **Fic**
Cates, K. The Secret Remedy Book **E**
Cooney, B. Miss Rumphius **E**
Couloumbis, A. Getting near to baby (5 and up) **Fic**
Gordon, A. The Gorillas of Gill Park (4 and up) **Fic**
Horvath, P. The trolls (3-6) **Fic**
Howard, E. F. Aunt Flossie's hats (and crab cakes later) **E**
Koss, A. G. Stolen words (4 and up) **Fic**
Lester, H. Something might happen **E**
Lisle, J. T. The lost flower children (4-6) **Fic**
MacLachlan, P. Seven kisses in a row (2-4) **Fic**
Major, K. Aunt Olga's Christmas postcards **E**
Prigger, M. S. Aunt Minnie McGranahan **E**
Ross, A. In the quiet (5 and up) **Fic**
Weeks, S. Jumping the scratch (5 and up) **Fic**
Wiggin, K. D. S. Rebecca of Sunnybrook Farm (4 and up) **Fic**
Wright, B. R. Nothing but trouble (4 and up) **Fic**

Authors, American—*Continued*

Lasky, K. A brilliant streak: the making of Mark Twain (4 and up) **92**

Lowry, L. Looking back (5 and up) **92**

Marciano, J. B. Bemelmans **92**

Marcus, L. S. Side by side (4 and up) **070.5**

McGinty, A. B. Meet Daniel Pinkwater (1-3) **92**

McGinty, A. B. Meet Eve Bunting (1-3) **92**

McGinty, A. B. Meet Jane Yolen (1-3) **92**

Medina, J. Tomás Rivera (k-2) **92**

Nixon, J. L. The making of a writer **92**

Paulsen, G. Caught by the sea (5 and up) **92**

Paulsen, G. How Angel Peterson got his name (5 and up) **92**

Paulsen, G. My life in dog years (4 and up) **92**

Peet, B. Bill Peet: an autobiography (4 and up) **92**

Seidman, D. Jerry Spinelli (5 and up) **92**

Spinelli, J. Knots in my yo-yo string (4 and up) **92**

The wand in the word (6 and up) **813.009**

Wilder, L. I. A Little House traveler (5 and up) **92**

Wilder, L. I. West from home (6 and up) **92**

Yep, L. The lost garden (5 and up) **92**

Younger, B. Purple mountain majesties: the story of Katharine Lee Bates and "America the beautiful" (2-4) **92**

Authors, Danish

Hesse, K. The young Hans Christian Andersen (2-4) **92**

Varmer, H. Hans Christian Andersen (5 and up) **92**

Yolen, J. The perfect wizard [biography of Hans Christian Andersen] (2-4) **92**

Authors, English

Boekhoff, P. M. J.K. Rowling (4-6) **92**

Chippendale, L. A. Triumph of the imagination: the story of writer J.K. Rowling (5 and up) **92**

Cooling, W. D is for Dahl (4 and up) **823.009**

King-Smith, D. Chewing the cud (5 and up) **92**

Rosen, M. Dickens (5 and up) **92**

Stanley, D. Charles Dickens (4 and up) **92**

The wand in the word (6 and up) **813.009**

Winter, J. Beatrix: various episodes from the life of Beatrix Potter (k-3) **92**

Authors, Mexican

Mora, P. A library for Juana: the world of Sor Juana Inés (2-4) **92**

Authors, Scottish

Murphy, J. Across America on an emigrant train [biography of Robert Louis Stevenson] (5 and up) **92**

Authors, Yiddish

Silverman, E. Sholom's treasure [biography of Sholem Aleichem] (k-3) **92**

Authorship

See also Creative writing; Journalism

Bauer, M. D. What's your story? (5 and up) **808.3**

Christelow, E. What do authors do? (1-3) **808**

Fletcher, R. How writers work (4 and up) **808**

Freedman, J. Sid Fleischman (5 and up) **92**

Harrison, D. L. Writing stories (4 and up) **808.3**

Leedy, L. Look at my book (k-3) **808**

Lester, J. On writing for children & other people **92**

Otfinoski, S. Extraordinary short story writing (5 and up) **808.3**

Stevens, J. From pictures to words (k-3) **741.6**

Trueit, T. S. Keeping a journal (5 and up) **808**

Young, S. Writing with style (5 and up) **808**

See/See also pages in the following book(s):

Lester, H. Author (k-3) **92**

Fiction

Blegvad, L. Kitty and Mr. Kipling (3-5) **Fic**

Child, L. Clarice Bean spells trouble (3-5) **Fic**

Clements, A. The school story (4 and up) **Fic**

Crew, G. Troy Thompson's excellent peotry book (4 and up) **Fic**

DiSalvo-Ryan, D. The sloppy copy slipup (2-4) **Fic**

Hahn, M. D. Daphne's book (5 and up) **Fic**

Howe, J. It came from beneath the bed! (3-5) **Fic**

Kladstrup, K. The book of story beginnings (4 and up) **Fic**

Kroll, S. Patches: lost and found **E**

Lisle, J. T. How I became a writer and Oggie learned to drive (4 and up) **Fic**

Nelson, T. Ruby electric (5 and up) **Fic**

O'Malley, K. Once upon a cool motorcycle dude **E**

Snyder, Z. K. Libby on Wednesdays (5 and up) **Fic**

Autism

Baldwin, C. Autism (4-6) **616.89**

Fiction

Choldenko, G. Al Capone does my shirts (5 and up) **Fic**

Automata *See* Robots

Automobile accidents *See* Traffic accidents

Automobile racing

Buckley, J., Jr. NASCAR (4 and up) **796.72**

Dooling, M. The great horseless carriage race (2-4) **796.72**

Rex, M. My race car (k-1) **629.228**

Fiction

Floca, B. The racecar alphabet **E**

Automobile travel

Brown, D. Alice Ramsey's grand adventure (k-3) **92**

Fiction

Coy, J. Vroomaloom zoom **E**

Automobile travel—Fiction—*Continued*

Koralek, J. Night ride to Nanna's   **E**

Walters, V. Are we there yet, Daddy?   **E**

Williams, V. B. Stringbean's trip to the shining sea   **E**

Automobiles

Court, R. How to draw cars and trucks (4-6)   **743**

Mitchell, J. S. Crashed, smashed, and mashed (3-6)   **629.2**

Rex, M. My race car (k-1)   **629.228**

Fiction

Aroner, M. Clink, clank, clunk!   **E**

Barton, B. My car   **E**

Fleming, I. Chitty chitty bang bang (4-6)   **Fic**

Gibbons, F. Mama and me and the Model-T   **E**

Hurd, T. Sleepy Cadillac   **E**

Hurd, T. Zoom City   **E**

Peck, R. Here lies the librarian   **Fic**

Root, P. Rattletrap car   **E**

Steen, S. Car wash   **E**

Folklore

Lyons, M. E. Roy makes a car (k-3)   **398.2**

Touring

See Automobile travel

Autumn

Gerber, C. Leaf jumpers   **E**

Maestro, B. Why do leaves change color? (k-3)   **582.16**

Robbins, K. Autumn leaves (3-6)   **582.16**

Fiction

Hall, Z. Fall leaves fall!   **E**

Partridge, E. Moon glowing   **E**

Spinelli, E. I know it's autumn   **E**

Poetry

Florian, D. Autumnblings   **811**

Autumn leaves. Robbins, K.   **582.16**

Autumn Street. Lowry, L.   **Fic**

Autumnblings. Florian, D.   **811**

AV market place   **371.3025**

Avery, Ben

Lullaby: Wisdom seeker (4-6)   **741.5**

Avi

Abigail takes the wheel (2-4)   **Fic**

The barn (4 and up)   **Fic**

Blue heron (5 and up)   **Fic**

The Book Without Words (5 and up)   **Fic**

Crispin (5 and up)   **Fic**

Don't you know there's a war on? (4 and up)   **Fic**

The end of the beginning (3-5)   **Fic**

Finding Providence: the story of Roger Williams (2-4)   **92**

The good dog (4-6)   **Fic**

How I got my English A

In Tripping over the lunch lady and other school stories p17-28   **S C**

Midnight magic (5 and up)   **Fic**

Never mind! (5 and up)   **Fic**

Poppy (3-5)   **Fic**

Prairie school (2-4)   **Fic**

S.O.R. losers (5 and up)   **Fic**

The secret school (4 and up)   **Fic**

Silent movie   **E**

Strange happenings (5 and up)   **S C**

Contents: Bored Tom; Babette the beautiful; Curious; The shoemaker and Old Scratch; Simon

The true confessions of Charlotte Doyle (6 and up)   **Fic**

What do fish have to do with anything? and other stories (4 and up)   **S C**

Contents: What do fish have to do with anything?; The goodness of Matt Kaizer; Talk to me; Teacher tamer; Pets; What's inside; Fortune cookie

Aviation *See* Aeronautics

Aviators *See* Air pilots

Awake. Lee, T.

In Swan sister; fairy tales retold   **S C**

Awani Indians *See* Miwok Indians

Awards, Literary *See* Literary prizes

Awesome ocean science!. Littlefield, C. A.   **551.46**

Awful Ogre's awful day. Prelutsky, J.   **811**

Axtell, David

(il) We're going on a lion hunt. See We're going on a lion hunt   **E**

Aylesworth, Jim

The full belly bowl   **E**

The Gingerbread man (k-3)   **398.2**

Goldilocks and the three bears (k-3)   **398.2**

Old black fly   **E**

The tale of Tricky Fox (k-3)   **398.2**

Ayliffe, Alex

(il) Mayo, M. Choo choo clickety-clack!   **E**

Ayres, Katherine

Macaroni boy (5 and up)   **Fic**

Ayto, John

(ed) Brewer's dictionary of phrase and fable. See Brewer's dictionary of phrase and fable   **803**

Ayto, Russell

(il) Jones, U. The witch's children   **E**

Azarian, Mary

A farmer's alphabet   **E**

A gardener's alphabet   **E**

(il) Connor, L. Miss Bridie chose a shovel   **E**

(il) Hurwitz, J. Faraway summer   **Fic**

(il) Lunge-Larsen, L. The race of the Birkebeiners   **398.2**

(il) Martin, J. B. Snowflake Bentley [biography of Wilson Alwyn Bentley]   **92**

(il) Pollock, P. When the moon is full   **811**

(il) Saul, C. P. Barn cat   **E**

Azerbaijan

King, D. C. Azerbaijan (5 and up)   **947.5**

The **Aztec** empire. Stein, R. C.   **972**

Aztecs

Kimmel, E. A. Montezuma and the fall of the Aztecs (3-5)   **972**

Sonneborn, L. The ancient Aztecs (5 and up)   **972**

Tanaka, S. Lost temple of the Aztecs (4 and up)   **972**

Folklore

Kimmel, E. A. The two mountains (3-5)   **398.2**

Azuma, Kiyohiko
    Yotsuba&! (2-4)   **741.5**

B

Baba Yaga. Afanas´ev, A. N.
    In Afanas´ev, A. N. Russian fairy tales p194-
    95   **398.2**

Baba Yaga [another story]. Afanas´ev, A. N.
    In Afanas´ev, A. N. Russian fairy tales p363-
    65   **398.2**

Baba Yaga and the brave youth. Afanas´ev, A. N.
    In Afanas´ev, A. N. Russian fairy tales p76-
    79   **398.2**

Baba Yaga and Vasilisa the brave. Mayer, M.
        398.2

Babbitt, Natalie
    The Devil's other storybook (4-6)   **S C**
    Contents: The fortunes of Madame Organza; Justice; The sol-
dier; Boating; How Akbar went to Bethlehem; The signpost; Lessons; The fall and rise of Bathbone; Simple sentences; The ear
    The Devil's storybook (4-6)   **S C**
    Contents: Wishes; The very pretty lady; The harps of Heaven;
The imp in the basket; Nuts; A palindrome; Ashes; Perfection;
The rose and the minor demon; The power of speech
    The eyes of the Amaryllis (5 and up)   **Fic**
    Kneeknock Rise (4-6)   **Fic**
    Ouch! (k-3)   **398.2**
    The search for delicious (5 and up)   **Fic**
    Tuck everlasting (5 and up)   **Fic**
    (il) Worth, V. All the small poems and fourteen
    more   **811**
    (il) Worth, V. Peacock and other poems   **811**

Babe. King-Smith, D.   **Fic**

The **Babe** & I. Adler, D. A.   **E**

Babette the beautiful. Avi
    In Avi. Strange happenings; five tales of
    transformation   **S C**

Babies *See* Infants

Babies in the library!. Marino, J.   **027.62**

Babies on the go. Ashman, L.   **E**

The **baboon** and the shark. Climo, S.
    In Climo, S. Monkey business; stories from
    around the world   **398.2**

Baboons
Fiction
    Banks, K. Baboon   **E**
    Olaleye, I. Bitter bananas   **E**

Baboushka and the three kings. Robbins, R.
        398.2

Babushka's doll. Polacco, P.   **E**

Babushka's Mother Goose. Polacco, P.   **398.8**

Baby. MacLachlan, P.   **Fic**

Baby bat's lullaby. Mitchard, J.   **E**

Baby Bear's chairs. Yolen, J.   **E**

The **baby** beebee bird. Massie, D. R.   **E**

Baby Beluga. Raffi   **782.42**

Baby Bird's first nest. Asch, F.   **E**

Baby Brains. James, S.   **E**

Baby danced the polka. Beaumont, K.   **E**

Baby Duck's new friend. Asch, F.   **E**

The **baby** goes beep. O'Connell, R.   **E**

Baby knows best. Henderson, K.   **E**

Baby koala. Lang, A.   **599.2**

The **baby** on the way. English, K.   **E**

Baby on the way. Sears, W.   **612.6**

Baby radar. Nye, N. S.   **E**

Baby rattlesnake. Moroney, L.   **398.2**

Baby says. Steptoe, J.   **E**

The **baby** sister. De Paola, T.   **E**

The **Baby-sitter's** Club: Kristy's great idea. Mar-
    tin, A. M.   **741.5**

Baby sloth. Lang, A.   **599.3**

Baby talk. Hindley, J.   **E**

Baby whales drink milk. Esbensen, B. J.
        599.5

Baby whale's journey. London, J.   **E**

The **baby** who loved pumpkins. Lester, J.
    In Lester, J. The last tales of Uncle Remus
    p46-48   **398.2**

The **Babylonia** princes vex. Graham, L. B.
    In Graham, L. B. How God fix Jonah p132-
    36   **398.2**

Babymouse. Holm, J. L.   **741.5**

The **baby's** bedtime book   **808.81**

The **baby's** book of baby animals   **808.81**

The **baby's** game book. Wilner, I.   **398.8**

The **baby's** good morning book   **808.81**

The **Baby's** lap book   **398.8**

The **baby's** playtime book (k-1)   **811.008**

Babysitters
Fiction
    Gorbachev, V. Ms. Turtle the babysitter   **E**
    Harris, R. H. Don't forget to come back!   **E**

Babysitting
    Raatma, L. Safety for babysitters (4 and up)
        649

Bacarole for paper and bones. Anderson, M. T.
    In Shelf life: stories by the book p127-49
        S C

Baccalario, Pierdomenico
    The door to time (4-6)   **Fic**

Bach, Johann Sebastian, 1685-1750
About
    Winter, J. Sebastian: a book about Bach (k-3)
        92

    See/See also pages in the following book(s):
    Krull, K. Lives of the musicians (4 and up)
        920

The **bachelor** and the bean. Fowles, S.   **398.2**

Bachrach, Susan D.
    Tell them we remember (5 and up)   **940.53**

Back home. Pinkney, G. J.   **E**

Back in the spaceship again. Sands, K.   **016.8**

Backyard buddies [series]
    Ross, M. E. Millipedeology   **595.6**
    Ross, M. E. Spiderology   **595.4**

Bacon, Josephine
    Cooking the Israeli way
    In Easy menu ethnic cookbooks   **641.5**

Bacon, Paul
  (il) Golenbock, P. Teammates [biography of Jackie Robinson] **92**
  (il) Sandburg, C. The Sandburg treasury **818**

Bacon, Quentin
  (il) Lagasse, E. Emeril's there's a chef in my family! **641.5**

Bacteria
  Berger, M. Germs make me sick! (k-3) **616.9**

Bacteriologists
  Tocci, S. Alexander Fleming (5 and up) **92**

The **bad** baby-sitter. Stine, R. L.
  In Stine, R. L. The haunting hour p20-37 **S C**

The **bad** beginning. Snicket, L. **Fic**

A **bad** case of stripes. Shannon, D. **E**

Bad day at Riverbend. Van Allsburg, C. **E**

Bad Heart Buffalo, Amos
  The life and death of Crazy Horse (5 and up) **92**

Bad man from Brodie. Nixon, J. L.
  In Nixon, J. L. Ghost town; seven ghostly stories p102-24 **S C**

The **bad** wife. Afanas'ev, A. N.
  In Afanas'ev, A. N. Russian fairy tales p56-57 **398.2**

The **Baddies'** goodies. See McAllister, A. Barkus, Sly and the golden egg **E**

The **badger** and the magic fan. Sakade, F.
  In Sakade, F. Japanese children's favorite stories **398.2**

Badgers
Fiction
  Brett, J. Honey . . . honey . . . lion! **E**
  Bunting, E. Can you do this, Old Badger? **E**
  Eckert, A. W. Incident at Hawk's Hill (6 and up) **Fic**
  Hoban, R. Bedtime for Frances **E**

Badoe, Adwoa
  The pot of wisdom: Ananse stories **398.2**
  <small>Includes the following stories: Why Ananse lives on the ceiling; Ananse and the feeding pot; Ananse becomes the owner of stories; Ananse the even-handed judge; Ananse the forgetful guest; The mat confidences; Ananse and the pot of wisdom; Ananse and the singing cloak; Why pig has a short snout; Ananse and the birds</small>

Baek, Matthew J.
  (il) Kushner, L. In God's hands **E**

Baer, Lore, 1938-
About
  Adler, D. A. Hiding from the Nazis (2-4) **940.53**

Baez, Joan
  See/See also pages in the following book(s):
  Orgill, R. Shout, sister, shout! (6 and up) **920**

Baghdad (Iraq)
  Gaag, N. v. d. Baghdad (3-6) **956.7**

Bagnold, Enid
  National Velvet (5 and up) **Fic**

Baguley, Kitt
  (jt. auth) Winter, J. K. Venezuela **987**

Bahamas
Poetry
  Greenfield, E. Under the Sunday tree (2-4) **811**

Bahamas
  Barlas, R. Bahamas (5 and up) **972.96**
  Hintz, M. The Bahamas (5 and up) **972.96**
  Lourie, P. First dive to shark dive **797.2**

Bahrampour, Ali
  Otto, the story of a mirror **E**

Bahrawi, Nazry
  (jt. auth) Levy, P. Puerto Rico **972.95**

Bahti, Tom
  (il) Baylor, B. When clay sings **970.004**

Baicker, Karen
  You can do it too! **E**

Bailer, Darice
  Arkansas
  In World Almanac Library of the States series **973**

  Connecticut
  In World Almanac Library of the States series **973**

Bailey, Jacqui
  Charged up (2-4) **333.79**
  Monster bones (2-4) **567.9**
  Sun up, sun down (2-4) **525**

Bailey, Peter
  (il) Finney, P. I, Jack **Fic**
  (il) Pullman, P. The scarecrow and his servant **Fic**

Baja California (Mexico: Peninsula)
Fiction
  O'Dell, S. The black pearl (6 and up) **Fic**

Bake and make amazing cakes. MacLeod, E. **641.8**

Bake and make amazing cookies. MacLeod, E. **641.8**

The **bake** shop ghost. Ogburn, J. K. **E**

Baker, Alia Muhammad
About
  Winter, J. The librarian of Basra **E**

Baker, Augusta
  (jt. auth) Greene, E. Storytelling **372.6**

Baker, Barbara
  Anna shares **E**
  Digby and Kate and the beautiful day **E**

Baker, Charles
  (jt. auth) Rembert, W. Don't hold me back **92**

Baker, Christopher W.
  Scientific visualization (5 and up) **006**

Baker, Ella, 1903-1986
  See/See also pages in the following book(s):
  Pinkney, A. D. Let it shine (4 and up) **920**

Baker, Florence von Sass, 1841-1916
  See/See also pages in the following book(s):
  Atkins, J. How high can we climb? (5 and up) **920**

Baker, Jeannie
  Home **E**
  Where the forest meets the sea **E**
  Window **E**

Baker, Josephine, 1906-1975
Fiction
Schroeder, A. Ragtime Tumpie   E
Baker, Karen
(il) Knock at a star. See Knock at a star
     811.008
Baker, Keith
Big fat hen   **398.8**
Little Green   E
The magic fan   E
Meet Mr. and Mrs. Green   E
Quack and count   E
Baker, Leslie
You bad dog!   E
Baker, Olaf
Where the buffaloes begin (2-4)   Fic
Baker, Pamela J.
My first book of sign (k-3)   **419**
Baker, Rosalie F.
In a word (5 and up)   **422**
(jt. auth) Rembert, W. Don't hold me back
     92

Bakers and bakeries
Fiction
Ogburn, J. K. The bake shop ghost   E
The **baker's** dozen. Forest, H.   **398.2**
Baking
See also Bread; Cake
Fiction
Priceman, M. How to make an apple pie and
see the world   E
Smalls, I. My Pop Pop and me   E
Bakotahl. San Souci, R.
In San Souci, R. Dare to be scared; thirteen
stories to chill and thrill   S C
Balaam (Biblical figure)
About
Paterson, K. The angel and the donkey (3-5)
     222
Balance. English, J.
In Girls got game; sports stories and poems
     810.8
Balanchine, George, 1904-1983
See/See also pages in the following book(s):
Schubert, L. Ballet of the elephants   **791.8**
Balboa, Vasco Núñez de, 1475-1519
About
Otfinoski, S. Vasco Nuñez de Balboa (5 and up)
     92
See/See also pages in the following book(s):
Fritz, J. Around the world in a hundred years (4
and up)   **910.4**
Bald eagle
Gibbons, G. Soaring with the wind (k-3)
     598
Morrison, G. Bald eagle (2-4)   **598**
Patent, D. H. The bald eagle returns (4 and up)
     598
Wilcox, C. Bald eagles (3-6)   **598**
The **bald** eagle returns. Patent, D. H.   **598**
The **Bald** Mountain monster. San Souci, R.
In San Souci, R. Dare to be scared; thirteen
stories to chill and thrill   S C

Baldak Borisievich. Afanas´ev, A. N.
In Afanas´ev, A. N. Russian fairy tales p90-
96   **398.2**
Baldwin, Carol
Asthma (4-6)   **616.2**
Autism (4-6)   **616.89**
Sickle cell disease (4-6)   **616.1**
Balian, Lorna
Humbug witch   E
Balit, Christina
Atlantis (2-4)   **398.2**
(il) Mitton, J. Once upon a starry night
     523.8
(il) Mitton, J. Zodiac   **398**
(il) Rock, L. Everlasting stories   **220.9**
Ball, Jacqueline A.
New York
In World Almanac Library of the States series
     973
Ball, Johnny
Go figure! (4 and up)   **793.74**
Ball, Mary *See* Washington, Mary Ball, 1708-
1789
The **ballad** of Lucy Whipple. Cushman, K.
     Fic
The **ballad** of the pirate queens. Yolen, J.   **811**
The **ballad** of Valentine. Jackson, A.   E
Ballard, Carol
The skeleton and muscular system (5 and up)
     612.7
Ballard, Robert D.
Ghost liners (4 and up)   **910.4**
Ballard, Robert D., 1942-
About
Hill, C. M. Robert Ballard (5 and up)   **92**
See/See also pages in the following book(s):
Talking with adventurers (4-6)   **920**
Ballard, Robin
My day, your day   E
Ballerina!. Sís, P.   E
Ballerina flying. Brandenberg, A.   E
Ballerino Nate. Bradley, K. B.   E
Ballet
Augustyn, F. Footnotes (5 and up)   **792.8**
Frith, M. Hooray for ballet! (2-4)   **792.8**
Isadora, R. On your toes   E
Rubin, S. G. Degas and the dance (3-6)   **92**
Schorer, S. Put your best foot forward (4 and
up)   **792.8**
Schubert, L. Ballet of the elephants   **791.8**
Siegel, S. C. To dance: a ballerina's graphic
novel (4 and up)   **741.5**
Varriale, J. Kids dance (4 and up)   **792.8**
Fiction
Allen, D. Dancing in the wings   E
Auch, M. J. Peeping Beauty   E
Bradley, K. B. Ballerino Nate   E
Brandenberg, A. Ballerina flying   E
Deans, S. B. Every day and all the time (5 and
up)   Fic
Gauch, P. L. Tanya and the red shoes   E
Geras, A. Time for ballet   E
Holabird, K. Angelina Ballerina   E

Ballet—Fiction—*Continued*

Isadora, R. Lili at ballet   E
Isadora, R. Max   E
Jacobson, J. Winnie (dancing) on her own (2-4)   **Fic**
Kinerk, R. Clorinda   E
Lasky, K. Dancing through fire (4-6)   **Fic**
Marshall, J. Swine Lake   E
Maybarduk, L. James the dancing dog   E
Newsome, J. Dream dancer   E
Samuels, B. Dolores on her toes   E
Sís, P. Ballerina!   E
Whelan, G. The turning (5 and up)   **Fic**
Yep, L. Angelfish (5 and up)   **Fic**
Young, A. Belinda, the ballerina   E

Ballet dancers

Tallchief, M. Tallchief (3-5)   **92**

Ballet of the elephants. Schubert, L.   **791.8**

Ballet Tech School (New York, N.Y.)

Varriale, J. Kids dance (4 and up)   **792.8**

Balliett, Blue

Chasing Vermeer (5 and up)   **Fic**

Balloons

Levine, S. The ultimate balloon book (5 and up)   **745.594**
Priceman, M. Hot air   E

Fiction

Coerr, E. The big balloon race   E
Du Bois, W. P. The twenty-one balloons (5 and up)   **Fic**
Lamorisse, A. The red balloon   E
Nolen, J. Harvey Potter's balloon farm   E
Sakai, K. Emily's balloon   E

Balloons, Dirigible *See* Airships

Ballpark. Curlee, L.   **796.357**

Ballparks *See* Stadiums

Baloney (Henry P.). Scieszka, J.   E

Baltimore (Md.)

Fiction

Hahn, M. D. Anna all year round (3-5)   **Fic**

Baltimore Orioles (Baseball team)

Herman, G. Cal Ripken, Jr. (1-3)   **92**

Balto and the great race. Kimmel, E. C.   **636.7**

La **Bamba**. Soto, G.

In Soto, G. Baseball in April, and other stories p81-89   **S C**

Bambi. Salten, F.   **Fic**

Banana

Landau, E. Bananas (2-4)   **634**

Bancroft, Ann

See/See also pages in the following book(s):
Atkins, J. How high can we climb? (5 and up)   **920**

Bancroft, Henrietta

Animals in winter (k-1)   **591.56**

A **band** of angels. Hopkinson, D.   E

The **bandit**. Kimmel, E. A.

In Kimmel, E. A. The adventures of Hershel of Ostropol p16-18   **398.2**

Bandit's moon. Fleischman, S.   **Fic**

Bands (Music)

Fiction

Hurd, T. Mama don't allow   E

Bang, Molly

Goose   E
The Grey Lady and the Strawberry Snatcher   E
My light (1-3)   **621.47**
Nobody particular (4 and up)   **363.7**
The paper crane   E
Ten, nine, eight   E
When Sophie gets angry—really, really angry   E
(il) Bang-Campbell, M. Little Rat sets sail   E
(il) Livingstone, S. Harley   E

Bang-Campbell, Monika

Little Rat sets sail   E

Bania, Michael

Kumak's fish   E

Bank credit cards *See* Credit cards

Bank debit cards *See* Debit cards

Banks, Kate

And if the moon could talk   E
Baboon   E
The cat who walked across France   E
Close your eyes   E
Dillon Dillon (4 and up)   **Fic**
A gift from the sea   E
The great blue house   E
The night worker   E

Banks, Lynne Reid

The Indian in the cupboard (5 and up)   **Fic**

Banks and banking

Debit cards

See Debit cards

Banned books *See* Books—Censorship

Banneker, Benjamin, 1731-1806

About

Ferris, J. What are you figuring now? a story about Benjamin Banneker (3-5)   **92**
Hinman, B. Benjamin Banneker (5 and up)   **92**
Pinkney, A. D. Dear Benjamin Banneker (2-4)   **92**
Wadsworth, G. Benjamin Banneker (3-5)   **92**

Fiction

McGill, A. Molly Bannaky   E

Bannerman, Helen

The story of Little Babaji   E
Story of Little Black Sambo; adaptation. See Lester, J. Sam and the tigers   E

Bannon, Kay T.

(jt. auth) Bushyhead, R. H. Yonder mountain   **398.2**

Bantam of the opera. Auch, M. J.   E

Bányai, István

The other side   E
Zoom   E

Banyan tree

Bash, B. In the heart of the village (3-5)   **583**

Baptists

See also Mennonites

Barancik, Sue

Guide to collective biographies for children and young adults   **016.9**

Barasch, Lynne
A country schoolhouse   E
Knockin' on wood [biography of Peg Leg Bates] (2-4)   **92**
Radio rescue   E
The reluctant flower girl   E
(jt. auth) Cutler, J. Common sense and fowls   **Fic**

Barber, Daniel Wynn
Tiger in the snow
  In Beware!; R.L. Stine picks his favorite scary stories p127-37   **808.8**

Barber, Nicola
Islamic empires (4 and up)   **704**
Istanbul (3-6)   **949.6**
Music: an A-Z guide (4 and up)   **780.3**
(jt. auth) Ganeri, A. The young person's guide to the opera   **792.5**

Barberie, Heather
(il) Burgess, R. Be a clown!   **791.3**
(il) Thibault, T. Kids' easy quilting projects   **746.46**

Barbers and barbershops
Fiction
Mitchell, M. K. Uncle Jed's barbershop   E
Tarpley, N. Bippity Bop barbershop   E

Barbie. Soto, G.
  In Soto, G. Baseball in April, and other stories p33-42   **S C**

Barbour, Karen
Mr. Williams   E
(il) Herrera, J. F. Laughing out loud, I fly   **811**
(jt. auth) Lester, J. Let's talk about race   **305.8**
(il) Marvelous math. See Marvelous math   **811.008**

Bard of Avon: the story of William Shakespeare. Stanley, D.   **822.3**

Bardhan-Quallen, Sudipta
AIDS (4-6)   **616.97**
The Mexican-American War (5 and up)   **973.6**

Bardsley, John, d. 1999
Fiction
Gerstein, M. Sparrow Jack   E

Bare bones children's services. Steele, A. T.   **027.62**

The **Barefoot** book of Buddhist tales. See Chödzin, S. The wisdom of the crows and other Buddhist tales   **294.3**

Barenblat, Rachel
Massachusetts
  In World Almanac Library of the States series   **973**
Washington
  In World Almanac Library of the States series   **973**
Wisconsin
  In World Almanac Library of the States series   **973**

Baret, Jeanne, 1740-1807?
See/See also pages in the following book(s):
Atkins, J. How high can we climb? (5 and up)   **920**

Baring, Maurice
The blue rose
  In Shedlock, M. L. The art of the story-teller p204-12   **372.6**

Bark, George. Feiffer, J.   E

Barkin, Carol
(jt. auth) James, E. How to write terrific book reports   **808**

Barkley, James
(il) Armstrong, W. H. Sounder   **Fic**

Barkus, Sly and the golden egg. McAllister, A.   E

Barlas, Robert
Bahamas (5 and up)   **972.96**
Latvia (5 and up)   **947.9**
Uganda (5 and up)   **967.6**

Barn. Atwell, D.   E

The **barn**. Avi   Fic

The **barn** burner. Willis, P.   Fic

Barn cat. Saul, C. P.   E

Barn dance!. Martin, B.   E

The **barn** owls. Johnston, T.   E

Barn raising. Brown, C. M.   E

Barn savers. High, L. O.   E

Barnard, Alan
(il) Tanaka, S. New dinos   **567.9**

Barnard, Bryn
Outbreak (5 and up)   **614.4**
(il) Nye, B. Bill Nye the science guy's great big book of tiny germs   **579**
(il) Redmond, S.-R. Tentacles!   **594**

Barner, Bob
Bug safari   E
Dem bones (k-3)   **611**
Fish wish   E

Barnes, Harold
The proud cock
  In Shedlock, M. L. The art of the story-teller p191-94   **372.6**

Barnes, Karen
(il) Berger, M. Why don't haircuts hurt?   **612**

Barnes, Trevor
Archaeology (5 and up)   **930.1**

Barnett, Ida B. Wells- *See* Wells-Barnett, Ida B., 1862-1931

Barnett, Moneta
(il) Greenfield, E. Sister   Fic

Barns
Fiction
Brown, C. M. Barn raising   E
High, L. O. Barn savers   E

Barnum, Jay Hyde
(il) Tunis, J. R. The Kid from Tomkinsville   Fic

Barnum, P. T. (Phineas Taylor), 1810-1891
Fiction
Prince, A. J. Twenty-one elephants and still standing   E

Barnum, Phineas Taylor *See* Barnum, P. T. (Phineas Taylor), 1810-1891

Barnyard banter. Fleming, D.   E

Barton, Byron—*Continued*
  (il) Kalan, R. Jump, frog, jump!   **E**
  (il) Sharmat, M. W. Gila monsters meet you at the airport   **E**
  (il) Simon, S. The paper airplane book
     745.592

Barton, Clara, 1821-1912
About
  Koestler-Grack, R. A. The story of Clara Barton (2-4)   **92**

Barton, Jill
  (il) Hest, A. Guess who, Baby Duck!   **E**
  (il) King-Smith, D. Lady Lollipop   **Fic**
  (il) Root, P. Rattletrap car   **E**
  (il) Waddell, M. It's quacking time!   **E**

Barton, Otis
About
  Matsen, B. The incredible record-setting deep-sea dive of the bathysphere (4 and up)
     551.46

Bartone, Elisa
  Peppe the lamplighter   **E**

Bartram, John, 1699-1777
About
  Ray, D. K. Flower hunter [biography of William Bartram] (3-5)   **92**

Bartram, William, 1739-1823
About
  Ray, D. K. Flower hunter [biography of William Bartram] (3-5)   **92**

Baseball
    See also Negro leagues; Softball
  Buckley, J., Jr. Play ball! (3-6)   **796.357**
  Coleman, J. W. Baseball for everyone (4-6)
     796.357
  Curlee, L. Ballpark (3-6)   **796.357**
  Geng, D. Play-by-play baseball (5 and up)
     796.357
  Gibbons, G. My baseball book (k-2)
     796.357
  Isadora, R. Nick plays baseball (k-3)
     796.357
  Kennedy, M. Baseball (4 and up)   **796.357**
  Kisseloff, J. Who is baseball's greatest pitcher? (5 and up)   **796.357**
  Krasner, S. Play ball like the hall of famers (5 and up)   **796.357**
  Krasner, S. Play ball like the pros (5 and up)
     796.357
  McKissack, P. C. Black diamond (6 and up)
     796.357
  Moss, M. Mighty Jackie: the strike out queen
     E
  Ritter, L. S. Leagues apart (2-4)   **796.357**
  Smith, C. R. Diamond life (2-4)   **796.357**
  Smyth, I. The young baseball player (4 and up)
     796.357
  Stewart, M. Long ball (4 and up)   **796.357**
  Weatherford, C. B. A Negro league scrapbook (4 and up)   **796.357**
  See/See also pages in the following book(s):
  Bauer, C. F. Celebrations p1-24   **808.8**
Biography
  Adler, D. A. Lou Gehrig (2-4)   **92**

Adler, D. A. A picture book of Jackie Robinson (1-3)   **92**
Cline-Ransome, L. Satchel Paige (2-4)   **92**
Ford, C. T. Jackie Robinson (2-4)   **92**
Ford, C. T. Roberto Clemente (5 and up)
     92
Golenbock, P. Hank Aaron (1-3)   **92**
Golenbock, P. Teammates [biography of Jackie Robinson] (1-4)   **92**
Green, M. Y. A strong right arm: the story of Mamie "Peanut" Johnson (4 and up)   **92**
Herman, G. Cal Ripken, Jr. (1-3)   **92**
Lipsyte, R. Heroes of baseball (4 and up)
     796.357
Marlin, J. Mickey Mantle (4 and up)   **92**
Márquez, H. Roberto Clemente (4 and up)
     92
Robinson, S. Promises to keep: how Jackie Robinson changed America (4 and up)   **92**
Viola, K. Lou Gehrig (4 and up)   **92**
Winter, J. Beisbol! Latino baseball pioneers and legends (3-6)   **920**
Winter, J. Roberto Clemente (2-4)   **92**
Fiction
Bildner, P. Shoeless Joe & Black Betsy   **E**
Burleigh, R. Home run   **E**
Chabon, M. Summerland (5 and up)   **Fic**
Christopher, M. The dog that called the pitch (2-4)   **Fic**
Cohen, B. Thank you, Jackie Robinson (4-6)
     Fic
Corbett, S. Free baseball (5 and up)   **Fic**
Corey, S. Players in pigtails   **E**
Curtis, G. The bat boy & his violin   **E**
Gutman, D. Shoeless Joe & me (4 and up)
     Fic
Hopkinson, D. Girl wonder   **E**
Hurwitz, J. Baseball fever (3-5)   **Fic**
Isadora, R. Max   **E**
Jennings, P. Out standing in my field (4-6)
     Fic
Johnson, A. Just like Josh Gibson   **E**
Kessler, L. P. Here comes the strikeout   **E**
Kovalski, M. Take me out to the ball game
     E
Lupica, M. Heat (5 and up)   **Fic**
Mochizuki, K. Baseball saved us   **E**
Rappaport, D. Dirt on their skirts   **E**
Ritter, J. H. The boy who saved baseball (5 and up)   **Fic**
Ritter, J. H. Over the wall (6 and up)   **Fic**
Roberts, K. My 13th season (5 and up)   **Fic**
Slote, A. Finding Buck McHenry (4-6)   **Fic**
Slote, A. Hang tough, Paul Mather (4-6)
     Fic
Smith, R. K. Bobby Baseball (4-6)   **Fic**
Tavares, M. Mudball   **E**
Tunis, J. R. The Kid from Tomkinsville (5 and up)   **Fic**
Uhlberg, M. Dad, Jackie, and me   **E**
Poetry
Extra innings (4 and up)   **811.008**
Thayer, E. L. Casey at the bat   **811**

Baseball cards
Fiction
Slote, A. The trading game (4-6)   **Fic**

Baseball fever. Hurwitz, J.   **Fic**

Baseball for everyone. Coleman, J. W.   **796.357**

Baseball in April. Soto, G.
In Soto, G. Baseball in April, and other stories p13-22   **S C**

Baseball in April, and other stories. Soto, G.   **S C**

Baseball saved us. Mochizuki, K.   **E**

Baseman, Gary
(il) Harris, J. Strong stuff   **398.2**

Bash, Barbara
Ancient ones (3-5)   **585**
Desert giant (3-5)   **583**
In the heart of the village (3-5)   **583**
Urban roosts: where birds nest in the city (1-4)   **598**
(il) Sayre, A. P. Dig, wait, listen   **E**
(il) Schaefer, L. M. What's up, what's down?   **E**

Bashō *See* Matsuo, Bashō, 1644-1694

Basho and the river stones. Myers, T.   **E**

Basic rights *See* Civil rights

Basket making
Fiction
Ray, M. L. Basket moon   **E**

Basket moon. Ray, M. L.   **E**

Basketball
Cooper, F. Jump! [biography of Michael Jordan] (k-3)   **92**
Gibbons, G. My basketball book (k-2)   **796.323**
Jordan, D. Salt in his shoes   **E**
Kuklin, S. Hoops with Swoopes (k-3)   **796.323**
Stewart, M. Jackie Stiles (4 and up)   **92**
Thomas, K. How basketball works (5 and up)   **796.323**
Fiction
Coy, J. Strong to the hoop   **E**
Richardson, C. K. The real slam dunk (2-4)   **Fic**
Soto, G. Taking sides (5 and up)   **Fic**
Poetry
Burleigh, R. Hoops   **811**
Smith, C. R. Hoop kings   **811**
Smith, C. R. Hoop queens   **811**

Basketball's new wave [series]
Stewart, M. Jackie Stiles   **92**

Baskets
Fiction
Belton, S. Beauty, her basket   **E**
Raven, M. Circle unbroken   **E**

Baskin, Nora Raleigh
What every girl (except me) knows (4 and up)   **Fic**

Basman, Michael
Chess for kids (4 and up)   **794.1**

Bass, L. G.
A three hat day   **E**

Bass, Scott
Kayaking (4-6)   **797.1**

Bassett, Jeni
(il) Kroll, S. The biggest pumpkin ever   **E**

Bassil, Andrea
Vincent van Gogh (4 and up)   **92**

The **bat** boy & his violin. Curtis, G.   **E**

Bat loves the night. Davies, N.   **E**

The **bat-poet**. Jarrell, R.   **Fic**

Bateman, Colin
Running with the Reservoir Pups (5 and up)   **Fic**

Bateman, Teresa
April foolishness   **E**
The Bully Blockers Club   **E**
The dragon at the well
In Fire and wings: dragon tales from East and West p1-14   **S C**
Farm flu   **E**
Harp o' gold   **E**
Red, white, blue, and Uncle who? (4 and up)   **929.9**
Waiting for a white knight
In Fire and wings: dragon tales from East and West p137-40   **S C**

Bates, Amy June
(il) English, K. Speak to me   **E**
(il) Hopkinson, D. Susan B. Anthony   **92**

Bates, Ivan
Five little ducks (k-2)   **782.42**
(il) Hindley, J. Do like a duck does!   **E**

Bates, Katharine Lee
America the beautiful   **E**

Bates, Katharine Lee, 1859-1929
About
Younger, B. Purple mountain majesties: the story of Katharine Lee Bates and "America the beautiful" (2-4)   **92**

Bates, Peg Leg, 1907-1998
About
Barasch, L. Knockin' on wood [biography of Peg Leg Bates] (2-4)   **92**

Bateson, Catherine
Stranded in Boringsville (5 and up)   **Fic**

Bath, K. P.
The secret of Castle Cant (5 and up)   **Fic**

Bathrooms
Fiction
Elya, S. M. Oh no, gotta go!   **E**
History
Lauber, P. What you never knew about tubs, toilets & showers (2-4)   **391**

Baths
Ehrlich, F. Does an elephant take a bath?   **E**
Fiction
Meister, C. Tiny's bath   **E**
Wood, A. King Bidgood's in the bathtub   **E**
History
Lauber, P. What you never knew about tubs, toilets & showers (2-4)   **391**
Poetry
The Fish is me (k-2)   **811.008**

Bathtub science. Levine, S.   **507.8**

Batmanglij, Najmieh
See/See also pages in the following book(s):
Major, J. S. Caravan to America p[1]-13 (4 and up)   **920**

Bats
Dornfeld, M. Bats (3-6)   **599.4**
Earle, A. Zipping, zapping, zooming bats (k-3)   **599.4**
Gibbons, G. Bats (k-3)   **599.4**
Markle, S. Little lost bat   **599.4**
Markle, S. Outside and inside bats (2-4)   **599.4**
Pringle, L. P. Bats! (3-5)   **599.4**

Fiction
Appelt, K. Bats around the clock   **E**
Cannon, J. Stellaluna   **E**
Davies, N. Bat loves the night   **E**
Jarrell, R. The bat-poet (2-4)   **Fic**
Jarvis, R. The oaken throne (5 and up)   **Fic**
Mitchard, J. Baby bat's lullaby   **E**
Oppel, K. Silverwing (5 and up)   **Fic**

Bats around the clock. Appelt, K.   **E**

Batten, John D. (John Dickson)
(il) Jacobs, J. English fairy tales   **398.2**

Batten, Mary
Aliens from Earth (3-6)   **577**
Anthropologist: scientist of the people (4 and up)   **301**

Battered children *See* Child abuse

Battered women *See* Abused women

Battering of wives *See* Wife abuse

Batting after Sophie. Macy, S.
In Girls got game; sports stories and poems   **810.8**

The **battle** for Bornholm. Lunge-Larsen, L.
In Lunge-Larsen, L. The hidden folk; stories of fairies, dwarves, selkies, and other secret beings p28-31   **398.2**

The **battle** for St. Michaels. McCully, E. A.   **E**

The **battle** of birds. Philip, N.
In Philip, N. Celtic fairy tales p15-26   **398.2**

The **battle** of Chihaya Castle. Kimmel, E. A.
In Kimmel, E. A. Sword of the samurai; adventure stories from Japan p53-62   **Fic**

The **Battle** of Gettysburg and Lincoln's Gettysburg Address. Ford, C. T.   **973.7**

The **Battle** of the Little Bighorn. Uschan, M. V.   **973.8**

Bauer, Caroline Feller
Caroline Feller Bauer's new handbook for storytellers   **372.6**
Celebrations   **808.8**
Leading kids to books through crafts   **027.62**
Leading kids to books through magic   **027.62**
Leading kids to books through puppets   **027.62**
Marika the snowmaiden
In Snowy day: stories and poems p45-49   **808.8**
The poetry break   **372.6**
Read for the fun of it   **027.62**
This way to books   **028.5**

(ed) Snowy day: stories and poems. See Snowy day: stories and poems   **808.8**

Bauer, Joan
Clean sweep
In Shelf life: stories by the book p151-64   **S C**

Bauer, Marion Dane
A bear named Trouble (3-6)   **Fic**
The blue ghost (2-4)   **Fic**
The double-digit club (3-5)   **Fic**
The good deed
In Shelf life: stories by the book p109-26   **S C**
If you were born a kitten (k-1)   **591.3**
Jason's bears   **E**
On my honor (4 and up)   **Fic**
Runt (4 and up)   **Fic**
What's your story? (5 and up)   **808.3**
Wind (k-2)   **551.51**

Baum, L. Frank
The Wizard of Oz (3-6)   **Fic**

Baumfree, Isabella *See* Truth, Sojourner, d. 1883

Bausum, Ann
Dragon bones and dinosaur eggs: a photobiography of Roy Chapman Andrews (5 and up)   **92**
Freedom Riders (5 and up)   **323.1**
Our country's presidents (5 and up)   **920**

Baviera, Rocco
(il) Bruchac, J. A boy called Slow: the true story of Sitting Bull   **92**

Bavin (Clark R.) National Fish and Wildlife Forensics Laboratory *See* National Fish and Wildlife Forensics Laboratory

Bavsi's feast. Geras, A.
In Geras, A. My grandmother's stories; a collection of Jewish folk tales p1-8   **398.2**

Bawden, Nina
Granny the Pag (4 and up)   **Fic**
Humbug (4 and up)   **Fic**

Baxter, Kathleen A.
Gotcha!   **028.1**

Baxter, Roberta
Chemical reaction (4 and up)   **540**
Computers (3-5)   **004**

Baya, baya, lulla-by-a. McDonald, M.   **E**

Bayer, Jane
A my name is Alice   **E**

Bayley, Nicola
(il) Kipling, R. The jungle book: Mowgli's story   **S C**

Baylor, Byrd
The desert is theirs (1-4)   **577.5**
Hawk, I'm your brother   **E**
The way to start a day (1-4)   **204**
When clay sings (1-4)   **970.004**

Baynes, Pauline
(jt. auth) Koralek, J. The coat of many colors   **222**
(il) Lewis, C. S. The lion, the witch, and the wardrobe   **Fic**

Bazler, Judith A.
More science projects for all students   **507.8**

Bears—Fiction—*Continued*

Moss, M. Don't forget I love you   E
Muth, J. J. Zen shorts   E
Paver, M. Wolf brother (5 and up)   Fic
Peet, B. Big bad Bruce   E
Rosen, M. We're going on a bear hunt   E
Ryder, J. Big Bear Ball   E
Stanley, D. Goldie and the three bears   E
Tafuri, N. Mama's Little Bears   E
Waddell, M. Can't you sleep, Little Bear?   E
Waddell, M. Snow bears   E
Wallace, N. E. Seeds! Seeds! Seeds!   E
Walters, C. Time to sleep, Alfie Bear   E
Ward, L. K. The biggest bear   E
Wilson, K. Bear snores on   E
Wiseman, B. Morris and Boris at the circus   E
Yolen, J. Baby Bear's chairs   E

Folklore

Aylesworth, J. Goldilocks and the three bears (k-3)   398.2
Barton, B. The three bears (k-1)   398.2
Bruchac, J. How Chipmunk got his stripes (k-3)   398.2
Galdone, P. The three bears (k-2)   398.2
Marshall, J. Goldilocks and the three bears (k-2)   398.2
San Souci, R. Two bear cubs (k-3)   398.2
Stevens, J. Tops and bottoms (k-3)   398.2

The **bears** on Hemlock Mountain. Dalgliesh, A.   Fic
The **bears** on Hemlock mountain. Dalgliesh, A.
   In You read to me & I'll read to you; 20th-century stories to share p180-99   E
Beast feast. Florian, D.   811
The **beasties**. Sleator, W.   Fic
Beasts in a pit. Afanas'ev, A. N.
   In Afanas'ev, A. N. Russian fairy tales p498   398.2
A **beasty** story. Martin, B.   E

Beaton, Clare
(il) Blackstone, S. Secret seahorse   E
(il) Blackstone, S. Who are you, baby kangaroo?   E

Beatrice doesn't want to. Numeroff, L. J.   E
Beatrix: various episodes from the life of Beatrix Potter. Winter, J.   92

Beattie, Owen
Buried in ice (4 and up)   998

Beatty, Patricia
Turn homeward, Hannalee (5 and up)   Fic

Beatty, Richard
Boron
   In The Elements   546
Manganese
   In The Elements   546
Phosphorus
   In The Elements   546
Sulfur
   In The Elements   546

Beaumont, Karen
Baby danced the polka   E
Duck, duck, goose!   E
I ain't gonna paint no more!   E

Beaumont, Le Prince de *See* Le Prince de Beaumont, Madame, 1711-1780

Beautiful blackbird. Bryan, A.   398.2
The **beautiful** butterfly. Sierra, J.   398.2
The **beautiful** Christmas tree. Zolotow, C.   E
The **beautiful** girl of the moon tower. Hamilton, V.
   In Hamilton, V. The people could fly; American black folktales p53-59   398.2
Beautiful warrior. McCully, E. A.   E
Beauty. Wallace, B.   Fic
Beauty and the beast. Brett, J.   398.2
Beauty and the beast. Le Prince de Beaumont, Madame
   In Princess stories; a classic illustrated edition   398.2
Beauty and the beast. Mayer, M.   398.2
Beauty and the Beast. Steig, J.
   In Steig, J. A handful of beans; six fairy tales p33-58   398.2
Beauty and the beast. Villeneuve, M. d.
   In The Blue fairy book p100-19   398.2
Beauty, her basket. Belton, S.   E
The **Beauty** of the beast (4-6)   811.008
Beauty shops

Fiction
Wells, R. Ruby's beauty shop   E
Beaver pond, moose pond. Arnosky, J.   E
Beavers
Rounds, G. Beaver (k-3)   599.3

Fiction
Arnosky, J. Beaver pond, moose pond   E
Folklore
Bruchac, J. Turtle's race with Beaver (k-3)   398.2
Bebop Express. Panahi, H. L.   E
Because of Winn-Dixie. DiCamillo, K.   Fic
Because of you. Hennessy, B. G.   E

Bechtold, Lisze
Edna's tale   E
(il) Kuskin, K. Toots the cat   811

Beck, Peggy
GlobaLinks: resources for world studies, grades K-8   016.9

Beck, Scott
Pepito the brave   E

Becker, Beverley C.
Hit list for children 2   016.8

Becker, Helaine
Boredom blasters (4-6)   793
Funny business (5 and up)   792

Becker, John E.
Gray whales (4-6)   599.5

Beckett, Wendy
A child's book of prayer in art (3-6)   242

Becoming a citizen. Hamilton, J.   323.6
Becoming butterflies. Rockwell, A. F.   595.7
Becoming Joe DiMaggio. Testa, M.   811
Becoming Naomi León. Ryan, P. M.   Fic
Bed-knob and broomstick. Norton, M.   Fic

Bedard, Michael
The wolf of Gubbio (3-6)   **398.2**

Beddows, Eric
(il) Fleischman, P. I am phoenix: poems for two voices   **811**
(il) Fleischman, P. Joyful noise: poems for two voices   **811**

Bedford, David
The way I love you   E

Bedford, F. D.
(il) Barrie, J. M. Peter Pan   **Fic**

Bedore, Bernie
The mufferaw catfish
In Bauer, C. F. Celebrations; read-aloud holiday and theme book programs p85-86   **808.8**

Bedtime
Maccarone, G. A child's good night prayer   E

Fiction
Anderson, C. Bedtime!   E
Asch, F. Barnyard lullaby   E
Bang, M. Ten, nine, eight   E
Banks, K. And if the moon could talk   E
Bogan, P. Goodnight Lulu   E
Branford, H. Little Pig Figwort can't get to sleep   E
Brown, M. W. A child's good night book   E
Brown, M. W. Little Fur family   E
Cook, S. Good night pillow fight   E
Cooper, E. A good night walk   E
Coy, J. Vroomaloom zoom   E
Dewdney, A. Llama, llama red pajama   E
Doyle, M. One, two, three O'Leary   E
Eilenberg, M. Cowboy Kid   E
Emberley, E. Go away, big green monster!   E
Fox, M. Sleepy bears   E
Geisert, A. Lights out   E
Hest, A. Kiss good night   E
Hoban, R. Bedtime for Frances   E
Hurd, T. Sleepy Cadillac   E
Jones, S. L. Time to say goodnight   E
Kanevsky, P. Sleepy boy   E
Kloske, G. Once upon a time, the end   E
Kono, E. E. Hula lullaby   E
Krauss, R. Goodnight goodnight sleepyhead   E
Lewis, K. Good night, Harry   E
Lum, K. What! cried Granny   E
MacLachlan, P. Who loves me?   E
Markes, J. Shhhhh! Everybody's sleeping   E
Medearis, A. S. Snug in Mama's arms   E
Mitchard, J. Baby bat's lullaby   E
Mitton, T. Goodnight me, goodnight you   E
Moon, N. Tick-tock, drip-drop!   E
Mortensen, D. D. Good night engines   E
Pow, T. Tell me one thing, Dad   E
Rathmann, P. 10 minutes till bedtime   E
Rohmann, E. Clara and Asha   E
Saltzberg, B. Cornelius P. Mud, are you ready for bed?   E
Schwartz, A. Some babies   E
Scotton, R. Russell the sheep   E
Spinelli, E. Night shift daddy   E
Tafuri, N. Goodnight, my duckling   E

Thomas, S. M. Good night, Good Knight   E
Waddell, M. Can't you sleep, Little Bear?   E
Walters, C. Time to sleep, Alfie Bear   E
Whybrow, I. The noisy way to bed   E
Wilcoxen, C. Niccolini's song   E
Wolff, F. It is the wind   E
Wood, D. Piggies   E
Yolen, J. How do dinosaurs say goodnight?   E

Poetry
Myers, T. Dark sparkle tea (2-4)   **811**

Bedtime!. Anderson, C.   E

Bedtime for Frances. Hoban, R.   E

Bee-bim bop!. Park, L. S.   E

Bee culture *See* Beekeeping

The **bee-man** of Orn. Stockton, F.   **Fic**

The **bee** tree. Polacco, P.   E

Beebe, William, 1877-1962
About
Matsen, B. The incredible record-setting deep-sea dive of the bathysphere (4 and up)   **551.46**

Beecher family
About
Fritz, J. Harriet Beecher Stowe and the Beecher preachers (5 and up)   **92**

Beegu. Deacon, A.   E

Beeke, Tiphanie
(il) Bruss, D. Book! book! book!   E
(il) Mackall, D. D. First day   E
(il) Morrow, T. J. Mommy loves her baby   E
(il) Whybrow, I. The noisy way to bed   E

Beekeeping
Fiction
Kessler, C. The best beekeeper of Lalibela   E

Beekman's big deal. De Guzman, M.   **Fic**

Beeler, Selby B.
Throw your tooth on the roof (k-3)   **398**

Been to yesterdays: poems of a life. Hopkins, L. B.   **811**

Beep beep, vroom vroom!. Murphy, S. J.   **515**

Bees
See also Beekeeping
Cole, J. The magic school bus inside a beehive (2-4)   **595.7**
Glaser, L. Brilliant bees (k-3)   **595.7**
Heiligman, D. Honeybees (k-3)   **595.7**
Markle, S. Outside and inside killer bees (2-4)   **595.7**
Micucci, C. The life and times of the honeybee (2-4)   **595.7**
Miller, S. S. Ants, bees, and wasps of North America (4-6)   **595.7**
Rockwell, A. F. Honey in a hive (k-3)   **595.7**
Sayre, A. P. The bumblebee queen (1-3)   **595.7**

Fiction
McDonald, M. Ant and Honey Bee, what a pair!   E
Polacco, P. The bee tree   E

Bemelmans, Ludwig, 1898-1962
About
Marciano, J. B. Bemelmans   **92**
Ben-Ami, Doron
(il) Byars, B. C. Tornado   **Fic**
Ben and me. Lawson, R.   **Fic**
Ben-'Ezer, Ehud
Hosni the dreamer (2-4)   **398.2**
Ben Franklin's almanac. Fleming, C. **92**
Ben over night. Ellis, S.   **E**
Benatar, Raquel
Isabel Allende (3-5)   **92**
Benchley, Nathaniel
A ghost named Fred   **E**
Benchmark all stars [series]
Bradley, M. Lance Armstrong **92**
Bendall-Brunello, John
(il) Braun, T. My goose Betsy **E**
Bender, Howard
(il) Pellowski, M. The art of making comic
books   **741.5**
Bender, Lionel
Invention (4 and up)   **609**
Bender, Robert
(il) Greene, R. G. Barnyard song **E**
(il) Hall, K. Ribbit riddles   **793.73**
Beneath a blue umbrella: rhymes. Prelutsky, J.
    811
Benedict, of Nursia, Saint *See* Benedict, Saint,
Abbot of Monte Cassino
Benedict, Saint, Abbot of Monte Cassino
About
Norris, K. The holy twins: Benedict and Scho-
lastica (3-5)   **92**
Beneduce, Ann
Jack and the beanstalk (2-4) **398.2**
(ed) Joy to the world. See Joy to the world
    808.8
Benga, Ota, d. 1916
Fiction
McNamee, G. Sparks (4-6)   **Fic**
Benizara and Kakezara. MacDonald, M. R.
In MacDonald, M. R. Celebrate the world;
twenty tellable folktales for multicultural
festivals p10-19   **372.6**
Benjamin, of Tudela, 12th cent.
Fiction
Shulevitz, U. The travels of Benjamin of Tudela
(4 and up)   **Fic**
Benjamin and the caliph. Jaffe, N.
In Jaffe, N. and Zeitlin, S. J. While standing
on one foot; puzzle stories and wisdom
tales from the Jewish tradition p33-37
    296.1
Benjamin ben Jonah *See* Benjamin, of Tudela,
12th cent.
Benjamin Franklin (2-4)   **92**
Bennett, Erin Susanne
(il) Stroud, B. The patchwork path **E**
Bennett, Jill
(comp) Grandad's tree. See Grandad's tree
    811.008

Bennett, Nneka
(il) Lasky, K. Vision of beauty: the story of Sarah Breedlove Walker   **92**
Benny and the binky. Lindgren, B. **E**
Ben's dream. Van Allsburg, C. **E**
Ben's trumpet. Isadora, R.   **E**
Benson, Kathleen
(jt. auth) Haskins, J. African beginnings **960**
(jt. auth) Haskins, J. Bound for America
    326
(jt. auth) Haskins, J. Out of the darkness
    305.8
Benson, Patrick
(il) Grahame, K. The wind in the willows
    Fic
(il) Newman, M. Mole and the baby bird **E**
(il) Waddell, M. Owl babies   **E**
(il) Wise, W. Christopher Mouse **Fic**
Bentley, Wilson Alwyn, 1865-1931
About
Martin, J. B. Snowflake Bentley [biography of
Wilson Alwyn Bentley] (k-3) **92**
Benton, Gail
Ready-to-go storytimes   **027.62**
Beowulf
Kimmel, E. A. The hero Beowulf (3-6)
    398.2
Beowulf. Osborne, M. P.
In Osborne, M. P. Favorite medieval tales p8-
16   **398.2**
Beowulf against Grendel. Nye, R.
In Bauer, C. F. Celebrations; read-aloud holi-
day and theme book programs p105-08
    808.8
The **berbalangs**. San Souci, R.
In San Souci, R. Even more short & shivery;
thirty spine-tingling stories p20-23
    398.2
Berberick, Nancy Varian
A song for Croaker Nordge
In A Glory of unicorns p127-43 **S C**
Bercaw, Edna Coe
Halmoni's day   **E**
Bereavement
Brown, L. K. When dinosaurs die (k-3)
    155.9
Dennison, A. Our dad died (4 and up)
    155.9
Krementz, J. How it feels when a parent dies (4
and up)   **155.9**
Fiction
Brisson, P. I remember Miss Perry **E**
Carson, J. You hold me and I'll hold you **E**
Deans, S. B. Every day and all the time (5 and
up)   **Fic**
Demas, C. Saying goodbye to Lulu **E**
Edwards, M. Papa's latkes   **E**
Martino, C. A. Rosa, sola (4-6) **Fic**
Roberts, K. My 13th season (5 and up) **Fic**
Roberts, W. D. The one left behind (5 and up)
    Fic
Rosen, M. Michael Rosen's sad book **E**
Schick, E. Mama   **E**
Tolan, S. S. Listen! (4 and up) **Fic**

Bereavement—Fiction—*Continued*
Wiles, D. Each little bird that sings (4-6)
Fic

Berenstain, Jan
(jt. auth) Berenstain, S. Down a sunny dirt road
92

Berenstain, Stan
Down a sunny dirt road (4 and up)   **92**

Berenzy, Alix
Sammy the classroom guinea pig   **E**
(il) A Glory of unicorns. See A Glory of unicorns   **S C**
(il) Guiberson, B. Z. Into the sea   **597.92**
(il) My kingdom for a horse. See My kingdom for a horse   **811.008**

Berg, Elizabeth
Senegal (5 and up)   **966.3**

Berg, Michelle
(il) Sidman, J. Meow ruff   **811**

Bergen, David
Life-size dinosaurs (3-6)   **567.9**

Berger, Barbara
All the way to Lhasa (k-3)   **398.2**

Berger, Gilda
Celebrate! (4 and up)   **296.4**
(jt. auth) Berger, M. Do stars have points?
523
(jt. auth) Berger, M. Do whales have belly buttons?   **599.5**
(jt. auth) Berger, M. How do flies walk upside down?   **595.7**
(jt. auth) Berger, M. Penguins swim but don't get wet   **591.7**
(jt. auth) Berger, M. The real Vikings   **948**
(jt. auth) Berger, M. Why don't haircuts hurt?
612

Berger, Melvin
Chirping crickets (k-3)   **595.7**
Do stars have points? (2-4)   **523**
Do whales have belly buttons? (2-4)   **599.5**
Germs make me sick! (k-3)   **616.9**
How do flies walk upside down? (3-5)
595.7
Look out for turtles! (k-3)   **597.92**
Penguins swim but don't get wet (2-4)
591.7
The real Vikings (4 and up)   **948**
Spinning spiders (k-3)   **595.4**
Switch on, switch off (k-3)   **537**
Why don't haircuts hurt? (2-4)   **612**
Why I sneeze, shiver, hiccup, and yawn (k-3)
612.7

Bergman, Mara
Snip snap!   **E**

Berkowitz, Robert E.
(jt. auth) Eisenberg, M. Teaching information & technology skills   **025.5**

Berman, Ruth
American bison (3-6)   **599.64**
Sharks (3-6)   **597**

Bermuda
Karwoski, G. Miracle (4-6)   **972.9**

Bernadorne, Francis *See* Francis, of Assisi, Saint, 1182-1226

Bernard, Nancy Stone
(jt. auth) Smith, S. T. Valley of the Kings
932

Bernardin, James
(il) Haddix, M. P. Say what?   **Fic**
(il) Kimmel, E. A. A horn for Louis [biography of Louis Armstrong]   **92**
(il) Kinsey-Warnock, N. Lumber camp library
Fic

Bernier-Grand, Carmen T.
César (3-6)   **811**
Juan Bobo (k-2)   **398.2**
Contents: The best way to carry water; A pig in Sunday clothes; Do not sneeze, do not scratch . . . do not eat; A dime a jug

Bernstein, Nina
Magic by the book (4-6)   **Fic**

Bernstein, Zena
(il) O'Brien, R. C. Mrs. Frisby and the rats of NIMH   **Fic**

Berries
See also Cranberries; Strawberries
Gibbons, G. The berry book (k-3)   **634**
Fiction
Degen, B. Jamberry   **E**
Sloat, T. Berry magic   **E**

Berry, Holly
(il) Old MacDonald had a farm. See Old MacDonald had a farm   **782.42**
(il) Rascol, S. I. The impudent rooster   **398.2**
(il) Stanley, D. Roughing it on the Oregon Trail
Fic

Berry, James
A nest full of stars (2-5)   **821**

Berry, Lynne
Duck skates   **E**

The **berry** book. Gibbons, G.   **634**

Berry magic. Sloat, T.   **E**

Berta: a remarkable dog. Lottridge, C. B.   **Fic**

Bertrand, Lynne
Granite baby   **E**

Besheer, Margaret
(jt. auth) Janin, H. Saudi Arabia   **953.8**

Beshore, George W.
Science in ancient China (4 and up)   **509**
Science in early Islamic culture (4 and up)
509

Bess. Schwartz, A.
In Schwartz, A. Scary stories 3; more tales to chill your bones p27-29   **398.2**

Bess and Bella. Haas, I.   **E**

Bess Call. San Souci, R.
In San Souci, R. Cut from the same cloth; American women of myth, legend, and tall tale p13-18   **398.2**

Bessie Smith and the night riders. Stauffacher, S.
E

Best, Cari
Are you going to be good?   **E**
Goose's story   **E**
Sally Jean, the Bicycle Queen   **E**
Shrinking Violet   **E**
Three cheers for Catherine the Great   **E**

The **best** beekeeper of Lalibela. Kessler, C. **E**

Best best friends. Chodos-Irvine, M. **E**

The **best** birthday parties ever!. Ross, K. **793.2**

Best books

Adventuring with books **011.6**

Barr, C. Best books for children: preschool through grade 6 **011.6**

The Best in children's books **028.1**

Freeman, J. Books kids will sit still for 3 **011.6**

Helbig, A. Dictionary of American children's fiction, 1995-1999 **028.5**

Kaleidoscope **011.6**

Notable social studies trade books for young people **016.3**

Outstanding science trade books for students K-12 **016.5**

Silvey, A. 100 best books for children **011.6**

What do children and young adults read next? **016.8**

Best books for children: preschool through grade 6. Barr, C. **011.6**

The **best** boy in the world. Schwartz, A.
In Schwartz, A. All of our noses are here, and other noodle tales p38-57 **398.2**

The **best** cat in the world. Newman, L. **E**

The **best** Christmas pageant ever. Robinson, B. **Fic**

Best friends. Kellogg, S. **E**

Best friends. San Souci, R.
In San Souci, R. Double-dare to be scared: another thirteen chilling tales **S C**

Best friends forever!. Torres, L. **745.5**

The **Best** in children's books **028.1**

The **Best** in children's nonfiction **028.1**

The **best** of Latino heritage 1996-2002. Schon, I. **011.6**

The **best** of times. Tang, G. **513**

The **best** picnic ever. Jarrett, C. **E**

The **best** place. Meddaugh, S. **E**

The **best** seat in second grade. Kenah, K. **E**

The **best** time of day. Spinelli, E. **E**

The **best** way to carry water. Bernier-Grand, C. T.
In Bernier-Grand, C. T. Juan Bobo; four folktales from Puerto Rico p6-12 **398.2**

Betancourt, Jeanne
My name is brain Brian (4-6) **Fic**

Betcha!. Murphy, S. J. **519.5**

Bethune, Mary Jane McLeod, 1875-1955
See/See also pages in the following book(s):
Pinkney, A. D. Let it shine (4 and up) **920**

Betsy-Tacy. Lovelace, M. H. **Fic**

Better wait till Martin comes. Hamilton, V.
In Hamilton, V. The people could fly; American black folktales p133-37 **398.2**

Between earth & sky. Bruchac, J. **398.2**

Between heaven and earth. Norman, H. **398.2**

Beware! (4 and up) **808.8**

Beware of kissing Lizard Lips. Shalant, P. **Fic**

The **bewitching** of Sea Pink. Climo, S.
In Climo, S. Magic & mischief; tales from Cornwall p75-84 **398.2**

Beyond Old MacDonald. Hoce, C. **811**

Beyond the Deepwoods. Stewart, P. **Fic**

Beyond the fringe. Maguire, G.
In A Glory of unicorns p45-57 **S C**

Beyond the great mountains. Young, E. **811**

Beyond the mango tree. Zemser, A. B. **Fic**

Beyond the ridge. Goble, P. **Fic**

The **BFG**. Dahl, R. **Fic**

Bhargava, Neirah
(il) Jani, M. What you will see inside a Hindu temple **294.5**

Bhend, Käthi
(il) Johansen, H. Henrietta and the golden eggs **E**

Bhopal. Bryan, N. **363.7**

Bhopal Union Carbide Plant Disaster, Bhopal, India, 1984
Bryan, N. Bhopal (5 and up) **363.7**

Bi-racial people *See* Racially mixed people

Bial, Raymond
Amish home (3-5) **289.7**
Ghost towns of the American West (3-6) **978**
A handful of dirt (3-6) **577.5**
One-room school (3-5) **370.9**
Portrait of a farm family (4 and up) **630.1**
The strength of these arms (4 and up) **326**
Tenement (4 and up) **974.7**
The Underground Railroad (4 and up) **326**
Where Washington walked (3-6) **92**
With needle and thread (4 and up) **746.46**

Bianco, Margery Williams
The velveteen rabbit (2-4) **Fic**

Bible
The Holy Bible [King James Bible. Oxford Univ. Press] **220.5**
The Holy Bible: new revised standard version **220.5**

Bible
Natural history
Bible. Selections. Animals of the Bible (1-4) **220.8**

Bible. O.T. Pentateuch
See also Torah

Bible. O.T. Psalms
Lindbergh, R. On morning wings (k-3) **223**

Bible. N.T.
The Christmas story **232.9**
The Easter story **232.9**

Bible. O.T. Ecclesiastes
To every thing there is a season **223**

Bible. O.T. Genesis
The story of the creation (k-3) **222**

Bible. Selections
Animals of the Bible (1-4) **220.8**
Tomie dePaola's book of Bible stories **220.9**

Bible (as subject)
Brown, A. The Bible and Christianity (5 and up) **220**

Bible (as subject)—*Continued*

Feiler, B. S. Walking the Bible   **222**

The **Bible** and Christianity. Brown, A.   **220**

The **Bible** for children from Good Books. Watts, M.   **220.9**

Bible stories

Bible. N.T. The Easter story   **232.9**

Bible. O.T. Genesis. The story of the creation (k-3)   **222**

Bible. Selections. Tomie dePaola's book of Bible stories   **220.9**

Chaikin, M. Angels sweep the desert floor (4 and up)   **296.1**

De Paola, T. Mary, the mother of Jesus (3-5)   **232.91**

De Paola, T. The miracles of Jesus (k-3)   **232.9**

De Regniers, B. S. David and Goliath   **222**

Fisher, L. E. David and Goliath (k-3)   **222**

Geisert, A. The ark (k-3)   **222**

Goldin, B. D. Journeys with Elijah (4 and up)   **222**

Graham, L. B. How God fix Jonah (4 and up)   **398.2**

Hoffman, M. Animals of the Bible (2-4)   **220.9**

Koralek, J. The coat of many colors (k-3)   **222**

Lepp, R. David: Shepard's song, vol. 1 (3-5)   **741.5**

Lester, J. When the beginning began (4 and up)   **296.1**

Lottridge, C. B. Stories from the life of Jesus (4 and up)   **232.9**

Manushkin, F. Miriam's cup (k-3)   **222**

Marzollo, J. Daniel in the lion's den (k-3)   **224**

Marzollo, J. Miriam and her brother Moses (k-3)   **222**

Marzollo, J. Ruth and Naomi (k-3)   **222**

McKissack, P. C. Let my people go (4 and up)   **221.9**

Paterson, J. B. Images of God (5 and up)   **231**

Paterson, K. The angel and the donkey (3-5)   **222**

Pinkney, J. Noah's ark (k-3)   **222**

Rock, L. Everlasting stories (3-6)   **220.9**

Sasso, S. E. But God remembered (3-5)   **221.9**

Sasso, S. E. Cain & Abel (k-3)   **222**

Spier, P. Noah's ark (k-2)   **222**

Thompson, L. Love one another (1-3)   **232.9**

Ward, E. M. Old Testament women (5 and up)   **221.9**

Watts, M. The Bible for children from Good Books (3-6)   **220.9**

Wildsmith, B. Exodus   **222**

Winthrop, E. He is risen: the Easter story (k-3)   **232.9**

Words of gold (4 and up)   **220.9**

Bibliographic instruction

Miller, P. Library skills   **025.5**

Stover, L. F. Magical library lessons   **027.62**

Bibliography

See also Books

Best books

See Best books

Bickel, Cindy

(jt. auth) Nagda, A. W. Chimp math   **529**

(jt. auth) Nagda, A. W. Polar bear math   **513**

(jt. auth) Nagda, A. W. Tiger math   **511**

Bicycle book. Gibbons, G.   **629.227**

The **bicycle** man. Say, A.   **E**

Bicycle racing

Armstrong, K. R. Lance Armstrong (1-3)   **92**

Donovan, S. Lance Armstrong (2-4)   **92**

Bicycles

See also Cycling

Gibbons, G. Bicycle book (k-3)   **629.227**

Haduch, B. Go fly a bike! (4-6)   **629.227**

Fiction

Best, C. Sally Jean, the Bicycle Queen   **E**

Mollel, T. M. My rows and piles of coins   **E**

Bicycles and bicycling *See* Cycling

Bidner, Jenni

The kids' guide to digital photography (5 and up)   **775**

Bierhorst, John

Is my friend at home? (1-4)   **398.2**

Includes the following stories: Roasted ears; Why mouse walks softly; Beetle's new life; Winter story; The racer; Why peaches are sweet; Coyote breaks his leg

The people with five fingers (k-3)   **398.2**

Bierman, Carol

Journey to Ellis Island (3-5)   **325.73**

Bies, Don

(il) Reynolds, D. W. Star wars: the visual dictionary   **791.43**

Biesty, Stephen

Egypt in spectacular cross-section (4 and up)   **932**

Rome: in spectacular cross section (4 and up)   **937**

Big & little. Jenkins, S.   **591.4**

Big and little. Miller, M.   **E**

Big, bad, and a little bit scary (k-3)   **811.008**

Big bad Bruce. Peet, B.   **E**

Big bad sixteen. Thomas, J. C.

In Thomas, J. C. The skull talks back and other haunting tales   **398.2**

The **big** balloon race. Coerr, E.   **E**

Big Bear Ball. Ryder, J.   **E**

Big blue whale. Davies, N.   **599.5**

Big book of rescue vehicles. Bingham, C.   **629.04**

Big book of trains (4-6)   **625.1**

Big Brown Bear's up and down day. McPhail, D. M.   **E**

The **big** brown box. Russo, M.   **E**

The **Big** cabbage

In Stockings of buttermilk: American folktales p87   **398.2**

Big cats. Patent, D. H.   **599.75**

Big cats. Simon, S. **599.75**

Big day on the river. Wilson, S. **E**

The big dinin'. Van Laan, N.
In Van Laan, N. With a whoop and a holler; a bushel of lore from way down south p27-31 **398.2**

Big Dipper *See* Ursa Major

The Big Dipper. Branley, F. M. **523.8**

Big dogs. Altman, L. J. **636.7**

Big fat hen. Baker, K. **398.8**

Big fat Little Lit (2-4) **741.5**

Big game hunting *See* Hunting

Big green drawing book, Ed Emberley's. Emberley, E. **741.2**

The big house. Coman, C. **Fic**

Big Jabe. Nolen, J. **E**

Big Jack and Little Jack
In The Jack tales p67-75 **398.2**

Big Jimmy's Kum Kau Chinese take-out. Lewin, T. **E**

Big Momma makes the world. Root, P. **E**

Big numbers. Packard, E. **513**

Big Pig and Little Pig. McPhail, D. M. **E**

Big Pig, Little Pig, Speckled Pig, and Runt. Sierra, J.
In Sierra, J. Can you guess my name?; traditional tales around the world p11-15 **398.2**

Big red barn. Brown, M. W. **E**

Big red drawing book, Ed Emberley's. Emberley, E. **741.2**

The big rivers. Hiscock, B. **551.48**

The big snow. Hader, B. **E**

Big talk. Fleischman, P. **811**

Big tracks, little tracks. Selsam, M. E. **591.5**

Big Tree People. Bruchac, J.
In Bruchac, J. and Bruchac, J. When the Chenoo howls; native American tales of terror **398.2**

Big wheels. Rockwell, A. F. **E**

Bigda, Diane
(il) Park, L. S. Mung-mung! **413**

Bigfoot bird. Curry, J. L.
In Curry, J. L. The wonderful sky boat and other Native American tales of the Southeast p51-53 **398.2**

Bigger, Better, BEST!. Murphy, S. J. **516**

The biggest bear. Ward, L. K. **E**

The biggest pumpkin ever. Kroll, S. **E**

The biggest soap. Schaefer, C. L. **E**

Biggest, strongest, fastest. Jenkins, S. **590**

The biggest test in the universe. Poydar, N. **E**

Biggs, Brian
(il) Draanen, W. v. Shredderman: Secret identity **Fic**

Bigmama's. Crews, D. **92**

Bigotry *See* Toleration

The bijli. San Souci, R.
In San Souci, R. A terrifying taste of short & shivery; thirty creepy tales p35-38 **398.2**

Bildner, Phil
Shoeless Joe & Black Betsy **E**

Bileck, Marvin
(jt. auth) Scheer, J. Rain makes applesauce **E**

Bilingual books
English-Japanese
Carle, E. Where are you going? To see my friend! **E**
English-Spanish
Ada, A. F. Gathering the sun (2-4) **811**
Alarcón, F. X. From the bellybutton of the moon and other summer poems (2-4) **811**
Alarcón, F. X. Iguanas in the snow and other winter poems (2-4) **811**
Alarcón, F. X. Laughing tomatoes and other spring poems (2-4) **811**
Alarcón, F. X. Poems to dream together (3-5) **811**
Ancona, G. The piñata maker: El piñatero (k-3) **745.594**
Argueta, J. Moony Luna **E**
Argueta, J. A movie in my pillow (3-6) **861**
Arrorró mi niño (k-3) **398.8**
Arroz con leche (k-3) **782.42**
Benatar, R. Isabel Allende (3-5) **92**
Brusca, M. C. Three friends. Tres amigos **E**
Campos, T. Muffler man **E**
Colato Laínez, R. Playing loteria **E**
Cool salsa (5 and up) **811.008**
Cruz, A. The woman who outshone the sun (k-3) **398.2**
Cumpiano, I. Quinito's neighborhood **E**
De colores and other Latin-American folk songs for children (k-3) **782.42**
De Paola, T. Marco's colors **E**
Diez deditos. Ten little fingers & other play rhymes and action songs from Latin America (k-3) **782.42**
Dorros, A. Radio Man. Don Radio **E**
Eastman, P. D. Are you my mother? **E**
Ehlert, L. Cuckoo. Cucú (k-3) **398.2**
Ehlert, L. Moon rope. Un lazo a la luna (k-3) **398.2**
Elya, S. M. Eight animals on the town **E**
Fiestas: a year of Latin American songs of celebration (k-3) **782.42**
Garza, C. L. Family pictures **E**
Garza, C. L. In my family (k-3) **305.8**
Garza, C. L. Magic windows **305.8**
Garza, X. Lucha libre: the Man in the Silver Mask (2-5) **Fic**
González, R. Antonio's card **E**
Guy, G. F. Fiesta! **E**
Guy, G. F. Siesta **E**
Hayes, J. Little Gold Star (k-3) **398.2**
Herrera, J. F. Laughing out loud, I fly **811**
Herrera, J. F. The upside down boy (k-3) **92**
Hinojosa, T. Cada niño/Every child (k-3) **782.42**

Bilingual books—English-Spanish—*Continued*
Jiménez, F. The Christmas gift: El regalo de
Navidad **E**
Mamá Goose (k-2) **398.8**
Mora, P. Uno, dos, tres: one, two, three **E**
Pérez, A. I. My diary from here to there (2-4)
Fic
Pérez, A. I. My very own room **E**
Perl, L. Piñatas and paper flowers (4 and up)
394.26
¡Pio peep! (k-3) **398.8**
Reiser, L. The lost ball: la pelota perdida **E**
Reiser, L. Tortillas and lullabies. Tortillas y
cancioncitas **E**
Rohmer, H. Uncle Nacho's hat (k-3) **398.2**
Seuss, Dr. The cat in the hat **E**
Shahan, S. Spicy hot colors: colores picantes
E
Tortillitas para mamá and other nursery rhymes
398.8
Vigil-Piñón, E. Marina's muumuu **E**
Wáchale! poetry and prose on growing up
Latino in America (5 and up) **810.8**
Winter, J. Diego [biography of Diego Rivera]
(k-3) **92**
You're on!: seven plays in English and Spanish
(4 and up) **812.008**
English-Spanish—Bibliography
Dale, D. C. Bilingual children's books in En-
glish and Spanish **011.6**
English-Thai
MacDonald, M. R. The girl who wore too much
(k-3) **398.2**
English-Tibetan
Rose, N. C. Tibetan tales for little Buddhas
(k-3) **398.2**
Bilingual children's books in English and Spanish.
Dale, D. C. **011.6**

Bill, Buffalo *See* Buffalo Bill, 1846-1917
Bill. Reaver, C. **Fic**
Bill and Pete. De Paola, T. **E**
Bill Greenfield and the cold day. Bruchac, J.
In Bruchac, J. Tell me a tale; a book about
storytelling p23-27 **372.6**
Bill Grogan's goat. Hoberman, M. A. **782.42**
Bill Nye the science guy's great big book of tiny
germs. Nye, B. **579**
Bill of rights (U.S.) *See* United States. Constitu-
tion. 1st-10th amendments
Bill Pickett, rodeo ridin' cowboy. Pinkney, A. D.
92
Bill, the talking mule.
In Thomas, J. C. The skull talks back and
other haunting tales **398.2**

Billingsley, Franny
The Folk Keeper (5 and up) **Fic**
Well wished (4-6) **Fic**

Billion (The number)
Schwartz, D. M. How much is a million? **E**
Billy and the rebel. Hopkinson, D. **E**
Billy Clikk: creach battler. Crilley, M. **Fic**

The **billy** goat and the vegetable garden. González,
L. M.
In González, L. M. Señor Cat's romance and
other favorite stories from Latin America
p29-33 **398.2**
Billy Mosby's nightride. San Souci, R.
In San Souci, R. Short & shivery; thirty chilling tales p103-11 **398.2**
Billy Yank & Johnny Reb. Beller, S. P. **973.7**
Billywise. Nicholls, J. **E**
Binch, Caroline
(il) Hoffman, M. Amazing Grace **E**
(il) Hoffman, M. Starring Grace **Fic**
Bindon, John
(il) Lessem, D. The fastest dinosaurs **567.9**
(il) Lessem, D. Feathered dinosaurs **567.9**
(il) Lessem, D. Flying giants of dinosaur time
567.9
(il) Lessem, D. Sea giants of dinosaur time
567.9
(il) Lessem, D. The smartest dinosaurs
567.9
Bing, Christopher
(il) Longfellow, H. W. Paul Revere's ride
811
(il) Thayer, E. L. Casey at the bat **811**
Bing bang boing. Florian, D. **811**
Bing: paint day. Dewan, T. **E**
Bingham, Caroline
Airplane (k-3) **629.133**
Big book of rescue vehicles (k-3) **629.04**
Fire truck (k-3) **628.9**
Monster machines (k-3) **621.8**
Bingham, Edith
(il) Bauer, C. F. The poetry break **372.6**
Bingham, Jane
Why do families break up? (4 and up)
306.89

The **binnacle** boy. Fleischman, P.
In Fleischman, P. Graven images; three sto-
ries **S C**
Binnorie. Jacobs, J.
In Jacobs, J. English fairy tales p50-53
398.2
Binns, T. B.
Winston Churchill (5 and up) **92**
Biodiversity. Patent, D. H. **333.95**
Bioengineered foods *See* Food—Biotechnology
Biography
Bibliography
Barancik, S. Guide to collective biographies for
children and young adults **016.9**
From biography to history **016.8**
Biography for beginners: world explorers (3-5)
920.003

Biography from ancient civilizations [series]
Gedney, M. The life and times of Buddha
294.3

Biological diversity
Gallant, R. A. The wonders of biodiversity (5
and up) **333.95**
Patent, D. H. Biodiversity (5 and up)
333.95

Birds—Flight—*Continued*
See/See also pages in the following book(s):
Bishop, N. The secrets of animal flight (3-6)
591.47

Folklore
Bryan, A. Beautiful blackbird (k-3) **398.2**
Hamilton, V. When birds could talk & bats could sing (3-5) **398.2**
Kimmel, E. A. The birds' gift (k-3) **398.2**
Martin, R. The language of birds (2-4)
398.2
Norman, H. Between heaven and earth (4 and up) **398.2**
Polacco, P. Luba and the wren (k-3) **398.2**
Spirin, G. The tale of the Firebird (2-4)
398.2

Migration
See/See also pages in the following book(s):
Simon, S. Ride the wind (4-6) **591.56**
Nests
Bash, B. Urban roosts: where birds nest in the city (1-4) **598**
Winer, Y. Birds build nests (k-3) **598**
Poetry
Fleischman, P. I am phoenix: poems for two voices (4 and up) **811**
Florian, D. On the wing **811**
Wings on the wind (k-3) **811.008**
Yolen, J. Fine feathered friends (3-5) **811**
Yolen, J. Wild wings (3-6) **811**
Protection
Patent, D. H. The bald eagle returns (4 and up)
598
Salmansohn, P. Saving birds (5 and up)
333.95
North America
Peterson, R. T. A field guide to the birds of eastern and central North America (5 and up)
598
West (U.S.)
Peterson, R. T. A field guide to western birds (5 and up) **598**
Birds build nests. Winer, Y. **598**
The **Bird's** Christmas Carol. Wiggin, K. D. S.
Fic
The **birds'** gift. Kimmel, E. A. **398.2**
Birds' nests *See* Birds—Nests
Birds of prey
See also names of birds of prey
Evert, L. Birds of prey (3-6) **598**
Laubach, C. M. Raptor! a kid's guide to birds of prey (4 and up) **598**
Birdsall, Jeanne
The Penderwicks (3-6) **Fic**
Birdseye, Debbie Holsclaw
Under our skin (4 and up) **305.8**
What I believe (4 and up) **200**
Birdseye, Tom
(jt. auth) Birdseye, D. H. Under our skin
305.8
(jt. auth) Birdseye, D. H. What I believe
200
Birdsongs
Johnson, S. A. Songbirds (3-6) **598**

See/See also pages in the following book(s):
Sayre, A. P. Secrets of sound (4 and up)
591.59
Birney, Betty G.
The seven wonders of Sassafras Springs (3-6)
Fic
Birth *See* Childbirth
Birth, Multiple *See* Multiple birth
Birth customs
Onyefulu, I. Welcome Dede! (k-3) **392**
Birth rate
See also Population
Birtha, Becky
Grandmama's pride **E**
Birthday piñata. Delacre, L.
In Delacre, L. Salsa stories p44-54 **S C**
Birthday pony. Haas, J. **Fic**
The **birthday** room. Henkes, K. **Fic**
Birthday zoo. Rose, D. L. **E**
Birthdays
Elya, S. M. F is for fiesta **E**
Lankford, M. D. Birthdays around the world (3-5) **394.2**
Ross, K. The best birthday parties ever! (2-4)
793.2
Trawicky, B. Anniversaries and holidays
394.26
Fiction
Best, C. Three cheers for Catherine the Great
E
Brust, B. W. The great tulip trade **E**
Bunting, E. Flower garden **E**
Cheng, A. The lemon sisters **E**
Chodos-Irvine, M. Best best friends **E**
Danziger, P. It's Justin Time, Amber Brown
E
Flack, M. Ask Mr. Bear **E**
Graham, B. Oscar's half birthday **E**
Horse, H. Little Rabbit lost **E**
Hutchins, P. There's only one of me! **E**
Krensky, S. Lionel's birthday **E**
Porte, B. A. Harry's birthday **E**
Potter, G. Chloe's birthday . . . and me **E**
Rose, D. L. Birthday zoo **E**
Segal, L. G. Morris the artist **E**
Tryon, L. Albert's birthday **E**
Wright, B. R. The blizzard **E**
Zolotow, C. Mr. Rabbit and the lovely present
E
Birthdays around the world. Lankford, M. D.
394.2
Biscuit's new trick. Capucilli, A. **E**
Bishop, Nic
Digging for bird-dinosaurs (4 and up) **567.9**
The secrets of animal flight (3-6) **591.47**
(il) Cowley, J. Red-eyed tree frog **E**
(il) Jackson, E. B. Looking for life in the universe **576.8**
(il) Montgomery, S. The snake scientist
597.96
(il) Montgomery, S. The tarantula scientist
595.4

Bisignano, Alphonse
  Cooking the Italian way
    In Easy menu ethnic cookbooks   **641.5**
Bismarck (Battleship)
  McGowen, T. Sink the Bismarck (5 and up)
              940.54
Bison
  Berman, R. American bison (3-6)   **599.64**
  Freedman, R. Buffalo hunt (4 and up)
             970.004
  Perry, P. J. Buffalo (3-6)   **599.64**
           Fiction
  Arnosky, J. Grandfather Buffalo   **E**
  Baker, O. Where the buffaloes begin (2-4)
           Fic
           Folklore
  Goble, P. Buffalo woman (2-4)   **398.2**
Bisson, Terry
  (jt. auth) Spinner, S. Be first in the universe
           Fic
Biswas, Pulak
  (il) Ravishankar, A. Tiger on a tree   **E**
A **bit** more Bert. Ahlberg, A.   **E**
Bitter bananas. Olaleye, I.   **E**
Bitter dumplings. Lee, J. M.   **E**
Bittle. MacLachlan, P.   **E**
Bix, Cynthia Overbeck
  (jt. auth) Rauzon, M. J. Water, water every-
    where   **551.48**
Biyera well. MacDonald, M. R.
  In MacDonald, M. R. Look back and see;
    twenty lively tales for gentle tellers p90-
    94   **372.6**
Björk, Christina
  Linnea in Monet's garden (3-5)   **Fic**
  Linnea's almanac (2-5)   **508**
  Vendela in Venice (4 and up)   **Fic**
Bjorklund, Ruth
  Alaska
    In It's my state! [series]   **973**
  Asthma (4 and up)   **616.2**
  Food-borne illnesses (4 and up)   **615.9**
  Massachusetts
    In It's my state! [series]   **973**
  Montana
    In It's my state! [series]   **973**
  New Mexico
    In It's my state! [series]   **973**
  South Dakota
    In It's my state! [series]   **973**
Björkman, Steve
  (il) Murphy, S. J. Coyotes all around   **519**
  (il) Murphy, S. J. The Grizzly Gazette   **513**
  (il) Murphy, S. J. Safari Park   **512**
  (il) Murphy, S. J. Same old horse   **E**
  (il) Wallace, C. One nosy pup   **E**
Black, Angela
  (jt. auth) Sheehan, S. Jamaica   **972.92**
  (jt. auth) Torchinskiĭ, O. Russia   **947**
Black Americans *See* African Americans
The **Black** Americans: a history in their own
  words, 1619-1983   **305.8**
Black and white. Macaulay, D.   **E**

Black art (Magic) *See* Witchcraft
Black authors
    See also African American authors
Black authors and illustrators of books for chil-
  dren and young adults. Murphy, B. T.
           920.003
Black authors and illustrators of children's books.
  See Murphy, B. T. Black authors and illustra-
  tors of books for children and young adults
           920.003
Black bear. Swinburne, S. R.   **599.78**
Black Beauty. Sewell, A.   **Fic**
Black Beauty [excerpt]. Sewell, A.
  In Horse tales   **S C**
Black Books Galore!—guide to great African
  American children's books about boys. Rand,
  D.   **016.3058**
The **Black** Bull of Norroway
  In The Blue fairy book p380-84   **398.2**
The **Black** Bull of Norroway. Huck, C. S.
           398.2
Black Bull of Norroway. Jacobs, J.
  In Jacobs, J. English fairy tales p242-48
           398.2
The **black** bull of Norroway. Philip, N.
  In Philip, N. Celtic fairy tales p67-72
           398.2
The **Black** Canary. Curry, J. L.   **Fic**
Black cat. Myers, C.   **E**
The **black** cat. Philip, N.
  In Philip, N. Celtic fairy tales p92-104
           398.2
Black cowboy, wild horses. Lester, J.   **E**
Black diamond. McKissack, P. C.   **796.357**
The **black** dog. Schwartz, A.
  In Schwartz, A. Scary stories 3; more tales to
    chill your bones p17-19   **398.2**
The **black** dragon princess. Kang, H.
  In Fire and wings: dragon tales from East and
    West p103-11   **S C**
Black eagles. Haskins, J.   **629.13**
The **Black** experience in children's books
           016.3058
The **black** ferris. Bradbury, R.
  In Beware!; R.L. Stine picks his favorite
    scary stories p3-17   **808.8**
The **black** fox. San Souci, R.
  In San Souci, R. A terrifying taste of short &
    shivery; thirty creepy tales p137-40
           398.2
Black hands, white sails. McKissack, P. C.
           639.2
Black holes (Astronomy)
  Rau, D. M. Black holes (3-5)   **523.8**
Black is brown is tan. Adoff, A.   **E**
Black Jack. Garfield, L.   **Fic**
Black literature (American) *See* American litera-
  ture—African American authors

Black magic (Witchcraft) *See* Magic

Black music
    See also African American music

Black musicians
    See also African American musicians

Black on white. Hoban, T.   **E**

The **black** pearl. O'Dell, S.   **Fic**

Black poetry (American) *See* American poetry—African American authors

The **black** snake. Olson, A. N.
    In Olson, A. N. and Schwartz, H. Ask the bones: scary stories from around the world p99-104   **398.2**

The **Black** soldier. Clinton, C.   **355**

The **Black** Stallion. Farley, W.   **Fic**

Black stars [series]
    Sullivan, O. R. African American inventors   **920**
    Sullivan, O. R. African American millionaires   **920**
    Wilkinson, B. S. African American women writers   **810.9**

Black whiteness. Burleigh, R.   **998**

Black women of the Old West. Katz, W. L.   **978**

Blackall, Sophie
    (il) Barrows, A. Ivy + Bean   **Fic**
    (il) Bridges, S. Y. Ruby's wish   **E**
    (il) Rosoff, M. Meet wild boars   **E**

Blackbeard, 1680?-1718
    Fiction
    Kimmel, E. A. Blackbeard's last fight   **E**

The **Blackbirch** kid's visual reference of the United States (4 and up)   **973**

The **Blackbirch** kid's visual reference of the world (5 and up)   **910**

The **Blackbirch** treasury of American poetry (5 and up)   **811.008**

Blackburn, G. Meredith
    (comp) Index to poetry for children and young people. See Index to poetry for children and young people   **808.81**

Blackburn, Lorraine A.
    (comp) Index to poetry for children and young people. See Index to poetry for children and young people   **808.81**

Blackfoot Indians *See* Siksika Indians

Blacklock, Dyan
    The Roman Army (4 and up)   **937**

Blacks
    Bibliography
    The Black experience in children's books   **016.3058**
    Biography
    See also African Americans—Biography
    Fiction
    Daly, N. Where's Jamela?   **E**
    Medearis, A. S. Seven spools of thread   **E**
    Poetry
    Dawes, K. S. N. I saw your face (3-5)   **811**

    United States
    See African Americans

Blacks in art
    See also African Americans in art

Blacks in literature
    See also African Americans in literature

The **blacksmith** and the Devil. Lester, J.
    In Lester, J. The last tales of Uncle Remus p141-47   **398.2**

Blacksmithing
    Fisher, L. E. The blacksmiths (4 and up)   **682**
    See/See also pages in the following book(s):
    Lyons, M. E. Catching the fire: Philip Simmons, blacksmith (4 and up)   **92**

Blackstone, Margaret
    This is soccer (k-2)   **796.334**

Blackstone, Stella
    My granny went to market   **E**
    Secret seahorse   **E**
    Storytime (k-1)   **398.2**
    Contents: The cock, the mouse and the little red hen; The gingerbread man; The ugly duckling; Goldilocks and the three bears; The timid hare
    Who are you, baby kangaroo?   **E**

Blackwater. Bunting, E.   **Fic**

Blackwater Ben. Durbin, W.   **Fic**

Blackwell's Island. Graff, S.   **Fic**

Blackwood, Gary L.
    Debatable deaths (4 and up)   **920**
    Enigmatic events (4 and up)   **904**
    Legends or lies? (4 and up)   **398.2**
    Perplexing people (4 and up)   **920**
    Second sight (5 and up)   **Fic**
    The Shakespeare stealer (5 and up)   **Fic**

The **bladder,** the straw, and the shoe. Afanas´ev, A. N.
    In Afanas´ev, A. N. Russian fairy tales p590   **398.2**

Blades, boards & scooters. Thomas, K.   **796.2**

Blake, Quentin
    Tell me a picture   **750**
    (il) Cooling, W. D is for Dahl   **823.009**
    (il) Dahl, R. The BFG   **Fic**
    (il) Dahl, R. The enormous crocodile   **Fic**
    (il) Dahl, R. The magic finger   **Fic**
    (il) Dahl, R. Matilda   **Fic**
    (il) Fleischman, S. Here comes McBroom!   **Fic**
    (il) Rosen, M. Michael Rosen's sad book   **E**
    (il) Yeoman, J. The Seven voyages of Sinbad the Sailor   **398.2**

Blake, Robert J.
    Akiak   **E**
    Togo   **E**

Blakemore, Catherine
    Faraway places   **011.6**

Blakey, Michael L.
    See/See also pages in the following book(s):
    Talking with adventurers (4-6)   **920**

Blakey, Nancy
    Go outside! (3-6)   **790.1**

Blind, Dogs for the *See* Guide dogs

The **blinded** giant. Jacobs, J.
    In Jacobs, J. English fairy tales p303-04
                      398.2

Bliss, Harry
    (il) Cronin, D. Diary of a worm   **E**
    (il) Harris, R. H. Don't forget to come back!
                      E
    (il) McGhee, A. Mrs. Watson wants your teeth
                      E

Blister. Shreve, S. R.   **Fic**

Blitt, Barry
    (jt. auth) Kloske, G. Once upon a time, the end
                      E

The **blizzard**. Wright, B. R.   **E**

Blizzards
Fiction
    Clifford, E. Help! I'm a prisoner in the library
    (3-5)   **Fic**
    Steig, W. Brave Irene   **E**

Blobaum, Cindy
    Geology rocks! (4-6)   **551**
    Insectigation! (3-6)   **595.7**

Bloch, Serge
    (il) Morgenstern, S. H. A book of coupons
                      Fic

Block city. Stevenson, R. L.   **E**

Blomgren, Jennifer
    Where do I sleep?   **E**

Blood, Charles L.
    The goat in the rug   **E**

Blood
    Showers, P. A drop of blood (k-3)   **612.1**
Circulation
    See also Cardiovascular system
Diseases
    See also Leukemia

The **blood-drawing** ghost. San Souci, R.
    In San Souci, R. Even more short & shivery;
    thirty spine-tingling stories p38-43
                      398.2

Blood on the river. Carbone, E. L.   **Fic**

Bloom, Lloyd
    (il) MacLachlan, P. Arthur, for the very first
    time   **Fic**
    (il) Recorvits, H. Goodbye, Walter Malinski
                      Fic

Bloom, Suzanne
    The bus for us   **E**
    A splendid friend, indeed   **E**
    (il) Bunting, E. Girls A to Z   **E**
    (il) Bunting, E. My special day at Third Street
    School   **E**

Bloomability. Creech, S.   **Fic**

Bloomer, Amelia Jenks, 1818-1894
About
    Corey, S. You forgot your skirt, Amelia Bloom-
    er (k-2)   **92**

Blos, Joan W.
    A gathering of days: a New England girl's jour-
    nal, 1830-32 (6 and up)   **Fic**

Blowers, Helene
    Weaving a library Web   **025.04**

Blue, Rose
    (jt. auth) Naden, C. J. Belle Starr and the Wild
    West   **92**

Blue. Byars, B. C.
    In Byars, B. C. and others. My dog, my hero
    p31-36   **S C**

Blue Beard. Perrault, C.
    In The Blue fairy book p290-95   **398.2**

Blue collar workers *See* Working class

A **blue-eyed** daisy. Rylant, C.   **Fic**

Blue eyes better. Wallace-Brodeur, R.   **Fic**

The **Blue** fairy book (4-6)   **398.2**

The **blue** ghost. Bauer, M. D.   **Fic**

Blue heron. Avi   **Fic**

Blue jasmine. Sheth, K.   **Fic**

Blue Jay and Swallow take the heat. Hamilton, V.
    In Hamilton, V. When birds could talk & bats
    could sing; the adventures of Bruh Spar-
    row, Sis Wren, and their friends p19-25
                      398.2

Blue jays
    Rockwell, A. F. Two blue jays   **E**

Blue moon soup. Goss, G.   **641.8**

Blue Moose. Pinkwater, D. M.
    In You read to me & I'll read to you; 20th-
    century stories to share p233-39   **E**

Blue potatoes, orange tomatoes. Creasy, R.
                      635

The **blue** rose. Baring, M.
    In Shedlock, M. L. The art of the story-teller
    p204-12   **372.6**

Blue silver. Sandburg, C.
    In Sandburg, C. More Rootabaga stories
    p156-58   **S C**
    also in Sandburg, C. The Sandburg treasury;
    prose and poetry for young people p159-
    60   **818**

A **blue** so blue. Dumont, J.-F.   **E**

Blue willow. Gates, D.   **Fic**

Blueberries for Sal. McCloskey, R.   **E**

Blueberries for the queen. Paterson, K.   **E**

Blues journey. Myers, W. D.   **811**

Blues music
    See also Jazz music
    Lester, J. The blues singers (5 and up)   **920**
Fiction
    Myers, W. D. The blues of Flats Brown   **E**
    Stauffacher, S. Bessie Smith and the night riders
                      E
Poetry
    Myers, W. D. Blues journey   **811**

The **blues** of Flats Brown. Myers, W. D.   **E**

The **blues** singers. Lester, J.   **920**

Bluestem. Arrington, F.   **Fic**

Bluford, Guion S., 1942-
    See/See also pages in the following book(s):
    Haskins, J. Black eagles (5 and up)   **629.13**

Bodybuilding (Weight lifting) *See* Weight lifting

Bodyscope [series]
Macnair, P. A. Movers & shapers   **612.7**

Boekhoff, P. M.
J.K. Rowling (4-6)   **92**
Lasers (3-5)   **621.36**

Bogacki, Tomek
(il) Jenkins, E. Five creatures   **E**

Bogan, Paulette
Goodnight Lulu   **E**
(il) Reynolds, A. Chicks and salsa   **E**

The **Boggart**. Cooper, S.   **Fic**

Bogs *See* Marshes; Wetlands

Bohannon, Lisa Frederiksen
The American Revolution (5 and up)   **973.3**

Boing!. Bruel, N.   **E**

Bolam, Emily
(il) Ehrlich, F. Does an elephant take a bath?   **E**
(il) Ehrlich, H. M. Louie's goose   **E**
(il) Ziefert, H. Little Red Riding Hood   **398.2**

The **bold** knight, the apples of youth, and the water of life. Afanas´ev, A. N.
In Afanas´ev, A. N. Russian fairy tales p314-20   **398.2**

Bolden, Tonya
The champ! [biography of Muhammad Ali] (2-5)   **92**
Maritcha [biography of Maritcha Rémond Lyons] (4 and up)   **92**
Rock of ages (3-5)   **811**
Tell all the children our story (5 and up)   **305.8**
Portraits of African-American heroes (4 and up)   **920**
(ed) 33 things every girl should know about women's history. See 33 things every girl should know about women's history   **305.4**

Boles, Philana Marie
Little divas (5 and up)   **Fic**

Boling, Katharine
January 1905 (5 and up)   **Fic**
New year be coming! (k-3)   **811**

Bollard, John K.
Scholastic children's thesaurus (4 and up)   **423**

Bolliger, Max
The happy troll   **E**

Bolognese, Don
(il) Avi. Abigail takes the wheel   **Fic**
(il) Brenner, B. Wagon wheels   **E**

Bolotin, Norm
Civil War A to Z (4 and up)   **973.7**

Bolshevism *See* Communism

Bombardment. Bruchac, J.
In Sports shorts   **S C**

Bonaparte, Napoleon *See* Napoleon I, Emperor of the French, 1769-1821

Bonaparte. Chall, M. W.   **E**

Bonar, Samantha
Comets (4 and up)   **523.6**

Bond, Felicia
(il) Brown, M. W. Big red barn   **E**
(il) Kramer, S. How to think like a scientist   **507**
(il) Numeroff, L. J. If you give a mouse a cookie   **E**

Bond, Higgins
(il) Berger, M. Do whales have belly buttons?   **599.5**

Bond, Michael
A bear called Paddington (2-5)   **Fic**

Bond, Nancy
A string in the harp (6 and up)   **Fic**

Bond, Rebecca
This place in the snow   **E**

The **bone** detectives. Jackson, D. M.   **614**

Boneless. San Souci, R.
In San Souci, R. Short & shivery; thirty chilling tales p127-32   **398.2**

Bones
Barner, B. Dem bones (k-3)   **611**
Simon, S. Bones (4 and up)   **612.7**
           Fiction
Steig, W. The amazing bone   **E**

Bones, bones, dinosaur bones. Barton, B.   **E**

The **bones** of Fred Mcfee. Bunting, E.   **E**

Bones rock!. Larson, P. L.   **560**

Bonfires and broomsticks. Norton, M.
In Norton, M. Bed-knob and broomstick   **Fic**

Bonk, John J.
Dustin Grubbs (5 and up)   **Fic**

Bonner, Hannah
When bugs were big, plants were strange, and tetrapods stalked the earth (3-6)   **560**

Bonners, Susan
Edwina victorious (3-5)   **Fic**

Bonny, Anne, b. 1700
           Poetry
Yolen, J. The ballad of the pirate queens (3-5)   **811**

Bonsall, Crosby Newell
The case of the hungry stranger   **E**
The day I had to play with my sister   **E**
Mine's the best   **E**
Who's a pest?   **E**
Who's afraid of the dark?   **E**

Bony-Legs. Cole, J.   **398.2**

Boo Mama. McKissack, P. C.
In McKissack, P. C. The dark-thirty; Southern tales of the supernatural p78-94   **S C**

Book!. George, K. O.   **E**

A **book** about design. Gonyea, M.   **745.4**

A **book** about God. Fitch, F. M.   **231**

Book awards *See* Literary prizes

Book! book! book!. Bruss, D.   **E**

Book illustration *See* Illustration of books

Book industry
       See also Publishers and publishing

A **book** of coupons. Morgenstern, S. H.   **Fic**

The **Book** of knowledge. See The New book of knowledge   **031**

Botany

See also Plants

VanCleave, J. P. Janice VanCleave's plants (5 and up) **580.7**

United States

See Plants—United States

Bott, C. J.

The bully in the book and in the classroom **371.5**

Bottner, Barbara

Rosa's room **E**

The Scaredy Cats **E**

Wallace's lists **E**

Bouchard, Dave

The gift of reading **372.4**

Bouchard, Jocelyne

(il) Love, A. The kids book of the Far North **998**

Boucher, Jerry

(il) Wilcox, C. Bald eagles **598**

Boudicca *See* Boadicea, Queen, d. 62

Bouki dances the kokioko

In The Magic orange tree, and other Haitian folktales p79-86 **398.2**

Bouki over a barrel. Doucet, S. A.

In Doucet, S. A. Lapin plays possum: trickster tales from the Louisiana Bayou p3-22 **398.2**

Boulanger, Nadia, 1887-1979

See/See also pages in the following book(s):

Krull, K. Lives of the musicians (4 and up) **920**

Bound for America. Haskins, J. **326**

Bound for America. Meltzer, M. **325.73**

Bound for Oregon. Van Leeuwen, J. **Fic**

The **Bourbon** Street musicians. Price, K. **398.2**

Bourseiller, Philippe

(il) Burleigh, R. Volcanoes **551.2**

Boursin, Didier

Easy origami (4 and up) **745.54**

Boutilier, Nancy

The rhythm of strong

In Girls got game; sports stories and poems **810.8**

What the cat contemplates while pretending to clean herself

In Girls got game; sports stories and poems **810.8**

Bow, Patricia

Chimpanzee rescue (5 and up) **599.8**

Bow wow meow meow. Florian, D. **811**

Bowden, Rob

Energy (5 and up) **333.79**

Food and farming (5 and up) **363.8**

Jerusalem (3-6) **956.94**

The Nile (5 and up) **962**

Waste (5 and up) **363.7**

Bowdish, Lynea

Brooklyn, Bugsy, and me (3-5) **Fic**

Bowen, Betsy

(il) Lunge-Larsen, L. The troll with no heart in his body and other tales of trolls from Norway **398.2**

(il) Van Laan, N. Shingebiss **398.2**

Bowen, Gary

Stranded at Plimoth Plantation, 1626 (4 and up) **974.4**

Bower, Tamara

How the Amazon queen fought the prince of Egypt (3-6) **Fic**

Bowers, Tim

(il) Numeroff, L. J. Sometimes I wonder if poodles like noodles **811**

Bowers, Vivien

Crazy about Canada! (4-6) **971**

Wow Canada! (3-6) **971**

Bowles, Ann

See/See also pages in the following book(s):

Talking with adventurers (4-6) **920**

Bowling

Fiction

Gutman, D. The million dollar strike (4-6) **Fic**

The **bowmen** and the sisters. Garland, S.

In Garland, S. Children of the dragon; selected tales from Vietnam p50-58 **398.2**

Box Turtle at Long Pond. George, W. T. **E**

Boxes

Fiction

Russo, M. The big brown box **E**

The **boxes.** Sleator, W. **Fic**

Boxes for Katje. Fleming, C. **E**

Boxing

Biography

Adler, D. A. Joe Louis (2-4) **92**

Bolden, T. The champ! [biography of Muhammad Ali] (2-5) **92**

Haskins, J. Champion: the story of Muhammad Ali (3-5) **92**

Shange, N. Muhammad Ali: the man who could float like a butterfly and sting like a bee (k-3) **92**

Fiction

Kroeger, M. K. Paperboy **E**

The **boxing** lesson. Soto, G.

In Soto, G. Petty crimes **S C**

A **boy,** a dog, and a frog. Mayer, M. **E**

The **boy** and the North Wind. Lunge-Larsen, L.

In Lunge-Larsen, L. The troll with no heart in his body and other tales of trolls from Norway p49-55 **398.2**

A **boy** called Slow: the true story of Sitting Bull. Bruchac, J. **92**

Boy fossil. Conrad, P.

In Conrad, P. Our house **S C**

The **boy** of the three-year nap. Snyder, D. **398.2**

The **boy** on Fairfield Street: how Ted Geisel grew up to become Dr. Seuss. Krull, K. **92**

The **boy,** the bear, the baron, the bard. Rogers, G. **E**

Boy, were we wrong about dinosaurs!. Kudlinski, K. V. **567.9**

The **boy** who became a lion, a falcon, and an ant. Lunge-Larsen, L.
 In Lunge-Larsen, L. The troll with no heart in his body and other tales of trolls from Norway p23-31 **398.2**

The **boy** who cried wolf. Hennessy, B. G. **398.2**

The **boy** who drew birds: a story of John James Audubon. Davies, J. **92**

The **boy** who drew cats. Hodges, M. **398.2**

The **boy** who killed the hill. Curry, J. L.
 In Curry, J. L. Hold up the sky: and other Native American tales from Texas and the Southern Plains p120-22 **398.2**

The **boy** who lived with the seals. Martin, R. **398.2**

The **boy** who loved to draw: Benjamin West. Brenner, B. **92**

The **boy** who loved words. Schotter, R. **E**

The **boy** who saved baseball. Ritter, J. H. **Fic**

The **boy** who saved Cleveland. Giblin, J. **Fic**

The **boy** who spoke dog. Morgan, C. **Fic**

The **boy** who took care of the pigs. Brenner, A.
 In Bauer, C. F. Celebrations; read-aloud holiday and theme book programs p152-54 **808.8**

The **boy** who tried to fool his father. Sierra, J.
 In Sierra, J. Nursery tales around the world p29-31 **398.2**

The **boy** who wanted the moon. Washington, D. L.
 In Washington, D. L. A pride of African tales

The **boy** who wouldn't obey: a Mayan legend. Rockwell, A. F. **398.2**

Boy with a wolf's foot. Aiken, J.
 In Aiken, J. Shadows and moonshine; stories **S C**

Boynton, Sandra
 Dog train (k-3) **782.42**
 Philadelphia chickens (k-3) **782.42**

Boys
 Madaras, L. The "what's happening to my body?" book for boys (4 and up) **613.9**
 Rand, D. Black Books Galore!—guide to great African American children's books about boys **016.3058**

Books and reading
 Knowles, E. Boys and literacy **028.5**
 Odean, K. Great books for boys **028.1**

Employment
 See Child labor

Boys, Teenage *See* Teenagers

Boys and literacy. Knowles, E. **028.5**

Boys' Choir of Harlem
 O holy night. See O holy night **782.28**
 Smith, C. R. Perfect harmony (4 and up) **811**

The **boys** of San Joaquin. Smith, D. J. **Fic**

A **boy's** Thanksgiving Day. See Child, L. M. F.
 Over the river and through the wood **811**

The **boys'** war. Murphy, J. **973.7**

Boz *See* Dickens, Charles, 1812-1870

Brace, Eric
 (il) Newquist, H. P. The great brain book **612.8**
 (il) Solheim, J. It's disgusting—and we ate it! **641.3**

The **bracelet.** Uchida, Y. **E**

Bradamante. Yolen, J.
 In Yolen, J. Not one damsel in distress; world folktales for strong girls p84-94 **398.2**

Bradberry, Sarah
 Kids knit! (5 and up) **746.43**

Bradburn, Frances Bryant
 Output measures for school library media programs **027.8**

Bradbury, Judy
 Children's book corner **372.4**

Bradbury, Ray
 The black ferris
  In Beware!; R.L. Stine picks his favorite scary stories p3-17 **808.8**

Bradby, Marie
 Momma, where are you from? **E**
 More than anything else **E**

Bradford, June
 (il) MacLeod, E. Bake and make amazing cakes **641.8**
 (il) MacLeod, E. Bake and make amazing cookies **641.8**
 (il) Sadler, J. A. Christmas crafts from around the world **745.594**
 (il) Sadler, J. A. Embroidery **746.44**
 (il) Sadler, J. A. Making fleece crafts **746**
 (il) Storms, B. Quilting **746.46**

Bradford, Karleen
 You can't rush a cat **E**

Bradley, Kimberly Brubaker
 Ballerino Nate **E**
 Energy makes things happen (k-3) **531**
 Forces make things move (k-3) **531**
 Pop! (k-1) **530.4**
 The President's daughter (3-5) **Fic**
 Ruthie's gift (3-5) **Fic**
 Weaver's daughter (4 and up) **Fic**

Bradley, Michael
 Lance Armstrong (4-6) **92**

Bradman, Tony
 Daddy's lullaby **E**

Brady, Hana
   About
 Levine, K. Hana's suitcase (4 and up) **940.53**

Bragg, Linda Wallenberg
 Fundamental gymnastics (5 and up) **796.44**

Brahms, Johannes, 1833-1897
 See/See also pages in the following book(s):
 Krull, K. Lives of the musicians (4 and up) **920**

A **Braid** of lives (4 and up)   **970.004**
Braille, Louis, 1809-1852
    About
Adler, D. A. A picture book of Louis Braille (1-3)   **92**
Freedman, R. Out of darkness: the story of Louis Braille (4 and up)   **92**
Braille books *See* Blind—Books and reading
Brain
Funston, S. It's all in your head (3-6)   **612.8**
Newquist, H. P. The great brain book (5 and up)   **612.8**
Simon, S. The brain (4 and up)   **612.8**
    Diseases
See also Stroke
Brainboy and the Deathmaster. Seidler, T.   **Fic**
Brainstorm!. Tucker, T.   **609**
Braman, Arlette N.
Kids around the world cook! (4-6)   **641.5**
Brand, Dionne
Earth magic (4 and up)   **811**
Brand new readers [series]
Friend, C. Eddie the raccoon   **E**
Brandenberg, Alexa
Ballerina flying   **E**
Brandenburg, Jim
Sand and fog (4 and up)   **968.8**
To the top of the world (4 and up)   **599.77**
(il) Swinburne, S. R. Once a wolf   **333.95**
Brandon *See* Brendan, Saint, the Voyager, ca. 483-577
Branford, Henrietta
Fire, bed, & bone (5 and up)   **Fic**
Little Pig Figwort can't get to sleep   **E**
Branley, Franklyn Mansfield
Air is all around you (k-1)   **551.5**
The Big Dipper (k-1)   **523.8**
Day light, night light (k-3)   **535**
Down comes the rain (k-3)   **551.57**
Earthquakes (k-3)   **551.2**
Flash, crash, rumble, and roll (k-3)   **551.55**
Floating in space (k-3)   **629.45**
The International Space Station (k-3)   **629.44**
Is there life in outer space? (k-3)   **576.8**
Mission to Mars (k-3)   **629.45**
The moon seems to change (k-3)   **523.3**
The planets in our solar system (k-3)   **523.4**
Snow is falling (k-1)   **551.57**
The sun, our nearest star (k-2)   **523.7**
Sunshine makes the seasons (k-3)   **508.2**
What makes a magnet? (k-3)   **538**
What the moon is like (k-3)   **523.3**
Branton, Ann
(comp) The Children's song index, 1978-1993. See The Children's song index, 1978-1993   **782.42**
Braren, Loretta Trezzo
(il) Hauser, J. F. Kids' crazy concoctions   **745.5**
Braun, Eric
Canada in pictures (5 and up)   **971**
Braun, Sebastien
(jt. auth) Ford, B. First snow   **E**

Braun, Trudi
My goose Betsy   **E**
Brave as a mountain lion. Scott, A. H.   **E**
Brave, brave mouse. Morgan, M.   **E**
Brave Charlotte. Stohner, A.   **E**
Brave dogs, gentle dogs. Urbigkit, C.   **636.7**
Brave Harriet [biography of Harriet Quimby] Moss, M.   **92**
Brave Irene. Steig, W.   **E**
The **brave** laborer. Afanas'ev, A. N.
In Afanas'ev, A. N. Russian fairy tales p276-77   **398.2**
The **brave** little seamstress. Osborne, M. P.   **398.2**
Brave little tailor. Grimm, J.
In The Blue fairy book p304-12   **398.2**
Brave Margaret. San Souci, R.   **398.2**
The **brave** widow. Philip, N.
In Philip, N. Horse hooves and chicken feet: Mexican folktales p54-58   **398.2**
Brave woman counts coup. Yolen, J.
In Yolen, J. Not one damsel in distress; world folktales for strong girls p38-43   **398.2**
Bravo! brava! a night at the opera. Siberell, A.   **792.5**
Bray-Moffatt, Naia
Gymnastics school (k-3)   **796.44**
Brazil
Galvin, I. F. Brazil (4 and up)   **981**
Heinrichs, A. Brazil (5 and up)   **981**
Reiser, R. Brazil (2-4)   **981**
Richard, C. Brazil (5 and up)   **981**
Streissguth, T. Brazil in pictures (5 and up)   **981**
    Fiction
Ibbotson, E. Journey to the river sea (5 and up)   **Fic**
    Social life and customs
Ancona, G. Carnaval (3-6)   **394.25**
Brazil in pictures. Streissguth, T.   **981**
Bread
Jones, J. Knead it, punch it, bake it! (3-6)   **641.8**
Morris, A. Bread, bread, bread (k-1)   **641.8**
    Fiction
Kleven, E. Sun bread   **E**
Bread, bread, bread. Morris, A.   **641.8**
Break a leg!. Friedman, L.   **792**
Break-of-day book [series]
Sharmat, M. W. Nate the Great   **E**
The **breaker** boys. Hughes, P.   **Fic**
Breakfast at Danny's Diner. Stamper, J. B.   **E**
Breakfast for Jack. Schories, P.   **E**
Breakfasts
    Fiction
Weston, T. Hey, pancakes!   **E**
Breaking through. Jiménez, F.   **Fic**
Breaking trail. Bell, J.   **Fic**
Breakout at the bug lab. Horowitz, R.   **E**

Brinkerhoff, Shirley
Why can't I learn like everyone else? (5 and up)
371.9

Brisson, Pat
I remember Miss Perry **E**
Mama loves me from away **E**
The summer my father was ten **E**
Tap-dance fever **E**

Britain. Fuller, B. **941**

British Cameroons See Cameroon

British Columbia
Fiction
Horvath, P. Everything on a waffle (4 and up)
Fic

Broach, Elise
Shakespeare's secret (5 and up) **Fic**

Broberg, Catherine
Kenya in pictures (5 and up) **967.62**

The **Broccoli** tapes. Slepian, J. **Fic**

Brock, C. E. (Charles Edmond)
(il) Nesbit, E. The railway children **Fic**

Brock, Charles Edmond See Brock, C. E.
(Charles Edmond), 1870-1938

Brockmeier, Kevin
Grooves (4 and up) **Fic**

Brodie, Carolyn S.
(jt. auth) Latrobe, K. H. The children's literature
dictionary **028.5**

Broekel, Ray
Hocus pocus: magic you can do (3-5) **793.8**
(jt. auth) White, L. B. Shazam! simple science
magic **793.8**

Brøgger, Lilian
(il) Varmer, H. Hans Christian Andersen **92**

Broken chain. Soto, G.
In Soto, G. Baseball in April, and other stories p1-12 **S C**

Broken song. Lasky, K. **Fic**

Bromann, Jennifer
Storytime action! **027.62**

Bronchial asthma See Asthma

Brontë, Charlotte, 1816-1855
See/See also pages in the following book(s):
Krull, K. Lives of the writers (4 and up)
920

Brontë, Emily, 1818-1848
See/See also pages in the following book(s):
Krull, K. Lives of the writers (4 and up)
920

Bronx Zoo
Zoehfeld, K. W. Wild lives (5 and up)
590.73

The **bronze** bow. Speare, E. G. **Fic**

The **Bronze** ring
In The Blue fairy book p1-11 **398.2**

Bronzes
Fritz, J. Leonardo's horse (4 and up) **730.9**

Brook, Larry
Daily life in ancient and modern Timbuktu (4
and up) **966.23**

Brooker, Kyrsten
(il) Lewis, J. P. Isabella Abnormella and the
very, very finicky Queen of Trouble **E**
(il) McKissack, P. C. Precious and the Boo Hag
E
(il) Newman, L. Runaway dreidel! **E**

Brookfield, Karen
Book (4 and up) **070.5**

Brooklyn (New York, N.Y.)
Fiction
Avi. Don't you know there's a war on? (4 and
up) **Fic**
Bowdish, L. Brooklyn, Bugsy, and me (3-5)
Fic
Estes, E. The Alley (4-6) **Fic**
Giff, P. R. All the way home (4 and up)
Fic
Giff, P. R. A house of tailors (5 and up)
Fic
Goode, D. The most perfect spot **E**
Schirripa, S. R. Nicky Deuce (4-6) **Fic**
Shalant, P. When pirates came to Brooklyn (4
and up) **Fic**
Uhlberg, M. Dad, Jackie, and me **E**

Brooklyn Bridge (New York, N.Y.)
Curlee, L. Brooklyn Bridge (3-6) **624.2**
Fiction
Prince, A. J. Twenty-one elephants and still
standing **E**

Brooklyn, Bugsy, and me. Bowdish, L. **Fic**

Brooklyn Dodgers (Baseball team)
Golenbock, P. Teammates [biography of Jackie
Robinson] (1-4) **92**

Brooks, Bruce
Everywhere (4 and up) **Fic**

Brooks, Bruce, 1950-
See/See also pages in the following book(s):
Author talk (4 and up) **028.5**

Brooks, Erik
(il) Climo, S. Monkey business **398.2**

Brooks, Gwendolyn
See/See also pages in the following book(s):
Wilkinson, B. S. African American women writ-
ers (4 and up) **810.9**

Brooks, Jeremy
A world of prayers (1-4) **242**

Brooks, Joe
(il) King, C. Oh, freedom! **323.1**

Brooks, Walter R.
Freddy the detective (3-5) **Fic**

Brooms
Fiction
Willard, N. Sweep dreams **E**

Brother and sister. San Souci, R.
In San Souci, R. Short & shivery; thirty chilling tales p117-22 **398.2**

Brother Wolf. Taylor, H. P. **398.2**

Brothers
Giblin, J. Good brother, bad brother [biography
of John Wilkes Booth and Edwin Booth] (5
and up) **92**
Fiction
Blume, J. Tales of a fourth grade nothing (3-6)
Fic

Brown, Marc Tolon—*Continued*
(jt. auth) Brown, L. K. Visiting the art museum
708
(jt. auth) Brown, L. K. What's the big secret?
613.9
(jt. auth) Brown, L. K. When dinosaurs die
155.9
(il) Read-aloud rhymes for the very young. See Read-aloud rhymes for the very young
821.008
(comp) Scared silly! See Scared silly! **810.8**
(il) Sierra, J. Wild about books **E**

Brown, Marcia
Once a mouse (k-3) **398.2**
Stone soup (k-3) **398.2**
(il) Cendrars, B. Shadow **841**
(il) Perrault, C. Cinderella **398.2**
(il) Sing a song of popcorn. See Sing a song of popcorn **808.81**

Brown, Marcia, 1918-
See/See also pages in the following book(s):
Marcus, L. S. A Caldecott celebration **741.6**

Brown, Margaret Tobin See Brown, Molly, 1867-1932

Brown, Margaret Wise
Another important book **E**
Big red barn **E**
Bunny's noisy book **E**
A child's good night book **E**
The fierce yellow pumpkin **E**
The good little bad little pig **E**
Goodnight moon **E**
Little Fur family **E**
The little island **E**
The little scarecrow boy **E**
The runaway bunny **E**
Two little trains **E**
Where have you been? **E**

Brown, Mary Barrett
(il) Esbensen, B. J. Tiger with wings **598**

Brown, Molly, 1867-1932
About
Landau, E. Heroine of the Titanic: the real unsinkable Molly Brown (5 and up) **92**

Brown, Oliver, 1919-1961
About
Good, D. L. Brown v. Board of Education (4-6) **344**
Somervill, B. A. Brown v. Board of Education (5 and up) **344**

Brown, Risa W.
(jt. auth) Stein, B. L. Running a school library media center **027.8**

Brown, Rod
(il) Lester, J. From slave ship to freedom road **326**

Brown, Roslind Varghese
Tunisia (5 and up) **961.1**

Brown, Ruth
A dark, dark tale **E**
Ten seeds **E**

Brown, William Wells, 1815-1884
See/See also pages in the following book(s):
Currie, S. Escapes from slavery (5 and up) **326**

Brown angels. Myers, W. D. **811**
Brown bear, brown bear what do you see? Martin, B. **E**
The **brown** bear of the Green Glen. Philip, N.
In Philip, N. Celtic fairy tales p36-43 **398.2**
Brown honey in broomwheat tea. Thomas, J. C. **811**

Brown paper school book [series]
Burns, M. The book of think **153.4**
Burns, M. The I hate mathematics! book **513**

Brown v. Board of Education. Good, D. L. **344**
Brown v. Board of Education. Somervill, B. A. **344**

Browne, Anthony
Into the forest **E**
My dad **E**
My mom **E**
Piggybook **E**
The shape game **E**
Voices in the park **E**
Willy the dreamer **E**

Browne, Jane
(il) Cooper, S. Frog **E**

Brownell, Shawn
(il) Peacock, C. A. Mommy far, Mommy near **E**

The **browney** at the grocer's. Andersen, H. C.
In Andersen, H. C. The swan's stories p99-107 **S C**

Browning, Robert
The Pied Piper of Hamelin **821**

The **Browns** take the day off. Schwartz, A.
In Schwartz, A. There is a carrot in my ear, and other noodle tales p9-14 **398.2**

Brownstone, David M.
Frontier America (5 and up) **973.03**

Bruchac, James
(jt. auth) Bruchac, J. How Chipmunk got his stripes **398.2**
(jt. auth) Bruchac, J. Raccoon's last race **398.2**
(jt. auth) Bruchac, J. Turtle's race with Beaver **398.2**
(jt. auth) Bruchac, J. When the Chenoo howls **398.2**

Bruchac, Joseph
The arrow over the door (4-6) **Fic**
Between earth & sky (3-5) **398.2**
Bombardment
In Sports shorts **S C**
A boy called Slow: the true story of Sitting Bull (1-3) **92**
Children of the longhouse (4 and up) **Fic**
Crazy Horse's vision **E**
The dark pond (5 and up) **Fic**
The first strawberries (k-3) **398.2**
The great ball game (k-3) **398.2**
How Chipmunk got his stripes (k-3) **398.2**
Pushing up the sky: seven Native American plays for children (3-5) **812**

Bruchac, Joseph—*Continued*
Contents: Gluskabe and Old Man Winter; Star sisters; Possum's tail; Wihio's duck dance; Pushing up the sky; The cannibal monster; The strongest one

Raccoon's last race (k-3) **398.2**
Skeleton man (4 and up) **Fic**
Tell me a tale (5 and up) **372.6**
Includes the following stories: Coyote's name; Bill Greenfield and the cold day; How the Adirondacks got their name; Can you pluck my rooster?; The wisdom of Princess Maya; Bring in the chickens; Yiyi the Spider and the stick sap man; Straightening the mind of Tadadaho; The seventh boy; The creation of Gluskabe; The other half of the blanket; The three young crows

Thirteen moons on a turtle's back **811**
The Trail of Tears (2-4) **970.004**
Turtle's race with Beaver (k-3) **398.2**
When the Chenoo howls (4-6) **398.2**
Contents: The Stone Giant; The Flying Head; Ugly-face; Chenoo; Amankamek; Keewahkwee; Yakwawiak; Man Bear; The Spreaders; Aglebemu; Big Tree People; Toad Woman

Whisper in the dark (5 and up) **Fic**
The winter people (5 and up) **Fic**
(jt. auth) Caduto, M. J. Keepers of the night **398.2**

Bruchac, Margaret M.
(jt. auth) Grace, C. O. 1621 **394.26**

Bruder, Mikyla
Button girl (5 and up) **745.5**

Bruegel, Pieter *See* Brueghel, Pieter, the Elder, 1522?-1569

Brueghel, Pieter, the Elder, 1522?-1569
Fiction
Shafer, A. C. The fantastic journey of Pieter Bruegel (4 and up) **Fic**

Bruel, Nick
Boing! **E**

Bruh Alligator and Bruh Deer. Hamilton, V.
In Hamilton, V. The people could fly; American black folktales p26-30 **398.2**

Bruh Alligator meets Trouble. Hamilton, V.
In Hamilton, V. The people could fly; American black folktales p35-42 **398.2**

Bruh Buzzard and Fair Maid. Hamilton, V.
In Hamilton, V. When birds could talk & bats could sing; the adventures of Bruh Sparrow, Sis Wren, and their friends p27-31 **398.2**

Bruh Lizard and Bruh Rabbit. Hamilton, V.
In Hamilton, V. The people could fly; American black folktales p31-34 **398.2**

Bruh Possum & the snake. McGill, A.
In McGill, A. Sure as sunrise; stories of Bruh Rabbit & his walkin' talkin' friends **398.2**

Bruh Rabbit and the tar baby girl. Hamilton, V. **398.2**

Bruh Rabbit's mystery bag. McGill, A.
In McGill, A. Sure as sunrise; stories of Bruh Rabbit & his walkin' talkin' friends **398.2**

Bruh Wolf and Bruh Rabbit join together. Hamilton, V.
In Hamilton, V. A ring of tricksters; animal tales from America, the West Indies, and Africa p39-43 **398.2**

Brun-Cosme, Nadine
No, I want daddy! **E**
Brundibar. Kushner, T. **E**
Brunhoff, Jean de
The story of Babar, the little elephant **E**
Brunkus, Denise
(il) Park, B. Junie B. Jones and her big fat mouth **Fic**
(il) Swallow, P. C. Groundhog gets a say **E**
(il) Winters, K. My teacher for President **E**
Bruno, Iacopo
(il) Baccalario, P. The door to time **Fic**
Bruno Munari's zoo. Munari, B. **E**
Brusca, María Cristina
Three friends. Tres amigos **E**
Bruss, Deborah
Book! book! book! **E**
Brust, Beth Wagner
The great tulip trade **E**
Brutschy, Jennifer
Just one more story **E**
Bryan, Ashley
Ashley Bryan's African tales, uh-huh (4-6) **398.2**
Beautiful blackbird (k-3) **398.2**
Sing to the sun **811**
Tortoise, Hare, and the sweet potatoes
In Bauer, C. F. Celebrations; read-aloud holiday and theme book programs p231-34 **808.8**
(comp) All night, all day. See All night, all day **782.25**
(il) Ashley Bryan's ABC of African-American poetry. See Ashley Bryan's ABC of African-American poetry **811.008**
(il) Berry, J. A nest full of stars **821**
(il) Giovanni, N. The sun is so quiet **811**
(il) Graham, L. B. How God fix Jonah **398.2**
(il) Hughes, L. Carol of the brown king **811**
(comp) The Night has ears. See The Night has ears **398.9**
(il) Salting the ocean. See Salting the ocean **811.008**

Bryan, Ashley, 1923-
See/See also pages in the following book(s):
Marcus, L. S. Ways of telling **741.6**
Bryan, Mike
(jt. auth) Herman, G. Cal Ripken, Jr. **92**
Bryan, Nichol
Los Alamos wildfires (5 and up) **363.34**
Bhopal (5 and up) **363.7**
Chernobyl (5 and up) **363.7**
Danube (5 and up) **363.7**
Exxon Valdez oil spill (5 and up) **363.7**
Love Canal (5 and up) **363.7**
Bryan, Robin
(jt. auth) Blowers, H. Weaving a library Web **025.04**
Bryant, Jennifer
Georgia's bones [biography of Georgia O'Keefe] (k-3) **92**
Bryant, Michael
(il) Grimes, N. Come Sunday **811**

Buildings in disguise. Arbogast, J. M.   **720**

Built for speed. Thompson, S. E.   **599.75**

Built for speed [series]
Murdico, S. J. Concorde   **629.133**

Bukhtan Bukhtanovich. Afanas′ev, A. N.
In Afanas′ev, A. N. Russian fairy tales p168-70   **398.2**

Bulfinch, Thomas
Bulfinch's mythology   **201**

Bulfinch's mythology. Bulfinch, T.   **201**

Bull Run, 1st Battle of, 1861
Fiction
Fleischman, P. Bull Run (6 and up)   **Fic**

Bulla, Clyde Robert
The chalk box kid   **E**
Daniel's duck   **E**
The Paint Brush Kid (2-4)   **Fic**
The story of Valentine's Day (k-3)   **394.26**
The sword in the tree (3-5)   **Fic**
A tree is a plant (k-2)   **582.16**
What makes a shadow? (k-1)   **535**

Buller, Laura
A faith like mine (4 and up)   **200**
Myths and monsters (5 and up)   **398**

Bullfights
Fiction
Leaf, M. The story of Ferdinand   **E**
Wojciechowska, M. Shadow of a bull (6 and up)   **Fic**

Bullies
Bott, C. J. The bully in the book and in the classroom   **371.5**
Winkler, K. Bullying (5 and up)   **371.5**
Fiction
Evangelista, B. Gifted (5 and up)   **Fic**
Nordin, S. In the wild (4 and up)   **Fic**
Tacang, B. Bully-be-gone (3-6)   **Fic**

Bullock, Mike
Lions, tigers, and bears, vol. 1: Fear and pride (2-4)   **741.5**

Bulls
Fiction
Leaf, M. The story of Ferdinand   **E**

Bulls-eye: a photobiography of Annie Oakley. Macy, S.   **92**

Bully-be-gone. Tacang, B.   **Fic**

The **Bully** Blockers Club. Bateman, T.   **E**

Bully for you, Teddy Roosevelt!. Fritz, J.   **92**

The **bully** in the book and in the classroom. Bott, C. J.   **371.5**

Bullying. Winkler, K.   **371.5**

The **bumblebee** queen. Sayre, A. P.   **595.7**

Bumperboy loses his marbles. Huey, D.   **741.5**

The **bumpy** little pumpkin. Cuyler, M.   **E**

The **bun.** Afanas′ev, A. N.
In Afanas′ev, A. N. Russian fairy tales p447-49   **398.2**

The **bun.** Sierra, J.
In Sierra, J. Nursery tales around the world p17-21   **398.2**

Bunnicula. Howe, D.   **Fic**

The **bunny** who found Easter. Zolotow, C.   **E**

Bunny's noisy book. Brown, M. W.   **E**

Bunting, Anne Eve *See* Bunting, Eve, 1928-

Bunting, Eve
Blackwater (5 and up)   **Fic**
The bones of Fred Mcfee   **E**
Butterfly house   **E**
Can you do this, Old Badger?   **E**
Cheyenne again   **E**
Christmas cricket   **E**
Dandelions   **E**
December   **E**
Flower garden   **E**
Fly away home   **E**
Girls A to Z   **E**
How many days to America?   **E**
Jin Woo   **E**
Little Bear's little boat   **E**
The memory string   **E**
My special day at Third Street School   **E**
Nasty, stinky sneakers (4-6)   **Fic**
Night tree   **E**
One candle   **E**
One green apple   **E**
A picnic in October   **E**
Secret place   **E**
Sing a song of piglets (k-2)   **811**
Smoky night   **E**
So far from the sea   **E**
Some frog! (2-4)   **Fic**
Someday a tree   **E**
Spying on Miss Müller (5 and up)   **Fic**
That's what leprechauns do   **E**
Train to Somewhere   **E**
The Wall   **E**
The Wednesday surprise   **E**

Bunting, Eve, 1928-
About
McGinty, A. B. Meet Eve Bunting (1-3)   **92**

Bunyan, Paul (Legendary character)
Kellogg, S. Paul Bunyan (k-3)   **398.2**
Rounds, G. Ol' Paul, the mighty logger (3-6)   **398.2**
Wood, A. The Bunyans   **E**

The **Bunyans.** Wood, A.   **E**

Buonarotti, Michelangelo *See* Michelangelo Buonarroti, 1475-1564

Buonarroti, Michel Angelo *See* Michelangelo Buonarroti, 1475-1564

Buranbaeva, Oksana
(jt. auth) Beliaev, E. Dagestan   **947.5**

Burbank, Jon
Nepal (5 and up)   **954.96**

Burch, Robert
Ida Early comes over the mountain (4 and up)   **Fic**
Queenie Peavy (5 and up)   **Fic**

Burd Janet. Yolen, J.
In Yolen, J. Not one damsel in distress; world folktales for strong girls p48-56   **398.2**

Burenushka, the little red cow. Afanas′ev, A. N.
In Afanas′ev, A. N. Russian fairy tales p146-50   **398.2**

Buzzard's will. Marshall, J.
   In Marshall, J. Rats on the range and other
     stories p72-80   **S C**
Buzzeo, Toni
   Dawdle Duckling   **E**
   The sea chest   **E**
   Terrific connections with authors, illustrators,
     and storytellers   **372.6**
By the dawn's early light. Kroll, S.   **782.42**
By the Great Horn Spoon!. Fleischman, S.   **Fic**
Byam, Michéle
   Arms & armor (4 and up)   **355.8**
Byard, Carole
   (il) Greenfield, E. Africa dream   **E**
   (il) Williams, S. A. Working cotton   **E**
Byars, Betsy Cromer
   The burning questions of Bingo Brown (4 and
     up)   **Fic**
   Cracker Jackson (5 and up)   **Fic**
   The Cybil war (4-6)   **Fic**
   The dark stairs (4 and up)   **Fic**
   The Golly sisters go West   **E**
   The house of wings (4-6)   **Fic**
   The keeper of the doves (4 and up)   **Fic**
   Little Horse (1-3)   **Fic**
   Me Tarzan (3-5)   **Fic**
   My brother, Ant   **E**
   My dog, my hero (3-6)   **S C**
   Contents: Smiley; Bear; Munchkin; Old Dog; Buster; Blue;
Little Bit; Dopey
   The not-just-anybody family (5 and up)   **Fic**
   The pinballs (5 and up)   **Fic**
   The SOS file (3-5)   **Fic**
   The summer of the swans (5 and up)   **Fic**
   Tornado (2-4)   **Fic**
Byars, Betsy Cromer, 1928-
     About
   Cammarano, R. Betsy Byars (4 and up)   **92**
"Bye-Bye"
   In The Magic orange tree, and other Haitian
     folktales p189-93   **398.2**
Byers, Ann
   Neil Armstrong (4 and up)   **92**
Bynum, Eboni
   Jamari's drum   **E**
Byrd, Richard Evelyn, 1888-1957
     About
   Burleigh, R. Black whiteness (3-5)   **998**
Byrd, Robert
   Finn MacCoul and his fearless wife (k-3)
     398.2
   The hero and the minotaur (3-6)   **398.2**
   Leonardo, beautiful dreamer (3-6)   **92**
   Saint Francis and the Christmas donkey   **E**
Byrd, Samuel
   (il) Adler, D. A. A picture book of Harriet Tub-
     man   **92**
   (il) Livingston, M. C. Keep on singing   **811**

C

C D B. Steig, W.   **793.73**
C D C? Steig, W.   **793.73**

Cabban, Vanessa
   (il) Freedman, C. Gooseberry Goose   **E**
The **cabin** faced west. Fritz, J.   **Fic**
Cabin on Trouble Creek. Van Leeuwen, J.
     Fic
Cabinet officers
   See also Prime ministers
The **cabinetmakers**. Fisher, L. E.   **684.1**
Cabinetwork
   Fisher, L. E. The cabinetmakers (4 and up)
     684.1
Cable, Annette
   (il) Sweeney, J. Me and my amazing body
     611
Cable railroads
   See also Street railroads
     Fiction
   Burton, V. L. Maybelle, the cable car   **E**
Cabot, John, 1450-1498
   See/See also pages in the following book(s):
   Fritz, J. Around the world in a hundred years (4
     and up)   **910.4**
Cabot, Meg
   Connie Hunter Williams, psychic teacher
   In Friends; stories about new friends, old
     friends, and unexpectedly true friends
     S C
Cabral, Pedro Alvares, 1460?-1526?
   See/See also pages in the following book(s):
   Fritz, J. Around the world in a hundred years (4
     and up)   **910.4**
Cabrera, Cozbi A.
   (il) Belton, S. Beauty, her basket   **E**
Cabrera, Jane
   If you're happy and you know it   **E**
   Mommy, carry me please!   **E**
   Old Mother Hubbard (k-2)   **398.8**
A **cache** of jewels and other collective nouns.
   Heller, R.   **428**
Cactus
   Bash, B. Desert giant (3-5)   **583**
   Guiberson, B. Z. Cactus hotel (k-3)   **583**
     Fiction
   Keats, E. J. Clementina's cactus   **E**
Cactus hotel. Guiberson, B. Z.   **583**
Cada niño/Every child. Hinojosa, T.   **782.42**
Caddie Woodlawn. Brink, C. R.   **Fic**
Caduto, Michael J.
   Keepers of the night   **398.2**
   Includes the following stories: How the bat came to be; Moth,
the fire dancer; Oot-Kwah-Tah, the seven star dancers; Chipmunk
and the Owl Sisters; The great Lacrosse game; How Grizzly Bear
climbed the mountain
Caesar's antlers. Hansen, B.   **Fic**
Caffey, Donna
   Yikes-lice! (k-3)   **616.5**
Cahoon, Heather
   (il) Tang, G. Math fables   **513**
Cain (Biblical figure)
     About
   Sasso, S. E. Cain & Abel (k-3)   **222**

Cain, David
(il) Cobb, V. Science experiments you can eat
      507.8
(il) Martin, L. C. Nature's art box   **745.5**
Cain & Abel. Sasso, S. E.   **222**
Cairns, Julia
(il) Chamberlin, M. Mama Panya's pancakes
      E
(il) Grandad's tree. See Grandad's tree
      811.008
(il) Unobagha, U. C. Off to the sweet shores of
    Africa and other talking drum rhymes   **811**
Cairo (Egypt)
           Fiction
Heide, F. P. The day of Ahmed's secret   **E**
Cajuns
           Fiction
Thomassie, T. Feliciana Feyra LeRoux   **E**
           Folklore
San Souci, R. Six foolish fishermen (k-3)
      398.2
    Social life and customs
Hoyt-Goldsmith, D. Mardi Gras: a Cajun coun-
    try celebration (3-5)   **394.25**
Cake
MacLeod, E. Bake and make amazing cakes
    (4-6)   **641.8**
           Fiction
Ogburn, J. K. The bake shop ghost   **E**
Sperring, M. The fairytale cake   **E**
The **cake** tree. Sierra, J.
    In Sierra, J. Can you guess my name?; tradi-
    tional tales around the world p91-95
      398.2

Calabro, Marian
The perilous journey of the Donner Party (5 and
    up)   **978**
Calavera abecedario. Winter, J.   **E**
A **Caldecott** celebration. Marcus, L. S.   **741.6**
Caldecott Medal
Marcus, L. S. A Caldecott celebration   **741.6**
The Newbery and Caldecott awards   **028.5**
Newbery and Caldecott Medal books, 1966-1975
    028.5
Newbery and Caldecott Medal books, 1976-1985
    028.5
Caldecott Medal titles
Azarian, Mary See Martin, J. B. Snowflake
    Bentley (biography of Wilson Alwyn Bentley)
    92
Bemelmans, Ludwig See Bemelmans, L. Made-
    line's rescue   **E**
Brown, Marcia See Brown, M. Once a mouse
    398.2
Brown, Marcia See Brown, M. Stone soup
    398.2
Brown, Marcia See Cendrars, B. Shadow
    841
Brown, Marcia See Perrault, C. Cinderella
    398.2
Burton, Virginia Lee See Burton, V. L. The lit-
    tle house   **E**
Cooney, Barbara See Cooney, B. Chanticleer
    and the fox   **E**

Cooney, Barbara See Hall, D. Ox-cart man
    E
Diaz, David See Bunting, E. Smoky night   **E**
Dillon, L. and Dillon D. See Musgrove, M.
    Ashanti to Zulu: African traditions   **960**
Dillon, Leo See Aardema, V. Why mosquitoes
    buzz in people's ears   **398.2**
Duvoisin, Roger See Tresselt, A. R. White
    snow, bright snow   **E**
Egielski, Richard See Yorinks, A. Hey, Al
    E
Emberley, Ed See Emberley, B. Drummer Hoff
    398.8
Gammell, Stephen See Ackerman, K. Song and
    dance man   **E**
Gerstein, Mordicai See Gerstein, M. The man
    who walked between the towers   **E**
Goble, Paul See Goble, P. The girl who loved
    wild horses   **398.2**
Hader, Berta See Hader, B. The big snow   **E**
Haley, Gail E. See Haley, G. E. A story, a story
    398.2
Henkes, Kevin See Henkes, K. Kitten's first full
    moon   **E**
Hogrogian, Nonny See Hogrogian, N. One fine
    day   **398.2**
Hogrogian, Nonny See Leodhas, S. N. Always
    room for one more   **782.42**
Hyman, Trina Schart See Hodges, M. Saint
    George and the dragon   **398.2**
Jones, Elizabeth Orton See Field, R. Prayer for
    a child   **242**
Keats, Ezra Jack See Keats, E. J. The snowy
    day   **E**
Lathrop, Dorothy P. See Bible. Selections. Ani-
    mals of the Bible   **220.8**
Lent, Blair See Mosel, A. The funny little wom-
    an   **398.2**
Lobel, Arnold See Lobel, A. Fables   **Fic**
Macaulay, David See Macaulay, D. Black and
    white   **E**
McCloskey, Robert See McCloskey, R. Make
    way for ducklings   **E**
McCloskey, Robert See McCloskey, R. Time of
    wonder   **E**
McCully, Emily See McCully, E. A. Mirette on
    the high wire   **E**
McDermott, Gerald See McDermott, G. Arrow
    to the sun   **398.2**
Monresor, Beni See De Regniers, B. S. May I
    bring a friend?   **E**
Ness, Evaline See Ness, E. Sam, Bangs &
    Moonshine   **E**
Politi, Leo See Politi, L. Song of the swallows
    E
Provensen, A. and Provensen M See Provensen,
    A. The glorious flight: across the Channel
    with Louis Blériot, July 25, 1909   **92**
Raschka, Christopher See Juster, N. The hello,
    goodbye window   **E**
Rathmann, Peggy See Rathmann, P. Officer
    Buckle and Gloria   **E**
Rohmann, Eric See Rohmann, E. My friend
    Rabbit   **E**
Rojankovsky, Feodor See Langstaff, J. M. Frog
    went a-courtin'   **782.42**

Caldecott Medal titles—*Continued*

Say, Allen *See* Say, A. Grandfather's journey **E**

Schoenherr, John *See* Yolen, J. Owl moon **E**

Sendak, Maurice *See* Sendak, M. Where the wild things are **E**

Shulevitz, Uri *See* Ransome, A. The Fool of the World and the flying ship **398.2**

Sidjakov, Nicolas *See* Robbins, R. Baboushka and the three kings **398.2**

Simont, Marc *See* Udry, J. M. A tree is nice **E**

Slobodkin, Louis *See* Thurber, J. Many moons **Fic**

Small, David *See* St. George, J. So you want to be president? **973**

Spier, Peter *See* Spier, P. Noah's ark **222**

Steig, William *See* Steig, W. Sylvester and the magic pebble **E**

Taback, Simms *See* Taback, S. Joseph had a little overcoat **E**

Van Allsburg, Chris *See* Van Allsburg, C. Jumanji **E**

Van Allsburg, Chris *See* Van Allsburg, C. The Polar Express **E**

Ward, Lynd Kendall *See* Ward, L. K. The biggest bear **E**

Weisgard, L. *See* Brown, M. W. The little island **E**

Wiesner, David *See* Wiesner, D. Tuesday **E**

Wisniewski, David *See* Wisniewski, D. Golem **398.2**

Young, Ed *See* Young, E. Lon Po Po **398.2**

Zelinsky, Paul O. *See* Zelinsky, P. O. Rapunzel **398.2**

Caldwell, Ben
Fantasy! cartooning (5 and up) **741.5**

Caleb & Kate. Steig, W. **E**

Calendars
See also Days
Chase's calendar of events **394.26**
Kummer, P. K. The calendar (4 and up) **529**
Maestro, B. The story of clocks and calendars (3-6) **529**
Trawicky, B. Anniversaries and holidays **394.26**

See/See also pages in the following book(s):
Bauer, C. F. Celebrations p1-24 **808.8**

Calhoun, Dia
The Phoenix Dance (5 and up) **Fic**

Calhoun, Mary
Cross-country cat **E**
Flood **E**

Calico's cousins. Tildes, P. L. **636.8**

California
Burgan, M. California
In It's my state! [series] **973**
Heinrichs, A. California
In America the beautiful, second series **973**
Ingram, S. California
In World Almanac Library of the States series **973**

Antiquities
Thompson, S. E. Death trap (4 and up) **560**
Fiction
Fleischman, S. The Giant Rat of Sumatra (4 and up) **Fic**
Gates, D. Blue willow (4 and up) **Fic**
Koss, A. G. Stranger in Dadland (5 and up) **Fic**
Ly, M. Home is east (5 and up) **Fic**
McCully, E. A. Squirrel and John Muir **E**
Nelson, T. Ruby electric (5 and up) **Fic**
Pérez, L. K. First day in grapes **E**
Politi, L. Song of the swallows **E**
Ryan, P. M. Esperanza rising (5 and up) **Fic**
Smith, D. J. The boys of San Joaquin (5 and up) **Fic**
Soto, G. Baseball in April, and other stories (5 and up) **S C**
Uchida, Y. A jar of dreams (5 and up) **Fic**
Warner, S. This isn't about the money (5 and up) **Fic**
Folklore
Ryan, P. M. Nacho and Lolita (2-4) **398.2**
Gold discoveries
Leeper, D. R. The diary of David R. Leeper (4 and up) **92**
O'Donnell, K. The gold rush (4 and up) **979.4**

Gold discoveries—Fiction
Cushman, K. The ballad of Lucy Whipple (5 and up) **Fic**
Fleischman, S. Bandit's moon (4-6) **Fic**
Fleischman, S. By the Great Horn Spoon! (4-6) **Fic**
Kay, V. Gold fever **E**
Yep, L. The journal of Wong Ming-Chung (4 and up) **Fic**
History
Doak, R. S. California
In Voices from colonial America [series] **973.2**

California. Doak, R. S.
In Voices from colonial America [series] **973.2**

The **caliph** and the cobbler. Kimmel, E. A.
In Kimmel, E. A. The spotted pony: a collection of Hanukkah stories p50-55 **398.2**

Calisthenics *See* Gymnastics
Call, Greg
(il) Rappaport, D. Victory or death! **973.3**
Call, Ken
(il) Armstrong, K. R. Lance Armstrong **92**
Call it courage. Sperry, A. **Fic**
The **call** of the wild. London, J. **Fic**
Callan, Lyndall
(jt. auth) Rappaport, D. Dirt on their skirts **E**

The **caller**. San Souci, R.
In San Souci, R. Dare to be scared; thirteen stories to chill and thrill **S C**
Calmenson, Stephanie
Good for you! (k-1) **811**
Kindergarten kids (k-1) **811**

Calmenson, Stephanie—*Continued*
Rosie (k-3)   **636.7**
Welcome, baby! (k-1)   **811**
(jt. auth) Cole, J. Crazy eights and other card games   **795.4**
(jt. auth) Cole, J. Why did the chicken cross the road? and other riddles, old and new
                                                 793.73
(comp) The Eentsy, weentsy spider: fingerplays and action rhymes. See The Eentsy, weentsy spider: fingerplays and action rhymes
                                                 796.1
(comp) Miss Mary Mack and other children's street rhymes. See Miss Mary Mack and other children's street rhymes   **796.1**
(comp) Pat-a-cake and other play rhymes. See Pat-a-cake and other play rhymes   **398.8**

Calvert, Patricia
The ancient Celts (5 and up)   **936**
The ancient Inca (5 and up)   **985**
Vasco da Gama (5 and up)   **92**
Zebulon Pike (5 and up)   **92**

Cam Jansen and the mystery of the stolen diamonds. Adler, D. A.   **Fic**

Cambodian Americans
Fiction
Ly, M. Home is east (5 and up)   **Fic**

The **Cambridge** guide to children's books in English   **028.5**

Camels
Jango-Cohen, J. Camels (3-6)   **599.63**
Poetry
Carryl, C. E. The camel's lament   **E**
The **camel's** lament. Carryl, C. E.   **E**

Cameras
Price, S. Click! fun with photography (4 and up)
                                                 771

Cameron, Ann
Colibri (5 and up)   **Fic**
Gloria's way (2-4)   **Fic**
The stories Julian tells (2-4)   **Fic**

Cameron, Eileen
Canyon (3-5)   **811**

Cameron, Eleanor
The court of the stone children (5 and up)
                                                 Fic
The wonderful flight to the Mushroom Planet (4-6)   **Fic**

Cameron, Marie
(il) Chödzin, S. The wisdom of the crows and other Buddhist tales   **294.3**

Cameron, Scott
(il) De Regniers, B. S. David and Goliath
                                                 222
(il) Nichol, B. Beethoven lives upstairs   **Fic**

Cameroon
Fiction
Alexander, L. The fortune-tellers   **E**
Folklore
See Folklore—Cameroon

Cammarano, Rita
Betsy Byars (4 and up)   **92**

Camp Fat. Konigsburg, E. L.
In Konigsburg, E. L. Altogether, one at a time p29-59   **S C**

Campbell, Ann
The New York Public Library amazing space (5 and up)   **520**

Campbell, Bebe Moore
Sometimes my mommy gets angry   **E**

Campbell, Mary, fl. 1764
Fiction
Durrant, L. The beaded moccasins (5 and up)
                                                 Fic

Campbell, Nicola I.
Shi-shi-etko   **E**

Campbell, Rod
Dear zoo   **E**

Camper, Cathy
Bugs before time (4 and up)   **560**

Campfire tale. San Souci, R.
In San Souci, R. Double-dare to be scared: another thirteen chilling tales   **S C**

Camping
Fiction
Evangelista, B. Gifted (5 and up)   **Fic**
Gilson, J. 4B goes wild (4-6)   **Fic**
Lasky, K. Lucille camps in   **E**
Naylor, P. R. The fear place (5 and up)   **Fic**
Partridge, E. Whistling   **E**
Say, A. The lost lake   **E**
Williams, V. B. Three days on a river in a red canoe   **E**
Yep, L. Skunk scout (4-6)   **Fic**
Poetry
George, K. O. Toasting marshmallows (3-5)
                                                 811

Campos, Tito
Muffler man   **E**

Campoy, F. Isabel
Rosa Raposa   **E**
(comp) Mamá Goose. See Mamá Goose
                                                 398.8
(comp) ¡Pio peep! See ¡Pio peep!   **398.8**

Camps
Fiction
Vail, R. Daring to be Abigail (4-6)   **Fic**
Can you cuddle like a koala? Butler, J.   **E**
Can you do this, Old Badger? Bunting, E.   **E**
Can you draw me? Stine, R. L.
In Stine, R. L. The haunting hour p138-53
                                                 S C
Can you find it? Cressy, J.   **750**
Can you guess my name? Sierra, J.   **398.2**
Can you pluck my rooster? Bruchac, J.
In Bruchac, J. Tell me a tale; a book about storytelling p38-42   **372.6**
Can you see the chalkboard? Silverstein, A.
                                                 617.7
Can you see what I see? Wick, W.   **793.73**
Canada
Bowers, V. Crazy about Canada! (4-6)   **971**
Bowers, V. Wow Canada! (3-6)   **971**
Braun, E. Canada in pictures (5 and up)
                                                 971

Carbon dioxide greenhouse effect *See* Greenhouse effect

Carbone, Elisa Lynn
Blood on the river (5 and up)   **Fic**
Storm warriors (4 and up)   **Fic**

Card games
Cole, J. Crazy eights and other card games (3-5)
     795.4
King, D. Games (5 and up)   **794**
Ward, A. Card games for kids (3-6)   **795.4**

Card games for kids. Ward, A.   **795.4**

Cardinal and Bruh Deer. Hamilton, V.
In Hamilton, V. When birds could talk & bats could sing; the adventures of Bruh Sparrow, Sis Wren, and their friends p47-53
     398.2

Cardiovascular system
See also Heart
Simon, S. The heart (4 and up)   **612.1**

Cards, Debit *See* Debit cards

Care, Medical *See* Medical care

Career day. Rockwell, A. F.   **E**

Careers *See* Occupations

The **caretaker**. Taback, S.
In Taback, S. Kibitzers and fools; tales my zayda (grandfather) told me   **398.2**

Caribbean region
Antiquities
Macaulay, D. Ship (4 and up)   **387.2**
Fiction
Cherry, L. The sea, the storm, and the mangrove tangle   **E**
Gershator, D. Kallaloo!   **E**
Lessac, F. Island counting 1 2 3   **E**
Taylor, T. The cay (5 and up)   **Fic**
Taylor, T. Timothy of the cay (5 and up)
     Fic
Folklore
See Folklore—Caribbean region
Poetry
Berry, J. A nest full of stars (2-5)   **821**
Social life and customs
Temko, F. Traditional crafts from the Caribbean (4 and up)   **745.5**

Caribou
Quinlan, S. E. Caribou (3-6)   **599.65**
Fiction
Root, P. If you want to see a caribou   **E**

Carle, Eric
10 little rubber ducks   **E**
The art of Eric Carle   **741.6**
Do you want to be my friend?   **E**
Does a kangaroo have a mother, too?   **E**
From head to toe   **E**
The grouchy ladybug   **E**
A house for Hermit Crab   **E**
Mister Seahorse   **E**
The mixed-up chameleon   **E**
"Slowly, slowly, slowly," said the sloth   **E**
Today is Monday (k-3)   **782.42**
The very busy spider   **E**
The very clumsy click beetle   **E**
The very hungry caterpillar   **E**
The very lonely firefly   **E**

The very quiet cricket   **E**
Where are you going? To see my friend!   **E**
See/See also pages in the following book(s):
Marcus, L. S. Ways of telling   **741.6**
(il) Eric Carle's animals, animals. See Eric Carle's animals, animals   **808.81**
(il) Eric Carle's dragons dragons and other creatures that never were. See Eric Carle's dragons and other creatures that never were   **808.81**
(il) Martin, B. Brown bear, brown bear what do you see?   **E**
(il) Martin, B. Panda bear, panda bear, what do you see?   **E**
(il) Martin, B. Polar bear, polar bear, what do you hear?   **E**

Carling, Amelia Lau
Mama & Papa have a store   **E**
Sawdust carpets   **E**

Carl's sleepy afternoon. Day, A.   **E**

Carlson, Laurie M.
Boss of the plains [biography of John Batterson Stetson] (k-3)   **92**

Carlson, Lori M.
(ed) Cool salsa. See Cool salsa   **811.008**
(comp) You're on!: seven plays in English and Spanish. See You're on!: seven plays in English and Spanish   **812.008**

Carlson, Maria
(jt. auth) Prokofiev, S. Peter and the wolf   **E**

Carlson, Nancy L.
Get up and go!   **E**
Harriet and the roller coaster   **E**
Henry's show and tell   **E**
Hooray for Grandparent's Day   **E**
I like me!   **E**

Carlson, Natalie Savage
The family under the bridge (3-5)   **Fic**

Carlstrom, Nancy White
Giggle-wiggle wake-up!   **E**
Jesse Bear, what will you wear?   **E**
Thanksgiving Day at our house (k-2)   **811**
Who said boo? (k-3)   **811**

Carman, Patrick
The Dark Hills divide (5 and up)   **Fic**

Carmen Teresa's gift. Delacre, L.
In Delacre, L. Salsa stories p71-75   **S C**

Carmi, Giora
(il) Kimmel, E. A. The Chanukkah guest   **E**
(il) Schwartz, H. A journey to paradise and other Jewish tales   **398.2**

Carmine. Sweet, M.   **E**

Carney, Patrick
(il) Kreger, C. Cheese   **637**
(il) Kreger, C. Jelly beans   **641.8**

Carney, William, 1840-1908
About
Clinton, C. Hold the flag high (2-4)   **973.7**

Carnival
Ancona, G. Carnaval (3-6)   **394.25**
Gulevich, T. Encyclopedia of Easter, Carnival, and Lent (5 and up)   **394.26**
Hoyt-Goldsmith, D. Mardi Gras: a Cajun country celebration (3-5)   **394.25**

Carry me!. Wells, R.   **E**

Carrying the running-aways. Hamilton, V.
In Hamilton, V. The people could fly; American black folktales p141-46   **398.2**

Carryl, Charles E.
The camel's lament   **E**

Cars (Automobiles) *See* Automobiles

Carson, Jo
You hold me and I'll hold you   **E**

Carson, Kit, 1809-1868
Fiction
Osborne, M. P. Adaline Falling Star (5 and up)   **Fic**

Carson, Mary Kay
The Wright Brothers for kids (4 and up)   **629.13**

Carson, Rachel, 1907-1964
About
Ehrlich, A. Rachel: the story of Rachel Carson (2-4)   **92**
Gow, M. Rachel Carson (5 and up)   **92**

Carter, Abby
(il) Jacobson, J. Andy Shane and the very bossy Dolores Starbuckle   **E**
(il) Kenah, K. The best seat in second grade   **E**
(il) Lindbergh, R. My hippie grandmother   **E**

Carter, Alden R.
I'm tougher than diabetes! (2-4)   **616.4**

Carter, Carol S.
(il) Carter, A. R. I'm tougher than diabetes!   **616.4**

Carter, David A.
One red dot   **E**

Carter, Don
(il) Lillegard, D. Wake up house!   **811**

Carter, Howard, 1874-1939
About
Frank, J. The tomb of the boy king (3-6)   **932**

Carter, James Earl *See* Carter, Jimmy, 1924-

Carter, Jimmy, 1924-
About
Kent, D. Jimmy Carter (4 and up)   **92**

Carter family
About
Rappaport, D. The school is not white! (1-3)   **379**

Cartlidge, Michelle
(il) Morgan, M. Brave, brave mouse   **E**

Cartography *See* Maps

Cartooning. Roche, A.   **741.5**

Cartoons and comics
Becker, H. Funny business (5 and up)   **792**
Caldwell, B. Fantasy! cartooning (5 and up)   **741.5**
Giarrano, V. Comics crash course (5 and up)   **741.5**
Hart, C. Kids draw anime (3-6)   **741.5**
Hart, C. Kids draw Manga Shoujo (1-4)   **741.5**
Hart, C. Mecha mania (5 and up)   **741.5**

Mayne, D. Draw your own cartoons! (3-6)   **741.5**
Pellowski, M. The art of making comic books (5 and up)   **741.5**
Roche, A. Cartooning (3-6)   **741.5**
Fiction
Clements, A. Lunch money (4-6)   **Fic**

Carts *See* Carriages and carts

Cartwheel to the moon. Di Pasquale, E.   **811**

Carus, Marianne
(ed) Celebrate Cricket. See Celebrate Cricket   **808.8**
(ed) Di Pasquale, E. Cartwheel to the moon   **811**
(ed) Fire and wings: dragon tales from East and West. See Fire and wings: dragon tales from East and West   **S C**

Carver, George Washington, 1864?-1943
About
Adler, D. A. A picture book of George Washington Carver (1-3)   **92**
Mitchell, B. A pocketful of goobers: a story about George Washington Carver (3-5)   **92**

Carville, James
Lu and the swamp ghost   **E**

Carving, Wood *See* Wood carving

Casanova, Mary
The hunter (k-3)   **398.2**
One-dog canoe   **E**

Case, James F., 1926-
About
Collard, S. B., III. A firefly biologist at work (4-6)   **595.7**

Case closed. Meltzer, M.   **363.2**

A **case** for Jenny Archer. Conford, E.   **Fic**

A **case** of mistaken identity. Taback, S.
In Taback, S. Kibitzers and fools; tales my zayda (grandfather) told me   **398.2**

The **case** of the Baker Street Irregular. Newman, R.   **Fic**

The **case** of the boiled egg. Jaffe, N.
In Jaffe, N. and Zeitlin, S. J. While standing on one foot; puzzle stories and wisdom tales from the Jewish tradition p18-22   **296.1**

The **case** of the hungry stranger. Bonsall, C. N.   **E**

The **case** of the missing monkey. Rylant, C.   **E**

The **Case** of the uncooked eggs
In The Magic orange tree, and other Haitian folktales p49-55   **398.2**

Caseley, Judith
On the town   **E**

Caselli, Giovanni
In search of Pompeii (3-5)   **937**
(il) Morley, J. Egyptian myths   **299**

Casey, Carolyn
Mary Cassatt (2-4)   **92**

Casey, Patricia
One day at Wood Green Animal Shelter   **E**

Casey at the bat. Thayer, E. L.   **811**

Cash-Walsh, Tina
(il) D'Amico, J. The healthy body cookbook
641.5
(il) D'Amico, J. The math chef **641.5**
(il) D'Amico, J. The science chef **641.3**

Casil, Amy Sterling
Hantavirus (4-6) **616.9**

Casilla, Robert
(il) Adler, D. A. A picture book of Jackie Robinson **92**
(il) Adler, D. A. A picture book of Jesse Owens **92**
(il) Adler, D. A. A picture book of John F. Kennedy **92**
(il) Adler, D. A. A picture book of Thurgood Marshall **92**
(il) Hines, G. Midnight forests [biography of Gifford Pinchot] **92**
(il) Marsden, C. Mama had to work on Christmas **Fic**
(il) Pérez, L. K. First day in grapes **E**

Casolino, Peter
(il) Englart, M. R. Helicopters **629.133**

Cassatt, Mary, 1844-1926
About
Casey, C. Mary Cassatt (2-4) **92**
O'Connor, J. Mary Cassatt (2-4) **92**

Cassels, Jean
(il) Dewey, J. Once I knew a spider **E**

Cassidy, Cathy
Dizzy (5 and up) **Fic**
Indigo Blue (5 and up) **Fic**

Cassie's journey. Harvey, B. **Fic**

Castañeda, Omar S.
Abuela's weave **E**

Castaway cats. Wheeler, L. **E**

Castedo, Elena
Luck
In You're on!: seven plays in English and Spanish p84-99 **812.008**

Casteret, Elisabeth, 1905-1940
See/See also pages in the following book(s):
Atkins, J. How high can we climb? (5 and up) **920**

Castle. Gravett, C. **728.8**

Castle diary. Platt, R. **Fic**

Castle in the air. Jones, D. W. **Fic**

The **castle** in the attic. Winthrop, E. **Fic**

The **castle** of the fly. Afanas'ev, A. N.
In Afanas'ev, A. N. Russian fairy tales p25-26 **398.2**

A **castle** on Viola Street. DiSalvo-Ryan, D. **E**

Castle under siege!. Solway, A. **621.8**

Castle waiting. Medley, L. **741.5**

Castles
Adams, S. Castles & forts (5 and up) **355.7**
Cole, J. Ms. Frizzle's adventures: medieval castle (2-4) **728.8**
Gravett, C. Castle (4 and up) **728.8**
Macaulay, D. Castle (4 and up) **728.8**
Martin, A. Knights & castles (5 and up) **940.1**
Solway, A. Castle under siege! (3-5) **621.8**

Steele, P. Castles (4 and up) **728.8**
Fiction
Platt, R. Castle diary (4 and up) **Fic**

Castles & forts. Adams, S. **355.7**

Castles, caves, and honeycombs. Ashman, L.
E

Cat and Dog and the return of the dead
In The Magic orange tree, and other Haitian folktales p65-68 **398.2**

Cat and Mouse. Lester, J.
In Lester, J. When the beginning began; stories about God, the creatures, and us p31-32 **296.1**

Cat and Rat. Yolen, J.
In Yolen, J. Meow; cat stories from around the world **398.2**

Cat and Rat. Young, E. **398.2**

The **cat** and the cuckoo. Hughes, T. **821**

The **cat** and the fox. Aesop
In Yolen, J. Meow; cat stories from around the world **398.2**

The **cat** and the hen. Aesop
In Yolen, J. Meow; cat stories from around the world **398.2**

The **cat** and the mouse. Jacobs, J.
In Jacobs, J. English fairy tales p187-88 **398.2**
In De Paola, T. Tomie dePaola's Favorite nursery tales p114-16 **398.2**

The **cat** and the parrot. Sierra, J.
In Sierra, J. Nursery tales around the world p33-37 **398.2**

The **Cat** and the Rat. Hamilton, V.
In Hamilton, V. A ring of tricksters; animal tales from America, the West Indies, and Africa p33-37 **398.2**

Cat crafts. Hendry, L. **745.5**

The **cat** goes fiddle-i-fee. Galdone, P. **398.8**

The **cat** in the hat. Seuss, Dr. **E**

The **Cat** in the Hat beginner book dictionary (k-3)
423

Cat 'n mouse
In The Jack tales p127-34 **398.2**

Cat poems. Crawley, D. **811**

Cat running. Snyder, Z. K. **Fic**

The **cat** that walked by himself. Kipling, R.
In Kipling, R. Just so stories **S C**

The **Cat** that went a-traveling
In Stockings of buttermilk: American folktales p91-94 **398.2**

The **cat,** the cock, and the fox. Afanas'ev, A. N.
In Afanas'ev, A. N. Russian fairy tales p86-88 **398.2**

The **cat** who got carried away. Ahlberg, A.
Fic

The **cat** who liked potato soup. Farish, T. **E**

The **cat** who thought she was a dog & the dog who thought he was a cat. Singer, I. B.
In Singer, I. B. Stories for children p308-12 **S C**

The **cat** who walked across France. Banks, K.
E

The **cat** who went to heaven. Coatsworth, E. J.
Fic

The **cat** who wished to be a man. Alexander, L.
Fic

The **cat** with the beckoning paw. MacDonald, M. R.

In MacDonald, M. R. When the lights go out; twenty scary tales to tell p115-17
372.6

The **cat** with the yellow star. Rubin, S. G.
940.53

Catalano, Dominic
(il) Aroner, M. Clink, clank, clunk! **E**

Catalanotto, Peter
Emily's art **E**
Kitten red, yellow, blue **E**
(il) Berger, G. Celebrate! **296.4**
(il) Lyon, G. E. Mother to tigers [biography of Helen Martini] **92**

Cataloging
Cataloging correctly for kids **025.3**
Fritz, D. A. Cataloging with AACR2 and MARC21 **025.3**
Gorman, M. The concise AACR2 **025.3**
See/See also pages in the following book(s):
Building a special collection of children's literature in your library **025.2**

Cataloging correctly for kids **025.3**

Cataloging with AACR2 and MARC21. Fritz, D. A. **025.3**

Cataloging with AACR2R and USMARC. *See* Fritz, D. A. Cataloging with AACR2 and MARC21 **025.3**

Catalogs *See* Audiovisual materials—Catalogs; School libraries—Catalogs

Catalogs, Library *See* Library catalogs

Catalogs, Subject *See* Subject catalogs

Catapult
Gurstelle, W. The art of the catapult (5 and up) **623.4**

Catching the fire: Philip Simmons, blacksmith. Lyons, M. E. **92**

Caterpillars
Heiligman, D. From caterpillar to butterfly (k-1) **595.7**
Latimer, J. P. Caterpillars (4 and up) **595.7**
Fiction
Carle, E. The very hungry caterpillar **E**
Keller, H. Farfallina & Marcel **E**
Swope, S. Gotta go! Gotta go! **E**

Cates, Karin
A far-fetched story **E**
The Secret Remedy Book **E**

Cathedrals
Macaulay, D. Building the book Cathedral (4 and up) **726**
Macaulay, D. Cathedral: the story of its construction (4 and up) **726**

Catherine II, the Great, Empress of Russia, 1729-1796
See/See also pages in the following book(s):
Krull, K. Lives of extraordinary women (4 and up) **920**
Meltzer, M. Ten queens (5 and up) **920**

Catherine, called Birdy. Cushman, K. **Fic**

Catholics
Fiction
Littman, S. Confessions of a closet Catholic (5 and up) **Fic**

The **Catlady**. King-Smith, D. **Fic**

Catlett, Elizabeth
(il) Johnson, J. W. Lift every voice and sing **782.42**

Cato, Vivienne
The Torah and Judaism (5 and up) **222**

Catrow, David
(il) Beaumont, K. I ain't gonna paint no more! **E**
(il) Carville, J. Lu and the swamp ghost **E**
(il) Child, L. M. F. Over the river and through the wood **811**
(il) Katz, A. Take me out of the bathtub and other silly dilly songs **782.42**
(il) Orloff, K. K. I wanna iguana **E**
(il) Simms, L. Rotten teeth **E**

Cats
Clutton-Brock, J. Cat (4 and up) **599.75**
George, J. C. How to talk to your cat (2-4) **636.8**
Gibbons, G. Cats (k-3) **636.8**
Hendry, L. Cat crafts (4-6) **745.5**
Holub, J. Why do cats meow? (k-2) **636.8**
Jeffrey, L. S. Cats (3-5) **636.8**
Lauber, P. The true-or-false book of cats (k-3) **636.8**
Simon, S. Cats (1-4) **636.8**
Tildes, P. L. Calico's cousins (k-3) **636.8**
Fiction
Alexander, L. The cat who wished to be a man (4-6) **Fic**
Alexander, L. How the cat swallowed thunder **E**
Armstrong, A. Whittington (4-6) **Fic**
Arnold, M. D. Heart of a tiger **E**
Asch, F. Mr. Maxwell's mouse **E**
Baker, B. Digby and Kate and the beautiful day **E**
Banks, K. The cat who walked across France **E**
Beames, M. Night cat **E**
Bechtold, L. Edna's tale **E**
Bottner, B. The Scaredy Cats **E**
Bradford, K. You can't rush a cat **E**
Brett, J. Annie and the wild animals **E**
Brown, R. A dark, dark tale **E**
Calhoun, M. Cross-country cat **E**
Catalanotto, P. Kitten red, yellow, blue **E**
Cleary, B. Socks (3-5) **Fic**
Coatsworth, E. J. The cat who went to heaven (4 and up) **Fic**
Cooper, E. Magic thinks big **E**
Cooper, H. Pumpkin soup **E**
Duncan, L. I walk at night **E**
Egielski, R. Slim and Jim **E**
Ehlert, L. Feathers for lunch **E**
Ehlert, L. Top cat **E**
Farish, T. The cat who liked potato soup **E**
Fine, A. The diary of a killer cat (2-4) **Fic**
Fleming, D. Buster **E**
Fleming, D. Mama cat has three kittens **E**

Cats—Fiction—*Continued*

Fox, P. One-eyed cat (5 and up)	**Fic**
Freeman, M. The trouble with cats (2-4)	**Fic**
Freeman, M. Who stole Halloween? (4-6)	
	Fic
Gág, W. Millions of cats	**E**
Gantos, J. Rotten Ralph	**E**
Godwin, L. Happy and Honey	**E**
Gretz, S. Riley and Rose in the picture	**E**
Harper, D. Telling time with Big Mama Cat	
	E
Henkes, K. Kitten's first full moon	**E**
Hesse, K. The cats in Krasinski Square	**E**
Hoberman, M. A. The two sillies	**E**
Howe, J. Houndsley and Catina	**E**
Jenkins, E. Five creatures	**E**
Keats, E. J. Hi, cat!	**E**
Kehret, P. Don't tell anyone (5 and up)	**Fic**
King-Smith, D. The Catlady (2-4)	**Fic**
King-Smith, D. The nine lives of Aristotle (2-4)	
	Fic
Kitamura, S. Comic adventures of Boots	**E**
Kitamura, S. Me and my cat?	**E**
Kuskin, K. So what's it like to be a cat?	**E**
Lawson, J. Audrey and Barbara	**E**
Lawson, J. The Klondike cat	**E**
Le Guin, U. K. Catwings (2-4)	**Fic**
Leopold, N. S. C. K is for kitten	**E**
MacLachlan, P. Bittle	**E**
MacLachlan, P. Who loves me?	**E**
Manders, J. Señor Don Gato	**E**
McCarty, P. Hondo and Fabian	**E**
Meggs, L. P. Go home!	**E**
Murphy, S. J. Hamster champs (1-3)	**516**
Myers, C. Black cat	**E**
Myers, W. D. Three swords for Granada (3-6)	
	Fic
Nagda, A. W. Meow means mischief (2-4)	
	Fic
Naylor, P. R. The grand escape (4-6)	**Fic**
Neville, E. C. It's like this, Cat (5 and up)	
	Fic
Newberry, C. T. April's kittens	**E**
Newman, L. The best cat in the world	**E**
Newsome, J. Night walk	**E**
Potter, B. The story of Miss Moppet	**E**
Raschka, C. Like likes like	**E**
Ruelle, K. G. The Thanksgiving beast feast	
	E
Ryder, J. Come along, kitten	**E**
Rylant, C. Moonlight: the Halloween cat	**E**
Rylant, C. Mr. Putter and Tabby pour the tea	
	E
Sachs, M. The four ugly cats in apartment 3D (3-5)	**Fic**
Samuels, B. Dolores on her toes	**E**
Saul, C. P. Barn cat	**E**
Schachner, J. B. The Grannyman	**E**
Selden, G. The cricket in Times Square (3-6)	
	Fic
Seuss, Dr. The cat in the hat	**E**
Slepian, J. The Broccoli tapes (5 and up)	
	Fic
Snyder, Z. K. The witches of Worm (5 and up)	
	Fic
Soto, G. Chato's kitchen	**E**
Thomson, P. Drat that fat cat!	**E**

Varon, S. Chicken and Cat	**E**
Viorst, J. The tenth good thing about Barney	
	E
Voake, C. Ginger	**E**
Wells, R. Yoko	**E**
Wheeler, L. Castaway cats	**E**

Folklore

Galdone, P. Puss in boots (k-2)	**398.2**
Hodges, M. The boy who drew cats (k-3)	
	398.2
Hodges, M. Dick Whittington and his cat (k-3)	
	398.2
Light, S. Puss in boots (k-3)	**398.2**
MacDonald, M. R. Fat cat (k-3)	**398.2**
MacDonald, M. R. Mabela the clever (k-3)	
	398.2
Perrault, C. Puss in boots (k-3)	**398.2**
Shepard, A. King O' the Cats (k-3)	**398.2**
So, M. Gobble, gobble, slip, slop	**398.2**
Yolen, J. Meow (k-3)	**398.2**
Young, E. Cat and Rat (k-3)	**398.2**

Poetry

Alter, A. The three little kittens (k-1)	**398.8**
Crawley, D. Cat poems (2-4)	**811**
Florian, D. Bow wow meow meow	**811**
Galdone, P. Three little kittens	**398.8**
Kuskin, K. Toots the cat (k-3)	**811**
Sidman, J. Meow ruff (1-3)	**811**

Cats, Wild *See* Wild cats

Cat's baptism

In The Magic orange tree, and other Haitian folktales p123-26   **398.2**

Cat's cradle *See* String figures

Cat's cradle. Aiken, J.

In Aiken, J. Shadows and moonshine; stories   **S C**

The **cats** in Krasinski Square. Hesse, K.   **E**

Catskin. Jacobs, J.

In Jacobs, J. English fairy tales p403-08   **398.2**

Catskinella. Hamilton, V.

In Hamilton, V. Her stories; African American folktales, fairy tales, and true tales p23-27   **398.2**

Catskins

In Grandfather tales; American-English folk tales p106-14   **398.2**

Cattle

See also Bulls

Aliki. Milk from cow to carton (k-3)	**637**
Gibbons, G. The milk makers (k-3)	**637**
Steele, C. Cattle ranching in the American West (5 and up)	**978**

Fiction

Arnold, M. D. Prancing, dancing Lily	**E**
Cronin, D. Click, clack, moo	**E**
Kinerk, R. Clorinda	**E**
Macaulay, D. Black and white	**E**
Pedersen, J. Millie wants to play!	**E**
Root, P. Kiss the cow	**E**
Seymour, T. Hunting the white cow	**E**
Smith, L. When Moon fell down	**E**

Folklore

Cooper, S. The silver cow (1-4)	**398.2**

Cattle ranching in the American West. Steele, C. **978**

Catwings. Le Guin, U. K. **Fic**

Catwings. Le Guin, U. K.
  also in You read to me & I'll read to you; 20th-century stories to share p113-23 **E**

Caught by the sea. Paulsen, G. **92**

The Cauld Lad of Hilton. Jacobs, J.
  In Jacobs, J. English fairy tales p200-02 **398.2**

Cauley, Lorinda Bryan
  Clap your hands **E**
  (il) Kipling, R. The elephant's child **Fic**

The causes of the Civil War. Anderson, D.
  In Anderson, D. World Almanac library of the Civil War [Series] **973.7**

Cave, Kathryn
  One child, one seed **E**

Cave drawings and paintings
  See also Rock drawings, paintings, and engravings

Cave paintings to Picasso. Sayre, H. M. **709**

Caves
  Brimner, L. D. Caves (2-4) **551.4**
  Kramer, S. Caves (4-6) **551.4**

The cay. Taylor, T. **Fic**

Cazet, Denys
  Elvis the rooster almost goes to heaven **E**
  The octopus **E**
  The perfect pumpkin pie **E**

CD-ROMs
Reviews
Adamson, L. G. Literature connections to American history, K-6 **016.973**
Adamson, L. G. Literature connections to world history, K-6 **016.9**

Ceban, Bonnie J.
  Hurricanes, typhoons, and cyclones (4 and up) **551.55**
  Tornadoes (4 and up) **551.55**

Cecil, Randy
  (il) Kimmel, E. A. The runaway tortilla **398.2**
  (il) Sayre, A. P. One is a snail, ten is a crab **E**
  (il) Stenmark, V. The singing chick **E**
  (il) Wilson, S. Big day on the river **E**

Cecilia's year. Abraham, S. G. **Fic**

The Cegua. San Souci, R.
  In San Souci, R. Short & shivery; thirty chilling tales p41-47 **398.2**

Celebrate!. Berger, G. **296.4**

Celebrate Cricket **808.8**

Celebrate the 50 states. Leedy, L. **973**

Celebrate the states **973**

Celebrate the world. MacDonald, M. R. **398.2**

Celebrate with books. Blass, R. J. **028.1**

Celebrating a Quinceañera. Hoyt-Goldsmith, D. **392**

Celebrating Chinese New Year. Hoyt-Goldsmith, D. **394.26**

Celebrating culture in your library [series]
  Pavon, A.-E. 25 Latino craft projects **027.62**

Celebrating Hanukkah. Hoyt-Goldsmith, D. **296.4**

Celebrating Passover. Hoyt-Goldsmith, D. **296.4**

Celebrating Ramadan. Hoyt-Goldsmith, D. **297.3**

Celebrations. Bauer, C. F. **808.8**

Celebrations. Kindersley, A. **394.26**

Celebrations. Livingston, M. C. **811**

Celia Cruz, Queen of salsa. Chambers, V. **92**

Cello *See* Violoncellos

The cello of Mr. O. Cutler, J. **E**

Celtic fairy tales. Philip, N. **398.2**

Celtic memories. Matthews, C. **398.2**

Celtic mythology
  Matthews, C. Celtic memories (3-6) **398.2**

Celts
  Calvert, P. The ancient Celts (5 and up) **936**
Folklore
  Philip, N. Celtic fairy tales (4 and up) **398.2**

Cendrars, Blaise
  Shadow (1-3) **841**

Cendrillon. San Souci, R. **398.2**

Censorship
  Becker, B. C. Hit list for children 2 **016.8**
  Pipkin, G. At the schoolhouse gate **373.1**

Centipedes
  Blaxland, B. Centipedes, millipedes, and their relatives (3-6) **595.6**
  Povey, K. D. Centipede (3-5) **595.6**

Centipedes, millipedes, and their relatives. Blaxland, B. **595.6**

Central America
  Shields, C. J. Central America: facts and figures (4 and up) **972.8**

Central heating. Singer, M. **811**

Central High School (Little Rock, Ark.)
  O'Neill, L. Little Rock (5 and up) **370**

Central Pacific Railroad
  Halpern, M. Railroad fever (4-6) **385.09**
  Houghton, G. The Transcontinental Railroad (5 and up) **385.09**
  Landau, E. The transcontinental railroad (5 and up) **385.09**
  Thompson, L. The transcontinental railroad (4-6) **385.09**
Fiction
  Yin. Coolies **E**

Central Park (New York, N.Y.)
Fiction
  Godwin, L. Central Park serenade **E**

Central Park serenade. Godwin, L. **E**

Central Utah Relocation Center
  Tunnell, M. O. The children of Topaz (5 and up) **940.53**

The century. See Jennings, P. The century for young people **909.82**

Century farm. Peterson, C. **630.1**

The **century** for young people. Jennings, P.
909.82

Cepeda, Joe
  (il) Aardema, V. Koi and the kola nuts
      398.2
  (il) Coy, J. Vroomaloom zoom   **E**
  (il) Lester, J. What a truly cool world! **E**
  (il) Montes, M. Juan Bobo goes to work
      398.2
  (il) Pattison, D. S. The journey of Oliver K.
    Woodman   **E**
  (il) Reiche, D. I, Freddy   **Fic**
  (il) Thomas, E. The red blanket   **E**
  (il) Yacowitz, C. Pumpkin fiesta   **E**

Cephalopods
  Blaxland, B. Octopuses, squids, and their relatives (3-6)   **594**
Cephalopods: octopuses, squids, and their relatives. See Blaxland, B. Octopuses, squids, and
  their relatives   **594**

Ceramics
  Ellis, M. Ceramics for kids (3-6)   **738.1**
Ceramics for kids. Ellis, M.   **738.1**

Ceratosaurus and other horned meat-eaters.
  Schomp, V.
  In Schomp, V. Prehistoric world [series]
      567.9

Cerebral palsy
  Gold, J. C. Cerebral palsy (4 and up) **616.8**
  Gray, S. H. Living with cerebral palsy (4 and
  up)   **362.1**
  Pimm, P. Living with cerebral palsy (3-5)
      362.4

        Fiction
  Mikaelsen, B. Petey (5 and up)   **Fic**

Cerebrovascular disease *See* Stroke

Cerf, Bennett
  Book of riddles
  In Cerf, B. Riddles and more riddles!
      793.73
  More riddles
  In Cerf, B. Riddles and more riddles!
      793.73
  Riddles and more riddles!   **793.73**

Cerisier, Emmanuel
  (il) Burleigh, R. The sea   **551.46**

Cerullo, Mary M.
  Coral reef (4 and up)   **577.7**
  Life under ice (3-5)   **578.7**
  Sea turtles: ocean nomads (4 and up)
      597.92
  The truth about dangerous sea creatures (3-5)
      591.7
  The truth about great white sharks (4 and up)
      597

Cervantes Saavedra, Miguel de
  Don Quixote; adaptation. See Kimmel, E. A.
  Don Quixote and the windmills   **E**

Cervantes Saavedra, Miguel de, 1547-1616
  See/See also pages in the following book(s):
  Krull, K. Lives of the writers (4 and up)
      920

César. Bernier-Grand, C. T.   **811**

Cézanne, Paul, 1839-1906
        About
  Burleigh, R. Paul Cezanne (4 and up) **92**

Cha, Chue
  (il) Cha, D. Dia's story cloth   **305.8**

Cha, Dia
  Dia's story cloth (3-5)   **305.8**

Cha, Nhia Thao
  (il) Cha, D. Dia's story cloth   **305.8**

Chabon, Michael
  Summerland (5 and up)   **Fic**

Chaconas, Dori
  Christmas mouseling   **E**
  Cork & Fuzz   **E**
  One little mouse   **E**

Chagall, Marc, 1887-1985
        About
  Markel, M. Dreamer from the village [biography
  of Marc Chagall] (k-3)   **92**

Chagoya, Enrique
  See/See also pages in the following book(s):
  Just like me p2-3   **920**

Chahrour, Janet
  Zap! blink! taste! think! (5 and up) **507.8**

Chaikin, Miriam
  Angel secrets (4 and up)   **296.1**
  Angels sweep the desert floor (4 and up)
      296.1
  Don't step on the sky (k-3)   **811**
  Menorahs, mezuzas, and other Jewish symbols
  (5 and up)   **296.4**

Chaikovsky, P. I. *See* Tchaikovsky, Peter Ilich,
  1840-1893

The **chain** letter. Schumacher, J.   **Fic**

A **chair** for my mother. Williams, V. B. **E**

Chairs
        Fiction
  Williams, V. B. A chair for my mother **E**
  Yolen, J. Baby Bear's chairs   **E**

Chaka, Zulu Chief, 1787?-1828
        About
  Stanley, D. Shaka, king of the Zulus (4 and up)
      92

Chalk, Gary
  (il) Jacques, B. Redwall   **Fic**

The **chalk** box kid. Bulla, C. R.   **E**

The **chalk** doll. Pomerantz, C.   **E**

Chall, Marsha Wilson
  Bonaparte   **E**

Challoner, Jack
  Hurricane & tornado (4 and up) **551.55**

Chamberlain, Margaret
  (il) Grindley, S. It's my school   **E**

Chamberlin, Mary
  Mama Panya's pancakes   **E**

Chamberlin, Richard
  (jt. auth) Chamberlin, M. Mama Panya's pancakes   **E**

Chambers, Roland
  Rooftop rocket party   **E**

Chambers, Tina
  (il) Platt, R. Shipwreck   **910.4**

Chief: the life of Peter J. Ganci, a New York City firefighter. Ganci, C.   **92**

Chiggers. Jarrow, G.   **616.9**

Chilcoat, George W.
(jt. auth) Tunnell, M. O. The children of Topaz
                              940.53

Child, Lauren
Clarice Bean spells trouble (3-5)   **Fic**
I am too absolutely small for school   **E**
The princess and the pea in miniature   **E**

Child, Lydia Maria Francis
Over the river and through the wood (k-2)
                              811

Child abuse
See also Child sexual abuse
Newman, S. P. Child slavery in modern times (5 and up)   **326**
Fiction
Byars, B. C. Cracker Jackson (5 and up)
                              Fic
Coman, C. What Jamie saw (5 and up)   **Fic**
Lowry, L. Gossamer (5 and up)   **Fic**
Neufeld, J. Almost a hero (5 and up)   **Fic**
White, R. Tadpole (4 and up)   **Fic**

Child and mother *See* Mother-child relationship

Child and parent *See* Parent-child relationship

Child artists
—I never saw another butterfly—   **741.9**

Child care
See also Babysitting

Child care centers *See* Day care centers

Child labor
Bartoletti, S. C. Growing up in coal country (5 and up)   **331.3**
Bartoletti, S. C. Kids on strike! (5 and up)
                              331.8
Brown, D. Kid Blink beats the world (2-4)
                              331.3
Freedman, R. Kids at work (5 and up)
                              331.3
Newman, S. P. Child slavery in modern times (5 and up)   **326**
Fiction
Beatty, P. Turn homeward, Hannalee (5 and up)
                              Fic
Boling, K. January 1905 (5 and up)   **Fic**
D'Adamo, F. Iqbal (5 and up)   **Fic**
Howard, E. The gate in the wall (5 and up)
                              Fic

Child molesting *See* Child sexual abuse

Child of Faerie. Kimberly, G.
In A Glory of unicorns p165-82   **S C**

Child of the owl. Yep, L.   **Fic**

Child psychiatry
See also Autism

Child sexual abuse
See/See also pages in the following book(s):
Jukes, M. It's a girl thing (5 and up)
                              305.23
Fiction
Weeks, S. Jumping the scratch (5 and up)
                              Fic

Child slavery in modern times. Newman, S. P.
                              326

Childbirth
See also Multiple birth
Bauer, M. D. If you were born a kitten (k-1)
                              591.3
Butler, D. H. My mom's having a baby! (2-4)
                              612.6
Cole, J. How you were born (k-2)   **612.6**
Cole, J. When you were inside Mommy (k-1)
                              612.6
Frasier, D. On the day you were born   **E**
Harris, R. H. It's not the stork! (k-3) **612.6**
Harris, R. H. It's so amazing! (2-4)   **612.6**
Pringle, L. P. Everybody has a bellybutton (k-3)
                              612.6
Rosenberg, M. B. Mommy's in the hospital having a baby (k-1)   **362.1**
Sears, W. Baby on the way (k-2)   **612.6**
Fiction
English, K. The baby on the way   **E**
Harris, R. H. Happy birth day!   **E**
Lund, D. Tell me my story, Mama   **E**

Childe Rowland. Jacobs, J.
In Jacobs, J. English fairy tales p120-26
                              398.2

Childlessness
See also Infertility

Children
See also Abandoned children; African American children; Boys; Girls; Infants; Internet and children; Runaway children
Hoose, P. M. We were there, too! (5 and up)
                              973
A Life like mine (3-6)   **305.23**
The Milestones Project   **305.23**
Abuse
See Child abuse
Adoption
See Adoption
Books and reading
Feinberg, B. Welcome to Lizard Motel
                              028.5
Larson, J. C. Bringing mysteries alive for children and young adults   **028.5**
Simpson, M. S. Storycraft   **372.6**
Sutherland, Z. Children & books   **028.5**
Books and reading—Bibliography
Van Orden, P. J. Library service to children
                              027.62
Employment
See Child labor
Pictorial works
Kindersley, B. Children just like me (3-6)
                              305.23
Canada
Kurelek, W. A prairie boy's summer (3-5)
                              971.27
Kurelek, W. A prairie boy's winter (3-5)
                              971.27
United States
Cole, S. To be young in America (5 and up)
                              973

Children's literature—History and criticism—
Continued
The Norton anthology of children's literature
808.8
Stephens, C. G. Coretta Scott King Award
books **028.5**
Sutherland, Z. Children & books **028.5**
Yolen, J. Touch magic **028.5**
Study and teaching
Buzzeo, T. Terrific connections with authors, illustrators, and storytellers **372.6**
Ellis, S. From reader to writer **372.6**
Scales, P. R. Teaching banned books **323.44**
The **children's** literature dictionary. Latrobe, K. H.
028.5
Children's literature in the elementary school
028.5
Children's moneymaking projects *See* Moneymaking projects for children
Children's Museum (Boston, Mass.)
Simonds, N. Moonbeams, dumplings & dragon boats **394.26**
Children's museums. Norris, J. **069**
Children's night sky atlas. Scagell, R. **520**
Children's poetry
See also Lullabies; Nonsense verses; Nursery rhymes; Tongue twisters
The **Children's** song index, 1978-1993 **782.42**
Children's traditional games. Sierra, J. **796**
Children's writings
—I never saw another butterfly— **741.9**
The Palm of my heart **811.008**
Rising voices (5 and up) **810.8**
Salting the ocean (4 and up) **811.008**
A **children's** zoo. Hoban, T. **E**
Childress, Diana
The War of 1812 (5 and up) **973.5**
A **child's** book of art: great pictures, first words.
Micklethwait, L. **701**
A **child's** book of prayer in art. Beckett, W.
242
A **child's** calendar. Updike, J. **811**
A **child's** Christmas in Wales. Thomas, D.
828
A **child's** garden of verses. Stevenson, R. L.
821
A **child's** good night book. Brown, M. W. **E**
A **child's** good night prayer. Maccarone, G. **E**
A **child's** introduction to poetry. Driscoll, M.
808.81
Childtimes: a three-generation memoir. Greenfield, E. **920**
Chile
Winter, J. K. Chile (5 and up) **983**
Chil's song. Kipling, R.
In Kipling, R. The jungle book: the Mowgli stories **S C**
Chimp math. Nagda, A. W. **529**
Chimpanzees
Bow, P. Chimpanzee rescue (5 and up)
599.8

Goodall, J. The chimpanzees I love (4 and up)
599.8
Goodall, J. My life with the chimpanzees (3-6)
92
Goodall, J. With love (4 and up) **599.8**
Nagda, A. W. Chimp math (2-4) **529**
Fiction
Alborough, J. Tall **E**
Browne, A. Willy the dreamer **E**
Durango, J. Cha-cha chimps **E**
Hoban, L. Arthur's Christmas cookies **E**
Mallat, K. Mama love **E**
The **chimpanzees** I love. Goodall, J. **599.8**
Chin, Beverly Ann
(ed) The Dictionary of characters in children's literature. See The Dictionary of characters in children's literature **028.5**
Chin, Jason
(il) Jango-Cohen, J. Chinese New Year
394.26
Chin-Lee, Cynthia
Amelia to Zora (4 and up) **920**
Ch'in Shih-huang, Emperor of China, 259-210 B.C.
Tomb
Dean, A. Terra-cotta soldiers (4 and up)
931
O'Connor, J. The emperor's silent army (4 and up) **931**
China
Asher, S. China (2-4) **951**
Dramer, K. People's Republic of China (5 and up) **951**
Ferroa, P. G. China (5 and up) **951**
Fritz, J. China homecoming (6 and up)
951.05
Fritz, J. Homesick: my own story (5 and up)
92
Ma Yan. The diary of Ma Yan (5 and up)
951.05
Antiquities
Dean, A. Terra-cotta soldiers (4 and up)
931
O'Connor, J. The emperor's silent army (4 and up) **931**
Shuter, J. Ancient China (4-6) **931**
Civilization
Anderson, D. Ancient China (4 and up)
709.51
Cole, J. Ms. Frizzle's adventures: Imperial China (2-4) **931**
Cotterell, A. Ancient China (4 and up) **931**
Schomp, V. The ancient Chinese (5 and up)
931
Shuter, J. Ancient China (4-6) **931**
Stefoff, R. The Asian empires (5 and up)
950
Communism
See Communism—China
Fiction
Alexander, L. The remarkable journey of Prince Jen (5 and up) **Fic**
Brett, J. Daisy comes home **E**
Bridges, S. Y. Ruby's wish **E**
Cheng, A. Shanghai messenger (3-6) **Fic**

China—Fiction—*Continued*

Compestine, Y. C. The runaway rice cake   **E**
DeJong, M. The house of sixty fathers (4-6)
       Fic
Demi. The emperor's new clothes   **E**
Demi. The greatest power   **E**
Demi. Kites   **E**
Gower, C. Long-Long's New Year   **E**
Hill, E. S. Bird Boy (2-4)   **Fic**
Hill, E. S. Chang and the bamboo flute (3-5)
       Fic
Lee, J. M. Bitter dumplings   **E**
McCaughrean, G. The kite rider (5 and up)
       Fic
McCully, E. A. Beautiful warrior   **E**
Muth, J. J. Stone soup (k-3)   **398.2**
Okimoto, J. D. The White Swan express   **E**
Partridge, E. Oranges on Golden Mountain
       E
Poole, A. L. The pea blossom   **E**
Roome, D. R. The elephant's pillow   **E**
Tsubakiyama, M. Mei-Mei loves the morning
       E
Tucker, K. The seven Chinese sisters   **E**
Wilkinson, C. Dragon keeper (5 and up)   **Fic**
Young, E. Monkey King   **E**
Young, E. My Mei Mei   **E**

Folklore
See Folklore—China
History
Cole, J. Ms. Frizzle's adventures: Imperial China (2-4)   **931**
Stefoff, R. The Asian empires (5 and up)
       950
History—1949-1976—Personal narratives
Jiang, J.-l. Red scarf girl (6 and up)   **951.05**
Zhang, A. Red land, yellow river (5 and up)
       951.05
Poetry
Young, E. Beyond the great mountains (4 and up)   **811**
Religion
Fisher, L. E. The gods and goddesses of ancient China (3-6)   **299**
Science
See Science—China
Social life and customs
Demi. Happy, happy Chinese New Year! (k-3)
       394.26
Temko, F. Traditional crafts from China (4 and up)   **745.5**

China homecoming. Fritz, J.   **951.05**
Chinatown (New York, N.Y.)
Fiction
Mak, K. My Chinatown   **E**
Chincoteague Island (Va.)
Fiction
Henry, M. Misty of Chincoteague (4 and up)
       Fic
Chinese
Fiction
Carling, A. L. Mama & Papa have a store
       E
Carling, A. L. Sawdust carpets   **E**

United States—Fiction

Namioka, L. Yang the youngest and his terrible ear (4-6)   **Fic**
Yep, L. Dragon's gate (6 and up)   **Fic**
Yep, L. The journal of Wong Ming-Chung (4 and up)   **Fic**
The **Chinese** American family album. Hoobler, D.
       305.8

Chinese Americans
     See also Chinese—United States
Hoobler, D. The Chinese American family album   **305.8**
Kuklin, S. How my family lives in America (k-3)   **305.8**
Yep, L. The lost garden (5 and up)   **92**
Fiction
Cheng, A. Honeysuckle house (3-5)   **Fic**
Cheng, A. The key collection (3-5)   **Fic**
Cheng, A. Shanghai messenger (3-6)   **Fic**
Chinn, K. Sam and the lucky money   **E**
Coerr, E. Chang's paper pony   **E**
Currier, K. S. Kai's journey to Gold Mountain (4 and up)   **Fic**
Hall, B. E. Henry and the kite dragon   **E**
Katz, K. My first Chinese New Year   **E**
Lee, M. Landed   **Fic**
Lee, M. Nim and the war effort   **E**
Lewin, T. Big Jimmy's Kum Kau Chinese take-out   **E**
Lin, G. Dim sum for everyone!   **E**
Look, L. Henry's first-moon birthday   **E**
Look, L. Love as strong as ginger   **E**
Look, L. Ruby Lu, brave and true (1-3)   **Fic**
Look, L. Uncle Peter's amazing Chinese wedding   **E**
Lord, B. B. In the Year of the Boar and Jackie Robinson (4-6)   **Fic**
Louie, T. O. Raymond's perfect present   **E**
Mak, K. My Chinatown   **E**
Martin, N. Flight of the Fisherbird (5 and up)
       Fic
Partridge, E. Oranges on Golden Mountain
       E
Peacock, C. A. Mommy far, Mommy near   **E**
Thong, R. One is a drummer   **E**
Thong, R. Red is a dragon   **E**
Wong, J. S. Apple pie 4th of July   **E**
Yang, B. Hannah is my name   **E**
Yee, L. Millicent Min, girl genius (5 and up)
       Fic
Yep, L. The amah (5 and up)   **Fic**
Yep, L. Angelfish (5 and up)   **Fic**
Yep, L. Child of the owl (5 and up)   **Fic**
Yep, L. Dragonwings (5 and up)   **Fic**
Yep, L. The magic paintbrush (3-5)   **Fic**
Yep, L. Skunk scout (4-6)   **Fic**
Yep, L. Thief of hearts (5 and up)   **Fic**
Yep, L. The traitor (5 and up)   **Fic**
Yep, L. When the circus came to town (3-5)
       Fic
Yin. Coolies   **E**
Young, E. My Mei Mei   **E**
Social life and customs
Hoyt-Goldsmith, D. Celebrating Chinese New Year (3-5)   **394.26**

Chinese Americans—Social life and customs—
Continued

Waters, K. Lion dancer: Ernie Wan's Chinese New Year (k-3)   **394.26**

Chinese art

Anderson, D. Ancient China (4 and up)   **709.51**

Chinese civilization *See* China—Civilization

Chinese cooking

See/See also pages in the following book(s):

Simonds, N. Moonbeams, dumplings & dragon boats (4 and up)   **394.26**

A **Chinese** fairy tale. Housman, L.

In Bauer, C. F. Celebrations; read-aloud holiday and theme book programs p4-11   **808.8**

Chinese language

Lee, H. V. 1, 2, 3 go! (k-3)   **495.1**
Lee, H. V. At the beach (k-3)   **495.1**
Young, E. Voices of the heart   **179**

The **Chinese** mirror. Ginsburg, M.   **398.2**

Chinese New Year

Bledsoe, K. E. Chinese New Year crafts (2-4)   **745.594**
Demi. Happy, happy Chinese New Year! (k-3)   **394.26**
Hoyt-Goldsmith, D. Celebrating Chinese New Year (3-5)   **394.26**
Jango-Cohen, J. Chinese New Year (1-3)   **394.26**
Waters, K. Lion dancer: Ernie Wan's Chinese New Year (k-3)   **394.26**

See/See also pages in the following book(s):

Simonds, N. Moonbeams, dumplings & dragon boats (4 and up)   **394.26**

Fiction

Chinn, K. Sam and the lucky money   **E**
Compestine, Y. C. The runaway rice cake   **E**
Gower, C. Long-Long's New Year   **E**
Katz, K. My first Chinese New Year   **E**
Lin, G. The year of the dog (3-5)   **Fic**
Wong, J. S. This next New Year   **E**
Yep, L. When the circus came to town (3-5)   **Fic**

Chinese New Year crafts. Bledsoe, K. E.   **745.594**

The **Chinese** Red Riding Hood. Chang, I. C.

In Womenfolk and fairy tales p14-19   **398.2**

Chinese science *See* Science—China

Chinn, Karen

Sam and the lucky money   **E**

Chinook Indians

Folklore

Martin, R. The boy who lived with the seals (1-4)   **398.2**
Taylor, H. P. Coyote places the stars (k-3)   **398.2**

Chipmunk and the Owl Sisters. Caduto, M. J.

In Caduto, M. J. and Bruchac, J. Keepers of the night; Native American stories and nocturnal activities for children p93-96   **398.2**

Chipmunks

Folklore

Bruchac, J. How Chipmunk got his stripes (k-3)   **398.2**

Chippendale, Lisa A.

Triumph of the imagination: the story of writer J.K. Rowling (5 and up)   **92**

Chippewa Indians *See* Ojibwa Indians

Chips. San Souci, R.

In San Souci, R. Even more short & shivery; thirty spine-tingling stories p94-99   **398.2**

Chirping crickets. Berger, M.   **595.7**

Chisholm, Shirley, 1924-2005

See/See also pages in the following book(s):

Pinkney, A. D. Let it shine (4 and up)   **920**

Chitty chitty bang bang. Fleming, I.   **Fic**

Chivalry

See also Medieval civilization
Bulfinch, T. Bulfinch's mythology   **201**

Chloe's birthday . . . and me. Potter, G.   **E**

Cho, Michael

(il) Ali, D. Media madness   **302.23**

Chocolate, Debbi

Kwanzaa (3-5)   **394.26**
My first Kwanzaa book (k-2)   **394.26**

Chocolate

Burleigh, R. Chocolate (3-6)   **641.3**
MacLeod, E. Chock full of chocolate (4-6)   **641.6**

Chocolate fever. Smith, R. K.   **Fic**

Chodos-Irvine, Margaret

Best best friends   **E**
Ella Sarah gets dressed   **E**
(il) Wong, J. S. Apple pie 4th of July   **E**
(il) Wong, J. S. Buzz   **E**
(jt. auth) Wong, J. S. Hide & seek   **E**

Chödzin, Sherab

The wisdom of the crows and other Buddhist tales (4 and up)   **294.3**

Choi, Sook Nyul

Halmoni and the picnic   **E**
Year of impossible goodbyes (5 and up)   **Fic**

Choi, Yangsook

(il) Cheng, A. The key collection   **Fic**
(il) Lee, M. Nim and the war effort   **E**
(il) Park, F. Good-bye, 382 Shin Dang Dong   **E**
(il) Wong, J. S. This next New Year   **E**

Choldenko, Gennifer

Al Capone does my shirts (5 and up)   **Fic**
Notes from a liar and her dog (5 and up)   **Fic**

Choo choo clickety-clack!. Mayo, M.   **E**

Choosing books for children. Hearne, B. G.   **028.5**

Chopin, Frédéric, 1810-1849

See/See also pages in the following book(s):

Krull, K. Lives of the musicians (4 and up)   **920**

Chorao, Kay

D is for drums (k-3)   **975.5**
Here comes Kate   **E**

Chorao, Kay—*Continued*

Pig and Crow   **E**

(comp) The baby's bedtime book. See The baby's bedtime book   **808.81**

(comp) The baby's book of baby animals. See The baby's book of baby animals   **808.81**

(comp) The baby's good morning book. See The baby's good morning book   **808.81**

(comp) The Baby's lap book. See The Baby's lap book   **398.8**

(comp) The baby's playtime book. See The baby's playtime book   **811.008**

Choreographers

Glover, S. Savion!: my life in tap (5 and up)   **92**

Reich, S. José! [biography of José Limón] (2-4)   **92**

Chorlton, Windsor

Woolly mammoth (4 and up)   **569**

Chrisp, Peter

Ancient Egypt revealed (4 and up)   **932**

Ancient Rome (4 and up)   **709.37**

Mesopotamia (5 and up)   **935**

Town and country life (5 and up)   **940.1**

Warfare (5 and up)   **355**

Welcome to the Globe (1-3)   **822.3**

Christ *See* Jesus Christ

Christelow, Eileen

Five little monkeys jumping on the bed   **E**

Vote! (k-3)   **324**

What do authors do? (1-3)   **808**

What do illustrators do? (1-3)   **741.6**

Christensen, Bonnie

The daring Nellie Bly (3-5)   **92**

Woody Guthrie, poet of the people (3-6)   **92**

(il) Osborne, M. P. Pompeii   **937**

Christian X, King of Denmark, 1870-1947
Fiction
Deedy, C. A. The yellow star (3-5)   **Fic**

Christian, Peggy

If you find a rock (k-3)   **552**

Christian, Rebecca

Cooking the Spanish way

In Easy menu ethnic cookbooks   **641.5**

Christian holidays

See also Lent

Christian life
Fiction
De Paola, T. Pascual and the kitchen angels   **E**

Paterson, K. Preacher's boy (5 and up)   **Fic**

Tolan, S. S. Save Halloween! (5 and up)   **Fic**

Christian saints

Brown, D. Across a dark and wild sea [biography of Saint Columba] (2-5)   **92**

De Paola, T. Patrick: patron saint of Ireland (k-3)   **92**

Demi. The legend of Saint Nicholas (3-6)   **92**

Hodges, M. Joan of Arc (2-4)   **92**

Kennedy, R. F. Saint Francis of Assisi (2-4)   **271**

Mulvihill, M. The treasury of saints and martyrs (5 and up)   **920**

Norris, K. The holy twins: Benedict and Scholastica (3-5)   **92**

Pandell, K. Saint Francis sings to Brother Sun (4 and up)   **271**

Poole, J. Joan of Arc (2-4)   **92**

Sabuda, R. Saint Valentine (1-3)   **92**

Stanley, D. Joan of Arc (4 and up)   **92**

Visconti, G. Clare and Francis (4 and up)   **271**

Christiana, David

(il) Bath, K. P. The secret of Castle Cant   **Fic**

(il) Levine, G. C. Fairy dust and the quest for the egg   **Fic**

Christianity

See also Protestantism

Brown, A. The Bible and Christianity (5 and up)   **220**

Self, D. Christianity (5 and up)   **230**

See/See also pages in the following book(s):

Osborne, M. P. One world, many religions (4 and up)   **200**
Fiction
Howe, J. Kaddish for Grandpa in Jesus' name, amen   **E**

Speare, E. G. The bronze bow (6 and up)   **Fic**

Christiansen, Lee

(il) Kurtz, J. Water hole waiting   **E**

Christie, Gregory

(il) Bolden, T. The champ! [biography of Muhammad Ali]   **92**

(il) Bolden, T. Rock of ages   **811**

(il) Frame, J. A. Yesterday I had the blues   **E**

(il) Joosse, B. M. Hot city   **E**

(il) Khan, R. Ruler of the courtyard   **E**

(il) Medina, T. Love to Langston   **811**

(il) Miller, W. Richard Wright and the library card   **E**

(il) The Palm of my heart. See The Palm of my heart   **811.008**

(il) Richards, B. Keep climbing, girls   **E**

(il) Rockwell, A. F. Only passing through: the story of Sojourner Truth   **92**

(il) Sherman, P. The sun's daughter   **398.2**

(il) Williams, M. Brothers in hope   **Fic**

Christina, Queen of Sweden, 1626-1689

See/See also pages in the following book(s):

Meltzer, M. Ten queens (5 and up)   **920**

Christmas

Barth, E. Holly, reindeer, and colored lights (3-6)   **394.26**

A Christmas treasury (2-4)   **808.8**

Erlbach, A. Merry Christmas, everywhere! (k-3)   **394.26**

Hoyt-Goldsmith, D. Las Posadas (3-5)   **394.26**

Joy to the world (4 and up)   **808.8**

Lankford, M. D. Christmas around the world (3-5)   **394.26**

Christmas—*Continued*

McKissack, P. C. Christmas in the big house, Christmas in the quarters (4 and up) **394.26**

Sabuda, R. The Christmas alphabet **E**

See/See also pages in the following book(s):

Bauer, C. F. Celebrations p1-24 **808.8**

Fiction

Anaya, R. A. The farolitos of Christmas **E**

Antle, N. Sam's Wild West Christmas **E**

Brett, J. Who's that knocking on Christmas Eve (k-2) **398.2**

Brett, J. The wild Christmas reindeer **E**

Buck, P. S. Christmas day in the morning **E**

Bunting, E. Christmas cricket **E**

Bunting, E. December **E**

Bunting, E. Night tree **E**

Carlson, N. S. The family under the bridge (3-5) **Fic**

Chaconas, D. Christmas mouseling **E**

Climo, S. Cobweb Christmas **E**

De Paola, T. An early American Christmas **E**

De Paola, T. Guess who's coming to Santa's for dinner? **E**

De Paola, T. The night of Las Posadas **E**

Dunrea, O. Bear Noel **E**

Duval, K. The Three Bears' Christmas **E**

Fine, A. The true story of Christmas (4 and up) **Fic**

Fox, M. Wombat divine **E**

Frazee, M. Santa Claus, the world's number one toy expert **E**

Hamilton, V. The bells of Christmas (4-6) **Fic**

Harvey, B. My prairie Christmas (2-4) **Fic**

Hoban, L. Arthur's Christmas cookies **E**

Hoffmann, E. T. A. Nutcracker (4 and up) **Fic**

Houston, G. The year of the perfect Christmas tree **E**

Jiménez, F. The Christmas gift: El regalo de Navidad **E**

Kain, K. The Nutcracker **E**

Kimmel, E. C. My penguin Osbert **E**

Klise, K. Shall I knit you a hat? **E**

Koppe, S. The Nutcracker (3-5) **Fic**

Major, K. Aunt Olga's Christmas postcards **E**

Marsden, C. Mama had to work on Christmas (2-4) **Fic**

Palatini, M. Three French hens **E**

Pinkney, A. D. Mim's Christmas jam **E**

Polacco, P. Christmas tapestry (2-4) **Fic**

Polacco, P. The trees of the dancing goats **E**

Polacco, P. Welcome Comfort **E**

Potter, B. The tailor of Gloucester **E**

Robinson, B. The best Christmas pageant ever (4-6) **Fic**

Rosen, M. J. Elijah's angel (2-4) **Fic**

Ryan, P. M. There was no snow on Christmas Eve **E**

Rylant, C. Christmas in the country **E**

Santiago, E. A doll for Navidades **E**

Say, A. Tree of cranes **E**

Schulman, J. The nutcracker (4 and up) **Fic**

Seibold, J. O. Olive the other reindeer **E**

Seuss, Dr. How the Grinch stole Christmas **E**

Soto, G. Too many tamales **E**

Thayer, J. The puppy who wanted a boy **E**

Van Allsburg, C. The Polar Express **E**

Wells, R. Morris's disappearing bag **E**

Wiggin, K. D. S. The Bird's Christmas Carol (3-5) **Fic**

Wojciechowski, S. The Christmas miracle of Jonathan Toomey **E**

Ziefert, H. Home for Navidad **E**

Zolotow, C. The beautiful Christmas tree **E**

Folklore

De Paola, T. The clown of God (k-3) **398.2**

De Paola, T. The legend of the poinsettia (k-3) **398.2**

Robbins, R. Baboushka and the three kings (1-4) **398.2**

Poetry

Christmas poems **808.81**

Christmas presents (k-3) **811.008**

Grimes, N. Under the Christmas tree (k-3) **811**

Moore, C. C. The night before Christmas (k-3) **811**

Prelutsky, J. It's Christmas (1-3) **811**

Songs

Coots, J. F. Santa Claus is comin' to town (k-3) **782.42**

Wales

Thomas, D. A child's Christmas in Wales **828**

The **Christmas** alphabet. Sabuda, R. **E**

The **Christmas** apple. Sawyer, R.

In Bauer, C. F. Celebrations; read-aloud holiday and theme book programs p259-64 **808.8**

Christmas around the world. Lankford, M. D. **394.26**

Christmas carols *See* Carols

Christmas crafts from around the world. Sadler, J. A. **745.594**

Christmas cricket. Bunting, E. **E**

Christmas day in the morning. Buck, P. S. **E**

Christmas decorations

Sadler, J. A. Christmas crafts from around the world (4-6) **745.594**

Christmas fantasy. Hijuelos, O.

In You're on!: seven plays in English and Spanish p108-31 **812.008**

Christmas gift. Jiménez, F.

In Jiménez, F. The circuit: stories from the life of a migrant child p51-56 **S C**

The **Christmas** gift: El regalo de Navidad. Jiménez, F. **E**

Christmas in the big house, Christmas in the quarters. McKissack, P. C. **394.26**

Christmas in the country. Rylant, C. **E**

The **Christmas** miracle of Jonathan Toomey. Wojciechowski, S. **E**

Christmas mouseling. Chaconas, D. **E**

Cinderella's rat. Meddaugh, S. E

Cipher and telegraph codes
Fiction
Barasch, L. Radio rescue E

Ciphers
Janeczko, P. B. Top secret (4 and up) 652
Circle dogs. Henkes, K. E
The **circle** of days. Lindbergh, R. 242
Circle opens quartet [series]
Pierce, T. Magic steps Fic
Circle unbroken. Raven, M. E
The **circlemaker**. Schur, M. Fic
The **circuit**. Jiménez, F.
In Jiménez, F. The circuit: stories from the life of a migrant child p73-83 S C
The **circuit**: stories from the life of a migrant child. Jiménez, F. S C
Circulatory system See Cardiovascular system
Circumnavigation See Voyages around the world
Circus
Helfer, R. The world's greatest elephant (1-3) 791.3
Schubert, L. Ballet of the elephants 791.8
Fiction
Clements, A. Circus family dog E
Corder, Z. Lionboy (4 and up) Fic
Dodds, D. A. Where's Pup? E
Ehlert, L. Circus E
Fleischman, P. Sidewalk circus E
Hoff, S. Oliver E
Horvath, P. When the circus came to town (4-6) Fic
Priceman, M. Emeline at the circus E
Seuss, Dr. If I ran the circus E
Wiseman, B. Morris and Boris at the circus E
Yep, L. When the circus came to town (3-5) Fic
Circus dreams. San Souci, R.
In San Souci, R. Double-dare to be scared: another thirteen chilling tales S C
Circus family dog. Clements, A. E
Cirrone, Dorian
Finding high-jump fame
In Sports shorts S C
Cities and towns
Geisert, B. Mountain town E
Fiction
Raschka, C. New York is English, Chattanooga is Creek E
Growth
See also Urbanization
Cities of the world [series]
Stein, R. C. Berlin 943
Cities through time [series]
Brook, L. Daily life in ancient and modern Timbuktu 966.23
Citizenship
Hamilton, J. Becoming a citizen (3-5) 323.6

Citrus fruits
See also Oranges
City: a story of Roman planning and construction. Macaulay, D. 711
The **city** ABC book. Milich, Z. E
City and town life
Freedman, R. Immigrant kids (4 and up) 325.73
Sandler, M. W. Straphanging in the USA (5 and up) 388.4
Fiction
Bunting, E. Secret place E
Burleigh, R. Messenger, messenger E
Burton, V. L. The little house E
Ferris, J. Much ado about Grubstake (5 and up) Fic
Fleischman, P. Seedfolks (4 and up) Fic
Fleischman, P. Sidewalk circus E
Grant, K. Sofie and the city E
Guest, E. H. Iris and Walter E
Jonas, A. Round trip E
Joosse, B. M. Hot city E
Keats, E. J. Apt. 3 E
Maitland, B. Moo in the morning E
Myers, C. Black cat E
Myers, C. Fly! E
Neubecker, R. Wow! city! E
Stewart, S. The journey E
U'Ren, A. Mary Smith E
Varon, S. Chicken and Cat E
Zolotow, C. The beautiful Christmas tree E
Poetry
Grimes, N. A pocketful of poems (k-3) 811
Moore, L. Mural on Second Avenue, and other city poems (k-3) 811
Rosten, N. A city is (k-3) 811
Stone bench in an empty park (4 and up) 811.008
City by numbers. Johnson, S. E
City chicken. Dorros, A. E
City colors. Milich, Z. E
A **city** is. Rosten, N. 811
City of angels. Jaskol, J. 979.4
The **city** of Ember. DuPrau, J. Fic
City planning
Rome
Macaulay, D. City: a story of Roman planning and construction (4 and up) 711
City signs. Milich, Z. E
Civil disorders See Riots
Civil engineering
See also Structural engineering
Fantastic feats and failures (4 and up) 624.1
Macaulay, D. City: a story of Roman planning and construction (4 and up) 711
Macaulay, D. Underground (5 and up) 624
Sullivan, G. Built to last (5 and up) 624
Civil rights
See also African Americans—Civil rights; Women's rights
Krull, K. A kid's guide to America's Bill of Rights (4 and up) 342

Civil rights demonstrations
Fiction
McKissack, P. C. Abby takes a stand (2-4)
Fic
Weatherford, C. B. Freedom on the menu **E**
Civil War
United States
See United States—History—1861-1865,
Civil War
Civil War. Stanchak, J. E.
973.7
[Grolier 10v set] (5 and up) **973.7**
Civil War A to Z. Bolotin, N. **973.7**
The **Civil** War at sea. Anderson, D.
In Anderson, D. World Almanac library of
the Civil War [Series] **973.7**
The **Civil** War in the East (1861-1863). Anderson,
D.
In Anderson, D. World Almanac library of
the Civil War [Series] **973.7**
The **Civil** War in the West (1861-1863). Ander-
son, D.
In Anderson, D. World Almanac library of
the Civil War [Series] **973.7**
Civil War library [series]
Ford, C. T. African-American soldiers in the
Civil War **973.7**
Ford, C. T. The American Civil War **973.7**
Ford, C. T. The Battle of Gettysburg and Lin-
coln's Gettysburg Address **973.7**
Ford, C. T. Daring women of the Civil War
973.7
Ford, C. T. Lincoln, slavery, and the Emancipa-
tion Proclamation **973.7**
Civilization
See also names of continents, countries,
states, etc., with the subdivision Civilization,
e.g. United States—Civilization
Encyclopedias
Brimson, S. Nations of the world (5 and up)
909
Civilization, Ancient See Ancient civilization
Civilization, Classical See Classical civilization
Civilization, Medieval See Medieval civilization
Civilization, Sumerian See Sumerians
Civilization and science See Science and civiliza-
tion
Cixi See Tz'u-hsi, Empress dowager of China,
1835-1908
Clairvoyance
Fiction
Blackwood, G. L. Second sight (5 and up)
Fic
Wright, B. R. Crandall's castle (4 and up)
Fic
Clambake. Peters, R. M. **970.004**
Clap your hands. Cauley, L. B. **E**
Clare, of Assisi, Saint, 1194-1253
About
Visconti, G. Clare and Francis (4 and up)
271
Clare and Francis. Visconti, G. **271**

Clarice Bean spells trouble. Child, L. **Fic**
Clark, Clara Gillow
Hill Hawk Hattie (5 and up) **Fic**
Clark, Eugenie
About
Ross, M. E. Fish watching with Eugenie Clark
(4 and up) **92**
Clark, Warren
(il) Graydon, S. Made you look **659.1**
(il) Swanson, D. Nibbling on Einstein's brain
500
Clark, William, 1770-1838
About
Blumberg, R. The incredible journey of Lewis
and Clark (5 and up) **978**
Kimmel, E. C. As far as the eye can reach (4
and up) **978**
Schanzer, R. How we crossed the West (3-5)
978
Fiction
Myers, L. Lewis and Clark and me (3-6)
Fic
**Clark R. Bavin National Fish and Wildlife Fo-
rensics Laboratory** See National Fish and
Wildlife Forensics Laboratory
Clarke, Barry
Amphibian (4 and up) **597.8**
The **class** artist. Karas, G. B. **E**
Class clown. Hurwitz, J. **Fic**
Class cootie. San Souci, R.
In San Souci, R. Double-dare to be scared:
another thirteen chilling tales **S C**
Classical antiquities
See also Greece—Antiquities; Rome—An-
tiquities
Classical art See Roman art
Classical civilization
See also Rome—Civilization
Greene, J. D. Slavery in ancient Greece and
Rome (5 and up) **326**
Classical music See Music
Classical mythology
See also Eros (Greek deity); Psyche (Greek
deity)
Aliki. The gods and goddesses of Olympus (2-5)
292
Colum, P. The Golden Fleece and the heroes
who lived before Achilles (5 and up) **292**
Craft, M. Cupid and Psyche (4 and up) **292**
Hamilton, E. Mythology (5 and up) **292**
Low, A. The Macmillan book of Greek gods
and heroes (3-6) **292**
Mayer, M. Pegasus (4-6) **292**
McCaughrean, G. Greek gods and goddesses
(4-6) **292**
McCaughrean, G. Greek myths (4-6) **292**
McCaughrean, G. Hercules (5 and up) **292**
McCaughrean, G. Odysseus (5 and up) **292**
McCaughrean, G. Perseus (5 and up) **292**
Mitton, J. Once upon a starry night (k-3)
523.8
Osborne, M. P. Favorite Greek myths (3-6)
292

Clewer, Carolyn
Kids can knit (4 and up)   **746.43**
Click-clack. San Souci, R.
   In San Souci, R. Double-dare to be scared:
   another thirteen chilling tales   **S C**
Click, clack, moo. Cronin, D.   **E**
Click! fun with photography. Price, S.   **771**
Click here. Vega, D.   **Fic**
Clifford, Eth
Help! I'm a prisoner in the library (3-5)   **Fic**
The remembering box (3-5)   **Fic**
Clifton, Lucille
Everett Anderson's 1-2-3   **E**
The times they used to be (4 and up)   **Fic**
Climate
   See also Greenhouse effect; Meteorology;
   Weather
Arnold, C. El Niño (4 and up)   **551.6**
Climo, Shirley
Cobweb Christmas   **E**
The Egyptian Cinderella (k-3)   **398.2**
The Korean Cinderella (k-3)   **398.2**
Magic & mischief (4 and up)   **398.2**
Includes the following stories: The giant of Castle Treen; The
very old woman and the Piskey; The widow and the Spriggans
of Trencrom Hill; Tom Trevorrow and the Knackers; Pleasing
Betty Stoggs; The changeling of Brea Vean; The bewitching of
Sea Pink; The mermaid of Zennor; The cornish teeny-tiny; Duffy
and the Bucca
Monkey business (3-6)   **398.2**
Cline-Ransome, Lesa
Satchel Paige (2-4)   **92**
Clink, clank, clunk!. Aroner, M.   **E**
Clinton, Catherine
The Black soldier (5 and up)   **355**
Hold the flag high (2-4)   **973.7**
(comp) I, too, sing America. See I, too, sing
   America   **811.008**
The cloak. Jaffe, N.
   In Jaffe, N. and Zeitlin, S. J. The cow of no
   color: riddle stories and justice tales from
   around the world p23-26   **398.2**
Clocks and watches
Borden, L. Sea clocks (3-6)   **526**
Duffy, T. The clock (4 and up)   **681.1**
Gardner, R. It's about time! Science projects
   (3-6)   **529**
Koscielniak, B. About time (3-5)   **529**
Lasky, K. The man who made time travel (3-5)
   526
Maestro, B. The story of clocks and calendars
   (3-6)   **529**
Older, J. Telling time (k-3)   **529**
Fiction
Danziger, P. It's Justin Time, Amber Brown
   E
Harper, D. Telling time with Big Mama Cat
   E
Clockwork. Pullman, P.   **Fic**
Cloning
Nardo, D. Cloning [Science on the edge series]
   (5 and up)   **660.6**
Clorinda. Kinerk, R.   **E**
Close your eyes. Banks, K.   **E**

Clothing and dress
   See also Children's clothing; Coats; Cos-
   tume
Corey, S. You forgot your skirt, Amelia Bloom-
   er (k-2)   **92**
Rowland-Warne, L. Costume (4 and up)   **391**
Fiction
Brett, J. The hat   **E**
Chodos-Irvine, M. Ella Sarah gets dressed   **E**
Fleming, C. This is the baby   **E**
Gilson, J. Bug in a rug (2-4)   **Fic**
Kuskin, K. Under my hood I have a hat   **E**
Neitzel, S. The jacket I wear in the snow   **E**
Taback, S. Joseph had a little overcoat   **E**
Valckx, C. Lizette's green sock   **E**
Vigil-Piñón, E. Marina's muumuu   **E**
The cloud book. De Paola, T.   **551.57**
Cloud dance. Locker, T.   **E**
Cloud forests
Collard, S. B., III. Forest in the clouds (2-4)
   577.3
Cloud weavers. Krasno, R.   **398.2**
Clouds
Branley, F. M. Down comes the rain (k-3)
   551.57
De Paola, T. The cloud book (k-3)   **551.57**
Fiction
Locker, T. Cloud dance   **E**
Wiesner, D. Sector 7   **E**
The clouds above. Crane, J.   **741.5**
Cloudy with a chance of meatballs. Barrett, J.
   In You read to me & I'll read to you; 20th-
   century stories to share p97-104   **E**
Clowes, Martin
(jt. auth) Woodford, C. Atoms and molecules
   540
The clown of God. De Paola, T.   **398.2**
Clowns
Becker, H. Funny business (5 and up)   **792**
Burgess, R. Be a clown! (3-6)   **791.3**
Fiction
Dodds, D. A. Where's Pup?   **E**
Clutton-Brock, Juliet
Cat (4 and up)   **599.75**
Cneut, Carll
(il) Swope, S. Jack and the seven deadly giants
   Fic
Coal miners
Fiction
Kehret, P. The ghost's grave (5 and up)   **Fic**
A **coal** miner's bride. Bartoletti, S. C.   **Fic**
Coal mines and mining
Bartoletti, S. C. Growing up in coal country (5
   and up)   **331.3**
Fiction
Almond, D. Kit's wilderness (5 and up)   **Fic**
Bartoletti, S. C. A coal miner's bride (4 and up)
   Fic
Easton, R. A real American (5 and up)   **Fic**
Hughes, P. The breaker boys (5 and up)   **Fic**
Coalson, Glo
(il) Scott, A. H. Brave as a mountain lion   **E**
(il) Scott, A. H. On Mother's lap   **E**

Colón, Raúl—*Continued*
 (il) Winter, J. Roberto Clemente **92**
 (il) Yolen, J. Mightier than the sword **398.2**
Colonial and revolutionary times. Burgan, M.
  973.2

Colonial craftsmen [series]
 Fisher, L. E. The architects **720.9**
 Fisher, L. E. The blacksmiths **682**
 Fisher, L. E. The cabinetmakers **684.1**
 Fisher, L. E. The doctors **610.9**
 Fisher, L. E. The hatters **646**
 Fisher, L. E. The limners **759.13**
 Fisher, L. E. The papermakers **676**
 Fisher, L. E. The peddlers **381**
 Fisher, L. E. The printers **686.2**
 Fisher, L. E. The shoemakers **685**
 Fisher, L. E. The silversmiths **739.2**
 Fisher, L. E. The tanners **675**
 Fisher, L. E. The weavers **677**
 Fisher, L. E. The wigmakers **391**

Colonial craftsmen and the beginnings of American industry. Tunis, E. **680**
Colonial days. King, D. C. **973.2**

Colonial leaders [series]
 Hinman, B. Benjamin Banneker **92**
Colonial living. Tunis, E. **973.2**

Colonial Williamsburg (Williamsburg, Va.)
 Chorao, K. D is for drums (k-3) **975.5**

Color
 Crews, D. Freight train **E**
 De Paola, T. Marco's colors **E**
 Ehlert, L. Color farm **E**
 Ehlert, L. Color zoo **E**
 Farndon, J. Color (3-6) **535.6**
 Fleming, D. Lunch **E**
 Gardner, R. Dazzling science projects with light
  and color (4-6) **535**
 Hoban, T. Colors everywhere **E**
 Hoban, T. Is it red? Is it yellow? Is it blue?
  E
 Hoban, T. Of colors and things **E**
 Levine, S. The optics book (4 and up) **535**
 McMillan, B. Growing colors **E**
 Milich, Z. City colors **E**
 Pinkney, S. L. A rainbow all around me **E**
 Seeger, L. V. Lemons are not red **E**
 Shahan, S. Spicy hot colors: colores picantes
  E
 Shannon, G. White is for blueberry **E**
 Sís, P. Ballerina! **E**
 Thong, R. Red is a dragon **E**
 Wood, A. The deep blue sea **E**
 See/See also pages in the following book(s):
 Luxbacher, I. The jumbo book of art (4 and up)
  702.8

Fiction
 Catalanotto, P. Kitten red, yellow, blue **E**
 Dewan, T. Bing: paint day **E**
 Dumont, J.-F. A blue so blue **E**
 Dunbar, P. Flyaway Katie **E**
 Feiffer, K. Double pink **E**
 Guy, G. F. Siesta **E**
 Lionni, L. Little blue and little yellow **E**
 Martin, B. A beasty story **E**

 Martin, B. Brown bear, brown bear what do you
  see? **E**
 Ziefert, H. Lunchtime for a purple snake **E**
 Zolotow, C. Mr. Rabbit and the lovely present
  E

Poetry
 Larios, J. H. Yellow elephant **811**
 O'Neill, M. L. D. Hailstones and halibut bones
  (k-3) **811**
Color farm. Ehlert, L. **E**
Color in art
 Gogh, V. v. Vincent's colors (k-3) **759.9492**
Color me a rhyme. Yolen, J. **811**
Color me dark. McKissack, P. C. **Fic**
The **color** of home. Hoffman, M. **E**
The **color** of my words. Joseph, L. **Fic**
Color zoo. Ehlert, L. **E**
Colorado
 Altman, L. J. Colorado
  In It's my state! [series] **973**
 Blashfield, J. F. Colorado
  In America the beautiful, second series
  973
 Elias, M. Colorado
  In World Almanac Library of the States series
  973

Fiction
 Avi. The secret school (4 and up) **Fic**
 Barron, T. A. High as a hawk **E**
 Ferris, J. Much ado about Grubstake (5 and up)
  Fic
 Oswald, N. Nothing here but stones (5 and up)
  Fic

Colorado River (Colo.-Mexico)
 Waldman, S. The last river (3-6) **978**
Colorful, captivating coral reefs. Patent, D. H.
  577.7

Colors everywhere. Hoban, T. **E**
Colosseum (Rome, Italy)
 Nardo, D. Roman amphitheaters (5 and up)
  725

Coltrane, John
 (jt. auth) Raschka, C. John Coltrane's Giant
  steps **E**
Colum, Padraic
 The Golden Fleece and the heroes who lived be-
  fore Achilles (5 and up) **292**
Columba, Saint, 521-597
About
 Brown, D. Across a dark and wild sea [biogra-
  phy of Saint Columba] (2-5) **92**
Columbia (Space shuttle)
 Cole, M. D. The Columbia space shuttle disaster
  (4 and up) **629.44**
Columbia. See Cole, M. D. The Columbia space
  shuttle disaster **629.44**
The **Columbia** space shuttle disaster. Cole, M. D.
  629.44

Columbus, Christopher
About
 Fritz, J. Where do you think you're going,
  Christopher Columbus? (2-4) **92**

Composition (Rhetoric) *See* Rhetoric

Compost
  Glaser, L. Compost! (k-2)   **363.7**
  Lavies, B. Compost critters (4 and up)
    591.7

Compost critters. Lavies, B.   **591.7**

Compton's encyclopedia & fact-index   **031**

Compton's yearbook. See Compton's encyclopedia & fact-index   **031**

Compulsory labor *See* Slavery

Computation, Approximate *See* Approximate computation

Computer-assisted instruction
  Eisenberg, M. Teaching information & technology skills   **025.5**

Computer-based information systems *See* Information systems

Computer games
    Fiction
  Pratchett, T. Only you can save mankind (5 and up)   **Fic**

Computer modeling *See* Computer simulation

Computer models *See* Computer simulation

Computer network resources *See* Internet resources

Computer networks
  See also Internet
  Gordon, R. S. Teaching the Internet in libraries
    025.04

Computer simulation
  Baker, C. W. Scientific visualization (5 and up)
    006

Computer software industry
  Woog, A. Bill Gates (4 and up)   **92**

Computers
  See also Data processing
  Barrett, J. R. Teaching and learning about computers   **004**
  Baxter, R. Computers (3-5)   **004**
    History
  Sherman, J. The history of the personal computer (4 and up)   **004**

Computers and children
  Haycock, K. Neal-Schuman authoritative guide to kids' search engines, subject directories, and portals   **025.04**

Con artists *See* Swindlers and swindling

Concentration camps
  See also Holocaust, 1933-1945; Japanese Americans—Evacuation and relocation, 1942-1945

Concepts
  See also Shape
  Freymann, S. Food for thought   **E**

The **conch** bearer. Divakaruni, C. B.   **Fic**

The **concise** AACR2. Gorman, M.   **025.3**

Concord (Mass.), Battle of, 1775
  Fradin, D. B. Let it begin here! (2-4)   **973.3**
  Krensky, S. Paul Revere's midnight ride (2-4)
    973.3

Concorde. Murdico, S. J.   **629.133**

Conduct of life
  MacGregor, C. Think for yourself (3-6)   **170**
  McIntyre, T. The behavior survival guide for kids (5 and up)   **158**
  Rimm, S. B. See Jane win for girls (5 and up)
    305.23
  Rosenthal, A. K. Cookies   **E**
    Fiction
  Muth, J. J. The three questions   **E**
    Literary collections
  I can make a difference   **808.8**

Cone, Molly
  Come back, salmon (3-6)   **639.3**

Conejito. MacDonald, M. R.   **398.2**

Conestoga wagons. Ammon, R.   **388.3**

Confectionery
  Kreger, C. Jelly beans (2-4)   **641.8**

Confessions of a closet Catholic. Littman, S.
    Fic

Conflict, Ethnic *See* Ethnic relations

Conford, Ellen
  Annabel the actress starring in "Gorilla my dreams" (2-4)   **Fic**
  A case for Jenny Archer (2-4)   **Fic**
  In your hat
    In Shelf life: stories by the book   **S C**

Confucianism
  See/See also pages in the following book(s):
  Osborne, M. P. One world, many religions (4 and up)   **200**

Confucius
    About
  Freedman, R. Confucius (4 and up)   **92**

Congo (Brazzaville) *See* Congo (Republic)

Congo (Republic)
  Heale, J. Democratic Republic of the Congo (5 and up)   **967.51**
  Willis, T. Democratic Republic of the Congo (5 and up)   **967.51**
    Fiction
  Smith, R. Cryptid hunters (5 and up)   **Fic**

Congress (U.S.) *See* United States. Congress

The **Congress**. Horn, G.   **328**

The **conjure** brother. McKissack, P. C.
  In Beware!; R.L. Stine picks his favorite scary stories p19-33   **808.8**
  In McKissack, P. C. The dark-thirty; Southern tales of the supernatural p66-77   **S C**

The **Conjure** wives
  In Diane Goode's book of scary stories & songs p42-47   **398.2**

The **conjure** wives. MacDonald, M. R.
  In MacDonald, M. R. When the lights go out; twenty scary tales to tell p79-85
    372.6

Conjuring *See* Magic tricks

Conlan, Kathy
  Under the ice (4 and up)   **578.7**

Conly, Jane Leslie
  Crazy lady! (5 and up)   **Fic**
  Racso and the rats of NIMH (4 and up)   **Fic**
  While no one was watching (5 and up)   **Fic**

Connecticut

Bailer, D. Connecticut
In World Almanac Library of the States series
973

Burgan, M. Connecticut
In It's my state! [series] **973**

McNair, S. Connecticut
In America the beautiful, second series
973

Sherrow, V. Connecticut
In Celebrate the states **973**

Fiction

Dalgliesh, A. The courage of Sarah Noble (2-4)
Fic

History—1600-1775, Colonial period—Fiction
Speare, E. G. The witch of Blackbird Pond (6 and up) **Fic**

Connecting fathers, children, and reading. Herb, S. **028.5**

Connery, Jeff
(il) Levine, S. Bathtub science **507.8**

Connie Hunter Williams, psychic teacher. Cabot, M.
In Friends; stories about new friends, old friends, and unexpectedly true friends
S C

Conniff, Richard
Rats! (3-6) **599.35**

Connolly, Maureen, 1934-1969
See/See also pages in the following book(s):
Krull, K. Lives of the athletes (4 and up)
920

Connor, Leslie
Miss Bridie chose a shovel **E**

Conover, Chris
Over the hills & far away **E**

Conrad, Pam
My Daniel (5 and up) **Fic**
Our house (4 and up) **S C**
Prairie songs (5 and up) **Fic**
Stonewords (5 and up) **Fic**

Conservation movement *See* Environmental movement

Conservation of forests *See* Forest conservation

Conservation of natural resources
See also Forest conservation; Nature conservation; Wildlife conservation

Conservationists
Hines, G. Midnight forests [biography of Gifford Pinchot] (3-5) **92**

Constellations
Mitton, J. Once upon a starry night (k-3)
523.8
Mitton, J. Zodiac (2-4) **398**
Rey, H. A. Find the constellations (3-6)
523.8
VanCleave, J. P. Janice VanCleave's constellations for every kid (4 and up) **523.8**

The **Constitution**. Finkelman, P. **342**

Constitutional history
Finkelman, P. The Constitution (4 and up)
342

United States
Fritz, J. Shhh! we're writing the Constitution (2-4) **342**
Maestro, B. A more perfect union (2-4) **342**

Constitutional rights *See* Civil rights

Construction *See* Building

Construction equipment
Fiction
Rockwell, A. F. Good morning, Digger **E**

Construction workers
Fiction
Roth, S. L. Hard hat area **E**
Zimmerman, A. G. Dig! **E**

Construction zone. Hoban, T. **621.8**
Construction zone. Hudson, C. W. **690**

Consumer credit
See also Credit cards

Containers, Box *See* Boxes

Contaminated food *See* Food contamination

The **contest**. Hogrogian, N. **398.2**

Contests
Fiction
Catalanotto, P. Emily's art **E**
Lester, H. Three cheers for Tacky **E**

The **Continuum** encyclopedia of children's literature **028.5**

Contributions to the study of science fiction and fantasy [series]
Sands, K. Back in the spaceship again
016.8

Conundrums *See* Riddles

Conversation
Verdick, E. Words are not for hurting (k-2)
177

Convicts *See* Prisoners

The **convicts**. Lawrence, I. **Fic**

Conway, David
The most important gift of all **E**

Cook, Bernadine
The little fish that got away **E**

Cook, Deanna F.
Kids' pumpkin projects (2-4) **745.5**

Cook, James, 1728-1779
Fiction
Hesse, K. Stowaway (5 and up) **Fic**

Cook, Sally
Good night pillow fight **E**

Cook, Scott
(il) Doucet, S. A. Lapin plays possum: trickster tales from the Louisiana Bayou **398.2**
(il) Fox, F. G. Jean Laffite and the big ol' whale **E**
(il) Van Laan, N. With a whoop and a holler
398

Cook-a-doodle-doo!. Stevens, J. **E**

The **cookcamp**. Paulsen, G. **Fic**

Cooke, Trish
Full, full, full of love **E**

Cookies
MacLeod, E. Bake and make amazing cookies (4-6) **641.8**

Cookies—*Continued*
Rosenthal, A. K. Cookies E

Fiction
Hutchins, P. The doorbell rang E
Lewis, P. No more cookies! E

Cooking

See also Baking; Eggs; Vegetarian cooking
Arnold, A. The adventurous chef: Alexis Soyer (3-5) **92**
Braman, A. N. Kids around the world cook! (4-6) **641.5**
Cobb, V. Science experiments you can eat (5 and up) **507.8**
Crespo, C. The secret life of food (4 and up) **641.5**
D'Amico, J. The coming to America cookbook (5 and up) **641.5**
D'Amico, J. The healthy body cookbook (4 and up) **641.5**
D'Amico, J. The math chef (4-6) **641.5**
D'Amico, J. The science chef (4-6) **641.3**
Easy menu ethnic cookbooks [series] (5 and up) **641.5**
Gillies, J. The Kids Can Press jumbo cookbook (4 and up) **641.5**
Goss, G. Blue moon soup (4-6) **641.8**
Hopkinson, D. Fannie in the kitchen (k-3) **641.5**
Ichord, L. F. Skillet bread, sourdough, and vinegar pie (3-5) **641.5**
Katzen, M. Salad people and more real recipes (k-3) **641.5**
Kids' first cookbook (k-3) **641.5**
Lagasse, E. Emeril's there's a chef in my family! (5 and up) **641.5**
Locricchio, M. The international cookbook for kids (5 and up) **641.5**
MacLeod, E. Chock full of chocolate (4-6) **641.6**
Pentland, P. Kitchen science (4 and up) **641.3**
Taylor, G. George Crum and the Saratoga chip (2-4) **92**
Walker, B. M. The Little House cookbook (5 and up) **641.5**
Warshaw, H. The sleepover cookbook (4 and up) **641.5**
Webb, L. S. Holidays of the world cookbook for students (5 and up) **641.5**
See/See also pages in the following book(s):
Cook, D. F. Kids' pumpkin projects (2-4) **745.5**
Erlbach, A. Merry Christmas, everywhere! (k-3) **394.26**
Gibbons, G. The berry book (k-3) **634**
Griffin, M. The sleepover book (3-6) **793.2**
King, D. C. Colonial days (3-6) **973.2**
King, D. C. Pioneer days (3-6) **978**
King, D. C. Wild West days (3-6) **978**
King, D. C. World War II days (3-6) **940.53**
Souter, G. Perfect parties (2-5) **793.2**

Fiction
Cazet, D. The perfect pumpkin pie E
Chamberlin, M. Mama Panya's pancakes E

De Paola, T. Pascual and the kitchen angels E
Fusco Castaldo, N. Pizza for the queen E
Hester, D. Grandma Lena's big ol' turnip E
Park, L. S. Bee-bim bop! E
Reynolds, A. Chicks and salsa E
Stevens, J. Cook-a-doodle-doo! E

Cooks and prophecies. Aiken, J.
In Aiken, J. Shadows and moonshine; stories S C

Cool beaded jewelry. Scheunemann, P. **745.58**
Cool chemistry concoctions. Rhatigan, J. **540.7**
Cool clay projects. Scheunemann, P. **731.4**
Cool crafts [series]
Price, P. S. Cool rubber stamp art **761**
Price, P. S. Cool scrapbooks **745.593**
Scheunemann, P. Cool beaded jewelry **745.58**
Scheunemann, P. Cool clay projects **731.4**
Wagner, L. Cool melt & pour soap **668**
Wagner, L. Cool painted stuff **745.7**
A **cool** drink of water. Kerley, B. **363.6**
Cool melons—turn to frogs!: the life and poems of Issa [Kobayashi] Gollub, M. **92**
Cool melt & pour soap. Wagner, L. **668**
A **cool** moonlight. Johnson, A. **Fic**
Cool painted stuff. Wagner, L. **745.7**
Cool rubber stamp art. Price, P. S. **761**
Cool salsa (5 and up) **811.008**
Cool scrapbooks. Price, P. S. **745.593**
Cool story programs for the school-age crowd. Reid, R. **028.5**

Cooley, Brian
Make-a-saurus (4 and up) **567.9**

Coolies. Yin E

Cooling, Wendy
D is for Dahl (4 and up) **823.009**

Cooney, Barbara
Chanticleer and the fox E
Eleanor [biography of Eleanor Roosevelt] (k-3) **92**
Miss Rumphius E
(il) Hall, D. Ox-cart man E
(il) Houston, G. The year of the perfect Christmas tree E
(il) McLerran, A. Roxaboxen E
(il) Ray, M. L. Basket moon E
(il) Tortillitas para mamá and other nursery rhymes. See Tortillitas para mamá and other nursery rhymes **398.8**

Coons, Jason
(il) Levine, S. The optics book **535**

Cooper, Chris
Arsenic
In The Elements **546**

Cooper, Elisha
Dance! (2-4) **792.8**
A good night walk E
Ice cream (k-3) **637**
Magic thinks big E

Cooper, Floyd
Coming home [biography of Langston Hughes] (k-3) **92**
Jump! [biography of Michael Jordan] (k-3) **92**
Mandela (2-4) **92**
(il) Greenfield, E. Grandpa's face **E**
(il) Grimes, N. Meet Danitra Brown **811**
(jt. auth) Haskins, J. African beginnings **960**
(il) Haskins, J. Bound for America **326**
(il) McKissack, P. C. Ma Dear's aprons **E**
(il) Merrill, J. The Girl Who Loved Caterpillars **E**
(il) Pass it on. See Pass it on **811.008**
(il) Schroeder, A. Satchmo's blues **E**
(il) Thomas, J. C. Brown honey in broomwheat tea **811**
(il) Thomas, J. C. I have heard of a land **E**
(il) Vander Zee, R. Mississippi morning **E**

Cooper, Gail
New virtual field trips **025.5**

Cooper, Garry
(jt. auth) Cooper, G. New virtual field trips **025.5**

Cooper, Helen
Chestnut gray
In Horse tales **S C**
Pumpkin soup **E**

Cooper, Ilene
Jewish holidays all year round (4 and up) **296.4**

Cooper, Martha
(il) Waters, K. Lion dancer: Ernie Wan's Chinese New Year **394.26**

Cooper, Michael L.
Dust to eat (4 and up) **973.917**

Cooper, Robert
Croatia (5 and up) **949.7**

Cooper, Susan
The Boggart (4 and up) **Fic**
Frog **E**
The grey king (5 and up) **Fic**
King of shadows (5 and up) **Fic**
The magician's boy (2-4) **Fic**
Over sea, under stone (5 and up) **Fic**
The silver cow (1-4) **398.2**

Cooper, Susan, 1935-
See/See also pages in the following book(s):
Ellis, S. From reader to writer **372.6**

Coots, John Frederick
Santa Claus is comin' to town (k-3) **782.42**

Copeland, Gregory
(il) Collier, J. L. The Tecumseh you never knew **92**

Copernicus, Nicolaus, 1473-1543
About
Fradin, D. B. Nicolaus Copernicus (3-6) **92**
Ingram, S. Nicolaus Copernicus (5 and up) **92**

Copper. Lisle, R. **Fic**

Coppinger, Tom
Curse in reverse **E**

Coppola, Angela
(il) Chryssicas, M. K. I love yoga **613.7**

Copsey, Sue
(jt. auth) Kindersley, B. Children just like me **305.23**

Copyright
See also Fair use (Copyright)
Butler, R. P. Copyright for teachers and librarians **346.04**
Complete copyright **346.04**
Crews, K. D. Copyright law for librarians and educators **346.04**

Copyright essentials for librarians and educators. See Crews, K. D. Copyright law for librarians and educators **346.04**

Copyright for teachers and librarians. Butler, R. P. **346.04**

Copyright law for librarians and educators. Crews, K. D. **346.04**

Coral reef. Cerullo, M. M. **577.7**

Coral reefs and islands
Arnold, C. A walk on the Great Barrier Reef (3-5) **578.7**
Cerullo, M. M. Coral reef (4 and up) **577.7**
Collard, S. B., III. On the coral reefs (4-6) **577.7**
Collard, S. B., III. One night in the Coral Sea (3-5) **593.6**
Patent, D. H. Colorful, captivating coral reefs (2-4) **577.7**
Fiction
Barner, B. Fish wish **E**
Blackstone, S. Secret seahorse **E**

Coraline. Gaiman, N. **Fic**

Corals
Collard, S. B., III. One night in the Coral Sea (3-5) **593.6**

Corazones Valientes (Organization)
Reiser, L. Tortillas and lullabies. Tortillas y cancioncitas **E**

Corbett, Sue
Free baseball (5 and up) **Fic**

Corbishley, Mike
Ancient Rome (5 and up) **937**
The Middle Ages (5 and up) **940.1**

Corder, Zizou
Lionboy (4 and up) **Fic**

Cordi, Kevin
(jt. auth) Sima, J. Raising voices **027.62**

Cordsen, Carol Foskett
The milkman **E**

Corduroy. Freeman, D. **E**

Coretta Scott King Award
The Coretta Scott King Awards book, 1970-1999 **028.5**
Stephens, C. G. Coretta Scott King Award books **028.5**

Coretta Scott King Award books. Stephens, C. G. **028.5**

The **Coretta** Scott King Awards book, 1970-1999 **028.5**

Corey, Shana
Players in pigtails **E**
You forgot your skirt, Amelia Bloomer (k-2) **92**

Counting

See also Numbers

Alda, A. Arlene Alda's 1 2 3	E
Anderson, L. Tea for ten	E
Anno, M. Anno's counting book	E
Baker, K. Big fat hen	398.8
Baker, K. Quack and count	E
Bang, M. Ten, nine, eight	E
Barry, F. Duckie's ducklings	E
Bates, I. Five little ducks (k-2)	782.42
Blackstone, S. My granny went to market	E
Brown, M. W. Another important book	E
Brown, R. Ten seeds	E
Brusca, M. C. Three friends. Tres amigos	E
Carle, E. 10 little rubber ducks	E
Carter, D. A. One red dot	E
Cave, K. One child, one seed	E
Chaconas, D. One little mouse	E
Christelow, E. Five little monkeys jumping on the bed	E
Doyle, M. One, two, three O'Leary	E
Elya, S. M. Eight animals on the town	E
Falwell, C. Turtle splash!	E
Feelings, M. Moja means one	E
Fleming, D. Count!	E
Freymann, S. Food for thought	E
Freymann, S. One lonely sea horse	E
Geisert, A. Pigs from 1 to 10	E
Geisert, A. Roman numerals I to MM (k-3)	513
Giganti, P., Jr. Each orange had 8 slices	E
Giganti, P., Jr. How many snails?	E
Golding, K. Counting kids	E
Guy, G. F. Fiesta!	E
Hoban, T. 26 letters and 99 cents	E
Hoban, T. Let's count	E
Huck, C. S. A creepy countdown	E
Hutchins, P. 1 hunter	E
Hutchins, P. Ten red apples	E
Johnson, S. City by numbers	E
Jonas, A. Splash!	E
Katz, K. Mommy hugs	E
Katz, K. Ten tiny tickles	E
Keats, E. J. Over in the meadow	E
Kellogg, S. Give the dog a bone (k-3)	782.42
Langstaff, J. M. Over in the meadow (k-2)	782.42
Lee, H. V. 1, 2, 3 go! (k-3)	495.1
Lessac, F. Island counting 1 2 3	E
Leuck, L. One witch	E
Lobel, A. One lighthouse, one moon	E
Macdonald, S. Look whooo's counting	E
Mannis, C. A. One leaf rides the wind	E
Martin, B. Chicka chicka 1, 2, 3	E
Merriam, E. 12 ways to get to 11 (k-3)	510
Milich, Z. City 1 2 3	E
Mora, P. Uno, dos, tres: one, two, three	E
Morales, Y. Just a minute (k-3)	398.2
Moss, L. Zin! zin! zin! a violin	E
Murphy, S. J. Coyotes all around (1-3)	519
Murphy, S. J. Jack the builder (k-1)	513
Murphy, S. J. Just enough carrots (k-1)	513
Murphy, S. J. Leaping lizards	E
Murphy, S. J. Mall mania (k-2)	513

Newcome, Z. Head, shoulders, knees, and toes	E
Pallotta, J. Ocean counting	E
Pomeroy, D. One potato	E
Raschka, C. Five for a little one	E
Reiser, L. Ten puppies	E
Rockwell, A. F. 100 school days	E
Rose, D. L. One nighttime sea	E
Rubin, A. How many fish?	E
Saul, C. P. Barn cat	E
Sayre, A. P. One is a snail, ten is a crab	E
Schertle, A. 1, 2, I love you	E
Schmandt-Besserat, D. The history of counting (4 and up)	513
Schumaker, W. In my garden	E
Schwartz, D. M. On beyond a million (2-4)	513
Sendak, M. One was Johnny	E
Shea, P. D. Ten mice for Tet! (k-3)	394.26
Tang, G. Math fables (k-1)	513
Tang, G. Math-terpieces (2-4)	510
Thompson, L. Little Quack	E
Thong, R. One is a drummer	E
Tudor, T. 1 is one	E
Wadsworth, O. A. Over in the meadow	E
Walsh, E. S. Mouse count	E
Wells, R. Emily's first 100 days of school	E
Williams, S. Let's go visiting	E
Wilson, A. Over in the grasslands	E
Wilson, K. A frog in the bog	E
Winter, J. Josefina	E
Wise, W. Ten sly piranhas	E
Wong, J. S. Hide & seek	E
Wormell, C. Teeth, tails, & tentacles	E
Yolen, J. Count me a rhyme (3-5)	811
Zelinsky, P. O. Knick-knack paddywhack! (k-3)	782.42
Ziefert, H. A dozen ducklings lost and found	E

Counting books *See* Counting

Counting kids. Golding, K.   E

Countries of the world [series]

Kazem, H. Afghanistan	958.1
NgCheong-Lum, R. France	944

Country and western music *See* Country music

The **country** bunny and the little gold shoes. Heyward, D.   E

Country life

See also Mountain life

Barbour, K. Mr. Williams	E
Crews, D. Bigmama's (k-3)	92

Fiction

Birney, B. G. The seven wonders of Sassafras Springs (3-6)	Fic
Burch, R. Ida Early comes over the mountain (4 and up)	Fic
Creech, S. Ruby Holler (4 and up)	Fic
Dorros, A. City chicken	E
Dudley, D. L. The bicycle man (4-6)	Fic
Guest, E. H. Iris and Walter	E
Hobbs, V. Defiance (5 and up)	Fic
Hopkinson, D. Saving Strawberry Farm	E
Lindbergh, R. The visit	E
Martin, B. Barn dance!	E

Country life—Fiction—*Continued*
Morgan, N. Chicken friend (5 and up)   **Fic**
Peck, R. Here lies the librarian   **Fic**
Peck, R. The teacher's funeral (5 and up)
                                            Fic
Rylant, C. Christmas in the country   **E**
Schertle, A. Down the road   **E**
Sorensen, V. E. Miracles on Maple Hill (4 and
    up)   **Fic**
Waddell, M. Tiny's big adventure   **E**
Country music
George-Warren, H. Honky-tonk heroes & hillbil-
    ly angels (3-6)   **920**
    Fiction
Paterson, K. Come sing, Jimmy Jo (5 and up)
                                            Fic
A **country** schoolhouse. Barasch, L.   **E**
The **country** under the water. Curry, J. L.
    In Curry, J. L. The wonderful sky boat and
        other Native American tales of the
        Southeast p121-24   **398.2**
Courage
    Fiction
Hearne, B. G. Seven brave women   **E**
Morgan, M. Brave, brave mouse   **E**
Sperry, A. Call it courage (5 and up)   **Fic**
Spinelli, J. Wringer (4 and up)   **Fic**
Steig, W. Brave Irene   **E**
The **courage** of Sarah Noble. Dalgliesh, A.
                                            Fic
The **courageous** princess. Espinosa, R.   **741.5**
The **courier**. Delacre, L.
    In Delacre, L. Golden tales; myths, legends,
        and folktales from Latin America p65-68
                                            398.2
Courlander, Harold
    Cow-tail switch, and other West African stories
        (4-6)   **398.2**
Court, Rob
    How to draw cars and trucks (4-6)   **743**
The **court** jester's last wish. Jaffe, N.
    In Jaffe, N. and Zeitlin, S. J. While standing
        on one foot; puzzle stories and wisdom
        tales from the Jewish tradition p23-25
                                            296.1
The **court** of the stone children. Cameron, E.
                                            Fic
Courts and courtiers
    See also Princesses; Queens
    Aliki. A medieval feast (2-5)   **940.1**
Courtship (Animal behavior) *See* Animal court-
    ship
Cousins, Lucy
    Hooray for fish!   **E**
Cousins
    Fiction
Allison, J. Gilda Joyce, psychic investigator (5
    and up)   **Fic**
Boles, P. M. Little divas (5 and up)   **Fic**
Greenwald, S. Rosy Cole's worst ever, best yet
    tour of New York City (3-5)   **Fic**
Hamilton, V. Cousins (5 and up)   **Fic**
Keller, H. What a hat!   **E**
Koss, A. G. Strike two (4 and up)   **Fic**

White, R. Belle Prater's boy (5 and up)   **Fic**
Wright, B. R. Crandall's castle (4 and up)
                                            Fic
Cousins in the castle. Wallace, B. B.   **Fic**
Covered wagons, bumpy trails. Kay, V.   **E**
Coverlets *See* Quilts
Coville, Bruce
    The guardian of memory
        In A Glory of unicorns p1-28   **S C**
    Jennifer Murdley's toad (4-6)   **Fic**
    Jeremy Thatcher, dragon hatcher (4-6)   **Fic**
    Juliet Dove, Queen of Love (4-6)   **Fic**
    A life in miniature
        In Swan sister; fairy tales retold   **S C**
    The skull of truth (4-6)   **Fic**
    Thor's wedding day (4 and up)   **Fic**
    William Shakespeare's A midsummer night's
        dream (5 and up)   **822.3**
    William Shakespeare's Hamlet (5 and up)
                                            822.3
    William Shakespeare's Macbeth (5 and up)
                                            822.3
    William Shakespeare's Romeo and Juliet (5 and
        up)   **822.3**
    William Shakespeare's Twelfth night (5 and up)
                                            822.3
    (comp) A Glory of unicorns. See A Glory of
        unicorns   **S C**
Coville, Katherine
    Story hour
        In A Glory of unicorns p97-112   **S C**
    (il) San Souci, R. More short & shivery
                                            398.2
    (il) San Souci, R. Short & shivery   **398.2**
The **cow**. Kimmel, E. A.
    In Kimmel, E. A. The adventures of Hershel
        of Ostropol p44-51   **398.2**
The **cow** of no color. Jaffe, N.
    In Jaffe, N. and Zeitlin, S. J. The cow of no
        color: riddle stories and justice tales from
        around the world p10-13   **398.2**
The **cow** of no color: riddle stories and justice
    tales from around the world. Jaffe, N.
                                            398.2
The **cow-tail** switch. Courlander, H.
    In Courlander, H. and Herzog, G. Cow-tail
        switch, and other West African stories
        p5-12   **398.2**
Cow-tail switch, and other West African stories.
    Courlander, H.   **398.2**
The **coward**. Kimmel, E. A.
    In Kimmel, E. A. Sword of the samurai; ad-
        venture stories from Japan p23-30
                                            Fic
Cowboy country. Scott, A. H.   **978**
Cowboy dreams. Appelt, K.   **E**
Cowboy José. Elya, S. M.   **E**
Cowboy Kid. Eilenberg, M.   **E**
Cowgirl Kate and Cocoa. Silverman, E.   **E**
Cowhands
    Ancona, G. Charro (3-6)   **972**
    Freedman, R. In the days of the vaqueros (4 and
        up)   **636.2**

Cuffari, Richard
(il) Cohen, B. Thank you, Jackie Robinson
    Fic

Cullen, Catherine Ann
Thirsty baby   **E**

Cullinan, Bernice E.
(ed) The Continuum encyclopedia of children's literature. See The Continuum encyclopedia of children's literature   **028.5**

Cullum, Carolyn N.
The storytime sourcebook   **027.62**

Cultural anthropology *See* Ethnology

Cultural atlas for young people [series]
Corbishley, M. Ancient Rome   **937**
Corbishley, M. The Middle Ages   **940.1**
Powell, A. Ancient Greece   **938**
Wood, M. Ancient America   **970.01**

Cultural pluralism *See* Multiculturalism

Culture crafts [series]
Temko, F. Traditional crafts from Africa
    745.5
Temko, F. Traditional crafts from China
    745.5
Temko, F. Traditional crafts from Japan
    745.5
Temko, F. Traditional crafts from Mexico and Central America   **745.5**
Temko, F. Traditional crafts from native North America   **745.5**
Temko, F. Traditional crafts from the Caribbean
    745.5

Culture in India. Guile, M.   **954**
Culture in Malaysia. Guile, M.   **959.5**
Culture in Vietnam. Guile, M.   **959.7**

Cultures of the past [series]
Stein, R. C. The Aztec empire   **972**

Cultures of the world [series]
Abazov, R. Tajikistan   **958.6**
Barlas, R. Bahamas   **972.96**
Barlas, R. Latvia   **947.9**
Barlas, R. Uganda   **967.6**
Beliaev, E. Dagestan   **947.5**
Berg, E. Senegal   **966.3**
Brown, R. V. Tunisia   **961.1**
Burbank, J. Nepal   **954.96**
Cheong-Lum, R. N. Haiti   **972.94**
Cooper, R. Croatia   **949.7**
DuBois, J. Colombia   **986.1**
DuBois, J. Greece   **949.5**
DuBois, J. Israel   **956.94**
DuBois, J. Korea   **951.9**
Esbenshade, R. S. Hungary   **943.9**
Ferroa, P. G. China   **951**
Foley, E. Dominican Republic   **972.93**
Foley, E. Ecuador   **986.6**
Foley, E. El Salvador   **972.84**
Fuller, B. Britain   **941**
Fuller, B. Germany   **943**
Gan, D. Sweden   **948.5**
Gascoigne, I. Papua New Guinea   **995.3**
Gofen, E. Argentina   **982**
Goodman, J. Thailand   **959.3**
Hassig, S. M. Iraq   **956.7**

Heale, J. Democratic Republic of the Congo
    967.51
Heale, J. Poland   **943.8**
Heale, J. Portugal   **946.9**
Heale, J. Tanzania   **967.8**
Hestler, A. Yemen   **953.3**
Janin, H. Saudi Arabia   **953.8**
Jermyn, L. Belize   **972.82**
Jermyn, L. Guyana   **988.1**
Jermyn, L. Paraguay   **989.2**
Jermyn, L. Uruguay   **989.5**
King, D. C. Azerbaijan   **947.5**
King, D. C. Kyrgyzstan   **958.4**
King, D. C. Serbia and Montenegro   **949.7**
Knowlton, M. Albania   **949.65**
Knowlton, M. Macedonia   **949.7**
Knowlton, M. Turkmenistan   **958.5**
Knowlton, M. Uzbekistan   **958.7**
Kohen, E. Spain   **946**
Kott, J. Nicaragua   **972.85**
Layton, L. Singapore   **959.57**
Levy, P. Ghana   **966.7**
Levy, P. Ireland   **941.5**
Levy, P. Nigeria   **966.9**
Levy, P. Puerto Rico   **972.95**
Levy, P. Scotland   **941.1**
Levy, P. Switzerland   **949.4**
Malcolm, P. Libya   **961.2**
McGaffey, L. Honduras   **972.83**
O'Shea, M. Kuwait   **953.67**
Pang, G.-C. Canada   **971**
Pang, G.-C. Mongolia   **951.7**
Pateman, R. Denmark   **948.9**
Pateman, R. Egypt   **962**
Pateman, R. Kenya   **967.62**
Rajendra, V. Australia   **994**
Rajendra, V. Iran   **955**
Reilly, M.-J. Mexico   **972**
Richard, C. Brazil   **981**
Rosmarin, I. South Africa   **968**
Seah, A. Vietnam   **959.704**
Seffal, R. Niger   **966.26**
Seward, P. Morocco   **964**
Seward, P. Netherlands   **949.2**
Sheehan, P. Côte d'Ivoire   **966.68**
Sheehan, P. Luxembourg   **949.35**
Sheehan, P. Moldova   **947.6**
Sheehan, S. Austria   **943.6**
Sheehan, S. Cuba   **972.91**
Sheehan, S. Guatemala   **972.81**
Sheehan, S. Jamaica   **972.92**
Sheehan, S. Malta   **945**
Sheehan, S. Pakistan   **954.91**
Sheehan, S. Zimbabwe   **968.91**
Sioras, E. Czech Republic   **943.7**
Smelt, R. New Zealand   **993**
South, C. Syria   **956.91**
Spilling, M. Cyprus   **956.93**
Spilling, M. Estonia   **947.9**
Srinivasan, R. India   **954**
Tope, L. R. R. Philippines   **959.9**
Torchinskiĭ, O. Russia   **947**
Wanasundera, N. P. Sri Lanka   **954.93**
Winter, J. K. Chile   **983**
Winter, J. K. Italy   **945**
Winter, J. K. Venezuela   **987**
Yin, S. M. Myanmar   **959.1**

Cumming, David
The Nile (4 and up)   **962**

Cummings, Linda
(comp) Talking with adventurers. See Talking with adventurers   **920**

Cummings, Michael
(il) In the hollow of your hand. See In the hollow of your hand   **782.42**

Cummings, Pat
Ananse and the lizard (k-3)   **398.2**
Angel baby   **E**
(il) MacDonald, M. R. Pickin' peas   **398.2**
(il) Stolz, M. Go fish   **Fic**
(comp) Talking with adventurers. See Talking with adventurers   **920**
(ed) Talking with artists [I-III] See Talking with artists [I-III]   **741.6**

Cummings, Priscilla
Saving Grace (5 and up)   **Fic**

Cummins, Julie
Tomboy of the air: daredevil pilot Blanche Stuart Scott (3-6)   **92**
(jt. auth) Munro, R. The inside-outside book of libraries   **027**

Cumpiano, Ina
Quinito's neighborhood   **E**

Cunha, Stephen F.
(jt. auth) Bockenhauer, M. H. Our fifty states   **973**

Cunnane, Kelly
For you are a Kenyan child   **E**

Cunnie Anansi does some good. Hamilton, V.
In Hamilton, V. A ring of tricksters; animal tales from America, the West Indies, and Africa p59-71   **398.2**

Cunnie Rabbit and Spider make a match. Hamilton, V.
In Hamilton, V. A ring of tricksters; animal tales from America, the West Indies, and Africa p75-83   **398.2**

Cunningham, Kelley
(il) Myers, T. Dark sparkle tea   **811**

Cunningham, Kevin
Arthur Ashe (5 and up)   **92**
Condoleezza Rice (5 and up)   **92**

Cupid (Roman deity) See Eros (Greek deity)

Cupid and Psyche. Craft, M.   **292**

Cupples, Pat
(il) Romanek, T. The technology book for girls and other advanced beings   **600**
(il) Wyatt, V. The math book for girls and other beings who count   **510**

Curie, Maria Sklodowska See Curie, Marie, 1867-1934

Curie, Marie, 1867-1934
About
MacLeod, E. Marie Curie (5 and up)   **92**
McClafferty, C. K. Something out of nothing [biography of Marie Curie] (5 and up)   **92**
Poynter, M. Marie Curie: discoverer of radium (4 and up)   **92**

Curiosities and wonders
See also Monsters
Blackwood, G. L. Enigmatic events (4 and up)   **904**
Curlee, L. Seven wonders of the ancient world (3-6)   **709.01**
Guinness book of records   **032.02**
Masoff, J. Oh, yuck! (4 and up)   **031.02**

Curious. Avi
In Avi. Strange happenings; five tales of transformation   **S C**

Curious George. Rey, H. A.   **E**

Curlee, Lynn
Ballpark (3-6)   **796.357**
Brooklyn Bridge (3-6)   **624.2**
Capital (3-6)   **975.3**
Liberty (3-6)   **974.7**
Parthenon (3-6)   **726**
Seven wonders of the ancient world (3-6)   **709.01**

Currency. Kummer, P. K.   **332.4**

Currey, Anna
(il) Moss, M. Don't forget I love you   **E**

Curriculum materials centers See Instructional materials centers

Currie, Stephen
Escapes from slavery (5 and up)   **326**

Currier, Katrina Saltonstall
Kai's journey to Gold Mountain (4 and up)   **Fic**

Curry, Jane Louise
The Black Canary (5 and up)   **Fic**
Hold up the sky: and other Native American tales from Texas and the Southern Plains (4 and up)   **398.2**
Contents: The beginning of the world; Coyote makes the sun; Why Bear waddles when he walks; The quarrel between Wind and Thunder; Thunderbird Woman, Skiwis, and Little Big-Belly Boy; The monsters and the flood; Coyote and the seven brothers; Slaying the monsters; Hold up the sky; Coyote and Mouse; Coyote and the smallest snake; Coyote flies with the geese; Coyote frees the buffalo; The great meatball; The fight between the animals and insects; How Rabbit stole Mountain Lion's teeth; Fox and Possum; Sendeh sings to the prairies dogs; The deserted children; Mountain lion and the four sisters; How Poor Boy won his wife; The ghost woman; The boy who killed the hill; White Fox; The tonkawa and the bear; Young Boy Chief and his sister

The wonderful sky boat and other Native American tales of the Southeast (4 and up)   **398.2**
Contents: The creation of the world; The Crying Place; First Woman; The great flood; Stonecoat; The coming of corn; The rabbit who stole fire; Rabbit's horse; Rabbit and Wildcat; How Rabbit stole Otter's coat; How Alligator's nose was broken; Heron and Hummingbird; Bigfoot bird; Opossum and her children; Fox and Crawfish; How the biters and stingers got their poison; Why the buzzard is bald; The Ice Man; Lodge Boy, Wild Boy, and the Monster Woman; Keeper of the animals; The three owls; The wonderful sky boat; The old people who turned into bears; Panther and Little Sister; The country under the water

Curry, Tom
(il) Lowell, S. The bootmaker and the elves   **398.2**
(il) Wojciechowski, S. A fine St. Patrick's day   **E**

Curry-Rood, Leah
(jt. auth) Raines, S. C. Story stretchers for infants, toddlers, and twos   **372.4**

Curse in reverse. Coppinger, T.   E
The **curse** of the blue figurine. Bellairs, J.   **Fic**
Curse of the pharaohs. Hawass, Z. A.   **932**
Curtis, Carolyn
   I took the moon for a walk   E
Curtis, Christopher Paul
   Bucking the Sarge (5 and up)   **Fic**
   Bud, not Buddy (4 and up)   **Fic**
   Mr. Chickee's funny money (3-6)   **Fic**
   The Watsons go to Birmingham—1963 (4 and up)   **Fic**
Curtis, Edward S.
   (il) Weave little stars into my sleep. See Weave little stars into my sleep   **782.42**
Curtis, Gavin
   The bat boy & his violin   E
Curtis, Jamie Lee
   I'm gonna like me   E
   Tell me again about the night I was born   E
Curtsinger, Bill
   (il) Cerullo, M. M. Life under ice   **578.7**
Curzon, Susan Carol
   Managing change   **025.1**
Cushites
   Sonneborn, L. The ancient Kushites (5 and up)   **939**
Cushman, Doug
   Inspector Hopper   E
   Mystery at the Club Sandwich   E
   (il) Lexau, J. M. Crocodile and hen   **398.2**
   (il) Simon, S. Let's try it out in the air   **533**
   (il) Simon, S. Let's try it out in the water   **532**
   (il) Williams, B. Albert's impossible toothache   E
   (il) Wood, D. What dads can't do   E
Cushman, Karen
   The ballad of Lucy Whipple (5 and up)   **Fic**
   Catherine, called Birdy (6 and up)   **Fic**
   Matilda Bone (5 and up)   **Fic**
   The midwife's apprentice (6 and up)   **Fic**
   Rodzina (5 and up)   **Fic**
Cushman, Karen, 1941-
See/See also pages in the following book(s):
   Author talk (4 and up)   **028.5**
Custer, Elizabeth Bacon
   The diary of Elizabeth Bacon Custer (5 and up)   **973.8**
Custer, George Armstrong, 1839-1876
About
   Anderson, P. C. George Armstrong Custer (4 and up)   **92**
   Custer, E. B. The diary of Elizabeth Bacon Custer (5 and up)   **973.8**
   Uschan, M. V. The Battle of the Little Bighorn (5 and up)   **973.8**
Cut from the same cloth. San Souci, R.   **398.2**
Cut-paper play!. Henry, S.   **745.54**
Cutler, Jane
   The cello of Mr. O   E
   Common sense and fowls (3-5)   **Fic**
   Rats! (3-5)   **Fic**
   Rose and Riley   E

Cuts, scrapes, scabs, and scars. Silverstein, A.   **617.1**
"Cutta cord-la". Lester, J.
   In Lester, J. The last tales of Uncle Remus p115-19   **398.2**
Cuyler, Margery
   100th day worries   E
   The bumpy little pumpkin   E
The **Cybil** war. Byars, B. C.   **Fic**
Cycles [series]
   Ross, M. E. Earth cycles   **525**
Cycling
   See also Bicycles; Mountain biking
   Bradley, M. Lance Armstrong (4-6)   **92**
   Gibbons, G. Bicycle book (k-3)   **629.227**
Fiction
   Best, C. Sally Jean, the Bicycle Queen   E
   Burleigh, R. Messenger, messenger   E
   Mills, C. Gus and Grandpa and the two-wheeled bike   E
   Say, A. The bicycle man   E
   Shannon, D. Duck on a bike   E
Cyclones
   See also Hurricanes
   Ceban, B. J. Hurricanes, typhoons, and cyclones (4 and up)   **551.55**
Cyprus
   Spilling, M. Cyprus (5 and up)   **956.93**
Cyrus, Kurt
   Hotel deep (3-5)   **811**
   (il) Anderson, M. T. Whales on stilts   **Fic**
   (il) Bunting, E. The bones of Fred Mcfee   E
Cystic fibrosis
   Gold, S. D. Cystic fibrosis (4 and up)   **616.3**
Czech, Kenneth P.
   Snapshot (5 and up)   **770.9**
Czech Republic
   Sioras, E. Czech Republic (5 and up)   **943.7**
Czechoslovakia
   See also Czech Republic
Czekaj, Jef
   Grampa & Julie: Shark hunters (2-4)   **741.5**

D

D is for Dahl. Cooling, W.   **823.009**
D is for drums. Chorao, K.   **975.5**
D.N.A. *See* DNA
D.W. all wet. Brown, M. T.   E
Da Gama, Vasco *See* Gama, Vasco da, 1469-1524
The **Da Trang** crab. Terada, A. M.
   In Terada, A. M. Under the starfruit tree; folktales from Vietnam p37-41   **398.2**
Da Vinci, Leonardo *See* Leonardo, da Vinci, 1452-1519
Dabcovich, Lydia
   The polar bear son (k-3)   **398.2**
   (il) Milord, S. The ghost on the hearth   E
Dacey, Bob
   (il) Manushkin, F. Miriam's cup   **222**
Dad, Jackie, and me. Uhlberg, M.   E

D'Adamo, Francesco
Iqbal (5 and up)   **Fic**

Daddy Boogey. San Souci, R.
In San Souci, R. Double-dare to be scared: another thirteen chilling tales   **S C**

Daddy loves his baby. *See* Morrow, T. J. Mommy loves her baby   **E**

Daddy makes the best spaghetti. Hines, A. G.   **E**

Daddy's lullaby. Bradman, T.   **E**

Daft Jack. Doherty, B.
In Doherty, B. The famous adventures of Jack p26-49   **398.2**

Dagestan (Russia)
Beliaev, E. Dagestan (5 and up)   **947.5**

Dahl, Roald
The BFG (4-6)   **Fic**
The enormous crocodile (2-4)   **Fic**
James and the giant peach (4-6)   **Fic**
The magic finger (2-4)   **Fic**
also in You read to me & I'll read to you; 20th-century stories to share p10-25   **E**
Matilda (4-6)   **Fic**
Vile verses (4-6)   **821**
The witches
In Beware!; R.L. Stine picks his favorite scary stories p101-19   **808.8**
About
Cooling, W. D is for Dahl (4 and up)   **823.009**

Dahlia. McClintock, B.   **E**

Daily life in a Plains Indian village, 1868. Terry, M. B. H.   **970.004**

Daily life in ancient and modern Timbuktu. Brook, L.   **966.23**

Daily life on a Southern plantation, 1853. Erickson, P.   **975**

Dairying
Aliki. Milk from cow to carton (k-3)   **637**
Gibbons, G. The milk makers (k-3)   **637**
Peterson, C. Extra cheese, please! (k-3)   **637**

Daisy comes home. Brett, J.   **E**

Dakos, Kalli
Put your eyes up here (2-4)   **811**

Dakota Indians
See also Oglala Indians
Bruchac, J. A boy called Slow: the true story of Sitting Bull (1-3)   **92**
See/See also pages in the following book(s):
Ehrlich, A. Wounded Knee: an Indian history of the American West (6 and up)   **970.004**
Freedman, R. Indian chiefs (6 and up)   **920**
Fiction
Sneve, V. D. H. High Elk's treasure   **Fic**

Dalai Lama XIV, 1935-
About
Demi. The Dalai Lama (3-6)   **92**

Dale, Doris Cruger
Bilingual children's books in English and Spanish   **011.6**

Daley, Michael J.
Space station rat (4-6)   **Fic**

Dalfunka, where the rich live forever. Singer, I. B.
In Singer, I. B. Stories for children p254-59   **S C**

Dalgleish, Sharon
Cleaning the air (3-6)   **363.7**
Managing the land (3-6)   **333.73**
Protecting forests (3-6)   **333.75**
Protecting wildlife (3-6)   **333.95**
Renewing energy (3-6)   **333.79**
Saving water (3-6)   **363.6**

Dalgliesh, Alice
The bears on Hemlock Mountain (1-4)   **Fic**
In You read to me & I'll read to you; 20th-century stories to share p180-99   **E**
The courage of Sarah Noble (2-4)   **Fic**

Dall, Mary Doerfler
Little Hands create! (k-2)   **745.5**

Dalston, Teresa R.
(jt. auth) Hallam, A. Managing budgets and finances   **025.1**

Daly, Jude
Fair, Brown & Trembling (k-3)   **398.2**
(il) Hofmeyr, D. The star-bearer   **299**
(il) Roome, D. R. The elephant's pillow   **E**
(il) Williams, S. Imani's music   **E**

Daly, Niki
My dad   **E**
Once upon a time   **E**
Ruby sings the blues   **E**
Where's Jamela?   **E**
(il) Borden, L. The greatest skating race   **Fic**
(il) Gregorowski, C. Fly, eagle, fly!   **398.2**

D'Amico, Carmela
Ella the Elegant Elephant   **E**

D'Amico, Joan
The coming to America cookbook (5 and up)   **641.5**
The healthy body cookbook (4 and up)   **641.5**
The math chef (4-6)   **641.5**
The science chef (4-6)   **641.3**

D'Amico, Steven
(jt. auth) D'Amico, C. Ella the Elegant Elephant   **E**

Dams
See/See also pages in the following book(s):
Macaulay, D. Building big (5 and up)   **720**

Dance
See also Ballet; Tap dancing
Cooper, E. Dance! (2-4)   **792.8**
Grau, A. Dance (4 and up)   **792.8**
Jones, B. T. Dance (k-3)   **792.8**
Fiction
Arnold, M. D. Prancing, dancing Lily   **E**
Durango, J. Cha-cha chimps   **E**
Gray, L. M. My mama had a dancing heart   **E**
Martin, B. Barn dance!   **E**
McKissack, P. C. Mirandy and Brother Wind   **E**
Michelson, R. Happy feet   **E**
Ryder, J. Big Bear Ball   **E**
Say, A. Music for Alice   **E**
Schroeder, A. Ragtime Tumpie   **E**

Dance—Fiction—*Continued*

Wilson, K. Hilda must be dancing   E

Winthrop, E. Dumpy La Rue   E

The **dance** of Elegba. Jaffe, N.

In Jaffe, N. and Zeitlin, S. J. The cow of no color: riddle stories and justice tales from around the world p76-83   **398.2**

Dance of the continents. Gallant, R. A.   **551.1**

Dancers

See also African American dancers; Ballet dancers

Reich, S. José! [biography of José Limón] (2-4)   **92**

Fiction

Levy, E. Seventh grade tango (5 and up)   **Fic**

Dancing *See* Dance

The **dancing** dead of Shark Island. San Souci, R.

In San Souci, R. Even more short & shivery; thirty spine-tingling stories p24-28   **398.2**

Dancing in Cadillac light. Holt, K. W.   **Fic**

Dancing in the wings. Allen, D.   E

Dancing teepees: poems of American Indian youth (3-5)   **897**

Dancing through fire. Lasky, K.   **Fic**

Dandelions

Posada, M. Dandelions (2-4)   **583**

Dandelions. Bunting, E.   E

D'Andrea, Domenick

(il) Farley, W. The Black Stallion   **Fic**

Dangerous animals

Lewin, T. Tooth and claw (4 and up)   **590**

Wilkes, A. Dangerous creatures (5 and up)   **591.6**

Dangerous creatures. Wilkes, A.   **591.6**

Dangerous crossing. Krensky, S.   **Fic**

Dangerous hill. San Souci, R.

In San Souci, R. A terrifying taste of short & shivery; thirty creepy tales p73-76   **398.2**

Dangles and bangles. Haab, S.   **745.5**

Daniel (Biblical figure)

About

Marzollo, J. Daniel in the lion's den (k-3)   **224**

Daniel, Alan

(il) Howe, D. Bunnicula   **Fic**

(il) Naylor, P. R. The grand escape   **Fic**

Daniel Handler [biography of Lemony Snicket] Haugen, H. M.   **92**

Daniel in the lion's den. Marzollo, J.   **224**

Daniel's duck. Bulla, C. R.   E

Danilo the Luckless. Afanas'ev, A. N.

In Afanas'ev, A. N. Russian fairy tales p255-61   **398.2**

Danish authors *See* Authors, Danish

Dann, Geoff

(il) Gravett, C. Castle   **728.8**

(il) Gravett, C. Knight   **940.1**

(il) Greenaway, T. Jungle   **577.3**

Danny and the dinosaur. Hoff, S.   E

Danube. Bryan, N.   **363.7**

Danziger, Paula

Amber Brown is not a crayon (2-4)   **Fic**

It's Justin Time, Amber Brown   E

P.S. Longer letter later (5 and up)   **Fic**

Snail mail no more (5 and up)   **Fic**

United Tates of America (4 and up)   **Fic**

Daphne Eloise Slater, who's tall for her age. Willner-Pardo, G.   **Fic**

Daphne's book. Hahn, M. D.   **Fic**

Darby. Fuqua, J. S.   **Fic**

The **dare**. Naidoo, B.

In Naidoo, B. Out of bounds: seven stories of conflict and hope p1-17   **S C**

Dare to be scared. San Souci, R.   **S C**

D'Argo, Laura

(il) Carson, M. K. The Wright Brothers for kids   **629.13**

The **daring** escape of Ellen Craft. Moore, C.   **92**

The **daring** Nellie Bly. Christensen, B.   **92**

Daring to be Abigail. Vail, R.   **Fic**

Daring women of the Civil War. Ford, C. T.   **973.7**

Dark Ages *See* Middle Ages

The **dark** dark house. San Souci, R.

In San Souci, R. Dare to be scared; thirteen stories to chill and thrill   **S C**

A **dark,** dark tale. Brown, R.   E

The **Dark** Hills divide. Carman, P.   **Fic**

The **dark** pond. Bruchac, J.   **Fic**

The **dark** portal. Jarvis, R.   **Fic**

Dark sparkle tea. Myers, T.   **811**

The **dark-thirty**. McKissack, P. C.   **S C**

Darling, Kathy

Lions (3-6)   **599.75**

(jt. auth) Cobb, V. You gotta try this!   **507.8**

Darling, Louis

(il) Butterworth, O. The enormous egg   **Fic**

(il) Cleary, B. Ellen Tebbits   **Fic**

(il) Cleary, B. Henry Huggins   **Fic**

(il) Cleary, B. The mouse and the motorcycle   **Fic**

(il) Cleary, B. Otis Spofford   **Fic**

(il) Cleary, B. Ramona the pest   **Fic**

Darling, Tara

(il) Darling, K. Lions   **599.75**

The **darning** needle. Andersen, H. C.

In Andersen, H. C. The swan's stories p69-77   **S C**

Darrow, Sharon

Old Thunder and Miss Raney   E

Darwin, Beatrice

(il) Cleary, B. Socks   **Fic**

Darwin, Charles, 1809-1882

About

Lawson, K. Darwin and evolution for kids (4 and up)   **92**

Darwin, Charles, 1809-1882—About—_Continued_
Sís, P. The tree of life: a book depicting the life of Charles Darwin, naturalist, geologist & thinker (4 and up) **92**

Darwin and evolution for kids. Lawson, K. **92**

Darwinism _See_ Evolution

Darzee's chant. Kipling, R.
_In_ Kipling, R. The jungle book: the Mowgli stories **S C**

Dasch, E. Julius (Ernest Julius)
(ed) Explorers. See Explorers **920.003**

Dash, Joan
The longitude prize [biography of John Harrison] (5 and up) **92**
The world at her fingertips: the story of Helen Keller (5 and up) **92**

Data processing
See also Artificial intelligence
Barrett, J. R. Teaching and learning about computers **004**

Data storage and retrieval systems _See_ Information systems

Data transmission systems
See also Computer networks; Electronic mail systems

Datlow, Ellen
(ed) Swan sister. See Swan sister **S C**

Daugherty, James Henry
Andy and the lion **E**

Daughter and stepdaughter. Afanas´ev, A. N.
_In_ Afanas´ev, A. N. Russian fairy tales p278-79 **398.2**

Daughters and fathers _See_ Father-daughter relationship

Daughters and mothers _See_ Mother-daughter relationship

D'Aulaire, Edgar Parin
(il) Key, F. S. The Star-Spangled Banner **782.42**

D'Aulaire, Ingri
Persephone
_In_ Bauer, C. F. Celebrations; read-aloud holiday and theme book programs p199-202 **808.8**
(il) Key, F. S. The Star-Spangled Banner **782.42**

D'Aulnoy, Madame _See_ Aulnoy, Madame d', 1650 or 51-1705

Dauntless Little John
_In_ Diane Goode's book of scary stories & songs p38-41 **398.2**

Dávalos, Felipe
(il) Wardlaw, L. Punia and the King of Sharks **398.2**

Dave, Vijay
(il) Jani, M. What you will see inside a Hindu temple **294.5**

Dave at night. Levine, G. C. **Fic**

Davenier, Christine
(il) Best, C. Sally Jean, the Bicycle Queen **E**
(il) Bridges, M. P. I love the rain! **E**

(il) Guest, E. H. Iris and Walter **E**
(il) Havill, J. I heard it from Alice Zucchini **811**
(il) In every tiny grain of sand. See In every tiny grain of sand **204**
(il) Swanson, S. M. The first thing my mama told me **E**

Dave's down-to-earth rock shop. Murphy, S. J. **511.3**

Davick, Linda
(il) Madaras, L. Ready, set, grow! **613.9**

David, King of Israel
About
De Regniers, B. S. David and Goliath **222**
Fisher, L. E. David and Goliath (k-3) **222**
See/See also pages in the following book(s):
Meltzer, M. Ten kings (5 and up) **920**
Fiction
Lepp, R. David: Shepard's song, vol. 1 (3-5) **741.5**

David and Goliath. De Regniers, B. S. **222**
David and Goliath. Fisher, L. E. **222**
David gets his drum. Francis, P. **E**
David he no fear. Graham, L. B.
_In_ Graham, L. B. How God fix Jonah p34-38 **398.2**

David-Neel, Alexandra, 1868-1969
About
Brown, D. Far beyond the garden gate: Alexandra David-Neel's journey to Lhasa (3-5) **92**

David: Shepard's song, vol. 1. Lepp, R. **741.5**
David's drawings. Falwell, C. **E**

Davidson, Andrew
(il) Hughes, T. The iron giant **Fic**

Davidson, George
About
Morrison, T. The coast mappers (5 and up) **623.89**

Davidson, Rebecca Piatt
All the world's a stage **E**

Davie, Helen
(il) Bancroft, H. Animals in winter **591.56**
(il) Goldin, A. R. Ducks don't get wet **598**
(il) Pfeffer, W. Dolphin talk **599.5**
(il) Tatham, B. Penguin chick **598**
(il) Zoehfeld, K. W. What lives in a shell? **591.4**

Davies, Jacqueline
The boy who drew birds: a story of John James Audubon (2-4) **92**

Davies, Nicola
Bat loves the night **E**
Big blue whale (k-3) **599.5**
Ice bear (k-3) **599.78**
One tiny turtle (k-3) **597.92**
Poop (2-5) **573.4**
Surprising sharks (k-3) **597**

Dávila, Claudia
(il) Becker, H. Boredom blasters **793**
(il) Becker, H. Funny business **792**
(il) Mason, A. Move it! **531**
(il) Mason, A. Touch it! **530.4**

Davis, Benjamin O., Jr.
See/See also pages in the following book(s):
Haskins, J. Black eagles (5 and up)   **629.13**

Davis, Jack E.
(il) Sierra, J. Monster Goose   **811**

Davis, Jane
Crochet (5 and up)   **746.43**

Davis, Lambert
(il) Esbensen, B. J. Baby whales drink milk   **599.5**
(il) Hamilton, V. The bells of Christmas   **Fic**
(il) Rylant, C. The journey   **591.56**

Davis, Lucile
Alabama
In America the beautiful, second series   **973**
Puerto Rico
In America the beautiful, second series   **973**

Davis, Michele Ivy
Evangeline Brown and the Cadillac Motel (4-6)   **Fic**

Davis, Nancy
(il) Graham, J. B. Flicker flash   **811**

Davis, Rich
(il) Meister, C. Tiny's bath   **E**

Davis, Yvonne
(il) MacDonald, M. R. The girl who wore too much   **398.2**
(il) MacDonald, M. R. The round book   **782.42**

Davy Crockett. Osborne, M. P.
In Osborne, M. P. American tall tales p3-13   **398.2**

Davy Crockett saves the world. Schanzer, R.   **E**

Dawdle Duckling. Buzzeo, T.   **E**

Dawes, Kwame Senu Neville
I saw your face (3-5)   **811**

Dawn, Evening, and Midnight. Afanas'ev, A. N.
In Afanas'ev, A. N. Russian fairy tales p457-63   **398.2**

Day, Alexandra
Carl's sleepy afternoon   **E**

Day, Betsy
(il) Johnson, G. Paper-folding fun!   **745.54**
(il) Press, J. Around-the-world art & activities   **745.5**

Day, Frances Ann
Latina and Latino voices in literature   **810.9**

Day, Kenrick L.
(il) Kramer, S. Caves   **551.4**

Day, Larry
(jt. auth) Jurmain, S. George did it [biography of George Washington]   **92**
(il) Pitzer, S. Not afraid of dogs   **E**

Day
See also Night
Bailey, J. Sun up, sun down (2-4)   **525**
Murphy, S. J. It's about time! (k-2)   **529**
Fiction
George, J. C. Morning, noon, and night   **E**
Ormerod, J. Miss Mouse's day   **E**

Schwartz, A. A glorious day   **E**
Spinelli, E. The best time of day   **E**
Tafuri, N. What the sun sees   **E**
Viorst, J. Alexander and the terrible, horrible, no good, very bad day   **E**
Williams, V. B. Lucky song   **E**

A **day** at the New Amsterdam Theatre. Amendola, D.   **792.6**

Day care centers
See also Nursery schools
Fiction
Ballard, R. My day, your day   **E**
Cole, J. When Mommy and Daddy go to work   **E**

The **day** I got lost. Singer, I. B.
In Singer, I. B. Stories for children p115-21   **S C**

The **day** I had to play with my sister. Bonsall, C. N.   **E**

A **day** in the life of Murphy. Provensen, A.   **E**

The **day** Jimmy's boa ate the wash. Noble, T. H.   **E**

Day light, night light. Branley, F. M.   **535**

The **day** Ocean came to visit. Wolkstein, D.   **398.2**

The **day** of Ahmed's secret. Heide, F. P.   **E**

Day of Atonement *See* Yom Kippur

Day of the Dead *See* All Souls' Day

Day of the Dead. Gnojewski, C.   **394.26**

Day of the Dead. Hoyt-Goldsmith, D.   **394.26**

Day of the Dead. Johnston, T.   **E**

The **day** puffins netted Hid-Well. Norman, H.
In Norman, H. The girl who dreamed only geese, and other tales of the Far North   **398.2**

Day that changed America [series]
Tanaka, S. Earthquake!   **979.4**

The **day** the animals came. Weller, F. W.   **E**

The **day** the babies crawled away. Rathmann, P.   **E**

The **day** the horses came. Butcher, G.
In Girls got game; sports stories and poems   **810.8**

The **daydreamer.** Afanas'ev, A. N.
In Afanas'ev, A. N. Russian fairy tales p161   **398.2**

Dayrell, Elphinstone
Why the Sun and the Moon live in the sky (k-3)   **398.2**

Days
Fiction
Lobel, A. One lighthouse, one moon   **E**
Days like this   **811.008**
Days of Jubilee. McKissack, P. C.   **973.7**
Days of the Dead. Lasky, K.   **394.26**
Days of the ducklings. McMillan, B.   **598**
Days to celebrate. Hopkins, L. B.   **051**

Dazzling science projects with light and color. Gardner, R.   **535**

De Angeli, Marguerite Lofft
The door in the wall (4-6)   **Fic**

Dead flies. Conrad, P.
   In Conrad, P. Our house   **S C**
The **dead** hand. Schwartz, A.
   In Schwartz, A. Scary stories 3; more tales to
     chill your bones p35-38   **398.2**
The **dead** mother. San Souci, R.
   In San Souci, R. More short & shivery; thirty
     terrifying tales p143-47   **398.2**
Deadly disasters [series]
   Ceban, B. J. Hurricanes, typhoons, and cyclones
     551.55
   Ceban, B. J. Tornadoes   **551.55**
   Miller, M. Hurricane Katrina strikes the Gulf
     Coast   **363.34**
   Reed, J. Earthquakes   **551.2**
The **deadly** violin. San Souci, R.
   In San Souci, R. Even more short & shivery;
     thirty spine-tingling stories p125-27
     398.2

Deaf
   Adler, D. A. A picture book of Helen Keller
     (1-3)   **92**
   Dash, J. The world at her fingertips: the story of
     Helen Keller (5 and up)   **92**
   Garrett, L. Helen Keller (5 and up)   **92**
   Haughton, E. Living with deafness (3-5)
     362.4
   Koestler-Grack, R. A. The story of Helen Keller
     (2-4)   **92**
   Lawlor, L. Helen Keller: rebellious spirit (5 and
     up)   **92**
   MacLeod, E. Helen Keller (3-6)   **92**
     Fiction
   Millman, I. Moses goes to school   **E**
   Riskind, M. Apple is my sign (5 and up)
     Fic
   Smith, D. J. The boys of San Joaquin (5 and
     up)   **Fic**
   Uhlberg, M. Dad, Jackie, and me   **E**
    Means of communication
    See also Sign language
Deafness
   Haughton, E. Living with deafness (3-5)
     362.4
Dealing with dragons. Wrede, P. C.   **Fic**
Dean, Arlan
   Terra-cotta soldiers (4 and up)   **931**
Dean, Tanya
   Theodor Geisel [Dr. Seuss] (4 and up)   **92**
Deans, Sis Boulos
   Every day and all the time (5 and up)   **Fic**
Dear America [series]
   Bartoletti, S. C. A coal miner's bride   **Fic**
   Hesse, K. A light in the storm   **Fic**
   Lasky, K. Dreams in the golden country   **Fic**
   McDonald, M. All the stars in the sky   **Fic**
   McKissack, P. C. Color me dark   **Fic**
   McKissack, P. C. A picture of Freedom   **Fic**
   Turner, A. W. Love thy neighbor   **Fic**
Dear Benjamin Banneker. Pinkney, A. D.   **92**
Dear Juno. Pak, S.   **E**
Dear Mr. Henshaw. Cleary, B.   **Fic**
Dear Mrs. LaRue. Teague, M.   **E**

Dear Papa. Ylvisaker, A.   **Fic**
Dear Whiskers. Nagda, A. W.   **Fic**
Dear zoo. Campbell, R.   **E**
Death
   Blackwood, G. L. Debatable deaths (4 and up)
     920
   Brown, L. K. When dinosaurs die (k-3)
     155.9
   Krementz, J. How it feels when a parent dies (4
     and up)   **155.9**
   See/See also pages in the following book(s):
   Gellman, M. Lost & found (4-6)   **155.9**
     Fiction
   Aliki. The two of them   **E**
   Barron, T. A. Where is Grandpa?   **E**
   Baskin, N. R. What every girl (except me)
     knows (4 and up)   **Fic**
   Brisson, P. I remember Miss Perry   **E**
   Brooks, B. Everywhere (4 and up)   **Fic**
   Bunting, E. Blackwater (5 and up)   **Fic**
   Carson, J. You hold me and I'll hold you   **E**
   Clark, C. G. Hill Hawk Hattie (5 and up)
     Fic
   Clifford, E. The remembering box (3-5)   **Fic**
   Conly, J. L. Crazy lady! (5 and up)   **Fic**
   Couloumbis, A. Getting near to baby (5 and up)
     Fic
   Creech, S. Walk two moons (6 and up)   **Fic**
   Danziger, P. United Tates of America (4 and
     up)   **Fic**
   De Paola, T. Nana Upstairs & Nana Downstairs
     E
   Demas, C. Saying goodbye to Lulu   **E**
   DiSalvo-Ryan, D. A dog like Jack   **E**
   Fletcher, R. Fig pudding (4 and up)   **Fic**
   Fletcher, R. Flying solo (5 and up)   **Fic**
   Hamilton, V. Cousins (5 and up)   **Fic**
   Harris, R. H. Goodbye, Mousie   **E**
   Henkes, K. Sun & Spoon (4 and up)   **Fic**
   Hobbs, V. Defiance (5 and up)   **Fic**
   Howe, J. Kaddish for Grandpa in Jesus' name,
     amen   **E**
   Johnston, T. That summer   **E**
   Kornblatt, M. Izzy's place (4-6)   **Fic**
   Koss, A. G. Stolen words (4 and up)   **Fic**
   Lowry, L. A summer to die (5 and up)   **Fic**
   MacLachlan, P. Baby (5 and up)   **Fic**
   McGhee, A. Snap (5 and up)   **Fic**
   Miles, M. Annie and the Old One (1-4)   **Fic**
   Napoli, D. J. Flamingo dream   **E**
   Neufeld, J. Almost a hero (5 and up)   **Fic**
   Newman, L. The best cat in the world   **E**
   Park, B. Mick Harte was here (4-6)   **Fic**
   Paterson, K. Bridge to Terabithia (4 and up)
     Fic
   Polikoff, B. G. Life's a funny proposition, Hora-
     tio (5 and up)   **Fic**
   Recorvits, H. Goodbye, Walter Malinski (3-6)
     Fic
   Ross, A. In the quiet (5 and up)   **Fic**
   Rylant, C. Missing May (5 and up)   **Fic**
   Slepian, J. The Broccoli tapes (5 and up)
     Fic
   Smith, D. B. A taste of blackberries (4-6)
     Fic

Death—Fiction—*Continued*

Snyder, Z. K. Spyhole secrets (4 and up)
Fic

Viorst, J. The tenth good thing about Barney
E

Wallace-Brodeur, R. Blue eyes better (4-6)
Fic

Warner, S. This isn't about the money (5 and up)
Fic

Wiles, D. Each little bird that sings (4-6)
Fic

Ylvisaker, A. Dear Papa (4 and up)
Fic

Zolotow, C. The old dog
E

Poetry

Grimes, N. What is goodbye? (4 and up)
811

Death and disease. Woolf, A.
610.9

Death and the two friends. San Souci, R.

In San Souci, R. Even more short & shivery; thirty spine-tingling stories p110-12
398.2

Death at Devil's Bridge. DeFelice, C. C.
Fic

Death forgiven. Jiménez, F.

In Jiménez, F. The circuit: stories from the life of a migrant child p57-60
S C

Death of a miser. Afanas´ev, A. N.

In Afanas´ev, A. N. Russian fairy tales p268
398.2

The **death** of the cock. Afanas´ev, A. N.

In Afanas´ev, A. N. Russian fairy tales p17-19
398.2

Death of the iron horse. Goble, P.
E

Death take him hand off pican heart. Graham, L. B.

In Graham, L. B. How God fix Jonah p91-95
398.2

Death trap. Thompson, S. E.
560

Death Valley. Levinson, N. S.
577.5

The **death** waltz. San Souci, R.

In San Souci, R. Short & shivery; thirty chilling tales p133-38
398.2

Debatable deaths. Blackwood, G. L.
920

Debit cards

Hall, M. Credit cards and checks (3-5)
332.7

Debon, Nicolas

Four pictures by Emily Carr (4 and up)
92

Decades of the 20th Century [series]. Feinstein, S.
909.82

The **deceitful** heron. Lee, J. M.

In Lee, J. M. I once was a monkey; stories Buddha told
294.3

December. Bunting, E.
E

Decision making

See also Problem solving

Declaration of Independence *See* United States. Declaration of Independence

The **Declaration** of Independence
973.3

Declaring independence. Miller, B. M.
973.3

Decoration Day *See* Memorial Day

Decorative arts

Tunis, E. Colonial craftsmen and the beginnings of American industry (4 and up)
680

Deeds, Sharon

(ed) The New books kids like. *See* The New books kids like
011.6

Deedy, Carmen Agra

The yellow star (3-5)
Fic

Deem, James M.

Bodies from the ash (4 and up)
937

Bodies from the bog (4 and up)
930.1

Deep diving vehicles *See* Submersibles

Deep sea diving *See* Submarine diving

Deer

See also Reindeer

Patent, D. H. White-tailed deer (2-4)
599.65

Fiction

Rawlings, M. K. The yearling (6 and up)
Fic

Salten, F. Bambi (4-6)
Fic

Deer hunting. Sanfield, S.

In Sanfield, S. The adventures of High John the Conqueror
398.2

Deer woman. San Souci, R.

In San Souci, R. Even more short & shivery; thirty spine-tingling stories p5-8
398.2

Deere, Kathleen

(jt. auth) Feinberg, S. Running a parent/child workshop
027.62

Deeter, Catherine

(il) Walker, A. Langston Hughes, American poet
92

DeFelice, Cynthia C.

The apprenticeship of Lucas Whitaker (5 and up)
Fic

Death at Devil's Bridge (5 and up)
Fic

The ghost and Mrs. Hobbs (4-6)
Fic

The ghost of Fossil Glen (4-6)
Fic

The missing manatee (5 and up)
Fic

Old Granny and the bean thief
E

The real, true Dulcie Campbell
E

Weasel (4 and up)
Fic

Defense mechanisms (Zoology) *See* Animal defenses

Defiance. Hobbs, V.
Fic

DeFord, Deborah H.

Maine

In World Almanac Library of the States series
973

Degas, Edgar, 1834-1917

About

Cocca-Leffler, M. Edgar Degas: paintings that dance (2-4)
92

Rubin, S. G. Degas and the dance (3-6)
92

Degas, Hilaire Germain Edgar *See* Degas, Edgar, 1834-1917

Degas and the dance. Rubin, S. G.
92

Degen, Bruce

Jamberry
E

(il) Carlstrom, N. W. Jesse Bear, what will you wear?
E

Degen, Bruce—*Continued*
- (il) Coerr, E. The Josefina story quilt   **E**
- (il) Cole, J. The magic school bus and the electric field trip   **621.3**
- (il) Cole, J. The magic school bus at the waterworks   **551.48**
- (il) Cole, J. The magic school bus explores the senses   **612.8**
- (il) Cole, J. The magic school bus: in the time of the dinosaurs   **567.9**
- (il) Cole, J. The magic school bus inside a beehive   **595.7**
- (il) Cole, J. The magic school bus inside a hurricane   **551.55**
- (il) Cole, J. The magic school bus inside the Earth   **551.1**
- (il) Cole, J. The magic school bus inside the human body   **612**
- (il) Cole, J. The magic school bus, lost in the solar system   **523**
- (il) Cole, J. The magic school bus on the ocean floor   **591.7**
- (il) Cole, J. Ms. Frizzle's adventures: medieval castle   **728.8**
- (il) Yolen, J. Commander Toad and the voyage home   **E**

DeGroat, Diane
- (il) Gilson, J. Bug in a rug   **Fic**
- (il) Koss, A. G. How I saved Hanukkah   **Fic**

Deities *See* Gods and goddesses

DeJong, Meindert
- The house of sixty fathers (4-6)   **Fic**
- The wheel on the school (4-6)   **Fic**

Del Negro, Janice
- Willa and the wind   **E**

Delacre, Lulu
- Golden tales (5 and up)   **398.2**
  Contents: How the sea was born; Guanina; The eleven thousand Virgins; The laughing skull; Sención, the Indian girl; When the sun and the moon were children; How the rainbow was born; The miracle of Our Lady of Guadalupe; El Dorado; Manco Capac and the rod of gold; Kákuy; The courier
- Rafi and Rosi   **E**
- Salsa stories (4-6)   **S C**
  Contents: New Years Day; A carpet for Holy Week; At the beach; The night of San Juan; Teatime; Birthday piñata; The Lord of Miracles; Aguinaldo; Carmen Teresa's gift
- Arroz con leche. See Arroz con leche   **782.42**
- (comp) Arrorró mi niño. See Arrorró mi niño   **398.8**
- (il) González, L. M. Señor Cat's romance and other favorite stories from Latin America   **398.2**

Delahunty, Andrew
- Barron's first thesaurus (1-5)   **423**

Delaney, Joseph
- The last apprentice: Revenge of the witch (5 and up)   **Fic**

Delaney, M. C. (Michael Clark)
- Birdbrain Amos (3-5)   **Fic**

Delano, Marfe Ferguson
- American heroes (5 and up)   **920**
- Genius [biography of Albert Einstein] (5 and up)   **92**
- Inventing the future: a photobiography of Thomas Alva Edison (5 and up)   **92**

Delaware
- Blashfield, J. F. Delaware
  In America the beautiful, second series   **973**
- Fontes, J. Delaware
  In World Almanac Library of the States series   **973**
- King, D. C. Delaware
  In It's my state! [series]   **973**
  Fiction
- Hesse, K. A light in the storm (5 and up)   **Fic**
  History
- Hossell, K. Delaware
  In Voices from colonial America [series]   **973.2**

Delaware. Hossell, K.
  In Voices from colonial America [series]   **973.2**

Delaware Bay (Del. and N.J.)
- Crenson, V. Horseshoe crabs and shorebirds (2-4)   **577.7**

Delaware Indians
  Fiction
- Durrant, L. The beaded moccasins (5 and up)   **Fic**

Delinquency, Juvenile *See* Juvenile delinquency

Delton, Judy
- Angel's mother's wedding (3-5)   **Fic**

Dem bones. Barner, B.   **611**

Demarest, Chris L.
- Firefighters A to Z (k-1)   **628.9**
- Hurricane hunters! (k-3)   **551.55**
- (il) Murphy, S. J. Beep beep, vroom vroom!   **515**
- (il) Stamper, J. B. Breakfast at Danny's Diner   **E**

Demas, Corinne
- Saying goodbye to Lulu   **E**

DeMauro, Lisa
- Thomas Edison. See Thomas Edison   **92**

Demi
- Buddha (4-6)   **294.3**
- Buddha stories (3-6)   **294.3**
- The Dalai Lama (3-6)   **92**
- The donkey and the rock (k-3)   **398.2**
- The emperor's new clothes   **E**
- The empty pot (k-3)   **398.2**
- Gandhi (3-6)   **92**
- The greatest power   **E**
- Happy, happy Chinese New Year! (k-3)   **394.26**
- The hungry coat (k-3)   **398.2**
- In the eyes of the cat   **895.6**
- Jesus (3-6)   **232.9**
- King Midas (2-4)   **398.2**
- Kites   **E**
- The legend of Saint Nicholas (3-6)   **92**
- Mother Teresa (3-6)   **92**
- Muhammad (4 and up)   **297**

Democratic Republic of the Congo. Heale, J.   **967.51**

Democratic Republic of the Congo. Willis, T.   **967.51**

The **demon** in the wine cellar. Schwartz, H.
  In Schwartz, H. and Rush, B. A coat for the
    moon and other Jewish tales p22-25
                                                  398.2
Demoniac possession
                         Fiction
  Paver, M. Wolf brother (5 and up)   **Fic**
The **demonic** double. Schwartz, H.
  In Schwartz, H. Invisible kingdoms; Jewish
    tales of angels, spirits, and demons p49-
    56   **398.2**
Demonstrations
    See also Civil rights demonstrations; Riots
Dendy, Leslie A.
  Guinea pig scientists (5 and up)   **616**
Denmark
  Pateman, R. Denmark (5 and up)   **948.9**
                         Fiction
  Bredsdorff, B. The Crow-girl (4 and up)   **Fic**
  Deedy, C. A. The yellow star (3-5)   **Fic**
  Lowry, L. Number the stars (4 and up)   **Fic**
                         Folklore
    See Folklore—Denmark
Dennis, Wesley
  (il) Henry, M. Brighty of the Grand Canyon
                                               Fic
  (il) Henry, M. Justin Morgan had a horse
                                               Fic
  (il) Henry, M. King of the wind   **Fic**
Dennis, Yvonne Wakim
  Children of native America today (3-6)
                                           970.004
  Sequoyah, 1770?-1843 (3-6)   **92**
Dennison, Allie
  (jt. auth) Dennison, A. Our dad died   **155.9**
Dennison, Amy
  Our dad died (4 and up)   **155.9**
Dennison, David
  (jt. auth) Dennison, A. Our dad died   **155.9**
Denominations, Protestant *See* Protestant church-
  es
Denslow, Sharon Phillips
  Georgie Lee (2-4)   **Fic**
  In the snow   **E**
Denslow, William Wallace
  (il) Baum, L. F. The Wizard of Oz   **Fic**
Dent, Charlie, 1919-1994
                         About
  Fritz, J. Leonardo's horse (4 and up)   **730.9**
Dentistry
  Keller, L. Open wide (k-3)   **617.6**
Dentists
                         Fiction
  Steig, W. Doctor De Soto   **E**
Denton, Carey
  (jt. auth) Glenn, J. The treasury of family games
                                               793
Denton, Kady MacDonald
  (il) Masurel, C. Two homes   **E**
Denton, Terry
  (il) Fox, M. Night noises   **E**
DePalma, Mary Newell
  A grand old tree   **E**

DePaola, Tomie *See* De Paola, Tomie, 1934-
Depression (Psychology)
    See also Manic-depressive illness
  Gold, S. D. Bipolar disorder and depression (4
    and up)   **616.89**
  Roy, J. R. Depression (4 and up)   **616.85**
                         Fiction
  Bell, J. Breaking trail (5 and up)   **Fic**
Depressions
                         1929
    See Great Depression, 1929-1939
Derby, Ethel Roosevelt, 1891-1977
                         Fiction
  Bradley, K. B. The President's daughter (3-5)
                                               Fic
DerKazarian, Susan
  You have head lice! (k-2)   **616.5**
DeRoy, Craig
  (il) Polland, B. K. We can work it out
                                             303.6
Derzipilski, Kathleen
  Arizona
    In It's my state! [series]   **973**
  Beetles (3-6)   **595.7**
Desai Hidier, Tanuja
  Shashikala: a brief history of love and khadi
    In Friends; stories about new friends, old
      friends, and unexpectedly true friends
                                               S C
Desegregation *See* Segregation
Desegregation in education *See* School integra-
  tion
Desert animals
    See also Camels
  Arnosky, J. Watching desert wildlife (3-6)
                                             591.7
                         Fiction
  Johnston, T. Desert song   **E**
  Ketteman, H. Armadilly chili   **E**
  Sayre, A. P. Dig, wait, listen   **E**
Desert ecology
  Bash, B. Desert giant (3-5)   **583**
  Baylor, B. The desert is theirs (1-4)   **577.5**
  Brandenburg, J. Sand and fog (4 and up)
                                             968.8
  Guiberson, B. Z. Cactus hotel (k-3)   **583**
  Johansson, P. The dry desert (3-5)   **577.5**
  Johnson, R. L. A walk in the desert (3-6)
                                             577.5
  Lesser, C. Storm on the desert (2-4)   **577.5**
  Levinson, N. S. Death Valley (1-3)   **577.5**
  Stille, D. R. Deserts (2-4)   **577.5**
  Wright-Frierson, V. A desert scrapbook (3-5)
                                             577.5
Desert giant. Bash, B.   **583**
The **desert** is theirs. Baylor, B.   **577.5**
Desert plants
    See also Cactus
A **desert** scrapbook. Wright-Frierson, V. **577.5**
Desert song. Johnston, T.   **E**

El **Dia** de los Muertos. Marcantonio, P. S.
In Marcantonio, P. S. Red ridin' in the hood;
and other cuentos **S C**

Diabetes
Carter, A. R. I'm tougher than diabetes! (2-4)
616.4
Haney, J. Juvenile diabetes (4 and up)
616.4
Peacock, C. A. Sugar was my best food (3-6)
362.1
Pirner, C. W. Even little kids get diabetes (k-1)
616.4
Semple, C. M. Diabetes (4 and up) **616.4**
Silverstein, A. Diabetes (3-5) **616.4**
Fiction
Morgan, N. Chicken friend (5 and up) **Fic**
Zemser, A. B. Beyond the mango tree (5 and
up) **Fic**

Diagram Group
Junior science diagrams on file. See Junior science diagrams on file **507**

Diakité, Penda
I lost my tooth in Africa **E**

Dial-a-ghost. Ibbotson, E. **Fic**

Dial easy-to-read [series]
Antle, N. Sam's Wild West Christmas **E**
Ehrlich, A. Leo, Zack, and Emmie together
again **E**
Hall, K. Creepy riddles **793.73**
Hall, K. Dino riddles **793.73**
Hall, K. Mummy riddles **793.73**
Hall, K. Ribbit riddles **793.73**
Hall, K. Snakey riddles **793.73**
Hall, K. Stinky riddles **793.73**
Hall, K. Turkey riddles **793.73**
Herman, G. Cal Ripken, Jr. **92**
Holub, J. Why do birds sing? **598**
Holub, J. Why do cats meow? **636.8**
Holub, J. Why do dogs bark? **636.7**
Holub, J. Why do horses neigh? **636.1**
Holub, J. Why do rabbits hop? **636.9**
Holub, J. Why do snakes hiss? **597.96**
Horowitz, R. Breakout at the bug lab **E**
Krensky, S. Lionel's birthday **E**
Marshall, E. Fox and his friends **E**
Marshall, E. Three by the sea **E**
McMullan, K. Pearl and Wagner: two good
friends **E**
Parks, R. I am Rosa Parks **92**
Van Leeuwen, J. Tales of Oliver Pig **E**

Diamond, Donna
(jt. auth) Clifford, E. The remembering box
Fic
(il) Paterson, K. Bridge to Terabithia **Fic**

Diamond life. Smith, C. R. **796.357**

Diane Goode's book of scary stories & songs
(2-5) **398.2**

Diaries
Truet, T. S. Keeping a journal (5 and up)
808
Fiction
Cruise, R. Fiona's private pages (5 and up)
Fic
Gantos, J. Heads or tails (5 and up) **Fic**
Parker, T. T. Sienna's scrapbook (3-5) **Fic**

Wilson, N. H. Mountain pose (5 and up)
Fic
The **diary** of a killer cat. Fine, A. **Fic**
Diary of a spider. Cronin, D. **E**
Diary of a wombat. French, J. **E**
Diary of a worm. Cronin, D. **E**
The **diary** of a young girl. Frank, A. **92**
The **diary** of a young girl: the definitive edition.
Frank, A. **92**
The **diary** of David R. Leeper. Leeper, D. R.
92
The **diary** of Elizabeth Bacon Custer. Custer, E.
B. **973.8**
The **diary** of Ma Yan. Ma Yan **951.05**
The **diary** of Melanie Martin; or, How I survived
Matt the Brat, Michelangelo, and the Leaning
Tower of Pizza. Weston, C. **Fic**
Dias, Bartholomeu, 1450?-1500
See/See also pages in the following book(s):
Fritz, J. Around the world in a hundred years (4
and up) **910.4**
Dia's story cloth. Cha, D. **305.8**
Diaz, Bartholomeu *See* Dias, Bartholomeu,
1450?-1500
Diaz, David
(il) Andrews-Goebel, N. The pot that Juan built
[biography of Juan Quezada] **92**
(il) Bernier-Grand, C. T. César **811**
(il) Brown, M. W. The little scarecrow boy
E
(il) Bunting, E. December **E**
(il) Bunting, E. Smoky night **E**
(il) Creech, S. The Wanderer **Fic**
(il) Krull, K. Wilma unlimited: how Wilma Rudolph became the world's fastest woman
92
(il) Soto, G. Neighborhood odes **811**
(il) Wilbur, R. The disappearing alphabet
811
DiCamillo, Kate
Because of Winn-Dixie (4 and up) **Fic**
Mercy Watson to the rescue **E**
The miraculous journey of Edward Tulane (3-6)
Fic
The tale of Despereaux (3-6) **Fic**
Dicey and Orpus. San Souci, R.
In San Souci, R. Even more short & shivery;
thirty spine-tingling stories p89-93
398.2
Dicey's song. Voigt, C. **Fic**
Dick Whittington and his cat. Hodges, M.
398.2
Dickens, Charles, 1812-1870
About
Rosen, M. Dickens (5 and up) **92**
Stanley, D. Charles Dickens (4 and up) **92**
See/See also pages in the following book(s):
Krull, K. Lives of the writers (4 and up)
920
Dickinson, Emily
Emily Dickinson
In The Blackbirch treasury of American poet-
ry p101-45 **811.008**

Dickinson, Emily—*Continued*
I'm nobody! who are you? (3-6) **811**
(jt. auth) Winter, J. Emily Dickinson's letters to
the world **811**

Dickinson, Emily, 1830-1886
About
Winter, J. Emily Dickinson's letters to the world
(k-3) **811**
See/See also pages in the following book(s):
Krull, K. Lives of the writers (4 and up)
920

Dickinson, Peter
Inside Grandad (4 and up) **Fic**
Unicorn
In Horse tales **S C**

Dictionaries *See* Encyclopedias and dictionaries

Dictionaries, Picture *See* Picture dictionaries

Dictionary of American children's fiction, 1995-
1999. Helbig, A. **028.5**

The **Dictionary** of characters in children's literature **028.5**

The **Dictionary** of folklore (4 and up) **398**

Did dinosaurs have feathers? Zoehfeld, K. W.
568

Did the rabbi have a head? Kimmel, E. A.
In Kimmel, E. A. The spotted pony: a collection of Hanukkah stories p43-46
398.2

Did you say pears? Alda, A. **E**

Didrikson, Babe *See* Zaharias, Babe Didrikson,
1911-1956

Diego [biography of Diego Rivera] Winter, J.
92

Diehn, Gwen
Making books that fly, fold, wrap, hide, pop up,
twist, and turn (4 and up) **736**
Nature smart (3-6) **745.5**

Diet
See also Eating customs
Fiction
Sharmat, M. Gregory, the terrible eater **E**

Diez deditos. Ten little fingers & other play
rhymes and action songs from Latin America
(k-3) **782.42**

The **difference** between babies & cookies. Hanson,
M. E. **E**

Dig!. Zimmerman, A. G. **E**

Dig, wait, listen. Sayre, A. P. **E**

Digby. Hazen, B. S. **E**

Digby and Kate and the beautiful day. Baker, B.
E

Digestion
Simon, S. Guts (4 and up) **612.3**

Digger man. Zimmerman, A. G. **E**

Digging for bird-dinosaurs. Bishop, N. **567.9**

Digging for the past [series]
Scarre, C. The Palace of Minos at Knossos
728.8
Smith, S. T. Valley of the Kings **932**

Digging up the past [series]
Dean, A. Terra-cotta soldiers **931**

Digital photography
Bidner, J. The kids' guide to digital photography (5 and up) **775**

Dillon, Diane
(il) Aardema, V. Who's in Rabbit's house?
398.2
(il) Aardema, V. Why mosquitoes buzz in people's ears **398.2**
(il) Bible. O.T. Ecclesiastes. To every thing
there is a season **223**
(il) Brown, M. W. Two little trains **E**
(il) Brown, M. W. Where have you been? **E**
(jt. auth) Dillon, L. Rap a tap tap **E**
(il) Greenfield, E. Honey, I love, and other love
poems **811**
(il) Hamilton, V. The girl who spun gold
398.2
(il) Hamilton, V. Her stories **398.2**
(il) Hamilton, V. Many thousand gone **326**
(il) Hamilton, V. The people could fly [Ameri-
can black folktales] **398.2**
(il) Hamilton, V. The people could fly [the picture book] **398.2**
(il) Musgrove, M. Ashanti to Zulu: African traditions **960**
(il) Norman, H. Between heaven and earth
398.2
(il) Norman, H. The girl who dreamed only
geese, and other tales of the Far North
398.2
(il) Paterson, K. The tale of the mandarin ducks
398.2
(il) Verdi, G. Aïda **792.5**
(il) Verne, J. 20,000 leagues under the sea
Fic
(il) Willard, N. Pish, posh, said Hieronymus
Bosch **811**

Dillon, Eilís
Saint Patrick and the snakes
In Bauer, C. F. Celebrations; read-aloud holiday and theme book programs p170-71
808.8

Dillon, Lee
(il) Willard, N. Pish, posh, said Hieronymus
Bosch **811**

Dillon, Leo
Rap a tap tap **E**
(il) Aardema, V. Who's in Rabbit's house?
398.2
(il) Aardema, V. Why mosquitoes buzz in people's ears **398.2**
(il) Bible. O.T. Ecclesiastes. To every thing
there is a season **223**
(il) Brown, M. W. Two little trains **E**
(il) Brown, M. W. Where have you been? **E**
(jt. auth) Burns, K. Mansa Musa **Fic**
(il) Greenfield, E. Honey, I love, and other love
poems **811**
(il) Hamilton, V. The girl who spun gold
398.2
(il) Hamilton, V. Her stories **398.2**
(il) Hamilton, V. Many thousand gone **326**
(il) Hamilton, V. The people could fly [Ameri-
can black folktales] **398.2**
(il) Hamilton, V. The people could fly [the picture book] **398.2**

Dinosaurs—Fiction—*Continued*

Whybrow, I. Harry and the bucketful of dinosaurs   **E**

Yolen, J. How do dinosaurs say goodnight?   **E**

Poetry

Dinosaurs: poems (3-5)   **811.008**

Prelutsky, J. Tyrannosaurus was a beast (2-5)   **811**

Wise, W. Dinosaurs forever (k-3)   **811**

Dinosaurs all around. Arnold, C.   **567.9**

Dinosaurs at the ends of the earth. Floca, B.   **567.9**

Dinosaurs divorce. Brown, L. K.   **306.89**

Dinosaurs forever. Wise, W.   **811**

Dinosaurs of the world (5 and up)   **567.9**

The **dinosaurs** of Waterhouse Hawkins. Kerley, B.   **92**

Dinosaurs: poems (3-5)   **811.008**

Dinosaurs to the rescue!. Brown, L. K.   **363.7**

Dinosaurs with feathers. Arnold, C.   **568**

Diphtheria

Kimmel, E. C. Balto and the great race (3-5)   **636.7**

Margulies, P. Diphtheria (4-6)   **616.9**

Direction (Theater) *See* Theater—Production and direction

Direction sense

See also Navigation

Dirigible balloons *See* Airships

Dirt on their skirts. Rappaport, D.   **E**

The **dirty** cowboy. Timberlake, A.   **E**

Disabled *See* Handicapped

DiSalvo-Ryan, DyAnne

A castle on Viola Street   **E**

A dog like Jack   **E**

Grandpa's corner store   **E**

The sloppy copy slipup (2-4)   **Fic**

Uncle Willie and the soup kitchen   **E**

(il) Fritz, J. George Washington's mother   **92**

(il) Fritz, J. You want women to vote, Lizzie Stanton?   **92**

(il) Rosen, M. J. Our eight nights of Hanukkah   **296.4**

The **disappearing** alphabet. Wilbur, R.   **811**

Disaster in the Indian Ocean, Tsunami 2004. Torres, J. A.   **909.83**

Disaster planning. Halsted, D. D.   **025.8**

Disaster relief

Halsted, D. D. Disaster planning   **025.8**

Disasters

See also Accidents; Natural disasters

Blackwood, G. L. Enigmatic events (4 and up)   **904**

Discoveries (in geography) *See* Exploration

Discovering African American art for children. See Rolling, J. H., Jr. Come look with me: discovering African American art for children   **704**

Discovering Central America [series]

Shields, C. J. Belize   **972.82**

Shields, C. J. Central America: facts and figures   **972.8**

Shields, C. J. Honduras   **972.83**

Discovering cultures [series]

Asher, S. China   **951**

De Capua, S. Colombia   **986.1**

De Capua, S. Dominican Republic   **972.93**

De Capua, S. Korea   **951.9**

De Capua, S. Peru   **985**

De Capua, S. Russia   **947**

Gordon, S. Australia   **994**

Gordon, S. Cuba   **972.91**

Gordon, S. Germany   **943**

Gordon, S. Great Britain   **941**

Gordon, S. Greece   **949.5**

Gordon, S. Philippines   **959.9**

Gordon, S. Poland   **943.8**

Malone, M. G. Italy   **945**

Murphy, P. Canada   **971**

Murphy, P. India   **954**

Murphy, P. Ireland   **941.5**

Murphy, P. Nigeria   **966.9**

Murphy, P. South Africa   **968**

Parker, L. K. Egypt   **962**

Parker, L. K. Spain   **946**

Rau, D. M. Iraq   **956.7**

Rau, D. M. Singapore   **959.57**

Roy, J. R. Israel   **956.94**

Roy, J. R. Jamaica   **972.92**

Discovering the Caribbean [series]

Hernandez, R. Trinidad & Tobago   **972.983**

Discovering the Inca Ice Maiden. Reinhard, J.   **930.1**

Discovering women artists for children. See Coyne, J. T. Come look with me: discovering women artists for children   **704**

The **discovery** of the Americas. Maestro, B.   **970.01**

Discrimination

See also Sex discrimination

Discrimination in education

See also Segregation in education

Disease germs *See* Bacteria

Disease update [series]

Silverstein, A. The flu and pneumonia update   **616.2**

Diseases

See also Chickenpox; Sick *also* names of specific diseases and groups of diseases; and subjects with the subdivision *Diseases*

Barnard, B. Outbreak (5 and up)   **614.4**

Bjorklund, R. Food-borne illnesses (4 and up)   **615.9**

Dishonesty *See* Honesty

Disney (Walt) Productions *See* Walt Disney Productions

A **disorderly** table. Goldin, B. D.

In Goldin, B. D. Journeys with Elijah; eight tales of the Prophet p21-28   **222**

Dispezio, Michael A.

Eye-popping optical illusions (4-6)   **152.14**

Optical illusion magic (4 and up)   **152.14**

Displaced persons *See* Refugees

Ditchfield, Christin
Golf (2-4)	**796.352**
Memorial Day (2-4)	**394.26**
Tennis (2-4)	**796.342**
Wrestling (2-4)	**796.8**

DiTerlizzi, Tony
Jimmy Zangwow's out-of-this-world, moon pie adventure **E**
(il) Howitt, M. B. The spider and the fly **821**
(il) Johnston, T. Alien & Possum: hanging out **E**

Divakaruni, Chitra Banerjee
The conch bearer (5 and up) **Fic**

Dive!. Earle, S. A. **551.46**

Dive to the deep ocean. Kovacs, D. **623.8**

Diversity, Biological *See* Biological diversity

Divide and ride. Murphy, S. J. **513**

Dividing the goose. Afanas´ev, A. N.
In Afanas´ev, A. N. Russian fairy tales p579-80 **398.2**

Diving
Yoo, P. Sixteen years in sixteen seconds [biography of Sammy Lee] (2-4) **92**

Diving, Scuba *See* Scuba diving

Diving, Submarine *See* Submarine diving

Division
Murphy, S. J. Divide and ride (1-3)	**513**
Murphy, S. J. Jump, kangaroo, jump! (1-3)	**513**

Fiction
Hutchins, P. The doorbell rang **E**

DiVito, Anna
(il) Holub, J. Why do birds sing?	**598**
(il) Holub, J. Why do cats meow?	**636.8**
(il) Holub, J. Why do horses neigh?	**636.1**
(il) Holub, J. Why do rabbits hop?	**636.9**
(il) Holub, J. Why do snakes hiss?	**597.96**
(il) Krull, K. A kid's guide to America's Bill of Rights	**342**

Divorce
See also Remarriage
Bingham, J. Why do families break up? (4 and up)	**306.89**
Brown, L. K. Dinosaurs divorce (k-3)	**306.89**
Krementz, J. How it feels when parents divorce (4 and up)	**306.89**
Rogers, F. Divorce (k-2)	**306.89**

Fiction
Alvarez, J. How Tía Lola came to visit/stay (4 and up)	**Fic**
Bateman, C. Running with the Reservoir Pups (5 and up)	**Fic**
Bateson, C. Stranded in Boringsville (5 and up)	**Fic**
Boles, P. M. Little divas (5 and up)	**Fic**
Bunting, E. Some frog! (2-4)	**Fic**
Cleary, B. Dear Mr. Henshaw (4 and up)	**Fic**
Cleary, B. Strider (4 and up)	**Fic**
Johnson, A. Songs of faith (5 and up)	**Fic**

Koss, A. G. Stranger in Dadland (5 and up) **Fic**
Lisle, J. T. How I became a writer and Oggie learned to drive (4 and up)	**Fic**
Ly, M. Home is east (5 and up)	**Fic**
Masurel, C. Two homes	**E**
Rodowsky, C. F. Spindrift (5 and up)	**Fic**
Schotter, R. Missing Rabbit	**E**
Williams, V. B. Scooter (3-5)	**Fic**
Zimmer, T. V. Sketches from a spy tree (3-6)	**Fic**

Dixon, Dougal
Dougal Dixon's amazing dinosaurs (3-6)	**567.9**
Dougal Dixon's dinosaurs (4 and up)	**567.9**

Dixon, Norma
Lowdown on earthworms (3-5) **592**

Dizzy. Cassidy, C. **Fic**

DK biography [series]
Garrett, L. Helen Keller	**92**
Sawyer, K. K. Anne Frank	**92**

DK eyewitness books [series]
Adams, S. Titanic	**910.4**
Adams, S. World War I	**940.3**
Adams, S. World War II	**940.53**
Ardley, N. Music	**784.19**
Bender, L. Invention	**609**
Brookfield, K. Book	**070.5**
Buckley, J., Jr. NASCAR	**796.72**
Burnie, D. Bird	**598**
Burnie, D. Tree	**582.16**
Byam, M. Arms & armor	**355.8**
Challoner, J. Hurricane & tornado	**551.55**
Clarke, B. Amphibian	**597.8**
Clutton-Brock, J. Cat	**599.75**
Cotterell, A. Ancient China	**931**
Cribb, J. Money	**332.4**
Gamlin, L. Evolution	**576.8**
Grau, A. Dance	**792.8**
Gravett, C. Castle	**728.8**
Gravett, C. Knight	**940.1**
Greenaway, T. Jungle	**577.3**
Halley, N. Farm	**630.1**
Hill, D. Witches & magic-makers	**133.4**
Hornby, H. Soccer	**796.334**
James, S. Ancient Rome	**937**
Lane, B. Crime and detection	**364**
Langley, A. Medieval life	**940.1**
Macquitty, M. Shark	**597**
Margeson, S. M. Viking	**948**
Matthews, R. Explorer	**910.4**
McCarthy, C. Reptile	**597.9**
McIntosh, J. Archeology	**930.1**
Murdoch, D. H. North American Indian	**970.004**
Nahum, A. Flying machine	**629.133**
Newmark, A. Chemistry	**540**
Parker, S. Electricity	**537**
Parker, S. Seashore	**577.7**
Pearson, A. Ancient Greece	**938**
Platt, R. Shipwreck	**910.4**
Redmond, I. Gorilla, monkey & ape	**599.8**
Rowland-Warne, L. Costume	**391**
Stanchak, J. E. Civil War	**973.7**
Stott, C. Space exploration	**629.4**
Symes, R. F. Crystal & gem	**548**

Dogs—*Continued*

Fiction

Alborough, J. Some dogs do	E
Appelt, K. Bubba and Beau, best friends	E
Armstrong, W. H. Sounder (5 and up)	**Fic**
Avi. The good dog (4-6)	**Fic**
Baker, B. Digby and Kate and the beautiful day	E
Baker, L. You bad dog!	E
Barracca, D. The adventures of Taxi Dog	E
Bartoletti, S. C. Nobody's diggier than a dog	E
Bedford, D. The way I love you	E
Bemelmans, L. Madeline's rescue	E
Blake, R. J. Akiak	E
Branford, H. Fire, bed, & bone (5 and up)	**Fic**
Buehner, C. Superdog	E
Byars, B. C. My dog, my hero (3-6)	**S C**
Byars, B. C. Tornado (2-4)	**Fic**
Capucilli, A. Biscuit's new trick	E
Carlson, N. L. Harriet and the roller coaster	E
Cazet, D. The octopus	E
Chall, M. W. Bonaparte	E
Christopher, M. The dog that called the pitch (2-4)	**Fic**
Cleary, B. Strider (4 and up)	**Fic**
Clements, A. Circus family dog	E
Cronin, D. Wiggle	E
Day, A. Carl's sleepy afternoon	E
De Paola, T. Marco's colors	E
De Paola, T. Meet the Barkers	E
Demas, C. Saying goodbye to Lulu	E
DiCamillo, K. Because of Winn-Dixie (4 and up)	**Fic**
DiSalvo-Ryan, D. A dog like Jack	E
Dodd, E. Dog's noisy day	E
Dodds, D. A. Where's Pup?	E
Dunbar, P. Dog Blue	E
Estes, E. Ginger Pye (4-6)	**Fic**
Faller, R. The adventures of Polo	E
Feiffer, J. Bark, George	E
Fine, A. Notso hotso (2-4)	**Fic**
Finney, P. I, Jack (3-6)	**Fic**
Fleming, D. Buster	E
Frank, J. The toughest cowboy	E
French, J. Pete the sheep-sheep	E
Gardiner, J. R. Stone Fox (2-5)	**Fic**
Gipson, F. B. Old Yeller (6 and up)	**Fic**
Godwin, L. Happy and Honey	E
Graham, B. Let's get a pup, said Kate	E
Gretz, S. Riley and Rose in the picture	E
Harlow, J. H. Star in the storm	**Fic**
Harper, D. Sit, Truman!	E
Harvey, A. Dog eared	E
Hazen, B. S. Digby	E
Henkes, K. Circle dogs	E
Henkes, K. Protecting Marie (5 and up)	**Fic**
Herman, R. A. Gomer & Little Gomer	E
Hesse, K. Sable (2-4)	**Fic**
Hobbs, V. Sheep (3-5)	**Fic**
Howe, J. Houndsley and Catina	E
Howe, J. It came from beneath the bed! (3-5)	**Fic**
Huneck, S. Sally goes to the beach	E
Hurd, T. Art dog	E
Jenkins, E. That new animal	E
Johnson, P. B. On top of spaghetti	E
Kalman, M. Smartypants (Pete in school)	E
Kasza, K. The dog who cried wolf	E
Keller, H. Sophie's window	E
Kellogg, S. Pinkerton, behave!	E
King, S. M. Mutt dog!	E
Labatt, M. Pizza for Sam	E
Lee, C. Good dog, Paw!	E
Leedy, L. Mapping Penny's world	E
Leonard, E. A coyote's in the house (5 and up)	**Fic**
London, J. Sled dogs run	E
Lottridge, C. B. Berta: a remarkable dog (3-5)	**Fic**
Loupy, C. Hugs and kisses	E
Lowry, L. Stay! (5 and up)	**Fic**
MacLachlan, P. Bittle	E
Maybarduk, L. James the dancing dog	E
McCarty, P. Hondo and Fabian	E
McKay, H. Dog Friday (4-6)	**Fic**
McKissack, P. C. Tippy Lemmey (2-4)	**Fic**
Meddaugh, S. Martha speaks	E
Meister, C. Tiny's bath	E
Meyers, S. Puppies! Puppies! Puppies!	E
Middleton, C. Do you still love me?	E
Miller, S. S. Three more stories you can read to your dog	E
Morgan, C. The boy who spoke dog (5 and up)	**Fic**
Myers, L. Lewis and Clark and me (3-6)	**Fic**
Myers, W. D. The blues of Flats Brown	E
Myers, W. D. Three swords for Granada (3-6)	**Fic**
Naylor, P. R. Shiloh (4-6)	**Fic**
Newman, L. Hachiko waits (3-5)	**Fic**
Newsome, J. Night walk	E
O'Connor, J. The perfect puppy for me	E
Peet, B. The whingdingdilly	E
Pennac, D. Dog (3-5)	**Fic**
Pilkey, D. The Hallo-wiener	E
Pitzer, S. Not afraid of dogs	E
Provensen, A. A day in the life of Murphy	E
Rathmann, P. Officer Buckle and Gloria	E
Rawls, W. Where the red fern grows (4 and up)	**Fic**
Reaver, C. Bill (5 and up)	**Fic**
Reiser, L. Hardworking puppies	E
Reiser, L. Ten puppies	E
Rodowsky, C. F. The next-door dogs (2-4)	**Fic**
Rodowsky, C. F. Not my dog (2-4)	**Fic**
Ryder, J. Come along, kitten	E
Rylant, C. Henry and Mudge	E
Schories, P. Breakfast for Jack	E
Sebestyen, O. Out of nowhere (5 and up)	**Fic**
Seibold, J. O. Olive the other reindeer	E
Sendak, M. Higglety pigglety pop! (2-4)	**Fic**
Shannon, D. Good boy, Fergus!	E
Shannon, G. Tippy-toe chick, go!	E
Sherlock, P. Letters from Wolfie (5 and up)	**Fic**
Shyer, M. F. Fleabiscuit sings! (3-5)	**Fic**
Simont, M. The stray dog	E

Dogs—Fiction—*Continued*

Staples, S. F. The green dog (4-6)   **Fic**

Steig, W. Caleb & Kate   **E**

Steig, W. Dominic (3-5)   **Fic**

Stolz, M. A dog on Barkham Street (4-6)   **Fic**

Sweet, M. Carmine   **E**

Taylor, T. The trouble with Tuck (5 and up)   **Fic**

Teague, M. Dear Mrs. LaRue   **E**

Thayer, J. The puppy who wanted a boy   **E**

Thomas, J. R. The comeback dog (3-5)   **Fic**

Timberlake, A. The dirty cowboy   **E**

Tolan, S. S. Listen! (4 and up)   **Fic**

Turner, P. S. Hachiko   **E**

Van Allsburg, C. The garden of Abdul Gasazi   **E**

Van Allsburg, C. The sweetest fig   **E**

Vande Velde, V. Smart dog (4-6)   **Fic**

Wallace, B. A dog called Kitty (4-6)   **Fic**

Wallace, C. One nosy pup   **E**

Wallace, C. Turkeys together   **E**

Wells, R. McDuff moves in   **E**

Wright, B. R. Nothing but trouble (4 and up)   **Fic**

Yang, J. Joey and Jet   **E**

Zimmerman, A. G. Dig!   **E**

Zimmerman, A. G. My dog Toby   **E**

Zion, G. Harry the dirty dog   **E**

Zolotow, C. The old dog   **E**

Poetry

Florian, D. Bow wow meow meow   **811**

George, K. O. Little Dog and Duncan (k-2)   **811**

George, K. O. Little dog poems (k-2)   **811**

Gottfried, M. Good dog (k-3)   **811**

Johnston, T. It's about dogs (2-4)   **811**

Sidman, J. Meow ruff (1-3)   **811**

Songs

Kellogg, S. Give the dog a bone (k-3)   **782.42**

Dogs, Wild *See* Wild dogs

Dogs for the blind *See* Guide dogs

A **dog's** gotta do what a dog's gotta do. Singer, M.   **636.7**

Dog's noisy day. Dodd, E.   **E**

Dogsong. Paulsen, G.   **Fic**

Dōhaku's head. Kimmel, E. A.

In Kimmel, E. A. Sword of the samurai; adventure stories from Japan p5-10   **Fic**

Doherty, Berlie

Fairy tales (4-6)   **398.2**

Contents: Cinderella; The sleeping beauty in the forest; Rumpelstiltskin; Rapunzel; Snow White; Aladdin and the enchanted lamp; Little Red Riding Hood; The fire-bird; Hansel and Gretel; Frog prince; The wild swans

The famous adventures of Jack (3-5)   **398.2**

Includes the following stories: The king of the herrings; Daft Jack; The magic castle and the apples of immortality; Jack and the golden snuffbox; Jack the Giant Killer

Doherty, Craig A.

The thirteen colonies [series] (4-6)   **973.2**

Doherty, Katherine M.

(jt. auth) Doherty, C. A. The thirteen colonies [series]   **973.2**

Doll, Carol Ann

Managing and analyzing your collection   **025.2**

Doll. Wolff, V. E.

In Friends; stories about new friends, old friends, and unexpectedly true friends   **S C**

A **doll** for Navidades. Santiago, E.   **E**

The **doll** in the garden. Hahn, M. D.   **Fic**

The **doll** people. Martin, A. M.   **Fic**

The **doll** with the yellow star. McDonough, Y. Z.   **Fic**

The **dollar** watch and the five jack-rabbits. Sandburg, C.

In Sandburg, C. Rootabaga stories p106-13   **S C**

also in Sandburg, C. The Sandburg treasury; prose and poetry for young people p57-61   **818**

The **dollhouse** murders. Wright, B. R.   **Fic**

Dollhouses

Fiction

Godden, R. The doll's house (2-4)   **Fic**

Dolls

Markel, M. Cornhusk, silk, and wishbones (3-6)   **688.7**

Fiction

Field, R. Hitty: her first hundred years (4 and up)   **Fic**

Godden, R. The doll's house (2-4)   **Fic**

Martin, A. M. The doll people (3-5)   **Fic**

McClintock, B. Dahlia   **E**

McDonough, Y. Z. The doll with the yellow star (3-5)   **Fic**

Newsome, J. Dream dancer   **E**

Polacco, P. Babushka's doll   **E**

Pomerantz, C. The chalk doll   **E**

Russo, M. The trouble with Baby   **E**

Rylant, C. The ticky-tacky doll   **E**

Waugh, S. The Mennyms (5 and up)   **Fic**

Zolotow, C. William's doll   **E**

The **doll's** house. Godden, R.   **Fic**

Dolores on her toes. Samuels, B.   **E**

Dolphin talk. Pfeffer, W.   **599.5**

Dolphins

Berger, M. Do whales have belly buttons? (2-4)   **599.5**

Dudzinski, K. Meeting dolphins (4 and up)   **599.5**

Montgomery, S. Encantado (4 and up)   **599.5**

Pfeffer, W. Dolphin talk (k-2)   **599.5**

Domaine, Helena

Robotics (4-6)   **629.8**

Domenico, Gino

(il) Amendola, D. A day at the New Amsterdam Theatre   **792.6**

Domestic animals

See also Pets

Tafuri, N. Spots, feathers, and curly tails   **E**

Fiction

Armstrong, A. Whittington (4-6)   **Fic**

Asch, F. Barnyard lullaby   **E**

Bateman, T. Farm flu   **E**

Doolittle, Michael J.—*Continued*
(il) Goodman, S. Ultimate field trip 5
        629.45

The **door** in the wall. De Angeli, M. L.   **Fic**

The **door** to time. Baccalario, P.   **Fic**

The **doorbell** rang. Hutchins, P.   **E**

Doors. Munro, R.   **E**

Dopey. Byars, B. C.
In Byars, B. C. and others. My dog, my hero
    p42-47   **S C**

Dorjee, Yeshi *See* Yeshi Dorjee

Dork in disguise. Gorman, C.   **Fic**

Dorling Kindersley animal encyclopedia (4 and up)   **590.3**

Dorling Kindersley children's illustrated encyclopedia

Dorling Kindersley readers [series]
Chrisp, P. Welcome to the Globe   **822.3**
Hayden, K. Horse show   **798.2**

The **Dorling** Kindersley science encyclopedia. See The DK science encyclopedia   **503**

Dornfeld, Margaret
Bats (3-6)   **599.4**
Wisconsin
  In It's my state! [series]   **973**

Dorris, Michael
Morning Girl (4 and up)   **Fic**
Sees Behind Trees (4 and up)   **Fic**

Dorros, Arthur
Abuela   **E**
Ant cities (k-3)   **595.7**
City chicken   **E**
Feel the wind (k-3)   **551.51**
Follow the water from brook to ocean (k-3)
    551.48
Julio's magic   **E**
Radio Man. Don Radio   **E**
(il) Wyler, R. Magic secrets   **793.8**

The **dot**. Reynolds, P.   **E**

Dot & Jabber and the big bug mystery. Walsh, E. S.   **E**

Dotlich, Rebecca Kai
Grandpa loves   **E**
Over in the pink house (k-3)   **811**

Dots, spots, speckles, and stripes. Hoban, T.   **E**

Doty, Eldon
(il) Muller, E. P. While you're waiting for the food to come   **507.8**

Doubilet, David
See/See also pages in the following book(s):
Talking with adventurers (4-6)   **920**

The **double** dare. San Souci, R.
In San Souci, R. Dare to be scared; thirteen
    stories to chill and thrill   **S C**

Double-dare to be scared: another thirteen chilling tales. San Souci, R.   **S C**

The **double-digit** club. Bauer, M. D.   **Fic**

Double dutch. Chambers, V.   **796.2**

Double life. Richards, J.   **Fic**

Double pink. Feiffer, K.   **E**

Double the ducks. Murphy, S. J.   **513**

Doucet, Sharon Arms
Lapin plays possum: trickster tales from the
    Louisiana Bayou (4-6)   **398.2**
Contents: Bouki over a barrel; Lapin plays possum; Lapin tangles with Tee Tar Bébé

Dougal Dixon's amazing dinosaurs. Dixon, D.
    567.9

Dougal Dixon's dinosaurs. Dixon, D.   **567.9**

Douglas fir
Bash, B. Ancient ones (3-5)   **585**

Douglass, Frederick, 1817?-1895
About
McKissack, P. C. Frederick Douglass (2-4)
    92

Douglass, Susan L.
Ramadan (1-3)   **297.3**

The **dove** dove. Terban, M.   **793.73**

Doves *See* Pigeons

Dovey Coe. Dowell, F. O.   **Fic**

Dowdle, Mary
(il) Friedman, L. Break a leg!   **792**

Dowell, Frances O'Roark
Chicken boy (4 and up)   **Fic**
Dovey Coe (5 and up)   **Fic**
The secret language of girls (5 and up)   **Fic**
Where I'd like to be (4 and up)   **Fic**

Down a sunny dirt road. Berenstain, S.   **92**

Down by the bay. Raffi   **782.42**

Down by the station. Hillenbrand, W.   **782.42**

Down comes the rain. Branley, F. M.   **551.57**

Down Cut Shin Creek. Appelt, K.   **027**

Down syndrome
Routh, K. Down syndrome (5 and up)
    616.85

Down the road. Schertle, A.   **E**

Down to the sea in ships. Sturges, P.   **811**

Downen, Thomas W.
(comp) School Library Journal's best. See
    School Library Journal's best   **027.8**

Downer, Ann
Hatching magic (4 and up)   **Fic**

Downing, Julie
(il) Le Guin, U. K. Tom Mouse   **E**
(il) Park, L. S. The firekeeper's son   **E**

Dowson, Nick
Tigress   **E**

Doyle, Beverly
(il) Batten, M. Aliens from Earth   **577**

Doyle, Malachy
One, two, three O'Leary   **E**
Tales from old Ireland (3-6)   **398.2**
Contents: The children of Lir; Fair, Brown, and Trembling; The twelve wild geese; Lusmore and the fairies; Son of an otter, son of a wolf; The soul cages; Oisin in Tir na nOG

A **dozen** ducklings lost and found. Ziefert, H.
    E

Dr. Jenner and the speckled monster. Marrin, A.
    614.5

Dr. Martin Luther King, Jr. Adler, D. A.   **92**

Dr. Seuss *See* Seuss, Dr.

Draanen, Wendelin van
Flipped (6 and up)   **Fic**

Draanen, Wendelin van—*Continued*

Sammy Keyes and the hotel thief (4 and up) **Fic**

Shredderman: Attack of the tagger
In Draanen, W. v. Shredderman: Secret identity

Shredderman: Secret identity (3-5) **Fic**

The **dragon** at the well. Bateman, T.
In Fire and wings: dragon tales from East and West p1-14 **S C**

Dragon bones and dinosaur eggs: a photobiography of Roy Chapman Andrews. Bausum, A. **92**

Dragon rider. Funke, C. C. **Fic**

The **dragon** woke and stretched. Yolen, J.
In Yolen, J. Here there be dragons p23 **810.8**

Dragonfield. Yolen, J.
In Yolen, J. Here there be dragons p52-83 **810.8**

Dragons

Gibbons, G. Behold . . . the dragons! (k-3) **398**

Penner, L. R. Dragons (3-5) **398.2**

Fiction

Coville, B. Jeremy Thatcher, dragon hatcher (4-6) **Fic**

De Paola, T. The knight and the dragon **E**

Downer, A. Hatching magic (4 and up) **Fic**

Fire and wings: dragon tales from East and West (4 and up) **S C**

Funke, C. C. Dragon rider (5 and up) **Fic**

Gannett, R. S. My father's dragon (1-4) **Fic**

Grahame, K. The reluctant dragon (3-5) **Fic**

Gray, L. Falcon's egg (3-5) **Fic**

Kent, J. There's no such thing as a dragon **E**

Mayhew, J. The knight who took all day **E**

Nolen, J. Raising dragons **E**

San Souci, R. Kenneth Grahame's The reluctant dragon (2-4) **Fic**

Thayer, J. The popcorn dragon **E**

Thomas, S. M. Good night, Good Knight **E**

Tucker, K. The seven Chinese sisters **E**

Wilkinson, C. Dragon keeper (5 and up) **Fic**

Wrede, P. C. Dealing with dragons (6 and up) **Fic**

Yolen, J. Here there be dragons (5 and up) **810.8**

Zinnen, L. The dragons of Spratt, Ohio (5 and up) **Fic**

Folklore

Hodges, M. Saint George and the dragon (2-5) **398.2**

Poetry

Prelutsky, J. The dragons are singing tonight (2-5) **811**

The **dragons** are singing tonight. Prelutsky, J. **811**

The **dragon's** boy. Yolen, J. **Fic**

The **dragon's** boy. Yolen, J.
also in Yolen, J. Here there be dragons p90-113 **810.8**

Dragon's coo. MacLachlan, P.
In Fire and wings: dragon tales from East and West p25-31 **S C**

Dragons dragons and other creatures that never were, Eric Carle's **808.81**

Dragon's gate. Yep, L. **Fic**

The **dragons** of Spratt, Ohio. Zinnen, L. **Fic**

Dragonwagon, Crescent

And then it rained . . . **E**

Dragonwings. Yep, L. **Fic**

Drake, Jane

The kids campfire book (4-6) **796.5**

The kids winter handbook (4 and up) **790.1**

(jt. auth) Love, A. Kids and grandparents: an activity book **790.1**

(jt. auth) Love, A. The kids book of the Far North **998**

(jt. auth) Love, A. The kids book of the night sky **520**

Drama

See also American drama

Collections

Shepard, A. Stories on stage **812**

Indexes

Play index **808.82**

Dramer, Kim

People's Republic of China (5 and up) **951**

Draper, Allison Stark

Polio (5 and up) **616.8**

Draper, Judith

My first horse and pony book (k-3) **636.1**

Drat that fat cat!. Thomson, P. **E**

The **draug**. San Souci, R.
In San Souci, R. More short & shivery; thirty terrifying tales p22-26 **398.2**

[**Draw** 50 series]. Ames, L. J. **743**

Draw your own cartoons!. Mayne, D. **741.5**

Drawing

Ames, L. J. [Draw 50 series] (4 and up) **743**

Caldwell, B. Fantasy! cartooning (5 and up) **741.5**

Court, R. How to draw cars and trucks (4-6) **743**

Emberley, E. Ed Emberley's big green drawing book (2-5) **741.2**

Emberley, E. Ed Emberley's big red drawing book (2-5) **741.2**

Emberley, E. Ed Emberley's drawing book: make a world (2-5) **741.2**

Emberley, E. Ed Emberley's drawing book of faces (2-5) **743**

Emberley, E. Ed Emberley's fingerprint drawing book (2-5) **741.2**

Emberley, E. Ed Emberley's great thumbprint drawing book (2-5) **741.2**

Giarrano, V. Comics crash course (5 and up) **741.5**

Hart, C. Kids draw anime (3-6) **741.5**

Hart, C. Kids draw Manga Shoujo (1-4) **741.5**

Hart, C. Mecha mania (5 and up) **741.5**

Mayne, D. Draw your own cartoons! (3-6) **741.5**

Drawing—*Continued*

Pericoli, M. See the city (4 and up) **741.9**
Roche, A. Cartooning (3-6) **741.5**
Temple, K. Drawing (5 and up) **741.2**
Zemke, D. 2 is for Toucan (3-5) **741.2**
See/See also pages in the following book(s):
Luxbacher, I. The jumbo book of art (4 and up) **702.8**

Fiction

Falwell, C. David's drawings **E**
Johnson, C. Harold and the purple crayon **E**
Kleven, E. The paper princess **E**
Kroll, S. Patches: lost and found **E**
Mills, C. Ziggy's blue-ribbon day **E**
Reynolds, P. The dot **E**
Reynolds, P. Ish **E**
Williams, V. B. Cherries and cherry pits **E**

Drawing book: make a world, Ed Emberley's. Emberley, E. **741.2**

Drawing book of faces, Ed Emberley's. Emberley, E. **743**

Drawing lessons from a bear. McPhail, D. M. **E**

Drawson, Blair
(il) Hovey, K. Arachne speaks **811**

The **dream**. Schwartz, A.
In Schwartz, A. Scary stories 3; more tales to chill your bones p53-54 **398.2**

Dream dancer. Newsome, J. **E**

A **dream** in the road. Storni, A.
In You're on!: seven plays in English and Spanish p100-07 **812.008**

The **dream** keeper and other poems. Hughes, L. **811**

A **dream** of freedom. McWhorter, D. **323.1**

Dreamer from the village [biography of Marc Chagall] Markel, M. **92**

Dreaming in black and white. Jung, R. **Fic**

Dreams

See also Sleep

Fiction

Asch, F. Moonbear's dream **E**
Banks, K. Close your eyes **E**
Briggs, R. The snowman **E**
Cole, B. Fair Monaco **E**
Lowry, L. Gossamer (5 and up) **Fic**
Ramirez, A. Napi **E**
Ringgold, F. Tar Beach **E**
Van Allsburg, C. Ben's dream **E**
Van Allsburg, C. Just a dream **E**
Van Allsburg, C. The sweetest fig **E**
Wiesner, D. Free fall **E**

Poetry

Wong, J. S. Night garden (3-6) **811**

Dreams in the golden country. Lasky, K. **Fic**

Dreifuss, Donald
(il) Ziefert, H. A dozen ducklings lost and found **E**

Drescher, Henrik
(il) Sierra, J. The gruesome guide to world monsters **398**

Dress *See* Clothing and dress

Dressen-McQueen, Stacey
(il) Cruise, R. Little Mamá forgets **E**

(il) Fleming, C. Boxes for Katje **E**
(il) Schaefer, C. L. The biggest soap **E**

Dressmaking
See also Needlework

Dreyer, Francis
(jt. auth) Plisson, P. Lighthouses **387.1**

Drez, Ronald J.
Remember D-day (5 and up) **940.54**

Drinking. Pringle, L. P. **362.292**

The **drinking** gourd. Monjo, F. N. **E**

Drinking problem *See* Alcoholism

Drip, drop. Weeks, S. **E**

The **dripping** cutlass. Olson, A. N.
In Olson, A. N. and Schwartz, H. Ask the bones: scary stories from around the world p92-98 **398.2**

Driscoll, Michael
A child's introduction to poetry (4 and up) **808.81**

Driven from the land. Meltzer, M. **978**

Dronzek, Laura
(il) Henkes, K. Oh! **E**
(il) Shannon, G. Tippy-toe chick, go! **E**
(il) Shannon, G. White is for blueberry **E**

A **drop** of blood. Showers, P. **612.1**

A **drop** of water. Wick, W. **553.7**

Drop Star. San Souci, R.
In San Souci, R. Cut from the same cloth; American women of myth, legend, and tall tale p21-26 **398.2**

Droughts
Cooper, M. L. Dust to eat (4 and up) **973.917**

Fiction

Hamilton, V. Drylongso (3-5) **Fic**
Jackson, A. Rainmaker (5 and up) **Fic**
Peterson, J. W. Don't forget Winona **E**

Folklore

Aardema, V. Bringing the rain to Kapiti Plain (k-3) **398.2**

Drug abuse
See/See also pages in the following book(s):
Jukes, M. It's a girl thing (5 and up) **305.23**

Drug trade, Illicit *See* Drug traffic

Drug traffic
Fiction
DeFelice, C. C. Death at Devil's Bridge (5 and up) **Fic**

Drugs and crime
See also Drug traffic

Druids and Druidism
Fiction
Farmer, N. The Sea of Trolls (5 and up) **Fic**

Drummer Hoff. Emberley, B. **398.8**

Drummond, Allan
Liberty! **E**
(il) Borden, L. The journey that saved Curious George [biography of Margret Rey and H. A. Rey] **92**

Drummond, Karen Eich
(jt. auth) D'Amico, J. The coming to America
cookbook **641.5**
(jt. auth) D'Amico, J. The healthy body cookbook **641.5**
(jt. auth) D'Amico, J. The math chef **641.5**
(jt. auth) D'Amico, J. The science chef
641.3

Drums
Fiction
Bearden, R. Li'l Dan, the drummer boy E
Bynum, E. Jamari's drum E
Francis, P. David gets his drum E
The **dry** desert. Johansson, P. **577.5**
Drylongso. Hamilton, V. **Fic**
Du Bois, William Pène
The twenty-one balloons (5 and up) **Fic**
(il) Zolotow, C. William's doll E
DuBois, Jill
Colombia (5 and up) **986.1**
Greece (5 and up) **949.5**
Israel (5 and up) **956.94**
Korea (5 and up) **951.9**
Dubois, Philippe J.
Birds (5 and up) **598**
Dubowski, Cathy East
A horse named Seabiscuit (2-4) **798.4**
Dubowski, Mark
(jt. auth) Dubowski, C. E. A horse named
Seabiscuit **798.4**
Duck & Goose. Hills, T. E
Duck-billed platypus See Platypus
Duck, duck, goose!. Beaumont, K. E
Duck for President. Cronin, D. E
Duck in the truck. Alborough, J. E
Duck on a bike. Shannon, D. E
Duck skates. Berry, L. E
The **duck** with golden eggs. Afanas´ev, A. N.
In Afanas´ev, A. N. Russian fairy tales p541-
44 **398.2**
Duckie's ducklings. Barry, F. E
Duckling. Magloff, L. **598**
Ducks
Baker, K. Quack and count E
Brenner, B. Chibi (k-3) **598**
Goldin, A. R. Ducks don't get wet (k-3)
598
Magloff, L. Duckling (k-2) **598**
McMillan, B. Days of the ducklings (2-4)
598
Watts, B. Duck (k-3) **598**
Fiction
Alborough, J. Duck in the truck E
Aruego, J. The last laugh E
Asch, F. Baby Duck's new friend E
Barry, F. Duckie's ducklings E
Berry, L. Duck skates E
Buzzeo, T. Dawdle Duckling E
Cooper, H. Pumpkin soup E
Cronin, D. Duck for President E
Cronin, D. Giggle, giggle, quack E
Ginsburg, M. The chick and the duckling E
Grindley, S. Mucky Duck E

Hest, A. Guess who, Baby Duck! E
Hills, T. Duck & Goose E
Hindley, J. Do like a duck does! E
Hutchins, P. We're going on a picnic! E
James, S. Little One Step E
King-Smith, D. Funny Frank (3-5) **Fic**
Luthardt, K. Peep! E
McCloskey, R. Make way for ducklings E
Murphy, M. I kissed the baby E
Peters, L. W. Cold little duck, duck, duck E
Polacco, P. John Philip Duck E
Potter, B. The tale of Jemima Puddle-duck
E
Shannon, D. Duck on a bike E
Simmons, J. Come along, Daisy! E
Sloat, T. I'm a duck! E
Tafuri, N. Goodnight, my duckling E
Tafuri, N. Have you seen my duckling? E
Thompson, L. Little Quack E
Waddell, M. Farmer duck E
Waddell, M. It's quacking time! E
Ziefert, H. A dozen ducklings lost and found
E
Folklore
Paterson, K. The tale of the mandarin ducks
(1-3) **398.2**
Van Laan, N. Shingebiss (2-4) **398.2**
Songs
Bates, I. Five little ducks (k-2) **782.42**
Raffi. Five little ducks (k-2) **782.42**
Whippo, W. Little white duck (k-2) **782.42**
Ducks don't get wet. Goldin, A. R. **598**
Dudley, David L.
The bicycle man (4-6) **Fic**
Dudzinski, Kathleen
Meeting dolphins (4 and up) **599.5**
Due, Linnea A.
Cream puff
In Girls got game; sports stories and poems
810.8
Duel. Grossman, D. **Fic**
Duey, Kathleen
Lara and the gray mare (4-6) **Fic**
Duffey, Betsy
Dopey
In Byars, B. C. and others. My dog, my hero
p42-47 **S C**
Spotlight on Cody (2-4) **Fic**
(jt. auth) Byars, B. C. My dog, my hero
S C
(jt. auth) Byars, B. C. The SOS file **Fic**
Duffy, Daniel M.
(il) Cohen, B. Molly's pilgrim E
Duffy, Trent
The clock (4 and up) **681.1**
Duffy and the Bucca. Climo, S.
In Climo, S. Magic & mischief; tales from
Cornwall p111-22 **398.2**
Duffy and the devil. Philip, N.
In Philip, N. Celtic fairy tales p78-85
398.2
Dufour, Daniel
(il) Plisson, P. Lighthouses **387.1**

Dyer, Brooke
　(il) Wilson, K. Mama always comes home　E
Dyer, Jane
　(il) Appelt, K. Oh my baby, little one　E
　(il) Ashman, L. Babies on the go　E
　(il) Goss, G. Blue moon soup　**641.8**
　(il) Krauss, R. Goodnight goodnight sleepyhead
　　　E
　(il) Krull, K. A woman for president [biography
　　of Victoria C. Woodhull]　**92**
　(il) Lewis, R. A. I love you like crazy cakes
　　　E
　(il) Rosenthal, A. K. Cookies　**E**
　(il) Spinelli, E. Sophie's masterpiece　**E**
　(il) Talking like the rain. See Talking like the
　　rain　**821.008**
　(il) Yolen, J. The three bears holiday rhyme
　　book　**811**
Dyslexia
　Landau, E. Dyslexia (5 and up)　**616.85**
　Wiltshire, P. Dyslexia (5 and up)　**616.85**
　　　　　　　Fiction
　Betancourt, J. My name is brain Brian (4-6)
　　　Fic
Dyson, Marianne J.
　Home on the moon (4 and up)　**629.45**

　　　　　　　E

E-Mail. Brimner, L. D.　**004.6**
E-mail: a magic mouse guide. Ward-Johnson, C.
　　　004.6
E-mail systems See Electronic mail systems
E.S.P. See Extrasensory perception
Each little bird that sings. Wiles, D.　**Fic**
Each living thing. Ryder, J.　**E**
Each orange had 8 slices. Giganti, P., Jr.　**E**
Each peach pear plum. Ahlberg, J.　**E**
Eager, Edward
　Half magic (4-6)　**Fic**
　Magic or not? (4-6)　**Fic**
　Seven-day magic (4-6)　**Fic**
Eager. Fox, H.　**Fic**
Eagles
　　　See also Bald eagle
　Penny, M. Golden eagle (k-3)　**598**
　　　　　　　Folklore
　Gregorowski, C. Fly, eagle, fly! (k-3)　**398.2**
Ear
　Simon, S. Eyes and ears (4 and up)　**612.8**
The **ear**. Babbitt, N.
　In Babbitt, N. The Devil's other storybook
　　p73-81　**S C**
The **Ear**, the Eye, and the Arm. Farmer, N.
　　　Fic
Earhart, Amelia, 1898-1937
　　　　　　　About
　Adler, D. A. A picture book of Amelia Earhart
　　(1-3)　**92**
　Lauber, P. Lost star: the story of Amelia Earhart
　　(5 and up)　**92**

　　　　　　　Fiction
　Ryan, P. M. Amelia and Eleanor go for a ride
　　　E
Earl Mar's daughter. Jacobs, J.
　In Jacobs, J. English fairy tales p159-63
　　　398.2
Earle, Ann
　Zipping, zapping, zooming bats (k-3)　**599.4**
Earle, Sylvia A.
　Dive! (4-6)　**551.46**
　Sea critters (k-3)　**591.7**
Earle, Sylvia A., 1935-
　See/See also pages in the following book(s):
　Atkins, J. How high can we climb? (5 and up)
　　　920
The **earliest** Americans. Sattler, H. R.　**970.01**
An **early** American Christmas. De Paola, T.　**E**
Early bird nature books [series]
　Patent, D. H. White-tailed deer　**599.65**
　Walker, S. M. Fireflies　**595.7**
Early experiences [series]
　Ehrlich, F. Does an elephant take a bath?　**E**
Early humans. Gallant, R. A.　**599.93**
Early I can read book [series]
　Bonsall, C. N. Who's afraid of the dark?　**E**
　Robins, J. Addie meets Max　**E**
Early moon. Sandburg, C.
　In Sandburg, C. The Sandburg treasury; prose
　　and poetry for young people p161-207
　　　818
Earth
　　　　　　　Gravity
　　　See Gravity
Earth
　Bailey, J. Sun up, sun down (2-4)　**525**
　Frasier, D. On the day you were born　**E**
　Gallant, R. A. Earth's place in space (5 and up)
　　　525
　Gibbons, G. Planet earth/inside out (k-3)
　　　550
　Gibbons, G. The reasons for seasons (k-3)
　　　525
　Karas, G. B. On Earth (k-2)　**525**
　Miller, R. Earth and the moon (5 and up)
　　　525
　Ross, M. E. Earth cycles (k-3)　**525**
　Simon, S. Earth: our planet in space (4 and up)
　　　525
　　　　　　　Fiction
　Glaser, L. Our big home　**E**
　　　　　　Internal structure
　Cole, J. The magic school bus inside the Earth
　　(2-4)　**551.1**
　Gallant, R. A. Structure (5 and up)　**551.1**
　　　　　　　Poetry
　Singer, M. Footprints on the roof (4 and up)
　　　811
Earth and the moon. Miller, R.　**525**
Earth cycles. Ross, M. E.　**525**
Earth Day-hooray!. Murphy, S. J.　**513**
Earth from above for young readers. Arthus-
　Bertrand, Y.　**779**
Earth magic. Brand, D.　**811**

Earth science for every kid, Janice VanCleave's. VanCleave, J. P. **550**

Earth sciences

See also Geology

Lauber, P. You're aboard Spaceship Earth (k-3) **550**

VanCleave, J. P. Janice VanCleave's earth science for every kid (4 and up) **550**

Earthenware *See* Pottery

Earthquack!. Palatini, M. **E**

Earthquake sea waves *See* Tsunamis

Earthquake terror. Kehret, P. **Fic**

Earthquakes

Branley, F. M. Earthquakes (k-3) **551.2**

Grace, C. O. Forces of nature (4 and up) **551.2**

Reed, J. Earthquakes (4 and up) **551.2**

Silverstein, A. Plate tectonics (5 and up) **551.1**

Simon, S. Earthquakes (3-6) **551.2**

Tanaka, S. Earthquake! (4 and up) **979.4**

Walker, S. M. Earthquakes (3-6) **551.2**

Fiction

Kehret, P. Earthquake terror (4-6) **Fic**

Earth's place in space. Gallant, R. A. **525**

Earth's wild winds. Friend, S. **551.51**

Earthshake. Peters, L. W. **811**

Earthworks [series]

Gallant, R. A. Atmosphere **551.51**

Gallant, R. A. Plates **551.1**

Gallant, R. A. Structure **551.1**

Gallant, R. A. Water **553.7**

Harrison, D. L. Glaciers **551.3**

Harrison, D. L. Volcanoes: nature's incredible fireworks **551.2**

Earthworms, leeches, and sea worms. Blaxland, B. **592**

Eason, Alethea

The unicorns of Kabustan

In A Glory of unicorns p115-24 **S C**

East, Stella

(il) Trottier, M. The paint box **E**

East *See* Asia

East (Near East) *See* Middle East

East Africa

Feelings, M. Jambo means hello **E**

Feelings, M. Moja means one **E**

Fiction

Whelan, G. Listening for lions (5 and up) **Fic**

East Indians

Fiction

Sheth, K. Blue jasmine (5 and up) **Fic**

United States—Fiction

Fleming, C. Lowji discovers America (3-5) **Fic**

Nagda, A. W. Meow means mischief (2-4) **Fic**

East of the sun and west of the moon [story] Asbjornsen, P. C.

In The Blue fairy book p19-29 **398.2**

also in Womenfolk and fairy tales p111-26 **398.2**

Easter

See also Lent

Barth, E. Lilies, rabbits, and painted eggs (3-6) **394.26**

Bible. N.T. The Easter story **232.9**

Fisher, A. L. The story of Easter (3-5) **394.26**

Gibbons, G. Easter (k-3) **394.26**

Gulevich, T. Encyclopedia of Easter, Carnival, and Lent (5 and up) **394.26**

Landau, E. Easter (2-4) **394.26**

Thompson, L. Love one another (1-3) **232.9**

Winthrop, E. He is risen: the Easter story (k-3) **232.9**

Fiction

Carling, A. L. Sawdust carpets **E**

Heyward, D. The country bunny and the little gold shoes **E**

Polacco, P. Chicken Sunday **E**

Polacco, P. Rechenka's eggs **E**

Zolotow, C. The bunny who found Easter **E**

Folklore

Kimmel, E. A. The birds' gift (k-3) **398.2**

Poetry

Grimes, N. At Jerusalem's gate (5 and up) **811**

Easter Island

Arnold, C. Easter Island (5 and up) **996**

Underwood, D. The Easter Island statues (3-6) **996**

The **Easter** Island statues. Underwood, D. **996**

The **Easter** story. Bible. N.T. **232.9**

Eastern Africa *See* East Africa

Eastman, Dianne

(il) Bowers, V. Crazy about Canada! **971**

(il) Bowers, V. Wow Canada! **971**

(il) Thomas, L. Ha! Ha! Ha! **793.73**

Eastman, Mary Huse

Index to fairy tales. See Index to fairy tales **398.2**

Eastman, P. D. (Philip D.)

Are you my mother? **E**

The Cat in the Hat beginner book dictionary. See The Cat in the Hat beginner book dictionary **423**

Eastman, Philip D. *See* Eastman, P. D. (Philip D.), 1909-1986

Easton, Richard

A real American (5 and up) **Fic**

Eastwood, John

(il) King-Smith, D. The Catlady **Fic**

(il) King-Smith, D. Funny Frank **Fic**

Easy math puzzles. Adler, D. A. **793.74**

Easy menu ethnic cookbooks [series] (5 and up) **641.5**

Easy origami. Boursin, D. **745.54**

Eat your vegetables. Marshall, J.

In Marshall, J. Rats on the roof, and other stories p41-47 **S C**

Eating *See* Dining

The **eating** competition. Lunge-Larsen, L.
    In Lunge-Larsen, L. The troll with no heart in
    his body and other tales of trolls from
    Norway p69-75   **398.2**

Eating customs
    See also Table etiquette
  Lauber, P. What you never knew about fingers,
    forks, & chopsticks (2-4)   **394.1**
  Solheim, J. It's disgusting—and we ate it! (4
    and up)   **641.3**

Eating the alphabet. Ehlert, L.   **E**

Eating up Gladys. Zemach, M.   **E**

Eating with trolls. Yolen, J.
    In Yolen, J. Mightier than the sword; world
    folktales for strong boys p28-35
        398.2

Ebbeler, Jeffrey
  (il) Hill, S. L. Punxsutawney Phyllis   **E**

Ebola virus
  Bueche, S. The Ebola virus (4-6)   **616.9**

Echinoderms
  Blaxland, B. Sea stars, sea urchins, and their
    relatives (3-6)   **593.9**
Echinoderms: sea stars, sea urchins, and their rel-
    atives. See Blaxland, B. Sea stars, sea ur-
    chins, and their relatives   **593.9**

Eckert, Allan W.
  Incident at Hawk's Hill (6 and up)   **Fic**

Ecological movement *See* Environmental movement

Ecology
    See also Biological diversity; Environmen-
    tal protection; Food chains (Ecology); Habitat
    (Ecology) types of ecology
  Gibbons, G. Marshes & swamps (k-3)   **577.6**
  Goodman, S. Seeds, stems, and stamens (2-4)
        581.4
  Lorbiecki, M. Planet patrol (3-5)   **577**
  Pollock, S. Ecology (4 and up)   **577**
  VanCleave, J. P. Janice Vancleave's ecology for
    every kid (4 and up)   **577**
  Wright-Frierson, V. An island scrapbook (3-5)
        508
  See/See also pages in the following book(s):
  Patent, D. H. Biodiversity (5 and up)
        333.95
        Fiction
  Cherry, L. The sea, the storm, and the mangrove
    tangle   **E**
  Sleator, W. The beasties (6 and up)   **Fic**

Ecology, Human *See* Human ecology

Ecosystems in action [series]
  Patent, D. H. Life in a grassland   **577.4**

Ecuador
  Foley, E. Ecuador (5 and up)   **986.6**
  Lourie, P. Lost treasure of the Inca (4 and up)
        986.6

Ed Emberley's big green drawing book. Emberley,
  E.   **741.2**

Ed Emberley's big red drawing book. Emberley,
  E.   **741.2**

Ed Emberley's drawing book: make a world.
  Emberley, E.   **741.2**

Ed Emberley's drawing book of faces. Emberley,
  E.   **743**

Ed Emberley's fingerprint drawing book.
  Emberley, E.   **741.2**

Ed Emberley's great thumbprint drawing book.
  Emberley, E.   **741.2**

Eddie & the gang with no name [series]
  Bateman, C. Running with the Reservoir Pups
        Fic

Eddie the raccoon. Friend, C.   **E**

Edelman, Marian Wright
  (ed) I can make a difference. See I can make a
    difference   **808.8**

Edelman, Rob
  The War of 1812 (5 and up)   **973.5**

Edens, Cooper
  (comp) Princess stories. See Princess stories
        398.2

Ederle, Gertrude, 1905-2003
        About
  Adler, D. A. America's champion swimmer:
    Gertrude Ederle (2-4)   **92**
  See/See also pages in the following book(s):
  Krull, K. Lives of the athletes (4 and up)
        920

Edge chronicles [series]
  Stewart, P. Beyond the Deepwoods   **Fic**

Edison, Thomas A. (Thomas Alva), 1847-1931
        About
  Delano, M. F. Inventing the future: a
    photobiography of Thomas Alva Edison (5
    and up)   **92**
  Dooling, M. Young Thomas Edison (1-3)   **92**
  Thomas Edison (2-4)   **92**

Edliq, Emily S.
  (il) Levine, S. Shocking science   **537**

Edmonds, Marie
        About
  Grace, C. O. Forces of nature (4 and up)
        551.2

Edna's tale. Bechtold, L.   **E**

Ed's terrestrials. Sava, S. C.   **741.5**

Education
    See also Internet in education; Schools;
    Teaching
        Fiction
  Bridges, S. Y. Ruby's wish   **E**
  Elvgren, J. R. Josias, hold the book   **E**
        History
  Woolf, A. Education (5 and up)   **940.1**
        Social aspects
  Stanley, J. Children of the Dust Bowl (5 and
    up)   **371.9**
        United States—History
  Bial, R. One-room school (3-5)   **370.9**
  Fisher, L. E. The schoolmasters (4 and up)
        370.9
  Loeper, J. J. Going to school in 1776 (4 and up)
        370.9
  See/See also pages in the following book(s):
  Freedman, R. Children of the wild West (4 and
    up)   **978**

Egyptian language
Donoughue, C. The mystery of the hieroglyphs (4 and up) **493**
Giblin, J. The riddle of the Rosetta Stone (5 and up) **493**

Egyptian mummies. Pemberton, D. **393**

Egyptian mythology
Fisher, L. E. The gods and goddesses of ancient Egypt (3-6) **299**
Hofmeyr, D. The star-bearer (3-5) **299**
Morley, J. Egyptian myths (4 and up) **299**

Egyptian myths. Morley, J. **299**

Egyptian science *See* Science—Egypt

Ehlert, Lois
Circus **E**
Color farm **E**
Color zoo **E**
Cuckoo. Cucú (k-3) **398.2**
Eating the alphabet **E**
Feathers for lunch **E**
Growing vegetable soup **E**
Hands **E**
Leaf Man **E**
Market day **E**
Mole's hill **E**
Moon rope. Un lazo a la luna (k-3) **398.2**
Nuts to you! **E**
Pie in the sky **E**
Planting a rainbow **E**
Red leaf, yellow leaf (k-3) **582.16**
Snowballs **E**
Top cat **E**
Waiting for wings **E**
(il) Martin, B. Chicka chicka 1, 2, 3 **E**
(il) Martin, B. Chicka chicka boom boom **E**

Ehrlich, Amy
Leo, Zack, and Emmie together again **E**
Rachel: the story of Rachel Carson (2-4) **92**
Thumbelina **E**
Wounded Knee: an Indian history of the American West (6 and up) **970.004**

Ehrlich, Fred
Does an elephant take a bath? **E**

Ehrlich, H. M.
Louie's goose **E**

Eichenberg, Fritz
Ape in a cape **E**
(il) Sandburg, C. Rainbows are made: poems **811**
(il) Sewell, A. Black Beauty **Fic**

Eight animals on the town. Elya, S. M. **E**

Eilenberg, Max
Cowboy Kid **E**

Einstein, Albert, 1879-1955
About
Brown, D. Odd boy out: young Albert Einstein (2-4) **92**
Delano, M. F. Genius [biography of Albert Einstein] (5 and up) **92**
Lassieur, A. Albert Einstein (5 and up) **92**
MacLeod, E. Albert Einstein (4 and up) **92**
Severance, J. B. Einstein (5 and up) **92**
Sullivan, A. M. Albert Einstein (4 and up) **92**

Einzig, Susan
(il) Pearce, P. Tom's midnight garden **Fic**

Eisenberg, Lisa
(jt. auth) Hall, K. Creepy riddles **793.73**
(jt. auth) Hall, K. Dino riddles **793.73**
(jt. auth) Hall, K. Mummy riddles **793.73**
(jt. auth) Hall, K. Ribbit riddles **793.73**
(jt. auth) Hall, K. Snakey riddles **793.73**
(jt. auth) Hall, K. Stinky riddles **793.73**
(jt. auth) Hall, K. Turkey riddles **793.73**

Eisenberg, Michael
Teaching information & technology skills **025.5**

Eitan, Ora
(il) Mallett, D. Inch by inch **782.42**

El Dorado. Delacre, L.
In Delacre, L. Golden tales; myths, legends, and folktales from Latin America p47-51 **398.2**

El-Hamamsy, Salwa
(jt. auth) Pateman, R. Egypt **962**

El Niño Current
Arnold, C. El Niño (4 and up) **551.6**

El Salvador
Foley, E. El Salvador (5 and up) **972.84**

El-Shabazz, El-Hajj Malik *See* Malcolm X, 1925-1965

Elbert's bad word. Wood, A. **E**

Elderly
See also Old age

The **elders** of Chelm & Genendel's key. Singer, I. B.
In Singer, I. B. Stories for children p3-7 **S C**

Eleanor, of Aquitaine, Queen, consort of Henry II, King of England, 1122?-1204
See/See also pages in the following book(s):
Krull, K. Lives of extraordinary women (4 and up) **920**
Meltzer, M. Ten queens (5 and up) **920**
Fiction
Konigsburg, E. L. A proud taste for scarlet and miniver (5 and up) **Fic**

Eleanor [biography of Eleanor Roosevelt] Cooney, B. **92**

Elections
Christelow, E. Vote! (k-3) **324**
Hamilton, J. Running for office (3-5) **324**
Fiction
Beard, D. B. Operation Clean Sweep (3-6) **Fic**
Cronin, D. Duck for President **E**

Electric apparatus and appliances
Bartholomew, A. Electric mischief (4-6) **621.31**

Electric fish. Landau, E. **597**

Electric Girl. Brennan, M. **741.5**

Electric lines
See/See also pages in the following book(s):
Macaulay, D. Underground (5 and up) **624**

Electric mischief. Bartholomew, A. **621.31**

Electric power

Cole, J. The magic school bus and the electric field trip (2-4) **621.3**

Electric power plants

See also Nuclear power plants

Electric railroads

See also Street railroads

Electricity

Bailey, J. Charged up (2-4) **333.79**

Bang, M. My light (1-3) **621.47**

Bartholomew, A. Electric mischief (4-6) **621.31**

Berger, M. Switch on, switch off (k-3) **537**

Cole, J. The magic school bus and the electric field trip (2-4) **621.3**

Farndon, J. Electricity (3-6) **537**

Gardner, R. Energizing science projects with electricity and magnetism (4-6) **537**

Lauw, D. Electricity (3-6) **537**

Levine, S. Shocking science (5 and up) **537**

Meiani, A. Electricity (4 and up) **537**

Parker, S. Electricity (4 and up) **537**

VanCleave, J. P. Janice VanCleave's electricity (4 and up) **537**

Woodford, C. Electricity (5 and up) **537**

Electronic data processing *See* Data processing

Electronic mail systems

Brimner, L. D. E-Mail (2-4) **004.6**

Ward-Johnson, C. E-mail: a magic mouse guide (k-3) **004.6**

Electronic toys

See also Computer games

Elementary school libraries

See also Children's libraries

Exploring science in the library **027.8**

The **Elements** [Benchmark Bks. series] (5 and up) **546**

Elements [Grolier] (5 and up) **546**

Elena the Wise. Afanas´ev, A. N.

In Afanas´ev, A. N. Russian fairy tales p545-49 **398.2**

Elena's serenade. Geeslin, C. **E**

Elephant and Frog go courting. Bryan, A.

In Bryan, A. Ashley Bryan's African tales, uh-huh p13-19 **398.2**

An **elephant** in the backyard. Sobol, R. **636.9**

The **elephant** prince. Novesky, A. **294.5**

Elephant quest. Lewin, T. **591.9**

Elephant rescue. Morgan, J. **599.67**

Elephants

Arnold, K. Elephants can paint, too! (k-3) **599.67**

Helfer, R. The world's greatest elephant (1-3) **791.3**

Morgan, J. Elephant rescue (5 and up) **599.67**

Schubert, L. Ballet of the elephants **791.8**

Sobol, R. An elephant in the backyard (k-3) **636.9**

See/See also pages in the following book(s):

Sayre, A. P. Secrets of sound (4 and up) **591.59**

Fiction

Brunhoff, J. d. The story of Babar, the little elephant **E**

Chorao, K. Here comes Kate **E**

Cushman, D. Mystery at the Club Sandwich **E**

D'Amico, C. Ella the Elegant Elephant **E**

Hoff, S. Oliver **E**

Kipling, R. The elephant's child **Fic**

Lewis, K. Good night, Harry **E**

Lobel, A. Uncle Elephant **E**

McGrory, A. Kidogo **E**

Prince, A. J. Twenty-one elephants and still standing **E**

Pullman, P. The firework-maker's daughter (4 and up) **Fic**

Roome, D. R. The elephant's pillow **E**

Root, B. Gumbrella **E**

Schertle, A. 1, 2, I love you **E**

Seuss, Dr. Horton hatches the egg **E**

Seuss, Dr. Horton hears a Who! **E**

Folklore

Young, E. Seven blind mice (k-3) **398.2**

Elephants can paint, too!. Arnold, K. **599.67**

The **elephant's** child. Kipling, R. **Fic**

The **elephant's** child. Kipling, R.

also in Kipling, R. Just so stories **S C**

The **elephant's** pillow. Roome, D. R. **E**

The **elevator**. Sleator, W.

In Beware!; R.L. Stine picks his favorite scary stories p87-99 **808.8**

Elevator magic. Murphy, S. J. **513**

Eleven. Myracle, L. **Fic**

The **eleven** thousand Virgins. Delacre, L.

In Delacre, L. Golden tales; myths, legends, and folktales from Latin America p15-18 **398.2**

Elffers, Joost

(jt. auth) Freymann, S. How are you peeling? **E**

(jt. auth) Freymann, S. One lonely sea horse **E**

Elias *See* Elijah (Biblical figure)

Elias, Marie Louise

(jt. auth) Kohen, E. Spain **946**

Elias, Megan

Colorado

In World Almanac Library of the States series **973**

Eliason, Mike

(il) Buckley, J., Jr. Play ball! **796.357**

Elijah (Biblical figure)

About

Goldin, B. D. Journeys with Elijah (4 and up) **222**

Elijah and the three brothers. Goldin, B. D.

In Goldin, B. D. Journeys with Elijah; eight tales of the Prophet p39-47 **222**

Elijah the slave. Singer, I. B.

In Singer, I. B. Stories for children p206-09 **S C**

Elijah's angel. Rosen, M. J. **Fic**

Emberley, Michael—*Continued*
  (il) Harris, R. H. Sweet Jasmine, nice Jackson
    612.6
  (il) Hoberman, M. A. You read to me, I'll read
    to you [very short fairy tales to read together]
    E
  (il) Hoberman, M. A. You read to me, I'll read
    to you [very short Mother Goose tales to read
    together] **811**
  (il) Hoberman, M. A. You read to me, I'll read
    to you [very short stories to read together]
    811

Emblems *See* Signs and symbols
Emblems, National *See* National emblems
Embroidery
  Cobb, M. A sampler view of colonial life (2-5)
    746.44
  Nicholas, K. Kids embroidery (3-6)   **746.44**
  Sadler, J. A. Embroidery (4-6)   **746.44**
  Sadler, J. A. Embroidery
    also in Sadler, J. A. The jumbo book of
      needlecrafts   **746.4**

Embryology
    See also Fertilization in vitro; Fetus; Repro-
      duction

Emeline at the circus. Priceman, M.   **E**
Emelya the simpleton. Afanas´ev, A. N.
  In Afanas´ev, A. N. Russian fairy tales p46-
    48   **398.2**

Emergency!. Gibbons, G.   **363.34**
Emergency relief *See* Disaster relief
An **emerging** world power (1900-1929). Stanley,
  G. E.   **973.91**
Emeril's there's a chef in my family!. Lagasse, E.
    641.5

Emigrants *See* Immigrants
Emigration *See* Immigration and emigration
Emily Dickinson's letters to the world. Winter, J.
    811
Emily Post's The guide to good manners for kids.
  Post, P.   **395**
Emily's art. Catalanotto, P.   **E**
Emily's balloon. Sakai, K.   **E**
Emily's first 100 days of school. Wells, R.   **E**
Emma Dilemma and the new nanny. Hermes, P.
    Fic
Emma in charge. McPhail, D. M.   **E**
Emma's rug. Say, A.   **E**
Emma's yucky brother. Little, J.   **E**
Emmett's pig. Stolz, M.   **E**
Emotions
  Aliki. Feelings (k-3)   **152.4**
  Freymann, S. How are you peeling?   **E**
  Young, E. Voices of the heart   **179**
Fiction
  Frame, J. A. Yesterday I had the blues   **E**
  Seeger, L. V. Walter was worried   **E**
  Spinelli, E. When you are happy   **E**
Emperador's new clothes. Marcantonio, P. S.
  In Marcantonio, P. S. Red ridin' in the hood;
    and other cuentos   **S C**

The **emperor** lays an egg. Guiberson, B. Z.
    598
The **emperor** penguin. Noonan, D.   **598**
The **emperor's** egg. Jenkins, M.   **598**
The **emperor's** new clothes. Andersen, H. C.
  In Andersen, H. C. Hans Christian Andersen's
    Fairy Tales   **S C**
  also in De Paola, T. Tomie dePaola's Favor-
    ite nursery tales p87-95   **398.2**
The **emperor's** new clothes. Demi   **E**
The **emperor's** new clothes. Sedgwick, M.   **E**
The **emperor's** new clothes [illustrated by Angela
  Barrett] Andersen, H. C.   **E**
The **emperor's** new clothes [illustrated by Virginia
  Lee Burton] Andersen, H. C.   **E**
The **emperor's** silent army. O'Connor, J.   **931**
Empire State Building (New York, N.Y.)
  Macaulay, D. Unbuilding (4 and up)   **690**
Fiction
  Hopkinson, D. Sky boys   **E**
  Kirk, C. A. Sky dancers   **E**
  Wiesner, D. Sector 7   **E**
Employees
Training
    See also Apprentices
Employment of children *See* Child labor
Employment of women *See* Women—Employ-
  ment
The **empty** mirror. Collier, J. L.   **Fic**
The **empty** pot. Demi   **398.2**
Encantado. Montgomery, S.   **599.5**
The **enchanted** castle. Nesbit, E.   **Fic**
The **Enchanted** horse
  In The Arabian nights entertainments p358-89
    398.2
The **Enchanted** prince
  In Stockings of buttermilk: American folktales
    p95-103   **398.2**
The **enchanted** princess. Afanas´ev, A. N.
  In Afanas´ev, A. N. Russian fairy tales p600-
    11   **398.2**
The **enchanted** ring. Afanas´ev, A. N.
  In Afanas´ev, A. N. Russian fairy tales p31-
    37   **398.2**
The **enchanted** spring. Schwartz, H.
  In Schwartz, H. and Rush, B. A coat for the
    moon and other Jewish tales p8-11
    398.2
Enchantment of the world, second series
  Augustin, B. Iraq   **956.7**
  Augustin, B. United Arab Emirates   **953**
  Blashfield, J. F. England   **942**
  Blauer, E. South Africa   **968**
  Burgan, M. Belgium   **949.3**
  Dramer, K. People's Republic of China   **951**
  Foster, L. M. Kuwait   **953.67**
  Foster, L. M. Oman   **953**
  Greenblatt, M. Afghanistan   **958.1**
  Heinrichs, A. Australia   **994**
  Heinrichs, A. Brazil   **981**
  Heinrichs, A. Japan   **952**
  Hintz, M. Algeria   **965**

Environment

See also Environmental degradation

Environmental degradation

Burnie, D. Endangered planet (5 and up)
333.95

Environmental disasters [series]

Bryan, N. Los Alamos wildfires   363.34
Bryan, N. Bhopal   363.7
Bryan, N. Chernobyl   363.7
Bryan, N. Exxon Valdez oil spill   363.7
Bryan, N. Love Canal   363.7

Environmental movement

Pringle, L. P. The environmental movement (5 and up)   363.7

Environmental pollution *See* Pollution

Environmental protection

Bang, M. Nobody particular (4 and up)
363.7

Brown, L. K. Dinosaurs to the rescue! (k-3)
363.7

Dalgleish, S. Managing the land (3-6)
333.73

Pringle, L. P. The environmental movement (5 and up)   363.7

Fiction

Hiaasen, C. Flush (5 and up)   Fic
Hiaasen, C. Hoot (5 and up)   Fic
Van Allsburg, C. Just a dream   E

Environmental sciences

Lorbiecki, M. Planet patrol (3-5)   577

The **epic** of Gilgamesh. McCaughrean, G.
398.2

An **epidemic** of ducks. Sanfield, S.

In Sanfield, S. The adventures of High John the Conqueror   398.2

Epidemics

Barnard, B. Outbreak (5 and up)   614.4

Fiction

Anderson, L. H. Fever, 1793 (5 and up)   Fic
Giblin, J. The boy who saved Cleveland (3-5)
Fic

Epidemics! Deadly diseases throughout history [series]

Casil, A. S. Hantavirus   616.9
Draper, A. S. Polio   616.8
Isle, M. Malaria   616.9
Margulies, P. Diphtheria   616.9
Ramen, F. SARS   614.5

Epigrams

See also Proverbs; Quotations

Epiphany

Hoyt-Goldsmith, D. Three Kings Day (3-5)
394.26

Fiction

Vidal, B. Federico and the Magi's gift   E

Epossumondas. Salley, C.   398.2

Equations

Murphy, S. J. Safari Park (2-4)   512

Equestrianism *See* Horsemanship

Erandi's braids. Madrigal, A. H.   E

Eratosthenes, 3rd cent. B.C.

About

Lasky, K. The librarian who measured the earth [biography of Eratosthenes] (2-5)   92

Erdrich, Louise

The birchbark house (5 and up)   Fic
The game of silence (5 and up)   Fic

Eric Carle's animals, animals   808.81

Eric Carle's dragons dragons and other creatures that never were   808.81

Erickson, Darren

(il) Kelly, E. J. Paper airplanes   745.592
(il) Ross, M. E. Millipedeology   595.6
(il) Ross, M. E. Spiderology   595.4

Erickson, Paul

Daily life on a Southern plantation, 1853 (4 and up)   975

Eriksson, Eva

Molly goes shopping   E
(il) Lindgren, B. Julia wants a pet   E

Eriksson, Inga-Karin

(il) Björk, C. Vendela in Venice   Fic

Ering, Timothy Basil

(il) DiCamillo, K. The tale of Despereaux
Fic

Erlbach, Arlene

The kids' invention book (4 and up)   608
The kids' volunteering book (4-6)   302
Merry Christmas, everywhere! (k-3)   394.26
Sidewalk games around the world (3-5)
796.1

Erlbach, Herb

(jt. auth) Erlbach, A. Merry Christmas, everywhere!   394.26

Erlbruch, Wolf

(il) Oh, no! Where are my pants? and other disasters. See Oh, no! Where are my pants? and other disasters   811.008

Ernst, Linda L.

Lapsit services for the very young II   027.62

Ernst, Lisa Campbell

Goldilocks returns   E
Little Red Riding Hood: a newfangled prairie tale (k-3)   398.2
Sam Johnson and the blue ribbon quilt   E
The turn-around upside-down alphabet book
E
Zinnia and Dot   E

Eros (Greek deity)

Craft, M. Cupid and Psyche (4 and up)   292

Esbaum, Jill

Ste-e-e-eamboat a-comin'!   E

Esbensen, Barbara Juster

Baby whales drink milk (k-1)   599.5
Sponges are skeletons (k-3)   593.4
Swing around the sun (2-4)   811
Tiger with wings (2-4)   598

Esbenshade, Richard S.

Hungary (5 and up)   943.9

Escape. Haddix, M. P.

In Shelf life: stories by the book   S C

Escape! [biography of Harry Houdini] Fleischman, S.   92

Excavations (Archeology)—*Continued*
Greece
Scarre, C. The Palace of Minos at Knossos (4 and up)   **728.8**
Iraq
Shuter, J. Mesopotamia (4-6)   **935**
United States
Quigley, M. Mesa Verde (4-6)   **978.8**

Exceptional children
See also Wild children

The **executioner's** daughter. Williams, L. E.
                    Fic

Exercise
See also Physical fitness; Weight lifting
Carle, E. From head to toe   **E**
Carlson, N. L. Get up and go!   **E**
Rockwell, L. The busy body book (k-1)   **612**

Exhibitions
See also Fairs

Exiles *See* Refugees

Exner, Carol R.
Practical puppetry A-Z   **791.5**

Exodus. Wildsmith, B.   **222**

Expanding universe *See* Universe

Expansion of America [series]
Thompson, L. The transcontinental railroad
                    385.09

Experimenting with science [series]
Meiani, A. Air   **533**
Meiani, A. Chemistry   **540.7**
Meiani, A. Electricity   **537**
Meiani, A. Light   **535**
Meiani, A. Magnetism   **538**
Meiani, A. Water   **532**

Experts, Incorporated. Weeks, S.
In Tripping over the lunch lady and other school stories p30-40   **S C**

Exploding ants. Settel, J.   **591.5**

Exploration
Kimmel, E. C. The look-it-up book of explorers (5 and up)   **920**
Matthews, R. Explorer (4 and up)   **910.4**
Stefoff, R. Exploration (5 and up)   **910.4**
Encyclopedias
Explorers and exploration (5 and up)   **910.4**

Exploration and conquest. Maestro, B.   **970.01**

Exploration and settlement. Steins, R.   **970.01**

Explorers
Atkins, J. How high can we climb? (5 and up)
                    920
Calvert, P. Vasco da Gama (5 and up)   **92**
Calvert, P. Zebulon Pike (5 and up)   **92**
Faber, H. Samuel de Champlain (5 and up)
                    92
Ferris, J. Arctic explorer: the story of Matthew Henson (3-6)   **92**
Fritz, J. Around the world in a hundred years (4 and up)   **910.4**
Fritz, J. Where do you think you're going, Christopher Columbus? (2-4)   **92**
Goodman, J. E. Despite all obstacles: La Salle and the conquest of the Mississippi (4 and up)   **92**

Goodman, J. E. A long and uncertain journey: the 27,000 mile voyage of Vasco da Gama (4 and up)   **92**
Johnson, D. Onward [biography of Matthew Henson] (5 and up)   **92**
Kimmel, E. C. The look-it-up book of explorers (5 and up)   **920**
Kostyal, K. M. Trial by ice: a photobiography of Sir Ernest Shackleton (4 and up)   **92**
Levinson, N. S. Magellan and the first voyage around the world (5 and up)   **92**
Matthews, R. Explorer (4 and up)   **910.4**
Meltzer, M. Francisco Pizarro (5 and up)   **92**
Otfinoski, S. Juan Ponce de Leon (5 and up)
                    92
Otfinoski, S. Vasco Nuñez de Balboa (5 and up)
                    92
Sís, P. Follow the dream [biography of Christopher Columbus] (k-3)   **92**
Dictionaries
Biography for beginners: world explorers (3-5)
                    920.003
Explorers (5 and up)   **920.003**
Encyclopedias
Explorers and exploration (5 and up)   **910.4**
Explorers (5 and up)   **920.003**
Explorers and exploration (5 and up)   **910.4**

Explorers of new worlds [series]
Brennan, K. Sir Edmund Hillary, modern day explorer   **92**

Exploring cultures of the world [series]
Galvin, I. F. Brazil   **981**
Markham, L. Colombia   **986.1**

Exploring life science (4-6)   **570**

Exploring our solar system. Ride, S. K.   **523.2**

Exploring planet earth [series]
Friend, S. Earth's wild winds   **551.51**

Exploring Saturn. Bortolotti, D.   **523.4**

Exploring science in the library   **027.8**

Exploring technology (5 and up)   **603**

Exploring the deep, dark sea. Gibbons, G.
                    551.46

Exploring tough issues [series]
Bingham, J. Why do families break up?
                    306.89
Woolf, A. Why are people terrorists?   **303.6**

Express yourself!. Raimondo, J.   **709.04**

Expressionism (Art)
Raimondo, J. Express yourself! (1-5)   **709.04**

Extinct animals
See also Prehistoric animals; Rare animals

Extinct cities
See also Ghost towns

The **extinguished** lights. Singer, I. B.
In Singer, I. B. The power of light; eight stories for Hanukkah p13-20   **S C**
also in Singer, I. B. Stories for children p15-21   **S C**

Extra cheese, please!. Peterson, C.   **637**

Extra innings (4 and up)   **811.008**

Extraordinary African-Americans. Altman, S.
                    920

Extraordinary Asian Americans and Pacific Islanders. Sinnott, S. **920**

Extraordinary Asian-Pacific Americans. See Sinnott, S. Extraordinary Asian Americans and Pacific Islanders **920**

Extraordinary Black Americans. See Altman, S. Extraordinary African-Americans **920**

An **extraordinary** life. Pringle, L. P. **595.7**

Extraordinary patriots of the United States of America. Robinson Masters, N. **920**

Extraordinary people [series]
Altman, S. Extraordinary African-Americans **920**
Robinson Masters, N. Extraordinary patriots of the United States of America **920**
Sinnott, S. Extraordinary Asian Americans and Pacific Islanders **920**

Extraordinary short story writing. Otfinoski, S. **808.3**

Extrasensory perception
See also Clairvoyance
Fiction
Christopher, M. The dog that called the pitch (2-4) **Fic**
Lester, J. The old African (3-6) **Fic**
Sleator, W. Into the dream (5 and up) **Fic**
Snyder, Z. K. The magic nation thing (4 and up) **Fic**

Extraterrestrial beings
Fiction
Deacon, A. Beegu **E**
Johnston, T. Alien & Possum: hanging out **E**
Saint-Exupéry, A. d. The little prince **Fic**
Spinner, S. Be first in the universe (4-6) **Fic**
Waugh, S. Space race (4-6) **Fic**

Extravehicular activity (Space flight)
Vogt, G. Spacewalks (4 and up) **629.45**

Exxon Valdez (Ship)
Bryan, N. Exxon Valdez oil spill (5 and up) **363.7**

Exxon Valdez oil spill. Bryan, N. **363.7**

Eye
Silverstein, A. Can you see the chalkboard? (3-5) **617.7**
Simon, S. Eyes and ears (4 and up) **612.8**

Eye-popping optical illusions. Dispezio, M. A. **152.14**

Eyeglasses
Fiction
Giff, P. R. Watch out, Ronald Morgan! **E**
Smith, L. Glasses: who needs 'em? **E**

Eyes and ears. Simon, S. **612.8**

Eyes, nose, fingers and toes. Hindley, J. **E**

Eyes, nose, fingers, toes. See Krauss, R. Goodnight goodnight sleepyhead **E**

Eyes of marriage. Terada, A. M.
In Terada, A. M. Under the starfruit tree; folktales from Vietnam p64-68 **398.2**

The **eyes** of the Amaryllis. Babbitt, N. **Fic**

Eyes on the universe. Reed, G. **520**

Eyewitness readers [series]
Maynard, C. Micromonsters **579**
Wallace, K. Tale of a tadpole **597.8**

Eyewitness rocks & minerals. Symes, R. F. **549**

Eyewitness science [series]
Burnie, D. Light **535**

F

F E G: ridiculous stupid poems for intelligent children. Hirsch, R. **821**

F is for fiesta. Elya, S. M. **E**

F.W. prep [series]
Otfinoski, S. Extraordinary short story writing **808.3**

Fa Mulan. San Souci, R. **398.2**

Faber, Harold
Samuel de Champlain (5 and up) **92**

Fables
Brett, J. Town mouse, country mouse (k-3) **398.2**
Brown, M. Once a mouse (k-3) **398.2**
Cooney, B. Chanticleer and the fox **E**
Galdone, P. The monkey and the crocodile (k-2) **398.2**
McClintock, B. Animal fables from Aesop (1-4) **398.2**
Morpurgo, M. The McElderry book of Aesop's fables (k-2) **398.2**
Pinkney, J. Aesop's fables **398.2**
Poole, A. L. The ant and the grasshopper (k-3) **398.2**
Scieszka, J. Squids will be squids **E**
Tomie dePaola's Favorite nursery tales (k-3) **398.2**
Ward, H. The hare and the tortoise (k-3) **398.2**
Ward, H. The rooster and the fox **E**
Ward, H. Unwitting wisdom (3-6) **398.2**
Wormell, C. Mice, morals, & monkey business (k-3) **398.2**
Young, E. Seven blind mice (k-3) **398.2**

Fables. Lobel, A. **Fic**

Fabulous fractions. Long, L. **513**

Face
Jackson, D. M. In your face (3-6) **611**

Face in art
Dawes, K. S. N. I saw your face (3-5) **811**
Emberley, E. Ed Emberley's drawing book of faces (2-5) **743**
Robert, F. Find a face **E**

Face painting
Silver, P. Face painting (4-6) **745.5**

The **faces** of the Czar. Geras, A.
In Geras, A. My grandmother's stories; a collection of Jewish folk tales p9-15 **398.2**

Facklam, Margery
Lizards: weird and wonderful (3-6) **597.95**
Spiders and their web sites (3-6) **595.4**

Factorials
  Anno, M. Anno's mysterious multiplying jar (2-5) **512**

Factories
Fiction
  Brockmeier, K. Grooves (4 and up) **Fic**
  McCully, E. A. The bobbin girl (3-5) **Fic**
  Paterson, K. Lyddie (5 and up) **Fic**

Facts, Miscellaneous *See* Curiosities and wonders

The **facts** and fictions of Minna Pratt. MacLachlan, P. **Fic**

Facts on File science library [series]
  Bazler, J. A. More science projects for all students **507.8**

Fagan, Eleanora *See* Holiday, Billie, 1915-1959

Faidley, Warren
  (il) Kramer, S. Lightning **551.56**

Fair, Brown & Trembling. Daly, J. **398.2**

Fair, Brown, and Trembling. Doyle, M.
  In Doyle, M. Tales from old Ireland p16-29 **398.2**

Fair, Brown, and Trembling. Philip, N.
  In Philip, N. Celtic fairy tales p27-35 **398.2**

Fair Monaco. Cole, B. **E**

Fair use (Copyright)
  Butler, R. P. Copyright for teachers and librarians **346.04**

Fair weather. Peck, R. **Fic**

Fair-weather Pig. Marshall, J.
  In Marshall, J. Rats on the range and other stories p51-56 **S C**

Fairies
  Allen, J. Fantasy encyclopedia (4 and up) **398**
Fiction
  Augarde, S. The Various (5 and up) **Fic**
  Colfer, E. Artemis Fowl (5 and up) **Fic**
  Kimmel, E. A. Hershel and the Hanukkah goblins **E**
  Levine, G. C. Fairy dust and the quest for the egg (3-5) **Fic**
  McGraw, E. J. The moorchild (4 and up) **Fic**
  Shannon, D. Alice the fairy **E**

Fairs
Fiction
  Crews, D. Night at the fair **E**
  Wells, R. Wingwalker (3-6) **Fic**

Fairy dust and the quest for the egg. Levine, G. C. **Fic**

Fairy ointment. Jacobs, J.
  In Jacobs, J. English fairy tales p208-10 **398.2**

Fairy tales
  See also Fantasy fiction
  Afanas´ev, A. N. Russian fairy tales (4 and up) **398.2**
  Andersen, H. C. The emperor's new clothes [illustrated by Virginia Lee Burton] **E**
  Andersen, H. C. The emperor's new clothes [illustrated by Angela Barrett] **E**

Andersen, H. C. Fairy tales of Hans Christian Andersen (3-6) **S C**
Andersen, H. C. Hans Christian Andersen's Fairy Tales (4 and up) **S C**
Andersen, H. C. The princess and the pea [illustrated by Dorothee Duntze] (k-3) **Fic**
Andersen, H. C. The swan's stories **S C**
Andersen, H. C. Tales of Hans Christian Andersen (4 and up) **S C**
Andersen, H. C. Thumbeline **E**
The Arabian nights entertainments (5 and up) **398.2**
Aylesworth, J. The full belly bowl **E**
Babbitt, N. Ouch! (k-3) **398.2**
Barrie, J. M. Peter Pan (3-5) **Fic**
Barry, D. Peter and the starcatchers (5 and up) **Fic**
Bateman, T. Harp o' gold **E**
Bell, A. The Snow Queen **E**
Beneduce, A. Jack and the beanstalk (2-4) **398.2**
Bianco, M. W. The velveteen rabbit (2-4) **Fic**
The Blue fairy book (4-6) **398.2**
Brett, J. Beauty and the beast (1-3) **398.2**
Brett, J. Trouble with trolls **E**
Calhoun, D. The Phoenix Dance (5 and up) **Fic**
Child, L. The princess and the pea in miniature **E**
Cinderella (2-4) **398.2**
Climo, S. The Egyptian Cinderella (k-3) **398.2**
Climo, S. The Korean Cinderella (k-3) **398.2**
Cole, J. Bony-Legs (k-3) **398.2**
Collodi, C. The adventures of Pinocchio (3-6) **Fic**
Cooper, S. The magician's boy (2-4) **Fic**
Coppinger, T. Curse in reverse **E**
Craft, M. F. Sleeping Beauty (2-4) **398.2**
Daly, J. Fair, Brown & Trembling (k-3) **398.2**
De Paola, T. Adelita (k-3) **398.2**
Demi. The emperor's new clothes **E**
DiCamillo, K. The tale of Despereaux (3-6) **Fic**
Doherty, B. Fairy tales (4-6) **398.2**
Doherty, B. The famous adventures of Jack (3-5) **398.2**
Dunrea, O. Hanne's quest (3-5) **Fic**
Ehrlich, A. Thumbelina **E**
Elya, S. M. Fairy trails **E**
Ernst, L. C. Goldilocks returns **E**
Fearnley, J. Mr. Wolf's pancakes **E**
Galdone, P. The elves and the shoemaker (k-2) **398.2**
Galdone, P. The gingerbread boy (k-2) **398.2**
Galdone, P. Puss in boots (k-2) **398.2**
Gerstein, M. Carolinda clatter! **E**
Grahame, K. The reluctant dragon (3-5) **Fic**
Grimm, J. Hansel and Gretel (3-6) **398.2**
Hamilton, V. The girl who spun gold (k-3) **398.2**
Hautzig, D. The Nutcracker ballet **E**
Hayes, J. Little Gold Star (k-3) **398.2**

Fairy tales—*Continued*

Hickox, R. The golden sandal (k-3)   **398.2**

Hoberman, M. A. You read to me, I'll read to you [very short fairy tales to read together]   **E**

Hoffmann, E. T. A. Nutcracker (4 and up)   **Fic**

Hooks, W. H. Moss gown (k-3)   **398.2**

Huck, C. S. The Black Bull of Norroway (2-4)   **398.2**

Huck, C. S. Princess Furball (1-3)   **398.2**

Hughes, S. Ella's big chance   **E**

Index to fairy tales   **398.2**

Jackson, E. B. Cinder Edna   **E**

Jacobs, J. English fairy tales (4-6)   **398.2**

Kain, K. The Nutcracker   **E**

Karlin, B. James Marshall's Cinderella (k-2)   **398.2**

Kellogg, S. Jack and the beanstalk (k-3)   **398.2**

Kimmel, E. A. Iron John (2-5)   **398.2**

Kimmel, E. A. The runaway tortilla (k-3)   **398.2**

Kimmel, E. A. Seven at one blow (k-3)   **398.2**

Kimmel, E. A. Three sacks of truth (2-4)   **398.2**

Kloske, G. Once upon a time, the end   **E**

Koppe, S. The Nutcracker (3-5)   **Fic**

Krudop, W. The man who caught fish   **E**

Lesser, R. Hansel and Gretel (k-3)   **398.2**

Levine, G. C. The princess test (4 and up)   **Fic**

Light, S. Puss in boots (k-3)   **398.2**

Long, L. The lady & the lion (2-4)   **398.2**

Louie, A.-L. Yeh-Shen (2-4)   **398.2**

Lowell, S. The bootmaker and the elves (k-3)   **398.2**

Lunge-Larsen, L. The hidden folk (3-5)   **398.2**

MacDonald, G. At the back of the North Wind (4-6)   **Fic**

MacDonald, G. The light princess (3-6)   **Fic**

MacDonald, G. The princess and the goblin (3-6)   **Fic**

Mahy, M. The seven Chinese brothers (1-3)   **398.2**

Marcantonio, P. S. Red ridin' in the hood (3-5)   **S C**

Marshall, J. Hansel and Gretel (k-2)   **398.2**

Martin, R. The language of birds (2-4)   **398.2**

Martin, R. The storytelling princess   **E**

Mayer, M. The adventures of Tom Thumb (1-4)   **398.2**

Mayer, M. Baba Yaga and Vasilisa the brave (3-5)   **398.2**

Mayer, M. Beauty and the beast (1-4)   **398.2**

McClintock, B. Cinderella (2-4)   **398.2**

McClintock, B. Molly and the magic wishbone   **E**

Meddaugh, S. Cinderella's rat   **E**

Medley, L. Castle waiting (5 and up)   **741.5**

Merrill, J. The Girl Who Loved Caterpillars   **E**

Mills, L. A. Thumbelina   **E**

Mitchell, S. The nightingale (2-4)   **Fic**

Ogburn, J. K. The magic nesting doll   **E**

O'Malley, K. Once upon a cool motorcycle dude   **E**

Osborne, M. P. The brave little seamstress (k-3)   **398.2**

Osborne, M. P. Kate and the beanstalk (k-3)   **398.2**

Osborne, W. Sleeping Bobby (k-3)   **398.2**

Perrault, C. Cinderella (k-3)   **398.2**

Perrault, C. Puss in boots (k-3)   **398.2**

Philip, N. Celtic fairy tales (4 and up)   **398.2**

Philip, N. The pirate princess and other fairy tales (4-6)   **398.2**

Pinkney, J. The little match girl   **E**

Pinkney, J. The nightingale (2-4)   **Fic**

Pinkney, J. The ugly duckling   **E**

Polacco, P. Luba and the wren (k-3)   **398.2**

Poole, A. L. The pea blossom   **E**

Price, K. The Bourbon Street musicians (3-5)   **398.2**

Princess stories (2-4)   **398.2**

Prokofiev, S. Peter and the wolf   **E**

Pullman, P. Aladdin and the enchanted lamp (3-5)   **398.2**

Pullman, P. The scarecrow and his servant (4-6)   **Fic**

Roberts, L. Little Red   **E**

Ruskin, J. The king of the Golden River   **Fic**

San Souci, R. Brave Margaret (k-3)   **398.2**

San Souci, R. Cendrillon (k-3)   **398.2**

San Souci, R. Kenneth Grahame's The reluctant dragon (2-4)   **Fic**

San Souci, R. Little Gold Star (2-4)   **398.2**

San Souci, R. A weave of words (3-5)   **398.2**

San Souci, R. The well at the end of the world   **E**

Sandburg, C. More Rootabaga stories   **S C**

Sandburg, C. Rootabaga stories   **S C**

Sanderson, R. The crystal mountain (3-5)   **398.2**

Schroeder, A. Smoky Mountain Rose   **E**

Schulman, J. The nutcracker (4 and up)   **Fic**

Scieszka, J. The Frog Prince continued   **E**

Sedgwick, M. The emperor's new clothes   **E**

Seidler, T. The steadfast tin soldier (1-4)   **Fic**

Sendak, M. Outside over there   **E**

Setterington, K. The wild swans (4-6)   **Fic**

Shannon, M. The red wolf   **E**

Shepard, A. The princess mouse (k-3)   **398.2**

Shulevitz, U. The golden goose (k-3)   **398.2**

Sierra, J. The gift of the Crocodile (k-3)   **398.2**

Silverman, E. Raisel's riddle (k-3)   **398.2**

Smith, L. Pinocchio, the boy   **E**

Sperring, M. The fairytale cake   **E**

Spirin, G. The tale of the Firebird (2-4)   **398.2**

Stanley, D. Bella at midnight (5 and up)   **Fic**

Stanley, D. The Giant and the beanstalk   **E**

Stanley, D. Rumpelstiltskin's daughter   **E**

Steig, J. A handful of beans (k-3)   **398.2**

Stockton, F. The bee-man of Orn (2-4)   **Fic**

Family life—Fiction—*Continued*

Curtis, C. P. The Watsons go to Birmingham—1963 (4 and up) **Fic**

Cushman, K. The ballad of Lucy Whipple (5 and up) **Fic**

Cutler, J. Rats! (3-5) **Fic**

De Paola, T. Guess who's coming to Santa's for dinner? **E**

DeFelice, C. C. The real, true Dulcie Campbell **E**

Delton, J. Angel's mother's wedding (3-5) **Fic**

Diakité, P. I lost my tooth in Africa **E**

Dowell, F. O. Chicken boy (4 and up) **Fic**

Estes, E. The Moffats (4-6) **Fic**

Feiffer, J. A room with a zoo (3-5) **Fic**

Fine, A. The true story of Christmas (4 and up) **Fic**

Fleischman, S. Bo & Mzzz Mad (5 and up) **Fic**

Fletcher, R. Fig pudding (4 and up) **Fic**

Flournoy, V. The patchwork quilt **E**

Ford, C. Scout (5 and up) **Fic**

Fox, P. The stone-faced boy (4-6) **Fic**

Frame, J. A. Yesterday I had the blues **E**

Franklin, K. L. Lone wolf (4 and up) **Fic**

Gantos, J. Heads or tails (5 and up) **Fic**

Garden, N. Molly's family **E**

Geisert, B. Prairie summer (4-6) **Fic**

Gibbons, F. Mama and me and the Model-T **E**

Gibbons, F. Mountain wedding **E**

Gleeson, L. Cuddle time

Goode, D. Thanksgiving is here! **E**

Graham, B. Oscar's half birthday **E**

Greene, S. Falling into place (3-5) **Fic**

Greene, S. Queen Sophie Hartley (3-5) **Fic**

Greenwald, S. Rosy Cole's worst ever, best yet tour of New York City (3-5) **Fic**

Griessman, A. The fire **E**

Gwaltney, D. Homefront (5 and up) **Fic**

Haddix, M. P. Say what? (2-4) **Fic**

Hahn, M. D. Anna all year round (3-5) **Fic**

Hahn, M. D. Daphne's book (5 and up) **Fic**

Halpern, S. Introducing . . . Sasha Abramowitz (5 and up) **Fic**

Hamilton, V. The bells of Christmas (4-6) **Fic**

Hamilton, V. M.C. Higgins, the great (5 and up) **Fic**

Hamilton, V. Time pieces (5 and up) **Fic**

Hannigan, K. Ida B (4-6) **Fic**

Heide, F. P. Sami and the time of the troubles **E**

Henkes, K. The birthday room (5 and up) **Fic**

Henkes, K. Olive's ocean (5 and up) **Fic**

Hermes, P. Emma Dilemma and the new nanny (2-4) **Fic**

Hesse, K. Just Juice (3-5) **Fic**

Holm, J. L. Our only May Amelia (5 and up) **Fic**

Hooks, B. Homemade love **E**

Hopkinson, D. Pioneer summer (2-4) **Fic**

Horvath, P. The Pepins and their problems (3-6) **Fic**

Horvath, P. The trolls (3-6) **Fic**

Horvath, P. When the circus came to town (4-6) **Fic**

Hughes, S. Olly and me **E**

Hurst, C. O. You come to Yokum (3-5) **Fic**

Hurwitz, J. Oh no, Noah! (2-4) **Fic**

Hurwitz, J. Rip-roaring Russell (2-4) **Fic**

Hutchins, P. There's only one of me! **E**

Jenkins, E. Five creatures **E**

Joosse, B. M. A houseful of Christmas **E**

Joseph, L. The color of my words (5 and up) **Fic**

Karim, R. Kindle me a riddle **E**

Karr, K. Man of the family (4 and up) **Fic**

Kelly, K. Lucy Rose, here's the thing about me (2-4) **Fic**

Kuskin, K. I am me **E**

Lasky, K. Lucille camps in **E**

L'Engle, M. Meet the Austins (5 and up) **Fic**

Levitin, S. Journey to America (4 and up) **Fic**

Lindsey, K. Sweet potato pie **E**

Little, J. From Anna (4-6) **Fic**

Love, D. A. A year without rain (5 and up) **Fic**

Lowry, L. Anastasia Krupnik (4-6) **Fic**

MacLachlan, P. All the places to love **E**

MacLachlan, P. Journey (4 and up) **Fic**

MacLachlan, P. Seven kisses in a row (2-4) **Fic**

MacLean, C. K. Mary Margaret and the perfect pet plan (3-5) **Fic**

Madden, K. Gentle's Holler (5 and up) **Fic**

Marsden, C. Silk umbrellas (3-6) **Fic**

Martin, A. M. Here today (5 and up) **Fic**

Mason, S. The Quigleys at large (2-4) **Fic**

McElmurry, J. I'm not a baby! **E**

McKay, H. Saffy's angel (5 and up) **Fic**

Mills, C. Trading places (3-5) **Fic**

Moranville, S. B. Over the river (5 and up) **Fic**

Myracle, L. Eleven (4 and up) **Fic**

Namioka, L. Yang the youngest and his terrible ear (4-6) **Fic**

Naylor, P. R. Starting with Alice (3-6) **Fic**

Nesbit, E. The railway children (4-6) **Fic**

Nixon, J. L. Laugh till you cry (5 and up) **Fic**

Ormerod, J. Lizzie nonsense **E**

Parr, T. The family book **E**

Paterson, K. Come sing, Jimmy Jo (5 and up) **Fic**

Paterson, K. Preacher's boy (5 and up) **Fic**

Peck, R. Fair weather (5 and up) **Fic**

Pérez, A. I. My very own room **E**

Pinkney, A. D. Mim's Christmas jam **E**

Polacco, P. When lightning comes in a jar (2-4) **Fic**

Rand, G. Sailing home (2-4) **Fic**

Rattigan, J. K. Dumpling soup **E**

Recorvits, H. Goodbye, Walter Malinski (3-6) **Fic**

Riggio, A. Smack dab in the middle **E**

Rocklin, J. Strudel stories (4 and up) **Fic**

Ryan, P. M. Becoming Naomi León (5 and up) **Fic**

Family life—Fiction—*Continued*
Rylant, C. A blue-eyed daisy (5 and up)
Fic
Rylant, C. A fine white dust (5 and up)   Fic
Rylant, C. The relatives came   E
Schlein, M. The story about me   E
Sebestyen, O. Words by heart (5 and up)
Fic
Shreve, S. R. Blister (4 and up)   Fic
Shreve, S. R. The flunking of Joshua T. Bates
(3-5)   Fic
Smith, D. J. The boys of San Joaquin (5 and
up)   Fic
Smith, R. K. The war with Grandpa (4-6)
Fic
Sorensen, V. E. Miracles on Maple Hill (4 and
up)   Fic
Spinelli, E. When you are happy   E
Spinelli, J. Loser (4 and up)   Fic
St. Anthony, J. The summer Sherman loved me
Fic
Turner, A. W. Dust for dinner   E
Uchida, Y. A jar of dreams (5 and up)   Fic
Uchida, Y. Journey home (5 and up)   Fic
Van Leeuwen, J. Going West   E
Van Leeuwen, J. Tales of Oliver Pig   E
Walter, M. P. Justin and the best biscuits in the
world (3-6)   Fic
Waugh, S. The Mennyms (5 and up)   Fic
Weston, C. The diary of Melanie Martin; or,
How I survived Matt the Brat, Michelangelo,
and the Leaning Tower of Pizza (3-6)   Fic
Weston, M. Act I, act II, act normal (5 and up)
Fic
Weston, T. Hey, pancakes!   E
White, R. Tadpole (4 and up)   Fic
Whittenberg, A. Sweet Thang (5 and up)
Fic
Wiles, D. Each little bird that sings (4-6)
Fic
Williams, V. B. A chair for my mother   E
Williams, V. B. "More more more" said the
baby   E
Willis, P. The barn burner (5 and up)   Fic
Wilson, S. Big day on the river   E
Winthrop, E. Squashed in the middle   E
Woodson, J. We had a picnic this Sunday past
E
Yep, L. The amah (5 and up)   Fic
Ylvisaker, A. Dear Papa (4 and up)   Fic
Poetry
Grandad's tree (k-3)   811.008
Grimes, N. What is goodbye? (4 and up)
811
The Kingfisher book of family poems (3-6)
821.008
Singer, M. Family reunion (k-3)   811
Smith, H. A. The way a door closes (4 and up)
811
Thomas, J. C. Crowning glory (k-3)   811
A **family** of demons. Schwartz, H.
In Schwartz, H. and Rush, B. A coat for the
moon and other Jewish tales p66-67
398.2
A **family** of poems   808.81
Family pictures. Garza, C. L.   E

Family reunion. Singer, M.   811
Family reunions
Fiction
Polacco, P. When lightning comes in a jar (2-4)
Fic
Family trees [series]
Stefoff, R. The primate order   599.8
Zabludoff, M. The insect class   595.7
The **family** under the bridge. Carlson, N. S.
Fic
Famines
Fiction
Giff, P. R. Nory Ryan's song (5 and up)
Fic
Hazen, B. S. Katie's wish   E
The **famous** adventures of Jack. Doherty, B.
398.2
Famous first facts. Kane, J. N.   031.02
Famous inventors [series]
Ford, C. T. Benjamin Franklin   92
Famous people [series]
Woog, A. Bill Gates   92
Famous wagon trails. Steele, C.   978
Fancher, Lou
(il) Duncan, L. I walk at night   E
(il) Krull, K. The boy on Fairfield Street: how
Ted Geisel grew up to become Dr. Seuss
92
(il) Osborne, M. P. New York's bravest   E
(il) Panahi, H. L. Bebop Express   E
(il) Paolilli, P. Silver seeds   811
(il) Wolkstein, D. The day Ocean came to visit
398.2
Fancy dress *See* Costume
Fanelli, Sara
(il) Collodi, C. The adventures of Pinocchio
Fic
Fang, Linda
The Ch'i-lin purse (5 and up)   398.2
Contents: The Ch'i-lin purse; Dog steals and Rooster crows;
Two Miss Peonys; The Ho Shi jade; The prime minister and the
General; The clever magistrate; Mr. Yeh's New Year; The mira-
cle doctor; The royal bridegroom
Fannie in the kitchen. Hopkinson, D.   641.5
Fanny's dream. Buehner, C.   E
Fantasic physical science experiments [series]
Gardner, R. Dazzling science projects with light
and color   535
Fantastic farm machines. Peterson, C. 631.3
Fantastic feats and failures (4 and up) 624.1
Fantastic fiction *See* Fantasy fiction
The **fantastic** journey of Pieter Bruegel. Shafer, A.
C.   Fic
Fantastic physical science experiments [series]
Gardner, R. Energizing science projects with
electricity and magnetism   537
Gardner, R. Jazzy science projects with sound
and music   534
Gardner, R. Sensational science projects with
simple machines   621.8
Fantastic! wow! and unreal!. Heller, R. 428
Fantasy! cartooning. Caldwell, B.   741.5
Fantasy encyclopedia. Allen, J.   398

Fantasy fiction

See also Fairy tales; Science fiction

Abbott, T. Kringle (5 and up)   **Fic**

Aiken, J. Shadows and moonshine (4 and up)   **S C**

Alexander, L. The Arkadians (5 and up)   **Fic**

Alexander, L. The book of three (5 and up)   **Fic**

Alexander, L. The foundling and other tales of Prydain (5 and up)   **S C**

Alexander, L. Gypsy Rizka (5 and up)   **Fic**

Alexander, L. The high king (5 and up)   **Fic**

Almond, D. Skellig (5 and up)   **Fic**

Anderson, J. L. May Bird and The Ever After (5 and up)   **Fic**

Augarde, S. The Various (5 and up)   **Fic**

Babbitt, N. The search for delicious (5 and up)   **Fic**

Babbitt, N. Tuck everlasting (5 and up)   **Fic**

Banks, L. R. The Indian in the cupboard (5 and up)   **Fic**

Barron, T. A. The lost years of Merlin (6 and up)   **Fic**

Bath, K. P. The secret of Castle Cant (5 and up)   **Fic**

Baum, L. F. The Wizard of Oz (3-6)   **Fic**

Bell, H. The wizard test (5 and up)   **Fic**

Billingsley, F. The Folk Keeper (5 and up)   **Fic**

Billingsley, F. Well wished (4-6)   **Fic**

Bond, N. A string in the harp (6 and up)   **Fic**

Boston, L. M. The children of Green Knowe (4-6)   **Fic**

Carman, P. The Dark Hills divide (5 and up)   **Fic**

Carroll, L. Alice through the looking glass (4 and up)   **Fic**

Carroll, L. Alice's adventures in Wonderland (4 and up)   **Fic**

Carroll, L. Alice's adventures in Wonderland, and Through the looking glass (4 and up)   **Fic**

Chabon, M. Summerland (5 and up)   **Fic**

Colfer, E. Artemis Fowl (5 and up)   **Fic**

Collins, S. Gregor the Overlander (4 and up)   **Fic**

Cooper, S. The grey king (5 and up)   **Fic**

Cooper, S. Over sea, under stone (5 and up)   **Fic**

Coville, B. Jennifer Murdley's toad (4-6)   **Fic**

Coville, B. Jeremy Thatcher, dragon hatcher (4-6)   **Fic**

Coville, B. The skull of truth (4-6)   **Fic**

Dahl, R. James and the giant peach (4-6)   **Fic**

Donaldson, J. The Giants and the Joneses (3-5)   **Fic**

Eager, E. Half magic (4-6)   **Fic**

Eager, E. Magic or not? (4-6)   **Fic**

Eager, E. Seven-day magic (4-6)   **Fic**

Etchemendy, N. The power of Un (4 and up)   **Fic**

Farmer, N. The Sea of Trolls (5 and up)   **Fic**

Flanagan, J. Ranger's apprentice (5 and up)   **Fic**

Fleischman, S. The 13th floor (4-6)   **Fic**

Funke, C. C. Dragon rider (5 and up)   **Fic**

Gannett, R. S. My father's dragon (1-4)   **Fic**

Haptie, C. Otto and the flying twins (4 and up)   **Fic**

Hardinge, F. Fly by night (5 and up)   **Fic**

Hodges, M. Gulliver in Lilliput (3-6)   **Fic**

Ibbotson, E. The secret of platform 13 (5 and up)   **Fic**

Jacques, B. Redwall (6 and up)   **Fic**

James, M. Shoebag (5 and up)   **Fic**

Jansson, T. Moominsummer madness (4-6)   **Fic**

Jarrell, R. The animal family (4 and up)   **Fic**

Jarvis, R. The dark portal (5 and up)   **Fic**

Johnston, T. The spoon in the bathroom wall (3-5)   **Fic**

Jones, D. W. Castle in the air (6 and up)   **Fic**

Jones, D. W. Howl's moving castle (6 and up)   **Fic**

Jones, D. W. Mixed magics (5 and up)   **S C**

Joyce, W. George shrinks   **E**

Juster, N. The phantom tollbooth (5 and up)   **Fic**

Kendall, C. The Gammage Cup (5 and up)   **Fic**

Langrish, K. Troll Fell (5 and up)   **Fic**

Langton, J. The fledgling (5 and up)   **Fic**

Le Guin, U. K. Catwings (2-4)   **Fic**

Le Guin, U. K. A wizard of Earthsea (6 and up)   **Fic**

L'Engle, M. A wrinkle in time (5 and up)   **Fic**

Levine, G. C. Ella enchanted (5 and up)   **Fic**

Levine, G. C. The two princesses of Bamarre (5 and up)   **Fic**

Lewis, C. S. The lion, the witch, and the wardrobe (4 and up)   **Fic**

Lofting, H. The voyages of Doctor Dolittle (4 and up)   **Fic**

McGraw, E. J. The moorchild (4 and up)   **Fic**

Myers, W. D. Three swords for Granada (3-6)   **Fic**

Nesbit, E. The enchanted castle (4-6)   **Fic**

Nesbit, E. Five children and it (4-6)   **Fic**

Norton, M. Bed-knob and broomstick (3-6)   **Fic**

Norton, M. The borrowers (3-6)   **Fic**

Pearce, P. Tom's midnight garden (4 and up)   **Fic**

Philbrick, W. R. REM world (4 and up)   **Fic**

Pierce, T. Magic steps (5 and up)   **Fic**

Prue, S. Cold Tom (5 and up)   **Fic**

Pullman, P. I was a rat! (4 and up)   **Fic**

Rodda, E. Rowan of Rin (4-6)   **Fic**

Rowling, J. K. Harry Potter and the sorcerer's stone (4 and up)   **Fic**

Ruby, L. The Wall and the Wing (5 and up)   **Fic**

Sabuda, R. Alice's adventures in Wonderland   **E**

Sage, A. Magyk (5 and up)   **Fic**

Fantasy fiction—*Continued*
Scieszka, J. Knights of the kitchen table (3-5)
Fic
Sendak, M. In the night kitchen   E
Sendak, M. Where the wild things are   E
Stewart, P. Beyond the Deepwoods (4-6)
Fic
Tolkien, J. R. R. The hobbit, or, There and back
again (4 and up)   Fic
Travers, P. L. Mary Poppins (4-6)   Fic
Winthrop, E. The castle in the attic (4-6)
Fic
Yorinks, A. Hey, Al   E
Bibliography
Lynn, R. N. Fantasy literature for children and
young adults   **016.8**
History and criticism
Colbert, D. The magical worlds of Harry Potter
(5 and up)   **823.009**
Kronzek, A. Z. The sorcerer's companion (4 and
up)   **823.009**
The wand in the word (6 and up)   **813.009**
Fantasy for children. *See* Lynn, R. N. Fantasy lit-
erature for children and young adults
016.8

Fantasy in art
Caldwell, B. Fantasy! cartooning (5 and up)
741.5

Fantasy literature for children and young adults.
Lynn, R. N.   **016.8**

Far beyond the garden gate: Alexandra David-
Neel's journey to Lhasa. Brown, D.   **92**

A **far-fetched** story. Cates, K.   E

Far-out science projects with height and depth.
Gardner, R.   **530.8**

Faraway home. Kurtz, J.   E

Faraway places. Blakemore, C.   **011.6**

Faraway summer. Hurwitz, J.   **Fic**

Fardell, John
The 7 professors of the Far North (4 and up)
Fic

Farfallina & Marcel. Keller, H.   E

Faricy, Patrick
(il) Hopkinson, D. Pioneer summer   **Fic**

Farish, Terry
The cat who liked potato soup   E

Farley, Carol J.
Sim Chung and the dragon king
In Fire and wings: dragon tales from East and
West p87-94   **S C**

Farley, Walter
The Black Stallion (4 and up)   **Fic**

Farlow, James Orville
Bringing dinosaur bones to life (5 and up)
567.9

Farm animals *See* Domestic animals

Farm engines *See* Agricultural machinery

Farm flu. Bateman, T.   E

Farm laborers *See* Agricultural laborers

Farm life
Azarian, M. A farmer's alphabet   E
Bial, R. Portrait of a farm family (4 and up)
630.1

Peterson, C. Century farm (k-3)   **630.1**
Splear, E. L. Growing seasons (3-5)   **630.1**
Fiction
Avi. The barn (4 and up)   **Fic**
Bateman, T. April foolishness   E
Bradley, K. B. Ruthie's gift (3-5)   **Fic**
Brown, C. M. Barn raising   E
Brown, M. W. Big red barn   E
Buck, P. S. Christmas day in the morning   E
Buehner, C. Fanny's dream   E
Cleary, B. The hullabaloo ABC   E
Denslow, S. P. Georgie Lee (2-4)   **Fic**
Easton, R. A real American (5 and up)   **Fic**
Ehlert, L. Market day   E
Fisher, D. C. Understood Betsy (4-6)   **Fic**
Fleischman, S. Here comes McBroom! (3-5)
Fic
Friedrich, E. Leah's pony   E
Gammell, S. Once upon MacDonald's farm
E
Geisert, B. Prairie summer (4-6)   **Fic**
Griffith, H. V. Grandaddy's place   E
Haas, J. Hurry!   E
Hamilton, V. Drylongso (3-5)   **Fic**
Hesse, K. Out of the dust (5 and up)   **Fic**
Hurwitz, J. Faraway summer (4-6)   **Fic**
King-Smith, D. The golden goose (2-4)   **Fic**
Kinsey-Warnock, N. Nora's ark   E
Lindsey, K. Sweet potato pie   E
Lobel, A. A treeful of pigs   E
Lottridge, C. B. Berta: a remarkable dog (3-5)
Fic
MacLachlan, P. All the places to love   E
Maitland, B. Moo in the morning   E
McGill, A. Molly Bannaky   E
Noble, T. H. The day Jimmy's boa ate the wash
E
Nolen, J. Harvey Potter's balloon farm   E
Nolen, J. Raising dragons   E
Paterson, K. Park's quest (5 and up)   **Fic**
Paulsen, G. Alida's song (5 and up)   **Fic**
Paulsen, G. The winter room (5 and up)   **Fic**
Pinkney, G. J. Back home   E
Porter, P. P. The crazy man (5 and up)   **Fic**
Provensen, A. A day in the life of Murphy
E
Reynolds, A. Chicks and salsa   E
Rostoker-Gruber, K. Rooster can't cock-a-
doodle-doo   E
Sandburg, C. The Huckabuck family and how
they raised popcorn in Nebraska and quit and
came back   E
Schnur, S. Spring thaw   E
Seredy, K. The Good Master (4-6)   **Fic**
Seymour, T. Hunting the white cow   E
Spinelli, E. The best time of day   E
Tafuri, N. This is the farmer   E
Thomas, J. R. The comeback dog (3-5)   **Fic**
Turner, A. W. Dust for dinner   E
Waddell, M. Farmer duck   E
Wallace, B. Beauty (4-6)   **Fic**
Wallace, B. A dog called Kitty (4-6)   **Fic**
Poetry
Hoce, C. Beyond Old MacDonald (k-3)   **811**
Songs
Old MacDonald had a farm (k-2)   **782.42**

Father-son relationship—Fiction—*Continued*
Kirk, C. A. Sky dancers   E
Koss, A. G. Stranger in Dadland (5 and up)   Fic
Lawlor, L. He will go fearless (5 and up)   Fic
London, J. Do your ABC's Little Brown Bear   E
London, J. Giving thanks   E
Martin, D. Piggy and Dad go fishing   E
McBratney, S. Guess how much I love you   E
Michelson, R. Happy feet   E
Norac, C. My daddy is a giant   E
Partridge, E. Whistling   E
Ray, M. L. Basket moon   E
Say, A. The lost lake   E
Smith, R. K. Bobby Baseball (4-6)   Fic
Steig, W. Pete's a pizza   E
Uhlberg, M. Dad, Jackie, and me   E
Vander Zee, R. Mississippi morning   E
Walvoord, L. Razzamadaddy   E

Fathers
    See also Stepfathers
Dennison, A. Our dad died (4 and up)   155.9
Herb, S. Connecting fathers, children, and reading   028.5
Fiction
Bradman, T. Daddy's lullaby   E
Browne, A. Into the forest   E
Browne, A. My dad   E
Campos, T. Muffler man   E
Carle, E. Mister Seahorse   E
Daly, N. My dad   E
Isadora, R. At the crossroads   E
Mills, C. Alex Ryan, stop that! (5 and up)   Fic
Morrow, T. J. Mommy loves her baby   E
Napoli, D. J. Flamingo dream   E
Nelson, T. Ruby electric (5 and up)   Fic
Numeroff, L. J. What mommies do best   E
Rockwell, A. F. Father's Day   E
Weigel, J. Atomic Ace   E
Wood, D. What dads can't do   E
Woodson, J. Visiting day   E
Ylvisaker, A. Dear Papa (4 and up)   Fic
Poetry
In daddy's arms I am tall   811.008
Smith, H. A. The way a door closes (4 and up)   811

Fathers, Single parent *See* Single parent family
Fathers and sons *See* Father-son relationship
Father's Day
Fiction
Rockwell, A. F. Father's Day   E
Fatigue
    See also Chronic fatigue syndrome
Fatus, Sophie
(il) Lupton, H. Riddle me this!   793.73
(il) MacDonald, M. R. A hen, a chick, and a string guitar   398.2
Faulkner, Matt
(il) St. George, J. You're on your way, Teddy Roosevelt!   92

Fauteux, Nicole
(jt. auth) Simon, S. Let's try it out in the air   533
(jt. auth) Simon, S. Let's try it out in the water   532
(jt. auth) Simon, S. Let's try it out with towers and bridges   624.1
Favorite children's authors and illustrators   920.003
Favorite Greek myths. Osborne, M. P.   292
Favorite medieval tales. Osborne, M. P.   398.2
Favorite Norse myths. Osborne, M. P.   293
Favorite nursery tales, Tomie dePaola's   398.2
A **fawn** in the grass. Ryder, J.   E
Fazio, Wende
Saudi Arabia (2-4)   953.8
West Virginia
    In America the beautiful, second series   973
FBI *See* United States. Federal Bureau of Investigation
The **FBI** director. Ingram, S.   363.2
Fear
Crist, J. J. What to do when you're scared & worried (5 and up)   152.4
Heide, F. P. Some things are scary   E
Fiction
Blume, J. Otherwise known as Sheila the Great (4-6)   Fic
Bonsall, C. N. Who's afraid of the dark?   E
Bottner, B. The Scaredy Cats   E
Ellis, S. Ben over night   E
Emberley, E. Go away, big green monster!   E
Guilloppé, A. One scary night   E
Khan, R. Ruler of the courtyard   E
Lester, H. Something might happen   E
Lin, G. Olvina flies   E
Martin, B. The ghost-eye tree   E
Martin, J. B. Grandmother Bryant's pocket   E
Mayer, M. There's a nightmare in my closet   E
Moodie, F. Noko and the night monster   E
Pitzer, S. Not afraid of dogs   E
Rodowsky, C. F. The next-door dogs (2-4)   Fic
Williams, L. The little old lady who was not afraid of anything   E
The **fear** place. Naylor, P. R.   Fic
Fearless Fernie. Soto, G.   811
Fearless Jack. Johnson, P. B.   398.2
Fearnley, Jan
Mr. Wolf's pancakes   E
Watch out!   E
The **fearsome** inn. Singer, I. B.
    In Singer, I. B. Stories for children p290-307   S C
Feast of Lights *See* Hanukkah
The **feather** of Finist, the Bright Falcon. Afanas´ev, A. N.
    In Afanas´ev, A. N. Russian fairy tales p580-88   398.2

Fertilization in vitro, Human *See* Fertilization in vitro

Festivals

Ancona, G. The fiestas (2-4)   **394.26**

Fiestas: a year of Latin American songs of celebration (k-3)   **782.42**

The Folklore of world holidays   **394.26**

Jones, L. Kids around the world celebrate! (4-6)   **394.26**

Junior worldmark encyclopedia of world holidays (5 and up)   **394.26**

Kindersley, A. Celebrations (3-5)   **394.26**

MacDonald, M. R. Celebrate the world   **398.2**

Moehn, H. World holidays (3-6)   **394.26**

    Bibliography

Matthew, K. I. Neal-Schuman guide to celebrations & holidays around the world   **394.26**

    Fiction

Blumenthal, D. Ice palace   **E**

    History

Aliki. A medieval feast (2-5)   **940.1**

    Poetry

Livingston, M. C. Festivals   **811**

    China

Simonds, N. Moonbeams, dumplings & dragon boats (4 and up)   **394.26**

    United States

Ancona, G. Fiesta U.S.A. (k-3)   **394.26**

Festivals [series]

Marchant, K. Id-ul-Fitr   **297.3**

Fetus

Pringle, L. P. Everybody has a bellybutton (k-3)   **612.6**

Fever, 1793. Anderson, L. H.   **Fic**

Fiammenghi, Gioia

(il) Smith, R. K. Chocolate fever   **Fic**

Fiction

    See also Adventure fiction; Fairy tales; Fantasy fiction; Horror fiction; Mystery fiction; School stories; Science fiction; Sea stories; Short stories; War stories

Fiddle-i-fee. Hillenbrand, W.   **782.42**

The **fiddler.** San Souci, R.

    In San Souci, R. A terrifying taste of short & shivery; thirty creepy tales p15-19   **398.2**

The **fiddler** in hell. Afanas´ev, A. N.

    In Afanas´ev, A. N. Russian fairy tales p180-82   **398.2**

The **fiddler** in the cave. Philip, N.

    In Philip, N. Celtic fairy tales p119-20   **398.2**

The **Fiddler** Man. Medearis, A. S.

    In Medearis, A. S. Haunts; five hair-raising tales p1-8   **S C**

Fiddling with fire. Olson, A. N.

    In Olson, A. N. and Schwartz, H. Ask the bones: scary stories from around the world p46-52   **398.2**

Field, Elinor Whitney

(ed) Newbery Medal books, 1922-1955. See Newbery Medal books, 1922-1955   **028.5**

Field, Eugene

Wynken, Blynken, and Nod   **811**

Field, Rachel

Hitty: her first hundred years (4 and up)   **Fic**

Prayer for a child (k-2)   **242**

Field athletics *See* Track athletics

A **field** guide to the birds. See Peterson, R. T. A field guide to the birds of eastern and central North America   **598**

A **field** guide to the birds of eastern and central North America. Peterson, R. T.   **598**

A **field** guide to western birds. Peterson, R. T.   **598**

Field Museum of Natural History

Relf, P. A dinosaur named Sue: the story of the colossal fossil: the world's most complete T. rex   **567.9**

Field trips

Cooper, G. New virtual field trips   **025.5**

Field trips. Arnosky, J.   **508**

Fields of fury. McPherson, J. M.   **973.7**

The **fierce** yellow pumpkin. Brown, M. W.   **E**

Fieser, Stephen

(il) Schwartz, H. Invisible kingdoms   **398.2**

Fiesta!. Guy, G. F.   **E**

Fiesta femenina. Gerson, M.-J.   **398.2**

Fiesta U.S.A. Ancona, G.   **394.26**

The **fiestas.** Ancona, G.   **394.26**

Fiestas: a year of Latin American songs of celebration (k-3)   **782.42**

Fifty words about plants. See Armentrout, D. 50 words about plants   **580**

Fig pudding. Fletcher, R.   **Fic**

The **fight** between the animals and insects. Curry, J. L.

    In Curry, J. L. Hold up the sky: and other Native American tales from Texas and the Southern Plains p77-80   **398.2**

Fight for freedom. Bobrick, B.   **973.3**

The **figure** skating book. Wilkes, D.   **796.91**

Figuring out Frances. Willner-Pardo, G.   **Fic**

Filan, Patricia Rosten

(jt. auth) Rosten, N. A city is   **811**

Files and filing

ALA filing rules   **025.3**

Filial piety. Shedlock, M. L.

    In Shedlock, M. L. The art of the story-teller p229-32   **372.6**

Fill, bowl! Fill!

    In The Jack tales p89-95   **398.2**

Fillmore, Parker

Clever Manka

    In Womenfolk and fairy tales p146-55   **398.2**

Financial planning, Personal *See* Personal finance

Find a face. Robert, F.   **E**

Find the constellations. Rey, H. A.   **523.8**

Find where the wind goes. Jemison, M. C.   **92**

Finding Buck McHenry. Slote, A.   **Fic**

Finding high-jump fame. Cirrone, D.
In Sports shorts   **S C**

Finding out about holidays [series]
Gnojewski, C. Day of the Dead   **394.26**
Landau, E. Easter   **394.26**
Landau, E. St. Patrick's Day   **394.26**
Landau, E. Valentine's day   **394.26**

Finding Providence: the story of Roger Williams.
Avi   **92**

Finding things *See* Lost and found possessions

Fine, Anne
The diary of a killer cat (2-4)   **Fic**
Notso hotso (2-4)   **Fic**
The true story of Christmas (4 and up)   **Fic**
Up on cloud nine (5 and up)   **Fic**

Fine, Edith Hope
Gary Paulsen (5 and up)   **92**

Fine, Howard
(il) Palatini, M. Piggie pie!   **E**
(il) Shaw, N. Raccoon tune   **E**
(il) Wright, C. Steamboat Annie and the thousand-pound catfish   **E**

Fine arts *See* Arts

Fine feathered friends. Yolen, J.   **811**

A **fine** St. Patrick's day. Wojciechowski, S.   **E**

A **fine** white dust. Rylant, C.   **Fic**

The **finger**. Schwartz, H.
In Schwartz, H. A journey to paradise and other Jewish tales p32-35   **398.2**

The **finger** Lock. MacDonald, M. R.
In MacDonald, M. R. Celebrate the world; twenty tellable folktales for multicultural festivals p128-34   **372.6**

Finger play
Arrorró mi niño (k-3)   **398.8**
Brown, M. T. Play rhymes   **796.1**
Diez deditos. Ten little fingers & other play rhymes and action songs from Latin America (k-3)   **782.42**
The Eentsy, weentsy spider: fingerplays and action rhymes   **796.1**
Hoberman, M. A. The eensy-weensy spider (k-3)   **782.42**
Newcome, Z. Head, shoulders, knees, and toes   **E**
Pat-a-cake and other play rhymes   **398.8**
This little piggy   **398.8**
Wilner, I. The baby's game book   **398.8**

Finishing blocks and deadly hook shots. Trueman, T.
In Sports shorts   **S C**

Fink, Mike, 1770-1823?
Fiction
Kellogg, S. Mike Fink (k-3)   **398.2**

Fink, Sam
(il) The Declaration of Independence. See The Declaration of Independence   **973.3**

Finkelman, Paul
The Constitution (4 and up)   **342**

Finland
McNair, S. Finland (5 and up)   **948.97**

Folklore
See Folklore—Finland

Finley, Carol
The art of African masks (5 and up)   **391**

Finn MacCool *See* Finn MacCumhaill, 3rd cent.

Finn MacCool and the Scottish giant. Philip, N.
In Philip, N. Celtic fairy tales p73-77   **398.2**

Finn Maccoul. Osborne, M. P.
In Osborne, M. P. Favorite medieval tales p1-7   **398.2**

Finn MacCoul and his fearless wife. Byrd, R.   **398.2**

Finn MacCumhaill, 3rd cent.
Fiction
Byrd, R. Finn MacCoul and his fearless wife (k-3)   **398.2**
Souhami, J. Mrs. McCool and the giant Cuhullin (k-3)   **398.2**

Finney, Patricia
I, Jack (3-6)   **Fic**

Finnish Americans
Fiction
Holm, J. L. Our only May Amelia (5 and up)   **Fic**

Fiona's private pages. Cruise, R.   **Fic**

Fiore, Carole D.
Fiore's summer library reading program handbook   **027.62**

Fiore, Peter
(il) Kroll, S. The Boston Tea Party   **973.3**

Fiore, Peter M.
(il) Borden, L. Touching the sky: the flying adventures of Wilbur and Orville Wright   **92**

Fiore's summer library reading program handbook. Fiore, C. D.   **027.62**

Fir, Douglas *See* Douglas fir

The **fir** tree. Andersen, H. C.
In Andersen, H. C. The swan's stories p123-41   **S C**

Fire
Poetry
Singer, M. Central heating (4 and up)   **811**

The **fire**. Griessman, A.   **E**

Fire!. Masoff, J.   **628.9**

Fire and wings: dragon tales from East and West (4 and up)   **S C**

Fire, bed, & bone. Branford, H.   **Fic**

The **fire-bird**. Doherty, B.
In Doherty, B. Fairy tales   **398.2**

A **fire** engine for Ruthie. Newman, L.   **E**

Fire engines
Bingham, C. Fire truck (k-3)   **628.9**
Fiction
Sís, P. Fire truck   **E**

Fire fighters
Beil, K. M. Fire in their eyes (4 and up)   **628.9**
Demarest, C. L. Firefighters A to Z (k-1)   **628.9**
Ganci, C. Chief: the life of Peter J. Ganci, a New York City firefighter (3-6)   **92**

Fischer, Hans
(il) Grimm, J. The Bremen town musicians
398.2

Fish, Helen Dean
(ed) Bible. Selections. Animals of the Bible
220.8

Fish. Jeffrey, L. S. **639.34**

The **fish** and the ring. Jacobs, J.
In Jacobs, J. English fairy tales p189-92
398.2

Fish culture
See also Aquariums

Fish is fish. Lionni, L. **E**

The **Fish** is me (k-2) **811.008**

A **fish** story. San Souci, R.
In San Souci, R. A terrifying taste of short &
shivery; thirty creepy tales p25-29
398.2

Fish watching with Eugenie Clark. Ross, M. E.
92

Fish wish. Barner, B. **E**

Fisher, Aileen Lucia
The story goes on **E**
The story of Easter (3-5) **394.26**

Fisher, Cynthia
(il) Adler, D. A. Easy math puzzles **793.74**

Fisher, Dorothy Canfield
Thanksgiving Day
In Bauer, C. F. Celebrations; read-aloud holi-
day and theme book programs p243-48
808.8
Understood Betsy (4-6) **Fic**

Fisher, Jeff
(il) Adler, D. A. A picture book of Amelia Earhart **92**

Fisher, Leonard Everett
The ABC exhibit **E**
The architects (4 and up) **720.9**
The blacksmiths (4 and up) **682**
The cabinetmakers (4 and up) **684.1**
David and Goliath (k-3) **222**
The doctors (4 and up) **610.9**
The gods and goddesses of ancient China (3-6)
299
The gods and goddesses of ancient Egypt (3-6)
299
Gods and goddesses of the ancient Maya (3-6)
299
Gods and goddesses of the ancient Norse (3-6)
293
The hatters (4 and up) **646**
The limners (4 and up) **759.13**
The Oregon Trail (4 and up) **979.5**
The papermakers (4 and up) **676**
The peddlers (4 and up) **381**
The printers (4 and up) **686.2**
The schoolmasters (4 and up) **370.9**
The shoemakers (4 and up) **685**
The silversmiths (4 and up) **739.2**
The tanners (4 and up) **675**
To bigotry, no sanction (4 and up) **296**
The weavers (4 and up) **677**
The wigmakers (4 and up) **391**

(il) If you ever meet a whale. See If you ever
meet a whale **811.008**
(il) Kimmel, E. A. Don Quixote and the windmills **E**
(il) Kimmel, E. A. The hero Beowulf **398.2**
(il) Kimmel, E. A. The spotted pony: a collection of Hanukkah stories **398.2**
(il) Kimmel, E. A. The three princes **398.2**
(il) Kimmel, E. A. The two mountains
398.2
(il) Livingston, M. C. Celebrations **811**
(il) Livingston, M. C. Festivals **811**
(il) Rogasky, B. Dybbuk **398.2**

Fisher, Mel
About
Matsen, B. The incredible search for the treasure
ship Atocha (4 and up) **910.4**

Fisher, Valorie
My big brother **E**

Fisheries *See* Commercial fishing

The **fisherman** and the chamberlain. Yolen, J.
In Yolen, J. Mightier than the sword; world
folktales for strong boys p52-55
398.2

The **fisherman** and the silver fish. Schwartz, H.
In Schwartz, H. and Rush, B. A coat for the
moon and other Jewish tales p54-59
398.2

Fishes
See also Aquariums; Codfish; Coelacanth;
Eels; Goldfish; Rays (Fishes); Salmon
Jeffrey, L. S. Fish (3-5) **639.34**
Landau, E. Electric fish (2-4) **597**
Pfeffer, W. What's it like to be a fish? (k-1)
597
Ross, M. E. Fish watching with Eugenie Clark
(4 and up) **92**
Rubin, A. How many fish? **E**
Fiction
Carle, E. Mister Seahorse **E**
Cousins, L. Hooray for fish! **E**
Lionni, L. Fish is fish **E**
Lionni, L. Swimmy **E**
Rohmann, E. Clara and Asha **E**
Wise, W. Ten sly piranhas **E**
Wright, C. Steamboat Annie and the thousand-
pound catfish **E**
Folklore
Partridge, E. Kogi's mysterious journey (k-3)
398.2

Fishing
Arnosky, J. Hook, line, & seeker (4 and up)
799.1
McMillan, B. Going fishing (2-4) **949.12**
McMillan, B. Salmon summer (2-4) **639.2**
See/See also pages in the following book(s):
Bauer, C. F. Celebrations p1-24 **808.8**
Fiction
Bania, M. Kumak's fish **E**
Cook, B. The little fish that got away **E**
DeFelice, C. C. Death at Devil's Bridge (5 and
up) **Fic**
DeFelice, C. C. The missing manatee (5 and up)
Fic
Dewey, A. Splash! **E**

Folklore—*Continued*

Denmark

MacDonald, M. R. Fat cat (k-3) 398.2

East Africa

Aardema, V. Who's in Rabbit's house? (k-3) 398.2

Martin, F. Clever Tortoise (k-3) 398.2

Egypt

Climo, S. The Egyptian Cinderella (k-3) 398.2

England

See Folklore—Great Britain

Ethiopia

Kurtz, J. Fire on the mountain (1-4) 398.2

Laird, E. When the world began (3-6) 398.2

Europe

Bulfinch, T. Bulfinch's mythology 201

Osborne, M. P. Favorite medieval tales (4 and up) 398.2

Finland

Shepard, A. The princess mouse (k-3) 398.2

France

Brett, J. Beauty and the beast (1-3) 398.2

Brown, M. Stone soup (k-3) 398.2

Galdone, P. Puss in boots (k-2) 398.2

Kimmel, E. A. Three sacks of truth (2-4) 398.2

Light, S. Puss in boots (k-3) 398.2

Mayer, M. Beauty and the beast (1-4) 398.2

McClintock, B. Cinderella (2-4) 398.2

Perrault, C. Cinderella (k-3) 398.2

Perrault, C. Puss in boots (k-3) 398.2

Germany

Babbitt, N. Ouch! (k-3) 398.2

Craft, M. F. Sleeping Beauty (2-4) 398.2

Galdone, P. The elves and the shoemaker (k-2) 398.2

Grimm, J. The Bremen town musicians (k-3) 398.2

Grimm, J. Hansel and Gretel (3-6) 398.2

Hettinga, D. R. The Brothers Grimm (5 and up) 92

Hodges, M. The hero of Bremen (3-5) 398.2

Hyman, T. S. Little Red Riding Hood (k-2) 398.2

Kimmel, E. A. Iron John (2-5) 398.2

Kimmel, E. A. Seven at one blow (k-3) 398.2

Lesser, R. Hansel and Gretel (k-3) 398.2

Long, L. The lady & the lion (2-4) 398.2

Marshall, J. Hansel and Gretel (k-2) 398.2

Marshall, J. Red Riding Hood (k-2) 398.2

Orgel, D. The Bremen town musicians and other animal tales from Grimm (3-5) 398.2

Osborne, W. Sleeping Bobby (k-3) 398.2

Puttapipat, N. The musicians of Bremen (k-3) 398.2

Shulevitz, U. The golden goose (k-3) 398.2

Watts, B. Jorinda and Jorindel (k-3) 398.2

Zelinsky, P. O. Rumpelstiltskin (k-4) 398.2

Ziefert, H. Little Red Riding Hood (k-2) 398.2

Ghana

Cummings, P. Ananse and the lizard (k-3) 398.2

McDermott, G. Anansi the spider (k-3) 398.2

Mollel, T. M. Ananse's feast (k-3) 398.2

Great Britain

Beneduce, A. Jack and the beanstalk (2-4) 398.2

Bodger, J. Tales of court and castle (5 and up) 398.2

Climo, S. Magic & mischief (4 and up) 398.2

Doherty, B. The famous adventures of Jack (3-5) 398.2

Galdone, P. The teeny-tiny woman (k-2) 398.2

Hodges, M. Dick Whittington and his cat (k-3) 398.2

I saw Esau 398.8

Jacobs, J. English fairy tales (4-6) 398.2

Kellogg, S. Jack and the beanstalk (k-3) 398.2

Kellogg, S. The three sillies (k-3) 398.2

Kimmel, E. A. The hero Beowulf (3-6) 398.2

Marshall, J. The three little pigs (k-2) 398.2

Opie, I. A. The lore and language of schoolchildren 398

Osborne, M. P. Kate and the beanstalk (k-3) 398.2

Philip, N. Celtic fairy tales (4 and up) 398.2

Shepard, A. King O' the Cats (k-3) 398.2

Zemach, M. The three little pigs (k-2) 398.2

Greece

Manna, A. L. Mr. Semolina-Semolinus (1-3) 398.2

Haiti

MacDonald, A. Please, Malese! (k-3) 398.2

The Magic orange tree, and other Haitian folktales (5 and up) 398.2

Hawaii

Martin, R. The Shark God (k-3) 398.2

Wardlaw, L. Punia and the King of Sharks (k-3) 398.2

India

Brown, M. Once a mouse (k-3) 398.2

Galdone, P. The monkey and the crocodile (k-2) 398.2

So, M. Gobble, gobble, slip, slop 398.2

Weitzman, D. L. Rama and Sita (3-6) 398.2

Young, E. Seven blind mice (k-3) 398.2

Indonesia

Sierra, J. The gift of the Crocodile (k-3) 398.2

Iraq

Henderson, K. Lugalbanda: 398.2

Hickox, R. The golden sandal (k-3) 398.2

McCaughrean, G. The epic of Gilgamesh (5 and up) 398.2

Ireland

Byrd, R. Finn MacCoul and his fearless wife (k-3) 398.2

Daly, J. Fair, Brown & Trembling (k-3) 398.2

De Paola, T. Jamie O'Rourke and the big potato (k-3) 398.2

Doyle, M. Tales from old Ireland (3-6) 398.2

Folklore—Puerto Rico—*Continued*

Montes, M. Juan Bobo goes to work (k-3) **398.2**

Romania

Philip, N. Noah and the Devil (k-3) **398.2**

Rascol, S. I. The impudent rooster (k-3) **398.2**

Russia

See also Folklore—Ukraine

Afanas'ev, A. N. Russian fairy tales (4 and up) **398.2**

Cole, J. Bony-Legs (k-3) **398.2**

Ginsburg, M. Clay boy (k-3) **398.2**

Martin, R. The language of birds (2-4) **398.2**

Mayer, M. Baba Yaga and Vasilisa the brave (3-5) **398.2**

McCaughrean, G. Grandma Chickenlegs (k-3) **398.2**

Polacco, P. Luba and the wren (k-3) **398.2**

Ransome, A. The Fool of the World and the flying ship (k-3) **398.2**

Robbins, R. Baboushka and the three kings (1-4) **398.2**

Sanderson, R. The Golden Mare, the Firebird, and the magic ring (3-5) **398.2**

Shepard, A. The sea king's daughter (3-6) **398.2**

Spirin, G. The tale of the Firebird (2-4) **398.2**

Scotland

Huck, C. S. The Black Bull of Norroway (2-4) **398.2**

Lupton, H. Pirican Pic and Pirican Mor (k-3) **398.2**

South Africa

Seeger, P. Abiyoyo (k-3) **398.2**

Southern States

Bushyhead, R. H. Yonder mountain (k-3) **398.2**

Curry, J. L. Hold up the sky: and other Native American tales from Texas and the Southern Plains (4 and up) **398.2**

Curry, J. L. The wonderful sky boat and other Native American tales of the Southeast (4 and up) **398.2**

Doucet, S. A. Lapin plays possum: trickster tales from the Louisiana Bayou (4-6) **398.2**

Grandfather tales (4 and up) **398.2**

The Jack tales (4-6) **398.2**

MacDonald, M. R. Pickin' peas (k-3) **398.2**

Salley, C. Epossumondas (k-3) **398.2**

San Souci, R. Little Gold Star (2-4) **398.2**

San Souci, R. The talking eggs (k-3) **398.2**

Thomas, J. C. What's the hurry, Fox? (k-3) **398.2**

Van Laan, N. With a whoop and a holler (4 and up) **398**

Wooldridge, C. N. Wicked Jack (k-3) **398.2**

Spain

Sierra, J. The beautiful butterfly (k-3) **398.2**

Thailand

MacDonald, M. R. The girl who wore too much (k-3) **398.2**

Tibet (China)

Berger, B. All the way to Lhasa (k-3) **398.2**

Demi. The donkey and the rock (k-3) **398.2**

Rose, N. C. Tibetan tales for little Buddhas (k-3) **398.2**

Turkey

Demi. The hungry coat (k-3) **398.2**

Johnson-Davies, D. Goha the wise fool (2-4) **398.2**

Ukraine

Brett, J. The mitten (k-2) **398.2**

Kimmel, E. A. The birds' gift (k-3) **398.2**

Tresselt, A. R. The mitten (k-2) **398.2**

United States

Forest, H. The baker's dozen (k-3) **398.2**

Galdone, J. The tailypo (k-3) **398.2**

Keats, E. J. John Henry (k-3) **398.2**

Lester, J. John Henry (k-3) **398.2**

Lyons, M. E. Roy makes a car (k-3) **398.2**

Osborne, M. P. American tall tales (3-6) **398.2**

San Souci, R. Cut from the same cloth (4 and up) **398.2**

San Souci, R. The secret of the stones (k-3) **398.2**

San Souci, R. Six foolish fishermen (k-3) **398.2**

Schwartz, A. More scary stories to tell in the dark (4 and up) **398.2**

Schwartz, A. Scary stories 3 (4 and up) **398.2**

Schwartz, A. Scary stories to tell in the dark (4 and up) **398.2**

Stockings of buttermilk: American folktales (4 and up) **398.2**

Thomas, J. C. The six fools (k-3) **398.2**

Willey, M. Clever Beatrice (k-3) **398.2**

Vietnam

Garland, S. Children of the dragon (3-6) **398.2**

Lee, J. M. Toad is the uncle of heaven (k-3) **398.2**

Terada, A. M. Under the starfruit tree (4-6) **398.2**

Wales

Cooper, S. The silver cow (1-4) **398.2**

West Africa

Aardema, V. Anansi does the impossible! (k-3) **398.2**

Aardema, V. Why mosquitoes buzz in people's ears (k-3) **398.2**

Badoe, A. The pot of wisdom: Ananse stories **398.2**

Courlander, H. Cow-tail switch, and other West African stories (4-6) **398.2**

Graham, L. B. How God fix Jonah (4 and up) **398.2**

Wagué Diakité, B. The hatseller and the monkeys (k-3) **398.2**

Wagué Diakité, B. The hunterman and the crocodile (2-4) **398.2**

West Indies

Hamilton, V. The girl who spun gold (k-3) **398.2**

See/See also pages in the following book(s):

Hamilton, V. A ring of tricksters (3-6) **398.2**

The **footless** champion and the handless champion. Afanas'ev, A. N.
  In Afanas'ev, A. N. Russian fairy tales p269-73   **398.2**

Footnotes. Augustyn, F.   **792.8**

Footprints on the roof. Singer, M.   **811**

Footsteps. Schwartz, A.
  In Schwartz, A. Scary stories 3; more tales to chill your bones p20-21   **398.2**

Footwear *See* Shoes

For laughing out loud   **811.008**

For Pete's sake. Walsh, E. S.   **E**

For you are a Kenyan child. Cunnane, K.   **E**

Forbes, Esther
  Johnny Tremain (5 and up)   **Fic**

The **Forbidden** apple
  In The Magic orange tree, and other Haitian folktales p171-75   **398.2**

The **forbidden** schoolhouse [biography of Prudence Crandall] Jurmain, S.   **92**

Force and energy
  Bradley, K. B. Energy makes things happen (k-3)   **531**
  Bradley, K. B. Forces make things move (k-3)   **531**
  Mason, A. Move it! (k-2)   **531**

Forced labor *See* Slavery

Forces make things move. Bradley, K. B.   **531**

Forces of nature. Grace, C. O.   **551.2**

Ford, Bernette
  First snow   **E**

Ford, Carin T.
  African-American soldiers in the Civil War (4-6)   **973.7**
  The American Civil War (4-6)   **973.7**
  Andy Warhol (2-4)   **92**
  The Battle of Gettysburg and Lincoln's Gettysburg Address (4-6)   **973.7**
  Benjamin Franklin (1-3)   **92**
  Daring women of the Civil War (3-5)   **973.7**
  Jackie Robinson (2-4)   **92**
  Lincoln, slavery, and the Emancipation Proclamation (4-6)   **973.7**
  Roberto Clemente (5 and up)   **92**
  Slavery and the underground railroad (3-5)   **326**

Ford, Christine
  Scout (5 and up)   **Fic**

Ford, George
  (jt. auth) Coles, R. The story of Ruby Bridges   **370**
  (il) Giovanni, N. Ego-tripping and other poems for young people   **811**

Ford, H. J. (Henry Justice)
  (il) The Arabian nights entertainments. See The Arabian nights entertainments   **398.2**
  (il) The Blue fairy book. See The Blue fairy book   **398.2**

Ford, Michael
  (jt. auth) Boynton, S. Dog train   **782.42**
  (jt. auth) Boynton, S. Philadelphia chickens   **782.42**

Forecasting
  See also Weather forecasting

Foreign population *See* Immigrants

Foreigners *See* Immigrants

Foreman, Michael
  (il) Baum, L. F. The Wizard of Oz   **Fic**
  (il) Borden, L. The little ships   **E**
  (il) Grahame, K. The wind in the willows   **Fic**
  (il) Morpurgo, M. Arthur, high king of Britain   **Fic**
  (il) Morpurgo, M. Sir Gawain and the Green Knight   **398.2**

Forensic sciences
  Jackson, D. M. The bone detectives (5 and up)   **614**
  Jackson, D. M. The wildlife detectives (4 and up)   **363.2**
  Lane, B. Crime and detection   **364**
  Mattern, J. Forensics (5 and up)   **363.2**
  Pentland, P. Forensic science (4 and up)   **363.2**
  Platt, R. Forensics (5 and up)   **363.2**

Forensics. Mattern, J.   **363.2**

Forensics. Platt, R.   **363.2**

Forest, Heather
  The baker's dozen (k-3)   **398.2**

Forest animals
  George, L. B. In the woods: who's been here?   **E**
  Swinburne, S. R. The woods scientist (4 and up)   **591.7**

Forest conservation
  Dalgleish, S. Protecting forests (3-6)   **333.75**

Forest ecology
  See also Rain forest ecology
  Bash, B. Ancient ones (3-5)   **585**
  Beil, K. M. Fire in their eyes (4 and up)   **628.9**
  Brenner, B. One small place in a tree (2-4)   **577.3**
  Burnie, D. Shrublands (5 and up)   **577.3**
  Collard, S. B., III. Forest in the clouds (2-4)   **577.3**
  Johansson, P. The forested Taiga (3-5)   **577.3**
  Johansson, P. The temperate forest (3-5)   **577.3**
  Johnson, R. L. A walk in the boreal forest (3-6)   **577.3**
  Johnson, R. L. A walk in the deciduous forest (3-6)   **577.3**
  Morrison, G. Oak tree (3-6)   **583**
  Patent, D. H. Fire: friend or foe (4 and up)   **577.2**
  Pfeffer, W. A log's life (k-3)   **577.3**
  Simon, S. Wildfires (3-6)   **577.2**

Forest fires
  Beil, K. M. Fire in their eyes (4 and up)   **628.9**
  Landau, E. Smokejumpers (3-6)   **628.9**
  Morrison, T. Wildfire (4-6)   **634.9**
  Patent, D. H. Fire: friend or foe (4 and up)   **577.2**

Fossils—*Continued*

Thompson, S. E. Death trap (4 and up) **560**

Zoehfeld, K. W. Did dinosaurs have feathers? (k-3) **568**

Zoehfeld, K. W. Dinosaur parents, dinosaur young (4 and up) **567.9**

Fiction

Ewart, C. Fossil **E**

Fossils tell of long ago. Aliki **560**

Foster, John

(comp) My first Oxford book of animal poems. See My first Oxford book of animal poems **808.81**

Foster, Leila Merrell

Kuwait (5 and up) **953.67**

Oman (5 and up) **953**

Foster, Stephen Collins, 1826-1864

See/See also pages in the following book(s):

Krull, K. Lives of the musicians (4 and up) **920**

Foster home care

Fiction

Byars, B. C. The pinballs (5 and up) **Fic**

Dowell, F. O. Where I'd like to be (4 and up) **Fic**

Giff, P. R. Pictures of Hollis Woods (5 and up) **Fic**

Lowry, L. Gossamer (5 and up) **Fic**

Nixon, J. L. A family apart (5 and up) **Fic**

Paterson, K. The great Gilly Hopkins (5 and up) **Fic**

Polacco, P. Welcome Comfort **E**

Quattlebaum, M. Grover G. Graham and me (4 and up) **Fic**

Sebestyen, O. Out of nowhere (5 and up) **Fic**

Wolfson, J. What I call life (5 and up) **Fic**

Poetry

Woodson, J. Locomotion (4 and up) **811**

The **founders**. Fradin, D. B. **920**

The **foundling**. Alexander, L.

In Alexander, L. The foundling and other tales of Prydain p5-14 **S C**

The **foundling** and other tales of Prydain. Alexander, L. **S C**

Fountain, Joanna F.

(ed) Cataloging correctly for kids. See Cataloging correctly for kids **025.3**

The **four** corners of the sky. Zeitlin, S. J. **201**

Four dollars and fifty cents. Kimmel, E. A. **E**

The **four-footed** horror. Olson, A. N.

In Olson, A. N. and Schwartz, H. Ask the bones: scary stories from around the world p37-41 **398.2**

Four hairs from the beard of the Devil

In The Magic orange tree, and other Haitian folktales p43-48 **398.2**

Four perfect pebbles. Perl, L. **940.53**

Four pictures by Emily Carr. Debon, N. **92**

The **four** questions. Schwartz, L. S. **296.4**

Four seasons make a year. Rockwell, A. F. **E**

The **four** ugly cats in apartment 3D. Sachs, M. **Fic**

Fourth of July

Giblin, J. Fireworks, picnics, and flags (3-6) **394.26**

Hess, D. The Fourth of July (4-6) **394.26**

Fiction

Wong, J. S. Apple pie 4th of July **E**

The **fourth** question. Chu, V.

In Fire and wings: dragon tales from East and West p55-64 **S C**

Fowles, Shelley

The bachelor and the bean (k-3) **398.2**

Fox, Dan

(ed) A treasury of children's songs. See A treasury of children's songs **782.42**

Fox, F. G. (Frank G.)

Jean Laffite and the big ol' whale **E**

Fox, Helen

Eager (5 and up) **Fic**

Fox, Mem

Hattie and the fox **E**

Hunwick's egg **E**

Koala Lou **E**

Night noises **E**

Reading magic **028.5**

Sleepy bears **E**

Sophie **E**

Tough Boris **E**

Where is the green sheep? **E**

Wombat divine **E**

Fox, Paula

One-eyed cat (5 and up) **Fic**

The slave dancer (5 and up) **Fic**

The stone-faced boy (4-6) **Fic**

Fox and Crawfish. Curry, J. L.

In Curry, J. L. The wonderful sky boat and other Native American tales of the Southeast p59-60 **398.2**

Fox and his friends. Marshall, E. **E**

Fox and Possum. Curry, J. L.

In Curry, J. L. Hold up the sky: and other Native American tales from Texas and the Southern Plains p84-88 **398.2**

The **fox** and the crab. Sierra, J.

In Sierra, J. Nursery tales around the world p81-83 **398.2**

The **fox** and the crane. Afanas'ev, A. N.

In Afanas'ev, A. N. Russian fairy tales p171-72 **398.2**

The **fox** and the lobster. Afanas'ev, A. N.

In Afanas'ev, A. N. Russian fairy tales p310 **398.2**

The **fox** and the woodcock. Afanas'ev, A. N.

In Afanas'ev, A. N. Russian fairy tales p171 **398.2**

The **fox** and the woodpecker. Afanas'ev, A. N.

In Afanas'ev, A. N. Russian fairy tales p199 **398.2**

The **fox** as midwife. Afanas'ev, A. N.

In Afanas'ev, A. N. Russian fairy tales p191-92 **398.2**

The **fox** as mourner. Afanas'ev, A. N.

In Afanas'ev, A. N. Russian fairy tales p437-38 **398.2**

The **fox** confessor. Afanas'ev, A. N.
In Afanas'ev, A. N. Russian fairy tales p72-
74 **398.2**

Fox-Davies, Sarah
(il) Davies, N. Bat loves the night **E**
(il) Waddell, M. Snow bears **E**

The **fox** physician. Afanas'ev, A. N.
In Afanas'ev, A. N. Russian fairy tales p15-
17 **398.2**

The **fox**, the hare, and the cock. Afanas'ev, A. N.
In Afanas'ev, A. N. Russian fairy tales p192-
94 **398.2**

The **Fox** went out on a chilly night (k-3)
782.42

Foxes
Greenaway, T. Wolves, wild dogs, and foxes (4
and up) **599.77**
Fiction
Brun-Cosme, N. No, I want daddy! **E**
Campoy, F. I. Rosa Raposa **E**
Church, C. One smart goose **E**
Cooney, B. Chanticleer and the fox **E**
Fox, M. Hattie and the fox **E**
Gliori, D. No matter what **E**
Hindley, J. Do like a duck does! **E**
Hutchins, P. Rosie's walk **E**
Kasza, K. My lucky day **E**
Marshall, E. Fox and his friends **E**
McAllister, A. Barkus, Sly and the golden egg
E
McKissack, P. C. Flossie & the fox **E**
McPhail, D. M. Piggy's pancake parlor (1-3)
Fic
Myers, T. Basho and the river stones **E**
Nikola-Lisa, W. Setting the turkeys free **E**
Palatini, M. Three French hens **E**
Tompert, A. Grandfather Tang's story **E**
Waring, R. Hungry hen **E**
Folklore
Aylesworth, J. The tale of Tricky Fox (k-3)
398.2
Hogrogian, N. One fine day (k-3) **398.2**
Knutson, B. Love and roast chicken (k-3)
398.2
Songs
The Fox went out on a chilly night (k-3)
782.42

Fraction action. Leedy, L. **513**
Fraction fun. Adler, D. A. **513**
Fractions
Adler, D. A. Fraction fun (2-4) **513**
Leedy, L. Fraction action (k-3) **513**
Long, L. Fabulous fractions (3-6) **513**
Murphy, S. J. Jump, kangaroo, jump! (1-3)
513
Nagda, A. W. Polar bear math (2-4) **513**
Fractured fairy tales. Lohnes, M. **812**
Fradin, Dennis B.
The founders (4 and up) **920**
Ida B. Wells (5 and up) **92**
Let it begin here! (2-4) **973.3**
Nicolaus Copernicus (3-6) **92**
The planet hunters (5 and up) **523.4**
Samuel Adams (6 and up) **92**
The signers (4 and up) **920**

With a little luck (5 and up) **509**
(jt. auth) Fradin, J. B. 5,000 miles to freedom
326

Fradin, Judith Bloom
5,000 miles to freedom **326**
(jt. auth) Fradin, D. B. Ida B. Wells **92**

The **fragrance** of paradise. Goldin, B. D.
In Goldin, B. D. Journeys with Elijah; eight
tales of the Prophet p49-56 **222**

Frame, Jeron Ashford
Yesterday I had the blues **E**

Frampton, David
(il) Carrick, C. Whaling days **639.2**
(il) Fleischman, P. Bull Run **Fic**
(il) Grimes, N. At Jerusalem's gate **811**

France
Landau, E. France (2-4) **944**
Nardo, D. France (5 and up) **944**
NgCheong-Lum, R. France (4 and up) **944**
Fiction
Banks, K. The cat who walked across France
E
Chall, M. W. Bonaparte **E**
Knight, J. Charlotte in Giverny (3-6) **Fic**
Maguire, G. The good liar (4 and up) **Fic**
Morpurgo, M. Waiting for Anya (5 and up)
Fic
Polacco, P. The butterfly (2-4) **Fic**
Potter, G. Chloe's birthday . . . and me **E**
Rappaport, D. The secret seder (2-4) **E**
Schnur, S. The shadow children (5 and up)
Fic
Wells, R. The miraculous tale of the two Maries
E
Folklore
See Folklore—France
History—1328-1589, House of Valois
Hodges, M. Joan of Arc (2-4) **92**
Poole, J. Joan of Arc (2-4) **92**
Stanley, D. Joan of Arc (4 and up) **92**

Francie. English, K. **Fic**

Francis, of Assisi, Saint
Canticle of the sun; adaptation. See Lindbergh,
R. The circle of days **242**

Francis, of Assisi, Saint, 1182-1226
About
Kennedy, R. F. Saint Francis of Assisi (2-4)
271
Pandell, K. Saint Francis sings to Brother Sun
(4 and up) **271**
Visconti, G. Clare and Francis (4 and up)
271
Fiction
Byrd, R. Saint Francis and the Christmas don-
key **E**
Legends
Bedard, M. The wolf of Gubbio (3-6) **398.2**
Egielski, R. Saint Francis and the wolf (1-3)
398.2

Francis, Panama
David gets his drum **E**

Franck, Irene M.
(jt. auth) Brownstone, D. M. Frontier America
973.03

Freedman, Russell—*Continued*

Indian chiefs (6 and up)   **920**

An Indian winter (6 and up)   **978**

Kids at work (5 and up)   **331.3**

Lincoln: a photobiography (5 and up)   **92**

Out of darkness: the story of Louis Braille (4 and up)   **92**

The voice that challenged a nation [biography of Marian Anderson] (5 and up)   **92**

The Wright brothers: how they invented the airplane   **92**

See/See also pages in the following book(s):

Author talk (4 and up)   **028.5**

(jt. auth) Bad Heart Buffalo, A. The life and death of Crazy Horse   **92**

Freedom, Academic *See* Academic freedom

Freedom. Sanfield, S.

In Sanfield, S. The adventures of High John the Conqueror   **398.2**

Freedom like sunlight. Lewis, J. P.   **811**

Freedom marches for civil rights *See* Civil rights demonstrations

Freedom of information

See also Censorship

Freedom on the menu. Weatherford, C. B.   **E**

Freedom Riders. Bausum, A.   **323.1**

Freedom river [biography of John P. Parker] Rappaport, D.   **92**

Freedom roads: searching for the Underground Railroad. Hansen, J.   **973.7**

Freedom struggle. Rossi, A.   **973.7**

Freedom Summer. Wiles, D.   **E**

Freeman, Don

Corduroy   **E**

Earl the squirrel   **E**

Freeman, Judy

Books kids will sit still for 3   **011.6**

Freeman, Martha

The trouble with cats (2-4)   **Fic**

Who stole Halloween? (4-6)   **Fic**

Freeze frame. Macy, S.   **796.98**

Freight train. Crews, D.   **E**

Fremont, David

(il) Proimos, J. The grade school zone   **S C**

French, Jackie

Diary of a wombat   **E**

Pete the sheep-sheep   **E**

French, Martin

(jt. auth) Miller, N. Stompin' at the Savoy [biography of Norma Miller]   **92**

French, Simon

Where in the world (5 and up)   **Fic**

French, Vivian

Growing frogs (k-3)   **597.8**

French and Indian War *See* United States—History—1755-1763, French and Indian War

French artists *See* Artists, French

French Cameroons *See* Cameroon

French language

Vocabulary

Jocelyn, M. ABC x 3   **E**

French poetry

Cendrars, B. Shadow (1-3)   **841**

Fresco painting *See* Mural painting and decoration

Freshwater animals

Aliki. My visit to the aquarium (k-3)   **639.34**

Aquatic life of the world (4 and up)   **578.7**

Freymann, Saxton

Dog food   **E**

Fast food   **E**

Food for thought   **E**

How are you peeling?   **E**

One lonely sea horse   **E**

Friar, Joanne H.

(il) Purmell, A. Apple cider making days   **E**

Frida [Kahlo] Winter, J.   **92**

Frida Kahlo and Diego Rivera: their lives and ideas. Sabbeth, C.   **92**

The **Friday** nights of Nana. Hest, A.   **E**

Fridell, Ron

The search for poison-dart frogs (4-6)   **597.8**

Friedman, Debra

Picture this (4-6)   **770**

Friedman, Ina R.

How my parents learned to eat   **E**

Friedman, Judith

(il) Stanek, M. I speak English for my mom   **Fic**

Friedman, Lise

Break a leg! (4 and up)   **792**

Friedman, Robin

The silent witness (k-3)   **973.7**

Friedrich, Elizabeth

Leah's pony   **E**

Friend, Catherine

Eddie the raccoon   **E**

Friend, Sandra

Earth's wild winds (5 and up)   **551.51**

The **friend**. Stewart, S.   **E**

A **friend** called Anne. Lee, C. A.   **940.53**

The **friend** who changed my life. Ryan, P. M.

In Friends; stories about new friends, old friends, and unexpectedly true friends   **S C**

The **Friendly** demon

In Stockings of buttermilk: American folktales p56-61   **398.2**

Friends, Imaginary *See* Imaginary playmates

Friends, Society of *See* Society of Friends

Friends (5 and up)   **S C**

Friendship

Brown, L. K. How to be a friend (k-3)   **158**

Rogers, F. Making friends (k-1)   **158**

Fiction

Aliki. We are best friends   **E**

Barrows, A. Ivy + Bean (1-3)   **Fic**

Baskin, N. R. What every girl (except me) knows (4 and up)   **Fic**

Bateson, C. Stranded in Boringsville (5 and up)   **Fic**

Bauer, M. D. The double-digit club (3-5)   **Fic**

Friendship—Fiction—*Continued*

Betancourt, J. My name is brain Brian (4-6)
    Fic
Blegvad, L. Kitty and Mr. Kipling (3-5) **Fic**
Bloom, S. A splendid friend, indeed **E**
Bottner, B. Wallace's lists **E**
Byars, B. C. The Cybil war (4-6) **Fic**
Byars, B. C. The pinballs (5 and up) **Fic**
Cameron, A. Gloria's way (2-4) **Fic**
Caple, K. The friendship tree **E**
Carle, E. Where are you going? To see my friend! **E**
Carville, J. Lu and the swamp ghost **E**
Chaconas, D. Cork & Fuzz **E**
Cheaney, J. B. My friend, the enemy (5 and up)
    Fic
Cheng, A. Honeysuckle house (3-5) **Fic**
Cheng, A. The lace dowry (4 and up) **Fic**
Child, L. Clarice Bean spells trouble (3-5)
    Fic
Chodos-Irvine, M. Best best friends **E**
Cohen, B. Thank you, Jackie Robinson (4-6)
    Fic
Collier, J. L. Me and Billy (5 and up) **Fic**
Cox, J. Butterfly buddies (2-4) **Fic**
Cox, J. That crazy Eddie and the science project of doom (2-4) **Fic**
Creech, S. Heartbeat (4 and up) **Fic**
Creech, S. Walk two moons (6 and up) **Fic**
Cutler, J. Rose and Riley **E**
Daly, N. Once upon a time **E**
Danziger, P. Amber Brown is not a crayon (2-4)
    Fic
Danziger, P. P.S. Longer letter later (5 and up)
    Fic
Danziger, P. Snail mail no more (5 and up)
    Fic
Danziger, P. United Tates of America (4 and up) **Fic**
Dowell, F. O. Chicken boy (4 and up) **Fic**
Dowell, F. O. The secret language of girls (5 and up) **Fic**
Dowell, F. O. Where I'd like to be (4 and up)
    Fic
Ehrlich, A. Leo, Zack, and Emmie together again **E**
English, K. Hot day on Abbott Avenue **E**
Falwell, C. David's drawings **E**
Farish, T. The cat who liked potato soup **E**
Fine, A. Up on cloud nine (5 and up) **Fic**
Ford, C. Scout (5 and up) **Fic**
Franklin, K. L. Lone wolf (4 and up) **Fic**
Freymann, S. One lonely sea horse **E**
Friends (5 and up) **S C**
Giff, P. R. All the way home (4 and up)
    Fic
Giff, P. R. Lily's crossing (4 and up) **Fic**
Gorbachev, V. That's what friends are for **E**
Gordon, A. The Gorillas of Gill Park (4 and up)
    Fic
Grant, K. Sofie and the city **E**
Greene, B. Philip Hall likes me, I reckon maybe (4-6) **Fic**
Gretz, S. Riley and Rose in the picture **E**
Guest, E. H. Iris and Walter **E**
Haas, I. Bess and Bella **E**
Hahn, M. D. Daphne's book (5 and up) **Fic**

Hale, M. The truth about sparrows (5 and up)
    Fic
Hamilton, V. The planet of Junior Brown (6 and up) **Fic**
Henkes, K. Words of stone (5 and up) **Fic**
Hest, A. Mr. George Baker **E**
Holt, K. W. When Zachary Beaver came to town (5 and up) **Fic**
Horvath, P. When the circus came to town (4-6)
    Fic
Howe, J. Horace and Morris but mostly Dolores
    E
Howe, J. Houndsley and Catina **E**
Howe, J. Pinky and Rex **E**
Hurwitz, J. The hot & cold summer (3-5)
    Fic
Hurwitz, J. Oh no, Noah! (2-4) **Fic**
Jacobson, J. Winnie (dancing) on her own (2-4)
    Fic
Jennings, P. The weeping willow (2-4) **Fic**
Johnston, T. Alien & Possum: hanging out
    E
Karr, K. Worlds apart (4 and up) **Fic**
Keller, H. Farfallina & Marcel **E**
Kellogg, S. Best friends **E**
Kimmel, E. C. Visiting Miss Caples (6 and up)
    Fic
Konigsburg, E. L. Jennifer, Hecate, Macbeth, William McKinley, and me, Elizabeth (4-6)
    Fic
Konigsburg, E. L. The view from Saturday (4 and up) **Fic**
Koss, A. G. The girls (5 and up) **Fic**
Krumgold, J. Onion John (5 and up) **Fic**
Kurtz, J. The storyteller's beads (5 and up)
    Fic
Lairla, S. Abel and the wolf **E**
Levy, E. Seventh grade tango (5 and up)
    Fic
Lisle, J. T. Afternoon of the elves (4-6) **Fic**
Lovelace, M. H. Betsy-Tacy (2-4) **Fic**
Lowry, L. Autumn Street (4 and up) **Fic**
Lowry, L. Number the stars (4 and up) **Fic**
Lowry, L. Rabble Starkey (5 and up) **Fic**
Mackel, K. MadCat (5 and up) **Fic**
Marsden, C. Moon runner (3-5) **Fic**
Marshall, J. George and Martha **E**
Martin, A. M. A corner of the universe (5 and up) **Fic**
McGhee, A. Snap (5 and up) **Fic**
McMullan, K. Pearl and Wagner: two good friends **E**
McNamee, G. Sparks (4-6) **Fic**
Mead, A. Madame Squidley and Beanie (3-5)
    Fic
Morgan, N. Chicken friend (5 and up) **Fic**
Murray, M. The slightly true story of Cedar B. Hartley (5 and up) **Fic**
Mwangi, M. The Mzungu boy (5 and up)
    Fic
Myracle, L. Eleven (4 and up) **Fic**
Nagda, A. W. Dear Whiskers (2-4) **Fic**
Naylor, P. R. Starting with Alice (3-6) **Fic**
O'Dell, K. Agnes Parker . . . girl in progress (4 and up) **Fic**
Orgel, D. The devil in Vienna (6 and up)
    Fic

The **frog** princess. Kimmel, E. A. **398.2**

Frog rescue. Hamilton, G. **597.8**

Frog went a-courtin'. Langstaff, J. M. **782.42**

Froggy learns to swim. London, J. **E**

Frogs

 See also Toads

 Arnosky, J. All about frogs (k-3) **597.8**

 Dewey, J. Poison dart frogs (3-5) **597.8**

 French, V. Growing frogs (k-3) **597.8**

 Fridell, R. The search for poison-dart frogs (4-6) **597.8**

 Gibbons, G. Frogs (k-3) **597.8**

 Hamilton, G. Frog rescue (5 and up) **597.8**

 Llewellyn, C. Frog (k-3) **597.8**

 Magloff, L. Frog (k-2) **597.8**

 Noonan, D. The frog (2-4) **597.8**

 Patent, D. H. Flashy fantastic rain forest frogs (k-3) **597.8**

 Pfeffer, W. From tadpole to frog (k-1) **597.8**

 Schwabacher, M. Frogs (3-6) **597.8**

 Wallace, K. Tale of a tadpole (k-1) **597.8**

 Winer, Y. Frogs sing songs (k-3) **597.8**

Fiction

 Asch, F. Baby Bird's first nest **E**

 Cooper, S. Frog **E**

 Cowley, J. Red-eyed tree frog **E**

 Delacre, L. Rafi and Rosi **E**

 Gorbachev, V. Ms. Turtle the babysitter **E**

 Grobler, P. Hey, frog! **E**

 Kalan, R. Jump, frog, jump! **E**

 Leedy, L. The great graph contest **E**

 Lionni, L. Fish is fish **E**

 Lobel, A. Frog and Toad are friends **E**

 London, J. Froggy learns to swim **E**

 Mayer, M. A boy, a dog, and a frog **E**

 Napoli, D. J. The prince of the pond (4-6) **Fic**

 Potter, B. The tale of Mr. Jeremy Fisher **E**

 Scieszka, J. The Frog Prince continued **E**

 Wiesner, D. Tuesday **E**

 Wilson, K. A frog in the bog **E**

Folklore

 Heo, Y. The green frogs (k-3) **398.2**

 Kimmel, E. A. The frog princess (2-4) **398.2**

Songs

 Langstaff, J. M. Frog went a-courtin' (k-3) **782.42**

Frogs sing songs. Winer, Y. **597.8**

The **frogs** wore red suspenders. Prelutsky, J. **811**

Frolka Stay-at-Home. Afanas'ev, A. N.

 In Afanas'ev, A. N. Russian fairy tales p299-302 **398.2**

From Anna. Little, J. **Fic**

From biography to history **016.8**

From caterpillar to butterfly. Heiligman, D. **595.7**

From cover to cover. Horning, K. T. **028.1**

From egg to butterfly. Zemlicka, S. **595.7**

From head to toe. Carle, E. **E**

From pictures to words. Stevens, J. **741.6**

From rags to riches. Sills, L. **391**

From reader to writer. Ellis, S. **372.6**

From slave ship to freedom road. Lester, J. **326**

From slave to soldier. Hopkinson, D. **E**

From spider webs to man-made silk. Allman, T. **595.4**

From tadpole to frog. Pfeffer, W. **597.8**

From the bellybutton of the moon and other summer poems. Alarcón, F. X. **811**

From the mixed-up files of Mrs. Basil E. Frankweiler. Konigsburg, E. L. **Fic**

Froman, Nan

 What's that bug? (4-6) **595.7**

Frontier America. Brownstone, D. M. **973.03**

Frontier and pioneer life

 Anderson, W. T. Pioneer girl: the story of Laura Ingalls Wilder (2-4) **92**

 Greenwood, B. A pioneer sampler (4 and up) **971.3**

 Halpern, M. Railroad fever (4-6) **385.09**

 Houghton, G. The Transcontinental Railroad (5 and up) **385.09**

 Kellogg, S. Johnny Appleseed (k-3) **92**

 Landau, E. The transcontinental railroad (5 and up) **385.09**

 Lowery, L. Aunt Clara Brown (2-4) **92**

 Moses, W. Johnny Appleseed (3-6) **92**

 Rounds, G. Sod houses on the Great Plains (k-3) **693**

 Stanley, G. E. The European settlement of North America (1492-1763) (5 and up) **973.2**

 Steele, C. Famous wagon trails (5 and up) **978**

 Steele, C. Pioneer life in the American West (5 and up) **978**

 Stefoff, R. First frontier (4 and up) **973.5**

 Thompson, L. The transcontinental railroad (4-6) **385.09**

 Walker, B. M. The Little House cookbook (5 and up) **641.5**

Fiction

 Arrington, F. Bluestem (4-6) **Fic**

 Arrington, F. Prairie whispers (5 and up) **Fic**

 Auch, M. J. Journey to nowhere (4 and up) **Fic**

 Avi. The barn (4 and up) **Fic**

 Avi. Prairie school (2-4) **Fic**

 Bradley, K. B. Weaver's daughter (4 and up) **Fic**

 Brenner, B. Wagon wheels **E**

 Brink, C. R. Caddie Woodlawn (4-6) **Fic**

 Bunting, E. Dandelions **E**

 Byars, B. C. The Golly sisters go West **E**

 Cannon, A. E. Charlotte's Rose (5 and up) **Fic**

 Conrad, P. Prairie songs (5 and up) **Fic**

 Couloumbis, A. The misadventures of Maude March (5 and up) **Fic**

 Cushman, K. The ballad of Lucy Whipple (5 and up) **Fic**

 Dalgliesh, A. The courage of Sarah Noble (2-4) **Fic**

 DeFelice, C. C. Weasel (4 and up) **Fic**

Galdone, Paul—*Continued*

Henny Penny (k-2)	**398.2**
The little red hen (k-2)	**398.2**
The monkey and the crocodile (k-2)	**398.2**
Puss in boots (k-2)	**398.2**
The teeny-tiny woman (k-2)	**398.2**
The three bears (k-2)	**398.2**
The three Billy Goats Gruff (k-2)	**398.2**
Three little kittens	**398.8**
(il) Bulla, C. R. The sword in the tree	**Fic**
(il) Galdone, J. The tailypo	**398.2**

Galford, Ellen

Hatshepsut (4 and up)	**92**
The trail West (5 and up)	**978**

Galilei, Galileo, 1564-1642
About

Panchyk, R. Galileo for kids (5 and up)	**92**
Sís, P. Starry messenger [biography of Galileo Galilei]	**92**
Steele, P. Galileo (4 and up)	**92**

Galileo *See* Galilei, Galileo, 1564-1642

Galileo for kids. Panchyk, R.   **92**

Galimoto. Williams, K. L.   **E**

Gall, Alice

Bucephalus: a king's horse
In Horse tales   **S C**

Gall, Chris

(il) Bates, K. L. America the beautiful   **E**

Gall, Susan B.

Junior worldmark encyclopedia of the nations. See Junior worldmark encyclopedia of the nations   **910.3**

(ed) Junior Worldmark encyclopedia of the states. See Junior Worldmark encyclopedia of the states   **973.03**

(ed) The Lincoln Library of Greek & Roman mythology. See The Lincoln Library of Greek & Roman mythology   **292**

Gall, Timothy L.

Junior worldmark encyclopedia of the nations. See Junior worldmark encyclopedia of the nations   **910.3**

(ed) Junior Worldmark encyclopedia of the states. See Junior Worldmark encyclopedia of the states   **973.03**

(ed) The Lincoln Library of Greek & Roman mythology. See The Lincoln Library of Greek & Roman mythology   **292**

Gallagher, Saelig

(il) Burnett, F. H. The secret garden	**Fic**
(il) Pullman, P. The firework-maker's daughter	**Fic**
(il) Wilde, O. The selfish giant	**Fic**

Gallant, Jonathan R.

The tales fossils tell (5 and up)   **560**

Gallant, Roy A.

Atmosphere (5 and up)	**551.51**
Dance of the continents (5 and up)	**551.1**
Early humans (5 and up)	**599.93**
Earth's place in space (5 and up)	**525**
The ever changing atom (5 and up)	**539.7**
Fossils (3-5)	**560**
The origins of life (5 and up)	**576.8**
Plates (5 and up)	**551.1**

Space stations (3-5)	**629.44**
Structure (5 and up)	**551.1**
The treasure of inheritance (5 and up)	**576.5**
Water [Earthworks series] (5 and up)	**553.7**
[Kaleidoscope series] (3-5)	**551.48**
The wonders of biodiversity (5 and up)	**333.95**

Galleries, Art *See* Art museums

Galloway, Priscilla

Archers, alchemists, and 98 other medieval jobs you might have loved or loathed (3-6)   **940.1**

Gallymanders! Gallymanders!
In Grandfather tales; American-English folk tales p18-28   **398.2**

Galvin, Irene Flum

Brazil (4 and up)   **981**

Gama, Vasco da, 1469-1524
About

Calvert, P. Vasco da Gama (5 and up)   **92**

Goodman, J. E. A long and uncertain journey: the 27,000 mile voyage of Vasco da Gama (4 and up)   **92**

See/See also pages in the following book(s):

Fritz, J. Around the world in a hundred years (4 and up)   **910.4**

The **game** of silence. Erdrich, L.   **Fic**

The **Game** of Sunken Places. Anderson, M. T.   **Fic**

Game protection

See also Birds—Protection

Jackson, D. M. The wildlife detectives (4 and up)   **363.2**

Games

See also Card games; Computer games; Indoor games; Singing games; Sports; Word games and names of individual games

Anna Banana: 101 jump-rope rhymes	**398.8**
Becker, H. Boredom blasters (4-6)	**793**
Erlbach, A. Sidewalk games around the world (3-5)	**796.1**
Glenn, J. The treasury of family games (5 and up)	**793**
Miss Mary Mack and other children's street rhymes	**796.1**
Rhatigan, J. Run, jump, hide, slide, splash (2-6)	**796**
Ripoll, O. Play with us (3-5)	**793**
Sierra, J. Children's traditional games	**796**
Williamson, S. Summer fun!	**790.1**
Wilner, I. The baby's game book	**398.8**
Wise, L. The way cool license plate book (4 and up)	**793.7**

See/See also pages in the following book(s):

Griffin, M. The sleepover book (3-6)	**793.2**
Love, A. Kids and grandparents: an activity book (3-6)	**790.1**
Ross, K. The best birthday parties ever! (2-4)	**793.2**
Warshaw, H. Get out! (3-6)	**790.1**

Fiction

Anderson, M. T. The Game of Sunken Places (5 and up)   **Fic**

Colato Laínez, R. Playing loteria   **E**

Geronimo, Apache Chief, 1829-1909
See/See also pages in the following book(s):
Ehrlich, A. Wounded Knee: an Indian history of
the American West (6 and up)   **970.004**

Gerontology

   See also Old age

Gershator, David
Kallaloo!   **E**

Gershator, Phillis
Kotoshi the dragon doctor
  In Fire and wings: dragon tales from East and
     West p117-23   **S C**
Zzzng! Zzzng! Zzzng! (k-3)   **398.2**
(jt. auth) Gershator, D. Kallaloo!   **E**

Gershwin, George, 1898-1937
See/See also pages in the following book(s):
Krull, K. Lives of the musicians (4 and up)
     920

Gerson, Mary-Joan
Fiesta femenina (4 and up)   **398.2**
Contents: Rosha and the sun; The hungry goddess; The legend
of Tangu Yuh; Why the moon is free; Green bird; Blanca Flor;
The Virgin of Guadalupe; Malintzin of the Mountain
Why the sky is far away (k-3)   **398.2**

Gerstein, Mordicai
Carolinda clatter!   **E**
The man who walked between the towers   **E**
Sparrow Jack   **E**
What Charlie heard [biography of Charles Edward Ives] (k-3)   **92**
The wild boy (k-3)   **92**
(il) Kimmel, E. A. The jar of fools: eight Hanukkah stories from Chelm   **S C**
(il) Silverman, E. Sholom's treasure [biography
  of Sholem Aleichem]   **92**

Get on board: the story of the Underground Railroad. Haskins, J.   **326**

Get out!. Warshaw, H.   **790.1**

Get up and go!. Carlson, N. L.   **E**

Getting near to baby. Couloumbis, A.   **Fic**

Getting ready for bed *See* Bedtime

Getting to know the world's greatest artists [se-
ries]
Venezia, M. Diego Velázquez   **92**

Gettysburg (Pa.), Battle of, 1863
Ford, C. T. The Battle of Gettysburg and Lin-
  coln's Gettysburg Address (4-6)   **973.7**
Murphy, J. The long road to Gettysburg (5 and
  up)   **973.7**
       Fiction
Gauch, P. L. Thunder at Gettysburg (3-5)
     Fic
Hopkinson, D. Billy and the rebel   **E**
Osborne, M. P. My brother's keeper (3-5)
     Fic

Getz, David
Frozen man (5 and up)   **930.1**

Ghana
Levy, P. Ghana (5 and up)   **966.7**
       Fiction
Medearis, A. S. Seven spools of thread   **E**

Folklore
  See Folklore—Ghana
    Social life and customs
Onyefulu, I. Welcome Dede! (k-3)   **392**

Ghana Empire
McKissack, P. C. The royal kingdoms of Ghana,
  Mali, and Songhay (5 and up)   **966.2**

Ghazi, Suhaib Hamid
Ramadan (k-3)   **297.3**

Gherman, Beverly
Norman Rockwell (4 and up)   **92**

Ghiuselev, Iassen
(il) Collodi, C. The adventures of Pinocchio
     Fic
(il) Ruskin, J. The king of the Golden River
     Fic

The **ghost** and Mrs. Hobbs. DeFelice, C. C.
     Fic

Ghost at the window. McAllister, M.   **Fic**

Ghost dance
See/See also pages in the following book(s):
Ehrlich, A. Wounded Knee: an Indian history of
  the American West (6 and up)   **970.004**

The **ghost-eye** tree. Martin, B.   **E**

Ghost girl. Ray, D.   **Fic**

The **ghost** in Room 11. Wright, B. R.   **Fic**

Ghost liners. Ballard, R. D.   **910.4**

A **ghost** named Fred. Benchley, N.   **E**

The **ghost** of Fossil Glen. DeFelice, C. C.   **Fic**

The **ghost** of Misery Hill. San Souci, R.
  In San Souci, R. Short & shivery; thirty chill-
    ing tales p139-43   **398.2**

The **ghost** on Saturday night. Fleischman, S.
     Fic

The **ghost** on the hearth. Milord, S.   **E**

Ghost poems (1-4)   **821.008**

The **ghost** sitter. Griffin, P. R.   **Fic**

Ghost stories
Almond, D. Kit's wilderness (5 and up)   **Fic**
Bauer, M. D. The blue ghost (2-4)   **Fic**
Benchley, N. A ghost named Fred   **E**
Cazet, D. The perfect pumpkin pie   **E**
Collier, J. L. The empty mirror (5 and up)
     Fic
Conrad, P. Stonewords (5 and up)   **Fic**
DeFelice, C. C. The ghost and Mrs. Hobbs (4-6)
     Fic
DeFelice, C. C. The ghost of Fossil Glen (4-6)
     Fic
Diane Goode's book of scary stories & songs
  (2-5)   **398.2**
Fleischman, S. The ghost on Saturday night
  (3-5)   **Fic**
Fleischman, S. The midnight horse (3-6)   **Fic**
Galdone, P. The teeny-tiny woman (k-2)
     398.2
Griffin, P. R. The ghost sitter (4 and up)
     Fic
Hahn, M. D. The doll in the garden (4-6)
     Fic
Hahn, M. D. The old Willis place (5 and up)
     Fic

Giants in the land. Appelbaum, D. K. 634.9

Giants of science [series]

Allman, T. J. Robert Oppenheimer 92

Ingram, S. Nicolaus Copernicus 92

Krull, K. Isaac Newton 92

Giarrano, Vince

Comics crash course (5 and up) 741.5

Gibbon, Rebecca

(il) Burg, B. Outside the lines 811

(il) Corey, S. Players in pigtails E

Gibbons, Faye

Mama and me and the Model-T E

Mountain wedding E

Gibbons, Gail

Apples (k-3) 634

The art box (k-1) 702.8

Bats (k-3) 599.4

Beacons of light: lighthouses (k-3) 387.1

Behold . . . the dragons! (k-3) 398

The berry book (k-3) 634

Bicycle book (k-3) 629.227

Boat book (k-3) 387.2

Cats (k-3) 636.8

Chicks & chickens (k-3) 636.5

Dogs (k-3) 636.7

Easter (k-3) 394.26

Emergency! (k-3) 363.34

Exploring the deep, dark sea (k-3) 551.46

Fire! Fire! (k-3) 628.9

Frogs (k-3) 597.8

Giant pandas (k-3) 599.78

Gulls—gulls—gulls (k-3) 598

Halloween is— (k-3) 394.26

Horses! (k-3) 636.1

How a house is built (k-3) 690

Knights in shining armor (k-3) 940.1

Marshes & swamps (k-3) 577.6

The milk makers (k-3) 637

Monarch butterfly (k-3) 595.7

The moon book (k-3) 523.3

My baseball book (k-2) 796.357

My basketball book (k-2) 796.323

My football book (k-2) 796.332

My soccer book (k-2) 796.334

Nature's green umbrella (k-3) 577.3

Owls (k-3) 598

Penguins! (k-3) 598

Pigs (k-3) 636.4

Planet earth/inside out (k-3) 550

The planets (k-3) 523.4

Polar bears (k-3) 599.78

The puffins are back! (k-3) 598

The pumpkin book (k-3) 635

Rabbits, rabbits, & more rabbits! (k-3) 599.3

The reasons for seasons (k-3) 525

Sea turtles (k-3) 597.92

The seasons of Arnold's apple tree E

Sharks (k-3) 597

Soaring with the wind (k-3) 598

St. Patrick's Day (k-3) 394.26

Sun up, sun down (k-3) 523.7

Sunken treasure (k-3) 910.4

Tell me, tree (k-3) 582.16

Thanksgiving Day (k-3) 394.26

Valentine's Day (k-3) 394.26

Weather forecasting (k-3) 551.63

Weather words and what they mean (k-3) 551.6

Wolves (k-3) 599.77

Giblin, James

The boy who saved Cleveland (3-5) Fic

The dwarf, the giant, and the unicorn (3-5) 398.2

Fireworks, picnics, and flags (3-6) 394.26

Good brother, bad brother [biography of John Wilkes Booth and Edwin Booth] (5 and up) 92

The mystery of the mammoth bones (4 and up) 569

The riddle of the Rosetta Stone (5 and up) 493

Secrets of the Sphinx (4 and up) 932

Gideon the cutpurse. Buckley-Archer, L. Fic

Giff, Patricia Reilly

All the way home (4 and up) Fic

Don't tell the girls (4 and up) 92

A house of tailors (5 and up) Fic

Kidnap at the Catfish Cafe (3-5) Fic

Lily's crossing (4 and up) Fic

Nory Ryan's song (5 and up) Fic

Pictures of Hollis Woods (5 and up) Fic

Watch out, Ronald Morgan! E

Willow run (4 and up) Fic

Gifford, Clive

The Kingfisher geography encyclopedia (4 and up) 910.3

Pollution (4 and up) 363.7

Spies (5 and up) 327.12

A **gift** from the sea. Banks, K. E

Gift horse. Crebbin, J.

In Horse tales S C

A **gift** of gracias. Alvarez, J. E

The **gift** of reading. Bouchard, D. 372.4

The **gift** of the Crocodile. Sierra, J. 398.2

Gift pig. Aiken, J.

In Aiken, J. Shadows and moonshine; stories S C

Gifted. Evangelista, B. Fic

Gifted children

Fiction

Evangelista, B. Gifted (5 and up) Fic

Yee, L. Millicent Min, girl genius (5 and up) Fic

Gifts

Fiction

Best, C. Three cheers for Catherine the Great E

Borden, L. The last day of school (2-4) Fic

Helldorfer, M. C. Hog music E

Louie, T. O. Raymond's perfect present E

Santiago, E. A doll for Navidades E

Giganti, Paul, Jr.

Each orange had 8 slices E

How many snails? E

Giggle, giggle, quack. Cronin, D. E

Giggle-wiggle wake-up!. Carlstrom, N. W. E

Gila monsters meet you at the airport. Sharmat, M. W. E

Gilbert, W. S. (William Schwenck), 1836-1911
See/See also pages in the following book(s):
Krull, K. Lives of the musicians (4 and up)
920

Gilbert, William Schwenck *See* Gilbert, W. S.
(William Schwenck), 1836-1911

Gilberto and the Wind. Ets, M. H. **E**

Gilchrist, Jan Spivey
(il) Greenfield, E. Honey, I love **811**
(il) Greenfield, E. Me & Neesie **E**
(il) Greenfield, E. Nathaniel talking **811**

Gilchrist, Jane E.
(ed) Cataloging correctly for kids. See Cataloging correctly for kids **025.3**

Gilda Joyce, psychic investigator. Allison, J.
Fic

Gildart, Leslie S.
Louisiana
In World Almanac Library of the States series
973

Gilgamesh
McCaughrean, G. The epic of Gilgamesh (5 and up) **398.2**

Gilgamesh the hero. See McCaughrean, G. The epic of Gilgamesh **398.2**

Gill, Margery
(il) Cooper, S. Over sea, under stone **Fic**

Gilles de la Tourette's syndrome *See* Tourette syndrome

Gillespie, Haven
(jt. auth) Coots, J. F. Santa Claus is comin' to town **782.42**

Gillespie, Jessie
(il) Wiggin, K. D. S. The Bird's Christmas Carol **Fic**

Gillespie, John Thomas
The children's and young adult literature handbook **011.6**
The Newbery/Printz companion **028.5**
(jt. auth) Barr, C. Best books for children: preschool through grade 6 **011.6**

Gilley, Jeremy
Peace one day **303.6**

Gillie, Oliver
Cancer (5 and up) **616.99**

Gillies, Judi
The jumbo vegetarian cookbook (4 and up)
641.5
The Kids Can Press jumbo cookbook (4 and up)
641.5

Gilliland, Judith Heide
Strange birds (3-6) **Fic**
(jt. auth) Heide, F. P. The day of Ahmed's secret **E**
(jt. auth) Heide, F. P. Sami and the time of the troubles **E**

Gilman, Laura Anne
Grail quest: the Camelot spell (5 and up)
Fic

Gilson, Jamie
4B goes wild (4-6) **Fic**
Bug in a rug (2-4) **Fic**
Do bananas chew gum? (4-6) **Fic**

Hello, my name is Scrambled Eggs (4 and up)
Fic
Stink Alley (4 and up) **Fic**

Ginger. Voake, C. **E**
Ginger Pye. Estes, E. **Fic**
Gingerbread baby. Brett, J. **398.2**
The **gingerbread** boy. Egielski, R. **398.2**
The **gingerbread** boy. Galdone, P. **398.2**
The **Gingerbread** man. Aylesworth, J. **398.2**
The **gingerbread** man. Blackstone, S.
In Blackstone, S. Storytime; first tales for sharing **398.2**
The **gingerbread** man. Kimmel, E. A. **398.2**
The **gingerbread** man. Sierra, J.
In Sierra, J. Nursery tales around the world p3-9 **398.2**

The **gingi**. McKissack, P. C.
In McKissack, P. C. The dark-thirty; Southern tales of the supernatural p95-110 **S C**

Ginsburg, Max
(il) Taylor, M. D. The friendship **Fic**
(il) Taylor, M. D. Mississippi bridge **Fic**

Ginsburg, Mirra
The chick and the duckling **E**
The Chinese mirror (k-3) **398.2**
Clay boy (k-3) **398.2**
Good morning, chick **E**

Giovanni, Nikki
Ego-tripping and other poems for young people (5 and up) **811**
Rosa [biography of Rosa Parks] (3-5) **92**
Spin a soft black song: poems for children (3-6)
811
The sun is so quiet (k-3) **811**
See/See also pages in the following book(s):
Wilkinson, B. S. African American women writers (4 and up) **810.9**

Gipsies *See* Gypsies

Gipson, Frederick Benjamin
Old Yeller (6 and up) **Fic**

Giraffes
Anderson, J. Giraffes (k-2) **599.63**
Leach, M. Giraffe (3-5) **599.63**

Giraudon, David
(il) Arthus-Bertrand, Y. Earth from above for young readers **779**
(il) Burleigh, R. Volcanoes **551.2**

The **girl** and the puma. Yolen, J.
In Yolen, J. Not one damsel in distress; world folktales for strong girls p27-32
398.2

The **girl** from Chimel. Menchú, R. **92**
A **girl** in the attic. Metzger, L.
In Swan sister; fairy tales retold **S C**
A **girl** named Disaster. Farmer, N. **Fic**
Girl of Kosovo. Mead, A. **Fic**
The **girl** on the high-diving horse. High, L. O.
E
The **girl** who dreamed only geese. Norman, H.
In Norman, H. The girl who dreamed only geese, and other tales of the Far North
398.2

The **girl** who dreamed only geese, and other tales of the Far North. Norman, H. **398.2**

The **Girl** Who Loved Caterpillars. Merrill, J. **E**

The **girl** who loved wild horses. Goble, P. **398.2**

The **girl** who married a star. Curry, J. L.
In Curry, J. L. The wonderful sky boat and other Native American tales of the Southeast p68-73 **398.2**

The **girl** who spun gold. Hamilton, V. **398.2**

The **girl** who stood on a grave. Schwartz, A.
In Beware!; R.L. Stine picks his favorite scary stories p185-87 **808.8**

The **girl** who watched in the nighttime. Norman, H.
In Norman, H. The girl who dreamed only geese, and other tales of the Far North **398.2**

The **girl** who waters basil and the very inquisitive prince. García Lorca, F.
In You're on!: seven plays in English and Spanish p62-83 **812.008**

The **girl** who wore too much. MacDonald, M. R. **398.2**

The **girl** with the green ear [excerpt] Mahy, M.
In You read to me & I'll read to you; 20th-century stories to share p167-70 **E**

The **girl** with the silver eyes. Roberts, W. D. **Fic**

Girl wonder. Hopkinson, D. **E**

Girls
Jukes, M. Growing up: it's a girl thing (4 and up) **612.6**
Jukes, M. It's a girl thing (5 and up) **305.23**
Madaras, L. The "what's happening to my body" book for girls (4 and up) **613.9**
Movsessian, S. Puberty girl (4 and up) **612.6**
Rimm, S. B. See Jane win for girls (5 and up) **305.23**
Sills, L. From rags to riches (5 and up) **391**
Books and reading
Odean, K. Great books for girls **028.1**
Employment
See Child labor
Health and hygiene
Cheung, L. W. Y. Be healthy! it's a girl thing (5 and up) **613**
Poetry
Richards, B. Keep climbing, girls **E**

Girls, Teenage *See* Teenagers

The **girls**. Koss, A. G. **Fic**

Girls A to Z. Bunting, E. **E**

Girls got game (5 and up) **810.8**

The **girls'** room. Shreve, S. R.
In Tripping over the lunch lady and other school stories p133-56 **S C**

Girls think of everything. Thimmesh, C. **920**

The **Girls'** World book of jewelry: 50 cool designs to make. Newcomb, R. **745.594**

Girouard, Patrick
(il) Caffey, D. Yikes-lice! **616.5**

GIs *See* Soldiers—United States

Gittings, Jane
(jt. auth) Robert, F. Find a face **E**

Give me a crab, John. Philip, N.
In Philip, N. Celtic fairy tales p66 **398.2**

Give me liberty!. Freedman, R. **973.3**

Give the dog a bone. Kellogg, S. **782.42**

The **giver**. Lowry, L. **Fic**

Giving thanks. London, J. **E**

Giving thanks. Swamp, J. **299.7**

The **Gizzard**
In The Magic orange tree, and other Haitian folktales p99-112 **398.2**

Glaciers
Harrison, D. L. Glaciers (k-3) **551.3**
Simon, S. Icebergs and glaciers (3-6) **551.3**

Gladiators
Watkins, R. R. Gladiator (4 and up) **937**

Glanzman, Louis S.
(il) Lindgren, A. Pippi Longstocking **Fic**

Glaser, Linda
Bridge to America (4-6) **Fic**
Brilliant bees (k-3) **595.7**
Compost! (k-2) **363.7**
Our big home **E**

Glass, Andrew
(il) Kimmel, E. A. Grizz! **E**
(il) Mollel, T. M. Ananse's feast **398.2**
(il) Price, K. The Bourbon Street musicians **398.2**
(il) Zimmer, T. V. Sketches from a spy tree **Fic**

Glassblowing
Fiction
Geeslin, C. Elena's serenade **E**

Glasser, Robin Preiss
(il) Weitzman, J. P. You can't take a balloon into the Metropolitan Museum **E**

Glasses: who needs 'em? Smith, L. **E**

Glazer, Tom
(jt. auth) Johnson, P. B. On top of spaghetti **E**

Gleeson, Libby
Cuddle time

Gleitzman, Morris
Toad rage (3-6) **Fic**

Glenn, Jim
The treasury of family games (5 and up) **793**

Glenn, John, 1921-
About
Ashby, R. Rocket man [biography of John Glenn] (4-6) **92**
Bredeson, C. John Glenn returns to orbit (4 and up) **629.4**

Gliori, Debi
Flora's surprise! **E**
Mr. Bear's new baby **E**
No matter what **E**

Global warming *See* Greenhouse effect

Global warming. Oxlade, C. **363.7**

Global warming. Parks, P. J. **363.7**

Global warming. Pringle, L. P. **363.7**

GlobaLinks: resources for world studies, grades K-8. Beck, P. **016.9**

Globe Theatre (London, England)

 See also Shakespeare's Globe (London, England)

 Aliki. William Shakespeare & the Globe (4 and up) **822.3**

 Chrisp, P. Welcome to the Globe (1-3) **822.3**

Fiction

 Cooper, S. King of shadows (5 and up) **Fic**

Gloria's way. Cameron, A. **Fic**

A **glorious** day. Schwartz, A. **E**

The **glorious** flight: across the Channel with Louis Blériot, July 25, 1909. Provensen, A. **92**

A **Glory** of unicorns (5 and up) **S C**

Glossaries *See* Encyclopedias and dictionaries

Glossop, Jennifer

 (jt. auth) Gillies, J. The jumbo vegetarian cookbook **641.5**

 (jt. auth) Gillies, J. The Kids Can Press jumbo cookbook **641.5**

Glover, Savion

 Savion!: my life in tap (5 and up) **92**

Gluskabe and Old Man Winter. Bruchac, J.

 In Bruchac, J. Pushing up the sky: seven Native American plays for children p11-23 **812**

Gnat Stokes and the Foggy Bottom Swamp Queen. Keehn, S. M. **Fic**

Gnojewski, Carol

 Cinco de Mayo crafts (2-4) **745.594**

 Day of the Dead (2-4) **394.26**

Go away, big green monster!. Emberley, E. **E**

Go figure!. Ball, J. **793.74**

Go fish. Stolz, M. **Fic**

Go fly a bike!. Haduch, B. **629.227**

Go free or die: a story about Harriet Tubman. Ferris, J. **92**

Go! Go! Maria!. Harris, R. H. **612.6**

Go home!. Meggs, L. P. **E**

Go I know not whither, bring back I know not what. Afanas´ev, A. N.

 In Afanas´ev, A. N. Russian fairy tales p504-20 **398.2**

Go in and out the window. See A treasury of children's songs **782.42**

Go outside!. Blakey, N. **790.1**

Go to sleep, Groundhog!. Cox, J. **E**

Go wild in New York City. Matsen, B. **974.7**

Goal. Burleigh, R. **811**

The **goat** in the rug. Blood, C. L. **E**

The **goat** shedding on one side. Afanas´ev, A. N.

 In Afanas´ev, A. N. Russian fairy tales p312-13 **398.2**

Goats

 Polacco, P. G is for goat **E**

Fiction

 Blood, C. L. The goat in the rug **E**

 Gorbachev, V. That's what friends are for **E**

 Jordan, R. Lost Goat Lane (5 and up) **Fic**

 Palatini, M. The three silly billies **E**

 Polacco, P. Oh, look! **E**

 Sharmat, M. Gregory, the terrible eater **E**

Folklore

 Galdone, P. The three Billy Goats Gruff (k-2) **398.2**

 Rounds, G. Three billy goats Gruff (k-3) **398.2**

Songs

 Hoberman, M. A. Bill Grogan's goat (k-3) **782.42**

Gobble, gobble, slip, slop. So, M. **398.2**

Gobborn Seer. Jacobs, J.

 In Jacobs, J. English fairy tales p275-78 **398.2**

Goble, Paul

 All our relatives (5 and up) **970.004**

 Beyond the ridge (2-4) **Fic**

 Buffalo woman (2-4) **398.2**

 Crow chief (2-4) **398.2**

 Death of the iron horse **E**

 The girl who loved wild horses (k-3) **398.2**

 The legend of the White Buffalo Woman (3-5) **398.2**

 Mystic horse (2-4) **398.2**

 Remaking the earth (2-4) **398.2**

 Song of creation (k-3) **242**

 Storm Maker's tipi (2-5) **398.2**

The **goblin** spider. San Souci, R.

 In San Souci, R. Short & shivery; thirty chilling tales p160-65 **398.2**

The **Goblins** at the bathhouse

 In Diane Goode's book of scary stories & songs p54-61 **398.2**

God

 Fitch, F. M. A book about God (k-3) **231**

 Lindbergh, R. On morning wings (k-3) **223**

 Paterson, J. B. Images of God (5 and up) **231**

Fiction

 Lester, J. What a truly cool world! **E**

God battles the Queen of the Waters. Lester, J.

 In Lester, J. When the beginning began; stories about God, the creatures, and us p7-10 **296.1**

God confronts Adam, the Woman, and the Snake. Lester, J.

 In Goldin, B. D. Journeys with Elijah; eight tales of the Prophet p87-92 **296.1**

 also in Lester, J. When the beginning began; stories about God, the creatures, and us p87-92 **296.1**

God creates Adam. Lester, J.

 In Lester, J. When the beginning began; stories about God, the creatures, and us p59-63 **296.1**

God creates Woman. Lester, J.
   In Lester, J. When the beginning began; stories about God, the creatures, and us p64-68   **296.1**

God learns how to create. Lester, J.
   In Lester, J. When the beginning began; stories about God, the creatures, and us p1-5   **296.1**

God make a road down in the sea. Graham, L. B.
   In Graham, L. B. How God fix Jonah p71-77   **398.2**

God make plenty chop. Graham, L. B.
   In Graham, L. B. How God fix Jonah p154-56   **398.2**

God makes people. Lester, J.
   In Lester, J. When the beginning began; stories about God, the creatures, and us p49-57   **296.1**

God returns to Heaven. Lester, J.
   In Lester, J. When the beginning began; stories about God, the creatures, and us p93-95   **296.1**

God wash the world and start again. Graham, L. B.
   In Graham, L. B. How God fix Jonah p44-51   **398.2**

Godden, Rumer
   The doll's house (2-4)   **Fic**

Goddesses *See* Gods and goddesses

Godfrey, Neale S.
   Neale S. Godfrey's ultimate kids' money book (5 and up)   **332.024**

Gods and goddesses
   See also Religions names of individual gods and goddesses
   Fisher, L. E. The gods and goddesses of ancient China (3-6)   **299**
   Tchana, K. H. Changing Woman and her sisters (5 and up)   **398.2**
   See/See also pages in the following book(s):
   Hamilton, E. Mythology (5 and up)   **292**

The **gods** and goddesses of ancient China. Fisher, L. E.   **299**

The **gods** and goddesses of ancient Egypt. Fisher, L. E.   **299**

The **gods** and goddesses of Olympus. Aliki   **292**

Gods and goddesses of the ancient Maya. Fisher, L. E.   **299**

Gods and goddesses of the ancient Norse. Fisher, L. E.   **293**

Godwin, Laura
   Barnyard prayers (k-2)   **811**
   Central Park serenade   **E**
   Happy and Honey   **E**
   (jt. auth) Martin, A. M. The doll people   **Fic**

Goedeken, Kathy
   (il) Cohen, S. Fire on ice   **92**

Goembel, Ponder
   (il) Wheeler, L. Castaway cats   **E**
   (il) Wheeler, L. Old Cricket   **E**

Gofen, Ethel
   Argentina (5 and up)   **982**

Gogh, Vincent van
   Vincent's colors (k-3)   **759.9492**

Gogh, Vincent van, 1853-1890
   About
   Bassil, A. Vincent van Gogh (4 and up)   **92**
   Rubin, S. G. The yellow house (2-4)   **759.4**

Goin' someplace special. McKissack, P. C.   **E**

Going fishing. McMillan, B.   **949.12**

Going home. Mohr, N.   **Fic**

Going north. Harrington, J. N.   **E**

Going to Cervières. MacDonald, M. R.
   In MacDonald, M. R. Celebrate the world; twenty tellable folktales for multicultural festivals p202-09   **372.6**

Going to school in 1776. Loeper, J. J.   **370.9**

Going to the hospital. Rogers, F.   **362.1**

Going west!. Johmann, C.   **978**

Going West. Van Leeuwen, J.   **E**

Gold, Alison Leslie
   Memories of Anne Frank (5 and up)   **92**

Gold, John Coopersmith
   Cerebral palsy (4 and up)   **616.8**

Gold, Michael
   (il) Cobb, V. Fireworks   **662**
   (jt. auth) Cobb, V. Junk food   **664**
   (il) Cobb, V. Sneakers   **685**

Gold, Susan Dudley
   Attention deficit disorder (4 and up)   **616.85**
   Bipolar disorder and depression (4 and up)   **616.89**
   Cystic fibrosis (4 and up)   **616.3**
   Multiple sclerosis (4 and up)   **616.8**
   Sickle cell disease (4 and up)   **616.1**

The **gold** Cadillac. Taylor, M. D.   **Fic**

Gold fever. Kay, V.   **E**

The **Gold** in the chimney
   In Stockings of buttermilk: American folktales p73-77   **398.2**

Gold mines and mining
   See also Klondike River valley (Yukon)—Gold discoveries
   Fiction
   Coerr, E. Chang's paper pony   **E**
   Ferris, J. Much ado about Grubstake (5 and up)   **Fic**
   Fleischman, S. Bo & Mzzz Mad (5 and up)   **Fic**

Gold rush *See* California—Gold discoveries

The **gold** rush. O'Donnell, K.   **979.4**

The **gold-threaded** dress. Marsden, C.   **Fic**

The **golden** arm. Jacobs, J.
   In Jacobs, J. English fairy tales p138-39   **398.2**

The **golden** arm. San Souci, R.
   In San Souci, R. More short & shivery; thirty terrifying tales p103-08   **398.2**

The **golden** ball. Jacobs, J.
   In Jacobs, J. English fairy tales p234-37   **398.2**

Gooch, Randall—*Continued*
(il) Temko, F. Traditional crafts from the Caribbean **745.5**

Good, Diane L.
Brown v. Board of Education (4-6) **344**

Good advice. Afanas'ev, A. N.
In Afanas'ev, A. N. Russian fairy tales p289-91 **398.2**

Good and evil

Fiction
Cooper, S. The grey king (5 and up) **Fic**
Cooper, S. Over sea, under stone (5 and up) **Fic**

Poetry
Wicked poems (4 and up) **811.008**
Good babies. Myers, T. **E**

Good Blanche, bad Rose, and the talking eggs. Hamilton, V.
In Hamilton, V. Her stories; African American folktales, fairy tales, and true tales p28-32 **398.2**

Good books, good times! (1-3) **811.008**
Good boy, Fergus!. Shannon, D. **E**
Good brother, bad brother [biography of John Wilkes Booth and Edwin Booth] Giblin, J. **92**

Good-bye, 382 Shin Dang Dong. Park, F. **E**
A **good** day's fishing. Prosek, J. **E**
The **good** deed. Bauer, M. D.
In Shelf life: stories by the book p109-26 **S C**
The **good** dog. Avi **Fic**
Good dog. Gottfried, M. **811**
Good dog, Paw!. Lee, C. **E**
Good enough to eat. Rockwell, L. **613.2**
The **good** fight. Ambrose, S. E. **940.53**
Good for you!. Calmenson, S. **811**
Good in she heart. Graham, L. B.
In Graham, L. B. How God fix Jonah p23-28 **398.2**
Good King Wenceslas. Neale, J. M. **782.28**
The **good** liar. Maguire, G. **Fic**
The **good** little bad little pig. Brown, M. W. **E**
Good luck, Mrs. K!. Borden, L. **E**
The **Good** Master. Seredy, K. **Fic**
Good morning, chick. Ginsburg, M. **E**
Good morning, Digger. Rockwell, A. F. **E**
Good morning, garden. Brenner, B. **E**
Good night engines. Mortensen, D. D. **E**
A **good** night for freedom. Morrow, B. O. **E**
Good night, Good Knight. Thomas, S. M. **E**
Good night, Gorilla. Rathmann, P. **E**
Good night, Harry. Lewis, K. **E**
Good night, Maman. Mazer, N. F. **Fic**
Good night pillow fight. Cook, S. **E**
A **good** night walk. Cooper, E. **E**
Good Queen Bess: the story of Elizabeth I of England. Stanley, D. **92**

Good thing you're not an octopus!. Markes, J. **E**

Goodall, Jane
The chimpanzees I love (4 and up) **599.8**
My life with the chimpanzees (3-6) **92**
With love (4 and up) **599.8**

Goodall, Jane, 1934-
See/See also pages in the following book(s):
Talking with adventurers (4-6) **920**

Goodbye, Charley. Buchanan, J. **Fic**
Goodbye, Mousie. Harris, R. H. **E**
Goodbye, Vietnam. Whelan, G. **Fic**
Goodbye, Walter Malinski. Recorvits, H. **Fic**

Goode, Diane
The most perfect spot **E**
Thanksgiving is here! **E**
(il) Diane Goode's book of scary stories & songs. See Diane Goode's book of scary stories & songs **398.2**
(il) Rylant, C. Christmas in the country **E**
(il) Rylant, C. When I was young in the mountains **E**

Goodell, Jon
(il) Kimmel, E. A. Zigazak! **E**
Goode's school atlas. See Goode's world atlas **912**

Goode's world atlas (4 and up) **912**

Goodman, Jim
Thailand (5 and up) **959.3**

Goodman, Joan E.
Despite all obstacles: La Salle and the conquest of the Mississippi (4 and up) **92**
A long and uncertain journey: the 27,000 mile voyage of Vasco da Gama (4 and up) **92**

Goodman, Susan
Claws, coats, and camouflage (2-4) **591.4**
Seeds, stems, and stamens (2-4) **581.4**
Skyscraper (2-5) **720**
The truth about poop (2-5) **573.4**
Ultimate field trip 5 (4 and up) **629.45**

The **goodness** of Matt Kaizer. Avi
In Avi. What do fish have to do with anything? and other stories p35-59 **S C**

Goodnight goodnight sleepyhead. Krauss, R. **E**
Goodnight Lulu. Bogan, P. **E**
Goodnight me, goodnight you. Mitton, T. **E**
Goodnight moon. Brown, M. W. **E**
Goodnight, my duckling. Tafuri, N. **E**

Goodsell, Joan
(ed) Sears list of subject headings. See Sears list of subject headings **025.4**

Goodyear, Charles, 1800-1860
See/See also pages in the following book(s):
Fradin, D. B. With a little luck (5 and up) **509**

Gooney Bird Greene. Lowry, L. **Fic**
Goose. Bang, M. **E**
The **goose** girl. Grimm, J.
In The Blue fairy book p266-73 **398.2**
Gooseberry Goose. Freedman, C. **E**

The **grade** school zone. Proimos, J.
In Tripping over the lunch lady and other school stories p85-92 **S C**

Graef, Renée
(il) Schulman, J. The nutcracker **Fic**

Graff, Serena
Blackwell's Island (5 and up) **Fic**

Graham, Bette Nesmith, 1924-1980
See/See also pages in the following book(s):
Thimmesh, C. Girls think of everything (5 and up) **920**

Graham, Bob
Let's get a pup, said Kate **E**
Max **E**
Oscar's half birthday **E**
(il) King-Smith, D. The nine lives of Aristotle **Fic**

Graham, Joan Bransfield
Flicker flash **811**
Splish splash **811**

Graham, John
Hands-on science. See Hands-on science **507.8**

Graham, Lorenz B.
How God fix Jonah (4 and up) **398.2**
Contents: How God fix Jonah [story]; Good in she heart; He no be keeper for him brother; David he no fear; Don't nobody sing; God wash the world and start again; Samson he weak for woman palaver; Hongry catch the foolish boy; Pican in river grass; God make a road down in the sea; They be slaves too long; She got hard head you know; Death take him hand off pican heart; The Shushan king love peace; Yam-leaf greens and rice; Old Satan try Job plenty; Brothers got bad heart for Joseph; Wise sword find true mommy; The Babylonia princes vex; Joshua be God's man; Every man heart lay down; Small boy teach wise men; God make plenty chop

Graham, Margaret Bloy
(il) Zion, G. Harry the dirty dog **E**

Graham, Mark
(il) Ryder, J. My father's hands **E**

Grahame, Kenneth
The reluctant dragon (3-5) **Fic**
The wind in the willows (4-6) **Fic**

Grahame, Kenneth, 1859-1932
Adaptations
San Souci, R. Kenneth Grahame's The reluctant dragon (2-4) **Fic**

Grail
Fiction
Sutcliff, R. The light beyond the forest (4 and up) **398.2**

Grail quest: the Camelot spell. Gilman, L. A. **Fic**

Grajnert, Paul
(jt. auth) Heale, J. Poland **943.8**

Gralley, Jean
The moon came down on Milk Street **E**

Gramatky, Hardie
Little Toot **E**

Grammar
See also English language—Grammar

Grampa & Julie: Shark hunters. Czekaj, J. **741.5**

Grand, Carmen T. Bernier- *See* Bernier-Grand, Carmen T.

Grand Canyon (Ariz.)
Weintraub, A. The Grand Canyon (2-4) **557**
Fiction
Henry, M. Brighty of the Grand Canyon (4 and up) **Fic**

Grand Central Terminal (New York, N.Y.)
Kalman, M. Next stop, Grand Central **E**

The **grand** escape. Naylor, P. R. **Fic**

The **Grand** Inquisitor. Jaffe, N.
In Jaffe, N. and Zeitlin, S. J. While standing on one foot; puzzle stories and wisdom tales from the Jewish tradition p7-10 **296.1**

A **grand** old tree. DePalma, M. N. **E**

The **grand** parade. Lester, J.
In Lester, J. When the beginning began; stories about God, the creatures, and us p43-48 **296.1**

Grandaddy's place. Griffith, H. V. **E**

Grandad's tree (k-3) **811.008**

Grandfather and I. Buckley, H. E. **E**

Grandfather Bear is hungry. MacDonald, M. R.
In MacDonald, M. R. Look back and see; twenty lively tales for gentle tellers p126-29 **372.6**

Grandfather Buffalo. Arnosky, J. **E**

Grandfather tales (4 and up) **398.2**

Grandfather Tang's story. Tompert, A. **E**

Grandfathers
Fiction
Ackerman, K. Song and dance man **E**
Aliki. The two of them **E**
Appelt, K. Where, where is Swamp Bear? **E**
Barasch, L. A country schoolhouse **E**
Barron, T. A. Where is Grandpa? **E**
Bartek, M. Funerals & fly fishing (4 and up) **Fic**
Bowdish, L. Brooklyn, Bugsy, and me (3-5) **Fic**
Bradford, K. You can't rush a cat **E**
Brooks, B. Everywhere (4 and up) **Fic**
Buckley, H. E. Grandfather and I **E**
Bunting, E. Butterfly house **E**
Byars, B. C. The house of wings (4-6) **Fic**
Creech, S. Heartbeat (4 and up) **Fic**
De Guzman, M. The bamboozlers (5 and up) **Fic**
De Paola, T. Now one foot, now the other **E**
De Paola, T. Tom **E**
Dickinson, P. Inside Grandad (4 and up) **Fic**
DiSalvo-Ryan, D. Grandpa's corner store **E**
Dotlich, R. K. Grandpa loves **E**
Fox, M. Sophie **E**
French, S. Where in the world (5 and up) **Fic**
George, J. C. Charlie's raven (5 and up) **Fic**
Gower, C. Long-Long's New Year **E**
Greenfield, E. Grandpa's face **E**
Griffith, H. V. Grandaddy's place **E**
Haas, J. Sugaring **E**
Hest, A. Guess who, Baby Duck! **E**

Grandmothers—Fiction—*Continued*

Polacco, P. When lightning comes in a jar (2-4) **Fic**

Reiser, L. Cherry pies and lullabies **E**

Reiser, L. Tortillas and lullabies. Tortillas y cancioncitas **E**

Roberts, L. Little Red **E**

Root, P. The name quilt **E**

Rylant, C. The ticky-tacky doll **E**

Schirripa, S. R. Nicky Deuce (4-6) **Fic**

Schlein, M. The story about me **E**

Siegelson, K. L. In the time of the drums **E**

Spinelli, E. Wanda's monster **E**

Spinner, S. It's a miracle! **E**

Stock, C. Gugu's house **E**

Voigt, C. Dicey's song (6 and up) **Fic**

Wild, M. Our granny **E**

Willner-Pardo, G. Figuring out Frances (4-6) **Fic**

Wilson, N. H. Mountain pose (5 and up) **Fic**

Woodson, J. Coming on home soon **E**

Yep, L. Child of the owl (5 and up) **Fic**

Yolen, J. Off we go! **E**

Poetry

Love to mamá (3-6) **811.008**

Grandmother's tale. Singer, I. B.

In Singer, I. B. Zlateh the goat, and other stories p21-23 **398.2**

Grandpa buys a pumpkin egg. Schwartz, A.

In Schwartz, A. There is a carrot in my ear, and other noodle tales p44-57 **398.2**

Grandpa loves. Dotlich, R. K. **E**

Grandpa misses the boat. Schwartz, A.

In Schwartz, A. All of our noses are here, and other noodle tales p18-21 **398.2**

Grandparents

Rotner, S. Lots of grandparents! (k-1) **306.8**

See/See also pages in the following book(s):

Bauer, C. F. Celebrations p1-24 **808.8**

Fiction

Carlson, N. L. Hooray for Grandparent's Day **E**

Creech, S. Walk two moons (6 and up) **Fic**

Haas, J. Hurry! **E**

Hamanaka, S. Grandparents song **E**

Juster, N. The hello, goodbye window **E**

Kinsey-Warnock, N. Nora's ark **E**

Nagda, A. W. Meow means mischief (2-4) **Fic**

Rylant, C. Christmas in the country **E**

Wiles, D. Love, Ruby Lavender (4-6) **Fic**

Grandparents song. Hamanaka, S. **E**

Grandpa's corner store. DiSalvo-Ryan, D. **E**

Grandpa's face. Greenfield, E. **E**

Grandpré, Mary

(il) Buzzeo, T. The sea chest **E**

(il) Rowling, J. K. Harry Potter and the sorcerer's stone **Fic**

(il) Willard, N. Sweep dreams **E**

Granfield, Linda

America votes (4-6) **324**

Grange, Red, 1903-1991

See/See also pages in the following book(s):

Krull, K. Lives of the athletes (4 and up) **920**

Granite baby. Bertrand, L. **E**

Granny the Pag. Bawden, N. **Fic**

Granny Torrelli makes soup. Creech, S. **Fic**

The **Grannyman**. Schachner, J. B. **E**

Granström, Brita

(il) Henderson, K. Baby knows best **E**

(il) Hindley, J. Baby talk **E**

(il) Hindley, J. Eyes, nose, fingers and toes **E**

(il) Lewis, P. No more cookies! **E**

Grant, Karima

Sofie and the city **E**

Grants for school libraries. Hall-Ellis, S. D. **025.1**

Grants-in-aid

Anderson, C. Write grants, get money **025.1**

Grantsmanship for small libraries and school library media centers **025.1**

Hall-Ellis, S. D. Grants for school libraries **025.1**

Grantsmanship for small libraries and school library media centers **025.1**

Grape thief. Franklin, K. L. **Fic**

The **grapes** of math. Tang, G. **793.74**

The **graphic** alphabet. Pelletier, D. **E**

Graphic fiction *See* Graphic novels

Graphic methods

Leedy, L. The great graph contest **E**

Nagda, A. W. Tiger math (2-4) **511**

Graphic novels

Avery, B. Lullaby: Wisdom seeker (4-6) **741.5**

Azuma, K. Yotsuba&! (2-4) **741.5**

Big fat Little Lit (2-4) **741.5**

Brennan, M. Electric Girl (5 and up) **741.5**

Bullock, M. Lions, tigers, and bears, vol. 1: Fear and pride (2-4) **741.5**

Crane, J. The clouds above (3-5) **741.5**

Crilley, M. Akiko pocket-size, vol. 1 (3-5) **741.5**

Czekaj, J. Grampa & Julie: Shark hunters (2-4) **741.5**

De Campi, A. Kat & Mouse: Teacher torture (4-6) **741.5**

Di Fiori, L. Jackie and the Shadow Snatcher (k-3) **741.5**

Espinosa, R. The courageous princess (3-5) **741.5**

Goscinny. Asterix the Gaul (4 and up) **741.5**

Gownley, J. Amelia rules! (4 and up) **741.5**

Guibert, E. Sardine in outer space (3-5) **741.5**

Hastings, J. Terrabella Smoot and the unsung monsters (k-3) **741.5**

Hergé. The adventures of Tintin, vol. 1 (4 and up) **741.5**

Holm, J. L. Babymouse (3-5) **741.5**

Huey, D. Bumperboy loses his marbles (2-4) **741.5**

Great American memorials—*Continued*
Ashabranner, B. K. Remembering Korea
951.9

Great-aunts *See* Aunts
The **great** ball game. Bruchac, J. **398.2**
Great Barrier Reef (Australia)
Arnold, C. A walk on the Great Barrier Reef
(3-5) **578.7**
The **great** blue house. Banks, K. **E**
The **Great** Blue Yonder. Shearer, A. **Fic**
Great books about things kids love. Odean, K.
028.1
Great books for babies and toddlers. Odean, K.
028.1
Great books for boys. Odean, K. **028.1**
Great books for girls. Odean, K. **028.1**
The **Great** Brain. Fitzgerald, J. D. **Fic**
The **great** brain book. Newquist, H. P. **612.8**
Great Britain

See also England
Fuller, B. Britain (5 and up) **941**
Gordon, S. Great Britain (2-4) **941**
Fiction
Aiken, J. The wolves of Willoughby Chase (5
and up) **Fic**
Almond, D. Kit's wilderness (5 and up) **Fic**
Bagnold, E. National Velvet (5 and up) **Fic**
Bond, M. A bear called Paddington (2-5)
Fic
Boston, L. M. The children of Green Knowe
(4-6) **Fic**
Burgess, M. Kite (5 and up) **Fic**
Burnett, F. H. A little princess (4-6) **Fic**
Burnett, F. H. The secret garden (4-6) **Fic**
Cassidy, C. Dizzy (5 and up) **Fic**
Cassidy, C. Indigo Blue (5 and up) **Fic**
Cooper, S. Over sea, under stone (5 and up)
Fic
Cottrell Boyce, F. Millions (5 and up) **Fic**
Cushman, K. Catherine, called Birdy (6 and up)
Fic
Cushman, K. Matilda Bone (5 and up) **Fic**
Cushman, K. The midwife's apprentice (6 and
up) **Fic**
De Angeli, M. L. The door in the wall (4-6)
Fic
Horowitz, A. Stormbreaker (5 and up) **Fic**
Howard, E. The gate in the wall (5 and up)
Fic
Ibbotson, E. Dial-a-ghost (4-6) **Fic**
King-Smith, D. The Catlady (2-4) **Fic**
McKay, H. Dog Friday (4-6) **Fic**
Morgan, N. Chicken friend (5 and up) **Fic**
Nesbit, E. The enchanted castle (4-6) **Fic**
Nesbit, E. Five children and it (4-6) **Fic**
Nesbit, E. The railway children (4-6) **Fic**
Sewell, A. Black Beauty (4-6) **Fic**
Vining, E. G. Adam of the road (5 and up)
Fic
Waugh, S. The Mennyms (5 and up) **Fic**
Whelan, G. Listening for lions (5 and up)
Fic
Wiseman, D. Jeremy Visick (5 and up) **Fic**

Folklore
See Folklore—Great Britain
History—0-1066
Crossley-Holland, K. The world of King Arthur
and his court (5 and up) **942.01**
History—0-1066—Fiction
Avi. The Book Without Words (5 and up)
Fic
History—1154-1399, Plantagenets
Tanaka, S. In the time of knights (4 and up)
942.03
History—1154-1399, Plantagenets—Fiction
Avi. Crispin (5 and up) **Fic**
Branford, H. Fire, bed, & bone (5 and up)
Fic
History—1485-1603, Tudors
Adams, S. Elizabeth I (4 and up) **92**
Mannis, C. A. The Queen's progress [biography
of Elizabeth I] (3-5) **92**
Stanley, D. Good Queen Bess: the story of Eliz-
abeth I of England (4 and up) **92**
See/See also pages in the following book(s):
Rosen, M. Shakespeare (6 and up) **822.3**
History—1485-1603, Tudors—Fiction
Blackwood, G. L. The Shakespeare stealer (5
and up) **Fic**
Curry, J. L. The Black Canary (5 and up)
Fic
Lasky, K. Elizabeth I (4 and up) **Fic**
History—1714-1837—Fiction
Buckley-Archer, L. Gideon the cutpurse (5 and
up) **Fic**
Lawrence, I. The wreckers (5 and up) **Fic**
Woodruff, E. The Ravenmaster's secret (5 and
up) **Fic**
History—19th century
See also Industrial revolution
Kings and rulers
Fritz, J. Can't you make them behave, King
George? [biography of George III, King of
Great Britain] (2-4) **92**
Mannis, C. A. The Queen's progress [biography
of Elizabeth I] (3-5) **92**
Stanley, D. Good Queen Bess: the story of Eliz-
abeth I of England (4 and up) **92**
Politics and government—20th century
Binns, T. B. Winston Churchill (5 and up)
92

Prime ministers
See Prime ministers—Great Britain
Great building feats [series]
DuTemple, L. A. The New York subways
388.4
DuTemple, L. A. The Pantheon **726**
Great building stories of the past. Kent, P.
624

Great cities of the world [series]
Barber, N. Istanbul **949.6**
Bowden, R. Jerusalem **956.94**
Gaag, N. v. d. Baghdad **956.7**
Rowe, P. Toronto **971**
Stacey, G. London **942.1**
Great Depression, 1929-1939
Appelt, K. Down Cut Shin Creek (4 and up)
027

Great Depression, 1929-1939—*Continued*

Cooper, M. L. Dust to eat (4 and up)
973.917

Freedman, R. Children of the Great Depression
305.23

Meltzer, M. Driven from the land (4 and up)
978

Stanley, J. Children of the Dust Bowl (5 and up)
371.9

Fiction

Adler, D. A. The Babe & I **E**

Alexander, L. The Gawgon and The Boy (5 and up) **Fic**

Ayres, K. Macaroni boy (5 and up) **Fic**

Bornstein, R. L. Butterflies and lizards, Beryl and me (4 and up) **Fic**

Burch, R. Ida Early comes over the mountain (4 and up) **Fic**

Carville, J. Lu and the swamp ghost **E**

Cummings, P. Saving Grace (5 and up) **Fic**

Curtis, C. P. Bud, not Buddy (4 and up) **Fic**

Friedrich, E. Leah's pony **E**

Griffin, A. Hannah, divided (4 and up) **Fic**

Hale, M. The truth about sparrows (5 and up) **Fic**

Haseley, D. The amazing thinking machine (4 and up) **Fic**

Hesse, K. Out of the dust (5 and up) **Fic**

Hopkinson, D. Saving Strawberry Farm **E**

Jackson, A. Rainmaker (5 and up) **Fic**

Peck, R. A long way from Chicago (5 and up) **Fic**

Peck, R. A year down yonder (5 and up) **Fic**

Recorvits, H. Goodbye, Walter Malinski (3-6) **Fic**

Snyder, Z. K. Cat running (4 and up) **Fic**

Stewart, S. The gardener **E**

Taylor, M. D. Let the circle be unbroken (4 and up) **Fic**

Taylor, M. D. Song of the trees (4 and up) **Fic**

Turner, A. W. Dust for dinner **E**

Wells, R. Wingwalker (3-6) **Fic**

Willis, P. The barn burner (5 and up) **Fic**

Wyatt, L. J. Poor is just a starting place (5 and up) **Fic**

Great escapes [series]

Currie, S. Escapes from slavery **326**

Great explorations [series]

Calvert, P. Vasco da Gama **92**

Calvert, P. Zebulon Pike **92**

Faber, H. Samuel de Champlain **92**

Meltzer, M. Francisco Pizarro **92**

Otfinoski, S. Juan Ponce de Leon **92**

Otfinoski, S. Vasco Nuñez de Balboa **92**

Great explorers book [series]

Goodman, J. E. Despite all obstacles: La Salle and the conquest of the Mississippi **92**

Goodman, J. E. A long and uncertain journey: the 27,000 mile voyage of Vasco da Gama **92**

The **great** fire. Murphy, J. **977.3**

The **great** flood. Curry, J. L.
In Curry, J. L. The wonderful sky boat and other Native American tales of the Southeast p14-17 **398.2**

The **great** frog race and other poems. George, K. O. **811**

The **great** fuzz frenzy. Stevens, J. **E**

The **great** Gilly Hopkins. Paterson, K. **Fic**

The **Great** Googlestein museum mystery. Van Leeuwen, J. **Fic**

Great-Grandfather Dragon's tale. Yolen, J.
In Yolen, J. Here there be dragons p3-22 **810.8**

The **great** graph contest. Leedy, L. **E**

Great horned owl *See* Owls

The **great** horseless carriage race. Dooling, M. **796.72**

Great ideas of science [series]

Johnson, R. L. Genetics **576.5**

Great journeys [series]

Haskins, J. Out of the darkness **305.8**

Meltzer, M. Bound for America **325.73**

Meltzer, M. Driven from the land **978**

The **great** kapok tree. Cherry, L. **E**

The **great** Lacrosse game. Caduto, M. J.
In Caduto, M. J. and Bruchac, J. Keepers of the night; Native American stories and nocturnal activities for children p97-99 **398.2**

Great Lakes region

Fiction

Holling, H. C. Paddle-to-the-sea (4-6) **Fic**

Root, P. If you want to see a caribou **E**

Great life stories [series]

Binns, T. B. Winston Churchill **92**

Lassieur, A. Albert Einstein **92**

The **great** little Madison. Fritz, J. **92**

The **great** meatball. Curry, J. L.
In Curry, J. L. Hold up the sky: and other Native American tales from Texas and the Southern Plains p73-76 **398.2**

The **great** migration. Lawrence, J. **759.13**

Great minds of science [series]

Anderson, M. J. Aristotle **92**

Gow, M. Rachel Carson **92**

Poynter, M. Marie Curie: discoverer of radium **92**

Reed, J. Leonardo da Vinci: genius of art and science **92**

Tocci, S. Alexander Fleming **92**

Great Plains

History

Levey, R. H. Dust bowl! (1-3) **363.34**

Meltzer, M. Driven from the land (4 and up) **978**

Great record breakers in nature [series]

Weintraub, A. The Grand Canyon **557**

The **Great** Red Cat. MacDonald, M. R.
In MacDonald, M. R. When the lights go out; twenty scary tales to tell p47-60 **372.6**

Greene, Bette

Philip Hall likes me, I reckon maybe (4-6)
Fic

Summer of my German soldier (6 and up)
Fic

Greene, Charles Sumner, 1868-1957
About

Thorne-Thomsen, K. Greene & Greene for kids [biography of Charlie & Henry Greene] (5 and up) **92**

Greene, Ellin

The little golden lamb (k-3) **398.2**
Storytelling **372.6**

Greene, Henry Mather, 1870-1954
About

Thorne-Thomsen, K. Greene & Greene for kids [biography of Charlie & Henry Greene] (5 and up) **92**

Greene, Jacqueline Dembar

Slavery in ancient Greece and Rome (5 and up) **326**

Greene, Meg

Louis Sachar (5 and up) **92**

Greene, Rhonda Gowler

Barnyard song **E**

Greene, Stephanie

Falling into place (3-5) **Fic**
Moose's big idea (1-3) **Fic**
Owen Foote, frontiersman (2-4) **Fic**
Queen Sophie Hartley (3-5) **Fic**

Greene & Greene for kids [biography of Charlie & Henry Greene] Thorne-Thomsen, K. **92**

Greenfeld, Howard

After the Holocaust (6 and up) **940.53**
The hidden children (4 and up) **940.53**

Greenfield, Eloise

Africa dream **E**
Childtimes: a three-generation memoir (4 and up) **920**
Grandpa's face **E**
Honey, I love (k-2) **811**
Honey, I love, and other love poems (2-4)
811
Me & Neesie **E**
Nathaniel talking (2-4) **811**
Sister (4 and up) **Fic**
Under the Sunday tree (2-4) **811**

Greenhouse effect

Oxlade, C. Global warming (5 and up)
363.7
Parks, P. J. Global warming (5 and up)
363.7
Pringle, L. P. Global warming (4 and up)
363.7

Greenkid. Yolen, J.

In Swan sister; fairy tales retold **S C**

Greenseid, Diane

(il) Dragonwagon, C. And then it rained . . .
E
(il) Gershator, D. Kallaloo! **E**
(il) Woodson, J. We had a picnic this Sunday past **E**

Greenstein, Elaine

Ice cream cones for sale! (k-3) **637**

One little lamb **E**
One little seed **E**
(il) Goldin, B. D. While the candles burn
296.4

Greenwald, Sheila

Rosy Cole's worst ever, best yet tour of New York City (3-5) **Fic**

Greenwillow read-alone books [series]

Prelutsky, J. It's Christmas **811**
Prelutsky, J. It's Thanksgiving **811**
Prelutsky, J. It's Valentine's Day **811**

Greenwood, Barbara

A pioneer sampler (4 and up) **971.3**

Greeting card making. Hufford, D. **745.59**

Greeting cards

Hufford, D. Greeting card making (3-5)
745.59

Gregor the Overlander. Collins, S. **Fic**

Gregorowski, Christopher

Fly, eagle, fly! (k-3) **398.2**

Gregory, Adair

(jt. auth) Peacock, C. A. Sugar was my best food **362.1**

Gregory, Kyle Carney

(jt. auth) Peacock, C. A. Sugar was my best food **362.1**

Gregory, the terrible eater. Sharmat, M. **E**

Gretz, Susanna

Riley and Rose in the picture **E**

Grey, Mini

Traction Man is here! **E**

Grey. San Souci, R.

In San Souci, R. Double-dare to be scared: another thirteen chilling tales **S C**

The **grey** king. Cooper, S. **Fic**

The **Grey** Lady and the Strawberry Snatcher. Bang, M. **E**

Grief. Andersen, H. C.

In Andersen, H. C. The swan's stories p79-83
S C

Griego, Margot C.

(comp) Tortillitas para mamá and other nursery rhymes. See Tortillitas para mamá and other nursery rhymes **398.8**

Griessman, Annette

The fire **E**

Grifalconi, Ann

The village of round and square houses (k-3)
398.2
The village that vanished **E**
(il) Clifton, L. Everett Anderson's 1-2-3 **E**
(il) Dorros, A. Julio's magic **E**
(il) Myers, W. D. Patrol **E**

Griffin, Adele

Hannah, divided (4 and up) **Fic**
The other Shepards (6 and up) **Fic**

Griffin, Margot

The sleepover book (3-6) **793.2**

Griffin, Peni R.

The ghost sitter (4 and up) **Fic**
Switching well (5 and up) **Fic**

Grose, Helen Mason
  (il) Wiggin, K. D. S. Rebecca of Sunnybrook
  Farm   **Fic**

Grossman, David
  Duel (5 and up)   **Fic**

Grossman, Laurie M.
  Children of Israel (2-4)   **956.94**

The **grouchy** ladybug. Carle, E.   **E**

Ground-hogs *See* Marmots

Groundhog Day
          Fiction
  Cox, J. Go to sleep, Groundhog!   **E**
  Hill, S. L. Punxsutawney Phyllis   **E**

Groundhog gets a say. Swallow, P. C. **E**

Groundhog's dance. Sierra, J.
  In Sierra, J. Nursery tales around the world
    p93-95   **398.2**

Grover G. Graham and me. Quattlebaum, M.
                          Fic

Growing colors. McMillan, B.   **E**

Growing frogs. French, V.   **597.8**

Growing like me. Rockwell, A. F.   **E**

Growing seasons. Splear, E. L.   **630.1**

Growing up. Singer, I. B.
  In Singer, I. B. Stories for children p217-30
                        S C

Growing up. Soto, G.
  In Soto, G. Baseball in April, and other sto-
    ries p97-107   **S C**

Growing up in coal country. Bartoletti, S. C.
                        331.3

Growing up in pioneer America, 1800 to 1890.
  Josephson, J. P.   **978**

Growing up in revolution and the new nation,
  1775 to 1800. Miller, B. M.   **973.3**

Growing up: it's a girl thing. Jukes, M. **612.6**

Growing up stories [series]
  Harris, R. H. Go! Go! Maria!   **612.6**
  Harris, R. H. Hello Benny! What it's like to be
    a baby   **612.6**
  Harris, R. H. Sweet Jasmine, nice Jackson
                        612.6

Growing up wild: wolves. Markle, S. **599.77**

Growing up with science (5 and up)   **503**

Growing vegetable soup. Ehlert, L.   **E**

Growth
  Harris, R. H. Go! Go! Maria! (k-3) **612.6**
  Harris, R. H. Hello Benny! What it's like to be
    a baby (k-3)   **612.6**
  Parker, S. Reproduction (5 and up) **612.6**
  Rockwell, A. F. Growing like me   **E**
  Saltz, G. Amazing you (k-1)   **612.6**
          Fiction
  Brown, M. W. Another important book **E**
  Bunting, E. Little Bear's little boat **E**
  Greenstein, E. One little seed   **E**
  Keller, H. Farfallina & Marcel   **E**
  McElmurry, J. I'm not a baby!   **E**
  Swanson, S. M. The first thing my mama told
    me   **E**

Gruber, Franz Xaver, 1787-1863
         About
  Thuswaldner, W. Silent night holy night (k-3)
                        782.28

Gruen, John
  (il) Nicholas, K. Kids embroidery **746.44**
  (il) Ronci, K. Kids crochet   **746.43**

The **gruesome** guide to world monsters. Sierra, J.
                        398

The **grumbling** old woman. Afanas'ev, A. N.
  In Afanas'ev, A. N. Russian fairy tales p340-
    41   **398.2**

Grupper, Jonathan
  Destination: Australia (3-6)   **591.9**
  Destination: deep sea (3-6)   **591.7**
  Destination: rain forest (3-6)   **577.3**
  Destination: Rocky Mountains (3-6) **978**

Grutter, Alexandra
         About
  Collard, S. B., III. On the coral reefs (4-6)
                        577.7

Guanina. Delacre, L.
  In Delacre, L. Golden tales; myths, legends,
    and folktales from Latin America p7-12
                        398.2

The **guardian** of memory. Coville, B.
  In A Glory of unicorns p1-28   **S C**

Guarino, Deborah
  Is your mama a llama?   **E**

Guatemala
  Menchú, R. The girl from Chimel (4 and up)
                        92
  Sheehan, S. Guatemala (5 and up) **972.81**
          Fiction
  Carling, A. L. Mama & Papa have a store
                        E
  Carling, A. L. Sawdust carpets   **E**
  Castañeda, O. S. Abuela's weave   **E**
  Ichikawa, S. My pig Amarillo   **E**

Guayaki Indians
  Batten, M. Anthropologist: scientist of the peo-
    ple (4 and up)   **301**

Guback, Georgia
  Luka's quilt   **E**

La **güera**. Soto, G.
  In Soto, G. Petty crimes   **S C**

Guernsey, JoAnn Bren
  (jt. auth) Brandenburg, J. Sand and fog
                        968.8
  (jt. auth) Brandenburg, J. To the top of the
    world   **599.77**

Guess, George *See* Sequoyah, 1770?-1843

Guess how much I love you. McBratney, S. **E**

Guess who? Miller, M.   **E**

Guess who, Baby Duck!. Hest, A.   **E**

Guess who's coming to Santa's for dinner? De
  Paola, T.   **E**

Guest, Elissa Haden
  Iris and Walter   **E**

Guests from Gibbet Island. San Souci, R.
  In San Souci, R. Even more short & shivery;
    thirty spine-tingling stories p44-48
                        398.2

Guevara, Susan
  (il) Lillegard, D. Tiger, tiger   E
  (il) Soto, G. Chato's kitchen   E
  (il) Yolen, J. Not one damsel in distress
                               398.2

Guggenheim (Solomon R.) Museum *See* Solomon R. Guggenheim Museum

Gugu's house. Stock, C.   E

La Guiablesse. San Souci, R.
  In San Souci, R. Even more short & shivery; thirty spine-tingling stories p33-37
                               398.2

Guiberson, Brenda Z.
  Cactus hotel (k-3)   **583**
  The emperor lays an egg (k-3)   **598**
  Into the sea (k-3)   **597.92**
  Mud city (2-4)   **598**
  Rain, rain, rain forest (k-3)   **577.3**

Guibert, Emmanuel
  Sardine in outer space (3-5)   **741.5**

Guida, Liisa Chauncy
  (jt. auth) Tomecek, S. Moon   **523.3**

Guide dogs
  Kent, D. Animal helpers for the disabled (4 and up)   **636.088**
  Patent, D. H. The right dog for the job (2-4)
                               362.4

Guide to collective biographies for children and young adults. Barancik, S.   **016.9**

Guide to reference books for school media centers. See Safford, B. R. Guide to reference materials for school media centers   **011.6**

Guide to reference materials for school media centers. Safford, B. R.   **011.6**

Guidoux, Valérie
  (jt. auth) Dubois, P. J. Birds   **598**

Guile, Melanie
  Culture in India (4 and up)   **954**
  Culture in Malaysia (4 and up)   **959.5**
  Culture in Vietnam (4 and up)   **959.7**

Guilloppé, Antoine
  One scary night   E

Guilt
Fiction
Bunting, E. Blackwater (5 and up)   **Fic**

Guinea Fowl and Rabbit get justice. Courlander, H.
  In Courlander, H. and Herzog, G. Cow-tail switch, and other West African stories p87-94   **398.2**

Guinea pig scientists. Dendy, L. A.   **616**

Guinea pigs
  Hansen, E. Guinea pigs (3-6)   **636.9**
  Holub, J. Why do rabbits hop? (k-2)   **636.9**
  Jeffrey, L. S. Hamsters, gerbils, guinea pigs, rabbits, ferrets, mice, and rats (3-5)   **636.9**
  King-Smith, D. I love guinea pigs (k-3)
                               636.9

Fiction
Berenzy, A. Sammy the classroom guinea pig
                               E
Hurwitz, J. PeeWee's tale (2-4)   **Fic**
Kroll, S. Patches: lost and found   E
Meade, H. John Willy and Freddy McGee   E

Wells, R. Felix feels better   E
Folklore
Knutson, B. Love and roast chicken (k-3)
                               398.2

Guinness book of records   **032.02**

Guinness book of world records. See Guinness book of records   **032.02**

Guinness world records. See Guinness book of records   **032.02**

Guji Guji. Chen, C.-Y.   E

Gulevich, Tanya
  Encyclopedia of Easter, Carnival, and Lent (5 and up)   **394.26**

Gullahs
Fiction
Belton, S. Beauty, her basket   E
Raven, M. Circle unbroken   E
Siegelson, K. L. In the time of the drums   E
Poetry
Boling, K. New year be coming! (k-3)   **811**

Gulliver in Lilliput. Hodges, M.   **Fic**

Gulls
  Gibbons, G. Gulls—gulls—gulls (k-3)   **598**

Gulls—gulls—gulls. Gibbons, G.   **598**

"Gulp!". San Souci, R.
  In San Souci, R. Double-dare to be scared: another thirteen chilling tales   **S C**

Gumbrella. Root, B.   E

The **gun.** Naidoo, B.
  In Naidoo, B. Out of bounds: seven stories of conflict and hope p96-119   **S C**

Gündisch, Karin
  How I became an American (4 and up)   **Fic**

Gunnella
  (jt. auth) McMillan, B. The problem with chickens   E

The **gunny** wolf. Sierra, J.
  In Sierra, J. Nursery tales around the world p87-91   **398.2**

Gunter, Veronika Alice
  The ultimate indoor games book (3-6)   **793**
  (jt. auth) Rhatigan, J. Cool chemistry concoctions   **540.7**

Gurstelle, William
  The art of the catapult (5 and up)   **623.4**

Gurvin, Abe
  (il) Chahrour, J. Zap! blink! taste! think!
                               507.8

Gus and Grandpa and the two-wheeled bike. Mills, C.   E

Gustafson, Dana
  (il) Haskins, J. Count your way through the Arab world   **909**

Gustafson, Scott
  (il) Barrie, J. M. Peter Pan   **Fic**

Gustavson, Adam
  (il) Borden, L. The A+ custodian   E
  (il) Borden, L. Good luck, Mrs. K!   E
  (jt. auth) Borden, L. The last day of school
                               Fic

Guthrie, Woody
  This land is your land (k-3)   **782.42**

Guthrie, Woody, 1912-1967
About
Christensen, B. Woody Guthrie, poet of the people (3-6) **92**
Neimark, A. E. There ain't nobody that can sing like me: the life of Woody Guthrie (5 and up) **92**

See/See also pages in the following book(s):
Krull, K. Lives of the musicians (4 and up) **920**

Gutman, Dan
The homework machine (4-6) **Fic**
Ice skating (5 and up) **796.91**
The million dollar strike (4-6) **Fic**
Shoeless Joe & me (4 and up) **Fic**

Guts. Simon, S. **612.3**

Guy, Ginger Foglesong
Fiesta! **E**
Siesta **E**

Guyana
Jermyn, L. Guyana (5 and up) **988.1**
Morrison, M. Guyana (5 and up) **988.1**

Gwaltney, Doris
Homefront (5 and up) **Fic**

Gwendolen. Mayer, M.
In Mayer, M. Women warriors; myths and legends of heroic women p43-49 **398**

Gymnastics
Bragg, L. W. Fundamental gymnastics (5 and up) **796.44**
Bray-Moffatt, N. Gymnastics school (k-3) **796.44**
Jackman, J. Gymnastics (4 and up) **796.44**

Gymnastics school. Bray-Moffatt, N. **796.44**

Gynecology *See* Women—Health and hygiene

Gypsies
Fiction
Alexander, L. Gypsy Rizka (5 and up) **Fic**

Gypsy Rizka. Alexander, L. **Fic**

H

Ha! Ha! Ha!. Thomas, L. **793.73**

Haab, Michelle
(jt. auth) Haab, S. Dangles and bangles **745.5**

Haab, Sherri
Dangles and bangles (5 and up) **745.5**

Haas, Irene
Bess and Bella **E**

Haas, Jessie
Birthday pony (2-4) **Fic**
Hurry! **E**
Jigsaw pony (2-4) **Fic**
Runaway Radish (2-4) **Fic**
Scamper and the horse show **E**
Sugaring **E**

Haban, Rita D.
How proudly they wave (4 and up) **929.9**

Habetrot and Scantlie Mab. Jacobs, J.
In Jacobs, J. English fairy tales p396-400 **398.2**

Habitat (Ecology)
See also types of ecology, e.g. Desert ecology; Marine ecology
Arnosky, J. Crinkleroot's guide to knowing animal habitats (k-3) **591.7**
Fleming, D. Where once there was a wood (k-2) **639.9**
Habitats of the world (5 and up) **577**
Jenkins, S. I see a kookaburra! (k-3) **591.7**
Stetson, E. Kids' easy-to-create wildlife habitats (2-4) **639.9**
Toft, K. M. The world that we want (k-3) **577**
VanCleave, J. P. Janice Vancleave's ecology for every kid (4 and up) **577**

Habitats of the world (5 and up) **577**

Hachiko. Turner, P. S. **E**

Hachiko waits. Newman, L. **Fic**

Had gadya (k-3) **296.4**

Haddix, Margaret Peterson
Escape
In Shelf life: stories by the book **S C**
Say what? (2-4) **Fic**

Hader, Berta
The big snow **E**

Hader, Elmer Stanley
(jt. auth) Hader, B. The big snow **E**

Haduch, Bill
Go fly a bike! (4-6) **629.227**
Science fair success secrets (5 and up) **507.8**

Haefele, Steve
(il) Cobb, V. Squirts and spurts **507.8**

Hafiz, the stone-cutter. Shedlock, M. L.
In Shedlock, M. L. The art of the story-teller p179-82 **372.6**

Hafner, Marylin
(il) Berger, M. Germs make me sick! **616.9**
(il) Horvath, P. The Pepins and their problems **Fic**
(il) Lasky, K. Lucille camps in **E**
(il) Pocket poems. See Pocket poems **811.008**
(il) Prelutsky, J. It's Christmas **811**
(il) Prelutsky, J. It's Thanksgiving **811**
(il) Ross, P. Meet M and M **E**

Hague, Michael
(il) Barrie, J. M. Peter Pan **Fic**
(il) Baum, L. F. The Wizard of Oz **Fic**
(il) Bianco, M. W. The velveteen rabbit **Fic**
(il) Grahame, K. The reluctant dragon **Fic**
(il) Lofting, H. The voyages of Doctor Dolittle **Fic**

Hahn, Mary Downing
Anna all year round (3-5) **Fic**
Daphne's book (5 and up) **Fic**
The doll in the garden (4-6) **Fic**
The Gentleman Outlaw and me—Eli (5 and up) **Fic**
Hear the wind blow (5 and up) **Fic**
The old Willis place (5 and up) **Fic**
Stepping on the cracks (5 and up) **Fic**
Time for Andrew (5 and up) **Fic**
Wait till Helen comes (4-6) **Fic**

Haiku

Chaikin, M. Don't step on the sky (k-3) **811**

Grimes, N. A pocketful of poems (k-3) **811**
Mannis, C. A. One leaf rides the wind **E**
Prelutsky, J. If not for the cat (1-4) **811**
Stone bench in an empty park (4 and up) **811.008**
See/See also pages in the following book(s):
Gollub, M. Cool melons—turn to frogs!: the life and poems of Issa [Kobayashi] (3-6) **92**
Hailstones and halibut bones. O'Neill, M. L. D. **811**

Hair

Swain, R. F. Hairdo! (1-4) **391**
Watters, D. Where's Mom's hair? (2-4) **616.99**
Fiction
Madrigal, A. H. Erandi's braids **E**
Poetry
Thomas, J. C. Crowning glory (k-3) **811**
Hairdo!. Swain, R. F. **391**

Hairston, Martha

(il) Burns, M. The I hate mathematics! book **513**
The **hairy** hands. San Souci, R.
In San Souci, R. A terrifying taste of short & shivery; thirty creepy tales p52-57 **398.2**
Hairy, scary, ordinary. Cleary, B. P. **428**
The **hairy** toe. Van Laan, N.
In Van Laan, N. Teeny tiny tingly tales **E**

Haiti

Cheong-Lum, R. N. Haiti (5 and up) **972.94**
Hintz, M. Haiti (5 and up) **972.94**
Fiction
Elvgren, J. R. Josias, hold the book **E**
Lotu, D. Running the road to ABC **E**
Temple, F. Tonight, by sea (6 and up) **Fic**
Williams, K. L. Painted dreams **E**
Folklore
See Folklore—Haiti

Hakim, Joy

A history of US (5 and up) **973**

Haldane, Suzanne

(jt. auth) Left Hand Bull, J. Lakota hoop dancer **970.004**

Hale, Christy

(il) Hearne, B. G. Who's in the hall? **E**
(il) It rained all day that night. *See* It rained all day that night **811.008**
(il) Kirk, C. A. Sky dancers **E**
(il) Stuve-Bodeen, S. Elizabeti's doll **E**

Hale, James Graham

(il) Branley, F. M. Down comes the rain **551.57**
(il) Zoehfeld, K. W. How mountains are made **551.4**

Hale, Marian

The truth about sparrows (5 and up) **Fic**

Haley, Amanda

(il) Frith, M. Hooray for ballet! **792.8**

Haley, Gail E.

A story, a story (k-3) **398.2**

(il) Konigsburg, E. L. Altogether, one at a time **S C**
The **Half-a-Moon** Inn. Fleischman, P. **Fic**
Half-chick. *See* Barnes, H. The proud cock
Half magic. Eager, E. **Fic**
Half-Moon investigations. Colfer, E. **Fic**
Half-past midnight. San Souci, R.
In San Souci, R. Double-dare to be scared: another thirteen chilling tales **S C**

Halilbegovich, Nadja

My childhood under fire (5 and up) **949.7**

Hall, Bruce Edward

Henry and the kite dragon **E**

Hall, Donald

Ox-cart man **E**
(ed) The Oxford book of children's verse in America. *See* The Oxford book of children's verse in America **811.008**
(ed) The Oxford illustrated book of American children's poems. *See* The Oxford illustrated book of American children's poems **811.008**

Hall, Eleanor J.

Recycling (5 and up) **363.7**

Hall, Greg

(il) Thomas, K. How hockey works **796.962**

Hall, Katy

Creepy riddles (k-2) **793.73**
Dino riddles (k-2) **793.73**
Mummy riddles (k-2) **793.73**
Ribbit riddles (k-2) **793.73**
Snakey riddles (k-2) **793.73**
Stinky riddles (k-2) **793.73**
Turkey riddles (k-2) **793.73**

Hall, Margaret

Credit cards and checks (3-5) **332.7**
Money (3-5) **332.4**
Your allowance (3-5) **332.024**

Hall, Melanie W.

(il) Christmas presents. *See* Christmas presents **811.008**
(il) Fishman, C. On Hanukkah **296.4**
(il) Fishman, C. On Passover **296.4**
(il) Fishman, C. On Rosh Hashanah and Yom Kippur **296.4**
(il) Hanukkah lights. *See* Hanukkah lights **811.008**

Hall, Nelson

(il) Reynolds, D. W. Star wars: the visual dictionary **791.43**

Hall, Ruby Bridges *See* Bridges, Ruby

Hall, Susan

Using picture storybooks to teach literary devices v3 **016.8**

Hall, Zoe

The apple pie tree (k-1) **634**
Fall leaves fall! **E**

Hall-Ellis, Sylvia Dunn

Grants for school libraries **025.1**
Grantsmanship for small libraries and school library media centers. *See* Grantsmanship for small libraries and school library media centers **025.1**

Hallam, Arlita
  Managing budgets and finances   **025.1**

Hallensleben, Georg
  (il) Banks, K. And if the moon could talk **E**
  (il) Banks, K. Baboon   **E**
  (il) Banks, K. The cat who walked across France   **E**
  (il) Banks, K. Close your eyes   **E**
  (il) Banks, K. A gift from the sea   **E**
  (il) Banks, K. The great blue house   **E**
  (il) Banks, K. The night worker   **E**

Hallett, Mark
  (il) Hehner, B. Ice Age cave bear   **569**
  (il) Hehner, B. Ice Age mammoth   **569**
  (il) Hehner, B. Ice Age sabertooth   **569**

Halley, Ned
  Farm (4 and up)   **630.1**

The **Hallo-wiener**. Pilkey, D.   **E**

Halloween
  Barth, E. Witches, pumpkins, and grinning ghosts (3-6)   **394.26**
  Gibbons, G. Halloween is— (k-3)   **394.26**
  See/See also pages in the following book(s):
  Bauer, C. F. Celebrations p1-24   **808.8**
Fiction
  Bunting, E. The bones of Fred Mcfee   **E**
  Cazet, D. The perfect pumpkin pie   **E**
  De Groat, D. Trick or treat, smell my feet   **E**
  Fleming, D. Pumpkin eye   **E**
  Freeman, M. Who stole Halloween? (4-6)   **Fic**
  Hubbell, W. Pumpkin Jack   **E**
  Huck, C. S. A creepy countdown   **E**
  Kroll, S. The biggest pumpkin ever   **E**
  Leuck, L. One witch   **E**
  Marshall, E. Space case   **E**
  Martin, B. Trick or treat?   **E**
  Pilkey, D. The Hallo-wiener   **E**
  Rylant, C. Moonlight: the Halloween cat   **E**
  Serfozo, M. Plumply, dumply pumpkin   **E**
  Seuling, B. Robert and the back-to-school special (2-4)   **Fic**
  Thompson, J. Scary Godmother (k-3)   **741.5**
  Tolan, S. S. Save Halloween! (5 and up)   **Fic**
  Zolotow, C. A tiger called Thomas   **E**
Poetry
  Behn, H. Halloween (1-3)   **811**
  Carlstrom, N. W. Who said boo? (k-3)   **811**
  Halloween howls (k-3)   **811.008**
  Merriam, E. Spooky A B C (3-6)   **811**
Halloween ABC. See Merriam, E. Spooky A B C   **811**

The **Halloween** dance. Stine, R. L.
  In Stine, R. L. The haunting hour p2-19   **S C**

Halloween howls (k-3)   **811.008**

Halloween is—. Gibbons, G.   **394.26**

The **Halloween** pony. San Souci, R.
  In San Souci, R. Short & shivery; thirty chilling tales p166-70   **398.2**

The **Halloween** spirit. San Souci, R.
  In San Souci, R. Dare to be scared; thirteen stories to chill and thrill   **S C**

Halls, Kelly Milner
  Dinosaur mummies (5 and up)   **567.9**
  Wild dogs (5 and up)   **599.77**

Halmoni and the picnic. Choi, S. N.   **E**

Halmoni's day. Bercaw, E. C.   **E**

Halperin, Wendy Anderson
  (il) Aylesworth, J. The full belly bowl   **E**
  (il) Cates, K. The Secret Remedy Book   **E**
  (il) Chall, M. W. Bonaparte   **E**
  (il) Lindbergh, R. The visit   **E**
  (il) Seymour, T. Hunting the white cow   **E**

Halpern, Monica
  Railroad fever (4-6)   **385.09**

Halpern, Shari
  (il) Hall, Z. The apple pie tree   **634**
  (il) Hall, Z. Fall leaves fall!   **E**
  (il) Sturges, P. I love planes!   **E**
  (il) Sturges, P. I love school!   **E**
  (il) Sturges, P. I love trains!   **E**

Halpern, Sue
  Introducing . . . Sasha Abramowitz (5 and up)   **Fic**

Halsey, Megan
  (il) Appelt, K. Where, where is Swamp Bear?   **E**
  (il) Chin-Lee, C. Amelia to Zora   **920**
  (il) Older, J. Telling time   **529**
  (il) Rockwell, A. F. Becoming butterflies   **595.7**
  (jt. auth) Rockwell, A. F. Four seasons make a year   **E**
  (il) Rockwell, A. F. Little shark   **597**
  (il) Rockwell, A. F. One bean   **635**
  (il) Rockwell, A. F. Two blue jays   **E**

Halstead, Virginia
  (il) Spectacular science. See Spectacular science   **811.008**

Halsted, Deborah D.
  Disaster planning   **025.8**

Ham radio stations See Amateur radio stations

Hamanaka, Sheila
  All the colors of the earth   **E**
  Grandparents song   **E**
  (il) Hurwitz, J. Class clown   **Fic**

Hamer, Fannie Lou Townsend, 1917-1977
  See/See also pages in the following book(s):
  Pinkney, A. D. Let it shine (4 and up)   **920**

Hamilton, Clive See Lewis, C. S. (Clive Staples), 1898-1963

Hamilton, Edith
  Mythology (5 and up)   **292**

Hamilton, Garry
  Frog rescue (5 and up)   **597.8**

Hamilton, Janice
  Mexico in pictures (5 and up)   **972**

Hamilton, John
  Becoming a citizen (3-5)   **323.6**
  How a bill becomes a law (3-5)   **328**
  Running for office (3-5)   **324**
  Tsunamis (2-4)   **551.46**

Hamilton, Meredith
  (il) Driscoll, M. A child's introduction to poetry   **808.81**

Hamilton, Virginia
  The bells of Christmas (4-6) **Fic**
  Bruh Rabbit and the tar baby girl (k-3)
       398.2
  Cousins (5 and up) **Fic**
  Drylongso (3-5) **Fic**
  The girl who spun gold (k-3) **398.2**
  Her stories (4 and up) **398.2**
  Includes the following stories: Little Girl and Buh Rabby;
Lena and Big One Tiger; Marie and Redfish; Miz Hattie gets
some company; Catskinella; Good Blanche, bad Rose, and the
talking eggs; Mary Belle and the mermaid; Mom Bett and the lit-
tle ones a-glowing; Who you!; Macie and boo hag; Lonna and
Cat Woman; Malindy and little devil; Woman and Man started
even; Luella and the tame parrot; The mer-woman out of the sea;
Annie Christmas
  The house of Dies Drear (5 and up) **Fic**
  In the beginning; creation stories from around
    the world (5 and up) **201**
  M.C. Higgins, the great (5 and up) **Fic**
  Many thousand gone (5 and up) **326**
  The people could fly [American black folktales]
    (5 and up)
       398.2
  [the picture book] (3-6) **398.2**
  Plain City (5 and up) **Fic**
  The planet of Junior Brown (6 and up) **Fic**
  A ring of tricksters (3-6) **398.2**
  Time pieces (5 and up) **Fic**
  Wee Winnie Witch's Skinny **E**
  When birds could talk & bats could sing (3-5)
       398.2
  Zeely (4 and up) **Fic**
Hamilton, Virginia, 1936-2002
  See/See also pages in the following book(s):
  Ellis, S. From reader to writer **372.6**
Hamlet. Packer, T.
  In Packer, T. Tales from Shakespeare p31-47
       822.3
Hamlet, William Shakespeare's. Coville, B.
       822.3
Hamlin, Janet
  (il) Radin, R. Y. Escape to the forest **Fic**
Hamlyn reference [series]
  Ward, A. Card games for kids **795.4**
Hamm, Mia
  Winners never quit! **E**
Hammurabi, King of Babylonia
  See/See also pages in the following book(s):
  Meltzer, M. Ten kings (5 and up) **920**
Hampton, Wilborn
  Kennedy assassinated! (5 and up) **973.922**
Hamster champs. Murphy, S. J. **516**
Hamsters
  Hinds, K. Hamsters and gerbils (3-6) **636.9**
  Holub, J. Why do rabbits hop? (k-2) **636.9**
  Jeffrey, L. S. Hamsters, gerbils, guinea pigs,
    rabbits, ferrets, mice, and rats (3-5) **636.9**
  Rockwell, A. F. My pet hamster (k-2) **636.9**
       Fiction
  Kenah, K. The best seat in second grade **E**
  Murphy, S. J. Hamster champs (1-3) **516**
  Rathmann, P. 10 minutes till bedtime **E**
  Reiche, D. I, Freddy (3-5) **Fic**
  Wallace, C. One nosy pup **E**
Hamsters and gerbils. Hinds, K. **636.9**

Hamsters, gerbils, guinea pigs, rabbits, ferrets,
  mice, and rats. Jeffrey, L. S. **636.9**
Han, Oki S.
  (il) Myers, T. Basho and the river stones **E**
Han, Suzanne Crowder
  The rabbit's tail (k-3) **398.2**
Hana in the time of the tulips. Noyes, D. **E**
Hana's suitcase. Levine, K. **940.53**
Hancock, John, 1737-1793
       About
  Fritz, J. Will you sign here, John Hancock?
    (2-4) **92**
Hand
  Aliki. My hands (k-1) **612**
  The **hand** of death. Olson, A. N.
  In Olson, A. N. and Schwartz, H. Ask the
    bones: scary stories from around the
    world p105-09 **398.2**
  The **hand** of fate. San Souci, R.
  In San Souci, R. Even more short & shivery;
    thirty spine-tingling stories p140-43
       398.2
  The **hand** of the necromancer. Strickland, B.
       Fic
Handbook for storytellers. See Bauer, C. F. Caro-
  line Feller Bauer's new handbook for story-
  tellers **372.6**
Handel, George Frideric, 1685-1759
       About
  Anderson, M. T. Handel, who knew what he
    liked (4-6) **92**
Handel, who knew what he liked. Anderson, M.
  T. **92**
Handelsman, J. B.
  (il) Fritz, J. Who's that stepping on Plymouth
    Rock? **974.4**
A **handful** of beans. Steig, J. **398.2**
A **handful** of dirt. Bial, R. **577.5**
Handicapped
  See also Mentally handicapped; Physically
  handicapped
  Barasch, L. Knockin' on wood [biography of
    Peg Leg Bates] (2-4) **92**
       Fiction
  Jung, R. Dreaming in black and white (5 and
    up) **Fic**
  Stauffacher, S. Harry Sue (5 and up) **Fic**
  Wait, L. Wintering well (5 and up) **Fic**
       Fiction—Bibliography
  Ward, M. Voices from the margins **016.8**
Handicapped and animals See Animals and the
  handicapped
Handicapped children
  See also Mentally handicapped children;
  Physically handicapped children
Handicraft
  See also Leather work; Nature craft
  Anderson, M. Amazing Leonardo da Vinci in-
    ventions you can build yourself **92**
  Bauer, C. F. Leading kids to books through
    crafts **027.62**
  Bledsoe, K. E. Chinese New Year crafts (2-4)
       745.594

Hands-on science (4-6)   **507.8**

The **handshake**. Lunge-Larsen, L.
  In Lunge-Larsen, L. The troll with no heart in
    his body and other tales of trolls from
    Norway p43-47   **398.2**

Handsprings. Florian, D.   **811**

Handwriting
                    Fiction
  Cleary, B. Muggie Maggie (2-4)   **Fic**

Handy crafts [series]
  Souter, G. Paints plus   **745.7**
  Souter, G. Perfect parties   **793.2**

Haney, Johannah
  Juvenile diabetes (4 and up)   **616.4**
  Michigan
    In It's my state! [series]   **973**

Hang tough, Paul Mather. Slote, A.   **Fic**

Hannah, divided. Griffin, A.   **Fic**

Hannah is my name. Yang, B.   **E**

Hannah's collections. Jocelyn, M.   **E**

Hanne's quest. Dunrea, O.   **Fic**

Hannigan, Katherine
  Ida B (4-6)   **Fic**

Hans Brinker; or, The silver skates. Dodge, M. M.
                                              Fic

Hans Christian Andersen's Fairy Tales. Andersen,
  H. C.   **S C**

Hansel and Gretel. Doherty, B.
  In Doherty, B. Fairy tales   **398.2**

Hansel and Gretel. Grimm, J.   **398.2**

Hansel and Gretel. Lesser, R.   **398.2**

Hansel and Gretel. Marshall, J.   **398.2**

Hansel and Gretel. Steig, J.
  In Steig, J. A handful of beans; six fairy tales
    p61-82   **398.2**

Hansel and Grettel. Grimm, J.
  In The Blue fairy book p251-58   **398.2**

Hansen, Brooks
  Caesar's antlers (5 and up)   **Fic**

Hansen, Elvig
  Guinea pigs (3-6)   **636.9**

Hansen, Joyce
  African princess (5 and up)   **920**
  Freedom roads: searching for the Underground
    Railroad (5 and up)   **973.7**

Hansen-Krening, Nancy
  (ed) Kaleidoscope. See Kaleidoscope   **011.6**

Hanson, Mary Elizabeth
  The difference between babies & cookies   **E**

Hanson, Peter E.
  (il) Mitchell, B. A pocketful of goobers: a story
    about George Washington Carver   **92**

Hanson, Rick
  (il) Haskins, J. Count your way through Israel
                                              956.94

Hantavirus. Casil, A. S.   **616.9**

Hantavirus infections
  Casil, A. S. Hantavirus (4-6)   **616.9**

Hantula, Richard
  (jt. auth) Asimov, I. The life and death of stars
                                              523.8

(jt. auth) Asimov, I. The Milky Way and other
  galaxies   **523.1**

Hanukkah
  Fishman, C. On Hanukkah (k-3)   **296.4**
  Goldin, B. D. While the candles burn (4 and up)
                                              296.4
  A Hanukkah treasury   **296.4**
  Hoyt-Goldsmith, D. Celebrating Hanukkah (3-5)
                                              296.4
  Podwal, M. H. The menorah story (k-3)
                                              296.4
  Rosen, M. J. Our eight nights of Hanukkah
    (k-3)   **296.4**
  Simon, N. The story of Hanukkah (2-4)
                                              296.4
                    Fiction
  Bunting, E. One candle   **E**
  Edwards, M. Papa's latkes   **E**
  Howland, N. Latkes, latkes, good to eat   **E**
  Kimmel, E. A. The Chanukkah guest   **E**
  Kimmel, E. A. Hershel and the Hanukkah gob-
    lins   **E**
  Kimmel, E. A. The jar of fools: eight Hanukkah
    stories from Chelm (4 and up)   **S C**
  Kimmel, E. A. Zigazak!   **E**
  Koss, A. G. How I saved Hanukkah (3-5)
                                              Fic
  Melmed, L. K. Moishe's miracle   **E**
  Newman, L. Runaway dreidel!   **E**
  Polacco, P. The trees of the dancing goats **E**
  Rosen, M. J. Elijah's angel (2-4)   **Fic**
  Singer, I. B. The power of light (4 and up)
                                              S C
  Spinner, S. It's a miracle!   **E**
                    Folklore
  Adler, D. A. Chanukah in Chelm (k-3)
                                              398.2
  Kimmel, E. A. The spotted pony: a collection of
    Hanukkah stories (3-6)   **398.2**
                    Poetry
  Hanukkah lights (k-3)   **811.008**
                    Songs
  Roth, S. L. Hanukkah, oh Hanukkah (k-2)
                                              782.42

A **Hanukkah** Eve in Warsaw. Singer, I. B.
  In Singer, I. B. Stories for children p53-70
                                              S C

A **Hanukkah** evening in my parents' house. Singer, I. B.
  In Singer, I. B. The power of light; eight sto-
    ries for Hanukkah p3-9   **S C**
  also in Singer, I. B. Stories for children p155-
    59   **S C**

Hanukkah in the poorhouse. Singer, I. B.
  In Singer, I. B. The power of light; eight sto-
    ries for Hanukkah p75-87   **S C**
  also in Singer, I. B. Stories for children p271-
    82   **S C**

Hanukkah lights (k-3)   **811.008**

Hanukkah, oh Hanukkah. Roth, S. L.   **782.42**

A **Hanukkah** treasury   **296.4**

Hapipi, Rafiz
  (jt. auth) Foley, E. El Salvador   **972.84**

Happiness
Fiction
Bolliger, M. The happy troll   **E**

Happy and Honey. Godwin, L.   **E**

Happy bees. Yorinks, A.   **E**

Happy birth day!. Harris, R. H.   **E**

Happy birthday, Martin Luther King. Marzollo, J.   **92**

The **happy** egg. Krauss, R.   **E**

Happy, happy Chinese New Year!. Demi   **394.26**

Happy Honey [series]
Godwin, L. Happy and Honey   **E**

Happy New Year! Kung-Hsi Fa-ts'ai! See Demi. Happy, happy Chinese New Year!   **394.26**

The **happy** troll. Bolliger, M.   **E**

Haptie, Charlotte
Otto and the flying twins (4 and up)   **Fic**

Harada, Violet H.
Assessing learning   **027.8**

Inquiry learning through librarian-teacher partnerships   **371.1**

Harbors
Crews, D. Harbor   **E**

The **Harcourt** Brace student thesaurus (4 and up)   **423**

Hard hat area. Roth, S. L.   **E**

The **hard-times** jar. Smothers, E. F.   **E**

Harding, R. R.
(jt. auth) Symes, R. F. Crystal & gem   **548**

Hardinge, Frances
Fly by night (5 and up)   **Fic**

Hardworking puppies. Reiser, L.   **E**

Hardy Hardhead
In The Jack tales p96-105   **398.2**

The **hare** and the lion. See Aardema, V. Rabbit makes a monkey of lion   **398.2**

The **hare** and the tortoise. Sierra, J.
In Sierra, J. Nursery tales around the world p75   **398.2**

The **hare** and the tortoise. Ward, H.   **398.2**

Hargittai, Magdolna
Cooking the Hungarian way
In Easy menu ethnic cookbooks   **641.5**

Hargraves, Orin
(jt. auth) Seward, P. Morocco   **964**

Hariton, Anca
(il) Glaser, L. Compost!   **363.7**

(il) Richards, J. A fruit is a suitcase for seeds   **581.4**

Harlem (New York, N.Y.)
Fiction
Collier, B. Uptown   **E**

Michelson, R. Happy feet   **E**

Ringgold, F. Tar Beach   **E**

Taylor, D. A. Sweet music in Harlem   **E**
Poetry
Myers, W. D. Harlem   **811**

Harlem Renaissance
The entrance place of wonders (3-5)   **811.008**

Harley. Livingstone, S.   **E**

Harlin, Gregory
(il) Krensky, S. Dangerous crossing   **Fic**

(il) Krensky, S. Paul Revere's midnight ride   **973.3**

Harlow, Joan Hiatt
Si-Ling and the dragon
In Fire and wings: dragon tales from East and West p32-42   **S C**

Star in the storm   **Fic**

Harmon, Charles T.
(jt. auth) Symons, A. K. Protecting the right to read   **025.2**

Harmonicas
Fiction
McCloskey, R. Lentil   **E**

Harms, Jeanne McLain
Picture books to enhance the curriculum   **011.6**

Harness, Cheryl
Abe Lincoln goes to Washington, 1837-1865 (2-4)   **92**

George Washington (3-5)   **92**

Mark Twain and the queens of the Mississippi (3-5)   **92**

The remarkable Benjamin Franklin (2-4)   **92**

The revolutionary John Adams (3-6)   **92**

They're off! (3-5)   **383**

Harold. Schwartz, A.
In Beware!; R.L. Stine picks his favorite scary stories p179-84   **808.8**

also in Schwartz, A. Scary stories 3; more tales to chill your bones p30-34   **398.2**

Harold and the purple crayon. Johnson, C.   **E**

Harp o' gold. Bateman, T.   **E**

Harp of fishbones. Aiken, J.
In Aiken, J. Shadows and moonshine; stories   **S C**

The **harp** that sang. Frost, G.
In Swan sister; fairy tales retold   **S C**

Harper, Charise Mericle
Imaginative inventions (k-3)   **609**

Harper, Dan
Sit, Truman!   **E**

Telling time with Big Mama Cat   **E**

Harper, Jamie
(il) Warner, S. Only Emma   **Fic**

The **harps** of Heaven. Babbitt, N.
In Babbitt, N. The Devil's storybook p21-35   **S C**

Harpster, Steve
(il) Levine, S. Wonderful weather   **551.5**

Harrah, Madge
Blind Boone (5 and up)   **92**

Harriet and the Promised Land. Lawrence, J.   **811**

Harriet and the roller coaster. Carlson, N. L.   **E**

Harriet Beecher Stowe and the Beecher preachers. Fritz, J.   **92**

Harriet, the spy. Fitzhugh, L.   **Fic**

Harrington, Janice N.
Going north   **E**

Hawaii
Doak, R. S. Hawaii
In World Almanac Library of the States series
973

Hintz, M. Hawaii
In America the beautiful, second series
973

Fiction
Guback, G. Luka's quilt **E**
Kono, E. E. Hula lullaby **E**
Rattigan, J. K. Dumpling soup **E**
Salisbury, G. Lord of the deep (5 and up)
Fic

Slepian, J. The Broccoli tapes (5 and up)
Fic

Folklore
See Folklore—Hawaii

History
Stanley, F. The last princess: the story of Princess Ka'iulani of Hawai'i (4 and up) **92**

Hawass, Zahi A.
Curse of the pharaohs (5 and up) **932**
Tutankhamun (3-6) **932**

Hawes, Louise
Willem de Kooning (2-4) **92**

Hawk, I'm your brother. Baylor, B. **E**

Hawkes, Kevin
(il) Anderson, M. T. Handel, who knew what he liked **92**
(il) Bauer, M. D. Jason's bears **E**
(il) Bertrand, L. Granite baby **E**
(il) A Christmas treasury. See A Christmas treasury **808.8**
(il) Fleischman, P. Sidewalk circus **E**
(il) Fleischman, P. Weslandia **E**
(il) Ibbotson, E. Dial-a-ghost **Fic**
(il) Ibbotson, E. The haunting of Granite Falls **Fic**
(il) Ibbotson, E. Journey to the river sea **Fic**
(il) Ibbotson, E. The star of Kazan **Fic**
(il) Lasky, K. The librarian who measured the earth [biography of Eratosthenes] **92**
(il) Lasky, K. The man who made time travel **526**
(il) Lasky, K. Marven of the Great North Woods **E**
(il) Pullman, P. I was a rat! **Fic**

Hawkins, Benjamin Waterhouse
About
Kerley, B. The dinosaurs of Waterhouse Hawkins (3-5) **92**

Hawks
Mudd-Ruth, M. Hawks & falcons (3-6) **598**
Fiction
Baylor, B. Hawk, I'm your brother **E**

Hawks & falcons. Mudd-Ruth, M. **598**

Hawthorne, Nathaniel
Lady Eleanore's mantle; adaptation. See San Souci, R. Lady Eleanore's mantle

Hayashi, Nancy
(il) Spinelli, E. I know it's autumn **E**
(il) Spinelli, E. Wanda's monster **E**

Haycock, Ken
Neal-Schuman authoritative guide to kids' search engines, subject directories, and portals
025.04

Hayden, Kate
Horse show (1-3) **798.2**

Hayes, Ann
Meet the orchestra (k-3) **784.2**

Hayes, Joe
Little Gold Star (k-3) **398.2**
A spoon for every bite **E**

Hays, Anna Jane
Ready, set, preschool! **E**

Hays, Michael
(il) Schmandt-Besserat, D. The history of counting **513**
(il) Seeger, P. Abiyoyo **398.2**
(il) Taylor, M. D. The gold Cadillac **Fic**

The **Haystack** Cricket and how things are different up in the moon towns. Sandburg, C.
In Sandburg, C. More Rootabaga stories p113-18 **S C**
also in Sandburg, C. The Sandburg treasury; prose and poetry for young people p139-42 **818**

Haywood, Karen Diane
Georgia
In It's my state! [series] **973**

Hazardous waste sites
See also Love Canal Chemical Waste Landfill (Niagara Falls, N.Y.)

Hazen, Barbara Shook
Digby **E**
Katie's wish **E**

The **HBJ** student thesaurus. See The Harcourt Brace student thesaurus **423**

He is risen: the Easter story. Winthrop, E.
232.9

He Lion, Bruh Bear and Bruh Rabbit. Hamilton, V.
In Hamilton, V. The people could fly; American black folktales p5-12 **398.2**

He no be keeper for him brother. Graham, L. B.
In Graham, L. B. How God fix Jonah p29-33 **398.2**

He will go fearless. Lawlor, L. **Fic**

He Zhihong
(il) Gower, C. Long-Long's New Year **E**

Head, body, legs. Paye, W.-L. **398.2**

Head, shoulders, knees, and toes. Newcome, Z.
E

The **headless** cupid. Snyder, Z. K. **Fic**

The **Headless** Horseman rides tonight. Prelutsky, J.
811

The **headrest.** San Souci, R.
In San Souci, R. More short & shivery; thirty terrifying tales p130-33 **398.2**

Heads of state
See also Kings and rulers; Presidents; Prime ministers

Heads or tails. Gantos, J. **Fic**

Heale, Jay
Democratic Republic of the Congo (5 and up)
967.51
Poland (5 and up) **943.8**
Portugal (5 and up) **946.9**
Tanzania (5 and up) **967.8**
The **healing** truth. Lay, K.
In A Glory of unicorns p145-62 **S C**
Health
> *See also* Hygiene; Physical fitness

Miller, E. The monster health book (2-4)
613.7
Health alert [series]
Bjorklund, R. Asthma **616.2**
Bjorklund, R. Food-borne illnesses **615.9**
Brill, M. T. Alzheimer's disease **616.8**
Haney, J. Juvenile diabetes **616.4**
Hicks, T. A. Allergies **616.97**
Hoffmann, G. Mononucleosis **616.9**
Roy, J. R. Depression **616.85**
Health care *See* Medical care
Health issues [series]
Lennard-Brown, S. Asthma **616.2**
Wiltshire, P. Dyslexia **616.85**
Health matters [series]
Baldwin, C. Asthma **616.2**
Baldwin, C. Autism **616.89**
Baldwin, C. Sickle cell disease **616.1**
Health watch [series]
Burnett, G. L. Muscular dystrophy **616.7**
Gold, J. C. Cerebral palsy **616.8**
Gold, S. D. Attention deficit disorder **616.85**
Gold, S. D. Bipolar disorder and depression
616.89
Gold, S. D. Cystic fibrosis **616.3**
Gold, S. D. Multiple sclerosis **616.8**
Gold, S. D. Sickle cell disease **616.1**
Semple, C. M. Diabetes **616.4**
The **healthy** body cookbook. D'Amico, J.
641.5
Heap, Sue
What shall we play? **E**
(il) Eilenberg, M. Cowboy Kid **E**
Hear that train whistle blow!. Meltzer, M.
385.09
Hear the wind blow. Hahn, M. D. **Fic**
Hear your heart. Showers, P. **612.1**
Heard, Georgia
(ed) This place I know. See This place I know
811.008
Hearing
Farndon, J. Sound and hearing (3-6) **534**
Simon, S. Eyes and ears (4 and up) **612.8**
Hearing impaired
> *See also* Deaf

Hearn, Diane Dawson
(il) Levinson, N. S. Death Valley **577.5**
(il) Levinson, N. S. North Pole, South Pole
998
Hearn, Lafcadio
The old woman and her dumpling
In Womenfolk and fairy tales p44-50
398.2

The old woman and her dumpling; adaptation.
See Mosel, A. The funny little woman
398.2
Hearne, Betsy Gould
Choosing books for children **028.5**
Seven brave women **E**
Who's in the hall? **E**
Heart
Showers, P. Hear your heart (k-3) **612.1**
Simon, S. The heart (4 and up) **612.1**
Heart and soul: the story of Florence Nightingale.
Gorrell, G. K. **92**
Heart attack *See* Heart diseases
Heart diseases
Burnett, G. L. Muscular dystrophy (4 and up)
616.7
Heart of a tiger. Arnold, M. D. **E**
Heart to heart (5 and up) **811.008**
Heartbeat. Creech, S. **Fic**
Hearts, cupids, and red roses. Barth, E.
394.26
Heat
Gardner, R. Really hot science projects with
temperature (3-6) **536**
Poetry
Singer, M. Central heating (4 and up) **811**
Heat. Lupica, M. **Fic**
Heaven. Johnson, A. **Fic**
Heaven Eyes. Almond, D. **Fic**
The **heavenly** court. Schwartz, H.
In Schwartz, H. A journey to paradise and
other Jewish tales p24-25 **398.2**
Heavy-duty science projects with weight. Gardner,
R. **530.8**
Hebrew language
Groner, J. S. My first Hebrew word book (k-2)
492.4
Heckedy Peg. Wood, A. **E**
Hedgehogs
Fiction
Brett, J. The hat **E**
Potter, B. The tale of Mrs. Tiggy-Winkle **E**
The **Hedley** Kow. Jacobs, J.
In Jacobs, J. English fairy tales p271-74
398.2
Hegi, Ursula
Trudi & Pia **E**
Hehner, Barbara
First on the moon (4 and up) **629.45**
Ice Age cave bear (5 and up) **569**
Ice Age mammoth (5 and up) **569**
Ice Age sabertooth (5 and up) **569**
(jt. auth) Bierman, C. Journey to Ellis Island
325.73
Heide, Florence Parry
The day of Ahmed's secret **E**
Sami and the time of the troubles **E**
The shrinking of Treehorn (2-5) **Fic**
also in You read to me & I'll read to you;
20th-century stories to share p56-65
E
Some things are scary **E**

Heidi. Spyri, J.   **Fic**

The **Heifer** hide
  In The Jack tales p161-71   **398.2**

Height, Dorothy I., 1912-
See/See also pages in the following book(s):
  Pinkney, A. D. Let it shine (4 and up)   **920**

Heiligman, Deborah
  From caterpillar to butterfly (k-1)   **595.7**
  High hopes [biography of John F. Kennedy] (4
    and up)   **92**
  Honeybees (k-3)   **595.7**
  The New York Public Library kid's guide to re-
    search (5 and up)   **025.5**

Heilman, Carl
  (il) Weber, S. Two in the wilderness   **508**

Heinemann, Sue
  The New York Public Library amazing women
    in American history (5 and up)   **305.4**

Heinlen, Marieka
  (il) Verdick, E. Words are not for hurting
                                          177

Heinrichs, Ann
  Australia (5 and up)   **994**
  Brazil (5 and up)   **981**
  California
    In America the beautiful, second series
                                          973
  Florida
    In America the beautiful, second series
                                          973
  Indiana
    In America the beautiful, second series
                                          973
  Japan (5 and up)   **952**
  New York
    In America the beautiful, second series
                                          973
  Ohio
    In America the beautiful, second series
                                          973
  Pennsylvania
    In America the beautiful, second series
                                          973
  Texas
    In America the beautiful, second series
                                          973
  The Underground Railroad (2-4)   **326**
  Vermont
    In America the beautiful, second series
                                          973

Hekeke. San Souci, R.
  In San Souci, R. Cut from the same cloth;
    American women of myth, legend, and
    tall tale p103-09   **398.2**

Helbig, Alethea
  Dictionary of American children's fiction, 1995-
    1999   **028.5**
  Many peoples, one land   **016.8**

Helen Keller: rebellious spirit. Lawlor, L.   **92**

The **Helen** Oxenbury nursery collection (k-3)
                                           398.8

Helfer, Ralph
  The world's greatest elephant (1-3)   **791.3**

Helicopters
  Englart, M. R. Helicopters (2-4)   **629.133**

Hellard, Susan
  (il) McAllister, A. Take a kiss to school   **E**

Helldorfer, Mary Claire
  Hog music   **E**

Heller, Julek
  (il) Mayer, M. Women warriors   **398.2**

Heller, Lora
  Sign language for kids (3-6)   **419**

Heller, Ruth
  Behind the mask (k-2)   **428**
  A cache of jewels and other collective nouns
    (k-2)   **428**
  Chickens aren't the only ones (k-1)   **591.4**
  Fantastic! wow! and unreal! (k-2)   **428**
  Kites sail high: a book about verbs (k-2)
                                          428
  Many luscious lollipops: a book about adjectives
    (k-2)   **428**
  Merry-go-round (k-2)   **428**
  Mine, all mine (k-2)   **428**
  Up, up and away (k-2)   **428**
  (il) Climo, S. The Egyptian Cinderella   **398.2**
  (il) Climo, S. The Korean Cinderella   **398.2**
  (il) Creasy, R. Blue potatoes, orange tomatoes
                                          635
  (il) Merriam-Webster's primary dictionary. See
    Merriam-Webster's primary dictionary   **423**

Hello Benny! What it's like to be a baby. Harris,
  R. H.   **612.6**

Hello! good-bye!. Aliki   **395**

The **hello**, goodbye window. Juster, N.   **E**

Hello, hello!. Schlein, M.   **E**

Hello, Kate!. Schwartz, A.
  In Schwartz, A. Scary stories 3; more tales to
    chill your bones p15-16   **398.2**

Hello, my name is Scrambled Eggs. Gilson, J.
                                           Fic

Hello, snow!. Vestergaard, H.   **E**

Hello sunshine, good night moonlight (k-3)
                                           811.008

Hello world!. Stojic, M.   **413**

Hellweg, Paul
  The American Heritage children's thesaurus
    (4-6)   **423**

Help! I'm a prisoner in the library. Clifford, E.
                                           Fic

Helquist, Brett
  (il) Balliett, B. Chasing Vermeer   **Fic**
  (il) Howe, J. It came from beneath the bed!
                                          Fic
  (il) Snicket, L. The bad beginning   **Fic**

A **hen,** a chick, and a string guitar. MacDonald,
  M. R.   **398.2**

Hen and Frog. Bryan, A.
  In Bryan, A. Ashley Bryan's African tales,
    uh-huh p43-53   **398.2**

Henderson, Douglas
  Asteroid impact (3-5)   **567.9**

Henderson, Kathy
  Baby knows best   **E**
  Lugalbanda: **398.2**

Herbert, Janis
The American Revolution for kids (4-6)
973.3

Herbie Jones. Kline, S. **Fic**

Herbst, Judith
The history of transportation (5 and up) **388**

Hercegovina *See* Bosnia and Hercegovina

Hercules (Legendary character)
Burleigh, R. Hercules (3-6) **292**
Harris, J. Strong stuff (4 and up) **398.2**
McCaughrean, G. Hercules (5 and up) **292**
See/See also pages in the following book(s):
Colum, P. The Golden Fleece and the heroes
who lived before Achilles (5 and up) **292**
Hamilton, E. Mythology (5 and up) **292**

Herd, Richard
About
Grace, C. O. Forces of nature (4 and up)
551.2

Here comes Grandma!. Lord, J. **E**

Here comes Kate. Chorao, K. **E**

Here comes McBroom!. Fleischman, S. **Fic**

Here comes Mother Goose **398.8**

Here comes the strikeout. Kessler, L. P. **E**

Here is the African savanna. Dunphy, M.
577.4

Here there be dragons. Yolen, J. **810.8**

Here today. Martin, A. M. **Fic**

Here we all are. De Paola, T. **92**

Hereafterthis. Jacobs, J.
In Jacobs, J. English fairy tales p230-33
398.2

Heredity
Gallant, R. A. The treasure of inheritance (5 and
up) **576.5**

Hergé
The adventures of Tintin, vol. 1 (4 and up)
741.5

Herman, Gail
Cal Ripken, Jr. (1-3) **92**

Herman, R. A. (Ronnie Ann)
Gomer & Little Gomer **E**

Hermes, Patricia
Emma Dilemma and the new nanny (2-4)
Fic
Summer secrets (5 and up) **Fic**

Hermit crabs *See* Crabs

Hernandez, Romel
Trinidad & Tobago (4 and up) **972.983**

Hernández de la Cruz, Maria
(il) Endredy, J. The journey of Tunuri and the
Blue Deer **398.2**

Hernandez-Divers, Sonia
Geckos (3-6) **639.3**

A **hero** and the holocaust: the story of Janusz
Korczak and his children. Adler, D. A.
92

The **hero** and the minotaur. Byrd, R. **398.2**

The **hero** Beowulf. Kimmel, E. A. **398.2**

The **hero** of Bremen. Hodges, M. **398.2**

Herobear and the Kid, vol. 1: The Inheritance.
Kunkel, M. **741.5**

Heroes. Mochizuki, K. **E**

Heroes [series]
McCaughrean, G. Hercules **292**
McCaughrean, G. Odysseus **292**
McCaughrean, G. Perseus **292**

Heroes and heroines
Mayer, M. Women warriors (5 and up)
398.2
Fiction
McLeod, B. SuperHero ABC **E**

Heroes of American History [series]
Ford, C. T. Jackie Robinson **92**

Heroes of baseball. Lipsyte, R. **796.357**

Heroine of the Titanic: the real unsinkable Molly
Brown. Landau, E. **92**

Heroines *See* Heroes and heroines

Heroism *See* Courage

Herold, Maggie Rugg
A very important day **E**

Heron and Hummingbird. Curry, J. L.
In Curry, J. L. The wonderful sky boat and
other Native American tales of the
Southeast p47-50 **398.2**

Herons
Fiction
Avi. Blue heron (5 and up) **Fic**
Ramirez, A. Napi **E**

Herrera, Juan Felipe
Laughing out loud, I fly **811**
The upside down boy (k-3) **92**

Herrera, Juan Felipe, 1948-
About
Herrera, J. F. The upside down boy (k-3)
92

Hershel and the Hanukkah goblins. Kimmel, E. A.
E

Hershel and the nobleman. Jaffe, N.
In Jaffe, N. and Zeitlin, S. J. While standing
on one foot; puzzle stories and wisdom
tales from the Jewish tradition p56-61
296.1

Hershel goes to heaven. Kimmel, E. A.
In Kimmel, E. A. The adventures of Hershel
of Ostropol p61-62 **398.2**

Hershele and Hanukkah. Singer, I. B.
In Singer, I. B. The power of light; eight stories for Hanukkah p63-72 **S C**
also in Singer, I. B. Stories for children p184-
93 **S C**

Herxheimer, Sophie
(il) Clayton, S. P. Tales told in tents **398.2**

Herzegovina *See* Bosnia and Hercegovina

Herzog, George
(jt. auth) Courlander, H. Cow-tail switch, and
other West African stories **398.2**

He's got the whole world in his hands. Nelson, K.
782.25

Heslop, Michael
(il) Cooper, S. The grey king **Fic**

Hess, Debra
  Florida
    In It's my state! [series]   **973**
  The Fourth of July (4-6)   **394.26**
  The Liberty Bell (3-5)   **974.8**
  South Carolina
    In It's my state! [series]   **973**
  The Statue of Liberty (3-5)   **974.7**
  The White House (3-5)   **975.3**

Hesse, Karen
  The cats in Krasinski Square   **E**
  Come on, rain!   **E**
  Just Juice (3-5)   **Fic**
  Letters from Rifka (5 and up)   **Fic**
  A light in the storm (5 and up)   **Fic**
  Out of the dust (5 and up)   **Fic**
  Sable (2-4)   **Fic**
  Stowaway (5 and up)   **Fic**
  Witness (6 and up)   **Fic**
  The young Hans Christian Andersen (2-4)
    92

Hest, Amy
  The Friday nights of Nana   **E**
  Guess who, Baby Duck!   **E**
  Kiss good night   **E**
  Mr. George Baker   **E**
  The purple coat   **E**
  When Jessie came across the sea   **E**

Hester, Denia
  Grandma Lena's big ol' turnip   **E**

Hestler, Anna
  Yemen (5 and up)   **953.3**

Hettinga, Donald R.
  The Brothers Grimm (5 and up)   **92**

Heuser, Randy
  (jt. auth) Kunkel, M. Land of Sokmunster
    741.5

Hewett, Richard
  (il) Arnold, C. The ancient cliff dwellers of
    Mesa Verde   **970.004**
  (il) Arnold, C. Dinosaur mountain   **567.9**
  (il) Arnold, C. Dinosaurs all around   **567.9**
  (il) Arnold, C. Stories in stone   **709.01**

Hewitson, Jennifer
  (il) Wong, J. S. The rainbow hand   **811**

Hewitt, Kathryn
  (il) Bunting, E. Flower garden   **E**
  (il) Krull, K. Lives of extraordinary women
    920
  (il) Krull, K. Lives of the athletes   **920**
  (il) Krull, K. Lives of the musicians   **920**
  (il) Krull, K. Lives of the presidents   **920**
  (il) Krull, K. Lives of the writers   **920**

Hewitt, Sally
  Solid, liquid, or gas? (k-3)   **530.4**

Hewitt Anderson's great big life. Nolen, J.   **E**

Hey, Al. Yorinks, A.   **E**

Hey, frog!. Grobler, P.   **E**

Hey! listen to this   **028.5**

Hey, pancakes!. Weston, T.   **E**

Heyer, Carol
  (il) O'Malley, K. Once upon a cool motorcycle
    dude   **E**

Heyman, Ken
  (il) Morris, A. Bread, bread, bread   **641.8**
  (il) Morris, A. Hats, hats, hats   **391**

Heyward, DuBose
  The country bunny and the little gold shoes
    E

Hi, cat!. Keats, E. J.   **E**

Hi, Harry!. Waddell, M.   **E**

Hiaasen, Carl
  Flush (5 and up)   **Fic**
  Hoot (5 and up)   **Fic**

Hiawatha. Longfellow, H. W.   **811**

Hibernation
        Fiction
  Fleming, D. Time to sleep   **E**

Hickman, Pamela M.
  Animals and their mates (3-5)   **591.56**
  Animals and their young (3-5)   **591.56**
  Animals in motion (3-5)   **591.47**

Hickox, Rebecca
  The golden sandal (k-3)   **398.2**

Hicks, Barbara Jean
  Jitterbug jam   **E**

Hicks, Betty
  Busted! (5 and up)   **Fic**
  Out of order (4-6)   **Fic**

Hicks, Terry Allan
  Allergies (4 and up)   **616.97**
  Nevada
    In It's my state! [series]   **973**
  New Hampshire
    In It's my state! [series]   **973**

The **hidden** alphabet. Seeger, L. V.   **E**

Hidden child. Millman, I.   **940.53**

The **hidden** children. Greenfeld, H.   **940.53**

The **hidden** folk. Lunge-Larsen, L.   **398.2**

Hidden worlds: looking through a scientist's microscope. Kramer, S.   **502.8**

Hide and seek. Vos, I.   **Fic**

Hide and seek fog. Tresselt, A. R.   **E**

Hidier, Tanuja Desai *See* Desai Hidier, Tanuja

Hiding from the Nazis. Adler, D. A.   **940.53**

Hiding to survive. Rosenberg, M. B.   **940.53**

Hiera. Mayer, M.
  In Mayer, M. Women warriors; myths and legends of heroic women p27-29   **398**

Hieroglyphics
  Coulter, L. Secrets in stone   **497**
  Donoughue, C. The mystery of the hieroglyphs (4 and up)   **493**
  Giblin, J. The riddle of the Rosetta Stone (5 and up)   **493**
  Rumford, J. Seeker of knowledge [biography of Jean François Champollion] (3-5)   **92**

Higglety pigglety pop!. Sendak, M.   **Fic**

High, Linda Oatman
  Barn savers   **E**
  The girl on the high-diving horse   **E**

High as a hawk. Barron, T. A.   **E**

High Elk's treasure. Sneve, V. D. H.   **Fic**

High hopes [biography of John F. Kennedy]
Heiligman, D. **92**
High John the Conqueror, The adventures of.
Sanfield, S. **398.2**
The **high** king. Alexander, L. **Fic**
High-rise private eyes [series]
Rylant, C. The case of the missing monkey
E

High school libraries
See also Young adults' libraries
High tech *See* Technology
High Walker. Thomas, J. C.
In Thomas, J. C. The skull talks back and
other haunting tales **398.2**
A **higher** truth. Jaffe, N.
In Jaffe, N. and Zeitlin, S. J. The cow of no
color: riddle stories and justice tales from
around the world p110-13 **398.2**
Highways *See* Roads
Hiiaka. San Souci, R.
In San Souci, R. Cut from the same cloth;
American women of myth, legend, and
tall tale p121-28 **398.2**
Hijuelos, Oscar
Christmas fantasy
In You're on!: seven plays in English and
Spanish p108-31 **812.008**
Hiking
See also Walking
Weber, S. Two in the wilderness (4 and up)
508
Hilda must be dancing. Wilson, K. **E**
Hildebrandt, Ziporah
This is our Seder (k-3) **296.4**
Hill, Barbara W.
Cooking the English way
In Easy menu ethnic cookbooks **641.5**
Hill, Christine M.
Robert Ballard (5 and up) **92**
Hill, Douglas
Witches & magic-makers (4 and up) **133.4**
Hill, Elizabeth Starr
Bird Boy (2-4) **Fic**
Chang and the bamboo flute (3-5) **Fic**
Hill, Kim
About
Batten, M. Anthropologist: scientist of the peo-
ple (4 and up) **301**
Hill, Kirkpatrick
The year of Miss Agnes (3-5) **Fic**
Hill, Susan
Ruby bakes a cake **E**
Hill, Susanna Leonard
Punxsutawney Phyllis **E**
Hill Hawk Hattie. Clark, C. G. **Fic**
Hillary, Sir Edmund
About
Brennan, K. Sir Edmund Hillary, modern day
explorer (4 and up) **92**
Coburn, B. Triumph on Everest: a
photobiography of Sir Edmund Hillary (4 and
up) **92**

See/See also pages in the following book(s):
Krull, K. Lives of the athletes (4 and up)
920

Hillel the Wise. Jaffe, N.
In Jaffe, N. and Zeitlin, S. J. While standing
on one foot; puzzle stories and wisdom
tales from the Jewish tradition p91-95
296.1
Hillenbrand, Will
Down by the station (k-2) **782.42**
Fiddle-i-fee (k-3) **782.42**
(il) Cuyler, M. The bumpy little pumpkin **E**
(il) Doyle, M. One, two, three O'Leary **E**
(il) Hickox, R. The golden sandal **398.2**
(il) Root, P. Kiss the cow **E**
(il) Sierra, J. Preschool to the rescue **E**
(il) This little piggy. See This little piggy
398.8
(il) Wooldridge, C. N. Wicked Jack **398.2**
Hills, Tad
Duck & Goose **E**
Himalaya. Neale, J. **Fic**
Himalaya Mountains
Fiction
Neale, J. Himalaya (5 and up) **Fic**
Tenzing Norbu. Secret of the snow leopard
E
Himelblau, Linda
The trouble begins (4 and up) **Fic**
Himler, Ronald
(il) Adler, D. A. A picture book of Samuel Adams **92**
(il) Bunting, E. Fly away home **E**
(il) Bunting, E. Someday a tree **E**
(il) Bunting, E. Train to Somewhere **E**
(il) Bunting, E. The Wall **E**
(il) Coerr, E. Sadako and the thousand paper
cranes [biography of Sadako Sasaki] **92**
(il) Cohen, M. My big brother **E**
(il) Fritz, J. Why not, Lafayette? **92**
(il) Kroll, S. William Penn **92**
(il) Lawlor, L. The school at Crooked Creek
Fic
(il) Newman, L. The best cat in the world
E
(il) Scheer, J. A Thanksgiving turkey **E**
(il) Sneve, V. D. H. The Apaches **970.004**
(il) Sneve, V. D. H. The Cherokees **970.004**
(il) Sneve, V. D. H. The Cheyennes
970.004
(il) Sneve, V. D. H. The Hopis **970.004**
(il) Sneve, V. D. H. The Navajos **970.004**
(il) Sneve, V. D. H. The Nez Percé **970.004**
(il) Sneve, V. D. H. The Seminoles **970.004**
(il) Turner, A. W. Nettie's trip South **Fic**
(il) Wright, B. R. The blizzard **E**
Himmelman, John
Frog in a bog **E**
A pill bug's life (k-2) **595.3**
Hindenburg (Airship)
O'Brien, P. The Hindenburg (4 and up)
629.133
Hindley, Judy
Baby talk **E**
Do like a duck does! **E**

Hirschi, Ron
  Searching for grizzlies (3-5)   **599.78**
Hirschmann, Kris
  Lice (4-6)   **616.5**
  Montana
  In World Almanac Library of the States series
     973
  Pollution (5 and up)   **363.7**
  Solar energy (5 and up)   **333.79**
  South Dakota
  In World Almanac Library of the States series
     973
  Utah
  In World Almanac Library of the States series
     973
Hiscock, Bruce
  The big rivers (2-4)   **551.48**
  (il) Swinburne, S. R. Turtle tide   **597.92**
  (il) Swinburne, S. R. Wings of light   **595.7**
Hispanic American poetry *See* American poetry—Hispanic American authors
Hispanic Americans
  Wáchale! poetry and prose on growing up
    Latino in America (5 and up)   **810.8**
       Biography
  Winter, J. Beisbol! Latino baseball pioneers and
    legends (3-6)   **920**
       Drama
  You're on!: seven plays in English and Spanish
    (4 and up)   **812.008**
       Fiction
  Abraham, S. G. Cecilia's year (4 and up)
     Fic
  Dorros, A. Abuela   **E**
  Garza, C. L. Family pictures   **E**
  Griessman, A. The fire   **E**
  Hayes, J. A spoon for every bite   **E**
  Marcantonio, P. S. Red ridin' in the hood (3-5)
     S C
  Soto, G. Taking sides (5 and up)   **Fic**
  Weller, F. W. The day the animals came   **E**
       Folklore
  Hayes, J. Little Gold Star (k-3)   **398.2**
  Kimmel, E. A. The runaway tortilla (k-3)
     398.2
  San Souci, R. Little Gold Star (2-4)   **398.2**
       Poetry
  Argueta, J. A movie in my pillow (3-6)   **861**
  Love to mamá (3-6)   **811.008**
  Soto, G. Neighborhood odes (4-6)   **811**
       Social life and customs
  Ancona, G. Fiesta U.S.A. (k-3)   **394.26**
  Hoyt-Goldsmith, D. Las Posadas (3-5)
     394.26
  Pavon, A.-E. 25 Latino craft projects   **027.62**
Historic buildings
  See also Literary landmarks
Historic sites
       Fiction
  Parker, T. T. Sienna's scrapbook (3-5)   **Fic**
Historical chronology
  Tomaselli-Moschovitis, V. Junior timelines on
    file   **902**

History
  See also Military history; World history
       Bibliography
  Adamson, L. G. Literature connections to world
    history, K-6   **016.9**
  From biography to history   **016.8**
       Miscellanea
  Blackwood, G. L. Enigmatic events (4 and up)
     904
       Study and teaching
  Johnson, M. Primary sources in the library
     027.8
History in art [series]
  Anderson, D. Ancient China   **709.51**
  Barber, N. Islamic empires   **704**
  Chrisp, P. Ancient Rome   **709.37**
  January, B. Native Americans   **709.7**
  Langley, A. Ancient Egypt   **932**
  Langley, A. Ancient Greece   **709.38**
History maker bios [series]
  Waxman, L. H. Colin Powell   **92**
The **history** of counting. Schmandt-Besserat, D.
     513
The **history** of everyday life. Landau, E.   **609**
The **history** of food. Jango-Cohen, J.   **641.3**
The **History** of Jack the giant killer
  In The Blue fairy book p374-79   **398.2**
History of space exploration [series]
  Kerrod, R. Space probes   **629.43**
  Kerrod, R. Space shuttles   **629.44**
  Kerrod, R. Space stations   **629.44**
The **history** of the Internet. Sherman, J.   **004.6**
The **history** of the personal computer. Sherman, J.
     004
The **history** of Tom Thumb. Jacobs, J.
  In Jacobs, J. English fairy tales p140-46
     398.2
The **history** of transportation. Herbst, J.   **388**
A **history** of US. Hakim, J.   **973**
The **History** of Whittington
  In The Blue fairy book p206-13   **398.2**
Hitchcock, Sue
  (il) Beames, M. Night cat   **E**
Hitty: her first hundred years. Field, R.   **Fic**
Hitz, Demi *See* Demi, 1942-
HIV disease *See* AIDS (Disease)
Hmong (Asian people)
  Cha, D. Dia's story cloth (3-5)   **305.8**
       Fiction
  Brown, J. Little Cricket (4-6)   **Fic**
       Folklore
  Blia Xiong. Nine-in-one, Grr! Grr! (k-2)
     398.2
Ho, Minfong
  Hush!   **E**
  Peek!   **E**
The **Ho-Shih** jade. Fang, L.
  In Fang, L. The Ch'i-lin purse; a collection of
    ancient Chinese stories p39-50   **398.2**
Hoang Anh. Hoyt-Goldsmith, D.   **305.8**
Hoare, Ben
  Temperate grasslands (5 and up)   **577.4**

Hoban, Lillian
Arthur's Christmas cookies — E
Silly Tilly's Thanksgiving dinner — E
(il) Hurwitz, J. Rip-roaring Russell — Fic

Hoban, Russell
Bedtime for Frances — E

Hoban, Tana
26 letters and 99 cents — E
Black on white — E
A children's zoo — E
Colors everywhere — E
Construction zone (k-2) — 621.8
Dots, spots, speckles, and stripes — E
Exactly the opposite — E
I read signs (k-2) — 659.1
Is it larger? Is it smaller? — E
Is it red? Is it yellow? Is it blue? — E
Is it rough? Is it smooth? Is it shiny? — E
Let's count — E
Look book — E
Of colors and things — E
Over, under & through, and other spatial concepts — E
Shadows and reflections — E
Shapes, shapes, shapes — E
So many circles, so many squares — E
White on black — E
See/See also pages in the following book(s):
Marcus, L. S. Ways of telling — 741.6

The **hobbit,** or, There and back again. Tolkien, J. R. R. — Fic

Hobbs, Dan
(il) Bowers, V. Wow Canada! — 971

Hobbs, Valerie
Defiance (5 and up) — Fic
Sheep (3-5) — Fic

Hobbs, Will
Jackie's Wild Seattle (5 and up) — Fic
Jason's gold (5 and up) — Fic
Kokopelli's flute (5 and up) — Fic

Hoberman, Mary Ann
Bill Grogan's goat (k-3) — 782.42
The eensy-weensy spider (k-3) — 782.42
Mary had a little lamb (k-2) — 782.42
Miss Mary Mack — 398.8
There once was a man named Michael Finnegan (k-3) — 782.42
The two sillies — E
You read to me, I'll read to you [very short fairy tales to read together] — E
[very short Mother Goose tales to read together] (k-3) — 811
[very short stories to read together] (k-3) — 811

Hoboes *See* Tramps

The **Hoboken** chicken emergency. Pinkwater, D. M. — Fic

The **Hobyahs.** Jacobs, J.
In Jacobs, J. English fairy tales p336-42 — 398.2

The **Hobyahs.** MacDonald, M. R.
In MacDonald, M. R. When the lights go out; twenty scary tales to tell p96-103 — 372.6

Hoce, Charley
Beyond Old MacDonald (k-3) — 811

Hockey
Etue, E. Hayley Wickenheiser (4 and up) — 92
Foley, M. Fundamental hockey (5 and up) — 796.962
Kennedy, M. Ice hockey (4 and up) — 796.962
Thomas, K. How hockey works (3-6) — 796.962

Hocus pocus: magic you can do. Broekel, R. — 793.8

Hodge, Susie
Pablo Picasso (4 and up) — 92

Hodges, C. Walter
(il) Serraillier, I. The silver sword — Fic

Hodges, Margaret
The boy who drew cats (k-3) — 398.2
Dick Whittington and his cat (k-3) — 398.2
Excalibur
In Hodges, M. and Malory, Sir T. Merlin and the making of the king — 398.2
Gulliver in Lilliput (3-6) — Fic
The hero of Bremen (3-5) — 398.2
Joan of Arc (2-4) — 92
The kitchen knight (3-6) — 398.2
The Lady of the Lake
In Hodges, M. and Malory, Sir T. Merlin and the making of the king — 398.2
Merlin and the making of the king (3-6) — 398.2
Saint George and the dragon (2-5) — 398.2
The sword in the stone
In Hodges, M. and Malory, Sir T. Merlin and the making of the king — 398.2

Hodges, Sarah Margaret *See* Hodges, Margaret

Hoestlandt, Jo
Star of fear, star of hope — E

Hoeye, Michael
Time stops for no mouse (5 and up) — Fic

Hofer, Ernst
(il) Setterington, K. The wild swans — Fic

Hofer, Nelly
(il) Setterington, K. The wild swans — Fic

Hoff, Syd
Danny and the dinosaur — E
Oliver — E
Sammy the seal — E
(il) Schwartz, A. I saw you in the bathtub, and other folk rhymes — 398.2

Hoffman, Lawrence A.
What you will see inside a synagogue (3-6) — 296.4

Hoffman, Mary
Amazing Grace — E
Animals of the Bible (2-4) — 220.9
The color of home — E
Starring Grace (3-5) — Fic

Hoffman, Nina Kiriki
Chambers of the heart
In Swan sister; fairy tales retold **S C**

Hoffmann, E. T. A. (Ernst Theodor Amadeus)
Nutcracker (4 and up) **Fic**
The Nutcracker; adaptation. See Koppe, S. The Nutcracker **Fic**
The nutcracker and the King of Mice; adaptation. See Schulman, J. The nutcracker **Fic**

Hoffmann, Frank W. (Frank William)
(ed) Grantsmanship for small libraries and school library media centers. See Grantsmanship for small libraries and school library media centers **025.1**

Hoffmann, Gretchen
Mononucleosis (4 and up) **616.9**

Hoffmeister, Adolf
Brundibar; adaptation. See Kushner, T. Brundibar **E**

Hofmeyr, Dianne
The star-bearer (3-5) **299**

The **hog**. Philip, N.
In Philip, N. Horse hooves and chicken feet: Mexican folktales p18 **398.2**

The **hog**. Schwartz, A.
In Schwartz, A. Scary stories 3; more tales to chill your bones p80-81 **398.2**

Hog-eye. Meddaugh, S. **E**

Hog music. Helldorfer, M. C. **E**

Hogan, Sophie
(il) Watters, D. Where's Mom's hair? **616.99**

Hogrogian, Nonny
The contest (k-3) **398.2**
One fine day (k-3) **398.2**
(il) Leodhas, S. N. Always room for one more **782.42**

Hoichi the earless. San Souci, R.
In San Souci, R. A terrifying taste of short & shivery; thirty creepy tales p118-22 **398.2**

Hokusai (Katsushika Hokusai), 1760-1849
About
Ray, D. K. Hokusai (3-6) **92**
Fiction
Place, F. The old man mad about drawing (3-6) **Fic**

Holabird, Katharine
Angelina Ballerina **E**

Holbrook, Belinda
String stories **027.62**

"Hold him, Tabb!"**. San Souci, R.
In San Souci, R. More short & shivery; thirty terrifying tales p1-4 **398.2**

Hold the flag high. Clinton, C. **973.7**

Hold up the sky. Curry, J. L.
In Curry, J. L. Hold up the sky: and other Native American tales from Texas and the Southern Plains p53-55 **398.2**

Hold up the sky: and other Native American tales from Texas and the Southern Plains. Curry, J. L. **398.2**

Holdcroft, Tina
(il) Pinchuk, A. Make amazing toy and game gadgets **745.592**

Holden, Caroline
(il) The Kingfisher book of funny poems. See The Kingfisher book of funny poems **821.008**

Holes. Sachar, L. **Fic**

Holiday, Billie, 1915-1959
See/See also pages in the following book(s):
Lester, J. The blues singers (5 and up) **920**

Holiday cooking around the world
In Easy menu ethnic cookbooks **641.5**

Holiday histories [series]
Jordan, D. Juneteenth **394.26**

Holiday House reader [series]
Adler, D. A. Dr. Martin Luther King, Jr. **92**
Caple, K. The friendship tree **E**
Levinson, N. S. Death Valley **577.5**
Ruelle, K. G. The Thanksgiving beast feast **E**
Wallace, C. One nosy pup **E**
Wallace, C. Turkeys together **E**

Holidays
See also Christmas; Father's Day; Fourth of July; Kwanzaa; Memorial Day; Mother's Day; New Year; Saint Patrick's Day; Thanksgiving Day; Valentine's Day
Bauer, C. F. Celebrations p1-24 **808.8**
Chase's calendar of events **394.26**
The Folklore of world holidays **394.26**
Irvine, J. How to make holiday pop-ups (3-6) **736**
Jones, L. Kids around the world celebrate! (4-6) **394.26**
Junior worldmark encyclopedia of world holidays (5 and up) **394.26**
Kindersley, A. Celebrations (3-5) **394.26**
Moehn, H. World holidays (3-6) **394.26**
Perl, L. Piñatas and paper flowers (4 and up) **394.26**
Trawicky, B. Anniversaries and holidays **394.26**
Webb, L. S. Holidays of the world cookbook for students (5 and up) **641.5**
Bibliography
Blass, R. J. Celebrate with books **028.1**
Matthew, K. I. Neal-Schuman guide to celebrations & holidays around the world **394.26**
Poetry
Hines, A. G. Winter lights (k-3) **811**
Livingston, M. C. Celebrations **811**
Yolen, J. The three bears holiday rhyme book (k-2) **811**

Holidays, Hindu *See* Hindu holidays

Holidays, Jewish *See* Jewish holidays

Holidays of the world cookbook for students. Webb, L. S. **641.5**

Holland, Gay W.
(il) Glaser, L. Brilliant bees **595.7**
(il) Sayre, A. P. The hungry hummingbird **598**

Holland *See* Netherlands

Hollein, Max
   (jt. auth) Hollein, N. Matisse   **92**

Hollein, Nina
   Matisse (3-5)   **92**

Holling, Holling C.
   Paddle-to-the-sea (4-6)   **Fic**

Holly, reindeer, and colored lights. Barth, E.
     394.26

Hollyer, Belinda
   (comp) The Kingfisher book of family poems.
   See The Kingfisher book of family poems
     821.008

Hollywood (Calif.)
Fiction
   Leonard, E. A coyote's in the house (5 and up)
     Fic

Holm, Anne
   I am David (6 and up)   **Fic**

Holm, Jennifer L.
   Babymouse (3-5)   **741.5**
   Follow the water
    In Shelf life: stories by the book   **S C**
   My best friend
    In Friends; stories about new friends, old
    friends, and unexpectedly true friends
     S C
   Our only May Amelia (5 and up)   **Fic**

Holm, Matthew
   (jt. auth) Holm, J. L. Babymouse   **741.5**

Holm, Sharon Lane
   (il) Erlbach, A. Merry Christmas, everywhere!
     394.26
   (il) Erlbach, A. Sidewalk games around the
   world   **796.1**
   (il) Ross, K. The best birthday parties ever!
     793.2

Holocaust, 1933-1945
    See also Holocaust survivors; World War,
   1939-1945—Jews
   Adler, D. A. A hero and the holocaust: the story
   of Janusz Korczak and his children (3-5)
     92
   Adler, D. A. Hiding from the Nazis (2-4)
     940.53
   Bachrach, S. D. Tell them we remember (5 and
   up)   **940.53**
   Frank, A. The diary of a young girl (6 and up)
     92
   Frank, A. The diary of a young girl: the defini-
   tive edition (6 and up)   **92**
   Gold, A. L. Memories of Anne Frank (5 and
   up)   **92**
   Greenfeld, H. After the Holocaust (6 and up)
     940.53
   Hurwitz, J. Anne Frank: life in hiding (3-5)
     92
   Koestler-Grack, R. A. The story of Anne Frank
   (2-4)   **92**
   Leapman, M. Witnesses to war (5 and up)
     940.53
   Lee, C. A. A friend called Anne (4 and up)
     940.53

   Levine, K. Hana's suitcase (4 and up)
     940.53
   Meltzer, M. Never to forget: the Jews of the
   Holocaust (6 and up)   **940.53**
   Meltzer, M. Rescue: the story of how Gentiles
   saved Jews in the Holocaust (6 and up)
     940.53
   Mochizuki, K. Passage to freedom (3-6)
     940.53
   Poole, J. Anne Frank (2-4)   **92**
   Rol, R. v. d. Anne Frank, beyond the diary (5
   and up)   **92**
   Rubin, S. G. The cat with the yellow star (3-6)
     940.53
   Rubin, S. G. The flag with fifty-six stars (3-5)
     940.53
   Russo, M. Always remember me (3-5)
     940.53
   Sawyer, K. K. Anne Frank (5 and up)   **92**
   Talbott, H. Forging freedom (4 and up)
     940.53
   Warren, A. Surviving Hitler (5 and up)
     940.53
   Whiteman, D. B. Lonek's journey (5 and up)
     940.53
Fiction
   Ackerman, K. The night crossing (3-5)   **Fic**
   Bunting, E. One candle   **E**
   Deedy, C. A. The yellow star (3-5)   **Fic**
   Hesse, K. The cats in Krasinski Square   **E**
   Hoestlandt, J. Star of fear, star of hope   **E**
   Jung, R. Dreaming in black and white (5 and
   up)   **Fic**
   Mazer, N. F. Good night, Maman (5 and up)
     Fic
   McDonough, Y. Z. The doll with the yellow star
   (3-5)   **Fic**
   Orgel, D. The devil in Vienna (6 and up)
     Fic
   Orlev, U. The island on Bird Street (5 and up)
     Fic
   Orlev, U. The man from the other side (6 and
   up)   **Fic**
   Radin, R. Y. Escape to the forest (3-6)   **Fic**
   Rappaport, D. The secret seder (2-4)   **E**
   Roy, J. R. Yellow star (5 and up)   **Fic**
   Sachs, M. Lost in America (5 and up)   **Fic**
   Schnur, S. The shadow children (5 and up)
     Fic
   Vos, I. Anna is still here (4 and up)   **Fic**
   Vos, I. Hide and seek (4 and up)   **Fic**
Personal narratives
   Greenfeld, H. The hidden children (4 and up)
     940.53
   Holocaust memories (5 and up)   **940.53**
   Krinitz, E. N. Memories of survival (6 and up)
     940.53
   Millman, I. Hidden child (4 and up)   **940.53**
   Perl, L. Four perfect pebbles (6 and up)
     940.53
   Reiss, J. The upstairs room (5 and up)   **92**
   Rosenberg, M. B. Hiding to survive (5 and up)
     940.53
Study and teaching
   Schroeder, P. W. Six million paper clips (5 and
   up)   **940.53**

Holocaust memories (5 and up)   **940.53**

Holocaust Museum (U.S.) *See* United States Holocaust Memorial Museum

Holocaust survivors
> Greenfeld, H. After the Holocaust (6 and up)
>   **940.53**

Holt, Kimberly Willis
> Dancing in Cadillac light (5 and up)   **Fic**
> Mister and me (3-5)   **Fic**
> When Zachary Beaver came to town (5 and up)
>   **Fic**

Holtz, Eric Siegfried
> Georgia
> *In* World Almanac Library of the States series
>   **973**

Holub, Joan
> The garden that we grew   **E**
> Why do birds sing? (k-2)   **598**
> Why do cats meow? (k-2)   **636.8**
> Why do dogs bark? (k-2)   **636.7**
> Why do horses neigh? (k-2)   **636.1**
> Why do rabbits hop? (k-2)   **636.9**
> Why do snakes hiss? (k-2)   **597.96**
> (il) Horowitz, R. Breakout at the bug lab   **E**

The Holy Bible [King James Bible. Oxford Univ. Press] Bible   **220.5**

The Holy Bible: new revised standard version. Bible   **220.5**

Holy Grail *See* Grail

The holy twins: Benedict and Scholastica. Norris, K.   **92**

Holyfield, John
> (il) Smothers, E. F. The hard-times jar   **E**
> (il) Stauffacher, S. Bessie Smith and the night riders   **E**

Holyoke, Nancy
> A smart girl's guide to manners (3-6)   **395**

Holzer, Harold
> The president is shot! (5 and up)   **973.7**

Hom, Nancy
> *See/See also pages in the following book(s):*
> Just like me p2-3   **920**
> (il) Blia Xiong. Nine-in-one, Grr! Grr!   **398.2**

Home
> Ashman, L. Castles, caves, and honeycombs
>   **E**

Poetry
> Home to me (3-5)   **811.008**

Home. Baker, J.   **E**

Home among the giants. Norman, H.
> *In* Norman, H. The girl who dreamed only geese, and other tales of the Far North
>   **398.2**

Home for Navidad. Ziefert, H.   **E**

The home fronts in the Civil War. Anderson, D.
> *In* Anderson, D. World Almanac library of the Civil War [Series]   **973.7**

Home is east. Ly, M.   **Fic**

Home life *See* Family life

Home on the moon. Dyson, M. J.   **629.45**

Home run. Burleigh, R.   **E**

Home to me (3-5)   **811.008**

Home video systems
> *See also* Video recording

Homecoming. Voigt, C.   **Fic**

Homefront. Gwaltney, D.   **Fic**

Homeless bird. Whelan, G.   **Fic**

Homeless persons
> *See also* Refugees; Runaway children; Runaway teenagers; Tramps

Fiction
> Bunting, E. December   **E**
> Bunting, E. Fly away home   **E**
> Fenner, C. The king of dragons (5 and up)
>   **Fic**
> Howe, J. Dew drop dead (4-6)   **Fic**
> King, S. M. Mutt dog!   **E**
> McPhail, D. M. The teddy bear   **E**
> Neufeld, J. Almost a hero (5 and up)   **Fic**
> Spinelli, J. Maniac Magee (5 and up)   **Fic**

Homemade love. Hooks, B.   **E**

Homer

Adaptations
> Osborne, M. P. The gray-eyed goddess (4 and up)   **883**
> Osborne, M. P. The land of the dead (4 and up)
>   **883**
> Osborne, M. P. The one-eyed giant (4 and up)
>   **883**
> Osborne, M. P. Return to Ithaca (4 and up)
>   **883**
> Osborne, M. P. Sirens and sea monsters (4 and up)   **883**

Homer Price. McCloskey, R.   **Fic**

Homesick: my own story. Fritz, J.   **92**

Homosexuality
> Snow, J. E. How it feels to have a gay or lesbian parent (5 and up)   **306.8**

Fiction
> Richardson, J. And Tango makes three   **E**

Homosexuals, Female *See* Lesbians

Hondo and Fabian. McCarty, P.   **E**

Honduras
> McGaffey, L. Honduras (5 and up)   **972.83**
> Shields, C. J. Honduras (4 and up)   **972.83**

Honest pretzels. Katzen, M.   **641.5**

The honest-to-goodness truth. McKissack, P. C.
>   **E**

Honesty
> *See also* Truthfulness and falsehood

Fiction
> McKissack, P. C. The honest-to-goodness truth
>   **E**

Honey
> Micucci, C. The life and times of the honeybee (2-4)   **595.7**
> Rockwell, A. F. Honey in a hive (k-3)
>   **595.7**

Honey . . . honey . . . lion!. Brett, J.   **E**

Honey, I love. Greenfield, E.   **811**

Honey, I love, and other love poems. Greenfield, E.   **811**

Honey in a hive. Rockwell, A. F.   **595.7**

The **honey** jar. Menchú, R.   398.2

Honeybee culture *See* Beekeeping

Honeybees. Heiligman, D.   595.7

Honeyguides (Birds)
Miller, S. S. Woodpeckers, toucans, and their kin (4-6)   598
Fiction
Brett, J. Honey . . . honey . . . lion!   E

Honeysuckle house. Cheng, A.   Fic

Hong, Lily Toy
Two of everything (k-3)   398.2

Hongry catch the foolish boy. Graham, L. B.
In Graham, L. B. How God fix Jonah p61-66   398.2

Honky-tonk heroes & hillbilly angels. George-Warren, H.   920

Honoring our ancestors (3-6)   759.13

Hoobler, Dorothy
The African American family album (5 and up)   305.8
The Chinese American family album   305.8
The Cuban American family album   305.8
The German American family album (5 and up)   305.8
The Irish American family album (5 and up)   305.8
The Italian American family album (5 and up)   305.8
The Japanese American family album (5 and up)   305.8
The Jewish American family album (5 and up)   305.8
The Mexican American family album (5 and up)   305.8
The Scandinavian American family album (5 and up)   305.8
We are Americans (5 and up)   325.73

Hoobler, Thomas
(jt. auth) Hoobler, D. The African American family album   305.8
(jt. auth) Hoobler, D. The Chinese American family album   305.8
(jt. auth) Hoobler, D. The Cuban American family album   305.8
(jt. auth) Hoobler, D. The German American family album   305.8
(jt. auth) Hoobler, D. The Irish American family album   305.8
(jt. auth) Hoobler, D. The Italian American family album   305.8
(jt. auth) Hoobler, D. The Japanese American family album   305.8
(jt. auth) Hoobler, D. The Jewish American family album   305.8
(jt. auth) Hoobler, D. The Mexican American family album   305.8
(jt. auth) Hoobler, D. The Scandinavian American family album   305.8
(jt. auth) Hoobler, D. We are Americans   325.73

Hood, Robin (Legendary character) *See* Robin Hood (Legendary character)

Hoodwinked. Howard, A.   E

Hoofbeats [series]
Duey, K. Lara and the gray mare   Fic

Hoofbeats, claws, & rippled fins (3-6)   811.008

Hook, line, & seeker. Arnosky, J.   799.1

Hooks, Bell
Be boy buzz   E
Homemade love   E

Hooks, William H.
Moss gown (k-3)   398.2

Hoop kings. Smith, C. R.   811

Hoop queens. Smith, C. R.   811

Hooper, Meredith
Antarctic journal (3-6)   591.9

Hoops. Burleigh, R.   811

Hoops with Swoopes. Kuklin, S.   796.323

Hooray for ballet!. Frith, M.   792.8

Hooray for Diffendoofer Day!. Seuss, Dr.   E

Hooray for fish!. Cousins, L.   E

Hooray for Grandparent's Day. Carlson, N. L.   E

Hooray for me!. Charlip, R.   E

Hoose, Phillip M.
We were there, too! (5 and up)   973

Hoot. Hiaasen, C.   Fic

Hoover, Herbert, 1874-1964
Fiction
Ray, D. Ghost girl (5 and up)   Fic

Hoover, Lou Henry, 1874-1944
Fiction
Ray, D. Ghost girl (5 and up)   Fic

Hoover Dam (Ariz. and Nev.)
Mann, E. Hoover Dam (4 and up)   627

Hooway for Wodney Wat. Lester, H.   E

The **Hope** Bakery. Wynne-Jones, T.
In Wynne-Jones, T. Some of the kinder planets: stories p25-35   S C

Hopi Indians
Sneve, V. D. H. The Hopis (3-5)   970.004
Folklore
Bierhorst, J. Is my friend at home? (1-4)   398.2

Hopkins, Dianne McAfee
(jt. auth) Zweizig, D. Lessons from Library Power   027.8

Hopkins, Lee Bennett
Been to yesterdays: poems of a life (4 and up)   811
Days to celebrate (3-5)   051
Pass the poetry, please!   372.6
(comp) Christmas presents. See Christmas presents   811.008
(comp) Dinosaurs: poems. See Dinosaurs: poems   811.008
(comp) Extra innings. See Extra innings   811.008
(comp) Good books, good times! See Good books, good times!   811.008
(comp) Got geography! See Got geography!   811.008
(comp) Halloween howls. See Halloween howls   811.008

Hopkins, Lee Bennett—*Continued*
(comp) Hanukkah lights. See Hanukkah lights **811.008**
(comp) Home to me. See Home to me **811.008**
(comp) Lives: poems about famous Americans. See Lives: poems about famous Americans **811.008**
(comp) Marvelous math. See Marvelous math **811.008**
(comp) My America. See My America **811.008**
(comp) Oh, no! Where are my pants? and other disasters. See Oh, no! Where are my pants? and other disasters **811.008**
(comp) Opening days. See Opening days **811.008**
(comp) A Pet for me. See A Pet for me **811.008**
(comp) Sandburg, C. Rainbows are made: poems **811**
(comp) Spectacular science. See Spectacular science **811.008**
(comp) Sports! sports! sports! See Sports! sports! sports! **811.008**

Hopkins, Lee Bennett, 1938-
See/See also pages in the following book(s):
Author talk (4 and up) **028.5**

Hopkinson, Deborah
Apples to Oregon **E**
A band of angels **E**
Billy and the rebel **E**
Birdie's lighthouse (1-3) **Fic**
Fannie in the kitchen (k-3) **641.5**
From slave to soldier **E**
Girl wonder **E**
Maria's comet **E**
A packet of seeds **E**
Pioneer summer (2-4) **Fic**
Saving Strawberry Farm **E**
Shutting out the sky (5 and up) **974.7**
Sky boys **E**
Susan B. Anthony (2-4) **92**
Sweet Clara and the freedom quilt **E**
Up before daybreak **331.7**

Hopper, Edward, 1882-1967
About
Spangenburg, R. Edward Hopper (2-4) **92**

Hopper, Grace, 1906-1992
See/See also pages in the following book(s):
Thimmesh, C. Girls think of everything (5 and up) **920**

Hopscotch
Lankford, M. D. Hopscotch around the world (3-5) **796.2**

Hopscotch around the world. Lankford, M. D. **796.2**

Hopscotch love. Grimes, N. **811**

Horace. Keller, H. **E**

Horace and Morris but mostly Dolores. Howe, J. **E**

Horacek, Judy
(il) Fox, M. Where is the green sheep? **E**

Horacek, Petr
Silly Suzy Goose **E**

Horenstein, Henry
A is for—? **E**

Horn, Geoffrey
The Congress (5 and up) **328**
The presidency (5 and up) **352.23**
The Supreme Court (5 and up) **347**

A **horn** for Louis [biography of Louis Armstrong] Kimmel, E. A. **92**

Hornby, Hugh
Soccer (4 and up) **796.334**

Horning, Kathleen T.
From cover to cover **028.1**

Horning, Sandra
The giant hug **E**

Horns. Afanas´ev, A. N.
In Afanas´ev, A. N. Russian fairy tales p292-94 **398.2**

Horoscopes
See/See also pages in the following book(s):
Chahrour, J. Zap! blink! taste! think! (5 and up) **507.8**

Horowitz, Anthony
The Devil and his boy (5 and up) **Fic**
Public enemy number two (5 and up) **Fic**
Stormbreaker (5 and up) **Fic**

Horowitz, Ruth
Breakout at the bug lab **E**

Horrible Harry in room 2B. Kline, S. **Fic**

Horror fiction
Beware! (4 and up) **808.8**
Bruchac, J. Whisper in the dark (5 and up) **Fic**
Gutman, D. The million dollar strike (4-6) **Fic**
Jarvis, R. The alchemist's cat (5 and up) **Fic**
MacDonald, M. R. When the lights go out **372.6**
San Souci, R. Dare to be scared (4 and up) **S C**
San Souci, R. Double-dare to be scared: another thirteen chilling tales (4 and up) **S C**
Schwartz, A. In a dark, dark room, and other scary stories (k-2) **398.2**
Schwartz, A. More scary stories to tell in the dark (4 and up) **398.2**
Schwartz, A. Scary stories 3 (4 and up) **398.2**
Schwartz, A. Scary stories to tell in the dark (4 and up) **398.2**
Sleator, W. The beasties (6 and up) **Fic**
Stine, R. L. The haunting hour (4 and up) **S C**
Thomas, J. C. The skull talks back and other haunting tales (4 and up) **398.2**
Van Laan, N. Teeny tiny tingly tales **E**

Horse, Harry
Little Rabbit lost **E**
(il) King-Smith, D. Chewing the cud **92**

Horse & pony breeds. Ransford, S. **636.1**

Horse & pony care. Ransford, S. **636.1**

Horse and toad
> *In* The Magic orange tree, and other Haitian folktales p143-50   **398.2**

Horse crafts. Hendry, L.   **745.5**

Horse hooves and chicken feet. Philip, N.
> *In* Philip, N. Horse hooves and chicken feet: Mexican folktales p36   **398.2**

Horse hooves and chicken feet: Mexican folktales. Philip, N.   **398.2**

A **horse** named Seabiscuit. Dubowski, C. E.   **798.4**

Horse racing
> Dubowski, C. E. A horse named Seabiscuit (2-4)   **798.4**

Horse show. Hayden, K.   **798.2**

Horse show handbook for kids. Kimball, C.   **798.2**

Horse showing for kids. *See* Kimball, C. Horse show handbook for kids   **798.2**

Horse tales (4 and up)   **S C**

Horseback riding *See* Horsemanship

Horsemanship
> *See also* Rodeos
> Draper, J. My first horse and pony book (k-3)   **636.1**
> Gibbons, G. Horses! (k-3)   **636.1**
> Hayden, K. Horse show (1-3)   **798.2**
> Kimball, C. Horse show handbook for kids (4 and up)   **798.2**
> Ransford, S. The Kingfisher illustrated horse & pony encyclopedia (4 and up)   **636.1**
> Richter, J. Riding for kids (3-5)   **798.2**
> > **Fiction**
> Haas, J. Birthday pony (2-4)   **Fic**
> Haas, J. Scamper and the horse show   **E**

Horsepower. Peterson, C.   **636.1**

Horses
> Budiansky, S. The world according to horses (4 and up)   **636.1**
> Draper, J. My first horse and pony book (k-3)   **636.1**
> Gibbons, G. Horses! (k-3)   **636.1**
> Hendry, L. Horse crafts (4-6)   **745.5**
> Holub, J. Why do horses neigh? (k-2)   **636.1**
> Jeffrey, L. S. Horses (3-5)   **636.1**
> Lauber, P. The true-or-false book of horses (k-3)   **636.1**
> Peterson, C. Horsepower (k-3)   **636.1**
> Peterson, C. Wild horses (3-6)   **599.66**
> Ransford, S. Horse & pony breeds (4 and up)   **636.1**
> Ransford, S. Horse & pony care (4 and up)   **636.1**
> Ransford, S. The Kingfisher illustrated horse & pony encyclopedia (4 and up)   **636.1**
> Ryden, H. Wild horses I have known (4 and up)   **599.66**
> Simon, S. Horses (2-4)   **636.1**
> > **Fiction**
> Armstrong, J. Magnus at the fire   **E**
> Bagnold, E. National Velvet (5 and up)   **Fic**
> Byars, B. C. Little Horse (1-3)   **Fic**
> Coerr, E. Chang's paper pony   **E**
> Cowley, J. Where horses run free   **E**

Duey, K. Lara and the gray mare (4-6)   **Fic**
Farley, W. The Black Stallion (4 and up)   **Fic**
Gilliland, J. H. Strange birds (3-6)   **Fic**
Haas, J. Birthday pony (2-4)   **Fic**
Haas, J. Jigsaw pony (2-4)   **Fic**
Haas, J. Runaway Radish (2-4)   **Fic**
Haas, J. Scamper and the horse show   **E**
Haas, J. Sugaring   **E**
Henry, M. Justin Morgan had a horse (4 and up)   **Fic**
Henry, M. King of the wind (4 and up)   **Fic**
Henry, M. Misty of Chincoteague (4 and up)   **Fic**
Horse tales (4 and up)   **S C**
Lawson, R. Mr. Revere and I (5 and up)   **Fic**
Lester, J. Black cowboy, wild horses   **E**
London, J. Mustang canyon   **E**
Meister, C. My pony Jack   **E**
Murphy, S. J. Same old horse   **E**
Polacco, P. Mrs. Mack   **E**
Porter, P. P. Sky (3-5)   **Fic**
Rounds, G. Once we had a horse   **E**
Sewell, A. Black Beauty (4-6)   **Fic**
Silverman, E. Cowgirl Kate and Cocoa   **E**
Wallace, B. Beauty (4-6)   **Fic**
Ward, L. K. The silver pony (2-4)   **Fic**
Wilson, D. L. I rode a horse of milk white jade (6 and up)   **Fic**

Folklore
Cohen, C. L. The mud pony (k-3)   **398.2**
Goble, P. The girl who loved wild horses (k-3)   **398.2**
Goble, P. Mystic horse (2-4)   **398.2**
Hausman, G. Horses of myth (4 and up)   **398.2**

Poetry
My kingdom for a horse (2-4)   **811.008**

Horses of myth. Hausman, G.   **398.2**

Horseshoe crabs and shorebirds. Crenson, V.   **577.7**

Hort, Lenny
> How many stars in the sky?   **E**
> The seals on the bus (k-2)   **782.42**

Horton hatches the egg. Seuss, Dr.   **E**

Horton hatches the egg. Seuss, Dr.
> *also in* You read to me & I'll read to you; 20th-century stories to share p36-55   **E**

Horton hears a Who!. Seuss, Dr.   **E**

Horvath, Polly
> Everything on a waffle (4 and up)   **Fic**
> The Pepins and their problems (3-6)   **Fic**
> The trolls (3-6)   **Fic**
> When the circus came to town (4-6)   **Fic**

Hosking, Wayne
> Asian kites (3-6)   **629.133**

Hosni the dreamer. Ben-'Ezer, E.   **398.2**

Hospitals
> Rogers, F. Going to the hospital (k-2)   **362.1**
> Rosenberg, M. B. Mommy's in the hospital having a baby (k-1)   **362.1**

Hossell, Karen
Delaware
In Voices from colonial America [series]
973.2

The **hot** & cold summer. Hurwitz, J.   **Fic**

Hot air. Priceman, M.   **E**

Hot city. Joosse, B. M.   **E**

Hot day on Abbott Avenue. English, K.   **E**

Hot potato (k-2)   **811.008**

Hotel deep. Cyrus, K.   **811**

Hotels and motels
Fiction
Davis, M. I. Evangeline Brown and the Cadillac Motel (4-6)   **Fic**
Fleischman, P. The Half-a-Moon Inn (4-6)   **Fic**
Polacco, P. John Philip Duck   **E**
Thompson, K. Kay Thompson's Eloise   **E**

Hottest, coldest, highest, deepest. Jenkins, S.
910

Houdini, Harry, 1874-1926
About
Fleischman, S. Escape! [biography of Harry Houdini] (5 and up)   **92**
Krull, K. Houdini (2-4)   **92**
MacLeod, E. Harry Houdini (4-6)   **92**
Fiction
Burleigh, R. The secret of the great Houdini
E

Hough, Charlotte Woodyatt
The magic pencil
In Bauer, C. F. Celebrations; read-aloud holiday and theme book programs p12-14
808.8

Houghton, Gillian
Mildred Taylor (5 and up)   **92**
The Transcontinental Railroad (5 and up)
385.09

Houlihan, Dorothy F.
(jt. auth) Marino, J. Mother Goose time
027.62

Houndsley and Catina. Howe, J.   **E**

The **House** at Pooh Corner. Milne, A. A.   **Fic**

The **house** at Pooh Corner. Milne, A. A.
also in Milne, A. A. The complete tales of Winnie-the-Pooh p163-344   **Fic**
also in Milne, A. A. The world of Pooh; the complete Winnie-the-Pooh and The House at Pooh Corner p153-314   **Fic**

A **house** for Hermit Crab. Carle, E.   **E**

The **house** of Dies Drear. Hamilton, V.   **Fic**

The **house** of sixty fathers. DeJong, M.   **Fic**

A **house** of tailors. Giff, P. R.   **Fic**

The **house** of wings. Byars, B. C.   **Fic**

The **house** on the hill. Asbjornsen, P. C.
In De Paola, T. Tomie dePaola's Favorite nursery tales p122-26   **398.2**

The **house** that Jack built. Winter, J.   **398.8**

The **house** with a clock in its walls. Bellairs, J.
Fic

A **houseful** of Christmas. Joosse, B. M.   **E**

Household employees
Fiction
Parish, P. Amelia Bedelia   **E**
Stewart, S. The friend   **E**

Household moving *See* Moving

Household pests
See also Cockroaches

Houses
Barton, B. Building a house (k-1)   **690**
Gibbons, G. How a house is built (k-3)   **690**
Rounds, G. Sod houses on the Great Plains (k-3)   **693**
Fiction
Banks, K. The great blue house   **E**
Burton, V. L. The little house   **E**
DiSalvo-Ryan, D. A castle on Viola Street
E
Lobel, A. Ming Lo moves the mountain   **E**
Poetry
Lillegard, D. Wake up house! (k-2)   **811**

Housman, Laurence
A Chinese fairy tale
In Bauer, C. F. Celebrations; read-aloud holiday and theme book programs p4-11
808.8

Houston, Gloria
My great-aunt Arizona   **E**
The year of the perfect Christmas tree   **E**

Houston, James A.
Frozen fire (6 and up)   **Fic**

Houston, Samuel, 1793-1863
About
Fritz, J. Make way for Sam Houston (4 and up)
92

Hovey, Kate
Arachne speaks (4 and up)   **811**

Hovland, Pamela
(jt. auth) Dugan, J. ABC NYC   **E**

How a bill becomes a law. Hamilton, J.   **328**

How a house is built. Gibbons, G.   **690**

How a husband weaned his wife from fairy tales. Afanas´ev, A. N.
In Afanas´ev, A. N. Russian fairy tales p308
398.2

How a skyscraper and a railroad train got picked up and carried away from Pig's Eye Valley far in the Pickax Mountains. Sandburg, C.
In Sandburg, C. More Rootabaga stories p141-46   **S C**
also in Sandburg, C. The Sandburg treasury; prose and poetry for young people p152-54   **818**

How a warty toad became an emperor. Sierra, J.
In Sierra, J. Can you guess my name?; traditional tales around the world p69-72
398.2

How Akbar went to Bethlehem. Babbitt, N.
In Babbitt, N. The Devil's other storybook p33-39   **S C**

How Alligator's nose was broken. Curry, J. L.
In Curry, J. L. The wonderful sky boat and other Native American tales of the Southeast p44-46   **398.2**

How I got my English A. Avi
In Tripping over the lunch lady and other school stories p17-28 **S C**

How I saved Hanukkah. Koss, A. G. **Fic**

How Ijapa the tortoise tricked the hippopotamus. Sierra, J.
In Sierra, J. Can you guess my name?; traditional tales around the world p51-53 **398.2**

How it feels to be adopted. Krementz, J. **362.7**

How it feels to have a gay or lesbian parent. Snow, J. E. **306.8**

How it feels when a parent dies. Krementz, J. **155.9**

How it feels when parents divorce. Krementz, J. **306.89**

How Jack went to seek his fortune. Jacobs, J.
also in Jacobs, J. English fairy tales p34-36 **398.2**
In De Paola, T. Tomie dePaola's Favorite nursery tales p118-21 **398.2**

How Jack went to seek his fortune. Sierra, J.
In Sierra, J. Can you guess my name?; traditional tales around the world p25-[29] **398.2**

How Johnny the Wham sleeps in money all the time and Joe the Wimp shines and sees things. Sandburg, C.
In Sandburg, C. More Rootabaga stories p63-68 **S C**
also in Sandburg, C. The Sandburg treasury; prose and poetry for young people p117-20 **818**

How little Lori visited Times Square. Vogel, A. **E**

How many days to America? Bunting, E. **E**

How many fish? Rubin, A. **E**

How many miles to Bethlehem? Crossley-Holland, K. **232.9**

How many snails? Giganti, P., Jr. **E**

How many stars in the sky? Hort, L. **E**

How men first played the game of ball. Curry, J. L.
In Curry, J. L. The wonderful sky boat and other Native American tales of the Southeast p74-81 **398.2**

How mountains are made. Zoehfeld, K. W. **551.4**

How much? Lewin, T. **381**

How much can a bare bear bear? Cleary, B. P. **428**

How much is a million? Schwartz, D. M. **E**

How my family lives in America. Kuklin, S. **305.8**

How my parents learned to eat. Friedman, I. R. **E**

How Nehemiah got free. Hamilton, V.
In Hamilton, V. The people could fly; American black folktales p147-50 **398.2**

How Pink Peony sent Spuds, the Ballplayer, up to pick four moons. Sandburg, C.
In Sandburg, C. More Rootabaga stories p77-81 **S C**
also in Sandburg, C. The Sandburg treasury; prose and poetry for young people p124-26 **818**

How Poor Boy won his wife. Curry, J. L.
In Curry, J. L. Hold up the sky: and other Native American tales from Texas and the Southern Plains p107-13 **398.2**

How proudly they wave. Haban, R. D. **929.9**

How Rabbit stole Mountain Lion's teeth. Curry, J. L.
In Curry, J. L. Hold up the sky: and other Native American tales from Texas and the Southern Plains p81-83 **398.2**

How rabbit stole Otter's coat. Curry, J. L.
In Curry, J. L. The wonderful sky boat and other Native American tales of the Southeast p39-43 **398.2**

How Rag Bag Mammy kept her secret while the wind blew away the Village of Hat Pins. Sandburg, C.
In Sandburg, C. More Rootabaga stories p25-30 **S C**
also in Sandburg, C. The Sandburg treasury; prose and poetry for young people p100-02 **818**

How Santa got his job. Krensky, S. **E**

How six pigeons came back to Hatrack the Horse after many accidents and six telegrams. Sandburg, C.
In Sandburg, C. More Rootabaga stories p31-36 **S C**
also in Sandburg, C. The Sandburg treasury; prose and poetry for young people p103-06 **818**

How six umbrellas took off their straw hats to show respect to the one big umbrella. Sandburg, C.
In Sandburg, C. More Rootabaga stories p41-46 **S C**
also in Sandburg, C. The Sandburg treasury; prose and poetry for young people p107-10 **818**

How Soko brought debt to Ashanti. Courlander, H.
In Courlander, H. and Herzog, G. Cow-tail switch, and other West African stories p103-06 **398.2**

How tall, how short, how faraway. Adler, D. A. **530.8**

How the Adirondacks got their name. Bruchac, J.
In Bruchac, J. Tell me a tale; a book about storytelling p27-29 **372.6**

How the alphabet was made. Kipling, R.
In Kipling, R. Just so stories **S C**

How the animals lost their tails and got them back traveling from Philadelphia to Medicine Hat. Sandburg, C.
In Sandburg, C. Rootabaga stories p164-76 **S C**

How the animals lost their tails and got them back traveling from Philadelphia to Medicine Hat—*Continued*

    also in Sandburg, C. The Sandburg treasury; prose and poetry for young people p81-86   **818**

How the bat came to be. Caduto, M. J.

    In Caduto, M. J. and Bruchac, J. Keepers of the night; Native American stories and nocturnal activities for children p21-22   **398.2**

How the Bee became. Hughes, T.

    In Hughes, T. How the Whale became and other stories   **S C**

How the biters and stingers got their poison. Curry, J. L.

    In Curry, J. L. The wonderful sky boat and other Native American tales of the Southeast p61-63   **398.2**

How the camel got his hump. Kipling, R.

    In Kipling, R. Just so stories   **S C**

How the Cat became. Hughes, T.

    In Hughes, T. How the Whale became and other stories   **S C**

How the cat swallowed thunder. Alexander, L.   **E**

How the critters got groceries. McGill, A.

    In McGill, A. Sure as sunrise; stories of Bruh Rabbit & his walkin' talkin' friends   **398.2**

How the Dao people came to be. Terada, A. M.

    In Terada, A. M. Under the starfruit tree; folktales from Vietnam p54-58   **398.2**

How the Donkey became. Hughes, T.

    In Hughes, T. How the Whale became and other stories   **S C**

How the Elephant became. Hughes, T.

    In Hughes, T. How the Whale became and other stories   **S C**

How the first letter was written. Kipling, R.

    In Kipling, R. Just so stories   **S C**

How the five rusty rats helped find a new village. Sandburg, C.

    In Sandburg, C. Rootabaga stories p21-27   **S C**

    also in Sandburg, C. The Sandburg treasury; prose and poetry for young people p19-23   **818**

How the Fox came to be where it is. Hughes, T.

    In Hughes, T. How the Whale became and other stories   **S C**

How the gecko came to be. Terada, A. M.

    In Terada, A. M. Under the starfruit tree; folktales from Vietnam p69-71   **398.2**

How the Grinch stole Christmas. Seuss, Dr.   **E**

How the Hare became. Hughes, T.

    In Hughes, T. How the Whale became and other stories   **S C**

How the hat ashes shovel helped Snoo Foo. Sandburg, C.

    In Sandburg, C. Rootabaga stories p80-82   **S C**

How the hot ashes shovel helped Snoo Foo. Sandburg, C.

    In Sandburg, C. The Sandburg treasury; prose and poetry for young people p45-46   **818**

How the Hyena became. Hughes, T.

    In Hughes, T. How the Whale became and other stories   **S C**

How the leopard got his spots. Kipling, R.

    In Kipling, R. Just so stories   **S C**

How the narwhal got its tusk. Norman, H.

    In Norman, H. The girl who dreamed only geese, and other tales of the Far North   **398.2**

How the Polar Bear became. Hughes, T.

    In Hughes, T. How the Whale became and other stories   **S C**

How the Potato Face Blind man enjoyed himself on a fine spring morning. Sandburg, C.

    In Sandburg, C. Rootabaga stories p34-38   **S C**

    also in Sandburg, C. The Sandburg treasury; prose and poetry for young people p25-26   **818**

How the rainbow was born. Delacre, L.

    In Delacre, L. Golden tales; myths, legends, and folktales from Latin America p37-39   **398.2**

How the rhinoceros got his skin. Kipling, R.

    In Kipling, R. Just so stories   **S C**

How the rooster got his crown. Poole, A. L.   **398.2**

How the sea was born. Delacre, L.

    In Delacre, L. Golden tales; myths, legends, and folktales from Latin America p3-5   **398.2**

How the three wild babylonian baboons went away in the rain eating bread and butter. Sandburg, C.

    In Sandburg, C. More Rootabaga stories p37-40   **S C**

    also in Sandburg, C. The Sandburg treasury; prose and poetry for young people p106-07   **818**

How the tiger got its stripes. Garland, S.

    In Garland, S. Children of the dragon; selected tales from Vietnam p4-10   **398.2**

How the tiger got its stripes. Terada, A. M.

    In Terada, A. M. Under the starfruit tree; folktales from Vietnam p7-9   **398.2**

How the Tortoise became. Hughes, T.

    In Hughes, T. How the Whale became and other stories   **S C**

How the Whale became. Hughes, T.

    In Hughes, T. How the Whale became and other stories   **S C**

How the Whale became and other stories. Hughes, T.   **S C**

How the whale got his throat. Kipling, R.

    In Kipling, R. Just so stories   **S C**

How the witch was caught. Lester, J.

    In Lester, J. The last tales of Uncle Remus p66-70   **398.2**

How they bring back the Village of Cream Puffs when the wind blows it away. Sandburg, C.
In Sandburg, C. Rootabaga stories p14-20
S C

also in Sandburg, C. The Sandburg treasury; prose and poetry for young people p17-19
818

How they broke away to go to the Rootabaga Country. Sandburg, C.
In Sandburg, C. Rootabaga stories p3-13
S C

also in Sandburg, C. The Sandburg treasury; prose and poetry for young people p10-16
818

How they play driedel in Chelm. Kimmel, E. A.
In Kimmel, E. A. The jar of fools: eight Hanukkah stories from Chelm p5-8 **S C**

How Tía Lola came to visit/stay. Alvarez, J.
Fic

How Tinktum Tidy recruited an army for the king. Lester, J.
In Lester, J. The last tales of Uncle Remus p82-88
398.2

How to bargain with a dragon. Stine, R. L.
In Stine, R. L. The haunting hour p48-65
S C

How to be a friend. Brown, L. K. **158**
How to be a nature detective. See Selsam, M. E. Big tracks, little tracks
591.5

How to cook a gooseberry fool. Vaughan, M.
In Easy menu ethnic cookbooks **641.5**

How to cross a pond. Singer, M. **811**

How-to-do-it manuals for librarians [series]
Curzon, S. C. Managing change **025.1**
Halsted, D. D. Disaster planning **025.8**

How-to-do-it manuals for libraries [series]
Cuddy, C. Using PDAs in libraries **004**
Duncan, D. I-search for success **001.4**
Duncan, D. I-Search, you search, we all learn to research **001.4**
Ernst, L. L. Lapsit services for the very young II **027.62**
Feinberg, S. Running a parent/child workshop **027.62**
Hallam, A. Managing budgets and finances **025.1**
Herb, S. Connecting fathers, children, and reading **028.5**
Nespeca, S. M. Library programming for families with young children **027.62**
Stein, B. L. Running a school library media center **027.8**
Symons, A. K. Protecting the right to read **025.2**

How-to-do-it manuals for school and public librarians [series]
Herb, S. Using children's books in preschool settings **372.4**

How to do "The three bears" with two hands. Minkel, W. **791.5**

How to draw cars and trucks. Court, R. **743**
How to eat fried worms. Rockwell, T. **Fic**
How to get your child to love reading. Codell, E. R. **028.5**

How to make an apple pie and see the world. Priceman, M. **E**
How to make holiday pop-ups. Irvine, J. **736**
How to play tennis. Williams, V. **796.342**
How to really fool yourself. Cobb, V. **152.1**
How to survive in Antarctica. Bledsoe, L. J. **998**
How to talk to your cat. George, J. C. **636.8**
How to talk to your dog. George, J. C. **636.7**
How to tell corn fairies if you see 'em. Sandburg, C.
In Sandburg, C. Rootabaga stories p157-63
S C

also in Sandburg, C. The Sandburg treasury; prose and poetry for young people p81-86
818

How to think like a scientist. Kramer, S. **507**
How to write terrific book reports. James, E.
808
How to write your best book report. See James, E. How to write terrific book reports **808**

How Turtle's back was cracked. Ross, G.
398.2

How two sweetheart dippies sat in the moonlight on a lumberyard fence and heard about the Sooners and the Boomers. Sandburg, C.
In Sandburg, C. More Rootabaga stories p101-09 **S C**
also in Sandburg, C. The Sandburg treasury; prose and poetry for young people p134-39
818

How Uncle Rabbit tricked Uncle Tiger. González, L. M.
In González, L. M. Señor Cat's romance and other favorite stories from Latin America p35-41
398.2

How we crossed the West. Schanzer, R. **978**
How will we get to the beach? Luciani, B. **E**
How writers work. Fletcher, R. **808**
How you were born. Cole, J. **612.6**

Howard, Arthur
Hoodwinked **E**
(il) Appelt, K. Bubba and Beau, best friends
E
(il) Byars, B. C. The SOS file **Fic**
(il) Cuyler, M. 100th day worries **E**
(il) Rylant, C. Mr. Putter and Tabby pour the tea **E**

Howard, Elizabeth Fitzgerald
Aunt Flossie's hats (and crab cakes later) **E**
Virgie goes to school with us boys
E
[story]
also in You read to me & I'll read to you; 20th-century stories to share p66-74
E

Howard, Ellen
The gate in the wall (5 and up) **Fic**
Howard, Paul
(il) Cooke, T. Full, full, full of love **E**
Howe, Deborah
Bunnicula (4-6) **Fic**

Hughes, Langston—_Continued_
The dream keeper and other poems (5 and up)
811
Langston Hughes (5 and up) **811**
Hughes, Langston, 1902-1967
About
Burleigh, R. Langston's train ride (1-4) **92**
Cooper, F. Coming home [biography of Langston Hughes] (k-3) **92**
Walker, A. Langston Hughes, American poet (2-5) **92**
See/See also pages in the following book(s):
Krull, K. Lives of the writers (4 and up)
920

Poetry
Medina, T. Love to Langston (3-5) **811**
Hughes, Meredith Sayles
Spill the beans and pass the peanuts: legumes (4 and up) **583**
Yes, we have bananas (4 and up) **634**
Hughes, Monica
See/See also pages in the following book(s):
Ellis, S. From reader to writer **372.6**
Hughes, Neal
(il) Sachar, L. Marvin Redpost, kidnapped at birth? **Fic**
Hughes, Pat
The breaker boys (5 and up) **Fic**
Hughes, Richard
Nothing
_In_ Bauer, C. F. Celebrations; read-aloud holiday and theme book programs p144-45
808.8

Hughes, Shirley
Annie Rose is my little sister **E**
Ella's big chance **E**
Olly and me **E**
Out and about **E**
Rhymes for Annie Rose (k-2) **821**
Stories by firelight **E**
Hughes, Ted
The cat and the cuckoo (3-6) **821**
How the Whale became and other stories (4-6)
S C
Contents: Why the Owl behaves as it does; How the Whale became; How the Fox came to be where it is; How the Polar Bear became; How the Hyena became; How the Tortoise became; How the Bee became; How the Cat became; How the Donkey became; How the Hare became; How the Elephant became
The iron giant (4-6) **Fic**
Hughes-Hassell, Sandra
Collection management for youth **025.2**
(ed) The Information-powered school. See The Information-powered school **027.8**
Hugs and kisses. Loupy, C. **E**
Huguenots
Fiction
Kirkpatrick, K. A. Escape across the wide sea (5 and up) **Fic**
Hula lullaby. Kono, E. E. **E**
Huliska-Beith, Laura
(il) Johnson, A. Violet's music **E**
(il) Lear, E. Edward Lear **821**
(il) Wheeler, L. Bubble gum, bubble gum **E**

Hull, Richard
(il) Viorst, J. Sad underwear and other complications **811**
The **hullabaloo** ABC. Cleary, B. **E**
The **human** alphabet **E**
Human anatomy
See also Human body
Berger, M. Why don't haircuts hurt? (2-4)
612
Cole, J. The magic school bus inside the human body (2-4) **612**
Gray, S. H. The human body [series] (3-6)
612
Sweeney, J. Me and my amazing body (k-2)
611
VanCleave, J. P. Janice VanCleave's the human body for every kid (4 and up) **612**
Walker, R. Body (4 and up) **611**
Walker, R. The Kingfisher first human body encyclopedia (3-5) **612**
Human body
Rau, D. M. What's inside me? [series] (k-3)
612
Human body [series]
Ballard, C. The skeleton and muscular system
612.7
Parker, S. The lungs and respiratory system
612.2
Human body for every kid, Janice VanCleave's.
VanCleave, J. P. **612**
Human ecology
See/See also pages in the following book(s):
Swamp, J. Giving thanks (k-3) **299.7**
Fiction
Baker, J. Window **E**
Human fertility
See also Infertility
Human geography
Arthus-Bertrand, Y. Earth from above for young readers (4 and up) **779**
Smith, D. J. If the world were a village (3-5)
304.6
Human impact. Vogel, C. G. **333.91**
Human influence on nature
Burnie, D. Endangered planet (5 and up)
333.95
Vogel, C. G. Human impact (5 and up)
333.91
See/See also pages in the following book(s):
Patent, D. H. Biodiversity (5 and up)
333.95
Human origins
See also Evolution; Fossil hominids; Prehistoric peoples
Gallant, R. A. Early humans (5 and up)
599.93
Human relations _See_ Interpersonal relations
Humbug. Bawden, N. **Fic**
Humbug witch. Balian, L. **E**

Hummingbird and Little Breeze. Hamilton, V.
  In Hamilton, V. When birds could talk & bats could sing; the adventures of Bruh Sparrow, Sis Wren, and their friends p33-39
  398.2

Hummingbird nest. George, K. O.   **E**

Hummingbirds
  Kelly, I. It's a hummingbird's life (k-3)   **598**
  Sayre, A. P. The hungry hummingbird (k-3)
  598

Fiction
  Baker, K. Little Green   **E**
  George, K. O. Hummingbird nest   **E**

Humor *See* Wit and humor

Humorists
  Keating, F. Will Rogers: an American legend (k-3)   **92**

Humorous poetry
  Brown, C. Dutch sneakers and flea keepers (2-4)
  811
  Ciardi, J. You read to me, I'll read to you
  811
  Dahl, R. Vile verses (4-6)   **821**
  Florian, D. In the swim   **811**
  Florian, D. Laugh-eteria   **811**
  For laughing out loud   **811.008**
  Hirsch, R. F E G: ridiculous stupid poems for intelligent children (5 and up)   **821**
  The Kingfisher book of funny poems (4 and up)
  821.008
  Numeroff, L. J. Sometimes I wonder if poodles like noodles (k-3)   **811**
  Prelutsky, J. It's raining pigs & noodles (3-6)
  811
  Prelutsky, J. The new kid on the block: poems (3-6)   **811**
  Prelutsky, J. A pizza the size of the sun (3-6)
  811
  Prelutsky, J. Rolling Harvey down the hill (1-3)
  811
  Prelutsky, J. Something big has been here (3-5)
  811
  Shields, C. D. Almost late to school and more school poems (2-4)   **811**
  Shields, C. D. Lunch money and other poems about school (2-4)   **811**
  Silverstein, S. Falling up   **811**
  Silverstein, S. A light in the attic   **811**
  Silverstein, S. Runny Babbit   **811**
  Silverstein, S. Where the sidewalk ends   **811**
  Viorst, J. Sad underwear and other complications (3-6)   **811**
  Wise, W. Zany zoo (k-3)   **811**

The **hundredth** skull. San Souci, R.
  In San Souci, R. A terrifying taste of short & shivery; thirty creepy tales p43-45
  398.2

Hundreth day worries. See Cuyler, M. 100th day worries   **E**

Huneck, Stephen
  Sally goes to the beach   **E**

Hungarian Americans
Fiction
  Karr, K. Man of the family (4 and up)   **Fic**

Hungary
  Esbenshade, R. S. Hungary (5 and up)
  943.9
Fiction
  Cheng, A. The lace dowry (4 and up)   **Fic**
  Seredy, K. The Good Master (4-6)   **Fic**
  Seredy, K. The white stag (4-6)   **Fic**

Hunger
Fiction
  Namioka, L. The hungriest boy in the world
  E

The **hungriest** boy in the world. Namioka, L.
  E

The **hungry** coat. Demi   **398.2**

Hungry ghosts. San Souci, R.
  In San Souci, R. Dare to be scared; thirteen stories to chill and thrill   **S C**

The **hungry** goddess. Gerson, M.-J.
  In Gerson, M.-J. Fiesta femenina; celebrating women in Mexican folktale   **398.2**

Hungry hen. Waring, R.   **E**

The **hungry** hummingbird. Sayre, A. P.   **598**

Hungry Spider and the Turtle. Courlander, H.
  In Courlander, H. and Herzog, G. Cow-tail switch, and other West African stories p107-12   **398.2**

Hunt, Charlotte Dumaresq *See* Demi, 1942-

Hunt, Robert
  (il) Bercaw, E. C. Halmoni's day   **E**

Hunt, Scott
  (il) Testa, M. Becoming Joe DiMaggio   **811**

Hunter, Anne
  (il) Larios, J. H. Have you ever done that?
  811

Hunter, Mollie
  The mermaid summer (4 and up)   **Fic**

Hunter, Norman
  The unexpected banquet
  In Bauer, C. F. Celebrations; read-aloud holiday and theme book programs p45-51
  808.8

Hunter, Ryan Ann
  Take off! (k-3)   **629.13**

The **hunter**. Casanova, M.   **398.2**

The **hunter** in the haunted forest. San Souci, R.
  In San Souci, R. Short & shivery; thirty chilling tales p112-16   **398.2**

The **hunterman** and the crocodile. Wagué Diakité, B.   **398.2**

Hunting
  See also Tracking and trailing
Fiction
  Dahl, R. The magic finger (2-4)   **Fic**
  Rosen, M. We're going on a bear hunt   **E**

Hunting song of the Seeonee pack. Kipling, R.
  In Kipling, R. The jungle book: the Mowgli stories   **S C**

Hunting the white cow. Seymour, T.   **E**

Hunwick's egg. Fox, M.   **E**

Hurd, Clement
  (il) Brown, M. W. Goodnight moon   **E**
  (il) Brown, M. W. The runaway bunny   **E**

Hyman, Flo, 1954-1986
See/See also pages in the following book(s):
Krull, K. Lives of the athletes (4 and up)
920

Hyman, Teresa L.
Pyramids (3-6) **726**

Hyman, Trina Schart
Little Red Riding Hood (k-2) **398.2**
(il) Alexander, L. The fortune-tellers **E**
(il) Brink, C. R. Caddie Woodlawn **Fic**
(il) Christmas poems. See Christmas poems
808.81
(il) Cohen, B. Canterbury tales **821**
(il) Fritz, J. Why don't you get a horse, Sam
Adams? **92**
(il) Fritz, J. Will you sign here, John Hancock?
92
(il) Garland, S. Children of the dragon
398.2
(il) Hodges, M. The kitchen knight **398.2**
(il) Hodges, M. Merlin and the making of the
king **398.2**
(il) Hodges, M. Saint George and the dragon
398.2
(il) Kimmel, E. A. The adventures of Hershel of
Ostropol **398.2**
(il) Kimmel, E. A. Hershel and the Hanukkah
goblins **E**
(il) Kimmel, E. A. Iron John **398.2**
(il) Lasky, K. The night journey **Fic**
(il) Medearis, A. S. Haunts **S C**
(il) Rogasky, B. The golem **398.2**
(il) Tchana, K. H. Changing Woman and her
sisters **398.2**
(il) Tchana, K. H. Sense Pass King **398.2**
(il) Thomas, D. A child's Christmas in Wales
828
(il) Updike, J. A child's calendar **811**
(il) Winter poems. See Winter poems
808.81

Hymns
See also Spirituals (Songs)
Pinkney, G. J. Music from our Lord's holy
heaven (2-4) **264**

Hynes, Margaret
Rocks & fossils (5 and up) **552**

Hypatia, ca. 370-415
About
Love, D. A. Of numbers and stars [biography of
Hypatia] (2-4) **92**

Hyperactive children
See also Attention deficit disorder

Hypnotism
Fiction
Auch, M. J. I was a third grade science project
(2-4) **Fic**

I

I ain't gonna paint no more!. Beaumont, K. **E**
I am David. Holm, A. **Fic**
I am me. Kuskin, K. **E**

I am not going to school today. Harris, R. H.
E
I am phoenix: poems for two voices. Fleischman,
P. **811**
I am Rosa Parks. Parks, R. **92**
I am the darker brother **811.008**
I am the turkey. Spirn, M. **E**
I am too absolutely small for school. Child, L.
E
I and you and don't forget who. Cleary, B. P.
428
I can make a difference **808.8**
I can read book [series]
Bernier-Grand, C. T. Juan Bobo **398.2**
Bonsall, C. N. The case of the hungry stranger
E
Bonsall, C. N. Who's a pest? **E**
Brenner, B. Wagon wheels **E**
Bulla, C. R. Daniel's duck **E**
Byars, B. C. The Golly sisters go West **E**
Cazet, D. Elvis the rooster almost goes to heav-
en **E**
Christmas presents **811.008**
Coerr, E. The big balloon race **E**
Coerr, E. Chang's paper pony **E**
Coerr, E. The Josefina story quilt **E**
Cushman, D. Inspector Hopper **E**
Gorbachev, V. Ms. Turtle the babysitter **E**
Halloween howls **811.008**
Hanukkah lights **811.008**
Hazen, B. S. Digby **E**
Hill, S. Ruby bakes a cake **E**
Hoban, L. Arthur's Christmas cookies **E**
Hoban, L. Silly Tilly's Thanksgiving dinner
E
Hoff, S. Oliver **E**
Hoff, S. Sammy the seal **E**
Hurd, E. T. Johnny Lion's book **E**
Kenah, K. The best seat in second grade **E**
Kessler, L. P. Here comes the strikeout **E**
Kessler, L. P. Kick, pass, and run **E**
Kessler, L. P. Last one in is a rotten egg **E**
Lexau, J. M. Crocodile and hen **398.2**
Little, J. Emma's yucky brother **E**
Lobel, A. Frog and Toad are friends **E**
Lobel, A. Grasshopper on the road **E**
Lobel, A. Mouse soup **E**
Lobel, A. Mouse tales **E**
Lobel, A. Owl at home **E**
Lobel, A. Small pig **E**
Lobel, A. Uncle Elephant **E**
Maestro, M. Geese find the missing piece
793.73
Maestro, M. What do you hear when cows sing?
793.73
McCully, E. A. The grandma mix-up **E**
Minarik, E. H. Little Bear **E**
Minarik, E. H. No fighting, no biting! **E**
Monjo, F. N. The drinking gourd **E**
Paterson, K. Marvin one too many **E**
A Pet for me **811.008**
Porte, B. A. Harry's birthday **E**
Prelutsky, J. It's snowing! it's snowing! **811**
Schwartz, A. All of our noses are here, and oth-
er noodle tales **398.2**

Ibbotson, Eva—*Continued*
  Journey to the river sea (5 and up)   **Fic**
  The secret of platform 13 (5 and up)   **Fic**
  The star of Kazan (5 and up)   **Fic**
Ibn Battuta, 1304-1377
          About
  Rumford, J. Traveling man: the journey of Ibn
    Battuta, 1325-1354 (3-6)   **92**
Ibn Ezra and the archbishop. Kimmel, E. A.
  In Kimmel, E. A. The spotted pony: a collec-
    tion of Hanukkah stories p12-17
                   398.2
Ibo (African people) *See* Igbo (African people)
Ice
          Fiction
  Appelbaum, D. K. Cocoa ice   **E**
Ice Age cave bear. Hehner, B.   **569**
Ice Age mammoth. Hehner, B.   **569**
Ice Age sabertooth. Hehner, B.   **569**
Ice bear. Davies, N.   **599.78**
Ice cream, ices, etc.
  Cooper, E. Ice cream (k-3)   **637**
  Fleisher, P. Ice cream treats (4 and up)
                   641.8
  Greenstein, E. Ice cream cones for sale! (k-3)
                   637
Ice cream. Cooper, E.   **637**
Ice cream cones for sale!. Greenstein, E.   **637**
Ice cream treats. Fleisher, P.   **641.8**
Ice drift. Taylor, T.   **Fic**
Ice hockey *See* Hockey
Ice hockey. Kennedy, M.   **796.962**
The **Ice** Man. Curry, J. L.
  In Curry, J. L. The wonderful sky boat and
    other Native American tales of the
    Southeast p82-85   **398.2**
Ice palace. Blumenthal, D.   **E**
Ice skating
  Cohen, S. Fire on ice (4 and up)   **92**
  Gutman, D. Ice skating (5 and up)   **796.91**
  Isadora, R. Sophie skates (k-3)   **796.91**
  Wilkes, D. The figure skating book (4 and up)
                   796.91
          Fiction
  Borden, L. The greatest skating race (2-5)
                   Fic
  Dodge, M. M. Hans Brinker; or, The silver
    skates (4 and up)   **Fic**
  Keller, H. Pearl's new skates   **E**
Ice story. Kimmel, E. C.   **998**
Icebergs
  Simon, S. Icebergs and glaciers (3-6)   **551.3**
Icebergs and glaciers. Simon, S.   **551.3**
Iceland
  McMillan, B. Going fishing (2-4)   **949.12**
          Fiction
  McMillan, B. The problem with chickens   **E**
Ichikawa, Satomi
  La La Rose   **E**
  My pig Amarillo   **E**
  (il) Gauch, P. L. Tanya and the red shoes   **E**
  (il) Lisle, J. T. The lost flower children   **Fic**

Ichord, Loretta Frances
  Skillet bread, sourdough, and vinegar pie (3-5)
                   641.5
Id-ul-Fitr. Marchant, K.   **297.3**
Ida B. Hannigan, K.   **Fic**
Ida Early comes over the mountain. Burch, R.
                   Fic
Idaho
  Edwards, K. Idaho
    In World Almanac Library of the States series
                   973
  George, C. Idaho
    In America the beautiful, second series
                   973
  George, L. Idaho
    In America the beautiful, second series
                   973
  Sanders, D. Idaho
    In It's my state! [series]   **973**
Idioms *See* English language—Idioms
Iditarod dream. Wood, T.   **798.8**
Iditarod Trail Sled Dog Race, Alaska
  Miller, D. S. The great serum race (3-5)
                   798.8
          Fiction
  Blake, R. J. Akiak   **E**
If I ran the circus. Seuss, Dr.   **E**
If I ran the zoo. Seuss, Dr.   **E**
If I were a Rockefeller. Taback, S.
  In Taback, S. Kibitzers and fools; tales my
    zayda (grandfather) told me   **398.2**
If I were in charge of the world and other worries.
  Viorst, J.   **811**
If not for the cat. Prelutsky, J.   **811**
If the shoe fits. Soto, G.   **E**
If the shoe fits. Soto, G.
  In Soto, G. Petty crimes   **S C**
If the shoe fits. Whipple, L.   **811**
If the world were a village. Smith, D. J.
                   304.6
If you don't like it don't listen. Afanas'ev, A. N.
  In Afanas'ev, A. N. Russian fairy tales p345-
    48   **398.2**
If you ever get lost. Porte, B. A.   **Fic**
If you ever meet a whale (3-5)   **811.008**
If you find a rock. Christian, P.   **552**
If you give a mouse a cookie. Numeroff, L. J.
                   E
If you made a million. Schwartz, D. M.   **E**
If you want to see a caribou. Root, P.   **E**
If you were born a kitten. Bauer, M. D.   **591.3**
If you were there in 1776. Brenner, B.   **973.3**
. . . **if** your name was changed at Ellis Island.
  Levine, E.   **325.73**
If you're happy and you know it. Cabrera, J.
                   E
If you're happy and you know it!. Ormerod, J.
                   E
Igbo (African people)
          Fiction
  Siegelson, K. L. In the time of the drums   **E**

Imaginary playmates
Fiction
Greenfield, E. Me & Neesie   E
Henkes, K. Jessica   E
Rohmann, E. Clara and Asha   E

Imagination
Feinberg, B. Welcome to Lizard Motel
    028.5
Fiction
Ahlberg, A. The shopping expedition   E
Colón, R. Orson blasts off!   E
Crumpacker, B. Alexander's pretending day
    E
Dorros, A. Abuela   E
Dunbar, P. Flyaway Katie   E
Gelman, R. G. Doodler doodling   E
Grey, M. Traction Man is here!   E
Krauss, R. A very special house   E
McLerran, A. Roxaboxen   E
McNaughton, C. Once upon an ordinary school
    day   E
Ness, E. Sam, Bangs & Moonshine   E
Ormerod, J. Lizzie nonsense   E
Shannon, D. Alice the fairy   E
Thomson, S. L. Imagine a day   E
Van Allsburg, C. The mysteries of Harris
    Burdick   E

Imaginative inventions. Harper, C. M.   609
Imagine that!. Raimondo, J.   709.04
Imani's music. Williams, S.   E
Imershein, Betsy
    (il) Howe, J. When you go to kindergarten
    372.2

Imitating nature [series]
Allman, T. From spider webs to man-made silk
    595.4

Immigrant kids. Freedman, R.   325.73
Immigrants
Fiction
Aliki. Painted words: Marianthe's story one
    E
Atwell, D. The Thanksgiving door   E
Avi. Silent movie   E
Bartoletti, S. C. A coal miner's bride (4 and up)
    Fic
Brown, J. Little Cricket (4-6)   Fic
Bunting, E. One green apple   E
Bunting, E. A picnic in October   E
Cannon, A. E. Charlotte's Rose (5 and up)
    Fic
Cheng, A. Honeysuckle house (3-5)   Fic
Cohen, B. Molly's pilgrim   E
Connor, L. Miss Bridie chose a shovel   E
Currier, K. S. Kai's journey to Gold Mountain
    (4 and up)   Fic
Easton, R. A real American (5 and up)   Fic
French, S. Where in the world (5 and up)
    Fic
Gerstein, M. Sparrow Jack   E
Giff, P. R. A house of tailors (5 and up)
    Fic
Glaser, L. Bridge to America (4-6)   Fic
Grant, K. Sofie and the city   E
Gündisch, K. How I became an American (4
    and up)   Fic

Hazen, B. S. Katie's wish   E
Herold, M. R. A very important day   E
Hesse, K. Letters from Rifka (5 and up)   Fic
Hest, A. When Jessie came across the sea   E
Himelblau, L. The trouble begins (4 and up)
    Fic
Hoffman, M. The color of home   E
Hughes, P. The breaker boys (5 and up)   Fic
Lasky, K. Dreams in the golden country (4 and
    up)   Fic
Lee, M. Landed   Fic
Mak, K. My Chinatown   E
Nagda, A. W. Dear Whiskers (2-4)   Fic
Napoli, D. J. The king of Mulberry Street (5
    and up)   Fic
Nolan, J. The St. Patrick's Day shillelagh   E
Oberman, S. The always prayer shawl   E
Oswald, N. Nothing here but stones (5 and up)
    Fic
Park, F. Good-bye, 382 Shin Dang Dong   E
Partridge, E. Oranges on Golden Mountain
    E
Pérez, A. I. My diary from here to there (2-4)
    Fic
Rael, E. O. Rivka's first Thanksgiving   E
Recorvits, H. My name is Yoon   E
Russell, B. T. Maggie's Amerikay   E
Sachs, M. Lost in America (5 and up)   Fic
Sheth, K. Blue jasmine (5 and up)   Fic
Woodruff, E. The memory coat   E
Yang, B. Hannah is my name   E
Poetry
Argueta, J. A movie in my pillow (3-6)   861
United States
Bial, R. Tenement (4 and up)   974.7
Hopkinson, D. Shutting out the sky (5 and up)
    974.7

Immigration and emigration
    See also Children of immigrants; Immi-
    grants; Refugees names of countries with the
    subdivision *Immigration and emigration*; and
    names of nationality groups
    See/See also pages in the following book(s):
Bauer, C. F. Celebrations p1-24   808.8
Immortality
    See also Future life
Immunization *See* Vaccination
Imogene's antlers. Small, D.   E
The **imp** in the basket. Babbitt, N.
    In Babbitt, N. The Devil's storybook p37-46
    S C
Imperial Trans-Antarctic Expedition (1914-
    1917)
Kimmel, E. C. Ice story (4 and up)   998
An **important** question. Taback, S.
    In Taback, S. Kibitzers and fools; tales my
    zayda (grandfather) told me   398.2
Impostures and imposture
Blackwood, G. L. Perplexing people (4 and up)
    920
Impressionism (Art)
Raimondo, J. Picture this! (1-5)   759.05
Sabbeth, C. Monet and the impressionists for
    kids (5 and up)   759.05

Infants—Fiction—*Continued*

Hindley, J. Baby talk	E
Hopkinson, D. A packet of seeds	E
James, S. Baby Brains	E
Jenkins, E. That new animal	E
Katz, K. Ten tiny tickles	E
Lewis, R. A. I love you like crazy cakes	E
Lindgren, B. Benny and the binky	E
Look, L. Henry's first-moon birthday	E
MacLachlan, P. Baby (5 and up)	Fic
MacLachlan, P. Bittle	E
Markes, J. I can't talk yet, but when I do...	E
Meyers, S. This is the way a baby rides	E
Milord, S. Love that baby!	E
Myers, T. Good babies	E
O'Connell, R. The baby goes beep	E
Quattlebaum, M. Grover G. Graham and me (4 and up)	Fic
Rathmann, P. The day the babies crawled away	E
Russo, M. Come back, Hannah!	E
Schlein, M. The story about me	E
Schwartz, A. Some babies	E
Steptoe, J. Baby says	E
Swift, F. Old blue buggy	E
Van Leeuwen, J. Benny & beautiful baby Delilah	E
Wheeler, L. Te amo, Bebé, little one	E
Wild, M. Midnight babies	E
Williams, V. B. "More more more" said the baby	E

Poetry

Calmenson, S. Welcome, baby! (k-1)	811

Infertility

Orr, T. Test tube babies (5 and up)   **618.1**

Influenza

Silverstein, A. The flu and pneumonia update (5 and up)   **616.2**

Fiction

Bateman, T. Farm flu	E
Collier, J. L. The empty mirror (5 and up)	Fic

Information networks

   See also Computer networks; Internet

Information please almanac, atlas & yearbook   **031.02**

Information power. American Association of School Librarians   **027.8**

The **Information-powered** school   **027.8**

Information resources

   See also Internet resources

Information society

   See also Information technology

Information storage and retrieval systems *See* Information systems

Information systems

Wolinsky, A. Internet power research using the Big6 approach (5 and up)   **025.04**

Information technology

Farmer, L. S. J. Technology-infused instruction for the educational community   **025.5**

Informational picture books for children. Cianciolo, P. J.   **028.1**

Ingemanson, Donna

   (il) Schorer, S. Put your best foot forward   **792.8**

Ingman, Bruce

   (il) Feiffer, K. Double pink   E

Ingpen, Robert R.

About

Cox, S. M. Pictures telling stories	741.6
(il) Barrie, J. M. Peter Pan	Fic
(il) Collodi, C. The adventures of Pinocchio	Fic
(il) Rosen, M. Dickens	92
(il) Rosen, M. Shakespeare	822.3
(il) Thuswaldner, W. Silent night holy night	782.28

Ingraham, Erick

(il) Calhoun, M. Cross-country cat	E
(il) Calhoun, M. Flood	E

Ingram, Jay

   (jt. auth) Funston, S. It's all in your head   **612.8**

Ingram, Scott

California

   In World Almanac Library of the States series   **973**

The FBI director (2-4)   **363.2**

Kansas

   In World Almanac Library of the States series   **973**

New Jersey

   In World Almanac Library of the States series   **973**

Nicolaus Copernicus (5 and up)   **92**

Oregon

   In America the beautiful, second series   **973**

   In World Almanac Library of the States series   **973**

Pennsylvania

   In World Almanac Library of the States series   **973**

Injuries *See* Accidents; First aid; Wounds and injuries

Innerst, Stacy

   (il) Krull, K. M is for music   E

Innocenti, Roberto

   (il) Collodi, C. The adventures of Pinocchio   Fic

   (il) Lewis, J. P. The Last Resort   Fic

Inns *See* Hotels and motels

Innuit *See* Inuit

Inoculation *See* Vaccination

Inquiry learning through librarian-teacher partnerships. Harada, V. H.   **371.1**

Insane *See* Mentally ill

The **insect** class. Zabludoff, M.   **595.7**

Insect facts and folklore. Kite, L. P.   **595.7**

Insectigation!. Blobaum, C.   **595.7**

Insectivorous plants *See* Carnivorous plants

Insectlopedia. Florian, D.   **811**

Insects

   See also Ants; Butterflies; Grasshoppers; Moths; Wasps

Insects—*Continued*

Berger, M. How do flies walk upside down? (3-5) **595.7**

Blobaum, C. Insectigation! (3-6) **595.7**

Camper, C. Bugs before time (4 and up) **560**

Froman, N. What's that bug? (4-6) **595.7**

Hipp, A. Orchid mantises (3-5) **595.7**

Hipp, A. Peanut-head bugs (3-5) **595.7**

Insects and spiders of the world (5 and up) **595.7**

Jackson, D. M. The bug scientists (4 and up) **595.7**

Johnson, J. Simon & Schuster children's guide to insects and spiders (4 and up) **595.7**

Kite, L. P. Insect facts and folklore (4 and up) **595.7**

Pascoe, E. Bugs (4 and up) **595.7**

Rockwell, A. F. Bugs are insects (k-3) **595.7**

Stewart, M. Maggots, grubs, and more (4-6) **595.7**

VanCleave, J. P. Janice VanCleave's insects and spiders (4 and up) **595.7**

VanCleave, J. P. Janice VanCleave's play and find out about bugs (k-2) **595.7**

Zabludoff, M. The insect class (5 and up) **595.7**

See/See also pages in the following book(s):

Arnosky, J. Field trips (3-6) **508**

Bishop, N. The secrets of animal flight (3-6) **591.47**

Fiction

Barner, B. Bug safari **E**

Cushman, D. Inspector Hopper **E**

Greenberg, D. Bugs! **E**

McDonald, M. Insects are my life **E**

Walsh, E. S. Dot & Jabber and the big bug mystery **E**

Wilson, K. A frog in the bog **E**

Poetry

Fleischman, P. Joyful noise: poems for two voices (4 and up) **811**

Florian, D. Insectlopedia **811**

Singer, M. Fireflies at midnight (2-4) **811**

Insects and spiders of the world (5 and up) **595.7**

Insects are my life. McDonald, M. **E**

Inside Grandad. Dickinson, P. **Fic**

Inside, inside, inside. Meade, H. **E**

Inside mouse, outside mouse. George, L. B. **E**

Inside out. Jiménez, F.

In Jiménez, F. The circuit: stories from the life of a migrant child p14-26 **S C**

The **inside-outside** book of libraries. Munro, R. **027**

Inside the Alamo. Murphy, J. **976.4**

Inside the Titanic. Marschall, K. **910.4**

Insignia

See also National emblems

Inspector Hopper. Cushman, D. **E**

Instruction *See* Teaching

Instructional materials *See* Teaching—Aids and devices

Instructional materials centers

See also School libraries

American Association of School Librarians. Information power **027.8**

Bradburn, F. B. Output measures for school library media programs **027.8**

Harada, V. H. Assessing learning **027.8**

Hughes-Hassell, S. Collection management for youth **025.2**

The Information-powered school **027.8**

Martin, A. M. 7 steps to an award-winning school library program **027.8**

Safford, B. R. Guide to reference materials for school media centers **011.6**

Stein, B. L. Running a school library media center **027.8**

Van Orden, P. J. Selecting books for the elementary school library media center **025.2**

Where do I start? **025.1**

The Whole school library handbook **027.8**

Integration in education *See* School integration

Intellectual freedom

See also Academic freedom

Intellectual freedom manual **323.44**

Symons, A. K. Protecting the right to read **025.2**

Intellectual freedom manual **323.44**

Intelligence, Artificial *See* Artificial intelligence

Interest groups *See* Lobbying

The **international** cookbook for kids. Locricchio, M. **641.5**

The **International** Space Station. Branley, F. M. **629.44**

International Wildlife Conservation Park (New York, N.Y.) *See* Bronx Zoo

Internet

See also Internet resources

Buzzeo, T. Terrific connections with authors, illustrators, and storytellers **372.6**

Cooper, G. New virtual field trips **025.5**

Kazunas, C. The Internet for kids (2-4) **004.6**

Sherman, J. The history of the Internet (4 and up) **004.6**

Internet and children

Raatma, L. Safety on the Internet (4 and up) **025.04**

The **Internet** for kids. Kazunas, C. **004.6**

Internet in education

Johnson, C. Using internet primary sources to teach critical thinking skills in the sciences **025.04**

Internet library [series]

Wolinsky, A. Internet power research using the Big6 approach **025.04**

Internet power research using the Big6 approach. Wolinsky, A. **025.04**

Internet resources

See also subjects with the subdivision *Internet resources,* for materials about information available on the Internet on a subject, e.g. *Job hunting—Internet resources*

Craver, K. W. Creating cyber libraries **027.8**

Is it larger? Is it smaller? Hoban, T.　　　**E**

Is it red? Is it yellow? Is it blue? Hoban, T.
　　　E

Is it rough? Is it smooth? Is it shiny? Hoban, T.
　　　E

Is my friend at home? Bierhorst, J.　　　**398.2**

Is something wrong? Schwartz, A.
　　In Schwartz, A. Scary stories 3; more tales to
　　　chill your bones p82　　　**398.2**

Is that a rash? Silverstein, A.　　　**616.5**

Is there life in outer space? Branley, F. M.
　　　576.8

Is your mama a llama? Guarino, D.　　　**E**

**Isaac Asimov's 21st century library of the uni-
　verse** [series]
　　Asimov, I. The Milky Way and other galaxies
　　　523.1

Isaacs, Anne
　　Swamp Angel　　　**E**

Isabel. Meyer, C.　　　**Fic**

Isabel of the whales. Velmans, H.　　　**Fic**

Isabella I, Queen of Spain, 1451-1504
　　See/See also pages in the following book(s):
　　Krull, K. Lives of extraordinary women (4 and
　　　up)　　　**920**
　　Meltzer, M. Ten queens (5 and up)　　　**920**
　　　　　Fiction
　　Meyer, C. Isabel (4 and up)　　　**Fic**

Isabella Abnormella and the very, very finicky
　　Queen of Trouble. Lewis, J. P.　　　**E**

Isadora, Rachel
　　At the crossroads　　　**E**
　　Ben's trumpet　　　**E**
　　Lili at ballet　　　**E**
　　Max　　　**E**
　　Nick plays baseball (k-3)　　　**796.357**
　　On your toes　　　**E**
　　Sophie skates (k-3)　　　**796.91**
　　What a family!　　　**E**
　　(il) Andersen, H. C. The little match girl
　　　Fic
　　(il) Hopkinson, D. Saving Strawberry Farm
　　　E
　　(il) McKissack, P. C. Flossie & the fox　　　**E**

Ish. Reynolds, P.　　　**E**

Islam
　　Barber, N. Islamic empires (4 and up)　　　**704**
　　Demi. Muhammad (4 and up)　　　**297**
　　Douglass, S. L. Ramadan (1-3)　　　**297.3**
　　Ganeri, A. Muslim festivals throughout the year
　　　(3-6)　　　**297.3**
　　Ghazi, S. H. Ramadan (k-3)　　　**297.3**
　　Hoyt-Goldsmith, D. Celebrating Ramadan (3-5)
　　　297.3
　　Khan, A. K. What you will see inside a mosque
　　　(3-6)　　　**297.3**
　　Marchant, K. Id-ul-Fitr (3-5)　　　**297.3**
　　Petrini, C. M. What makes me a Muslim? (3-5)
　　　297.3
　　See/See also pages in the following book(s):
　　Osborne, M. P. One world, many religions (4
　　　and up)　　　**200**

Islamic art
　　Barber, N. Islamic empires (4 and up)　　　**704**
Islamic countries
　　　　　Civilization
　　Beshore, G. W. Science in early Islamic culture
　　　(4 and up)　　　**509**
Islamic empires. Barber, N.　　　**704**
Island counting 1 2 3. Lessac, F.　　　**E**
An **island** grows. Schaefer, L. M.　　　**E**
Island of fear. San Souci, R.
　　In San Souci, R. More short & shivery; thirty
　　　terrifying tales p68-74　　　**398.2**
Island of hope. Sandler, M. W.　　　**325.73**
Island of the Blue Dolphins. O'Dell, S.　　　**Fic**
Island of the lost children. Osborne, M. P.
　　In Osborne, M. P. Favorite medieval tales
　　　p25-33　　　**398.2**
The **island** on Bird Street. Orlev, U.　　　**Fic**
An **island** scrapbook. Wright-Frierson, V.　　　**508**
Islands
　　　　　Fiction
　　Brown, M. W. The little island　　　**E**
　　Buzzeo, T. The sea chest　　　**E**
　　MacLachlan, P. Baby (5 and up)　　　**Fic**
　　Martin, J. B. On Sand Island　　　**E**
　　Schaefer, L. M. An island grows　　　**E**
Isle, Mick
　　Malaria (5 and up)　　　**616.9**
Isles, Joanna
　　(il) Stevenson, R. L. A child's garden of verses
　　　821
Israel
　　　See also Jerusalem
　　DuBois, J. Israel (5 and up)　　　**956.94**
　　Grossman, L. M. Children of Israel (2-4)
　　　956.94
　　Roy, J. R. Israel (2-4)　　　**956.94**
Israel and the werewolf. San Souci, R.
　　In San Souci, R. A terrifying taste of short &
　　　shivery; thirty creepy tales p114-17
　　　398.2
Israel-Arab conflicts
　　Ellis, D. Three wishes (5 and up)　　　**956.94**
　　Senker, C. The Arab-Israeli conflict (5 and up)
　　　956.04
Issues in focus today [series]
　　Winkler, K. Bullying　　　**371.5**
Istanbul (Turkey)
　　Barber, N. Istanbul (3-6)　　　**949.6**
It. Van Laan, N.
　　In Van Laan, N. Teeny tiny tingly tales　　　**E**
It came from beneath the bed!. Howe, J.　　　**Fic**
It couldn't be worse!. Van Kampen, V.　　　**398.2**
It is the wind. Wolff, F.　　　**E**
It is time to go to sleep. Schwartz, A.
　　In Schwartz, A. There is a carrot in my ear,
　　　and other noodle tales p58-63　　　**398.2**
It looked like spilt milk. Shaw, C.　　　**E**
It rained all day that night (3-6)　　　**811.008**
The **Italian** American family album. Hoobler, D.
　　　305.8

Italian Americans

Hoobler, D. The Italian American family album
(5 and up) **305.8**

Fiction

Bartone, E. Peppe the lamplighter **E**

Bunting, E. A picnic in October **E**

Creech, S. Replay (5 and up) **Fic**

Hall, B. E. Henry and the kite dragon **E**

Martino, C. A. Rosa, sola (4-6) **Fic**

Napoli, D. J. The king of Mulberry Street (5
and up) **Fic**

Schirripa, S. R. Nicky Deuce (4-6) **Fic**

Smith, D. J. The boys of San Joaquin (5 and
up) **Fic**

Poetry

Testa, M. Becoming Joe DiMaggio (4 and up)
811

Italian artists *See* Artists, Italian

Italiano, Bob

(il) Pascoe, E. Scholastic kid's almanac
031.02

Italy

Behnke, A. Italy in pictures (5 and up) **945**

Malone, M. G. Italy (2-4) **945**

Winter, J. K. Italy (5 and up) **945**

Fiction

Alexander, L. The rope trick (4 and up) **Fic**

Avi. Midnight magic (5 and up) **Fic**

Barrett, T. On Etruscan time (5 and up) **Fic**

Bedard, M. The wolf of Gubbio (3-6) **398.2**

De Paola, T. Strega Nona: an old tale **E**

Egielski, R. Saint Francis and the wolf (1-3)
398.2

Fusco Castaldo, N. Pizza for the queen **E**

Radunsky, V. The mighty asparagus **E**

Weston, C. The diary of Melanie Martin; or,
How I survived Matt the Brat, Michelangelo,
and the Leaning Tower of Pizza (3-6) **Fic**

Folklore

See Folklore—Italy

Social life and customs

Potter, G. The year I didn't go to school **E**

Italy in pictures. Behnke, A. **945**

It's a girl thing. Jukes, M. **305.23**

It's a hummingbird's life. Kelly, I. **598**

It's a miracle!. Spinner, S. **E**

It's about dogs. Johnston, T. **811**

It's about time!. Murphy, S. J. **529**

It's about time! Science projects. Gardner, R.
529

It's all in your head. Funston, S. **612.8**

It's Christmas. Prelutsky, J. **811**

It's disgusting—and we ate it!. Solheim, J.
641.3

It's "Him!". Schwartz, A.

In Schwartz, A. Scary stories 3; more tales to
chill your bones p84-85 **398.2**

It's Justin Time, Amber Brown. Danziger, P.
E

It's like this, Cat. Neville, E. C. **Fic**

It's my school. Grindley, S. **E**

It's my state! [series] (4 and up) **973**

It's not the stork!. Harris, R. H. **612.6**

It's perfectly normal. Harris, R. H. **613.9**

It's quacking time!. Waddell, M. **E**

It's raining pigs & noodles. Prelutsky, J. **811**

It's science! [series]

Hewitt, S. Solid, liquid, or gas? **530.4**

It's snowing!. Dunrea, O. **E**

It's snowing! it's snowing!. Prelutsky, J. **811**

It's so amazing!. Harris, R. H. **612.6**

It's Thanksgiving. Prelutsky, J. **811**

It's Valentine's Day. Prelutsky, J. **811**

Ivan the Cow's Son. Afanas'ev, A. N.

In Afanas'ev, A. N. Russian fairy tales p234-
49 **398.2**

Ivan the peasant's son and the thumb-sized man.
Afanas'ev, A. N.

In Afanas'ev, A. N. Russian fairy tales p262-
68 **398.2**

Ivan the Simpleton. Afanas'ev, A. N.

In Afanas'ev, A. N. Russian fairy tales p142-
45 **398.2**

Ivanko, John D.

(jt. auth) Ajmera, M. Be my neighbor **307**

(jt. auth) Ajmera, M. To be an artist **700**

Ivanko the bear's son. Afanas'ev, A. N.

In Afanas'ev, A. N. Russian fairy tales p221-
23 **398.2**

Ivanushka the Little Fool. Afanas'ev, A. N.

In Afanas'ev, A. N. Russian fairy tales p62-
65 **398.2**

I've seen the promised land [biography of Martin
Luther King] Myers, W. D. **92**

Ives, Charles Edward, 1874-1954

About

Gerstein, M. What Charlie heard [biography of
Charles Edward Ives] (k-3) **92**

See/See also pages in the following book(s):

Krull, K. Lives of the musicians (4 and up)
920

Ives, David

Scrib (5 and up) **Fic**

Ivory Coast

Sheehan, P. Côte d'Ivoire (5 and up) **966.68**

The **ivory** cups. Lunge-Larsen, L.

In Lunge-Larsen, L. The hidden folk; stories
of fairies, dwarves, selkies, and other secret beings p14-17 **398.2**

Ivy + Bean. Barrows, A. **Fic**

Iwai, Melissa

(il) Mortensen, D. D. Good night engines **E**

(il) Spinelli, E. Night shift daddy **E**

Iwamatsu, Atushi Jun

Crow Boy **E**

Umbrella **E**

Iwamura, Kazuo

(jt. auth) Carle, E. Where are you going? To see
my friend! **E**

Izzy's place. Kornblatt, M. **Fic**

Jamaica
  Roy, J. R. Jamaica (2-4)   **972.92**
  Sheehan, S. Jamaica (5 and up)   **972.92**
              Fiction
  Pomerantz, C. The chalk doll   **E**

Jamaican poetry
  Berry, J. A nest full of stars (2-5)   **821**

Jamaica's find. Havill, J.   **E**

Jamari's drum. Bynum, E.   **E**

Jamberry. Degen, B.   **E**

Jambo means hello. Feelings, M.   **E**

James, Ann
  (il) Bedford, D. The way I love you   **E**
  (il) Wild, M. Midnight babies   **E**

James, Curtis
  (il) Linda Brown, you are not alone. See Linda
    Brown, you are not alone   **323.1**
  (jt. auth) Rappaport, D. The school is not white!
                        379

James, Elizabeth
  How to write terrific book reports (4 and up)
                      808

James, Mary
  Shoebag (5 and up)   **Fic**

James, Simon
  Ancient Rome   **937**
  Baby Brains   **E**
  Little One Step   **E**
  (comp) Days like this. See Days like this
                   811.008

James and the giant peach. Dahl, R.   **Fic**

James Marshall's Cinderella. Karlin, B. **398.2**

James Marshall's Mother Goose   **398.8**

James the dancing dog. Maybarduk, L.   **E**

James Towne: struggle for survival. Sewall, M.
                   975.5

Jamestown (Va.)
  Sewall, M. James Towne: struggle for survival
    (3-5)   **975.5**
              History
  Karwoski, G. Miracle (4-6)   **972.9**
  Rosen, D. New beginnings (4-6)   **975.5**
      History—Fiction
  Carbone, E. L. Blood on the river (5 and up)
                    Fic

Jamestown and the Virginia Colony. See Rosen,
  D. New beginnings   **975.5**

Jamie O'Rourke and the big potato. De Paola, T.
                    398.2

Jamie O'Rourke and the pooka. De Paola, T.
                      E

Jane gets a donkey. Schwartz, A.
  In Schwartz, A. All of our noses are here,
    and other noodle tales p8-17   **398.2**

Jane grows a carrot. Schwartz, A.
  In Schwartz, A. There is a carrot in my ear,
    and other noodle tales p40-43   **398.2**

Janeczko, Paul B.
  Top secret (4 and up)   **652**
  Wing nuts (2-4)   **811**
  (comp) The Place my words are looking for.
    See The Place my words are looking for
                   811.008

  (comp) Poetry from A to Z. See Poetry from A
    to Z   **808.1**
  (comp) A Poke in the I. See A Poke in the I
                   811.008
  (comp) Stone bench in an empty park. See
    Stone bench in an empty park   **811.008**

Jango-Cohen, Judith
  Armadillos (3-6)   **599.3**
  Camels (3-6)   **599.63**
  Chinese New Year (1-3)   **394.26**
  The history of food (5 and up)   **641.3**
  Kangaroos (3-6)   **599.2**
  Octopuses (3-6)   **594**
  Porcupines (3-6)   **599.35**
  Rhinoceroses (3-6)   **599.66**

Jani, Mahendra
  What you will see inside a Hindu temple (3-6)
                   294.5

Jani, Vandana
  (jt. auth) Jani, M. What you will see inside a
    Hindu temple   **294.5**

Janice VanCleave's 201 awesome, magical, bizarre & incredible experiments. VanCleave, J.
  P.   **507.8**

Janice VanCleave's 202 oozing, bubbling, dripping & bouncing experiments. VanCleave, J.
  P.   **507.8**

Janice VanCleave's 203 icy, freezing, frosty, cool
  & wild experiments. VanCleave, J. P.
                   507.8

Janice VanCleave's constellations for every kid.
  VanCleave, J. P.   **523.8**

Janice VanCleave's earth science for every kid.
  VanCleave, J. P.   **550**

Janice Vancleave's ecology for every kid.
  VanCleave, J. P.   **577**

Janice VanCleave's electricity. VanCleave, J. P.
                   537

Janice VanCleave's food and nutrition for every
  kid. VanCleave, J. P.   **613.2**

Janice VanCleave's geometry for every kid.
  VanCleave, J. P.   **516**

Janice VanCleave's guide to more of the best science fair projects. VanCleave, J. P.   **507.8**

Janice VanCleave's guide to the best science fair
  projects. VanCleave, J. P.   **507.8**

Janice VanCleave's insects and spiders.
  VanCleave, J. P.   **595.7**

Janice VanCleave's oceans for every kid.
  VanCleave, J. P.   **551.46**

Janice VanCleave's plants. VanCleave, J. P.
                  580.7

Janice VanCleave's play and find out about bugs.
  VanCleave, J. P.   **595.7**

Janice VanCleave's play and find out about math.
  VanCleave, J. P.   **513**

Janice VanCleave's play and find out about nature. VanCleave, J. P.   **570**

Janice VanCleave's rocks and minerals.
  VanCleave, J. P.   **552**

Janice VanCleave's science around the year.
  VanCleave, J. P.   **507.8**

Jarrett, Clare
The best picnic ever   E

Jarrow, Gail
Chiggers (4-6)   **616.9**

Jarvis, Robin
The alchemist's cat (5 and up)   **Fic**
The dark portal (5 and up)   **Fic**
The oaken throne (5 and up)   **Fic**

Jaskiel, Stan
(il) Hauser, J. F. Wow! I'm reading!   **372.4**
(il) Mahren, S. Make your own teddy bears &
    bear clothes!   **745.592**

Jaskol, Julie
City of angels (2-4)   **979.4**

Jason's bears. Bauer, M. D.   E

Jason's gold. Hobbs, W.   **Fic**

Jasper, Richard P.
(jt. auth) Halsted, D. D. Disaster planning
     025.8

Jataka stories
Demi. Buddha stories (3-6)   **294.3**
Galdone, P. The monkey and the crocodile (k-2)
     398.2
Lee, J. M. I once was a monkey (4 and up)
     294.3

Jay, Alison
ABC: a child's first alphabet book   E
(il) Curtis, C. I took the moon for a walk   E
(il) Lewis, J. P. A world of wonders   **811**
(il) Sedgwick, M. The emperor's new clothes
     E

Jazz A-B-Z. Marsalis, W.   **781.65**

Jazz music
     See also Blues music
Marsalis, W. Jazz A-B-Z (5 and up)   **781.65**
Raschka, C. John Coltrane's Giant steps   E
     Fiction
Daly, N. Ruby sings the blues   E
Miller, W. Rent party jazz   E
Panahi, H. L. Bebop Express   E

Jazz musicians
Collier, J. L. The Louis Armstrong you never
    knew (4 and up)   **92**
Kimmel, E. A. A horn for Louis [biography of
    Louis Armstrong] (2-4)   **92**
Marsalis, W. Jazz A-B-Z (5 and up)   **781.65**
Pinkney, A. D. Duke Ellington (2-4)   **92**
Raschka, C. Mysterious Thelonious   E
     Fiction
Taylor, D. A. Sweet music in Harlem   E

Jazzy science projects with sound and music.
    Gardner, R.   **534**

The **jealous** husband. Terada, A. M.
     In Terada, A. M. Under the starfruit tree;
     folktales from Vietnam p10-13   **398.2**

Jean and Jeannette. Sierra, J.
     In Sierra, J. Can you guess my name?; tradi-
     tional tales around the world p83-88
     398.2

Jean-Bart, Leslie
(il) Coy, J. Strong to the hoop   E

Jean Laffite and the big ol' whale. Fox, F. G.
     E

Jeanne d'Arc, Saint *See* Joan, of Arc, Saint,
    1412-1431

Jeans (Clothing)
     Fiction
Brockmeier, K. Grooves (4 and up)   **Fic**

Jeffers, Susan
(il) Ehrlich, A. Thumbelina   E
(il) Leopold, N. S. C. K is for kitten   E
(il) Longfellow, H. W. Hiawatha   **811**
(il) Paterson, K. Blueberries for the queen   E
(il) Wells, R. McDuff moves in   E

Jefferson, Thomas, 1743-1826
     About
Adler, D. A. A picture book of Thomas Jeffer-
    son (1-3)   **92**
     Fiction
Fleming, C. The hatmaker's sign   E
     Homes and haunts
Richards, N. Monticello (4-6)   **975.5**

Jeffrey, Laura S.
All about Braille (2-4)   **411**
Birds (3-5)   **636.6**
Cats (3-5)   **636.8**
Dogs (3-5)   **636.7**
Fish (3-5)   **639.34**
Hamsters, gerbils, guinea pigs, rabbits, ferrets,
    mice, and rats (3-5)   **636.9**
Horses (3-5)   **636.1**

Jellies. George, T. C.   **593.5**

Jelly beans. Kreger, C.   **641.8**

Jellyfishes
George, T. C. Jellies (2-4)   **593.5**
King, D. C. Jellyfish (3-6)   **593.5**

Jemison, Mae C.
Find where the wind goes (5 and up)   **92**
     About
Alagna, M. Mae Jemison (4 and up)   **92**

Jenkins, Emily
Five creatures   E
That new animal   E

Jenkins, Leonard
(il) Burleigh, R. Langston's train ride   **92**
(il) Holt, K. W. Mister and me   **Fic**
(il) Kessler, C. The best beekeeper of Lalibela
     E
(il) Morrow, B. O. A good night for freedom
     E
(il) Myers, W. D. I've seen the promised land
    [biography of Martin Luther King]   **92**
(il) Myers, W. D. Malcolm X   **92**
(il) Thomas, J. C. The skull talks back and other
    haunting tales   **398.2**

Jenkins, Martin
The emperor's egg (k-3)   **598**

Jenkins, Steve
Actual size (k-3)   **591.4**
Almost gone   **591.68**
Big & little (k-2)   **591.4**
Biggest, strongest, fastest (k-2)   **590**
Hottest, coldest, highest, deepest (k-2)   **910**
I see a kookaburra! (k-3)   **591.7**
Life on earth: the story of evolution (3-6)
     576.8
Move!   E

Jenkins, Steve—*Continued*
Prehistoric actual size (k-3)   **560**
The top of the world (2-4)   **796.52**
What do you do when something wants to eat you? (k-3)   **591.47**
What do you do with a tail like this? (k-3)   **573.8**
(il) Collard, S. B., III. Animal dads   **591.56**
(il) Collard, S. B., III. Making animal babies   **571.8**
(il) Guiberson, B. Z. Rain, rain, rain forest   **577.3**
(il) Pfeffer, W. Wiggling worms at work   **592**
(il) Rockwell, A. F. Bugs are insects   **595.7**
(il) Rose, D. L. Into the A, B, sea   **591.7**
(il) Rose, D. L. One nighttime sea   **E**

Jenner, Edward, 1749-1823
About
Marrin, A. Dr. Jenner and the speckled monster (5 and up)   **614.5**

Jennie's hat. Keats, E. J.   **E**

Jennifer, Hecate, Macbeth, William McKinley, and me, Elizabeth. Konigsburg, E. L.   **Fic**

Jennifer Murdley's toad. Coville, B.   **Fic**

Jennings, Patrick
Flit
    In Friends; stories about new friends, old friends, and unexpectedly true friends   **S C**
Out standing in my field (4-6)   **Fic**
The weeping willow (2-4)   **Fic**

Jennings, Peter
The century for young people (4 and up)   **909.82**

Jennings, Richard W.
My life of crime (5 and up)   **Fic**
Orwell's luck (5 and up)   **Fic**

Jensen, Julie
Fundamental volleyball (5 and up)   **796.325**

Jensen, Julie M.
(ed) The Best in children's nonfiction. See The Best in children's nonfiction   **028.1**

Jenssen, Hans
(il) Reynolds, D. W. Star wars: incredible cross sections   **791.43**

Jeong, Kyoung-Sim
(il) Kim, S.-U. Korean children's favorite stories   **398.2**

Jerabek, Ann
(jt. auth) Hall-Ellis, S. D. Grants for school libraries   **025.1**

Jeram, Anita
(il) Hest, A. Kiss good night   **E**
(il) King-Smith, D. All pigs are beautiful   **636.4**
(il) King-Smith, D. I love guinea pigs   **636.9**
(il) McBratney, S. Guess how much I love you   **E**

Jeremy Thatcher, dragon hatcher. Coville, B.   **Fic**

Jeremy Visick. Wiseman, D.   **Fic**

Jermyn, Leslie
Belize (5 and up)   **972.82**

Guyana (5 and up)   **988.1**
Paraguay (5 and up)   **989.2**
Uruguay (5 and up)   **989.5**
(jt. auth) Cheong-Lum, R. N. Haiti   **972.94**
(jt. auth) DuBois, J. Colombia   **986.1**
(jt. auth) Foley, E. Dominican Republic   **972.93**
(jt. auth) Foley, E. Ecuador   **986.6**
(jt. auth) Gan, D. Sweden   **948.5**
(jt. auth) Gofen, E. Argentina   **982**
(jt. auth) Reilly, M.-J. Mexico   **972**
(jt. auth) Richard, C. Brazil   **981**
(jt. auth) Sheehan, S. Cuba   **972.91**
(jt. auth) South, C. Syria   **956.91**
(jt. auth) Srinivasan, R. India   **954**
(jt. auth) Winter, J. K. Italy   **945**

Jerome, Karen A.
(il) McMahon, P. Just add one Chinese sister   **E**

Jerusalem
Bowden, R. Jerusalem (3-6)   **956.94**
Fiction
Grossman, D. Duel (5 and up)   **Fic**
Poetry
Podwal, M. H. Jerusalem sky (3-5)   **811**

Jerusalem sky. Podwal, M. H.   **811**

Jesse Bear, what will you wear? Carlstrom, N. W.   **E**

Jessica. Henkes, K.   **E**

The **jester**. Afanas'ev, A. N.
    In Afanas'ev, A. N. Russian fairy tales p151-55   **398.2**

Jesus Christ
About
Bible. N.T. The Easter story   **232.9**
De Paola, T. The miracles of Jesus (k-3)   **232.9**
Demi. Jesus (3-6)   **232.9**
Lottridge, C. B. Stories from the life of Jesus (4 and up)   **232.9**
Mayer, M. Seeing Jesus in His own words   **232.9**
Thompson, L. Love one another (1-3)   **232.9**
Wildsmith, B. Jesus (k-3)   **232.9**
Winthrop, E. He is risen: the Easter story (k-3)   **232.9**
Fiction
Menotti, G. C. Amahl and the night visitors (2-4)   **Fic**
Speare, E. G. The bronze bow (6 and up)   **Fic**
Wildsmith, B. A Christmas story   **E**
Nativity
Bible. N.T. The Christmas story   **232.9**
Byrd, R. Saint Francis and the Christmas donkey   **E**
Chaconas, D. Christmas mouseling   **E**
Crossley-Holland, K. How many miles to Bethlehem? (k-3)   **232.9**
Milligan, B. Brigid's cloak (k-3)   **398.2**
Ryan, P. M. There was no snow on Christmas Eve   **E**
Poetry
Grimes, N. At Jerusalem's gate (5 and up)   **811**

Jews—Fiction—*Continued*

Morpurgo, M. Waiting for Anya (5 and up) **Fic**

Napoli, D. J. The king of Mulberry Street (5 and up) **Fic**

Oberman, S. The always prayer shawl **E**

Orgel, D. The devil in Vienna (6 and up) **Fic**

Orlev, U. The island on Bird Street (5 and up) **Fic**

Oswald, N. Nothing here but stones (5 and up) **Fic**

Polacco, P. The butterfly (2-4) **Fic**

Polacco, P. Chicken Sunday **E**

Polacco, P. Christmas tapestry (2-4) **Fic**

Polacco, P. The keeping quilt **E**

Polacco, P. Mrs. Katz and Tush **E**

Polacco, P. The trees of the dancing goats **E**

Propp, V. W. When the soldiers were gone (3-5) **Fic**

Radin, R. Y. Escape to the forest (3-6) **Fic**

Rael, E. O. Rivka's first Thanksgiving **E**

Rappaport, D. The secret seder (2-4) **E**

Rocklin, J. Strudel stories (4 and up) **Fic**

Rosen, M. J. Elijah's angel (2-4) **Fic**

Roy, J. R. Yellow star (5 and up) **Fic**

Sachs, M. Lost in America (5 and up) **Fic**

Schur, M. The circlemaker (5 and up) **Fic**

Shalant, P. When pirates came to Brooklyn (4 and up) **Fic**

Shulevitz, U. The travels of Benjamin of Tudela (4 and up) **Fic**

Silverman, E. When the chickens went on strike **E**

Singer, I. B. The fools of Chelm and their history (4 and up) **Fic**

Singer, I. B. The power of light (4 and up) **S C**

Singer, I. B. Stories for children (4 and up) **S C**

Taback, S. Joseph had a little overcoat **E**

Taylor, S. All-of-a-kind family (4-6) **Fic**

Vos, I. Anna is still here (4 and up) **Fic**

Vos, I. Hide and seek (4 and up) **Fic**

Woodruff, E. The memory coat **E**

Zalben, J. B. Unfinished dreams (5 and up) **Fic**

Folklore

Adler, D. A. Chanukah in Chelm (k-3) **398.2**

Fowles, S. The bachelor and the bean (k-3) **398.2**

Geras, A. My grandmother's stories (3-5) **398.2**

Jaffe, N. The way meat loves salt (k-3) **398.2**

Kimmel, E. A. Gershon's monster **398.2**

Kimmel, E. A. The spotted pony: a collection of Hanukkah stories (3-6) **398.2**

Oberman, S. Solomon and the ant; (5 and up) **398.2**

Schwartz, H. Before you were born (k-3) **398.2**

Schwartz, H. A coat for the moon and other Jewish tales (4 and up) **398.2**

Schwartz, H. Invisible kingdoms (3-5) **398.2**

Schwartz, H. A journey to paradise and other Jewish tales (3-5) **398.2**

Silverman, E. Raisel's riddle (k-3) **398.2**

Singer, I. B. Zlateh the goat, and other stories (4 and up) **398.2**

Souhami, J. The little, little house (k-2) **398.2**

Taback, S. Kibitzers and fools (k-3) **398.2**

History

Waldman, N. Masada (4 and up) **933**

Legends

See Jewish legends

Persecutions

See also Holocaust, 1933-1945; World War, 1939-1945—Jews—Rescue

Rites and ceremonies

See Judaism—Customs and practices

Czechoslovakia

Rubin, S. G. The cat with the yellow star (3-6) **940.53**

Europe

Greenfeld, H. The hidden children (4 and up) **940.53**

Rosenberg, M. B. Hiding to survive (5 and up) **940.53**

France

Millman, I. Hidden child (4 and up) **940.53**

Germany

Perl, L. Four perfect pebbles (6 and up) **940.53**

Rubin, S. G. The flag with fifty-six stars (3-5) **940.53**

Russo, M. Always remember me (3-5) **940.53**

Netherlands

Adler, D. A. Hiding from the Nazis (2-4) **940.53**

Frank, A. The diary of a young girl (6 and up) **92**

Frank, A. The diary of a young girl: the definitive edition (6 and up) **92**

Gold, A. L. Memories of Anne Frank (5 and up) **92**

Hurwitz, J. Anne Frank: life in hiding (3-5) **92**

Koestler-Grack, R. A. The story of Anne Frank (2-4) **92**

Lee, C. A. A friend called Anne (4 and up) **940.53**

Poole, J. Anne Frank (2-4) **92**

Reiss, J. The upstairs room (5 and up) **92**

Rol, R. v. d. Anne Frank, beyond the diary (5 and up) **92**

Sawyer, K. K. Anne Frank (5 and up) **92**

Poland

Krinitz, E. N. Memories of survival (6 and up) **940.53**

Whiteman, D. B. Lonek's journey (5 and up) **940.53**

United States

Bierman, C. Journey to Ellis Island (3-5) **325.73**

Fisher, L. E. To bigotry, no sanction (4 and up) **296**

Hoobler, D. The Jewish American family album (5 and up) **305.8**

Johnson, Angela
Bird (5 and up)   Fic
A cool moonlight (5 and up)   Fic
Heaven (6 and up)   Fic
I dream of trains   E
Just like Josh Gibson   E
The other side   811
Songs of faith (5 and up)   Fic
Tell me a story, Mama   E
Tripping over the lunch lady
   In Tripping over the lunch lady and other
     school stories p1-15   S C
Violet's music   E

Johnson, Carolyn
Using internet primary sources to teach critical
   thinking skills in the sciences   025.04

Johnson, Cathy Ann
(il) Smalls, I. My Pop Pop and me   E

Johnson, Crockett
Ellen's lion
   In You read to me & I'll read to you; 20th-
     century stories to share p171-89   E
Harold and the purple crayon   E
(il) Cook, B. The little fish that got away   E
(il) Krauss, R. The carrot seed   E
(il) Krauss, R. The happy egg   E

Johnson, David
(il) Cohn, A. L. Abraham Lincoln   92
(il) Martin, J. B. On Sand Island   E

Johnson, Dinah
Quinnie Blue   E

Johnson, Dolores
Onward [biography of Matthew Henson] (5 and
   up)   92

Johnson, Donald B. (Donald Barton)
Henry hikes to Fitchburg   E

Johnson, Gillian
Thora (4-6)   Fic
(il) Maybarduk, L. James the dancing dog   E

Johnson, Ginger
Paper-folding fun! (3-5)   745.54

Johnson, James Weldon
Lift every voice and sing   782.42

Johnson, Jinny
Simon & Schuster children's guide to insects
   and spiders (4 and up)   595.7
Simon & Schuster children's guide to sea creatures (4 and up)   591.7

Johnson, Krista
(il) O'Reilly, G. Slangalicious   427

Johnson, Larry
(il) Walter, M. P. Alec's primer   E

Johnson, Layne
(il) Cowley, J. Where horses run free   E
(il) Knowlton, L. L. A young man's dance
     E

Johnson, Mamie, 1935-
About
Green, M. Y. A strong right arm: the story of
   Mamie "Peanut" Johnson (4 and up)   92

Johnson, Mary
Primary sources in the library   027.8

Johnson, Milton
(il) O'Dell, S. The black pearl   Fic

Johnson, Pamela
(il) Aiken, J. Shadows and moonshine   S C

Johnson, Paul Brett
Fearless Jack (k-3)   398.2
Jack outwits the giants (k-3)   398.2
On top of spaghetti   E
(il) McDonald, M. Insects are my life   E

Johnson, Peanut *See* Johnson, Mamie, 1935-

Johnson, Rebecca L.
Genetics (5 and up)   576.5
A walk in the boreal forest (3-6)   577.3
A walk in the deciduous forest (3-6)   577.3
A walk in the desert (3-6)   577.5
A walk in the prairie (3-6)   577.4
A walk in the tundra (3-6)   577.5

Johnson, Robert, 1911-1938
See/See also pages in the following book(s):
Lester, J. The blues singers (5 and up)   920

Johnson, Stephen
Alphabet city   E
City by numbers   E
(il) Burleigh, R. Goal   811
(il) Burleigh, R. Hoops   811
(il) Look, L. Love as strong as ginger   E
(il) Siebert, D. Tour america   811

Johnson, Steve
(il) Duncan, L. I walk at night   E
(il) Krull, K. The boy on Fairfield Street: how
   Ted Geisel grew up to become Dr. Seuss
     92
(il) Osborne, M. P. New York's bravest   E
(il) Panahi, H. L. Bebop Express   E
(il) Paolilli, P. Silver seeds   811
(il) Scieszka, J. The Frog Prince continued
     E
(il) Wolkstein, D. The day Ocean came to visit
     398.2

Johnson, Sylvia A.
Crows (3-6)   598
Ferrets (3-6)   636.9
Mapping the world (4 and up)   912
Songbirds (3-6)   598

Johnson-Davies, Denys
Goha the wise fool (2-4)   398.2

Johnston, Robert D. (Robert Dougall)
The making of America (5 and up)   973

Johnston, Tony
Alice Nizzy Nazzy, the Witch of Santa Fe
     E
Alien & Possum: hanging out   E
Any small goodness (4 and up)   Fic
The barn owls   E
Day of the Dead   E
Desert song   E
It's about dogs (2-4)   811
The quilt story   E
The spoon in the bathroom wall (3-5)   Fic
The tale of Rabbit and Coyote (k-3)   398.2
That summer   E
Uncle Rain Cloud   E
The whole green world   E

Johnston, William J., b. 1850
Fiction
Wisler, G. C. Mr. Lincoln's drummer (4 and up)
     Fic

Johnstone, Leslie
(jt. auth) Levine, S. Backyard science **507.8**
(jt. auth) Levine, S. Bathtub science **507.8**
(jt. auth) Levine, S. Kitchen science **507.8**
(jt. auth) Levine, S. The optics book **535**
(jt. auth) Levine, S. The science of sound & music **534**
(jt. auth) Levine, S. Shocking science **537**
(jt. auth) Levine, S. Wonderful weather **551.5**

Jokes
Brewer, P. You must be joking! (3-6) **818**
Cerf, B. Riddles and more riddles! **793.73**
Hall, K. Ribbit riddles (k-2) **793.73**
Kessler, L. P. Old Turtle's 90 knock-knocks, jokes, and riddles (1-3) **793.73**
Thomas, L. Ha! Ha! Ha! (3-6) **793.73**

Jomo & the Dakini queen. Rose, N. C.
In Rose, N. C. Tibetan tales for little Buddhas **398.2**

Jon Agee's palindromania!. Agee, J. **793.73**

Jonas, Ann
The quilt **E**
Reflections **E**
Round trip **E**
Splash! **E**

Jonell, Lynne
Let's play rough **E**
When Mommy was mad **E**

Jones, Mother, 1830-1930
About
Bartoletti, S. C. Kids on strike! (5 and up) **331.8**
Koestler-Grack, R. A. The story of Mother Jones (2-4) **92**

Jones, Bill T.
Dance (k-3) **792.8**

Jones, Carol
(il) Old MacDonald had a farm. See Old MacDonald had a farm **782.42**

Jones, Casey, 1863-1900
Fiction
Johnson, A. I dream of trains **E**

Jones, Charlotte Foltz
Westward ho! (5 and up) **920**

Jones, David
Mighty robots (5 and up) **629.8**

Jones, Diana Wynne
Castle in the air (6 and up) **Fic**
Howl's moving castle (6 and up) **Fic**
Mixed magics (5 and up) **S C**
Includes the following stories: Warlock at the wheel; The sage of theare; Carol Oneir's hundredth dream; Stealer of souls

Jones, Dolores Blythe
(ed) Building a special collection of children's literature in your library. See Building a special collection of children's literature in your library **025.2**

Jones, Douglas B.
(il) Cordsen, C. F. The milkman **E**
(il) Thimmesh, C. Madam president **920**

Jones, Elizabeth Orton
(il) Field, R. Prayer for a child **242**

Jones, Evan
(jt. auth) Jones, J. Knead it, punch it, bake it! **641.8**

Jones, Joe, 1896-1987
About
Haskins, J. Out of the darkness (5 and up) **305.8**

Jones, John Paul, 1747-1792
About
Haugen, B. John Paul Jones (4 and up) **92**

Jones, Judith
Knead it, punch it, bake it! (3-6) **641.8**

Jones, Lynda
Kids around the world celebrate! (4-6) **394.26**

Jones, Mary
(il) Peacock, C. A. Sugar was my best food **362.1**

Jones, Mary Harris *See* Jones, Mother, 1830-1930

Jones, Pattie Ridley
(jt. auth) Greenfield, E. Childtimes: a three-generation memoir **920**

Jones, Randy
(il) Leacock, E. Places in time **911**

Jones, Sally Lloyd
Time to say goodnight **E**

Jones, Tim Wynne- *See* Wynne-Jones, Tim

Jones, Ursula
The witch's children **E**

Jonkel, Charles
About
Patent, D. H. A polar bear biologist at work (4 and up) **599.78**

Joosse, Barbara M.
Hot city **E**
A houseful of Christmas **E**
Mama, do you love me? **E**
Papa, do you love me? **E**

Joplin, Scott, 1868-1917
See/See also pages in the following book(s):
Krull, K. Lives of the musicians (4 and up) **920**

Jordan, Deloris
Salt in his shoes **E**

Jordan, Denise
Juneteenth (1-3) **394.26**

Jordan, Michael, 1963-
About
Cooper, F. Jump! [biography of Michael Jordan] (k-3) **92**
Jordan, D. Salt in his shoes **E**

Jordan, Rosa
Lost Goat Lane (5 and up) **Fic**

Jordan, Roslyn M.
(jt. auth) Jordan, D. Salt in his shoes **E**

Jordan, Sandra
(jt. auth) Greenberg, J. Action Jackson [biography of Jackson Pollock] **92**
(jt. auth) Greenberg, J. Frank O. Gehry **92**

Jorinda and Jorindel. Watts, B. **398.2**

Jorisch, Stephane
(il) Brisson, P. I remember Miss Perry **E**

Juan, Ana—*Continued*
(il) Winter, J. Frida [Kahlo]   **92**
Juan and the pinto bean stalk. Marcantonio, P. S.
In Marcantonio, P. S. Red ridin' in the hood; and other cuentos   **S C**
Juan Bobo. Bernier-Grand, C. T.   **398.2**
Juan Bobo and the three-legged pot. González, L. M.
In González, L. M. Señor Cat's romance and other favorite stories from Latin America p15-19   **398.2**
Juan Bobo goes to work. Montes, M.   **398.2**
Juana Inés de la Cruz, 1651-1695
About
Mora, P. A library for Juana: the world of Sor Juana Inés (2-4)   **92**
Jubb, Kendahl Jan
(il) Patent, D. H. Big cats   **599.75**
(il) Patent, D. H. Colorful, captivating coral reefs   **577.7**
(il) Patent, D. H. Flashy fantastic rain forest frogs   **597.8**
(il) Patent, D. H. Slinky, scaly, slithery snakes   **597.96**
Jubilee Singers (Musical group)
Fiction
Hopkinson, D. A band of angels   **E**
Judaism
Cato, V. The Torah and Judaism (5 and up)   **222**
Hoffman, L. A. What you will see inside a synagogue (3-6)   **296.4**
Keene, M. Judaism (5 and up)   **296**
Woog, A. What makes me a Jew? (3-5)   **296.4**
See/See also pages in the following book(s):
Osborne, M. P. One world, many religions (4 and up)   **200**
Customs and practices
Chaikin, M. Menorahs, mezuzas, and other Jewish symbols (5 and up)   **296.4**
Fiction
Howe, J. Kaddish for Grandpa in Jesus' name, amen   **E**
The **judge**. Zemach, H.   **E**
Judges
Adler, D. A. A picture book of Thurgood Marshall (1-3)   **92**
Fiction
Zemach, H. The judge   **E**
The **judge's** house. Stine, R. L.
In Beware!; R.L. Stine picks his favorite scary stories p55-75   **808.8**
Judkis, Jim
(il) Rogers, F. Divorce   **306.89**
(il) Rogers, F. Going to the hospital   **362.1**
(il) Rogers, F. Making friends   **158**
Judy Moody. McDonald, M.   **Fic**
Juettner, Bonnie
Energy (5 and up)   **333.79**
Molecules (4 and up)   **540**
The **juggler** of Notre Dame. Sawyer, R.
In Sawyer, R. The way of the storyteller p273-81   **372.6**

Jukes, Mavis
Growing up: it's a girl thing (4 and up)   **612.6**
It's a girl thing (5 and up)   **305.23**
No one is going to Nashville
In You read to me & I'll read to you; 20th-century stories to share p84-96   **E**
(jt. auth) Cheung, L. W. Y. Be healthy! it's a girl thing   **613**
Julia wants a pet. Lindgren, B.   **E**
Julie. George, J. C.   **Fic**
Julie of the wolves. George, J. C.   **Fic**
Juliet Dove, Queen of Love. Coville, B.   **Fic**
Julio's magic. Dorros, A.   **E**
Julius, the baby of the world. Henkes, K.   **E**
Jumanji. Van Allsburg, C.   **E**
The **jumbo** book of art. Luxbacher, I.   **702.8**
The **jumbo** book of drama. Dunleavy, D.   **792**
The **jumbo** book of needlecrafts (4-6)   **746.4**
The **jumbo** book of paper crafts. Lewis, A.   **745.54**
The **jumbo** vegetarian cookbook. Gillies, J.   **641.5**
Jump! [biography of Michael Jordan] Cooper, F.   **92**
Jump at de sun: the story of Zora Neale Hurston. Porter, A. P.   **92**
Jump, frog, jump!. Kalan, R.   **E**
Jump in. Ruiz, D.
In You're on!: seven plays in English and Spanish p42-61   **812.008**
Jump into science [series]
Heiligman, D. Honeybees   **595.7**
Jump, kangaroo, jump!. Murphy, S. J.   **513**
Jump rope *See* Rope skipping
Jump rope rhymes
Anna Banana: 101 jump-rope rhymes   **398.8**
Chambers, V. Double dutch (4 and up)   **796.2**
Dotlich, R. K. Over in the pink house (k-3)   **811**
Sierra, J. Schoolyard rhymes (k-3)   **398.8**
Jump ship to freedom. Collier, J. L.   **Fic**
The **jumpers**. Andersen, H. C.
In Andersen, H. C. Hans Christian Andersen's Fairy Tales   **S C**
also in Andersen, H. C. The swan's stories p47-51   **S C**
Jumping the scratch. Weeks, S.   **Fic**
June 29, 1999. Wiesner, D.   **E**
Junebug. Mead, A.   **Fic**
Juneteenth
Jordan, D. Juneteenth (1-3)   **394.26**
Leeper, A. Juneteenth (3-5)   **394.26**
Nelson, V. M. Juneteenth (2-4)   **394.26**
Jung, Reinhardt
Dreaming in black and white (5 and up)   **Fic**
Jungle. Greenaway, T.   **577.3**
The **jungle** book: Mowgli's story. Kipling, R.   **S C**

The **jungle** book: the Mowgli stories. Kipling, R.
S C

Junie B. Jones and her big fat mouth. Park, B.
Fic

Junior high school catalog. *See* Middle and junior high school library catalog **011.6**

Junior science diagrams on file **507**

Junior science experiments on file (3-5) **507.8**

Junior state maps on file (4 and up) **973**

Junior timelines on file. Tomaselli-Moschovitis, V. **902**

Junior worldmark encyclopedia of the nations (5 and up) **910.3**

Junior Worldmark encyclopedia of the states (5 and up) **973.03**

Junior worldmark encyclopedia of world holidays (5 and up) **394.26**

Junk food. Cobb, V. **664**

Jupiter (Planet)
Simon, S. Destination: Jupiter (3-6) **523.4**

Jurmain, Suzanne
The forbidden schoolhouse [biography of Prudence Crandall] (5 and up) **92**
George did it [biography of George Washington] (2-4) **92**

The **jury**. Jaffe, N.
In Jaffe, N. and Zeitlin, S. J. The cow of no color: riddle stories and justice tales from around the world p47-51 **398.2**

Just a dream. Van Allsburg, C. **E**

Just a minute. Morales, Y. **398.2**

Just add one Chinese sister. McMahon, P. **E**

Just around the corner. Stevenson, J. **811**

Just delicious. Schwartz, A.
In Schwartz, A. Scary stories 3; more tales to chill your bones p12-14 **398.2**

Just enough and not too much. Zemach, K. **E**

Just enough carrots. Murphy, S. J. **513**

Just in case. Viorst, J. **E**

Just Juice. Hesse, K. **Fic**

Just like Josh Gibson. Johnson, A. **E**

Just like me **920**

Just one ghost. Terada, A. M.
In Terada, A. M. Under the starfruit tree; folktales from Vietnam p128-29 **398.2**

Just one more story. Brutschy, J. **E**

The **just** reward. Afanas'ev, A. N.
In Afanas'ev, A. N. Russian fairy tales p39-40 **398.2**

Just so stories. Kipling, R. **S C**

Just the facts [series]
Burnfield, A. Multiple sclerosis **616.8**
Gillie, O. Cancer **616.99**
Parker, S. Allergies **616.97**
Pigache, P. ADHD **616.85**
Routh, K. Down syndrome **616.85**
Routh, K. Meningitis **616.8**

Juster, Norton
The hello, goodbye window **E**
The phantom tollbooth (5 and up) **Fic**

Justice. Babbitt, N.
In Babbitt, N. The Devil's other storybook p11-17 **S C**

Justice. McKissack, P. C.
In McKissack, P. C. The dark-thirty; Southern tales of the supernatural p22-34 **S C**

The **Justice** League. Levithan, D.
In Friends; stories about new friends, old friends, and unexpectedly true friends **S C**

Justin and the best biscuits in the world. Walter, M. P. **Fic**

Justin Morgan had a horse. Henry, M. **Fic**

Juvenile delinquency
See also Gangs
Fiction
Sachar, L. Holes (5 and up) **Fic**

Juvenile diabetes. Haney, J. **616.4**

K

K is for kitten. Leopold, N. S. C. **E**

Kaa's hunting. Kipling, R.
In Kipling, R. The jungle book: Mowgli's story p56-107 **S C**
also in Kipling, R. The jungle book: the Mowgli stories **S C**

The **kabil's** donkey. Kimmel, E. A.
In Kimmel, E. A. The spotted pony: a collection of Hanukkah stories p19-23 **398.2**

Kachurek, Sandra J.
George W. Bush (4 and up) **92**

Kaddish for Grandpa in Jesus' name, amen. Howe, J. **E**

Kaddo's wall. Courlander, H.
In Courlander, H. and Herzog, G. Cow-tail switch, and other West African stories p13-24 **398.2**

Kadohata, Cynthia
Kira-Kira (5 and up) **Fic**
Weedflower **Fic**

Kafirs (African people) *See* Zulu (African people)

Kahanamoku, Duke, 1890-1968
See/See also pages in the following book(s):
Krull, K. Lives of the athletes (4 and up) **920**

Kahl, Jonathan D.
National Audubon Society first field guide: weather (4 and up) **551.5**

Kahlo, Frida, 1907-1954
About
Frith, M. Frida Kahlo (2-4) **92**
Laidlaw, J. A. Frida Kahlo (5 and up) **92**
Sabbeth, C. Frida Kahlo and Diego Rivera: their lives and ideas (5 and up) **92**
Winter, J. Frida [Kahlo] (k-3) **92**

Kahumbu, Paula
(jt. auth) Hatkoff, I. Owen & Mzee **599.63**

Kain, Karen
The Nutcracker **E**

Kai's journey to Gold Mountain. Currier, K. S.
Fic

Kaiulani, Princess of Hawaii, 1875-1899
About
Stanley, F. The last princess: the story of Princess Ka'iulani of Hawai'i (4 and up) **92**

Kajikawa, Kimiko
Yoshi's feast (k-3) **398.2**

Kákuy. Delacre, L.
In Delacre, L. Golden tales; myths, legends, and folktales from Latin America p59-63
398.2

Kalan, Robert
Jump, frog, jump! **E**

Kaleidoscope **011.6**

Kaleidoscope [series]
Gallant, R. A. Fossils **560**
Gallant, R. A. Space stations **629.44**
Gallant, R. A. Water **551.48**

Kaleidoscope Kids book [series]
Johmann, C. Going west! **978**

Kalis, Jennifer
(il) O'Connor, J. Mary Cassatt **92**

Kallaloo!. Gershator, D. **E**

Kallen, Stuart A.
Gems (4 and up) **553.8**
Mummies (4 and up) **393**
Spiders (4 and up) **595.4**
(jt. auth) Boekhoff, P. M. J.K. Rowling **92**
(jt. auth) Boekhoff, P. M. Lasers **621.36**

Kalman, Maira
Fireboat (k-3) **974.7**
Next stop, Grand Central **E**
Smartypants (Pete in school) **E**

Kalz, Jill
Mount Everest (4-6) **954.96**

Kaminski, Robert
(jt. auth) Sierra, J. Children's traditional games
796

Kaminsky, Karol
(il) Press, J. ArtStarts for little hands! **745.5**

Kamishibai man. Say, A. **E**

Kane, Joseph Nathan
Famous first facts **031.02**

Kaner, Etta
Animals migrating (2-4) **591.5**

Kanevsky, Polly
Sleepy boy **E**

Kang, Hildi
The black dragon princess
In Fire and wings: dragon tales from East and West p103-11 **S C**

Kang, Johanna
(il) Hoestlandt, J. Star of fear, star of hope
E

Kangaroos
Burt, D. Kangaroos (3-6) **599.2**
Jango-Cohen, J. Kangaroos (3-6) **599.2**
Noonan, D. The kangaroo (2-4) **599.2**
Fiction
Bruel, N. Boing! **E**
Payne, E. Katy No-Pocket **E**

Kanji-jo, the nestlings. MacDonald, M. R.
In MacDonald, M. R. Look back and see; twenty lively tales for gentle tellers p24-36 **372.6**

Kansas
Ingram, S. Kansas
In World Almanac Library of the States series
973
King, D. C. Kansas
In It's my state! [series] **973**
Robinson Masters, N. Kansas
In America the beautiful, second series
973
Fiction
Hopkinson, D. Pioneer summer (2-4) **Fic**
Kimmel, E. C. To the frontier (4 and up)
Fic
Kochenderfer, L. The victory garden (5 and up)
Fic

Kanu above and Kanu below. MacDonald, M. R.
In MacDonald, M. R. The storyteller's start-up book; finding, learning, performing, and using folktales including twelve tellable tales p167-75 **372.6**

Kaplan, Elizabeth
The tundra (4-6) **551.4**

Kaplan, Gisela T.
(jt. auth) Rajendra, V. Iran **955**

Karas, G. Brian
Atlantic **E**
The class artist **E**
On Earth (k-2) **525**
(il) Beeler, S. B. Throw your tooth on the roof
398
(jt. auth) Best, C. Are you going to be good?
E
(il) Dakos, K. Put your eyes up here **811**
(il) Elya, S. M. F is for fiesta **E**
(il) Elya, S. M. Oh no, gotta go! **E**
(il) Fleming, C. Muncha! Muncha! Muncha!
E
(il) Hort, L. The seals on the bus **782.42**
(il) McDonald, M. Ant and Honey Bee, what a pair! **E**
(il) McDonald, M. Baya, baya, lulla-by-a **E**
(il) Mills, C. 7 x 9 = trouble! **Fic**
(il) Murphy, S. J. Elevator magic **513**
(il) Rylant, C. The case of the missing monkey
E
(il) Stanley, D. Saving Sweetness **E**
(il) Steen, S. Car wash **E**
(il) Williams, A. Tiny tortilla **E**

Karate
Rielly, R. L. Karate for kids (4 and up)
796.8
Fiction
Leary, M. Karate girl **E**
Nevius, C. Karate hour **E**

Karate for kids. Rielly, R. L. **796.8**

Karate girl. Leary, M. **E**

Karate hour. Nevius, C. **E**

The **Karate** Kid. Soto, G.
In Soto, G. Baseball in April, and other stories p69-80 **S C**

Kelly, Christie Watts—_Continued_
   (jt. auth) Sears, W. What baby needs   **649**
Kelly, Emery J.
   Paper airplanes (4 and up)   **745.592**
Kelly, Irene
   It's a hummingbird's life (k-3)   **598**
Kelly, John
   The mystery of Eatum Hall   **E**
Kelly, Joseph
   (il) Kerrin, J. S. Martin Bridge: ready for take-off!   **Fic**
Kelly, Katy
   Lucy Rose, here's the thing about me (2-4)   **Fic**
Kelly, Sheila M.
   (jt. auth) Rotner, S. Lots of grandparents!   **306.8**
Kelsey, Elin
   Strange new species   **578**
Kemp, Moira
   (il) McCaughrean, G. Grandma Chickenlegs   **398.2**
Kemp-Welch, Lucy Elizabeth
   (il) Sewell, A. Black Beauty   **Fic**
Kenah, Katharine
   The best seat in second grade   **E**
Kendall, Carol
   The Gammage Cup (5 and up)   **Fic**
Kendall, Russ
   (il) Waters, K. On the Mayflower   **974.4**
   (il) Waters, K. Samuel Eaton's day   **974.4**
   (il) Waters, K. Sarah Morton's day   **974.4**
Kenna, Kathleen
   A people apart (4 and up)   **289.7**
Kennebec Indians _See_ Abnaki Indians
Kennedy, Caroline
   (ed) A family of poems. See A family of poems   **808.81**
Kennedy, Dorothy M. (Dorothy Mintzlaff)
   (comp) Knock at a star. See Knock at a star   **811.008**
   (comp) Talking like the rain. See Talking like the rain   **821.008**
Kennedy, Doug
   (il) San Souci, R. Six foolish fishermen   **398.2**
Kennedy, John F. (John Fitzgerald), 1917-1963
About
   Adler, D. A. A picture book of John F. Kennedy (1-3)   **92**
   Heiligman, D. High hopes [biography of John F. Kennedy] (4 and up)   **92**
   Sommer, S. John F. Kennedy (5 and up)   **92**
   See/See also pages in the following book(s):
   St. George, J. In the line of fire (4 and up)   **364.1**
Kennedy, Mike
   Baseball (4 and up)   **796.357**
   Ice hockey (4 and up)   **796.962**
   (jt. auth) Stewart, M. Long ball   **796.357**
Kennedy, Robert Francis
   Saint Francis of Assisi (2-4)   **271**

Kennedy, X. J.
   (comp) Knock at a star. See Knock at a star   **811.008**
   (comp) Talking like the rain. See Talking like the rain   **821.008**
Kennedy assassinated!. Hampton, W.   **973.922**
Kenneth Grahame's The reluctant dragon. San Souci, R.   **Fic**
Kennett, David
   (il) Blacklock, D. The Roman Army   **937**
Kenny, Kevin _See_ Krull, Kathleen, 1952-
Kensuke's kingdom. Morpurgo, M.   **Fic**
Kent, Deborah
   Animal helpers for the disabled (4 and up)   **636.088**
   Athletes with disabilities (4 and up)   **371.9**
   Jimmy Carter (4 and up)   **92**
   Maine
      _In_ America the beautiful, second series   **973**
   New Mexico
      _In_ America the beautiful, second series   **973**
   Tennessee
      _In_ America the beautiful, second series   **973**
   Utah
      _In_ America the beautiful, second series   **973**
   Wyoming
      _In_ America the beautiful, second series   **973**
Kent, Jack
   There's no such thing as a dragon   **E**
Kent, Peter
   Great building stories of the past (4 and up)   **624**
Kentley, Eric
   Story of the Titanic (4 and up)   **910.4**
Kentucky
   Appelt, K. Down Cut Shin Creek (4 and up)   **027**
   Gaines, A. Kentucky
      _In_ It's my state! [series]   **973**
   Pollock, M. H. Kentucky
      _In_ World Almanac Library of the States series   **973**
   Stein, R. C. Kentucky
      _In_ America the beautiful, second series   **973**
Fiction
   Byars, B. C. The keeper of the doves (4 and up)   **Fic**
   Creech, S. Chasing Redbird (5 and up)   **Fic**
   Wyatt, L. J. Poor is just a starting place (5 and up)   **Fic**
Kenya
   Broberg, C. Kenya in pictures (5 and up)   **967.62**
   Hatkoff, I. Owen & Mzee (k-3)   **599.63**
   Pateman, R. Kenya (5 and up)   **967.62**
Fiction
   Chamberlin, M. Mama Panya's pancakes   **E**
   Conway, D. The most important gift of all   **E**

Kimmel, Eric A.—*Continued*
Anansi and the talking melon (k-3) **398.2**
Anansi goes fishing (k-3) **398.2**
The birds' gift (k-3) **398.2**
Blackbeard's last fight **E**
The Chanukkah guest **E**
Don Quixote and the windmills **E**
Four dollars and fifty cents **E**
The frog princess (2-4) **398.2**
Gershon's monster **398.2**
The gingerbread man (k-2) **398.2**
Grizz! **E**
The hero Beowulf (3-6) **398.2**
Hershel and the Hanukkah goblins **E**
A horn for Louis [biography of Louis Armstrong] (2-4) **92**
Iron John (2-5) **398.2**
The jar of fools: eight Hanukkah stories from Chelm (4 and up) **S C**
Contents: The jar of fools; How they play dreidel in Chelm; Sweeter than honey, purer than oil; The Knight of the Golden Slippers; Silent Samson, the Maccabee; The magic spoon; The soul of a menorah; Wisdom for sale
Montezuma and the fall of the Aztecs (3-5) **972**
The rooster's antlers (k-3) **398.2**
The runaway tortilla (k-3) **398.2**
Seven at one blow (k-3) **398.2**
The spotted pony: a collection of Hanukkah stories (3-6) **398.2**
Includes the following stories: Ibn Ezra and the archbishop; The kabil's donkey; Leviathan and the fox; The wonderful shamir; Did the rabbi have a head?; The caliph and the cobbler; When Hershel eats; The spotted pony
Sword of the samurai (4 and up) **S C**
Includes the following stories: Dōhaku's head; The samurai and the dragon; The coward; Matajuro's training; The oxcart; The battle of Chihaya Castle; Tomoe Gozen; The burglar; Devil boy; The Rōnin and the tea master; No sword
Ten suns (2-4) **398.2**
The three princes (k-3) **398.2**
The three riddles
In Fire and wings: dragon tales from East and West p79-86 **S C**
Three sacks of truth (2-4) **398.2**
The two mountains (3-5) **398.2**
Wonders and miracles (4 and up) **296.4**
Zigazak! **E**
(ed) A Hanukkah treasury. See A Hanukkah treasury **296.4**

Kindergarten
Howe, J. When you go to kindergarten (k-1) **372.2**

Fiction
Cleary, B. Ramona the pest (3-5) **Fic**
Slate, J. Miss Bindergarten celebrates the 100th day of kindergarten **E**

Kindergarten kids. Calmenson, S. **811**

Kindersley, Anabel
Celebrations (3-5) **394.26**
(jt. auth) Kindersley, B. Children just like me **305.23**

Kindersley, Barnabas
Children just like me (3-6) **305.23**
(il) Kindersley, A. Celebrations **394.26**

Kindle me a riddle. Karim, R. **E**

Kinerk, Robert
Clorinda **E**

King, Andy
(il) Bragg, L. W. Fundamental gymnastics **796.44**
(il) Coleman, L. Fundamental soccer **796.334**
(il) Foley, M. Fundamental hockey **796.962**
(il) Geng, D. Play-by-play baseball **796.357**
(il) Jensen, J. Fundamental volleyball **796.325**
(il) Krause, P. Fundamental golf **796.352**
(il) Miller, M. Fundamental tennis **796.342**

King, B. B.
See/See also pages in the following book(s):
Lester, J. The blues singers (5 and up) **920**

King, Casey
Oh, freedom! (5 and up) **323.1**

King, Daniel
Games (5 and up) **794**

King, Dave
(il) Whalley, P. E. S. Butterfly & moth **595.7**

King, David C.
Azerbaijan (5 and up) **947.5**
Colonial days (3-6) **973.2**
Delaware
In It's my state! [series] **973**
Jellyfish (3-6) **593.5**
Kansas
In It's my state! [series] **973**
Kyrgyzstan (5 and up) **958.4**
New Jersey
In It's my state! [series] **973**
Pioneer days (3-6) **978**
Serbia and Montenegro (5 and up) **949.7**
Virginia
In It's my state! [series] **973**
Wild West days (3-6) **978**
World War II days (3-6) **940.53**

King, Elizabeth
Quinceañera (5 and up) **392**

King, Hazel
Carbohydrates for a healthy body (4-6) **613.2**

King, Martin Luther, Jr., 1929-1968
About
Adler, D. A. Dr. Martin Luther King, Jr. (1-3) **92**
Farris, C. My brother Martin [biography of Martin Luther King] (k-3) **92**
Marzollo, J. Happy birthday, Martin Luther King (k-3) **92**
Myers, W. D. I've seen the promised land [biography of Martin Luther King] (k-3) **92**
Rappaport, D. Martin's big words: the life of Dr. Martin Luther King, Jr. (k-3) **92**

King, Martin Luther, Jr.
I have a dream **323.1**

King, Riley B. *See* King, B. B.

King, Sandra
Shannon: an Ojibway dancer (3-6) **970.004**

King, Stephen Michael
Mutt dog! **E**

The **king** and the workman's daughter. Philip, N.
In Philip, N. Celtic fairy tales p105-12
398.2

King Arthur and his Knights of the Round Table.
Green, R. L. **398.2**

King Arthur and the Round Table. Talbott, H.
398.2

King Bear. Afanas'ev, A. N.
In Afanas'ev, A. N. Russian fairy tales p393-
98 **398.2**

King Bidgood's in the bathtub. Wood, A. **E**

King David is alive. Schwartz, H.
In Schwartz, H. Invisible kingdoms; Jewish
tales of angels, spirits, and demons p32-
34 **398.2**

King John and the Abbot of Canterbury. Jacobs,
J.
In Jacobs, J. English fairy tales p364-66
398.2

King Lear. Packer, T.
In Packer, T. Tales from Shakespeare p175-
192 **822.3**

King Midas. Demi **398.2**

King Midas. Stewig, J. W. **398.2**

King Midas and the golden touch. Craft, C.
398.2

The **King** o' the Cats. Jacobs, J.
In Jacobs, J. English fairy tales p372-74
398.2

King O' the Cats. Shepard, A. **398.2**

The **king** of dragons. Fenner, C. **Fic**

The **King** of England and his three sons. Jacobs,
J.
In Jacobs, J. English fairy tales p350-63
398.2

The **King** of Ireland's son. Philip, N.
In Philip, N. Celtic fairy tales p44-53
398.2

King of shadows. Cooper, S. **Fic**

King of the Cats. San Souci, R.
In San Souci, R. More short & shivery; thirty
terrifying tales p139-42 **398.2**

The **king** of the cats. Yolen, J.
In Yolen, J. Meow; cat stories from around
the world **398.2**

The **king** of the Golden River. Ruskin, J. **Fic**

The **king** of the herrings. Doherty, B.
In Doherty, B. The famous adventures of Jack
p6-25 **398.2**

King of the wind. Henry, M. **Fic**

King Peacock
In Stockings of buttermilk: American folktales
p47-50 **398.2**

King-Smith, Dick
All pigs are beautiful (k-3) **636.4**
Babe (3-5) **Fic**
The Catlady (2-4) **Fic**
Chewing the cud (5 and up) **92**
Funny Frank (3-5) **Fic**
The golden goose (2-4) **Fic**
I love guinea pigs (k-3) **636.9**
Lady Lollipop (3-5) **Fic**

The nine lives of Aristotle (2-4) **Fic**

King Solomon tests fate. Schwartz, H.
In Schwartz, H. A journey to paradise and
other Jewish tales p14-15 **398.2**

King Tut's tomb. Nardo, D. **932**

King who stood all night. Aiken, J.
In Aiken, J. Shadows and moonshine; stories
S C

The **Kingfisher** book of family poems (3-6)
821.008

The **Kingfisher** book of funny poems (4 and up)
821.008

The **Kingfisher** first human body encyclopedia.
Walker, R. **612**

The **Kingfisher** geography encyclopedia. Gifford,
C. **910.3**

The **Kingfisher** history encyclopedia (5 and up)
909

The **Kingfisher** illustrated horse & pony encyclopedia. Ransford, S. **636.1**

The **Kingfisher** illustrated nature encyclopedia.
Burnie, D. **508**

Kingfisher knowledge [series]
Adams, S. Castles & forts **355.7**
Barnes, T. Archaeology **930.1**
Burnie, D. Endangered planet **333.95**
Butterfield, M. Pirates & smugglers **910.4**
Gifford, C. Spies **327.12**
Hynes, M. Rocks & fossils **552**
Langley, A. Hurricanes, tsunamis, and other nat-
ural disasters **363.34**
Platt, R. Forensics **363.2**
Walker, R. Genes & DNA **576.5**
Wilkes, A. Dangerous creatures **591.6**

Kingfisher riding club [series]
Ransford, S. Horse & pony breeds **636.1**

The **Kingfisher** student atlas. Wilkinson, P.
912

Kingman, Lee
(ed) Newbery and Caldecott Medal books, 1966-
1975. See Newbery and Caldecott Medal
books, 1966-1975 **028.5**
(ed) Newbery and Caldecott Medal books, 1976-
1985. See Newbery and Caldecott Medal
books, 1976-1985 **028.5**

Kings and rulers
See also Queens
Meltzer, M. Ten kings (5 and up) **920**
Ross, S. Monarchs (5 and up) **940.1**
Stanley, D. Saladin: noble prince of Islam (4
and up) **92**
Fiction
Wood, A. King Bidgood's in the bathtub **E**

The **king's** ankus. Kipling, R.
In Kipling, R. The jungle book: the Mowgli
stories **S C**

The **king's** dragon. Yolen, J.
In Fire and wings: dragon tales from East and
West p112-16 **S C**
also in Yolen, J. Here there be dragons p84-
86 **810.8**

The **King's** fifth. O'Dell, S. **Fic**

The **King's** secret. Schwartz, H.
In Schwartz, H. and Rush, B. A coat for the
moon and other Jewish tales p48-51
398.2

Kingsley, Ben
(jt. auth) Ganeri, A. The young person's guide
to the orchestra **784.2**

Kinsey-Warnock, Natalie
Lumber camp library (3-5) **Fic**
Nora's ark **E**

Kiowa Indians
See/See also pages in the following book(s):
Freedman, R. Indian chiefs (6 and up) **920**

Kipling, Rudyard
A collection of Rudyard Kipling's Just so sto-
ries (3-6) **S C**
The elephant's child **Fic**
The jungle book: Mowgli's story (3-6) **S C**
The jungle book: the Mowgli stories (4 and up)
S C

Contents: Mowgli's brothers; Hunting song of the Seeonee
Pack; Kaa's hunting; Road song of the bandard-log; How fear
came; The law of the jungle; "Tiger-Tiger!"; Mowglie's song;
Letting in the jungle; Mowglie's song gainst people; The king's
ankus; The song of the little hunter; Red dog; Chil's song; The
spring running; The outsong; "Rikki-tikki-tavi"; Darzee's chant

Just so stories (3-6) **S C**

Contents: How the whale got his throat; How the camel got
his hump; How the rhinoceros got his skin; How the leopard got
his spots; The elephant's child; The sing-song of old man kangaroo; The beginning of the armadilloes; How the first letter was
written; How the alphabet was made; The crab that played with
the sea; The cat that walked by himself; The butterfly that
stamped

Rikki-tikki-tavi
In Kipling, R. The jungle book: the Mowgli
stories **S C**

Kipling, Rudyard, 1865-1936
Adaptations
Pinkney, J. Rikki-tikki-tavi **E**
Fiction
Blegvad, L. Kitty and Mr. Kipling (3-5) **Fic**

Kira-Kira. Kadohata, C. **Fic**

Kirk, Connie Ann
Sky dancers **E**

Kirk, Daniel
(il) Schlein, M. Hello, hello! **E**
(il) Stevenson, R. L. Block city **E**

Kirk, Steve
(il) Camper, C. Bugs before time **560**

Kirkpatrick, Katherine A.
Escape across the wide sea (5 and up) **Fic**

Kiss, Andrew
(il) Ruurs, M. Wild babies **591.3**

Kiss good night. Hest, A. **E**

Kiss kiss!. Wild, M. **E**

Kiss me. Sandburg, C.
In Sandburg, C. More Rootabaga stories
p152-55 **S C**
also in Sandburg, C. The Sandburg treasury;
prose and poetry for young people p158-
59 **818**

Kiss the cow. Root, P. **E**

Kisseloff, Jeff
Who is baseball's greatest pitcher? (5 and up)
796.357

Kitamura, Satoshi
Comic adventures of Boots **E**
Me and my cat? **E**

Kitchen, Bert
(il) Orgel, D. The Bremen town musicians and
other animal tales from Grimm **398.2**
(il) Tagholm, S. The rabbit **599.3**

Kitchen chemistry. See Gardner, R. Science project ideas about kitchen chemistry **540.7**

The **kitchen** knight. Hodges, M. **398.2**

Kitchen science. Levine, S. **507.8**

Kitchen science. Pentland, P. **641.3**

Kite, L. Patricia
Insect facts and folklore (4 and up) **595.7**

Kite. Burgess, M. **Fic**

The **kite** festival. Torres, L. **E**

The **kite** fighters. Park, L. S. **Fic**

Kite flying. Lin, G. **E**

The **kite** rider. McCaughrean, G. **Fic**

Kites
Hosking, W. Asian kites (3-6) **629.133**
Murphy, S. J. Let's fly a kite (k-3) **516**
Fiction
Demi. Kites **E**
Hall, B. E. Henry and the kite dragon **E**
Lin, G. Kite flying **E**
McCaughrean, G. The kite rider (5 and up)
Fic
Park, L. S. The kite fighters (4-6) **Fic**
Williams, V. B. Lucky song **E**

Kites sail high: a book about verbs. Heller, R.
428

Kit's wilderness. Almond, D. **Fic**

Kitten red, yellow, blue. Catalanotto, P. **E**

Kitten's first full moon. Henkes, K. **E**

Kitty and Mr. Kipling. Blegvad, L. **Fic**

KKK *See* Ku Klux Klan

Kladstrup, Kristin
The book of story beginnings (4 and up)
Fic

Klaffke, Ben
(il) Landau, E. Smokejumpers **628.9**

Klein, Suzanna
(il) Womenfolk and fairy tales. See Womenfolk
and fairy tales **398.2**

Kleven, Elisa
The paper princess **E**
Sun bread **E**
(il) De colores and other Latin-American folk
songs for children. See De colores and other
Latin-American folk songs for children
782.42
(il) Diez deditos. Ten little fingers & other play
rhymes and action songs from Latin America.
See Diez deditos. Ten little fingers & other
play rhymes and action songs from Latin
America **782.42**
(il) Dorros, A. Abuela **E**
(il) Fiestas: a year of Latin American songs of
celebration. See Fiestas: a year of Latin
American songs of celebration **782.42**
(il) Glaser, L. Our big home **E**

Knock at a star **811.008**

Knock . . . knock . . . knock. San Souci, R.
In San Souci, R. More short & shivery; thirty
terrifying tales p148-52 **398.2**

Knock on wood. Wong, J. S. **811**

Knockin' on wood [biography of Peg Leg Bates]
Barasch, L. **92**

Knots in my yo-yo string. Spinelli, J. **92**

Knots on a counting rope. Martin, B. **E**

Knotts, Bob
Martial arts (2-4) **796.8**
The Summer Olympics (2-4) **796.48**
Track and field (2-4) **796.42**
Weightlifting (2-4) **796.41**

Know Not. Afanas'ev, A. N.
In Afanas'ev, A. N. Russian fairy tales p97-
109 **398.2**

Knowles, Elizabeth
Boys and literacy **028.5**
More reading connections **028.5**
Talk about books! **372.4**

Knowlton, Laurie Lazzaro
A young man's dance **E**

Knowlton, MaryLee
Albania (5 and up) **949.65**
Macedonia (5 and up) **949.7**
Turkmenistan (5 and up) **958.5**
Uzbekistan (5 and up) **958.7**

Knuffle bunny. Willems, M. **E**

Knutson, Barbara
Love and roast chicken (k-3) **398.2**

Ko Kóngole. MacDonald, M. R.
In MacDonald, M. R. The storyteller's start-
up book; finding, learning, performing,
and using folktales including twelve
tellable tales p179-81 **372.6**

Koala Lou. Fox, M. **E**

Koalas
Lang, A. Baby koala (k-3) **599.2**
Fiction
Fox, M. Koala Lou **E**

Kobayashi, Issa, 1763-1827
About
Gollub, M. Cool melons—turn to frogs!: the life
and poems of Issa [Kobayashi] (3-6) **92**

Koch, Kenneth
(comp) Talking to the sun: an illustrated anthology of poems for young people. See Talking
to the sun: an illustrated anthology of poems
for young people **808.81**

Kochalka, James
Peanutbutter & Jeremy's best book ever (4 and
up) **741.5**

Kochel, Marcia Agness
(jt. auth) Baxter, K. A. Gotcha! **028.1**

Kochenderfer, Lee
The victory garden (5 and up) **Fic**

Kodaira, Machiyo
(il) Newman, L. Hachiko waits **Fic**

Koerber, Nora
(il) Kimmel, E. C. Balto and the great race
636.7

Koestler-Grack, Rachel A.
The story of Anne Frank (2-4) **92**
The story of Clara Barton (2-4) **92**
The story of Eleanor Roosevelt (2-4) **92**
The story of Harriet Tubman (2-4) **92**
The story of Helen Keller (2-4) **92**
The story of Mother Jones (2-4) **92**

Kogan, Deborah *See* Ray, Deborah Kogan, 1940-

Kogi's mysterious journey. Partridge, E. **398.2**

Koh, Angeline
(jt. auth) Heale, J. Portugal **946.9**

Kohen, Elizabeth
Spain (5 and up) **946**

Kohn, Alexander
(jt. auth) Chödzin, S. The wisdom of the crows
and other Buddhist tales **294.3**

Koi and the kola nuts. Aardema, V. **398.2**

Koizumi, Yakumo *See* Hearn, Lafcadio, 1850-
1904

Koja, Kathe
Lupe
In Swan sister; fairy tales retold **S C**

Kokopelli's flute. Hobbs, W. **Fic**

Kolanovic, Dubravka
(il) Ross, M. Wake up sleepy head! **811**

Koller, Jackie French
One monkey too many **E**

Komodo dragon
Fiction
Sís, P. Komodo! **E**

Konigsburg, E. L.
Altogether, one at a time (4-6) **S C**
Contents: Inviting Jason; The Night of the Leonids; Camp Fat;
Momma at the Pearly Gates
From the mixed-up files of Mrs. Basil E.
Frankweiler (4-6) **Fic**
Jennifer, Hecate, Macbeth, William McKinley,
and me, Elizabeth (4-6) **Fic**
A proud taste for scarlet and miniver (5 and up)
Fic
TalkTalk **028.5**
Up from Jericho Tel (5 and up) **Fic**
The view from Saturday (4 and up) **Fic**
See/See also pages in the following book(s):
Author talk (4 and up) **028.5**

Kono, Erin Eitter
Hula lullaby **E**

Kooning, Willem de *See* De Kooning, Willem,
1904-1997

Koppe, Susanne
The Nutcracker (3-5) **Fic**

Kops, Deborah
(jt. auth) Pascoe, E. Scholastic kid's almanac
031.02

Koralek, Jenny
The coat of many colors (k-3) **222**
Night ride to Nanna's **E**

Korczak, Janusz, 1878-1942
About
Adler, D. A. A hero and the holocaust: the story
of Janusz Korczak and his children (3-5)
92

Kraus, Robert
Whose mouse are you?   E
Krause, Peter
Fundamental golf (5 and up)   796.352
Krauss, Ruth
Bears   E
The carrot seed   E
Goodnight goodnight sleepyhead   E
The happy egg   E
A very special house   E
Krautwurst, Terry
Night science for kids (4-6)   591.5
(jt. auth) Diehn, G. Nature smart   745.5
Kreger, Claire
Cheese (2-4)   637
Jelly beans (2-4)   641.8
Kreiter, Eshel
John Singer Sargent (2-4)   92
Krementz, Jill
How it feels to be adopted (4 and up)
                                         362.7
How it feels when a parent dies (4 and up)
                                         155.9
How it feels when parents divorce (4 and up)
                                         306.89
Krenina, Katya
(il) Kimmel, E. A. The birds' gift   398.2
Krensky, Stephen
Dangerous crossing (2-4)   Fic
How Santa got his job   E
Lionel's birthday   E
Paul Revere's midnight ride (2-4)   973.3
Kress, Stephen W.
(jt. auth) Salmansohn, P. Saving birds
                                         333.95
Krinitz, Esther Nisenthal
Memories of survival (6 and up)   940.53
Krishnaswami, Uma
Monsoon   E
Kristina, Queen of Sweden, 1626-1689 *See*
Christina, Queen of Sweden, 1626-1689
Kristo, Janice V.
(ed) Adventuring with books. See Adventuring
with books   011.6
Kroeger, Mary Kay
Paperboy   E
Krog, Hazlitt
(jt. auth) Shulman, M. Attack of the killer video
book   778.59
Kroll, Steven
The biggest pumpkin ever   E
The Boston Tea Party (3-5)   973.3
By the dawn's early light (3-5)   782.42
Ellis Island (3-5)   325.73
Patches: lost and found   E
William Penn (3-5)   92
Krommes, Beth
(il) Lunge-Larsen, L. The hidden folk   398.2
(il) Martin, J. B. The lamp, the ice, and the boat
called Fish   998
(il) Root, P. Grandmother Winter   E
(il) The Sun in me. See The Sun in me
                                         811.008

Kronheimer, Ann
(il) King-Smith, D. The golden goose   Fic
Kronosaurus and other sea creatures. Schomp, V.
In Schomp, V. Prehistoric world [series]
                                         567.9
Kronzek, Allan Zola
The sorcerer's companion (4 and up)
                                         823.009
Kronzek, Elizabeth
(jt. auth) Kronzek, A. Z. The sorcerer's compan-
ion   823.009
Krudop, Walter
The man who caught fish   E
(il) Burleigh, R. Black whiteness   998
(il) Lasky, K. Born in the breezes: the seafaring
of Joshua Slocum   92
Kruglik, Gerald
(jt. auth) Bottner, B. Wallace's lists   E
Krull, Kathleen
The book of rock stars (4 and up)   920
The boy on Fairfield Street: how Ted Geisel
grew up to become Dr. Seuss (k-3)   92
Harvesting hope: the story of Cesar Chavez
(2-4)   92
Houdini (2-4)   92
Isaac Newton (5 and up)   92
A kid's guide to America's Bill of Rights (4
and up)   342
Leonardo da Vinci (5 and up)   92
Lives of extraordinary women (4 and up)
                                           920
Lives of the artists (4 and up)   920
Lives of the athletes (4 and up)   920
Lives of the musicians (4 and up)   920
Lives of the presidents (4 and up)   920
Lives of the writers (4 and up)   920
M is for music   E
The night the Martians landed (3-6)   791.44
A pot o' gold (3-6)   820.8
Supermarket (k-3)   381
Wilma unlimited
In You read to me & I'll read to you; 20th-
century stories to share p105-12   E
Wilma unlimited: how Wilma Rudolph became
the world's fastest woman (2-4)   92
A woman for president [biography of Victoria
C. Woodhull] (3-5)   92
(ed) I hear America singing! See I hear America
singing!   782.42
Krumgold, Joseph
Onion John (5 and up)   Fic
Krupinski, Loretta
(il) Maestro, B. Why do leaves change color?
                                         582.16
Krush, Beth
(il) Enright, E. Gone-Away Lake   Fic
(il) Sorensen, V. E. Miracles on Maple Hill
                                           Fic
Krush, Joe
(il) Enright, E. Gone-Away Lake   Fic
(il) Sorensen, V. E. Miracles on Maple Hill
                                           Fic
Ku Klux Klan
Fiction
Hesse, K. Witness (6 and up)   Fic

Langstaff, John M.—*Continued*
Oh, a-hunting we will go (k-2)   **782.42**
Over in the meadow (k-2)   **782.42**
(jt. auth) Wiseman, A. S. Making music
    784.19

Langston, Laura
Remember, Grandma?   **E**

Langston Hughes, American poet. Walker, A.
    92

Langston's train ride. Burleigh, R.   **92**

Langton, Jane
The fledgling (5 and up)   **Fic**

Language and languages
See also Sign language

Language arts
See also Creative writing

Language games *See* Literary recreations

The **language** of birds. Martin, R.   **398.2**

Language of the birds. Yolen, J.
In Yolen, J. Mightier than the sword; world
folktales for strong boys p39-45
    398.2

Languages
Vocabulary
See Vocabulary

Lanino, Deborah
(il) Hopkinson, D. Maria's comet   **E**

Lankford, Mary D.
Birthdays around the world (3-5)   **394.2**
Christmas around the world (3-5)   **394.26**
Dominoes around the world (3-5)   **795.3**
Hopscotch around the world (3-5)   **796.2**

Lanquetin, Anne-Sophie
(il) Ochiltree, D. Sixteen runaway pumpkins
    E

The **lantuch**. Singer, I. B.
In Singer, I. B. Stories for children p231-36
    S C

Lantz, Paul
(il) Gates, D. Blue willow   **Fic**

Laos
Folklore
See Folklore—Laos

Lapin plays possum. Doucet, S. A.
In Doucet, S. A. Lapin plays possum: trickster tales from the Louisiana Bayou p23-
40   **398.2**

Lapin plays possum: trickster tales from the Louisiana Bayou. Doucet, S. A.   **398.2**

Lapin tangles with Tee Tar Bébé. Doucet, S. A.
In Doucet, S. A. Lapin plays possum: trickster tales from the Louisiana Bayou p41-
62   **398.2**

The **Laplander's** drum. Olson, A. N.
In Olson, A. N. and Schwartz, H. Ask the
bones: scary stories from around the
world p53-59   **398.2**

Lapsit services for the very young II. Ernst, L. L.
    027.62

Lara and the gray mare. Duey, K.   **Fic**

LaReau, Jenna
(il) Janeczko, P. B. Top secret   **652**

Large print books
Erdrich, L. The birchbark house   **Fic**
McGraw, E. J. The moorchild   **Fic**

Larios, Julie Hofstrand
Have you ever done that? (k-3)   **811**
Yellow elephant   **811**

Larky Mavis. Cole, B.   **E**

Laroche, Giles
(il) Sturges, P. Bridges are to cross   **624.2**
(il) Sturges, P. Down to the sea in ships
    811
(il) Sturges, P. Sacred places   **203**

Larsen, Janet
(il) Terada, A. M. Under the starfruit tree
    398.2

Larsen, Lise Lunge- *See* Lunge-Larsen, Lise

Larson, Heidi
(jt. auth) Morris, A. Tsunami   **959.3**

Larson, Jeanette C.
Bringing mysteries alive for children and young
adults   **028.5**

Larson, Peter L.
Bones rock! (5 and up)   **560**

Lasers
Boekhoff, P. M. Lasers (3-5)   **621.36**

Lasky, Kathryn
Before I was your mother   **E**
Born in the breezes: the seafaring of Joshua Slo-
cum (3-6)   **92**
A brilliant streak: the making of Mark Twain (4
and up)   **92**
Broken song (5 and up)   **Fic**
Dancing through fire (4-6)   **Fic**
Days of the Dead (4-6)   **394.26**
Dreams in the golden country (4 and up)
    Fic
Elizabeth I (4 and up)   **Fic**
Interrupted journey (3-6)   **639.9**
John Muir (3-5)   **92**
The librarian who measured the earth [biography
of Eratosthenes] (2-5)   **92**
Love that baby! (k-2)   **305.23**
Lucille camps in   **E**
The man who made time travel (3-5)   **526**
Marie Antoinette (4 and up)   **Fic**
Marven of the Great North Woods   **E**
The most beautiful roof in the world (4 and up)
    577.3
The night journey (4 and up)   **Fic**
Vision of beauty: the story of Sarah Breedlove
Walker (3-5)   **92**
A voice of her own: the story of Phillis
Wheatley, slave poet (3-5)   **92**

The **lass** who went out at the cry of dawn.
Leodhas, S. N.
In Womenfolk and fairy tales p83-92
    398.2

Lassieur, Allison
Albert Einstein (5 and up)   **92**
The ancient Greeks (5 and up)   **938**
The ancient Romans (5 and up)   **937**

The **last** apprentice: Revenge of the witch. Delaney, J. **Fic**

Last dance at the Dew Drop Inn. Medearis, A. S.
In Medearis, A. S. Haunts; five hair-raising tales p16-21 **S C**

The **last** day of school. Borden, L. **Fic**

The **last** of the dragons. Nesbit, E.
In Fire and wings: dragon tales from East and West p124-36 **S C**

Last one in is a rotten egg. Kessler, L. P. **E**

The **last** princess: the story of Princess Ka'iulani of Hawai'i. Stanley, F. **92**

The **Last** Resort. Lewis, J. P. **Fic**

The **last** river. Waldman, S. **978**

The **last** tales of Uncle Remus. Lester, J. **398.2**

The **Last** tiger in Haiti
In The Magic orange tree, and other Haitian folktales p183-87 **398.2**

The **last** treasure. Anderson, J. **Fic**

Latchkey children
Mediavilla, C. Creating the full-service homework center in your library **027.4**

Lathrop, Dorothy P.
(il) Bible. Selections. Animals of the Bible **220.8**
(il) Field, R. Hitty: her first hundred years **Fic**

Latimer, Jonathan P.
Butterflies (4 and up) **595.7**
Caterpillars (4 and up) **595.7**

Latin America
Bibliography
Schon, I. The best of Latino heritage 1996-2002 **011.6**

Fiction
Hurwitz, J. New shoes for Silvia **E**
Vidal, B. Federico and the Magi's gift **E**

Folklore
See Folklore—Latin America
Social life and customs
Fiestas: a year of Latin American songs of celebration (k-3) **782.42**

Latin American literature
Bibliography
Schon, I. Recommended books in Spanish for children and young adults, 2000 through 2004 **011.6**

Latina and Latino voices in literature. Day, F. A. **810.9**

Latino biography library [series]
Ford, C. T. Roberto Clemente **92**

Latinos (U.S.) *See* Hispanic Americans

Latkes, latkes, good to eat. Howland, N. **E**

Latrobe, Kathy Howard
The children's literature dictionary **028.5**

Latter-day Saints *See* Church of Jesus Christ of Latter-day Saints

Latvia
Barlas, R. Latvia (5 and up) **947.9**

Laubach, Christyna M.
Raptor! a kid's guide to birds of prey (4 and up) **598**

Laubach, René
(jt. auth) Laubach, C. M. Raptor! a kid's guide to birds of prey **598**

Lauber, Patricia
Be a friend to trees (k-3) **582.16**
Flood (4 and up) **551.48**
Lost star: the story of Amelia Earhart (5 and up) **92**
The true-or-false book of cats (k-3) **636.8**
The true-or-false book of dogs (k-3) **636.7**
The true-or-false book of horses (k-3) **636.1**
Volcano: the eruption and healing of Mount St. Helens (4 and up) **551.2**
What you never knew about fingers, forks, & chopsticks (2-4) **394.1**
What you never knew about tubs, toilets & showers (2-4) **391**
Who came first (5 and up) **970.01**
Who eats what? (k-3) **577**
You're aboard Spaceship Earth (k-3) **550**

Laugh-eteria. Florian, D. **811**

Laugh till you cry. Nixon, J. L. **Fic**

Laughing Gravy Design (Firm)
Ward-Johnson, C. E-mail: a magic mouse guide **004.6**

Laughing out loud, I fly. Herrera, J. F. **811**

The **laughing** skull. Delacre, L.
In Delacre, L. Golden tales; myths, legends, and folktales from Latin America p21-23 **398.2**

Laughing tomatoes and other spring poems. Alarcón, F. X. **811**

Laughlin, Kay
(comp) The Children's song index, 1978-1993. See The Children's song index, 1978-1993 **782.42**

Laughter. San Souci, R.
In San Souci, R. Double-dare to be scared: another thirteen chilling tales **S C**

Laura Secord: a story of courage. Lunn, J. L. S. **Fic**

Lauré, Jason
(jt. auth) Blauer, E. South Africa **968**

Laurent, Richard
(il) Bauer, C. F. Leading kids to books through magic **027.62**
(il) Bauer, C. F. Leading kids to books through puppets **027.62**

Lauter, Richard
(il) Smith, R. K. The war with Grandpa **Fic**

Lautrec, Henri de Toulouse- *See* Toulouse-Lautrec, Henri de, 1864-1901

Lauw, Darlene
Electricity (3-6) **537**
Light (3-6) **535**
Water (3-6) **553.7**
Weather (3-6) **551.5**

Lavallee, Barbara
(il) Joosse, B. M. Mama, do you love me? **E**

Lavallee, Barbara—*Continued*
  (il) Mora, P. Uno, dos, tres: one, two, three
      E
  (il) Schertle, A. All you need for a beach **E**
  (il) Schertle, A. All you need for a snowman
      E

Lavender, David Sievert
  Snowbound (4 and up)   **978**

Lavender. San Souci, R.
  In San Souci, R. Short & shivery; thirty chill-
    ing tales p155-59   **398.2**

Lavies, Bianca
  Compost critters (4 and up)   **591.7**

Law, Ruth, b. 1887
      About
  Brown, D. Ruth Law thrills a nation (k-3)
      629.13

Law, Westley Wallace, 1923-2002
      About
  Haskins, J. Delivering justice [biography of
    Westley Wallace Law] (2-4)   **92**

Law
  Donovan, S. Making laws (4-6)   **328**
  Hamilton, J. How a bill becomes a law (3-5)
      328

Law for K-12 libraries and librarians. Torrans, L.
  A.   **344**

The **law** of the jungle. Kipling, R.
  In Kipling, R. The jungle book: the Mowgli
    stories   **S C**

Lawlor, Laurie
  He will go fearless (5 and up)   **Fic**
  Helen Keller: rebellious spirit (5 and up) **92**
  The school at Crooked Creek (3-5)   **Fic**

Lawlor, Veronica
  (il) I was dreaming to come to America. See I
    was dreaming to come to America **325.73**

Lawrence, Iain
  The convicts (5 and up)   **Fic**
  Lord of the nutcracker men (5 and up) **Fic**
  The wreckers (5 and up)   **Fic**

Lawrence, Jack
  (jt. auth) Bullock, M. Lions, tigers, and bears,
    vol. 1: Fear and pride   **741.5**

Lawrence, Jacob
  The great migration   **759.13**
  Harriet and the Promised Land   **811**

Lawrence, Jacob, 1917-2000
      About
  Duggleby, J. Story painter: the life of Jacob
    Lawrence (4 and up)   **92**

Lawrence, John
  This little chick   **E**
  (il) Butterworth, C. Sea horse   **597**
  (il) Waddell, M. Tiny's big adventure **E**

Lawson, Janet
  Audrey and Barbara   **E**

Lawson, Julie
  The Klondike cat   **E**

Lawson, Kristan
  Darwin and evolution for kids (4 and up)
      92

Lawson, Robert
  Ben and me (5 and up)   **Fic**
  Mr. Revere and I (5 and up)   **Fic**
  Rabbit Hill (3-6)   **Fic**
  (il) Atwater, R. T. Mr. Popper's penguins
      Fic
  (il) Leaf, M. The story of Ferdinand **E**
  (il) Vining, E. G. Adam of the road **Fic**

Lawton, Clive
  Hiroshima (5 and up)   **940.54**

Lawyers
    See also Judges

Lay, Kathryn
  The healing truth
    In A Glory of unicorns p145-62 **S C**

Layton, Lesley
  Singapore (5 and up)   **959.57**

Layton, Neal
  (il) Davies, N. Poop   **573.4**
  (il) Grindley, S. Mucky Duck   **E**
  (il) Wicked poems. See Wicked poems
      811.008

Lazan, Marion Blumenthal
  (jt. auth) Perl, L. Four perfect pebbles
      940.53

Lazare, Jerry
  (il) Burch, R. Queenie Peavy   **Fic**

Lazy Heinz. Grimm, J.
  In Bauer, C. F. Celebrations; read-aloud holi-
    day and theme book programs p140-43
      808.8

Lazy Jack. Jacobs, J.
  In Jacobs, J. English fairy tales p152-54
      398.2

The **lazy** maiden. Afanas'ev, A. N.
  In Afanas'ev, A. N. Russian fairy tales p423-
    25   **398.2**

Lazy Tok. Skipper, M.
  In Bauer, C. F. Celebrations; read-aloud holi-
    day and theme book programs p137-40
      808.8

Le Guin, Ursula K.
  Catwings (2-4)   **Fic**
  also in You read to me & I'll read to you;
    20th-century stories to share p113-23
      E
  Tom Mouse   **E**
  A wizard of Earthsea (6 and up)   **Fic**

Le Jars, David
  (il) Hands-on science. See Hands-on science
      507.8

Le Prince de Beaumont, Madame
  Beauty and the beast
    In Princess stories; a classic illustrated edition
      398.2
  Prince Hyacinth and the dear little princess
    In The Blue fairy book p12-18 **398.2**

Le Sieg, Theo *See* Seuss, Dr.

Le Tord, Bijou
  (il) Pandell, K. Saint Francis sings to Brother
    Sun   **271**

Leach, Michael
  Giraffe (3-5)   **599.63**

Leonard, Tom
  (il) Brenner, B. One small place in a tree
    577.3

Leonardo, da Vinci, 1452-1519
About
  Anderson, M. Amazing Leonardo da Vinci inventions you can build yourself **92**
  Byrd, R. Leonardo, beautiful dreamer (3-6)
    92
  Fritz, J. Leonardo's horse (4 and up) **730.9**
  Krull, K. Leonardo da Vinci (5 and up) **92**
  O'Connor, B. Leonardo da Vinci (5 and up)
    92
  Reed, J. Leonardo da Vinci: genius of art and science (5 and up) **92**
  Stanley, D. Leonardo da Vinci (4 and up)
    92

Leonardo, beautiful dreamer. Byrd, R. **92**
Leonardo da Vinci: genius of art and science. Reed, J. **92**
Leonardo, the terrible monster. Willems, M. **E**
Leonardo's horse. Fritz, J. **730.9**
Leon's story. Tillage, L. **92**
Leopold, Nikia Speliakos Clark
  K is for kitten **E**
Lepp, Royden
  David: Shepard's song, vol. 1 (3-5) **741.5**
Leprechauns
Fiction
  Bunting, E. That's what leprechauns do **E**
  Edwards, P. D. The leprechaun's gold **E**
The **leprechaun's** gold. Edwards, P. D. **E**
Leprince de Beaumont, Madame *See* Le Prince de Beaumont, Madame, 1711-1780
Lerner, Carol
  Butterflies in the garden (k-3) **595.7**
Lesbians
Fiction
  Garden, N. Molly's family **E**
  González, R. Antonio's card **E**
Less than zero. Murphy, S. J. **513**
Lessac, Frané
  Island counting 1 2 3 **E**
  (il) Melmed, L. K. New York, New York
    974.7
  (il) Pomerantz, C. The chalk doll **E**
  (il) Singer, M. On the same day in March
    551.6
Lessem, Don
  The fastest dinosaurs (2-4) **567.9**
  Feathered dinosaurs (2-4) **567.9**
  Flying giants of dinosaur time (2-4) **567.9**
  Scholastic dinosaurs A to Z (4 and up)
    567.9
  Sea giants of dinosaur time (2-4) **567.9**
  The smartest dinosaurs (2-4) **567.9**
Lesser, Carolyn
  Storm on the desert (2-4) **577.5**
Lesser, Rika
  Hansel and Gretel (k-3) **398.2**
Lessons. Babbitt, N.
  In Babbitt, N. The Devil's other storybook
    p47-52 **S C**

Lessons from Library Power. Zweizig, D.
    027.8
Lester, Alison
  Are we there yet? **E**
  Snow pony [excerpt]
    In Horse tales **S C**
Lester, Helen
  Author (k-3) **92**
  Hooway for Wodney Wat **E**
  Something might happen **E**
  Three cheers for Tacky **E**
Lester, Julius
  Black cowboy, wild horses **E**
  The blues singers (5 and up) **920**
  From slave ship to freedom road (4 and up)
    326
  John Henry (k-3) **398.2**
  The last tales of Uncle Remus (4 and up)
    398.2
    Contents: Why the cricket has elbows on his legs; Why the earth is mostly water; The origin of the ocean; Brer Rabbit and Miss Nancy; The old king and the new king; Brer Bear comes to the community; The snake; A ghost story; Brer Bear exposes Brer Rabbit; Brer Rabbit teaches Brer Bear to comb his hair; Why Brer Possum has no hair on his tail; Why Brer Possum loves peace; The baby who loved pumpkins; Impty-Umpty and the blacksmith; The angry woman; Brer Rabbit throws a party; Why Brer Fox's legs are black; How the witch was caught; The man who almost married a witch; Why dogs are tame; How Tinktum Tidy recruited an army for the king; Why guinea fowls are speckled; Why the Guineas stay awake; Brer Fox and the white grapes; Why the hawk likes to eat chickens; The little boy and his dogs; The man and the wild cattle; "Cutta cord-la"; Why Brer Bull growls and grumbles; Brer Rabbit, King Polecat, and the gingercakes; The fool; How Brer Lion lost his hair; The man and the boots; Why the goat has a short tail; Brer Buzzard and Brer Crow; The blacksmith and the Devil; Why chickens scratch in the dirt; Brer Rabbit and Aunt Nancy; The adventures of Simon and Susanna
  Let's talk about race (k-3) **305.8**
  The old African (3-6) **Fic**
  On writing for children & other people **92**
  Sam and the tigers **E**
  To be a slave (6 and up) **326**
  What a truly cool world! **E**
  When the beginning began (4 and up) **296.1**
    Contents: God learns how to create; God battles the Queen of the Waters; Sun and Moon; Strange creatures; The Angel of Death; Cat and Mouse; Leviathan and Fox; Crown learns a lesson; The grand parade; God makes people; God creates Adam; God creates Woman; Adam marries; The Snake; The Woman, Adam, and the fruit; God confronts Adam, the Woman, and the Snake; God returns to Heaven
Lester, Mike
  A is for salad **E**
Let it shine. Pinkney, A. D. **920**
Let me play. Blumenthal, K. **796**
Let my people go. McKissack, P. C. **221.9**
Let the circle be unbroken. Taylor, M. D. **Fic**
Let the games begin!. Ajmera, M. **796**
Let there be light (3-6) **242**
Let's count. Hoban, T. **E**
Let's fly a kite. Murphy, S. J. **516**
Let's get a pup, said Kate. Graham, B. **E**
Let's go rock collecting. Gans, R. **552**
Let's go visiting. Williams, S. **E**
Let's play rough. Jonell, L. **E**
Let's-read-and-find-out science [series]
  Bancroft, H. Animals in winter **591.56**

Leukemia

Coerr, E. Sadako [biography of Sadako Sasaki] (1-4)   **92**

Coerr, E. Sadako and the thousand paper cranes [biography of Sadako Sasaki] (3-6)   **92**

Westcott, P. Living with leukemia (3-5)   **362.1**

Fiction

Slote, A. Hang tough, Paul Mather (4-6)   **Fic**

Levey, Judith S.

(ed) Macmillan first dictionary. See Macmillan first dictionary   **423**

(ed) Scholastic first dictionary. See Scholastic first dictionary   **423**

Levey, Richard H.

Dust bowl! (1-3)   **363.34**

Leviathan and Fox. Lester, J.

In Lester, J. When the beginning began; stories about God, the creatures, and us p34-38   **296.1**

Leviathan and the fox. Jaffe, N.

In Jaffe, N. and Zeitlin, S. J. While standing on one foot; puzzle stories and wisdom tales from the Jewish tradition p11-17   **296.1**

Leviathan and the fox. Kimmel, E. A.

In Kimmel, E. A. The spotted pony: a collection of Hanukkah stories p25-31   **398.2**

Levin, Betty

Shadow-catcher (5 and up)   **Fic**

Levine, Ellen

. . . if your name was changed at Ellis Island (3-5)   **325.73**

Levine, Gail Carson

Dave at night (5 and up)   **Fic**

Ella enchanted (5 and up)   **Fic**

Fairy dust and the quest for the egg (3-5)   **Fic**

The princess test (4 and up)   **Fic**

The two princesses of Bamarre (5 and up)   **Fic**

Levine, Karen

Hana's suitcase (4 and up)   **940.53**

Levine, Laura

(il) George-Warren, H. Honky-tonk heroes & hillbilly angels   **920**

(il) George-Warren, H. Shake, rattle, & roll   **920**

Levine, Shar

Backyard science (3-5)   **507.8**

Bathtub science (3-5)   **507.8**

Kitchen science (3-5)   **507.8**

The optics book (4 and up)   **535**

The science of sound & music (4 and up)   **534**

Shocking science (5 and up)   **537**

The ultimate balloon book (5 and up)   **745.594**

Wonderful weather (2-4)   **551.5**

Levinson, Nancy Smiler

Death Valley (1-3)   **577.5**

Magellan and the first voyage around the world (5 and up)   **92**

North Pole, South Pole (k-3)   **998**

Levitas, Mitchel

(ed) A Nation challenged. See A Nation challenged   **973.931**

Levithan, David

The Justice League

In Friends; stories about new friends, old friends, and unexpectedly true friends   **S C**

(ed) Friends. See Friends   **S C**

Levitin, Sonia

Journey to America (4 and up)   **Fic**

The return (6 and up)   **Fic**

Levittown (N.Y.)

Fiction

Conrad, P. Our house (4 and up)   **S C**

Levy, Constance

Splash! (3-6)   **811**

Levy, Debbie

The Vietnam War (5 and up)   **959.704**

Levy, Elizabeth

My life as a fifth-grade comedian (4-6)   **Fic**

Seventh grade tango (5 and up)   **Fic**

Levy, Patricia

Ghana (5 and up)   **966.7**

Ireland (5 and up)   **941.5**

Nigeria (5 and up)   **966.9**

Puerto Rico (5 and up)   **972.95**

Scotland (5 and up)   **941.1**

Switzerland (5 and up)   **949.4**

Lewin, Betsy

Animal snackers (k-3)   **811**

(il) Cronin, D. Click, clack, moo   **E**

(il) Cronin, D. Duck for President   **E**

(il) Cronin, D. Giggle, giggle, quack   **E**

(il) Joosse, B. M. A houseful of Christmas   **E**

(il) Kuskin, K. So what's it like to be a cat?   **E**

(jt. auth) Lewin, T. Elephant quest   **591.9**

(jt. auth) Lewin, T. Gorilla walk   **599.8**

(jt. auth) Lewin, T. Top to bottom down under   **994**

(il) Prigger, M. S. Aunt Minnie McGranahan   **E**

(il) Silverman, E. Cowgirl Kate and Cocoa   **E**

(il) Weeks, S. Two eggs, please   **E**

(il) Winthrop, E. Dumpy La Rue   **E**

(il) Winthrop, E. Promises   **E**

Lewin, Ted

Big Jimmy's Kum Kau Chinese take-out   **E**

Elephant quest (3-6)   **591.9**

Gorilla walk (4 and up)   **599.8**

How much? (k-3)   **381**

Lost city (2-4)   **985**

Market! (k-3)   **381**

Tooth and claw (4 and up)   **590**

Top to bottom down under (2-4)   **994**

(il) Barron, T. A. High as a hawk   **E**

(il) Bartone, E. Peppe the lamplighter   **E**

(il) Borden, L. A. Lincoln and me   **E**

(il) Bunting, E. One green apple   **E**

(il) Heide, F. P. The day of Ahmed's secret   **E**

Lexau, Joan M.
Crocodile and hen (k-2)   **398.2**
Who took the farmer's [hat]?   **E**

Lexington (Mass.), Battle of, 1775
Fradin, D. B. Let it begin here! (2-4)   **973.3**
Krensky, S. Paul Revere's midnight ride (2-4)
                                                         973.3
Poetry
Longfellow, H. W. Paul Revere's ride   **811**

Li Chi slays the serpent. Yolen, J.
In Yolen, J. Not one damsel in distress; world
folktales for strong girls p33-37
                                                       398.2

Liano, Dante
(jt. auth) Menchú, R. The girl from Chimel
                                                          92
(jt. auth) Menchú, R. The honey jar   **398.2**

Liao, Jimmy
(jt. auth) Thomson, S. L. The sound of colors
                                                           E

Libby on Wednesdays. Snyder, Z. K.   **Fic**

Liberia
Fiction
Zemser, A. B. Beyond the mango tree (5 and
up)   **Fic**
Folklore
See Folklore—Liberia

Liberty. Curlee, L.   **974.7**

Liberty!. Drummond, A.   **E**

Liberty Bell
Hess, D. The Liberty Bell (3-5)   **974.8**
The **Liberty** Bell. Hess, D.   **974.8**

Liberty or death. Maestro, B.   **973.3**

Liberty rising. Shea, P. D.   **974.7**

The **librarian** of Basra. Winter, J.   **E**

The **librarian** who measured the earth [biography
of Eratosthenes] Lasky, K.   **92**

Librarians
Appelt, K. Down Cut Shin Creek (4 and up)
                                                         027
Winter, J. The librarian of Basra   **E**
Ethics
Ethics in school librarianship   **174**
Fiction
Peck, R. Here lies the librarian   **Fic**
Williams, S. Library Lil   **E**

Libraries
See also Instructional materials centers;
Public libraries
Duncan, D. I-search for success   **001.4**
Duncan, D. I-Search, you search, we all learn to
research   **001.4**
Heiligman, D. The New York Public Library
kid's guide to research (5 and up)   **025.5**
Malam, J. Library (4 and up)   **027**
Munro, R. The inside-outside book of libraries
(2-4)   **027**
Winter, J. The librarian of Basra   **E**
Administration
Curzon, S. C. Managing change   **025.1**
MacDonell, C. Essential documents for school
libraries   **025.1**

Thelen, L. N. Essentials of elementary library
management   **025.1**
See/See also pages in the following book(s):
Stein, B. L. Running a school library media cen-
ter   **027.8**
Automation
Cuddy, C. Using PDAs in libraries   **004**
Censorship
Intellectual freedom manual   **323.44**
Symons, A. K. Protecting the right to read
                                                       025.2
Collection development
Doll, C. A. Managing and analyzing your col-
lection   **025.2**
Hughes-Hassell, S. Collection management for
youth   **025.2**
Fiction
Bruss, D. Book! book! book!   **E**
Clifford, E. Help! I'm a prisoner in the library
(3-5)   **Fic**
Joosse, B. M. Hot city   **E**
Mora, P. Tomás and the library lady   **E**
Numeroff, L. J. Beatrice doesn't want to   **E**
Sierra, J. Wild about books   **E**
Law and legislation
Torrans, L. A. Law for K-12 libraries and librar-
ians   **344**
Public relations
Flowers, H. F. Public relations for school library
media programs   **021.7**
Special collections
Building a special collection of children's litera-
ture in your library   **025.2**

Libraries, Children's *See* Children's libraries

Libraries, School *See* School libraries

Libraries, Young adults' *See* Young adults' libraries

Libraries and community
Lukenbill, W. B. Community resources in the
school library media center   **025.2**
Schuckett, S. Political advocacy for school librarians   **027.8**

Libraries and students
Mediavilla, C. Creating the full-service home-
work center in your library   **027.4**
Steele, A. T. Bare bones children's services
                                                       027.62

**Libraries Unlimited professional guides in
school librarianship** [series]
Johnson, C. Using internet primary sources to
teach critical thinking skills in the sciences
                                                       025.04

The **library.** Stewart, S.   **E**
The **library** card. Spinelli, J.   **S C**

Library catalogs
ALA filing rules   **025.3**

Library finance
Hallam, A. Managing budgets and finances
                                                       025.1

A **library** for Juana: the world of Sor Juana Inés.
Mora, P.   **92**

Library instruction *See* Bibliographic instruction
Library Lil. Williams, S.   **E**

Library materials *See* Library resources

The **Library** of Alexandria. Trumble, K.   **027**

Library of American lives and times [series]
Anderson, P. C. George Armstrong Custer   **92**
Butler, M. G. Sojourner Truth   **92**
Pierce, M. A. Robert Fulton and the development of the steamboat   **92**

Library of astronaut biographies [series]
Byers, A. Neil Armstrong   **92**
Orr, T. Alan Shepard   **92**

Library of author biographies [series]
Freedman, J. Sid Fleischman   **92**
Greene, M. Louis Sachar   **92**
Houghton, G. Mildred Taylor   **92**
Seidman, D. Jerry Spinelli   **92**

Library policies *See* Libraries—Administration

Library Power (Program)
The Information-powered school   **027.8**
Zweizig, D. Lessons from Library Power   **027.8**

Library programming for families with young children. Nespeca, S. M.   **027.62**

Library resources
    Conservation and restoration
Halsted, D. D. Disaster planning   **025.8**

Library science
Malam, J. Library (4 and up)   **027**

Library service to children. Van Orden, P. J.   **027.62**

Library services to children *See* Children's libraries

Library services to young adults *See* Young adults' libraries

Library skills. Miller, P.   **025.5**

Libya
Malcolm, P. Libya (5 and up)   **961.2**

Lice
Caffey, D. Yikes-lice! (k-3)   **616.5**
DerKazarian, S. You have head lice! (k-2)   **616.5**
Hirschmann, K. Lice (4-6)   **616.5**

Lieblich, Irene
(il) Singer, I. B. The power of light   **S C**

Lies, Brian
(il) Landau, E. Popcorn   **641.3**

Lies and other tall tales. Myers, C.   **398.2**

Life, Kay
(il) Cleary, B. Muggie Maggie   **Fic**
(il) Hurst, C. O. You come to Yokum   **Fic**

Life
   See also Death
    Origin
Gallant, R. A. The origins of life (5 and up)   **576.8**

Life (Biology)
   See also Reproduction

Life after death *See* Future life

The **life** and death of Crazy Horse. Freedman, R.   **92**

The **life** and death of stars. Asimov, I.   **523.8**

The **life** and times of Buddha. Gedney, M.   **294.3**

The **life** and times of the ant. Micucci, C.   **595.7**

The **life** and times of the honeybee. Micucci, C.   **595.7**

The **life** and times of the peanut. Micucci, C.   **641.3**

Life balance [series]
Andrews, L. W. Meditation   **158**
Landau, E. Dyslexia   **616.85**
Trueit, T. S. ADHD   **616.85**
Trueit, T. S. Keeping a journal   **808**

Life cycle of a mushroom. Royston, A.   **579.6**

Life cycle of an oak tree. Royston, A.   **583**

Life cycles [series]
Noonan, D. The butterfly   **595.7**
Noonan, D. The emperor penguin   **598**
Noonan, D. The frog   **597.8**
Noonan, D. The green turtle   **597.92**
Noonan, D. The kangaroo   **599.2**

Life in a grassland. Patent, D. H.   **577.4**

A **life** in miniature. Coville, B.
   In Swan sister; fairy tales retold   **S C**

Life in the temperate grasslands. Toupin, L.   **577.4**

A **Life** like mine (3-6)   **305.23**

Life on earth: the story of evolution. Jenkins, S.   **576.8**

Life on other planets
Branley, F. M. Is there life in outer space? (k-3)   **576.8**
Jackson, E. B. Looking for life in the universe (4 and up)   **576.8**
Skurzynski, G. Are we alone? (5 and up)   **576.8**
    Fiction
Scieszka, J. Baloney (Henry P.)   **E**

Life-Saving Service (U.S.) *See* United States. Life-Saving Service

Life sciences
    Encyclopedias
Exploring life science (4-6)   **570**

Life-size dinosaurs. Bergen, D.   **567.9**

Life under ice. Cerullo, M. M.   **578.7**

Life's a funny proposition, Horatio. Polikoff, B. G.   **Fic**

Lifesaving
   See also First aid

Lift every voice and sing. Johnson, J. W.   **782.42**

Light, Steven
Puss in boots (k-3)   **398.2**

Light
Branley, F. M. Day light, night light (k-3)   **535**
Burnie, D. Light (4 and up)   **535**
Cobb, V. I see myself (k-2)   **535**
Farndon, J. Light and optics (3-6)   **535**
Gardner, R. Dazzling science projects with light and color (4-6)   **535**
Lauw, D. Light (3-6)   **535**

Littlefield, Cindy A.
Awesome ocean science! (3-5)   **551.46**

The **littlest** wolf. Brimner, L. D.   **E**

Littlewood, Karin
(il) Conway, D. The most important gift of all
   E
(il) Hoffman, M. The color of home   **E**

Littman, Sarah
Confessions of a closet Catholic (5 and up)
   Fic

Litzinger, Rosanne
(il) Berger, M. Chirping crickets   **595.7**
(il) Greene, E. The little golden lamb   **398.2**
(il) Kimmel, E. A. The frog princess   **398.2**
(il) Sachs, M. The four ugly cats in apartment
3D   **Fic**

Liu, Jae Soo
Yellow umbrella   **E**

Liu, Lesley
(il) Hill, E. S. Bird Boy   **Fic**
(il) Hill, E. S. Chang and the bamboo flute
   Fic

Lives of extraordinary women. Krull, K.   **920**

Lives of the artists. Krull, K.   **920**

Lives of the artists [series]
Bassil, A. Vincent van Gogh   **92**
Hodge, S. Pablo Picasso   **92**

Lives of the athletes. Krull, K.   **920**

Lives of the musicians. Krull, K.   **920**

Lives of the presidents. Krull, K.   **920**

Lives of the writers. Krull, K.   **920**

Lives: poems about famous Americans (4 and up)
   811.008

The **living** rain forest. Kratter, P.   **591.7**

Living well [series]
Gray, S. W. Living with asthma   **616.2**
Gray, S. H. Living with cerebral palsy
   362.1
Gray, S. H. Living with juvenile rheumatoid arthritis   **616.7**
Raatma, L. Safety for babysitters   **649**
Raatma, L. Safety in your neighborhood
   613.6
Raatma, L. Safety on the Internet   **025.04**

Living with asthma. Gray, S. W.   **616.2**

Living with blindness. Westcott, P.   **362.4**

Living with cerebral palsy. Gray, S. H.   **362.1**

Living with cerebral palsy. Pimm, P.   **362.4**

Living with deafness. Haughton, E.   **362.4**

Living with juvenile rheumatoid arthritis. Gray, S. H.   **616.7**

Living with leukemia. Westcott, P.   **362.1**

Livingston, Myra Cohn
Celebrations   **811**
Festivals   **811**
Keep on singing (k-3)   **811**
Poem-making (4 and up)   **372.6**
(comp) Christmas poems. See Christmas poems
   808.81
(comp) If you ever meet a whale. See If you
ever meet a whale   **811.008**

Livingstone, Star
Harley   **E**

Lizard music. Pinkwater, D. M.   **Fic**

Lizards
Facklam, M. Lizards: weird and wonderful (3-6)
   597.95
Schafer, S. Lizards (3-6)   **639.3**
Fiction
Leedy, L. The great graph contest   **E**
Murphy, S. J. Leaping lizards   **E**
Shannon, G. Lizard's guest   **E**

Lizards, frogs, and pollywogs. Florian, D.   **811**

Lizard's guest. Shannon, G.   **E**

Lizards: weird and wonderful. Facklam, M.
   597.95

Lizette's green sock. Valckx, C.   **E**

Lizzie at last. Mills, C.   **Fic**

Llama, llama red pajama. Dewdney, A.   **E**

Llamas
Fiction
Dewdney, A. Llama, llama red pajama   **E**
Guarino, D. Is your mama a llama?   **E**
Livingstone, S. Harley   **E**

Llewellyn, Claire
Butterfly (k-3)   **595.7**
Frog (k-3)   **597.8**
Oranges (k-3)   **641.3**

Lloyd, Megan
(il) Berger, M. Look out for turtles!   **597.92**
(il) Branley, F. M. Earthquakes   **551.2**
(il) Guiberson, B. Z. Cactus hotel   **583**
(il) Kimmel, E. A. The gingerbread man
   398.2
(il) Kimmel, E. A. Seven at one blow   **398.2**
(il) Williams, L. The little old lady who was not
afraid of anything   **E**

Lobbying
Schuckett, S. Political advocacy for school librarians   **027.8**

Lobel, Anita
Alison's zinnia   **E**
One lighthouse, one moon   **E**
(il) Davidson, R. P. All the world's a stage
   E
(il) Geras, A. My grandmother's stories
   398.2
(il) Henkes, K. So happy!   **E**
(il) Huck, C. S. The Black Bull of Norroway
   398.2
(il) Huck, C. S. Princess Furball   **398.2**
(il) Lobel, A. On Market Street   **E**
(il) Lobel, A. A treeful of pigs   **E**

Lobel, Arnold
Fables (3-5)   **Fic**
Frog and Toad are friends   **E**
Grasshopper on the road   **E**
Ming Lo moves the mountain   **E**
Mouse soup   **E**
Mouse tales   **E**
On Market Street   **E**
Owl at home   **E**
Small pig   **E**
A treeful of pigs   **E**
Uncle Elephant   **E**

Lobel, Arnold—*Continued*
(il) The Arnold Lobel book of Mother Goose. See The Arnold Lobel book of Mother Goose
398.8
(il) Bass, L. G. A three hat day **E**
(il) Prelutsky, J. The Headless Horseman rides tonight **811**
(il) Prelutsky, J. Nightmares: poems to trouble your sleep **811**
(il) Prelutsky, J. Tyrannosaurus was a beast
811
(il) The Random House book of poetry for children. See The Random House book of poetry for children **821.008**
(il) Van Leeuwen, J. Tales of Oliver Pig **E**

Locker, Thomas
Cloud dance **E**
John Muir, America's naturalist (2-4) **92**
Walking with Henry **E**
(l) Bruchac, J. Between earth & sky **398.2**
(il) Bruchac, J. Thirteen moons on a turtle's back **811**

Lockhart, Laura
(jt. auth) Duncan, D. I-search for success
001.4
(jt. auth) Duncan, D. I-Search, you search, we all learn to research **001.4**

Lockouts *See* Strikes

Lockwood, Sophie
Polar Bears (5 and up) **599.78**
Sea turtles (4 and up) **597.92**

Locomotion. Woodson, J. **811**

Locomotives
Zimmermann, K. R. Steam locomotives (4 and up) **385**

Locricchio, Matthew
The international cookbook for kids (5 and up)
641.5

Lodge Boy, Wild Boy, and the Monster Woman. Curry, J. L.
In Curry, J. L. The wonderful sky boat and other Native American tales of the Southeast p86-90 **398.2**

Loehle, Richard
(il) Tucker, T. Brainstorm! **609**

Loeper, John J.
Going to school in 1776 (4 and up) **370.9**

Loertscher, David V.
(ed) The Whole school library handbook. See The Whole school library handbook **027.8**

Loft the enchanter. San Souci, R.
In San Souci, R. More short & shivery; thirty terrifying tales p115-20 **398.2**

Lofting, Hugh
The voyages of Doctor Dolittle (4 and up)
Fic

Lofts, Pamela
(il) Fox, M. Hunwick's egg **E**
(il) Fox, M. Koala Lou **E**

Logan, Claudia
The 5,000-year-old puzzle (2-4) **932**

Logging *See* Lumber and lumbering

A **log's** life. Pfeffer, W. **577.3**

Lohnes, Marilyn
Fractured fairy tales **812**

Lomas Garza, Carmen *See* Garza, Carmen Lomas, 1948-

Lon Po Po. Young, E. **398.2**

London, Jack
The call of the wild (5 and up) **Fic**
White Fang (5 and up) **Fic**

London, Jack, 1876-1916
See/See also pages in the following book(s):
Krull, K. Lives of the writers (4 and up)
920

London, Jonathan
Baby whale's journey **E**
Do your ABC's Little Brown Bear **E**
Froggy learns to swim **E**
Giving thanks **E**
Mustang canyon **E**
Sled dogs run **E**
A truck goes rattley-bumpa **E**
(jt. auth) Bruchac, J. Thirteen moons on a turtle's back **811**

London (England)
Stacey, G. London (4 and up) **942.1**
Fiction
Alcock, V. The cuckoo sister (6 and up)
Fic
Curry, J. L. The Black Canary (5 and up)
Fic
Garfield, L. Black Jack (6 and up) **Fic**
Garfield, L. Smith (6 and up) **Fic**
Horowitz, A. The Devil and his boy (5 and up)
Fic
Jarvis, R. The alchemist's cat (5 and up)
Fic
Naidoo, B. The other side of truth (5 and up)
Fic
Newman, R. The case of the Baker Street Irregular (5 and up) **Fic**
Sturtevant, K. At the sign of the star (5 and up)
Fic
Woodruff, E. The Ravenmaster's secret (5 and up) **Fic**

London (England). Tower *See* Tower of London (England)

Lone wolf. Franklin, K. L. **Fic**

Lonek's journey. Whiteman, D. B. **940.53**

Long, Laurel
The lady & the lion (2-4) **398.2**
(il) Ogburn, J. K. The magic nesting doll **E**

Long, Loren
(il) Byars, B. C. My dog, my hero **S C**
(il) Johnson, A. I dream of trains **E**
(il) Piper, W. The little engine that could **E**
(il) Schmidt, G. D. The wonders of Donal O'Donnell **398.2**
(il) Weller, F. W. The day the animals came
E
(il) Whitman, W. When I heard the learn'd astronomer **E**

Long, Lynette
Fabulous fractions (3-6) **513**
Marvelous multiplication (3-6) **513**
Measurement mania (3-6) **530.8**

Long, Melinda
How I became a pirate   **E**

Long, Sylvia
(il) Aston, D. H. An egg is quiet   **591.4**
(il) Sylvia Long's Mother Goose. See Sylvia
Long's Mother Goose   **398.8**

A **long** and uncertain journey: the 27,000 mile
voyage of Vasco da Gama. Goodman, J. E.
     92

Long ball. Stewart, M.   **796.357**

The **long** horse. Lunge-Larsen, L.
In Lunge-Larsen, L. The hidden folk; stories
of fairies, dwarves, selkies, and other secret beings p52-54   **398.2**

Long-Long's New Year. Gower, C.   **E**

The **long-nosed** goblins. Sakade, F.
In Sakade, F. Japanese children's favorite stories   **398.2**

The **long** road to Gettysburg. Murphy, J.
     973.7

A **long** way from Chicago. Peck, R.   **Fic**

The **longest** summer on record. Conrad, P.
In Conrad, P. Our house   **S C**

Longevity
See also Old age

Longfellow, Henry Wadsworth
Henry Wadsworth Longfellow
In The Blackbirch treasury of American poet-
ry p239-83   **811.008**
Hiawatha   **811**
Paul Revere's ride   **811**

Longitude
Borden, L. Sea clocks (3-6)   **526**
Dash, J. The longitude prize [biography of John
Harrison] (5 and up)   **92**
Lasky, K. The man who made time travel (3-5)
     526

The **longitude** prize [biography of John Harrison]
Dash, J.   **92**

Lonna and Cat Woman. Hamilton, V.
In Hamilton, V. Her stories; African American folktales, fairy tales, and true tales
p56-60   **398.2**

Look, Lenore
Henry's first-moon birthday   **E**
Love as strong as ginger   **E**
Ruby Lu, brave and true (1-3)   **Fic**
Uncle Peter's amazing Chinese wedding   **E**

Look at my book. Leedy, L.   **808**

Look back and see. MacDonald, M. R.   **372.6**

Look back and see [story] MacDonald, M. R.
In MacDonald, M. R. Look back and see;
twenty lively tales for gentle tellers p11-
23   **372.6**

Look book. Hoban, T.   **E**

The **look-it-up** book of explorers. Kimmel, E. C.
     920

Look out for turtles!. Berger, M.   **597.92**

Look to the North. George, J. C.   **E**

Look whooo's counting. Macdonald, S.   **E**

Looking back. Lowry, L.   **92**

Looking for home. MacDonald, M. R.
In MacDonald, M. R. When the lights go out;
twenty scary tales to tell p29-32
     372.6

Looking for life in the universe. Jackson, E. B.
     576.8

Looking for seabirds. Webb, S.   **598**

Looking to get married. McGill, A.
In McGill, A. Sure as sunrise; stories of Bruh
Rabbit & his walkin' talkin' friends
     398.2

Loons
Fiction
Banks, K. Dillon Dillon (4 and up)   **Fic**

Loose tooth. Schaefer, L. M.   **E**

Lopes, Tom
(il) Baker, R. F. In a word   **422**

Lopez, Loretta
(il) Elya, S. M. Say hola to Spanish, otra vez
     463

Lorbiecki, Marybeth
Planet patrol (3-5)   **577**
Sister Anne's hands   **E**

Lorca, Federico García *See* García Lorca,
Federico, 1898-1936

Lord, Bette Bao
In the Year of the Boar and Jackie Robinson
(4-6)   **Fic**

Lord, Janet
Here comes Grandma!   **E**

Lord, John Vernon
The giant jam sandwich   **E**

Lord, Richard
(jt. auth) Levy, P. Switzerland   **949.4**

The **Lord** of Miracles. Delacre, L.
In Delacre, L. Salsa stories p55-61   **S C**

Lord of the deep. Salisbury, G.   **Fic**

Lord of the nutcracker men. Lawrence, I.   **Fic**

Lord's Day *See* Sabbath

The **lore** and language of schoolchildren. Opie, I.
A.   **398**

Los Alamos wildfires
Bryan, N. Los Alamos wildfires (5 and up)
     363.34

Los Angeles (Calif.)
Jaskol, J. City of angels (2-4)   **979.4**
Fiction
Bunting, E. Smoky night   **E**
Currier, K. S. Kai's journey to Gold Mountain
(4 and up)   **Fic**
Johnston, T. Any small goodness (4 and up)
     Fic
Woods, B. The red rose box (5 and up)   **Fic**

Loser. Spinelli, J.   **Fic**

Losers. Stine, R. L.
In Stine, R. L. The haunting hour p122-37
     S C

Losing things *See* Lost and found possessions

Losleben, Elie
(jt. auth) Malcolm, P. Libya   **961.2**

Love that baby!. Lasky, K.   305.23
Love that baby!. Milord, S.   E
Love that dog. Creech, S.   Fic
Love thy neighbor. Turner, A. W.   Fic
Love to Langston. Medina, T.   811
Love to mamá (3-6)   811.008
Lovelace, Maud Hart
    Betsy-Tacy (2-4)   Fic
Lovers. Andersen, H. C.
    In Andersen, H. C. The swan's stories p53-58
        S C
The **lovers** of Dismal Swamp. San Souci, R.
    In San Souci, R. Short & shivery; thirty chilling tales p123-26   398.2
Low, Alice
    The Macmillan book of Greek gods and heroes (3-6)   292
Low, William
    (il) Hall, B. E. Henry and the kite dragon   E
Lowdown on earthworms. Dixon, N.   592
Lowe, Joy L.
    (jt. auth) Matthew, K. I. Neal-Schuman guide to celebrations & holidays around the world   394.26
Lowell, Susan
    The bootmaker and the elves (k-3)   398.2
Lowenstein, Felicia
    All about sign language (2-4)   419
Lower East Side (New York, N.Y.)
    Bial, R. Tenement (4 and up)   974.7
    Hopkinson, D. Shutting out the sky (5 and up)   974.7
Lowery, Linda
    Aunt Clara Brown (2-4)   92
Lowji discovers America. Fleming, C.   Fic
Lowman, Margaret
        About
    Lasky, K. The most beautiful roof in the world (4 and up)   577.3
Lowry, Lois
    Anastasia Krupnik (4-6)   Fic
    Autumn Street (4 and up)   Fic
    Gathering blue (5 and up)   Fic
    The giver (6 and up)   Fic
    Gooney Bird Greene (2-4)   Fic
    Gossamer (5 and up)   Fic
    Looking back (5 and up)   92
    Messenger (6 and up)   Fic
    Number the stars (4 and up)   Fic
    The one hundredth thing about Caroline (5 and up)   Fic
    Rabble Starkey (5 and up)   Fic
    Stay! (5 and up)   Fic
    A summer to die (5 and up)   Fic
    Your move, J.P.! (5 and up)   Fic
    See/See also pages in the following book(s):
    Author talk (4 and up)   028.5
Loy, Roy Chan Yoon
    (il) Lauw, D. Electricity   537
    (il) Lauw, D. Light   535
Loyalists, American *See* American Loyalists
Lu and the swamp ghost. Carville, J.   E

Luba and the wren. Polacco, P.   398.2
Lubar, David
    Science friction
       In Tripping over the lunch lady and other school stories p60-82   S C
    Two left feet, two left hands, and too left on the bench
       In Sports shorts   S C
Lubin, Leonard B.
    (il) Conly, J. L. Racso and the rats of NIMH
        Fic
Lucas, Cedric
    (il) Miller, W. Night golf   E
Luciani, Brigitte
    How will we get to the beach?   E
Lucille camps in. Lasky, K.   E
Luck. Castedo, E.
    In You're on!: seven plays in English and Spanish p84-99   812.008
Lucky 13. Street, M.   795.4
Lucky leaf. O'Malley, K.   E
Lucky pennies and hot chocolate. Shields, C. D.   E
Lucky song. Williams, V. B.   E
Lucky stars. Frank, L. K.   Fic
Lucy Rose, here's the thing about me. Kelly, K.   Fic
Luella and the tame parrot. Hamilton, V.
    In Hamilton, V. Her stories; African American folktales, fairy tales, and true tales p75-77   398.2
Luka's quilt. Guback, G.   E
Lukenbill, W. Bernard
    Community resources in the school library media center   025.2
Lullabies
    All the pretty little horses (k-2)   782.42
    Arrorró mi niño (k-3)   398.8
    Asch, F. Barnyard lullaby   E
    The baby's bedtime book   808.81
    Fishing for a dream   782.42
    Ho, M. Hush!   E
    Hush, little baby (k-2)   782.42
    In the hollow of your hand   782.42
    Pinkney, B. Hush, little baby (k-2)   782.42
    Seeger, P. One grain of sand (k-1)   782.42
    Weave little stars into my sleep (2-4)   782.42
        Fiction
    McDonald, M. Baya, baya, lulla-by-a   E
    Wilcoxen, C. Niccolini's song   E
Lullaby. San Souci, R.
    In San Souci, R. Even more short & shivery; thirty spine-tingling stories p105-09   398.2
Lullaby: Wisdom seeker. Avery, B.   741.5
Lulu's busy day. Uff, C.   E
Lulu's hat. Meddaugh, S.   Fic
Lum, Bernice
    (il) Murphy, S. J. Mighty Maddie   389
    (il) Rockwell, A. F. My pet hamster   636.9

Lum, Kate
What! cried Granny   **E**

Lumber and lumbering
Appelbaum, D. K. Giants in the land (2-4)
     634.9

Fiction

Arnold, C. The terrible Hodag and the animal catchers   **E**
Durbin, W. Blackwater Ben (5 and up)   **Fic**
Kinsey-Warnock, N. Lumber camp library (3-5)   **Fic**
Lasky, K. Marven of the Great North Woods   **E**

Lumber camp library. Kinsey-Warnock, N.   **Fic**

Lunar bases
Cole, M. D. Moon base (4 and up)   **629.4**

Lunar expeditions See Space flight to the moon

Lunch. Fleming, D.   **E**

Lunch money. Clements, A.   **Fic**

Lunch money and other poems about school. Shields, C. D.   **811**

Lunchtime for a purple snake. Ziefert, H.   **E**

Lund, Deb
Tell me my story, Mama   **E**

Lundquist, David R.
(jt. auth) Peterson, C. Fantastic farm machines
     631.3

Lunge-Larsen, Lise
The hidden folk (3-5)   **398.2**
Contents: The ivory cups; Tulips and parsley; The nisse's revenge; The battle for Bornholm; The wedding feast; The silver king; The long horse; Playing the fourth part; The selkie wife
The race of the Birkebeiners (3-5)   **398.2**
The troll with no heart in his body and other tales of trolls from Norway (3-6)   **398.2**
Contents: The Three Billy Goats Gruff; The boy who became a lion, a falcon, and an ant; Butterball; The handshake; The boys and the North Wind; The white cat in the Dovre Mountain; The sailors and the troll; The eating competition; The troll with no heart in his body

Lungs
Parker, S. The lungs and respiratory system (5 and up)   **612.2**

Diseases

See also Asthma

Lunn, Janet Louise Swoboda
Laura Secord: a story of courage (3-5)   **Fic**

Lupe. Koja, K.
In Swan sister; fairy tales retold   **S C**

Lupica, Mike
Heat (5 and up)   **Fic**

Lupton, Hugh
Pirican Pic and Pirican Mor (k-3)   **398.2**
Riddle me this! (2-4)   **793.73**

Lusitania (Steamship)
Preston, D. Remember the Lusitania (5 and up)
     940.4

Lusmore and the fairies. Doyle, M.
In Doyle, M. Tales from old Ireland p42-51
     398.2

Lutey and the mermaid. Philip, N.
In Philip, N. Celtic fairy tales p60-65
     398.2

Luthardt, Kevin
Peep!   **E**

The **lutin**. San Souci, R.
In San Souci, R. A terrifying taste of short & shivery; thirty creepy tales p39-42
     398.2

Lutoniushka. Afanas´ev, A. N.
In Afanas´ev, A. N. Russian fairy tales p336-37
     398.2

Luxbacher, Irene
The jumbo book of art (4 and up)   **702.8**

Luxembourg
Sheehan, P. Luxembourg (5 and up)   **949.35**

Ly, Many
Home is east (5 and up)   **Fic**

Lyddie. Paterson, K.   **Fic**

Lyga, Allyson A. W.
Graphic novels in your media center   **025.2**

Lyga, Barry
(jt. auth) Lyga, A. A. W. Graphic novels in your media center   **025.2**

Lying See Truthfulness and falsehood

Lyle, Lyle, crocodile. Waber, B.   **E**

Lynch, P. J.
(il) Hest, A. When Jessie came across the sea   **E**
(il) Stockton, F. The bee-man of Orn   **Fic**
(il) Wojciechowski, S. The Christmas miracle of Jonathan Toomey   **E**

Lynch, Wayne
Penguins! (4 and up)   **598**
(jt. auth) Evert, L. Birds of prey   **598**
(il) Lang, A. Baby koala   **599.2**

Lynn, Ruth Nadelman
Fantasy literature for children and young adults
     016.8

Lyon, George Ella
Mother to tigers [biography of Helen Martini] (k-3)   **92**
Weaving the rainbow   **E**

Lyons, Maritcha Rémond, 1848-1929
About
Bolden, T. Maritcha [biography of Maritcha Rémond Lyons] (4 and up)   **92**

Lyons, Mary E.
Catching the fire: Philip Simmons, blacksmith (4 and up)   **92**
Letters from a slave girl (6 and up)   **Fic**
Roy makes a car (k-3)   **398.2**

Lyons, Oren
(il) Sneve, V. D. H. High Elk's treasure   **Fic**

M

M.C. Higgins, the great. Hamilton, V.   **Fic**

M is for music. Krull, K.   **E**

Ma Dear's aprons. McKissack, P. C.   **E**

Ma Yan
The diary of Ma Yan (5 and up)   **951.05**

Maarsen, Jacqueline van
(jt. auth) Lee, C. A. A friend called Anne
     940.53

Maass, Robert
  When spring comes (k-2)   **508.2**
  (il) Rosenberg, M. B. Mommy's in the hospital
    having a baby   **362.1**
Mabela the clever. MacDonald, M. R.   **398.2**
Mabinogion
  See/See also pages in the following book(s):
  Bulfinch, T. Bulfinch's mythology   **201**
Mable Riley. Jocelyn, M.   **Fic**
Macaroni boy. Ayres, K.   **Fic**
Macaulay, David
  Angelo   **E**
  Black and white   **E**
  Building big (5 and up)   **720**
  Building the book Cathedral (4 and up)   **726**
  Castle (4 and up)   **728.8**
  Cathedral: the story of its construction (4 and
    up)   **726**
  City: a story of Roman planning and construc-
    tion (4 and up)   **711**
  Mill (4 and up)   **690**
  Mosque (4 and up)   **726**
  The new way things work (4 and up)   **600**
  Pyramid (4 and up)   **726**
  Rome antics (4 and up)   **945**
  Ship (4 and up)   **387.2**
  Shortcut   **E**
  Unbuilding (4 and up)   **690**
  Underground (5 and up)   **624**
  Why the chicken crossed the road   **E**
Macbeth. Packer, T.
  In Packer, T. Tales from Shakespeare p67-83
        822.3
Macbeth, William Shakespeare's. Coville, B.
        822.3
Maccabees, Feast of the *See* Hanukkah
Maccarone, Grace
  A child's good night prayer   **E**
MacCarthy, Patricia
  (il) Mahy, M. 17 kings and 42 elephants   **E**
MacDonald, Amy
  Please, Malese! (k-3)   **398.2**
MacDonald, Betty
  Mrs. Piggle-Wiggle (2-4)   **Fic**
MacDonald, George
  At the back of the North Wind (4-6)   **Fic**
  The light princess (3-6)   **Fic**
  The princess and the goblin (3-6)   **Fic**
MacDonald, Margaret Read
  Celebrate the world   **398.2**
  Conejito (k-3)   **398.2**
  Fat cat (k-3)   **398.2**
  The girl who wore too much (k-3)   **398.2**
  A hen, a chick, and a string guitar (k-2)
        398.2
  Look back and see   **372.6**
  Stories included are: The snow bunting's lullaby; Look back
  and see; Kanji-jo, the nestlings; Domingo siete; Turkey girl; Lit-
  tle Cricket's marriage; Please all . . . please none; Why Koala
  has no tale; Katchi Katchi Blue Jay; Biyera well; The strawber-
  ries of the little men; The elk and the wren; The bear-child; Two
  women hunt for ground squirrels; Quail song; Grandfather Bear
  is hungry; Tiny Mouse goes traveling; The singing turtle; The
  Teeny Weeny Bop; A penny and a half
  Mabela the clever (k-3)   **398.2**
  Pickin' peas (k-3)   **398.2**

The round book   **782.42**
Shake-it-up tales!   **372.6**
The storyteller's sourcebook   **398**
The storyteller's start-up book   **372.6**
  Stories included are: Turtle of Koka; The little old woman who
  lived in a vinegar bottle; Puchika Churika; Marsh Hawk; Gecko;
  Kudu break!; What are their names!; Aayoga with many excuses;
  Kanu above and Kanu below; Ko Kóngole; Ningun; Yonjwa
  seeks a bride
Three-minute tales   **398.2**
Tunjur! Tunjur! Tunjur! (k-2)   **398.2**
When the lights go out   **372.6**
  Stories included are: Little Buttercup; The Wee Little Tyke;
  Looking for home; Wicked John and the Devil; The Great Red
  Cat; The wizard clip; The tinker and the ghost; The conjure
  wives; Sop doll; The Hobyahs; Old Ben; Sam'l; The cat with the
  beckoning paw; Totanguak; The red silk handkerchief; The
  strange visitor; Who lives in the skull?
MacDonald, Ross
  Achoo! Bang! Crash!   **E**
  Another perfect day   **E**
Macdonald, Suse
  A was once an apple pie   **E**
  Alphabatics   **E**
  Look whooo's counting   **E**
  Sea shapes   **E**
MacDonell, Colleen
  Essential documents for school libraries
        025.1
MacEachern, Stephen
  (il) Thomas, K. The kids guide to money cent$
        332.024
Macedonia (Republic)
  Knowlton, M. Macedonia (5 and up)   **949.7**
MacGregor, Cynthia
  Jigsaw puzzle family (5 and up)   **306.8**
  Think for yourself (3-6)   **170**
Machine quilting *See* Quilting
Machinery
  See also Construction equipment; Mills
  Bingham, C. Monster machines (k-3)   **621.8**
  Hoban, T. Construction zone (k-2)   **621.8**
  Macaulay, D. The new way things work (4 and
    up)   **600**
  Rockwell, A. F. Big wheels   **E**
Machines, Simple *See* Simple machines
Machines at work. Barton, B.   **690**
Machines at work [series]
  Bingham, C. Airplane   **629.133**
  Bingham, C. Fire truck   **628.9**
Machu Picchu (Peru)
  Lewin, T. Lost city (2-4)   **985**
Macie and boo hag. Hamilton, V.
  In Hamilton, V. Her stories; African Ameri-
    can folktales, fairy tales, and true tales
    p51-55   **398.2**
Maciel, Amanda
  (jt. auth) Cohen, S. Fire on ice   **92**
Mack made movies [biography of Mack Sennett]
  Brown, D.   **92**
MacKain, Bonnie
  (il) Pinczes, E. J. One hundred hungry ants
        E
Mackall, Dandi Daley
  First day   **E**

Mackay, Donald A.
(il) Fox, P. The stone-faced boy   **Fic**

Mackel, Kathy
MadCat (5 and up)   **Fic**

Macken, JoAnn Early
Sing-along song   **E**

Mackenzie River (N.W.T.)
Harris, T. The Mackenzie River (5 and up)
    971

MacLachlan, Emily
(jt. auth) MacLachlan, P. Bittle   **E**
(jt. auth) MacLachlan, P. Painting the wind
    E

MacLachlan, Patricia
All the places to love   **E**
Arthur, for the very first time (4-6)   **Fic**
Baby (5 and up)   **Fic**
Bittle   **E**
Dragon's coo
    In Fire and wings: dragon tales from East and
      West p25-31   **S C**
The facts and fictions of Minna Pratt (4 and up)
    Fic
Journey (4 and up)   **Fic**
Painting the wind   **E**
Sarah, plain and tall (3-5)   **Fic**
Seven kisses in a row (2-4)   **Fic**
Who loves me?   **E**

MacLean, Christine Kole
Mary Margaret and the perfect pet plan (3-5)
    Fic

MacLean, Kerry Lee
Peaceful piggy meditation   **E**

MacLeod, Elizabeth
Albert Einstein (4 and up)   **92**
Bake and make amazing cakes (4-6)   **641.8**
Bake and make amazing cookies (4-6)   **641.8**
Chock full of chocolate (4-6)   **641.6**
Harry Houdini (4-6)   **92**
Helen Keller (3-6)   **92**
Marie Curie (5 and up)   **92**
(jt. auth) Skreslet, L. To the top of Everest
    796.52

The **Macmillan** book of Greek gods and heroes.
Low, A.   **292**

Macmillan dictionary for children (4-6)   **423**
Macmillan first dictionary (1-3)   **423**
Macmillan very first dictionary. See Macmillan
first dictionary   **423**

Macnair, Patricia Ann
Movers & shapers (3-5)   **612.7**

Macquitty, Miranda
Shark (4 and up)   **597**

Macramé
Sadler, J. A. Hemp jewelry (4-6)   **746.42**

Macy, Sue
Batting after Sophie
    In Girls got game; sports stories and poems
    810.8
Bulls-eye: a photobiography of Annie Oakley (4
and up)   **92**
Freeze frame (5 and up)   **796.98**
Swifter, higher, stronger (4 and up)   **796.48**

(ed) Girls got game. See Girls got game
    810.8

Mad as a wet hen! and other funny idioms.
Terban, M.   **423**

Madagascar
Bishop, N. Digging for bird-dinosaurs (4 and
up)   **567.9**

Madam president. Thimmesh, C.   **920**

Madama, John
(il) Peters, R. M. Clambake   **970.004**

Madame Squidley and Beanie. Mead, A.   **Fic**

Madaras, Area
(jt. auth) Madaras, L. The "what's happening to
my body" book for girls   **613.9**

Madaras, Lynda
Ready, set, grow! (3-6)   **613.9**
The "what's happening to my body?" book for
boys (4 and up)   **613.9**
The "what's happening to my body" book for
girls (4 and up)   **613.9**

Madavan, Vijay
Cooking the Indian way
    In Easy menu ethnic cookbooks   **641.5**

MadCat. Mackel, K.   **Fic**

Madden, Kerry
Gentle's Holler (5 and up)   **Fic**

Made in the U.S.A. [series]
Englart, M. R. Helicopters   **629.133**
Kreger, C. Cheese   **637**
Kreger, C. Jelly beans   **641.8**

A **made-to-order** suit. Taback, S.
    In Taback, S. Kibitzers and fools; tales my
      zayda (grandfather) told me   **398.2**

Made you look. Graydon, S.   **659.1**

Madeline. Bemelmans, L.   **E**

Madeline's rescue. Bemelmans, L.   **E**

Madison, James, 1751-1836
         About
Fritz, J. The great little Madison (5 and up)
    92

Madlenka. Sís, P.   **E**

Madonna, 1958-
See/See also pages in the following book(s):
Orgill, R. Shout, sister, shout! (6 and up)
    920

Madrigal, Antonio Hernandez
Erandi's braids   **E**

Madsen, Jim
(il) Smith, C. L. Indian shoes   **Fic**

Madsen, Mads Albert
         Fiction
Rand, G. Sailing home (2-4)   **Fic**

Maestro, Betsy
Coming to America: the story of immigration
(k-3)   **325.73**
The discovery of the Americas (2-4)   **970.01**
Exploration and conquest (2-4)   **970.01**
How do apples grow? (k-3)   **634**
Liberty or death (3-6)   **973.3**
A more perfect union (2-4)   **342**
The new Americans (2-4)   **973.2**
The story of clocks and calendars (3-6)   **529**
The story of money (3-5)   **332.4**

Maestro, Betsy—*Continued*

The story of religion (3-5)	**200**
The story of the Statue of Liberty (k-3)	**974.7**
Struggle for a continent (3-6)	**973.2**
Why do leaves change color? (k-3)	**582.16**

Maestro, Giulio

Riddle roundup (2-4)	**793.73**
(jt. auth) Maestro, B. The discovery of the Americas	**970.01**
(il) Maestro, B. Exploration and conquest	**970.01**
(il) Maestro, B. How do apples grow?	**634**
(il) Maestro, B. Liberty or death	**973.3**
(il) Maestro, B. A more perfect union	**342**
(il) Maestro, B. The new Americans	**973.2**
(il) Maestro, B. The story of clocks and calendars	**529**
(il) Maestro, B. The story of money	**332.4**
(il) Maestro, B. The story of religion	**200**
(il) Maestro, B. The story of the Statue of Liberty	**974.7**
(il) Maestro, B. Struggle for a continent	**973.2**
(jt. auth) Maestro, M. Geese find the missing piece	**793.73**
(jt. auth) Maestro, M. What do you hear when cows sing?	**793.73**
(il) Terban, M. Mad as a wet hen! and other funny idioms	**423**

Maestro, Marco

Geese find the missing piece (k-2)	**793.73**
What do you hear when cows sing? (k-2)	**793.73**

The **maestro** plays. Martin, B.   **E**

Magarian, La Verne J.
See/See also pages in the following book(s):
Major, J. S. Caravan to America p[1]-13 (4 and up)   **920**

Magellan, Ferdinand, 1480?-1521
About
Levinson, N. S. Magellan and the first voyage around the world (5 and up)   **92**
See/See also pages in the following book(s):
Fritz, J. Around the world in a hundred years (4 and up)   **910.4**

Magellan and the first voyage around the world. Levinson, N. S.   **92**

Maggie's Amerikay. Russell, B. T.   **E**

The **maggot**. San Souci, R.
In San Souci, R. Even more short & shivery; thirty spine-tingling stories p9-14   **398.2**

Maggots, grubs, and more. Stewart, M.   **595.7**

Magi
Fiction
Menotti, G. C. Amahl and the night visitors (2-4)   **Fic**
Vidal, B. Federico and the Magi's gift   **E**

Magic
Hill, D. Witches & magic-makers (4 and up)   **133.4**
Fiction
Avi. The Book Without Words (5 and up)   **Fic**

Bernstein, N. Magic by the book (4-6)   **Fic**
Billingsley, F. Well wished (4-6)   **Fic**
Bode, N. E. The Anybodies (5 and up)   **Fic**
Chabon, M. Summerland (5 and up)   **Fic**
Coville, B. Juliet Dove, Queen of Love (4-6)   **Fic**
Dahl, R. The magic finger (2-4)   **Fic**
Del Negro, J. Willa and the wind   **E**
Divakaruni, C. B. The conch bearer (5 and up)   **Fic**
Downer, A. Hatching magic (4 and up)   **Fic**
Fleischman, S. Mr. Mysterious & Company (5 and up)   **Fic**
Gilliland, J. H. Strange birds (3-6)   **Fic**
Gilman, L. A. Grail quest: the Camelot spell (5 and up)   **Fic**
Haptie, C. Otto and the flying twins (4 and up)   **Fic**
Hobbs, W. Kokopelli's flute (5 and up)   **Fic**
Howland, N. Latkes, latkes, good to eat   **E**
Jennings, R. W. Orwell's luck (5 and up)   **Fic**
Johnson, G. Thora (4-6)   **Fic**
Johnston, T. The spoon in the bathroom wall (3-5)   **Fic**
Jones, U. The witch's children   **E**
Keehn, S. M. Gnat Stokes and the Foggy Bottom Swamp Queen (5 and up)   **Fic**
Kitamura, S. Me and my cat?   **E**
Kladstrup, K. The book of story beginnings (4 and up)   **Fic**
Lillegard, D. Tiger, tiger   **E**
Lisle, R. Copper (3-6)   **Fic**
Martin, B. Trick or treat?   **E**
Meddaugh, S. The witch's walking stick   **E**
Melmed, L. K. Moishe's miracle   **E**
Pearce, P. The little gentleman (3-5)   **Fic**
Pullman, P. The firework-maker's daughter (4 and up)   **Fic**
Sage, A. Magyk (5 and up)   **Fic**
Van Allsburg, C. The garden of Abdul Gasazi   **E**
Van Allsburg, C. The sweetest fig   **E**
Van Allsburg, C. The widow's broom   **E**
Vande Velde, V. Wizard at work (3-6)   **Fic**
Willard, N. Sweep dreams   **E**
Yep, L. The magic paintbrush (3-5)   **Fic**

Magic. Afanas´ev, A. N.
In Afanas´ev, A. N. Russian fairy tales p399-404   **398.2**

Magic & mischief. Climo, S.   **398.2**

Magic Anansi. Hamilton, V.
In Hamilton, V. A ring of tricksters; animal tales from America, the West Indies, and Africa p53-57   **398.2**

The **magic** bean tree. Van Laan, N.   **398.2**

The **magic** bed-knob. Norton, M.
In Norton, M. Bed-knob and broomstick   **Fic**

The **magic** box. Afanas´ev, A. N.
In Afanas´ev, A. N. Russian fairy tales p164-68   **398.2**

The **magic** box. Sawyer, R.
In Sawyer, R. The way of the storyteller p219-25   **372.6**

The **magic** brocade. Yolen, J.
> *In* Yolen, J. Mightier than the sword; world folktales for strong boys p1-10   **398.2**

Magic by the book. Bernstein, N.   **Fic**

The **magic** castle and the apples of immortality. Doherty, B.
> *In* Doherty, B. The famous adventures of Jack p50-86   **398.2**

The **magic** crossbow. Terada, A. M.
> *In* Terada, A. M. Under the starfruit tree; folktales from Vietnam p120-25
> **398.2**

The **magic** eye. Nixon, J. L.
> *In* Nixon, J. L. Ghost town; seven ghostly stories p81-98   **S C**

The **magic** fan. Baker, K.   **E**

The **magic** finger. Dahl, R.   **Fic**

The **magic** finger. Dahl, R.
> *also in* You read to me & I'll read to you; 20th-century stories to share p10-25
> **E**

The **magic** gourd. Wagué Diakité, B.   **398.2**

Magic mouse guides [series]
> Ward-Johnson, C. E-mail: a magic mouse guide
> **004.6**

The **magic** nation thing. Snyder, Z. K.   **Fic**

The **magic** nesting doll. Ogburn, J. K.   **E**

Magic or not? Eager, E.   **Fic**

The **Magic** orange tree
> *In* The Magic orange tree, and other Haitian folktales p13-21   **398.2**

The **Magic** orange tree, and other Haitian folktales (5 and up)   **398.2**

The **magic** paintbrush. Yep, L.   **Fic**

The **magic** pencil. Hough, C. W.
> *In* Bauer, C. F. Celebrations; read-aloud holiday and theme book programs p12-14
> **808.8**

The **magic** school bus and the electric field trip. Cole, J.   **621.3**

The **magic** school bus at the waterworks. Cole, J.   **551.48**

The **magic** school bus explores the senses. Cole, J.   **612.8**

The **magic** school bus: in the time of the dinosaurs. Cole, J.   **567.9**

The **magic** school bus inside a beehive. Cole, J.   **595.7**

The **magic** school bus inside a hurricane. Cole, J.   **551.55**

The **magic** school bus inside the Earth. Cole, J.   **551.1**

The **magic** school bus inside the human body. Cole, J.   **612**

The **magic** school bus, lost in the solar system. Cole, J.   **523**

The **magic** school bus on the ocean floor. Cole, J.   **591.7**

Magic secrets. Wyler, R.   **793.8**

The **magic** seed. Jaffe, N.
> *In* Jaffe, N. and Zeitlin, S. J. The cow of no color: riddle stories and justice tales from around the world p55-58   **398.2**

The **magic** shirt. Afanas´ev, A. N.
> *In* Afanas´ev, A. N. Russian fairy tales p110-13   **398.2**

The **magic** spoon. Kimmel, E. A.
> *In* Kimmel, E. A. The jar of fools: eight Hanukkah stories from Chelm p27-34
> **S C**

Magic steps. Pierce, T.   **Fic**

The **magic** swan geese. Afanas´ev, A. N.
> *In* Afanas´ev, A. N. Russian fairy tales p349-51   **398.2**

The **magic** teakettle. Sakade, F.
> *In* Sakade, F. Japanese children's favorite stories

Magic thinks big. Cooper, E.   **E**

Magic tricks
> Bauer, C. F. Leading kids to books through magic   **027.62**
> Broekel, R. Hocus pocus: magic you can do (3-5)   **793.8**
> Burgess, R. Kids make magic!   **793.8**
> White, L. B. Shazam! simple science magic (3-6)   **793.8**
> Wyler, R. Magic secrets (k-2)   **793.8**

Magic windows. Garza, C. L.   **305.8**

Magical library lessons. Stover, L. F.   **027.62**

Magical math [series]
> Long, L. Fabulous fractions   **513**
> Long, L. Marvelous multiplication   **513**
> Long, L. Measurement mania   **530.8**

The **magical** Monkey King. Jiang, J.-l.   **398.2**

The **magical** worlds of Harry Potter. Colbert, D.
> **823.009**

Magicians
> Fleischman, S. Escape! [biography of Harry Houdini] (5 and up)   **92**
> Krull, K. Houdini (2-4)   **92**
> MacLeod, E. Harry Houdini (4-6)   **92**
> ### Fiction
> Agee, J. Milo's hat trick   **E**
> Alexander, L. The rope trick (4 and up)   **Fic**
> Avi. Midnight magic (5 and up)   **Fic**
> Bell, H. The wizard test (5 and up)   **Fic**
> Burleigh, R. The secret of the great Houdini
> **E**
> Cooper, S. The magician's boy (2-4)   **Fic**
> Fleischman, S. The midnight horse (3-6)   **Fic**
> Meddaugh, S. Lulu's hat (3-5)   **Fic**

The **magician's** boy. Cooper, S.   **Fic**

Magloff, Lisa
> Duckling (k-2)   **598**
> Frog (k-2)   **597.8**

Magnesium
> Uttley, C. Magnesium
> *In* The Elements   **546**

Magnetism
> Farndon, J. Magnetism (3-6)   **538**
> Gardner, R. Energizing science projects with electricity and magnetism (4-6)   **537**

Magnetism—*Continued*
Meiani, A. Magnetism (4 and up)   **538**

Magnets
Branley, F. M. What makes a magnet? (k-3)
   538

Magnus at the fire. Armstrong, J.   **E**

Magnuson, Diana
(il) Bruchac, J. The Trail of Tears   **970.004**

The **magpie's** nest. Jacobs, J.
In Jacobs, J. English fairy tales p193-95
   398.2

Maguire, Gregory
Beyond the fringe
In A Glory of unicorns p45-57   **S C**
The good liar (4 and up)   **Fic**
Seven spiders spinning (4-6)   **Fic**
Tea party ends in bloody massacre, film at 11
In Shelf life: stories by the book   **S C**

Magyk. Sage, A.   **Fic**

Mahomet *See* Muḥammad, d. 632

Mahren, Sue
Make your own teddy bears & bear clothes!
(3-6)   **745.592**

Mahurin, Matt
(il) Desimini, L. My beautiful child   **E**

Mahy, Margaret
17 kings and 42 elephants   **E**
The girl with the green ear [excerpt]
In You read to me & I'll read to you; 20th-
century stories to share p167-70   **E**
The seven Chinese brothers (1-3)   **398.2**

Mai-Wyss, Tatjana
(il) Cheng, A. The lemon sisters   **E**

Maiasaura and other duck-billed plant eaters.
Schomp, V.
In Schomp, V. Prehistoric world [series]
   567.9

The **Maiden** Tsar. Afanas'ev, A. N.
In Afanas'ev, A. N. Russian fairy tales p229-
34   **398.2**

Mail systems, Electronic *See* Electronic mail systems

Maine
DeFord, D. H. Maine
In World Almanac Library of the States series
   973
Hicks, T. A. Maine
In It's my state! [series]   **973**
Kent, D. Maine
In America the beautiful, second series
   973

Fiction
Buzzeo, T. The sea chest   **E**
Hopkinson, D. Birdie's lighthouse (1-3)   **Fic**
Martin, J. B. Grandmother Bryant's pocket
   E
McCloskey, R. Blueberries for Sal   **E**
McCloskey, R. One morning in Maine   **E**
McCloskey, R. Time of wonder   **E**
Wait, L. Wintering well (5 and up)   **Fic**

Maione, Heather Harms
(jt. auth) Napoli, D. J. Sly the Sleuth and the
pet mysteries   **Fic**

Mair, Jacqueline
(il) Philip, N. Horse hooves and chicken feet:
Mexican folktales   **398.2**
(il) Stockings of buttermilk: American folktales.
See Stockings of buttermilk: American folktales   **398.2**

Maitland, Barbara
Moo in the morning   **E**

Major, John S.
Caravan to America (4 and up)   **920**

Major, Kevin
Aunt Olga's Christmas postcards   **E**

Major inventions through history [series]
Herbst, J. The history of transportation   **388**
Jango-Cohen, J. The history of food   **641.3**
Landau, E. The history of everyday life   **609**

Mak, Kam
My Chinatown   **E**

Make-a-saurus. Cooley, B.   **567.9**

Make a world. See Emberley, E. Ed Emberley's
drawing book: make a world   **741.2**

Make amazing toy and game gadgets. Pinchuk, A.
   745.592

Make-believe playmates *See* Imaginary playmates

Make way for ducklings. McCloskey, R.   **E**

Make way for Sam Houston. Fritz, J.   **92**

Make your own teddy bears & bear clothes!.
Mahren, S.   **745.592**

Makeovers by Marcia. Mills, C.   **Fic**

Making animal babies. Collard, S. B., III
   571.8

Making books that fly, fold, wrap, hide, pop up,
twist, and turn. Diehn, G.   **736**

Making fleece crafts. Sadler, J. A.   **746**

Making friends. Rogers, F.   **158**

Making it home (4 and up)   **305.23**

Making laws. Donovan, S.   **328**

Making magic windows. Garza, C. L.   **736**

Making masks. Schwarz, R.   **646.4**

Making music. Wiseman, A. S.   **784.19**

Making musical things. See Wiseman, A. S. Making music   **784.19**

The **making** of a writer. Nixon, J. L.   **92**

The **making** of America. Johnston, R. D.   **973**

Making of America [series]
Anderson, D. The Cold War years   **973.92**
Steins, R. Exploration and settlement   **970.01**

Malam, John
Ancient Egyptian jobs (5 and up)   **932**
Ancient Greece (5 and up)   **938**
Library (4 and up)   **027**

Maland, Nick
(il) Bergman, M. Snip snap!   **E**
(il) Davies, N. Big blue whale   **599.5**

Malaria
Isle, M. Malaria (5 and up)   **616.9**
Fiction
Giblin, J. The boy who saved Cleveland (3-5)
   Fic

Malawi
Fiction
Williams, K. L. Galimoto   E
Malaysia
Guile, M. Culture in Malaysia (4 and up)
    959.5
Malcolm, Peter
Libya (5 and up)   961.2
Malcolm X, 1925-1965
About
Myers, W. D. Malcolm X (3-6)   92
Male, Alan
(il) Facklam, M. Lizards: weird and wonderful
    597.95
(il) Facklam, M. Spiders and their web sites
    595.4
Male role See Sex role
Mali
Fiction
Burns, K. Mansa Musa (4 and up)   Fic
Diakité, P. I lost my tooth in Africa   E
History
McKissack, P. C. The royal kingdoms of Ghana,
Mali, and Songhay (5 and up)   966.2
Wisniewski, D. Sundiata (1-4)   92
Malindy and little devil. Hamilton, V.
In Hamilton, V. Her stories; African Ameri-
can folktales, fairy tales, and true tales
p61-65   398.2
Malintzin of the Mountain. Gerson, M.-J.
In Gerson, M.-J. Fiesta femenina; celebrating
women in Mexican folktale   398.2
Mall mania. Murphy, S. J.   513
Mallat, Kathy
Mama love   E
Mallett, David
Inch by inch (k-2)   782.42
Mallory, Kenneth
Swimming with hammerhead sharks (4 and up)
    597
Malone, Margaret Gay
Italy (2-4)   945
Malone, Peter
(il) Crossley-Holland, K. How many miles to
Bethlehem?   232.9
(il) Crossley-Holland, K. The world of King Ar-
thur and his court   942.01
Malory, Sir Thomas
Morte d'Arthur; adaptation. See Hodges, M.
Merlin and the making of the king   398.2
Malta
Sheehan, S. Malta (5 and up)   945
Mama. Schick, E.   E
Mama & Papa have a store. Carling, A. L.   E
Mama always comes home. Wilson, K.   E
Mama and me and the Model-T. Gibbons, F.
    E
Mama cat has three kittens. Fleming, D.   E
Mama, do you love me? Joosse, B. M.   E
Mama don't allow. Hurd, T.   E

Mamá Goose (k-2)   398.8
Mama had to work on Christmas. Marsden, C.
    Fic
Mama love. Mallat, K.   E
Mama loves me from away. Brisson, P.   E
Mama Panya's pancakes. Chamberlin, M.   E
Mama's day. Ashman, L.   E
Mama's Little Bears. Tafuri, N.   E
Mammalabilia. Florian, D.   811
Mammals
See also Fossil mammals groups of mam-
mals; and names of mammals
Esbensen, B. J. Baby whales drink milk (k-1)
    599.5
Poetry
Florian, D. Mammalabilia   811
Mammals, Marine See Marine mammals
Mammoths
Aliki. Wild and woolly mammoths (k-3)
    569
Arnold, C. When mammoths walked the earth
(3-6)   569
Chorlton, W. Woolly mammoth (4 and up)
    569
Hehner, B. Ice Age mammoth (5 and up)
    569
Fiction
Martin, R. Will's mammoth   E
Man
Influence on nature
See Human influence on nature
Origin
See Human origins
Man, Fossil *See* Fossil hominids
Man, Prehistoric *See* Prehistoric peoples
The **man** and the boots. Lester, J.
In Lester, J. The last tales of Uncle Remus
p133-36   398.2
The **man** and the wild cattle. Lester, J.
In Lester, J. The last tales of Uncle Remus
p110-14   398.2
Man Bear. Bruchac, J.
In Bruchac, J. and Bruchac, J. When the
Chenoo howls; native American tales of
terror   398.2
The **man-eating** tigers of Sundarbans. Montgom-
ery, S.   599.75
The **man** from the other side. Orlev, U.   Fic
The **man** of influence. Fleischman, P.
In Fleischman, P. Graven images; three sto-
ries   S C
Man of the family. Karr, K.   Fic
The **man** who almost married a witch. Lester, J.
In Lester, J. The last tales of Uncle Remus
p71-76   398.2
The **man** who became a buzzard. Menchú, R.
In Menchú, R. and Liano, D. The honey jar
    398.2
The **man** who caught fish. Krudop, W.   E

The **man** who did not know fear. Afanas´ev, A. N.
In Afanas´ev, A. N. Russian fairy tales p325-27 **398.2**

The **man** who made time travel. Lasky, K. **526**

The **man** who married a seagull. Norman, H.
In Norman, H. The girl who dreamed only geese, and other tales of the Far North **398.2**

The **man** who walked between the towers. Gerstein, M. **E**

The **Man** who was afraid of nothing
In Diane Goode's book of scary stories & songs p26-31 **398.2**

The **man** who went to the far side of the moon: the story of Apollo 11 astronaut Michael Collins. Schyffert, B. U. **92**

Managing and analyzing your collection. Doll, C. A. **025.2**

Managing budgets and finances. Hallam, A. **025.1**

Managing change. Curzon, S. C. **025.1**

Managing the land. Dalgleish, S. **333.73**

Mancall, Jacqueline C.
(jt. auth) Hughes-Hassell, S. Collection management for youth **025.2**

Manchess, Gregory
(il) London, J. Giving thanks **E**
(il) Waldman, S. The last river **978**

Manco Capac and the rod of gold. Delacre, L.
In Delacre, L. Golden tales; myths, legends, and folktales from Latin America p55-57 **398.2**

Mandela, Nelson
About
Cooper, F. Mandela (2-4) **92**
Kramer, A. Mandela (4 and up) **92**
McDonough, Y. Z. Peaceful protest: the life of Nelson Mandela (2-5) **92**

Mandelbaum, Jack
About
Warren, A. Surviving Hitler (5 and up) **940.53**

Manders, John
Señor Don Gato **E**
(il) Arnold, M. D. Prancing, dancing Lily **E**
(il) Dodds, D. A. Minnie's Diner **E**
(il) Lauber, P. What you never knew about fingers, forks, & chopsticks **394.1**
(il) Lauber, P. What you never knew about tubs, toilets & showers **391**

Manfredi, Frederica
(il) De Campi, A. Kat & Mouse: Teacher torture **741.5**

Manganese
Beatty, R. Manganese
In The Elements **546**

Manhattan (New York, N.Y.)
Pericoli, M. See the city (4 and up) **741.9**

Manheimer, Ann S.
Martin Luther King Jr (5 and up) **92**

Maniac Magee. Spinelli, J. **Fic**

Manic-depressive illness
See also Depression (Psychology)
Gold, S. D. Bipolar disorder and depression (4 and up) **616.89**
Fiction
Calhoun, D. The Phoenix Dance (5 and up) **Fic**
Wilson, J. The illustrated Mum (5 and up) **Fic**

Mankell, Henning
Secrets in the fire (5 and up) **Fic**

Mankiller, Wilma
See/See also pages in the following book(s):
Krull, K. Lives of extraordinary women (4 and up) **920**

Manmade disasters [series]
Mayell, M. Tragedies of space exploration **363.1**

Mann, Elizabeth
Hoover Dam (4 and up) **627**
Tikal (4 and up) **972.81**

Manna, Anthony L.
Mr. Semolina-Semolinus (1-3) **398.2**

Manners *See* Etiquette

Manners. Aliki **395**

Manners and customs
See also Country life

Manning, Jane
(il) Climo, S. Cobweb Christmas **E**
(il) A Pet for me. See A Pet for me **811.008**
(il) Weeks, S. Drip, drop **E**

Mannis, Celeste A.
One leaf rides the wind **E**
The Queen's progress [biography of Elizabeth I] (3-5) **92**

Mansa Musa *See* Musa, d. 1337

Mansa Musa. Burns, K. **Fic**

Manson, Christopher
(il) Child, L. M. F. Over the river and through the wood **811**

Mantell, Paul
(jt. auth) Hart, A. Ancient Greece! **938**
(jt. auth) Hart, A. Knights & castles **940.1**

Mantle, Mickey, 1931-1995
About
Marlin, J. Mickey Mantle (4 and up) **92**

Manual workers *See* Working class

Manuel had a riddle. Hamilton, V.
In Hamilton, V. The people could fly; American black folktales p65-75 **398.2**

Manufactures
Slavin, B. Transformed (4 and up) **670**

Manushkin, Fran
Miriam's cup (k-3) **222**

Many luscious lollipops: a book about adjectives. Heller, R. **428**

Many, many weddings in one corner house. Sandburg, C.
In Sandburg, C. More Rootabaga stories p15-19 **S C**

Many, many weddings in one corner house—
Continued
   also in Sandburg, C. The Sandburg treasury; prose and poetry for young people p95-97   **818**
Many moons. Thurber, J.   **Fic**
Many peoples, one land. Helbig, A.   **016.8**
Many thousand gone. Hamilton, V.   **326**
Maple sugar

Fiction
   Haas, J. Sugaring   **E**
Mapping Penny's world. Leedy, L.   **E**
Mapping the world. Johnson, S. A.   **912**
Maps

   See also Atlases
   Johnson, S. A. Mapping the world (4 and up)
                                                                    912
   Morrison, T. The coast mappers (5 and up)
                                                                623.89

Fiction
   Hartman, G. As the crow flies   **E**
   Leedy, L. Mapping Penny's world   **E**
   Walters, V. Are we there yet, Daddy?   **E**
Maravich, Pete, 1948-1988
See/See also pages in the following book(s):
   Krull, K. Lives of the athletes (4 and up)
                                                                    920
The **marble** champ. Soto, G.
   In Soto, G. Baseball in April, and other stories p90-96   **S C**
Marcantonio, Patricia Santos
   Red ridin' in the hood (3-5)   **S C**
Marcellino, Fred
   I, crocodile   **E**
   (il) Babbitt, N. Ouch!   **398.2**
   (il) Bannerman, H. The story of Little Babaji
                                                                       E
   (il) Lear, E. The pelican chorus and other nonsense   **821**
   (il) Perrault, C. Puss in boots   **398.2**
   (il) Seidler, T. The steadfast tin soldier   **Fic**
   (il) Seidler, T. The Wainscott weasel   **Fic**
   (il) White, E. B. The trumpet of the swan
                                                                     Fic
Marchant, Kerena
   Id-ul-Fitr (3-5)   **297.3**
Marciano, John Bemelmans
   Bemelmans   **92**
Marco the Rich and Vasily the Luckless. Afanas'ev, A. N.
   In Afanas'ev, A. N. Russian fairy tales p213-20   **398.2**
Marco's colors. De Paola, T.   **E**
Marcus, Leonard S.
   A Caldecott celebration   **741.6**
   Side by side (4 and up)   **070.5**
   Storied city   **974.7**
   Ways of telling   **741.6**
   (ed) Author talk. See Author talk   **028.5**
   (ed) The wand in the word. See The wand in the word   **813.009**

Mardi Gras *See* Carnival
Mardi Gras: a Cajun country celebration. Hoyt-Goldsmith, D.   **394.25**
Maren, Julie
   (il) Chambers, V. Celia Cruz, Queen of salsa
                                                                      92
Margeson, Susan M.
   Viking (4 and up)   **948**
Margulies, Phillip
   Artificial intelligence (5 and up)   **006.3**
   Diphtheria (4-6)   **616.9**
Maria Morevna. Afanas'ev, A. N.
   In Afanas'ev, A. N. Russian fairy tales p553-62   **398.2**
Maria Theresa, Empress of Austria, 1717-1780
See/See also pages in the following book(s):
   Meltzer, M. Ten queens (5 and up)   **920**
Marianthe's story. See Aliki. Painted words: Marianthe's story one   **E**
Maria's comet. Hopkinson, D.   **E**
Marie and Redfish. Hamilton, V.
   In Hamilton, V. Her stories; African American folktales, fairy tales, and true tales p11-14   **398.2**
Marie Antoinette, Queen, consort of Louis XVI, King of France, 1755-1793
See/See also pages in the following book(s):
   Krull, K. Lives of extraordinary women (4 and up)   **920**

Fiction
   Lasky, K. Marie Antoinette (4 and up)   **Fic**
Marika the snowmaiden. Bauer, C. F.
   In Snowy day: stories and poems p45-49
                                                                   808.8
Marina's muumuu. Vigil-Piñón, E.   **E**
Marine animals

   See also Corals; Freshwater animals; Marine mammals
   Aliki. My visit to the aquarium (k-3)   **639.34**
   Arnold, C. A walk on the Great Barrier Reef (3-5)   **578.7**
   Arnosky, J. Hook, line, & seeker (4 and up)
                                                                   799.1
   Cerullo, M. M. Life under ice (3-5)   **578.7**
   Cerullo, M. M. The truth about dangerous sea creatures (3-5)   **591.7**
   Cole, J. The magic school bus on the ocean floor (2-4)   **591.7**
   Earle, S. A. Sea critters (k-3)   **591.7**
   Grupper, J. Destination: deep sea (3-6)
                                                                   591.7
   Johnson, J. Simon & Schuster children's guide to sea creatures (4 and up)   **591.7**
   Macdonald, S. Sea shapes   **E**
   Pallotta, J. Ocean counting   **E**
   Parker, S. Seashore (4 and up)   **577.7**
   Rose, D. L. Into the A, B, sea (k-3)   **591.7**
   Rose, D. L. Ocean babies (k-2)   **591.3**
   Rose, D. L. One nighttime sea   **E**
   Vogel, C. G. Ocean wildlife (5 and up)
                                                                   591.7

See/See also pages in the following book(s):
   Littlefield, C. A. Awesome ocean science! (3-5)
                                                                  551.46

Marine animals—_Continued_
Fiction
Cherry, L. The sea, the storm, and the mangrove
    tangle   **E**
Freymann, S. One lonely sea horse   **E**
Poetry
Cyrus, K. Hotel deep (3-5)   **811**
Florian, D. In the swim   **811**

Marine aquariums
Aliki. My visit to the aquarium (k-3)   **639.34**

Marine biology
Aquatic life of the world (4 and up)   **578.7**
Conlan, K. Under the ice (4 and up)   **578.7**
Gibbons, G. Exploring the deep, dark sea (k-3)
    551.46

Marine ecology
Cerullo, M. M. Coral reef (4 and up)   **577.7**
Collard, S. B., III. On the coral reefs (4-6)
    577.7
Littlefield, C. A. Awesome ocean science! (3-5)
    551.46

Marine mammal preservation. Thomas, P.
    639.9

Marine mammals
    See also Dolphins; Seals (Animals); Whales
Thomas, P. Marine mammal preservation (5 and
    up)   **639.9**

Marine plants
Cerullo, M. M. Life under ice (3-5)   **578.7**
Parker, S. Seashore (4 and up)   **577.7**
See/See also pages in the following book(s):
Littlefield, C. A. Awesome ocean science! (3-5)
    551.46

Marine pollution
    See also Oil spills
Conlan, K. Under the ice (4 and up)   **578.7**
Vogel, C. G. Human impact (5 and up)
    333.91

Marino, Gianna
Zoopa   **E**

Marino, Jane
Babies in the library!   **027.62**
Mother Goose time   **027.62**

Maritcha [biography of Maritcha Rémond Lyons]
Bolden, T.   **92**

Mark Twain and the queens of the Mississippi.
Harness, C.   **92**

The **Mark** Twain you never knew. Collier, J. L.
    92

Markel, Michelle
Cornhusk, silk, and wishbones (3-6)   **688.7**
Dreamer from the village [biography of Marc
    Chagall] (k-3)   **92**

Markes, Julie
Good thing you're not an octopus!   **E**
I can't talk yet, but when I do...   **E**
Shhhhh! Everybody's sleeping   **E**

Market day. Ehlert, L.   **E**

The **market** of miseries. Geras, A.
    _In_ Geras, A. My grandmother's stories; a col-
    lection of Jewish folk tales p57-67
    398.2

Markets
Lewin, T. How much? (k-3)   **381**
Lewin, T. Market! (k-3)   **381**
Fiction
Ehlert, L. Market day   **E**

Markham, Lois
Colombia (4 and up)   **986.1**

Markle, Sandra
Crocodiles (3-6)   **597.98**
Great white sharks (3-6)   **597**
Growing up wild: wolves (2-4)   **599.77**
Killer whales (3-6)   **599.5**
Lions (3-6)   **599.75**
Little lost bat   **599.4**
A mother's journey (k-3)   **598**
Outside and inside alligators (2-4)   **597.98**
Outside and inside bats (2-4)   **599.4**
Outside and inside big cats (2-4)   **599.75**
Outside and inside dinosaurs (2-4)   **567.9**
Outside and inside giant squid (2-4)   **594**
Outside and inside killer bees (2-4)   **595.7**
Outside and inside mummies (4 and up)
    393
Outside and inside rats and mice (2-4)
    599.35
Outside and inside sharks (2-4)   **597**
Outside and inside snakes (2-4)   **597.96**
Owls (3-6)   **598**
Polar bears (3-6)   **599.78**
Rescues! (4 and up)   **363.34**
Snakes (k-3)   **597.96**
Spiders (k-3)   **595.4**
Vultures (3-5)   **598**
Wolves (3-6)   **599.77**

Marks, Alan
(il) Goodall, J. With love   **599.8**
(il) Markle, S. Little lost bat   **599.4**
(il) Markle, S. A mother's journey   **598**

Marlin, John
Mickey Mantle (4 and up)   **92**

Marmots
Fiction
Cherry, L. How Groundhog's garden grew   **E**
Cox, J. Go to sleep, Groundhog!   **E**
Hill, S. L. Punxsutawney Phyllis   **E**
Swallow, P. C. Groundhog gets a say   **E**

Marooned [biography of Alexander Selkirk]
Kraske, R.   **92**

Marquette, Scott
America under attack (4 and up)   **973.931**
War of 1812 (4 and up)   **973.5**

Márquez, Herón
Roberto Clemente (4 and up)   **92**

Marrella, Maria Pia
(il) MacLachlan, P. Seven kisses in a row
    Fic

Marriage
    See also Divorce; Family; Remarriage;
    Weddings
Fiction
Buehner, C. Fanny's dream   **E**

Marriage customs and rites
Morris, A. Weddings (k-1)   **392**

Marrin, Albert
Dr. Jenner and the speckled monster (5 and up) **614.5**
Secrets from the rocks: dinosaur hunting with Roy Chapman Andrews (4 and up) **92**
Marriott, Pat
(il) Aiken, J. The wolves of Willoughby Chase **Fic**
Mars (Planet)
Simon, S. Destination: Mars (3-6) **523.4**
Exploration
Branley, F. M. Mission to Mars (k-3) **629.45**
Fiction
Pinkney, B. Cosmo and the robot **E**
Marsalis, Wynton
Jazz A-B-Z (5 and up) **781.65**
Marschall, Ken
Inside the Titanic (4 and up) **910.4**
(il) Ballard, R. D. Ghost liners **910.4**
Marsden, Carolyn
The gold-threaded dress (3-5) **Fic**
Mama had to work on Christmas (2-4) **Fic**
Moon runner (3-5) **Fic**
Silk umbrellas (3-6) **Fic**
Marsh, Carole S.
Asteroids, comets, and meteors (4-6) **523.6**
Marsh Hawk. MacDonald, M. R.
In MacDonald, M. R. The storyteller's start-up book; finding, learning, performing, and using folktales including twelve tellable tales p133-37 **372.6**
Marshal, William *See* Pembroke, William Marshal, Earl of, 1144?-1219
Marshall, Chris
(ed) Dinosaurs of the world. See Dinosaurs of the world **567.9**
Marshall, Edward
Fox and his friends **E**
Space case **E**
Three by the sea **E**
Marshall, Edward, 1942-1992
See also Marshall, James, 1942-1992
Marshall, Edward, 1598-1675
See/See also pages in the following book(s):
Marcus, L. S. Ways of telling **741.6**
Marshall, James
George and Martha **E**
Goldilocks and the three bears (k-2) **398.2**
Hansel and Gretel (k-2) **398.2**
Rats on the range and other stories (2-4) **S C**
Contents: Miss Mouse; When Pig went to heaven; When Pig took the wheel; Mouse party; Fair-weather Pig; When Pig got smart; Rats on the range; Buzzard's will
Rats on the roof, and other stories (2-4) **S C**
Contents: Rats on the roof; A sheepish tale; The mouse who got married; Eat your vegetables; Swan song; Ooh-la-la; Miss Jones
Red Riding Hood (k-2) **398.2**
Swine Lake **E**
The three little pigs (k-2) **398.2**
(jt. auth) Allard, H. Miss Nelson is missing! **E**

(il) James Marshall's Mother Goose. See James Marshall's Mother Goose **398.8**
(il) Karlin, B. James Marshall's Cinderella **398.2**
(il) Lear, E. The owl and the pussycat **821**
(il) Marshall, E. Fox and his friends **E**
(il) Marshall, E. Space case **E**
(il) Marshall, E. Three by the sea **E**
(il) Yolen, J. How beastly! **811**
Marshall, Samuel D.
About
Montgomery, S. The tarantula scientist (4 and up) **595.4**
Marshall, Thurgood, 1908-1993
About
Adler, D. A. A picture book of Thurgood Marshall (1-3) **92**
The **Marshall** Cavendish encyclopedia of health. See Encyclopedia of health **610.3**
The **Marshall** children's animal encyclopedia. See National Geographic animal encyclopedia **590.3**
Marshes
See also Swamp animals
Fiction
Himmelman, J. Frog in a bog **E**
Marshes & swamps. Gibbons, G. **577.6**
Marshfield dreams. Fletcher, R. **92**
Marstall, Bob
(il) Cleary, B. Mitch and Amy **Fic**
(il) Pringle, L. P. Crows!: strange and wonderful **598**
(il) Pringle, L. P. An extraordinary life **595.7**
Marsupials
Sill, C. P. About marsupials (k-2) **599.2**
Martha. Spirin, G. **E**
Martha speaks. Meddaugh, S. **E**
Martha's Vineyard (Mass.)
Fiction
DeFelice, C. C. Death at Devil's Bridge (5 and up) **Fic**
Martial arts
Knotts, B. Martial arts (2-4) **796.8**
Fiction
McCully, E. A. Beautiful warrior **E**
Shalant, P. Beware of kissing Lizard Lips (4-6) **Fic**
Martin, Alex
Knights & castles (5 and up) **940.1**
Martin, Ann M.
7 steps to an award-winning school library program **027.8**
The Baby-sitter's Club: Kristy's great idea (3-5) **741.5**
Belle Teal (4 and up) **Fic**
A corner of the universe (5 and up) **Fic**
The doll people (3-5) **Fic**
Here today (5 and up) **Fic**
Squirrel
In Friends; stories about new friends, old friends, and unexpectedly true friends **S C**

Martin, Ann M.—*Continued*

(jt. auth) Danziger, P. P.S. Longer letter later

Fic

(jt. auth) Danziger, P. Snail mail no more

Fic

(ed) Friends. See Friends **S C**

Martin, Ann M., 1955-

See/See also pages in the following book(s):

Author talk (4 and up) **028.5**

Martin, Bill

Barn dance! **E**

A beasty story **E**

Brown bear, brown bear what do you see?

E

Chicka chicka 1, 2, 3 **E**

Chicka chicka boom boom **E**

The ghost-eye tree **E**

Knots on a counting rope **E**

The maestro plays **E**

Panda bear, panda bear, what do you see? **E**

Polar bear, polar bear, what do you hear? **E**

Trick or treat? **E**

Martin, David

Piggy and Dad go fishing **E**

Martin, Francesca

Clever Tortoise (k-3) **398.2**

Martin, Gilles

(il) Dubois, P. J. Birds **598**

Martin, Jacqueline Briggs

Grandmother Bryant's pocket **E**

The lamp, the ice, and the boat called Fish (3-6)

998

On Sand Island **E**

Snowflake Bentley [biography of Wilson Alwyn Bentley] (k-3) **92**

Martin, Joseph Plumb, 1760-1850

About

Murphy, J. A young patriot (5 and up)

973.3

Martin, Laura C.

Nature's art box (4 and up) **745.5**

Recycled crafts box (3-6) **363.7**

Martin, Michael A.

Arizona

In World Almanac Library of the States series

973

Iowa

In World Almanac Library of the States series

973

Maryland

In World Almanac Library of the States series

973

Martin, Nora

Flight of the Fisherbird (5 and up) **Fic**

Martin, Pedro

(il) Murphy, S. J. Hamster champs **516**

Martin, Rafe

The boy who lived with the seals (1-4)

398.2

The language of birds (2-4) **398.2**

The Shark God (k-3) **398.2**

The storytelling princess **E**

Will's mammoth **E**

The world before this one (4 and up) **398.2**

Contents: Dangers; Moving; Gaqka, crow; The bow; The rock; Questions; New day; Two boys; Allies; Men's tales; Dream; Stories; The council; The people and the stone; Farewell

Martin, Sarah Catherine

Old Mother Hubbard. See Cabrera, J. Old Mother Hubbard **398.8**

Martin Bridge: ready for takeoff!. Kerrin, J. S.

Fic

Martin-Jourdenais, Norma Jean

(il) Check, L. Create your own candles

745.5

(il) Check, L. Little Hands paper plate crafts

745.54

(il) Henry, S. Cut-paper play! **745.54**

Martina, the little cockroach. González, L. M.

In González, L. M. Señor Cat's romance and other favorite stories from Latin America p21-27 **398.2**

Martinez, Ed

(il) Medina, J. Tomás Rivera **92**

(il) Soto, G. Too many tamales **E**

Martinez, Sergio

(il) Meltzer, M. Weapons & warfare **355**

(il) San Souci, R. Little Gold Star **398.2**

Martini, Helen, 1912-

About

Lyon, G. E. Mother to tigers [biography of Helen Martini] (k-3) **92**

Martinique

Folklore

See Folklore—Martinique

Martino, Carmela A.

Rosa, sola (4-6) **Fic**

Martins, George

(il) Giovanni, N. Spin a soft black song: poems for children **811**

Martin's big words: the life of Dr. Martin Luther King, Jr. Rappaport, D. **92**

Maruki, Toshi

Hiroshima no pika (5 and up) **940.54**

Marvelous math (4 and up) **811.008**

Marvelous Mattie [biography of Margaret Knight] McCully, E. A. **92**

The **marvelous** misadventures of Sebastian. Alexander, L. **Fic**

Marvelous multiplication. Long, L. **513**

Marven of the Great North Woods. Lasky, K.

E

Marvin one too many. Paterson, K. **E**

Marvin Redpost, kidnapped at birth? Sachar, L.

Fic

Marx, Trish

Everglades forever (3-6) **577.6**

(jt. auth) Borden, L. Touching the sky: the flying adventures of Wilbur and Orville Wright

92

Marxism

See also Communism

Mary, Blessed Virgin, Saint

About

De Paola, T. Mary, the mother of Jesus (3-5)

232.91

Wildsmith, B. Mary (k-3) **232.91**

McMahon, Patricia
Just add one Chinese sister   E

McMaster, Jack
(il) Busby, P. First to fly: how Wilbur & Orville Wright invented the airplane   92

McMillan, Bruce
Days of the ducklings (2-4)   598
Going fishing (2-4)   949.12
Growing colors   E
Mouse views   E
Nights of the pufflings (2-4)   598
Penguins at home (2-4)   598
The problem with chickens   E
Salmon summer (2-4)   639.2
Summer ice (3-6)   508
Wild flamingos (2-4)   598

McMillan, Terry, 1951-
See/See also pages in the following book(s):
Wilkinson, B. S. African American women writers (4 and up)   810.9

McMullan, Jim
(jt. auth) McMullan, K. I stink!   E
(il) McMullan, K. I'm mighty!   E
(il) McMullan, K. Papa's song   E

McMullan, Kate
I stink!   E
I'm mighty!   E
Papa's song   E
Pearl and Wagner: two good friends   E

McMullan, Margaret
How I found the Strong (5 and up)   Fic

McNair, Sylvia
Arkansas
In America the beautiful, second series
     973
Connecticut
In America the beautiful, second series
     973
Finland (5 and up)   948.97
Massachusetts
In America the beautiful, second series
     973
Nebraska
In America the beautiful, second series
     973
Rhode Island
In America the beautiful, second series
     973
U.S. Territories
In America the beautiful, second series
     973

McNamee, Graham
Sparks (4-6)   Fic

McNaughton, Colin
Once upon an ordinary school day   E

McNeely, Tom
(il) Goodman, J. E. Despite all obstacles: La Salle and the conquest of the Mississippi
     92
(il) Goodman, J. E. A long and uncertain journey: the 27,000 mile voyage of Vasco da Gama   92
(il) Mann, E. Tikal   972.81

McNicholas, June
Rats (4 and up)   636.9

McNicholas, Shelagh
(il) Geras, A. Time for ballet   E

McNulty, Faith
If you decide to go to the moon (k-3)
     629.45

McPhail, David M.
Big Brown Bear's up and down day   E
Big Pig and Little Pig   E
Drawing lessons from a bear   E
Edward and the pirates   E
Emma in charge   E
Mole music   E
My little brother   E
Piggy's pancake parlor (1-3)   Fic
Pigs aplenty, pigs galore!   E
Sisters   E
The teddy bear   E
(il) Byars, B. C. Little Horse   Fic
(il) Cullen, C. A. Thirsty baby   E
(il) Field, E. Wynken, Blynken, and Nod
     811
(il) Krull, K. A pot o' gold   820.8

McPhee, Andrew T.
AIDS (5 and up)   616.97

McPherson, James M.
Fields of fury (5 and up)   973.7

McSwigan, Marie
Snow treasure (3-6)   Fic

McWhorter, Diane
A dream of freedom (5 and up)   323.1

McWhorter, Heather
(il) Willey, M. Clever Beatrice   398.2

Me & Neesie. Greenfield, E.   E

Me and Billy. Collier, J. L.   Fic

Me and my amazing body. Sweeney, J.   611

Me and my cat? Kitamura, S.   E

Me and Rupert Goody. O'Connor, B.   Fic

Me and Uncle Romie. Hartfield, C.   E

Me baby, you baby. Wolff, A.   E

Me Tarzan. Byars, B. C.   Fic

Me too!. Arnold, K.   E

Mead, Alice
Crossing the Starlight Bridge (3-5)   Fic
Girl of Kosovo (5 and up)   Fic
Junebug (3-5)   Fic
Madame Squidley and Beanie (3-5)   Fic

Meade, Holly
Inside, inside, inside   E
John Willy and Freddy McGee   E
(il) Appelbaum, D. K. Cocoa ice   E
(il) Best, C. Goose's story   E
(il) Carlson, L. M. Boss of the plains [biography of John Batterson Stetson]   92
(il) Ho, M. Hush!   E
(il) Ho, M. Peek!   E
(il) Lindbergh, R. On morning wings   223

Meal planning *See* Nutrition

Mean soup. Everitt, B.   E

Measurement
See also Volume (Cubic content)
Adler, D. A. How tall, how short, how faraway (k-3)   530.8

Measurement—*Continued*

Gardner, R. Far-out science projects with height and depth (3-6) **530.8**

Gardner, R. Heavy-duty science projects with weight (3-6) **530.8**

Gardner, R. Super-sized science projects with volume (3-6) **530.8**

Leedy, L. Measuring Penny (1-3) **530.8**

Long, L. Measurement mania (3-6) **530.8**

Murphy, S. J. Bigger, Better, BEST! (k-3) **516**

Murphy, S. J. Polly's pen pal (k-3) **516**

Murphy, S. J. Room for Ripley (1-3) **530.8**

Schwartz, D. M. Millions to measure (2-4) **530.8**

Measurement mania. Long, L. **530.8**

Measures *See* Weights and measures

Measuring Penny. Leedy, L. **530.8**

Meatballs

Fiction

Johnson, P. B. On top of spaghetti **E**

Mecha mania. Hart, C. **741.5**

Mechanics

Pentland, P. Toy and game science (4 and up) **531**

Pinchuk, A. Make amazing toy and game gadgets (4 and up) **745.592**

Mechler, Gary

National Audubon Society first field guide: night sky (4 and up) **520**

Meddaugh, Susan

The best place **E**

Cinderella's rat **E**

Harry on the rocks **E**

Hog-eye **E**

Lulu's hat (3-5) **Fic**

Martha speaks **E**

The witch's walking stick **E**

Medearis, Angela Shelf

Haunts (4 and up) **S C**

Contents: The Fiddler Man; Scared silly; Last dance at the Dew Drop Inn; The rainmaker; Waiting for Mr. Chester

Seven spools of thread **E**

Snug in Mama's arms **E**

Media *See* Mass media

Media madness. Ali, D. **302.23**

Media workshop [series]

Pellowski, M. The art of making comic books **741.5**

Mediavilla, Cindy

Creating the full-service homework center in your library **027.4**

Medical care

Rogers, F. Going to the hospital (k-2) **362.1**

Fiction

Wells, R. Felix feels better **E**

Medicine

See also and names of diseases and groups of diseases

Encyclopedias

Encyclopedia of health (4 and up) **610.3**

History

Fisher, L. E. The doctors (4 and up) **610.9**

Green, J. Medicine (5 and up) **610.9**

Lindsay, J. The story of medicine (4-6) **610.9**

Woolf, A. Death and disease (5 and up) **610.9**

Research

Dendy, L. A. Guinea pig scientists (5 and up) **616**

Medicine, Veterinary *See* Veterinary medicine

Medieval architecture

Ross, S. Art and architecture (5 and up) **720.9**

Medieval art

Martin, A. Knights & castles (5 and up) **940.1**

Ross, S. Art and architecture (5 and up) **720.9**

Medieval civilization

Aliki. A medieval feast (2-5) **940.1**

Chrisp, P. Town and country life (5 and up) **940.1**

Chrisp, P. Warfare (5 and up) **355**

Cole, J. Ms. Frizzle's adventures: medieval castle (2-4) **728.8**

Corbishley, M. The Middle Ages (5 and up) **940.1**

Galloway, P. Archers, alchemists, and 98 other medieval jobs you might have loved or loathed (3-6) **940.1**

Gibbons, G. Knights in shining armor (k-3) **940.1**

Gravett, C. Knight (4 and up) **940.1**

Hart, A. Knights & castles (4 and up) **940.1**

Langley, A. Medieval life (4 and up) **940.1**

Martin, A. Knights & castles (5 and up) **940.1**

Ross, S. Monarchs (5 and up) **940.1**

Stefoff, R. The medieval world (5 and up) **909.07**

Woolf, A. Death and disease (5 and up) **610.9**

Woolf, A. Education (5 and up) **940.1**

A **medieval** feast. Aliki **940.1**

Medieval life. Langley, A. **940.1**

Medieval realms [series]

Chrisp, P. Town and country life **940.1**

Chrisp, P. Warfare **355**

Ross, S. Art and architecture **720.9**

Ross, S. Monarchs **940.1**

Woolf, A. Death and disease **610.9**

Woolf, A. Education **940.1**

The **medieval** world. Stefoff, R. **909.07**

Medina, Jane

Tomás Rivera (k-2) **92**

Medina, Tony

Love to Langston (3-5) **811**

Medio Pollito. Sierra, J.

In Sierra, J. Can you guess my name?; traditional tales around the world p31-[35] **398.2**

Meditation

Andrews, L. W. Meditation (5 and up) **158**

Fiction

MacLean, K. L. Peaceful piggy meditation **E**

The **memory** string. Bunting, E.   E

Memphis (Tenn.)
Fiction
Polacco, P. John Philip Duck   E

Menaseh's dream. Singer, I. B.
   In Singer, I. B. Stories for children p313-21
                            S C

Menashe and Rachel. Singer, I. B.
   In Singer, I. B. The power of light; eight stories for Hanukkah p31-39   S C
   also in Singer, I. B. Stories for children p122-29   S C

Menchú, Rigoberta
   The girl from Chimel (4 and up)   92
   The honey jar (4-6)   398.2
   See/See also pages in the following book(s):
   Krull, K. Lives of extraordinary women (4 and up)   920

Mendelson, Edward
   (ed) Lear, E. Edward Lear   821

Mendez, Simon
   (il) Llewellyn, C. Butterfly   595.7
   (il) Llewellyn, C. Frog   597.8

Meningitis
   Routh, K. Meningitis (5 and up)   616.8

Mennonites
   See also Amish
Kenna, K. A people apart (4 and up)   289.7
The **Mennyms**. Waugh, S.   Fic
The **menorah** story. Podwal, M. H.   296.4
Menorahs, mezuzas, and other Jewish symbols. Chaikin, M.   296.4

Menotti, Gian Carlo
   Amahl and the night visitors (2-4)   Fic

Menstruation
   Gravelle, K. The period book (4 and up)   612.6
   Jukes, M. Growing up: it's a girl thing (4 and up)   612.6
   See/See also pages in the following book(s):
   Jukes, M. It's a girl thing (5 and up)   305.23

Mental illness
Fiction
Hermes, P. Summer secrets (5 and up)   Fic
Weeks, S. So B. it (5 and up)   Fic

Mentally handicapped
Fiction
Conly, J. L. Crazy lady! (5 and up)   Fic
Martin, A. M. A corner of the universe (5 and up)   Fic
O'Connor, B. Me and Rupert Goody (4-6)   Fic
Weeks, S. So B. it (5 and up)   Fic

Mentally handicapped children
Fiction
Byars, B. C. The summer of the swans (5 and up)   Fic

Mentally ill
Fiction
Campbell, B. M. Sometimes my mommy gets angry   E
Lisle, J. T. Afternoon of the elves (4-6)   Fic

Porter, P. P. The crazy man (5 and up)   Fic
Meow. Yolen, J.   398.2
Meow means mischief. Nagda, A. W.   Fic
Meow ruff. Sidman, J.   811
The **mer-woman** out of the sea. Hamilton, V.
   In Hamilton, V. Her stories; African American folktales, fairy tales, and true tales p78-83   398.2

Mercado, Nancy E.
   (ed) Tripping over the lunch lady and other school stories. See Tripping over the lunch lady and other school stories   S C

Merchandising *See* Retail trade
The **merchant** and the poor man. Philip, N.
   In Philip, N. and Naḥman, of Bratslav. The pirate princess and other fairy tales   398.2

The **merchant's** daughter and the maidservant. Afanas'ev, A. N.
   In Afanas'ev, A. N. Russian fairy tales p327-31   398.2

The **merchant's** daughter and the slanderer. Afanas'ev, A. N.
   In Afanas'ev, A. N. Russian fairy tales p415-18   398.2

Mercury
Watt, S. Mercury
   In The Elements   546

Mercury (Planet)
Miller, R. Mercury and Pluto (5 and up)   523.4

Mercury and Pluto. Miller, R.   523.4
Mercury Project *See* Project Mercury
Mercy Watson to the rescue. DiCamillo, K.   E

Meret, Sasha
   (il) Feiler, B. S. Walking the Bible   222

Merkin, Richard
   (il) Ritter, L. S. Leagues apart   796.357

Merlin (Legendary character)
Hodges, M. Merlin and the making of the king (3-6)   398.2
Fiction
Barron, T. A. The lost years of Merlin (6 and up)   Fic
White, T. H. The sword in the stone (4 and up)   Fic
Yolen, J. The dragon's boy (5 and up)   Fic

Merlin and the making of the king. Hodges, M.   398.2

The **Mermaid**
   In Diane Goode's book of scary stories & songs p32-35   398.2

The **mermaid** of Zennor. Climo, S.
   In Climo, S. Magic & mischief; tales from Cornwall p89-95   398.2

The **mermaid** summer. Hunter, M.   Fic

Mermaids and mermen
San Souci, R. Sukey and the mermaid (1-4)   398.2
Fiction
Hunter, M. The mermaid summer (4 and up)   Fic
Johnson, G. Thora (4-6)   Fic

Mines and mineral resources
  See also Coal mines and mining
Mine's the best. Bonsall, C. N.   **E**
Ming Lo moves the mountain. Lobel, A.   **E**
Mingus, Cathi
  (il) Holyoke, N. A smart girl's guide to manners
                                                            395
Minka and Meanie. Cohn, R.
  In Friends; stories about new friends, old
    friends, and unexpectedly true friends
                                                            S C
Minkel, Walter
  How to do "The three bears" with two hands
                                                            791.5
Minnesota
  Hintz, M. Minnesota
  In America the beautiful, second series
                                                            973
  Pollock, M. H. Minnesota
  In World Almanac Library of the States series
                                                            973
                        Fiction
  Brown, J. Little Cricket (4-6)   **Fic**
  Durbin, W. Blackwater Ben (5 and up)   **Fic**
  Lasky, K. Marven of the Great North Woods
                                                            E
  Lovelace, M. H. Betsy-Tacy (2-4)   **Fic**
  Paulsen, G. The winter room (5 and up)   **Fic**
  Ylvisaker, A. Dear Papa (4 and up)   **Fic**
Minnie's Diner. Dodds, D. A.   **E**
Minor, Wendell
  Yankee Doodle America (2-4)   **973.3**
  (il) Aldrin, B. Reaching for the moon   **92**
  (il) Burleigh, R. Into the woods: John James
    Audubon lives his dream   **92**
  (il) Ehrlich, A. Rachel: the story of Rachel Car-
    son   **92**
  (il) George, J. C. Everglades   **975.9**
  (il) George, J. C. Julie   **Fic**
  (il) George, J. C. Morning, noon, and night
                                                            E
  (il) Turner, A. W. Abe Lincoln remembers
                                                            92
  (il) Zolotow, C. The seashore book   **E**
Minorities
  See also Ethnic relations
                     Bibliography
  Helbig, A. Many peoples, one land   **016.8**
  Kaleidoscope   **011.6**
  Steiner, S. F. Promoting a global community
    through multicultural children's literature
                                                            016.8
Minotaur (Greek mythology)
  Byrd, R. The hero and the minotaur (3-6)
                                                            398.2
Minstrels
                        Fiction
  Vining, E. G. Adam of the road (5 and up)
                                                            Fic
Minter, Daniel
  (il) Boling, K. New year be coming!   **811**
  (il) Coleman, E. The riches of Oseola McCarty
                                                            92

(il) Medearis, A. S. Seven spools of thread
                                                            E
Minty: a story of young Harriet Tubman.
  Schroeder, A.   **E**
Miracle. Karwoski, G.   **972.9**
The **miracle.** Kimmel, E. A.
  In Kimmel, E. A. The adventures of Hershel
    of Ostropol p32-36   **398.2**
The **miracle** doctor. Fang, L.
  In Fang, L. The Ch'i-lin purse; a collection of
    ancient Chinese stories p85-100   **398.2**
Miracle in Tent City. Jiménez, F.
  In Jiménez, F. The circuit: stories from the
    life of a migrant child p27-44   **S C**
The **miracle** of Our Lady of Guadalupe. Delacre,
  L.
  In Delacre, L. Golden tales; myths, legends,
    and folktales from Latin America p41-43
                                                            398.2
Miracles
                        Fiction
  Kushner, L. In God's hands   **E**
  Wells, R. The miraculous tale of the two Maries
                                                            E
                        Folklore
  De Paola, T. The clown of God (k-3)   **398.2**
The **miracles** of Jesus. De Paola, T.   **232.9**
Miracles on Maple Hill. Sorensen, V. E.   **Fic**
The **miraculous** pipe. Afanas'ev, A. N.
  In Afanas'ev, A. N. Russian fairy tales p425-
    27   **398.2**
The **miraculous** tale of the two Maries. Wells, R.
                                                            E
Miranda, Anne
  To market, to market   **E**
Mirandy and Brother Wind. McKissack, P. C.
                                                            E
Mirette on the high wire. McCully, E. A.   **E**
Miriam (Biblical figure)
                        About
  Manushkin, F. Miriam's cup (k-3)   **222**
  Marzollo, J. Miriam and her brother Moses
    (k-3)   **222**
Miriam and her brother Moses. Marzollo, J.
                                                            222
Miriam's cup. Manushkin, F.   **222**
Mirrors
                        Fiction
  Bahrampour, A. Otto, the story of a mirror
                                                            E
The **misadventures** of Maude March. Couloumbis,
  A.   **Fic**
Misadventures of Millicent Madding [series]
  Tacang, B. Bully-be-gone   **Fic**
Misakian, Jo Ellen Priest
  The essential school library glossary   **020**
Miscellaneous facts *See* Curiosities and wonders
The **miser.** Afanas'ev, A. N.
  In Afanas'ev, A. N. Russian fairy tales p58-
    59   **398.2**

Misty of Chincoteague [excerpt]. Henry, M.
In Horse tales **S C**

Mitakidou, Christodoula
(jt. auth) Manna, A. L. Mr. Semolina-Semolinus
398.2

Mitch and Amy. Cleary, B. **Fic**

Mitchard, Jacquelyn
Baby bat's lullaby **E**

Mitchell, Barbara
A pocketful of goobers: a story about George
Washington Carver (3-5) **92**
Shoes for everyone: a story about Jan
Matzeliger (3-5) **92**

Mitchell, Hetty
(il) Mitchell, B. Shoes for everyone: a story
about Jan Matzeliger **92**

Mitchell, Jackie, 1914-1987
About
Moss, M. Mighty Jackie: the strike out queen
E

Mitchell, Joyce Slayton
Crashed, smashed, and mashed (3-6) **629.2**

Mitchell, Margaree King
Uncle Jed's barbershop **E**

Mitchell, Maria, 1818-1889
Fiction
Hopkinson, D. Maria's comet **E**

Mitchell, Stephen
The nightingale (2-4) **Fic**

Mitchell, Tracy
(il) Avi. What do fish have to do with anything?
and other stories **S C**

Mites
Jarrow, G. Chiggers (4-6) **616.9**

The **mitten**. Brett, J. **398.2**

The **mitten**. Tresselt, A. R. **398.2**

Mitton, Jacqueline
Once upon a starry night (k-3) **523.8**
Zodiac (2-4) **398**

Mitton, Tony
Goodnight me, goodnight you **E**

Miwok Indians
Folklore
San Souci, R. Two bear cubs (k-3) **398.2**

Mixed beasts. Cox, K. **811**

Mixed magics. Jones, D. W. **S C**

Mixed race people *See* Racially mixed people

The **mixed-up** chameleon. Carle, E. **E**

The **mixed-up** feet and the silly bridegroom. Singer, I. B.
In Singer, I. B. Zlateh the goat, and other stories p39-50 **398.2**

Miz Hattie gets some company. Hamilton, V.
In Hamilton, V. Her stories; African American folktales, fairy tales, and true tales p15-19 **398.2**

Mizilca. Yolen, J.
In Yolen, J. Not one damsel in distress; world folktales for strong girls p57-63 **398.2**

Mizokawa, Donald T.
(ed) Kaleidoscope. See Kaleidoscope **011.6**

Mobs *See* Riots

Mochizuki, Ken
Baseball saved us **E**
Heroes **E**
Passage to freedom (3-6) **940.53**

Moctezuma *See* Montezuma II, Emperor of Mexico, ca. 1480-1520

Modarressi, Mitra
Yard sale! **E**
(il) Jones, J. Knead it, punch it, bake it!
641.8

Model airplanes *See* Airplanes—Models

Models and modelmaking
See also Airplanes—Models
Cooley, B. Make-a-saurus (4 and up) **567.9**
Simon, S. Let's try it out with towers and bridges (k-2) **624.1**

Modern art
1900-1999 (20th century)
See Art—20th century

Modern painting
Raczka, B. No one saw (k-3) **759.06**

Moehn, Heather
World holidays (3-6) **394.26**

The **Moffats**. Estes, E. **Fic**

Mogensen, Jan
(il) Kipling, R. The elephant's child **Fic**

Mohammed *See* Muḥammad, d. 632

Mohammedanism *See* Islam

Mohammedans *See* Muslims

Mohawk Indians
Swamp, J. Giving thanks (k-3) **299.7**
Fiction
Bruchac, J. Children of the longhouse (4 and up) **Fic**
Bruchac, J. Skeleton man (4 and up) **Fic**
Kirk, C. A. Sky dancers **E**

Mohr, Nicholasa
Going home (4-6) **Fic**

Mohr, Nicholasa, 1935-
See/See also pages in the following book(s):
Author talk (4 and up) **028.5**

Moishe's miracle. Melmed, L. K. **E**

Moja means one. Feelings, M. **E**

Mojave Desert (Calif.)
Fiction
Fleischman, S. Bo & Mzzz Mad (5 and up)
Fic

Moldova
Sheehan, P. Moldova (5 and up) **947.6**

Mole and the baby bird. Newman, M. **E**

Mole music. McPhail, D. M. **E**

Molecules
Juettner, B. Molecules (4 and up) **540**
Woodford, C. Atoms and molecules (5 and up)
540

Moles (Animals)
Fiction
Ehlert, L. Mole's hill **E**
McAllister, A. Take a kiss to school **E**
McPhail, D. M. Mole music **E**
Moon, N. Tick-tock, drip-drop! **E**

Moles (Animals)—Fiction—*Continued*
Newman, M. Mole and the baby bird   **E**
Pearce, P. The little gentleman (3-5)   **Fic**
Yee, W. H. Upstairs Mouse, downstairs Mole
   E

Mole's hill. Ehlert, L.   **E**

Molin, Paulette Fairbanks
American Indian stereotypes in the world of
children   **970.004**

Molinari, Fernando
(il) Benatar, R. Isabel Allende   **92**

Molk, Laurel
(il) Yolen, J. Off we go!   **E**

Mollel, Tololwa M. (Tololwa Marti)
Ananse's feast (k-3)   **398.2**
My rows and piles of coins   **E**
The orphan boy (k-3)   **398.2**

Mollusks
     See also Cephalopods; Slugs (Mollusks);
Snails; Squids
Blaxland, B. Snails, clams, and their relatives
(3-6)   **594**

Mollusks: snails, clams, and their relatives. See
Blaxland, B. Snails, clams, and their relatives
   594

Molly and the magic wishbone. McClintock, B.
   E

Molly Bannaky. McGill, A.   **E**

Molly Cottontail. San Souci, R.
In San Souci, R. Cut from the same cloth;
American women of myth, legend, and
tall tale p29-33   **398.2**

Molly goes shopping. Eriksson, E.   **E**

Molly Whuppie. De la Mare, W.
In Womenfolk and fairy tales p20-29
   398.2

Molly Whuppie. Jacobs, J.
In Jacobs, J. English fairy tales p127-31
   398.2

Molly Whuppie. Philip, N.
In Philip, N. Celtic fairy tales p86-91
   398.2

Molly Whuppie. Yolen, J.
In Yolen, J. Not one damsel in distress; world
folktales for strong girls p95-102
   398.2

Molly's family. Garden, N.   **E**
Molly's pilgrim. Cohen, B.   **E**

Molybdenum
Lepora, N. Molybdenum
In The Elements   **546**

Mom and Dad are palindromes. Shulman, M.
   E

Mom Bett and the little ones a-glowing. Hamilton,
V.
In Hamilton, V. Her stories; African American folktales, fairy tales, and true tales
p39-41   **398.2**

MoMA *See* Museum of Modern Art (New York,
N.Y.)

Mombourquette, Paul
(il) Lawson, J. The Klondike cat   **E**

Momma at the Pearly Gates. Konigsburg, E. L.
In Konigsburg, E. L. Altogether, one at a
time p61-79   **S C**

Momma, where are you from? Bradby, M.   **E**
Mommies say shhh!. Polacco, P.   **E**
Mommy, carry me please!. Cabrera, J.   **E**
Mommy far, Mommy near. Peacock, C. A.   **E**
Mommy hugs. Katz, K.   **E**
Mommy mine. Warnes, T.   **E**
Mommy's in the hospital having a baby. Rosen-
berg, M. B.   **362.1**
Momotarō and the island of ogres. Wada, S.
   398.2

Monaghan, Kathleen
You can weave! (4 and up)   **746.41**
Monarch butterfly. Gibbons, G.   **595.7**
Monarchs *See* Kings and rulers
Monarchs. Ross, S.   **940.1**

Monarchy
     See also Queens

Monasticism and religious orders for women
     See also Nuns

Monday's troll. Prelutsky, J.   **811**

Monet, Claude, 1840-1926
About
Kelley, T. Claude Monet: sunshine and
waterlilies (2-4)   **92**
Fiction
Björk, C. Linnea in Monet's garden (3-5)
   Fic

Monet and the impressionists for kids. Sabbeth, C.
   759.05

Money
     See also Paper money
Cribb, J. Money (4 and up)   **332.4**
Godfrey, N. S. Neale S. Godfrey's ultimate
kids' money book (5 and up)   **332.024**
Hall, M. Money (3-5)   **332.4**
Kummer, P. K. Currency (4 and up)   **332.4**
Leedy, L. Follow the money! (k-3)   **332.4**
Maestro, B. The story of money (3-5)   **332.4**
Fiction
Cottrell Boyce, F. Millions (5 and up)   **Fic**
Mollel, T. M. My rows and piles of coins   **E**

Money from a table. Kimmel, E. A.
In Kimmel, E. A. The adventures of Hershel
of Ostropol p19-27   **398.2**

Money-making projects for children
Kiefer, J. Jobs for kids (4 and up)   **650.1**
Fiction
Clements, A. Lunch money (4-6)   **Fic**

Money, money, money. Parker, N. W.   **769.5**

The **money** pig. Andersen, H. C.
In Andersen, H. C. The swan's stories p39-45
   S C

Monfried, Lucia
(comp) Diane Goode's book of scary stories &
songs. See Diane Goode's book of scary stories & songs   **398.2**

Mongolia
Pang, G.-C. Mongolia (5 and up)   **951.7**

Mongoose. Spinelli, J.
In Spinelli, J. The library card   **S C**

Mongooses
Fiction
Pinkney, J. Rikki-tikki-tavi   **E**

Monjo, F. N.
The drinking gourd   **E**

Monk, Thelonious, 1917-1982
About
Raschka, C. Mysterious Thelonious   **E**

Monkey accepts a challenge. Jiang, J.-L.
In Jiang, J.-l. The magical Monkey King; mischief in heaven p7-12   **398.2**

Monkey ancestors. Climo, S.
In Climo, S. Monkey business; stories from around the world   **398.2**

The **monkey** and the crocodile. Galdone, P.
   398.2

The **monkey** and the crocodile. Lee, J. M.
In Lee, J. M. I once was a monkey; stories Buddha told   **294.3**

Monkey as a Heavenly horse deity. Jiang, J.-L.
In Jiang, J.-l. The magical Monkey King; mischief in heaven p70-79   **398.2**

Monkey at the peach banquet. Jiang, J.-L.
In Jiang, J.-l. The magical Monkey King; mischief in heaven p92-97   **398.2**

Monkey becomes a student. Jiang, J.-L.
In Jiang, J.-l. The magical Monkey King; mischief in heaven p33-39   **398.2**

Monkey behind the waterfall. Jiang, J.-L.
In Jiang, J.-l. The magical Monkey King; mischief in heaven p13-18   **398.2**

Monkey business. Climo, S.   **398.2**

Monkey-dance and sparrow-dance. Sakade, F.
In Sakade, F. Japanese children's favorite stories   **398.2**

Monkey goes searching. Jiang, J.-L.
In Jiang, J.-l. The magical Monkey King; mischief in heaven p19-25   **398.2**

Monkey goes to a banquet. Jiang, J.-L.
In Jiang, J.-l. The magical Monkey King; mischief in heaven p86-90   **398.2**

Monkey goes to the sea. Jiang, J.-L.
In Jiang, J.-l. The magical Monkey King; mischief in heaven p54-61   **398.2**

Monkey in the Heavenly Peach Garden. Jiang, J.-L.
In Jiang, J.-l. The magical Monkey King; mischief in heaven p80-84   **398.2**

Monkey is captured. Jiang, J.-L.
In Jiang, J.-l. The magical Monkey King; mischief in heaven p111-16   **398.2**

The **monkey** keeper. Climo, S.
In Climo, S. Monkey business; stories from around the world   **398.2**

Monkey King. Young, E.   **E**

Monkey meets a demon. Jiang, J.-L.
In Jiang, J.-l. The magical Monkey King; mischief in heaven p47-53   **398.2**

Monkey meets a sage. Jiang, J.-L.
In Jiang, J.-l. The magical Monkey King; mischief in heaven p26-32   **398.2**

Monkey meets Magician Lang. Jiang, J.-L.
In Jiang, J.-l. The magical Monkey King; mischief in heaven p105-10   **398.2**

Monkey stew. Van Laan, N.
In Van Laan, N. With a whoop and a holler; a bushel of lore from way down south p11-12   **398.2**

The **monkey**, the rats, and the cheese. Climo, S.
In Climo, S. Monkey business; stories from around the world   **398.2**

Monkey transforms himself. Jiang, J.-L.
In Jiang, J.-l. The magical Monkey King; mischief in heaven p40-46   **398.2**

Monkey under attack. Jiang, J.-L.
In Jiang, J.-l. The magical Monkey King; mischief in heaven p98-104   **398.2**

Monkey visits Heaven. Jiang, J.-L.
In Jiang, J.-l. The magical Monkey King; mischief in heaven p62-69   **398.2**

The **Monkey** who asked for Misery
In The Magic orange tree, and other Haitian folktales p113-16   **398.2**

Monkeys

   See also Baboons
McDaniel, M. Monkeys (3-6)   **599.8**
Fiction
Buchanan, J. Goodbye, Charley (5 and up)
   Fic
Christelow, E. Five little monkeys jumping on the bed   **E**
Koller, J. F. One monkey too many   **E**
Kurtz, J. Water hole waiting   **E**
Rey, H. A. Curious George   **E**
Slobodkina, E. Caps for sale   **E**
Young, E. Monkey King   **E**
Folklore
Climo, S. Monkey business (3-6)   **398.2**
Galdone, P. The monkey and the crocodile (k-2)
   398.2
Jiang, J.-l. The magical Monkey King (3-5)
   398.2
Wagué Diakité, B. The hatseller and the monkeys (k-3)   **398.2**

Mono (Disease) *See* Mononucleosis

Mononucleosis
Hoffmann, G. Mononucleosis (4 and up)
   616.9

Monsoon. Krishnaswami, U.   **E**

Monsoons
Fiction
Krishnaswami, U. Monsoon   **E**

Monster bones. Bailey, J.   **567.9**

Monster Goose. Sierra, J.   **811**

The **monster** health book. Miller, E.   **613.7**

Monster machines. Bingham, C.   **621.8**

Monster museum. Singer, M.   **811**

The **monster** of Baylock. San Souci, R.
In San Souci, R. Even more short & shivery; thirty spine-tingling stories p70-75
   398.2

Monster trucks!. Todd, M.   **E**

Moon—_Continued_

Gibbons, G. The moon book (k-3)   **523.3**

McNulty, F. If you decide to go to the moon (k-3)   **629.45**

Miller, R. Earth and the moon (5 and up)   **525**

Simon, S. The moon (4 and up)   **523.3**

Tomecek, S. Moon (k-2)   **523.3**

Exploration

Cole, M. D. Moon base (4 and up)   **629.4**

Vogt, G. Apollo moonwalks (4 and up)   **629.45**

Fiction

Banks, K. And if the moon could talk   **E**

Chambers, R. Rooftop rocket party   **E**

Curtis, C. I took the moon for a walk   **E**

Gralley, J. The moon came down on Milk Street   **E**

Henkes, K. Kitten's first full moon   **E**

Murray, M. D. Little Wolf and the moon   **E**

Smith, L. When Moon fell down   **E**

Spinelli, E. Rise the moon   **E**

Tafuri, N. What the sun sees   **E**

Folklore

Dayrell, E. Why the Sun and the Moon live in the sky (k-3)   **398.2**

Ehlert, L. Moon rope. Un lazo a la luna (k-3)   **398.2**

Poetry

Pollock, P. When the moon is full (k-3)   **811**

The sun, the moon, and the stars (k-2)   **811.008**

Moon, Voyages to _See_ Space flight to the moon

The **moon**. Bredeson, C.   **523.3**

Moon base. Cole, M. D.   **629.4**

Moon bases _See_ Lunar bases

The **moon** book. Gibbons, G.   **523.3**

The **moon** came down on Milk Street. Gralley, J.   **E**

Moon glowing. Partridge, E.   **E**

Moon, have you met my mother? Kuskin, K.   **811**

Moon Indigo. See Shange, N. Ellington was not a street   **E**

Moon rope. Un lazo a la luna. Ehlert, L.   **398.2**

Moon runner. Marsden, C.   **Fic**

The **moon** seems to change. Branley, F. M.   **523.3**

Moonbeams, dumplings & dragon boats. Simonds, N.   **394.26**

Moonbear's dream. Asch, F.   **E**

Moonlight: the Halloween cat. Rylant, C.   **E**

Moonshine in the mustard pot. Aiken, J.

_In_ Aiken, J. Shadows and moonshine; stories   **S C**

Moony Luna. Argueta, J.   **E**

The **moorchild**. McGraw, E. J.   **Fic**

Moore, Ann

See/See also pages in the following book(s):

Thimmesh, C. Girls think of everything (5 and up)   **920**

Moore, Bobbie

(il) King, D. C. Colonial days   **973.2**

Moore, Cathy

The daring escape of Ellen Craft (1-3)   **92**

Moore, Clement Clarke

The night before Christmas (k-3)   **811**

Moore, Cyd

(il) Newman, L. A fire engine for Ruthie   **E**

(il) Schotter, R. Missing Rabbit   **E**

Moore, Ella Sheppard, 1851-1914

Fiction

Hopkinson, D. A band of angels   **E**

Moore, Gustav

(il) Ross, M. E. Earth cycles   **525**

Moore, Inga

(il) Grahame, K. The wind in the willows   **Fic**

(il) Horse tales. See Horse tales   **S C**

Moore, Lilian

I'm small and other verses (k-2)   **811**

Mural on Second Avenue, and other city poems (k-3)   **811**

(jt. auth) Charlip, R. Hooray for me!   **E**

Moore, Margie

(il) Hill, S. Ruby bakes a cake   **E**

(il) London, J. Do your ABC's Little Brown Bear   **E**

Moose

DuTemple, L. A. North American moose (3-6)   **599.65**

Estigarribia, D. Moose (3-6)   **599.65**

Fiction

Arnosky, J. Beaver pond, moose pond   **E**

Greene, S. Moose's big idea (1-3)   **Fic**

Haseley, D. The invisible moose   **E**

Van Laan, N. Moose tales   **E**

Wiseman, B. Morris and Boris at the circus   **E**

Moose and Hildy [series]

Greene, S. Moose's big idea   **Fic**

Moose tales. Van Laan, N.   **E**

Moose's big idea. Greene, S.   **Fic**

Mora, Pat

Doña Flor   **E**

A library for Juana: the world of Sor Juana Inés (2-4)   **92**

Tomás and the library lady   **E**

Uno, dos, tres: one, two, three   **E**

(ed) Love to mamá. See Love to mamá   **811.008**

Moral and philosophic stories _See_ Fables

Moral philosophy _See_ Ethics

Morales, Rodolfo, 1925-2001

See/See also pages in the following book(s):

Just like me p2-3   **920**

Morales, Yuyi

Just a minute (k-3)   **398.2**

(il) Krull, K. Harvesting hope: the story of Cesar Chavez   **92**

Moranville, Sharelle Byars

Over the river (5 and up)   **Fic**

Mordan, C. B.

(il) Avi. Silent movie   **E**

Morrison, Marion
Colombia (5 and up)   **986.1**
Costa Rica (5 and up)   **972.86**
Guyana (5 and up)   **988.1**

Morrison, Taylor
The coast mappers (5 and up)   **623.89**
Wildfire (4-6)   **634.9**

Morrison, Toni
Remember (3-5)   **379**

Morrison, Toni, 1931-
About
Haskins, J. Toni Morrison (4 and up)   **92**

Morris's disappearing bag. Wells, R.   **E**

Morrow, Barbara Olenyik
A good night for freedom   **E**

Morrow, Tara Jaye
Mommy loves her baby   **E**

Morse, Jenifer Corr
(jt. auth) Pascoe, E. Scholastic kid's almanac   **031.02**

Morse, Susan
(jt. auth) Swinburne, S. R. The woods scientist   **591.7**

Mortensen, Denise Dowling
Good night engines   **E**

Morticians *See* Undertakers and undertaking

Morton, Robert
(il) Greenaway, T. Wolves, wild dogs, and foxes   **599.77**

Mose. Osborne, M. P.
In Osborne, M. P. American tall tales p51-61   **398.2**

Mosel, Arlene
The funny little woman (k-2)   **398.2**
Tikki Tikki Tembo (k-2)   **398.2**

Moser, Barry
The three little pigs (k-3)   **398.2**
(il) George, K. O. Hummingbird nest   **E**
(il) Hamilton, V. In the beginning; creation stories from around the world   **201**
(il) Hamilton, V. A ring of tricksters   **398.2**
(il) Hamilton, V. Wee Winnie Witch's Skinny   **E**
(il) Hamilton, V. When birds could talk & bats could sing   **398.2**
(il) Harper, D. Sit, Truman!   **E**
(il) Harper, D. Telling time with Big Mama Cat   **E**
(il) I can make a difference. See I can make a difference   **808.8**
(il) Johnston, T. That summer   **E**
(il) Kipling, R. Just so stories   **S C**
(il) Lasky, K. A brilliant streak: the making of Mark Twain   **92**
(il) MacLachlan, P. Journey   **Fic**
(il) Palatini, M. Earthquack!   **E**
(il) Rylant, C. Appalachia   **974**
(il) Thayer, E. L. Casey at the bat   **811**
(il) Twain, M. The adventures of Tom Sawyer   **Fic**

Moser, Cara
(il) Harper, D. Sit, Truman!   **E**
(il) Harper, D. Telling time with Big Mama Cat   **E**

Moser, Diane
(jt. auth) Spangenburg, R. Edward Hopper   **92**
(jt. auth) Spangenburg, R. Georgia O'Keeffe   **92**

Moses (Biblical figure)
About
Chaikin, M. Angels sweep the desert floor (4 and up)   **296.1**
Marzollo, J. Miriam and her brother Moses (k-3)   **222**
Wildsmith, B. Exodus   **222**

Moses, Will
Johnny Appleseed (3-6)   **92**
(il) Will Moses Mother Goose. See Will Moses Mother Goose   **398.8**

Moses goes to school. Millman, I.   **E**

Moses supposes his toeses are roses and 7 other silly old rhymes. Patz, N.   **398.8**

Moslem countries *See* Islamic countries

Moslemism *See* Islam

Moslems *See* Muslims

Mosque. Macaulay, D.   **726**

Mosques
Khan, A. K. What you will see inside a mosque (3-6)   **297.3**
Design and construction
Macaulay, D. Mosque (4 and up)   **726**

Mosquito bite. Siy, A.   **595.7**

Mosquitoes
Siy, A. Mosquito bite (3-5)   **595.7**
Folklore
Aardema, V. Why mosquitoes buzz in people's ears (k-3)   **398.2**
Gershator, P. Zzzng! Zzzng! Zzzng! (k-3)   **398.2**

Moss, Carol (Carol Marie)
Science in ancient Mesopotamia (4 and up)   **509**

Moss, Lloyd
Zin! zin! zin! a violin   **E**

Moss, Marissa
Amelia's 6th-grade notebook (4-6)   **Fic**
Brave Harriet [biography of Harriet Quimby] (k-3)   **92**
Mighty Jackie: the strike out queen   **E**
(il) Schwartz, D. M. G is for googol   **510**

Moss, Miriam
Don't forget I love you   **E**

Moss, Onawumi Jean
(jt. auth) McKissack, P. C. Precious and the Boo Hag   **E**

Moss gown. Hooks, W. H.   **398.2**

Mosses
Pascoe, E. Plants without seeds (2-5)   **586**

Most, Bernard
ABC T-Rex   **E**
How big were the dinosaurs   **E**
Whatever happened to the dinosaurs?   **E**

The **most** amazing dinosaur. Stevenson, J.   **E**

The **most** beautiful roof in the world. Lasky, K.   **577.3**

The **most** important gift of all. Conway, D. E

The **most** perfect spot. Goode, D. E

The **most** precious thing. Jaffe, N.
In Jaffe, N. and Zeitlin, S. J. While standing on one foot; puzzle stories and wisdom tales from the Jewish tradition p26-32
296.1

The **most** useful slave. Hamilton, V.
In Hamilton, V. The people could fly; American black folktales p160-65 **398.2**

Motels *See* Hotels and motels

Moth, the fire dancer. Caduto, M. J.
In Caduto, M. J. and Bruchac, J. Keepers of the night; Native American stories and nocturnal activities for children p43-45
398.2

Mother and child *See* Mother-child relationship

Mother and daughter. Soto, G.
In Soto, G. Baseball in April, and other stories p60-68 **S C**

The **mother** and death. San Souci, R.
In San Souci, R. A terrifying taste of short & shivery; thirty creepy tales p141-45
398.2

Mother-child relationship
Fiction
Appelt, K. Oh my baby, little one E
Ashman, L. Mama's day E
Cabrera, J. Mommy, carry me please! E
Campbell, B. M. Sometimes my mommy gets angry E
Crumpacker, B. Alexander's pretending day
E
Dewdney, A. Llama, llama red pajama E
Fearnley, J. Watch out! E
Forward, T. What did you do today? E
Katz, K. Mommy hugs E
Kono, E. E. Hula lullaby E
McDonald, M. Baya, baya, lulla-by-a E
Medearis, A. S. Snug in Mama's arms E
Peacock, C. A. Mommy far, Mommy near E
Russo, M. Come back, Hannah! E
Scott, A. H. On Mother's lap E
Warnes, T. Mommy mine E
Wheeler, L. Te amo, Bebé, little one E
Wild, M. Kiss kiss! E
Wilson, K. Mama always comes home E
Woodson, J. Coming on home soon E

Mother-daughter relationship
Fiction
Bradby, M. Momma, where are you from?
E
Brisson, P. Mama loves me from away E
Brun-Cosme, N. No, I want daddy! E
Cassidy, C. Dizzy (5 and up) Fic
Gray, L. M. My mama had a dancing heart
E
Johnson, A. Tell me a story, Mama E
Johnston, T. The quilt story E
Joosse, B. M. Mama, do you love me? E
Madrigal, A. H. Erandi's braids E
Paratore, C. The wedding planner's daughter (4-6) Fic
Pomerantz, C. The chalk doll E
Reiser, L. Cherry pies and lullabies E

Reiser, L. Tortillas and lullabies. Tortillas y cancioncitas E
Rodgers, M. Freaky Friday (4 and up) Fic
St. Anthony, J. The summer Sherman loved me
Fic
Stanek, M. I speak English for my mom (2-4)
Fic
Stauffacher, S. Harry Sue (5 and up) Fic
Wilson, J. The illustrated Mum (5 and up)
Fic
Winthrop, E. Promises E

Mother Goose
The Arnold Lobel book of Mother Goose
398.8
Here comes Mother Goose **398.8**
James Marshall's Mother Goose **398.8**
My very first Mother Goose **398.8**
The neighborhood Mother Goose **398.8**
Polacco, P. Babushka's Mother Goose **398.8**
The Real Mother Goose **398.8**
Sylvia Long's Mother Goose **398.8**
Tomie dePaola's Mother Goose **398.8**
Will Moses Mother Goose **398.8**

Mother Goose time. Marino, J. **027.62**

Mother Jones *See* Jones, Mother, 1830-1930

Mother of the waters
In The Magic orange tree, and other Haitian folktales p151-56 **398.2**

Mother-son relationship
Fiction
González, R. Antonio's card E
Goode, D. The most perfect spot E
McKissack, P. C. Ma Dear's aprons E
Moss, M. Don't forget I love you E
Say, A. Tree of cranes E
Shannon, D. No, David! E
Zolotow, C. The seashore book E

Mother Teresa. Demi 92

Mother to tigers [biography of Helen Martini] Lyon, G. E. 92

Mothers
See also Stepmothers
Carrick, C. Mothers are like that E
Fiction
Aliki. Welcome, little baby E
Baskin, N. R. What every girl (except me) knows (4 and up) Fic
Browne, A. My mom E
Browne, A. Piggybook E
Charlip, R. Sleepytime rhyme E
Curtis, C. P. Bucking the Sarge (5 and up)
Fic
Dunrea, O. It's snowing! E
Hicks, B. Busted! (5 and up) Fic
Jonell, L. When Mommy was mad E
Lasky, K. Before I was your mother E
Louie, T. O. Raymond's perfect present E
Mallat, K. Mama love E
Martin, A. M. Here today (5 and up) Fic
Mead, A. Madame Squidley and Beanie (3-5)
Fic
Morrow, T. J. Mommy loves her baby E
Numeroff, L. J. What mommies do best E
Schick, E. Mama E
Ziefert, H. Home for Navidad E

Mothers—*Continued*

Poetry

Love to mamá (3-6)   **811.008**

Wong, J. S. The rainbow hand (4-6)   **811**

Mothers, Single parent *See* Single parent family

Mothers and daughters *See* Mother-daughter relationship

Mothers and sons *See* Mother-son relationship

Mothers are like that. Carrick, C.   **E**

Mother's clothes. Soto, G.

     In Soto, G. Petty crimes   **S C**

Mother's Day

Fiction

Rockwell, A. F. Mother's Day   **E**

A **mother's** journey. Markle, S.   **598**

Moths

     See also Caterpillars

Whalley, P. E. S. Butterfly & moth (4 and up)   **595.7**

Motion

Mason, A. Move it! (k-2)   **531**

Motion picture actors *See* Actors

Motion picture producers and directors

Brown, D. Mack made movies [biography of Mack Sennett] (2-4)   **92**

Motion pictures

     See also Musicals

Motivation (Psychology)

     See also Wishes

Mouly, Françoise

(ed) Big fat Little Lit. See Big fat Little Lit   **741.5**

Mount Everest (China and Nepal)

Brennan, K. Sir Edmund Hillary, modern day explorer (4 and up)   **92**

Coburn, B. Triumph on Everest: a photobiography of Sir Edmund Hillary (4 and up)   **92**

Kalz, J. Mount Everest (4-6)   **954.96**

Skreslet, L. To the top of Everest (4 and up)   **796.52**

Venables, S. To the top (5 and up)   **796.52**

Mount Saint Helens (Wash.)

Lauber, P. Volcano: the eruption and healing of Mount St. Helens (4 and up)   **551.2**

Mountain biking

Schoenherr, A. Mountain biking (4-6)   **796.6**

Mountain childers. San Souci, R.

     In San Souci, R. Double-dare to be scared: another thirteen chilling tales   **S C**

Mountain life

Appelt, K. Down Cut Shin Creek (4 and up)   **027**

Geisert, B. Mountain town   **E**

Fiction

Dowell, F. O. Dovey Coe (5 and up)   **Fic**

Gibbons, F. Mama and me and the Model-T   **E**

Gibbons, F. Mountain wedding   **E**

O'Connor, B. Me and Rupert Goody (4-6)   **Fic**

Ray, M. L. Basket moon   **E**

Mountain lion and the four sisters. Curry, J. L.

     In Curry, J. L. Hold up the sky: and other Native American tales from Texas and the Southern Plains p103-06   **398.2**

Mountain lions *See* Pumas

Mountain pose. Wilson, N. H.   **Fic**

Mountain town. Geisert, B.   **E**

Mountain wedding. Gibbons, F.   **E**

Mountaineering

Brennan, K. Sir Edmund Hillary, modern day explorer (4 and up)   **92**

Coburn, B. Triumph on Everest: a photobiography of Sir Edmund Hillary (4 and up)   **92**

Skreslet, L. To the top of Everest (4 and up)   **796.52**

Venables, S. To the top (5 and up)   **796.52**

Fiction

Barron, T. A. High as a hawk   **E**

Neale, J. Himalaya (5 and up)   **Fic**

Mountains

     See also Adirondack Mountains (N.Y.); Himalaya Mountains; Ozark Mountains; Rocky Mountains

Simon, S. Mountains (3-6)   **551.4**

Zoehfeld, K. W. How mountains are made (k-3)   **551.4**

Fiction

Lobel, A. Ming Lo moves the mountain   **E**

Mouse *See* Mice

Mouse and mouser. Jacobs, J.

     In Jacobs, J. English fairy tales p54-56   **398.2**

The **mouse** and the cat. Yolen, J.

     In Yolen, J. Meow; cat stories from around the world   **398.2**

The **mouse** and the motorcycle. Cleary, B.   **Fic**

Mouse count. Walsh, E. S.   **E**

A **mouse** in the house. Hassett, J.   **E**

Mouse mess. Riley, L. A.   **E**

Mouse party. Marshall, J.

     In Marshall, J. Rats on the range and other stories p43-50   **S C**

Mouse soup. Lobel, A.   **E**

Mouse tales. Lobel, A.   **E**

The **mouse** that snored. Waber, B.   **E**

The **mouse** tower. San Souci, R.

     In San Souci, R. More short & shivery; thirty terrifying tales p83-87   **398.2**

Mouse views. McMillan, B.   **E**

The **mouse** who got married. Marshall, J.

     In Marshall, J. Rats on the roof, and other stories p29-39   **S C**

The **mousetrap**. Olson, A. N.

     In Olson, A. N. and Schwartz, H. Ask the bones: scary stories from around the world p78-84   **398.2**

Mouth organs *See* Harmonicas

Move it!. Mason, A.   **531**

A **movie** in my pillow. Argueta, J.   **861**

Moving

Fiction

Auch, M. J. Wing nut (5 and up) **Fic**

Bateson, C. Stranded in Boringsville (5 and up) **Fic**

Bottner, B. Rosa's room **E**

Bowdish, L. Brooklyn, Bugsy, and me (3-5) **Fic**

Cassidy, C. Indigo Blue (5 and up) **Fic**

Daly, N. Where's Jamela? **E**

Danziger, P. Amber Brown is not a crayon (2-4) **Fic**

De Guzman, M. Beekman's big deal (5 and up) **Fic**

Fleming, C. Lowji discovers America (3-5) **Fic**

Hale, M. The truth about sparrows (5 and up) **Fic**

Harrington, J. N. Going north **E**

Hurwitz, J. Oh no, Noah! (2-4) **Fic**

Kelly, K. Lucy Rose, here's the thing about me (2-4) **Fic**

Lewis, M. Morgy makes his move (2-4) **Fic**

Ly, M. Home is east (5 and up) **Fic**

Nixon, J. L. Laugh till you cry (5 and up) **Fic**

Patron, S. Maybe yes, maybe no, maybe maybe (3-5) **Fic**

Polikoff, B. G. Why does the coqui sing? (5 and up) **Fic**

Sharmat, M. W. Gila monsters meet you at the airport **E**

Shreve, S. R. Blister (4 and up) **Fic**

Siebold, J. My nights at the Improv (4 and up) **Fic**

Snyder, Z. K. Spyhole secrets (4 and up) **Fic**

Williams, V. B. Scooter (3-5) **Fic**

Moving still. Jiménez, F.
In Jiménez, F. The circuit: stories from the life of a migrant child p113-34 **S C**

Movsessian, Shushann

Puberty girl (4 and up) **612.6**

Mowglie's song. Kipling, R.
In Kipling, R. The jungle book: the Mowgli stories **S C**

Mowglie's song gainst people. Kipling, R.
In Kipling, R. The jungle book: the Mowgli stories **S C**

Mowgli's brothers. Kipling, R.
In Kipling, R. The jungle book: Mowgli's story p10-50 **S C**
also in Kipling, R. The jungle book: the Mowgli stories **S C**

Mozambique

Fiction

Farmer, N. A girl named Disaster (6 and up) **Fic**

Mankell, H. Secrets in the fire (5 and up) **Fic**

Mozart, Johann Chrysostom Wolfgang Amadeus *See* Mozart, Wolfgang Amadeus, 1756-1791

Mozart, Wolfgang Amadeus, 1756-1791

About

Sís, P. Play, Mozart, play! (k-2) **92**
See/See also pages in the following book(s):
Krull, K. Lives of the musicians (4 and up) **920**

Mr. Bear's new baby. Gliori, D. **E**

Mr. Brown washes his underwear. Schwartz, A.
In Schwartz, A. There is a carrot in my ear, and other noodle tales p28-38 **398.2**

Mr. Chickee's funny money. Curtis, C. P. **Fic**

Mr. Fox. Jacobs, J.
In Jacobs, J. English fairy tales p145-51 **398.2**
In Womenfolk and fairy tales p30-35 **398.2**

Mr. George Baker. Hest, A. **E**

Mr. Gumpy's outing. Burningham, J. **E**

Mr. Lincoln's drummer. Wisler, G. C. **Fic**

Mr. Lincoln's way. Polacco, P. **E**

Mr. Lucky straw. Sakade, F.
In Sakade, F. Japanese children's favorite stories **398.2**

Mr. Maxwell's mouse. Asch, F. **E**

Mr. Miacca
In Diane Goode's book of scary stories & songs p48-51 **398.2**

Mr. Miacca. Jacobs, J.
In Jacobs, J. English fairy tales p164-66 **398.2**

Mr. Mysterious & Company. Fleischman, S. **Fic**

Mr. Popper's penguins. Atwater, R. T. **Fic**

Mr. Putter and Tabby pour the tea. Rylant, C. **E**

Mr. Rabbit and the lovely present. Zolotow, C. **E**

Mr. Revere and I. Lawson, R. **Fic**

Mr. Semolina-Semolinus. Manna, A. L. **398.2**

Mr. Tucket. Paulsen, G. **Fic**

Mr. Vinegar. Jacobs, J.
In Jacobs, J. English fairy tales p37-40 **398.2**

Mr. Wolf's pancakes. Fearnley, J. **E**

Mr. Yeh's New Year. Fang, L.
In Fang, L. The Ch'i-lin purse; a collection of ancient Chinese stories p71-84 **398.2**

Mrs. Biddlebox. Smith, L. **E**

Mrs. Chicken and the hungry crocodile. Paye, W.-L. **398.2**

Mrs. Frisby and the rats of NIMH. O'Brien, R. C. **Fic**

Mrs. Katz and Tush. Polacco, P. **E**

Mrs. Mack. Polacco, P. **E**

Mrs. McCool and the giant Cuhullin. Souhami, J. **398.2**

Mrs. Moonlight (Senora de Luna). San Souci, R.
In San Souci, R. Dare to be scared; thirteen stories to chill and thrill **S C**

Mrs. Piggle-Wiggle. MacDonald, B. **Fic**

Mrs. Watson wants your teeth. McGhee, A.   **E**

Ms. Frizzle's adventures: medieval castle. Cole, J.
728.8

Ms. Turtle the babysitter. Gorbachev, V.   **E**

Much ado about Grubstake. Ferris, J.   **Fic**

Much ado about nothing. Packer, T.
In Packer, T. Tales from Shakespeare p49-65
822.3

Mucky Duck. Grindley, S.   **E**

Mud city. Guiberson, B. Z.   **598**

Mud matters. Dewey, J.   **553.6**

The **mud** pony. Cohen, C. L.   **398.2**

Mud pony [excerpt]. Cohen, C. L.
In Horse tales   **S C**

Mudball. Tavares, M.   **E**

Mudd-Ruth, Maria
Hawks & falcons (3-6)   **598**
Owls (3-6)   **598**

Mufaro's beautiful daughters. Steptoe, J.   **398.2**

The **mufferaw** catfish. Bedore, B.
In Bauer, C. F. Celebrations; read-aloud holiday and theme book programs p85-86
808.8

Muffler man. Campos, T.   **E**

Muggie Maggie. Cleary, B.   **Fic**

Muḥammad, d. 632
About
Demi. Muhammad (4 and up)   **297**

Muhammad ibn 'Abd Allāh ibn Baṭūṭah *See* Ibn Battuta, 1304-1377

Muhammadanism *See* Islam

Muhammedans *See* Muslims

Muir, John, 1838-1914
About
Lasky, K. John Muir (3-5)   **92**
Locker, T. John Muir, America's naturalist (2-4)
92
Fiction
McCully, E. A. Squirrel and John Muir   **E**

The **mule** drivers who lost their feet. Philip, N.
In Philip, N. Horse hooves and chicken feet: Mexican folktales p44-45   **398.2**

Muller, Eric Paul
While you're waiting for the food to come (3-6)
507.8

Mullins, Patricia
(il) Fox, M. Hattie and the fox   **E**

Mulock, Julian
(il) Froman, N. What's that bug?   **595.7**

The **mulombe**. San Souci, R.
In San Souci, R. A terrifying taste of short & shivery; thirty creepy tales p95-100
398.2

Multiculturalism
Bibliography
Kaleidoscope   **011.6**

Multimedia materials *See* Audiovisual materials

Multiple birth
Jackson, D. M. Twin tales (4 and up)   **618.2**

Multiple sclerosis
Burnfield, A. Multiple sclerosis (5 and up)
616.8
Gold, S. D. Multiple sclerosis (4 and up)
616.8

Multiplication
Leedy, L. 2 x 2 = boo! (k-3)   **513**
Long, L. Marvelous multiplication (3-6)   **513**
Murphy, S. J. Double the ducks (k-1)   **513**
Tang, G. The best of times (2-4)   **513**
Fiction
Dodds, D. A. Minnie's Diner   **E**
Stamper, J. B. Breakfast at Danny's Diner   **E**

Multiracial people *See* Racially mixed people

Mulvihill, Margaret
The treasury of saints and martyrs (5 and up)
920

Mummies
Deem, J. M. Bodies from the bog (4 and up)
930.1
Getz, D. Frozen man (5 and up)   **930.1**
Kallen, S. A. Mummies (4 and up)   **393**
Markle, S. Outside and inside mummies (4 and up)   **393**
Pemberton, D. Egyptian mummies (4 and up)
393
Reinhard, J. Discovering the Inca Ice Maiden (5 and up)   **930.1**
Tanaka, S. Mummies (4 and up)   **393**
Tanaka, S. Secrets of the mummies (4 and up)
393
Taylor, J. H. Mummy (5 and up)   **932**
Wilcox, C. Mummies, bones & body parts (5 and up)   **393**

Mummies, bones & body parts. Wilcox, C.
393

Mummy. Taylor, J. H.   **932**

Mummy riddles. Hall, K.   **793.73**

The **mummy's** dream. Stine, R. L.
In Stine, R. L. The haunting hour p66-79
S C

Munari, Bruno
Bruno Munari's zoo   **E**

Muncha! Muncha! Muncha!. Fleming, C.   **E**

Munchkin. Byars, B. C.
In Byars, B. C. and others. My dog, my hero p16-19   **S C**

Mung-mung!. Park, L. S.   **413**

Municipal planning *See* City planning

Muñoz, Claudio
(il) Branford, H. Little Pig Figwort can't get to sleep   **E**
(il) Newsome, J. Dream dancer   **E**
(il) Newsome, J. Night walk   **E**

Muñoz, William
(il) Patent, D. H. Animals on the trail with Lewis and Clark   **978**
(il) Patent, D. H. The bald eagle returns
598
(il) Patent, D. H. Biodiversity   **333.95**
(il) Patent, D. H. Fire: friend or foe   **577.2**
(il) Patent, D. H. The Lewis and Clark trail
978
(il) Patent, D. H. Life in a grassland   **577.4**

Murphy, Stuart J.—*Continued*
Same old horse   E
Seaweed soup (k-3)   **511.3**
Sluggers' car wash (1-3)   **513**
The sundae scoop (1-3)   **511**

Murray, Marjorie Dennis
Little Wolf and the moon   E

Murray, Martine
The slightly true story of Cedar B. Hartley (5 and up)   **Fic**

Musa, d. 1337
See/See also pages in the following book(s):
Meltzer, M. Ten kings (5 and up)   **920**
Fiction
Burns, K. Mansa Musa (4 and up)   **Fic**

Muscles
Simon, S. Muscles (4 and up)   **612.7**

Muscular dystrophy
Burnett, G. L. Muscular dystrophy (4 and up)   **616.7**

Musculoskeletal system
See also Bones; Muscles
Ballard, C. The skeleton and muscular system (5 and up)   **612.7**
Macnair, P. A. Movers & shapers (3-5)   **612.7**
Parker, S. The skeleton and muscles (5 and up)   **612.7**

Muse, Daphne
(ed) The entrance place of wonders. See The entrance place of wonders   **811.008**

Museum ABC   E

Museum of Modern Art (New York, N.Y.)
Fiction
Scieszka, J. Seen Art?   **Fic**

Museum shapes   E

Museum trip. Lehman, B.   E

Museums
See also Art museums appropriate subjects with the subdivision *Museums;* and names of galleries and museums
Norris, J. Children's museums   **069**
Fiction
Cameron, E. The court of the stone children (5 and up)   **Fic**
Howe, J. Pinky and Rex   E
Stevenson, J. The most amazing dinosaur   E

Musgrove, Margaret
Ashanti to Zulu: African traditions (3-6)   **960**

Mushrooms
See also Fungi
Royston, A. Life cycle of a mushroom (k-3)   **579.6**

Music
Aliki. Ah, music! (k-3)   **780**
Ardley, N. A young person's guide to music (5 and up)   **780**
Krull, K. M is for music   E
Nathan, A. Meet the musicians (5 and up)   **780**
Parker, S. The science of sound (4 and up)   **534**

Sabbeth, A. Rubber-band banjos and a java jive bass (4 and up)   **781**
Analysis, appreciation
See Music appreciation
Dictionaries
Barber, N. Music: an A-Z guide (4 and up)   **780.3**
Fiction
Johnson, A. Violet's music   E
McPhail, D. M. Mole music   E
Schuch, S. A symphony of whales   E
Williams, S. Imani's music   E
Poetry
Carnival of the animals   **811.008**
Smith, C. R. Perfect harmony (4 and up)   **811**

Music, African American *See* African American music

Music, Gospel *See* Gospel music

Music. Ardley, N.   **784.19**

Music appreciation
Ganeri, A. The young person's guide to the orchestra (4 and up)   **784.2**

Music for Alice. Say, A.   E

Music from our Lord's holy heaven. Pinkney, G. J.   **264**

Musical instruments
Ardley, N. Music (4 and up)   **784.19**
Ganeri, A. The young person's guide to the orchestra (4 and up)   **784.2**
Hayes, A. Meet the orchestra (k-3)   **784.2**
Koscielniak, B. The story of the incredible orchestra (2-4)   **784.2**
Moss, L. Zin! zin! zin! a violin   E
Sabbeth, A. Rubber-band banjos and a java jive bass (4 and up)   **781**
Wiseman, A. S. Making music (3-6)   **784.19**
Fiction
Cox, J. My family plays music   E

Musicals
Boynton, S. Philadelphia chickens (k-3)   **782.42**

The **musician.** Terada, A. M.
In Terada, A. M. Under the starfruit tree; folktales from Vietnam p132-34   **398.2**

Musicians
See also Composers
George-Warren, H. Honky-tonk heroes & hillbilly angels (3-6)   **920**
George-Warren, H. Shake, rattle, & roll (4 and up)   **920**
Nathan, A. Meet the musicians (5 and up)   **780**
Fiction
Alexander, L. The marvelous misadventures of Sebastian (4 and up)   **Fic**
Brutschy, J. Just one more story   E
Conover, C. Over the hills & far away   E
Cox, J. My family plays music   E
Cutler, J. The cello of Mr. O   E
Edwards, P. D. The leprechaun's gold   E
Fenner, C. Yolonda's genius (4-6)   **Fic**
Francis, P. David gets his drum   E

Musicians—Fiction—*Continued*

Frank, L. K. Lucky stars (5 and up)   **Fic**

French, S. Where in the world (5 and up)   **Fic**

Isadora, R. Ben's trumpet   **E**

MacLachlan, P. The facts and fictions of Minna Pratt (4 and up)   **Fic**

Martin, B. The maestro plays   **E**

Folklore

Shepard, A. The sea king's daughter (3-6)   **398.2**

Musicians, African American *See* African American musicians

The **musicians** of Bremen. Puttapipat, N.   **398.2**

Musicians of the sun. McDermott, G.   **398.2**

Muskrats

Fiction

Chaconas, D. Cork & Fuzz   **E**

Musleah, Rahel

Why on this night?   **296.4**

Muslim countries *See* Islamic countries

Muslim festivals throughout the year. Ganeri, A.   **297.3**

Muslimism *See* Islam

Muslims

Fiction

Bunting, E. One green apple   **E**

United States

Wolf, B. Coming to America (3-5)   **305.8**

Mustang canyon. London, J.   **E**

Muth, Jon J.

Stone soup (k-3)   **398.2**

The three questions   **E**

Zen shorts   **E**

(il) Charlip, R. Why I will never ever ever ever have enough time to read this book   **E**

(il) A family of poems. See A family of poems   **808.81**

(il) Hesse, K. Come on, rain!   **E**

(il) Hest, A. Mr. George Baker   **E**

(il) Kimmel, E. A. Gershon's monster   **398.2**

Mutsmag

In Grandfather tales; American-English folk tales p40-51   **398.2**

Mutt dog!. King, S. M.   **E**

Mwangi, Meja

The Mzungu boy (5 and up)   **Fic**

My 13th season. Roberts, K.   **Fic**

My America (4 and up)   **811.008**

My America [series]

Osborne, M. P. My brother's keeper   **Fic**

My baseball book. Gibbons, G.   **796.357**

My basketball book. Gibbons, G.   **796.323**

My beautiful child. Desimini, L.   **E**

My best friend. Holm, J. L.

In Friends; stories about new friends, old friends, and unexpectedly true friends   **S C**

My big brother. Cohen, M.   **E**

My big brother. Fisher, V.   **E**

My big feet out for a walk. Thacker, N.

In Girls got game; sports stories and poems   **810.8**

My big toe

In Diane Goode's book of scary stories & songs p12-13   **398.2**

My brother, Ant. Byars, B. C.   **E**

My brother Martin [biography of Martin Luther King] Farris, C.   **92**

My brother, my sister, and I. Watkins, Y. K.   **Fic**

My brother Sam is dead. Collier, J. L.   **Fic**

My brother's keeper. Osborne, M. P.   **Fic**

My car. Barton, B.   **E**

My childhood under fire. Halilbegovich, N.   **949.7**

My Chinatown. Mak, K.   **E**

My dad. Browne, A.   **E**

My dad. Daly, N.   **E**

My daddy is a giant. Norac, C.   **E**

My Daniel. Conrad, P.   **Fic**

My day, your day. Ballard, R.   **E**

My diary from here to there. Pérez, A. I.   **Fic**

My dog, my hero. Byars, B. C.   **S C**

My dog Toby. Zimmerman, A. G.   **E**

My family plays music. Cox, J.   **E**

My father's dragon. Gannett, R. S.   **Fic**

My father's hands. Ryder, J.   **E**

My feet. Aliki   **612**

My first book of sign. Baker, P. J.   **419**

My first Chinese New Year. Katz, K.   **E**

My first Hebrew word book. Groner, J. S.   **492.4**

My first horse and pony book. Draper, J.   **636.1**

My first I can read book [series]

Bonsall, C. N. The day I had to play with my sister   **E**

Bonsall, C. N. Mine's the best   **E**

Capucilli, A. Biscuit's new trick   **E**

Schaefer, L. M. Loose tooth   **E**

My first Kwanzaa book. Chocolate, D.   **394.26**

My first Oxford book of animal poems (1-4)   **808.81**

My first word book. Wilkes, A.   **E**

My five senses. Aliki   **612.8**

My football book. Gibbons, G.   **796.332**

My friend Rabbit. Rohmann, E.   **E**

My friend, the enemy. Cheaney, J. B.   **Fic**

My goose Betsy. Braun, T.   **E**

My grandma is coming to town. Hines, A. G.   **E**

My grandmother's stories. Geras, A.   **398.2**

My granny went to market. Blackstone, S.   **E**

My great-aunt Arizona. Houston, G.   **E**

My hands. Aliki   **612**

My health [series]

Silverstein, A. Allergies   **616.97**

My health—*Continued*

Silverstein, A. Burns and blisters **617.1**
Silverstein, A. Can you see the chalkboard?
617.7
Silverstein, A. Common colds **616.2**
Silverstein, A. Cuts, scrapes, scabs, and scars
617.1
Silverstein, A. Diabetes **616.4**
Silverstein, A. Is that a rash? **616.5**
Silverstein, A. Physical fitness **613.7**
Silverstein, A. Scoliosis **616.7**
Silverstein, A. Sleep **612.8**
Silverstein, A. Tooth decay and cavities
617.6
Silverstein, A. Vaccinations **615**

My hippie grandmother. Lindbergh, R. **E**

My imaginary friend. Stine, R. L.
In Stine, R. L. The haunting hour p110-21
S C

My kingdom for a horse (2-4) **811.008**

My life as a fifth-grade comedian. Levy, E.
Fic

My life in dog years. Paulsen, G. **92**

My life of crime. Jennings, R. W. **Fic**

My life with the chimpanzees. Goodall, J. **92**

My light. Bang, M. **621.47**

My little brother. McPhail, D. M. **E**

My lucky day. Kasza, K. **E**

My mama had a dancing heart. Gray, L. M. **E**

My man Blue. Grimes, N. **811**

My Mei Mei. Young, E. **E**

My mom. Browne, A. **E**

My mom's having a baby!. Butler, D. H.
612.6

My mother got married (and other disasters). Park,
B. **Fic**

My name is America [series]
Bartoletti, S. C. The journal of Finn Reardon
Fic
Durbin, W. The journal of Sean Sullivan
Fic
Myers, W. D. The journal of Joshua Loper
Fic
Myers, W. D. The journal of Scott Pendleton
Collins **Fic**
Rinaldi, A. The journal of Jasper Jonathan
Pierce, a pilgrim boy **Fic**
Yep, L. The journal of Wong Ming-Chung
Fic

My name is brain Brian. Betancourt, J. **Fic**

My name is Georgia [biography of Georgia
O'Keeffe] Winter, J. **92**

My name is Yoon. Recorvits, H. **E**

My nights at the Improv. Siebold, J. **Fic**

My own self. Jacobs, J.
In Jacobs, J. English fairy tales p238-41
398.2

My parents think I'm sleeping: poems. Prelutsky,
J. **811**

My penguin Osbert. Kimmel, E. C. **E**

My pet hamster. Rockwell, A. F. **636.9**

My pig Amarillo. Ichikawa, S. **E**

My pony Jack. Meister, C. **E**

My Pop Pop and me. Smalls, I. **E**

My prairie Christmas. Harvey, B. **Fic**

My race car. Rex, M. **629.228**

My rotten redheaded older brother. Polacco, P.
E

My rows and piles of coins. Mollel, T. M. **E**

My season with penguins. Webb, S. **598**

My side of the mountain trilogy. George, J. C.
Fic

My soccer book. Gibbons, G. **796.334**

My special day at Third Street School. Bunting, E.
E

My swan sister. Vaz, K.
In Swan sister; fairy tales retold **S C**

My teacher for President. Winters, K. **E**

My thirteenth season. See Roberts, K. My 13th
season **Fic**

My very first Mother Goose **398.8**

My very own room. Pérez, A. I. **E**

My visit to the aquarium. Aliki **639.34**

My visit to the zoo. Aliki **590.73**

Myanmar
Yin, S. M. Myanmar (5 and up) **959.1**

Mycology *See* Fungi

Myers, Christopher
Black cat **E**
Fly! **E**
Lies and other tall tales **398.2**
Wings **E**
(il) Myers, W. D. Blues journey **811**
(il) Myers, W. D. Harlem **811**

Myers, Laurie
Lewis and Clark and me (3-6) **Fic**
(jt. auth) Byars, B. C. My dog, my hero
S C
(jt. auth) Byars, B. C. The SOS file **Fic**

Myers, Tim
Basho and the river stones **E**
Dark sparkle tea (2-4) **811**
Good babies **E**

Myers, Walter Dean
Amistad: a long road to freedom (5 and up)
326
Blues journey **811**
The blues of Flats Brown **E**
Brown angels **811**
Harlem **811**
The Harlem Hellfighters (5 and up) **940.4**
I've seen the promised land [biography of Mar-
tin Luther King] (k-3) **92**
The journal of Joshua Loper (5 and up) **Fic**
The journal of Scott Pendleton Collins (5 and
up) **Fic**
Malcolm X (3-6) **92**
Now is your time! (6 and up) **305.8**
Patrol **E**
Three swords for Granada (3-6) **Fic**
(jt. auth) Lawrence, J. The great migration
759.13

Myotte, Elsa
(il) Lottridge, C. B. Berta: a remarkable dog
Fic

Myracle, Lauren
Eleven (4 and up) **Fic**

Myriapods: centipedes, millipedes, and their relatives. See Blaxland, B. Centipedes, millipedes, and their relatives **595.6**

Myrtle. Pearson, T. C. **E**

The **mysteries** of Harris Burdick. Van Allsburg, C. **E**

The **mysterious** disappearance of Leon (I mean Noel). Raskin, E. **Fic**

The **mysterious** tadpole. Kellogg, S. **E**

Mysterious Thelonious. Raschka, C. **E**

Mysterious you [series]
Romanek, T. Zzz...: the most interesting book you'll ever read about sleep **612.8**

Mystery and detective stories See Mystery fiction

Mystery at the Club Sandwich. Cushman, D. **E**

Mystery fiction
Adler, D. A. Cam Jansen and the mystery of the stolen diamonds (2-4) **Fic**
Adler, D. A. Young Cam Jansen and the dinosaur game **E**
Allison, J. Gilda Joyce, psychic investigator (5 and up) **Fic**
Baccalario, P. The door to time (4-6) **Fic**
Balliett, B. Chasing Vermeer (5 and up) **Fic**
Bellairs, J. The curse of the blue figurine (5 and up) **Fic**
Bonsall, C. N. The case of the hungry stranger **E**
Broach, E. Shakespeare's secret (5 and up) **Fic**
Brockmeier, K. Grooves (4 and up) **Fic**
Brooks, W. R. Freddy the detective (3-5) **Fic**
Byars, B. C. The dark stairs [.] (4 and up) **Fic**
Cameron, E. The court of the stone children (5 and up) **Fic**
Colfer, E. Half-Moon investigations (4 and up) **Fic**
Conford, E. A case for Jenny Archer (2-4) **Fic**
Curtis, C. P. Mr. Chickee's funny money (3-6) **Fic**
Cushman, D. Inspector Hopper **E**
Cushman, D. Mystery at the Club Sandwich **E**
De Campi, A. Kat & Mouse: Teacher torture (4-6) **741.5**
DeFelice, C. C. The missing manatee (5 and up) **Fic**
Draanen, W. v. Sammy Keyes and the hotel thief (4 and up) **Fic**
Estes, E. The Alley (4-6) **Fic**
Freeman, M. Who stole Halloween? (4-6) **Fic**
Giff, P. R. Kidnap at the Catfish Cafe (3-5) **Fic**
Grossman, D. Duel (5 and up) **Fic**

Gutman, D. The million dollar strike (4-6) **Fic**
Hamilton, V. The house of Dies Drear (5 and up) **Fic**
Hoeye, M. Time stops for no mouse (5 and up) **Fic**
Horowitz, A. Public enemy number two (5 and up) **Fic**
Howe, D. Bunnicula (4-6) **Fic**
Howe, J. Dew drop dead (4-6) **Fic**
Ibbotson, E. The star of Kazan (5 and up) **Fic**
Konigsburg, E. L. Up from Jericho Tel (5 and up) **Fic**
Larson, J. C. Bringing mysteries alive for children and young adults **028.5**
Levin, B. Shadow-catcher (5 and up) **Fic**
Miller, K. Kiki Strike (5 and up) **Fic**
Napoli, D. J. Sly the Sleuth and the pet mysteries (2-4) **Fic**
Newman, R. The case of the Baker Street Irregular (5 and up) **Fic**
Raskin, E. The mysterious disappearance of Leon (I mean Noel) (4 and up) **Fic**
Raskin, E. The Westing game (5 and up) **Fic**
Richards, J. Double life (5 and up) **Fic**
Roberts, W. D. Scared stiff (5 and up) **Fic**
Roberts, W. D. The view from the cherry tree (5 and up) **Fic**
Rylant, C. The case of the missing monkey **E**
Sharmat, M. W. Nate the Great **E**
Sobol, D. J. Encyclopedia Brown, boy detective (3-5) **Fic**
Springer, N. The case of the missing marquess (5 and up) **Fic**
Strickland, B. The hand of the necromancer (5 and up) **Fic**
Wallace, B. B. Cousins in the castle (4-6) **Fic**
Wallace, B. B. The twin in the tavern (4-6) **Fic**
Walsh, E. S. Dot & Jabber and the big bug mystery **E**
Wright, B. R. The dollhouse murders (4 and up) **Fic**
Wright, B. R. The ghosts of Mercy Manor (4 and up) **Fic**
Wright, B. R. Nothing but trouble (4 and up) **Fic**
Wright, B. R. Princess for a week (2-4) **Fic**

The **mystery** of Eatum Hall. Kelly, J. **E**
The **mystery** of gravity. Parker, B. R. **531**
The **mystery** of the hieroglyphs. Donoughue, C. **493**
The **mystery** of the mammoth bones. Giblin, J. **569**
The **mystery** of the missing red mitten. See Kellogg, S. The missing mitten mystery **E**
Mystic horse. Goble, P. **398.2**

Mythical animals
See also Animals—Folklore; Dragons; Mermaids and mermen

National parks and reserves
  See also National monuments

National Railway Museum (Great Britain)
  Big book of trains. See Big book of trains
          625.1

National Science Teachers Association
  Outstanding science trade books for students K-12. See Outstanding science trade books for students K-12   **016.5**

National songs
United States
  Key, F. S. The Star-Spangled Banner   **782.42**

National songs, American *See* National songs—United States

National Velvet. Bagnold, E.   **Fic**

Nations of the world. Brimson, S.   **909**

Native American art
  Baylor, B. When clay sings (1-4)   **970.004**
  January, B. Native Americans (4 and up)
          709.7
  Temko, F. Traditional crafts from native North America (4 and up)   **745.5**

Native American dance
  Left Hand Bull, J. Lakota hoop dancer (3-6)
          970.004
Fiction
  Smith, C. L. Jingle dancer   **E**

Native American literature
  Weave little stars into my sleep (2-4)
          782.42

Native American women
  Tallchief, M. Tallchief (3-5)   **92**

Native Americans
  See also Taino Indians; Zapotec Indians names of Native American peoples and linguistic families
  A Braid of lives (4 and up)   **970.004**
  Dennis, Y. W. Children of native America today (3-6)   **970.004**
  Goble, P. All our relatives (5 and up)
          970.004
  January, B. Native Americans (4 and up)
          709.7
  Molin, P. F. American Indian stereotypes in the world of children   **970.004**
  Murdoch, D. H. North American Indian (4 and up)   **970.004**
  Rising voices (5 and up)   **810.8**
  Steins, R. Exploration and settlement (5 and up)
          970.01
  Swamp, J. Giving thanks (k-3)   **299.7**
  Weber, E. N. R. Rattlesnake Mesa (4 and up)
          92
  Woods, G. Science of the early Americas (4 and up)   **509**
  See/See also pages in the following book(s):
  Freedman, R. Children of the wild West (4 and up)   **978**
  Peoples of the Americas (5 and up)   **970**
Antiquities
  Arnold, C. Stories in stone (4 and up)
          709.01
  Quigley, M. Mesa Verde (4-6)   **978.8**

  Sattler, H. R. The earliest Americans (5 and up)
          970.01
  Wood, M. Ancient America (5 and up)
          970.01
Biography
  Freedman, R. Indian chiefs (6 and up)   **920**
Dictionaries
  Patterson, L. Indian terms of the Americas
          970.004
Drama
  Bruchac, J. Pushing up the sky: seven Native American plays for children (3-5)   **812**
Dwellings
  Goble, P. Storm Maker's tipi (2-5)   **398.2**
Fiction
  Baker, O. Where the buffaloes begin (2-4)
          Fic
  Bruchac, J. The arrow over the door (4-6)
          Fic
  Campbell, N. I. Shi-shi-etko   **E**
  Dalgliesh, A. The courage of Sarah Noble (2-4)
          Fic
  Dorris, M. Sees Behind Trees (4 and up)
          Fic
  Goble, P. Beyond the ridge (2-4)   **Fic**
  Hobbs, W. Kokopelli's flute (5 and up)   **Fic**
  Karr, K. Worlds apart (4 and up)   **Fic**
  Martin, B. Knots on a counting rope   **E**
  O'Dell, S. Island of the Blue Dolphins (5 and up)   **Fic**
  O'Dell, S. Streams to the river, river to the sea (5 and up)   **Fic**
  Smith, C. L. Indian shoes (3-5)   **Fic**
  Speare, E. G. The sign of the beaver (5 and up)
          Fic
Folklore
  Bierhorst, J. The people with five fingers (k-3)
          398.2
  Bruchac, J. Between earth & sky (3-5)
          398.2
  Bruchac, J. How Chipmunk got his stripes (k-3)
          398.2
  Bruchac, J. When the Chenoo howls (4-6)
          398.2
  Caduto, M. J. Keepers of the night   **398.2**
  Curry, J. L. Hold up the sky: and other Native American tales from Texas and the Southern Plains (4 and up)   **398.2**
  Curry, J. L. The wonderful sky boat and other Native American tales of the Southeast (4 and up)   **398.2**
  De Paola, T. The legend of the Indian paintbrush (k-3)   **398.2**
  Delacre, L. Golden tales (5 and up)   **398.2**
  Goble, P. Buffalo woman (2-4)   **398.2**
  Goble, P. Crow chief (2-4)   **398.2**
  Goble, P. The girl who loved wild horses (k-3)
          398.2
  Goble, P. The legend of the White Buffalo Woman (3-5)   **398.2**
  Goble, P. Remaking the earth (2-4)   **398.2**
  Longfellow, H. W. Hiawatha   **811**
  McDermott, G. Coyote: a trickster tale from the American Southwest (k-3)   **398.2**
  McDermott, G. Jabuti the tortoise (k-3)
          398.2
  McDermott, G. Raven (k-3)   **398.2**

Nature study—_Continued_
Rhatigan, J. The kids' guide to nature adventures (3-6) **796.5**
See/See also pages in the following book(s):
Warshaw, H. Get out! (3-6) **790.1**

Nature upclose [series]
Himmelman, J. A pill bug's life **595.3**

Naturebooks [series]
Merrick, P. Cockroaches **595.7**

Nature's art box. Martin, L. C. **745.5**

Nature's green umbrella. Gibbons, G. **577.3**

Nature's predators [series]
Kallen, S. A. Spiders **595.4**

The **naughty** boy. Andersen, H. C.
_In_ Andersen, H. C. Hans Christian Andersen's Fairy Tales **S C**

Navaho Indians _See_ Navajo Indians

Navajo Indians
Roessel, M. Songs from the loom (3-6) **970.004**
Sneve, V. D. H. The Navajos (3-5) **970.004**
See/See also pages in the following book(s):
Ehrlich, A. Wounded Knee: an Indian history of the American West (6 and up) **970.004**
Fiction
Blood, C. L. The goat in the rug **E**
Miles, M. Annie and the Old One (1-4) **Fic**
O'Dell, S. Sing down the moon (5 and up) **Fic**

Naval history
See also Military history

Navigation
Lasky, K. The man who made time travel (3-5) **526**
Fiction
Frederick, H. V. The voyage of Patience Goodspeed (5 and up) **Fic**

Naylor, Phyllis Reynolds
The agony of Alice (5 and up) **Fic**
The fear place (5 and up) **Fic**
The grand escape (4-6) **Fic**
Peril in the Bessledorf Parachute Factory (4-6) **Fic**
Roxie and the Hooligans (3-5) **Fic**
Shiloh (4-6) **Fic**
Starting with Alice (3-6) **Fic**

NCTE bibliography series
Kaleidoscope **011.6**

Neal-Schuman authoritative guide to kids' search engines, subject directories, and portals. Haycock, K. **025.04**

Neal-Schuman guide to celebrations & holidays around the world. Matthew, K. I. **394.26**

Neale, J. M. (John Mason)
Good King Wenceslas (k-3) **782.28**

Neale, Jonathan
Himalaya (5 and up) **Fic**

Neale S. Godfrey's ultimate kids' money book. Godfrey, N. S. **332.024**

Near East _See_ Middle East

The **neat** line. Edwards, P. D. **E**

Neatness _See_ Cleanliness

Nebraska
Flocker, M. Nebraska
_In_ World Almanac Library of the States series **973**
McNair, S. Nebraska
_In_ America the beautiful, second series **973**
Sanders, D. Nebraska
_In_ It's my state! [series] **973**
Fiction
Bunting, E. Dandelions **E**
Conrad, P. My Daniel (5 and up) **Fic**
Conrad, P. Prairie songs (5 and up) **Fic**
LaFaye, A. Worth (5 and up) **Fic**
Ruckman, I. Night of the twisters (4 and up) **Fic**

Nebulae, Extragalactic _See_ Galaxies

Needham, Bobbe
(jt. auth) Diehn, G. Nature smart **745.5**

Needlework
See also Tapestry
The jumbo book of needlecrafts (4-6) **746.4**

Neel, Alexandra David- _See_ David-Neel, Alexandra, 1868-1969

Neely, Keith
(il) Krasner, S. Play ball like the hall of famers **796.357**

Negrin, Fabian
(il) Waters, F. Oscar Wilde's The selfish giant **Fic**

A **Negro** league scrapbook. Weatherford, C. B. **796.357**

Negro leagues
Weatherford, C. B. A Negro league scrapbook (4 and up) **796.357**

Neidigh, Sherry
(il) Evert, L. Birds of prey **598**

Neighborhood _See_ Community life

The **neighborhood** Mother Goose **398.8**

Neighborhood odes. Soto, G. **811**

Neimark, Anne E.
There ain't nobody that can sing like me: the life of Woody Guthrie (5 and up) **92**

Neitzel, Shirley
The jacket I wear in the snow **E**
Our class took a trip to the zoo **E**

Nelson, Annika
(il) Soto, G. Canto familiar **811**

Nelson, Drew
(jt. auth) Nelson, V. M. Juneteenth **394.26**

Nelson, Kadir
He's got the whole world in his hands (k-2) **782.25**
(il) Allen, D. Dancing in the wings **E**
(il) Grifalconi, A. The village that vanished **E**
(il) Grimes, N. Under the Christmas tree **811**
(il) Jordan, D. Salt in his shoes **E**
(il) Lee, S. Please, baby, please **E**
(il) Nolen, J. Big Jabe **E**

Nelson, Kadir—*Continued*
(il) Nolen, J. Hewitt Anderson's great big life
                                                      E
(il) Nolen, J. Thunder Rose   E
(il) Richardson, C. K. The real slam dunk
                                             Fic
(il) Shange, N. Ellington was not a street   E
Nelson, S. D.
The Star People   E
(il) Bruchac, J. Crazy Horse's vision   E
Nelson, Sharlene P.
Jedediah Smith (3-6)   92
Nelson, Ted W.
(jt. auth) Nelson, S. P. Jedediah Smith   92
Nelson, Theresa
And one for all (5 and up)   Fic
Ruby electric (5 and up)   Fic
Nelson, Vaunda Micheaux
Juneteenth (2-4)   **394.26**
Nepal
Burbank, J. Nepal (5 and up)   **954.96**
Fiction
Tenzing Norbu. Secret of the snow leopard
                                                      E

Nervous system
Berger, M. Why I sneeze, shiver, hiccup, and
yawn (k-3)   **612.7**
Simon, S. The brain (4 and up)   **612.8**
Diseases
See also Meningitis; Multiple sclerosis;
Tourette syndrome
Nesbit, E. (Edith)
The enchanted castle (4-6)   Fic
Five children and it (4-6)   Fic
The last of the dragons
In Fire and wings: dragon tales from East and
West p124-36   S C
The railway children (4-6)   Fic
Nesbit, Edith *See* Nesbit, E. (Edith), 1858-1924
Nespeca, Sue McCleaf
Library programming for families with young
children   **027.62**
Picture books plus   **028.5**
Ness, Evaline
Sam, Bangs & Moonshine   E
A **nest** full of stars. Berry, J.   **821**
Netherlands
Seward, P. Netherlands (5 and up)   **949.2**
Fiction
Borden, L. The greatest skating race (2-5)
                                                Fic
Brust, B. W. The great tulip trade   E
DeJong, M. The wheel on the school (4-6)
                                                Fic
Fleming, C. Boxes for Katje   E
Gilson, J. Stink Alley (4 and up)   Fic
Noyes, D. Hana in the time of the tulips   E
Propp, V. W. When the soldiers were gone (3-5)
                                                Fic
Vos, I. Anna is still here (4 and up)   Fic
Vos, I. Hide and seek (4 and up)   Fic
History—1940-1945, German occupation
Frank, A. The diary of a young girl (6 and up)
                                               92

Frank, A. The diary of a young girl: the defini-
tive edition (6 and up)   **92**
Reiss, J. The upstairs room (5 and up)   **92**
Nettie's trip South. Turner, A. W.   Fic
Nettleton, Pamela Hill
William Shakespeare (5 and up)   **822.3**
Networks, Computer *See* Computer networks
Neubecker, Robert
Wow! city!   E
Neufeld, John
Almost a hero (5 and up)   Fic
Neurology *See* Nervous system
**Neuwied, Maximilian Alexander Philipp, Prinz
von Wied-** *See* Wied, Maximilian, Prinz von,
1782-1867
Nevada
Hicks, T. A. Nevada
In It's my state! [series]   **973**
Stein, R. C. Nevada
In America the beautiful, second series
                                               973
Fiction
Cox, J. Weird stories from the Lonesome Café
(2-4)   Fic
Snyder, Z. K. The runaways (4 and up)   Fic
"**Never** far from you". San Souci, R.
In San Souci, R. Even more short & shivery;
thirty spine-tingling stories p52-56
                                             398.2
Never kick a slipper at the moon. Sandburg, C.
In Sandburg, C. Rootabaga stories p139-41
                                             S C
also in Sandburg, C. The Sandburg treasury;
prose and poetry for young people p71-
72   **818**
Never mind!. Avi   Fic
Never to forget: the Jews of the Holocaust.
Meltzer, M.   **940.53**
Neville, Emily Cheney
It's like this, Cat (5 and up)   Fic
Nevius, Carol
Karate hour   E
The **new** Americans. Maestro, B.   **973.2**
New Amsterdam Theatre (New York, N.Y.)
Amendola, D. A day at the New Amsterdam
Theatre (4 and up)   **792.6**
The **new** baby at your house. Cole, J.   **306.8**
New beginnings. Rosen, D.   **975.5**
The **New** book of knowledge   **031**
The **New** book of popular science (5 and up)
                                             503
The **New** books kids like   **011.6**
New dinos. Tanaka, S.   **567.9**
New England
Fiction
Alcott, L. M. Little women (5 and up)   Fic
Alcott, L. M. An old-fashioned Thanksgiving
(3-5)   Fic
Hall, D. Ox-cart man   E
Seidler, T. The dulcimer boy (4 and up)   Fic
Wiggin, K. D. S. Rebecca of Sunnybrook Farm
(4 and up)   Fic

New England

Folklore

See Folklore—New England

The **new** girl. Stewart, S.

In A Glory of unicorns p185-94   **S C**

New Hampshire

Hicks, T. A. New Hampshire

In It's my state! [series]   **973**

Mattern, J. New Hampshire

In World Almanac Library of the States series   **973**

Stein, R. C. New Hampshire

In America the beautiful, second series   **973**

Fiction

Banks, K. Dillon Dillon (4 and up)   **Fic**

Bertrand, L. Granite baby   **E**

Blos, J. W. A gathering of days: a New England girl's journal, 1830-32 (6 and up)   **Fic**

New handbook for storytellers, Caroline Feller Bauer's. Bauer, C. F.   **372.6**

New Jersey

Ingram, S. New Jersey

In World Almanac Library of the States series   **973**

King, D. C. New Jersey

In It's my state! [series]   **973**

Stein, R. C. New Jersey

In America the beautiful, second series   **973**

New Jersey

In Voices from colonial America [series]   **973.2**

The **new** kid on the block: poems. Prelutsky, J.   **811**

New Mexico

Bjorklund, R. New Mexico

In It's my state! [series]   **973**

Burgan, M. New Mexico

In World Almanac Library of the States series   **973**

Kent, D. New Mexico

In America the beautiful, second series   **973**

Fiction

Abraham, S. G. Cecilia's year (4 and up)   **Fic**

Hobbs, W. Kokopelli's flute (5 and up)   **Fic**

Johnston, T. Alice Nizzy Nazzy, the Witch of Santa Fe   **E**

The **new** mother. San Souci, R.

In San Souci, R. Even more short & shivery; thirty spine-tingling stories p76-82   **398.2**

New Orleans (La.)

Fiction

Miller, W. Rent party jazz   **E**

Russell, B. T. Maggie's Amerikay   **E**

Schroeder, A. Satchmo's blues   **E**

Race relations

Bridges, R. Through my eyes: the autobiography of Ruby Bridges (4 and up)   **92**

Coles, R. The story of Ruby Bridges (1-3)   **370**

The **New** Oxford treasury of children's poems (3-5)   **808.81**

The **New** Republic (1763-1815). Stanley, G. E.   **973.2**

New shoes for Silvia. Hurwitz, J.   **E**

New technologies for education. See Barron, A. E. Technologies for education   **371.3**

New virtual field trips. Cooper, G.   **025.5**

New visions for linking literature and mathematics. Whitin, D. J.   **372**

The **new** way things work. Macaulay, D.   **600**

New Year

Fiction

Rattigan, J. K. Dumpling soup   **E**

New Year, Chinese *See* Chinese New Year

New year be coming!. Boling, K.   **811**

New Year's Day. Delacre, L.

In Delacre, L. Salsa stories p1-7   **S C**

New Year's hats for the statues. Uchida, Y.

In Snowy day: stories and poems p3-11   **808.8**

New York (N.Y.)

See also Lower East Side (New York, N.Y.)

Dugan, J. ABC NYC   **E**

Marcus, L. S. Storied city   **974.7**

Matsen, B. Go wild in New York City (4 and up)   **974.7**

Melmed, L. K. New York, New York (k-3)   **974.7**

Winter, J. September roses   **E**

Fiction

Avi. Abigail takes the wheel (2-4)   **Fic**

Avi. Never mind! (5 and up)   **Fic**

Bartoletti, S. C. The journal of Finn Reardon (4 and up)   **Fic**

Bartone, E. Peppe the lamplighter   **E**

Chambers, R. Rooftop rocket party   **E**

De Guzman, M. Beekman's big deal (5 and up)   **Fic**

Dorros, A. Abuela   **E**

Egielski, R. The gingerbread boy (k-3)   **398.2**

Graff, S. Blackwell's Island (5 and up)   **Fic**

Gray, L. Falcon's egg (3-5)   **Fic**

Greenwald, S. Rosy Cole's worst ever, best yet tour of New York City (3-5)   **Fic**

Griffin, A. The other Shepards (6 and up)   **Fic**

Hall, B. E. Henry and the kite dragon   **E**

Haseley, D. The invisible moose   **E**

Herold, M. R. A very important day   **E**

Hopkinson, D. Sky boys   **E**

Hurwitz, J. PeeWee's tale (2-4)   **Fic**

Lakin, P. Fat chance Thanksgiving   **E**

Lasky, K. Dreams in the golden country (4 and up)   **Fic**

Levine, G. C. Dave at night (5 and up)   **Fic**

Lewis, J. P. The snowflake sisters   **E**

Lithgow, J. Micawber   **E**

Miller, K. Kiki Strike (5 and up)   **Fic**

Neville, E. C. It's like this, Cat (5 and up)   **Fic**

Osborne, M. P. New York's bravest   **E**

New York (N.Y.)—Fiction—*Continued*
Palatini, M. Three French hens   **E**
Potter, E. Olivia Kidney (3-6)   **Fic**
Raskin, E. The mysterious disappearance of Leon (I mean Noel) (4 and up)   **Fic**
Ritter, J. H. Over the wall (6 and up)   **Fic**
Roberts, W. D. The kidnappers (4 and up)   **Fic**
Ruby, L. The Wall and the Wing (5 and up)   **Fic**
Sawyer, R. Roller skates (4-6)   **Fic**
Selden, G. The cricket in Times Square (3-6)   **Fic**
Shyer, M. F. Fleabiscuit sings! (3-5)   **Fic**
Sís, P. Madlenka   **E**
Taylor, S. All-of-a-kind family (4-6)   **Fic**
Thompson, K. Kay Thompson's Eloise   **E**
Van Leeuwen, J. The Great Googlestein museum mystery (3-5)   **Fic**
Vogel, A. How little Lori visited Times Square   **E**
Waber, B. Lyle, Lyle, crocodile   **E**
Weitzman, J. P. You can't take a balloon into the Metropolitan Museum   **E**
Weller, F. W. The day the animals came   **E**

History
Brown, D. Kid Blink beats the world (2-4)   **331.3**
DuTemple, L. A. The New York subways (5 and up)   **388.4**
Weitzman, D. L. A subway for New York (4 and up)   **625.4**
See/See also pages in the following book(s):
Borden, L. Touching the sky: the flying adventures of Wilbur and Orville Wright (3-5)   **92**

Poetry
Rosten, N. A city is (k-3)   **811**

Race relations
Bolden, T. Maritcha [biography of Maritcha Rémond Lyons] (4 and up)   **92**

New York (N.Y.). Grand Central Terminal *See* Grand Central Terminal (New York, N.Y.)

New York (N.Y.). Statue of Liberty *See* Statue of Liberty (New York, N.Y.)

New York (N.Y.). World Trade Center *See* World Trade Center (New York, N.Y.)

New York (N.Y.) in literature
Marcus, L. S. Storied city   **974.7**

New York (State)
Ball, J. A. New York
In World Almanac Library of the States series   **973**
Elish, D. New York
In It's my state! [series]   **973**
Heinrichs, A. New York
In America the beautiful, second series   **973**

Fiction
Auch, M. J. Journey to nowhere (4 and up)   **Fic**
Blumenthal, D. Ice palace   **E**
George, J. C. My side of the mountain trilogy (5 and up)   **Fic**
Irving, W. Rip Van Winkle (5 and up)   **Fic**
O'Dell, S. Sarah Bishop (6 and up)   **Fic**

Ray, M. L. Basket moon   **E**

History
Burgan, M. New York, 1609-1776
In Voices from colonial America [series]   **973.2**

New York, 1609-1776. Burgan, M.
In Voices from colonial America [series]   **973.2**

New York City Public High School for Ballet
See Ballet Tech School (New York, N.Y.)

New York is English, Chattanooga is Creek. Raschka, C.   **E**

New York, New York. Melmed, L. K.   **974.7**

New York Public Library
The Black experience in children's books. See The Black experience in children's books   **016.3058**

The **New** York Public Library amazing space. Campbell, A.   **520**

The **New** York Public Library amazing women in American history. Heinemann, S.   **305.4**

New York Public Library answer books for kids series
Heinemann, S. The New York Public Library amazing women in American history   **305.4**

The **New** York Public Library kid's guide to research. Heiligman, D.   **025.5**

The **New** York subways. DuTemple, L. A.   **388.4**

New York Zoological Park *See* Bronx Zoo

New York's bravest. Osborne, M. P.   **E**

New Zealand
Smelt, R. New Zealand (5 and up)   **993**

Fiction
Morgan, C. The boy who spoke dog (5 and up)   **Fic**

Newberry, Clare Turlay
April's kittens   **E**

The **Newbery/Printz** companion. Gillespie, J. T.   **028.5**

The **Newbery** and Caldecott awards   **028.5**

Newbery and Caldecott Medal books, 1966-1975   **028.5**

Newbery and Caldecott Medal books, 1976-1985   **028.5**

Newbery Medal
Bostrom, K. L. Winning authors   **920**
Gillespie, J. T. The Newbery/Printz companion   **028.5**
The Newbery and Caldecott awards   **028.5**
Newbery and Caldecott Medal books, 1966-1975   **028.5**
Newbery and Caldecott Medal books, 1976-1985   **028.5**
Newbery Medal books, 1922-1955   **028.5**
Newbery Medal books, 1922-1955   **028.5**

Newbery Medal titles
Alexander, L. The high king   **Fic**
Armstrong, W. H. Sounder   **Fic**
Avi. Crispin   **Fic**
Blos, J. W. A gathering of days: a New England girl's journal, 1830-32   **Fic**

Newbery Medal titles—*Continued*

Brink, C. R. Caddie Woodlawn **Fic**
Byars, B. C. The summer of the swans **Fic**
Cleary, B. Dear Mr. Henshaw **Fic**
Coatsworth, E. J. The cat who went to heaven **Fic**
Cooper, S. The grey king **Fic**
Creech, S. Walk two moons **Fic**
Curtis, C. P. Bud, not Buddy **Fic**
Cushman, K. The midwife's apprentice **Fic**
De Angeli, M. L. The door in the wall **Fic**
DeJong, M. The wheel on the school **Fic**
DiCamillo, K. The tale of Despereaux **Fic**
Du Bois, W. P. The twenty-one balloons **Fic**
Estes, E. Ginger Pye **Fic**
Field, R. Hitty: her first hundred years **Fic**
Fleischman, P. Joyful noise: poems for two voices **811**
Fleischman, S. The whipping boy **Fic**
Forbes, E. Johnny Tremain **Fic**
Fox, P. The slave dancer **Fic**
Freedman, R. Lincoln: a photobiography **92**
George, J. C. Julie of the wolves **Fic**
Hamilton, V. M.C. Higgins, the great **Fic**
Henry, M. King of the wind **Fic**
Hesse, K. Out of the dust **Fic**
Kadohata, C. Kira-Kira **Fic**
Keith, H. Rifles for Watie **Fic**
Konigsburg, E. L. From the mixed-up files of Mrs. Basil E. Frankweiler **Fic**
Konigsburg, E. L. The view from Saturday **Fic**
Krumgold, J. Onion John **Fic**
Lawson, R. Rabbit Hill **Fic**
L'Engle, M. A wrinkle in time **Fic**
Lowry, L. The giver **Fic**
Lowry, L. Number the stars **Fic**
MacLachlan, P. Sarah, plain and tall **Fic**
Naylor, P. R. Shiloh **Fic**
Neville, E. C. It's like this, Cat **Fic**
O'Brien, R. C. Mrs. Frisby and the rats of NIMH **Fic**
O'Dell, S. Island of the Blue Dolphins **Fic**
Park, L. S. A single shard **Fic**
Paterson, K. Bridge to Terabithia **Fic**
Peck, R. A year down yonder **Fic**
Perkins, L. R. Criss cross **Fic**
Raskin, E. The Westing game **Fic**
Rylant, C. Missing May **Fic**
Sachar, L. Holes **Fic**
Sawyer, R. Roller skates **Fic**
Seredy, K. The white stag **Fic**
Sorensen, V. E. Miracles on Maple Hill **Fic**
Speare, E. G. The bronze bow **Fic**
Speare, E. G. The witch of Blackbird Pond **Fic**
Sperry, A. Call it courage **Fic**
Spinelli, J. Maniac Magee **Fic**
Taylor, M. D. Roll of thunder, hear my cry **Fic**
Treviño, E. B. d. I, Juan de Pareja **Fic**
Vining, E. G. Adam of the road **Fic**
Voigt, C. Dicey's song **Fic**
Willard, N. A visit to William Blake's inn **811**
Wojciechowska, M. Shadow of a bull **Fic**

Yates, E. Amos Fortune, free man **92**

Newbigging, Martha
(il) Galloway, P. Archers, alchemists, and 98 other medieval jobs you might have loved or loathed **940.1**
(il) Shulman, M. Attack of the killer video book **778.59**

Newcomb, Rain
The Girls' World book of jewelry: 50 cool designs to make (5 and up) **745.594**
(jt. auth) Rhatigan, J. Out-of-this-world astronomy **520**
(jt. auth) Rhatigan, J. Paper fantastic **745.54**
(jt. auth) Rhatigan, J. Prize-winning science fair projects for curious kids **507.8**
(jt. auth) Rhatigan, J. Run, jump, hide, slide, splash **796**
(jt. auth) Rhatigan, J. Stamp it! **761**

Newcome, Zita
Head, shoulders, knees, and toes **E**

Newfoundland
Fiction
Harlow, J. H. Star in the storm **Fic**

Newhouse, Maxwell
(il) Lunn, J. L. S. Laura Secord: a story of courage **Fic**

Newman, Colin
(il) Greenaway, T. Crabs **595.3**
(il) Greenaway, T. Whales **599.5**

Newman, Lesléa
The best cat in the world **E**
A fire engine for Ruthie **E**
Hachiko waits (3-5) **Fic**
Runaway dreidel! **E**
Where is bear? **E**

Newman, Marjorie
Mole and the baby bird **E**

Newman, Robert
The case of the Baker Street Irregular (5 and up) **Fic**

Newman, Shirlee Petkin
Child slavery in modern times (5 and up) **326**

Newmark, Ann
Chemistry (4 and up) **540**

Newquist, H. P. (Harvey P.)
The great brain book (5 and up) **612.8**

News!. Jacobs, J.
In Jacobs, J. English fairy tales p384-85 **398.2**

Newsboys *See* Newspaper carriers

Newsome, Jill
Dream dancer **E**
Night walk **E**

Newspaper carriers
Brown, D. Kid Blink beats the world (2-4) **331.3**
Fiction
Bartoletti, S. C. The journal of Finn Reardon (4 and up) **Fic**
Kroeger, M. K. Paperboy **E**
Pilkey, D. The paperboy **E**

Newspapers
See also Journalism
Fiction
Clements, A. The Landry News (4-6) **Fic**

Newton, Sir Isaac, 1642-1727
About
Krull, K. Isaac Newton (5 and up) **92**
See/See also pages in the following book(s):
Fradin, D. B. With a little luck (5 and up)
509

The **next-door** dogs. Rodowsky, C. F. **Fic**

Next-of-kin. Olson, A. N.
In Olson, A. N. and Schwartz, H. Ask the bones: scary stories from around the world p17-23 **398.2**

Next stop, Grand Central. Kalman, M. **E**

Nez Percé Indians
Englar, M. Chief Joseph, 1840-1904 (3-5)
92
Sneve, V. D. H. The Nez Percé (3-5)
970.004
See/See also pages in the following book(s):
Freedman, R. Indian chiefs (6 and up) **920**

Ngawang Lobsang Yishey Tenzing Gyatso *See* Dalai Lama XIV, 1935-

NgCheong-Lum, Roseline
France (4 and up) **944**

Nguyen, Chi Thien
Cooking the Vietnamese way
In Easy menu ethnic cookbooks **641.5**

Nibbling on Einstein's brain. Swanson, D. **500**

Nicaragua
Kott, J. Nicaragua (5 and up) **972.85**
Folklore
See Folklore—Nicaragua

Niccolini's song. Wilcoxen, C. **E**

Nichol, Barbara
Beethoven lives upstairs (3-5) **Fic**

Nicholas, Saint, Bishop of Myra
About
Demi. The legend of Saint Nicholas (3-6)
92

Nicholas, Kristin
Kids embroidery (3-6) **746.44**

Nicholas. Goscinny **Fic**

Nicholls, Calvin
(il) Martin, R. The world before this one
398.2

Nicholls, Judith
Billywise **E**
(comp) The Sun in me. *See* The Sun in me
811.008

Nichols, Margaret Irby
(jt. auth) Safford, B. R. Guide to reference materials for school media centers **011.6**

Nicholson, Dorinda Makanaōnalani
Remember World War II (5 and up) **940.53**

Nicholson, Sir William
(il) Bianco, M. W. The velveteen rabbit **Fic**

Nick plays baseball. Isadora, R. **796.357**

Nickel
Sparrow, G. Nickel
In The Elements **546**

Nicklaus, Carol
(il) Otfinoski, S. Speaking up, speaking out
808.5

Nicknames
Fiction
Korman, G. The sixth grade nickname game (4 and up) **Fic**

Niger
Seffal, R. Niger (5 and up) **966.26**

Nigeria
Levy, P. Nigeria (5 and up) **966.9**
Murphy, P. Nigeria (2-4) **966.9**
Fiction
Naidoo, B. The other side of truth (5 and up)
Fic
Folklore
See Folklore—Nigeria

Night
See also Bedtime; Day
Bailey, J. Sun up, sun down (2-4) **525**
Krautwurst, T. Night science for kids (4-6)
591.5
Murphy, S. J. It's about time! (k-2) **529**
Rose, D. L. One nighttime sea **E**
Fiction
Banks, K. And if the moon could talk **E**
Banks, K. The night worker **E**
Beames, M. Night cat **E**
Bonsall, C. N. Who's afraid of the dark? **E**
Brown, M. W. A child's good night book **E**
Brown, M. W. Goodnight moon **E**
Ford, B. First snow **E**
Fox, M. Night noises **E**
Juan, A. The Night Eater **E**
Shulevitz, U. So sleepy story **E**
Tafuri, N. What the sun sees **E**
Thompson, L. Polar bear night **E**
Weiss, N. Where does the brown bear go?
E
Folklore
Caduto, M. J. Keepers of the night **398.2**

Night at the fair. Crews, D. **E**

The **night** before Christmas. Moore, C. C. **811**

Night cat. Beames, M. **E**

The **night** crossing. Ackerman, K. **Fic**

The **Night** Eater. Juan, A. **E**

Night garden. Wong, J. S. **811**

Night golf. Miller, W. **E**

The **Night** has ears (k-3) **398.9**

The **night** it rained. Schwartz, A.
In Schwartz, A. In a dark, dark room, and other scary stories p42-49 **398.2**

The **night** journey. Lasky, K. **Fic**

Night noises. Fox, M. **E**

The **night** of Las Posadas. De Paola, T. **E**

No one is going to Nashville. Jukes, M.
In You read to me & I'll read to you; 20th-
century stories to share p84-96   **E**

No one saw. Raczka, B.   **759.06**

No sword. Kimmel, E. A.
In Kimmel, E. A. Sword of the samurai; ad-
venture stories from Japan p105-09
  Fic

No, thanks. Schwartz, A.
In Schwartz, A. Scary stories 3; more tales to
chill your bones p65   **398.2**

No turning back. Naidoo, B.   **Fic**

Noah (Biblical figure)
See/See also pages in the following book(s):
Brett, J. On Noah's ark   **E**

Noah and the Devil. Philip, N.   **398.2**

Noah hunts a wooly mammoth. Norman, H.
In Norman, H. The girl who dreamed only
geese, and other tales of the Far North
  398.2

Noah's ark
Geisert, A. The ark (k-3)   **222**
Pinkney, J. Noah's ark (k-3)   **222**
Spier, P. Noah's ark (k-2)   **222**
Fiction
Brett, J. On Noah's ark   **E**
Folklore
Philip, N. Noah and the Devil (k-3)   **398.2**

Noakes, Vivien
(ed) Lear, E. The complete verse and other nonsense   **821**

The **Nobel** book of answers (5 and up)   **001.4**

Nobel Prizes
The Nobel book of answers (5 and up)
  001.4

Noble, Trinka Hakes
The day Jimmy's boa ate the wash   **E**

Noble-Goodman, Katherine
Zebras (3-6)   **599.66**

The **nobleman** and the peasant. Afanas´ev, A. N.
In Afanas´ev, A. N. Russian fairy tales p59-
61   **398.2**

Nobles, Scott
(il) Bruder, M. Button girl   **745.5**

Nobody particular. Bang, M.   **363.7**

Nobody's diggier than a dog. Bartoletti, S. C.
  E

Nodey, the priest's grandson. Afanas´ev, A. N.
In Afanas´ev, A. N. Russian fairy tales p173-
77   **398.2**

Noise
MacDonald, R. Achoo! Bang! Crash!   **E**
Fiction
Cleary, B. The hullabaloo ABC   **E**
Dodd, E. Dog's noisy day   **E**
Mayo, M. Choo choo clickety-clack!   **E**
Waber, B. The mouse that snored   **E**

Noisy Nora. Wells, R.   **E**

The **noisy** way to bed. Whybrow, I.   **E**

Noko and the night monster. Moodie, F.   **E**

Nolan, Dennis
(il) Coville, B. William Shakespeare's A midsummer night's dream   **822.3**
(il) Coville, B. William Shakespeare's Romeo
and Juliet   **822.3**
(il) Kennedy, R. F. Saint Francis of Assisi
  271
(il) Ryan, P. M. There was no snow on Christmas Eve   **E**
(il) White, T. H. The sword in the stone
  Fic
(il) Yolen, J. The perfect wizard [biography of
Hans Christian Andersen]   **92**

Nolan, Janet
The St. Patrick's Day shillelagh   **E**

Nolen, Jerdine
Big Jabe   **E**
Harvey Potter's balloon farm   **E**
Hewitt Anderson's great big life   **E**
Max and Jax in second grade   **E**
Raising dragons   **E**
Thunder Rose   **E**

Noll, Cheryl Kirk
(il) King, D. C. World War II days   **940.53**

Nolting, Karen Stray
(jt. auth) Latimer, J. P. Butterflies   **595.7**
(jt. auth) Latimer, J. P. Caterpillars   **595.7**

Nome (Alaska)
Kimmel, E. C. Balto and the great race (3-5)
  636.7

Nonan-Mercado, Detch P.
(jt. auth) Tope, L. R. R. Philippines   **959.9**

Nonbook materials *See* Audiovisual materials

Nonsense verses
See also Limericks; Tongue twisters
Carroll, L. Jabberwocky (k-3)   **821**
Cox, K. Mixed beasts (3-5)   **811**
Florian, D. Bing bang boing   **811**
Lear, E. Edward Lear (4 and up)   **821**
Lear, E. The owl and the pussycat   **821**
Lear, E. The pelican chorus and other nonsense
  821
Macdonald, S. A was once an apple pie   **E**
Prelutsky, J. Beneath a blue umbrella: rhymes
(k-3)   **811**
Prelutsky, J. The frogs wore red suspenders
(k-3)   **811**
Prelutsky, J. Ride a purple pelican (k-3)   **811**
Prelutsky, J. Scranimals (2-5)   **811**
Silverstein, S. Falling up   **811**
Silverstein, S. A light in the attic   **811**
Silverstein, S. Where the sidewalk ends   **811**
Willard, N. A visit to William Blake's inn (2-5)
  811
Yolen, J. How beastly! (3-5)   **811**

Noon, Steve
(il) Kentley, E. Story of the Titanic   **910.4**

Noonan, Diana
The butterfly (2-4)   **595.7**
The emperor penguin (2-4)   **598**
The frog (2-4)   **597.8**
The green turtle (2-4)   **597.92**
The kangaroo (2-4)   **599.2**

Noonan, Julia
  (il) Mitchard, J. Baby bat's lullaby   **E**
The **noose**. Naidoo, B.
  In Naidoo, B. Out of bounds: seven stories of
    conflict and hope p18-49   **S C**
Norac, Carl
  My daddy is a giant   **E**
Nora's ark. Kinsey-Warnock, N.   **E**
Nordin, Sofia
  In the wild (4 and up)   **Fic**
Norman, Howard
  Between heaven and earth (4 and up)   **398.2**
  The girl who dreamed only geese, and other
    tales of the Far North (4 and up)   **398.2**
  Contents: The day puffins netted Hid-Well; Noah hunts a
wooly mammoth; Why the rude visitor was flung by walrus;
Uteritsoq and the duck-bill dolls; The wolverine's secret; The girl
who watched in the nighttime; The man who married a seagull;
Home among the giants; How the narwhal got its tusk; The girl
who dreamed only geese
Norris, Joann
  Children's museums   **069**
Norris, Kathleen
  The holy twins: Benedict and Scholastica (3-5)
    92
Norse mythology
  Fisher, L. E. Gods and goddesses of the ancient
    Norse (3-6)   **293**
  Hamilton, E. Mythology (5 and up)   **292**
  Osborne, M. P. Favorite Norse myths (4 and up)
    293
  Philip, N. Odin's family (4-6)   **293**
    Fiction
  Coville, B. Thor's wedding day (4 and up)
    Fic
  Farmer, N. The Sea of Trolls (5 and up)
    Fic
Norsemen *See* Vikings
North, John Ringling, 1903-1985
  See/See also pages in the following book(s):
  Schubert, L. Ballet of the elephants   **791.8**
North, Sterling
  Rascal (5 and up)   **599.7**
North American cranes. DuTemple, L. A.   **598**
North American historical atlases [series]
  Stefoff, R. First frontier   **973.5**
  Stefoff, R. The War of 1812   **973.5**
North American Indian. Murdoch, D. H.
    970.004
North American Indians *See* Native Americans
North American moose. DuTemple, L. A.
    599.65
North Carolina
  Gaines, A. North Carolina
    In It's my state! [series]   **973**
  Hintz, M. North Carolina
    In America the beautiful, second series
    973
  Rafle, S. North Carolina
    In World Almanac Library of the States series
    973
    Fiction
  Carbone, E. L. Storm warriors (4 and up)
    Fic
  Dowell, F. O. Dovey Coe (5 and up)   **Fic**

Madden, K. Gentle's Holler (5 and up)   **Fic**
Pinkney, G. J. Back home   **E**
Stauffacher, S. Bessie Smith and the night riders
    E
Taylor, T. Teetoncey (5 and up)   **Fic**
Weatherford, C. B. Freedom on the menu   **E**
    Natural history
  See Natural history—North Carolina
    Race relations
  Tillage, L. Leon's story (4 and up)   **92**
North Dakota
  Fontes, J. North Dakota
    In World Almanac Library of the States series
    973
  Hintz, M. North Dakota
    In America the beautiful, second series
    973
  Sanders, D. North Dakota
    In It's my state! [series]   **973**
North Dakota. Sanders, D.
    In It's my state! [series]   **973**
North Pole
  See also Arctic regions
  Ferris, J. Arctic explorer: the story of Matthew
    Henson (3-6)   **92**
  Johnson, D. Onward [biography of Matthew
    Henson] (5 and up)   **92**
  Levinson, N. S. North Pole, South Pole (k-3)
    998
    Fiction
  Van Allsburg, C. The Polar Express   **E**
North Pole, South Pole. Levinson, N. S.   **998**
North to freedom. See Holm, A. I am David
    Fic
Northern Ireland
    Fiction
  Bateman, C. Running with the Reservoir Pups
    (5 and up)   **Fic**
Northern lights *See* Auroras
Northern lights. Souza, D. M.   **538**
Northmen *See* Vikings
Northwest, Pacific *See* Pacific Northwest
Norton, Mary
  Bed-knob and broomstick (3-6)   **Fic**
  Bonfires and broomsticks
    In Norton, M. Bed-knob and broomstick
    Fic
  The borrowers (3-6)   **Fic**
  The magic bed-knob
    In Norton, M. Bed-knob and broomstick
    Fic
The **Norton** anthology of children's literature
    808.8
Norway
    Fiction
  McSwigan, M. Snow treasure (3-6)   **Fic**
  Myers, T. Good babies   **E**
    Folklore
  See Folklore—Norway
Nory Ryan's song. Giff, P. R.   **Fic**
Nose
    Fiction
  Brown, M. T. Arthur's nose   **E**

The **nun's** priest's tale. Cohen, B.
    In Cohen, B. Canterbury tales   **821**

Nurse Corps (Army) *See* United States. Army
Nurse Corps

Nursery rhymes
    See also Jump rope rhymes
Alter, A. The three little kittens (k-1)   **398.8**
The Arnold Lobel book of Mother Goose (k-2)
    398.8
Arrorró mi niño (k-3)   **398.8**
The baby's bedtime book   **808.81**
The baby's book of baby animals   **808.81**
The baby's good morning book   **808.81**
The Baby's lap book   **398.8**
The baby's playtime book (k-1)   **811.008**
Baker, K. Big fat hen   **398.8**
Brown, M. T. Play rhymes   **796.1**
Cabrera, J. Old Mother Hubbard (k-2)   **398.8**
Chapman, J. Sing a song of sixpence (k-1)
    398.8
Dunn, O. Hippety-hop, hippety-hay   **398.8**
Emberley, B. Drummer Hoff   **398.8**
Galdone, P. The cat goes fiddle-i-fee (k-1)
    398.8
Galdone, P. Three little kittens   **398.8**
The Helen Oxenbury nursery collection (k-3)
    398.8
Here comes Mother Goose   **398.8**
Hoberman, M. A. Miss Mary Mack   **398.8**
James Marshall's Mother Goose   **398.8**
Keats, E. J. Over in the meadow   **E**
Mamá Goose (k-2)   **398.8**
Marino, J. Mother Goose time   **027.62**
Miss Mary Mack and other children's street
rhymes   **796.1**
My very first Mother Goose   **398.8**
The neighborhood Mother Goose   **398.8**
Newcome, Z. Head, shoulders, knees, and toes
    E
The Orchard book of nursery rhymes   **398.8**
Pat-a-cake and other play rhymes   **398.8**
Patz, N. Moses supposes his toeses are roses
and 7 other silly old rhymes   **398.8**
¡Pio peep! (k-3)   **398.8**
Polacco, P. Babushka's Mother Goose   **398.8**
Prelutsky, J. Beneath a blue umbrella: rhymes
(k-3)   **811**
Prelutsky, J. The frogs wore red suspenders
(k-3)   **811**
Prelutsky, J. Ride a purple pelican (k-3)   **811**
Read-aloud rhymes for the very young (k-2)
    821.008
The Real Mother Goose   **398.8**
Scieszka, J. The book that Jack wrote (2-4)
    811
Spirin, G. A apple pie   **E**
Sylvia Long's Mother Goose   **398.8**
Taback, S. This is the house that Jack built
(k-3)   **398.8**
This little piggy   **398.8**
Tomie dePaola's Mother Goose   **398.8**
Tortillitas para mamá and other nursery rhymes
    398.8
Trapani, I. Mary had a little lamb (k-2)
    782.42
Wadsworth, O. A. Over in the meadow   **E**

Will Moses Mother Goose   **398.8**
Wilner, I. The baby's game book   **398.8**
Winter, J. The house that Jack built   **398.8**
Zemach, M. Some from the moon, some from
the sun (k-2)   **398.8**
    Dictionaries
The Oxford dictionary of nursery rhymes
    398.8
    Fiction
Edwards, P. D. The neat line   **E**
Hoberman, M. A. You read to me, I'll read to
you [very short Mother Goose tales to read
together] (k-3)   **811**

Nursery schools
    See also Day care centers; Preschool educa-
tion
Senisi, E. B. Hurray for pre-K!   **E**
    Fiction
Schaefer, C. L. Someone says   **E**

Nursery tales around the world. Sierra, J.
    398.2

Nurses
Gorrell, G. K. Heart and soul: the story of Flor-
ence Nightingale (5 and up)   **92**
Koestler-Grack, R. A. The story of Clara Barton
(2-4)   **92**
Wells, R. Mary on horseback [biography of
Mary Breckinridge] (4 and up)   **92**

Nutcracker. Hoffmann, E. T. A.   **Fic**

The **Nutcracker.** Kain, K.   **E**

The **Nutcracker.** Koppe, S.   **Fic**

The **nutcracker.** Schulman, J.   **Fic**

The **Nutcracker** ballet. Hautzig, D.   **E**

Nutik, the wolf pup. George, J. C.   **E**

Nutrition
    See also Diet; Eating customs
Cheung, L. W. Y. Be healthy! it's a girl thing
(5 and up)   **613**
D'Amico, J. The healthy body cookbook (4 and
up)   **641.5**
King, H. Carbohydrates for a healthy body (4-6)
    613.2
Miller, E. The monster health book (2-4)
    613.7
Rockwell, L. Good enough to eat (k-3)
    613.2
Royston, A. Proteins for a healthy body (4-6)
    613.2
Royston, A. Vitamins and minerals for a healthy
body (4-6)   **613.2**
VanCleave, J. P. Janice VanCleave's food and
nutrition for every kid (4 and up)   **613.2**

Nuts. Babbitt, N.
    In Babbitt, N. The Devil's storybook p47-51
    S C

Nuts! Nuts! Nuts!. Van Laan, N.
    In Van Laan, N. With a whoop and a holler;
a bushel of lore from way down south
p61-64   **398.2**

Nuts to you!. Ehlert, L.   **E**

Nutzhorn, Dorothea *See* Lange, Dorothea, 1895-
1965

Nye, Bill
Bill Nye the science guy's great big book of tiny germs (3-5) **579**

Nye, Naomi Shihab
Baby radar **E**
Come with me (3-6) **811**
(comp) Salting the ocean. See Salting the ocean **811.008**

Nye, Robert
Beowulf against Grendel
In Bauer, C. F. Celebrations; read-aloud holiday and theme book programs p105-08 **808.8**

Nzinga, Queen of Matamba, 1582-1663
See/See also pages in the following book(s):
Hansen, J. African princess (5 and up) **920**
Krull, K. Lives of extraordinary women (4 and up) **920**
Fiction
McKissack, P. C. Nzinga, warrior queen of Matamba (5 and up) **Fic**

Nzinga, warrior queen of Matamba. McKissack, P. C. **Fic**

O

Ó Flatharta, Antoine
Hurry and the monarch **E**

O holy night (k-3) **782.28**

Oak
Morrison, G. Oak tree (3-6) **583**
Pfeffer, W. A log's life (k-3) **577.3**
Royston, A. Life cycle of an oak tree (k-3) **583**

Oak tree. Morrison, G. **583**

The oaken throne. Jarvis, R. **Fic**

Oakley, Annie, 1860-1926
About
Macy, S. Bulls-eye: a photobiography of Annie Oakley (4 and up) **92**

Oakley, Mark
Thieves & kings (4 and up) **741.5**

Obama, Barack, 1961-
About
Brill, M. T. Barack Obama (5 and up) **92**

Obata, Chiura, 1888-1975
About
Ross, M. E. Nature art with Chiura Obata (4 and up) **92**

Oberman, Sheldon
The always prayer shawl **E**
Solomon and the ant; (5 and up) **398.2**

Obesity
Fiction
Holt, K. W. When Zachary Beaver came to town (5 and up) **Fic**

O'Brien, Anne Sibley
The legend of Hong Kil Dong, the Robin Hood of Korea (3-5) **741.5**
(il) Havill, J. Jamaica's find **E**
(il) Knight, M. B. Talking walls **909**
(il) Knight, M. B. Talking walls: the stories continue **909**

O'Brien, John
(il) Bateman, T. Red, white, blue, and Uncle who? **929.9**
(il) Blackstone, M. This is soccer **796.334**
(il) Shannon, G. More true lies **398.2**
(il) Terban, M. Funny you should ask **793.73**
(il) The Twelve days of Christmas. See The Twelve days of Christmas **782.28**

O'Brien, Patrick
The great ships (4 and up) **387.2**
The Hindenburg (4 and up) **629.133**
Megatooth! (k-3) **567**
(il) O'Malley, K. Captain Raptor and the moon mystery **E**

O'Brien, Robert C.
Mrs. Frisby and the rats of NIMH (4 and up) **Fic**

Occult sciences *See* Occultism

Occultism
See also Clairvoyance; Fortune telling
Fiction
Snyder, Z. K. The headless cupid (5 and up) **Fic**

Occupations
Bunting, E. Girls A to Z **E**
Miller, M. Guess who? **E**
Fiction
Catalanotto, P. Kitten red, yellow, blue **E**
Cumpiano, I. Quinito's neighborhood **E**
Rockwell, A. F. Career day **E**

Ocean
See also Atlantic Ocean; Seashore
Burleigh, R. The sea (5 and up) **551.46**
Cole, J. The magic school bus on the ocean floor (2-4) **591.7**
Littlefield, C. A. Awesome ocean science! (3-5) **551.46**
Scholastic atlas of oceans (4 and up) **551.46**
Simon, S. Oceans (3-6) **551.46**
Stille, D. R. Oceans (2-4) **551.46**
Poetry
Cyrus, K. Hotel deep (3-5) **811**

Ocean bottom
Collard, S. B., III. In the deep sea (4-6) **572**
Gibbons, G. Exploring the deep, dark sea (k-3) **551.46**
Matsen, B. The incredible record-setting deep-sea dive of the bathysphere (4 and up) **551.46**

Ocean currents
See also El Niño Current

Ocean travel
Paulsen, G. Caught by the sea (5 and up) **92**

Ocean waves
See also Tsunamis

Ocean wildlife. Vogel, C. G. **591.7**

Oceania
Fiction
Schaefer, C. L. The biggest soap **E**

Oceanographic submersibles *See* Submersibles

Oceanography

VanCleave, J. P. Janice VanCleave's oceans for every kid (4 and up)   **551.46**

Biography

Hill, C. M. Robert Ballard (5 and up)   **92**

Ochiltree, Dianne

Sixteen runaway pumpkins   **E**

O'Connell, Rebecca

The baby goes beep   **E**

O'Connor, Barbara

Fame and glory in Freedom, Georgia (4 and up)   **Fic**

Katherine Dunham (5 and up)   **92**

Leonardo da Vinci (5 and up)   **92**

Me and Rupert Goody (4-6)   **Fic**

Taking care of Moses (4-6)   **Fic**

O'Connor, Jane

The emperor's silent army (4 and up)   **931**

Mary Cassatt (2-4)   **92**

The perfect puppy for me   **E**

The **octopus**. Cazet, D.   **E**

Octopuses

Jango-Cohen, J. Octopuses (3-6)   **594**

Fiction

Cazet, D. The octopus   **E**

Octopuses, squids, and their relatives. Blaxland, B.   **594**

O'Cuilleanáin, Eilís Dillon *See* Dillon, Eilís, 1920-1994

O'Day, Anita, 1919-

See/See also pages in the following book(s):

Orgill, R. Shout, sister, shout! (6 and up)   **920**

Odd boy out: young Albert Einstein. Brown, D.   **92**

Oddities *See* Curiosities and wonders

Odean, Kathleen

Great books about things kids love   **028.1**

Great books for babies and toddlers   **028.1**

Great books for boys   **028.1**

Great books for girls   **028.1**

O'Dell, Kathleen

Agnes Parker . . . girl in progress (4 and up)   **Fic**

O'Dell, Scott

The black pearl (6 and up)   **Fic**

The captive (6 and up)   **Fic**

Island of the Blue Dolphins (5 and up)   **Fic**

The King's fifth (5 and up)   **Fic**

Sarah Bishop (6 and up)   **Fic**

Sing down the moon (5 and up)   **Fic**

Streams to the river, river to the sea (5 and up)   **Fic**

Odin's family. Philip, N.   **293**

Odon the giant. Sierra, J.

In Sierra, J. Nursery tales around the world p53-55   **398.2**

O'Donnell, Kerri

The gold rush (4 and up)   **979.4**

Odysseus (Greek mythology)

McCaughrean, G. Odysseus (5 and up)   **292**

Osborne, M. P. The gray-eyed goddess (4 and up)   **883**

Osborne, M. P. The land of the dead (4 and up)   **883**

Osborne, M. P. The one-eyed giant (4 and up)   **883**

Osborne, M. P. Return to Ithaca (4 and up)   **883**

Osborne, M. P. Sirens and sea monsters (4 and up)   **883**

See/See also pages in the following book(s):

Hamilton, E. Mythology (5 and up)   **292**

Fiction

Yolen, J. Odysseus in the serpent maze (4 and up)   **Fic**

Odysseus in the serpent maze. Yolen, J.   **Fic**

Of colors and things. Hoban, T.   **E**

Of numbers and stars [biography of Hypatia] Love, D. A.   **92**

Off limits. Sanfield, S.

In Sanfield, S. The adventures of High John the Conqueror   **398.2**

Off to the sweet shores of Africa and other talking drum rhymes. Unobagha, U. C.   **811**

Off we go!. Yolen, J.   **E**

Offenses against the person

See also Kidnapping

Office management

See also Files and filing

Officer Buckle and Gloria. Rathmann, P.   **E**

Ogburn, Jacqueline K.

The bake shop ghost   **E**

The magic nesting doll   **E**

(jt. auth) Long, L. The lady & the lion   **398.2**

Oglala Indians

Freedman, R. The life and death of Crazy Horse (5 and up)   **92**

See/See also pages in the following book(s):

Freedman, R. Indian chiefs (6 and up)   **920**

Fiction

Bruchac, J. Crazy Horse's vision   **E**

The **ogre** and the rooster. Sakade, F.

In Sakade, F. Japanese children's favorite stories   **398.2**

The **ogre's** arm. San Souci, R.

In San Souci, R. A terrifying taste of short & shivery; thirty creepy tales p46-51   **398.2**

Oh!. Henkes, K.   **E**

Oh, a-hunting we will go. Langstaff, J. M.   **782.42**

Oh, freedom!. King, C.   **323.1**

Oh, look!. Polacco, P.   **E**

Oh my baby, little one. Appelt, K.   **E**

Oh no, gotta go!. Elya, S. M.   **E**

Oh no, Noah!. Hurwitz, J.   **Fic**

Oh, no! Where are my pants? and other disasters (2-4)   **811.008**

Oh, the places you'll go!. Seuss, Dr.   **E**

Oh, yuck!. Masoff, J.   **031.02**

Ohio
Hart, J. Ohio
In It's my state! [series] **973**
Heinrichs, A. Ohio
In America the beautiful, second series
973
Martin, M. A. Ohio
In World Almanac Library of the States series
973
Fiction
DeFelice, C. C. Weasel (4 and up) **Fic**
Fleischman, P. The borning room (6 and up)
Fic
Giblin, J. The boy who saved Cleveland (3-5)
Fic
Hamilton, V. The bells of Christmas (4-6)
Fic
Hamilton, V. The house of Dies Drear (5 and up) **Fic**
Hamilton, V. Time pieces (5 and up) **Fic**
McCloskey, R. Lentil **E**
Pearsall, S. Crooked river (5 and up) **Fic**
Van Leeuwen, J. Cabin on Trouble Creek (4 and up) **Fic**
Van Leeuwen, J. Nothing here but trees **E**
Zinnen, L. The dragons of Spratt, Ohio (5 and up) **Fic**

Oil painting *See* Painting
Oil spills
Bryan, N. Exxon Valdez oil spill (5 and up)
363.7
Oisin in Tir na nOg. Doyle, M.
In Doyle, M. Tales from old Ireland p84-95
398.2
Ojibwa Indians
King, S. Shannon: an Ojibway dancer (3-6)
970.004
Fiction
Erdrich, L. The birchbark house (5 and up)
Fic
Erdrich, L. The game of silence (5 and up)
Fic
Pearsall, S. Crooked river (5 and up) **Fic**
Folklore
San Souci, R. Sootface (1-4) **398.2**
Van Laan, N. Shingebiss (2-4) **398.2**
O'Keeffe, Georgia, 1887-1986
About
Bryant, J. Georgia's bones [biography of Georgia O'Keefe] (k-3) **92**
Rodriguez, R. Through Georgia's eyes [biography of Georgia O'Keeffe] (k-3) **92**
Spangenburg, R. Georgia O'Keeffe (2-4) **92**
Winter, J. My name is Georgia [biography of Georgia O'Keeffe] (k-3) **92**
Okimoto, Jean Davies
The White Swan express **E**
Oklahoma
Martin, M. A. Oklahoma
In World Almanac Library of the States series
973
Reedy, J. Oklahoma
In America the beautiful, second series
973

Sanders, D. Oklahoma
In It's my state! [series] **973**
Fiction
Hesse, K. Out of the dust (5 and up) **Fic**
McCaughrean, G. Stop the train! (5 and up)
Fic
Peterson, J. W. Don't forget Winona **E**
Thomas, J. C. I have heard of a land **E**
Ol' Gally Mander. Van Laan, N.
In Van Laan, N. With a whoop and a holler; a bushel of lore from way down south p76-81 **398.2**
Ol' Master Biggety. Van Laan, N.
In Van Laan, N. With a whoop and a holler; a bushel of lore from way down south p43-46 **398.2**
Ol' Paul, the mighty logger. Rounds, G. **398.2**
Olaleye, Isaac
Bitter bananas **E**
Old, Wendie
To fly: the story of the Wright brothers (3-5)
92
Old age
Fiction
Arnosky, J. Grandfather Buffalo **E**
Auch, M. J. Wing nut (5 and up) **Fic**
Best, C. Are you going to be good? **E**
Bunting, E. Can you do this, Old Badger? **E**
Cannon, J. Verdi **E**
Cheng, A. The lemon sisters **E**
De Paola, T. Now one foot, now the other
E
Giff, P. R. Pictures of Hollis Woods (5 and up)
Fic
Greene, S. Queen Sophie Hartley (3-5) **Fic**
Hazen, B. S. Digby **E**
Hest, A. Mr. George Baker **E**
Holt, K. W. Dancing in Cadillac light (5 and up) **Fic**
Kimmel, E. C. Visiting Miss Caples (6 and up)
Fic
Knowlton, L. L. A young man's dance **E**
Langston, L. Remember, Grandma? **E**
Mikaelsen, B. Petey (5 and up) **Fic**
Miller, W. The piano **E**
Mills, C. Makeovers by Marcia (5 and up)
Fic
Rylant, C. Mr. Putter and Tabby pour the tea
E
Schachner, J. B. The Grannyman **E**
Old bag of bones. Stevens, J. **398.2**
Old Ben. MacDonald, M. R.
In MacDonald, M. R. When the lights go out; twenty scary tales to tell p104-08
372.6
Old black fly. Aylesworth, J. **E**
Old blue buggy. Swift, F. **E**
Old Cricket. Wheeler, L. **E**
Old Doctor Wango Tango. Van Laan, N.
In Van Laan, N. Teeny tiny tingly tales **E**
Old Dog. Byars, B. C.
In Byars, B. C. and others. My dog, my hero p20-24 **S C**
The **old** dog. Zolotow, C. **E**

Old Dry Frye
In Grandfather tales; American-English folk tales p100-05   **398.2**

Old Elm speaks. George, K. O.   **811**

An **old-fashioned** Thanksgiving. Alcott, L. M.   **Fic**

Old favors are soon forgotten. Afanas´ev, A. N.
In Afanas´ev, A. N. Russian fairy tales p273-75   **398.2**

Old Fire Dragaman
In The Jack tales p106-13   **398.2**

Old Granny and the bean thief. DeFelice, C. C.   **E**

The **old** king and the new king. Lester, J.
In Lester, J. The last tales of Uncle Remus p22-25   **398.2**

Old MacDonald had a farm (k-2)   **782.42**

The **old** man mad about drawing. Place, F.   **Fic**

The **old** man who made trees blossom. Sakade, F.
In Sakade, F. Japanese children's favorite stories   **398.2**

Old Mister Turtle gets a whipping. Hamilton, V.
In Hamilton, V. A ring of tricksters; animal tales from America, the West Indies, and Africa p91-95   **398.2**

Old Mother Hubbard. Cabrera, J.   **398.8**

Old Nan's ghost. San Souci, R.
In San Souci, R. A terrifying taste of short & shivery; thirty creepy tales p86-90   **398.2**

Old One-Eye
In Grandfather tales; American-English folk tales p205-07   **398.2**

The **old** people who turned into bears. Curry, J. L.
In Curry, J. L. The wonderful sky boat and other Native American tales of the Southeast p111-14   **398.2**

Old raw head. San Souci, R.
In San Souci, R. Even more short & shivery; thirty spine-tingling stories p144-46   **398.2**

Old Roaney
In Grandfather tales; American-English folk tales p195-204   **398.2**

Old Sally Cato. San Souci, R.
In San Souci, R. Cut from the same cloth; American women of myth, legend, and tall tale p67-73   **398.2**

Old Satan try Job plenty. Graham, L. B.
In Graham, L. B. How God fix Jonah p110-15   **398.2**

Old sow and the three shoats
In Grandfather tales; American-English folk tales p81-87   **398.2**

Old Testament women. Ward, E. M.   **221.9**

Old Thunder and Miss Raney. Darrow, S.   **E**

Old Turtle's 90 knock-knocks, jokes, and riddles. Kessler, L. P.   **793.73**

The **old** Willis place. Hahn, M. D.   **Fic**

The **old** witch. Jacobs, J.
In Jacobs, J. English fairy tales p312-17   **398.2**

The **old** woman and her dumpling. Hearn, L.
In Womenfolk and fairy tales p44-50   **398.2**

The **old** woman and her pig. Jacobs, J.
In Jacobs, J. English fairy tales p31-33   **398.2**

The **old** woman in a pumpkin shell. MacDonald, M. R.
In MacDonald, M. R. Celebrate the world; twenty tellable folktales for multicultural festivals p61-66   **372.6**

The **old** woman who ran away. Afanas´ev, A. N.
In Afanas´ev, A. N. Russian fairy tales p182-83   **398.2**

Old Yeller. Gipson, F. B.   **Fic**

Older, Jules
Telling time (k-3)   **529**

Ole & Trufa. Singer, I. B.
In Singer, I. B. Stories for children p249-53   **S C**

Olive the other reindeer. Seibold, J. O.   **E**

Oliver, Jenni
(il) Lowry, L. A summer to die   **Fic**

Oliver, Tony
(il) Winer, Y. Birds build nests   **598**
(il) Winer, Y. Frogs sing songs   **597.8**

Oliver. Hoff, S.   **E**

Oliver in the garden. See Beames, M. Night cat   **E**

Olivera, Francisco E.
(il) Cruz, A. The woman who outshone the sun   **398.2**

Olive's ocean. Henkes, K.   **Fic**

Olivia. Falconer, I.   **E**

Olivia Kidney. Potter, E.   **Fic**

Olly and me. Hughes, S.   **E**

Olson, Arielle North
Ask the bones: scary stories from around the world (4 and up)   **398.2**
Contents: The haunted forest; The murky secret; Next-of-kin; The bloody fangs; Ask the bones; The four-footed horror; Beginning with the ears; Fiddling with fire; The Laplander's drum; A night of terror; Nowhere to hide; The handkerchief; The mousetrap; The speaking head; The dripping cutlass; The black snake; The hand of death; The invisible guest; A trace of blood; The bridal gown; The greedy man and the goat; The evil eye

Olson, Steven P.
The trial of John T. Scopes (5 and up)   **345**

Olvina flies. Lin, G.   **E**

Olympic games
Fischer, D. The encyclopedia of the Summer Olympics (4 and up)   **796.48**
Knotts, B. The Summer Olympics (2-4)   **796.48**
Macy, S. Freeze frame (5 and up)   **796.98**
Macy, S. Swifter, higher, stronger (4 and up)   **796.48**
Woff, R. The ancient Greek Olympics (4 and up)   **796.48**

O'Malley, Kevin
Captain Raptor and the moon mystery   **E**

One lighthouse, one moon. Lobel, A.   **E**

One little lamb. Greenstein, E.   **E**

One little mouse. Chaconas, D.   **E**

One little seed. Greenstein, E.   **E**

One lonely sea horse. Freymann, S.   **E**

One monkey too many. Koller, J. F.   **E**

One morning in Maine. McCloskey, R.   **E**

"**One**, my darling, come to Mama"
In The Magic orange tree, and other Haitian folktales p165-70   **398.2**

One night in the Coral Sea. Collard, S. B., III   **593.6**

One nighttime sea. Rose, D. L.   **E**

One nosy pup. Wallace, C.   **E**

One Ox, Two Ox, Three Ox, and the Dragon King. Yolen, J.
In Yolen, J. Here there be dragons p118-47   **810.8**

One parent family *See* Single parent family

One potato. Pomeroy, D.   **E**

One red dot. Carter, D. A.   **E**

One riddle, one answer. Thompson, L.   **E**

One-room school. Bial, R.   **370.9**

One scary night. Guilloppé, A.   **E**

One small place by the sea. Brenner, B.   **577.6**

One small place in a tree. Brenner, B.   **577.3**

One smart goose. Church, C.   **E**

One smart skunk. Ziefert, H.   **E**

One thousand inventions & discoveries. See Bridgman, R. F. 1,000 inventions & discoveries   **609**

One tiny turtle. Davies, N.   **597.92**

One, two, I love you. See Schertle, A. 1, 2, I love you   **E**

One, two, three. See Mora, P. Uno, dos, tres: one, two, three   **E**

One, two, three go! See Lee, H. V. 1, 2, 3 go!   **495.1**

One, two, three O'Leary. Doyle, M.   **E**

One was Johnny. Sendak, M.   **E**

The **One** who would not listen to his own dream
In The Magic orange tree, and other Haitian folktales p71-74   **398.2**

One witch. Leuck, L.   **E**

One world, many religions. Osborne, M. P.   **200**

The **one** you don't see coming. Courlander, H.
In Courlander, H. and Herzog, G. Cow-tail switch, and other West African stories p31-40   **398.2**

O'Neill, Alexis
Estela's swap   **E**

O'Neill, Catharine
(il) Baker, B. Anna shares   **E**

O'Neill, Laurie
Little Rock (5 and up)   **370**

O'Neill, Mary Le Duc
Hailstones and halibut bones (k-3)   **811**

O'Neill, Ruth
Stealing dreams
In A Glory of unicorns p59-73   **S C**

Onion John. Krumgold, J.   **Fic**

Oniroku. Sierra, J.
In Sierra, J. Can you guess my name?; traditional tales around the world p55-[58]   **398.2**

Online catalogs
See also Libraries—Automation

Only a fair day's huntin'
In Grandfather tales; American-English folk tales p180-85   **398.2**

Only Emma. Warner, S.   **Fic**

Only passing through: the story of Sojourner Truth. Rockwell, A. F.   **92**

Only the names remain. Bealer, A. W.   **970.004**

Only you. Wells, R.   **E**

Only you can save mankind. Pratchett, T.   **Fic**

Onward [biography of Matthew Henson] Johnson, D.   **92**

Onyefulu, Ifeoma
Welcome Dede! (k-3)   **392**

Ooh-la-la. Marshall, J.
In Marshall, J. Rats on the roof, and other stories p55-61   **S C**

Oops! the manners guide for girls. See Holyoke, N. A smart girl's guide to manners   **395**

Oot-Kwah-Tah, the seven star dancers. Caduto, M. J.
In Caduto, M. J. and Bruchac, J. Keepers of the night; Native American stories and nocturnal activities for children p63-65   **398.2**

Open wide. Keller, L.   **617.6**

Opening days (4 and up)   **811.008**

Opera
Ganeri, A. The young person's guide to the opera (4 and up)   **792.5**
Siberell, A. Bravo! brava! a night at the opera (4 and up)   **792.5**
Fiction
Auch, M. J. Bantam of the opera   **E**
Stories, plots, etc.
Rosenberg, J. Sing me a story (4-6)   **792.5**
Verdi, G. Aïda (4 and up)   **792.5**

Operation Clean Sweep. Beard, D. B.   **Fic**

Operetta
See also Musicals

Opie, Iona Archibald
The lore and language of schoolchildren   **398**
See/See also pages in the following book(s):
Marcus, L. S. Ways of telling   **741.6**
(ed) Here comes Mother Goose. See Here comes Mother Goose   **398.8**
(ed) I saw Esau. See I saw Esau   **398.8**
(ed) My very first Mother Goose. See My very first Mother Goose   **398.8**
(ed) The Oxford book of children's verse. See The Oxford book of children's verse   **821.008**

Overland journeys to the Pacific

See also West (U.S.)—Exploration

Calabro, M. The perilous journey of the Donner Party (5 and up) **978**

Fisher, L. E. The Oregon Trail (4 and up) **979.5**

Johmann, C. Going west! (3-6) **978**

Lavender, D. S. Snowbound (4 and up) **978**

Leeper, D. R. The diary of David R. Leeper (4 and up) **92**

Steele, C. Famous wagon trails (5 and up) **978**

See/See also pages in the following book(s):

Freedman, R. Children of the wild West (4 and up) **978**

Fiction

Coerr, E. The Josefina story quilt **E**

Fleischman, S. Mr. Mysterious & Company (5 and up) **Fic**

Harvey, B. Cassie's journey (2-4) **Fic**

Hopkinson, D. Apples to Oregon **E**

Kay, V. Covered wagons, bumpy trails **E**

Lawlor, L. He will go fearless (5 and up) **Fic**

McDonald, M. All the stars in the sky (4 and up) **Fic**

Stanley, D. Roughing it on the Oregon Trail (2-4) **Fic**

Van Leeuwen, J. Bound for Oregon (4-6) **Fic**

Owen. Henkes, K. **E**

Owen & Mzee. Hatkoff, I. **599.63**

Owen Foote, frontiersman. Greene, S. **Fic**

Owens, Gail

(il) Byars, B. C. The Cybil war **Fic**

(il) Hurwitz, J. The adventures of Ali Baba Bernstein **Fic**

(il) Hurwitz, J. The hot & cold summer **Fic**

Owens, Jesse, 1913-1980

About

Adler, D. A. A picture book of Jesse Owens (1-3) **92**

See/See also pages in the following book(s):

Krull, K. Lives of the athletes (4 and up) **920**

Owl

In The Magic orange tree, and other Haitian folktales p29-36 **398.2**

The **owl** and the pussycat. Lear, E. **821**

Owl at home. Lobel, A. **E**

Owl babies. Waddell, M. **E**

Owl moon. Yolen, J. **E**

Owls

Esbensen, B. J. Tiger with wings (2-4) **598**

Gibbons, G. Owls (k-3) **598**

Markle, S. Owls (3-6) **598**

Mudd-Ruth, M. Owls (3-6) **598**

Sattler, H. R. The book of North American owls (4 and up) **598**

Fiction

Allen, J. I'm not cute! **E**

George, J. C. There's an owl in the shower (3-5) **Fic**

Hiaasen, C. Hoot (5 and up) **Fic**

Johnston, T. The barn owls **E**

Lobel, A. Owl at home **E**

Macdonald, S. Look whooo's counting **E**

Nicholls, J. Billywise **E**

Runton, A. Owly: The way home and The bittersweet summer (1-3) **741.5**

Waddell, M. Owl babies **E**

Yolen, J. Owl moon **E**

Owly: The way home and The bittersweet summer. Runton, A. **741.5**

Ox-cart man. Hall, D. **E**

The **ox** of the wonderful horns [story] Bryan, A.

In Bryan, A. Ashley Bryan's African tales, uh-huh p27-39 **398.2**

The **oxcart**. Kimmel, E. A.

In Kimmel, E. A. Sword of the samurai; adventure stories from Japan p41-51 **Fic**

Oxenbury, Helen

(il) Carroll, L. Alice through the looking glass **Fic**

(il) Carroll, L. Alice's adventures in Wonderland **Fic**

(il) Root, P. Big Momma makes the world **E**

(il) Rosen, M. We're going on a bear hunt **E**

(il) Trivizas, E. The three little wolves and the big bad pig **E**

(il) Waddell, M. Farmer duck **E**

Oxenbury, Helen, 1938-

See/See also pages in the following book(s):

Marcus, L. S. Ways of telling **741.6**

The **Oxford** book of children's verse **821.008**

The **Oxford** book of children's verse in America **811.008**

The **Oxford** companion to children's literature. Carpenter, H. **809**

The **Oxford** companion to fairy tales **398.2**

The **Oxford** dictionary of nursery rhymes **398.8**

The **Oxford** illustrated book of American children's poems **811.008**

Oxlade, Chris

Global warming (5 and up) **363.7**

A visit to England (1-4) **942**

A visit to Scotland (1-4) **941.1**

A visit to Wales (1-4) **942.9**

Oxygen

Farndon, J. Oxygen

In The Elements **546**

Ozark Mountains

Fiction

Rawls, W. Where the red fern grows (4 and up) **Fic**

P

P.S. Longer letter later. Danziger, P. **Fic**

Pablo remembers. Ancona, G. **394.26**

Palindromes—*Continued*

Fiction

Shulman, M. Mom and Dad are palindromes
     E

Pallotta, Jerry

Ocean counting   **E**

The **Palm** of my heart   **811.008**

Palmisciano, Diane

(il) Conford, E. A case for Jenny Archer
     Fic

Panahi, H. L.

Bebop Express   **E**

Panama

Lang, A. Baby sloth (k-3)   **599.3**

The **pancake**. Sierra, J.
  In Sierra, J. Nursery tales around the world
    p11-15   **398.2**

Panchyk, Richard

Archaeology for kids (5 and up)   **930.1**
Galileo for kids (5 and up)   **92**

Panda *See* Giant panda

Panda bear, panda bear, what do you see? Martin,
  B.   **E**

Panda rescue. Bortolotti, D.   **639.9**

Pandell, Karen

Journey through the northern rainforest (4 and
  up)   **578.7**
Saint Francis sings to Brother Sun (4 and up)
    271

Pandora (Legendary character)

Burleigh, R. Pandora (3-6)   **398.2**

Pang, Guek-Cheng

Canada (5 and up)   **971**
Mongolia (5 and up)   **951.7**
(jt. auth) Layton, L. Singapore   **959.57**

Pantheon (Rome, Italy)

DuTemple, L. A. The Pantheon (5 and up)
    726

Panther and Little Sister. Curry, J. L.
  In Curry, J. L. The wonderful sky boat and
    other Native American tales of the
    Southeast p115-20   **398.2**

Paolilli, Paul

Silver seeds (k-3)   **811**

Papa God and General Death
  In The Magic orange tree, and other Haitian
    folktales p75-78   **398.2**

Papa God and the Pintards. MacDonald, M. R.
  In MacDonald, M. R. Celebrate the world;
    twenty tellable folktales for multicultural
    festivals p193-97   **372.6**

"**Papa** God first, Man next, Tiger last"
  In The Magic orange tree, and other Haitian
    folktales p177-81   **398.2**

Papa God sends turtle doves
  In The Magic orange tree, and other Haitian
    folktales p87-90   **398.2**

Papa John's tall tale. Hamilton, V.
  In Hamilton, V. The people could fly; Ameri-
    can black folktales p76-80   **398.2**

Papagayo. McDermott, G.   **E**

Papago Indians

Baylor, B. The desert is theirs (1-4)   **577.5**

Paparone, Pamela

(il) Love, D. A. Of numbers and stars [biogra-
  phy of Hypatia]   **92**
(il) Roth, C. The little school bus   **E**

Papa's latkes. Edwards, M.   **E**

Papa's song. McMullan, K.   **E**

The **paper** airplane book. Simon, S.   **745.592**

Paper airplanes. Kelly, E. J.   **745.592**

Paper crafts

  See also Origami
Ancona, G. The piñata maker: El piñatero (k-3)
    745.594
Boursin, D. Easy origami (4 and up)   **745.54**
Check, L. Little Hands paper plate crafts (k-2)
    745.54
Diehn, G. Making books that fly, fold, wrap,
  hide, pop up, twist, and turn (4 and up)
    736
Garza, C. L. Making magic windows (3-6)
    736
Henry, S. Cut-paper play!   **745.54**
Hollein, N. Matisse (3-5)   **92**
Irvin, C. M. Paper cup mania (k-2)   **745.54**
Irvin, C. M. Paper plate mania (k-2)   **745.54**
Irvine, J. How to make holiday pop-ups (3-6)
    736
Johnson, G. Paper-folding fun! (3-5)   **745.54**
Kelly, E. J. Paper airplanes (4 and up)
    745.592
Lewis, A. The jumbo book of paper crafts (3-6)
    745.54
Rhatigan, J. Paper fantastic (3-6)   **745.54**
Simon, S. The paper airplane book (3-5)
    745.592

The **paper** crane. Bang, M.   **E**

Paper cup mania. Irvin, C. M.   **745.54**

Paper fantastic. Rhatigan, J.   **745.54**

Paper-folding fun!. Johnson, G.   **745.54**

Paper manufacture *See* Papermaking

Paper money

Parker, N. W. Money, money, money (3-5)
    769.5

Paper plate mania. Irvin, C. M.   **745.54**

The **paper** princess. Kleven, E.   **E**

Paperboy. Kroeger, M. K.   **E**

The **paperboy**. Pilkey, D.   **E**

The **papermakers**. Fisher, L. E.   **676**

Papermaking

Fisher, L. E. The papermakers (4 and up)
    676

Paprocki, Greg

(il) Tang, G. Math-terpieces   **510**

Papua New Guinea

Gascoigne, I. Papua New Guinea (5 and up)
    995.3

Parables

  See also Fables

Parades

Crews, D. Parade   **E**

Pennypacker, Sara
Stuart's cape (2-4)   **Fic**

Penobscot Indians
Fiction
Mead, A. Crossing the Starlight Bridge (3-5)
         Fic

Penraat, Jaap
About
Talbott, H. Forging freedom (4 and up)
         940.53

Pentagon (Va.) terrorist attack, 2001 *See* September 11 terrorist attacks, 2001

Pentland, Peter
Forensic science (4 and up)   **363.2**
Kitchen science (4 and up)   **641.3**
Party science (4 and up)   **507.8**
Toy and game science (4 and up)   **531**

A **people** apart. Kenna, K.   **289.7**

People at the center of [series]
Bardhan-Quallen, S. The Mexican-American War   **973.6**
Edelman, R. The War of 1812   **973.5**
Kupferberg, A. E. The Spanish-American War
         973.8

The **people** could fly [American black folktales] Hamilton, V.   **398.2**

The **people** could fly [story] Hamilton, V.
In Hamilton, V. The people could fly; American black folktales p166-73   **398.2**

The **people** could fly [the picture book] Hamilton, V.   **398.2**

People in the past [series]
Malam, J. Ancient Egyptian jobs   **932**

The **people** of Sparks. DuPrau, J.   **Fic**

People of the ancient world [series]
Calvert, P. The ancient Celts   **936**
Calvert, P. The ancient Inca   **985**
Lassieur, A. The ancient Greeks   **938**
Lassieur, A. The ancient Romans   **937**
Perl, L. The ancient Egyptians   **932**
Perl, L. The ancient Maya   **972**
Schomp, V. The ancient Chinese   **931**
Schomp, V. Ancient India   **934**
Schomp, V. Ancient Mesopotamia   **935**
Schomp, V. The Vikings   **948**
Sonneborn, L. The ancient Aztecs   **972**
Sonneborn, L. The ancient Kushites   **939**

The **people** of the trees. Climo, S.
In Climo, S. Monkey business; stories from around the world   **398.2**

People to know [series]
Fine, E. H. Gary Paulsen   **92**
Hill, C. M. Robert Ballard   **92**

The **people** with five fingers. Bierhorst, J.
         398.2

People's history [series]
Landau, E. Fleeing to freedom on the Underground Railroad   **973.7**
Miller, B. M. Declaring independence   **973.3**
Sullivan, G. Journalists at risk   **070**
Whitman, S. What's cooking?   **394.1**

People's history series
Miller, B. M. Buffalo gals   **978**

Peoples of Eastern Asia (5 and up)   **950**
Peoples of Europe (5 and up)   **940**
Peoples of the Americas (5 and up)   **970**
People's Republic of China *See* China
People's Republic of China. Dramer, K.   **951**
The **Pepins** and their problems. Horvath, P.
         Fic

Pepis, Aaron
(il) Khan, A. K. What you will see inside a mosque   **297.3**

Pepito the brave. Beck, S.   **E**
Peppe the lamplighter. Bartone, E.   **E**

Pequot Indians
Fiction
Ketchum, L. Where the great hawk flies (5 and up)   **Fic**

Percentage
Murphy, S. J. The Grizzly Gazette (1-3)
         513

Perception
See also Shape
Cobb, V. How to really fool yourself (5 and up)
         152.1

Pérez, Amada Irma
My diary from here to there (2-4)   **Fic**
My very own room   **E**

Pérez, L. King
First day in grapes   **E**

Perez, Lucia Angela
(il) Hayes, J. Little Gold Star   **398.2**
(il) Hinojosa, T. Cada niño/Every child
         782.42

Perfect harmony. Smith, C. R.   **811**
Perfect parties. Souter, G.   **793.2**

Perfect pets [series]
Altman, L. J. Big dogs   **636.7**
Altman, L. J. Parrots   **636.6**
Hinds, K. Hamsters and gerbils   **636.9**
Schafer, S. Lizards   **639.3**

The **perfect** pumpkin pie. Cazet, D.   **E**
The **perfect** puppy for me. O'Connor, J.   **E**
The **perfect** wizard [biography of Hans Christian Andersen] Yolen, J.   **92**

Perfection. Babbitt, N.
In Babbitt, N. The Devil's storybook p73-77
         S C

Performing arts
See also Dance

Pericoli, Matteo
See the city (4 and up)   **741.9**

Peril in the Bessledorf Parachute Factory. Naylor, P. R.   **Fic**

The **perilous** journey of the Donner Party. Calabro, M.   **978**

The **perilous** road. Steele, W. O.   **Fic**

The **period** book. Gravelle, K.   **612.6**

Perkins, Agnes
(jt. auth) Helbig, A. Dictionary of American children's fiction, 1995-1999   **028.5**
(jt. auth) Helbig, A. Many peoples, one land
         016.8

Perkins, Lynne Rae
All alone in the universe (5 and up)   Fic
Criss cross (6 and up)   Fic
Snow music   E
(il) Denslow, S. P. Georgie Lee   Fic

Perl, Lila
The ancient Egyptians (5 and up)   932
The ancient Maya (5 and up)   972
Four perfect pebbles (6 and up)   940.53
Piñatas and paper flowers (4 and up)   394.26

Pernu, Caryn
(jt. auth) Lewis, B. A. The kid's guide to social action   361.2

Perón, Eva, 1919-1952
See/See also pages in the following book(s):
Krull, K. Lives of extraordinary women (4 and up)   920

Perplexing people. Blackwood, G. L.   920

Perrault, Charles
Blue Beard
    In The Blue fairy book p290-95   398.2
Cinderella (k-3)   398.2
    In The Blue fairy book p64-71   398.2
    also in Princess stories; a classic illustrated edition   398.2
Little Thumb
    In The Blue fairy book p231-41   398.2
The master cat
    In The Blue fairy book p141-47   398.2
Puss in boots (k-3)   398.2
Puss in boots; adaptation. See Galdone, P. Puss in boots   398.2
Sleeping Beauty
    In Princess stories; a classic illustrated edition   398.2
The sleeping beauty in the wood
    In The Blue fairy book p54-63   398.2
Toads and diamonds
    In The Blue fairy book p274-77   398.2
(jt. auth) McClintock, B. Cinderella   398.2

Perrigo, Lynne
(jt. auth) Simpson, M. S. Storycraft   372.6

Perry, Matthew Calbraith, 1794-1858
About
Blumberg, R. Commodore Perry in the land of the Shogun (5 and up)   952

Perry, Phyllis J.
Buffalo (3-6)   599.64

Persephone. D'Aulaire, I.
    In Bauer, C. F. Celebrations; read-aloud holiday and theme book programs p199-202   808.8

Perseus (Greek mythology)
McCaughrean, G. Perseus (5 and up)   292
See/See also pages in the following book(s):
Hamilton, E. Mythology (5 and up)   292

Persia *See* Iran

Person, Diane Goetz
(ed) The Continuum encyclopedia of children's literature. See The Continuum encyclopedia of children's literature   028.5

Personal appearance
See/See also pages in the following book(s):
Griffin, M. The sleepover book (3-6)   793.2

Personal conduct *See* Conduct of life
Personal digital assistants
Cuddy, C. Using PDAs in libraries   004
Personal finance
Godfrey, N. S. Neale S. Godfrey's ultimate kids' money book (5 and up)   332.024
Hall, M. Credit cards and checks (3-5)   332.7
Hall, M. Your allowance (3-5)   332.024
Schwartz, D. M. If you made a million   E
Thomas, K. The kids guide to money cent$ (4-6)   332.024

Personal hygiene *See* Hygiene
Personal names
Onyefulu, I. Welcome Dede! (k-3)   392
Fiction
Henkes, K. Chrysanthemum   E
Hurwitz, J. The adventures of Ali Baba Bernstein (2-4)   Fic
Swanson, S. M. The first thing my mama told me   E
Folklore
Mosel, A. Tikki Tikki Tembo (k-2)   398.2

Peru
De Capua, S. Peru (2-4)   985
Antiquities
Reinhard, J. Discovering the Inca Ice Maiden (5 and up)   930.1
Folklore
    See Folklore—Peru

Pesach *See* Passover

A **Pet** for me (k-3)   811.008

Pete the sheep. See French, J. Pete the sheep-sheep   E

Pete the sheep-sheep. French, J.   E

Peter I, the Great, Emperor of Russia, 1672-1725
About
Stanley, D. Peter the Great (4 and up)   92

Peter II, Emperor of Russia, 1715-1730
See/See also pages in the following book(s):
Meltzer, M. Ten kings (5 and up)   920

Peter and the starcatchers. Barry, D.   Fic

Peter and the wolf. Prokofiev, S.   E

Peter and Wendy. See Barrie, J. M. Peter Pan   Fic

Peter Pan. Barrie, J. M.   Fic

Peters, Lisa Westberg
Cold little duck, duck, duck   E
Earthshake (3-5)   811

Peters, Russell M.
Clambake (3-6)   970.004

Petersen, David
Australia (2-4)   994

Petersham, Maud
(il) Sandburg, C. More Rootabaga stories   S C
(il) Sandburg, C. Rootabaga stories   S C

Petersham, Miska
(il) Sandburg, C. More Rootabaga stories   S C
(il) Sandburg, C. Rootabaga stories   S C

Peterson, Cris
Century farm (k-3) **630.1**
Extra cheese, please! (k-3) **637**
Fantastic farm machines (k-3) **631.3**
Horsepower (k-3) **636.1**
Wild horses (3-6) **599.66**

Peterson, Jeanne Whitehouse
Don't forget Winona **E**

Peterson, Roger Tory
A field guide to the birds of eastern and central North America (5 and up) **598**
A field guide to western birds (5 and up) **598**

Peterson, Virginia Marie
(jt. auth) Peterson, R. T. A field guide to the birds of eastern and central North America **598**

Peterson field guides for young naturalists [series]
Latimer, J. P. Butterflies **595.7**
Latimer, J. P. Caterpillars **595.7**

Pete's a pizza. Steig, W. **E**

Petey. Mikaelsen, B. **Fic**

Petit, Philippe, 1949-
About
Gerstein, M. The man who walked between the towers **E**

Petreycik, Rick
Rhode Island
In It's my state! [series] **973**

Petričič, Dušan
(il) Atkins, J. How high can we climb? **920**
(il) Dash, J. The longitude prize [biography of John Harrison] **92**

Petrini, Catherine M.
What makes me a Muslim? (3-5) **297.3**

Petroglyphs *See* Rock drawings, paintings, and engravings

Petrone, Valeria
(il) Murphy, S. J. Double the ducks **513**
(il) Serfozo, M. Plumply, dumply pumpkin **E**

Petrosino, Tamara
(il) Crawley, D. Cat poems **811**

Petry, Ann Lane
Tituba of Salem Village (6 and up) **Fic**

Pets

See also Domestic animals names of animals, e.g. *Cats; Dogs;* etc.
George, J. C. A tarantula in my purse (4-6) **92**

Fiction
Feiffer, J. A room with a zoo (3-5) **Fic**
Howard, A. Hoodwinked **E**
Kellogg, S. The mysterious tadpole **E**
Lindgren, B. Julia wants a pet **E**
Luthardt, K. Peep! **E**
MacLean, C. K. Mary Margaret and the perfect pet plan (3-5) **Fic**
Napoli, D. J. Sly the Sleuth and the pet mysteries (2-4) **Fic**
Orloff, K. K. I wanna iguana **E**
Poetry
A Pet for me (k-3) **811.008**

Pets. Avi
In Avi. What do fish have to do with anything? and other stories p121-50 **S C**

Pets and the handicapped *See* Animals and the handicapped

Petty crimes. Soto, G. **S C**

Petunia. Duvoisin, R. **E**

Peyton, K. M.
Pony in the dark [excerpt]
In Horse tales **S C**

Pfeffer, Wendy
Dolphin talk (k-2) **599.5**
From seed to pumpkin (k-1) **583**
From tadpole to frog (k-1) **597.8**
A log's life (k-3) **577.3**
Sounds all around (k-3) **534**
What's it like to be a fish? (k-1) **597**
Wiggling worms at work (k-3) **592**

Pferdehirt, Julia
Nothing at all
In Fire and wings: dragon tales from East and West p65-78 **S C**

Pham, LeUyen
(il) Bunting, E. Can you do this, Old Badger? **E**
(il) Chaconas, D. One little mouse **E**
(il) Katz, B. Once around the sun **811**
(il) Lasky, K. Before I was your mother **E**
(jt. auth) Macken, J. E. Sing-along song **E**

Pham, Viet Dinh
(il) Shea, P. D. Ten mice for Tet! **394.26**

A **phantom** at the wedding. Geras, A.
In Geras, A. My grandmother's stories; a collection of Jewish folk tales p76-87 **398.2**

The **phantom** tollbooth. Juster, N. **Fic**

Philadelphia (Pa.)
Fiction
Alexander, L. The Gawgon and The Boy (5 and up) **Fic**
Anderson, L. H. Fever, 1793 (5 and up) **Fic**
De Angeli, M. L. Thee, Hannah! (3-5) **Fic**
History
Murphy, J. An American plague (5 and up) **614.5**

Philadelphia chickens. Boynton, S. **782.42**

Philbrick, W. R. (W. Rodman)
REM world (4 and up) **Fic**
The young man and the sea (5 and up) **Fic**

Philip, Neil
Celtic fairy tales (4 and up) **398.2**
Contents: The battle of the birds; Fair, Brown, and Trembling; The brown bear of the Green Glen; The King of Ireland's son; The three blows; Rory the fox; Lutey and the mermaid; Give me a crab, John; The black bull of Norroway; Finn MacCool and the Scottish giant; Duffy and the devil; Molly Whuppie; The black cat; The king and the workman's daughter; The soul cages; The fiddler in the cave; The well at the world's end; The ship that went to America; The little bird; The tail

Horse hooves and chicken feet: Mexican folktales (4 and up) **398.2**
Contents: The flea; The story of the sun and the moon; The tailor who sold his soul to the Devil; The hog; Pedro the trickster; The shadow; Horse hooves and chicken feet; The seven oxen; The mule drivers who lost their feet; The two Marias; The priest who had a glimpse of glory; The brave widow; The endless tale; Cinder Juan

Physics

See also Nuclear physics

Gardner, R. Science projects about physics in the home (5 and up) **530**

Ross, M. E. Toy lab (3-6) **530**

Physiology

See also Human body

Berger, M. Why don't haircuts hurt? (2-4) **612**

Cole, J. The magic school bus inside the human body (2-4) **612**

Gray, S. H. The human body [series] (3-6) **612**

Rockwell, L. The busy body book (k-1) **612**

VanCleave, J. P. Janice VanCleave's the human body for every kid (4 and up) **612**

Walker, R. The Kingfisher first human body encyclopedia (3-5) **612**

Pianists

Reich, S. Clara Schumann (5 and up) **92**

The **piano**. Miller, W. **E**

Pianos

Fiction

Miller, W. The piano **E**

Pican in river grass. Graham, L. B.

In Graham, L. B. How God fix Jonah p67-70 **398.2**

Picasso, Pablo, 1881-1973

About

Hodge, S. Pablo Picasso (4 and up) **92**

Jacobson, R. Picasso (3-5) **92**

Scarborough, K. Pablo Picasso (5 and up) **92**

Pick-Goslar, Hannah

About

Gold, A. L. Memories of Anne Frank (5 and up) **92**

Pick, pull, snap!. Schaefer, L. M. **582**

Picketing *See* Strikes

Pickett, Bill, ca. 1860-1932

About

Pinkney, A. D. Bill Pickett, rodeo ridin' cowboy (k-3) **92**

Pickin' peas. MacDonald, M. R. **398.2**

A **picnic** in October. Bunting, E. **E**

A **picture** book of Amelia Earhart. Adler, D. A. **92**

A **picture** book of George Washington Carver. Adler, D. A. **92**

A **picture** book of Harriet Beecher Stowe. Adler, D. A. **92**

A **picture** book of Harriet Tubman. Adler, D. A. **92**

A **picture** book of Helen Keller. Adler, D. A. **92**

A **picture** book of Jackie Robinson. Adler, D. A. **92**

A **picture** book of Jesse Owens. Adler, D. A. **92**

A **picture** book of John F. Kennedy. Adler, D. A. **92**

A **picture** book of Louis Braille. Adler, D. A. **92**

A **picture** book of Sacagawea. Adler, D. A. **92**

A **picture** book of Samuel Adams. Adler, D. A. **92**

A **picture** book of Sojourner Truth. Adler, D. A. **92**

A **picture** book of Thomas Jefferson. Adler, D. A. **92**

A **picture** book of Thurgood Marshall. Adler, D. A. **92**

Picture books by Latino writers. York, S. **028.5**

Picture books for children

Carle, E. The art of Eric Carle **741.6**

Marcus, L. S. Side by side (4 and up) **070.5**

Marcus, L. S. Ways of telling **741.6**

Nespeca, S. M. Picture books plus **028.5**

Stevens, J. From pictures to words (k-3) **741.6**

York, S. Picture books by Latino writers **028.5**

Bibliography

Ammon, B. D. Worth a thousand words **011.6**

Blakemore, C. Faraway places **011.6**

Bromann, J. Storytime action! **027.62**

Cianciolo, P. J. Informational picture books for children **028.1**

Hall, S. Using picture storybooks to teach literary devices v3 **016.8**

Harms, J. M. Picture books to enhance the curriculum **011.6**

Lima, C. W. A to zoo **011.6**

Odean, K. Great books for babies and toddlers **028.1**

Indexes

Harms, J. M. Picture books to enhance the curriculum **011.6**

Picture books plus. Nespeca, S. M. **028.5**

Picture books to enhance the curriculum. Harms, J. M. **011.6**

Picture dictionaries

The American Heritage picture dictionary (k-1) **423**

The Cat in the Hat beginner book dictionary (k-3) **423**

DK illustrated Oxford dictionary (5 and up) **423**

Taback, S. Simms Taback's big book of words **E**

A **picture** of Freedom. McKissack, P. C. **Fic**

Picture puzzler. Westray, K. **152.14**

Picture that! [series]

Galford, E. The trail West **978**

Martin, A. Knights & castles **940.1**

Picture this. Friedman, D. **770**

Picture this!. Raimondo, J. **759.05**

Picture writing

See also Hieroglyphics

Pictures for Miss Josie. Belton, S. **E**

Pinkney, Jerry—*Continued*
(il) Hurwitz, J. New shoes for Silvia   **E**
(il) Kipling, R. The jungle book: the Mowgli stories   **S C**
(jt. auth) Lester, J. Black cowboy, wild horses   **E**
(il) Lester, J. John Henry   **398.2**
(il) Lester, J. The last tales of Uncle Remus   **398.2**
(il) Lester, J. Sam and the tigers   **E**
(il) McKissack, P. C. Goin' someplace special   **E**
(il) McKissack, P. C. Mirandy and Brother Wind   **E**
(il) Pinkney, G. J. Back home   **E**
(il) Pinkney, G. J. Music from our Lord's holy heaven   **264**
(il) San Souci, R. The talking eggs   **398.2**
(il) Schroeder, A. Minty: a story of young Harriet Tubman   **E**
(il) Taylor, M. D. Song of the trees   **Fic**

Pinkney, Jerry, 1939-
See/See also pages in the following book(s):
Marcus, L. S. Ways of telling   **741.6**

Pinkney, Myles C.
(il) Pinkney, G. J. Music from our Lord's holy heaven   **264**
(il) Pinkney, S. L. A rainbow all around me   **E**
(il) Pinkney, S. L. Read and rise   **E**
(il) Pinkney, S. L. Shades of black   **E**

Pinkney, Sandra L.
A rainbow all around me   **E**
Read and rise   **E**
Shades of black   **E**

Pinkwater, Daniel Manus
Blue Moose
In You read to me & I'll read to you; 20th-century stories to share p233-39   **E**
Fat men from space (3-6)   **Fic**
The Hoboken chicken emergency (3-6)   **Fic**
Lizard music (4 and up)   **Fic**

Pinkwater, Daniel Manus, 1941-
About
McGinty, A. B. Meet Daniel Pinkwater (1-3)   **92**

Pinkwater, Jill
(il) Pinkwater, D. M. The Hoboken chicken emergency   **Fic**

Pinkwater, Manus *See* Pinkwater, Daniel Manus, 1941-

Pinky and Rex. Howe, J.   **E**
Pinocchio. Young, E.   **Fic**
Pinocchio. See Collodi, C. The adventures of Pinocchio   **Fic**
Pinocchio, the boy. Smith, L.   **E**
¡Pio peep! (k-3)   **398.8**
Pioneer days. King, D. C.   **978**
Pioneer girl: the story of Laura Ingalls Wilder. Anderson, W. T.   **92**
Pioneer life *See* Frontier and pioneer life
Pioneer life in the American West. Steele, C.   **978**
A **pioneer** sampler. Greenwood, B.   **971.3**

A **pioneer** story. See Greenwood, B. A pioneer sampler   **971.3**
Pioneer summer. Hopkinson, D.   **Fic**
The **pious** cat. Yolen, J.
In Yolen, J. Meow; cat stories from around the world   **398.2**
Piper, Watty
The little engine that could   **E**
The **Piper** of Harmonia. Marcantonio, P. S.
In Marcantonio, P. S. Red ridin' in the hood; and other cuentos   **S C**
Pipkin, Gloria
At the schoolhouse gate   **373.1**
Pippi Longstocking. Lindgren, A.   **Fic**
The **pirate.** San Souci, R.
In San Souci, R. More short & shivery; thirty terrifying tales p97-102   **398.2**
The **pirate.** Schwartz, A.
In Schwartz, A. In a dark, dark room, and other scary stories p50-59   **398.2**
The **pirate** princess. Philip, N.
In Philip, N. and Naḥman, of Bratslav. The pirate princess and other fairy tales   **398.2**
The **pirate** princess. Yolen, J.
In Yolen, J. Not one damsel in distress; world folktales for strong girls p64-77   **398.2**
The **pirate** princess and other fairy tales. Philip, N.   **398.2**
Pirates
Butterfield, M. Pirates & smugglers (5 and up)   **910.4**

Fiction
Barry, D. Peter and the starcatchers (5 and up)   **Fic**
Fleischman, S. The 13th floor (4-6)   **Fic**
Fleischman, S. The Giant Rat of Sumatra (4 and up)   **Fic**
Fox, M. Tough Boris   **E**
Kimmel, E. A. Blackbeard's last fight   **E**
Long, M. How I became a pirate   **E**
Masefield, J. Jim Davis (5 and up)   **Fic**
McPhail, D. M. Edward and the pirates   **E**
Stevenson, R. L. Treasure Island (6 and up)   **Fic**

Poetry
Yolen, J. The ballad of the pirate queens (3-5)   **811**

Pirates & smugglers. Butterfield, M.   **910.4**
Pirican Pic and Pirican Mor. Lupton, H.   **398.2**
Pirner, Connie White
Even little kids get diabetes (k-1)   **616.4**
Pish, posh, said Hieronymus Bosch. Willard, N.   **811**
Pistolis, Donna Reidy
Hit list. See Becker, B. C. Hit list for children 2   **016.8**
Pitcairn, Ansel
(il) Bolden, T. Portraits of African-American heroes   **920**

Pitcher, Molly, 1754-1832
About
Rockwell, A. F. They called her Molly Pitcher (3-5) **92**

Pitzer, Susanna
Not afraid of dogs **E**

Piven, Hanoch
What presidents are made of (2-4) **920**

Pizarro, Francisco, ca. 1475-1541
About
Meltzer, M. Francisco Pizarro (5 and up) **92**

Pizza
Fiction
Fusco Castaldo, N. Pizza for the queen **E**

Pizza for Sam. Labatt, M. **E**

Pizza for the queen. Fusco Castaldo, N. **E**

A **pizza** the size of the sun. Prelutsky, J. **811**

Place, François
The old man mad about drawing (3-6) **Fic**
(il) Stevenson, R. L. The strange case of Dr. Jekyll and Mr. Hyde **Fic**

The **Place** my words are looking for (4 and up) **811.008**

Place names *See* Geographic names

Place value (Mathematics)
Murphy, S. J. Earth Day-hooray! (1-3) **513**

Places. Thomson, R. **704.9**

Places in time. Leacock, E. **911**

Plain, Nancy
(jt. auth) Custer, E. B. The diary of Elizabeth Bacon Custer **973.8**

Plain City. Hamilton, V. **Fic**

Planet earth/inside out. Gibbons, G. **550**

The **planet** hunters. Fradin, D. B. **523.4**

The **planet** of Junior Brown. Hamilton, V. **Fic**

Planet patrol. Lorbiecki, M. **577**

Planet under pressure [series]
Gifford, C. Pollution **363.7**
Mason, P. Poverty **362.5**

Planets
See also names of planets
Branley, F. M. The planets in our solar system (k-3) **523.4**
Cole, J. The magic school bus, lost in the solar system (2-4) **523**
Croswell, K. Ten worlds (5 and up) **523.4**
Dussling, J. Planets (1-3) **523.4**
Fradin, D. B. The planet hunters (5 and up) **523.4**
Gibbons, G. The planets (k-3) **523.4**
Ride, S. K. Exploring our solar system (4 and up) **523.2**
Rockwell, A. F. Our stars (k-2) **523.8**

The **planets** in our solar system. Branley, F. M. **523.4**

Plant conservation
See also Scarecrows

Plant ecology
Souza, D. M. Plant invaders (3-5) **581.6**

Plant introduction
Batten, M. Aliens from Earth (3-6) **577**

Plant invaders. Souza, D. M. **581.6**

Plantation life
Bial, R. The strength of these arms (4 and up) **326**
Erickson, P. Daily life on a Southern plantation, 1853 (4 and up) **975**
McKissack, P. C. Christmas in the big house, Christmas in the quarters (4 and up) **394.26**

Planting a rainbow. Ehlert, L. **E**

Plants
See also Ferns; Flowers; Mosses
Armentrout, D. 50 words about plants (3-5) **580**
Brown, R. Ten seeds **E**
Goodman, S. Seeds, stems, and stamens (2-4) **581.4**
Pascoe, E. Plants with seeds (2-5) **580**
Schaefer, L. M. Pick, pull, snap! (k-3) **582**
VanCleave, J. P. Janice VanCleave's plants (5 and up) **580.7**

Ecology
See Plant ecology
Fiction
Fleischman, P. Weslandia **E**
United States
Patent, D. H. Plants on the trail with Lewis and Clark (4 and up) **978**

Plants, Industrial *See* Factories

Plants on the trail with Lewis and Clark. Patent, D. H. **978**

Plants with seeds. Pascoe, E. **580**

Plants without seeds. Pascoe, E. **586**

Plate tectonics
Gallant, R. A. Dance of the continents (5 and up) **551.1**
Gallant, R. A. Plates (5 and up) **551.1**
Silverstein, A. Plate tectonics (5 and up) **551.1**

Plateosaurus and other early long-necked planteaters. Schomp, V.
In Schomp, V. Prehistoric world [series] **567.9**

Plates. Gallant, R. A. **551.1**

Platinum
Wood, I. Platinum
In The Elements **546**

Plato
Timaeus. See Balit, C. Atlantis **398.2**
Timaeus. See Balit, C. Atlantis **398.2**

Platt, Richard
Castle diary (4 and up) **Fic**
Eureka! (4 and up) **609**
Forensics (5 and up) **363.2**
Shipwreck (4 and up) **910.4**

Platypus
Collard, S. B. Platypus, probably **599.2**
Fiction
Riddell, C. Platypus **E**

Play
Fiction
Colón, R. Orson blasts off! **E**
Heap, S. What shall we play? **E**

Poetry

See also African poetry; American poetry; Animals—Poetry; Christmas—Poetry; English poetry; French poetry; Japanese poetry; Native Americans—Poetry; Scottish poetry; Spanish poetry and types of poetry; subjects with the subdivision *Poetry*

Frost, H. Spinning through the universe (4 and up)　**Fic**

See/See also pages in the following book(s):

Bauer, C. F. This way to books　**028.5**

Collections

The baby's bedtime book　**808.81**
The baby's book of baby animals　**808.81**
The baby's good morning book　**808.81**
The Beauty of the beast (4-6)　**811.008**
Christmas poems　**808.81**
Driscoll, M. A child's introduction to poetry (4 and up)　**808.81**
Eric Carle's animals, animals　**808.81**
Eric Carle's dragons dragons and other creatures that never were　**808.81**
A family of poems　**808.81**
Fishing for a dream　**782.42**
The Helen Oxenbury nursery collection (k-3)　**398.8**
Hello sunshine, good night moonlight (k-3)　**811.008**
Hot potato (k-2)　**811.008**
A kick in the head　**811.008**
The Kingfisher book of family poems (3-6)　**821.008**
My first Oxford book of animal poems (1-4)　**808.81**
The New Oxford treasury of children's poems (3-5)　**808.81**
Once upon a poem (3-6)　**808.81**
Poems for the very young (k-3)　**821.008**
Poetry by heart (3-5)　**821.008**
Sing a song of popcorn　**808.81**
Stone bench in an empty park (4 and up)　**811.008**
The Sun in me (2-4)　**811.008**
Talking to the sun: an illustrated anthology of poems for young people　**808.81**
War and the pity of war (5 and up)　**808.81**
Wicked poems (4 and up)　**811.008**
Winter poems　**808.81**
A Zooful of animals　**808.81**

Fiction

Creech, S. Love that dog (4 and up)　**Fic**
Crew, G. Troy Thompson's excellent peotry book (4 and up)　**Fic**
Jarrell, R. The bat-poet (2-4)　**Fic**
Montenegro, L. N. A bird about to sing　**E**
Myers, T. Basho and the river stones　**E**
Scieszka, J. Science verse　**E**

History and criticism

Driscoll, M. A child's introduction to poetry (4 and up)　**808.81**

Indexes

Index to children's poetry　**808.81**
Index to poetry for children and young people　**808.81**

Study and teaching

Bauer, C. F. The poetry break　**372.6**

Hopkins, L. B. Pass the poetry, please!　**372.6**
Livingston, M. C. Poem-making (4 and up)　**372.6**
The **poetry** break. Bauer, C. F.　**372.6**
Poetry by heart (3-5)　**821.008**

Poetry for young people [series]

Frost, R. Robert Frost　**811**
Hughes, L. Langston Hughes　**811**
Lear, E. Edward Lear　**821**
Sandburg, C. Carl Sandburg　**811**

Poetry from A to Z (5 and up)　**808.1**
Poetry matters. Fletcher, R.　**808.1**

Poets

See also Women poets

Gollub, M. Cool melons—turn to frogs!: the life and poems of Issa [Kobayashi] (3-6)　**92**
Herrera, J. F. The upside down boy (k-3)　**92**

Poets, American

Burleigh, R. Langston's train ride (1-4)　**92**
Cooper, F. Coming home [biography of Langston Hughes] (k-3)　**92**
Kerley, B. Walt Whitman (4 and up)　**92**
Lasky, K. A voice of her own: the story of Phillis Wheatley, slave poet (3-5)　**92**
Niven, P. Carl Sandburg: adventures of a poet (3-6)　**92**
Walker, A. Langston Hughes, American poet (2-5)　**92**

Pogány, Willy

(il) Colum, P. The Golden Fleece and the heroes who lived before Achilles　**292**

Pohaha. San Souci, R.

In San Souci, R. Cut from the same cloth; American women of myth, legend, and tall tale p87-91　**398.2**

Pohrt, Tom

(il) Frank, J. The tomb of the boy king　**932**
(il) Pearce, P. The little gentleman　**Fic**

Poison dart frogs. Dewey, J.　**597.8**

Poisonous animals

See also Rattlesnakes

A **Poke** in the I (4 and up)　**811.008**
Poker Face the Baboon and Hot Dog the Tiger. Sandburg, C.

In Sandburg, C. Rootabaga stories p39-43　**S C**

also in Sandburg, C. The Sandburg treasury; prose and poetry for young people p27-29　**818**

Polacco, Patricia

Babushka's doll　**E**
Babushka's Mother Goose　**398.8**
The bee tree　**E**
The butterfly (2-4)　**Fic**
Chicken Sunday　**E**
Christmas tapestry (2-4)　**Fic**
G is for goat　**E**
John Philip Duck　**E**
The keeping quilt　**E**
Luba and the wren (k-3)　**398.2**
Mommies say shhh!　**E**

Polacco, Patricia—*Continued*

Mr. Lincoln's way	E
Mrs. Katz and Tush	E
Mrs. Mack	E
My rotten redheaded older brother	E
Oh, look!	E
Pink and Say	E
Rechenka's eggs	E
Thank you, Mr. Falker	E
The trees of the dancing goats	E
Welcome Comfort	E
When lightning comes in a jar (2-4)	Fic
(il) Thayer, E. L. Casey at the bat	811

Poland

Gordon, S. Poland (2-4)	943.8
Heale, J. Poland (5 and up)	943.8
Hintz, M. Poland (5 and up)	943.8

Fiction

Hesse, K. The cats in Krasinski Square   E

Orlev, U. The island on Bird Street (5 and up)   Fic

Roy, J. R. Yellow star (5 and up)   Fic

Polar bear

Davies, N. Ice bear (k-3)	599.78
Gibbons, G. Polar bears (k-3)	599.78
Lockwood, S. Polar Bears (5 and up)	599.78
Markle, S. Polar bears (3-6)	599.78
Miller, D. S. A polar bear journey (2-4)	599.78
Nagda, A. W. Polar bear math (2-4)	513
Patent, D. H. A polar bear biologist at work (4 and up)	599.78
Patent, D. H. Polar bears (3-6)	599.78
Ryder, J. A pair of polar bears (k-2)	599.78

Fiction

Bloom, S. A splendid friend, indeed	E
Thompson, L. Polar bear night	E

Folklore

Dabcovich, L. The polar bear son (k-3)   398.2

A **polar** bear biologist at work. Patent, D. H.   599.78

A **polar** bear journey. Miller, D. S.   599.78

Polar bear math. Nagda, A. W.   513

Polar bear night. Thompson, L.   E

Polar bear, polar bear, what do you hear? Martin, B.   E

The **polar** bear son. Dabcovich, L.   398.2

Polar expeditions *See* Antarctica—Exploration

The **Polar** Express. Van Allsburg, C.   E

Polar regions

    See also Antarctica; Arctic regions; North Pole; South Pole

Conlan, K. Under the ice (4 and up)   578.7

Poles apart. Scott, E.   998

Police

Meltzer, M. Case closed (5 and up)   363.2

Polikoff, Barbara Garland

Life's a funny proposition, Horatio (5 and up)   Fic

Why does the coqui sing? (5 and up)   Fic

Polio. Draper, A. S.   616.8

Poliomyelitis

Draper, A. S. Polio (5 and up)   **616.8**

Kehret, P. Small steps: the year I got polio (4-6)   **92**

Fiction

Giff, P. R. All the way home (4 and up)   Fic

Polish Americans

Fiction

Bartoletti, S. C. A coal miner's bride (4 and up)   Fic

Cushman, K. Rodzina (5 and up)   Fic

Recorvits, H. Goodbye, Walter Malinski (3-6)   Fic

Polish refugees

Fiction

Serraillier, I. The silver sword (5 and up)   Fic

Politi, Leo

Song of the swallows   E

Political action committees *See* Lobbying

Political activists

Fiction

Bonners, S. Edwina victorious (3-5)   Fic

Political advocacy for school librarians. Schuckett, S.   027.8

Political campaigns *See* Politics

Politicians

United States

Brill, M. T. Barack Obama (5 and up)   92

Politics

Christelow, E. Vote! (k-3)   324

Hamilton, J. Running for office (3-5)   324

Politics, Practical *See* Politics

Polizzotti, Mark

(jt. auth) Hoestlandt, J. Star of fear, star of hope   E

Pollack, Pam

Virginia

   In World Almanac Library of the States series   973

Pollak, Barbara

(il) Haab, S. Dangles and bangles   745.5

Polland, Barbara K.

We can work it out (k-3)   303.6

Pollard, Simon

(il) Markle, S. Spiders   595.4

Pollock, Jackson, 1912-1956

About

Greenberg, J. Action Jackson [biography of Jackson Pollock] (3-6)   92

Pollock, Miriam Heddy

Minnesota

   In World Almanac Library of the States series   973

Pollock, Paul Jackson *See* Pollock, Jackson, 1912-1956

Pollock, Penny

The Turkey Girl (3-5)   398.2

When the moon is full (k-3)   811

Pollock, Steve

Ecology (4 and up)   577

Pollution

See also Air pollution; Environmental protection; Marine pollution; Water pollution

Bang, M. Nobody particular (4 and up)
          363.7
Bryan, N. Love Canal (5 and up) **363.7**
Gifford, C. Pollution (4 and up) **363.7**
Hirschmann, K. Pollution (5 and up) **363.7**

Fiction

Bunting, E. Someday a tree   **E**
Van Allsburg, C. Just a dream **E**

Pollution control industry

See also Recycling

Polyglot materials

Park, L. S. Mung-mung! (k-2) **413**
Park, L. S. Yum! Yuck! (k-2) **413**
Stojic, M. Hello world! (k-2) **413**

Polynesia

Fiction

Sperry, A. Call it courage (5 and up) **Fic**

Polynesians

Webster, C. Polynesians (3-5) **996**

Pomerantz, Charlotte

The chalk doll   **E**
The piggy in the puddle
 In You read to me & I'll read to you; 20th-
  century stories to share p26-30 **E**

Pomeroy, Diana

One potato   **E**
Wildflower ABC   **E**

Pompeii (Extinct city)

Caselli, G. In search of Pompeii (3-5) **937**
Deem, J. M. Bodies from the ash (4 and up)
          937
Osborne, M. P. Pompeii   **937**

Ponce de Leon, Juan, 1460?-1521

About

Otfinoski, S. Juan Ponce de Leon (5 and up)
          92

See/See also pages in the following book(s):
Fritz, J. Around the world in a hundred years (4
 and up)   **910.4**

Pond. Morrison, G.   **577.6**

Pond ecology

Morrison, G. Pond (2-4)   **577.6**

Fiction

Fleming, D. In the small, small pond **E**

Pond watching with Ann Morgan. Ross, M. E.
          92

Ponds

Poetry

Sidman, J. Song of the water boatman (3-5)
          811

Pony express

Harness, C. They're off! (3-5) **383**

Pony in the dark [excerpt]. Peyton, K. M.
 In Horse tales   **S C**

Poole, Amy Lowry

The ant and the grasshopper (k-3) **398.2**
How the rooster got his crown (k-3) **398.2**
The pea blossom   **E**

Poole, Josephine

Anne Frank (2-4)   **92**

Joan of Arc (2-4)   **92**

Poop. Davies, N.   **573.4**

Poor

Bial, R. Tenement (4 and up) **974.7**
Hopkinson, D. Shutting out the sky (5 and up)
          974.7

Poor is just a starting place. Wyatt, L. J. **Fic**

The **poor** wretch. Afanas´ev, A. N.
 In Afanas´ev, A. N. Russian fairy tales p177-
  79   **398.2**

Pop!. Bradley, K. B.   **530.4**

Pop art

Ford, C. T. Andy Warhol (2-4) **92**

Popcorn

De Paola, T. The popcorn book (k-3) **641.3**
Landau, E. Popcorn (2-4)   **641.3**

Popcorn. Stevenson, J.   **811**

The **popcorn** book. De Paola, T. **641.3**

The **popcorn** dragon. Thayer, J. **E**

Popp, K. Wendy

(il) Lorbiecki, M. Sister Anne's hands **E**

Popp, Wendy

(il) Bunting, E. One candle   **E**

Poppleton. Rylant, C.   **E**

Poppy. Avi   **Fic**

Popular authors series

Bostrom, K. L. Winning authors **920**
McElmeel, S. L. 100 most popular children's
 authors   **810.3**
McElmeel, S. L. 100 most popular picture book
 authors and illustrators   **810.3**

Popular mechanics for kids [series]

Pinchuk, A. Make amazing toy and game gadgets   **745.592**
Thomas, K. Blades, boards & scooters **796.2**

Popular music

See also Blues music; Country music; Gospel music; Rock music

Orgill, R. Shout, sister, shout! (6 and up)
          920

Popular science: science year by year **509**

Popular series fiction for K-6 readers. Thomas, R.
 L.   **016.8**

Population

Smith, D. J. If the world were a village (3-5)
          304.6

Porcupines

Jango-Cohen, J. Porcupines (3-6) **599.35**

Fiction

Moodie, F. Noko and the night monster **E**

Pordes, Laurence

(il) Brookfield, K. Book   **070.5**

Porte, Barbara Ann

Harry's birthday   **E**
If you ever get lost (2-4)   **Fic**

Porter, A. P.

Jump at de sun: the story of Zora Neale Hurston
 (4 and up)   **92**

Porter, Janice Lee

(il) Lowery, L. Aunt Clara Brown **92**

Porter, Pamela Paige

The crazy man (5 and up)   **Fic**

Presidents
Fiction
Bradley, K. B. The President's daughter (3-5)
Fic
Winters, K. My teacher for President **E**
United States
Adler, D. A. George Washington (5 and up)
92
Adler, D. A. A picture book of John F. Kennedy (1-3) **92**
Adler, D. A. A picture book of Thomas Jefferson (1-3) **92**
Bausum, A. Our country's presidents (5 and up)
920
Bial, R. Where Washington walked (3-6) **92**
Cohn, A. L. Abraham Lincoln (k-3) **92**
Freedman, R. Franklin Delano Roosevelt (5 and up) **92**
Freedman, R. Lincoln: a photobiography (5 and up) **92**
Fritz, J. Bully for you, Teddy Roosevelt! (5 and up) **92**
Fritz, J. The great little Madison (5 and up)
92
Harness, C. Abe Lincoln goes to Washington, 1837-1865 (2-4) **92**
Harness, C. George Washington (3-5) **92**
Harness, C. The revolutionary John Adams (3-6)
92
Heiligman, D. High hopes [biography of John F. Kennedy] (4 and up) **92**
Horn, G. The presidency (5 and up) **352.23**
Jurmain, S. George did it [biography of George Washington] (2-4) **92**
Kachurek, S. J. George W. Bush (4 and up)
92
Kent, D. Jimmy Carter (4 and up) **92**
Kraft, B. H. Theodore Roosevelt (5 and up)
92
Krull, K. Lives of the presidents (4 and up)
920
Piven, H. What presidents are made of (2-4)
920
Rubel, D. Scholastic encyclopedia of the presidents and their times (5 and up) **920**
Sommer, S. John F. Kennedy (5 and up) **92**
St. George, J. John & Abigail Adams (6 and up)
92
St. George, J. So you want to be president? (3-6) **973**
Stanley, G. E. America in today's world (1969-2004) (5 and up) **973.92**
Sullivan, G. Abraham Lincoln (4 and up)
92
Turner, A. W. Abe Lincoln remembers (k-3)
92
Winters, K. Abraham Lincoln: the boy who loved books (k-2) **92**
United States—Assassination
St. George, J. In the line of fire (4 and up)
364.1
United States—Election
The encyclopedia of U.S. presidential elections (5 and up) **324**
Granfield, L. America votes (4-6) **324**
Landau, E. The 2000 presidential election (2-5)
324

United States—Mothers
Fritz, J. George Washington's mother (1-3)
92
United States—Spouses
See Presidents' spouses—United States
The **President's** daughter. Bradley, K. B. **Fic**
Presidents' spouses
United States
Cooney, B. Eleanor [biography of Eleanor Roosevelt] (k-3) **92**
Fleming, C. Our Eleanor (5 and up) **92**
Freedman, R. Eleanor Roosevelt (5 and up)
92
Koestler-Grack, R. A. The story of Eleanor Roosevelt (2-4) **92**
St. George, J. John & Abigail Adams (6 and up)
92
Wallner, A. Abigail Adams (1-3) **92**
Press, Judy
All around town! (k-2) **307**
Around-the-world art & activities (k-2)
745.5
ArtStarts for little hands! (k-2) **745.5**
The kids' natural history book (3-5) **745.5**
The little hands big fun craft book **745.5**
Press
See also Newspapers
Pressure groups *See* Lobbying
Preston, Diana
Remember the Lusitania (5 and up) **940.4**
Pretty Penny. Yolen, J.
In Yolen, J. Not one damsel in distress; world folktales for strong girls p44-47
398.2
Price, Anne
(ed) Middle and junior high school library catalog. See Middle and junior high school library catalog **011.6**
Price, Kathy
The Bourbon Street musicians (3-5) **398.2**
Price, Pamela S.
Cool rubber stamp art (4-6) **761**
Cool scrapbooks (4-6) **745.593**
Price, Susanna
Click! fun with photography (4 and up) **771**
Price-Groff, Claire
Illinois
In It's my state! [series] **973**
Priceman, Marjorie
Emeline at the circus **E**
Hot air **E**
How to make an apple pie and see the world
E
(il) For laughing out loud. See For laughing out loud **811.008**
(il) Moss, L. Zin! zin! zin! a violin **E**
(il) Ogburn, J. K. The bake shop ghost **E**
Prichard, Mari
(jt. auth) Carpenter, H. The Oxford companion to children's literature **809**
A **pride** of African tales. Washington, D. L.
398.2

The **priest** who had a glimpse of glory. Philip, N.
In Philip, N. Horse hooves and chicken feet:
Mexican folktales p53   **398.2**

The **priest's** laborer. Afanas´ev, A. N.
In Afanas´ev, A. N. Russian fairy tales p332
398.2

Prigger, Mary Skillings
Aunt Minnie McGranahan   **E**

Primary physical science [series]
Mason, A. Move it!   **531**
Mason, A. Touch it!   **530.4**

Primary source history of the United States [series]
Stanley, G. E. America in today's world (1969-2004)   **973.92**
Stanley, G. E. An emerging world power (1900-1929)   **973.91**
Stanley, G. E. The European settlement of North America (1492-1763)   **973.2**
Stanley, G. E. The New Republic (1763-1815)   **973.2**

Primary sources in American history [series]
Houghton, G. The Transcontinental Railroad
385.09
O'Donnell, K. The gold rush   **979.4**

Primary sources in the library. Johnson, M.
027.8

Primates
Collard, S. B., III. In the wild (4-6)   **591.68**
Redmond, I. Gorilla, monkey & ape (4 and up)
599.8
Stefoff, R. The primate order (5 and up)
599.8

Primavera, Elise
(il) Fritz, J. Make way for Sam Houston   **92**
(il) Nolen, J. Raising dragons   **E**

The **prime** minister and the General. Fang, L.
In Fang, L. The Ch'i-lin purse; a collection of
ancient Chinese stories p51-62   **398.2**

Prime ministers
Great Britain
Binns, T. B. Winston Churchill (5 and up)
92

Primm, E. Russell
(ed) Favorite children's authors and illustrators.
See Favorite children's authors and illustrators
920.003

Prince, April Jones
Twenty-one elephants and still standing   **E**

Prince Danila Govorila. Afanas´ev, A. N.
In Afanas´ev, A. N. Russian fairy tales p351-56   **398.2**

Prince Darling
In The Blue fairy book p278-89   **398.2**

Prince Edward Island
Fiction
Montgomery, L. M. Anne of Green Gables (5
and up)   **Fic**

Prince Hyacinth and the dear little princess. Le
Prince de Beaumont, Madame
In The Blue fairy book p12-18   **398.2**

Prince Ivan and Byely Polyanin. Afanas´ev, A. N.
In Afanas´ev, A. N. Russian fairy tales p475-82   **398.2**

Prince Ivan and Princess Martha. Afanas´ev, A. N.
In Afanas´ev, A. N. Russian fairy tales p79-86   **398.2**

Prince Ivan, the firebird, and the gray wolf.
Afanas´ev, A. N.
In Afanas´ev, A. N. Russian fairy tales p612-24   **398.2**

The **prince** of the pond. Napoli, D. J.   **Fic**

Prince Rama and the monkey chieftain. Climo, S.
In Climo, S. Monkey business; stories from
around the world   **398.2**

Prince Rooster. Jaffe, N.
In Jaffe, N. and Zeitlin, S. J. While standing
on one foot; puzzle stories and wisdom
tales from the Jewish tradition p70-75
296.1

The **Prince** who ran away. Rockwell, A. F.
294.3

Princes and princesses *See* Princesses

The **princess** and the goblin. MacDonald, G.
Fic

The **princess** and the pea. Andersen, H. C.
also in Andersen, H. C. Hans Christian Andersen's Fairy Tales   **S C**
also in Princess stories; a classic illustrated
edition   **398.2**
also in De Paola, T. Tomie dePaola's Favorite nursery tales p64-67   **398.2**

The **princess** and the pea [illustrated by Dorothee
Duntze] Andersen, H. C.   **Fic**

The **princess** and the pea in miniature. Child, L.
E

The **princess** and the vagabone. Sawyer, R.
In Sawyer, R. The way of the storyteller
p319-33   **372.6**

Princess for a week. Wright, B. R.   **Fic**

Princess Furball. Huck, C. S.   **398.2**

The **princess** in the mirror. Jaffe, N.
In Jaffe, N. and Zeitlin, S. J. While standing
on one foot; puzzle stories and wisdom
tales from the Jewish tradition p38-44
296.1

The **princess** knight. Funke, C. C.   **E**

The **princess** mouse. Shepard, A.   **398.2**

Princess of Canterbury. Jacobs, J.
In Jacobs, J. English fairy tales p425-28
398.2

The **princess** on the glass hill. Asbjornsen, P. C.
In The Blue fairy book p332-41   **398.2**

The **princess** on the pea. Andersen, H. C.
In Shedlock, M. L. The art of the story-teller
p259-60   **372.6**

Princess stories (2-4)   **398.2**

Princess tales [series]
Levine, G. C. The princess test   **Fic**

The **princess** test. Levine, G. C.   **Fic**

Princess tombi-ende and the frog. Sierra, J.
In Sierra, J. Can you guess my name?; traditional tales around the world p63-[67]
398.2

The **princess** who never smiled. Afanas'ev, A. N.
In Afanas'ev, A. N. Russian fairy tales p360-63 **398.2**

The **princess** who wanted to solve riddles. Afanas'ev, A. N.
In Afanas'ev, A. N. Russian fairy tales p115-17 **398.2**

Princesses
Hansen, J. African princess (5 and up) **920**
Stanley, F. The last princess: the story of Princess Ka'iulani of Hawai'i (4 and up) **92**

Fiction
DeFelice, C. C. The real, true Dulcie Campbell **E**
Funke, C. C. The princess knight **E**
King-Smith, D. Lady Lollipop (3-5) **Fic**
Levine, G. C. The two princesses of Bamarre (5 and up) **Fic**
McKissack, P. C. Nzinga, warrior queen of Matamba (5 and up) **Fic**
Shannon, M. The red wolf **E**
Vande Velde, V. Wizard at work (3-6) **Fic**

Pringle, Laurence P.
Bats! (3-5) **599.4**
Come to the ocean's edge (k-3) **577.7**
Crows!: strange and wonderful (2-4) **598**
Dog of discovery (4-6) **978**
Drinking (5 and up) **362.292**
The environmental movement (5 and up) **363.7**
Everybody has a bellybutton (k-3) **612.6**
An extraordinary life (5 and up) **595.7**
Global warming (4 and up) **363.7**
Sharks!: strange and wonderful (3-5) **597**
Snakes! (3-5) **597.96**
Strange animals, new to science (4 and up) **591.68**
Whales! strange and wonderful (3-5) **599.5**

The **printers**. Fisher, L. E. **686.2**

Printing
History
Fisher, L. E. The printers (4 and up) **686.2**

Prints
Pomeroy, D. One potato **E**

Printup, Erwin
(il) Swamp, J. Giving thanks **299.7**

Prisoners
Fiction
Brisson, P. Mama loves me from away **E**
Lawrence, I. The convicts (5 and up) **Fic**
Stauffacher, S. Harry Sue (5 and up) **Fic**
Woodson, J. Visiting day **E**

Prisoners of war, German *See* German prisoners of war

Prize-winning science fair projects for curious kids. Rhatigan, J. **507.8**

Prizes, Literary *See* Literary prizes

Probabilities
Murphy, S. J. Probably pistachio (k-3) **519.2**

Probably pistachio. Murphy, S. J. **519.2**

Probing volcanoes. Lindop, L. **551.2**

Problem drinking *See* Alcoholism

Problem solving
Burns, M. The book of think (4 and up) **153.4**

The **problem** with chickens. McMillan, B. **E**

Professional growth series
Where do I start? **025.1**

Professions
See also Occupations

Programmed instruction
See also Computer-assisted instruction

Prohibition
Fiction
Reaver, C. Bill (5 and up) **Fic**

Proimos, James
The grade school zone
In Tripping over the lunch lady and other school stories p85-92 **S C**

Project Apollo
Bredeson, C. The moon (4 and up) **523.3**
Vogt, G. Apollo moonwalks (4 and up) **629.45**

Project Apollo *See* Apollo project

Project Mercury
Ashby, R. Rocket man [biography of John Glenn] (4-6) **92**

Project UltraSwan. Osborn, E. **598**

Prokofiev, Sergey
Peter and the wolf **E**

Prokofiev, Sergey, 1891-1953
See/See also pages in the following book(s):
Krull, K. Lives of the musicians (4 and up) **920**

Promises. Winthrop, E. **E**

Promises to keep: how Jackie Robinson changed America. Robinson, S. **92**

Promoting a global community through multicultural children's literature. Steiner, S. F. **016.8**

Propp, Vera W.
When the soldiers were gone (3-5) **Fic**

Prosek, James
A good day's fishing **E**

Prosmitsky, Jenya
(il) Cleary, B. P. Hairy, scary, ordinary **428**

Protecting forests. Dalgleish, S. **333.75**

Protecting Marie. Henkes, K. **Fic**

Protecting the right to read. Symons, A. K. **025.2**

Protecting wildlife. Dalgleish, S. **333.95**

Protection of birds *See* Birds—Protection

Protection of environment *See* Environmental protection

Protection of game *See* Game protection

Protection of wildlife *See* Wildlife conservation

Proteins
Royston, A. Proteins for a healthy body (4-6) **613.2**

Proteins for a healthy body. Royston, A. **613.2**

Puerto Ricans—United States—_Continued_
Kuklin, S. How my family lives in America
(k-3)   **305.8**
Puerto Rico
Burgan, M. Puerto Rico and outlying territories
_In_ World Almanac Library of the States series
                                        973
Davis, L. Puerto Rico
_In_ America the beautiful, second series
                                        973
Levy, P. Puerto Rico (5 and up)   **972.95**
Fiction
Delacre, L. Rafi and Rosi   **E**
Mohr, N. Going home (4-6)   **Fic**
Polikoff, B. G. Why does the coqui sing? (5 and
up)   **Fic**
Santiago, E. A doll for Navidades   **E**
Wallner, A. Sergio and the hurricane   **E**
Folklore
See Folklore—Puerto Rico

Puerto Rico and outlying territories. Burgan, M.
_In_ World Almanac Library of the States series
                                        973
Puffins
Gibbons, G. The puffins are back! (k-3)   **598**
McMillan, B. Nights of the pufflings (2-4)
                                        598
The **puffins** are back!. Gibbons, G.   **598**
Pullen, Zachary
(il) Frank, J. The toughest cowboy   **E**
Pullman, Philip
Aladdin and the enchanted lamp (3-5) **398.2**
Clockwork (4 and up)   **Fic**
The firework-maker's daughter (4 and up)
                                        Fic
I was a rat! (4 and up)   **Fic**
The scarecrow and his servant (4-6)   **Fic**
Pulver, Robin
Punctuation takes a vacation   **E**
Pumas
Fiction
Bledsoe, L. J. Cougar canyon (4 and up)
                                        Fic
Mora, P. Doña Flor   **E**
Naylor, P. R. The fear place (5 and up) **Fic**
Pumping iron _See_ Weight lifting
Pumpkin
Cave, K. One child, one seed   **E**
Cook, D. F. Kids' pumpkin projects (2-4)
                                        745.5
Gibbons, G. The pumpkin book (k-3)   **635**
Pfeffer, W. From seed to pumpkin (k-1)
                                        583
Fiction
Arnold, M. D. The pumpkin runner   **E**
Brown, M. W. The fierce yellow pumpkin   **E**
Holub, J. The garden that we grew   **E**
Hubbell, W. Pumpkin Jack   **E**
Kroll, S. The biggest pumpkin ever   **E**
Ochiltree, D. Sixteen runaway pumpkins   **E**
Serfozo, M. Plumply, dumply pumpkin   **E**
Titherington, J. Pumpkin, pumpkin   **E**
Wallace, N. E. Pumpkin day!   **E**
Yacowitz, C. Pumpkin fiesta   **E**

The **pumpkin** book. Gibbons, G.   **635**
The **pumpkin** child. MacDonald, M. R.
_In_ MacDonald, M. R. Celebrate the world;
twenty tellable folktales for multicultural
festivals p52-60   **372.6**
Pumpkin day!. Wallace, N. E.   **E**
Pumpkin eye. Fleming, D.   **E**
Pumpkin fiesta. Yacowitz, C.   **E**
The **Pumpkin** Giant
_In_ Diane Goode's book of scary stories &
songs p14-19   **398.2**
Pumpkin Jack. Hubbell, W.   **E**
Pumpkin, pumpkin. Titherington, J.   **E**
The **pumpkin** runner. Arnold, M. D.   **E**
Pumpkin soup. Cooper, H.   **E**
Punctuation
Terban, M. Punctuation power! (4 and up)
                                        428
Fiction
Pulver, R. Punctuation takes a vacation   **E**
Punctuation power!. Terban, M.   **428**
Punctuation takes a vacation. Pulver, R. **E**
Punia and the King of Sharks. Wardlaw, L.
                                        398.2
Puns
Terban, M. Funny you should ask (3-5)
                                      793.73
Punxsutawney Phyllis. Hill, S. L.   **E**
Puppets and puppet plays
Bauer, C. F. Leading kids to books through pup-
pets   **027.62**
Champlin, C. Storytelling with puppets
                                      372.6
Exner, C. R. Practical puppetry A-Z   **791.5**
Lohnes, M. Fractured fairy tales   **812**
Minkel, W. How to do "The three bears" with
two hands   **791.5**
Potter, G. The year I didn't go to school **E**
Fiction
Collodi, C. The adventures of Pinocchio (3-6)
                                        Fic
Harrison, B. Theo (5 and up)   **Fic**
Keats, E. J. Louie   **E**
Young, E. Pinocchio (3-6)   **Fic**
Puppies! Puppies! Puppies!. Meyers, S. **E**
The **puppy** who wanted a boy. Thayer, J. **E**
Puritans
Fiction
Gilson, J. Stink Alley (4 and up)   **Fic**
Speare, E. G. The witch of Blackbird Pond (6
and up)   **Fic**
Purmell, Ann
Apple cider making days   **E**
The **purple** coat. Hest, A.   **E**
Purple mountain majesties: the story of Katharine
Lee Bates and "America the beautiful". Youn-
ger, B.   **92**
Pushing up the sky. Bruchac, J.
_In_ Bruchac, J. Pushing up the sky: seven Na-
tive American plays for children p57-65
                                        812

Quilting—*Continued*

Storms, B. Quilting

also in Sadler, J. A. The jumbo book of needlecrafts   **746.4**

Thibault, T. Kids' easy quilting projects (3-6)   **746.46**

Quilts

Bial, R. With needle and thread (4 and up)   **746.46**

Hines, A. G. Pieces (k-3)   **811**

Hines, A. G. Winter lights (k-3)   **811**

Fiction

Cates, K. A far-fetched story   **E**

Coerr, E. The Josefina story quilt   **E**

Ernst, L. C. Sam Johnson and the blue ribbon quilt   **E**

Flournoy, V. The patchwork quilt   **E**

Guback, G. Luka's quilt   **E**

Hopkinson, D. Sweet Clara and the freedom quilt   **E**

Johnston, T. The quilt story   **E**

Johnston, T. That summer   **E**

Jonas, A. The quilt   **E**

Polacco, P. The keeping quilt   **E**

Root, P. The name quilt   **E**

Stroud, B. The patchwork path   **E**

Woodson, J. Show way   **E**

Quimby, Harriet, 1875-1912

About

Moss, M. Brave Harriet [biography of Harriet Quimby] (k-3)   **92**

Quinceañera (Social custom)

Hoyt-Goldsmith, D. Celebrating a Quinceañera (3-5)   **392**

King, E. Quinceañera (5 and up)   **392**

Quinito's neighborhood. Cumpiano, I.   **E**

Quinlan, Susan E.

Caribou (3-6)   **599.65**

Quinnie Blue. Johnson, D.   **E**

Quotations

See also Proverbs

Bartlett, J. Familiar quotations   **808.88**

R

Raatma, Lucia

Safety for babysitters (4 and up)   **649**

Safety in your neighborhood (4 and up)   **613.6**

Safety on the Internet (4 and up)   **025.04**

The **rabbi** is so smart, or How Chelm got bigger. Taback, S.

In Taback, S. Kibitzers and fools; tales my zayda (grandfather) told me   **398.2**

Rabbi Leib & the witch Cunegunde. Singer, I. B.

In Singer, I. B. Stories for children p89-97   **S C**

Rabbit (Legendary character)

Johnston, T. The tale of Rabbit and Coyote (k-3)   **398.2**

The **rabbit** and the moon. Sakade, F.

In Sakade, F. Japanese children's favorite stories   **398.2**

Rabbit and Wildcat. Curry, J. L.

In Curry, J. L. The wonderful sky boat and other Native American tales of the Southeast p35-38   **398.2**

Rabbit Hill. Lawson, R.   **Fic**

Rabbit makes a monkey of lion. Aardema, V.   **398.2**

The **rabbit** who crossed the sea. Sakade, F.

In Sakade, F. Japanese children's favorite stories   **398.2**

The **rabbit** who stole fire. Curry, J. L.

In Curry, J. L. The wonderful sky boat and other Native American tales of the Southeast p25-30   **398.2**

Rabbits

Gibbons, G. Rabbits, rabbits, & more rabbits! (k-3)   **599.3**

Holub, J. Why do rabbits hop? (k-2)   **636.9**

Jeffrey, L. S. Hamsters, gerbils, guinea pigs, rabbits, ferrets, mice, and rats (3-5)   **636.9**

Tagholm, S. The rabbit (2-4)   **599.3**

Fiction

Adams, R. Watership Down (6 and up)   **Fic**

Bianco, M. W. The velveteen rabbit (2-4)   **Fic**

Brown, M. W. Bunny's noisy book   **E**

Brown, M. W. Goodnight moon   **E**

Brown, M. W. The runaway bunny   **E**

Carlson, N. L. Harriet and the roller coaster   **E**

Dewan, T. Bing: paint day   **E**

DiCamillo, K. The miraculous journey of Edward Tulane (3-6)   **Fic**

Fleming, C. Muncha! Muncha! Muncha!   **E**

Ford, B. First snow   **E**

Gliori, D. Flora's surprise!   **E**

Henkes, K. So happy!   **E**

Heyward, D. The country bunny and the little gold shoes   **E**

Horse, H. Little Rabbit lost   **E**

Jennings, R. W. Orwell's luck (5 and up)   **Fic**

Keller, H. What a hat!   **E**

Klise, K. Shall I knit you a hat?   **E**

Lawson, R. Rabbit Hill (3-6)   **Fic**

Lee, H. B. While we were out   **E**

McBratney, S. Guess how much I love you   **E**

McMullan, K. Pearl and Wagner: two good friends   **E**

Moon, N. Tick-tock, drip-drop!   **E**

Peet, B. Huge Harold   **E**

Potter, B. The tale of Peter Rabbit   **E**

Raschka, C. Five for a little one   **E**

Rohmann, E. My friend Rabbit   **E**

Segal, J. Carrot soup   **E**

Wallace, N. E. Pumpkin day!   **E**

Wallace, N. E. Recycle every day!   **E**

Wells, R. Carry me!   **E**

Wells, R. Emily's first 100 days of school   **E**

Wells, R. Morris's disappearing bag   **E**

Wells, R. Read to your bunny   **E**

Wells, R. Ruby's beauty shop   **E**

Zolotow, C. The bunny who found Easter   **E**

Rabbits—Fiction—*Continued*
Zolotow, C. Mr. Rabbit and the lovely present
    E

Folklore
Hamilton, V. Bruh Rabbit and the tar baby girl
(k-3)   **398.2**
Han, S. C. The rabbit's tail (k-3)   **398.2**
MacDonald, M. R. Conejito (k-3)   **398.2**
MacDonald, M. R. Pickin' peas (k-3)   **398.2**
McDermott, G. Zomo the Rabbit (k-3)   **398.2**
Stevens, J. Tops and bottoms (k-3)   **398.2**
Wagué Diakité, B. The magic gourd (2-4)
    398.2
Ward, H. The hare and the tortoise (k-3)
    398.2

Rabbit's horse. Curry, J. L.
In Curry, J. L. The wonderful sky boat and
    other Native American tales of the
    Southeast p31-34   **398.2**
Rabbits, rabbits, & more rabbits!. Gibbons, G.
    599.3

The **rabbit's** tail. Han, S. C.   **398.2**

Rabble Starkey. Lowry, L.   **Fic**

Rabinovitch, Sholem *See* Sholem Aleichem,
1859-1916

Rabinowitz, Sholem Yakov *See* Sholem
Aleichem, 1859-1916

Rabinowitz, Solomon *See* Sholem Aleichem,
1859-1916

Raccoon tune. Shaw, N.   **E**

Raccoons
North, S. Rascal (5 and up)   **599.7**
Fiction
Friend, C. Eddie the raccoon   **E**
Hill, S. Ruby bakes a cake   **E**
Shaw, N. Raccoon tune   **E**
Folklore
Bruchac, J. Raccoon's last race (k-3)   **398.2**
Taylor, H. P. Brother Wolf (k-3)   **398.2**
Raccoon's last race. Bruchac, J.   **398.2**

Race, Pat
(il) Symons, A. K. Protecting the right to read
    025.2

Race awareness
Molin, P. F. American Indian stereotypes in the
    world of children   **970.004**
The **race** of the Birkebeiners. Lunge-Larsen, L.
    398.2

Race relations
    See also Ethnic relations; Multiculturalism
    names of countries, cities, etc., with the sub-
    division *Race relations*
Fiction
English, K. Francie (5 and up)   **Fic**
Fuqua, J. S. Darby (4 and up)   **Fic**
Hermes, P. Summer secrets (5 and up)   **Fic**
Jordan, R. Lost Goat Lane (5 and up)   **Fic**
Lorbiecki, M. Sister Anne's hands   **E**
Martin, A. M. Belle Teal (4 and up)   **Fic**
Mwangi, M. The Mzungu boy (5 and up)
    Fic
Pinkney, A. D. Fishing day   **E**
Raschka, C. Yo! Yes?   **E**
Reeder, C. Across the lines (5 and up)   **Fic**

Robinet, H. G. Walking to the bus-rider blues (5
    and up)   **Fic**
Rodman, M. A. Yankee girl (4 and up)   **Fic**
Sebestyen, O. Words by heart (5 and up)
    Fic
Spinelli, J. Maniac Magee (5 and up)   **Fic**
Taylor, M. D. The friendship (4 and up)
    Fic
Taylor, M. D. The gold Cadillac (4 and up)
    Fic
Taylor, M. D. Mississippi bridge (4 and up)
    Fic
Taylor, M. D. The road to Memphis (4 and up)
    Fic
Taylor, M. D. The well (4 and up)   **Fic**
Taylor, T. The cay (5 and up)   **Fic**
Taylor, T. Timothy of the cay (5 and up)
    Fic
Vander Zee, R. Mississippi morning   **E**
Weatherford, C. B. Freedom on the menu   **E**
Wiles, D. Freedom Summer   **E**
Woodson, J. The other side   **E**
The **racecar** alphabet. Floca, B.   **E**
The **racer.** Bierhorst, J.
    In Bierhorst, J. Is my friend at home?; Pueblo
    fireside tales   **398.2**
Races of people *See* Ethnology
Rachel: the story of Rachel Carson. Ehrlich, A.
    92
Racial balance in schools *See* School integration
Racially mixed people
Brill, M. T. Barack Obama (5 and up)   **92**
Taylor, G. George Crum and the Saratoga chip
    (2-4)   **92**
Fiction
Adoff, A. Black is brown is tan   **E**
Curry, J. L. The Black Canary (5 and up)
    Fic
Graham, B. Oscar's half birthday   **E**
Hamanaka, S. Grandparents song   **E**
Hamilton, V. Plain City (5 and up)   **Fic**
O'Connor, B. Me and Rupert Goody (4-6)
    Fic
Osborne, M. P. Adaline Falling Star (5 and up)
    Fic
Paterson, K. Jip (5 and up)   **Fic**
Yep, L. Angelfish (5 and up)   **Fic**
Yep, L. Thief of hearts (5 and up)   **Fic**
Racism
Lester, J. Let's talk about race (k-3)   **305.8**
Rackham, Arthur
(il) Irving, W. Rip Van Winkle   **Fic**
Racso and the rats of NIMH. Conly, J. L.   **Fic**
Raczka, Bob
More than meets the eye (k-3)   **750**
No one saw (k-3)   **759.06**
Unlikely pairs (4 and up)   **750**
Rader, Laura
(il) Markes, J. I can't talk yet, but when I do...
    E
Radin, Ruth Yaffe
Escape to the forest (3-6)   **Fic**
Radio Man. Don Radio. Dorros, A.   **E**
Radio rescue. Barasch, L.   **E**

Radio stations, Amateur *See* Amateur radio stations

Radioactive elements. Jackson, T.
In The Elements   **546**

Radioactive waste disposal
Scarborough, K. Nuclear waste (5 and up)
    363.7

Radioactivity
Nardo, D. Atoms (3-5)   **539.7**

Radunsky, Vladimir
The mighty asparagus   **E**
One   **E**
What does peace feel like?   **E**
(il) Martin, B. The maestro plays   **E**

Rael, Elsa Okon
Rivka's first Thanksgiving   **E**

Raffi
Baby Beluga (k-2)   **782.42**
Down by the bay (k-2)   **782.42**
Five little ducks (k-2)   **782.42**

Raffi songs to read [series]
Raffi. Baby Beluga   **782.42**
Raffi. Down by the bay   **782.42**
Raffi. Five little ducks   **782.42**

Rafi and Rosi. Delacre, L.   **E**

Rafle, Sarah
North Carolina
In World Almanac Library of the States series
    973

The **raft**. LaMarche, J.   **E**

Rafting (Sports)
Fiction
LaMarche, J. The raft   **E**
Wilson, S. Big day on the river   **E**

Rage *See* Anger

Raglin, Tim
(il) Coville, B. William Shakespeare's Twelfth night   **822.3**
(il) Elya, S. M. Cowboy José   **E**

Ragtime Tumpie. Schroeder, A.   **E**

Raible, Alton
(il) Snyder, Z. K. The Egypt game   **Fic**
(il) Snyder, Z. K. The headless cupid   **Fic**
(il) Snyder, Z. K. The witches of Worm   **Fic**

Railroad fever. Halpern, M.   **385.09**

Railroads
Barton, B. Trains (k-1)   **625.1**
Big book of trains (4-6)   **625.1**
Crews, D. Freight train   **E**
Simon, S. Seymour Simon's book of trains (k-3)
    625.1
Zimmermann, K. R. All aboard! (5 and up)
    385
Fiction
Brown, M. W. Two little trains   **E**
Crews, D. Shortcut   **E**
Durbin, W. The journal of Sean Sullivan (5 and up)   **Fic**
Goble, P. Death of the iron horse   **E**
Johnson, A. I dream of trains   **E**
Macaulay, D. Black and white   **E**
Nesbit, E. The railway children (4-6)   **Fic**
Panahi, H. L. Bebop Express   **E**

Piper, W. The little engine that could   **E**
Ray, M. L. All aboard!   **E**
Sturges, P. I love trains!   **E**
Wilcoxen, C. Niccolini's song   **E**
Yep, L. Dragon's gate (6 and up)   **Fic**
History
Halpern, M. Railroad fever (4-6)   **385.09**
Houghton, G. The Transcontinental Railroad (5 and up)   **385.09**
Landau, E. The transcontinental railroad (5 and up)   **385.09**
Meltzer, M. Hear that train whistle blow! (5 and up)   **385.09**
Murphy, J. Across America on an emigrant train [biography of Robert Louis Stevenson] (5 and up)   **92**
Thompson, L. The transcontinental railroad (4-6)
    385.09
Poetry
Booth, P. Crossing (k-3)   **811**
Songs
Hillenbrand, W. Down by the station (k-2)
    782.42

Railroads, Cable *See* Cable railroads

The **railway** children. Nesbit, E.   **Fic**

Raimondo, Joyce
Express yourself! (1-5)   **709.04**
Imagine that! (1-5)   **709.04**
Picture this! (1-5)   **759.05**

Rain
See also Droughts
Branley, F. M. Down comes the rain (k-3)
    551.57
Fiction
Bridges, M. P. I love the rain!   **E**
Dragonwagon, C. And then it rained . . .   **E**
Hesse, K. Come on, rain!   **E**
Ray, M. L. Red rubber boot day   **E**
Shannon, D. The rain came down   **E**
Stojic, M. Rain   **E**
Weeks, S. Drip, drop   **E**
Winter, J. Elsina's clouds   **E**
Poetry
Evans, L. Rain song (k-1)   **811**
Sidman, J. Meow ruff (1-3)   **811**

Rain. Stojic, M.   **E**

Rain & hail. See Branley, F. M. Down comes the rain   **551.57**

The **rain** came down. Shannon, D.   **E**

Rain forest animals
Kratter, P. The living rain forest (k-3)   **591.7**
Fiction
Witte, A. The parrot Tico Tango   **E**

Rain forest ecology
Fusco Castaldo, N. Rainforests (2-5)   **577.3**
Gibbons, G. Nature's green umbrella (k-3)
    577.3
Greenaway, T. Jungle (4 and up)   **577.3**
Grupper, J. Destination: rain forest (3-6)
    577.3
Jackson, T. Tropical forests (5 and up)
    577.3
Johansson, P. The tropical rain forest (3-5)
    577.3

Rain forest ecology—*Continued*
Lasky, K. The most beautiful roof in the world (4 and up) **577.3**
Pandell, K. Journey through the northern rainforest (4 and up) **578.7**
Patent, D. H. Garden of the spirit bear (3-5) **599.78**
Stille, D. R. Tropical rain forest (2-4) **577.3**

Rain forests
Collard, S. B., III. In the rain forest canopy (4-6) **578**
Grupper, J. Destination: rain forest (3-6) **577.3**
Lang, A. Baby sloth (k-3) **599.3**
Patent, D. H. Flashy fantastic rain forest frogs (k-3) **597.8**
Fiction
Baker, J. Where the forest meets the sea **E**
Cherry, L. The great kapok tree **E**
Cowley, J. Red-eyed tree frog **E**
Olaleye, I. Bitter bananas **E**
Rain makes applesauce. Scheer, J. **E**
Rain May and Captain Daniel. *See* Bateson, C. Stranded in Boringsville **Fic**
Rain player. Wisniewski, D. **E**
Rain, rain, rain forest. Guiberson, B. Z. **577.3**
Rain song. Evans, L. **811**
A **rainbow** all around me. Pinkney, S. L. **E**
The **rainbow** hand. Wong, J. S. **811**
Rainbows are made: poems. Sandburg, C. **811**
Raines, Shirley C.
Story stretchers for infants, toddlers, and twos **372.4**

Rainey, Ma, 1886-1939
See/See also pages in the following book(s):
Orgill, R. Shout, sister, shout! (6 and up) **920**

Rainfall *See* Rain
Rainforests. Fusco Castaldo, N. **577.3**
Rainmaker. Jackson, A. **Fic**
The **rainmaker.** Medearis, A. S.
In Medearis, A. S. Haunts; five hair-raising tales p22-31 **S C**
Raisel's riddle. Silverman, E. **398.2**
Raising dragons. Nolen, J. **E**
Raising voices. Sima, J. **027.62**
Rajendra, Rudi
(jt. auth) Rajendra, V. Iran **955**
Rajendra, Sundran
(jt. auth) Rajendra, V. Australia **994**
Rajendra, Vijeya
Australia (5 and up) **994**
Iran (5 and up) **955**
Rakitin, Sarah
(il) Burgess, R. Kids make magic! **793.8**
(il) Dall, M. D. Little Hands create! **745.5**
(il) Littlefield, C. A. Awesome ocean science! **551.46**

The **ram** in the chile patch. Sierra, J.
In Sierra, J. Nursery tales around the world p47-51 **398.2**

The **ram,** the cat, and the twelve wolves. Afanas'ev, A. N.
In Afanas'ev, A. N. Russian fairy tales p196-98 **398.2**
The **ram** who lost half his skin. Afanas'ev, A. N.
In Afanas'ev, A. N. Russian fairy tales p188-91 **398.2**
Ramá, Sue
(il) Park, L. S. Yum! Yuck! **413**
Râma (Hindu deity)
Weitzman, D. L. Rama and Sita (3-6) **398.2**
Rama and Sita. Weitzman, D. L. **398.2**
Ramadan
Douglass, S. L. Ramadan (1-3) **297.3**
Ghazi, S. H. Ramadan (k-3) **297.3**
Hoyt-Goldsmith, D. Celebrating Ramadan (3-5) **297.3**
The **Ramayana** and Hinduism. Ganeri, A. **294.5**
Rambé and Ambé. Yolen, J.
In Yolen, J. Meow; cat stories from around the world **398.2**
Ramen, Fred
SARS (4-6) **614.5**
Ramirez, Antonio
Napi **E**
Ramirez, José
(il) Cumpiano, I. Quinito's neighborhood **E**
Ramon, Ilan, 1954-2003
About
Stone, T. L. Ilan Ramon, Israel's first astronaut (3-5) **92**
Ramona the pest. Cleary, B. **Fic**
Ramos Nieves, Ernesto
(il) Bernier-Grand, C. T. Juan Bobo **398.2**
Rampersad, Arnold
(ed) Hughes, L. Langston Hughes **811**
The **Ramsay** scallop. Temple, F. **Fic**
Ramsey, Alice Huyler, d. 1983
About
Brown, D. Alice Ramsey's grand adventure (k-3) **92**
Ranch life
Freedman, R. In the days of the vaqueros (4 and up) **636.2**
King, D. C. Wild West days (3-6) **978**
Steele, C. Cattle ranching in the American West (5 and up) **978**
Rand, Donna
Black Books Galore!—guide to great African American children's books about boys **016.3058**
Rand, Gloria
Mary was a little lamb **E**
Sailing home (2-4) **Fic**
Rand, Ted
(il) Blumenthal, D. Ice palace **E**
(il) Bunting, E. The memory string **E**
(il) Bunting, E. Night tree **E**
(il) Bunting, E. Secret place **E**
(il) Cheng, A. Anna the bookbinder **E**
(il) Cleary, B. The hullabaloo ABC **E**
(il) George, J. C. Nutik, the wolf pup **E**

Raschka, Christopher—*Continued*
(il) Zeitlin, S. J. The four corners of the sky
201

Rascol, Sabina I.
The impudent rooster (k-3)   **398.2**

Rashkin, Rachel
Feeling better (4 and up)   **616.89**

Raskin, Ellen
The mysterious disappearance of Leon (I mean
Noel) (4 and up)   **Fic**
The Westing game (5 and up)   **Fic**

Rathmann, Peggy
10 minutes till bedtime   **E**
The day the babies crawled away   **E**
Good night, Gorilla   **E**
Officer Buckle and Gloria   **E**

Rats
Conniff, R. Rats! (3-6)   **599.35**
Jeffrey, L. S. Hamsters, gerbils, guinea pigs,
rabbits, ferrets, mice, and rats (3-5)   **636.9**
Markle, S. Outside and inside rats and mice
(2-4)   **599.35**
McNicholas, J. Rats (4 and up)   **636.9**
          Fiction
Bang-Campbell, M. Little Rat sets sail   **E**
Conly, J. L. Racso and the rats of NIMH (4 and
up)   **Fic**
Crocker, C. The tale of the swamp rat (4 and
up)   **Fic**
Daley, M. J. Space station rat (4-6)   **Fic**
Egielski, R. Slim and Jim   **E**
Jarvis, R. The dark portal (5 and up)   **Fic**
McPhail, D. M. Big Brown Bear's up and down
day   **E**
Meddaugh, S. Cinderella's rat   **E**
O'Brien, R. C. Mrs. Frisby and the rats of
NIMH (4 and up)   **Fic**
Stevenson, J. The most amazing dinosaur   **E**
          Folklore
Young, E. Cat and Rat (k-3)   **398.2**

Rats!. Cutler, J.   **Fic**

Rats on the range. Marshall, J.
In Marshall, J. Rats on the range and other
stories p63-71   **S C**

Rats on the range and other stories. Marshall, J.
    S C

Rats on the roof. Marshall, J.
In Marshall, J. Rats on the roof, and other
stories p7-17   **S C**

Rats on the roof, and other stories. Marshall, J.
    S C

Rattigan, Jama Kim
Dumpling soup   **E**

Rattlesnake Mesa. Weber, E. N. R.   **92**

Rattlesnakes
          Folklore
Moroney, L. Baby rattlesnake (k-2)   **398.2**

Rattletrap car. Root, P.   **E**

Rau, Dana Meachen
Black holes (3-5)   **523.8**
Iraq (2-4)   **956.7**
The Milky Way and other galaxies (3-5)
    523.1
Singapore (2-4)   **959.57**

A star in my orange   **E**
What's inside me? [series] (k-3)   **612**

Rauzon, Mark J.
Water, water everywhere (k-3)   **551.48**

Raven, Margot
Circle unbroken   **E**

Raven. McDermott, G.   **398.2**

The **raven** and the lobster. Afanas'ev, A. N.
In Afanas'ev, A. N. Russian fairy tales p612
    398.2

The **raven** and the star fruit. Garland, S.
In Garland, S. Children of the dragon; selected tales from Vietnam p38-49   **398.2**

The **Ravenmaster's** secret. Woodruff, E.   **Fic**

Ravens
          Fiction
George, J. C. Charlie's raven (5 and up)
    Fic
Woodruff, E. The Ravenmaster's secret (5 and
up)   **Fic**

Ravishankar, Anushka
Tiger on a tree   **E**

Rawlings, Marjorie Kinnan
The yearling (6 and up)   **Fic**

Rawls, Wilson
Where the red fern grows (4 and up)   **Fic**

Ray, Deborah Kogan
Flower hunter [biography of William Bartram]
(3-5)   **92**
Hokusai (3-6)   **92**
(il) Coerr, E. Chang's paper pony   **E**
(il) Harvey, B. Cassie's journey   **Fic**
(il) Harvey, B. My prairie Christmas   **Fic**
(il) Johnston, T. The barn owls   **E**

Ray, Delia
Ghost girl (5 and up)   **Fic**

Ray, Jane
Adam and Eve and the Garden of Eden (k-3)
    222
(il) Bible. O.T. Genesis. The story of the creation   **222**
(il) Doherty, B. Fairy tales   **398.2**
(il) Henderson, K. Lugalbanda: **398.2**

Ray, Mary Lyn
All aboard!   **E**
Basket moon   **E**
Red rubber boot day   **E**

Ray, Virginia Lawrence
School wide book events   **027.8**

Rayevsky, Robert
(il) Hodges, M. Joan of Arc   **92**
(il) Kimmel, E. A. Three sacks of truth
    398.2

Raymond's perfect present. Louie, T. O.   **E**

Rays (Fishes)
Walker, S. M. Rays (3-6)   **597**

Rayyan, Omar
(il) Ghazi, S. H. Ramadan   **297.3**
(il) Stewig, J. W. King Midas   **398.2**

Razzamadaddy. Walvoord, L.   **E**

Reaching for the moon. Aldrin, B.   **92**

Read, Mary, 1680-1721
    Poetry
    Yolen, J. The ballad of the pirate queens (3-5)
        811
Read a rhyme, write a rhyme (2-4)   **811.008**
The **read-aloud** handbook. Trelease, J.   **028.5**
Read-aloud rhymes for the very young (k-2)
        821.008
Read and rise. Pinkney, S. L.   **E**
Read and wonder [series]
    King-Smith, D. All pigs are beautiful   **636.4**
    King-Smith, D. I love guinea pigs   **636.9**
Read for the fun of it. Bauer, C. F.   **027.62**
Read to your bunny. Wells, R.   **E**
Readers' theater
    Shepard, A. Stories on stage   **812**
Reading
    Bouchard, D. The gift of reading   **372.4**
    Bradbury, J. Children's book corner   **372.4**
    Hauser, J. F. Wow! I'm reading! (k-2)
        372.4
    Herb, S. Using children's books in preschool
      settings   **372.4**
    Pinkney, S. L. Read and rise   **E**
    Fiction
    Bunting, E. The Wednesday surprise   **E**
    Daly, N. Once upon a time   **E**
    Gilson, J. Do bananas chew gum? (4-6)   **Fic**
    Hest, A. Mr. George Baker   **E**
    Park, F. The royal bee   **E**
    Paterson, K. Marvin one too many   **E**
    Polacco, P. Thank you, Mr. Falker   **E**
    Walter, M. P. Alec's primer   **E**
Reading activities. Miller, P.   **025.5**
Reading activities series
    Totten, K. Seasonal storytime crafts   **372.6**
Reading interests of children *See* Children—
    Books and reading
Reading Is Fundamental, Inc.
    The art of reading. See The art of reading
        741.6
Reading magic. Fox, M.   **028.5**
Reading raps. Soltan, R.   **027.62**
Ready for chapters [series]
    Hopkinson, D. Pioneer summer   **Fic**
    McKissack, P. C. Tippy Lemmey   **Fic**
Ready, set, grow!. Madaras, L.   **613.9**
Ready, set, preschool!. Hays, A. J.   **E**
Ready-to-go storytimes. Benton, G.   **027.62**
Ready-to-read [series]
    Hopkinson, D. Billy and the rebel   **E**
Ready-to-read stories of famous Americans [series]
    Hopkinson, D. Susan B. Anthony   **92**
A **real** American. Easton, R.   **Fic**
Real estate
    See also Land tenure
The **Real** Mother Goose   **398.8**
The **real** slam dunk. Richardson, C. K.   **Fic**
The **real** thief. Steig, W.   **Fic**

The **real,** true Dulcie Campbell. DeFelice, C. C.
        E
The **real** Vikings. Berger, M.   **948**
Really hot science projects with temperature.
    Gardner, R.   **536**
Really wild life of insects [series]
    Hipp, A. Orchid mantises   **595.7**
    Hipp, A. Peanut-head bugs   **595.7**
Reardon, Mary
    (il) McSwigan, M. Snow treasure   **Fic**
The **reasons** for seasons. Gibbons, G.   **525**
Reaver, Chap
    Bill (5 and up)   **Fic**
Rebecca of Sunnybrook Farm. Wiggin, K. D. S.
        Fic
Rebels against slavery. McKissack, P. C.   **326**
Rebuilding the body. Fullick, A.   **617.9**
RebuildingBooks, relationships, divorce and beyond [series]
    MacGregor, C. Jigsaw puzzle family   **306.8**
Recess at 20 below. Aillaud, C. L.   **371.2**
Rechenka's eggs. Polacco, P.   **E**
Recipes *See* Cooking
Recipes for art and craft materials. Sattler, H. R.
        745.5
Reconstruction (1865-1876)
    Fiction
    Robinet, H. G. Forty acres and maybe a mule (4
      and up)   **Fic**
Recorvits, Helen
    Goodbye, Walter Malinski (3-6)   **Fic**
    My name is Yoon   **E**
Recreation
    See also Amusements
    Drake, J. The kids winter handbook (4 and up)
        790.1
Recreations, Literary *See* Literary recreations
Recycle every day!. Wallace, N. E.   **E**
Recycled crafts box. Martin, L. C.   **363.7**
Recycling
    Hall, E. J. Recycling (5 and up)   **363.7**
    Martin, L. C. Recycled crafts box (3-6)
        363.7
    Murphy, S. J. Earth Day-hooray! (1-3)   **513**
    See/See also pages in the following book(s):
    Glaser, L. Compost! (k-2)   **363.7**
    Fiction
    Wallace, N. E. Recycle every day!   **E**
The **red** balloon. Lamorisse, A.   **E**
The **red** blanket. Thomas, E.   **E**
The **red** book. Lehman, B.   **E**
Red Cap. Wisler, G. C.   **Fic**
Red Cloud, Sioux Chief, 1822-1909
    See/See also pages in the following book(s):
    Ehrlich, A. Wounded Knee: an Indian history of
      the American West (6 and up)   **970.004**
    Freedman, R. Indian chiefs (6 and up)   **920**
Red Cross of the United States *See* American
    Red Cross

Richard Wright and the library card. Miller, W.
E

Richards, Beah
Keep climbing, girls
E

Richards, Jean
A fruit is a suitcase for seeds (k-2)
581.4

Richards, Justin
Double life (5 and up)
Fic

Richards, Norman
Monticello (4-6)
975.5

Richardson, Charisse K.
The real slam dunk (2-4)
Fic

Richardson, Justin
And Tango makes three
E

The **riches** of Oseola McCarty. Coleman, E.
92

Richter, Judy
Riding for kids (3-5)
798.2

Riddell, Chris
Platypus
E
(il) Andersen, H. C. The swan's stories
S C
(il) Platt, R. Castle diary
Fic
(jt. auth) Stewart, P. Beyond the Deepwoods
Fic

Riddle, Sue
(il) Swope, S. Gotta go! Gotta go!
E

Riddle me this!. Lupton, H.
793.73

The **riddle** of the Rosetta Stone. Giblin, J.
493

Riddle roundup. Maestro, G.
793.73

The **riddle** tale of freedom. Hamilton, V.
In Hamilton, V. The people could fly; American black folktales p156-59
398.2

Riddles
Adler, D. A. Easy math puzzles (2-4)
793.74
Brewer, P. You must be joking! (3-6)
818
Cerf, B. Riddles and more riddles!
793.73
Cole, J. Why did the chicken cross the road? and other riddles, old and new (3-5)
793.73
Hall, K. Creepy riddles (k-2)
793.73
Hall, K. Dino riddles (k-2)
793.73
Hall, K. Ribbit riddles (k-2)
793.73
Hall, K. Snakey riddles (k-2)
793.73
Hall, K. Stinky riddles (k-2)
793.73
Kessler, L. P. Old Turtle's 90 knock-knocks, jokes, and riddles (1-3)
793.73
Lewis, J. P. Scien-trickery (2-4)
811
Lupton, H. Riddle me this! (2-4)
793.73
Maestro, G. Riddle roundup (2-4)
793.73
Maestro, M. Geese find the missing piece (k-2)
793.73
Maestro, M. What do you hear when cows sing? (k-2)
793.73
Shannon, G. More stories to solve (3 and up)
398.2
Shannon, G. Still more stories to solve (3 and up)
398.2
Shannon, G. Stories to solve (3 and up)
398.2
Terban, M. The dove dove (3-5)
793.73
Terban, M. Funny you should ask (3-5)
793.73

Thomas, L. Ha! Ha! Ha! (3-6)
793.73
Fiction
Karim, R. Kindle me a riddle
E
Thompson, L. One riddle, one answer
E

Riddles. Afanas'ev, A. N.
In Afanas'ev, A. N. Russian fairy tales p29-30
398.2

Riddles and more riddles!. Cerf, B.
793.73

Ride, Sally K.
Exploring our solar system (4 and up)
523.2

Ride a purple pelican. Prelutsky, J.
811

Ride the wind. Simon, S.
591.56

Riding *See* Horsemanship

Riding for kids. Richter, J.
798.2

Riding the century. Siy, A.
In Sports shorts
S C

Rielly, Robin L.
Karate for kids (4 and up)
796.8

Rieth, Elizabeth
(jt. auth) Johmann, C. Bridges!
624.2
(jt. auth) Johmann, C. Going west!
978

Rifles for Watie. Keith, H.
Fic

Riggio, Anita
Smack dab in the middle
E

Right and wrong. Afanas'ev, A. N.
In Afanas'ev, A. N. Russian fairy tales p202-08
398.2

The **right** dog for the job. Patent, D. H.
362.4

Rights, Civil *See* Civil rights

Riglietti, Serena
(il) Cooper, S. The magician's boy
Fic

Rikki-tikki-tavi. Kipling, R.
In Kipling, R. The jungle book: the Mowgli stories
S C

Rikki-tikki-tavi. Pinkney, J.
E

Riley, Linnea Asplind
Mouse mess
E

Riley and Rose in the picture. Gretz, S.
E

Riley-Webb, Charlotte
(il) The entrance place of wonders. See The entrance place of wonders
811.008
(il) Lindsey, K. Sweet potato pie
E
(il) Miller, W. Rent party jazz
E

Rimm, Sylvia B.
See Jane win for girls (5 and up)
305.23

Rinaldi, Ann
The journal of Jasper Jonathan Pierce, a pilgrim boy (4 and up)
Fic

A **ring** of tricksters. Hamilton, V.
398.2

Ringgold, Faith
Tar Beach
E
(il) O holy night. See O holy night
782.28

Rio Grande valley
Lourie, P. Rio Grande (4 and up)
976.4

Riordan, James
King Arthur (5 and up)
398.2

Riots
Fiction
Bunting, E. Smoky night
E

Rip-roaring Russell. Hurwitz, J.
Fic

Rip Van Winkle. Irving, W.
Fic

Roberts, Willo Davis—*Continued*
The view from the cherry tree (5 and up)
Fic

Robert's snow. Lin, G.   E

Robertson, Barbara
(jt. auth) Robertson, J. C. The kids' building
workshop   694

Robertson, J. Craig
The kids' building workshop (3-6)   694

Robertson, Keith
Henry Reed, Inc. (4-6)   Fic

Robin Hood (Legendary character)
Creswick, P. Robin Hood (5 and up)   398.2
Fiction
Springer, N. Rowan Hood, outlaw girl of Sher-
wood Forest (4 and up)   Fic

Robin Hood and his merry men. Osborne, M. P.
In Osborne, M. P. Favorite medieval tales
p60-66   398.2

Robinet, Harriette Gillem
Forty acres and maybe a mule (4 and up)
Fic
Walking to the bus-rider blues (5 and up)
Fic

Robins, Joan
Addie meets Max   E

Robinson, Aminah Brenda Lynn
(il) Fox, M. Sophie   E
(il) Rosen, M. J. Elijah's angel   Fic
(il) Rosen, M. J. A school for Pompey Walker
Fic

Robinson, Barbara
The best Christmas pageant ever (4-6)   Fic

Robinson, Bill, 1878-1949
About
Dillon, L. Rap a tap tap   E

Robinson, Bill Bojangles *See* Robinson, Bill,
1878-1949

Robinson, Charles
(il) Burnett, F. H. The secret garden   Fic
(il) Levitin, S. Journey to America   Fic
(il) Smith, D. B. A taste of blackberries Fic
(il) Stevenson, R. L. A child's garden of verses
821
(il) Uchida, Y. Journey home   Fic

Robinson, Jackie, 1919-1972
About
Adler, D. A. A picture book of Jackie Robinson
(1-3)   92
Ford, C. T. Jackie Robinson (2-4)   92
Golenbock, P. Teammates [biography of Jackie
Robinson] (1-4)   92
Robinson, S. Promises to keep: how Jackie Rob-
inson changed America (4 and up)   92
See/See also pages in the following book(s):
Krull, K. Lives of the athletes (4 and up)
920
Fiction
Uhlberg, M. Dad, Jackie, and me   E

Robinson, Sharon
Promises to keep: how Jackie Robinson changed
America (4 and up)   92

Robinson Masters, Nancy
Extraordinary patriots of the United States of
America (5 and up)   920
Georgia
In America the beautiful, second series
973
Kansas
In America the beautiful, second series
973

Robotics *See* Robots
Robots
Domaine, H. Robotics (4-6)   629.8
Jones, D. Mighty robots (5 and up)   629.8
Sonenklar, C. Robots rising (3-5)   629.8
Fiction
Craig, J. Jimmy Coates: assassin? (5 and up)
Fic
Fox, H. Eager (5 and up)   Fic
Pinkney, B. Cosmo and the robot   E

Robots rising. Sonenklar, C.   629.8

Robusti, Marietta *See* Tintoretto, Marietta, d.
1590

Roca, François
(jt. auth) Prince, A. J. Twenty-one elephants and
still standing   E

Roche, Art
Cartooning (3-6)   741.5

Roche, Denis
Little Pig is capable   E
(il) London, J. A truck goes rattley-bumpa E

Rochelle, Belinda
(ed) Words with wings. See Words with wings
811.008

Rock, Lois
Everlasting stories (3-6)   220.9
(comp) Words of gold. See Words of gold
220.9

Rock and roll music *See* Rock music

Rock collecting. See Gans, R. Let's go rock collecting   552

Rock drawings, paintings, and engravings
Arnold, C. Stories in stone (4 and up)
709.01

Rock music
Boynton, S. Dog train (k-3)   782.42
George-Warren, H. Shake, rattle, & roll (4 and
up)   920
Fiction
Appelt, K. Bats around the clock   E

Rock musicians
Krull, K. The book of rock stars (4 and up)
920
Rappaport, D. John's secret dreams [biography
of John Lennon] (4 and up)   92
Fiction
Thiesing, L. The Aliens are coming!   E

Rock of ages. Bolden, T.   811

Rock paintings *See* Rock drawings, paintings, and
engravings

Rocking donkey. Aiken, J.
In Aiken, J. Shadows and moonshine; stories
S C

Rocklin, Joanne
Strudel stories (4 and up)   Fic

Rockman, Connie C.
(ed) Ninth book of junior authors and illustrators. See Ninth book of junior authors and illustrators **920.003**

Rocks
Christian, P. If you find a rock (k-3) **552**
Farndon, J. Rocks and minerals (4 and up) **549**
Hynes, M. Rocks & fossils (5 and up) **552**
Symes, R. F. Eyewitness rocks & minerals (5 and up) **549**
Trueit, T. S. Rocks, gems, and minerals (4 and up) **552**
VanCleave, J. P. Janice VanCleave's rocks and minerals (4 and up) **552**

Collectors and collecting
Gans, R. Let's go rock collecting (k-2) **552**
Hurst, C. O. Rocks in his head **E**
Murphy, S. J. Dave's down-to-earth rock shop (k-3) **511.3**

Fiction
Banks, K. A gift from the sea **E**

Rocks & fossils. Hynes, M. **552**
Rocks and minerals. Farndon, J. **549**
Rocks, gems, and minerals. Trueit, T. S. **552**
Rocks in his head. Hurst, C. O. **E**

Rockwell, Anne F.
100 school days **E**
Becoming butterflies (k-2) **595.7**
Big wheels **E**
The boy who wouldn't obey: a Mayan legend (2-4) **398.2**
Bugs are insects (k-3) **595.7**
Career day **E**
Father's Day **E**
Four seasons make a year **E**
Good morning, Digger **E**
Growing like me **E**
Honey in a hive (k-3) **595.7**
Little shark (k-2) **597**
Mother's Day **E**
My pet hamster (k-2) **636.9**
One bean (k-2) **635**
Only passing through: the story of Sojourner Truth (3-5) **92**
Our earth (k-2) **910**
Our stars (k-2) **523.8**
The Prince who ran away (3-6) **294.3**
Thanksgiving Day **E**
They called her Molly Pitcher (3-5) **92**
The toolbox **E**
Two blue jays **E**
Valentine's Day **E**

Rockwell, Harlow
(jt. auth) Rockwell, A. F. The toolbox **E**

Rockwell, Lizzy
The busy body book (k-1) **612**
Good enough to eat (k-3) **613.2**
(il) Rockwell, A. F. 100 school days **E**
(il) Rockwell, A. F. Career day **E**
(il) Rockwell, A. F. Father's Day **E**
(il) Rockwell, A. F. Mother's Day **E**
(il) Rockwell, A. F. Thanksgiving Day **E**
(il) Rockwell, A. F. Valentine's Day **E**

Rockwell, Norman, 1894-1978
About
Gherman, B. Norman Rockwell (4 and up) **92**
Roy, J. R. Norman Rockwell (2-4) **92**

Rockwell, Thomas
How to eat fried worms (3-6) **Fic**

Rocky Mountains
Grupper, J. Destination: Rocky Mountains (3-6) **978**

Rodanas, Kristina
(il) Bealer, A. W. Only the names remain **970.004**
(il) Bushyhead, R. H. Yonder mountain **398.2**

Rodda, Emily
Rowan of Rin (4-6) **Fic**

Rodeos
Pinkney, A. D. Bill Pickett, rodeo ridin' cowboy (k-3) **92**

Rodgers, Mary
Freaky Friday (4 and up) **Fic**

Rodman, Mary Ann
My best friend **E**
Yankee girl (4 and up) **Fic**

Rodowsky, Colby F.
The next-door dogs (2-4) **Fic**
Not my dog (2-4) **Fic**
Spindrift (5 and up) **Fic**

Rodriguez, Edel
(il) Shange, N. Muhammad Ali: the man who could float like a butterfly and sting like a bee **92**

Rodriguez, Rachel
Through Georgia's eyes [biography of Georgia O'Keeffe] (k-3) **92**

Rodzina. Cushman, K. **Fic**

Roebling, John Augustus
About
Curlee, L. Brooklyn Bridge (3-6) **624.2**

Roebling, Washington Augustus, 1837-1926
About
Curlee, L. Brooklyn Bridge (3-6) **624.2**

Roessel, David
(ed) Hughes, L. Langston Hughes **811**

Roessel, Monty
Songs from the loom (3-6) **970.004**

Rogasky, Barbara
Dybbuk **398.2**
The golem (4 and up) **398.2**
(comp) Winter poems. See Winter poems **808.81**

Rogers, Fred
Divorce (k-2) **306.89**
Going to the hospital (k-2) **362.1**
Making friends (k-1) **158**

Rogers, Gregory
The boy, the bear, the baron, the bard **E**

Rogers, Jacqueline
(il) Byars, B. C. The not-just-anybody family **Fic**
(il) San Souci, R. Even more short & shivery **398.2**

Rome (Italy)
Description and travel
Macaulay, D. Rome antics (4 and up)   **945**
Fiction
Macaulay, D. Angelo   **E**
Rome antics. Macaulay, D.   **945**
Romeo and Juliet. Packer, T.
In Packer, T. Tales from Shakespeare p139-153   **822.3**
Romeo and Juliet, William Shakespeare's. Coville, B.   **822.3**
Ronci, Kelli
Kids crochet (4 and up)   **746.43**
The **rōnin** and the tea master. Kimmel, E. A.
In Kimmel, E. A. Sword of the samurai; adventure stories from Japan p95-103   **Fic**
The **roof** of leaves. Washington, D. L.
In Washington, D. L. A pride of African tales
Rooftop rocket party. Chambers, R.   **E**
Rookie read-about health [series]
DerKazarian, S. You have head lice!   **616.5**
Room for Ripley. Murphy, S. J.   **530.8**
A **room** with a zoo. Feiffer, J.   **Fic**
Roome, Diana Reynolds
The elephant's pillow   **E**
A **roomful** of ghosts. Schwartz, H.
In Schwartz, H. Invisible kingdoms; Jewish tales of angels, spirits, and demons p27-31   **398.2**
Roop, Connie
(ed) Leeper, D. R. The diary of David R. Leeper   **92**
(jt. auth) Roop, P. Sojourner Truth   **92**
(jt. auth) Roop, P. Take command, Captain Farragut!   **92**
Roop, Peter
Sojourner Truth (3-6)   **92**
Take command, Captain Farragut! (4-6)   **92**
(ed) Leeper, D. R. The diary of David R. Leeper   **92**
Roosa, Karen
Beach day   **E**
Roosevelt, Eleanor, 1884-1962
About
Cooney, B. Eleanor [biography of Eleanor Roosevelt] (k-3)   **92**
Fleming, C. Our Eleanor (5 and up)   **92**
Freedman, R. Eleanor Roosevelt (5 and up)   **92**
Koestler-Grack, R. A. The story of Eleanor Roosevelt (2-4)   **92**
See/See also pages in the following book(s):
Krull, K. Lives of extraordinary women (4 and up)   **920**
Fiction
Ryan, P. M. Amelia and Eleanor go for a ride   **E**
Roosevelt, Franklin D. (Franklin Delano), 1882-1945
About
Freedman, R. Franklin Delano Roosevelt (5 and up)   **92**

Roosevelt, Theodore, 1858-1919
About
Fritz, J. Bully for you, Teddy Roosevelt! (5 and up)   **92**
Kraft, B. H. Theodore Roosevelt (5 and up)   **92**
Fiction
Bradley, K. B. The President's daughter (3-5)   **Fic**
The **rooster** and the fox. Ward, H.   **E**
The **rooster** and the mouse. Sierra, J.
In Sierra, J. Nursery tales around the world p69-71   **398.2**
Rooster can't cock-a-doodle-doo. Rostoker-Gruber, K.   **E**
Roosters
Fiction
Auch, M. J. Bantam of the opera   **E**
Cazet, D. Elvis the rooster almost goes to heaven   **E**
Pearson, T. C. Bob   **E**
Rostoker-Gruber, K. Rooster can't cock-a-doodle-doo   **E**
Ward, H. The rooster and the fox   **E**
Folklore
Poole, A. L. How the rooster got his crown (k-3)   **398.2**
Rascol, S. I. The impudent rooster (k-3)   **398.2**
The **rooster's** antlers. Kimmel, E. A.   **398.2**
Root, Barry
Gumbrella   **E**
(il) Appelt, K. Cowboy dreams   **E**
(il) Burleigh, R. Messenger, messenger   **E**
(il) Farish, T. The cat who liked potato soup   **E**
(il) Godwin, L. Central Park serenade   **E**
Root, Kimberly Bulcken
(il) Fisher, D. C. Understood Betsy   **Fic**
(il) Hodges, M. Gulliver in Lilliput   **Fic**
(il) Hopkinson, D. Birdie's lighthouse   **Fic**
(il) Martin, R. The storytelling princess   **E**
(il) McDonough, Y. Z. The doll with the yellow star   **Fic**
(il) Peterson, J. W. Don't forget Winona   **E**
Root, Phyllis
Big Momma makes the world   **E**
Grandmother Winter   **E**
If you want to see a caribou   **E**
Kiss the cow   **E**
The name quilt   **E**
Rattletrap car   **E**
Rootabaga stories. Sandburg, C.   **S C**
Rootabaga stories. Sandburg, C.
also in Sandburg, C. The Sandburg treasury; prose and poetry for young people p9-160   **818**
Rope skipping
Chambers, V. Double dutch (4 and up)   **796.2**
Fiction
English, K. Hot day on Abbott Avenue   **E**
Rope skipping rhymes *See* Jump rope rhymes
The **rope** trick. Alexander, L.   **Fic**

Royalty *See* Kings and rulers; Princesses; Queens

Royston, Angela
Life cycle of a mushroom (k-3) **579.6**
Life cycle of an oak tree (k-3) **583**
Proteins for a healthy body (4-6) **613.2**
Vitamins and minerals for a healthy body (4-6) **613.2**
Water (k-3) **553.7**

Rozinski, Robert
(il) Jackson, D. M. The wildlife detectives **363.2**

Rubber-band banjos and a java jive bass. Sabbeth, A. **781**

Rubber stamp printing
Price, P. S. Cool rubber stamp art (4-6) **761**
Rhatigan, J. Stamp it! (3-6) **761**

Rubel, David
Scholastic atlas of the United States (4 and up) **912**
Scholastic encyclopedia of the presidents and their times (5 and up) **920**

Rubel, Nicole
Twice as nice (k-3) **306.8**
(il) Gantos, J. Rotten Ralph **E**
(il) Hall, K. Dino riddles **793.73**
(il) Hall, K. Mummy riddles **793.73**

Rubin, Alan
How many fish? **E**

Rubin, Susan Goldman
Art against the odds (5 and up) **700**
The cat with the yellow star (3-6) **940.53**
Degas and the dance (3-6) **92**
The flag with fifty-six stars (3-5) **940.53**
The yellow house (2-4) **759.4**

Ruby, Laura
Lily's ghosts (5 and up) **Fic**
The Wall and the Wing (5 and up) **Fic**

Ruby bakes a cake. Hill, S. **E**

Ruby electric. Nelson, T. **Fic**

Ruby Holler. Creech, S. **Fic**

Ruby Lu, brave and true. Look, L. **Fic**

Ruby sings the blues. Daly, N. **E**

Ruby's beauty shop. Wells, R. **E**

Ruby's wish. Bridges, S. Y. **E**

Ruckman, Ivy
Night of the twisters (4 and up) **Fic**

Rudolph, Wilma, 1940-1994
About
Krull, K. Wilma unlimited: how Wilma Rudolph became the world's fastest woman (2-4) **92**

See/See also pages in the following book(s):
Krull, K. Lives of the athletes (4 and up) **920**

Rueda, Claudia
(il) Ryan, P. M. Nacho and Lolita **398.2**

Ruelle, Karen Gray
The Thanksgiving beast feast **E**

Ruffins, Reynold
(il) Lotu, D. Running the road to ABC **E**
(il) Sierra, J. The gift of the Crocodile **398.2**

(il) Sloat, T. There was an old lady who swallowed a trout **E**

Rugs and carpets
Fiction
Blood, C. L. The goat in the rug **E**
Say, A. Emma's rug **E**

Ruhl, Greg
In the time of knights (4 and up) **942.03**
(il) Hehner, B. First on the moon **629.45**
(il) Tanaka, S. Lost temple of the Aztecs **972**
(il) Tanaka, S. Secrets of the mummies **393**

Ruins *See* Excavations (Archeology)

The **ruins** of Gorlan. See Flanagan, J. Ranger's apprentice **Fic**

Ruiz, Denise
Jump in
In You're on!: seven plays in English and Spanish p42-61 **812.008**

Ruler of the courtyard. Khan, R. **E**

Rulers *See* Kings and rulers; Queens

Rumford, James
Seeker of knowledge [biography of Jean François Champollion] (3-5) **92**
Sequoyah (1-4) **92**
Traveling man: the journey of Ibn Battuta, 1325-1354 (3-6) **92**

Rumpelstiltskin. Doherty, B.
In Doherty, B. Fairy tales **398.2**

Rumpelstiltskin. Grimm, J.
In De Paola, T. Tomie dePaola's Favorite nursery tales p46-52 **398.2**

Rumpelstiltskin. Steig, J.
In Steig, J. A handful of beans; six fairy tales p9-31 **398.2**

Rumpelstiltskin. Zelinsky, P. O. **398.2**

Rumpelstiltskin's daughter. Stanley, D. **E**

Rumpelstiltzkin. Grimm, J.
In The Blue fairy book p96-99 **398.2**

Run, jump, hide, slide, splash. Rhatigan, J. **796**

The **runaway** bunny. Brown, M. W. **E**

Runaway children
Fiction
Naidoo, B. No turning back (5 and up) **Fic**
Snyder, Z. K. The runaways (4 and up) **Fic**
Willis, P. The barn burner (5 and up) **Fic**

The **runaway** children. Sierra, J.
In Sierra, J. Can you guess my name?; traditional tales around the world p97-101 **398.2**

Runaway dreidel!. Newman, L. **E**

Runaway Radish. Haas, J. **Fic**

The **runaway** rice cake. Compestine, Y. C. **E**

Runaway teenagers
Fiction
Johnson, A. Bird (5 and up) **Fic**

The **runaway** tortilla. Kimmel, E. A. **398.2**

The **runaways.** Snyder, Z. K. **Fic**

Running
Fiction
Arnold, M. D. The pumpkin runner **E**

S

Safety education—*Continued*
Raatma, L. Safety on the Internet (4 and up)
025.04

Fiction
Rathmann, P. Officer Buckle and Gloria **E**
Safety for babysitters. Raatma, L. **649**
Safety in your neighborhood. Raatma, L.
613.6
Safety measures *See* Accidents—Prevention
Safety on the Internet. Raatma, L. **025.04**
Saffell, David C., ed
The encyclopedia of U.S. presidential elections.
See The encyclopedia of U.S. presidential
elections **324**
Safford, Barbara Ripp
Guide to reference materials for school media
centers **011.6**
Saffy's angel. McKay, H. **Fic**
A **saga**. Russell, J.
In Shedlock, M. L. The art of the story-teller
p165-67 **372.6**
Sage, Angie
Magyk (5 and up) **Fic**
The **sage** of theare. Jones, D. W.
In Jones, D. W. Mixed magics **S C**
Sail away. Crews, D. **E**
Sailing

Fiction
Bang-Campbell, M. Little Rat sets sail **E**
Creech, S. The Wanderer (5 and up) **Fic**
Crews, D. Sail away **E**
Mead, A. Junebug (3-5) **Fic**
Sailing home. Rand, G. **Fic**
Sailors
Lasky, K. Born in the breezes: the seafaring of
Joshua Slocum (3-6) **92**
The **sailors** and the troll. Lunge-Larsen, L.
In Lunge-Larsen, L. The troll with no heart in
his body and other tales of trolls from
Norway p63-67 **398.2**
Sailors' life *See* Seafaring life
Saint Crispin's follower. Fleischman, P.
In Fleischman, P. Graven images; three sto-
ries **S C**
Saint-Exupéry, Antoine de
The little prince **Fic**
Saint Francis and the Christmas donkey. Byrd, R.
E
Saint Francis and the wolf. Egielski, R. **398.2**
Saint Francis of Assisi. Kennedy, R. F. **271**
Saint Francis sings to Brother Sun. Pandell, K.
271
Saint George and the dragon. Hodges, M.
398.2
Saint Helens, Mount (Wash.) *See* Mount Saint
Helens (Wash.)
Saint Patrick and the snakes. Dillon, E.
In Bauer, C. F. Celebrations; read-aloud holi-
day and theme book programs p170-71
808.8

Saint Patrick's Day
Barth, E. Shamrocks, harps, and shillelaghs
(3-6) **394.26**
Gibbons, G. St. Patrick's Day (k-3) **394.26**
Landau, E. St. Patrick's Day (2-4) **394.26**
See/See also pages in the following book(s):
Bauer, C. F. Celebrations p1-24 **808.8**
Fiction
Wojciechowski, S. A fine St. Patrick's day
E
Saint Valentine. Sabuda, R. **92**
Saint Valentine's Day *See* Valentine's Day
Saints
See also Christian saints
Fiction
Alvarez, J. A gift of gracias **E**
Sakade, Florence
Japanese children's favorite stories (2-4)
398.2
Contents: Peach boy; The magic teakettle; Monkey-dance and
sparrow dance; The long-nosed goblins; The rabbit and the
moon; The tongue-cut sparrow; Silly Saburo; The toothpick war-
riors; The Sticky-sticky pine; The spider weaver; Little one-inch;
The badger and the magic fan; Mr. Lucky straw; Why the jelly-
fish has no bones; The old man who made trees blossom; The
crab and the monkey; The ogre and the rooster; The rabbit who
crossed the sea; The grateful statues; The bobtail monkey
Sakai, Komako
Emily's balloon **E**
Sakurai, Gail
Asian-Americans in the old West (4 and up)
978
Sakyamuni *See* Gautama Buddha
Sal Fink. San Souci, R.
In San Souci, R. Cut from the same cloth;
American women of myth, legend, and
tall tale p51-55 **398.2**
Salad people and more real recipes. Katzen, M.
641.5
Saladin, Sultan of Egypt and Syria, 1137-1193
About
Stanley, D. Saladin: noble prince of Islam (4
and up) **92**
Saladin: noble prince of Islam. Stanley, D. **92**
Salem (Mass.)
Fiction
Petry, A. L. Tituba of Salem Village (6 and up)
Fic
History
Jackson, S. The witchcraft of Salem Village (4
and up) **133.4**
Roach, M. K. In the days of the Salem witch-
craft trials (4 and up) **133.4**
Salerno, Steven
(il) Anderson, C. Bedtime! **E**
(il) Franco, B. Mathematickles **811**
Sales, Auction *See* Auctions
Salisbury, Graham
Lord of the deep (5 and up) **Fic**
Salley, Coleen
Epossumondas (k-3) **398.2**
Sally Ann Thunder Ann Whirlwind. Osborne, M.
P.
In Osborne, M. P. American tall tales p15-23
398.2

Sally Ann Thunder Ann Whirlwind Crockett. Kellogg, S. **398.2**

Sally goes to the beach. Huneck, S. **E**

Sally Jean, the Bicycle Queen. Best, C. **E**

Salmansohn, Pete
  Saving birds (5 and up) **333.95**

Salmon
  Cone, M. Come back, salmon (3-6) **639.3**
  McMillan, B. Salmon summer (2-4) **639.2**

Salmon summer. McMillan, B. **639.2**

Salmonson, Jessica Amanda
  The ugly unicorn
    In A Glory of unicorns p79-94 **S C**

Salsa stories. Delacre, L. **S C**

Salt
  Kurlansky, M. The story of salt (3-6) **553.6**

Salt. Afanas'ev, A. N.
    In Afanas'ev, A. N. Russian fairy tales p40-44 **398.2**

Salt in his shoes. Jordan, D. **E**

Salten, Felix
  Bambi (4-6) **Fic**

Salting the ocean (4 and up) **811.008**

Saltz, Gail
  Amazing you (k-1) **612.6**

Saltzberg, Barney
  Cornelius P. Mud, are you ready for bed? **E**
  (il) Murphy, S. J. Sluggers' car wash **513**

Salvage
  Mitchell, J. S. Crashed, smashed, and mashed (3-6) **629.2**

Sam, Joe *See* JoeSam

Sam and Jane go camping. Schwartz, A.
    In Schwartz, A. There is a carrot in my ear, and other noodle tales p16-26 **398.2**

Sam and Sooky
    In Grandfather tales; American-English folk tales p150-55 **398.2**

Sam and the lucky money. Chinn, K. **E**

Sam and the tigers. Lester, J. **E**

Sam, Bangs & Moonshine. Ness, E. **E**

Sam Johnson and the blue ribbon quilt. Ernst, L. C. **E**

Sam who never forgets. Rice, E. **E**

Same old horse. Murphy, S. J. **E**

The **same** stuff as stars. Paterson, K. **Fic**

Sami and the time of the troubles. Heide, F. P. **E**

Sam'l. MacDonald, M. R.
    In MacDonald, M. R. When the lights go out; twenty scary tales to tell p109-14 **372.6**

Sammy and the dinosaurs. See Whybrow, I. Harry and the bucketful of dinosaurs **E**

Sammy Keyes and the hotel thief. Draanen, W. v. **Fic**

Sammy the classroom guinea pig. Berenzy, A. **E**

Sammy the seal. Hoff, S. **E**

Samora, John
  (il) Cano-Murillo, K. The crafty diva's lifestyle makeover **745.5**

A **sampler** view of colonial life. Cobb, M. **746.44**

Sampson, Michael R.
  (jt. auth) Martin, B. Chicka chicka 1, 2, 3 **E**
  (jt. auth) Martin, B. Trick or treat? **E**

Sam's girl friend. Schwartz, A.
    In Schwartz, A. All of our noses are here, and other noodle tales p58-63 **398.2**

Sam's new pet. Schwartz, A.
    In Schwartz, A. Scary stories 3; more tales to chill your bones p55-56 **398.2**

Sam's Wild West Christmas. Antle, N. **E**

Samson he weak for woman palaver. Graham, L. B.
    In Graham, L. B. How God fix Jonah p52-60 **398.2**

Samuel (Biblical figure)
Fiction
  Lepp, R. David: Shepard's song, vol. 1 (3-5) **741.5**

Samuel Eaton's day. Waters, K. **974.4**

Samuels, Barbara
  Dolores on her toes **E**

Samuelson, Mary Lou
  (jt. auth) Schlaepfer, G. G. Pythons and boas **597.96**

The **samurai** and the dragon. Kimmel, E. A.
    In Kimmel, E. A. Sword of the samurai; adventure stories from Japan p11-21 **Fic**

The **samurai** maiden. Yolen, J.
    In Yolen, J. Not one damsel in distress; world folktales for strong girls p78-83 **398.2**

San Francisco (Calif.)
Description
  Wilder, L. I. West from home (6 and up) **92**

Fiction
  Burton, V. L. Maybelle, the cable car **E**
  English, K. Speak to me **E**
  Freeman, M. The trouble with cats (2-4) **Fic**
  Lee, M. Landed **Fic**
  Partridge, E. Oranges on Golden Mountain **E**
  Snyder, Z. K. The magic nation thing (4 and up) **Fic**
  Yang, B. Hannah is my name **E**
  Yep, L. Child of the owl (5 and up) **Fic**
  Yep, L. Dragonwings (5 and up) **Fic**
  Yep, L. Thief of hearts (5 and up) **Fic**
History
  Tanaka, S. Earthquake! (4 and up) **979.4**

San Nicolas Island (Calif.)
Fiction
  O'Dell, S. Island of the Blue Dolphins (5 and up) **Fic**

San Souci, Daniel
  (il) Kimmel, E. A. Montezuma and the fall of the Aztecs **972**
  (il) London, J. Mustang canyon **E**

San Souci, Daniel—*Continued*

(il) San Souci, R. Sootface   **398.2**

(il) San Souci, R. Two bear cubs   **398.2**

San Souci, Robert

Brave Margaret (k-3)   **398.2**

Cendrillon (k-3)   **398.2**

Cut from the same cloth (4 and up)   **398.2**

Contents: The Star Maiden; Bess Call; Drop Star; Molly Cottontail; Annie Christmas; Susanna and Simon; Sal Fink; Sweet Betsey from Pike; Old Sally Cato; Pale-Face Lightning; Pohaha; Sister Fox and Brother Coyote; Hekeke; Otoonah; Hiiaka

Dare to be scared (4 and up)   **S C**

Contents: Nighttown; The dark dark house; The caller; The double dare; Space is the place; Ants; The Halloween spirit; The Bald Mountain monster; Playland; Smoke; Mrs. Moonlight (Senora de Luna); Hungry ghosts; Bakotahl

Double-dare to be scared: another thirteen chilling tales (4 and up)   **S C**

Contents: Campfire tale; Best friends; The quilt; Circus dreams; Rosalie; Mountain childers; Class cootie; Half-past midnight; Laughter; Click-clack; Daddy Boogey; Grey; "Gulp!"

Even more short & shivery (4 and up)

    398.2

Contents: Appointment in Samarra; Deer woman; The maggot; Witch woman; The berbalangs; The dancing dead of Shark Island; "That I see, but this I sew"; La Guiablesse; The blood-drawing ghost; Guests from Gibbet Island; The haunted house; "Never far from you"; The rose elf; The wind rider; The skull that spoke; The monster of Baylock; The new mother; Rokuro-Kubi; Dicey and Orpus; Chips; The skeleton's revenge; Lullaby; Death and the two friends; Forest ghosts; A Carolina banshee; The deadly violin; A night of terrors; The sending; The hand of fate; Old raw head

Fa Mulan (2-4)   **398.2**

The faithful friend (2-4)   **398.2**

Kenneth Grahame's The reluctant dragon (2-4)

    Fic

Little Gold Star (2-4)   **398.2**

More short & shivery (4 and up)   **398.2**

Contents: "Hold him, Tabb!"; The witches' eyes; The duppy; Two snakes; The draug; The vampire cat; Windigo Island; The haunted inn; The rolling head; The Croglin Grange vampire; The Yara; "Me, myself"; Island of fear; Three who sought death; Sister Death and the healer; The mouse tower; The devil and Tom Walker; The greedy daughter; The pirate; The golden arm; The serpent woman; Loft the enchanter; The accursed house; Escape up the tree; The headrest; The thing in the woods; King of the Cats; The dead mother; Knock . . . knock . . . knock . . .; Twice surprised

The secret of the stones (k-3)   **398.2**

Short & shivery (4 and up)   **398.2**

Contents: The robber bridegroom; Jack Frost; The waterfall of ghosts; The ghost's cap; The witch cat; The green mist; The Cegua; The ghostly little girl; The midnight mass of the Dead; Tailypo; Lady Eleanore's mantle; The soldier and the vampire; The skeleton's dance; Scared to death; Swallowed alive; The deacon's ghost; Nuckelavee; The adventure of the German student; Billy Mosby's night ride; The hunter in the haunted forest; Brother and sister; The lovers of Dismal Swamp; Boneless; The death waltz; The ghost of Misery Hill; The loup-garou; The golem; Lavender; The goblin spider; The Halloween pony

Six foolish fishermen (k-3)   **398.2**

Sootface (1-4)   **398.2**

Sukey and the mermaid (1-4)   **398.2**

The talking eggs (k-3)   **398.2**

A terrifying taste of short & shivery (4 and up)

    398.2

Contents: Crooker waits; Yara-ma-yha-who; The fata; The fiddler; Land-otter; A fish story; Apparitions; The bijli; The lutin; The hundredth skull; The ogre's arm; The hairy hands; The snow husband; The zimwi; Witchbirds; Dangerous hill; The witch's head; Dinkins is dead; Old Nan's ghost; The interrupted wedding; The mulombe; The haunted grove; The tiger woman; Peacock's ghost; Israel and the werewolf; Hoichi the earless; A snap of the fingers; Narrow escape; The black fox; The mother and death

The twins and the Bird of Darkness (3-6)

    398.2

Two bear cubs (k-3)   **398.2**

A weave of words (3-5)   **398.2**

The well at the end of the world   **E**

Sanchez, Enrique O.

(il) Castañeda, O. S. Abuela's weave   **E**

(il) O'Neill, A. Estela's swap   **E**

(il) Santiago, E. A doll for Navidades   **E**

Sanctuary movement

See also Refugees

Sand

See also Quicksand

Sand and fog. Brandenburg, J.   **968.8**

Sand Creek, Battle of, 1864

See/See also pages in the following book(s):

Ehrlich, A. Wounded Knee: an Indian history of the American West (6 and up)   **970.004**

Sandburg, Carl

Abe Lincoln grows up

In Sandburg, C. The Sandburg treasury; prose and poetry for young people p383-477

    818

Carl Sandburg (4 and up)   **811**

In The Blackbirch treasury of American poetry p9-52   **811.008**

Early moon

In Sandburg, C. The Sandburg treasury; prose and poetry for young people p161-207

    818

The haystack cricket and how things are different up in the moon towns

also in Sandburg, C. The Sandburg treasury; prose and poetry for young people p139-42   **818**

How Rag Bag Mammy kept her secret while the wind blew away the Village of Hat Pins

also in Sandburg, C. The Sandburg treasury; prose and poetry for young people p100-02   **818**

The Huckabuck family and how they raised popcorn in Nebraska and quit and came back

    E

More Rootabaga stories   **S C**

Contents: The skyscraper to the moon and how the green rat with the rheumatism ran a thousand miles twice; Slipfoot and how he nearly always never gets what he goes after; Many, many weddings in one corner house; Shush Shush, the big buff banty hen who laid an egg in the postmaster's hat; How Rag Bag Mammy kept her secret while the wind blew away the Village of Hat Pins; How six pigeons came back to Hatrack the Horse after many accidents and six telegrams; How the three wild babylonian baboons went away in the rain eating bread and butter; How six umbrellas took off their straw hats to show respect to the one big umbrella; How Bozo the Button Buster busted all his buttons when a mouse came; How Googler and Gaggler, the two Christmas babies, came home with monkey wrenches; How Johnny the Wham sleeps in money all the time and Joe the Wimp shines and sees things; How Deep Red Roses goes back and forth between the clock and the looking glass; How Pink Peony sent Spuds, the Ballplayer, up to pick four moons; How Dippy the Wisp and Slip Me Liz came in the moonshine where the Potato Face Blind Man sat with his accordion; How Hot Balloons and his pigeon daughter crossed over into the Rootabaga country; How two sweetheart dippies sat in the moonlight on a lumberyard fence and heard about the Sooners and the Boomers; The Haystack Cricket and how things are different up in the moon towns; Why the big ball game between Hot Grounders and the Grand Standers was a hot game; The Huckabuck Family and how

Sandburg, Carl—*Continued*

they raised popcorn in Nebraska and quit and came back; Yang Yang and Hoo Hoo, or the song of the left foot of the shadow of the goose in Oklahoma; How a skyscraper and a railroad train got picked up and carried away from Pig's Eye Valley far in the Pickax Mountains; Pig wisps; Kiss me; Blue silver

Prairie-town boy

In Sandburg, C. The Sandburg treasury; prose and poetry for young people p263-382
818

Rainbows are made: poems (5 and up)   **811**

Rootabaga stories   **S C**

Contents: How they broke away to go to the Rootabaga Country; How they bring back the Village of Cream Puffs when the wind blows it away; How the five rusty rats helped find a new village; The Potato Face Blind Man who lost the diamond rabbit on his gold accordion; How the Potato Face Blind Man enjoyed himself on a fine spring morning; Poker Face the Baboon and Hot Dog the Tiger; The Toboggan-to-the-Moon dream of the Potato Face Blind Man; How Gimme the Ax found out about the Zigzag Railroad and who made it zigzag; The story of Blixie Bimber and the power of the gold buckskin whincher; The story of Jason Squiff and why he had a popcorn hat, popcorn mittens and popcorn shoes; The story of Rags Habakuk, the two blue rats, and the circus man who came with spot cash money; The wedding procession of the Rag Doll and the Broom Handle and who was in it; How the hat ashes shovel helped Snoo Foo; Three boys with jugs of molasses and secret ambitions; How Bimbo the Snip's thumb stuck to his nose when the wind changed; The two skyscrapers who decided to have a child; The dollar watch and the five jack-rabbits; The wooden Indian and the Shaghorn Buffalo; The White Horse Girl and Blue Wind Boy; What six girls with balloons told the Gray Man on Horseback; How Henry Haggleyhoagly played the guitar with his mittens on; Never kick a slipper at the moon; Sand flat shadows; How to tell corn fairies if you see 'em; How the animals lost their tails and got them back traveling from Philadelphia to Medicine Hat

also in Sandburg, C. The Sandburg treasury; prose and poetry for young people p9-160   **818**

The Sandburg treasury (5 and up)   **818**

Wind song

In Sandburg, C. The Sandburg treasury; prose and poetry for young people p209-61
818

(jt. auth) Niven, P. Carl Sandburg: adventures of a poet   **92**

Sandburg, Carl, 1878-1967
About

Niven, P. Carl Sandburg: adventures of a poet (3-6)   **92**

See/See also pages in the following book(s):

Krull, K. Lives of the writers (4 and up)
920

The **Sandburg** treasury. Sandburg, C.   **818**

Sanders, Doug

Idaho

In It's my state! [series]   **973**

Missouri

In It's my state! [series]   **973**

Nebraska

In It's my state! [series]   **973**

North Dakota

In It's my state! [series]   **973**

Oklahoma

In It's my state! [series]   **973**

Utah

In It's my state! [series]   **973**

Sanders, Nancy I.

A kid's guide to African American history (4-6)
305.8

Sanderson, Ruth

The crystal mountain (3-5)   **398.2**

The Golden Mare, the Firebird, and the magic ring (3-5)   **398.2**

(il) Sleator, W. Into the dream   **Fic**

Sandflat shadows. Sandburg, C.

In Sandburg, C. The Sandburg treasury; prose and poetry for young people p73-77
818

Sandford, John

(il) Arnold, C. The terrible Hodag and the animal catchers   **E**

(il) Medearis, A. S. Snug in Mama's arms
E

Sandin, Joan

(il) Bulla, C. R. Daniel's duck   **E**

(il) Little, J. From Anna   **Fic**

Sandler, Martin W.

Island of hope (5 and up)   **325.73**

On the waters of the USA (5 and up)   **387.2**

Straphanging in the USA (5 and up)   **388.4**

Trapped in ice! (5 and up)   **639.2**

The **Sandman**. Andersen, H. C.

In Andersen, H. C. Hans Christian Andersen's Fairy Tales   **S C**

Sands, Karen

Back in the spaceship again   **016.8**

Sanfield, Steve

The adventures of High John the Conqueror (4 and up)   **398.2**

Contents: Master's walking stick; Just possum; "You better not do it"; In a box; Off limits; John wins a bet; This one and that one; Who's the fool now; George's dream; Deer hunting; John's memory; Freedom; An epidemic of ducks; John in court; Tops and bottoms; The Christmas turkey

Santa Claus

Demi. The legend of Saint Nicholas (3-6)
92

Fiction

Abbott, T. Kringle (5 and up)   **Fic**

Antle, N. Sam's Wild West Christmas   **E**

De Paola, T. Guess who's coming to Santa's for dinner?   **E**

Duval, K. The Three Bears' Christmas   **E**

Frazee, M. Santa Claus, the world's number one toy expert   **E**

Krensky, S. How Santa got his job   **E**

Polacco, P. Welcome Comfort   **E**

Seibold, J. O. Olive the other reindeer   **E**

Van Allsburg, C. The Polar Express   **E**

Poetry

Moore, C. C. The night before Christmas (k-3)
811

Songs

Coots, J. F. Santa Claus is comin' to town (k-3)
782.42

Santa Claus is comin' to town. Coots, J. F.
782.42

Santa Claus, the world's number one toy expert. Frazee, M.   **E**

Santa Fe (N.M.)
Fiction

De Paola, T. The night of Las Posadas   **E**

Saving the pennies. Geras, A.
    In Geras, A. My grandmother's stories; a collection of Jewish folk tales p41-47
                      398.2

Saving water. Dalgleish, S.   **363.6**

Savion!: my life in tap. Glover, S.   **92**

Sawdust carpets. Carling, A. L.   **E**

Sawyer, Kem Knapp
    Anne Frank (5 and up)   **92**

Sawyer, Ruth
    The Christmas apple
    In Bauer, C. F. Celebrations; read-aloud holiday and theme book programs p259-64
                      808.8
    Roller skates (4-6)   **Fic**
    The way of the storyteller   **372.6**
    <small>Stories included are: Wee Meg Barnileg and the fairies; The magic box; Señora, will you snip? Señora will you sew?; The peddler of Ballaghadereen; Where one is fed a hundred can dine; A matter of brogues; The juggler of Notre Dame; The deserted mine; The legend of Saint Elizabeth; The princess and the vagabone; The bird who spoke three times</small>

Say, Allen
    Allison   **E**
    The bicycle man   **E**
    Emma's rug   **E**
    Grandfather's journey   **E**
    Kamishibai man   **E**
    The lost lake   **E**
    Music for Alice   **E**
    Tea with milk   **E**
    Tree of cranes   **E**
    (il) Friedman, I. R. How my parents learned to eat   **E**
    (il) Snyder, D. The boy of the three-year nap
                      398.2

Say hola to Spanish, otra vez. Elya, S. M.
                      463

Say what? Haddix, M. P.   **Fic**

Saying goodbye to Lulu. Demas, C.   **E**

Sayles, Elizabeth
    (il) Ackerman, K. The night crossing   **Fic**

Sayre, April Pulley
    Army ant parade (k-3)   **595.7**
    The bumblebee queen (1-3)   **595.7**
    Dig, wait, listen   **E**
    The hungry hummingbird (k-3)   **598**
    One is a snail, ten is a crab   **E**
    Secrets of sound (4 and up)   **591.59**
    Shadows   **E**
    Stars beneath your bed (k-3)   **551.51**

Sayre, Henry M.
    Cave paintings to Picasso (5 and up)   **709**

Sayre, Jeff
    (jt. auth) Sayre, A. P. One is a snail, ten is a crab   **E**

Scagell, Robin
    Children's night sky atlas (5 and up)   **520**

Scales, Pat R.
    Teaching banned books   **323.44**

Scamper and the horse show. Haas, J.   **E**

The **Scandinavian** American family album. Hoobler, D.   **305.8**

Scandinavian Americans
    Hoobler, D. The Scandinavian American family album (5 and up)   **305.8**

Scandinavians
    See also Vikings

Scarborough, Kate
    Nuclear waste (5 and up)   **363.7**
    Pablo Picasso (5 and up)   **92**

The **scarecrow** and his servant. Pullman, P.
                      Fic

Scarecrows
    Fiction
    Brown, K. The scarecrow's hat   **E**
    Brown, M. W. The little scarecrow boy   **E**
    Pullman, P. The scarecrow and his servant (4-6)   **Fic**

The **scarecrow's** hat. Brown, K.   **E**

Scared silly! (k-3)   **810.8**

Scared silly. Medearis, A. S.
    In Medearis, A. S. Haunts; five hair-raising tales p9-15   **S C**

Scared stiff. Roberts, W. D.   **Fic**

Scared to death. San Souci, R.
    In San Souci, R. Short & shivery; thirty chilling tales p78-83   **398.2**

The **Scaredy** Cats. Bottner, B.   **E**

Scarre, Christopher
    The Palace of Minos at Knossos (4 and up)
                      728.8

Scary Godmother. Thompson, J.   **741.5**

Scary stories 3. Schwartz, A.   **398.2**

Scary stories to tell in the dark. Schwartz, A.
                      398.2

Scathach. Mayer, M.
    In Mayer, M. Women warriors; myths and legends of heroic women p31-36   **398**

Schaap, Phil
    (jt. auth) Marsalis, W. Jazz A-B-Z   **781.65**

Schachner, Judith Byron
    The Grannyman   **E**
    (il) Alexander, L. How the cat swallowed thunder   **E**
    (il) Napoli, D. J. The prince of the pond   **Fic**

Schaefer, Carole Lexa
    The biggest soap   **E**
    Someone says   **E**

Schaefer, Lola M.
    An island grows   **E**
    Loose tooth   **E**
    Pick, pull, snap! (k-3)   **582**
    This is the sunflower   **E**
    What's up, what's down?   **E**

Schafer, Susan
    Lizards (3-6)   **639.3**

Schanzer, Rosalyn
    Davy Crockett saves the world   **E**
    George vs. George (3-6)   **973.3**
    How we crossed the West (3-5)   **978**
    (il) Lauber, P. The true-or-false book of cats   **636.8**

Schanzer, Rosalyn—*Continued*
  (il) Lauber, P. The true-or-false book of dogs
    636.7
  (il) Lauber, P. The true-or-false book of horses
    636.1
Schecter, David
  (jt. auth) Cruz, A. The woman who outshone the
    sun   **398.2**
  (ed) Garza, C. L. In my family   **305.8**
  (ed) Garza, C. L. Magic windows   **305.8**
Schecter, Ellen
  The family Haggadah   **296.4**
Scheer, Julian
  Rain makes applesauce   E
  A Thanksgiving turkey   E
Scheffler, Axel
  (il) Donaldson, J. The snail and the whale E
Schertle, Alice
  1, 2, I love you   E
  All you need for a beach   E
  All you need for a snowman   E
  Down the road   E
  ¡Pio peep! See ¡Pio peep!   **398.8**
Scheuer, Philip
  (il) Haduch, B. Science fair success secrets
    507.8
Scheunemann, Pam
  Cool beaded jewelry (4-6)   **745.58**
  Cool clay projects (4-6)   **731.4**
Schick, Eleanor
  Mama   E
Schick, Joel
  (il) Sachar, L. Wayside School gets a little
    stranger   Fic
Schindler, S. D.
  (il) Antle, N. Sam's Wild West Christmas E
  (il) Armstrong, A. Whittington   Fic
  (il) Berger, M. Spinning spiders   **595.4**
  (il) Hall, K. Creepy riddles   **793.73**
  (il) Helldorfer, M. C. Hog music   E
  (il) Kay, V. Covered wagons, bumpy trails
    E
  (il) Kay, V. Gold fever   E
  (il) Krensky, S. How Santa got his job E
  (il) Kudlinski, K. V. Boy, were we wrong about
    dinosaurs!   **567.9**
  (il) Kurlansky, M. The cod's tale   **639.2**
  (il) Kurlansky, M. The story of salt   **553.6**
  (il) Le Guin, U. K. Catwings   Fic
  (il) Leuck, L. One witch   E
  (il) Murphy, S. J. Betcha!   **519.5**
  (il) Rockwell, A. F. Honey in a hive   **595.7**
  (il) Spinelli, E. Three pebbles and a song E
  (il) Walters, V. Are we there yet, Daddy? E
Schirripa, Steven R.
  Nicky Deuce (4-6)   Fic
Schlaepfer, Gloria G.
  The Louisiana Purchase (5 and up)   **973.4**
  Pythons and boas (4 and up)   **597.96**
Schlein, Lonnie
  (ed) A Nation challenged. See A Nation chal-
    lenged   **973.931**
Schlein, Miriam
  Hello, hello!   E

The story about me   E
Schmandt-Besserat, Denise
  The history of counting (4 and up)   **513**
Schmidt, Gary D.
  Anson's way (5 and up)   Fic
  The wonders of Donal O'Donnell (3-6)
    398.2
  (jt. auth) Kushner, L. In God's hands E
Schmidt, Karen
  (il) Nolen, J. Max and Jax in second grade
    E
Schmidt, Suzy
  (jt. auth) Cohn, A. L. Abraham Lincoln **92**
Schmitzer, Jeanne Cannella
  (jt. auth) Appelt, K. Down Cut Shin Creek
    027
Schneider, Katy
  (il) MacLachlan, P. Painting the wind E
Schneider, Rex
  (il) Dickinson, E. I'm nobody! who are you?
    811
Schnur, Steven
  The shadow children (5 and up)   Fic
  Spring   E
  Spring thaw   E
  Winter   E
Schoenherr, Alicia
  Mountain biking (4-6)   **796.6**
Schoenherr, John
  (il) Eckert, A. W. Incident at Hawk's Hill
    Fic
  (il) George, J. C. Julie of the wolves Fic
  (il) Morey, W. Gentle Ben   Fic
  (il) North, S. Rascal   **599.7**
  (il) Yolen, J. Owl moon   E
Schoenherr, Rusty
  (jt. auth) Schoenherr, A. Mountain biking
    796.6
The **scholar** Be. Terada, A. M.
  In Terada, A. M. Under the starfruit tree;
    folktales from Vietnam p42-49   **398.2**
Scholastic achievement *See* Academic achieve-
ment
Scholastic atlas of oceans (4 and up)   **551.46**
Scholastic atlas of the United States. Rubel, D.
    912
Scholastic atlas of the world (4 and up)   **912**
Scholastic atlas of weather (5 and up)   **551.5**
Scholastic children's dictionary (3-5)   **423**
Scholastic children's encyclopedia (4 and up)
    031
Scholastic children's thesaurus. Bollard, J. K.
    423
Scholastic dictionary of idioms. Terban, M.
    423
Scholastic dictionary of spelling. Terban, M.
    428
Scholastic dinosaurs A to Z. Lessem, D.
    567.9
Scholastic encyclopedia of the presidents and their
    times. Rubel, D.   **920**

School stories—*Continued*

McNamee, G. Sparks (4-6)　　　　　**Fic**

McNaughton, C. Once upon an ordinary school day　　　　　**E**

Mead, A. Madame Squidley and Beanie (3-5)　　　　　**Fic**

Millman, I. Moses goes to school　　　　　**E**

Mills, C. 7 x 9 = trouble! (2-4)　　　　　**Fic**

Mills, C. Alex Ryan, stop that! (5 and up)　　　　　**Fic**

Mills, C. Lizzie at last (5 and up)　　　　　**Fic**

Mills, C. Makeovers by Marcia (5 and up)　　　　　**Fic**

Mills, C. Trading places (3-5)　　　　　**Fic**

Mills, C. Ziggy's blue-ribbon day　　　　　**E**

Morgenstern, S. H. A book of coupons (3-5)　　　　　**Fic**

Moss, M. Amelia's 6th-grade notebook (4-6)　　　　　**Fic**

Nagda, A. W. Dear Whiskers (2-4)　　　　　**Fic**

Naylor, P. R. The agony of Alice (5 and up)　　　　　**Fic**

Naylor, P. R. Starting with Alice (3-6)　　　　　**Fic**

Nixon, J. L. Laugh till you cry (5 and up)　　　　　**Fic**

Noble, T. H. The day Jimmy's boa ate the wash　　　　　**E**

O'Dell, K. Agnes Parker . . . girl in progress (4 and up)　　　　　**Fic**

Park, B. Junie B. Jones and her big fat mouth (2-4)　　　　　**Fic**

Paterson, K. Marvin one too many　　　　　**E**

Peck, R. Lost in cyberspace (5 and up)　　　　　**Fic**

Pérez, L. K. First day in grapes　　　　　**E**

Polacco, P. Mr. Lincoln's way　　　　　**E**

Poydar, N. The biggest test in the universe　　　　　**E**

Pulver, R. Punctuation takes a vacation　　　　　**E**

Rathmann, P. Officer Buckle and Gloria　　　　　**E**

Ray, D. Ghost girl (5 and up)　　　　　**Fic**

Reynolds, P. The dot　　　　　**E**

Rockwell, A. F. 100 school days　　　　　**E**

Rockwell, A. F. Career day　　　　　**E**

Rockwell, A. F. Mother's Day　　　　　**E**

Rockwell, A. F. Thanksgiving Day　　　　　**E**

Rockwell, A. F. Valentine's Day　　　　　**E**

Rodman, M. A. Yankee girl (4 and up)　　　　　**Fic**

Rosenberry, V. Vera's first day of school　　　　　**E**

Rylant, C. The ticky-tacky doll　　　　　**E**

Sachar, L. Wayside School gets a little stranger (3-6)　　　　　**Fic**

Schwartz, A. Things I learned in second grade　　　　　**E**

Scott, A. H. Brave as a mountain lion　　　　　**E**

Seuling, B. Robert and the back-to-school special (2-4)　　　　　**Fic**

Seuss, Dr. Hooray for Diffendoofer Day!　　　　　**E**

Shalant, P. Beware of kissing Lizard Lips (4-6)　　　　　**Fic**

Shreve, S. R. The flunking of Joshua T. Bates (3-5)　　　　　**Fic**

Shreve, S. R. Trout and me (5 and up)　　　　　**Fic**

Siebold, J. My nights at the Improv (4 and up)　　　　　**Fic**

Simms, L. Rotten teeth　　　　　**E**

Snyder, Z. K. Libby on Wednesdays (5 and up)　　　　　**Fic**

Spinelli, J. Loser (4 and up)　　　　　**Fic**

Spinelli, J. There's a girl in my hammerlock (5 and up)　　　　　**Fic**

Spirn, M. I am the turkey　　　　　**E**

Sturges, P. I love school!　　　　　**E**

Tolan, S. S. Save Halloween! (5 and up)　　　　　**Fic**

Tripping over the lunch lady and other school stories (4 and up)　　　　　**S C**

Vega, D. Click here (5 and up)　　　　　**Fic**

Wells, R. Emily's first 100 days of school　　　　　**E**

Wells, R. Timothy's tales from Hilltop School　　　　　**E**

Wells, R. Yoko　　　　　**E**

Weston, M. Act I, act II, act normal (5 and up)　　　　　**Fic**

Whittenberg, A. Sweet Thang (5 and up)　　　　　**Fic**

Wild, M. Tom goes to kindergarten　　　　　**E**

Willner-Pardo, G. Daphne Eloise Slater, who's tall for her age (2-4)　　　　　**Fic**

Winerip, M. Adam Canfield of the Slash (5 and up)　　　　　**Fic**

Wright, B. R. The ghost in Room 11 (3-5)　　　　　**Fic**

Yee, L. Millicent Min, girl genius (5 and up)　　　　　**Fic**

Zalben, J. B. Unfinished dreams (5 and up)　　　　　**Fic**

The **school** story. Clements, A.　　　　　**Fic**

School survival guide [series]

James, E. How to write terrific book reports　　　　　**808**

School trips *See* Field trips

School wide book events. Ray, V. L.　　　　　**027.8**

The **schoolmasters**. Fisher, L. E.　　　　　**370.9**

Schools

See also Education; Nursery schools; Public schools

Fiction

See School stories

Poetry

Calmenson, S. Kindergarten kids (k-1)　　　　　**811**

Dakos, K. Put your eyes up here (2-4)　　　　　**811**

Shields, C. D. Almost late to school and more school poems (2-4)　　　　　**811**

Shields, C. D. Lunch money and other poems about school (2-4)　　　　　**811**

Alaska

Aillaud, C. L. Recess at 20 below (k-3)　　　　　**371.2**

United States—History

Bial, R. One-room school (3-5)　　　　　**370.9**

Loeper, J. J. Going to school in 1776 (4 and up)　　　　　**370.9**

Schorer, Suki

Put your best foot forward (4 and up)　　　　　**792.8**

Schories, Pat

Breakfast for Jack　　　　　**E**

(il) Capucilli, A. Biscuit's new trick　　　　　**E**

Schotter, Roni

The boy who loved words　　　　　**E**

Missing Rabbit　　　　　**E**

Schraff, Anne E.
Harriet Tubman (5 and up)   **92**

Schram, Peninnah
(ed) Oberman, S. Solomon and the ant;   **398.2**

Schroder, Mark
(il) Nelson, V. M. Juneteenth   **394.26**
(il) Wadsworth, G. Cesar Chavez   **92**

Schroeder, Alan
Minty: a story of young Harriet Tubman   **E**
Ragtime Tumpie   **E**
Satchmo's blues   **E**
Smoky Mountain Rose   **E**

Schroeder, Becky
See/See also pages in the following book(s):
Thimmesh, C. Girls think of everything (5 and up)   **920**

Schroeder, Peter W.
Six million paper clips (5 and up)   **940.53**

Schroeder-Hildebrand, Dagmar
(jt. auth) Schroeder, P. W. Six million paper clips   **940.53**

Schubert, Leda
Ballet of the elephants   **791.8**

Schuch, Steve
A symphony of whales   **E**

Schuckett, Sandy
Political advocacy for school librarians   **027.8**

Schuett, Stacey
(il) Branley, F. M. Day light, night light   **535**
(il) Bulla, C. R. A tree is a plant   **582.16**
(il) Edwards, M. Papa's latkes   **E**
(il) Halloween howls. See Halloween howls   **811.008**
(il) Lakin, P. Fat chance Thanksgiving   **E**
(il) Murray, M. D. Little Wolf and the moon   **E**
(il) Schnur, S. Spring thaw   **E**
(il) Younger, B. Purple mountain majesties: the story of Katharine Lee Bates and "America the beautiful"   **92**

Schulman, Janet
The nutcracker (4 and up)   **Fic**
(ed) You read to me & I'll read to you. See You read to me & I'll read to you [20th-century stories to share]   **E**

Schumacher, Julie
The chain letter (5 and up)   **Fic**

Schumaker, Ward
In my garden   **E**

Schumann, Clara, 1819-1896
About
Reich, S. Clara Schumann (5 and up)   **92**
See/See also pages in the following book(s):
Krull, K. Lives of the musicians (4 and up)   **920**

Schur, Maxine
The circlemaker (5 and up)   **Fic**

Schwabacher, Martin
Butterflies (3-6)   **595.7**
Frogs (3-6)   **597.8**

Schwartz, Alvin
All of our noses are here, and other noodle tales (k-2)   **398.2**
Contents: Jane gets a donkey; Grandpa misses the boat; All of our noses are here; The best boy in the world; Sam's girl friend
Busy buzzing bumblebees and other tongue twisters (k-2)   **808.88**
Ghosts! (k-2)   **398.2**
Contents: The haunted house; Susie; A little green bottle; The umbrella; Three little ghosts; The teeny-tiny woman; Ghost, get lost
The girl who stood on a grave
In Beware!; R.L. Stine picks his favorite scary stories p185-87   **808.8**
Harold
In Beware!; R.L. Stine picks his favorite scary stories p179-84   **808.8**
I saw you in the bathtub, and other folk rhymes (k-2)   **398.2**
In a dark, dark room, and other scary stories (k-2)   **398.2**
Contents: The teeth; In the graveyard; The green ribbon; In a dark, dark room; The night it rained; The pirate
More scary stories to tell in the dark (4 and up)   **398.2**
Scary stories 3 (4 and up)   **398.2**
Scary stories to tell in the dark (4 and up)   **398.2**
There is a carrot in my ear, and other noodle tales (k-2)   **398.2**
Contents: The Browns take the day off; Sam and Jane go camping; Mr. Brown washes his underwear; Jane grows a carrot; Grandpa buys a pumpkin egg; It is time to go to sleep
The wendigo
In Schwartz, A. Scary stories to tell in the dark p49-53   **398.2**

Schwartz, Amy
Begin at the beginning   **E**
A glorious day   **E**
Some babies   **E**
Things I learned in second grade   **E**
What James likes best   **E**
(il) Hest, A. The purple coat   **E**

Schwartz, Betty Ann
(ed) My kingdom for a horse. See My kingdom for a horse   **811.008**

Schwartz, Daniel Bennett
(il) Byars, B. C. The house of wings   **Fic**

Schwartz, David M.
G is for googol (4 and up)   **510**
How much is a million?   **E**
If you made a million   **E**
Millions to measure (2-4)   **530.8**
On beyond a million (2-4)   **513**
Q is for quark (4 and up)   **500**

Schwartz, Howard
Before you were born (k-3)   **398.2**
A coat for the moon and other Jewish tales (4 and up)   **398.2**
Contents: The Queen of the Sea; The enchanted spring; The lamp on the mountain; The underground world; The demon in the wine cellar; The rusty plate; The witch Barusha; The Sabbath walking stick; Amsha the giant; The king's secret; The fisherman and the silver fish; The weaving that saved the prince; A family of demons; The royal artists and the clever king; A coat for the moon
Invisible kingdoms (3-5)   **398.2**

The **selkie** wife. Lunge-Larsen, L.
   In Lunge-Larsen, L. The hidden folk; stories of fairies, dwarves, selkies, and other secret beings p64-68   **398.2**

Selkirk, Alexander, 1676-1721
About
Kraske, R. Marooned [biography of Alexander Selkirk] (5 and up)   **92**

Selsam, Millicent Ellis
   Big tracks, little tracks (k-3)   **591.5**

Seltzer, Meyer
   (il) White, L. B. Shazam! simple science magic   **793.8**

Selway, Martina
   (jt. auth) Whitford, R. Little yoga   **613.7**

Selznick, Brian
   The wild prince
   In Friends; stories about new friends, old friends, and unexpectedly true friends   **S C**
   (il) Clements, A. Frindle   **Fic**
   (il) Clements, A. The school story   **Fic**
   (il) Conrad, P. Our house   **S C**
   (il) Godwin, L. Barnyard prayers   **811**
   (il) Kerley, B. The dinosaurs of Waterhouse Hawkins   **92**
   (il) Kerley, B. Walt Whitman   **92**
   (il) Martin, A. M. The doll people   **Fic**
   (il) Ryan, P. M. Amelia and Eleanor go for a ride   **E**
   (il) Ryan, P. M. When Marian sang: the true recital of Marian Anderson, the voice of a century   **92**
   (il) Seidler, T. The dulcimer boy   **Fic**
   (il) Wells, R. Wingwalker   **Fic**

Seminole Indians
Andryszewski, T. The Seminoles (4-6)   **970.004**
Sneve, V. D. H. The Seminoles (3-5)   **970.004**

Semiramis. Mayer, M.
   In Mayer, M. Women warriors; myths and legends of heroic women p21-24   **398**

Semmelweis, Ignác Fülöp, 1818-1865
See/See also pages in the following book(s):
Fradin, D. B. With a little luck (5 and up)   **509**

Sempé
   (il) Goscinny. Nicholas   **Fic**

Semple, Carol McCormick
   Diabetes (4 and up)   **616.4**

Sención, the Indian girl. Delacre, L.
   In Delacre, L. Golden tales; myths, legends, and folktales from Latin America p25-27   **398.2**

Sendak, Maurice
   Alligators all around   **E**
   Chicken soup with rice   **E**
   Higglety pigglety pop! (2-4)   **Fic**
   In the night kitchen   **E**
   One was Johnny   **E**
   Outside over there   **E**
   Pierre   **E**

   also in You read to me & I'll read to you; 20th-century stories to share p240-48   **E**
   Where the wild things are   **E**
About
Kushner, T. The art of Maurice Sendak   **741.6**
See/See also pages in the following book(s):
Marcus, L. S. A Caldecott celebration   **741.6**
Marcus, L. S. Ways of telling   **741.6**
   (il) DeJong, M. The house of sixty fathers   **Fic**
   (il) DeJong, M. The wheel on the school   **Fic**
   (il) Hoffmann, E. T. A. Nutcracker   **Fic**
   (il) I saw Esau. See I saw Esau   **398.8**
   (il) Jarrell, R. The animal family   **Fic**
   (il) Jarrell, R. The bat-poet   **Fic**
   (il) Joslin, S. What do you do, dear?   **395**
   (il) Joslin, S. What do you say, dear?   **395**
   (il) Krauss, R. Bears   **E**
   (il) Krauss, R. A very special house   **E**
   (il) Kushner, T. The art of Maurice Sendak   **741.6**
   (il) Kushner, T. Brundibar   **E**
   (il) MacDonald, G. The light princess   **Fic**
   (il) Marshall, J. Swine Lake   **E**
   (il) Minarik, E. H. Little Bear   **E**
   (il) Minarik, E. H. No fighting, no biting!   **E**
   (il) Singer, I. B. Zlateh the goat, and other stories   **398.2**
   (il) Vogel, A. How little Lori visited Times Square   **E**
   (il) Zolotow, C. Mr. Rabbit and the lovely present   **E**

Sendeh sings to the prairie dogs. Curry, J. L.
   In Curry, J. L. Hold up the sky: and other Native American tales from Texas and the Southern Plains p89-94   **398.2**

The **sending.** San Souci, R.
   In San Souci, R. Even more short & shivery; thirty spine-tingling stories p136-39   **398.2**

Seneca Indians
Folklore
Bruchac, J. Turtle's race with Beaver (k-3)   **398.2**
Martin, R. The world before this one (4 and up)   **398.2**
Taylor, H. P. Brother Wolf (k-3)   **398.2**

Senegal
Berg, E. Senegal (5 and up)   **966.3**

Senisi, Ellen B.
   Hurray for pre-K!   **E**

Senker, Cath
   The Arab-Israeli conflict (5 and up)   **956.04**
   Rosalind Franklin (5 and up)   **92**

Sennett, Mack, 1880-1960
About
Brown, D. Mack made movies [biography of Mack Sennett] (2-4)   **92**

Senning, Cindy Post
   (jt. auth) Post, P. Emily Post's The guide to good manners for kids   **395**

Shange, Ntozake
Ellington was not a street   E
Muhammad Ali: the man who could float like a butterfly and sting like a bee (k-3)   92

Shannon, David
Alice the fairy   E
A bad case of stripes   E
Duck on a bike   E
Good boy, Fergus!   E
No, David!   E
The rain came down   E
(il) Long, M. How I became a pirate   E
(il) Martin, R. The boy who lived with the seals   398.2
(il) Martin, R. The Shark God   398.2
(il) Wood, A. The Bunyans   E
(il) Yolen, J. The ballad of the pirate queens   811

Shannon, George
Busy in the garden (k-2)   811
Lizard's guest   E
More stories to solve (3 and up)   398.2
More true lies (3-6)   398.2
Still more stories to solve (3 and up)   398.2
Stories to solve (3 and up)   398.2
Tippy-toe chick, go!   E
Tomorrow's alphabet   E
White is for blueberry   E

Shannon, Margaret
The red wolf   E

Shannon: an Ojibway dancer. King, S.   970.004

Shansa Mutongo Shima. Washington, D. L.
In Washington, D. L. A pride of African tales

Shape
Adler, D. A. Shape up! (2-4)   516
Ehlert, L. Color farm   E
Ehlert, L. Color zoo   E
Emberley, E. The wing on a flea   E
Hoban, T. Is it red? Is it yellow? Is it blue?   E
Hoban, T. Shapes, shapes, shapes   E
Hoban, T. So many circles, so many squares   E
Jenkins, S. Big & little (k-2)   591.4
Macdonald, S. Sea shapes   E
Murphy, S. J. Captain Invincible and the space shapes (k-3)   516
Museum shapes   E
Rau, D. M. A star in my orange   E
      Fiction
Henkes, K. Circle dogs   E

The **shape** game. Browne, A.   E

Shape up!. Adler, D. A.   516

Shapes, shapes, shapes. Hoban, T.   E

Shaping the earth. Patent, D. H.   550

Sharing the soup. Jaffe, N.
In Jaffe, N. and Zeitlin, S. J. The cow of no color: riddle stories and justice tales from around the world p104-09   398.2

The **Shark** God. Martin, R.   398.2

Sharkabet. Troll, R.   597

Sharkey, Niamh
(il) Doyle, M. Tales from old Ireland   398.2

Sharks
Arnold, C. Giant shark: megalodon, prehistoric super predator (3-6)   567
Arnosky, J. All about sharks (k-3)   597
Berman, R. Sharks (3-6)   597
Cerullo, M. M. The truth about great white sharks (4 and up)   597
Davies, N. Surprising sharks (k-3)   597
Gibbons, G. Sharks (k-3)   597
Macquitty, M. Shark (4 and up)   597
Mallory, K. Swimming with hammerhead sharks (4 and up)   597
Markle, S. Great white sharks (3-6)   597
Markle, S. Outside and inside sharks (2-4)   597
O'Brien, P. Megatooth! (k-3)   567
Pringle, L. P. Sharks!: strange and wonderful (3-5)   597
Rockwell, A. F. Little shark (k-2)   597
Simon, S. Sharks (2-4)   597
Troll, R. Sharkabet (k-3)   597
      Folklore
Martin, R. The Shark God (k-3)   398.2
Wardlaw, L. Punia and the King of Sharks (k-3)   398.2

Sharks and other sea monsters. Sabuda, R.   560

Sharks!: strange and wonderful. Pringle, L. P.   597

Sharmat, Marjorie Weinman
Gila monsters meet you at the airport   E
I'm not Oscar's friend anymore
In Bauer, C. F. Celebrations; read-aloud holiday and theme book programs p282-85   808.8
Nate the Great   E

Sharmat, Mitchell
Gregory, the terrible eater   E

Sharp, William
(il) Spyri, J. Heidi   Fic

Shashikala: a brief history of love and khadi. Desai Hidier, T.
In Friends; stories about new friends, old friends, and unexpectedly true friends   S C

Shattil, Wendy
(il) Jackson, D. M. The wildlife detectives   363.2

Shaw, Charles
It looked like spilt milk   E

Shaw, Nancy
Raccoon tune   E
Sheep in a jeep   E

Shawnee Indians
Collier, J. L. The Tecumseh you never knew (4 and up)   92

She got hard head you know. Graham, L. B.
In Graham, L. B. How God fix Jonah p84-89   398.2

Shea, Pegi Deitz
Liberty rising (2-4)   974.7
Ten mice for Tet! (k-3)   394.26

Shearer, Alex
The Great Blue Yonder (5 and up)   Fic

Shecter, Ben
 (il) Benchley, N. A ghost named Fred **E**
Shed, Greg
 (il) Bunting, E. Butterfly house **E**
 (il) Bunting, E. Dandelions **E**
Shedlock, Marie L.
 The art of the story-teller **372.6**
 Includes the following stories: Filial piety; The folly of panic;
Hafiz, the stone-cutter; Snegourka; The true spirit of a festival
day
Sheehan, Patricia
 Côte d'Ivoire (5 and up) **966.68**
 Luxembourg (5 and up) **949.35**
 Moldova (5 and up) **947.6**
Sheehan, Sean
 Austria (5 and up) **943.6**
 Cuba (5 and up) **972.91**
 Guatemala (5 and up) **972.81**
 Jamaica (5 and up) **972.92**
 Malta (5 and up) **945**
 Pakistan (5 and up) **954.91**
 Turkey (5 and up) **956.1**
 Zimbabwe (5 and up) **968.91**
 (jt. auth) Powell, A. Ancient Greece **938**
Sheep
 Urbigkit, C. A young shepherd (k-3) **636.3**
    Fiction
 Caple, K. The friendship tree **E**
 Fox, M. Where is the green sheep? **E**
 French, J. Pete the sheep-sheep **E**
 Greenstein, E. One little lamb **E**
 Hobbs, V. Sheep (3-5) **Fic**
 Lewis, K. Little Baa **E**
 Livingstone, S. Harley **E**
 Lyon, G. E. Weaving the rainbow **E**
 Rand, G. Mary was a little lamb **E**
 Scotton, R. Russell the sheep **E**
 Shaw, N. Sheep in a jeep **E**
 Stohner, A. Brave Charlotte **E**
    Folklore
 Aardema, V. Borreguita and the coyote (k-3)
    398.2
 Greene, E. The little golden lamb (k-3)
    398.2
 Hennessy, B. G. The boy who cried wolf (k-2)
    398.2
    Songs
 Hoberman, M. A. Mary had a little lamb (k-2)
    782.42
 Trapani, I. Mary had a little lamb (k-2)
    782.42
Sheep dogs
 Urbigkit, C. Brave dogs, gentle dogs (k-3)
    636.7
Sheep herders *See* Shepherds
Sheep in a jeep. Shaw, N. **E**
The **sheep-pig**. See King-Smith, D. Babe **Fic**
The **sheep,** the fox, and the wolf. Afanas'ev, A. N.
 In Afanas'ev, A. N. Russian fairy tales p275-
 76 **398.2**
A **sheepish** tale. Marshall, J.
 In Marshall, J. Rats on the roof, and other
 stories p19-27 **S C**
Sheila Rae, the brave. Henkes, K. **E**

Sheinkin, Steve
 The American Revolution (4 and up) **973.3**
Shelf life: stories by the book (5 and up) **S C**
She'll be comin' 'round the mountain. Sturges, P.
    782.42
Shellfish
 See also Crabs; Mollusks
Shells
 Zoehfeld, K. W. What lives in a shell? (k-1)
    591.4
Shelter dogs. Kehret, P. **636.7**
Shelters, Animal *See* Animal shelters
Shemiaka the judge. Afanas'ev, A. N.
 In Afanas'ev, A. N. Russian fairy tales p625-
 27 **398.2**
Shepard, Aaron
 King O' the Cats (k-3) **398.2**
 Master man (k-3) **398.2**
 The princess mouse (k-3) **398.2**
 The sea king's daughter (3-6) **398.2**
 Stories on stage **812**
Shepard, Alan B., Jr.
    About
 Orr, T. Alan Shepard (4 and up) **92**
Shepard, Ernest H. (Ernest Howard)
 (il) Grahame, K. The reluctant dragon **Fic**
 (il) Milne, A. A. The complete tales of Winnie-
 the-Pooh **Fic**
 (il) Milne, A. A. The House at Pooh Corner
    Fic
 (il) Milne, A. A. Now we are six **821**
 (il) Milne, A. A. When we were very young
    821
 (il) Milne, A. A. Winnie-the-Pooh **Fic**
 (il) Milne, A. A. The world of Pooh **Fic**
Shepard, Mary Eleanor
 (il) Travers, P. L. Mary Poppins **Fic**
Shepherd, Amanda
 (il) MacLachlan, P. Who loves me? **E**
Shepherd, Donna Walsh *See* Walsh Shepherd,
 Donna, 1948-
The **shepherd** who fought for a princess.
 Skurzynski, G.
 In Fire and wings: dragon tales from East and
 West p95-102 **S C**
The **shepherdess** and the chimney sweep. Ander-
 sen, H. C.
 In Andersen, H. C. The swan's stories p85-97
    S C
Shepherds
 Urbigkit, C. A young shepherd (k-3) **636.3**
    Folklore
 Ben-'Ezer, E. Hosni the dreamer (2-4) **398.2**
The **shepherd's** disguise. Jaffe, N.
 In Jaffe, N. and Zeitlin, S. J. While standing
 on one foot; puzzle stories and wisdom
 tales from the Jewish tradition p50-55
    296.1
Sheppard, Ella *See* Moore, Ella Sheppard, 1851-
 1914
Shepperson, Rob
 (il) Coman, C. The big house **Fic**

Sherlock, Patti
Letters from Wolfie (5 and up)   **Fic**

Sherman, Gale W.
(jt. auth) Ammon, B. D. Worth a thousand words   **011.6**

Sherman, Josepha
The history of the Internet (4 and up)   **004.6**
The history of the personal computer (4 and up)   **004**

Sherman, Ori
(il) Schwartz, L. S. The four questions   **296.4**

Sherman, Pat
The sun's daughter (2-4)   **398.2**

Sherman, Patsy O., 1930-
See/See also pages in the following book(s):
Thimmesh, C. Girls think of everything (5 and up)   **920**

Sherman, Whitney
(il) Jaffe, N. The cow of no color: riddle stories and justice tales from around the world   **398.2**

Sheth, Kashmira
Blue jasmine (5 and up)   **Fic**

Shetterly, Will
Little Red and the Big Bad
In Swan sister; fairy tales retold   **S C**

Shhh! we're writing the Constitution. Fritz, J.   **342**

Shhhhh! Everybody's sleeping. Markes, J.   **E**

Shi-shi-etko. Campbell, N. I.   **E**

Shields, Carol Diggory
Almost late to school and more school poems (2-4)   **811**
English, fresh squeezed! (4 and up)   **811**
Lucky pennies and hot chocolate   **E**
Lunch money and other poems about school (2-4)   **811**

Shields, Charles J.
Belize (4 and up)   **972.82**
Central America: facts and figures (4 and up)   **972.8**
Honduras (4 and up)   **972.83**

Shih Huang-ti, Emperor of China *See* Ch'in Shih-huang, Emperor of China, 259-210 B.C.

Shikibu, Murasaki *See* Murasaki Shikibu, b. 978?

Shillinglaw, Bruce
(jt. auth) Zoehfeld, K. W. Dinosaur parents, dinosaur young   **567.9**

Shiloh. Naylor, P. R.   **Fic**

Shimin, Symeon
(il) Hamilton, V. Zeely   **Fic**
(il) Krumgold, J. Onion John   **Fic**

Shine, Andrea
(il) Brisson, P. The summer my father was ten   **E**

Shingebiss. Van Laan, N.   **398.2**

Ship. Macaulay, D.   **387.2**

Ship ahoy!. Sís, P.   **E**

The **ship** that went to America. Philip, N.
In Philip, N. Celtic fairy tales p125-36   **398.2**

Shipbuilding
History
Appelbaum, D. K. Giants in the land (2-4)   **634.9**

Shipping
United States
Sandler, M. W. On the waters of the USA (5 and up)   **387.2**

Ships
See also Steamboats
Barton, B. Boats (k-1)   **387.2**
Collicutt, P. This boat (k-2)   **387.2**
Crews, D. Harbor   **E**
Gibbons, G. Boat book (k-3)   **387.2**
O'Brien, P. The great ships (4 and up)   **387.2**
Sandler, M. W. On the waters of the USA (5 and up)   **387.2**
Sís, P. Ship ahoy!   **E**
Fiction
Avi. Abigail takes the wheel (2-4)   **Fic**

Shipton, Paul
The pig scrolls (5 and up)   **Fic**

Shipwrecked!: the true adventures of a Japanese boy [biography of Manjiro Nakahama] Blumberg, R.   **92**

Shipwrecks
Adams, S. Titanic (4 and up)   **910.4**
Ballard, R. D. Ghost liners (4 and up)   **910.4**
Gibbons, G. Sunken treasure (k-3)   **910.4**
Kentley, E. Story of the Titanic (4 and up)   **910.4**
Macaulay, D. Ship (4 and up)   **387.2**
Marschall, K. Inside the Titanic (4 and up)   **910.4**
Matsen, B. The incredible search for the treasure ship Atocha (4 and up)   **910.4**
Platt, R. Shipwreck (4 and up)   **910.4**
Fiction
Agee, J. Terrific   **E**
Lawrence, I. The wreckers (5 and up)   **Fic**
Meddaugh, S. Harry on the rocks   **E**

A **shlemiel** and a shlimazel. Taback, S.
In Taback, S. Kibitzers and fools; tales my zayda (grandfather) told me   **398.2**

Shlemiel the businessman. Singer, I. B.
In Singer, I. B. Stories for children p130-38   **S C**

Shocking science. Levine, S.   **537**

Shoe industry
Mitchell, B. Shoes for everyone: a story about Jan Matzeliger (3-5)   **92**

Shoebag. James, M.   **Fic**

Shoeless Joe & Black Betsy. Bildner, P.   **E**

Shoeless Joe & me. Gutman, D.   **Fic**

Shoeless Joe Jackson *See* Jackson, Joe, 1888-1951

The **shoemaker** and Old Scratch. Avi
In Avi. Strange happenings; five tales of transformation   **S C**

Shoemakers
Fisher, L. E. The shoemakers (4 and up)   **685**

Shoes
  Miller, M. Whose shoe?   **E**
  Morris, A. Shoes, shoes, shoes (k-1)   **391**
  Yue, C. Shoes (4 and up)   **391**
        Fiction
  Hurwitz, J. New shoes for Silvia   **E**
  Soto, G. If the shoe fits   **E**
  Winthrop, E. Shoes   **E**
Shoes for everyone: a story about Jan Matzeliger.
  Mitchell, B.   **92**
Shoes, shoes, shoes. Morris, A.   **391**
Shohet, Marti
  (il) Sattler, H. R. Recipes for art and craft mate-
  rials   **745.5**
Sholem Aleichem, 1859-1916
        About
  Silverman, E. Sholom's treasure [biography of
  Sholem Aleichem] (k-3)   **92**
        Adaptations
  Silverman, E. When the chickens went on strike
      E
Sholom Aleichem *See* Sholem Aleichem, 1859-
  1916
Sholom's treasure [biography of Sholem
  Aleichem] Silverman, E.   **92**
The **shoot-out.** Nixon, J. L.
  In Nixon, J. L. Ghost town; seven ghostly
  stories p3-15   **S C**
The **shooting** of Dan McGrew. Service, R. W.
      811

Shooting stars *See* Meteors
Shopping
        Fiction
  Ahlberg, A. The shopping expedition   **E**
  Elya, S. M. Bebe goes shopping   **E**
  Eriksson, E. Molly goes shopping   **E**
  Lobel, A. On Market Street   **E**
The **shopping** expedition. Ahlberg, A.   **E**
Shore, Diane ZuHone
  This is the dream (2-4)   **811**
Short & shivery. San Souci, R.   **398.2**
Short stories
  Aiken, J. Shadows and moonshine (4 and up)
      S C
  Alexander, L. The foundling and other tales of
  Prydain (5 and up)   **S C**
  Andersen, H. C. Hans Christian Andersen's
  Fairy Tales (4 and up)   **S C**
  Andersen, H. C. The swan's stories   **S C**
  Avi. Strange happenings (5 and up)   **S C**
  Avi. What do fish have to do with anything?
  and other stories (4 and up)   **S C**
  Babbitt, N. The Devil's other storybook (4-6)
      S C
  Babbitt, N. The Devil's storybook (4-6)   **S C**
  Byars, B. C. My dog, my hero (3-6)   **S C**
  Conrad, P. Our house (4 and up)   **S C**
  Fire and wings: dragon tales from East and
  West (4 and up)   **S C**
  Fleischman, P. Graven images (5 and up)
      S C
  Friends (5 and up)   **S C**
  A Glory of unicorns (5 and up)   **S C**
  Horse tales (4 and up)   **S C**

Hughes, S. Stories by firelight   **E**
Hughes, T. How the Whale became and other
  stories (4-6)   **S C**
Jiménez, F. The circuit: stories from the life of
  a migrant child (5 and up)   **S C**
Jones, D. W. Mixed magics (5 and up)   **S C**
Kimmel, E. A. The jar of fools: eight Hanukkah
  stories from Chelm (4 and up)   **S C**
Kimmel, E. A. Sword of the samurai (4 and up)
      S C
Kipling, R. A collection of Rudyard Kipling's
  Just so stories (3-6)   **S C**
Kipling, R. The jungle book: Mowgli's story
  (3-6)   **S C**
Kipling, R. The jungle book: the Mowgli stories
  (4 and up)   **S C**
Kipling, R. Just so stories (3-6)   **S C**
Konigsburg, E. L. Altogether, one at a time
  (4-6)   **S C**
Marcantonio, P. S. Red ridin' in the hood (3-5)
      S C
Marshall, J. Rats on the range and other stories
  (2-4)   **S C**
Marshall, J. Rats on the roof, and other stories
  (2-4)   **S C**
McKissack, P. C. The dark-thirty (4 and up)
      S C
Medearis, A. S. Haunts (4 and up)   **S C**
Naidoo, B. Out of bounds: seven stories of con-
  flict and hope (5 and up)   **S C**
Nixon, J. L. Ghost town   **S C**
San Souci, R. Dare to be scared (4 and up)
      S C
San Souci, R. Double-dare to be scared: another
  thirteen chilling tales (4 and up)   **S C**
Sandburg, C. More Rootabaga stories   **S C**
Sandburg, C. Rootabaga stories   **S C**
Shelf life: stories by the book (5 and up)
      S C
Singer, I. B. The power of light (4 and up)
      S C
Singer, I. B. Stories for children (4 and up)
      S C
Soto, G. Baseball in April, and other stories (5
  and up)   **S C**
Soto, G. Petty crimes (5 and up)   **S C**
Spinelli, J. The library card (4 and up)   **S C**
Sports shorts (5 and up)   **S C**
Stine, R. L. The haunting hour (4 and up)
      S C
Swan sister (5 and up)   **S C**
Tripping over the lunch lady and other school
  stories (4 and up)   **S C**
Van Laan, N. Teeny tiny tingly tales   **E**
Wynne-Jones, T. Some of the kinder planets:
  stories (4 and up)   **S C**
You read to me & I'll read to you [20th-century
  stories to share]   **E**
Short story
  Otfinoski, S. Extraordinary short story writing (5
  and up)   **808.3**
Shortall, Leonard W.
  (il) Sobol, D. J. Encyclopedia Brown, boy de-
  tective   **Fic**
  (il) Stolz, M. A dog on Barkham Street   **Fic**
Shortcut. Crews, D.   **E**

Simont, Marc—*Continued*
- (il) Byars, B. C. My brother, Ant   **E**
- (il) Lord, B. B. In the Year of the Boar and Jackie Robinson   **Fic**
- (il) Sharmat, M. W. Nate the Great   **E**
- (il) Udry, J. M. A tree is nice   **E**

Simple machines
- Gardner, R. Sensational science projects with simple machines (4-6)   **621.8**
- Solway, A. Castle under siege! (3-5)   **621.8**

Simple sentences. Babbitt, N.
- *In* Babbitt, N. The Devil's other storybook p63-71   **S C**

Simply sewing. Sadler, J. A.   **646.2**

Simply sewing. Sadler, J. A.
- *also in* Sadler, J. A. The jumbo book of needlecrafts   **746.4**

Simpson, Carol
- (ed) Ethics in school librarianship. See Ethics in school librarianship   **174**

Simpson, Martha Seif
- Storycraft   **372.6**

Sims, Blanche
- (il) Cox, J. Butterfly buddies   **Fic**
- (il) Cox, J. That crazy Eddie and the science project of doom   **Fic**

Simulation, computer *See* Computer simulation

Sinbad the Sailor, The Seven voyages of. Yeoman, J.   **398.2**

Sing a song of piglets. Bunting, E.   **811**

Sing a song of popcorn   **808.81**

Sing a song of sixpence. Chapman, J.   **398.8**

Sing-along song. Macken, J. E.   **E**

Sing-along stories [series]
- Hoberman, M. A. Mary had a little lamb   **782.42**

Sing down the moon. O'Dell, S.   **Fic**

Sing me a story. Rosenberg, J.   **792.5**

The **sing-song** of old man kangaroo. Kipling, R.
- *In* Kipling, R. Just so stories   **S C**

Sing to the sun. Bryan, A.   **811**

Singapore
- Layton, L. Singapore (5 and up)   **959.57**
- Rau, D. M. Singapore (2-4)   **959.57**

Singer, Beverly R.
- (comp) Rising voices. See Rising voices   **810.8**

Singer, Isaac Bashevis
- The fools of Chelm and their history (4 and up)   **Fic**
- The power of light (4 and up)   **S C**
  - Contents: A Hanukkah evening in my parents' house; The extinguished lights; The parakeet named Dreidel; Menashe and Rachel; The squire; The power of light; Hershele and Hanukkah; Hanukkah in the poorhouse
- Shrewd Todie and Lyzer the miser
  - *In* Bauer, C. F. Celebrations; read-aloud holiday and theme book programs p121-25   **808.8**
- The snow in Chelm
  - *In* Snowy day: stories and poems p25-29   **808.8**
- Stories for children (4 and up)   **S C**
  - Contents: The elders of Chelm & Genendel's key; A tale of three wishes; The extinguished lights; Mazel & Shlimazel; Why Noah chose the dove; Zlateh the goat; A Hanukkah Eve in Warsaw; The fools of Chelm & the stupid carp; The wicked city; Rabbi Leib & the witch Cunegunde; The parakeet named Dreidel; Lemel & Tzipa; The day I got lost; Menashe & Rachel; Shlemiel the businessman; Joseph & Koza; A Hanukkah evening in my parents' house; Tsirtsur & Peziza; Naftali the storyteller & his horse, Sus; Hershele & Hanukkah; When Shlemiel went to Warsaw; Elijah the slave; The power of light; Growing up; The Lantuch; Utzel & his daughter, Poverty; The squire; Ole & Trufa; Dalfunka, where the rich live forever; Topiel & Tekla; Hanukkah in the poorhouse; Shrewd Todie & Lyzer the miser; The fearsome inn; The cat who thought she was a dog & the dog who thought he was a cat; Menaseh's dream; Tashlik
- Zlateh the goat, and other stories (4 and up)   **398.2**
  - Contents: Fool's paradise; Grandmother's tale; The snow in Chelm; The mixed-up feet and the silly bridegroom; The first shlemiel; The Devil's trick; Zlateh the goat

Singer, Isaac Bashevis, 1904-1991
- *See/See also pages in the following book(s):*
- Krull, K. Lives of the writers (4 and up)   **920**

Singer, Marilyn
- Central heating (4 and up)   **811**
- Creature carnival (2-4)   **811**
- A dog's gotta do what a dog's gotta do (3-6)   **636.7**
- Family reunion (k-3)   **811**
- Fireflies at midnight (2-4)   **811**
- First position
  - *In* Sports shorts   **S C**
- Footprints on the roof (4 and up)   **811**
- How to cross a pond (3-6)   **811**
- Monster museum (2-4)   **811**
- On the same day in March (k-3)   **551.6**

Singers
- *See also* African American singers
- Chambers, V. Celia Cruz, Queen of salsa (2-4)   **92**
- Christensen, B. Woody Guthrie, poet of the people (3-6)   **92**
- Neimark, A. E. There ain't nobody that can sing like me: the life of Woody Guthrie (5 and up)   **92**
- Orgill, R. Shout, sister, shout! (6 and up)   **920**

Fiction
- Auch, M. J. Bantam of the opera   **E**
- Curry, J. L. The Black Canary (5 and up)   **Fic**
- Daly, N. Ruby sings the blues   **E**

Singing
Fiction
- Bolliger, M. The happy troll   **E**
- Stenmark, V. The singing chick   **E**

The **Singing** bone
- *In* The Magic orange tree, and other Haitian folktales p91-97   **398.2**

The **singing** chick. Stenmark, V.   **E**

Singing games
- Sierra, J. Schoolyard rhymes (k-3)   **398.8**

The **singing** tortoise. Courlander, H.
- *In* Courlander, H. and Herzog, G. Cow-tail switch, and other West African stories p65-72   **398.2**

The **singing** tree and the talking bird. Afanas´ev, A. N.
>*In* Afanas´ev, A. N. Russian fairy tales p184-88   **398.2**

The **singing** turtle. MacDonald, M. R.
>*In* MacDonald, M. R. Look back and see; twenty lively tales for gentle tellers p137-46   **372.6**

Single parent family
Fiction
Birdsall, J. The Penderwicks (3-6)   **Fic**
Greenfield, E. Sister (4 and up)   **Fic**
Hicks, B. Busted! (5 and up)   **Fic**
Lowry, L. The one hundredth thing about Caroline (5 and up)   **Fic**
Thomas, E. The red blanket   **E**

A **single** shard. Park, L. S.   **Fic**

Sink the Bismarck. McGowen, T.   **940.54**

Sinnott, Susan
>Extraordinary Asian Americans and Pacific Islanders (5 and up)   **920**

Sino-Japanese Conflict, 1937-1945
Fiction
DeJong, M. The house of sixty fathers (4-6)   **Fic**

Sioras, Efstathia
>Czech Republic (5 and up)   **943.7**

Siouan Indians
>*See also* Dakota Indians; Oglala Indians

Sioux Indians *See* Dakota Indians

Sir Edmund Hillary, modern day explorer. Brennan, K.   **92**

Sir Gammer Vans. Jacobs, J.
>*In* Jacobs, J. English fairy tales p261-63   **398.2**

Sir Gawain and the Green Knight. Morpurgo, M.   **398.2**

Sir Gawain and the Green Knight. Osborne, M. P.
>*In* Osborne, M. P. Favorite medieval tales p50-59   **398.2**

Sirens and sea monsters. Osborne, M. P.   **883**

Sirrell, Terry
>(il) Masoff, J. Oh, yuck!   **031.02**

Sís, Peter
Ballerina!   **E**
Dinosaur!   **E**
Fire truck   **E**
Follow the dream [biography of Christopher Columbus] (k-3)   **92**
Komodo!   **E**
Madlenka   **E**
Play, Mozart, play! (k-2)   **92**
Ship ahoy!   **E**
A small tall tale from the far Far North   **E**
Starry messenger [biography of Galileo Galilei]   **92**
Tibet   **951**
The train of states (2-4)   **973**
The tree of life: a book depicting the life of Charles Darwin, naturalist, geologist & thinker (4 and up)   **92**
Trucks, trucks, trucks   **E**
(il) Bolliger, M. The happy troll   **E**

(il) Fleischman, S. The 13th floor   **Fic**
(il) Fleischman, S. The midnight horse   **Fic**
(il) Fleischman, S. The whipping boy   **Fic**
(il) Prelutsky, J. The dragons are singing tonight   **811**
(il) Prelutsky, J. The gargoyle on the roof   **811**
(il) Prelutsky, J. Monday's troll   **811**
(il) Prelutsky, J. Scranimals   **811**
(il) Shannon, G. More stories to solve   **398.2**
(il) Shannon, G. Still more stories to solve   **398.2**
(il) Shannon, G. Stories to solve   **398.2**

Sister. Greenfield, E.   **Fic**

Sister Alionushka, brother Ivanushka. Afanas´ev, A. N.
>*In* Afanas´ev, A. N. Russian fairy tales p406-10   **398.2**

Sister Anne's hands. Lorbiecki, M.   **E**

Sister Death and the healer. San Souci, R.
>*In* San Souci, R. More short & shivery; thirty terrifying tales p78-82   **398.2**

Sister Fox and Brother Coyote. San Souci, R.
>*In* San Souci, R. Cut from the same cloth; American women of myth, legend, and tall tale p93-99   **398.2**

Sisters
Fiction
Alcock, V. The cuckoo sister (6 and up)   **Fic**
Arrington, F. Bluestem (4-6)   **Fic**
Barasch, L. The reluctant flower girl   **E**
Birdsall, J. The Penderwicks (3-6)   **Fic**
Boling, K. January 1905 (5 and up)   **Fic**
Buzzeo, T. The sea chest   **E**
Byars, B. C. The keeper of the doves (4 and up)   **Fic**
Cheng, A. The lemon sisters   **E**
Couloumbis, A. Getting near to baby (5 and up)   **Fic**
Greenfield, E. Sister (4 and up)   **Fic**
Griffin, A. The other Shepards (6 and up)   **Fic**
Haas, J. Jigsaw pony (2-4)   **Fic**
Levine, G. C. The two princesses of Bamarre (5 and up)   **Fic**
Lindbergh, R. The visit   **E**
Lisle, J. T. The lost flower children (4-6)   **Fic**
Lowry, L. A summer to die (5 and up)   **Fic**
McPhail, D. M. Sisters   **E**
Numeroff, L. J. The Chicken sisters   **E**
Patron, S. Maybe yes, maybe no, maybe maybe (3-5)   **Fic**
Peterson, J. W. Don't forget Winona   **E**
Potter, G. Chloe's birthday . . . and me   **E**
Roberts, W. D. The one left behind (5 and up)   **Fic**
Rodowsky, C. F. Spindrift (5 and up)   **Fic**
Samuels, B. Dolores on her toes   **E**
Sendak, M. Outside over there   **E**
Tucker, K. The seven Chinese sisters   **E**
Wilson, J. The illustrated Mum (5 and up)   **Fic**
Young, E. My Mei Mei   **E**
Zemach, M. Eating up Gladys   **E**

Smith, Charles W. G.
(jt. auth) Laubach, C. M. Raptor! a kid's guide to birds of prey **598**

Smith, Craig
(il) Crew, G. Troy Thompson's excellent peotry book **Fic**

Smith, Cynthia Leitich
Indian shoes (3-5) **Fic**
Jingle dancer **E**

Smith, D. James
The boys of San Joaquin (5 and up) **Fic**

Smith, David J.
If the world were a village (3-5) **304.6**

Smith, Dick King- *See* King-Smith, Dick, 1922-

Smith, Doris Buchanan
A taste of blackberries (4-6) **Fic**

Smith, Elwood H.
(il) Goodman, S. The truth about poop **573.4**

Smith, Heather
(jt. auth) Rhatigan, J. Sure-to-win science fair projects **507.8**

Smith, Henrietta M.
(ed) The Coretta Scott King Awards book, 1970-1999. See The Coretta Scott King Awards book, 1970-1999 **028.5**

Smith, Hope Anita
The way a door closes (4 and up) **811**

Smith, Janice Lee
The kid next door and other headaches (2-4) **Fic**

Smith, Jessie Willcox
(il) MacDonald, G. The princess and the goblin **Fic**
(il) Spyri, J. Heidi **Fic**

Smith, Jos. A. *See* Smith, Joseph A., 1936-

Smith, Joseph A.
(il) Armstrong, J. Audubon **92**
(il) Fleischman, S. Bandit's moon **Fic**
(il) Gellman, M. How do you spell God? **200**
(il) Ginsburg, M. Clay boy **398.2**
(il) Haas, J. Hurry! **E**
(il) Haas, J. Sugaring **E**
(il) Huck, C. S. A creepy countdown **E**
(il) Rubin, S. G. The yellow house **759.4**

Smith, Lane
Glasses: who needs 'em? **E**
Pinocchio, the boy **E**
(il) Dahl, R. James and the giant peach **Fic**
(il) Merriam, E. Spooky A B C **811**
(il) Scieszka, J. Baloney (Henry P.) **E**
(il) Scieszka, J. Knights of the kitchen table **Fic**
(il) Scieszka, J. Math curse **E**
(il) Scieszka, J. Science verse **E**
(jt. auth) Scieszka, J. Seen Art? **Fic**
(jt. auth) Scieszka, J. Squids will be squids **E**
(jt. auth) Scieszka, J. The Stinky Cheese Man and other fairly stupid tales **E**
(il) Scieszka, J. The true story of the 3 little pigs **E**

(jt. auth) Seuss, Dr. Hooray for Diffendoofer Day! **E**

Smith, Linda
Mrs. Biddlebox **E**
When Moon fell down **E**

Smith, Maggie
(il) Fleming, C. This is the baby **E**
(il) George, K. O. Book! **E**
(il) Markes, J. Good thing you're not an octopus! **E**
(il) Roosa, K. Beach day **E**

Smith, Martha
(jt. auth) Knowles, E. Boys and literacy **028.5**
(jt. auth) Knowles, E. More reading connections **028.5**
(jt. auth) Knowles, E. Talk about books! **372.4**

Smith, Owen
(il) Armstrong, J. Magnus at the fire **E**

Smith, Robert Kimmel
Bobby Baseball (4-6) **Fic**
Chocolate fever (4-6) **Fic**
The war with Grandpa (4-6) **Fic**

Smith, Roland
Cryptid hunters (5 and up) **Fic**

Smith, Stuart Tyson
Valley of the Kings (4 and up) **932**

Smith, Theresa
(il) Gershator, P. Zzzng! Zzzng! Zzzng! **398.2**

Smith, Wendy
(il) Ross, M. E. Fish watching with Eugenie Clark **92**
(il) Ross, M. E. Pond watching with Ann Morgan **92**

Smith, Whitney
Flag lore of all nations (4 and up) **929.9**

Smith, William Jay
Around my room (k-3) **811**

Smith. Garfield, L. **Fic**

Smith-Griswold, Wendy
(il) Ross, M. E. Nature art with Chiura Obata **92**

The **smith,** the weaver, and the harper. Alexander, L.
In Alexander, L. The foundling and other tales of Prydain p65-72 **S C**

Smoke. San Souci, R.
In San Souci, R. Dare to be scared; thirteen stories to chill and thrill **S C**

Smokejumpers. Landau, E. **628.9**

Smoking lessons. McCormick, P.
In Friends; stories about new friends, old friends, and unexpectedly true friends **S C**

Smoky Mountain Rose. Schroeder, A. **E**

Smoky night. Bunting, E. **E**

Smothers, Ethel Footman
The hard-times jar **E**

Smuggling
Butterfield, M. Pirates & smugglers (5 and up) **910.4**

Smuggling of drugs *See* Drug traffic

Smyth, Ian
The young baseball player (4 and up)
796.357

The **snail** and the whale. Donaldson, J.   **E**

Snail mail no more. Danziger, P.   **Fic**

Snails
Fiction
Avi. The end of the beginning (3-5)   **Fic**
Donaldson, J. The snail and the whale   **E**
Leedy, L. The great graph contest   **E**
Waddell, M. Hi, Harry!   **E**

Snails, clams, and their relatives. Blaxland, B.
594

The **snake**. Lester, J.
In Lester, J. The last tales of Uncle Remus
p28-33   **398.2**
also in Lester, J. When the beginning began;
stories about God, the creatures, and us
p73-80   **296.1**

The **snake** princess. Terada, A. M.
In Terada, A. M. Under the starfruit tree;
folktales from Vietnam p14-17   **398.2**

The **snake** scientist. Montgomery, S.   **597.96**

Snakes
See also Pythons; Rattlesnakes
Holub, J. Why do snakes hiss? (k-2)   **597.96**
Markle, S. Outside and inside snakes (2-4)
597.96
Markle, S. Snakes (k-3)   **597.96**
Montgomery, S. The snake scientist (4 and up)
597.96
Patent, D. H. Slinky, scaly, slithery snakes (k-3)
597.96
Pringle, L. P. Snakes! (3-5)   **597.96**
Fiction
Aruego, J. The last laugh   **E**
Cannon, J. Verdi   **E**
Noble, T. H. The day Jimmy's boa ate the wash
   E
Spohn, K. Turtle and Snake's day at the beach
   E
Ungerer, T. Crictor   **E**
Walsh, E. S. Mouse count   **E**

Snakey riddles. Hall, K.   **793.73**

Snap. McGhee, A.   **Fic**

Snap books crafts [series]
Hufford, D. Greeting card making   **745.59**

A **snap** of the fingers. San Souci, R.
In San Souci, R. A terrifying taste of short &
shivery; thirty creepy tales p123-29
398.2

Snapshot. Czech, K. P.   **770.9**

Snapshots: Images of People and Places in History [series]
MacLeod, E. Helen Keller   **92**

Sneakers
Cobb, V. Sneakers (3-5)   **685**

Sneed, Brad
(il) Arnold, M. D. The pumpkin runner   **E**
(il) Schroeder, A. Smoky Mountain Rose   **E**

Snegourka. Shedlock, M. L.
In Shedlock, M. L. The art of the story-teller
p195-97   **372.6**

Sneve, Virginia Driving Hawk
The Apaches (3-5)   **970.004**
The Cherokees (3-5)   **970.004**
The Cheyennes (3-5)   **970.004**
High Elk's treasure   **Fic**
The Hopis (3-5)   **970.004**
The Navajos (3-5)   **970.004**
The Nez Percé (3-5)   **970.004**
The Seminoles (3-5)   **970.004**
(comp) Dancing teepees: poems of American Indian youth. See Dancing teepees: poems of American Indian youth   **897**

Snicket, Lemony
The bad beginning (4 and up)   **Fic**
Lemony Snicket: the unauthorized autobiography (4 and up)   **Fic**

Snicket, Lemony, 1970-
About
Haugen, H. M. Daniel Handler [biography of Lemony Snicket] (4 and up)   **92**

Snip snap!. Bergman, M.   **E**

Snodgrass, Mary Ellen
(jt. auth) Patterson, L. Indian terms of the Americas   **970.004**

The **snotty** goat. Afanas´ev, A. N.
In Afanas´ev, A. N. Russian fairy tales p200-02   **398.2**

Snow, Judith E.
How it feels to have a gay or lesbian parent (5 and up)   **306.8**

Snow, Scott
(il) Kimmel, E. C. To the frontier   **Fic**

Snow
Branley, F. M. Snow is falling (k-1)   **551.57**
Martin, J. B. Snowflake Bentley [biography of Wilson Alwyn Bentley] (k-3)   **92**
Waldman, N. The snowflake (k-3)   **551.48**
Fiction
Berry, L. Duck skates   **E**
Bond, R. This place in the snow   **E**
Briggs, R. The snowman   **E**
Buehner, C. Snowmen at night   **E**
Burton, V. L. Katy and the big snow   **E**
Cheng, A. The lemon sisters   **E**
Denslow, S. P. In the snow   **E**
Dunrea, O. It's snowing!   **E**
Ehlert, L. Snowballs   **E**
Fenner, C. Snowed in with Grandmother Silk (2-4)   **Fic**
Fleming, D. The first day of winter   **E**
Ford, B. First snow   **E**
Henkes, K. Oh!   **E**
Keats, E. J. The snowy day   **E**
Lewis, J. P. The snowflake sisters   **E**
Lin, G. Robert's snow   **E**
McCully, E. A. First snow   **E**
Neitzel, S. The jacket I wear in the snow   **E**
Perkins, L. R. Snow music   **E**
Root, P. Grandmother Winter   **E**
Schertle, A. All you need for a snowman   **E**
Shulevitz, U. Snow   **E**
Tresselt, A. R. White snow, bright snow   **E**

Snow—Fiction—*Continued*

Vestergaard, H. Hello, snow!　　　　　　**E**

Waddell, M. Snow bears　　　　　　　　**E**

Yee, W. H. Tracks in the snow　　　　　**E**

Poetry

Quattlebaum, M. Winter friends (k-2)　　**811**

Snow bears. Waddell, M.　　　　　　　**E**

The **snow** bunting's lullaby. MacDonald, M. R.

In MacDonald, M. R. Look back and see; twenty lively tales for gentle tellers p3-10　　**372.6**

The **snow** husband. San Souci, R.

In San Souci, R. A terrifying taste of short & shivery; thirty creepy tales p58-61　　**398.2**

The **snow** in Chelm. Singer, I. B.

also in Singer, I. B. Zlateh the goat, and other stories p29-34　　**398.2**

In Snowy day: stories and poems p25-29　　**808.8**

Snow is falling. Branley, F. M.　　　　**551.57**

The **snow** monkey and the boar. Climo, S.

In Climo, S. Monkey business; stories from around the world　　**398.2**

Snow music. Perkins, L. R.　　　　　　**E**

Snow pony [excerpt]. Lester, A.

In Horse tales　　　　　　　　　　　**S C**

The **Snow** Queen. Bell, A.　　　　　　**E**

Snow treasure. McSwigan, M.　　　　　**Fic**

Snow White. Doherty, B.

In Doherty, B. Fairy tales　　　　　　**398.2**

Snow-White and Rose-Red. Grimm, J.

In The Blue fairy book p259-65　　　　**398.2**

Snow White and the fox. Afanas'ev, A. N.

In Afanas'ev, A. N. Russian fairy tales p283-84　　**398.2**

Snow White and the seven dwarfs. Grimm, J.

In Princess stories; a classic illustrated edition　　**398.2**

Snowballs. Ehlert, L.　　　　　　　　**E**

Snowboarding

Thomas, K. Blades, boards & scooters (5 and up)　　**796.2**

Woods, B. Snowboarding (4-6)　　　　**796.9**

Snowbound. Lavender, D. S.　　　　　**978**

Snowed in with Grandmother Silk. Fenner, C.　　**Fic**

The **snowflake**. Waldman, N.　　　　　**551.48**

Snowflake Bentley [biography of Wilson Alwyn Bentley] Martin, J. B.　　**92**

The **snowflake** sisters. Lewis, J. P.　　　**E**

The **snowman**. Andersen, H. C.

In Andersen, H. C. The swan's stories p109-21　　**S C**

The **snowman**. Briggs, R.　　　　　　**E**

Snowmen at night. Buehner, C.　　　　**E**

The **snowy** day. Keats, E. J.　　　　　**E**

Snowy day: stories and poems (2-4)　　**808.8**

Snug in Mama's arms. Medearis, A. S.　　**E**

Snyder, Dianne

The boy of the three-year nap (1-3)　　**398.2**

Snyder, Midori

Golden fur [y]

In Swan sister; fairy tales retold　　　**S C**

Snyder, Zilpha Keatley

Cat running (4 and up)　　　　　　　**Fic**

The Egypt game (5 and up)　　　　　**Fic**

The ghosts of Rathburn Park (5 and up)　**Fic**

The headless cupid (5 and up)　　　　**Fic**

Libby on Wednesdays (5 and up)　　　**Fic**

The magic nation thing (4 and up)　　**Fic**

The runaways (4 and up)　　　　　　**Fic**

Spyhole secrets (4 and up)　　　　　**Fic**

The Unseen (5 and up)　　　　　　　**Fic**

The witches of Worm (5 and up)　　　**Fic**

So, Meilo

Gobble, gobble, slip, slop　　　　　　**398.2**

(il) The 20th century children's poetry treasury. See The 20th century children's poetry treasury　　**811.008**

(il) The Beauty of the beast. See The Beauty of the beast　　**811.008**

(il) Ó Flatharta, A. Hurry and the monarch　　**E**

(il) Okimoto, J. D. The White Swan express　　**E**

(il) Sierra, J. Tasty baby belly buttons　　**398.2**

(il) Simonds, N. Moonbeams, dumplings & dragon boats　　**394.26**

(il) Singer, M. Central heating　　　　**811**

(il) Singer, M. Footprints on the roof　　**811**

(il) Singer, M. How to cross a pond　　**811**

So B. it. Weeks, S.　　　　　　　　　**Fic**

So far from the bamboo grove. Watkins, Y. K.　　**Fic**

So far from the sea. Bunting, E.　　　　**E**

So happy!. Henkes, K.　　　　　　　　**E**

So many circles, so many squares. Hoban, T.　　**E**

So many dynamos! and other palindromes. Agee, J.　　**793.73**

So say the little monkeys. Climo, S.

In Climo, S. Monkey business; stories from around the world　　**398.2**

So sleepy story. Shulevitz, U.　　　　　**E**

So what's it like to be a cat? Kuskin, K.　　**E**

So you want to be an inventor? St. George, J.　　**609**

So you want to be president? St. George, J.　　**973**

Soap

Rhatigan, J. Soapmaking (3-6)　　　　**668**

Wagner, L. Cool melt & pour soap (4-6)　　**668**

Fiction

Schaefer, C. L. The biggest soap　　　**E**

Soap, soap, soap

In Grandfather tales; American-English folk tales p130-36　　**398.2**

Soapmaking. Rhatigan, J.　　　　　　**668**

Soaring with the wind. Gibbons, G.　　**598**

Sobol, Donald J.

Encyclopedia Brown, boy detective (3-5)　**Fic**

Sobol, Richard
An elephant in the backyard (k-3) **636.9**
(il) Hudson, C. W. Construction zone **690**

Soccer
Blackstone, M. This is soccer (k-2) **796.334**
Coleman, L. Fundamental soccer (5 and up)
 796.334
Gibbons, G. My soccer book (k-2) **796.334**
Hamm, M. Winners never quit! **E**
Hornby, H. Soccer (4 and up) **796.334**
Fiction
Avi. S.O.R. losers (5 and up) **Fic**
Poetry
Burleigh, R. Goal (k-3) **811**

Social anthropology *See* Ethnology

Social classes
 See also Working class

Social problems
Lewis, B. A. The kid's guide to social action (4 and up) **361.2**

Social sciences
Bibliography
Notable social studies trade books for young people **016.3**

Society of Friends
Kroll, S. William Penn (3-5) **92**
Woog, A. What makes me a Quaker? (3-5)
 289.6
Fiction
Bruchac, J. The arrow over the door (4-6)
 Fic
De Angeli, M. L. Thee, Hannah! (3-5) **Fic**

Socks. Cleary, B. **Fic**

Sod houses on the Great Plains. Rounds, G.
 693

Sodium chloride *See* Salt

Sody Sallyraytus
 In Grandfather tales; American-English folk tales p75-80 **398.2**

Sody sallyraytus. Sierra, J.
 In Sierra, J. Nursery tales around the world p41-45 **398.2**

Soentpiet, Chris K.
(il) Barron, T. A. Where is Grandpa? **E**
(il) Bradby, M. Momma, where are you from?
 E
(il) Bradby, M. More than anything else **E**
(il) Bunting, E. Jin Woo **E**
(il) Bunting, E. So far from the sea **E**
(il) Farris, C. My brother Martin [biography of Martin Luther King] **92**
(il) McGill, A. Molly Bannaky **E**
(il) Yin. Coolies **E**

Sofie and the city. Grant, K. **E**

Softball
Fiction
Koss, A. G. Strike two (4 and up) **Fic**
Mackel, K. MadCat (5 and up) **Fic**

Sogabe, Aki
(il) Hodges, M. The boy who drew cats
 398.2
(il) Namioka, L. The hungriest boy in the world
 E

(il) Partridge, E. Kogi's mysterious journey
 398.2
(il) Partridge, E. Oranges on Golden Mountain
 E

Soil. Pascoe, E. **577.5**

Soil ecology
Bial, R. A handful of dirt (3-6) **577.5**
Lavies, B. Compost critters (4 and up)
 591.7
Pascoe, E. Soil (k-3) **577.5**

Soils
Bial, R. A handful of dirt (3-6) **577.5**

Sojourner Truth *See* Truth, Sojourner, d. 1883

Solar energy
Bang, M. My light (1-3) **621.47**
Hirschmann, K. Solar energy (5 and up)
 333.79

Solar radiation
 See also Greenhouse effect

Solar system
Berger, M. Do stars have points? (2-4) **523**
Branley, F. M. The planets in our solar system (k-3) **523.4**
Croswell, K. Ten worlds (5 and up) **523.4**
Ride, S. K. Exploring our solar system (4 and up) **523.2**
Simon, S. Our solar system (3-6) **523.2**
VanCleave, J. P. Janice VanCleave's solar system (4 and up) **523.2**

The **soldier.** Babbitt, N.
 In Babbitt, N. The Devil's other storybook p19-23 **S C**

The **soldier** and the king. Afanas'ev, A. N.
 In Afanas'ev, A. N. Russian fairy tales p563-67 **398.2**

The **soldier** and the vampire. San Souci, R.
 In San Souci, R. Short & shivery; thirty chilling tales p68-72 **398.2**

Soldier Jack
 In The Jack tales p172-79 **398.2**

Soldiers
United States
Beller, S. P. Billy Yank & Johnny Reb (5 and up) **973.7**

A **soldier's** life in the Civil War. Anderson, D.
 In Anderson, D. World Almanac library of the Civil War [Series] **973.7**

A **soldier's** riddle. Afanas'ev, A. N.
 In Afanas'ev, A. N. Russian fairy tales p117-18 **398.2**

Soledad. Jiménez, F.
 In Jiménez, F. The circuit: stories from the life of a migrant child p9-13 **S C**

Solheim, James
It's disgusting—and we ate it! (4 and up)
 641.3

Solid, liquid, or gas? Hewitt, S. **530.4**

Solitaire (Game)
Street, M. Lucky 13 (4 and up) **795.4**

Solomon, Heather
(il) Del Negro, J. Willa and the wind **E**

Solomon and the ant;. Oberman, S. **398.2**

Solomon R. Guggenheim Museum
Fiction
Van Leeuwen, J. The Great Googlestein museum mystery (3-5) **Fic**

Soltan, Rita
Reading raps **027.62**

Solway, Andrew
Castle under siege! (3-5) **621.8**
(jt. auth) Biesty, S. Rome: in spectacular cross section **937**

Somalia
Fiction
Hoffman, M. The color of home **E**

Soman, David
(il) Johnson, A. Tell me a story, Mama **E**
(il) Levy, C. Splash! **811**

Some babies. Schwartz, A. **E**

Some dogs do. Alborough, J. **E**

Some frog!. Bunting, E. **Fic**

Some from the moon, some from the sun. Zemach, M. **398.8**

Some of the kinder planets [story] Wynne-Jones, T.
In Wynne-Jones, T. Some of the kinder planets: stories p101-17 **S C**

Some of the kinder planets: stories. Wynne-Jones, T. **S C**

Some smug slug. Edwards, P. D. **E**

Some things are scary. Heide, F. P. **E**

Someday a tree. Bunting, E. **E**

Someone says. Schaefer, C. L. **E**

Somervill, Barbara A.
Brown v. Board of Education (5 and up) **344**

Something about the author **920.003**

Something about the author: autobiography series **920.003**

Something big has been here. Prelutsky, J. **811**

Something funny happened at the library. Reid, R. **027.62**

Something might happen. Lester, H. **E**

Sometimes I wonder if poodles like noodles. Numeroff, L. J. **811**

Sometimes I'm Bombaloo. Vail, R. **E**

Sometimes my mommy gets angry. Campbell, B. M. **E**

Sommer, Shelley
John F. Kennedy (5 and up) **92**

A **son** of Adam. Jacobs, J.
In Jacobs, J. English fairy tales p328-29 **398.2**

Son of an otter, son of a wolf. Doyle, M.
In Doyle, M. Tales from old Ireland p52-67 **398.2**

The **son** of the wind. Bryan, A.
In Bryan, A. Ashley Bryan's African tales, uh-huh p136-71 **398.2**

Sonenklar, Carol
Robots rising (3-5) **629.8**

Song and dance man. Ackerman, K. **E**

A **song** for Croaker Nordge. Berberick, N. V.
In A Glory of unicorns p127-43 **S C**

Song of creation. Goble, P. **242**

The **song** of Roland. Osborne, M. P.
In Osborne, M. P. Favorite medieval tales p34-41 **398.2**

The **song** of the little hunter. Kipling, R.
In Kipling, R. The jungle book: the Mowgli stories **S C**

Song of the swallows. Politi, L. **E**

Song of the trees. Taylor, M. D. **Fic**

Song of the water boatman. Sidman, J. **811**

Songbirds. Johnson, S. A. **598**

Songhai Empire
McKissack, P. C. The royal kingdoms of Ghana, Mali, and Songhay (5 and up) **966.2**

Songs
See also Carols; National songs; Popular music; Spirituals (Songs)
Bates, I. Five little ducks (k-2) **782.42**
Boynton, S. Dog train (k-3) **782.42**
Boynton, S. Philadelphia chickens (k-3) **782.42**
Cabrera, J. If you're happy and you know it **E**
Carle, E. Today is Monday (k-3) **782.42**
Child, L. M. F. Over the river and through the wood (k-2) **811**
Coots, J. F. Santa Claus is comin' to town (k-3) **782.42**
Diez deditos. Ten little fingers & other play rhymes and action songs from Latin America (k-3) **782.42**
The Eentsy, weentsy spider: fingerplays and action rhymes **796.1**
Fiestas: a year of Latin American songs of celebration (k-3) **782.42**
Guthrie, W. This land is your land (k-3) **782.42**
Had gadya (k-3) **296.4**
Hillenbrand, W. Down by the station (k-2) **782.42**
Hinojosa, T. Cada niño/Every child (k-3) **782.42**
Hoberman, M. A. Bill Grogan's goat (k-3) **782.42**
Hoberman, M. A. The eensy-weensy spider (k-3) **782.42**
Hoberman, M. A. Mary had a little lamb (k-2) **782.42**
Hoberman, M. A. There once was a man named Michael Finnegan (k-3) **782.42**
Hort, L. The seals on the bus (k-2) **782.42**
Johnson, J. W. Lift every voice and sing **782.42**
Johnson, P. B. On top of spaghetti **E**
Katz, A. Take me out of the bathtub and other silly dilly songs (k-3) **782.42**
MacDonald, M. R. The round book **782.42**
Mallett, D. Inch by inch (k-2) **782.42**
Manders, J. Señor Don Gato **E**
Raffi. Baby Beluga (k-2) **782.42**
Raffi. Down by the bay (k-2) **782.42**
Raffi. Five little ducks (k-2) **782.42**

Sounds

Fiction

Maitland, B. Moo in the morning   **E**

Sounds all around. Pfeffer, W.   **534**

Soup. Peck, R. N.   **Fic**

Soups

Goss, G. Blue moon soup (4-6)   **641.8**

Souter, Gillian

Paints plus (2-5)   **745.7**

Perfect parties (2-5)   **793.2**

South, Coleman

Syria (5 and up)   **956.91**

South (U.S.) *See* Southern States

South Africa

Blauer, E. South Africa (5 and up)   **968**

Murphy, P. South Africa (2-4)   **968**

Rosmarin, I. South Africa (5 and up)   **968**

Fiction

Daly, N. Where's Jamela?   **E**

Isadora, R. At the crossroads   **E**

Naidoo, B. No turning back (5 and up)   **Fic**

Winter, J. Elsina's clouds   **E**

Folklore

See Folklore—South Africa

Politics and government

Cooper, F. Mandela (2-4)   **92**

Kramer, A. Mandela (4 and up)   **92**

McDonough, Y. Z. Peaceful protest: the life of Nelson Mandela (2-5)   **92**

Race relations

Cooper, F. Mandela (2-4)   **92**

Kramer, A. Mandela (4 and up)   **92**

McDonough, Y. Z. Peaceful protest: the life of Nelson Mandela (2-5)   **92**

Race relations—Fiction

Naidoo, B. Journey to Jo'burg (5 and up)   **Fic**

Naidoo, B. Out of bounds: seven stories of conflict and hope (5 and up)   **S C**

Social life and customs

Cave, K. One child, one seed   **E**

South American animals. Arnold, C.   **591.9**

South American Indians *See* Native Americans—South America

South Carolina

Hess, D. South Carolina

In It's my state! [series]   **973**

Stein, R. C. South Carolina

In America the beautiful, second series   **973**

Volkwein, A. South Carolina

In World Almanac Library of the States series   **973**

Fiction

Fuqua, J. S. Darby (4 and up)   **Fic**

Karr, K. Worlds apart (4 and up)   **Fic**

O'Connor, B. Taking care of Moses (4-6)   **Fic**

South Dakota

Bjorklund, R. South Dakota

In It's my state! [series]   **973**

Hirschmann, K. South Dakota

In World Almanac Library of the States series   **973**

McDaniel, M. South Dakota

In Celebrate the states   **973**

Walsh Shepherd, D. South Dakota

In America the beautiful, second series   **973**

Fiction

Arrington, F. Prairie whispers (5 and up)   **Fic**

Love, D. A. A year without rain (5 and up)   **Fic**

Turner, A. W. Grasshopper summer (4-6)   **Fic**

South Pacific Region *See* Oceania

South Pole

See also Antarctica

Levinson, N. S. North Pole, South Pole (k-3)   **998**

South Sea Islands *See* Oceania

South Seas *See* Oceania

Southern Africa

Fiction

Grifalconi, A. The village that vanished   **E**

Southern Rhodesia *See* Zimbabwe

Southern States

Folklore

See Folklore—Southern States

Race relations

Bausum, A. Freedom Riders (5 and up)   **323.1**

Southwaite, Wendy

Orange pony [excerpt]

In Horse tales   **S C**

Southwest, New *See* Southwestern States

Southwest Pacific Region *See* Oceania

Southwestern States

Freedman, R. In the days of the vaqueros (4 and up)   **636.2**

Natural history

See Natural history—Southwestern States

Souza, D. M. (Dorothy M.)

Freaky flowers (5 and up)   **582.13**

Northern lights (4-6)   **538**

Plant invaders (3-5)   **581.6**

What is a fungus? (5 and up)   **579.5**

Sovereigns *See* Kings and rulers; Queens

Soviet Union

See also Russia

Fiction

Whelan, G. The turning (5 and up)   **Fic**

Soyer, Alexis, 1809-1858

About

Arnold, A. The adventurous chef: Alexis Soyer (3-5)   **92**

Space, Outer *See* Outer space

Space and time

Fiction

Conrad, P. Stonewords (5 and up)   **Fic**

Griffin, P. R. Switching well (5 and up)   **Fic**

Hahn, M. D. The doll in the garden (4-6)   **Fic**

Hahn, M. D. Time for Andrew (5 and up)   **Fic**

Spanish literature
Bibliography
Schon, I. Recommended books in Spanish for children and young adults, 2000 through 2004
011.6

Spanish poetry
Collections
Messengers of rain and other poems from Latin America (3-6) **861.008**

Sparks, Timothy *See* Dickens, Charles, 1812-1870

Sparks. McNamee, G. **Fic**

Sparks fly upward. Matas, C. **Fic**

Sparrow, Giles
Iron
In The Elements **546**
Nickel
In The Elements **546**

Sparrow Jack. Gerstein, M. **E**

Sparrows
Fiction
Gerstein, M. Sparrow Jack **E**
Hansen, B. Caesar's antlers (5 and up) **Fic**

Sparrow's luck!. MacDonald, M. R.
In MacDonald, M. R. Celebrate the world; twenty tellable folktales for multicultural festivals p162-71 **372.6**

Spastic paralysis *See* Cerebral palsy

Speak to me. English, K. **E**

Speaking *See* Public speaking

The **speaking** head. Olson, A. N.
In Olson, A. N. and Schwartz, H. Ask the bones: scary stories from around the world p85-91 **398.2**

Speaking up, speaking out. Otfinoski, S. **808.5**

Speare, Elizabeth George
The bronze bow (6 and up) **Fic**
The sign of the beaver (5 and up) **Fic**
The witch of Blackbird Pond (6 and up)
Fic

Spears, Rick
(il) Halls, K. M. Dinosaur mummies **567.9**

Special collections in libraries *See* Libraries—Special collections

Spectacular science (2-4) **811.008**

Spectacular science projects series
VanCleave, J. P. Janice VanCleave's insects and spiders **595.7**
VanCleave, J. P. Janice VanCleave's plants
580.7
VanCleave, J. P. Janice VanCleave's rocks and minerals **552**
VanCleave, J. P. Janice VanCleave's weather
551.5

The **specter** from the magician's museum. See Strickland, B. John Bellairs's Lewis Barnavelt in The specter from the magician's museum
Fic

Speech disorders
Fiction
Lester, H. Hooway for Wodney Wat **E**

Speed
Gardner, R. Split-second science projects with speed (3-6) **531**

Speedy facts [series]
Berger, M. Penguins swim but don't get wet
591.7

The **speedy** messenger. Afanas´ev, A. N.
In Afanas´ev, A. N. Russian fairy tales p124-30 **398.2**

Speirs, John
(il) Murphy, S. J. It's about time! **529**
(il) Myers, W. D. Three swords for Granada
Fic

Speleology *See* Caves

Spellers
Terban, M. Scholastic dictionary of spelling (4 and up) **428**

Spells *See* Magic

Spencer, Russ
Skateboarding (4-6) **796.22**

Spengler, Margaret
(il) Buzzeo, T. Dawdle Duckling **E**
(il) Tekavec, H. Storm is coming! **E**

Spenser, Edmund
Faerie Queene; adaptation. See Hodges, M. Saint George and the dragon **398.2**

Sperring, Mark
The fairytale cake **E**

Sperry, Armstrong
Call it courage (5 and up) **Fic**

Spicy hot colors: colores picantes. Shahan, S.
E

The **spider**. Afanas´ev, A. N.
In Afanas´ev, A. N. Russian fairy tales p75-76 **398.2**

The **spider** and the fly. Howitt, M. B. **821**

The **spider** monkey's close shave. Climo, S.
In Climo, S. Monkey business; stories from around the world **398.2**

The **spider** weaver. Sakade, F.
In Sakade, F. Japanese children's favorite stories **398.2**

Spiderology. Ross, M. E. **595.4**

Spiders
See also Tarantulas
Allman, T. From spider webs to man-made silk (4 and up) **595.4**
Berger, M. Spinning spiders (k-3) **595.4**
Facklam, M. Spiders and their web sites (3-6)
595.4
Insects and spiders of the world (5 and up)
595.7
Johnson, J. Simon & Schuster children's guide to insects and spiders (4 and up) **595.7**
Kallen, S. A. Spiders (4 and up) **595.4**
Markle, S. Spiders (k-3) **595.4**
Murawski, D. Spiders and their webs (2-5)
595.4
Ross, M. E. Spiderology (3-6) **595.4**
Sill, C. P. About arachnids (k-3) **595.4**
Simon, S. Spiders (4 and up) **595.4**
VanCleave, J. P. Janice VanCleave's insects and spiders (4 and up) **595.7**
Fiction
Carle, E. The very busy spider **E**
Climo, S. Cobweb Christmas **E**

Spiders—Fiction—*Continued*

Dewey, J. Once I knew a spider   **E**

Maguire, G. Seven spiders spinning (4-6)
   Fic

Spinelli, E. Sophie's masterpiece   **E**

White, E. B. Charlotte's web (3-6)   **Fic**

Poetry

Howitt, M. B. The spider and the fly (k-3)
   821

Songs

Hoberman, M. A. The eensy-weensy spider
(k-3)   **782.42**

Spiders and their web sites. Facklam, M.
   595.4

Spiders and their webs. Murawski, D.   **595.4**

Spiegel, Beth

(il) Bottner, B. Rosa's room   **E**

Spiegelman, Art

(ed) Big fat Little Lit. See Big fat Little Lit
   741.5

Spier, Peter

Noah's ark (k-2)   **222**

(il) The Fox went out on a chilly night. See The
Fox went out on a chilly night   **782.42**

(il) Key, F. S. The Star-Spangled Banner
   782.42

Spies

Gifford, C. Spies (5 and up)   **327.12**

Fiction

Horowitz, A. Stormbreaker (5 and up)   **Fic**

Spill the beans and pass the peanuts: legumes.
Hughes, M. S.   **583**

Spilling, Michael

Cyprus (5 and up)   **956.93**

Estonia (5 and up)   **947.9**

Spin a soft black song: poems for children. Giovanni, N.   **811**

Spindrift. Rodowsky, C. F.   **Fic**

Spinelli, Eileen

The best time of day   **E**

I know it's autumn   **E**

Night shift daddy   **E**

Rise the moon   **E**

Sophie's masterpiece   **E**

Three pebbles and a song   **E**

Wanda's monster   **E**

When you are happy   **E**

Spinelli, Jerry

Crash (5 and up)   **Fic**

Knots in my yo-yo string (4 and up)   **92**

The library card (4 and up)   **S C**

Includes the following stories: Mongoose; Brenda; Sonseray;
April Mendez

Loser (4 and up)   **Fic**

Maniac Magee (5 and up)   **Fic**

There's a girl in my hammerlock (5 and up)
   Fic

Wringer (4 and up)   **Fic**

Spinelli, Jerry, 1941-

About

Seidman, D. Jerry Spinelli (5 and up)   **92**

Spinner, Stephanie

Be first in the universe (4-6)   **Fic**

It's a miracle!   **E**

Spinning spiders. Berger, M.   **595.4**

Spinning through the universe. Frost, H.   **Fic**

Spiral-bound. Renier, A.   **741.5**

Spirin, Gennadiï

A apple pie   **E**

Martha   **E**

The tale of the Firebird (2-4)   **398.2**

(il) Beneduce, A. Jack and the beanstalk
   398.2

(il) Bible. N.T. The Christmas story   **232.9**

(il) Bible. N.T. The Easter story   **232.9**

(il) Bodkin, O. The crane wife   **398.2**

(il) Joy to the world. See Joy to the world
   808.8

(il) Shepard, A. The sea king's daughter
   398.2

Spirits *See* Angels

Spirituals (Songs)

   See also Gospel music

All night, all day   **782.25**

Nelson, K. He's got the whole world in his
hands (k-2)   **782.25**

Pinkney, G. J. Music from our Lord's holy
heaven (2-4)   **264**

This little light of mine (k-3)   **782.25**

Spirn, Michele

I am the turkey   **E**

Splash!. Dewey, A.   **E**

Splash!. Jonas, A.   **E**

Splash!. Levy, C.   **811**

Splear, Elsie Lee

Growing seasons (3-5)   **630.1**

A **splendid** friend, indeed. Bloom, S.   **E**

Splish splash. Graham, J. B.   **811**

Split-second science projects with speed. Gardner,
R.   **531**

Spohn, Kate

Turtle and Snake's day at the beach   **E**

Spoken memories. See Aliki. Painted words:
Marianthe's story one   **E**

Sponges

Esbensen, B. J. Sponges are skeletons (k-3)
   593.4

Sponges are skeletons. Esbensen, B. J.   **593.4**

Spooks a-hunting

In Diane Goode's book of scary stories &
songs p6-11   **398.2**

Spooky A B C. Merriam, E.   **811**

A **spoon** for every bite. Hayes, J.   **E**

The **spoon** in the bathroom wall. Johnston, T.
   Fic

Sports

   See also Games; Winter sports

Ajmera, M. Let the games begin! (3-5)   **796**

Girls got game (5 and up)   **810.8**

Encyclopedias

Scholastic visual sports encyclopedia (4 and up)
   796.03

Fiction

Sports shorts (5 and up)   **S C**

Poetry

Opening days (4 and up)   **811.008**

Stars—*Continued*
Fiction
Hort, L. How many stars in the sky?   **E**
Nelson, S. D. The Star People   **E**
Folklore
Park, J. J. The love of two stars (k-3)   **398.2**
Taylor, H. P. Coyote places the stars (k-3)
     398.2
Poetry
The sun, the moon, and the stars (k-2)
     811.008
Stars beneath your bed. Sayre, A. P.   **551.51**
The **stars** in the sky. Jacobs, J.
   In Jacobs, J. English fairy tales p380-83
     398.2
The **stars** will still shine. Rylant, C.   **E**
Start to finish [series]
   Zemlicka, S. From egg to butterfly   **595.7**
Starting life [series]
   Llewellyn, C. Butterfly   **595.7**
   Llewellyn, C. Frog   **597.8**
Starting with Alice. Naylor, P. R.   **Fic**
Statesmen
   See also Politicians
Ashby, R. Rocket man [biography of John
   Glenn] (4-6)   **92**
Waxman, L. H. Colin Powell (2-5)   **92**
United States
Cunningham, K. Condoleezza Rice (5 and up)
     92
Fradin, D. B. The founders (4 and up)   **920**
Fradin, D. B. The signers (4 and up)   **920**
Statistics
Information please almanac, atlas & yearbook
     031.02
The World almanac and book of facts
     031.02
Statue of Liberty (New York, N.Y.)
Curlee, L. Liberty (3-6)   **974.7**
Hess, D. The Statue of Liberty (3-5)   **974.7**
Maestro, B. The story of the Statue of Liberty
   (k-3)   **974.7**
Shea, P. D. Liberty rising (2-4)   **974.7**
Fiction
Bunting, E. A picnic in October   **E**
Drummond, A. Liberty!   **E**
Staub, Leslie
(il) Lives: poems about famous Americans. See
   Lives: poems about famous Americans
     811.008
Staudenmaier, Eric
(il) Crespo, C. The secret life of food   **641.5**
Stauffacher, Sue
The angel and other stories (3-5)   **398.2**
Bessie Smith and the night riders   **E**
Donuthead (4-6)   **Fic**
Harry Sue (5 and up)   **Fic**
Stavans, Ilan
(ed) Wáchale! poetry and prose on growing up
   Latino in America. See Wáchale! poetry and
   prose on growing up Latino in America
     810.8

Stavros-Lanning, Mary Ann
(il) Gulevich, T. Encyclopedia of Easter, Carni-
   val, and Lent   **394.26**
Stawicki, Andrew
(il) Kenna, K. A people apart   **289.7**
Stay!. Lowry, L.   **Fic**
Ste-e-e-eamboat a-comin'!. Esbaum, J.   **E**
The **steadfast** tin soldier. Andersen, H. C.
   In Andersen, H. C. The swan's stories p27-37
     S C
The **steadfast** tin soldier. Seidler, T.   **Fic**
Stealer of souls. Jones, D. W.
   In Jones, D. W. Mixed magics   **S C**
Stealing dreams. O'Neill, R.
   In A Glory of unicorns p59-73   **S C**
Steam engines
Zimmermann, K. R. Steam locomotives (4 and
   up)   **385**
Steam locomotives. Zimmermann, K. R.   **385**
Steam navigation
   See also Navigation
Steam-shovels
Fiction
Burton, V. L. Mike Mulligan and his steam
   shovel   **E**
Zimmerman, A. G. Digger man   **E**
Steamboat Annie and the thousand-pound catfish.
   Wright, C.   **E**
Steamboats
Harness, C. Mark Twain and the queens of the
   Mississippi (3-5)   **92**
Pierce, M. A. Robert Fulton and the develop-
   ment of the steamboat (4 and up)   **92**
Fiction
Esbaum, J. Ste-e-e-eamboat a-comin'!   **E**
Steckel, Michele
(il) The Milestones Project. See The Milestones
   Project   **305.23**
Steckel, Richard
(il) The Milestones Project. See The Milestones
   Project   **305.23**
Steel construction
Fiction
Kirk, C. A. Sky dancers   **E**
Steele, Anitra T.
Bare bones children's services   **027.62**
Steele, Christy
Cattle ranching in the American West (5 and
   up)   **978**
Famous wagon trails (5 and up)   **978**
Pioneer life in the American West (5 and up)
     978
Steele, Philip
Castles (4 and up)   **728.8**
Galileo (4 and up)   **92**
Steele, William Owen
The perilous road (5 and up)   **Fic**
Steen, Sandra
Car wash   **E**
Steen, Susan
(jt. auth) Steen, S. Car wash   **E**

Steffens, Lincoln
Christmas pony
  In Horse tales   **S C**

Stefoff, Rebecca
Alaska
  In Celebrate the states   **973**
The ancient Mediterranean (5 and up)   **938**
The ancient Near East (5 and up)   **939**
The Asian empires (5 and up)   **950**
Exploration (5 and up)   **910.4**
First frontier (4 and up)   **973.5**
The medieval world (5 and up)   **909.07**
The primate order (5 and up)   **599.8**
The War of 1812 (4 and up)   **973.5**
(jt. auth) Scarre, C. The Palace of Minos at Knossos   **728.8**

Stegosaurus and other plate-backed plant-eaters.
Schomp, V.
  In Schomp, V. Prehistoric world [series]   **567.9**

Steig, Jeanne
A handful of beans (k-3)   **398.2**
<small>Contents: Rumpelstiltskin; Beauty and the Beast; Hansel and Gretel; Little Red Riding Hood; The frog prince; Jack and the beanstalk</small>

Steig, William
Abel's island (3-5)   **Fic**
The amazing bone   **E**
Amos & Boris
  In You read to me & I'll read to you; 20th-century stories to share p2-9   **E**
Brave Irene   **E**
C D B   **793.73**
C D C?   **793.73**
Caleb & Kate   **E**
Doctor De Soto   **E**
Dominic (3-5)   **Fic**
Pete's a pizza   **E**
Potch & Polly   **E**
The real thief (3-5)   **Fic**
Sylvester and the magic pebble   **E**
When everybody wore a hat   **E**
(il) Steig, J. A handful of beans   **398.2**

Steig, William, 1907-2003
See/See also pages in the following book(s):
Marcus, L. S. A Caldecott celebration   **741.6**
Marcus, L. S. Ways of telling   **741.6**

Stein, Barbara L.
Running a school library media center   **027.8**

Stein, R. Conrad
The Aztec empire (4 and up)   **972**
Berlin (5 and up)   **943**
Kentucky
  In America the beautiful, second series   **973**
Nevada
  In America the beautiful, second series   **973**
New Hampshire
  In America the beautiful, second series   **973**
New Jersey
  In America the beautiful, second series   **973**

South Carolina
  In America the beautiful, second series   **973**
Valley Forge (4-6)   **973.3**
Washington, D.C.
  In America the beautiful, second series   **973**

Stein, Ross S.
About
Grace, C. O. Forces of nature (4 and up)   **551.2**

Steiner, Stanley F.
Promoting a global community through multicultural children's literature   **016.8**

Steinhardt, Bernice
(jt. auth) Krinitz, E. N. Memories of survival   **940.53**

Steins, Richard
Exploration and settlement (5 and up)   **970.01**

Stellaluna. Cannon, J.   **E**

Steltzer, Ulli
Building an igloo (3-6)   **728**

Stem cell research
Tesar, J. Stem cells (5 and up)   **616**

Stem cells. Tesar, J.   **616**

Stemple, Adam
(jt. auth) Yolen, J. Apple for the teacher   **782.42**

Stemple, Jane H. Yolen *See* Yolen, Jane

Stemple, Jason
(il) Yolen, J. Color me a rhyme   **811**
(il) Yolen, J. Count me a rhyme   **811**
(il) Yolen, J. Fine feathered friends   **811**
(il) Yolen, J. Wild wings   **811**

Stenmark, Victoria
The singing chick   **E**

Step into reading [series]
Bruchac, J. The Trail of Tears   **970.004**
Brust, B. W. The great tulip trade   **E**
Hautzig, D. The Nutcracker ballet   **E**
Redmond, S.-R. Tentacles!   **594**

A **Stepchild** that was treated mighty bad
  In Stockings of buttermilk: American folktales p17-26   **398.2**

Stepchildren
Fiction
Hahn, M. D. Wait till Helen comes (4-6)   **Fic**

Stepfamilies
MacGregor, C. Jigsaw puzzle family (5 and up)   **306.8**
Fiction
Cohn, R. The Steps (5 and up)   **Fic**
Greene, S. Falling into place (3-5)   **Fic**
Hicks, B. Out of order (4-6)   **Fic**
Park, B. My mother got married (and other disasters) (4-6)   **Fic**
Zimmer, T. V. Sketches from a spy tree (3-6)   **Fic**

Stepfathers
Fiction
Freeman, M. The trouble with cats (2-4)   **Fic**
Johnson, A. Bird (5 and up)   **Fic**

Stewart, Melissa
  Maggots, grubs, and more (4-6)   **595.7**
  Science in ancient India (4 and up)   **509**
  Sloths (3-6)   **599.3**

Stewart, Paul
  Beyond the Deepwoods (4-6)   **Fic**
  Midnight over Sanctaphrax. See note under
    In Stewart, P. and Riddell, C. Beyond the
      Deepwoods   **Fic**
  Stormchaser
    In Stewart, P. and Riddell, C. Beyond the
      Deepwoods

Stewart, Sarah
  The friend   **E**
  The gardener   **E**
  The journey   **E**
  The library   **E**

Stewart, Sean
  The new girl
    In A Glory of unicorns p185-94   **S C**

Stewig, John W.
  King Midas (2-4)   **398.2**

The **Sticky-sticky** pine. Sakade, F.
    In Sakade, F. Japanese children's favorite sto-
      ries   **398.2**

Stiekel, Bettina
  (ed) The Nobel book of answers. See The Nobel
    book of answers   **001.4**

Stiles, Jackie, 1978-
About
  Stewart, M. Jackie Stiles (4 and up)   **92**

Still and ugly Bat. Hamilton, V.
    In Hamilton, V. When birds could talk & bats
      could sing; the adventures of Bruh Spar-
      row, Sis Wren, and their friends p11-16
      398.2

Still more stories to solve. Shannon, G.   **398.2**

Stille, Darlene R.
  Deserts (2-4)   **577.5**
  Grasslands (2-4)   **577.4**
  Oceans (2-4)   **551.46**
  Tropical rain forest (2-4)   **577.3**
  Trucks (2-4)   **629.224**

Stine, R. L.
  The haunting hour (4 and up)   **S C**
  Contents: The Halloween dance; The bad baby-sitter; Revenge
of the snowman; How to bargain with a dragon; The mummy's
dream; Are we there yet?; Take me with you; My imaginary
friend; Losers; Can you draw me?
  Joe is not a monster
    In Beware!; R.L. Stine picks his favorite
      scary stories p121-25   **808.8**
  The judge's house
    In Beware!; R.L. Stine picks his favorite
      scary stories p55-75   **808.8**
  The surprise guest
    In Beware!; R.L. Stine picks his favorite
      scary stories p39-53   **808.8**
  The terrifying adventures of the golem
    In Beware!; R.L. Stine picks his favorite
      scary stories p147-67   **808.8**
  (comp) Beware! See Beware!   **808.8**

Stink. McDonald, M.   **Fic**

Stink Alley. Gilson, J.   **Fic**

Stinker from space. Service, P. F.   **Fic**

The **Stinky** Cheese Man and other fairly stupid
  tales. Scieszka, J.   **E**

Stinky riddles. Hall, K.   **793.73**

Stinky spirits. MacDonald, M. R.
    In MacDonald, M. R. Celebrate the world;
      twenty tellable folktales for multicultural
      festivals p149-58   **372.6**

Stock, Catherine
  Gugu's house   **E**
  (il) Herold, M. R. A very important day   **E**
  (il) Howe, J. Kaddish for Grandpa in Jesus'
    name, amen   **E**
  (il) Mills, C. Gus and Grandpa and the two-
    wheeled bike   **E**
  (il) Walter, M. P. Justin and the best biscuits in
    the world   **Fic**
  (il) Williams, K. L. Galimoto   **E**
  (il) Williams, K. L. Painted dreams   **E**

Stockdale, Susan
  Carry me! (k-2)   **591.56**

Stockings of buttermilk: American folktales (4 and
  up)   **398.2**

Stockton, Frank
  The bee-man of Orn (2-4)   **Fic**

Stoeke, Janet Morgan
  A hat for Minerva Louise   **E**
  Waiting for May   **E**

Stohner, Anu
  Brave Charlotte   **E**

Stojic, Manya
  Hello world! (k-2)   **413**
  Rain   **E**

The **stolen** bairn and the Sidh. Leodhas, S. N.
    In Womenfolk and fairy tales p1-13   **398.2**

Stolen words. Koss, A. G.   **Fic**

Stolz, Mary
  A dog on Barkham Street (4-6)   **Fic**
  Emmett's pig   **E**
  Go fish (2-4)   **Fic**

Stompin' at the Savoy [biography of Norma Mil-
  ler] Miller, N.   **92**

Stone, Kazuko G.
  (il) Gollub, M. Cool melons—turn to frogs!: the
    life and poems of Issa [Kobayashi]   **92**

Stone, Lynn M.
  Tigers (3-6)   **599.75**

Stone, Tanya Lee
  Ilan Ramon, Israel's first astronaut (3-5)   **92**

The **stone**. Alexander, L.
    In Alexander, L. The foundling and other
      tales of Prydain p17-26   **S C**

Stone Age farmers beside the sea. Arnold, C.
    936.1

Stone bench in an empty park (4 and up)
    811.008

The **stone-faced** boy. Fox, P.   **Fic**

Stone Fox. Gardiner, J. R.   **Fic**

The **Stone** Giant. Bruchac, J.
    In Bruchac, J. and Bruchac, J. When the
      Chenoo howls; native American tales of
      terror   **398.2**

The **stone** monkey. Climo, S.
    In Climo, S. Monkey business; stories from around the world   **398.2**

Stone Monkey is born. Jiang, J.-L.
    In Jiang, J.-l. The magical Monkey King; mischief in heaven p1-6   **398.2**

Stone soup. Blackstone, S.
    In Blackstone, S. Storytime; first tales for sharing   **398.2**

Stone soup. Brown, M.   **398.2**

Stone soup. Muth, J. J.   **398.2**

Stonecoat. Curry, J. L.
    In Curry, J. L. The wonderful sky boat and other Native American tales of the Southeast p18-22   **398.2**

Stones in water. Napoli, D. J.   **Fic**

Stonewall [biography of Stonewall Jackson] Fritz, J.   **92**

Stoneware *See* Pottery

Stonewords. Conrad, P.   **Fic**

Stop the train!. McCaughrean, G.   **Fic**

Stores *See* Retail trade; Supermarkets

Storied city. Marcus, L. S.   **974.7**

Stories by firelight. Hughes, S.   **E**

Stories for children. Singer, I. B.   **S C**

Stories from the life of Jesus. Lottridge, C. B.   **232.9**

Stories in rhyme
    Aardema, V. Bringing the rain to Kapiti Plain (k-3)   **398.2**
    Ahlberg, J. Each peach pear plum   **E**
    Alborough, J. Duck in the truck   **E**
    Alborough, J. Some dogs do   **E**
    Appelt, K. Bats around the clock   **E**
    Appelt, K. Cowboy dreams   **E**
    Appelt, K. Oh my baby, little one   **E**
    Ashman, L. Castles, caves, and honeycombs   **E**
    Ashman, L. Mama's day   **E**
    Aylesworth, J. Old black fly   **E**
    Baker, K. Little Green   **E**
    Barracca, D. The adventures of Taxi Dog   **E**
    Bateman, T. April foolishness   **E**
    Bateman, T. Farm flu   **E**
    Bayer, J. A my name is Alice   **E**
    Beaumont, K. Duck, duck, goose!   **E**
    Beaumont, K. I ain't gonna paint no more!   **E**
    Bemelmans, L. Madeline   **E**
    Bemelmans, L. Madeline's rescue   **E**
    Berry, L. Duck skates   **E**
    Blackstone, S. My granny went to market   **E**
    Blackstone, S. Secret seahorse   **E**
    Blackstone, S. Who are you, baby kangaroo?   **E**
    Blomgren, J. Where do I sleep?   **E**
    Brenner, B. Good morning, garden   **E**
    Brown, M. W. Another important book   **E**
    Brown, M. W. Big red barn   **E**
    Brown, M. W. Goodnight moon   **E**
    Brown, M. W. Where have you been?   **E**
    Buehner, C. Snowmen at night   **E**
    Bunting, E. The bones of Fred Mcfee   **E**
    Bunting, E. Butterfly house   **E**
    Bunting, E. Flower garden   **E**
    Burleigh, R. Messenger, messenger   **E**
    Butler, J. Can you cuddle like a koala?   **E**
    Carlstrom, N. W. Jesse Bear, what will you wear?   **E**
    Casanova, M. One-dog canoe   **E**
    Cauley, L. B. Clap your hands   **E**
    Chaconas, D. One little mouse   **E**
    Charlip, R. Sleepytime rhyme   **E**
    Chesworth, M. Alphaboat   **E**
    Cleary, B. The hullabaloo ABC   **E**
    Clifton, L. Everett Anderson's 1-2-3   **E**
    Conover, C. Over the hills & far away   **E**
    Cook, S. Good night pillow fight   **E**
    Cordsen, C. F. The milkman   **E**
    Cronin, D. Wiggle   **E**
    Cullen, C. A. Thirsty baby   **E**
    Cummings, P. Angel baby   **E**
    Curtis, C. I took the moon for a walk   **E**
    Curtis, J. L. I'm gonna like me   **E**
    Davidson, R. P. All the world's a stage   **E**
    Degen, B. Jamberry   **E**
    Denslow, S. P. In the snow   **E**
    Dewdney, A. Llama, llama red pajama   **E**
    Dillon, L. Rap a tap tap   **E**
    Dodds, D. A. Minnie's Diner   **E**
    Dodds, D. A. Where's Pup?   **E**
    Donaldson, J. The snail and the whale   **E**
    Doyle, M. One, two, three O'Leary   **E**
    Durango, J. Cha-cha chimps   **E**
    Ehlert, L. Feathers for lunch   **E**
    Ehlert, L. Market day   **E**
    Ehlert, L. Nuts to you!   **E**
    Ehlert, L. Top cat   **E**
    Ehlert, L. Waiting for wings   **E**
    Elya, S. M. Bebe goes shopping   **E**
    Elya, S. M. Cowboy José   **E**
    Elya, S. M. Eight animals on the town   **E**
    Elya, S. M. F is for fiesta   **E**
    Elya, S. M. Fairy trails   **E**
    Elya, S. M. Oh no, gotta go!   **E**
    Esbaum, J. Ste-e-e-eamboat a-comin'!   **E**
    Ewart, C. Fossil   **E**
    Falwell, C. Turtle splash!   **E**
    Fisher, A. L. The story goes on   **E**
    Fleming, C. This is the baby   **E**
    Fleming, D. Barnyard banter   **E**
    Fleming, D. In the small, small pond   **E**
    Fleming, D. In the tall, tall grass   **E**
    Fleming, D. Pumpkin eye   **E**
    Fox, M. Sleepy bears   **E**
    Fox, M. Where is the green sheep?   **E**
    Freymann, S. One lonely sea horse   **E**
    George, K. O. Book!   **E**
    George, K. O. Hummingbird nest   **E**
    George, K. O. Up!   **E**
    Gliori, D. No matter what   **E**
    Godwin, L. Central Park serenade   **E**
    Gralley, J. The moon came down on Milk Street   **E**
    Greenberg, D. Bugs!   **E**
    Greene, R. G. Barnyard song   **E**
    Guarino, D. Is your mama a llama?   **E**
    Hamanaka, S. Grandparents song   **E**
    Hindley, J. Baby talk   **E**
    Hindley, J. Do like a duck does!   **E**
    Hindley, J. Eyes, nose, fingers and toes   **E**

Stories in rhyme—*Continued*

Ho, M. Peek!	E
Hoberman, M. A. The two sillies	E
Holub, J. The garden that we grew	E
Huck, C. S. A creepy countdown	E
Hughes, S. Out and about	E
Hutchins, P. Ten red apples	E
Jackson, A. The ballad of Valentine	E
Johnston, T. The whole green world	E
Jones, S. L. Time to say goodnight	E
Kalan, R. Jump, frog, jump!	E
Kay, V. Covered wagons, bumpy trails	E
Kinerk, R. Clorinda	E
Kleven, E. Sun bread	E
Koller, J. F. One monkey too many	E
Kraus, R. Whose mouse are you?	E
Krauss, R. Goodnight goodnight sleepyhead	
	E
Kuskin, K. Under my hood I have a hat	E
Lawrence, J. This little chick	E
Leopold, N. S. C. K is for kitten	E
Lessac, F. Island counting 1 2 3	E
Leuck, L. One witch	E
Lewis, J. P. Isabella Abnormella and the very, very finicky Queen of Trouble	E
Lindbergh, R. My hippie grandmother	E
Lindbergh, R. Our nest	E
Lindbergh, R. The visit	E
Lithgow, J. Micawber	E
Lobel, A. On Market Street	E
London, J. A truck goes rattley-bumpa	E
Lord, J. V. The giant jam sandwich	E
Mackall, D. D. First day	E
Mahy, M. 17 kings and 42 elephants	E
Mallat, K. Mama love	E
Markes, J. Shhhhh! Everybody's sleeping	E
Martin, B. Barn dance!	E
Martin, B. A beasty story	E
Martin, B. Brown bear, brown bear what do you see?	E
Martin, B. Chicka chicka 1, 2, 3	E
Martin, B. Chicka chicka boom boom	E
Martin, B. Panda bear, panda bear, what do you see?	E
Martin, B. Polar bear, polar bear, what do you hear?	E
McPhail, D. M. Pigs aplenty, pigs galore!	E
Medearis, A. S. Snug in Mama's arms	E
Meister, C. My pony Jack	E
Meyers, S. Everywhere babies	E
Meyers, S. This is the way a baby rides	E
Miranda, A. To market, to market	E
Mitchard, J. Baby bat's lullaby	E
Mitton, T. Goodnight me, goodnight you	E
Mora, P. Uno, dos, tres: one, two, three	E
Morrow, T. J. Mommy loves her baby	E
Mortensen, D. D. Good night engines	E
Moss, L. Zin! zin! zin! a violin	E
Murphy, S. J. Leaping lizards	E
Neitzel, S. The jacket I wear in the snow	E
Neitzel, S. Our class took a trip to the zoo	
	E
Nevius, C. Karate hour	E
Newman, L. Runaway dreidel!	E
Newman, L. Where is bear?	E
Nicholls, J. Billywise	E
Ochiltree, D. Sixteen runaway pumpkins	E

Ormerod, J. If you're happy and you know it!	
	E
Panahi, H. L. Bebop Express	E
Park, L. S. Bee-bim bop!	E
Peet, B. Huge Harold	E
Peters, L. W. Cold little duck, duck, duck	E
Pinczes, E. J. One hundred hungry ants	E
Polacco, P. G is for goat	E
Raschka, C. Five for a little one	E
Rathmann, P. The day the babies crawled away	
	E
Ravishankar, A. Tiger on a tree	E
Rex, M. Truck Duck	E
Riley, L. A. Mouse mess	E
Roosa, K. Beach day	E
Rose, D. L. Birthday zoo	E
Roth, C. The little school bus	E
Ryan, P. M. There was no snow on Christmas Eve	E
Ryder, J. Big Bear Ball	E
Ryder, J. Come along, kitten	E
Ryder, J. Each living thing	E
Ryder, J. A fawn in the grass	E
Rylant, C. The stars will still shine	E
Saul, C. P. Barn cat	E
Sayre, A. P. Shadows	E
Schaefer, L. M. Loose tooth	E
Schaefer, L. M. This is the sunflower	E
Schertle, A. 1, 2, I love you	E
Schertle, A. All you need for a beach	E
Sedgwick, M. The emperor's new clothes	E
Sendak, M. Chicken soup with rice	E
Sendak, M. Pierre	E
Serfozo, M. Plumply, dumply pumpkin	E
Seuss, Dr. And to think that I saw it on Mulberry Street	E
Seuss, Dr. The cat in the hat	E
Seuss, Dr. Green eggs and ham	E
Seuss, Dr. Hooray for Diffendoofer Day!	E
Seuss, Dr. Horton hatches the egg	E
Seuss, Dr. Horton hears a Who!	E
Seuss, Dr. How the Grinch stole Christmas	
	E
Seuss, Dr. If I ran the circus	E
Seuss, Dr. If I ran the zoo	E
Seuss, Dr. McElligot's pool	E
Seuss, Dr. Oh, the places you'll go!	E
Shaw, N. Raccoon tune	E
Shaw, N. Sheep in a jeep	E
Sierra, J. Preschool to the rescue	E
Sierra, J. Thelonius Monster's sky-high fly pie	
	E
Sierra, J. Wild about books	E
Slate, J. Miss Bindergarten celebrates the 100th day of kindergarten	E
Sloat, T. I'm a duck!	E
Sloat, T. There was an old lady who swallowed a trout	E
Small, D. George Washington's cows	E
Smalls, I. My Pop Pop and me	E
Smith, L. Mrs. Biddlebox	E
Smith, L. When Moon fell down	E
Spinelli, E. The best time of day	E
Spinelli, E. I know it's autumn	E
Spinelli, E. Night shift daddy	E
Spinelli, E. Rise the moon	E
Stewart, S. The library	E

The **story** of Blixie Bimber and the power of the gold buckskin whincher. Sandburg, C.
In Sandburg, C. Rootabaga stories p55-59
S C

also in Sandburg, C. The Sandburg treasury; prose and poetry for young people p33-36 **818**

The **story** of Clara Barton. Koestler-Grack, R. A. **92**

The **story** of clocks and calendars. Maestro, B. **529**

The **story** of Easter. Fisher, A. L. **394.26**

The **story** of Eleanor Roosevelt. Koestler-Grack, R. A. **92**

The **story** of Ferdinand. Leaf, M. **E**

The **story** of Hanukkah. Simon, N. **296.4**

The **story** of Harriet Tubman. Koestler-Grack, R. A. **92**

The **story** of Helen Keller. Koestler-Grack, R. A. **92**

The **story** of Jason Squiff and why he had a popcorn hat, popcorn mittens and popcorn shoes. Sandburg, C.
In Sandburg, C. Rootabaga stories p60-66
S C

also in Sandburg, C. The Sandburg treasury; prose and poetry for young people p36-39 **818**

The **story** of Jumping Mouse. Steptoe, J. **398.2**

The **story** of Le Nuong. Terada, A. M.
In Terada, A. M. Under the starfruit tree; folktales from Vietnam p99-101 **398.2**

The **story** of Little Babaji. Bannerman, H. **E**

The **story** of medicine. Lindsay, J. **610.9**

The **story** of Miss Moppet. Potter, B. **E**

The **story** of money. Maestro, B. **332.4**

The **story** of Monticello. See Richards, N. Monticello **975.5**

The **story** of Mother Jones. Koestler-Grack, R. A. **92**

The **story** of Passover. Simon, N. **296.4**

The **story** of Pretty Goldilocks. Aulnoy, Madame d'
In The Blue fairy book p193-205 **398.2**

The **Story** of Prince Ahmed and the Fairy Paribanou
In The Blue fairy book p342-73 **398.2**

The **story** of Rags Habakuk, the two blue rats, and the circus man who came with spot cash money. Sandburg, C.
In Sandburg, C. Rootabaga stories p67-72
S C

also in Sandburg, C. The Sandburg treasury; prose and poetry for young people p39-42 **818**

The **story** of religion. Maestro, B. **200**

The **story** of Ruby Bridges. Coles, R. **370**

The **story** of salt. Kurlansky, M. **553.6**

Story of science [series]
Gallant, J. R. The tales fossils tell **560**

Gallant, R. A. Dance of the continents **551.1**

Gallant, R. A. Early humans **599.93**

Gallant, R. A. Earth's place in space **525**

Gallant, R. A. The ever changing atom **539.7**

Gallant, R. A. The origins of life **576.8**

Gallant, R. A. The treasure of inheritance **576.5**

Gallant, R. A. The wonders of biodiversity **333.95**

Parker, B. R. The mystery of gravity **531**

Reed, G. Eyes on the universe **520**

The **Story** of Sidi-Nouman
In The Arabian nights entertainments p331-45 **398.2**

The **Story** of the barber's fifth brother
In The Arabian nights entertainments p196-208 **398.2**

The **Story** of the barber's sixth brother
In The Arabian nights entertainments p209-15 **398.2**

Story of the blind Baba-Abdalla
In The Arabian nights entertainments p320-30 **398.2**

The **story** of the creation. Bible. O.T. Genesis **222**

The **Story** of the envious man and of him who was envied
In The Arabian nights entertainments p86-101 **398.2**

The **Story** of the first calender, son of a king
In The Arabian nights entertainments p68-74 **398.2**

The **Story** of the first old man and of the hind
In The Arabian nights entertainments p13-18 **398.2**

The **Story** of the fisherman
In The Arabian nights entertainments p23-28 **398.2**

The **story** of the hormigo tree. Menchú, R.
In Menchú, R. and Liano, D. The honey jar **398.2**

The **Story** of the husband and the parrot
In The Arabian nights entertainments p32-33 **398.2**

The **story** of the incredible orchestra. Koscielniak, B. **784.2**

The **Story** of the merchant and the genius
In The Arabian nights entertainments p6-12 **398.2**

The **Story** of the second calender, son of a king
In The Arabian nights entertainments p75-85 **398.2**

The **Story** of the second old man and of the two black dogs
In The Arabian nights entertainments p19-22 **398.2**

The **story** of the Statue of Liberty. Maestro, B. **974.7**

The **story** of the sun and the moon. Philip, N.
In Philip, N. Horse hooves and chicken feet: Mexican folktales p8-15 **398.2**

Stoyles, Pennie
  (jt. auth) Pentland, P. Forensic science **363.2**
  (jt. auth) Pentland, P. Kitchen science **641.3**
  (jt. auth) Pentland, P. Party science **507.8**
  (jt. auth) Pentland, P. Toy and game science
  531

Straightening the mind of Tadadaho. Bruchac, J.
  In Bruchac, J. Tell me a tale; a book about storytelling p71-76 **372.6**

Stranded at Plimoth Plantation, 1626. Bowen, G.
  974.4

Stranded in Boringsville. Bateson, C. **Fic**

Strange animals, new to science. Pringle, L. P.
  591.68

Strange birds. Gilliland, J. H. **Fic**

The **strange** case of Dr. Jekyll and Mr. Hyde. Stevenson, R. L. **Fic**

Strange creatures. Lester, J.
  In Lester, J. When the beginning began; stories about God, the creatures, and us p18-24 **296.1**

A **strange** encounter. Terada, A. M.
  In Terada, A. M. Under the starfruit tree; folktales from Vietnam p95-98 **398.2**

Strange happenings. Avi **S C**

Strange Mr. Satie. Anderson, M. T. **92**

The **strange** visitor. Jacobs, J.
  In Jacobs, J. English fairy tales p177-80
  398.2

The **strange** visitor. MacDonald, M. R.
  In MacDonald, M. R. When the lights go out; twenty scary tales to tell p133-42
  372.6

The **stranger**. Van Allsburg, C. **E**

Stranger in Dadland. Koss, A. G. **Fic**

Strangers. Schwartz, A.
  In Schwartz, A. Scary stories 3; more tales to chill your bones p79 **398.2**

Strangers on the shore. Wynne-Jones, T.
  In Wynne-Jones, T. Some of the kinder planets: stories p49-65 **S C**

Straphanging in the USA. Sandler, M. W.
  388.4

Strauss, Rochelle
  Tree of life (5 and up) **578**

Stravinsky, Igor, 1882-1971
  See/See also pages in the following book(s):
  Krull, K. Lives of the musicians (4 and up)
  920
  Schubert, L. Ballet of the elephants **791.8**

The **Straw** ox
  In De Paola, T. Tomie dePaola's Favorite nursery tales p75-82 **398.2**

Strawberries
Fiction
  Bang, M. The Grey Lady and the Strawberry Snatcher **E**
Folklore
  Bruchac, J. The first strawberries (k-3)
  398.2

The **strawberries** of the little men. MacDonald, M. R.
  In MacDonald, M. R. Look back and see; twenty lively tales for gentle tellers p95-102 **372.6**

The **stray** dog. Simont, M. **E**

Streams to the river, river to the sea. O'Dell, S. **Fic**

Street, Michael
  Lucky 13 (4 and up) **795.4**

Street, Pat
  (jt. auth) Leedy, L. There's a frog in my throat
  428

Street gangs *See* Gangs

Street people *See* Homeless persons

Street railroads
  See also Cable railroads
  Sandler, M. W. Straphanging in the USA (5 and up) **388.4**

Streets of gold [biography of Mary Antin] Wells, R. **92**

Strega Nona: an old tale. De Paola, T. **E**

Streiffert, Kristi
  (jt. auth) Kott, J. Nicaragua **972.85**

Streissguth, Thomas
  Brazil in pictures (5 and up) **981**

The **strength** of these arms. Bial, R. **326**

Stretchy library lessons [series]
  Miller, P. Library skills **025.5**
  Miller, P. Reading activities **025.5**
  Miller, P. Research skills **025.5**

Strevens-Marzo, Bridget
  (il) Wild, M. Kiss kiss! **E**

Strickland, Brad
  The hand of the necromancer (5 and up)
  Fic
  John Bellairs's Lewis Barnavelt in The specter from the magician's museum (5 and up)
  Fic

Strickland, Tessa
  (comp) One earth, one spirit. See One earth, one spirit **242**

Strider. Cleary, B. **Fic**

Strike two. Koss, A. G. **Fic**

Strikes
  Bartoletti, S. C. Kids on strike! (5 and up)
  331.8
  Brown, D. Kid Blink beats the world (2-4)
  331.3
Fiction
  Koss, A. G. Strike two (4 and up) **Fic**
  McCully, E. A. The bobbin girl (3-5) **Fic**

String beans. Hurwitz, J.
  In Bauer, C. F. Celebrations; read-aloud holiday and theme book programs p65-67
  808.8

String figures
  Holbrook, B. String stories **027.62**
Fiction
  Fleischman, P. Lost! **Fic**

A **string** in the harp. Bond, N. **Fic**

String stories. Holbrook, B. **027.62**

Subways—*Continued*

Fiction

Pinkney, A. D. Mim's Christmas jam   **E**

Reid, B. The Subway mouse   **E**

Suen, A. Subway   **E**

Success

> *See also* Academic achievement

Rimm, S. B. See Jane win for girls (5 and up)
    305.23

Such things happen. Schwartz, A.

> *In* Schwartz, A. Scary stories 3; more tales to chill your bones p39-43   **398.2**

Sudan

Fiction

Williams, M. Brothers in hope (3-5)   **Fic**

Suen, Anastasia

Red light, green light   **E**

Subway   **E**

Suffrage

> *See also* Women—Suffrage

Sugar

> *See also* Maple sugar

Sugar was my best food. Peacock, C. A.
    362.1

Sugaring. Haas, J.   **E**

Sugihara, Chiune *See* Sugihara, Sempo, 1900-1986

Sugihara, Sempo, 1900-1986

About

Mochizuki, K. Passage to freedom (3-6)
    940.53

Suicide

Fiction

Fine, A. Up on cloud nine (5 and up)   **Fic**

Suitcase. Walter, M. P.   **Fic**

Sukey and the mermaid. San Souci, R.   **398.2**

Suki's kimono. Uegaki, C.   **E**

Sulfur *See* Sulphur

Sullivan, Anne Marie

Albert Einstein (4 and up)   **92**

Sullivan, Sir Arthur, 1842-1900

> *See/See also pages in the following book(s):*

Krull, K. Lives of the musicians (4 and up)
    920

Sullivan, George

Abraham Lincoln (4 and up)   **92**

Built to last (5 and up)   **624**

Journalists at risk (5 and up)   **070**

Sullivan, Michael

Fundamentals of children's services   **027.62**

Sullivan, Otha Richard

African American inventors (5 and up)   **920**

African American millionaires   **920**

Sulphur

Beatty, R. Sulfur

> *In* The Elements   **546**

Sultanate of Oman *See* Oman

Sumerians

Shuter, J. Mesopotamia (4-6)   **935**

> *See/See also pages in the following book(s):*

Moss, C. Science in ancient Mesopotamia (4 and up)   **509**

Summer

Kurelek, W. A prairie boy's summer (3-5)
    971.27

Fiction

English, K. Hot day on Abbott Avenue   **E**

Hesse, K. Come on, rain!   **E**

Joosse, B. M. Hot city   **E**

Staples, S. F. The green dog (4-6)   **Fic**

Poetry

Alarcón, F. X. From the bellybutton of the moon and other summer poems (2-4)   **811**

Florian, D. Summersaults   **811**

Summer camps *See* Camps

Summer fun!. Williamson, S.   **790.1**

Summer ice. McMillan, B.   **508**

The **summer** my father was ten. Brisson, P.   **E**

Summer of my German soldier. Greene, B.
    Fic

The **summer** of the swans. Byars, B. C.   **Fic**

The **Summer** Olympics. Knotts, B.   **796.48**

Summer secrets. Hermes, P.   **Fic**

The **summer** Sherman loved me. St. Anthony, J.
    Fic

A **summer** to die. Lowry, L.   **Fic**

Summerland. Chabon, M.   **Fic**

Summersaults. Florian, D.   **811**

Sun

Bailey, J. Sun up, sun down (2-4)   **525**

Branley, F. M. The sun, our nearest star (k-2)
    523.7

Gibbons, G. Sun up, sun down (k-3)   **523.7**

Fiction

Asch, F. The sun is my favorite star   **E**

Kleven, E. Sun bread   **E**

Tafuri, N. What the sun sees   **E**

Folklore

Dayrell, E. Why the Sun and the Moon live in the sky (k-3)   **398.2**

Poetry

The sun, the moon, and the stars (k-2)
    811.008

Sun (in religion, folklore, etc.) *See* Sun worship

Sun & Spoon. Henkes, K.   **Fic**

Sun and Moon. Lester, J.

> *In* Lester, J. When the beginning began; stories about God, the creatures, and us p11-17   **296.1**

Sun bread. Kleven, E.   **E**

The **Sun** in me (2-4)   **811.008**

The **sun** is my favorite star. Asch, F.   **E**

The **sun** is so quiet. Giovanni, N.   **811**

The **sun,** our nearest star. Branley, F. M.
    523.7

The **Sun,** the Moon, and the Raven. Afanas'ev, A. N.

> *In* Afanas'ev, A. N. Russian fairy tales p588-89   **398.2**

The **sun,** the moon, and the stars (k-2)
    811.008

Sun up, sun down. Bailey, J.   **525**

Sun up, sun down. Gibbons, G.   **523.7**

Sun worship
    Baylor, B. The way to start a day (1-4)   **204**
The **sundae** scoop. Murphy, S. J.   **511**
Sundiata *See* Keita, Soundiata, d. 1255
Sundiata. Wisniewski, D.   **92**
The **sunflower** family. Winner, C.   **583**
Sunflowers
    Fiction
    Schaefer, L. M. This is the sunflower   **E**
Sunken treasure. Gibbons, G.   **910.4**
Sunny Boy!. Fleming, C.   **E**
The **sun's** daughter. Sherman, P.   **398.2**
Super science concoctions. Hauser, J. F.   **507.8**
Super-sized science projects with volume. Gardner, R.   **530.8**
Supercroc and the origin of crocodiles. Sloan, C.   **567.9**
Superdog. Buehner, C.   **E**
Supermarkets
    Krull, K. Supermarket (k-3)   **381**
Supernatural
    Fiction
    Avi. The Book Without Words (5 and up)   **Fic**
    Avi. Strange happenings (5 and up)   **S C**
    Cooper, S. The Boggart (4 and up)   **Fic**
    Delaney, J. The last apprentice: Revenge of the witch (5 and up)   **Fic**
    Farmer, N. A girl named Disaster (6 and up)   **Fic**
    Fleischman, P. Graven images (5 and up)   **S C**
    Gaiman, N. Coraline (5 and up)   **Fic**
    Graff, S. Blackwell's Island (5 and up)   **Fic**
    Jarvis, R. The oaken throne (5 and up)   **Fic**
    Pullman, P. Clockwork (4 and up)   **Fic**
    Schwartz, H. Invisible kingdoms (3-5)   **398.2**
    Snyder, Z. K. The Unseen (5 and up)   **Fic**
    Wiseman, D. Jeremy Visick (5 and up)   **Fic**
    Poetry
    Prelutsky, J. Monday's troll (2-5)   **811**
Superstition
    Fiction
    Babbitt, N. Kneeknock Rise (4-6)   **Fic**
    Schumacher, J. The chain letter (5 and up)   **Fic**
    Poetry
    Wong, J. S. Knock on wood (3-5)   **811**
Supreme Court (U.S.) *See* United States. Supreme Court
The **Supreme** Court. Horn, G.   **347**
Sure as sunrise. McGill, A.   **398.2**
Sure-to-win science fair projects. Rhatigan, J.   **507.8**
Suriname
    Fridell, R. The search for poison-dart frogs (4-6)   **597.8**
The **surprise** guest. Stine, R. L.
    In Beware!; R.L. Stine picks his favorite scary stories p39-53   **808.8**
Surprising sharks. Davies, N.   **597**

Surrealism
    Raimondo, J. Imagine that! (1-5)   **709.04**
Surveying
    Morrison, T. The coast mappers (5 and up)   **623.89**
Survival after airplane accidents, shipwrecks, etc.
    Kraske, R. Marooned [biography of Alexander Selkirk] (5 and up)   **92**
    Markle, S. Rescues! (4 and up)   **363.34**
    Fiction
    Morgan, C. The boy who spoke dog (5 and up)   **Fic**
    Morpurgo, M. Kensuke's kingdom (4 and up)   **Fic**
    Steig, W. Abel's island (3-5)   **Fic**
    Taylor, T. The cay (5 and up)   **Fic**
    Taylor, T. Timothy of the cay (5 and up)   **Fic**
    Wheeler, L. Castaway cats   **E**
    Wyss, J. D. The Swiss family Robinson (5 and up)   **Fic**
Surviving Hitler. Warren, A.   **940.53**
Susan laughs. Willis, J.   **E**
Susanna and Simon. San Souci, R.
    In San Souci, R. Cut from the same cloth; American women of myth, legend, and tall tale p43-48   **398.2**
Susannah and the elders. Jaffe, N.
    In Jaffe, N. and Zeitlin, S. J. The cow of no color: riddle stories and justice tales from around the world p40-46   **398.2**
Susie. Schwartz, A.
    In Schwartz, A. Ghosts!; ghostly tales from folklore p13-19   **398.2**
Sustainable world [series]
    Bowden, R. Energy   **333.79**
    Bowden, R. Food and farming   **363.8**
    Bowden, R. Waste   **363.7**
Sutcliff, Rosemary
    The light beyond the forest (4 and up)   **398.2**
    The road to Camlann (4 and up)   **398.2**
    The sword and the circle (4 and up)   **398.2**
Sutcliffe, Justin
    (il) Calmenson, S. Rosie   **636.7**
Sutcliffe, Mandy
    (il) Koralek, J. Night ride to Nanna's   **E**
    (il) Mitton, T. Goodnight me, goodnight you   **E**
Sutherland, Jonathan
    (jt. auth) Canwell, D. African Americans in the Vietnam War   **959.704**
Sutherland, Zena
    Children & books   **028.5**
    (ed) The Best in children's books. See The Best in children's books   **028.1**
    (comp) The Orchard book of nursery rhymes. See The Orchard book of nursery rhymes   **398.8**
Sutton, Wendy K.
    (jt. auth) Bouchard, D. The gift of reading   **372.4**

Suu Kyi *See* Aung San Suu Kyi

Swahili language
  Feelings, M. Jambo means hello   **E**
  Feelings, M. Moja means one   **E**

Swain, Holly
  (il) The Kingfisher book of family poems. See The Kingfisher book of family poems   **821.008**

Swain, Ruth Freeman
  Hairdo! (1-4)   **391**

Swallow, Pamela Curtis
  Groundhog gets a say   **E**

Swallowed alive. San Souci, R.
  In San Souci, R. Short & shivery; thirty chilling tales p84-87   **398.2**

Swallows
Fiction
  Politi, L. Song of the swallows   **E**
Folklore
  Ryan, P. M. Nacho and Lolita (2-4)   **398.2**

Swamp, Jake
  Giving thanks (k-3)   **299.7**

Swamp Angel. Isaacs, A.   **E**

Swamp animals
  Arnosky, J. Wild and swampy (2-4)   **591.7**

Swamps *See* Marshes; Wetlands

Swan, Erin Pembrey
  Penguins: from emperors to macaronis (4-6)   **598**

Swan sister (5 and up)   **S C**

Swan song. Marshall, J.
  In Marshall, J. Rats on the roof, and other stories p49-53   **S C**

Swans
  Osborn, E. Project UltraSwan (4 and up)   **598**
Fiction
  Pinkney, J. The ugly duckling   **E**
  Watts, B. The ugly duckling   **E**
  White, E. B. The trumpet of the swan (3-6)   **Fic**

The **swan's** stories. Andersen, H. C.   **S C**

Swanson, Diane
  Nibbling on Einstein's brain (5 and up)   **500**

Swanson, Susan Marie
  The first thing my mama told me   **E**

Swarner, Kristina
  (il) Schwartz, H. Before you were born   **398.2**

Swartz, Leslie
  (jt. auth) Simonds, N. Moonbeams, dumplings & dragon boats   **394.26**

Swearingen, Greg
  (il) Donaldson, J. The Giants and the Joneses   **Fic**

Sweaterweather. Varon, S.   **741.5**

Sweden
  Gan, D. Sweden (5 and up)   **948.5**
Fiction
  Lindgren, A. Pippi Longstocking (3-6)   **Fic**

Sweeney, Joan
  Me and my amazing body (k-2)   **611**

Sweep dreams. Willard, N.   **E**

Sweet, Melissa
  Carmine   **E**
  (il) Appelt, K. Bats around the clock   **E**
  (il) Calmenson, S. Good for you!   **811**
  (jt. auth) Calmenson, S. Kindergarten kids   **811**
  (il) Calmenson, S. Welcome, baby!   **811**
  (il) Carlstrom, N. W. Giggle-wiggle wake-up!   **E**
  (il) Davies, J. The boy who drew birds: a story of John James Audubon   **92**
  (il) Hines, A. G. My grandma is coming to town   **E**
  (il) Howe, J. Pinky and Rex   **E**
  (il) Knight, J. Charlotte in Giverny   **Fic**
  (il) Logan, C. The 5,000-year-old puzzle   **932**
  (il) Rupp, R. Weather   **551.6**
  (il) Rylant, C. Moonlight: the Halloween cat   **E**
  (il) Thimmesh, C. Girls think of everything   **920**
  (il) Thimmesh, C. The sky's the limit   **500**
  (il) Yolen, J. Baby Bear's chairs   **E**

Sweet Betsey from Pike. San Souci, R.
  In San Souci, R. Cut from the same cloth; American women of myth, legend, and tall tale p57-64   **398.2**

Sweet Clara and the freedom quilt. Hopkinson, D.   **E**

Sweet Jasmine, nice Jackson. Harris, R. H.   **612.6**

Sweet music in Harlem. Taylor, D. A.   **E**

Sweet potato pie. Lindsey, K.   **E**

A **sweet** year. Podwal, M. H.   **296.4**

Sweeter than honey, purer than oil. Kimmel, E. A.
  In Kimmel, E. A. The jar of fools: eight Hanukkah stories from Chelm p9-12   **S C**

The **sweetest** fig. Van Allsburg, C.   **E**

Sweets *See* Confectionery

Swiatkowska, Gabriela
  (il) Recorvits, H. My name is Yoon   **E**

Swift, Fran
  Old blue buggy   **E**

Swift, Hildegarde Hoyt
  The little red lighthouse and the great gray bridge   **E**

Swift, Jonathan
  Gulliver's travels; adaptation. See Hodges, M. Gulliver in Lilliput   **Fic**

Swifter, higher, stronger. Macy, S.   **796.48**

Swimming
Biography
  Adler, D. A. America's champion swimmer: Gertrude Ederle (2-4)   **92**
Fiction
  Cooper, S. Frog   **E**
  Kessler, L. P. Last one in is a rotten egg   **E**
  London, J. Froggy learns to swim   **E**

Swimming with hammerhead sharks. Mallory, K.   **597**

Swimmy. Lionni, L.   **E**

Swinburne, Stephen R.
Black bear (3-5)   **599.78**
Bobcat: North America's cat (4 and up)   **599.75**
Coyote (4-6)   **599.77**
Once a wolf (4 and up)   **333.95**
Safe, warm, and snug (k-3)   **591.56**
Turtle tide (2-4)   **597.92**
Wings of light (k-3)   **595.7**
The woods scientist (4 and up)   **591.7**

Swindlers and swindling
Fiction
Collier, J. L. Me and Billy (5 and up)   **Fic**
De Guzman, M. The bamboozlers (5 and up)   **Fic**

Swine Lake. Marshall, J.   **E**

The **swineherd**. Andersen, H. C.
In Andersen, H. C. Hans Christian Andersen's Fairy Tales   **S C**
In Shedlock, M. L. The art of the story-teller p235-42   **372.6**

Swing around the sun. Esbensen, B. J.   **811**

The **Swiss** family Robinson. Wyss, J. D.   **Fic**

Switch on, switch off. Berger, M.   **537**

Switching well. Griffin, P. R.   **Fic**

Switzerland
Levy, P. Switzerland (5 and up)   **949.4**
Fiction
Creech, S. Bloomability (5 and up)   **Fic**
Spyri, J. Heidi (4 and up)   **Fic**

Swoopes, Sheryl, 1971-
About
Kuklin, S. Hoops with Swoopes (k-3)   **796.323**

Swope, Sam
The Araboolies of Liberty Street
In You read to me & I'll read to you; 20th-century stories to share p78-83   **E**
Gotta go! Gotta go!   **E**
Jack and the seven deadly giants (3-5)   **Fic**

The **sword**. Alexander, L.
In Alexander, L. The foundling and other tales of Prydain p53-62   **S C**

The **sword** and the circle. Sutcliff, R.   **398.2**

The **sword** in the stone. Hodges, M.
In Hodges, M. and Malory, Sir T. Merlin and the making of the king   **398.2**

The **sword** in the stone. Osborne, M. P.
In Osborne, M. P. Favorite medieval tales p17-24   **398.2**

The **sword** in the stone. White, T. H.   **Fic**

The **sword** in the tree. Bulla, C. R.   **Fic**

Sword of the samurai. Kimmel, E. A.   **S C**

Sylvada, Peter
(il) Schuch, S. A symphony of whales   **E**

Sylvester and the magic pebble. Steig, W.   **E**

Sylvia Long's Mother Goose   **398.8**

Symbiosis
Aruego, J. Weird friends (k-3)   **577.8**

Symbolism of numbers
See also Numbers

Symbols *See* Signs and symbols

Symbols of America [series]
Hess, D. The Fourth of July   **394.26**
Hess, D. The Liberty Bell   **974.8**
Hess, D. The Statue of Liberty   **974.7**

Symes, R. F.
Crystal & gem (5 and up)   **548**
Eyewitness rocks & minerals (5 and up)   **549**

Symmetry
Murphy, S. J. Let's fly a kite (k-3)   **516**

Symons, Ann K.
Protecting the right to read   **025.2**

A **symphony** of whales. Schuch, S.   **E**

Syria
South, C. Syria (5 and up)   **956.91**

T

T-H-U-P-P-P-P-P-P-P!. Schwartz, A.
In Schwartz, A. Scary stories 3; more tales to chill your bones p86-88   **398.2**

T is for terrible. McCarty, P.   **E**

Taback, Simms
Joseph had a little overcoat   **E**
Kibitzers and fools (k-3)   **398.2**
Contents: The sign; A made-to-order suit; Chicken soup; A philosophical dispute; The umbrella; An important question; A shlemiel and a shlimazel; Two brothers; A case of mistaken identity; The caretaker; The restaurant; If I were a Rockefeller; The rabbi is so smart, or How Chelm got bigger
Simms Taback's big book of words   **E**
There was an old lady who swallowed a fly   **782.42**
This is the house that Jack built (k-3)   **398.8**
(il) Hall, K. Snakey riddles   **793.73**
(il) Hennessy, B. G. Road builders   **625.7**
(il) McGovern, A. Too much noise   **398.2**

Tabei, Junko, 1939-
See/See also pages in the following book(s):
Atkins, J. How high can we climb? (5 and up)   **920**

Table etiquette
Lauber, P. What you never knew about fingers, forks, & chopsticks (2-4)   **394.1**

The **tablecloth**. Geras, A.
In Geras, A. My grandmother's stories; a collection of Jewish folk tales p24-33   **398.2**

Tabletop scientist [series]
Parker, S. The science of air   **533**
Parker, S. The science of sound   **534**
Parker, S. The science of water   **532**

Tableware
Lauber, P. What you never knew about fingers, forks, & chopsticks (2-4)   **394.1**

Tacang, Brian
Bully-be-gone (3-6)   **Fic**

Tadgell, Nicole
(il) Elvgren, J. R. Josias, hold the book   **E**

Tadjo, Véronique
  (ed) Talking drums. See Talking drums   **896**
Tadpole. White, R.   **Fic**
Tadpoles *See* Frogs
Tafuri, Nancy
  Five little chicks   **E**
  Goodnight, my duckling   **E**
  Have you seen my duckling?   **E**
  Mama's Little Bears   **E**
  Silly little goose!   **E**
  Spots, feathers, and curly tails   **E**
  This is the farmer   **E**
  What the sun sees   **E**
  You are special, Little one   **E**
  (il) Denslow, S. P. In the snow   **E**
Tagholm, Sally
  The rabbit (2-4)   **599.3**
Tai chi morning. Grimes, N.   **811**
The **tail**. Philip, N.
  In Philip, N. Celtic fairy tales p[140]
    398.2
The **tailor** of Gloucester. Potter, B.   **E**
The **tailor** who sold his soul to the Devil. Philip,
  N.
  In Philip, N. Horse hooves and chicken feet:
    Mexican folktales p16   **398.2**
Tailoring
    Fiction
  Potter, B. The tailor of Gloucester   **E**
The **tailypo**. Galdone, J.   **398.2**
Tailypo. San Souci, R.
  In San Souci, R. Short & shivery; thirty chill-
    ing tales p58-61   **398.2**
Taino Indians
    Fiction
  Dorris, M. Morning Girl (4 and up)   **Fic**
'Tain't so
  In Diane Goode's book of scary stories &
    songs p22-25   **398.2**
**Taitu, Empress, consort of Menelik II, Negus of
  Ethiopia, d. 1918**
  See/See also pages in the following book(s):
  Hansen, J. African princess (5 and up)   **920**
Taiwanese Americans
    Fiction
  Lin, G. The year of the dog (3-5)   **Fic**
  Wahl, J. Candy shop   **E**
Tajikistan
  Abazov, R. Tajikistan (5 and up)   **958.6**
Takabayashi, Mari
  I live in Tokyo (k-3)   **952**
Takahashi, Denise Y.
  (il) Pandell, K. Journey through the northern
    rainforest   **578.7**
Takahashi, Kiyoshi
  (il) Tokuda, Y. I'm a pill bug   **595.3**
Takaya, Julia
  (jt. auth) Brenner, B. Chibi   **598**
Take a kiss to school. McAllister, A.   **E**
Take command, Captain Farragut!. Roop, P.
    92

Take me out of the bathtub and other silly dilly
  songs. Katz, A.   **782.42**
Take me out to the ball game. Kovalski, M.
    E

Take me with you. Stine, R. L.
  In Stine, R. L. The haunting hour p96-109
    S C
Take off!. Hunter, R. A.   **629.13**
Taking care of Moses. O'Connor, B.   **Fic**
Taking sides. Soto, G.   **Fic**
Talbott, Hudson
  Excalibur (3-5)   **398.2**
  Forging freedom (4 and up)   **940.53**
  King Arthur and the Round Table (3-5)
    398.2
  (il) Fritz, J. Leonardo's horse   **730.9**
  (il) Fritz, J. The Lost Colony of Roanoke
    975.6
  (il) Woodson, J. Show way   **E**
Tale of a tadpole. Wallace, K.   **597.8**
The **tale** of a youth who set out to learn what fear
  was. Grimm, J.
  In The Blue fairy book p86-95   **398.2**
The **tale** of Despereaux. DiCamillo, K.   **Fic**
The **tale** of Jemima Puddle-duck. Potter, B.   **E**
The **tale** of Mr. Jeremy Fisher. Potter, B.   **E**
The **tale** of Mrs. Tiggy-Winkle. Potter, B.   **E**
The **tale** of Mrs. Tittlemouse. Potter, B.   **E**
The **tale** of Peter Rabbit. Potter, B.   **E**
The **tale** of Pigling Bland. Potter, B.   **E**
The **tale** of Rabbit and Coyote. Johnston, T.
    398.2
The **tale** of Squirrel Nutkin. Potter, B.   **E**
The **tale** of the Firebird. Spirin, G.   **398.2**
The **tale** of the mandarin ducks. Paterson, K.
    398.2
The **tale** of the swamp rat. Crocker, C.   **Fic**
A **tale** of three wishes. Singer, I. B.
  In Singer, I. B. Stories for children p8-14
    S C
The **tale** of Timmy Tiptoes. Potter, B.   **E**
The **tale** of Tricky Fox. Aylesworth, J.   **398.2**
The **tale** of two bad mice. Potter, B.   **E**
The **talent** show. Edwards, M.   **Fic**
The **tales** fossils tell. Gallant, J. R.   **560**
Tales from old Ireland. Doyle, M.   **398.2**
Tales from Shakespeare. Lamb, C.   **822.3**
Tales from Shakespeare. Packer, T.   **822.3**
Tales from the House of Bunnicula [series]
  Howe, J. It came from beneath the bed!   **Fic**
Tales of a fourth grade nothing. Blume, J.   **Fic**
Tales of court and castle. Bodger, J.   **398.2**
Tales of Hans Christian Andersen. Andersen, H.
  C.   **S C**
Tales of Oliver Pig. Van Leeuwen, J.   **E**
Tales told in tents. Clayton, S. P.   **398.2**

Tennessee—*Continued*

Kent, D. Tennessee

In America the beautiful, second series
973

Peck, B. Tennessee

In World Almanac Library of the States series
973

Petreycik, R. Tennessee

In It's my state! [series]   **973**

Fiction

Bradley, K. B. Weaver's daughter (4 and up)
Fic

Dowell, F. O. Where I'd like to be (4 and up)
Fic

Isaacs, A. Swamp Angel   **E**

Keehn, S. M. Gnat Stokes and the Foggy Bottom Swamp Queen (5 and up)   **Fic**

McKissack, P. C. Abby takes a stand (2-4)
Fic

McKissack, P. C. Goin' someplace special   **E**

McKissack, P. C. Tippy Lemmey (2-4)   **Fic**

Steele, W. O. The perilous road (5 and up)
Fic

Tenniel, Sir John

(il) Carroll, L. Alice's adventures in Wonderland
Fic

(il) Carroll, L. Alice's adventures in Wonderland, and Through the looking glass   **Fic**

Tennis

Ditchfield, C. Tennis (2-4)   **796.342**

Miller, M. Fundamental tennis (5 and up)
796.342

Williams, V. How to play tennis (5 and up)
796.342

Biography

Cunningham, K. Arthur Ashe (5 and up)   **92**

Fiction

Christopher, M. Tennis ace (3-6)   **Fic**

Tennis ace. Christopher, M.   **Fic**

Tentacles!. Redmond, S.-R.   **594**

The **tenth** good thing about Barney. Viorst, J.
E

The **tenth** good thing about Barney. Viorst, J.

also in You read to me & I'll read to you; 20th-century stories to share p31-35
E

Tenure of land *See* Land tenure

Tenzing Norbu

Secret of the snow leopard   **E**

Terada, Alice M.

Under the starfruit tree (4-6)   **398.2**

Stories included are: Under the starfruit tree; How the tiger got its stripes; The jealous husband; The snake princess; Mister Thirty; Tam and Cam; The Da Trang crab; The scholar Be; The war between gods; How the Dao people came to be; The worm and the snail; Eyes of marriage; How the gecko came to be; Truong Ba and the butcher's skin; The general; The tea server from heaven; Trial in the dragon's palace; A strange encounter; The story of Le Nuong; Rice cakes for the new year; Two brothers; The lady of stone; The magic crossbow; They ran to me; Just one ghost; The grateful tombstone; The musician

Terban, Marvin

Building your vocabulary (4 and up)   **428**

The dove dove (3-5)   **793.73**

Funny you should ask (3-5)   **793.73**

Mad as a wet hen! and other funny idioms (3-5)
423

Punctuation power! (4 and up)   **428**

Scholastic dictionary of idioms (4 and up)
423

Scholastic dictionary of spelling (4 and up)
428

Tereshichka. Afanas´ev, A. N.

In Afanas´ev, A. N. Russian fairy tales p389-93   **398.2**

Terezin (Czechoslovakia: Concentration camp)

—I never saw another butterfly—   **741.9**

Rubin, S. G. The cat with the yellow star (3-6)
940.53

Term paper writing *See* Report writing

Terra-cotta soldiers. Dean, A.   **931**

Terrabella Smoot and the unsung monsters. Hastings, J.   **741.5**

The **terrible** black snake's revenge. Uchida, Y.

In Bauer, C. F. Celebrations; read-aloud holiday and theme book programs p172-76
808.8

The **Terrible** Head. Lang, A.

In The Blue fairy book p182-92   **398.2**

The **terrible** Hodag and the animal catchers. Arnold, C.   **E**

Terrific connections with authors, illustrators, and storytellers. Buzzeo, T.   **372.6**

The **terrifying** adventures of the golem. Stine, R. L.

In Beware!; R.L. Stine picks his favorite scary stories p147-67   **808.8**

A **terrifying** taste of short & shivery. San Souci, R.   **398.2**

Terrorism

Marquette, S. America under attack (4 and up)
973.931

A Nation challenged (4 and up)   **973.931**

Stewart, G. Terrorism (4 and up)   **303.6**

Woolf, A. Why are people terrorists? (4 and up)
303.6

Fiction

Horowitz, A. Stormbreaker (5 and up)   **Fic**

Terrorist attacks, September 11, 2001 *See* September 11 terrorist attacks, 2001

Terry, Michael Bad Hand

Daily life in a Plains Indian village, 1868 (4 and up)   **970.004**

Terry, Will

(il) Ketteman, H. Armadilly chili   **E**

Tesar, Jenny

Stem cells (5 and up)   **616**

The **test**. Jaffe, N.

In Jaffe, N. and Zeitlin, S. J. The cow of no color; riddle stories and justice stories from around the world p134-36   **398.2**

Test tube babies. Orr, T.   **618.1**

Test tube fertilization *See* Fertilization in vitro

Testa, Maria

Almost forever (3-5)   **Fic**

Becoming Joe DiMaggio (4 and up)   **811**

The **testimony** of the fly. Jaffe, N.

In Jaffe, N. and Zeitlin, S. J. The cow of no color; riddle stories and justice tales from around the world p32-39   **398.2**

Testing, testing 1 . . . 2 . . . 3. LaFaye, A.
In Shelf life: stories by the book p55-66
S C

Tests *See* Examinations

Teton Indians
Left Hand Bull, J. Lakota hoop dancer (3-6)
970.004

Texas
Altman, L. J. Texas
In It's my state! [series] **973**
Barenblat, R. Texas
In World Almanac Library of the States series
973
Heinrichs, A. Texas
In America the beautiful, second series
973
Fiction
Ford, C. Scout (5 and up) **Fic**
Gipson, F. B. Old Yeller (6 and up) **Fic**
Griffin, P. R. Switching well (5 and up) **Fic**
Holt, K. W. Dancing in Cadillac light (5 and up) **Fic**
Holt, K. W. When Zachary Beaver came to town (5 and up) **Fic**
History
Murphy, J. Inside the Alamo (5 and up)
976.4
Teitelbaum, M. Texas, 1527-1836
In Voices from colonial America [series]
973.2

Texas, 1527-1836. Teitelbaum, M.
In Voices from colonial America [series]
973.2

Textile industry
Hopkinson, D. Up before daybreak **331.7**
History
Macaulay, D. Mill (4 and up) **690**

Thacker, Nola
My big feet out for a walk
In Girls got game; sports stories and poems
810.8

Thai Americans
Fiction
Marsden, C. The gold-threaded dress (3-5)
Fic

Thailand
Goodman, J. Thailand (5 and up) **959.3**
Morris, A. Tsunami (3-5) **959.3**
Sobol, R. An elephant in the backyard (k-3)
636.9
Fiction
Ho, M. Hush! **E**
Ho, M. Peek! **E**
Krudop, W. The man who caught fish **E**
Marsden, C. Silk umbrellas (3-6) **Fic**
Folklore
See Folklore—Thailand

Thank you, Jackie Robinson. Cohen, B. **Fic**
Thank you, Mr. Falker. Polacco, P. **E**
Thanks, Mom!. Emberley, E. **E**
The **Thanksgiving** beast feast. Ruelle, K. G. **E**
Thanksgiving Day
Barth, E. Turkeys, Pilgrims, and Indian corn (3-6)
394.26

Gibbons, G. Thanksgiving Day (k-3) **394.26**
Grace, C. O. 1621 (3-5) **394.26**
See/See also pages in the following book(s):
Bauer, C. F. Celebrations p1-24 **808.8**
Fiction
Alcott, L. M. An old-fashioned Thanksgiving (3-5) **Fic**
Atwell, D. The Thanksgiving door **E**
Bunting, E. How many days to America? **E**
Cohen, B. Molly's pilgrim **E**
Goode, D. Thanksgiving is here! **E**
Hoban, L. Silly Tilly's Thanksgiving dinner
E
Lakin, P. Fat chance Thanksgiving **E**
Rael, E. O. Rivka's first Thanksgiving **E**
Rockwell, A. F. Thanksgiving Day **E**
Ruelle, K. G. The Thanksgiving beast feast
E
Scheer, J. A Thanksgiving turkey **E**
Spirn, M. I am the turkey **E**
Poetry
Child, L. M. F. Over the river and through the wood (k-2) **811**
Prelutsky, J. It's Thanksgiving (1-3) **811**
Thanksgiving Day. Fisher, D. C.
In Bauer, C. F. Celebrations; read-aloud holiday and theme book programs p243-48
808.8
Thanksgiving Day. Rockwell, A. F. **E**
Thanksgiving Day at our house. Carlstrom, N. W.
811
The **Thanksgiving** door. Atwell, D. **E**
Thanksgiving is here!. Goode, D. **E**
A **Thanksgiving** turkey. Scheer, J. **E**
Thapar, Valmik
Tiger (3-5) **599.75**
Tharlet, Eve
(jt. auth) Loupy, C. Hugs and kisses **E**
(il) Luciani, B. How will we get to the beach?
E
That crazy Eddie and the science project of doom. Cox, J. **Fic**
That new animal. Jenkins, E. **E**
That one, Anansi. Hamilton, V.
In Hamilton, V. A ring of tricksters; animal tales from America, the West Indies, and Africa p47-51 **398.2**
That summer. Johnston, T. **E**
Thatch, Edward *See* Blackbeard, 1680?-1718
That's what friends are for. Gorbachev, V. **E**
That's what leprechauns do. Bunting, E. **E**
Thayer, Ernest Lawrence
Casey at the bat **811**
Thayer, Jane
The popcorn dragon **E**
The puppy who wanted a boy **E**
Theater
See also Acting; Musicals; Readers' theater
Amendola, D. A day at the New Amsterdam Theatre (4 and up) **792.6**
Fiction
Aliki. A play's the thing **E**
Best, C. Shrinking Violet **E**

Theater—Fiction—*Continued*
Blackwood, G. L. The Shakespeare stealer (5 and up)   **Fic**
Bonk, J. J. Dustin Grubbs (5 and up)   **Fic**
Creech, S. Replay (5 and up)   **Fic**
De Paola, T. Stagestruck   **E**
Hoffman, M. Amazing Grace   **E**
Horowitz, A. The Devil and his boy (5 and up)   **Fic**
Spirn, M. I am the turkey   **E**
Waber, B. Evie & Margie   **E**
Weston, M. Act I, act II, act normal (5 and up)   **Fic**

Production and direction
Dunleavy, D. The jumbo book of drama (4 and up)   **792**
Friedman, L. Break a leg! (4 and up)   **792**
Great Britain
See/See also pages in the following book(s):
Rosen, M. Shakespeare (6 and up)   **822.3**

Theatrical costume *See* Costume

Thee, Hannah!. De Angeli, M. L.   **Fic**

Theft
Fiction
Jennings, R. W. My life of crime (5 and up)   **Fic**
MacDonald, M. R. Tunjur! Tunjur! Tunjur! (k-2)   **398.2**

Thelen, Laurie Noble
Essentials of elementary library management   **025.1**

Thelen, Mary
(il) Broekel, R. Hocus pocus: magic you can do   **793.8**

Thelonius Monster's sky-high fly pie. Sierra, J.   **E**

Theo. Harrison, B.   **Fic**

Therapy, Psychological *See* Psychotherapy

There ain't nobody that can sing like me: the life of Woody Guthrie. Neimark, A. E.   **92**

There is a carrot in my ear, and other noodle tales. Schwartz, A.   **398.2**

There once was a man named Michael Finnegan. Hoberman, M. A.   **782.42**

There was an old lady who swallowed a fly. Taback, S.   **782.42**

There was an old lady who swallowed a trout. Sloat, T.   **E**

There was no snow on Christmas Eve. Ryan, P. M.   **E**

There's a dead person following my sister around. Vande Velde, V.   **Fic**

There's a frog in my throat. Leedy, L.   **428**

There's a girl in my hammerlock. Spinelli, J.   **Fic**

There's a nightmare in my closet. Mayer, M.   **E**

There's an owl in the shower. George, J. C.   **Fic**

There's no such thing as a dragon. Kent, J.   **E**
There's only one of me!. Hutchins, P.   **E**

Therizinosaurus and other colossal-clawed plant-eaters. Schomp, V.
In Schomp, V. Prehistoric world [series]   **567.9**

These shoes of mine. Soto, G.
In You're on!: seven plays in English and Spanish p12-32   **812.008**
Theseus (Greek mythology)
Byrd, R. The hero and the minotaur (3-6)   **398.2**
See/See also pages in the following book(s):
Colum, P. The Golden Fleece and the heroes who lived before Achilles (5 and up)   **292**
Hamilton, E. Mythology (5 and up)   **292**
They be slaves too long. Graham, L. B.
In Graham, L. B. How God fix Jonah p78-83   **398.2**
They call me Woolly. DuQuette, K.   **590**
They called her Molly Pitcher. Rockwell, A. F.   **92**
They ran to me. Terada, A. M.
In Terada, A. M. Under the starfruit tree; folktales from Vietnam p126   **398.2**
They're off!. Harness, C.   **383**
Thibault, Terri
Kids' easy quilting projects (3-6)   **746.46**
Thick-head. Yolen, J.
In Yolen, J. Mightier than the sword; world folktales for strong boys p46-51   **398.2**
The **thief.** Afanas´ev, A. N.
In Afanas´ev, A. N. Russian fairy tales p590-93   **398.2**
The **thief** and the pig. Jaffe, N.
In Jaffe, N. and Zeitlin, S. J. The cow of no color: riddle stories and justice tales from around the world p28-31   **398.2**
Thief of hearts. Yep, L.   **Fic**
Thiesing, Lisa
The Aliens are coming!   **E**
Thieves
Fiction
Buckley-Archer, L. Gideon the cutpurse (5 and up)   **Fic**
DeFelice, C. C. Old Granny and the bean thief   **E**
Fleischman, S. Bandit's moon (4-6)   **Fic**
Fleischman, S. The ghost on Saturday night (3-5)   **Fic**
Fleischman, S. The whipping boy (5 and up)   **Fic**
Garfield, L. Smith (6 and up)   **Fic**
Lindgren, A. Ronia, the robber's daughter (4-6)   **Fic**
Steig, W. The real thief (3-5)   **Fic**
Thieves & kings. Oakley, M.   **741.5**
Thimmesh, Catherine
Girls think of everything (5 and up)   **920**
Madam president (4 and up)   **920**
The sky's the limit (5 and up)   **500**
Team moon (5 and up)   **629.45**
The **thing** in the woods. San Souci, R.
In San Souci, R. More short & shivery; thirty terrifying tales p134-38   **398.2**

Things I learned in second grade. Schwartz, A.
E

Things will never be the same. De Paola, T.
92

Think for yourself. MacGregor, C.   170

Thinking *See* Thought and thinking

Thirsty baby. Cullen, C. A.   E

The **thirteen** colonies [series]. Doherty, C. A.
973.2

Thirteen moons on a turtle's back. Bruchac, J.
811

The **thirteenth** floor. See Fleischman, S. The 13th
floor   Fic

Thirty three things every girl should know about
women's history. See 33 things every girl
should know about women's history   305.4

This boat. Collicutt, P.   387.2

This is our Seder. Hildebrandt, Z.   296.4

This is soccer. Blackstone, M.   796.334

This is the baby. Fleming, C.   E

This is the dream. Shore, D. Z.   811

This is the farmer. Tafuri, N.   E

This is the house that Jack built. Sierra, J.
In Sierra, J. Nursery tales around the world
p59-63   398.2

This is the house that Jack built. Taback, S.
398.8

This is the sunflower. Schaefer, L. M.   E

This is the way a baby rides. Meyers, S.   E

This isn't about the money. Warner, S.   Fic

This land is your land. Guthrie, W.   782.42

This little chick. Lawrence, J.   E

This little light of mine (k-3)   782.25

This little piggy   398.8

This next New Year. Wong, J. S.   E

This one and that one. Sanfield, S.
In Sanfield, S. The adventures of High John
the Conqueror   398.2

This place I know (3-5)   811.008

This place in the snow. Bond, R.   E

This time, Tempe Wick? Gauch, P. L.   Fic

This truck. Collicutt, P.   E

This way to books. Bauer, C. F.   028.5

Thomas, Dylan
A child's Christmas in Wales   828

Thomas, Eliza
The red blanket   E

Thomas, Jane Resh
The comeback dog (3-5)   Fic

Thomas, Joyce Carol
Brown honey in broomwheat tea (k-3)   811
Crowning glory (k-3)   811
I have heard of a land   E
The six fools (k-3)   398.2
The skull talks back and other haunting tales (4
and up)   398.2
Contents: Big, bad Sixteen; Bill, the talking mule; High Walk-
er; The witch who could slip off her skin; The skull talks back;
The haunted house
What's the hurry, Fox? (k-3)   398.2

(ed) Linda Brown, you are not alone. See Linda
Brown, you are not alone   323.1

Thomas, Keltie
Blades, boards & scooters (5 and up)   796.2
How basketball works (5 and up)   796.323
How hockey works (3-6)   796.962
The kids guide to money cent$ (4-6)
332.024

Thomas, Lyn
Ha! Ha! Ha! (3-6)   793.73

Thomas, Middy Chilman
(il) Lowry, L. Gooney Bird Greene   Fic

Thomas, Peggy
Marine mammal preservation (5 and up)
639.9

Thomas, Rebecca L.
Popular series fiction for K-6 readers   016.8

Thomas, Shelley Moore
Good night, Good Knight   E

Thomas, Valerie
See/See also pages in the following book(s):
Thimmesh, C. Girls think of everything (5 and
up)   920

Thomas, W. Jenkyn (William Jenkyn)
Arthur in the cave
In Shedlock, M. L. The art of the story-teller
p173-78   372.6

Thomas, William Jenkyn *See* Thomas, W.
Jenkyn (William Jenkyn)

Thomas Edison (2-4)   92

Thomassie, Tynia
Feliciana Feyra LeRoux   E

Thompson, Carol
(il) Butler, D. H. My mom's having a baby!
612.6
(il) Forward, T. What did you do today?   E
(il) Hamm, M. Winners never quit!   E
(il) Swift, F. Old blue buggy   E

Thompson, Ellen
(il) Duffey, B. Spotlight on Cody   Fic

Thompson, Jeffrey
(il) Longfellow, H. W. Paul Revere's ride
811

Thompson, Jill
Scary Godmother (k-3)   741.5

Thompson, John
(il) Lewis, J. P. Freedom like sunlight   811
(il) McKissack, P. C. Christmas in the big
house, Christmas in the quarters   394.26

Thompson, K. Dyble
(il) Di Pasquale, E. Cartwheel to the moon
811

Thompson, Karmen
(il) Hayes, A. Meet the orchestra   784.2

Thompson, Kay
Kay Thompson's Eloise   E

Thompson, Lauren
Little Quack   E
Love one another (1-3)   232.9
One riddle, one answer   E
Polar bear night   E

Thompson, Linda
The transcontinental railroad (4-6)   385.09

Thompson, Margot
(il) Strauss, R. Tree of life   **578**

Thompson, Sharon Elaine
Built for speed (5 and up)   **599.75**
Death trap (4 and up)   **560**

Thomson, Bill
(il) Nevius, C. Karate hour   **E**

Thomson, Pat
Drat that fat cat!   **E**

Thomson, Ruth
Creatures (2-5)   **704.9**
Families (2-5)   **704.9**
Places (2-5)   **704.9**
Portraits (2-5)   **757**

Thomson, Sarah L.
Amazing whales! (1-3)   **599.5**
Imagine a day   **E**
The sound of colors   **E**

Thong, Roseanne
One is a drummer   **E**
Red is a dragon   **E**

Thora. Johnson, G.   **Fic**

Thoreau, Henry David, 1817-1862
Fiction
Johnson, D. B. Henry hikes to Fitchburg   **E**
Locker, T. Walking with Henry   **E**

Thorne-Thomsen, Kathleen
Greene & Greene for kids [biography of Charlie
& Henry Greene] (5 and up)   **92**

Thorpe, James Francis *See* Thorpe, Jim, 1888-
1953

Thorpe, Jim, 1888-1953
See/See also pages in the following book(s):
Krull, K. Lives of the athletes (4 and up)
   920

Thought and thinking
See also Perception
Burns, M. The book of think (4 and up)
   153.4

Thoughts of a drought dragon. McCaughrean, G.
In Fire and wings: dragon tales from East and
West p15-24   **S C**

Threatened species *See* Endangered species

The **three** bears. Barton, B.   **398.2**

The **three** bears. Galdone, P.   **398.2**

The **three** bears. Jacobs, J.
In De Paola, T. Tomie dePaola's Favorite
nursery tales p55-61   **398.2**

The **Three** Bears' Christmas. Duval, K.   **E**

The **three** bears holiday rhyme book. Yolen, J.
   811

The **three** billy goats gruff. Asbjornsen, P. C.
In De Paola, T. Tomie dePaola's Favorite
nursery tales p42-45   **398.2**

The **three** Billy Goats Gruff. Galdone, P.
   398.2

The **Three** Billy Goats Gruff. Lunge-Larsen, L.
In Lunge-Larsen, L. The troll with no heart in
his body and other tales of trolls from
Norway p17-21   **398.2**

Three billy goats Gruff. Rounds, G.   **398.2**

The **three** blows. Philip, N.
In Philip, N. Celtic fairy tales p54-56
   398.2

Three boys with jugs of molasses and secret ambitions. Sandburg, C.
In Sandburg, C. Rootabaga stories p83-92
   S C
also in Sandburg, C. The Sandburg treasury;
prose and poetry for young people p46-
51   **818**

Three by the sea. Marshall, E.   **E**

Three cheers for Catherine the Great. Best, C.
   E

Three cheers for Tacky. Lester, H.   **E**

The **three** chicharrones. Marcantonio, P. S.
In Marcantonio, P. S. Red ridin' in the hood;
and other cuentos   **S C**

The **three** cows. Jacobs, J.
In Jacobs, J. English fairy tales p300-02
   398.2

Three days on a river in a red canoe. Williams, V.
B.   **E**

Three Eileschpijjel stories
In Stockings of buttermilk: American folktales
p78-80   **398.2**

Three feathers. Jacobs, J.
In Jacobs, J. English fairy tales p256-60
   398.2

Three Foots. Van Laan, N.
In Van Laan, N. With a whoop and a holler;
a bushel of lore from way down south
p91-94   **398.2**

Three French hens. Palatini, M.   **E**

Three friends in a forest. Lee, J. M.
In Lee, J. M. I once was a monkey; stories
Buddha told   **294.3**

Three friends. Tres amigos. Brusca, M. C.   **E**

The **three** geese. Sierra, J.
In Sierra, J. Can you guess my name?; traditional tales around the world p17-21
   398.2

A **three** hat day. Bass, L. G.   **E**

The **three** heads of the well. Jacobs, J.
In Jacobs, J. English fairy tales p218-22
   398.2

The **three** kingdoms. Afanas'ev, A. N.
In Afanas'ev, A. N. Russian fairy tales p49-
53   **398.2**

The **three** kingdoms, copper, silver, and golden.
Afanas'ev, A. N.
In Afanas'ev, A. N. Russian fairy tales p375-
87   **398.2**

Three Kings Day. Hoyt-Goldsmith, D.   **394.26**

The **three** little kittens. Alter, A.   **398.8**

Three little kittens. Galdone, P.   **398.8**

The **three** little piggies and Old Mister Fox. Sierra, J.
In Sierra, J. Can you guess my name?; traditional tales around the world p3-[9]
   398.2

The **three** little pigs. Blackstone, S.
  In Blackstone, S. Storytime; first tales for sharing **398.2**
The **three** little pigs. Jacobs, J.
  In De Paola, T. Tomie dePaola's Favorite nursery tales p34-38 **398.2**
The **three** little pigs. Kellogg, S. **398.2**
The **three** little pigs. Marshall, J. **398.2**
The **three** little pigs. Moser, B. **398.2**
The **three** little pigs. Zemach, M. **398.2**
The **three** little wolves and the big bad pig. Trivizas, E. **E**
Three-minute tales. MacDonald, M. R. **398.2**
Three more stories you can read to your dog. Miller, S. S. **E**
The **three** owls. Curry, J. L.
  In Curry, J. L. The wonderful sky boat and other Native American tales of the Southeast p97-104 **398.2**
Three pebbles and a song. Spinelli, E. **E**
The **three** pennies. Afanas'ev, A. N.
  In Afanas'ev, A. N. Russian fairy tales p113-14 **398.2**
The **three** pigs. Sierra, J.
  In Sierra, J. Nursery tales around the world p97-101 **398.2**
The **three** pigs. Wiesner, D. **E**
The **three** princes. Kimmel, E. A. **398.2**
The **three** questions. Muth, J. J. **E**
The **three** riddles. Kimmel, E. A.
  In Fire and wings: dragon tales from East and West p79-86 **S C**
Three sacks of truth. Kimmel, E. A. **398.2**
The **three** sillies. Jacobs, J.
  In Jacobs, J. English fairy tales p21-25 **398.2**
The **three** sillies. Kellogg, S. **398.2**
The **three** sisters who were entrapped into a mountain. Asbjornsen, P. C.
  In Womenfolk and fairy tales p156-63 **398.2**
Three strong women. Stamm, C.
  In Womenfolk and fairy tales p93-105 **398.2**
Three swords for Granada. Myers, W. D. **Fic**
Three who sought death. San Souci, R.
  In San Souci, R. More short & shivery; thirty terrifying tales p75-77 **398.2**
Three wise men (Magi) *See* Magi
Three wishes. Ellis, D. **956.94**
The **three** wishes. Jacobs, J.
  In Jacobs, J. English fairy tales p318-20 **398.2**
The **three** wishes. Zemach, M. **398.2**
The **three** wives of Nenpetro. Jaffe, N.
  In Jaffe, N. and Zeitlin, S. J. The cow of no color: riddle stories and justice tales from around the world p84-87 **398.2**
The **three** young crows. Bruchac, J.
  In Bruchac, J. Tell me a tale; a book about storytelling p116-17 **372.6**

Thrift *See* Saving and investment
Through my eyes: the autobiography of Ruby Bridges. Bridges, R. **92**
Through the eyes of your ancestors. Taylor, M. **929**
Through the looking glass. Carroll, L.
  In Carroll, L. Alice's adventures in Wonderland, and Through the looking glass **Fic**
Through the looking-glass and what Alice found there. See Carroll, L. Alice through the looking glass **Fic**
Throw Mountains. Courlander, H.
  In Courlander, H. and Herzog, G. Cow-tail switch, and other West African stories p113-18 **398.2**
Throw your tooth on the roof. Beeler, S. B. **398**
Thumbelina. Ehrlich, A. **E**
Thumbelina. Mills, L. A. **E**
Thumbeline. Andersen, H. C. **E**
Thumbeline. Andersen, H. C.
  In Andersen, H. C. Hans Christian Andersen's Fairy Tales **S C**
Thunder at Gettysburg. Gauch, P. L. **Fic**
Thunder Rose. Nolen, J. **E**
Thunderbird Woman, Skiwis, and Little Big-Belly Boy. Curry, J. L.
  In Curry, J. L. Hold up the sky: and other Native American tales from Texas and the Southern Plains p22-31 **398.2**
Thunderstorms
  Branley, F. M. Flash, crash, rumble, and roll (k-3) **551.55**
  Lesser, C. Storm on the desert (2-4) **577.5**
Thurber, James
  Many moons (1-4) **Fic**
Thuswaldner, Werner
  Silent night holy night (k-3) **782.28**
Tibet (China)
  Brown, D. Far beyond the garden gate: Alexandra David-Neel's journey to Lhasa (3-5) **92**
  Demi. The Dalai Lama (3-6) **92**
  Kummer, P. K. Tibet (5 and up) **951**
  Sís, P. Tibet **951**

Folklore
  See Folklore—Tibet (China)
Tibetan tales for little Buddhas. Rose, N. C. **398.2**
Tick-tock, drip-drop!. Moon, N. **E**
The **ticky-tacky** doll. Rylant, C. **E**
Tidal waves, Seismic *See* Tsunamis
Tide pool ecology
  Brenner, B. One small place by the sea (2-4) **577.6**
Tied to Zelda. Rice, D.
  In Tripping over the lunch lady and other school stories p158-77 **S C**

Tiegreen, Alan
  (il) Anna Banana: 101 jump-rope rhymes. See Anna Banana: 101 jump-rope rhymes **398.8**
  (il) Cole, J. Crazy eights and other card games **795.4**
  (il) Cole, J. Why did the chicken cross the road? and other riddles, old and new **793.73**
  (il) The Eentsy, weentsy spider: fingerplays and action rhymes. See The Eentsy, weentsy spider: fingerplays and action rhymes **796.1**
  (il) Miss Mary Mack and other children's street rhymes. See Miss Mary Mack and other children's street rhymes **796.1**
  (il) Pat-a-cake and other play rhymes. See Pat-a-cake and other play rhymes **398.8**
  (il) Smith, R. K. Bobby Baseball **Fic**
  (il) Street, M. Lucky 13 **795.4**

Tierra del Fuego (Argentina and Chile)
  Lourie, P. Tierra del Fuego (4 and up) **982**

A **tiger** called Thomas. Zolotow, C. **E**

Tiger in the snow. Barber, D. W.
  In Beware!; R.L. Stine picks his favorite scary stories p127-37 **808.8**

Tiger math. Nagda, A. W. **511**

Tiger on a tree. Ravishankar, A. **E**

Tiger rescue. Bortolotti, D. **333.95**

"Tiger! tiger!". Kipling, R.
  In Kipling, R. The jungle book: Mowgli's story p114-51 **S C**
  also in Kipling, R. The jungle book: the Mowgli stories **S C**

Tiger, tiger. Lillegard, D. **E**

Tiger with wings. Esbensen, B. J. **598**

The **tiger** woman. San Souci, R.
  In San Souci, R. A terrifying taste of short & shivery; thirty creepy tales p104-08 **398.2**

Tigers
  Bortolotti, D. Tiger rescue (4 and up) **333.95**
  Montgomery, S. The man-eating tigers of Sundarbans (4 and up) **599.75**
  Nagda, A. W. Tiger math (2-4) **511**
  Stone, L. M. Tigers (3-6) **599.75**
  Thapar, V. Tiger (3-5) **599.75**
    Fiction
  Arnold, M. D. Heart of a tiger **E**
  Banks, K. Close your eyes **E**
  Bannerman, H. The story of Little Babaji **E**
  Dowson, N. Tigress **E**
  Lester, J. Sam and the tigers **E**
  Lillegard, D. Tiger, tiger **E**
  Ravishankar, A. Tiger on a tree **E**
    Folklore
  Blia Xiong. Nine-in-one, Grr! Grr! (k-2) **398.2**
  Han, S. C. The rabbit's tail (k-3) **398.2**

Tightrope walking
  Gerstein, M. The man who walked between the towers **E**
    Fiction
  McCully, E. A. Mirette on the high wire **E**

Tigress. Dowson, N. **E**

Tikal. Mann, E. **972.81**

Tikki Tikki Tembo. Mosel, A. **398.2**

Tildes, Phyllis Limbacher
  Calico's cousins (k-3) **636.8**

Tillage, Leon
  Leon's story (4 and up) **92**

Tilley, Debbie
  (il) Gellman, M. Lost & found **155.9**
  (il) Hanson, M. E. The difference between babies & cookies **E**
  (il) Jukes, M. Growing up: it's a girl thing **612.6**
  (il) Jukes, M. It's a girl thing **305.23**

Timberlake, Amy
  The dirty cowboy **E**

Timbuktu (Mali) *See* Tombouctou (Mali)

Time
    See also Day; Night
  Duffy, T. The clock (4 and up) **681.1**
  Gardner, R. It's about time! Science projects (3-6) **529**
  Koscielniak, B. About time (3-5) **529**
  Maestro, B. The story of clocks and calendars (3-6) **529**
  Murphy, S. J. It's about time! (k-2) **529**
  Nagda, A. W. Chimp math (2-4) **529**
  Older, J. Telling time (k-3) **529**
  Skurzynski, G. On time (4 and up) **529**
    Fiction
  Charlip, R. Why I will never ever ever ever have enough time to read this book **E**
  Danziger, P. It's Justin Time, Amber Brown **E**
  Harper, D. Telling time with Big Mama Cat **E**

Time. Courlander, H.
  In Courlander, H. and Herzog, G. Cow-tail switch, and other West African stories p73-78 **398.2**

Time and space *See* Space and time

Time flies. Rohmann, E. **E**

Time for Andrew. Hahn, M. D. **Fic**

Time for ballet. Geras, A. **E**

Time for kids biographies [series]
  Benjamin Franklin **92**
  Thomas Edison **92**

Time of wonder. McCloskey, R. **E**

Time pieces. Hamilton, V. **Fic**

Time quest book [series]
  Beattie, O. Buried in ice **998**

Time stops for no mouse. Hoeye, M. **Fic**

Time to say goodnight. Jones, S. L. **E**

Time to sleep. Fleming, D. **E**

Time to sleep, Alfie Bear. Walters, C. **E**

Time-traveling twins [series]
  Stanley, D. Roughing it on the Oregon Trail **Fic**

Time Warp Trio [series]
  Scieszka, J. Knights of the kitchen table **Fic**

The **times** they used to be. Clifton, L. **Fic**

The **timid** hare. Blackstone, S.
In Blackstone, S. Storytime; first tales for
   sharing   **398.2**

Timmons, Dan
  (il) Patterson, L. Indian terms of the Americas
      970.004

Timothy of the cay. Taylor, T.   **Fic**

Timothy's tales from Hilltop School. Wells, R.
      E

Tin
  Gray, L. Tin
   In The Elements   **546**

Tincknell, Cathy
  (jt. auth) Kelly, J. The mystery of Eatum Hall
      E

The **tinderbox**. Andersen, H. C.
  In Andersen, H. C. Hans Christian Andersen's
   Fairy Tales   **S C**

Tinkelman, Murray
  (il) Dinosaurs: poems. See Dinosaurs: poems
      811.008

The **tinker** and the ghost. MacDonald, M. R.
  In MacDonald, M. R. When the lights go out;
   twenty scary tales to tell p69-78
      372.6

Tintoretto, Marietta, d. 1590
     Fiction
  Trottier, M. The paint box   **E**

Tiny Mouse goes traveling. MacDonald, M. R.
  In MacDonald, M. R. Look back and see;
   twenty lively tales for gentle tellers
   p130-36   **372.6**

Tiny tortilla. Williams, A.   **E**

Tiny's bath. Meister, C.   **E**

Tiny's big adventure. Waddell, M.   **E**

The **Tipitaka** and Buddhism. Ganeri, A.   **294.3**

Tippy Lemmey. McKissack, P. C.   **Fic**

Tippy-toe chick, go!. Shannon, G.   **E**

Titanic (Steamship)
  Adams, S. Titanic (4 and up)   **910.4**
  Kentley, E. Story of the Titanic (4 and up)
      910.4
  Marschall, K. Inside the Titanic (4 and up)
      910.4
  See/See also pages in the following book(s):
  Hill, C. M. Robert Ballard (5 and up)   **92**
  Landau, E. Heroine of the Titanic: the real
   unsinkable Molly Brown (5 and up)   **92**

Titeliture. Sierra, J.
  In Sierra, J. Can you guess my name?; traditional tales around the world p45-48
      398.2

Titherington, Jeanne
  Pumpkin, pumpkin   **E**

Titty Mouse and Tatty Mouse. Jacobs, J.
  In Jacobs, J. English fairy tales p81-84
      398.2

Tituba
     Fiction
  Petry, A. L. Tituba of Salem Village (6 and up)
      Fic

Tituba of Salem Village. Petry, A. L.   **Fic**

Tlingit Indians
     Fiction
  Wisniewski, D. The wave of the Sea-Wolf
      E
     Folklore
  Kimmel, E. A. The frog princess (2-4)
      398.2

Tô, Ngoc Trang
  (il) Shea, P. D. Ten mice for Tet!   **394.26**

To be a slave. Lester, J.   **326**

To be an artist. Ajmera, M.   **700**

To be young in America. Cole, S.   **973**

To bigotry, no sanction. Fisher, L. E.   **296**

To dance: a ballerina's graphic novel. Siegel, S. C.
      741.5

To every thing there is a season. Bible. O.T. Ecclesiastes   **223**

To have and to hold. Jiménez, F.
  In Jiménez, F. The circuit: stories from the
   life of a migrant child p96-112   **S C**

To market, to market. Miranda, A.   **E**

To the beach!. Ashman, L.   **E**

To the frontier. Kimmel, E. C.   **Fic**

To the top. Venables, S.   **796.52**

To the top of Everest. Skreslet, L.   **796.52**

To the top of the world. Brandenburg, J.
      599.77

To your good health!
  In Shedlock, M. L. The art of the story-teller
   p183-90   **372.6**

Toad is the uncle of heaven. Lee, J. M. **398.2**

Toad rage. Gleitzman, M.   **Fic**

Toad Woman. Bruchac, J.
  In Bruchac, J. and Bruchac, J. When the
   Chenoo howls; native American tales of
   terror   **398.2**

Toads
     Fiction
  Coville, B. Jennifer Murdley's toad (4-6)
      Fic
  Gleitzman, M. Toad rage (3-6)   **Fic**
  Lobel, A. Frog and Toad are friends   **E**
  Sayre, A. P. Dig, wait, listen   **E**
  Yolen, J. Commander Toad and the voyage
   home (.)   **E**
     Folklore
  Lee, J. M. Toad is the uncle of heaven (k-3)
      398.2

Toads and diamonds. Perrault, C.
  In The Blue fairy book p274-77   **398.2**

Toasting marshmallows. George, K. O.   **811**

Tobago *See* Trinidad and Tobago

Tobe killed a bear
  In Stockings of buttermilk: American folktales
   p88-90   **398.2**

Tobin, Nancy
  (il) Adler, D. A. Fraction fun   **513**
  (il) Adler, D. A. How tall, how short, how faraway   **530.8**
  (il) Adler, D. A. Shape up!   **516**

The **Toboggan-to-the-Moon** dream of the Potato Face Blind Man. Sandburg, C.
In Sandburg, C. Rootabaga stories p44-47
S C
also in Sandburg, C. The Sandburg treasury; prose and poetry for young people p29-30 **818**

Tocci, Salvatore
Alexander Fleming (5 and up) **92**
Alpine tundra (4 and up) **577.5**
Arctic tundra (4 and up) **577.5**

Today is Monday. Carle, E. **782.42**

Todd, Mark
Monster trucks! **E**

Todd, Mary Ellen, 1843-1924
Fiction
Van Leeuwen, J. Bound for Oregon (4-6)
Fic

Toddler time. Simon, F. **821**

Toddlers
Harris, R. H. Sweet Jasmine, nice Jackson (k-3) **612.6**

Toddy, Irving
(il) Bunting, E. Cheyenne again **E**

Todo o nada. MacDonald, M. R.
In MacDonald, M. R. Celebrate the world; twenty tellable folktales for multicultural festivals p24-29 **372.6**

Toft, Kim Michelle
The world that we want (k-3) **577**

Toft, Lis
(il) Cameron, A. Gloria's way **Fic**

Togo. Blake, R. J. **E**

Tokuda, Yukihisa
I'm a pill bug (k-2) **595.3**

Tolan, Stephanie S.
Listen! (4 and up) **Fic**
Save Halloween! (5 and up) **Fic**

Toleration
Fiction
Wahl, J. Candy shop **E**

Tolkien, J. R. R. (John Ronald Reuel)
The hobbit, or, There and back again (4 and up) **Fic**

Tolkien, J. R. R. (John Ronald Reuel), 1892-1973
See/See also pages in the following book(s):
Ellis, S. From reader to writer **372.6**

Tolkien, John Ronald Reuel *See* Tolkien, J. R. R. (John Ronald Reuel), 1892-1973

Tolstoy, Leo, graf
Three questions; adaptation. See Muth, J. J. The three questions **E**

Toltecs
See also Aztecs

Tom. De Paola, T. **E**

Tom goes to kindergarten. Wild, M. **E**

Tom Hickathrift. Jacobs, J.
In Jacobs, J. English fairy tales p264-70 **398.2**

Tom Mouse. Le Guin, U. K. **E**

Tom Tit Tot. Jacobs, J.
In Jacobs, J. English fairy tales p13-20 **398.2**

Tom Treverrow and the Knackers. Climo, S.
In Climo, S. Magic & mischief; tales from Cornwall p35-44 **398.2**

Tomás and the library lady. Mora, P. **E**

Tomaselli-Moschovitis, Valerie
Junior timelines on file **902**

The **tomb** of the boy king. Frank, J. **932**

Tombaugh, Clyde, 1906-1997
See/See also pages in the following book(s):
Fradin, D. B. With a little luck (5 and up) **509**

Tombouctou (Mali)
Brook, L. Daily life in ancient and modern Timbuktu (4 and up) **966.23**

Tomboy of the air: daredevil pilot Blanche Stuart Scott. Cummins, J. **92**

Tomecek, Steve
Moon (k-2) **523.3**
What a great idea! (4 and up) **609**

Tomes, Margot
(il) Fritz, J. And then what happened, Paul Revere? **92**
(il) Fritz, J. Homesick: my own story **92**
(il) Fritz, J. What's the big idea, Ben Franklin? **92**
(il) Fritz, J. Where do you think you're going, Christopher Columbus? **92**
(il) Fritz, J. Where was Patrick Henry on the 29th of May? **92**
(il) Gauch, P. L. Aaron and the Green Mountain Boys **E**
(il) Gauch, P. L. This time, Tempe Wick? **Fic**
(il) Snowy day: stories and poems. See Snowy day: stories and poems **808.8**

Tomie dePaola's book of Bible stories. Bible. Selections **220.9**

Tomie dePaola's Favorite nursery tales (k-3) **398.2**

Tomie dePaola's Mother Goose **398.8**

Tomoe Gozen. Kimmel, E. A.
In Kimmel, E. A. Sword of the samurai; adventure stories from Japan p63-72 **Fic**

Tomorrow's alphabet. Shannon, G. **E**

Tompert, Ann
Grandfather Tang's story **E**

Tom's midnight garden. Pearce, P. **Fic**

The **tomten.** Lindgren, A.
In You read to me & I'll read to you; 20th-century stories to share p229-32 **E**

The **tongue-cut** sparrow. Sakade, F.
In Sakade, F. Japanese children's favorite stories **398.2**

Tongue twisters
Schwartz, A. Busy buzzing bumblebees and other tongue twisters (k-2) **808.88**

Tonight, by sea. Temple, F. **Fic**

Tower of London (England)
Fiction
Woodruff, E. The Ravenmaster's secret (5 and up) **Fic**

Town and country life. Chrisp, P. **940.1**

Town mouse, country mouse. Brett, J. **398.2**

Town planning *See* City planning

Townesend, Frances Eliza Hodgson Burnett *See* Burnett, Frances Hodgson, 1849-1924

Towns *See* Cities and towns

Toy and game science. Pentland, P. **531**

Toy lab. Ross, M. E. **530**

Toys
Pentland, P. Toy and game science (4 and up) **531**
Pinchuk, A. Make amazing toy and game gadgets (4 and up) **745.592**
Ross, M. E. Toy lab (3-6) **530**
Fiction
Bianco, M. W. The velveteen rabbit (2-4) **Fic**
Carle, E. 10 little rubber ducks **E**
DiCamillo, K. The miraculous journey of Edward Tulane (3-6) **Fic**
Ehrlich, H. M. Louie's goose **E**
Eilenberg, M. Cowboy Kid **E**
Grey, M. Traction Man is here! **E**
Havill, J. Jamaica's find **E**
Herman, R. A. Gomer & Little Gomer **E**
Howe, J. Pinky and Rex **E**
Lewis, P. No more cookies! **E**
Milne, A. A. The complete tales of Winnie-the-Pooh (1-4) **Fic**
Milne, A. A. The House at Pooh Corner (1-4) **Fic**
Milne, A. A. Winnie-the-Pooh (1-4) **Fic**
Milne, A. A. The world of Pooh (1-4) **Fic**
Schotter, R. Missing Rabbit **E**
Seidler, T. The steadfast tin soldier (1-4) **Fic**
Whybrow, I. Harry and the bucketful of dinosaurs **E**
Williams, K. L. Galimoto **E**

A **trace** of blood. Olson, A. N.
In Olson, A. N. and Schwartz, H. Ask the bones: scary stories from around the world p118-24 **398.2**

Track and field. Knotts, B. **796.42**

Track athletics
See also Running
Adler, D. A. A picture book of Jesse Owens (1-3) **92**
Knotts, B. Track and field (2-4) **796.42**
Biography
Krull, K. Wilma unlimited: how Wilma Rudolph became the world's fastest woman (2-4) **92**
Fiction
Mills, C. Ziggy's blue-ribbon day **E**

Tracking and trailing
Selsam, M. E. Big tracks, little tracks (k-3) **591.5**

Tracks in the snow. Yee, W. H. **E**

Traction Man is here!. Grey, M. **E**

Tractors
Fiction
Burton, V. L. Katy and the big snow **E**

Trade-off. Nixon, J. L.
In Nixon, J. L. Ghost town; seven ghostly stories p129-40 **S C**

Trades *See* Occupations

The **trading** game. Slote, A. **Fic**

Trading places. Mills, C. **Fic**

Traditional crafts from Africa. Temko, F. **745.5**

Traditional crafts from China. Temko, F. **745.5**

Traditional crafts from Japan. Temko, F. **745.5**

Traditional crafts from Mexico and Central America. Temko, F. **745.5**

Traditional crafts from native North America. Temko, F. **745.5**

Traditional crafts from the Caribbean. Temko, F. **745.5**

Traffic accidents
Fiction
Bruchac, J. Whisper in the dark (5 and up) **Fic**

Trafficking in drugs *See* Drug traffic

Tragedies of space exploration. Mayell, M. **363.1**

The **Trail** of Tears. Bruchac, J. **970.004**

The **trail** West. Galford, E. **978**

Trailblazer biography [series]
Harrah, M. Blind Boone **92**
Manheimer, A. S. Martin Luther King Jr **92**
Márquez, H. Roberto Clemente **92**
O'Connor, B. Katherine Dunham **92**
O'Connor, B. Leonardo da Vinci **92**

Trailing *See* Tracking and trailing

The **train** of states. Sís, P. **973**

Train to Somewhere. Bunting, E. **E**

Trains, Railroad *See* Railroads

Trains. Barton, B. **625.1**

The **traitor**. Yep, L. **Fic**

Tramps
Fiction
Carlson, N. S. The family under the bridge (3-5) **Fic**

The **Transcontinental** Railroad. Houghton, G. **385.09**

The **transcontinental** railroad. Landau, E. **385.09**

The **transcontinental** railroad. Thompson, L. **385.09**

Transplantation of organs, tissues, etc.
Fullick, A. Rebuilding the body (5 and up) **617.9**

Transportation
Ammon, R. Conestoga wagons (2-5) **388.3**
Freymann, S. Fast food **E**
Fiction
Lord, J. Here comes Grandma! **E**

Trick or treat, smell my feet. De Groat, D.　**E**

Tricks

　　See also Magic tricks

Trillion (The number)

　Schwartz, D. M. How much is a million?　**E**

Trimble, Stephen

　(il) Dewey, J. Mud matters　**553.6**

Trinidad

Poetry

　Brand, D. Earth magic (4 and up)　**811**

Trinidad and Tobago

　Hernandez, R. Trinidad & Tobago (4 and up)
　　　972.983

Tripp, Irving

　(jt. auth) Stanley, J. Little Lulu, vol. 1: My din-
　　ner with Lulu　**741.5**

Tripping over the lunch lady. Johnson, A.

　In Tripping over the lunch lady and other
　　school stories p1-15　**S C**

Tripping over the lunch lady and other school sto-
　ries (4 and up)　**S C**

Triumph of the imagination: the story of writer
　J.K. Rowling. Chippendale, L. A.　**92**

Triumph on Everest: a photobiography of Sir Ed-
　mund Hillary. Coburn, B.　**92**

Trivas, Irene

　(il) Blume, J. The Pain and the Great One
　　　E

Trivia *See* Curiosities and wonders

Trivizas, Eugene

　The three little wolves and the big bad pig
　　　E

Trojan War

　See/See also pages in the following book(s):
　Hamilton, E. Mythology (5 and up)　**292**

Troll, Ray

　Sharkabet (k-3)　**597**

Troll Fell. Langrish, K.　**Fic**

The **troll** with no heart in his body. Lunge-Larsen,
　L.

　In Lunge-Larsen, L. The troll with no heart in
　　his body and other tales of trolls from
　　Norway p77-87　**398.2**

The **troll** with no heart in his body and other tales
　of trolls from Norway. Lunge-Larsen, L.
　　　398.2

Trolley cars *See* Street railroads

The **trolls**. Horvath, P.　**Fic**

Trombley, Richard

　(il) Kelly, E. J. Paper airplanes　**745.592**

Tropical forests. Jackson, T.　**577.3**

Tropical memories. Belpré, P.

　In You're on!: seven plays in English and
　　Spanish p34-41　**812.008**

The **tropical** rain forest. Johansson, P.　**577.3**

Tropical rain forest. Stille, D. R.　**577.3**

Tropical rain forests *See* Rain forests

Trottier, Maxine

　The paint box　**E**

The **trouble**. Schwartz, A.

　In Schwartz, A. Scary stories 3; more tales to
　　chill your bones p69-76　**398.2**

Trouble don't last. Pearsall, S.　**Fic**

The **trouble** with Baby. Russo, M.　**E**

The **trouble** with cats. Freeman, M.　**Fic**

Trouble with trolls. Brett, J.　**E**

The **trouble** with Tuck. Taylor, T.　**Fic**

Troupe, Quincy

　Little Stevie Wonder (k-3)　**92**

Trout and me. Shreve, S. R.　**Fic**

Troy Thompson's excellent peotry book. Crew, G.
　　　Fic

Truck. Crews, D.　**E**

Truck Duck. Rex, M.　**E**

A **truck** goes rattley-bumpa. London, J.　**E**

The **trucker**. Weatherby, B.　**E**

Trucks

　Barton, B. Trucks (k-1)　**629.224**

　Collicutt, P. This truck　**E**

　Court, R. How to draw cars and trucks (4-6)
　　　743

　Crews, D. Truck　**E**

　Hennessy, B. G. Road builders (k-2)　**625.7**

　Robbins, K. Trucks (k-2)　**629.224**

　Simon, S. Seymour Simon's book of trucks
　　(k-3)　**629.224**

　Stille, D. R. Trucks (2-4)　**629.224**

Fiction

　London, J. A truck goes rattley-bumpa　**E**

　Sís, P. Trucks, trucks, trucks　**E**

　Todd, M. Monster trucks!　**E**

　Weatherby, B. The trucker　**E**

Trucks. Robbins, K.　**629.224**

Trucks. Stille, D. R.　**629.224**

Trucks, trucks, trucks. Sís, P.　**E**

Trudi & Pia. Hegi, U.　**E**

True book [series]

　Brimner, L. D. Caves　**551.4**

　Brimner, L. D. E-Mail　**004.6**

　Brimner, L. D. The World Wide Web
　　　025.04

　Ditchfield, C. Golf　**796.352**

　Ditchfield, C. Memorial Day　**394.26**

　Ditchfield, C. Tennis　**796.342**

　Ditchfield, C. Wrestling　**796.8**

　Fazio, W. Saudi Arabia　**953.8**

　Flanagan, A. K. The Pueblos　**970.004**

　Flanagan, A. K. The Zunis　**970.004**

　January, B. Ireland　**941.5**

　Kazunas, C. The Internet for kids　**004.6**

　Knotts, B. Martial arts　**796.8**

　Knotts, B. The Summer Olympics　**796.48**

　Knotts, B. Track and field　**796.42**

　Knotts, B. Weightlifting　**796.41**

　Landau, E. Apples　**634**

　Landau, E. Bananas　**634**

　Landau, E. Corn　**633.1**

　Landau, E. Electric fish　**597**

　Landau, E. France　**944**

　Landau, E. Wheat　**633.1**

　Petersen, D. Australia　**994**

　Squire, A. Cheetahs　**599.75**

Twins

Harris, R. H. Sweet Jasmine, nice Jackson (k-3) **612.6**

Jackson, D. M. Twin tales (4 and up) **618.2**

Rubel, N. Twice as nice (k-3) **306.8**

Fiction

Avi. Never mind! (5 and up) **Fic**

Baccalario, P. The door to time (4-6) **Fic**

Boling, K. January 1905 (5 and up) **Fic**

Bruchac, J. Children of the longhouse (4 and up) **Fic**

Cleary, B. Mitch and Amy (3-5) **Fic**

Creech, S. Ruby Holler (4 and up) **Fic**

De Paola, T. Meet the Barkers **E**

Haas, J. Jigsaw pony (2-4) **Fic**

Mills, C. Trading places (3-5) **Fic**

Roberts, W. D. The one left behind (5 and up) **Fic**

Seidler, T. The dulcimer boy (4 and up) **Fic**

Smith, R. Cryptid hunters (5 and up) **Fic**

Spinner, S. Be first in the universe (4-6) **Fic**

Wallace, B. B. The twin in the tavern (4-6) **Fic**

Zimmer, T. V. Sketches from a spy tree (3-6) **Fic**

The **twins** and the Bird of Darkness. San Souci, R. **398.2**

Twins make holes in your clothes and send ants. Menchú, R.
In Menchú, R. and Liano, D. The honey jar **398.2**

Twister. Beard, D. B. **E**

Two bear cubs. San Souci, R. **398.2**

Two blue jays. Rockwell, A. F. **E**

Two brothers. Taback, S.
In Taback, S. Kibitzers and fools; tales my zayda (grandfather) told me **398.2**

Two brothers. Terada, A. M.
In Terada, A. M. Under the starfruit tree; folktales from Vietnam p109-14 **398.2**

The **Two** donkeys
In The Magic orange tree, and other Haitian folktales p23-28 **398.2**

Two dreamers. Soto, G.
In Soto, G. Baseball in April, and other stories p23-32 **S C**

Two eggs, please. Weeks, S. **E**

The **Two** frogs
In Shedlock, M. L. The art of the story-teller p213-15 **372.6**

Two homes. Masurel, C. **E**

Two hundred and one awesome, magical, bizarre & incredible experiments, Janice Van Cleave's. See VanCleave, J. P. Janice VanCleave's 201 awesome, magical, bizarre & incredible experiments **507.8**

Two hundred and three icy, freezing, frosty, cool & wild experiments, Janice Van Cleave's. See VanCleave, J. P. Janice VanCleave's 203 icy, freezing, frosty, cool & wild experiments **507.8**

Two hundred and two oozing, bubbling, dripping & bouncing experiments, Janice VanCleave's. See VanCleave, J. P. Janice VanCleave's 202 oozing, bubbling, dripping & bouncing experiments **507.8**

Two in the wilderness. Weber, S. **508**

Two Ivans, soldier's sons. Afanas'ev, A. N.
In Afanas'ev, A. N. Russian fairy tales p463-75 **398.2**

The **two** Johns. Hamilton, V.
In Hamilton, V. The people could fly; American black folktales p81-89 **398.2**

Two kinds of luck. Afanas'ev, A. N.
In Afanas'ev, A. N. Russian fairy tales p501-04 **398.2**

Two left feet, two left hands, and too left on the bench. Lubar, D.
In Sports shorts **S C**

Two little trains. Brown, M. W. **E**

Two lost babes
In Grandfather tales; American-English folk tales p162-69 **398.2**

The **two** Marias. Philip, N.
In Philip, N. Horse hooves and chicken feet: Mexican folktales p46-50 **398.2**

The **two** Miss Peonys. Fang, L.
In Fang, L. The Ch'i-lin purse; a collection of ancient Chinese stories p27-38 **398.2**

The **two** mountains. Kimmel, E. A. **398.2**

Two of everything. Hong, L. T. **398.2**

The **two** of them. Aliki **E**

Two old women's bet
In Grandfather tales; American-English folk tales p160-61 **398.2**

Two out of the sack. Afanas'ev, A. N.
In Afanas'ev, A. N. Russian fairy tales p321-24 **398.2**

The **two** princesses of Bamarre. Levine, G. C. **Fic**

The **two** rivers. Afanas'ev, A. N.
In Afanas'ev, A. N. Russian fairy tales p172 **398.2**

The **two** sillies. Hoberman, M. A. **E**

The **two** skyscrapers who decided to have a child. Sandburg, C.
In Sandburg, C. Rootabaga stories p101-05 **S C**
also in Sandburg, C. The Sandburg treasury; prose and poetry for young people p55-57 **818**

Two snakes. San Souci, R.
In San Souci, R. More short & shivery; thirty terrifying tales p16-21 **398.2**

Two thousand presidential election. See Landau, E. The 2000 presidential election **324**

Two times two equals boo! See Leedy, L. 2 x 2 = boo! **513**

The **Two** witches
In Stockings of buttermilk: American folktales
p27-28 **398.2**
Two women hunt for ground squirrels. MacDonald, M. R.
In MacDonald, M. R. Look back and see;
twenty lively tales for gentle tellers
p115-20 **372.6**
Tyler on prime time. Atinsky, S. **Fic**
The **typewriter**. Naidoo, B.
In Naidoo, B. Out of bounds: seven stories of
conflict and hope p72-95 **S C**
Typhoons
See also Hurricanes
Ceban, B. J. Hurricanes, typhoons, and cyclones
(4 and up) **551.55**
Typography *See* Printing
Tyrannosaurus and other giant meat-eaters.
Schomp, V.
In Schomp, V. Prehistoric world [series]
567.9
Tyrannosaurus was a beast. Prelutsky, J. **811**
Tz'u-hsi, Empress dowager of China, 1835-1908
See/See also pages in the following book(s):
Krull, K. Lives of extraordinary women (4 and
up) **920**

U

U.F.O.'s *See* Unidentified flying objects
U.S. Fish and Wildlife Service. Forensics Laboratory *See* National Fish and Wildlife Forensics Laboratory
U.S. Holocaust Memorial Museum *See* United
States Holocaust Memorial Museum
U.S.S.R. *See* Soviet Union
U.S. Space Camp (Huntsville, Ala.)
Goodman, S. Ultimate field trip 5 (4 and up)
629.45
U.S. Territories. McNair, S.
In America the beautiful, second series
973
Uchida, Yoshiko
The bracelet **E**
A jar of dreams (5 and up) **Fic**
Journey home (5 and up) **Fic**
Journey to Topaz (5 and up) **Fic**
New Year's hats for the statues
In Snowy day: stories and poems p3-11
808.8
The terrible black snake's revenge
In Bauer, C. F. Celebrations; read-aloud holiday and theme book programs p172-76
808.8
Uderzo
(jt. auth) Goscinny. Asterix the Gaul **741.5**
Udry, Janice May
A tree is nice **E**
Uegaki, Chieri
Suki's kimono **E**
Uff, Caroline
Lulu's busy day **E**

UFOs *See* Unidentified flying objects
Uganda
Barlas, R. Uganda (5 and up) **967.6**
The **ugly** duckling. Blackstone, S.
In Blackstone, S. Storytime; first tales for
sharing **398.2**
The **ugly** duckling. Pinkney, J. **E**
The **ugly** duckling. Watts, B. **E**
Ugly-face. Bruchac, J.
In Bruchac, J. and Bruchac, J. When the
Chenoo howls; native American tales of
terror **398.2**
The **ugly** unicorn. Salmonson, J. A.
In A Glory of unicorns p79-94 **S C**
Uhlberg, Myron
Dad, Jackie, and me **E**
Ukraine
Kummer, P. K. Ukraine (5 and up) **947.7**
Folklore
See Folklore—Ukraine
Ulrich, George
(il) Murphy, S. J. Divide and ride **513**
The **ultimate** balloon book. Levine, S.
745.594
Ultimate field trip 5. Goodman, S. **629.45**
The **ultimate** indoor games book. Gunter, V. A.
793
Ultimate kids' money book, Neale S. Godfrey's.
Godfrey, N. S. **332.024**
Uluru, Australia's Aboriginal heart. Arnold, C.
994
Uluru-Kata Tjuta National Park (Australia)
Arnold, C. Uluru, Australia's Aboriginal heart
(5 and up) **994**
Ulysses Moore [series]
Baccalario, P. The door to time **Fic**
Umansky, Kaye
The silver spoon of Solomon Snow (5 and up)
Fic
Umbrella. Iwamatsu, A. J. **E**
The **umbrella.** Schwartz, A.
In Schwartz, A. Ghosts!; ghostly tales from
folklore p38-43 **398.2**
The **umbrella.** Taback, S.
In Taback, S. Kibitzers and fools; tales my
zayda (grandfather) told me **398.2**
Umbrellas and parasols
Fiction
Iwamatsu, A. J. Umbrella **E**
Liu, J. S. Yellow umbrella **E**
Unanana and the elephant. Arnott, K.
In Womenfolk and fairy tales p127-34
398.2
Unborn child *See* Fetus
Unbuilding. Macaulay, D. **690**
Uncle Andy's. Warhola, J. **E**
Uncle Elephant. Lobel, A. **E**
Uncle Jed's barbershop. Mitchell, M. K. **E**
Uncle Monkey and the ghosts. Climo, S.
In Climo, S. Monkey business; stories from
around the world **398.2**

Uncle Nacho's hat. Rohmer, H.   **398.2**
Uncle Rain Cloud. Johnston, T.   **E**
Uncle Willie and the soup kitchen. DiSalvo-Ryan, D.   **E**
Uncles
          Fiction
Cox, J. Weird stories from the Lonesome Café (2-4)   **Fic**
DiSalvo-Ryan, D. Uncle Willie and the soup kitchen   **E**
Garza, X. Lucha libre: the Man in the Silver Mask (2-5)   **Fic**
Gilson, J. Bug in a rug (2-4)   **Fic**
Hartfield, C. Me and Uncle Romie   **E**
Henkes, K. The birthday room (5 and up)   **Fic**
Hobbs, W. Jackie's Wild Seattle (5 and up)   **Fic**
Horvath, P. Everything on a waffle (4 and up)   **Fic**
Johnston, T. Uncle Rain Cloud   **E**
Lobel, A. Uncle Elephant   **E**
Look, L. Uncle Peter's amazing Chinese wedding   **E**
MacLachlan, P. Seven kisses in a row (2-4)   **Fic**
Martin, A. M. A corner of the universe (5 and up)   **Fic**
Martin, N. Flight of the Fisherbird (5 and up)   **Fic**
Mitchell, M. K. Uncle Jed's barbershop   **E**
Nichol, B. Beethoven lives upstairs (3-5)   **Fic**
Schirripa, S. R. Nicky Deuce (4-6)   **Fic**
Yep, L. Skunk scout (4-6)   **Fic**

Under my hood I have a hat. Kuskin, K.   **E**
Under our skin. Birdseye, D. H.   **305.8**
Under the Christmas tree. Grimes, N.   **811**
Under the ice. Conlan, K.   **578.7**
Under the royal palms. Ada, A. F.   **92**
Under the spell of the moon   **741.6**
Under the starfruit tree. Terada, A. M.   **398.2**
Under the starfruit tree [story] Terada, A. M.
   In Terada, A. M. Under the starfruit tree; folktales from Vietnam p3-6   **398.2**
Under the Sunday tree. Greenfield, E.   **811**
Under the Watson's porch. Shreve, S. R.   **Fic**
Under the wild western sky. Arnosky, J.   **578**
Under the wire. Jiménez, F.
   In Jiménez, F. The circuit: stories from the life of a migrant child p1-8   **S C**
Underground. Macaulay, D.   **624**
Underground railroad
Adler, D. A. A picture book of Harriet Tubman (1-3)   **92**
Bial, R. The Underground Railroad (4 and up)   **326**
Ferris, J. Go free or die: a story about Harriet Tubman (3-5)   **92**
Ford, C. T. Slavery and the underground railroad (3-5)   **326**
Hamilton, V. Many thousand gone (5 and up)   **326**

Hansen, J. Freedom roads: searching for the Underground Railroad (5 and up)   **973.7**
Haskins, J. Get on board: the story of the Underground Railroad (5 and up)   **326**
Heinrichs, A. The Underground Railroad (2-4)   **326**
Koestler-Grack, R. A. The story of Harriet Tubman (2-4)   **92**
Landau, E. Fleeing to freedom on the Underground Railroad (5 and up)   **973.7**
Rappaport, D. Freedom river [biography of John P. Parker] (2-5)   **92**
Schraff, A. E. Harriet Tubman (5 and up)   **92**
          Fiction
McKissack, P. C. A picture of Freedom (4 and up)   **Fic**
Monjo, F. N. The drinking gourd   **E**
Morrow, B. O. A good night for freedom   **E**
Pearsall, S. Trouble don't last (5 and up)   **Fic**
Stroud, B. The patchwork path   **E**
Vande Velde, V. There's a dead person following my sister around (4 and up)   **Fic**
Winter, J. Follow the drinking gourd   **E**
          Poetry
Lawrence, J. Harriet and the Promised Land   **811**

The **underground** world. Schwartz, H.
   In Schwartz, H. and Rush, B. A coat for the moon and other Jewish tales p18-20   **398.2**

Understanding diseases and disorders [series]
Bardhan-Quallen, S. AIDS   **616.97**
Understanding issues [series]
Stewart, G. Terrorism   **303.6**
Understood Betsy. Fisher, D. C.   **Fic**
Undertakers and undertaking
          Fiction
Wiles, D. Each little bird that sings (4-6)   **Fic**
Underwater exploration
Earle, S. A. Dive! (4-6)   **551.46**
Gibbons, G. Exploring the deep, dark sea (k-3)   **551.46**
Kovacs, D. Dive to the deep ocean (4 and up)   **623.8**
Macaulay, D. Ship (4 and up)   **387.2**
Matsen, B. The incredible record-setting deep-sea dive of the bathysphere (4 and up)   **551.46**

Underwater exploration devices *See* Submersibles
Underwood, Deborah
The Easter Island statues (3-6)   **996**
Undocumented aliens *See* Illegal aliens
The **unexpected** banquet. Hunter, N.
   In Bauer, C. F. Celebrations; read-aloud holiday and theme book programs p45-51   **808.8**
Unfinished dreams. Zalben, J. B.   **Fic**
Ungerer, Tomi
Crictor   **E**

Ungerer, Tomi—*Continued*

No kiss for mother

  In You read to me & I'll read to you; 20th-century stories to share p207-18   **E**

  (il) Brown, J. Flat Stanley   **E**

UNICEF

Kindersley, A. Celebrations   **394.26**

Unicorn. Dickinson, P.

  In Horse tales   **S C**

Unicorns

Fiction

A Glory of unicorns (5 and up)   **S C**

The **unicorns** of Kabustan. Eason, A.

  In A Glory of unicorns p115-24   **S C**

Unidentified flying objects

Fiction

Sleator, W. Into the dream (5 and up)   **Fic**

Union of South Africa *See* South Africa

Union of Soviet Socialist Republics *See* Soviet Union

Union Pacific Railroad Company

Halpern, M. Railroad fever (4-6)   **385.09**

Houghton, G. The Transcontinental Railroad (5 and up)   **385.09**

Landau, E. The transcontinental railroad (5 and up)   **385.09**

Thompson, L. The transcontinental railroad (4-6)   **385.09**

The **Union** victory (July 1863-1865). Anderson, D.

  In Anderson, D. World Almanac library of the Civil War [Series]   **973.7**

United Arab Emirates

Augustin, B. United Arab Emirates (5 and up)   **953**

United no more!. Rappaport, D.   **973.7**

United Republic of Cameroon *See* Cameroon

United States

America the beautiful, second series (5 and up)   **973**

The Blackbirch kid's visual reference of the United States (4 and up)   **973**

Bockenhauer, M. H. Our fifty states (4 and up)   **973**

Celebrate the states   **973**

It's my state! [series] (4 and up)   **973**

Leedy, L. Celebrate the 50 states (k-3)   **973**

Sís, P. The train of states (2-4)   **973**

World Almanac Library of the States series (4 and up)   **973**

Yorinks, A. Quilt of states (5 and up)   **973**

Biography

Delano, M. F. American heroes (5 and up)   **920**

Robinson Masters, N. Extraordinary patriots of the United States of America (5 and up)   **920**

Biography—Poetry

Lives: poems about famous Americans (4 and up)   **811.008**

Colonies

  See United States—Territories and possessions

Constitutional history

  See Constitutional history—United States

Description and travel

Brown, D. Alice Ramsey's grand adventure (k-3)   **92**

Murphy, J. Across America on an emigrant train [biography of Robert Louis Stevenson] (5 and up)   **92**

Wilder, L. I. A Little House traveler (5 and up)   **92**

Emigration

  See United States—Immigration and emigration

Encyclopedias

Junior Worldmark encyclopedia of the states (5 and up)   **973.03**

The student encyclopedia of the United States (5 and up)   **973.03**

Exploration

  See also West (U.S.)—Exploration

Foreign population

  See Immigrants—United States

Foreign relations

Stanley, G. E. An emerging world power (1900-1929) (5 and up)   **973.91**

Foreign relations—Japan

Blumberg, R. Commodore Perry in the land of the Shogun (5 and up)   **952**

Foreign relations—Middle East

Marquette, S. America under attack (4 and up)   **973.931**

Government

  See United States—Politics and government

Historical geography

Leacock, E. Journeys in time (4 and up)   **973**

Leacock, E. Places in time (4 and up)   **911**

History

  See also West (U.S.)—History

Hakim, J. A history of US (5 and up)   **973**

Hoose, P. M. We were there, too! (5 and up)   **973**

Johnston, R. D. The making of America (5 and up)   **973**

Leacock, E. Journeys in time (4 and up)   **973**

See/See also pages in the following book(s):

Parker, N. W. Money, money, money (3-5)   **769.5**

History—1600-1775, Colonial period

Avi. Finding Providence: the story of Roger Williams (2-4)   **92**

Burgan, M. Colonial and revolutionary times (5 and up)   **973.2**

Doherty, C. A. The thirteen colonies [series] (4-6)   **973.2**

Fisher, L. E. The blacksmiths (4 and up)   **682**

Fisher, L. E. The doctors (4 and up)   **610.9**

Fisher, L. E. The printers (4 and up)   **686.2**

Fritz, J. Where was Patrick Henry on the 29th of May? (2-4)   **92**

Maestro, B. The new Americans (2-4)   **973.2**

Maestro, B. Struggle for a continent (3-6)   **973.2**

United States—History—1861-1865, Civil War—*Continued*

Ford, C. T. Lincoln, slavery, and the Emancipation Proclamation (4-6) **973.7**

Freedman, R. Lincoln: a photobiography (5 and up) **92**

Friedman, R. The silent witness (k-3) **973.7**

Fritz, J. Stonewall [biography of Stonewall Jackson] (4 and up) **92**

Giblin, J. Good brother, bad brother [biography of John Wilkes Booth and Edwin Booth] (5 and up) **92**

McKissack, P. C. Days of Jubilee (5 and up) **973.7**

McPherson, J. M. Fields of fury (5 and up) **973.7**

Murphy, J. The boys' war (5 and up) **973.7**

Rappaport, D. United no more! (4 and up) **973.7**

Stanchak, J. E. Civil War (4 and up) **973.7**

Sullivan, G. Abraham Lincoln (4 and up) **92**

Turner, A. W. Abe Lincoln remembers (k-3) **92**

History—1861-1865, Civil War—Fiction

Bearden, R. Li'l Dan, the drummer boy **E**

Beatty, P. Turn homeward, Hannalee (5 and up) **Fic**

Blackwood, G. L. Second sight (5 and up) **Fic**

Fleischman, P. Bull Run (6 and up) **Fic**

Hahn, M. D. Hear the wind blow (5 and up) **Fic**

Hesse, K. A light in the storm (5 and up) **Fic**

Hopkinson, D. Billy and the rebel **E**

Hopkinson, D. From slave to soldier **E**

Ives, D. Scrib (5 and up) **Fic**

Keith, H. Rifles for Watie (6 and up) **Fic**

Matas, C. The war within (5 and up) **Fic**

McMullan, M. How I found the Strong (5 and up) **Fic**

Osborne, M. P. My brother's keeper (3-5) **Fic**

Polacco, P. Pink and Say **E**

Reeder, C. Across the lines (5 and up) **Fic**

Steele, W. O. The perilous road (5 and up) **Fic**

Wisler, G. C. Mr. Lincoln's drummer (4 and up) **Fic**

Wisler, G. C. Red Cap (4 and up) **Fic**

History—1861-1865, Civil War—Reconstruction

See Reconstruction (1865-1876)

History—1861-1865, Civil War—Women

Ford, C. T. Daring women of the Civil War (3-5) **973.7**

History—1865-1898—Fiction

Lawlor, L. He will go fearless (5 and up) **Fic**

Robinet, H. G. Forty acres and maybe a mule (4 and up) **Fic**

History—1898, War of 1898

See Spanish-American War, 1898

History—1919-1933

Stanley, G. E. An emerging world power (1900-1929) (5 and up) **973.91**

History—1939-1945, World War

See World War, 1939-1945—United States

History—1945-

Anderson, D. The Cold War years (5 and up) **973.92**

Stanley, G. E. America in today's world (1969-2004) (5 and up) **973.92**

History—Bibliography

Adamson, L. G. Literature connections to American history, K-6 **016.973**

History—Dictionaries

Kane, J. N. Famous first facts **031.02**

History—Encyclopedias

Brownstone, D. M. Frontier America (5 and up) **973.03**

History—Poetry

Katz, B. We the people (5 and up) **811**

Immigration and emigration

See also Immigrants—United States

Anderson, D. Arriving at Ellis Island (5 and up) **325.73**

Bierman, C. Journey to Ellis Island (3-5) **325.73**

D'Amico, J. The coming to America cookbook (5 and up) **641.5**

Freedman, R. Immigrant kids (4 and up) **325.73**

Hoobler, D. We are Americans (5 and up) **325.73**

I was dreaming to come to America (4 and up) **325.73**

Kroll, S. Ellis Island (3-5) **325.73**

Levine, E. . . . if your name was changed at Ellis Island (3-5) **325.73**

Maestro, B. Coming to America: the story of immigration (k-3) **325.73**

Meltzer, M. Bound for America (5 and up) **325.73**

Sandler, M. W. Island of hope (5 and up) **325.73**

Wells, R. Streets of gold [biography of Mary Antin] (3-6) **92**

Maps

Junior state maps on file (4 and up) **973**

Rubel, D. Scholastic atlas of the United States (4 and up) **912**

National songs

See National songs—United States

Poetry

Bates, K. L. America the beautiful **E**

My America (4 and up) **811.008**

Siebert, D. Tour america (3-6) **811**

Politics and government

Horn, G. The presidency (5 and up) **352.23**

Politics and government—1775-1783, Revolution

The Declaration of Independence **973.3**

Fradin, D. B. The signers (4 and up) **920**

Freedman, R. Give me liberty! (5 and up) **973.3**

St. George, J. The journey of the one and only Declaration of Independence (2-4) **973.3**

Politics and government—1783-1809

Fradin, D. B. The founders (4 and up) **920**

Politics and government—1861-1865

Armentrout, D. The Emancipation Proclamation (4 and up) **973.7**

Uttley, Colin
Magnesium
   In The Elements   **546**
Utzel & his daughter, Poverty. Singer, I. B.
   In Singer, I. B. Stories for children p237-41
           S C

Uyehara, Elizabeth
(il) Thompson, L. Love one another   **232.9**
Uzbekistan
Knowlton, M. Uzbekistan (5 and up)   **958.7**

V

V.C.R.'s *See* Video recording
V.D. *See* Sexually transmitted diseases
Vaccination
Silverstein, A. Vaccinations (3-5)   **615**
Vagabonds *See* Tramps
Vagrants *See* Tramps
Vail, Rachel
The crush
   In Tripping over the lunch lady and other
      school stories p120-30   **S C**
Daring to be Abigail (4-6)   **Fic**
Sometimes I'm Bombaloo   **E**
(jt. auth) Avi. Never mind!   **Fic**
Valckx, Catharina
Lizette's green sock   **E**
Valdez (Ship) *See* Exxon Valdez (Ship)
Valentine, Saint
About
Sabuda, R. Saint Valentine (1-3)   **92**
Valentines
Fiction
Jackson, A. The ballad of Valentine   **E**
Valentine's Day
Barth, E. Hearts, cupids, and red roses (3-6)
           394.26
Bulla, C. R. The story of Valentine's Day (k-3)
           394.26
Gibbons, G. Valentine's Day (k-3)   **394.26**
Landau, E. Valentine's day (2-4)   **394.26**
See/See also pages in the following book(s):
Bauer, C. F. Celebrations p1-24   **808.8**
Fiction
Rockwell, A. F. Valentine's Day   **E**
Poetry
Prelutsky, J. It's Valentine's Day (1-3)   **811**
Valerie & Walter's best books for children. Lewis,
   V. V.   **028.5**
Valério, Geraldo
(il) MacDonald, M. R. Conejito   **398.2**
(il) Spinelli, E. When you are happy   **E**
Valley Forge. Stein, R. C.   **973.3**
Valley of the Kings. Smith, S. T.   **932**
The **vampire**. Afanas'ev, A. N.
   In Afanas'ev, A. N. Russian fairy tales p593-
     98   **398.2**
The **vampire** cat. San Souci, R.
   In San Souci, R. More short & shivery; thirty
     terrifying tales p27-32   **398.2**

Vampires
Fiction
Sfar, J. Little Vampire goes to school (2-4)
           741.5
Van Allsburg, Chris
Bad day at Riverbend   **E**
Ben's dream   **E**
The garden of Abdul Gasazi   **E**
Jumanji   **E**
Just a dream   **E**
The mysteries of Harris Burdick   **E**
The Polar Express   **E**
The stranger   **E**
The sweetest fig   **E**
The widow's broom   **E**
The wreck of the Zephyr   **E**
The wretched stone   **E**
The Z was zapped   **E**
Zathura   **E**
See/See also pages in the following book(s):
Marcus, L. S. A Caldecott celebration   **741.6**
Van Beethoven, Ludwig *See* Beethoven, Ludwig
   van, 1770-1827
Van der Meer, Jan *See* Vermeer, Johannes, 1632-
   1675
Van Dusen, Chris
(jt. auth) DiCamillo, K. Mercy Watson to the
   rescue   **E**
Van Gelder, Richard George
(jt. auth) Bancroft, H. Animals in winter
           591.56
Van Gogh, Vincent *See* Gogh, Vincent van, 1853-
   1890
Van Kampen, Vlasta
It couldn't be worse! (k-3)   **398.2**
Van Laan, Nancy
The hairy toe
   In Van Laan, N. Teeny tiny tingly tales   **E**
It
   In Van Laan, N. Teeny tiny tingly tales   **E**
The magic bean tree (k-3)   **398.2**
Moose tales   **E**
Old Doctor Wango Tango
   In Van Laan, N. Teeny tiny tingly tales   **E**
Shingebiss (2-4)   **398.2**
Teeny tiny tingly tales   **E**
When winter comes   **E**
With a whoop and a holler (4 and up)   **398**
Includes the following stories: One cold day; Monkey stew;
Fool John; Possum plays dead; The big dinin'; The watermillion
patch; Ol' Mister Biggety; How come Ol' Buzzard boards; Mis-
ter Grumpy rides the clouds; Nuts! Nuts! Nuts!; We hunted and
we hollered; Ol' Gally Mander; Jack runs off; Three Foots
Van Leeuwen, Jean
Benny & beautiful baby Delilah   **E**
Bound for Oregon (4-6)   **Fic**
Cabin on Trouble Creek (4 and up)   **Fic**
Going West   **E**
The Great Googlestein museum mystery (3-5)
           Fic
Nothing here but trees   **E**
Tales of Oliver Pig   **E**
Van Orden, Phyllis J.
Library service to children   **027.62**
Selecting books for the elementary school li-
   brary media center   **025.2**

Van Wright, Cornelius
(il) Chinn, K. Sam and the lucky money   E
(il) Miller, W. Zora Hurston and the chinaberry tree   **92**
(il) Rappaport, D. We are the many   **920**
(il) Smith, C. L. Jingle dancer   E
(il) Tsubakiyama, M. Mei-Mei loves the morning   E

Van Zyle, Jon
(il) London, J. Baby whale's journey   E
(il) London, J. Sled dogs run   E
(il) Miller, D. S. Arctic lights, arctic nights   **591.4**
(il) Miller, D. S. The great serum race   **798.8**
(il) Miller, D. S. A polar bear journey   **599.78**
(il) Miller, D. S. River of life   **577.6**

VanCleave, Janice Pratt
Janice VanCleave's 201 awesome, magical, bizarre & incredible experiments (4 and up)   **507.8**
Janice VanCleave's 202 oozing, bubbling, dripping & bouncing experiments (4 and up)   **507.8**
Janice VanCleave's 203 icy, freezing, frosty, cool & wild experiments (4 and up)   **507.8**
Janice VanCleave's constellations for every kid (4 and up)   **523.8**
Janice VanCleave's earth science for every kid (4 and up)   **550**
Janice Vancleave's ecology for every kid (4 and up)   **577**
Janice VanCleave's electricity (4 and up)   **537**
Janice VanCleave's food and nutrition for every kid (4 and up)   **613.2**
Janice VanCleave's geometry for every kid (4 and up)   **516**
Janice VanCleave's guide to more of the best science fair projects (4 and up)   **507.8**
Janice VanCleave's guide to the best science fair projects (4 and up)   **507.8**
Janice VanCleave's insects and spiders (4 and up)   **595.7**
Janice VanCleave's oceans for every kid (4 and up)   **551.46**
Janice VanCleave's plants (5 and up)   **580.7**
Janice VanCleave's play and find out about bugs (k-2)   **595.7**
Janice VanCleave's play and find out about math (k-2)   **513**
Janice VanCleave's play and find out about nature (k-2)   **570**
Janice VanCleave's rocks and minerals (4 and up)   **552**
Janice VanCleave's science around the year (4 and up)   **507.8**
Janice VanCleave's solar system (4 and up)   **523.2**
Janice VanCleave's the human body for every kid (4 and up)   **612**
Janice VanCleave's weather (4 and up)   **551.5**

Vande Velde, Vivian
Smart dog (4-6)   Fic
There's a dead person following my sister around (4 and up)   Fic
Three good deeds (3-5)   Fic
Wizard at work (3-6)   Fic

Vandenbroeck, Fabricio
(il) Johnston, T. Uncle Rain Cloud   E

Vander Zee, Ruth
Mississippi morning   E

Vanderbilt, Cornelius, 1794-1877
Fiction
Stowell, P. The greatest potatoes   E

Vanishing species *See* Endangered species

The **Various**. Augarde, S.   Fic

Varmer, Hjørdis
Hans Christian Andersen (5 and up)   **92**

Varon, Sara
Chicken and Cat   E
Sweaterweather (3-5)   **741.5**

Varriale, Jim
Kids dance (4 and up)   **792.8**

Vasconcellos, Daniel
(il) Christopher, M. The dog that called the pitch   Fic

Vasilisa the Beautiful. Afanas´ev, A. N.
In Afanas´ev, A. N. Russian fairy tales p439-47   **398.2**

Vathanaprida, Supaporn
(jt. auth) MacDonald, M. R. The girl who wore too much   **398.2**

Vaughan, Marcia
How to cook a gooseberry fool
In Easy menu ethnic cookbooks   **641.5**

Vaz, Katherine
My swan sister
In Swan sister; fairy tales retold   S C

VCRs *See* Video recording

VD *See* Sexually transmitted diseases

Vecchione, Patrice
(ed) Whisper and shout. See Whisper and shout   **811.008**

Vega, Denise
Click here (5 and up)   Fic

Vegetable gardening
Creasy, R. Blue potatoes, orange tomatoes (3-5)   **635**

See/See also pages in the following book(s):
Cook, D. F. Kids' pumpkin projects (2-4)   **745.5**

Fiction
Ehlert, L. Growing vegetable soup   E

Vegetables
See also names of vegetables
Creasy, R. Blue potatoes, orange tomatoes (3-5)   **635**
Ehlert, L. Eating the alphabet   E
McMillan, B. Growing colors   E
Fiction
Wiesner, D. June 29, 1999   E

Vegetarian cooking
Gillies, J. The jumbo vegetarian cookbook (4 and up)   **641.5**

A **Very** happy donkey
   In The Magic orange tree, and other Haitian
      folktales p157-63 **398.2**
The **very** hungry caterpillar. Carle, E. **E**
A **very** important day. Herold, M. R. **E**
The **very** lonely firefly. Carle, E. **E**
The **very** old woman and the Piskey. Climo, S.
   In Climo, S. Magic & mischief; tales from
      Cornwall p15-20 **398.2**
The **very** pretty lady. Babbitt, N.
   In Babbitt, N. The Devil's storybook p13-20
      S C
The **very** quiet cricket. Carle, E. **E**
A **very** special house. Krauss, R. **E**
Vespucci, Amerigo, 1451-1512
See/See also pages in the following book(s):
   Fritz, J. Around the world in a hundred years (4
      and up) **910.4**
Vestergaard, Hope
   Hello, snow! **E**
Veterinarians
   Fiction
   Lee, C. Good dog, Paw! **E**
Veterinary medicine
   Jackson, D. M. ER vets (5 and up) **636.089**
Vicksburg (Miss.)
   Siege, 1863
   Fraser, M. A. Vicksburg—the battle that won
      the Civil War (4 and up) **973.7**
Vicksburg—the battle that won the Civil War.
   Fraser, M. A. **973.7**
Victims of crimes
   See also Abused women
Victor *See* Wild Boy of Aveyron, d. 1828
Victoria, Queen of Great Britain, 1819-1901
See/See also pages in the following book(s):
   Krull, K. Lives of extraordinary women (4 and
      up) **920**
The **victory** garden. Kochenderfer, L. **Fic**
Victory or death!. Rappaport, D. **973.3**
Vidal, Beatriz
   Federico and the Magi's gift **E**
   (il) Aardema, V. Bringing the rain to Kapiti
      Plain **398.2**
   (il) Alvarez, J. A gift of gracias **E**
   (il) Mora, P. A library for Juana: the world of
      Sor Juana Inés **92**
   (il) Van Laan, N. The magic bean tree
      398.2
Video cassette recorders and recording *See* Vid-
   eo recording
Video games
   Fiction
   Seidler, T. Brainboy and the Deathmaster (5 and
      up) **Fic**
Video recording
   Shulman, M. Attack of the killer video book (5
      and up) **778.59**
Videorecorders *See* Video recording
Videotape recorders and recording *See* Video
   recording

Vienna (Austria)
   Fiction
   Ibbotson, E. The star of Kazan (5 and up)
      Fic
Vietnam
   Guile, M. Culture in Vietnam (4 and up)
      959.7
   Seah, A. Vietnam (5 and up) **959.704**
   Fiction
   Keller, H. Grandfather's dream **E**
   Folklore
   See Folklore—Vietnam
   Social life and customs
   Huynh, Q. N. The land I lost: adventures of a
      boy in Vietnam (5 and up) **92**
   Huynh, Q. N. Water buffalo days (3-5) **92**
Vietnam Veterans Memorial (Washington, D.C.)
   Fiction
   Bunting, E. The Wall **E**
Vietnam War, 1961-1975
   Canwell, D. African Americans in the Vietnam
      War (5 and up) **959.704**
   Levy, D. The Vietnam War (5 and up)
      959.704
   Fiction
   Myers, W. D. Patrol **E**
   Nelson, T. And one for all (5 and up) **Fic**
   Sherlock, P. Letters from Wolfie (5 and up)
      Fic
   Testa, M. Almost forever (3-5) **Fic**
Vietnamese
   Fiction
   Whelan, G. Goodbye, Vietnam (4 and up)
      Fic

      United States—Fiction
   Gilson, J. Hello, my name is Scrambled Eggs (4
      and up) **Fic**
Vietnamese Americans
   Hoyt-Goldsmith, D. Hoang Anh (3-5) **305.8**
   Fiction
   Himelblau, L. The trouble begins (4 and up)
      Fic
   Paterson, K. Park's quest (5 and up) **Fic**
Vietnamese New Year
   Shea, P. D. Ten mice for Tet! (k-3) **394.26**
The **view** from Saturday. Konigsburg, E. L.
      Fic
The **view** from the cherry tree. Roberts, W. D.
      Fic
Vigil-Piñón, Evangelina
   Marina's muumuu **E**
Viking easy-to-read [series]
   Adler, D. A. Young Cam Jansen and the dino-
      saur game **E**
   Chaconas, D. Cork & Fuzz **E**
   Holub, J. The garden that we grew **E**
   Meister, C. My pony Jack **E**
   Meister, C. Tiny's bath **E**
   Spohn, K. Turtle and Snake's day at the beach
      E
   Ziefert, H. Little Red Riding Hood **398.2**
Vikings
   Berger, M. The real Vikings (4 and up) **948**
   Margeson, S. M. Viking (4 and up) **948**

Von Schmidt, Eric
(il) Fleischman, S. By the Great Horn Spoon!
               Fic
(il) Fleischman, S. Mr. Mysterious & Company
               Fic

Vos, Ida
Anna is still here (4 and up)   **Fic**
Hide and seek (4 and up)   **Fic**

Vossmeyer, Gabriele
(jt. auth) Fuller, B. Germany   **943**

Vote!. Christelow, E.   **324**

Voting *See* Elections

The **voyage** of Patience Goodspeed. Frederick, H. V.   **Fic**

Voyages and travels
 See also Travel
Rumford, J. Traveling man: the journey of Ibn Battuta, 1325-1354 (3-6)   **92**
      Fiction
Bahrampour, A. Otto, the story of a mirror
               E
Blackstone, S. My granny went to market **E**
Corder, Z. Lionboy (4 and up)   **Fic**
Helldorfer, M. C. Hog music   **E**
Hobbs, W. Jason's gold (5 and up) **Fic**
Ketchum, L. Orphan journey home (4-6) **Fic**
Kirkpatrick, K. A. Escape across the wide sea (5 and up)   **Fic**
Krensky, S. Dangerous crossing (2-4) **Fic**
Lin, G. Olvina flies   **E**
Priceman, M. How to make an apple pie and see the world   **E**
Say, A. Grandfather's journey   **E**
Shafer, A. C. The fantastic journey of Pieter Bruegel (4 and up)   **Fic**
Shulevitz, U. The travels of Benjamin of Tudela (4 and up)   **Fic**
Weston, C. The diary of Melanie Martin; or, How I survived Matt the Brat, Michelangelo, and the Leaning Tower of Pizza (3-6) **Fic**
      Poetry
Lewis, J. P. A world of wonders (3-5) **811**

Voyages around the world
Lasky, K. Born in the breezes: the seafaring of Joshua Slocum (3-6)   **92**
Levinson, N. S. Magellan and the first voyage around the world (5 and up)   **92**
      Fiction
Hesse, K. Stowaway (5 and up)   **Fic**
The **voyages** of Doctor Dolittle. Lofting, H.
               Fic

Vroomaloom zoom. Coy, J.   **E**

Vultures
Markle, S. Vultures (3-5)   **598**

W

Waber, Bernard
Evie & Margie   **E**
Ira sleeps over   **E**
A lion named Shirley Williamson   **E**
Lyle, Lyle, crocodile   **E**
The mouse that snored   **E**

Wáchale! poetry and prose on growing up Latino in America (5 and up)   **810.8**

Wada, Stephanie
Momotarō and the island of ogres (3-6)
              398.2

Waddell, Martin
Can't you sleep, Little Bear?   **E**
Farmer duck   **E**
Hi, Harry!   **E**
It's quacking time!   **E**
Owl babies   **E**
Snow bears   **E**
Tiny's big adventure   **E**

Wadsworth, Ginger
Benjamin Banneker (3-5)   **92**
Cesar Chavez (2-4)   **92**

Wadsworth, Olive A.
Over in the meadow   **E**

Wagner, Lisa
Cool melt & pour soap (4-6)   **668**
Cool painted stuff (4-6)   **745.7**

Wagon wheels. Brenner, B.   **E**

Wagons *See* Carriages and carts

Wagué Diakité, Baba
The hatseller and the monkeys (k-3) **398.2**
The hunterman and the crocodile (2-4)
              398.2
The magic gourd (2-4)   **398.2**
(il) Badoe, A. The pot of wisdom: Ananse stories   **398.2**
(il) Bynum, E. Jamari's drum   **E**

Wahl, Jan
Candy shop   **E**

Waichulaitis, Trisha
(jt. auth) Benton, G. Ready-to-go storytimes
             027.62

The **Wainscott** weasel. Seidler, T. **Fic**

Wait, Lea
Wintering well (5 and up)   **Fic**

Wait! No paint!. Whatley, B.   **E**

Wait till Helen comes. Hahn, M. D. **Fic**

Waiting for a white knight. Bateman, T.
 In Fire and wings: dragon tales from East and West p137-40   **S C**

Waiting for Anya. Morpurgo, M. **Fic**

Waiting for May. Stoeke, J. M.   **E**

Waiting for Mr. Chester. Medearis, A. S.
 In Medearis, A. S. Haunts; five hair-raising tales p32-37   **S C**

Waiting for wings. Ehlert, L.   **E**

Wake up house!. Lillegard, D.   **811**

Wake up sleepy head!. Ross, M.   **811**

Wakefield, Ruth
See/See also pages in the following book(s):
Thimmesh, C. Girls think of everything (5 and up)   **920**

Wakim, Yvonne
(jt. auth) Molin, P. F. American Indian stereotypes in the world of children **970.004**

Waldee, Lynne Marie
Cooking the French way
 In Easy menu ethnic cookbooks **641.5**

Waldman, Neil
Masada (4 and up)   933
Out of the shadows (5 and up)   92
The snowflake (k-3)   551.48
(il) Schecter, E. The family Haggadah   296.4

Waldman, Stuart
The last river (3-6)   978

Wales
Oxlade, C. A visit to Wales (1-4)   942.9
Fiction
Bond, N. A string in the harp (6 and up)
                                               Fic
Cooper, S. The grey king (5 and up)   Fic
Kimmel, E. C. In the stone circle (5 and up)
                                               Fic

Folklore
See Folklore—Wales

A **walk** in the boreal forest. Johnson, R. L.
                                             577.3
A **walk** in the deciduous forest. Johnson, R. L.
                                             577.3
A **walk** in the desert. Johnson, R. L.   577.5
A **walk** in the prairie. Johnson, R. L.   577.4
A **walk** in the tundra. Johnson, R. L.   577.5
Walk on!. Frazee, M.   E
A **walk** on the Great Barrier Reef. Arnold, C.
                                             578.7
Walk two moons. Creech, S.   Fic

Walker, Alice
Langston Hughes, American poet (2-5)   92

Walker, Barbara Muhs
The Little House cookbook (5 and up)
                                             641.5

Walker, C. J., Madame, 1867-1919
About
Lasky, K. Vision of beauty: the story of Sarah
Breedlove Walker (3-5)   92
McKissack, P. C. Madam C.J. Walker (1-3)
                                               92

Walker, David
(il) Meyers, S. Puppies! Puppies! Puppies!   E

Walker, Lester
Carpentry for children (4 and up)   694

Walker, Madame C. J. *See* Walker, C. J., Madame, 1867-1919

Walker, Pamela
Science experiments on file (5 and up)
                                             507.8

Walker, Richard
Body (4 and up)   611
Genes & DNA (5 and up)   576.5
The Kingfisher first human body encyclopedia
(3-5)   612

Walker, Sally M.
Earthquakes (3-6)   551.2
Fireflies (k-3)   595.7
Fossil fish found alive (5 and up)   597
Hippos (3-6)   599.63
Rays (3-6)   597

Walker, Sarah Breedlove *See* Walker, C. J., Madame, 1867-1919

Walking
Fiction
Cooper, E. A good night walk   E
Frazee, M. Walk on!   E
Johnson, D. B. Henry hikes to Fitchburg   E
Walking the Bible. Feiler, B. S.   222
Walking to the bus-rider blues. Robinet, H. G.
                                              Fic
Walking with Henry. Locker, T.   E
The **Wall**. Bunting, E.   E
The **Wall** and the Wing. Ruby, L.   Fic
Wall painting *See* Mural painting and decoration
Wallace, Barbara Brooks
Cousins in the castle (4-6)   Fic
Ghosts in the gallery (5 and up)   Fic
The twin in the tavern (4-6)   Fic

Wallace, Bill
Beauty (4-6)   Fic
A dog called Kitty (4-6)   Fic
Skinny-dipping at Monster Lake (4 and up)
                                              Fic

Wallace, Carol
One nosy pup   E
Turkeys together   E

Wallace, Daisy *See* Cuyler, Margery
(ed) Ghost poems. See Ghost poems
                                           821.008

Wallace, John
(il) Bauer, M. D. Wind   551.51
(il) Hello sunshine, good night moonlight. See
Hello sunshine, good night moonlight
                                           811.008

Wallace, Karen
I am an ankylosaurus (k-2)   567.9
Tale of a tadpole (k-1)   597.8

Wallace, Nancy Elizabeth
Pumpkin day!   E
Recycle every day!   E
Seeds! Seeds! Seeds!   E
(comp) The sun, the moon, and the stars. See
The sun, the moon, and the stars   811.008

Wallace-Brodeur, Ruth
Blue eyes better (4-6)   Fic
Wallace's lists. Bottner, B.   E

Wallner, Alexandra
Abigail Adams (1-3)   92
Grandma Moses (k-3)   92
Sergio and the hurricane   E
(il) Adler, D. A. A picture book of Helen Keller
                                               92
(il) Adler, D. A. A picture book of Louis Braille
                                               92
(il) Adler, D. A. A picture book of Thomas Jefferson
                                               92
(il) The Farmer in the dell. See The Farmer in
the dell   782.42

Wallner, John C.
(il) Adler, D. A. A picture book of Helen Keller
                                               92
(il) Adler, D. A. A picture book of Louis Braille
                                               92
(il) Adler, D. A. A picture book of Thomas Jefferson
                                               92

Ward, Adam
Card games for kids (3-6)　　**795.4**

Ward, April
(il) Fletcher, R. A writing kind of day　　**811**

Ward, Elaine M.
Old Testament women (5 and up)　　**221.9**

Ward, Helen
The hare and the tortoise (k-3)　　**398.2**
The rooster and the fox　　**E**
Unwitting wisdom (3-6)　　**398.2**

Ward, John
(il) Sanfield, S. The adventures of High John the Conqueror　　**398.2**

Ward, Lynd Kendall
The biggest bear　　**E**
The silver pony (2-4)　　**Fic**
(il) Coatsworth, E. J. The cat who went to heaven　　**Fic**
(il) Swift, H. H. The little red lighthouse and the great gray bridge　　**E**
(il) Wyss, J. D. The Swiss family Robinson　　**Fic**

Ward, Marilyn
Voices from the margins　　**016.8**

Ward-Johnson, Chris
E-mail: a magic mouse guide (k-3)　　**004.6**

Wardlaw, Lee
The desk
In Tripping over the lunch lady and other school stories p97-117　　**S C**
Punia and the King of Sharks (k-3)　　**398.2**

Warfare. Chrisp, P.　　**355**

Warhol, Andy, 1928?-1987
About
Ford, C. T. Andy Warhol (2-4)　　**92**
Warhola, J. Uncle Andy's　　**E**

Warhola, James
Uncle Andy's　　**E**

Waring, Richard
Hungry hen　　**E**

Warlock at the wheel. Jones, D. W.
In Jones, D. W. Mixed magics　　**S C**

Warner, Sally
Only Emma (2-4)　　**Fic**
This isn't about the money (5 and up)　　**Fic**

Warnes, Tim
Mommy mine　　**E**

Warnick, Elsa
(il) Simon, S. Ride the wind　　**591.56**

Warren, Andrea
Orphan train rider (4 and up)　　**362.7**
Surviving Hitler (5 and up)　　**940.53**
We rode the orphan trains (4 and up)　　**362.7**

Warren, Elizabeth V.
(jt. auth) Coleman, J. W. Baseball for everyone　　**796.357**

Warshaw, Hallie
Get out! (3-6)　　**790.1**
The sleepover cookbook (4 and up)　　**641.5**
Zany rainy days (2-5)　　**793**

Washakie, Shoshone Chief, 1797-1900
See/See also pages in the following book(s):
Freedman, R. Indian chiefs (6 and up)　　**920**

Washburn, Lucia
(il) George, J. C. Look to the North　　**E**
(il) Zoehfeld, K. W. Did dinosaurs have feathers?　　**568**
(il) Zoehfeld, K. W. Dinosaur babies　　**567.9**

Washington, Booker T., 1856-1915
About
McKissack, P. C. Booker T. Washington (1-3)　　**92**

Fiction
Bradby, M. More than anything else　　**E**

Washington, Donna L.
A pride of African tales (3-5)　　**398.2**
Contents: Anansi's fishing expedition; The boy who wanted the moon; Shansa Mutongo Shima; The roof of leaves; The wedding basket; The talking skull

Washington, George, 1732-1799
About
Adler, D. A. George Washington (5 and up)　　**92**
Bial, R. Where Washington walked (3-6)　　**92**
Chandra, D. George Washington's teeth　　**E**
Ferrie, R. The world turned upside down (5 and up)　　**973.3**
Fritz, J. George Washington's mother (1-3)　　**92**
Harness, C. George Washington (3-5)　　**92**
Jurmain, S. George did it [biography of George Washington] (2-4)　　**92**

Fiction
Small, D. George Washington's cows　　**E**

Washington, Mary Ball, 1708-1789
About
Fritz, J. George Washington's mother (1-3)　　**92**

Washington (D.C.)
Curlee, L. Capital (3-6)　　**975.3**
Figueroa, A. Washington D. C.
In World Almanac Library of the States series　　**973**
Stein, R. C. Washington, D.C.
In America the beautiful, second series　　**973**

Fiction
Blackwood, G. L. Second sight (5 and up)　　**Fic**
Cummings, P. Saving Grace (5 and up)　　**Fic**
Kelly, K. Lucy Rose, here's the thing about me (2-4)　　**Fic**

Washington (George) Bridge (N.Y. and N.J.)
See George Washington Bridge (N.Y. and N.J.)

Washington (State)
Barenblat, R. Washington
In World Almanac Library of the States series　　**973**
Blashfield, J. F. Washington
In America the beautiful, second series　　**973**
Otfinoski, S. Washington
In It's my state! [series]　　**973**

Fiction
Holm, J. L. Our only May Amelia (5 and up)　　**Fic**
Kehret, P. The ghost's grave (5 and up)　　**Fic**

Watson, Wendy
(il) Bierhorst, J. Is my friend at home?
398.2
(il) Hesse, K. The cats in Krasinski Square
E
(il) Showers, P. Sleep is for everyone   **612.8**
The **Watsons** go to Birmingham—1963. Curtis, C.
P.   **Fic**

Watt, Susan
Cobalt
In The Elements   **546**
Mercury
In The Elements   **546**

Wattenberg, Jane
Henny-Penny (k-3)   **398.2**

Watters, Debbie
Where's Mom's hair? (2-4)   **616.99**

Watters, Emmett
(jt. auth) Watters, D. Where's Mom's hair?
616.99

Watters, Haydn
(jt. auth) Watters, D. Where's Mom's hair?
616.99

Watts, Barrie
Duck (k-3)   **598**

Watts, Bernadette
Jorinda and Jorindel (k-3)   **398.2**
The ugly duckling   **E**
(il) Bell, A. The Snow Queen   **E**

Watts, James
(il) Curry, J. L. Hold up the sky: and other Native American tales from Texas and the Southern Plains   **398.2**
(il) Curry, J. L. The wonderful sky boat and other Native American tales of the Southeast
398.2

Watts, Leslie Elizabeth
(il) Bradford, K. You can't rush a cat   **E**

Watts, Murray
The Bible for children from Good Books (3-6)
220.9

Watts, Sharon
(il) Stowell, P. The greatest potatoes   **E**

Watts, Suzanne
(il) Wilson, K. Hilda must be dancing   **E**

Watts library [series]
Carruthers, M. W. The Hubble Space Telescope
522
Greene, J. D. Slavery in ancient Greece and Rome   **326**
Kennedy, M. Baseball   **796.357**
Kennedy, M. Ice hockey   **796.962**
Kent, D. Animal helpers for the disabled
636.088
Kent, D. Athletes with disabilities   **371.9**
Landau, E. The transcontinental railroad
385.09
McPhee, A. T. AIDS   **616.97**
Nardo, D. Greek temples   **726**
Nardo, D. Roman amphitheaters   **725**
Nelson, S. P. Jedediah Smith   **92**
Newman, S. P. Child slavery in modern times
326

Schlaepfer, G. G. The Louisiana Purchase
973.4
Schlaepfer, G. G. Pythons and boas   **597.96**
Sherman, J. The history of the Internet
004.6
Sherman, J. The history of the personal computer   **004**
Sonneborn, L. The Mormon Trail   **978**
Souza, D. M. Freaky flowers   **582.13**
Souza, D. M. Plant invaders   **581.6**
Souza, D. M. What is a fungus?   **579.5**
Trueit, T. S. Rocks, gems, and minerals   **552**

Watts reference [series]
Barber, N. Music: an A-Z guide   **780.3**
The encyclopedia of U.S. presidential elections
324
Fischer, D. The encyclopedia of the Summer Olympics   **796.48**

Waugh, Sylvia
The Mennyms (5 and up)   **Fic**
Space race (4-6)   **Fic**
The **wave** of the Sea-Wolf. Wisniewski, D.   **E**

Waxman, Laura Hamilton
Colin Powell (2-5)   **92**
The **way** a door closes. Smith, H. A.   **811**
The **way** cool license plate book. Wise, L.
793.7
The **way** I love you. Bedford, D.   **E**
The **way** meat loves salt. Jaffe, N.   **398.2**
The **way** of the storyteller. Sawyer, R.   **372.6**
The **way** things work. See Macaulay, D. The new way things work   **600**
The **way** to start a day. Baylor, B.   **204**
Ways of telling. Marcus, L. S.   **741.6**
Wayside School gets a little stranger. Sachar, L.
Fic
We are Americans. Hoobler, D.   **325.73**
We are best friends. Aliki   **E**
We are still here: Native Americans today [series]
King, S. Shannon: an Ojibway dancer
970.004
Peters, R. M. Clambake   **970.004**
Roessel, M. Songs from the loom   **970.004**
We are the many. Rappaport, D.   **920**
We can work it out. Polland, B. K.   **303.6**
We had a picnic this Sunday past. Woodson, J.
E
We hunted and we hollered. Van Laan, N.
In Van Laan, N. With a whoop and a holler; a bushel of lore from way down south p65   **398.2**
We organized. McKissack, P. C.
In McKissack, P. C. The dark-thirty; Southern tales of the supernatural p17-21   **S C**
We rode the orphan trains. Warren, A.   **362.7**
We the people. Katz, B.   **811**
We the people [series]
Heinrichs, A. The Underground Railroad
326
We were there, too!. Hoose, P. M.   **973**

Wealth

See also Success

Fiction

Hayes, J. A spoon for every bite   **E**

Roberts, W. D. The kidnappers (4 and up)

    Fic

Weapons

See also Armor

Byam, M. Arms & armor (4 and up)   **355.8**

Meltzer, M. Weapons & warfare (5 and up)

    355

Weapons & warfare. Meltzer, M.   **355**

Weasel. DeFelice, C. C.   **Fic**

Weasels

Fiction

Seidler, T. The Wainscott weasel (4-6)   **Fic**

Weate, Jeremy

A young person's guide to philosophy (5 and up)   **100**

Weather

See also Meteorology

Challoner, J. Hurricane & tornado (4 and up)

    551.55

Cole, J. The magic school bus inside a hurricane (2-4)   **551.55**

Gibbons, G. Weather words and what they mean (k-3)   **551.6**

Kahl, J. D. National Audubon Society first field guide: weather (4 and up)   **551.5**

Lauw, D. Weather (3-6)   **551.5**

Levine, S. Wonderful weather (2-4)   **551.5**

Rupp, R. Weather (4 and up)   **551.6**

Simon, S. Weather (3-6)   **551.5**

Singer, M. On the same day in March (k-3)

    551.6

VanCleave, J. P. Janice VanCleave's weather (4 and up)   **551.5**

Weather forecasting

Breen, M. The kids' book of weather forecasting (4 and up)   **551.63**

Demarest, C. L. Hurricane hunters! (k-3)

    551.55

Gibbons, G. Weather forecasting (k-3)

    551.63

Weather words and what they mean. Gibbons, G.

    551.6

Weatherby, Brenda

The trucker   **E**

Weatherby, Mark Alan

(il) Weatherby, B. The trucker   **E**

Weatherford, Carole Boston

Freedom on the menu   **E**

A Negro league scrapbook (4 and up)

    796.357

Remember the bridge   **811**

Weave little stars into my sleep (2-4)   **782.42**

A **weave** of words. San Souci, R.   **398.2**

The **weaver** of Yzad. Goldin, B. D.

In Goldin, B. D. Journeys with Elijah; eight tales of the Prophet p29-37   **222**

The **weavers**. Fisher, L. E.   **677**

Weaver's daughter. Bradley, K. B.   **Fic**

Weaving

Fisher, L. E. The weavers (4 and up)   **677**

Monaghan, K. You can weave! (4 and up)

    746.41

Roessel, M. Songs from the loom (3-6)

    970.004

Fiction

Castañeda, O. S. Abuela's weave   **E**

Lyon, G. E. Weaving the rainbow   **E**

Weaving a library Web. Blowers, H.   **025.04**

The **weaving** that saved the Prince. Schwartz, H.

In Schwartz, H. and Rush, B. A coat for the moon and other Jewish tales p62-64

    398.2

Weaving the rainbow. Lyon, G. E.   **E**

Web sites

Blowers, H. Weaving a library Web   **025.04**

Haycock, K. Neal-Schuman authoritative guide to kids' search engines, subject directories, and portals   **025.04**

Lindsay, D. Dave's quick n' easy web pages (5 and up)   **005.7**

Selfridge, B. A Kid's guide to creating web pages for home and school (5 and up)

    005.7

Webb, Lois Sinaiko

Holidays of the world cookbook for students (5 and up)   **641.5**

Webb, Ray

(il) Brook, L. Daily life in ancient and modern Timbuktu   **966.23**

Webb, Sophie

Looking for seabirds (4 and up)   **598**

My season with penguins (4 and up)   **598**

Weber, Bruce

(jt. auth) Glover, S. Savion!: my life in tap

    92

Weber, EdNah New Rider

Rattlesnake Mesa (4 and up)   **92**

Weber, Jill

(il) Bateman, T. Harp o' gold   **E**

Weber, Mark

(il) Philip, N. The pirate princess and other fairy tales   **398.2**

Weber, Sandra

Two in the wilderness (4 and up)   **508**

Webster, Christine

Polynesians (3-5)   **996**

Webster's elementary dictionary. See Merriam-Webster's elementary dictionary   **423**

Webster's New World children's dictionary (3-5)

    423

The **wedding** basket. Washington, D. L.

In Washington, D. L. A pride of African tales

    398.2

The **wedding** feast. Lunge-Larsen, L.

In Lunge-Larsen, L. The hidden folk; stories of fairies, dwarves, selkies, and other secret beings p34-38   **398.2**

The **wedding** planner's daughter. Paratore, C.

    Fic

The **wedding** procession of the Rag Doll and the Broom Handle and who was in it. Sandburg, C.

In Sandburg, C. Rootabaga stories p75-79

S C

also in Sandburg, C. The Sandburg treasury; prose and poetry for young people p43-45 **818**

Weddings

See also Marriage customs and rites

Fiction

Barasch, L. The reluctant flower girl **E**
Delton, J. Angel's mother's wedding (3-5) **Fic**
Gibbons, F. Mountain wedding **E**
Look, L. Uncle Peter's amazing Chinese wedding **E**
Paratore, C. The wedding planner's daughter (4-6) **Fic**

Weddings. Morris, A. **392**

Wedman, Belgin K.
(il) Novesky, A. The elephant prince **294.5**

The **Wednesday** surprise. Bunting, E. **E**

The **wee** bannock. Jacobs, J.

In Jacobs, J. English fairy tales p286-90 **398.2**

The **Wee** Little Tyke. MacDonald, M. R.

In MacDonald, M. R. When the lights go out; twenty scary tales to tell p21-28 **372.6**

Wee Meg Barnileg and the fairies. Sawyer, R.

In Sawyer, R. The way of the storyteller p205-16 **372.6**

The **wee**, wee mannie. Jacobs, J.

In Jacobs, J. English fairy tales p393-95 **398.2**

Wee Winnie Witch's Skinny. Hamilton, V. **E**

Weeks, Sarah
Drip, drop **E**
Experts, Incorporated
In Tripping over the lunch lady and other school stories p30-40 **S C**
Jumping the scratch (5 and up) **Fic**
Regular Guy (4-6) **Fic**
So B. it (5 and up) **Fic**
Two eggs, please **E**

The **weeping** willow. Jennings, P. **Fic**

Wehlage, Gary
(jt. auth) Zweizig, D. Lessons from Library Power **027.8**

Wehrman, Richard
(il) Han, S. C. The rabbit's tail **398.2**

Weigel, Jeff
Atomic Ace **E**

Weight lifting
Knotts, B. Weightlifting (2-4) **796.41**

Weights and measures
See also Metric system; Volume (Cubic content)
Murphy, S. J. Mighty Maddie (k-2) **389**
Schwartz, D. M. Millions to measure (2-4) **530.8**

Weihs, Erika
(il) Chaikin, M. Menorahs, mezuzas, and other Jewish symbols **296.4**
(il) Simon, N. The story of Passover **296.4**

Weill, Cynthia
(jt. auth) Shea, P. D. Ten mice for Tet! **394.26**

Weinhaus, Karen Ann
(il) Schwartz, A. All of our noses are here, and other noodle tales **398.2**
(il) Schwartz, A. There is a carrot in my ear, and other noodle tales **398.2**

Weinstein, Julius
About
Bierman, C. Journey to Ellis Island (3-5) **325.73**

Weintraub, Aileen
The Grand Canyon (2-4) **557**

Weird friends. Aruego, J. **577.8**

Weird stories from the Lonesome Café. Cox, J. **Fic**

Weisgard, Leonard
(il) Brown, M. W. The little island **E**
(il) Dalgliesh, A. The courage of Sarah Noble **Fic**

Weiss, Alta, 1890-1964
Fiction
Hopkinson, D. Girl wonder **E**

Weiss, Emil
(il) Neville, E. C. It's like this, Cat **Fic**

Weiss, Erich *See* Houdini, Harry, 1874-1926

Weiss, Karen
(il) Press, J. All around town! **307**

Weiss, Nicki
Where does the brown bear go? **E**

Weissberger, Ela
(jt. auth) Rubin, S. G. The cat with the yellow star **940.53**

Weissman, Annie
Do tell! **027.62**

Weissman, Bari
(il) Heiligman, D. From caterpillar to butterfly **595.7**

Weissmuller, Johnny, 1904-1984
See/See also pages in the following book(s):
Krull, K. Lives of the athletes (4 and up) **920**

Weitzman, David L.
Rama and Sita (3-6) **398.2**
A subway for New York (4 and up) **625.4**

Weitzman, Jacqueline Preiss
You can't take a balloon into the Metropolitan Museum **E**

Welcome, baby!. Calmenson, S. **811**

Welcome Comfort. Polacco, P. **E**

Welcome Dede!. Onyefulu, I. **392**

Welcome, little baby. Aliki **E**

Welcome to Lizard Motel. Feinberg, B. **028.5**

Welcome to the Globe. Chrisp, P. **822.3**

The **well.** Taylor, M. D. **Fic**

The **well** at the end of the world. San Souci, R. **E**

The **well** at the world's end. Philip, N.
In Philip, N. Celtic fairy tales p121-24
398.2

The **Well** of the World's End. Jacobs, J.
In Jacobs, J. English fairy tales p211-15
398.2

Well wished. Billingsley, F. **Fic**

Weller, Frances Ward
The day the animals came **E**

Welles, Toby
(il) Duffy, T. The clock **681.1**

Wellesley, Charles *See* Brontë, Charlotte, 1816-1855

Wellington, Monica
Apple farmer Annie **E**

Wells, Daryl, 1969-
See/See also pages in the following book(s):
Just like me p2-3 **920**

Wells, Ida B. *See* Wells-Barnett, Ida B., 1862-1931

Wells, Rosemary
Carry me! **E**
Emily's first 100 days of school **E**
Felix feels better **E**
Mary on horseback [biography of Mary Breckinridge] (4 and up) **92**
McDuff moves in **E**
The miraculous tale of the two Maries **E**
Morris's disappearing bag **E**
Noisy Nora **E**
Only you **E**
Read to your bunny **E**
Ruby's beauty shop **E**
Shy Charles **E**
Streets of gold [biography of Mary Antin] (3-6) **92**
Timothy's tales from Hilltop School **E**
Wingwalker (3-6) **Fic**
Yoko **E**
(il) Here comes Mother Goose. See Here comes Mother Goose **398.8**
(il) My very first Mother Goose. See My very first Mother Goose **398.8**
(il) Stolz, M. Emmett's pig **E**
(jt. auth) Tallchief, M. Tallchief **92**

Wells, Rosemary, 1943-
See/See also pages in the following book(s):
Marcus, L. S. Ways of telling **741.6**

Wells-Barnett, Ida B., 1862-1931
About
Fradin, D. B. Ida B. Wells (5 and up) **92**
See/See also pages in the following book(s):
Pinkney, A. D. Let it shine (4 and up) **920**
Wilkinson, B. S. African American women writers (4 and up) **810.9**

Welton, Jude
Henri Matisse (5 and up) **92**

Welzl, Jan
Fiction
Sís, P. A small tall tale from the far Far North
E

Wemberly worried. Henkes, K. **E**

The **wendigo**. Schwartz, A.
In Schwartz, A. Scary stories to tell in the dark p49-53 **398.2**

Wenzel, David
(il) Murphy, S. J. More or less **513**

We're going on a bear hunt. Rosen, M. **E**
We're going on a lion hunt **E**
We're going on a picnic!. Hutchins, P. **E**

The **werewolf**. Osborne, M. P.
In Osborne, M. P. Favorite medieval tales p42-49 **398.2**

Wertz, Michael
(il) Cerullo, M. M. The truth about dangerous sea creatures **591.7**
(il) Cerullo, M. M. The truth about great white sharks **597**

Weslandia. Fleischman, P. **E**

West, Benjamin, 1738-1820
About
Brenner, B. The boy who loved to draw: Benjamin West (k-3) **92**

West, Rick C.
See/See also pages in the following book(s):
Talking with adventurers (4-6) **920**

West (U.S.)
Geisert, B. Mountain town **E**
Naden, C. J. Belle Starr and the Wild West (5 and up) **92**
Scott, A. H. Cowboy country (k-3) **978**
Children
See Children—West (U.S.)
Exploration
See also Overland journeys to the Pacific
Blumberg, R. The incredible journey of Lewis and Clark (5 and up) **978**
Blumberg, R. York's adventures with Lewis and Clark (5 and up) **978**
Calvert, P. Zebulon Pike (5 and up) **92**
Kimmel, E. C. As far as the eye can reach (4 and up) **978**
Patent, D. H. Animals on the trail with Lewis and Clark (4 and up) **978**
Patent, D. H. The Lewis and Clark trail (4 and up) **978**
Patent, D. H. Plants on the trail with Lewis and Clark (4 and up) **978**
Pringle, L. P. Dog of discovery (4-6) **978**
Waldman, S. The last river (3-6) **978**
See/See also pages in the following book(s):
Schanzer, R. How we crossed the West (3-5)
978
St. George, J. Sacagawea (4-6) **92**
Fiction
Appelt, K. Cowboy dreams **E**
Byars, B. C. The Golly sisters go West **E**
Durbin, W. The journal of Sean Sullivan (5 and up) **Fic**
Fleischman, S. The ghost on Saturday night (3-5) **Fic**
Frank, J. The toughest cowboy **E**
Hahn, M. D. The Gentleman Outlaw and me—Eli (5 and up) **Fic**
Harvey, B. Cassie's journey (2-4) **Fic**
Harvey, B. My prairie Christmas (2-4) **Fic**

Where Washington walked. Bial, R.   92

Where, where is Swamp Bear? Appelt, K.   E

Where's Jamela? Daly, N.   E

Where's Mary's hat? Barroux, S.   E

Where's Mom's hair? Watters, D.   616.99

Where's Pup? Dodds, D. A.   E

Where's the science here? [series]

   Cobb, V. Fireworks   662

   Cobb, V. Junk food   664

   Cobb, V. Sneakers   685

While no one was watching. Conly, J. L.   Fic

While standing on one foot. Jaffe, N.   296.1

While the candles burn. Goldin, B. D.   296.4

While we were out. Lee, H. B.   E

While you're waiting for the food to come. Muller, E. P.   507.8

The **whingdingdilly**. Peet, B.   E

The **whipping** boy. Fleischman, S.   Fic

Whipple, Catherine

   (il) King, S. Shannon: an Ojibway dancer   970.004

Whipple, Laura

   If the shoe fits (5 and up)   811

   (comp) Eric Carle's animals, animals. See Eric Carle's animals, animals   808.81

   (comp) Eric Carle's dragons dragons and other creatures that never were. See Eric Carle's dragons dragons and other creatures that never were   808.81

Whippo, Walt

   Little white duck (k-2)   782.42

Whisper and shout (4 and up)   811.008

Whisper in the dark. Bruchac, J.   Fic

Whistling. Partridge, E.   E

Whitcraft, James E.

   (il) Farlow, J. O. Bringing dinosaur bones to life   567.9

White, E. B. (Elwyn Brooks)

   Charlotte's web (3-6)   Fic

   Stuart Little (3-6)   Fic

   The trumpet of the swan (3-6)   Fic

White, E. B. (Elwyn Brooks), 1899-1985

   See/See also pages in the following book(s):

   Krull, K. Lives of the writers (4 and up)   920

White, Elwyn Brooks *See* White, E. B. (Elwyn Brooks), 1899-1985

White, Laurence B.

   Shazam! simple science magic (3-6)   793.8

   (jt. auth) Broekel, R. Hocus pocus: magic you can do   793.8

White, Linda

   I could do that! [biography of Esther Hobart Morris] (2-4)   92

White, Maureen

   (jt. auth) Latrobe, K. H. The children's literature dictionary   028.5

White, Ruth

   Belle Prater's boy (5 and up)   Fic

   Tadpole (4 and up)   Fic

White, T. H. (Terence Hanbury)

   The sword in the stone (4 and up)   Fic

The **White** Cat. Aulnoy, Madame d'

   In The Blue fairy book p157-73   398.2

The **white** cat in the Dovre Mountain. Lunge-Larsen, L.

   In Lunge-Larsen, L. The troll with no heart in his body and other tales of trolls from Norway p57-61   398.2

The **white** duck. Afanas'ev, A. N.

   In Afanas'ev, A. N. Russian fairy tales p342-45   398.2

White Fang. London, J.   Fic

White Fox. Curry, J. L.

   In Curry, J. L. Hold up the sky: and other Native American tales from Texas and the Southern Plains p123-27   398.2

The **White** Horse Girl and the Blue Wind Boy. Sandburg, C.

   In Sandburg, C. Rootabaga stories p121-26   S C

   also in Sandburg, C. The Sandburg treasury; prose and poetry for young people p63-65   818

White House (Washington, D.C.)

   Grace, C. O. The White House (3-6)   975.3

   Hess, D. The White House (3-5)   975.3

White is for blueberry. Shannon, G.   E

The **White** Mountains. Christopher, J.   Fic

White on black. Hoban, T.   E

White snow, bright snow. Tresselt, A. R.   E

The **white** stag. Seredy, K.   Fic

The **White** Swan express. Okimoto, J. D.   E

White-tailed deer. Patent, D. H.   599.65

White tiger, blue serpent. Tseng, G.   398.2

Whitebear Whittington

   In Grandfather tales; American-English folk tales p52-64   398.2

Whiteblack the penguin sees the world. Rey, M.   E

Whiteman, Dorit Bader

   Lonek's journey (5 and up)   940.53

Whitford, Rebecca

   Little yoga (k-1)   613.7

Whitin, David Jackman

   New visions for linking literature and mathematics   372

Whitin, Phyllis

   (jt. auth) Whitin, D. J. New visions for linking literature and mathematics   372

Whitman, Sylvia

   What's cooking? (5 and up)   394.1

Whitman, Walt

   Walt Whitman

   In The Blackbirch treasury of American poetry p193-237   811.008

   When I heard the learn'd astronomer   E

Whitman, Walt, 1819-1892

About

   Kerley, B. Walt Whitman (4 and up)   92

Whittenberg, Allison

   Sweet Thang (5 and up)   Fic

Whittington, Richard, d. 1423
Legends
Hodges, M. Dick Whittington and his cat (k-3)
398.2

Whittington. Armstrong, A. **Fic**

Whittington and his cat. Jacobs, J.
In Jacobs, J. English fairy tales p167-76
398.2

Whittling *See* Wood carving

Who are you, baby kangaroo? Blackstone, S.
E

Who came first. Lauber, P. **970.01**

Who eats what? Lauber, P. **577**

Who is baseball's greatest pitcher? Kisseloff, J.
796.357

Who lives in the skull? MacDonald, M. R.
In MacDonald, M. R. When the lights go out;
twenty scary tales to tell p143-47
372.6

Who loves me? MacLachlan, P. **E**

Who said boo? Carlstrom, N. W. **811**

Who stole Halloween? Freeman, M. **Fic**

Who took the farmer's [hat]? Lexau, J. M. **E**

Who was the woman who wore the hat? Patz, N.
811

Who wrote that? [series]
Cammarano, R. Betsy Byars **92**
Dean, T. Theodor Geisel **92**

Who you!. Hamilton, V.
In Hamilton, V. Her stories; African American folktales, fairy tales, and true tales
p45-50 **398.2**

The **whole** green world. Johnston, T. **E**

The **Whole** school library handbook **027.8**

Whole story [series]
Stevenson, R. L. The strange case of Dr. Jekyll
and Mr. Hyde **Fic**

Whooping cranes *See* Cranes (Birds)

Who's a pest? Bonsall, C. N. **E**

Who's afraid of the dark? Bonsall, C. N. **E**

Who's in Rabbit's house? Aardema, V. **398.2**

Who's in the hall? Hearne, B. G. **E**

Who's that knocking on Christmas Eve. Brett, J.
398.2

Who's that stepping on Plymouth Rock? Fritz, J.
974.4

Who's the fool now. Sanfield, S.
In Sanfield, S. The adventures of High John
the Conqueror **398.2**

Whose baby am I? Butler, J. **E**

Whose mouse are you? Kraus, R. **E**

Whose shoe? Miller, M. **E**

Why a monkey's not a man. Climo, S.
In Climo, S. Monkey business; stories from
around the world **398.2**

Why Ananse lives on the ceiling. Badoe, A.
In Badoe, A. The pot of wisdom: Ananse stories **398.2**

Why are people terrorists? Woolf, A. **303.6**

Why Bear waddles when he walks. Curry, J. L.
In Curry, J. L. Hold up the sky: and other
Native American tales from Texas and
the Southern Plains p15-19 **398.2**

Why Brer Bull growls and grumbles. Lester, J.
In Lester, J. The last tales of Uncle Remus
p119-23 **398.2**

Why Brer Fox's legs are black. Lester, J.
In Lester, J. The last tales of Uncle Remus
p64-66 **398.2**

Why Brer Possum has no hair on his tail. Lester,
J.
In Lester, J. The last tales of Uncle Remus
p41-44 **398.2**

Why Brer Possum loves peace. Lester, J.
In Lester, J. The last tales of Uncle Remus
p44-46 **398.2**

Why Bush Cow and Elephant are bad friends.
Bryan, A.
In Bryan, A. Ashley Bryan's African tales,
uh-huh p54-69 **398.2**

Why can't I learn like everyone else? Brinkerhoff,
S. **371.9**

Why chickens scratch in the dirt. Lester, J.
In Lester, J. The last tales of Uncle Remus
p147-49 **398.2**

Why did the chicken cross the road? and other
riddles, old and new. Cole, J. **793.73**

Why do birds sing? Holub, J. **598**

Why do cats meow? Holub, J. **636.8**

Why do dogs bark? Holub, J. **636.7**

Why do families break up? Bingham, J.
306.89

Why do horses neigh? Holub, J. **636.1**

Why do leaves change color? Maestro, B.
582.16

Why do rabbits hop? Holub, J. **636.9**

Why do snakes hiss? Holub, J. **597.96**

Why does the coqui sing? Polikoff, B. G. **Fic**

Why dogs are tame. Lester, J.
In Lester, J. The last tales of Uncle Remus
p76-82 **398.2**

Why don't haircuts hurt? Berger, M. **612**

Why don't you get a horse, Sam Adams? Fritz, J.
92

Why Frog and Snake never play together. Bryan,
A.
In Bryan, A. Ashley Bryan's African tales,
uh-huh p81-92 **398.2**

Why guinea fowls are speckled. Lester, J.
In Lester, J. The last tales of Uncle Remus
p88-93 **398.2**

Why I cough, sneeze, shiver, hiccup & yawn. See
Berger, M. Why I sneeze, shiver, hiccup, and
yawn **612.7**

Why I sneeze, shiver, hiccup, and yawn. Berger,
M. **612.7**

Why I will never ever ever ever have enough time
to read this book. Charlip, R. **E**

Why Koala has no tale. MacDonald, M. R.
   In MacDonald, M. R. Look back and see;
    twenty lively tales for gentle tellers p74-
    80   **372.6**

Why mosquitoes buzz in people's ears. Aardema,
V.   **398.2**

Why mouse walks softly. Bierhorst, J.
   In Bierhorst, J. Is my friend at home?; Pueblo
    fireside tales   **398.2**

Why Noah chose the dove. Singer, I. B.
   In Singer, I. B. Stories for children p41-44
        S C

Why not, Lafayette? Fritz, J.   **92**

Why on this night? Musleah, R.   **296.4**

Why peaches are sweet. Bierhorst, J.
   In Bierhorst, J. Is my friend at home?; Pueblo
    fireside tales   **398.2**

Why pig has a short snout. Badoe, A.
   In Badoe, A. The pot of wisdom: Ananse sto-
    ries   **398.2**

Why the big ball game between Hot Grounders
and the Grand Standers was a hot game.
Sandburg, C.
   In Sandburg, C. More Rootabaga stories
    p119-22   **S C**
   also in Sandburg, C. The Sandburg treasury;
    prose and poetry for young people p142-
    44   **818**

Why the buzzard is bald. Curry, J. L.
   In Curry, J. L. The wonderful sky boat and
    other Native American tales of the
    Southeast p64-67   **398.2**

Why the cat falls on her feet. Yolen, J.
   In Yolen, J. Meow; cat stories from around
    the world   **398.2**

Why the chicken crossed the road. Macaulay, D.
        E

Why the cricket has elbows on his legs. Lester, J.
   In Lester, J. The last tales of Uncle Remus
    p3-8   **398.2**

Why the earth is mostly water. Lester, J.
   In Lester, J. The last tales of Uncle Remus
    p8-12   **398.2**

Why the elders are the four corners of the universe. Menchú, R.
   In Menchú, R. and Liano, D. The honey jar
        398.2

Why the goat has a short tail. Lester, J.
   In Lester, J. The last tales of Uncle Remus
    p136-38   **398.2**

Why the Guineas stay awake. Lester, J.
   In Lester, J. The last tales of Uncle Remus
    p93-94   **398.2**

Why the hawk likes to eat chickens. Lester, J.
   In Lester, J. The last tales of Uncle Remus
    p98-102   **398.2**

Why the jellyfish has no bones. Sakade, F.
   In Sakade, F. Japanese children's favorite sto-
    ries   **398.2**

Why the moon is free. Gerson, M.-J.
   In Gerson, M.-J. Fiesta femenina; celebrating
    women in Mexican folktale   **398.2**

Why the Owl behaves as it does. Hughes, T.
   In Hughes, T. How the Whale became and
    other stories   **S C**

Why the rude visitor was flung by walrus. Norman, H.
   In Norman, H. The girl who dreamed only
    geese, and other tales of the Far North
        398.2

Why the sea is salt. Asbjørnsen, P. C.
   In The Blue fairy book p136-40   **398.2**

Why the sky is far away. Gerson, M.-J.   **398.2**

Why the Sun and the Moon live in the sky.
Dayrell, E.   **398.2**

Why Tiger is angry at Cat. Yolen, J.
   In Yolen, J. Meow; cat stories from around
    the world   **398.2**

Why you can see a rainbow when deer are born.
Menchú, R.
   In Menchú, R. and Liano, D. The honey jar
        398.2

Whybrow, Ian
  Harry and the bucketful of dinosaurs   **E**
  The noisy way to bed   **E**

Wick, Walter
  Can you see what I see?   **793.73**
  A drop of water (4-6)   **553.7**
  I spy   **793.73**
  Walter Wick's Optical tricks (4 and up)
        152.14

The **wicked** city. Singer, I. B.
   In Singer, I. B. Stories for children p77-88
        S C

Wicked Jack. Wooldridge, C. N.   **398.2**

Wicked John and the Devil
   In Grandfather tales; American-English folk
    tales p29-39   **398.2**

Wicked John and the Devil. MacDonald, M. R.
   In MacDonald, M. R. When the lights go out;
    twenty scary tales to tell p33-46
        372.6

Wicked poems (4 and up)   **811.008**

The **wicked** sisters. Afanas'ev, A. N.
   In Afanas'ev, A. N. Russian fairy tales p356-
    60   **398.2**

Wickenheiser, Hayley, 1978-
        About
  Etue, E. Hayley Wickenheiser (4 and up)   **92**

Wickstrom, Sylvie
  I love you, Mister Bear   **E**
  (il) Murphy, S. J. Room for Ripley   **530.8**
  (il) Schaefer, L. M. Loose tooth   **E**

Widder, Edith
        About
  Collard, S. B., III. In the deep sea (4-6)
        572

The **wide** open grasslands. Johansson, P.   **577.4**

Widener, Terry
  (il) Adler, D. A. America's champion swimmer:
    Gertrude Ederle   **92**
  (il) Adler, D. A. The Babe & I   **E**
  (il) Adler, D. A. Lou Gehrig   **92**
  (il) Adler, D. A. Joe Louis   **92**
  (il) Hopkinson, D. Girl wonder   **E**

Wilderness survival

Fiction

Eckert, A. W. Incident at Hawk's Hill (6 and up) **Fic**

Fleischman, P. Lost! **Fic**

George, J. C. Julie of the wolves (6 and up) **Fic**

George, J. C. My side of the mountain trilogy (5 and up) **Fic**

Houston, J. A. Frozen fire (6 and up) **Fic**

Neale, J. Himalaya (5 and up) **Fic**

Nordin, S. In the wild (4 and up) **Fic**

O'Dell, S. Island of the Blue Dolphins (5 and up) **Fic**

Wildfires

Bryan, N. Los Alamos wildfires (5 and up) **363.34**

Morrison, T. Wildfire (4-6) **634.9**

Wildfires. Simon, S. **577.2**

Wildflower ABC. Pomeroy, D. **E**

Wildflowers around the year. Ryden, H. **582.13**

Wildlife

Lewin, T. Tooth and claw (4 and up) **590**

Wildlife conservation

See also Birds—Protection; Game protection

Bortolotti, D. Panda rescue (4 and up) **639.9**

Bortolotti, D. Tiger rescue (4 and up) **333.95**

Bow, P. Chimpanzee rescue (5 and up) **599.8**

Collard, S. B., III. In the wild (4-6) **591.68**

Cone, M. Come back, salmon (3-6) **639.3**

Dalgleish, S. Protecting wildlife (3-6) **333.95**

Fleming, D. Where once there was a wood (k-2) **639.9**

Fridell, R. The search for poison-dart frogs (4-6) **597.8**

Hamilton, G. Frog rescue (5 and up) **597.8**

Hoyt, E. Whale rescue (5 and up) **599.5**

Lasky, K. Interrupted journey (3-6) **639.9**

Morgan, J. Elephant rescue (5 and up) **599.67**

Peterson, C. Wild horses (3-6) **599.66**

Salmansohn, P. Saving birds (5 and up) **333.95**

Stetson, E. Kids' easy-to-create wildlife habitats (2-4) **639.9**

Swinburne, S. R. Once a wolf (4 and up) **333.95**

Thomas, P. Marine mammal preservation (5 and up) **639.9**

Turner, P. S. Gorilla doctors (5 and up) **333.95**

Fiction

Bledsoe, L. J. Cougar canyon (4 and up) **Fic**

Collard, S. B., III. Butterfly count **E**

McCully, E. A. Hurry! (2-4) **Fic**

The **wildlife** detectives. Jackson, D. M. **363.2**

Wildsmith, Brian

ABC **E**

A Christmas story **E**

Exodus **222**

Jesus (k-3) **232.9**

Mary (k-3) **232.91**

Wiles, Deborah

Each little bird that sings (4-6) **Fic**

Freedom Summer **E**

Love, Ruby Lavender (4-6) **Fic**

Wiley, his mama, and the Hairy Man. Hamilton, V.

In Hamilton, V. The people could fly; American black folktales p90-103 **398.2**

Wilhelmina, Queen of the Netherlands, 1880-1962

Fiction

Paterson, K. Blueberries for the queen **E**

Wilkes, Angela

Dangerous creatures (5 and up) **591.6**

My first word book **E**

Wilkes, Debbi

The figure skating book (4 and up) **796.91**

Wilkinson, Brenda Scott

African American women writers (4 and up) **810.9**

Wilkinson, Carole

Dragon keeper (5 and up) **Fic**

Wilkinson, Philip

Buddhism (4 and up) **294.3**

Gandhi (4 and up) **92**

The Kingfisher student atlas (5 and up) **912**

Will Moses Mother Goose **398.8**

Will Rogers: an American legend. Keating, F. **92**

Will you sign here, John Hancock? Fritz, J. **92**

Willa and the wind. Del Negro, J. **E**

Willans, Tom

Wait! I want to tell you a story **E**

Willard, Nancy

Pish, posh, said Hieronymus Bosch (2-5) **811**

Sweep dreams

A visit to William Blake's inn (2-5) **811**

Willems, Mo

Don't let the pigeon drive the bus! **E**

Knuffle bunny **E**

Leonardo, the terrible monster **E**

Willey, Margaret

Clever Beatrice (k-3) **398.2**

William Shakespeare & the Globe. Aliki **822.3**

William Shakespeare's A midsummer night's dream. Coville, B. **822.3**

William Shakespeare's Hamlet. Coville, B. **822.3**

William Shakespeare's Macbeth. Coville, B. **822.3**

William Shakespeare's Romeo and Juliet. Coville, B. **822.3**

William Shakespeare's Twelfth night. Coville, B. **822.3**

Williams, Arlene

Tiny tortilla **E**

Williams, Barbara
Albert's impossible toothache   **E**
World War II, Pacific (5 and up)   **940.54**

Williams, Berkeley
(il) Grandfather tales. See Grandfather tales
     398.2
(il) The Jack tales. See The Jack tales   **398.2**

Williams, Brian
(jt. auth) Wood, M. Ancient America   **970.01**

Williams, Garth
(il) Brown, M. W. Little Fur family   **E**
(il) Carlson, N. S. The family under the bridge
     Fic
(il) Hoban, R. Bedtime for Frances   **E**
(il) Prelutsky, J. Beneath a blue umbrella:
rhymes   **811**
(il) Prelutsky, J. Ride a purple pelican   **811**
(il) Selden, G. The cricket in Times Square
     Fic
(il) Stolz, M. Emmett's pig   **E**
(il) Walker, B. M. The Little House cookbook
     641.5
(il) White, E. B. Charlotte's web   **Fic**
(il) White, E. B. Stuart Little   **Fic**
(il) Wilder, L. I. Little house in the big woods
     Fic

Williams, Jay
The practical princess
In You read to me & I'll read to you; 20th-
century stories to share p219-28   **E**

Williams, Jennifer
(il) Williams, V. B. Stringbean's trip to the
shining sea   **E**

Williams, Karen Lynn
Galimoto   **E**
Painted dreams   **E**

Williams, Laura E.
The executioner's daughter (6 and up)   **Fic**

Williams, Linda
The little old lady who was not afraid of anything   **E**

Williams, Lucinda
See/See also pages in the following book(s):
Orgill, R. Shout, sister, shout! (6 and up)
     920

Williams, Marcia
Hooray for inventors! (3-5)   **609**

Williams, Mary
Brothers in hope (3-5)   **Fic**

Williams, Richard
(il) Kline, S. Herbie Jones   **Fic**

Williams, Roger, 1604?-1683
     About
Avi. Finding Providence: the story of Roger
Williams (2-4)   **92**

Williams, Sam
(il) Maccarone, G. A child's good night prayer
     E
(il) Peters, L. W. Cold little duck, duck, duck
     E
(il) Shannon, G. Busy in the garden   **811**
(il) Wilner, I. The baby's game book   **398.8**

Williams, Serena
(jt. auth) Williams, V. How to play tennis
     796.342

Williams, Sherley Anne
Working cotton   **E**

Williams, Sheron
Imani's music   **E**

Williams, Sophy
(il) Pullman, P. Aladdin and the enchanted lamp
     398.2

Williams, Sue
Let's go visiting   **E**

Williams, Suzanne
Library Lil   **E**

Williams, Venus
How to play tennis (5 and up)   **796.342**

Williams, Vera B.
Amber was brave, Essie was smart (3-5)
     811
A chair for my mother   **E**
Cherries and cherry pits   **E**
Lucky song   **E**
"More more more" said the baby   **E**
Scooter (3-5)   **Fic**
Stringbean's trip to the shining sea   **E**
Three days on a river in a red canoe   **E**
(il) Charlip, R. Hooray for me!   **E**

Williams-Andriani, Renée
(il) Conford, E. Annabel the actress starring in
"Gorilla my dreams"   **Fic**
(jt. auth) Hall, K. Stinky riddles   **793.73**
(il) Murphy, S. J. Earth Day-hooray!   **513**
(il) Murphy, S. J. Mall mania   **513**
(il) Sears, W. Baby on the way   **612.6**
(il) Sears, W. What baby needs   **649**

William's doll. Zolotow, C.   **E**

Williamson, Susan
Summer fun!   **790.1**

Williamson Little Hands book [series]
Check, L. Little Hands paper plate crafts
     745.54
Dall, M. D. Little Hands create!   **745.5**
Hauser, J. F. Wow! I'm reading!   **372.4**
Press, J. All around town!   **307**
Press, J. Around-the-world art & activities
     745.5
Press, J. ArtStarts for little hands!   **745.5**
Press, J. The little hands big fun craft book
     745.5

Willis, Jeanne
Susan laughs   **E**

Willis, Patricia
The barn burner (5 and up)   **Fic**

Willis, Terri
Democratic Republic of the Congo (5 and up)
     967.51

Willner-Pardo, Gina
Daphne Eloise Slater, who's tall for her age
(2-4)   **Fic**
Figuring out Frances (4-6)   **Fic**

Willoughby-Herb, Sara
(jt. auth) Herb, S. Connecting fathers, children,
and reading   **028.5**

Winkler, Kathleen
Bullying (5 and up)   **371.5**
Winner, Cherie
The sunflower family (3-6)   **583**
Winners never quit!. Hamm, M.   **E**
Winnie (dancing) on her own. Jacobson, J.
    Fic
Winnie-the-Pooh. Milne, A. A.   **Fic**
Winnie-the-Pooh. Milne, A. A.
    also in Milne, A. A. The complete tales of
      Winnie-the-Pooh p1-159   **Fic**
    also in Milne, A. A. The world of Pooh; the
      complete Winnie-the-Pooh and The
      House at Pooh Corner p7-149   **Fic**
Winning authors. Bostrom, K. L.   **920**
Winter, Jane Kohen
Chile (5 and up)   **983**
Italy (5 and up)   **945**
Venezuela (5 and up)   **987**
Winter, Jeanette
Beatrix: various episodes from the life of
    Beatrix Potter (k-3)   **92**
Calavera abecedario   **E**
Elsina's clouds   **E**
Emily Dickinson's letters to the world (k-3)
    811
Follow the drinking gourd   **E**
The house that Jack built   **398.8**
Josefina   **E**
The librarian of Basra   **E**
Mama   **E**
My name is Georgia [biography of Georgia
    O'Keeffe] (k-3)   **92**
Niño's mask   **E**
Sebastian: a book about Bach (k-3)   **92**
September roses   **E**
(il) Johnston, T. Day of the Dead   **E**
(il) Winter, J. Diego [biography of Diego Rive-
    ra]   **92**
Winter, Jonah
Beisbol! Latino baseball pioneers and legends
    (3-6)   **920**
Diego [biography of Diego Rivera] (k-3)   **92**
Frida [Kahlo] (k-3)   **92**
Roberto Clemente (2-4)   **92**
Winter, Susan
(il) Ryder, J. Come along, kitten   **E**
(il) Simon, F. Toddler time   **821**
Winter
Bancroft, H. Animals in winter (k-1)   **591.56**
Kurelek, W. A prairie boy's winter (3-5)
    971.27
Schnur, S. Winter   **E**
        Fiction
Blumenthal, D. Ice palace   **E**
Fleming, D. The first day of winter   **E**
Fleming, D. Time to sleep   **E**
Freedman, C. Gooseberry Goose   **E**
Hader, B. The big snow   **E**
Hughes, S. Stories by firelight   **E**
Kuskin, K. Under my hood I have a hat   **E**
Root, P. Grandmother Winter   **E**
Spinelli, E. Three pebbles and a song   **E**
Van Laan, N. When winter comes   **E**

        Poetry
Alarcón, F. X. Iguanas in the snow and other
    winter poems (2-4)   **811**
Florian, D. Winter eyes   **811**
Hines, A. G. Winter lights (k-3)   **811**
Prelutsky, J. It's snowing! it's snowing! (1-3)
    811
Quattlebaum, M. Winter friends (k-2)   **811**
Winter poems   **808.81**
Winter eyes. Florian, D.   **811**
Winter friends. Quattlebaum, M.   **811**
Winter lights. Hines, A. G.   **811**
The **winter** people. Bruchac, J.   **Fic**
Winter poems   **808.81**
The **winter** room. Paulsen, G.   **Fic**
Winter sports
    See also Olympic games; Snowboarding
Macy, S. Freeze frame (5 and up)   **796.98**
Winter story. Bierhorst, J.
    In Bierhorst, J. Is my friend at home?; Pueblo
      fireside tales   **398.2**
Wintering well. Wait, L.   **Fic**
Winters, Kay
Abraham Lincoln: the boy who loved books
    (k-2)   **92**
My teacher for President   **E**
Winthrop, Elizabeth
The castle in the attic (4-6)   **Fic**
Dumpy La Rue   **E**
He is risen: the Easter story (k-3)   **232.9**
Promises   **E**
Shoes   **E**
Squashed in the middle   **E**
Winyan Ohitika. Mayer, M.
    In Mayer, M. Women warriors; myths and
      legends of heroic women p67-69   **398**
Wisconsin
Barenblat, R. Wisconsin
    In World Almanac Library of the States series
    973
Blashfield, J. F. Wisconsin
    In America the beautiful, second series
    973
Dornfeld, M. Wisconsin
    In It's my state! [series]   **973**
Zeinert, K. Wisconsin
    In Celebrate the states   **973**
        Fiction
Brink, C. R. Caddie Woodlawn (4-6)   **Fic**
Hannigan, K. Ida B (4-6)   **Fic**
Wilder, L. I. Little house in the big woods (4-6)
    Fic
Wisdom for sale. Kimmel, E. A.
    In Kimmel, E. A. The jar of fools: eight Ha-
      nukkah stories from Chelm p42-55
    S C
The **wisdom** of Princess Maya. Bruchac, J.
    In Bruchac, J. Tell me a tale; a book about
      storytelling p46-51   **372.6**
The **wisdom** of the crows and other Buddhist
    tales. Chödzin, S.   **294.3**

Wise, Leonard
The way cool license plate book (4 and up)
793.7

Wise, William
Christopher Mouse (3-5)   **Fic**
Dinosaurs forever (k-3)   **811**
Ten sly piranhas   **E**
Zany zoo (k-3)   **811**

The **wise** dove. Lee, J. M.
   In Lee, J. M. I once was a monkey; stories
     Buddha told   **294.3**

The **wise** fools of Chelm. Jaffe, N.
   In Jaffe, N. and Zeitlin, S. J. While standing
     on one foot; puzzle stories and wisdom
     tales from the Jewish tradition p62-65
      296.1

The **wise** king. Jaffe, N.
   In Jaffe, N. and Zeitlin, S. J. The cow of no
     color: riddle stories and justice tales from
     around the world p118-21   **398.2**

The **wise** little girl. Afanas'ev, A. N.
   In Afanas'ev, A. N. Russian fairy tales p252-
     55   **398.2**

The **wise** maiden and the seven robbers.
   Afanas'ev, A. N.
   In Afanas'ev, A. N. Russian fairy tales p134-
     40   **398.2**

Wise men (Magi) *See* Magi

The **wise** men of Gotham. Jacobs, J.
   In Jacobs, J. English fairy tales p418-24
      398.2

The **wise** old shepherd. Rouse, W. H. D.
   In Shedlock, M. L. The art of the story-teller
     p216-21   **372.6**

Wise sword find true mommy. Graham, L. B.
   In Graham, L. B. How God fix Jonah p126-
     31   **398.2**

The **wise** wife. Afanas'ev, A. N.
   In Afanas'ev, A. N. Russian fairy tales p521-
     28   **398.2**

Wiseman, Ann Sayre
Making music (3-6)   **784.19**

Wiseman, Bernard
Morris and Boris at the circus   **E**

Wiseman, David
Jeremy Visick (5 and up)   **Fic**

Wishes
Fiction
Billingsley, F. Well wished (4-6)   **Fic**
McClintock, B. Molly and the magic wishbone
      E
Folklore
Zemach, M. The three wishes (k-2)   **398.2**

Wishes. Babbitt, N.
   In Babbitt, N. The Devil's storybook p3-11
      S C

Wisler, G. Clifton
Mr. Lincoln's drummer (4 and up)   **Fic**
Red Cap (4 and up)   **Fic**

Wisniewski, David
Golem (3-5)   **398.2**
Rain player   **E**
Sundiata (1-4)   **92**

The wave of the Sea-Wolf   **E**
(il) Clements, A. Workshop   **621.9**
(il) Shepard, A. Master man   **398.2**
(il) Siddals, M. M. I'll play with you   **E**

Wit and humor
   See also Humorous poetry; Jewish wit and
    humor; Jokes; Puns
Becker, H. Funny business (5 and up)   **792**
Brewer, P. You must be joking! (3-6)   **818**
Schwartz, A. All of our noses are here, and oth-
    er noodle tales (k-2)   **398.2**
Schwartz, A. There is a carrot in my ear, and
    other noodle tales (k-2)   **398.2**

The **witch** Barusha. Schwartz, H.
   In Schwartz, H. and Rush, B. A coat for the
     moon and other Jewish tales p32-34
      398.2

The **witch** cat. San Souci, R.
   In San Souci, R. Short & shivery; thirty chill-
     ing tales p28-34   **398.2**

The **witch** family. Estes, E.   **Fic**

The **witch** of Blackbird Pond. Speare, E. G.
      Fic

The **witch** who could slip off her skin. Thomas, J.
   C.
   In Thomas, J. C. The skull talks back and
     other haunting tales   **398.2**

Witch woman. San Souci, R.
   In San Souci, R. Even more short & shivery;
     thirty spine-tingling stories p15-19
      398.2

Witchbirds. San Souci, R.
   In San Souci, R. A terrifying taste of short &
     shivery; thirty creepy tales p68-72
      398.2

Witchcraft
   See also Magic
Hill, D. Witches & magic-makers (4 and up)
      133.4
Jackson, S. The witchcraft of Salem Village (4
    and up)   **133.4**
Meltzer, M. Witches and witch-hunts (4 and up)
      133.4
Roach, M. K. In the days of the Salem witch-
    craft trials (4 and up)   **133.4**
Fiction
Bellairs, J. The house with a clock in its walls
    (5 and up)   **Fic**
Jarvis, R. The alchemist's cat (5 and up)
      Fic
Konigsburg, E. L. Jennifer, Hecate, Macbeth,
    William McKinley, and me, Elizabeth (4-6)
      Fic
Norton, M. Bed-knob and broomstick (3-6)
      Fic
Petry, A. L. Tituba of Salem Village (6 and up)
      Fic
Snyder, Z. K. The witches of Worm (5 and up)
      Fic
Speare, E. G. The witch of Blackbird Pond (6
    and up)   **Fic**
Strickland, B. John Bellairs's Lewis Barnavelt in
    The specter from the magician's museum (5
    and up)   **Fic**
Van Allsburg, C. The widow's broom   **E**

The **witchcraft** of Salem Village. Jackson, S.
133.4

Witches

Fiction

Balian, L. Humbug witch   **E**
Coppinger, T. Curse in reverse   **E**
De Paola, T. Strega Nona: an old tale   **E**
Delaney, J. The last apprentice: Revenge of the witch (5 and up)   **Fic**
Estes, E. The witch family (4-6)   **Fic**
Hamilton, V. Wee Winnie Witch's Skinny   **E**
Howard, A. Hoodwinked   **E**
Johnston, T. Alice Nizzy Nazzy, the Witch of Santa Fe   **E**
Jones, U. The witch's children   **E**
King-Smith, D. The nine lives of Aristotle (2-4)   **Fic**
Leuck, L. One witch   **E**
Meddaugh, S. The witch's walking stick   **E**
Myers, T. Good babies   **E**
Palatini, M. Piggie pie!   **E**
Peet, B. Big bad Bruce   **E**
Peet, B. The whingdingdilly   **E**
Rowling, J. K. Harry Potter and the sorcerer's stone (4 and up)   **Fic**
Steig, W. Caleb & Kate   **E**
Vande Velde, V. Three good deeds (3-5)   **Fic**
Wood, A. Heckedy Peg   **E**

The **witches**. Dahl, R.
In Beware!; R.L. Stine picks his favorite scary stories p101-19   **808.8**

Witches & magic-makers. Hill, D.   **133.4**
Witches and witch-hunts. Meltzer, M.   **133.4**

The **witches'** eyes. San Souci, R.
In San Souci, R. More short & shivery; thirty terrifying tales p5-10   **398.2**

The **witches** of Worm. Snyder, Z. K.   **Fic**

Witches, pumpkins, and grinning ghosts. Barth, E.   **394.26**

The **witch's** children. Jones, U.   **E**

The **witch's** head. San Souci, R.
In San Souci, R. A terrifying taste of short & shivery; thirty creepy tales p77-81   **398.2**

The **witch's** walking stick. Meddaugh, S.   **E**

With a little luck. Fradin, D. B.   **509**

With a whoop and a holler. Van Laan, N.   **398**

With love. Goodall, J.   **599.8**

With needle and thread. Bial, R.   **746.46**

Witness. Hesse, K.   **Fic**

Witnesses to war. Leapman, M.   **940.53**

Witschonke, Alan
(il) Mann, E. Hoover Dam   **627**

Witte, Anna
The parrot Tico Tango   **E**

Wittlinger, Ellen
Wet hens
In Shelf life: stories by the book   **S C**

Wittwer, Hala
(il) Yolen, J. Meow   **398.2**

Wizard at work. Vande Velde, V.   **Fic**

The **wizard** clip. MacDonald, M. R.
In MacDonald, M. R. When the lights go out; twenty scary tales to tell p61-68   **372.6**

A **wizard** of Earthsea. Le Guin, U. K.   **Fic**
The **Wizard** of Oz. Baum, L. F.   **Fic**
The **wizard** test. Bell, H.   **Fic**

Woff, Richard
The ancient Greek Olympics (4 and up)   **796.48**

Wojciechowska, Maia
Shadow of a bull (6 and up)   **Fic**

Wojciechowski, Susan
The Christmas miracle of Jonathan Toomey   **E**
A fine St. Patrick's day   **E**

Wolcott, Dyanna
(il) Kuskin, K. I am me   **E**

Wolf, Bernard
Coming to America (3-5)   **305.8**

The **wolf**. Afanas´ev, A. N.
In Afanas´ev, A. N. Russian fairy tales p312   **398.2**

Wolf and birds and the Fish-Horse. Hamilton, V.
In Hamilton, V. The people could fly; American black folktales p43-49   **398.2**

A **wolf** and Little Daughter. Hamilton, V.
In Hamilton, V. The people could fly; American black folktales p60-64   **398.2**

The **wolf** and the goat. Afanas´ev, A. N.
In Afanas´ev, A. N. Russian fairy tales p249-51   **398.2**

Wolf brother. Paver, M.   **Fic**

Wolf children *See* Wild children

The **wolf** girl. Schwartz, A.
In Schwartz, A. Scary stories 3; more tales to chill your bones p47-50   **398.2**

The **wolf** of Gubbio. Bedard, M.   **398.2**

The **wolf** who cried boy. Hartman, B.   **E**

Wolfe, Art
(il) Pandell, K. Journey through the northern rainforest   **578.7**

Wolff, Ashley
Me baby, you baby   **E**
(il) Raffi. Baby Beluga   **782.42**
(il) Ryder, J. Each living thing   **E**
(il) Slate, J. Miss Bindergarten celebrates the 100th day of kindergarten   **E**
(il) Sturges, P. She'll be comin' 'round the mountain   **782.42**

Wolff, Ferida
It is the wind   **E**

Wolff, Virginia Euwer
Doll
In Friends; stories about new friends, old friends, and unexpectedly true friends   **S C**
Water
In Girls got game; sports stories and poems   **810.8**

Wolfram, von Eschenbach
Parzival; adaptation. See Paterson, K. Parzival   **398.2**

The **wolf's** chicken stew. Kasza, K. **E**

Wolfsgruber, Linda
(il) Lottridge, C. B. Stories from the life of Jesus **232.9**

Wolfson, Jill
What I call life (5 and up) **Fic**

Wolfson, Ron
(jt. auth) Hoffman, L. A. What you will see inside a synagogue **296.4**

Wolinsky, Art
Internet power research using the Big6 approach (5 and up) **025.04**

Wolk-Stanley, Jessica
(il) Campbell, A. The New York Public Library amazing space **520**
(il) Cobb, V. How to really fool yourself **152.1**

Wolkstein, Diane
The day Ocean came to visit (k-3) **398.2**
(comp) The Magic orange tree, and other Haitian folktales. See The Magic orange tree, and other Haitian folktales **398.2**

The **wolverine's** secret. Norman, H.
In Norman, H. The girl who dreamed only geese, and other tales of the Far North **398.2**

Wolves
Brandenburg, J. To the top of the world (4 and up) **599.77**
George, M. Wolves (1-3) **599.77**
Gibbons, G. Wolves (k-3) **599.77**
Greenaway, T. Wolves, wild dogs, and foxes (4 and up) **599.77**
Markle, S. Growing up wild: wolves (2-4) **599.77**
Markle, S. Wolves (3-6) **599.77**
Swinburne, S. R. Once a wolf (4 and up) **333.95**

Fiction
Avi. The good dog (4-6) **Fic**
Bauer, M. D. Runt (4 and up) **Fic**
Brimner, L. D. The littlest wolf **E**
Fearnley, J. Mr. Wolf's pancakes **E**
Gaiman, N. The wolves in the walls **E**
George, J. C. Julie (6 and up) **Fic**
George, J. C. Julie of the wolves (6 and up) **Fic**
George, J. C. Look to the North **E**
George, J. C. Nutik, the wolf pup **E**
Hartman, B. The wolf who cried boy **E**
Kasza, K. The dog who cried wolf **E**
Kasza, K. The wolf's chicken stew **E**
Kelly, J. The mystery of Eatum Hall **E**
Lairla, S. Abel and the wolf **E**
Marshall, J. Swine Lake **E**
Meddaugh, S. The best place **E**
Meddaugh, S. Hog-eye **E**
Murray, M. D. Little Wolf and the moon **E**
Numeroff, L. J. The Chicken sisters **E**
Palatini, M. Piggie pie! **E**
Paver, M. Wolf brother (5 and up) **Fic**
Prokofiev, S. Peter and the wolf **E**
Roberts, L. Little Red **E**
Roche, D. Little Pig is capable **E**

Scieszka, J. The true story of the 3 little pigs **E**
Sweet, M. Carmine **E**
Trivizas, E. The three little wolves and the big bad pig **E**
Whatley, B. Wait! No paint! **E**

Folklore
Bedard, M. The wolf of Gubbio (3-6) **398.2**
Egielski, R. Saint Francis and the wolf (1-3) **398.2**
Ernst, L. C. Little Red Riding Hood: a newfangled prairie tale (k-3) **398.2**
Hamilton, V. Bruh Rabbit and the tar baby girl (k-3) **398.2**
Hennessy, B. G. The boy who cried wolf (k-2) **398.2**
Hyman, T. S. Little Red Riding Hood (k-2) **398.2**
Kellogg, S. The three little pigs (k-3) **398.2**
Marshall, J. Red Riding Hood (k-2) **398.2**
Marshall, J. The three little pigs (k-2) **398.2**
Moser, B. The three little pigs (k-3) **398.2**
Taylor, H. P. Brother Wolf (k-3) **398.2**
Young, E. Lon Po Po (1-3) **398.2**
Zemach, M. The three little pigs (k-2) **398.2**
Ziefert, H. Little Red Riding Hood (k-2) **398.2**

Wolves and the mermaids. Aiken, J.
In Aiken, J. Shadows and moonshine; stories **S C**

The **wolves** in the walls. Gaiman, N. **E**
The **wolves** of Willoughby Chase. Aiken, J. **Fic**

Wolves, wild dogs, and foxes. Greenaway, T. **599.77**

The **Woman,** Adam, and the fruit. Lester, J.
In Lester, J. When the beginning began; stories about God, the creatures, and us p81-85 **296.1**

Woman and Man started even. Hamilton, V.
In Hamilton, V. Her stories; African American folktales, fairy tales, and true tales p69-74 **398.2**

A **woman** for president [biography of Victoria C. Woodhull] Krull, K. **92**

The **woman** in the snow. McKissack, P. C.
In McKissack, P. C. The dark-thirty; Southern tales of the supernatural p55-65 **S C**

The **woman** who flummoxed the fairies. Leodhas, S. N.
In Womenfolk and fairy tales p135-45 **398.2**

The **woman** who outshone the sun. Cruz, A. **398.2**

Woman's way. Afanas´ev, A. N.
In Afanas´ev, A. N. Russian fairy tales p599 **398.2**

Wombat divine. Fox, M. **E**

Wombats
Fiction
Fox, M. Wombat divine **E**
French, J. Diary of a wombat **E**

The **wondrous** wonder, the marvelous marvel. Afanas´ev, A. N.
In Afanas´ev, A. N. Russian fairy tales p13-15   **398.2**

Wong, Janet S.
Apple pie 4th of July   **E**
Buzz   **E**
Hide & seek   **E**
Knock on wood (3-5)   **811**
Night garden (3-6)   **811**
The rainbow hand (4-6)   **811**
This next New Year   **E**

Wong, Nicole E.
(il) Wahl, J. Candy shop   **E**

Wood, Audrey
The Bunyans   **E**
The deep blue sea   **E**
Elbert's bad word   **E**
Heckedy Peg   **E**
King Bidgood's in the bathtub   **E**
The napping house   **E**
(jt. auth) Wood, D. Piggies   **E**

Wood, Bruce Robert
(jt. auth) Wood, A. The deep blue sea   **E**

Wood, Clare
(il) Pringle, L. P. Everybody has a bellybutton   **612.6**

Wood, Don
Piggies   **E**
(il) Wood, A. Elbert's bad word   **E**
(il) Wood, A. Heckedy Peg   **E**
(il) Wood, A. King Bidgood's in the bathtub   **E**
(il) Wood, A. The napping house   **E**

Wood, Douglas
What dads can't do   **E**

Wood, Elaine
(jt. auth) Walker, P. Science experiments on file   **507.8**

Wood, Grant, 1892-1942
About
Duggleby, J. Artist in overalls: the life of Grant Wood (4 and up)   **92**

Wood, Ian
Platinum
In The Elements   **546**

Wood, Marion
Ancient America (5 and up)   **970.01**

Wood, Michele
See/See also pages in the following book(s):
Just like me p2-3   **920**
(il) Igus, T. I see the rhythm   **780.89**

Wood, Ted
Iditarod dream (4 and up)   **798.8**

Wood, Tim
The Renaissance (4 and up)   **940.2**

Wood carving
Fiction
Bulla, C. R. Daniel's duck   **E**
Dorros, A. Julio's magic   **E**
Wojciechowski, S. The Christmas miracle of Jonathan Toomey   **E**

Wood lice *See* Woodlice

Wood thrush
Cherry, L. Flute's journey (2-4)   **598**

Woodchucks *See* Marmots

Wooden, Lenny
(il) San Souci, R. A terrifying taste of short & shivery   **398.2**

The **wooden** bowl. Vittorini, D.
In Bauer, C. F. Celebrations; read-aloud holiday and theme book programs p68-70   **808.8**

The **wooden** Indian and the Shaghorn Buffalo. Sandburg, C.
In Sandburg, C. Rootabaga stories p114-17   **S C**
also in Sandburg, C. The Sandburg treasury; prose and poetry for young people p61-62   **818**

Woodford, Chris
Atoms and molecules (5 and up)   **540**
Electricity (5 and up)   **537**

Wooding, Sharon
(il) Garden, N. Molly's family   **E**

Woodlice
Himmelman, J. A pill bug's life (k-2)   **595.3**
Tokuda, Y. I'm a pill bug (k-2)   **595.3**

Woodpeckers
Miller, S. S. Woodpeckers, toucans, and their kin (4-6)   **598**

Woodpeckers, toucans, and their kin. Miller, S. S.   **598**

Woodruff, Elvira
The memory coat   **E**
The Ravenmaster's secret (5 and up)   **Fic**

Woods, Bob
Snowboarding (4-6)   **796.9**

Woods, Brenda
The red rose box (5 and up)   **Fic**

Woods, Geraldine
Science in ancient Egypt (4 and up)   **509**
Science of the early Americas (4 and up)   **509**

Woods *See* Forests and forestry

The **woods** scientist. Swinburne, S. R.   **591.7**

Woodson, Jacqueline
Beanie
In Girls got game; sports stories and poems   **810.8**
Coming on home soon   **E**
Locomotion (4 and up)   **811**
The other side   **E**
Show way   **E**
Visiting day   **E**
We had a picnic this Sunday past   **E**

Woodwork
See also Carpentry
Robertson, J. C. The kids' building workshop (3-6)   **694**
Schwarz, R. Birdhouses (4-6)   **690**

Woody Guthrie, poet of the people. Christensen, B.   **92**

Woog, Adam
Bill Gates (4 and up)   **92**

World of animals [series]
   Halls, K. M. Wild dogs   **599.77**

World of biomes [series]
   Johansson, P. The forested Taiga   **577.3**
   Johansson, P. The frozen tundra   **577.5**
   Johansson, P. The temperate forest   **577.3**
   Johansson, P. The tropical rain forest   **577.3**

The **world** of King Arthur and his court. Crossley-
   Holland, K.   **942.01**

World of mammals [series]
   Lockwood, S. Polar Bears   **599.78**

The **world** of Pooh. Milne, A. A.   **Fic**

A **world** of prayers. Brooks, J.   **242**

World of reptiles [series]
   Lockwood, S. Sea turtles   **597.92**

The **world** of storytelling. Pellowski, A.   **372.6**

A **world** of wonders. Lewis, J. P.   **811**

The **world** that we want. Toft, K. M.   **577**

World Trade Center (New York, N.Y.)
See/See also pages in the following book(s):
   Gerstein, M. The man who walked between the
   towers   **E**

**World Trade Center (New York, N.Y.) terrorist
attack, 2001**
   See also September 11 terrorist attacks,
   2001

The **world** turned upside down. Ferrie, R.
    973.3

World War, 1914-1918
   Adams, S. World War I (4 and up)   **940.3**
   Gay, K. World War I (5 and up)   **940.3**
   Myers, W. D. The Harlem Hellfighters (5 and
   up)   **940.4**
Fiction
   Lawrence, I. Lord of the nutcracker men (5 and
   up)   **Fic**
Naval operations
   Preston, D. Remember the Lusitania (5 and up)
    940.4

World War, 1939-1945
   Adams, S. World War II (4 and up)   **940.53**
   Ambrose, S. E. The good fight (5 and up)
    940.53
   Tanaka, S. Attack on Pearl Harbor (4 and up)
    940.54
   Williams, B. World War II, Pacific (5 and up)
    940.54
Aerial operations
See/See also pages in the following book(s):
   Haskins, J. Black eagles (5 and up)   **629.13**
Battles, sieges, etc.
   See World War, 1939-1945—Aerial opera-
   tions; World War, 1939-1945—Campaigns;
   World War, 1939-1945—Naval operations
Campaigns
   See also names of battles, campaigns,
   sieges, etc.
Campaigns—France
   Drez, R. J. Remember D-day (5 and up)
    940.54
Children
   Leapman, M. Witnesses to war (5 and up)
    940.53

   Tunnell, M. O. The children of Topaz (5 and
   up)   **940.53**
Fiction
   Avi. Don't you know there's a war on? (4 and
   up)   **Fic**
   Borden, L. Across the blue Pacific (2-5)   **Fic**
   Borden, L. The greatest skating race (2-5)
    Fic
   Borden, L. The little ships   **E**
   Buchanan, J. Goodbye, Charley (5 and up)
    Fic
   Bunting, E. Spying on Miss Müller (5 and up)
    Fic
   Cheaney, J. B. My friend, the enemy (5 and up)
    Fic
   Deedy, C. A. The yellow star (3-5)   **Fic**
   Fleming, C. Boxes for Katje   **E**
   Giff, P. R. Lily's crossing (4 and up)   **Fic**
   Giff, P. R. Willow run (4 and up)   **Fic**
   Greene, B. Summer of my German soldier (6
   and up)   **Fic**
   Gwaltney, D. Homefront (5 and up)   **Fic**
   Hahn, M. D. Stepping on the cracks (5 and up)
    Fic
   Harrison, B. Theo (5 and up)   **Fic**
   Kadohata, C. Weedflower   **Fic**
   Kochenderfer, L. The victory garden (5 and up)
    Fic
   Lee, M. Nim and the war effort   **E**
   Levitin, S. Journey to America (4 and up)
    Fic
   Lisle, J. T. The art of keeping cool (5 and up)
    Fic
   Lowry, L. Autumn Street (4 and up)   **Fic**
   Lowry, L. Number the stars (4 and up)   **Fic**
   Maguire, G. The good liar (4 and up)   **Fic**
   Mazer, N. F. Good night, Maman (5 and up)
    Fic
   McSwigan, M. Snow treasure (3-6)   **Fic**
   Mochizuki, K. Baseball saved us   **E**
   Morpurgo, M. Waiting for Anya (5 and up)
    Fic
   Myers, W. D. The journal of Scott Pendleton
   Collins (5 and up)   **Fic**
   Napoli, D. J. Stones in water (5 and up)
    Fic
   Orlev, U. The island on Bird Street (5 and up)
    Fic
   Orlev, U. The man from the other side (6 and
   up)   **Fic**
   Park, L. S. When my name was Keoko (5 and
   up)   **Fic**
   Paterson, K. Blueberries for the queen   **E**
   Paulsen, G. The cookcamp (5 and up)   **Fic**
   Paulsen, G. The quilt (5 and up)   **Fic**
   Polacco, P. The butterfly (2-4)   **Fic**
   Serraillier, I. The silver sword (5 and up)
    Fic
   Uchida, Y. The bracelet   **E**
   Watkins, Y. K. My brother, my sister, and I (6
   and up)   **Fic**
   Watkins, Y. K. So far from the bamboo grove
   (6 and up)   **Fic**
   Woodson, J. Coming on home soon   **E**

Wyss, Thelma Hatch
Bear dancer (5 and up)   **Fic**

X

X-treme disasters that changed America [series]
Levey, R. H. Dust bowl!   **363.34**
Ximen Bao and the river spirit. Jaffe, N.
In Jaffe, N. and Zeitlin, S. J. The cow of no
color: riddle stories and justice tales from
around the world p18-22   **398.2**
Xuan YongSheng
(il) Kimmel, E. A. The rooster's antlers
398.2
(il) Kimmel, E. A. Ten suns   **398.2**

Y

Yaccarino, Dan
(il) Brown, M. W. The good little bad little pig
E
(il) Henkes, K. Circle dogs   **E**
(il) MacLachlan, P. Bittle   **E**
(il) Nye, N. S. Come with me   **811**
(il) Zimmerman, A. G. Trashy town   **E**
Yachts and yachting
See also Sailing
Yacowitz, Caryn
Pumpkin fiesta   **E**
Yakami. Mayer, M.
In Mayer, M. Women warriors; myths and
legends of heroic women p61-64   **398**
Yakwawiak. Bruchac, J.
In Bruchac, J. and Bruchac, J. When the
Chenoo howls; native American tales of
terror   **398.2**
Yallery Brown. Jacobs, J.
In Jacobs, J. English fairy tales p249-55
398.2
Yam-leaf greens and rice. Graham, L. B.
In Graham, L. B. How God fix Jonah p104-
09   **398.2**
Yang, Belle
Hannah is my name   **E**
Yang, James
Joey and Jet   **E**
Yang the youngest and his terrible ear. Namioka,
L.   **Fic**
Yang Yang and Hoo Hoo. Sandburg, C.
In Sandburg, C. The Sandburg treasury; prose
and poetry for young people p149-51
818
Yang Yang and Hoo Hoo, or the song of the left
foot of the shadow of the goose in Oklahoma.
Sandburg, C.
In Sandburg, C. More Rootabaga stories
p133-38   **S C**
The **Yangtze**. Waterlow, J.   **951.2**
Yangtze River valley (China)
Waterlow, J. The Yangtze (4 and up)   **951.2**
Yankee Doodle America. Minor, W.   **973.3**

Yankee girl. Rodman, M. A.   **Fic**
Yao (African people)
Fiction
Grifalconi, A. The village that vanished   **E**
Yao Jour. MacDonald, M. R.
In MacDonald, M. R. Celebrate the world;
twenty tellable folktales for multicultural
festivals p175-81   **372.6**
The **Yara**. San Souci, R.
In San Souci, R. More short & shivery; thirty
terrifying tales p57-60   **398.2**
Yara-ma-yha-who. San Souci, R.
In San Souci, R. A terrifying taste of short &
shivery; thirty creepy tales p6-11
398.2
Yard sale!. Modarressi, M.   **E**
Yard sales *See* Garage sales
Yardley, Joanna
(il) Uchida, Y. The bracelet   **E**
Yaroslava
(il) Tresselt, A. R. The mitten   **398.2**
Yates, Elizabeth
Amos Fortune, free man (4 and up)   **92**
A **year** down yonder. Peck, R.   **Fic**
The **year** I didn't go to school. Potter, G.   **E**
Year of festivals [series]
Ganeri, A. Hindu festivals throughout the year
294.5
Ganeri, A. Muslim festivals throughout the year
297.3
Year of impossible goodbyes. Choi, S. N.   **Fic**
The **year** of Miss Agnes. Hill, K.   **Fic**
The **year** of the perfect Christmas tree. Houston,
G.   **E**
A **year** without rain. Love, D. A.   **Fic**
The **yearling**. Rawlings, M. K.   **Fic**
Yee, Lisa
Millicent Min, girl genius (5 and up)   **Fic**
Yee, Paul
See/See also pages in the following book(s):
Ellis, S. From reader to writer   **372.6**
Yee, Wong Herbert
Tracks in the snow   **E**
Upstairs Mouse, downstairs Mole   **E**
(il) Friend, C. Eddie the raccoon   **E**
Yeh-Shen. Louie, A.-L.   **398.2**
The **yellow** dwarf. Aulnoy, Madame d'
In The Blue fairy book p30-50   **398.2**
Yellow fever
Murphy, J. An American plague (5 and up)
614.5
Fiction
Anderson, L. H. Fever, 1793 (5 and up)   **Fic**
The **yellow** house. Rubin, S. G.   **759.4**
The **yellow** star. Deedy, C. A.   **Fic**
Yellow star. Roy, J. R.   **Fic**
Yellow umbrella. Liu, J. S.   **E**
Yellow umbrella books for early readers [series]
Rubin, A. How many fish?   **E**
Yemen
Hestler, A. Yemen (5 and up)   **953.3**

Yeoman, John
The Seven voyages of Sinbad the Sailor (5 and up) **398.2**

Yep, Laurence
The amah (5 and up) **Fic**
Angelfish (5 and up) **Fic**
Child of the owl (5 and up) **Fic**
Dragon's gate (6 and up) **Fic**
Dragonwings (5 and up) **Fic**
Hiroshima (4 and up) **Fic**
The journal of Wong Ming-Chung (4 and up) **Fic**
The Khan's daughter (3-5) **398.2**
The lost garden (5 and up) **92**
The magic paintbrush (3-5) **Fic**
Skunk scout (4-6) **Fic**
Thief of hearts (5 and up) **Fic**
The traitor (5 and up) **Fic**
When the circus came to town (3-5) **Fic**
See/See also pages in the following book(s):
Author talk (4 and up) **028.5**

Yes, we have bananas. Hughes, M. S. **634**

Yeshi Dorjee
See/See also pages in the following book(s):
Major, J. S. Caravan to America p[1]-13 (4 and up) **920**

Yeshi's luck. Rose, N. C.
In Rose, N. C. Tibetan tales for little Buddhas **398.2**

Yesterday I had the blues. Frame, J. A. **E**

Yezerski, Thomas
A full hand **E**
(il) Cohen, M. Mimmy and Sophie all around the town **Fic**
(il) Cutler, J. Rose and Riley **E**
(il) Rodowsky, C. F. Not my dog **Fic**

Yikes-lice!. Caffey, D. **616.5**

Yin
Coolies **E**

Yin, Saw Myat
Myanmar (5 and up) **959.1**

Yiyi the Spider and the stick sap man. Bruchac, J.
In Bruchac, J. Tell me a tale; a book about storytelling p67-70 **372.6**

Ylvisaker, Anne
Dear Papa (4 and up) **Fic**

Yo! Yes? Raschka, C. **E**

Yo-yos
Fiction
Egielski, R. Slim and Jim **E**

Yockteng, Rafael
(il) Messengers of rain and other poems from Latin America. See Messengers of rain and other poems from Latin America **861.008**

Yoga
Chryssicas, M. K. I love yoga (3-5) **613.7**
Whitford, R. Little yoga (k-1) **613.7**

Yoko. Wells, R. **E**

Yolen, Jane
Apple for the teacher (4 and up) **782.42**
Baby Bear's chairs **E**
The ballad of the pirate queens (3-5) **811**
Color me a rhyme (3-5) **811**

Commander Toad and the voyage home (.) **E**
Count me a rhyme (3-5) **811**
The dragon's boy (5 and up) **Fic**
Fine feathered friends (3-5) **811**
Greenkid
In Swan sister; fairy tales retold **S C**
Here there be dragons (5 and up) **810.8**
Includes the following stories: Great-Grandfather Dragon's tale; The dragon woke and stretched; "Story," the old man said; Cockfight; Dragonfield; The king's dragon; The dragon's boy; One Ox, Two Ox, Three Ox, and the Dragon King
How beastly! (3-5) **811**
How do dinosaurs say goodnight? **E**
The king's dragon
In Fire and wings: dragon tales from East and West p112-16 **S C**
Meow (k-3) **398.2**
Mightier than the sword (4 and up) **398.2**
Contents: The magic brocade; The young man protected by the river; The devil with the three golden hairs; Eating with trolls; Knee-high man; Language of the birds; Thick-head; The fisherman and the chamberlain; Jack and his companions; The truthful shepherd; And who cured the princess?; The false knight on the road; Hired hands; Mighty mikko
Not one damsel in distress (4 and up) **398.2**
Contents: Atalanta the huntress; Nana Miriam; Fitcher's bird; The girl and the puma; Li Chi slays the serpent; Brave woman counts coup; Pretty Penny; Burd Janet; Mizilca; The pirate princess; The samurai maiden; Bradamante; Molly Whuppie
Odysseus in the serpent maze (4 and up) **Fic**
Off we go! **E**
Owl moon **E**
The perfect wizard [biography of Hans Christian Andersen] (2-4) **92**
The three bears holiday rhyme book (k-2) **811**
Touch magic **028.5**
Wild wings (3-6) **811**
About
McGinty, A. B. Meet Jane Yolen (1-3) **92**
(ed) This little piggy. See This little piggy **398.8**

Yolonda's genius. Fenner, C. **Fic**

Yom Kippur
Fishman, C. On Rosh Hashanah and Yom Kippur (k-3) **296.4**

Yona and the river demon. Schwartz, H.
In Schwartz, H. Invisible kingdoms; Jewish tales of angels, spirits, and demons p43-48 **398.2**

Yonder mountain. Bushyhead, R. H. **398.2**

Yonjwa seeks a bride. MacDonald, M. R.
In MacDonald, M. R. The storyteller's start-up book; finding, learning, performing, and using folktales including twelve tellable tales p195-99 **372.6**

Yoo, Paula
Sixteen years in sixteen seconds [biography of Sammy Lee] (2-4) **92**

Yorinks, Adrienne
Quilt of states (5 and up) **973**

Yorinks, Arthur
Happy bees **E**
Hey, Al **E**

York, ca. 1775-ca. 1815
About
Blumberg, R. York's adventures with Lewis and
Clark (5 and up)   **978**
York, Pat
The fish's story
In Swan sister; fairy tales retold   **S C**
York, Sherry
Children's and young adult literature by Latino
writers   **028.5**
Picture books by Latino writers   **028.5**
York's adventures with Lewis and Clark.
Blumberg, R.   **978**
Yorktown (Va.)
History—Siege, 1781
Ferrie, R. The world turned upside down (5 and
up)   **973.3**
Yoruba (African people)
Folklore
Gershator, P. Zzzng! Zzzng! Zzzng! (k-3)
                                                398.2

Yoshida, Hideo C.
See/See also pages in the following book(s):
Just like me p2-3   **920**
Yoshikawa, Sachiko
(il) Walvoord, L. Razzamadaddy   **E**
Yoshina, Joan M.
(jt. auth) Harada, V. H. Assessing learning
                                                027.8
(jt. auth) Harada, V. H. Inquiry learning through
librarian-teacher partnerships   **371.1**
Yoshi's feast. Kajikawa, K.   **398.2**
Yotsuba&!. Azuma, K.   **741.5**
You and me together. Kerley, B.   **E**
You are special, Little one. Tafuri, N.   **E**
You are the scientist [series]
Ross, M. E. Toy lab   **530**
You bad dog!. Baker, L.   **E**
"You better not do it". Sanfield, S.
In Sanfield, S. The adventures of High John
the Conqueror   **398.2**
You can do it too!. Baicker, K.   **E**
You can weave!. Monaghan, K.   **746.41**
You can write [series]
Roy, J. R. You can write using good grammar
                                                428
You can write using good grammar. Roy, J. R.
                                                428
You can't rush a cat. Bradford, K.   **E**
You can't take a balloon into the Metropolitan
Museum. Weitzman, J. P.   **E**
You come to Yokum. Hurst, C. O.   **Fic**
You forgot your skirt, Amelia Bloomer. Corey, S.
                                                92
You gotta try this!. Cobb, V.   **507.8**
You have head lice!. DerKazarian, S.   **616.5**
You hold me and I'll hold you. Carson, J.   **E**
You may be the next . . . Schwartz, A.
In Schwartz, A. Scary stories 3; more tales to
chill your bones p89   **398.2**
You must be joking!. Brewer, P.   **818**

You read to me & I'll read to you [20th-century
stories to share]   **E**
You read to me, I'll read to you. Ciardi, J.
                                                811
You read to me, I'll read to you [very short fairy
tales to read together] Hoberman, M. A.
                                                E
You read to me, I'll read to you [very short Moth-
er Goose tales to read together] Hoberman,
M. A.   **811**
You read to me, I'll read to you [very short stories
to read together] Hoberman, M. A.   **811**
You want women to vote, Lizzie Stanton? Fritz, J.
                                                92
Younde goes to town. Courlander, H.
In Courlander, H. and Herzog, G. Cow-tail
switch, and other West African stories
p59-64   **398.2**
Young, Amy
Belinda, the ballerina   **E**
(il) Meister, C. My pony Jack   **E**
Young, Ed
Beyond the great mountains (4 and up)   **811**
Cat and Rat (k-3)   **398.2**
Lon Po Po (1-3)   **398.2**
Monkey King   **E**
My Mei Mei   **E**
Pinocchio (3-6)   **Fic**
Seven blind mice (k-3)   **398.2**
The sons of the Dragon King (3-5)   **398.2**
Voices of the heart   **179**
What about me? (k-3)   **398.2**
(il) Casanova, M. The hunter   **398.2**
(il) Coerr, E. Sadako [biography of Sadako
Sasaki]   **92**
(il) Frost, R. Birches   **811**
(il) Grimes, N. Tai chi morning   **811**
(il) Johnston, T. Desert song   **E**
(il) Louie, A.-L. Yeh-Shen   **398.2**
(il) Olaleye, I. Bitter bananas   **E**
(il) Pollock, P. The Turkey Girl   **398.2**
Young, Jackie
(jt. auth) Blakley Kinsler, G. Crocheting
                                                746.43
Young, Mary O'Keefe
(il) Moore, C. The daring escape of Ellen Craft
                                                92
Young, Sarah
(il) Words of gold. See Words of gold
                                                220.9
Young, Sue
Writing with style (5 and up)   **808**
Young adult literature
Bibliography
Bott, C. J. The bully in the book and in the
classroom   **371.5**
Children's books: awards & prizes   **028.5**
Cox Clark, R. E. Tantalizing tidbits for middle
schoolers   **028.5**
Day, F. A. Latina and Latino voices in literature
                                                810.9
Gillespie, J. T. The children's and young adult
literature handbook   **011.6**
Helbig, A. Many peoples, one land   **016.8**

Z

Zhang, Ange
Red land, yellow river (5 and up)   **951.05**

Zhang, Christopher Zhong-yuan
(il) Park, F. The royal bee   **E**

Ziefert, Harriet
A dozen ducklings lost and found   **E**
Home for Navidad   **E**
Little Red Riding Hood (k-2)   **398.2**
Lunchtime for a purple snake   **E**
One smart skunk   **E**

Zigazak!. Kimmel, E. A.   **E**

Ziggy's blue-ribbon day. Mills, C.   **E**

Zimbabwe
Fiction
Farmer, N. The Ear, the Eye, and the Arm (6 and up)   **Fic**
Farmer, N. A girl named Disaster (6 and up)   **Fic**
Stock, C. Gugu's house   **E**

Zimmer, Dirk
(il) Cole, J. Bony-Legs   **398.2**
(il) Coppinger, T. Curse in reverse   **E**
(il) Maguire, G. Seven spiders spinning   **Fic**
(il) Schwartz, A. In a dark, dark room, and other scary stories   **398.2**

Zimmer, Tracie Vaughn
Sketches from a spy tree (3-6)   **Fic**

Zimmerman, Andrea Griffing
Dig!   **E**
Digger man   **E**
My dog Toby   **E**
Trashy town   **E**

Zimmermann, Karl R.
All aboard! (5 and up)   **385**
Steam locomotives (4 and up)   **385**

The **zimwi**. San Souci, R.
In San Souci, R. A terrifying taste of short & shivery; thirty creepy tales p62-67   **398.2**

Zin! zin! zin! a violin. Moss, L.   **E**

Zinc
Gray, L. Zinc
In The Elements   **546**

Zinnen, Linda
The dragons of Spratt, Ohio (5 and up)   **Fic**

Zinnia and Dot. Ernst, L. C.   **E**

Zion, Gene
Harry the dirty dog   **E**

Zipes, Jack David
(ed) The Norton anthology of children's literature. See The Norton anthology of children's literature   **808.8**
(ed) The Oxford companion to fairy tales. See The Oxford companion to fairy tales   **398.2**

Zipping, zapping, zooming bats. Earle, A.   **599.4**

Zlateh the goat. Singer, I. B.
In Singer, I. B. Stories for children p45-52   **S C**
also in Singer, I. B. Zlateh the goat, and other stories p79-90   **398.2**

Zlateh the goat, and other stories. Singer, I. B.   **398.2**

Zodiac
Kimmel, E. A. The rooster's antlers (k-3)   **398.2**
Mitton, J. Zodiac (2-4)   **398**
Young, E. Cat and Rat (k-3)   **398.2**

Zoehfeld, Kathleen Weidner
Did dinosaurs have feathers? (k-3)   **568**
Dinosaur babies (k-3)   **567.9**
Dinosaur parents, dinosaur young (4 and up)   **567.9**
How mountains are made (k-3)   **551.4**
What is the world made of? (k-3)   **530.4**
What lives in a shell? (k-1)   **591.4**
Wild lives (5 and up)   **590.73**
(jt. auth) Nye, B. Bill Nye the science guy's great big book of tiny germs   **579**

Zoell, Bob
(il) Hirsch, R. F E G: ridiculous stupid poems for intelligent children   **821**

Zolotow, Charlotte
The beautiful Christmas tree   **E**
The bunny who found Easter   **E**
Mr. Rabbit and the lovely present   **E**
The old dog   **E**
The seashore book   **E**
Seasons (k-3)   **811**
Sleepy book   **E**
A tiger called Thomas   **E**
When the wind stops   **E**
William's doll   **E**

Zolotow, Charlotte, 1915-
See/See also pages in the following book(s):
Marcus, L. S. Ways of telling   **741.6**

Zomo the Rabbit. McDermott, G.   **398.2**

A **Zooful** of animals   **808.81**

Zoologists
Miles, V. Wild science (5 and up)   **591.68**

Zoology
United States
See Animals—United States

Zoom. Bányai, I.   **E**

Zoom City. Hurd, T.   **E**

Zoos
Aliki. My visit to the zoo (k-3)   **590.73**
Collard, S. B., III. In the wild (4-6)   **591.68**
Lyon, G. E. Mother to tigers [biography of Helen Martini] (k-3)   **92**
Munari, B. Bruno Munari's zoo   **E**
Zoehfeld, K. W. Wild lives (5 and up)   **590.73**

Fiction
Bauer, M. D. A bear named Trouble (3-6)   **Fic**
Hoff, S. Sammy the seal   **E**
Neitzel, S. Our class took a trip to the zoo   **E**
Rathmann, P. Good night, Gorilla   **E**
Rice, E. Sam who never forgets   **E**
Rose, D. L. Birthday zoo   **E**
Seuss, Dr. If I ran the zoo   **E**
Waber, B. A lion named Shirley Williamson   **E**